COMPLETE PRONUNCIATION KEY

The pronunciation of each word is shown just after the word, in this way: **ab.bre.vi.ate** (ə.brē′vi.āt). The letters and signs used are pronounced as in the words below. The mark ′ is placed after a syllable with primary or strong accent, as in the example above. The mark ′ after a syllable shows a secondary or lighter accent, as in **ab.bre.vi.a.tion** (ə.brē′vi.ā′shən).

Some words, taken from foreign languages, are spoken with sounds that otherwise do not occur in English. Symbols for these sounds are given at the end of the table as "Foreign Sounds."

a	hat, cap	**i**	it, pin	**s**	say, yes
ā	age, face	**ī**	ice, five	**sh**	she, rush
ã	care, air			**t**	tell, it
ä	father, far	**j**	jam, enjoy	**th**	thin, both
		k	kind, seek	**ŧħ**	then, smooth
b	bad, rob	**l**	land, coal		
ch	child, much	**m**	me, am	**u**	cup, son
d	did, red	**n**	no, in	**u̇**	put, book
		ng	long, bring	**ü**	rule, move
e	let, best			**ū**	use, music
ē	equal, see	**o**	hot, rock		
ėr	term, learn	**ō**	open, go	**v**	very, save
		ô	order, all	**w**	will, woman
f	fat, if	**oi**	oil, toy	**y**	you, yet
g	go, bag	**ou**	out, now	**z**	zero, breeze
h	he, how			**zh**	measure, seizure
		p	pet, cup		
		r	run, try		

ə occurs only in unaccented syllables and represents the sound of *a* in *a*bout, *e* in tak*e*n, *i* in penc*i*l, *o* in lem*o*n, and *u* in circ*u*s.

FOREIGN SOUNDS

Y as in French *lune*, German *süss*. Pronounce ē as in *equal* with the lips rounded for ü as in *rule*.

œ as in French *peu*, German *könig*. Pronounce ā as in *age* with the lips rounded for ō as in *open*.

N as in French *bon*. The N is not pronounced, but shows that the vowel before it is nasalized.

H as in German *ach*, Scottish *loch*. Pronounce k without closing the breath passage.

COMMON SPELLINGS OF ENGLISH SOUNDS

The table below shows the different sounds of the English language and the commonest spellings for those sounds. After each symbol, the various spellings for that sound are boldface in each example. The spellings have been grouped into three sections to indicate position of occurrence of the sound (initial, medial, and terminal, but in some cases examples do not exist or are so rare as not to merit entry) and each of these sections is separated from the others after each symbol by a dash. This table will help the user who is unfamiliar with English spelling avoid errors in spelling and will help him find entries of whose spelling he is uncertain.

SYMBOL:	SPELLING:
a	**a**t, **a**lmond, **au**nt — h**a**t, pl**ai**d, h**a**lf, s**a**lmon, l**au**gh, mer**i**ngue
ā	**a**ge, **ai**d, **ay**, **aye**, **ei**ght, **e**lite, **é**clair — c**a**me, m**ai**d, g**ao**l, g**au**ge, alc**ay**de, br**ea**k, v**ei**n, cr**e**pe, f**e**te, r**e**gime, convey**a**nce — br**ae**, s**ay**, y**ea**, w**ei**gh, th**ey**, attach**é**, dossi**er**, bouqu**et**
ã	**a**rea, **Aa**ron, **ae**rial, **ai**r, **e**re, **Ei**re, **ey**rie — c**a**re, ch**ai**r, pr**ay**er, wh**e**re, p**ea**r, th**ei**r
ä	**a**rgue, **aa**rdvark, **a**lmond, **a**lms, **au**nt, enc**o**re, **ah** — f**a**ther, **A**frik**aa**ns, h**a**lf, c**a**lm, l**au**gh, serge**a**nt — br**a**, sp**a**, b**aa**
b	**b**ad — ra**b**id, ra**bb**it — we**b**, tu**b**e, e**bb**
ch	**ch**ild — ar**ch**er, Appala**ch**ian, scrat**ch**y, righ**t**eous, ques**t**ion, fu**t**ure — ri**ch**, avalan**ch**e, wa**tch**
d	**d**id — rea**d**y, la**dd**er — di**d**, ma**d**e, a**dd**, fille**d**
e	**a**ny, **ae**sthetic, **e**lbow, **é**migré — m**a**ny, s**ai**d, s**ay**s, l**e**t, br**ea**d, h**ei**fer, l**eo**pard, fri**e**nd, assaf**oe**tida, b**u**ry
ē	**Ae**sop, **e**qual, **ea**t, **ee**l, **ei**ther, **ey**rie, **oe**sophagus — C**ae**sar, m**e**ter, t**ea**m, w**ea**k, w**ee**k, rec**ei**ve, p**eo**ple, ma**chi**ne, beli**e**ve, ph**oe**nix — alg**ae**, qu**ay**, t**ea**, b**ee**, k**ey**, Mar**ie**
ėr	**ear**th, **er**mine, **er**r, **ir**k, **Ir**ving, **ur**n — p**ear**l, st**er**n, f**ir**st, st**ir**ring, w**or**d, w**or**ry, j**our**ney, t**ur**n, b**ur**row, m**yr**tle — f**ir**, sh**irr**, entrepren**eur**, chauff**eur**, f**ur**, b**urr**
ər	p**o**larize, advert**i**se, avoird**u**pois, arm**o**ry, acr**ea**ge, **a**pron — li**ar**, moth**er**, chauff**eur**, elix**ir**, hon**or**, hon**our**, acr**e**, aug**ur**, zeph**yr**
f	**f**at, **ph**rase — sel**f**ish, roo**f**ing, e**ff**ort, go**ph**er, telephone roo**f**, cara**f**e, o**ff**, gira**ff**e, lau**gh**, syl**ph**
g	**g**o, **gh**ost, **gu**est — ec**z**ema, au**g**er, ba**gg**y, a**gh**ast, ro**gu**ish — le**g**, e**gg**, Pittsbur**gh**, ro**gu**e
h	**h**e, **wh**o — a**h**ead
hw	**wh**eat — a**wh**ile
i	**Ae**neas, **E**ngland, **i**t — c**a**bbage, pala**e**ography, pr**e**tty, b**ee**n, b**i**t, s**ie**ve, w**o**men, b**u**sy, b**ui**ld, h**y**mn — Attl**ee**, all**ey**, Missour**i**, zombi**e**, Anni**e**, happ**y**
ī	**ai**sle, **ay**e, **ay**, **ei**der, **ei**ther, **eye**, **i**ce — h**ei**ght, g**ey**ser, n**i**ce, t**ie**d, h**i**gher, b**uy**er, fl**y**ing — assag**ai**, alk**ali**, l**ie**, h**igh**, b**uy**, sk**y**, r**ye**
j	**g**em, **gi**aour, **j**am — lo**dg**ing, sol**di**er, ad**j**oin, ver**d**ure, tra**g**ic, exa**gg**erate, alle**g**iance, Geor**g**ia, a**j**ar — bri**dg**e, aven**g**e
k	**c**oat, **ch**emistry, **k**ind, **qu**eue — a**c**re, a**cc**ount, Ba**cch**us, an**ch**or, bu**ck**et, a**cqu**ire, o**k**ra, li**qu**or — zin**c**, monar**ch**, a**ch**e, ba**ck**, sa**cqu**e, par**k**, fol**k**, mas**qu**e
l	**l**and, **ll**ama, **Ll**oyd — fe**l**t, bu**ll**et — contro**l**, boi**l**, ru**l**e, te**ll**, bagate**ll**e, ki**ln**
m	**m**e — dra**m**a, plu**mb**er, com**m**on — drach**m**, paradig**m**, cal**m**, drea**m**, ho**m**e, cli**mb**, sole**mn**
n	**gn**aw, **kn**ife, **mn**emonic, **n**o — si**gn**ing, ma**n**y, ma**nn**er — si**gn**, colog**n**e, pa**n**, go**n**e, An**n**e
ng	i**nk**, fi**ng**er, si**ng**er — lo**ng**, to**ng**ue
o	**o**dd — w**a**tch, h**o**t
ō	**o**pen, **oa**ts, **oh**, **ow**n, **owe** — m**au**ve, chauff**eu**r, y**eo**man, s**ew**ing, b**o**ne, b**oa**t, g**oe**s, f**o**lk, br**oo**ch, s**ou**l — b**eau**, s**ew**, domin**o**, Eskim**o**, wh**oa**, coc**oa**, t**oe**, th**ough**, l**ow**
ô	**a**ll, **au**tomobile, **aw**e, **aw**l, **o**rder, **ou**ght — w**ar**m, w**a**lk, t**au**ght, b**aw**l, n**or**th, br**oa**d, reserv**oi**r, b**ough**t — Ut**ah**, Ark**a**nsas, Es**au**, l**aw**
oi	**oi**l — b**oi**l, r**oy**al, bu**oy**ant — Illin**oi**s, Iroqu**oi**s, b**oy**, bu**oy**
ou	**ou**t, **ow**l — gi**a**our, sauerkr**au**t, h**ou**se, p**ow**der — b**ough**, n**ow**
p	**p**lay — ma**p**le, ha**pp**y — cu**p**, ro**p**e, hicc**ough**
r	**r**un, **rh**ythm, **wr**ong — p**r**ay, car**r**y, cata**rrh**al — ca**r**, ca**r**e, pa**rr**, bu**rr**, cata**rrh**
s	**c**ent, **p**sychology, **s**ay, **sc**ent, **sch**ism — a**c**id, mer**c**y, pea**c**eful, mo**s**t, de**sc**ent — ni**ce**, ga**s**, cur**se**, acquie**sce**
sh	**ch**auffeur, **Ch**icago, **psh**aw, **s**ure, **sch**ist, **sh**e — o**ce**an, ma**ch**ine, spe**c**ial, in**s**ure, con**sc**ience, nau**se**ous, a**sh**es, ten**s**ion, is**s**ue, mi**ss**ion, na**t**ion — douche, ca**sh**
t	**pt**omaine, **t**ell, **Th**omas — me**t**er, Es**th**er, bu**tt**on, sto**pp**ed, bough**t**, yach**t**, ca**t**, a**te**, Sco**tt**, dine**tte**
th	**th**in — e**th**ics — wi**th**, brea**th**, absin**th**e
th	**th**en — fa**th**er — smoo**th**, brea**the**
u	**o**ven, **u**p — c**o**me, d**oe**s, fl**oo**d, tr**ou**ble, c**u**p
ū	**eu**genic, **Eu**rope, **ewe**, **ewe**r, **u**se, **yo**u, **yu**le — b**eau**ty, f**eu**d, p**ew**ter, c**u**re, m**u**sic — q**ueue**, f**ew**, adi**eu**, vi**ew**, em**u**, c**ue**
ů	w**o**lf, b**o**som, g**oo**d, sh**ou**ld, f**u**ll
ū	**oo**ze, **ou**zel, **u**miak — man**eu**ver, Z**eu**s, l**ew**d, m**o**ve, f**oo**d, cr**ou**p, r**u**le, r**ue**ful, b**uh**l, fr**ui**t, bu**oy**ant — thr**ew**, adi**eu**, t**o**, sh**oe**, t**oo**, s**ou**, thr**ough**, gn**u**, bl**ue**, b**uoy**, tw**o**, Si**oux**
v	**v**ery — li**v**er, fli**vv**er — o**f**, ha**ve**
w	**w**ill — **ch**oir, **qu**ick, s**u**ite, a**w**ake
y	**y**es — a**z**alea, op**i**nion, halle**l**ujah, can**y**on
z	**X**erxes, **z**ero — di**s**cern, ea**s**y, **sc**issors, o**z**one, pu**zz**le — ha**s**, ro**se**, ad**z**, ad**ze**, bu**zz**
zh	**j**abot — re**g**ime, mea**s**ure, divi**s**ion, a**z**ure, bra**z**ier — gara**ge**
ə	**a**lone, **e**ffect, **e**ssential, **o**blige, **o**ccasion, **u**pon — **I**saac, **a**bacus, fount**ai**n, mom**e**nt, flag**eo**let, penc**i**l, compl**e**te, caut**i**ous, circ**u**s, eth**y**l — sof**a**, pari**ah**, Miss**ou**ri, kimon**o**

THORNDIKE-BARNHART
Comprehensive Desk
Dictionary

THORNDIKE·BARNHART

Comprehensive Desk

Dictionary

EDITED BY

Clarence L. Barnhart

Editor of the Thorndike-Barnhart Dictionary Series,
The American College Dictionary,
The Dictionary of U.S. Army Terms and
The New Century Cyclopedia of Names

DOUBLEDAY & COMPANY, INC.

Garden City, New York

DICTIONARIES IN THIS SERIES

Thorndike-Barnhart Comprehensive Desk Dictionary
Thorndike-Barnhart Concise Dictionary
Thorndike-Barnhart Handy Dictionary
Thorndike-Barnhart Beginning Dictionary
Thorndike-Barnhart Junior Dictionary
Thorndike-Barnhart Advanced Junior Dictionary
Thorndike-Barnhart High School Dictionary

Library of Congress Catalog Card Number: 67–18142

TABLE OF CONTENTS

GENERAL EDITORIAL ADVISORY COMMITTEE

VII

SPECIAL EDITORS

OFFICE STAFF

IX

PREFACE

To put the proper word in the proper place or to comprehend fully what you read is not easy. Even the well-informed speaker, writer, or reader often turns to reference books to determine the spelling or pronunciation of a word, to learn its meaning, or to clear up some point of usage. Facts about words and advice on their use are either scattered in many places—in grammars, books of synonyms, technical handbooks—or brought together only in the largest dictionaries, books that are cumbersome to use and expensive to buy. This handy-size dictionary is designed to bring within the covers of *one* compact book the essential information about the basic vocabulary necessary to carry on the daily affairs of the English-speaking world.

Over 80,000 words are entered; they have been selected on the basis of word counts of over 30,000,000 words of text in every field of general interest. These 80,000 words make up 99 per cent of the words used in newspapers and magazines, in current fiction and nonfiction; they include all except the very technical terms used in textbooks. An understanding of these 80,000 words will give you a vocabulary larger than that of many college professors or business executives—more than adequate for all daily needs. Some 300,000 facts about the spelling, pronunciation, meanings, origin, and use of these words are given. A careful reading of the very complete notes on pages 1 to 7, explaining point by point how to use this dictionary, will make these facts easily accessible to you.

The arrangement of information provides the greatest possible amount of help to the user at the least cost of time and effort to him. To treat 80,000 words, each in its most useful way, involves thousands of subtle and complex problems. It is not sufficient merely to present in one fashion or another the important facts about a word; these should be made readily available and comprehensible to the person who seeks the dictionary's help. Accordingly, we have put all entries in *one alphabetical list*, put common meanings first, clearly numbered the definitions, used clear, precise language in the definitions, and made frequent use of explanatory phrases and sentences to clarify them.

The reader most frequently uses a dictionary to find out the meaning of a hard word as used in a book or article. An efficient dictionary offers the greatest possible number of words and meanings without sacrificing full explanations of idiomatic uses and expressions. Space is at such a premium that information of little value to the users of the dictionary must be excluded, yet all relevant and needed information must be included. In the selection and arrangement of the definitions, *A Semantic Count of English Words* by Professor Irving Lorge and Professor E. L. Thorndike has been invaluable. In that study, every meaning in approximately 5,000,000 words of text in 29 different types of sources (such as the *Encyclopædia Britannica*, standard novels, and works of nonfiction) was counted and keyed to the meanings listed in the monumental *Oxford English Dictionary*. The value of such a count to a dictionary editor in selecting meanings, in allotting the amount of space for definitions and illustrative sentences, and in the arrangement of the definitions is evident. In addition, by using word counts of the general vocabulary, especially *The Teacher's Word Book of 30,000 Words* by Professor Thorndike and Professor Lorge, counts made of the vocabulary of various special technical and scientific subjects, and the glossaries and indexes of over 300 nonfiction books (five each in 60 different fields of knowledge), we have been able to include all but rare, archaic, obsolete, and excessively technical words and meanings.

The modern writer who has something to say, and takes some thought as to how he will say it, seeks effective control over a basic vocabulary of some 30,000 words (a vocabulary nearly twice as large as that used by Shakespeare). Many of these words —the so-called simple words, such as *set, run, off, about, from*—are extraordinarily complex, with many shades of meaning and numerous idiomatic uses which can be made clear only by the liberal use of explanatory sentences and phrases. Careful and full explanation of these words, the function words of the language, is usually sacrificed in dictionaries in order to include as many words as possible. In this dictionary we have paid special attention to the explanation of function words so that the writer may have at hand a catalogue of the rich variety of ways in which they are used.

Some writers and speakers affect the use of big words which often obscure the meaning of what they write and say. Certainly a writer or speaker who uses many words not in this dictionary can expect to be understood by only a limited few. If it is necessary to use such words—and it may be—they should be explained by the writer or speaker. Meanings labeled *Chem.*, *Physics*, *Biol.*, and *Law* are those used chiefly in these various fields and, unless the term is one used frequently in high-school texts, they will be understood readily only by chemists, physicists, biologists, and lawyers. Meanings labeled *Archaic*, *Obsolete*, or *Poetic* are inappropriate for a writer addressing modern English readers unless he wants to give an archaic or poetic flavor to his writing. Meanings labeled *Colloq.* are appropriate in all but formal writing. Before using a word with an unfamiliar meaning the writer should consider whether there is a restrictive label just after the definition number or the part of speech.

Writers, particularly beginning writers, frequently overuse favorite words. For such writers and others interested in developing a more varied vocabulary, we give over 5,000 synonym and antonym lists keyed to the proper definitions, so that they may, if they desire, choose a simpler or more fitting word or avoid overusing one word.

In addition to the synonym lists there are hundreds of notes describing in some detail cases of conflicting usage so that the person who consults the dictionary may decide which usage he prefers. Often the usage notes discuss general principles of style and language so that the writer, speaker, or reader has at his elbow a concise discussion of many of the most important results of a hundred years of linguistic study. These notes are by Professor Porter G. Perrin, whose *Writer's Guide and Index to English* is well known in the colleges and universities of this country.

In addition to the usage notes there are four special sections designed to give practical help to our users. The first section, written by Professor Charles C. Fries (author of the standard *American English Grammar*) and Professor Aileen Traver Kitchin, gives the fundamental principles of modern American English grammar and is based upon scientific studies of American English as it is used today. The second section, on punctuation, is written by Professor Albert H. Marckwardt of the University of Michigan, author of the *Scribner Handbook of English*, which is used in colleges and universities as a standard guide. The third section, describing the fundamental rules for the preparation of manuscript for tne typesetter, has been prepared by a copy editor (Ethel M. Ryan of Doubleday) and an editor (W. D. Halsey, the managing editor for this dictionary) and will give many practical hints to writers. The fourth section, giving forms and styles for social and business letter-writing (the one form of composition we are all certain to practice), by Professor John A. Kouwenhoven of Barnard College, is authoritative and easy to follow. These special sections offer practical advice as well as a general discussion of principles and will be useful to anyone interested in the art of writing or speaking good English.

The speaker has one need over and above the needs of the writer: he must be furnished with acceptable pronunciations which can be used on all occasions in every part of the country. A dictionary, however, cannot be a substitute for the judgment and good taste of the speaker. He must decide the appropriateness to his purpose, his audience, and the occasion of the words and pronunciations that he uses. But a dictionary can be faithful in recording good present-day American English, and can set forth the more important variant pronunciations in use in the principal regions of the country. Professor Greet and Professor Hubbell, the special editors in charge of pronunciation, have ensured that these aims are carried out.

This dictionary employs a pronunciation key that is easy to learn and to remember. The symbols in the key are listed and explained on the inside of the front and back covers. Outside of the very frequent so-called short and long vowels (as in hat, let, it, hot, cup; āge, ēqual, īce, ōpen, ūse) there are only eight symbols for the user to learn (see the section How to Use This Dictionary, pages 1 to 7). One of these symbols, ə, is called *schwa* and is used to denote the neutral sound of a vowel in an unaccented syllable. It is the sound of *a* in about, *e* in taken, *i* in pencil, *o* in lemon, and *u* in circus. The use of only one symbol for this somewhat variable sound is the approved practice of modern phonetics. This special symbol (ə) for unaccented syllables has proved useful in radio as an aid in teaching broadcasters to avoid the overstressing of unaccented syllables which results in an unnatural or exaggerated pronunciation. It has also been employed in the widely used Thorndike-Century school-dictionary series for over fifteen years, with beneficial results in teaching pupils pronunciation.

A notion of the original meaning of a word will often give the reader a better understanding of it. This dictionary includes word origins generously and a reading of them may prove both profitable and interesting. To know that *acronym* is made up of Greek words meaning "tip name," that originally *abduct* meant "lead away," that *conduct* meant "lead to," that *assert* meant "join to" gives the reader, writer, or speaker an insight into the development of meaning and enables him to recognize familiar elements in new words. The word origins are concerned with the earliest form and meaning of a word, especially the meaning. They have been specially prepared by Professors Hall, Moulton, and Ward and have been carefully checked by Professor Kemp Malone. Users of this dictionary will find them readable and authoritative.

The contributions of America to the English language have not hitherto been recognized in dictionaries because the facts have not been available. For some years, however, Dr. M. M. Mathews has been compiling a historical dictionary of Americanisms (words American in origin), for the University of Chicago Press. We have carefully read the galleys of this scholarly work and have had the benefit of Dr. Mathews' advice in labeling all of the Americanisms in this dictionary. For the first time in a dictionary of this kind we label words and meanings that American English has contributed to the English vocabulary, such as *abalone, anesthesia, appendicitis, gangster, kitchenette, lowbrow, molasses, oscar, party line, phony,* and many others are evidence of the growth and vitality of American English.

The making of a reliable dictionary—a record of existing usage—is, or should be, the work of many scholars and editors working together. In framing the policies of this book we have had advice and help from twenty-eight scholars on the Editorial Advisory Committee. Many of them—those who were my associates on *The Thorndike-Century Senior Dictionary*—have worked with me for fifteen years. For their conscientious, helpful, and friendly advice I am much indebted, and especially to W. Cabell Greet, who, as its chairman, has given freely of his time and knowledge to the work of the committee.

The special editors (listed on page ix) have had charge of special sections of the book—pronunciation, etymology, Americanisms, new words, and usage notes— and have made these sections a convenient and authoritative guide to modern standard American usage. To Professor Lorge, I am indebted for the right to use the *English Semantic Count* which has been greatly expanded and brought up to date with a special count of the 570 commonest words, *here used for the first time.* Finally, I have had the right to use material from *The Thorndike-Century Senior Dictionary, The New Century Dictionary, The Dictionary of Americanisms,* and *The Dictionary of American English.* The selection and organization of material from these varied sources, the rewriting of definitions to make them more understandable, and the addition of modern words and meanings have been the work of the office staff and the special editors. We have tried to approach the language problems of this dictionary in the spirit of the late E. L. Thorndike, psychologist, and the late Leonard Bloomfield, linguist. I believe they would have been pleased to know that a permanent editorial staff has been set up to apply to dictionaries the results of scientific research on language and vocabulary. On behalf of all my associates I express the hope that the assemblage of such a wealth of material from so many sources will result in a reference tool of great value to the users of American English today.

Clarence L. Barnhart

HOW TO USE THIS DICTIONARY

1. The order in which information is given about a word (see **ability,** below) is as follows: (1) the word spelled in boldface type, (2) its pronunciation, (3) part of speech, (4) any irregular inflected forms (plural, past tense, etc.), (5) definitions of its meanings arranged under the appropriate parts of speech, (6) the origin of the word, or etymology, (7) synonyms keyed to the definitions, and (8) usage notes telling you about preferred forms of usage, awkward forms, good written style, and similar matters.

a·bil·i·ty (ə·bil′ə·ti), *n., pl.* **-ties. 1.** power to do or act in any relation: *give according to your ability.* **2.** skill: *mechanical ability.* **3.** power to do some special thing; talent: *musical ability, natural abilities.* [< F < L. See ABLE.] —**Syn. 1.** capacity. **2.** cleverness. **3.** aptitude. ▷ Ability is followed by *to* and an infinitive rather than *of* (*ability to do,* not *of doing*) or *in* and a substantive: *ability to design buildings; ability in arithmetic.*

How to Find a Word

2. One Alphabetical List. You merely need to know the order of the letters of the alphabet to find a word in this dictionary. All main entries are in one long alphabetical list so that you have only one place to look to find a word. Look at column 1, page 33; words in the common vocabulary (A, a (the letter), a (the article), aardvark, abacá, aback, abacus, etc.), technical terms (abaft), proper names (Aachen, Aaron), chemical symbols (A), abbreviations (a., A.B.), and prefixes (a-¹, a-², ab-) are in one list.

3. Homographs (words spelled exactly alike but of different origin) have a small number raised a little above the line after each entry to remind you to look at the other entries spelled in the same way if you do not find the information you are seeking under the first one.

mail¹ (māl), *n.* **1.** letters, papers, parcels, etc., sent by the postal system. **2.** system by which they are sent, managed by the Post Office Department. —*v.* send by mail; put in a mailbox. —*adj.* of mail. [< OF *male* wallet < Gmc.] —**mail′a·ble,** *adj. Am.* —**mail′er,** *n.*

mail² (māl), *n.* **1.** armor made of metal rings, or small loops of chain, linked together. **2.** armor; protective covering. —*v.* cover or protect with mail. [< OF < L *macula* a mesh in network] —**mailed,** *adj.*

When looking up cross references as from **bore³** to **bear¹** be sure to look under the right homograph.

bore³ (bôr; bōr), *v. pt. of* **bear¹.**
bear¹ (bãr), *v.* **bore** or (*Archaic*) **bare, borne** or **born, bear·ing. 1.** carry: *bear a burden.* . . .
bear² (bãr), *n., adj., v.,* **beared, bear·ing.** —*n.* **1.** a large, clumsy, quadruped animal. . . .

4. Main and Subordinate Entries. In this dictionary, main entries always appear on the left-hand margin in large boldface type. On page 33, the first four main entries in column 2 are **abandon, abandoned, abase, abash.** Both **abbrev.** and its variant **abbr.** are main entries; so is **abbreviation.** Subordinate entries on page 33 are idioms (**taken aback** under **aback**), derivatives or run-ons (**abbreviator** under **abbreviate**), inflected forms (**-cat·ed,**

-cat·ing under **abdicate**). Subordinate entries are put in a smaller-sized boldface type.

5. Derivatives (words formed from root words + suffixes) **as Main Entries or Subordinate Entries.** Note that derivative entries are sometimes entered as main entries and sometimes as subordinate entries. Derivatives formed with *-ly, -ness, -er, -able, -less, -like,* and less frequently *-tion, -ity,* and *-al,* are often printed in smaller boldface type at the very end of the definition of the word from which they are derived, because the meaning and the pronunciation can easily be obtained by combining the root with the suffix. Entries of this kind are called run-on entries. Sometimes, however, a derivative is very frequently used, has specialized meanings, or is hard to recognize as a derivative; in such cases the derivative is listed as a main entry (contrast **abbreviation,** a main entry, with **abbreviator,** a run-on entry).

6. Derivatives formed from root words + prefixes (*un-, non-,* etc.) are listed under the prefix without a definition if they are easy to understand by combining the meaning of the prefix with that of the root word. Certain common prefixes such as **non-, un-, over-,** and **re-** have long lists of such words. If a word beginning with one of the common prefixes is not in the list of words under the prefix, look in the proper place in the main entry list for it. Thus, **nonadhesive** can be found under **non-** (the meaning of the word is merely *not adhesive*). If further information is desired, **adhesive** may be looked up and "not" added to the beginning of each of its definitions. **Noncombatant,** however, has a specialized meaning and will be found in the main alphabetical list.

7. Idioms are phrases or expressions, such as *chip on one's shoulder,* that cannot be fully understood from the ordinary meanings of the words which combine to form them. Look for an idiom under its most important word. Thus, **feather in one's cap** is placed under the noun definitions of **feather;** feather one's nest is under the verb definitions of **feather.**

feath·er (feth′ər), *n.* **1.** one of the light, thin growths that cover a bird's skin. **2.** something like a feather in shape or lightness. **3.** feather in one's cap, thing to be proud of. **4. in fine, good,** or **high feather,** in good health, high spirits, etc. —*v.* **1.** supply or cover with feathers. **2.** grow like feathers. **3.** move like feathers. **4.** join by a tongue and groove. **5.** turn the edge of a blade in the direction of movement. **6.** feather one's nest, take advantage of chances to get rich. [OE *fether*] —**feath′ered,** *adj.* —**feath′er·less,** *adj.* —**feath′er·like′,** *adj.*

8. Guide Words are words printed at the top of each column in heavy black letters. The one at the top of the left column is the same as the first entry word on the page; the one at the top of the right column is the same as the last entry word on the page. All the main entries that fall alphabetically between the guide words can be found on that page. By using the guide words to see whether or not an entry is on a particular page you can save much time in locating desired entries.

1

How to Use This Dictionary for Spelling

9. Words of one syllable are printed solid (**each**); words of more than one syllable are separated into syllables by centered dots (**ab·di·cate, ea·ger, re·ly**). Syllabication of the printed or written word is determined partly by speech (but note that the syllables in the pronunciation sometimes, as in **double**, differ from those in the entry word), partly by the component parts (root + affixes) of which the word has been formed, and partly by the conventions of printers and writers. When more than one pronunciation is given for a word, the syllabication shown is ordinarily that of the first pronunciation.

reb·el (*n., adj.* reb′əl; *v.* ri·bel′), *n., adj., v.* . . . The dot in the entry word represents the point at which a word may normally be broken at the end of a written or printed line. In printed matter and formal writing, however, it is not considered good practice to break a word so that a single letter stands alone on one line ($^{a-}_{bed}$ or $^{i-}_{deologically}$ or sleep$^{-}_y$). Short words, such as **able**, should stand unbroken on one line or the other; long ones should be broken as near the middle as possible (**ideologi-cally**); hyphenated compounds (**double-cross**) are best broken only at the hyphen.

10. Variant Spellings. Often there are two or more ways of spelling the same word in English; both ways are current and in good use and it is merely a question of your preference or the preference (if you know it) of the person to or for whom you are writing. We record all of the common variant spellings. When two or more variants are close enough to be seen in the same eye-span they are entered together, and we put first the one that is simpler or is more common in American usage. If the variant spellings must be entered in different parts of the dictionary, we give them at the end of the preferred entry. Under the variant, we refer the user of the dictionary to the preferred form.

adz, adze (adz), *n.* . . . .
la·bor, *esp. Brit.* **la·bour** (lā′bər), *n.* . . . .
en·close (en·klōz′), *v.,* –closed, –clos·ing. 1. shut in on all sides; surround. 2. put a wall or fence around. 3. put in an envelope along with a letter, etc. 4. contain. Also, **inclose.**
in·close (in·klōz′), *v.,* –closed, –clos·ing. en·close.

11. Inflected Forms (the plurals of nouns, the forms of the verb, and the comparatives and superlatives of adjectives) are sometimes difficult to spell. All inflected forms in which there is any change in the root are given immediately after the pronunciation, so that the person seeking to determine their spelling or syllabication may find them quickly and easily. Notice the syllabication of inflected forms in the examples given.

ba·by (bā′bi), *n., pl.* –bies, *adj., v.,* –bied, –by·ing. . . .
need·y (nēd′i), *adj.,* need·i·er, need·i·est. . . .

How to Use the Pronunciations

12. The Standard for the Selection of Pronunciations. The system of indicating pronunciation used in this dictionary is intended to present as clearly as possible pronunciations customarily heard from educated speakers of English in the United States. You will use this dictionary, perhaps, for the purpose of finding what

are the acceptable pronunciations of a certain word, or of finding whether the one which you have been using or hearing is one which is generally accepted or which prevails in a large section of the country. The purpose of this dictionary is to record social custom, with due regard for regional differences, not to impose the pronunciation of one section upon the whole country, or to prescribe or dictate innovations which some individuals might think desirable.

Since fashions in pronunciation change from time to time, it is not sufficient for a dictionary to establish a list of pronunciations and continue using them forever. Authorities have never agreed on all matters of pronunciation, nor can they be expected to agree as to the time when some new pronunciation may be considered to have established itself. For example, when the word *balcony* was borrowed into English from Italian, educated speakers accented the word on the second syllable; but English speakers who did not know Italian tended to treat the word as an English noun and accent it on the first syllable. Such a pronunciation was long considered vulgar, and was objected to by teachers and authors of textbooks. The question may now be considered settled for that particular word. It would be eccentric and indefensible pedantry to accent the word in English on the second syllable simply because such an accent was historically justified. Pronunciation is constantly changing. Some pronunciations that once were common, as (kun′i) for *cony*, are now rarely used. New pronunciations, as (ad·vér′tiz·mənt) for *advertisement*, gradually come into wide use and often force older pronunciations into obscurity. This dictionary has included variant pronunciations, sometimes not recorded elsewhere, which its editors have reason to believe are now part of the language. Examples of changed or changing pronunciations that are recorded are:

dol·drum (dol′drəm; dōl′–)
hom·i·cide (hom′ə·sīd; hō′mə–)
ig·no·ra·mus (ig′nə·rā′məs; –ram′əs)
ja·bot (zha·bō′; zhab′ō; jab′ō)
pre·mo·ni·tion (prē′mə·nish′ən; prem′ə–)

In preparing the work on pronunciation, it was our purpose to have and to use the advice of the best available authorities of the past and present. For the first, the recommended pronunciations of the best existing dictionaries were consulted and compared. Only one who has worked on such a task can realize how widely good authorities may sometimes differ. To any naïve questioner who asks, "What does the dictionary say?" as if "the dictionary" were a sort of Olympian abstraction, an experienced lexicographer can only reply, "What dictionary, and which edition of it?" For the second, authorities to advise on the present state of pronunciation, a group of 28 were chosen. All the members of this committee are well known as scholars in their own professions. They represent all parts of the United States, and many different types of training and points of view. An experienced and skilled phonetician was entrusted with the task of carrying out the policies on pronunciation laid down by the group of advisers.

It is not possible to present in a dictionary all pronunciations that may be heard from cultivated speakers, but we have tried in each case to give the best-established American pronunciation and the commonest acceptable variants.

It is not even possible in a dictionary to give all the possible varying pronunciations used by the same speaker. A dictionary must present its material one word at a time, but we do not speak one word at a time. Even such a simple question as "How do you pronounce *the?*" can never have a single answer. One's pronunciation of this word and of other words depends on neighboring sounds, accent, speed of utterance, and, in many cases, on the style of discourse: formal, informal, colloquial, etc. The pronunciations are, as far as is possible when words must be treated in isolation, those of educated informal speech. The fact that a particular pronunciation is given first does not indicate that it is "more correct." We put the more frequent pronunciation first, wherever this can be ascertained, but usage is often rather evenly divided and in many instances the relative frequency of the variants can only be guessed at.

13. Regional Variations in Pronunciation. Although the United States is the most homogeneous speech community of comparable size in the world, there are nevertheless certain rather noticeable differences in the usage of different parts of the country. Educated speakers do not pronounce English in exactly the same way in Chicago, New York, Boston, and Atlanta. It is the task of special phonetic dictionaries to record these differences in minute detail; but even a general dictionary must include the more important regional variations in pronunciation. A careful use of symbols will make it unnecessary to enter some of these variants separately. For example, speakers from eastern New England and from the North Central states will not pronounce the key word *ärm* with the same vowels. But if each pronounces in every word respelled with (ä) the same vowel he uses in the key word, his pronunciation will be correct and appropriate to his own usage. In the more important instances where this device is not sufficient, as in the case of words like *forest* and *hoarse* (see below), the respellings include as many entries as are necessary to record the facts.

For our purposes here the various speech areas in the United States can be roughly grouped into five main areas—Northern (from western New England to, and including, the Midwest), Midland (from southern New Jersey and northern Delaware and Maryland westward to the Ohio Valley), Southern (from southern Delaware and Maryland southward and westward to Texas), Eastern New England, and Metropolitan New York. Little detailed information is available on pronunciation in the western part of the country.

a. Pronunciation of "r." In this dictionary (r) has been recorded in the pronunciations wherever *r* occurs in the spelling, as in far·ther (fär′thər), since a majority of the speakers of American English pronounce it in all positions. In eastern New England, metropolitan New York, and the many areas of the coastal South, however, (r) is often not pronounced when final or when followed by a consonant. If the reader is a native of one of these "r-less" regions, he should, of course, pronounce (r) only where it is natural for him.

b. Pronunciation of "o" in "log," "loft," "broth," "cost," "forest," "on," "prong." Before certain consonants, the pronunciation of a historical "short *o*" varies in American English between the limits of the (o) in *hot* and the (ô) in *law*. All words in which this variation occurs have been given two pronunciations, the first being the one which the editors consider more common in America as a whole.

log (lôg; log). . . .
loft (lôft; loft). . . .
doff (dof; dôf). . . .
broth (brôth; broth). . . .
cost (kôst; kost). . . .

for·est (fôr′ist; for′–). . . .
on (on; ôn). . . .
prong (prông; prong). . . .

A number of words spelled with *wa* or *ua* vary in the same fashion:

swamp (swomp; swômp). . . .
war·rant (wôr′ənt; wor′–). . . .
quar·rel (kwôr′əl; kwor′–). . . .

c. Pronunciation of "o" in "for" and "four." A distinction in the pronunciation of such pairs of words as *for* (fôr), *four* (fôr; fōr) and *horse* (hôrs), *hoarse* (hôrs; hōrs) is heard in some parts of the United States, particularly in eastern New England and the South. In other parts of the country, such pairs of words are more often pronounced identically, so that *horse* and *hoarse* are both (hôrs), rather than (hôrs) and (hōrs), respectively. Words in which such a distinction is made are recorded as follows:

mourn·ing (môr′ning; mōr′–). . . .

Compare this with the pronunciation for morning:

morn·ing (môr′ning). . . .

d. Pronunciation of "a" in "ask" and "command." The pronunciation of *a* in words like ask and command varies between (a) and (ä) and a vowel intermediate between the two (heard also in the eastern New England pronunciation of *barn, car*, etc.). In this dictionary such words are recorded as follows:

ask (ask; äsk). . . .
com·mand (kə-mand′; –mänd′). . . .

e. Pronunciation of "a" in "fat" and "man." The reader may find that he pronounces one vowel in fat and a much longer one of a different quality in man. There has been a tendency in many parts of the United States to lengthen an original "short *a*" before certain consonants and to change its quality. The longer vowel (in the speech of some breaking into a diphthong) has not been recorded in this dictionary because the facts about its occurrence are not yet fully known:

fat (fat). . . .
man (man). . . .

f. Pronunciation of "o" in "stop" and "lodge." The lengthening of "short *a*" referred to in paragraph e. above has been paralleled in some parts of America by a lengthening of an original "short *o*" under similar conditions, as in the word lodge. The result of this in the "r-less" parts of the South has been to make pairs of words like *lodge* and *large* identical in pronunciation. This longer vowel has not been separately recorded in this dictionary:

stop (stop). . . .
lodge (loj). . . .

g. Pronunciation of vowels before "r" as in "clear" and "poor." There is a variation in American speech in the pronunciation of long vowels before (r). Vowels followed by (r) tend to shorten, so that ea is pronounced (ē) in *clean*, but in *clear*, in the speech of many Americans, it becomes (i) or a vowel intermediate in quality between (ē) and (i). Words like *clear* may have the vowel of *beat* or of *bit*, and words like *poor* may have the vowel of *boot* or of *bush* in different sections of the country. Such words, in which the vowel is shortened by a following (r), have been recorded with the shortened vowel, but the variants with the longer vowel should be assumed to exist in all cases.

clear (klir). . . .
poor (pùr). . . .

h. Pronunciation of vowels before "r" in "dare" and "dairy." The exact quality of the vowel in words like dare and dairy varies considerably in cultivated American speech. Variation exists between vowels close to (e) or to (a) and a long vowel intermediate in quality between them. In New England and the coastal South words like dairy, which are not derived from forms in which the (r) is final, often have a vowel close to (ā), while in some parts of New England and the coastal South this type of pronunciation may even be heard in dare and hair. The symbol (ā) is used in this dictionary to cover all these variants:

dare (dâr). . . .
dair·y (dâr′i). . . .

i. Pronunciation of "y" in "city" and "happy." In this dictionary we have shown (i) as the final vowel of words like city and happy, but a good many people pronounce a longer vowel approaching (ē) (in the speech of those who use the shorter vowel one would hear no distinction between pairs of words like candid and candied):

cit·y (sit′i). . . .
hap·py (hap′i). . . .

j. Pronunciation of "wh" in "whale" and "which." In the speech of many cultivated people no distinction is heard in pairs of words like whale, wail and which, witch, all of which are pronounced with a simple (w). In the pronunciations in this dictionary words spelled with wh have been recorded as (hw), but (w) should be assumed as an equally acceptable variant in each case:

whale (hwāl). . . .
which (hwich). . . .

The Pronunciation Key

14. Function of Letters of the Alphabet. The letters of the alphabet are directions to produce sounds: the letters used in bet direct us to utter a different set of sounds than are called for by the letters in sad. Since English spelling habits are very conservative and have not kept pace with the changes in pronunciation, the directions are often ambiguous: the ea in steak directs us to say ā and the ea in meat to say ē; the ei in receive directs us to say ē but the ei in vein to say ā. The 26 letters of the alphabet occur in over 200 different spelling combinations directing us to say some 40 English sounds.

15. Basis of the Pronunciation Key. The inconsistencies and conservatism of English spelling make necessary a system of giving clear directions to say the proper sounds. This can be done by assigning one sound only to a letter (a as in bat), combination of letters (ch as in much), or a letter modified by a diacritic (ā as in bate) to distinguish it from other sounds indicated by the same letter (ā as in care, ä as in far). There are in the key 43 symbols to represent the speech sounds of English.

16. Diacritical Marks. The first step in learning to read the pronunciations is to learn the key. There are only 13 special symbols for English sounds; five of these are the so-called long vowels, ā, ē, ī, ō, ū; these symbols are well known and common to most dictionary systems and will cause little trouble. The "short" vowels, a, e, i, o, and u, left unmarked since they are approximately 40 per cent of all vowel sounds, occur chiefly in closed syllables (those with a consonant following a vowel, as in hat, bet, sit, hot, cut). There is no more reason to mark these common vowel symbols than there is to mark d or n or b with a diacritic.

17. The special symbols that must be learned are ä as in far, ā as in care, ė as in her, ô as in order, th as in then (contrast with th in thin), ü as in put, ü as in rule, and ə as in about (ə·bout′). These symbols are put in an abbreviated key at the bottom of every other page so that you may refer to them quickly and learn them easily. See also the full pronunciation key on the front and back end-sheets.

How to Find the Pronunciations

18. The pronunciation is entered in parentheses after the main entry.

ab·a·tis (ab′ə·tis). . . .

19. If there are two (or more) main entries, pronounced the same, the pronunciation follows the second (or last) variant spelling or form.

adz, adze (adz). . . .

20. If a variant form is pronounced differently from the main entry, the proper pronunciation follows directly after each word. In most cases, it is necessary to give only the differing part of the variant pronunciation.

bro·mine (brō′mēn; –min), **bro·min** (–min). . . .

21. If the words that make up a phrase are entered separately and pronunciations are given there, no pronunciation is entered for the phrase.

benefit of clergy. . . .

22. Difficult inflected forms are pronounced in the entry, unless they are separately entered.

for·mu·la (fôr′myə·lə), n., pl. –las, –lae (–lē). . . .

hoof (hüf; hůf), n., pl. hoofs or (Rare) hooves. **hooves** (hüvz; hůvz), n. Rare. pl. of hoof. . . .

23. Run-ons are pronounced when they involve a change in pronunciation from the main entry that is not clear from the syllabication and stress alone.

ge·om·e·try (ji·om′ə·tri), n. branch of mathematics that deals with lines, angles, surfaces, and solids. . . . —**ge·o·met·ric** (jē′ə·met′rik), adj.

cli·mate (klī′mit), n. 1. the kind of weather a place has. . . . —**cli·mat·ic** (kli·mat′ik), adj.

24. When a run-on has the variants of the entry word, and these are variants of stress, the run-on is entered with the stress of the first pronunciation, although either pronunciation is correct.

con·trite (kən·trīt′; kon′trīt). . . . —**con·trite′ly**, adv. —**con·trite′ness**, n.

25. Some words are differently pronounced depending on their grammatical function in a particular context. These pronunciations have been labeled in accordance with the parts of speech shown in the entry.

mod·er·ate (adj., n. mod′ər·it; v. mod′ər·āt). . . .

26. Foreign pronunciations, when considered helpful, are given with a label after the American pronunciation.

au grat·in (ō grat′ən, grä′tən; Fr. ō grä·tan′). . . .

Although it has been considered by some to be fashionable or "more correct" to retain foreign pronunciations, particularly those of French words, the best rule to follow on the pronunciation of foreign words is—if a good, usable Anglicized pronunciation exists, use it! In the pronunciation of foreign words and phrases in this dictionary, emphasis has been placed on providing the reader with a pronunciation he may use comfortably, as (ôr' dérv') for *hors d'oeuvre*. Where a foreign pronunciation is also commonly used, that, too, has been provided and labeled, as (*Fr.* ôr dœ'vrə). See **Bund, concierge, debris.**

27. Accent is indicated in the pronunciations by the symbol ' for the heavier or primary accent, and ' for the lighter or secondary accent, placed *after* the syllable which is to be accented.

hes·i·ta·tion (hez'ə·tā'shən). . . . Some words may be correctly accented in more than one way. Two (or more) pronunciations are given for such words.

ab·do·men (ab'də·mən; ab·dō'mən). . . .

How to Locate a Meaning

28. Order of Definitions. The meanings of words are arranged according to the frequency of their use. Meanings that are used most frequently are put first and those that are less frequent, such as archaic or technical meanings, come last.

If the meaning to be looked up is a common one the reader should scan the first few definitions of the entry. In neutral, *adj.,* the most common meanings are 1–4, and the less frequent chemical, electrical, and biological meanings are given later. This arrangement of definitions according to frequency enables the reader to find various meanings quickly and easily.

neu·tral (nū'trəl; nū'-), *adj.* **1.** on neither side in a quarrel or war. **2.** of or belonging to a neutral country or neutral zone: *a neutral port.* **3.** neither one thing nor the other; indefinite. **4.** having little or no color; grayish. **5.** *Chem.* neither acid nor alkaline. **6.** *Elect.* neither positive nor negative. **7.** *Biol.* neuter. . . .

29. Ways in Which Meanings Are Given. Meanings of words are given in one of the following four ways or some combination of them: descriptive statements (**abatis**), synonyms (**abattoir**), pictures (def. 2 of **abdomen**), explanatory examples (**alive**). Hard words or technical terms with only one or two meanings can be explained by using the first three methods; words with many meanings or closely related meanings require explanatory examples to clarify the meanings.

ab·a·tis (ab'ə·tis), *n., pl.* **ab·a·tis.** barricade of trees cut down and placed with their sharpened branches directed toward an enemy. . . .

ab·at·toir (ab'ə·twär; -twôr), *n.* slaughterhouse. . . .

ab·do·men (ab'də·mən; ab-dō'mən), *n.* **1.** *Anat., Zool.* the part of the body containing the stomach and other digestive organs; belly. **2.** *Zool.* the last of the three parts of the body of an insect or crustacean. . . .

Abdomen (def. 2)

a·live (ə·līv'), *adj.* **1.** living; not dead: *the man is alive.* **2.** in continued activity or operation: *keep the principles of liberty alive.* **3.** of all living: *happiest man alive.* . . .

30. Function of Explanatory Sentences. Many relation words (prepositions, adverbs, linking verbs) cannot be understood readily by merely giving a definition. Consider the importance of the explanatory examples in distinguishing the first two definitions of about: "of"; concerned with" and "in connection with." These very frequent words with a complex network of meanings are difficult to use idiomatically, and great care is taken in this dictionary to make their various meanings clear.

a·bout (ə·bout'), *prep.* **1.** of; concerned with: *a book about bridges.* **2.** in connection with: *something queer about him.* . . .

31. Fitting the Definition into the Context. The best test of the adequacy of a definition is to fit the definition into a context in place of the hard word. If the definition makes the context clear to the reader, the dictionary has done its work well. Find the appropriate definition for the italicized word in the sentences containing the word *encore* at the end of this paragraph by running down the list of definitions for **encore** given below. Notice how the clear numbering of the definitions helps you to find the different senses quickly. "The singer tried hard to get an *encore.*" "Three *encores* are enough for any performer to give."

en·core (äng'kôr; -kōr; än'-), *interj., n., v.,* -cored, -cor·ing. —*interj.* once more; again. —*n.* **1.** demand by the audience for the repetition of a song, etc., or for another appearance of the performer or performers. **2.** repetition of a song, etc., in response to such a demand. **3.** an additional song, etc., given in response to such a demand. —*v.* make such a demand for (a performer, etc.) by applauding. [< F]

32. Special Constructions. A number of words are followed by certain prepositions (**accede**) and some have different meanings with different prepositions (**abound**). These prepositional usages should be learned as an integral part of the definition to avoid incorrect constructions in speech and writing. In this dictionary they are entered in italic type and enclosed in parentheses at the end of the definition.

ac·cede (ak·sēd'), *v.,* -ced·ed, -ced·ing. **1.** give consent (*to*): *please accede to my request.* **2.** become a party (*to*): *our government acceded to the treaty.* **3.** attain (*to* an office or dignity); come (*to*): *the king's oldest son acceded to the throne.* . . .

a·bound (ə·bound'), *v.* **1.** be plentiful: *fish abound in the ocean.* **2.** be rich (*in*): *America abounds in oil.* **3.** be well supplied (*with*): *the ocean abounds with fish.* . . .

33. Definitions with Restrictive Labels. Not all words or meanings are used by every speaker or writer of English on every occasion. The great body of English is common to all users of the language but some meanings are used chiefly by members of certain trades and professions (subject labels), others are common only in certain geographical areas (*Dial., Am., Brit.*), still others are used only on certain occasions—in speaking and in informal, but not in formal, writing (*Colloq.*)—and others are the half-remembered common words of former generations (*Archaic, Obs., Poetic*) which are chiefly found in literary use or in old books. The chief labels are:

a. *Colloq.* = *Colloquial,* which merely means that the word or meaning is more common in speech than in writing. Colloquial English is good English as used in conversation and in those kinds of writing which resemble conversation, and is appropriate for all but the most formal occasions.

get·a·way (get'ə·wā'), *n. Colloq.* **1.** act of getting away; escape. **2.** start of a race.

b. *Slang* arises from a desire for novelty or for vivid emphasis or for unconventionality. Many slang words have short lives, but some prove more useful and become a part of the general colloquial and familiar vocabulary. Until they do, slang words and meanings should be avoided on formal occasions.

Veep (vēp), *n. Slang.* **1.** Vice-president of the United States. **2. veep,** any vice-president.

c. *Law, Elect., Bot., Physics, Electronics,* and similar labels are subject labels and indicate that the word or meaning is used chiefly by the members of a particular profession or trade.

an·dro·gen (an′drə·jən), *n. Biochem.* any substance that induces or strengthens masculine characteristics, as a male sex hormone. . . .

ad·i·a·bat·ic (ad′i·ə·bat′ik; ā′dī-), *adj. Physics.* without transmission (gain or loss) of heat.

d. *Trademark* indicates that a word or meaning is a proprietary name owned by a particular company and valued by it as identifying its product. Sometimes a trademark by common use and wide application to related products becomes a part of the common vocabulary; aspirin was formerly a trademark. Great care has been taken to label trademarks but failure to include the label does not mean that the word is not a trademark.

Plex·i·glas (plek′sə·glas′; -gläs′), *n. Trademark.* a light, transparent thermoplastic, often used in place of glass. [< *pl(astic)* + *(fl) exi(ble)* + *glas(s)*]

as·pi·rin (as′pə·rin), *n.* drug for headaches, colds, etc., C₉H₈O₄. It is the acetate of salicylic acid. [from trademark]

ko·dak (kō′dak), *n., v.,* –daked, –dak·ing. *Am.* —*n.* 1. a small camera with rolls of film on which photographs are taken. 2. Kodak, *Trademark.* a small camera made by the Eastman Kodak Company. —*v.* take photographs with a kodak. —ko′dak·er, *n.*

e. *Dial. = Dialect.* A word or meaning used only in a certain geographical area or by a certain group.

a·nent (ə·nent′), *prep.* 1. *Archaic or Scot.* concerning. 2. *Brit. Dial.* beside. . . .

f. *Poetic.* A word or meaning found only in poetry or in prose that has some qualities of poetry.

ope (ōp), *v.,* oped, op·ing, *Poetic.* open.

g. *Archaic.* A word or meaning rare except in books written in, or in the style of, an earlier period.

a·vaunt (ə·vônt′; ə·vänt′), *interj. Archaic.* begone! get out! go away! . . .

h. *Obs. = Obsolete.* A word or meaning not used at all at the present time. It exists only in old books or books about the past.

cap·ti·vate (kap′tə·vāt), *v.,* –vat·ed, –vat·ing. 1. hold captive by beauty or interest; charm; fascinate. 2. *Obs.* capture. —cap′ti·va′tion, *n.* —cap′ti·va′tor, *n.* —Syn. 1. enchant, entrance.

i. *Am. = Americanism.* A word or meaning originating in the United States, although its use may have spread throughout the English-speaking world.

a·board (ə·bôrd′; ə·bōrd′), *adv.* 1. in or on a ship. 2. *Am.* in or on a train, bus, airplane, etc. . . .

OK, O.K. (ō′kā′), *adj., adv., v.,* OK′d, OK′ing; O.K.′d, O.K.′ing; *n., pl.* OK's; O.K.'s. *Am., Colloq.* —*adj., adv.* all right; correct; approved. —*v.* endorse; approve. —*n.* approval. . . .

j. *Am., S.W.* An Americanism which originated in and is chiefly used in the southwestern United States.

a·do·be (ə·dō′bē), *n. Am., S.W.* 1. sun-dried clay or mud. 2. a brick or bricklike piece of such material, used in building. —*adj.* built or made of sun-dried bricks: *an adobe house.* . . .

k. *Am., S.* An Americanism which originated in and is chiefly used in the southern United States.

pone (pōn), *n. Am., S.* 1. bread made of corn meal. 2. loaf or cake of this bread. . . .

l. *Am., W.* An Americanism which originated in and is chiefly used in the western United States.

ro·de·o (rō′di·ō; rō·dā′ō), *n., pl.* –de·os. *Am.* 1. contest or exhibition of skill in roping cattle, riding horses, etc. 2. *W.* the driving together of cattle. . . .

Both definitions 1 and 2 are Americanisms but definition 2 is used chiefly in the West.

m. *U.S.* A word used more commonly in the United States than in other parts of the English-speaking world, but which originated elsewhere than in the United States.

bowling alley, *U.S.* a long, narrow, enclosed floor for bowling.

n. *Brit. = Briticism.* A word or meaning more common in Great Britain and the British Empire than in the rest of the English-speaking world.

ac·cu·mu·la·tor (ə·kū′myə·lā′tər), *n.* 1. one that accumulates. 2. *Brit.* a storage battery.

o. Common non-English words from other languages used only or chiefly for special purposes, or by people familiar with other languages, are labeled with the name of the language before the definition.

gar·çon (gär·sôɴ′), *n., pl.* –çons (-sôɴ′). *French.* 1. a young man; boy. 2. servant. 3. waiter.

ad in·fi·ni·tum (ad in′fə·nī′təm), *Latin.* without limit; forever.

Word Origins (Etymologies)

34. Selection of Word Origins. We give the origin for all root words when this origin is known. The origin of derivative words may be obtained by referring back to the root word. The origin of the word accession (from a Latin verb that breaks down into the component parts *ad-* to + *cedere* come) may be learned by referring to the root word accede.

35. Placement of Word Origins. The origin of a word is put immediately after all the definitions, in square brackets. Notice that only the ultimate form of the word is ordinarily given and that the various intermediate forms, of interest chiefly to the scholar, that a word acquired as it passed through various languages are ignored, so that a readable and concise history of the word can be given in a streamlined form, with essential information only, for the general reader.

accost . . . . [< F < Ital. < LL, < L *ad-* to + *costa* side, rib]

This word origin may be read "accost comes from a French word borrowed from an Italian word which came from a Late Latin word which in turn was formed from the Latin elements *ad-* meaning 'to' and *costa* meaning 'side' or 'rib.' " The sign < means "from" and may be variously read "comes from," "borrowed from," "taken from," "derived from," or "formed from." The etymologies can be easily read if you read the sign < as "from" and expand the abbreviation of the language. See the complete etymology key on the inside front cover for an explanation of the abbreviations and symbols used in the etymologies.

36. Omitted Forms. For those persons specially interested in the form of words in the various languages a comma is inserted after the abbreviation of the language to show that a form exists in that language which is either exactly or somewhat like the English form. Notice the comma after the *L* in the word origin for **adjacent:**

[< L, < *ad-* near + *jacere* to lie]

This word origin should be read "*adjacent* comes from a Latin word, somewhat similar in form to the English word *adjacent.* It was formed of two parts in Latin—*ad-* and *jacere* which meant 'to lie near.' " Or more simply it may be read "*adjacent* comes ultimately from the two Latin words *ad-* and *jacere,* meaning 'to lie near.' " Many dictionaries lay stress upon giving the actual language form in Latin but we have given rather the root or ultimate meaning in Latin, since the meaning of the parts in Latin may help the reader to understand the meaning in English and give the user of the dictionary some idea of the make-up or composition of the word. The plus sign (+) is used to unite the two parts of a word in these cases.

37. Breaking down Ultimate Form into Component Parts. Breaking down words into their component parts will often help the user to get a root or core meaning of the word and will enable him to understand other words. Consider the two word origins for reduce and produce:

reduce . . . . [< L, < *re-* back + *ducere* bring]
produce . . . . [< L, < *pro-* forth + *ducere* bring]

38. Cross References. Sometimes there is information entered elsewhere in the dictionary that the reader will find useful in reading and understanding a particular word origin. Cross references to such entries are given in small capital letters. For example, words formed from a foreign word and an English word element can be understood better if you understand the English word element. In such cases the word element is given in small capital letters.

biology . . . . [< Gk. *bios* life + –LOGY]
Often there is additional information in another etymology carrying the history of a word farther back. To avoid repetition, cross references in small capital letters are given to the entry where there is fuller information.

eleemosynary . . . . [< LL, < L *eleemosyna* ALMS]
alms . . . . [< VL < L < Gk. *eleemosyne* compassion < *eleos* mercy]
By cross-referring to alms from the etymology of eleemosynary, the reader finds that the Latin word *eleemosyna* meaning "alms" comes from the Greek word *eleemosyne* meaning "compassion," which was derived from the Greek word *eleos* meaning "mercy." Thus, the words eleemosynary and alms have their common derivation in the Greek word *eleos.*

39. Doublets. Because the English vocabulary has borrowed so widely from other languages, there are pairs of words, called doublets, which, though quite different in form in English, go back to the same earlier word.

fragile . . . . [< L *fragilis;* akin to *frangere* break. Doublet of FRAIL.]
frail . . . . [< OF < L *fragilis.* Doublet of FRAGILE.]

Thus, the Latin word *fragilis,* which came into English directly as *fragile,* but was altered in passing through Old French to give us *frail,* is the common ancestor of both these words.

40. Words of Scandinavian Origin. Words taken from the languages of the North and recorded in Old and Middle English are placed together under the generic term Scandinavian (Scand.), and, normally, the Old Norse form is cited. When no Old Norse form is recorded, the Scandinavian language in which the form cited occurs is indicated in parentheses.

skirt . . . . [< Scand. *skyrta* shirt]
skull . . . . [< Scand. (dial. Norw.) *skul* shell]

Synonyms

41. Synonyms are given for words which a speaker or writer may overuse, and for which a substitute word is therefore often desirable. They are also given in order to sharpen definitions and to help the reader distinguish between words which may look or sound alike but be very different in meaning (*council* and *counsel; accede* and *exceed*). These lists are keyed to specific definition numbers and parts of speech, since synonyms exist only for specific meanings of particular words. In able, below, *capable* may be used in place of *able* in the sense of "having ordinary power to do" but not strictly in the sense of "talented." For the second meaning of **able**, which is "talented, clever," either of the two synonyms may be substituted: *an expert lawyer, a skillful lawyer.* The third meaning is concerned with the manner or effect of something done, not with potentiality or present capacity: *an able speech, an effective speech.* By using care to choose synonyms that fit in the right contexts you will learn to use words more precisely and more effectively.

a·ble (āʹbəl), *adj.,* **a·bler, a·blest. 1.** having ordinary capacity, power, or means to do: *a man able to work.* **2.** having more power or skill than most others have; talented; clever: *a supreme court justice should be an able lawyer.* **3.** competently done: *an able speech.* [< OF < L *habilis* easily held or handled < *habere* hold] —**Syn. 1.** capable. **2.** expert, skillful. **3.** effective. —**Ant. 1.** incapable.

Usage Notes

42. Usage notes are given at the end of certain entries, and are preceded by a heavy black arrow. These discussions are concerned with such points as good idiomatic usage, substandard or awkward usage, problems of spelling, grammar, punctuation, literary style, and the nature of language. They are designed to help you make the best possible choice of two or more ways of expression.

con·tin·u·al (kən·tinʹyü·əl), *adj.* **1.** never stopping. . . . ➤ **continual, continuous.** *Continual* means "frequently or closely repeated": *Dancing requires continual practice. Continuous* means "without interruption": *a continuous procession of cars.*

AMERICAN ENGLISH GRAMMAR

Charles C. Fries and Aileen Traver Kitchin

All of us wish to speak and write "good English." For more than a century its teaching has been one of the major concerns of our educational system. To its study all pupils are required to give a large portion of their school time and it is the one required subject of the school curriculum that enjoys almost unanimous support from the general public and school authorities.

Nevertheless, in spite of this general agreement as to its importance, many of us do not understand what "good English" really is. Many of us would doubtless agree with the statement that "a sound knowledge of grammar is important to a person who desires to speak good English." But what do we mean by "knowledge of grammar"? And how is it linked to "good English"? In order to answer these questions we must first of all understand the meaning and purpose or grammar as a science.

THE RELATIONSHIP BETWEEN GRAMMAR AND USAGE

One of the chief purposes of a scientific study of the grammar of any language is to identify and describe the forms and patterns of the language as they are actually used in various situations and by various groups of speakers of the language. The "rules" and "laws" of scientific grammar are not rules and laws in the common sense of something that must be obeyed; rather they are general statements which attempt to describe the ways in which a particular language operates in order to fulfill its communicative function. They are based on careful observation of the language itself and are valid only in so far as they are accurate generalizations. They do not in any way determine or affect the way in which the language is used by its speakers; they are, on the contrary, entirely determined by this usage.

This may sound rather different from the grammar with which most of us are familiar, for we have learned not about the scientific grammar described above, but about the so-called "prescriptive" or "normative" grammar which seeks to impart skill in language (1) through the prescribing of rules for correct usage which are often based, not on what is actually in accepted use in the language, but on what some "authority" thinks should be used, and (2) through the analysis of sentences by a study of clauses, phrases, and parts of speech. It is the tendency of this type of grammar to attempt to fit the language to the rules, rather than the rules to the language. It is because of this tendency that we often encounter a great divergence between the language we actually use, and which we hear being used by educated people, and the language which the "rules of grammar" tell us we should use. In cases of this kind, the scientific grammarian will often insist that the rules are wrong, not the speaker.

For ordinary purposes, if we ignore the special differences that separate the speech of New England, the South, and the Middle West, we do have in the United States a set of language habits, broadly conceived, in which the major matters of the political, social, economic, educational, and religious life of this country are carried on. This set of language habits has thus achieved considerable prestige and therefore furnishes the English usage which it is the obligation of our schools to teach.

HOW OUR LANGUAGE OPERATES

Linguistic forms

Our language is made up of forms (all words are forms, and so also are such elements as "-ing" and "-s" which indicate inflection, plural number, and so forth), and these can be separated roughly into two classes:

The first class includes the words which stand for the things, the acts, the qualities, judgments, times, places, etc. of which we are conscious in the world about us, words like *cat, man, faith, honor; walk, sit, think; big, little, good, slow.* These words are classified, on the basis of the forms which each has, as nouns, verbs, and adjectives. Such words constitute the "lexicon" of the language and are said to have "lexical" meaning. Words such as *here, now,* and *slowly* may also be included in the lexicon, since, in a sense, they are labels for time, place, and manner.

The second class includes forms which do not in themselves stand for things, acts, etc., but which serve to show the relationship between the things, acts, etc. represented by the first class. This class includes words like *the, in, between, of, shall, might.* These words play an essential part in the mechanics or the grammar of our language. They are said to have "relational" or "grammatical" rather than "lexical" meaning and hence are called grammatical items.

In the sentence "The little boy is sitting on a big chair," the words *little, boy, sit, big, chair* belong to the first class and are part of the English lexicon, while *the, is, -ing, on,* and *a* are grammatical items (and are, except for "-ing," of the type called function words).

Relationships of Linguistic Forms

A study of the way these lexical and grammatical forms are used in English involves four chief matters:

A. The first matter to be considered is the kinds of utterances or sentences we make, which may be called the "sentence patterns" of English.

1. There are in English only three major sentence patterns: the statement or report ("John gave a kitten to his brother"), the question ("What did John give his brother?"), and the request or command ("Give the cat to John!").

2. There are many minor sentence patterns, among which are: conventionalized cries ("Ouch!"), answers to questions ("Where is John?" "Downtown."), calls ("Oh, John!"), and exclamations ("What a beautiful cat!").

B. The second matter to be considered is the means we use to indicate in a sentence the performer of the act, the thing affected by the act, and the one to or for whom the act is performed.

John/ gave/ his brother/ a cat.
His brother/ gave/ John/ a cat.

C. The third matter is the way in which we indicate "character," that is, the way in which we describe the things about which we speak.

> John, *who is much older*, gave his *little* brother a *Persian* cat.

D. The fourth of the main points to be considered in a study of English is the means by which we state the variety of times, aspects, moods, and conditions under which an action is performed, that is, the various verb forms and verbal expressions which we have at our disposal to express different types of action.

> John *gave* his brother a cat.
> Tommy *is going to feed* the cat.
> Tommy *feeds* the cat every morning.
> John *has given* his brother a cat.
> John *would give* his brother a cat, *if* he *could find* just the right kind.

Linguistic forms and English grammar

The study of English grammar is a study of the devices English uses to indicate relationships such as those stated above in paragraphs A, B, C, and D. For this purpose our language uses the following three important devices:

A. The Device of Word Order

In the earlier stages of English the relationships between the lexical items in an utterance were indicated to a large extent by the forms of words or inflections. A noun, for instance, had one form when it was used as the subject in a sentence, another form when it was used as direct object, and still another form when it was used as indirect object. As the language changed over the years, however, many of these inflectional forms were gradually lost and word-order patterns became progressively more significant as signals.

1. **The Chief Positions of Noun and Verb in Statements.**

a. Position before the verb. In the sentence "The boy killed the bear," notice that the starting point of the action, the performer of the act or subject, is indicated by the position of that noun *before* the verb. The fact that it is position primarily that signals the subject is illustrated by the following sentence in which, although the words are gibberish, one can easily pick out the subject of the sentence as "mirl" (we are aided here, of course, by the fact that *mirl*, like *boy*, has one of the chief formal characteristics of a noun in that it is preceded by *the*).

> The mirl sooled the pogle.

In some sentences more than one noun precedes the verb but there are various signals which indicate which of the nouns is the subject.

> The *boy's dog* is sitting on the chair.
> In the *afternoon* the little *boy* played in the garden.
> The older *boy*, a handsome *chap*, came to call.
> The *boy* and his *sister* played in the garden.
> The *bread, butter,* and *cheese* were on the table.
> The *stone house* on the corner belongs to John's grandfather.

b. Position after the verb.

If a single noun follows the verb and if it refers to the *same* person or thing as the subject noun, it is an identifying noun:

> John's brother is a *surgeon*.

If a single noun follows the verb and does not refer to the same person or thing as the subject noun, then it represents the end point of the action, the person or thing affected by the act, the direct object.

> The boys crossed the *river*.

Sometimes two nouns follow the verb. In these instances there are also various signals which indicate which noun is "direct object" and which is "indirect object," or "object complement."

> They call the *baby Corky*.
> The children need *shoes* and *underwear*.
> John gave his little *brother* an *apple*.

In this section we have seen how the order of words serves as a device to indicate the relationships discussed in paragraph B on page xxv above, namely, the performer of the act, the person or thing affected by the act, and the one to or for whom the act is performed. We have seen that in English statements, position before the verb is "subject" position, while position after the verb is "object" position, with the indirect object preceding the direct object.

2. **The Chief Positions of a Noun and a Modifier.**

a. Single-word modifiers. Single-word modifiers of a noun (such as adjectives, noun adjuncts) precede the words they modify, but word-group modifiers (phrases and clauses) follow the words they modify.

When a single word with the characteristics of an adjective (that is, inflection with *-er* or *-est* or use with *more* or *most* for comparison) precedes a noun, it is a modifier of that noun.

> a *beautiful* view   a *prettier* girl

When two nouns are used together, often with a word like *the, a, these* before the first noun, the first noun modifies the second. In such cases there is no formal indication of the fact that the first noun is used as a modifier except its position before the second noun.

> a *brick* wall   the *meat* bill
> my *college* course   *school* spirit

In some constructions there are frequently two or even more modifiers for a single noun.

> *fair* and *beautiful* children
> an *easy, accurate* manner

When two or more modifiers are not leveled, the word-order pattern shows the direction of the modification.

> in *reasonably good* health
> *high moral* character

b. Word-group modifiers. In English there are also modifiers that are made up of groups of words. These word-group modifiers immediately follow the words they modify.

> the cat *in the chair*
> a trip *by air*
> the community *where he lived*
> the environment *in which they grew up*

Subordinate clauses are generally introduced by function words like *which, who, that*, but frequently these function words are omitted and then the position of the clause after the noun is all that indicates its function of modifying the noun. Position without function word is sufficient.

Any information *you can send me* will be appreciated.

B. The Uses of Function Words

A second important device for indicating relationships between the lexical items in our language is the use of function words. Some of the more important classes of function words are (a) prepositions (the function words that are used with nouns or pronouns), (b) auxiliaries (the function words that are used with verbs), (c) the words modifying adjectives that become function words of degree, and (d) conjunctions (words which have as one of their functions the signaling of relationship between clauses).

1. Function Words Used with Substantives.

The nine function words most frequently used with substantives are *at, by, for, from, in, of, on, to, with.* These nine occur in about 90 per cent of all constructions using function words with substantives. Other important function words are *about, after, against, before, between, near, over, since, through, under,* and *among.* There are also combinations such as *into, onto, without, within.* Such groups of words as *on account of, for the sake of,* and *in view of* operate frequently as single units and are considered a kind of compound preposition.

These function words bring substantives (primarily nouns) into several types of grammatical relationships. Only the most frequent are illustrated here. Through function words a noun is made to modify (a) another noun ("the cat *on* the chair is John's"), (b) a verb ("the cat is sitting *on* the chair"), (c) a verb and a noun simultaneously ("the little boy received a present *from* his brother"), (d) an adjective ("arithmetic was very difficult *for* John's little brother"), (e) the subject, and the modifying noun stands after the verb *to be* and the phrase functions as a predicate adjective ("but he is happy and *without* a care in the world").

2. Function Words Used with Verbs.

There are two types of function words used with verbs: (a) those that are used with verbal substantives or infinitives (the name of an action, as *run, walk, play*) and (b) those that are used with verbal adjectives, that is, present participles (*playing*) and past participles (*played*).

a. Function Words Used with the Infinitive.

(1) *To.* The function word *to* is frequently called the "sign" of the infinitive, and certainly in present-day English the infinitive is most often preceded by the word *to. To* brings the infinitive into several types of relationships, only a few of which are illustrated here: (a) as a verb or sentence modifier, expressing purpose ("the little boy is running *to see* his new cat"), (b) as object of such verbs as *want, wish, try,* etc. ("he wants *to pull* the cat's tail"), (c) with a substantive preceding, the whole expression serving as an object ("John wants him *to quit* pulling the cat's tail"), (d) as modifier of a noun ("John has a tendency *to preach* to his little brother"), (e) as a modifier of an adjective ("the cat was unable *to escape*").

(2) *Do.* While *do* still retains its lexical meaning of "perform" or "accomplish" in such expressions as "what is John going to *do* tonight?", it more frequently operates simply as a function word: (a) in questions ("*do* you know the name of John's little brother?") and (b) with negative

verbs ("I *don't* know his name"). Two other uses of *do* are (c) the emphatic *do* ("but I *do* like cats") and (d) *do* as a substitute verb, referring to a previously used verb ("John likes cats better than I *do*").

(3) *Shall* and *will,* the so-called auxiliaries of the future tense. *Shall* and *will* are function words used to indicate that the action expressed takes place in the future. Actually, however, English has many different ways of expressing the future, as in "John leaves tomorrow" and "John is going to leave tomorrow." For a discussion of the problems in the use of *shall* and *will,* see their entries in the main text of this dictionary.

(4) *Be.* The function word *be* in its various forms used with *to* and an infinitive may express "plan" or "appointment," as in "he *is to leave*" and "he *was to leave*." With *about* to and an infinitive, as in "he *is about to leave*" and "he *was about to leave*," it expresses an immediate future. With *going to* and an infinitive, as in "he *is going to leave*" and "he *was going to leave*," it expresses near future.

(5) *Have + to.* In the sentence "John has to leave tomorrow," the phrase *has to leave* expresses "obligation" or "necessity" for going somewhere. In such uses as this the verb *have* is said to be a function word of necessity.

(6) *Used + to,* for customary action. In a sentence such as "he *used to sit* there every sunny afternoon," the word *used* is said to be a function word expressing customary action in the past.

(7) *May, might, can, could, would, should, must, ought to* + the infinitive. These words, the so-called modal auxiliaries, are function words used primarily to express attitudes toward the action or state indicated by the infinitive (attitudes such as permission, obligation, possibility, and doubt: "Can I go to the movies this afternoon, Mother?", "You ought to drive slowly when it's slippery," "It may rain tomorrow," "His statement could be true, but I don't really believe it").

b. Function Words Used with Participles.

(1) *Be* in its various forms, with the present participle (the progressive form of the verb). This combination of the function word *be* and the present participle of a verb is used primarily in expressions with a definite time for the action ("I *am writing* a letter to John right now") as opposed to the habitual or general time of the simple tense form ("I *write* a letter to John every Sunday" and "the sun *rises* in the east"). At other times the participle after the verb *be* has more of the quality of an adjective than of an action ("John's departure *was exciting*").

(2) *Keep,* in its various forms, with the present participle, expresses continuous or repetitive action, as in "he *kept writing* furiously all morning" and "the two boys *kept singing* off key."

(3) *Be,* in its various forms, with the past participle, sometimes signals action and sometimes an adjectival quality. Observe the difference in "my knowledge of little boys is very *limited*" and "the kitten *was frightened* by the storm." To call both these verb phrases examples of the passive voice is somewhat misleading. Although the grammatical form of both is exactly the same, only the second one can really be called "passive"; the subject of the sentence is the "receiver" of the act only when an agent of the action is expressed either in the sentence or in the context. The term "passive," therefore, really applies to the meaning of the sentence rather than to the grammatical form of the verb.

(4) *Have*, in its various forms, with the past participle (the perfect tenses). *Have* + the past participle signals that an action has occurred and stands completed within a period of time considered to be the present, as in "what *have* you *done* today, my dear?" and "I *have washed* my hair and I *have baked* a pie." *Had* + the past participle indicates that an act occurred and was completed before some other time in the past, as in "I *had* just *washed* my hair when John came to call."

c. Function Words Used with Adjectives.

(1) *More* and *most*, function words of comparison. At earlier stages of the English language, adjectives were compared by the inflectional endings –*er* (comparative), –*est* (superlative), but for several centuries the function words *more* and *most* have been replacing the older inflectional forms. Today, many of the adjectives are still inflected for the comparative and superlative (*longer, longest; prettier, prettiest*), but most unfamiliar words, new words, and the more learned words are compared by the use of function words (*more beautiful, most beautiful*).

(2) When standing before an adjective, certain words serve simply to intensify or to tone down the adjective which they precede. Notice how the word *pretty* in "a pretty girl" means one thing, while in the expression "a pretty bad girl" it has lost the meaning it had previously and serves only to intensify the adjective *bad*. The intensifier that we use most frequently is the word *very*, as in "that was a *very* good play" and "he was a *very* able speaker." Other words commonly used to intensify or tone down adjectives are *stark* ("stark mad"), *dead* ("dead sure"), *precious* ("precious few"), and *good* ("a good long time"). Many such words end in –*ly*, as in "*practically* impossible," "*perfectly* able," "not *really* necessary," and "*entirely* alone."

d. Function Words Used with Word Groups.

The particular function words with which we will be concerned here are those that join sentences and clauses, that is to say, word groups in which there are two essential elements: (a) a substantive and (b) a verb with inflection for tense (a finite verb). The most frequently used conjunctions are *and, that, which, if, who, as, what, when, while, where*, and *so*. Traditionally the conjunctions are classified into two groups, "coördinating" and "subordinating." But this classification is not particularly important. Each of these function words signals a particular relationship between the clauses which it joins, and what is important is the precise nature of the relationship. For example, it has frequently been said that the conjunction *and* can be used only in an "additive" sense. An examination of the actual usage of educated speakers of English, however, reveals that the function word *and* indicates much more than simple addition. As a matter of fact, when simple addition is meant between the word groups, *also* is frequently added to *and* to make that meaning perfectly clear.

> Her father has been out of work for several months, *and* he is *also* in very poor physical condition.

And is consistently found in the following uses:

(1) Adversative or contrasting use of *and*, as in "John is a blond and Tommy is a brunette."

(2) *And* can introduce a consequence or a result, as in "there was not enough milk, *and* Tommy gave his to the kitten."

(3) *And* can introduce the concluding clause of a condition, as in "give a child a kitten *and* he will entertain himself for hours."

e. **Three Miscellaneous Function Words: it, there, and one.**

The words *it* and *there* (unstressed) operate as "pattern filling" words in certain sentence types.

> *It* rains very frequently.
> Is *it* raining now?
> *There* was an old man at the gate.
> Was *there* anybody home?
> *One* (the function word as distinct from the numeral) appears very frequently with adjectives.
> (Of dresses) I like the two red *ones*.
> (Of books) One good *one* is "War and Peace."

C. The Uses of the Forms of Words

Of all the inflections that our language originally had, only six are left in present-day English. Of these six, only two are vigorously alive; the other four are dying.

1. The Two Major or Live Inflections.

a. **The forms for number.** The contrast of forms to signal plural and singular has, in English, practically disappeared in all parts of speech except nouns and pronouns. The –*s* ending is today the regular plural inflection for the vast majority of nouns. Among those nouns not forming the plural by adding –*s* (irregular plurals) are a few very common and much-used words from older English (*men, feet, teeth, children*). Also some foreign words still maintain the inflectional forms of the language from which they come (*data, alumni, phenomena*).

Since at the present time so few words in English other than nouns have any distinctive forms for number, agreement in number has nearly passed out of the language. The only possibilities for number concord in present-day English are (a) in the use of *this, that, these,* and *those* as modifiers of other words (*this book, these books*), (b) in the use of *am, is, are, was, were,* and of the present indicative third-person singular –*s* of other verbs (*I am, we are; he walks, they walk*), and (c) in the use of the third-person pronouns when they refer to substantives already mentioned ("I had a *book* but I lost *it*; I had two *books* but I lost *them*"). There are situations in present-day English where even the very few number-forms that still survive in verbs are not used in accord with the demand of a formal concord of number. A collective noun like *family* may be followed by a plural verb whenever the meaning stresses the individuals that make up the group rather than the group itself ("My family *are* all going out this evening, each one to a different place"). We often choose the form of the verb in accordance with the meaning of the word rather than in accordance with its form.

The indefinite pronouns (*none, any, everyone, everybody, nobody, anyone, anybody*) are much like collective words. *None* and *any* already occur consistently with both the singular and the plural forms of the verb. The others, although they are still immediately followed by the singular form of the verb, frequently appear with a pronoun referring to them in the plural, as in "did *everyone* have *their* books?" There was a time in the language when the collective nouns were at this same stage of development, that is, they were always immediately followed by a singular form of the verb, but the pronoun referring to them would occur in the plural. Similarly, when a subject consists of two or more words joined by *and* which refer to things that are felt as a unit the verb frequently has a singular form, as in "the organization and work of this office is very complex."

b. The forms for tense. The forms of words which distinguish the past tense of the verb from the present tense provide the second most important use of inflection in modern English. Within the past-tense form there is now no distinction for number or for person except in the verb *to be* in which *was* is used with singulars (except second person) and *were* with plurals (I *walked*, we *walked*, but I *was*, we *were*).

The particular form which has become the pattern for the past tense in present-day English is the suffix which is regularly spelled *-ed* (*raised, saved, raced, walked, nodded, wanted*). In English these "regular" verbs comprise the great body of verbs in the language. In this regular pattern there is no difference in form between the past tense and the past participle (I *walked*, I have *walked*).

There are, however, several groups of verbs that have not yet adjusted themselves to the pattern of tense inflection in present-day English. Among these are such verbs as *bite, drive, freeze, fly, drink, sing, shine, strike, fight, find, be, go, do, sell, teach, think, bring,* and *spend*.

2. Four Minor Inflections, Remnants of Older Patterns.

While the inflections for number and tense are still vigorously alive in the language, the inflections for the so-called "possessive" and "objective" cases, for comparison of adjectives, and for person and mood in the verb are gradually dying out.

a. The genitive inflection. The term "genitive" is used here because this form is frequently used to indicate a relationship other than that of possession or ownership: *John's hat, the man's coat, John's teacher, the man's physician, in a month's time, three days' grace, in a woman's college.*

This genitive inflection of nouns has tended to be displaced by the use of the function word *of,* until, in present-day English, the proportion of inflected genitive forms to this use of *of* is very small indeed; for instance, *the king of England, the effect of heat on rubber, the color of that paint.*

(1) The genitive form of pronouns. Although the genitive inflections of nouns have been largely displaced by the use of the function word *of,* genitive inflections of pronouns still persist. Most pronouns have two genitive forms, one which is used before nouns in so-called "attributive" position ("This is *our* house"), and one which stands alone in so-called "absolute" position ("This house is *ours*"). Not all the pronouns have two forms for the attributive and absolute position. *His* remains unchanged in both positions ("*his* book; the book is *his*").

The genitive forms of the pronouns are used in combination with *self (myself, ourselves),* except for *themselves* and *himself,* which have the objective forms *them* and *him* rather than the genitive forms *their* and *his.*

b. The objective forms. Only six "objective" forms remain in present-day English: *me, us, her, him, them, whom.* These forms do not today constitute effective signals of relationships but usually simply accompany the signals of position. Thus *Who* did you call? rather than *Whom* did you call? It's *me,* rather than It's *I,* is the frequent answer to the question Who's there?

c. The inflection for comparison. *More* and *most* occur more frequently than the inflec-

tional forms *-er* and *-est* for the comparative and superlative of adjectives. The comparative form is not now restricted to use when two things only are being compared, with the superlative being used when more than two things are involved. Speakers of English now use the comparative form in definite statements of comparison with *than* ("John is *older than* all the other children") and use the superlative form in statements without *than* regardless of the number of people or things involved ("John is the *smartest*").

d. Forms for person and mood.

(1) Person. In discussions of grammar the term "person" refers to distinctions which indicate whether the subject of a verb is the one speaking (first person), the one spoken to (second person), or the one spoken of (third person). The pronouns which make this distinction in their forms are therefore called personal pronouns. *I* and *we* are first-person pronouns; *you* is a second-person pronoun; and *he, she, it,* and *they* are third-person pronouns. In older English, verbs as well as pronouns had person-forms. Such a person-form of the verb could be used in a sentence in which no subject was expressed. In present-day English all that is left of the person-forms of the verbs are the present singular forms *am* for the first person and *is* for the third person, and the *-s* ending to indicate the third-person singular present of other verbs, *walks, eats, reads.* With the loss of the older person-forms of the verb, we must look in present-day English to the subject itself to determine the person. Except in commands and requests, English verbs do not now stand alone with no subject expressed. If no noun is used as subject, one of the personal pronouns is used ("*They* live in the country, but *we* live in the city").

(2) Mood. The disappearance of the inflections for the "subjunctive" mood has been accompanied by greatly increased use of the function words known as modal auxiliaries, *may, might, should,* etc. ("I might go" and "he should come soon").

The verb *be* retains today more forms that are distinctly subjunctive than any other verb in present-day English.

The president recommended that they *be* moved to another office.

I asked that my request *be* granted.

If their mother *were* well, the children could go to school.

Actually, however, in situations where such subjunctive forms could be used, they appear less than 20 per cent of the time.

It is evident that such a short study as this can only touch some of the intricacies of the English language, but even from this brief survey we can see that the mechanics of English have changed over the years. Of the three devices used to express grammatical relationships, word order, function words, and inflection, the last is now of much less importance than it formerly was. The first two devices, on the other hand, have become increasingly vigorous, taking over in many instances the functions of inflection. It should always be kept in mind that English, like all languages, is in a constant state of change and that, as has happened many times in the past, forms, use of words, and ways of expressing relationships which are now considered to be "good English" may very well become the "vulgar English" of the future.

PUNCTUATION

Albert H. Marckwardt

Speech is the primary or basic form of language. Writing is a secondary form which has developed only recently, relatively speaking, in the history of mankind. Speech communicates meaning in part by means of sounds of distinctive quality—the vowel of *pit* as distinct from that of *pet* or of *peat*. Speech also employs stress, intonation, or cadence, and pauses between utterances as an integral part of its communicative mechanism.

Most systems of writing are based almost wholly upon the phonetic quality of the speech sounds included in the language. But this is not enough. The four words *we, are, going,* and *now* may be uttered in that order as a plain statement of fact, as a question, or excitedly as an exclamation. In writing, as illustrated by the examples below, the pointing or punctuation is the only means even of suggesting these totally different meanings, clearly indicated in speech by stress and intonation:

We are going now.
We are going now?
We are going now!

The relative length of pause between words may also have a considerable bearing upon meaning. Again the written language has developed certain mechanical ways of differentiating possibly confusing situations. Note the difference between:

the English teaching-staff
the English-teaching staff

In the former example, we may be referring to a staff which is of English, rather than French, German, or some other nationality; in the latter example, we mean the staff which teaches English, without reference to the nationality of its members.

Punctuation thus becomes in a sense an auxiliary to systems of writing, lending to the written word some of the color and body that pause, pitch, and stress add to the spoken.

The word *punctuation* goes back ultimately to Latin *punctus,* "a point," and we may say as well that the purpose of punctuation is to give point to what is written. Isolated words, in and by themselves, are not language. Rarely do they communicate meaning. By putting certain words together and by separating these words from other combinations, marks of punctuation are vital to communication. They might almost be called road markers along the highway of written thought; they guide the reader's mind from point to point in a passage of writing very much as road signs and speed limits channel and control the flow of automobile traffic. Too much punctuation, like needless starting and stopping on the road, can be irritating; too little punctuation, like an unmarked highway, can cause a reader to lose his way completely.

There are, of course, certain marks of punctuation which have no equivalents in the pauses, stresses, or intonation turns of spoken English. Among these are the apostrophe, quotation marks, and the hyphen in some of its uses. The chief use of these marks is often primarily mechanical, as with the hyphen when it is used to break a word at the end of a line or to form compound words (such as *forty-seven*). Another function is to indicate meanings which are in spoken English made clear by the syntax of the sentence, as when *you are* is combined into *you're.* A more detailed discussion of when and how these marks of punctuation should be used will be found below.

Punctuation That Terminates. It is impossible to speak or write ordinary English without using sentences, and it is impossible to speak or write a sentence without giving it an ending. In speech this ending is usually marked by a decided pause; in writing, by a punctuation mark calling for a full stop. A few writers, including Don Marquis's famous archy the cockroach, have sought to write without using punctuation at the close of a sentence, but in such cases these writers have then simply had to devise some means other than punctuation to indicate the end of a sentence. As illustrated below, archy may not have used terminal points, but he nevertheless found it necessary to separate his sentences (or units of language) by putting each one on a different line:

"expression is the need of my soul
i was once a vers libre bard
but i died and my soul went into the
    body of a cockroach
it has given me a new outlook upon
    life"

Most sentences, including this one, are declarations or statements of a fact or condition. Sentences of this kind are terminated by a period. Such sentences are usually grammatically complete, which means that they contain a subject-verb sequence (*John works.*). But we will do well to recall that meaning rather than grammatical analysis is the prime factor in determining what is a sentence. The affirmative replies below are punctuated with periods, indicating a full-stop termination:

"Will you be home by bedtime?" asked
    John's mother.
"Yes."
"Will you have your homework done?"
"Certainly."

The one-word replies here suggest, of course, "Yes, I will be home" and "Certainly I will have my homework done." Inasmuch as this is entirely clear from the one-word statements, these may be properly treated as sentences and closed with periods.

Sentences which ask questions are usually terminated by a question mark. Two examples of such sentences as this are provided by the mother's words above. Note, however, that the same meaning may be conveyed even when the sentences are rearranged as below:

"You will be home by bedtime?"
"You will have your homework done?"

Though normally this word-order pattern is associated with a declarative statement, a speaker may convert it into a question by selecting and employing the appropriate intonation pattern. The use of the question mark performs the same function for the written language. On the other hand, a sentence which is actually a command or request will often be put in question form as a matter of politeness:

Will you be sure to have these letters done by five.

Will you please close the door.

Although a question mark may be used with sentences of this kind, the intent is clearly not interrogative, and a period is more often used.

Sentences which are outright commands may be followed either by a period or an exclamation point, depending on the tone which the writer intends to suggest:

You must be home by five!

You must be home by five.

Both of these sentences convey the meaning of a direct order, but the latter one suggests by its punctuation the intonation pattern of a simple or factual statement rather than an emphatic tone of command.

Some sentences may be exclamations and are in this use followed by exclamation points:

What weather to have for our vacation!

Of all the marks of punctuation indicating a full stop, this one is probably the least used by most people. It is also the one most easily misused. When it is properly and sparingly employed, it conveys a sense of great emphasis, of what might almost be called visual shock; but if it is too often used, it will lose its effect. Before finally deciding to use an exclamation point, one should consider very carefully whether a particular sentence would not be more appropriately concluded by a period. In the jargon of many proofreaders, an exclamation point is called a "bang," and it is the mark of a good writer that he uses it in such a way as not to diminish by too frequent use the explosive force which this suggests.

Punctuation That Joins. Thus far we have dealt with sentences so simple in structure as to require little or no internal punctuation. However, when we begin to deal with two or more related thoughts, we may find ourselves writing compound sentences consisting of at least two main clauses, each of which is itself the grammatical equivalent of a sentence. Because punctuation is an effective way of showing the organization of words into groups, it is often employed as a link between clauses. Clauses may be thus joined in a sentence by a conjunction alone, by a comma alone, by a comma and a conjunction, by a semicolon, or by a semicolon with a conjunction. The kind of punctuation employed in linking separate clauses is dependent upon the closeness of relationship in idea between the compound members and upon the degree of separation which the writer wishes to suggest. Short, closely related clauses require little linking punctuation. Contrasted ideas should usually be separated by some pointing. If the clauses themselves contain a good deal of internal punctuation, a stronger linking element, usually a semicolon, is appropriate. In the illustrative examples below, the elements of linkage in each sentence have been placed in brackets:

He graduated on Friday [and] by Monday morning he was married.

I came [,] I saw [,] I conquered.

He sued for damages at once [, and] his lawyer assured him that his case was a good one.

The foreign minister protested that an apology was not enough [;] his country would insist on reparations.

Stirred by the speaker's tales of insults and injuries to their fellow country-

men abroad, the young men cried out for war [; but] in the little villages in the hills, their wives and mothers prayed for peace.

Because of the bad roads, we arrived much later than we had intended [;] consequently, there was almost no time left for swimming.

Probably most ordinary writing will require the use of no more linking than the first three of the methods here illustrated, especially if the writer is using open, fairly informal punctuation. The third method, comma and conjunction, is very widely employed. The semicolon is, however, one of the basic and most useful marks of punctuation, and may be used (indeed, some authorities have insisted that it must be used) between any main clauses not linked by a conjunction.

Punctuation That Introduces. We do not always begin a sentence or statement by immediately naming the principal person or thing it concerns. Sometimes we find it helpful to begin with a subordinate idea or bit of information, thus placing the principal statement in its proper frame of reference. When this is done, a comma is helpful in showing that the initial group of words is a logically related unit and in suggesting that it has some bearing upon what is to come. This is true even when the introductory element is no more than a single word. Although introductory phrases and clauses are not always punctuated, at least a comma is sometimes necessary to avoid ambiguity, as in the following:

True to his promise, the next day Charles returned the book.

Other examples of introductory punctuation follow:

Midway through one of the smaller rooms, still questing for an elusive presence, she caught sight of someone that she knew.

In those early days, after it became a custom for each family to prepare its own Christmas potion, the quality of the drink depended upon the wealth of the host.

Spring having come, robins are seen frequently.

Mr. Norris, I want to congratulate you on your splendid record.

Oh, he's somewhat of a nuisance.

Yes, now you have the correct answer.

After introductory clauses and phrases of a somewhat formal or extended nature, the colon is used. The colon also usually follows the salutation of a business letter.

Punctuation That Inserts. At times there may be inserted within a sentence certain clauses, phrases, or words which add useful but not absolutely essential information to the idea or statement as a whole. Because they do not affect the central meaning of the sentence which includes them, elements of this kind are termed nonrestrictive. In spoken English, these are marked by intonations and sometimes by pauses. In writing, they are set off from the rest of the sentence by punctuation. In the examples listed below, the nonrestrictive elements have been bracketed:

The king [, who feared a surprise attack,] insisted on mobilization.

John Jones [, a newspaper reporter,] was present.

The boxer [, bleeding,] struggled to his feet.

In these examples, commas have been used to set off the nonrestrictive elements; they are unquestionably the marks of punctuation used most frequently for this purpose. However, there are cases where dashes or parentheses may be used instead of commas. Dashes are most often found in fairly informal writing where the nonrestrictive element conveys information closely related to the word or words immediately preceding:

> The dogs—all eight of them—were at our throats.

Parentheses, on the other hand, are chiefly used where the information conveyed by the nonrestrictive element is related only slightly to the sentence as a whole:

> The prime minister (who was related to the royal family) did not appear for the ceremony.

Special caution must be exercised to place the commas, or whatever other marks of punctuation are used, at *both* extremities of the parenthetical expression.

One must be very careful, however, to distinguish between nonrestrictive elements such as these, which are set off by punctuation, and restrictive elements which establish some important condition or limitation to the meaning of the sentence of which they are a part. Restrictive clauses and phrases are not set off by punctuation. In the following sentences the restrictive elements have been bracketed:

> Dogs [who bite people] are not welcome here.
> The night [before Christmas] is called Christmas Eve.

The bracketed elements above have a definite bearing on the meaning of the entire sentences which include them. They could not be omitted from the sentences of which they are a part without changing the meaning considerably, if indeed the statements could then be said to have left any of the intended meaning at all.

Series Punctuation. When a number of coördinate items—words, phrases, or clauses—modify a single sentence-element, the members of such a series are indicated in the spoken language by the intonation. In writing it is equally necessary to mark the various items in a series. This function is regularly performed by the comma. Examples of punctuation between coördinate elements in series are bracketed below:

> The unceasing [,] shrill [,] nerve-shattering whine of the shells broke the soldier's will to fight.
> Life became for him an unending torture of bitterness [,] recrimination [,] and frustrated ambition.

If the last two in a series of coördinate elements are separated by a conjunction, a comma may or may not be used. In formal punctuation, as in the last example immediately above, the comma is used; in less formal punctuation, as illustrated below, no comma is used:

> The speech was long, dull and meaningless.

In the same way, a series of adjectives are regularly separated by commas, but only if they are really coördinate:

> He was an ambitious, successful young man.

Here *ambitious* and *successful* are coördinate, whereas neither is really coördinate with *young*, for both of them are felt as modifying not *man* alone, but the combination *young man*.

Punctuation That Unifies. It is often necessary to show that two or more words are being used as a unit in modifying another word or words in a sentence, or that a prefix is being attached to a particular word to give it another meaning. This is done, in most cases, through use of the hyphen. In the examples immediately following, the hyphen is used to form unit modifiers:

> A three-year-old child can seldom swim.
> The freedom-hating mercenaries swept into the city.

In the following example, the hyphen is used to unite a prefix and verb. Observe that without the hyphen in *re-dress* there would be the possibility of some confusion:

> If you will re-dress in more suitable clothes, we will see if we can't get him to redress the wrong done to you.

The hyphen is always used in uniting a prefix to a proper name:

> It is obvious that he must have pro-German sympathies, but for that reason alone, one can scarcely be certain that he is anti-French.

The apostrophe is used to indicate that letters have been omitted in combining two words into a single word:

> I couldn't [could not] be there.
> If we're [we are] not careful, we'll [we will] spend more than we earn.
> I'm [I am] not sure that I can keep the appointment.

Punctuation That Indicates Exact Speech. Exact and direct quotation of spoken or written words is usually indicated in writing by quotation marks around the quoted passage. When a paraphrase or summary of a speech or written selection is given, quotation marks are never used, except for those parts of the paraphrase or summary taken verbatim from the original. Quotations which are being cited within quotations are indicated by single rather than double quotation marks:

> The witness took the stand and said: "As I recall it, he said, 'I won't come with you.' Perhaps I am wrong. He may have said he didn't want to come with me."

If a quoted passage is so long that it is broken into paragraphs, quotation marks are put only at the beginning of each paragraph until the last one, which has them also at the end. Any interruptions within the quotation of such an extended passage are, of course, placed outside of quotation marks. It is also possible, when citing an extended passage from a book or other written material, to indicate clearly in the wording of the introduction that the material is being quoted and then to indent from six to ten spaces from either margin until the quotation has been completed. This is recommended only, however, for passages of considerable length. Quotation marks are not necessary where this block style is used.

Punctuation That Indicates Possession. The apostrophe is used to indicate the possessive or genitive form of all nouns and a few indefinite pronouns:

> It is man's duty to defend the right.
> That looks like a child's toy.
> One's instincts are not always the best guide.

In some styles of punctuation, words ending with an *s* or a sound close to it take only an apostrophe; in other styles, such words take an apostrophe and another *s* to form the possessive. For example:

> John Adams' house.

or

> John Adams's house.

However, plural forms ending in *s* take only the apostrophe:

> The cows' condition is deplorable.
> The countries' various resolutions were futile.

The apostrophe is frequently omitted in the names of organizations when the possessive case is implied, and in certain geographic designations:

> Citizens League
> Actors Equity Association
> Teachers College
> Pikes Peak

Punctuation for Special Purposes. Certain marks of punctuation have special uses which are not covered by any of the foregoing sections. Most of these uses are very well known, but mention should be made of them. The period, for example, indicates abbreviation:

> *Dr.* for *Doctor.*
> *Ave.* for *Avenue.*

These and most other common abbreviations will be found entered in the main body of this dictionary and may be used in all cases where abbreviation is proper.

Letters used alone, figures, and words used as examples of themselves all form their plurals by adding an apostrophe plus *s:*

> It is a well-known fact that the *e*'s are the most frequently used of all the letters of the English alphabet.
> The *7*'s and the *9*'s are the figures he transcribes best.
> The *and*'s and *but*'s in his speech irritate me.

Quotation marks are widely used for titles of articles in periodicals, or for chapters or other divisions of a book, the title of the entire book or periodical being distinguished, as noted below, by being put in italic type.

In some written passages it is desirable, for the sake of emphasis or distinctness, to employ italic type. Titles, whether of books, publications, musical selections, or works of art, words from other languages, and words or letters spoken of as words or letters are generally italicized. (On this last point, observe the illustrative examples immediately preceding this paragraph.) In manuscript or typescript, italics are indicated by underlining:

> I suppose you have read War and Peace.
> It is a de facto, not a de jure government.

In written English it is often necessary to indicate that a word has been broken at the end of a line and carried over to the beginning of the next line. This may be done by placing a hyphen at the end of any syllable within the word to be broken unless (1) the word is extremely short (it is seldom desirable to break such words as *money, plenty,* or *early*) or (2) the break would leave a single letter hanging at the end or beginning of one of the two lines involved (never break such words as *emit, adore,* or *heady*). The points at which all words in this dictionary may be broken are indicated in their form of entry.

What Is "Good" Punctuation? Many rules have been formulated for the use of the various marks of punctuation, and people have thought that by simply memorizing these rules they might find a key to good writing. Unfortunately, as teachers of punctuation will be among the first to point out, this is not the case. By acting as a visual aid, punctuation can help one to comprehend a carefully thought out piece of writing, but it cannot supply meaning. If a written composition, be it a letter, set of directions, or a critical essay, seems to lack precision and directness, the writer will do well to consider first of all whether it is properly organized, not whether it is properly punctuated. Ordinarily, meaningful and well-organized writing is not hard to punctuate. One's style of punctuation is generally determined by the type and purpose of the writing. Compared to a sports story in the daily paper, a treatise on physics will be marked by more complex constructions, and accordingly, a greater amount of punctuation. This does not mean that one kind or style of punctuation is better than another. It simply indicates that the precise distinctions in thought and meaning which concern the scholar and scientist require more detailed, complex statement, and hence more detailed and complex punctuation, than the factual, comparatively simple story of a baseball game. The former type of writing is designed to compress a maximum amount of exact and complicated information within a limited space. The purpose of the latter is to provide a simple, easily readable account which will entertain and inform its readers. In both instances, the punctuation has the same function: to aid the writer in conveying his particular message to his readers. Punctuation that performs this function is "good" punctuation; when punctuation fails to realize this aim it is faulty.

A full explanation of each mark of punctuation dealt with in this preface will be found in the main alphabetical list under the entry on each mark. For information on rules of capitalization see the special note under that entry in the main body of the book.

WRITING AND EDITING: MANUSCRIPT TO PRINTED PAGE

Ethel M. Ryan and W. D. Halsey

The first and most obvious requirement of a publishable piece of writing is that it should have something to say which will be interesting or useful to its readers. A second requirement is that it should be prepared in a fashion which will enable the editor or typesetter to work with it. There can be no question that many articles, stories, and book-length manuscripts which were otherwise acceptable have failed to find a publisher simply because their authors neglected to meet this second requirement. An article which is scrawled in pencil on odd bits of paper may contain information fully as important as one which is neatly typed, but it has far less chance of ever appearing in print. Not only is it harder (and thus more expensive) to set such manuscript in type, but there is also the possibility that serious errors may creep into it through misreading of illegible characters. Good common sense will tell us that final manuscript should be as easy for the editor and typesetter to work with as possible.

Even though one may not be a professional writer, many of us today have occasion to work with editors and typesetters on material which will appear in print. It may be that one will have made a speech which is to be printed in a newspaper or magazine, written an article which is to appear in the publication of some society or group, prepared a feature article or news story for a company or school newspaper, or written a short piece of advertising copy for one's business. Regardless of the nature of the material, and whether one is a professional writer or amateur, it is desirable to prepare it and work on it according to the rules outlined below. These rules and principles apply to work by writers, editors, and typesetters all over the United States; their purpose is to produce good printed work.

How to Prepare a Manuscript

Typewritten Manuscript. It is standard practice today to type material which is to be submitted to a magazine or book publisher. In preparing final manuscript for this purpose, an author should pay careful attention to the following:

(1) Use a good quality of bond paper in one of the standard sizes (the most often used, and probably the best, size measures 8½ by 11 inches). A poor grade of paper, particularly one which permits the letters to show through, makes a manuscript hard to read and work on; paper cut in an odd size often makes a manuscript difficult to file.

(2) Use a black typewriter ribbon and change it for a new one as soon as it fails to produce letters which are sharp and clear on the page. More than one manuscript has been rejected with the notation that its typed characters were too faint to read.

(3) Make an original and two carbons in final typing. The original should always be sent to the publisher; the carbons safeguard the writer against possible loss of his manuscript in the mail or elsewhere.

(4) Type on one side of the paper only, use double-spacing between the lines, and leave a margin of at least one inch at the top, bottom, and each side of every page. If in any doubt as to the desirable margin, leave slightly more than one inch, but once the margin has been established, observe it consistently on every page thereafter to the end of the manuscript.

(5) The author should enter his name and complete address in the upper left-hand corner of the first page. Some authors repeat this information in the same place on every subsequent page, while others insert only their names or the title of their work; although this reduces the possibility of confusing pages from one manuscript with those from another, it is not absolutely necessary. The endorsement of the first page, however, is essential on any manuscript submitted for publication. Moreover, unless a publisher has specifically requested or already accepted a manuscript, it is desirable to enclose return postage.

(6) Some typewriters have slightly larger type than others and for this reason produce slightly fewer characters within a line of a given length than a machine using smaller type. A manuscript may be typed in either size, but it is important that a writer should not switch from one to the other within the same manuscript. If he does so he will make it difficult to estimate the number of pages which the manuscript will require in print.

(7) Manuscript pages should always be consecutively numbered. Do not number each chapter or section as a unit by itself; number the pages of a manuscript as a whole in one sequence through to the last page. The page numbers should be clearly typed or written (some writers use a number-stamping machine) in the top margin of each page.

(8) If a short section is being extracted from the work of another author, or if particular works are being cited as sources of information, specific credit should be given either in the body of the manuscript or in a footnote. If the quoted material is only a few words or one or two lines in length, it may be set off by quotation marks; if it is longer, it should be typed as a separate section in block form with an indention of at least six spaces at the beginning and end of each line in the block.

(9) Minor changes in manuscript may be typed or made in ink between the lines, but a page which is heavily marked should be retyped. The reason for adding and correcting material between the lines on manuscript is that the typesetter reads the copy line by line in setting, and material which is entered marginally makes his work enormously more difficult. This is, as the reader will note in a later part of this pref-

ace, exactly the reverse of work in proof, in which all corrections are made marginally. The
following example will show how a manuscript should be corrected:

a publishable pence of writing is that it

should have somthing to say which will be

interesting or useful to its readers. A

second requirement is that it should be

prepare in a fashion which will enable the
                                or typesetter
editor to work with it. There can be no

question that many articles, stories, and

booklength manuscripts which were other-

wise acceptable have failed to find a pub-

lisher simply because there authors neglec-

   ted to meet this second requirement; an

article which is scrawled in pencil on odd
bits of paper
may contain information fully as important

and well presented as one which is neatly

typed; but it has far less chance ever of

appearing in print. Not only is it harder
                                              such
(and thus more expensive) to set manuscript

in type, there there is also the possibility

(10) Particularly with book-length manuscripts, an editor will often suggest deletions, rewriting of certain sections, or other alterations. After these have been discussed and, where desirable, incorporated into the manuscript, the writer's work is sent to the copy editor. It is the copy editor's responsibility to read the manuscript for error in factual data, grammatical construction, sequence, punctuation, capitalization, and consistency. The copy editor in most publishing houses is guided in doing this by a style manual which gives the rules which that particular publisher wishes to observe in these matters, and the writer will usually find that consistent observance of these rules greatly improves his manuscript.

Handwritten Manuscript. Manuscripts in longhand are now confined almost entirely to classroom compositions or themes, and even here (particularly at the graduate level in universities) typing is usually preferable, and often required. However, in those cases where longhand manuscript is acceptable, the following rules should be observed:

(1) Write with a medium-pointed pen in black or dark blue ink. Take special pains to write legibly, and be sure that the letters are grouped so that each word may easily be read as a unit.

(2) Use paper which will take ink without blurring. Be sure it is heavy enough so that the writing will not show through the back. Standard theme paper with lines about one half inch apart is preferred in many schools and colleges.

(3) Leave a margin of at least one inch at each side of every page, write on only one side of each sheet, and number the pages consecutively in the top margin.

How to Work in Proof

An author will often see his work in print for the first time when the publisher or printer sends him what are called galley proofs. These are long sheets (usually covering the equivalent of two or three pages in a printed book) on which is made an inked impression from the slugs or pieces of type while they are in the trays, or galleys, in which they are stored until all copy has been set and all corrections made. In most cases, the printer will already have proofread the galleys and the amount of correction which the author will have to make may therefore be very slight. The rules which an author should follow in working on galleys are given below:

(1) Check for typographical errors and correct them where found. Other errors should, of course, also be corrected at this time, but a careful author does not submit final manuscript which contains very many errors. Authors should not at this stage make corrections which involve merely a reworking or polishing of language. It costs an author little or nothing to move his pen, but it can cost a publisher hundreds of dollars to make the changes thus called for. Typesetters and compositors do not charge for the correction of typographical errors, but an unreasonable number of additional changes (or "author's alterations") will, and quite justly, result in an increased charge for typesetting and composition.

(2) Answer all queries made on the proofs by the proofreader or editor. These will be found written in the margins next to the section of copy to which they apply. If the answer to a query is "no," and if the copy is correct as set, it is enough simply to cross out the query. If it is "yes," or if some additional comment is required, this should be written below the query and circled. If the query requires insertion or change in copy, this should be done in the fashion outlined in the example on page xxxviii.

(3) Each proof should be initialed in the upper right-hand corner by the author after he has finished checking it. This will inform the printer that the author has checked it and noted the corrections which should be made.

(4) All corrections should be made in ink, and great care should be taken to see that they are legibly written.

(5) Each correction should be made in the margin next to the line to which it applies. This is the exact reverse of the interlinear method of correction preferred for manuscripts, and it is extremely important that authors follow this preferred practice in marking galleys. The reason for it is that the compositor, in working on galleys, looks only at the margins of the proof; a change which is not clearly indicated there may well, for this reason, be overlooked.

Following is a list of the special symbols most often used by editors and proofreaders in marking proof sheets. Also shown is a galley proof in which these marks have been properly used to make corrections.

HOW TO CORRECT PROOF

It does not appear that the earliest printers had any method of correcting errors, before the form was on the press. The learned The learned correctors of the first two centuries of printing were not proof readers in our sense, they were rather what we should term office editors. Their labors were chiefly to see that the proof corresponded to the copy, but that the printed page was correct in its latinity, that the words were there, and that the sense was right. They cared but little about orthography, bad letters or purely printers errors, and when the text seemed to them wrong they consulted fresh authorities or altered it on their own responsibility. Good proofs in the modern sense, were impossible until professional readers were employed, men who had first a printer's education, and then spent many years in the correction of proof. The orthography of English, which for the past century has undergone little change, was very fluctuating until after the publication of Johnson's Dictionary, and capitals, which have been used with considerable regularity for the past 80 years, were previously used on the miss or hit plan. The approach to regularity, so far as we have may be attributed to the growth of a class of professional proof readers, and it is to them that we owe the correctness of modern printing. More errors have been found in the Bible than in any other one work. For many generations it was frequently the case that Bibles were brought out stealthily, from fear of governmental interference. They were frequently printed from imperfect texts, and were often modified to meet the views of those who publised them. The story is related that a certain woman in Germany, who was the wife of a printer, and had become disgusted with the continual assertion of the superiority of man over woman which she had heard, hurried into the composing room while her husband was at supper and altered a sentence in the Bible, which he was printing, so that it read Narr instead of Herr, thus making the verse read "And he shall be thy fool" instead of "And he shall be thy lord." The word not was omitted by Barker, the king's printer in England in 1632, in printing the seventh commandment. He was fined £3,000 on this account.

PROOFREADERS' MARKS

∧	Make correction indicated in margin.
Stet	Retain crossed-out word or letter; let it stand.
....	Retain words under which dots appear; write "Stet" in margin.
Stet	
✗	Appears battered; examine.
≡	Straighten lines.
∨∧∨	Unevenly spaced; correct spacing.
∥	Line up; i.e., make lines even with other matter.
run in	Make no break in the reading; no ¶
no ¶	No paragraph; sometimes written "run in."
out see copy	Here is an omission; see copy.
¶	Make a paragraph here.
tr	Transpose words or letters as indicated.
ℐ	Take out matter indicated; dele.
ℐ	Take out character indicated and close up.
¢	Line drawn through a cap means lower case.
℗	Upside down; reverse.
⌒	Close up; no space.
#	Insert a space here.
⊥	Push down this space.
⌷	Indent line one em.
[	Move this to the left.
]	Move this to the right.

⎤	Raise to proper position.
⎦	Lower to proper position.
⫽⫽⫽	Hair space letters.
w.f.	Wrong font; change to proper font.
Qu?	Is this right?
l.c.	Put in lower case (small letters).
s.c.	Put in small capitals.
Caps	Put in capitals.
C&s.c.	Put in caps and small caps.
rom.	Change to Roman.
ital.	Change to Italic.
≡	Under letter or word means caps.
=	Under letter or word, small caps.
—	Under letter or word means Italic.
∼∼	Under letter or word, bold face.
⹁/	Insert comma.
;/	Insert semicolon.
:/	Insert colon.
⊙	Insert period.
/?/	Insert interrogation mark.
(!)	Insert exclamation mark.
/=/	Insert hyphen.
⹊	Insert apostrophe.
❦❧	Insert quotation marks.
ℓ	Insert superior letter or figure.
⋀	Insert inferior letter or figure.
[/]	Insert brackets.
(/)	Insert parenthesis.
—/m	One-em dash.
≝/m	Two-em parallel dash.

LETTER WRITING: BUSINESS AND PERSONAL

John A. Kouwenhoven

Letter writing is the one kind of writing in which all of us engage and which most directly concerns the personal welfare of each of us. One may never write a novel or a play, but one is virtually certain to write letters when seeking a job, when applying for entrance to a college, or when announcing a birth or a wedding. In business particularly, the ability to write a letter which is brief, neat, and to the point is one of the most valuable skills one can have.

The two most frequently used classifications for letters are (1) business letters and (2) personal letters. The chief rules of style and form for both of these classifications are covered below. Anyone who applies these rules will be able to write a satisfactory letter for almost any occasion if he will bear in mind that a letter builds in the mind of its reader, particularly if he is a person whom one has never met, a picture of its writer's personality and habits. A letter which is free of smudges and erasures, and in which the points to be covered have been well thought out and concisely stated, cannot help but convey a good impression of its writer. Some carelessness or untidiness may be forgiven in personal letters to one's friends and relatives (although it is surely more courteous to prepare a neat letter), but in business a poor letter may create in its reader's mind so unflattering an image of the writer as to defeat one's whole purpose in writing.

(1) *Addresses should be written clearly on the envelope.* The name and address of the person being written to should be centered on the envelope; the address (and often the name) of the person writing the letter may be placed in the upper left-hand corner of the envelope. Postal zone numbers, where obtainable, should be included after the name of the city. Instructions for special handling, such as "Air Mail" or "Special Delivery," should be noted on the envelope. It is helpful to the post office if the address of the recipient can be double spaced with the name of the State on the line below the name of the city. If the name of the State is abbreviated (this dictionary gives standard abbreviations, where these exist, for the names of the various States), the abbreviation should be clearly written. However, it is never wrong to write out the name of the State in full, and many people prefer to do so. If a line in the address is required in order to indicate an apartment number or particular department of a company, this should be indicated in the lower left-hand corner of the envelope:

return address ➤	R. N. Jackson 27 West Street Portsmouth 7 New Hampshire
special in- structions ➤	Air Mail
envelope address ➤	Mr. John L. Jones 970 West 4th Street New York 17 New York
additional address ➤	Apartment 3A

(2) *Use as good a grade of stationery as possible.* Good paper costs very little more than poor paper, and vastly improves the appearance of any letter. Printed letterheads are, of course, common on business stationery, and increasingly so on personal stationery, but a perfectly satisfactory letter may be written on plain paper of good quality. Many styles and sizes of stationery exist, but the standard ones are always easily obtainable and proper. Two standard business sizes are 8½ by 11 inches and 6 by 9 inches.

(3) *Typewritten letters: business and personal.* In business correspondence the typewritten letter is standard; in the United States, typed personal letters between friends or relatives are increasingly common, and usually welcome because of greater legibility. Longhand is perhaps preferable in the earlier stages of a friendship, and should probably always be used for invitations, acknowledgments, or other social correspondence of a formal nature. Letters expressing condolence, or otherwise concerning particularly deep sentiment or feeling, should also be written in longhand.

(4) *Margins should be generous and letters centered on the page.* Unless there is some particular reason for not doing so, it is customary to single space the heading, the inside address, and each separate paragraph of a typewritten letter. Two spaces should be left between the single-spaced paragraphs in the body of a letter. If a line in the inside address is so long as to spoil the appearance of the address as a whole, it may be made into two lines. If the line being broken deals with something which must be treated as a unit, the lower line may be indented two spaces:

> The Southern New England
> Commodity Shipping Co.
> 127 Worth Street
> Hartford 37, Connecticut

Note that the name of the State in the inside address is ordinarily written on the same line as the city, unlike the practice preferred for the envelope address. However, if this handling should produce an address which is out of balance, the State may be dropped to the next line:

> Mr. Joseph L. Jones
> Yazoo City
> Mississippi

A little care in the placement of the heading, the inside address, and the body of the copy will enable one to put even a very short letter on paper as large as 8½ by 11 inches in such a way as to create an effect which is pleasing to the eye; a letter which is cramped almost entirely in the upper half of the sheet suggests to its recipient that its writer either didn't know when he started how much he wanted to say, or that he was simply too lazy to try to make the letter attractive.

BUSINESS LETTERS

Most business letters written in the United States today use a modification of the block style.

This pattern for the arrangement of a letter forms, as the name suggests, "blocks" of typescript with no indention on the left. Because it enables a typist to begin a maximum number of lines flush with the left-hand margin, a minimum amount of time is lost in hitting the space bar or tabular key for indentions. In its most extreme form, every unit of the letter (heading, inside address, body paragraphs, etc.) is blocked to the left, but this arrangement, although extremely efficient from the mechanical point of view, tends to produce a letter too heavily weighted on the left to be attractive. For this reason, most companies today use a modification of this extreme style, which permits some indention.

In the pattern letters shown below, a modified block style is used. In the first one, which shows how to write a letter on a sheet which does not contain a printed letterhead, the heading is blocked in the upper right-hand portion of the sheet so as to align with the right-hand margin of the letter. Such a heading should be placed with some regard to the length of the letter as a whole, so that in a short letter the heading will be closer to the middle of the page than in a long letter, but in no case should the heading on a sheet which measures 8½ by 11 inches be more than about three inches or less than one and one half inches from the top of the page. When a sheet with printed letterhead is being used, only the date needs to be inserted. As shown in the second pattern letter below, this is usually put in from three to six lines below the letterhead and aligned with the right-hand margin.

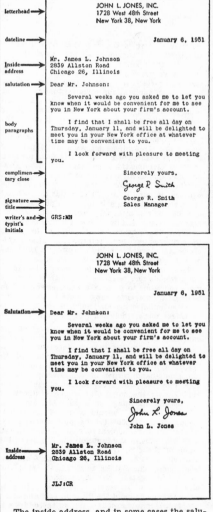

Any of the three letters on this page would be acceptable for all ordinary business purposes. The second one deviates further from the most extreme block style in that it uses indentions for the paragraphs in the main body of the letter.

Some firms, and many professional men, may use the salutation Dear Sir: or Dear Mr. Johnson: at the opening of the letter, and put the full inside address two to five lines below the signature flush with the left-hand margin, as shown in the third letter on this page. This type of letter, which may also be used as a formal personal letter, retains all the information required for the carbon copy in a business letter, but manages to have at the same time some of the appearance of a personal letter.

The inside address, and in some cases the salutation, should include any title (and sometimes the academic or honorary degree) which is held by the recipient of the letter. Where no other title applies or is called for, it is correct to use Mr., Mrs., or Miss (the last is used in letters to women whose marital status is unknown or who are known to be single, and to whom no academic or professional title may be applied). If it is not known whether the person being written to is a man or a woman, it is proper to use Mr. before the name. The abbreviations Mr. and Mrs. are always used, and the abbreviation Dr. is entirely permissible; it is perhaps safest to write out all other titles in full. Many doctors in fields other than medicine prefer the use of Mr. in the salutation, as do many professors and other people in the academic world. Where preferences of this kind are known, they should, of course, be followed; where no preference is known, it is safest to use a title.

Where a letter is being sent to a company or organization, and there is no need to specify a particular individual, the salutation (which is always followed in business letters by a colon) may read Gentlemen: or Dear Sirs:. If the points dealt with by the letter may be expected to concern a particular department of the company, this may be noted two lines below the inside address and two lines above the salutation:

> John L. Jones, Inc.
> 1728 West 48th Street
> New York 38, New York

double spaced ➤
> Attention: Personnel Department

double spaced ➤
> Gentlemen:

If some particular subject is involved, this may be noted as follows:

> John L. Jones, Inc.
> 1728 West 48th Street
> New York 38, New York

> Subject: Display Advertising

> Gentlemen:

The complimentary close in business letters has been vastly simplified from the elaborate forms which once prevailed. The two forms now most often used in the United States are probably *Sincerely yours* and *Yours truly*, both of which may be varied slightly, as with *Very truly yours* or *Yours sincerely*. Official correspondence, or correspondence with some distinguished person, may use *Respectfully yours* or *Very respectfully*. Only the first letter of the first word is capitalized in a complimentary close, and the phrase as a whole is always followed by a comma.

Signatures to business letters are usually placed immediately over the name in typescript, beneath which the title or position of the person signing the letter is also often indicated. The block style is entirely proper here, and is used in the examples below:

Sincerely yours,

John Smith

John Smith
Advertising Manager

Sincerely yours,

J. L. Jones, Inc.

John Smith

John Smith
Advertising Manager

The chief purpose of a business letter is to convey information of some sort to its recipient, but a business letter also provides, through its carbon copy or copies (some firms regularly make several carbon copies of certain kinds of correspondence), a record of the matters dealt with and decisions made, with the name and address of the person written to, the date of writing, and the name and position of the person writing. It is customary to show the initials of both writer and typist at the left-hand margin two lines below the signature. The initials of the writer are placed first: JS:mn, JS/mn, JS:MN, and JS/MN are four acceptable ways of doing this.

Although the various styles and conventions which have been covered above are acceptable for any kind of business use, it is probable that the "house style" of a particular company or organization will be found to require a slightly different handling of certain parts of a letter. The difference will not, in all probability, be very great; very few companies in the United States now follow a style of correspondence which is not based upon the same principles as have been used in preparing the patterns here shown. However, it is always advisable for a person just starting his employment with a particular company to familiarize himself with the particular style preferred by his employer, either by asking questions of those who know the style or by glancing over letters which have gone out under the letterhead of that company.

PERSONAL LETTERS

Many letters to one's friends and relatives constitute a kind of informal written conversation. To a great extent, therefore, the standards for spoken conversation may be applied to such letters. One may be extremely informal, and even casual, with a classmate or other close friend in one's own generation; with an older person, such as a teacher, one's letter, although still informal, would properly and naturally have a more respectful tone. A young man is perhaps equally anxious to please his fiancée and her mother, but he will hardly attempt to do so with the same kind of letter. Here, as in conversation, common sense and good taste are the best possible guides.

Personal letters between people who regularly write each other need no heading other than the date; letters between people who are not closely acquainted, or who write each other infrequently, should include the address in the heading. Not everyone keeps an address book, and failure to give one's address may make it impossible for an occasional correspondent to reply to one's letter.

The salutation in a personal letter may range from great informality (Dear Joe,) to comparative formality (Dear Mr. Jones:). The comma (or sometimes a dash) may be used with very informal salutations, while the colon is placed after those which are more formal. In cases which require great formality, as with an older person whom one knows only slightly, the form My dear Mr. Jones: is often used. The complimentary close, like the salutation, may range from the extreme informality of Yours, to the formality of Sincerely yours.

Many personal letters to editors of newspapers or the like are written as "open letters," which means that the writer will permit (and usually hopes for) their publication in a newspaper or some other medium of public information. Such letters are one means of drawing general attention to some matter of public interest. They should be well organized and written in a courteous, dignified manner, although if criticism of some public policy is the purpose of the letter it may (and should) be forthrightly expressed. The preferred form for addressing the editor of a particular paper may be determined by looking at the letter column of that paper.

One type of personal correspondence for which certain very definite rules exist is that known as social correspondence. An invitation to a party or to a wedding is a form of social correspondence, and the first (and possibly most important) rule for the recipient of such an invitation is that he should acknowledge it. The form of the acknowledgment may range from an informal note to a highly formal one cast in the third person. Examples of all of these are shown below.

Note that the formal acceptance follows the same arrangement as the note of invitation. If an engraved note of invitation is being used, it is desirable to seek and follow the advice of the engraver as to the style of type, the size and kind of stationery, and the arrangement of the lines.

Dear Mary,

My cousin Karen will be staying with us for a few days next week and I have planned a buffet supper for her on Thursday evening at seven o'clock so that she may meet my friends. I should be delighted if you could join us. I hope you will let me know that you can.

Yours,
Barbara

Mr. and Mrs. Jonathan L. Jones
request the pleasure
of the company of
Miss Barbara L. Smith
at a reception
in honor of
Miss Karen Newton,
on Friday, the twelfth of May,
at eight o'clock in the evening,
R.S.V.P.

Dear Barbara,

Thank you for your very kind invitation to the buffet supper you are giving next Thursday for your cousin. I shall be very happy indeed to come, and look forward with pleasure to meeting the cousin you have told me so much about.

Cordially yours,
Mary

Miss Barbara L. Smith accepts with pleasure the very kind invitation of Mr. and Mrs. Jonathan L. Jones to a reception in honor of Miss Karen Newton on Friday, the twelfth of May at eight o'clock in the evening.

SPECIAL FORMS OF ADDRESS

Listed below are various forms of address and salutation which may be used for letters to various public officials, religious dignitaries, and the like. The complimentary close which is used for these various letters may be any one of the various formal types: "Respectfully yours," "Very truly yours," or "Sincerely yours." A Catholic writing to a dignitary of the Roman Catholic Church will usually add "in Christ" if he uses either the first or third of the forms listed. Slight deviations from these forms are permissible if they do not alter the respectful tone of the letter; when in doubt it is desirable to follow without any change the forms here shown:

Dignitary Being Addressed	Inside Address	Salutation	Complimentary Close
President of the United States	The President The White House Washington 25, D.C.	Sir: (formal) My dear Mr. President: (less formal)	Very respectfully yours,
Member of the Cabinet	The Honorable (full name) Secretary of State Washington 25, D.C.	Sir: (formal) My dear Mr. Secretary: (less formal)	Very truly yours,
Senator of the United States (or of a State)	The Honorable (full name) United States (or State) Senate Washington 25, D.C. (or capital city and State)	Sir: (formal) My dear Senator (name): (less formal)	Very truly yours,
Congressman	The Honorable (full name) House of Representatives Washington 25, D.C.	Sir: (formal) My dear Mr. (name): (less formal)	Very truly yours,

Dignitary Being Addressed	Inside Address	Salutation	Complimentary Close
American Ambassador	The Honorable (full name) American Ambassador London, England	Sir: (formal) My dear Mr. Ambassador: (less formal)	Very truly yours,
Justice (or Chief Justice) of the Supreme Court of the United States (or of a State)	The Honorable (full name) Associate (or Chief) Justice of the United States (or State) Supreme Court Washington 25, D.C. (or city and State)	Sir: (formal) My dear Mr. Justice: (less formal)	Very truly yours,
Governor of a State	The Honorable (full name) Governor of (State) (capital city and State)	Sir: (formal) My dear Governor (name): (less formal)	Very truly yours,
Member of a State Legislature (except a State Senate)	The Honorable (full name) Member of Assembly (or other name of legislature) (capital city and State)	Sir: (formal) My dear Mr. (name): (less formal)	Very truly yours,
Judge (except of a Supreme Court)	The Honorable (full name) (name of court) (city and State)	Sir: (formal) My dear Judge (name): (less formal)	Very truly yours,
Mayor	The Honorable (full name) Mayor of (city) (city and State)	Sir: (formal) My dear Mr. Mayor: (less formal)	Very truly yours,
Foreign Ambassador or Minister	His Excellency (full name) Ambassador of (country) Washington, D.C.	My dear Mr. Ambassador:	Very truly yours,
American (or foreign) Consul	(full name), Esq. American (or other) Consul (city and State or country)	My dear Mr. Consul:	Very truly yours,
Cardinal of the Roman Catholic Church	His Eminence (first name) Cardinal (last name) Archbishop (or other title) of (city, etc.) (city and State)	Your Eminence:	Respectfully yours, (in Christ is usually added if the writer is a Catholic)
Bishop of the Roman Catholic Church	The Most Reverend (full name) Bishop of (diocese) (city and state)	Your Excellency:	Sincerely yours,
Bishop of the Methodist Church	Bishop (full name) (city and state)	Dear Bishop (name):	Sincerely yours,
Bishop of the Protestant Episcopal Church	The Right Reverend (full name) Bishop of (diocese) (city and state)	Dear Bishop (name):	Sincerely yours,
Monsignor of the Roman Catholic Church	The Right Reverend Msgr. (full name) (city and state)	Right Reverend Monsignor:	Sincerely yours,
Protestant Minister	Rev. (full name) (street address, city, and State)	My dear Mr. (surname):	Sincerely yours,
Roman Catholic Priest	The Reverend (full name) (street address, city, and State)	My dear Father (surname):	Sincerely yours,
Rabbi	Rabbi (full name) (street address, city, and State)	My dear Rabbi (surname):	Sincerely yours,

Note: Wherever full name is called for above, initials and last name may also be used.

A DICTIONARY
OF THE
ENGLISH LANGUAGE

A, a (ā), *n., pl.* A's; a's. **1.** the first letter of the alphabet. **2.** *Music.* the sixth note in the scale of C major.

a (ə; *stressed* ā), *adj. or indefinite article.* **1.** any: *a tree.* **2.** one: *a pound of butter.* **3.** a certain; a particular: *two at a time.* **4.** to or for each: *ten dollars a day.* **5.** a single: *not a one.* [var. of *an¹*] ➤ A is used before words pronounced with an initial consonant sound whether or not that consonant is shown by the spelling, as in *a man, a year, a union, a hospital.* Now we usually write *a hotel* or *a historian* but some people use *an* in such cases.

a-¹, *prefix.* not; without, as in *atonal,* without tone. [< Gk.; *a*– becomes *an*– before a vowel or *h*] ➤ a– is of Greek origin and is used in words taken directly, or through Latin, from Greek, as in *apathy.* It is also used as a naturalized English prefix in new formations, as in *achromatic.* a–, called alpha privative, corresponds to English un– and Latin in–.

a-², *prefix.* **1.** in; on; to, as in *abed.* **2.** in the act of ——ing, as in *a-fishing.* [OE *an, on*]

A, 1. *Physics.* angstrom unit. **2.** *Chem.* argon.

a., 1. about. **2.** acre; acres. **3.** adjective.

A 1, *Colloq.* A one.

Aa·chen (ä′ʜᴇn), *n.* city in W Germany. French, Aix-la-Chapelle.

aard·vark (ärd′värk′), *n.* a burrowing African mammal that eats ants and termites. [< Afrikaans < Dutch *aarde* earth + *vark* pig]

Aardvark (ab. 6 ft. long)

Aar·on (âr′ən), *n. Bible.* the brother of Moses and first high priest of the Jews.

ab-, *prefix.* from; away; off, as in *abnormal, abduct, abjure.* [< L ab, prep.; *ab*– appears as *a*– before *m* and *v*, and *abs*– before *c* and *t*. Akin to Greek *apo*– from, and English *of* and *off*.]

A.B., Bachelor of Arts. Also, **B.A.**

a·ba·cá (ä′bə·kä′), *n.* **1.** hemp made from the fibers of a Philippine banana plant; Manila hemp. **2.** the plant itself. [< Malay]

a·back (ə·bak′), *adv.* **1.** toward the back. **2.** taken aback, suddenly surprised.

ab·a·cus (ab′ə·kəs), *n., pl.* -cus·es, -ci (-sī) frame with rows of counters or beads that slide back and forth, used for calculating. [< L < Gk. *abax*]

a·baft (ə·baft′; ə·bäft′), *Naut.* —*prep.* back of; behind. —*adv.* toward or at the stern.

ab·a·lo·ne (ab′ə·lō′nē), *n. Am.* an edible mollusk, with a large, rather flat shell lined with mother-of-pearl. [< Am. Sp. *abulón* < Am. Ind. *aulun*]

a·ban·don¹ (ə·ban′dən), *v.* **1.** give up entirely: *abandon a career.* **2.** leave without intending to return to; desert: *abandon one's home.* **3.** yield (oneself) completely to a feeling, impulse, etc.): *abandon oneself to grief.* [< OF *a bandon* at liberty] —a·ban′don·er, *n.* —a·ban′don·ment, *n.* —**Syn. 1.** renounce, relinquish. **3.** forsake. **3.** succumb, surrender.

a·ban·don² (ə·ban′dən), *n.* freedom from conventional restraint. [< F]

a·ban·doned (ə·ban′dənd), *adj.* **1.** deserted; forsaken. **2.** shamelessly wicked. —a·ban′doned·ly, *adv.*

a·base (ə·bās′), *v.,* a·based, a·bas·ing. make lower in rank, condition, or character; degrade: *a traitor abases himself.* [< OF < LL, < L *ad*– + LL *bassus* low] —a·base′ment, *n.*

a·bash (ə·bash′), *v.* embarrass and confuse. [< OF *esbair* be astonished] —a·bashed′, *adj.* —a·bash′ment, *n.* —**Syn.** disconcert, chagrin.

a·bate (ə·bāt′), *v.,* a·bat·ed, a·bat·ing. **1.** make less: *the medicine abated his pain.* **2.** become less: *the storm has abated.* **3.** *Law.* put an end to (a nuisance, an action, or a writ). **4.** deduct. **5.** omit. [< OF *abatre* beat down] —a·bat′a·ble, *adj.* —a·bate′ment, *n.* —a·bat′er, *n.* —**Syn. 1, 2.** decrease, diminish.

ab·a·tis (ab′ə·tis), *n., pl.* ab·a·tis. barricade of trees cut down and placed with their sharpened branches directed toward an enemy. [< F]

ab·at·toir (ab′ə·twär; -twôr), *n.* slaughterhouse. [< F]

ab·ba·cy (ab′ə·si), *n., pl.* -cies. **1.** position, term of office, or district of an abbot. **2.** an abbey. [< LL *abbatia.* See ABBOT.]

ab·bé (ab′ā; a·bā′), *n.* in France: **1.** an abbot. **2.** any clergyman, esp. a priest. [< F]

ab·bess (ab′is), *n.* woman at the head of a community of nuns. [< OF < LL *abbatissa*]

ab·bey (ab′i), *n., pl.* -beys. **1.** the building or buildings where monks or nuns live a religious life ruled by an abbot or abbess; a monastery or convent. **2.** the monks or nuns as a group. **3.** building that was once an abbey or a part of an abbey. [< OF < LL *abbatia*]

ab·bot (ab′ət), *n.* man at the head of an abbey of monks. [OE < LL < LGk. < Aramaic *abbā* father] —ab′bot·ship, *n.*

abbrev., abbr., abbreviation.

ab·bre·vi·ate (ə·brē′vi·āt), *v.,* -at·ed, -at·ing. **1.** make (a word or phrase) shorter so that a part stands for the whole: *abbreviate "hour" to "hr."* **2.** make briefer. [< L, < *ad*– + *brevis* short. Doublet of ABRIDGE.] —ab·bre′vi·a·tor, *n.* —**Syn. 2.** condense.

ab·bre·vi·a·tion (ə·brē′vi·ā′shən), *n.* **1.** shortened form of a word or phrase standing for the whole: *"in." is an abbreviation of "inch."* **2.** act of shortening; abridgment. ➤ **period with abbreviation.** Naturally a writer intends to use a period after an abbreviation and omitting it is a careless slip, but a pretty common careless slip. Some publishers do not use a period after an abbreviation that is to be followed by a colon (as *i.e.:*). There is a growing tendency today not to use a period after an abbreviation that ends with the last letter of the word abbreviated, that is, a word which really is a contraction: *Dr, Mr, Mrs, vs, Wm.* This is more common in British than in American usage.

ABC (ā′bē′sē′), *n., pl.* ABC's. **1.** elementary principles. **2.** ABC's, the alphabet.

ab·di·cate (ab′də·kāt), *v.,* -cat·ed, -cat·ing. **1.** give up or renounce formally: *the king abdicated*

āge, cāre, fär; ēqual, tėrm; īce; ōpen, ôrder; pùt, rüle, ūse; ᵺ, then; ə=a in about.

his throne. **2.** renounce office or power: *why did the king abdicate?* [< L, < *ab-* away + *dicare* proclaim] —**ab′di·ca′tion,** *n.* —**ab′di·ca′tor,** *n.*

ab·do·men (ab′də·mən; ab-dō′mən), *n.* **1.** *Anat., Zool.* the part of the body containing the stomach and other digestive organs; belly. **2.** *Zool.* the last of the three parts of the body of an insect or crustacean. [< L]

HEAD
THORAX
ABDOMEN

Abdomen (def. 2)

ab·dom·i·nal (ab·dom′ə-nəl), *adj.* of, in, or for the abdomen. —**ab·dom′i·nal·ly,** *adv.*

ab·duce (ab·dūs′; -dūs′), *v.,* –duced, –duc·ing. lead away; abduct.

ab·duct (ab·dukt′), *v.* **1.** carry away (a person) unlawfully or by force; kidnap. **2.** pull (a part of the body) away from its usual position. [< L, < *ab-* away + *ducere* lead] —**ab·duc′tion,** *n.* —**ab·duc′tor,** *n.* —**Ant.** 2. adduct.

a·beam (ə·bēm′), *adv.* directly opposite to the middle part of a ship's side.

a·bed (ə·bed′), *adv.* in bed.

A·bel (ā′bəl), *n. Bible.* second son of Adam and Eve, killed by his older brother Cain.

Ab·é·lard (ab′ə·lärd), *n.* Pierre, 1079–1142, French philosopher and teacher.

Ab·er·deen (ab′ər·dēn′), *n.* city in E Scotland. —**Ab·er·do·ni·an** (ab′ər·dō′ni·ən), *adj., n.*

ab·er·rant (ab·er′ənt), *adj.* deviating from what is regular, normal, or right. [< L, < *ab-* away + *errare* wander] —**ab·er′rance, ab·er′ran·cy,** *n.*

ab·er·ra·tion (ab′ər·ā′shən), *n.* **1.** deviation from the right path or usual course of action. **2.** deviation from a standard or type. **3.** temporary mental disorder. **4.** the failure of rays of light coming from one point to converge to one focus. —**ab′er·ra′tion·al,** *adj.*

a·bet (ə·bet′), *v.,* a·bet·ted, a·bet·ting. encourage or help, esp. in something wrong. [< OF *abeter* arouse < L *ad-* + Frankish *bētan* cause to bite] —**a·bet′ment,** *n.* —**a·bet′tor, a·bet′ter,** *n.* —**Syn.** support, assist.

a·bey·ance (ə·bā′əns), *n.* temporary inactivity: *hold the question in abeyance.* [< AF < OF *abeance* expectation < L *ad-* at + VL *batare* gape] —**a·bey′ant,** *adj.*

ab·hor (ab·hôr′), *v.,* –horred, –hor·ring. feel disgust or hate for; detest. [< L, < *ab-* from + *horrere* shrink] —**ab·hor′rer,** *n.* —**Syn.** loathe, abominate. —**Ant.** admire.

ab·hor·rence (ab·hôr′əns; -hor′–), *n.* **1.** a feeling of very great dislike. **2.** something detested.

ab·hor·rent (ab·hôr′ənt; -hor′–), *adj.* **1.** causing horror; disgusting; repugnant (*to*). **2.** feeling disgust or hate (*of*). **3.** remote in character (*from*). —**ab·hor′rent·ly,** *adv.*

a·bide (ə·bīd′), *v.,* a·bode or a·bid·ed, a·bid·ing. **1.** continue to stay. **2.** dwell. **3.** put up with: *she cannot abide dirt.* **4.** wait for. **5.** endure. **6.** abide by, a. accept and follow out. b. remain faithful to. [OE *ābidan* stay on, and *onbīdan* wait for] —**a·bid′er,** *n.* —**Syn.** 3. bear, stand.

a·bid·ing (ə·bīd′ing), *adj.* continuing; lasting. —**a·bid′ing·ly,** *adv.* —**a·bid′ing·ness,** *n.*

Ab·i·djan (ab′i·jän′), *n.* capital of the Ivory Coast Republic, in the SE part.

a·bil·i·ty (ə·bil′ə·ti), *n., pl.* –ties. **1.** power to do or act in any relation: *give according to your ability.* **2.** skill: *mechanical ability.* **3.** power to do some special thing; talent: *musical ability, natural abilities.* [< F < L. See ABLE.] —**Syn.** 1. capacity. 2. cleverness. 3. aptitude. ➤ *Ability* is followed by *to* and an infinitive rather than *of* (*ability to do,* not *of doing*) or *in* and a noun: *ability to design buildings; ability in arithmetic.*

ab·ject (ab′jekt; ab·jekt′), *adj.* **1.** wretched; miserable. **2.** deserving contempt. [< L, < *ab-* down + *jacere* throw] —**ab·jec′tion,** *n.* —**ab·ject·ly** (ab·jekt′li; ab′jekt·li), *adv.* —**ab·ject′ness,** *n.* —**Syn.** 2. contemptible, despicable.

ab·jure (ab·jur′), *v.,* –jured, –jur·ing. renounce on oath; repudiate. [< L, < *ab-* away + *jurare* swear] —**ab′ju·ra′tion,** *n.* —**ab·jur·a-**

to·ry (ab·jur′ə·tô′ri, -tō′–), *adj.* —**ab·jur′er,** *n.* —**Syn.** forswear.

abl., ablative.

ab·la·tive (ab′lə·tiv), *n.* **1.** the case in Latin expressing removal or separation. **2.** a word or construction in this case. [< L *ablativus* < *ab-* away + *ferre* carry]

a·blaze (ə·blāz′), *adv., adj.* blazing.

a·ble (ā′bəl), *adj.,* a·bler, a·blest. **1.** having ordinary capacity, power, or means to do: *a man able to work.* **2.** having more power or skill than most others have; talented; clever: *a supreme court justice should be an able lawyer.* **3.** competently done: *an able speech.* [< OF < L *habilis* easily held or handled < *habere* hold] —**Syn.** 1. capable. 2. expert, skillful. 3. effective. —**Ant.** 1. incapable.

-able, *suffix.* **1.** that can be ——ed; able to be ——ed: *obtainable = that can be obtained.* **2.** likely to or suitable for: *comfortable = suitable for comfort.* **3.** inclined to: *peaceable = inclined to peace.* **4.** deserving to be ——ed: *lovable = deserving to be loved.* See **-ible.** [< OF < L *-abilis*] ➤ The common and useful suffix **-able** appears in a number of words with the spelling **-ible.** *-able* is the living suffix and is much more frequent than *-ible* and should be used in coining occasional words like *jumpable.* *-able* is attached to verbs (*actable*), nouns (*actionable*), and even verbal phrases (*get-at-able*) to form adjectives.

a·ble-bod·ied (ā′bəl·bod′id), *adj.* physically fit and competent; strong and healthy.

Able Day, *Am.* day of the Bikini atom bomb test, June 30, 1946. Also, **A-day.** [< *able,* the signaler's word for the letter *a,* + *day*]

a·bloom (ə·blüm′), *adv., adj.* in bloom.

ab·lu·tion (ab·lü′shən), *n.* **1.** a washing of one's person. **2.** washing or cleansing as a religious ceremony of purification. **3.** the liquid used. [< L, < *ab-* away + *luere* wash]

a·bly (ā′bli), *adv.* with skill or ability.

ab·ne·gate (ab′nə·gāt), *v.,* –gat·ed, –gat·ing. deny (anything) to oneself; renounce; give up. [< L, < *ab-* off, away + *negare* deny] —**ab′ne·ga′tion,** *n.* —**ab′ne·ga′tor,** *n.*

ab·nor·mal (ab·nôr′məl), *adj.* deviating from the normal, the standard, or a type; markedly irregular; unusual. [< AB- from + NORMAL] —**ab·nor′mal·ly,** *adv.* —**ab·nor′mal·ness,** *n.* —**Syn.** exceptional.

ab·nor·mal·i·ty (ab′nôr·mal′ə·ti), *n., pl.* –ties. **1.** abnormal thing. **2.** abnormal condition.

a·board (ə·bôrd′; ə·bōrd′), *adv.* **1.** in or on a ship. **2.** *Am.* in or on a train, bus, airplane, etc. **3.** all aboard, everybody on (conductor's call directing passengers to enter a train, bus, etc.). **4.** alongside. —*prep.* on board of.

a·bode (ə·bōd′), *n.* place to live in; dwelling. —*v.* pt. and pp. of abide. [OE *ābād*]

a·bol·ish (ə·bol′ish), *v.* do away with (a law, institution, or custom) completely: *abolish slavery.* [< F *abolir* < L *abolere* destroy] —**a·bol′ish·a·ble,** *adj.* —**a·bol′ish·er,** *n.* —**a·bol′ish·ment,** *n.* —**Syn.** suppress.

ab·o·li·tion (ab′ə·lish′ən), *n.* **1.** act or fact of abolishing. **2.** *Am., Hist.* suppression of Negro slavery. —**ab′o·li′tion·ism,** *n.* —**ab′o·li′tion·ist,** *n.*

ab·o·ma·sum (ab′ə·mā′səm), **ab·o·ma·sus** (-səs), *n.* the fourth stomach of cows, sheep, and other cud-chewing animals. [< L]

A-bomb (ā′bom′), *n.* the atomic bomb.

a·bom·i·na·ble (ə·bom′nə·bəl; ə·bom′ə·nə-), *adj.* **1.** causing disgust; loathsome. **2.** unpleasant. —**a·bom′i·na·ble·ness,** *n.* —**a·bom′i·na·bly,** *adv.* —**Syn.** 1. detestable, odious, revolting.

a·bom·i·nate (ə·bom′ə·nāt), *v.,* –nat·ed, –nat·ing. **1.** feel disgust for; abhor; detest. **2.** dislike. [< L, deplore as an ill omen, < *ab-* off + *ominari* prophesy < *omen* omen] —**a·bom′i·na′tor,** *n.* —**Syn.** 1. loathe, despise, hate.

a·bom·i·na·tion (ə·bom′ə·nā′shən), *n.* **1.** a disgusting thing. **2.** a shamefully wicked action or custom. **3.** a feeling of disgust.

ab·o·rig·i·nal (ab′ə·rij′ə·nəl), *adj.* **1.** existing from the beginning; first; original; native: ab-

original inhabitants. 2. of the earliest known inhabitants. —*n.* any one of the earliest known inhabitants. —**ab'o·rig'i·nal·ly,** *adv.*

ab·o·rig·i·nes (ab'ə·rij'ə·nēz), *n., pl.* of **aborigine.** 1. the earliest known inhabitants of a country. 2. the native animals and plants of a region. [< L, < *ab origine* from the beginning]

a·bort (ə·bôrt'), *v.* 1. miscarry. 2. fail to develop. 3. check the development of. [< L, < *ab*-amiss + *oriri* be born]

a·bor·tion (ə·bôr'shən), *n.* 1. birth that occurs before the embryo has developed enough to live; miscarriage. 2. something that has failed to develop properly. —**a·bor'tion·al,** *adj.*

a·bor·tion·ist (ə·bôr'shən·ist), *n. Am.* person who produces criminal abortions.

a·bor·tive (ə·bôr'tiv), *adj.* 1. coming to nothing; unsuccessful. 2. born before the right time. —**a·bor'tive·ly,** *adv.* —**a·bor'tive·ness,** *n.*

a·bound (ə·bound'), *v.* 1. be plentiful: *fish abound in the ocean.* 2. be rich (*in*): *America abounds in oil.* 3. be well supplied (*with*): *the ocean abounds with fish.* [< OF < L, < *ab*- off + *undare* rise in waves < *unda* a wave] —**a·bound'ing,** *adj.* —**a·bound'ing·ly,** *adv.*

a·bout (ə·bout'), *prep.* 1. of; concerned with: *a book about bridges.* 2. in connection with: *something queer about him.* 3. somewhere near: *he was about five miles from home.* 4. approximating; near: *about my size.* 5. on every side of; around: *a fence about the garden.* 6. on (one's person); with: *she has no money about her.* 7. on the point of; ready: *a plane about to take off.* 8. here and there in or on: *scatter papers about the room.* —*adv.* 1. nearly; almost: *about full.* 2. somewhere near: *loiter about.* 3. all around; in every direction: *the boy looked about.* 4. here and there: *scatter papers about.* 5. in the opposite direction: *face about.* 6. doing: *he knows what he is about.* 7. one after another; by turns: *turn about is fair play.* [OE *onbūtan* on the outside of] ➤ **about (at about).** *At about* is a common colloquial doubling of prepositions: *I got there at about three o'clock.* In writing we should ordinarily choose the more accurate of the two: *I got there at three o'clock,* or *I got there about three o'clock. About* is usually the one intended.

a·bout-face (*n.* ə·bout'fās'; *v.* ə·bout'fās'), *n., v.,* **-faced, -fac·ing.** —*n.* a turning or going in the opposite direction. —*v.* turn or go in the opposite direction.

a·bove (ə·buv'), *adv.* 1. in or at a higher place; overhead: *the sky is above.* 2. on the upper side or on top: *leaves dark above and light below.* 3. higher in rank or power: *the courts above.* 4. in or from a direction thought of as higher: *there's good fishing above.* 5. earlier, in a book or article: *said above.* 6. in heaven. —*prep.* 1. in or to a higher place than: *birds fly above the earth.* 2. higher than; over: *a captain is above a sergeant.* 3. superior to: *above mean actions.* 4. more than: *the weight is above a ton.* 5. beyond: *the first corner above the school.* —*adj.* written above. —*n.* the above, something that is written above. [OE *abufan*] ➤ **Above** is primarily a preposition (*above the clouds*) or adverb (*the statements made above—above* modifying the verb *made*). Its common use as an adverb, as in *the story told above* (that is, on the same page or on a preceding page), would be avoided by most writers in favor of *the story I have told* . . . or some such expression. The use of *above* as an adjective (*the above statements*) or noun (*the above is confirmed* . . .) is better limited to business writing and reference works. This sentence shows how crude *above* as a noun may sound in an inappropriate context: *In answer to the above I would say that the children didn't grow up with the right parents.*

a·bove·board (ə·buv'bôrd'; -bōrd'), *adv., adj.* without tricks or concealment.

ab o·vo (ab ō'vō), *Latin.* from the beginning.

ab·ra·ca·dab·ra (ab'rə·kə·dab'rə), *n.* 1. a mystical word used in incantations, or as a charm to ward off diseases. 2. gibberish. [< L]

a·brade (ə·brād'), *v.,* **a·brad·ed, a·brad·ing.** wear away by rubbing; scrape off. [< L, < *ab*- off + *radere* scrape] —**a·brad'er,** *n.*

A·bra·ham (ā'brə·ham; -həm), *n. Bible.* the ancestor of the Hebrews. Gen. 12–25.

a·bra·sion (ə·brā'zhən), *n.* 1. place scraped or worn by rubbing. 2. act of abrading.

a·bra·sive (ə·brā'siv; -ziv), *n.* a substance used for grinding, smoothing, or polishing, as sandpaper. —*adj.* tending to abrade.

a·breast (ə·brest'), *adv., adj.* 1. side by side. 2. abreast of or with, up with; alongside of: *keep abreast of what is going on.*

a·bridge (ə·brij'), *v.,* **a·bridged, a·bridg·ing.** 1. make shorter by using fewer words. 2. make less: *abridge the rights of citizens.* 3. deprive (*of*): *abridge citizens of their rights.* [< OF *abregier* < L, < *ad*- + *brevis* short. Doublet of ABBREVIATE.] —**a·bridg'a·ble, a·bridge'a·ble,** *adj.* —**a·bridged',** *adj.* —**a·bridg'er,** *n.*

a·bridg·ment, *occas. Brit.* **a·bridge·ment** (ə·brij'mənt), *n.* 1. condensed form of a book, long article, etc. 2. an abridging.

a·broad (ə·brôd'), *adv.* 1. in or to a foreign land or lands: *go abroad.* 2. out in the open air. 3. going around; current: *a rumor is abroad.* 4. far and wide. 5. in error.

ab·ro·gate (ab'rə·gāt), *v.,* **-gat·ed, -gat·ing.** 1. abolish or annul (a law or custom) by an authoritative act; repeal. 2. do away with. [< L, < *ab*- away + *rogare* demand] —**ab'ro·ga'tion,** *n.* —**ab'ro·ga'tor,** *n.*

a·brupt (ə·brupt'), *adj.* 1. sudden; unexpected: *an abrupt turn.* 2. very steep. 3. (of speech or manners) short or sudden; blunt. 4. (of style) disconnected. [< L *abruptus* < *ab*- off + *rumpere* break] —**a·brupt'ly,** *adv.* —**a·brupt'ness,** *n.* —Syn. 3. brusque, curt.

Ab·sa·lom (ab'sə·ləm), *n. Bible.* David's favorite son, who rebelled against him.

ab·scess (ab'ses; -sis), *n.* a collection of pus in the tissues of some part of the body. [< L *abscessus* < *ab*- away + *cedere* go] —**ab'scessed,** *adj.*

ab·scis·sa (ab·sis'ə), *n., pl.* **-scis·sas, -scis·sae** (-sis'ē). *Math.* line running from left to right on a graph that defines a point in a system of coördinates. [< L (*linea*) *abscissa* (line) cut off]

ab·scond (ab·skond'), *v.* go away suddenly and secretly; go off and hide. [< L, < *ab*- away + *condere* store] —**ab·scond'er,** *n.* —Syn. flee.

ab·sence (ab'səns), *n.* 1. a being away: *absence from work.* 2. time of being away: *an absence of two weeks.* 3. a being without; lack: *absence of light.* 4. absent-mindedness.

absence of mind, inattentiveness.

ab·sent (*adj.* ab'sənt; *v.* ab·sent'), *adj.* 1. not present (at a place); away: *John is absent today.* 2. not existing; lacking: *snow is absent in some countries.* 3. absent-minded. —*v.* take or keep (oneself) away: *absent oneself from class.* [< L *absens* < *ab*- away + *esse* to be] —**ab·sent'er,** *n.* —**ab'sent·ness,** *n.*

ab·sen·tee (ab'sən·tē'), *n.* one who is absent or remains absent. —*adj. Am.* of or for a voter or voters permitted to vote by mail. —**ab'sen·tee'ism,** *n.*

ab·sent·ly (ab'sənt·li), *adv.* absent-mindedly.

ab·sent-mind·ed (ab'sənt·mīn'did), *adj.* not paying attention to what is going on around one. —**ab'sent-mind'ed·ly,** *adv.* —**ab'sent-mind'ed·ness,** *n.* —Syn. inattentive.

ab·sinthe, ab·sinth (ab'sinth), *n.* a bitter, green liqueur flavored with wormwood and anise. [< F < L < Gk. *apsinthion* wormwood]

ab·so·lute (ab'sə·lüt), *adj.* 1. complete; entire: *absolute ignorance.* 2. not mixed with anything else; pure: *absolute alcohol.* 3. free from imperfection; perfect: *absolute purity.* 4. free from control or restrictions: *absolute liberty.* 5. not compared with anything else: *absolute velocity.* 6. real; actual. 7. certain; infallible: *absolute proof.* 8. *Gram.* forming a part of a sentence, but not connected with it grammatically. In "The train being late, we missed the boat," *the* *train being late* is an absolute construction. —*n.* the absolute, that which is absolute. [< L *absolutus,* pp. See ABSOLVE.] —**ab′so·lute′ness,** *n.*

ab·so·lute·ly (ab′sə·lüt′li; emphatic ab′sə·lüt′li), *adv.* 1. completely. 2. *Am., Colloq.* positively. 3. *U.S. Slang.* yes. ➤ In speech **absolutely** has become generalized to mean "very" or "quite": *he is absolutely the finest fellow I know* —and in slang means simply "yes." It is sometimes a useful word to put force into dialogue but would be out of place in most writing, except in its original meaning of "completely, unconditionally."

absolute zero, temperature at which substances would have no heat whatever; –273.13° centigrade or –459.72° Fahrenheit.

ab·so·lu·tion (ab′sə·lü′shən), *n.* 1. remission of guilt and punishment for sin by a priest after the sinner confesses and does penance. 2. act of declaring such remission. 3. formula declaring remission of sin. 4. release from consequences or penalties. —Syn. 1. forgiveness.

ab·so·lut·ism (ab′sə·lüt·iz′əm), *n.* government whose ruler has unrestricted power; despotism. —**ab′so·lut·ist,** *n., adj.* —**ab′so·lut·is′tic,** *adj.*

ab·solve (ab·solv′; –zolv′), *v.,* –solved, –solving. 1. declare (a person) free from sin, guilt, or blame. 2. set free (from a promise or duty). 3. remit (sin). [< L, < *ab–* from + *solvere* loosen] —**ab·solv′a·ble,** *adj.* —**ab·sol′vent,** *adj., n.* —**ab·solv′er,** *n.* —Syn. 1. exonerate, acquit. 2. release, exempt. 3. forgive.

ab·sorb (ab·sôrb′; –zôrb′), *v.* 1. take in or suck up (liquids): *a blotter absorbs ink.* 2. swallow up; assimilate. 3. interest very much: *the circus absorbed the boys.* 4. take up by chemical or molecular action: *charcoal absorbs gases.* 5. take (digested food, oxygen, etc.) into the blood stream by osmosis. [< L, < *ab–* from + *sorbere* suck in] —**ab·sorb′a·ble,** *adj.* —**ab·sorb′a·bil′i·ty,** *n.* —**ab·sorb′er,** *n.*

ab·sorbed (ab·sôrbd′; –zôrbd′), *adj.* very much interested. —**ab·sorb·ed·ly** (ab·sôr′bid·li; –zôr′–), *adv.* —**ab·sorb′ed·ness,** *n.*

ab·sorb·ent (ab·sôr′bənt; –zôr′–), *adj.* absorbing or capable of absorbing. —*n.* any thing or substance that absorbs.

ab·sorb·ing (ab·sôr′bing; –zôr′–), *adj.* extremely interesting. —**ab·sorb′ing·ly,** *adv.*

ab·sorp·tion (ab·sôrp′shən; –zôrp′–), *n.* 1. an absorbing. 2. great interest (in something). 3. process of taking digested food, oxygen, etc., into the blood stream by osmosis. —**ab·sorp′tive,** *adj.* —**ab·sorp′tive·ness,** *n.*

ab·stain (ab·stān′), *v.* do without something voluntarily; refrain (*from*): *abstain from smoking.* [< F < L, < *ab–* off + *tenere* hold] —**ab·stain′er,** *n.* —Syn. forbear, cease.

ab·ste·mi·ous (ab·stē′mi·əs), *adj.* moderate in eating and drinking; temperate. [< L, < *ab–* off + unrecorded *temum* intoxicating drink] —**ab·ste′mi·ous·ly,** *adv.* —**ab·ste′mi·ous·ness,** *n.*

ab·sten·tion (ab·sten′shən), *n.* act of abstaining; abstinence. —**ab·sten′tious,** *adj.*

ab·sti·nence (ab′stə·nəns), *n.* 1. partly or entirely giving up certain pleasures, food, drink, etc. 2. act or practice of refraining (*from*): *abstinence from smoking.* 3. total abstinence, a refraining from the use of any alcoholic liquor. —**ab′sti·nent,** *adj.* —**ab′sti·nent·ly,** *adv.* —Syn. 1, 2. abstention.

ab·stract (*adj.* ab′strakt, ab·strakt′; *v.* ab·strakt′ for 1, 3, 4, ab′strakt for 2; *n.* ab′strakt), *adj.* 1. thought of apart from any particular object or real thing; not concrete: *an abstract number.* 2. expressing a quality that is thought of apart from any particular object or real thing: *"goodness" is an abstract noun.* 3. ideal; theoretical. 4. hard to understand; difficult. 5. pertaining to art that avoids the representation of realities and all ordinary conventional designs. —*v.* 1. think of (a quality) apart from a particular object or real thing having that quality. 2. make an abstract of; summarize. 3. remove, esp. dishonestly. 4. withdraw attention. —*n.* 1. a short statement giving the main ideas of an article, book, etc.; summary. 2. in the ab-

stract, in theory rather than in practice. [< L *abstractus* < *ab–* away + *trahere* draw] —**ab·stract′er,** *n.* —**ab′stract·ly,** *adv.* —**ab′stract·ness,** *n.* —Ant. *adj.* 1. concrete.

ab·stract·ed (ab·strak′tid), *adj.* absent-minded. —**ab·stract′ed·ly,** *adv.* —**ab·stract′ed·ness,** *n.* —Syn. inattentive, preoccupied.

ab·strac·tion (ab·strak′shən), *n.* 1. idea of a quality thought of apart from any particular object or real thing having that quality. 2. formation of such an idea. 3. removal. 4. absence of mind. 5. a work of abstract art.

ab·struse (ab·strüs′), *adj.* hard to understand. [< L *abstrusus* < *ab–* away + *trudere* thrust] —**ab·struse′ly,** *adv.* —**ab·struse′ness,** *n.* —Syn. profound, recondite. —Ant. obvious.

ab·surd (ab·sérd′; –zėrd′), *adj.* plainly not true or sensible; foolish; ridiculous. [< L *absurdus* out of tune, senseless] —**ab·surd′ly,** *adv.* —**ab·surd′ness,** *n.*

ab·surd·i·ty (ab·sér′də·ti; –zėr′–), *n., pl.* –ties. 1. something absurd. 2. an absurd quality or condition; folly.

a·bun·dance (ə·bun′dəns), *n.* great plenty; full supply. [< OF < L. See ABOUND.] —Syn. profusion, superfluity.

a·bun·dant (ə·bun′dənt), *adj.* more than enough; very plentiful. —**a·bun′dant·ly,** *adv.*

a·buse (*v.* ə·büz′; *n.* ə·büs′), *v.,* a·bused, a·bus·ing, *n.* —*v.* 1. put to a wrong or bad use; misuse: *abuse a privilege.* 2. treat badly; mistreat: *abuse a child.* 3. use harsh and insulting language to. —*n.* 1. a wrong or improper use. 2. harsh or severe treatment of a person. 3. harsh and insulting language. 4. a corrupt practice or custom. [< F < L *abusus* < *ab–* away + *uti* use] —**a·bus′er,** *n.* —Syn. *v.* 1. misapply. 2. maltreat. 3. revile.

a·bu·sive (ə·bü′siv; –ziv), *adj.* 1. using harsh or insulting language. 2. containing abuse. —**a·bu′sive·ly,** *adv.* —**a·bu′sive·ness,** *n.*

a·but (ə·but′), *v.,* a·but·ted, a·but·ting. 1. touch at one end or edge; end (*on* or *against*): *our house abuts on the street.* 2. join at a boundary; border (*on* or *upon*): *his land abuts upon mine.* [< OF]

a·but·ment (ə·but′mənt), *n.* 1. a support for an arch or bridge. 2. the point or place where the support joins the thing supported.

a·but·ting (ə·but′ing), *adj.* adjacent.

a·bysm (ə·biz′əm), *n.* an abyss. [< OF *abisme*]

a·bys·mal (ə·biz′məl), *adj.* too deep to be measured; bottomless. —**a·bys′mal·ly,** *adv.*

a·byss (ə·bis′), *n.* 1. a bottomless or immeasurably deep space. 2. the lowest depths of anything. 3. the bottomless pit (hell). [< L < Gk., < *a–* without + *byssos* bottom] —Syn. 1. chasm.

Abutment: A, arch abutments; B, current abutments.

A·bys·sin·i·a (ab′ə·sin′i·ə), *n.* Ethiopia. —**Ab′ys·sin′i·an,** *adj., n.*

Ac, *Chem.* actinium.

A.C., a.c., *Elect.* alternating current.

a·ca·cia (ə·kā′shə), *n.* 1. any of a genus of trees native to warm regions, several species of which yield gum arabic. 2. *Am.* the locust tree of North America. [< L < Gk. *akakia* a thorny Egyptian tree]

ac·a·dem·ic (ak′ə·dem′ik), **ac·a·dem·i·cal** (–ə·kəl), *adj.* 1. of or having to do with schools, colleges, and their studies. 2. *Am.* concerned with general rather than commercial, technical, or professional education. 3. scholarly. 4. theoretical. 5. following rules and traditions; formal. —**ac′a·dem′i·cal·ly,** *adv.*

academic freedom, *Am.* the freedom of a teacher to state the truth as he sees it without fear of losing his position or standing.

a·cad·e·mi·cian (ə·kad′ə·mish′ən; ak′ə·də–), *n.* member of a society for encouraging literature, science, or art.

a·cad·e·my (ə·kad′ə·mi), *n., pl.* –mies. 1. high school, esp. a private high school. 2. school for instruction in a particular art or science: *a mili-tary academy.* 3. society of authors, scholars, scientists, artists, etc., for encouraging litera-ture, science, or art. [< L < Gk. *Akademeia* the grove where Plato taught]

A·ca·di·a (ə·kā'di·ə), *n.* a former French ter-ritory in SE Canada. —A·ca'di·an, *n., adj.*

a·can·thus (ə·kan'thəs), *n., pl.* –thus·es, –thi (-thī). 1. a prickly plant with large, toothed leaves that grows in Medi-terranean regions. 2. an architectural ornament imitating these leaves. [< L < Gk., < *ake* thorn]

a cap·pel·la (ä' kə-pel'ə), *Music.* without instrumental accom-paniment. [< Ital., in the manner of chapel (music)]

Acanthus: A, leaf of plant; B, ornament.

acc., 1. account. 2. accusative.

ac·cede (ak·sēd'), *v.,* –ced·ed, –ced·ing. 1. give consent (to): *please accede to my request.* 2. be-come a party (to): *our government acceded to the treaty.* 3. attain (to an office or dignity); come (to): *the king's oldest son acceded to the throne.* [< L, < *ad–* to + *cedere* come] —ac·ced'-ence, *n.* —ac·ced'er, *n.* —Syn. 1. agree, assent.

ac·cel·er·an·do (ak·sel'ər·an'dō), *adv., adj. Music.* gradually increasing in speed. [< Ital.]

ac·cel·er·ate (ak·sel'ər·āt), *v.,* –at·ed, –at·ing. 1. go or cause to go faster. 2. cause to happen sooner; hasten. 3. *Physics.* change the speed or velocity of (a moving object). [< L, < *ad–* + *celer* swift] —ac·cel'er·a'tive, *adj.*

ac·cel·er·a·tion (ak·sel'ər·ā'shən), *n.* 1. an accelerating or being accelerated. 2. change in velocity, either a gradual increase (positive ac-celeration) or decrease (negative acceleration). 3. rate of change in the velocity of a moving body.

ac·cel·er·a·tor (ak·sel'ər·ā'tər), *n.* 1. thing that accelerates. 2. a device for opening and closing the throttle of an automobile. 3. cyclotron.

ac·cent (*n.* ak'sent; *v.* ak'sent, ak·sent'), *n.* 1. special force or emphasis given to a syllable or a word in pronouncing it. 2. a mark to indicate special force or emphasis. 3. characteristic man-ner of pronunciation: *a foreign accent.* 4. ac-cents, tone of voice: *in soothing accents.* 5. a mark to indicate vowel quality in foreign lan-guages, as acute (´), grave (`), or circumflex (^). 6. emphasis on certain words or syllables in a line of poetry to give them rhythm. 7. *Music.* emphasis on certain notes or chords. —*v.* 1. pro-nounce or mark with an accent. 2. emphasize; accentuate. [< L *accentus* < *ad–* to + *canere* sing] ➤ **accents.** French words in English some-times keep the accent marks with which they are spelled in their original language: *café, outré, attaché; crêpe, tête-à-tête; à la mode.* Words that are used frequently in English usually drop the accent marks after a time unless the marks are necessary to indicate pronunciation (as in *café, attaché*).

ac·cen·tu·al (ak·sen'chü·əl), *adj.* 1. of or formed by accent. 2. (of poetry) using stress in-stead of quantity. —ac·cen'tu·al·ly, *adv.*

ac·cen·tu·ate (ak·sen'chü·āt), *v.,* –at·ed, –at-ing. 1. emphasize. 2. pronounce or mark with an accent. —ac·cen'tu·a'tion, *n.*

ac·cept (ak·sept'), *v.* 1. take or receive (some-thing offered): *accept a gift.* 2. agree to; consent to: *accept a proposal.* 3. take as true or satis-factory; believe: *accept an excuse.* 4. receive (a thing or person) with favor; approve: *Einstein's new theory was widely accepted.* 5. undertake as a responsibility: *accept a position as cashier.* 6. *Com.* sign and promise to pay: *accept a note.* [< L *acceptare* < *ad–* to + *capere* take] —ac-cept'er, *esp. in Com.,* ac·cep'tor, *n.* —Syn. 2. accede, assent to. 3. acknowledge, recognize. 5. assume. ➤ See usage note under **except.**

ac·cept·a·ble (ak·sep'tə·bəl), *adj.* worth ac-cepting; satisfactory. —ac·cept'a·bil'i·ty, ac-

cept'a·ble·ness, *n.* —ac·cept'a·bly, *adv.* —Syn. agreeable, welcome.

ac·cept·ance (ak·sep'təns), *n.* 1. act of ac-cepting. 2. state of being accepted; favorable reception; approval. 3. *Com.* a. agreement as to terms, esp. to pay a draft or bill of exchange when it is due. b. the draft or bill itself.

ac·cep·ta·tion (ak'sep·tā'shən), *n.* usual meaning; generally accepted meaning.

ac·cess (ak'ses), *n.* 1. right to approach, enter, or use; admission: *access to the library.* 2. condi-tion of being easy or hard to reach: *access to the mountain town was difficult.* 3. way or means of approach: *access to powerful men.* 4. an at-tack (of disease). 5. outburst (of anger). 6. in-crease. [< L *accessus* < *ad–* to + *cedere* come]

ac·ces·sa·ry (ak·ses'ə·ri), *n., pl.* –ries, *adj. Esp. Law.* accessory. —ac·ces'sa·ri·ly, *adv.* —ac-ces'sa·ri·ness, *n.*

ac·ces·si·ble (ak·ses'ə·bəl), *adj.* 1. that can be entered or reached. 2. easy to get at; easy to reach. 3. accessible to, capable of being influ-enced by. 4. that can be obtained. —ac·ces'si-bil'i·ty, *n.* —ac·ces'si·bly, *adv.* —Syn. 1. ap-proachable. 3. susceptible. 4. available.

ac·ces·sion (ak·sesh'ən), *n.* 1. act of attaining to a right, office, etc. 2. a yielding or agreeing (to a plan, opinion, demand, etc.); consent. 3. an increase; addition. 4. thing added. —ac·ces'sion-al, *adj.* —Syn. 1. attainment. 2. assent.

ac·ces·so·ry (ak·ses'ə·ri), *n., pl.* –ries, *adj.* —*n.* 1. an extra thing added to help something of more importance; subordinate part or detail. 2. person who helps an offender against the law, without being present at the time of the offense, by encouraging the offender (an accessory be-fore the fact) or shielding him (an accessory after the fact). —*adj.* 1. helping something more important; subsidiary. 2. *Law.* giving aid as an accessory. Also, *esp. Law,* accessary. —ac·ces'-so·ri·ly, *adv.* —ac·ces'so·ri·ness, *n.* —Syn. *n.* 2. accomplice.

ac·ci·dence (ak'sə·dəns), *n.* part of grammar dealing with word order and those changes in words that show case, number, tense, etc.

ac·ci·dent (ak'sə·dənt), *n.* 1. an undesirable or unfortunate happening: *an automobile acci-dent.* 2. an unexpected or unintentional happen-ing: *their meeting was an accident.* 3. chance: *we met by accident.* 4. a nonessential. [< L *accidens* < *ad–* to + *cadere* fall]

ac·ci·den·tal (ak'sə·den'təl), *adj.* 1. happen-ing by chance; unexpected. 2. nonessential; inci-dental. 3. *Music.* of or having to do with an ac-cidental. —*n. Music.* a sign used to show a change of pitch after the key signature and be-fore the note to be changed. —ac'ci·den'tal·ly, *adv.* —ac'ci·den'tal·ness, *n.* —Syn. *adj.* 1. for-tuitous, unintentional, casual.

ac·ci·dent-prone (ak'sə·dənt·prōn'), *adj.* tending to have accidents.

ac·claim (ə·klām'), *v.* 1. show satisfaction and approval of by words or sounds; applaud. 2. an-nounce with signs of approval; hail. —*n.* shout or show of approval; applause. [< L, < *ad–* to + *clamare* cry out] —ac·claim'er, *n.*

ac·cla·ma·tion (ak'lə·mā'shən), *n.* 1. shout of approval by a crowd; applause. 2. oral vote.

ac·cli·mate (ə·klī'mit; ak'lə·māt), *v.,* –mat-ed, –mat·ing. *Esp. U.S.* accustom or become ac-customed to a new climate or to new conditions. [< F *acclimater.* See CLIMATE.] —ac·cli'mat-a·ble (ə·klī'mit·ə·bəl), *adj.* —ac·cli·ma·tion (ak'lə·mā'shən), *n. Am.*

ac·cli·ma·tize (ə·klī'mə·tīz), *v.,* –tized, –tiz-ing. *Esp. Brit.* acclimate. —ac·cli'ma·tiz'a·ble, *adj.* —ac·cli'ma·ti·za'tion, *n.*

ac·cliv·i·ty (ə·kliv'ə·ti), *n., pl.* –ties. an up-ward slope, as of ground. [< L, < *ad–* toward + *clivus* rising ground]

ac·co·lade (ak'ə·lād'; -läd'), *n.* 1. a ceremony used in making a man a knight. 2. honor; praise. [< F < Pg. *acolada* an embrace about the neck < L *ad–* to + *collum* neck]

ac·com·mo·date (ə·kom'ə·dāt), *v.,* –dat·ed, –dat·ing. 1. have room for; hold comfortably. 2.

do a kindness or favor to; oblige. 3. furnish with lodging and sometimes with food as well. 4. supply; furnish. 5. *Am.* provide (a person) with (a loan of) money. 6. make fit; make suitable. 7. reconcile; adjust. [< L, < *ad– + com–* with + *modus* measure] —ac·com′mo·da′tor, *n.* —Syn. 4. provide, equip.

ac·com·mo·dat·ing (ə·kom′ə·dāt′ing), *adj.* obliging. —ac·com′mo·dat′ing·ly, *adv.*

ac·com·mo·da·tion (ə·kom′ə·dā′shən), *n.* 1. lodging and sometimes food as well: *the hotel has accommodations for one hundred.* 2. help; favor; convenience. 3. *Am.* loan. 4. willingness to help out. 5. adjustment; adaptation. 6. settlement of differences; reconciliation.

accommodation train, *Am.* train that stops at all or nearly all stations.

ac·com·mo·da·tive (ə·kom′ə·dā′tiv), *adj.* obliging. —ac·com′mo·da′tive·ness, *n.*

ac·com·pa·ni·ment (ə·kum′pə·ni·mənt), *n.* 1. something incidental that goes along with something else. 2. *Music.* a supplementary part added to support the main part. —Syn. 1. adjunct.

ac·com·pa·nist (ə·kum′pə·nist), *n. Music.* one who plays an accompaniment.

ac·com·pa·ny (ə·kum′pə·ni), *v.,* –nied, –ny·ing. 1. go along with: *accompany a friend on a walk.* 2. be or happen in connection with: *fire is accompanied by heat.* 3. cause to be attended by; supplement (*with*): *accompany a speech with gestures.* 4. play or sing a musical accompaniment for or to. [< F *accompagner < à to + compagne* COMPANION] —ac·com′pa·ni·er, *n.* —Syn. 1. attend, escort. —Ant. 1. avoid.

ac·com·plice (ə·kom′plis), *n.* person who aids another in committing an unlawful act. [earlier *a complice* a confederate < F *complice* < L, < *com–* together with + *plicare* fold]

ac·com·plish (ə·kom′plish), *v.* 1. succeed in completing; carry out: *accomplish a purpose.* 2. finish; actually do: *accomplish nothing.* [< OF < LL, < *ad– + complere* fill up] —ac·com′plish·a·ble, *adj.* —ac·com′plish·er, *n.* —Syn. 1, 2. achieve, effect, complete, fulfill.

ac·com·plished (ə·kom′plisht), *adj.* 1. done; carried out; completed. 2. expert; skilled. 3. skilled in social arts and graces.

ac·com·plish·ment (ə·kom′plish·mənt), *n.* 1. an accomplishing or being accomplished. 2. thing accomplished; achievement. 3. skill in some social art or grace: *good manners are a desirable accomplishment.* —Syn. 1. completion. 2, 3. acquirement, attainment.

ac·cord (ə·kôrd′), *v.* 1. be in harmony; agree: *his report accords with yours.* 2. grant (a favor, request, etc.): *accord Tom praise for good work.* —*n.* 1. agreement; harmony: *opinions in accord.* 2. an informal agreement between nations. 3. harmony of color, pitch, or tone. 4. of one's own accord, all together. [< OF < VL *acchordare* bring into harmony < L *ad–* to + *chorda* string] —ac·cord′a·ble, *adj.* —ac·cord′er, *n.* —Syn. *v.* 1. correspond, harmonize.

ac·cord·ance (ə·kôr′dəns), *n.* agreement; harmony: *in accordance with the plan.*

ac·cord·ant (ə·kôr′dənt), *adj.* agreeing; in harmony (*with* or *to*). —ac·cord′ant·ly, *adv.*

ac·cord·ing (ə·kôr′ding), *adv.* 1. according to, a. in agreement with: *according to his promise.* b. in proportion to: *spend according to your income.* c. on the authority of: *according to this book.* 2. according as, in proportion as. 3. accordingly. —*adj.* in harmony.

ac·cord·ing·ly (ə·kôr′-ding·li), *adv.* 1. in agreement with something that has been stated; suitably. 2. for this reason; therefore.

Boy playing an accordion

ac·cor·di·on (ə·kôr′di·ən), *n.* a portable musical wind instrument with a bellows, metallic reeds, and keys. —*adj.* having folds like the

bellows of an accordion. [< G < Ital. *accordare* harmonize] —ac·cor′di·on·ist, *n.*

ac·cost (ə·kôst′; ə·kost′), *v.* approach and speak to first. [< F < Ital. < LL, < L *ad–* to + *costa* side, rib] —Syn. address, greet.

ac·couche·ment (ə·küsh′mənt; *Fr.* ä·küsh-mäN′), *n.* confinement for childbirth. [< F]

ac·count (ə·kount′), *n.* 1. detailed or explanatory statement: *please give an account of your trip.* 2. reason: *do not lie on any account.* 3. consideration: *take into account.* 4. value; worth: *of no account.* 5. regard; behalf: *don't wait on my account.* 6. profit; advantage: *turn to account.* 7. statement of money received and paid out. 8. a record of business dealings between a bank and a depositor. 9. a periodic record of purchases for which a customer is billed. 10. **call to account,** a. demand an explanation of. b. scold; reprimand. 11. **on account,** as part payment. 12. **on account of,** a. because of. b. for the sake of. 13. **take account of,** a. make allowance for; consider. b. make a note of; note. 14. **take into account,** make allowance for; consider. [< OF. See ACCOUNT, v.] —*v.* 1. give a statement of money received or paid out. 2. **account for,** a. give a reason for; explain. b. answer for. 3. hold to be; consider: *Solomon was accounted wise.* [< OF *aconter* count up < LL, < L *ad– + computare* compute] —Syn. *n.* 1. report, description, narrative.

ac·count·a·ble (ə·koun′tə·bəl), *adj.* 1. responsible. 2. explainable. —ac·count′a·bil′i·ty, ac·count′a·ble·ness, *n.* —ac·count′a·bly, *adv.*

ac·count·an·cy (ə·koun′tən·si), *n.* the examining or keeping of business accounts.

ac·count·ant (ə·koun′tənt), *n.* person who examines or manages business accounts.

ac·count·ing (ə·koun′ting), *n.* theory or system of keeping, analyzing, and interpreting business accounts.

ac·cou·ter, *esp. Brit.* **ac·cou·tre** (ə·kü′tər), *v.,* –tered, –ter·ing; –tred, –tring. to outfit or equip; array. [< F *accoutrer*]

ac·cou·ter·ments, *esp. Brit.* **ac·cou·tre·ments** (ə·kü′tər·mənts), *n.pl.* 1. a soldier's equipment with the exception of his weapons and clothing. 2. personal equipment; outfit.

Ac·cra (ə·krä′), *n.* seaport in W Africa, capital of Ghana.

ac·cred·it (ə·kred′it), *v.* 1. give (a person) credit (for something): *accredit her with kindness.* 2. *Am.* consider (a thing) as belonging or due (to a person): *we accredit the invention of the telephone to Bell.* 3. accept as worth believing; trust: *Einstein is an accredited authority in mathematics.* 4. give authority to. 5. send or provide with credentials: *an accredited representative.* 6. recognize as coming up to an official standard: *an accredited high school.* [< F *accréditer*] —Syn. 1, 2. credit, attribute. 4. authorize.

ac·cre·tion (ə·krē′shən), *n.* 1. growth in size. 2. a growing together of separate things. 3. an increase in size by natural growth or gradual external addition. 4. thing added; addition. 5. a whole that results from such growths or additions. —ac·cre′tive, *adj.*

ac·cru·al (ə·krü′əl), *n.* 1. an accruing. 2. amount accrued or accruing.

ac·crue (ə·krü′), *v.,* –crued, –cru·ing. come as a natural product or result. [< F < L, < *ad–* to + *crescere* grow] —ac·crue′ment, *n.*

acct., 1. account. 2. accountant.

ac·cu·mu·late (ə·kü′myə·lāt), *v.,* –lat·ed, –lat·ing. 1. collect or heap up little by little: *accumulate a fortune.* 2. grow into a heap or mass. [< L, < *ad–* up + *cumulus* heap] —Syn. 1. gather, amass. 2. increase, accrue.

ac·cu·mu·la·tion (ə·kü′myə·lā′shən), *n.* 1. gradual collection. 2. material collected; mass.

ac·cu·mu·la·tive (ə·kü′myə·lā′tiv; –lə·tiv), *adj.* tending to accumulate; collective. —ac·cu′mu·la′tive·ly, *adv.* —ac·cu′mu·la′tive·ness, *n.*

ac·cu·mu·la·tor (ə·kü′myə·lā′tər), *n.* 1. one that accumulates. 2. *Brit.* a storage battery.

ac·cu·ra·cy (ak′yə·rə·si), *n.* condition of being without errors or mistakes. —Syn. correctness.

ac·cu·rate (ak′yə·rit), *adj.* **1.** making few or no errors: *an accurate observer.* **2.** without errors or mistakes; exact: *accurate measure.* [< L, < *ad-* to + *cura* care] —**ac′cu·rate·ly,** *adv.* —**ac′cu·rate·ness,** *n.* —**Syn. 1.** careful, precise.

ac·curs·ed (ə·kėr′sid; ə·kėrst′), **ac·curst** (ə·kėrst′), *adj.* **1.** detestable; abominable. **2.** under a curse. —**ac·curs·ed·ly** (ə·kėr′sid·li), *adv.*

accus., accusative.

ac·cu·sa·tion (ak′yŭ·zā′shən), *n.* **1.** a charge of wrongdoing. **2.** the offense charged. **3.** act of accusing.

ac·cu·sa·tive (ə·kū′zə·tiv), *Gram.* —*n.* **1.** the objective case. **2.** word used as an object of a verb or preposition. —*adj.* showing the direct object; objective. —**ac·cu′sa·tive·ly,** *adv.*

ac·cu·sa·to·ry (ə·kū′zə·tô′ri; -tō′-), *adj.* containing an accusation; accusing.

ac·cuse (ə·kūz′), *v.,* **-cused, -cus·ing. 1.** charge with some crime, offense, etc. **2.** find fault with; blame. [< OF < L *accusare* < *ad-* to + *causa* cause] —**Syn. 1.** denounce, arraign. —**ac·cus′er,** *n.* —**ac·cus′ing·ly,** *adv.*

ac·cus·tom (ə·kus′təm), *v.* make familiar by use or habit; get used. [< OF *acostumer*] —**Syn.** habituate, familiarize.

ac·cus·tomed (ə·kus′təmd), *adj.* usual; customary. —**ac·cus′tomed·ness,** *n.*

ace (ās), *n.* **1.** a playing card, domino, or side of a die having a single spot. **2.** a single spot. **3.** a point won by a single stroke in tennis and certain other games. **4.** an expert. **5.** a combat pilot who has shot down five or more enemy planes. —*adj.* of very high quality; expert. [< OF *as* < L, smallest unit (of coinage, measure, etc.)]

a·cer·bi·ty (ə·sėr′bə·ti), *n., pl.* **-ties. 1.** sharpness of taste; sourness. **2.** harshness of manner; severity. [< F < L, < *acerbus* bitter]

ac·e·tab·u·lum (as′ə·tab′yə·ləm), *n., pl.* **-la** (-lə). *Anat.* a socket. [< L, cup-shaped holder for vinegar, < *acetum* vinegar] —**ac′e·tab′u·lar,** *adj.*

ac·et·an·i·lid (as′ət·an′ə·lid), **ac·et·an·i·lide** (-ə·līd; -ə·lid), *n. Chem.* a white, crystalline drug, $C_6H_5NH·COCH_3$, used in medicines to relieve pain and lessen fever.

ac·e·tate (as′ə·tāt), *n. Chem.* any salt or ester of acetic acid. —**ac′e·tat′ed,** *adj.*

a·ce·tic (ə·sē′tik; ə·set′ik), *adj.* of or derived from vinegar or acetic acid. [< L *acetum* vinegar]

acetic acid, a very sour, colorless acid, CH_3COOH, present in vinegar.

a·cet·i·fy (ə·set′ə·fī), *v.,* **-fied, -fy·ing.** turn into vinegar. —**a·cet′i·fi·ca′tion,** *n.*

ac·e·tone (as′ə·tōn), *n.* a colorless, volatile, inflammable liquid, $CH_3·CO·CH_3$, used as a solvent and in making varnishes, etc.

ac·e·tyl·cho·line (as′ə·til·kō′lēn; -lin), *n.* chemical compound that transmits nerve impulses.

a·cet·y·lene (ə·set′ə·lēn; -lin), *n.* a colorless gas, C_2H_2, that burns with a bright light and very hot flame, used for lighting and, combined with oxygen, for welding metals.

ac·e·tyl·sal·i·cyl·ic acid (as′ə·til·sal′ə·sil′ik; ə·sē′təl-), aspirin.

A·chae·a (ə·kē′ə), **A·cha·ia** (ə·kā′ə), *n.* country in ancient Greece, in the S part. —**A·chae′an, A·cha′ian,** *adj., n.*

A·cha·tes (ə·kā′tēz), *n.* **1.** the faithful companion of Aeneas. **2.** a faithful companion.

ache (āk), *v.,* **ached, ach·ing,** *n.* —*v.* **1.** be in continued pain. **2.** *Colloq.* wish very much. —*n.* **1.** a dull, steady pain. [OE *acan*] —**ach′ing·ly,** *adv.* —**Syn.** *v.* **1.** hurt. **2.** long, yearn.

a·chene (ā·kēn′), *n. Bot.* any small, dry, hard fruit consisting of one seed with a thin outer covering that does not burst when ripe. Also, **akene.** [< NL < Gk., < *a-* not + *chainein* gape; because it ripens without bursting]

Ach·er·on (ak′ər·on), *n. Class. Myth.* **1.** river in Hades. **2.** the lower world; Hades.

a·chieve (ə·chēv′), *v.,* **a·chieved, a·chiev·ing. 1.** bring to a successful end; accomplish: *achieve one's purpose.* **2.** get by effort: *achieve distinction.* [< OF, < (*venir*) a chief (come) to a head] —**a·chiev′a·ble,** *adj.* —**a·chiev′er,** *n.* —**Syn. 1.**

finish, complete, effect. **2.** gain, attain. —**Ant. 1.** fail.

a·chieve·ment (ə·chēv′mənt), *n.* **1.** thing achieved. **2.** act of achieving. —**Syn. 1.** accomplishment, feat, exploit.

A·chil·les (ə·kil′ēz), *n. Gk. Legend.* hero of the Greeks at the siege of Troy. No weapon could injure Achilles anywhere, except in the heel. —**Ach·il·le·an** (ak′ə·lē′ən), *adj.*

ach·ro·mat·ic (ak′rə·mat′ik), *adj.* transmitting white light without breaking it up into the colors of the spectrum. [< Gk., < *a-* without + *chroma* color] —**ach′ro·mat′i·cal·ly,** *adv.*

ac·id (as′id), *n.* **1.** *Chem.* a compound that yields hydrogen ions when dissolved in water, usually reacts with a base to form salt and water, and turns blue litmus paper red. **2.** substance having a sour taste. —*adj.* **1.** *Chem.* of or having the properties of an acid. **2.** sour; sharp; biting. [< L *acidus* sour] —**ac′id·ly,** *adv.* —**ac′id·ness,** *n.*

a·cid·ic (ə·sid′ik), *adj.* forming acid.

a·cid·i·fy (ə·sid′ə·fī), *v.,* **-fied, -fy·ing. 1.** make or become sour. **2.** change into an acid. —**a·cid′i·fi·ca′tion,** *n.* —**a·cid′i·fi′er,** *n.*

a·cid·i·ty (ə·sid′ə·ti), *n., pl.* **-ties.** acid quality or condition; sourness.

ac·i·do·sis (as′ə·dō′sis), *n.* a harmful condition in which the blood and tissues are less alkaline than is normal.

acid test, a thorough test.

a·cid·u·late (ə·sij′ə·lāt), *v.,* **-lat·ed, -lat·ing.** make slightly acid or sour. —**a·cid′u·la′tion,** *n.*

a·cid·u·lous (ə·sij′ə·ləs), *adj.* slightly acid or sour. —**a·cid′u·lous·ly,** *adv.* —**a·cid′u·lous·ness,** *n.*

ack-ack (ak′ak′), *n. Slang.* anti-aircraft fire. [British radio operator's code word for AA (anti-aircraft)]

ac·knowl·edge (ak·nol′ij), *v.,* **-edged, -edg·ing. 1.** admit to be true. **2.** recognize the authority or claims of. **3.** express appreciation of (a gift, favor, etc.). **4.** make known the receipt of: *acknowledge a letter.* **5.** recognize or certify in legal form: *acknowledge a deed.* [blend of obs. *acknow* admit + *knowledge*, v., admit] —**ac·knowl′edge·a·ble,** *adj.* —**ac·knowl′edged·ly,** *adv.* —**ac·knowl′edg·er,** *n.* —**Syn. 1.** concede. **2.** accept. —**Ant. 1.** deny. **2.** reject.

ac·knowl·edg·ment, *occas. Brit.* **ac·knowl·edge·ment** (ak·nol′ij·mənt), *n.* **1.** thing given or done to show that one has received a gift, favor, message, etc. **2.** act of admitting the existence or truth of anything. **3.** recognition of authority or claims. **4.** expression of thanks. **5.** official certificate in legal form. —**Syn. 2.** admission. **3.** acceptance.

ac·me (ak′mē), *n.* the highest point. [< Gk. *akme* point] —**Syn.** apex.

ac·ne (ak′nē), *n.* a skin disease in which the oil glands in the skin become clogged and inflamed, often causing pimples. [? < Gk. *akme* point]

ac·o·lyte (ak′ə·līt), *n.* **1.** altar boy. **2.** attendant; assistant. **3.** *Rom. Cath. Ch.* person ordained to the fourth and highest of the minor orders. [< Med.L < Gk. *akolouthos* follower]

ac·o·nite (ak′ə·nīt), *n.* **1.** any of a genus of poisonous plants, with blue, purple, or yellow flowers shaped like hoods, including wolf's-bane and monkshood. **2.** drug used to relieve inflammation and pain, obtained from one of these plants. [< F < L < Gk. *akoniton*]

a·corn (ā′kôrn; ā′kərn), *n.* the nut, or fruit, of an oak tree. [OE *æcern*]

a·cous·tic (ə·küs′tik), **a·cous·ti·cal** (-tə·kəl), *adj.* **1.** having to do with the sense or the organs of hearing. **2.** having to do with the science of sound. **3.** exploded by sound: *an acoustic mine.* [< F < Gk. *akoustikos* having to do with hearing < *akouein* hear] —**a·cous′ti·cal·ly,** *adv.*

a·cous·tics (ə·küs′tiks), *n.* **1.** (*pl. in use*) the qualities of a room, hall, auditorium, etc., that determine how well sounds can be heard in it;

acoustic qualities. 2. *Physics.* (*sing. in use*) science of sound.

ac·quaint (ə·kwānt′), *v.* 1. inform (a person about a thing): *acquaint him with your intention.* 2. make more or less familiar: *acquaint oneself with the facts.* 3. **be acquainted with,** have personal knowledge of: *he is acquainted with my father.* [< OF *acointer* < LL, < L *ad-* to + *cognitus* known < *com* with + *gnoscere* come to know] —**Syn.** 1. tell. 2. familiarize.

ac·quaint·ance (ə·kwān′təns), *n.* 1. person known to one, but not a close friend. 2. knowledge of persons or things gained from experience with them. —**ac·quaint′ance·ship,** *n.*

ac·qui·esce (ak′wi·es′), *v.,* **-esced, -esc·ing.** give consent by keeping silent; submit quietly: *we acquiesced in their plan.* [< F < L, < *ad-* to + *quiescere* to rest] —**ac′qui·esc′ing·ly,** *adv.*

ac·qui·es·cence (ak′wi·es′əns), *n.* consent without making objections; submitting quietly.

ac·qui·es·cent (ak′wi·es′ənt), *adj.* submitting with apparent consent. —**ac′qui·es′cent·ly,** *adv.*

ac·quire (ə·kwīr′), *v.,* **-quired, -quir·ing.** 1. receive or get as one's own: *acquire land.* 2. get by one's own efforts or actions: *acquire an education.* [< L, < *ad-* to + *quaerere* seek] —**ac·quir′a·ble,** *adj.* —**ac·quir′er,** *n.* —**Syn.** 1. obtain. 2. gain, win.

ac·quire·ment (ə·kwīr′mənt), *n.* 1. act of acquiring. 2. something acquired; attainment.

ac·qui·si·tion (ak′wə·zish′ən), *n.* 1. act of acquiring. 2. thing acquired.

ac·quis·i·tive (ə·kwiz′ə·tiv), *adj.* fond of acquiring; likely to get and keep. —**ac·quis′i·tive·ly,** *adv.* —**ac·quis′i·tive·ness,** *n.*

ac·quit (ə·kwit′), *v.,* **-quit·ted, -quit·ting.** 1. declare (a person) not guilty (of an offense). 2. set free (from a duty, an obligation, etc.). 3. conduct (oneself): *the soldiers acquitted themselves well in battle.* 4. pay off or settle (a debt, claim, etc.). [< OF, < *a-* + *quitte* free < L *quietus* quiet] —**ac·quit′ter,** *n.* —**Syn.** 1. exonerate. 2. release. 3. behave. —**Ant.** 1. condemn.

ac·quit·tal (ə·kwit′əl), *n.* 1. a setting free by declaring not guilty; discharge; release. 2. performance (of a duty, obligation, etc.).

ac·quit·tance (ə·kwit′əns), *n.* 1. release from a debt or obligation. 2. payment of a debt. 3. a written acknowledgment.

a·cre (ā′kər), *n.* 1. a measure of land, 160 square rods or 43,560 square feet. 2. **acres,** lands; property. [OE *æcer* field]

A·cre (ä′kər; ā′kər), *n.* seaport in NW Palestine, important during the Crusades.

a·cre·age (ā′kər·ij), *n.* 1. number of acres. 2. piece of land sold by the acre.

ac·rid (ak′rid), *adj.* 1. sharp or stinging to the nose, mouth, or skin. 2. sharp or irritating in manner. [< L *acer* sharp] —**a·crid·i·ty** (ə·krid′ə·ti), **ac′rid·ness,** *n.* —**ac′rid·ly,** *adv.*

Ac·ri·lan (ak′rə·lan), *n. Trademark.* a synthetic, wrinkle-resistant fiber, resembling wool in texture.

ac·ri·mo·ni·ous (ak′rə·mō′ni·əs), *adj.* caustic and stinging; bitter. —**ac′ri·mo′ni·ous·ly,** *adv.* —**ac′ri·mo′ni·ous·ness,** *n.*

ac·ri·mo·ny (ak′rə·mō′ni), *n., pl.* **-nies.** sharpness or bitterness in temper, language, or manner. [< L *acrimonia* < *acer* sharp]

ac·ro·bat (ak′rə·bat), *n.* person who can perform on a trapeze, a tightrope, etc. [< F < Gk., < *akros* tip (of the toes) + *-batos* going] —**ac′ro·bat′ic,** *adj.* —**ac′ro·bat′i·cal·ly,** *adv.*

ac·ro·bat·ics (ak′rə·bat′iks), *n.pl.* 1. gymnastic feats. 2. feats like those of an acrobat.

ac·ro·gen (ak′rə·jən), *n. Bot.* plant growing only at the apex, such as the ferns and mosses. [< Gk. *akros* tip + *-genes* born] —**ac·ro·gen·ic** (ak′rə·jen′ik), **a·crog·e·nous** (ə·kroj′ə·nəs), *adj.* —**a·crog′e·nous·ly,** *adv.*

ac·ro·meg·a·ly (ak′rō·meg′ə·li), *n.* a disease in which the head, hands, and feet become permanently enlarged. [< F, < Gk. *akros* tip + *megas* big] —**ac·ro·me·gal·ic** (ak′rō·mə·gal′ik), *adj.*

ac·ro·nym (ak′rə·nim), *n.* word formed from the first letters or syllables of other words, as UNESCO. [< Gk. *akros* tip + *onyma* name]

a·crop·o·lis (ə·krop′ə·lis), *n.* the high, fortified part of an ancient Greek city, esp. the Acropolis of Athens. [< Gk., < *akros* highest part of + *polis* city]

a·cross (ə·krôs′; ə·kros′), *prep.* 1. from side to side of; over: *a bridge laid across a river.* 2. on or to the other side of; beyond: *across the sea.* 3. into contact with: *come across a new word.* 4. **across the board,** without any exceptions. —*adv.* 1. from one side to the other: *what is the distance across?* 2. from side to side; crosswise: *with arms across.* 3. on or to the other side: *when are you going across?* 4. **come across,** *U.S. Colloq.* a. pay up; hand over. b. own up; admit.

a·cros·tic (ə·krôs′tik; ə·kros′-), *n.* a composition in verse or an arrangement of words in which the first, last, or certain other letters of each line, taken in order, spell a word or phrase.—*adj.* of or forming an acrostic. [< L < Gk., < *akros* tip + *stichos* row] —**a·cros′ti·cal·ly,** *adv.*

ac·ry·lo·ni·trile (ak′rə·lō·ni′trəl), *n.* a colorless, inflammable, poisonous liquid, CH_2:CH·CN. It is used in making certain kinds of synthetic rubber, fabrics, etc.

**North
East
West
South**

Acrostic

act (akt), *n.* 1. thing done; deed: *an act of kindness.* 2. process of doing: *in the act of stealing.* 3. a main division of a play or opera. 4. one of several performances on a program: *the trained dog's act.* 5. a legislative decision; law: *an act of Congress.* 6. a legal document proving that something has been done. —*v.* 1. put forth effort: *act at once.* 2. perform specific duties or functions: *act as counsel for the committee.* 3. behave: *act tired.* 4. behave like: *act the fool.* 5. have an effect or influence: *yeast acts on dough.* 6. play a part; perform in a theater. 7. act as or for, take the place of; do the work of. 8. **act up,** *Am., Colloq.* a. behave badly. b. play tricks; make mischief. [< L *actus* a doing and *actum* (thing) done < *agere* to do] —**act′a·ble,** *adj.* —**Syn.** *n.* 5. decree, statute. ▶**act.** In the sense "to behave," *act* is a linking verb, so that its meaning can be completed by an adjective: *he acts old, he acts older than he is.*

ACTH, *n.* a hormone used in treating arthritis, rheumatic fever, etc.

act·ing (ak′ting), *adj.* 1. temporarily taking another's place and doing his duties. 2. that acts or functions. 3. arranged for the use of actors.

ac·tin·ic (ak·tin′ik), *adj.* 1. of actinism. 2. producing chemical changes by radiation. [< Gk. *aktis* ray]

ac·tin·ism (ak′tən·iz·əm), *n.* property in light that causes chemical changes.

ac·tin·i·um (ak·tin′i·əm), *n.* a radioactive chemical element, Ac, somewhat like radium, found in pitchblende.

ac·ti·no·zo·an (ak′tə·nə·zō′ən), *n. Zool.* sea animal belonging to the group that includes corals, sea anemones, etc.

ac·tion (ak′shən), *n.* 1. process of acting: *a machine in action.* 2. activity: *a soldier is a man of action.* 3. thing done; act. 4. **actions,** conduct; behavior. 5. exertion of power or force; influence: *the action of wind on a ship's sails.* 6. way of moving or working; movement: *a motor with an easy action.* 7. the working parts of a machine, instrument, etc. 8. a minor battle. 9. combat between military forces. 10. series of events in a story or play. 11. a lawsuit. 12. **take action,** a. become active. b. start working. c. start a lawsuit; sue. [< F < L *actio.* See ACT.] —**ac′tion·less,** *adj.*

ac·tion·a·ble (ak′shən·ə·bəl), *adj.* justifying a lawsuit. —**ac′tion·a·bly,** *adv.*

ac·ti·vate (ak′tə·vāt), *v.,* **-vat·ed, -vat·ing.** 1. make active. 2. *Physics.* make radioactive. 3. *Chem.* make capable of reacting or of speeding up a reaction. 4. purify (sewage) by treating it with air and bacteria. —**ac′ti·va′tion,** *n.* —**ac′ti·va′tor,** *n.*

ac·tive (ak′tiv), *adj.* 1. acting; working: *an active volcano.* 2. moving rather quickly; lively. 3. showing much or constant action: *an active market.* 4. real; effective: *take an active part.* 5. causing action or change. 6. *Gram.* showing the subject of a verb as acting. In "He broke the window," *broke* is in the active voice. —*n.* the active voice. [< F < L *activus*. See ACT.] —*ac'*-**tive·ly,** *adv.* —**ac'tive·ness,** *n.* —**Syn.** *adj.* 2. nimble, quick. 3. vigorous, energetic. ≫ A verb is in the active voice when its subject is the doer of the action: "Jimmy's father *gave* him a car" as contrasted with the passive verb in "Jimmy *was given* a car by his father."

active duty or **service,** 1. military service with full pay and regular duties. 2. service in the armed forces in time of war.

ac·tiv·i·ty (ak·tiv'ə·ti), *n., pl.* **–ties.** 1. state of being active: *mental activity.* 2. action; doing: *the activities of enemy spies.* 3. vigorous action; liveliness: *no activity in the market.* 4. thing to do; sphere of action: *outside activities.* 5. anything active; active force.

act of God, a sudden, unforeseeable, and uncontrollable action of natural forces, such as flood, storm, or earthquake.

ac·tor (ak'tər), *n.* 1. person who acts on the stage, in moving pictures, or in a broadcast. 2. person who acts; a doer.

ac·tress (ak'tris), *n.* a female actor.

Acts (akts), or **Acts of the Apostles,** *n.* the fifth book of the New Testament.

ac·tu·al (ak'chŭ·əl), *adj.* 1. existing as a fact; real: *the actual as opposed to the imaginary.* 2. now existing; present; current: *the actual state of affairs.* [< F < LL < L *actus* a doing. See ACT.] —**ac'tu·al·ness,** *n.* —**Syn.** 1. true, genuine.

ac·tu·al·i·ty (ak'chŭ·al'ə·ti), *n., pl.* **–ties.** 1. actual existence. 2. actual thing; fact.

ac·tu·al·ize (ak'chŭ·əl·īz), *v.,* **–ized, –iz·ing.** make actual. —**ac'tu·al·i·za'tion,** *n.*

ac·tu·al·ly (ak'chŭ·əl·i), *adv.* really; in fact.

ac·tu·ar·y (ak'chŭ·er'i), *n., pl.* **–ar·ies.** person whose work is figuring values, rates, etc., for insurance companies. See ACT.] —**ac·tu·ar·i·al** (ak'chŭ·ãr'i·əl), *adj.* —**ac'tu·ar'i·al·ly,** *adv.*

ac·tu·ate (ak'chŭ·āt), *v.,* **–at·ed, –at·ing.** 1. put into action. 2. influence to act. [< LL, < L *actus* action] —**ac'tu·a'tion,** *n.* —**ac'tu·a'tor,** *n.*

a·cu·i·ty (ə·kū'ə·ti), *n.* sharpness; acuteness. [< Med.L < OF *aguëté* < *agu* sharp < L *acutus*]

a·cu·men (ə·kū'mən), *n.* sharpness and quickness in seeing and understanding; keen insight. [< L, < *acuere* sharpen]

a·cute (ə·kūt'), *adj.* 1. having a sharp point. 2. sharp and severe: *an acute fuel shortage.* 3. brief and severe: *an acute attack of appendicitis.* 4. keen: *an acute sense of smell.* 5. intense; poignant: *acute jealousy.* 6. (of sounds) high in pitch; shrill. 7. having the mark (ˊ) over it. —*n.* acute accent. [< L < *acuere* sharpen] —**a·cute'ly,** *adv.* —**a·cute'ness,** *n.*

acute accent, mark (ˊ) used to show the quality of a vowel, as in French *abbé,* or to show stress, as in Spanish *adiós.*

acute angle, *Geom.* angle less than a right angle.

ad (ad), *n. Am., Colloq.* advertisement. ≫ Ad is the clipped form of *advertisement,* has only one *d,* and should not be followed by a period. Like other clipped words it belongs to informal and familiar speech and writing.

ad–, *prefix.* to; toward, as in *admit, administer, adverb, advert.* [< L *ad,* prep.; appears also, by assimilation to the following consonant, as *ac–, af–, ag–, al–, an–, ap–, ar–, as–, at–,* and, by reduction before *sc, sp, st,* as *a–*]

A.D., in the year of the Lord; since Christ was born: *Augustus lived from 63 B.C. to 14 A.D.* [for LL *anno domini*]

ad·age (ad'ij), *n.* a brief, familiar proverb; an old saying. [< F < L *adagium*]

a·da·gio (ə·dä'jō; –zhi·ō), *adv., adj., n., pl.* **–gios.** *Music.* —*adv.* slowly. —*adj.* slow. —*n.* a slow part in a piece of music. [< Ital. *ad agio* at ease]

Ad·am (ad'əm), *n. Bible.* the first man.

ad·a·mant (ad'ə·mant), *n.* substance too hard to be cut or broken. —*adj.* 1. too hard to be cut or broken. 2. unyielding; firm; immovable. [< OF *adamaunt* the hardest stone (= diamond) < L < Gk., < *a–* not + *damaein* subdue]

ad·a·man·tine (ad'ə·man'tin; –tēn; –tīn), *adj.* adamant; impenetrable; unyielding.

Ad·ams (ad'əmz), *n.* 1. **John,** 1735–1826, second president of the United States, 1797–1801. 2. **John Quincy,** 1767–1848, sixth president of the United States, 1825–29, son of John Adams.

Adam's apple, the lump in the front of the throat formed by the thyroid cartilage.

a·dapt (ə·dapt'), *v.* 1. make fit or suitable; adjust: *adapt oneself to a new job.* 2. modify or alter for a different use: *adapt a novel for the stage.* [< L, < *ad–* to + *aptare* fit] —**a·dapt'**-**er,** *n.* —**Syn.** 1. accommodate.

a·dapt·a·ble (ə·dap'tə·bəl), *adj.* 1. easily changed to fit different conditions. 2. changing easily to fit different conditions. —**a·dapt'**-**a·bil'i·ty, a·dapt'a·ble·ness,** *n.*

ad·ap·ta·tion (ad'əp·tā'shən), *n.* 1. adjustment to new or different circumstances. 2. result of altering for a different use. 3. *Biol.* change in structure, form, or habits to fit different conditions. —**ad'ap·ta'tion·al,** *adj.*

a·dap·tive (ə·dap'tiv), *adj.* 1. that can adapt. 2. showing adaptation. —**a·dap'tive·ly,** *adv.* —**a·dap'tive·ness,** *n.*

A-day (ā'dā'), *n., adj. Am.* Able Day.

add (ad), *v.* 1. join (one thing to another); put together; put with: *add another stone to the pile.* 2. find the sum of: *add 8 and 2 and you have 10.* 3. make or form an addition; increase: *add to our pleasure.* 4. say further. [< L, < *ad–* to + *dare* put] —**add'a·ble, add'i·ble,** *adj.* —**add'er,** *n.*

ad·dax (ad'aks), *n.* a large antelope of Arabia and N Africa. [< L < an African word]

ad·den·dum (ə·den'dəm), *n., pl.* **–da** (–də). 1. thing to be added. 2. things added; appendix.

ad·der (ad'ər), *n.* 1. a small, poisonous snake of Europe. 2. a small, harmless snake of North America. 3. puff adder. [OE *nœdre;* in ME a *nadder* was taken as *an adder*]

ad·der's-tongue (ad'ərz·tung'), *n.* 1. a variety of small fern with a fruiting spike. 2. *Am.* the dogtooth violet.

ad·dict (*n.* ad'ikt; *v.* ə·dikt'), *n.* person who is a slave or devotee to a habit. —*v.* give (oneself) over, as to a habit. [< L, < *ad–* to + *dicere* say] —**ad·dic'tion,** *n.*

ad·dict·ed (ə·dik'tid), *adj.* slavishly following (a habit, practice); strongly inclined.

Ad·dis Ab·a·ba (ad'is ab'ə·bə), the capital of Ethiopia, in E Africa.

Ad·di·son (ad'ə·sən), *n.* **Joseph,** 1672–1719, English essayist, poet, and statesman. —**Ad·di·so·ni·an** (ad'ə·sō'ni·ən), *adj.*

ad·di·tion (ə·dish'ən), *n.* 1. act or process of adding. 2. result of adding; thing added. 3. *Am.* part added to a building. 4. *Am.* a. land added to existing holdings. b. recent extension of the residential section of a city. 5. **in addition to,** besides; also. [< F < L. See ADD.]

ad·di·tion·al (ə·dish'ən·əl), *adj.* added; supplementary. —**ad·di'tion·al·ly,** *adv.*

ad·di·tive (ad'ə·tiv), *adj.* 1. to be added. 2. *Gram.* linking and making equal two or more elements of a sentence. In "the dog and the cat," *and* is an additive element. —*n.* 1. an additive word or element. 2. a chemical compound or other substance added to anything to increase its effectiveness.

ad·dle (ad'əl), *v.,* **–dled, –dling,** *adj.* —*v.* 1. make or become confused. 2. make or become rotten. —*adj.* muddled; confused, as in addlebrain, addleheaded, etc. [OE *adela* liquid filth]

ad·dress (ə·dres'; *esp. for n. defs. 3 and 4,* ad'res), *n., v.,* **–dressed** or **–drest, –dress·ing.** —*n.* 1. a speech, esp. a formal one: *the President's inaugural address.* 2. an expression of views in writing transmitted to an authority: *an address from the colonists to the king, listing grievances.* 3. place at which a person, business, etc., receives mail. **4.** the writing on an envelope, package, etc., that shows where it is to be sent. **5.** manner in conversation. **6.** skill; adroitness. **7. addresses,** attention paid in courtship. —*v.* **1.** direct speech or writing to: *the President addressed the nation over the radio.* **2.** use titles or other forms in speaking or writing to: *how do you address a mayor?* **3.** direct to the attention: *address a warning to a friend.* **4.** apply (oneself) in speech (to a person): *he addressed himself to the chairman.* **5.** write on (a letter, package, etc.) where it is to be sent. **6.** apply or devote (oneself); direct one's energies: *he addressed himself to the task of doing his homework.* [< F *adresser* direct to < OF < L, < *ad-* to + *directus* straight] —**ad·dress′er, ad·dres′sor,** *n.* ≽ **addresses.** When the various parts of a person's address are written on the same line, they are separated by commas: *Miss Louise Finney, 48 Adirondack View, Middlebury, Vermont; Mr. Davis was a native of Carroll County, Va., and a graduate of the College of William and Mary.*

ad·dress·ee (ə·dres·ē′; ad′res·ē′), *n. Am.* person to whom a letter, etc., is addressed.

ad·duce (ə·düs′; ə·dūs′), *v.,* **–duced, –duc·ing.** offer as a reason; give as proof or evidence. [< L, < *ad–* to + *ducere* lead]

ad·duct (ə·dukt′), *v. Physiol.* pull (a part of the body) inward toward the main axis. [< L *adductus,* pp. See ADDUCE.] —**ad·duc′tive,** *adj.* —**ad·duc′tor,** *n.* —**Ant.** abduct.

ad·duc·tion (ə·duk′shən), *n.* **1.** an adducing. **2.** *Physiol.* an adducting.

Ad·e·laide (ad′ə·lād), *n.* city in S Australia.

A·den (äd′ən, ā′dən), *n.* **1.** territory in SW Arabia, under British control. **2.** British colony there. **3.** seaport and capital of the colony. —**A·den·ese** (ā′dən·ēz; –ēs′; ä′–), *adj.*

Ad·e·nau·er (ad′ə·nou′ər), *n.* **Konrad,** born 1876, German statesman; chancellor of West Germany from 1949 to 1963.

ad·e·noid (ad′ə·noid), **ad·e·noi·dal** (ad′ə·noi′dəl), *adj.* **1.** of the lymphatic glands. **2.** glandular.

ad·e·noids (ad′ə·noidz), *n.pl.* growths of glandular tissue in the part of the throat behind the nose, that often interfere with natural breathing and speaking. [< Gk., < *aden* gland]

ad·ept (*n.* ad′ept, ə·dept′; *adj.* ə·dept′), *n.* a thoroughly skilled person; expert. —*adj.* thoroughly skilled. [< L *adeptus* < *ad–* to + *apisci* get] —**a·dept′ly,** *adv.* —**a·dept′ness,** *n.*

ad·e·qua·cy (ad′ə·kwə·si), *n.* as much as is needed for a particular purpose; sufficiency.

ad·e·quate (ad′ə·kwit), *adj.* **1.** as much as is needed; fully sufficient: *means adequate to the object.* **2.** suitable; competent: *an adequate person for the job.* [< L, < *ad–* to + *aequus* equal] —**ad′e·quate·ly,** *adv.* —**ad′e·quate·ness,** *n.* —**Syn. 1.** enough, requisite, needful.

ad·here (ad·hir′), *v.,* **–hered, –her·ing. 1.** stick fast (to): *mud adheres to your shoes.* **2.** hold closely or firmly (to): *adhere to a plan.* **3.** be devoted (to): *most people adhere to the church of their parents.* [< L, < *ad–* to + *haerere* stick]

ad·her·ence (ad·hir′əns), *n.* **1.** steady attachment or loyalty (to a person, group, belief, etc.). **2.** a holding to and following closely.

ad·her·ent (ad·hir′ənt), *n.* faithful supporter. —*adj.* adhering. —**ad·her′ent·ly,** *adv.*

ad·he·sion (ad·hē′zhən), *n.* **1.** act or state of adhering; a sticking fast. **2.** following and supporting; faithfulness. **3.** agreement; assent. **4.** *Physics.* the attraction that holds molecules together. **5.** *Pathol.* the growing together of tissues that should be separate.

ad·he·sive (ad·hē′siv; –ziv), *adj.* **1.** holding fast; adhering easily; sticky. **2.** smeared with a sticky substance for holding (something) fast: *adhesive tape.* —*n. U.S.* gummed tape used to hold bandages in place. —**ad·he′sive·ly,** *adv.* —**ad·he′sive·ness,** *n.*

ad hoc (ad hok′), for a certain purpose; special. [< L, for this]

ad·i·a·bat·ic (ad′i·ə·bat′ik; ā′dī–), *adj. Physics.* without transmission (gain or loss) of heat. —**ad′i·a·bat′i·cal·ly,** *adv.*

a·dieu (ə·dü′; ə·dū′), *interj., n., pl.* **a·dieus, a·dieux** (ə·düz′; ə·dūz′). —*interj.* good-by; farewell. —*n.* a farewell. [< F *à dieu* to God]

ad in·fi·ni·tum (ad in′fə·nī′təm), *Latin.* without limit; forever.

ad in·te·rim (ad in′tə·rim), *Latin.* **1.** in the meantime. **2.** temporary.

a·di·os (ä′di·ōs′; ad′i–), *Am., S.W.* —*interj.* good-by. —*n.* a farewell. [< Sp. *a dios* to God]

ad·i·pose (ad′ə·pōs), *adj.* fatty. —*n.* animal fat. [< NL < L *adeps* fat] —**ad′i·pose·ness, ad·i·pos·i·ty** (ad′ə·pos′ə·ti), *n.*

Ad·i·ron·dacks (ad′ə·ron′daks), or **Adi·rondack Mountains,** *n.pl.* a mountain range in NE New York.

adj., 1. adjective. **2.** adjunct. **3.** adjustment.

ad·ja·cen·cy (ə·jā′sən·si), *n., pl.* **–cies. 1.** nearness. **2.** that which is adjacent.

ad·ja·cent (ə·jā′sənt), *adj.* lying near or close; adjoining: *the garage is adjacent to our house.* [< L, < *ad–* near + *jacere* to lie] —**ad·ja′cent·ly,** *adv.* —**Syn.** bordering, neighboring. —**Ant.** distant.

adjacent angles, *Geom.* two angles that have the same vertex and the same line as one of their sides. In the diagram, ADB and BDC are adjacent angles.

ad·jec·ti·val (aj′ik·tī′vəl; aj′ik·ti·vəl), *adj.* of or used as an adjective. —**ad′jec·ti′val·ly,** *adv.*

ad·jec·tive (aj′ik·tiv), *Gram.* —*n.* a word used to qualify or limit a noun or pronoun. A descriptive adjective shows a quality or condition as belonging to the noun or pronoun named, as, a *blue* shirt, a *wrecked* car. A limiting adjective points out in some way the noun or pronoun named, or indicates quantity or number, as, *this* pencil, *his* book, *any* person, *twenty-five* cents. —*adj.* **1.** of an adjective. **2.** used as an adjective. [< L *adjectivus* that is added to < *ad–* to + *jacere* throw] —**ad′jec·tive·ly,** *adv.* ≽ **adjective. 1. forms of adjectives.** Many adjectives have come down from an early period of the language (*high, handsome, civil*) and many have been made and are still being made by adding a suffix to a noun or verb. Some suffixes that are still active are: *–able* (*–ible*), as in *translatable; dirigible; –ed,* as in *sugared,* and usually in adjectives that are compound words: *four-footed, well-lighted; –escent,* as in *florescent; –ese,* as in *Burmese, journalese; –ful,* as in *playful, soulful; –ish,* as in *babyish, cattish, womanish; –less,* as in *harmless, fearless; –like,* as in *birdlike; –y,* as in *cranky, dreamy, corny.* **2. position of adjectives.** According to its position in a sentence, an adjective is either attributive or predicate: *Attributive* adjectives are placed next to their nouns, usually preceding as in the *tiny* brook, *horseless* carriages. *Predicate* adjectives come after some form of the verb *be* or some other linking verb (*taste, feel, turn, . . .*)*:* the day is *warm,* the train was *crowded,* that pie smells *good,* for a while I felt *bad.* **3. comparison of adjectives.** A greater degree of the quality named by an adjective is shown by adding *–er* or *–est* to the adjective or by placing *more* or *most* before it: *warm, warmer* or *more warm, warmest* or *most warm.*

ad·join (ə·join′), *v.* **1.** be next to; be in contact with: *Canada adjoins the United States.* **2.** be next or close to each other; be in contact. [< OF *ajoindre* < L, < *ad–* to + *jungere* join] —**ad·join′ing,** *adj.*

ad·journ (ə·jėrn′), *v.* **1.** put off until a later time: *the club adjourned consideration of the question.* **2.** suspend the meeting of to a future time or to another place: *the judge adjourned the court for two hours.* **3.** stop business or proceedings for a time: *the court adjourned from Friday until Monday.* **4.** *Colloq.* go to another place. [< OF *ajorner* < *a–* for (< L *ad–*) + *jorn* day < LL *diurnum,* unit. < L *dies* day]

ad·journ·ment (ə·jėrn′mənt), *n.* **1.** act of adjourning. **2.** time during which a court, law-making body, etc., is adjourned.

Adjt., Adjutant.

ad·judge (ə·juj′), *v.,* **–judged, –judg·ing. 1.** decree or declare by law: *the accused man was* *adjudged guilty.* **2.** condemn or sentence by law: *the thief was adjudged to prison for two years.* **3.** decide or settle by law; judge. **4.** award or assign by law. [< OF *ajugier* < L, < *ad–* to + *judicare* judge. Doublet of ADJUDICATE.] —**adjudge′a·ble,** *adj.*

ad·ju·di·cate (ə·jü′də·kāt), *v.,* **–cat·ed, –cat·ing. 1.** decide or settle by law. **2.** act as judge. [< L *adjudicatus,* pp. Doublet of ADJUDGE.] —**ju′di·ca′tion,** *n.* —**ad·ju′di·ca′tive,** *adj.* —**ad·ju′di·ca′tor,** *n.*

ad·junct (aj′ungkt), *n.* **1.** something added that is less important or not necessary, but helpful. **2.** a subordinate colleague. **3.** *Gram.* word or phrase qualifying or modifying another word or phrase. [< L *adjunctus,* pp. of *adjungere* join to. See ADJOIN.] —**ad·junc′tive,** *adj.* —**ad·junc′tive·ly,** *adv.*

ad·jure (ə·jür′), *v.,* **–jured, –jur·ing. 1.** command or charge (a person) on oath or under some penalty (to do something). **2.** ask earnestly or solemnly. [< L, < *ad–* to + *jurare* swear] —**ad·ju·ra·tion** (aj′ú·rā′shən), *n.* —**ad·jur·a·to·ry** (ə·jür′ə·tô′ri; –tō′–), *adj.* —**ad·jur′er,** **ad·ju′ror,** *n.*

ad·just (ə·just′), *v.* **1.** fit or adapt (one thing to another): *adjust a seat to the height of a child.* **2.** regulate for use: *adjust a radio dial.* **3.** arrange satisfactorily; settle: *adjust a difference of opinion.* **4.** accommodate oneself; get used: *adjust well to army life.* [< F *ajuster* < a– (< L *ad–*) + *juste* right < L *justus*] —**ad·just′a·ble,** *adj.* —**ad·just′a·bly,** *adv.* —**ad·just′ed,** *adj.* —**ad·just′er, ad·jus′tor,** *n.*

ad·just·ment (ə·just′mənt), *n.* **1.** act or process of adjusting. **2.** orderly arrangement of parts or elements. **3.** means of adjusting. **4.** settlement of a dispute, a claim, etc.

ad·ju·tan·cy (aj′ə·tən·si), *n., pl.* **–cies.** rank or position of an adjutant in the army.

ad·ju·tant (aj′ə·tənt), *n.* **1.** army officer who assists a commanding officer by sending out orders, writing letters, giving messages, etc. **2.** helper; assistant. **3.** a very large species of stork of India and Africa. —*adj.* helping. [< L *adjutans,* ult. < *ad–* to + *juvare* help] —**ad′ju·tant·ship′,** *n.*

adjutant general, *pl.* **adjutants general.** adjutant of a division or a larger military unit.

ad-lib (ad·lib′), *v.,* **–libbed, –lib·bing.** *Colloq.* make up and insert as one speaks, performs, or acts; extemporize freely. [< L *ad libitum* at pleasure]

ad lib·i·tum (ad lib′ə·təm), *Music.* a direction to change, omit, or expand a passage as much as the player wishes. [< NL, at pleasure]

Adm., Admiral; Admiralty.

ad·min·is·ter (ad·min′əs·tər), *v.* **1.** manage or conduct as chief agent or steward; direct: *administer a government department.* **2.** put in force; dispense: *administer relief.* **3.** supply or give: *administer punishment to a person.* **4.** offer or tender (an oath). **5.** *Law.* settle or take charge of (an estate). **6.** act as administrator. **7.** be helpful; add something; contribute. [< L, < *ad–* + *ministrare* serve < *minister* servant] —**ad·min·is·tra·ble** (ad·min′əs·trə·bəl), *adj.* —**ad·min·is·trant** (ad·min′əs·trənt), *n.*

ad·min·is·trate (ad·min′əs·trāt), *v.,* **–trat·ed, –trat·ing.** *U.S.* administer.

ad·min·is·tra·tion (ad·min′əs·trā′shən), *n.* **1.** management (of a business, public affairs, etc.). **2.** the conducting of the governmental duties of a state, esp. its executive functions. **3. a.** the officials charged with the execution of law and the management of public affairs. **b.** *Am.* the President of the United States and his Cabinet. **4. a.** the period of office of these officials. **b.** *Am.* the term or terms during which a President holds office. **5.** a giving out, applying, or dispensing (medicine, justice, etc.).

ad·min·is·tra·tive (ad·min′əs·trā′tiv), *adj.* executive. —**ad·min′is·tra′tive·ly,** *adv.*

ad·min·is·tra·tor (ad·min′əs·trā′tər), *n.* **1.** person who administers. **2.** *Law.* person appointed by a court to take charge of or settle

an estate. —**ad·min′is·tra′tor·ship,** *n.* —**Syn. 1.** manager, director, executive.

ad·min·is·tra·trix (ad·min′əs·trā′triks), *n.* *Law.* woman administrator.

ad·mi·ra·ble (ad′mə·rə·bəl), *adj.* **1.** worth admiring. **2.** excellent; very good. —**ad′mi·ra·ble·ness,** *n.* —**ad′mi·ra·bly,** *adv.*

ad·mi·ral (ad′mə·rəl), *n.* **1.** commander in chief of a fleet. **2.** naval officer having the highest rank. **3.** admiral, vice-admiral, or rear admiral. **4.** flagship. [earlier *amiral* < OF < Ar. *amīr* al chief of the; akin to AMIR]

ad·mi·ral·ty (ad′mə·rəl·ti), *n., pl.* **–ties. 1.** law or court dealing with affairs of the sea and ships. **2.** in England, the government department in charge of naval affairs. **3.** the Admiralty, official building of the British commissioners for naval affairs, in London.

ad·mi·ra·tion (ad′mə·rā′shən), *n.* **1.** a feeling of wonder, pleasure, and approval. **2.** delight at something fine or beautiful. **3.** one that is admired. **4.** *Archaic.* wonder.

ad·mire (ad·mīr′), *v.,* **–mired, –mir·ing. 1.** regard with wonder, approval, and delight. **2.** feel or express admiration. **3.** *U.S.* like. **4.** *Archaic.* wonder at. [< L, < *ad–* at + *mirari* wonder]

ad·mir·er (ad·mīr′ər), *n.* **1.** person who admires. **2.** man who is in love with a woman.

ad·mir·ing (ad·mīr′ing), *adj.* full of admiration. —**ad·mir′ing·ly,** *adv.*

ad·mis·si·ble (ad·mis′ə·bəl), *adj.* **1.** that can be permitted or considered; allowable. **2.** *Law.* allowable as evidence. **3.** having the right to enter or use. —**ad·mis′si·bil′i·ty, ad·mis′si·ble·ness,** *n.* —**ad·mis′si·bly,** *adv.*

ad·mis·sion (ad·mish′ən), *n.* **1.** act of allowing (a person, animal, etc.) to enter: *admission of aliens into a country.* **2.** power or right to enter or use an office, place, etc. **3.** price paid for the right to enter. **4.** acceptance into an office or position. **5.** confession of an error or a crime. **6.** an acknowledging; accepting as true or valid. **7.** fact or point acknowledged; something accepted as true or valid. **8.** *Am.* formal receiving of a State into the Union. **9.** admission to the bar, *Am.* the granting of authority to practice as a lawyer.

ad·mis·sive (ad·mis′iv), *adj.* tending to admit.

ad·mit (ad·mit′), *v.,* **–mit·ted, –mit·ting. 1.** acknowledge: *admit a mistake.* **2.** accept as true or valid. **3.** allow to enter or use; let in. **4.** give the right to enter. **5.** allow; permit. **6.** be capable (of): *his answer admits of no reply.* **7.** have room for: *the harbor admits three ships.* **8.** *U.S.* let attain to a position, privilege, etc. **9.** *Am.* receive (a State) into the Union. **10.** admit to the bar, *Am.* give authority to practice law. [< L, < *ad–* to + *mittere* let go] —**ad·mit′ter,** *n.* —**Syn. 2.** recognize.

ad·mit·tance (ad·mit′əns), *n.* **1.** right to go in. **2.** act of admitting. **3.** actual entrance.

ad·mit·ted·ly (ad·mit′id·li), *adv.* without denial; by general consent.

ad·mix (ad·miks′), *v.* add in mixing; mix in.

ad·mix·ture (ad·miks′chər), *n.* **1.** act of mixing; mixture. **2.** anything added in mixing. [< L *admixtus* < *ad–* in addition + *miscere* mix]

ad·mon·ish (ad·mon′ish), *v.* **1.** advise against something; warn: *the policeman admonished him not to drive too fast.* **2.** reprove gently: *admonish a student for careless work.* **3.** urge strongly; advise. **4.** recall to a duty overlooked or forgotten; remind. [< *admonition*] —**ad·mon′ish·er,** *n.* —**ad·mon′ish·ing·ly,** *adv.* —**ad·mon′ish·ment,** *n.*

ad·mo·ni·tion (ad′mə·nish′ən), *n.* an admonishing; warning. [< L, < *ad–* to + *monere* warn]

ad·mon·i·to·ry (ad·mon′ə·tô′ri; –tō′–), *adj.* admonishing; warning.

a·do (ə·dü′), *n.* stir; bustle. [ME *at do* to do]

a·do·be (ə·dō′bē), *Am., S.W.* —*n.* **1.** sun-dried clay or mud. **2.** a brick or bricklike piece of such material, used in building. —*adj.* built or made of sun-dried bricks: *an adobe house.* [< Sp., < *adobar* to daub < Gmc.]

ad·o·les·cence (ad'ə·les'əns), *n.* **1.** growth from childhood to manhood (from 14 to 25) or womanhood (from 12 to 21). **2.** period or time of this growth; youth.

ad·o·les·cent (ad'ə·les'ənt), *n.* person from about 12 to about 22 years of age. —*adj.* **1.** growing up from childhood to maturity. **2.** of or characteristic of adolescents. [< L *adolescens* < *ad-* to + *alescere* grow]

A·don·is (ə·don'is; ə·dō'nis), *n.* **1.** *Class. Myth.* a handsome young man loved by Aphrodite (Venus). **2.** a handsome young man.

a·dopt (ə·dopt'), *v.* **1.** take for one's own. **2.** accept formally: *the legislature adopted the committee's report.* **3.** take (a child of other parents) and bring up as one's own. **4.** take (a person) into close relationship. [< L, < *ad-* to + *optare* choose] —**a·dopt'a·ble,** *adj.* —**a·dopt'-a·bil'i·ty,** *n.* —**a·dopt'er,** *n.* —**a·dop'tion,** *n.*

a·dop·tive (ə·dop'tiv), *adj.* **1.** tending to adopt. **2.** related by adoption. —**a·dop'tive·ly,** *adv.*

a·dor·a·ble (ə·dôr'ə·bəl; ə·dōr'-), *adj.* **1.** worthy of being adored. **2.** *Colloq.* lovely; delightful. —**a·dor'a·ble·ness, a·dor'a·bil'i·ty,** *n.* —**a·dor'a·bly,** *adv.*

ad·o·ra·tion (ad'ə·rā'shən), *n.* **1.** worship. **2.** highest respect; devoted love.

a·dore (ə·dôr'; ə·dōr'), *v.,* **a·dored, a·dor·ing. 1.** respect very highly; love very greatly. **2.** *Colloq.* like very much. **3.** worship. [< OF < L, < *ad-* to + *orare* pray] —**a·dor'er,** *n.* —**a·dor'ing,** *adj.* —**a·dor'ing·ly,** *adv.* —**Syn. 1.** revere, idolize. **3.** venerate.

a·dorn (ə·dôrn'), *v.* **1.** add beauty to; make greater the splendor or honor of. **2.** put ornaments on; decorate. [< OF < L, < *ad-* + *ornare* fit out] —**a·dorn'er,** *n.* —**a·dorn'ing·ly,** *adv.*

a·dorn·ment (ə·dôrn'mənt), *n.* **1.** thing that adds beauty; decoration. **2.** act of adorning.

ad·re·nal (ə·drē'nəl), *Anat., Zool.* —*adj.* **1.** near or on the kidney. **2.** of or from the adrenal glands. —*n.* an adrenal gland. [< L *ad-* near + *renes* kidneys]

adrenal gland, *Anat., Zool.* one of the two endocrine glands above the kidneys; suprarenal gland.

ad·ren·al·in (ə·dren'əl·in), **ad·ren·al·ine** (-in; -ēn), *n.* **1.** hormone secreted by the adrenal glands. **2. Adrenalin,** *Trademark.* a white, crystalline drug prepared from this hormone, used to stimulate the heart and stop bleeding.

A·dri·at·ic Sea (ā'dri·at'ik), arm of the Mediterranean between Yugoslavia and Italy.

a·drift (ə·drift'), *adv., adj.* **1.** drifting. **2.** swayed by any chance impulse; at a loss.

a·droit (ə·droit'), *adj.* expert in the use of the hands or the mind; skillful: *a teacher adroit in asking questions.* [< F à *droit* rightly < L *ad-* to + *directus* straight] —**a·droit'ly,** *adv.* —**a·droit'ness,** *n.* —**Syn.** clever, dexterous, deft.

ad·sorb (ad·sôrb'; -zôrb'), *v.* gather (a gas, liquid, or dissolved substance) on a surface in a condensed layer. [< L *ad-* to + *sorbere* suck in] —**ad·sorb'ent,** *adj., n.*

ad·sorp·tion (ad·sôrp'shən; -zôrp'-), *n.* an adsorbing or being adsorbed. —**ad·sorp'tive,** *adj.*

ad·u·late (aj'ə·lāt), *v.,* -**lat·ed,** -**lat·ing.** flatter excessively. [< L *adulatus*] —**ad'u·la'tion,** *n.* —**ad'u·la'tor,** *n.* —**ad·u·la·to·ry** (aj'ə·lə·tô'ri; -tō'-), *adj.*

a·dult (ə·dult'; ad'ult), *adj.* **1.** having reached full size and strength; grown-up. **2.** of or for adults. —*n.* **1.** grown-up person. **2.** a full-grown plant or animal. [< L *adultus* < *ad-* to + *alescere* grow up] —**a·dult'hood, a·dult'ness,** *n.*

a·dul·ter·ant (ə·dul'tər·ənt), *n.* substance used in adulterating. —*adj.* adulterating.

a·dul·ter·ate (ə·dul'tər·āt), *v.,* -**at·ed,** -**at·ing.** make lower in quality by adding inferior or impure materials: *adulterate milk with water.* [< L *adulteratus,* ult. < *ad-* + *alter* other, different] —**a·dul'ter·a'tion,** *n.* —**a·dul'ter·a'tor,** *n.* —**Syn.** debase.

a·dul·ter·er (ə·dul'tər·ər), *n.* person, esp. a man, guilty of adultery.

a·dul·ter·ess (ə·dul'tər·is; -tris), *n.* woman guilty of adultery.

a·dul·ter·y (ə·dul'tər·i), *n., pl.* -**ter·ies.** voluntary sexual relations of a married person with any other than the lawful mate. —**a·dul'ter·ous,** *adj.* —**a·dul'ter·ous·ly,** *adv.*

ad·um·brate (ad·um'brāt; ad'əm·brāt), *v.,* -**brat·ed,** -**brat·ing. 1.** foreshadow. **2.** conceal partially; overshadow. [< L, < *ad-* + *umbra* shade] —**ad'um·bra'tion,** *n.*

adv., **1.** adverb. **2.** adverbial. **3.** advertisement.

ad va·lo·rem (ad və·lô'rəm; -lō'-), (of merchandise) in proportion to the value. [< Med.L]

ad·vance (ad·vans'; -väns'), *v.* -**vanced,** -**vanc·ing,** *n., adj.* —*v.* **1.** move forward: *the troops advanced.* **2.** bring forward: *the troops were advanced.* **3.** make progress; improve: *we advance in knowledge.* **4.** help forward; further: *advance a cause.* **5.** raise to a higher rank; promote: *advance him from lieutenant to captain.* **6.** rise in rank; be promoted: *advance in one's profession.* **7.** raise (prices): *advance the price of milk.* **8.** rise in price: *the stock advanced three points.* **9.** make earlier; hasten: *advance the time of the meeting.* **10.** supply beforehand: *advance a salesman funds for expenses.* **11.** lend (money), esp. on security: *advance a loan.* **12.** put forward; suggest: *advance an opinion.* —*n.* **1.** movement forward. **2.** a step forward; progress. **3.** a rise in price. **4.** the furnishing of money or goods before they are due or as a loan. **5.** the money or goods furnished. **6. advances,** personal approaches toward another or others to settle a difference, to make an acquaintance, etc. **7.** a forward position. **8. in advance, a.** in front; ahead. **b.** ahead of time. —*adj.* **1.** going before. **2.** ahead of time. [< OF *avancier* < LL, < L *ab-* from + *ante* before] —**ad·vanc'er,** *n.* —**Syn.** *v.* **1.** progress. **12.** present, offer, propose.

ad·vanced (ad·vanst'; -vänst'), *adj.* **1.** in front of others; forward. **2.** *Am.* beyond most others. **3.** far along in life; very old.

ad·vance·ment (ad·vans'mənt; -väns'-), *n.* **1.** movement forward; advance. **2.** progress; improvement. **3.** promotion.

ad·van·tage (ad·van'tij; -vän'-), *n., v.,* -**taged,** -**tag·ing.** —*n.* **1.** any favorable condition, circumstance, or opportunity; means helpful in getting something desired. **2. take advantage of, a.** use to help or benefit oneself. **b.** impose upon. **3.** better or superior position. **4.** the result of a better position. **5. to advantage,** to a good effect; with a useful effect. **6.** the first point scored in a tennis game after deuce. —*v.* give an advantage to; help; benefit. [< OF, < *avant* before < LL. See ADVANCE.] —**Syn.** *n.* **3.** superiority, ascendancy. **4.** benefit, gain, profit.

ad·van·ta·geous (ad'vən·tā'jəs), *adj.* giving advantage; profitable. —**ad'van·ta'geous·ly,** *adv.* —**ad'van·ta'geous·ness,** *n.*

ad·vent (ad'vent), *n.* **1.** coming; arrival. **2. Advent, a.** the birth of Christ. **b.** the season of devotion including the four Sundays before Christmas. **3. Second Advent,** the coming of Christ at the Last Judgment. [< L, < *ad-* to + *venire* come]

Ad·vent·ism (ad'ven·tiz·əm; ad·ven'-), *n. Am.* belief that the second coming of Christ is near at hand. —**Ad'vent·ist,** *n. Am.*

ad·ven·ti·tious (ad'ven·tish'əs), *adj.* **1.** coming from outside. **2.** *Bot., Zool.* appearing in an unusual position or place. —**ad'ven·ti'tious·ly,** *adv.* —**ad'ven·ti'tious·ness,** *n.*

ad·ven·tive (ad·ven'tiv), *adj. Bot., Zool.* **1.** introduced into a new environment. **2.** not native, though growing with cultivation.

ad·ven·ture (ad·ven'chər), *n., v.,* -**tured,** -**tur·ing.** —*n.* **1.** an exciting or unusual experience. **2.** a bold and difficult undertaking, usually exciting and somewhat dangerous. **3.** seeking excitement or danger: *spirit of adventure.* **4.** business undertaking; commercial speculation. **5.** *Obs.* peril. —*v.* venture; dare. [< OF < L. See ADVENT.]

ad·ven·tur·er (ad·ven'chər·ər), *n.* **1.** person who seeks or has adventures. **2.** soldier who sold his services to the highest bidder. **3.** person who schemes to get money, social position, etc. **4.** speculator.

ad·ven·ture·some (ad·ven′chər·səm), *adj.* bold and daring; adventurous.

ad·ven·tur·ess (ad·ven′chər·is), *n.* 1. woman who schemes to get money, social position, etc. 2. woman adventurer.

ad·ven·tur·ous (ad·ven′chər·əs), *adj.* 1. fond of adventures; ready to take risks; daring. 2. full of risk; dangerous. —**ad·ven′tur·ous·ly,** *adv.* —**ad·ven′tur·ous·ness,** *n.*

ad·verb (ad′vẽrb), *n. Gram.* word that extends or limits the meaning of verbs but is also used to qualify adjectives or other adverbs, esp. as to place, time, manner, or degree. *Soon, here, very, gladly,* and *not* are adverbs. [< L, < *ad-* to + *verbum* verb] —**ad·ver·bi·al** (ad·vẽr′bi·əl), *adj.* —**ad·ver′bi·al·ly,** *adv.* ➤ **adverbs. 1. forms.** Some adverbs have forms that have developed from Old English forms without a special adverbial sign: *now, quite, since, then, there, where;* but most adverbs are adjectives or participles plus the ending *–ly:* he rowed *badly,* she was *deservedly* popular, *surely* you heard that. There are a number of adverbs with the same forms as adjectives, most of them going back to Old English adverbs that ended in *–e* (an ending which has disappeared) instead of to those that ended in *–lice* (which gives us the current *–ly*). Some of these are: *cheap, close, deep, even, first, high, loud, much, near, right, slow, smooth, tight, well, wrong.* Most of these adverbs also have forms in *–ly* too, so that we can write "He sang *loud*" or "He sang *loudly.*" The *–ly* forms are preferred in formal English although the shorter forms are frequently used in informal and familiar writing. **2. comparison of adverbs.** A greater degree of the quality named by the adverb is shown by adding *–er* or *–est* to an adverb or by placing *more* or *most* before it: *hard, harder, hardest; slow, slower, slowest;* or *slowly, more slowly, most slowly.* Most adverbs of more than one syllable are compared with *more* and *most.*

ad·ver·sar·y (ad′vẽr·ser′i), *n., pl.* **–sar·ies.** 1. unfriendly opponent; enemy. 2. person or group on the other side in a contest. —**Syn.** 1. foe. 2. contestant, opponent, antagonist.

ad·ver·sa·tive (ad·vẽr′sə·tiv), *adj.* (of words, etc.) expressing contrast or opposition. *But* and *yet* are adversative conjunctions.

ad·verse (ad·vẽrs′; ad′vẽrs), *adj.* 1. unfriendly in purpose; hostile: *adverse criticism.* 2. unfavorable; harmful. 3. acting in a contrary direction; opposing: *adverse winds.* [< L *adversus.* See ADVERT.] —**ad·verse′ly,** *adv.* —**ad·verse′ness,** *n.* —**Syn.** 1. inimical. —**Ant.** 2. favorable.

ad·ver·si·ty (ad·vẽr′sə·ti), *n., pl.* **–ties.** 1. condition of unhappiness, misfortune, or distress. 2. stroke of misfortune.

ad·vert (ad·vẽrt′), *v.* direct attention; refer (to): *advert to the need for more parks.* [< L, < *ad-* to + *vertere* turn] —**Syn.** allude.

ad·vert·ent (ad·vẽr′tənt), *adj.* attentive; heedful. —**ad·vert′ence,** *n.* —**ad·vert′en·cy,** *n.*

ad·ver·tise, *esp. Brit.* **ad·ver·tize** (ad′vẽr·tīz; ad′vẽr·tīz′), *v.,* **–tised, –tis·ing;** *esp. Brit.* **–tized, –tiz·ing.** 1. give public notice of: *advertise a house for sale.* 2. ask by public notice (for): *advertise for a job.* 3. make generally known. 4. inform. 5. praise the good qualities of (a product, etc.) in order to promote sales. 6. issue advertising: *it pays to advertise.* 7. call attention to (oneself). [< obs. F *advertir* < L. See ADVERT.] —**ad′ver·tis′er,** *esp. Brit.* **ad′ver·tiz′er,** *n.*

ad·ver·tise·ment, *esp. Brit.* **ad·ver·tize·ment** (ad′vẽr·tīz′mənt; ad·vẽr′tis·mənt; –tiz–), *n.* a public notice or announcement, as in a newspaper or magazine, or over the radio.

ad·ver·tis·ing, *esp. Brit.* **ad·ver·tiz·ing** (ad′vẽr·tīz′ing), *n.* 1. business of preparing, publishing, or circulating advertisements. 2. advertisements.

ad·vice (ad·vīs′), *n.* 1. opinion about what should be done. 2. **advices,** information; news. [< obs. F *advis,* var. of *avis* < L *ad-* + *visum* thing seen] —**Syn.** 1. counsel. 2. report, word.

ad·vis·a·ble (ad·vīz′ə·bəl), *adj.* to be recommended; wise; sensible. —**ad·vis′a·bil′i·ty,** **ad·vis′a·ble·ness,** *n.* —**ad·vis′a·bly,** *adv.*

ad·vise (ad·vīz′), *v.,* **–vised, –vis·ing.** 1. give advice to; counsel: *advise him to be cautious.* 2. give advice: *I shall act as you advise.* 3. give notice; inform: *we were advised of the dangers.* 4. talk over plans; consult (*with): he advised with his friends.* [< OF *aviser* < *avis* opinion. See ADVICE.] —**Syn.** 1. caution, admonish, warn. 2. recommend. 3. notify, acquaint, tell. 4. confer.

ad·vised (ad·vīzd′), *adj.* planned and considered. —**ad·vis·ed·ness** (ad·vīz′id·nis), *n.*

ad·vis·ed·ly (ad·vīz′id·li), *adv.* after careful consideration; deliberately.

ad·vise·ment (ad·vīz′mənt), *n.* careful consideration: *take a case under advisement.*

ad·vis·er, ad·vi·sor (ad·vīz′ər), *n.* 1. person who gives advice. 2. teacher who is appointed to advise students. ➤ **Adviser** has been the more common spelling, but the *–or* form is being increasingly used. Either is correct.

ad·vi·so·ry (ad·vīz′ə·ri), *adj.* 1. having power to advise. 2. containing advice. —*n.* bulletin or report to advise of developments, as of the movement and direction of a hurricane.

ad·vo·ca·cy (ad′və·kə·si), *n.* speaking in favor; public recommendation; support.

ad·vo·cate (*v.* ad′və·kāt; *n.* ad′və·kit, –kāt), *v.,* **–cat·ed, –cat·ing,** *n.* —*v.* speak in favor of; recommend publicly: *he advocates building more schools.* —*n.* 1. person who pleads or argues for: *an advocate of peace.* 2. lawyer who pleads in a law court. [< L, < *ad-* to + *vocare* call] —**ad′vo·ca′tion,** *n.* —**ad′vo·ca′tor,** *n.*

adz, adze (adz), *n.* tool somewhat like an ax but with a blade set across the end of the handle and curving inward. [OE *adesa*]

X, Cooper's adz; Y, Carpenter's adz

AEC, A.E.C., Atomic Energy Commission.

ae·dile (ē′dīl), *n.* official in charge of public buildings, games, streets, and markets in ancient Rome. Also, **edile.** [< L, < *aedes* building]

A.E.F., American Expeditionary Forces.

Ae·ge·an Sea (i·jē′ən), arm of the Mediterranean between Greece and Turkey.

ae·gis (ē′jis), *n.* 1. *Gk. Myth.* the shield of Zeus, used also by Athena. 2. protection. 3. patronage. Also, **egis.** [< L < Gk. *aigis*]

Ae·ne·as (i·nē′əs), *n. Class. Legend.* Trojan hero who escaped from Troy and settled in Italy.

ae·o·li·an harp or **lyre** (ē·ō′li·ən), a boxlike stringed instrument that produces musical sounds when currents of air blow across it.

Ae·o·lus (ē′ə·ləs), *n. Gk. Myth.* god of the winds. —**Ae·o·li·an** (ē·ō′li·ən), *adj.*

ae·on (ē′ən; ē′on), *n.* an indefinitely long period of time. Also, **eon.** [< L < Gk. *aion*]

aer·ate (ãr′āt; ā′ər·āt), *v.,* **–at·ed, –at·ing.** 1. expose to air. 2. expose to and mix with air. 3. fill with a gas, esp. carbon dioxide. 4. expose to chemical action with oxygen. [< L *aer* < Gk., air] —**aer·a′tion,** *n.* —**aer′a·tor,** *n.*

aer·i·al (*adj.* ãr′i·əl, ā·ir′i·əl; *n.* ãr′i·əl), *adj.* 1. in the air. 2. of or pertaining to the air. 3. like air; thin and light as air. 4. ideal; imaginary. 5. growing in the air. 6. relating to aircraft. —*n.* wire or wires used in radio or television for sending out or receiving electric waves. [< L *aerius* < Gk., < *aer* air] —**aer′i·al·ly,** *adv.*

aer·i·al·ist (ãr′i·əl·ist), *n.* performer on a trapeze; aerial acrobat.

aer·ie, aer·y (ãr′i; ir′i), *n., pl.* **aer·ies.** 1. the lofty nest of an eagle or other bird of prey. 2. young eagles or other birds of prey. 3. house, castle, etc., built in a high place. Also, **eyrie, eyry.** [< Med.L *aeria* < OF < L *area* AREA or *atrium* ATRIUM]

aer·i·fy (ãr′ə·fī; ā·ir′–), *v.,* **–fied, –fy·ing.** 1. convert into vapor. 2. aerate. —**aer′i·fi·ca′tion,** *n.*

aer·o (ãr′ō), *adj.* of or for aircraft.

aero–, *word element.* **1.** air; of the air. **2.** gas; of gas or gases. **3.** of or for aircraft. [< Gk. *aer* air]

aer·obe (ãr′ōb; ā′ər-ōb), *n.* any microörganism that lives in or grows on oxygen. [< NL < Gk. *aer* air + *bios* life] —aer·o′bic, *adj.* —aer·o′bi·cal·ly, *adv.*

aer·o·drome (ãr′ə-drōm), *n. Brit.* airdrome.

aer·o·dy·nam·ics (ãr′ō-dī-nam′iks; –dī–), *n.* the branch of physics that deals with the forces exerted by air or other gases in motion. —aer′o·dy·nam′ic, *adj.*

aer·o·lite (ãr′ə-līt), *n.* a stone meteorite. [< F, < Gk. *aer* air + *lithos* stone]

aer·o·me·chan·ics (ãr′ō-mə-kan′iks), *n.* science of the motion and equilibrium of air and other gases; aerodynamics and aerostatics. —aer′o·me·chan′ic, aer′o·me·chan′i·cal, *adj.*

aer·o·naut (ãr′ə-nôt), *n.* **1.** pilot of an airship or balloon; balloonist. **2.** person who travels in an airship or balloon. [< F, < Gk. *aer* air + *nautes* sailor]

aer·o·nau·tics (ãr′ə-nô′tiks), *n.* science or art having to do with the design, manufacture, and operation of aircraft. —aer′o·nau′tic, aer′o·nau′ti·cal, *adj.* —aer′o·nau′ti·cal·ly, *adv.*

aer·o·pause (ãr′ə-pôz), *n.* limit of man's penetration in the upper atmosphere. This limit has virtually ceased to exist. [< AERO– + Gk. *pausis* a ceasing]

aer·o·plane (ãr′ə-plān), *n. Esp. Brit.* airplane. ➤ See airplane for usage note.

aer·o·space (ãr′ə-spās), *n.* **1.** earth's envelope of air and the space enclosing it. **2.** science, technology, and industry dealing with the flight of rockets, missiles, vehicles, etc., through the atmosphere or through space: *studies in aerospace.*

aer·o·stat (ãr′ə-stat), *n.* any lighter-than-air aircraft, as a balloon or dirigible. [< AERO– + Gk. *statos* standing]

aer·o·stat·ics (ãr′ə-stat′iks), *n.* branch of physics that deals with the equilibrium of air and other gases, and with the equilibrium of solid objects floating in air and other gases. —aer′o·stat′ic, aer′o·stat′i·cal, *adj.*

aer·o·train (ãr′ə-trān′), *n.* a high-speed train that combines the characteristics of the hovercraft and the monorail.

Aes·chy·lus (es′kə-ləs), *n.* 525–456 B.C., Greek tragic poet and dramatist.

Aes·cu·la·pi·us (es′kyə-lā′pi-əs), *n. Roman Myth.* god of medicine and healing. —Aes′cu·la′pi·an, *adj.*

Ae·sop (ē′səp; ē′sop), *n.* 620?–560? B.C., Greek writer of fables. —Ae·so·pi·an (ē-sō′pi-ən), *adj.*

aes·thete (es′thēt), *n.* **1.** person who pretends to care a great deal about beauty. **2.** person who is sensitive to or loves beauty. Also, esthete. [< Gk. *aisthetes* one who perceives]

aes·thet·ic (es·thet′ik), *adj.* **1.** Also, aes·thet′i·cal. having to do with the beautiful, as distinguished from the useful, scientific, etc. **2.** (of persons) sensitive to beauty. **3.** (of things) pleasing; artistic. Also, esthetic. —aes·thet′i·cal·ly, *adv.*

aes·thet·ics (es·thet′iks), *n.* study of beauty in art and nature; philosophy of beauty; theory of the fine arts. Also, esthetics.

aet., aetat., at the age of.

ae·ther (ē′thər), *n.* **1.** space beyond the earth's atmosphere. **2.** invisible elastic substance formerly supposed to be distributed through all space and to conduct light waves, electric waves, etc. Also, ether. [< L < Gk.]

ae·the·re·al (i·thir′i·əl), *adj.* ethereal.

ae·ti·ol·o·gy (ē′ti·ol′ə·ji), *n.* etiology. —ae·ti·o·log·i·cal (ē′ti·ə·loj′ə·kəl), *adj.*

Aet·na (et′nə), *n.* Mount. See Etna, Mount.

AF, Anglo-French.

A.F., a.f., *Physics, Electronics.* audio frequency.

a·far (ə·fär′), *adv.* **1.** from a distance: *see from afar.* **2.** far away: *stand afar off.*

a·feard, a·feared (ə·fird′), *adj. Archaic* or *Dial.* frightened; afraid.

af·fa·ble (af′ə-bəl), *adj.* **1.** easy to speak to or approach; courteous, friendly, and pleasant. **2.** gracious; mild; benign. [< F < L *affabilis* easy to speak to < *ad–* to + *fari* speak] —af′fa·bil′i·ty, af′fa·ble·ness, *n.* —af′fa·bly, *adv.*

af·fair (ə·fãr′), *n.* **1.** anything done or to be done. **2.** affairs, matters of interest, esp. business matters. **3.** particular action or event (referred to in vague terms): *a jolly affair.* **4.** private concern: *that's my affair.* **5.** thing: *this machine is a complicated affair.* **6.** a romance. [< OF *a faire* to do < L *ad* to + *facere* to do] —Syn. 1. activity. 3. happening.

af·fect¹ (ə·fekt′), *v.* **1.** have an effect on; influence, esp. injuriously: *disease affects the body.* **2.** stir the emotions of. [< L *affectus* < *ad–* to + *facere* do] —Syn. 2. touch ➤ affect, effect. Since most people make no distinction in pronouncing the first vowel of these words, the spelling is likely to be confused. *Affect* is nearly always a verb, meaning "to influence": *this will affect the lives of thousands. Effect* is most commonly a noun, meaning "result": *the effects of this will be felt by thousands. Effect* is also a verb in formal English, meaning to "bring about": *the change was effected peaceably.*

af·fect² (ə·fekt′), *v.* **1.** pretend to have or feel: *affect ignorance.* **2.** be fond of; like: *she affects old furniture.* **3.** assume, use, or frequent by preference: *he affects carelessness in dress.* **4.** (of animals and plants) inhabit naturally. [< F < L *affectare* strive for < *ad–* to + *facere* do] —af·fect′er, *n.* —Syn. 1. feign, simulate.

af·fec·ta·tion (af′ek·tā′shən; –ik–), *n.* **1.** behavior that is not natural. **2.** outward appearance; pretense.

af·fect·ed¹ (ə·fek′tid), *adj.* **1.** influenced. **2.** influenced injuriously. **3.** moved emotionally.

af·fect·ed² (ə·fek′tid), *adj.* **1.** put on for effect; unnatural. **2.** behaving, speaking, writing, etc., unnaturally for effect. —af·fect′ed·ly, *adv.* —af·fect′ed·ness, *n.* —Syn. 1. artificial.

af·fect·ing (ə·fek′ting), *adj.* causing emotion. —af·fect′ing·ly, *adv.*

af·fec·tion (ə·fek′shən), *n.* **1.** friendly feeling; tenderness; love. **2.** feeling; inclination. **3.** disease; unhealthy condition. **4.** *Archaic.* disposition; tendency. —Syn. 1. fondness.

af·fec·tion·ate (ə·fek′shən·it), *adj.* **1.** having affection; warmly attached. **2.** showing affection. —af·fec′tion·ate·ly, *adv.* —af·fec′tion·ate·ness, *n.* —Syn. 1. devoted, tender.

af·fec·tive (ə·fek′tiv), *adj.* of the feelings; emotional.

af·fer·ent (af′ər·ənt), *adj.* (of nerves or blood vessels) carrying inward to a central organ or point. [< L, < *ad–* to + *ferre* bring]

af·fi·ance (ə·fī′əns), *v.,* –anced, –anc·ing. pledge solemnly, esp. in marriage; betroth. [< OF *afiancer* ult. < L *ad–* to + *fidus* faithful]

af·fi·da·vit (af′ə·dā′vit), *n.* statement written down and sworn to be true. An affidavit is usually made before a judge or notary public. [< Med.L, he has stated on oath]

af·fil·i·ate (*v.* ə·fil′i·āt; *n.* ə·fil′i·it, –āt), *v.,* –at·ed, –at·ing, *n.* —*v.* **1.** *Am.* connect in close association: *affiliated clubs.* **2.** *Am.* associate oneself (*with*): *affiliate with a political party.* **3.** bring into relationship; adopt. —*n.* organization or group associated with other similar bodies. [< LL, < L *ad–* + *filius* son]

af·fil·i·a·tion (ə·fil′i·ā′shən), *n.* **1.** *Am.* association; relation. **2.** act of affiliating.

af·fin·i·ty (ə·fin′ə·ti), *n., pl.* –ties. **1.** natural attraction to a person or liking for a thing: *an affinity for dancing.* **2.** person to whom one is especially attracted. **3.** relationship by marriage. **4.** relation; connection. **5.** resemblance; likeness. **6.** *Chem.* force that attracts certain chemical elements to others and keeps them combined. [< F < L, < *ad–* on + *finis* boundary]

af·firm (ə·fėrm′), *v.* **1.** declare to be true; assert. **2.** confirm; ratify: *the higher court affirmed the lower court's decision.* **3.** *Law.* declare solemnly, but without taking an oath. [< OF < L, < *ad–* + *firmus* strong] —af·firm′a·ble, *adj.* —af·firm′a·bly, *adv.* —af·firm′er, *n.*

af·fir·ma·tion (af′ər·mā′shən), *n.* **1.** *Law.* solemn declaration, equivalent to taking an oath, made by a person whose conscience forbids his taking an oath. **2.** a positive statement; assertion. **3.** act of confirming.

af·firm·a·tive (ə·fėr′mə·tiv), *adj.* asserting that a fact is so. —*n.* **1.** word or statement that gives assent or agrees. **2. the affirmative,** the side arguing in favor of a question being debated. —**af·firm′a·tive·ly,** *adv.*

af·fix (*v.* ə·fiks′; *n.* af′iks), *v.* **1.** make firm or fix (one thing to or on another). **2.** add at the end. **3.** make an impression of (a seal, etc.). **4.** connect with; attach: *affix blame.* —*n.* **1.** thing affixed. **2.** a prefix, suffix, or infix. *Un–* and *–ly* are affixes. [< Med.L *affixare,* ult. < L *ad–* to + *figere* fix] —**af·fix′er,** *n.*

af·fla·tus (ə·flā′təs), *n.* divinely imparted knowledge; inspiration. [< L, *= ad–* on + *flare* blow]

af·flict (ə·flikt′), *v.* cause pain to; trouble greatly; distress. [< L *afflictus* < *ad–* upon + *fligere* dash] —**af·flict′er,** *n.* —**Syn.** torment.

af·flic·tion (ə·flik′shən), *n.* **1.** state of pain or distress. **2.** cause of pain, trouble, or distress. —**Syn. 1.** misery, wretchedness. **2.** misfortune.

af·flu·ence (af′lū·əns), *n.* **1.** wealth. **2.** abundant supply. [< F < L, < *ad–* to + *fluere* flow]

af·flu·ent (af′lū·ənt), *adj.* **1.** very wealthy. **2.** abundant; plentiful. —*n.* stream flowing into a larger stream, etc. —**af′flu·ent·ly,** *adv.*

af·ford (ə·fôrd′; ə·fōrd′), *v.* **1.** spare the money for: *we can't afford a new car.* **2.** spare: *can you afford the time?* **3.** manage: *I can't afford to take the chance.* **4.** furnish from natural resources; yield: *some trees afford resin.* **5.** yield or give as an effect or a result; provide: *reading affords pleasure.* [OE *geforthian* further, accomplish] —**af·ford′a·ble,** *adj.*

af·fray (ə·frā′), *n.* a noisy quarrel; fight in public; brawl. [< OF *affrei,* ult. < L *ex–* out of + unrecorded Frankish *frithu* peace]

af·front (ə·frunt′), *n.* **1.** a word or act expressing openly intentional disrespect. **2.** a slight or injury to one's dignity. —*v.* **1.** insult openly; offend purposely. **2.** confront. [< OF < VL < L *ad frontem* on the forehead] —**af·front′er,** *n.*

Af·ghan (af′gən; -gan), *n.* **1.** native of Afghanistan. **2. afghan,** blanket or shawl made of knitted or crocheted wool. —*adj.* of Afghanistan or its people.

Af·ghan·i·stan (af-gan′ə·stan), *n.* country in SW Asia.

a·fi·cio·na·do (ə·fē′syə·nä′dō), *n., pl.* -dos. **1.** person who takes a very great interest in bullfighting, but who is not a bullfighter. **2.** person who is very enthusiastic about anything. [< Sp., lit., fond of < *aficion* < L *affectio* < *affectus,* pp. See AFFECT².]

a·field (ə·fēld′), *adv.* **1.** on or in the field; to the field. **2.** away from home; away. **3.** out of the way; astray.

a·fire (ə·fir′), *adv., adj.* on fire; burning.

A.F.L., A.F. of L., *Am.* American Federation of Labor, a group of trade unions. It was merged with the CIO in December, 1955.

a·flame (ə·flām′), *adv., adj.* on fire.

a·float (ə·flōt′), *adv., adj.* **1.** floating. **2.** on shipboard; at sea. **3.** adrift. **4.** flooded. **5.** going around: *rumors of an outbreak were afloat.*

a·flut·ter (ə·flut′ər), *adv., adj.* fluttering.

a·foot (ə·fut′), *adv., adj.* **1.** on foot; walking. **2.** going on; in progress: *mischief afoot.*

a·fore (ə·fôr′; ə·fōr′), *adv., prep., conj. Archaic, Dial., or Naut.* before.

a·fore·men·tioned (ə·fôr′men′shənd; ə·fōr′–), *adj.* spoken of before; mentioned above.

a·fore·said (ə·fôr′sed′; ə·fōr′–), *adj.* spoken of before; mentioned above.

a·fore·thought (ə·fôr′thôt′; ə·fōr′–), *adj.* thought of beforehand; deliberately planned.

a·fore·time (ə·fôr′tīm′; ə·fōr′–), *adv.* in time past; formerly. —*adj.* former.

a for·ti·o·ri (ā fôr′shi·ô′rī; –ō′–; –rī), *Latin.* for a still stronger reason; all the more.

a·foul (ə·foul′), *adv., adj.* **1.** *Am.* in a tangle, in collision; entangled. **2. run afoul of,** get into difficulties with.

a·fraid (ə·frād′), *adj.* feeling fear; frightened. [orig. pp. of archaic *v. affray* frighten]

af·reet, af·rit (af′rēt; ə·frēt′), *n.* in Arabian myths, a powerful evil demon or giant. [< Ar. *'ifrīt*]

a·fresh (ə·fresh′), *adv.* once more; again.

Af·ri·ca (af′rə·kə), *n.* continent south of Europe; the second largest continent.

Af·ri·can (af′rə·kən), *adj.* **1.** of or from Africa. **2.** of or belonging to the black race of Africa. —*n.* **1.** a native of Africa. **2.** a Negro.

Af·ri·kaans (af′rə·käns′; –känz′), *n.* variety of Dutch spoken in South Africa; South African Dutch

Af·ri·kan·er (af′rə·kan′ər), **Af·ri·kan·der** (-kan′dər), *n.* a native, white South African, usually of Dutch or Huguenot descent.

aft (aft; äft), *adv. Naut.* at, near, or toward the stern; abaft. [OE *æftan* from behind]

af·ter (af′tər; äf′–), *prep.* **1.** behind in place: *in line one after another.* **2.** next to; following: *day after day.* **3.** in pursuit of; in search of: *run after him.* **4.** about; concerning: *your aunt asked after you.* **5.** later in time than: *after supper.* **6.** because of: *after the selfish way she acted, who could like her?* **7.** in spite of: *after all her suffering she is still cheerful.* **8.** imitating; in imitation of: *a fable after the manner of Aesop.* **9.** lower in rank or importance: *a captain comes after a general.* **10.** according to: *act after one's own ideas.* **11.** for: *named after his cousin.* **12. look after,** see after, take care of. —*adv.* **1.** behind: *follow after.* **2.** later: *three hours after.* —*adj.* **1.** later; subsequent: *in after years he regretted the mistakes of his boyhood.* **2.** *Naut.* nearer or toward the stern: *after sails.* —*conj.* later than the time that: *after he goes, we shall eat.* [OE *æfter* more to the rear, later]

af·ter·birth (af′tər·bėrth′; äf′–), *n.* placenta and membranes that enveloped the fetus, expelled from the uterus after childbirth.

af·ter·burn·er (af′tər·bėr′nər; äf′–), *n.* (in the engine of a jet plane) a device which supplies additional fuel to the exhaust and reignites it, thus increasing the thrust of the plane so that bursts of very high speed can be obtained.

af·ter·deck (af′tər·dek′; äf′–), *n. Naut.* deck toward or at the stern of a ship.

af·ter·ef·fect (af′tər·i·fekt′; äf′–), *n.* result or effect that follows later.

af·ter·glow (af′tər·glō′; äf′–), *n.* **1.** glow after something bright has gone. **2.** glow in the sky after sunset.

af·ter·im·age (af′tər·im′ij; äf′–), *n.* sensation that persists or recurs after the stimulus is withdrawn.

af·ter·math (af′tər·math; äf′–), *n.* result; consequence. [< *after* + dial. *math* a mowing]

af·ter·most (af′tər·mōst; äf′–), *adj.* **1.** *Naut.* nearest the stern. **2.** hindmost; last.

af·ter·noon (*n.* af′tər·nün′, äf′–; *adj.* af′tər·nün′, äf′–), *n.* the part of the day between noon and evening. —*adj.* of, in, or suitable for the afternoon.

af·ter·thought (af′tər·thôt′; äf′–), *n.* **1.** thought that comes after the time when it could have been used. **2.** later thought or explanation.

af·ter·ward (af′tər·wərd; äf′–), **af·ter·wards** (-wərdz), *adv.* later.

Ag, *Chem.* silver.

A.G., **1.** Adjutant General. **2.** Attorney General.

a·gain (ə·gen′; *esp. Brit.,* ə·gān′), *adv.* **1.** once more; another time: *try again.* **2.** in return; in reply: *answer again.* **3.** to the same place or person; back: *bring us word again.* **4.** moreover; besides: *again, I must say.* **5.** on the other hand: *it might rain, and again it might not.* **6. again and again,** often; frequently. **7.** as much again,

ãge, cãre, fär; ēqual, tẽrm; īce; ōpen, ôrder; pŭt, rüle, ūse; tⁱⁱ, then; ə=a in about.

twice as much. [OE *ongegn* < *on-* on + *gegn* direct]

a·gainst (ə·genst′; *esp. Brit.* ə·gänst′), *prep.* **1.** in an opposite direction to, so as to meet; upon; toward: *sail against the wind.* **2.** in opposition to: *against reason.* **3.** directly opposite to; facing: *over against the wall.* **4.** in contrast to or with: *the ship appeared against the sky.* **5.** in contact with: *lean against a wall.* **6.** in preparation for: *against a rainy day.* **7.** in defense from: *a fire is a protection against cold.* [see AGAIN]

Ag·a·mem·non (ag′ə·mem′non; -nən), *n.* *Gk. Legend.* king of Mycenae and leader of the Greeks in the Trojan War.

A·ga·ña (ä·gän′yə), *n.* capital of Guam.

a·gape (ə·gāp′; ə·gap′), *adv., adj.* with the mouth wide open, as in wonder or eagerness.

a·gar-a·gar (ä′gər·ä′gər; ag′ər·ag′ər), *n.* a gelatinlike extract obtained from certain seaweeds, used in making cultures for bacteria, fungi, etc. [< Malay]

a·gar·ic (ag′ə·rik; ə·gar′ik), *n.* any of several fungi, including mushrooms and toadstools. [< L < Gk., < *Agaria*, place name]

Ag·as·siz (ag′ə·si), *n.* **(Jean) Louis** (Rodolphe), 1807–1873, American naturalist, born in Switzerland.

ag·ate (ag′it), *n.* **1.** a variety of quartz with variously colored stripes or clouded colors. **2.** *Am.* a playing marble that looks like this. **3.** *Am.* a size of printing type (5½ point). [< F < L < Gk. *achates*] —**ag′ate·like′**, *adj.*

a·ga·ve (ə·gā′vē), *n.* any of several North American desert plants (the century plant, sisal, etc.). Soap, alcoholic drinks, and rope are made from some kinds of agave. [< NL < Gk. *Agaue*, fem. proper name, noble]

age (āj), *n., v.*, **aged, ag·ing** or **age·ing.** —*n.* **1.** length of life: *he died at the age of eighty.* **2.** a period in life attained: *middle age.* **3.** latter part of life: *the wisdom of age.* **4.** of age, 21 years old or over and having full legal rights. **5.** the full or average term of life: *the age of a horse is from 25 to 30 years.* **6.** *Psychol.* the mental, physiological, emotional, etc., development of an individual as compared with the average development of individuals of his chronological age. **7.** a period of history: *the golden age.* **8.** generation: *ages yet unborn.* **9.** *Colloq.* a long time: *I haven't seen you for an age.* —*v.* **1.** grow old: *he ages rapidly.* **2.** make old: *age wine.* [< OF *aage* < VL *aetaticum* < L *aetas* age]

-age, *suffix.* **1.** act of, as in *breakage.* **2.** collection of; group of, as in *baggage.* **3.** condition of; rank of, as in *peerage.* **4.** cost of, as in *postage.* **5.** home of, as in *orphanage.* [< OF < L *-aticum* < Gk.]

a·ged (ā′jid *for 1 and 3*; ājd *for 2*), *adj.* **1.** having lived a long time; old. **2.** of the age of 3. characteristic of old age. —**a′ged·ly**, *adv.*

age·less (āj′lis), *adj.* never growing old.

age·long (āj′lông′; -long′), *adj.* lasting a long time.

a·gen·cy (ā′jən·si), *n., pl.* **-cies. 1.** means; action. **2.** business of a person or company that has the authority to act for another. **3.** office of such a person or company.

a·gen·da (ə·jen′də), *n.pl., sing.* **-dum** (-dəm). **1.** things to be done. **2.** (*sometimes sing. in use*) list of items of business to be considered, as at a meeting. [< L, things to be done]

a·gent (ā′jənt), *n.* **1.** person or company that has the authority to act for another. **2.** person who does things. **3.** active power or cause that produces an effect. **4.** means; instrument. **5.** *Colloq.* a traveling salesman. **6.** *Am.* a station agent or ticket agent. **7.** *Chem.* substance that is capable of causing a reaction. [< L, < *agere* do] —**a·gen′tial** (ā·jen′shəl), *adj.* —Syn. **1.** representative, intermediary.

ag·er·a·tum (aj′ər·ā′təm; ə·jer′ə-), *n.* any of several plants of the aster family with small, dense flower heads, usually blue. [< NL < Gk., < *a-* without + *geras* old age]

ag·glom·er·ate (*v.* ə·glom′ər·āt; *n., adj.* ə·glom′ər·it, -āt), *v.*, **-at·ed, -at·ing,** *n., adj.* —*v.* gather together in a mass. —*n.* mass; collec-

tion; cluster. —*adj.* packed together in a mass. [< L, < *ad-* + *glomus* ball] —**ag·glom′er·a′tive,** *adj.*

ag·glom·er·a·tion (ə·glom′ər·ā′shən), *n.* **1.** an agglomerating. **2.** agglomerated condition. **3.** mass of things gathered together.

ag·glu·ti·nate (*v.* ə·glü′tə·nāt; *adj.* ə·glü′tə·nit, -nāt), *v.*, **-nat·ed, -nat·ing,** *adj.* —*v.* **1.** stick or join together, as with glue. **2.** form (words) by joining words, or words and affixes, together. —*adj.* stuck or joined together: "*never-to-be-forgotten*" is an agglutinate word. [< L, < *ad-* to + *gluten* glue] —**ag·glu′ti·na′tion,** *n.* —**ag·glu′ti·na′tive,** *adj.*

ag·gran·dize (ə·gran′dīz; ag′rən·dīz), *v.*, **-dized, -diz·ing.** increase, as in power, wealth, rank, etc.; make greater. [< F *agrandir*, ult. < L *ad-* + *grandis* great] —**ag·gran·dize·ment** (ə·gran′diz·mənt), *n.* —**ag·gran′diz·er,** *n.*

ag·gra·vate (ag′rə·vāt), *v.*, **-vat·ed, -vat·ing. 1.** make worse or more severe. **2.** *Colloq.* annoy; irritate; provoke. [< L, < *ad-* on, to + *gravis* heavy. Doublet of AGGRIEVE.] —**ag′gra·vat′ing,** *adj.* —**ag′gra·vat′ing·ly,** *adv.* —**ag′gra·va′tion,** *n.* —**ag′gra·va′tive·ly,** *adv.* —**ag′gra·va′tor,** *n.* —Syn. **1.** intensify, increase.

ag·gre·gate (*v.* ag′rə·gāt; *n., adj.* ag′rə·git, -gāt), *v.*, **-gat·ed, -gat·ing,** *n., adj.* —*v.* **1.** gather together in a mass or group; collect; unite. **2.** *Colloq.* amount to. —*n.* **1.** mass of separate things joined together; collection. **2.** in the aggregate, together; as a whole. —*adj.* **1.** gathered together in one mass or group. **2.** total. [< L *aggregatus* < *ad-* + *grex* flock] —**ag′gre·gate·ly,** *adv.* —**ag′gre·ga′tive,** *adj.*

ag·gre·ga·tion (ag′rə·gā′shən), *n.* collection of separate things into one mass or whole.

ag·gress (ə·gres′), *v.* take the first step in an attack or quarrel.

ag·gres·sion (ə·gresh′ən), *n.* **1.** first step in an attack or quarrel; an unprovoked attack. **2.** practice of making assaults or attacks. [< L *aggressio* < *ad-* to + *gradi* to step]

ag·gres·sive (ə·gres′iv), *adj.* **1.** beginning an attack or quarrel. **2.** *U.S.* active; energetic. —**ag·gres′sive·ly,** *adv.* —**ag·gres′sive·ness,** *n.*

ag·gres·sor (ə·gres′ər), *n.* one that begins an attack or quarrel.

ag·grieve (ə·grēv′), *v.*, **-grieved, -griev·ing.** injure unjustly; cause grief or trouble to. [< OF *agrever* < L. Doublet of AGGRAVATE.]

a·ghast (ə·gast′; ə·gäst′), *adj.* filled with horror; frightened; terrified. [pp. of obs. *agast* terrify; akin to GHOST]

ag·ile (aj′əl), *adj.* moving quickly and easily; active; lively; nimble. [< L *agilis* < *agere* move] —**ag′ile·ly,** *adv.* —**ag′ile·ness,** *n.* —Syn. sprightly, spry, brisk, quick.

a·gil·i·ty (ə·jil′ə·ti), *n.* ability to move quickly and easily; nimbleness.

ag·i·tate (aj′ə·tāt), *v.*, **-tat·ed, -tat·ing. 1.** move or shake violently. **2.** disturb; excite (the feelings or the thoughts). **3.** argue about; discuss vigorously. **4.** keep arguing and discussing to arouse public interest: *agitate for a shorter working day.* [< L *agitatus* < *agere* drive, move] —**ag′i·tat′ed·ly,** *adv.*

ag·i·ta·tion (aj′ə·tā′shən), *n.* **1.** a violent moving or shaking. **2.** disturbed, upset, or troubled state. **3.** argument or discussion to arouse public interest. —Syn. **3.** debate.

ag·i·ta·tor (aj′ə·tā′tər), *n.* **1.** person who tries to make people discontented with things as they are. **2.** device for shaking or stirring.

a·glow (ə·glō′), *adv., adj.* glowing.

ag·no·men (ag·nō′mən), *n., pl.* **-nom·i·na** (-nom′ə·nə). **1.** additional name given to a person by the ancient Romans in allusion to some quality or achievement. **2.** any additional name. [< L, < *ad-* to + *nomen* name] —**ag·nom·i·nal** (ag·nom′ə·nəl), *adj.*

ag·nos·tic (ag·nos′tik), *n.* person who believes that nothing is known or can be known about the existence of God or about things outside of human experience. —*adj.* of agnostics or their beliefs. [< Gk., < *a-* not + *gnostos* (to be) known] —**ag·nos′ti·cal·ly,** *adv.*

ag·nos·ti·cism (ag·nos′tə·siz·əm), *n.* the belief or intellectual attitude of agnostics.

a·go (ə·gō′), *adj.* gone by; past (always after the noun): *a year ago.* —*adv.* in the past: *he went long ago.* [OE *āgān* gone by]

a·gog (ə·gog′), *adj.* eager; curious; excited. —*adv.* with eagerness, curiosity, or excitement. [? < F en *gogues* in happy mood]

a·gon·ic (ā·gon′ik; ə·gon′-), *adj.* not forming an angle. [< Gk., < *a*- without + *gonia* angle]

ag·o·nize (ag′ə·nīz), *v.*, -nized, -niz·ing. 1. feel very great pain. 2. pain very much; torture. 3. strive painfully; struggle. —ag′o·niz′ing, *adj.* —ag′o·niz′ing·ly, *adv.*

ag·o·ny (ag′ə·ni), *n.*, *pl.* -nies. 1. great pain or suffering. 2. intense mental suffering. 3. the struggle often preceding death. [< LL < Gk. *agonia* struggle] —**Syn.** 1, 2. anguish, torment.

ag·o·ra (ag′ə·rə), *n.*, *pl.* -rae (-rē). market place in an ancient Greek city. [< Gk.]

ag·o·ra·pho·bi·a (ag′ə·rə·fō′bi·ə), *n.* a morbid fear of open spaces.

a·gou·ti (ə·gü′ti), *n.*, *pl.* -tis, -ties. a rodent of tropical America related to the guinea pig, but having longer legs. [< F < Sp. < native Indian name]

A·gra (ä′grə), *n.* city in N India; site of the Taj Mahal.

Agouti (18 in. long)

a·grar·i·an (ə·grār′i·ən), *adj.* 1. having to do with land, its use, or its ownership. 2. for the support and advancement of the interests of farmers. 3. agricultural. —*n.* person who favors a redistribution of land. [< L *agrarius < ager* field] —a·grar′i·an·ism, *n.*

a·gree (ə·grē′), *v.*, a·greed, a·gree·ing. 1. have the same opinion or opinions: *I agree with you.* 2. be in harmony; correspond (*with*): *your story agrees with mine.* 3. get along well together. 4. consent (*to*): *he agreed to accompany us.* 5. come to an understanding, esp. in settling a dispute. 6. have a good effect on; suit (*with*): *this food does not agree with me.* 7. *Gram.* have the same number, case, gender, person, etc. (*with*): *that verb agrees with its subject.* [< OF, < a *gre* to (one's) liking < L *ad*- to + *gratus* pleasing] —**Syn.** 2. coincide, match, tally. ➤ agree to, agree with. One agrees *to* a plan and agrees *with* a person.

a·gree·a·ble (ə·grē′ə·bəl), *adj.* 1. to one's liking; pleasing: *agreeable manners.* 2. ready to agree; willing to agree: *agreeable to a suggestion.* 3. in agreement; suitable (*to*): *music agreeable to the occasion.* —a·gree′a·bil′i·ty, a·gree′a·ble·ness, *n.* —a·gree′a·bly, *adv.*

a·greed (ə·grēd′), *adj.* 1. fixed by common consent. 2. of like mind; agreeing.

a·gree·ment (ə·grē′mənt), *n.* 1. consent. 2. sameness of opinion. 3. harmony; correspondence. 4. an agreeing; an understanding reached by two or more nations, persons, or groups of persons among themselves. 5. *Gram.* correspondence of words with respect to number, case, gender, person, etc.

ag·ri·cul·tur·al (ag′rə·kul′chər·əl), *adj.* 1. having to do with farming; of agriculture. 2. *Am.* promoting the interests or the study of agriculture. —ag′ri·cul′tur·al·ly, *adv.*

ag·ri·cul·tur·al·ist (ag′rə·kul′chər·əl·ist), *n.* *U.S.* agriculturist.

ag·ri·cul·ture (ag′rə·kul′chər), *n.* farming; the raising of crops and livestock; science or art of cultivating the ground. [< L, < *ager* field + *cultura* cultivation]

ag·ri·cul·tur·ist (ag′rə·kul′chər·ist), *n.* 1. farmer. 2. an expert in farming.

ag·ri·mo·ny (ag′rə·mō′ni), *n.*, *pl.* -nies. plant with slender stalks of feathery leaves and yellow flowers, whose roots are used as an astringent. [< L < Gk. *argemone*]

ag·ro·nom·ics (ag′rə·nom′iks), *n.* art or science of managing farmland.

a·gron·o·my (ə·gron′ə·mi), *n.* branch of agriculture dealing with crop production; husbandry. [< Gk., < *agros* land + *nemein* manage] —ag·ro·nom·ic (ag′rə·nom′ik), ag′ro·nom′i·cal, *adj.* —a·gron′o·mist, *n.*

a·ground (ə·ground′), *adv., adj.* on the ground; on the bottom in shallow water.

agt., agent.

a·gue (ā′gū), *n.* 1. malarial fever characterized by intermittent fits of sweating and shivering. 2. fit of shivering; chill. [< OF < L *acuta* (*febris*) severe (fever)] —a′gu·ish, *adj.*

ah (ä), *interj.* exclamation of pain, surprise, pity, joy, etc.

a·ha (ä·hä′), *interj.* exclamation of triumph, satisfaction, surprise, etc.

A·hab (ā′hab), *n. Bible.* king of Israel who was led into idolatry by his wife Jezebel.

a·head (ə·hed′), *adv.* 1. in front; before: *walk ahead of me.* 2. *Am.*, *Colloq.* forward; onward: *go ahead with this work.* 3. *Am.* in an advanced or successful position or state. 4. *Am.* in advance: *ahead of his times.* 5. be ahead, *Am.*, *Colloq.* be to the good. 6. get ahead, *Am.*, *Colloq.* succeed. 7. get ahead of, surpass.

a·hem (ə·hem′), *interj.* a sound made to attract attention, express doubt, gain time, etc.

a·hoy (ə·hoi′), *interj.* a call used by sailors to hail persons at a distance.

ai (ī), *n., pl.* ais (īz). a three-toed sloth of South America.

aid (ād), *v.* give support to; help: *the Red Cross aids flood victims.* —*n.* 1. help; support. 2. helper; assistant. 3. *U.S.* aide-de-camp. [< OF *aidier* < L, < *ad*- to + *juvare* help] —aid′er, *n.* —aid′less, *adj.* —**Syn.** *v.* assist.

aid-de-camp (ād′də·kamp′), *n.*, *pl.* aids-de-camp. *U.S.* an aide-de-camp.

aide (ād), *n.* 1. aide-de-camp. 2. assistant, especially to a person of high rank.

aide-de-camp (ād′də·kamp′), *n.*, *pl.* aides-de-camp. army or navy officer who acts as an assistant to a superior officer. [< F]

ai·grette (ā′gret; ā·gret′), *n.* 1. tuft of feathers worn as an ornament on the head. 2. anything shaped or used like this. 3. egret. [< F. See EGRET.]

Aigrette of feathers

ail (āl), *v.* 1. be the matter with; trouble: *what ails the man?* 2. be ill; feel sick: *he is ailing.* [OE *eglan*]

ai·lan·thus (ā·lan′thəs), *n.* an Asiatic tree with many leaflets and clusters of small, bad-smelling, greenish flowers. [< NL < Amboinan *aylanto* tree of heaven; form infl. by Gk. *anthos* flower]

ai·ler·on (ā′lər·on), *n.* a movable part of an airplane wing, usually part of the trailing edge, used primarily to maintain lateral balance while flying. [< F, dim. of *aile* < L *ala* wing]

ail·ment (āl′mənt), *n.* a slight sickness.

aim (ām), *v.* 1. point or direct (a gun, blow, etc.) in order to hit a target: *aim a gun.* 2. direct one's efforts: *man aims at happiness.* 3. *U.S.* intend: *I aim to go.* 4. *U.S.* try: *he aims to be helpful.* —*n.* 1. act of aiming. 2. direction aimed in; line of sighting. 3. mark aimed at; target. 4. purpose; intention. [< OF *esmer* < L *aestimare* appraise, and OF *aesmer* < VL *adaestimare*] —aim′er, *n.* —**Syn.** *n.* 4. intent, object.

aim·less (ām′lis), *adj.* without purpose. —aim′less·ly, *adv.* —aim′less·ness, *n.*

ain't (ānt), *Dial.* or *Illiterate.* contraction of the phrases: a. am not. b. are not; is not. c. have not; has not. ➤ Ain't is not acceptable in formal English. Even in informal English its use is subject to sharp criticism. Nevertheless it is often heard, usually in substandard speech, but sometimes from educated speakers tenacious of old ways and perhaps resentful of bookish authority. *Ain't I* or *an't I* is or would be a convenient contraction of *am not I.* (Compare *don't*

I, haven't I, etc.) It is surprising that neither is completely acceptable.

Ai·nu (ī′nü), *n.* member of an aboriginal, light-skinned race in N Japan, now becoming extinct.

air (ãr), *n.* 1. the mixture of gases that surrounds the earth; atmosphere. Air is a mixture of nitrogen, oxygen, argon, helium, and other inert gases. 2. space overhead; sky: *birds fly in the air.* 3. a light wind; breeze. 4. melody; tune. 5. public mention: *he gave air to his feelings.* 6. general character or appearance of anything: *an air of mystery.* 7. bearing; manner: *an air of importance.* 8. airs, unnatural or affected manners. 9. medium through which radio waves travel. 10. in the air, a. going around: *wild rumors were in the air.* b. uncertain. 11. on the air, broadcasting. 12. up in the air, a. uncertain. b. *Colloq.* very angry or excited. —*v.* 1. put out in the air; let air through: *air clothes.* 2. make known; mention publicly: *do not air your troubles.* —*adj.* 1. conducting or supplying air: *air duct.* 2. compressing or confining air: *air valve.* 3. using or worked by compressed air: *air drill.* 4. relating to aviation; done by means of aircraft: *air photography.* [< OF < L < Gk. *aer*]

air-, *word element:* 1. air, as in *air-breathing.* 2. by air, as in *air-blown.* 3. of air, as in *airphobia.* 4. against air, as in *airproof.*

air base, headquarters and airport for military aircraft.

air bladder, sac in most fishes and various animals and plants, filled with air.

air-borne (ãr′bôrn′; –bōrn′), *adj.* 1. carried in aircraft or gliders. 2. carried by air.

air brake, *Am.* brake operated by a piston or pistons worked by compressed air.

air brush, device operated by compressed air that is used to spray paint on a surface.

air·burst (ãr′bėrst′), *n.* an exploding of a shell or bomb, now esp. an atomic bomb, in the air rather than on the ground or under water.

air castle, daydream.

air chamber, any compartment filled with air, esp. one in a hydraulic engine.

air coach, aircraft with low passenger rates, made possible by elimination of luxuries.

air-con·di·tion (ãr′kən-dish′ən), *v. Am.* 1. supply with the equipment for air conditioning. 2. treat (air) by means of air conditioning.

air conditioner, a machine for air-conditioning buildings, rooms, trains, etc.

air conditioning, *Am.* a means of treating air in buildings to free it from dust, etc., and to regulate its humidity and temperature.

air-cool (ãr′kül′), *v.* 1. remove heat produced in motor cylinders by combustion, friction, etc., by blowing air on. 2. remove heat in a room by blowing cool air in. —**air′-cooled′**, *adj.*

air·craft (ãr′kraft′; –kräft′), *n., pl.* **-craft**. 1. machine for air navigation that is supported in air by buoyancy (such as a balloon) or by dynamic action (such as an airplane). 2. such machines collectively or as a class.

aircraft carrier, warship designed as a base for aircraft.

air·drome (ãr′drōm′), *n.* airport. Also, *esp. Brit.* aerodrome. [< AIR- + Gk. *dromos* race course]

air drop, system of dropping food, supplies, etc., from aircraft, esp. to allies behind enemy lines, in occupied territory, etc. —**air′drop′**, *v.*

Aire·dale (ãr′dāl), *n.* a large terrier having a wiry brown or tan coat with dark markings. [< *Airedale* in Yorkshire, England]

air field, landing field of an airport.

air·foil (ãr′foil′), *n.* any surface, such as a wing, rudder, etc., designed to help lift or control an aircraft.

air force, 1. branch of the military or naval forces that uses aircraft. 2. Air Force, a separate branch of the armed forces of the U.S. that includes aviation personnel, equipment, etc. 3. group of fliers for military aircraft.

air·frame (ãr′frām′), *n.* the structural part of an airplane, ballistic missile, etc., apart from propulsion and guidance components.

air hole, 1. *Am.* open space in the ice on a

river, pond, etc. 2. air pocket.

air·i·ly (ãr′ə·li), *adv.* in an airy manner.

air·i·ness (ãr′i·nis), *n.* airy quality.

air·ing (ãr′ing), *n.* 1. exposure to air for drying, etc. 2. a walk, ride, etc. in the open air. 3. exposure to public discussion, criticism, etc.: *the proposed ordinance is due for an airing.*

air lane, a regular route used by aircraft.

air·less (ãr′lis), *adj.* 1. without fresh air; stuffy. 2. without a breeze.

air lift, system of using aircraft for passenger transportation and freight conveyance to a place when land approaches are closed.

air·lift (ãr′lift′), *v.* transport by air lift.

air line, *Am.* 1. system of transportation of people and things by aircraft. 2. company operating such a system. —**air′-line′**, *adj. Am.*

air liner, large airplane or airship for carrying many passengers.

air lock, an airtight compartment between places where there is a difference in air pressure.

air mail, *Am.* 1. system of sending mail by aircraft. 2. mail so sent. —**air′-mail′**, *adj. Am.*

air·man (ãr′mən), *n., pl.* **-men**. 1. pilot of an aircraft. 2. one of the crew of an aircraft.

air-mind·ed (ãr′mīn′did), *adj.* 1. interested in aviation. 2. fond of traveling by air. —**air′-mind′ed·ness**, *n.*

air·plane (ãr′plān′), *n.* a mechanically driven heavier-than-air aircraft supported in flight by the action of the air flowing past or thrusting upward on its fixed wings. Also, *esp. Brit.* aeroplane. ➤ airplane, aeroplane. For several years these two words competed for general usage, but in the United States at least *airplane* is both the official and popular form.

air pocket, a vertical current or condition in the air that causes a sudden drop of an airplane.

air·port (ãr′pôrt′; –pōrt′), *n.* tract of land or water where aircraft can land or take off, with facilities for shelter and repair.

air pressure, pressure of the atmosphere.

air pump, apparatus for forcing air in or drawing air out of something.

air raid, attack by enemy aircraft.

air rifle, *Am.* gun worked by compressed air.

air sac, an air-filled space in the body of a bird, connected with the lungs.

air service, 1. transportation of people or things by aircraft. 2. airforce (def. 1).

air·ship (ãr′ship′), *n.* dirigible.

air·sick (ãr′sik′), *adj.* sick as a result of traveling by air. —**air′sick′ness**, *n.*

air·space (ãr′spās′), *n.* the atmosphere as used by aircraft, esp. that part of it regarded as under the control of a particular country, etc.

air speed, speed of an aircraft measured by its greater movement than that of the air.

air·strip (ãr′strip′), *n.* a paved or cleared strip on which aircraft land and take off.

air·tight (ãr′tīt′), *adj.* 1. so tight that no air or gas can get in or out. 2. having no weak points open to an opponent's attack.

air-to-air (ãr′tü·ãr′), *adj.* 1. launched from a flying aircraft, etc., to intercept and destroy another flying aircraft, etc.: *air-to-air rockets.* 2. between two flying aircraft: *air-to-air refueling.*

air·way (ãr′wā′), *n.* 1. route for aircraft. 2. passage for air.

air·wor·thy (ãr′wėr′тн̇i), *adj.* fit or safe for service in the air. —**air′wor′thi·ness**, *n.*

air·y (ãr′i), *adj.*, **air·i·er**, **air·i·est**. 1. like air; not solid or substantial. 2. light as air; graceful; delicate. 3. light in manner; light-hearted; gay. 4. open to currents of air; breezy. 5. reaching high into the air; lofty. 6. of air; in the air. 7. unnatural; affected.

aisle (īl), *n.* 1. passage between rows of seats in a hall, theater, school, etc. 2. any long or narrow passageway, as in a store. 3. part of a church at the side of the main part, separated from it by columns or piers. 4. nave. [< OF < L *ala* wing; infl. in form by *isle* and in meaning by *alley*] —**aisled** (īld), *adj.*

Aix-la-Cha·pelle (āks′lä·shä·pel′), *n.* French name of Aachen.

a·jar[1] (ə·jär′), *adj., adv.* partly opened. [ME *on char* on the turn; OE *cerr* turn]

a·jar[2] (ə·jär′), *adv., adj.* not in harmony. [< *a–* in + *jar* discord]

A·jax (ā′jaks), *n.* Gk. Legend. Greek hero at the siege of Troy.

a·kene (ā·kēn′), *n.* achene.

a·kim·bo (ə·kim′bō), *adj., adv.* with the hand on the hip and the elbow bent outward. [ME *in kene bowe*, appar., in keen bow, at a sharp angle]

a·kin (ə·kin′), *adj.* **1.** related by blood: *your cousins are akin to you.* **2.** alike; similar. [for *of kin*]

Boy with arms akimbo

Ak·ron (ak′rən), *n.* city in NE Ohio.

-al[1], *suffix.* of; like; having the nature of, as in *ornamental.* [< L *–alis, -ale* pertaining to]

-al[2], *suffix.* act of ——ing, as in *refusal.* [< L *-ale*, neut. of *-alis*]

Al, *Chem.* aluminum.

a la (ä′lə), *French* **à la** (ä lä), after; according to.

Ala., Alabama.

Al·a·bam·a (al′ə·bam′ə), *n.* Am. a Southern State of the United States. *Capital:* Montgomery. *Abbrev.:* Ala. —**Al′a·bam′an, Al·a·bam·i·an** (al′ə·bam′i·ən), *adj., n.*

al·a·bam·ine (al′ə·bam′ēn; –in), *n. Chem.* a rare, unisolated element. [< *Alabama*]

al·a·bas·ter (al′ə·bas′tər; –bäs′–), *n.* **1.** a smooth, white, translucent variety of gypsum. **2.** a variety of calcite, often banded like marble. —*adj.* Also, **al·a·bas·trine** (al′ə·bas′trin; –bäs′–). of or like alabaster. [< L < Gk. *alabast(r)os* an alabaster box]

à la carte (ä′ lə kärt′), with a stated price for each dish. [< F]

a·lack (ə·lak′), **a·lack·a·day** (ə·lak′ə·dā′), *interj. Archaic.* exclamation of sorrow or regret; alas.

a·lac·ri·ty (ə·lak′rə·ti), *n.* **1.** brisk and eager action; liveliness. **2.** cheerful willingness. [< L, < *alacer* brisk] —**a·lac′ri·tous**, *adj.* —Ant. **1.** languor.

A·lad·din (ə·lad′ən), *n.* a youth in *The Arabian Nights*, who found a magic lamp and a magic ring.

à la king (ä′ lə king′), *Am.* creamed with pimiento or green pepper: *chicken à la king.*

Al·a·me·da (al′ə·mē′də; –mā′–), *n.* city in W California.

al·a·me·da (al′ə·mā′də), *n., Am., Esp. S.W.* promenade with trees, esp. poplars, on each side. [< Sp., < *alamo* poplar]

Al·a·mo (al′ə·mō), *n.* a mission in San Antonio, Texas. After a siege, the Mexicans finally captured it from the Americans on March 6, 1836.

à la mode, a la mode (ä′ lə mōd′; al′ə–), *adv.* **1.** according to the prevailing fashion; in style. **2.** *Cookery.* **a.** (of desserts) served with ice cream. **b.** (of beef) cooked with vegetables. [< F]

Al·a·ric (al′ə·rik), *n.* 370?–410 A.D., king of the Visigoths who captured Rome in 410 A.D.

a·larm (ə·lärm′), *n.* **1.** sudden fear or fright. **2.** a warning of approaching danger. **3.** thing that gives such a warning. **4.** call to arms or action. **5.** a device that makes noise to warn or awaken people. —*v.* **1.** fill with sudden fear. **2.** warn (anyone) of approaching danger. **3.** call to arms. [< OF < Ital., < *all'arme!* to arms!]

alarm clock, clock that can be set to make a noise at any desired time.

a·larm·ing (ə·lär′ming), *adj.* that alarms; frightening. —**a·larm′ing·ly**, *adv.*

a·larm·ist (ə·lär′mist), *n.* person who is easily alarmed or alarms others needlessly or on very slight grounds. —**a·larm·ism** (ə·lär′miz·əm), *n.*

a·lar·um (ə·lar′əm; ə·lär′–), *n. Archaic.* alarm.

a·las (ə·las′; ə·läs′), *interj.* exclamation of sorrow, grief, regret, pity, or dread. [< OF *a ah + las* miserable < L *lassus* weary]

Alas., Alaska.

A·las·ka (ə·las′kə), *n.* the largest State of the United States, in NW North America, formerly (until 1958) a territory. *Capital:* Juneau. —**A·las′kan**, *adj., n.*

Alaska Highway, a highway that extends from Dawson Creek, British Columbia, Canada, to Fairbanks, Alaska.

a·late (ā′lāt), **a·lat·ed** (–id), *adj.* having wings or winglike parts. [< L, < *ala* wing]

alb (alb), *n.* a white linen robe worn by Roman Catholic and some Anglican priests at the Eucharist. [< L (*vestis*) *alba* white (robe)]

al·ba·core (al′bə·kôr; –kōr), *n., pl.* **-cores** or (*esp. collectively*) **-core.** a long-finned, edible fish related to the tuna, found in the Atlantic. [< Pg. < Ar. *al-bakūra*]

Al·ba·ni·a (al·bā′ni·ə; –bān′yə), *n.* country in Europe, between Yugoslavia and Greece. —**Al·ba′ni·an**, *adj., n.*

Al·ba·ny (ôl′bə·ni), *n.* capital of New York State, on the Hudson River.

al·ba·tross (al′bə·trôs; –tros), *n.* any of various webfooted sea birds related to the petrel. [var. of obs. *alcatras* frigate bird <Sp. < Pg. < Ar. *al-qādus* the bucket < Gk. *kados* < Phoenician]

Albatross (30 in. long)

al·be·it (ôl·bē′it), *conj.* although; even though. [ME *al be it* although it be]

Al·ber·ta (al·bér′tə), *n.* province in W Canada.

al·bi·no (al·bī′nō), *n., pl.* **-nos. 1.** person who congenitally lacks pigmentation. Albinos have a pale skin, light hair, and pink eyes. **2.** any animal or plant that has pale, defective coloring. [< Pg., < *albo* < L *albus* white] —**al·bin·ic** (al·bin′ik), *adj.* —**al·bi·nism** (al′bə·niz·əm), *n.*

Al·bi·on (al′bi·ən), *n. Poetic.* England.

al·bum (al′bəm), *n.* **1.** book with blank pages for pictures, stamps, etc. **2.** case for phonograph records. [< L, tablet, neut. of *albus* white]

al·bu·men (al·bū′mən), *n.* **1.** white of an egg, consisting mostly of albumin dissolved in water. **2.** *Chem.* albumin. **3.** *Bot.* endosperm. [< L *albumen* < *albus* white]

al·bu·min (al·bū′mən), *n. Chem.* any of a class of proteins soluble in water and found in the white of egg and in many other animal and plant tissues and juices, esp. $C_{72}H_{112}N_{18}O_{22}S$. [< L. See ALBUMEN.]

al·bu·mi·nous (al·bū′mə·nəs), **al·bu·mi·nose** (–nōs), *adj.* of, like, or containing albumin.

Al·bu·quer·que (al′bə·kér′kē), *n.* city in central New Mexico.

al·caide, al·cayde (al·kād′), *n.* **1.** governor of a Spanish fortress. **2.** warden of a Spanish prison. [< Sp. < Ar. *al-qā'id* the commander]

Al·can Highway (al′kan), Alaska Highway.

Al·ca·traz (al′kə·traz), *n.* **1.** island in San Francisco Bay. **2.** former U.S. penitentiary there.

al·ca·zar (al′kə·zär; al·kaz′ər), *n.* palace of the Spanish Moors. [< Ar. *al-qaṣr* the castle < L *castrum* fort]

al·che·mist (al′kə·mist), *n.* in the Middle Ages, a man who studied alchemy. —**al′che·mis′tic, al′che·mis′ti·cal**, *adj.*

al·che·my (al′kə·mi), *n.* **1.** medieval chemistry, esp. the search for a process by which baser metals could be turned into gold. **2.** magic power or process for changing one thing into another. [< OF < Med.L < Ar. *al-kimiyā'*, < LGk. *chymeia* < Gk. *chyma* molten metal] —**al·chem·ic** (al·kem′ik), **al·chem′i·cal**, *adj.* —**al·chem′i·cal·ly**, *adv.*

al·co·hol (al′kə·hôl; –hol), *n.* **1.** the colorless liquid, C_2H_5OH, in wine, beer, whiskey, gin, etc., that makes them intoxicating; grain alcohol; ethyl alcohol. Alcohol is used in medicine, in manufacturing, and as a fuel. **2.** any intoxicating liquor containing this liquid. **3.** *Chem.* any of a group of similar organic compounds. Alcohols contain a hydroxyl group and react with organic acids to form esters. [< Med.L (orig., "fine powder," then "essence") < Ar. *al-kuḥl* powdered antimony]

al·co·hol·ic (al'kə·hôl'ik; –hol'–), *adj.* **1.** of alcohol. **2.** containing alcohol. **3.** suffering from the excessive use of alcoholic liquors. —*n.* person suffering from alcoholism.

al·co·hol·ism (al'kə·hôl·iz'əm; –hol–), *n.* **1.** a disease having as its chief symptom the inability to drink alcoholic liquors in moderation. **2.** a diseased condition caused by drinking too much alcoholic liquor.

Al·co·ran (al'kō·rän'; –ran'), *n.* the Koran.

al·cove (al'kōv), *n.* **1.** small room opening out of a larger room. **2.** part in a wall set back from the rest. **3.** summerhouse. [< F < Sp. < Ar. *al-qubba* the vaulted chamber]

Ald., Aldm., Alderman.

al·de·hyde (al'də·hīd), *n.* **1.** a transparent, colorless liquid, CH₃CHO, with a suffocating smell, produced by the partial oxidation of ordinary alcohol. **2.** any similar organic compound. —**al'de·hy'dic,** *adj.*

Al·den (ôl'dən), *n.* **John,** 1599?–1687, one of the Pilgrims who settled at Plymouth, Mass.

al·der (ôl'dər), *n.* any of several trees and shrubs that usually grow in wet land and have clusters of catkins. [OE *alor*]

al·der·man (ôl'dər·mən), *n.,* *pl.* **-men. 1.** *U.S.* member of a council that governs a city. An alderman is usually elected by the voters of a certain ward or district and represents them on the council. **2.** in English and Irish cities, a member of a city or county council next in rank to the mayor. [see ELDER¹] —**al'der·man·cy, al'der·man·ship',** *n.* —**al·der·man·ic** (ôl'dər·man'ik), *adj.*

Alder

Al·der·ney (ôl'dər·ni), *n.,* *pl.* **-neys. 1.** one of a group of British islands in the English Channel. **2.** one of a breed of dairy cattle.

Al·drin (al'drin), *n.* *Trademark.* a very powerful organic insecticide, distantly related to DDT.

ale (āl), *n.* a heavy, bitter beer, fermented from hops and malt. [OE *alu*]

a·lee (ə·lē'), *adv., adj.* *Naut.* on or toward the side of a ship that is away from the wind. [< Scand., < *ā* on + *hlē* shelter, lee]

ale·house (āl'hous'), *n.* place where ale or beer is sold; saloon.

A·le·mán (ä'lā·män'), *n.* **Miguel,** born 1902, president of Mexico 1946–1952.

a·lem·bic (ə·lem'bik), *n.* **1.** a glass or metal container formerly used in distilling. **2.** something that transforms or refines. [< Med.L < Ar. *al anbïq* the still < Gk. *ambïx* cup]

A·len·çon (ä·län·sôn' *for 1;* ə·len'sən, –son *for 2*), *n.* **1.** city in NW France. **2.** lace made there.

A·lep·po (ə·lep'ō), *n.* city in NW Syria.

a·lert (ə·lėrt'), *adj.* **1.** watchful; wide-awake. **2.** brisk; active; nimble. —*n.* **1.** a signal warning of an air attack. **2.** a signal to troops, etc., to be ready for action. **3. on the alert,** on the lookout; watchful; wide-awake. —*v.* warn against and prepare for an approaching air attack. [< F < Ital. *all' erta* on the watch, ult. < L *erigere* raise up] —**a·lert'ly,** *adv.* —**a·lert'ness,** *n.* —Syn. *adj.* **1.** attentive. —Ant. *adj.* **1.** heedless.

Al·e·ut (al'i·üt), *n.* *Am.* an Eskimo native of the Aleutian Islands.

A·leu·tians (ə·lü'shənz), or **Aleutian Islands,** *n.pl.* chain of many small islands SW of Alaska, belonging to the United States.

ale·wife (āl'wīf'), *n.,* *pl.* **-wives.** *Am.* a sea fish related to the herring and the shad.

Al·ex·an·der the Great (al'ig·zan'dər; –zän'–), 356–323 B.C., king of Macedonia from 336 to 323 B.C.

Al·ex·an·dri·a (al'ig·zan'dri·ə; –zän'–), *n.* seaport in N Egypt, on the Mediterranean.

Al·ex·an·dri·an (al'ig·zan'dri·ən; –zän'–),

adj. **1.** of Alexandria. **2.** of Alexander the Great. **3.** of Alexandrine verse.

Al·ex·an·drine (al'ig·zan'drin; –drēn; –zän'–), *n.* line of poetry having six iambic feet, with a caesura (pause) after the third foot.

al·fal·fa (al·fal'fə), *n.* *Esp. U.S.* a plant of the pea family much grown in western United States for pasture and forage; lucerne. [< Sp. < Ar. *al-faṣ faṣah* the best kind of fodder]

Al·fred (al'frid), *n.* ("*Alfred the Great*") 849–899 A.D., king of the West Saxons, 871–899 A.D.

al·fres·co, al fres·co (al·fres'kō), *adv., adj.* in the open air; outdoors. [< Ital.]

alg., algebra.

al·ga (al'gə), *n., pl.* **-gae** (–jē). one of the algae. —**al·gal** (al'gəl), *adj.*

al·gae (al'jē), *n.pl.* group of plants that have chlorophyll but do not have true stems, roots, or leaves. Some algae are single-celled and form scum on rocks; others, such as the seaweeds, are very large. [< L, seaweed]

al·ge·bra (al'jə·brə), *n.* branch of mathematics in which quantities are denoted by letters, negative numbers as well as ordinary numbers are used, and problems are solved in the form of equations. [< Med.L < Ar. *al-jebr* the bone setting; hence, reduction] —**al·ge·bra·ic** (al'jə·brā'ik), **al'ge·bra'i·cal,** *adj.* —**al'ge·bra'i·cal·ly,** *adv.*

al·ge·bra·ist (al'jə·brā'ist), *n.* expert in algebra.

Al·ge·ri·a (al·jir'i·ə), *n.* country in N Africa, formerly under French control. It became independent in 1962. —**Al·ge'ri·an, Al·ge·rine** (al'jə·rēn), *adj., n.*

Al·giers (al·jirz'), *n.* **1.** capital of Algeria. **2.** Algeria.

Al·gon·qui·an (al·gong'ki·ən; –kwi·ən), *n. Am.* **1.** the most widespread linguistic stock of American Indians. **2.** an Indian belonging to an Algonquian tribe. —*adj.* of or belonging to this linguistic stock.

Al·gon·quin (al·gong'kin; –kwin), **Al·gon·kin** (al·gong'kin), *n. Am.* **1.** member of a family of tribes of the Algonquian linguistic stock. **2.** the language of any of these tribes. **3.** any Algonquian.

Al·ham·bra (al·ham'brə), *n.* palace of the Moorish kings at Granada, Spain.

a·li·as (ā'li·əs), *n., pl.* **-li·as·es,** *adv.* —*n.* an assumed name. —*adv.* with the assumed name of. [< L, at another time]

al·i·bi (al'ə·bī), *n., pl.* **-bis,** *v.,* **-bied, -bi·ing.** —*n.* **1.** *Law.* plea or fact that a person accused of a certain offense was elsewhere when the offense was committed. **2.** *Am., Colloq.* an excuse. —*v. Am., Colloq.* make an excuse. [< L, elsewhere]

al·ien (āl'yən; ā'li·ən), *n.* **1.** person who is not a citizen of the country in which he lives. **2.** foreigner; stranger. —*adj.* **1.** of another country; foreign. **2.** opposed; hostile (*to* or *from*): *ideas alien to our way of thought.* **3.** entirely different; not in agreement. [< L, < *alius* other]

al·ien·a·ble (āl'yən·ə·bəl; ā'li·ən–), *adj.* capable of being transferred to another owner. —**al'ien·a·bil'i·ty,** *n.*

al·ien·ate (āl'yən·āt; ā'li·ən–), *v.,* **-at·ed, -at·ing. 1.** turn away in feeling or affection; make unfriendly. **2.** transfer the ownership of (property) to another. —**al'ien·a'tion,** *n.*

al·ien·ist (āl'yən·ist; ā'li·ən–), *n.* psychiatrist, esp. one who testifies in court. [< F < L *alienus* insane]

a·light¹ (ə·līt'), *v.,* **a·light·ed** or (*Poetic*) **a·lit, a·light·ing. 1.** get down; get off, as from horseback. **2.** come down from the air and settle: *a bird alights on a tree.* **3.** come upon by chance; happen to find. [OE *ālīhtan*] —Syn. **1.** dismount.

a·light² (ə·līt'), *adv., adj.* lighted up: *her face was alight with joy.* [OE *āliht* illuminated]

a·lign (ə·līn'), *v.* **1.** bring into line; adjust to a line: *align the sights of a gun.* **2.** form in line: *the troops aligned.* **3.** join with others in or against a cause: *Germany was aligned with Japan in World War II.* Also, **aline.** [< F, < *a*- to + *ligner* < L, < *linea* line] —**a·lign'er,** *n.* —**a·lign'ment,** *n.*

a·like (ə·līk′), adv. 1. in the same way. 2. similarly; equally. —adj. like one another; similar. [OE gelīc, onlīc]

al·i·ment (al′ə·mənt), n. nourishment; food. [< L alimentum < alere nourish] —al·i·men·tal (al′ə·men′təl), adj. —al′i·men′tal·ly, adv.

al·i·men·ta·ry (al′ə·men′tə·ri; -men′tri), adj. 1. having to do with food and nutrition. 2. nourishing; nutritious. 3. providing support.

alimentary canal, the digestive tract of any animal, extending from the mouth to the anus.

al·i·men·ta·tion (al′ə·men·tā′shən), n. 1. nutrition. 2. support. —al·i·men·ta·tive (al′ə·men′tə·tiv), adj.

al·i·mo·ny (al′ə·mō′ni), n. money that a man must pay his wife or ex-wife, legally separated from him. [< L alimonia < alere nourish]

a·line (ə·līn′), v., a·lined, a·lin·ing. align. —a·line′ment, n. —a·lin′er, n.

al·i·quant (al′ə·kwənt), adj. Math. not dividing a number without a remainder: 5 is an aliquant part of 14. [< L, < alius other + quantus how much]

al·i·quot (al′ə·kwət), adj. Math. dividing a number without a remainder: 3 is an aliquot part of 12. [< L, < alius some + quot how many]

a·lit (ə·lit′), v. Poetic. pt. and pp. of alight¹.

a·live (ə·līv′), adj. 1. living; not dead: the man is alive. 2. in continued activity or operation: keep the principles of liberty alive. 3. of all living: happiest man alive. 4. active; sprightly; lively. 5. alive to, awake to; sensitive to. 6. alive with, full of; swarming with; thronged with. 7. look alive! hurry up! be quick! [OE on life in life] —a·live′ness, n.

a·liz·a·rin (ə·liz′ə·rin), **a·liz·a·rine** (-rin; -rēn), n. a red dye, C₁₄H₈O₄, prepared from coal tar, formerly obtained from madder. [< F, < alizari < Sp. < Ar. al-ʻaṣāra the extract]

al·ka·li (al′kə·lī), n., pl. -lis, -lies. 1. Chem. any base or hydroxide that is soluble in water, neutralizes acids and forms salts with them, and turns red litmus blue. 2. any salt or mixture of salts that neutralizes acids. Some desert soils contain much alkali. [< MF < Ar. al-qalī the ashes of saltwort (a genus of plants)]

al·ka·line (al′kə·līn; -lin), adj. 1. of or like an alkali. 2. Am., W. impregnated with alkali. —al·ka·lin·i·ty (al′kə·lin′ə·ti), n.

alkaline-earth metals, Chem. group of elements including calcium, strontium, barium, magnesium, and radium.

alkaline earths, Chem. oxides of the alkaline-earth metals.

al·ka·lize (al′kə·līz), v., -lized, -liz·ing. make alkaline. —al′ka·li·za′tion, n.

al·ka·loid (al′kə·loid), n. Chem. any organic base containing nitrogen. Many alkaloids from plants are drugs, such as cocaine, strychnine, morphine, and quinine. —adj. noting or pertaining to an alkaloid. —al′ka·loi′dal, adj.

all (ôl), adj. 1. the whole of: all Europe. 2. every one of: all men. 3. the greatest possible: with all speed. 4. any; any whatever: the prisoner denied all connection with the crime. 5. nothing but; only: all words and no thought. 6. all in, Am., Colloq. weary; worn out. —pron. 1. (pl. in use) the whole number; everyone: all of us are going. 2. (sing. in use) the whole quantity; everything: all that glitters is not gold. —n. 1. everything one has: he lost his all in the fire. 2. above all, before everything else. 3. after all, all things considered; nevertheless. 4. all but, almost; nearly. 5. all in all, a. everything. b. completely. 6. at all, a. under any conditions. b. in any way. 7. in all, altogether: 100 men in all. —adv. 1. wholly; entirely: the cake is all gone. 2. each; apiece: the score was one all. 3. at, Am., Colloq. as much as; no less than. [OE eall] ≫ **all (of).** Colloquially and familiarly all is followed by of in many constructions where the of is not necessary and would not be used in formal writing: all [of] the milk was spilled. All of is usual with a pronoun: all of them went home.

Al·lah (al′ə; ä′lə), n. the Mohammedan name of the Supreme Being.

all-A·mer·i·can (ôl′ə·mer′ə·kən), Am. —adj. 1. representing the whole United States. 2. made up entirely of Americans or American elements. 3. selected as the best in the United States. —n. an all-American person, esp. a player on a team.

all-a·round (ôl′ə·round′), adj. Am., Colloq. able to do many things; useful in many ways. —all′-a·round′ness, n. Am.

al·lay (ə·lā′), v., -layed, -lay·ing. 1. put at rest; quiet: his fears were allayed by the news of the safety of his family. 2. relieve; check: her fever was allayed by the medicine. 3. make less. [OE ālecgan] —al·lay′er, n. —al·lay′ment, n. —Syn. 1. pacify, calm.

all clear, signal indicating the end of an air raid or other danger. —all′-clear′, adj.

al·le·ga·tion (al′ə·gā′shən), n. 1. assertion without proof. 2. act of alleging; assertion: the lawyer's allegation was proved. 3. assertion made as a plea or excuse.

al·lege (ə·lej′), v., -leged, -leg·ing. 1. assert without proof: the alleged theft never happened. 2. state positively: this man alleges that his watch has been stolen. 3. give or bring forward as a reason, etc. [< AF alegier < L ex- + litigare strive, sue; with sense of L allegare charge] —al·lege′a·ble, adj. —al·leg′er, n. —Syn. 2. affirm. 3. produce, cite.

al·leg·ed·ly (ə·lej′id·li), adv. according to what is or has been alleged.

Al·le·ghe·nies (al′ə·gā′niz; al′ə·gā′niz), or **Allegheny Mountains,** n.pl. a mountain range in Pennsylvania, Maryland, Virginia, and West Virginia. —Al·le·ghe·ni·an (al′ə·gā′ni·ən), n., adj.

al·le·giance (ə·lē′jəns), n. 1. the loyalty owed by a citizen to his country or by a subject to his ruler. 2. loyalty; faithfulness; devotion. [ME ligeaunce < OF, < lige liege]

al·le·gor·i·cal (al′ə·gôr′ə·kəl; -gor′-), **al·le·gor·ic** (-ik), adj. using allegory. —al′le·gor′i·cal·ly, adv. —al′le·gor′i·cal·ness, n.

al·le·go·rist (al′ə·gô′rist; -gō′-; al′ə·gə·rist), n. one who uses allegories.

al·le·go·rize (al′ə·gə·rīz), v., -rized, -riz·ing. 1. make into allegory. 2. treat or interpret as an allegory. 3. use allegory. —al·le·go·ri·za·tion (al′ə·gôr′ə·zā′shən; -gor′ə-), n. —al′le·go·riz′er, n.

al·le·go·ry (al′ə·gō′ri; -gō′-), n., pl. -ries. 1. story which is told to explain or teach something: Bunyan's "The Pilgrim's Progress" is an allegory. 2. emblem (def. 1). [< L < Gk., < allos other + agoreuein speak]

al·le·gro (ə·lā′grō; ə·leg′rō), adj., adv., n., pl. -gros. Music. —adj. quick; lively. —adv. in allegro time. —n. a movement in such time. [< Ital. < L alacer brisk]

al·le·lu·ia (al′ə·lü′yə), interj. liturgical form of hallelujah, meaning "praise ye the Lord." —n. hymn of praise to the Lord. [< L < Gk. < Heb. hallēlūjāh praise ye Jehovah]

al·ler·gic (ə·lér′jik), adj. 1. of allergy. 2. having an allergy.

al·ler·gy (al′ər·ji), n., pl. -gies. unusual sensitiveness to a particular substance, as certain pollens and dusts. [< NL < Gk. allos different, strange + ergon action]

al·le·vi·ate (ə·lē′vi·āt), v., -at·ed, -at·ing. make easier to endure (suffering of the body or mind). [< LL, < L ad- up + levis light] —al·le′vi·a′tion, n. —al·le′vi·a′tive, adj., n. —al·le′vi·a′tor, n. —Syn. allay, mitigate.

al·ley¹ (al′i), n., pl. -leys. 1. Am. a narrow back street. 2. Brit. a narrow street. 3. path in a park or garden, bordered by trees. 4. a long, narrow enclosed place for bowling. [< OF alee a going]

al·ley² (al′i), n., pl. -leys. a large, choice playing marble. [short for alabaster]

al·ley·way (al′i·wā′), n. Am. 1. a narrow lane in a city or town. 2. a narrow passageway.

All Fools' Day, April 1, April Fools' Day.

all fours, 1. all four legs of an animal. 2. arms and legs of a person; hands and knees.

āge, cāre, fär; ēqual, tėrm; īce; ōpen, ôrder; pút, rüle, ūse; th, then; ə=a in about.

All·hal·lows (ôl′hal′ōz), *n.* Nov. 1, All Saints' Day.

al·li·ance (ə·lī′əns), *n.* **1.** union formed by agreement; joining of interests. An alliance may be a joining of family interests by marriage, a joining of national interests by treaty, etc. **2.** nations, persons, etc., who belong to such a union. **3.** association; connection. **4.** similarity in structure or descent. [< OF, < *alier* unite < L, < *ad-* to + *ligare* bind]

al·lied (ə·līd′; al′īd), *adj.* **1.** united by agreement or treaty: *allied nations.* **2.** associated: *allied banks.* **3.** connected by nature; akin: *allied animals.* **4.** Allied, of the Allies.

Al·lies (al′īz; ə·līz′), *n.pl.* **1.** nations that fought against Germany and Austria in World War I. **2.** nations that fought against Germany, Italy, and Japan in World War II.

al·li·ga·tor (al′ə-gā′tər), *n.* **1.** an American reptile, similar to the crocodile but having a shorter and flatter head. **2.** leather prepared from its skin. **3.** *Mil.* amphibian vehicle for carrying troops ashore, etc. [< Sp. *el lagarto* the lizard < L *lacertus* lizard]

Alligator (12 ft. long)

alligator pear, avocado.

al·lit·er·ate (ə·lit′ər·āt), *v.,* **-at·ed, -at·ing. 1.** begin with the same letter or sound. **2.** use alliteration. [< L *ad-* to + *litera* letter] **—al·lit′er·a′tor,** *n.*

al·lit·er·a·tion (ə·lit′ər·ā′shən), *n.* repetition of the same first letter or sound in a group of words or line of poetry; initial rhyme. *Example:* the sun sank slowly. **—al·lit′er·a′tive,** *adj.* **—al·lit′er·a′tive·ly,** *adv.* **—al·lit′er·a′tive·ness,** *n.*

al·lo·cate (al′ə·kāt), *v.,* **-cat·ed, -cat·ing. 1.** assign or allot, as a share, portion, etc. **2.** locate. [< Med.L, < L *ad-* to, at + *locare* to place] **—al′lo·ca′tion,** *n.* **—Syn. 1.** distribute.

al·lo·path (al′ə·path), *n.* **1.** doctor who uses allopathy. **2.** person who favors allopathy.

al·lop·a·thist (ə·lop′ə·thist), *n.* **1.** doctor who uses allopathy. **2.** person who favors allopathy.

al·lop·a·thy (ə·lop′ə·thi), *n.* method of treating a disease by using remedies to produce effects different from those caused by the disease treated (opposite of *homeopathy*). [< G < Gk. *allos* other + -PATHY] **—al·lo·path·ic** (al′ə-path′ik), *adj.* **—al′lo·path′i·cal·ly,** *adv.*

al·lo·phone (al′ə·fōn), *n. Phonet.* one of the several individual sounds belonging to a single phoneme. The *t* in *take* and the *t* in *try* are allophones of the phoneme *t.* [< Gk. *allos* other + *phone* sound]

al·lot (ə·lot′), *v.,* **-lot·ted, -lot·ting. 1.** divide and distribute in parts or shares: *the profits have all been allotted.* **2.** appropriate to a special purpose. **3.** assign as a share: *the teacher allotted work to each student.* [< OF *aloter.* See LOT.] **—al·lot′ta·ble,** *adj.* **—al·lot′ter,** *n.*

al·lot·ment (ə·lot′mənt), *n.* **1.** division and distribution in parts or shares. **2.** share.

al·lo·trope (al′ə·trōp), *n.* an allotropic form.

al·lo·trop·ic (al′ə·trop′ik), **al·le·trop·i·cal** (-ə·kəl), *adj.* occurring in two or more forms that differ in physical and chemical properties but not in the kind of atoms of which they are composed. **—al′lo·trop′i·cal·ly,** *adv.*

al·lot·ro·py (ə·lot′rə·pi), **al·lot·ro·pism** (-piz′əm), *n.* the property or fact of being allotropic. [< Gk., < *allos* other + *tropos* way]

all-out (ôl′out′), *adj.* greatest possible.

al·low (ə·lou′), *v.* **1.** permit: *smoking is not allowed.* **2.** let have; give: *he is allowed two dollars a week.* **3.** admit; acknowledge; recognize: *allow a claim.* **4.** add or subtract to make up for something: *allow an extra hour for traveling time.* **5.** permit to happen, esp. through carelessness or neglect: *allow a mine disaster.* **6.** *U.S. Dial.* say or think. **7.** allow for, take into consideration; provide for. [< OF *alouer* < L *allaudare* (< *ad-* + *laudare* praise) and *allo-*

care ALLOCATE] **—al·low′er,** *n.* **—Syn. 1.** let. **2.** grant, yield, assign.

al·low·a·ble (ə·lou′ə·bəl), *adj.* **1.** allowed by law or by a person in authority. **2.** permitted by the rules of the game; not forbidden. **—al·low′a·ble·ness,** *n.* **—al·low′a·bly,** *adv.*

al·low·ance (ə·lou′əns), *n., v.,* **-anced, -anc·ing. —n. 1.** definite portion or amount given out: *a weekly allowance of $12.* **2.** subtraction or addition to make up for something: *an allowance on a used car.* **3.** an allowing: *allowance of a claim.* **4.** tolerance: *allowance of slavery.* **5.** make allowance for, take into consideration: *make allowance for a person's youth.* **—v.** put upon an allowance; to limit (supplies, food, etc.) to a fixed, regular amount.

al·low·ed·ly (ə·lou′id·li), *adv.* admittedly.

al·loy (*n.* al′oi, ə·loi′; *v.* ə·loi′), *n.* **1.** an inferior metal mixed with a more valuable one. **2.** metal made by the fusion of two or more metals, or a metal and a nonmetal. **3.** any injurious addition: *no happiness is without alloy.* **—v. 1.** make into an alloy. **2.** lower in value by mixing with an inferior metal: *alloy gold with copper.* **3.** make worse; debase: *happiness alloyed by misfortune.* [< OF *alei* < L, < *ad-* to + *ligare* bind. Doublet of ALLY.]

all-pur·pose (ôl′pėr′pəs), *adj.* that can be used for any end: *all-purpose thread.*

all right, 1. without error; correct. **2.** yes. **3.** certainly. **4.** in good health. **5.** satisfactory. **≫** See alright for usage note.

all-round (ôl′round′), *adj. Colloq.* **1.** all-around. **2.** extending everywhere around.

All Saints' Day, Nov. 1, a church festival honoring all the saints; Allhallows.

all·spice (ôl′spīs′), *n.* **1.** a spice supposed to have a flavor like a mixture of cinnamon, nutmeg, and cloves. **2.** the berry of the West Indian pimento tree that it is made from.

all-star (ôl′stär′), *adj. Am.* composed of the best players or performers.

al·lude (ə·lüd′), *v.,* **-lud·ed, -lud·ing.** refer indirectly; mention slightly (*to*): *do not mention or even allude to his failure.* [< L, < *ad-* with + *ludere* play]

al·lure (ə·lür′), *v.,* **-lured, -lur·ing,** *n.* **—v. 1.** fascinate; charm. **2.** tempt by some advantage. **—n.** attractiveness. [< OF *alurer* LURE] **—al·lure′ment,** *n.* **—al·lur′er,** *n.*

al·lur·ing (ə·lür′ing), *adj.* **1.** tempting. **2.** attractive. **—al·lur′ing·ly,** *adv.* **—al·lur′ing·ness,** *n.*

al·lu·sion (ə·lü′zhən), *n.* an indirect or casual reference; slight mention. **≫** See illusion for usage note.

al·lu·sive (ə·lü′siv), *adj.* containing allusions. **—al·lu′sive·ly,** *adv.* **—al·lu′sive·ness,** *n.*

al·lu·vi·al (ə·lü′vi·əl), *adj.* consisting of or forming alluvium. **—n.** alluvial soil.

al·lu·vi·um (ə·lü′vi·əm), *n., pl.* **-vi·ums, -vi·a** (-vi·ə). sand, mud, etc., left by flowing water. [< L, < *ad-* up + *luere* wash]

al·ly (*v.* ə·lī′; *n.* al′ī, ə·lī′), *v.,* **-lied, -ly·ing,** *n., pl.* **-lies. —v. 1.** unite by formal agreement, as by marriage, treaty, or league (*to* or *with*): *France allied herself with England.* **2.** connect by some relation, as of likeness, kinship, or friendship. **3.** enter into an alliance. **—n. 1.** person or nation united with another for some special purpose. **2.** a related animal, plant, or thing. **3.** helper; supporter. See also Allies. [< OF *alier* < L, < *ad-* to + *ligare* bind. Doublet of ALLOY.]

al·ma ma·ter, Al·ma Ma·ter (al′mə mä′tər; äl′-; al′mə mā′tər), person's school, college, or university. [< L, nourishing mother]

al·ma·nac (ôl′mə·nak), *n.* table or book of tables containing a calendar, astronomical data, etc. [< Med.L < Sp. < Ar. *almanākh,* appar. < LGk. *almenichiakon* calendar]

al·might·y (ôl·mīt′i), *adj.* **1.** having supreme power; all-powerful. **2.** *U.S. Colloq.* great; very. **—adv.** *U.S. Colloq.* exceedingly. **—n.** the Almighty, God. **—al·might′i·ly,** *adv.* **—al·might′i·ness,** *n.* **—Syn.** *adj.* **1.** omnipotent.

almighty dollar, *Am., Colloq.* money thought of as all-powerful.

al·mond (ä′mənd; am′ənd), n. 1. the nut, or seed, of a peachlike fruit growing in warm regions. 2. tree that it grows on. [< OF *almande* < L < Gk. *amygdale*] —al′mond·like′, adj.

al·mon·er (al′mən·ər; ä′mən-), n. one who distributes alms for a king, monastery, etc. [< OF *almosnier* < VL *alemosynarius* of ALMS]

al·mon·ry (al′mən·ri; ä′mən-), n., pl. -ries. place where alms are distributed.

al·most (ôl′mōst; ôl·mōst′), adv. nearly. [OE *eal mãst* nearly]

alms (ämz), n.pl. (*sometimes sing. in use*) money or gifts to help the poor. [< VL < L < Gk. *eleemosyne* compassion < *eleos* mercy]

alms·giv·ing (ämz′giv′ing), n., adj. giving help to the poor. —alms′giv′er, n.

alms·house (ämz′hous′), n. 1. Brit. house endowed by private charity for the poor to live in. 2. U.S. house maintained at public expense for the poor to live in.

al·oe (al′ō), n., pl. -oes. 1. plant having a long spike of flowers and thick, narrow leaves, that grows in South Africa and other warm, dry climates. 2. aloes (*sing. in use*), a bitter drug made from the leaves of this plant. 3. U.S. the century plant. Cf. agave. [< L < Gk.]

a·loft (ə·lôft′; ə·loft′), adv., adj. 1. far above the earth; high up. 2. high above the deck of a ship. [< Scand. *ã lopti* in the air]

a·lo·ha (ə·lō′ə; ä·lō′hä), n., interj. Hawaiian. salutation meaning: a. welcome. b. good-by.

a·lone (ə·lōn′), adj. 1. apart from other persons or things; solitary: *he was alone.* 2. without anyone else; only: *he alone remained.* 3. without anything more. 4. unique. 5. leave alone, not bother. 6. let alone, a. not bother. b. not to mention. —adv. only; merely; exclusively. [ME *al one* all (completely) one] —a·lone′ness, n. —Syn. adj. 1. lone, isolated.

a·long (ə·lông′; ə·long′), prep. on or by the whole length of; lengthwise of: *walk along a river.* —adv. 1. lengthwise: *cars parked along by the stadium.* 2. with progressive motion; onward: *let us walk along.* 3. in company; together (*with*): *I'll go along with you.* 4. U.S. going with one as a companion: *he took his dog along.* 5. Am., Colloq. (of time) some way on. 6. all along, all the time. 7. be along, Am., Colloq. catch up with others. 8. get along, a. Am., Colloq. manage with at least some success. b. agree. c. go away. d. advance. e. succeed; prosper. [OE *andlang*]

a·long·shore (ə·lông′shôr′; ə·long′-; -shôr′), adv. near or along the shore.

a·long·side (ə·lông′sīd′; ə·long′-), adv. at the side; side by side: *anchor alongside.* —prep. by the side of; beside: *alongside the wharf.*

a·loof (ə·lüf′), adv. at a distance; withdrawn; apart: *he stood aloof from the others.* —adj. unsympathetic; indifferent: *an aloof attitude.* [< a- on + *loof* windward, prob. < Du. *loef*] —a·loof′ly, adv. —a·loof′ness, n.

a·loud (ə·loud′), adv. 1. loud enough to be heard; not in a whisper: *read aloud.* 2. in a loud voice; loudly. —Syn. 1. audibly.

al·pac·a (al·pak′ə), n. 1. a variety of llama with long, soft, silky hair or wool. 2. its wool. 3. cloth made from this wool. [< Sp. < Ar. *al* the + Peruvian *paco* alpaca]

al·pen·horn (al′pən·hôrn′), **alp·horn** (alp′hôrn′), n. long, powerful horn used in Switzerland for military signals, etc. [< G]

al·pen·stock (al′pən·stok′), n. a strong staff with an iron point, used in climbing mountains. [< G]

al·pha (al′fə), n. 1. the first letter of the Greek alphabet (Α, α). 2. the first; beginning.

al·pha·bet (al′fə·bet), n. 1. series of characters or signs representing sounds, used in writing a language. 2. letters of a language arranged in the customary order. 3. elementary principles. [< LL < Gk., < *alpha* A + *beta* B]

al·pha·bet·i·cal (al′fə·bet′ə·kəl), **al·pha·bet·ic** (-bet′ik), adj. 1. arranged in the order of the alphabet. 2. of the alphabet. 3. using an alphabet. —al′pha·bet′i·cal·ly, adv.

al·pha·bet·ize (al′fə·bə·tīz), v., -ized, -iz-

ing. 1. arrange in alphabetical order. 2. express by an alphabet. —al·pha·bet·i·za·tion (al′fə·bet′ə·zā′shən), n. —al′pha·bet·iz′er, n.

alpha particle, Physics. a positively charged particle consisting of two protons and two neutrons, released in the disintegration of radioactive substances, as radium.

alpha ray, Physics. stream of alpha particles.

Al·pine (al′pīn; -pin), adj. 1. of the Alps. 2. alpine. a. of high mountains. b. very high.

Alps (alps), n.pl. a mountain system in S Europe, famous for its beautiful scenery.

al·read·y (ôl·red′i), adv. before this time; by this time; even now: *the house is already full.* [for *all ready*] ➤ All ready, as distinguished from already, is used as an adjective phrase meaning "quite or completely ready": *the men were all ready to start their next job.*

al·right (ôl·rīt′), adv. all right. ➤ All right is the correct spelling of both the adjective phrase (*He is all right*) and the sentence adverb meaning, "Yes, certainly" (*All right, I'll come*). Alright is a natural analogy with *altogether* and *already*, but at present is found only in advertising, comic strips, familiar writing, etc.

Al·sace (al′sãs; -sas; al·sãs′), n. region in NE France. —Al·sa·tian (al·sã′shən), adj.

Al·sace-Lor·raine (al′sãs-lə·rãn′; al′sas-), n. Alsace and Lorraine, region in NE France; part of Germany, 1871–1919 and 1940–44.

al·so (ôl′sō), adv. in addition; too. [OE *ealswā* all so, quite so] —Syn. besides, likewise, furthermore. ➤ Also is a weak connective; ordinarily *and* will do its work better: *he came with tents, cooking things, and* [better than *also*] *about fifty pounds of photographic equipment.*

alt., 1. alternate. 2. altitude.

al·tar (ôl′tər), n. 1. table or stand in the most sacred part of a church, synagogue, or temple. In Christian churches the altar is used in the Communion service or in celebrating Mass. 2. an elevated structure on which sacrifices are offered to a deity. 3. lead to the altar, marry. [< LL, < L *altus* high]

altar boy, person who helps a priest during certain religious services, esp. Mass.

al·tar·piece (ôl′tər·pēs′), n. a decorated panel or wall behind or above an altar.

al·ter (ôl′tər), v. 1. make different in some respect without changing into something else: *alter a dress.* 2. become different: *her whole outlook has altered.* 3. Am., Colloq. castrate or spay (an animal). [< OF < LL, < L *alter* other]

al·ter., alteration.

al·ter·a·ble (ôl′tər·ə·bəl), adj. that can be altered. —al′ter·a·bil′i·ty, al′ter·a·ble·ness, n. —al′ter·a·bly, adv.

al·ter·a·tion (ôl′tər·ā′shən), n. 1. result of altering; change. 2. act of altering.

al·ter·a·tive (ôl′tər·ā′tiv), adj. 1. causing change. 2. Med. gradually restoring the healthy bodily functions. —n. Med. remedy that gradually restores health.

al·ter·cate (ôl′tər·kāt; al′-), v., -cat·ed, -cat·ing. dispute angrily; quarrel. [< L, < *alter* other]

al·ter·ca·tion (ôl′tər·kā′shən; al′-), n. an angry dispute; quarrel.

al·ter e·go (ôl′tər ē′gō; al′tər; eg′ō), 1. another aspect of one's nature. 2. a very intimate friend. [< L, trans. of Gk. *heteros ego*]

al·ter·nate (v. ôl′tər·nāt, al′-; adj., n. ôl′tər·nit, al′-), v., -nat·ed, -nat·ing, adj., n. —v. 1. occur by turns; first one and then the other; happen or be arranged by turns. 2. arrange by turns; do by turns: *alternate work and pleasure.* 3. take turns: *Lucy and her sister will alternate in setting the table.* 4. interchange regularly. 5. Elect. reverse direction at regular intervals. 6. produce or be operated by such a current. —adj. 1. placed or occurring by turns; first one and then the other. 2. every other. 3. reciprocal. 4.

Alternate leaves

Bot. placed singly at different heights along a stem, as leaves. —*n.* **Am.** person appointed to take the place of another if necessary; substitute. [< L, < *alternus* every second < *alter* other] —**al′ter·nate·ly,** *adv.* —**al′ter·nate·ness,** *n.*

alternating current, electric current that reverses its direction at regular intervals.

al·ter·na·tion (ôl′tər·nā′shən; al′-), *n.* act of alternating; occurring by turns.

al·ter·na·tive (ôl·tér′nə·tiv; al-), *adj.* **1.** giving or requiring a choice between only two things: *alternative results of two different actions.* **2.** (less strictly) giving a choice from among more than two things: *several alternative suggestions.* —*n.* **1.** choice between two things: *he had the alternative of going home or staying all night.* **2.** (less strictly) choice from among more than two things. **3.** one of the things to be chosen: *we have no alternative but to leave.* —**al·ter′na·tive·ly,** *adv.* —**al·ter′na·tive·ness,** *n.* —**Syn.** *n.* 1, 2. choice, selection. ➤ Alternative comes from the Latin *alternus,* "every second," i.e., "the second of two"; some formal writers, in deference to the word's origin, confine its meaning to "one of two possibilities," but it is commonly used to mean one of several possibilities.

al·ter·na·tor (ôl′tər·nā′tər; al′-), *n.* dynamo or generator for producing an alternating electric current.

al·the·a, al·thae·a (al·thē′ə), *n.* rose of Sharon, a shrub like the mallow. [< L < Gk. *althaia* wild mallow,? < *althainein* heal]

alt·horn (alt′hôrn′), *n.* a brass musical instrument similar to the French horn. Also, **alto horn.**

al·though, al·tho (ôl·thō′), *conj.* though. [ME *al thogh* even though] —**Syn.** despite, albeit. ➤ Altho is appropriate in familiar writing, but should not be used in formal writing.

al·tim·e·ter (al·tim′ə·tər; al′tə·mē′tər), *n.* any instrument for measuring altitudes, as a quadrant, sextant, or device for aircraft navigation (an aneroid barometer, radar, etc.).

al·ti·tude (al′tə·tüd; -tūd), *n.* **1.** the vertical height above sea level, the earth's surface, or some other reference plane. **2.** elevation or high place: *mountain altitude.* **3.** height. **4.** high position, power, etc. **5.** the vertical distance from the base of a geometrical figure to its highest point. **6.** the angular distance of a star, etc., above the horizon. [< L, < *altus* high]

al·to (al′tō), *n., pl.* **-tos,** *adj. Music.* —*n.* **1. a.** the lowest female voice; contralto. **b.** the highest male voice. **2.** singer with such a voice. **3.** an alto part. **4.** instrument playing such a part. —*adj.* of, sung by, or composed for an alto. [< Ital. < L *altus* high]

al·to·geth·er (ôl′tə·geth′ər), *adv.* **1.** wholly; entirely: *altogether wicked.* **2.** on the whole: *altogether, I'm sorry it happened.* **3.** all included: *altogether there were 14 books.* —*n.* a whole; general effect. [ME *altogeder*] —**Syn.** *adv.* 1. completely. ➤ **all together** as distinguished from altogether is used as an adjective phrase meaning "everyone in a group": *they went out all together.*

alto horn, althorn.

al·tru·ism (al′trü·iz·əm), *n.* unselfish devotion to the interests and welfare of others, esp. as a principle of action. [< F *altruisme* < Ital. *altrui* of or for others < L *alter* other] —**al′tru·ist,** *n.*

al·tru·is·tic (al′trü·is′tik), *adj.* having regard for the well-being and best interests of others; unselfish. —**al′tru·is′ti·cal·ly,** *adv.*

al·um (al′əm), *n.* **1.** an astringent crystalline substance, KAl(SO₄)₂·12H₂O, a double sulfate of aluminum and potassium, used in dyeing, medicine, etc. **2.** *Chem.* one of a class of double sulfates analogous to the potassium alum. **3.** aluminum sulfate, Al₂(SO₄)₃·18H₂O. [< OF < L *alumen*]

a·lu·mi·na (ə·lü′mə·nə), *n. Chem.* aluminum oxide, Al₂O₃, occurring in clay. [< NL < L *alumen* alum]

a·lu·mi·nous (ə·lü′mə·nəs), *adj.* **1.** of or containing alum. **2.** of or containing aluminum.

a·lu·mi·num (ə·lü′mə·nəm), *esp. Brit.* **al·u·min·ium** (al′yə·min′yəm), *n.* a silver-white, very light, ductile metal that resists tarnish and is used for making utensils, instruments, etc. It is a metallic element that occurs in nature only in combination. [< ALUMINA]

a·lum·na (ə·lum′nə), *n., pl.* **-nae** (-nē). *Am.* a woman graduate or former student of a school, college, or university. Cf. alumnus.

a·lum·nus (ə·lum′nəs), *n., pl.* **-ni** (-nī). *Am.* **1.** graduate or former student of a school, college, or university. **2.** *Colloq.* a former member, as of a baseball team. [< L, foster child, < *alere* nourish]

al·ve·o·lar (al·vē′ə·lər), *adj. Anat., Zool.* **a.** of or pertaining to a socket, as of a tooth. **b.** of or pertaining to the air cells of the lungs. **2.** *Phonet.* formed by touching the tip of the tongue to or bringing it near the alveoli. English *t* and *d* are alveolar sounds.

al·ve·o·late (al·vē′ə·lit; -lāt), *adj.* deeply pitted. —al·ve′o·la′tion, *n.*

al·ve·o·li (al·vē′ə·lī), *n.pl.* **1.** *Phonet.* ridge behind and above the upper front teeth. **2.** pl. of alveolus.

al·ve·o·lus (al·vē′ə·ləs), *n., pl.* **-li** (-lī). *Anat., Zool.* **1.** a little cell or cavity, as the air cells of the lungs, etc. **2.** socket of a tooth. [< L, dim. of *alveus* cavity]

al·way (ôl′wā), *adv. Archaic.* always.

al·ways (ôl′wiz; -wāz), *adv.* **1.** all the time; continually: *mother is always cheerful.* **2.** every time; at all times: *he always comes home on Saturday.* [all + way] —**Syn.** 1. forever, unceasingly, perpetually.

a·lys·sum (ə·lis′əm), *n.* **1.** a plant of the mustard family, having small white or yellow flowers. **2.** sweet alyssum. [< NL < Gk. *alysson,* name of a plant thought to cure rabies]

am (am; *unstressed* əm), *v.* the first person singular, present indicative of be. [OE *eom*]

Am, *Chem.* americium.

AM, A.M., amplitude modulation.

Am., **1.** America; American. **2.** Americanism.

A.M., Master of Arts. Also, **M.A.**

a.m., A.M., 1. before noon. **2.** time from midnight to noon. [for L *ante meridiem*] ➤ A.m. and p.m. are usually written in small letters except in headlines and tables. In consecutive writing they are used only with figures for specific hours: *from 2 to 4 a.m.*

A.M.A., A.M.A., AMA, American Medical Association.

a·mah (ä′mə; am′ə), *n.* in India, etc., a nurse.

a·main (ə·mān′), *adv.* **1.** at full speed. **2.** with full force; violently. **3.** in haste.

a·mal·gam (ə·mal′gəm), *n.* **1.** an alloy of mercury with some other metal or metals, used for filling teeth, silvering mirrors, etc. **2.** mixture; blend. [< Med.L, apparently < L < Gk. *malagma* emollient < *malassein* soften]

a·mal·gam·ate (ə·mal′gə·māt), *v.,* **-at·ed, -at·ing. 1.** unite together; combine. **2.** alloy (one or more metals) with mercury. —a·mal′gam·a·ble (ə·mal′gəm·ə·bəl), *adj.* —a·mal′gam·a′tive, *adj.* —a·mal′gam·a′tor, *n.*

a·mal·gam·a·tion (ə·mal′gə·mā′shən), *n.* mixture; combination; blend; union.

a·man·u·en·sis (ə·man′yü·en′sis), *n., pl.* **-ses** (-sēz). person who writes what another says, or copies what another has written. [< L, < (*servus*) *a manu* secretary]

am·a·ranth (am′ə·ranth), *n.* **1.** *Poetic.* an imaginary flower that never fades. **2.** any of a large genus of plants, esp. some with colorful flowers. [< L < Gk. *amarantos* everlasting < *a-* not + *marainein* wither; infl. by Gk. *anthos* flower]

am·a·ran·thine (am′ə·ran′thin; -thīn), *adj.* **1.** of the amaranth. **2.** never-fading; undying. **3.** purplish-red.

Am·a·ril·lo (am′ə·ril′ō), *n.* city in NW Texas.

am·a·ryl·lis (am′ə·ril′is), *n.* a bulbous plant related to the lily, with large red, white, or purple flowers. See picture on next page. [< L < Gk., typical name of a country girl]

a·mass (ə·mas′), *v.* **1.** collect or accumulate

for oneself: *amass a fortune.* 2. collect into a mass or heap. [< OF, < a– to + *masse* MASS] —a·mass′a·ble, *adj.* —a·mass′er, *n.* —a·mass′ment, *n.*

am·a·teur (am′ə·chûr; –chər; –tyûr; am′ə·tér′), *n.* 1. person who does something for pleasure, not for money or as a profession. 2. person who does something rather poorly. 3. athlete who is not a professional. —*adj.* 1. of amateurs; made or done by amateurs. 2. being an amateur: *amateur pianist.* [< F < L *amator* < *amare* love] —am′a·teur′ish, —am′a·teur′ish·ly, *adv.* —am′a·teur′ish·ness, *n.* —am′a·teur·ship′, *n.*

Amaryllis
(2 to 4 ft. high)

am·a·teur·ism (am′ə·chûr·iz′əm; –chər–; –tyûr–; am′ə·tér′iz·əm), *n.* 1. amateurish way of doing things. 2. position of an amateur.

am·a·to·ry (am′ə·tô′ri; –tō′–), *adj.* of love; causing love; having to do with making love or with lovers. [< L *amatorius* < *amare* love]

a·maze (ə·māz′), *v.*, **a·mazed, a·maz·ing,** *n.* —*v.* 1. surprise greatly; strike with sudden wonder. 2. *Obs.* stun; bewilder. —*n.* *Poetic.* amazement. [OE *āmasian*] —Syn. *v.* 1. astonish, astound.

a·mazed (ə·māzd′), *adj.* greatly surprised. —a·maz·ed·ly (ə·māz′id·li), *adv.* —a·maz′ed·ness, *n.*

a·maze·ment (ə·māz′mənt), *n.* great surprise; sudden wonder; astonishment.

a·maz·ing (ə·māz′ing), *adj.* very surprising; wonderful; astonishing. —*adv.* *Am., Colloq.* wonderfully. —a·maz′ing·ly, *adv.*

Am·a·zon (am′ə·zon; –zən), *n.* 1. the largest river in the world, flowing from the Andes Mountains in NW South America across Brazil to the Atlantic. 2. *Gk. Legend.* one of a race of women warriors living near the Black Sea. 3. amazon, a warlike or masculine woman. —Am·a·zo·ni·an (am′ə·zō′ni·ən), *adj.*

am·bas·sa·dor (am·bas′ə·dər; –dôr), *n.* 1. the highest representative sent by one government or ruler to another who speaks and acts in behalf of his government. 2. official messenger with a special errand. Also, embassador. [< F < Ital. *ambasciatore*] —am·bas·sa·do·ri·al (am·bas′ə·dô′ri·əl; –dō′–), *adj.* —am·bas′sa·dor·ship′, *n.*

am·bas·sa·dress (am·bas′ə·dris), *n.* 1. a woman ambassador. 2. wife of an ambassador.

am·ber (am′bər), *n.* 1. a hard, translucent, yellow or yellowish-brown fossil resin of pine trees, used for jewelry, etc. 2. color of amber. —*adj.* 1. made of amber. 2. yellow; yellowish-brown. [< OF < Ar. ′*anbar* ambergris]

am·ber·gris (am′bər·grēs; –gris), *n.* a waxy intestinal concretion of the sperm whale, used esp. as a fixative in perfumes. [< F *ambre gris* gray amber]

ambi–, *prefix.* around; round about; on both sides, as in *ambidexterity.* [< L; also (before vowels) amb–; (before p) am–]

am·bi·dex·ter·i·ty (am′bə·deks·ter′ə·ti), *n.* 1. ability to use both hands equally well. 2. unusual skillfulness. 3. deceitfulness.

am·bi·dex·trous (am′bə·dek′strəs), *adj.* 1. able to use both hands equally well. 2. very skillful. 3. deceitful; double-dealing. [< LL < L *ambi–* both + *dexter* right] —am′bi·dex′trous·ly, *adv.* —am′bi·dex′trous·ness, *n.*

am·bi·ent (am′bi·ənt), *adj.* surrounding. [< L *ambiens* < *ambi–* around + *ire* go]

am·bi·gu·i·ty (am′bə·gū′ə·ti), *n., pl.* –ties. 1. possibility of two or more meanings. 2. an ambiguous word or expression.

am·big·u·ous (am·big′yū·əs), *adj.* 1. having more than one possible meaning. 2. of uncertain meaning or nature. 3. obscure. [< L *ambiguus* < *ambi–* in two ways + *agere* drive] —am·big′u·ous·ly, *adv.* —am·big′u·ous·ness, *n.* —Syn. 1. equivocal. 2. puzzling. 3. vague.

am·bi·tion (am·bish′ən), *n.* 1. strong desire for fame or honor; seeking after a high position or great power. 2. thing strongly desired or sought after. [< L *ambitio* a canvassing for votes < *ambi–* around + *ire* go] —am·bi′tion·less, *adj.* —Syn. 1. aspiration, longing.

am·bi·tious (am·bish′əs), *adj.* 1. having or guided by ambition. 2. arising from or showing ambition. 3. strongly desirous; eager (of): *ambitious of power.* 4. showy; pretentious. —am·bi′tious·ly, *adv.* —am·bi′tious·ness, *n.*

am·biv·a·lence (am·biv′ə·ləns), *n.* coexistence of contrary tendencies or feelings, as in the mind. —am·biv′a·lent, *adj.*

am·ble (am′bəl), *n., v.,* –bled, –bling. —*n.* 1. gait of a horse in which both legs on one side are moved at the same time. 2. easy, slow pace in walking. —*v.* 1. walk at a slow, easy pace. 2. (of a horse) move at an amble. [< OF < L *ambulare* walk] —am′bler, *n.* —am′bling·ly, *adv.*

am·bro·sia (am·brō′zhə), *n.* 1. *Class. Myth.* food of the ancient Greek and Roman gods. 2. something especially pleasing to taste or smell. [< L < Gk., < a– not + *brotos* mortal] —am·bro′sial, am·bro′sian, *adj.* —am·bro′sial·ly, *adv.*

am·bu·lance (am′byə·ləns), *n.* a vehicle, boat, or airplane equipped to carry sick or wounded persons. [< F, < (*hôpital*) *ambulant* walking (hospital)]

am·bu·lant (am′byə·lənt), *adj.* walking.

am·bu·late (am′byə·lāt), *v.,* –lat·ed, –lat·ing. walk; move about. —am′bu·la′tion, *n.*

am·bu·la·to·ry (am′byə·lə·tô′ri; –tō′–), *adj., n., pl.* –ries. —*adj.* 1. of or fitted for walking. 2. moving from place to place. 3. *Med.* able to walk. 4. not permanent; changeable. —*n.* covered place for walking; cloister.

am·bus·cade (am′bəs·kād′), *n., v.,* –cad·ed, –cad·ing. ambush. [< F < Ital. *imboscata* < *imboscare* AMBUSH] —am′bus·cad′er, *n. Am.*

am·bush (am′bûsh), *n.* 1. soldiers or other enemies hidden to make a surprise attack. 2. place where they are hidden. 3. act or condition of lying in wait. —*v.* 1. attack from an ambush. 2. wait in hiding to make a surprise attack. 3. put (soldiers or other persons) in hiding for a surprise attack. [< OF *embusche,* ult. < *en–* in + *busche* bush] —am′bush·er, *n.* —am′bush-like′, *adj.* —am′bush·ment, *n.*

a·me·ba (ə·mē′bə), *n., pl.* –bas, –bae (–bē). amoeba. —a·me′ba-like′, *adj.* —a·me′ban, *adj.*

a·me·bic (ə·mē′bik), *adj.* amoebic.

a·me·boid (ə·mē′boid), *adj.* amoeboid.

a·meer (ə·mir′), *n.* amir.

a·me·lio·ra·ble (ə·mēl′yə·rə·bəl; ə·mēl′li·ə–), *adj.* that can be improved.

a·me·lio·rate (ə·mēl′yə·rāt; ə·mēl′li·ə–), *v.,* –rat·ed, –rat·ing. make or become better; improve: *new housing ameliorated living conditions in the slums.* [< F *améliorer,* ult. < LL, < L *melior* better] —a·mel′io·ra′tion, *n.* —a·mel′io·ra′tive, *adj.* —a·mel′io·ra′tor, *n.*

a·men (ā′men′; ä′men′), *interj.* 1. be it so; said after a prayer or wish and used as an expression of assent. 2. *Colloq.* an expression of approval. —*n.* the word amen. [< L < Gk. < Heb., truth, certainty < *āman* strengthen]

a·me·na·ble (ə·mē′nə·bəl; ə·men′ə–), *adj.* 1. open to suggestion or advice: *amenable to persuasion.* 2. accountable; answerable: *amenable to the law.* [< AF, < a– to + *mener* lead < L *minare* drive] —a·me′na·bil′i·ty, a·me′na·ble·ness, *n.* —a·me′na·bly, *adv.*

amen corner, *Am.* 1. a place in a church where formerly the deacons sat who led the responsive amens during the service. 2. *Colloq.* any rallying place.

a·mend (ə·mend′), *v.* 1. change the form of (a law, bill, or motion, etc.) by addition, omission, etc. 2. change for the better; improve: *amend one's conduct.* 3. free from faults; correct: *amend the spelling of a word.* 4. to become better, as by reform or by regaining health. [< OF < L, < *ex–* out of + *mendum* fault] —a·mend′a·ble, *adj.* —a·mend′er, *n.*

a·mend·ment (ə·mend′mənt), *n.* 1. change

age, câre, fär; ēqual, tèrm; īce; ōpen, ôrder; pùt, rüle, ūse; tḥ, then; ə=a in about.

made in a law, bill, motion, etc. **2.** change for the better; improvement. **3.** change made to remove an error; correction. **4.** *Am.* article added to the Constitution of the United States.

a·mends (ə·mendz′), *n.pl.* (*sometimes sing. in use*) compensation for a loss or injury.

a·men·i·ty (ə·men′ə·ti; ə·mē′nə-), *n., pl.* -**ties.** **1.** amenities, pleasing manners or courteous acts that lead to agreeable social relations. **2.** pleasant feature. **3.** pleasantness; agreeableness. [< L, < *amoenus* pleasant]

am·ent (am′ənt; ā′mənt), *n. Bot.* a long, slender spike covered with rows of bracts having flowers of one sex and no petals; catkin. [< L *amentum* thong]

Amer., America; American.

a·merce (ə·mèrs′), *v.,* a·merced, a·merc·ing. **1.** punish by an arbitrary or discretionary fine. **2.** punish by any penalty. [< AF, < *a merci* at the mercy (of)] —a·merce′a·ble, *adj.* —a·merce′ment, *n.* —a·merc′er, *n.*

A·mer·i·ca (ə·mer′ə·kə), *n.* **1.** *Am.* the United States of America. **2.** North America. **3.** North America and South America; the Western Hemisphere. **4.** South America.

A·mer·i·can (ə·mer′ə·kən), *adj.* **1.** *Am.* of, having to do with, or in the United States: *an American citizen.* **2.** of or in the Western Hemisphere: *the Amazon and other American rivers.* **3.** *Am., Biol.* native only to the United States: *American eagle, American aloe.* —*n.* **1.** *Am.* citizen of the United States, or of the earlier British colonies, not belonging to one of the aboriginal races. **2.** native or inhabitant of the Western Hemisphere. **3.** *Am.* American language.

A·mer·i·ca·na (ə·mer′ə·kä′nə; -kan′ə; -kā′-nə), *n.pl.* collection of objects or documents about America, esp. its history.

A·mer·i·can·ism (ə·mer′ə·kən·iz′əm), *n. Am.* **1.** devotion or loyalty to the United States, its customs, traditions, etc. **2.** a word, phrase, or idiom originating in the United States, as *almighty dollar, amen corner.* **3.** custom or trait peculiar to the United States. **4.** thing considered typically American.

A·mer·i·can·ize (ə·mer′ə·kən·īz), *v.,* -ized, -iz·ing. *Am.* make or become American in habits, customs, or character. —A·mer′i·can·i·za′tion, A·mer′i·can·iz′ing, *n. Am.* —A·mer′i·can·ized, *adj. Am.*

American English, the form of English spoken and written in the United States.

American plan, *Am.* system used in hotels where one price covers room, board, and service (distinguished from *European plan*).

American Revolution, 1. war fought by the American colonies from 1775 to 1783 to gain their independence from England. **2.** series of protests and acts of the American colonists from 1763 to 1783 against England's attempts to increase her power over them.

a·mer·i·ci·um (am′ər·ish′i·əm), *n. Chem.* an artificial, radioactive metallic element, Am.

Am·er·ind (am′ər·ind), *n. Am.* the American Indian. —Am′er·in′di·an, *adj., n. Am.*

am·e·thyst (am′ə·thist), *n.* **1.** a purple or violet variety of quartz, used as a precious stone. **2.** violet-colored corundum, used for jewelry. [< OF < L < Gk. *amethystos* < a- not + *methy* wine; thought to prevent intoxication] —am′e·thyst·like′, *adj.*

a·mi·a·ble (ā′mi·ə·bəl), *adj.* good-natured and friendly; pleasant and agreeable: *an amiable disposition.* [< OF < LL *amicabilis* < L *amicus* friend. Doublet of AMICABLE.] —a′mi·a·bil′i·ty, a′mi·a·ble·ness, *n.* —a′mi·a·bly, *adv.*

am·i·ca·ble (am′ə·kə·bəl), *adj.* peaceable; friendly. [< LL *amicabilis* < L *amicus* friend. Doublet of AMIABLE.] —am′i·ca·bil′i·ty, am′i·ca·ble·ness, *n.* —am′i·ca·bly, *adv.*

am·ice (am′is), *n.* an oblong piece of linen covering the shoulders, worn by priests at Mass. [< OF < L *amictus* cloak]

a·mi·cus cu·ri·ae (ə·mī′kəs kyûr′i·ē; ə·mē′-kəs kyûr′i·ī), *Law.* person with no interest in a case who is called in to advise the judge. [< NL, friend of the court]

a·mid (ə·mid′), **a·midst** (ə·midst′), *prep.* in the midst or middle of; among.

am·ide (am′īd; -id), **am·id** (-id), *n. Chem.* a compound produced by replacing one or more of the hydrogen atoms of ammonia by univalent acid radicals. —a·mid·ic (ə·mid′ik), *adj.*

a·mid·ships (ə·mid′ships), **a·mid·ship** (-ship), *adv.* in or toward the middle of a ship; halfway between the bow and stern.

Am·i·ens (am′i·ənz; *Fr.* ä·myaɴ′), *n.* city in N France, on the Somme River.

a·mi·go (ə·mē′gō), *n. Am., S.W.* a friend. [< Sp. < L *amicus*]

a·mine (ə·mēn′; am′in), **am·in** (am′in), *n. Chem.* a compound produced by replacing one or more of the hydrogen atoms of ammonia by univalent hydrocarbon radicals.

a·mi·no acids (ə·mē′nō; am′ə·nō), *Chem.* complex organic compounds of nitrogen that combine in various ways to form proteins.

a·mir (ə·mir′), *n.* in Mohammedan countries, a commander, ruler, or prince. Also, ameer. [< Ar., commander. Cf. ADMIRAL.]

Am·ish (am′ish; ä′mish), *n., pl.* Am·ish, *adj. Am.* —*n.* member of a strict Mennonite sect, founded in the 17th century. —*adj.* of this sect or its members. —Am′ish·man′, *n. Am.*

a·miss (ə·mis′), *adv.* **1.** in a faulty manner; wrongly. **2.** take amiss, be offended at. —*adj.* improper; wrong: *it is not amiss to ask advice.* [ME *a mis* by (way of) fault. See MISS[1].]

am·i·to·sis (am′ə·tō′sis), *n. Biol.* simple or direct method of cell division. —am′i·tot′ic (am′ə·tot′ik), *adj.* —am′i·tot′i·cal·ly, *adv.*

am·i·ty (am′ə·ti), *n., pl.* -**ties.** peace and friendship; friendly relations: *treaty of amity.* [< MF *amitié,* ult. < L *amicus* friend]

'Am·man (a·man′), *n.* capital of Jordan, in the N part.

am·me·ter (am′mē′tər; am′ē′tər), *n. Elect.* instrument for measuring in amperes the strength of an electric current. [< *am*(pere) + –METER]

am·mo·nia (ə·mō′nyə; ə·mō′ni·ə), *n.* **1.** a colorless, pungent gas, NH_3, consisting of nitrogen and hydrogen. **2.** this gas dissolved in water, NH_4OH. [< NL; so named because obtained from sal *ammoniac*]

am·mo·ni·ac (ə·mō′ni·ak), *adj.* Also, am·mo·ni·a·cal (am′ə·nī′ə·kəl). of or like ammonia. —*n.* gum ammoniac. [< L < Gk. *ammoniakon;* applied to a salt obtained near the shrine of Ammon in Libya]

am·mo·nite (am′ə·nīt), *n.* one of the spiraled fossil shells of an extinct mollusk. [< NL *ammonites* < Med.L *cornu Ammonis* horn of Ammon (Egyptian god)]

am·mo·ni·um (ə·mō′ni·əm), *n. Chem.* the radical NH_4, which never appears in a free state by itself, but acts as a unit in chemical reactions.

Ammonite

ammonium chloride, NH_4Cl, colorless crystals or white powder used in medicine, in printing cloth, etc.; sal ammoniac.

ammonium hydroxide, alkali formed when ammonia gas dissolves in water, NH_4OH.

am·mu·ni·tion (am′yə·nish′ən), *n.* **1.** bullets, shells, gunpowder, etc., for guns or other weapons. **2.** thing or things that can be shot or thrown. **3.** means of attack or defense. [< obs. F *amunition,* used for *munition*]

am·ne·sia (am·nē′zhə), *n.* loss of memory caused by injury to the brain, by disease, or by shock. [< NL < Gk., < a- not + *mnasthai* remember] —am·ne·sic (am·nē′sik; -zik), am·nes·tic (am·nes′tik), *adj.*

am·nes·ty (am′nes·ti), *n., pl.* -**ties,** *v.,* -**tied,** -**ty·ing.** —*n.* a general pardon for past offenses against a government. —*v.* give amnesty to; pardon. [< L < Gk. *amnestia* < a- not + *mnasthai* remember]

am·ni·on (am′ni·ən), *n., pl.* -**ni·ons,** -**ni·a** (-ni·ə) *Zool.* a membrane lining the sac which encloses a fetus. [< Gk., dim. of *amnos* lamb] —am·ni·ot·ic (am′ni·ot′ik), *adj.*

a·moe·ba (ə·mē′bə), *n.*, *pl.* **-bas, -bae** (-bē). *Zool.* microscopic one-celled animal that moves by forming temporary projections that are constantly changing. Also, **ameba.** [< Gk. *amoibe* change] —**a·moe′ba·like′**, *adj.* —**a·moe′ban**, *adj.*

a·moe·bic (ə·mē′bik), *adj.* **1.** of or like an amoeba or amoebas. **2.** caused by amoebas. Also, **amebic.**

a·moe·boid (ə·mē′boid), *adj.* of or like an amoeba. Also, **ameboid.**

a·mok (ə·muk′; ə·mok′), *n.* a mental disturbance of the Malays, characterized by a period of depression followed by a murderous frenzy. —*adv.* amuck.

a·mong (ə·mung′), *prep.* **1.** in the number or class of: *that book is the best among modern novels.* **2.** by, with, or through the whole of: *political unrest among the people.* **3.** in contact or association with: *he fell among thieves.* **4.** surrounded by: *a house among the trees.* **5.** in comparison with: *one among many.* **6.** by or for distribution to; to each of: *divide the money among them.* **7.** by the mutual or reciprocal action of: *they fought among themselves.* **8.** by the combined action of: *settle it among yourselves.* [OE *amang* < *on* (ge)*mang* in a crowd] ➤ See between for usage note.

a·mongst (ə·mungst′), *prep.* among.

a·mor·al (ā·môr′əl; ā·mor′-; a-), *adj.* not involving any question of morality; nonmoral. [< *a-* not + *moral*] —**a·mo·ral·i·ty** (ā′mə·ral′-ə·ti; am′ə-), *n.* —**a·mor′al·ly**, *adv.*

am·o·rous (am′ə·rəs), *adj.* **1.** inclined to love: *an amorous disposition.* **2.** in love. **3.** showing love; loving. **4.** having to do with love or courtship: *amorous poems.* [< OF, < *amour* love < L *amor*] —**am′o·rous·ly**, *adv.* —**am′o·rous·ness**, *n.* —**Syn. 2.** enamored. **3.** fond, devoted.

a·mor·phism (ə·môr′fiz·əm), *n.* amorphous condition.

a·mor·phous (ə·môr′fəs), *adj.* **1.** *Chem.* not crystallized. Glass is amorphous; sugar is crystalline. **2.** of no particular kind or type. **3.** having no definite form; shapeless. [< Gk., < *a-* without + *morphe* shape] —**a·mor′phous·ly**, *adv.* —**a·mor′phous·ness**, *n.*

am·or·tize, *esp. Brit.* **am·or·tise** (am′ər-tīz; ə·môr′tīz), *v.*, **-tized, -tiz·ing;** *esp. Brit.* **-tised, -tis·ing.** set aside money regularly for future payment of (a debt, etc.). [< OF *amortir* deaden < *a-* to + *mort* death < L *mors*] —**am′or·tiz′a·ble,** *esp. Brit.* **am′or·tis′a·ble,** *adj.* —**am·or·ti·za·tion,** *esp. Brit.* **am·or·ti·sa·tion** (am′ər-tə·zā′shən; ə·môr′-), **a·mor·tize·ment,** *esp. Brit.* **a·mor·tise·ment** (ə·môr′tiz·mənt), *n.*

A·mos (ā′məs), *n.* **1.** a Hebrew prophet who lived about 760 B.C. **2.** book of the Old Testament.

a·mount (ə·mount′), *n.* **1.** sum; total: *amount of the day's sales.* **2.** the full effect, value, or extent: *the amount of evidence against him is this.* **3.** quantity viewed as a whole: *a great amount of intelligence.* **4.** principal plus interest. —*v.* **1.** be equal; reach (*to*): *the debt amounted to $50.* **2.** be equivalent in quantity, value, force, effect, etc. (*to*): *his answer amounted to a threat.* [< OF, < *a mont* up; lit. to the mountain. See MOUNT.] ➤ **amount, number.** *Amount* is used of things viewed in the bulk, weight, or sums; *number* is used of things that can be counted: *an amount of milk* (but *a number of cans of milk*).

a·mour (ə·mur′), *n.* **1.** a love affair. **2.** an illicit love affair. [< OF, prob. < Pr. < L *amor* love]

A·moy (ä·moi′; ə-), *n.* **1.** seaport on an island near the SE coast of China. **2.** the island.

amp., *Elect.* **1.** amperage. **2.** ampere.

am·per·age (am′pər·ij; am·pir′-), *n. Elect.* strength of a current measured in amperes.

am·pere (am′pir; am·pir′), *n. Elect.* unit for measuring the strength of an electric current. It is the current one volt can send through a resistance of one ohm. [for A. M. *Ampère*, French physicist]

am·per·sand (am′pər·sand), *n.* the character &, meaning "and." [alter. of *and per se = and*, & by itself = and] ➤ Used chiefly in business

correspondence and reference works. In addressing firms, use the form they habitually use (. . . *and Company* or . . . *& Company*), and in quoting, follow your original carefully.

amphi-, *word element.* **1.** around; on both sides, as in *amphitheater.* **2.** in two ways; of two kinds, as in *amphibious.* [< Gk.]

Am·phib·i·a (am·fib′i·ə), *n.pl. Zool.* class of cold-blooded vertebrates with moist, scaleless skin, including frogs, toads, newts, salamanders, etc. Their young usually develop as tadpoles that have gills and live in water.

am·phib·i·an (am·fib′i·ən), *n.* **1.** animal that lives on land and in water. **2.** one of the Amphibia. **3.** plant that grows on land or in water. **4.** aircraft that can take off from and alight on land or water. **5.** *Mil.* tank for use both on land and in water. —*adj.* **1.** able to live both on land and in water. **2.** able to take off and alight on either land or water.

am·phib·i·ous (am·fib′i·əs), *adj.* **1.** able to live both on land and in water. **2.** suited for use on land or water: *an amphibious tank.* **3.** having two qualities, kinds, natures, or parts. **4.** by the combined action of land, water, and air forces: *amphibious attack.* [< L < Gk., < *amphi-* both + *bios* life] —**am·phib′i·ous·ly**, *adv.* —**am·phib′i·ous·ness**, *n.*

am·phi·the·a·ter, *esp. Brit.* **am·phi·the·a·tre** (am′fə·thē′ə·tər), *n.* **1.** a circular or oval building with rows of seats rising around a central open space. **2.** something resembling an amphitheater in shape. [< L < Gk., < *amphi-* on all sides + *theatron* theater] —**am·phi·the·at·ric** (am′fə·thi·at′rik), **am′phi·the·at′ri·cal,** *adj.* —**am′phi·the·at′ri·cal·ly**, *adv.*

am·pho·ra (am′fə·rə), *n., pl.* **-rae** (-rē). tall two-handled jar, used by the ancient Greeks and Romans. [< L < Gk., < *amphi-* on both sides + *phoreus* bearer; with ref. to handles]

am·ple (am′pəl), *adj.*, **-pler, -plest. 1.** fully sufficient for any purpose: *ample food for the table.* **2.** large in extent or degree: *give ample praise.* **3.** large; big; roomy: *an ample room.* **4.** more than enough. [< F < L *amplus*] —**am′ple·ness**, *n.* —**Syn. 1.** abundant, plentiful, copious, liberal. —**Ant. 1.** insufficient.

am·plex·i·caul (am·plek′sə·kôl), *adj.* clasping the stem, as some leaves do at their bases. [< NL, < L *amplexus* an embrace + *caulis* stem]

am·pli·fi·ca·tion (am′plə·fə·kā′shən), *n.* **1.** act of amplifying; expansion. **2.** detail, example, etc., that amplifies a statement, narrative, etc. **3.** an expanded statement, etc. —**am′pli·fi·ca′tive,** **am·plif·i·ca·to·ry** (am·plif′ə·kə·tô′ri; -tō′-), *adj.*

am·pli·fi·er (am′plə·fī′ər), *n.* **1.** person or thing that amplifies. **2.** *Elect.* device for strengthening electrical impulses, as a radio vacuum tube.

am·pli·fy (am′plə·fī), *v.*, **-fied, -fy·ing. 1.** make fuller and more extensive; expand; enlarge. **2.** expand by giving details, examples, comparisons, etc.; develop fully: *amplify a theory.* **3.** *Elect.* increase the strength of (a sound or an electrical impulse). [< F < L, < *amplus* ample + *facere* make]

am·pli·tude (am′plə·tüd; -tūd), *n.* **1.** width; breadth; size. **2.** abundance; fullness, as of intelligence, understanding, etc. **3.** *Physics.* one half the range of symmetric vibrations. **4.** *Elect.* the peak strength of an alternating current in a given cycle. [< L *amplitudo.* See AMPLE.]

amplitude modulation, *Electronics.* purposeful alteration of the amplitude of radio waves. Ordinary broadcasting uses amplitude modulation. Cf. **frequency modulation.**

am·ply (am′pli), *adv.* in an ample manner; to an ample degree; liberally; sufficiently.

am·poule (am′pül; -pül), **am·pule** (am′-pül), *n.* small glass tube or bulb filled with a drug and hermetically sealed. [< F < L *ampulla* jar, dim. of *amphora.* See AMPHORA.]

am·pu·tate (am′pyə·tāt), *v.*, **-tat·ed, -tat·ing.** cut off (contrasted with *excise*). [< L, < *ambi-* about + *putare* prune] —**am′pu·ta′tion**, *n.* —**am′pu·ta′tor**, *n.*

āge, câre, fär; ēqual, térm; īce; ōpen, ôrder; pùt, rüle, ūse; th, then; ə=a in about.

am·pu·tee (am'pyə·tē'), *n.* one who has undergone an amputation, as of an arm or leg.

Am·ster·dam (am'stər·dam), *n.* important seaport and capital of the Netherlands.

amt., amount.

a·muck (ə·muk'), *adv.* **1.** in a murderous frenzy. **2.** run amuck, run about in a murderous frenzy. Also, amok. [< Malay *amoq*]

am·u·let (am'yə·lit), *n.* some object worn as a magic charm against evil or harm. [< L *amuletum*]

A·mur (ä·múr'), *n.* river in NE Asia.

a·muse (ə·mūz'), *v.*, **a·mused, a·mus·ing. 1.** cause to laugh or smile: *amuse an audience.* **2.** keep pleasantly interested; entertain: *new toys amuse children.* [< OF *amuser* divert, < *a–* + *muser* stare] —**a·mus'a·ble,** *adj.* —**a·mus'er,** *n.*

a·mused (ə·mūzd'), *adj.* pleasantly entertained. —**a·mus·ed·ly** (ə·mūz'id·li), *adv.*

a·muse·ment (ə·mūz'mənt), *n.* **1.** condition of being amused. **2.** thing that amuses.

a·mus·ing (ə·mūz'ing), *adj.* **1.** entertaining. **2.** causing laughter, smiles, etc. —**a·mus'ing·ly,** *adv.* —**a·mus'ing·ness,** *n.*

Am·vets (am'vets'), *n. Am.* American Veterans of World War II, an organization founded in 1944.

am·yl (am'il), *n. Chem.* group of carbon and hydrogen atoms, $-C_5H_{11}$, that acts as a unit in forming compounds. [< L < Gk. *amylon* starch, orig., unground < *a–* not + *myle* mill] —**a·myl'ic** (ə·mil'ik), *adj.*

am·yl·ase (am'ə·lās), *n. Biochem.* enzyme in saliva, pancreatic juice, etc., or in parts of plants, that helps to change starch into sugar. [< *amyl*]

an¹ (an; *unstressed* ən), *adj. or indefinite article.* **1.** one; any: *an apple.* **2.** each; every: *twice an hour.* Cf. **a.** [OE (unstressed) *ān* (before vowels)] ➤ See a for usage note.

an², **an'** (an; *unstressed* ən), *conj.* **1.** *Dial. or Colloq.* and. **2.** *Archaic or Dial.* if. [var. of *and*]

an–, *prefix.* not; without, as in *anhydrous.* [var. of *a–¹* before vowels and *h*]

–an, *suffix.* **1.** of or having to do with, as in *republican.* **2.** native or inhabitant of, as in *American.* [< L *–ānus*]

An·a·bap·tist (an'ə·bap'tist), *n.* member of a Protestant sect opposing infant baptism and requiring adult baptism. —**An'a·bap'tism,** *n.*

a·nab·o·lism (ə·nab'ə·liz·əm), *n. Biol.* constructive metabolism in which matter is changed into the tissues of a living animal or plant (opposite of *catabolism*). [coined from *metabolism* by substitution of Gk. *ana–* up] —**an·a·bol·ic** (an'ə·bol'ik), *adj.*

a·nach·ro·nism (ə·nak'rə·niz·əm), *n.* **1.** act of putting a person, thing, or event in some time where it does not belong. It would be an anachronism to speak of Julius Caesar as telephoning. **2.** something placed or occurring out of its proper time. [< F < Gk., < *ana–* backwards + *chronos* time]

a·nach·ro·nis·tic (ə·nak'rə·nis'tik), *adj.* having or involving an anachronism.

a·nach·ro·nous (ə·nak'rə·nəs), *adj.* placed or occurring out of the proper time. —**a·nach'ro·nous·ly,** *adv.*

an·a·co·lu·thon (an'ə·kə·lü'thon), *n.*, *pl.* **–tha** (–thə). change from one grammatical construction to another within the same sentence for greater force. [< LL < Gk., < *an–* not + *akolouthos* following] —**an'a·co·lu'thic,** *adj.*

an·a·con·da (an'ə·kon'də), *n.* **1.** a very large tropical snake that crushes its prey in its coils; water boa. **2.** any large snake that crushes its prey in its folds, such as the python.

a·nad·ro·mous (ə·nad'rə·məs), *adj. Zool.* going up rivers from the sea to spawn. [< LGk., < *ana–* up + *dromos* a running]

a·nae·mi·a (ə·nē'mi·ə), *n.* anemia. —**a·nae'mic,** *adj.*

an·aer·obe (an·âr'ōb; an·ā'ər·ōb), *n.* **1.** organism that cannot live in the presence of free oxygen. **2.** organism that can live without free oxygen. —**an'aer·o'bic,** *adj.* —**an'aer·o'bi·cal·ly,** *adv.*

an·aes·the·sia (an'əs·thē'zhə), *n. Am.* anesthesia.

an·aes·thet·ic (an'əs·thet'ik), *adj., n. Am.* anesthetic.

an·aes·the·tist (ə·nes'thə·tist), *n.* anesthetist.

an·aes·the·tize (ə·nes'thə·tīz), *v.*, **–tized, –tiz·ing.** anesthetize. —**an·aes·the·ti·za·tion** (ə·nes'thə·tə·zā'shən; an'əs·thet'ə–), *n.*

an·a·gram (an'ə·gram), *n.* **1.** word or phrase formed from another by transposing the letters. *Example:* lived—devil. **2.** anagrams (*sing. in use*), game in which players make words by changing and adding letters. [< NL < Gk. *ana-grammatizein* transpose letters < *ana–* up or back + *gramma* letter]

a·nal (ā'nəl), *adj.* of or near the anus.

an·a·lects (an'ə·lekts), *n.pl.* literary extracts or fragments forming a collection. [< L < Gk. *analekta* < *ana–* up + *legein* pick]

an·al·ge·si·a (an'əl·jē'zi·ə; –si·ə; –zhə; –shə), *n.* insensibility to pain without losing consciousness. [< NL < Gk., < *an–* not + *algeein* feel pain]

an·al·ge·sic (an'əl·jē'zik; –sik), *adj.* of or causing analgesia. —*n.* medicine or other agent that causes analgesia.

an·a·log·i·cal (an'ə·loj'ə·kəl), **an·a·log·ic** (–loj'ik), *adj.* using analogy; having to do with analogy. —**an'a·log'i·cal·ly,** *adv.*

a·nal·o·gize (ə·nal'ə·jīz), *v.*, **–gized, –giz·ing. 1.** explain by analogy. **2.** use analogy. —**a·nal·o·gist** (ə·nal'ə·jist), *n.*

a·nal·o·gous (ə·nal'ə·gəs), *adj.* **1.** corresponding in some way; similar; comparable. **2.** *Biol.* corresponding in function, but not in structure and origin. —**a·nal'o·gous·ly,** *adv.* —**a·nal'o·gous·ness,** *n.*

an·a·logue, an·a·log (an'ə·lôg; –log), *n.* something analogous.

analogue computer, a calculating machine or automatic control which deals directly with physical quantities (weights, voltages, etc.) rather than a numerical code.

a·nal·o·gy (ə·nal'ə·ji), *n.*, *pl.* **–gies. 1.** likeness in some ways between things that are otherwise unlike; similarity. **2.** comparison of such things: *it is risky to argue by analogy.* **3.** *Biol.* correspondence in function but not in structure and origin. [< L < Gk. *analogia*] ➤ One says **analogy** *between* things, and that one thing has analogy *to* or *with* another. See also **metaphor.**

a·nal·y·sis (ə·nal'ə·sis), *n.*, *pl.* **–ses** (–sēz). **1.** separation of a thing into parts; examination of a thing's parts to find out their essential features: *analysis of a book.* **2.** *Chem.* **a.** intentional separation of a substance into its ingredients or elements to determine their amount and nature. **b.** the determination of the kind or amount of one or more of the constituents of a substance, whether actually obtained in separate form or not. **3.** statement of the results of an analysis. [< Med.L < Gk., a breaking up, < *ana–* up + *lyein* loose]

an·a·lyst (an'ə·list), *n.* **1.** one who analyzes. **2.** one who practices psychoanalysis.

an·a·lyt·ic (an'ə·lit'ik), **an·a·lyt·i·cal** (–ə·kəl), *adj.* of or using analysis. —**an'a·lyt'i·cal·ly,** *adv.*

an·a·lyt·ics (an'ə·lit'iks), *n.* mathematical or algebraic analysis.

an·a·lyze, *esp. Brit.* **an·a·lyse** (an'ə·līz), *v.*, **–lyzed, –lyz·ing;** *esp. Brit.* **–lysed, –lys·ing. 1.** separate into its parts. **2.** examine the parts or elements of critically; find out the essential features of: *analyze an argument.* **3.** examine carefully and in detail. **4.** *Chem.* subject to analysis. —**an'a·lyz'a·ble,** *esp. Brit.* **an'a·lys'a·ble,** *adj.* —**an'a·ly·za'tion,** *esp. Brit.* **an'a·ly·sa'tion,** *n.* —**an'a·lyz'er,** *esp. Brit.* **an'a·lys'er,** *n.*

An·a·ni·as (an'ə·nī'əs), *n.* **1.** *Bible.* liar who was struck dead for this fault. Acts 5:1–10. **2.** *Colloq.* any liar.

an·a·pest, an·a·paest (an'ə·pest), *n.* measure or foot in poetry consisting of two unaccented syllables followed by an accented syllable. [< L < Gk. *anapaistos* < *ana–* back + *paiein* strike] —**an'a·pes'tic, an'a·paes'tic,** *adj.*, *n.*

an·a·phor·ic pronoun (an′ə-fôr′ik; -for′-), *Gram.* word which refers to a previously mentioned word, phrase, etc. In "I couldn't get a large book, so I got two small ones," *ones* is an anaphoric pronoun.

an·ar·chism (an′ər-kiz·əm), *n.* 1. the political theory that all systems of government and law are harmful and prevent individuals from reaching their greatest development. 2. practice or support of this doctrine. 3. terrorism; lawlessness.

an·ar·chist (an′ər-kist), *n.* person who wants to overthrow established governments and have a world without rulers and laws. —**an′ar·chis′tic,** *adj.*

an·ar·chy (an′ər-ki), *n.* 1. absence of a system of government and law. 2. confusion; lawlessness. [< Gk., < *an-* without + *archos* ruler] —**an·ar·chic** (an·är′kik), **an·ar′chi·cal,** *adj.* —**an·ar′chi·cal·ly,** *adv.*

anat., 1. anatomical. 2. anatomy.

a·nath·e·ma (ə·nath′ə·mə), *n., pl.* -**mas.** 1. a solemn curse by church authorities excommunicating some person from the church. 2. denouncing and condemning some person or thing as evil; curse. 3. person or thing accursed. 4. thing that is detested and condemned. [< L < Gk., thing devoted, esp. to evil, < *ana-* up + *tithenai* set]

a·nath·e·ma·tize (ə·nath′ə·mə·tīz), *v.,* -**tized,** -**tiz·ing.** denounce; curse. —**a·nath′e·ma·ti·za′tion,** *n.* —**a·nath′e·ma·tiz′er,** *n.*

An·a·to·li·a (an′ə·tō′li·ə), *n.* Asia Minor. —**An′a·to′li·an,** *adj., n.*

an·a·tom·i·cal (an′ə·tom′ə·kəl), **an·a·tom·ic** (-tom′ik), *adj.* of or having to do with anatomy. —**an′a·tom′i·cal·ly,** *adv.*

a·nat·o·mist (ə·nat′ə·mist), *n.* 1. an expert in anatomy. 2. person who dissects or analyzes.

a·nat·o·mize (ə·nat′ə·mīz), *v.,* -**mized,** -**miz·ing.** 1. divide into parts to study the structure; dissect. 2. examine the parts of; analyze. —**a·nat′o·mi·za′tion,** *n.*

a·nat·o·my (ə·nat′ə·mi), *n., pl.* -**mies.** 1. structure of an animal or plant. 2. science of the structure of animals and plants. 3. dissecting of animals or plants to study their structure. 4. examination of the parts or elements of a thing; analysis. [< LL < Gk., < *ana-* up + *tomos* cutting]

anc., ancient.

-ance, *suffix.* 1. act or fact of ——ing, as in *avoidance.* 2. quality or state of being ——ed, as in *annoyance.* 3. quality or state of being ——ant, as in *importance.* 4. thing that ——s, as in *conveyance.* 5. what is ——ed, as in *contrivance.* [< F < L *-antia, -entia*]

an·ces·tor (an′ses·tər), *n.* 1. person from whom one is descended (opposite of *descendant*). 2. *Biol.* early form from which the species or group in question has descended. 3. the precursor of a later type. [< OF *ancestre* < L *antecessor* < *ante* before + *cedere* go] —**Syn.** 1. forefather.

an·ces·tral (an·ses′trəl), *adj.* 1. of or pertaining to ancestors: *the ancestral home of the Pilgrims was England.* 2. inherited from ancestors. —**an·ces′tral·ly,** *adv.*

an·ces·tress (an′ses·tris), *n.* a woman ancestor.

an·ces·try (an′ses·tri), *n., pl.* -**tries.** 1. line of descent from ancestors; lineage. 2. honorable descent. 3. parents, grandparents, and other ancestors.

an·chor (ang′kər), *n.* 1. shaped piece of iron attached to a chain or rope and used to hold a ship in place. 2. thing for holding something else in place. 3. something that makes a person feel safe and secure. 4. at anchor, held by an anchor. 5. cast anchor, drop the anchor. —*v.* 1. hold in place by an anchor: *anchor a ship.* 2. drop anchor; stop or stay in place by using an anchor. 3. hold in

Anchor

place; fix firmly. [< Gk. *ankyra*] —**an′chor·less,** *adj.* —**an′chor·like′,** *adj.*

an·chor·age (ang′kər·ij), *n.* 1. place to anchor. 2. money paid for the right to anchor. 3. an anchoring or being anchored. 4. something to hold on to or depend on.

an·cho·ress (ang′kə·ris), *n.* a woman anchorite.

an·cho·rite (ang′kə·rīt), **an·cho·ret** (ang′kə·rit; -ret), *n.* 1. person who lives alone in a solitary place for religious meditation. 2. hermit. [< Med.L < LL < Gk. *anachoretes,* < *ana-* back + *choreein* withdraw] —**an·cho·rit·ic** (ang′kə·rit′ik), **an·cho·ret·ic** (-ret′ik), *adj.*

an·cho·vy (an′chō·vi; -chə·vi; an·chō′vi), *n., pl.* -**vies.** a very small fish that looks somewhat like a herring. Anchovies are pickled or made into a paste. [< Sp. and Pg. *anchova* < VL *apiuva* < Gk. *aphye*]

an·cienne no·blesse (äN·syen′ nō·bles′), *French.* 1. the old nobility before the French Revolution. 2. the old nobility.

an·cien ré·gime (äN·syaN′ rā·zhēm′), *French.* 1. the social and political structure of France before the Revolution of 1789. 2. the old order of things.

an·cient (ān′shənt), *adj.* 1. pertaining to the period of history before the fall of the Western Roman Empire (476 A.D.). 2. existing or occurring in time long past: *ancient records.* 3. of great age; very old: *an ancient city.* 4. having to do with the ancients. 5. old-fashioned; antique. —*n.* 1. a very old person. 2. **the ancients,** a. people who lived long ago, such as the Greeks and Romans. b. the classical authors of ancient times. [< OF *ancien* < LL, < L *ante* before] —**an′cient·ness,** *n.*

an·cient·ly (ān′shənt·li), *adv.* in ancient times.

an·cil·lar·y (an′sə·ler′i), *adj.* 1. subordinate. 2. assisting. [< L, < *ancilla* handmaid]

an·con (ang′kon), *n., pl.* **an·co·nes** (ang·kō′nēz). 1. elbow. 2. projection like a bracket, used to support a cornice. [< L < Gk. *ankon* bend] —**an·co·nal** (ang′kə·nəl), **an·co·ne·al** (ang·kō′ni·əl), *adj.*

-ancy, *suffix.* variant of *-ance,* as in *infancy.*

and (and; *unstressed* ənd, ən), *conj.* 1. as well as: *nice and cold.* 2. added to; with: *ham and eggs.* 3. as a result: *the sun came out and the grass dried.* 4. *Colloq.* to: *try and come.* [OE] ➤ **And** is a coördinating conjunction, that is, it connects words, phrases, or clauses of equal grammatical value.

An·da·lu·sia (an′də·lü′zhə; -shə), *n.* region in S Spain. —**An′da·lu′sian,** *adj., n.*

an·dan·te (an·dan′tē; än·dän′tā), *Music.* —*adj.* moderately slow. —*adv.* in andante time. —*n.* piece in andante time. [< Ital., < *andare* walk]

An·der·sen (an′dər·sən), *n.* Hans Christian, 1805–1875, Danish writer of fairy tales.

An·des (an′dēz), *n.pl.* mountain system in W South America. —**An·de·an** (an·dē′ən; an′di-), *adj., n.*

and·i·ron (and′ī′ərn), *n.* one of a pair of metal supports for wood burned in a fireplace. [< OF *andier; -iron* by association with *iron*]

and/or, both or either. ➤ And/or is primarily a business and legal locution. It is useful when three alternatives exist (both circumstances mentioned or either one of the two).

An·dor·ra (an·dôr′ə; -dor′ə), *n.* 1. a small country between France and Spain. 2. its capital.

An·drew (an′drü), *n. Bible.* one of Jesus' apostles.

an·dro·gen (an′drə·jən), *n. Biochem.* any substance that induces or strengthens masculine characteristics, as a male sex hormone. [< Gk. *aner* (*andr-*) male + *-genes* gene, produced] —**an·dro·gen·ic** (an′drə·jen′ik), *adj.*

an·drog·y·nous (an·droj′ə·nəs), *adj.* 1. *Bot.* having male and female flowers in the same cluster. 2. hermaphroditic. [< L < Gk., < *aner* (*andr-*) man + *gyne* woman] —**an·drog′y·ny,** *n.*

An·drom·a·che (an·drom'ə·kē), *n.* Gk. Legend. the loyal wife of Hector.

an·ec·dot·age (an'ik·dōt'ij), *n.* **1.** anecdotes. **2.** talkative old age. [for def. 2, see DOTAGE]

an·ec·do·tal (an'ik·dō'təl; an'ik·dō'təl), *adj.* of anecdotes; containing anecdotes.

an·ec·dote (an'ik·dōt), *n.* short account of some interesting incident or event. [< Med.L < Gk. *anekdota* (things) unpublished < *an*– not + *ek*– out + *didonai* give] —**an·ec·dot·ic** (an'-ik·dot'ik), **an'ec·dot'i·cal**, *adj.*

a·ne·mi·a (ə·nē'mi·ə), *n.* deficiency of the blood; insufficiency of red corpuscles or hemoglobin in the blood. Also, **anaemia.** [< NL < Gk. *anaimia* lack of blood < *an*– not + *haima* blood] —**a·ne·mic** (ə·nē'mik), *adj.*

an·e·mom·e·ter (an'ə·mom'ə·tər), *n.* instrument for measuring the velocity or pressure of the wind. [< Gk. *anemos* wind + –METER] —**a·ne·mo·met·ric** (an'ə·mō·met'rik), **an'e·mo·met'ri·cal**, *adj.*

a·nem·o·ne (ə·nem'ə·nē), *n.* **1.** plant with small white flowers that blossoms early in the spring. **2.** plant of the same genus with much larger, bright-red, blue, or white flowers. **3.** sea anemone. [< L < Gk., wind flower, < *anemos* wind]

a·nent (ə·nent'), *prep.* **1.** Archaic or Scot. concerning. **2.** Dial. beside. [OE *on emn*, *on efn* on even (ground with)]

an·er·oid (an'ər·oid), *adj.* using no fluid. —*n.* an aneroid barometer. [< F *anéroïde* < Gk. *a*– without + LGk. *neros* water]

Sea anemone.

aneroid barometer, barometer that works by the pressure of air on the elastic lid of a box containing no air.

an·es·the·sia (an'əs·thē'zhə), *n.* Am. entire (general) or partial (local) loss of sensation by means of ether, chloroform, hypnotism, etc., or as the result of hysteria, paralysis, or disease. Also, **anaesthesia.** [< NL < Gk., < *an*– without + *aisthesis* sensation]

an·es·thet·ic (an'əs·thet'ik), Am. —*n.* substance that causes anesthesia, as ether. —*adj.* **1.** causing anesthesia. **2.** of or with anesthesia: *anesthetic effects.* Also, **anaesthetic.** —**an'es·thet'i·cal·ly**, *adv.*

an·es·the·tist (ə·nes'thə·tist), *n.* person whose work is giving anesthetics during operations, etc. Also, **anaesthetist.**

an·es·the·tize (ə·nes'thə·tīz), *v.*, **–tized, –tiz·ing.** make unable to feel pain, touch, cold, etc.; make insensible. Also, **anaesthetize.** —**an·es·the·ti·za·tion** (ə·nes'thə·tə·zā'shən; an'əs·thet'ə–), *n.* —**an·es'the·tiz'er**, *n.*

an·eu·rysm, an·eu·rism (an'yə·riz·əm), *n.* Pathol. a permanent swelling of an artery, due to pressure of the blood on a part weakened by disease or injury. [< Gk. *aneurysma* dilatation, < *ana*– up + *eurys* wide] —**an'eu·rys'mal, an'eu·ris'mal**, *adj.*

a·new (ə·nū'; ə·nū'), *adv.* **1.** once more; again: *to arm anew.* **2.** in a new form or way. [OE *ofniowe.* See NEW.]

an·gel (ān'jəl), *n.* **1.** Theol. one of an order of spiritual beings that are attendants and messengers of God. **2.** conventional representation of such a being. **3.** person as good or lovely as an angel. **4.** any spirit, either good or bad. **5.** Am., Slang. person who pays for producing a play. **6.** an old English coin in use between 1465 and 1634. [< L < Gk. *angelos* messenger]

angel cake, or **angel food cake,** Am. delicate, white, spongy cake made of the whites of eggs, sugar, and a little flour.

an·gel·fish (ān'jəl·fish'), *n., pl.* **–fish·es** or (*esp. collectively*) **–fish. 1.** shark with large pectoral fins that extend like wings. **2.** any of several showy tropical fish.

an·gel·ic (an·jel'ik), **an·gel·i·cal** (–ə·kəl), *adj.* **1.** of angels; heavenly. **2.** like an angel; pure; innocent; good and lovely. —**an·gel'i·cal·ly**, *adv.*

an·gel·i·ca (an·jel'ə·kə), *n.* perennial plant of the same family as the carrot, used in cooking, in medicine, etc. [< Med.L; named from its use as an antidote]

An·ge·li·co (an·jel'ə·kō), *n.* Fra, 1387–1455, Italian painter.

An·ge·lus (an'jə·ləs), *n.* **1.** prayer said by Roman Catholics in memory of Christ's assuming human form. **2.** bell rung at morning, noon, and night as a signal for Roman Catholics to say this prayer. [from first word in service]

an·ger (ang'gər), *n.* the feeling one has toward something that hurts, opposes, offends, or annoys; wrath. —*v.* **1.** make angry. **2.** become angry: *he angers easily.* [< Scand. *angr* grief] —**Syn.** *n.* fury, rage.

an·gi·na (an·jī'nə; *in Med. often* an'jə·nə), *n.* **1.** any inflammatory disease of the throat, such as quinsy, croup, or mumps. **2.** angina pectoris. [< L, quinsy, < *angere* choke]

angina pec·to·ris (pek'tə·ris), serious disease of the heart that causes sharp chest pains and a feeling of being suffocated.

an·gi·o·sperm (an'ji·ō·spérm'), *n.* plant having its seeds enclosed in an ovary; a flowering plant. [< NL, < Gk. *angeion* vessel + *sperma* seed] —**an'gi·o·sper'mous**, *adj.*

an·gle¹ (ang'gəl), *n., v.,* **–gled, –gling.** —*n.* **1.** Geom. **a.** space between two lines or surfaces that meet. **b.** figure formed by two such lines or surfaces. **c.** difference in direction between two such lines or surfaces. **2.** corner. **3.** point of view. **4.** one aspect of something; phase. —*v.* **1.** Am. move at an angle. **2.** turn or bend at an angle. **3.** present with bias or prejudice. [< F < L *angulus*] —**an'gled**, *adj.*

ACUTE　RIGHT　OBTUSE

an·gle² (ang'gəl), *v.,* **–gled, –gling. 1.** fish with a hook and line. **2.** scheme to get: *she angled for an invitation to his party by flattering him.* [OE *angel* fishhook] —**an'gler**, *n.*

angle iron, a triangular strip of iron or steel.

angle of incidence. See incidence, def. 3.

angle of reflection. See reflection, def. 8.

An·gles (ang'gəlz), *n.pl.* a Germanic tribe that settled in England in the fifth century A.D. —**An·gli·an** (ang'gli·ən), *adj., n.*

an·gle·worm (ang'gəl·wèrm'), *n.* earthworm.

An·gli·can (ang'glə·kən), *adj.* **1.** of or having to do with the Church of England or other churches of the same faith elsewhere. **2.** Esp. U.S. English. —*n.* member of an Anglican church. —**An'gli·can·ism**, *n.*

An·gli·cism (ang'glə·siz·əm), *n.* **1.** U.S. a Briticism. **2.** custom or trait peculiar to the English.

An·gli·cize, an·gli·cize (ang'glə·sīz), *v.,* **–cized, –ciz·ing.** make or become English in form, pronunciation, habits, customs, or character. *Chauffeur* and *garage* are French words that have been Anglicized. —**An'gli·ci·za'tion, an'gli·ci·za'tion**, *n.*

an·gling (ang'gling), *n.* act or art of fishing with a rod and line.

Anglo–, *word element.* **1.** English, as in *Anglo-Catholic church.* **2.** English and, as in *the Anglo-American alliance.*

An·glo-A·mer·i·can (ang'glō·ə·mer'ə·kən), Am. —*adj.* **1.** English and American. **2.** of Anglo-Americans. **3.** S.W. non-Spanish. —*n.* an American, esp. a U.S., citizen of English descent.

An·glo-E·gyp·tian Sudan (ang'glō·i·jip'-shən), former country in NE Africa. Now called Sudan.

An·glo-French (ang'glō·french'), *adj.* of or having to do with England and France together. —*n.* the dialect of French spoken by the Normans in England (esp. 1066–c1154); Anglo-Norman; Norman-French.

An·glo·ma·ni·a (ang'glə·mā'ni·ə), *n.* Am. craze for English institutions and customs, esp. for imitating them. —**An'glo·ma'ni·ac**, *n.*

An·glo-Nor·man (ang'glō·nôr'mən), *n.* **1.** one of the Normans who lived in England after its conquest in 1066. **2.** descendant of an English

Norman. 3. Anglo-French. —*adj.* English and Norman.

An·glo·phile (ang′glə·fīl), **An·glo·phil** (-fīl), *n.* person who greatly likes or admires England or the English.

An·glo-Sax·on (ang′glō-sak′sən), *n.* 1. member of the English-speaking world. 2. person of English descent. 3. plain English. 4. world English. 5. Englishman of the fifth to twelfth centuries. 6. his speech. —*adj.* 1. of the Anglo-Saxons. 2. of Anglo-Saxon.

An·go·ra (ang-gô′rə, -gō′-; *for* 3, *also* ang′-gə·rə), *n.* 1. variety of long-haired cat. 2. variety of goat with long, silky hair. 3. Ankara.

an·gos·tu·ra (ang′gəs·túr′ə; -tyūr′ə), *n.* 1. the bitter bark of a South American tree. 2. Angostura, *Trademark.* a type of bitters, prepared from water, alcohol, gentian, etc. [for *Angostura,* now Ciudad Bolivar, Venezuela]

an·gry (ang′grĭ), *adj.,* **-gri·er, -gri·est.** 1. feeling or showing anger: *an angry reply.* 2. raging or stormy: *angry sky.* 3. moved by anger: *angry words.* 4. inflamed and sore: *an infected cut looks angry.* —*an′gri·ly, adv.* —*an′gri·ness, n.* —**Syn.** 1. furious, infuriated.

ang·strom unit (ang′strəm), or **angstrom,** *n. Physics.* one ten-millionth of a millimeter, a unit of measurement of the wave lengths of various radiations, as of light.

an·guish (ang′gwĭsh), *n.* very great pain or grief. [< OF < L *angustia* tightness < *angustus* narrow] —**Syn.** agony, torment.

an·guished (ang′gwĭsht), *adj.* 1. suffering anguish. 2. full of anguish; showing anguish.

an·gu·lar (ang′gyə·lər), *adj.* 1. having angles; sharp-cornered. 2. measured by an angle. In the diagram, the angular distance of P from Q, when measured from O, is the angle X. 3. not plump; gaunt. 4. stiff and awkward. —*an′gu·lar·ly, adv.* —*an′gu·lar·ness, n.*

an·gu·lar·i·ty (ang′gyə·lar′ə·tĭ), *n., pl.* **-ties.** 1. angular quality or form. 2. an angular part; an angle.

an·hy·dride (an-hī′drīd; -drĭd), **an·hy·drid** (-drĭd), *n. Chem.* any oxide that unites with water to form an acid or base.

an·hy·drous (an-hī′drəs), *adj. Chem.* 1. without water. 2. containing no water of crystallization. [< Gk., < *an-* without + *hydor* water]

an·ile (an′īl; ā′nīl), *adj.* old-womanish. [< L < *anus* old woman]

an·i·line (an′ə·lĭn; -līn), **an·i·lin** (-lĭn), *n.* a colorless liquid, $C_6H_5NH_2$, obtained from coal tar and esp. from nitrobenzene ($C_6H_5NO_2$), used in making dyes, etc. —*adj.* made from aniline.

a·nil·i·ty (ə·nĭl′ə·tĭ), *n., pl.* **-ties.** 1. anile condition. 2. an anile act or notion.

an·i·mad·ver·sion (an′ə·mad·vėr′zhən; -shən), *n.* 1. observation often implying reproof. 2. act of criticizing; censure; criticism.

an·i·mad·vert (an′ə·mad·vėrt′), *v.* make criticisms; express blame. [< L, < *animum* mind + *ad-* to + *vertere* turn] —*an′i·mad·vert′er, n.*

an·i·mal (an′ə·məl), *n.* 1. any living thing that is not a plant. Most animals can move about, while most plants cannot; most animals cannot make their own food from carbon dioxide, water, nitrogen, etc., while most plants can. 2. an inferior living being, as distinguished from man; brute; beast. 3. person like a brute or beast. —*adj.* 1. of animals. 2. like an animal; pertaining to the physical part of man's nature. [< L, < *anima* life, breath]

an·i·mal·cule (an′ə·mal′kūl), *n.* a minute or microscopic animal. [< NL *animalculum,* dim. of L *animal*] —*an′i·mal′cu·lar, adj.*

an·i·mal·ism (an′ə·məl·ĭz′əm), *n.* 1. animal existence, nature, or enjoyment. 2. doctrine that human beings are mere animals without souls. —*an′i·mal·ist, n.* —*an′i·mal·is′tic, adj.*

an·i·mal·i·ty (an′ə·mal′ə·tĭ), *n.* 1. animal nature or character in man. 2. animal life.

animal magnetism, hypnotism; mesmerism.

animal spirits, natural liveliness.

an·i·mate (*v.* an′ə·māt; *adj.* an′ə·mĭt), *v.,* **-mat·ed, -mat·ing,** *adj.* —*v.* 1. give life to; make alive. 2. make lively, gay, or vigorous. 3. inspire; encourage. 4. put into action; cause to act or work. —*adj.* 1. living; alive: *all plants and animals are animate.* 2. lively; gay; vigorous. [< L, < *anima* life, breath] —*an′i·mate·ly, adv.* —*an′i·mat′er, an′i·ma′tor, n.* —*an′i·ma′tion, n.*

an·i·mat·ed (an′ə·māt′ĭd), *adj.* 1. lively; gay. 2. living. —*an′i·mat′ed·ly, adv.*

animated cartoon, series of drawings arranged to be photographed and shown like a motion picture. Each drawing shows a slight change from the one before it.

an·i·mat·ing (an′ə·māt′ing), *adj.* giving life to; making lively; inspiring; encouraging. —*an′i·mat′ing·ly, adv.*

an·i·mism (an′ə·mĭz·əm), *n.* the belief that animals, trees, rocks, and other natural objects have souls. [< L *anima* life] —*an′i·mist, n.* —*an′i·mis′tic, adj.*

an·i·mos·i·ty (an′ə·mos′ə·tĭ), *n., pl.* **-ties.** violent hatred; active enmity.

an·i·mus (an′ə·məs), *n.* 1. violent hatred; ill will; active dislike or enmity. 2. moving spirit; intention. [< L, spirit]

an·i·on (an′ī′ən), *n. Physical Chem.* 1. a negatively charged ion that moves toward the positive pole in electrolysis. 2. atom or group of atoms having a negative charge. [< Gk., (thing) going up, < *ana-* up + *ienai* go]

an·ise (an′ĭs), *n.* 1. plant of the carrot family grown for its fragrant seeds. 2. the seed. [< OF < L < Gk. *anison*]

an·i·seed (an′ə·sēd; an′ĭs·sēd′), *n.* seed of anise, used as a flavoring or in medicine.

An·jou (an′jü), *n.* a former duchy in W France.

An·ka·ra (ang′kə·rə; äng′-), *n.* capital of Turkey since 1923. Also, Angora.

an·kle (ang′kəl), *n.* 1. joint that connects the foot and the leg. 2. part of the leg between this joint and the calf. [< Scand. Cf. Dan. *ankel*.]

an·kle·bone (ang′kəl·bōn′), *n. Anat.* talus.

an·klet (ang′klĭt), *n.* 1. a short sock. 2. band, often ornamental, worn around the ankle.

an·ky·lo·sis (ang′kə·lō′sĭs), *n.* 1. *Anat.* a growing together of bones as a result of disease or injury. 2. *Pathol.* stiffness of a joint caused by this. [< NL < Gk., < *ankyloein* stiffen < *ankylos* crooked] —*an·ky·lot·ic* (ang′kə·lot′ik), *adj.*

an·na (an′ə), *n.* in India: a. one-sixteenth of a rupee. b. a coin having this value.

an·nal·ist (an′əl·ĭst), *n.* writer of annals. —*an′nal·is′tic, adj.*

an·nals (an′əlz), *n.pl.* 1. a written account of events year by year. 2. historical records; history. [< L, < *annus* year]

An·nam (ə·nam′; an′am), *n.* a former French protectorate in Indo-China, now part of Viet-Nam. —**An·na·mese** (an′ə·mēz′; -mēs′), *adj., n.*

An·nap·o·lis (ə·nap′ə·lĭs), *n.* seaport and capital of Maryland, site of the U.S. Naval Academy.

Anne (an), *n.* 1665–1714, queen of Great Britain and Ireland, 1702–14.

an·neal (ə·nēl′), *v.* toughen (glass, metals, etc.) by heating and then cooling; temper. [OE *anǣlan* < *an-* on + *ǣlan* burn] —*an·neal′er, n.*

an·ne·lid (an′ə·lĭd), *Zool.* —*n.* one of the phylum of segmented worms, as the earthworms and leeches. —*adj.* of or having to do with annelids. [< F < OF *annel* ring < L *anellus,* double dim. of *anus* ring] —*an·nel·i·dan* (ə·nel′ə·dən), *adj., n.*

an·nex (*v.* ə·neks′; *n.* an′eks), *v.* 1. to join or add to a larger thing: *the United States annexed Texas in 1845.* 2. attach as an attribute or consequence. 3. *Colloq.* take as one's own; appropriate. —*n.* 1. something annexed; an added part. 2. a supplementary building. [< Med. L, < L *annexus* < *ad-* to + *nectere* bind] —*an·nex′a·ble, adj.* —*an·nex′ment, n.*

an·nex·a·tion (an′ik·sā′shən; -ek-), *n.* 1. an

āge, cāre, fär; ēqual, tėrm; īce, ōpen, ôrder; pút, rüle, ūse; tʰ, then; ə=a in about.

annexing or being annexed. 2. something annexed. —**an'nex·a'tion·ist,** n.

An·nie Oak·ley (an'i ōk'li), Am., Slang. a free pass to a play, etc. Also, Oakley. [after Annie Oakley, 1860–1926, a noted woman marksman; in allusion to the resemblance between a punched pass and a small target used by her]

an·ni·hi·la·ble (ə·nī'ə·lə·bəl), n. that can be annihilated. —**an·ni'hi·la·bil'i·ty,** n.

an·ni·hi·late (ə·nī'ə·lāt), v., -lat·ed, -lat·ing. 1. destroy completely; wipe out of existence. 2. bring to ruin or confusion. [< LL, < L ad- + nihil nothing] —**an·ni'hi·la'tion,** n. —**an·ni'hi·la'-tive,** adj. —**an·ni'hi·la'tor,** n.

an·ni·ver·sa·ry (an'ə·vėr'sə·ri), n., pl. -ries, adj. —n. 1. the yearly return of a date: a birthday is an anniversary. 2. celebration of the yearly return of a date. —adj. 1. celebrated each year at the same date. 2. having to do with an anniversary: an anniversary gift. [< L, returning annually, < annus year + vertere turn]

an·no Dom·i·ni (an'ō dom'ə·nī), in the year of our Lord; any year of the Christian Era. Abbrev.: A.D.

an·no·tate (an'ō·tāt), v., -tat·ed, -tat·ing. 1. provide with explanatory notes or comments. 2. make explanatory notes or comments. [< L, < ad- + nota note] —**an'no·ta'tor,** n.

an·no·ta·tion (an'ō·tā'shən), n. 1. act of annotating. 2. note of explanation.

an·nounce (ə·nouns'), v., -nounced, -nounc-ing. 1. give formal or public notice of: announce a wedding in the papers. 2. make known; make evident. 3. make known the presence or arrival of: announce a guest. [< OF < L, < ad- + nuntius messenger] —**an·nounce'ment,** n.

an·nounc·er (ə·noun'sər), n. person who announces, esp. on a radio or television broadcast.

an·noy (ə·noi'), v. 1. make angry; disturb; trouble: annoy by teasing. 2. hurt; harm; molest: annoy the enemy by raids. [< OF anuier < LL, < L in odio in hatred] —**an·noy'er,** n. —Syn. 1. irritate, bother, vex, irk, tease.

an·noy·ance (ə·noi'əns), n. 1. an annoying. 2. a being annoyed. 3. thing that annoys. —Syn. 3. bother, pest.

an·noy·ing (ə·noi'ing), adj. disturbing. —**an·noy'ing·ly,** adv. —**an·noy'ing·ness,** n.

an·nu·al (an'yū·əl), adj. 1. coming once a year: annual celebration. 2. of or for a year; yearly: an annual salary of $3,000. 3. accomplished during a year: the earth's annual course around the sun. 4. Bot. living but one year or season. —n. 1. an annual publication. 2. plant that lives one year or season. [< OF < LL, < L annus year] —**an'nu·al·ly,** adv.

an·nu·i·tant (ə·nū'ə·tənt; -nū'-), n. person who receives an annuity.

an·nu·i·ty (ə·nū'ə·ti; -nū'-), n., pl. -ties. 1. sum of money paid every year. 2. right to receive or duty to pay such a yearly sum. 3. investment that provides a fixed yearly income. [< F < Med. L, < L annus year]

an·nul (ə·nul'), v., -nulled, -nul·ling. destroy the force of; make void: annul a marriage. [< LL, < L ad- + nullus none] —**an·nul'la·ble,** adj. —**an·nul'ler,** n. —**an·nul'ment,** n.

an·nu·lar (an'yə·lər), adj. ringlike; ring-shaped; ringed. [< L, < annulus ring] —**an·nu-lar·i·ty** (an'yə·lar'ə·ti), n. —**an'nu·lar·ly,** adv.

an·nu·let (an'yə·lit), n. 1. a little ring. 2. Archit. a ringlike molding of wood, stone, etc. [< L annulus ring]

an·nu·lus (an'yə·ləs), n., pl. -li (-lī), -lus·es. a ringlike part, band, or space. [< L annulus, dim. of anus ring]

an·num (an'əm), n. year.

an·nun·ci·ate (ə·nun'shi·āt; -si-), v., -at·ed, -at·ing. make known; announce. [< Med.L < L, < ad- to + nuntius messenger]

an·nun·ci·a·tion (ə·nun'si·ā'shən; -shi-), n. 1. announcement. 2. the Annunciation, a. the angel Gabriel's announcement to the Virgin Mary that she was to be the mother of Christ. Luke 1:26–33. b. Lady Day.

an·nun·ci·a·tor (ə·nun'shi·ā'tər; -si-), n. Am. an electric signaling device or indicator.

A No. 1, Am., Colloq. A one.

an·ode (an'ōd), n. positive electrode. [< Gk., < ana- up + hodos way] —**an·od·ic** (an·od'ik), adj.

an·o·dyne (an'ə·dīn), n. anything that relieves pain. —adj. soothing. [< L < Gk., < an- without + odyne pain]

a·noint (ə·noint'), v. 1. put oil on; rub with ointment; smear. 2. consecrate by applying oil. [< OF enoint < L, < in- on + unguere smear] —**a·noint'er,** n. —**a·noint'ment,** n.

a·nom·a·lous (ə·nom'ə·ləs), adj. departing from the common rule; irregular; abnormal. [< LL < Gk., < an- not + homalos even] —**a·nom'a·lous·ly,** adv. —**a·nom'a·lous·ness,** n.

a·nom·a·ly (ə·nom'ə·li), n., pl. -lies. 1. departure from a common rule; irregularity. 2. something abnormal. —**a·nom·a·lism** (ə·nom'ə·liz-əm), n.

a·non (ə·non'), adv. 1. in a little while; soon. 2. at another time; again. 3. ever and anon, now and then. [OE on ān into one, on āne in one, at once]

anon., anonymous.

an·o·nym·i·ty (an'ə·nim'ə·ti), n. state of being anonymous.

a·non·y·mous (ə·non'ə·məs), adj. 1. of unknown or unacknowledged authorship: an anonymous letter, pamphlet, etc. 2. having no name; nameless. [< Gk., < an- without + dial. onyma name] —**a·non'y·mous·ly,** adv.

a·noph·e·les (ə·nof'ə·lēz), n., pl. -les. mosquito that can transmit malaria.

an·oth·er (ə·nuth'ər), adj. 1. an additional; one more: have another glass of milk. 2. different; not the same: that is another matter entirely. —pron. 1. one more; an additional one: have another. 2. a different one: I don't like this book, give me another. 3. one of the same kind: his father is a scholar, and he is another. [for an other]

ans., answer; answered.

An·schluss (än'shlŭs), n. German. union, esp. that of Germany and Austria in 1938.

an·ser·ine (an'sər·īn; -in), **an·ser·ous** (—əs), adj. 1. of, like, or pertaining to a goose or geese. 2. stupid; foolish. [< L, < anser goose]

an·swer (an'sər; än'-), n. 1. words spoken or written in reply to a question: the boy gave a quick answer. 2. thing done in return: a nod was her only answer. 3. solution to a problem, as in mathematics. —v. 1. reply to: he answered my question. 2. make answer; reply: I asked him a question, but he would not answer. 3. reply or respond by act: he knocked on the door, but no one answered. 4. act or move in response to: she answered the doorbell. 5. serve: his poor excuse will not answer. 6. be accountable or responsible: you must answer for your mistakes. 7. correspond (to): this house answers to his description. 8. answer back, Colloq. make an insolent reply. [OE andswaru < and- against + swerian swear] —**an'swer·er,** n. —Syn. n. 1. rejoinder, retort, return. -v. 1, 2. retort, rejoin.

an·swer·a·ble (an'sər·ə·bəl; än'-), adj. 1. responsible. 2. that can be answered. 3. Archaic. corresponding. —**an'swer·a·ble·ness,** n. —**an'-swer·a·bly,** adv.

answering service, an agency that cuts in on the telephone circuits of its clients to answer calls, etc. in their absence.

ant (ant), n. any member of a family of small hymenopterous insects that live with others in colonies. [OE ǣmete] —**ant'like',** adj.

-ant, suffix. 1. ——ing, as in buoyant, compliant, triumphant. 2. one that ——s, as in assistant. See also -ent. [< F < L -ans, -ens]

Ant. Line shows actual length.

ant., 1. antiquary. 2. antonym.

Ant·a·buse (an'tə·būs), n. Trademark. drug used to combat alcoholism by making a person feel ill after drinking alcoholic liquor.

ant·ac·id (ant·as'id), adj. neutralizing acids; counteracting acidity. —n. substance that neutralizes acids, such as baking soda.

an·tag·o·nism (an·tag′ə·niz·əm), *n.* active opposition; hostility.

an·tag·o·nist (an·tag′ə·nist), *n.* one who fights, struggles, or contends with another. —Syn. opponent, adversary, foe, enemy.

an·tag·o·nis·tic (an·tag′ə·nis′tik), *adj.* acting against each other. —**an·tag′o·nis′ti·cal·ly,** *adv.* —Syn. opposing, conflicting, hostile.

an·tag·o·nize (an·tag′ə·nīz), *v.,* –nized, –nizing. 1. make an enemy of; arouse dislike in. 2. oppose. [< Gk., < *anti-* against + *agon* contest] —**an·tag′o·niz′er,** *n.*

ant·arc·tic (ant·ärk′tik; –är′tik), *adj.* of or near the South Pole or the south polar region. —*n.* the south polar region.

Ant·arc·ti·ca (ant·ärk′tə·kə; –är′tə–), or **Ant·arctic Continent,** *n.* land around or near the South Pole.

Antarctic Circle, the imaginary boundary of the south polar region, running parallel to the equator at 23°30′ north of the South Pole.

Antarctic Ocean, ocean of the south polar region.

Antarctic Zone, region between the Antarctic Circle and the South Pole.

ant bear, 1. a large, shaggy, gray anteater of South America. 2. aardvark.

an·te (an′tē), *n., v.,* –ted or –teed, –te·ing. —*n. Am.* stake in the game of poker that every player must put up before receiving a hand or drawing new cards. —*v. Colloq.* 1. *Am.* put (one's stake) into the pool. 2. pay (one's share). [see ANTE–]

ante–, *prefix.* before, as in *antenatal, anteroom.* [< L]

ant·eat·er (ant′ēt′ər), *n.* a mammal with a long, slender, sticky tongue, such as the pangolin or ant bear, that feeds on ants.

an·te·bel·lum (an′ti·bel′əm), *adj.* 1. before the war. 2. *Am.* before the Civil War. [< L, before the war]

an·te·ced·ence (an′tə·sēd′əns), *n.* 1. a going before; precedence; priority. 2. apparent motion of a planet from east to west.

an·te·ced·ent (an′tə·sēd′ənt), *adj.* coming or happening before; preceding; previous: *an event antecedent to this one.* —*n.* 1. a previous thing or event. 2. antecedents, a. the past life or history. b. ancestors. 3. *Gram.* word, phrase, or clause that is referred to by a pronoun. In "The dog that killed the rat is brown," *dog* is the antecedent of *that.* 4. *Math.* the first term in any ratio; the first or third term in a proportion. [< L, < *ante–* before + *cedere* go] —**an′te·ced′ent·ly,** *adv.* —Syn. *adj.* prior, earlier.

an·te·cham·ber (an′ti·chām′bər), *n.* anteroom.

an·te·date (an′ti·dāt; an′ti·dāt′), *v.,* –dat·ed, –dat·ing, *n.* —*v.* 1. be or happen before. 2. give too early a date to. —*n.* 1. a prior date. 2. date earlier than the true date.

an·te·di·lu·vi·an (an′ti·di·lü′vi·ən), *adj.* 1. before the Flood. 2. very old; old-fashioned. —*n.* 1. person who lived before the Flood. 2. a very old person. 3. an old-fashioned person. [< ANTE– + L *diluvium* deluge]

an·te·lope (an′tə·lōp), *n., pl.* –lope, –lopes. 1. a cud-chewing, deerlike animal related to cattle, sheep, and goats. 2. *Am.* pronghorn. [< OF < Med.L < LGk. *antholops*]

an·te me·rid·i·em (an′tē mə·rid′i·əm), before noon. *Abbrev.:* a.m., A.M. [< L, before midday]

an·te·na·tal (an′ti·nā′təl), *adj.* before birth.

an·ten·na (an·ten′ə), *n., pl.* –ten·nae (–ten′ē) *for 1;* –ten·nas *for 2.* 1. *Zool.* one of two feelers on the head of an insect, lobster, etc. 2. *Radio, Television.* aerial. [< L, orig., sail yard]

an·te·nup·tial (an′ti·nup′shəl), *adj.* before marriage.

an·te·pe·nult (an′ti·pē′nult; –pi·nult′), *n.* the third syllable, counting back from the end of a word. In *an te ri or, te* is the antepenult.

an·te·pe·nul·ti·mate (an′ti·pi·nul′tə·mit), *adj.* third from the end. —*n.* antepenult.

an·te·ri·or (an·tir′i·ər), *adj.* 1. toward the

front; fore. 2. going before; earlier; previous. [< L, comparative of *ante* before] —**an·te·ri·or·i·ty** (an·tir′i·ôr′ə·ti; –or′–), **an·te′ri·or·ness,** *n.*

an·te·room (an′ti·rüm′; –rüm′), *n.* a small room leading to a larger one; a waiting room.

an·them (an′thəm), *n.* 1. song of praise, devotion, or patriotism: *the national anthem.* 2. piece of sacred music, usually with words from some passage in the Bible. [< VL < LL < Gk. *antiphona* antiphon. Doublet of ANTIPHON.]

an·ther (an′thər), *n. Bot.* part of the stamen that bears the pollen. [< NL < Gk., < *anthos* flower]

ANTHER
STAMEN

Anthers

an·ther·id·i·um (an′thər·id′i·əm), *n., pl.* –id·i·a (–id′i·ə). *Bot.* part of a fern, moss, etc., that produces male reproductive cells. —**an′ther·id′i·al,** *adj.*

an·thol·o·gy (an·thol′ə·ji), *n., pl.* –gies. 1. collection of poems or prose selections from various authors. 2. collection of epigrams from various authors. [< L < Gk., < *anthos* flower + *legein* gather] —**an·tho·log·i·cal** (an′thə·loj′ə·kəl), *adj.* —**an·thol′o·gist,** *n.*

an·tho·zo·an (an′thə·zō′ən), *n.* any sea anemone, coral, or other polyp with radial segments. —*adj.* of such polyps.

an·thra·cene (an′thrə·sēn), *n.* a colorless, crystalline compound, $C_{14}H_{10}$, used in making alizarin dyes.

an·thra·cite (an′thrə·sīt), *n.* coal that burns with very little smoke or flame; hard coal. [< L < Gk., name of a gem, < *anthrax* charcoal] —**an·thra·cit·ic** (an′thrə·sit′ik), *adj.*

an·thrax (an′thraks), *n., pl.* –thra·ces (–thrə·sēz). an infectious, often fatal, disease of cattle, sheep, etc., that may be transmitted to human beings. [< LL < Gk., carbuncle, live coal]

anthrop–, anthropological; anthropology.

anthropo–, *word element.* man; human being; human, as in *anthropology, anthropometry.* [< Gk. *anthropos*]

an·thro·poid (an′thrə·poid), *adj.* manlike; resembling man. —*n.* a manlike ape. Chimpanzees and gorillas are anthropoids. —**an′thro·poi′dal,** *adj.*

an·thro·pol·o·gy (an′thrə·pol′ə·ji), *n.* science that deals with the origin, development, races, customs, and beliefs of mankind. —**an·thro·po·log·i·cal** (an′thrə·pə·loj′ə·kəl), **an·thro·po·log·ic** (–ik), *adj.* —**an′thro·po·log′i·cal·ly,** *adv.* —**an′thro·pol′o·gist,** *n.*

an·thro·pom·e·try (an′thrə·pom′ə·tri), *n.* branch of anthropology that deals with the measurement of the human body. —**an·thro·po·met·ric** (an′thrə·pə·met′rik), **an′thro·po·met′·ri·cal,** *adj.* —**an′thro·pom′e·trist,** *n.*

an·thro·po·mor·phic (an′thrə·pə·môr′fik), *adj.* attributing human form or qualities to gods or things. —**an′thro·po·mor′phi·cal·ly,** *adv.*

an·thro·po·mor·phism (an′thrə·pə·môr′fiz·əm), *n.* an attributing of human form or qualities to gods or things. —**an′thro·po·mor′phist,** *n.*

an·ti (an′tī; –ti), *n., pl.* –tis. *Colloq.* person opposed to some plan, idea, party, etc.

anti–, *prefix.* 1. against; opposed to, as in *anti-British.* 2. rival, as in *antipope.* 3. not; the opposite of, as in *antisocial.* 4. preventing or counteracting, as in *antirust.* 5. preventing, curing, or alleviating, as in *antituberculosis.* [< Gk.; also (before vowels and *h*), *ant–*] ➤ Anti– is hyphened only before root words beginning with *i* and before proper nouns: *anti-imperialistic, anti-intellectual, anti-British, anti-Semitic. Anti–* is pronounced an′ti or often, more emphatically, an′tī.

an·ti·air·craft (an′ti·ãr′kraft′; –kräft′), *adj.* used in defense against enemy aircraft.

an·ti·bi·ot·ic (an′ti·bī·ot′ik), *n.* product of an organism, as penicillin, that works against harmful microörganisms.

an·ti·bod·y (an'ti·bod'i), n., pl. **-bod·ies.** one of a class of substances in the blood, etc., that destroy or weaken bacteria or neutralize toxins.

an·tic (an'tik), n., adj., v., **-ticked, -tick·ing.** —n. 1. Often, antics. a grotesque gesture or action; a silly trick; caper. 2. Archaic. clown. —adj. Archaic. grotesque. —v. perform antics; caper. [< Ital. antico old (with sense of grottesco grotesque) < L antiquus ancient]

An·ti·christ (an'ti·krīst'), n. the great enemy or opponent of Christ.

an·tic·i·pate (an·tis'ə·pāt), v., **-pat·ed, -pat·ing.** 1. look forward to; expect: anticipate a good vacation. 2. use or realize in advance; foresee: anticipate the disaster. 3. consider or mention before the proper time: anticipate a point in his argument. 4. take care of ahead of time: anticipate a person's wishes. 5. be before (another) in thinking, acting, etc. 6. cause to happen sooner; hasten. [< L anticipatus < ante before + capere take] —**an·tic'i·pa'tor,** n.

an·tic·i·pa·tion (an·tis'ə·pā'shən), n. 1. act of anticipating; foretaste; use, realization, or action in advance. 2. expectation.

an·tic·i·pa·tive (an·tis'ə·pā'tiv), adj. tending to anticipate; having anticipation (of).

an·tic·i·pa·to·ry (an·tis'ə·pə·tô'ri; -tō'-), adj. anticipating. —**an·tic'i·pa·to'ri·ly,** adv.

an·ti·cler·i·cal (an'ti·kler'ə·kəl), adj. opposed to the influence of the church and clergy in public affairs. —**an'ti·cler'i·cal·ism,** n.

an·ti·cli·max (an'ti·klī'maks), n. 1. an abrupt descent from the important to the trivial. 2. descent (in importance, interest, etc.) contrasting with a previous rise. —**an·ti·cli·mac·tic** (an'ti·klī·mak'tik), adj.

an·ti·co·lo·ni·al (an'ti·kə·lō'ni·əl), adj. opposed to colonialism. —**an'ti·co·lo'ni·al·ism,** n.

an·ti·co·lo·ni·al·ist (an'ti·kə·lō'ni·ə·list), n. an opponent of colonialism. —adj. anticolonial.

an·ti·cy·clone (an'ti·sī'klōn), n. winds moving around and away from a center of high pressure, which also moves. —**an·ti·cy·clon·ic** (an'ti·sī·klon'ik), adj.

an·ti·dote (an'ti·dōt), n. 1. medicine or remedy that counteracts a poison. 2. remedy for any evil. [< L < Gk. antidoton (thing) given against < anti- against + didonai give] —**an'ti·dot'al,** adj. —**an'ti·dot'al·ly,** adv.

An·tie·tam (an·tē'təm), n. small creek in Maryland near which a major battle of the Civil War was fought in 1862.

an·ti·freeze (an'ti·frēz'), n. Am. substance added to a liquid to prevent it from freezing.

an·ti·fric·tion (an'ti·frik'shən), n. prevention or reduction of friction.

an·ti·gen (an'tə·jən), n. any substance that stimulates the production of antibodies.

An·ti·gua (an·tē'gə; -gwə), n. island SE of Puerto Rico, in the West Indies.

an·ti·his·ta·mine (an'ti·his'tə·mēn; -min), n. a chemical compound used against certain allergies and against symptoms of a cold.

an·ti·knock (an'ti·nok'), n. any material added to the fuel of an internal-combustion engine to reduce noise during its operation.

An·til·les (an·til'ēz), n.pl. chain of islands in the West Indies, including Cuba, Hispaniola, Puerto Rico, and smaller islands near by.

an·ti·log·a·rithm (an'ti·lôg'ə·rith·əm; -log'-), n. Math. number corresponding to a given logarithm.

an·ti·ma·cas·sar (an'ti·mə·kas'ər), n. a small covering to protect the back or arms of a chair, sofa, etc. [< anti- against + macassar a hair oil from Macassar]

an·ti·mis·sile (an'ti·mis'əl), adj. used in defense against ballistic missiles, rockets, etc.

an·ti·mo·ny (an'tə·mō'ni), n. Chem. a metallic, crystalline element, Sb, with a bluish-white luster, used chiefly in alloys and medicinal compounds. [< Med.L antimonium]

An·ti·och (an'ti·ok), n. city in Turkey, the former capital of ancient Syria.

an·ti·pas·to (än'tē·päs'tō), n., pl. **-tos.** Ital-

ian. an appetizer consisting of fish, meats, etc.

an·tip·a·thet·ic (an·tip'ə·thet'ik; an'ti·pə-), **an·tip·a·thet·i·cal** (-ə·kəl), adj. contrary or opposed in nature or disposition. —**an·tip'a·thet'i·cal·ly,** adv.

an·tip·a·thy (an·tip'ə·thi), n., pl. **-thies.** 1. intense or fixed dislike; a feeling against. 2. object of intense dislike. [< L < Gk., < anti- against + pathos feeling]

an·ti·phon (an'tə·fon), n. verses sung or chanted by two groups alternately in a church service. [< LL < Gk. antiphona sounding in response < anti- opposed to + phone sound. Doublet of ANTHEM.] —**an·tiph·o·nal** (an·tif'ə·nəl), adj. —**an·tiph'o·nal·ly,** adv.

an·tip·o·dal (an·tip'ə·dəl), adj. 1. on the opposite side of the earth. 2. directly opposite; exactly contrary: antipodal ideas.

an·ti·pode (an'tə·pōd), n. the direct opposite.

an·tip·o·des (an·tip'ə·dēz), n.pl. 1. two places on directly opposite sides of the earth. 2. (sometimes sing. in use) place on the opposite side of the earth. 3. persons who live on the opposite sides of the earth. 4. two opposites or contraries: forgiveness and revenge are antipodes. 5. (sometimes sing. in use) the direct opposite. [< L < Gk., < anti- opposite to + pous foot] —**an·tip·o·de·an** (an·tip'ə·dē'ən), adj., n.

an·ti·pro·ton, an·ti·pro·ton (an'ti·prō'ton), n. a tiny particle of the same mass as a proton, but negatively charged, created when a proton hits a neutron.

an·ti·py·ret·ic (an'ti·pi·ret'ik), Med. —adj. checking or preventing fever. —n. any medicine or remedy for checking or preventing fever.

an·ti·quar·i·an (an'tə·kwâr'i·ən), adj. having to do with antiques or antiquaries. —n. antiquary. —**an'ti·quar'i·an·ism,** n.

an·ti·quar·y (an'tə·kwer'i), n., pl. **-quar·ies.** student or collector of antiques.

an·ti·quate (an'tə·kwāt), v., **-quat·ed, -quat·ing.** make old-fashioned or out-of-date.

an·ti·quat·ed (an'tə·kwāt'id), adj. 1. old-fashioned; out-of-date. 2. old. —**an'ti·quat'ed·ness,** n.

an·tique (an·tēk'), adj. 1. old-fashioned; out-of-date. 2. of or belonging to ancient Greece or Rome. 3. of or from times long ago; ancient. 4. in the style of times long ago. —n. 1. something made long ago. 2. antique style, usually of Greek or Roman art. 3. Printing. style of type. This line is in antique. [< L antiquus < ante before] —**an·tique'ly,** adv. —**an·tique'ness,** n.

an·tiq·ui·ty (an·tik'wə·ti), n., pl. **-ties.** 1. oldness; great age. 2. times long ago; early ages of history; the period from 5000 B.C. to 476 A.D. 3. people of long ago. 4. antiquities, a. things from times long ago. b. customs and life of olden times.

an·ti·ra·chit·ic (an'ti·rə·kit'ik), adj. preventing or curing rickets.

an·ti·sa·loon (an'ti·sə·lün'), adj. Am. opposed to the sale of intoxicating liquor.

an·ti·scor·bu·tic (an'ti·skôr·bū'tik), Med. —adj. preventing or curing scurvy. —n. remedy for scurvy.

an·ti·Sem·i·tism (an'ti·sem'ə·tiz·əm), n. dislike or hatred for Jews; prejudice against Jews. —**an·ti·Sem·ite** (an'ti·sem'īt; -sē'mīt), n. —**an·ti·Se·mit·ic** (an'ti·sə·mit'ik), adj.

an·ti·sep·sis (an'tə·sep'sis), n. 1. prevention of infection. 2. method or medicine that prevents infection.

an·ti·sep·tic (an'tə·sep'tik), adj. preventing infection. —n. substance, as iodine, mercurochrome, etc., that prevents infection. —**an'ti·sep'ti·cal·ly,** adv.

an·ti·slav·er·y (an'ti·slāv'ər·i), n. opposed to slavery; against slavery.

an·ti·so·cial (an'ti·sō'shəl), adj. 1. harmful to the public welfare; against the common good. 2. averse to social relations.

an·ti·stro·phe (an·tis'trə·fē), n. 1. part of an ancient Greek ode sung by the chorus when moving from left to right. 2. stanza following a strophe and usually in the same meter. [< LL

< Gk., < *anti-* against + *strephein* turn] —an·ti·stroph·ic (an'ti·strof'ik), *adj.*

an·ti·tank (an'ti·tangk'), *adj. Mil.* designed for use against armored vehicles, esp. tanks.

an·tith·e·sis (an·tith'ə·sis), *n., pl.* -ses (-sēz). 1. the direct opposite: *hate is the antithesis of love.* 2. contrast of ideas. 3. opposition; contrast (*of* or *between*): *antithesis of theory and fact.* [< L < Gk., < *anti-* against + *tithenai* set]

an·ti·thet·ic (an'tə·thet'ik), an·ti·thet·i·cal (-ə·kəl), *adj.* 1. of or using antithesis. 2. contrasted; opposite. —an'ti·thet'i·cal·ly, *adv.*

an·ti·tox·ic (an'ti·tok'sik), *adj.* 1. counteracting diseases or poisonings caused by toxins. 2. having to do with or like an antitoxin.

an·ti·tox·in (an'ti·tok'sən), an·ti·tox·ine (-sən; -sēn), *n.* 1. substance formed in the body to counteract a disease or poison. 2. a serum containing antitoxin.

an·ti·trades (an'ti·trādz'), *n.pl.* winds that blow in a direction opposite to the trade winds on a level above them and descend beyond the trade-wind belt.

an·ti·trust (an'ti·trust'), *adj. Am.* opposed to large corporations that control the trade practices of certain kinds of business.

ant·ler (ant'lər), *n.* 1. a branched horn of a deer or similar animal. 2. branch of such a horn. [< OF *antoillier* < L *ante* before + *oculus* eye]

ant lion, *n.* 1. insect whose larva digs a pit, where it lies in wait to catch ants, etc. 2. its larva.

An·toi·nette (an'twə·net'), *n.* Marie, 1755–1793, wife of Louis XVI of France.

An·to·ni·nus (an'tə·nī'nəs), *n.* Marcus Aurelius, 121–180 A.D., Roman emperor 161–180 A.D. and Stoic philosopher.

An·to·ni·us (an·tō'ni·əs), *n.* Marcus (*Mark Antony*), 83?–30 B.C., Roman general, friend of Julius Caesar, and rival of Augustus.

an·to·nym (an'tə·nim), *n.* word that means the opposite of another word (contrasted with synonym): *"hot" is the antonym of "cold."* [< Gk., < *anti-* opposite to + dial. *onyma* word]

Ant·werp (ant'wérp), *n.* seaport in NW Belgium.

A number 1, *Am., Colloq.* A one.

a·nus (ā'nəs), *n. Anat., Zool.* an opening at the lower end of the alimentary canal. [< L, orig., ring]

an·vil (an'vəl), *n., v.,* -viled, -vil·ing; esp. Brit. -villed, -vil·ling. —*n.* 1. an iron or steel block on which metals are hammered and shaped. 2. *Anat.* incus. —*v.* form or shape on or as on an anvil. [OE *anfilt*]

anx·i·e·ty (ang·zī'ə·ti), *n., pl.* -ties. 1. anxious state or feeling; troubled, worried, or uneasy feeling. 2. eager desire: *anxiety to succeed.* —Syn. 1. apprehension, dread, misgiving.

anx·ious (angk'shəs; ang'-), *adj.* 1. uneasy because of thoughts or fears of what may happen; troubled; worried. 2. eagerly desiring; wishing very much. 3. attended by uneasiness or anxiety. [< L *anxius* troubled < *angere* choke, cause distress] —anx'ious·ly, *adv.* —anx'ious·ness, *n.* —Syn. 1. concerned, apprehensive, solicitous.

anxious seat or bench, 1. *Am.* seat near the pulpit at a revival meeting for those who are troubled about their religious life. 2. uneasy or troubled condition.

an·y (en'i), *adj.* 1. one (no matter which) out of many: *any book will do.* 2. some: *have you any fresh fruit?* 3. every: *any child knows that.* 4. even one; even a little; even one or two: *he was forbidden to go to any house.* 5. in no matter what quantity or number: *have you any sugar?* 6. enough to be noticed: *he had hardly any money.* —*pron.* 1. any person or thing; any part: *keep the cake; I don't want any.* 2. some: *have you any?* —*adv.* in some extent or degree; at all: *has the sick child improved any?* [OE *ænig*] ➤ Any is used primarily as an adjective (*any member of the family, any dog is a good dog*), but also as a pronoun (*any* will do). In comparison of things of the same class, idiom calls for *any other*: "This book is better than *any*

other on the subject"; but: "I think a movie is more entertaining than *any* book" (not the same class of things). See also anyone.

an·y·bod·y (en'i·bod'i), *pron., n., pl.* -bod·ies. 1. any person; anyone: *has anybody been here?* 2. an important person: *is he anybody?*

an·y·how (en'i·hou), *adv.* 1. in any way whatever. 2. in any case. 3. at least. 4. carelessly.

an·y·one (en'i·wun; -wən), *pron.* any person; anybody. ➤ Anyone is written as one word when the stress is on the *any*, and as two when the stress is on the *one*: *Anyone* (en'i·wun) *would know that. I'd like any one* (en·i wun') *of them.*

an·y·place (en'i·plās), *adv. Colloq.* anywhere.

an·y·thing (en'i·thing), *pron.* any thing. —*n.* a thing of any kind whatever. —*adv.* at all.

an·y·way (en'i·wā), *adv.* 1. in any way whatever. 2. in any case. 3. carelessly.

an·y·where (en'i·hwãr), *adv.* in, at, or to any place.

an·y·wise (en'i·wīz), *adv.* in any way; at all.

An·zac (an'zak), *n.* soldier from Australia or New Zealand.

AN·ZUS (an'zus), *n.* Australia, New Zealand, and the U.S. acting collectively for the purpose of mutual defense in the Pacific.

A one (ā' wun'), *Colloq.* first-rate; first-class; excellent. Also, A 1; A No. 1 or A number 1, *Am.*

a·o·rist (ā'ə·rist), *n. Gram.* 1. a tense of Greek verbs indicating simple past time. [< Gk. *aoristos* < *a-* not + *horizein* to limit < *horos* boundary]

a·or·ta (ā·ôr'tə), *n., pl.* -tas, -tae (-tē). *Anat.* the main artery that conveys blood from the left side of the heart to all parts of the body except the lungs. [< NL or Med.L < Gk. *aorte*] —a·or'·tic, a·or'tal, *adj.*

a·ou·dad (ä'ụ·dad), *n.* a wild sheep of northern Africa. [< F < Berber *audad*]

A.P., AP, *Am.* Associated Press.

a·pace (ə·pās'), *adv.* swiftly; quickly; fast.

A·pach·e (ə·pach'ē), *n., pl.* A·pach·es, A·pach·e. member of a tribe of warlike, nomadic Indians living in the SW United States.

a·pache (ə·päsh'; ə·pash'), *n.* one of a band of roughs and criminals of Paris, Brussels, etc. [< F; special use of *Apache*]

ap·a·nage (ap'ə·nij), *n.* appanage.

ap·a·re·jo (ap'ə·rā'hō), *n., pl.* -jos. *Am., S.W.* a kind of packsaddle. [< Sp.]

a·part (ə·pärt'), *adv.* 1. to pieces; in pieces; in separate parts: *take the watch apart.* 2. away from each other: *keep the dogs apart.* 3. to one side; aside: *he stood apart from the others.* 4. separately; independently: *view each idea apart.* [< F *à part* to the side. See PART.] —a·part'ness, *n.*

a·part·heid (ä·pärt'hāt), *n. South African.* racial segregation. [Du., separateness < *apart* separate < F *à part*]

a·part·ment (ə·pärt'mənt), *n.* 1. *Am.* a set of rooms in a building for a single household. 2. *U.S.* a single room.

ap·a·thet·ic (ap'ə·thet'ik), ap·a·thet·i·cal (-ə·kəl), *adj.* 1. with little interest or desire for action; indifferent. 2. lacking in feeling. —ap'a·thet'i·cal·ly, *adv.*

ap·a·thy (ap'ə·thi), *n., pl.* -thies. 1. lack of interest or desire for activity; indifference. 2. lack of feeling. [< L < Gk., < *a-* without + *pathos* feeling]

ape (āp), *n., v.,* aped, ap·ing. —*n.* 1. any of various large, tailless monkeys that can stand almost erect and walk on two feet. Chimpanzees, gorillas, orang-utans, and gibbons are apes. 2. any monkey. 3. person who imitates or mimics. —*v.* imitate; mimic. [OE *apa*] —ape'like', *adj.*

Ap·en·nines (ap'ə·nīnz), *n.pl.* mountain system extending north and south in Italy.

a·pe·ri·ent (ə·pir'i·ənt), *Med.* —*adj.* laxative. —*n.* a mild laxative. [< L, < *aperire* open]

a·pe·ri·tif, a·pé·ri·tif (ä·pā·rē·tēf'; *Fr.* ä·pā·rē·tēf'), *n. French.* 1. alcoholic drink taken as an appetizer. 2. appetizer.

ap·er·ture (ap'ər·chủr; -chər), *n.* 1. an opening; gap; hole. 2. in a telescope, camera, etc., the diameter of the exposed part of a lens. [< L *apertura* < *aperire* open. Doublet of OVERTURE.] —**ap′er·tured,** *adj.*

a·pet·al·ous (ā·pet′əl·əs), *adj. Bot.* having no petals.

a·pex (ā′peks), *n., pl.* **a·pex·es, ap·i·ces.** 1. the highest point; tip. 2. climax. [< L]

a·pha·sia (ə·fā′zhə), *n. Pathol.* loss of the ability to use or understand words. [< NL < Gk., < *a*– not + *phanai* speak] —**a·pha·si·ac** (ə·fā′zi·ak), *adj., n.* —**a·pha·sic** (ə·fā′zik; –sik), *adj., n.*

a·phe·li·on (ə·fē′li·ən; a–), *n., pl.* **–li·a** (–li·ə). *Astron.* point most distant from the sun, in the orbit of a planet or comet. [< NL < Gk. *apo*– away from + *helios* sun]

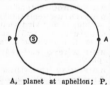

A, planet at aphelion; P, same planet at perihelion; S, sun.

a·phid (ā′fid; af′id),
a·phis (ā′fis; af′is), *n., pl.* **a·phids; aph·i·des** (af′ə·dēz). a very small insect that lives by sucking juices from plants; plant louse. [< NL *aphis*] —**a·phid·i·an** (ə·fid′i·ən), *adj., n.*

aph·o·rism (af′ə·riz·əm), *n.* a short sentence stating a general truth; maxim; proverb. [< Med.L < Gk. *aphorismos* definition < *apo*– off + *horizein* to limit < *horos* boundary] —**aph′o·rist,** *n.* —**aph′o·ris′tic,** *adj.* —**aph′o·ris′ti·cal·ly,** *adv.*

aph·ro·dis·i·ac (af′rə·diz′i·ak), *Med.* —*adj.* exciting sexual desire; erotic. —*n.* an aphrodisiac drug or food.

Aph·ro·di·te (af′rə·dī′tē), *n.* the Greek goddess of love and beauty, identified by the Romans with Venus.

a·pi·ar·y (ā′pi·er′i), *n., pl.* **–ar·ies.** place where bees are kept. [< L, < *apis* bee] —**a·pi·a·rist** (ā′pi·ə·rist), *n.*

ap·i·cal (ap′ə·kəl; ā′pə–), *adj.* of or at the apex; forming the apex. —**ap′i·cal·ly,** *adv.*

ap·i·ces (ap′ə·sēz; ā′pə–), *n.* pl. of apex.

a·pi·cul·ture (ā′pə·kul′chər), *n.* the raising and caring for bees; beekeeping. [< L *apis* bee + E *culture*] —**a′pi·cul′tur·al,** *adj.* —**a′pi·cul′tur·ist,** *n.*

a·piece (ə·pēs′), *adv.* for each one; each.

ap·ish (āp′ish), *adj.* 1. like an ape. 2. senselessly imitative. 3. foolish; silly. —**ap′ish·ly,** *adv.* —**ap′ish·ness,** *n.*

a·plen·ty (ə·plen′ti), *adv. Colloq.* in plenty.

a·plomb (ə·plom′), *n.* self-possession; poise. [< F, < *à plomb* according to the plummet. See PLUMB.]

a·poc·a·lypse (ə·pok′ə·lips), *n.* 1. revelation. 2. the Apocalypse, last book of the New Testament. [< L < Gk., < *apo*– off, un– + *kalyptein* cover]

a·poc·a·lyp·tic (ə·pok′ə·lip′tik), **a·poc·a·lyp·ti·cal** (–tə·kəl), *adj.* 1. of the Apocalypse. 2. like a revelation; giving a revelation. —**poc′a·lyp′ti·cal·ly,** *adv.*

a·poc·o·pe (ə·pok′ə·pē), *n.* the dropping out of the last sound, syllable, or letter in a word. *Th′* for *the* is an example of apocope. [< L < Gk., < *apo*– off + *koptein* cut]

A·poc·ry·pha (ə·pok′rə·fə), *n.pl.* 1. fourteen books included in the Roman Catholic Bible, but not accepted as genuine by Jews and Protestants. 2. apocrypha, writings or statements of doubtful authorship or authority.

a·poc·ry·phal (ə·pok′rə·fəl), *adj.* 1. of doubtful authorship or authority. 2. false; counterfeit; sham. 3. Apocryphal, of the Apocrypha. —**a·poc′ry·phal·ly,** *adv.* —**a·poc′ry·phal·ness,** *n.*

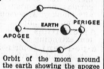

Orbit of the moon around the earth showing the apogee

ap·o·gee (ap′ə·jē), *n.* 1. furthermost point; highest point. 2. *Astron.* point most distant from the earth in the orbit of a planet, comet,

etc. [< F < Gk., < *apo*– away from + *ge* or *gaia* earth] —**ap′o·ge′al, ap′o·ge′an,** *adj.*

A·pol·lo (ə·pol′ō), *n., pl.* **–los.** 1. the Greek and Roman god of the sun, poetry, music, prophecy, and healing. 2. an extremely handsome young man.

A·pol·lyon (ə·pol′yən), *n. Bible.* the Devil.

ap·o·lo·get·ic (ə·pol′ə·jet′ik), **ap·o·lo·get·i·cal** (–ə·kəl), *adj.* 1. making an apology; expressing regret; acknowledging a fault; excusing failure. 2. defending by speech or writing. —**a·pol′o·get′i·cal·ly,** *adv.*

ap·o·lo·get·ics (ə·pol′ə·jet′iks), *n.* branch of theology that deals with the defense of Christianity on the basis of reason.

ap·o·lo·gi·a (ap′ə·lō′ji·ə), *n.* statement in defense or justification; apology.

a·pol·o·gist (ə·pol′ə·jist), *n.* person who defends an idea, belief, religion, etc., in speech or writing; a defender.

a·pol·o·gize (ə·pol′ə·jīz), *v.* **–gized, –giz·ing.** 1. make an apology; express regret. 2. make a defense in speech or writing. —**a·pol′o·giz′er,** *n.*

ap·o·logue (ap′ə·lôg; –log), *n.* fable with a moral: *Aesop's fables are apologues.*

a·pol·o·gy (ə·pol′ə·ji), *n., pl.* **–gies.** 1. words of regret for an offense or accident. 2. defense in speech or writing: *an apology for the Christian religion.* 3. a poor substitute; makeshift. [< L < Gk. *apologia* a speech in defense, ult. < *apo*– off + *legein* speak] —**Syn.** 2. justification.

ap·o·phthegm (ap′ə·them), *n.* apothegm. —**ap·o·phtheg·mat·ic** (ap′ə·theg·mat′ik), **ap′·o·phtheg·mat′i·cal,** *adj.*

ap·o·plec·tic (ap′ə·plek′tik), *adj.* Also, **ap′o·plec′ti·cal.** 1. of or causing apoplexy. 2. suffering from apoplexy. 3. showing symptoms of a tendency to apoplexy. —*n.* person who has or is likely to have apoplexy. —**ap′o·plec′ti·cal·ly,** *adv.*

ap·o·plex·y (ap′ə·plek′si), *n. Pathol.* sudden loss or impairment of the power to feel or think or move, caused by injury to the brain when a blood vessel breaks or the blood supply becomes obstructed. [< LL < Gk. *apoplexia*, < *apo*– off, from + *plessein* strike]

a·port (ə·pôrt′; ə·pōrt′), *adv. Naut.* to the port side; to the left.

a·pos·ta·sy (ə·pos′tə·si), *n., pl.* **–sies.** complete forsaking of one's religion, faith, principles, or political party. [< LL < Gk., < *apo*– away from + *stenai* stand]

a·pos·tate (ə·pos′tāt; –tit), *n.* person guilty of apostasy. —*adj.* guilty of apostasy; unfaithful.

a·pos·ta·tize (ə·pos′tə·tīz), *v.*, **–tized, –tiz·ing.** forsake completely one's religion, faith, principles, or political party.

a pos·te·ri·o·ri (ā pos·tir′i·ô′rī; –rī; –ō′–), from particular cases to a general rule. 2. based on actual observation or experience. [< Med.L, from what comes after] —**Ant.** 1, 2. a priori.

a·pos·tle (ə·pos′əl), *n.* 1. Apostle, one of the twelve disciples chosen by Christ to go forth and preach the gospel to all the world. 2. any early Christian leader or missionary. 3. the first Christian missionary to any country or region. 4. leader of any reform movement or belief. 5. *Am.* one of the council of twelve officials of the Mormon Church who help administer the affairs of the church. [< L < Gk. *apostolos* messenger < *apo*– off + *stellein* send] —**a·pos′tle·ship,** *n.*

Apostles' Creed, statement of belief that contains the fundamental doctrines of Christianity.

ap·os·tol·ic (ap′əs·tol′ik), **ap·os·tol·i·cal** (–ə·kəl), *adj.* 1. of or having to do with apostles, esp. the twelve Apostles. 2. according to the beliefs and teachings of the Apostles. 3. of the Pope; papal. —**ap′os·tol′i·cal·ly,** *adv.* —**ap·os·tol·i·cism** (ap′əs·tol′ə·siz·əm), *n.* —**a·pos·to·lic·i·ty** (ə·pos′tə·lis′ə·ti), *n.*

Apostolic See, bishopric of the Pope.

a·pos·tro·phe[1] (ə·pos′trə·fē), *n.* sign (′) used to show: a. omission of one or more letters, as in *o'er* for *over, thro'* for *through.* b. the possessive forms of nouns, as in *John's book, the lions' den.*

c. certain plurals, as in *two o's, four 9's in 9,999.* [< F < LL < Gk. *apostrophos* (*prosodia*) omission (mark) < *apostrephein* avert, get rid of. See APOSTROPHE².] ▶ The **apostrophe** is used: (1) to indicate genitive (possessive) case of nouns and of the indefinite pronouns (*anyone, nobody, someone*): *Dorothy's first picture, the companies' original charters, everybody's business;* (2) to show the omission of one or more letters in contractions: *can't, I'm, I'll, it's* [it is]; (3) in plurals of figures, letters of the alphabet, and words being discussed as words: *three e's, the 1920's, the first of the two that's* (there is a growing tendency to omit this apostrophe); (4) to show that certain sounds represented in the usual spelling were not spoken: *Good mornin'.*

a·pos·tro·phe² (ə·pos′trə·fē), *n.* words addressed to an absent person as if he were present or to a thing or idea as if it could appreciate them. [< LL < Gk., < *apo-* away from + *strephein* turn] —**ap·os·troph·ic** (ap′əs·trof′ik), *adj.*

a·pos·tro·phize (ə·pos′trə·fīz), *v.,* –**phized,** –**phiz·ing.** 1. stop in a speech, poem, etc., and address some person or thing, usually with emotion. 2. address an apostrophe to. 3. mark with an apostrophe.

apothecaries' measure, system of units used in the U.S. in compounding and dispensing liquid drugs.

apothecaries' weight, system of weights used in mixing drugs and filling prescriptions.

a·poth·e·car·y (ə·poth′ə·ker′i), *n., pl.* –**car·ies.** 1. druggist. 2. *Brit., Obs.* person who prescribed medicines and sold them. [< LL *apothecarius* warehouseman, < L *apotheca* storehouse < Gk., < *apo-* away + *tithenai* put]

ap·o·thegm (ap′ə·them), *n.* a short, forceful saying; maxim. Also, **apophthegm.** [< Gk. *apophthegma* < *apo-* forth + *phthengesthai* utter] —**ap·o·theg·mat·ic** (ap′ə·theg·mat′ik), **ap′o·theg·mat′i·cal,** *adj.* —**ap′o·theg·mat′i·cal·ly,** *adv.*

a·poth·e·o·sis (ə·poth′i·ō′sis; ap′ə·thē′ə·sis), *n., pl.* –**ses** (–sēz). 1. raising of a human being to the rank of a god; deification. 2. glorification; exaltation. 3. a glorified ideal. [< L < Gk., ult. < *apo-* + *theos* god]

a·poth·e·o·size (ə·poth′i·ə·sīz; ap′ə·thē′ə·sīz), *v.,* –**sized,** –**siz·ing.** 1. make a god of; deify. 2. glorify; exalt.

app., 1. apparent; apparently. 2. appendix.

Ap·pa·la·chi·ans (ap′ə·lā′chi·ənz, –lach′i-ənz; –lā′chənz, –lach′ənz), or **Appalachian Mountains,** *n.pl.* chief mountain system of E North America, extending from Quebec to Alabama.

ap·pall, ap·pal (ə·pôl′), *v.,* –**palled,** –**pall·ing.** fill with horror; dismay; terrify. [< OF *apallir* become or make pale < *a-* (< L *ad-*) + *pale* PALE¹]

ap·pall·ing (ə·pôl′ing), *adj.* dismaying; terrifying; horrifying. —**ap·pall′ing·ly,** *adv.*

ap·pa·nage (ap′ə·nij), *n.* 1. land, property, or money set aside to support the younger children of kings, princes, etc. 2. person's assigned portion; rightful property. 3. a natural accompaniment; adjunct. Also, **apanage.** [< F, < *apaner* give bread to, ult. < L *ad-* + *panis* bread]

ap·pa·ra·tus (ap′ə·rā′təs; –rat′əs), *n., pl.* –**tus, –tus·es.** 1. things necessary to carry out a purpose or for a particular use: *chemical apparatus.* 2. any complex appliance or piece of machinery for a particular purpose. [< L, preparation, < *ad-* + *parare* make ready]

ap·par·el (ə·par′əl), *n., v.,* –**eled, –el·ing;** *esp. Brit.* –**elled, –el·ling.** —*n.* 1. clothing; dress. 2. *Archaic.* equipment. —*v.* clothe; dress up. [< OF, < *apareiller* clothe, ult. < L *ad-* + *par* equal] —Syn. *n.* 1. raiment, garb, attire.

ap·par·ent (ə·par′ənt; ə·pâr′-), *adj.* 1. plain to see; so plain that one cannot help seeing it; easily understood. 2. according to appearances; seeming: *the apparent truth was really a lie.* 3. entitled to inherit a throne, title, etc.: *heir apparent.* 4. visible to the sight. [< OF < L, < *ad-* to + *parere* come in sight] —**ap·par′ent-**

ness, *n.* —Syn. 1. evident, unmistakable, certain, obvious.

ap·par·ent·ly (ə·par′ənt·li; ə·pâr′–), *adv.* 1. seemingly. 2. clearly; plainly; obviously.

ap·pa·ri·tion (ap′ə·rish′ən), *n.* 1. ghost; phantom. 2. appearance of something strange, remarkable, or unexpected. 3. act of appearing; appearance. —**ap′pa·ri′tion·al,** *adj.*

ap·peal (ə·pēl′), *n.* 1. attraction; interest. 2. an earnest request; call for help, favor, mercy, etc. 3. *Law.* **a.** a request to have a case heard again before a higher court or judge. **b.** right to have a case heard again. 4. a call to a recognized authority for proof or decision: *an appeal to truth.* —*v.* 1. be attractive, interesting, or enjoyable. 2. make an earnest request; apply for help, sympathy, etc. 3. *Law.* **a.** ask that a case be taken to a higher court or judge to be heard again. **b.** apply for a retrial of (a case) before a higher court. 4. call on a recognized authority for a decision. [< OF < L, *ad-* up + *pellare* call] —**ap·peal′a·ble,** *adj.* —**ap·peal′er,** *n.* —**ap·peal′ing,** *adj.* —**ap·peal′ing·ly,** *adv.* —**ap·peal′ing·ness,** *n.* —Syn. *n.* 2. plea, entreaty, petition, solicitation.

ap·pear (ə·pir′), *v.* 1. be seen; come in sight: *the sun appeared on the horizon.* 2. seem; look: *he appears very old.* 3. be published: *the book appeared in the autumn.* 4. present oneself publicly or formally: *appear on the stage.* 5. become known to the mind: *it appears that we must go.* 6. stand before an authority: *appear in court.* [< OF < L, < *ad-* + *parere* come in sight] —**ap·pear′er,** *n.*

ap·pear·ance (ə·pir′əns), *n.* 1. act of appearing. 2. the coming into court of a party to a law suit. 3. outward look; aspect. 4. outward show or seeming: *keep up appearances.* 5. apparition. —Syn. 3. air, mien, countenance. 4. semblance, guise.

ap·pease (ə·pēz′), *v.,* –**peased,** –**peas·ing.** 1. satisfy, as an appetite or desire: *appease one's hunger.* 2. make calm; quiet. 3. give in to the demands of (esp. a potential enemy): *Chamberlain appeased Hitler at Munich.* [< OF, < *a* to (< L *ad-*) + *pais* peace < L *pax*] —**ap·peas′a·ble,** *adj.* —**ap·pease′ment,** *n.* —**ap·peas′er,** *n.* —**ap·peas′ing·ly,** *adv.*

ap·pel·lant (ə·pel′ənt), *n.* person who appeals. —*adj.* appellate.

ap·pel·late (ə·pel′it), *adj.* 1. appealed to. 2. having the power to reëxamine and reverse the decisions of a lower court. [< L *appellatus,* pp. See APPEAL.]

ap·pel·la·tion (ap′ə·lā′shən), *n.* 1. name; title. 2. act or mode of naming.

ap·pel·la·tive (ə·pel′ə·tiv), *n.* 1. name; title. 2. a common noun. —*adj.* that names. —**ap·pel′la·tive·ly,** *adv.*

ap·pend (ə·pend′), *v.* add; attach. [< L, < *ad-* on + *pendere* hang]

ap·pend·age (ə·pen′dij), *n.* 1. thing attached; addition. 2. *Biol.* any of various external or subordinate parts, such as a leg, fin, tail, etc. —**ap·pend′aged,** *adj.*

ap·pend·ant, ap·pend·ent (ə·pen′dənt), *adj.* added; attached. —*n.* appendage; addition.

ap·pen·dec·to·my (ap′ən·dek′tə·mi), *n., pl.* –**mies.** *Am., Surg.* removal of the vermiform appendix by surgical operation.

ap·pen·di·ci·tis (ə·pen′də·sī′tis), *n. Am., Pathol.* inflammation of the vermiform appendix.

ap·pen·dix (ə·pen′diks), *n., pl.* –**dix·es, –di·ces** (–də·sēz). 1. addition at the end of a book or document. 2. outgrowth of some part of the body, esp. the vermiform appendix. [< L. See APPEND.] ▶ The English plural *appendixes* is rapidly overtaking the Latin *appendices* and is more frequent except in quite formal usage.

ap·per·cep·tion (ap′ər·sep′shən), *n.* 1. *Psychol.* assimilation of a new perception by means of a mass of ideas already in the mind. 2. clear perception; full understanding. [< F < NL. See PERCEPTION.] —**ap′per·cep′tive,** *adj.* —**ap′per·cep′tive·ly,** *adv.*

ap·per·tain (ap′ər·tān′), *v.* belong as a part;

pertain; relate. [< OF < LL, < L *ad-* to + *per-tinere* PERTAIN]

ap·pe·tite (ap′ə·tīt), *n.* 1. desire for food. 2. desire to satisfy a need. [< OF < L *appetitus* < *ad-* + *petere* seek] —**Syn.** 1, 2. hunger, craving, longing.

ap·pe·tiz·er (ap′ə·tīz′ər), *n.* something that arouses the appetite or gives relish to food.

ap·pe·tiz·ing (ap′ə·tīz′ing), *adj.* exciting the appetite. —**ap′pe·tiz′ing·ly,** *adv.*

ap·plaud (ə·plôd′), *v.* 1. express approval by clapping hands, shouting, etc. 2. express approval of in this way. 3. approve; praise. [< L, < *ad-* + *plaudere* clap] —**ap·plaud′er,** *n.* —**Syn.** 2. acclaim.

ap·plause (ə·plôz′), *n.* 1. approval expressed by clapping the hands, shouting, etc. 2. approval; praise. —**Syn.** 2. commendation.

ap·ple (ap′əl), *n.* 1. the firm, fleshy fruit of a tree of the rose family widely grown in temperate regions. 2. the tree. 3. any of various other fruits or fruitlike products, as the oak apple. [OE *æppel*]

ap·ple·jack (ap′əl·jak′), *n.* Am. an intoxicating liquor distilled from apple cider.

ap·ple·sauce (ap′əl·sôs′), *n.* 1. Am. apples cut in pieces and cooked with sugar and water until soft. 2. Slang. nonsense.

ap·pli·ance (ə·plī′əns), *n.* 1. thing like a tool, small machine, etc., used in doing something; device. 2. an applying.

ap·pli·ca·ble (ap′lə·kə·bəl; ə·plik′ə-), *adj.* capable of being applied. —**ap′pli·ca·bil′i·ty,** ap′pli·ca·ble·ness, *n.* —**ap′pli·ca·bly,** *adv.* —**Syn.** appropriate, suitable, fitting.

ap·pli·cant (ap′lə·kənt), *n.* person who applies (for money, position, help, office, etc.).

ap·pli·ca·tion (ap′lə·kā′shən), *n.* 1. act of putting to use; use. 2. act of applying or putting on. 3. ways of using; reference; relevancy. 4. thing applied. 5. a making of a request. 6. a request. 7. continued effort; close attention. —**ap′pli·ca′tive,** ap·pli·ca·to·ry (ap′lə·kə·tô′ri, -tō′-), *adj.*

ap·plied (ə·plīd′), *adj.* put to practical use.

ap·pli·qué (ap′lə·kā′), *n., v.,* -quéd, -qué·ing, *adj.* —*n.* ornaments made of one material sewed or otherwise fastened on another. —*v.* trim or ornament with appliqué. —*adj.* trimmed in this way. [< F, < *appliquer* APPLY]

ap·ply (ə·plī′), *v.,* -plied, -ply·ing. 1. put: *apply paint to a house.* 2. put to practical use: *apply a law.* 3. be useful or suitable; fit: *when does this rule apply?* 4. use for a special purpose: *apply a sum of money to charity.* 5. Appliqué make a request: *apply for a job.* 6. use (a word or words) appropriately with reference to a person or thing: *apply a nickname.* 7. set to work and stick to it: *he applied himself to learning French.* [< OF *aplier* < L, < *ad-* on + *plicare* fold, lay] —**ap·pli′er,** *n.* —**Syn.** 5. petition, solicit.

ap·pog·gia·tu·ra (ə·poj′ə·tur′ə; -tyur′ə), *n.* Music. grace note. [< Ital., < *appoggiare* lean, ult. < L *ad-* on + < *podium* PODIUM]

ap·point (ə·point′), *v.* 1. name for an office or position; choose: *this man was appointed postmaster.* 2. decide on; set: *appoint a time for the meeting.* 3. fix; prescribe: *God appointed death as punishment for sin.* 4. furnish; equip: *a well-appointed office.* [< OF *apointer,* ult. < L *ad-* to + *punctum* a POINT] —**ap·point′a·ble,** *adj.* —**ap·point′er,** *n.* —**Syn.** 1. designate. 4. supply.

ap·point·ee (ə·poin′tē′; ap′oin·tē′; ə·poin′tē), *n.* person appointed.

ap·poin·tive (ə·poin′tiv), *adj.* Am. filled by appointment. —**ap·poin′tive·ly,** *adv.*

ap·point·ment (ə·point′mənt), *n.* 1. act of naming for an office or position; choosing. 2. office or position. 3. act of ordaining. 4. engagement to be somewhere or to meet someone. 5. appointments, furniture; equipment. —**Syn.** 2. post.

Ap·po·mat·tox (ap′ə·mat′əks), *n.* village in C Virginia where Lee surrendered to Grant, April 9, 1865.

ap·por·tion (ə·pôr′shən; ə·pōr′-), *v.* divide and give out in fair shares; distribute according to some rule. [< F, ult. < L *ad-* to + *portio* portion] —**ap·por′tion·er,** *n.* —**ap·por′tion·ment,** *n.*

ap·pose (ə·pōz′), *v.,* -posed, -pos·ing. 1. put next; place side by side. 2. put (one thing to another). [< F, < *a-* to + *poser* put, POSE] —**ap·pos′a·ble,** *adj.*

ap·po·site (ap′ə·zit), *adj.* appropriate; suitable; apt. [< L *appositus* < *ad-* near + *ponere* place] —**ap′po·site·ly,** *adv.* —**ap′po·site·ness,** *n.*

ap·po·si·tion (ap′ə·zish′ən), *n.* 1. act of putting side by side. 2. Gram. a. a placing together in the same grammatical relation. b. relation of two words or phrases when the second is added to the first as an explanation. In ''Mr. Brown, our neighbor, has a new car,'' *Mr. Brown* and *neighbor* are in apposition. 3. position side by side. —**ap′po·si′tion·al,** *adj.* —**ap′po·si′tion·al·ly,** *adv.*

ap·pos·i·tive (ə·poz′ə·tiv), Gram. —*n.* noun added to another noun as an explanation; phrase or clause in apposition. —*adj.* placed in apposition. —**ap·pos′i·tive·ly,** *adv.*

ap·prais·al (ə·prāz′əl), *n.* 1. an appraising. 2. estimate of the value.

ap·praise (ə·prāz′), *v.,* -praised, -prais·ing. 1. estimate the value, amount, quality, etc., of. 2. set a price on; fix the value of. [< *praise,* ? after *prize³, apprize²*] —**ap·prais′a·ble,** *adj.* —**ap·praise′ment,** *n.* —**ap·prais′er,** *n.* —**ap·prais′ing·ly,** *adv.*

ap·pre·ci·a·ble (ə·prē′shi·ə·bəl; -shə·bəl), *adj.* enough to be felt or estimated. —**ap·pre′ci·a·bly,** *adv.*

ap·pre·ci·ate (ə·prē′shi·āt), *v.,* -at·ed, -at·ing. 1. recognize the worth or quality of; think highly of: *appreciate good food.* 2. be thankful for. 3. be sensitive to: *a blind man cannot appreciate color.* 4. make or form an estimate of the value or worth of: *appreciate knowledge.* 5. value or estimate correctly. 6. Am. raise (currency, property, etc.) in value. 7. Am. rise in value. [< L *apretiatus* appraised < *ad-* + *pretium* price. Doublet of APPRIZE².] —**ap·pre′ci·a′tor,** *n.* —**ap·pre·ci·a·to·ry** (ə·prē′shi·ə·tô′ri; -tō′-; -shə-), *adj.* —**Syn.** 1. esteem, prize. 4. appraise.

ap·pre·ci·a·tion (ə·prē′shi·ā′shən), *n.* 1. a valuing. 2. sympathetic understanding. 3. favorable criticism. 4. Am. a rise in value.

ap·pre·ci·a·tive (ə·prē′shi·ā′tiv; -shə·tiv), *adj.* having or showing appreciation. —**ap·pre′ci·a′tive·ly,** *adv.* —**ap·pre′ci·a′tive·ness,** *n.*

ap·pre·hend (ap′ri·hend′), *v.* 1. anticipate with fear; dread. 2. arrest. 3. understand. [< L, < *ad-* upon + *prehendere* seize]

ap·pre·hen·si·ble (ap′ri·hen′sə·bəl), *adj.* capable of being apprehended. —**ap′pre·hen′si·bil′i·ty,** *n.*

ap·pre·hen·sion (ap′ri·hen′shən), *n.* 1. expectation of evil; fear; dread. 2. arrest. 3. understanding. 4. opinion; notion.

ap·pre·hen·sive (ap′ri·hen′siv), *adj.* 1. afraid; anxious; worried. 2. quick to understand; able to learn. —**ap′pre·hen′sive·ly,** *adv.* —**ap′pre·hen′sive·ness,** *n.*

ap·pren·tice (ə·pren′tis), *n., v.,* -ticed, -tic·ing. —*n.* 1. person learning a trade or art. In return for instruction the apprentice agrees to work for his master a certain length of time with little or no pay. 2. beginner; learner. —*v.* bind or take as an apprentice. [< OF *aprentis* < *aprendre* learn. See APPREHEND.] —**ap·pren′tice·ment,** *n.* —**ap·pren′tice·ship,** *n.*

ap·prise¹, ap·prize¹ (ə·prīz′), *v.,* -prised, -pris·ing; -prized, -priz·ing. inform; notify; advise. [< F *appris,* pp. of *apprendre* learn. See APPREHEND.]

ap·prize², ap·prise² (ə·prīz′), *v.,* -prized, -priz·ing; -prised, -pris·ing. appraise. [< OF < L *appretiare.* Doublet of APPRECIATE.] —**ap·prize′ment,** ap·prise′ment, *n.* —**ap·priz′er,** ap·pris′er, *n.*

ap·proach (ə·prōch′), *v.* 1. come near or nearer to: *approach the gate.* 2. come near: *winter ap-*

proaches. **3.** come near in quality, character, or state: *approach manhood.* **4.** make advances or overtures to. **5.** *Am.* make overtures to (a person) in an effort to bribe or corrupt him. **6.** bring near to something. —*n.* **1.** act of coming near. **2.** way by which a place or a person can be reached; access. **3.** approximation; likeness. **4.** approach or approaches, a. advance; overture. b. *Am.* advance made to a person in an effort to influence his actions improperly. **5.** *Golf.* stroke toward the green. [< OF *aprochier* << LL, < L *ad-* to + *prope* near] —**ap·proach′a·ble,** *adj.* —**ap·proach′a·bil′i·ty, ap·proach′a·ble·ness,** *n.*

ap·pro·ba·tion (ap′rə·bā′shən), *n.* **1.** approval. **2.** sanction. [< L, < *approbare* APPROVE]

ap·pro·pri·ate (*adj.* ə·prō′pri·it; *v.* ə·prō′pri·āt), *adj., v.,* -at·ed, -at·ing. —*adj.* suitable; proper: *clothes appropriate for school wear.* —*v.* **1.** set apart for some special use: *appropriate money for roads.* **2.** take for oneself. [< LL, < *ad-* to + *proprius* one's own] —**ap·pro′pri·ate·ly,** *adv.* —**ap·pro′pri·ate·ness,** *n.* —**ap·pro′pri·a·tive,** *adj.* —**ap·pro′pri·a′tor,** *n.* —Syn. *adj.* fitting, meet. —*v.* **1.** allot.

ap·pro·pri·a·tion (ə·prō′pri·ā′shən), *n.* **1.** sum of money or other thing appropriated. **2.** an appropriating. **3.** being appropriated.

ap·prov·al (ə·prüv′əl), *n.* **1.** approving; favorable opinion. **2.** consent; sanction. **3.** on approval, with permission to return (an article purchased). —Syn. **1.** commendation.

ap·prove (ə·prüv′), *v.,* -proved, -prov·ing. **1.** think or speak well of; be pleased with. **2.** speak or think favorably (*of*); commend. **3.** sanction; consent to: *Congress approved the bill.* **4.** prove to be; show. [< OF < L, < *ad-* to + *probus* good] —**ap·prov′a·ble,** *adj.* —**ap·prov′er,** *n.* —**ap·prov′ing·ly,** *adv.* —Syn. **1.** praise, laud, like. **3.** authorize, endorse, ratify, uphold.

approx., approximately.

ap·prox·i·mate (*adj.* ə·prok′sə·mit; *v.* ə·prok′sə·māt), *adj., v.,* -mat·ed, -mat·ing. —*adj.* **1.** nearly correct. **2.** very like. **3.** very near. —*v.* **1.** come near to; approach: *the crowd approximated a thousand people.* **2.** come near; be almost equal: *approximate the truth.* **3.** bring near. [< L, < *ad-* to + *proximus* nearest < *prope* near] —**ap·prox′i·mate·ly,** *adv.*

ap·prox·i·ma·tion (ə·prok′sə·mā′shən), *n.* **1.** an approximating; approach. **2.** nearly correct amount; close estimate.

ap·pur·te·nance (ə·pér′tə·nəns), *n.* **1.** an added thing; accessory. **2.** a minor right or privilege. [< AF. See APPERTAIN.]

ap·pur·te·nant (ə·pér′tə·nənt), *adj.* pertaining; belonging (*to*).

Apr., April.

a·pri·cot (ā′prə·kot; ap′rə-), *n.* **1.** a roundish, orange-colored fruit somewhat like both a peach and a plum. **2.** tree that it grows on. **3.** pale orange-yellow. [earlier *apricock* (< Pg. *albricoque*), later infl. by F *abricot* < Pg. < Sp. < Ar. < Gk. < L, < *prae* before + *coquere* cook, ripen]

A·pril (ā′prəl), *n.* the fourth month of the year, containing 30 days. [< L *aprilis*]

April fool, person who gets fooled on April 1.

April Fools′ Day, April 1, a day observed by fooling people with tricks and jokes.

a pri·o·ri (ā pri·ô′rī; ā prī·ô′rī; -ō′-), **1.** from a general rule to a particular case. **2.** based on opinion or theory rather than on actual observation or experience. [< Med.L, from (something) previous] —Ant. **1, 2,** a posteriori.

a·pron (ā′prən), *n.* **1.** garment worn over the front part of the body to cover or protect clothes. **2.** something resembling an apron in use or shape. [< OF *naperon,* dim. of *nape* < L *nappa* napkin; ME *a napron* taken as *an apron*]

ap·ro·pos (ap′rə·pō′), *adv.* **1.** fittingly; opportunely. **2.** apropos of, concerning; with regard to. —*adj.* fitting; suitable. [< F *à propos* to the purpose]

apse (aps), *n. Archit.* a semicircular or many-sided arched or vaulted recess in a church, usually at the east end. [< L < Gk. *hapsis* loop, arch < *haptein* fasten]

apt (apt), *adj.* **1.** fitted by nature; likely: *apt to make mistakes.* **2.** suitable; fitting: *an apt reply.* **3.** quick to learn: *an apt pupil.* [< L *aptus* joined, fitted] —**apt′ly,** *adv.* —**apt′ness,** *n.* —Syn. **1.** prone, inclined, liable. **2.** apposite, appropriate. **3.** clever, bright. ➤ See likely for usage note.

apt., *pl.* **apts.** apartment.

ap·ter·ous (ap′tər·əs), *adj. Zool.* wingless.

ap·ter·yx (ap′tər·iks), *n., pl.* -ter·yx·es (-tər·ik·siz). any of several wingless birds of New Zealand with hairlike feathers, now almost extinct; kiwi. [< NL, < *a-* without + Gk. *pteryx* wing]

ap·ti·tude (ap′tə·tüd; -tūd), *n.* **1.** natural tendency; ability. **2.** readiness in learning; quickness to understand. **3.** special fitness. [< LL *aptitudo.* See APT.]

Aq., aq., water. [< L *aqua*]

aq·ua for·tis (ak′wə fôr′tis; ā′kwə), nitric acid. [< L, strong water]

aq·ua·lung (ak′wə·lung′), *n.* a diving device consisting of cylinders of compressed air strapped to the diver's back and a glass mask placed over the eyes and nose. The supply of air to the diver is regulated automatically by a valve.

aq·ua·ma·rine (ak′wə·mə·rēn′), *n.* **1.** a transparent, bluish-green precious stone, a variety of beryl. **2.** bluish green. [< F < L *aqua marina* sea water]

aq·ua·plane (ak′wə·plān′), *n., v.,* -planed, -plan·ing. —*n.* a wide board on which a person rides for sport as he is towed by a speeding motorboat. —*v.* ride on such a board for sport. [< L *aqua* water + E *plane*[1]]

aq·ua re·gi·a (ak′wə rē′ji·ə; ā′kwə), mixture of nitric acid and hydrochloric acid. [< NL, royal water; because it dissolves gold]

a·quar·i·um (ə·kwãr′i·əm), *n., pl.* a·quar·i·ums, a·quar·i·a (ə·kwãr′i·ə). **1.** pond, tank, or glass bowl in which living fish, water animals, and water plants are kept. **2.** place where collections of living fish, etc., are exhibited. [< L, of water, < *aqua* water]

A·quar·i·us (ə·kwãr′i·əs), *n., gen.* A·quar·i·i (ə·kwãr′i·ī). **1.** a northern constellation supposed to represent a man pouring water out of a vase. **2.** the 11th sign of the zodiac.

a·quat·ic (ə·kwat′ik; ə·kwot′-), *adj.* **1.** growing or living in water. **2.** taking place in or on water: *aquatic sports.* —*n.* **1.** plant or animal that lives in water. **2.** aquatics, sports that take place in or on water. —**a·quat′i·cal·ly,** *adv.*

aq·ua·tint (ak′wə·tint′), *n.* **1.** process in which spaces, not lines, are etched by acid. **2.** etching made by this process.

aq·ua vi·tae (ak′wə vī′tē; ā′kwə), **1.** alcohol. **2.** brandy; whiskey, etc. [< NL, water of life]

aq·ue·duct (ak′wə·dukt), *n.* **1.** an artificial channel or large pipe for bringing water from a distance. **2.** structure that supports such a channel or pipe. **3.** *Anat.* canal or passage in the body. [< L, < *aqua* water + *ducere* lead, convey]

a·que·ous (ā′kwi·əs; ak′wi-), *adj.* **1.** of water; like water; watery. **2.** containing water.

aqueous humor, watery liquid that fills the space in the eye between the cornea and the lens.

aq·ui·line (ak′wə·līn′; -lin), *adj.* **1.** of or like an eagle. **2.** curved like an eagle's beak; hooked. [< L, < *aquila* eagle]

A·qui·nas (ə·kwī′nəs), *n.* **Saint Thomas,** 1225?-1274, Roman Catholic theologian and philosopher.

Aq·ui·taine (ak′wə·tān; ak′wə·tān′), *n.* region in SW France.

Ar, *Chem.* argon.

Ar., Arabic.

Ar·ab (ar′əb), *n.* **1.** native or inhabitant of Arabia; member of a Semitic race now widely scattered over SW and S Asia and N, E, and central Africa. **2.** one of a breed of swift, graceful horses. —*adj.* of the Arabs or Arabia.

ar·a·besque (ar′ə·besk′), *n.* an elaborate and fanciful design of flowers, leaves, geometrical figures, etc. —*adj.* **1.** carved or painted in arabesque. **2.** elaborate; fanciful. [< F < Ital. *ara-besco* < *Arabo* Arab]

A·ra·bi·a (ə·rā′bi·ə), *n.* a large peninsula in SW Asia. —**A·ra′bi·an**, *adj., n.*

Arabian Sea, part of the Indian Ocean between Arabia and India.

Ar·a·bic (ar′ə·bik), *adj.* of or coming from the Arabs; belonging to Arabia. —*n.* the Semitic language of the Arabs.

Arabic numerals or **figures,** figures 1, 2, 3, 4, 5, 6, 7, 8, 9, 0.

ar·a·ble (ar′ə·bəl), *adj.* fit for plowing: *arable land.* [< L, < *arare* plow]

Arab League, a loose confederation, since 1945, of Egypt, Iraq, Lebanon, Saudi Arabia, Syria, Jordan, Yemen, and other Arab states.

a·rach·nid (ə·rak′nid), *n.* any of a large group of small arthropods including spiders, scorpions, mites, etc. [< Gk. *arachne* spider, web] —**a·rach·ni·dan** (ə·rak′nə·dən), *adj., n.*

Ar·a·gon (ar′ə·gon), *n.* region in NE Spain, formerly a kingdom.

A·ral Sea (ar′əl), or **Lake Aral,** inland sea in SW Soviet Union, near the Caspian Sea.

Aram., Aramaic.

Ar·a·ma·ic (ar′ə·mā′ik), *n.* a Semitic language or group of dialects, including Syriac and the language spoken in Palestine at the time of Christ. —*adj.* of or in Aramaic.

Ar·a·rat (ar′ə·rat), *n.* mountain in E Turkey.

ar·ba·lest, ar·ba·list (är′bə·list), *n.* powerful crossbow with a steel bow. [< OF *arba-leste* < LL, < L *arcus* bow + *ballista* military engine, ult. < Gk. *bal-lein* throw] —**ar′ba-lest·er, ar′ba·list·er,** *n.*

Man using an arbalest

ar·bi·ter (är′bə·tər), *n.* **1.** person chosen to decide a dispute. **2.** person with full power to decide. [< L, orig., one who approaches (two disputants) < *ad—* up to + *baetere* go] —Syn. **1.** judge, umpire, arbitrator.

ar·bi·tra·ble (är′bə·trə·bəl), *adj.* capable of being decided by arbitration.

ar·bit·ra·ment (är·bit′rə·mənt), *n.* decision by an arbitrator or arbiter.

ar·bi·trar·y (är′bə·trer′i), *adj.* **1.** based on one's own wishes, notions, or will; not going by rule or law. **2.** capricious. **3.** tyrannical. —**ar·bi·trar·i·ly** (är′bə·trer′ə·li; *emphatic* är′bə·trār′ə·li), *adv.* —**ar′bi·trar′i·ness,** *n.* —Syn. **2.** willful. **3.** despotic, dictatorial.

ar·bi·trate (är′bə·trāt), *v.,* –**trat·ed,** –**trat·ing. 1.** give a decision in a dispute; act as arbiter. **2.** settle by arbitration. **3.** submit to arbitration. [< L, < *arbiter* ARBITER] —**ar′bi·tra′tive,** *adj.*

ar·bi·tra·tion (är′bə·trā′shən), *n.* settlement of a dispute by the decision of somebody chosen to be a judge, umpire, or arbiter. —**ar′bi·tra′tion·al,** *adj.*

ar·bi·tra·tor (är′bə·trā′tər), *n.* person chosen to decide a dispute. —**ar′bi·tra′tor·ship,** *n.* —Syn. judge, umpire.

ar·bi·tress (är′bə·tris), *n.* woman arbiter.

ar·bor¹, *esp. Brit.* **ar·bour** (är′bər), *n.* a shady place formed by trees or shrubs or by vines growing on latticework. [< AF *erber* < L, < *herba* plant]

ar·bor² (är′bər), *n.* the main shaft or axle of a machine. [< F *arbre*]

Arbor Day, *Am.* day observed in many States of the United States by planting trees.

ar·bo·re·al (är·bô′ri·əl; –bō′–), *adj.* **1.** of or like trees. **2.** living in or among trees: *an arboreal animal.*

ar·bo·res·cent (är′bə·res′ənt), *adj.* like a tree in structure or growth; branching.

ar·bo·re·tum (är′bə·rē′təm), *n., pl.* –**tums,** –**ta** (–tə). botanical garden of trees and shrubs. [< L]

ar·bor vi·tae (är′bər vī′tē), an evergreen tree of the pine family often planted for hedges. [< L, tree of life]

ar·bu·tus (är·būt′əs), *n.* **1.** *Am.* plant that has clusters of fragrant pink or white flowers and grows in patches on the ground; Mayflower; trailing arbutus. **2.** shrub or tree of the heath family, that has clusters of large white flowers and scarlet berries. [< L]

arc (ärk), *n., v.,* arced (ärkt), arc·ing (är′king), or arcked, arck·ing. —*n.* **1.** any part of a circle or other curved line. **2.** *Elect.* a curved stream of brilliant light or sparks formed as a current jumps from one conductor to another. —*v.* form an electric arc. [< L *arcus* bow]

Arc (ärk), *n.* **Jeanne d′.** See Joan of Arc.

ar·cade (är·kād′), *n.* **1.** passageway with an arched roof. **2.** any covered passageway. **3.** row of arches supported by columns. [< F < Pr. *arcado* < OPr. *arca* ARCH¹] —**ar·cad′ed,** *adj.*

Arcs of circles

Ar·ca·di·a (är·kā′di·ə), *n.* a mountain district in the S part of ancient Greece, famous for the simple, contented life of its people. —**Ar·ca′di·an,** *adj., n.*

Ar·ca·dy (är′kə·di), *n. Poetic.* Arcadia.

ar·ca·num (är·kā′nəm), *n., pl.* –**nums,** –**na** (–nə). a secret; mystery. [< L, (thing) hidden, < *arca* chest]

arch¹ (ärch), *n.* **1.** a curved structure that bears the weight of the material above it. **2.** monument forming an arch or arches. **3.** archway. **4.** instep. **5.** something like an arch. —*v.* **1.** bend into an arch; curve. **2.** furnish with an arch. **3.** form an arch over; span. [< OF, < VL *arca,* irreg. var. of L *arcus* bow] —**arched,** *adj.*

arch² (ärch), *adj.* **1.** chief. **2.** playfully mischievous. [< *arch–*] —**arch′ly,** *adv.* —**arch′ness,** *n.*

arch–, *prefix.* chief; principal, as in *archbishop, archduke, archfiend.* [< L < Gk. *arch(e)–, archi–* < *archein* be first, lead]

arch., **1.** archaic; archaism. **2.** Arch., Archbishop. **3.** Also, **archit.** architecture.

ar·chae·ol·o·gy (är′ki·ol′ə·ji), *n.* study of the people, customs, and life of the remote past by excavating and classifying the remains of ancient cities, tools, monuments, etc. Also, **archeology.** [< Gk., < *archaios* ancient + *logos* discourse] —**ar·chae·o·log·i·cal** (är′ki·ə·loj′ə·kəl), **ar′chae·o·log′ic,** *adj.* —**ar′chae·o·log′i·cal·ly,** *adv.* —**ar′chae·ol′o·gist,** *n.*

ar·cha·ic (är·kā′ik), *adj.* **1.** no longer in general use. **2.** old-fashioned; out-of-date. **3.** ancient. [< Gk. *archaikos,* ult. < *arche* beginning] —**ar·cha′i·cal·ly,** *adv.*

ar·cha·ism (är′ki·iz·əm; –kā–), *n.* **1.** word or expression no longer in general use. *In sooth* is an archaism meaning *in truth.* **2.** use of something out of date in language or art. —**ar′cha·ist,** *n.* —**ar′cha·is′tic,** *adj.*

arch·an·gel (ärk′ān′jəl), *n.* angel of a higher rank. [< L < Gk. See ARCH–, ANGEL.]

Arch·an·gel (ärk′ān′jəl), *n.* seaport in N Russia, on the White Sea.

arch·bish·op (ärch′bish′əp), *n.* bishop of the highest rank.

arch·bish·op·ric (ärch′bish′əp·rik), *n.* **1.** church district governed by an archbishop. **2.** position, rank, or dignity of an archbishop.

arch·dea·con (ärch′dē′kən), *n.* assistant to a bishop in the Church of England. —**arch·dea·con·ate** (ärch′dē′kən·it), *n.* —**arch′dea′con·ship,** *n.*

arch·dea·con·ry (ärch′dē′kən·ri), *n., pl.* –**ries.** position, rank, or residence of an archdeacon.

arch·di·o·cese (ärch′dī′ə·sis; –sēs), *n.* church district governed by an archbishop.

arch·du·cal (ärch′dü′kəl; –dū′–), *adj.* of an archduke or an archduchy.

arch·duch·ess (ärch′duch′is), *n.* **1.** wife or widow of an archduke. **2.** princess of the former ruling house of Austria.

arch·duch·y (ärch′duch′i), *n., pl.* –**duch·ies.** territory under the rule of an archduke or archduchess.

arch·duke (ärch′dük′; -dūk′), *n*. prince of the former ruling house of Austria.

ar·che·go·ni·um (är′kə·gō′ni·əm), *n*., *pl.* -ni·a (-ni·ə). *Bot.* the female reproductive organ in ferns, mosses, etc. [< NL, ult. < Gk. *arche* beginning + *gonos* race] —ar′che·go′ni·al, *adj.* —ar·che·go·ni·ate (är′kə·gō′ni·it; -āt), *adj.*

ar·che·ol·o·gy (är′ki·ol′ə·ji), *n*. archaeology. —ar·che·o·log·i·cal (är′ki·ə·loj′ə·kəl), ar′che·o·log′ic, *adj.* —ar′che·o·log′i·cal·ly, *adv.* —ar′che·ol′o·gist, *n*.

arch·er (är′chər), *n*. 1. person who shoots with a bow and arrows. 2. Archer, Sagittarius. [< AF < L, < *arcus* bow]

arch·er·y (är′chər·i), *n*. 1. practice or art of shooting with bows and arrows. 2. archers. 3. weapons of an archer.

ar·che·type (är′kə·tīp), *n*. an original model or pattern from which copies are made, or out of which later forms develop. [< L < Gk.] —ar·che·typ·al (är′kə·tīp′əl), ar·che·typ·i·cal (är′kə·tīp′ə·kəl), *adj.*

arch·fiend (ärch′fēnd′), *n*. 1. chief fiend. 2. Satan.

ar·chi·e·pis·co·pal (är′ki·i·pis′kə·pəl), *adj.* of an archbishop.

ar·chi·e·pis·co·pate (är′ki·i·pis′kə·pit; -pāt), *n*. archbishopric.

Ar·chi·me·des (är′kə·mē′dēz), *n*. 287?–212 B.C., Greek mathematician, physicist, and inventor. —Ar·chi·me·de·an (är′kə·mē′di·ən; -mə·dē′ən), *adj.*

ar·chi·pel·a·go (är′kə·pel′ə·gō), *n*., *pl.* -gos, -goes. 1. sea having many islands in it. 2. group of many islands. [< Ital., < *arci*- chief (ult. < Gk. *archi*-) + *pelago* sea (ult. < Gk. *pelagos*); orig., the Aegean]

archit., architecture.

ar·chi·tect (är′kə·tekt), *n*. 1. person whose profession is to design buildings and superintend their construction. 2. person skilled in architecture. 3. maker; creator. [< L < Gk., *archi*- chief + *tekton* builder]

ar·chi·tec·ton·ic (är′kə·tek·ton′ik), *adj.* 1. having to do with architecture, construction, or design. 2. showing skill in construction or design. 3. directive.

ar·chi·tec·ture (är′kə·tek′chər), *n*. 1. science or art of building, including design, construction, and decorative treatment. 2. style or special manner of building: *Greek architecture made much use of columns.* 3. construction. 4. a building; structure. —ar′chi·tec′tur·al, *adj.* —ar′chi·tec′tur·al·ly, *adv.* —Syn. 4. edifice.

ar·chi·trave (är′kə·trāv), *n*. 1. the main beam resting on the top of a column. See the diagram of entablature. 2. the molding around a door, window, etc. [< Ital., < *archi*- chief (ult. < Gk.) + *trave* beam (< L *trabs*)]

ar·chives (är′kīvz), *n.pl.* 1. place where public records or historical documents are kept. 2. public records or historical documents. [< L < Gk. *archeia* < *arche* government] —ar·chi·val, *adj.* —ar·chi·vist (är′kə·vist), *n*.

ar·chon (är′kon), *n*. chief magistrate in ancient Athens. —ar′chon·ship, *n*.

arch·priest (ärch′prēst′), *n*. 1. chief priest. 2. chief assistant to a bishop and dean of a cathedral chapter. —arch′priest′hood, *n*.

arch·way (ärch′wā′), *n*. 1. passageway with an arch above it. 2. an arch covering a passageway.

arc lamp or **light**, *Am.* lamp in which the light comes from an electric arc.

arc·tic (ärk′tik; är′tik), *adj.* 1. of or near the North Pole or the north polar region. 2. extremely cold; frigid. —*n*. 1. the north polar region. 2. arctics, *Am.* warm, waterproof overshoes. [< L < Gk. *arktikos* of the Bear (constellation) < *arktos* bear]

Arctic Circle, arctic circle, 1. imaginary boundary of the north polar region running parallel to the equator at 23°30′ south of the North Pole. 2. the polar region surrounded by this parallel.

Arctic Ocean, ocean of the north polar region.

Arctic Zone, region between the Arctic Circle and the North Pole.

Arc·tu·rus (ärk·tür′əs; -tyur′-), *n*. a very bright star in the northern sky.

ar·den·cy (är′dən·si), *n*. being ardent.

ar·dent (är′dənt), *adj.* 1. full of zeal; very enthusiastic; eager. 2. burning; fiery; hot. 3. glowing. [< F < L, < *ardere* burn] —ar′dent·ly, *adv.* —ar′dent·ness, *n*. —Syn. 1. fervent, keen. —Ant. 1. indifferent.

ar·dor, *esp. Brit.* **ar·dour** (är′dər), *n*. 1. warmth of emotion; great enthusiasm. 2. burning heat. [< L, < *ardere* burn] —Syn. 1. fervor, zeal. —Ant. 1. indifference.

ar·du·ous (är′jü·əs), *adj.* 1. hard to do; requiring much effort; difficult. 2. using up much energy; strenuous. 3. hard to climb; steep. [< L *arduus* steep] —ar′du·ous·ly, *adv.* —ar′du·ous·ness, *n*.

are[1] (är; *unstressed* ər), *v*. plural of the present indicative of *be*: *we are, you are, they are.* [OE (Northumbrian) *aron*]

are[2] (âr; är), *n*. in the metric system, a surface measure equal to 100 square meters, or 119.6 square yards. [< F < L *area* AREA]

ar·e·a (âr′i·ə), *n*. 1. amount of surface; extent of surface: *an area of 600 square feet.* 2. extent; range; scope. 3. region: *the Rocky Mountain area.* 4. level space. 5. *Brit.* sunken space at the entrance of a cellar or basement. [< L, piece of level ground] —ar′e·al, *adj.* —Syn. 3. tract.

ar·e·a·way (âr′i·ə·wā′), *n*. *Am.* area serving as a passageway between buildings.

a·re·na (ə·rē′nə), *n*. 1. space where contests or shows take place. 2. any place of conflict and trial. [< later var. of L *harena* sand; because floor of Roman arenas was sand]

ar·e·na·ceous (ar′ə·nā′shəs), *adj.* sandy.

aren't (ärnt), are not.

Ar·es (âr′ēz), *n*. the Greek god of war, identified with the Roman god Mars.

ar·ga·li (är′gə·li), *n*., *pl.* -li. 1. a large wild sheep of Asia with big curved horns. 2. the bighorn, or other wild sheep.

ar·gent (är′jənt), *n*. *Archaic or Poetic.* silver. —*adj.* silvery. [< F < L *argentum*]

Ar·gen·ti·na (är′jən·tē′nə), *n*. country in S South America. —Ar·gen·tine (är′jən·tēn; -tīn), *adj.*, *n*. —Ar·gen·tin·e·an (är′jən·tin′i·ən), *n*., *adj.*

ar·gil (är′jil), *n*. clay, esp. potter's clay. [< F < L < Gk., < *argos* shining]

Ar·give (är′jiv; -gīv), *n*., *adj.* Greek.

Ar·go (är′gō), *n*. *Gk. Legend.* ship in which Jason and his companions sailed in search of the Golden Fleece.

ar·gon (är′gon), *n*. *Chem.* a colorless, odorless, inert gas, A or Ar, an element that forms a very small part of the air. Argon is used in electric light bulbs and radio tubes. [< NL < Gk. *argos* idle < *a*- without + *ergon* work]

Ar·go·naut (är′gə·nôt), *n*. 1. *Gk. Legend.* one of the men who sailed with Jason in search of the Golden Fleece. 2. *Am.* person who went to California in 1849 in search of gold. —Ar′go·nau′tic, *adj.*

Ar·gonne (är′gon), *n*. forest in NE France; site of battles in World War I.

ar·go·sy (är′gə·si), *n*., *pl.* -sies. 1. large merchant ship. 2. fleet of such ships. [< Ital. *Ragusea* ship of Ragusa, Italian port formerly trading extensively with England]

ar·got (är′gō; -gət), *n*. jargon or slang used by a group of persons: *argot of thieves.* [< F] —ar·got·ic (är·got′ik), *adj.*

ar·gue (är′gū), *v*., -gued, -gu·ing. 1. discuss with someone who disagrees. 2. bring forward reasons for or against: *argue a question.* 3. persuade by giving reasons: *he argued me into going.* 4. try to prove by reasoning; maintain: *Columbus argued that the world was round.* 5. indicate; show; prove: *her rich clothes argue her to be wealthy.* 6. raise objections; dispute. [< OF

< L, < *arguere* make clear] —ar′gu·a·ble, *adj.* —ar′gu·er, *n.* —Syn. 1. debate. 5. demonstrate, denote, imply.

ar·gu·ment (är′gyə·mənt), *n.* 1. discussion by persons who disagree. 2. process of reasoning. 3. reason or statement intended to persuade or convince. 4. short statement of what is in a book, poem, etc. —Syn. 1. debate.

ar·gu·men·ta·tion (är′gyə·men·tā′shən), *n.* 1. process of arguing. 2. discussion.

ar·gu·men·ta·tive (är′gyə·men′tə·tiv), *adj.* 1. fond of arguing. 2. controversial. —ar′gu·men′ta·tive·ly, *adv.* —ar′gu·men′ta·tive·ness, *n.*

Ar·gus (är′gəs), *n.* 1. *Gk. Legend.* giant with a hundred eyes, killed by Hermes. 2. a watchful guardian.

Ar·gus-eyed (är′gəs·īd′), *adj.* watchful.

a·ri·a (ä′ri·ə), *n.* air or melody; melody for a single voice with instrumental or vocal accompaniment. [< Ital. < L *aer* air < Gk.]

Ar·i·ad·ne (ar′i·ad′nē), *n. Gk. Legend.* daughter of a king of Crete, who gave Theseus a ball of thread to help him find his way out of the Labyrinth of the Minotaur.

Ar·i·an¹ (ãr′i·ən; ar′-), *adj.* of or pertaining to Arius or his doctrines. —*n.* believer in the doctrines of Arius. —Ar′i·an·ism, *n.*

Ar·i·an² (ãr′i·ən; ar′-), *adj., n.* Aryan.

ar·id (ar′id), *adj.* 1. dry; barren: *desert lands are arid.* 2. dull; uninteresting. [< L, < *arere* be dry] —a·rid·i·ty (ə·rid′ə·ti), ar′id·ness, *n.* —ar′id·ly, *adv.* —Syn. 2. lifeless.

Ar·ies (ãr′ēz; -i·ēz), *n., gen.* A·ri·e·tis (ə·rī′ə·tis). 1. a northern constellation that was thought of as arranged in the shape of a ram. 2. the first sign of the zodiac; the Ram.

a·right (ə·rīt′), *adv.* correctly; rightly.

ar·il (ar′il), *n. Bot.* accessory covering of certain seeds. [< NL < Med.L *arilli* raisins]

ar·il·late (ar′ə·lāt), *adj. Bot.* having an aril.

a·rise (ə·rīz′), *v.,* a·rose, a·ris·en, a·ris·ing. 1. rise up; get up: *the audience arose.* 2. move upward: *vapors arose from the swamp.* 3. come into being or action; come about; appear; begin: *a great wind arose, accidents arise from carelessness.* 4. originate. 5. rebel. [OE *ārīsan*] —Syn. 2. ascend, mount. ➤ See rise for usage note.

Ar·is·ti·des (ar′əs·tī′dēz), *n.* 530?–468? B.C., Athenian statesman and general.

ar·is·toc·ra·cy (ar′əs·tok′rə·si), *n., pl.* –cies. 1. a ruling body of nobles; nobility. 2. any class that is superior because of birth, intelligence, culture, or wealth; upper class. 3. government in which a privileged upper class rules. 4. country or state having such a government. 5. government by the best citizens. [< LL < Gk., < *aristos* best + *krateein* rule]

a·ris·to·crat (ə·ris′tə·krat; ar′is-), *n.* 1. person who belongs to the aristocracy; noble. 2. person who has the tastes, opinions, manners, etc., of the upper classes. 3. person who favors government by an aristocracy.

a·ris·to·crat·ic (ə·ris′tə·krat′ik; ar′is-), **a·ris·to·crat·i·cal** (-ə·kəl), *adj.* 1. belonging to the upper classes. 2. like an aristocrat in manners; proud. 3. having to do with an aristocracy. —a·ris′to·crat′i·cal·ly, *adv.*

Ar·is·toph·a·nes (ar′əs·tof′ə·nēz), *n.* 448?–385? B.C., Greek writer of comedies.

Ar·is·tot·le (ar′əs·tot′əl), *n.* 384–322 B.C., Greek philosopher. —Ar·is·to·te·lian (ar′is·tə·tēl′yən; -tē′li·ən), *adj., n.* —Ar′is·to·te′lian·ism, *n.*

arith., arithmetic; arithmetical.

a·rith·me·tic (ə·rith′mə·tik), *n.* 1. science of positive, real numbers; art of computing by figures. 2. textbook or handbook of arithmetic. [< L < Gk. *arithmetike* < *arithmos* number] —ar·ith·met·i·cal (ar′ith·met′ə·kəl), *adj.* —ar′ith·met′i·cal·ly, *adv.*

arithmetical progression. See progression (def. 2).

a·rith·me·ti·cian (ə·rith′mə·tish′ən; ar′ith-), *n.* expert in arithmetic.

Ar·i·us (ãr′i·əs; ə·rī′əs), *n.* d. 336 A.D., Alexan-

drian priest who asserted that Christ the Son was subordinate to God the Father.

Ariz., Arizona.

Ar·i·zo·na (ar′ə·zō′nə), *n.* a Southwestern State of the United States. *Capital:* Phoenix. *Abbrev.:* Ariz. —Ar′i·zo′nan, Ar·i·zo·ni·an (ar′-ə·zō′ni·ən), *adj., n.*

ark (ärk), *n.* 1. *Bible.* the large boat in which Noah saved himself, his family, and a pair of each kind of animal from the Flood. 2. *Colloq.* any large, clumsy boat. 3. *Bible.* the repository of the Jewish tables of the law. [< L *arca* chest]

Ark., Arkansas.

Ar·kan·sas (är′kən·sô *for 1;* är′kən·sô, är·kan′zəs *for 2*), *n.* 1. a Southern State of the United States. *Capital:* Little Rock. *Abbrev.:* Ark. 2. river flowing from C Colorado SE into the Mississippi. —Ar·kan·san (är·kan′zən), *n., adj.*

Ar·ling·ton (är′ling·tən), *n.* the largest national cemetery in the United States, in NE Virginia.

arm¹ (ärm), *n.* 1. part of the human body between the shoulder and the hand. 2. forelimb of an animal. 3. anything resembling an arm in shape or use: *the arm of a chair, an arm of the sea.* 4. power; authority. 5. arm in arm, with arms linked. 6. with open arms, cordially. [OE *earm*] —arm′less, *adj.*

arm² (ärm), *n.* 1. weapon. See arms. 2. branch of the military service, such as the infantry, artillery, cavalry, etc. —*v.* 1. supply with weapons. 2. prepare for war. 3. provide with a protective covering. [< L *arma,* pl.] —arm′er, *n.*

ar·ma·da (är·mä′də; -mā′-), *n.* 1. fleet of warships. 2. fleet of airplanes. 3. the Armada, the Spanish fleet sent to attack England in 1588. [< Sp. < L *armata* < *armare* to arm. Doublet of ARMY.]

ar·ma·dil·lo (är′mə·dil′ō), *n., pl.* –los. any of several small burrowing animals of South America and southern North America, with an armorlike shell of bony plates. [< Sp., dim. of *armado* armed (one) < L, < *armare* arm]

Armadillo
(total length 2 ½ ft.)

Ar·ma·ged·don (är′mə·ged′ən), *n. Bible.* 1. place of a great and final conflict between the forces of good and evil. Rev. 16:16. 2. any great and final conflict.

ar·ma·ment (är′mə·mənt), *n.* 1. war equipment and supplies. 2. the army, navy, and other military forces of a nation. 3. process of equipping or arming for war.

ar·ma·ture (är′mə·chúr; -chər), *n.* 1. armor. 2. a protective covering. 3. wire wound round and round a cable. 4. *Elect.* a. piece of soft iron placed in contact with the poles of a magnet. b. a revolving part of an electric relay, buzzer, etc. c. a movable part of an electric relay, buzzer, etc. [< L *armatura* < *armare* arm. Doublet of ARMOR.]

arm·chair (ärm′chãr′), *n.* chair with side pieces to support a person's arms or elbows.

Ar·me·ni·a (är·mē′ni·ə; -mēn′yə), *n.* a former country of W Asia, now divided among Turkey, Iran, and the Soviet Union. —Ar·me′ni·an, *adj., n.*

arm·ful (ärm′fúl), *n., pl.* –fuls. as much as one arm or both arms can hold.

arm·hole (ärm′hōl′), *n.* hole for the arm in a garment.

Ar·min·i·us (är·min′i·əs), *n.* 1560–1609, Dutch Protestant theologian who denied Calvin's doctrine of predestination. —Ar·min′i·an, *adj., n.*

ar·mi·stice (är′mə·stis), *n.* temporary stop in fighting; truce. [< NL *armistitium* < L *arma* arms + *sistere* stop, stand]

Armistice Day, Nov. 11, the anniversary of the end of World War I. See Veterans Day.

arm·let (ärm′lit), *n.* 1. an ornamental band for the upper arm. 2. a small inlet.

ar·mor, *esp. Brit.* **ar·mour** (är′mər), *n.* 1. a covering worn to protect the body in fighting. 2. any kind of protective covering. 3. *Am.* the steel or iron plates or other protective covering of a warship or fortification. —*v.* cover or protect with armor. [< OF *armeüre* < L *armatura* < *armare* arm. Doublet of ARMATURE.]

ar·mor·bear·er (är′mər-bâr′-ər), *n.* attendant who carried the armor or weapons of a warrior.

ar·mored, *esp. Brit.* **ar·moured** (är′mərd), *adj.* covered or protected with armor.

ar·mor·er, *esp. Brit.* **ar·mour·er** (är′mər-ər), *n.* 1. person who made or repaired armor. 2. manufacturer of firearms. 3. man in charge of firearms.

ar·mo·ri·al (är-mô′ri-əl; -mō′-), *adj.* of coats of arms or heraldry.

armorial bearings, the design of a coat of arms.

armor plate, steel or iron plating to protect warships, forts, etc. —**ar′mor-plat′ed,** *adj.*

ar·mor·y, *esp. Brit.* **ar·mour·y** (är′mər-i), *n., pl.* -mor·ies; *esp. Brit.* -mour·ies. 1. place where weapons are kept. 2. *Am.* place where weapons are made. 3. a building with a drill hall, offices, etc., for militia.

Armor: A, Helmet; B, Gorget; C, Gauntlet.

arm·pit (ärm′pit′), *n.* the hollow under the arm at the shoulder.

arms (ärmz), *n.pl.* 1. weapons. 2. fighting; war. 3. symbols and designs used in heraldry or by governments. 4. **bear arms,** serve as a soldier.

ar·my (är′mi), *n., pl.* -mies. 1. a large, organized group of soldiers trained and armed for war. 2. Often, **Army.** the military organization of a nation, exclusive of its navy. 3. any organized group of people: *the Salvation Army.* 4. a very large number; multitude. [< OF < L *armata.* Doublet of ARMADA.] —Syn. 1. troops. 4. throng, host.

army worm, *Am.* caterpillar that travels in large numbers and is destructive to crops.

ar·ni·ca (är′nə-kə), *n.* 1. a healing liquid used on bruises, sprains, etc., prepared from the dried flowers, leaves, or roots of a plant of the aster family. 2. the plant itself. [< NL]

Ar·nold (är′nəld), *n.* Benedict, 1741–1801, American general in the Revolutionary War who turned traitor.

a·roint (ə-roint′), *interj. Archaic.* begone!

a·ro·ma (ə-rō′mə), *n.* 1. fragrance; spicy odor. 2. distinctive fragrance or flavor; subtle quality. [< L < Gk., spice]

ar·o·mat·ic (ar′ə-mat′ik), *adj.* fragrant. —*n.* fragrant plant or substance. —**ar′o·mat′i·cal·ly,** *adv.*

a·rose (ə-rōz′), *v.* pt. of arise.

a·round (ə-round′), *adv., prep.* 1. in a circle about: *travel around the world.* 2. closely surrounding: *she had a coat around her shoulders.* 3. on all sides of: *woods lay around the house.* 4. *U.S. Colloq.* here and there in: *he leaves his books around the house.* 5. *U.S. Colloq.* somewhere near: *play around the house.* 6. *U.S. Colloq.* near in amount, number, etc., to: *that hat cost around five dollars.* 7. on the far side of: *just around the corner.* 8. **around the clock,** without stopping, closing, etc.: *work around the clock.* —*adv.* 1. in a circle. 2. in circumference: *the tree measures four feet around.* 3. on all sides: *a dense fog lay around.* 4. *U.S.* here and there: *we walked around to see the town.* 5. *U.S. Colloq.* somewhere near: *wait around awhile.* 6. in the opposite direction: *turn around.* ➤ See **round** for distinction in use between *around* and *round.*

a·rouse (ə-rouz′), *v.,* a·roused, a·rous·ing. 1. awaken. 2. stir to action; excite. —a·rous·al (ə-rouz′əl), *n.* —a·rous′er, *n.* —Syn. 2. stimulate, kindle.

ar·peg·gi·o (är-pej′i-ō; -pej′ō), *n., pl.* -gi·os. *Music.* a. the sounding of the notes of a chord in rapid succession instead of together. b. chord

sounded in this way. [< Ital., < *arpa* harp < Gmc.]

ar·que·bus (är′kwə-bəs), *n.* harquebus.

ar·raign (ə-rān′), *v.* 1. *Law.* bring before a court for trial. 2. call in question; find fault with. [< AF *arainer* < VL, < L *ad-* to + *ratio* account] —**ar·raign′er,** *n.* —**ar·raign′ment,** *n.*

ar·range (ə-rānj′), *v.,* -ranged, -rang·ing. 1. put in the proper order. 2. settle (a dispute). 3. come to an agreement. 4. plan; prepare. 5. adapt (a piece of music) to voices or instruments for which it was not written. [< OF, < *a* to + *rang* rank[1] < Gmc.] —**ar·range′a·ble,** *adj.* —**ar·rang′er,** *n.* —Syn. 1. group, sort, classify, organize. 2. adjust. 4. devise. —Ant. 1. jumble.

ar·range·ment (ə-rānj′mənt), *n.* 1. a putting or being put in proper order. 2. way or order in which things or persons are put. 3. adjustment; settlement. 4. Usually, **arrangements.** plan; preparation. 5. something arranged in a particular way, as a piece of music.

ar·rant (ar′ənt), *adj.* thoroughgoing; downright. [var. of *errant*] —**ar′rant·ly,** *adv.*

ar·ras (ar′əs), *n.* kind of tapestry. [named for *Arras,* a city in France]

ar·ray (ə-rā′), *v.* 1. arrange in order. 2. dress in fine clothes; adorn. —*n.* 1. order: *in battle array.* 2. display of persons or things. 3. military force; soldiers. 4. clothes; dress: *bridal array.* [< OF *a* to + *rei* order < Gmc.] —**ar·ray′er,** *n.* —Syn. *v.* 1. marshal. —*n.* 1. formation. 3. troops. 4. attire.

ar·ray·al (ə-rā′əl), *n.* an arraying; array.

ar·rear·age (ə-rir′ij), *n.* debts; arrears.

ar·rears (ə-rirz′), *n.pl.* 1. debts. 2. unfinished work. 3. in arrears, behind in payments, work, etc. [< OF *arere* < LL *ad retro* to the rear]

ar·rest (ə-rest′), *v.* 1. seize by legal authority. 2. catch and hold. 3. stop; check. —*n.* 1. a seizing by legal authority. 2. a stopping; checking. 3. any device for arresting motion in a mechanism. [< OF < VL, < L *ad-* + *re-* back + *stare* stand] —**ar·rest′er,** *n.* —**ar·rest′ment,** *n.* —Syn. *v.* 1. apprehend. 2. capture. 3. halt.

ar·riv·al (ə-rīv′əl), *n.* 1. act of arriving; a coming. 2. person or thing that arrives.

ar·rive (ə-rīv′), *v.,* -rived, -riv·ing. 1. reach the end of a journey; come to a place. 2. reach a point in any course of action: *arrive at a decision.* 3. be successful. 4. come, as a time, opportunity, etc.; occur. [< OF *ar(r)iver* < VL, < L *ad ripam* to the shore] —Ant. 1. depart. 3. fail.

ar·ro·gance (ar′ə-gəns), *n.* overbearing pride; haughtiness.

ar·ro·gant (ar′ə-gənt), *adj.* too proud; haughty. [< L, < *ad-* to + *rogare* ask] —**ar′ro·gant·ly,** *adv.* —Syn. overbearing, presumptuous. —Ant. humble.

ar·ro·gate (ar′ə-gāt), *v.,* -gat·ed, -gat·ing. 1. claim or take without right. 2. attribute or assign without good reasons. [< L, < *ad-* to + *rogare* ask] —**ar′ro·ga′tion,** *n.* —**ar′ro·ga′tor,** *n.*

ar·ron·disse·ment (ä-rôn′dēs·män′), *n., pl.* -ments (-män′). in France, the largest administrative subdivision of a department.

ar·row (ar′ō), *n.* 1. a slender, pointed shaft or stick for shooting from a bow. 2. anything resembling an arrow in shape or speed. 3. a sign (→) used to show direction or position. [OE *arwe*]

ar·row·head (ar′ō-hed′), *n.* 1. head or tip of an arrow. 2. plant with leaves shaped like arrowheads.

ar·row·root (ar′ō-rüt′; -rüt′), *n. Am.* 1. an easily digested starch made from the roots of a tropical American plant. 2. the plant itself.

Indian arrowhead

ar·row·wood (ar′ō-wud′), *n. Am.* viburnum or other shrub with a tough, straight stem.

ar·roy·o (ə-roi′ō), *n., pl.* -roy·os. *Am., S.W.* 1. the dry bed of a stream; gully. 2. a small river. [< Sp. < L *arrugia* mine shaft]

ar·se·nal (är′sə-nəl), *n.* a building for storing

or manufacturing weapons and ammunition for an army or navy. [< Ital. < Ar. *dār aṣ-ṣinā'a* house (of) the manufacturing]

ar·se·nate (är'sə·nāt; –nit), *n. Chem.* a salt of arsenic acid. **Arsenate of lead** is a poison that is used to kill insects.

ar·se·nic (*n.* är'sə·nik; *adj.* är·sen'ik), *n.* 1. a grayish-white chemical element, As, having a metallic luster and volatilizing when heated. 2. a violent poison that is a compound of this element, As₂O₃, a white, tasteless powder. —*adj.* Also, **ar·sen'i·cal.** of or containing arsenic. [< Gk. *arsenikon* < Heb. < OPers., golden]

ar·son (är'sən), *n.* the crime of intentionally setting fire to a building or other property. [< OF < LL *arsio* a burning < L *ardere* burn]

art¹ (ärt), *n.* 1. branch of learning appealing to the imagination, esp. drawing, painting, and sculpture, also architecture, poetry, music, dancing, etc. 2. these branches of learning as a group. 3. branch of learning that depends more on special practice than on general principles: *writing compositions is an art; grammar is a science.* 4. branch or division of learning: *literature is one of the liberal arts.* 5. skill. 6. human skill. 7. some kind of skill or practical application of skill: *cooking is a household art.* 8. principles; methods. 9. skillful act. 10. trick. [< OF < L *ars*]

art² (ärt), *v. Archaic or Poetic.* are. "Thou art" means "You are." [OE *eart*]

art., 1. article. 2. artillery. 3. artist.

Ar·te·mis (är'tə·mis), *n. Gk. Myth.* the goddess of the hunt, of the forests, of wild animals, and of the moon, identified by the Romans with Diana.

ar·te·ri·al (är·tir'i·əl), *adj.* 1. *Anat.* pertaining to or resembling the arteries. 2. *Physiol.* pertaining to the bright-red blood of the arteries. 3. having a main channel with many branches. —*ar·te'ri·al·ly, adv.*

ar·te·ri·o·scle·ro·sis (är·tir'i·ō·sklə·rō'sis), *n.* a hardening of the walls of the arteries that makes circulation of the blood difficult.

ar·ter·y (är'tər·i), *n., pl.* –ter·ies. 1. any of the blood vessels or tubes that carry blood from the heart to all parts of the body. 2. a main road; important channel. [< L < Gk. *arteria*]

ar·te·sian well (är·tē'zhən), a deep-drilled well. [< F *artésien* of Artois, province where such wells first existed]

art·ful (ärt'fəl), *adj.* 1. crafty; deceitful. 2. skillful; clever. 3. artificial. —*art'ful·ly, adv.* —*art'ful·ness, n.*

ar·thri·tis (är·thrī'tis), *n.* inflammation of a joint or joints. —*ar·thrit·ic* (är·thrit'ik), *adj.*

ar·thro·pod (är'thrə·pod), *n.* any of a phylum of invertebrate animals having segmented legs, such as the insects, arachnids, and crustaceans. —*ar·throp·o·dous* (är·throp'ə·dəs), *adj.*

Ar·thur (är'thər), *n.* 1. a legendary king of ancient Britain who gathered about him a famous group of knights. 2. Chester A., 1830–1886, the 21st president of the U.S., 1881–1885.

Ar·thu·ri·an (är·thûr'i·ən; –thyûr'–), *adj.* of King Arthur and his knights.

ar·ti·choke (är'ti·chōk), *n.* 1. a thistlelike plant whose flowering head is cooked and eaten. 2. the flowering head. 3. Jerusalem artichoke. [< Ital. < Provençal < Ar. *al-kharshūf*]

ar·ti·cle (är'tə·kəl), *n., v.,* –cled, –cling. —*n.* 1. a literary composition, complete in itself, but forming part of a magazine, newspaper, or book. 2. clause in a contract, treaty, statute, etc. 3. particular thing; item: *bread is a main article of food.* 4. one of the words *a, an,* or *the* or the corresponding words in certain other languages. *A* and *an* are indefinite articles; *the* is the definite article. —*v.* 1. bind by contract: *an apprentice articled to serve for seven years.* 2. bring charges; accuse. [< F < L *articulus,* dim. of *artus* joint]

ar·tic·u·lar (är·tik'yə·lər), *adj.* of the joints: *arthritis is an articular disease.*

ar·tic·u·late (*adj.* är·tik'yə·lit; *v.* är·tik'yə·lāt), *adj., v.,* –lat·ed, –lat·ing. —*adj.* 1. uttered in distinct syllables or words. 2. capable of speaking. 3. made up of distinct parts; distinct;

4. jointed; segmented. —*v.* 1. speak distinctly. 2. unite by joints. 3. fit together in a joint. [< L *articulatus* divided into single joints. See ARTICLE.] —*ar·tic'u·late·ly, adv.* —*ar·tic'u·late·ness, n.* —*ar·tic'u·la'tive, adj.* —*ar·tic'u·la'tor, n.*

ar·tic·u·la·tion (är·tik'yə·lā'shən), *n.* 1. way of speaking; enunciation. 2. an articulate sound. 3. joint. 4. act or manner of connecting by a joint or joints.

ar·ti·fact, ar·te·fact (är'tə·fakt), *n.* 1. anything made by human skill or work. 2. an artificial product. [< L *ars* art + *factus* made]

ar·ti·fice (är'tə·fis), *n.* 1. a clever stratagem or trick. 2. trickery; craft. 3. *Obs.* workmanship. [< F < L *artificium* < *arti–* art + *facere* make]

ar·tif·i·cer (är·tif'ə·sər), *n.* 1. skilled workman; craftsman. 2. maker.

ar·ti·fi·cial (är'tə·fish'əl), *adj.* 1. made by human skill or labor; not natural. 2. made as a substitute for or in imitation of; not real. 3. assumed; false; affected. 4. *Obs.* artful. —*ar'ti·fi'cial·ly, adv.* —*ar'ti·fi'cial·ness, n.*

ar·ti·fi·ci·al·i·ty (är'tə·fish'i·al'ə·ti), *n., pl.* –ties. 1. artificial quality or condition. 2. something unnatural or unreal.

ar·til·ler·y (är·til'ər·i), *n.* 1. mounted guns; cannon, as distinguished from small arms. 2. part of an army that uses and manages cannon. 3. science of ballistics and gunnery. [< OF, < *artiller* equip, ult. < *a–* + *tire* order]

ar·til·ler·y·man (är·til'ər·i·mən), **ar·til·ler·ist** (–ər·ist), *n., pl.* –men; –ists. *U.S.* soldier who belongs to the artillery.

ar·ti·san (är'tə·zən), *n.* workman skilled in some industry or trade; craftsman. [< F < Ital. *artigiano* < L *ars* art] —*Syn.* mechanic.

art·ist (är'tist), *n.* 1. person who paints pictures. 2. person who is skilled in any of the fine arts, such as sculpture, music, or literature. 3. person who does work with skill and good taste. [< F < Ital. *artista* < VL, < L *ars* art]

ar·tiste (är·tēst'), *n. French.* a very skillful performer or worker.

ar·tis·tic (är·tis'tik), **ar·tis·ti·cal** (–tə·kəl), *adj.* 1. of art or artists. 2. done with skill and good taste. 3. having good color and design. 4. having or showing appreciation of beauty. —*ar·tis'ti·cal·ly, adv.*

art·ist·ry (är'tis·tri), *n., pl.* –ries. artistic work; workmanship of an artist.

art·less (ärt'lis), *adj.* 1. without any trickery or deceit; simple. 2. natural. 3. without art; unskilled; ignorant. —*art'less·ly, adv.* —*art'less·ness, n.*

art·y (är'ti), *adj.,* art·i·er, art·i·est. *Colloq.* trying to be artistic. —*art'i·ness, n.*

ar·um (ār'əm), *n.* 1. a plant having heart-shaped or sword-shaped leaves and a partly hooded flower cluster. 2. calla lily. [< L < Gk. *aron*]

–ary, *suffix.* 1. place for ——, as in *library.* 2. collection of ——, as in *statuary.* 3. person or thing that is, does, belongs to, etc., ——, as in *commentary.* 4. of or pertaining to ——, as in *legendary.* 5. being; having the nature of ——, as in *supplementary.* 6. characterized by ——, as in *honorary.* [< L *–arius* or (neut.) *–arium*]

Ar·y·an (ār'i·ən; ar'–), *n.* 1. the assumed prehistoric language from which the Indo-European languages are derived. 2. person who spoke this language. 3. descendant of this prehistoric group of people. 4. in Nazi use, a non-Jew. —*adj.* 1. Indo-European. 2. of the Aryans. Also, **Arian.**

as¹ (az; *unstressed* əz), *adv.* 1. to the same degree or extent; equally: *as black as coal.* 2. for example: *some animals, as dogs and cats, eat meat.* —*conj.* 1. to the same degree or extent that: *she worked just so much as she was told to.* 2. in the same way that: *run as I do.* 3. during the time that; when; while: *she sang as she worked.* 4. because: *he was well paid, as he had done the work well.* 5. though: *brave as they were, the danger made them afraid.* 6. that the result was: *the child so marked the picture as to spoil it.* 7. **as for, as to,** about; concerning; referring to. 8. **as if, as though,** as it would be if. **9. as yet,** up to this time; so far. —*prep. Am.* in the character of; doing the work of: *who will act as teacher?* —*pron.* **1.** a condition or fact that: *she is very careful, as her work shows.* **2.** that: *do the same thing as I do.* [OE (unstressed) *ealswā* quite so. See ALSO.] ➤ **1.** as to and as for are often clumsy substitutes for a single preposition, usually *about* or *of.* **2.** For the conflict between as and like, see like[1]. **3.** As occurs most commonly as a conjunction, introducing several kinds of clauses: Degree or Manner: *... as far as I could.* Time = While: *As I was coming, he was going out.* Attendant Circumstance: *He told stories as we went along.* Cause: *As it was getting dark, we made for home.* Such a handy word is of course much used in speech, which often prefers counter words to more exact ones. But the very variety of possible uses makes *as* a problem in written English. It is necessary in comparisons (*We went as far as he did*) and for attendant circumstance (*As we walked along he told us stories*) though *while* is preferable if the emphasis is on the time or the action (*While we were walking along he told us stories*). As is weak in the sense of *because.* Usually *since,* more exact and emphatic in the sentence given here, or *because,* most emphatic, a little formal, would be better in writing and certainly would be better in formal English: *As it was almost time to go, we were getting more and more exasperated.* ➤ See also **because.**

as[2] (as), *n., pl.* **as·ses** (as'iz). **1.** ancient Roman pound, equal to twelve ounces. **2.** ancient Roman coin, worth a few cents. [< L]

As, *Chem.* arsenic.

AS, A.S., Anglo-Saxon.

as·a·fet·i·da, as·a·foet·i·da (as'ə-fet'ə-də), *n.* gum resin with a garliclike odor, used in medicine to prevent spasms. Also, **assafetida, assafoetida.** [< Med.L, < *asa* (< Pers. *azā*) mastic + L *fetidus* stinking]

as·bes·tos, as·bes·tus (as-bes'təs; az-), *n.* **1.** a mineral, a silicate of calcium and magnesium, that does not burn or conduct heat, usually occurring in fibers. **2.** a fireproof fabric made of these fibers. [< OF < L < Gk. *asbestos* unquenchable (orig., of quicklime), < *a-* not + *sbennunai* quench]

as·cend (ə·send'), *v.* **1.** go up; rise; move upward. **2.** climb; go to or toward the top of. **3.** go toward the source or beginning. **4.** go back in time. **5.** slope upward. [< L *ascendere* < *ad-* up + *scandere* climb] —**as·cend'a·ble, as·cend'i·ble,** *adj.* —**as·cend'er,** *n.* —Syn. **2.** scale.

as·cend·ance, as·cend·ence (ə·sen'dəns), *n.* ascendancy.

as·cend·an·cy, as·cend·en·cy (ə·sen'dən·si), *n.* controlling influence.

as·cend·ant, as·cend·ent (ə·sen'dənt), *adj.* **1.** ascending; rising. **2.** superior; dominant; ruling; controlling. —*n.* position of power; controlling influence.

as·cen·sion (ə·sen'shən), *n.* **1.** act of ascending; ascent. **2.** Ascension, **a.** the bodily passing of Christ from earth to heaven. **b.** Also, Ascension Day, a church festival in honor of this on the fortieth day after Easter. —**as·cen'sion·al,** *adj.*

As·cen·sion (ə·sen'shən), *n.* a British island in the S Atlantic.

as·cent (ə·sent'), *n.* **1.** act of going up; a rising. **2.** a climbing; upward movement. **3.** a going back toward a source or beginning. **4.** place or way that slopes up.

as·cer·tain (as'ər·tān'), *v.* find out with certainty; determine. [< OF, < *a-* + *certain* CERTAIN] —**as'cer·tain'a·ble,** *adj.* —**as'cer·tain'a·ble·ness, as'cer·tain·a·bil'i·ty,** *n.* —**as'cer·tain'a·bly,** *adv.* —**as'cer·tain'ment,** *n.*

as·cet·ic (ə·set'ik), *n.* **1.** person who practices unusual self-denial and devotion, or severe discipline of self for religious reasons. **2.** person who refrains from pleasures and comforts. —*adj.* Also, **as·cet'i·cal.** refraining from pleasures and comforts; self-denying. [< Gk., < *askeein* exercise; hence, discipline] —**as·cet'i·cal·ly,** *adv.*

as·cet·i·cism (ə·set'ə·siz·əm), *n.* **1.** life or habits of an ascetic. **2.** doctrine that by abstinence and self-denial a person can train himself to be in conformity with God's will.

as·cid·i·an (ə·sid'i·ən), *n. Zool.* sea animal with a tough saclike covering.

as·cid·i·um (ə·sid'i·um), *n., pl.* **-cid·i·a** (-sid'i·ə). *Bot.* a baglike or pitcherlike part. [< NL < Gk. *askidion,* dim. of *askos* bag]

a·scor·bic acid (ā·skôr'bik; ə-), *Biochem.* vitamin C, $C_6H_8O_6$.

as·cot (as'kət; -kot), *n.* necktie with broad ends, tied so that the ends may be laid flat, one across the other.

Man wearing an ascot tie

as·cribe (əs·krīb'), *v.,* **-cribed, -crib·ing. 1.** assign; attribute: *the police ascribed the automobile accident to fast driving.* **2.** consider as belonging: *men have ascribed their own characteristics to their gods.* [< OF < L, < *ad-* to + *scribere* write] —**as·crib'a·ble,** *adj.*

as·crip·tion (əs·krip'shən), *n.* **1.** act of ascribing. **2.** statement or words ascribing something.

a·sep·sis (ə·sep'sis; ā-), *n.* **1.** aseptic condition. **2.** aseptic methods or treatment.

a·sep·tic (ə·sep'tik; ā-), *adj.* free from germs causing infection. —**a·sep'ti·cal·ly,** *adv.*

a·sex·u·al (ā·sek'shü·əl), *adj. Biol.* **1.** having no sex. **2.** independent of sexual processes: *reproduction by spore formation is asexual.* —**a·sex·u·al·i·ty** (ā·sek'shü·al'ə·ti), *n.* —**a·sex'u·al·ly,** *adv.*

As·gard (as'gärd; az'-; äs'-), *n. Scand. Myth.* the home of the Norse gods and heroes.

ash[1] (ash), *n.* **1.** what remains of a thing after it has been thoroughly burned. **2.** powdered lava. [OE *æsce* ashes]

ash[2] (ash), *n.* **1.** timber or shade tree that has straight-grained wood. **2.** its tough, springy wood. [OE *æsc* the tree]

a·shamed (ə·shāmd'), *adj.* **1.** feeling shame. **2.** unwilling because of shame. —**a·sham·ed·ly** (ə·shām'id·li), *adv.* —**a·sham'ed·ness,** *n.*

ash·en[1] (ash'ən), *adj.* **1.** like ashes; pale as ashes. **2.** of ashes.

ash·en[2] (ash'ən), *adj.* **1.** of the ash tree. **2.** made from the wood of the ash tree.

ash·es (ash'iz), *n.pl.* **1.** what remains of a thing after it has been burned. **2.** remains; dead body.

ash·lar, ash·ler (ash'lər), *n.* **1.** a square stone used in building. **2.** masonry made of ashlars. [< OF < VL *axillarium* < *axis* plank]

a·shore (ə·shôr'; ə·shōr'), *adv., adj. Naut.* **1.** to the shore. **2.** on the shore.

Ash·to·reth (ash'tə·reth), *n.* Astarte.

Ash Wednesday, the first day of Lent.

ash·y (ash'i), *adj.,* **ash·i·er, ash·i·est. 1.** like ashes; pale as ashes. **2.** of ashes. **3.** covered with ashes.

A·sia (ā'zhə; ā'shə), *n.* the largest continent. China and India are in Asia.

Asia Minor, peninsula of W Asia, between the Black Sea and the Mediterranean. Also, **Anatolia.**

Asian flu or **Asiatic flu,** a kind of influenza caused by a new strain of virus, first identified in Hong Kong in early 1957.

A·si·at·ic (ā'zhi·at'ik; ā'shi-), **A·sian** (ā'zhən; ā'shən), *adj.* of or having to do with Asia or its people. —*n.* native of Asia. —**A'si·at'i·cal·ly,** *adv.*

a·side (ə·sīd'), *adv.* **1.** on one side; to one side; away: *move the table aside.* **2.** *Am.* out of one's thoughts, consideration, etc.: *put one's troubles aside.* **3. aside from,** *Am.* **a.** apart from. **b.** *Colloq.* except for. —*n.* actor's remark that the other actors are not supposed to hear.

as·i·nine (as'ə·nīn), *adj.* **1.** like an ass. **2.** stupid; silly. [< L, < *asinus* ass] —**as'i·nine·ly,** *adv.*

as·i·nin·i·ty (as'ə·nin'ə·ti), *n., pl.* **-ties.** stupidity; silliness.

ask (ask; äsk), v. 1. try to find out by words; inquire: *why don't you ask?* 2. seek the answer to: *ask any questions you wish, ask the way.* 3. put a question to; inquire of: *ask him.* 4. try to get by words; request: *ask a favor.* 5. claim; demand: *ask too high a price for a house.* 6. invite. 7. need; require. 8. *U.S. Colloq.* publish the banns of (a person or persons). [OE *āscian*] **—ask′er**, n. —Syn. 3. query, question, interrogate. 4. solicit. 5. require, exact.

a·skance (ə·skans′), **a·skant** (ə·skant′), adv. 1. with suspicion. 2. sideways.

a·skew (ə·skū′), adv., adj. to one side; turned or twisted the wrong way.

a·slant (ə·slant′; ə·slänt′), adv. in a slanting direction. —prep. slantingly across. —adj. slanting.

a·sleep (ə·slēp′), adj. 1. sleeping. 2. in a condition of sleep. 3. dull; inactive. 4. numb: *my foot is asleep.* 5. dead. —adv. into a condition of sleep.

a·slope (ə·slōp′), adv., adj. at a slant.

asp[1] (asp), n. 1. any of several small, poisonous snakes of Africa, esp. the Egyptian cobra. 2. a small, poisonous snake of Europe; adder. [< L < Gk. *aspis*]

asp[2] (asp), n. *Poetic.* aspen. [OE *æspe*]

as·par·a·gus (əs·par′ə·gəs), n. 1. a perennial plant of the lily family having scalelike leaves and stems with many branches. 2. the green tender shoots of one species, used as a vegetable. [< L < Gk. *asparagos*]

as·pect (as′pekt), n. 1. look; appearance: *aspect of the countryside.* 2. countenance; expression: *the solemn aspect of a judge.* 3. one side or part or view (of a subject): *various aspects of a plan.* 4. direction anything faces. 5. side fronting in a given direction: *the southern aspect of a house.* 6. relative position of planets as determining their supposed influence upon human affairs. [< L, < *ad*- at + *specere* look]

as·pen (as′pən), n. a poplar tree whose leaves tremble and rustle in the slightest breeze. —adj. 1. of this tree. 2. quivering; trembling. [earlier meaning "of the ASP[2]"]

as·per·i·ty (as·per′ə·ti), n., pl. **-ties.** roughness; harshness; severity. [< OF < L, < *asper* rough]

as·perse (əs·pèrs′), v., **-persed, -pers·ing.** spread damaging or false reports about; slander. [< L *aspersus* < *ad*- on + *spargere* sprinkle] —as·pers′er, n.

as·per·sion (əs·pèr′zhən; -shən), n. damaging or false report; slander.

as·phalt (as′fôlt; -falt), **as·phal·tum** (as·fal′təm), n. 1. a dark-colored substance, much like tar, found in various parts of the world or obtained by evaporating petroleum. 2. mixture of this substance with crushed rock, used for pavements, roofs, etc. [< LL < Gk. *asphaltos* < Semitic] —as·phal′tic, adj.

as·pho·del (as′fə·del), n. 1. plant of the lily family with spikes of white or yellow flowers. 2. *Gk. Myth.* flower of the Greek paradise. 3. *Poetic.* daffodil. [< L < Gk. *asphodelos*]

as·phyx·i·a (as·fik′si·ə), n. suffocation or unconscious condition caused by lack of oxygen and excess of carbon dioxide in the blood. [< NL < Gk., < *a*- without + *sphyxis* pulse < *sphyzein* throb]

as·phyx·i·ate (as·fik′si·āt), v., **-at·ed, -at·ing.** suffocate because of lack of oxygen. —as·phyx′i·a′tion, n. —as·phyx′i·a′tor, n.

as·pic (as′pik), n. kind of jelly made from meat, tomato juice, etc. [< F]

as·pi·dis·tra (as′pə·dis′trə), n. plant with large, green leaves and very small flowers, used as a house plant. [< NL < Gk. *aspis* shield + *astron* star]

as·pir·ant (əs·pīr′ənt; as′pə·rənt), n. person who aspires; person who seeks a position of honor. —adj. aspiring.

as·pi·rate (v. as′pə·rāt; adj., n. as′pə·rit), v., **-rat·ed, -rat·ing,** adj., n. *Phonet.* —v. pronounce with a breathing or h-sound. The *h* in *hot* is aspirated. —adj. pronounced with a breathing or

h-sound. —n. an aspirated sound. [< L *aspiratus.* See ASPIRE.]

as·pi·ra·tion (as′pə·rā′shən), n. 1. earnest desire; longing. 2. act of drawing air into the lungs; breathing. 3. *Phonet.* a. an aspirating (of sounds). b. an aspirated sound. 4. withdrawal by suction.

as·pi·ra·tor (as′pə·rā′tər), n. apparatus or device employing suction.

as·pire (əs·pīr′), v., **-pired, -pir·ing.** 1. have an ambition for something; desire earnestly. 2. rise. [< L, < *ad*- toward + *spirare* breathe] —as·pir′er, n. —as·pir′ing·ly, adv.

as·pi·rin (as′pə·rin), n. drug for headaches, colds, etc., $C_9H_8O_4$. It is the acetate of salicylic acid. [from trademark]

a·squint (ə·skwint′), adv., adj. sideways.

ass (as), n. 1. a long-eared mammal of the horse family, serving as a patient, sure-footed beast of burden when domesticated; donkey. 2. stupid fool; silly person. [OE *assa* < OWelsh < L *asinus*]

as·sa·fet·i·da, as·sa·foet·i·da (as′ə·fet′ə·də), n. asafetida.

as·sa·gai, as·se·gai (as′ə·gī), n., pl. **-gais.** a slender spear or javelin of hard wood, used by some African tribes. [< Sp. < Ar. *az-zaghāyah* < Berber]

as·sail (ə·sāl′), v. 1. set upon with violence; attack. 2. set upon vigorously with arguments, abuse, etc. [< OF < VL < L *ad*- at + *salire* leap] —as·sail′a·ble, adj. —as·sail′er, n. —as·sail′ment, n.

as·sail·ant (ə·sāl′ənt), n. person who attacks. —adj. assailing.

as·sas·sin (ə·sas′ən), n. murderer, esp. one hired to murder. [< F < Ital. < Ar. *hashshāshīn* HASHISH eaters; with ref. to fanatics who murdered while under the influence of hashish]

as·sas·si·nate (ə·sas′ə·nāt), v., **-nat·ed, -nat·ing.** kill by a sudden or secret attack; murder. —as·sas′si·na′tion, n. —as·sas′si·na′tor, n.

as·sault (ə·sôlt′), n. 1. a sudden, vigorous attack; attack. 2. *Law.* an attempt or offer to do violence to another. 3. *Mil.* final phase of an attack; close hand-to-hand fighting. —v. make an assault on. [< OF, < L *ad*- at + *saltare* leap] —as·sault′a·ble, adj. —as·sault′er, n. —Syn. n. 1. onslaught, charge.

as·say (v. ə·sā′; n. ə·sā′, as′ā), v. 1. analyze (an ore, alloy, etc.) to find out the quantity of gold, silver, or other metal in it. 2. try; test; examine. 3. *Am.* (of ore) contain, as shown by analysis, a certain proportion of metal. 4. *Archaic.* attempt. —n. 1. analysis of an ore, alloy, etc., to find out the amount of metal in it. 2. trial; test; examination. 3. the substance analyzed or tested. 4. a list of the results of assaying an ore, drug, etc. [< OF *a(s)sayer,* ult. < LL, < VL *exagere* weigh] —as·say′a·ble, adj. —as·say′er, n.

as·sem·blage (ə·sem′blij), n. 1. group of persons gathered together; assembly. 2. collection; group. 3. a bringing or coming together; meeting. 4. a putting or fitting together, as parts of a machine.

as·sem·ble (ə·sem′bəl), v., **-bled, -bling.** 1. gather or bring together. 2. come together; meet. 3. *Am.* put or fit together. [< OF *as(s)embler* < VL *assimulare* bring together < L, compare, ult. < *ad*- to + *similis* like, or *simul* together] —as·sem′bler, n. —Syn. 2. congregate.

as·sem·bly (ə·sem′bli), n., pl. **-blies.** 1. an assembling. 2. a being assembled. 3. group of people gathered together for some purpose; meeting. 4. a reception. 5. a ball. 6. a lawmaking group. 7. a putting or fitting together. 8. signal on a bugle or drum for troops to form in ranks. 9. Assembly, in some States, the lower branch of the State legislature. —Syn. 1. gathering. 3. convention, congregation. 6. legislature.

assembly line, *Am.* row of workers and machines along which work is successively passed until the final product is made.

as·sem·bly·man, As·sem·bly·man (ə·sem′bli·mən), n., pl. **-men.** *U.S.* member of a lawmaking group.

as·sent (ə·sent′), v. express agreement; agree.

—*n.* acceptance of a proposal, statement, etc.; agreement. [< OF < L, < *ad-* along with + *sentire* feel, think] —as·sent'er, *n.* —as·sent'-ing·ly, *adv.*

as·sert (ə·sèrt'), *v.* 1. state positively; declare. 2. insist on (a right, a claim, etc.); defend. 3. assert oneself, put oneself forward; refuse to be ignored. [< L, < *ad-* to + *serere* join] —as·sert'-a·ble, as·sert'i·ble, *adj.* —as·sert'er, as·ser'tor, *n.* —Syn. 1. affirm, aver, maintain.

as·ser·tion (ə·sèr'shən), *n.* 1. positive statement; declaration. 2. act of asserting.

as·ser·tive (ə·sèr'tiv), *adj.* too confident and certain; positive. —as·ser'tive·ly, *adv.* —as·ser'-tive·ness, *n.*

as·sess (ə·ses'), *v.* 1. estimate the value of (property or income) for taxation. 2. fix the amount of (a tax, fine, damages, etc.). 3. put a tax or fine on (a person, property, etc.). 4. portion out as a tax; apportion. [< OF < VL *assessare* fix a tax < L *assidere* < *ad-* by + *sedere* sit] —as·sess'a·ble, *adj.*

as·sess·ment (ə·ses'mənt), *n.* 1. act of assessing. 2. amount assessed.

as·ses·sor (ə·ses'ər), *n.* person who assesses taxes. —as·ses'sor·ship, *n.*

as·set (as'et), *n.* 1. something having value. 2. a single item of property.

as·sets (as'ets), *n.pl.* 1. things of value; property. 2. property that can be used to pay debts. [< OF *asez* enough < L *ad-* to + *satis* enough]

as·sev·er·ate (ə·sev'ər·āt), *v.*, **-at·ed, -at·ing.** declare solemnly; state positively. [< L, < *ad-* + *severus* serious] —as·sev'er·a'tion, *n.*

as·si·du·i·ty (as'ə·dū'ə·ti; -dū'ə-), *n.*, *pl.* **-ties.** careful and steady attention; diligence.

as·sid·u·ous (ə·sij'ù·əs), *adj.* careful and attentive; diligent. [< L, < *assidere* sit at. See ASSESS.] —as·sid'u·ous·ly, *adv.* —as·sid'u·ous·ness, *n.*

as·sign (ə·sīn'), *v.* 1. give as a share. 2. appoint, as to a post or duty. 3. name definitely; fix; set. 4. refer; ascribe; attribute. 5. transfer or hand over (property, a right, etc.) legally. —*n.* person to whom property, a right, etc., is legally transferred. [< OF < L, < *ad-* to, for + *signum* mark] —as·sign'a·ble, *adj.* —as·sign'a·bil'i·ty, *n.* —as·sign'a·bly, *adv.* —as·sign'er, *n.* —Syn. *v.* 1. allot. 3. designate.

as·sig·na·tion (as'ig·nā'shən), *n.* 1. appointment for a meeting. 2. illicit meeting of lovers. 3. legal transfer of property, a right, etc. 4. an allotting.

as·sign·ee (ə·sī·nē'; as'ə·nē'), *n.* person to whom some property, right, etc., is legally transferred.

as·sign·ment (ə·sīn'mənt), *n.* 1. something assigned. 2. *Am.* duty, task, position, etc., given to one to perform or fill. 3. an assigning. 4. legal transfer of some property, right, etc.

as·sign·or (ə·sī·nôr'; as'ə·nôr'), *n.* person who legally transfers to another some property, right, etc.

as·sim·i·la·ble (ə·sim'ə·lə·bəl), *adj.* that can be assimilated. —as·sim'i·la·bil'i·ty, *n.*

as·sim·i·late (ə·sim'ə·lāt), *v.*, **-lat·ed, -lat·ing.** 1. absorb; digest. 2. be absorbed. 3. make like. 4. liken; compare. 5. be like. [< L, < *ad-* to + *similis* like] —as·sim'i·la'tion, *n.* —as·sim'i·la'tor, *n.* —Syn. 1. incorporate.

as·sim·i·la·tive (ə·sim'ə·lā'tiv), *adj.* assimilating. —as·sim'i·la·tive·ness, *n.*

as·sist (ə·sist'), *v.* 1. help; aid. 2. be associated with as an assistant. —*n. Am.*, Baseball. help given in putting a runner out. [< F < L, < *ad-* by + *sistere* take a stand] —as·sist'er, *Law* as·sis'tor, *n.*

as·sist·ance (ə·sis'təns), *n.* help; aid.

as·sist·ant (ə·sis'tənt), *n.* helper; aid. —*adj.* helping; assisting. —as·sist'ant·ship, *n.*

assistant professor, *Am.* teacher ranking below a professor.

as·size (ə·sīz'), *n.* 1. session of a law court. 2. verdict; judgment. 3. assizes, periodical sessions of court held in each county of England. [< OF

as(s)ise < *aseeir* < VL *assedere* sit at. See ASSESS.]

assn., Assn., association.

assoc., associate; association.

as·so·ci·ate (*v.* ə·sō'shi·āt; *n., adj.* ə·sō'shi·it, -āt), *v.*, **-at·ed, -at·ing, *n., adj.*** —*v.* 1. connect in thought. 2. join as a companion, partner, or friend. 3. join; combine; unite. 4. combine for a common purpose. 5. keep company (with). —*n.* 1. thing connected in thought with another. 2. companion; partner; friend. 3. member without full rights and privileges. —*adj.* 1. joined in companionship, interest, action, etc. 2. admitted to some, but not all, rights and privileges, etc. [< L, < *ad-* to + *socius* companion] —as·so'ci·ate·ship', *n.* —as·so'ci·a'tor, *n.* —Syn. *n.* 2. ally, colleague, comrade. —*adj.* 1. allied.

as·so·ci·a·tion (ə·sō'si·ā'shən; -shi-), *n.* 1. an associating or being associated. 2. group of people joined together for some purpose; society. 3. companionship; partnership; friendship. 4. connection of ideas in thought. —as·so'ci·a'tion·al, *adj.* —Syn. 1. alliance. 2. club.

association football, soccer.

as·so·ci·a·tive (ə·sō'shi·ā'tiv), *adj.* 1. tending to associate. 2. pertaining to association. —as·so'ci·a·tive·ly, *adv.*

as·soil (ə·soil'), *v. Archaic.* 1. absolve. 2. atone for. [< F < L *absolvere* ABSOLVE]

as·so·nance (as'ə·nəns), *n.* 1. resemblance in sound. 2. a substitute for rhyme in which the vowels are alike but the consonants are different, as in *brave—vain, lone—show.* [< F < L, < *ad-* to + *sonare* sound] —as'so·nant, *adj.*, *n.* —as·so·nan·tal (as'ə·nan'təl), *adj.*

as·sort (ə·sôrt'), *v.* 1. sort out; classify; arrange in sorts. 2. furnish with various sorts. 3. agree; suit; match. 4. associate. [< F, < *a-* to (< L *ad-*) + *sorte* SORT] —as·sort'er, *n.* —as·sort'ment, *n.*

as·sort·ed (ə·sôr'tid), *adj.* 1. selected so as to be of different kinds; various. 2. arranged by kinds; classified.

asst., Asst., assistant.

as·suage (ə·swāj'), *v.*, **-suaged, -suag·ing.** 1. make easier or milder: *assuage pain.* 2. grow easier or milder. 3. make less: *assuage thirst.* [< OF *assuagier*, ult. < L *ad-* + *suavis* sweet] —as·suage'ment, *n.*

as·sume (ə·süm'), *v.*, **-sumed, -sum·ing.** 1. take upon oneself; undertake. 2. take on; put on. 3. appropriate; usurp. 4. pretend. 5. take for granted; suppose. [< L, < *ad-* to + *sumere* take] —as·sum'a·ble, *adj.* —as·sum'a·bly, *adv.* —as·sum'ed·ly, *adv.* —as·sum'er, *n.* —Syn. 4. feign, simulate. 5. presume.

as·sum·ing (ə·süm'ing), *adj.* taking too much on oneself; presumptuous.

as·sump·tion (ə·sump'shən), *n.* 1. act of assuming. 2. thing assumed. 3. presumption; arrogance; unpleasant boldness. 4. **the Assumption, a.** the bodily taking of the Virgin Mary from earth to heaven after her death. **b.** a church festival in honor of this on August 15. —Syn. 2. hypothesis, conjecture.

as·sur·ance (ə·shúr'əns), *n.* 1. a making sure or certain. 2. positive declaration inspiring confidence. 3. security; certainty; confidence. 4. self-confidence. 5. impudence; too much boldness. 6. *Brit.* insurance. —Syn. 2. guarantee. 5. audacity, presumption.

as·sure (ə·shúr'), *v.*, **-sured, -sur·ing.** 1. make sure or certain. 2. make confident. 3. tell positively. 4. make safe; secure. 5. make safe against loss; insure. [< OF *aseürer* < VL < L *ad-* + *securus* safe, SECURE] —as·sur'a·ble, *adj.* —as·sur'er, *n.* —Syn. 1. ascertain. 2. encourage. 3. state. 4. ensure.

as·sured (ə·shúrd'), *adj.* 1. sure; certain. 2. confident; bold. 3. insured against loss. —*n.* 1. person who is the beneficiary of an insurance policy. 2. person whose life or property is insured. —as·sur·ed·ly (ə·shúr'id·li), *adv.* —as·sur'ed·ness, *n.*

As·syr·i·a (ə·sir'i·ə), *n.* an ancient country in SW Asia. —As·syr'i·an, *adj.*, *n.*

age, cāre, fär; ēqual, tèrm; īce; ōpen, ôrder; pùt, rüle, ūse; th, then; ə=a in about.

As·tar·te (as·tär′tē), *n.* Phoenician goddess of fertility and love. The Hebrews called her **Ashtoreth**.

as·ter (as′tər), *n.* **1.** *Bot.* any plant of a widespread genus whose daisylike blossoms are really compact heads of florets surrounded by small leaves or bracts. **2.** plant of some allied genus, as the China aster. [< L < Gk., star] **—as′ter·like′**, *adj.*

as·ter·isk (as′tər·isk), *n.* a star-shaped mark (*) used in printing and writing to call attention to a footnote, indicate an omission, etc. **—***v.* mark with an asterisk. [< LL < Gk., dim. of *aster* star]

a·stern (ə·stern′), *adv.* **1.** at or toward the rear of a ship. **2.** backward. **3.** behind.

as·ter·oid (as′tər·oid), *n.* **1.** any of the very numerous small planets revolving about the sun between the orbit of Mars and the orbit of Jupiter. **2.** any starfish. **—as′ter·oi′dal**, *adj.*

asth·ma (az′mə; as′–), *n.* a chronic disease that causes difficulty in breathing, a feeling of suffocation, and coughing. [< Gk., panting, < *azein* breathe hard]

asth·mat·ic (az·mat′ik; as–), *adj.* **1.** of or pertaining to asthma. **2.** suffering from asthma. **—***n.* person suffering from asthma. **—asth·mat′i·cal·ly**, *adv.*

as·tig·mat·ic (as′tig·mat′ik), *adj.* **1.** having astigmatism. **2.** pertaining to astigmatism. **3.** correcting astigmatism. **—as′tig·mat′i·cal·ly**, *adv.*

a·stig·ma·tism (ə·stig′mə·tiz·əm), *n.* defect of the eye or of a lens whereby rays of light fail to converge to a focus, thus making objects look indistinct or imperfect. [< *a–* without + Gk. *stigma* point]

a·stir (ə·ster′), *adv., adj.* in motion.

as·ton·ish (əs·ton′ish), *v.* surprise greatly; amaze. [var. of *astoun* < OF *estoner* < VL *extonare*. Cf. L *attonare*.] **—as·ton′ished·ly**, *adv.* **—as·ton′ish·er**, *n.* **—Syn.** astound.

as·ton·ish·ing (əs·ton′ish·ing), *adj.* very surprising; amazing. **—as·ton′ish·ing·ly**, *adv.*

as·ton·ish·ment (əs·ton′ish·mənt), *n.* **1.** great surprise; amazement; sudden wonder. **2.** anything that causes great surprise.

as·tound (əs·tound′), *v.* surprise very greatly; amaze. [earlier *astoun*, var. of *astony* ASTONISH] **—as·tound′ing**, *adj.* **—as·tound′ing·ly**, *adv.*

a·strad·dle (ə·strad′əl), *adv., adj.* astride.

as·tra·gal (as′trə·gəl), *n. Archit.* a small, convex molding cut into the form of a string of beads.

as·trag·a·lus (as·trag′ə·ləs), *n., pl.* **–li** (–lī). *Anat.* the uppermost bone of the tarsus; anklebone; talus. [< L < Gk. *astragalos*]

as·tra·khan, as·tra·chan (as′trə·kən), *n.* **1.** the curly furlike wool on the skin of young lambs from Astrakhan, a district in E European Russia. **2.** a woolen cloth resembling it. [named for *Astrakhan*]

as·tral (as′trəl), *adj.* of the stars; starry. [< LL, < *astrum* star < Gk. *astron*]

a·stray (ə·strā′), *adj., adv.* out of the right way. **—Syn.** straying.

a·stride (ə·strīd′), *adj., adv.* **1.** with one leg on each side. **2.** with legs far apart. **—***prep.* with one leg on each side of (something).

as·trin·gent (əs·trin′jənt), *adj.* **1.** having the property of shrinking or contracting. **2.** severe. **—***n.* substance that shrinks tissues and checks the flow of blood by contracting blood vessels, as alum. [< L, < *ad–* to + *stringere* bind] **—as·trin·gen·cy** (əs·trin′jən·si), *n.* **—as·trin′gent·ly**, *adv.*

astrol., astrologer; astrology.

as·tro·labe (as′trə·lāb), *n.* an astronomical instrument formerly used for measuring the altitude of the sun or stars. [< OF < Med.L < Gk. *astrolabon*, orig., star-taking < *astron* star + *lambanein* take]

as·trol·o·ger (əs·trol′ə·jər), *n.* person who claims to interpret the influence of the stars and planets on persons, events, etc.

as·trol·o·gy (əs·trol′ə·ji), *n.* **1.** false science that claims to interpret the influence of the stars

and planets on persons, events, etc. **2.** *Archaic.* practical astronomy. **—as·tro·log·i·cal** (as′trə·loj′ə·kəl), **as′tro·log′ic**, *adj.* **—as′tro·log′i·cal·ly**, *adv.*

astron., astronomer; astronomical; astronomy.

as·tro·naut (as′trə·nôt), *n.* a pilot or member of a crew of a space ship.

as·tro·nau·tics (as′trə·nô′tiks), *n.* science that deals with travel in outer space. **—as′tro·nau′ti·cal, as′tro·nau′tic**, *adj.*

as·tron·o·mer (əs·tron′ə·mər), *n.* expert in astronomy.

as·tro·nom·i·cal (as′trə·nom′ə·kəl), **as·tro·nom·ic** (–nom′ik), *adj.* **1.** of astronomy; having to do with astronomy. **2.** extremely large. **—as′tro·nom′i·cal·ly**, *adv.*

astronomical year, period of the earth's revolution around the sun; solar year.

as·tron·o·my (əs·tron′ə·mi), *n.* science of the sun, moon, planets, stars, and other heavenly bodies, their composition, motions, positions, distances, sizes, etc. [< L < Gk., < *astron* star + *nomos* distribution]

as·tro·phys·ics (as′trō·fiz′iks), *n.* branch of astronomy that deals with the physical and chemical characteristics of heavenly bodies. **—as′tro·phys′i·cal**, *adj.* **—as′tro·phys·i·cist** (as′trō·fiz′ə·sist), *n.*

as·tute (əs·tüt′; –tūt′), *adj.* sagacious; shrewd; crafty. [< L, < *astus* sagacity] **—as·tute′ly**, *adv.* **—as·tute′ness**, *n.*

A·sun·ción (ä·sün·syon′), *n.* capital of Paraguay.

a·sun·der (ə·sun′dər), *adj.* apart; separate. **—***adv.* in pieces; into separate parts.

a·sy·lum (ə·sī′ləm), *n.* **1.** institution for the support and care of the insane, blind, orphans, or other classes of unfortunate persons. **2.** an inviolable refuge, as formerly for debtors and criminals. [< L < Gk. *asylon* refuge < *a–* without + *syle* right of seizure] **—Syn. 2.** sanctuary.

a·sym·me·try (ā·sim′ə·tri; a–), *n.* lack of symmetry. **—a·sym·met·ric** (ā′sə·met′rik; as′ə–), **a′sym·met′ri·cal**, *adj.* **—a′sym·met′ri·cal·ly**, *adv.*

as·ymp·tote (as′im·tōt), *n. Math.* a straight line that continually approaches a curve, but does not meet it within a finite distance. **—as·ymp·tot·ic** (as′im·tot′ik), **as′ymp·tot′i·cal**, *adj.* **—as′ymp·tot′i·cal·ly**, *adv.*

at (at; *unstressed* ət, it), *prep.* **1.** in; on; by; near: *at school, at the front door.* **2.** to; toward; in the direction of: *aim at the mark, look at me.* **3.** in a place or condition of: *at war.* **4.** on or near the time of: *at midnight.* **5.** through; by way of: *smoke came out at the chimney.* **6.** doing; trying to do: *at work.* **7.** because of; by reason of: *the shipwrecked sailors were happy at the arrival of the rescue ship.* **8.** for: *two books at a dollar each.* **9.** according to: *at will.* **10.** from: *the sick man got good treatment at the hands of his doctor.* [OE *æt*]

at., **1.** atmosphere. **2.** atomic.

At·a·lan·ta (at′ə·lan′tə), *n.* Gk. *Legend.* a maiden famous for her beauty and her speed in running.

at·a·vism (at′ə·viz·əm), *n.* **1.** resemblance to a remote ancestor. **2.** reversion to a primitive type. [< L *atavus* ancestor] **—at′a·vist**, *n.* **—at′a·vis′tic**, *adj.* **—at′a·vis′ti·cal·ly**, *adv.*

a·tax·i·a (ə·tak′si·ə), *n.* inability to coördinate voluntary movements; irregularity in bodily functions or muscular movements. [< NL, Gk., < *a–* without + *taxis* order] **—a·tax′ic**, *adj.*

A·te (ā′tē), *n.* the Greek goddess of blind recklessness, later regarded as an avenging goddess.

–ate[1], *suffix.* **1.** of or pertaining to, as in *collegiate.* **2.** having; containing, as in *compassionate.* **3.** having the form of; like, as in *stellate.* **4.** become, as in *maturate.* **5.** cause to be, as in *alienate.* **6.** produce, as in *ulcerate.* **7.** supply or treat with, as in *aerate.* **8.** combine with, as in *oxygenate.* [< L *–atus, –atum*, pp. endings]

–ate[2], *suffix. Chem.* a salt formed by the action of an ——ic acid on a base, as in *sulfate.* [special use of *–ate[1]*]

–ate³, *suffix.* office, rule, or condition of, as in *caliphate, magistrate.* [< L *–atus,* from 4th declension nouns]

at·el·ier (at′əl·yā), *n.* workshop; studio. [< F, orig., pile of chips, < OF *astele* chip, ult. < L *astula*]

Ath·a·na·sius (ath′ə·nā′shəs), *n.* Saint, 296?–373 A.D., bishop of Alexandria, one of the chief opponents of the Arian doctrine. **—Ath·a·na·sian** (ath′ə·nā′zhən), *adj.*

a·the·ism (ā′thi·iz·əm), *n.* **1.** belief that there is no God. **2.** godless living. [< F, < Gk. *atheos* denying the gods < *a–* without + *theos* a god] **—a′the·ist,** *n.*

a·the·is·tic (ā′thi·is′tik), **a·the·is·ti·cal** (–tə·kəl), *adj.* of atheism or atheists. **—a′the·is′ti·cal·ly,** *adv.*

A·the·na (ə·thē′nə), **A·the·ne** (–nē), *n.* the Greek goddess of wisdom, arts, industries, and prudent warfare, identified with the Roman goddess Minerva. Also, **Pallas, Pallas Athena.**

ath·e·nae·um, ath·e·ne·um (ath′ə·nē′əm), *n. Am.* **1.** a scientific or literary club. **2.** a reading room; library.

Ath·ens (ath′ənz), *n.* **1.** capital of Greece, in the SE part. Athens was famous in ancient times for its art and literature. **2.** *Am.* city compared to Athens because it is a center of art and literature. **—A·the·ni·an** (ə·thē′ni·ən), *adj., n.*

a·thirst (ə·thèrst′), *adj.* **1.** thirsty. **2.** eager.

ath·lete (ath′lēt), *n.* person trained in exercises of physical strength, speed, and skill. [< L < Gk., < *athlon* prize]

athlete's foot, *Am.* a contagious skin disease of the feet, caused by a fungus.

ath·let·ic (ath·let′ik), *adj.* **1.** active and strong. **2.** of, like, or suited to an athlete. **3.** for athletes. **4.** having to do with active games and sports. **—ath·let′i·cal·ly,** *adv.*

ath·let·i·cism (ath·let′ə·siz·əm), *n.* **1.** the practice of athletics. **2.** athletic quality or behavior.

ath·let·ics (ath·let′iks), *n.* **1.** (*usually construed as pl.*) exercises of strength, speed, and skill; active games and sports: *athletics include baseball and basketball.* **2.** (*usually construed as sing.*) the principles of athletic training: *athletics is recommended for every student.*

at·home (ət·hōm′), *n.* an informal reception, usually in the afternoon.

a·thwart (ə·thwôrt′), *adv.* crosswise; across from side to side. **—prep. 1.** across. **2.** across the line or course of. **3.** in opposition to; against.

a·tilt (ə·tilt′), *adj., adv.* tilted.

a·tin·gle (ə·ting′gəl), *adj.* tingling.

–ation, *suffix.* **1.** act or state of ——ing, as in *admiration.* **2.** condition or state of being ——ed, as in *agitation.* **3.** result of ——ing, as in *civilization.* [< L *–atio*]

–ative, *suffix.* **1.** tending to, as in *talkative.* **2.** having to do with, as in *qualitative.* [< L *–ativus*]

At·lan·ta (at·lan′tə), *n.* the capital of Georgia, in the N part.

At·lan·tic (at·lan′tik), *n.* ocean east of North and South America, extending to Europe and Africa. **—adj. 1.** of, on, or near the Atlantic Ocean. **2.** *Am.* of or on the Atlantic coast of the U.S. **3.** having to do with NATO and its member nations. **4.** of or pertaining to the Atlas Mountains.

Atlantic Charter, the joint declaration of President Roosevelt and Prime Minister Churchill on August 14, 1941.

Atlantic City, a resort in SE New Jersey.

At·lan·tis (at·lan′tis), *n.* a legendary sunken island in the Atlantic.

at·las (at′ləs), *n.* **1.** book of maps. **2.** book of plates or tables illustrating any subject. **3. Atlas,** *Gk. Legend.* giant who supported the heavens on his shoulders.

Atlas Mountains, mountain range in NW Africa.

at·mos·phere (at′məs·fir), *n.* **1.** air that surrounds the earth; air. **2.** air in any given place: *a damp atmosphere.* **3.** mass of gases that surrounds any heavenly body. **4.** *Physics.* a unit of pressure equal to 14.69 pounds per square inch. **5.** surrounding influence. [< NL < Gk. *atmos* vapor + *sphaira* sphere]

at·mos·pher·ic (at′məs·fer′ik), *adj.* Also, **at′mos·pher′i·cal. 1.** of, in, or having to do with the atmosphere. **2.** caused, produced, or worked by the atmosphere. **—n. atmospherics,** radio static. **—at′mos·pher′i·cal·ly,** *adv.*

at. no., *Physics, Chem.* atomic number.

at·oll (at′ol; ə·tol′), *n.* a ring-shaped coral island enclosing or partly enclosing a lagoon. [? < Malayalam *aḍal* uniting]

Atoll

at·om (at′əm), *n.* **1.** *Physics, Chem.* the smallest particle of a chemical element that can take part in a chemical reaction without being permanently changed. **2.** a very small particle; tiny bit. [< L < Gk. *atomos* indivisible < *a–* not + *tomos* a cutting]

a·tom·ic (ə·tom′ik), **a·tom·i·cal** (–ə·kəl), *adj.* **1.** of or having to do with atoms. **2.** extremely small; minute. **—a·tom′i·cal·ly,** *adv.*

atomic age, era marked by the first use of atomic energy.

atomic bomb, atom bomb, bomb that uses the splitting of atoms to cause an explosion of tremendous force, accompanied by a blinding light. Also, **A-bomb.**

atomic clock, a highly accurate clock, that is run by controlled radio waves.

atomic energy, energy generated through alteration of an atomic nucleus by fission, etc.

atomic furnace, *Nuclear Physics.* reactor.

atomic number, *Physics, Chem.* number used in describing an element and giving its relation to other elements. It is the number of positive charges on the nucleus of an atom of the element.

atomic pile or **reactor.** See reactor.

atomic submarine, submarine powered by a reactor.

atomic theory or **hypothesis,** *Physics, Chem.* theory that all matter is composed of atoms, esp. the modern theory that an atom is made of a nucleus of neutrons and protons around which electrons speed.

atomic weight, *Physics, Chem.* the relative weight of an atom of an element, using oxygen or hydrogen as a standard of comparison.

at·om·ize (at′om·īz), *v.,* **–ized,** **–iz·ing. 1.** separate into atoms. **2.** change (a liquid) into a fine spray. **—at′om·i·za′tion,** *n.* **—at′om·iz′er,** *n.*

atom smasher, cyclotron.

a·ton·al (ā·tōn′əl), *adj. Music.* without tone. **—a·ton′al·ism,** *n.* **—a·ton′al·is′tic,** *adj.* **—a·to·nal·i·ty** (ā′tō·nal′ə·ti), *n.* **—a·ton′al·ly,** *adv.*

a·tone (ə·tōn′), *v.,* **a·toned, a·ton·ing.** make up; make amends (*for*). [< *atonement*] **—a·ton′er,** *n.*

a·tone·ment (ə·tōn′mənt), *n.* **1.** giving satisfaction for a wrong, loss, or injury; amends. **2.** the **Atonement,** reconciliation of God with sinners through the sufferings and death of Christ. [< *at onement* a being at one, i.e., in accord]

a·top (ə·top′), *adv.* on or at the top. **—prep.** on the top of.

at·ra·bil·ious (at′rə·bil′yəs), **at·ra·bil·iar** (–bil′yər), *adj.* **1.** melancholy; hypochondriac. **2.** bad-tempered. [< L *atra bilis* black bile]

a·tri·um (ā′tri·əm), *n.,* *pl.* **a·tri·a** (ā′tri·ə). **1.** the main room of an ancient Roman house. **2.** hall; court. **3.** *Anat.* auricle. [< L]

a·tro·cious (ə·trō′shəs), *adj.* **1.** very wicked or cruel; very savage or brutal. **2.** *Colloq.* very bad; abominable. **—a·tro′cious·ly,** *adv.* **—a·tro′cious·ness,** *n.*

a·troc·i·ty (ə·tros′ə·ti), *n.,* *pl.* **–ties. 1.** very great wickedness or cruelty. **2.** very cruel or brutal act. **3.** *Colloq.* very bad blunder. [< L, < *atrox* fierce < *ater* dark]

āge, cāre, fär; ēqual, tèrm; īce, ōpen, ôrder; pút, rüle, üse; tħ, then; ə=a in about.

at·ro·phy (at′rə-fĭ), *n.*, *v.*, **-phied**, **-phy·ing.** —*n.* a wasting away of a part or parts of the body. —*v.* waste away. [< LL < Gk., < *a*- without + *trophe* nourishment] —a·troph·ic (ə-trŏf′ĭk), *adj.* —at′ro·phied, *adj.*

at·ro·pine (at′rə-pēn; -pin), **at·ro·pin** (-pin), *n.* a poisonous drug, $C_{17}H_{23}NO_3$, obtained from belladonna and similar plants, that relaxes muscles and dilates the pupil of the eye. [< NL *Atropa* belladonna < Gk. *Atropos* one of the Fates]

at·tach (ə-tach′), *v.* 1. fasten (to). 2. join. 3. assign; appoint. 4. affix: *attach one's signature to a document.* 5. attribute. 6. fasten itself; belong: *the blame attaches to you.* 7. bind by affection. 8. take (person or property) by legal authority. [< OF *atachier* < L *ad*- to + Gmc. ancestor of OF *tache* a fastening, a nail. See TACK.] —at·tach′a·ble, *adj.* —at·tached′, *adj.*

at·ta·ché (at′ə-shā′; *esp.* Brit. ə·tash′ā), *n.* person belonging to the official staff of an ambassador or minister to a foreign country. [< F. See ATTACH.] —at′ta·ché′ship, *n.*

at·tach·ment (ə-tach′mənt), *n.* 1. an attaching. 2. a being attached. 3. thing attached. 4. means of attaching; fastening. 5. bond arising from affection and regard. 6. legal taking of a person or property.

at·tack (ə-tak′), *v.* 1. use force or weapons on to hurt. 2. talk or write against. 3. begin to work vigorously on. 4. act harmfully on. 5. make an attack. —*n.* 1. sudden occurrence of illness, discomfort, etc. 2. act or fact of attacking. [< F < Ital. *attaccare.* See ATTACH.] —at·tack′a·ble, *adj.* —at·tack′er, *n.* —Syn. *v.* 1. assail, assault, beset. 2. criticize, blame.

at·tain (ə-tān′), *v.* 1. arrive at in due course; reach, as by effort or progress. 2. gain; accomplish. 3. attain to, succeed in coming to or getting. [< OF *ataindre* < VL, < *ad*- to + *tangere* touch] —at·tain′a·ble, *adj.* —at·tain′a·bil′i·ty, at·tain′a·ble·ness, *n.* —at·tain′er, *n.* —Syn. 2. achieve.

at·tain·der (ə-tān′dər), *n.* loss of property and civil rights as the result of being sentenced to death or being outlawed. [< OF *ataindre* attain; infl. by F *taindre* TAINT]

at·tain·ment (ə-tān′mənt), *n.* 1. act or fact of attaining. 2. something attained. 3. accomplishment; ability.

at·taint (ə-tānt′), *v.* 1. condemn to death and loss of property and civil rights. 2. disgrace. —*n.* disgrace. [< OF *ataint*, pp. of *ataindre* ATTAIN] —at·taint′ment, *n.*

at·tar (at′ər), *n.* perfume made from the petals of roses or other flowers. [< Pers. < Ar. *'iṭr*]

at·tempt (ə-tempt′), *v.* 1. make an effort at; try. 2. try to take or destroy (life, etc.). —*n.* 1. a putting forth of effort to accomplish something, esp. something difficult. 2. an attack, as on one's life. [< L, < *ad*- + *temptare* try] —at·tempt′a·ble, *adj.* —at·tempt′a·bil′i·ty, *n.* —at·tempt′er, *n.* —Syn. *v.* 1. essay, endeavor.

at·tend (ə-tend′), *v.* 1. be present at. 2. give care and thought; pay attention. 3. apply oneself. 4. go with; accompany. 5. go with as a result. 6. wait on; care for; tend. 7. be ready; wait. [< OF < L, < *ad*- toward + *tendere* stretch] —at·tend′er, *n.* —Syn. 6. serve. —Ant. 2. disregard.

at·tend·ance (ə-ten′dəns), *n.* 1. act of attending. 2. persons attending.

at·tend·ant (ə-ten′dənt), *adj.* 1. waiting on another to help or serve. 2. going with as a result; accompanying. 3. present: *attendant hearers.* —*n.* 1. person who waits on another, such as a servant. 2. accompanying thing or event. 3. person who is present.

at·ten·tion (ə-ten′shən), *n.* 1. act or fact of attending. 2. ability to give care and thought. 3. care and thought. 4. courtesy. 5. attentions, acts of devotion of a suitor. 6. military attitude of readiness. 7. come to attention, take a straight and still position. 8. stand at attention, stand straight and still. —*interj.* command to soldiers to come to attention. [< L *attentio.* See ATTEND.] —Syn. *n.* 3. application, concentration, heed. 4. deference, civility.

at·ten·tive (ə-ten′tĭv), *adj.* 1. giving attention. 2. courteous; polite. —at·ten′tive·ly, *adv.* —at·ten′tive·ness, *n.*

at·ten·u·ate (ə-ten′yủ-āt), *v.*, **-at·ed**, **-at·ing.** 1. make or become thin or slender. 2. weaken; reduce. 3. make less dense; dilute. [< L, < *ad*- + *tenuis* thin] —at·ten′u·a′tion, *n.*

at·test (ə-test′), *v.* 1. give proof or evidence of. 2. declare to be true or genuine; certify. 3. bear witness; testify. [< L, < *ad*- to + *testis* witness] —at·tes·ta·tion (at′es-tā′shən), *n.* —at·test′er, at·tes′tor, *n.*

at·tic (at′ĭk), *n.* 1. space just below the roof in a house. 2. a low story above an entablature or main cornice of a building. [< F < L *Atticus* Attic < Gk.]

At·tic (at′ĭk), *adj.* 1. of Attica; of Athens; Athenian. 2. simple; elegant; refined.

At·ti·ca (at′ə-kə), *n.* district in ancient Greece which included Athens.

At·ti·la (at′ə-lə), *n.* died 453 A.D., king of the Huns from 433–453 A.D.

at·tire (ə-tīr′), *v.*, **-tired**, **-tir·ing**, *n.* dress; array. [< OF *atirer* arrange < *a*- to (< L *ad*-) + *tire* row < Gmc.] —at·tire′ment, *n.* —at·tir′er, *n.*

at·ti·tude (at′ə-tüd; -tūd), *n.* 1. disposition or manner toward a person or thing. 2. position of the body appropriate to an action, purpose, emotion, etc. [< F < Ital. < LL *aptitudo* APTITUDE] —Syn. 2. posture, pose.

at·ti·tu·di·nize (at′ə-tü′də-nīz; -tū′-), *v.*, **-nized**, **-niz·ing.** pose for effect. —at′ti·tu′di·niz′er, *n.*

At·tlee (at′lĭ), *n.* Clement Richard, born 1883, British prime minister 1945–1951.

at·tor·ney (ə-tėr′nĭ), *n.*, *pl.* **-neys.** 1. person who has power to act for another. 2. lawyer. [< OF *atourné*, pp. of *atourner* assign, appoint < *a*- to + *tourner* TURN] —at·tor′ney·ship, *n.* —Syn. 1. agent.

attorney at law, lawyer.

attorney general, *n.*, *pl.* **attorneys general, attorney generals.** 1. the chief law officer of a country. 2. *Am.* **a.** the chief law officer of the United States. **b.** the chief law officer of a State of the United States.

at·tract (ə-trakt′), *v.* 1. draw to oneself: *a magnet attracts iron.* 2. be pleasing to; win the attention and liking of. [< L *attractus* < *ad*- to + *trahere* draw] —at·tract′a·ble, *adj.* —at·tract′a·bil′i·ty, *n.* —at·trac′tor, at·tract′er, *n.* —Syn. allure, fascinate.

at·trac·tion (ə-trak′shən), *n.* 1. act or power of attracting. 2. thing that delights or attracts people. 3. charm; fascination. 4. *Physics.* the force exerted by molecules on one another, which holds them together.

at·trac·tive (ə-trak′tĭv), *adj.* 1. pleasing; winning attention and liking. 2. attracting. —at·trac′tive·ly, *adv.* —at·trac′tive·ness, *n.* —Syn. 1. alluring, magnetic.

at·trib·ute (*v.* ə-trĭb′ūt; *n.* at′rə-būt), *v.*, **-ut·ed**, **-ut·ing**, *n.* —*v.* consider (something) as belonging or appropriate (to a person or thing). —*n.* 1. a quality considered as belonging to a person or thing; a characteristic. 2. an object considered appropriate to a person, rank, or office; symbol. 3. adjective; word or phrase used as an adjective. [< L, < *ad*- to + *tribuere* assign, orig., divide among the tribes < *tribus* tribe] —at·trib′ut·a·ble, *adj.* —at·trib′ut·er, at·trib′u·tor, *n.* —Syn. *v.* ascribe, credit. —*n.* 1. trait.

at·tri·bu·tion (at′rə-bū′shən), *n.* 1. act of attributing. 2. thing attributed.

at·trib·u·tive (ə-trĭb′yə-tĭv), *adj.* 1. expressing a quality or attribute. 2. that attributes. 3. of or like an attribute. —*n.* an attributive word. In the phrase "big brown dog," *big* and *brown* are attributives. —at·trib′u·tive·ly, *adv.* —at·trib′u·tive·ness, *n.* ▶ **attributive.** An adjective that stands before its noun is attributive (a *blue shirt*), as contrasted with a predicate adjective (the shirt is *blue*).

at·tri·tion (ə-trĭsh′ən), *n.* 1. wearing away by friction. 2. any gradual process of wearing down: *war of attrition.* [< L *attritio* < *ad*-against + *terere* rub]

at·tune (ə·tün´; ə·tün´), *v.*, **-tuned, -tun·ing.** tune. **—at·tune´ment,** *n.*

at. wt., *Physics, Chem.* atomic weight.

Au, *Chem.* gold.

au·burn (ô´bərn), *n., adj.* reddish brown. [< OF *auborne* < L *alburnus* whitish < *albus* white; appar. confused with *brown*]

Auck·land (ôk´lənd), *n.* an important seaport in N New Zealand.

auc·tion (ôk´shən), *n.* 1. a public sale in which each thing is sold to the highest bidder. 2. auction bridge. **—v.** sell at an auction. [< L *auctio* < *augere* increase]

auction bridge, a variety of bridge in which the players bid for the privilege of declaring the trump or no trumps.

auc·tion·eer (ôk´shən·ir´), *n.* man who conducts auctions. **—v.** sell at an auction.

au·da·cious (ô·dā´shəs), *adj.* 1. bold; daring. 2. too bold; impudent. [< F, < *audace* daring (n.) < L *audacia*, ult. < *audere* dare] **—au·da´cious·ly,** *adv.* **—au·da´cious·ness,** *n.*

au·dac·i·ty (ô·das´ə·ti), *n., pl.* **-ties.** 1. boldness; reckless daring. 2. rude boldness.

au·di·ble (ô´də·bəl), *adj.* capable of being heard. [< Med.L, < L *audire* hear] **—au´di·bil´i·ty, au´di·ble·ness,** *n.* **—au´di·bly,** *adv.*

au·di·ence (ô´di·əns), *n.* 1. people gathered in a place to hear or see. 2. any person within hearing. 3. chance to be heard; hearing. 4. formal interview with a person of high rank. 5. act or fact of hearing. 6. *Am.* the readers of a book, newspaper, or magazine. [< OF < L *audientia* hearing < *audire* hear]

au·di·o (ô´di·ō), *adj.* having to do with electronic frequencies that are audible, as sound waves. [< L, I hear]

audio frequency, *Physics, Electronics.* frequency of sound vibrations from about 20 to about 20,000 cycles per second.

au·di·o·phile (ô´di·ə·fīl´), *n.* person who makes a hobby of high-fidelity sound reproduction.

au·dit (ô´dit), *n.* 1. an official examination or check of accounts. 2. statement of an account that has been examined and checked authoritatively. **—v.** 1. examine and check (accounts) officially. 2. *U.S.* attend (a course) as an auditor. [< L *auditus* a hearing < *audire* hear]

au·di·tion (ô·dish´ən), *n.* 1. act of hearing. 2. power or sense of hearing. 3. a hearing to test the voice of a singer, speaker, etc. **—v.** *U.S.* give (a person) an audition.

au·di·tor (ô´də·tər), *n.* 1. hearer; listener. 2. person who audits accounts. 3. *U.S.* one who attends a college course, but not for credit toward a degree. **—au´di·tor·ship´,** *n.*

au·di·to·ri·um (ô´də·tô´ri·əm; -tō´-), *n., pl.* **-to·ri·ums, -to·ri·a** (-tô´ri·ə; -tō´-). 1. a large room for an audience in a church, theater, school, etc. 2. *Am.* a building especially designed for the giving of lectures, concerts, etc.

au·di·to·ry (ô´də·tô´ri; -tō´-), *adj., n., pl.* **-ries. —adj.** of or having to do with hearing, the sense of hearing, or the organs of hearing. **—n.** 1. audience. 2. auditorium.

Au·du·bon (ô´də·bon), *n.* John James, 1785–1851, American ornithologist and artist.

Aug., August.

au·ger (ô´gər), *n.* tool for boring holes in wood. [OE *nafugār*, orig., a nave borer < *nafu* nave of a wheel + *gār* spear; ME *a nauger* taken as *an auger*]

aught¹ (ôt), *n.* anything: *you may go for aught I care.* **—adv.** at all: *help came too late to avail aught.* [OE *āwiht* < *ā*- ever + *wiht* a thing]

aught² (ôt), *n.* zero; cipher; nothing. [see NAUGHT; *a naught* taken as *an aught*]

aug·ment (ôg·ment´), *v.* increase; enlarge. [< L, < *augere* increase] **—aug·ment´a·ble,** *adj.* **—aug·men·ta´tion,** *n.* **—aug·ment´a·tive,** *adj.* **—aug·ment´er,** *n.*

Augers

au grat·in (ō grat´ən, grä´tən; *Fr.* ō grätaṉ´), French. cooked with crumbs or cheese, or both.

Augs·burg (ôgz´bėrg), *n.* city in SW Germany.

au·gur (ô´gər), *n.* 1. priest in ancient Rome who made predictions and gave advice. 2. prophet; fortuneteller. **—v.** 1. predict; foretell. 2. be a sign. [< L, appar. increase, growth (of crops), personified in ritual service, < *augere* increase]

au·gu·ry (ô´gyə·ri), *n., pl.* **-ries.** 1. art or practice of foretelling the future. 2. indication; sign; omen.

Au·gust (ô´gəst), *n.* the 8th month of the year, containing 31 days. [after *Augustus*]

au·gust (ô·gust´), *adj.* inspiring reverence and admiration; majestic; venerable. [< L, < unrecorded *augus* increase, power < *augere* to increase] **—au·gust´ly,** *adv.* **—au·gust´ness,** *n.*

Au·gus·ta (ô·gus´tə), *n.* capital of Maine, in the SW part.

Au·gus·tan age (ô·gus´tən), *n.* 1. period of Latin literature from 27 B.C. to 14 A.D. 2. period of English literature from 1700 to 1750.

Au·gus·tine (ô´gəs·tēn; ô·gus´tin), *n.* 1. Saint, 354–430 A.D., bishop of N Africa and one of the great leaders in the early Christian church. 2. Saint, died 604 A.D., Roman monk sent to preach Christianity in England in 597 A.D. **—Au·gus·tin·i·an** (ô´gəs·tin´i·ən), *adj., n.*

Au·gus·tus (ô·gus´təs), *n.* (*Augustus Caesar*), 63 B.C.–14 A.D., title of Gaius Octavianus (Octavian) as first emperor of Rome, 27 B.C.–14 A.D. **—Au·gus´tan,** *adj.*

auk (ôk), *n.* northern sea bird with short wings used only as paddles. [< Scand. *ālka*]

auk·let (ôk´lit), *n.* small kind of auk.

auld (ôld), *adj. Scot.* old.

auld lang syne (ôld´ lang sīn´; zīn´), *Scot.* old times; long ago in one's life.

aunt (ant; änt), *n.* 1. sister of one's father or mother. 2. uncle's wife. [< OF < L *amita* father's sister]

au·ra (ô´rə), *n., pl.* **au·ras, au·rae** (ô´rē). something supposed to come from a person or thing and surround him or it as an atmosphere. [< L < Gk.]

au·ral (ô´rəl), *adj.* of the ear; having to do with hearing. **—au´ral·ly,** *adv.*

Au·re·li·us (ô·rē´li·əs; ô·rēl´yəs), *n.* See Antoninus.

au·re·ole (ô´ri·ōl), **au·re·o·la** (ô·rē´ə·lə), *n.* 1. encircling radiance; halo. 2. a ring of light surrounding the sun. [< L *aureola* (*corona*) golden (crown) < *aurum* gold]

Au·re·o·my·cin (ô´ri·ō·mī´sin), *n. Trademark.* drug related to streptomycin, used to check or kill bacteria and viruses. [< L *aureus* golden + Gk. *mykes* fungus; from its color]

au re·voir (ō rə·vwär´), good-by; till I see you again. [< F; *revoir* < L, < *re*- again + *videre* see]

au·ri·cle (ô´rə·kəl), *n.* 1. *Anat.* a. chamber of the heart that receives the blood from the veins. b. outer part of the ear. 2. an earlike part. [< L *auricula,* dim. of *auris* ear] **—au´ri·cled,** *adj.*

au·ric·u·lar (ô·rik´yə·lər), *adj.* 1. of or near the ear. 2. said privately. 3. perceived by the sense of hearing. 4. shaped like an ear. 5. having to do with an auricle of the heart. **—au·ric´u·lar·ly,** *adv.*

au·rif·er·ous (ô·rif´ər·əs), *adj.* yielding gold. [< L, < *aurum* gold + *ferre* bear] **—au·rif´er·ous·ly,** *adv.*

au·rochs (ô´roks), *n., pl.* **-rochs.** 1. European bison, now almost extinct. 2. extinct wild ox. [< G *auerochs*]

Au·ro·ra (ô·rô´rə; -rō´-), *n.* 1. *Class. Myth.* goddess of the dawn. 2. aurora, a. dawn. b. streamers or bands of light appearing in the sky at night. **—au·ro´ral,** *adj.* **—au·ro´ral·ly,** *adv.*

aurora aus·tra·lis (ôs·trā´lis), streamers or bands of light appearing in the southern sky at night.

aurora bo·re·a·lis (bô'ri·al'is; -ā'lis; bō'-), streamers or bands of light appearing in the northern sky at night.

aus·pice (ôs'pis), n., pl. **aus·pi·ces** (ôs'pə·siz). 1. divination or prophecy, esp. one made from the flight of birds. 2. omen; sign. 3. favorable circumstance; indication of success. 4. auspices, patronage. [< F < L auspicium < avis bird + specere look at. See def. 1.]

aus·pi·cious (ôs·pish'əs), adj. 1. with signs of success; favorable. 2. fortunate. —**aus·pi'cious·ly,** adv. —**aus·pi'cious·ness,** n.

Aus·ten (ôs'tən), n. Jane, 1775–1817, English novelist.

aus·tere (ôs·tir'), adj. 1. harsh to the feelings; stern in manner. 2. strict in self-discipline or in self-restraint. 3. severely simple. 4. sour. [< L < Gk. austeros < auein dry] —**aus·tere'ly,** adv.

aus·ter·i·ty (ôs·ter'ə·ti), n., pl. **-ties.** 1. sternness; severity. 2. austerities, severe practices.

Aus·tin (ôs'tən), n. capital of Texas, in the C part.

aus·tral (ôs'trəl), adj. 1. southern. 2. Austral, a. Australian. b. Australasian. [< L, < auster the south wind; akin to EAST]

Aus·tral·a·sia (ôs'tral·ā'zhə; -shə), n. Australia, Tasmania, New Zealand, and nearby islands. —**Aus'tral·a'sian,** adj., n.

Aus·tral·ia (ôs·trāl'yə), n. 1. continent SE of Asia. 2. Commonwealth of, British dominion that includes this continent and Tasmania. —**Aus·tral'ian,** adj., n.

Aus·tral·ian ballot (ôs·trāl'yən), Am. ballot with the names of all candidates on it, which is marked secretly.

Aus·tri·a (ôs'tri·ə), n. country in central Europe. —**Aus'tri·an,** adj., n.

Aus·tri·a-Hun·ga·ry (ôs'tri·ə·hung'gə·ri), n. a former monarchy in central Europe. —**Aus-tro-Hun·gar·i·an** (ôs'trō·hung·gâr'i·ən), adj.

au·tar·chy (ô'tär·ki), n., pl. **-chies.** 1. autocracy. 2. autarky. —**au·tar'chic, au·tar'chi·cal,** adj.

au·tar·ky (ô'tär·ki), n., pl. **-kies.** independence of imports from other nations. —**au·tar'ki·cal,** adj. —**au'tar·kist,** n.

au·then·tic (ô·then'tik), **au·then·ti·cal** (-tə·kəl), adj. 1. reliable: an authentic count. 2. genuine: an authentic signature. 3. authoritative. [< L < Gk., < auto- by oneself + hentes one who acts] —**au·then'ti·cal·ly,** adv.

au·then·ti·cate (ô·then'tə·kāt), v., **-cat·ed, -cat·ing.** 1. establish the truth of. 2. establish the authorship of. —**au·then'ti·ca'tion,** n. —**au·then'ti·ca'tor,** n.

au·then·tic·i·ty (ô'then·tis'ə·ti), n. 1. reliability. 2. genuineness.

au·thor (ô'thər), n. 1. person who writes books, stories, or articles. 2. an author's publications: have you read this author? 3. person who creates or begins anything. [< OF < L auctor < augere increase] —**Syn.** 1. writer. 3. creator.

au·thor·ess (ô'thər·is), n. a woman author.

au·thor·i·tar·i·an (ə·thôr'ə·tār'i·ən; -thor'-), adj. favoring obedience to authority instead of individual freedom. —n. person who supports authoritarian principles. —**au·thor'i·tar'i·an·ism,** n.

au·thor·i·ta·tive (ə·thôr'ə·tā'tiv; ə·thor'-), adj. 1. having authority; officially ordered. 2. commanding: authoritative tones. 3. that ought to be believed or obeyed. —**au·thor'i·ta'tive·ly,** adv. —**au·thor'i·ta'tive·ness,** n.

au·thor·i·ty (ə·thôr'ə·ti; ə·thor'-), n., pl. **-ties.** 1. legal power to enforce obedience. 2. the authorities, a. officials of the government. b. persons in control. 3. influence that creates respect and confidence. 4. source of correct information or wise advice. 5. expert on some subject. [< F < L auctoritas] —**Syn.** 1. control, jurisdiction, dominion. 3. prestige.

au·thor·ize (ô'thər·īz), v., **-ized, -iz·ing.** 1. give power or right to. 2. make legal; sanction. 3. give authority for; justify. —**au'thor·i·za'tion,** n. —**au'thor·iz'er,** n. —**Syn.** 1. empower.

au·thor·ized (ô'thər·īzd), adj. 1. having authority. 2. supported by authority.

Authorized Version, the English translation of the Bible published in 1611; the King James Version.

au·thor·ship (ô'thər·ship), n. 1. occupation of an author. 2. source; origin.

au·to (ô'tō), n., pl. **au·tos.** Am. automobile.

auto-, word element. 1. self, as in autobiography, auto-intoxication. 2. automobile, as in autobus. [< Gk.; also (before vowels and h), aut-]

Au·to·bahn (ou'tō·bän'), n., pl. **-bah·nen** (-bä'nən). in Germany, a four-lane highway with no speed limit.

au·to·bi·og·ra·phy (ô'tə·bī·og'rə·fi; -bī-), n., pl. **-phies.** story of a person's life written by himself. —**au'to·bi·og'ra·pher,** n. —**au·to·bi·o·graph·ic** (ô'tə·bī'ə·graf'ik), **au'to·bi'o·graph'·i·cal,** adj. —**au'to·bi'o·graph'i·cal·ly,** adv. **>** See **biography** for usage note.

au·to·clave (ô'tə·klāv), n. a strong, closed vessel used for sterilizing, cooking, etc. [< F, < auto- self + L clavis key]

auto court, Am. motel.

au·toc·ra·cy (ô·tok'rə·si), n., pl. **-cies.** 1. government having absolute power over its citizens. 2. absolute authority; unlimited power over a group. —**au·to·crat·ic** (ô'tə·krat'ik), **au'to·crat'i·cal,** adj. —**au'to·crat'i·cal·ly,** adv.

au·to·crat (ô'tə·krat), n. 1. ruler having absolute power over his subjects. 2. person having unlimited power over a group of persons. [< Gk., < auto- self + kratos strength]

au·to·da·fé (ô'tō·də·fā'; ou'-), n., pl. **au·tos-da·fé.** public ceremony accompanying the passing of sentence by the Spanish Inquisition. [< Pg., act of the faith, < L actus and fides]

au·to·gi·ro, au·to·gy·ro (ô'tə·jī'rō), n., pl. **-ros.** airplane with a horizontal propeller that enables the airplane to go straight up or down. [< Sp. < Gk. auto- self + gyros circle]

au·to·graph (ô'tə·graf; -gräf), n. 1. person's signature. 2. something written in a person's own handwriting. —v. 1. write one's signature in or on. 2. write with one's own hand.

au·to·mat (ô'tə·mat), n. restaurant in which food is obtained from compartments that open when coins are inserted in slots. [short for automatic]

au·to·mate (ô'tə·māt), v., **-mat·ed, -mat·ing.** to convert to or make use of automation. [< automation]

au·to·mat·ic (ô'tə·mat'ik), adj. 1. moving or acting by itself: automatic pump. 2. Physiol. a. done unconsciously, as certain muscular reactions. b. independent of external stimuli, as the beating of the heart. 3. of a firearm, pistol, etc., utilizing the recoil, or part of the force of the explosions, to eject the cartridge shell, introduce a new cartridge, etc. —n. 1. a. any automatic gun. b. Am. an automatic pistol or rifle. 2. an automatic machine or device. [see AUTOMATON] —**au'to·mat'i·cal·ly,** adv.

au·to·ma·tion (ô'tə·mā'shən), n. method or technique of making a manufacturing process, a production line, etc., operate more automatically by the use of self-regulating controls in machinery. [< autom(atic) + (oper)ation]

au·tom·a·tism (ô·tom'ə·tiz·əm), n. 1. action not controlled by the will. 2. automatic quality.

au·tom·a·ton (ô·tom'ə·ton; -tən), n., pl. **-tons, -ta** (-tə). 1. person or animal whose actions are purely mechanical. 2. machine that has its motive power concealed. 3. thing able to move itself. [< Gk., acting by one's self]

au·to·mo·bile (n. ô'tə·mə·bēl, ô'tə·mə·bēl', -mō'bēl; adj. ô'tə·mō'bil, -bēl; v. ô'tə·mə·bēl', -mō'bēl), n., adj., v., **-biled, -bil·ing.** Am. —n. motorcar; car that carries its own engine. —adj. self-moving: an automobile torpedo. —v. travel by automobile. [< F. See MOBILE.]

au·to·mo·bil·ist (ô'tə·mə·bēl'ist; -mō'bil·ist), n. person who uses an automobile.

au·to·mo·tive (ô'tə·mō'tiv), adj. 1. of automobiles. 2. self-moving.

au·to·nom·ic (ô'tə·nom'ik), **au·to·nom·i·cal** (-ə·kəl), adj. autonomous.

autonomic system, the ganglia and nerves that control digestive and other involuntary reactions.

au·ton·o·mous (ô·ton′ə·məs), *adj.* **1.** self-governing; independent. **2.** *Biol.* reacting independently. **3.** *Bot.* spontaneous. —**au·ton′o·mous·ly,** *adv.*

au·ton·o·my (ô·ton′ə·mi), *n., pl.* **-mies. 1.** power or right of self-government. **2.** a self-governing community. [< Gk., < *auto-* of oneself + *nomos* law] —**au·ton′o·mist,** *n.*

au·top·sy (ô′top·si; ô′təp-), *n., pl.* **-sies.** medical examination of a dead body to find the cause of death. [< NL < Gk., < *auto-* for oneself + *opsis* a seeing]

au·to·sug·ges·tion (ô′tō·səg·jes′chən; -sə·jes′-), *n. Psychol.* suggestion to oneself of ideas that produce actual effects.

au·tumn (ô′təm), *n.* **1.** season of the year between summer and winter. **2.** season of maturity. —*adj.* of autumn; coming in autumn. [< L *autumnus*] —**au·tum·nal** (ô·tum′nəl), *adj.*

autumnal equinox. See equinox.

aux·il·ia·ry (ôg·zil′yə·ri; -zil′ə-), *adj., n., pl.* **-ries.** —*adj.* **1.** helping; assistant. **2.** additional. —*n.* **1.** helper; aid. **2.** auxiliary verb. **3.** auxiliaries, foreign or allied troops that help the army of a nation at war. [< L, < *auxilium* aid]

auxiliary verb, verb used to form the tenses, moods, or voices of other verbs, such as *be, can, do, have,* and *may: I am* going; *he will* go; *they are* lost; *they were* lost.

A.V., Authorized Version.

a·vail (ə·vāl′), *v.* **1.** be of use or value to; help; benefit. **2.** avail oneself of, take advantage of; make use of. —*n.* **1.** help; benefit. **2.** efficacy for a purpose; use. [appar. < *a-* to (< OF < L *ad-*) + *vail* < F < L *valere* be worth]

a·vail·a·ble (ə·vāl′ə·bəl), *adj.* **1.** that can be used. **2.** that can be had. **3.** *Law.* efficacious; valid. —**a·vail′a·bil′i·ty, a·vail′a·ble·ness,** *n.* —**a·vail′a·bly,** *adv.*

av·a·lanche (av′ə·lanch; -länch), *n., v.,* **-lanched, -lanch·ing.** —*n.* **1.** a large mass of snow and ice, or of dirt and rocks, sliding or falling down a mountainside. **2.** anything like an avalanche. —*v.* slide down in or like an avalanche. [< F < Swiss F *lavenche,* infl. by F *avaler* go down < *à val* < L *ad vallem* to the valley]

a·vant-garde (ä·vän·gärd′), *n.* in art, literature, music, etc., those who are most experimental and inventive in a particular period. —*adj.* experimental and inventive. [< F < *avant* forward + *garde* guard] —**a·vant′-gard′ist,** *n.*

av·a·rice (av′ə·ris), *n.* greedy desire for money. [< OF < L, < *avarus* greedy] —**av·a·ri·cious** (av′ə·rish′əs), *adj.* —**av′a·ri′cious·ly,** *adv.* —**av′a·ri′cious·ness,** *n.* —Ant. generosity.

a·vast (ə·vast′; ə·väst′), *interj. Naut.* stop! stay! [prob. < Du. *houd vast* hold fast]

a·vaunt (ə·vônt′; ə·vänt′), *interj. Archaic.* go away! [< F < L *ab ante* forward, in front]

a·ve (ä′vā; ā′vē), *interj.* hail! farewell! —*n.* Ave, the prayer Ave Maria. [< L]

Ave., ave., Avenue; avenue.

A·ve Ma·ri·a (ä′vā mə·rē′ə; ā′vē), **A·ve Mar·y** (ā′vē mār′i), **1.** "Hail Mary!", the first words of the Latin form of a prayer of the Roman Catholic Church. **2.** the prayer.

a·venge (ə·venj′), *v.,* **a·venged, a·veng·ing. 1.** get revenge for. **2.** get revenge on behalf of. **3.** get revenge. [< OF, < *a-* to (< L *ad-*) + *vengier* < L *vindicare* punish < *vindex* champion] —**a·venge′ment,** *n.* —**a·veng′er,** *n.*

av·e·nue (av′ə·nū; -nū), *n.* **1.** *Am.* wide or main street. **2.** road or walk bordered by trees. **3.** way of approach or departure; passage. **4.** *Am.* a city thoroughfare, running at right angles to others properly called "streets." [< F, fem. pp. of *avenir* < L, < *ad-* to + *venire* come]

a·ver (ə·vėr′), *v.,* **a·verred, a·ver·ring. 1.** state to be true; assert. **2.** *Law.* prove; justify. [< OF, ult. < L *ad-* to + *verus* true] —**a·ver′ment,** *n.*

av·er·age (av′rij; av′ər·ij), *n., adj., v.,* **-aged, -ag·ing.** —*n.* **1.** quantity found by dividing the sum of all the quantities by the number of quantities: *the average of 3, 5, and 10 is 6.* **2.** usual kind or quality; ordinary amount or rate. —*adj.* **1.** obtained by averaging; being an aver-

age: *an average price.* **2.** usual; ordinary: *average intelligence.* —*v.* **1.** find the average of. **2.** amount on an average to. **3.** do on an average: *he averages six hours work a day.* **4.** divide among several proportionately. [< F *avarie* damage to ship or cargo < Ar. *'awārīya* damage from sea water. In E extended to "equal distribution" (at first, "of loss").] —**av′er·age·ly,** *adv.* —**av′er·ag·er,** *n.*

A·ver·nus (ə·vėr′nəs), *n. Rom. Myth.* the lower world; Hades. —**A·ver′nal,** *adj.*

a·verse (ə·vėrs′), *adj.* opposed; unwilling. [< L *aversus.* See AVERT.] —**a·verse′ly,** *adv.* —**a·verse′ness,** *n.*

a·ver·sion (ə·vėr′zhən; -shən), *n.* **1.** strong or fixed dislike; antipathy. **2.** object of dislike. **3.** unwillingness.

a·vert (ə·vėrt′), *v.* **1.** prevent; avoid. **2.** turn away; turn aside. [< OF < LL, < L *ab-* from + *vertere* turn] —**a·vert′ed·ly,** *adv.* —**a·vert′i·ble, a·vert′a·ble,** *adj.* —**a·vert′er,** *n.*

A·ves (ā′vēz), *n.pl. Zool.* class of vertebrates comprising the birds. [< L]

A·ves·ta (ə·ves′tə), *n.* the sacred writings of the ancient Zoroastrianism. —**A·ves′tan,** *adj.*

a·vi·ar·y (ā′vi·er′i), *n., pl.* **-ar·ies.** place where many birds are kept. [< L, < *avis* bird]

a·vi·a·tion (ā′vi·ā′shən; av′i-), *n.* flying in airplanes; art or science of navigating aircraft. [< F, < L *avis* bird]

a·vi·a·tor (ā′vi·ā′tər; av′i-), *n.* person who flies an airplane; airplane pilot.

a·vi·a·tress (ā′vi·ā′tris; av′i-), *n.* aviatrix.

a·vi·a·trix (ā′vi·ā′triks; av′i-), *n.* a woman aviator.

av·id (av′id), *adj.* eager; greedy. [< L *avidus* < *avere* desire eagerly] —**a·vid·i·ty** (ə·vid′ə·ti), *n.* —**av′id·ly,** *adv.*

A·vi·gnon (à·vē·nyôn′), *n.* city in SE France; residence of the popes, 1309–1377.

a·vi·on·ics (ā·vi·on′iks), *n.* science of adapting electronic devices to aviation, rocketry, and astronautics. [< *avi*(ation) + (electr)*onics*]

av·o·ca·do (av′ə·kä′dō; ä′və-), *n., pl.* **-dos. 1.** *Am.* a pear-shaped tropical fruit with a dark-green skin; alligator pear. **2.** tree that it grows on. [< Sp., var. of *aguacate* < Mexican *ahuacatl*]

av·o·ca·tion (av′ə·kā′shən), *n.* **1.** minor occupation; hobby. **2.** *Colloq.* regular business; occupation. [< L, < *ab-* away + *vocare* to call]

av·o·cet, av·o·set (av′ə·set), *n.* a web-footed wading bird. [< F < Ital. *avosetta*]

a·void (ə·void′), *v.* **1.** keep out of the way of. **2.** *Law.* make void; annul. [< AF var. of OF *esvuidier* empty, quit < *es-* out (< L *ex-*) + *vuidier* < VL *vocitare* empty] —**a·void′a·ble,** *adj.* —**a·void′a·bly,** *adv.* —**a·void′ance,** *n.*

av·oir·du·pois (av′ər·də·poiz′), *n.* **1.** avoirdupois weight. **2.** *Am., Colloq.* a person's weight. [< OF *avoir de pois* (goods that) have weight < L *habere* have, *de* of, and *pensum* weight]

avoirdupois weight, system of weighing in which a pound containing sixteen ounces is used.

A·von (ā′von; av′ən), *n.* river in C England.

a·vouch (ə·vouch′), *v.* **1.** declare to be true. **2.** guarantee. **3.** acknowledge; affirm. [< OF *avochier* < *a-* + *vochier.* See VOUCH.]

a·vow (ə·vou′), *v.* declare frankly or openly; confess; admit; acknowledge. [< OF, < *a-* (< L *ad-*) + *vouer* < VL *votare* vow] —**a·vow′er,** *n.*

a·vow·al (ə·vou′əl), *n.* frank or open declaration; confession; admission.

a·vowed (ə·voud′), *adj.* openly declared; admitted; acknowledged. —**a·vow·ed·ly** (ə·vou′id·li), *adv.* —**a·vow′ed·ness,** *n.*

a·vun·cu·lar (ə·vung′kyə·lər), *adj.* **1.** of an uncle. **2.** like an uncle. [< L *avunculus* mother's brother, dim. of *avus* grandfather]

a·wait (ə·wāt′), *v.* **1.** wait for; look forward to. **2.** be ready for; be in store for. **3.** wait; be expectant. [< OF, < *a-* for (< L *ad-*) + *waitier* wait < Gmc.] —**a·wait′er,** *n.* —Syn. **1.** expect.

a·wake (ə·wāk′), *v.,* **a·woke** or **a·waked, a·wak·ing,** *adj.* —*v.* wake up; arouse. —*adj.* not asleep; alert. [OE *āwacian* + OE *onwæcnan*]

a·wak·en (ə·wāk′ən), v. wake up; arouse. —a·wak′en·er, n.

a·wak·en·ing (ə·wāk′ən·ing), adj. arousing. —n. 1. act of awaking. 2. Am., Obs. a religious revival.

a·ward (ə·wôrd′), v. 1. give after careful consideration; grant. 2. decide or settle by law; adjudge. —n. 1. something given after careful consideration; prize. 2. Law. decision by a judge. [< AF var. of OF esguarder observe, decide < L ex- from + wardare guard < Gmc.] —a·ward′a·ble, adj. —a·ward′er, n.

a·ware (ə·wâr′), adj. knowing; realizing; conscious. [OE gewær] —a·ware′ness, n.

a·wash (ə·wosh′; ə·wôsh′), adv., adj. 1. just covered with water. 2. washed over. 3. floating.

a·way (ə·wā′), adv. 1. from a place; to a distance. 2. at a distance; far. 3. in another direction; aside: turn away. 4. out of one's possession: he gave his boat away. 5. out of existence: the sounds died away. 6. without stopping; continuously: she worked away at her job. 7. without hesitation; at once. 8. away back, Am., Colloq. far back in space or time. 9. away with, a. take away. b. go away. 10. do away with, a. put an end to; get rid of. b. kill. —adj. 1. at a distance; far. 2. absent; gone. [OE onweg]

awe (ô), n., v., awed, aw·ing. —n. great fear and wonder; fear and reverence. —v. 1. cause to feel awe; fill with awe. 2. influence or restrain by awe. [< Scand. agi] —aw′less, awe′less, adj.

a·weigh (ə·wā′), adj. Naut. raised off the bottom: anchors aweigh.

awe·some (ô′səm), adj. 1. causing awe. 2. showing awe; awed. —awe′some·ly, adv. —awe′some·ness, n.

awe-struck (ô′struk′), **awe-strick·en** (ô′strik′ən), adj. filled with awe.

aw·ful (ô′fəl), adj. 1. dreadful; terrible: an awful storm. 2. Colloq. very bad, great, ugly, etc. 3. deserving great respect and reverence. 4. filling with awe; impressive. —adv. Am., Colloq. very: he was awful mad. [< awe + -ful] —aw′ful·ness, n. —Syn. adj. 1. fearful. 3. sublime, grand. 4. imposing. ▶ In formal English awful means "inspiring with awe." In familiar English it is a general utility word of disapproval: awful manners. As a result awe-inspiring has taken its place.

aw·ful·ly (ô′fli; ô′fəl·i), adv. 1. dreadfully; terribly. 2. Colloq. very.

a·while (ə·hwīl′), adv. for a short time.

awk·ward (ôk′wərd), adj. 1. clumsy; not graceful or skillful. 2. not well-suited to use. 3. not easy to manage or deal with. 4. embarrassing. [< obs. awk perversely, in the wrong way (< Scand. öfugr turned the wrong way) + -ward] —awk′ward·ly, adv. —awk′ward·ness, n. —Syn. 4. trying, disconcerting. —Ant. 2. handy.

awl (ôl), n. tool used for making small holes in leather or wood. [OE æl]

awn (ôn), n. Bot. one of the bristly hairs forming the beard on a head of barley, oats, etc. [< Scand. ögn chaff] —awned, adj. —awn′less, adj.

awn·ing (ôn′ing), n. a rooflike shelter of canvas, etc., over a door, window, porch, etc.

a·woke (ə·wōk′), v. pt. and pp. of awake.

A.W.O.L., a.w.o.l. (ā′wôl, or pronounced as initials), Am., Mil. absent without leave.

a·wry (ə·rī′), adv., adj. 1. with a twist or turn to one side. 2. wrong. [< a on, in + wry]

ax, axe (aks), n., pl. ax·es, v., axed, ax·ing. —n. 1. tool with a bladed head on a handle, used for chopping, etc. 2. battle-ax. —v. cut or shape with an ax. [OE æx] —ax′like′, adj.

ax·es¹ (ak′sēz), n. pl. of axis.

ax·es² (ak′siz), n. pl. of ax.

ax·i·al (ak′si·əl), **ax·ile** (ak′sil; -sīl), adj. 1. of an axis; forming an axis. 2. on or around an axis. —ax′i·al·ly, adv.

ax·il (ak′sil), n. Bot. angle between the upper side of a leaf or stem and the supporting stem or branch. [< L axilla armpit]

ax·il·la (ak·sil′ə), n., pl. ax·il·lae (ak·sil′ē). 1. Anat. armpit. 2. Bot. axil. [< L]

ax·il·lar·y (ak′sə·ler′i), adj. 1. of or near the armpit. 2. Bot. in or growing from an axil.

ax·i·om (ak′si·əm), n. 1. statement seen to be true without proof; self-evident truth. 2. established principle. [< L < Gk., < axios worthy] —ax·i·o·mat·ic (ak′si·ə·mat′ik), ax′i·o·mat′i·cal, adj. —ax′i·o·mat′i·cal·ly, adv.

ax·is (ak′sis), n., pl. ax·es (ak′sēz). 1. imaginary or real line that passes through an object and about which the object turns or seems to turn. 2. central or principal line around which parts are arranged regularly. 3. central or principal structure extending lengthwise. 4. important line of relation: the Berlin-Rome axis. 5. the Axis, Germany, Italy, Japan, and their allies, before the end of World War II. [< L]

ax·le (ak′səl), n. 1. bar on which or with which a wheel turns. 2. axletree. [OE eaxl shoulder, eax axle; ? infl. by Scand. öxl axle] —ax′led, adj.

ax·le·tree (ak′səl·trē′), n. crossbar that connects two opposite wheels.

Ax·min·ster (aks′min·stər), n. a velvetlike carpet.

ay¹ (ā), adv. always; ever. Also, aye. [< Scand. ei]

ay² (ī), adv., n. yes. Also, aye.

a·yah (ä′yə), n. a native maid or nurse in India. [< Hind. < Pg. aia governess]

aye¹ (ā), adv. always; ever.

aye² (ī), adv., n. yes. [OE gī YEA]

aye-aye (ī′ī′), n. a squirrellike lemur of Madagascar.

Aye-aye (total length 3 ft.; height 8 in.)

a·za·le·a (ə·zāl′yə), n. 1. shrub with many showy flowers, resembling rhododendrons. 2. the flower. [< NL < Gk., dry, < azein parch]

az·i·muth (az′ə·məth), n. Astron. the angular distance east or west from the north point. The azimuth of the North Star is 0 degrees. [< F < Ar. as-sumūt the ways < samt way] —az·i·muth·al (az′ə·muth′əl; -mū′thəl), adj. —az′i·muth′al·ly, adv.

A·zores (ə·zôrz′; ə·zōrz′; ā′zôrz; ā′zōrz), n.pl. group of islands in the Atlantic west of and belonging to Portugal.

A·zov (ä·zôf′; ā′zov), n. Sea of, a small sea in S European Russia, connected with the Black Sea by a narrow channel.

Az·tec (az′tek), n. member of a highly civilized people who ruled Mexico before its conquest by the Spaniards in 1519. —adj. of the Aztecs. —Az′tec·an, adj.

az·ure (azh′ər; ā′zhər), n. 1. blue; sky blue. 2. the blue sky. 3. a blue pigment. —adj. blue; sky-blue. [< OF l'azur the azure < Ar. < Pers. lajward lapis lazuli]

az·u·rite (azh′ə·rīt), n. a blue copper ore. It is a basic carbonate of copper, $2CuCO_3 \cdot Cu(OH)_2$.

B

B, b (bē), *n., pl.* **B's; b's. 1.** the second letter of the alphabet. **2.** *Music.* the seventh note in the scale of C major.

B, *Chem.* boron.

B., 1. Bay. 2. Bible. 3. British.

b., 1. base. 2. bass. 3. bay. 4. book. 5. born.

Ba, *Chem.* barium.

B.A., Bachelor of Arts. Also, **A.B.**

baa (bä), *n., v.,* **baaed, baa·ing.** bleat.

Ba·al (bā′əl; bāl), *n., pl.* **Ba·al·im** (bā′əl·im). 1. the chief god of the Canaanites and Phoenicians. 2. a false god. —**Ba′al·ism,** *n.* —**Ba′al·ist, Ba·al·ite** (bā′əl·īt), *n.*

bab·bitt (bab′it), or **Babbitt metal,** *n. Am.* alloy of tin, antimony, and copper, used in bearings to lessen friction.

Bab·bitt (bab′it), *n. Am.* a self-satisfied businessman who readily conforms to middle-class ideas of respectability and business success. —**bab·bitt·ry** (bab′it·ri), *n.*

bab·ble (bab′əl), *v.,* **–bled, –bling,** *n.* —*v.* **1.** make indistinct sounds like a baby. **2.** talk or speak foolishly. **3.** talk too much; tell secrets. **4.** murmur. —*n.* **1.** talk that cannot be understood. **2.** foolish talk. **3.** murmur. [ME *babel;* imit.] —**bab′ble·ment,** *n.* —**bab′bler,** *n.* —**bab′bling·ly,** *adv.*

babe (bāb), *n.* **1.** baby. **2.** an innocent or inexperienced person.

Ba·bel (bā′bəl; bab′əl), *n.* **1.** Babylon, where, according to the Bible, the building of a lofty tower intended to reach heaven was begun and a confusion of the language of the people took place. Gen. 11:1–9. **2.** Also, **babel. a.** confusion of sounds; noise. **b.** place of noise and confusion. [< Heb.]

ba·bies'-breath, ba·by's-breath (bā′biz-breth′), *n.* a tall herb bearing numerous small, fragrant, white or pink flowers.

ba·boo, ba·bu (bä′bü), *n., pl.* **–boos; –bus. 1.** a Hindu title meaning "Mr." **2.** native of India with a smattering of English education. **3.** an Indian clerk who writes English. [< Hind. *babu*]

ba·boon (ba·bün′), *n.* any of various (usually) large, fierce monkeys of Arabia and Africa, with a doglike face and a short tail. [< OF *babouin* stupid person]

ba·by (bā′bi), *n., pl.* **–bies,** *adj., v.,* **–bied, –by·ing.** —*n.* **1.** a very young child. **2.** the youngest of a family or group. **3.** person who acts like a baby. **4.** something unusually small for its kind. **5.** *Am., Slang.* term of praise or approval applied to a person or thing. —*adj.* **1.** of or for a baby. **2.** young. **3.** small for its kind; small. **4.** childish. —*v.* treat as a baby; pamper. [ME *babi*] —**ba′by·hood,** *n.* —**ba′by·ish,** *adj.* —**ba′by·ish·ly,** *adv.* —**ba′by·ish·ness,** *n.* —**ba′by·like′,** *adj.*

Baboon (body 2 ft. high, 2 ft. long; tail 18 in.)

Bab·y·lon (bab′ə·lən; –lon), *n.* **1.** capital of ancient Babylonia, noted for its wealth, magnificence, and wickedness. **2.** any rich or wicked city.

Bab·y·lo·ni·a (bab′ə·lō′ni·ə), *n.* an ancient empire in SW Asia, from 2800 to 1000 B.C. —**Bab′y·lo′ni·an,** *adj., n.*

ba·by·sit (bā′bi·sit′), *v.,* **–sat, –sit·ting.** *Colloq.* take care of a child during the temporary absence of its parents. —**baby sitter.**

bac·ca·lau·re·ate (bak′ə·lô′ri·it), *n.* **1.** degree of bachelor given by a college or university. **2.** Also, **baccalaureate sermon.** *Am.* sermon delivered to a graduating class at commencement. [< Med.L, < *baccalarius*]

bac·ca·rat, bac·ca·ra (bak′ə·rä; bak′ə·rä′), *n.* kind of card game played for money. [< F]

bac·cha·nal (bak′ə·nəl; –nal), *adj.* having to do with Bacchus or his worship. —*n.* **1.** worshiper of Bacchus. **2.** a drunken reveler. **3.** a drunken revelry. **4.** Bacchanals, the Bacchanalia. [< L, < *Bacchus* god of wine < Gk. *Bakchos*]

Bac·cha·na·li·a (bak′ə·nā′li·ə; –nāl′yə), *n., pl.* **1.** a wild, noisy Roman festival in honor of Bacchus. **2.** bacchanalia, a drunken revelry; orgy. —**bac′cha·na′li·an,** *adj., n.*

bac·chant (bak′ənt), *n., pl.* **bac·chants, bac·chan·tes** (bə·kan′tēz). **1.** priest or worshiper of Bacchus. **2.** a drunken reveler. —**bac·chan·tic** (bə·kan′tik), *adj.*

bac·chan·te (bə·kan′tē; bə·kant′; bak′ənt), *n.* priestess or woman worshiper of Bacchus.

Bac·chic (bak′ik), *adj.* **1.** of Bacchus or his worship. **2.** Also, **bacchic.** drunken; riotous.

Bac·chus (bak′əs), *n. Class. Myth.* god of wine. The Greeks also called him Dionysus.

Bach (bäн), *n.* Johann Sebastian, 1685–1750, German composer of music and organist.

bach·e·lor (bach′ə·lər; bach′lər), *n.* **1.** man who has not married. **2.** person who has the first degree of a college or university. **3.** a young knight who served under the banner of another. [< OF < Med.L *baccalarius,* appar., small landowner] —**bach·e·lor·dom** (bach′ə·lər·dəm; bach′lər–), *n. Am.* —**bach′e·lor·hood′,** *n.* —**bach′e·lor·ship′,** *n.*

bach·e·lor-at-arms (bach′ə·lər·ət·ärmz′; bach′lər–), *n., pl.* **bach·e·lors-at-arms.** bachelor (def. 3).

bach·e·lor's-but·ton (bach′ə·lərz·but′ən; bach′lərz–), *n.* **1.** cornflower. **2.** any of several button-shaped flowers or the plants that bear them.

ba·cil·lus (bə·sil′əs), *n., pl.* **–cil·li** (–sil′ī). *Bacteriol.* **1.** any of the rod-shaped bacteria. **2.** any of the bacteria. [< LL, dim. of *baculus* rod]

back¹ (bak), *n.* **1.** part of a person's body opposite to his face or to the front part of his body. **2.** the upper part of an animal's body from the neck to the end of the backbone. **3.** the backbone. **4.** part opposite the front. **5.** part of a chair, couch, etc., that supports the back of a person sitting down. **6.** that part of a garment which covers any part of the body thought of as a back. **7.** the less used part: *the back of the hand.* **8.** player whose position is behind the front line in certain games. **9. behind one's back,** without one's knowing it. —*v.* **1.** support; help. **2.** move backward. **3.** endorse. **4.** bet on. **5.** get upon the back of; mount. **6.** make or be a back for. **7.** of the wind, move counterclockwise with respect to the compass. **8. back and fill, a.** move in a zigzag way. **b.** *U.S. Colloq.* keep changing one's mind. **9. back down,** give up; withdraw. **10. back out** or **out of,** *Colloq.* **a.** withdraw from an undertaking. **b.** break a promise. **11. back up, a.** *Am.* move backward. **b.** support; help. **12. back water,** *Am.* retreat; withdraw. —*adj.* **1.** opposite the front; away from one. **2.** at, in, to, or toward an earlier place, position, etc. **3.** belonging to the past. **4.** overdue. **5.** *Phonet.* pronounced at the back of the mouth. **6.** *Am.* in distant or frontier regions: *back country.* [OE *bæc*] —**back′less,** *adj.* —Syn. *v.* **3.** uphold, second. —*adj.* **1.** rear, hinder. —Ant. *v.* **3.** oppose.

back² (bak), *adv.* **1.** to or toward the rear; behind. **2.** in or toward the past. **3.** in return. **4.** in the place from which it (he, she, etc.) came: *put the books back.* **5.** in reserve. **6.** in check. **7. back of,** *U.S. Colloq.* **a.** in the rear of; behind. **b.** supporting; helping. **8. go back on,** *Colloq.* break a promise. [var. of *aback*]

back·bite (bak′bīt′), *v.,* **–bit, –bit·ten** or

(*Colloq.*) –bit, –bit·ing. slander (an absent person). —**back′bit′er**, *n.* —**back′bit′ing**, *n.*

back·bone (bak′bōn′), *n.* 1. the main bone along the middle of the back in vertebrates; the spine. 2. anything resembling a backbone. 3. the most important part; chief support. 4. strength of character. —**back′boned′**, *adj.*

back·door (bak′dōr′; –dōr′), *adj.* secret; sly.

back·drop (bak′drop′), *n.* 1. curtain at the back of a stage. 2. background.

back·er (bak′ər), *n.* person who backs or supports another person, some plan or idea, etc.

back·field (bak′fēld′), *n. Am.* 1. *Football.* players behind the front line; quarterback, two halfbacks, and fullback. 2. *Baseball.* the outfield.

back·fire (bak′fīr′), *n., v.,* –fired, –fir·ing. —*n.* 1. explosion of gas occurring too soon or in the wrong place in a gasoline engine, etc. 2. *Am.* fire set to check a forest or prairie fire by burning off the area in front of it. 3. an adverse reaction. —*v.* 1. explode prematurely. 2. *Am.* set a backfire. 3. have adverse results.

back formation, a word formed on analogy with other words and usually needed to serve as a different part of speech. *Typewrite* is a back formation from *typewriter.* ▶ A number of back formations, like *diagnose* from *diagnosis,* have made their way into the common vocabulary, but some modern ones are formed in fun, like *burgle,* and are used either in humor or in a derogatory sense, like *orate.*

back·gam·mon (bak′gam′ən; bak′gam′ən), *n.* game for two played on a special board, with pieces moved according to the throw of dice. [< *back¹,* adj. + *gammon* game; because the men are sometimes set back]

back·ground (bak′ground′), *n.* 1. part of a picture or scene toward the back. 2. surface against which things are seen or upon which things are made or placed. 3. earlier conditions or events that help to explain some later condition or event. 4. the past experience, knowledge, and training of a person. 5. the accompanying music or sound effects in a play, motion picture, etc. 6. **in the background,** out of sight.

back·hand (bak′hand′), *n.* 1. stroke made with back of the hand turned outward. 2. handwriting in which the letters slope to the left. —*adj.* backhanded.

back·hand·ed (bak′han′did), *adj.* 1. done or made with the back of the hand turned outward. 2. slanting to the left. 3. awkward; clumsy. 4. indirect; insincere. —**back′hand′ed·ly**, *adv.*

back·ing (bak′ing), *n.* 1. support; help. 2. supporters; helpers. 3. back part supporting or strengthening something.

back·lash (bak′lash′), *n.* 1. the jarring reaction of a machine or mechanical device. 2. movement between worn or loosely fitting parts. 3. any sudden unfavorable reaction.

back·log (bak′lôg′; –log′), *n. Am.* 1. a large log at the back of a wood fire. 2. a reserve of orders, commitments, etc., that have not yet been filled.

back number, *Colloq.* 1. an old issue of a magazine or newspaper. 2. *Am.* an old-fashioned and out-of-date person or thing.

back seat, *Am., Colloq.* place of inferiority or insignificance.

back·sheesh, back·shish (bak′shēsh), *n.* baksheesh.

back·side (bak′sīd′), *n.* 1. back. 2. rump.

back·slide (bak′slīd′), *v.,* –slid, –slid·den or –slid, –slid·ing. slide back into wrongdoing; lose one's enthusiasm for religion or the church. —**back′slid′er**, *n.*

back·stage (bak′stāj′), *adv.* 1. in the dressing rooms of a theater. 2. toward the rear of a stage. —*adj.* happening, located, etc., backstage.

back·stay (bak′stā′), *n.* 1. *Naut.* rope extending from the top of the mast to the ship's side. 2. *Mach.* a supporting or checking device.

back·stop (bak′stop′), *n.* 1. fence or screen used in various games to keep the ball from going too far away. 2. player who stops balls in various games.

back·stroke (bak′strōk′), *n.* 1. a swimming stroke made with the swimmer lying on his back. 2. a backhanded stroke.

back talk, *U.S. Colloq.* talking back; impudent answers.

back·track (bak′trak′), *v. Am.* 1. go back over a course or path. 2. withdraw from an undertaking, position, etc. —*Syn.* 1. return.

back·ward (bak′wərd), *adv.* Also, **back′wards.** 1. toward the back: *walk backward.* 2. with the back first. 3. toward the starting point. 4. opposite to the usual way; in the reverse way: *read backward.* 5. from better to worse. 6. toward the past. —*adj.* 1. directed toward the back: *a backward glance.* 2. with the back first. 3. reversed; returning. 4. done in reverse order. 5. from better to worse; retrogressive. 6. reaching back into the past. 7. slow in development; dull. 8. behind time; late. 9. shy; bashful. [ME *bakward* < *bak* BACK¹ + –WARD] —**back′ward·ly**, *adv.* —**back′ward·ness**, *n.*

back·wash (bak′wosh′; –wôsh′), *n.* 1. water thrown back by oars, paddle wheels, the passing of a ship, etc. 2. backward current.

back·wa·ter (bak′wô′tər; –wot′ər), *n.* 1. water held or pushed back. 2. a sluggish, stagnant condition; backward place. 3. backwash.

back·woods (bak′wùdz′), *n.pl. Am.* uncleared regions far away from towns. —*adj.* Also, **back′wood′.** 1. of the backwoods. 2. crude; rough. —**back′woods′man**, *n. Am.*

ba·con (bā′kən), *n.* salted and smoked meat from the back and sides of a hog. [< OF < Gmc.]

Ba·con (bā′kən), *n.* Francis, 1561–1626, English essayist, statesman, and philosopher. —**Ba·co·ni·an** (bā–kō′ni·ən), *adj., n.*

bac·te·ri·a (bak·tir′i·ə), *n.pl.* microscopic vegetable organisms, usually single-celled and having no chlorophyll, multiplying by fission and spore formation. Various species of bacteria are concerned in fermentation and putrefaction, the production of disease, etc. —**bac·te′ri·al**, *adj.* —**bac·te′ri·al·ly**, *adv.*

SPHERE ROD SPIRAL
Bacteria

bac·te·ri·cide (bak·tir′ə·sīd), *n.* substance that destroys bacteria. [< *bacterium* + –*cide* < L –*cida* killer < *caedere* kill] —**bac·te′ri·cid′al**, *adj.*

bacteriol., bacteriology.

bac·te·ri·ol·o·gy (bak·tir′i·ol′ə·ji), *n.* science that deals with bacteria. [< *bacterium* + –LOGY] —**bac·te·ri·o·log·i·cal** (bak·tir′i·ə·loj′ə·kəl), *adj.* —**bac·te′ri·ol′o·gist**, *n.*

bac·te·ri·o·phage (bak·tir′i·ə·fāj), *n.* bactericide produced within the body and normally present in the intestines, urine, blood, etc. [< *bacterium* + –*phage* eating < Gk. *phagein* eat]

bac·te·ri·um (bak·tir′i·əm), *n., pl.* –te·ri·a (–tir′i·ə). one of the bacteria. [< NL < Gk. *baktērion,* dim. of *baktron*]

Bac·tri·an camel (bak′tri·ən), camel with two humps.

bad¹ (bad), *adj.,* worse, worst, *n., adv.* —*adj.* 1. not as it ought to be; not good. 2. evil; wicked. 3. disagreeable; painful. 4. harmful. 5. sick; injured. 6. unfavorable: *he came at a bad time.* 7. worthless: *a bad check.* 8. incorrect; faulty. 9. not valid. 10. rotten; spoiled: *a bad egg.* 11. *Am.* hostile; dangerous; murderous. —*n.* 1. that which is bad; bad condition, quality, etc. 2. be in bad, *Am., Slang.* be in disfavor (of or over). —*adv.* badly. [orig. pp. of OE *bædan* defile] —**bad′ness**, *n.* —*Syn. adj.* 1. inferior, poor. 2. sinful. 4. injurious. 8. defective, imperfect. 11. vicious. ▶ **Bad** is usually the adjective, though *badly* is used in the predicate (either: I feel *bad* or I feel *badly*); *badly* is usually the adverb, but *bad* is colloquially used: He draws *badly* (colloq. *bad*). *Worse, worst,* the comparative and superlative of *bad,* were originally used in comparing *evil* and *ill;* when *bad* acquired the meaning of these words, *worse* and *worst* were used for it too.

bad² (bad), *v.* pt. of bid (defs. 1, 2).

bade (bad, bād), *v.* pt. of bid.

badge (baj), *n.*, *v.*, **badged, badg·ing.** —*n.* **1.** a token or device worn as a sign of occupation, authority, achievements, or membership. **2.** symbol; sign. —*v.* furnish with a badge or as with a badge. [ME *bage*] —**badge′less,** *adj.*

badg·er (baj′ər), *n.* **1.** any of various burrowing carnivorous mammals of Europe and America related to the weasels. **2.** its fur. —*v.* keep on teasing or annoying; torment by nagging. [? < *badge;* with ref. to white spot on head]

bad·i·nage (bad′ə·näzh′; bad′ə·nij), *n.* joking; banter. [< F, < *badiner* banter < *badin* silly < VL *batāre* gape]

Bad Lands, *Am.* the rugged, barren region in SW South Dakota and NW Nebraska.

bad·ly (bad′li), *adv.* **1.** in a bad manner. **2.** *Colloq.* greatly; much.

bad·min·ton (bad′min·tən), *n.* game like tennis, but played with a feathered cork instead of a ball. [named for Duke of Beaufort's estate]

bad·tem·pered (bad′tem′pərd), *adj.* having a bad temper or disposition.

baf·fle (baf′əl), *v.*, **-fled, -fling,** *n.* —*v.* **1.** be too hard for (a person) to understand or solve. **2.** hinder; thwart. **3.** struggle without success. —*n.* a wall or screen for hindering or changing the flow of air, water, etc. —**baf′fle·ment,** *n.* —**baf′fler,** *n.* —**baf′fling,** *adj.*

bag (bag), *n.*, *v.*, **bagged, bag·ging.** —*n.* **1.** container made of paper, cloth, leather, etc., that can be closed at the top. **2.** sac in an animal's body. **3.** something suggesting a bag by its use or shape, as a valise, suitcase, udder, etc. **4.** game killed or caught by a hunter. **5.** *Am.* a base in baseball. **6. bag and baggage,** with all one's belongings; entirely. **7. hold the bag,** *Colloq.* a. be left empty-handed. b. be left to take the blame, responsibility, etc. **8. in the bag,** *Am., Colloq.* assured. —*v.* **1.** put in a bag. **2.** swell; bulge. **3.** hang loosely. **4.** kill or catch in hunting. **5.** *Slang.* catch; take; steal. [< Scand. *baggi* pack] —**Syn.** *n.* **1.** sack, pouch. —*v.* **4.** capture.

ba·gasse (bə·gas′), *n. Am.* pulp of sugar cane after the juice has been extracted. [< F < Pr. *bagasso* husks]

bag·a·telle (bag′ə·tel′), *n.* **1.** a mere trifle. **2.** game somewhat like billiards. [< F < Ital. *bagatella,* dim. of *baga* berry]

Bag·dad, Bagh·dad (bag′dad), *n.* capital of Iraq, on the Tigris River.

bag·gage (bag′ij), *n.* **1.** the trunks, bags, suitcases, etc., that a person takes with him when he travels. **2.** *Brit.* the portable equipment of an army. **3.** a lively young woman. **4.** a worthless woman. [< OF, < *bagues* bundles]

bag·ging (bag′ing), *n.* material for making bags.

bag·gy (bag′i), *adj.*, **-gi·er, -gi·est. 1.** swelling; bulging. **2.** hanging loosely. —**bag′gi·ly,** *adv.* —**bag′gi·ness,** *n.*

bagn·io (ban′yō; bän′-), *n.*, *pl.* **bagn·ios. 1.** prison. **2.** house of prostitution; brothel. [< Ital. < L *balneum* < Gk. *balaneion* bath]

bag·pipe (bag′pīp), *n.* Often, **bagpipes.** a shrill-toned musical instrument made of a windbag and pipes, now used chiefly in Scotland. —**bag′pip′er,** *n.*

ba·guette, ba·guet (ba·get′), *n.* gem that is cut in a narrow oblong shape. [< F < Ital., ult. < L *baculum* staff]

Ba·gui·o (bag′i·ō), *n.* a mountain city in the N Philippines; summer capital.

Scottish bagpipe

Ba·ha·mas (bə·hä′məz; -hā′-), or **Bahama Islands,** *n.pl.* group of islands in the West Indies, a member of the British Commonwealth.

Bah·rain, Bah·rein (bä·rān′), group of islands in the Persian Gulf, under British control.

bail[1] (bāl), *n.* **1.** guarantee necessary to set a person free from arrest until he is to appear for trial. **2.** amount guaranteed. **3.** person or persons who stand ready to pay the money guaranteed. **4. go bail for,** supply bail for. —*v.*

obtain the freedom of (a person under arrest) by guaranteeing to pay bail. [< OF, custody, < *baillier* deliver < L *bajulāre* carry] —**bail′a·ble,** *adj.* —**bail′ment,** *n.*

bail[2] (bāl), *n.* **1.** the arched handle of a kettle or pail. **2.** a hooplike support. [prob. < Scand. *beygla*]

bail[3] (bāl), *n.* scoop or pail used to throw water out of a boat. —*v.* **1.** throw (water) out of a boat with a pail, a dipper, or any other container. **2.** dip water from. **3. bail out,** drop from an airplane in a parachute. [< F *baille* < L *bajulus* carrier] —**bail′er,** *n.*

bail[4] (bāl), *n. Cricket.* either of two small bars that form the top of a wicket. [< OF, barrier]

bail·ie (bāl′i), *n.* official of a Scottish town or city corresponding to an English alderman. [< OF *bailli,* var. of *bailif* BAILIFF]

bail·iff (bāl′if), *n.* **1.** assistant to a sheriff. **2.** officer of a court who has charge of prisoners while they are in the courtroom. **3.** overseer or steward of an estate. **4.** in England, the chief magistrate in certain towns. [< OF *baillif* < *baillir* govern. See BAIL[1].]

bail·i·wick (bāl′i·wik), *n.* **1.** district over which a bailiff or bailie has authority. **2.** a person's field of knowledge, work, or authority. [< *bailie* + *wick* office < OE *wīce*]

bails·man (bālz′mən), *n.*, *pl.* **-men.** *Law.* person who gives bail.

bairn (bârn), *n. Scot.* child. [OE *bearn*]

bait (bāt), *n.* **1.** anything, esp. food, used to attract fish or other animals so that they may be caught. **2.** thing used to tempt or attract. —*v.* **1.** put bait on (a hook) or in (a trap). **2.** tempt; attract. **3.** set dogs to attack and worry (a bull, bear, etc.) for sport. **4.** torment or worry by unkind or annoying remarks. **5.** stop and feed. [< Scand. *beita* cause to bite] —**bait′er,** *n.*

baize (bāz), *n.* a thick woolen cloth used for curtains, table covers, etc. [< F *baies,* pl. of *bai* chestnut-colored < L *badius*]

bake (bāk), *v.*, **baked, bak·ing,** *n.* —*v.* **1.** cook (food) by dry heat without exposing it directly to the fire. **2.** dry or harden by heat. **3.** become baked: *cookies bake quickly.* —*n.* **1.** a baking. **2.** *Am.* a social gathering at which a meal is served. [OE *bacan*]

Ba·ke·lite (bā′kə·līt), *n. Trademark.* an artificial material used to make beads, electric insulators, etc.

bak·er (bāk′ər), *n.* **1.** person who makes or sells baked goods. **2.** *Am.* a small portable oven.

Bak·er (bāk′ər), *n.* Mount, mountain in NW Washington.

Baker Day, *Am.* day of the second Bikini atom bomb test, July 25, 1946. [< *baker,* the signaler's word for the letter *b,* + *day*]

Baker Island, a small island in the Pacific near the equator, belonging to the U.S.

baker's dozen, thirteen.

bak·er·y (bāk′ər·i), *n.*, *pl.* **-er·ies.** a baker's shop.

bak·ing (bāk′ing), *n.* **1.** act or process of baking. **2.** amount baked at one time; batch.

baking powder, *Am.* mixture of soda and cream of tartar, or of other substances, used instead of yeast to raise biscuits, cakes, etc.

baking soda, *Am.* sodium bicarbonate.

bak·sheesh, bak·shish (bak′shēsh), *n.* money given as a tip in Egypt, Turkey, India, etc. Also, **backsheesh, backshish.** [< Pers. *bakhshish* < *bakhshidan* give]

Ba·ku (bä·kü′), *n.* seaport in S Soviet Union, on the Caspian Sea.

bal., balance.

Ba·laam (bā′ləm), *n. Bible.* a prophet who was rebuked by the ass he rode.

bal·a·lai·ka (bal′ə·lī′kə), *n.* a Russian musical instrument somewhat like a guitar. [< Russ.]

bal·ance (bal′əns), *n.*, *v.*, **-anced, -anc·ing.** —*n.* **1.** instrument for weighing. **2.** equality in weight, amount, force, effect, etc. **3.** comparison as to weight, amount, importance, etc.; estimate.

4. harmony; proportion. 5. steady condition or position; steadiness. 6. anything that counteracts the effect, weight, etc., of something else. 7. difference between the debit and credit sides of an account. 8. *Am., Colloq.* part that is left over; remainder. 9. wheel that regulates the rate of movement of a clock or watch. 10. preponderating weight, amount, or power. 11. a balancing movement in dancing. 12. **in the balance,** undecided. —*v.* 1. weigh in a balance. 2. make or be equal in weight, amount, force, effect, etc. 3. compare the value, importance, etc., of. 4. make or be proportionate to. 5. bring into or keep in a steady condition or position. 6. counteract the effect, influence, etc., of; make up for. 7. make the debit and credit sides of (an account) equal. 8. be equal in the debit and credit sides of an account. 9. hesitate; waver. [< OF < LL *bilanx* two-scaled < *bi-* two + *lanx* scale²] —**bal′ance·a·ble,** *adj.* —**bal′anc·er,** *n.* —Syn. *n.* 1. scale, scales. 5. poise. 8. rest, surplus. —*v.* 5. steady. 6. offset.

balanced diet, diet having the correct amounts of all kinds of foods necessary for health.

balance of power, even distribution of power among nations or groups of nations.

balance of trade, difference in value between the imports and the exports of a country.

balance sheet, a written statement showing the profits and losses, the assets and liabilities, and the net worth of a business.

bal·a·ta (bal′ə·tə), *n.* 1. a tropical tree whose dried gumlike juice is used in making chewing gum, etc. 2. the juice. [< Sp.]

Bal·bo·a (bal·bō′ə), *n.* Vasco de, 1475?–1517, Spanish adventurer, discovered the Pacific, 1513.

bal·brig·gan (bal·brig′ən), *n.* a knitted cotton cloth, used for stockings, underwear, etc. [orig. made at *Balbriggan,* Ireland]

bal·co·ny (bal′kə·ni), *n., pl.* **-nies.** 1. a projecting platform with an entrance from an upper floor of a building. 2. a gallery in a theater or hall. [< Ital., < *balco* scaffold < OHG *balcho* beam] —**bal′co·nied,** *adj.*

bald (bôld), *adj.* 1. wholly or partly without hair on the head. 2. without its natural covering. 3. bare; plain. 4. undisguised. 5. having white on the head. [ME *balled,* appar. < obs. *ball* white spot] —**bald′ly,** *adv.* —**bald′ness,** *n.*

bald eagle, *Am.* a large, powerful eagle with white feathers on its head, neck, and tail.

Bal·der, **Bal·dr** (bôl′dər), *n.* the Norse god of light, beauty, goodness, wisdom, and peace.

bal·der·dash (bôl′dər·dash), *n.* nonsense.

bald·pate (bôld′pāt′), *n.* 1. person who has a bald head. 2. *Am.* kind of duck. —**bald′pat′ed,** *adj.* —**bald′pat′ed·ness,** *n.*

bal·dric (bôl′drik), *n.* belt for a sword, horn, etc., hung from one shoulder to the opposite side of the body. [akin to MHG *balderich* girdle]

bale¹ (bāl), *n., v.,* **baled, bal·ing.** —*n.* a large bundle of merchandise securely wrapped or bound for shipping or storage: *a bale of cotton.* —*v.* make into bales. [prob. < Flem. < OF < OHG *balla* BALL¹] —**bal′er,** *n.*

bale² (bāl), *n. Poetic or Archaic.* 1. evil; harm. 2. sorrow; pain. [OE *bealu*]

Bal·e·ar·ic Islands (bal′i·ar′ik; bə·lir′ik), a group of Spanish islands in the W Mediterranean.

bale·ful (bāl′fəl), *adj.* evil; harmful. —**bale′ful·ly,** *adv.* —**bale′ful·ness,** *n.*

Ba·li (bä′li), *n.* island in SE Indonesia, south of Borneo. —**Ba·li·nese** (bä′lə·nēz′; -nēs′), *adj., n.*

balk (bôk), *v.* 1. stop short and stubbornly refuse to go on. 2. thwart; hinder; check. 3. fail to use; let slip; miss. 4. *Am., Baseball.* make a balk. [< *n.*] —*n.* 1. hindrance; check; defeat. 2. blunder; mistake. 3. ridge between furrows; strip left unplowed. 4. a large beam or timber.

5. *Am., Baseball.* failure of a pitcher to complete a pitch he has started. Also, **baulk.** [OE *balca* ridge] —**balk′er,** *n.* —**balk′ing,** *n., adj.*

Bal·kan (bôl′kən), *adj.* 1. having to do with the Balkan Peninsula. 2. having to do with the Balkan States, or the people of these states. —*n.* the Balkans, the Balkan States.

Balkan Mountains, mountain range in the Balkan Peninsula.

Balkan Peninsula, peninsula in SE Europe.

Balkan States, Yugoslavia, Rumania, Bulgaria, Albania, Greece, and European Turkey.

balk·y (bôk′i), *adj.* **balk·i·er, balk·i·est.** 1. stopping short and stubbornly refusing to go on. 2. likely to balk. —**Ant.** 1. submissive.

ball¹ (bôl), *n.* 1. anything round or roundish. 2. game in which some kind of ball is thrown, hit, or kicked. 3. ball in motion: *a fast ball.* 4. baseball. 5. *Am.* baseball pitched too high, too low, or not over the plate, that the batter does not strike at. 6. bullet. 7. something that is somewhat like a ball. 8. globe; sphere; the earth. 9. **play ball,** *Colloq.* a. begin a game or start it again after stopping. b. get busy; get active. c. *Am.* work together; join in partnership. —*v.* make or form into a ball. [< Scand. *böllr*]

ball² (bôl), *n.* a large, formal party for dancing. [< F *bal* < *baler* dance < LL *ballāre*]

bal·lad (bal′əd), *n.* 1. a simple song. 2. a narrative poem, esp. one that tells a popular legend. [< OF < Pr. *balada* dancing song]

bal·last (bal′əst), *n.* 1. something heavy carried in a ship to steady it. 2. weight carried by a balloon or dirigible to control it. 3. anything which steadies a person or thing. 4. gravel or crushed rock used in making the bed for a road or railroad track. —*v.* 1. furnish with ballast. 2. give steadiness to. 3. load or weigh down. [appar. < Scand. (ODan.) *barlast* < *bar* bare + *last* load] —**bal′last·er,** *n.*

ball bearing, 1. bearing in which the shaft turns upon a number of loose metal balls to lessen friction. 2. one of the metal balls.

bal·le·ri·na (bal′ə·rē′nə), *n., pl.* **-nas.** a woman ballet dancer. [< Ital.]

bal·let (bal′ā; ba·lā′), *n.* 1. an elaborate dance by a group on a stage. 2. the dancers. [< F, dim. of *bal* dance. See BALL².]

bal·lis·ta (bə·lis′tə), *n., pl.* **-tae** (-tē). an ancient military machine for throwing stones and other missiles. [< L, < Gk. *ballein* throw]

ballistic missile, projectile powered by a rocket engine or engines but reaching its target as a result of

Ballista

aim at the time of launching, used esp. as a long-range weapon of offense.

bal·lis·tics (bə·lis′tiks), *n.* science that deals with the motion of projectiles, such as bullets and shells. —**bal·lis′tic,** *adj.* —**bal·lis′ti·cal·ly,** *adv.* —**bal·lis·ti·cian** (bal′is·tish′ən), *n.*

bal·lo·net (bal′ə·net′), *n.* a small bag inside a balloon or airship that holds air or gas to regulate ascent or descent. [< F, dim. of *ballon* BALLOON]

bal·loon (bə·lün′), *n.* an airtight bag filled with some gas lighter than air, so that it will rise and float in the air. —*v.* 1. ride in a balloon. 2. swell out like a balloon. [< Ital. *ballone* < *balla* BALL¹] —**bal·loon′ist,** *n.*

bal·lot (bal′ət), *n., v.,* **-lot·ed, -lot·ing.** —*n.* 1. piece of paper or other object used in voting. 2. the total number of votes cast. —*v.* vote by ballots. [< Ital. *ballotta,* dim. of *balla* BALL¹]

ballot box, *Am.* box into which voters put their ballots after they have voted.

ball·play·er (bôl′plā′ər), *n.* 1. a baseball player. 2. person who plays ball.

ball·room (bôl′rüm′; -rüm′), *n.* a large room for dancing.

bal·ly·hoo (n. bal′i·hü; v. bal′i·hü, bal′i·hü′), n., pl. -hoos, v., -hooed, -hoo·ing. Slang. —n. 1. Am. noisy advertising. 2. uproar; outcry. —v. Am. advertise noisily. —bal′ly·hoo′er, n.

balm (bäm), n. 1. a fragrant ointment or oil used in anointing or for healing or soothing. 2. anything that heals or soothes. 3. an aromatic fragrance; sweet odor. 4. a fragrant, oily, sticky substance obtained from certain kinds of trees. 5. a fragrant plant of the same family as mint. [< OF < L balsamum BALSAM]

balm of Gilead, 1. a fragrant ointment prepared from the resin of a small evergreen tree. 2. the tree itself. 3. Am. the balsam poplar. 4. Am. the balsam fir.

balm·y¹ (bäm′i), adj., balm·i·er, balm·i·est. 1. mild and soothing. 2. fragrant. —balm′i·ly, adv. —balm′i·ness, n. —Syn. 1. bland, temperate.

balm·y² (bäm′i), adj., balm·i·er, balm·i·est. Brit. Slang. silly; crazy. [var. of barmy] —balm′i·ly, adv. —balm′i·ness, n.

ba·lo·ney (bə·lō′ni), n. Am., Slang. nonsense. Also, boloney.

bal·sa (bôl′sə; bäl′-), n. 1. a tropical American tree with very lightweight wood. 2. the wood. 3. a raft or float. [< Sp., raft]

bal·sam (bôl′səm), n. 1. an ointment or preparation for healing or soothing. 2. a fragrant, oily, sticky substance obtained from certain kinds of trees. 3. tree that yields balsam; balsam fir. 4. a garden plant with seed vessels that burst open violently when ripe. 5. anything that heals or soothes. [< L < Gk. balsamon] —bal·sam·ic (bôl·sam′ik; bal-), adj. —bal·sam′i·cal·ly, adv.

balsam fir, Am. 1. an evergreen tree of North America that yields turpentine. 2. its wood.

balsam poplar, Am. a species of poplar grown as a shade tree.

Bal·tic (bôl′tik), adj. 1. of the Baltic Sea. 2. of the Baltic States.

Baltic Sea, sea in N Europe, north of Germany and southeast of Sweden.

Baltic States, Estonia, Latvia, Lithuania, and, sometimes, Finland.

Bal·ti·more (bôl′tə·môr; -mōr), n. city in N Maryland, on Chesapeake Bay.

Baltimore oriole, Am. a North American bird with orange and black feathers.

Ba·lu·chi·stan (bə·lü′chə·stän′; bə·lü′chə·stän), n. former country between India and Iran, on the Arabian Sea, now partly in Pakistan.

bal·us·ter (bal′əs·tər), n. a pillarlike support for a railing. [< F < Ital. < L < Gk. balaustion pomegranate blossom; from the shape]

Baluster and balustrade

bal·us·trade (bal′əs·trād′), n. row of balusters and the railing on them. [< F, < Ital. balustro BALUSTER] —bal′us·trad′ed, adj.

Bal·zac (bal′zak; bôl′-), n. Honoré de, 1799-1850, French novelist.

bam·bi·no (bam·bē′nō), n., pl. -ni (-ni). 1. baby; little child. 2. image or picture of the baby Jesus. [< Ital., dim. of bambo silly]

bam·boo (bam·bü′), n., pl. -boos. any of various woody or treelike tropical or semitropical grasses whose stiff, hollow stems are used for making canes, furniture, and even houses. [< Du. bamboes, prob. < Malay]

Bamboo Curtain, an imaginary wall, separating Communist China from the rest of the world, behind which strict censorship and secrecy are enforced.

bam·boo·zle (bam·bü′zəl), v., -zled, -zling. Colloq. 1. impose upon; cheat; trick. 2. puzzle. —bam·boo′zle·ment, n. —bam·boo′zler, n.

ban (ban), v., banned, ban·ning, n. —v. 1. prohibit; forbid. 2. place a ban on; pronounce a curse on. —n. 1. the forbidding of an act or speech by authority of the law, the church, or public opinion. 2. a solemn curse by the church. 3. sentence of outlawry. [< Scand. banna forbid]

ba·nal (bā′nəl; bə·nal′; -näl′; ban′əl), adj. commonplace; trite. [< F, < ban proclamation. < Gmc.; orig. sense, "of feudal service"; later, "open to the community"] —ba·nal·i·ty (bə·nal′ə·ti; bā-; ba-), n. —ba′nal·ly, adv. —Syn. hackneyed.

ba·nan·a (bə·nan′ə), n. 1. a slightly curved, yellow or red fruit with firm, creamy flesh. 2. a treelike tropical plant on which bananas grow in large clusters. [< Pg. or Sp.]

band¹ (band), n. 1. number of persons or animals joined or acting together. 2. group of musicians playing various instruments together. 3. Am., W. drove or flock of animals; herd. 4. a thin, flat strip of material for binding, trimming, or some other purpose. 5. stripe. 6. collar with two strips hanging in front, worn by certain clergymen. 7. Radio. a particular range of wave lengths in broadcasting. —v. 1. unite in a group. 2. put a band on. 3. mark with stripes. [< F bande, ult. < Gmc.] —Syn. n. 1. company, party, gang, group, crew.

band² (band), n. anything that ties, binds, or unites. [< Scand. band + F bande < Gmc.]

band·age (ban′dij), n., v., -aged, -ag·ing. —n. strip of cloth or other material used in binding up and dressing a wound, injured leg or arm, etc. —v. bind, tie up, or dress with a bandage. [< F, < bande BAND¹] —band′ag·er, n.

ban·dan·na, ban·dan·a (ban·dan′ə), n. a large, colored handkerchief. [prob. < Hind. bāndhnū tie-dyeing]

band·box (band′boks′), n. a light cardboard box to put hats, collars, etc., in.

ban·deau (ban·dō′; ban′dō), n., pl. -deaux (-dōz′; -dōz). 1. band worn about the head. 2. a narrow band. [< F bandeau, dim. of bande band², ult. < Gmc.]

ban·de·role, ban·de·rol (ban′də·rōl), n. a small flag. [< F < Ital., < bandiera BANNER]

ban·di·coot (ban′də·küt), n. 1. a very large rat of India, about two feet long. 2. a ratlike marsupial of Australia. [< Indian dial. pandikokku pig-rat]

ban·dit (ban′dit), n., pl. ban·dits, ban·dit·ti (ban·dit′i). highwayman; robber. [< Ital. bandito, pp. of bandire banish, proscribe, ult. < Gmc.; akin to BAN] —ban′dit·ry, n. —Syn. outlaw, brigand, desperado.

band·mas·ter (band′mas′tər; -mäs′-), n. leader of a band of musicians.

ban·do·leer, ban·do·lier (ban′də·lir′), n. a shoulder belt having loops for carrying cartridges. [< F < Sp., < banda BAND¹]

bands·man (bandz′mən), n., pl. -men. member of a band of musicians.

band·stand (band′stand′), n. an outdoor platform, usually roofed, for band concerts.

band·wag·on (band′wag′ən), n. Am. 1. wagon that carries a musical band in a parade. 2. Colloq. the winning side in a political campaign.

ban·dy (ban′di), v., -died, -dy·ing, n., pl. -dies, adj. —v. 1. throw back and forth; toss about. 2. give and take; exchange: bandy words. —n. Esp. Brit. the game of hockey. —adj. curved outward. [cf. F bander bandy, se bander band together]

ban·dy-leg·ged (ban′di·leg′id; -legd′), adj. having legs that curve outward; bowlegged.

bane (bān), n. 1. cause of death or harm. 2. thing that ruins or spoils. [OE bana murderer]

bane·ful (bān′fəl), adj. deadly; harmful. —bane′ful·ly, adv. —bane′ful·ness, n.

Banff (bamf), n. a resort in SW Canada.

bang¹ (bang), n. 1. a sudden, loud noise. 2. a violent, noisy blow. 3. vigor; impetus. 4. U.S. Colloq. kick; thrill. —v. 1. make a sudden loud noise. 2. hit with violent and noisy blows; strike noisily. 3. shut with noise; slam. 4. handle roughly. —adv. 1. suddenly and loudly. 2. violently and noisily. [? < Scand. banga to hammer]

bang² (bang), Am. —n. 1. fringe of banged hair. 2. bangs, hair cut straight over the forehead. —v. cut squarely across. [short for bangtail docked tail (of a horse)]

Bang·kok (bang′kok), n. capital of Thailand.

āge, cāre, fär; ēqual, tėrm; īce; ōpen, ôrder; pût, rüle, ûse; ŧħ, then; ə=a in about.

ban·gle (bang′gəl), *n.* ring worn around the wrist, arm, or ankle. [< Hind. *bangri* glass bracelet]

Ban·gui (bang′gē), *n.* capital of Central African Republic, in the SW part.

ban·ian (ban′yən), *n.* 1. banyan. 2. a Hindu merchant of a caste that eats no meat. [< Pg., prob. < Ar. *banyān* < Gujarati (a language of western India), ult. < Skt. *vaṇij* merchant]

ban·ish (ban′ish), *v.* 1. condemn to leave a country; exile. 2. force to go away; send away; drive away. [< OF < LL *bannire* ban < Gmc.] —**ban′ish·er,** *n.* —**ban′ish·ment,** *n.* —Syn. 1. expel, outlaw.

ban·is·ter (ban′is·tər), *n.* 1. baluster. 2. banisters, balustrade of a staircase. [var. of *baluster*]

ban·jo (ban′jō), *n., pl.* –jos, –joes. *Am.* a stringed musical instrument of the guitar class, played with the fingers or a plectrum. [alter. of *bandore* < Sp. < LL < Gk. *pandoura* 3-stringed instrument] —**ban′jo·ist,** *n.*

Man playing a banjo

bank¹ (bangk), *n.* 1. a long pile or heap. 2. ground bordering a river, lake, etc. 3. a shallow place in a body of water; shoal. 4. slope. 5. the lateral inclination of an airplane when making a turn. —*v.* 1. border with a bank or ridge. 2. form into a bank; pile or heap up. 3. slope. 4. make (an airplane) bank. 5. cover (a fire) with ashes or fresh fuel so that it will burn long and slowly. 6. *Am.* protect, esp. against the cold, by piling earth against. [prob. < Scand.] —**banked,** *adj.* —Syn. *n.* 1. ridge, mound. 3. bar.

bank² (bangk), *n.* 1. an institution for keeping, lending, exchanging, and issuing money. 2. the office of such an institution. 3. fund of money out of which the dealer or manager in gambling games pays his losses. 4. stock of pieces from which players draw in games. 5. any place where reserve supplies are kept, as of blood plasma for transfusions. —*v.* 1. keep a bank. 2. keep money in a bank. 3. put (money) in a bank. 4. bank on, *Am., Colloq.* depend on; be sure of. [< F < Ital. *banca,* orig., bench < Gmc.] —**bank′a·ble,** *adj.*

bank³ (bangk), *n.* 1. bench for rowers in a galley. 2. row or tier of oars. 3. row of keys on an organ, typewriter, etc. 4. row of things. —*v.* arrange in rows. [< OF < LL *bancus* < Gmc.; akin to BENCH] —**banked,** *adj.*

bank account, money in a bank that can be withdrawn by a depositor.

bank·book (bangk′bùk′), *n.* a depositor's book in which a bank keeps a record of his account.

bank·er (bangk′ər), *n.* 1. person or company that keeps a bank. 2. dealer in a gambling game.

bank·ing (bangk′ing), *n.* business of a bank.

bank note, note issued by a bank that must be paid on demand, circulating as money.

bank·rupt (bangk′rupt), *n.* person who is declared by a law court to be unable to pay his debts and whose property is distributed among his creditors. —*adj.* 1. declared legally unable to pay debts. 2. at the end of one's resources; destitute. 3. wanting; lacking. 4. of bankrupts. —*v.* make bankrupt. [< F < Ital. *bancarotta* bankruptcy < *banca* bank² + *rotta,* fem. pp. of *rompere* break < L *rumpere*]

bank·rupt·cy (bangk′rupt·si; –rəp·si), *n., pl.* –cies. bankrupt condition.

ban·ner (ban′ər), *n.* 1. flag. 2. piece of cloth with some design or words on it, attached by its upper edge to a pole or staff. —*adj. Am.* leading; foremost. [< OF *baniere* < LL *bandum* < Gmc.] —**ban′nered,** *adj.* —Syn. *n.* 1, 2. ensign, standard.

banns (banz), *n.pl.* public notice, given three times in church, that a certain man and woman are to be married. [var. of *bans* proclamations]

ban·quet (bang′kwit), *n., v.,* –quet·ed, –quet·ing. —*n.* 1. feast. 2. a formal dinner with speeches. —*v.* 1. give a banquet to. 2. enjoy a banquet. [< F < Ital. *banchetto,* dim. of *banco* bench < Gmc.] —**ban′quet·er,** *n.*

ban·quette (bang·ket′), *n.* 1. platform along the inside of a parapet or trench for gunners. 2. *Am., Louisiana.* sidewalk. [< F]

ban·shee, ban·shie (ban′shē; ban·shē′), *n. Irish and Scot.* spirit whose wails mean that there will soon be a death in the family. [< Irish *bean sidhe* woman of the fairies]

ban·tam (ban′təm), *n.* 1. Often, Bantam. a small-sized kind of fowl. 2. a small person who is fond of fighting. —*adj.* light in weight; small. [prob. named for *Bantam,* city in Java]

ban·tam·weight (ban′təm·wāt′), *n.* boxer who weighs 118 pounds or less.

ban·ter (ban′tər), *n.* playful teasing; joking. —*v.* 1. tease playfully. 2. talk in a joking way. —**ban′ter·er,** *n.* —**ban′ter·ing·ly,** *adv.*

Ban·tu (ban′tü), *n., pl.* –tu, –tus, *adj.* —*n.* 1. member of a large group of Negroid tribes living in central and S Africa. 2. any of the languages of these tribes. —*adj.* of these tribes or their languages.

ban·yan (ban′yən), *n.* a fig tree of India whose branches have hanging roots that grow down to the ground and take root. Also, **banian.**

ban·zai (bän′zī′), *interj.* a Japanese greeting or patriotic cheer. It means "May you live ten thousand years!"

Bap., Bapt., Baptist.

bap·tism (bap′tiz·əm), *n.* 1. rite or sacrament of dipping a person into water or sprinkling water on him, as a sign of the washing away of sin and of admission into the Christian church. 2. experience that cleanses a person or introduces him into a new kind of life. —**bap·tis·mal** (bap·tiz′məl), *adj.* —**bap·tis′mal·ly,** *adv.*

Bap·tist (bap′tist), *n.* 1. member of a Christian church that believes in baptism by dipping the whole person under water. 2. person who baptizes, as **John the Baptist.** —*adj.* of or having to do with the Baptists.

bap·tis·ter·y (bap′tis·tər·i; –tis·tri), **bap·tist·ry** (bap′tis·tri), *n., pl.* –ter·ies; –ries. a building, or a part of a church, in which baptism is administered.

bap·tize (bap·tīz′; bap′tīz), *v.,* –tized, –tiz·ing. 1. dip into water or sprinkle with water, in baptism. 2. purify; cleanse. 3. christen. [< OF < LL < Gk., < *baptein* dip] —**bap·tiz′er,** *n.*

bar (bär), *n., v.,* barred, bar·ring, *prep.* —*n.* 1. an evenly shaped piece of some solid, longer than it is wide or thick: *bar of soap.* 2. pole or rod put across a door, gate, window, etc., to fasten or shut off something. 3. anything that blocks the way or prevents progress. 4. band of color; stripe. 5. unit of rhythm in music. 6. line between two such units on a musical staff. 7. counter where drinks are served to customers. 8. place containing such a counter. 9. railing around the place where lawyers sit in a court. 10. profession of a lawyer. 11. lawyers as a group. 12. place where an accused person stands in a law court. 13. law court. 14. anything like a law court: *the bar of public opinion.* 15. *U.S.* metal part of a horse's bit. —*v.* 1. put bars across; fasten or shut off with a bar. 2. block; obstruct. 3. exclude; forbid. 4. mark with stripes or bands of color. —*prep.* except; excluding: *the best student, bar none.* [< OF < VL *barra* thick ends of bushes (collectively) < Celtic] —Syn. *n.* 3. barrier, obstacle, obstruction.

BAR, Browning Automatic Rifle.

bar., 1. barometer; barometric. 2. barrel.

barb (bärb), *n.* 1. point projecting backward from the main point, as of a fishhook. 2. *Bot., Zool.* a beardlike growth or part. —*v.* furnish with barbs. [< F < L *barba* beard] —**barbed,** *adj.* —**barb′less,** *adj.*

BARBS

Bar·ba·dos (bär·bā′dōz; bär′bə·dōz), *n.* British island in the West Indies.

bar·bar·i·an (bär·bãr′i·ən), *n.* 1. person who is not civilized. 2. foreigner differing from the speaker or writer in language and customs. 3. person without sympathy for culture or art. —*adj.* 1. not civilized; barbarous. 2. differing from the speaker or writer in language and customs. —**bar·bar′i·an·ism,** *n.*

Barbs (def. 1)

bar·bar·ic (bär·bar′ik), *adj.* 1. uncivilized; rough and rude. 2. of or like that of barbarians. 3. crudely rich or splendid. [< L < Gk., < *barbaros* foreign] —**bar·bar′i·cal·ly,** *adv.*

bar·ba·rism (bär′bə·riz·əm), *n.* 1. condition of uncivilized people. 2. a barbarous act, custom, or trait. 3. use of a word or expression not in accepted use. 4. word or expression not in accepted use, as "his'n" for *his.*

bar·bar·i·ty (bär·bar′ə·ti), *n., pl.* –ties. 1. brutal cruelty. 2. act of cruelty. 3. barbaric manner, taste, or style.

bar·ba·rize (bär′bə·riz), *v.,* –rized, –riz·ing. make or become barbarous. —**bar′ba·ri·za′tion,** *n.*

bar·ba·rous (bär′bə·rəs), *adj.* 1. not civilized. 2. rough; rude. 3. savagely cruel; brutal. 4. crude; harsh. 5. differing from the language and customs of the speaker or writer. 6. filled with words or expressions not in accepted use. [< L < Gk. *barbaros* foreign, appar. orig., stammering] —**bar′ba·rous·ly,** *adv.* —**bar′ba·rous·ness,** *n.* —Syn. 1. barbarian. —Ant. 2. cultured.

Bar·ba·ry (bär′bə·ri), *n.* the Mohammedan countries west of Egypt on the N coast of Africa.

Barbary ape, a tailless monkey that lives in N Africa and on the Rock of Gibraltar.

Barbary States, Morocco, Algeria, Tunis, and Tripoli.

bar·be·cue (bär′bə·kū), *n., v.,* –cued, –cu·ing. —*n.* 1. *Am.* a. feast at which animals are roasted whole. b. food at such a feast. c. device on which the food is prepared. 2. animal roasted whole. 3. meat roasted before an open fire. —*v.* 1. roast (an animal) whole. 2. roast (meat) before an open fire. 3. cook (meat or fish) in a highly flavored sauce. [< Sp. < Haitian *barboka* framework of sticks]

barbed wire, or **barb·wire** (bärb′wir′), *n. Am.* wire with sharp points on it every few inches, used for fences, etc.

bar·bel (bär′bəl), *n.* 1. a long, thin growth hanging from the mouths of some fishes. 2. fish having such growths. [< OF < LL *barbellus,* dim. of *barbus* a kind of fish < L *barba* beard]

BARBELS

bar·ber (bär′bər), *n.* person whose business is cutting hair, shaving men, and trimming beards. —*v.* cut the hair of; shave; trim the beard of. [< AF < L *barba* beard]

bar·ber·ry (bär′ber′i; –bər·i), *n., pl.* –ries. 1. shrub with sour red berries. 2. the berry.

bar·ber·shop (bär′bər·shop′), *n. Am.* shop where barbers work.

bar·bi·can (bär′bə·kən), *n.* tower for defense built over a gate or bridge to a city or castle. [< OF < Med.L *barbicana*]

bar·bi·tal (bär′bə·tôl; –tal), *n.* a drug containing barbituric acid, used as a sedative or hypnotic.

bar·bi·tu·rate (bär·bich′ə·rāt, –rit; bär′bə·tūr′āt, –it, –tyúr′–), *n. Chem.* salt or ester of barbituric acid.

bar·bi·tu·ric acid (bär′bə·tūr′ik; –tyúr′–), *Chem.* an acid, $C_4H_4O_3N_2$, much used as the basis of sedatives and hypnotics.

bar·ca·role, bar·ca·rolle (bär′kə·rōl), *n.* 1. a Venetian boat song. 2. music imitating such a song. [< F < Ital. *barcarola* boatman's song < *barca* boat]

Bar·ce·lo·na (bär′sə·lō′nə), *n.* seaport in NE Spain.

bard (bärd), *n.* 1. an ancient Celtic poet and singer. 2. poet. [< Scotch Gaelic and Irish] —**bard′ic,** *adj.*

bare¹ (bär), *adj.,* bar·er, bar·est, *v.,* bared, bar·ing. —*adj.* 1. without covering; not clothed; naked. 2. with the head uncovered. 3. not concealed; not disguised; open. 4. not furnished; empty. 5. plain; unadorned. 6. much worn; threadbare. 7. just enough and no more; mere. 8. lay bare, uncover; expose; reveal. —*v.* make bare; uncover; reveal. [OE *bær*] —**bare′ness,** *n.* —**bar′er,** *n.*

bare² (bär), *v. Archaic.* pt. of **bear¹.**

bare·back (bär′bak′), *adv., adj.* on a horse's bare back. —**bare′backed′,** *adj.*

bare·faced (bär′fāst′), *adj.* 1. with the face bare. 2. not disguised. 3. shameless; impudent. —**bare·fac·ed·ly** (bär′fās′id·li; –fāst′li), *adv.* —**bare′fac′ed·ness,** *n.*

bare·foot (bär′fút′), *adj., adv.* without shoes and stockings. —**bare′foot′ed,** *adj.*

bare·hand·ed (bär′han′did), *adj.* 1. without any covering on the hands. 2. with empty hands.

bare·head·ed (bär′hed′id), *adj., adv.* wearing nothing on the head. —**bare′head′ed·ness,** *n.*

bare·leg·ged (bär′leg′id; –legd′), *adj.* without stockings.

bare·ly (bär′li), *adv.* 1. only just; scarcely: *barely enough.* 2. nakedly. 3. openly; plainly.

bar·gain (bär′gin), *n.* 1. agreement to trade or exchange. 2. something offered for sale cheap or bought cheap. 3. a good trade or exchange. 4. **into the bargain,** besides; also. —*v.* 1. try to get good terms. 2. make a bargain; come to terms. 3. trade. 4. **bargain for,** be ready for; expect. [< OF *bargaigne*] —**bar′gain·er,** *n.* —Syn. *n.* 1. contract, transaction.

barge (bärj), *n., v.,* barged, barg·ing. —*n.* 1. a large, flat-bottomed boat for carrying freight. 2. a large boat used for excursions, pageants, etc. 3. a large motorboat or rowboat used by the commanding officer of a flagship. 4. houseboat. —*v.* 1. carry by barge. 2. move clumsily like a barge. 3. *Colloq.* push oneself rudely. [< OF < L < Gk. *baris* boat used on Nile] —**barge′man,** *n.*

bar·ite (bär′it; bar′–), *n.* native barium sulfate. Also, **barytes.**

bar·i·tone (bar′ə·tōn), *n.* 1. a male voice between tenor and bass. 2. part to be sung by such a voice. 3. person who sings this part. 4. a musical instrument that has the quality or range of this voice. —*adj.* of or for a baritone. Also, **barytone.** [< Gk., < *barys* deep + *tonos* pitch]

bar·i·um (bar′i·əm; bar′–), *n. Chem.* a soft, silvery-white metallic element, Ba. [< NL < Gk. *barytes* weight] —**bar′ic,** *adj.*

barium sulfate, a sulfate of barium, $BaSO_4$.

bark¹ (bärk), *n.* the tough outside covering of the trunk, branches, and roots of trees and plants —*v.* 1. strip the bark from (a tree, etc.). 2. cover with bark. 3. scrape the skin from (shins, knuckles, etc.). [< Scand. *börkr*] —**bark′er,** *n.* —**bark′less,** *adj.*

bark² (bärk), *n.* 1. the short, sharp sound that a dog makes. 2. a sound like this. —*v.* 1. make this sound or one like it. 2. shout sharply; speak gruffly. 3. *Colloq.* cough. 4. *Am., Slang.* act as barker. [OE *beorcan*] —Syn. *n.* 1. yelp, bay.

bark³ (bärk), *n.* 1. ship with three masts, square-rigged on the first two masts and fore-and-aft-rigged on the other. 2. *Poetic.* boat; ship. Also, **barque.** [< F < Ital. < LL *barca*]

bar·keep·er (bär′kēp′ər), *Am.* **bar·keep** (bär′kēp′), *n.* man who tends a bar where alcoholic drinks are sold.

bar·ken·tine, bar·kan·tine (bär′kən·tēn), *n. Am.* a three-masted ship with the foremast square-rigged and the other masts fore-and-aft-rigged. Also, **barquentine.** [< bark³; modeled on *brigantine*]

bark·er (bär′kər), *n.* 1. one that barks. 2. *U.S.* person who stands in front of a store, show, etc., urging people to go in.

Bark·ley (bärk′li), *n.* Alben William, 1877–1956. vice-president of the U.S. 1949–1953.

bar·ley (bär′li), *n.* 1. the seed or grain of a cereal grass used for food and for making malt. 2. plant yielding this grain. [OE *bærlic*]

Bar·ley·corn (bär′li·kôrn′), *n.* John, a name for intoxicating liquor.

barm (bärm), *n.* a foamy yeast that forms on malt liquors while they are fermenting. [OE *beorma*]

bar·maid (bär′mād′), *n.* woman who works in a bar, serving drinks to customers.

āge, câre, fär; ēqual, tėrm; īce; ōpen, ôrder; pút, rüle, ūse; ŧħ, then; ə=a in about.

bar·man (bär′mən), *n.*, *pl.* **-men.** barkeeper.

barm·y (bär′mi), *adj.*, **barm·i·er, barm·i·est.** 1. full of barm; fermenting. 2. *Colloq.* silly.

barn (bärn), *n.* 1. a building for storing hay, grain, etc. 2. *Am.* such a building which has the added use of sheltering cows, horses, etc. [OE *bærn* < *bere* barley + *ærn* place]

bar·na·cle (bär′nə·kəl), *n.* a crustacean that attaches itself to rocks, the bottoms of ships, etc. [< OF *bernac*]

barn dance, *Am.* 1. dance held in a barn. 2. a lively dance resembling a polka.

barn·storm (bärn′stôrm′), *v. Am., Colloq.* act plays, make speeches, etc., in small towns and country districts. **—barn′storm′er,** *n. Am.* **—barn′storm′ing,** *adj., n. Am.*

Barnacles (2 to 6 in. long)

Bar·num (bär′nəm), *n.* Phineas Taylor, 1810–1891, American showman.

barn·yard (bärn′yärd′), *n. Am.* yard around a barn for livestock, etc.

bar·o·graph (bar′ə·graf; -gräf), *n.* instrument that automatically records changes in air pressure. [< Gk. *baros* weight + -GRAPH] **—bar′o·graph′ic,** *adj.*

ba·rom·e·ter (bə·rom′ə·tər), *n.* 1. an instrument for measuring the pressure of the atmosphere, and thus determining the height above sea level, probable changes in the weather, etc. 2. something that indicates changes. [< Gk. *baros* weight + -METER] **—bar·o·met·ric** (bar′ə·met′rik), **bar′o·met′ri·cal,** *adj.* **—bar′o·met′ri·cal·ly,** *adv.*

bar·on (bar′ən), *n.* 1. nobleman in Great Britain ranking next below a viscount. 2. nobleman in other countries having a similar rank. 3. *Am.* a powerful merchant or financier. [< OF < L *barō* man, fellow] **—ba·ro·ni·al** (bə·rō′ni·əl), *adj.*

bar·on·age (bar′ən·ij), *n.* 1. all the barons. 2. the nobility. 3. rank or title of a baron.

bar·on·ess (bar′ən·is), *n.* 1. wife or widow of a baron. 2. woman whose rank is equal to that of a baron.

bar·on·et (bar′ən·it; -et), *n.* 1. member of a hereditary order of honor in Great Britain ranking next below a baron and next above a knight. 2. title indicating this rank. **—bar′on·et·cy,** *n.*

bar·o·ny (bar′ə·ni), *n.*, *pl.* **-nies.** 1. lands of a baron. 2. rank or title of a baron.

ba·roque (bə·rōk′; -rok′), *adj.* 1. artistically irregular; tastelessly odd; ornate; fantastic; grotesque. 2. irregular in shape. **—n.** *Art.* a. a baroque style. b. something in a baroque style. [< F < Pg. *barroco* irregular]

bar·o·scope (bar′ə·skōp), *n.* instrument for showing changes in the pressure or density of the air. [< Gk. *baros* weight + E -*scope* instrument for viewing < Gk. *skopein* look at] **—ba·ro·scop·ic** (bar′ə·skop′ik), **bar′o·scop′i·cal,** *adj.*

ba·rouche (bə·rüsh′), *n.* a four-wheeled carriage with two seats facing each other and a folding top. [< dial. G < Ital. < L *birotus* two-wheeled < *bi-* two + *rota* wheel]

barque (bärk), *n.* bark³.

bar·quen·tine (bär′kən·tēn), *n.* barkentine.

bar·rack (bar′ək), *n.* Usually, **barracks.** 1. a building or group of buildings for soldiers to live in. 2. a large, plain building in which many people live. **—v.** lodge in barracks. [< F < Ital. *baracca*]

barracks bag, *Mil.* a cloth sack for holding clothing and equipment of military personnel.

bar·ra·cu·da (bar′ə·kü′də), *n.*, *pl.* **-da, -das.** a large, voracious fish of the seas near the West Indies. [< Sp. < West Indian name]

bar·rage (bə·räzh′ *for n.* 1 *and a; bär′ij for n.* 2), *n., v.,* **-raged, -rag·ing. —n.** 1. barrier of artillery fire to check the enemy or to protect one's own soldiers in advancing or retreating. 2. artificial bar in a river; dam. **—v.** fire at with artillery. [< F, < *barrer* BAR]

bar·ra·try (bar′ə·tri), *n.* fraud or gross negligence of a ship's officer or seaman against owners, insurers, etc. [< OF, < *barater* exchange, cheat] **—bar′ra·trous,** *adj.*

barred (bärd), *adj.* 1. having bars: *a barred window.* 2. marked with stripes.

bar·rel (bar′əl), *n., v.,* **-reled, -rel·ing;** *esp. Brit.* **-relled, -rel·ling. —n.** 1. container with round, flat top and bottom and slightly curved sides, usually made of thick boards held together by hoops. 2. amount that a barrel can hold. 3. something somewhat like a barrel: *the barrel of a drum.* 4. the metal tube of a gun. **—v.** put in barrels. [< OF *baril,* prob. < VL *barra* bar, stave] **—Syn.** *n.* 1. cask.

barrel organ, a hand organ.

bar·ren (bar′ən), *adj.* 1. not producing anything. 2. not able to bear offspring. 3. fruitless; unprofitable. 4. without interest; dull. **—n.** Usually, **barrens.** *Am.* barren stretch of land. [< OF *baraine*] **—bar′ren·ly,** *adv.* **—bar′ren·ness,** *n.* **—Syn.** *adj.* 1, 2. unproductive, sterile.

bar·rette (bə·ret′), *n.* a clasp, used by women or girls for holding the hair in place.

bar·ri·cade (bar′ə·kād′; bar′ə·kād), *n., v.,* **-cad·ed, -cad·ing. —n.** 1. a rough, hastily made barrier for defense. 2. any barrier or obstruction. **—v.** block or obstruct with a barricade. [< F, appar. < Pr. *barricada* < *barrica* cask; orig., made of casks. See BARREL.] **—bar′ri·cad′er,** *n.*

Bar·rie (bar′i), *n.* Sir James M., 1860–1937, Scottish writer of novels and plays.

bar·ri·er (bar′i·ər), *n.* 1. something that stands in the way; something stopping progress or preventing approach. 2. something that keeps apart. [< AF < LL, < *barra* BAR]

bar·ring (bär′ing), *prep.* except; not including.

bar·ris·ter (bar′is·tər), *n.* lawyer in England who can plead in any court. [< *bar* + -*ster*] **—bar·ris·te·ri·al** (bar′is·tir′i·əl), *adj.*

bar·room (bär′rüm′; -rum′), *n. Am.* room with a bar for the sale of alcoholic drinks.

bar·row¹ (bar′ō), *n.* 1. frame with two short shafts for handles at each end, used for carrying a load. 2. wheelbarrow. 3. handcart. [OE *bearwe;* akin to BEAR¹]

bar·row² (bar′ō), *n.* mound of earth or stones over an ancient grave. [OE *beorg*]

Bar·row (bar′ō), *n.* Point, northernmost point of land in Alaska.

bar sinister, supposed sign of illegitimacy.

Bart., Baronet.

bar·tend·er (bär′ten′dər), *n. Am.* man who serves alcoholic drinks to customers at a bar.

bar·ter (bär′tər), *v.* 1. trade by exchanging one kind of goods for other goods without using money. 2. exchange. **—n.** 1. act of bartering. 2. exchange. 3. something bartered. [< OF *barater* exchange; akin to BARRATRY] **—bar′ter·er,** *n.*

bar·ti·zan (bär′tə·zən; bär′tə·zan′), *n.* a small overhanging turret on a wall or tower. [alter. of *bratticing* < *brattice* parapet < OF, prob. < OE *brittisc* British (type of fortification)]

Bar·ton (bär′tən), *n.* Clara, 1821–1912, American woman who organized the American Red Cross in 1881.

ba·ry·tes (bə·rī′tēz), *n.* barite.

bar·y·tone (bar′ə·tōn), *n., adj.* baritone.

bas·al (bās′əl), *adj.* 1. of or at the base; forming the base. 2. fundamental; basic. **—bas′al·ly,** *adv.*

basal metabolism, *Physiol.* amount of energy used by an animal at rest.

ba·salt (bə·sôlt′; bas′ôlt), *n.* a hard, dark-colored rock of volcanic origin. [< LL *basaltēs,* a manuscript corruption of L *basanītēs* < Gk., < *basanos* touchstone]

bas·cule (bas′kül), *n.* device that works like a seesaw. In a bascule **bridge** the rising part is counterbalanced by a weight. [< F, seesaw, ult. < *battre* beat (infl. by *bas* low) + *cul* posterior]

base¹ (bās), *n., v.,* **based, bas·ing. —n.** 1. part of a thing on which it rests; bottom. 2. a fundamental principle; basis. 3. the principal element; essential part. 4. a. part of a column on which the shaft rests. b. part at the bottom of a wall or monument. 5. *Bot., Zool.* a. part of an animal or plant organ nearest its point of attachment. b. the point of attachment. 6. *Chem.* a compound that reacts with an acid to form a salt. Calcium hydroxide is a base. 7. station or goal in certain games, such as baseball. 8. starting place. 9. *Mil.* place from which an army, air force, or navy operates and from which supplies are obtained; headquarters. 10. *Math.* number that is a starting point for a system of numeration or logarithms. 11. *Geom.* line or surface forming that part of a figure on which it is supposed to stand. 12. *Surveying.* line used as the starting point. —*v.* 1. make or form a base or foundation for. 2. establish; found (on): *his large business was based on good service.* [< OF < L < Gk. *basis* base; lit., a step] —Syn. *n.* 2. groundwork.

Base (def. 5)

base² (bās), *adj.*, bas·er, bas·est, *n.* —*adj.* 1. morally low; mean; selfish; cowardly. 2. fit for an inferior person or thing; menial; unworthy. 3. *Archaic.* of humble birth or origin. 4. coarse in quality. 5. having little comparative value; inferior. 6. debased; counterfeit. 7. deep or grave in sound. —*n.* the lowest male voice; bass. [< OF < LL *bassus* low] —base′ly, *adv.* —base′ness, *n.* —Syn. *adj.* 1. abject, ignoble. 3. common.

base·ball (bās′bôl′), *n. Am.* 1. game played with bat and ball by two teams of nine players each on a field with four bases. 2. ball used in this game.

base·board (bās′bôrd′; -bōrd′), *n. Am.* 1. line of boards around the walls of a room, next to the floor. 2. board forming the base of anything.

base·born (bās′bôrn′), *adj.* 1. born of humble parents. 2. illegitimate.

base hit, *Am.* successful hitting of the baseball by a batter so that he gets at least to first base without the help of an error.

Ba·sel (bä′zəl), *n.* city in NW Switzerland.

base·less (bās′lis), *adj.* groundless. —base′less·ness, *n.*

base line, 1. line used as a base. 2. *Am.* line between bases.

base·ment (bās′mənt), *n.* 1. story of a building partly or wholly below ground. 2. the lowest division of the wall of a building.

ba·ses¹ (bā′sēz), *n.* pl. of basis.

ba·ses² (bās′iz), *n.* pl. of base¹.

bash (bash), *Dial. and Slang.* —*v.* strike with a smashing blow. —*n.* a smashing blow. [? imit.]

bash·ful (bash′fəl), *adj.* uneasy and awkward in the presence of strangers; shy. [< *bash*, v. (var. of *abash*) + *-ful*] —bash′ful·ly, *adv.* —bash′ful·ness, *n.* —Syn. timid.

bas·ic (bās′ik), *adj.* 1. of or at the base; forming the base; fundamental. 2. *Chem.* a. relating to, having the nature of, or containing a base. b. alkaline. —bas′i·cal·ly, *adv.*

Basic English, or **Basic,** *n.* a copyrighted system of simplified English having a vocabulary of 850 words used according to a simplified English grammar.

bas·il (baz′əl), *n. Am.* a sweet-smelling plant of the same family as mint, used in cooking. [< OF < L < Gk. *basilikon* royal]

bas·i·lar (bas′ə·lər), **bas·i·lar·y** (-ler′i), *adj.* at the base.

ba·sil·i·ca (bə·sil′ə·kə), *n.* 1. in ancient Rome, an oblong building with a broad nave separated from side aisles by rows of columns. 2. an early Christian church built in this form. [< L < Gk. *basilike (oikia)* royal (house) < *basileus* king] —ba·sil′i·can, *adj.*

bas·i·lisk (bas′ə·lisk; baz′-), *n.* 1. *Class. Legend.* a fabled reptile whose breath and look were thought to be fatal. 2. *Zool.* a crested lizard of tropical America. [< L < Gk. *basiliskos*, dim. of *basileus* king]

ba·sin (bā′sən), *n.* 1. a wide, shallow bowl; bowl. 2. an amount that a basin can hold. 3. a hollow place containing water. 4. a roundish valley or hollow. 5. all the land drained by a river and the streams that flow into it. [< OF *bacin* < LL *baccinum* < *bacca* water vessel] —ba′sined, *adj.* —ba′sin·like′, *adj.*

ba·sis (bā′sis), *n., pl.* -ses (-sēz). 1. main part; base. 2. a fundamental principle or set of principles; foundation. 3. the principal ingredient. 4. a starting point. [< L < Gk. See BASE¹.]

bask (bask; bäsk), *v.* warm oneself pleasantly. [< Scand. *bathask* bathe oneself] —bask′er, *n.*

bas·ket (bas′kit; bäs′-), *n.* 1. container made of twigs, grasses, fibers, strips of wood, etc., woven together. 2. amount that a basket holds. 3. anything resembling or shaped like a basket. 4. the structure beneath a balloon for carrying passengers or ballast. 5. *Am.* net shaped like a basket, used as a goal in basketball. 6. *Am.* score made in basketball by tossing the ball through a ring into the basket. —bas′ket·like′, *adj.*

bas·ket·ball (bas′kit·bôl′; bäs′-), *n. Am.* 1. game played with a large, round leather ball by two teams of five players each. The players try to toss the ball through a ring into a net shaped like a basket. 2. the ball used.

bas·ket·ry (bas′kit·ri; bäs′-), *n.* 1. basketwork; baskets. 2. art of making baskets.

bas·ket·work (bas′kit·werk′; bäs′-), *n.* work woven like a basket; wickerwork.

Basque (bask), *n.* 1. member of a race living in the Pyrenees in S France and in N Spain. 2. their language. 3. **basque,** a woman's waist extending over the hips. —*adj.* having to do with the Basques or their language.

bas-re·lief (bä′ri·lēf′, bas′-; bä′ri·lēf, bas′-), *n.* carving or sculpture in which the figures project only slightly from the background. [< F < Ital. *basso-rilievo* low relief]

bass¹ (bās), *adj.* 1. low or deep in sound. 2. *Music.* of or for the lowest part. —*n. Music.* 1. the lowest male voice. 2. singer with such a voice. 3. lowest part in harmonized music. 4. instrument for such a part. [var. of *base²*; after Ital. *basso*]

bass² (bas), *n., pl.* bass·es (*esp. collectively*) bass. any of various spiny-finned fishes, living in fresh water or in the ocean, as the black bass. [var. of *barse* perch; OE *bears*]

bass³ (bas), *n.* 1. basswood. 2. *Bot.* bast. [alter. of *bast*]

bass drum (bās), *Music.* a large drum that makes a deep, low sound when struck.

bas·set (bas′it), or **basset hound,** *n.* dog with short legs and a long body, like a dachshund, but larger and heavier. [< F, dim. of *bas* low]

bas·si·net (bas′ə·net′; bas′ə·net), *n.* 1. a basketlike cradle. 2. a baby carriage of similar shape. [< F, dim. of *bassin* BASIN]

bas·so (bas′ō; bäs′ō), *n., pl.* -sos, -si (-si), *adj. Music.* —*n.* singer with a bass voice. —*adj.* bass¹. [< Ital. See BASE².]

bas·soon (bə·sün′; ba-), *n. Music.* a deep-toned wind instrument with a doubled wooden tube and a curved metal mouthpiece. [< F < Ital. *bassone* < *basso* bass] —bas·soon′ist, *n.*

bass viol (bās), *Music.* a deep-toned stringed instrument like a very large violin.

Man playing a bassoon

bass·wood (bas′wůd′), *n.* 1. Also, **basswood tree.** a. *Am.* linden tree. b. the tulip tree. 2. *Am.* wood of either of these trees. —*adj. Am.* made of basswood.

bast (bast), *n.* 1. *Bot.* the inner layer of the bark that contains cells for carrying sap. 2. the tough fibers in this inner layer. [OE *bæst*]

bas·tard (bas′tərd), *n.* 1. child whose parents are not married to each other; illegitimate child. 2. anything inferior or spurious. —*adj.* 1. born of parents who are not married to each other. 2.

spurious; inferior. 3. irregular or unusual in shape, size, style, etc. [< OF < (fils de) bast packsaddle (child)] —bas′tar·dy, n.

baste[1] (bāst), v., bast·ed, bast·ing. drip or pour melted fat or butter on (meat, etc.) while roasting.

baste[2] (bāst), v., bast·ed, bast·ing. sew with long stitches to hold the cloth until the final sewing. [< OF bastir, < Gmc. Cf. OHG bestan tie up, sew with bast.] —bast′er, n.

baste[3] (bāst), v., bast·ed, bast·ing. beat; thrash. [< Scand. beysta]

Bas·tille (bas·tēl′), n. 1. an old fort in Paris used as a prison, destroyed by a mob on July 14, 1789. 2. bastille, bastile, prison. [< F < LL bastilia < bastire build]

bas·ti·na·do (bas′tə·nā′dō), n., pl. -does, v., -doed, -do·ing. —n. 1. a beating with a stick, esp. on the soles of the feet. 2. stick; cudgel. —v. beat or flog with a stick. [< Sp. bastonada < baston cudgel, ult. < Gmc.]

bast·ings (bās′tingz), n.pl. long, loose stitches to hold the cloth in place until the final sewing.

bas·tion (bas′chən; -ti·ən), n. 1. a projecting part of a fortification. 2. defense; fortification. [< F < Ital. bastione < bastire build. See BASTILLE.] —bas′tioned, adj.

Ba·su·to·land (bə·sü′tō·land′), n. territory in S Africa under British control.

bat[1] (bat), n., v., bat·ted, bat·ting. —n. 1. a stout wooden stick or club, used to hit the ball in baseball, etc. 2. act of batting. 3. turn at batting. 4. Colloq. stroke; blow. 5. Slang. a wild, gay time; spree. 6. at bat, Am. in the batter's position. —v. 1. hit with a bat; hit. 2. Am., Baseball. hit safely balls served by the pitcher. [OE batt]

bat[2] (bat), n. a nocturnal flying mammal characterized by modified forelimbs which serve as wings. [< Scand. (Dan.) -bakke] —bat′like′, adj.

bat[3] (bat), v., bat·ted, bat·ting. wink. [< OF < L battuere beat]

bat., batt., 1. battalion. 2. battery.

Ba·taan (bə·tän′; -tan′), n. peninsula near Manila in the Philippines; surrender of U.S. troops to Japanese, 1942.

Ba·ta·vi·a (bə·tā′vi·ə), n. former name of Djakarta as capital of the Dutch East Indies.

batch (bach), n. 1. quantity of bread made at one baking. 2. quantity of anything made as one lot. 3. number of persons or things taken together. [ME bacche < OE bacan bake]

bate (bāt), v., bat·ed, bat·ing. 1. abate; lessen. 2. with bated breath, holding the breath in great fear, awe, etc. [var. of abate]

ba·teau (ba·tō′), n., pl. -teaux (-tōz′). Am. a light boat with a flat bottom and tapering ends. [< F, ult. < OE bāt BOAT]

bath (bath; bäth), n., pl. baths (bathz; bäthz). 1. a washing of the body. 2. water, etc., for a bath. 3. a tub, room, or other place for bathing. 4. resort with baths for medical treatment. 5. liquid in which something is washed or dipped. 6. container holding the liquid. [OE bæth]

Bath (bath; bäth), n. city in SW England.

bathe (bāth), v., bathed, bath·ing. 1. take a bath. 2. give a bath to. 3. apply water to; wash or moisten with any liquid. 4. go in swimming. 5. cover; surround. [OE bathian] —bath′er, n.

bath·house (bath′hous′; bäth′-), n. 1. building fitted up for bathing. 2. Am. building containing dressing rooms for swimmers.

ba·thos (bā′thos), n. 1. a ludicrous descent from the lofty or elevated to the commonplace in writing or speech; anticlimax. 2. excessive or insincere pathos. [< Gk., depth] —ba·thet·ic (bə·thet′ik), adj.

bath·robe (bath′rōb′; bäth′-), n. Am. a long, loose garment worn to and from the bath.

bath·room (bath′rüm′; -rům′; bäth′-), n. 1. room fitted up for taking baths, etc. 2. toilet.

bath·tub (bath′tub′; bäth′-), n. Am. tub to bathe in.

bath·y·sphere (bath′ə·sfir′), n. a watertight chamber with glass windows, in which men can go deep down in the sea to study animal and

plant life. [< Gk. bathys deep + E -sphere < Gk. sphaira sphere]

ba·tik (bə·tēk′; bat′ik), n. 1. method of making designs on cloth by covering with wax the parts not to be dyed. 2. cloth dyed in this way. 3. design formed in this way. —adj. 1. made by batik; made of batik. 2. like batik; brightly or gaily colored. Also, battik. [< Malay]

ba·tiste (bə·tēst′), n. a fine, thin, cotton cloth. [< F Baptiste, prob. from name of maker]

ba·ton (ba·ton′; bə-), n. 1. a staff or stick used as a symbol of office or authority. 2. stick used by the leader of an orchestra or band for beating time to the music. [< F]

Bat·on Rouge (bat′ən rüzh′), capital of Louisiana, in the SE part, on the Mississippi.

ba·tra·chi·an (bə·trā′ki·ən), Zool. —adj. 1. of or belonging to the division of vertebrates consisting of tailless amphibians, as frogs and toads. 2. like frogs and toads. —n. a tailless amphibian. [< Gk. batrachos frog]

bat·tal·ion (bə·tal′yən), n. 1. U.S. Mil. tactical unit comprising two or more companies, usually commanded by a major and forming part of a regiment. 2. large part of an army organized to act together. 3. army. 4. organized group. 5. battalions, armies. [< F < Ital. battaglione, dim. of battaglia BATTLE]

bat·ten[1] (bat′ən), v. 1. grow fat. 2. fatten. 3. feed greedily. [< Scand. batna < bati improvement] —bat′ten·er, n.

bat·ten[2] (bat′ən), n. 1. board used for flooring. 2. strip of wood nailed across parallel boards to strengthen them, cover cracks, etc. —v. fasten or strengthen with strips of wood. [var. of baton]

bat·ter[1] (bat′ər), v. 1. beat with repeated blows; pound. 2. damage by hard use. [< bat[1]]

bat·ter[2] (bat′ər), n. mixture of flour, milk, eggs, etc., beaten together for use in cookery. [prob. < OF, < batre BAT[3]]

bat·ter[3] (bat′ər), n. player whose turn it is to bat in baseball, cricket, etc.

battering ram, 1. a military machine with a heavy horizontal beam used in ancient times for battering down walls, gates, etc. 2. any heavy object similarly used.

bat·ter·y (bat′ər·i), n., pl. -ter·ies. 1. set of similar or connected things. 2. Elect. set of one or more cells that produce current. 3. Mil. a. set of big guns for combined action in attack or defense. b. these guns together with the soldiers and equipment for them. c. platform or fortification equipped with big guns. 4. Am., Baseball. the pitcher and the catcher together. 5. Law. the unlawful beating of another person. 6. any act of beating or battering. [< F, < battre beat. See BAT[3], BATTLE.]

bat·tik (bat′ik), n., adj. batik.

bat·ting (bat′ing), n. Am. cotton or wool pressed into thin layers.

bat·tle (bat′əl), n., v., -tled, -tling. —n. 1. fight between armies or navies. 2. fighting; war. 3. fight; contest. —v. 1. take part in a battle. 2. fight; struggle; contend. [< OF < LL battalia < L battuere beat] —bat′tler, n.

bat·tle-ax, bat·tle-axe (bat′əl·aks′), n. ax used as a weapon in war.

battle cruiser, a large, fast warship, not so heavily armored as a battleship.

battle cry, 1. shout of soldiers in battle. 2. motto or slogan in any contest.

bat·tle·dore (bat′əl·dôr; -dōr), n. a small racket used to hit a shuttlecock back and forth in the game of battledore and shuttlecock.

battle fatigue, neurosis from anxiety during combat.

bat·tle·field (bat′əl·fēld′), **bat·tle·ground** (bat′əl·ground′), n. place where a battle is fought or has been fought.

bat·tle·ment (bat′əl·mənt), n. 1. wall with indentations for men to shoot through. 2. Archit. wall built like this for ornament. [ult. < OF bastiller fortify]

Battlement for defense

bat·tle·ship (bat′əl·ship′), *n.* one of a class of the largest and most heavily armored warships.

bat·ty (bat′i), *adj.*, **-ti·er**, **-ti·est**. 1. batlike. 2. *U.S. Slang.* crazy; queer.

bau·ble (bô′bəl), *n.* a showy trifle having no real value. [< OF *babel* toy]

baulk (bôk), *v.*, *n.* balk.

baux·ite (bôk′sīt; bō′zīt), *n.* a claylike mineral from which aluminum is obtained. [from Les *Baux*, France]

Ba·var·i·a (bə·vãr′i·ə), *n.* a state in SW Germany. —**Ba·var′i·an**, *n.*, *adj.*

bawd (bôd), *n.* procurer; procuress; person who keeps a brothel. [< OF *baud* gay < Gmc.]

bawd·ry (bôd′ri), *n.* obscenity; lewdness.

bawd·y (bôd′i), *adj.*, **bawd·i·er**, **bawd·i·est**. lewd; obscene. —**bawd′i·ly**, *adv.* —**bawd′i·ness**, *n.*

bawl (bôl), *n.* 1. a noisy shout at the top of one's voice. 2. a loud crying. —*v.* 1. shout or cry out in a noisy way. 2. cry loudly. 3. bawl out, *Am.*, *Slang.* reprimand. [prob. < Med.L *baulare* bark] —**bawl′er**, *n.* —**Syn.** *v.* 2. weep.

bay[1] (bā), *n.* part of a sea or lake, extending into the land. [< OF *baie* < Gmc.]

bay[2] (bā), *n. Archit.* space or division of a wall or building between columns, pillars, etc. 2. space with a window or set of windows in it, projecting out from a wall. 3. bay window. [< F *baie* opening < VL *batare* gape]

bay[3] (bā), *n.* 1. the long, deep bark of a dog. 2. stand made by a hunted animal to face pursuers when escape is impossible. 3. similar stand made by a person against persecution, etc. 4. position of pursuers or enemy kept off. —*v.* bark; bark at. [< OF *bayer*, prob. < VL *batare* gape] —**bay′er**, *n.*

bay[4] (bā), *n.* 1. a small evergreen tree with smooth, shiny leaves; laurel tree. 2. bays, a. laurel wreath worn by poets or victors. b. honor; renown; fame. [< OF *baie* < L *baca* berry]

bay[5] (bā), *n.* 1. reddish brown. 2. a reddish-brown horse. —*adj.* reddish-brown. [< OF *bai* < L *badius*]

bay·ber·ry (bā′ber′i), *n.*, *pl.* **-ries**. 1. a. *Am.* a North American shrub with grayish-white berries coated with wax. b. one of the berries. 2. a tropical American tree whose leaves contain an oil used in bay rum.

bay·o·net (bā′ə·nit; -net), *n.*, *v.*, **-net·ed**, **-net·ing**. —*n.* blade for piercing or stabbing, attached to a gun. —*v.* pierce or stab with a bayonet. [< F *baionnette*; named for *Bayonne*, France]

bay·ou (bī′ü), *n.*, *pl.* **-ous**. *Am.* a marshy inlet or outlet of a lake, river, or gulf in the southern United States. [< Louisiana F < Choctaw *bayuk* small stream]

bay rum, a fragrant liquid originally made from the leaves of a tree growing in the West Indies, used in medicine and cosmetics.

bay window, window or set of windows projecting out from a wall.

ba·zaar, **ba·zar** (bə·zär′), *n.* 1. street or streets full of shops. 2. place for the sale of many kinds of goods. 3. sale held for some charity, a worthy cause, etc. [< F < Ar. < Pers. *bāzār*]

ba·zoo·ka (bə·zü′kə), *n. Am.*, *Mil.* rocket gun used against tanks. [from resemblance to trombonelike instrument created and named by Bob Burns, American humorist]

B.B.C., British Broadcasting Corporation.

bbl., *pl.* **bbls.** barrel.

B-bop (bē′bop′), *n. Slang.* bebop.

B.C., 1. before Christ; before the birth of Christ. 350 B.C. is 100 years earlier than 250 B.C. 2. British Columbia.

bd., *pl.* **bds.** 1. board. 2. bond. 3. bound.

be (bē), *v.*, *pres. indic. sing.* am, are, is, *pl.* are; *pt. indic. sing.* was, were, was, *pl.* were; *pp.* been; *ppr.* be·ing. 1. have reality; exist; live. 2. take place; happen. 3. remain; continue. 4. equal; represent. 5. *Be* is used as a linking verb between a subject and a predicate modifier or to form infinitives and participial phrases: *you will be late, try to be just.* 6. *Be* is used as an auxiliary verb;

with: a. the present participle of another verb to form the progressive tense: *he is building a house.* b. the past participle of another verb to form the passive voice: *the date was fixed.* [OE *bēon*] ≫ Older usage of be survives in stock phrases, as "the powers that be," and in non-standard spoken English, as in "You ain't (sometimes be'n't) going, be you?" Nonstandard spoken English also continues to use was in the plural, as in "*Was* the Adamses there?," which would have been good informal usage 200 years ago. ≫ a. be as linking verb. Be is the most common linking verb, linking, without adding specifically a meaning of its own, a subject and a predicate nominative or adjective: *Jerome was the secretary* [predicate nominative]. *She is sick* [predicate adjective]. b. as auxiliary verb. Forms of be are used with the present participles of other verbs to form the progressive tense form: *I am asking, he was asking, you will be asking.* Forms of be with past participles form the passive voice: *I am asked, you will be asked, he was asked.* c. as verb of complete predication. *Be* is a verb of complete predication when indicating states or positions: *I am tired, the fire was just across the street.*

be-, *prefix.* 1. thoroughly; all around, as in *bespatter*. 2. at; on; to; for; about; against, as in *bewail*. 3. make, as in *belittle*. 4. provide with, as in *bespangle*. [OE, unstressed form of bī by]

Be, *Chem.* beryllium.

B/E, **b.e.**, bill of exchange.

beach (bēch), *n.* the almost flat shore of sand or little stones at the edge of the sea, a river, or a large lake. —*v.* run or draw (a boat) ashore. —**beach′less**, *adj.* —**Syn.** *n.* strand, coast, seashore.

beach·comb·er (bēch′kōm′ər), *n.* 1. a vagrant or loafer on beaches. 2. *U.S.* a long wave rolling in from the ocean.

beach·head (bēch′hed′), *n. Mil.* the first position established by an invading army on a hostile shore.

bea·con (bē′kən), *n.* 1. fire or light used as a signal to guide or warn. 2. a radio signal for guiding aviators through fogs, storms, etc. 3. a tall tower for a signal; lighthouse. —*v.* 1. give light to; guide; warn. 2. shine brightly. 3. supply with beacons. [OE *bēacn*] —**bea′con·less**, *adj.*

bead (bēd), *n.* 1. a small ball or bit of glass, metal, etc., with a hole through it, so that it can be strung on a thread with others like it. 2. beads, a. string of beads. b. a rosary. 3. say, tell, or count one's beads, say prayers, using a rosary. 4. any small, round object like a drop or bubble: *beads of sweat.* 5. *Am.* the front sight of a rifle. 6. a narrow, semicircular molding. —*v.* 1. put beads on; ornament with beads. 2. form beads. [OE *bedu* prayer. See def. 2b.] —**bead′ed**, *adj.*

bead·ing (bēd′ing), *n.* 1. trimming made of beads threaded into patterns. 2. a narrow trimming. 3. pattern or edge on woodwork, silver, etc., made of small beads. 4. a narrow, semicircular molding.

bea·dle (bē′dəl), *n.* a minor officer in the Church of England. [OE *bydel*]

bead·y (bēd′i), *adj.*, **bead·i·er**, **bead·i·est**. 1. small, round, and shiny. 2. trimmed with beads. 3. covered with drops or bubbles.

bea·gle (bē′gəl), *n.* a small hunting dog with short legs and drooping ears. [ME *begle*]

beak (bēk), *n.* 1. a bird's bill, esp. one that is strong and hooked and useful in striking or tearing. 2. a similar part in other animals. 3. the projecting bow of an ancient warship. 4. a spout. [< OF < L *beccus* < Celtic] —**beaked** (bēkt; bēk′id), *adj.* —**beak′less**, *adj.* —**beak′like′**, *adj.*

beak·er (bēk′ər), *n.* 1. a large cup or drinking glass. 2. contents of a beaker. 3. a thin glass or metal cup used in laboratories. [< Scand. *bikarr*]

Beaker (def. 3)

beam (bēm), *n.* 1. a large, long piece of timber, ready for use in building. 2. a similar piece of metal or stone. 3. the main horizontal support of a building or ship. 4. part of a plow by which it is pulled. 5. the crosswise bar of a balance, from the ends of which the scales or pans are suspended. 6. the balance itself. 7. ray or rays of light or heat; ray. 8. a bright look or smile. 9. a radio signal directed in a straight line, used to guide aviators, sailors, etc. 10. *Radio*. a. the maximum range at which a loudspeaker is effective. b. angle which gives the maximum performance to a microphone, amplifier, etc. 11. *Naut*. side of a ship, or the direction at right angles to the keel, with reference to wind, sea, etc. 12. the greatest width of a ship. 13. on her beam's ends, almost capsizing. 14. on the beam, a. of a ship, broadside. b. of an aircraft, in the right path by the directing signals. c. *Slang*. just right; exactly. —*v*. 1. send out rays of light; shine. 2. smile radiantly. 3. direct (a broadcast): *beam programs at Russia*. [OE *bēam* tree, piece of wood, ray of light] —**beamed**, *adj*. —**beam'less**, *adj*. —**beam'like'**, *adj*.

beam·ing (bēm'ing), *adj*. 1. shining; bright. 2. smiling brightly. —**beam'ing·ly**, *adv*.

bean (bēn), *n*. 1. a smooth, kidney-shaped seed used as a vegetable. 2. the long pod containing such seeds. 3. plant that beans grow on. 4. any seed shaped somewhat like a bean. 5. *Am., Slang*. head. —*v. Am., Slang*. hit on the head. [OE *bēan*]

bean·ball (bēn'bôl'), *n. Am., Slang*. a baseball thrown by the pitcher so as to hit or attempt to hit the batter's head. —**bean'ball'er**, *n*.

bear¹ (bãr), *v*., bore or (*Archaic*) bare, borne or born, bear·ing. 1. carry: *bear a burden*. 2. support: *bear the weight of the roof*. 3. put up with; endure: *he can't bear the noise*. 4. undergo; experience: *bear pain*. 5. produce; yield: *bear fruit*. 6. give birth to; have (offspring): *bear a child*. 7. have a connection or effect; relate: *his story does not bear on the question*. 8. behave; conduct. 9. bring forward; give: *bear witness to what happened*. 10. have; hold. 11. have as an identification or characteristic: *a coat bearing marks of hard wear*. 12. have as a duty, right, privilege, etc.: *bear sway over an empire*. 13. press; push. 14. move; go; tend in direction: *the ship bore north*. 15. lie; be situated: *the land bore due north of the ship*. 16. allow; permit: *the accident bears two explanations*. 17. bear down, a. put pressure on. b. approach; move toward. 18. bear out, support; prove. 19. bear up, keep one's courage; not lose hope or faith. 20. bear with, put up with; be patient with. [OE *beran*] —Syn. 1. bring, convey. 2. sustain. 3. abide, tolerate, brook. 10. cherish, harbor. 13. thrust, drive. ➤ See borne for usage note.

bear² (bãr), *n., adj., v.*, beared, bear·ing. —*n*. 1. a large, clumsy, quadruped animal that has coarse hair and a very short tail. 2. a gruff or surly person. 3. person who tries to lower prices in the stock market, etc. 4. Bear, *Astron*. one of two northern groups of stars; the Little Bear or the Great Bear. —*adj*. having to do with lowering prices in the stock market, etc. —*v*. operate for a decline in stocks, etc. [OE *bera*]

bear·a·ble (bãr'ə·bəl), *adj*. that can be borne; endurable. —**bear'a·ble·ness**, *n*. —**bear'a·bly**, *adv*.

beard (bird), *n*. 1. hair growing on a man's face. 2. something resembling or suggesting this, as the chin tuft of a goat. 3. hairs on the heads of plants like oats, barley, and wheat; awns. —*v*. face boldly; defy. [OE] —**beard'ed**, *adj*. —**beard'less**, *adj*. —**beard'less·ness**, *n*. —**beard'like'**, *adj*.

bear·er (bãr'ər), *n*. 1. person or thing that carries. 2. person who holds or presents a check, draft, or note for payment. 3. tree or plant that produces fruit or flowers. 4. holder of a rank or office. 5. pallbearer.

A, bearded wheat; B, beardless wheat.

bear·ing (bãr'ing), *n*. 1. act of a person or thing that bears. 2. act, power, or season of bearing offspring or fruit. 3. way of standing, sitting, walking, etc.; manner: *a military bearing*. 4. reference; relation: *the question has no bearing on the problem*. 5. direction; position in relation to other things: *he got his bearings from*

the sun. 6. part of a machine on which another part turns or slides. 7. a supporting part. 8. a single device in a coat of arms. —Syn. 1. sustaining. 3. behavior, air, conduct.

bear·ish (bãr'ish), *adj*. 1. like a bear; rough; surly. 2. aiming at or tending to lower prices in the stock market, etc. 3. not hopeful or confident; pessimistic. —**bear'ish·ly**, *adv*. —**bear'ish·ness**, *n*.

bear·skin (bãr'skin'), *n*. fur of a bear.

beast (bēst), *n*. 1. any animal except man, esp. a four-footed animal. 2. a coarse, dirty, or brutal person. 3. the beastly nature in human beings. [< OF < LL *besta*] —**beast'like'**, *adj*.

beast·ly (bēst'li), *adj*., -li·er, -li·est, *adv*. —*adj*. 1. like a beast; brutal; coarse. 2. *Brit. Colloq*. annoying; irksome. —*adv. Brit. Colloq*. annoyingly. —**beast'li·ness**, *n*.

beat (bēt), *v*., beat, beat·en or beat, beat·ing, *n., adj*. —*v*. 1. strike again and again; strike; whip; thrash. 2. throb: *her heart beats fast with joy*. 3. drive by blows; force by blows: *he beat off the savage dog*. 4. defeat; overcome. 5. *Colloq*. baffle. 6. *Am., Colloq*. cheat; swindle. 7. make flat; shape with a hammer: *beat gold into gold leaf*. 8. make flat by much walking; tread (a path). 9. mix by stirring; mix by striking with a fork, spoon, or other utensil: *beat eggs*. 10. move up and down; flap: *the bird beat its wings*. 11. make a sound by being struck: *the drums beat loudly*. 12. mark (time) with drumsticks or by tapping with hands or feet: *beat a tattoo*. 13. show musical beat by a stroke of the hand, etc. 14. go through in a hunt. 15. move against the wind by a zigzag course: *the sailboat beat along the coast*. 16. *Colloq*. win. 17. beat a retreat, a. run away; retreat. b. sound a retreat on a drum. 18. beat up, *Am., Colloq*. attack; thrash. —*n*. 1. stroke or blow made again and again: *the beat of a drum*. 2. *Music*. a. unit of time or accent: *three beats to a measure*. b. stroke of the hand, baton, etc., showing a musical beat. 3. a regular route or round made by a policeman or watchman. 4. *Am., Colloq*. person, thing, or event that wins. 5. *Am*. in journalism, the securing and publishing of news ahead of one's competitors. —*adj. Am., Colloq*. 1. exhausted. 2. overcome by astonishment; taken aback. [OE *bēatan*] —**beat'er**, *n*. —Syn. *v*. 1. smite, pommel, flog. 4. vanquish, conquer. 16. surpass, outdo.

beat·en (bēt'ən), *v*. pp. of beat. —*adj*. 1. whipped; thrashed. 2. shaped by blows of a hammer. 3. much walked on or traveled: *beaten path*. 4. defeated; overcome. 5. exhausted.

be·a·tif·ic (bē'ə·tif'ik), *adj*. making blessed; blissful. [< L *beatificus* < *beare* bless + *facere* make] —**be·a·tif'i·cal·ly**, *adv*.

be·at·i·fy (bi·at'ə·fī), *v*., -fied, -fy·ing. 1. make supremely happy; bless. 2. declare (a dead person) by a decree of the Pope to be among the blessed in heaven. —**be·at'i·fi·ca'tion**, *n*.

beat·ing (bēt'ing), *n*. 1. act of one that beats. 2. whipping; thrashing. 3. defeat. 4. throbbing.

be·at·i·tude (bi·at'ə·tūd; -tūd), *n*. 1. supreme happiness; bliss. 2. blessing. 3. the Beatitudes, verses in the Bible beginning "Blessed are the poor in spirit." Matt. 5:3–12. [< L *beatitudo* < *beare* bless]

beat·nik (bēt'nik), *n*. a person who lives in a free and easy, unconventional way; Bohemian.

beat-up (bēt'up'), *adj. Am., Slang*. in very bad condition; showing evidence of hard use.

beau (bō), *n., pl.* beaus, beaux (bōz). 1. a suitor; lover. 2. dandy; fop. [< F, handsome, < L *bellus* fine] —**beau'ish**, *adj*. —Syn. 1. swain. 2. dude.

Beau·fort scale (bō'fərt), an internationally used scale of wind velocities, ranging from 0 (calm) to 12 (hurricane).

beau geste (bō zhest'), *pl*. beaux gestes (bō zhest'). 1. a graceful or kindly act. 2. *French*. pretense of kindness merely for effect.

beau·te·ous (bū'tē·əs), *adj. Esp. Poetic*. beautiful. —**beau'te·ous·ly**, *adv*. —**beau'te·ous·ness**, *n*.

beau·ti·ful (bū'tə·fəl), *adj*. very pleasing to see or hear; delighting the mind or senses. —**beau'ti·ful·ly**, *adv*. —**beau'ti·ful·ness**, *n*.

beau·ti·fy (bū'tə·fī), v., –fied, –fy·ing. make or become beautiful or more beautiful. —**beau'ti·fi·ca'tion**, n. —**beau'ti·fi'er**, n. —Syn. ornament, decorate, adorn.

beau·ty (bū'ti), n., pl. –ties. 1. good looks. 2. quality that pleases in flowers, pictures, music, etc. 3. quality that pleases the intellect or moral sense. 4. a beautiful person, animal, or thing, esp. a beautiful woman. [< OF beauté < beau beautiful. See BEAU.] —Syn. 2. loveliness.

beauty parlor or **shop**, Am. place where women have their hair, skin, and fingernails cared for.

beaux-arts (bō·zär'), n.pl. French. fine arts; painting, sculpture, music, etc.

bea·ver[1] (bē'vər), n. 1. an amphibious rodent with a broad, flat tail, noted for its ingenuity in damming streams with mud, branches, etc. 2. its soft brown fur. 3. a man's high silk hat. [OE beofor] —**bea'ver·like'**, adj.

bea·ver[2] (bē'vər), n. 1. the movable lower part of a helmet. 2. visor of a helmet. 3. Slang. beard. [< OF bavière, orig., bib < bave saliva]

be·bop (bē'bop'), n. Slang. a fad in popular music, based on unusual rhythms, dissonance, and lack of formalism. Also, bop, B-bop.

B, beaver.

be·calm (bi·käm'), v. 1. prevent from moving by lack of wind. 2. make calm.

be·came (bi·kām'), v. pt. of become.

be·cause (bi·kôz'), conj. for the reason that; since. —adv. because of, by reason of; on account of: we did not go because of the rain. [ME bicause by cause] —Syn. conj. inasmuch as, for. ➤ Because introduces a subordinate clause, giving the reason for the independent statement: because we were late we hurried. Since and as can be used in such clauses, but they are less definite, more casual, and are more characteristic of easy speech than of writing. For, which also introduces reasons, is more formal.

be·chance (bi·chans'; –chäns'), v., –chanced, –chanc·ing. happen; happen to; befall.

Bech·u·a·na·land (bech'ü·ä'nə·land'), n. former district in S Africa under British control. Now called **Botswana**.

beck (bek), n. 1. motion of the head or hand meant as a call or command. 2. at one's beck and call, a. ready whenever wanted. b. under one's complete control. —v. beckon to.

Beck·et (bek'it), n. Saint Thomas à, 1118?–1170, archbishop of Canterbury.

beck·on (bek'ən), v. signal (to a person) by a motion of the head or hand. —n. a beckoning gesture. [OE bēcnan] —**beck'on·er**, n.

be·cloud (bi·kloud'), v. obscure.

be·come (bi·kum'), v., be·came, be·come, be·com·ing. 1. come to be; grow to be. 2. be suitable for; suit. 3. become of, happen to: what will become of her? [OE becuman] ➤ Become is primarily a linking verb with little meaning of its own, chiefly connecting a subject with a predicate adjective or noun: he became a doctor.

be·com·ing (bi·kum'ing), adj. 1. fitting; suitable; appropriate: becoming conduct for a gentleman. 2. that looks well: a becoming dress. —**be·com'ing·ly**, adv. —**be·com'ing·ness**, n. —Syn. 1. proper, meet, seemly.

Becque·rel rays (bek'rel), invisible rays given off by radioactive substances.

bed (bed), n., v., bed·ded, bed·ding. —n. 1. mattress. 2. bedstead. 3. anything to sleep or rest on. 4. the use of a bed: bed and board. 5. any place where people or animals rest or sleep. 6. flat base on which anything rests; foundation. 7. ground under a body of water: the bed of a river. 8. piece of ground in which plants are grown. 9. such a piece and the plants in it. 10. layer; stratum: a bed of coal. —v. 1. provide with a bed. 2. put to bed. 3. go to bed. 4. fix or set in a permanent position; embed. 5. plant in a garden bed. 6. form a compact layer. 7. lay flat; lay in order. [OE bedd] —**bed'less**, adj. —**bed'like'**, adj. —Syn. n. 3. couch, berth.

be·daze (bi·dāz'), v., –dazed, –daz·ing. stupefy.

be·daz·zle (bi·daz'əl), v., –zled, –zling. dazzle completely; confuse. —**be·daz'zle·ment**, n.

bed·bug (bed'bug'), n. a small, flat blood-sucking hemipterous insect.

bed·cham·ber (bed'chām'bər), n. bedroom.

bed·clothes (bed'klōz'; –klōthz'), n.pl. sheets, blankets, quilts, etc.

bed·ding (bed'ing), n. 1. sheets, blankets, quilts, etc.; bedclothes. 2. material for beds. 3. foundation; bottom layer.

be·deck (bi·dek'), v. adorn; decorate.

be·dev·il (bi·dev'əl), v., –iled, –il·ing; esp. Brit. –illed, –il·ling. 1. trouble greatly; torment. 2. confuse completely; muddle. 3. put under a spell; bewitch. —**be·dev'il·ment**, n.

be·dew (bi·dū'; –dū'), v. wet with dew or with drops like dew.

bed·fast (bed'fast'; –fäst'), adj. bedridden.

bed·fel·low (bed'fel'ō), n. 1. sharer of one's bed. 2. associate.

be·dight (bi·dīt'), v., –dight, –dight or –dight-ed, –dight·ing. adj. Archaic. —v. adorn; array. —adj. adorned; arrayed.

be·dim (bi·dim'), v., –dimmed, –dim·ming. make dim; darken; obscure. —Syn. overcast.

be·di·zen (bi·dī'zən; –diz'ən), v. ornament with showy finery. —**be·di'zen·ment**, n.

bed·lam (bed'ləm), n. 1. uproar; confusion. 2. insane asylum; madhouse. 3. Bedlam, insane asylum in London. [alter. of Bethlehem. See def. 3.]

Bed·ou·in (bed'ü·in), n. 1. a wandering Arab who lives in the deserts of Arabia, Syria, or northern Africa. 2. wanderer; nomad.

bed·pan (bed'pan'), n. 1. Am. pan used as a toilet by sick people in bed. 2. pan filled with hot coals for warming a bed.

be·drag·gle (bi·drag'əl), v., –gled, –gling. make limp and soiled, as with dirt. —**be·drag'gle·ment**, n.

bed·rid·den (bed'rid'ən), **bed·rid** (–rid'), adj. confined to bed for a long time because of sickness or weakness.

bed·rock (bed'rok'), n. 1. Am. solid rock beneath the soil and looser rocks. 2. firm foundation. 3. the lowest level; bottom. 4. Am. fundamental or essential part.

bed·room (bed'rüm'; –rüm'), n. room to sleep in.

bed·side (bed'sīd'), n. side of a bed.

bed·spread (bed'spred'), n. Am. cover for a bed, usually decorative.

bed·stead (bed'sted; –stid), n. the wooden or metal framework of a bed.

bed·time (bed'tīm'), n. time to go to bed.

bee (bē), n. 1. any of various hymenopterous insects, esp. the common honeybee, producing honey and wax, and forming highly organized colonies. 2. any of various similar insects. 3. Am. a gathering for work or amusement: a husking bee. [OE bēo]

Worker honeybee (ab. ¾ actual size).

bee·bread (bē'bred'), n. a brownish, bitter substance consisting of pollen, or pollen mixed with honey, used by bees as food.

beech (bēch), n. 1. a tree with smooth, gray bark and glossy leaves that bears a sweet edible nut. 2. its wood. [OE bēce] —**beech'en**, adj.

beech·nut (bēch'nut'), n. the small, triangular nut of the beech tree.

beef (bēf), n., pl. beeves (bēvz) (for 2) or beefs (for 5), v. —n. 1. meat from a steer, cow, or bull. 2. steer, cow, or bull when full-grown and fattened for food. 3. Colloq. strength; muscle. 4. Colloq. weight. 5. Am., Colloq. complaint; grievance. —v. 1. Am., Slang. complain loudly. 2. beef up, Slang. strengthen: beef up defenses. [< OF boef < L bos ox] —**beef'less**, adj.

āge, cãre, fär; ēqual, tėrm; īce; ōpen, ôrder; pùt, rüle, ūse; th, then; ə=a in about.

beef·steak (bēf′stāk′), n. slice of beef for broiling or frying.

beef·y (bēf′i), adj., beef·i·er, beef·i·est. strong; muscular; solid. —beef′i·ness, n.

bee·hive (bē′hīv′), n. 1. hive or house for bees. 2. a busy, swarming place.

bee·line (bē′līn′), n. Am. straightest way or line between two places.

Be·el·ze·bub (bi·el′zə·bub), n. 1. Bible. the Devil. 2. a devil.

been (bin; rarely bēn), v. pp. of be.

beer (bir), n. 1. an alcoholic drink made from malt and usually hops. 2. drink made from roots or plants, as root beer. [OE bēor]

Beer·she·ba (bir·shē′bə; bir′shi–), n. town near the S boundary of Arab Palestine.

beer·y (bir′i), adj., beer·i·er, beer·i·est. 1. of or like beer. 2. caused by beer. —beer′i·ness, n.

beest·ings (bēs′tingz), n.pl. the first milk from a cow after it has given birth to a calf. [OE bȳsting < bēost beestings]

bees·wax (bēz′waks′), n. wax given out by bees, from which they make their honeycomb. —v. rub, polish, or treat with beeswax.

beet (bēt), n. 1. thick root of a plant. Red beets are eaten as vegetables. Sugar is made from white beets. 2. the plant. The leaves are sometimes eaten as greens. [< L beta]

Bee·tho·ven (bā′tō·vən), n. Ludwig van, 1770–1827, German musical composer.

bee·tle[1] (bē′təl), n. 1. any of an order of insects with two hard, shiny cases to cover the wings when folded. 2. any similar insect. [OE bitela < bītan bite]

bee·tle[2] (bē′təl), n., v., -tled, -tling. —n. 1. a heavy wooden mallet. 2. a wooden household utensil for beating or mashing. —v. pound with a beetle. [OE bíetel < bēatan beat]

bee·tle[3] (bē′təl), v., -tled, -tling, adj. —v. project; overhang. —adj. projecting; overhanging. [< beetle-browed]

bee·tle-browed (bē′təl·broud′), adj. 1. having overhanging eyebrows. 2. scowling; sullen. [ME bitel biting < brow. See BEETLE[1].]

beeves (bēvz), n. pl. of beef (def. 2).

be·fall (bi·fôl′), v., -fell, -fall·en, -fall·ing. 1. happen to. 2. happen. —Syn. 2. occur.

be·fit (bi·fit′), v., -fit·ted, -fit·ting. be suitable for; be proper for; be suited to. —be·fit′ting, adj. —be·fit′ting·ly, adv.

be·fog (bi·fog′; -fôg′), v., -fogged, -fog·ging. surround with fog; make foggy; obscure; confuse.

be·fore (bi·fôr′; -fōr′), prep. 1. in front of; in advance of; ahead of: walk before me. 2. earlier than: come before five o'clock. 3. rather than; sooner than: I will die before giving in. 4. in the presence or sight of: stand before the king. —adv. 1. in front; in advance; ahead: go before. 2. earlier: come at five o'clock, not before. 3. until now; in the past: I didn't know that before. —conj. 1. previously to the time when: before she goes. 2. rather than; sooner than: I will die before I give in. [OE beforan]

be·fore·hand (bi·fôr′hand′; -fōr′-), adv., adj. ahead of time; in advance.

be·foul (bi·foul′), v. 1. make dirty; cover with filth. 2. entangle.

be·friend (bi·frend′), v. act as a friend to.

be·fud·dle (bi·fud′əl), v., -dled, -dling. stupefy; confuse, esp. with alcoholic drink.

beg (beg), v., begged, beg·ging. 1. ask for (food, money, clothes, etc.) as a charity. 2. ask help or charity. 3. ask earnestly or humbly. 4. ask formally and courteously. 5. beg off, get free by pleading. 6. beg the question, take for granted the very thing argued about. [OE bedecian] —Syn. 3. entreat, implore.

be·gan (bi·gan′), v. pt. of begin.

be·get (bi·get′), v., be·got or (Archaic) be·gat, be·got·ten or be·got, be·get·ting. 1. become the father of. 2. cause to be; produce. —be·get′ter, n.

beg·gar (beg′ər), n. 1. person who lives by begging. 2. a very poor person. 3. fellow. —v. 1. bring to poverty. 2. make seem poor. —beg·gar·dom (beg′ər·dəm), beg′gar·hood, n.

beg·gar·ly (beg′ər·li), adj. fit for a beggar; poor. —beg′gar·li·ness, n.

beg·gar's-lice (beg′ərz·līs′), **beg·gar·lice** (beg′ər·līs′), n. Am. 1. (pl. in use) burs or seeds of various plants that stick to clothes. 2. (pl. or sing. in use) weed on which such burs or seeds grow.

beg·gar's-ticks (beg′ərz·tiks′), **beg·gar·ticks** (beg′ər·tiks′), n. sing. or pl. beggar's-lice.

beg·gar·y (beg′ər·i), n. very great poverty.

be·gin (bi·gin′), v., be·gan, be·gun, be·gin·ning. 1. do the first part; do the first part of; start. 2. come into being; bring into being; originate. 3. be near; come near: that suit doesn't even begin to fit you. [OE beginnan] —Syn. 1. commence. 2. arise.

be·gin·ner (bi·gin′ər), n. 1. person who is doing something for the first time; person who lacks skill and experience. 2. person who begins anything. —Syn. 1. amateur, novice.

be·gin·ning (bi·gin′ing), n. 1. a commencing, start. 2. time when anything begins. 3. first part. 4. first cause; source; origin. —adj. that begins. —Syn. n. 1. initiation. —Ant. n. 1. end.

be·gird (bi·gėrd′), v., -girt (-gėrt′) or -gird·ed, -gird·ing. surround; encircle.

be·gone (bi·gôn′; -gon′), interj., v. be gone; go away; depart.

be·go·ni·a (bi·gō′ni·ə; -gōn′yə), n. a tropical plant with handsome leaves and waxy flowers. [from Michel Bégon, patron of botany]

be·got (bi·got′), v. pt. and pp. of beget.

be·got·ten (bi·got′ən), v. pp. of beget.

be·grime (bi·grīm′), v., -grimed, -grim·ing. make grimy; make dirty.

be·grudge (bi·gruj′), v., -grudged, -grudg·ing. envy (somebody) the possession of; be reluctant to give (something); grudge. —be·grudg′ing·ly, adv.

be·guile (bi·gīl′), v., -guiled, -guil·ing. 1. deceive; cheat. 2. take away from deceitfully or cunningly. 3. entertain; amuse. 4. while away (time) pleasantly. —be·guil′er, n. —be·guil′ing·ly, adv. —Syn. 1. delude. 3. divert, charm.

be·gun (bi·gun′), v. pp. of begin.

be·half (bi·haf′; -häf′), n. 1. side; interest; favor: his friends will act in his behalf. 2. in behalf of, in the interest of; for. 3. on behalf of, a. as a representative of. b. in behalf of. [ME behalve beside, on the side of]

be·have (bi·hāv′), v., -haved, -hav·ing. 1. act. 2. conduct (oneself or itself) in a certain way. 3. act well; do what is right.

be·hav·ior, esp. Brit. **be·hav·iour** (bi·hāv′yər), n. 1. way of acting; conduct; actions; acts. 2. manners; deportment. —Syn. 2. demeanor.

be·hav·ior·ism (bi·hāv′yər·iz·əm), n. doctrine that the objective acts of persons and animals are the chief or only subject matter of scientific psychology. —be·hav′ior·ist, n. —be·hav′ior·is′tic, adj. —be·hav′ior·is′ti·cal·ly, adv.

be·head (bi·hed′), v. cut off the head of.

be·held (bi·held′), v. pt. and pp. of behold.

be·he·moth (bi·hē′məth; bē′ə-), n. Bible. a huge animal mentioned in Job 40:15–24. [< Heb. b′hēmōth, pl. of b′hēmah beast]

be·hest (bi·hest′), n. command; order. [OE hǣs promise]

be·hind (bi·hīnd′), prep. 1. at the back of; in the rear of: behind the door. 2. at or on the far side of: behind the hill. 3. concealed by: vile treachery lurked behind his smooth manners. 4. inferior to; less advanced than. 5. later than; after: behind one's usual time. 6. remaining after: the dead man left a family behind him. 7. in support of; supporting: his friends are behind him. —adv. 1. at or toward the back; in the rear. 2. farther back in place or time. 3. in arrears. 4. not on time; slow; late. [OE behindan. See BE-, HIND[1].]

be·hind·hand (bi·hīnd′hand′), adv., adj. 1. behind time; late. 2. behind others in progress; backward; slow. 3. in debt.

be·hold (bi·hōld′), v., be·held, be·hold·ing, interj. 1. see; look at. 2. look; take notice. [OE behealdan] —be·hold′er, n. —Syn. 1. observe.

be·hold·en (bi·hōl′dən), *adj.* indebted.

be·hoof (bi·hüf′), *n.* use; advantage; benefit. [OE *behōf* need]

be·hoove (bi·hüv′), *esp. Brit.* **be·hove** (bi·hōv′), *v.*, **–hooved, –hoov·ing; –hoved, –hov·ing.** 1. be necessary for. 2. be proper for. [OE *behōfian* to need]

beige (bāzh), *n., adj.* pale brown. [< F]

be·ing (bē′ing), *n.* 1. life; existence. 2. nature; constitution: *her whole being thrilled to the music.* 3. that which exists. 4. person; living creature. —*adj.* that is; present: *the time being.*

Bei·rut (bā′rüt; bā·rüt′), *n.* capital of Lebanon.

be·jew·el (bi·jü′əl), *v.*, **–eled, –el·ing;** *esp. Brit.* **–elled, –el·ling.** adorn with jewels.

be·la·bor, *esp. Brit.* **be·la·bour** (bi·lā′bər), *v.* 1. beat vigorously. 2. abuse; ridicule.

be·lat·ed (bi·lāt′id), *adj.* 1. delayed; too late. 2. overtaken by darkness. —**be·lat′ed·ly,** *adv.* —**be·lat′ed·ness,** *n.*

be·lay (bi·lā′), *v.*, **be·layed, be·lay·ing.** 1. *Naut.* fasten (a rope) by winding it around a pin or cleat. 2. *Colloq.* stop. [OE *belecgan.* See BE–, LAY¹.]

belaying pin, *Naut.* pin around which ropes can be wound and fastened.

belch (belch), *v.* 1. throw out gas from the stomach through the mouth. 2. throw out with force: *the volcano belched fire.* —*n.* act of belching. [cf. OE *bealcian*] —**belch′er,** *n.*

Belaying pins with ropes on them

bel·dam (bel′dəm), **bel·dame** (–dəm; –dām′), *n.* 1. an old woman. 2. an ugly old woman. [< *bel–* grand– (< OF, < *belle* fair) + *dam* DAME]

be·lea·guer (bi·lē′gər), *v.* 1. besiege. 2. surround. [< Du. *belegeren* < *leger* camp] —**be·lea′guered,** *adj.* —**be·lea′guer·er,** *n.* —**be·lea′guer·ment,** *n.*

Be·lém (bə·lem′), *n.* seaport in NE Brazil. Also, **Pará.**

Bel·fast (bel′fast; –fäst), *n.* seaport and capital of Northern Ireland.

bel·fry (bel′fri), *n., pl.* **–fries.** 1. tower for a bell or bells. 2. space for the bell in a tower. [< OF *berfrei* < Gmc.] —**bel·fried** (bel′frid), *adj.*

Belg., Belgium; Belgian.

Belgian Congo, former Belgian colony in C Africa, now called the Congo.

Bel·gium (bel′jəm), *n.* a small country in W Europe. —**Bel·gian** (bel′jən), *adj., n.*

Bel·grade (bel′grād; bel·grād′), *n.* capital of Yugoslavia, on the Danube River.

Be·li·al (bē′li·əl; bēl′yəl), *n.* the devil.

be·lie (bi·lī′), *v.*, **–lied, –ly·ing.** 1. give a false idea of; misrepresent. 2. show to be false; prove to be mistaken. 3. lie about. 4. be false to. —**be·li′er,** *n.*

be·lief (bi·lēf′), *n.* 1. what is held true; thing believed; opinion. 2. acceptance as true or real. 3. faith; trust: *he expressed his belief in the boy's honesty.* 4. religious faith. [ME *bileafe.* Cf. OE *gelēafa.*] —Syn. 1. conviction, view.

be·lieve (bi·lēv′), *v.*, **–lieved, –liev·ing.** 1. accept as true or real. 2. have faith in (a person or thing); trust. 3. think (somebody) tells the truth. 4. have religious belief. 5. think; suppose. [ME *bileve(n).* Cf. OE *gelīefan.*] —**be·liev′a·ble,** *adj.* —**be·liev′a·ble·ness,** *n.* —**be·liev′er,** *n.*

be·lit·tle (bi·lit′əl), *v.*, **–lit·tled, –lit·tling.** *Am.* 1. cause to seem little, unimportant, or less important; speak slightingly of. 2. make small. —**be·lit′tle·ment,** *n.* —**be·lit′tler,** *n. Am.* —Syn. 1. depreciate, disparage.

bell (bel), *n.* 1. a hollow metal cup that makes a musical sound when struck by a clapper or hammer. 2. sound of a bell. 3. stroke of a bell every half hour to tell time on shipboard. —*v.* 1. put a bell on. 2. swell out like a bell. [OE *belle*] —**bell′less,** *adj.* —**bell′like′,** *adj.*

Bell (bel), *n.* **Alexander Graham,** 1847–1922, American scientist who invented the telephone.

bel·la·don·na (bel′ə·don′ə), *n.* 1. a poisonous plant with black berries and red flowers. 2. drug made from this plant. [< Ital., fair lady]

bell·boy (bel′boi′), *n. Am.* man or boy whose work is carrying hand baggage and doing errands for the guests of a hotel or club.

bell buoy, *Naut.* buoy with a bell rung by the movement of the waves.

belle (bel), *n.* 1. a beautiful woman or girl. 2. the prettiest or most admired woman or girl. [< F, fem. of *beau.* See BEAU.]

belles-let·tres (bel′let′rə), *n.pl.* the finer forms of literature. [< F] —**bel·let·rist** (bel′let′-rist), *n.* —**bel·le·tris·tic** (bel′le·tris′tik), *adj.*

bell·hop (bel′hop′), *n. Am., Colloq.* bellboy.

bel·li·cose (bel′ə·kōs), *adj.* warlike; fond of fighting. [< L *bellicosus* < *bellum* war] —**bel′li·cose′ly,** *adv.* —**bel·li·cos·i·ty** (bel′ə·kos′ə·ti), *n.*

bel·lig·er·ence (bə·lij′ər·əns), *n.* 1. fondness for fighting. 2. fighting; war.

bel·lig·er·en·cy (bə·lij′ər·ən·si), *n.* 1. state of being at war. 2. belligerence.

bel·lig·er·ent (bə·lij′ər·ənt), *adj.* 1. fond of fighting; warlike. 2. at war; engaged in war; fighting. 3. having to do with nations or persons at war. —*n.* nation or person at war. [< L, < *bellum* war + *gerere* wage] —**bel·lig′er·ent·ly,** *adv.* —Syn. *adj.* 1. hostile, pugnacious.

bel·low (bel′ō), *v.* 1. roar as a bull does. 2. shout loudly or angrily. 3. make a loud, deep noise; roar. —*n.* 1. such a roar. 2. any noise made by bellowing. [OE *bylgan*] —**bel′low·er,** *n.*

bel·lows (bel′ōz; –əs), *n. sing. or pl.* 1. instrument for producing a strong current of air, used for blowing fires or sounding an organ. 2. the folding part of a camera, behind the lens. [OE *belgas;* akin to BELLY]

bell·weth·er (bel′weth′ər), *n.* 1. a male sheep that wears a bell and leads the flock. 2. person or thing that sets a standard or example for a group.

bel·ly (bel′i), *n., pl.* **–lies,** *v.*, **–lied, –ly·ing.** —*n.* 1. the lower part of the human body that contains the stomach and bowels; abdomen. 2. under part of an animal's body. 3. stomach. 4. the bulging part of anything; hollow space in a bulging part. —*v.* swell out; bulge. [OE *belg*]

be·long (bi·lông′; –long′), *v.* 1. have one's or its proper place: *that book belongs on this shelf.* 2. belong to, a. be the property of. b. be a part of; be connected with. c. be a member of. [ME *bilonge(n)* < *bi–* BE– + *longen* belong, ult. < OE *gelang* belonging to]

be·long·ing (bi·lông′ing; –long′–), *n.* 1. something that belongs. 2. **belongings,** things that belong to a person; possessions.

be·lov·ed (bi·luv′id; –luvd′), *adj.* dearly loved; dear. —*n.* person who is loved; darling.

be·low (bi·lō′), *adv.* 1. in a lower place; to a lower place. 2. in a lower rank; further down in a scale. 3. on a lower floor or deck; downstairs. 4. on earth. 5. in hell. 6. after in a book or article. —*prep.* 1. lower than; under: *below the third floor.* 2. less than; lower in rank or degree than: *four degrees below freezing.* 3. unworthy of: *below contempt.* [ME *bilooghe* by low]

belt (belt), *n.* 1. strip of leather, cloth, etc., worn around the body to hold in or support clothes or weapons. 2. any broad strip or band. 3. region having distinctive characteristics; zone: *the cotton belt.* 4. an endless band that moves the wheels and pulleys it passes over. 5. below the belt, a. foul; unfair. b. foully; unfairly. —*v.* 1. put a belt around. 2. fasten on with a belt. 3. beat with a belt. 4. hit. [OE, appar. ult. < L *balteus* girdle] —**belt′ed,** *adj.* —**belt′less,** *adj.*

belt·ing (bel′ting), *n.* 1. material for making belts. 2. belts.

belt·way (belt′wā′), *n.* an express highway that goes around a city, congested area, etc.

be·mire (bi·mīr′), *v.*, **–mired, –mir·ing.** 1. make dirty with mud. 2. sink in mud.

be·moan (bi·mōn′), *v.* 1. lament; bewail.

be·muse (bi·mūz′), *v.*, **–mused, –mus·ing.** confuse; bewilder; stupefy.

Ben·a·dryl (ben′ə·dril), *n. Trademark.* a synthetic drug used to relieve allergies such as hay fever, etc.

Be·na·res (bə-nä′riz), *n.* city in E India, on the Ganges; sacred city of the Hindus.

bench (bench), *n.* 1. a long seat, usually of wood or stone. 2. work table of a carpenter. 3. seat where judges sit in a law court. 4. judge or group of judges sitting in a law court. 5. position as a judge. 6. law court. 7. a raised level tract of land. 8. **on the bench, a.** sitting in a law court as a judge. **b.** sitting among the substitute players. —*v.* 1. furnish with benches. 2. assign a seat on a bench. 3. take (a player) out of a game. [OE *benc*] —**bench′less,** *adj.*

bench warrant, *Law.* a written order from a judge or law court to arrest a person.

bend (bend), *v.,* **bent** or (*Archaic*) **bend·ed, bend·ing,** *n.* —*v.* 1. make, be, or become curved or crooked. 2. stoop; bow. 3. force to submit. 4. submit. 5. turn in a certain direction; direct (mind or effort). 6. *Naut.* fasten (a sail, rope, etc.). —*n.* 1. part that is not straight; curve; turn. 2. stoop; bow. 3. knot for tying two ropes together or tying a rope to something else. 4. **the bends,** *U.S. Colloq.* cramps caused by changing too suddenly from high air pressure to ordinary air pressure. [OE *bendan* bind, band] —**bend′-a·ble,** *adj.* —**Syn.** *v.* 1. turn, twist, warp. 2. incline. 5. apply. –*n.* 1. crook, angle, twist.

bend·er (ben′dər), *n.* 1. person or thing that bends. 2. *Am., Slang.* a drinking spree.

be·neath (bi-nēth′), *adv.* below; underneath. —*prep.* 1. below; under; lower than. 2. unworthy of; worthy not even of: *beneath contempt.* [OE *beneothan < be-* by + *neothan* below]

ben·e·dic·i·te (ben′ə-dis′ə-tē), *interj.* Latin word that means *Bless you!* or *Bless us!* or *Bless me!* —*n.* 1. invocation of a blessing. 2. **Benedicite,** hymn of praise to God. [< L, < *bene* well + *dicere* say]

ben·e·dict (ben′ə-dikt), *n.* 1. a recently married man, esp. one who was a bachelor for a long time. 2. a married man. [< *Benedick*, character in Shakespeare's *Much Ado About Nothing*]

Ben·e·dict (ben′ə-dikt), *n.* Saint, 480?–543?, Italian founder of the Benedictine order.

Ben·e·dic·tine (ben′ə-dik′tin, –tēn, –tīn for *n. 1 and adj.;* ben′ə-dik′tēn for *n.* 2), *n.* 1. monk or nun following the rules of Saint Benedict or the order founded by him. 2. a kind of liqueur. —*adj.* of Saint Benedict or a religious order following his rules.

ben·e·dic·tion (ben′ə-dik′shən), *n.* 1. the asking of God's blessings at the end of a church service. 2. blessing. [< L *benedictio.* See BENEDICTE.] —**ben′e·dic′tion·al,** *adj.* —**ben·e·dic·to·ry** (ben′ə-dik′tə-ri), *adj.*

ben·e·fac·tion (ben′ə-fak′shən), *n.* 1. a doing good; kind act. 2. benefit conferred.

ben·e·fac·tor (ben′ə-fak′tər; ben′ə-fak′-), *n.* person who does money or kindly help. [< L, < *bene* well + *facere* do]

ben·e·fac·tress (ben′ə-fak′tris; ben′ə-fak′-), *n.* a woman benefactor.

ben·e·fice (ben′ə-fis), *n.* a permanent office or position created by proper ecclesiastical authority and consisting of a sacred duty and the income that goes with it. [< OF < L *beneficium* benefit. See BENEFACTOR.]

be·nef·i·cence (bə-nef′ə-səns), *n.* 1. kindness; doing good. 2. a kindly act; gift.

be·nef·i·cent (bə-nef′ə-sənt), *adj.* kind; doing good. —**be·nef′i·cent·ly,** *adv.*

ben·e·fi·cial (ben′ə-fish′əl), *adj.* helpful; productive of good: *sunshine and moisture are beneficial to plants.* —**ben′e·fi′cial·ly,** *adv.* —**ben′e·fi′cial·ness,** *n.*

ben·e·fi·ci·ar·y (ben′ə-fish′i·er′i; –fish′ər·i), *n., pl.* **-ar·ies.** 1. person who receives benefit. 2. person who receives money or property from an insurance policy, a will, etc.

ben·e·fit (ben′ə-fit), *n., v.,* **-fit·ed, -fit·ing.** —*n.* 1. anything which is for the good of a person or thing; advantage. 2. act of kindness; favor. 3. money paid to the sick, disabled, etc. 4. performance at the theater, a game, etc., to raise money which goes to a worthy cause. —*v.* 1. give benefit

to; be good for. 2. receive good; profit. [< AF *benfet < L benefactum.* See BENEFACTOR.] —**ben′e·fit·er,** *n.* —**Syn.** *n.* 1. profit, help.

benefit of clergy, 1. privilege of being tried in church courts instead of regular courts. 2. services or approval of the church.

Ben·e·lux (ben′ə-luks), *n.* the economic union of Belgium, the Netherlands, and Luxembourg, since 1948.

be·nev·o·lence (bə-nev′ə-ləns), *n.* 1. good will; kindly feeling. 2. act of kindness; something good that is done; generous gift. [< OF < L, < *bene* well + *velle* wish]

be·nev·o·lent (bə-nev′ə-lənt), *adj.* kindly; charitable. —**be·nev′o·lent·ly,** *adv.* —**Syn.** generous, bountiful. —**Ant.** malevolent, unkind.

Ben·gal (ben-gôl′; beng–), *n.* 1. former province of NE India now divided into West Bengal (republic of India) and East Bengal (republic of Pakistan). 2. **Bay of,** bay between India and Burma.

Ben·ga·lese (ben′gə-lēz′; –lēs′; beng′–), *n., pl.* –lese, *adj.* —*n.* native of Bengal. —*adj.* of Bengal, its people, or their language.

be·night·ed (bi-nīt′id), *adj.* 1. not knowing right and wrong; ignorant. 2. overtaken by night. —**be·night′ed·ness,** *n.*

be·nign (bi-nīn′), *adj.* 1. gentle; kindly: *a benign old lady.* 2. favorable; mild: *a benign climate.* 3. *Med.* doing no harm; not dangerous: *a benign tumor.* [< OF < L *benignus < bene* well + *-gnus* born] —**be·nign′ly,** *adv.* —**Syn.** 1. gracious. 2. salutary. —**Ant.** 3. malignant.

be·nig·nant (bi-nig′nənt), *adj.* 1. kindly; gracious. 2. favorable; beneficial. —**be·nig·nan·cy** (bi-nig′nən·si), *n.* —**be·nig′nant·ly,** *adv.*

be·nig·ni·ty (bi-nig′nə·ti), *n., pl.* –ties. 1. kindliness; graciousness. 2. a kind act; favor.

ben·i·son (ben′ə·zən; –sən), *n.* blessing. [< OF *beneison < L benedictio*]

Ben·ja·min (ben′jə·mən), *n.* 1. *Bible.* the youngest and favorite son of Jacob. 2. one of the twelve tribes of Israel.

ben·ny (ben′i), *n., pl.* –nies. *Am., Slang.* a pill of Benzedrine or some similar drug.

bent[1] (bent), *v.* pt. and pp. of **bend.** —*adj.* 1. not straight; curved; crooked. 2. strongly inclined; determined. —*n.* 1. bent condition. 2. capacity of enduring. 3. inclination; tendency. —**Syn.** *adj.* 2. resolved, bound, set. –*n.* 3. bias.

bent[2] (bent), *n.* 1. Also, **bent grass.** a stiff, wiry grass that grows on sandy or waste land. 2. *Archaic.* heath; moor. [OE *beonet*]

Ben·tham (ben′thəm; –təm), *n.* Jeremy, 1748–1832, English philosopher and jurist.

Ben·ton (ben′tən), *n.* **Thomas Hart,** born 1889, American painter.

be·numb (bi-num′), *v.* 1. make numb. 2. stupefy; deaden.

Ben·ze·drine (ben′zə·drēn; –drin), *n. Trademark.* a drug, $C_9H_{13}N$, that causes wakefulness.

ben·zene (ben′zēn; ben·zēn′), *n. Chem.* a colorless, volatile, inflammable liquid, C_6H_6, obtained chiefly from coal tar and used for removing grease and in making dyes.

ben·zine (ben′zēn; ben·zēn′), *n.* a colorless, volatile, inflammable liquid consisting of a mixture of hydrocarbons obtained in distilling petroleum, used in cleaning, dyeing, etc.

ben·zo·ate (ben′zō·āt; –it), *n. Chem.* salt or ester of benzoic acid.

ben·zo·ic acid (ben·zō′ik), *Chem.* an acid, C_6H_5COOH, occurring in benzoin, cranberries, etc., used as an antiseptic or as a food preservative.

ben·zo·in (ben′zō·in; –zoin; ben·zō′in), *n.* 1. a fragrant resin obtained from certain species of trees of Java, Sumatra, etc., used in perfume and medicine. 2. substance somewhat like camphor made from this resin. [< F < Sp. or Pg. < Ar. *lubān jāwī* incense of Java]

ben·zol (ben′zôl; –zol), *n.* 1. benzene, C_6H_6. 2. liquid containing about 70 per cent of benzene and 20 to 30 per cent of toluene.

Be·o·wulf (bā′ə·wulf), *n.* 1. an Old English epic poem, probably composed in England about 700 A.D. 2. hero of this poem.

be·queath (bi·kwēth′; –kwēth′), v. 1. give or leave (property, etc.) by a will. 2. hand down to posterity. [OE *becwethan* < *be*- to, for + *cwethan* say] —**be·queath′ment**, n.

be·queath·al (bi·kwēth′əl), n. a bequeathing.

be·quest (bi·kwest′), n. 1. something bequeathed; legacy. 2. act of bequeathing.

be·rate (bi·rāt′), v. –rat·ed, –rat·ing. scold sharply. —**Syn.** upbraid, reprimand.

Ber·ber (bėr′bər), n. 1. member of a race living in N Africa, west of Egypt. 2. their language. —adj. of the Berbers or their language.

be·reave (bi·rēv′), v., be·reaved or be·reft (bi·reft′), be·reav·ing. 1. deprive (of) ruthlessly; rob: *bereft of hope.* 2. leave desolate. [OE *berēafian* < *be*- away + *rēafian* rob] —**be·reave′ment**, n. —**be·reav′er**, n.

be·ret (bə·rā′; ber′ā), n. a soft, round woolen cap. [< F. See BIRETTA.]

berg (bėrg), n. iceberg.

ber·ga·mot (bėr′gə·mot), n. 1. a pear-shaped variety of orange. 2. oil obtained from its rind, used in perfume. [< F < Ital., appar. < Turk. *begarmudi* prince's pear]

Ber·gen (bėr′gən), n. seaport in SW Norway.

Ber·ge·rac (bâr′zhə·räk), n. Cyrano de, 1619–1655, French dramatist and poet, hero of a famous play by Rostand.

ber·i·ber·i (ber′i·ber′i), n. disease affecting the nerves, accompanied by weakness, loss of weight, and wasting away. [< Singhalese (the lang. of Ceylon), reduplication of *beri* weakness]

Ber·ing Sea (bir′ing; bâr′–), sea in the N Pacific, between Alaska and Siberia.

Bering Strait, strait between Bering Sea and the Arctic Ocean.

ber·ke·li·um (bėr·kē′li·əm), n. Chem. a radioactive element, Bk, produced by the cyclotron at the University of California. [< *Berkeley*, California (site of the University)]

Berk·shires (bėrk′shirz; –shərz), or **Berkshire Hills**, n.pl. range of hills and mountains in W Massachusetts.

Ber·lin (bėr·lin′), n. capital of East Germany and the former capital of Germany, in the N part.

berm (bėrm), n. Am. 1. bank of a canal opposite the towing path. 2. the side of a road. [< F *berme* < MDu. and G]

Ber·mu·da (bər·mū′də), **Bermudas**, n. group of British islands in the Atlantic, 580 miles east of North Carolina. —**Ber·mu·di·an** (bər·mū′di·ən), adj., n.

Bermuda onion, a large, mild onion grown in Bermuda, Texas, and California.

Ber·mu·das (bər·mū′dəz), n.pl. Colloq., or **Bermuda shorts**, short trousers that end an inch or two above the knee.

Bern, **Berne** (bėrn; bern), n. capital of Switzerland, in the W part.

Ber·nard (bėr′nərd; bər·närd′), n. Saint, 1090–1153, French abbot.

Bern·hardt (bėrn′härt), n. Sarah, 1845–1923, French actress.

ber·ry (ber′i), n., pl. –ries, v., –ried, –ry·ing. —n. 1. a small, juicy fruit with many seeds, as the strawberry. 2. a dry seed or kernel, as of wheat. 3. *Bot.* a simple fruit with the seeds in the pulp and a skin or rind, as grapes or tomatoes. —v. 1. gather or pick berries. 2. produce berries. [OE *berie*]

ber·serk (bėr′sėrk; bėr·sėrk′), adj., adv. in a frenzy. [< Scand. *berserkr* wild warrior]

berth (bėrth), n. 1. Am. place to sleep on a ship, train, or airplane. 2. a ship's place at a wharf. 3. place for a ship to anchor conveniently or safely. 4. appointment; position; job. 5. give a wide berth to, keep well away from. —v. 1. put in a berth; provide with a berth. 2. have or occupy a berth. [? < *bear*[1]]

ber·tha (bėr′thə), n. a woman's wide collar

that often extends over the shoulders. [named for *Berthe*, mother of Charlemagne]

Ber·til·lon system (bėr′tə·lon), system of identifying persons, esp. criminals, by a record of individual measurements and physical peculiarities, esp. by fingerprinting. [from A. *Bertillon*, French anthropologist]

ber·yl (ber′əl), n. a very hard mineral, usually green or greenish-blue, a silicate of beryllium and aluminum. Emeralds and aquamarines are beryls. [< L < Gk. *beryllos*]

be·ryl·li·um (bə·ril′i·əm), n. Chem. a rare metallic element, Be; glucinum.

be·seech (bi·sēch′), v., –sought or –seeched, –seech·ing. ask earnestly; beg. [ME *biseche(n)* < *be*- thoroughly + *seche(n)* seek] —**be·seech′er**, n. —**be·seech′ing·ly**, adv. —**Syn.** entreat.

be·seem (bi·sēm′), v. 1. be proper for; be fitting to. 2. be seemly or fitting.

be·set (bi·set′), v., –set, –set·ting. 1. attack on all sides; assail. 2. surround; hem in. 3. set; stud: *a bracelet beset with gems.* [OE *besettan* < *be*- around + *settan* set] —**Syn.** 1. besiege. 2. encompass.

be·set·ting (bi·set′ing), adj. habitually attacking: *laziness is her besetting sin.*

be·shrew (bi·shrü′), v. Archaic. call down evil upon; curse mildly.

be·side (bi·sīd′), prep. 1. by the side of; near; close to: *we sat beside the fire.* 2. in addition to: *other men beside ourselves.* 3. compared with: *beside his efforts ours seem small.* 4. away from; aside from: *beside the point.* 5. beside oneself, out of one's senses. —adv. besides. [OE *be sīdan* by side]

be·sides (bi·sīdz′), adv. 1. moreover; further: *he didn't want to quarrel; besides, he had come to enjoy himself.* 2. in addition: *we tried two other ways besides.* 3. otherwise; else: *he is ignorant of politics, whatever he may know besides.* —prep. 1. in addition to; over and above: *besides our own members.* 2. except; other than: *we spoke of no one besides you.*

be·siege (bi·sēj′), v., –sieged, –sieg·ing. 1. make a long-continued attempt to get possession of (a place) by armed force: *besiege a city.* 2. crowd around. 3. overwhelm with requests, questions, etc. —**be·siege′ment**, n. —**be·sieg′er**, n.

be·smear (bi·smir′), v. smear over.

be·smirch (bi·smėrch′), v. make dirty; soil; sully. —**be·smirch′er**, n. —**be·smirch′ment**, n.

be·som (bē′zəm), n. 1. broom made of twigs. 2. the broom plant. [OE *besma*]

be·sot (bi·sot′), v., –sot·ted, –sot·ting. 1. make foolish; stupefy. 2. intoxicate. —**be·sot′ted·ly**, adv. —**be·sot′ted·ness**, n.

be·sought (bi·sôt′), v. pt. and pp. of beseech.

be·span·gle (bi·spang′gəl), v., –gled, –gling. adorn with or as with spangles.

be·spat·ter (bi·spat′ər), v. 1. spatter all over; soil by spattering. 2. slander. —**be·spat′ter·er**, n. —**be·spat′ter·ment**, n.

be·speak (bi·spēk′), v., –spoke or (Archaic) –spake, –spo·ken or –spoke, –speak·ing. 1. engage in advance; order; reserve: *bespeak tickets for a play.* 2. give evidence of; indicate: *a neat appearance bespeaks care.* 3. Poetic. speak to.

be·spec·ta·cled (bi·spek′tə·kəld), adj. wearing glasses.

be·spread (bi·spred′), v., –spread, –spreading. spread over.

be·sprin·kle (bi·spring′kəl), v., –kled, –kling. sprinkle all over.

Bes·sa·ra·bi·a (bes′ə·rā′bi·ə), n. region in E Europe, under Russian control after World War II. —**Bes′sa·ra′bi·an**, adj., n.

Bes·se·mer process (bes′ə·mər), method of making steel by burning out carbon and impurities in molten iron with a blast of air.

best (best), adj. (superlative of good). 1. the most desirable, valuable, superior, etc. 2. the greatest advantage, usefulness, etc.: *the best*

Man wearing a beret

Besom

thing to do. **3.** largest: *the best part of the day.* **4.** chief: *a best seller.* —*adv. (superlative of* well[1]*).* **1.** in the most excellent way; most thoroughly. **2.** in the highest degree. **3.** had best, should; ought to; will be wise to. —*n.* **1.** the best thing or state. **2.** one's highest, finest, utmost, etc.: *to look one's best.* **3.** at best, under the most favorable circumstances. **4.** get the best of, defeat. **5.** make the best of, do as well as possible with. —*v.* outdo; defeat. [OE *betst*]

be·stead (bi·sted'), *v.,* -stead·ed, -stead·ed or -stead, -stead·ing, *adj.* —*v.* help; assist; serve. —*adj.* placed; situated. [< *be-* + *stead,* v., help]

bes·tial (bes'chəl; best'yəl), *adj.* **1.** beastly; brutal; vile. **2.** of beasts. [< L, < *bestia*] —**bes·ti·al·i·ty** (bes'chi·al'ə·ti; -ti·al'-), *n.* —**bes'tial·ly,** *adv.* —Syn. **1.** brutish.

be·stir (bi·stér'), *v.,* -stirred, -stir·ring. stir up; rouse to action; exert.

best man, chief attendant of the bridegroom at a wedding.

be·stow (bi·stō'), *v.* **1.** give as a gift; give; confer. **2.** make use of; apply. **3.** *Archaic.* put safely; put; place. **4.** *Archaic.* find quarters for; lodge. —**be·stow'a·ble,** *adj.* —**be·stow'al,** *n.*

be·strad·dle (bi·strad'əl), *v.,* -dled, -dling. bestride; straddle.

be·strew (bi·strü'), *v.,* -strewed, -strewed or -strewn, -strew·ing. **1.** strew. **2.** strew (things) around; scatter about. **3.** lie scattered over.

be·stride (bi·strīd'), *v.,* -strode or -strid, -strid·den or -strid, -strid·ing. **1.** get on, sit on, or stand over with one leg on each side. **2.** stride across; step over.

best seller, *Am.* **1.** anything, esp. a book, that has a very large sale. **2.** author of such a book.

bet (bet), *v.,* bet or bet·ted, bet·ting, *n.* —*v.* **1.** promise (money or a certain thing) to another if he is right and you are wrong. **2.** make a bet. —*n.* **1.** act of betting; wager. **2.** the money or thing promised. **3.** thing to bet on. —Syn. *n.* **1.** stake.

be·ta (bā'tə; bē'-), *n.* **1.** the second letter of the Greek alphabet (B, β). **2.** the second of a series.

be·take (bi·tāk'), *v.* -took, -tak·en, -tak·ing. betake oneself, a. go: *betake oneself to the mountains.* b. apply oneself.

beta particle, *Physics.* an electron, esp. one in a stream of electrons.

beta rays, *Physics.* stream of electrons from radium and other radioactive substances.

be·ta·tron (bā'tə·tron; bē'-), *n.* apparatus in which electrons are accelerated to high speeds.

be·tel (bē'təl), *n.* kind of pepper plant of the East Indies, the leaves of which are chewed by people in Asia. [< Pg. < Malayalam *veṭṭila*]

Be·tel·geuse (bē'təl·jüz; bet'əl·jœz), *n.* a very large reddish star in the constellation Orion. [< F, ? < Ar. *bit-al-jāuza* shoulder of the giant]

betel nut, the orange-colored nut of a tropical Asiatic palm tree.

betel palm, Asiatic palm tree on which the betel nut grows.

bête noire (bāt' nwär'), thing or person dreaded or detested. [< F, black beast]

Beth·a·ny (beth'ə·ni), *n.* village in E Palestine, near Jerusalem.

Beth·el (beth'əl), *n.* ancient town in E Palestine, near Jerusalem.

beth·el (beth'əl), *n.* **1.** a holy place. **2.** church or chapel for seamen. [< Heb., house of God]

be·think (bi·thingk'), *v.,* -thought, -think·ing. **1.** think about; consider. **2.** remember.

Beth·le·hem (beth'li·əm; -lə·hem), *n.* birthplace of Jesus, six miles south of Jerusalem.

be·tide (bi·tīd'), *v.,* -tid·ed, -tid·ing. **1.** happen to. **2.** happen. [ME *betide(n)* < *be-* + *tiden* happen]

be·times (bi·tīmz'), *adv.* **1.** early. **2.** soon. [ME *bitime* by time]

be·to·ken (bi·tō'kən), *v.* be a sign or token of; indicate; show. —**be·to'ken·er,** *n.*

be·took (bi·tůk'), *v.* pt. of betake.

be·tray (bi·trā'), *v.* **1.** give away to the enemy. **2.** be unfaithful to. **3.** mislead; deceive. **4.** give

away (a secret); disclose unintentionally. **5.** reveal; show. **6.** seduce. [ME *bitraien* < *be-* (intensive) + *traie(n)* betray < OF < L *tradere* hand over] —**be·tray'al,** *n.* —**be·tray'er,** *n.*

be·troth (bi·trōth'; -trôth'), *v.* promise in marriage; engage. [ME *betrouthe(n),* var. of *betreuthien* < *be-* + *treuthe,* OE *trēowth* pledge] —**be·troth'ment,** *n.*

be·troth·al (bi·trōth'əl; -trôth'-), *n.* promise of marriage; engagement.

be·trothed (bi·trōthd'; -trôtht'), *n.* person engaged to be married.

bet·ter[1] (bet'ər), *adj. (comparative of good).* **1.** more desirable, useful, etc., than another. **2.** of superior quality. **3.** less sick. **4.** larger: *the better part of a week.* —*adv. (comparative of* well[1]*).* **1.** in a superior manner. **2.** in a higher degree; more. **3.** better off, in better circumstances. **4.** had better, should; ought to; will be wise to. **5.** think better of, think over and change one's mind. —*n.* **1.** a better person, thing, or state. **2.** advantage. **3.** betters, one's superiors. **4.** get or have the better of, be superior to; defeat. —*v.* **1.** make or become better; improve. **2.** do better than; surpass. [OE *betera*] —**bet'ter·er,** *n.* —Syn. *v.* **1.** advance, ameliorate.

bet·ter[2], **bet·tor** (bet'ər), *n.* person who bets.

bet·ter·ment (bet'ər·mənt), *n.* **1.** improvement. **2.** Usually, betterments, *Am., Law.* an improvement of real estate property.

be·tween (bi·twēn'), *prep.* **1.** in the space or time separating (two points, objects, etc.): *between New York and Chicago.* **2.** in the range or part separating: *shades between pink and red.* **3.** from one to the other of; connecting: *relation between ideas.* **4.** involving; having to do with: *war between two countries.* **5.** by the combined action of: *they caught twelve fish between them.* **6.** in the combined possession of: *they own the property between them.* —*adv.* **1.** in the intervening space or time. **2.** in an intermediate position or relation. [OE *betwēonum* < *be-* by + *twā* two] ► between, among. Among implies more than two objects: *They distributed food among the survivors.* In its most exact use, *between* implies only two: *The teacher divided the books between Tom and Jim.* If between is used of more than two it suggests the individuals involved more than the situation: *The family of seven hadn't a pair of shoes between them.* ► between you and me. Since the object of a preposition is grammatically in the accusative case, the correct form is *between you and me, for you and me, to you and me* (or when the pronouns are objects of a verb, "He will take *you and me.*"). *Between you and I* is frequently used—reversing the usual colloquial tendency to use *me* (as in *It's me*), perhaps because the speakers remember the prohibition against *It's me* and carry over the taboo to a different contruction.

be·twixt (bi·twikst'), *prep., adv.* **1.** between. **2.** betwixt and between, neither one nor the other. [OE *betweox*]

Bev (bev), *n. Am.* billion electron volts.

Bev·an (bev'ən), *n.* Aneurin, 1897–1960, the leader of a faction of the British Labour Party. —**Bev'an·ism,** *n.* —**Bev'an·ite,** *n.*

bev·a·tron (bev'ə·tron), *n. Am.* a high-energy cyclotron.

bev·el (bev'əl), *n., v.,* -eled, -el·ing; *esp. Brit.* -elled, -el·ling, *adj.* —*n.* **1.** the angle that one line or surface makes with another when not at right angles. **2.** instrument or tool for drawing angles, etc. —*v.* cut a square edge to a sloping edge; make slope. —*adj.* slanting; oblique.

Bevel

bev·er·age (bev'ər·ij; bev'rij), *n.* a liquid used or prepared for drinking. Milk, tea, coffee, beer, and wine are beverages. [< OF *bevrage* < *bevre* drink < L *bibere*]

bev·y (bev'i), *n., pl.* bev·ies. **1.** a flock of birds. **2.** a small group.

be·wail (bi·wāl'), *v.* mourn; lament. —**be·wail'er,** *n.* —**be·wail'ing·ly,** *adv.*

be·ware (bi·wâr′), v. be on one's guard against; be careful. [< phrase be ware! See WARY.]

be·wil·der (bi·wil′dər), v. confuse completely; puzzle; perplex. —**be·wil′dered**, adj. —**be·wil′dered·ly**, adv. —**be·wil′der·ing**, adj. —**be·wil′der·ing·ly**, adv. —**be·wil′der·ment**, n.

be·witch (bi·wich′), v. 1. put under a spell. 2. charm; fascinate. —**be·witch′er**, n. —**be·witch′er·y**, n. —**be·witch′ing**, adj. —**be·witch′ing·ly**, adv. —**be·witch′ment**, n. —Syn. 2. enchant, captivate.

be·wray (bi·rā′), v. Archaic. 1. betray. 2. reveal. [ME bewreie(n) < be- + wreie(n) < OE wrēgan accuse]

bey (bā), n., pl. **beys**. 1. governor of a Turkish province. 2. Turkish title of respect. 3. native ruler of Tunis. [< Turk. beg]

be·yond (bi·yond′), prep. 1. on or to the farther side of: beyond the barn. 2. farther on than: beyond the hill. 3. later than: they stayed beyond the time set. 4. out of the reach, range, or understanding of: the dying man was beyond help. 5. more than; exceeding: a price beyond what I can pay. 6. in addition to; besides: I will pay nothing beyond the stated price. —adv. farther away: beyond were the hills. —n. the beyond, the great beyond, life after death. [OE begeondan < be- at, near + geondan beyond]

be·zique (bə·zēk′), n. card game somewhat like pinochle. [< F bésigue]

b.f., bf., boldface (type).

bg., pl. **bgs.,** bag.

Bhu·tan (bü·tan′), n. small kingdom between Tibet and NE India.

bi-, prefix. 1. twice, as in biannual. 2. doubly, as in bipinnate. 3. two, as in bicuspid. 4. Chem. denoting the presence of two parts or equivalents of a constituent indicated, as in bicarbonate. [< L, < bis]

Bi, Chem. bismuth.

bi·an·nu·al (bī·an′yū·əl), adj. occurring twice a year. —**bi·an′nu·al·ly**, adv.

bi·as (bī′əs), n., adj., adv., v., **bi·ased, bi·as·ing**; esp. Brit. **bi·assed, bi·as·sing**. —n. 1. a slanting or oblique line. Cloth is cut on the bias when it is cut diagonally across the weave. 2. opinion before there is basis for it; prejudice; a leaning of the mind. —adj. slanting across the threads of cloth; oblique; diagonal. —adv. obliquely. —v. influence, usually not fairly. [< F biais slant < VL biaxius having a double axis] —Syn. n. inclination, bent, partiality.

bi·ax·i·al (bī·ak′si·əl), adj. having two axes.

bib (bib), n. 1. cloth worn under the chin by babies and small children to protect their clothing. 2. part of an apron above the waist. [< bib drink, ? < L bibere]

bi·be·lot (bib′lō; Fr. bē·blō′), n. a small object of curiosity, beauty, or rarity. [< F]

Bi·ble (bī′bəl), n. 1. the collection of sacred writings of the Christian religion, comprising the Old and New Testaments. 2. the Old Testament in the form received by the Jews. 3. the sacred writings of any religion. 4. bible, book accepted as an authority. [< Med.L < Gk. biblia, pl. dim. of biblos book] ➤ **Bible**, referring to the Christian scriptures, is capitalized but not italicized: "You will find it in the Bible." Bible in the sense of an authoritative book is not capitalized: "Gray's Manual, the botanist's bible, ..."

Bib·li·cal, bib·li·cal (bib′lə·kəl), adj. 1. of or in the Bible. 2. according to the Bible. —**Bib′li·cal·ly, bib′li·cal·ly**, adv.

bib·li·og·ra·phy (bib′li·og′rə·fi), n., pl. **-phies**. 1. list of books, articles, etc., about a subject or person. 2. list of books, articles, etc., by a certain author. 3. study of the authorship, editions, dates, etc., of books, articles, etc. [< Gk., < biblion book + graphein write] —**bib′li·og′ra·pher**, n. —**bib·li·o·graph·ic** (bib′li·ə·graf′ik), **bib′li·o·graph′i·cal**, adj. —**bib′li·o·graph′i·cal·ly**, adv.

bib·li·o·ma·ni·a (bib′li·ō·mā′ni·ə), n. craze for collecting books. —**bib·li·o·ma·ni·ac** (bib′li·ō·mā′ni·ak), n., adj.

bib·li·o·phile (bib′li·ə·fīl), **bib·li·o·phil** (-fīl), n. lover of books. [< F, < Gk. biblion book + philos loving]

bib·u·lous (bib′yə·ləs), adj. 1. fond of drinking alcoholic liquor. 2. absorbent. [< L bibulus < bibere drink] —**bib′u·lous·ly**, adv.

bi·cam·er·al (bī·kam′ər·əl), adj. having or consisting of two legislative assemblies. [< bi- two + L camera chamber. See CAMERA.]

bi·car·bo·nate (bī·kär′bə·nit; -nāt), n. salt of carbonic acid that contains a base and hydrogen.

bicarbonate of soda, sodium bicarbonate.

bi·cen·te·nar·y (bī·sen′tə·ner′i; bī′sen·ten′ər·i), adj., n., pl. **-nar·ies**. bicentennial.

bi·cen·ten·ni·al (bī′sen·ten′i·əl), adj. 1. having to do with a period of 200 years. 2. recurring every 200 years. —n. 1. a 200th anniversary. 2. its celebration.

bi·ceps (bī′seps), n. any muscle having two heads or origins, esp.: a. the large muscle in the front part of the upper arm. b. the large muscle in the back of the thigh. [< L, two-headed, < bi- two + caput head]

bi·chlo·ride (bī·klō′rīd; -rid; -klō′-), **bi·chlo·rid** (-rid), n. Chem. 1. compound containing two atoms of chlorine combined with another element or radical. 2. bichloride of mercury.

bichloride of mercury, an extremely poisonous, white substance, HgCl₂, used in solution as an antiseptic, in medicine, and in dyeing.

bick·er (bik′ər), v., n. quarrel. [ME biker(en)]

bi·cus·pid (bī·kus′pid), n. a double-pointed tooth. —adj. Also, **bi·cus·pi·date** (bī·kus′pə·dāt). having two points. [< bi- two + L cuspis point]

bi·cy·cle (bī′sə·kəl; -sik′əl), n., v., **-cled, -cling**. —n. a metal frame with two wheels, handles for steering, and a seat for the rider. —v. ride a bicycle. [< F. See BI-, CYCLE.] —**bi′cy·cler**, Am., **bi′cy·clist**, n.

bid (bid), v., **bade** or **bad** (for 1, 2) or **bid** (for 3–10), **bid·den** or **bid, bid·ding**, n. —v. 1. command. 2. say; tell: bid him farewell. 3. Archaic. invite. 4. proclaim; declare. 5. bid fair, seem likely; have a good chance. 6. offer. 7. offer a price; state a price. 8. state as what one proposes to make or to win in some card game. 9. bid in, Am. buy at auction, to keep for the owner. 10. bid up, raise the price of by bidding more. —n. 1. a bidding. 2. an offer. 3. Am., Colloq. an invitation. 4. amount offered. 5. amount bid in a card game. 6. an attempt to secure, achieve, etc. 7. appeal: a bid for sympathy. [OE biddan ask; meaning infl. by OE bēodan offer] —**bid′da·ble**, adj. —**bid′der**, n. —Syn. v. 1. order, direct. 6. proffer, tender.

bid·ding (bid′ing), n. 1. command. 2. invitation. 3. offers at an auction. 4. in card games, bids collectively.

bid·dy (bid′i), n., pl. **-dies**. hen.

bide (bīd), v., **bode** or **bid·ed, bid·ed, bid·ing**. 1. Archaic or Dial. dwell; abide. 2. Archaic or Dial. continue; wait. 3. Archaic or Dial. bear; endure. 4. bide one's time, wait for a good chance. [OE bīdan] —**bid′er**, n.

bi·en·ni·al (bī·en′i·əl), adj. 1. occurring every two years. 2. Bot. lasting two years. —n. 1. event that occurs every two years. 2. Bot. plant that lives two years. [< L biennium < bi- two + annus year] —**bi·en′ni·al·ly**, adv.

bier (bir), n. movable stand on which a coffin or dead body is placed. [OE bēr < beran bear¹]

biff (bif), n., v. Am., Colloq. hit; slap.

bi·fid (bī′fid), adj. divided into two parts by a cleft. [< L bifidus < bi- two + findere cleave]

bi·fo·cal (bī·fō′kəl), adj. 1. having two focuses. 2. Am. (used of glasses) having two parts, the upper for far vision, the lower for near vision. —n. 1. Usually, bifocals, Am. pair of glasses having bifocal lenses. 2. bifocal lens.

bi·fur·cate (v., adj. bī′fər·kāt, bī·fėr′kāt; adj. also -kit), v., **-cat·ed, -cat·ing**, adj. —v. divide into two branches. —adj. divided into two branches; forked. [< Med.L, < L bi- two + furca fork] —**bi′fur·cate·ly**, adv. —**bi′fur·ca′tion**, n.

big (big), *adj.*, **big·ger, big·gest**, *adv.* —*adj.* 1. great in extent, amount, size, etc.; large. 2. grown up. 3. *Am.*, *Colloq.* important; great. 4. full; loud: *a big voice.* 5. boastful: *big talk.* 6. pregnant. —*adv.* boastfully. [ME; orig. uncert.] —**big′ly**, *adv.* —**big′ness**, *n.* —Syn. *adj.* 1. huge.

big·a·my (big′ə·mi), *n.* having two wives or two husbands at the same time. [< F, < *bigame* < Med.L, < *bi*– twice + Gk. *gamos* married] —**big′a·mist**, *n.* —**big′a·mous**, *adj.* —**big′a·mous·ly**, *adv.*

Big Dipper, group of stars in the constellation of Ursa Major.

big game, 1. large animals sought by hunters, such as elephants, tigers, or lions. 2. very important thing that is sought.

big-heart·ed (big′här′tid), *adj.* kindly; generous.

big·horn (big′hôrn′), *n.*, *pl.* **–horn, –horns.** *Am.* a wild, grayish-brown sheep of the Rocky Mountains, with large, curved horns.

bight (bīt), *n.* 1. a long curve in a coastline. 2. bay¹. 3. bend; angle; corner. 4. the loop of a rope. 5. slack of rope between the fastened ends. [OE *byht*]

big·no·ni·a (big·nō′ni·ə), *n. Am.* vine with showy, trumpet-shaped orange flowers. [< NL; named for Abbé *Bignon*]

big·ot (big′ət), *n.* a bigoted person. [< F]

big·ot·ed (big′ət·id), *adj.* sticking to an opinion, belief, party, etc., without reason and not tolerating other views; intolerant. —**big′ot·ed·ly**, *adv.* —Syn. narrow-minded.

big·ot·ry (big′ət·ri), *n.*, *pl.* **–ries.** bigoted conduct or attitude; prejudice. —Syn. intolerance.

big top, *Am.* main tent of a circus.

big·wig (big′wig′), *n. Colloq.* an important person.

bi·jou (bē′zhū), *n.*, *pl.* **–joux** (–zhūz). 1. a jewel. 2. something small and fine. [< F]

bi·ju·gate (bī′jū·gāt; bī·jū′gāt), **bi·ju·gous** (bī′jū·gəs), *adj.* having two pairs of leaflets. [< *bi*– two + L *jugatus* yoked]

bike (bīk), *n.*, *v.*, **biked, bik·ing.** *Am.*, *Colloq.* bicycle.

Bi·ki·ni (bi·kē′ni), *n.* atoll in the Marshall Islands in the W Pacific, where atomic bomb tests took place.

bi·ki·ni (bi·kē′ni), *n.* a woman's very abbreviated bathing costume, in two pieces.

bi·la·bi·al (bī·lā′bi·əl), *adj.* 1. *Bot.* having two lips. 2. *Phonet.* formed by both lips. —*n.* sound formed by both lips, as *b, p, m,* and *w.*

bi·la·bi·ate (bī·lā′bi·āt; –it), *adj. Bot.* having an upper and a lower lip.

bi·lat·er·al (bī·lat′ər·əl), *adj.* 1. having two sides. 2. on two sides. 3. affecting or influencing two sides. —**bi·lat′er·al·ism, bi·lat′er·al·ness**, *n.* —**bi·lat′er·al·ly**, *adv.*

Bil·ba·o (bil·bä′ō), *n.* seaport in N Spain.

bil·ber·ry (bil′ber′i), *n.*, *pl.* **–ries.** 1. an edible berry much like a blueberry. 2. shrub that it grows on. [appar. alter. of Scand. (Dan.) *bölle·bær* after *berry*]

bil·bo (bil′bō), *n.*, *pl.* **–boes.** Usually **bilboes.** a long iron bar with sliding shackles and a lock.

bile (bīl), *n.* 1. a bitter, yellow or greenish liquid secreted by the liver and stored in the gall bladder to aid digestion. 2. ill humor; anger. [< F < L *bilis*]

bilge (bilj), *n.*, *v.*, **bilged, bilg·ing.** —*n.* 1. *Naut.* a. the lowest part of a ship's hold. b. bottom of a ship's hull. 2. bilge water. 3. the bulging part of a barrel. 4. *Colloq.* nonsense. —*v.* 1. spring a leak. 2. bulge; swell out.

bilge water, dirty water that collects in the bottom of a ship.

bil·i·ar·y (bil′i·er′i), *adj.* 1. of bile. 2. carrying bile. 3. bilious.

bi·lin·gual (bī·ling′gwəl), *adj.* 1. able to speak one's own language and another equally well. 2. containing or written in two languages. —**bi·lin′gual·ism**, *n.* —**bi·lin′gual·ly**, *adv.*

bil·ious (bil′yəs), *adj.* 1. having to do with bile. 2. suffering from or caused by some trouble with bile or the liver. 3. peevish; cross; bad-tempered. —**bil′ious·ly**, *adv.* —**bil′ious·ness**, *n.*

bilk (bilk), *v.* 1. avoid payment of; elude. 2. defraud; cheat; deceive. —*n.* 1. fraud; deception. 2. person who avoids paying his bills; swindler. —**bilk′er**, *n.*

bill¹ (bil), *n.* 1. account of money owed for work done or things supplied. 2. *U.S.* piece of paper money: *a dollar bill.* 3. a written or printed public notice; advertisement; poster; handbill. 4. a written or printed statement; list of items. 5. a theater program. 6. *Am.* entertainment in a theater. 7. a proposed law presented to a law-making body. 8. bill of exchange. 9. *Law.* a written request or complaint presented to a court. —*v.* 1. send a bill to. 2. enter in a bill. 3. *Am.* consign (freight) by rail to a destination. 4. announce by bills or public notice. 5. post bills or on. 6. list on a theatrical program. [< Anglo-L *billa*, alter. of Med.L *bulla* document, seal, BULL²] —**bill′a·ble**, *adj.* —**bill′er**, *n.* —Syn. 1. invoice. 2. placard, circular, bulletin.

bill² (bil), *n.* 1. the horny mouth of a bird; beak. 2. anything shaped somewhat like a bird's bill. —*v.* 1. join beaks; touch bills. 2. show affection. [OE *bile*]

bill³ (bil), *n.* 1. spear with a hook-shaped blade. 2. Also, **billhook**. tool for pruning or cutting. [OE *bil*]

bil·la·bong (bil′ə·bong), *n. Australia.* a branch of a river flowing away from the main stream.

bill·board (bil′bôrd′; –bōrd′), *n. Am.* sign-board for posting advertisements or notices.

bil·let¹ (bil′it), *n.*, *v.*, **–let·ed, –let·ing.** —*n.* 1. *Mil.* written order to provide board and lodging for a soldier. 2. place where a soldier is lodged. 3. job; position. —*v. Mil.* assign to quarters by billet. [< OF *billette*, dim. of *bille* bill¹]

bil·let² (bil′it), *n.* 1. a thick stick of wood. 2. bar of iron or steel. [< F *billette*, dim. of *bille* log, tree trunk]

bil·let-doux (bil′i·dū′; bil′ā–), *n.*, *pl.* **bil·lets-doux** (bil′i·dūz′; bil′ā–). a love letter. [< F]

bill·fold (bil′fōld′), *n. Am.* a folding pocket-book for money.

bill·head (bil′hed′), *n.* name and business address printed at the top of a sheet of paper.

bill·hook (bil′hûk′), *n.* bill³ (def. 2).

bil·liard (bil′yərd), *adj.* of or for billiards. —*n.* point made by hitting the balls in billiards.

bil·liards (bil′yərdz), *n.* game played with balls on a special table. A long stick called a cue is used in hitting the balls. [< F *billard(s)*, dim. of *bille* log, tree trunk] —**bil′liard·ist**, *n. Am.*

bil·lings·gate (bil′ingz·gāt′; *esp. Brit.* bil′ingz-git), *n.* vulgar, abusive language.

bil·lion (bil′yən), *n.*, *adj.* 1. *Am.* in the United States and France, one thousand millions. 2. in Great Britain and Germany, one million millions. [< F, < *bi*– two (i.e., to the second power) + (*mi*)*llion* million] —**bil′lionth**, *adj.*, *n.*

bil·lion·aire (bil′yən·ãr′), *n. Am.* person who owns a billion dollars, francs, marks, etc.

bill of attainder, a legal act depriving a person of property and civil rights because of a sentence of death or outlawry.

bill of exchange, written order to pay a certain sum of money to a specified person.

bill of fare, list of the articles of food served or that can be served at a meal.

bill of health, certificate stating whether or not there are infectious diseases on a ship or in a port.

bill of lading, receipt given by a railroad, express agency, etc., showing a list of goods delivered to it for transportation.

bill of rights, 1. statement of the fundamental rights of the people of the nation. 2. **Bill of Rights**, *Am.* the first ten amendments to the Constitution of the United States.

bill of sale, written statement transferring ownership of something from seller to buyer.

bil·low (bil′ō), *n.* 1. a great wave or surge of the sea. 2. any great wave. —*v.* 1. rise or roll in big waves. 2. swell out. [< Scand. *bylgja*]

bil·low·y (bil′ō·i), *adj.*, **–low·i·er, –low·i·est.** 1. rising or rolling in big waves. 2. swelling out; bulging. —**bil′low·i·ness**, *n.*

bil·ly (bil′i), *n.*, *pl.* **–lies.** *Am.* club; stick.

billy goat, *Colloq.* a male goat.

bi·me·tal·lic (bī′mə·tal′ik), *adj.* **1.** using two metals. **2.** of or based on bimetallism.

bi·met·al·lism (bī·met′əl·iz·əm), *n.* use of both gold and silver at a fixed relative value as the basis of the money system of a nation. —bi·met′al·list, *n.*

bi·month·ly (bī·munth′li), *adj., n., pl.* -lies, *adv.* —*adj.* **1.** happening once every two months. **2.** happening twice a month. —*n.* magazine published bimonthly. —*adv.* **1.** once every two months. **2.** twice a month.

bin (bin), *n., v.,* binned, bin·ning. —*n.* box or enclosed place for holding grain, coal, etc. —*v.* store in a bin. [OE *binn*]

bi·na·ry (bī′nə·ri), *adj., n., pl.* -ries. —*adj.* consisting of two; involving two; dual. —*n.* a whole composed of two. [< L *binarius* < *bini* two at a time]

binary star, *Astron.* pair of stars that revolve around a common center of gravity.

bi·nate (bī′nāt), *adj. Bot.* growing in pairs; double. —bi′nate·ly, *adv.*

bind (bīnd), *v.,* bound, bind·ing, *n.* —*v.* **1.** tie together; hold together; fasten. **2.** stick together. **3.** hold by some force; restrain. **4.** hold by a promise, love, duty, etc.; oblige: *she was bound to help.* **5.** put under legal obligation: *bound to keep the peace.* **6.** put a bandage on. **7.** put a band or wreath around. **8.** fasten (sheets of paper) into a cover. **9.** constipate. —*n.* anything that binds or ties. [OE *bindan*] —Syn. *v.* **1.** connect, attach. **4.** obligate, constrain.

bind·er (bīn′dər), *n.* **1.** person or thing that binds. **2.** cover for holding loose sheets of paper together. **3.** *Am.* machine that cuts grain and ties it in bundles.

bind·er·y (bīn′dər·i), *n., pl.* -er·ies. *Am.* place where books are bound.

bind·ing (bīn′ding), *n.* **1.** a making fast, securing, or uniting. **2.** the covering of a book. **3.** strip protecting or ornamenting an edge. **4.** substance that binds. —*adj.* **1.** that binds, fastens, or connects. **2.** having force or power to hold to some agreement, pledge, etc.; obligatory. —bind′ing·ly, *adv.* —bind′ing·ness, *n.*

binding energy, *Nuclear Physics.* energy necessary to break a particular atomic nucleus into its smaller component parts.

bind·weed (bīnd′wēd′), *n.* plant that twines around the stems of other plants.

bin·go (bing′gō), *n.* a game derived from lotto.

bin·na·cle (bin′ə·kəl), *n.* box or stand that contains a ship's compass, placed near the man who is steering. [alter. of *bittacle* < Sp. or Pg. < L *habitaculum* dwelling place < *habitare* dwell]

bin·o·cle (bin′ə·kəl), *n.* binocular.

bi·noc·u·lar (bə·nok′yə·lər, bī–), *adj.* **1.** using both eyes. **2.** for both eyes. —*n.* Often, binoculars, a field glass or opera glass for both eyes. [< L *bini* two at a time + *oculi* eyes] —bi·noc′u·lar·i·ty, *n.* —bi·noc′u·lar·ly, *adv.*

bi·no·mi·al (bī·nō′mi·əl), *adj.* consisting of two terms. —*n.* expression or name consisting of two terms. 8a + 2b is a binomial. [< LL *binomius* having two names < *bi–* two + *nomen* name] —bi·no′mi·al·ly, *adv.*

biochem., biochemistry.

bi·o·chem·is·try (bī′ō·kem′is·tri), *n.* chemistry of living animals and plants; biological chemistry. [< Gk. *bios* life + E *chemistry*] —bi·o·chem·i·cal (bī′ō·kem′ə·kəl), bi′o·chem′ic, *adj.* —bi′o·chem′i·cal·ly, *adv.* —bi′o·chem′ist, *n.*

biog., biographer; biographical; biography.

bi·o·gen·e·sis (bī′ō·jen′ə·sis), bi·og·e·ny (bī·oj′ə·ni), *n. Biol.* theory that living things can be produced only by other living things. [< Gk. *bios* life + E *genesis*] —bi·o·ge·net·ic (bī′ō·jə·net′ik), *adj.* —bi′o·ge·net′i·cal·ly, *adv.*

bi·og·ra·phy (bī·og′rə·fi, bī–), *n., pl.* -phies. **1.** the written story of a person's life. **2.** part of literature that consists of biographies. [< L < Gk., < *bios* life + *graphein* write] —bi·og′ra-

pher, *n.* —bi·o·graph·i·cal (bī′ə·graf′ə·kəl), bi′o·graph′ic, *adj.* —bi′o·graph′i·cal·ly, *adv.* ▶ A *biography* is the life of a person written by someone else; an *autobiography* is the life of a person written by himself.

biol., biology.

bi·o·log·i·cal (bī′ə·loj′ə·kəl), bi·o·log·ic (–loj′ik), *adj.* **1.** of plant and animal life. **2.** having to do with biology. —bi′o·log′i·cal·ly, *adv.*

biological warfare, a waging of war by using disease germs, etc., against the enemy.

bi·ol·o·gy (bī·ol′ə·ji), *n.* science of life or living matter in all its forms and phenomena; study of the origin, reproduction, structure, etc., of plant and animal life. [< Gk. *bios* life + –LOGY] —bi·ol′o·gist, *n.*

bi·om·e·try (bī·om′ə·tri), *n.* **1.** measurement of life; calculation of the probable duration of human life. **2.** Also, **bi·o·met·rics** (bī′ə·met′riks). branch of biology that deals with living things by measurements and statistics. [< Gk. *bios* life + E *–metry* < Gk. *metron* measure] —bi·o·met·ric (bī′ə·met′rik), bi′o·met′ri·cal, *adj.* —bi′o·met′ri·cal·ly, *adv.*

bi·on·ics (bī·on′iks), *n.* the study of the anatomy and physiology of animals as a basis for new or improved electronic devices or methods.

bi·par·ti·san (bī·pär′tə·zən), *adj.* of or representing two political parties. —bi·par′ti·san·ship′, *n.*

bi·par·tite (bī·pär′tīt), *adj.* **1.** having two parts. **2.** *Bot.* divided into two parts nearly to the base. —bi·par′tite·ly, *adv.* —bi·par·ti·tion (bī′pär·tish′ən), *n.*

bi·par·ty (bī′pär′ti), *adj.* combining two different political groups, etc.

bi·ped (bī′ped), *Zool.* —*n.* animal having two feet. —*adj.* having two feet. [< L, < *bi–* two + *pes* foot]

bi·pet·al·ous (bī·pet′əl·əs), *adj. Bot.* having two petals.

bi·pin·nate (bī·pin′āt), *adj. Bot.* doubly pinnate.

bi·plane (bī′plān′), *n.* airplane having two wings, one above the other.

birch (bėrch), *n.* **1.** tree whose smooth bark peels off in thin layers. **2.** its close-grained wood, often used in making furniture. **3.** bundle of birch twigs or a birch stick, used for whipping. —*v.* whip with a birch; flog. [OE *bierce*] —birch·en (bėr′chən), *adj.*

Bipinnate leaf

birch·bark (bėrch′bärk′), *n.* **1.** bark of a birch tree. **2.** Also, **birchbark canoe.** *Am.* canoe made of birchbark. —*adj.* made of or covered with birchbark.

bird (bėrd), *n.* **1.** any of a class of warm-blooded vertebrates having a body covered with feathers and the forelimbs modified to form wings by means of which most species fly. **2.** bird hunted for sport. **3.** *Am., Slang.* a fellow; guy. **4.** *Slang.* a hissing sound of disapproval. **5.** *Am., Slang.* a ballistic missile. [OE *bridd, bird*]

bird dog, *Am.* dog trained to find or bring back birds for hunters.

bird·ie (bėr′di), *n.* **1.** a little bird. **2.** *Am.* score of one stroke less than par for any hole on a golf course.

bird·lime (bėrd′līm′), *n.* a sticky substance smeared on twigs to catch small birds.

bird·man (bėrd′man′; –mən), *n., pl.* -men. *Colloq.* aviator.

bird of paradise, bird of New Guinea noted for its magnificent plumage.

bird of passage, 1. bird that flies from one region to another as the seasons change. **2.** *Colloq.* person who roams from place to place.

bird of prey, any of a group of flesh-eating birds, including eagles, hawks, vultures, etc.

bird's-eye (bėrdz′i′), *adj.* **1.** seen from above or from a distance; general: *a bird's-eye view.* **2.** having markings somewhat like birds' eyes.

bi·ret·ta (bə·ret′ə), *n.* a stiff, square cap with three upright projecting pieces, worn by Roman Catholic priests. [< Ital., ult. < LL *birretum* cap, dim. of *birrus* cloak]

birl (bérl), *v. Am.* among lumberjacks, to revolve a log in the water while standing on it.

Bir·ming·ham (bér′ming·əm *for 1;* bėr′ming·ham *for 2),* *n.* 1. city in W England. 2. city in C Alabama.

Biretta

birth (bėrth), *n.* 1. coming into life; being born. 2. beginning; origin. 3. a bringing forth. 4. natural inheritance: *a musician by birth.* 5. descent; family: *he was a man of humble birth.* 6. noble family or descent. 7. that which is born. 8. give birth to, a. bear; bring forth. b. be the origin or cause of. [ME *birthe,* prob. < Scand. *byrth*] —Syn. 5. parentage, extraction.

birth·day (bėrth′dā′), *n.* 1. day on which a person was born. 2. day on which a thing began. 3. anniversary of the day on which a person was born, or on which a thing began.

birth·mark (bėrth′märk′), *n.* spot or mark on the skin that was there at birth.

birth·place (bėrth′plās′), *n.* 1. place where a person was born. 2. place of origin.

birth rate, proportion of the number of births per year to the total population or to some other stated number.

birth·right (bėrth′rīt′), *n.* right belonging to a person because of any fact about his birth.

birth·stone (bėrth′stōn′), *n.* jewel associated with a certain month of the year.

Bis·cay (bis′kā; -kī), *n.* Bay of, bay N of Spain and W of France, part of the Atlantic.

bis·cuit (bis′kit), *n., pl.* **-cuits, -cuit.** 1. *Am.* a kind of bread in small soft cakes, made with baking powder, soda, etc. 2. *Brit.* cracker. 3. a pale brown. [< OF *bescuit* < bes twice (< L *bis*) + *cuit,* pp. of *cuire* cook (< L *coquere*)]

bi·sect (bī·sekt′), *v.* 1. divide into two parts. 2. *Geom.* divide into two equal parts. [< *bi-* two + L *sectus,* pp. of *secare* cut] —**bi·sec′tion,** *n.* —**bi·sec′tion·al,** *adj.* —**bi·sec′tion·al·ly,** *adv.* —**bi·sec′tor,** *n.*

bish·op (bish′əp), *n.* 1. clergyman of high rank who has certain spiritual duties and who administers the affairs of a church district. 2. one of the pieces in the game of chess. [< VL (*e*)*biscopus,* var. of L *episcopus* < Gk. *episkopos* overseer < *epi* on, over + *skopos* watcher] —**bish′op·less,** *adj.*

D

A B C

The line DB bisects the angle ADC.

bish·op·ric (bish′əp·rik), *n.* 1. position, office, or rank of bishop. 2. diocese.

Bis·marck (biz′märk), *n.* 1. Otto von, 1815-1898, German statesman. 2. capital of North Dakota, in the S part.

Bismarck Archipelago, group of islands NE of New Guinea, governed by Australia.

bis·muth (biz′məth), *n. Chem.* a brittle, reddish-white metallic element, Bi, used in medicine. [< G] —**bis′muth·al,** *adj.*

bi·son (bī′sən; -zən), *n., pl.* **-son.** 1. the American buffalo, a wild ox with a big, shaggy head and strong front legs. 2. the European buffalo, slightly larger than the American buffalo and now almost extinct. [< L < Gmc.]

bisque (bisk), *n.* a smooth, creamy soup. [< F]

bis·sex·tile (bi·seks′til), *n.* leap year. —*adj.* containing the extra day of leap year. [< L *bissextilis* (*annus*) leap (year) < *bis* twice + *sextus* sixth. The Julian calendar added an extra day after the *sixth* day before the calends of March.]

bis·ter, bis·tre (bis′tər), *n.* 1. a dark-brown coloring matter made from soot. 2. a dark brown. [< F *bistre*] —**bis′tered, bis′tred,** *adj.*

bi·sul·fate, bi·sul·phate (bī·sul′fāt), *n. Chem.* salt of sulfuric acid in which half of the hydrogen is replaced by a metal.

bi·sul·fide, bi·sul·phide (bī·sul′fīd; -fīd), **bi·sul·fid, bi·sul·phid** (-fīd), *n. Chem.* disulfide.

bit¹ (bit), *n., v.,* **bit·ted, bit·ting.** —*n.* 1. part of a bridle that goes in a horse's mouth. 2. anything that curbs or restrains. 3. the biting or cutting part of a tool. 4. tool for boring or drilling that usually fits into a handle called a brace. 5. part of a key that goes into a lock and makes it turn. —*v.* 1. put a bit in the mouth of; bridle. 2. curb; restrain. [OE *bite* a bite < *bītan* bite]

bit² (bit), *n.* 1. a small piece; small amount. 2. somewhat; a little. 3. *Colloq.* short time. 4. *Am. Colloq.* 12½ cents. 5. *Am., Slang.* a piece of stage business; routine. 6. **do one's bit,** do one's share. [OE *bita* < *bītan* bite] —Syn. 1. particle, speck.

bitch (bich), *n.* 1. a female dog, wolf, or fox. 2. vulgar term of contempt for a woman. [OE *bicce*]

bite (bīt), *n., v.,* **bit, bit·ten** (bit′ən) or **bit, bit·ing.** —*n.* 1. a piece bitten off; bit of food. 2. food. 3. act of biting. 4. result of a bite, wound, sting, etc. 5. a sharp, smarting pain. 6. tight hold. 7. action of acid in eating into a metal, etc. 8. *Am., Slang.* the amount or percentage of money, etc. taken from a total received, earned, etc.: *the tax bite.* —*v.* 1. seize, cut into, or cut off with the teeth. 2. cut; pierce. 3. wound with teeth, fangs, etc.; sting. 4. nip; snap: *a dog biting at fleas.* 5. cause a sharp, smarting pain to. 6. take a tight hold on; grip: *the wheels bite the rails.* 7. take a bait; be caught. 8. cheat; trick. 9. eat into: *acid bites metal.* 10. **bite the dust,** fall slain; be vanquished. [OE *bītan*] —**bit′er,** *n.*

bit·ing (bīt′ing), *adj.* 1. sharp; cutting. 2. sarcastic; sneering. —**bit′ing·ly,** *adv.*

bitt (bit), *Naut.* —*n.* a strong post on a ship's deck to which ropes, cables, etc., are fastened. —*v.* put (ropes, cables, etc.) around the bitts. [var. of *bit¹*]

bit·ter (bit′ər), *adj.* 1. having a sharp, harsh, unpleasant taste like quinine. 2. hard to admit or bear. 3. harsh or cutting, as words. 4. causing pain; sharp; severe. 5. of weather, very cold. 6. expressing grief, pain, misery, etc. —*n.* that which is bitter; bitterness. —*v.* make or become bitter. [OE *biter;* akin to BITE] —**bit′ter·ish,** *adj.* —**bit′ter·ly,** *adv.* —**bit′ter·ness,** *n.* —Syn. *adj.* 1. acrid. 2. painful, distressing. 3. caustic.

bit·tern (bit′ərn), *n.* a small kind of heron that lives in marshes and has a peculiar booming cry. [< OF *butor*]

bit·ter·root (bit′ər·rüt′; -rút′), *n. Am.* a small plant with pink flowers, found in the northern Rocky Mountains.

bit·ters (bit′ərz), *n.pl.* a liquid, usually alcoholic, flavored with some bitter plant.

bit·ter·sweet (*n.* bit′ər·swēt′; *adj.* bit′ər·swēt′), *n.* 1. a climbing plant with purple flowers and poisonous, scarlet berries. 2. *Am.* a climbing shrub of North America, with greenish flowers, and scarlet arils growing from orange capsules. —*adj.* both bitter and sweet.

bi·tu·men (bi·tü′mən; -tū′-; bich′ú-), *n.* mineral that will burn, such as asphalt, petroleum, naphtha, etc. [< L] —**bi·tu·mi·noid** (bi·tü′mə·noid; -tū′-), *adj.* —**bi·tu′mi·nous,** *adj.*

bituminous coal, coal that burns with much smoke and a yellow flame; soft coal.

bi·va·lent (bī·vā′lənt; biv′ə-), *adj. Chem.* having a valence of two. [< *bi-* two + L *valens,* ppr. of *valere* be worth] —**bi·va·lence** (bī·vā′ləns; biv′ə-), **bi·va′len·cy,** *n.*

bi·valve (bī′valv′), *Zool.* —*n.* any mollusk whose shell consists of two parts hinged together, as oysters and clams. —*adj.* having two parts hinged together. —**bi′valved′, bi·val·vu·lar** (bī·val′vyə·lər), *adj.*

biv·ou·ac (biv′ú·ak; biv′wak), *n., v.,* **-acked, -ack·ing.** camp outdoors. [< F, prob. < Swiss G *biwache* < *bī* by + *wache* watch]

bi·week·ly (bī·wēk′li), *adj., n., pl.* **-lies,** *adv.* —*adj.* 1. happening once every two weeks. 2. happening twice a week; semiweekly. —*n.* newspaper or magazine published biweekly. —*adv.* 1. once every two weeks. 2. twice a week; semiweekly.

bi·zarre (bi·zär′), *adj.* odd; queer; fantastic; grotesque. [< F < Sp., brave, < Basque *bezar* beard] —**bi·zarre′ly**, *adv.* —**bi·zarre′ness**, *n.*

Bi·zet (bē·zā′), *n.* Georges, 1838–1875, French musical composer who wrote the opera *Carmen.*

Bi·zo·ni·a (bī·zō′ni·ə; bĭ–), **Bi·zone** (bī′zōn′), *n.* territory in W Germany occupied by British and American forces after World War II.

bk., 1. bank. 2. bark. 3. block. 4. book.

bl., 1. *pl.* **bls.** bale. 2. *pl.* **bls.** barrel.

blab (blab), *v.,* **blabbed, blab·bing,** *n.* —*v.* tell (secrets); talk too much. —*n.* 1. blabbing talk; chatter. 2. person who blabs. —**blab′ber**, *n.*

black (blak), *adj.* 1. opposite of white. 2. without any light; very dark. 3. clad in black. 4. having a dark skin. 5. Negro. 6. dirty; filthy. 7. dismal; gloomy. 8. sullen; angry. 9. evil; wicked. 10. calamitous; disastrous. 11. indicating blame or disgrace. —*n.* 1. opposite of white. 2. black coloring matter. 3. black clothes; mourning. 4. person who has dark skin. 5. Negro. —*v.* 1. make or become black. 2. put blacking on (shoes, etc.). 3. become temporarily blind or unconscious. [OE *blæc*] —**black′en**, *v.* —**black′ly**, *adv.* —**black′ness**, *n.* —**Syn.** *adj.* 2. dusky.

black·a·moor (blak′ə·mür), *n.* 1. a Negro. 2. a dark-skinned person. [var. of *black Moor*]

black art, evil magic.

black·ball (blak′bôl′), *v.* 1. vote against. 2. ostracize. —*n.* a vote against a person or thing. —**black′ball′er**, *n.*

black bass, *Am.* a North American game fish that lives in fresh water.

black bear, 1. *Am.* a large American bear. 2. a large Asiatic bear.

black·ber·ry (blak′ber′ĭ), *n., pl.* **–ries,** *v.,* **–ried, –ry·ing.** —*n.* 1. a small, black or dark-purple, edible fruit of certain bushes and vines. 2. a thorny bush or vine that it grows on. —*v.* gather blackberries.

black·bird (blak′bėrd′), *n.* 1. *Am.* any American bird so named because the male is mostly black, as the red-winged blackbird. 2. any similar bird, as the European blackbird.

black·board (blak′-bôrd′; –bōrd′), *n.* a dark, smooth surface for writing or drawing on with chalk or crayon.

Red-winged blackbird (9 in. long)

Black Death, a violent plague that spread through Asia and Europe in the 14th century.

black·en (blak′ən), *v.,* **–ened, –en·ing.** 1. make or become black. 2. speak evil of. —**black′en·er**, *n.* —**Syn.** 1. darken. 2. slander, defame.

black eye, 1. bruise around an eye. 2. *Colloq.* cause of disgrace or discredit.

black-eyed Su·san (blak′ĭd′ sü′zən), *Am.* a yellow daisy with a black center.

black·face (blak′fās′), *n.* 1. *Am.* Negro minstrel; actor made up as a Negro. 2. *Am.* theatrical entertainment given by blackfaces. 3. printing type with thick, heavy lines. —*adj.* having a black face.

Black·foot (blak′fût′), *n., pl.* **–feet** (–fēt′), **–foot,** *adj. Am.* —*n.* 1. confederacy of Algonquian Indians of the northern plains and Canada. 2. their language. 3. an Algonquian Indian. —*adj.* or having to do with the Blackfeet or their language.

Black Forest, mountains covered with forests in SW Germany.

black·guard (blag′ärd; –ərd), *n.* scoundrel. —*v.* abuse with vile language. [< *black + guard*] —**black′guard·ism**, *n.* —**black·guard·ly** (blag′ərd·li), *adj.*

Black Hand, *Am.* a secret society organized to commit blackmail and crimes of violence.

black·head (blak′hed′), *n.* 1. *Am.* a small, black-tipped lump in a pore of the skin. 2. any of various birds that have a black head. 3. disease that attacks turkeys.

black-heart·ed (blak′här′tid), *adj.* evil.

Black Hills, mountains in W South Dakota and NE Wyoming.

black·ing (blak′ing), *n.* black polish used on shoes, stoves, etc.

black·ish (blak′ish), *adj.* somewhat black.

black·jack (blak′jak′), *n.* 1. *Am.* club with a flexible handle, used as a weapon. 2. a large drinking cup or jug. 3. the black flag of a pirate. —*v.* 1. *Am.* hit (a person) with a blackjack. 2. coerce. —**black′jack′**, *adj. Am.*

black lead, graphite.

black·leg (blak′leg′), *n.* 1. *Colloq.* swindler. 2. *Brit.* strikebreaker. 3. an infectious, usually fatal disease of cattle and sheep.

black letter, a printing type with thick, heavy lines. —**black′-let′ter,** *adj.*

black list, list of persons who are believed to deserve punishment, blame, suspicion, etc.

black·list (blak′list′), *v.* put on a black list.

black magic, evil magic.

black·mail (blak′māl′), *v.* get or try to get blackmail from. —*n.* 1. money obtained from a person by threatening to tell something bad about him. 2. act of blackmailing. [< *black + mail* rent, tribute, coin < OF *maille* < *mail, medaille* coin, medal] —**black′mail′er**, *n.*

Black Ma·ri·a (mə·rī′ə), *Am., Colloq.* police patrol wagon.

black mark, mark of criticism or punishment.

black market, the selling of goods at illegal prices or in illegal quantities.

black mar·ket·eer (mär′kə·tir′), one who deals on the black market.

Black Muslim, member of an American Negro minority group of the 1960's preaching a form of Islam, Negro racial superiority, and total segregation between Negroes and whites.

black nightshade, plant with white flowers, poisonous, black berries, and poisonous leaves.

black oak, *Am.* 1. any of various American oaks, having dark bark and foliage. 2. its wood.

black·out (blak′out′), *n.* 1. a turning off of all the lights on the stage of a theater. 2. a turning out or concealing of all the lights of a city, district, etc., as a protection against an air raid. 3. *Aviation.* temporary blindness or unconsciousness experienced by a pilot, resulting from rapid changes in velocity or direction.

black out, 1. darken completely. 2. *Aviation.* experience a blackout.

black pepper, 1. a seasoning with a hot taste. It is made by grinding the berries of a plant. 2. the plant itself.

Black Sea, sea between Turkey and S Russia.

black sheep, a worthless member of a decent family; scoundrel.

Black Shirt, 1. an Italian Fascist. 2. member of any fascist organization, esp. one using black shirts as part of their uniforms.

black·smith (blak′smith′), *n.* man who works with iron. Blacksmiths mend tools and shoe horses. [with ref. to black metals, e.g., iron]

black·snake (blak′snāk′), *n. Am.* 1. a harmless, dark-colored snake of North America. 2. a heavy whip made of braided leather.

black spruce, 1. *Am.* a North American evergreen tree with dark-green foliage. 2. its light, soft wood.

Black·stone (blak′stōn; –stən), *n.* Sir William, 1723–1780, English legal writer and judge.

black·thorn (blak′thôrn′), *n.* a thorny European shrub of the peach family that has dark-purple, plumlike fruit called sloes.

black walnut, *Am.* 1. an oily nut that is good to eat. 2. the tall tree that it grows on. 3. its dark-brown wood, often used for furniture.

black widow, *Am.* a very poisonous spider, so called from its color and its habit of eating its mate.

blad·der (blad′ər), *n.* 1. *Anat., Zool.* a soft, thin bag in the body that secretes urine from the kidneys. 2. anything like this. [OE *blǣdre*] —**blad′der·like′**, *adj.* —**blad′der·y**, *adj.*

blad·der·wort (blad′ər·wėrt′), *n.* any of

various plants with yellow flowers. Some varieties float on the water; others take root in mud.

blade (blād), *n.* 1. the cutting part of anything like a knife or sword. 2. sword. 3. swordsman. 4. a smart or dashing fellow. 5. leaf of grass. 6. *Bot.* the flat, wide part of a leaf; leaf. 7. a flat, wide part of anything: *the blade of a paddle.* 8. the wide, flat part of a bone: *the shoulder blade.* 9. *Phonet.* the front, flat part of the tongue. [OE *blæd*] —**blad′ed**, *adj.* —**blade′less**, *adj.* —**blade′like′**, *adj.*

blain (blān), *n. Pathol.* an inflamed swelling or sore; blister; pustule. [OE *blegen*]

Blake (blāk), *n.* William, 1757–1827, English poet and artist.

blam·a·ble (blām′ə·bəl), *adj.* deserving blame. —**blam′a·ble·ness**, *n.* —**blam′a·bly**, *adv.*

blame (blām), *v.*, **blamed**, **blam·ing**, *n.* —*v.* 1. hold responsible (for something bad or wrong). 2. find fault with. 3. **be to blame**, deserve blame. —*n.* 1. responsibility for something bad or wrong. 2. fault. 3. finding fault. [< OF < L < Gk. *blasphemein*, ? < *blapsis* harm + –*phemos* speaking] —**blame′ful**, *adj.* —**blame′ful·ly**, *adv.* —**blame′ful·ness**, *n.* —**blame′less**, *adj.* —**blame′less·ly**, *adv.* —**blame′less·ness**, *n.* —**blam′er**, *n.* —Syn. *v.* 1. accuse. 2. censure. —*n.* 1. guilt. 3. censure, condemnation, reproach. —Ant. *v.* 1. absolve. 2. praise.

blame·wor·thy (blām′wėr′ᵺi), *adj.* deserving blame. —**blame′wor′thi·ness**, *n.*

blanch (blanch; blänch), *v.* 1. make white; bleach: *almonds are blanched.* 2. turn white or pale: *blanch with fear.* [< OF *blanchir* < *blanc* white, BLANK] —**blanch′er**, *n.*

blanc·mange (blə·mänzh′), *n.* a sweet dessert made of milk thickened with gelatin, cornstarch, etc. [< OF *blanc-manger* white food]

bland (bland), *adj.* 1. mild; gentle; soothing: *a bland spring breeze.* 2. agreeable; polite. [< L *blandus* soft] —**bland′ly**, *adv.* —**bland′ness**, *n.* —Syn. 1. soft, balmy. 2. suave, urbane.

blan·dish (blan′dish), *v.* coax; flatter. [< F < L *blandiri* flatter < *blandus* soft] —**blan′dish·er**, *n.* —**blan′dish·ment**, *n.*

blank (blangk), *n.* 1. space left empty or to be filled in: *leave a blank after each word.* 2. paper with spaces to be filled in: *an application blank.* 3. an empty or vacant place. 4. piece of metal prepared to be stamped or filed into a coin, key, or the like. —*adj.* 1. not written or printed on: *blank paper.* 2. with spaces to be filled in: *a blank check.* 3. empty; vacant. 4. without interest or meaning; dull. 5. complete; absolute: *blank stupidity.* 6. lacking some usual feature: *a blank cartridge.* [< F *blanc* white, shining < Gmc.] —**blank′ly**, *adv.* —**blank′ness**, *n.* —Syn. *adj.* 3. void, bare.

blank check, a signed check that allows the bearer to fill in the amount.

blan·ket (blang′kit), *n.* 1. a soft, heavy covering woven from wool or cotton, used to keep people or animals warm. 2. anything like a blanket. —*v.* 1. cover with a blanket. 2. cover; hinder; obscure. 3. apply to uniformly: *a law that blankets all commercial activities.* —*adj.* covering several or all: *a blanket insurance policy.* [< OF *blankete* < *blanc* white] —**blan′ket·less**, *adj.*

blank verse, 1. unrhymed poetry having five iambic feet in each line. 2. unrhymed poetry.

blare (blãr), *v.*, **blared**, **blar·ing**, *n.* —*v.* 1. make a loud, harsh sound: *the trumpets blared.* 2. utter harshly or loudly. —*n.* 1. a loud, harsh sound. 2. brilliance of color; glare. [< MDu. *blaren*]

blar·ney (blär′ni), *n.*, *v.*, **–neyed**, **–ney·ing.** —*n.* flattering, coaxing talk. —*v.* flatter; coax. [< *Blarney stone,* stone in a castle in Ireland, said to give skill in flattery to those who kiss it] —**blar′ney·er**, *n.*

bla·sé (blä·zā′; blä′zā), *adj.* tired of pleasures; bored. [< F, pp. of *blaser* exhaust with pleasure]

blas·pheme (blas·fēm′), *v.*, **–phemed**, **–phem·ing.** 1. speak about (God or sacred things) with abuse or contempt; utter blasphemy. 2. speak evil of. [< OF < L *blasphemare.* See BLAME.] —**blas·phem′er**, *n.*

blas·phe·my (blas′fə·mi), *n.*, *pl.* **–mies.** abuse or contempt for God or sacred things. —**blas′phe·mous**, *adj.* —**blas′phe·mous·ly**, *adv.* —**blas′phe·mous·ness**, *n.* —Syn. profanity.

blast (blast; bläst), *n.* 1. a strong sudden rush of wind or air: *the icy blasts of winter.* 2. the blowing of a trumpet, horn, etc. 3. sound so made. 4. current of air used in smelting, etc. 5. charge of dynamite, gunpowder, etc., that blows up rocks, earth, etc. 6. a blasting; explosion. 7. cause of withering, blight, or ruin. 8. **in full blast,** in full operation. —*v.* 1. blow up (rocks, earth, etc.) with dynamite, gunpowder, etc. 2. wither; blight; ruin. [OE *blæst*] —**blast′er**, *n.* —Syn. *v.* 2. destroy.

blast·ed (blas′tid; bläs′–), *adj.* 1. withered; blighted; ruined. 2. damned; cursed.

blast furnace, *Metall.* furnace in which ores are smelted by blowing a strong current of air into the furnace to make a very great heat.

blas·tu·la (blas′chủ·lə), *n.*, *pl.* **–lae** (–lē). *Embryol.* embryo of an animal. [< NL, dim. of Gk. *blastos* sprout, germ] —**blas′tu·lar**, *adj.*

blat (blat), *v.*, **blat·ted**, **blat·ting.** 1. cry like a calf or sheep; bleat. 2. *Colloq.* say loudly and foolishly; blurt out. [imit.]

bla·tant (blā′tənt), *adj.* 1. noisy; loudmouthed. 2. showy in dress, manner, etc. [coined by Spenser < L *blatire* babble] —**bla′tan·cy**, *n.* —**bla′tant·ly**, *adv.* —Syn. 1. clamorous.

blaze¹ (blāz), *n.*, *v.*, **blazed**, **blaz·ing.** —*n.* 1. a bright flame or fire. 2. an intense light; glare. 3. bright display. 4. a violent outburst: *a blaze of temper.* —*v.* 1. burn with a bright flame; be on fire. 2. show bright colors or lights. 3. make a bright display. 4. burst out in anger or excitement. [OE *blæse*] —**blaz′ing·ly**, *adv.* —Syn. *n.* 1. conflagration. 2. brightness.

blaze² (blāz), *n.*, *v.*, **blazed**, **blaz·ing.** —*n.* 1. mark made on a tree by chipping off a piece of bark. 2. a white spot on the face of a horse, cow, etc. —*v.* mark (a tree, trail, etc.) by chipping off a piece of the bark. [< LG *bläse*]

blaze³ (blāz), *v.*, **blazed**, **blaz·ing.** make known; proclaim. [< MDu. *blasen*]

blaz·er (blāz′ər), *n.* a bright-colored jacket.

Blazon

bla·zon (blā′zən), *v.* 1. make known; proclaim. 2. decorate; adorn. 3. describe or paint (a coat of arms). 4. display; show. —*n.* 1. coat of arms. 2. description or painting of a coat of arms. 3. display; show. [< OF *blason* shield] —**bla′zon·er**, *n.* —**bla′zon·ment**, **bla′zon·ry**, *n.*

bldg., *pl.* **bldgs.** building.

bleach (blēch), *v.* 1. whiten by exposing to sunlight or by using chemicals. 2. turn white. —*n.* 1. chemical used in bleaching. 2. act of bleaching. [OE *blǣcean;* akin to BLEAK]

bleach·er (blēch′ər), *n.* 1. person who bleaches. 2. thing that bleaches or is used in bleaching. 3. bleachers, *Am.* low-priced, often roofless seats at outdoor sports.

bleak (blēk), *adj.* 1. swept by winds; bare. 2. chilly; cold. 3. dreary; dismal. [ME *bleke* pale. Cf. OE *blǣc, blāc.*] —**bleak′ly**, *adv.* —**bleak′ness**, *n.* —Syn. 1. desolate. 2. raw.

blear (blir), *adj.* dim; blurred. —*v.* make dim or blurred. [ME *blere(n)*]

blear-eyed (blir′īd′), *adj.* having blear eyes.

blear·y (blir′i), *adj.*, **blear·i·er**, **blear·i·est.** dim; blurred. —**blear′i·ness**, *n.*

bleat (blēt), *n.* cry made by a sheep, goat, or calf, or a sound like it. —*v.* make such a cry. [OE *blǣtan*] —**bleat′er**, *n.* —**bleat′ing·ly**, *adv.*

bleed (blēd), *v.*, **bled** (bled), **bleed·ing.** 1. lose blood. 2. shed one's blood; suffer wounds or death. 3. take blood from: *doctors used to bleed sick people.* 4. lose sap, juice, etc. 5. take sap, juice, etc., from. 6. feel pity, sorrow, or grief. 7. get money away from by extortion. [OE *blēdan* < *blōd* blood]

bleed·er (blēd′ər), *n.* person who bleeds very easily because the blood fails to clot.

blem·ish (blem′ish), *n.* stain; spot; scar: *a blemish on the skin.* —*v.* **1.** stain; spot; scar. **2.** injure; mar: *blemish one's reputation.* [< OF *ble(s)mir* make livid] —**blem′ish·er,** *n.* —Syn. *v.* **1.** deface, disfigure. **2.** tarnish, sully.

blench¹ (blench), *v.* draw back; shrink away. [appar. OE *blencan* deceive] —**blench′er,** *n.*

blench² (blench), *v.* **1.** turn pale. **2.** make white. [var. of *blanch*]

blend (blend), *v.,* **blend·ed** or **blent, blend·ing,** *n.* —*v.* **1.** mix together thoroughly so that the things mixed cannot be distinguished. **2.** make by mixing several kinds together. **3.** shade into each other, little by little; merge. **4.** go well together; harmonize. —*n.* **1.** thorough mixture. **2.** mixture of several kinds: *a blend of coffee.* **3.** a word made by fusing two words, often with a syllable in common, as *cinemactress. Blotch* is a blend of *blot* and *botch.* [pt. of OE *blandan*] —**blend′er,** *n.* —Syn. *v.* **1.** mingle, combine.

bless (bles), *v.,* **blessed** or **blest, bless·ing. 1.** make holy or sacred. **2.** ask God's favor for. **3.** wish good to. **4.** make happy or successful. **5.** praise; glorify. **6.** guard; protect. **7.** make the sign of the cross over. [OE *blētsian* consecrate (i.e., with blood) < *blōd* blood] —**bless′er,** *n.*

bless·ed (bles′id; blest), *adj.* **1.** holy; sacred. **2.** beatified. **3.** happy; successful. **4.** in heaven. **5.** annoying; cursed. —**bless′ed·ly,** *adv.* —**bless′ed·ness,** *n.*

Blessed Virgin, the Virgin Mary.

bless·ing (bles′ing), *n.* **1.** prayer asking God to show His favor. **2.** giving of God's favor. **3.** wish for happiness or success. **4.** anything that makes one happy or contented. —Syn. **1.** invocation.

blew (blü), *v.* pt. of **blow².**

blight (blīt), *n.* **1.** any disease that causes plants to wither or decay. **2.** insect or fungus that causes such a disease. **3.** anything that causes destruction or ruin. —*v.* **1.** cause to wither or decay. **2.** destroy; ruin.

blimp (blimp), *n. Colloq.* a small, nonrigid dirigible airship. [appar. from Type *B limp,* designation for "limp dirigible"]

blind (blīnd), *adj.* **1.** not able to see. **2.** lacking discernment, understanding, or judgment. **3.** not controlled by reason: *blind fury.* **4.** made without thought or good sense: *a blind guess.* **5.** covered; hidden. **6.** without an opening: *a blind wall.* **7.** with only one opening: *a blind alley.* **8.** of or for blind persons. —*v.* **1.** make unable to see temporarily or permanently. **2.** darken; dim; cover; conceal. **3.** rob of power to understand or judge. —*n.* **1.** something that keeps out light or hinders sight. **2.** anything that conceals an action or purpose. **3.** *Am.* a hiding place for a hunter. **4.** any hiding place. [OE] —**blind′ing,** *adj.* —**blind′ing·ly,** *adv.* —**blind′ly,** *adv.* —**blind′ness,** *n.* —Syn. *adj.* **1.** sightless. **4.** heedless, oblivious, unmindful.

blind·er (blīn′dər), *n.* **1.** one that blinds. **2.** a blinker for a horse.

blind flying, directing an airplane by instruments only.

blind·fold (blīnd′fōld′), *v.* cover the eyes of. —*adj.* **1.** with the eyes covered. **2.** reckless. —*n.* thing covering the eyes. [OE *blindfellian* < *blind* blind + *fell,* var. of *fiell* fall; infl. by *fold*]

Blinders (def. 2)

blind spot, 1. *Anat.* a round spot on the retina of the eye that is not sensitive to light. **2.** matter on which a person does not know that he is prejudiced or poorly informed. **3.** *Radio.* an area of poor reception.

blink (blingk), *v.* **1.** look with the eyes opening and shutting: *blink at a sudden light.* **2.** wink: *blink one's eyes.* **3.** shine with an unsteady light: *a lantern blinked in the darkness.* **4.** blink at, look with indifference at; ignore. —*n.* **1.** a blinking. **2.** glimpse. [ME *blenken*] —**blink′ing·ly,** *adv.*

blink·er (blingk′ər), *n.* **1.** a leather flap to keep a horse from seeing sidewise; blinder. **2.** a warning signal with flashing lights.

blip (blip), *n.* image on a radar screen.

bliss (blis), *n.* **1.** great happiness; perfect joy. **2.** the joy of heaven; blessedness. [OE *bliths* < *blithe* blithe] —**bliss′ful,** *adj.* —**bliss′ful·ly,** *adv.* —**bliss′ful·ness,** *n.* —Syn. **1.** ecstasy, rapture.

blis·ter (blis′tər), *n.* **1.** a little baglike place under the skin filled with watery matter, often caused by burns or rubbing. **2.** a similar swelling on a surface. —*v.* **1.** raise a blister on. **2.** become covered with blisters. **3.** attack with sharp words. [< OF *blestre* tumor, lump, prob. < Gmc.] —**blis′ter·y,** *adj.*

blithe (blīth; blīth), *adj.* gay; happy; cheerful. [OE *blīthe*] —**blithe′ly,** *adv.* —**blithe′ness,** *n.*

blithe·some (blīth′səm; blīth′–), *adj.* gay; happy; cheerful. —**blithe′some·ly,** *adv.* —**blithe′some·ness,** *n.*

blitz (blits), *n.* **1.** blitzkreig. **2.** a sudden, violent attack using many airplanes and tanks. **3.** any sudden violent attack. —*v.* attack by blitz. [< G, lightning]

blitz·krieg (blits′krēg′), *n.* warfare in which the offensive is extremely rapid, violent, and hard to resist. [< G, lightning war]

bliz·zard (bliz′ərd), *n.* a violent, blinding snowstorm with a very strong wind and very great cold. [var. of *blizzer* blow, shot; orig., flash, blaze. Cf. OE *blysian* burn.]

bloat (blōt), *v.* swell up; puff up. [< *bloat,* adj., soft < Scand. *blautr*]

blob (blob), *n.* a small lump; bubble; drop.

bloc (blok), *n.* a member or members of a group combined for a purpose, esp. a number of legislators: *the farm bloc.* [< F. See BLOCK.]

block (blok), *n.* **1.** a solid piece of wood, stone, metal, etc. **2.** obstruction; hindrance. **3.** *Sports.* a hindering of an opponent's play. **4.** *Am.* part of a city enclosed by streets on each side. **5.** length of one side of a city block. **6.** *Am.* number of buildings close together. **7.** group of things of the same kind: *a block of ten tickets for a play.* **8.** a short section of railroad track with signals for spacing trains. **9.** support for the neck of a person condemned to be beheaded. **10.** platform where things are put up for sale at an auction. **11.** pulley in a casing. **12.** mold on which things are shaped. **13.** piece of wood, etc., engraved for printing. —*v.* **1.** fill so as to prevent passage or progress. **2.** put things in the way of; obstruct; hinder. **3.** mount on a block. **4.** block in or out, plan roughly; outline. [< OF *bloc* < Gmc.] —**block′er,** *n.* —Syn. *v.* **2.** bar, blockade.

B, block (def. 11).

block·ade (blok·ād′), *n., v.,* **-ad·ed, -ad·ing.** —*n.* **1.** control of who or what goes into or out of a place by the use of an army or navy. **2.** army or navy used to blockade a place. **3.** anything that blocks up or obstructs. —*v.* **1.** put under blockade. **2.** obstruct. —**block·ad′er,** *n.*

blockade runner, *Am.* ship that tries to sneak into or out of a port that is being blockaded.

block and tackle, pulleys and ropes to lift or pull something.

block·bust·er (blok′bus′tər), *n. Colloq.* a very destructive aerial bomb that weighs two or more tons.

block·head (blok′hed′), *n.* a stupid person.

block·house (blok′hous′), *n.* **1.** *Am.* house of square logs, often with a jutting second story, having holes for guns. **2.** *Mil.* any small fortified building with ports for gunfire.

block·ish (blok′ish), *adj.* stupid; dull. —**block′ish·ly,** *adv.* —**block′ish·ness,** *n.*

block·y (blok′i), *adj.,* **block·i·er, block·i·est. 1.** like a block; chunky. **2.** having patches of light and shade.

blond, blonde (blond), *adj.* **1.** light-colored. **2.** having yellow or light-brown hair, blue or gray eyes, and light skin. —*n.* person having such hair, eyes, and skin. A man is a blond; a woman is a blonde. [< F < Gmc.] —**blond′ness, blonde′- ness,** *n.* —Syn. *adj.* 2. fair.

blood (blud), *n.* 1. the red liquid in the veins and arteries of the higher animals. 2. the corresponding liquid in lower animals. 3. juice; sap. 4. animal nature: *it stirred his blood.* 5. bloodshed; slaughter. 6. family; birth; relationship; parentage; descent. 7. high lineage, esp. royal lineage. 8. temper; state of mind: *there was bad blood between them.* 9. *Esp. Brit.* man of dash and spirit. 10. in cold blood, a. cruelly. b. on purpose. [OE *blōd*] —**blood′like′,** *adj.*

blood bank, 1. place for storage of blood. 2. the blood kept in storage.

blood brother, 1. brother by birth. 2. person who goes through a ceremony of mixing some of his blood with another person's.

blood count, count of the number of red and white corpuscles in a sample of a person's blood to see if it is normal.

blood·cur·dling (blud′kėrd′ling), *adj.* terrifying; horrible.

blood·ed (blud′id), *adj.* 1. *Am.* of good stock or breed. 2. having a certain kind of blood.

blood group, blood type.

blood·hound (blud′hound′), *n.* 1. one of a breed of large, powerful dogs with a keen sense of smell. 2. *Slang.* detective.

blood·less (blud′lis), *adj.* 1. without blood; pale. 2. without bloodshed. 3. without energy; spiritless. 4. cold-hearted; cruel. —**blood′less·ly,** *adv.* —**blood′less·ness,** *n.*

blood·let·ting (blud′let′ing), *n.* act of opening a vein to take out blood.

blood money, 1. money paid to have somebody killed. 2. money paid to compensate for killing somebody.

blood poisoning, a diseased condition of blood caused by poisonous matter or germs.

blood pressure, pressure of the blood against the inner walls of the blood vessels, varying with exertion, excitement, health, age, etc.

blood relation or **relative,** person related by birth.

blood·root (blud′rüt′; -rút′), *n. Am.* plant that has a red root, red sap, and a white flower.

blood·shed (blud′shed′), **blood·shed·ding** (-shed′ing), *n.* the shedding of blood.

blood·shot (blud′shot′), *adj.* of eyes, red and sore; tinged with blood.

blood·stained (blud′stānd′), *adj.* 1. stained with blood. 2. guilty of murder or bloodshed.

blood·stone (blud′stōn′), *n.* a semiprecious green stone with specks of red jasper scattered through it.

blood·suck·er (blud′suk′ər), *n.* 1. animal that sucks blood; leech. 2. person who gets all he can from others.

blood·thirst·y (blud′thérs′ti), *adj.* eager for bloodshed; cruel; murderous. —**blood′thirst′- i·ly,** *adv.* —**blood′thirst′i·ness,** *n.*

blood transfusion, injection of blood from one person or animal into another.

blood type, any one of four groups into which blood may be divided.

blood vessel, tube in the body through which the blood circulates, as an artery, vein, or capillary.

blood·y (blud′i), *adj.,* **blood·i·er, blood·i·est,** *v.,* **blood·ied, blood·y·ing.** —*adj.* 1. bleeding. 2. stained with blood. 3. with much bloodshed. 4. eager for bloodshed; cruel. 5. *Brit. Slang.* cursed; confounded. —*v.* 1. cause to bleed. 2. stain with blood. —**blood′i·ly,** *adv.* —**blood′i- ness,** *n.* —Syn. *adj.* 4. bloodthirsty, murderous.

bloom (blüm), *n.* 1. flower; blossom. 2. condition or time of flowering. 3. condition or time of greatest health, vigor, or beauty. 4. glow of health and beauty. 5. *Bot.* the powdery coating on some fruits and leaves. —*v.* 1. have flowers; open into flowers; blossom. 2. be in the condition or time of greatest health, vigor, or beauty. 3. glow with health and beauty. [< Scand. *blōm*] —**bloom′ing·ly,** *adv.* —Syn. *n.* 3. freshness, prime.

bloom·ers (blüm′ərz), *n.pl. Am.* a. loose trousers, gathered at the knee, worn by women and girls for physical training. b. underwear made like these. [first referred to in magazine published by Amelia J. Bloomer, 1851]

bloop·er (blüp′ər), *n. Am., Slang.* 1. a very foolish mistake; blunder. 2. *Baseball.* a ball hit high into the air.

blos·som (blos′əm), *n.* 1. flower, esp. of a plant that produces fruit. 2. condition or time of flowering. —*v.* 1. have flowers; open into flowers. 2. flourish; develop. [OE *blōstma*]

blot (blot), *v.,* **blot·ted, blot·ting,** *n.* —*v.* 1. spot with ink; stain. 2. dry (ink) with paper that soaks up ink. 3. blemish; disgrace. 4. blot out, a. hide; cover up. b. wipe out; destroy. —*n.* 1. spot of ink; stain of any kind. 2. blemish; disgrace. —**blot′less,** *adj.* —Syn. *v.* 3. sully.

blotch (bloch), *n.* 1. a large, irregular spot or stain. 2. place where the skin is red or broken out. —*v.* cover or mark with blotches. [blend of *blot* and *botch*] —**blotch′y,** *adj.*

blot·ter (blot′ər), *n.* 1. piece of blotting paper. 2. *Am.* book for writing down happenings, transactions, arrests, etc.

blotting paper, a soft paper used to dry writing by soaking up ink.

blouse (blous; blouz), *n.* 1. a loose shirtwaist worn by women and children. 2. loosely fitting garment for the upper part of the body: *sailors wear blouses.* 3. loosely fitting coat, worn as part of the undress uniform of the U.S. Army. 4. a kind of smock. [< F, < Pr., short (wool)] —**blouse′like′,** *adj.*

Blouse (def. 1)

blow¹ (blō), *n.* 1. a hard hit; knock; stroke. 2. a sudden happening that causes misfortune or loss; severe shock; misfortune. 3. a sudden attack or assault. [ME *blaw*] —Syn. 1. buffet. 2. calamity.

blow² (blō), *v.,* **blew, blown, blow·ing,** *n.* —*v.* 1. send forth a strong current of air. 2. move in a current; move rapidly or with power. 3. drive or carry by a current of air. 4. force a current of air into, through, or against. 5. clear or empty by forcing air through. 6. form or shape by air: *blow glass.* 7. make a sound by a current of air or steam: *the whistle blows at noon.* 8. puff up: *blown up with pride.* 9. swell with air: *to blow bubbles.* 10. break by an explosion. 11. be out of breath. 12. put out of breath. 13. exhale strongly. 14. *Colloq.* boast; brag. 15. of whales, spout air. 16. of flies, lay eggs in. 17. *Am., Slang.* spend (money, etc.) recklessly; squander. 18. melt (a fuse). 19. publish or spread (news). 20. blow in, *Am.* appear unexpectedly; drop in. 21. blow up, a. explode. b. fill with air. c. *Am., Colloq.* become very angry. d. *Colloq.* scold; abuse. e. arise; become stronger: *a storm suddenly blew up.* f. *Am., Colloq.* go to pieces, as from emotional stress. g. enlarge (a photograph). —*n.* 1. act or fact of forcing air into, through, or against something; blast. 2. a blowing. 3. gale of wind. [OE *blāwan*] —**blow′er,** *n.*

blow·fly (blō′flī′), *n., pl.* -flies. a two-winged fly that deposits its eggs on meat or in wounds.

blow·gun (blō′gun′), *n. Am.* tube through which a person blows arrows, darts, etc.

blow·hole (blō′hōl′), *n.* 1. hole where air or gas can escape. 2. hole for breathing, in the top of the head of whales and some other animals.

blown¹ (blōn), *adj.* 1. out of breath; exhausted. 2. tainted by flies; tainted; stale. 3. shaped by blowing. —*v.* pp. of **blow².**

blown² (blōn), *adj.* fully opened. [pp. of *blow* blossom, OE *blōwan*]

blow·out (blō′out′), *n.* 1. the bursting of the inner tube and casing of an automobile tire. 2. a sudden or violent escape of air, steam, etc. 3. the melting of an electric fuse caused by too much current. 4. *Slang.* big party or meal.

blow·pipe (blō′pīp′), *n.* 1. tube for blowing air or gas into a flame to increase the heat. 2. blowgun.

blow·torch (blō′tôrch′), *n. Am.* a small torch that shoots out a very hot flame.

blow·up (blō′up′), *n.* 1. explosion. 2. *Colloq.* outburst of anger. 3. *Am.* bankruptcy.

blow·y (blō′i), *adj.*, **blow·i·er**, **blow·i·est**. windy. —**blow′i·ness**, *n.*

blowz·y (blouz′i), *adj.*, **blowz·i·er**, **blowz·i·est**. 1. untidy; frowzy. 2. red-faced and coarse-looking. [< *blowze* wench, slattern]

blub·ber (blub′ər), *n.* 1. fat of whales and other sea animals. 2. noisy weeping. —*v.* weep noisily. —**blub′ber·er**, *n.* —**blub′ber·y**, *adj.*

bludg·eon (bluj′ən), *n.* short club with a heavy end. —*v.* 1. strike with a club. 2. bully; threaten. —**bludg′eon·er**, **bludg·eon·eer** (bluj′ən·ir′), *n.*

blue (blü), *n.*, *adj.*, **blu·er**, **blu·est**, *v.*, **blued**, **blu·ing** or **blue·ing**. —*n.* 1. the color of the clear sky in daylight. 2. a lighter or darker shade of this color. 3. something having this color; blue coloring matter, dye, or pigment. 4. **out of the blue**, completely unexpected. 5. **the blue**, a. the sky. b. the sea. 6. **the blues**. See **blues**. —*adj.* 1. having the color of the clear sky in daylight. 2. wearing blue clothes. 3. livid: *blue from cold.* 4. sad; gloomy; discouraged. —*v.* 1. make blue. 2. use bluing on. [< OF *bleu* < Gmc.] —**blue′ly**, *adv.* —**blue′ness**, *n.* —Syn. *adj.* 4. depressed, despondent, dejected.

Blue·beard (blü′bird′), *n.* a cruel man in an old legend who murdered six of his wives.

blue·bell (blü′bel′), *n.* any of various plants with flowers shaped like bells.

blue·ber·ry (blü′ber′i; -bər·i), *n.*, *pl.* -ries. *Am.* 1. a small, sweet, edible berry that has smaller seeds than the huckleberry. 2. the shrub that it grows on.

blue·bird (blü′bėrd′), *n. Am.* a small songbird of North America whose prevailing color is blue.

blue blood, aristocratic descent. —**blue′-blood′ed**, *adj.*

blue·bon·net (blü′bon′it), *n.* plant with blue flowers resembling sweet peas.

blue book, *Am.* book that lists socially prominent people.

blue·bot·tle (blü′bot′əl), *n.* 1. a large blowfly that has a blue abdomen and a hairy body. 2. any similar fly. 3. cornflower.

blue chip, 1. a poker chip of high value. 2. *Colloq.* anything of high value or quality. —**blue′-chip′**, *adj.*

blue·coat (blü′kōt′), *n.* 1. *Am.*, *Colloq.* policeman. 2. *Am.* (formerly) soldier in the army of the United States. —**blue′-coat′ed**, *adj.*

blue·fish (blü′fish′), *n.*, *pl.* -**fish·es** or (*esp. collectively*) -**fish**, a blue-and-silver salt-water edible fish of the Atlantic Coast.

blue·grass (blü′gras′; -gräs′), *n. Am.* any of various American grasses with bluish-green stems, esp. **Kentucky bluegrass.**

blue gum, eucalyptus.

blue·ing (blü′ing), *n.* bluing.

blue·ish (blü′ish), *adj.* bluish. —**blue′ish·ness**, *n.*

blue·jack·et (blü′jak′it), *n.* a sailor.

blue·jay (blü′jā′), *n. Am.* any of various North American jays, esp. a noisy, chattering bird with a crest and a blue back.

blue laws, *Am.* 1. severe laws for the regulation of religious and personal conduct in the colonies of Connecticut and New Haven. 2. any very strict and puritanical laws.

blue·nose, **Blue·nose** (blü′nōz′), *n. Am.* an excessively puritanical or inquisitive person.

blue·pen·cil (blü′pen′səl), *v.*, -**ciled**, -**cil·ing**; *esp. Brit.* -**cilled**, -**cil·ling.** change with a blue pencil; edit.

Bluejay (11 in. long)

blue·print (blü′print′), *n.* 1. photograph that shows white outlines on a blue background, used to make copies of building plans, maps, etc. 2. a detailed plan or outline of a project. —*v.* make a blueprint of.

blue ribbon, 1. first prize. 2. badge of a temperance society.

Blue Ridge, range of the Appalachian Moun-

tains, extending from E Pennsylvania to N Georgia.

blues (blüz), *n.pl. Am.* 1. depression of spirits; despondency. 2. a slow, melancholy jazz song.

blue-sky law (blü′ski′), *Am.*, *Colloq.* law to prevent the sale of worthless stocks and bonds.

blue·stock·ing (blü′stok′ing), *n.* *Colloq.* woman who displays great interest in intellectual or literary subjects. [because blue stockings were affected by a group of such women in London c 1750] —**blue′stock′ing·ism**, *n.*

blue streak, *Am.*, *Colloq.* with lightning speed: *she talks a blue streak.*

blu·et (blü′it), *n. Am.* small plant of the U.S., with pale bluish flowers.

bluff¹ (bluf), *n. Am.* a high, steep bank or cliff. —*adj.* 1. *Am.* rising with a straight, broad front. 2. abrupt, frank, and hearty in manner. [prob. < Du. *blaf* broad flat face] —**bluff′ly**, *adv.* —**bluff′ness**, *n.* —Syn. *adj.* 1. steep. 2. plain-spoken, unceremonious, blunt.

bluff² (bluf), *n.* 1. *Am.* show of pretended confidence, used to deceive or mislead. 2. threat that cannot be carried out. 3. person who bluffs. —*v. Am.* a. deceive by a show of pretended confidence. b. frighten with a threat that cannot be carried out. —**bluff′er**, *n. Am.*

blu·ing (blü′ing), *n. Am.* a blue liquid or powder put in water when rinsing clothes to keep white clothes from turning yellow. Also, **blueing.**

blu·ish (blü′ish), *adj.* somewhat blue. Also, **blueish.** —**blu′ish·ness**, *n.*

blun·der (blun′dər), *v.* 1. make a stupid mistake. 2. do clumsily or wrongly; bungle. 3. move clumsily or blindly; stumble. 4. blurt out. —*n.* a stupid mistake. —**blun′der·er**, *n.* —**blun′der·ing·ly**, *adv.* —Syn. *n.* bungle, oversight, slip.

blun·der·buss (blun′dər·bus), *n.* 1. a short gun with a wide muzzle, now no longer used. 2. person who blunders. [alter. of Du. *donderbus* thunder box]

blunt (blunt), *adj.* 1. without a sharp edge or point; dull. 2. plain-spoken; outspoken; frank. 3. slow in perceiving or understanding. —*v.* make or become blunt. —**blunt′ly**, *adv.* —**blunt′ness**, *n.* —Syn. *adj.* 2. candid, brusque. 3. obtuse.

blur (blėr), *v.*, **blurred**, **blur·ring**. —*v.* 1. make confused in form or outline: *mist blurred the hills.* 2. dim: *tears blurred my eyes.* 3. become dim or indistinct. 4. smear; blot; stain. —*n.* 1. a blurred condition; dimness. 2. thing seen dimly or indistinctly. 3. smear; blot; stain. [? var. of *blear*] —**blur′ry**, *adj.*

blurb (blėrb), *n. Am.* advertisement or announcement full of extremely high praise. [coined by Gelett Burgess, American humorist]

blurt (blėrt), *v.* say suddenly or without thinking: *blurt out a secret.* [imit.]

blush (blush), *n.* 1. a reddening of the skin caused by shame, confusion, or excitement. 2. rosy color. —*v.* 1. become red because of shame, confusion, or excitement. 2. be ashamed. 3. be or become rosy. [ME *blusche*(*n*). Cf. OE *blyscan* be red.] —**blush′er**, *n.* —**blush′ful**, *adj.* —**blush′ing·ly**, *adv.*

blus·ter (blus′tər), *v.* 1. storm or blow noisily and violently. 2. talk noisily and violently. 3. do or say noisily and violently. 4. make or get by blustering. —*n.* 1. stormy noise and violence. 2. noisy and violent talk. —**blus′ter·er**, *n.* —**blus′ter·ing·ly**, *adv.* —**blus′ter·y**, **blus′ter·ous**, *adj.*

blvd., boulevard.

bo·a (bō′ə), *n.*, *pl.* **bo·as**. 1. any of various large tropical American snakes that kill their prey by squeezing with their coils. 2. a long scarf made of fur or feathers, worn around a woman's neck. [< L (def. 1)]

boa constrictor, a large tropical American boa.

boar (bôr; bōr), *n.* 1. a male pig or hog. 2. the wild boar. [OE *bār*]

board (bôrd; bōrd), *n.* 1. a broad, thin piece of wood ready for use in building, etc. 2. a flat piece of wood used for some special purpose: *an ironing board.* 3. pasteboard. 4. table to serve food on; table. 5. food served on a table. 6. meals provided for pay. 7. *Am.* blackboard. 8. *Am.* stock exchange. 9. group of persons managing something; council. 10. side of a ship. 11. border; edge. 12. on board, *Am.* on a ship, train, etc. 13. the boards, the stage of a theater. —*v.* 1. cover with boards. 2. provide with regular meals, or room and meals, for pay. 3. get meals, or room and meals, for pay. 4. get on a ship. 5. *Am.* go on or into a vehicle. 6. come alongside of or against (a ship). —*adj.* made of boards. [OE *bord*]

board·er (bôr′dər; bōr′-), *n.* 1. person who pays for meals, or for room and meals, at another's house. 2. one of the men assigned to board an enemy ship.

board foot, *Am.* unit of measure equal to a board 1 foot square and 1 inch thick; 144 cu. in.

board·ing (bôr′ding; bōr′-), *n.* 1. boards. 2. structure made of boards.

boarding house, house where meals, or room and meals, are provided for pay.

boarding school, school where pupils are lodged and fed.

board measure, system for measuring logs and lumber. The unit is the board foot.

board·walk (bôrd′wôk′; bōrd′-), *n.* *U.S.* promenade made of boards, esp. along a beach.

boast (bōst), *v.* 1. praise oneself; brag. 2. brag about. 3. be proud. 4. have and be proud of: *our town boasts many fine parks.* —*n.* 1. praising oneself; bragging. 2. thing to be proud of. —boast′er, *n.* —boast′ing·ly, *adv.*

boast·ful (bōst′fəl), *adj.* 1. boasting. 2. fond of boasting. —boast′ful·ly, *adv.* —boast′ful·ness, *n.*

boat (bōt), *n.* 1. a small, open vessel for traveling on water. 2. ship. 3. a boat-shaped dish for gravy, sauce, etc. —*v.* 1. go in a boat. 2. put or carry in a boat. [OE *bāt*]

boat·house (bōt′hous′), *n.* house or shed for sheltering a boat or boats.

boat·ing (bōt′ing), *n.* rowing; sailing.

boat·load (bōt′lōd′), *n.* 1. as much or as many as a boat can hold or carry. 2. load that a boat is carrying.

boat·man (bōt′mən), *n., pl.* **-men.** man who manages or works on a boat.

boat·swain (bō′sən; *less often* bōt′swān′), *n.* a ship's officer in charge of anchors, ropes, rigging, etc. Also, bo's'n, bosun.

Bo·az (bō′az), *n. Bible.* the husband of Ruth.

bob[1] (bob), *n., v.,* **bobbed, bob·bing.** —*n.* a short, quick motion up and down, or to and fro. —*v.* move with short, quick motions.

bob[2] (bob), *n., v.,* **bobbed, bob·bing.** —*n.* 1. a short haircut. 2. a horse's docked tail. 3. weight on the end of a pendulum or plumb line. 4. a bait consisting of a knot of worms, rags, or the like. 5. float for a fishing line. —*v.* 1. cut (hair) short. 2. fish with a bob.

bob[3] (bob), *n., v.,* **bobbed, bob·bing.** —*n.* a light rap; tap. —*v.* rap lightly; tap.

bob[4] (bob), *n., pl.* **bob.** *Brit. Slang.* shilling.

bob·bin (bob′ən), *n.* reel or spool on which thread, yarn, etc., is wound. [< F *bobine*]

bob·ble (bob′əl), *n., v.,* **-bled, -bling.** —*n.* blunder; foolish error. —*v.* make a bobble.

bob·by (bob′i), *n., pl.* **-bies.** *Brit. Slang.* policeman. [for Sir *Robert* Peel, who improved the London police system]

bobby pin, metal hairpin whose prongs are close together.

bob·by·socks (bob′i·soks′), *n.pl. Colloq.* ankle-length socks, worn by young girls.

bob·by·sox·er (bob′i·sok′sər), *n. Colloq.* an adolescent girl, who follows every new fad.

bob·cat (bob′kat′), *n. Am.* wildcat; lynx.

bob·o·link (bob′ə·lingk), *n. Am.* an American songbird that lives in fields. [imit.]

bob·sled (bob′sled′), **bob·sleigh** (bob′slā′), *n., v.,* **-sled·ded, -sled·ding; -sleighed, -sleigh·ing.** *Am.* —*n.* 1. two short sleds fastened together by a plank. 2. either of the short sleds. 3. sled for coasting made of two pairs of runners connected

by a long board. —*v.* ride on a bobsled.

bob·stay (bob′stā′), *n.* rope or chain to hold a bowsprit down. See picture under bowsprit.

bob·tail (bob′tāl′), *n.* 1. a short tail; tail cut short. 2. animal having a bobtail. —*adj.* having a bobtail. —*v.* cut short the tail of.

bob·white (bob′hwīt′), *n. Am.* 1. an American quail that has a grayish body with brown and white markings. 2. its call.

Boc·cac·ci·o (bō·kä′chi·ō), *n.* Giovanni, 1313–1375, Italian poet and storywriter.

bock beer (bok), or **bock,** *n. Am.* a strong, dark beer, usually brewed in the spring. [< G *Bockbier* for *Einbocker Bier* beer of Einbeck, city in Germany]

bode[1] (bōd), *v.,* **bod·ed, bod·ing.** be a sign of. [OE *bodian* < *boda* messenger] —bode′ment, *n.* —Syn. portend, foreshadow.

bode[2] (bōd), *v.* pt. of bide.

bod·ice (bod′is), *n.* 1. the close-fitting waist of a dress. 2. a wide girdle worn over a dress and laced up the front. [var. of pl. of *body*, part of a dress]

Bodice (def. 2)

bod·i·ly (bod′ə·li), *adj.* of or in the body. —*adv.* 1. in person. 2. all together; as one group. —Syn. *adj.* corporeal, physical.

bod·kin (bod′kin), *n.* 1. a large, blunt needle. 2. a long hairpin. 3. a pointed tool for making holes.

Bodkin

bod·y (bod′i), *n., pl.* **bod·ies,** *v.,* **bod·ied, bod·y·ing.** —*n.* 1. the whole material part of a man, animal, or plant. 2. the main part or trunk of an animal, tree, etc. 3. the main part; larger part; bulk of anything. 4. a group of persons considered together; collection of persons or things: *a body of troops.* 5. *Colloq.* person. 6. dead person; corpse. 7. portion of matter; mass: *a lake is a body of water.* 8. matter; substance; density; substantial quality: *wine with an excellent body.* —*v.* 1. provide with a body; give substance to; embody. 2. **body forth, a.** give a real form to. **b.** be a sign of. [OE *bodig*] —bod′ied, *adj.*

bod·y·guard (bod′i·gärd′), *n.* 1. man or men who guard a person. 2. retinue; escort.

body politic, people forming a political group with an organized government.

Boe·o·tia (bē·ō′shə), *n.* district in ancient Greece, north of Athens. —Boe·o′tian, *n.*

Boer (bôr; bōr; bür), *n.* person of Dutch descent living in South Africa. [< Du., farmer]

bog (bog; bôg), *n., v.,* **bogged, bog·ging.** —*n.* soft, wet, spongy ground; marsh; swamp. —*v.* 1. sink or get stuck in a bog. 2. bog down, get stuck as if in mud. [< Irish or Scotch Gaelic *bogach* < *bog* soft] —bog′gish, *adj.* —bog′gy, *adj.* —bog′gi·ness, *n.*

bo·gey, bo·gie (bō′gi), *n., pl.* **-geys; -gies.** 1. bogy. 2. *Golf.* a. par. b. one stroke over par on a hole. 3. an unidentified aircraft. [from Colonel *Bogey,* imaginary partner]

bog·gle (bog′əl), *v.,* **-gled, -gling,** *n.* —*v.* 1. blunder; bungle; botch. 2. hold back; hesitate. 3. jump with fright; shy. 4. quibble; equivocate. —*n.* a boggling. —bog′gler, *n.*

Bo·go·tá (bō′gə·tä′), *n.* capital of Colombia.

bo·gus (bō′gəs), *adj. Am.* counterfeit; sham.

bo·gy (bō′gi), *n., pl.* **-gies.** 1. goblin; specter; evil spirit. 2. person or thing that is feared; bugaboo. Also, bogey, bogie. [< obs. *bog,* var. of *bug* bugbear]

Bo·he·mi·a (bō·hē′mi·ə), *n.* a former country in C Europe, now part of Czechoslovakia.

Bo·he·mi·an (bō·hē′mi·ən; -hēm′yən), *adj.* 1. of Bohemia or Bohemians. 2. free and easy; unconventional. —*n.* 1. native or inhabitant of Bohemia. 2. Often, **bohemian.** artist, writer, etc., who lives in a free and easy, unconventional way. 3. gypsy. —Bo·he′mi·an·ism, *n.*

boil[1] (boil), *v.* 1. bubble up and give off vapor. 2. cause to boil. 3. cook by boiling. 4. of a container, have its contents boil. 5. clean or sterilize by boiling. 6. make by boiling: *a boiled dinner.* 7. be very excited or angry. 8. move violently. 9. **boil down, a.** reduce by boiling. **b.** reduce by getting rid of unimportant parts. 10. **boil over, a.**

come to the boiling point and overflow. b. show excitement or anger. —n. 1. a boiling. 2. boiling condition. [< OF < L *bullire* form bubbles] —Syn. v. 1. seethe, simmer.

boil² (boil), n. a painful, red swelling on the skin, formed by pus around a hard core. [OE *býl(e)*]

boil·er (boil′ər), n. 1. container for heating liquids. 2. tank for making steam to heat buildings or drive engines. 3. tank for holding hot water.

boiling point, temperature at which a liquid boils.

Boi·se (boi′zē; -sē), n. capital of Idaho, in the SW part.

bois·ter·ous (bois′tər·əs; -trəs), adj. 1. abounding in rough and noisily cheerful activity. 2. violent; rough. —**bois′ter·ous·ly,** adv. —**bois′ter·ous·ness,** n.

bo·la (bō′lə), **bo·las** (bō′ləs), n. weapon consisting of stone or metal balls tied to cords. [< Sp. and Pg., ball, < L *bulla* bubble]

bold (bōld), adj. 1. without fear; daring. 2. showing or requiring courage: a bold act. 3. too free in manners; impudent. 4. striking; vigorous; clear: stand in bold outline against the sky. 5. steep; abrupt. 6. make bold, take the liberty; dare. [OE *bald*] —**bold′ly,** adv. —**bold′ness,** n. —Syn. 1. fearless, courageous, brave. 3. forward, impertinent, saucy. —Ant. 1. timid.

bold·face (bōld′fās′), n. heavy type that stands out clearly. **This line is in boldface.**

bole (bōl), n. Bot. trunk of a tree. [< Scand. *bolr*]

bo·le·ro (bə·lãr′ō), n., pl. -ros. 1. a lively Spanish dance in ¾ time. 2. music for it. 3. a short, loose jacket. [< Sp.]

Bol·i·var (bol′ə·vər), n. Simon, 1783-1830, Venezuelan general and statesman.

Bo·liv·i·a (bə·liv′i·ə), n. country in W South America. —**Bo·liv′i·an,** adj., n.

Bolero (def. 3)

boll (bōl), n. Bot. a rounded seed pod or capsule, as of cotton or flax. [var. of *bowl*]

boll weevil, Am. a long-billed beetle whose larva damages young cotton bolls.

boll·worm (bōl′wẽrm′), n. Am. larva that eats cotton bolls and the ears of corn.

bo·lo (bō′lō), n., pl. -los. a long, heavy knife, used in the Philippine Islands. [< Sp. < Philippine dial.]

Bo·lo·gna (bə·lōn′yə), n. city in N Italy.

bo·lo·gna sausage (bə·lō′ni; -nə), or **bologna,** n. a large sausage made of beef, veal, and pork.

bo·lo·ney (bə·lō′ni), n. 1. bologna sausage. 2. Am., Slang. baloney.

Bol·she·vik, bol·she·vik (bōl′shə·vik; bol′-), n., pl. -viks, -vi·ki (-vē′ki), adj. —n. 1. member of a radical political party in Russia that seized power in November, 1917. The Bolsheviks formed the Communist party in 1918. 2. an extreme radical. —adj. 1. of the Bolsheviks or Bolshevism. 2. extremely radical. [< Russ., < *bolshe* greater; with ref. to the majority of the party]

Bol·she·vism, bol·she·vism (bōl′shə·viz·əm; bol′-), n. 1. doctrines and methods of the Bolsheviks. 2. extreme radicalism.

Bol·she·vist, bol·she·vist (bōl′shə·vist; bol′-), n., adj. Bolshevik. —**Bol′she·vis′tic,** bol′she·vis′tic, adj. —**Bol′she·vis′ti·cal·ly,** bol′she·vis′ti·cal·ly, adv.

Bol·she·vize, bol·she·vize (bōl′shə·vīz; bol′-), v., -vized, -viz·ing. make Bolshevik. —**Bol′she·vi·za′tion, bol′she·vi·za′tion,** n.

bol·ster (bōl′stər), v. 1. support with a bolster; support. 2. keep from falling; prop: bolster up one's spirits. —n. 1. a long pillow for a bed. 2. pad; cushion. [OE] —**bol′ster·er,** n.

bolt¹ (bōlt), n. 1. rod with a head on one end and a screw thread for a nut on the other.

2. a sliding fastener for a door. 3. part of a lock moved by a key. 4. short arrow with a thick head. 5. discharge of lightning. 6. sudden start; a running away. 7. roll of cloth or wallpaper. 8. Am. refusal to support a candidate, platform, etc., of one's political party. —v. 1. fasten with a bolt. 2. dash away; run away. 3. Am. break away from one's political party or its candidates. 4. swallow (one's food) without chewing. —adv. bolt upright, stiff and straight. [OE, arrow] —**bolt′er,** n. —**bolt′less,** adj. —**bolt′like′,** adj.

bolt² (bōlt), v. 1. sift through a cloth or sieve. 2. examine carefully; separate. [< OF *bulter*]

bomb (bom), n. 1. container filled with an explosive charge or a chemical substance, usually dropped by aircraft, and exploded by contact or a time mechanism. 2. a sudden, unexpected happening. —v. attack with bombs; drop bombs on. [< F < Ital. < L < Gk. *bombos* boom¹]

bom·bard (bom·bärd′), v. 1. attack with heavy fire of shot and shell from big guns. 2. keep attacking vigorously. [< F *bombarder* < *bombarde* cannon. See BOMB.] —**bom·bard′er,** n. —**bom·bard′ment,** n.

bom·bar·dier (bom′bər·dir′), n. Mil. member of an airplane crew who operates the bombsight and the bomb-release mechanism.

bom·bast (bom′bast), n. fine-sounding language that is unsuitable. [< F < LL *bombax* cotton, var. of L *bombyx* silk < Gk.] —**bom·bas′tic,** bom·bas′ti·cal, adj. —**bom·bas′ti·cal·ly,** adv.

Bom·bay (bom·bā′), n. seaport in W India.

bomb bay, space in an airplane for bombs and from which they are dropped.

bomb·er (bom′ər), n. Mil. 1. a combat airplane used for dropping bombs on the enemy. 2. person who throws or drops bombs.

bomb·proof (bom′prüf′), adj. strong enough to be safe from bombs and shells.

bomb·shell (bom′shel′), n. 1. bomb. 2. a sudden unexpected happening; disturbing surprise.

bomb·sight (bom′sīt′), n. Mil. instrument used by a bombardier to aim bombs.

bo·na fide (bō′nə fīd; fī′dē), in good faith; genuine; without make-believe or fraud. [< L]

bo·nan·za (bə·nan′zə), n. Am. 1. accidental discovery of a rich mass of ore in a mine. 2. the mass itself. 3. Colloq. any rich source of profit. [< Sp., fair weather, prosperity, < L *bonus* good]

Bo·na·parte (bō′nə·pärt), n. Napoleon, 1769-1821, French general and emperor of France, 1804-1815. Also, Napoleon¹.

Bo·na·part·ism (bō′nə·pär′tiz·əm), n. rule of or adherence to the Bonapartes. —**Bo′na·part′ist,** n.

bon·bon (bon′bon′), n. piece of candy, often one with a fancy shape. [< F, good-good]

bond¹ (bond), n. 1. anything that ties, binds, or unites. 2. certificate issued by a government or company promising to pay back with interest the money borrowed. 3. written agreement by which a person says he will pay a certain sum of money if he, or another specified, does not perform certain duties properly. 4. person who acts as surety for another. 5. any agreement or binding engagement. 6. condition of goods placed in a warehouse until taxes are paid. 7. bonds, a. chains; shackles. b. imprisonment. —v. 1. Am. issue bonds on; mortgage. 2. convert into bonds: bond a debt. 3. Am. provide surety against financial loss by the act or default of: bond an employee. 4. put (goods) under bond. 5. bind or join firmly together. [var. of band²] —**bond′er,** n. —Syn. 1. link, tie. 4. security. 5. compact.

bond² (bond), adj. in slavery; captive; not free. [< Scand. *bōndi* peasant, orig., dweller]

bond·age (bon′dij), n. 1. lack of freedom; slavery. 2. condition of being under some power or influence. —Syn. 1. serfdom.

bond·ed (bon′did), adj. 1. secured by bonds. 2. put in a warehouse until taxes are paid.

bond·hold·er (bond′hōl′dər), n. person who owns bonds issued by a government or company. —**bond′hold′ing,** n., adj.

bond·man (bond′mən), *n., pl.* **-men. 1.** slave.
2. serf in the Middle Ages.

bonds·man (bondz′mən), *n., pl.* **-men.** person
who becomes responsible for another by bond.

bond·wom·an (bond′wŭm′ən), *n., pl.* **-wom·
en.** a woman slave.

bone (bōn), *n., v.*, **boned, bon·ing.** —*n.* **1.** *Anat.,
Zool.* **a.** one of the pieces of the skeleton of an
animal with a backbone. **b.** the hard substance of
which bones are made. **2.** any of various similar
substances, as ivory. **3. bones**, *a. U.S. Slang.* dice.
b. wooden clappers used in keeping time to
music. **c.** *Am.* end man in a minstrel show. **d.**
skeleton. —*v.* **1.** take bones out of. **2.** *Am., Colloq.*
study strenuously or diligently. [OE *bān*]
—**bone′less**, *adj.* —**bone′like′**, *adj.*

bone-dry (bōn′drī′), *adj.* **1.** dry as a bone;
completely dry. **2.** *Am.* with no intoxicating
drink whatever.

bone·head (bōn′hed′), *n. Am., Slang.* **1.** a very
stupid person. **2.** boner. —**bone′head′ed**, *adj.*

bon·er (bōn′ər), *n. Am., Slang.* a foolish mistake; stupid error; blunder.

bon·fire (bon′fīr′), *n.* fire built outdoors. [for
bone fire]

bon·ho·mie (bon′ə-mē′), *n.* good nature;
pleasant ways. [< F, < *bonhomme* good fellow]

ʔ·ni·to (bə-nē′tō), *n., pl.* **-tos, -toes.** type of
salt-water mackerel with very red edible flesh.
[< Sp., pretty, < L *bonus* good]

bon jour (bôn zhŭr′), *French.* good day.

bon mot (bôn mō′), *pl.* **bons mots** (bôn mōz′;
Fr. mō′). *French.* clever saying; witty remark.

Bonn (bon; *Ger.* bôn), *n.* capital of West Germany, on the Rhine River.

bon·net (bon′it), *n.* **1.** a head covering usually
tied under the chin with strings or ribbons, worn
by women and children. **2.** cap worn by men and
boys in Scotland. **3.** headdress of feathers worn
by American Indians. **4.** a covering that protects
a machine or chimney. —*v.* put a bonnet on.
[< OF, orig., fabric for hats]

bon·ny, bon·nie (bon′i), *adj.*, **-ni·er, -ni·est.
1.** rosy and pretty; handsome. **2.** fine; excellent.
3. healthy-looking. [ME *bonie*, appar. < OF *bon,
bonne* good < L *bonus*] —**bon′ni·ly**, *adv.* —**bon′·
ni·ness**, *n.*

bon soir (bôn swär′), *French.* good evening.

bo·nus (bō′nəs), *n.* something extra; thing
given in addition to what is due. [< L, good]

bon vo·yage (bôn vwä·yäzh′), *French.* good-
by; good luck; pleasant trip.

bon·y (bōn′i), *adj.*, **bon·i·er, bon·i·est. 1.** of or
like bone. **2.** full of bones. **3.** having big bones
that stick out. **4.** thin. —**bon′i·ness**, *n.*

boo (bü), *n., pl.* **boos**, *interj., v.*, **booed, boo·ing.**
—*n., interj.* sound made to show dislike or con-
tempt or to frighten. —*v.* **1.** make such a sound.
2. cry "boo" at.

boob (büb), *n. Am.* a stupid person; fool; dunce.
[see BOOBY]

boo·by (bü′bi), *n., pl.* **-bies.
1.** a stupid person; fool;
dunce. **2.** kind of large
sea bird. **3.** person who does
the worst in a game or contest. [prob. < Sp. *bobo* (defs.
1, 3) < L *balbus* stammer-
ing] —**boo′by·ish**, *adj.*

Booby (30 in. long)

booby trap, 1. trick arranged to annoy some un-
suspecting person. **2.** *Mil.* bomb arranged to
explode when an object is moved by an unwary
person.

boo·dle (bü′dəl), *n., v.*, **-dled, -dling.** *Am.,
Slang.* —*n.* **1.** lot; pack; crowd. **2.** graft; money
from bribes. —*v.* bribe. [< Du. *boedel* goods]
—**boo′dler**, *n.*

boog·ie-woog·ie (bŭg′i·wŭg′i), *n. Music.* a
form of instrumental blues characterized by bass
obbligato contrasting with melodic variations.

boo·hoo (bü′hü′), *n., pl.* **-hoos**, *v.*, **-hooed,
-hoo·ing.** —*n.* loud crying. —*v.* cry loudly.

book (bŭk), *n.* **1.** a written or printed work of
considerable length, esp. on sheets of paper
bound together. **2.** blank sheets bound together.

3. division of a literary work: *the books of the
Bible.* **4.** *Music.* words of an opera, operetta, etc.;
libretto. **5.** record of bets. **6.** something fastened
together like a book: *a book of tickets.* **7.** trick or
a number of tricks forming a set in a card game.
8. bring to book, a. demand an explanation
from. **b.** rebuke. **9. the Book**, the Bible. —*v.* **1.**
enter in a book or list. **2.** engage (a place, passage, etc.): *they booked two staterooms on the
steamship.* **3.** engage; make engagements for.
[OE *bōc*] —**book′er**, *n.* —**book′less**, *adj.* ▶ **Book**
refers especially to the contents, volume to the
physical appearance. A book may be in two or
more *volumes.*

book agent, *Am.* a book salesman, esp. one
who canvasses houses.

book·bind·er·y (bŭk′bīn′dər·i), *n., pl.* **-er·ies.**
Am. establishment for binding books.

book·case (bŭk′kās′), *n.* piece of furniture
with shelves for holding books.

book club, 1. group of persons who buy books
to be circulated within the group. **2.** a business
organization that supplies certain books regularly to subscribers.

book end, something placed at the end of a row
of books to hold them upright.

book·ie (bŭk′i), *n. Colloq.* bookmaker (def. 2).

book·ish (bŭk′ish), *adj.* **1.** fond of reading or
studying. **2.** knowing books better than real life.
3. of books. **4.** pedantic; formal. —**book′ish·ly**,
adv. —**book′ish·ness**, *n.*

book·keep·er (bŭk′kēp′ər), *n.* person who
keeps a record of business accounts.

book·keep·ing (bŭk′kēp′ing), *n.* work or art
of keeping a record of business accounts.

book learning or **knowledge**, knowledge
learned from books, not from real life. —**book-
learn·ed** (bŭk′lér′nid), *adj.*

book·let (bŭk′lit), *n.* a little book; thin book.

book·lore (bŭk′lôr′; -lōr′), *n.* book learning.

book·mak·er (bŭk′māk′ər), *n.* **1.** maker of
books. **2.** person who makes a business of betting
other peoples' money on horse races. —**book′·
mak′ing**, *n.*

book·mark (bŭk′märk′), *n.* something put between the pages of a book to mark the place.

book·plate (bŭk′plāt′), *n.* a label with the
owner's name or emblem on it, to paste in his
books.

book·rack (bŭk′rak′), *n.* **1.** rack for supporting an open book. **2.** rack for holding a number
of books.

book review, article written about a book,
discussing its merits, faults, etc.

book·sell·er (bŭk′sel′ər), *n.* person whose
business is selling books. —**book′sell′ing**, *n.*

book·stall (bŭk′stôl′), *n.* place where books
(usually secondhand) are sold.

book·stand (bŭk′stand′), *n.* **1.** bookrack. **2.**
Am. bookstall.

book·store (bŭk′stôr′; -stōr′), **book·shop**
(-shop′), *n. Am.* store where books are sold.

book·worm (bŭk′wérm′), *n.* **1.** insect larva
that gnaws the bindings or leaves of books. **2.**
person very fond of reading and studying.

boom[1] (büm), *n.* **1.** a deep hollow sound like the
roar of cannon or of big waves. **2.** *Am.* sudden
activity and increase in business, prices, or
values of property; rapid growth. **3.** *Am.* a vigorous pushing or urging. —*v.* **1.** *Am.* rush with
force or vigor. **2.** make a deep hollow sound: *the
big guns boomed.* **3.** utter with such a sound. **4.**
Am. increase suddenly in activity; grow rapidly.
5. *Am.* push or urge vigorously. —*adj. Am.* produced by a boom. [imit.]

boom[2] (büm), *n.* **1.** *Naut.* a long pole or beam,
used to extend the bottom of a sail or as the lifting pole of a derrick. **2.** *Am.* chain, cable, or line
of timbers that keeps logs from floating away.
[< Du., tree, pole]

boom·er·ang (büm′ər·ang), *n.* **1.** a curved
piece of wood, used as a weapon by Australian
natives, which can be so thrown that it returns
to the thrower. **2.** anything that recoils or reacts
to harm the doer or user. [< dial. of New South
Wales]

boom town, *Am.* town that has grown up suddenly.

boon[1] (bün), *n.* **1.** a blessing; great benefit. **2.** *Archaic.* something asked or granted as a favor. [< Scand. *bōn* petition] —**Syn. 1.** favor, gift.

boon[2] (bün), *adj.* **1.** jolly; gay; merry. **2.** *Poetic* kindly. [< OF *bon* good < L *bonus*]

boon·docks (bün′doks), *n.pl. Am., Dial.* a desolate place or area, as a swamp, scrub forest, etc.

boon·dog·gle (bün′dog′əl), *v.,* –**gled,** –**gling.** *Am., Slang.* do useless work. —**boon′dog′gler,** *n. Am.* —**boon′dog′gling,** *n. Am.*

Boone (bün), *n.* Daniel, 1735–1820, American pioneer in Kentucky.

boor (bùr), *n.* **1.** a rude, bad-mannered, or clumsy person. **2.** a farm laborer; peasant. [< LG *bur* or Du. *boer* farmer] —**boor′ish,** *adj.* —**boor′ish·ly,** *adv.* —**boor′ish·ness,** *n.*

boost (büst), *Am.* —*n.* a push or shove that helps a person in rising or advancing. —*v.* **1.** to lift or push from below or behind. **2.** speak favorably of. **3.** raise; increase: *boost prices.* **4.** cheer; hearten. [blend of *boom* and *hoist*]

boost·er (büs′tər), *n. Am., Slang.* one who or that which gives support to a person, cause, etc. —**boost′er·ism,** *n. Am.*

boot[1] (büt), *n.* **1.** a leather or rubber covering for the foot and leg. **2.** shoe that reaches above the ankle. **3.** a protecting apron or cover for the driver of an open carriage. **4.** kick. **5.** *Slang.* discharge; dismissal. **6.** *Slang.* a recruit in the U.S. Navy or Marines. —*v.* **1.** put boots on. **2.** kick. **3.** dismiss; discharge. [< OF *bote* < Gmc.]

boot[2] (büt), *n.* **to boot,** in addition; besides. [OE *bōt* advantage]

boot·black (büt′blak′), *n. Am.* person whose work is shining shoes and boots.

boot·ee (bü·tē′; *esp. for 1* büt′ē), *n. Am.* **1.** a baby's soft shoe. **2.** a woman's short boot.

booth (büth), *n., pl.* **booths** (büthz). **1.** place where goods are sold or shown at a fair, market, etc. **2.** a small, closed place for a telephone, motion-picture projector, etc. **3.** small, closed place for voting at elections. [< Scand. (ODan.) *bōth*]

Booth (büth), *n.,* William, 1829–1912, English clergyman who founded the Salvation Army.

boot·jack (büt′jak′), *n.* device to help in pulling off boots.

boot·leg (büt′leg′), *n., v.,* –**legged,** –**leg·ging,** *adj.* —*n. Am., Slang.* alcoholic liquor made or distributed illegally. —*v.* **1.** *Am.* sell or deal in illegally or secretly. **2.** *U.S.* transport goods secretly for illicit disposal. —*adj. Am.* made, transported, or sold illegally. [modern use from practice of smuggling liquor in boot legs] —**boot′leg′ger,** *n. Am.* —**boot′leg′ging,** *n.*

boot·less (büt′lis), *adj.* useless. —**boot′less·ly,** *adv.* —**boot′less·ness,** *n.*

boot·lick (büt′lik′), *v. Am., Slang.* curry favor with (a person); be a toady. —**boot′lick′er,** *n. Am.* —**boot′lick′ing,** *n. Am.*

boo·ty (bü′ti), *n., pl.* –**ties. 1.** things taken from the enemy in war. **2.** plunder. **3.** any valuable thing or things obtained; prize. [akin to BOOT[2]]

booze (büz), *n., v.,* **boozed, booz·ing.** *Colloq.* —*n.* **1.** intoxicating liquor. **2.** spree. —*v.* drink heavily. [prob. < MDu. *būzen* drink to excess]

booz·y (büz′i), *adj.,* **booz·i·er, booz·i·est.** drunk.

bop (bop), *n. Am., Slang.* bebop.

bo·rac·ic (bə·ras′ik), *adj. Chem.* boric.

bor·age (bėr′ij; bôr′–; bor′–), *n.* plant, native to S Europe with hairy leaves and blue or purplish flowers. [< AF *burage* < LL *burra* hair; with ref. to foliage]

bo·rate (*n.* bô′rāt, –rit, bō′–; *v.* bô′rāt, bō′–), *n., v.,* –**rat·ed,** –**rat·ing.** —*n. Chem.* salt or ester of boric acid. —*v.* treat with boric acid or borax.

bo·rax (bô′raks; –raks; bō′–), *n.* a white crystalline powder, Na₂B₄O₇·10H₂O, used as an antiseptic, in washing clothes, etc. [< OF < Med.L < Ar. < Pers. *bōrah*]

Bor·deaux (bôr·dō′), *n.* **1.** seaport in SW France. **2.** red or white wine made near Bordeaux.

bor·der (bôr′dər), *n.* **1.** a side, edge, or boundary of anything, or the part near it. **2.** frontier. **3.** strip on the edge of anything for strength or ornament. —*v.* **1.** form a border to; bound. **2.** put a border on; edge. **3. border on** or **upon,** a. be next to; adjoin. b. be close to; resemble. [< OF, < *bord* side < Gmc.] —**bor′dered,** *adj.* —**bor′der·less,** *adj.* —**Syn.** *n.* **1.** margin, rim, brink.

bor·der·land (bôr′dər·land′), *n.* **1.** land forming, or next to, a border. **2.** uncertain district or space.

bor·der·line (bôr′dər·līn′), *adj.* **1.** on a border or boundary. **2.** uncertain; in between.

bore[1] (bôr; bōr), *v.,* **bored, bor·ing,** *n.* —*v.* **1.** make a hole with a tool that keeps turning, or as a worm does in fruit. **2.** make (a hole, passage, entrance, etc.) by pushing through or digging out. **3.** bore a hole in; hollow out evenly. —*n.* **1.** hole made by a revolving tool. **2.** a hollow space inside a pipe, tube, or gun barrel. **3.** distance across the inside of a hole or tube. [OE *borian*] —**bor′er,** *n.* —**Syn.** *v.* **1.** pierce, perforate, drill.

bore[2] (bôr; bōr), *v.,* **bored, bor·ing,** *n.* —*v.* make weary by being dull or tiresome. —*n.* a dull, tiresome person or thing. —**Syn.** *v.* tire, fatigue.

bore[3] (bôr; bōr), *v.* pt. of **bear**[1].

bore[4] (bôr; bōr), *n.* a sudden, high tidal wave that rushes up a narrowing channel with great force. [< Scand. *bāra* wave]

bo·re·al (bô′ri·əl; bō′–), *adj.* **1.** northern. **2.** of Boreas.

Bo·re·as (bô′ri·əs; bō′–), *n.* the north wind. [< Gk.]

bore·dom (bôr′dəm; bōr′–), *n.* weariness caused by dull, tiresome people or events.

bore·some (bôr′səm; bōr′–), *adj.* dull; tiresome.

bo·ric (bô′rik; bō′–), *adj. Chem.* of or containing boron. Also, **boracic.**

boric acid, *Chem.* a white, crystalline substance, H₃BO₃, used as a mild antiseptic, to preserve food, etc.

born (bôrn), *adj.* **1.** brought into life; brought forth. **2.** by birth; by nature: *a born athlete.* —*v.* pp. of **bear**[1]. [pp. of *bear*[1]]

borne (bôrn; bōrn), *v.* pp. of **bear**[1]. ➤ **1. Borne** is the past participle of *bear* in most of its senses: *the ship was borne along by the breeze.* **2.** In the sense "give birth to," the past participle of *bear* is **borne** except in the very common passive when not followed by *by:* *She had borne five children. He was born in 1900.*

Bor·ne·o (bôr′ni·ō; bōr′–), *n.* island in the East Indies. Part of it is Malaysian, part is Indonesian.

bo·ron (bô′ron; bō′–), *n. Chem.* a nonmetallic element, B, found in borax. [blend of *borax* and *carbon*]

bor·ough (bėr′ō), *n.* **1.** *Am.* (in some States) an incorporated town smaller than a city. **2.** *Am.* one of the five divisions of New York City. **3.** town in England with a municipal corporation and a charter that guarantees the right of local self-government. **4.** town in England that sends representatives to Parliament. [OE *burg*]

bor·row (bôr′ō; bor′ō), *v.* **1.** get (something) from another person with the understanding that it must be returned. **2.** take and use as one's own; take. **3.** *Math.* in subtraction, to take from one denomination to add to the next lower. [OE *borgian* < *borg* pledge, surety] —**bor′row·er,** *n.*

borsch (bôrsch), **borscht** (bôrsht), *n.* a Russian soup containing beets.

bos·cage (bos′kij), *n.* a small woods; thicket. [< OF, < *bosc* < Frankish *busk* woods]

bosh (bosh), *n., interj. Colloq.* nonsense.

bosk·y (bos′ki), *adj.* **1.** wooded. **2.** shady. —**bosk′i·ness,** *n.*

bo's'n (bō′sən), *n. Naut.* boatswain.

Bos·ni·a (boz′ni·ə), *n.* district in W Yugoslavia. —**Bos′ni·an,** *adj., n.*

bos·om (bùz′əm; bü′zəm), *n.* **1.** the upper, front part of the human body; breast. **2.** part of a garment covering this. **3.** *Am.* a false shirt front; dickey. **4.** enclosure formed by the breast and arms. **5.** center or inmost part. **6.** heart, thought, affections, desires, etc. —*adj.* close; trusted: *a bosom friend.* —*v.* 1. embrace. 2. cherish. 3. keep in one's bosom; conceal. [OE *bōsm*]

Bos·po·rus (bos′pə·rəs), *n.* strait connecting the Black Sea and the Sea of Marmara.

boss[1] (bôs; bos), *Am.*, *Colloq.* —*n.* 1. person who hires workers or watches over or directs them; foreman; manager. 2. person who controls a political organization. —*v.* 1. be the boss of; direct; control. 2. be too overbearing. —*adj.* master; chief. [< Du. *baas*]

boss[2] (bôs; bos), *n.* 1. *Bot.*, *Zool.* a roundish protuberance on an animal or plant. 2. a raised ornament on a flat surface. 3. *Archit.* an ornamental projection or block. 4. any knoblike mass. —*v.* 1. decorate with bosses. 2. furnish with bosses. [< OF *boce*]

Boss (def. 2)

bos·sa no·va (bäs′ə nō′və), a dance music of Brazil that combines samba rhythm with jazz.

boss·ism (bôs′iz·əm; bos′-), *n. Am.* control by bosses, esp. political bosses.

boss·y[1] (bôs′i; bos′i), *adj.*, boss·i·er, boss·i·est. *Am.*, *Colloq.* fond of telling others what to do and how to do it; domineering.

boss·y[2] (bos′i; bôs′i), *n.*, *pl.* -sies. *Am.*, *Colloq.* calf or cow. [cf. L *bos* ox]

Bos·ton (bôs′tən; bos′-), *n.* seaport and capital of Massachusetts, in the E part. —**Bos·to·ni·an** (bôs·tō′ni·ən; bos-), *adj.*, *n.*

Boston terrier or **bull,** small, dark-brown dog with white markings and smooth, short hair.

bo·sun (bō′sən), *n.* boatswain.

Bos·well (boz′wel; -wəl), *n.* 1. James, 1740-1795, Scottish writer of a famous biography of Samuel Johnson. 2. any author of a biography of a close friend. —**Bos·well·i·an** (boz·wel′i·ən), *adj.*

bot (bot), *n.* larva of a botfly. It is a parasite of horses, cattle, and sheep. Also, bott.

bot., botany.

bo·tan·i·cal (bə·tan′ə·kəl), **bo·tan·ic** (-tan′ik), *adj.* 1. having to do with plants. 2. having to do with botany. [< Med.L < Gk. < *botane* plant] —**bo·tan′i·cal·ly,** *adv.*

bot·a·nize (bot′ə·nīz), *v.*, -nized, -niz·ing. 1. study plants where they grow. 2. collect plants for study. 3. explore the plant life of.

bot·a·ny (bot′ə·ni), *n.*, *pl.* -nies. 1. science of plants; study of plants and plant life. 2. textbook or manual of this science. 3. botanical facts. [< *botanic*] —**bot·a·nist** (bot′ə·nist), *n.*

Botany Bay, bay on the SE coast of Australia, near Sydney, site of a former penal colony.

botch (boch), *v.* 1. spoil by poor work; bungle. 2. patch or mend clumsily. —*n.* a clumsy patch. —**botch′er,** *n.* —**botch′er·y,** *n.* —**botch′y,** *adj.*

bot·fly (bot′flī′), *n.*, *pl.* -flies. fly whose larvae are parasites of horses, cattle, etc.

both (bōth), *adj.* the two together: *both houses are white.* —*pron.* the two together: *both belong to him.* —*adv.* together; alike; equally: *he can .sing and dance both.* —*conj.* together; alike; equally: *he is both strong and healthy.* [appar. < Scand. *bāther*] ➤ **Both** is a favorite colloquial way of emphasizing two-ness: *the twins were both there.* Strictly speaking, these *both*'s are redundant but they give emphasis.

both·er (both′ər), *n.* 1. worry; fuss; trouble. 2. person or thing that causes worry, fuss, or trouble. —*v.* 1. worry; fuss; trouble. 2. trouble oneself, as in an effort to do something. [appar. < Irish *bodhar* deaf] —**both′er·er,** *n.* —**Syn.** *v.* 1. annoy, vex.

both·er·a·tion (both′ər·ā′shən), *n.*, *interj.* *Colloq.* bother.

both·er·some (both′ər·səm), *adj.* causing worry or fuss; troublesome. —**Syn.** annoying.

Bo·tswa·na (bō·tswä′nä), *n.* country in S

Africa; formerly, the British protectorate of Bechuanaland.

bott (bot), *n.* bot.

Bot·ti·cel·li (bot′ə·chel′ē), *n.* Sandro, 1444?-1510, Italian painter.

bot·tle (bot′əl), *n.*, *v.*, -tled, -tling. —*n.* 1. container for holding liquids that has a narrow neck that can be closed with a stopper, and is usually without handles. 2. contents of a bottle. 3. amount that a bottle can hold. 4. **the bottle,** intoxicating liquor. —*v.* 1. put into bottles. 2. hold in; keep back; control. 3. **bottle up,** hold in; control. [< OF < VL *butticula,* dim. of LL *buttis* butt³] —**bot′tler,** *n.*

bot·tle·neck (bot′əl·nek′), *n.* 1. a narrow thoroughfare. 2. *Am.* **a.** a person or thing that hinders progress. **b.** situation in which progress is hindered.

bot·tom (bot′əm), *n.* 1. the lowest part; lowest rank. 2. part on which anything rests. 3. ground under water. 4. the low land along a river. 5. buttocks. 6. seat: *this chair needs a new bottom.* 7. power of endurance. 8. basis; foundation; origin. 9. keel or hull of a ship; ship. 10. at bottom, fundamentally. 11. be at the bottom of, be the cause of. —*v.* 1. put a seat on. 2. understand fully. 3. set upon a foundation; base; rest. —*adj.* 1. lowest; last. 2. underlying; fundamental. [OE *botm*] —**bot′tom·less,** *adj.*

bot·u·lism (boch′ə·liz·əm), *n.* poisoning caused by a toxin formed in food that has been infected by certain bacteria. [< L *botulus* sausage; orig. attributed esp. to sausages]

bou·clé (bü·klā′), *n.* a knitted cloth having a surface with tiny loops and curls. [< F, buckled]

bou·doir (bü′dwär; -dwôr; bü·dwär′; -dwôr′), *n.* a lady's private sitting room or dressing room. [< F, < *bouder* sulk]

bough (bou), *n.* 1. one of the main branches of a tree. 2. branch cut from a tree. [OE *bōg* bough, shoulder] —**bough′less,** *adj.*

bought (bôt), *v.* pt. and pp. of **buy.**

bought·en (bôt′ən), *adj. Dial.* bought.

bouil·lon (bùl′yon; -yən), *n.* a clear, thin soup. [< F, < *bouillir* boil < L *bullire*]

boul·der (bōl′dər), *n.* a large rock, rounded or worn by the action of water or weather. Also, **bowlder.** [for *boulderstone* < Scand. (Sw.) *bullersten* < *bullra* roar + *sten* stone]

Boulder Dam, Hoover Dam.

boul·e·vard (bùl′ə·värd; bü′lə-), *n.* a broad street. [< F < Gmc. See BULWARK.]

bounce (bouns), *v.*, bounced, bounc·ing, *n.* —*v.* 1. bound like a ball. 2. cause to bounce. 3. spring suddenly. 4. burst noisily, angrily, etc. 5. *Colloq.* throw out. 6. *Am.*, *Slang.* discharge from work or employment. —*n.* 1. a bound; a spring; a bouncing. 2. capacity to bound; resilience. 3. *Colloq.* liveliness. 4. a boasting; a bragging. 5. *Am.*, *Slang.* discharge from work or employment. [cf. Du. *bonzen* thump] —**bounc′-er,** *n.* —**Syn.** *v.* 3. leap.

bounc·ing (boun′sing), *adj.* 1. that bounces. 2. big; strong. 3. vigorous; healthy.

bound[1] (bound), *v.* pt. and pp. of **bind.** —*adj.* 1. put in covers: *a bound book.* 2. under obligation; obliged. 3. certain; sure. 4. determined; resolved. 5. **bound up in** or **with,** a. closely connected with. b. very devoted to. [pp. of *bind*]

bound[2] (bound), *v.* 1. leap; spring lightly along; jump: *bounding deer.* 2. leap or spring upward or onward. 3. spring back; bounce: *the ball bounded from the wall.* —*n.* 1. leap or spring upward or onward. 2. spring back; bounce. [< F *bondir* leap; orig., resound, ? < L *bombus.* See BOMB.]

bound[3] (bound), *n.* 1. Usually, **bounds.** boundary; limiting line; limit. 2. **bounds,** a. land on or near a boundary. b. area included within boundaries. —*v.* 1. limit as by bounds. 2. form the boundary or limit of. 3. name the boundaries of: *bound the State of Maine.* 4. have its boundary (on). [< OF < LL *butina*] —**bound′less,** *adj.* —**bound′less·ly,** *adv.* —**bound′less·ness,** *n.* —**Syn.** *n.* 1. border, confine.

bound[4] (bound), *adj.* ready or intending to go: *I am bound for home.* [< Scand. *būinn,* pp. of *būa* get ready]

bound·a·ry (boun'də·ri; -dri), *n.*, *pl.* –ries. a limiting line; limit; border.

bound·en (boun'dən), *adj.* 1. required; obligatory. 2. under obligation; obliged. [pp. of *bind*] —Syn. 2. indebted.

bound·er (boun'dər), *n. Esp. Brit. Colloq.* a rude, vulgar person; upstart; cad.

boun·te·ous (boun'ti·əs), *adj.* 1. generous; giving freely. 2. plentiful; abundant. —boun'·te·ous·ly, *adv.* —boun'te·ous·ness, *n.* —Syn. 1. liberal. 2. copious, ample.

boun·ti·ful (boun'tə·fəl), *adj.* bounteous. —boun'ti·ful·ly, *adv.* —boun'ti·ful·ness, *n.*

boun·ty (boun'ti), *n.*, *pl.* –ties. 1. generosity. 2. a generous gift. 3. a reward. [< OF < L *bonitas* < *bonus* good] —Syn. 1. munificence, liberality.

bou·quet (bō·kā', bü– *for 1;* bü·kā' *for 2*), *n.* 1. bunch of flowers. 2. characteristic fragrance; aroma. [< F, little wood, dim. of OF *bosc* wood. See BUSH¹.]

Bour·bon (bûr'bən, *occas.* bėr'– *for 1 and 2;* bėr'bən *for 3*), *n.* 1. member of a former royal family of France, Spain, Naples, and Sicily. 2. *Am.* an extreme conservative. 3. Also, *bourbon.* kind of whiskey. —Bour'bon·ism, *n.* —Bour'bon·ist, *n.*

bour·geois (bur·zhwä'; bûr'zhwä), *n.*, *pl.* –geois, *adj.* —n. 1. person of the middle class. 2. any property owner. —adj. 1. of the middle class. 2. like the middle class; ordinary. [< F < LL *burgensis* < *burgus* fort < Gmc.]

bour·geoi·sie (bůr'zhwä·zē'), *n.* 1. people of the middle class. 2. the opposite of the proletariat.

bourn¹, bourne¹ (bôrn; bōrn), *n.* brook. [OE *burna*]

bourn², bourne² (bôrn; bōrn; bůrn), *n.* 1. *Archaic.* boundary; limit. 2. goal. [< F *borne.* Akin to BOUND³.]

bourse (bůrs), *n.* stock exchange in Paris and other European cities. [< F, orig., purse, < LL *bursa* < Gk. *byrsa* hide]

bout (bout), *n.* 1. a trial of strength; contest. 2. a time of activity of any kind: *a long bout of house cleaning.* 3. a spell or fit of anything: *a bout of sickness.* [var. of *bought* a bending; turn; akin to BOW¹]

bou·ton·niere, bou·ton·nière (bü'tə·nyâr'), *n.* flower or flowers worn in a buttonhole. [< F, buttonhole. See BUTTON.]

bo·vine (bō'vīn; –vin), *adj.* 1. of an ox or cow; like an ox or cow. 2. slow; stupid. 3. without emotion; stolid. —n. ox, cow, etc. [< LL *bovinus* < L *bos* ox, cow]

bow¹ (bou), *v.* 1. bend the head or body in greeting, respect, worship, or submission. 2. show by bowing: *bow one's thanks.* 3. bend; stoop. 4. submit; yield. —n. act of bowing. [OE *būgan*] —bow'er, *n.* —Syn. *n.* nod, curtsy.

bow² (bō), *n.* 1. weapon for shooting arrows, consisting of a strip of elastic wood bent by a string. 2. curve; bend. 3. a bowknot: *a bow of ribbon.* 4. a slender rod with horsehairs stretched on it, for playing a violin, etc. 5. something curved; curved part, as a rainbow. —v. 1. curve; bend. 2. play (a violin, etc.) with a bow. [OE *boga*] —bow'less, *adj.* —bow'like', *adj.*

bow³ (bou), *n.* the forward part of a ship, boat, or airship. [prob. of LG or Scand. orig.; akin to BOUGH]

bowd·ler·ize (boud'lər·īz), *v.*, –ized, –iz·ing. expurgate. [for Dr. T. *Bowdler,* who published an expurgated Shakespeare in 1818] —bowd'ler·ism, *n.* —bowd'ler·i·za'tion, *n.*

bow·el (bou'əl), *n.* 1. *Anat.* a. an intestine. b. Usually, **bowels.** tube in the body into which food passes from the stomach; intestines. 2. **bowels,** a. inner part: *the bowels of the earth.* b. *Archaic.* pity; tender feelings. [< OF < L *botellus,* dim. of *botulus* sausage]

bow·er¹ (bou'ər), *n.* 1. shelter of leafy branches. 2. summerhouse or arbor. 3. *Archaic.* bedroom. [OE *būr* dwelling] —bow'er·like', *adj.*

bow·er² (bou'ər), *n.* the high card in certain games. [< G *bauer* jack (in cards); peasant]

bow·er·y (bou'ər·i), *adj.* leafy; shady.

bow·fin (bō'fin'), *n. Am.* a North American fresh-water ganoid fish.

bow·ie knife (bō'i; bü'i), *Am.* a long, single-edged hunting knife carried in a sheath. [named for Col. J. Bowie, U.S. pioneer]

bow·knot (bō'not'), *n.* a looped slipknot, such as is made in tying shoelaces, usually with loops and two ends.

Single bowknot

bowl¹ (bōl), *n.* 1. a hollow, rounded dish. 2. amount that a bowl can hold. 3. a hollow, rounded part: *the bowl of a spoon or a pipe.* 4. a large drinking cup. 5. drink. 6. drinking. 7. formation or structure shaped like a bowl, as an amphitheater. [OE *bolla*] —bowl'like', *adj.*

bowl² (bōl), *n.* 1. a wooden ball used in games. 2. a turn in the game of bowls. —v. 1. play the game of bowls; roll a ball in the game of bowls. 2. throw (the ball) to the batsman in the game of cricket. 3. roll or move along rapidly and smoothly. 4. **bowl down,** knock down. 5. **bowl over,** a. knock over. b. *Colloq.* make helpless and confused. [< F < L *bulla* ball, bubble] —bowl'er, *n.*

bowl·der (bōl'dər), *n.* boulder.

bow·leg (bō'leg'), *n.* an outward curve of the legs. —bow·leg·ged (bō'leg'id; –legd'), *adj.*

bow·line (bō'lən; –līn), *n.* 1. Also, **bowline knot.** knot used in making a loop. 2. *Naut.* rope to hold a sail steady when sailing into the wind.

Bowline knot

bowl·ing (bōl'ing), *n.* 1. game of bowls. 2. *U.S. and Canada.* tenpins. 3. playing the game of bowls.

bowling alley, *U.S.* a long, narrow, enclosed floor for bowling.

bowls (bōlz), *n.* 1. game played by rolling with a lopsided or weighted wooden ball toward a stationary ball. 2. ninepins or tenpins. [pl. of *bowl²*]

bow·man (bō'mən), *n.*, *pl.* –men. archer.

bow·shot (bō'shot'), *n.* distance that a bow will shoot an arrow.

bow·sprit (bou'sprit; bō'–), *n. Naut.* pole or spar projecting forward from the bow of a ship. Ropes from it help to steady sails and masts. [prob. < LG or Du. See BOW³, SPRIT.]

BOWSPRIT
BOBSTAY

bow·string (bō'string'), *n.* 1. a strong cord stretched from the ends of a bow. 2. cord like this.

box¹ (boks), *n.* 1. container made of wood, metal, paper, etc., to pack or put things in. 2. amount that a box can hold. 3. a small boxlike space with chairs at a theater, etc. 4. an enclosed space for a jury, witnesses, etc. 5. a small shelter. 6. anything shaped or used like a box. 7. a hollow part that encloses or protects some piece of machinery. 8. the driver's seat on a coach, carriage, etc. 9. *Am., Baseball.* place where the batter, or sometimes the pitcher or catcher, stands. 10. compartment for a horse in a stable or car. 11. space in a newspaper, magazine, etc. set off by enclosing lines. 12. a Christmas present; a present. 13. an awkward situation. 14. *Am.* cavity in a maple or pine for collecting sap or turpentine. 15. *Am.* receptacle in a post office for a subscriber's mail. —v. 1. pack in a box; put into a box. 2. provide with a box. 3. *Am.* make a box in a tree in which to collect sap or turpentine. 4. **box the compass,** a. name the points of the compass in order. b. go all the way around and end up where one started. 5. **box up,** shut in; keep from getting out. [specialization of meaning of *box³*] —box'like', *adj.* —Syn. *n.* 1. receptacle, chest, carton.

box² (boks), *n.* blow with the open hand or the fist, esp. on the ear. —v. 1. strike such a blow. 2. fight with the fists.

box³ (boks), *n.* 1. shrub or small, bushy tree that stays green all winter, much used for hedges, etc. 2. its hard, durable wood. [< L < Gk. *pyxos*]

box·car (boks'kär'), *n. Am.* a railroad freight car enclosed on all sides.

box elder, *Am.* a maple tree of North America, often grown for shade or ornament.

box·er (bok'sər), *n.* 1. man who fights with his fists in padded gloves according to special rules. 2. a dog with a smooth brown coat, related to the bulldog and terrier.

box·ing (bok'sing), *n.* act of fighting with the fists.

boxing gloves, padded gloves worn when boxing.

box office, 1. place where tickets are sold in a theater, hall, etc. 2. money taken in at the box office.

box score, *Am.* tabular record of the plays of a baseball game arranged by the players.

box seat, a seat in a box of a theater, etc.

box·wood (boks'wŭd'), *n. Am.* box³.

boy (boi), *n.* 1. a male child from birth to about eighteen. 2. a male servant, esp. a native servant in India, China, etc. 3. a familiar term for a man. —Syn. 1. lad, youngster, youth.

boy·cott (boi'kot), *v.* 1. combine against and have nothing to do with (a person, business, nation, etc.) as a means of intimidation or co-ercion. 2. refuse to buy or use (a product, etc.). —*n.* a boycotting. [for Captain *Boycott*, first man so treated] —boy'cott·er, *n.*

boy friend, *Am., Colloq.* a girl's sweetheart or steady male companion.

boy·hood (boi'hŭd), *n.* 1. time or condition of being a boy. 2. boys as a group.

boy·ish (boi'ish), *adj.* 1. of a boy. 2. like a boy. 3. like a boy's. 4. fit for a boy. —boy'ish·ly, *adv.* —boy'ish·ness, *n.*

boy scout, member of the Boy Scouts.

Boy Scouts, organization for boys that devel-ops manly qualities and usefulness to others.

boy·sen·ber·ry (boi'zən·ber'i), *n., pl.* -ries. *Am.* a purple berry like a blackberry in size and shape, and like a raspberry in flavor.

Br, *Chem.* bromine.

Br., Britain; British.

bra (brä), *n. Colloq.* brassière.

Bra·bant (brə·bant'; brä'bənt), *n.* region in the S Netherlands and N Belgium.

brace (brās), *n., v.,* braced, brac·ing. —*n.* 1. thing that holds parts together or in place, as a clamp, an iron frame to hold the ankle straight, etc. 2. anything that gives steadiness or rigidity. 3. pair; couple: *a brace of ducks.* 4. handle for a tool or drill used for boring. 5. either of these signs { } used to enclose words, figures, staves in music, etc. 6. braces, *Brit.* suspenders. 7. Often, braces. a metal wire used to straighten crooked teeth. [< v., but partly < OF *brace* the two arms] —*v.* 1. give strength or firmness; support. 2. hold or fix firmly in place. 3. brace up, *Am., Colloq.* summon one's strength or courage. 4. stimulate: *the cold air braced him.* 5. furnish with braces. 6. make tight or taut. [< OF *bracier* embrace < *brace* the two arms < L *bracchia*, pl. < Gk. *brachion*]

brace·let (brās'lit), *n.* band or chain worn for ornament around the wrist or arm. [< OF, dim. of *bracel* < L *bracchium* arm < Gk. *brachion*] —brace'let·ed, *adj.*

brac·er (brās'ər), *n.* 1. one that braces. 2. *U.S. Colloq.* stimulating drink.

brach·i·o·pod (brak'i·ə·pod'; brā'ki-), *n. Zool.* sea animal with upper and lower shells and a pair of armlike tentacles, one on each side of its mouth. [< NL < Gk. *brachion* arm + *pous* foot]

brach·y·ce·phal·ic (brak'i·sə·fal'ik), **brach·y·ceph·a·lous** (brak'i·sef'ə·ləs), *adj.* having a short, broad head. [< Gk. *brachys* short + *kephale* head]

brac·ing (brās'ing), *adj.* giving strength and energy; refreshing. —*n.* brace or braces. —brac'ing·ly, *adv.*

brack·en (brak'ən), *n. Brit.* 1. a large fern. 2. growth of these ferns. [ME *braken*, appar. < Scand.]

brack·et (brak'it), *n.* 1. a flat piece of stone, wood, or metal projecting from a wall as a sup-port for a shelf, a statue, etc. 2. support in the shape of a right triangle. 3. either of these signs [ ], used to enclose words or figures. 4. group thought of together or mentioned together: *in the low-income bracket.* —*v.* 1. support with brackets. 2. enclose within brackets. 3. think of together; mention together; group. [< F < Sp. *bragueta*, dim. of *braga* < L *bracae* breeches < Celtic] ▶ Brackets [ ] are rarely used in general writing and are not in the standard typewriter keyboard, but in much academic and professional writing they have specific and convenient uses. Brackets are primarily editorial marks, used to show where some explanation or comment has been added to the text, especially to quoted mat-ter. In quoting material *sic* in brackets is some-times used to indicate that an error was in the original: *"New Haven, Conneticut* [sic].*"* Or a correction may be inserted in brackets: *"When he was thirty-eight* [Actually he was forty-three] *he published his first novel."* In many of the usage notes in this dictionary, brackets are used in examples of faulty writing to enclose words that might better be left out, or to suggest an improved expression: *Throughout* [the course of] *the year I read such books as "Oliver Twist" and "Boots and Saddles." The continuously mov-ing belt makes a noise similar to* [like] *a cement mixer.*

brack·ish (brak'ish), *adj.* 1. somewhat salty. 2. distasteful; unpleasant. —brack'ish·ness, *n.*

bract (brakt), *n. Bot.* a small leaf at the base of a flower or flower stalk. [< L *bractea* thin metal plate] —brac·te·al (brak'ti·əl), *adj.* —bract'less, *adj.*

brad (brad), *n.* a small, thin nail with a small head. [var. of *brod* < Scand. *broddr* spike]

brad·awl (brad'ôl'), *n.* awl with a cutting edge for making holes for brads, etc.

brae (brā), *n. Scot.* slope; hillside.

brag (brag), *n., v.,* bragged, brag·ging. —*n.* 1. boast. 2. boasting. —*v.* boast. [cf. Scand. *bragga sig* recover heart] —brag'ger, *n.*

brag·ga·do·ci·o (brag'ə·dō'shi·ō), *n., pl.* -ci-os. 1. boasting; bragging. 2. boaster; braggart. [coined by Spenser as name of character in his *Faerie Queene*]

brag·gart (brag'ərt), *n.* boaster. —*adj.* boast-ful. [< F *bragard* < *braguer* brag]

Brah·ma (brä'mə *for 1*; brä'mə, brä'mə *for 2*), *n.* 1. in Hindu theology: a. the god of creation. b. impersonal and absolute divinity. 2. *Am.* species of cattle, originally imported from India.

Brah·man (brä'mən), *n., pl.* -mans. member of the priestly caste, the highest caste or class in India. Also, **Brahmin.** —**Brah·man·ic** (brä·man'ik), **Brah·man·i·cal**, *adj.* —**Brah'man·ism**, *n.* —**Brah'man·ist**, *n.*

Brah·min (brä'mən), *n., pl.* -min. 1. Brah-man. 2. a cultured, highly intellectual person, often snobbish. —**Brah·min·ic** (brä·min'ik), **Brah·min'i·cal**, *adj.* —**Brah'min·ism**, *n.*

Brahms (brämz), *n. Johannes*, 1833–1897, German composer of music.

braid (brād), *n.* 1. band formed by weaving to-gether three or more strands of hair, ribbon, straw, etc. 2. a narrow band of fabric used to trim or bind clothing. —*v.* 1. form by weaving together three or more strands of hair, etc. 2. trim or bind with braid. [OE *bregdan*] —braid'er, *n.* —Syn. *v.* 1. plait, entwine.

Braille, braille (brāl), *n.* system of writing and printing for blind people. The letters in Braille are made of raised points and are read by touching them. [for Louis *Braille*, French teacher of the blind]

brain (brān), *n.* 1. mass of nerve tissue en-closed in the skull or head of vertebrate animals. The brain is used in feeling and thinking. 2. large electronic computer. 3. *Slang.* very in-telligent person. 4. Usually, brains. mind; intelligence. —*v.* dash out the brains of. [OE *brægen*]

brain·less (brān'lis), *adj.* 1. without a brain.

2. stupid; foolish. —**brain′less·ly**, adv. —**brain′-less·ness**, n.

brain·pan (brān′pan′), n. cranium.

brain·sick (brān′sik′), adj. crazy; insane. —brain′sick′ly, adv. —brain′sick′ness, n.

brain storm, Colloq. a sudden inspired idea.

brain trust, Am. a group of experts acting as advisers to an administrator, a political leader, or an executive. —brain truster, Am.

brain·wash·ing (brān′wosh′ing; -wôsh′-), n. the process of purging a person's mind of his political, economic, and social ideas, so that he becomes willing to accept other views.

brain·y (brān′i), adj., brain·i·er, brain·i·est. Colloq. intelligent; clever. —brain′i·ness, n.

braise (brāz), v., braised, brais·ing. brown (meat) quickly and then cook it long and slowly in a covered pan with very little water. [< F braiser < braise hot charcoal < Gmc.]

brake[1] (brāk), n., v., braked, brak·ing. —n. 1. anything used to check by pressing or scraping or by rubbing against. 2. tool or machine for breaking up flax or hemp into fibers. —v. 1. slow up or stop by using a brake. 2. use a brake on. 3. break up (flax or hemp) into fibers. [< MLG or ODu. braeke; akin to BREAK]

brake[2] (brāk), n. a thick growth of bushes; thicket. [cf. MLG brake]

brake[3] (brāk), n. large, coarse fern. [prob. var. of bracken]

brake[4] (brāk), v. Archaic. pt. of break.

brake·man (brāk′mən), n., pl. -men. Am. man who works brakes and helps the conductor of a railroad train.

bram·ble (bram′bəl), n. 1. a prickly shrub of the rose family, such as the blackberry or raspberry. 2. any rough, prickly shrub. [OE brēmel < brōm BROOM] —bram′bly, adj.

bran (bran), n. the broken covering of wheat, rye, etc., separated from the flour. [< OF]

branch (branch; bränch), n. 1. part of a tree growing out from the trunk; any woody part of a tree above the ground except the trunk; bough; twig. 2. any division that resembles a branch of a tree: a branch of a river. 3. division; part: history is a branch of learning. 4. a local office: a branch of a bank. 5. a line of family descent. —v. 1. put out branches; spread in branches. 2. divide into branches. 3. branch out, a. put out branches. b. extend business, interests, activities, etc. [< OF branche < LL branca paw]

brand (brand), n. 1. piece of wood that is burning or partly burned. 2. mark made by burning the skin with a hot iron. Cattle and horses on big ranches are marked with brands to show who owns them. 3. Am., Western. herd of cattle with a distinctive brand. 4. an iron stamp for burning a mark. 5. a certain kind, grade, or make as indicated by a stamp, trademark, etc.: a brand of coffee. 6. trademark. 7. mark of disgrace. 8. Archaic and Poetic. sword. —v. 1. mark by burning the skin with a hot iron. 2. put a mark of disgrace on. [OE] —brand′er, n.

Bran·den·burg (bran′dən·bérg), n. 1. district in N Germany. 2. city in N Germany.

bran·died (bran′did), adj. prepared, mixed, or flavored with brandy.

bran·dish (bran′dish), v. wave or shake threateningly; flourish: brandish a sword. —n. threatening shake; flourish. [< OF brandir < brand sword < Gmc.] —brand′dish·er, n.

brand-new (brand′nü′; -nū′), **bran-new** (bran′nü′; -nū′), adj. very new; entirely new.

bran·dy (bran′di), n., pl. -dies, v., -died, -dy·ing. —n. 1. strong alcoholic liquor made from wine. 2. Am. similar alcoholic liquor made from fruit juice. —v. mix, flavor, or preserve with brandy. [< Du. brandewijn burnt (i.e., distilled) wine]

brant (brant), n., pl. brants or (esp. collectively) brant. a small, dark, wild goose.

brash (brash), adj. 1. hasty; rash. 2. impudent; saucy. —n. a rush or dash. —brash′y, adj.

bra·sier (brā′zhər), n. brazier.

Bra·sí·lia (brä-sē′lyä), n. capital of Brazil since 1960, in the C part.

brass (bras; bräs), n. 1. yellow metal that is an alloy of copper and zinc. 2. thing made of brass. 3. Also, **brasses**. the brass winds. 4. Colloq. shamelessness; impudence. 5. Am., Slang. high-ranking military officers (in allusion to their gold braid). —adj. made of brass. [OE bræs]

bras·sard (bras′ärd), n. 1. band worn above the elbow as a badge. 2. Also, bras·sart (bras′-ərt). armor for the upper part of the arm.[< F, < bras arm]

brass·ie, brass·y (bras′i; bräs′i), n., pl. brass·ies. golf club with a wooden head at the bottom of which is a metal plate.

bras·sière (brə-zir′), n. a bust support worn by women. [< F, bodice, < bras arm]

brass knuckles, Am. a protective metal device for the knuckles, used in fighting.

brass winds, metal musical instruments that are played by blowing, such as trumpets or trombones. —brass′-wind′, adj.

brass·y (bras′i; bräs′i), adj. brass·i·er, brass-i·est. 1. of or like brass. 2. loud and harsh. 3. Colloq. shameless; impudent. —brass′i·ness, n.

brat (brat), n. Contemptuous use. child. [cf. OE bratt cloak, covering]

bra·va·do (brə-vä′dō), n., pl. -does, -dos. a boastful defiance without much real desire to fight. [< Sp. bravada. See BRAVE.]

brave (brāv), adj., brav·er, brav·est, n., v., braved, brav·ing. —adj. 1. without fear; having courage. 2. making a fine appearance; showy. 3. Archaic. fine; excellent. —n. 1. a brave person. 2. Am. a North American Indian warrior. —v. 1. meet without fear. 2. dare; defy. [< F < Ital. bravo brave, bold < Sp., vicious (as applied to bulls), ? < L pravus] —brave′ly, adv. —brave′ness, n. —Syn. adj. 1. fearless, courageous, valiant. —Ant. adj. 1. cowardly, fearful.

brav·er·y (brāv′ər·i), n., pl. -er·ies. 1. fearlessness; courage. 2. showy dress; finery. —Syn. 1. intrepidity, boldness, daring, pluck.

bra·vo (brä′vō), interj., n., pl. -vos. —interj. well done! fine! —n. cry of "bravo!" [< Ital. See BRAVE.]

bra·vu·ra (brə-vyur′ə), n. 1. Music. piece requiring skill and spirit in the performer. 2. display of daring; dash; spirit. [< Ital., bravery. See BRAVE.]

braw (brô; brä), adj. Scot. 1. making a fine appearance; fine. 2. excellent; fine. [var. of brave]

brawl (brôl), n. noisy quarrel. —v. quarrel noisily. [ME brallen < brawl brawler]

brawn (brôn), n. muscle; firm, strong muscles; muscular strength. [< OF braon < Gmc.]

brawn·y (brôn′i), adj., brawn·i·er, brawn·i·est. strong; muscular. —brawn′i·ness, n. —Syn. sinewy, powerful.

bray (brā), n. 1. the loud, harsh sound made by a donkey. 2. noise like it. —v. 1. make a loud, harsh sound. 2. utter in a loud, harsh voice. [< F braire] —bray′er, n.

Braz., Brazil; Brazilian.

braze[1] (brāz), v., brazed, braz·ing. 1. cover or decorate with brass. 2. make like brass. [OE brasian < bræs brass]

braze[2] (brāz), v., brazed, braz·ing. solder with brass or other hard solder. [? < F braser < OF, burn]

bra·zen (brā′zən), adj. 1. made of brass. 2. like brass in color or strength. 3. loud and harsh. 4. shameless; impudent. —v. 1. make shameless or impudent. 2. brazen out or through, face boldly or shamelessly. [OE bræsen < bræs brass] —bra′zen·ly, adv. —bra′zen·ness, n.

bra·zier[1] (brā′zhər), n. a metal container to hold burning charcoal or coal, used for heating rooms. Also, brasier. [< F brasier < braise hot coals]

bra·zier[2] (brā′zhər), n. person who works with brass. Also, brasier. [< braze[1]]

Bra·zil (brə-zil′), n. largest country in South America. —Bra·zil·ian (brə-zil′yən), adj., n.

Brazil nut, a large, triangular nut of a tree growing in Brazil.

Braz·za·ville (braz'ə·vil), n. capital of the Congo, in the S part.

breach (brēch), n. 1. opening made by breaking down something solid; gap. 2. a broken or injured spot; break; rupture. 3. breaking (of a law, promise, duty, etc.); neglect. 4. breaking of friendly relations; quarrel. —v. break through; make an opening in. [< OF *breche* < Gmc.] —Syn. n. 1. fracture, crack, rent.

breach of promise, breaking of a promise to marry.

breach of the peace, public disturbance.

bread (bred), n. 1. food made of flour or meal mixed with milk or water and baked. 2. food; livelihood. 3. break bread, a. share a meal. b. take Communion. —v. cover with bread crumbs before cooking. [OE *brēad*] —**bread'less**, adj.

bread·board (bred'bôrd'; -bōrd'), n. 1. Am. board on which dough is kneaded, pastry is rolled, etc. 2. board on which bread is cut.

bread·fruit (bred'früt'), n. a large, round, starchy, tropical fruit of the Pacific Islands, much used, baked or roasted, for food.

bread line, Am. line of people waiting to get food given as charity or relief.

bread·stuff (bred'stuf'), n. Am. 1. grain, flour, or meal for making bread. 2. bread.

breadth (bredth; bretth), n. 1. how broad a thing is; distance across; width. 2. piece of a certain width: *a breadth of cloth*. 3. freedom from narrowness. 4. spaciousness; extent. [< OE *brǣdu* < *brād* broad] —Syn. 3. latitude, liberality, tolerance. 4. amplitude.

breadth·ways (bredth'wāz'; bretth'-), adv. in the direction of the breadth.

bread·win·ner (bred'win'ər), n. one who earns a living for those dependent on him.

break (brāk), v., **broke** or (Archaic) **brake, bro·ken** or (Archaic) **broke, break·ing,** n. —v. 1. make come to pieces by a blow or pull; divide into two or more parts. 2. come apart; crack; burst. 3. bruise; abrade. 4. interrupt; disturb: *break silence*. 5. Elect. open (a circuit). 6. destroy evenness, wholeness, etc.: *break a five-dollar bill*. 7. injure; damage; ruin; destroy. 8. cause to be declared invalid: *break a will*. 9. make or become bankrupt; ruin financially. 10. fail to keep; act against: *break a law*. 11. force one's way: *break into a house*. 12. come suddenly. 13. change suddenly. 14. Am. of stocks, bonds, etc., decline suddenly and sharply in price. 15. fail suddenly in health. 16. of a voice or wind instrument, change in register or tone. 17. Am., Baseball. of a pitch, swerve or curve at or near the plate. 18. lessen the force of. 19. become weak; give way. 20. of the heart, be overcome by grief. 21. stop; put an end to. 22. reduce in rank. 23. train to obey; tame: *break a colt*. 24. train away from a habit or practice: *break a child of lying*. 25. go beyond; exceed: *break a record*. 26. dig or plow (ground). 27. make known; reveal. 28. Am. make a rush towards; dash; run (for, to). 29. **break down,** a. have an accident; fail to work. b. collapse; become weak; lose one's health. c. begin to cry. 30. **break in,** a. prepare for work or use; train. b. enter by force. c. interrupt. 31. **break out,** a. start; begin. b. have pimples, rashes, etc., on the skin. 32. **break up,** Colloq. a. scatter. b. stop; put an end to. c. upset; disturb greatly. —n. 1. act or fact of breaking. 2. a broken place; gap, crack. 3. interruption. 4. act of forcing one's way out. 5. an abrupt or marked change. 6. Am. a sudden sharp decline in the prices of stocks, etc. 7. sharp change in direction of a pitched or bowled ball. 8. Am., Slang. an awkward remark; mistake in manners. 9. Am., Slang. chance; opportunity. 10. opening in an electric circuit. [OE *brecan*] —**break'a·ble,** adj. —Syn. v. 1. shatter, burst, smash. 2. split, splinter. 10. violate, disobey. —n. 1. rupture, shattering.

break·age (brāk'ij), n. 1. act of breaking; break. 2. damage or loss caused by breaking. 3. allowance made for such damage or loss.

break·down (brāk'doun'), n. 1. failure to work. 2. loss of health; collapse. 3. Am. a noisy, lively dance. 4. analysis, as of a total.

break·er (brāk'ər), n. 1. wave that breaks

into foam on the shore, rocks, etc. 2. machine for breaking things into smaller pieces.

break·fast (brek'fəst), n. the first meal of the day. —v. eat breakfast. [< *break* + *fast²*] —**break'fast·er,** n. —**break'fast·less,** adj.

break·neck (brāk'nek'), adj. likely to cause a broken neck; very dangerous.

break·through (brāk'thrü'), n. 1. Mil. an offensive operation that pierces a defensive system and reaches the unorganized area behind it. 2. a solving of the major problem or problems hindering some undertaking, esp. in science.

break·up (brāk'up'), n. 1. collapse; decay. 2. separation. 3. end.

break·wa·ter (brāk'wô'tər; -wot'ər), n. wall or barrier to break the force of waves.

bream (brēm), n., pl. **breams** or (esp. collectively) **bream.** 1. carp of inland European waters. 2. any of various related fishes. 3. Am. the common fresh-water sunfish. [< F *brême* < Gmc.]

breast (brest), n. 1. Anat. the upper, front part of the human body; chest. 2. Zool. the corresponding part in animals. 3. the upper, front part of a coat, dress, etc. 4. a front or forward part. 5. Anat., Zool. gland that gives milk. 6. heart; feelings. 7. **make a clean breast of,** confess completely. —v. U.S. struggle with; advance against; oppose; face. [OE *brēost*]

breast·bone (brest'bōn'), n. Anat., Zool. the thin, flat bone in the front of the chest to which the ribs are attached; sternum.

breast·pin (brest'pin'), n. Am. ornamental pin worn on the breast; brooch.

breast·plate (brest'plāt'), n. armor for the chest.

BREASTPLATE

breast·work (brest'wėrk'), n. a low, hastily built wall for defense.

breath (breth), n. 1. air drawn into and forced out of the lungs. 2. act of breathing. 3. moisture from breathing: *you can see your breath on a very cold day*. 4. ability to breathe easily: *out of breath*. 5. pause; respite. 6. a slight movement in the air; light breeze. 7. utterance; whisper. 8. life. 9. act of breathing out air without motion of the vocal cords, producing a hiss, puff, etc. 10. fragrance given off by flowers, etc. 11. **below** or **under one's breath,** in a whisper. [OE *brǣth* odor]

breathe (brēth), v., **breathed, breath·ing.** 1. draw (air) into the lungs and force it out. 2. stop for breath; rest; allow to rest and breathe. 3. put out of breath. 4. blow lightly. 5. say softly; whisper; utter. 6. be alive; live. 7. Phonet. utter with the breath and not with the voice. 8. draw into the lungs; inhale. 9. send out from the lungs; exhale. 10. send out; infuse: *breathe new life into tired soldiers*. 11. exhale an odor: *roses breathe fragrance*. 12. breathe again or freely, be relieved; feel easy. —**breath'a·ble,** adj.

breath·er (brēth'ər), n. 1. a short stop for breath; rest. 2. person or thing that breathes.

breath·ing (brēth'ing), n. 1. respiration. 2. a single breath. 3. time needed for a single breath. 4. remark; utterance. 5. a slight breeze. 6. aspiration; desire. 7. sound of the letter *h*.

breath·less (breth'lis), adj. 1. out of breath. 2. unable to breathe freely because of fear, interest, or excitement. 3. without breath; dead. 4. without a breeze. —**breath'less·ly,** adv. —**breath'less·ness,** n.

breath·tak·ing (breth'tāk'ing), adj. thrilling; exciting: *a breath-taking view*.

bred (bred), v. pt. and pp. of **breed.**

breech (brēch), n. 1. the lower part; back part. 2. part of a gun behind the barrel. 3. rump; buttocks. [OE *brēc*, gen. and dat. of *brōc*]

breech·cloth (brēch'klôth'; -kloth'), **breech·clout** (-klout'), n. Am. cloth worn as a loincloth, esp. by Indians.

breech·es (brich'iz), n.pl. 1. short trousers reaching from the waist to the knees. 2. Colloq. trousers. [OE *brēc*, pl. of *brōc* BREECH]

breeches buoy, *Naut.* pair of short canvas trousers fastened to a belt or life preserver. A breeches buoy slides along a rope on a pulley and is used to rescue people from sinking ships.

breech·ing (brich′ing; brēch′–), *n.* part of a harness that passes around a horse's rump.

breech·load·ing (brēch′lōd′ing), *adj.* of guns, loading from behind the barrel instead of at the mouth.

breed (brēd), *v.*, **bred, breed·ing,** *n.* —*v.* 1. produce (young). 2. raise (livestock, etc.). 3. produce; cause: *careless driving breeds accidents.* 4. be the native place or source of. 5. bring up; train. —*n.* 1. race; stock: *Jerseys and Guernseys are breeds of cattle.* 2. kind; sort. [OE *brēdan*] —breed′er, *n.* —Syn. *v.* 3. occasion. 5. educate.

breeder reactor or **pile,** *Nuclear Physics.* reactor which produces fissile material in excess of the amount required for the chain reaction.

breed·ing (brēd′ing), *n.* 1. producing offspring. 2. producing animals, esp. to get improved kinds. 3. bringing up; training; behavior; manners. 4. *Nuclear Physics.* the producing of a radioactive element at a rate exceeding the consumption of the original element used in the chain reaction.

breeze (brēz), *n.*, *v.*, **breezed, breez·ing.** —*n.* a light wind. —*v. Am., Colloq.* proceed easily or briskly. [< OSp. and Pg. *briza* northeast wind]

breez·y (brēz′i), *adj.*, **breez·i·er, breez·i·est.** 1. with light winds blowing. 2. brisk; lively; jolly. —breez′i·ly, *adv.* —breez′i·ness, *n.*

Brem·en (brem′ən; brā′mən), *n.* city in NW Germany.

Bren·ner Pass (bren′ər), a mountain pass in the Alps between Austria and Italy.

Bres·lau (brez′lou; bres′–), *n.* German name of Wroclaw. The name still has fairly wide usage.

Brest (brest), *n.* seaport in NW France.

Brest Li·tovsk (brest′ li·tôfsk′), city in W Russia.

breth·ren (breth′rən), *n.pl.* 1. brothers. 2. the fellow members of a church or society.

Bret·on (bret′ən), *n.* 1. native or inhabitant of Brittany. 2. language of Brittany. 3. Cape, the northeastern part of Nova Scotia. —*adj.* having to do with Brittany, its people, or their language.

breve (brēv), *n.* 1. curved mark (◡) put over a vowel or syllable to show that it is short. 2. *Music.* note equal to two whole notes. [< Ital. < L *brevis* short]

bre·vet (brə·vet′; *esp. Brit.* brev′it), *n.*, *v.*, **-vet·ted, -vet·ting; -vet·ed, -vet·ing.** —*n.* commission promoting an army officer to a higher rank without an increase in pay. —*v.* give rank by a brevet. [< F, dim. of *bref* letter. See BRIEF.]

bre·vi·ar·y (brē′vi·er′i; brev′i–), *n.*, *pl.* **-ar·ies.** book of prescribed prayers to be said daily by certain clergymen and religious of the Roman Catholic Church. [< L *breviarium* summary < *brevis* short]

brev·i·ty (brev′ə·ti), *n.*, *pl.* **-ties.** shortness; briefness. [< L, < *brevis* short] —Syn. conciseness, terseness. —Ant. verbosity.

brew (brü), *v.* 1. make (beer, ale, etc.) by soaking, boiling, and fermenting. 2. make (a drink) by soaking, boiling, or mixing. 3. bring about; plan; plot: *boys brewing mischief.* 4. begin to form; gather: *a storm is brewing.* —*n.* 1. drink brewed. 2. quantity brewed at one time. [OE *brēowan*] —brew′er, *n.*

brew·er·y (brü′ər·i; brür′i), *n.*, *pl.* **-er·ies.** place where beer, ale, etc., are brewed.

brew·ing (brü′ing), *n.* 1. preparing a brew. 2. amount brewed at one time.

Brezh·nev (brezh′nef), *n.* Leonid I., born 1906, secretary of the Russian Communist Party since October, 1964.

bri·ar (brī′ər), *n.* brier. —bri′ar·y, *adj.*

bri·ar·wood (brī′ər·wud′), *n.* brierwood.

bribe (brīb), *n.*, *v.*, **bribed, brib·ing.** —*n.* 1. anything given or offered to get a person to do something that he thinks is wrong to do. 2. reward for doing something that a person does not want to do. —*v.* 1. offer a bribe to. 2. influence by giving a bribe. 3. give bribes. [? < OF, bit of

bread given to a beggar] —brib′a·ble, *adj.* —brib′a·bil·i·ty, *n.* —brib′er, *n.*

brib·er·y (brīb′ər·i), *n.*, *pl.* **-er·ies.** 1. giving or offering a bribe. 2. taking a bribe.

bric-a-brac, bric-à-brac (brik′ə·brak′), *n.* interesting or curious knickknacks used as decorations. [< F]

brick (brik), *n.* 1. block of clay baked by sun or fire, used in building and paving. 2. bricks. 3. anything shaped like a brick. 4. *Slang.* a good fellow. —*adj.* made of bricks. —*v.* build or pave with bricks; wall in with bricks. [< F < MDu. *bricke*] —brick′like′, *adj.*

brick·bat (brik′bat′), *n.* 1. piece of broken brick. 2. *Colloq.* insult.

brick·lay·ing (brik′lā′ing), *n.* act or work of building with bricks. —brick′lay′er, *n.*

brick·work (brik′werk′), *n.* 1. thing made of bricks. 2. building with bricks; bricklaying.

brid·al (brīd′əl), *adj.* of a bride or a wedding. —*n.* wedding. [OE *brýdealo* bride ale] —brid′al·ly, *adv.* —Syn. *adj.* nuptial.

bridal wreath, a kind of spiraea.

bride (brīd), *n.* woman just married or about to be married. [OE *brýd*]

bride·groom (brīd′grüm′; -grum′), *n.* man just married or about to be married. [OE *brýdguma* < *brýd* bride + *guma* man; infl. by *groom*]

brides·maid (brīdz′mād′), *n.* young, usually unmarried woman who attends the bride at a wedding.

bride·well (brīd′wel; -wəl), *n.* house of correction; jail.

bridge¹ (brij), *n.*, *v.*, **bridged, bridg·ing.** —*n.* 1. structure built over a river, road, etc., so that people, trains, etc., can get across. 2. platform above the deck of a ship for the officer in command. 3. the upper, bony part of the nose. 4. mounting for false teeth fastened to real teeth near by. 5. a movable piece over which the strings of a violin, etc., are stretched. 6. any other thing like a bridge in form or use. —*v.* 1. build a bridge over. 2. extend over; span. 3. make a way over: *politeness will bridge many difficulties.* [OE *brycg*] —bridge′a·ble, *adj.* —bridge′less, *adj.*

bridge² (brij), *n.* 1. a card game for four players resembling whist, in which the dealer or his partner (the dummy) declares the trump, and the dealer plays both his own and his partner's hand. 2. auction bridge. 3. contract bridge.

bridge·head (brij′hed′), *n.* 1. fortification protecting the end of a bridge toward the enemy. 2. *Mil.* position obtained and held within enemy territory, used as a starting point for further attack. 3. either end of a bridge.

Bridge·port (brij′pôrt; -pōrt), *n.* city in SW Connecticut, on Long Island Sound.

bridge·work (brij′werk′), *n.* false teeth in a mounting fastened to real teeth near by.

bri·dle (brī′dəl), *n.*, *v.*, **-dled, -dling.** —*n.* 1. head part of a horse's harness, used to hold back or control a horse. 2. anything that holds back or checks. —*v.* 1. put a bridle on. 2. hold back; check; control. 3. hold the head up high with the chin drawn back to express pride, vanity, scorn, or anger. [OE *brídel, brigdels* < *bregdan* braid] —bri′dle·less, *adj.* —bri′dler, *n.* —Syn. *v.* 2. curb, restrain.

Bridle

brief (brēf), *adj.* 1. lasting only a short time. 2. using few words. —*n.* 1. short statement; summary. 2. *Law.* a. a writ. b. statement of the facts and the points of law of a case to be pleaded in court. 3. hold a brief for, argue for; support; defend. 4. in brief, in few words. —*v.* 1. make a brief of; summarize. 2. furnish with a brief. 3. *Brit. Law.* retain as a lawyer or counsel. 4. give a briefing to. [< OF < L *brevis* short] —brief′ly, *adv.* —brief′ness, *n.* —Syn. *adj.* 1. fleeting, transitory. 2. concise, succinct, terse.

brief case, flat container for carrying loose papers, books, drawings, etc.

brief·ing (brēf'ing), n. 1. a short summary of the details of a flight mission, given to the crew of a combat airplane just before it takes off. 2. any similar short, preparatory summary.

bri·er¹ (brī'ər), n. a thorny or prickly bush, esp. the wild rose. Also, briar. [OE brēr]

bri·er² (brī'ər), n. 1. white heath bush. Its root is used in making tobacco pipes. 2. tobacco pipe made of this. Also, briar. [< F bruyère heath < Celtic] —bri'er·y, adj.

bri·er·wood (brī'ər·wůd'), n. roots of the brier tree, often carved into tobacco pipes. Also, briarwood.

brig (brig), n. Naut.
a. a square-rigged ship with two masts.
b. U.S. prison on a warship. [short for brigantine]

Brig

bri·gade (bri·gād'), n., v., -gad·ed, -gad·ing. —n. 1. part of an army. It is usually made up of two or more regiments. 2. group of people organized for some purpose: a fire brigade puts out fires. —v. form into a brigade. [< F < Ital. brigata, ult. < briga strife]

brig·a·dier (brig'ə·dir'), n. brigadier general.

brigadier general, pl. **brigadier generals**. U.S. Mil. officer commanding a brigade, a wing of the Air Force, or an equivalent unit, ranking above a colonel and below a major general.

brig·and (brig'ənd), n. man who robs travelers on the road; robber; bandit. [< OF < Ital. brigante. See BRIGADE.] —brig'and·ish, adj.

brig·and·age (brig'ən·dij), **brig·and·ism** (-diz·əm), n. robbery; plundering.

brig·an·tine (brig'ən·tēn; -tin), n. big with the mainmast fore-and-aft-rigged. [< F < Ital. brigantino. See BRIGAND, BRIGADE.]

bright (brīt), adj. 1. giving much light; shining. 2. very light or clear. 3. quick-witted; clever. 4. intelligent. 5. vivid; glowing. 6. lively; gay; cheerful. 7. favorable. 8. famous; glorious. —adv. in a bright manner. [OE briht, beorht] —bright'ly, adv. —bright'ness, n. —Syn. adj. 1. beaming, gleaming, radiant. 3. smart, intelligent. 6. vivacious, animated. 7. promising.

bright·en (brīt'ən), v. 1. become bright or brighter. 2. make bright or brighter.

Bright's disease, Pathol. kidney disease characterized by albumin in the urine.

bril·liance (bril'yəns), **bril·lian·cy** (-yən·si), n. 1. great brightness; radiance; sparkle. 2. splendor; magnificence. 3. great ability.

bril·liant (bril'yənt), adj. 1. shining brightly; sparkling. 2. splendid; magnificent. 3. having great ability. —n. 1. diamond or other gem cut to sparkle brightly. 2. a very small size of type; 4 point. This line is set in brilliant. [< F brillant, ppr. of briller shine, ? < L beryllus beryl] —bril'liant·ly, adv. —bril'liant·ness, n.

bril·lian·tine (bril'yən·tēn'), n. Am. an oily liquid used to make the hair glossy.

brim (brim), n., v., brimmed, brim·ming. —n. 1. edge of a cup, bowl, etc.; rim. 2. the projecting edge of a hat. 3. edge bordering water. —v. fill to the brim; be full to the brim. [OE brim sea] —brim'less, adj.

brim·ful (brim'fůl'), adj. completely full.

brim·stone (brim'stōn'), n. sulfur. [ME brinston < brinn- burn + ston stone]

brin·dle (brin'dəl), adj. brindled. —n. 1. brindled color. 2. brindled animal. [< brindled]

brin·dled (brin'dəld), adj. gray, tan, or tawny with darker streaks and spots. [? akin to BRAND]

brine (brin), n. 1. very salty water. 2. salt lake or sea; ocean. [OE brȳne] —brin'ish, adj.

bring (bring), v., brought, bring·ing. 1. come with (some thing or person) from another place; take along to a place or person. 2. cause to come. 3. influence; lead. 4. Law. present before a court. 5. present (reasons, arguments, etc.); adduce. 6. sell for. 7. bring about, cause to happen. 8. bring around or round, a. restore to consciousness. b. convince; persuade. 9. bring forth, a.

give birth to; bear. b. reveal; show. 10. bring out, a. reveal; show. b. offer to the public. 11. bring to, a. restore to consciousness. b. stop; check. 12. bring up, a. care for in childhood. b. educate; train. c. suggest for action or discussion. d. stop suddenly. [OE bringan] —bring'er, n. —Syn. 1. convey, carry, bear.

bring·ing-up (bring'ing·up'), n. 1. care in childhood. 2. education; training.

brink (bringk), n. 1. edge at the top of a steep place. 2. on the brink of, very near. [ME; prob. < Scand.]

brink·man·ship (bringk'mən·ship), n. Colloq. urging of a policy even to the brink of war.

brin·y (brin'i), adj., brin·i·er, brin·i·est. of or like brine; salty. —brin'i·ness, n.

bri·quette, bri·quet (bri·ket'), n. a molded block, esp. of coal dust used for fuel. [< F]

Bris·bane (briz'bān; -bən), n. seaport in E Australia.

brisk (brisk), adj. 1. quick and active; lively. 2. keen; sharp. [? akin to BRUSQUE] —brisk'ly, adv. —brisk'ness, n. —Syn. 1. nimble, spry.

bris·ket (bris'kit), n. 1. meat from the breast of an animal. 2. breast of an animal. [< OF bruschet < Gmc.]

bris·tle (bris'əl), n., v., -tled, -tling. —n. a short, stiff hair. —v. 1. stand up straight: the angry dog's hair bristled. 2. cause (hair) to stand up straight; ruffle. 3. have one's hair stand up straight: the dog bristled. 4. show that one is aroused and ready to fight. 5. be thickly set: our path bristled with difficulties. [ME bristel] —bris'tly, adj. —bris'tli·ness, n.

bris·tle·tail (bris'əl·tāl'), n. a wingless insect having long, bristlelike appendages.

Bris·tol (bris'təl), n. seaport in SW England.

Bristol Channel, an inlet of the Atlantic, between SW England and Wales.

Brit., 1. Britain; British. 2. Briticism.

Brit·ain (brit'ən), n. England, Scotland, and Wales; Great Britain.

Bri·tan·ni·a (bri·tan'i·ə; -tan'yə), n. 1. Britain; Great Britain. 2. the British Empire.

Bri·tan·nic (bri·tan'ik), adj. British.

Brit·i·cism (brit'ə·siz·əm), n. Am. word or phrase peculiar to the British. Lift meaning elevator is a Briticism. Also, Am. Britishism.

Brit·ish (brit'ish), adj. 1. of Great Britain, the British Empire, or its people. 2. of or pertaining to the ancient Britons. —n. 1. (pl. in use) people of Great Britain or the British Empire collectively. 2. their language. [OE brittisc < Brittas Britons < Celtic]

British America, Am. 1. Canada. 2. (formerly) the British part of North America.

British Columbia, province in W Canada.

British Commonwealth of Nations, United Kingdom of Great Britain and Northern Ireland and the self-governing dominions (Canada, Australia, New Zealand, Ceylon, Ghana, Cyprus, etc.), the republics of India and Pakistan, and overseas colonies and dependencies, etc.; Commonwealth of Nations.

British East Africa, a former British territory in E Africa, including Kenya, Uganda, Tanganyika, and the island of Zanzibar.

British Empire, 1. originally, all the countries and colonies owing allegiance to the British crown, including the dominions, colonies, dependencies, etc. 2. now, the colonies, dependencies, etc., exclusive of the dominions and other autonomous units. The term now has no official use.

Brit·ish·er (brit'ish·ər), n. Am. Englishman.

British Guiana, former British colony in N South America. Now called Guyana.

British Honduras, British colony in Central America, SE of Mexico.

British India, all the territory in India formerly under British control or protection.

British Isles, Great Britain, Ireland, the Isle of Man, and other nearby islands.

Brit·ish·ism (brit'ish·iz·əm), n. Am. Briticism.

British thermal unit, amount of heat necessary to raise a pound of water one degree Fahrenheit at its maximum density.

British West Africa, a former British territory in W Africa, including Nigeria, the Gold Coast, etc.

British West Indies, British islands in the West Indies, including the Bahamas, Bermuda, and the British Virgin Islands.

Brit·on (brit′ən), n. 1. native or inhabitant of Great Britain or the British Empire. 2. member of a Celtic people who lived in S Britain long ago.

Brit·ta·ny (brit′ə·ni), n. region in NW France.

brit·tle (brit′əl), adj. very easily broken; breaking with a snap; apt to break. [ME britel < OE brēotan break] —brit′tle·ly, adv. —brit′tle·ness, n. —Syn. fragile, frail.

Br·no (bĕr′nō), n. city in central Czechoslovakia. Also, Brünn.

bro., Bro., pl. bros., Bros. brother.

broach (brōch), n. a pointed tool for making and shaping holes. —v. 1. open by making a hole. 2. begin to talk about: broach a subject. [< OF < L broccus projecting] —broach′er, n.

broad (brôd), adj. 1. large across; wide. 2. extensive: a broad experience. 3. not limited; liberal; tolerant: broad ideas. 4. main; general: broad outlines. 5. clear; full: broad daylight. 6. plain; plain-spoken. 7. coarse; not refined: broad jokes. 8. pronounced with the vocal passage open wide. The a in father is broad. —n. 1. the broad part of anything. 2. Slang. a woman. [OE brād] —broad′ish, adj. —broad′ly, adv.

broad·ax, broad·axe (brôd′aks′), n., pl. -axes. ax with a broad blade.

broad·cast (brôd′kast′; -käst′), v., -cast or -cast·ed, -cast·ing, n., adj., adv. —v. 1. send out by radio or television. 2. scatter widely. —n. 1. a sending out by radio or television. 2. speech, music, etc., sent out by radio or television. 3. a radio or television program. 4. a scattering far and wide. —adj. 1. sent out by radio or television. 2. scattered widely. —adv. over a wide surface. —broad′cast′er, n.

broad·cloth (brôd′klôth′; -kloth′), n. 1. a smooth, cotton or silk cloth, used in making shirts and dresses. 2. a smooth, closely woven woolen cloth, used in making men's suits. [orig. 2 yards "broad"]

broad·en (brôd′ən), v. 1. make broad or broader. 2. become broad or broader.

broad-gauge (brôd′gāj′), **broad-gauged** (-gājd′), adj. 1. having rails more than 56½ inches apart. 2. Am. broad-minded; liberal.

broad·loom (brôd′lüm′), adj. woven on a wide loom in one color: a broadloom carpet.

broad-mind·ed (brôd′mīn′did), adj. liberal; tolerant; not prejudiced or bigoted. —broad′-mind′ed·ly, adv. —broad′-mind′ed·ness, n.

broad·side (brôd′sīd′), n. 1. the whole side of a ship above the water line. 2. all the guns that can be fired from one side of a ship. 3. the firing of all these guns at the same time. 4. Colloq. violent attack. 5. Also, broad·sheet (brôd′shēt′). a large sheet of paper printed on one side only: broadsides announcing a big sale. —adv. with the side turned.

broad·sword (brôd′sôrd′; -sōrd′), n. sword with a broad, flat blade.

Broad·way (brôd′wā′), n. street running NE and SW through New York City.

Brob·ding·nag (brob′ding·nag), n. the land of giants in Swift's book Gulliver's Travels. —Brob′ding·nag′i·an, adj., n.

bro·cade (brō·kād′), n., v., -cad·ed, -cad·ing. —n. an expensive cloth woven with raised designs on it. —v. weave or decorate with raised designs. [< Sp., Pg. brocado, pp. of brocar embroider; akin to BROACH] —bro·cad′ed, adj.

broc·co·li (brok′ə·li), n. variety of cauliflower whose green branching stems and flower heads are used as a vegetable. [< Ital. (pl.) sprouts < L broccus projecting]

bro·chure (brō·shùr′), n. pamphlet. [< F, < brocher stitch]

bro·gan (brō′gən), n. a coarse, strong shoe. [< Irish, Scotch Gaelic, dim. of brōg shoe]

brogue[1] (brōg), n. 1. Irish accent or pronunciation of English. 2. accent or pronunciation peculiar to any dialect. [? specialization of meaning of brogue[2]]

brogue[2] (brōg), n. 1. a coarse, strong shoe. 2. shoe made for comfort and long wear. [< Irish, Scotch Gaelic brōg shoe]

broil[1] (broil), v. 1. cook by putting or holding near the fire. 2. make very hot. 3. be very hot. —n. 1. a broiling. 2. broiled meat, etc. [? < OF bruillir burn]

broil[2] (broil), v. engage in a broil; quarrel; fight. —n. an angry quarrel or struggle; brawl. [< F brouiller disorder]

broil·er (broil′ər), n. 1. Am. pan or rack for broiling. 2. a young chicken for broiling.

broke (brōk), v. 1. pt. of break. 2. Archaic. pp. of break. —adj. Slang. without money.

bro·ken (brō′kən), v. pp. of break. —adj. 1. crushed; in pieces. 2. destroyed. 3. ruined. 4. weakened. 5. tamed. 6. reduced to submission. 7. violated. 8. imperfectly spoken. 9. interrupted. 10. changing direction abruptly. —bro′ken·ly, adv. —bro′ken·ness, n.

bro·ken-heart·ed (brō′kən·här′tid), adj. crushed by sorrow or grief; heartbroken.

bro·ker (brō′kər), n. person who buys and sells stocks, bonds, grain, cotton, etc., for other people; agent. [< AF brocour tapster, retailer of wine; akin to BROACH]

bro·ker·age (brō′kər·ij), n. 1. business of a broker. 2. money charged by a broker for his services.

bro·mide (brō′mīd; -mid), n. 1. Also, bro·mid (brō′mid). Chem. compound of bromine with another element or radical. 2. potassium bromide, KBr, a drug used to calm nervousness, cause sleep, etc. 3. Am., Slang. a trite remark. [def. 3 has ref. to the effect of the drug]

bro·mid·ic (brō·mid′ik), adj. Am., Colloq. like a bromide; commonplace; trite.

bro·mine (brō′mēn; -min), **bro·min** (-min), n. Chem. a nonmetallic element, Br, somewhat like chlorine and iodine. Bromine is a dark-brown liquid that gives off an irritating vapor.

bron·chi (brong′kī), n. pl. of bronchus. 1. two main branches of the windpipe. 2. the smaller, branching tubes in the lungs.

bron·chi·a (brong′ki·ə), n.pl. the bronchi, esp. their smaller branches.

bron·chi·al (brong′ki·əl), adj. of the bronchi.

bron·chi·tis (brong·kī′tis), n. inflammation of the lining of the bronchial tubes. —bron·chit·ic (brong·kit′ik), adj.

bron·chus (brong′kəs), n., pl. -chi (-kī). one of the bronchi. [< NL < Gk. bronchos]

bron·co, bron·cho (brong′kō), n., pl. -cos; -chos. Am., Esp. W. and S.W. pony of the western United States. Broncos are often wild or only half tame. [< Sp., rough, rude]

bron·co·bust·er (brong′kō·bus′tər), n. Am., W. and S.W. Slang. one who breaks broncos to the saddle.

bron·to·sau·rus (bron′tə·sôr′əs), n. a huge, extinct dinosaur of America. [< NL < Gk. bronte thunder + sauros lizard]

Bronx (brongks), n. The, the northern borough of New York City.

Bronx cheer, Am., Slang. a contemptuous sound made by vibrating the tongue between the lips.

bronze (bronz), n., adj., v., bronzed, bronzing. —n. 1. a brown alloy of copper and tin. 2. a similar alloy of copper with zinc or other metals. 3. statue, medal, disk, etc., made of bronze. 4. yellowish brown; reddish brown. —adj. 1. made of bronze. 2. yellowish-brown; reddish-brown. —v. make or become bronze in color. [< F < Ital. bronzo bell metal] —bronz′y, adj.

Bronze Age, period after the Stone Age when bronze tools, weapons, etc., were used.

āge, cāre, fär; ēqual, tėrm; īce; ōpen, ôrder; pùt, rüle, ūse; tп, then; ə=a in about.

brooch (brōch; brüch), *n.* an ornamental pin having the point secured by a catch. [var. of *broach*, n.]

brood (brüd), *n.* 1. young birds hatched at one time in the nest or cared for together. 2. young who are cared for. 3. breed; kind. —*v.* 1. sit on in order to hatch. 2. hover over; hang close over. 3. think a long time about some one thing. 4. dwell on in thought: *for years he brooded vengeance.* [OE *brōd*] —**brood′ing·ly,** *adv.* —**brood′y,** *adj.*

brood·er (brüd′ər), *n.* 1. *Am.* a closed place that can be heated, used in raising chicks, etc. 2. one that broods.

brook[1] (brůk), *n.* a small natural stream of water. [OE *brōc*] —**Syn.** creek, rivulet.

brook[2] (brůk), *v.* put up with; endure; tolerate: *her pride would not brook such insults.* [OE *brūcan* use]

brook·let (brůk′lit), *n.* a little brook.

Brook·lyn (brůk′lən), *n.* borough of New York City, on Long Island.

brook trout, *Am.* a fresh-water game fish of the E part of North America.

broom (brüm; brům), *n.* 1. shrub with slender branches, small leaves, and yellow flowers. 2. a long-handled brush for sweeping. [OE *brōm*]

broom·corn (brüm′kôrn′; brům′–), *n.* *Am.* a tall plant resembling corn, with flower clusters having long, stiff stems used for making brooms.

broom·stick (brüm′stik′; brům′–), *n.* the long handle of a broom.

broth (brôth; broth), *n.* water in which meat has been boiled; thin soup. [OE]

broth·el (broth′əl; brôth′–; brŏth′–), *n.* house of prostitution. [ME, < OE *brēothan* go to ruin]

broth·er (bruth′ər), *n., pl.* **broth·ers, breth·ren,** *v.* —*n.* 1. son of the same parents. 2. a close friend; companion; countryman. 3. a fellow member of a group or association, as a church, union, etc. 4. member of a religious order who is not a priest. —*v.* address or treat as a brother. [OE *brōthor*]

broth·er·hood (bruth′ər·hůd), *n.* 1. bond between brothers; feeling of brother for brother. 2. persons joined as brothers; association of men with some common aim, characteristic, belief, profession, etc.

broth·er·in·law (bruth′ər·in·lô′), *n., pl.* **broth·ers·in·law.** 1. brother of one's husband or wife. 2. husband of one's sister. 3. husband of the sister of one's wife or husband.

broth·er·ly (bruth′ər·li), *adj.* 1. of a brother. 2. like a brother. 3. friendly; kindly; affectionate. —*adv.* like a brother. —**broth′er·li·ness,** *n.*

brougham (brüm; brü′əm; brō′əm), *n.* a closed carriage or automobile having an outside seat for the driver. [for Lord H. P. *Brougham*]

brought (brôt), *v.* pt. and pp. of **bring.**

brow (brou), *n.* 1. forehead. 2. arch of hair over the eye; eyebrow. 3. facial expression. 4. edge of a steep place; top of a slope. [OE *brū*]

brow·beat (brou′bēt′), *v.,* **–beat, –beat·en, –beat·ing.** frighten into doing something by overbearing looks or words; bully. —**brow′beat′-er,** *n.* —**Syn.** intimidate, domineer.

brown (broun), *n.* 1. color like that of toast, potato skins, and coffee. 2. paint or dye having this color. 3. something brown. —*adj.* 1. having this color. 2. dark-skinned; tanned. —*v.* make or become brown. [OE *brūn*] —**brown′ish,** *adj.* —**brown′ness,** *n.*

Brown (broun), *n.* **John,** 1800–1859, American abolitionist who attempted to incite a rebellion of the slaves but was captured at Harper's Ferry.

Brown·i·an movement or **motion** (broun′i·ən), *Physics.* a rapid oscillatory motion often observed in very minute particles suspended in water or other liquids.

brown·ie (broun′i), *n.* 1. a good-natured, helpful elf or fairy. 2. *Am.* a flat, sweet, chocolate cake with nuts, often in small squares.

Brown·ing (broun′ing), *n.* 1. **Elizabeth Barrett,** 1806–1861, English poet, wife of Robert Browning. 2. **Robert,** 1812–1889, English poet.

brown shirt, follower of Adolf Hitler; Nazi.

brown·stone (broun′stōn′), *n.* *Am.* reddish-brown sandstone, used as a building material.

brown study, condition of being absorbed in thought; serious reverie.

brown sugar, sugar that is not refined or only partly refined.

browse (brouz), *v.,* **browsed, brows·ing,** *n.* —*v.* 1. feed; graze. 2. read here and there in a book, library, etc. [< n., or < F *brouster* feed on buds and shoots] —*n.* tender shoots of shrubs. [appar. < MF *broust* bud, shoot < Gmc.] —**brows′er,** *n.*

Bruce (brüs), *n.* **Robert the,** 1274–1329, king of Scotland, 1306–29.

bru·in (brü′ən), *n.* bear. [< MDu., brown]

bruise (brüz), *v.,* **bruised, bruis·ing,** *n.* —*v.* 1. injure the outside of. 2. injure; hurt: *harsh words bruised her feelings.* 3. become bruised. 4. pound; crush. —*n.* 1. injury to the body, caused by a fall or a blow, that changes the color of the skin without breaking it. 2. injury to the outside of a fruit, vegetable, plant, etc. [fusion of OE *brÿsan* crush and OF *bruisier* break, shatter]

bruis·er (brüz′ər), *n.* 1. prize fighter. 2. *Colloq.* a bully.

bruit (brüt), *v.* spread a report or rumor of. [< OF, < *bruire* bray]

bru·nette, bru·net (brü·net′), *adj.* 1. dark-colored; having an olive color. 2. having dark-brown or black hair, brown or black eyes, and a dark skin. —*n.* person having such hair, eyes, and skin. A man with this complexion is a brunet; a woman is a brunette. [< F, dim. of *brun* brown < Gmc.]

Brun·hild (brün′hild), *n.* the young queen in the *Nibelungenlied* whom Siegfried wins as a bride for King Gunther by means of magic.

Brünn (bryn), *n.* Brno.

Bruns·wick (brunz′wik), *n.* 1. city in NW Germany. 2. a state in NW Germany.

brunt (brunt), *n.* main force or violence; hardest part.

brush[1] (brush), *n.* 1. tool for cleaning, rubbing, painting, etc., made of bristles, hair, or wires set in a stiff back or fastened to a handle. 2. a brushing; a rub with a brush. 3. a light touch in passing. 4. a short, brisk fight or quarrel. 5. the bushy tail of an animal, esp. of a fox. 6. *Elect.* piece of carbon, copper, etc., used to connect the electricity from the revolving part of a motor or generator to the outside circuit. 7. art or skill of an artist. —*v.* 1. clean, rub, paint, etc., with a brush; use a brush on. 2. wipe away; remove: *brush the tears away.* 3. touch lightly in passing. 4. move quickly. 5. **brush aside** or **away,** refuse to consider. 6. **brush up,** refresh one's knowledge. [< OF *broisse* < Gmc.] —**brush′er,** *n.* —**brush′y,** *adj.*

brush[2] (brush), *n.* 1. a. *U.S.* branches broken or cut off. b. thick growth of shrubs, bushes, small trees, etc. 2. *Am., S.W.* a thinly settled country; backwoods. [< OF *broche*] —**brush′y,** *adj.*

brush·wood (brush′wůd′), *n.* brush[2] (def. 1).

brusque (brusk), *adj.* abrupt in manner or speech; blunt. [< F < Ital. *brusco* coarse < LL *bruscus,* blend of *ruscum* broom and Gaulish *brucus* broom] —**brusque′ly,** *adv.* —**brusque′-ness,** *n.*

Brus·sels (brus′əlz), *n.* capital of Belgium, in the central part.

Brussels sprouts, 1. variety of cabbage that has many small heads growing along a stalk. 2. heads of this plant, used as a vegetable.

bru·tal (brü′təl), *adj.* coarse and savage; like a brute; cruel. —**bru′tal·ly,** *adv.*

bru·tal·i·ty (brü·tal′ə·ti), *n., pl.* **–ties.** 1. cruelty; savageness; coarseness: *whipping a tired horse is brutality.* 2. a cruel, savage, or coarse act. —**Syn.** 1. inhumanity, barbarity.

bru·tal·ize (brü′təl·īz), *v.,* **–ized, –iz·ing.** 1. make brutal: *war brutalizes many men.* 2. become brutal. —**bru′tal·i·za′tion,** *n.*

brute (brüt), *n.* 1. animal without power to reason. 2. a stupid, cruel, coarse, or sensual person. —*adj.* 1. without power to reason. 2. stupid; cruel; coarse; sensual. 3. unconscious: *the brute* *forces of nature.* [< F *brut* < L *brutus* heavy, dull]

brut·ish (brüt′ish), *adj.* stupid; coarse; savage; like a brute. —**brut′ish·ly,** *adv.* —**brut′ish·ness,** *n.*

Bru·tus (brü′təs), *n.* Marcus Junius, 85–42 B.C., Roman political leader and one of the men who killed Julius Caesar.

Bry·an (brī′ən), *n.* William Jennings, 1860–1925, American political leader and orator.

Bry·ant (brī′ənt), *n.* William Cullen, 1794–1878, American poet.

Bryn·hild (brin′hild), *n.* Brunhild.

bry·ol·o·gy (brī·ol′ə·ji), *n.* branch of botany that deals with mosses and liverworts. [< Gk. *bryon* moss + -LOGY] —**bry·o·log·i·cal** (brī′ə·loj′ə·kəl), *adj.* —**bry·ol′o·gist,** *n.*

bry·o·phyte (brī′ə·fīt), *n. Bot.* any of the mosses or liverworts. [< NL < Gk. *bryon* moss + *phyton* plant] —**bry·o·phyt·ic** (brī′ə·fit′ik), *adj.*

B.S., B.Sc., Bachelor of Science.

B.T.U., B.t.u., Btu, British thermal unit or units.

bu., bushel; bushels.

bub·ble (bub′əl), *n., v.,* –bled, –bling. —*n.* 1. a thin film of liquid enclosing air or gas. 2. a small globule of air in a solid or in a liquid. 3. act or process of bubbling; sound of bubbling. 4. plan or idea that looks good, but soon goes to pieces. —*v.* 1. have bubbles; make bubbles; look like water boiling. 2. make sounds like water boiling; gurgle. [ME *bobel*] —**bub′bling·ly,** *adv.* —**bub′bly,** *adj.*

bubble chamber, a small vessel filled with a superheated liquid, esp. pentane or hydrogen under pressure, through which subatomic particles make a bubbly track by means of which they may be isolated and identified.

bubble gum, a chewing gum which can be inflated so as to form a large bubble.

bu·bon·ic plague (bū·bon′ik), a very dangerous contagious disease, accompanied by fever, chills, and swelling of the lymphatic glands. It is carried to human beings by fleas from rats or squirrels. [< LL < Gk. *boubon* groin]

buc·cal (buk′əl), *adj. Anat.* 1. of the cheek. 2. of the sides of the mouth or the mouth. [< L *bucca* cheek, mouth]

buc·ca·neer (buk′ə·nir′), *n.* pirate; sea robber. [< F *boucanier* < *boucan* frame for curing meat, as done by the French in Haiti]

Bu·chan·an (bū·kan′ən; bə–), *n.* James, 1791–1868, 15th president of the U.S., 1857–61.

Bu·cha·rest (bü′kə·rest; bū′–), *n.* capital of Rumania, in the S part.

buck[1] (buk), *n.* 1. a male deer, goat, hare, rabbit, antelope, or sheep. 2. dandy. 3. *Colloq.* man. [coalescence of OE *buc* male deer and OE *bucca* male goat]

buck[2] (buk), *v.* 1. *Am., Colloq.* a. fight against; resist stubbornly. b. push or hit with the head; butt. c. rush at; charge against. 2. *Football.* charge into the opposing line with the ball. 3. *Am.* (of horses) jump into the air with back curved and come down with the front legs stiff. 4. buck up, *Colloq.* cheer up. —*n. Am.* a throw or attempt to throw by bucking. [special use of *buck*[1]] —**buck′er,** *n.*

buck[3] (buk), **pass the buck,** *Colloq.* shift the responsibility, work, etc., to someone else.

buck[4] (buk), *n., Am., Slang.* dollar.

buck·a·roo (buk′ə·rü; buk′ə·rü′), *n., pl.* -roos. *Am., S.W.* cowboy.

buck·board (buk′bôrd′; –bōrd′), *n. Am.* an open, four-wheeled carriage having the seat fastened to a platform of long, springy boards instead of a body and springs.

buck·et (buk′it), *n., v.,* -et·ed, -et·ing. —*n.* 1. pail made of wood or metal. 2. amount that a bucket can hold. 3. scoop of a dredging machine. 4. kick the bucket, *Slang.* die. —*v.* 1. lift or carry in a bucket or buckets. [appar. < AF *buket* wash tub, milk pail < OE *būc* vessel, pitcher]

buck·et·ful (buk′it·fůl), *n., pl.* -fuls. amount that a bucket can hold.

buck·eye (buk′ī′), *n. Am.* tree or shrub of the same family as the horse chestnut with showy clusters of small flowers, large divided leaves, and large brown seeds. [< *buck*[1] + *eye*; with ref. to mark on the seed]

Buck·ing·ham Palace (buk′ing·əm), official London residence of the British sovereign.

buck·le (buk′əl), *n., v.,* –led, –ling. —*n.* 1. catch or clasp used to fasten together the ends of a belt, strap, etc. 2. metal ornament for a shoe. 3. bend; bulge; kink; wrinkle. —*v.* 1. fasten together with a buckle. 2. bend; bulge; kink; wrinkle. 3. buckle down to, *Am.* work hard at. [< F < L *buccula* cheek strap on helmet, dim. of *bucca* cheek]

buck·ler (buk′lər), *n.* 1. a small, round shield. 2. protection; defense.

buck private, *Am., Slang.* a common soldier below the rank of private first class.

buck·ram (buk′rəm), *n.* a coarse cloth made stiff with glue or something like glue. [? ult. named for *Bukhāra* in central Asia]

buck·saw (buk′sô′), *n. Am.* saw set in a light frame and held with both hands.

buck·shot (buk′shot′), *n. Am.* large lead shot used for shooting large game such as deer.

buck·skin (buk′skin′), *n.* 1. a strong, soft leather, yellowish or grayish in color, made from the skins of deer or sheep. 2. buckskins, breeches made of buckskin. 3. *Am.* horse the color of buckskin.

buck·thorn (buk′thôrn′), *n. U.S.* 1. a small thorny tree or shrub with clusters of black berries. 2. a low, thorny tree that grows in southern United States.

buck·tooth (buk′tüth′), *n., pl.* -teeth. a large, protruding front tooth.

buck·wheat (buk′hwēt′), *n.* 1. plant with brown, triangular seeds and fragrant white flowers. 2. the seeds, used as food for animals or ground into flour.

bu·col·ic (bū·kol′ik), *adj.* 1. of shepherds; pastoral. 2. rustic; rural. —*n.* poem about shepherds. [< L < Gk. *boukolikos* rustic < *boukolos* shepherd] —**bu·col′i·cal·ly,** *adv.*

bud (bud), *n., v.,* bud·ded, bud·ding. —*n.* 1. a small swelling on a plant that will develop into a flower, leaf, or branch. 2. a partly opened flower. 3. beginning stage. 4. *Anat.* a small organ or part, as a taste bud. 5. nip in the bud, stop at the very beginning. —*v.* 1. put forth buds. 2. graft (a bud) from one kind of plant into the stem of a different kind. 3. begin to grow or develop. —**bud′der,** *n.* —**bud′less,** *adj.*

Bu·da·pest (bü′də·pest), *n.* capital of Hungary, on the Danube River.

Bud·dha (bůd′ə; bü′də), *n.* 563?–483? B.C., a great religious teacher of Asia. Also, Gautama.

Bud·dhism (bůd′iz·əm; bü′diz–), *n.* religion that originated in the sixth century B.C. in N India and spread widely over central, SE, and E Asia. —**Bud′dhist,** *n.* —**Bud·dhis′tic,** *adj.*

bud·dy (bud′i), *n., pl.* –dies. *Colloq.* 1. *Am.* comrade; pal. 2. a little boy.

budge (buj), *v.,* budged, budg·ing. move in the least: *he wouldn't budge from his chair.* [< F *bouger* stir < VL *bullicare* boil furiously < L *bullire* boil]

budg·et (buj′it), *n., v.,* -et·ed, -et·ing. —*n.* 1. estimate of the amount of money that can be spent, and the amounts to be spent for various purposes, in a given time. 2. stock or collection: *a budget of news.* —*v.* make a plan for spending. [< F *bougette,* dim. of *bouge* bag < L *bulga* < Celtic] —**budg·et·ar·y** (buj′ə·ter′i), *adj.*

Bue·nos Ai·res (bwā′nəs ī′riz; bō′nəs âr′ēz), capital of Argentina, on the Plata River.

buff[1] (buf), *n.* 1. a strong, soft, dull-yellow leather having a fuzzy surface. 2. soldier's coat. 3. dull yellow. 4. a polishing wheel covered with leather. 5. *Colloq.* bare skin. —*adj.* 1. made of buff leather. 2. dull-yellow. —*v.* polish with a buff. [< F *buffle* BUFFALO]

buff² (buf), *n. Am., Colloq.* devotee; fan (usually qualified) : *a model-train buff, football buff.*

buf·fa·lo (buf′ə·lō), *n., pl.* -loes, -los, or (*esp. collectively*) -lo, *v.,* -loed, -lo·ing. —*n.* 1. *Am.* the bison of America, a wild ox, the male of which has a big, shaggy head and strong front legs. 2. any of several kinds of oxen, as the tame water buffalo of India or the wild Cape buffalo of Africa. —*v. Am., Slang.* 1. intimidate or overawe. 2. puzzle; mystify. [< Ital. < L *bubalus* < Gk. *boubalos* wild ox]

Buf·fa·lo (buf′ə·lō), *n.* port in W New York State, on Lake Erie.

Buffalo Bill (*William F. Cody*), 1846–1917, American frontier scout and showman.

buffalo grass, *Am.* short grass of central and western North America.

buff·er¹ (buf′ər), *n.* anything that softens the shock of a blow. [< *buff* deaden force]

buff·er² (buf′ər), *n.* 1. person who polishes. 2. thing for polishing, covered with leather.

buffer state, a small country between two larger countries that are enemies or competitors.

buf·fet¹ (buf′it), *n., v.,* -fet·ed, -fet·ing. —*n.* 1. blow of the hand or fist. 2. knock; stroke; hurt. —*v.* 1. strike with the hand or fist. 2. knock about; strike; hurt. 3. fight; struggle. [< OF, dim. of *buffe* blow] —**buf′fet·er,** *n.*

buf·fet² (bu·fā′; bu–; bə–), *n.* 1. piece of dining-room furniture for holding dishes, silver, and table linen; sideboard. 2. counter where food and drinks are served. 3. restaurant with such a counter. [< F]

buffet supper or **lunch,** meal where the food is arranged on tables and buffet, and the guests serve themselves.

buf·foon (bu·fün′; bə–), *n.* person who amuses people with tricks, pranks, and jokes; clown. [< F < Ital. *buffone* < *buffa* jest] —**buf·foon·er·y** (bu·fün′ər·i; bə–), *n.* —**buf·foon′ish,** *adj.*

bug (bug), *n.* 1. crawling insect. 2. any insect or insectlike animal. 3. *Esp. Brit.* bedbug. 4. Often, **bugs,** *Am., Slang.* defect; fault. 5. *Am., Slang.* a small microphone used in wire tapping. 6. *Dial.* bugbear; bogy. [? < obs. Welsh *bwg* ghost]

bug·a·boo (bug′ə·bü), *n., pl.* -boos. imaginary thing feared. [< *bug* bogy + *boo,* interj.]

bug·bear (bug′bãr′), *n.* bugaboo. [< *bug* bogy + *bear²*]

bug·gy¹ (bug′i), *n., pl.* -gies. *Am.* a light carriage with one seat.

bug·gy² (bug′i), *adj.,* -gi·er, -gi·est. swarming with bugs.

bu·gle (bū′gəl), *n., v.,* -gled, -gling. —*n.* a musical instrument like a small trumpet, made of brass or copper, used in the army and navy for sounding calls and orders. —*v.* 1. blow a bugle. 2. direct or summon by blowing on a bugle. [< OF < L *buculus,* dim. of *bos* ox; with ref. to early hunting horns] —**bu′gler,** *n.*

Man blowing a bugle

buhl (būl), *n.* 1. wood inlaid with metal, tortoise shell, ivory, etc., in elaborate patterns. 2. furniture decorated with this. [< G spelling of F *Boule,* name of a cabinetmaker]

build (bild), *v.,* built or (*Archaic*) build·ed, build·ing, *n.* —*v.* 1. make by putting materials together; construct: *men build houses, dams, bridges, etc.* 2. form gradually; develop: *build a business.* 3. establish; base: *build a case on facts.* 4. rely; depend: *we can build on that man's honesty.* 5. make a structure: *he builds for a living.* —*n.* form, style, or manner of construction: *an elephant has a heavy build.* [OE *byldan* < *bold* dwelling] —**Syn.** *v.* 1. erect. 3. found.

build·er (bil′dər), *n.* 1. one who builds. 2. person whose business is building.

build·ing (bil′ding), *n.* 1. thing built, such as a house, factory, barn, etc. 2. business, art, or process of making houses, stores, ships, etc. —**Syn.** 1. edifice, structure.

build·up, build·up (bild′up′), *n.* 1. a building up; formation; development: *our build-up of military strength.* 2. *Colloq.* presentation of a person or thing with praise, fanfare, etc., esp. in advance of a performance or appearance.

built-in (bilt′in′), *adj.* built as part of the building: *a built-in bookcase.*

built-up (bilt′up′), *adj.* (of an area or land) having many houses or other buildings; urban or suburban rather than rural.

bulb (bulb), *n.* 1. *Bot.* a. a round, underground bud from which certain plants grow, as onions, tulips, and lilies. b. the thick part of an underground stem resembling a bulb; tuber: *a crocus bulb.* c. plant growing from a bulb. 2. *Elect.* a. the glass case of an incandescent lamp. b. an incandescent lamp. [< L < Gk. *bolbos* onion] —**bulb·ar** (bul′bər), *adj.* —**bulb′less,** *adj.*

bulb·ous (bul′bəs), *adj.* 1. having bulbs; growing from bulbs, as daffodils. 2. shaped like a bulb; rounded and swelling: *a bulbous nose.*

Bul·gar (bul′gär; bul′–; –gər), *n.* Bulgarian.

Bul·gar·i·a (bul·gãr′i·ə; bul–), *n.* country in SE Europe.

Bul·gar·i·an (bul·gãr′i·ən; bul–), *adj.* of or having to do with Bulgaria, its people, or their language. —*n.* 1. a native or inhabitant of Bulgaria. 2. language of Bulgaria.

bulge (bulj), *v.,* bulged, bulg·ing. —*v.* 1. swell outward. 2. cause to swell outward. —*n.* 1. an outward swelling. 2. *Slang.* advantage. 3. *Naut.* bilge. [< OF < L *bulga* bag] —**bulg′y,** *adj.* —**Syn.** *v.* 1. protrude. —*n.* 1. protuberance.

bulk (bulk), *n.* 1. size; large size. 2. largest part; main mass. 3. heap; pile. 4. **in bulk,** a. loose, not in packages. b. in large quantities. —*v.* 1. have size; be of importance. 2. grow large; swell. 3. cause to swell out. 4. pile in heaps. [< Scand. *būlki* heap] —**Syn.** *n.* 1. volume, magnitude.

bulk·head (bulk′hed′), *n.* 1. *Naut.* one of the upright partitions dividing a ship into watertight compartments to prevent sinking. 2. wall or partition built to hold back water, earth, rocks, air, etc. 3. *Am.* a flat or slanting door over a cellar entrance.

bulk·y (bul′ki), *adj.,* bulk·i·er, bulk·i·est. 1. taking up much space; large. 2. hard to handle; clumsy. —**bulk′i·ly,** *adv.* —**bulk′i·ness,** *n.* —**Syn.** 1. massive, ponderous. 2. unwieldy.

bull¹ (bul), *n.* 1. the male of beef cattle. 2. male of the whale, elephant, seal, walrus, and other large animals. 3. person who tries to raise prices in the stock market, etc. 4. *Am., Slang.* policeman. 5. *Am., Slang.* foolish talk. 6. *Am.* a bulldog. 7. **Bull, Taurus.** —*adj.* 1. male. 2. like a bull; large; strong; roaring. 3. having to do with rising prices in the stock market, etc. [OE *bula;* akin to BULLOCK] —**bull′ish,** *adj.* —**bull′ish·ly,** *adv.* —**bull′ish·ness,** *n.*

bull² (bul), *n.* a formal announcement or official order from the Pope. [< Med.L *bulla* document, seal < L, bubble]

Bull (bul), *n.* John, England or its people.

bull·dog (bul′dôg′; –dog′), *n., adj., v.,* –dogged, –dog·ging. —*n.* a heavily built dog with a large head and short hair, that is very muscular and courageous. —*adj.* like a bulldog's. —*v. Am., W.* throw (a steer, etc.) by grasping its horns and twisting its neck.

bull·doze (bul′dōz′), *v.,* –dozed, –doz·ing. *Am., Colloq.* frighten by violence or threats; bully.

bull·doz·er (bul′dōz′ər), *n. Am.* 1. a very powerful scraper or pusher for grading, road-building, etc. 2. *Colloq.* one who bulldozes.

bul·let (bul′it), *n.* a shaped piece of lead, steel, or other metal to be shot from a gun. [< F *boulette,* dim. of *boule* ball]

bul·le·tin (bul′ə·tən), *n.* 1. a short statement of news. Newspapers publish bulletins about the latest happenings. 2. magazine or newspaper appearing regularly, esp. one published by a club or society for its members. [< F < Ital. *bullettino,* double dim. of *bulla* BULL²]

bulletin board, *Am.* board on which notices are posted.

bul·let·proof (bul′it·prüf′), *adj.* made so that a bullet cannot go through.

bull·fight (bul′fīt′), *n.* fight between men and a bull in an enclosed arena. —**bull′fight′er,** *n.* —**bull′fight′ing,** *n.*

bull·finch (bul′finch′), *n.* a European songbird with handsome plumage and a short, stout bill. See p. 129 for picture.

bull·frog (bùl′frog′; –frôg′), *n. Am.* a large frog of North America that makes a loud croaking noise.

bull·head (bùl′hed′), *n. Am.* any of several American freshwater catfishes.

bull·head·ed (bùl′hed′id), *adj.* stupidly stubborn; obstinate. —**bull′head′ed·ness**, *n.*

bul·lion (bùl′yən), *n.* lumps, bars, etc., of gold or silver. [< AF *bullion* < *bouillir* boil; infl. by OF *billon* debased metal]

Bullfinch
(6 in. long)

bull·necked (bùl′nekt′), *adj.* having a thick neck.

bull·ock (bùl′ək), *n.* ox; steer.

bull pen, 1. pen for a bull or bulls. 2. *Am., Colloq.* place in which prisoners, suspects, etc., are temporarily confined. 3. *Baseball.* enclosure in which pitchers warm up during a game.

bull ring, an enclosed arena for bullfights.

bull's-eye (bùlz′ī′), *n.* 1. center of a target. 2. shot that hits it. 3. a lens shaped like a half-sphere to concentrate light. 4. a small lantern with such a lens.

bull terrier, a strong, active, white dog, a cross between a bulldog and a terrier.

bull·whip (bùl′hwip′), *n. Am., W.* whip made of rawhide, usually about 18 feet long.

bul·ly[1] (bùl′i), *n., pl.* –lies, *v.,* –lied, –ly·ing, *adj., interj.* —*n.* person who teases, frightens, or hurts smaller or weaker people. —*v.* 1. be a bully. 2. tease; frighten; hurt. —*adj. Am., Colloq.* fine; good. —*interj. Am., Colloq.* bravo! well done!

bul·ly[2] (bùl′i), or **bully beef,** *n.* canned or pickled beef. [? < F *bouilli* boiled beef]

bul·ly·rag (bùl′i·rag′), *v.,* –ragged, –rag·ging. *Dial. and Colloq.* bully; tease; abuse.

bul·rush (bùl′rush′), *n.* 1. a tall, slender plant that grows in wet places. 2. *Brit.* cattail.

bul·wark (bùl′wərk), *n.* 1. defense; protection. 2. earthwork or other wall for defense against the enemy. 3. Usually, **bulwarks.** *Naut.* a ship's side above the deck. —*v.* 1. defend; protect. 2. provide with a bulwark or bulwarks. [appar. < *bole* + *work;* akin to BOULEVARD]

bum (bum), *n., v.,* bummed, bum·ming, *adj.,* bum·mer, bum·mest. *Slang.* —*n.* 1. *Am.* a. an idle or good-for-nothing person; tramp. b. a drunken loafer. 2. spree. —*v.* 1. loaf. 2. drink heavily. 3. sponge on others; beg. 4. *Am.* get (something) by sponging on others. —*adj. Am.* of poor quality. —*bum′mer,* *n.*

bum·ble·bee (bum′bəl·bē′), *n.* a large bee with a thick, hairy body, usually banded with gold. Bumblebees live in colonies in nests in the ground. [< *bumble* buzz + *bee*]

Bumblebee (ab. ⅔ actual size)

bum·bling (bum′bling), *adj.* muddled; bungling. —**bum′bling·ly,** *adv.*

bump (bump), *v.* 1. push, throw, or strike (against something fairly large or solid). 2. move (along) with bumps. 3. hit or come against with heavy blows. 4. **bump off,** *Am., Slang.* kill; murder. —*n.* 1. a heavy blow or knock. 2. swelling caused by a bump. 3. any swelling or lump. [imit.]

bump·er (bump′ər), *n.* 1. *Am.* a bar or bars at the front or rear of a car or truck to keep it from being damaged if the vehicle is bumped. 2. cup or glass filled to the brim. —*adj.* unusually large: *a bumper crop.*

bump·kin (bump′kin), *n.* an awkward person from the country. [? < MDu. *bommekyn* little barrel]

bump·tious (bump′shəs), *adj.* unpleasantly assertive or conceited. [< *bump*] —**bump′tious·ly,** *adv.* —**bump′tious·ness,** *n.*

bump·y (bump′i), *adj.,* bump·i·er, bump·i·est. having bumps; causing bumps; rough. —**bump′i·ly,** *adv.* —**bump′i·ness,** *n.*

bun (bun), *n.* a slightly sweet roll.

bu·na (bü′nə; bü′–), *n. Chem.* an artificial rubber made from butadiene.

bunch (bunch), *n.* 1. group of things of the same kind growing or fastened together, placed together, or thought of together: *a bunch of grapes, a bunch of sheep.* 2. *Colloq.* a group of people. —*v.* 1. come together in one place. 2. bring together and make into a bunch. ▸ Bunch, in formal English, is limited to objects that grow together or can be fastened together, as *a bunch of carrots or roses, or keys,* and to expressions like *a bunch of cattle.* Colloquial and informal English holds to the older usage of *bunch,* applying it to a small collection of anything—including people.

bunch·y (bun′chi), *adj.,* bunch·i·er, bunch·i·est. 1. having bunches. 2. growing in bunches. —**bunch′i·ness,** *n.*

bun·co (bung′kō), *n., pl.* –cos, *v.,* –coed, –co·ing. *Am., Slang.* —*n.* 1. a dice game. 2. any swindling or confidence game. —*v.* swindle. Also, **bunko.** [short for *buncombe*]

bun·combe (bung′kəm), *n. Am.* insincere talk; humbug. Also, **bunkum.** [after Buncombe Co., N.C., whose congressman kept making pointless speeches "for Buncombe"]

Bund (bùnd; *Ger.* bùnt), *n., pl.* Bün·de (byn′də). *German.* society; league; association.

Bun·des·rat (bùn′dəs·rät′), *n.* the upper house of the legislature of West Germany.

Bun·des·tag (bùn′dəs·täk′), *n.* the lower, popularly elected house of the legislature of West Germany.

bun·dle (bun′dəl), *n., v.,* –dled, –dling. —*n.* 1. number of things tied or wrapped together. 2. parcel; package. 3. group; bunch. —*v.* 1. wrap or tie together; make into a bundle. 2. send or go in a hurry; hustle. 3. conduct a courtship, fully dressed, in bed. 4. **bundle up,** dress warmly. [cf. MDu. *bondel;* akin to BIND] —**bun′dler,** *n.*

bung (bung), *n.* 1. stopper for closing the hole in the side or end of a barrel, keg, or cask. 2. bunghole. —*v.* 1. close (a bunghole) with a stopper. 2. shut up in, or as in, a cask. 3. *Slang.* bruise. [prob. < MDu. *bonghe*]

bun·ga·low (bung′gə·lō), *n.* a one-story house. [< Hind. *banglā* of Bengal]

bung·hole (bung′hōl′), *n.* hole in the side or end of a barrel, keg, or cask through which it is filled and emptied.

bun·gle (bung′gəl), *v.,* –gled, –gling, *n.* —*v.* do or make (something) in a clumsy, unskillful way. —*n.* a clumsy, unskillful performance. —**bun′gler,** *n.* —**bun′gling·ly,** *adv.*

bun·ion (bun′yən), *n. Pathol.* painful, inflamed swelling on the foot, esp. on the first joint of the big toe.

bunk[1] (bungk), *n.* 1. a narrow bed set against a wall like a shelf. 2. *Colloq.* any place to sleep. —*v.* 1. *Colloq.* occupy a bunk. 2. sleep in rough quarters. [? < Scand. (Dan.) *bunke* heap]

bunk[2] (bungk), *n. Am., Slang.* humbug. [short for *buncombe*]

bunk·er (bungk′ər), *n.* 1. place or bin for coal on a ship. 2. a sandy hollow or mound of earth on a golf course, used as an obstacle.

Bunker Hill, hill in Charlestown, Massachusetts. An early battle of the American Revolution was fought near there on June 17, 1775.

bunk·house (bungk′hous′), *n. Am.* a rough building with sleeping quarters for laborers.

bun·kum (bung′kəm), *n. Am., Colloq.* buncombe.

bun·ny (bun′i), *n., pl.* –nies. *Colloq.* a. rabbit. b. *U.S.* squirrel.

Bun·sen burner (bun′sən), a gas burner with a very hot, blue flame, used in laboratories.

bunt (bunt), *v.* 1. strike with the head or horns, as a goat does. 2. push; shove. 3. *Am., Baseball.* hit (a pitch) lightly so that the ball goes to the ground and rolls only a short distance. —*n. Am., Baseball.* a. act of bunting. b. ball that is bunted. —**bunt′er,** *n.*

bun·ting[1] (bun′ting), *n.* 1. a thin cloth used for flags. 2. long pieces of cloth in flag colors and designs, used to decorate buildings and streets on holidays, etc.; flags.

bun·ting[2] (bun′ting), n. a small bird with a stout bill, somewhat like a sparrow.

Bun·yan (bun′yən), n. 1. **John**, 1628–1688, English preacher and religious writer who wrote *Pilgrim's Progress*. 2. **Paul**, imaginary hero of northwestern lumber camps.

buoy (boi; bū′i), n. *Naut.* 1. a floating object anchored in a certain place on the water to warn or guide. It marks hidden rocks or shallows, shows the safe part of the channel, etc. 2. life buoy. —v. 1. *Naut.* furnish with buoys; mark with a buoy. 2. keep from sinking. 3. hold up; sustain; encourage. [< OF or MDu. < L *boia* fetter]

buoy·an·cy (boi′ən·si; bū′yən–), n. 1. power to float: *wood has more buoyancy than iron.* 2. power to keep things afloat: *salt water has more buoyancy than fresh water.* 3. tendency to rise. 4. cheerfulness; hopefulness.

buoy·ant (boi′ənt; bū′yənt), adj. 1. able to float. 2. able to keep things afloat: *air is buoyant.* 3. tending to rise. 4. light-hearted; cheerful; hopeful. —**buoy′ant·ly**, adv.

bu·pres·tid beetle (bū·pres′tid), a beetle whose larvae poison cattle. [< L *buprestis* < Gk., poisonous beetle, lit., ox-burner]

bur (bėr), n., v., **burred, bur·ring.** —n. 1. a prickly, clinging seed case or flower. 2. plant or weed bearing burs. 3. person or thing that clings like a bur. —v. remove burs from. Also, **burr.** [prob. < Scand. (Dan.) *borre* burdock]

bur·bot (bėr′bət), n., pl. **-bots** or (esp. collectively) **-bot.** a fresh-water fish with a slender body, related to the cod. [< F *bourbotte* < L *barba* beard; infl. by F *bourbe* mud]

bur·den[1] (bėr′dən), n. 1. what is carried; a load (of things, care, work, duty, or sorrow). 2. thing hard to carry or bear; heavy load. 3. quantity of freight that a ship can carry; weight of a ship's cargo. —v. 1. put a burden on. 2. load too heavily; oppress. Also, *Archaic,* **burthen.** [OE *byrthen;* akin to BEAR[1]] —**Syn.** n. 2. weight, oppression.

bur·den[2] (bėr′dən), n. 1. main idea or message. 2. repeated verse in a song; chorus; refrain. [< OF *bourdon* humming, drone of bagpipe < LL *burda* pipe]

burden of proof, *Esp. Law.* obligation of proving something said to be true.

bur·den·some (bėr′dən·səm), adj. hard to bear; very heavy; oppressive. —**bur′den·some·ly,** adv. —**Syn.** oppressing, onerous.

bur·dock (bėr′dok′), n. a coarse weed with prickly burs and broad leaves. [< bur + dock[4]]

bu·reau (byŭr′ō), n., pl. **bu·reaus, bu·reaux** (byŭr′ōz). 1. *Am.* chest of drawers for clothes, often one with a mirror. 2. *Brit.* desk or writing table with drawers. 3. office: *a travel bureau.* 4. *Am.* subdivision of a government department: *the Weather Bureau.* [< F, desk (orig. cloth-covered) < OF *burel,* dim. of *bure* coarse woolen cloth < LL *burra*]

bu·reauc·ra·cy (byū·rok′rə·si), n., pl. **-cies.** 1. government by groups of officials. 2. officials administering the government. 3. concentration of power in administrative bureaus.

bu·reau·crat (byŭr′ə·krat), n. 1. official in a bureaucracy. 2. a formal pretentious government official. [blend of *bureau* + (*auto*)*crat*] —**bu′reau·crat′ic,** —**bu′reau·crat′i·cal,** adj. —**bu′reau·crat′i·cal·ly,** adv.

bu·rette, bu·ret (byū·ret′), n. a graduated glass tube with a valve at the bottom, for measuring out small amounts of a liquid or gas. [< F, dim. of *buire* vase]

burg (bėrg), n. *Am., Colloq.* town; city. [var. of *borough*]

bur·geon (bėr′jən), v., n. bud; sprout. [< OF *burjon,* appar. < Gmc.]

bur·gess (bėr′jis), n. 1. citizen of a borough. 2. *Am.* member of the lower house of the colonial legislature in Virginia or Maryland. [< OF < LL *burgensis* citizen. See BOURGEOIS.]

burgh (bėrg), n. a chartered town in Scotland; borough. [var. of *borough*] —**burgh′al,** adj.

burgh·er (bėr′gər), n. citizen of a burgh or town; citizen.

bur·glar (bėr′glər), n. person who breaks into a building at night to steal. [< Anglo-L *burglator,* ? partly < OE *burgbryce*]

bur·glar·i·ous (bėr·glâr′i·əs), adj. having to do with burglary. —**bur·glar′i·ous·ly,** adv.

bur·glar·ize (bėr′glər·īz), v., **-ized, -iz·ing.** *Am., Colloq.* commit burglary in.

bur·glar·proof (bėr′glər·prüf′), adj. so strong or safe that burglars cannot break in.

bur·glar·y (bėr′glər·i), n., pl. **-glar·ies.** *Law.* 1. act of breaking into a house, building, etc., at night to steal or commit some other crime. 2. act of breaking into a building to steal.

bur·gle (bėr′gəl), v., **-gled, -gling.** *Colloq.* burglarize.

bur·go·mas·ter (bėr′gə·mas′tər; –mäs′–), n. mayor of a town in the Netherlands, Flanders, or Germany. [< Du. *burgemeester* < *burg* borough + *meester* master]

Bur·gun·dy (bėr′gən·di), n., pl. **-dies.** 1. region in E France. 2. a red or white wine made there. —**Bur·gun·di·an** (bėr·gun′di·ən), adj., n.

bur·i·al (ber′i·əl), n. a burying. —adj. having to do with burying: *a burial service.*

burial ground, graveyard; cemetery.

Burke (bėrk), n. **Edmund,** 1729–1797, British statesman and orator.

burl (bėrl), n. 1. knot in wool, cloth, or wood. 2. a hard, round growth on the trunks of certain trees. —v. remove knots from. [< OF < LL *burra* flock of wool] —**burled,** adj. —**burl′er,** n.

bur·lap (bėr′lap), n. a coarse fabric made from jute or hemp, used to make bags, curtains, etc.

bur·lesque (bėr·lesk′), n., v., **-lesqued, -lesquing,** adj. —n. 1. a literary or dramatic composition in which a serious subject is treated ridiculously, or with mock solemnity. 2. *U.S.* a cheap, vulgar kind of vaudeville with dancing and horseplay. —v. imitate so as to ridicule. —adj. comical; making people laugh. [< F < Ital. *burlesco* < *burla* jest] —**bur·lesque′ly,** adv. —**bur·les′quer,** n. —**Syn.** n. 1. parody, take-off.

bur·ley, Bur·ley (bėr′li), n., pl. **-leys.** *Am.* kind of thin-leaved tobacco grown widely in Kentucky. [from a proper name]

bur·ly (bėr′li), adj., **-li·er, -li·est.** 1. strong; sturdy; big. 2. bluff; rough. [OE *borlīce* excellently] —**bur′li·ly,** adv. —**bur′li·ness,** n.

Bur·ma (bėr′mə), n. country in SE Asia, formerly a British dependency.

Burma Road, a highway from Burma to Chungking, China, used during World War II.

Bur·mese (bėr·mēz′; –mēs′), n., pl. **-mese,** adj. —n. 1. native of Burma. 2. language of Burma. —adj. of Burma, its people, or their language.

burn[1] (bėrn), v., **burned** or **burnt, burn·ing,** n. —v. 1. be on fire; be very hot; blaze; glow. 2. set on fire; cause to burn. 3. destroy or be destroyed by fire. 4. injure or be injured by fire, heat, or an acid. 5. make by fire, by a heated tool, etc.: *his cigar burned a hole in the rug.* 6. feel hot; give a feeling of heat to. 7. be very excited or eager. 8. inflame or be inflamed with anger, passion, etc. 9. give light: *lamps were burning in every room.* 10. sunburn; tan. 11. produce, harden, glaze, etc., by fire or heat: *burn bricks, burn lime.* 12. *Chem.* undergo or cause to undergo combustion; oxidize. 13. cauterize. —n. 1. injury caused by fire, heat, or an acid. 2. a burned place. [coalescence of OE *beornan* be on fire and OE *bærnan* consume with fire] —**burn′a·ble,** adj. —**Syn.** v. 1. flame. 2. ignite, fire.

burn[2] (bėrn), n. *Scot.* and *N.Eng.* a small stream; brook. [OE *burna*]

burn·er (bėr′nər), n. 1. part of a lamp, stove, etc., where flame is produced. 2. thing that burns. 3. man whose work is burning something.

burn·ing (bėr′ning), adj. glowing; hot. —**burn′ing·ly,** adv.

Burette

bur·nish (bér′nish), v., n. polish; shine. [< OF *burnir* make brown, polish < *brun* BROWN]

bur·noose, bur·nous (bér·nüs′; bér′nüs), n. cloak with a hood, worn by Moors and Arabs. [< F < Ar. *burnus*]

Burns (bérnz), n. Robert, 1759–1796, Scottish poet.

burn·sides, Burn·sides (bérn′sīdz′), n.pl. Am. growth of hair on cheeks but not on the chin. [for Gen. A. E. *Burnside*, American Civil War general]

burnt (bérnt), v. pt. and pp. of burn[1].

burp gun (bérp), a small, air-cooled, automatic machine gun, usually, of smaller caliber and having a higher rate of fire than a Thompson submachine gun.

burr[1] (bér), n. 1. bur. 2. a rough ridge or edge left by a tool on metal, wood, etc., after cutting or drilling it. 3. tool that resembles a burr: *dentists use tiny burrs*. 4. a rounded growth, as on a tree. —v. bur. [var. of *bur*]

burr[2] (bér), n. 1. rough pronunciation of r. 2. rough pronunciation: *a Scotch burr*. 3. a whirring sound. —v. 1. pronounce r roughly. 2. pronounce roughly. 3. make a whirring sound. [prob. imit.]

Burr (bér), n. Aaron, 1756–1836, vice-president of the United States, 1801–05.

bur·ro (bér′ō; bůr′ō), n., pl. -ros. Am., S.W. donkey. [< Sp., < *burrico* small horse < LL *burricus*]

bur·row (bér′ō), n. 1. hole dug in the ground by an animal for refuge or shelter. 2. similar dwelling or refuge. —v. 1. dig a hole in the ground. 2. live in burrows. 3. hide. 4. dig. 5. search: *burrow in the library for a book*. [cf. OE *beorg*; akin to BOROUGH, BURY] —bur′row·er, n.

bur·sa (bér′sə), n., pl. -sae (-sē), -sas. Anat., Zool. sac, esp. one containing a lubricating fluid; pouch; cavity. [< LL < Gk. *byrsa* wineskin] —bur′sal, adj.

bur·sar (bér′sər; -sär), n. treasurer of a college. [< Med.L *bursarius* < LL *bursa* purse]

bur·si·tis (bər·sī′tis), n. inflammation of a bursa.

burst (bérst), v., burst, burst·ing, n. —v. 1. break open; break out; fly apart suddenly with force; explode: *the bomb burst*. 2. break or give way because of grief or shock: *her heart almost burst with sadness*. 3. be very full: *after the harvest the barns were bursting with grain*. 4. go, come, do, etc., by force or suddenly: *he burst into the room*. 5. open or be opened suddenly or violently: *the trees burst into bloom*. 6. act or change suddenly in a way suggesting a break or explosion: *she burst into loud laughter*. 7. cause to break open or into pieces; shatter. —n. 1. bursting; split; explosion. 2. outbreak. 3. sudden and violent issuing forth. 4. sudden display of activity or energy: *a burst of speed*. 5. Mil. a series of shots fired by one pressure of the trigger of an automatic weapon. b. explosion of a projectile in the air or when it strikes the ground or target. [OE *berstan*] —burst′er, n.

bur·then (bér′thən), n., v. Archaic. burden[1].

bur·y (ber′i), v., bur·ied, bur·y·ing. 1. put (a dead body) in the earth, a tomb, etc. 2. perform a funeral service for. 3. cover up; hide. 4. plunge; sink. [OE *byrgan*] —bur′i·er, n. —Syn. 1. inter, entomb. 3. conceal, secrete.

bus (bus), n., pl. bus·es, bus·ses. automobile that carries passengers along a certain route; omnibus. [short for *omnibus*]

bus boy or **girl**, Am. waiter's assistant, who fills glasses, carries off dishes, etc.

bus·by (buz′bi), n., pl. -bies. a tall fur hat, worn by hussars in the British army.

bush[1] (bůsh), n. 1. a woody plant smaller than a tree, often with many separate branches starting from or near the ground. 2. something that resembles or suggests a bush. 3. Am. open forest; uncleared land: *take to the bush*. —v. 1. spread out like a

Busby

bush; grow thickly. 2. set (ground) with bushes; cover with bushes. [ME *busch, busk*]

bush[2] (bůsh), n. a bushing. —v. put a bushing in. [< MDu. *busse* BOX[1]]

bushed (bůsht), adj. Am., Colloq. worn-out.

bush·el[1] (bůsh′əl), n. 1. measure for grain, fruit, vegetables, and other dry things, equal to 4 pecks or 32 quarts. 2. container that holds a bushel. [< OF *boissiel*, dim. of *boisse* a measure]

bush·el[2] (bůsh′əl), v., -eled, -el·ing; esp. Brit. -elled, -el·ling. Am. repair or alter (clothing). —bush′el·er, esp. Brit. bush′el·ler, n.

Bu·shi·do, bu·shi·do (bů′shē·dō), n. moral code of feudal Japan; Japanese chivalry.

bush·ing (bůsh′ing), n. 1. a metal lining. 2. a removable metal lining used as a bearing.

bush·man (bůsh′mən), n., pl. -men. 1. settler in the Australian bush. 2. person who knows much about life in the bush. 3. Bushman, member of a South African tribe of roving hunters.

bush·mas·ter (bůsh′mas′tər; -mäs′-), n. a large, poisonous snake of tropical America.

bush pilot, Am. pilot who flies a small plane over relatively unsettled country, as Alaska.

bush·whack·er (bůsh′hwak′ər), n. Am. 1. frontiersman. 2. guerrilla fighter. —bush′-whack′ing, n.

bush·y (bůsh′i), adj., bush·i·er, bush·i·est. 1. spreading out like a bush; growing thickly. 2. overgrown with bushes. —bush′i·ness, n.

bus·i·ly (biz′ə·li), adv. in a busy manner.

busi·ness (biz′nis), n. 1. thing that one is busy at; work; occupation. 2. matter; affair. 3. activities of buying and selling; trade; commercial dealings. 4. commercial enterprise; industrial establishment: *a bakery business*. 5. right to act; concern: *that's not your business*. 6. action in a play; thing done to make a play seem like real life. [< *busy* + *-ness*] —Syn. 1. trade, profession.

business college or **school**, Am. school that gives training in shorthand, typewriting, bookkeeping, and other business subjects.

busi·ness·like (biz′nis·līk′), adj. having system and method; well-managed; practical.

busi·ness·man (biz′nis·man′), n., pl. -men. 1. man in business. 2. man who runs a business.

busi·ness·wom·an (biz′nis·wům′ən), n., pl. -wom·en. Am. 1. woman in business. 2. woman who runs a business.

bus·kin (bus′kin), n. 1. high shoe with a very thick sole, worn by Greek and Roman actors of tragedies. 2. tragedy; tragic drama. [cf. OF *brousequin*] —bus′kined, adj.

bus·man's holiday (bus′mənz), holiday spent in doing what one does at one's daily work.

buss (bus), v., n. Archaic or Dial. kiss.

bus·ses (bus′iz), n. pl. of bus.

bust[1] (bust), n. 1. statue of a person's head, shoulders, and chest. 2. the upper, front part of the body. 3. a woman's bosom. [< F < Ital. < L *bustum* funeral monument]

bust[2] (bust), n. 1. Substandard. burst. 2. Am., Slang. total failure; bankruptcy. 3. Am., Colloq. spree. —v. 1. Substandard. burst. 2. Slang. bankrupt; ruin. 3. Am., Slang. fail financially; become bankrupt. 4. Colloq. lower in rank. 5. Colloq. punch; hit. 6. train to obey; tame. 7. break up (a trust) into smaller companies. [var. of *burst*] ▷ Bust is the substandard form of *burst* in the sense of "exploding" or "breaking out." It is slang in the sense of "going broke" but is good English in *busting a bronco* or *busting a trust*.

bus·tard (bus′tərd), n. a large game bird of Africa, Europe, and Asia. [blend of OF *bistarde* and *oustarde*, both < L *avis tarda* slow bird]

bus·tle[1] (bus′əl), v., -tled, -tling, n. —v. 1. be noisily busy and in a hurry. 2. make (others) hurry or work hard. —n. noisy or excited activity. [? imit.] —bus′tler, n. —bus′tling·ly, adv. —Syn. n. stir, commotion, ado.

bus·tle[2] (bus′əl), n. pad used to puff out the upper back part of a woman's skirts. [? special use of *bustle*[1]]

bus·y (biz′i), adj., bus·i·er, bus·i·est, v., bus-ied, **bus·y·ing.** —*adj.* **1.** working; active. **2.** of a telephone line, in use. **3.** full of work or activity. **4.** prying into other people's affairs; meddling. —*v.* make busy; keep busy. [OE *bisig*] —**bus'y·ness,** *n.* —Syn. *adj.* **1.** employed, occupied.

bus·y·bod·y (biz'ē·bod'ĭ), *n., pl.* –**bod·ies.** person who pries into other people's affairs.

but (but; *unstressed* bət), *conj.* **1.** on the other hand; yet: *it rained, but I went anyway.* **2.** if not; unless; except that: *it never rains but it pours.* **3.** other than; otherwise than: *we cannot choose but hear.* **4.** that: *I don't doubt but he will come.* **5.** that not: *he is not so sick but he can eat.* **6.** who not; which not: *none sought his aid but were helped.* —*prep.* with the exception of: *he works every day but Sunday.* —*adv.* **1.** only; merely: *he is but a boy.* **2.** all but, nearly; almost. —*n.* objection: *not so many buts, please.* [OE *būtan* without, unless < *be*– + *ūtan* outside < *ūt* OUT] ➤ But is the natural coördinating conjunction to connect two contrasted (adversative) statements of equal grammatical rank. It is more natural than the heavy and formal *however* or *yet: He worked fast but accurately.* Two clauses separated by *but* should ordinarily be separated by a comma. The contrast in idea suggests the use of punctuation even when the clauses are relatively short: *I couldn't get the license number, but it was a New York plate.*

bu·ta·di·ene (bū'tə·dī'ēn; –dī·ēn'), *n. Chem.* **1.** a colorless gas, C_4H_6, used in making artificial rubber and as an anesthetic. **2.** its isomeric hydrocarbon.

bu·tane (bū'tān; bū·tān'), *n. Chem.* either of two isomeric hydrocarbons, C_4H_{10}, of the methane series. Both are inflammable gases.

butch·er (bùch'ər), *n.* **1.** man whose work is killing animals for food. **2.** man who sells meat. **3.** a brutal killer; murderer. **4.** *Am.* vender; peddler, esp. a man who goes through trains selling magazines, candy, etc. —*v.* **1.** kill (animals) for food. **2.** kill wholesale, needlessly, or cruelly. **3.** kill brutally; murder. **4.** spoil by poor work. [< OF *bocher* < *boc* he-goat, BUCK¹ < Gmc.] —**butch'er·er,** *n.*

butch·er·y (bùch'ər·ĭ), *n., pl.* –**er·ies. 1.** brutal killing; wholesale murder. **2.** slaughterhouse; butcher shop.

but·ler (but'lər), *n.* manservant in charge of the pantry and table service in a household; head servant. [< AF var. of OF *bouteillier* < *bouteille* BOTTLE] —**but'ler·ship,** *n.*

butler's pantry, a small room between the kitchen and dining room, for use by a butler, serving maid, etc.

butt¹ (but), *n.* **1.** the thicker end of anything, as a tool, weapon, ham, etc. **2.** end that is left; stub; stump. [akin to BUTTOCKS]

butt² (but), *n.* **1.** target. **2.** object of ridicule or scorn. **3.** an embankment of earth on which targets are placed for shooting practice. **4.** the **butts,** place to practice shooting. —*v.* join end to end; abut. [< F *bout* end < Gmc.]

butt³ (but), *v.* **1.** push or hit with the head. **2. butt in,** *Am., Colloq.* meddle; interfere. —*n.* push or hit with the head. [< OF *bouter* thrust < *bout* end < Gmc.] —**butt'er,** *n.*

butt⁴ (but), *n.* **1.** a large barrel for wine or beer. **2.** a liquid measure equal to 126 gallons. [< OF < LL *butta*]

butte (būt), *n. Am., W.* a steep hill standing alone.

but·ter (but'ər), *n.* **1.** the solid yellowish fat obtained from cream by churning. **2.** something like butter, as apple butter. —*v.* **1.** put butter on. **2.** *Colloq.* flatter. [< L < Gk. *boutyron*] —**but'ter·less,** *adj.*

but·ter·cup (but'ər·kup'), *n.* plant with bright-yellow flowers shaped like cups.

but·ter·fat (but'ər·fat'), *n.* fat in milk.

but·ter·fin·gers (but'ər·fing'gərz), *n. Colloq.* a careless or clumsy person.

but·ter·fish (but'ər·fish'), *n., pl.* –**fish·es** or (*esp. collectively*) –**fish.** a small, silvery fish, used for food.

but·ter·fly (but'ər·flī'), *n., pl.* –**flies. 1.** insect with a slender body and four large, usually

bright-colored, wings. **2.** person who suggests a butterfly by delicate beauty, bright clothes, fickleness, etc. [OE *buterflēoge.* See BUTTER, FLY¹.]

but·ter·milk (but'ər·milk'), *n.* an acid beverage obtained when butter is churned from cream.

but·ter·nut (but'ər·nut'), *n. Am.* **1.** an oily kind of walnut. **2.** tree that bears butternuts.

but·ter·scotch (but'ər·skoch'), *n.* candy made from brown sugar and butter. —*adj.* flavored with brown sugar and butter.

but·ter·y¹ (but'ər·ĭ), *adj.* **1.** like butter. **2.** containing butter; spread with butter.

but·ter·y² (but'ər·ĭ; but'rĭ), *n., pl.* –**ter·ies. 1.** storeroom, esp. for wines and liquors. **2.** pantry. [< OF, < *botte* BUTT⁴]

but·tocks (but'əks), *n.pl.* rump. [ME *buttok.* Cf. OE *buttuc* end, small piece of land]

but·ton (but'ən), *n.* **1.** knob or round piece fastened to clothing and other things to close them, decorate them, etc. **2.** anything that resembles or suggests a button, as the knob or disk pressed to ring an electric bell. **3. buttons,** *Brit. Colloq.* bellboy or page. —*v.* fasten with buttons; close with buttons. [< OF *boton* < *bouter* thrust. See BUTT³.] —**but'ton·er,** *n.* —**but'ton·less,** *adj.* —**but'ton·like',** *adj.*

but·ton·hole (but'ən·hōl'), *n., v.,* –**holed,** –**hol·ing.** —*n.* slit or loop through which a button is passed. —*v.* **1.** make buttonholes in. **2.** hold in conversation; force to listen.

but·ton·wood (but'ən·wùd'), *n. Am.* **1.** a tall plane tree with button-shaped fruit. **2.** its wood.

but·tress (but'ris), *n.* **1.** support built against a wall or building to strengthen it. See the picture under **flying buttress. 2.** support; prop. —*v.* **1.** strengthen with a buttress. **2.** support; prop. [< OF *bouterez* (pl.) < *bouter* thrust against. See BUTT³.]

bu·tyr·ic (bū·tir'ik), *adj. Chem.* of or derived from butyric acid. [< L *butyrum* butter]

butyric acid, *Chem.* colorless liquid, $C_4H_8O_2$, that has an unpleasant odor. It is formed by fermentation in rancid butter, cheese, etc.

bux·om (buk'səm), *adj.* plump and good to look at; healthy and cheerful. [ME *buhsum,* ? < OE *būgan* bend] —**bux'om·ly,** *adv.* —**bux'om·ness,** *n.*

buy (bī), *v.,* **bought, buy·ing,** *n.* —*v.* **1.** get by paying a price. **2.** buy things. **3.** get by sacrifice: *buy peace by surrender.* **4.** bribe. **5. buy off,** get rid of by paying money to. **6. buy out,** buy all the shares, rights, etc., of. **7. buy up,** buy all that one can of; buy. —*n.* **1.** *Colloq.* thing bought; a purchase. **2.** *Am., Colloq.* a bargain. [OE *bycgan*]

buy·er (bī'ər), *n.* **1.** person who buys. **2.** person whose work is buying goods for a department store or other business.

buyer's strike, a combined refusal of consumers to buy in protest against high prices.

buzz (buz), *n.* **1.** a humming sound made by flies, mosquitoes, or bees. **2.** a low, confused sound of many people talking quietly. **3.** whisper; rumor. —*v.* **1.** hum loudly. **2.** sound in a low, confused way. **3.** talk excitedly. **4.** utter or express by buzzing. **5.** whisper; rumor. **6.** fly a plane very fast and low over. **7. buzz about,** move about busily. **8. buzz off, a.** ring off on the telephone. **b.** *Brit. Colloq.* go away; leave. [imit.]

buz·zard (buz'ərd), *n.* **1.** any of various more or less heavily built diurnal birds of prey of the hawk family. **2.** turkey buzzard. [< OF *busart,* ult. < L *buteo* hawk]

buzz bomb, *Mil.* an aerial projectile that can be guided to a target where it explodes; robot bomb.

buzz·er (buz'ər), *n.* **1.** thing that buzzes. **2.** electrical device that makes a buzzing sound as a signal.

buzz saw, *Am.* a circular saw.

bx., *pl.* **bxs.** box.

by (bī), *prep.* **1.** near; beside: *by the house.* **2.** along; over; through: *go by the bridge.* **3.** through the act of; through the means, use, or efficacy of: *travel by airplane.* **4.** combined with in multiplication or relative dimensions: *a room ten by twenty feet.* **5.** in the measure of: *eggs by the dozen.* **6.** to the extent of: *larger by half.* **7.**

according to: *work by rule*. **8.** in relation to: *she did well by her children*. **9.** separately with: *two by two*. **10.** during: *by day*. **11.** not later than: *by six o'clock*. **12.** toward: *the island lies south by east from here*. —*adv*. **1.** at hand: *near by*. **2.** past (in space): *a car dashed by*. **3.** past (in time): *days gone by*. **4.** aside or away: *to put something by*. **5.** *Am., Colloq. Southern.* at, in, or into another's house when passing: *please come by and eat with me*. **6. by and by**, after a while. **7. b**,̣ **and large**, *Am*. in every way or aspect. —*n*. bye. [OE bī, unstressed *be*]

by-, *prefix*. **1.** secondary; minor; less important, as in *by-product*. **2.** near by, as in *bystander*.

bye (bī), *n*. **1.** odd man or condition of being the odd player in games where players are grouped in pairs. **2. by the bye**, incidentally. —*adj*. **1.** aside from the main point, subject, etc. **2.** secondary. **3.** incidental. [var. of *by*, prep.]

bye-bye (bī′bī′), *interj. Colloq.* good-by.

by-elec·tion (bī′i·lek′shən), *n*. a special election, not held at the time of the regular elections.

by·gone (bī′gôn′; -gon′), *adj*. past; former. —*n*. **1.** something in the past. **2.** the past.

by·law (bī′lô′), *n*. **1.** law made by a city, company, club, etc., for the control of its own affairs. **2.** a secondary law or rule; not one of the main rules. [< Scand. (Dan.) *bylov* < *by* town + *lov* LAW; meaning infl. by *by*-]

by-line (bī′līn′), *n. Am*. line at the beginning of a newspaper or magazine article giving the name of the writer.

by-name (bī′nām′), *n*. **1.** second name; surname. **2.** nickname.

by-pass (bī′pas′; -päs′), *n*. **1.** road, channel, pipe, etc., providing a secondary passage to be used instead of the main passage. **2.** *Elect.* a shunt. —*v*. **1.** provide a secondary passage for. **2.** go around. **3.** pass over the head of (a superior, etc.) to a higher authority. **4.** set aside or ignore (regulations, etc.) in order to reach a desired objective. **5.** get away from; avoid; escape: *bypass a question*. **6.** *Mil.* flank.

by-path (bī′path′; -päth′), *n*. a side path.

by-play (bī′plā′), *n*. action that is not part of the main action, esp. on the stage.

by-prod·uct (bī′prod′əkt), *n*. something produced in making or doing something else; not the main product.

by-road (bī′rōd′), *n*. a side road.

By·ron (bī′rən), *n*. George Gordon, Lord, 1788–1824, English poet. —**By·ron·ic** (bī·ron′ik), *adj*. —**By·ron′i·cal·ly**, *adv*.

by·stand·er (bī′stan′dər), *n*. person standing near or by; looker-on.

by·street (bī′strēt′), *n*. a side street.

by·word (bī′wėrd′), *n*. **1.** object of contempt; thing scorned. **2.** common saying; proverb.

Byz·an·tine (biz′ən·tēn; -tīn; bi·zan′tin), *adj*. having to do with Byzantium or a style of architecture developed there that uses round arches, crosses, circles, domes, and mosaics. —*n*. native or inhabitant of Byzantium.

Byzantine Empire, eastern part of the Roman Empire from 395 A.D. to 1453.

By·zan·ti·um (bi·zan′shi·əm; -ti·əm), *n*. ancient city where Istanbul now is.

C

C, c (sē), *n., pl*. **C's; c's. 1.** the third letter of the alphabet. **2.** the first note of the musical scale of C major. **3.** Roman numeral for 100.

C, 1. *Chem*. carbon. **2.** central. **3.** *Am., Colloq*. a hundred-dollar bill.

C., 1. Cape. **2.** Catholic. **3.** centigrade.

c., 1. carton; cartons. **2.** case. **3.** *Baseball*. catcher. **4.** cent; cents. **5.** center. **6.** centimeter. **7.** Also, **ca**, approximately. [L *circa* or *circum*] **8.** copyright. **9.** cubic.

Ca, *Chem*. calcium.

CAA, Civil Aeronautics Administration.

Caa·ba (kä′bə), *n*. Kaaba.

cab (kab), *n*. **1.** taxicab. **2.** carriage that can be hired, pulled by one horse. **3.** *Am*. the covered part of a locomotive where the engineer and fireman sit. **4.** an enclosed seat on a truck for the driver. [for *cabriolet*]

ca·bal (kə·bal′), *n., v.*, **-balled, -bal·ling.** —*n*. **1.** a small group of people working or plotting in secret. **2.** a secret scheme of such a group. —*v*. form such a group; conspire. [see CABALA] —Syn. *n*. **1.** faction, junto, conspiracy.

cab·a·la (kab′ə·lə; kə·bä′l-), *n*. **1.** a secret religious philosophy of the Jewish rabbis, based on a mystical interpretation of the Scriptures. **2.** a mystical belief. Also, **cabbala**. [< Med.L < Heb. *qabbalah* tradition] —**cab·a·lism** (kab′ə·liz·əm), *n*. —**cab′a·list**, *n*.

cab·a·lis·tic (kab′ə·lis′tik), **cab·a·lis·ti·cal** (-tə·kəl), *adj*. having a mystical meaning; secret. —**cab′a·lis′ti·cal·ly**, *adv*.

cab·al·le·ro (kab′əl·yâr′ō), *n., pl*. **-ros. 1.** *Am.*, W. gentleman or gallant. **2.** escort. [< Sp. < L *caballarius* horseman < *caballus* horse]

ca·ba·ña (kə·bä′nyə; -ban′ə), *n. Am., Orig. S.W.* **1.** cabin (def. 1). **2.** bathhouse. [< Sp. < LL *capanna*. Doublet of CABIN.]

cab·a·ret (kab′ə·rā′; kab′ə·rā), *n*. **1.** restaurant where an entertainment of singing and dancing is provided. **2.** the entertainment. [< F]

cab·bage (kab′ij), *n., v.*, **-baged, -bag·ing.** —*n*. vegetable whose leaves are closely folded into a round head that grows from a short stem. —*v*. form a head like a cabbage. [< F < Pr., ult. < L *caput* head]

cab·ba·la (kab′ə·lə; kə·bä′l-), *n*. cabala.

cab·by (kab′i), *n., pl*. **-bies.** *Colloq*. cabman.

cab·in (kab′ən), *n*. **1.** a small, roughly built house; hut. **2.** room in a ship. **3.** place for passengers in an airplane or airship. —*v*. **1.** live in a cabin. **2.** confine; cramp. [< F < LL *capanna*. Doublet of CABANA.] —Syn. *n*. **1.** shanty, shack.

cabin boy, boy whose work is waiting on the officers and passengers in a ship.

cab·i·net (kab′ə·nit), *n*. **1.** piece of furniture with shelves or drawers for holding dishes, etc. **2.** group of advisers chosen by the head of a nation to help him with the administration of the government. **3. the Cabinet,** *Am*. the cabinet of the President of the United States. **4.** a small, private room. —*adj*. **1.** of or having to do with a political cabinet. **2.** private. **3.** of such value, beauty, or size as to be suited for a private room or for keeping in a case. [< F < Ital. *gabinetto*, ult. < LL *cavea* CAGE]

cab·i·net·mak·er (kab′ə·nit·māk′ər), *n*. man who makes fine furniture and woodwork. —**cab′i·net-mak′ing**, *n*.

cab·i·net·work (kab′ə·nit·wėrk′), *n*. **1.** beautifully made furniture and woodwork. **2.** the making of such furniture and woodwork.

ca·ble (kā′bəl), *n., v.*, **-bled, -bling.** —*n*. **1.** a strong, thick rope, usually made of wires twisted together. **2.** cable's length. **3.** *Elect.* a protected bundle of wires to carry current. **4.** *Am*. cablegram. —*v*. **1.** tie or fasten with a cable. **2.** send a message under the ocean by cable. [< F < Pr. < L *capulum* halter]

Cable (def. 1)

cable car, *Am*. car pulled by a moving cable operated by a stationary engine.

ca·ble·gram (kā′bəl·gram), *n. Am*. telegram sent by cable.

cable's length, unit of measurement at sea, 720 ft. (U.S.); 607.56 ft. (British navy).

cab·man (kab′mən), *n., pl*. **-men.** a cab driver.

ca·boo·dle (kə·bü′dəl), *n. Am., Colloq*. group of people or things.

ca·boose (kə·bŭs′), *n.* **1.** *Am.* a small car on a freight train in which the trainmen can rest and sleep. **2.** kitchen on the deck of a ship. [< MLG *kabuse* cabin]

Cab·ot (kab′ət), *n.* **John,** 1450?–1498, Italian navigator who explored for England. He discovered the North American continent in 1497.

cab·ri·o·let (kab′ri·ə·lā′), *n.* **1.** automobile somewhat like a coupé, but having a folding top. **2.** a one-horse carriage with two wheels, and often with a folding top. [< F, < *cabrioler* leap < Ital. < L *caper* goat; from bouncing motion]

ca·ca·o (kə·kā′ō; -kā′ō), *n., pl.* **-ca·os. 1.** seeds from which cocoa and chocolate are made. **2.** the tropical American tree they grow on. [< Sp. < Mex. *caca-uatl*]

cach·a·lot (kash′ə·lot; -lō), *n.* sperm whale. [< F < Pg. < L *caccabus* pot]

cache (kash), *n., v.,* **cached, cach·ing. —n. 1.** a hiding place to store food or supplies. **2.** a hidden store of food or supplies. —*v.* put in a cache; hide. [< F, < *cacher* hide]

ca·chet (ka·shā′; kash′ā), *n.* **1.** a private seal or stamp. **2.** a distinguishing mark of quality or genuineness. [< F, < *cacher* hide]

cach·in·nate (kak′ə·nāt), *v.,* **-nat·ed, -nat·ing.** laugh loudly. [< L *cachinnatus*] —**cach′in·na′tion,** *n.*

ca·cique (kə·sēk′), *n.* **1.** a native chief in the West Indies, Mexico, etc. **2.** *Am., S.W.* a pompous political leader. [< Sp. < Haitian]

cack·le (kak′əl), *v.,* **-led, -ling,** *n.* —*v.* **1.** make a shrill, broken sound. **2.** laugh shrilly, harshly, and brokenly. **3.** chatter. —*n.* **1.** the shrill, broken sound that a hen makes after laying an egg. **2.** shrill, harsh, broken laughter. **3.** noisy chatter; silly talk. [ME *cakelen*; imit.]

ca·coph·o·ny (kə·kof′ə·ni), *n., pl.* **-nies.** harsh, clashing sound; dissonance; discord. [< NL < Gk., < *kakos* bad + *phone* sound] —**ca·coph′o·nous,** *adj.* —**ca·coph′o·nous·ly,** *adv.*

cac·tus (kak′təs), *n., pl.* **-tus·es, -ti** (-tī). plant whose thick, fleshy stems have spines but usually have no leaves. Most cactuses grow in very hot, dry regions. [< L < Gk. *kaktos*]

cad (kad), *n.* an ill-bred person. [< *caddie*]

ca·dav·er (kə·dav′ər; -dā′vər), *n.* dead body; corpse. [< L] —**ca·dav′er·ic,** *adj.*

Common cactus

ca·dav·er·ous (kə·dav′ər·əs), *adj.* **1.** of or like a cadaver. **2.** pale and ghastly. **3.** thin and worn. —**ca·dav′er·ous·ly,** *adv.* —**ca·dav′er·ous·ness,** *n.*

cad·die (kad′i), *n., v.,* **-died, -dy·ing.** —*n.* person who carries a golf player's clubs, etc. —*v.* help a golf player in this way. Also, **caddy.** [< F *cadet* CADET]

cad·dis fly (kad′is), a mothlike insect whose larvae (**caddis worms**) live under water in cocoons that are coated with sand, gravel, etc.

cad·dish (kad′ish), *adj.* ungentlemanly; illbred. —**cad′dish·ly,** *adv.* —**cad′dish·ness,** *n.*

cad·dy¹ (kad′i), *n., pl.* **-dies.** a small box, can, or chest. [< Malay *kati* a small weight]

cad·dy² (kad′i), *n., pl.* **-dies,** *v.,* **-died, -dy·ing.** caddie.

ca·dence (kā′dəns), **ca·den·cy** (-dən·si), *n., pl.* **-dences; -cies. 1.** rhythm. **2.** measure or beat of any rhythmical movement. **3.** fall of the voice. **4.** rising and falling sound; modulation. **5.** *Music.* series of chords, a trill, etc., that brings part of a piece of music to an end. [< F < Ital. See CADENZA.] —**ca′denced,** *adj.*

ca·den·za (kə·den′zə), *n. Music.* an elaborate flourish or showy passage near the end of an aria, concerto, etc. [< Ital. < L *cadentia* < *cadere* fall]

ca·det (kə·det′), *n.* **1.** a young man who is training to be an officer in the army or navy. **2.** a younger son or brother. [< F < Gascon *capdet* < L *capitellum,* dim. of *caput* head] —**ca·det′ship, ca·det·cy** (kə·det′si), *n.*

cadge (kaj), *v.,* **cadged, cadg·ing. 1.** *Dial.* peddle. **2.** *Colloq.* beg. —**cadg′er,** *n.*

ca·di (kä′di; kā′-), *n., pl.* **-dis.** a minor Mohammedan judge. Also, **kadi.** [< Ar. *qāḍī* judge]

Cá·diz (kə·diz′; kā′diz), *n.* seaport in SW Spain.

cad·mi·um (kad′mi·əm), *n. Chem.* a bluishwhite, ductile metallic element, Cd, resembling tin, used in making certain alloys. [< NL < L *cadmia* zinc ore < Gk. *kadmeia*] —**cad′mic,** *adj.*

Cad·mus (kad′məs), *n. Gk. Legend.* the founder of Thebes. —**Cad·me·an** (kad·mē′ən), *adj.*

ca·dre (kä′dər; *Mil.* kad′rē), *n.* **1.** framework. **2.** a permanent skeleton organization, esp. of officers of a military unit, that can be filled out as needed. [< F < Ital. < L *quadrum* square]

ca·du·ce·us (kə·dū′si·əs; -dū′-), *n., pl.* **-ce·i** (-sī·ī). staff carried by the god Hermes and by heralds in ancient Greece and Rome, now often used as an emblem of the medical profession. [< L < dial. Gk. *karykeion* herald's staff] —**ca·du′ce·an,** *adj.*

cae·cum (sē′kəm), *n., pl.* **-ca** (-kə). *Anat.* a cavity closed at one end, esp. the first part of the large intestine. [< L, blind (thing)] —**cae′cal,** *adj.*

Cae·sar (sē′zər), *n.* **1. Gaius Julius,** 102?–44 B.C., Roman general, statesman, and historian, conqueror of Gaul. **2.** a title of the Roman emperors from Augustus to Hadrian. **3.** an emperor. **4.** dictator; tyrant.

Cae·sar·e·an, Cae·sar·i·an (si·zâr′i·ən), *adj.* of Julius Caesar or the Caesars. —*n.* a Caesarean operation. Also, **Cesarean, Cesarian.**

Caesarean operation or **section,** operation by which a baby is removed from the uterus by cutting through the abdominal wall.

cae·si·um (sē′zi·əm), *n.* cesium.

cae·su·ra (si·zhŭr′ə; -zyŭr′ə), *n., pl.* **-sur·as, -sur·ae** (-zhŭr′ē; -zyŭr′ē). **1.** a break, esp. a sense pause, near the middle of a line in English poetry and in the middle of a foot in Greek and Latin poetry. **2.** a break. Also, **cesura.** [< L, cutting, < *caedere* cut] —**cae·sur′al,** *adj.*

ca·fé (ka·fā′; kə-), *n.* **1.** restaurant. **2.** coffee. **3.** *Am.* barroom. [< F. See COFFEE.]

caf·e·te·ri·a (kaf′ə·tir′i·ə), *n. Am.* restaurant where people wait on themselves. [< Mex. Sp., coffee shop]

caf·feine, caf·fein (kaf′ēn; kaf′i·in), *n.* a stimulating drug, $C_8H_{10}N_4O_2$, found in coffee and tea. [< F, < *café* coffee]

caf·tan (kaf′tən; kăf·tän′), *n.* a long tunic with a girdle, worn under the coat in Turkey, Egypt, etc. Also, **kaftan.** [< Turk.]

cage (kāj), *n., v.,* **caged, cag·ing.** —*n.* **1.** frame or place closed in with wires, bars, etc., for confining birds, wild animals, etc. **2.** thing shaped like a cage, as the closed platform of an elevator. **3.** prison. —*v.* put or keep in a cage. [< F < L *cavea* cell < *cavus* hollow]

cage·ling (kāj′ling), *n.* bird kept in a cage.

cage·y (kāj′i), *adj.* **cag·i·er, cag·i·est.** *Am., Slang.* shrewd; sharp. —**cag′i·ly,** *adv.* —**cag′i·ness,** *n.*

ca·hoot (kə·hüt′), *n., Am., Slang.* **1.** in cahoot or cahoots, in partnership, company or league. **2.** go cahoots, go into partnership.

cai·man (kā′mən), *n., pl.* **-mans.** cayman.

Cain (kān), *n.* **1.** the oldest son of Adam and Eve, who killed his brother Abel. **2.** murderer. **3. raise Cain,** *Am., Colloq.* make a great disturbance.

ca·ïque (kä·ēk′), *n.* a long, narrow Turkish rowboat, much used on the Bosporus.

cairn (kârn), *n.* pile of stones heaped up as a memorial, tomb, or landmark. [< Scotch Gaelic *carn* heap of stones] —**cairned** (kârnd), *adj.*

Cai·ro (kī′rō), *n.* capital of Egypt, in the NE part.

cais·son (kā′sən; -son), *n.* **1.** box for ammunition. **2.** wagon to carry ammunition. **3.** a watertight box or chamber in which men can work under water. **4.** a watertight float used in raising sunken ships. [< F, < *caisse* chest < L *capsa* box]

caisson disease, *Am.* the bends.

cai·tiff (kā'tif), *n.* a mean, bad person; coward. —*adj.* vile; cowardly; mean. [< OF < L *captivus* captive]

ca·jole (kə·jōl'), *v.*, **–joled, –jol·ing.** persuade by pleasant words, flattery, or false promises; coax. [< F *cajoler*] —**ca·jol'er,** *n.* —Syn. beguile.

ca·jol·er·y (kə·jōl'ər·i), *n., pl.* **–er·ies.** persuasion by smooth, deceitful words; flattery; coaxing.

cake (kāk), *n., v.,* **caked, cak·ing.** —*n.* 1. a baked mixture of flour, sugar, eggs, flavoring, and other things. 2. a flat, thin mass of dough baked or fried. 3. any small, flat mass of food fried on both sides: *a fish cake.* 4. a shaped mass: *a cake of soap.* —*v.* form into a solid mass. [prob. < Scand. *kaka*]

cakes and ale, pleasures of life.

cake·walk (kāk'wôk'), *Am. n.* a march or dance to music of American Negro origin, to see who could do the most graceful or eccentric steps. —*v.* do a cakewalk. —**cake'walk'er,** *n. Am.*

Cal., California.

cal·a·bash (kal'ə·bash), *n.* 1. gourd or fruit whose dried shell is used to make bottles, bowls, drums, rattles, etc. 2. a tropical plant or tree that it grows on. 3. bottle, bowl, etc., made from such a dried shell. [< F < Sp., prob. < Pers. *kharbuz* melon]

cal·a·boose (kal'ə·büs; kal'ə·büs'), *n. Am., Esp. Southern Colloq.* jail; prison. [< Sp. *calabozo* dungeon]

ca·la·di·um (kə·lā'di·əm), *n.* a tropical plant with large leaves. [< Malay *kelady*]

Cal·ais (ka·lā'; kal'ā), *n.* seaport in N France that is nearest England.

cal·a·mine (kal'ə·mīn; –min), *n.* native hydrous zinc silicate, $(ZnOH)_2SiO_3$. [< F < Med.L *calamina* < L *cadmia.* See CADMIUM.]

ca·lam·i·tous (kə·lam'ə·təs), *adj.* causing calamity; accompanied by calamity; disastrous. —**ca·lam'i·tous·ly,** *adv.* —**ca·lam'i·tous·ness,** *n.* —Syn. dire, deplorable, grievous.

ca·lam·i·ty (kə·lam'ə·ti), *n., pl.* **–ties.** 1. a great misfortune. 2. serious trouble; misery. [< L *calamitas*] —Syn. disaster, catastrophe.

cal·a·mus (kal'ə·məs), *n., pl.* **–mi** (–mī). 1. sweet flag. 2. its fragrant root. [< L < Gk. *kalamos* reed]

ca·lash (kə·lash'), *n.* 1. a light, low carriage that usually has a folding top. 2. a folding top or hood. 3. a kind of silk hood or bonnet formerly worn by women. [< F < Slavic]

Calash

cal·car·e·ous (kal·kãr'i·əs), *adj.* 1. of or containing lime or limestone. 2. of or containing calcium. [< L, < *calx* lime]

cal·ces (kal'sēz), *n.* pl. of **calx.**

cal·cif·er·ous (kal·sif'ər·əs), *adj. Chem.* containing calcite.

cal·ci·fy (kal'sə·fī), *v.,* **–fied, –fy·ing.** harden by the deposit of lime. [< L *calx* lime] —**cal'ci·fi·ca'tion,** *n.*

cal·ci·mine (kal'sə·mīn; –min), *n., v.,* **–mined, –min·ing.** —*n.* a white or colored liquid consisting of a mixture of water, coloring matter, glue, etc., used on ceilings and walls. —*v.* cover with calcimine. Also, **kalsomine.**

cal·cine (kal'sīn; –sin), *v.,* **–cined, –cin·ing.** 1. change to lime by heating. 2. burn to ashes or powder. —**cal·ci·na·tion** (kal'sə·nā'shən), *n.* —**cal·cin·a·to·ry** (kal·sin'ə·tô'ri; –tō'–; kal'sin–), *adj., n.*

cal·cite (kal'sīt), *n.* mineral composed of calcium carbonate, $CaCO_3$. It occurs as limestone, chalk, marble, etc.

cal·ci·um (kal'si·əm), *n. Chem.* a soft, silvery-white metallic element, Ca. It is a part of limestone, milk, bones, etc. [< L *calx* lime]

calcium carbide, *Chem.* a heavy gray substance, CaC_2, that reacts with water to form acetylene gas.

calcium carbonate, *Chem.* mineral, $CaCO_3$, occurring in rocks as marble and limestone and in animals as bones, shells, teeth, etc.

calcium chloride, *Chem.* compound of calcium and chlorine, $CaCl_2$, used in making artificial ice and chlorine.

cal·cu·la·ble (kal'kyə·lə·bəl), *adj.* 1. that can be calculated. 2. reliable. —**cal'cu·la·bly,** *adv.*

cal·cu·late (kal'kyə·lāt), *v.,* **–lat·ed, –lat·ing.** 1. find out by adding, subtracting, multiplying, or dividing; figure; compute. 2. find out beforehand by any process of reasoning; estimate. 3. *Am., Colloq.* rely; depend; count. 4. *Am., Colloq.* or *Dial.* plan; intend. 5. *Am., Colloq.* or *Dial.* think; believe; suppose. [< L, < *calculus* stone, used in counting, dim. of *calx* stone] —**cal'cu·la'tor,** *n.* ▶ **Calculate, guess,** and **reckon** are localisms for the *think, suppose, expect* of standard English.

calculated risk, venture or undertaking whose outcome can be estimated with some degree of confidence but not with certainty.

cal·cu·lat·ing (kal'kyə·lāt'ing), *adj.* 1. that calculates. 2. shrewd; careful. 3. scheming; selfish. —Syn. 2. crafty, astute.

cal·cu·la·tion (kal'kyə·lā'shən), *n.* 1. act of calculating. 2. result found by calculating. 3. careful thinking; deliberate planning. —**cal'cu·la'tive,** *adj.* —Syn. 3. forethought, prudence.

cal·cu·lus (kal'kyə·ləs), *n., pl.* **–li** (–lī), **–lus·es.** 1. a method of calculation in higher mathematics. 2. a stone that has formed in the body because of a diseased condition. Gallstones are calculi. [see CALCULATE]

Cal·cut·ta (kal·kut'ə), *n.* seaport in E India. Also, **cauldron.** [< OF < L *caldus* hot]

Cal·e·do·ni·a (kal'ə·dō'ni·ə), *n. Poetic.* Scotland. —**Cal'e·do'ni·an,** *adj.*

cal·en·dar (kal'ən·dər), *n.* 1. table showing the months, weeks, and days of the year. 2. system by which the beginning, length, and divisions of the year are fixed. 3. list; record; schedule: *a court calendar.* —*v.* enter in a calendar or list. [< AF < L *calendarium* account book < *calendae* calends (day bills were due).]

calendar day, the 24 hours from one midnight to the next midnight.

calendar month, month.

calendar year, period of 365 days (or in leap year, 366 days) that begins on January 1 and ends on December 31.

cal·en·der (kal'ən·dər), *n.* machine in which cloth, paper, etc., is smoothed and glazed by pressing between rollers. —*v.* make smooth and glossy by pressing in a calender. [< F < L < Gk. *kylindros* cylinder] —**cal'en·der·er,** *n.*

cal·ends (kal'əndz), *n.pl.* the first day of the month in the ancient Roman calendar. Also, **kalends.** [< L *calendae*]

ca·len·du·la (kə·len'jə·lə), *n.* kind of marigold with yellow or orange flowers. [< NL, dim. of *calendae* the calends]

calf¹ (kaf; käf), *n., pl.* **calves.** 1. a young cow or bull. 2. a young elephant, whale, seal, etc. 3. leather made from the skin of a calf. 4. *Colloq.* a silly boy. [OE *calf*]

calf² (kaf; käf), *n., pl.* **calves.** the thick, fleshy part of the back of the leg below the knee. [< Scand. *kālfi*]

calf·skin (kaf'skin'; käf'–), *n.* 1. skin of a calf. 2. leather made from it.

cal·i·ber, *esp. Brit.* **cal·i·bre** (kal'ə·bər), *n.* 1. diameter, esp. inside diameter. A .45-caliber revolver has a barrel with an inside diameter of 45/100 of an inch. 2. amount of ability. 3. amount of merit or importance. [< F < Ar. *qālib* mold]

cal·i·brate (kal'ə·brāt), *v.,* **–brat·ed, –brat·ing.** 1. determine, check, or rectify the scale of (a thermometer, gauge, or other measuring instrument). 2. find the caliber of. —**cal'i·bra'tion,** *n.* —**cal'i·bra'tor,** *n.*

cal·i·co (kal'ə·kō), *n., pl.* **–coes, –cos,** *adj.* —*n. Am.* a cotton cloth, usually with colored patterns printed on one side. —*adj.* 1. made of calico. 2. spotted in colors. [after *Calicut,* India]

Cal·i·cut (kal′ə·kut), *n.* seaport in SW India.

ca·lif (kā′lif; kal′if), *n.* caliph.

Calif., official abbreviation of California.

cal·if·ate (kal′ə·fāt; –fit; kā′lə–), *n.* caliphate.

Cal·i·for·nia (kal′ə·fôr′nyə; –fôr′ni·ə), *n.* 1. a Western State of the United States, on the Pacific coast. *Capital:* Sacramento. *Abbrev.:* Calif. 2. Gulf of, gulf east of Lower California. —Cal′i·for′nian, *adj., n.*

California poppy, *Am.* 1. a small poppy with finely divided leaves and colorful flowers. 2. its flower.

cal·i·for·ni·um (kal′ə·fôr′ni·əm), *n. Chem.* a radioactive element, Cf, produced by the bombardment of curium in the cyclotron at the University of California; the heaviest of known elements. [< *California*]

cal·i·per (kal′ə·pər), *n.* Usually, calipers. instrument used to measure the diameter or thickness of something. Also, **calliper**. [var. of *caliber*]

Calipers

ca·liph (kā′lif; kal′if), *n.* the head of a Moslem state. Also, **calif, khalif.** [< OF < Med.L < Ar. *khalīfa* successor, vicar]

cal·iph·ate (kal′ə·fāt; –fit; kā′lə–), *n.* rank, reign, government, or territory of a caliph. Also, califate.

cal·is·then·ic (kal′əs·then′ik), **cal·is·then·i·cal** (–ə·kəl), *adj.* of calisthenics. Also, **calisthenic, callisthenical.**

cal·is·then·ics (kal′əs·then′iks), *n.* 1. (*sing. in use*) the practice or art of calisthenic exercises. 2. (*pl. in use*) exercises to develop a strong and graceful body. Also, **callisthenics.** [< Gk. *kallos* beauty + *sthenos* strength]

calk[1] (kôk), *v.* fill up (a seam, crack, or joint) so that it will not leak; make watertight, as with oakum and tar. Also, **caulk.** [< OF < L *calcare* tread, press in] —calk′er, *n.*

calk[2] (kôk), *n.* 1. a projecting piece on a horseshoe to prevent slipping. 2. *Am.* a sharp, projecting piece of metal on the bottom of a shoe to prevent slipping. —*v.* put calks on. [< L *calx* heel or *calcar* spur] —calk′er, *n.*

call (kôl), *v.* 1. speak loudly; cry; shout: *he called from downstairs.* 2. (of a bird or animal) utter its cry. 3. signal: *the bugle called the men to assemble.* 4. rouse; waken: *call me in the morning.* 5. invite; command; summon: *obey when duty calls.* 6. ask to come; cause to come: *call off your dog, the assembly was called to order.* 7. get; bring: *call forth a reply.* 8. give a name to; term: *they called the baby John.* 9. consider; estimate: *they called the play a big hit.* 10. make a short visit or stop: *they called on us at home.* 11. read over: *the teacher called the roll.* 12. telephone (to). 13. demand payment of. 14. *Am.* demand for payment. 15. *Am.* demand a show of hands in poker. 16. *Am., Baseball.* a. declare (a game) ended: *the game was called on account of rain.* b. pronounce (a pitch) a strike or ball. 17. **call back,** a. recall. b. revoke. c. telephone to someone who has called previously. 18. **call down,** a. invoke. b. *Am., Colloq.* scold. 19. **call for,** go and get; stop and get. 20. **call off,** *Am.,* enumerate. 21. **call up,** a. bring to mind; bring back. b. telephone to. —*n.* 1. a shout; a cry. 2. the characteristic sound of a bird or other animal. 3. signal given by sound. 4. invitation; request; command; summons. 5. claim; demand: *a doctor is on call at all hours.* 6. need; occasion: *you have no call to meddle.* 7. a short visit or stop. 8. *Am.* demand for payment. 9. act of calling. 10. **on call,** *Am.* a. subject to payment on demand. b. ready. [OE. Cf. West Saxon *ceallian.*] —call′a·ble, *adj.* —Syn. *v.* 1. yell, shriek, scream. 5. bid. 8. designate.

cal·la (kal′ə), *n.* 1. Also, **calla lily.** plant with a large, petallike, white leaf around a thick spike of yellow florets. 2. a marsh plant with heart-shaped leaves. [< NL]

call·boy (kôl′boi′), *n.* 1. bellboy in a hotel, ship, etc. 2. boy who calls actors when they are supposed to go on the stage.

call·er (kôl′ər), *n.* 1. person who makes a short visit. 2. person who calls.

cal·lig·ra·phy (kə·lig′rə·fi), *n.* 1. handwriting. 2. beautiful handwriting. [< Gk., < *kallos* beauty + *graphein* write] —cal·lig′ra·pher, *n.* —cal·li·graph·ic (kal′ə·graf′ik), *adj.*

call·ing (kôl′ing), *n.* 1. business; occupation; profession. 2. invitation; command; summons.

calling card, *Am.* a small card with a person's name on it. It is used when visiting someone, to acknowledge gifts, etc.

cal·li·o·pe (kə·lī′ə·pē; *for 1, also* kal′i·ōp), *n.* 1. *Am.* musical instrument having a series of steam whistles played by pushing keys. 2. Calliope, the Muse of eloquence and heroic poetry. [< L < Gk. *kalliope* beautiful-voiced < *kallos* beauty + *ops* voice]

cal·li·per (kal′ə·pər), *n.* caliper.

cal·lis·then·ic (kal′əs·then′ik), **cal·lis·then·i·cal** (–ə·kəl), *adj.* calisthenic.

cal·lis·then·ics (kal′əs·then′iks), *n.* calisthenics.

call loan, *Am.* loan repayable on demand.

call money, money borrowed that must be paid back on demand.

cal·los·i·ty (kə·los′ə·ti), *n., pl.* –ties. 1. a hard thickening of the skin; callus. 2. lack of feeling; hardness of heart.

cal·lous (kal′əs), *adj.* 1. hard; hardened, as portions of the skin exposed to friction. 2. unfeeling; not sensitive. [< L, < *callus* hard skin] —cal′lous·ly, *adv.* —cal′lous·ness, *n.* —Syn. 2. insensible, unsusceptible. —Ant. 2. sensitive.

cal·low (kal′ō), *adj.* 1. young and inexperienced. 2. not fully developed. 3. (of birds) without feathers sufficiently developed for flight. [OE *calu* bald] —cal′low·ness, *n.* —Syn. 1. green.

cal·lus (kal′əs), *n., pl.* –lus·es. 1. a hard, thickened place on the skin. 2. a new growth to unite the ends of a broken bone. [see CALLOUS]

calm (käm), *adj.* 1. not stormy or windy; quiet; still; not moving. 2. peaceful; not excited. —*n.* 1. absence of motion or wind; quietness; stillness. 2. absence of excitement; peacefulness. —*v.* make or become calm. [< OF < Ital. < VL < Gk. *kauma* heat of the day; hence, time for rest, stillness] —calm′ly, *adv.* —calm′ness, *n.* —Syn. *adj.* 1. motionless, smooth, placid. 2. undisturbed, composed. —Ant. *adj.* 1. stormy. 2. excited.

cal·o·mel (kal′ə·mel; –məl), *n.* mercurous chloride, Hg_2Cl_2, a white, tasteless, crystalline powder, used in medicine as a cathartic, etc.

ca·lor·ic (kə·lôr′ik; –lor′–), *n.* heat. —*adj.* having to do with heat. —ca·lor·ic·i·ty (kal′ə·ris′ə·ti), *n.*

cal·o·rie, cal·o·ry (kal′ə·ri), *n., pl.* –ries. 1. *Physics.* unit of heat. The quantity of heat necessary to raise the temperature of a gram of water one degree centigrade is a small calorie. The quantity of heat necessary to raise the temperature of a kilogram of water one degree centigrade is a large calorie. 2. *Physiol.* a. unit of the energy supplied by food. It corresponds to a large calorie. An ounce of sugar will produce about a hundred such calories. b. quantity of food capable of producing such an amount of energy. [< F < L *calor* heat]

cal·o·rif·ic (kal′ə·rif′ik), *adj.* producing heat.

cal·o·rim·e·ter (kal′ə·rim′ə·tər), *n. Physics.* apparatus for measuring the quantity of heat.

cal·o·rim·e·try (kal′ə·rim′ə·tri), *n.* measurement of heat. —cal·o·ri·met·ric (kal′ə·rə·met′rik; kə·lôr′–; –lor′–), cal′o·ri·met′ri·cal, *adj.*

cal·u·met (kal′yə·met; kal′yə·met′), *n. Am.* a long, ornamented tobacco pipe smoked by the American Indians in ceremonies as a symbol of peace. [< F, ult. < L *calamus* < Gk. *kalamos* reed]

ca·lum·ni·ate (kə·lum′ni·āt), *v.,* –at·ed, –at·ing. say false and injurious things about; slander. —ca·lum′ni·a′tor, *n.*

ca·lum·ni·a·tion (kə·lum′ni·ā′shən), *n.* slander; calumny.

ca·lum·ni·ous (kə·lum′ni·əs), *adj.* slanderous. —ca·lum′ni·ous·ly, *adv.*

cal·um·ny (kal′əm·ni), *n., pl.* –nies. false statement made to injure someone's reputation; slander. [< L *calumnia*] —Syn. defamation.

Cal·va·ry (kal′və·ri), *n.* place near Jerusalem where Jesus died on the cross. Luke 23:33. [< L *calvaria* skull, trans. of Aram. *Gogoltha* Golgotha]

calve (kav; käv), *v.*, **calved, calv·ing.** give birth to a calf. [OE *calfian* < *calf* calf¹]

calves (kavz; kävz), *n.* pl. of calf¹ and calf².

Cal·vin (kal′vən), *n.* **John,** 1509–1564, French Protestant religious leader at Geneva.

Cal·vin·ism (kal′vən·iz·əm), *n.* religious teachings of Calvin and his followers. —**Cal′vin·ist,** *n.* —**Cal′vin·is′tic, Cal′vin·is′ti·cal,** *adj.*

calx (kalks), *n.*, *pl.* **calx·es, cal·ces** (kal′sēz). an ashy substance left after a metal or a mineral has been thoroughly roasted, burned, etc. [< L *calx* lime]

Cal·y·don (kal′ə·don), *n.* ancient city in W Greece. —**Cal·y·do·ni·an** (kal′ə·dō′ni·ən), *adj.*

Ca·lyp·so (kə·lip′sō), *n. Gk. Legend.* sea nymph who detained Odysseus on her island for seven years.

ca·lyp·so (kə·lip′sō), *n.* a type of improvised song that originated in the British West Indies.

ca·lyx (kā′liks; kal′iks), *n.*, *pl.* **ca·lyx·es, cal·y·ces** (kal′ə·sēz; kā′lə–). 1. *Bot.* the outer part of a flower that is a holder for the petals; the sepals. 2. *Anat., Zool.* a cuplike part. [< L < Gk. *kalyx* covering]

cam (kam), *n.* projection on a wheel or shaft that changes a regular circular motion into an irregular circular motion or into a back-and-forth motion. [< Du. *kam* cog, comb]

Cam: A, plunger down; B, plunger up.

ca·ma·ra·de·rie (kä′mə·rä′də·ri), *n.* comradeship. [< F. See COMRADE.]

cam·a·ril·la (kam′ə·ril′ə), *n.* cabal; clique. [< Sp., dim. of *cámara* chamber]

cam·ass, cam·as (kam′as), *n. Am.* plant of the lily family growing in the W United States. [< Am. Ind.]

cam·ber (kam′bər), *v.* arch slightly. —*n.* 1. a slight arch. 2. a slightly arching piece of timber. 3. the rise and fall of the curve of an airfoil. [< F *cambre* bent < L *camur* crooked]

cam·bi·um (kam′bi·əm), *n. Bot.* layer of soft, growing tissue between the bark and the wood of trees and shrubs. [< LL *cambium* exchange]

Cam·bo·di·a (kam·bō′di·ə), *n.* country in SE Asia, formerly under French influence.

Cam·bri·a (kam′bri·ə), *n.* old name of Wales.

Cam·bri·an (kam′bri·ən), *adj.* 1. Welsh. 2. having to do with an early geological period or group of rocks. —*n.* 1. Welshman. 2. an early geological period or group of rocks.

cam·bric (kām′brik), *n.* a fine, thin linen or cotton cloth. [after *Cambrai,* France]

cambric tea, *Am.* drink made of hot water, milk, sugar, and sometimes a little tea.

Cam·bridge (kām′brij), *n.* 1. city in SE England. 2. city in E Massachusetts, near Boston.

Cam·den (kam′dən), *n.* city in SW New Jersey.

came (kām), *v.* pt. of come.

cam·el (kam′əl), *n.* large animal with one or two humps on its back, used as a beast of burden. The Arabian camel, or dromedary, has one hump; the Bactrian camel of southern Asia has two humps. [< L < Gk. *kamelos* < Semitic]

ca·mel·lia (kə·mēl′yə; –mēl′li·ə), *n.* 1. shrub or tree with glossy leaves and waxy white or red flowers shaped like roses. 2. the flower. [for G. J. *Kamel,* missionary in Luzon]

ca·mel·o·pard (kə·mel′ə·pärd), *n.* a giraffe.

Cam·e·lot (kam′ə·lot), *n.* a legendary place in England where King Arthur had his palace.

camel's hair, 1. hair of a camel, used in making cloth, paintbrushes, etc. 2. cloth made of this hair or something like it.

Cam·em·bert (kam′əm·bâr), *n.* a rich, soft cheese.

cam·e·o (kam′i·ō), *n.*, *pl.* **–e·os.** a precious or semiprecious stone carved so that there is a raised part on a background. [< Ital.]

cam·er·a (kam′ər·ə), *n.*, *pl.* **–er·as** for 1, **–er·ae** (–ər·ē) for 2. 1. an apparatus in which photographic film or plates are exposed, the image being formed by means of a lens. 2. *Television.* part of the transmitter which converts images into electronic impulses for transmitting. 3. a judge's private office. 4. **in camera, a.** in a judge's private office. **b.** privately. [< L, arched chamber, arch < Gk. *kamara.* Doublet of CHAMBER.]

Cameo

cam·er·a·man (kam′ər·ə·man′; kam′rə–), *n.*, *pl.* **–men.** man who operates a camera, esp. a motion-picture camera.

Cam·er·oon (kam′ər·ün′), *n.* country in W Africa, including the former Cameroun and the S portion of the former Cameroons. Also, **Cameroun.**

Cam·er·oons (kam′ər·ünz′), *n.* former British trust territory, divided between Cameroon and Nigeria in 1961.

Cam·er·oun (kam′ər·ün′), *n.* 1. Cameroon. 2. former French trust territory now included in Cameroon.

cam·i·sole (kam′ə·sōl), *n.* 1. a woman's underwaist. 2. a loose jacket worn by women as a dressing gown. 3. a kind of strait jacket. [< F < Sp., < *camisa* shirt; akin to CHEMISE]

cam·o·mile (kam′ə·mīl), *n.* plant of the aster family with daisylike flowers. Its flowers and leaves are sometimes dried and used in medicine. Also, **chamomile.** [< L < Gk. *chamaimēlon* earth apple]

Ca·mor·ra (kə·môr′ə; –mor′ə), *n.* 1. a powerful secret political society formed in Naples, Italy, about 1820 that later was associated with blackmail, robbery, etc. 2. camorra, a similar secret society. —**Ca·mor′rist,** *n.*

cam·ou·flage (kam′ə·fläzh), *n.*, *v.*, **–flaged, –flag·ing.** —*n.* 1. disguise; deception. 2. in warfare, giving things a false appearance to deceive the enemy. —*v.* give a false appearance to in order to conceal; disguise. [< F, < *camoufler* disguise] —**cam′ou·flag′er,** *n.*

camp (kamp), *n.* 1. group of tents, huts, or other shelters where people live for a time. 2. a place where a camp is. 3. people living in a camp. 4. *Am.* one or more buildings, usually near a lake or in the woods, forming a temporary residence, esp. in summer. 5. living an outdoor life with very simple shelter; camping. 6. group of people who agree or work together. 7. military life. —*v.* 1. make a camp. 2. live in a camp for a time. 3. live simply without comforts for a time. 4. **camp out,** *Am.* **a.** spend the night outdoors. **b.** live in the open in a tent or camp. [< F < Ital. < L *campus* field] —**camp′er,** *n.*

cam·paign (kam·pān′), *n.* 1. series of related military operations for some special purpose. 2. series of connected activities to do or get something; planned course of action for some special purpose: *a campaign to raise money.* 3. *Am.* organized action in influencing voters in an election: *a political campaign.* —*v.* 1. take part in or serve in a campaign. 2. *Am.* conduct a political campaign. [< F *campagne* open country, ult. < L *campus* field] —**cam·paign′er,** *n.*

cam·pa·ni·le (kam′pə·nē′lē), *n.*, *pl.* **–ni·les, –ni·li** (–nē′lē). a bell tower. [< Ital., ult. < LL *campana* bell]

cam·pan·u·la (kam·pan′yə·lə), *n.* bluebell, Canterbury bell, or other similar plant with bell-shaped flowers. [< LL, dim. of *campana* bell]

camp chair, a lightweight, folding chair.

camp·fire (kamp′fīr′), *n.* 1. fire in a camp for warmth or cooking. 2. social gathering of soldiers, scouts, etc.

camp·ground (kamp′ground′), *n. Am.* 1. place where a camp is. 2. place where a camp meeting is held.

cam·phor (kam′fər), *n.* 1. a white, crystalline substance with a strong odor and a bitter taste, $C_{10}H_{16}O$, used in medicine, to protect clothes from moths, in the manufacture of celluloid, etc.

āge, câre, fär; ēqual, tėrm; īce; ōpen, ôrder; pùt, rüle, ūse; th, then; ə=a in about.

2. *Am.* camphor in alcohol; spirits of camphor. [< Med.L < Ar., ult. < Malay *kapur*] —**cam·phor·ic** (kam·fôr'ik; -for'-), *adj.*

cam·phor·ate (kam'fər·āt), *v.*, **-at·ed, -at·ing.** impregnate with camphor. —**cam'phor·at'ed,** *adj.*

camphor ball, a small ball made of camphor, naphthalene, etc., used to keep moths out of clothes, furniture, etc.

cam·pi·on (kam'pi·ən), *n.* plant with red or white flowers of the same family as the pink. [< L *campus* field]

camp meeting, *Am.* religious meeting held outdoors or in a tent, usually lasting several days.

camp·stool (kamp'stül'), *n.* a lightweight, folding seat.

cam·pus (kam'pəs), *n. Am.* grounds of a college, university, or school. [< L, field, plain]

can[1] (kan; *unstressed* kən), *v., pres. sing.* 1 **can,** 2 **can** or (*Archaic*) **canst,** 3 **can;** *pt.* **could.** 1. be able to. 2. know how to. 3. have the right to. 4. *Colloq.* be allowed to. 5. feel inclined to. [OE *can(n)* know, know how, can] ➤ **can, may.** 1. In formal English careful distinction is kept between the auxiliary *can* when it has the meaning of ability, "being able to," and *may,* with the meaning of permission: *You may go now. He can walk with crutches. You may if you can. May* also indicates possibility: *He may have been the one.* 2. In informal and colloquial English *may* occurs rather rarely except in the sense of possibility: *It may be all right for her, but not for me. Can* is generally used for both permission and ability: *Can I go now? You can if you want to. I can go 80 miles an hour with my car.* This is in such general usage that it should be regarded as good English in speaking and in informal writing.

can[2] (kan), *n., v.,* **canned, can·ning.** —*n.* 1. *Am.* a metal container: *a milk can.* 2. contents of a can. 3. drinking cup. 4. *Am.* a glass jar for canning at home. —*v.* 1. *Am.* preserve by putting in airtight cans or jars. 2. *Am., Slang.* dismiss from a job. [OE *canne*]

Can., Canada; Canadian.

Ca·naan (kā'nən), *n.* 1. region in Palestine between the Jordan River and the Mediterranean. 2. land of promise.

Ca·naan·ite (kā'nən·īt), *n.* inhabitant of Canaan before its conquest by the Hebrews.

Can·a·da (kan'ə·də), *n.* a British dominion, north of the United States.

Canada goose, the common wild goose of North America.

Ca·na·di·an (kə·nā'di·ən), *adj.* of Canada or its people. —*n.* native or inhabitant of Canada.

ca·naille (kə·nāl'; ka·nī'), *n.* rabble; riffraff. [< F < Ital. *canaglia,* ult. < L *canis* dog]

ca·nal (kə·nal'), *n., v.,* **-nalled, -nal·ling; -naled, -nal·ing.** —*n.* 1. waterway dug across land for navigation. 2. tube in the body or in a plant for carrying food, liquid, or air. 3. *Am., S.W.* a large irrigation ditch. 4. *Am.* a long arm of a large body of water. —*v.* 1. *Am.* make a canal through. 2. furnish with canals. [< L *canalis* trench, pipe. Doublet of CHANNEL.]

canal boat, a long, narrow boat used on canals.

ca·nal·i·za·tion (kə·nal'ə·zā'shən; kan'ə·lə-), *n.* 1. act of canalizing. 2. system of canals.

ca·nal·ize (kə·nal'īz; kan'ə·līz), *v.,* **-ized, -iz·ing.** 1. make a canal or canals through. 2. make into or like a canal.

Canal Zone, *Am.* Panama Canal and the land five miles on each side, governed by the U.S.

can·a·pé (kan'ə·pā; -pē), *n.* a cracker, thin piece of bread, etc., spread with a seasoned mixture of fish, cheese, etc. [< F, orig., a couch covered with mosquito netting. See CANOPY.]

ca·nard (kə·närd'), *n.* a false rumor; exaggerated report; hoax. [< F *canard* duck]

Ca·nar·ies (kə·när'iz), or **Canary Islands,** *n.pl.* group of Spanish islands in the Atlantic.

ca·nar·y (kə·när'i), *n., pl.* **-nar·ies.** 1. Also, **canary bird.** small, yellow songbird. Canaries

are often kept in cages. 2. Also, **canary yellow.** light yellow. 3. wine from the Canary Islands. —*adj.* light-yellow. [after the islands]

ca·nas·ta (kə·nas'tə), *n.* a card game.

Can·ber·ra (kan'ber·ə; -bər·ə), *n.* capital of Australia, in the SE part.

can·can (kan'kan), *n.* a dance by women marked by extravagant kicking. [< F]

can·cel (kan'səl), *v.,* **-celed, -cel·ing;** *esp. Brit.* **-celled, -cel·ling,** *n.* —*v.* 1. cross out; mark (something) so that it cannot be used. 2. cross out the same factor from the numerator and denominator of a fraction, or from the two sides of an equation. 3. do away with; abolish: *he canceled his order.* 4. make up for; balance. —*n.* 1. a canceling. 2. a canceled part. [< L *cancellare* cross out with latticed lines < *cancelli* cross bars] —**can'cel·a·ble,** *esp. Brit.* **can'cel·la·ble,** *adj.* —**can'cel·er,** *esp. Brit.* **can'cel·ler,** *n.* —Syn. *v.* 3. annul, nullify, revoke.

can·cel·la·tion (kan'sə·lā'shən), *n.* 1. a canceling or being canceled. 2. marks made when something is canceled or crossed out.

can·cer (kan'sər), *n.* 1. very harmful growth in the body; malignant tumor. Cancer tends to spread and destroy the healthy tissues and organs of the body. 2. evil or harmful thing that tends to spread. 3. **Cancer,** a. tropic of Cancer. b. a northern constellation that was thought of as arranged in the shape of a crab. c. the fourth sign of the zodiac. [< L *cancer* crab, tumor] —**can'cer·ous,** *adj.*

can·cer·o·gen·ic (kan'sər·ə·jen'ik), *adj.* carcinogenic.

can·de·la·bra (kan'də·lä'brə; -lä'-), *n.* 1. pl. of candelabrum. 2. (*pl. but taken as sing. with pl.* -bras) candelabrum.

can·de·la·brum (kan'də·lä'brəm; -lä'-), *n., pl.* **-bra** (-brə) or **-brums.** an ornamental candlestick with several branches for candles. [< L, < *candela* candle]

Candelabrum

can·des·cent (kan·des'ənt), *adj.* glowing with heat; incandescent. [< L *candescens* beginning to glow] —**can·des'cence,** *n.* —**can·des'cent·ly,** *adv.*

can·did (kan'did), *adj.* 1. frank; sincere. 2. fair; impartial. 3. *Obs.* white. 4. clear; pure. [< L *candidus* white] —**can'did·ly,** *adv.* —**can'did·ness,** *n.* —Syn. 1. truthful, straightforward.

can·di·da·cy (kan'də·də·si), *n.* being a candidate: *please support my candidacy for treasurer.*

can·di·date (kan'də·dāt; -dit), *n.* person who seeks, or is proposed for, some office or honor. [< L *candidatus* clothed in white (toga)] —**can'di·date·ship',** *n.*

can·di·da·ture (kan'də·də·chər; -dā'chər), *n. Brit.* candidacy.

candid camera, small camera with a fast lens for photographing persons unposed and often unaware.

can·died (kan'did), *adj.* 1. turned into sugar: *candied honey.* 2. cooked in sugar; covered with sugar. 3. made sweet or agreeable.

can·dle (kan'dəl), *n., v.,* **-dled, -dling.** —*n.* 1. stick of wax or tallow with a wick in it, burned to give light. 2. anything shaped or used like a candle. 3. unit for measuring the strength of a light. 4. **burn the candle at both ends,** use up one's strength and resources rapidly. 5. **not hold a candle to,** not compare with. —*v.* test (eggs) for freshness by holding them in front of a light. [< L *candela* < *candere* shine] —**can'dler,** *n.*

can·dle·ber·ry (kan'dəl·ber'i), *n., pl.* **-ries.** *Am.* 1. wax myrtle or bayberry. 2. its fruit.

can·dle·fish (kan'dəl·fish'), *n. Am.* an edible fish of the northwestern coast of America.

can·dle·light (kan'dəl·līt'), *n.* 1. light of a candle or candles. 2. time when candles are lighted; dusk; twilight; nightfall.

Can·dle·mas (kan'dəl·məs), *n.* February 2, a church festival in honor of the purification of the Virgin Mary. [OE *candelmæsse*]

candle power, light given by a standard candle, used as a unit for measuring light.

can·dle·stick (kan′dəl·stik′), **can·dle-hold·er** (-hōl′dər), *n.* holder for a candle, to make it stand up straight.

can·dor, *esp. Brit.* **can·dour** (kan′dər), *n.* 1. speaking openly what one really thinks; honesty in giving one's view or opinion. 2. fairness; impartiality. [< L, whiteness, purity < *candere* shine] —Syn. 1. frankness, sincerity.

can·dy (kan′di), *n., pl.* **-dies,** *v.,* **-died, -dy·ing.** —*n.* 1. sugar or syrup, cooked and flavored, then cooled and made into small pieces for eating. Chocolate, butter, milk, nuts, fruits, etc., are often added. 2. piece of this. —*v.* 1. turn into sugar. 2. cook in sugar; preserve by boiling in sugar. 3. make sweet or agreeable. [< F < Pers. *qand* sugar] —Syn. *n.* 1. confection, bonbon.

can·dy·tuft (kan′di·tuft′), *n.* plant with clusters of white, purple, or pink flowers.

cane (kān), *n., v.,* **caned, can·ing.** —*n.* 1. stick to help a person in walking; walking stick. 2. stick used to beat with. 3. a long, jointed stem, such as that of the bamboo. 4. plant having such stems. Sugar cane and bamboo are canes. 5. material made of such stems, used for furniture, chair seats, etc. 6. a slender stalk or stem. —*v.* 1. beat with a cane. 2. make or provide with cane. [< F < L. *kanna* reed]

cane·brake (kān′brāk′), *n. Am., Southern.* thicket or region of cane plants.

cane sugar, sugar made from sugar cane.

ca·nine (kā′nīn), *n.* 1. dog. 2. canine tooth. —*adj.* 1. of a dog; like a dog. 2. belonging to a group of meat-eating animals including dogs, foxes, and wolves. [< L, < *canis* dog]

canine tooth, one of the four pointed teeth next to the incisors.

Ca·nis Ma·jor (kā′nis mā′jər), group of stars SE of Orion that contains Sirius, the brightest of the stars.

Ca·nis Mi·nor (kā′nis mī′nər), group of stars SE of Orion, separated from Canis Major by the Milky Way.

can·is·ter (kan′is·tər), *n.* 1. a small box or can. 2. can filled with bullets that is shot from a cannon. [< L < Gk. *kanastron* basket]

can·ker (kang′kər), *n.* 1. a spreading sore, esp. one in the mouth. 2. disease of plants that causes slow decay. 3. anything that causes decay, rotting, or gradual eating away. —*v.* 1. infect or be infected with canker. 2. become malignant; decay. [< L *cancer* crab, gangrene]

can·ker·worm (kang′kər·wèrm′), *n. Am.* caterpillar that eats away the leaves of trees and plants.

can·na (kan′ə), *n.* 1. plant with large, pointed leaves and large, red, pink, or yellow flowers. 2. the flower. [< L, reed. See CANE.]

canned (kand), *adj. Am.* 1. put up and sealed for preservation. 2. *Slang.* recorded, as music.

can·nel (kan′əl), or **cannel coal,** *n.* soft coal in large lumps that burns with a bright flame. [appar. var. of *candle*]

can·ner (kan′ər), *n. Am.* person who cans food.

can·ner·y (kan′ər·i), *n., pl.* **-ner·ies.** *Am.* factory where meat, fish, fruit, vegetables, etc., are canned.

can·ni·bal (kan′ə·bəl), *n.* 1. person who eats human flesh. 2. animal that eats others of its own kind. —*adj.* of or like cannibals. [< Sp. *Caníbal* < *Caribe* Carib]

can·ni·bal·ism (kan′ə·bəl·iz′əm), *n.* practice of eating the flesh of one's own kind. —**can′ni·bal·is′tic,** *adj.* —**can′ni·bal·is′ti·cal·ly,** *adv.*

can·ni·bal·ize (kan′ə·bəl·īz), *v.,* **-ized, -iz·ing.** 1. assemble or repair (a vehicle, piece of machinery, etc.) by using parts from others which are useless as a whole. 2. take usable parts from (a vehicle, piece of machinery, etc.) to assemble or repair another.

can·ni·kin (kan′ə·kin), *n.* a small can; cup. [< *can²* + *-kin*]

can·ning (kan′ing), *n. Am.* the process or business of preserving food by putting it in air-tight cans or jars.

can·non (kan′ən), *n., pl.* **-nons** or (*esp. collectively*) **-non,** *v.* —*n.* 1. big mounted gun or

guns. 2. *Zool.* cannon bone. 3. the part of a bit that goes inside a horse's mouth; a smooth round bit. 4. *Brit.* carom. —*v.* 1. discharge cannon. 2. strike and rebound. 3. collide violently. 4. *Brit.* make a carom. [< F *canon* < Ital. < L < Gk. *kanna* reed]

can·non·ade (kan′ən·ād′), *n., v.,* **-ad·ed, -ad·ing.** —*n.* continued firing of cannons. —*v.* attack with cannons.

cannon ball, a large, iron or steel ball, formerly fired from cannons.

cannon bone, *Zool.* bone between the hock and fetlock.

can·non·eer (kan′ən·ir′), *n.* gunner.

can·non·ry (kan′ən·ri), *n., pl.* **-ries.** 1. continuous firing of cannons. 2. artillery.

can·not (kan′ot; kə·not′; kə-), *v.* can not.

can·ny (kan′i), *adj.,* **-ni·er, -ni·est.** *Scot.* 1. shrewd; cautious. 2. thrifty. [< *can¹*] —**can′ni·ly,** *adv.* —**can′ni·ness,** *n.*

ca·noe (kə·nü′), *n., v.,* **ca·noed, ca·noe·ing.** —*n.* light boat moved with paddles. —*v. Am.* paddle a canoe; go in a canoe. [< F < Sp. < Carib *kanoa*] —**ca·noe′ing,** *n. Am.*

can·on¹ (kan′ən), *n.* 1. law of a church; body of church law. 2. rule by which a thing is judged. 3. the official list of the books contained in the Bible; books of the Bible accepted by the church. 4. list of saints. 5. an official list. 6. part of the Mass coming after the offertory. 7. *Music.* a kind of composition in which the different participants begin the same melody one after another at regular intervals. [< L < Gk. *kanon*]

can·on² (kan′ən), *n.* 1. *Esp. Brit.* member of a group of clergymen belonging to a cathedral or collegiate church. 2. *Rom. Cath. Ch.* member of a group of clergymen living according to a certain rule. [< OF < L *canonicus* canonical < *canon* canon¹]

ca·ñon (kan′yən), *n. Am., S.W.* canyon.

ca·non·i·cal (kə·non′ə·kəl), *adj.* Also, **ca·non′ic.** 1. according to or prescribed by the laws of a church. 2. in the canon of the Bible. 3. authorized; accepted. —*n.* **canonicals,** clothes worn by a clergyman at a church service. —**ca·non′i·cal·ly,** *adv.* —**ca·non′i·cal·ness,** *n.*

canonical hours, the seven periods of the day for prayer and worship.

can·on·ize (kan′ən·īz), *v.,* **-ized, -iz·ing.** 1. declare (a dead person) to be a saint; place in the official list of the saints. 2. treat as a saint; glorify. 3. make or recognize as canonical. 4. authorize. —**can′on·i·za′tion,** *n.*

canon law, laws of a church governing ecclesiastical affairs.

can·on·ry (kan′ən·ri), *n., pl.* **-ries.** office or benefice of a canon.

can·o·py (kan′ə·pi), *n., pl.* **-pies,** *v.,* **-pied, -py·ing.** —*n.* 1. a covering fixed over a bed, throne, entrance, etc., or held over a person. 2. a rooflike covering; shelter; shade. 3. sky. —*v.* cover with a canopy. [< F < L < Gk. *konopeion* mosquito net < *konops* gnat]

canst (kanst), *v. Archaic.* 2nd pers. sing. present of can.

cant¹ (kant), *n.* 1. insincere talk; moral and religious statements that many people make, but few really believe or follow out. 2. whining or singsong speech like that of beggars. 3. peculiar language of a special group, using many strange words: *thieves' cant.* —*adj.* peculiar to a special group. —*v.* use cant. [< L *cantus* song]

cant² (kant), *n., v.* 1. slant; slope; bevel. 2. tip; tilt. 3. pitch; toss; throw with a sudden jerk. [prob. < MDu., MLG < OF < L *cant(h)us* corner, side < Celtic]

can't (kant; känt), cannot. ❯ **can't, mayn't.** *Can't* almost universally takes the place of the awkward *mayn't: Can't I go now?* ❯ **can't help (but).** This idiom illustrates differences between various levels of usage: Formal: *I cannot but feel sorry for him.* Informal: *I can't help feeling sorry for him.* Familiar, substandard: *I can't* *help but feel* sorry for him. The last is so commonly used in speaking and writing that perhaps it should be regarded as good English.

can·ta·bi·le (kän·tä′bi·lā), *Music.* —*adj.* in a smooth and flowing style; songlike. —*n.* a cantabile style, passage, or piece. [< Ital. < L *cantare* sing]

can·ta·loupe, can·ta·loup (kan′tə·lōp), *n.* a sweet, juicy melon with a hard, rough rind; muskmelon. [< F < Ital. *Cantalupo* place where first cultivated]

can·tan·ker·ous (kan·tang′kər·əs), *adj.* hard to get along with because ready to make trouble and oppose anything suggested; ill-natured. —**can·tan′ker·ous·ly,** *adv.* —**can·tan′ker·ous·ness,** *n.*

can·ta·ta (kan·tä′tə), *n.* story or play set to music to be sung by a chorus, but not acted. [< Ital. < L *cantare* sing]

can·teen (kan·tēn′), *n.* **1.** a small container for carrying water or other drinks. **2.** a military store where food, drinks, etc., are sold to soldiers and sailors. **3.** box of cooking utensils for use in camp. [< F < Ital. *cantina* cellar < LL *canthus* side]

Canteen

can·ter (kan′tər), *n.* gentle gallop. —*v.* gallop gently. [for *Canterbury gallop,* pace of pilgrims to Canterbury]

Can·ter·bur·y (kan′tər·ber′i), *n.* city in SE England.

Canterbury bell, plant with tall stalks of bell-shaped flowers, usually purplish-blue or white.

cant hook, *U.S.* pole with a movable hook at one end, used to grip and turn over logs.

can·ti·cle (kan′tə·kəl), *n.* a short song, hymn, or chant used in church services. [< L *canticulum* little song < *cantus* song]

can·ti·lev·er (kan′tə·lev′ər; -lē′vər), *n.* a large, projecting bracket or beam that is fastened at one end only.

cantilever bridge, bridge made of two cantilevers whose projecting ends meet but do not support each other.

can·tle (kan′təl), *n.* part of a saddle that sticks up at the back. [< OF < Med.L *cantellus* little corner]

can·to (kan′tō), *n., pl.* -tos. one of the main divisions of a long poem. A canto of a poem corresponds to a chapter of a novel. [< Ital. < L *cantus* song]

can·ton (kan′tən, -ton, kan·ton′ *for n. and v. 1;* kan·ton′, -tōn′, *esp. Brit.* -tün′ *for v. 2*), *n.* small part or political division of a country. Switzerland is made up of 22 cantons. —*v.* **1.** divide into cantons. **2.** allot quarters to. [< OF *canton* corner, portion. See CANT.[2]]

Can·ton (kan·ton′ *for 1;* kan′tən *for 2*), *n.* **1.** city in S China. **2.** city in NE Ohio.

Can·ton·ese (kan′tən·ēz′; -ēs′), *n., pl.* -ese. **1.** native or inhabitant of Canton, China. **2.** Chinese dialect spoken in or near Canton, China. —*adj.* of Canton, China, its people, or their dialect.

Canton flannel (kan′tən), a strong cotton cloth that is soft and fleecy on one side.

can·ton·ment (kan·ton′mənt; -tōn′-; *esp. Brit.* -tün′-), *n.* place where soldiers live; quarters. [< F]

can·tor (kan′tər; -tôr), *n.* **1.** man who leads the singing of a choir or congregation. **2.** soloist in a synagogue. [< L, singer, < *canere* sing]

Ca·nuck (kə·nuk′), *n., adj. Am., Slang.* **1.** Canadian. **2.** French Canadian.

can·vas (kan′vəs), *n.* **1.** a strong cloth made of cotton, flax, or hemp, used to make tents and sails. **2.** something made of canvas. **3.** sail or sails. **4.** piece of canvas on which an oil painting is painted. **5.** an oil painting. **6.** under canvas, **a.** in tents. **b.** with sails spread. —*adj.* made of canvas. [< OF < L *cannabis* hemp]

can·vas·back (kan′vəs·bak′), or **canvasback duck,** *n. Am.* a wild duck of North America with grayish feathers on its back.

can·vass (kan′vəs), *v.* **1.** examine carefully; examine. **2.** discuss. **3.** *Am.* go through (a city, district, etc.) asking for votes, orders, etc. **4.** *Am.* ask for votes, orders, etc. **5.** *Am.* examine and count the votes cast in an election. —*n.* **1.** act, fact, or process of canvassing. **2.** *Am.* an official scrutiny of votes. **3.** *Am.* personal visiting of homes or stores in a district to sell something. **4.** *Am.* a survey to determine sentiment for or against a candidate or a cause. [< *canvas,* orig., toss (someone) in a sheet, later, shake out, discuss] —**can′vass·er,** *n.*

can·yon (kan′yən), *n. Am., S.W.* a narrow valley with high, steep sides, usually with a stream at the bottom. Also, **cañon.** [< Sp. *cañón* tube, ult. < L *canna* cane]

caou·tchouc (kü′chùk; kou·chük′), *n.* the gummy, coagulated juice of various tropical plants; rubber. [< F < Sp. < S Am.Ind.]

cap (kap), *n., v.,* **capped, cap·ping.** —*n.* **1.** a close-fitting covering for the head with little or no brim. **2.** a special head covering worn to show rank, occupation, etc.: *a nurse's cap.* **3.** anything like a cap. **4.** the highest part; top. **5.** a small quantity of explosive in a wrapper or covering. **6. set one's cap for,** *Colloq.* try to get for a husband. —*v.* **1.** put a cap on. **2.** put a top on; cover the top of. **3.** do or follow with something as good or better: *each clown capped the other's last joke.* [< LL *cappa.* Cf. L *caput* head.]

cap., **1.** capacity. **2.** capital. **3.** capitalize. **4.** *pl.* caps. capital letter. **5.** chapter.

ca·pa·bil·i·ty (kā′pə·bil′ə·ti), *n., pl.* -ties. ability; power; fitness; capacity.

ca·pa·ble (kā′pə·bəl), *adj.* **1.** having capacity or qualifications to meet ordinary requirements; competent: *a capable teacher.* **2. capable of, a.** having ability, power, or fitness for: *capable of criticizing music.* **b.** open to; ready for: *a statement capable of many interpretations.* [< LL *capabilis* < L *capere* take] —**ca′pa·ble·ness,** *n.* —**ca′pa·bly,** *adv.* —**Syn. 1.** proficient, qualified, fitted.

ca·pa·cious (kə·pā′shəs), *adj.* able to hold much; roomy; large. —**ca·pa′cious·ly,** *adv.* —**ca·pa′cious·ness,** *n.* —**Syn.** spacious.

ca·pac·i·ty (kə·pas′ə·ti), *n., pl.* -ties. **1.** amount of room or space inside; largest amount that can be held by a container. **2.** power of receiving and holding: *the theater has a capacity of 400.* **3.** power of delivering electric current, power, etc. **4.** ability; power; fitness: *a great capacity for learning.* **5.** legal qualification. **6.** position; relation: *he acted in the capacity of guardian.* [< L *capacitas* < *capere* take] —**Syn. 1.** volume. **4.** competency. **6.** character.

cap-a-pie, cap-à-pie (kap′ə·pē′), *adv.* from head to foot; completely. [< F]

ca·par·i·son (kə·par′ə·sən), *n.* **1.** ornamental covering for a horse. **2.** rich dress; outfit. —*v.* dress richly; fit out. [< F < Pr. *capa* cape]

cape[1] (kāp), *n.* an outer garment, or part of one, without sleeves, worn falling loosely from the shoulders. [< F < Sp. < LL *cappa* cap]

cape[2] (kāp), *n.* **1.** point of land extending into the water. **2. the Cape,** the Cape of Good Hope. [< F < L *caput* head]

Cape buffalo, a large, savage buffalo of southern Africa.

cape·lin (kap′ə·lin), *n.* a small fish of the N Atlantic, used as bait for cod. [< F < Pr. *capelan* chaplain]

ca·per[1] (kā′pər), *n.* **1.** a playful leap or jump. **2.** prank; trick. —*v.* leap or jump about playfully. [< L *caper* he-goat] —**ca′per·er,** *n.* —**Syn.** *v.* skip, spring, gambol.

ca·per[2] (kā′pər), *n.* **1.** a prickly shrub of the Mediterranean region. **2.** capers, the green flower buds of this shrub, pickled and used for seasoning. [< L < Gk. *kapparis*]

cap·er·cail·lie (kap′ər·kāl′yi), **cap·er·cail·zie** (-kāl′yi; -kāl′zi), *n.* a large European grouse. [< Scotch Gaelic *capullcoille*]

Ca·per·na·um (kə·pėr′nā·əm; -ni-), *n.* ancient town in Palestine, on the **Sea of** Galilee.

Ca·pet (kā′pit; kap′ĭt), *n*, Hugh, 938?–996 A.D., king of France from 987 to 996 A.D. —**Ca·pe·tian** (kə-pē′shən), *adj., n.*

Cape Town, Cape·town (kāp′toun′), seaport near the S tip of Africa. The legislature for the Republic of South Africa meets there.

Cape Verde (kāp′ vérd′), 1. cape in extreme W Africa. 2. Cape Verde Islands, group of islands west of this cape, belonging to Portugal.

cap·ful (kap′fül), *n., pl.* **-fuls.** as much as a cap will hold.

ca·pi·as (kā′pi-əs; kap′i-), *n. Law.* writ ordering an officer to arrest a certain person. [< L *capias* you may take]

cap·il·lar·i·ty (kap′ə-lar′ə-ti), *n.* 1. capillary attraction or repulsion. 2. quality of having or causing capillary attraction or repulsion.

cap·il·lar·y (kap′ə-ler′i), *adj., n., pl.* **-lar·ies.** —*adj.* 1. hairlike; very slender. 2. of, by means of, or in a tube of fine bore. —*n.* Also, **capillary tube.** tube with a very slender, hairlike opening or bore. Capillaries join the end of an artery to the beginning of a vein. [< L *capillaris* of hair, hairlike < *capillus* hair]

capillary attraction, 1. force that raises the part of the surface of a liquid that is in contact with a solid. 2. ability of a porous substance to soak up a liquid. A blotter absorbs ink by means of capillary attraction.

cap·i·tal[1] (kap′ə-təl), *n.* 1. city where the government of a country or state is located. 2. A, B, C, D, or any similar large letter. 3. amount of money or property that a company or a person uses in carrying on a business. 4. source of power or advantage. 5. capitalists as a group. 6. **make capital of,** take advantage of; use to one's own advantage. —*adj.* 1. of or having to do with capital. 2. important; leading. 3. main; chief. 4. of the best kind; excellent. 5. (of letters) of the large kind used at the beginning of a sentence, or as the first letter of a proper name. 6. involving death; punishable by death. [< L *capitalis* chief, pertaining to the head < *caput* head] —**Syn.** *adj.* 2. foremost. 3. principal. 4. splendid. ➤ **Capital letters.** Certain uses of capitals, as at the beginning of sentences or for proper names, are conventions followed by everyone; certain others show divided usage or are matters of taste. In general, formal English tends to use more capitals than informal English. The principal uses of capitals in current writing are:

1. **Sentence Capitals.** The first word of a sentence is capitalized. In quotations, the first word of a quoted sentence or part of sentence is capitalized, but when the quotation is broken, the second quoted part of a sentence is not capitalized: *"The first time I came this way,"* he said, *"almost none of the roads were hard surfaced."*

2. **Proper Names.** Proper names and abbreviations of proper names are capitalized: names of people, places, races (*Indian, Negro, Caucasian*), languages (*French, Latin*), days of the week, months, companies, ships, institutions, fraternities, religious bodies, historical events (*the Revolutionary War*), documents (*the Constitution*).

3. **Lines of Poetry.** The first letter of a line of poetry is capitalized unless it was originally written without a capital.

4. **Titles of Articles, Books, etc.** The usual convention in English is to capitalize the first word, all nouns, pronouns, verbs, adjectives, and adverbs as well as prepositions that stand last or contain more than four (sometimes five) letters: *With Malice Toward Some; The Book of a Naturalist.*

5. **The Pronoun I Is Capitalized** (not from any sort of egotism, but simply because a small *i* is likely to be lost or to become attached to other words).

6. **Names of Relatives, Individuals.** Names of members of one's family (*my Father, my Brother Wren*—or *my father, my brother Wren*) are often capitalized in familiar writing as a mark of courtesy. A title and also nouns standing for

the name of a person in a high position are capitalized: *The President spoke.*

7. **References to Deity.** *God, Jesus,* nouns such as *Saviour,* and pronouns referring directly to a sacred figure are capitalized—though practice is divided on the pronouns.

8. **Street, River, Park, etc.** Usage is divided over capitalizing such words as *street, river, park, hotel, church* when they follow a proper name. Typically, books and conservative magazines would use capitals; more informal writing, in many magazines and most newspapers, would not: Formal: *the Mississippi River;* informal: *the Mississippi river.*

9. **Abstract Nouns.** Abstract nouns are likely to be capitalized, more in formal writing than in informal, when they are personified or when they refer to ideals or institutions: *the State has nothing to do with the Church, nor the Church with the State.*

cap·i·tal[2] (kap′ə-təl), *n.* the top part of a column, pillar, etc. [< L *capitellum,* dim. of *caput* head]

Capital

cap·i·tal·ism (kap′ə-təl·iz′-əm), *n.* 1. economic system based on private property, competition, and the production of goods for profit. 2. concentration of wealth with its power and influence in the hands of a few people. 3. possession of capital.

cap·i·tal·ist (kap′ə-təl·ist), *n.* 1. person whose money and property are used in carrying on business. 2. a wealthy person. 3. person who favors or supports capitalism. —*adj.* capitalistic.

cap·i·tal·is·tic (kap′ə-təl·is′tik), *adj.* 1. *Am.* of or having to do with capitalism or capitalists. 2. favoring or supporting capitalism. —**cap′i·tal·is′ti·cal·ly,** *adv.*

cap·i·tal·ize (kap′ə-təl·īz), *v.,* **-ized, -iz·ing.** 1. *Am.* write or print with a capital letter. 2. *Am.* invest in or provide with capital. 3. set the capital of (a company) at a certain amount. 4. turn into capital; use as capital. 5. *Am.* take advantage of; use to one's own advantage. —**cap′i·tal·i·za′tion,** *n.*

cap·i·tal·ly (kap′ə-təl·i), *adv.* 1. very well; excellently. 2. chiefly.

capital ship, a large warship; battleship.

cap·i·ta·tion (kap′ə-tā′shən), *n.* tax, fee, or charge of the same amount for every person.

Cap·i·tol (kap′ə-təl), *n.* 1. *Am.* the building at Washington, D.C., in which Congress meets. 2. Often, **capitol,** *Am.* the building in which a State legislature meets. 3. the ancient temple of Jupiter in Rome. [< L *Capitolium* chief temple (of Jupiter) < *caput* head]

ca·pit·u·late (kə-pich′ə-lāt), *v.,* **-lat·ed, -lat·ing.** surrender on certain terms or conditions: *the men in the fort capitulated upon the condition that they should go away unharmed.* [< Med.L, < *capitulare* draw up under separate heads, arrange in chapters < L *caput* head]

ca·pit·u·la·tion (kə-pich′ə-lā′shən), *n.* 1. a surrender on certain terms or conditions. 2. agreement; condition. 3. statement of the main facts of a subject; summary.

ca·pon (kā′pon; -pən), *n.* rooster specially raised to be eaten. It is castrated and fattened. [< OF < L *capo*]

ca·pote (kə-pōt′), *n.* 1. *Am.* a long cloak with a hood. 2. a close-fitting bonnet with strings. [< F]

Cap·pa·do·cia (kap′ə-dō′shə), *n.* ancient Roman province in E Asia Minor.

Ca·pri (kä′pri; kə-prē′), *n.* a small island in the Bay of Naples, Italy.

ca·pric·ci·o (kə-prē′chi-ō), *n., pl.* **-ci·os.** 1. caper; prank; caprice. 2. a lively piece of music in a free, irregular style. [< Ital., < *capro* goat < L *caper*]

ca·price (kə-prēs′), *n.* 1. sudden change of mind without reason; unreasonable notion or desire. 2. tendency to change suddenly and without reason. 3. *Music.* capriccio (def. 2). [< F

< Ital. *capriccio.* See CAPRICCIO.] —Syn. 1. whimsy, whim, humor, fancy.

ca·pri·cious (kə·prish′əs; -prē′shəs), *adj.* guided by one's fancy; changeable; fickle. —ca·pri′cious·ly, *adv.* —ca·pri′cious·ness, *n.*

Cap·ri·corn (kap′rə·kôrn), *n.* 1. tropic of Capricorn. 2. a southern constellation that was thought of as arranged in the shape of a goat. 3. the 10th sign of the zodiac.

cap·ri·ole (kap′ri·ōl), *n., v.,* -oled, -ol·ing. —*n.* 1. high leap made by a horse without moving forward. 2. a leap; caper. —*v.* 1. of a horse, make a high leap. 2. to leap; caper. [< F < Ital. *capriola,* ult. < *capro* goat. See CAPRICCIO.]

caps., capital letters.

cap·si·cum (kap′sə·kəm), *n.* 1. any of several plants with red or green pods containing seeds that usually have a hot, peppery taste. Green peppers, chilies, and pimientos are pods of different kinds of capsicum. 2. such pods prepared for seasoning or medicine. [< NL < L *capsa* box]

cap·size (kap·sīz′; kap′sīz), *v.,* -sized, -siz·ing. turn bottom side up; upset; overturn.

cap·stan (kap′stən), *n.* machine for lifting or pulling that stands upright. [< Pr. < L *capistrum* halter, < *capere* take]

capstan bar, pole used to turn a capstan.

cap·stone (kap′stōn′), *n.* top stone of a wall or other structure.

cap·su·lar (kap′sə·lər; -syə-), *adj.* 1. of or like a capsule. 2. in a capsule.

cap·sule (kap′səl; -syūl), *n.* 1. a small gelatin case for enclosing a dose of medicine. 2. part of a rocket that contains instruments, a man, etc., which is separated in flight from the motors and goes into orbit or is recovered at a later time. 3. a dry seedcase that opens when ripe. 4. *Anat.* a membrane enclosing an organ; membranous bag or sac. [< L *capsula,* dim. of *capsa* box]

Capsule

Capt., Captain.

cap·tain (kap′tən), *n.* 1. leader; chief. 2. an army officer ranking next below a major and next above a lieutenant. 3. a navy officer ranking next below a commodore and next above a commander. 4. commander of a ship. 5. leader of a team in sports. —*v.* lead or command as captain. [< OF < LL *capitaneus* chief < L *caput* head] —cap′tain·cy, *n.*

cap·tain·ship (kap′tən·ship), *n.* 1. rank, position, or authority of a captain. 2. ability as a captain; leadership.

cap·tan (kap′tan), *n.* powder used in solution on plants as a fungicide.

cap·tion (kap′shən), *n.* 1. *Am.* title or heading at the head of a page, article, chapter, etc., or under a picture. 2. a taking; a seizing. —*v. Am.* put a caption on. [< L *captio* a taking < *capere* take]

cap·tious (kap′shəs), *adj.* hard to please; faultfinding. [< L *captiosus,* ult. < *capere* take] —cap′tious·ly, *adv.* —cap′tious·ness, *n.*

cap·ti·vate (kap′tə·vāt), *v.,* -vat·ed, -vat·ing. 1. hold captive by beauty or interest; charm; fascinate. 2. *Obs.* capture. —cap′ti·vat′ing·ly, *adv.* —cap′ti·va′tion, *n.* —cap′ti·va′tor, *n.*

cap·tive (kap′tiv), *n.* prisoner. —*adj.* 1. held as a prisoner; made a prisoner. 2. captivated. [< L *captivus,* ult. < *capere* take]

captive audience, *Am.* group of persons who may be involuntarily subjected to an advertising appeal or other message, as passengers on a bus.

cap·tiv·i·ty (kap·tiv′ə·ti), *n., pl.* -ties. 1. a being in prison. 2. a being held or detained anywhere against one's will. —Syn. 2. bondage.

cap·tor (kap′tər), *n.* person who captures.

cap·ture (kap′chər), *v.,* -tured, -tur·ing, *n.* —*v.* make a prisoner of; take by force, skill, or trick; seize. [< n.] —*n.* 1. person or thing taken in this way. 2. act of capturing; fact of capturing or being captured. [< F < L *captura* taking < *capere* take] —cap′tur·er, *n.* —Syn. *v.* catch, apprehend. —*n.* 2. seizure, arrest.

cap·u·chin (kap′yŭ·chin; -shin), *n.* 1. a South American monkey with black hair on its head that looks like a hood. See the picture in col. 2. 2. a hooded cloak for women. 3. **Capuchin,**

Franciscan monk belonging to an order that wears a long, pointed hood or cowl.

car·put (kä′pət; kap′ət), *n., pl.* **cap·i·ta** (kap′ə·tə). *Anat.* head. [< L]

car (kär), *n.* 1. vehicle moving on wheels. 2. automobile. 3. *Am.* railroad vehicle for freight or passengers. 4. vehicle running on rails. 5. the closed platform of an elevator, balloon, etc., for carrying passengers. 6. *Poetic.* chariot. [< OF < L *carrus* two-wheeled cart] ➤ Car is a satisfactory and economical solution of the contest between *automobile, auto, motor car,* and other terms for a "gasoline-propelled pleasure vehicle."

Capuchin (body 1½ ft. long)

car·a·ba·o (kä′rə·bä′ō), *n., pl.* -ba·os. water buffalo of the Philippine Islands. [< Sp. < Malay *karbau*]

car·a·bi·neer, car·a·bi·nier (kar′ə·bə·nir′), *n.* cavalry soldier armed with a carbine. Also, **carbineer.**

ca·ra·ca·ra (kä′rə·kär′ə), *n.* a vulturelike bird of South America.

Ca·ra·cas (kə·rak′əs; -rä′kəs), *n.* capital of Venezuela.

car·a·cole (kar′ə·kōl), **car·a·col** (-kol), *n., v.,* -coled, -col·ing; -colled, -col·ling. —*n.* a half turn to the right or left, made by a horse and rider. —*v.* prance from side to side. [< F < Ital. < Sp. *caracol* spiral shell]

car·a·cul (kar′ə·kəl), *n.* the flat, loose, curly fur made from the skin of newborn lambs. Also, **karakul.** [< *Kara Kul,* lake in Turkestan]

ca·rafe (kə·raf′; -räf′), *n.* a glass water bottle. [< F < Ital. < Sp. < Ar. *gharrāf* drinking vessel]

car·a·mel (kar′ə·məl; -mel; kär′məl; kär·mel′), *n.* 1. burnt sugar used for coloring and flavoring. 2. a small block of chewy candy. [< F < Sp. *caramelo*]

car·a·pace (kar′ə·pās), *n.* shell on the back of a turtle, lobster, crab, etc. [< F < Sp. *carapacho*]

car·at (kar′ət), *n.* 1. unit of weight for precious stones, equal to ⅕ gram. 2. one 24th part. Also, **karat.** [< F < Ital. < Ar. < Gk. *keration* small horn-shaped bean used as a weight, dim. of *keras* horn]

car·a·van (kar′ə·van), *n.* 1. group of merchants, pilgrims, tourists, etc., traveling together for safety through a desert or a dangerous country. 2. a large, covered wagon for people or goods. 3. *Brit.* house on wheels. 4. van. [< F < Pers. *kārwān*]

car·a·van·sa·ry (kar′ə·van′sə·ri), **car·a·van·se·rai** (-rī; -rā), *n., pl.* -ries; -rais. 1. inn or hotel where caravans rest in the Orient. 2. *Am.* large inn or hotel. [< Pers., < *kārwān* caravan + *serāi* inn]

car·a·vel (kar′ə·vel), *n.* a small, fast ship of former times. Also, **carvel.** [< F *caravelle* < Ital. < LL *carabus* < Gk. *karabos* kind of light ship < ancient Macedonian]

car·a·way (kar′ə·wā), *n.* 1. plant yielding fragrant, spicy seeds used to flavor bread, rolls, cakes, etc. 2. its seeds. [< Med.L < Ar. *karawyā*]

car·bide (kär′bīd; -bid), *n. Chem.* 1. compound of carbon with a more electropositive element or radical. 2. calcium carbide.

car·bine (kär′bīn; -bēn), *n.* a short rifle or musket. [< F]

car·bi·neer (kär′bə·nir′), *n.* carabineer.

car·bo·hy·drate (kär′bō·hī′drāt), *n.* Chem. substance composed of carbon, hydrogen, and oxygen. Sugar and starch are carbohydrates. Carbohydrates are made from carbon dioxide and water by green plants in sunlight. [< *carbo(n)* + *hydrate*]

car·bo·lat·ed (kär′bə·lāt′id), *adj.* containing carbolic acid.

car·bol·ic acid (kär·bol′ik), *adj.* a very poisonous, corrosive, white, crystalline substance, C_6H_5OH, used in solution as a disinfectant and antiseptic; phenol.

car·bon (kär′bən), *n.* 1. *Chem.* a very common nonmetallic element, C. Diamonds and graphite are pure carbon; coal and charcoal are impure carbon. 2. *Elect.* piece of carbon used in batteries, arc lamps, etc. 3. piece of carbon paper. 4. copy made with carbon paper. [< F < L *carbo* coal]

carbon 12, the most abundant isotope of carbon, a stable isotope having a mass number of 12, now recognized as the official standard for atomic weights.

carbon 14, a radioactive form of carbon. The extent of its decay in wood, bone, etc. is evidence of the age of archaeological finds or geological formations in which organic matter occurs.

car·bo·na·ceous (kär′bə·nā′shəs), *adj.* of, like, or containing coal.

car·bon·ate (*n.* kär′bən·āt, –it; *v.* kär′bən·āt), *n., v., -at·ed, -at·ing. n. Chem.* a salt or ester of carbonic acid. —*v.* 1. change into a carbonate. 2. charge with carbon dioxide. Soda water is carbonated to make it fizz. —**car′bon·a′tion,** *n.*

carbon dioxide, a heavy, colorless, odorless gas, CO_2, present in the atmosphere.

car·bon·ic acid, acid made when carbon dioxide is dissolved in water, H_2CO_3.

carbonic-acid gas, carbon dioxide.

Car·bon·if·er·ous (kär′bən·if′ər·əs), *n.* 1. period when the warm, moist climate produced great forests, whose remains form the great coal beds. 2. rock and coal beds formed during this period. —*adj.* **carboniferous,** containing coal.

car·bon·ize (kär′bən·īz), *v., -ized, -iz·ing.* 1. change into carbon by burning. 2. cover or combine with carbon. —**car′bon·i·za′tion,** *n.*

carbon monoxide, a colorless, odorless, very poisonous gas, CO, formed when carbon burns with an insufficient supply of air.

carbon paper, thin paper having a preparation of carbon or other inky substance on one surface, used for making copies of letters, etc.

carbon tet·ra·chlo·ride (tet′rə·klō′rīd; –rid; –klō′–), a colorless, noninflammable liquid, CCl_4, often used in cleaning fluids.

car·bo·run·dum (kär′bə·run′dəm), *n. Am.* 1. an extremely hard compound of carbon and silicon, SiC, used for grinding, polishing, etc. 2. Carborundum, trademark for this abrasive. [< *carbo*(n) + (*co*)*rundum*]

car·boy (kär′boi), *n.* a very large, glass bottle, usually enclosed in basketwork or in a wooden box or crate to keep it from being broken. [< Pers. *qarābah* large flagon]

car·bun·cle (kär′bung·kəl), *n.* 1. a very painful, inflamed swelling under the skin. 2. a smooth, round garnet or other deep-red jewel. [< L *carbunculus* < *carbo* coal] —**car′bun·cled,** *adj.* —**car·bun·cu·lar** (kär·bung′kyə·lər), *adj.*

car·bu·ret (kär′bə·rāt; –byə·ret), *v., -ret·ed, -ret·ing; esp. Brit. -ret·ted, -ret·ting.* 1. mix (air or gas) with carbon compounds, such as gasoline, etc. 2. combine with carbon. -**car·bu·re·tion** (kär′bə·rā′shən; –byə·resh′ən), *n.*

car·bu·re·tor (kär′bə·rā′tər; –byə·ret′ər), *esp. Brit.* **car·bu·ret·tor** (kär′byə·ret′ər), *n.* device for mixing air with gasoline to make an explosive mixture.

car·ca·jou (kär′kə·jü; –zhü), *n. Am.* 1. the wolverine (animal). 2. American badger. [< Canadian F < Algonquian]

car·cass, car·case (kär′kəs), *n.* 1. dead body of an animal or, contemptuously, of a human being. 2. *Contemptuously.* a living body. 3. an unfinished framework or skeleton. [< F < Ital. *carcassa*]

car·cin·o·gen (kär·sin′ə·jən), *n.* any substance or agent that produces cancer.

car·cin·o·gen·ic (kär·sin′ə·jen′ik), *adj.* 1. tending to cause cancer. 2. caused by cancer. Also, **cancerogenic.**

car·ci·no·ma (kär′sə·nō′mə), *n., pl.* -mas, -ma·ta (–mə·tə). cancer. [< L < Gk. *karkinōma*]

card¹ (kärd), *n.* 1. piece of stiff paper or thin cardboard, usually small and rectangular. 2. one of a pack of cards used in playing games. 3. cards, a game played with such a pack. 4. *Colloq.* a queer or amusing person. 5. in or on the cards, likely to happen; possible. —*v.* 1. provide with a

card. 2. put on a card. [< F *carte* < L *charta.* Doublet of CHART.]

card² (kärd), *n.* a toothed tool or wire brush. —*v.* clean or comb with such a tool. [< F < Pr. < L *carrere* to card; infl. by L *carduus* thistle] —**card′er,** *n.*

car·da·mom, car·da·mum (kär′də·məm), or **car·da·mon** (–mən), *n.* 1. a spicy seed used as seasoning and in medicine. 2. the Asiatic plant that it grows on. [< L < Gk. *kardamomon*]

card·board (kärd′bôrd′; –bōrd′), *n.* a stiff material made of paper, used to make cards and boxes.

car·di·ac (kär′di·ak), *adj.* 1. of or having to do with the heart. 2. having to do with the upper part of the stomach. —*n.* medicine that stimulates the heart. [< L < Gk. *kardiakos* < *kardia* heart]

Car·diff (kär′dif), *n.* seaport in SE Wales.

car·di·gan (kär′də·gən), *n.* a knitted woolen jacket. [named for the Earl of *Cardigan* (1797–1868)]

car·di·nal (kär′də·nəl), *adj.* 1. of first importance; main. 2. bright-red. —*n.* 1. bright red. 2. one of the princes, or high officials, of the Roman Catholic Church, appointed by the Pope. 3. *Am.* cardinal bird. 4. cardinal number. [< L *cardinalis* chief, pertaining to a hinge < *cardo* hinge] —**car′di·nal·ly,** *adv.* —**car′di·nal·ship′,** *n.* —**Syn.** *adj.* 1. chief, principal.

car·di·nal·ate (kär′də·nəl·āt), *n.* position or rank of cardinal.

cardinal bird or **grosbeak,** or **cardinal,** *n. Am.* an American songbird that has bright-red feathers marked with black. It is a kind of finch.

cardinal flower, *Am.* 1. the bright-red flower of a North American plant. 2. the plant it grows on; the scarlet lobelia.

cardinal number or **numeral,** number that shows how many are meant. ➤ **Cardinal numbers,** like three, ten, 246, 9371, are the numbers used in counting and are contrasted with **ordinal numbers,** like 1st, 2nd, 24th, etc., which are used to indicate order or succession.

cardinal points, the four main directions of the compass; north, south, east, and west.

card·ing (kär′ding), *n.* preparation of the fibers of wool, cotton, flax, etc., for spinning by combing them.

car·di·o·graph (kär′di·ə·graf′; –gräf′), *n.* instrument that records the strength and nature of movements of the heart. [< Gk. *kardia* heart + –GRAPH] —**car′di·o·graph′ic,** *adj.* —**car·di·og·ra·phy** (kär′di·og′rə·fi), *n.*

card·play·ing (kärd′plā′ing), *n.* act, practice, or conventions of playing card games. —**card′play′er,** *n.*

cards (kärdz), *n.pl.* See card¹ (*n.* def. 3).

card·sharp (kärd′shärp′), **card·sharp·er** (kärd′shärp′ər), *n.* a dishonest professional cardplayer. —**card′sharp′ing,** *n.*

care (kär), *n., v., cared, car·ing.* —*n.* 1. burden of thought; worry. 2. serious attention; caution. 3. object of concern or attention. 4. watchful oversight; charge. 5. food, shelter, and protection. 6. have a care, be careful. 7. take care, be careful. 8. take care of, a. attend to; provide for. b. be careful of. c. *Colloq.* deal with. —*v.* 1. be concerned; feel an interest. 2. like; want; wish. 3. care for, a. be fond of; like. b. want; wish: *I don't care for any dessert tonight.* c. attend to; provide for. [OE *caru*] —**car′er,** *n.* —**Syn.** *n.* 1. anxiety, concern. 2. heed, regard. 4. custody, management.

CARE, Cooperative for American Remittances to Everywhere, Inc.

ca·reen (kə·rēn′), *v.* 1. lean to one side; tilt; tip. 2. lay (a ship) over on one side for cleaning, painting, repairing, etc. [< F < L *carina* keel] —**ca·reen′er,** *n.*

ca·reer (kə·rir′), *n.* 1. general course of action or progress through life. 2. way of living; occupation; profession. 3. speed; full speed. —*v.* rush along wildly; dash. —*adj. Am.* having to do with someone who has seriously followed a profession: *a career diplomat.* [< F *carrière* race course < L *carrus* wagon] —ca·reer'ist, *n.*

care·free (kãr'frē'), *adj.* without worry; happy; gay.

care·ful (kãr'fəl), *adj.* **1.** thinking what one says; watching what one does; cautious. **2.** done with thought or pains; exact; thorough. **3.** *Archaic.* anxious; worried. —care'ful·ly, *adv.* —care'ful·ness, *n.* —Syn. **1.** heedful, mindful, guarded. **2.** painstaking, particular.

care·less (kãr'lis), *adj.* **1.** not thinking what one says; not watching what one does. **2.** done without enough thought or pains; not exact or thorough. **3.** not troubling oneself. **4.** *Archaic.* without worry. —care'less·ly, *adv.* —care'less·ness, *n.* —Syn. **1.** inattentive, thoughtless. **2.** inaccurate, negligent. **3.** indifferent, unconcerned.

ca·ress (kə·res'), *n.* a touch or stroke to show affection; embrace; kiss. —*v.* touch or stroke to show affection; embrace; kiss. [< F < Ital. *carezza*, ult. < L *carus* dear] —ca·ress'a·ble, *adj.* —ca·ress'er, *n.* —ca·ress'ing·ly, *adv.*

car·et (kar'ət), *n.* mark (∧) to show where something should be put in, used in writing and in correcting proof. See proofreading marks on page 27 for example. [< L, there is wanting]

care·tak·er (kãr'tāk'ər), *n.* person who takes care of a person, place, or thing.

care·worn (kãr'wôrn'; -wōrn'), *adj.* showing signs of worry; tired; weary.

car·fare (kãr'fãr'), *n.* money to pay for riding on a streetcar, bus, etc.

car·go (kãr'gō), *n., pl.* **-goes, -gos.** load of goods carried on a ship. [< Sp., < *cargar* load, ult. < L *carrus* wagon]

Car·ib (kar'ib), *n.* **1.** member of an Indian tribe of NE South America. **2.** a language family found primarily in NE South America, and to a lesser extent in Central America and the West Indies. —Car'ib·an, *adj.*

Car·ib·be·an (kar'ə·bē'ən; kə·rib'i-), *n.* Also, **Caribbean Sea.** sea between Central America, the West Indies, and South America. —*adj.* **1.** of this sea or the islands in it. **2.** of the Caribs.

car·i·bou (kar'ə·bü), *n., pl.* **-bous** or (*esp. collectively*) **-bou.** *Am.* North American reindeer. [< Canadian F < Algonquian *xalibu* pawer]

car·i·ca·ture (kar'i-kə·chür; -chər), *n., v.,* **-tured, -tur·ing.** —*n.* **1.** picture, cartoon, description, etc., that ridiculously exaggerates the peculiarities or defects of a person or thing. **2.** art of making such pictures or descriptions. **3.** a very inferior imitation. —*v.* make a caricature of. [< F < Ital., < *caricare* overload] —car·i·ca·tur·al (kar'i·kə·chür·əl; -chər-; kar'i·kə·chür'əl), *adj.* —car'i·ca·tur'ist, *n.* —Syn. *n.* **1.** burlesque.

car·ies (kãr'ēz; -i·ēz), *n.* decay of teeth, bones, or tissues. [< L]

car·il·lon (kar'ə·lon; -lən; kə·ril'yən), *n., v.,* **-lonned, -lon·ning.** —*n.* **1.** set of bells arranged for playing melodies. **2.** melody played on such bells. **3.** part of an organ imitating the sound of bells. —*v.* play a carillon. [< F, ult. < L *quattuor* four; orig. consisted of four bells]

car·il·lon·neur (kar'ə·lə·nér'), *n.* person who plays a carillon.

car·i·ole (kar'i·ōl), *n.* **1.** a small carriage drawn by one horse. **2.** a covered cart. Also, **carriole.** [< F < Ital. < L *carrus* wagon]

car·i·ous (kãr'i·əs), *adj.* having caries; decayed. [< L *cariosus* < *caries* decay] —car·i·os·i·ty (kãr'i·os'ə·ti), car'i·ous·ness, *n.*

car·load (kãr'lōd'), *n.* as much as a car, esp. a railroad freight car, can hold or carry. —*adj. Am.* bought and sold by the carload.

Carls·bad Caverns (kärlz'bad), national park in SE New Mexico, famous for its huge limestone caverns.

Car·lyle (kär·līl'), *n.* **Thomas,** 1795–1881, British essayist and historian.

car·man (kär'mən), *n., pl.* **-men.** motorman or conductor of a streetcar.

Car·mel·ite (kär'məl·īt), *n.* a mendicant friar or nun of a religious order founded in the 12th century. —*adj.* of this order.

car·min·a·tive (kär·min'ə·tiv; kär'mə·nā'-tiv), *adj.* expelling gas from the stomach and intestines. —*n.* medicine that does this. [< L *carminatus* carded]

car·mine (kär'min; -mīn), *n.* **1.** deep red with a tinge of purple. **2.** light crimson. **3.** crimson coloring matter found in cochineal. —*adj.* **1.** deep-red with a tinge of purple. **2.** light-crimson. [< Med.L < Sp. *carmesi* CRIMSON]

car·nage (kär'nij), *n.* slaughter of a great number of people. [< F < Ital. *carnaggio* < *caro* flesh]

car·nal (kär'nəl), *adj.* **1.** worldly; not spiritual. **2.** bodily; sensual. [< L *carnalis* < *caro* flesh] —car·nal·i·ty (kär·nal'ə·ti), *n.* —car'nal·ly, *adv.*

car·na·tion (kär·nā'shən), *n.* **1.** a red, white, or pink flower with a spicy fragrance. **2.** the plant that it grows on. **3.** rosy pink. —*adj.* rosy-pink. [< F < Ital. *carnagione* flesh color. See CARNAGE.]

car·nel·ian (kär·nēl'yən), *n.* a red stone used in jewelry. Also, **cornelian.** [alter. of *cornelian*; infl. by L *caro* flesh]

car·ni·val (kär'nə·vəl), *n.* **1.** place of amusement or traveling show having merry-go-rounds, side shows, etc. **2.** feasting and merrymaking. **3.** time of feasting and merrymaking just before Lent. [< Ital. < Med.L < L *carnem levare* the putting away of flesh]

Car·niv·o·ra (kär·niv'ə·rə), *n.pl. Zool.* a large group of flesh-eating animals, including cats, dogs, lions, tigers, and bears.

car·ni·vore (kär'nə·vôr; -vōr), *n. Zool.* a flesh-eating animal. —car·niv·o·ral (kär·niv'ə-rəl), *adj.*

car·niv·o·rous (kär·niv'ə·rəs), *adj.* **1.** flesh-eating: *carnivorous animals.* **2.** of or having to do with the Carnivora. [< L *carnivorus* < *caro* flesh + *vorare* devour] —car·niv'o·rous·ly, *adv.* —car·niv'o·rous·ness, *n.*

car·ol (kar'əl), *n., v.,* **-oled, -ol·ing;** *esp. Brit.* **-olled, -ol·ling.** —*n.* **1.** song of joy. **2.** hymn: *Christmas carols.* —*v.* sing; sing joyously; praise with carols. [< OF *carole,* ? < L < Gk. *choraules* flute player] —car'ol·er, *esp. Brit.* car'ol·ler, *n.*

Car·o·li·na (kar'ə·lī'nə), *n.* **1.** an early American colony on the Atlantic coast. **2.** either North Carolina or South Carolina. **3.** **the Carolinas,** *Am.* North Carolina and South Carolina. —Car·o·lin·i·an (kar'ə·lin'i·ən), *adj., n.*

Car·o·line Islands (kar'ə·līn; -lin), group of over 500 islands in the W Pacific, near the equator; now under U.S. administration.

car·om (kar'əm), *n.* **1.** *Billiards.* shot in which the ball struck with the cue hits two balls, one after the other. **2.** a hitting and bouncing off. —*v.* **1.** make a carom. **2.** *Am.* hit and bounce off. Also, **carrom.** [< F < Sp. *carambola,* ? < Malay *carambil* name of fruit]

ca·rot·id (kə·rot'id), *Anat.* —*n.* either of two large arteries, one on each side of the neck, that carry blood to the head. —*adj.* having to do with these arteries. [< Gk. *karotides* < *karos* stupor (state produced by compression of carotids)]

ca·rous·al (kə·rouz'əl), *n.* **1.** noisy revelry. **2.** a drinking party.

ca·rouse (kə·rouz'), *n., v.,* **-roused, -rous·ing.** —*n.* a noisy feast; drinking party. —*v.* drink heavily; take part in noisy feasts or revels. [< obs. adv. < G *gar aus*(*trinken*) (drink) all up] —ca·rous'er, *n.*

car·ou·sel (kar'ə·sel'; -zel'), *n.* carrousel.

carp¹ (kärp), *v.* find fault with; complain. [< Scand. *karpa* wrangle] —carp'er, *n.* —carp'-ing·ly, *adv.* —Syn. cavil.

carp² (kärp), *n., pl.* **carps** or (*esp. collectively*) **carp. 1.** a fresh-water fish containing many bones that feeds mostly on plants. **2.** any of a group of similar fishes, including goldfish, minnows, chub, and dace. [< OF < Pr. < LL *carpa* < Gmc.]

carp., carpenter; carpentry.

car·pal (kär′pəl), *Anat.* —*adj.* of the carpus. —*n.* bone of the carpus. [< NL < Gk. *karpos* wrist]

Car·pa·thi·an Mountains (kär·pā′thi·ən), or **Carpathians**, *n.pl.* mountain system in E and C Europe, chiefly in Czechoslovakia and Poland.

car·pel (kär′pəl), *n. Bot.* a modified leaf from which a pistil of a flower is formed. [< Gk. *karpos* fruit] —**car·pel·lar·y** (kär′pə·ler′i), *adj.*

car·pen·ter (kär′pən·tər), *n.* man whose work is building with wood. —*v.* do such work. [< OF < LL *carpentarius* wagonmaker < L *carpentum* wagon]

car·pen·try (kär′pən·tri), *n.* work of a carpenter.

car·pet (kär′pit), *n.* 1. a heavy, woven fabric for covering floors and stairs. 2. a covering made of this fabric. 3. anything like a carpet. 4. **on the carpet**, *Colloq.* being scolded or rebuked. —*v.* cover with a carpet. [< OF *carpete* < L *carpere* card (wool)] —**car′pet·less**, *adj.*

car·pet·bag (kär′pit·bag′), *n.* traveling bag made of carpet.

car·pet·bag·ger (kär′pit·bag′ər), *n. Am.* Northerner who went to the South to get political or other advantages after the Civil War.

car·pet·ing (kär′pit·ing), *n.* 1. fabric for carpets. 2. carpets.

car·port (kär′pôrt; -pōrt), *n.* a roofed shelter for one or more automobiles, usually attached to a house and open on at least one side.

car·pus (kär′pəs), *n., pl.* -**pi** (-pī). *Anat.* 1. wrist. 2. bones of the wrist. [< NL < Gk. *karpos* wrist]

car·rack (kar′ək), *n. Archaic.* galleon. [< OF < Sp. < Ar. *qarāqir* (pl.)]

car·riage (kar′ij; *for* 7, *also* kar′i·ij), *n.* 1. vehicle moving on wheels, for carrying persons. 2. a wheeled passenger vehicle pulled by horses. 3. frame on wheels supporting a gun. 4. a moving part of a machine that supports some other part. 5. manner of holding the head and body; bearing. 6. act of carrying or transporting. 7. cost or price of carrying. 8. management; handling. [< OF *cariage* < *carier* CARRY]

car·ri·er (kar′i·ər), *n.* 1. person or thing that carries something: *mail carrier.* 2. thing to carry something in or on. 3. person or thing that carries or transmits a disease. 4. *Elect.* radio wave whose intensity is decreased or increased and whose frequency is regulated in transmitting a signal. 5. an aircraft carrier.

carrier pigeon, 1. *Colloq.* homing pigeon. 2. in technical use, one of a breed of large, heavy domestic pigeons.

car·ri·ole (kar′i·ōl), *n.* cariole.

car·ri·on (kar′i·ən), *n.* 1. dead and decaying flesh. 2. rottenness; filth. —*adj.* 1. dead and decaying. 2. feeding on dead and decaying flesh. 3. rotten. [< OF *caroigne* < VL < L *caries* decay]

Car·roll (kar′əl), *n.* Lewis, 1832–1898, English writer and mathematician. His real name was Charles L. Dodgson.

car·rom (kar′əm), *n., v.* carom.

car·rot (kar′ət), *n.* 1. plant that has a long, tapering, orange-red root eaten as a vegetable. 2. its root. [< F < L < Gk. *karoton*]

car·rot·y (kar′ət·i), *adj.* 1. like a carrot in color; orange-red. 2. red-haired.

car·rou·sel (kar′ə·sel′; -zel′), *n.* 1. *Am.* merry-go-round. 2. a kind of tournament to which dances, etc., were sometimes added. Also, **carousel.** [< F < Ital. *carosello* < L *carrus* cart]

car·ry (kar′i), *v.*, -**ried**, -**ry·ing**, *n., pl.* -**ries.** —*v.* 1. take from one place to another: *carry goods in a wagon.* 2. transfer in any manner; take or bring: *the ship carries goods to market.* 3. bear the weight of; hold up; support; sustain: *those columns carry the roof.* 4. hold (one's body and head) in a certain way. 5. capture; win. 6.

get (a motion or bill) passed or adopted. 7. continue; extend: *carry a road into the mountains.* 8. cover or reach to a certain distance: *his voice carries well.* 9. have the power of throwing or driving: *our guns could only carry ten miles.* 10. influence greatly; lead: *his acting carried the audience.* 11. have as a result; involve: *his judgment carries great weight.* 12. *Am.* a. keep in stock. b. keep on the account books of a business. 13. *Am.* extend credit to. 14. *Am.* sustain or perform (a melody or musical part): *carry the tune.* 15. *Southern U.S.* take; accompany: *carry Aunt Therese to the station.* 16. carry away, arouse strong feeling in. 17. carry off, a. win (a prize, honor, etc.). b. succeed with; pass off. 18. carry on, a. do; manage; conduct. b. go on with after being stopped. c. keep going; continue. d. *U.S. Colloq.* behave wildly or foolishly. 19. carry out, do; get done; accomplish; complete. —*n.* 1. distance covered; distance that something goes. 2. *Am.* a portage. [< OF < LL *carricare* < L *carrus* wagon, cart. Doublet of CHARGE.] —**Syn.** *v.* 1, 2. convey, transport, bring.

car·ry·all (kar′i·ôl′), *n. Am.* a lightweight covered carriage. [alter. of *cariole*]

car·ry·back, **car·ry′back** (kar′i·bak′), *n.* a credit on income tax in a given year as a result of previous overpayment or earlier losses not accounted for in computing the tax.

car·ry·o·ver (kar′i·ō′vər), *n.* part left over.

car·sick (kär′sik′), *adj.* nauseated by traveling in a car, train, etc.

Car·son City (kär′sən), capital of Nevada.

cart (kärt), *n.* 1. vehicle with two wheels, for carrying heavy loads. 2. a light wagon, used to deliver goods, etc. 3. a small vehicle on wheels, moved by hand. —*v.* carry in a cart. [OE *cræt* or < Scand. *kartr*] —**cart′er,** *n.*

cart·age (kärt′ij), *n.* 1. cost or price of carting. 2. act of carting.

carte blanche (kärt′ blänsh′), *French.* full authority; freedom to use one's own judgment.

car·tel (kär·tel′; kär′təl), *n.* 1. a large group of businesses that agree to fix prices and production. 2. a written agreement between countries at war for the exchange of prisoners or some other purpose. 3. a written challenge to a duel. [< F < Ital. *cartello* little CARD[1]]

Car·te·sian (kär·tē′zhən), *adj.* having to do with Descartes, or with his doctrines or methods. [< NL, < *Cartesius,* Latinized form of *Descartes*]

Car·thage (kär′thij), *n.* a powerful ancient city and seaport in N Africa, founded by the Phoenicians, destroyed by the Romans in 146 B.C. —**Car·tha·gin·i·an** (kär′thə·jin′i·ən), *adj., n.*

Car·thu·sian (kär·thü′zhən), *n.* member of an order of monks founded in 1086. —*adj.* of this order. [< *Chatrousse,* village where the first monastery of the order was]

car·ti·lage (kär′tə·lij), *n. Anat., Zool.* 1. the firm, tough, elastic, flexible substance forming parts of a skeleton; gristle. 2. part formed of this substance. The nose is supported by cartilages. [< F < L *cartilago*]

car·ti·lag·i·nous (kär′tə·laj′ə·nəs), *adj.* 1. of or like cartilage; gristly. 2. *Zool.* having the skeleton formed mostly of cartilage.

cart·load (kärt′lōd′), *n.* as much as a cart can hold or carry.

car·tog·ra·phy (kär·tog′rə·fi), *n.* the making of maps or charts. [< Med.L *charta* map + E -*graphy* drawing < Gk. *graphein* draw, write] —**car·tog′ra·pher,** *n.* —**car·to·graph·ic** (kär′tə·graf′ik), **car′to·graph′i·cal,** *adj.* —**car′to·graph′i·cal·ly,** *adv.*

car·ton (kär′tən), *n.* box made of pasteboard. [< F *carton* pasteboard < Ital., < *carta.* See CARD[1].]

car·toon (kär·tün′), *n.* 1. sketch or drawing that interests or amuses by showing persons, things, political events, etc., in an exaggerated way. 2. a full-size drawing of a design or painting, for a fresco, mosaic, tapestry, etc. 3. comic strip. 4. animated cartoon. —*v. Am.* make a cartoon of. [var. of *carton;* because drawn on paper] —**car·toon′ing,** *n. Am.* —**car·toon′ist,** *n.*

car·tridge (kär′trij), *n.* 1. case made of metal or cardboard for holding gunpowder. 2. roll of camera film. [alter. of *cartouche* (< F) a roll of paper]

cart wheel, 1. wheel of a cart. 2. a sidewise handspring or somersault.

carve (kärv), *v.,* **carved, carv·ing.** 1. cut into slices or pieces. 2. cut; make by cutting. 3. decorate with figures or designs cut on the surface. [OE *ceorfan*] —**carv′er,** *n.*

car·vel (kär′vəl), *n.* caravel.

carv·en (kär′vən), *adj. Poetic.* carved.

carv·ing (kär′ving), *n.* 1. act or art of one that carves. 2. carved work: *a wood carving.*

car·y·at·id (kar′i·at′id), *n., pl.* **–ids, –i·des** (–ə·dēz). statue of a woman used as a column. [< L < Gk. *Karyatides* women of Caryae] —**car′y·at′i·dal,** *adj.*

ca·sa·ba (kə·sä′bə), or **ca·saba melon,** *n. Am.* kind of muskmelon with a yellow rind. Also, **cassaba.** [after *Kasaba* near Smyrna, Asia Minor]

Caryatids

Cas·a·blan·ca (kas′ə·blang′kə; kä′sə·bläng′kə), *n.* seaport in NW Morocco.

Cas·a·no·va (kaz′ə·nō′və; kas′-), *n.* Giovanni Jacopo, 1725–1798, Italian adventurer.

cas·cade (kas·kād′), *n., v.,* **–cad·ed, –cad·ing.** —*n.* 1. a small waterfall. 2. anything like this. —*v.* fall in a cascade. [< F < Ital. *cascata* < L *cadere* fall]

Cascade Range, mountain range in NW United States, extending from N California to British Columbia.

cas·car·a (kas·kär′ə), *n. Am.* laxative made from the dried bark of a species of buckthorn. [< Sp., bark]

case[1] (kās), *n.* 1. instance; example: *a case of poor work.* 2. condition; situation; state: *a case of poverty.* 3. actual condition; real situation; true state: *that is the case.* 4. instance of a disease or injury: *a case of measles.* 5. person who has a disease or injury; patient. 6. *Law.* a. matter for a law court to decide. b. statement of facts for a law court to consider. 7. a convincing argument. 8. *Gram.* a. one of the forms of a noun, pronoun, or adjective used to show its relation to other words. b. relation shown by such a form. *I* is in the nominative case. 9. *Am., Slang.* a queer or unusual person. 10. in any case, under any circumstances; anyhow. 11. in case, if it should happen that; if; supposing. 12. in case of, in the event of. 13. in no case, under no circumstances. [< OF < L *casus* a falling, chance < *cadere* fall] ➤ Some of the commonest bits of deadwood in writing are various locutions with case. They are wordy and keep the real person or situation or thing (whatever the "case" stands for) one construction away from the reader: *Drinking went on moderately except in a few scattered cases.* [This was written of a convention. The "cases" would be delegates?]

case[2] (kās), *n., v.,* **cased, cas·ing.** —*n.* 1. thing to hold or cover something. 2. covering; sheath. 3. box. 4. quantity in a box. 5. frame: *a window fits in a case.* 6. tray for printing type, with a space for each letter. —*v.* put in a case; cover with a case. [< OF < L *capsa* box < *capere* hold]

case·hard·en (kās′här′dən), *v.* 1. *Metall.* harden (iron or steel) on the surface. 2. render callous; make unfeeling.

ca·se·in (kā′si·in; –sēn), *n. Biochem.* protein present in milk. Cheese is mostly casein. [< L *caseus* cheese]

case knife, 1. knife carried in a case. 2. table knife.

case·mate (kās′māt), *n.* 1. a shellproof vault; bombproof room. A casemate in the wall of a fort has holes for big guns to shoot through. 2. an armored enclosure protecting guns on a warship. [< F < Ital. *casamatta,* orig., round

house < L *casa* hut + *matta* round, spinning] —**case′mat·ed,** *adj.*

case·ment (kās′mənt), *n.* 1. a window opening on hinges like a door. 2. *Poetic.* any window. 3. casing; covering; frame. —**case′ment·ed,** *adj.*

ca·se·ous (kā′si·əs), *adj.* of or like cheese. [< L *caseus* cheese]

ca·sern, ca·serne (kə·zérn′), *n.* place for soldiers to live in a fortified town; barrack. [< F < Sp. *caserna* < L *quaterna* four each]

case·work (kās′werk′), *n.* 1. investigation and help by social workers of particular individuals, or families as units. 2. the occupation of doing this. —**case′work′er,** *n.*

cash[1] (kash), *n.* 1. ready money; coins and bills. 2. money, or an equivalent, as a check, paid at the time of buying something. —*v.* 1. get cash for. 2. give cash for. 3. cash in, *Am., Colloq.* a. in poker, etc., change (chips, etc.) into cash. b. pass away; die. 4. cash in on, *U.S. Colloq.* a. make a profit from. b. use to advantage. [< F *caisse* < Pr. < L *capsa* box, coffer]

cash[2] (kash), *n., pl.* **cash.** coin of small value, used in China, India, etc. [< Tamil *kasu*]

cash·book (kash′bûk′), *n.* book in which a record is kept of money received and paid out.

cash·ew (kash′ū; kə·shū′), *n.* 1. a small kidney-shaped nut. 2. the tropical American tree that it grows on. [< F < Brazilian Pg. *acajú* < Tupi]

cash·ier[1] (kash·ir′), *n.* person who has charge of money in a bank or business. [< F *caissier* treasurer. See CASH[1].]

cash·ier[2] (kash·ir′), *v.* dismiss from service; discharge in disgrace. [< Du. < F < L *quassare* shatter and LL *cassare* annul]

cash·mere (kash′mir), *n.* 1. a fine, soft wool from goats. 2. a costly kind of shawl made of this wool. 3. a fine, soft wool from sheep. 4. a fine, soft woolen cloth. [after *Kashmir*]

Cash·mere (kash·mir′; kash′mir), *n.* Kashmir.

cash register, *Am.* machine which records and shows the amount of a sale, usually with a drawer to hold money.

cas·ing (kās′ing), *n.* 1. thing put around something; covering; case. 2. *Am.* the part of a tire that encloses the inner tube. 3. *Am.* framework around a door or window.

ca·si·no (kə·sē′nō), *n., pl.* **–nos.** 1. a building or room for dancing, gambling, etc. 2. a card game. [< Ital., dim. of *casa* house < L *casa*]

cask (kask; käsk), *n.* 1. barrel. A cask may be large or small, and is usually made to hold liquids. 2. amount that a cask holds. [< Sp. *casco* skull, cask of wine, ult. < L *quassare* break]

cas·ket (kas′kit; käs′-), *n.* 1. a small box to hold jewels, letters, etc. 2. *Am.* coffin.

Cas·pi·an Sea (kas′pi·ən), an inland salt sea between Europe and Asia.

cas·sa·ba (kə·sä′bə), *n.* casaba.

Cas·san·dra (kə·san′drə), *n.* 1. *Gk. Legend.* a prophetess of ancient Troy, who was fated never to be believed. 2. person who prophesies misfortune, but is not believed.

cas·sa·va (kə·sä′və), *n.* 1. a tropical plant with starchy roots. 2. a nutritious starch from its roots; manioc. Tapioca is made from cassava. [< F < Sp. < Haitian *cacábi*]

cas·se·role (kas′ə·rōl), *n.* 1. a covered baking dish in which food can be both cooked and served. 2. food cooked and served in such a dish. [< F, < *casse* pan < VL *cattia* < Gk. *kyathion,* dim. of *kyathos* cup]

cas·sia (kash′ə; kas′i·ə), *n.* 1. an inferior kind of cinnamon. 2. the tree that produces it. 3. plant from whose leaves and pods the drug senna is obtained. 4. the pods or their pulp. [< L < Gk. < Heb. *q'tsi'āh*]

cas·si·no (kə·sē′nō), *n.* casino (def. 2).

Cas·si·o·pe·ia (kas′i·ə·pē′ə), *n.* 1. *Gk. Legend.* mother of an Ethiopian princess who was rescued from a sea monster by Perseus. 2. a northern constellation fancied to resemble Cassiopeia sitting in a chair.

cas·sock (kas′ək), *n.* a long outer garment, usually black, worn by a clergyman. [< F < Ital. *casacca*] —**cas′socked,** *adj.*

cas·so·war·y (kas⁣ʹə·wer′ĭ), *n.*, *pl.* **–war·ies.** a large bird of Australia and New Guinea, like an ostrich, but smaller. [< Malay *kasuari*]

cast (kast; käst), *v.*, **cast, cast·ing,** *n.*, *adj.* —*v.* 1. throw: *cast a fishing line.* 2. throw off; let fall: *the snake cast its skin.* 3. direct; turn: *he cast me a look.* 4. shape by pouring or squeezing into a mold to harden. 5. arrange (actors and parts in a play). 6. add; calculate. 7. cast a ballot, vote. 8. cast about, a. search; look. b. make plans. 9. cast down, a. turn downward; lower. b. make sad or discouraged. 10. cast out, drive away; banish; expel. 11. cast up, a. turn upward; raise. b. add up; find the sum of. —*n.* 1. act of throwing. 2. thing made by casting. 3. mold used in casting; mold. 4. actors in a play. 5. form; look; appearance. 6. kind; sort. 7. a slight amount of color; tinge. 8. a slight squint. —*adj.* (of a play) having all the actors chosen. [< Scand. *kasta* throw]

cas·ta·net (kas′tə·net′), *n.* a pair, or one of a pair, of instruments of hard wood or ivory like little cymbals, held in the hand and clicked together to beat time for dancing or music. [< Sp. *castaneta* < L *castanea* CHESTNUT]

cast·a·way (kastʹə·wā′; käst′–), *adj.* 1. thrown away; cast adrift. 2. outcast. —*n.* 1. shipwrecked person. 2. outcast.

caste (kast; käst), *n.* 1. any of the hereditary social classes into which the Hindus are divided. 2. an exclusive social group; distinct class. 3. a social system having class distinctions based on rank, wealth, position, etc. 4. lose caste, lose social rank or position. [< Sp. < Pg. *casta* race < L *castus* pure]

cas·tel·lat·ed (kasʹtə·lāt′ĭd), *adj.* having turrets and battlements. —**cas′tel·la′tion,** *n.*

cast·er (kasʹtər; käsʹ–), *n.* 1. person or thing that casts. 2. Also, *castor.* a. a small wheel on a piece of furniture to make it easier to move. b. bottle containing salt, mustard, vinegar, or other seasoning for table use. c. *Am.* stand or rack for such bottles.

cas·ti·gate (kasʹtə·gāt), *v.*, **–gat·ed, –gat·ing.** criticize severely; punish. [< L *castigatus,* ult. < *castus* pure] —**cas′-ti·ga′tion,** *n.* —**casʹti·ga′tor,** *n.*

Caster (def. 2a)

Cas·tile (kas·tēlʹ), *n.* 1. region in N and central Spain, formerly a kingdom. 2. Castile soap.

Cas·tile soap (kasʹtēl), a pure, hard soap made from olive oil.

Cas·til·ian (kas·tilʹyən), *adj.* of Castile, its people, or their language. —*n.* 1. Castilian Spanish, the accepted standard form of Spanish. 2. native or inhabitant of Castile.

cast·ing (kasʹting; käsʹ–), *n.* thing shaped by being poured into a mold to harden.

cast iron, a hard, brittle form of iron made by casting.

cast-i·ron (kastʹī′ərn; kästʹ–), *adj.* 1. made of cast iron. 2. hard; not yielding. 3. hardy; strong.

cas·tle (kasʹəl; käsʹ–), *n.*, *v.*, **–tled, –tling.** —*n.* 1. a building or group of buildings with thick walls, towers, and other defenses against attack. 2. palace that once had defenses against attack. 3. a large and imposing residence. 4. piece in the game of chess, shaped like a tower. —*v. Chess.* move the king two squares toward a castle and bring that castle to the square the king has passed over. [< L *castellum,* dim. of *castrum* fort. Doublet of CHATEAU.] —**cas′tled,** *adj.* —**Syn.** *n.* 1. fortress, citadel, stronghold. 3. mansion, château.

castle in the air, daydream.

cast-off (kastʹôf′; –ofʹ; kästʹ–), *adj.* thrown away; abandoned. —*n.* person or thing that has been cast off.

cas·tor¹ (kasʹtər; käsʹ–), *n.* caster (def. 2).

cas·tor² (kasʹtər; käsʹ–), *n.* 1. a hat made of beaver fur. 2. an oily substance with a strong odor, secreted by beavers. It is used in making perfume and in medicines. [< L < Gk. *kastor* beaver]

Cas·tor (kasʹtər; käsʹ–), *n.* 1. *Class. Myth.* the mortal twin brother of Pollux. 2. the fainter star of the two bright stars in the constellation called Gemini.

castor bean, *Am.* seed of the castor-oil plant.

castor oil, yellow oil obtained from castor beans, used as a cathartic, a lubricant, etc.

cas·tor-oil plant (kasʹtər-oilʹ; käsʹ–), a tall tropical plant from whose seeds castor oil is obtained.

cas·trate (kasʹtrāt), *v.*, **–trat·ed, –trat·ing.** 1. remove the male glands of. 2. mutilate; expurgate. [< L *castratus*] —**cas·tra′tion,** *n.*

Cas·tro (kasʹtrō), *n.* Fidel, born 1927, premier of Cuba since 1959.

cas·u·al (kazhʹu̇·əl), *adj.* 1. happening by chance; not planned or expected; accidental. 2. without plan or method. 3. careless; unconcerned; offhand. 4. uncertain; indefinite; vague. 5. occasional; irregular. A casual laborer does any kind of work that he can get. —*n.* 1. a casual laborer. 2. person occasionally receiving charity. 3. soldier temporarily separated from his unit. [< L *casualis* < *casus* chance] —**cas′u·al·ly,** *adv.* —**cas′u·al·ness,** *n.* —**Syn.** *adj.* 1. chance, fortuitous, unexpected. —**Ant.** *adj.* 1. expected. 2. planned; intentional.

cas·u·al·ty (kazhʹu̇·əl·tĭ), *n.*, *pl.* **–ties.** 1. accident. 2. an unfortunate accident; mishap. 3. soldier or sailor who has been wounded, killed, or lost. 4. person injured or killed in an accident.

cas·u·ist (kazhʹu̇·ist), *n.* 1. person who decides questions of right and wrong in regard to conduct, duty, etc. 2. person who reasons cleverly but falsely. [< F *casuiste* < L *casus* case]

cas·u·is·tic (kazhʹu̇·isʹtik), **cas·u·is·ti·cal** (–tə·kəl), *adj.* 1. of or like casuistry. 2. too subtle; sophistical. —**cas′u·isʹti·cal·ly,** *adv.*

cas·u·ist·ry (kazhʹu̇·is·trĭ), *n.*, *pl.* **–ries.** 1. act or process of deciding questions of right and wrong in regard to conduct, duty, etc. 2. clever but false reasoning.

cat (kat), *n.*, *v.*, **cat·ted, cat·ting.** —*n.* 1. a small animal often kept as a pet or for catching mice. 2. any animal of the group including cats, lions, tigers, leopards, etc. 3. *Am.* lynx. 4. animal something like a cat. 5. *Am.* catfish. 6. a mean, spiteful woman. 7. *Slang.* person devoted to swing music and to the cant that pertains to it. 8. cat-o'-nine-tails. 9. *Naut.* tackle for hoisting. —*v.* hoist (an anchor) and fasten it to a beam on the ship's side. [OE *catt* (male), *catte* (fem.), prob. < LL *cattus, catta*] —**catʹlike,** *adj.*

ca·tab·o·lism (kə·tabʹə·liz·əm), *n.* process of breaking down living tissues into simpler substances or waste matter, thereby producing energy. [prob. < *metabolism,* by substitution of *cata*– down] —**cat·a·bol·ic** (kat′ə·bolʹik), *adj.* —**cat′a·bolʹi·cal·ly,** *adv.*

cat·a·chre·sis (kat′ə·krēʹsis), *n.*, *pl.* **–ses** (–sēz). misuse of words. [< L < Gk. *katachresis* misuse < *kata–* amiss + *chresthai* use] —**cat·a·chres·tic** (kat′ə·kresʹtik), *adj.* —**cat′a·chresʹti·cal·ly,** *adv.*

cat·a·clysm (katʹə·kliz·əm), *n.* 1. a flood, earthquake, or any sudden, violent change in the earth. 2. any violent change. [< L < Gk. *kataklysmos* flood < *kata–* down + *klyzein* wash] —**cat·a·clys·mic** (kat′ə·klizʹmik), **cat·a·clys·mal** (–məl), *adj.* of or like a cataclysm; extremely sudden and violent. —**cat′a·clysʹmi·cal·ly,** *adv.*

cat·a·comb (katʹə·kōm), *n.* Usually, catacombs. an underground gallery forming a burial place. [< LL *catacumbae* < *cata* (< Gk.) *tumbas* among the tombs. See TOMB.]

cat·a·falque (katʹə·falk), *n.* stand or frame to support the coffin in which a dead person lies. [< F < Ital. *catafalco* < LL, < L *cata–* down + *jala* tower]

Cat·a·lan (katʹə·lan; –lən), *adj.* of Catalonia, its people, or their language. —*n.* 1. native or inhabitant of Catalonia. 2. language spoken in Catalonia.

cat·a·lep·sy (katʹə·lep′sĭ), **cat·a·lep·sis** (kat′ə·lepʹsis), *n.* kind of fit during which a person loses consciousness and power to feel and his muscles become rigid. [< LL < Gk. *katalepsis* seizure < *kata-* down + *lambanein* seize] —cat'·a·lep'tic, *adj., n.*

Cat·a·li·na (kat'ə·lē'nə), *n.* Santa Catalina.

cat·a·logue, cat·a·log (kat'ə·lôg; -log), *n., v.,* –logued, –logu·ing; –loged, –log·ing. —*n.* 1. a list, esp. a list arranged in alphabetical or other methodical order, with brief particulars concerning the names, articles, etc., listed. 2. *Am.* volume or booklet issued by a college or university listing rules, courses to be given, etc. —*v.* make a catalogue of; put in a catalogue. [< F < LL < Gk. *katalogos* list < *kata-* down + *legein* count] —cat'a·logu'er, cat'a·logu'ist; cat'a·log'er, cat'a·log'ist, *n.* ➤ catalogue, catalog. The spelling is divided, with the shorter form gaining. Nearly half the colleges now use *catalog* as the name of their annual bulletin of announcements.

Cat·a·lo·ni·a (kat'ə·lō'ni·ə), *n.* region in NE Spain.

ca·tal·pa (kə·tal'pə), *n. Am.* tree with large, heart-shaped leaves, bell-shaped flowers, and long pods. [< NL < Am.Ind. (Creek) *kutuhlpa*]

ca·tal·y·sis (kə·tal'ə·sis), *n., pl.* –ses (-sēz). *Chem.* the causing or speeding up of a chemical reaction by the presence of a substance that does not itself change. [< NL < Gk. *katalysis* dissolution < *kata-* down + *lyein* to loose] —cat·a·lyt·ic (kat'ə·lit'ik), *adj.* —cat'a·lyt'i·cal·ly, *adv.*

cat·a·lyst (kat'ə·list), *n.* substance that causes catalysis.

cat·a·lyze (kat'ə·līz), *v.,* –lyzed, –lyz·ing. act upon by catalysis. —cat'a·lyz'er, *n.*

cat·a·ma·ran (kat'ə·mə·ran'), *n. Am.* 1. boat with two hulls side by side. 2. raft made of pieces of wood lashed together. [< Tamil *katta-maram* tied tree]

Catamaran

cat·a·mount (kat'ə·mount'), *n. Am.* wildcat, such as a puma or lynx. [short for *catamountain* cat of (the) mountain]

Ca·ta·nia (kə·tän'yə; kä·tä'nyä), *n.* seaport in E Sicily.

cat·a·pult (kat'ə·pult), *n.* 1. an ancient weapon for shooting stones, arrows, etc. 2. *Brit.* slingshot. 3. device for launching an airplane from the deck of a ship. —*v.* shoot from a catapult; throw; hurl. [< L < Gk. *katapeltes,* prob. < *kata-* down + *pallein* hurl]

cat·a·ract (kat'ə·rakt), *n.* 1. a large, steep waterfall. 2. a violent rush or downpour of water; flood. 3. an opaque region in the lens or capsule of the eye that causes partial or total blindness. [< L < Gk. *kataraktes* < *kata-* down + *arassein* dash]

ca·tarrh (kə·tär'), *n.* an inflamed condition of a mucous membrane, usually that of the nose or throat, causing a discharge of mucus. [< F < L < Gk. *katarrhous* < *kata-* down + *rheein* flow] —ca·tarrh'al, *adj.*

ca·tas·tro·phe (kə·tas'trə·fē), *n.* 1. a sudden, widespread, or extraordinary disaster; great calamity or misfortune. 2. outcome; unhappy ending. 3. disastrous end; ruin. 4. sudden violent disturbance, esp. of the earth's surface. [< Gk. *katastrophe* overturning < *kata-* down + *strophein* turn] —cat·a·stroph·ic (kat'ə·strof'ik), *adj.* —Syn. 4. cataclysm.

Ca·taw·ba (kə·tô'bə), *n., pl.* –bas. *Am.* 1. a light-red grape. 2. a light wine made from it.

cat·bird (kat'bėrd'), *n. Am.* a slate-gray, American songbird that makes a sound like a cat mewing.

cat·boat (kat'bōt'), *n.* sailboat with one mast set far forward. It has no bowsprit or jib.

cat·call (kat'kôl'), *n.* a shrill cry or whistle to express disapproval. —*v.* 1. make catcalls. 2. attack with catcalls.

catch (kach), *v.,* caught, catch·ing, *n., adj.* —*v.* 1. take and hold; seize; capture. 2. take; get. 3. become caught. 4. become lighted; burn: *tinder catches easily.* 5. come on suddenly; surprise. 6.

Am. act as catcher in baseball. 7. catch on, *Am., Colloq.* a. understand; get the idea. b. become popular; be widely used or accepted. 8. catch up, a. come up even with a person or thing; overtake. b. pick up suddenly; snatch; grab. c. interrupt and annoy with criticisms or questions; heckle. d. hold up in loops. —*n.* 1. act of catching. 2. thing that catches. A fastener for a door or window is a catch. 3. thing caught. 4. *Colloq.* a good person to marry. 5. game of throwing and catching a ball. 6. *Music.* a short song sung by several persons or groups, beginning one after another. 7. *Am., Colloq.* a hidden or veiled condition in a plan, etc. —*adj.* 1. getting one's attention; arousing one's interest: *a catch phrase.* 2. tricky; deceptive: *a catch question.* [< OF *cachier* < LL *captiare* < L *capere* take. Doublet of CHASE[1].] —catch'a·ble, *adj.* —Syn. v. 1. grip, grasp, clutch, nab.

catch·all (kach'ôl'), *n. Am.* container for odds and ends.

catch·er (kach'ər), *n.* 1. person or thing that catches. 2. *Am.* a baseball player who stands behind the batter to catch the ball thrown by the pitcher.

catch·ing (kach'ing), *adj.* 1. contagious; infectious. 2. attractive; fascinating.

catch·pen·ny (kach'pen'i), *adj., n., pl.* –nies. —*adj.* showy but worthless or useless; made to sell quickly. —*n.* a catchpenny article.

catch·up (kech'əp; kach'–), *n. Now U.S.* sauce to use with meat, fish, etc. Tomato catchup is made of tomatoes, onions, salt, sugar, and spices. Also, catsup, ketchup.

catch·word (kach'wėrd'), *n.* 1. word or phrase used again and again for effect; slogan. 2. word so placed as to catch attention.

catch·y (kach'i), *adj.,* catch·i·er, catch·i·est. 1. easy to remember; attractive. 2. tricky; misleading; deceptive.

cat·e·chism (kat'ə·kiz·əm), *n.* 1. book of questions and answers about religion, used for teaching religious doctrine. 2. set of questions and answers about any subject. 3. a long or formal set of questions. —cat'e·chis'mal, *adj.*

cat·e·chist (kat'ə·kist), *n.* person who catechizes. —cat'e·chis'tic, cat'e·chis'ti·cal, *adj.* —cat'e·chis'ti·cal·ly, *adv.*

cat·e·chize, cat·e·chise (kat'ə·kīz), *v.,* –chized, –chiz·ing; –chised, –chis·ing. 1. teach by questions and answers. 2. question closely. [< L < Gk. *katechizein* teach orally < *kata-* thoroughly + *echein* sound] —cat'e·chi·za'tion, cat'e·chi·sa'tion, *n.* —cat'e·chiz'er, cat'e·chis'er, *n.*

cat·e·chu·men (kat'ə·kū'mən), *n.* person who is being taught the elementary facts of Christianity. [< LL < Gk. *katechoumenos* one being instructed. See CATECHIZE.] —cat'e·chu'me·nal, *adj.*

cat·e·gor·i·cal (kat'ə·gôr'ə·kəl; –gor'–), *adj.* 1. without conditions or qualifications; positive. 2. of or in a category. —cat'e·gor'i·cal·ly, *adv.* —cat'e·gor'i·cal·ness, *n.*

cat·e·go·ry (kat'ə·gō'ri; –gō'–), *n., pl.* –ries. group or division in a general system of classification; class. [< L < Gk. *kategoria* assertion < *kata-* down + *agoreuein* speak]

cat·e·nate (kat'ə·nāt), *v.,* –nat·ed, –nat·ing. connect in a series. [< L, < *catena* chain] —cat'e·na'tion, *n.*

ca·ter (kā'tər), *v.* 1. provide food or supplies. 2. supply means of enjoyment. [verbal use of *cater,* n., ME *acatour* buyer of provisions < F, < *acater* < LL *accaptare* acquire]

cat·er-cor·nered (kat'ər-kôr'nərd), *adj.* diagonal. —*adv.* diagonally. —*cater diagonally (< F *quatre* four) + *cornered*]

ca·ter·er (kā'tər·ər), *n.* person who provides food or supplies for parties, etc.

Caterpillar
(⅛ actual size)

cat·er·pil·lar (kat'ər·pil'ər), *n.* 1. wormlike form or larva of a butterfly or moth. 2. Caterpillar. *Trademark.* tractor that can travel over very rough ground on its two endless belts. [cf. OF *chatepelose* hairy cat]

cat·er·waul (kat′ər-wôl), *v.* howl like a cat; screech. —*n.* Also, **cat′er·waul′ing.** such a howl or screech. [ME *caterwrawe* < *cater*, appar., cat + *wrawe* wail, howl]

cat·fish (kat′fish′), *n., pl.* –fish·es or (*esp. collectively*) –fish. a scaleless fish with long, slender feelers around the mouth.

cat·gut (kat′gut′), *n.* a tough string made from the dried and twisted intestines of sheep or other animals, used for violin strings, tennis rackets, etc.

Cath., 1. Also, **cath.** Cathedral. 2. Catholic.

ca·thar·sis (kə-thär′sis), *n.* 1. *Med.* a purging. 2. an emotional purification or relief. [< NL < Gk. *katharsis*, ult. < *katharos* clean]

ca·thar·tic (kə-thär′tik), *n.* a strong laxative. Epsom salts and castor oil are cathartics. —*adj.* Also, **ca·thar′ti·cal.** strongly laxative.

Ca·thay (ka-thā′), *n. Poetic* or *Archaic.* China.

ca·the·dral (kə-thē′drəl), *n.* 1. the official church of a bishop. 2. a large or important church. —*adj.* 1. having a bishop's throne. 2. of or like a cathedral. 3. authoritative. [< Med.L < L < Gk. *kathedra* seat]

Catherine the Great, 1729–1796, empress of Russia from 1762 to 1796.

cath·e·ter (kath′ə-tər), *n. Med.* a slender metal or rubber tube to be inserted into a duct of the body. [< LL < Gk. *katheter* < *kata–* down + *hienai* send]

cath·ode (kath′ōd), *n.* negative electrode. The zinc case of a dry cell and the filament of a radio tube are cathodes. [< Gk. *kathodos* a way down < *kata–* down + *hodos* a way] —**ca·thod·ic** (kə-thod′ik), **ca·thod′i·cal,** *adj.*

cathode rays, invisible streams of electrons from the cathode in a vacuum tube. When cathode rays strike a solid substance, they produce X rays.

cath·o·lic (kath′ə-lik; kath′lik), *adj.* 1. of interest or use to all people; including all; universal. 2. having sympathies with all; broadminded; liberal. 3. of the whole Christian church. [< L < Gk. *katholikos* < *kata–* in respect to + *holos* whole] —**ca·thol·i·cal·ly** (kə-thol′ik-li), *adv.* —**Syn.** 1. all-embracing, general. 2. tolerant.

Cath·o·lic (kath′ə-lik; kath′lik), *adj.* 1. of the Christian church governed by the Pope; Roman Catholic. 2. of the ancient undivided Christian church, or of its present representatives. —*n.* member of either of these churches.

Ca·thol·i·cism (kə-thol′ə-siz-əm), **Cath·o·lic·i·ty** (kath′ə-lis′ə-ti), *n.* faith, doctrine, organization, and methods of the Roman Catholic Church.

cath·o·lic·i·ty (kath′ə-lis′ə-ti), **ca·thol·i·cism** (kə-thol′ə-siz-əm), *n.* 1. universality; wide prevalence. 2. broad-mindedness; liberalness.

ca·thol·i·cize (kə-thol′ə-sīz), *v.,* –cized, –cizing. make or become catholic; universalize.

cat·i·on (kat′ī′ən), *n.* positive ion. During electrolysis, cations move toward the cathode. [< Gk. *kation* going down < *kata–* down + *ienai* go]

cat·kin (kat′kin), *n.* the downy or scaly spike of flowers that grows on willows, birches, etc.; ament. [< Du. *katteken* little cat]

cat·mint (kat′mint′), *n. Brit.* catnip.

cat·nap (kat′nap′), *n., v.,* –napped, –nap·ping. —*n.* doze. —*v.* sleep or doze for a little while.

cat·nip (kat′nip), *n. Am.* kind of mint of which cats are fond. Also, *Brit.* catmint. [< *cat* + *nip,* var. of *nep* catnip < L *nepeta*]

Catkin

Ca·to (kā′tō), *n.* 1. Marcus Porcius, 234–149 B.C., Roman statesman and patriot. 2. his great-grandson, Marcus Porcius, 95–46 B.C., Roman statesman, soldier, and Stoic philosopher.

cat-o'-nine-tails (kat′ə-nīn′tālz′), *n., pl.* –tails. whip consisting of nine pieces of knotted cord fastened to a handle.

Cats·kills (kats′kilz), or **Catskill Mountains,** *n.pl.* a low mountain range in SE New York State.

cat's-paw, cats·paw (kats′pô′), *n.* 1. person used by another to do something unpleasant or dangerous. 2. a light breeze that ruffles a small stretch of water.

cat·sup (kech′əp; kat′səp), *n.* catchup.

cat·tail (kat′tāl′), *n.* 1. tall marsh plant with flowers in long, round, furry, brown spikes. 2. *Bot.* ament; catkin.

cat·tish (kat′ish), *adj.* 1. catlike. 2. catty. —**cat′tish·ly,** *adv.* —**cat′tish·ness,** *n.*

cat·tle (kat′əl), *n.* 1. *U.S.* cows, bulls, and steers; oxen. 2. farm animals; livestock. 3. low, worthless people. [< OF *catel* < L *capitale* property, CAPITAL¹. Doublet of CHATTEL.]

cat·tle·man (kat′əl-mən), *n., pl.* –men. *Am.* man who raises or takes care of cattle.

cat·ty (kat′i), *adj.,* –ti·er, –ti·est. 1. mean; spiteful. 2. catlike. 3. of cats. —**cat′ti·ly,** *adv.* —**cat′ti·ness,** *n.*

Ca·tul·lus (kə-tul′əs), *n.* Gaius Valerius, 87?–54? B.C., Roman lyric poet.

cat·walk (kat′wôk′), *n.* narrow place for walking on a bridge or in an airship.

Cau·ca·sia (kô-kā′zhə; –shə), *n.* region in S Russia, between the Black and Caspian Seas. Also, **Caucasus.**

Cau·ca·sian (kô-kā′zhən; –shən; –kazh′ən; –kash′ən), *n.* 1. member of the so-called white race, including the chief peoples of Europe, southwestern Asia, and northern Africa. 2. native of Caucasia. —*adj.* 1. of or having to do with the so-called white race. 2. of or having to do with Caucasia or its inhabitants.

Cau·ca·sus (kô′kə-səs), *n.* 1. mountain range in S Russia, between the Black and Caspian seas. 2. Caucasia.

cau·cus (kô′kəs), *n. Am.* a meeting of members or leaders of a political party to make plans, choose candidates, decide how to vote, etc. —*v.* hold a caucus. [? < Med.L *caucus* < Med.Gk. *kaukos,* a drinking vessel; "in allusion to the convivial feature" of the Caucus Club, a political club of the 18th century]

cau·dal (kô′dəl), *adj. Zool.* a. of, at, or near the tail. b. taillike. [< NL *caudalis* < L *cauda* tail] —**cau′dal·ly,** *adv.*

cau·date (kô′dāt), **cau·dat·ed** (–dāt-id), *adj.* having a tail.

cau·dle (kô′dəl), *n.* a warm drink for sick people; gruel sweetened and flavored with wine, ale, spices, etc. [< OF < L *calidus* warm]

caught (kôt), *v.* pt. and pp. of catch.

caul (kôl), *n.* membrane sometimes covering the head of a child at birth. [< OF *cale* a kind of little cap]

caul·dron (kôl′drən), *n.* caldron.

cau·li·flow·er (kô′lə-flou′ər; kol′i–), *n.* vegetable having a solid, white head with a few leaves around it. [half-trans. of NL *cauliflora* < *caulis* cabbage + *flos* flower]

cauliflower ear, *Am.* ear that has been misshapen by injuries received in boxing, etc.

caulk (kôk), *v.* calk¹. —**caulk′er,** *n.*

caus·al (kôz′əl), *adj.* 1. of a cause; being a cause. 2. having to do with cause and effect. 3. showing a cause or reason. —**caus′al·ly,** *adv.*

cau·sal·i·ty (kô-zal′ə-ti), *n., pl.* –ties. 1. relation of cause and effect; principle that nothing can happen or exist without a cause. 2. causal quality or agency.

cau·sa·tion (kô-zā′shən), *n.* 1. a causing or being caused. 2. whatever produces an effect; cause or causes. 3. relation of cause and effect; principle that nothing can happen or exist without a cause.

caus·a·tive (kôz′ə-tiv), *adj.* 1. being a cause; productive. 2. expressing causation. —**caus′a·tive·ly,** *adv.* —**caus′a·tive·ness,** *n.*

cause (kôz), *n., v.,* caused, caus·ing. —*n.* 1. whatever produces an effect; person or thing that makes something happen: *the earthquake was the cause of much damage.* 2. occasion for action; reason; ground; motive: *cause for celebration.* 3. good reason; reason enough: *he was angry without cause.* 4. subject or movement in which many people are interested and to which they give their support. 5. matter for a law court to decide; lawsuit. 6. **make common cause with,** join efforts with; side with. —*v.* produce as an effect; make happen; bring about. [< L *causa*] —**caus′a·ble,** *adj.* —**cause′less,** *adj.* —**caus′er,** *n.* —**Syn.** *n.* 2. incentive, inducement. —*v.* prompt, induce, occasion, effect.

cause cé·lè·bre (kōz′ sā·leb′rə), *French.* famous case (in law).

cau·se·rie (kō′zə·rē′), *n.* 1. an informal talk or discussion; chat. 2. short written article. [< F, < *causer* talk]

cause·way (kôz′wā′), *n.* 1. a raised road or path, usually built across wet ground, shallow water, etc. 2. a paved road; highway. —*v.* 1. provide with a causeway. 2. pave with cobbles or pebbles. [var. of *causey(way)* < OF < LL *calciata* paved way < L *calx* limestone]

caus·tic (kôs′tik), *n.* substance that burns or destroys flesh; corrosive substance. —*adj.* 1. that burns or destroys flesh; corrosive. 2. sarcastic; stinging; biting. [< L < Gk. *kaustikos*] —**caus′-ti·cal·ly,** *adv.* —**Syn.** *adj.* 2. satirical, cutting.

caustic soda, sodium hydroxide, NaOH.

cau·ter·ize (kô′tər·īz), *v.,* -**ized,** -**iz·ing.** burn with a hot iron or a caustic substance, esp. to prevent infection. —**cau′ter·i·za′tion,** *n.*

cau·ter·y (kô′tər·i), *n., pl.* -**ter·ies.** 1. a cauterizing. 2. instrument or substance used in cauterizing. [< L < Gk. *kauterion,* dim. of *kauter* branding iron]

cau·tion (kô′shən), *n.* 1. cautious behavior. 2. a warning. 3. *Am., Colloq.* a very unusual person or thing. —*v.* warn; urge to be careful. [< L *cautio < cavere* beware] —**Syn.** *n.* 1. prudence, wariness. 2. admonition, advice, counsel.

cau·tion·ar·y (kô′shən·er′i), *adj.* warning; urging to be careful.

cau·tious (kô′shəs), *adj.* very careful; taking care to be safe; never taking chances. —**cau′-tious·ly,** *adv.* —**cau′tious·ness,** *n.* —**Syn.** prudent, wary. —**Ant.** heedless, careless.

cav·al·cade (kav′əl·kād′; kav′əl·kād), *n.* procession of persons riding on horses or in carriages. [< F < Ital., < *cavalcare* ride horseback < LL, < L *caballus* horse]

cav·a·lier (kav′ə·lir′), *n.* 1. a courteous gentleman. 2. a courteous escort for a lady. 3. horseman; mounted soldier; knight. 4. Cavalier, person who supported Charles I of England in his struggle with Parliament from 1641 to 1649. —*adj.* 1. proud and scornful; haughty; arrogant. 2. free and easy; offhand. 3. Cavalier, of the Cavaliers. [< F < Ital. *cavalliere < cavallo* horse < L *caballus*] —**cav′a·lier′ly,** *adv.*

cav·al·ry (kav′əl·ri), *n., pl.* -**ries.** 1. soldiers who fight on horseback. 2. horsemen, horses, etc., collectively. [< F < Ital. *cavalleria* knighthood. See CAVALIER.] —**cav·al·ry·man** (kav′əl·ri·mən), *n.*

cave (kāv), *n., v.,* **caved, cav·ing.** —*n.* hollow space underground. —*v.* **cave in, a.** fall in; sink. **b.** cause to fall in; smash. **c.** *Colloq.* give in; yield; submit. [< F < L *cava* hollow (places)] —**Syn.** *n.* cavern, grotto, den.

ca·ve·at (kā′vi·at), *n.* 1. a warning. 2. *Law.* legal notice given to a law officer or some legal authority not to do something until the person giving notice can be heard. [< L *caveat* let him beware]

cave-in (kāv′in′), *n. Colloq.* 1. a caving in. 2. place where something has caved in.

cave man, 1. Also, **cave dweller.** man who lived in caves in prehistoric times. 2. a rough, crude man.

cav·ern (kav′ərn), *n.* a large cave. [< F < L *caverna < cavus* hollow]

cav·ern·ous (kav′ər·nəs), *adj.* 1. like a cavern; large and hollow. 2. full of caverns. —**cav′ern-ous·ly,** *adv.*

cav·i·ar, cav·i·are (kav′i·är; kä′vi-), *n.* 1. a salty relish made from the eggs of sturgeon or other large fish. 2. caviar to the general, too

good a thing to be appreciated by ordinary people. [< F < Ital. < Turk. *khaviar*]

cav·il (kav′əl), *v.,* -**iled,** -**il·ing;** *esp. Brit.* -**illed,** -**il·ling,** *n.* —*v.* find fault unnecessarily; raise trivial objections. —*n.* a petty objection. [< F < L *cavillari* jeer] —**cav′il·er,** *esp. Brit.* **cav′il·ler,** *n.* —**Syn.** *v.* carp, criticize.

cav·i·ty (kav′ə·ti), *n., pl.* -**ties.** 1. hole; hollow place: *a cavity in a tooth.* 2. *Anat.* enclosed space inside the body: *the abdominal cavity.* [< F < LL *cavitas* < L *cavus* hollow]

ca·vort (kə·vôrt′), *v. Am., Colloq.* prance about; jump around. [orig. unknown] —**ca·vort′er,** *n. Am.* —**ca·vort′ing,** *n., adj. Am.*

ca·vy (kā′vi), *n., pl.* -**vies.** a South American rodent of the family which includes the guinea pig.

caw (kô), *n.* the harsh cry made by a crow or raven. —*v.* make this cry. [imit.]

Cawn·pore (kôn′pôr; -pōr), **Cawn·pur** (-pûr), *n.* city in C India, on the Ganges River.

Cax·ton (kak′stən), *n.* **William,** 1422?-1491, first English printer.

cay (kā; kē), *n.* low island; reef; key.

cay·enne (kī·en′; kā-), or **cayenne pepper,** *n.* red pepper; very hot, biting powder made from seeds or fruit of a pepper plant. [after *Cayenne,* French Guiana]

cay·man (kā′mən), *n., pl.* -**mans.** a large alligator of tropical America. Also, **caiman.**

Ca·yu·ga (kā·ū′gə; kī-), *n., pl.* -**ga, -gas.** *Am.* member of a tribe of Iroquois Indians formerly living in W New York State.

cay·use (kī·ūs′), *n. Am., W.* 1. an Indian pony. 2. *Colloq.* any horse. [for the *Cayuse* Indians]

Cb, *Chem.* columbium.

cc., c.c., cubic centimeter; cubic centimeters.

Cd, *Chem.* cadmium.

Ce, *Chem.* cerium.

cease (sēs), *v.,* **ceased, ceas·ing.** 1. come to an end. 2. put an end or stop to. [< F < L *cessare*] —**Syn.** 1. discontinue, stop, quit, pause, desist.

cease-fire (sēs′fīr′), *n.* a halt in military operations, esp. for the purpose of discussing peace.

cease·less (sēs′lis), *adj.* never stopping; going on all the time; continual. —**cease′less·ly,** *adv.* —**Syn.** uninterrupted, unceasing, constant.

Ce·cro·pi·a moth (si·krō′pi·ə), *Am.* a large silkworm moth of the eastern United States.

ce·dar (sē′dər), *n.* 1. an evergreen tree with wide-spreading branches and fragrant, durable wood. 2. any of several trees with similar wood. 3. wood of any of these trees. —*adj. Am.* made of cedar. [< L < Gk. *kedros*]

ce·dar·bird (sē′dər·bėrd′), **cedar waxwing,** *n. Am.* a small American bird with a crest and small, red markings on its wings; waxwing.

Cedarbird (7 in. long)

cede (sēd), *v.,* **ced·ed, ced·ing.** give up; surrender; hand over to another. [< L *cedere* yield, go] —**Syn.** yield, relinquish, deliver. —**Ant.** keep, hold.

ce·dil·la (si·dil′ə), *n.* mark somewhat like a comma (ç) put under *c* in certain words to show that it has the sound of *s* before *a, o,* or *u.* *Example:* façade. [< Sp. < VL, dim. of L *zeta* < Gk., the letter *z*]

ceil (sēl), *v.* 1. put a ceiling in. 2. cover the ceiling of. [? < F < *ciel* canopy, sky < L *caelum* heaven]

ceil·ing (sēl′ing), *n.* 1. the inside, top covering of a room; surface opposite to the floor. 2. **a.** greatest height to which an airplane or airship can go under certain conditions. **b.** distance from the earth of the lowest clouds. 3. greatest height to which prices, wages, etc., are permitted to go. [< *ceil*]

cel·an·dine (sel′ən·dīn), *n.* plant with yellow flowers. [< OF < L < Gk., < *chelidon* swallow²]

Cel·a·nese (sel′ə·nēz′), *n. Trademark.* an acetate rayon material.

Cel·e·bes (sel′ə·bēz), *n.* a large island in E Indonesia. Now called **Sulawesi**.

cel·e·brant (sel′ə·brənt), *n.* 1. person who performs a ceremony or rite. 2. priest who performs Mass.

cel·e·brate (sel′ə·brāt), *v.*, **–brat·ed, –brat·ing.** 1. observe with the proper ceremonies or festivities. 2. perform publicly with the proper ceremonies and rites: *a priest celebrates Mass in church.* 3. make known publicly; proclaim. 4. praise; honor. 5. observe a festival or event with ceremonies or festivities. 6. *Colloq.* have a gay time. [< L *celebratus*] **—cel′e·bra′tor,** *n.* **—Syn.** 1, 2. solemnize. 4. laud. 5. commemorate.

cel·e·brat·ed (sel′ə·brāt′id), *adj.* famous; well-known. **—Syn.** noted, renowned, eminent.

cel·e·bra·tion (sel′ə·brā′shən), *n.* 1. act of celebrating. 2. whatever is done to celebrate something.

ce·leb·ri·ty (sə·leb′rə·ti), *n., pl.* **–ties.** 1. a famous person. 2. fame; being well known or much talked about.

ce·ler·i·ty (sə·ler′ə·ti), *n.* swiftness; speed. [< L, < *celer* swift]

cel·er·y (sel′ər·i; sel′ri), *n.* vegetable whose long stalks can be whitened by keeping them covered. Celery is usually eaten raw. [< F < dial. Ital. < L < Gk. *selinon* parsley]

ce·les·tial (sə·les′chəl), *adj.* 1. of the sky; having to do with the heavens. The sun, moon, planets, and stars are celestial bodies. 2. heavenly; divine. 3. **Celestial,** Chinese. **—n. Celestial,** Chinese. [< OF < L *caelestis* heavenly < *caelum* heaven] **—ce·les′tial·ly,** *adv.*

ce·li·ac (sē′li·ak), *adj. Anat.* coeliac.

cel·i·ba·cy (sel′ə·bə·si), *n., pl.* **–cies.** unmarried state; single life.

cel·i·bate (sel′ə·bit; –bāt), *n.* an unmarried person; person who takes a vow to lead a single life. **—adj.** unmarried; single. [< L *caelibatus* < *caelebs* unmarried]

cell (sel), *n.* 1. a small room in a prison, convent, etc. 2. a small, hollow place. Bees store honey in the cells of a honeycomb. 3. unit of living matter. Most cells have a nucleus near the center and are enclosed by a cell wall or membrane. 4. container holding materials for producing electricity by chemical action. 5. a small group that acts as a political, social, or religious unit for a larger, sometimes revolutionary, organization. [< L *cella* small room]

cel·lar (sel′ər), *n.* 1. an underground room or rooms, usually under a building and often used for storing food or fuel. 2. cellar for wines. 3. supply of wines. [< F < L *cellarium* < *cella* small room]

cel·lar·age (sel′ər·ij), *n.* 1. space in a cellar. 2. cellars. 3. charge for storage in a cellar.

cel·lar·er (sel′ər·ər), *n.* person who takes care of a cellar and the food or wines in it.

Cel·li·ni (chə·lē′ni), *n.* Benvenuto, 1500–1571, Italian artist.

cel·list, 'cel·list (chel′ist), *n.* person who plays the cello. Also, violoncellist.

cel·lo, 'cel·lo (chel′ō), *n., pl.* **–los.** instrument like a violin, but very much larger; bass violin. Also, violoncello.

cel·lo·phane (sel′ə·fān), *n.* 1. a transparent substance made from cellulose, used as a wrapping to keep food, candy, tobacco, etc., fresh and clean. 2. **Cellophane,** trademark for this substance. [< *cell(ul)o(se)* + Gk. *phanein* appear]

cel·lu·lar (sel′yə·lər), *adj.* 1. having to do with cells. 2. consisting of cells.

cel·lule (sel′ūl), *n.* a tiny cell. [< L *cellula*, dim. of *cella* small room]

cel·lu·loid (sel′yə·loid), *Am.* **—n.** 1. a hard, transparent substance made from cellulose and camphor. 2. **Celluloid,** trademark for this substance. **—adj.** pertaining to motion pictures.

cel·lu·lose (sel′yə·lōs), *n. Chem.* substance that forms the walls of plant cells; woody part of trees and plants. Cellulose is used to make paper, artificial silk, explosives, etc. [L *cellula* small cell]

Celt (selt; *esp. Brit.* kelt), *n.* member of a people to which the Irish, Highland Scotch, Welsh, and Bretons belong. The ancient Gauls and Britons were Celts. Also, **Kelt.**

Celt·ic (sel′tik; *esp. Brit.* kel′tik), *adj.* of the Celts or their language. **—n.** the group of languages spoken by the Celts, including Irish, Gaelic, Welsh, and Breton. Also, **Keltic.**

ce·ment (si·ment′), *n.* 1. substance made by burning clay and limestone. 2. this substance mixed with sand and water to make sidewalks, streets, floors, and walls and to hold stones or bricks together in building. 3. any soft substance that hardens and holds things together. 4. anything that joins together or unites. **—v.** 1. hold together with cement. 2. cover with cement. 3. join together; unite. [< OF < L *caementum* chippings of stone < *caedere* cut] **—ce·ment′er,** *n.*

cem·e·ter·y (sem′ə·ter′i), *n., pl.* **–ter·ies.** place for burying the dead; graveyard. [< LL < Gk. *koimeterion* < *koimaein* lull to sleep]

ce·no·bite (sē′nə·bīt; sen′ə–), *n.* member of a religious group living in a monastery or convent. [< LL *coenobita* < Gk. < *koinos* common + *bios* life] **—ce·no·bit·ic** (sē′nə·bit′ik; sen′ə–), **ce′no·bit′i·cal,** *adj.*

cen·o·taph (sen′ə·taf; –täf), *n.* monument erected in memory of a dead person whose body is elsewhere. [< L < Gk., < *kenos* empty + *taphos* tomb] **—cen′o·taph′ic,** *adj.*

cen·ser (sen′sər), *n.* container in which incense is burned. [< OF (*en*)*censier*, ult. < L *incensum* incense]

cen·sor (sen′sər), *n.* 1. person who examines and, if necessary, changes books, plays, motion pictures, etc., so as to make them satisfactory to the government or to the organization that employs him. 2. a Roman magistrate who took the census and told people how to behave. 3. person who tells others how they ought to behave. 4. person who likes to find fault. **—v.** act as censor; make changes in; take out part of (letters, etc.). [< L, < *censere* appraise] **—cen·so·ri·al** (sen·sô′ri·əl; –sō′–), *adj.*

cen·so·ri·ous (sen·sô′ri·əs; –sō′–), *adj.* too severely critical. **—cen·so′ri·ous·ly,** *adv.* **—cen·so′ri·ous·ness,** *n.* **—Syn.** hypercritical, carping.

cen·sor·ship (sen′sər·ship), *n.* 1. act or system of censoring. 2. position or work of a censor.

cen·sur·a·ble (sen′shər·ə·bəl), *adj.* worthy of censure. **—cen′sur·a·ble·ness, cen′sur·a·bil′i·ty,** *n.* **—cen′sur·a·bly,** *adv.*

cen·sure (sen′shər), *n., v.,* **–sured, –sur·ing.** **—n.** act or fact of blaming; expression of disapproval; criticism. **—v.** express disapproval of; blame; criticize. [< L *censura* < *censere* appraise] **—cen′sur·er,** *n.* **—Syn.** *n.* faultfinding, reproof, rebuke. *–v.* reprove, rebuke, reprimand.

cen·sus (sen′səs), *n.* an official count of the people of a country, with details as to age, sex, pursuits, etc. [< L, < *censere* appraise]

cent (sent), *n.* a coin, usually copper, of the United States and Canada, equal to the hundredth part of a dollar. [? < L *centesimus* hundredth]

cent., 1. centigrade. 2. central. 3. century.

cen·taur (sen′tôr), *n. Gk. Legend.* a monster that is half man and half horse. [< L < Gk. *kentauros*]

cen·ta·vo (sen·tä′vō), *n., pl.* **–vos.** a small coin used in Mexico, Cuba, the Philippines, etc., equal to the hundredth part of a peso. [< Am.Sp. See CENT.]

cen·te·nar·i·an (sen′tə·nār′i·ən), *n.* person who is 100 years old or more.

cen·te·nar·y (sen′tə·ner′i; sen·ten′ə·ri; *esp. Brit.* sen·tē′nə·ri), *n., pl.* **–nar·ies.** 1. period of 100 years. 2. 100th anniversary. [< L *centenarius* relating to a hundred < *centum* hundred]

cen·ten·ni·al (sen·ten′i·əl), *adj.* of or having to do with 100 years or the 100th anniversary. **—n.** 100th anniversary. [< L *centum* hundred + E (*bi*)*ennial*] **—cen·ten′ni·al·ly,** *adv.*

cen·ter (sen′tər), *n.* 1. a point within a circle or sphere equally distant from all of the circumference or surface. 2. the middle point, place, or part. 3. person, thing, or group in a middle position. 4. point toward which people or things go, or from which they come; main point. 5. player in the center of the line in football. 6. *Am.* player who starts play in basketball. 7. the political groups of a legislature having moderate opinions. —*v.* 1. place in or at the center. 2. collect at a center. 3. be at a center. Also, *esp. Brit.* centre. [< OF < L < Gk. *kentron* sharp point] ❯ Center around (or about) (the story *centers around* the theft of a necklace) is a colloquial idiom. The formal idiom is *center on* or *upon.*

center field, *Am., Baseball.* section of the outfield behind second base.

center of gravity, point in something around which its weight is evenly balanced.

cen·ter·piece (sen'tər·pēs'), *n.* an ornamental piece for the center of a dining table.

cen·tes·i·mal (sen·tes'ə·məl), *adj.* 1. 100th. 2. divided into 100ths. [< L *centesimus* hundredth] —**cen·tes'i·mal·ly,** *adv.*

centi-, *word element.* 1. 100. 2. 100th part of. [< L *centum* hundred]

cen·ti·grade (sen'tə·grād), *adj.* 1. divided into 100 degrees. 2. of or according to a centigrade thermometer. [< F < L *centum* hundred + *gradus* degree]

centigrade thermometer, thermometer having 0 for the temperature at which ice melts and 100 for the temperature at which water boils.

cen·ti·gram, *esp. Brit.* **cen·ti·gramme** (sen'tə·gram), *n.* ¹⁄₁₀₀ of a gram. [< F]

cen·ti·li·ter, *esp. Brit.* **cen·ti·li·tre** (sen'-tə·lē'tər), *n.* ¹⁄₁₀₀ of a liter. [< F]

cen·time (sän'tēm), *n.* ¹⁄₁₀₀ of a franc. [< F < L *centesimus* hundredth]

cen·ti·me·ter, *esp. Brit.* **cen·ti·me·tre** (sen'tə·mē'tər), *n.* ¹⁄₁₀₀ of a meter. [< F]

cen·ti·pede (sen'tə·pēd), *n.* a small wormlike animal with many pairs of legs. [< L *centipeda* < *centum* hundred + *pes* foot]

cen·tral (sen'trəl), *adj.* 1. of or being the center. 2. at or near the center. 3. from the center. 4. equally distant from all points; easy to get to or from. 5. main; chief. —*n. Am.* 1. a telephone exchange. 2. a telephone operator. [< L *centralis.* See CENTER.] —**cen'tral·ly,** *adv.* —**cen'tral·ness,** *n.* —Syn. *adj.* 5. leading, principal.

Central African Republic, republic in C Africa, N of the Congo, formerly part of French Equatorial Africa.

Central America, that part of North America between Mexico and South America. —**Central American.**

cen·tral·ize (sen'trəl·īz), *v.,* –ized, –iz·ing. 1. collect at a center; gather together. 2. bring or come under one control. —**cen'tral·i·za'tion,** *n.* —**cen'tral·iz'er,** *n.*

cen·tre (sen'tər), *n., v.,* –tred, –tring. *Esp. Brit.* center.

cen·tric (sen'trik), **cen·tri·cal** (–trə·kəl), *adj.* central. —**cen'tri·cal·ly,** *adv.* —**cen·tric·i·ty** (sen·tris'ə·ti), *n.*

cen·trif·u·gal (sen·trif'yə·gəl; –trif'ə–), *adj.* 1. moving away from the center. 2. making use of or acted upon by centrifugal force. [< NL, < E *centri–* center + L *fugere* flee] —**cen·trif'u·gal·ly,** *adv.*

centrifugal force or **action,** inertia of a body rotated around a center, tending to move it away from the center.

cen·tri·fuge (sen'trə·fūj), *n.* machine for separating cream from milk, bacteria from a fluid, etc., by means of centrifugal force. [< F]

cen·trip·e·tal (sen·trip'ə·təl), *adj.* 1. moving toward the center. 2. making use of or acted upon by centripetal force. [< NL, < E *centri–* center + L *petere* seek] —**cen·trip'e·tal·ly,** *adv.*

centripetal force or **action,** force that tends to move things toward the center around which they are turning.

cen·tu·ple (sen'tə·pəl; –tyə–), *adj., v.,* –pled,

–pling. —*adj.* 100 times as much or as many; hundredfold. —*v.* make 100 times as much or as many. [< F < LL *centuplus* hundredfold]

cen·tu·ri·on (sen·tùr'i·ən; –tyúr'–), *n.* commander of a group of about 100 soldiers in the ancient Roman army. [< L, < *centuria* CENTURY]

cen·tu·ry (sen'chə·ri), *n., pl.* –ries. 1. each 100 years, counting from some special time, such as the birth of Christ. 2. period of 100 years. 3. group of 100 people or things. 4. body of soldiers in the ancient Roman army. [< L *centuria* a division of a hundred units < *centum* hundred] ❯ Remember that the fifth century A.D. ran from the beginning of the year 401 to the end of the year 500, the nineteenth century from January 1, 1801, through December 31, 1900. That is, to name the century correctly, add one to the number of its hundred. Dates before Christ are figured like those after: the first century B.C. runs back from the birth of Christ through 100, the second century from 101 through 200, the fifth century from 401 through 500, and so on.

century plant, *Am.* a large, thick-leaved plant growing in Mexico and SW United States.

ce·phal·ic (sə·fal'ik), *adj.* 1. of the head. 2. near, on, or in the head. 3. toward the head. [< L < Gk., < *kephale* head]

ceph·a·lo·pod (sef'ə·lə·pod'), *n.* sea mollusk that has long, armlike tentacles around the mouth, a soft body, a pair of large eyes, and a sharp, birdlike beak. Cuttlefish and squids are cephalopods. —**ceph·a·lop·o·dan** (sef'ə·lop'ə·dən), *adj.*

ce·ram·ic (sə·ram'ik), *adj.* having to do with pottery, earthenware, porcelain, etc., or with making them. [< Gk., < *keramos* potter's clay]

ce·ram·ics (sə·ram'iks), *n.* 1. (*sing. in use*) art of making pottery, earthenware, porcelain, etc. 2. (*pl. in use*) articles made of pottery, earthenware, porcelain, etc. —**cer·a·mist** (ser'ə·mist), *n.*

Cer·ber·us (sér'bər·əs), *n.* 1. *Gk. and Roman Legend.* three-headed dog that guarded the entrance to Hades. 2. surly, watchful guard.

ce·re·al (sir'i·əl), *n.* 1. any grass that produces a grain used as food, as wheat, rice, oats, etc. 2. the grain. 3. a food made from the grain, as oatmeal and corn meal. —*adj.* of or having to do with grain or the grasses producing it. [< L *Cerealis* pertaining to Ceres]

cer·e·bel·lum (ser'ə·bel'əm), *n., pl.* –bel·lums, –bel·la (–bel'ə). *Anat., Zool.* part of the brain that controls the coördination of the muscles. [< L, dim. of *cerebrum* brain] —**cer·e·bel'lar,** *adj.*

cer·e·bral (ser'ə·brəl; se·rē'brəl), *adj.* 1. of the brain. 2. of the cerebrum. [< L *cerebrum* brain]

cerebral palsy, paralysis due to a lesion of the brain.

cer·e·brate (ser'ə·brāt), *v.,* –brat·ed, –brat·ing. use the brain; think. —**cer'e·bra'tion,** *n.*

cer·e·brum (ser'ə·brəm), *n., pl.* –brums, –bra (–brə). 1. *Anat.* part of the human brain that controls thought and voluntary muscular movements. 2. *Zool.* the corresponding part (anatomically) of the brain of any vertebrate. [< L]

cere·ment (sir'mənt), *n.* Usually, cerements. cloth or garment in which a dead person is wrapped for burial.

cer·e·mo·ni·al (ser'ə·mō'ni·əl), *adj.* 1. formal. 2. of or having to do with ceremony. —*n.* formal actions proper to an occasion. —**cer'e·mo'ni·al·ism,** *n.* —**cer'e·mo'ni·al·ist,** *n.* —**cer'e·mo'ni·al·ly,** *adv.*

cer·e·mo·ni·ous (ser'ə·mō'ni·əs), *adj.* 1. full of ceremony. 2. very formal; extremely polite. —**cer'e·mo'ni·ous·ly,** *adv.* —**cer'e·mo'ni·ous·ness,** *n.* —Syn. 2. stiff, precise.

cer·e·mo·ny (ser'ə·mō'ni), *n., pl.* –nies. 1. a special form or set of acts to be done on special occasions such as weddings, funerals, graduations, Christmas, or Easter. 2. any usage of politeness or civility. 3. very polite conduct. 4. a meaningless formality. 5. formality; formalities. [< L *caerimonia* rite]

(Centi-pede — Centipede (1 in. long))

Ce·res (sir'ēz), *n.* Roman goddess of agriculture, identified with the Greek goddess Demeter.

ce·rise (sə·rēz'; -rēs'), *n., adj.* bright, pinkish red. [< F *cerise* cherry < VL < LGk. *kerasia* < Gk. *kerasos* cherry tree]

ce·ri·um (sir'i·əm), *n. Chem.* a grayish metallic element, Ce. [< NL, from the asteroid *Ceres*]

cer·tain (sér'tən), *adj.* 1. sure: *certain to happen.* 2. settled; fixed: *at a certain hour.* 3. reliable; dependable. 4. definite but not named; some; one: *certain persons.* —*n.* for certain, surely; without a doubt. [< OF, ult. < L *certus* sure] —**cer'tain·ness,** *n.* —Syn. *adj.* 3. trustworthy, unfailing. 4. particular.

cer·tain·ly (sér'tən·li), *adv.* surely; without a doubt. —*interj.* surely! of course!

cer·tain·ty (sér'tən·ti), *n., pl.* **-ties.** 1. freedom from doubt. 2. a sure fact.

cer·tif·i·cate (*n.* sər·tif'ə·kit; *v.* sər·tif'ə·kāt), *n., v., -cat·ed, -cat·ing.* —*n.* 1. a written or printed statement that declares something to be a fact. 2. such a statement legally attested. —*v.* 1. give a certificate to. 2. authorize by a certificate. [< Med.L *certificatum.* See CERTIFY.] —**cer·ti·fi·ca·tion** (sér'tə·fə·kā'shən; sər·tif'ə-), *n.*

cer·ti·fy (sér'tə·fī), *v., -fied, -fy·ing.* 1. declare (something) true or correct by spoken, written, or printed statement. 2. guarantee the quality or value of. 3. assure; make certain. [< Med.L *certificare* < L *certus* sure + *facere* make] —**cer'ti·fi'a·ble,** *adj.* —**cer'ti·fi'er,** *n.*

cer·ti·o·ra·ri (sér'shi·ə·rār'ī; -rär'ī), *n. Law.* order from a higher court to a lower one, calling for the record of a case for review. [< LL, be informed. See CERTAIN.]

cer·ti·tude (sér'tə·tüd; -tūd), *n.* certainty; sureness. [< LL *certitudo.* See CERTAIN.]

ce·ru·le·an (sə·rü'li·ən), *adj., n.* sky-blue. [< L *caeruleus* dark blue]

Cer·van·tes (sər·van'tēz), *n.* Miguel de, 1547-1616, Spanish author who wrote *Don Quixote.*

cer·vi·cal (sér'və·kəl), *adj.* of the neck.

cer·vine (sér'vīn; -vin), *adj.* of or like a deer. [< L, < *cervus* deer]

cer·vix (sér'viks), *n., pl.* **cer·vix·es, cer·vi·ces** (sər·vī'sēz). 1. the neck, esp. the back of the neck. 2. a necklike part. [< L]

Ce·sar·e·an, Ce·sar·i·an (si·zãr'i·ən), *adj., n.* Caesarean.

ce·si·um (sē'zi·əm), *n. Chem.* a silvery metallic element, Cs. Also, **caesium.** [< NL, < L *caesius* bluish-gray]

ces·sa·tion (se·sā'shən), *n.* a ceasing or stopping. [< L, < *cessare* cease] —Syn. pause, lull.

ces·sion (sesh'ən), *n.* a handing over to another; ceding; giving up; surrendering. [< L *cessio* < *cedere* yield]

cess·pool (ses'pül'), *n.* 1. pool or pit for house drains to empty into. 2. filthy place.

ce·su·ra (sə·zhūr'ə; -zyūr'ə), *n.* caesura. —**ce·su'ral,** *adj.*

ce·ta·ce·an (sə·tā'shən), *adj.* Also, **ce·ta'ceous.** of or belonging to a group of mammals living in the water, including whales, dolphins, and porpoises. —*n.* animal that belongs to this group.

Cey·lon (si·lon'), *n.* island in the Indian Ocean, just off S India, a dominion in the British Commonwealth of Nations since 1948. —**Cey·lo·nese** (sē'lə·nēz'; -nēs'), *adj., n.*

Cé·zanne (sā·zan'; -zän'), *n.* Paul, 1839-1906, French painter.

cf., compare.

cg., centigram; centigrams.

ch., Ch., 1. chapter. 2. church.

Chad (chad), *n.* Lake, lake in N Africa.

Chad, a republic in C Africa, S of Libya, formerly part of N French Equatorial Africa.

chafe (chāf), *v.,* **chafed, chaf·ing,** *n.* —*v.* 1. rub to make warm. 2. wear or be worn away by

rubbing. 3. make or become sore by rubbing. 4. make angry. 5. become angry. —*n.* a chafing; irritation. [< OF *chaufer,* ult. < L, < *calere* to warm + *facere* make] —Syn. *v.* 4. irritate, gall.

chaf·er (chāf'ər), *n. Esp. Brit.* any of a group of beetles. [OE *ceafor*]

chaff¹ (chaf; chäf), *n.* 1. husks of wheat, oats, rye, etc., separated from grain by threshing. 2. worthless stuff; rubbish. [OE *ceaf*]

chaff² (chaf; chäf), *v.* banter; tease. —*n.* banter. —**chaff'er,** *n.*

chaf·fer (chaf'ər), *v.* dispute about a price; bargain. —*n.* bargaining. [ME *chaffare* < OE *cēap* bargain + *faru* journey] —**chaf'fer·er,** *n.*

chaf·finch (chaf'inch), *n.* a European songbird with a pleasant, short song, often kept as a cage bird. [OE *ceaffinc.* See CHAFF¹, FINCH.]

chaf·ing dish (chāf'ing), *Am.* pan with a heater under it, used to cook food at the table or to keep it warm.

cha·grin (shə·grin'), *n.* a feeling of disappointment, failure, or humiliation. —*v.* cause to feel chagrin. [< F, < OF *graignier* < *graim* sad, sorrowful] —Syn. *n.* mortification, dismay.

chain (chān), *n.* 1. series of links joined together. 2. series of things joined or linked together: *a mountain chain, a chain of happenings.* 3. anything that binds or restrains. 4. a measuring instrument like a chain. A surveyor's chain is 66 feet long; an engineer's chain is 100 feet long. 5. *Am.* number of similar restaurants, theaters, etc., owned and operated by one person or company. 6. **chains,** a. bonds; fetters. b. imprisonment; bondage. 7. *Chem.* a number of atoms of the same element linked together like a chain. —*v.* 1. join together or fasten with a chain. 2. bind; restrain. 3. keep in prison; make a slave of. [< OF *chaeine* < L *catena* chain]

chain gang, *Am.* gang of convicts, etc., chained together while at work outdoors.

chain mail, flexible armor made of metal rings linked together.

chain reaction, 1. *Physics.* process marked by an explosive release of atomic energy, as in the bombardment of unstable uranium nuclei by plutonium neutrons in the explosion of an atomic bomb, each uranium nucleus releasing a number of plutonium neutrons, which in turn split other uranium nuclei. 2. any series of events or happenings, each caused by the preceding one or ones. —**chain'-re·act'ing,** *adj.*

chain-smoke (chān'smōk'), *v.* smoke incessantly or heavily; smoke by lighting a cigarette or cigar from the one just smoked. —**chain'-smok'er,** *n.*

chain stitch, kind of sewing or crocheting in which each stitch makes a loop through which the next stitch is taken.

chain store, *Am.* one of a group of retail stores owned and operated by one company.

chair (chãr), *n.* 1. seat for one person that has a back and, sometimes, arms. 2. seat of position, dignity, or authority. 3. position or authority of a person who has such a seat. 4. chairman. 5. *Am.* electric chair. 6. **take the chair,** a. begin a meeting. b. be in charge of or preside at a meeting. —*v.* 1. put or carry in a chair. 2. put in a position of authority. 3. act as chairman of (a committee, etc.). [< OF *chaiere* < L < Gk. *kathedra* seat]

chair·man (chãr'mən), *n., pl.* **-men.** 1. person who presides at or is in charge of a meeting. 2. head of a committee. —**chair'man·ship,** *n.*

chair·wom·an (chãr'wum'ən), *n., pl.* **-wom·en.** a woman chairman.

chaise (shāz), *n.* a lightweight carriage, often one with a folding top. [< F *chaise* chair, var. of *chaire* CHAIR]

chaise longue (shāz' lông'; long'), chair with a long seat and a back at one end, somewhat like a couch. [< F, long chair]

chal·ced·o·ny (kal·sed'ə·ni; kal'sə·dō'ni), *n., pl.* **-nies.** variety of quartz that has a waxy luster and occurs in various colors and forms. [< L < Gk. *chalkedon*]

Chal·da·ic (kal·dā'ik), *adj., n.* Chaldean.

Chal·de·a (kal·dē′ə), *n.* ancient region in SW Asia, on the Tigris and Euphrates rivers. —**Chal·de′an**, *adj., n.*

Chal·dee (kal·dē′; kal′dē), *adj., n.* Chaldean.

cha·let (sha·lā′; shal′ā), *n.* 1. a house or villa with wide, overhanging eaves. 2. a herdsman's hut or cabin in the Swiss mountains. [< Swiss F]

chal·ice (chal′is), *n.* 1. cup. 2. cup that holds the wine used in the Communion service. 3. a cup-shaped flower. [< OF < L *calix* cup] —**chal·iced** (chal′ist), *adj.*

chalk (chôk), *n.* 1. soft limestone, made up mostly of very small fossil sea shells. 2. substance like chalk, used for writing or drawing on a blackboard. 3. piece of this substance. 4. a record of credit given. —*v.* 1. mark, write, or draw with chalk. 2. mix or rub with chalk; whiten with chalk. 3. score; record. 4. **chalk up,** a. *Am.* increase a price, score, etc.; mark up. b. write down; record. [< L *calx* lime] —**chalk′like′**, *adj.* —**chalk′y**, *adj.* —**chalk′i·ness**, *n.*

Chalice (def. 2)

chal·lenge (chal′inj), *v.*, **-lenged, -leng·ing,** *n.* —*v.* 1. call to fight, esp. call to fight in a duel. 2. invite or summon to a game or contest. 3. call on (a person, etc.) to answer and explain. 4. call in question; doubt; dispute. 5. object to (a juror, vote, etc.). 6. *Am.* object to (a certain person's vote) as illegal. 7. claim; demand: *a problem that challenges everyone's attention.* 8. make a challenge. —*n.* 1. call to fight, esp. in a duel. 2. call to a game or contest. 3. a demand to answer and explain: *"Who goes there?" is the guard's challenge.* 4. objection made, as to a juror or a vote. 5. *Am.* an objection that a voter is not qualified to vote. [< OF < L *calumnia* CALUMNY] —**chal′lenge·a·ble**, *adj.* —**chal′leng·er**, *n.*

chal·lis, chal·lie (shal′i), *n.* a lightweight plain or printed cloth, used for dresses.

cham·ber (chām′bər), *n.* 1. a room (in a house). 2. bedroom. 3. hall where a legislature or a governing body meets. 4. a legislative, judicial, or other like body. 5. a cavity: *the heart has four chambers.* 6. that part of the barrel of a gun which receives the charge. 7. place for a cartridge in the cylinder of a revolver. 8. **chambers,** a. *Brit.* set of rooms in a building to live in or use as offices. b. office of a lawyer or judge. —*v.* provide with a chamber. [< OF < L < Gk. *kamara* vaulted place. Doublet of CAMERA.] —**cham′bered**, *adj.*

cham·ber·lain (chām′bər·lin), *n.* 1. person who manages the household of a king or lord; steward. 2. a high official of a king's court. 3. treasurer: *city chamberlain.* [< OF < L *camera* vault + Gmc. *-ling*]

cham·ber·maid (chām′bər·mād′), *n.* maid who makes the beds, cleans the bedrooms, etc.

chamber music, music suited to a room or small hall; music for a trio, quartet, etc.

chamber of commerce, group of people organized to protect and promote business interests of a city, state, etc.

cham·bray (sham′brā), *n. Am.* a fine variety of gingham. [var. of *cambric*]

cha·me·le·on (kə·mē′li·ən; -mēl′yən), *n.* 1. lizard that can change the color of its skin. 2. a changeable or fickle person. [< L < Gk., lit., ground lion, < *chamai* on the ground, dwarf + *leon* lion] —**cha·me·le·on·ic** (kə·mē′li·on′ik), *adj.*

cham·ois (sham′i), *n., pl.* **-ois.** 1. a small, goatlike antelope that lives in the high mountains of Europe and SW Asia. 2. Also, **cham′my,** a soft leather made from the skin of sheep, goats, deer, etc. [< F < LL *camox*]

Chamois (2 ft. high at the shoulder)

cham·o·mile (kam′ə·mīl), *n.* camomile.

champ¹ (champ), *v.* 1. bite and chew noisily. 2. bite on impatiently. [? akin to *chap* CHOP²]

champ² (champ), *n. Am., Slang.* champion

cham·pagne (sham·pān′), *n.* 1. a sparkling, bubbling wine. 2. pale, brownish yellow.

cham·paign (sham·pān′), *n.* a wide plain, level, open country. —*adj.* level and open. [< OF *champagne.* See CAMPAIGN.]

cham·pi·on (cham′pi·ən), *n.* 1. person, animal, or thing that wins first place in a game or contest. 2. person who fights or speaks for another; defender; supporter. —*adj.* having won first place; ahead of all others. —*v.* fight or speak in behalf of; defend; support. [< OF < LL *campio* < *campus* field (i.e., of battle)] —**cham′pi·on·less**, *adj.* —**Syn.** *n.* 2. protector. *-v.* advocate.

cham·pi·on·ship (cham′pi·ən·ship′), *n.* 1. position of a champion; first place. 2. defense; support.

Cham·plain (sham·plān′), *n.* **Lake,** a long, narrow lake between New York and Vermont.

chance (chans; chäns), *n., v.,* **chanced, chanc·ing,** *adj.* —*n.* 1. opportunity: *the chance to go to college.* 2. possibility: *there's a chance he may go to college.* 3. probability: *the chances are that he will have enough money.* 4. fate; luck. 5. a risk. 6. a happening. 7. **by chance,** accidentally. —*v.* 1. happen. 2. *Colloq.* take the risk of; risk. —*adj.* not expected or planned; accidental; casual. [< OF < L *cadentia* a falling < *cadere* fall] —**Syn.** *n.* 3. likelihood. *-adj.* fortuitous, offhand, unexpected.

chan·cel (chan′səl; chän′-), *n.* space around the altar of a church, usually enclosed, used by the clergy and the choir. [< F < L *cancelli* grating]

chan·cel·ler·y (chan′sə·lər·i; -slə·ri; chän′-), *n., pl.* **-ler·ies.** 1. position of a chancellor. 2. office of a chancellor.

chan·cel·lor (chan′sə·lər; -slər; chän′-), *n.* 1. the title, esp. in Great Britain, of various high officials: *Chancellor of the Exchequer.* 2. *Am.* the chief judge of a court of chancery or equity in some States. 3. formerly, the prime minister in Germany or Austria. 4. the chief secretary of an embassy. 5. title of the president in certain universities. [< AF < L *cancellarius* officer stationed at tribunal. See CHANCEL.] —**chan′cel·lor·ship′**, *n.*

chan·cer·y (chan′sər·i; chän′-), *n., pl.* **-cer·ies.** 1. court of equity. 2. equity. 3. office where public records are kept. 4. office of a chancellor. 5. **in chancery,** a. in a court of equity. b. in a helpless position. [var. of CHANCELLERY]

chan·cre (shang′kər), *n.* ulcer or sore with a hard base. [< F. See CANKER.] —**chan′crous**, *adj.*

chan·de·lier (shan′də·lir′), *n.* fixture with branches for lights. [< F < VL *candelarius* < L *candela* CANDLE]

chan·dler (chan′dlər; chän′-), *n.* 1. maker or seller of candles. 2. dealer in groceries and supplies: *a ship chandler.* [< AF *chaundeler* < VL *candelarius* < L *candela* CANDLE]

Chang·chun (chäng′chŭn′), *n.* city in Manchuria.

change (chānj), *v.,* **changed, chang·ing,** *n.* —*v.* 1. make or become different. 2. put (something) in place of another; substitute. 3. take in place of. 4. give or get (money of a different sort) for. 5. take a different train, bus, etc. 6. put on other clothes. 7. put other clothing or covering on: *change a bed.* 8. give and take; exchange. 9. **change hands,** a. pass from one owner to another. b. substitute one hand for the other. —*n.* 1. act or fact of changing. 2. a changed condition or appearance. 3. *Music.* change of key; modulation. 4. variety; difference. 5. thing to be used in place of another of the same kind. 6. a second set of clothes. 7. money returned to a person when he has given an amount larger than the price of what he buys. 8. smaller pieces of money given in place of a large piece of money. 9. small coins. 10. Also, **'change.** exchange; place for trading in securities or commodities. 11. **changes,** different ways in which a set of bells can be rung. [< OF < LL *cambiare*] —**change′ful**, *adj.* —**change′ful·ness**, *n.* —**chang′er**, *n.* —**Syn.** *v.* 1. alter, transform, transmute. *-n.* 1. alteration. 2. transformation. 4. diversity. 5. substitute.

change·a·ble (chānj'ə·bəl), *adj.* 1. that can change; likely to change: *a changeable person.* 2. that can be changed; likely to be changed. 3. having a color or appearance that changes. —change'a·bil'i·ty, change'a·ble·ness, *n.* —change'a·bly, *adv.* —Syn. 1. inconstant. 2. alterable, variable, unstable, uncertain.

change·less (chānj'lis), *adj.* not changing; not likely to change; constant; steadfast. —change'less·ly, *adv.* —change'less·ness, *n.*

change·ling (chānj'ling), *n.* child secretly substituted for another.

change of venue, change of the place of a trial.

change·o·ver (chānj'ō'vər), *n.* a planned shift from one procedure of operation, manufacture, etc. to another.

chan·nel (chan'əl), *n., v.,* -neled, -nel·ing; *esp. Brit.* -nelled, -nel·ling. —*n.* 1. bed of a stream, river, etc. 2. body of water joining two larger bodies of water: *the English Channel.* 3. the deeper part of a waterway. 4. passage for liquids; groove. 5. means by which something is carried: *secret channels.* 6. *Radio.* a narrow band of frequencies. 7. course of action; line of doing things: *useful channels.* —*v.* form a channel in; cut out as a channel. [< OF < L *canalis* CANAL. Doublet of CANAL.]

Channel Islands, British islands near the NW coast of France; Alderney, Guernsey, Jersey, and Sark.

chant (chant; chänt), *n.* 1. song. 2. a short, simple song in which several syllables or words are sung in one tone, used in a church service. 3. psalm, prayer, or other song for chanting. 4. a singsong way of talking. —*v.* 1. sing. 2. sing to, or in the manner of, a chant. A choir chants psalms or prayers. 3. celebrate in song. 4. keep talking about; say over and over again. [< OF < L *cantare* < *canere* sing] —chant'er, *n.*

chant·ey, chant·y (shan'ti; chan'-), *n., pl.* -eys; -ies. song sung by sailors, in rhythm with the motions made during their work. Also, shanty. [alter. of F *chanter* sing. See CHANT.]

chan·ti·cleer (chan'tə·klir), *n.* rooster. [< OF, < *chanter* sing + *cler* clear]

cha·os (kā'os), *n.* 1. great confusion; complete disorder. 2. infinite space or formless matter before the universe existed. [< L < Gk.] —Syn. 1. disorganization, anarchy.

cha·ot·ic (kā·ot'ik), *adj.* in great confusion; very confused; completely disordered. —cha·ot'i·cal·ly, *adv.*

chap¹ (chap), *v.,* chapped, chap·ping, *n.* —*v.* crack open; make or become rough: *a person's lips often chap in cold weather.* —*n.* a place where the skin is chapped. [ME *chappe(n)* cut]

chap² (chap), *n. Colloq.* fellow; man; boy. [short for *chapman* a peddler; OE *cēapman* < *cēap* trade + *man* man]

chap³ (chap), *n.* chop (def. 2).

chap., 1. chapel. 2. chaplain. 3. chapter.

cha·pa·ra·jos (chä'pə·rä'hōs), **cha·pa·re·jos** (-rā'hōs), *n.pl. Am., S.W.* chaps. [< Mex. Sp.]

chap·ar·ral (chap'ə·ral'), *n. Am., S.W.* thicket of low shrubs, thorny bushes, etc. [< Sp., < *chaparro* evergreen oak]

chap·book (chap'bůk'), *n.* a small book or pamphlet of popular tales, ballads, etc., formerly sold on the streets.

chap·el (chap'əl), *n.* 1. a building for Christian worship, not so large as a church. 2. a small place for worship in a larger building. 3. room or building for worship in a palace, school, etc. 4. a religious service in a chapel. 5. *Brit.* a place for worship used by people who do not belong to an established church. [< OF < LL *cappella* orig., a shrine in which was preserved the *cappa* or cape of St. Martin]

chap·er·on, chap·er·one (shap'ər·ōn), *n., v.,* -oned, -on·ing. —*n.* a married woman or an older woman who accompanies a young unmarried woman in public for the sake of good form

and protection. —*v.* act as a chaperon to. [< F *chaperon* hood, protector. See CAPE¹.] —chap·er·on·age (shap'ər·ōn'ij), *n.*

chap·fall·en (chop'fôl'ən; chap'-), *adj.* dejected; discouraged. Also, chopfallen.

chap·lain (chap'lin), *n.* clergyman officially authorized to perform religious functions for a family, court, society, public institution, regiment, or warship. [< OF < LL *capellanus* < *cappella* CHAPEL] —chap'lain·cy, chap'lain·ship, *n.*

chap·let (chap'lit), *n.* 1. wreath worn on the head. 2. string of beads. 3. string of beads for keeping count in saying prayers, one third as long as a rosary. 4. prayers said with such beads. [< OF *chapelet,* dim. of *chapel* headdress. See CAP.] —chap'let·ed, *adj.*

chaps (chaps; shaps), *n.pl. Am., S. W.* strong leather trousers without a back, worn over other trousers, esp. by cowboys. Also, chaparajos, chaparejos.

chap·ter (chap'tər), *n.* 1. a main division of a book or other writing. 2. anything like a chapter; part; section. 3. *Am.* a local division of an organization; branch of a club, society, etc. 4. group of clergymen usually attached to a cathedral. 5. meeting of such a group. —*v.* divide into chapters; arrange in chapters. [< OF < L *capitulum,* dim. of *caput* head]

Cha·pul·te·pec (chə·pul'tə·pek), *n.* fort near Mexico City, scene of battle in Mexican War (1847) and site of international conference (1945) in World War II.

char¹ (chär), *v.,* charred, char·ring. 1. burn to charcoal. 2. scorch. [? < *charcoal*]

char² (chär), *n., v.,* charred, char·ring. *Esp. Brit.* —*n.* an odd job; chore. —*v.* 1. do odd jobs or chores. 2. do housework by the day or hour. Also, chare. [OE *cerr* turn, occasion]

char·ac·ter (kar'ik·tər), *n.* 1. all qualities or features possessed; kind; sort; nature. 2. moral strength or weakness; special way in which any person feels, thinks, and acts. 3. good character. 4. reputation. 5. good reputation. 6. special thing or quality that makes one person, animal, thing, or group different from others. 7. position; condition: *the treasurer of the club also serves in the character of secretary.* 8. person in a play or book. 9. *Colloq.* person who attracts attention because he is different or queer. 10. description of a person's qualities. 11. letter, mark, or sign used in writing or printing. A, a, +, −, 1, 2, and 3 are characters. —*v.* 1. inscribe; engrave. 2. describe. [< F < L < Gk. *charaktēr* instrument for marking < *charassein* engrave] —Syn. *n.* 2. personality, individuality, nature, temperament.

char·ac·ter·is·tic (kar'ik·tər·is'tik), *adj.* distinguishing from others; special. —*n.* a special quality or feature; whatever distinguishes one person or thing from others. —char'ac·ter·is'ti·cal·ly, *adv.* —Syn. *n.* attribute, trait.

char·ac·ter·ize (kar'ik·tər·īz), *v.,* -ized, -iz·ing. 1. describe the special qualities or features of (a person or thing); describe. 2. be a characteristic of; distinguish. 3. give character to. —char'ac·ter·i·za'tion, *n.* —char'ac·ter·iz'er, *n.* —Syn. 1. portray.

char·ac·ter·less (kar'ik·tər·lis), *adj.* 1. without a character. 2. without distinction; uninteresting.

cha·rade (shə·rād'), *n.* game of guessing a word from the descriptive or dramatic representation of each syllable or part, and of the whole. [< F < Pr. *charrada* < *charra* chatter]

char·coal (chär'kōl'), *n.* 1. black substance made by partly burning wood or bones in a place from which the air is shut out. 2. pencil made of charcoal for drawing. 3. drawing made with such a pencil. [ME *charcole*]

chare (chār), *n., v.,* chared, char·ing. *Esp. Brit.* char².

charge (chärj), *v.,* charged, charg·ing, *n.* —*v.* 1. load; fill: *a gun is charged with powder and*

āge, cāre, fär; ēqual, tẽrm; īce; ōpen, ôrder; půt, rüle, ūse; th, then; ə=a in about.

shot. **2.** restore the capacity of (an electric storage battery) by sending a direct current through it. **3.** give a task, duty, or responsibility to. **4.** give an order or command to; direct. **5.** accuse: *the driver was charged with speeding.* **6.** ask as a price; put on a price of. **7.** put down as a debt to be paid. **8.** make a violent final rush: *the soldiers charged the enemy.* **9. charge off,** a. subtract as a loss. b. put down as belonging: *a bad mistake must be charged off to experience.* —*n.* **1.** quantity needed to load or fill something, esp. the explosive used in firing a gun. **2.** task; duty; responsibility. **3.** care; management: *doctors and nurses have charge of sick people.* **4.** person, persons, or thing under the care or management of someone. **5.** order; command; direction. **6.** formal instruction or exhortation: *a judge's charge to the jury.* **7.** formal statement accusing a person of having broken the law, violated a rule, etc. **8.** price asked for or put on something. **9.** a debt to be paid. **10.** the violent final rush in an attack or assault. **11.** the military signal for attack. **12. in charge,** having the care or management. [< F < LL *carricare* load < L *carrus* wagon. Doublet of CARRY.] —Syn. *v.* **5.** indict, arraign. **8.** assault. —*n.* **3.** custody. **7.** indictment, complaint. **10.** assault, onset.

charge·a·ble (chär′jə·bəl), *adj.* **1.** that can be charged. **2.** liable to become a public charge.

char·gé d'af·faires (shär·zhā′ də·fār′), *pl.* **char·gés d'af·faires** (shär·zhāz′ də·fār′). *French.* deputy of a diplomat.

charg·er[1] (chär′jər), *n.* **1.** war horse. **2.** person or thing that charges.

charg·er[2] (chär′jər), *n. Archaic.* a large, flat dish; platter. [< OF, < *charger* CHARGE]

char·i·ly (châr′ə·li), *adv.* carefully; warily.

char·i·ness (châr′i·nis), *n.* chary quality.

char·i·ot (char′i·ət), *n.* **1.** a two-wheeled car pulled by horses, used in ancient times in fighting, racing, and processions. **2.** a four-wheeled carriage or coach. [< OF, < *char* CAR]

char·i·ot·eer (char′i·ət·ir′), *n.* person who drives a chariot.

char·i·ta·ble (char′ə·tə·bəl), *adj.* **1.** of charity. **2.** generous in giving help to poor or suffering people. **3.** kindly in judging people and their actions. —**char′i·ta·ble·ness,** *n.* —**char′i·ta·bly,** *adv.* —Syn. **2.** liberal, bountiful. **3.** tolerant.

char·i·ty (char′ə·ti), *n., pl.* **-ties. 1.** help given to the poor or suffering. **2.** act or work of charity. **3.** fund, institution, or organization for helping the poor or suffering. **4.** Christian love of one's fellow men. **5.** kindness in judging people. [< OF < L *caritas* dearness < *carus* dear] —Syn. **1.** philanthropy, beneficence.

char·la·tan (shär′lə·tən), *n.* person who pretends to have more knowledge or skill than he really has; quack. [< F < Ital. *ciarlatano*, ult. < Mongolian *dzar* proclaim, tell lies] —Syn. impostor, cheat.

char·la·tan·ism (shär′lə·tən·iz′əm), **char·la·tan·ry** (-tən·ri), *n.* quackery.

Char·le·magne (shär′lə·mān), *n.* 742?–814 A.D., king of the Franks from 768 to 814 A.D. and emperor of the Holy Roman Empire 800–814 A.D.

Charles I, 1. 1600–1649, king of England from 1625, executed in 1649. 2. Charlemagne.

Charles II, 1630–1685, king of England from 1660 to 1685, son of Charles I.

Charles·ton (chärlz′tən), *n.* **1.** capital of West Virginia, in the W part. **2.** seaport in SE South Carolina.

char·ley horse (chär′li), *Am., Colloq.* stiffness caused by straining a muscle.

Char·lotte (shär′lət), *n.* city in S North Carolina.

Char·lot·te A·ma·li·e (shär·lot′ə ə·mä′li·ə), seaport and capital of the Virgin Islands.

char·lotte russe (shär′lət rüs′), dessert made of a mold of sponge cake filled with whipped cream or custard. [< F, Russian charlotte (a type of dessert)]

Char·lottes·ville (shär′ləts·vil), *n.* city in C Virginia.

charm (chärm), *n.* **1.** power of delighting or

fascinating; attractiveness. **2.** a very pleasing quality or feature. **3.** a small ornament or trinket worn on a watch chain, bracelet, etc. **4.** word, verse, act, or thing supposed to have magic power to help or harm people. —*v.* **1.** please greatly; delight; fascinate; attract. **2.** act on as if by magic: *laughter charmed away his troubles.* **3.** give magic power to; protect as by a charm. [< OF < L *carmen* song, enchantment < *canere* sing] —**charm′er,** *n.* —**charm′less,** *adj.* —Syn. *n.* **1.** allurement. —*v.* **1.** captivate, entrance.

charm·ing (chär′ming), *adj.* very pleasing; delightful; fascinating; attractive. —**charm′ing·ly,** *adv.* —**charm′ing·ness,** *n.*

char·nel house (chär′nəl), place where dead bodies or bones are laid. [< OF < LL *carnale.* See CARNAL.]

Char·on (kār′ən), *n. Gk. Myth.* boatman who ferried the spirits of the dead across the river Styx to Hades.

chart (chärt), *n.* **1.** map, esp. a hydrographic or marine map. **2.** an outline map showing special conditions or facts: *a weather chart.* **3.** sheet giving information in lists, pictures, tables, or diagrams. **4.** such a list, table, picture, or diagram. —*v.* make a chart of; show on a chart. [< F < L *charta* < Gk. *chartes* leaf of paper. Doublet of CARD.] —**chart′less,** *adj.*

char·ter (chär′tər), *n.* **1.** a written grant of certain rights or privileges, esp. one by a ruler to his subjects, or by a legislature to a city or company, telling how it is to be organized and what it can do. **2.** a written order from the authorities of a society, giving to a group of persons the right to organize a new chapter, branch, or lodge. —*v.* **1.** give a charter to. **2.** hire; rent. [< OF < L *chartula,* dim. of *charta.* See CHART.] —**char′ter·er,** *n.* —**char′ter·less,** *adj.*

char·treuse (shär·trœz′; *for 2, also* shär·trüz′, -trüs′), *n.* **1.** a green, yellow, or white liqueur first made by Carthusian monks. **2.** a light, yellowish green. [< F, Carthusian]

char·wom·an (chär′wum′ən), *n., pl.* **-wom·en.** woman whose work is doing odd jobs by the day, esp. cleaning. [see CHAR[2]]

char·y (châr′i), *adj.,* **char·i·er, char·i·est. 1.** careful. **2.** shy. **3.** sparing; stingy. [OE *cearig* < *caru* care] —Syn. **1.** wary, cautious. **3.** frugal.

Cha·ryb·dis (kə·rib′dis), *n.* whirlpool in the strait between Sicily and Italy, opposite the rock Scylla. Charybdis sucked down ships.

chase[1] (chās), *v.,* **chased, chas·ing,** *n.* —*v.* **1.** run after to catch or kill. **2.** drive; drive away. **3.** hunt. **4.** follow; pursue. **5.** rush; hurry. —*n.* **1.** chasing. **2.** hunting as a sport. **3.** a hunted animal. **4.** give chase, run after; chase. [< OF *chacier* < LL *captiare.* Doublet of CATCH.] —**chas′er,** *n.*

chase[2] (chās), *v.,* **chased, chas·ing.** engrave; emboss. [var. of *enchase*] —**chas′er,** *n.*

chase[3] (chās), *n.* **1.** groove; furrow; trench. **2.** iron frame to hold type that is ready to print or make plates from. [< F < L *capsa* box]

chasm (kaz′əm), *n.* **1.** a deep opening or crack in the earth; gap. **2.** wide difference of feelings or interests between people or groups. [< L < Gk. *chasma*] —**chas·mal** (kaz′məl), *adj.* —Syn. **1.** fissure, gorge, cleft, breach, abyss.

chas·sis (shas′i; chas′i), *n., pl.* **chas·sis** (shas′iz; chas′-). **1.** frame, wheels, and machinery of a motor vehicle. **2.** main landing gear of an aircraft. [< F < VL *capsiceum* < L *capsa.* See CHASE[3].]

chaste (chāst), *adj.* **1.** pure; virtuous. **2.** decent; modest. **3.** simple in taste or style. [< OF < L *castus* pure] —**chaste′ly,** *adv.* —**chaste′ness,** *n.* —Syn. **1.** innocent. **3.** classic, refined. —Ant. **1.** immoral.

chas·ten (chās′ən), *v.* **1.** punish to improve. **2.** restrain from excess or crudeness. [< obs. v. *chaste* < F < L *castigare* make pure < *castus* pure] —**chas′ten·er,** *n.* —Syn. **1.** discipline.

chas·tise (chas·tīz′), *v.,* **-tised, -tis·ing.** punish by beating or thrashing. [< obs. *chaste* CHASTEN + *-ise*] —**chas·tise·ment** (chas′tiz·mənt; chas·tīz′-), *n.* —**chas·tis′er,** *n.*

chas·ti·ty (chas′tə·ti), *n.* **1.** purity; virtue.

2. decency; modesty. 3. simplicity of style or taste; absence of too much decoration.

chas·u·ble (chaz′yə·bəl; chas′-), *n.* a sleeveless outer vestment covering all other vestments, worn by the priest at Mass. [< F < LL *casubula* < L *casa* house; akin to CASSOCK]

CHASUBLE

chat (chat), *n., v.*, **chat·ted, chat·ting.** —*n.* 1. easy, familiar talk. 2. any of several birds with a chattering cry. —*v.* talk in an easy, familiar way. [short for *chatter*]

châ·teau (sha·tō′), *n., pl.* **-teaux** (-tōz′). in France: 1. a castle. 2. a large country house. [< F < L *castellum* CASTLE. Doublet of CASTLE.]

Châ·teau-Thier·ry (sha·tō′-tyâr′i; -tē′ə·ri′), *n.* town in N France, on the Marne River; site of several battles in World War I.

chat·e·laine (shat′ə·lān), *n.* 1. mistress or lady of a castle. 2. clasp to which keys, a purse, etc., may be attached. [< F, ult. < L *castellum* CASTLE]

Chat·ta·noo·ga (chat′ə·nü′gə), *n.* city in SE Tennessee, on the Tennessee River.

chat·tel (chat′əl), *n.* movable possession; piece of property that is not real estate. Furniture, automobiles, slaves, and animals are chattels. [< OF *chatel*. Doublet of CATTLE.]

chat·ter (chat′ər), *v.* 1. talk constantly, rapidly, and foolishly. 2. make quick, indistinct sounds: *monkeys chatter.* 3. utter rapidly or uselessly. 4. rattle together. —*n.* 1. quick, foolish talk. 2. quick, indistinct sounds. [imit.] —**chat′ter·er,** *n.*

chat·ter·box (chat′ər·boks′), *n.* person who talks all the time.

chat·ty (chat′i), *adj.,* **-ti·er, -ti·est.** 1. fond of friendly, familiar talk. 2. conversational. —**chat′ti·ly,** *adv.* —**chat′ti·ness,** *n.*

Chau·cer (chô′sər), *n.* Geoffrey, 1340?-1400, English poet, author of *The Canterbury Tales.* —**Chau·ce·ri·an** (chô·sir′i·ən), *adj.*

chauf·feur (shō′fər; shō·fér′), *n.* man whose work is driving an automobile. —*v.* act as a chauffeur to. [< F, stoker < *chauffer* to heat; term from days of steam automobiles]

chaunt (chônt; chänt), *n., v. Archaic.* chant.

chau·tau·qua, Chau·tau·qua (shə·tô′kwə), *n. Am.* assembly for education and entertainment by lectures, concerts, etc. —**chau·tau′quan, Chau·tau′quan,** *n., adj. Am.*

chau·vin·ism (shō′vən·iz·əm), *n.* boastful, warlike patriotism. [< F *chauvinisme;* after Nicolas *Chauvin,* overenthusiastic patriot] —**chau′vin·ist,** *n., adj.* —**chau′vin·is′tic,** *adj.* —**chau′vin·is′ti·cal·ly,** *adv.*

cheap (chēp), *adj.* 1. costing little. 2. costing less than it is worth. 3. charging low prices: *a cheap market.* 4. easily obtained. 5. of low value; common. 6. feel cheap, feel inferior and ashamed. —*adv.* at a low price; at small cost. [short for *good cheap* a good bargain; OE *cēap* price, bargain] —**cheap′ly,** *adv.* —**cheap′ness,** *n.* —**Syn.** *adj.* 1. inexpensive, low-priced. 5. poor, mean, inferior, paltry, worthless.

cheap·en (chēp′ən), *v.* make or become cheap. —**cheap′en·er,** *n.*

cheat (chēt), *v.* 1. deceive or trick; play or do business in a way that is not honest. 2. beguile. 3. elude. —*n.* 1. person who is not honest and does things to deceive and trick others. 2. fraud; trick. [var. of *escheat*] —**cheat′er,** *n.* —**cheat′ing·ly,** *adv.* —**Syn.** *v.* 1. swindle, dupe, defraud, fool. —*n.* 1. swindler, impostor, deceiver. 2. swindle, deception, hoax.

check (chek), *v.* 1. stop suddenly; control; restrain. 3. control to prevent error, fraud, etc. 4. rebuff; repulse; reverse. 5. examine or compare to prove true or right. 6. *Am.* agree or be similar in every detail on comparison: *the two accounts check.* 7. *Am.* get a check for; put a check on. 8. *Am.* write a check; draw a

check. 9. mark in a pattern of squares. 10. crack; split. 11. *Am.* send (baggage identified by means of a check) to a given destination. 12. in chess, have (an opponent's king) in check. 13. check in, a. arrive and register at a hotel, etc. b. *Am., Slang.* die. 14. check off, mark as checked and found true or right. 15. check out, a. pay one's bill at a hotel and leave. b. *Slang.* die. 16. check up, *Am.* examine or compare to prove true or correct. —*n.* 1. a sudden stop. 2. a holding back; control; restraint. 3. means of preventing error, fraud, etc. 4. any person, thing, or event that controls or holds back action. 5. rebuff; repulse; reverse. 6. an examination or comparison to prove something true or right. 7. mark to show that something has been checked and found true or right. 8. ticket or metal piece given in return for a coat, hat, baggage, package, etc., to show ownership. 9. *Am.* bill for a meal, etc. 10. Also, *Brit.* **cheque.** a written order directing a bank to pay money to the person named on it. 11. pattern of squares. 12. one of these squares. 13. fabric marked in squares. 14. crack; split. 15. in chess, position of an opponent's king when it is in danger and must be moved. 16. in check, held back; controlled. —*adj.* 1. used in checking. 2. marked in a pattern of squares. —*interj.* a call in the game of chess warning that an opponent's king is in danger and must be moved. [< OF *eschec* a check at chess < Pers. *shāh* king, king at chess] —**check′a·ble,** *adj.* —**check′er,** *n.* —**Syn.** *v.* 1. halt, block. 2. repress, curb, bridle. —*n.* 1. stoppage, repulse. 4. restriction, curb, bridle, obstruction, ocstacle, hindrance. 8. tag, token, coupon. ➤ **check, cheque.** *Cheque* is a British spelling and its use in the United States is likely to seem pretentious.

check·book (chek′bủk′), *n.* book of blank checks on a bank.

check·er (chek′ər), *v.* 1. mark in a pattern of squares of different colors. 2. mark off with patches different from one another. 3. have ups and downs; change; vary. —*n.* 1. pattern of squares. 2. one of these squares. 3. one of the flat, round pieces used in the game of checkers. Also, *Brit.* **chequer.** [< OF *escheker* chessboard]

check·er·board (chek′ər·bôrd′; -bôrd′), *n.* board marked in a pattern of 64 squares of two alternating colors, used in playing checkers or chess. Also, *Brit.* **chequerboard.**

check·ered (chek′ərd), *adj.* 1. marked in a pattern of many-colored squares. 2. marked in patches. 3. often changing; varied. Also, *Brit.* **chequered.**

check·ers (chek′ərz), *n.* game played on a checkerboard by two people. Each player has 12 round, flat pieces to move. Also, *Brit.* **chequers.**

checking account, *Am.* bank account against which checks may be drawn.

check·mate (chek′māt′), *v.,* **-mat·ed, -mat·ing,** *n.* —*v.* 1. make a move in chess that wins the game. 2. defeat completely. —*n.* 1. in chess, a move that ends the game by putting the opponent's king in inescapable check. 2. a complete defeat. [< OF *echec et mat* < Ar. *shāh māt* the king is dead]

check·off (chek′ôf′; -of′), *n. Am.* system of collecting union dues through wage deductions made by the employer.

check point, a gate, sentry box, etc. at which persons are stopped so that their passports or other documents, baggage, etc. may be examined.

check·rein (chek′rān′), *n.* a short rein to keep a horse from lowering its head.

check·up (chek′up′), *n.* 1. *Am.* a careful examination. 2. a thorough physical examination.

cheek (chēk), *n.* 1. side of the face below either eye. 2. anything suggesting the human cheek in form or position. 3. *Colloq.* saucy talk or behavior; impudence. [OE *cēce*]

cheek·bone (chēk′bōn′), *n.* bone just below either eye.

cheek·y (chēk′i), *adj.,* **cheek·i·er, cheek·i·est.** *Colloq.* saucy; impudent. —**cheek′i·ly,** *adv.* —**cheek′i·ness,** *n.*

cheep (chēp), *v.* make a short, sharp sound like

a young bird; chirp; peep. —*n.* such a sound. [imit.] —cheep′er, *n.*

cheer (chir), *n.* 1. joy; gladness; comfort; encouragement. 2. shout of encouragement, approval, praise, etc. 3. food. 4. state of mind; condition of feeling: "*Be of good cheer,*" *said the priest.* 5. *Archaic.* expression of face. —*v.* 1. fill with cheer; give joy to; gladden; comfort; encourage. 2. shout encouragement, approval, praise, etc. 3. urge on with cheers. 4. greet or welcome with cheers. 5. cheer up, don't be sad; be glad. [< F < LL *cara* face < Gk. *kara* head, face] —cheer′er, *n.* —Syn. *n.* 2. acclamation, shouting, applause. —*v.* 1. enliven, console. 2. applaud, acclaim.

cheer·ful (chir′fəl), *adj.* 1. full of cheer; joyful; glad: *a smiling, cheerful person.* 2. filling with cheer; pleasant; bright: *a cheerful, sunny room.* 3. willing: *a cheerful giver.* —cheer′ful·ly, *adv.* —cheer′ful·ness, *n.* —Syn. 1. cheery, joyous, gay, blithe. —Ant. 1. sad, depressed.

cheer·i·o (chir′i·ō), *interj., n., pl.* -i·os. *Esp. Brit. Colloq.* 1. hello! 2. good-by! 3. hurrah!

cheer·less (chir′lis), *adj.* without joy or comfort; gloomy; dreary. —cheer′less·ly, *adv.* —cheer′less·ness, *n.* —Syn. dismal, sad.

cheer·y (chir′i), *adj.,* cheer·i·er, cheer·i·est. cheerful; pleasant; bright; gay. —cheer′i·ly, *adv.* —cheer′i·ness, *n.*

cheese[1] (chēz), *n.* 1. solid food made from the thick part of milk. 2. mass of this pressed into shape. [< L *caseus*]

cheese[2] (chēz), *v.,* cheesed, chees·ing. *Slang.* 1. stop; leave off. 2. cheese it, look out! run away! [alter. of *cease*]

cheese cake, 1. dessert made of cheese, eggs, sugar, etc., baked together. 2. *Slang.* a. the photographing of a woman or women in such a fashion as to emphasize or reveal physical charms. b. such photographs.

cheese·cloth (chēz′klôth′; -kloth′), *n.* a thin, loosely woven cotton cloth.

chees·y (chēz′i), *adj.,* chees·i·er, chees·i·est. 1. of or like cheese. 2. *U.S. Slang.* poorly made; inferior. —chees′i·ness, *n.*

chee·tah (chē′tə), *n.* animal somewhat like a leopard, found in S Asia and Africa. Also, chetah. [< Hind. *chītā*]

chef (shef), *n.* 1. head cook. 2. cook. [< F. Doublet of CHIEF.]

Che·khov (chek′ôf; -of), *n.* Anton, 1860–1904, Russian dramatist and novelist.

che·la (kē′lə), *n., pl.* -lae (-lē). claw of a lobster, crab, scorpion, etc. It is like a pincer. [< L < Gk. *chele* claw]

Chel·sea (chel′si), *n.* borough in SW London.

chem., chemical; chemist; chemistry.

chem·i·cal (kem′ə·kəl), *adj.* 1. of chemistry. 2. made by or used in chemistry. —*n.* substance obtained by or used in a chemical process. Oxygen, sulfuric acid, bicarbonate of soda, borax, etc., are chemicals. —chem′i·cal·ly, *adv.*

che·mise (shə·mēz′), *n.* a loose, shirtlike undergarment worn by women and girls. [< F < LL *camisia* shirt < Celtic]

chem·ist (kem′ist), *n.* 1. expert in chemistry. 2. *Brit.* druggist. [var. of *alchemist*]

chem·is·try (kem′is·tri), *n., pl.* -tries. 1. science that deals with the characteristics of elements or simple substances, the changes that take place when they combine to form other substances, and the laws of their combination and behavior under various conditions. 2. application of this to a certain subject. [< *chemist*]

chem·ur·gy (kem′ér·ji), *n.* branch of applied chemistry that deals with the use of organic raw materials, such as casein and cornstalks, otherwise than for food, and especially in manufacturing.

che·nille (shə·nēl′), *n.* 1. a velvety cord, used in embroidery, fringe, etc. 2. fabric woven from this cord, used for rugs and curtains. [< F *chenille* caterpillar < L *canicula* little dog; from its furry look]

Che·ops (kē′ops), *n.* Egyptian king who lived about 2900 B.C., builder of a great pyramid. Also, Khufu.

cheque (chek), *n. Brit.* check (def. 10).

chequ·er (chek′ər), *v., n. Brit.* checker.

chequ·er·board (chek′ər·bôrd′; -bōrd′), *n. Brit.* checkerboard.

chequ·ered (chek′ərd), *adj. Brit.* checkered.

chequ·ers (chek′ərz), *n. Brit.* checkers.

Chequ·ers (chek′ərz), *n.* the official country residence of the prime minister of Great Britain, NW of London.

Cher·bourg (shär′bùrg), *n.* seaport in NW France.

cher·ish (cher′ish), *v.* 1. hold dear; treat with affection. 2. care for tenderly. 3. keep in mind; cling to. [< F *chérir* < *cher* dear < L *carus*] —cher′ish·er, *n.* —cher′ish·ing·ly, *adv.*

Cher·o·kee (cher′ə·kē; cher′ə·kē′), *n., pl.* -kee, -kees. *Am.* 1. member of a tribe of American Indians, now living mostly in Oklahoma. 2. their language.

che·root (shə·rüt′), *n.* cigar cut off square at both ends. [< F < Tamil *shuruttu* roll]

cher·ry (cher′i), *n., pl.* -ries, *adj.* 1. a small, round, juicy fruit with a stone or pit in it. 2. tree that it grows on. 3. its wood. 4. bright red. —*adj.* 1. made of this wood. 2. bright-red. [OE *ciris* < VL *cerisia* < LGk. *kerasia* < Gk. *kerasos* cherry tree. See CERISE.]

cher·ub (cher′əb), *n., pl.* cher·u·bim (cher′ə·bim; -yù·bim) *for 1 and 2,* cher·ubs *for 3 and 4.* 1. one of the second highest order of angels. 2. picture or statue of a child with wings, or of a child's head with wings. 3. beautiful, innocent, or good child. 4. person with a chubby, innocent face. [< Heb. *kerūb*] —che·ru·bic (chə·rü′bik), *adj.* —che·ru′bi·cal·ly, *adv.*

Cherub

Ches·a·peake Bay (ches′ə·pēk), bay of the Atlantic, in Maryland and Virginia.

Chesh·ire (chesh′ər; -ir), *n.* county in W England. Also, Chester.

chess (ches), *n.* game played on a chessboard by two people. Each player has 16 pieces to move in different ways. [< OF *esches* (pl.). See CHECK.]

chess·board (ches′bôrd′; -bōrd′), *n.* board marked in a pattern of 64 squares of two different colors, used in playing chess.

chess·man (ches′man′; -mən), *n., pl.* -men (-men′; -mən). one of the pieces used in playing chess.

chest (chest), *n.* 1. part of the body enclosed by ribs. 2. a large box with a lid, used for holding things: *a linen chest.* 3. piece of furniture with drawers. 4. place where money is kept; treasury. 5. the money itself. [< L < Gk. *kiste* box]

Ches·ter (ches′tər), *n.* 1. city in W England. 2. Cheshire.

Ches·ter·field (ches′tər·fēld′), *n.* 1. 4th Earl of, 1694–1773, English statesman who wrote witty and instructive letters to his son. 2. chesterfield, a single-breasted overcoat with the buttons hidden.

chest·nut (ches′nut; -nət), *n.* 1. large tree belonging to the same family as the beech, that bears sweet edible nuts in prickly burs. 2. nut of this tree. 3. wood of this tree. 4. horse chestnut. 5. reddish brown. 6. reddish-brown horse. 7. *Am., Colloq.* stale joke or story. —*adj.* reddish-brown. [< obs. *chesten* chestnut (< L < *kastanea* chestnut) + *nut*]

chest·y (ches′ti), *adj.,* chest·i·er, chest·i·est. *Am., Colloq.* pompous or self-assertive; conceited.

che·tah (chē′tə), *n.* cheetah.

chet·nik (chet′nik), *n., pl.* chet·ni·ci (chet-nē′tsē), -niks. one of a Yugoslav guerrilla force, most of which was active against the Nazis during the second World War. [< Serbian, < *cheta* band]

chev·a·lier (shev′ə·lir′), *n.* 1. *Archaic.* knight. 2. member of the lowest rank in the Legion of Honor of France. 3. in the old French nobility, a younger son. [< F, < *cheval* horse < L *caballus*. See CAVALIER.]

Chev·i·ot (chev′i·ət, chē′vi– *for 1;* shev′i·ət *for 2*), *n.* **1.** breed of sheep that originated in the Cheviot Hills. **2. cheviot,** a. a rough, woolen cloth. b. a cotton cloth like it.

Cheviot Hills, hills on the boundary between England and Scotland.

chev·ron (shev′rən), *n.* **1.** a cloth design consisting of stripes meeting at an angle, worn on the sleeve as an indication of rank (by noncommissioned officers, policemen, etc.) or of service or wounds in war. **2.** design shaped like an inverted V, used in coats of arms and in architecture. [< F, rafter, < *chèvre* goat < L *capra*]

chev·y (chev′i), *n., pl.* **chev·ies,** *v.,* **chev·ied, chev·y·ing.** *Brit.* —*n.* **1.** a hunting cry. **2.** hunt; chase. —*v.* **1.** hunt; chase. **2.** scamper; race. **3.** worry; harass. Also, *Brit.* **chivy, chivvy.**

chew (chü), *v.* **1.** crush or grind with the teeth. **2.** think over; consider. —*n.* **1.** chewing. **2.** thing chewed; piece for chewing. [OE *cēowan*] —**chew′er,** *n.* —Syn. *v.* **1.** munch, crunch, champ.

chewing gum, *Am.* gum prepared for chewing, usually sweetened and flavored with chicle.

che·wink (chi·wingk′), *Am.* finch of eastern and central North America whose cry sounds somewhat like its name. [imit.]

Chey·enne (shī·en′; –an′), *n.* capital of Wyoming, in the SE part.

Chey·enne (shī·en′), *n., pl.* –**enne,** –**ennes,** *adj.* —*n.* **1.** *Am.* member of an Algonquian tribe of American Indians, now living in Montana and Oklahoma. **2.** *Am.* this tribe. —*adj.* of this tribe.

chi (kī), *n.* the 22nd letter of the Greek alphabet (Χ, χ), written as *ch* in English, but sounded like *k*.

Chiang Kai-shek (chyäng′ kī′shek′; chyang′), born 1886, Chinese general and political leader.

Chi·an·ti (ki·än′ti; –an′–), *n.* a dry, red Italian wine.

chi·a·ro·scu·ro (ki·ä′rə·skyůr′ō), **chi·a·ro·o·scu·ro** (ki·ä′rə·ō·skyůr′ō), *n., pl.* –**ros.** **1.** treatment of light and shade in a picture. **2.** art using only light and shade in pictures. **3.** a sketch in black and white. [< Ital., clear-dark] —**chi·a′ro·scu′rist,** *n.*

chic (shēk; shik), *n.* style. —*adj.* **1.** stylish. **2.** *Am., Colloq.* clever; neat. [< F]

Chi·ca·go (shə·kô′gō; –kä′–), *n.* city in NE Illinois, on Lake Michigan; the second largest city in the United States. —**Chi·ca′go·an,** *n.*

chi·can·er·y (shi·kän′ər·i), *n., pl.* –**er·ies.** low trickery; unfair practice; quibbling. —Syn. deception, sophistry.

chic·o·ry (chik′ə·ri), *n., pl.* –**ries.** chicory.

chick (chik), *n.* **1.** young chicken. **2.** young bird. **3.** child. [var. of *chicken*]

chick·a·dee (chik′ə·dē), *n. Am.* a small bird with black, white, and gray feathers. [imit.]

Chickadee (5 in. long)

chick·en (chik′ən), *n.* **1.** the young of domestic fowl. **2.** *Am.* a domestic or barnyard fowl of any age. **3.** flesh of a chicken used for food. **4.** a young bird of certain other kinds. **5.** *U.S. Slang.* young or immature woman; young person. —*adj.* young; small. [OE *cīcen*]

chick·en-heart·ed (chik′ən·här′tid), *adj.* timid; cowardly.

chicken pox, a mild contagious disease of children accompanied by a rash on the skin.

chick·weed (chik′wēd′), *n.* a common weed whose leaves and seeds are eaten by birds.

chic·le (chik′əl), or **chicle gum,** *n. Am.* a tasteless, gumlike substance used in making chewing gum. It is the dried milky juice of a sapodilla tree of tropical America. [< Am.Sp. < Mex. *jiktli*]

chic·o·ry (chik′ə·ri), *n., pl.* –**ries. 1.** plant with bright-blue flowers whose leaves are used for salad. **2.** its root, roasted and used as a sub-stitute for coffee. Also, **chiccory.** [< F < L < Gk. *kichoreion*]

chide (chīd), *v.,* **chid·ed** or **chid** (chid); **chid·ed, chid,** or **chid·den** (chid′ən); **chid·ing.** reproach; blame; scold. [OE *cīdan*] —**chid′er,** *n.* —**chid′ing·ly,** *adv.* —Syn. rebuke, reprove.

chief (chēf), *n.* **1.** person highest in rank or authority; head of a group; leader. **2.** head of a tribe or clan. **3.** *Archaic.* the most important part; best part. **4. in chief,** at the head; of the highest rank or authority. —*adj.* **1.** highest in rank or authority; at the head; leading. **2.** most important; main. [< OF < L *caput* head. Doublet of CHEF.] —**chief′less,** *adj.* —Syn. *adj.* **2.** prime, essential, cardinal.

chief·ly (chēf′li), *adv.* **1.** mainly; mostly. **2.** first of all; above all.

chief·tain (chēf′tən), *n.* **1.** chief of a tribe or clan. **2.** leader; head of a group. [< OF < LL *capitanus.* See CAPTAIN.] —**chief′tain·cy, chief′-tain·ship,** *n.*

chif·fon (shi·fon′; shif′on), *n.* **1.** a very thin silk or rayon cloth, used for dresses. **2.** bit of ribbon, lace, or other feminine finery. [< F, < *chiffe* rag]

chif·fo·nier, chif·fon·nier (shif′ə·nir′), *n.* a high bureau or chest of drawers, often one with a mirror. [< F. See CHIFFON.]

chig·ger (chig′ər), *n.* **1.** *Am.* mite whose larvae stick to the skin and cause severe itching. **2.** chigoe. [alter. of *chigoe*]

chi·gnon (shēn′yon; *Fr.* shē·nyôN′), *n.* a roll of hair worn by women at the back of the head or on the nape of the neck. [< F]

chig·oe (chig′ō), **chig·o** (chig′ō), *n.* flea of the West Indies and South America. The female burrows under the skin of people and animals, where it causes severe itching and sores. [< WInd.]

Chi·hua·hua (chi·wä′wä), *n.* **1.** state in N Mexico. **2.** Also, **chihuahua,** *Am.* a very small dog of ancient Mexican breed.

chil·blain (chil′blān′), *n.* Usually, **chilblains.** an itching sore or redness on the hands or feet caused by cold. [< *chill* + *blain*] —**chil′blained′,** *adj.*

child (chīld), *n., pl.* **chil·dren** (chil′drən). **1.** baby; infant. **2.** boy or girl. **3.** son or daughter. **4.** descendant. **5.** person like a child in nearness, affection, interest, etc. **6.** an immature or childish person. **7.** result; product. **8. with child,** pregnant. [OE *cild*] —**child′less,** *adj.*

child·bear·ing (chīld′bãr′ing), *n.* giving birth to children.

child·bed (chīld′bed′), *n.* condition of a woman giving birth to a child.

child·birth (chīld′bérth′), *n.* giving birth to a child.

child·hood (chīld′hůd), *n.* condition or time of being a child.

child·ish (chīl′dish), *adj.* **1.** of a child. **2.** like a child. **3.** not suitable for a grown person; weak; silly; foolish. —**child′ish·ly,** *adv.* —**child′ish-ness,** *n.* —Syn. **2.** immature, infantile, babyish.

child·like (chīld′līk′), *adj.* **1.** like a child; innocent; frank; simple. **2.** suitable for a child.

chil·dren (chil′drən), *n.* pl. of **child.**

child's play, something very easy to do.

Chil·e (chil′ē), *n.* country in SW South America. —**Chil′e·an,** *adj., n.*

chil·e con car·ne (chil′ē kon kär′nē), *Am.* meat cooked with red peppers and, usually, beans. [< Sp., chili with meat]

Chile saltpeter, sodium nitrate, $NaNO_3$.

chil·i, chil·e, or **chil·li** (chil′ē), *n., pl.* **chil·ies; chil·es; chil·lies. 1.** *Am.* a hot-tasting pod of red pepper, used for seasoning. **2.** plant that it grows on, a tropical American shrub grown in the S part of the United States. **3.** *Am.* chile con carne. [< Sp. < Mex. *chilli*]

chili sauce, chilli sauce, *Am.* sauce made of red peppers, tomatoes, and spices, used on meat, fish, etc.

chill (chil), *n.* **1.** unpleasant coldness. **2.** sudden coldness of the body with shivering. **3.** unfriendliness; lack of heartiness. 4. depressing influence; discouraging feeling. 5. feeling cold; shivering. —*adj.* 1. unpleasantly cold. 2. cold in manner; unfriendly. 3. depressing; discouraging. —*v.* 1. make cold. 2. become cold; feel cold. 3. harden (metal) on the surface by sudden cooling. 4. depress; dispirit. [OE *ciele*] —chill′er, *n.* —chill′ing·ly, *adv.* —chill′ness, *n.*

chill·y (chil′i), *adj.*, chill·i·er, chill·i·est. 1. unpleasantly cool; rather cold. 2. cold in manner; unfriendly. —chill′i·ly, *adv.* —chill′i·ness, *n.* —Syn. 1. chill, raw.

chime (chīm), *n.*, *v.*, chimed, chim·ing. —*n.* 1. set of tuned bells to make musical sounds. 2. musical sound made by a set of tuned bells. 3. agreement; harmony. —*v.* 1. make musical sounds on (a set of tuned bells). 2. ring out musically: *the bells chimed midnight*. 3. agree; be in harmony. 4. say or utter in cadence or singsong. 5. **chime in**, a. be in harmony; agree. b. *Colloq.* join in. [< L < Gk. *kymbalon* CYMBAL]

chi·me·ra, chi·mae·ra (kə·mir′ə; kī–), *n.*, *pl.* -ras. 1. Often, **Chimera.** *Gk. Legend.* monster with a lion's head, a goat's body, and a serpent's tail, supposed to breathe out fire. 2. a horrible creature of the imagination. 3. an absurd idea; impossible notion; wild fancy. [< F < L < Gk. *chimaira* she-goat]

chi·mer·i·cal (kə·mer′ə·kəl; –mir′–; kī–), **chi·mer·ic** (–ik), *adj.* 1. unreal; imaginary. 2. absurd; impossible. 3. wildly fanciful; visionary.

chim·ney (chim′ni), *n.*, *pl.* -neys. 1. an upright structure to make a draft and carry away smoke. 2. part of this that rises above a roof. 3. glass tube put around the flame of a lamp. 4. crack or opening in a rock, mountain, volcano, etc. [< OF < LL *caminata* < L *caminus* oven < Gk. *kaminos*] —chim′ney·less, *adj.*

chimney corner, corner or side of a fireplace; place near the fire.

chimney sweep or **sweeper,** person whose work is cleaning out chimneys.

chimney swift, *Am.* bird of North America that often builds its nest in unused chimneys.

chim·pan·zee (chim′pan·zē′; chim·pan′zē), *n.* African manlike ape, smaller than a gorilla. [from native West African name]

chin (chin), *n.*, *v.*, chinned, chin·ning. —*n.* 1. the front of the lower jaw below the mouth. 2. *Am.*, *Slang.* talk. —*v.* 1. **chin oneself,** *Am.* hang by the hands from a bar and pull oneself up until one's chin is even with the bar. 2. *Am.*, *Slang.* talk; gossip. [OE *cin*]

Chi·na (chī′nə), *n.* a large country in E Asia.

chi·na (chī′nə), *n.* 1. a fine, white ware made of clay baked by a special process, first used in China. 2. dishes, vases, ornaments, etc., made of china. 3. dishes of any kind. —*adj.* made of china.

chi·na·ber·ry tree (chī′nə·ber′i), **china tree,** *Am.* 1. an ornamental tree with purple flowers and yellow fruit, especially used as a shade tree in the South. 2. soapberry of the S United States, Mexico, and the West Indies.

Chi·na·man (chī′nə·mən), *n.*, *pl.* -men. 1. native or inhabitant of China. 2. person of Chinese descent. ➤ See **Chinese** for usage note.

China Sea, part of the Pacific E and SE of Asia. Taiwan divides it into **South China Sea** and **East China Sea.**

Chi·na·town (chī′nə·toun′), *n. Am.* section of a city where Chinese live.

chi·na·ware (chī′nə·wār′), *n.* 1. dishes, vases, ornaments, etc., made of china. 2. dishes of any kind.

chin·ca·pin (ching′kə·pin), *n.* chinquapin.

chinch bug (chinch), *Am.* a small, black-and-white bug that does much damage to grain in dry weather. [< Sp. < L *cimex* bedbug]

Chinchilla (total length 15 in.)

chin·chil·la (chin·chil′ə), *n.* 1. a South American rodent that looks somewhat like a squirrel. 2. its very valuable soft, whitish-gray fur. 3. a thick woolen fabric woven in small,

closely set tufts, used for overcoats. [< Sp., dim. of *chinche* CHINCH BUG]

chine (chīn), *n.* 1. backbone; spine. 2. piece of an animal's backbone with the meat on it, for cooking. [< OF *eschine* < Gmc.]

Chi·nese (chī·nēz′; –nēs′), *n.*, *pl.* -nese, *adj.* —*n.* 1. native or inhabitant of China. 2. person of Chinese descent. 3. language of China. —*adj.* of China, its people, or their language. ➤ Chinese is preferred by natives of China (and others) to *Chinaman*, *Chinamen*, because of the belittling connotations of those words. Say *a Chinese*, *the Chinese.*

chink¹ (chingk), *n.* narrow opening; crack. —*v.* 1. fill up the chinks in. 2. make chinks in.

chink² (chingk), *n.* a short, sharp, ringing sound like coins or glasses hitting together. —*v.* 1. make such a sound. 2. cause to make such a sound. [imit.]

chin·ka·pin (ching′kə·pin), *n.* chinquapin.

Chi·nook (chi·nůk′; –nük′), *n.*, *pl.* -nook, -nooks. *Am.* 1. member of a group of American Indian tribes living along the Columbia River in NW United States. 2. dialect of Indian, French, and English. 3. **chinook,** a. *Am.* a warm, moist wind blowing from the sea to land in winter and spring in NW United States. b. *U.S.* a warm, dry wind that comes down from the Rocky Mountains.

chin·qua·pin (ching′kə·pin), *Am.* 1. a dwarf chestnut tree, whose nuts are good to eat. 2. an evergreen tree of California and Oregon that has a similar nut. 3. nut of either tree. Also, **chincapin, chinkapin.** [< Am.Ind. (Algonquian)]

chintz (chints), *n.* a cotton cloth printed in patterns of various colors and often glazed. [orig. pl., < Hind. *chint* < Skt. *citra* variegated]

chip (chip), *n.*, *v.*, chipped, chip·ping. —*n.* 1. a small, thin piece cut or broken off. 2. place where a small, thin piece has been cut or broken off. 3. a small, thin piece of food or candy, as potato chips. 4. a round, flat piece used for counting in games. 5. strip of wood, palm leaf, or straw used in making baskets or hats. 6. piece of dried dung. 7. **chip on one's shoulder,** *Am.*, *Colloq.* readiness to quarrel or fight. 8. **dry as a chip,** very dry. —*v.* 1. cut or break off in small, thin pieces. 2. shape by cutting at the surface or edge with an ax or chisel. 3. **chip in,** *Colloq.* a. *Am.* give (money or help). b. put in (a remark) when others are talking. [OE *(for) cippian*]

chip·munk (chip′mungk), *n. Am.* a small, striped American squirrel. [< Ojibwa *achitamo* squirrel]

chip·per (chip′ər), *adj. U.S. Colloq.* lively; cheerful.

Chip·pe·wa (chip′ə·wä; –wā; –wə), *n.*, *pl.* -wa, -was, *adj. Am.* Ojibwa.

chipping sparrow, a small sparrow of E and C North America.

chirk (chérk), *U.S. Colloq.* —*adj.* cheerful. —*v.* be or become cheerful. [OE *circian* roar]

chi·rog·ra·phy (kī·rog′rə·fi), *n.* handwriting. [< Gk. *cheir* hand + E *-graphy* writing < Gk. *graphein* write] —chi·rog′ra·pher, *n.* —chi·ro·graph·ic (kī′rə·graf′ik), chi′ro·graph′i·cal, *adj.*

chi·rop·o·dist (kə·rop′ə·dist; kī–), *n.* person who removes corns and treats other troubles of the feet.

chi·rop·o·dy (kə·rop′ə·di; kī–), *n.* work of a chiropodist. [< Gk. *cheir* hand + *pous* foot; orig. treatment of hands and feet]

chi·ro·prac·tic (kī′rə·prak′tik), *n.* 1. *Am.* treatment of diseases by manipulating the spine. 2. chiropractor. —*adj. Am.* having to do with the treatment of diseases by manipulating the spine. [< Gk. *cheir* hand + *praktikos* practical]

chi·ro·prac·tor (kī′rə·prak′tər), *n. Am.* person who treats disease by manipulating the spine.

chirp (chérp), *v.* 1. make a short, sharp sound such as some small birds and insects make. 2. utter with a chirp. —*n.* such a sound. [? var. of *chirk*] —chirp′er, *n.*

chirr (chér), *v.* make a shrill, trilling sound. —*n.* such a sound. Also, **churr.** [imit.]

chir·rup (chir'əp; chêr'-), v., -ruped, -rup·ing. chirp; chirp again and again. [< *chirp*]

chis·el (chiz'əl), n., v., -eled, -el·ing; esp. Brit. -elled, -el·ling. —n. a cutting tool with a sharp edge at the end of a strong blade, used to cut or shape wood, stone, or metal. —v. 1. cut or shape with a chisel. 2. U.S. Slang. use unfair practices; swindle. [< OF, ult. < L *caesus* < *caedere* cut]

chis·el·er, esp. Brit. **chis·el·ler** (chiz'əl·ər), n. 1. one that chisels. 2. Slang. a cheat.

chit[1] (chit), n. 1. child. 2. a saucy, forward girl. [akin to KITTEN. Cf. dial. *chit* puss.]

chit[2] (chit), n. voucher of a debt, as for food. [< Hind. *chitthi*]

chit-chat (chit'chat'), n. 1. friendly, informal talk; chat. 2. gossip. [< *chat*]

chi·tin (kī'tin), n. a horny substance forming the hard outer covering of beetles, lobsters, crabs, etc. [< F < Gk. *chiton* tunic]

chit·ter·ling (chit'ər·ling), n. Usually, chitterlings. part of the small intestine of pigs, cooked as food.

chiv·al·ric (shiv'əl·rik; shi·val'rik), adj. 1. having to do with chivalry. 2. chivalrous.

chiv·al·rous (shiv'əl·rəs), adj. 1. having the qualities of an ideal knight. 2. having to do with chivalry. —**chiv'al·rous·ly,** adv. —**chiv'al·rous·ness,** n. —Syn. 1. gallant, courteous, considerate.

chiv·al·ry (shiv'əl·ri), n. 1. qualities of an ideal knight, including bravery, honor, courtesy, respect for women, protection of the weak, generosity, and fairness to enemies. 2. rules and customs of knights in the Middle Ages; system of knighthood. 3. knights as a group. 4. gallant warriors or gentlemen. [< OF. See CHEVALIER.]

chive (chīv), or **chive garlic,** n. plant of the same family as the onion, with long, slender leaves used as seasoning. [< OF < L *caepa* onion]

chiv·vy, chiv·y (chiv'i), n., pl. chiv·vies; v., chiv·vied, chiv·vy·ing; chiv·ied, chiv·y·ing. Brit. chevy.

chlo·ral (klô'rəl; klō'-), n. Chem. 1. a colorless liquid, CCl₃CHO, made from chlorine and alcohol. 2. chloral hydrate.

chloral hydrate, Chem. a white, crystalline drug, CCl₃CH(OH)₂, that causes sleep.

chlo·rate (klô'rāt; -rit; klō'-), n. Chem. salt of chloric acid.

chlo·ric (klô'rik; klō'-), adj. Chem. of or containing chlorine.

chloric acid, Chem. acid, HClO₃, existing only as salts and in solution.

chlo·ride (klô'rīd; -rid; klō'-), **chlo·rid** (-rid), n. compound of chlorine with another element or radical; salt of hydrochloric acid.

chlo·rin·ate (klô'rə·nāt; klō'-), v., -at·ed, -at·ing. 1. combine or treat with chlorine. 2. disinfect with chlorine. —**chlo'rin·a'tion,** n.

chlo·rine (klô'rēn; -rin; klō'-), **chlo·rin** (-rin), n. Chem. a poisonous, greenish-yellow, gaseous chemical element, Cl, used in bleaching and disinfecting. It is very irritating to the nose, throat, and lungs. [< Gk. *chloros* green]

chlo·ro·form (klô'rə·fôrm; klō'-), n. Chem. CHCl₃, a colorless liquid with a sweetish smell, used as an anesthetic and to dissolve rubber, resin, wax, and many other substances. —v. 1. make unable to feel pain by giving chloroform. 2. kill with chloroform.

Chlo·ro·my·ce·tin (klô'rə·mī'sə·tin; klō'-), n. Trademark. an antibiotic drug, used chiefly against typhoid fever and certain types of pneumonia. [< *chloro-* green < Gk. *chloros*) + Gk. *mykes, -etos* fungus]

chlo·ro·phyll, chlo·ro·phyl (klô'rə·fil; klō'-), n. the green coloring matter of plants. In the presence of light it makes carbohydrates, such as starch, from carbon dioxide and water. [< Gk. *chloros* green + E *-phyll* leaf < Gk. *phyllon*]

chm., 1. Also, **chmn.** chairman. 2. checkmate.

chock (chok), n. 1. block; wedge. 2. Naut. a. block with two arms curving inward for a rope to pass through. b. one of the pieces of wood on which a boat rests. —v. 1. provide or fasten with chocks. 2. Naut. put (a boat) on chocks. —adv. as close or as tight as can be; quite. [appar. < OF *choque* log]

chock-full (chok'fŭl'), adj. as full as can be. Also, **chuck-full, choke-full.**

choc·o·late (chôk'lit; chok'-; chôk'ə·lit; chok'ə-), n. 1. preparation made by roasting and grinding cacao seeds. 2. drink made of chocolate with hot milk or water and sugar. 3. candy made of chocolate. 4. dark brown. —adj. 1. made of chocolate. 2. dark-brown. [< Sp. < Mex. *chocolatl*]

Choc·taw (chok'tô), n., pl. -taw, -taws, adj. —n. Am. member of a tribe of American Indians, now living mostly in Oklahoma. —adj. of this tribe.

choice (chois), n., adj., choic·er, choic·est. —n. 1. act of choosing: *make your choice.* 2. care in selecting: *her library showed choice and good taste.* 3. preference: *his choice was to stay at home.* 4. person or thing chosen. 5. power or chance to choose. 6. quantity and variety to choose from. 7. the best part. —adj. carefully chosen; of fine quality; excellent; superior. [< OF *chois* < Gmc.] —**choice'ly,** adv. —**choice'ness,** n. —Syn. 1. selection. 5. alternative, option. -adj. select, exquisite, fine, elegant.

choir (kwīr), n. 1. group of singers used in a church service. 2. part of a church set apart for such a group. 3. any group of singers. —v. sing all together at the same time. [< OF < L *chorus* CHORUS]

choke (chōk), v., choked, chok·ing, n. —v. 1. keep from breathing by squeezing or blocking up the throat. 2. be unable to breathe. 3. check or extinguish by cutting off the supply of air. 4. control; hold; suppress. 5. block; fill; clog. 6. **choke off,** put an end to; get rid of; stop. —n. 1. act or sound of choking. 2. valve that cuts off the supply of air in a gasoline engine. [var. of OE *acēocian*] —Syn. v. 1, 2. suffocate, stifle.

choke·damp (chōk'damp'), n. a heavy, suffocating gas, mainly carbon dioxide, that gathers in mines, old wells, etc.

choke-full (chōk'fŭl'), adj. chock-full.

chok·er (chōk'ər), n. 1. one that chokes. 2. Colloq. a. a high collar. b. a tight necklace.

chol·er (kol'ər), n. irritable disposition; anger. [< L < Gk. *cholera* cholera, appar. < *chole* bile]

chol·er·a (kol'ər·ə), n. an acute disease of the stomach and intestines, characterized by vomiting, cramps, and diarrhea. Summer cholera is not infectious. Asiatic cholera is infectious and often causes death. [< L < Gk. See CHOLER.]

chol·er·ic (kol'ər·ik), adj. easily made angry.

cho·les·ter·ol (kə·les'tər·ōl; -ol), n. Biochem. a white, crystalline substance, C₂₇H₄₅OH, a constituent of all animal fats, bile, gallstones, egg yolk, etc. It is important in metabolism.

choose (chüz), v., chose, cho·sen or (Obs.) chose, choos·ing. 1. make a choice: *you must choose.* 2. pick out; select from a number: *he chose a book from the library.* 3. prefer and decide; think fit: *he did not choose to go.* 4. **cannot choose but,** cannot do otherwise than. [OE *cēosan*] —**choos'er,** n. —Syn. 2. elect, prefer.

chop[1] (chop), v., chopped, chop·ping, n. —v. 1. cut by hitting with something sharp. 2. cut into small pieces. 3. make quick, sharp movements; jerk. 4. make by cutting. —n. 1. a cutting stroke. 2. slice of lamb, pork, veal, etc. There are rib, loin, and shoulder chops. 3. a short, irregular, broken motion of waves. [ME *choppe(n)*] —**chop'per,** n. —Syn. v. 1. hew, hack. 2. mince.

chop[2] (chop), n. 1. Usually, chops. jaw. 2. cheek. Also, **chap.** [< *chop*[1]]

chop[3] (chop), v., chopped, chop·ping. change suddenly; shift quickly. [? akin to *cheap* change. See CHEAP.]

chop·fall·en (chop'fôl'ən), adj. chapfallen.

chop·house (chop'hous'), n. restaurant that makes a specialty of serving chops, steaks, etc.

Cho·pin (shō'pan), n. Frédéric François, 1809-1849, Polish pianist and composer in France.

chop·py (chop'i), adj., -pi·er, -pi·est. 1. making

āge, cãre, fär; ēqual, tèrm; īce; ōpen, ôrder; put, rüle, ūse; th, then; ə=a in about.

quick, sharp movements; jerky. 2. moving in short, irregular, broken waves. [< *chop*[1]]

chop·stick (chop'stik'), *n.* one of the small sticks used to raise food to the mouth by the Chinese. [< Chinese Pidgin English *chop* quick + E *stick*[1]]

chop su·ey or **soo·y** (chop' sü'i), *Am.* fried or stewed meat and vegetables cut up and cooked together in a sauce. [alter. of Chinese word meaning "mixed pieces"]

cho·ral (*adj.* kô'rəl, kô'–; *n.* kô·ral', –räl', kô–, kô'rəl, kô'–), *adj.* **1.** of a choir or chorus. **2.** sung by a choir or chorus. —*n.* Also, **chorale.** **a.** a hymn tune. **b.** a simple hymn tune sung by the choir and congregation together. —**cho'ral·ly**, *adv.*

chord[1] (kôrd), *n.* combination of three or more musical notes sounded together in harmony. [var. of *cord*, var. of *accord*, n.]

chord[2] (kôrd), *n.* **1.** a straight line connecting two points on a circumference. **2.** *Anat.* cord (def. 4). **3.** string of a harp or other musical instrument. **4.** a feeling; emotion: *touch a sympathetic chord.* [< L < Gk. *chorde* gut, string of a musical instrument. Doublet of CORD.] —**chord'al**, *adj.*

AB and AC are chords.

chore (chôr, chōr), *n. U.S.* **1.** an odd job; small task. **2.** a difficult or disagreeable thing to do. [OE *cyrr*, var. of *cierr, cerr* turn, business]

cho·re·a (kô·rē'ə; kō–), *n.* a nervous disease characterized by involuntary twitching of the muscles; St. Vitus's dance. [< NL < Gk. *choreia* dance]

cho·re·og·ra·phy (kô'ri·og'rə·fi; kō'–), *esp.* *Brit.* **cho·reg·ra·phy** (kə·reg'rə·fi), *n.* **1.** art of planning the dances in a ballet. **2.** dancing; ballet dancing. [< Gk. *choreia* dance + E –*graphy* writing < Gk. *graphein* write] —**cho·re·o·graph·ic** (kô'ri·ə·graf'ik; kō–), *adj.* —**cho're·og'ra·pher**, *n.*

cho·ric (kô'rik), *adj.* of or for a chorus.

chor·is·ter (kôr'is·tər; kor'–), *n.* **1.** singer in a choir. **2.** boy who sings in a choir. **3.** *Am.* leader of a choir. [< Med.L *chorista* chorister < L *chorus* CHORUS]

chor·tle (chôr'təl), *v.*, –**tled**, –**tling**, *n.* –*v.* chuckle or snort with glee. —*n.* a gleeful chuckle or snort. [blend of *chuckle* and *snort*; coined by Lewis Carroll] —**chor'tler**, *n.*

cho·rus (kô'rəs; kō'–), *n.*, *pl.* –**rus·es**, *v.*, –**rused**, –**rus·ing**. —*n.* **1.** group of singers who sing together, such as a choir. **2.** song sung by many singers together. **3.** a musical composition to be sung by all singers together. **4.** the repeated part of a song coming after each stanza. **5.** a saying by many at the same time: *a chorus of noes.* **6.** group of singers and dancers. **7.** in chorus, all together at the same time. —*v.* sing or speak all at the same time. [< L < Gk. *choros* dance, band of dancers]

chose (chōz), *v.* pt. of choose.

cho·sen (chō'zən), *v.* pp. of choose. —*adj.* picked out; selected from a group.

Cho·sen (chō'sen'), *n.* Japanese name of Korea.

Chou En-lai (chou' en'lī'), born 1898, premier of the Chinese Communist government since 1949.

chow (chou), *n.* **1.** a medium-sized Chinese breed of dog with short, compact body, large head, and thick coat of one color, usually brown or black. **2.** *Am., Slang.* food. [short for Chinese Pidgin English *chow-chow*]

Chow

chow·der (chou'dər), *n.* *Am.* a thick soup or stew usually made of clams or fish with potatoes, onions, etc. [appar. < F *chaudière* pot, ult. < L *calidus* hot]

chow mein (chou' mān'), *Am.* fried noodles served with a thickened stew of onions, celery, meat, etc. [< Chinese, fried flour]

chres·tom·a·thy (kres·tom'ə·thi), *n.*, *pl.* –**thies.** collection of passages from literature or a foreign language. [< Gk., < *chrestos* useful + –*matheia* learning]

chrism (kriz'əm), *n.* consecrated oil, used by some churches in baptism and other sacred rites. [< L < Gk. *chrisma* < *chriein* anoint]

Christ (krīst), *n.* Jesus, the founder of the Christian religion. [< L < Gk. *christos* anointed]

chris·ten (kris'ən), *v.* **1.** admit to a Christian church by baptism; baptize. **2.** give a first name to at baptism. **3.** give a name to. **4.** *Colloq.* make the first use of. [OE *cristnian* make Christian < *cristen* Christian < L *christianus*]

Chris·ten·dom (kris'ən·dəm), *n.* **1.** the Christian part of the world. **2.** all Christians.

chris·ten·ing (kris'ən·ing; kris'ning), *n.* act or ceremony of baptizing and naming; baptism.

Chris·tian (kris'chən), *adj.* **1.** of Christ or His teachings. **2.** believing in Christ; belonging to the religion founded by Him. **3.** of Christians or Christianity. **4.** showing a gentle, humble, helpful spirit: *Christian charity.* **5.** human; not animal. **6.** *Colloq.* decent; respectable. —*n.* **1.** believer in Christ; follower of His example or teachings; member of the religion founded by Him. **2.** *Colloq.* a decent person. —**Chris'tian·ly**, *adj.*, *adv.*

Christian Era, time since the birth of Christ.

Chris·ti·an·i·a (kris'chi·an'i·ə; kris'ti·ä'-ni·ə), *n.* former name of Oslo.

Chris·ti·an·i·ty (kris'chi·an'ə·ti), *n.*, *pl.* –**ties.** **1.** religion taught by Christ and His followers; Christian religion. **2.** Christian beliefs or faith; Christian spirit or character. **3.** a particular Christian religious system.

Chris·tian·ize (kris'chən·īz), *v.*, –**ized**, –**iz-ing.** make Christian; convert to Christianity. —**Chris'tian·i·za'tion**, *n.* —**Chris'tian·iz'er**, *n.*

Christian name, first name; given name.

Christian Science, *Am.* religion and system of healing founded by Mary Baker Eddy in 1866. —**Christian Scientist**, *Am.*

Christ·like (krīst'līk'), *adj.* like Christ; that of Christ; showing the spirit of Christ. —**Christ'like'ness**, *n.*

Christ·ly (krīst'li), *adj.* of Christ; Christlike. —**Christ'li·ness**, *n.*

Christ·mas (kris'məs), *n.* the yearly celebration of the birth of Christ; December 25. [OE *Christes mœsse* Christ's MASS] —**Christ'mas·y**, **Christ'mas·sy**, *adj.*

Christmas Eve, the evening before Christmas.

Christ·mas·tide (kris'məs·tīd'), *n.* Christmas time.

chro·mate (krō'māt), *n.* *Chem.* salt of chromic acid.

chro·mat·ic (krō·mat'ik), *adj.* **1.** of color or colors. **2.** *Music.* progressing by half tones instead of by the regular intervals of the scale. [< L < Gk., < *chroma* color (in musical sense)] —**chro·mat'i·cal·ly**, *adv.*

chro·mat·ics (krō·mat'iks), **chro·ma·tol·o·gy** (krō'mə·tol'ə·ji), *n.* branch of science that deals with colors. —**chro·ma·tist** (krō'mə·tist), *n.*

chromatic scale, *Music.* scale divided equally into twelve half tones.

chro·ma·tin (krō'mə·tin), *n.* *Biol.* that part of the nucleus of an animal or plant cell which absorbs stains readily and comprises the chromosomes.

chrome (krōm), *n.* chromium, esp. as the source of various pigments (chrome green, chrome red, chrome yellow, etc.). [< F < Gk. *chroma* color]

chrome steel, **chromium steel**, a very hard, strong steel containing chromium.

chro·mic (krō'mik), *adj.* *Chem.* of or containing chromium.

chromic acid, acid, H_2CrO_4, existing only as salts and in solution.

chro·mi·um (krō'mi·əm), *n.* *Chem.* a shiny, hard, brittle metallic element, Cr, that does not rust or become dull easily when exposed to air. [< Gk. *chroma* color]

chro·mo·lith·o·graph (krō′mō-lith′ə·graf; –gräf), *n.* a colored picture printed from a series of stones or plates. —**chro·mo·li·thog·ra·pher** (krō′mō·li·thog′rə·fər), *n.* —**chro′mo·lith′o·graph′ic,** *adj.*

chro·mo·some (krō′mə·sōm), *n. Biol.* any of the microscopic filaments composed of chromatin that appear in an animal or plant cell during mitosis or division. Chromosomes are derived from the parents and carry the genes that determine heredity. [< Gk. *chroma* color + E –*some* body < Gk. *soma*]

chro·mo·sphere (krō′mə·sfir), *n.* a scarlet layer of gas around the sun.

Chron., *Bible.* Chronicles.

chron·ic (kron′ik), **chron·i·cal** (–ə·kəl), *adj.* 1. continuing a long time. 2. constant. 3. having had a disease, habit, etc., for a long time: *a chronic liar.* [< L < Gk., < *chronos* time] —**chron′i·cal·ly,** *adv.* —**Syn.** 3. habitual, inveterate, confirmed, hardened.

chron·i·cle (kron′ə·kəl), *n., v.,* –**cled,** –**cling.** —*n.* record of happenings in the order in which they happened. —*v.* record in a chronicle; write the history of; tell the story of. [< AF < L < Gk. *chronika* annals. See CHRONIC.] —**chron′i·cler,** *n.* —**Syn.** *n.* history, annals.

Chron·i·cles (kron′ə·kəlz), *n.pl.* two books of the Old Testament, called I and II Chronicles.

chron·o·log·i·cal (kron′ə·loj′ə·kəl), **chron·o·log·ic** (–loj′ik), *adj.* arranged in the order in which the events happened. —**chron′o·log′i·cal·ly,** *adv.*

chro·nol·o·gy (krə·nol′ə·ji), *n., pl.* –**gies.** 1. arrangement of time in periods; giving the exact dates of events arranged in the order in which they happened. 2. table or list that gives the exact dates of events arranged in the order in which they happened. —**chro·nol′o·gist, chro·nol′o·ger,** *n.*

chro·nom·e·ter (krə·nom′ə·tər), *n.* clock or watch that keeps very accurate time. —**chron·o·met·ric** (kron′ə·met′rik), **chron′o·met′ri·cal,** *adj.* —**chron′o·met′ri·cal·ly,** *adv.*

chrys·a·lid (kris′ə·lid), *n.* chrysalis. —*adj.* of a chrysalis.

chrys·a·lis (kris′ə·lis), *n., pl.* **chrys·a·lis·es, chrys·al·i·des** (kri·sal′ə·dēz). 1. form of an insect when it is in a case; pupa. 2. the case; cocoon. 3. stage of development or change. [< L < Gk. *chrysallis* golden sheath < *chrysos* gold]

chrys·an·the·mum (kri·san′thə·məm), *n.* 1. any of several cultivated plants of the aster family, which have showy, ball-shaped flowers in the autumn. 2. one of these flowers. [< L < Gk., < *chrysos* gold + *anthemon* flower]

chrys·o·lite (kris′ə·līt), *n.* a green or yellow semiprecious stone. [< L < Gk., < *chrysos* gold + *lithos* stone]

chub (chub), *n., pl.* **chubs** or (*esp. collectively*) **chub.** 1. a thick fresh-water fish, related to the carp. 2. *Am., Local.* any of various American fishes, such as the tautog, black bass, etc. [ME *chubbe*]

chub·by (chub′i), *adj.,* –**bi·er,** –**bi·est.** round and plump. —**chub′bi·ness,** *n.*

chuck[1] (chuk), *n., v.* 1. pat; tap. 2. throw; toss. [prob. imit.]

chuck[2] (chuk), *n.* 1. clamp. A chuck holds a tool or piece of work in a lathe. 2. cut of beef between the neck and the shoulder. [var. of *chock*]

chuck-full (chuk′fůl′), *adj.* chock-full.

chuck·le (chuk′əl), *v.,* **chuck·led, chuck·ling,** *n.* —*v.* 1. laugh to oneself. 2. cluck. —*n.* 1. a soft, quiet laugh. 2. cluck. [< *chuck* cluck; laugh; imit.] —**chuck′ler,** *n.*

chuck wagon, *Am., W.* wagon carrying provisions and cooking equipment for cowboys.

chug (chug), *n., v.,* **chugged, chug·ging.** —*n. Am.* a short, loud, explosive sound: *the chug of an engine's exhaust.* —*v.* 1. make such sounds. 2. *Am., Colloq.* move with such sounds. [imit.]

chuk·ker, chuk·kar (chuk′ər), *n.* one of the periods of play in polo. [< Hind. *chakar*]

chum (chum), *n., v.,* **chummed, chum·ming.** *Colloq.* —*n.* 1. a very close friend. 2. roommate. —*v.* 1. be very close friends. 2. room together.

chum·my (chum′i), *adj.,* –**mi·er,** –**mi·est.** *Colloq.* like a chum; very friendly. —**chum′mi·ly,** *adv.*

chump (chump), *n.* 1. *Colloq.* a foolish or stupid person; blockhead. 2. a short, thick block of wood. 3. a thick, blunt end. 4. *Slang.* the head.

Chung·king (chŭng′king′), *n.* city in C China, on the Yangtze River.

chunk (chungk), *n. Colloq.* 1. a thick piece or lump. 2. a stocky person, etc. [var. of *chuck*[2]]

chunk·y (chungk′i), *adj.,* **chunk·i·er, chunk·i·est.** *Colloq.* 1. like a chunk; short and thick. 2. stocky. —**chunk′i·ly,** *adv.* —**chunk′i·ness,** *n.*

church (chérch), *n.* 1. a building for public Christian worship or religious services. 2. public Christian worship or religious service in a church. 3. all Christians. 4. group of Christians with the same beliefs and under the same authority: *the Methodist Church.* 5. organization of a church; ecclesiastical authority or power. 6. profession of a clergyman. 7. any building, group, or organization like a church. —*adj.* of a church. [< Gk. *kyriakon* (doma) (house) of the Lord < *kyrios* lord < *kyros* power] —**church′less,** *adj.* —**church′like′,** *adj.* —**Syn.** *n.* 1. cathedral, temple, chapel. 4. denomination, sect.

church·go·er (chérch′gō′ər), *n.* person who goes to church regularly. —**church′go′ing,** *n.*

Church·ill (chérch′il; –əl), *n.* Sir Winston, 1874–1965, English statesman and writer, prime minister of England 1940–45 and 1951–55.

church·ly (chérch′li), *adj.* 1. of a church. 2. suitable for a church. —**church′li·ness,** *n.*

church·man (chérch′mən), *n., pl.* –**men.** 1. clergyman. 2. member of a church. —**church′man·ly,** *adv.* —**church′man·ship,** *n.*

Church of England, the Christian church in England that is recognized as a national institution by the government. Its head is the king or queen.

Church of Jesus Christ of Latter-day Saints, official name of the Mormon Church.

church·ward·en (chérch′wôr′dən), *n.* 1. a lay official in the Church of England or the Episcopal Church who manages the business, property, and money of a church. 2. *Colloq.* a clay tobacco pipe with a very long stem.

church·yard (chérch′yärd′), *n.* ground around a church, sometimes used as a burial ground.

churl (chérl), *n.* 1. a rude, surly person. 2. person of low birth; peasant. [OE *ceorl* freeman (of low rank)]

churl·ish (chér′lish), *adj.* rude; surly. —**churl′ish·ly,** *adv.* —**churl′ish·ness,** *n.*

churn (chérn), *n.* 1. container or machine in which cream or milk is made into butter by beating and shaking. 2. act or fact of stirring violently. —*v.* 1. stir or shake (cream or milk) in a churn. 2. make (butter) by using a churn. 3. stir violently; make or become foamy. 4. move as if beaten and shaken. [OE *cyrn*] —**churn′er,** *n.*

churr (chér), *v., n.* chirr.

chute (shūt), *n.* 1. *Am.* an inclined trough, tube, etc., for sliding or dropping things down to a lower level. 2. *Am.* rapids in a river. 3. a steep slope. 4. *Colloq.* parachute. [appar. blend of F *chute* fall (of water) and E *shoot*]

chut·ney, chut·nee (chut′ni), *n., pl.* –**neys;** –**nees.** a spicy sauce or relish made of fruits, herbs, pepper, etc. [< Hind. *chatni*]

chyle (kīl), *n.* a milky liquid composed of digested fat and lymph, formed from the chyme in the small intestine and carried from there into the veins. [< Med.L < Gk. *chylos* < *cheein* pour]

chyme (kīm), *n.* a pulpy, semiliquid mass into which food is changed by the action of the stomach. [< Med.L < Gk. *chymos* < *cheein* pour]

CIA, C.I.A., Central Intelligence Agency.

ci·bo·ri·um (si·bō′ri·əm; –bō′–), *n., pl.* –**bo-**

ri·a (-bō′ri·ə; -bō′-). **1.** vessel used to hold the consecrated bread of the Eucharist. **2.** a dome-shaped canopy over an altar. [< Med.L, < L, drinking cup, < Gk. *kiborion* cuplike seed vessel]

C.I.C., Counter Intelligence Corps.

ci·ca·da (si·kā′də; -kä′-), *n., pl.* **-das, -dae** (-dē). a large insect with transparent wings. The male makes a shrill sound in hot, dry weather. [< L]

Cicada
(ab. ⅓ actual size)

cic·a·trix (sik′ə·triks; si·kā′-), **cic·a·trice** (sik′ə·tris), *n., pl.* **cic·a·tri·ces** (sik′ə·trī′sēz). **1.** scar left by a healed wound. **2.** *Bot.* scar left on a tree or plant by a fallen leaf, seed, etc. [< L]

cic·a·trize (sik′ə·trīz), *v.,* **-trized, -triz·ing.** heal by forming a scar.

Cic·e·ro (sis′ə·rō), *n.* Marcus Tullius, 106–43 B.C., Roman orator, writer, and statesman. —**Cic·e·ro·ni·an** (sis′ə·rō′ni·ən), *adj.*

cic·e·ro·ne (sis′ə·rō′nē; chich′ə-), *n., pl.* **-ni** (-nē), **-nes** (-nēz). person who acts as a guide for sightseers. [< Ital. < L *Cicero* Cicero]

ci·der (sī′dər), *n.* **1.** juice pressed out of apples, used as a drink and in making vinegar. **2.** juice pressed from other fruits. [< OF < LL < Gk. < Heb. *shēkār* liquor]

ci·gar (si·gär′), *n.* a tight roll of tobacco leaves for smoking. [< Sp. *cigarro*]

cig·a·rette, cig·a·ret (sig′ə·ret′; sig′ə·ret), *n.* *Am.* a small roll of finely cut tobacco enclosed in a thin sheet of paper for smoking. [< F, dim. of *cigare* CIGAR]

cil·i·a (sil′i·ə), *n.pl., sing.* **cil·i·um** (sil′i·əm). **1.** eyelashes. **2.** *Zool.* very small hairlike projections. Some microscopic animals use cilia to move themselves or to set up currents in the surrounding water. [< L]

cil·i·ar·y (sil′i·er′i), *adj.* of or resembling cilia.

Cim·me·ri·an (si·mir′i·ən), *n.* one of a mythical people said to live in perpetual mists and darkness. —*adj.* very dark and gloomy.

cinch (sinch), *Am.* —*n.* **1.** a strong girth for fastening a saddle or pack on a horse. **2.** *Colloq.* a firm hold or grip. **3.** *Slang.* something sure and easy. —*v.* **1.** fasten on with a cinch; bind firmly. **2.** *Slang.* get a firm hold or grip on. [< Sp. < L *cincta* girdle < *cingere* bind]

cin·cho·na (sin·kō′nə), *n.* **1.** a small tree that grows in South America, the East Indies, India, and Java. **2.** its bitter bark, from which quinine is obtained; Peruvian bark. [< NL; named for Countess *Chinchón*, wife of a Spanish viceroy of Peru] —**cin·chon·ic** (sin·kon′ik), *adj.*

Cin·cin·nat·i (sin′sə·nat′i; -nat′ə), *n.* city in SW Ohio, on the Ohio River.

cinc·ture (singk′chər), *n.* **1.** belt; girdle. **2.** border; enclosure. [< L *cinctura* < *cingere* bind, gird]

cin·der (sin′dər), *n.* **1.** cinders, wood or coal partly burned and no longer flaming. **2.** piece of burned-up wood or coal. [OE *sinder*]

Cin·der·el·la (sin′dər·el′ə), *n.* **1.** heroine of a famous fairy tale. **2.** person whose real worth or beauty is not recognized.

cin·e·ma (sin′ə·mə), *n.* **1.** a motion picture. **2.** a motion-picture theater. **3.** the cinema, motion pictures. [short for *cinematograph*] —**cin·e·mat·ic** (sin′ə·mat′ik), *adj.* —**cin′e·mat′i·cal·ly,** *adv.*

Cin·e·ma·Scope (sin′ə·mə·skōp), *n.* *Trademark.* a motion-picture medium in which the use of a special lens on both a standard camera and projector gives the images greater depth when projected on a curved screen about 2½ times larger than an ordinary screen. [< *cinema* + *-scope* < NL, < Gk. *skopion* instrument for observing < Gk. *skopeein* look at]

cin·e·mat·o·graph (sin′ə·mat′ə·graf; -gräf), *n.* **1.** *Brit.* machine for projecting moving pictures on a screen. **2.** camera for taking moving pictures. Also, **kinematograph.** [< Gk. *kinema* motion + -GRAPH] —**cin′e·ma·tog′ra·phy,** *n.*

Cin·e·ram·a (sin′ər·äm·ə), *n.* Trademark. a motion-picture medium that uses a camera with

three lenses and a large curved screen to produce the illusion of three dimensions and a system whereby sound is reproduced from the direction of its original source. [< *cine(ma)* + (*pano*)*rama*]

cin·e·rar·i·um (sin′ə·rãr′i·əm), *n., pl.* **-rar·i·a** (-rãr′i·ə). place for keeping the ashes of cremated bodies. [< L]

cin·na·bar (sin′ə·bär), *n.* **1.** a reddish mineral that is the chief source of mercury; native mercuric sulfide. **2.** artificial mercuric sulfide, used as a red pigment in making paints, dyes, etc. **3.** bright red; vermilion. [< L < Gk. *kinnabari;* of Oriental orig.]

cin·na·mon (sin′ə·mən), *n.* **1.** spice made from the dried, reddish-brown inner bark of a laurel tree or shrub of the East Indies. **2.** this bark. **3.** tree or shrub yielding this bark. **4.** a light, reddish brown. —*adj.* **1.** flavored with cinnamon. **2.** light reddish-brown. [< F < LL < Gk. *kinnamon;* of Semitic orig.]

cinque·foil (singk′foil′), *n.* **1.** plant having small, yellow flowers and leaves divided into five parts. **2.** ornament in architecture, made of five connected semicircles or part circles. [< OF < L, < *quinque* five + *folium* leaf]

Cinquefoil

CIO, C.I.O., *Am.* Congress of Industrial Organizations. It was merged with the A.F.L. in December, 1955.

ci·on (sī′ən), *n.* scion (def. 2).

Ci·pan·go (si·pang′gō), *n.* *Poetic.* Japan.

ci·pher (sī′fər), *n.* **1.** zero; 0. **2.** person or thing of no importance. **3.** any Arabic numeral. **4.** method of secret writing which transposes the letters of a message according to a set pattern, or replaces the proper letters with substitutes called for in the system used, or combines both methods. **5.** something in secret writing. **6.** key to a method of secret writing. **7.** monogram. —*v.* **1.** do arithmetic. **2.** work by arithmetic. Also, **cypher.** [< Med.L < Ar. *ṣifr* empty. Doublet of ZERO.]

cir·ca (sèr′kə), *adv., prep.* about: *Mohammed was born circa 570 A.D.* [< L]

Cir·cas·sia (sər·kash′ə), *n.* region in S Russia, on the Black Sea. —**Cir·cas′sian,** *adj., n.*

Cir·ce (sèr′sē), *n.* *Gk. Legend.* an enchantress who changed men into swine. —**Cir·ce·an** (sər·sē′ən), *adj.*

cir·cle (sèr′kəl), *n., v.,* **-cled, -cling.** —*n.* **1.** line every point of which is equally distant from a point within called the center. **2.** a plane figure bounded by such a line. **3.** circlet, halo, crown, or anything shaped like a circle or part of one. **4.** a ring. **5.** set of seats in the balcony of a theater. **6.** a complete series or course; period; cycle. **7.** orbit of a heavenly body. **8.** period of revolution of a heavenly body. **9.** group of people held together by the same interests: *the family circle.* **10.** sphere of influence, action, etc. —*v.* **1.** go around in a circle; revolve around. **2.** form a circle around; surround; encircle. [< F < L *circulus,* dim. of *circus* ring] —**cir′cler,** *n.*

Circle

cir·clet (sèr′klit), *n.* **1.** a small circle. **2.** a round ornament worn on the head, neck, arm, or finger.

cir·cuit (sèr′kit), *n.* **1.** a going around; a trip around. **2.** way over which a person or group makes repeated journeys at certain times. Some judges make a circuit. **3.** part of the country through which such circuits are made. **4.** district under the jurisdiction of a circuit court. **5.** distance around any space. **6.** line enclosing any space. **7.** space enclosed. **8.** path over which an electric current flows. —*v.* make a circuit of; go in a circuit. [< L *circuitus* a going round < *circum* around + *ire* go] —**Syn.** *n.* **2.** route, course.

circuit court, court whose judges regularly hold court at certain places in a district.

cir·cu·i·tous (sər·kū′ə·təs), *adj.* roundabout; not direct. —**cir·cu′i·tous·ly,** *adv.* —**cir·cu′i·tous·ness,** *n.* —**Syn.** indirect, devious.

circuit rider, *Am.* a Methodist minister who rides from place to place over a circuit to preach.

cir·cu·lar (sér′kyə·lər), *adj.* 1. round like a circle. 2. moving in a circle; going around a circle. 3. having to do with a circle. 4. sent to each of a number of people: *a circular letter.* 5. roundabout; indirect. —*n.* letter, notice, or advertisement sent to each of a number of people. [< L *circularis.* See CIRCLE.] —**cir·cu·lar·i·ty** (sér′kyə·lar′ə·ti), *n.* —**cir′cu·lar·ly,** *adv.*

cir·cu·lar·ize (sér′kyə·lər·īz), *v.,* –ized, –iz·ing. 1. send circulars to. 2. make circular or round. —**cir′cu·lar·i·za′tion,** *n.* —**cir′cu·lar·iz′-er,** *n.*

circular saw, a thin disk with teeth in its edge, turned at high speed by machines.

cir·cu·late (sér′kyə·lāt), *v.,* –lat·ed, –lat·ing. 1. move in a circle or circuit; go around: *money circulates.* 2. send around from person to person or place to place. [< L *circulatus.* See CIRCLE.] —**cir′cu·la′tive,** *adj.* —**cir′cu·la′tor,** *n.* —**cir·cu·la·to·ry** (sér′kyə·lə·tô′ri; –tō′–), *adj.*

cir·cu·la·tion (sér′kyə·lā′shən), *n.* 1. a going around; a circulating. 2. movement of blood from the heart through the body and back to the heart. 3. a sending around of books, papers, news, etc., from person to person or place to place. 4. number of copies of a book, newspaper, magazine, etc., that are sent out during a certain time. 5. coins, notes, bills, etc., in use as money.

circum–, *prefix.* 1. round about; on all sides, as in *circumstance.* 2. in a circle; around, as in *circumnavigate.* [< L]

cir·cum·am·bi·ent (sér′kəm·am′bi·ənt), *adj.* surrounding; encircling. —**cir′cum·am′bi·ence,** **cir′cum·am′bi·en·cy,** *n.*

cir·cum·cise (sér′kəm·sīz), *v.,* –cised, –cis·ing. cut off the foreskin or internal labia of. [< L *circumcisus < circum* around + *caedere* cut] —**cir′cum·cis′er,** *n.* —**cir·cum·ci·sion** (sér′kəm·sizh′ən), *n.*

cir·cum·fer·ence (sər·kum′fər·əns), *n.* 1. the boundary line of a circle or of certain other surfaces. 2. the distance around. [< L *circumferentia < circum* around + *ferre* bear] —**cir·cum·fer·en·tial** (sər·kum′fər·en′shəl), *adj.*

cir·cum·flex (sér′kəm·fleks), *n.* a circumflex accent. —*adj.* 1. of or having a circumflex accent. 2. bent, bending, or winding around. [< L *circumflexus* bent around < *circum* around + *flectere* bend] —**cir·cum·flex·ion** (sér′kəm·flek′shən), *n.*

circumflex accent, mark (∧ or ∩) placed over a vowel to tell something about its pronunciation, as in the French words *fête* and *goût.*

cir·cum·flu·ent (sər·kum′flü·ənt), *adj.* flowing around; surrounding. [< L, < *circum* around + *fluere* flow]

cir·cum·fuse (sér′kəm·fūz′), *v.,* –fused, –fus·ing. 1. pour or spread around. 2. surround; suffuse. [< L *circumfusus < circum* around + *fundere* pour] —**cir′cum·fu′sion,** *n.*

cir·cum·lo·cu·tion (sér′kəm·lō·kū′shən), *n.* a roundabout way of speaking. [< L *circumlocutio < circum* around + *loqui* speak] —**cir·cum·loc·u·to·ry** (sér′kəm·lok′yə·tô′ri; –tō′–), *adj.*

cir·cum·nav·i·gate (sér′kəm·nav′ə·gāt), *v.,* –gat·ed, –gat·ing. sail around. [< L *circum·nav′-i·ga′tion,* *n.* —**cir′cum·nav′i·ga′tor,** *n.*

cir·cum·scribe (sér′kəm·skrīb′), *v.,* –scribed, –scrib·ing. 1. draw a line around; mark the boundaries of. 2. surround. 3. limit; restrict. 4. *Geom.* a. draw (a figure) around another figure so as to touch as many points as possible. b. be drawn around. [< L, < *circum* around + *scribere* write] —**cir′cum·scrib′er,** *n.* —*Syn.* 3. confine.

cir·cum·scrip·tion (sér′kəm·skrip′shən), *n.* 1. a circumscribing or being circumscribed. 2. thing that circumscribes. 3. inscription around a coin, medal, etc. 4. outline; boundary. 5. space circumscribed. 6. limitation; restriction.

cir·cum·spect (sér′kəm·spekt), *adj.* careful; cautious; prudent. [< L, < *circum* around + *specere* look] —**cir′cum·spec′tion,** *n.* —**cir′-cum·spec′tive,** *adj.* —**cir′cum·spect′ly,** *adv.* —**cir′cum·spect′ness,** *n.* —*Syn.* watchful, wary.

cir·cum·stance (sér′kəm·stans), *n.* 1. condition of an act or event. 2. fact or event, esp. in relation to others. 3. a particular or detail. 4. incident; occurrence. 5. **circumstances,** condition of affairs: *a rich person is in easy circumstances.* 6. **under no circumstances,** never; no matter what the conditions are. 7. **under the circumstances,** because of conditions; things being as they are or were. 8. *Archaic.* ceremony; display: *pomp and circumstance.* [< L *circumstantia* surrounding condition < *circum* around + *stare* stand] —**cir′cum·stanced,** *adj.*

cir·cum·stan·tial (sér′kəm·stan′shəl), *adj.* 1. depending on circumstances: *circumstantial evidence.* 2. incidental; not essential; not important. 3. giving full and exact details; complete: *a circumstantial report.* —**cir·cum·stan·ti·al·i·ty** (sér′kəm·stan′shi·al′ə·ti), **cir′cum·stan′tial·ness,** *n.* —**cir′cum·stan′tial·ly,** *adv.*

cir·cum·stan·ti·ate (sér′kəm·stan′shi·āt), *v.,* –at·ed, –at·ing. give the circumstances of; support or prove with details. —**cir′cum·stan′-ti·a′tion,** *n.*

cir·cum·vent (sér′kəm·vent′), *v.* 1. get the better of; defeat by trickery. 2. go around. 3. catch in a trap. [< L, < *circum* around + *venire* come] —**cir′cum·vent′er,** **cir′cum·ven′tor,** *n.* —**cir′cum·ven′tion,** *n.* —**cir′cum·ven′tive,** *adj.*

cir·cus (sér′kəs), *n.* 1. a traveling show of acrobats, clowns, horses, riders, and wild animals. 2. *Colloq.* an amusing person, thing, or event. 3. in ancient Rome, a round or oval space with rows of seats around it, one row above the other. [< L, ring]

cir·rho·sis (si·rō′sis), *n.* a diseased condition of the liver, kidneys, etc., due to excessive formation of connective tissue. [< NL < Gk. *kirrhos* orange-yellow] —**cir·rhot·ic** (si·rot′ik), *adj.*

cir·rus (sir′əs), *n., pl.* **cir·ri** (sir′ī). 1. a thin, fleecy cloud very high in the air. 2. *Bot.* a tendril. 3. *Zool.* a slender appendage. [< L *cirrus* curl]

cis·co (sis′kō), *n., pl.* **–coes, –cos.** *Am.* a whitefish or herring of the Great Lakes. [< Am.Ind.]

Cis·ter·cian (sis·tér′shən), *n.* member of a Benedictine order of monks and nuns founded in France in 1098. —*adj.* of this order.

cis·tern (sis′tərn), *n.* 1. reservoir or tank for storing water. 2. *Anat.* vessel or cavity of the body. [< L *cisterna < cista* box]

cit·a·del (sit′ə·dəl; –del), *n.* 1. fortress commanding a city. 2. a strongly fortified place; stronghold. 3. a strong, safe place; refuge. [< F < Ital. *cittadella,* dim. of *città* CITY]

ci·ta·tion (sī·tā′shən), *n.* 1. quotation or reference, esp. given as an authority for facts, opinions, etc. 2. specific mention in an official dispatch. 3. *Am.* public commendation or decoration for unusual achievement or gallant action, esp. in time of war. 4. summons to appear before a law court. —**ci·ta·to·ry** (sī′tə·tô′ri; –tō′–), *adj.*

cite (sīt), *v.,* cit·ed, cit·ing. 1. quote (a passage, book, or author), esp. as an authority. 2. refer to; mention as an example. 3. mention for bravery in war. 4. summon to appear before a law court. 5. arouse to action; summon. [< L *citare* summon < *ciere* set in motion]

cith·a·ra (sith′ə·rə), *n.* an ancient musical instrument somewhat like a lyre. [< L < Gk. *kithara.* Doublet of GUITAR and ZITHER.]

cith·er (sith′ər), *n.* 1. cithara. 2. cithern.

cith·ern (sith′ərn), *n.* a musical instrument somewhat like a guitar, popular in the 16th and 17th centuries. Also, **cittern.** [see CITTERN]

Girl playing a cithara

cit·i·zen (sit′ə·zən; –sən), *n.* 1. person who by birth or by choice is a member of a state or nation. 2. person who is not a soldier, policeman, etc.; civilian. 3. inhabitant of a city or town. [< AF *citisein < OF cite* CITY] —*Syn.* 1. national, subject. 3. resident.

cit·i·zen·ry (sit′ə·zən·ri; –sən–), *n., pl.* –ries. citizens as a group.

cit·i·zen·ship (sit′ə-zən-ship′; –sən-), n. 1. condition of being a citizen. 2. duties, rights, and privileges of a citizen.

cit·rate (sit′rāt; sī′trāt), n. Chem. salt or ester of citric acid.

cit·ric (sit′rik), adj. of or from fruits such as lemons, limes, oranges, etc.

citric acid, Chem. acid, $C_6H_8O_7$, from such fruits as lemons, limes, etc., used as a flavoring, as a medicine, and in making dyes.

cit·ron (sit′rən), n. 1. a pale-yellow fruit somewhat like a lemon but larger, less acid, and with a thicker rind. 2. the candied rind of this fruit, used in fruit cakes, plum pudding, candies, etc. 3. shrub or small tree that this fruit grows on. [< F < Ital. citrone < L citrus citrus tree]

cit·ron·el·la (sit′rən·el′ə), n. oil used in making perfume, soap, liniment, etc., and for keeping mosquitoes away. [< NL]

cit·rous (sit′rəs), adj. pertaining to fruits such as lemons, grapefruit, limes, oranges, etc.

cit·rus (sit′rəs), n. 1. any tree bearing lemons, limes, oranges, or similar fruit. 2. Also, Am., **citrus fruit.** fruit of such a tree. —adj. of such trees. [< L]

cit·tern (sit′ərn), n. cithern. [blend of L cithara CITHARA + E gittern]

cit·y (sit′i), n., pl. cit·ies, adj. —n. 1. a large and important town. 2. division of local government in the United States having a charter from the State that fixes its boundaries and powers, usually governed by a mayor and a board of aldermen or councilmen. 3. division of local government in Canada of the highest class. 4. people living in a city. —adj. 1. of a city. 2. in a city. [< OF < L civitas citizenship, state, city < civis citizen]

cit·y·bust·er (sit′i·bus′tər), n. Colloq. an atomic or hydrogen bomb.

city hall, Am. a building containing offices for the officials, bureaus, etc., of a city government.

city manager, Am. person appointed by a city council or commission to manage the government of a city. He is not elected by the people.

cit·y-state (sit′i·stāt′), n. an independent state consisting of a city and the territories depending on it.

Ciu·dad Tru·jil·lo (sū·thäth′ trū·hē′yō), n. former name of the capital of the Dominican Republic. Now called **Santo Domingo.**

civ·et (siv′it), n. 1. a yellowish secretion of certain glands of the civet cat. It has a musky odor and is used in making perfume. 2. Also, civet cat. a. a small, spotted animal of Africa, Europe, and Asia having glands that secrete a yellowish substance with a musky odor. b. any of certain similar animals. [< F < Ital. < Ar. zabād]

civ·ic (siv′ik), adj. 1. of a city. 2. of or having to do with citizenship. 3. of citizens. [< L civicus < civis citizen] —civ′i·cal·ly, adv.

civ·ics (siv′iks), n. Am. study of the duties, rights, and privileges of citizens.

civ·il (siv′əl), adj. 1. of a citizen or citizens; having to do with citizens. 2. of or having to do with the government, state, or nation: civil servants. 3. not military, naval, or connected with the church. Post offices are part of the civil service of the government. 4. polite; courteous. 5. pertaining to the private rights of individuals and to legal proceedings connected with these rights. [< L civilis < civis citizen] —Syn. 4. respectful, gracious, affable.

civil disobedience, refusal to obey the laws of the state, esp. by not paying taxes.

civil engineering, the planning and directing of the construction of bridges, roads, harbors, etc. —**civil engineer.**

ci·vil·ian (sə·vil′yən), n. person who is not a soldier or sailor. —adj. of civilians; not military or naval.

ci·vil·i·ty (sə·vil′ə·ti), n., pl. –ties. 1. politeness; courtesy. 2. act of politeness or courtesy. 3. Archaic. civilization.

civ·i·li·za·tion (siv′ə·lə·zā′shən), n. 1. act of civilizing. 2. process of becoming civilized; improvement in culture. 3. civilized condition; advanced stage in social development. 4. nations

and peoples that have reached advanced stages in social development. 5. the culture and ways of living of a race, nation, etc.: Chinese civilization.

civ·i·lize (siv′ə·līz), v., –lized, –liz·ing. 1. bring out of a savage or barbarian condition; train in culture, science, and art. 2. improve in culture and good manners; refine. See CIVIL, –IZE.] —civ′i·liz′a·ble, adj. —civ′i·liz′er, n.

civ·i·lized (siv′ə·līzd), adj. 1. trained in culture, art, and science. 2. of civilized nations or persons. 3. showing culture and good manners; refined.

civil law, law that regulates and protects private rights and is controlled and used by civil courts, not military courts.

civil liberty, right of a person to do and say what he pleases as long as he does not harm anyone else.

civ·il·ly (siv′ə·li), adv. 1. politely; courteously. 2. according to the civil law.

civil rights, Am. the rights of a citizen, esp. the rights guaranteed to citizens of the United States, irrespective of race or color, by the 13th and 14th amendments to the Constitution.

civil service, public service concerned with affairs not military, naval, legislative, or judicial. —**civil servant.**

civil war, 1. war between two groups of citizens of one nation. 2. **Civil War,** a. Am. war between the Northern and Southern States of the United States from 1861 to 1865. b. war between Charles I of England and Parliament, from 1642 to 1646 and from 1648 to 1652.

Cl, Chem. chlorine.

cl., 1. centiliter. 2. class. 3. clause.

clab·ber (klab′ər), n. thick, sour milk. —v. become thick in souring; curdle. [< Irish clabar curds, short for bainne clabair bonnyclabber (curdled milk)]

clack (klak), v. 1. make or cause to make a short, sharp sound. 2. chatter. —n. 1. short, sharp sound. 2. chatter. [imit.] —clack′er, n.

clad (klad), v. pt. and pp. of clothe.

claim (klām), v. 1. demand as one's own or one's right. 2. say one has and demand that others recognize (a right, title, possession, etc.); assert one's right to. 3. declare as a fact; say strongly; maintain. 4. require; call for; deserve. —n. 1. demand for something due; assertion of a right. 2. right or title to something. 3. something that is claimed. 4. Am. piece of public land that a settler or prospector marks out for himself. 5. assertion of something as a fact. [< OF < L clamare call, proclaim] —claim′a·ble, adj. —claim′er, n. —Syn. v. 2. exact.

claim·ant (klām′ənt), n. one who makes a claim.

clair·voy·ance (klâr·voi′əns), n. 1. power of knowing about things that are out of sight. 2. exceptional insight. [< F, < clair clear + voyant seeing] —clair·voy′ant, adj., n.

clam (klam), n., v., clammed, clam·ming. 1. mollusk somewhat like an oyster, with a shell in two halves. 2. Am., Slang. a close-mouthed or dull person. —v. Am. go out after clams; dig for clams. [appar. special use of clam pair of pincers; OE clamm fetter]

clam·ber (klam′bər), v. climb, using both hands and feet; climb awkwardly or with difficulty; scramble. —n. an awkward or difficult climb. [ME clambre(n)] —clam′ber·er, n.

clam·my (klam′i), adj., –mi·er, –mi·est. cold and damp. —clam′mi·ly, adv. —clam′mi·ness, n.

clam·or, esp. Brit. **clam·our** (klam′ər), n. 1. a loud noise; continual uproar; shouting. 2. a noisy demand or complaint. —v. 1. make a loud noise or continual uproar; shout. 2. demand or complain noisily. [< OF < L, < clamare cry out] —clam′or·er, esp. Brit. clam′our·er, n. —Syn. n. 1. outcry.

clam·or·ous (klam′ər·əs), adj. 1. noisy; shouting. 2. making noisy demands or complaints. —clam′or·ous·ly, adv. —clam′or·ous·ness, n.

clamp (klamp), n. 1. brace, band, wedge, or other device for holding things tightly together.

2. instrument for holding things tightly together temporarily. —v. fasten together with a clamp; put in a clamp; strengthen with a clamp. [< MDu. *klampe*]

clan (klan), *n.* **1.** group of related families that claim to be descended from a common ancestor. **2.** group of people closely joined together by some common interest. [< Scotch Gaelic *clann* family]

clan·des·tine (klan·des′tən), *adj.* secret; concealed; underhand. [< L *clandestinus*, ult. < *clam* secretly] —**clandes′tine·ly,** *adv.* —**clan·des′tine·ness,** *n.* —**Syn.** hidden, furtive, covert.

Clamp

clang (klang), *n.* a loud, harsh, ringing sound, as of metal being hit. —v. **1.** make a clang. **2.** strike together with a clang. [imit.]

clan·gor, *esp. Brit.* **clan·gour** (klang′gər; klang′ər), *n.* **1.** continued clanging. **2.** clang. —v. clang. [< L, < *clangere* clang] —**clan′gor·ous,** *adj.* —**clan′gor·ous·ly,** *adv.*

clank (klangk), *n.* a sharp, harsh sound like the rattle of a heavy chain. —v. **1.** make such a sound. **2.** cause to clank. [? < Du. *klank*]

clan·nish (klan′ish), *adj.* **1.** pertaining to a clan. **2.** closely united; not liking outsiders. —**clan′nish·ly,** *adv.* —**clan′nish·ness,** *n.*

clans·man (klanz′mən), *n., pl.* -**men.** member of a clan.

clap (klap), *n., v.,* **clapped, clap·ping.** —*n.* **1.** a sudden noise, such as a single burst of thunder, the sound of the hands struck together, or the sound of a loud slap. **2.** applause. —v. **1.** strike together loudly. **2.** applaud by striking the hands together. **3.** strike with a quick blow. **4.** put or place quickly and effectively. **5.** *Now Colloq.* make or arrange hastily. [OE *clæppan*]

clap·board (klab′ərd; klap′bôrd; -bōrd), *Am.* —*n.* a thin board, thicker along one edge than along the other, used to cover the outer walls of wooden buildings. —v. cover with clapboards.

clap·per (klap′ər), *n.* **1.** one that claps. **2.** part that strikes a bell. **3.** device for making noise.

clap·trap (klap′trap′), *n.* empty talk; an insincere remark. —*adj.* cheap and showy.

claque (klak), *n.* **1.** group of persons hired to applaud in a theater. **2.** group that applauds or follows another person for selfish reasons. [< F, < *claquer* clap]

clar·et (klar′ət), *n.* **1.** kind of red wine. **2.** a dark, purplish red. —*adj.* dark purplish-red. [< OF, light colored, < *cler* CLEAR]

clar·i·fy (klar′ə·fī), *v.,* -**fied, -fy·ing. 1.** make or become clear; purify: *clarify fat by straining it.* **2.** make clearer; explain. [< OF < LL *clarificare* < L *clarus* clear + *facere* make] —**clar′i·fi·ca′tion,** *n.* —**clar′i·fi′er,** *n.*

clar·i·net (klar′ə·net′), *n.* a wooden wind instrument played by means of holes and keys. [< F *clarinette,* dim. of *clarine* bell < L *clarus* clear] —**clar′i·net′ist, clar′i·net′tist,** *n.*

clar·i·on (klar′i·ən), *adj.* clear and shrill. —*n.* **1.** a kind of trumpet with clear, shrill tones. **2.** a clear, shrill sound. [< Med.L *clario* < L *clarus* clear]

clar·i·ty (klar′ə·ti), *n.* clearness.

Man playing a clarinet

clash (klash), *n.* **1.** a loud, harsh sound like that of two things running into each other, of striking metal, or of bells rung together but not in tune. **2.** strong disagreement; conflict. —v. **1.** strike with a clash. **2.** throw, shut, etc., with a clash. **3.** disagree strongly; conflict. [imit.] —**Syn.** *n.* **2.** discord.

clasp (klasp; kläsp), *n.* **1.** thing to fasten two parts or pieces together. **2.** a close hold with the arms or hands. **3.** a firm grip with the hand. —v. **1.** fasten together with a clasp. **2.** hold closely with the arms or hands. **3.** grip firmly with the hand. [ME *claspe(n)*] —**clasp′er,** *n.* —**Syn.** *v.* **1.** hook. **2.** embrace, hug. **3.** grasp, clutch.

class (klas; kläs), *n.* **1.** group of persons or things alike in some way; kind; sort. **2.** group of students taught together. **3.** a meeting of such

a group. **4.** *Am.* group of pupils entering a school together and graduating in the same year. **5.** rank or division of society: *the middle class.* **6.** system of ranks or divisions in society. **7.** *Mil.* group of draftees of the same age. **8.** high rank in society. **9.** grade; quality: *first class is the best way to travel.* **10.** *Slang.* excellence; style. **11.** group of animals or plants ranking below a phylum or subkingdom and above an order. —v. put or be in a class or group. [< L *classis* class, collection, fleet] —**class′a·ble,** *adj.* —**class′er,** *n.*

class., **1.** classic; classical. **2.** classified.

clas·sic (klas′ik), *adj.* **1.** of the highest grade or quality; excellent; first-class. **2.** of the literature, art, and life of ancient Greece and Rome. **3.** like this literature and art; simple, regular, and restrained. **4.** famous in literature or history. —*n.* **1.** work of literature or art of the highest quality. **2.** author or artist of acknowledged excellence. **3.** the classics, the literature of ancient Greece and Rome. [< L *classicus* < *classis* CLASS]

clas·si·cal (klas′ə·kəl), *adj.* **1.** classic. **2.** knowing the classics well. **3.** devoted to the classics. **4.** based on the classics. **5.** orthodox and sound, but not quite up to date: *classical physics.* **6.** *Music.* of high quality and enjoyed especially by serious students of music. —**clas′si·cal′i·ty,** *n.* —**clas′si·cal·ly,** *adv.* —**clas′si·cal·ness,** *n.*

clas·si·cism (klas′ə·siz·əm), **clas·si·cal·ism** (-kəl·iz′əm), *n.* **1.** principles of the literature and art of ancient Greece and Rome. **2.** adherence to these principles. **3.** knowledge of the literature of ancient Greece and Rome; classical scholarship. **4.** idiom or form from Greek or Latin introduced into another language.

clas·si·cist (klas′ə·sist), **clas·si·cal·ist** (-kəl·ist), *n.* **1.** follower of the principles of classicism in literature and art. **2.** expert in the literature of ancient Greece and Rome. **3.** person who urges the study of Greek and Latin.

clas·si·fi·ca·tion (klas′ə·fə·kā′shən), *n.* arrangement in classes or groups; a grouping according to some system. —**clas·si·fi·ca·to·ry** (klas′ə·fə·kə·tô′ri; -tō′-), *adj.*

clas·si·fied (klas′ə·fīd), *adj.* **1.** of certain public documents of the U.S., having a classification as secret, confidential, or restricted. **2.** *Slang.* secret.

classified ad, *Am.* want ad.

clas·si·fy (klas′ə·fī), *v.,* -**fied, -fy·ing.** arrange in classes or groups; group according to some system. —**clas′si·fi′a·ble,** *adj.* —**clas′si·fi′er,** *n.*

class·mate (klas′māt′; kläs′-), *n. Am.* member of the same class in school.

class·room (klas′rüm′; -rům′; kläs′-), *n.* room where classes meet in school; schoolroom.

clat·ter (klat′ər), *n.* **1.** a confused noise like that of many plates being struck together. **2.** noisy talk. —v. **1.** move or fall with confused noise; make a confused noise. **2.** talk fast and noisily. **3.** cause to clatter. [OE *clatrian*] —**clat′ter·er,** *n.* —**clat′ter·ing·ly,** *adv.*

clause (klôz), *n.* **1.** part of a sentence having a subject and predicate. In "He came before we left," "He came" is a **main clause,** and "before we left" is a **subordinate clause. 2.** a single provision of a law, treaty, or any other written agreement. [< Med.L *clausa* for L *clausula* close of a period < *claudere* close] —**claus′al,** *adj.* ▶ A **clause** is a part of a compound or complex sentence that ordinarily has a subject and a finite verb. **Compound** sentences have two coördinate clauses, of grammatically equal value, connected usually by *and, but, for,* or another coördinating conjunction: [First clause] *The drive for funds went well* [second clause] *and a large amount of money was accumulated.* **Complex** sentences have at least one main clause, grammatically capable of standing alone, and one or more subordinate clauses, joined to the main clause or clauses by *as, because, since, when,* or some other subordinating conjunction, or by a relative pronoun, *that, who, which:* [Main clause] *There are differences of opinion on the matter* [subordinate clause] *which cause a great deal of disharmony.*

claus·tro·pho·bi·a (klôs'trə·fō'bi·ə), *n.* morbid fear of enclosed spaces. [< NL., < L *claustrum* closed place + E *–phobia* fear (< Gk.)]

clave (klāv), *v. Archaic.* pt. of **cleave**².

clav·i·chord (klav'ə·kôrd), *n.* a stringed musical instrument with a keyboard. The piano developed from it. [< Med.L < L *clavis* key + *chorda* string]

clav·i·cle (klav'ə·kəl), *n. Anat., Zool.* collarbone. [< L *clavicula* bolt, dim. of *clavis* key] —cla·vic·u·lar (klə·vik'yə·lər), *adj.*

cla·vier (klə·vir'), *n.* any musical instrument with a keyboard, as the harpsichord and clavichord. [< G < F < L *clavis* key]

claw (klô), *n.* 1. a sharp, hooked nail on a bird's or animal's foot. 2. foot with such sharp, hooked nails. 3. pincers of lobsters, crabs, etc. 4. anything like a claw. 5. act of clawing. —*v.* scratch, tear, seize, or pull with claws or hands. [OE *clawu*]

clay (klā), *n.* 1. a stiff, sticky kind of earth, that can be easily shaped when wet and hardens after drying or baking. 2. earth. 3. human body. [OE *clǣg*] —clay·ey (klā'i), clay'ish, *adj.*

Clay (klā), *n.* Henry, 1777–1852, American statesman.

Claws of a bird

clay·more (klā'môr; –mōr), *n.* a heavy, two-edged sword, formerly used by Scottish Highlanders. [< Scotch Gaelic *claidheamh mor* great sword]

clean (klēn), *adj.* 1. free from dirt or filth; not soiled or stained. 2. pure; innocent. 3. having clean habits. 4. fit for food. 5. free from anything that mars or impedes; clear: *clean copy.* 6. of atomic weapons, causing little or no radioactive fall-out. 7. even; regular: *a clean cut.* 8. well-shaped; trim. 9. clever; skillful. 10. complete; entire; total. —*adv.* 1. completely; entirely; totally. 2. in a clean manner. —*v.* 1. make clean. 2. perform or undergo a process of cleaning. 3. remove in the process of cleaning. [OE *clǣne*] —clean'a·ble, *adj.* —clean'ness, *n.* —Syn. *adj.* 1. unstained, unsoiled. 2. chaste, virtuous. 5. spotless, immaculate. –*v.* 1. cleanse, scour, scrub, wash.

clean-cut (klēn'kut'), *adj.* 1. having clear, sharp outlines. 2. well-shaped. 3. clear; definite; distinct. 4. having a clear, definite character.

clean·er (klēn'ər), *n.* 1. person whose work is cleaning. 2. tool or machine for cleaning. 3. anything that removes dirt, grease, or stains.

clean·ly (*adj.* klen'li; *adv.* klēn'li), *adj.*, –li·er, –li·est, *adv.* —*adj.* clean; habitually clean. —*adv.* in a clean manner. —clean·li·ly (klēn'lə·li), *adv.* —clean·li·ness (klen'li·nis), *n.*

cleanse (klenz), *v.*, cleansed, cleans·ing. 1. make clean. 2. make pure. [OE *clǣnsian* < *clǣne* clean] —cleans'a·ble, *adj.* —cleans'er, *n.* —Syn. 1. clean. 2. purify.

clean·up (klēn'up'), *n.* 1. a cleaning up. 2. *Slang.* money made; profit.

clear (klir), *adj.* 1. not cloudy; bright; light. 2. transparent: *clear glass.* 3. having a pure, even color: *a clear blue.* 4. without stain or blemish. 5. that perceives distinctly: *a clear mind.* 6. easily seen, heard, or understood. 7. sure; certain. 8. not blocked or obstructed; open. 9. without touching; without being caught. 10. free from blame or guilt; innocent. 11. free from debts or charges. 12. without limitation; complete. —*v.* 1. make or become clear; get clear. 2. remove to leave a space. 3. pass by or over without touching or being caught. 4. make free from blame or guilt; prove to be innocent. 5. make as profit free from debts or charges. 6. get (a ship or cargo) free by meeting requirements on entering or leaving a port. 7. leave a port after doing this. 8. exchange (checks and bills) and settle accounts between different banks. 9. clear up. a. make or become clear. b. put in order by clearing. c. explain. d. become clear after a storm. —*adv.* 1. in a clear manner. 2. completely; entirely. —*n.* in the clear, a. between the outside parts. b. free. c. in plain text;

not in cipher or code. [< OF < L *clarus* clear] —clear'a·ble, *adj.* —clear'er, *n.* —clear'ly, *adv.* —clear'ness, *n.* —Syn. *adj.* 6. plain, distinct, evident, obvious, manifest, apparent, patent. –*v.* 4. absolve, acquit. —Ant. *adj.* 1. cloudy, dim. 2. opaque. 6. abstruse, ambiguous, unintelligible.

clear·ance (klir'əns), *n.* 1. act of making clear. 2. a clear space between two objects. 3. papers permitting a ship or aircraft to leave on a voyage or flight. 4. the settling of accounts between different banks.

clear-cut (klir'kut'), *adj.* 1. having clear, sharp outlines. 2. clear; definite; distinct.

clear-head·ed (klir'hed'id), *adj.* having or showing a clear understanding. —clear'-head'ed·ly, *adv.* —clear'-head'ed·ness, *n.*

clear·ing (klir'ing), *n. Am.* an open space of cleared land in a forest.

clearing house, place where banks exchange checks and bills and settle their accounts.

clear-sight·ed (klir'sīt'id), *adj.* 1. able to see clearly. 2. able to understand or think clearly. —clear'-sight'ed·ly, *adv.* —clear'-sight'ed·ness, *n.*

clear·sto·ry (klir'stô'ri; –stō'–), *n., pl.* –ries. clerestory.

cleat (klēt), *n.* 1. strip of wood or iron fastened across anything for support or for sure footing. 2. *Naut.* a. a small, wedge-shaped block fastened to a spar, etc., as a support, check, etc. b. piece of wood or metal used for securing ropes or lines. —*v.* fasten to or with a cleat. [ME *cleete*]

cleav·age (klēv'ij), *n.* 1. split; division. 2. way in which something splits or divides. 3. *Biol.* any of the series of divisions by which a fertilized egg develops into an embryo.

cleave¹ (klēv), *v.,* cleft or cleaved or clove, cleft or cleaved or clo·ven, cleav·ing. 1. split; divide. 2. pass through; pierce; penetrate. 3. make by cutting. [OE *clēofan*] —cleav'a·ble, *adj.*

cleave² (klēv), *v.,* cleaved or (*Archaic*) clave, cleaved, cleav·ing. stick; cling; be faithful. [OE *cleofian*]

cleav·er (klēv'ər), *n.* 1. one that cleaves. 2. cutting tool with a heavy blade and a short handle.

clef (klef), *n. Music.* symbol indicating the pitch of the notes on a staff. [< F < L *clavis* key]

cleft (kleft), *v.* pt. and pp. of **cleave**¹. —*adj.* split; divided. —*n.* a space or opening made by splitting; crack. [OE *geclyft*] —Syn. *n.* fissure, crevice, chink.

clem·a·tis (klem'ə·tis), *n.* vine with clusters of fragrant white or purple flowers. [< L < Gk., < *klema* vine branch]

Clem·en·ceau (klem'ən·sō'), *n.* Georges, 1841–1929, premier of France, 1906–09, 1917–20.

Clem·ens (klem'ənz), *n.* Samuel Langhorne, 1835–1910, the real name of Mark Twain.

clem·ent (klem'ənt), *adj.* 1. merciful. 2. mild. [< L *clemens*] —clem'en·cy, *n.* —clem'ent·ly, *adv.*

clench (klench), *v.* 1. close tightly together: *clench one's fists* in anger. 2. grasp firmly; grip tightly. 3. clinch (a nail, etc.). —*n.* firm grasp; tight grip. [OE (*be*)*clencan* hold fast]

Cle·o·pa·tra (klē'ə·pat'rə; –pā'trə; –pä'trə), *n.* 69?–30 B.C., last queen of ancient Egypt, 47–30 B.C.

clere·sto·ry (klir'stô'ri; –stō'–), *n., pl.* –ries. 1. the upper part of the wall of a church, having windows in it above the roofs of the aisles. 2. a similar structure in any building. Also, clear-story. [appar. < *clere* clear + *story*²]

cler·gy (klėr'ji), *n., pl.* –gies. persons ordained for religious work; ministers, pastors, and priests. [< OF *clergie*, ult. < LL *clericus* CLERIC]

cler·gy·man (klėr'ji·mən), *n., pl.* –men. member of the clergy; minister; pastor; priest.

cler·ic (kler'ik), *n.* clergyman. —*adj.* of a clergyman or the clergy. [< LL < Gk., < *kleros* clergy, orig., lot, allotment. Doublet of CLERK.]

cler·i·cal (kler'ə·kəl), *adj.* 1. of a clerk or clerks; for clerks. 2. of a clergyman or the clergy. 3. supporting the power or influence of the clergy in politics. —*n.* **1.** clergyman. **2.** supporter of the power or influence of the clergy in politics. —**cler′i·cal·ly,** *adv.*

cler·i·cal·ism (kler′ə·kəl·iz′em), *n.* power or influence of the clergy in politics. —**cler′i·cal·ist,** *n.*

clerk (klèrk; *Brit.* klärk), *n.* **1.** *Am.* person whose work is waiting on customers and selling goods in a store; salesman or saleswoman. **2.** person whose work is keeping records or accounts, copying letters, etc., in an office. **3.** official who keeps records and takes care of regular business in a law court, legislature, etc. **4.** layman who has minor church duties. **5.** *Esp. Law.* clergyman. **6.** *Archaic.* a scholar. —*v.* work as a clerk. [< LL *clericus.* Doublet of .CLERIC.] —**clerk′ly,** *adv.* —**clerk′li·ness,** *n.* —**clerk′ship,** *n.*

Cleve·land (klēv′lənd), *n.* **1.** city in NE Ohio, on Lake Erie. **2. (Stephen) Grover,** 1837–1908, the 22nd and 24th president of the United States 1885–89, 1893–97.

clev·er (klev′ər), *adj.* **1.** having a quick mind; bright; intelligent. **2.** skillful or expert in doing some particular thing. **3.** showing skill or intelligence. [ME *cliver*] —**clev′er·ly,** *adv.* —**clev′erness,** *n.* —**Syn. 1.** ingenious, smart. **2.** adroit. —**Ant. 1.** stupid. **2.** clumsy.

clev·is (klev′is), *n.* a U-shaped piece of metal with a bolt or pin through the ends. [akin to CLEAVE¹]

clew (klü), *n.* **1.** clue. **2.** ball of thread or yarn. —*v.* coil into a ball. [OE *cleowen*]

cli·ché (klē·shā′), *n.* a worn-out idea or trite expression. [< F, pp. of *clicher* stereotype]

click (klik), *n.* **1.** a light, sharp sound like that of a key turning in a lock. **2.** sound made by withdrawing the tongue from contact with some part of the mouth. **3.** pawl. —*v.* **1.** make a light, sharp sound. **2.** cause to make such a sound. **3.** *Slang.* be a success. [imit.] —**click′er,** *n.*

cli·ent (klī′ənt), *n.* **1.** person for whom a lawyer acts. **2.** customer. [< L *cliens;* akin to —*clinare* lean] —**cli·en·tal** (klī·en′təl, klī′ən·təl), *adj.* —**cli′ent·less,** *adj.*

cli·en·tele (klī′ən·tel′), *n.* **1.** clients; customers. **2.** number of clients. [< L *clientela*]

cliff (klif), *n.* a high, steep rock. [OE *clif*]

cli·mac·ter·ic (klī·mak′tər·ik; klī′mak·ter′ik), *n.* time when some important event occurs; crucial period. —*adj.* Also, **cli·mac·ter·i·cal** (klī′mak·ter′ə·kəl). of or like such a period; crucial [< L < Gk., < *klimakter* rung of a ladder < *klimax* ladder]

cli·mac·tic (klī·mak′tik), **cli·mac·ti·cal** (-tə·kəl), *adj.* of or forming a climax.

cli·mate (klī′mit), *n.* **1.** the kind of weather a place has, including conditions of heat and cold, moisture and dryness, clearness and cloudiness, wind and calm. **2.** intellectual and moral atmosphere. [< L < Gk. *klima* slope (of the earth) < *klinein* incline] —**cli·mat·ic** (klī·mat′ik), *adj.* —**cli·mat′i·cal·ly,** *adv.* —**Syn. 1.** clime.

cli·ma·tol·o·gy (klī′mə·tol′ə·ji), *n.* science that deals with climate. —**cli·ma·to·log·ic** (klī′mə·tə·loj′ik), **cli·ma·to·log′i·cal,** *adj.* —**cli′ma·tol′o·gist,** *n.*

cli·max (klī′maks), *n.* **1.** the highest point; point of greatest interest; most exciting part. **2.** arrangement of ideas in a rising scale of force and interest. —*v.* bring or come to a climax. [< LL < Gk. *klimax* ladder] —**Syn. n. 1.** peak, zenith, culmination.

climb (klīm), *v.,* **climbed** or (*Archaic*) **clomb, climb·ing,** *n.* —*v.* **1.** go up by using the hands or feet; ascend: *climb a ladder.* **2.** rise slowly with steady effort: *climb from poverty to wealth.* **3.** grow upward by holding on or twining around: *some vines climb.* **4. climb down,** a. go down by using the hands and feet. b. *Colloq.* give in; back down. —*n.* **1.** a climbing; ascent. **2.** place to be climbed. [OE *climban*] —**climb′a·ble,** *adj.* —**climb′er,** *n.* —**Syn. v. 1.** mount, scale.

clime (klīm), *n. Poetic.* **1.** country; region. **2.** climate. [< L *clima.* See CLIMATE.]

clinch (klinch), *v.* **1.** fasten (a driven nail, a bolt, etc.) firmly by bending over the part that projects. **2.** fasten (things) together in this way. **3.** fix firmly; settle decisively: *clinch a bargain.* **4.** *Am.* grasp tightly in fighting or wrestling. —*n.* **1.** a clinching. **2.** a tight grasp in fighting or wrestling. [var. of *clench*]

clinch·er (klin′chər), *n.* **1.** nail or bolt that is clinched. **2.** *Colloq.* argument, statement, etc., that is decisive.

cling (kling), *v.,* **clung, cling·ing,** *n.* —*v.* **1.** stick; hold fast. **2.** keep near. **3.** grasp; embrace. —*n.* act of clinging. [OE *clingan*] —**cling′er,** *n.* —**cling′ing·ly,** *adv.* —**cling′y,** *adj.*

cling·stone (kling′stōn′), *n. Am.* peach whose stone clings to the fleshy part.

clin·ic (klin′ik), *n.* **1.** place, usually connected with a hospital or medical school, where outpatients can receive medical treatment. **2.** practical instruction of medical students by examining or treating patients in a bed in the students' presence. [< L < Gk. *klinikos* of a bed < *kline* bed]

clin·i·cal (klin′ə·kəl), *adj.* **1.** of or having to do with a clinic. **2.** used or performed in a sickroom. **3.** having to do with the study of disease by observation of the patient. —**clin′i·cal·ly,** *adv.*

clink (klingk), *n.* **1.** a light, sharp, ringing sound like that of glasses hitting together. **2.** rhyme. —*v.* **1.** make a clink. **2.** cause to clink. [ME *clinke(n),* ? < Du. *klinken*]

clink·er (klingk′ər), *n.* **1.** a large, rough cinder. **2.** a very hard brick. —*v.* form clinkers. [< Du. *klinker* brick < *klinken* ring]

cli·nom·e·ter (klī·nom′ə·tər; klī–), *n.* instrument for measuring deviation from the horizontal. [< L –*clinare* incline + -METER]

Cli·o (klī′ō), *n. Gk. Myth.* the Muse of history.

clip¹ (klip), *v.,* **clipped, clip·ping,** *n.* —*v.* **1.** trim with shears or scissors; cut. **2.** cut the hair or fleece of. **3.** omit sounds in pronouncing. **4.** cut short; curtail. **5.** *Colloq.* move fast. **6.** *Colloq.* hit or punch sharply. **7.** cut pieces from a magazine, newspaper, etc. —*n.* **1.** act of clipping. **2.** anything clipped off. **3.** fast motion. **4.** *Colloq.* a sharp blow, etc. **5.** *Am., Colloq.* one time: *at one clip.* [ME *clippe(n),* prob. < Scand. *klippa*]

clip² (klip), *v.,* **clipped, clip·ping,** *n.* —*v.* hold tight; fasten. —*n.* **1.** thing used for clipping (things) together. **2.** a metal holder for cartridges on some firearms. [OE *clyppan* embrace]

clipped word, a shortened form made by dropping a syllable or more, as *ad* for *advertisement.* ➤ Clipped words are typical of shoptalk and familiar speech and often find their way into the general vocabulary. Many, like *gent* or *prof,* are out of place in writing.

clip·per (klip′ər), *n.* **1.** person who clips or cuts. **2.** Often, **clippers.** tool for cutting. **3.** *Am.* a sailing ship built and rigged for speed. **4.** a large, fast aircraft.

clip·ping (klip′ing), *n. Am.* piece cut out of a newspaper, magazine, etc.

clique (klēk; klik), *n.* a small, exclusive set or snobbish group of people. [< F, < *cliquer* click] —**cli′quish,** *adj.* —**cli′quish·ly,** *adv.* —**cli′quish·ness,** *n.*

cli·to·ris (klī′tə·ris; klit′ə–), *n. Anat.* in most mammals, a small organ of the female homologous to the penis of the male. [< NL < Gk., < *kleiein* shut]

clo·a·ca (klō·ā′kə), *n., pl.* -**cae** (-sē). **1.** sewer. **2.** privy. **3.** receptacle of moral filth. **4.** *Zool.* cavity in the body of birds, reptiles, amphibians, etc., into which the intestinal, urinary, and generative canals open. [< L, prob. < *cluere* purge] —**clo·a′cal,** *adj.*

cloak (klōk), *n.* **1.** a loose outer garment with or without sleeves. **2.** anything that hides or conceals. —*v.* **1.** cover with a cloak. **2.** hide. [< OF < LL *clocca,* orig., bell, < OIrish *cloc*]

cloak-and-dag·ger (klōk′ənd·dag′ər), *adj. Colloq.* associated or done with secrecy and violence.

cloak·room (klōk′rüm′; –rùm′), *n.* room where coats, hats, etc., can be left for a time.

clob·ber (klob′ər), *v. Am., Slang.* 1. attack violently. 2. *Sports.* defeat severely.

cloche (klōsh), *n.* a close-fitting hat for women. [< F, bell, ult. < LL *clocca*. See CLOCK¹.]

clock¹ (klok), *n.* instrument for measuring and showing time, esp. one that is not carried around like a watch. —*v.* 1. measure the time of. 2. record the time of. [< MDu. *clocke* < OF *cloque* or LL *clocca* < OIrish *cloc*] —**clock′er,** *n.*

clock² (klok), *n.* an ornamental pattern sewn or woven on the side of a stocking, extending up from the ankle. —*v.* ornament with clocks.

clock·wise (klok′wīz′), *adv., adj.* in the direction in which the hands of a clock move.

clock·work (klok′wėrk′), *n.* 1. machinery used to run a clock. 2. machinery like this. 3. like clockwork, with great regularity.

clod (klod), *n.* 1. lump of earth; lump. 2. earth; soil. 3. anything earthy. 4. a stupid person; blockhead. [OE *clod*] —**clod′dy,** *adj.*

clod·hop·per (klod′hop′ər), *n.* 1. a clumsy boor. 2. a large, heavy shoe.

clog (klog), *v.,* **clogged, clog·ging,** *n.* —*v.* 1. fill up; choke up. 2. become filled or choked up. 3. hinder; interfere; hold back. 4. dance by beating a heavy rhythm on the floor. —*n.* 1. thing that hinders or interferes. 2. a heavy shoe with a wooden sole. 3. a lighter shoe with a wooden sole, used in dancing. 4. dance in which wooden-soled shoes are worn. [ME *clogge* block]

clois·ter (klois′tər), *n.* 1. a covered walk along the wall of a building, with a row of pillars on the open side. 2. place of religious retirement; convent or monastery. 3. a quiet place shut away from the world. —*v.* shut away in a quiet place. [< OF < L *claustrum* closed place, lock < *claudere* close] —**clois·tral** (klois′trəl), *adj.*

clomb (klōm), *v. Archaic,* pt. and pp. of climb.

close¹ (klōz), *v.,* **closed, clos·ing,** *n.* —*v.* 1. shut. 2. stop up; fill; block: *close a gap.* 3. bring or come together: *close the ranks of troops.* 4. grapple. 5. surround; enclose. 6. come to terms; agree. 7. end; finish: *close a debate.* 8. close down, *Am.* shut completely. 9. close in, come near and shut in on all sides. 10. close out, *Am.* sell to get rid of. 11. close up, a. shut completely. b. bring or come nearer together. c. heal. d. *Am.* finish off; wind up. —*n.* end; finish. [< OF *clore* < L *claudere* close] —**Syn.** *v.* 7. conclude.

close² (klōs), *adj.,* **clos·er, clos·est,** *adv.* —*adj.* 1. with very little in between; near together; near. 2. fitting tightly; tight; narrow: *close quarters.* 3. having its parts near together; compact. 4. intimate; dear. 5. careful; exact: *a close translation.* 6. thorough; strict: *close attention.* 7. having little fresh air: *a close room.* 8. hard to breathe. 9. not fond of talking; keeping quiet about oneself. 10. secret; hidden. 11. strictly guarded; confined. 12. restricted; limited. 13. stingy. 14. hard to get; scarce. 15. nearly equal; almost even. 16. closed; shut; not open. 17. pronounced with the mouth or lips partly shut. —*adv.* in a close manner. [< OF *clos* < L *clausum* closed place < *claudere* close] —**close′ly,** *adv.* —**close′ness,** *n.* —**Syn.** *adj.* 3. dense.

close call (klōs), *Am., Colloq.* narrow escape.

closed-cir·cuit (klōzd′sėr′kit′), *adj.* denoting television broadcasting that is limited to a certain audience, as in a group of classrooms, etc.

closed shop, *Am.* factory or business that employs only members of labor unions.

close-fist·ed (klōs′fis′tid), *adj.* stingy. —**close′-fist′ed·ly,** *adv.* —**close′-fist′ed·ness,** *n.*

close-hauled (klōs′hôld′), *adj.* having sails set for sailing as nearly as possible in the direction from which the wind is blowing.

close-mouthed (klōs′mouthd′; -moutht′), *adj.* not fond of talking; reticent.

clos·et (kloz′it), *n.* 1. a small room used for storing clothes or household supplies. 2. a small, private room for prayer, study, or interviews. 3. a water closet; toilet. —*adj.* 1. private; secluded. 2. unpractical. —*v.* shut up in a private room for a secret talk. [< OF, dim. of *clos* < L *clausum* closed place < *claudere* to close]

close-up (klōs′up′), *n. Am.* 1. picture taken at close range. 2. a close view.

clo·sure (klō′zhər), *n.* 1. a closing. 2. a closed condition. 3. thing that closes. 4. end; finish; conclusion. 5. Also, *U.S.* cloture. way of ending a debate and getting an immediate vote on the question being discussed. [< OF < LL *clausura* < L *claudere* close]

clot (klot), *n., v.,* **clot·ted, clot·ting.** —*n.* a half-solid lump; thickened mass, as of coagulated blood. —*v.* form into clots. [OE *clott*]

cloth (klôth; kloth), *n., pl.* **cloths** (klôthz; kloths; klôths; kloths), *adj.* —*n.* 1. material made from wool, cotton, silk, linen, hair, etc., by weaving, knitting, or rolling and pressing. 2. piece of this material for some purpose, as a tablecloth. 3. the cloth, clergymen; the clergy. —*adj.* made of cloth. [OE *clāth*]

clothe (klōth), *v.,* **clothed** or **clad, cloth·ing.** 1. put clothes on; cover with clothes; dress. 2. provide with clothes. 3. cover. 4. provide; furnish; equip: *clothed with authority.* [OE *clāthian* < *clāth* cloth] —**Syn.** 1. attire, array, invest, robe, vest, garb. —**Ant.** 1. undress.

clothes (klōz; klōthz), *n.pl.* 1. covering for a person's body. 2. coverings for a bed. —**Syn.** 1. apparel, clothing, attire, garb.

clothes·horse (klōz′hôrs′; klōthz′-), *n.* frame to hang clothes on to dry or air them.

clothes·line (klōz′līn′; klōthz′-), *n.* rope or wire to hang clothes on to dry or air them.

clothes·pin (klōz′pin′; klōthz′-), *n. Am.* a wooden clip to hold clothes on a clothesline.

clothes tree, an upright pole with branches on which to hang coats and hats.

cloth·ier (klōth′yər; -i·ər), *n.* 1. seller or maker of clothing. 2. seller of cloth.

cloth·ing (klōth′ing), *n.* 1. clothes. 2. covering.

Clo·tho (klō′thō), *n. Gk. Myth.* one of the three Fates. Clotho spins the thread of life.

clo·ture (klō′chər), *n. U.S.* closure (def. 5). [< F < VL *clausitura.* See CLOSURE.]

cloud (kloud), *n.* 1. a white, gray, or almost black mass in the sky, made up of tiny drops of water. 2. mass of smoke or dust. 3. a great number of things moving close together: *a cloud of arrows.* 4. streak; spot. 5. anything that darkens or dims; cause of gloom, trouble, suspicion, or disgrace. 6. in the clouds, a. far above the earth. b. fanciful; theoretical. c. daydreaming; absent-minded. 7. under a cloud, a. under suspicion; in disgrace. b. in gloom or trouble. —*v.* 1. cover with a cloud or clouds. 2. grow cloudy. 3. streak; spot: *clouded marble.* 4. make or become gloomy, troubled, suspected, or disgraced. [OE *clūd* rock, hill] —**cloud′less,** *adj.*

cloud·burst (kloud′bėrst′), *n. Am.* a sudden, violent rainfall.

cloud chamber, a large vessel filled with a vapor, esp. a vapor of hydrogen and methyl alcohol, through which subatomic particles may be caused to move and thus permit themselves to be isolated and identified.

cloud seeding, the scattering of particles of carbon dioxide or certain other chemicals in clouds to produce rain.

cloud·y (kloud′i), *adj.,* **cloud·i·er, cloud·i·est.** 1. covered with clouds; having clouds in it. 2. of or like clouds. 3. not clear: *a cloudy liquid.* 4. streaked; spotted: *cloudy marble.* 5. confused; indistinct: *a cloudy notion.* 6. gloomy; frowning. —**cloud′i·ly,** *adv.* —**cloud′i·ness,** *n.*

clout (klout), *n. Colloq.* or *Dial.* —*n.* a blow, esp. with the hand. —*v.* strike, esp. with the hand; cuff. [OE *clūt* small piece of cloth or metal]

clove¹ (klōv), *n.* 1. a strong, fragrant spice obtained from the dried flower buds of a tropical tree. 2. the dried flower bud. 3. the tree. [ME *cloue* < OF *clou* < L *clavus* nail]

clove² (klōv), *n.* a small, separate section of a bulb: *a clove of garlic.* [OE *clufu*]

clove³ (klōv), *v.* pt. of cleave¹.

clo·ven (klō′vən), *v.* pp. of cleave¹. —*adj.* split; divided.

clo·ven-foot·ed (klō′vən·fut′id), *adj.* 1. having cloven feet. 2. devilish.

clo·ven-hoofed (klō′vən·hutf′; -hüft′), *adj.* 1. having cloven hoofs. 2. devilish.

clo·ver (klō′vər), *n.* a low plant with leaves in three small parts and rounded heads of small red, white, or purple flowers, grown as food for horses and cattle. [OE *clǣfre*]

clown (kloun), *n.* 1. man whose business is to amuse others by tricks and jokes. 2. a bad-mannered, awkward person. —*v.* act like a clown; play tricks and jokes; act silly. —**clown′ish**, *adj.* —**clown′ish·ly**, *adv.* —**clown′ish·ness**, *n.*

clown·er·y (kloun′ər·i), *n., pl.* **-er·ies.** tricks and jokes of a clown; clownish act.

cloy (kloi), *v.* 1. weary by too much, too sweet, or too rich food. 2. weary by too much of anything pleasant. [< MF *encloyer* < *clou* < L *clavus* nail] —**cloy′ing·ly**, *adv.* —**cloy′ing·ness**, *n.*

club (klub), *n., v.,* **clubbed, club·bing.** —*n.* 1. a heavy stick of wood, thicker at one end, used as a weapon. 2. stick or bat used to hit a ball in games. 3. group of people joined together for some special purpose: *a tennis club.* 4. a building or rooms used by a club. 5. a playing card with one or more black designs on it shaped like this: ♣. 6. **clubs,** the suit of cards marked with this design. —*v.* 1. beat or hit with a club. 2. join; unite; combine. [< Scand. *klubba*] —Syn. *n.* 1. cudgel. 3. association, society.

club·foot (klub′fût′), *n., pl.* **-feet.** 1. a deformed foot. 2. deformity of the foot caused by faulty development before birth. —**club′foot′ed**, *adj.*

club·house (klub′hous′), *n.* a building used by a club.

cluck (kluk), *n.* sound made by a hen calling her chickens. —*v.* make such a sound. [imit.]

clue (klū), *n.* guide to the solving of a mystery or problem. Also, *clew.* [var. of *clew;* OE *cliwen*]

clump (klump), *n.* 1. cluster: *a clump of trees.* 2. lump: *a clump of earth.* 3. sound of heavy, clumsy walking. —*v.* walk heavily and clumsily. [var. of OE *clympre* lump of metal] —**clump′y, clump′ish**, *adj.*

clum·sy (klum′zi), *adj.,* **-si·er, -si·est.** 1. not graceful or skillful; awkward. 2. not well-shaped or well-made. [< *clumse* be numb with cold, prob. < Scand.] —**clum′si·ly**, *adv.* —**clum′si·ness**, *n.* —Syn. 1. ungraceful, ungainly.

clung (klung), *v.* pt. and pp. of **cling.**

clus·ter (klus′tər), *n.* number of things of the same kind growing or grouped together. —*v.* form into a cluster; gather in clusters; group together closely. [OE] —**clus′ter·y**, *adj.*

clutch[1] (kluch), *n.* 1. a tight grasp. 2. a grasping claw, paw, hand, etc. 3. Usually, **clutches.** control; power. 4. device in a machine for connecting or disconnecting the engine or motor that makes it go. 5. lever or pedal that operates this device. —*v.* 1. grasp tightly. 2. seize eagerly; snatch. [var. of OE *clyccan* bend, clench]

clutch[2] (kluch), *n.* 1. nest of eggs. 2. brood of chickens. [var. of *cletch* < *cleck* hatch < Scand. *klekja*]

clut·ter (klut′ər), *n.* 1. a litter; confusion; disorder. 2. a loud clatter. —*v.* 1. litter with things. 2. clatter loudly. [< CLOT]

Cly·tem·nes·tra (klī′təm·nes′trə), *n. Gk. Legend.* wife of Agamemnon. She killed her husband and was killed by her son, Orestes.

Cm, *Chem.* curium.

cm., cm, centimeter; centimeters.

Cnos·sus (nos′əs), *n.* Knossos.

co-, *prefix.* 1. with; together: *coöperate = act with or together.* 2. joint; fellow: *coauthor = joint or fellow author.* 3. equally: *coextensive = equally extensive.* [< L, var. of *com-*]

Co, *Chem.* cobalt.

Co., co., 1. Company. 2. County.

C.O., 1. Commanding Officer. 2. *Colloq.* conscientious objector.

c.o., c/o, 1. in care of. 2. carried over.

coach (kōch), *n.* 1. a large, closed carriage with seats inside and often on top. 2. *Am.* a passenger car of a railroad train. 3. a closed automobile like a sedan. 4. *Am.* bus. 5. person who teaches or trains athletic teams, etc. 6. a private teacher who helps a student prepare for a special test. —*v.* 1. teach; train. 2. help to prepare for a

special test. [< Hung. *kocsi*] ▶ **Coach** as a verb is used either with persons (teams) or with the name of the sport as object: *he coaches baseball; he coached a winning team that fall.*

coach-and-four (kōch′ən·fôr′; -fōr′), *n.* coach pulled by four horses.

coach dog, Dalmatian.

coach·man (kōch′mən), *n., pl.* **-men.** man whose work is driving a coach or carriage.

co·ad·ju·tor (kō·aj′ə·tər; kō′ə·jü′tər), *n.* 1. assistant; helper. 2. bishop appointed to assist a bishop.

co·ag·u·late (kō·ag′yə·lāt), *v.,* **-lat·ed, -lat·ing.** change from a liquid into a thickened mass; thicken. [< L, < *coagulum* means of curdling < *co-* together + *agere* drive] —**co·ag′u·la′tion**, *n.* —**co·ag′u·la′tive**, *adj.* —**co·ag′u·la′tor**, *n.*

coal (kōl), *n.* 1. a black mineral that burns and gives off heat, composed mostly of carbon. It is formed from partly decayed vegetable matter under great pressure in the earth. 2. piece of this mineral. 3. piece of wood, coal, etc., burning, partly burned, or all burned. 4. charcoal. —*v.* 1. supply with coal. 2. take in a supply of coal. [OE *col* (def. 3)]

co·a·lesce (kō′ə·les′), *v.,* **-lesced, -lesc·ing.** 1. grow together. 2. unite into one body, mass, party, etc.; combine. [< L, < *co-* together + *alescere* grow] —**co′a·les′cence**, *n.* —**co′a·les′cent**, *adj.*

coal gas, 1. gas made from coal, used for heating and lighting. 2. gas given off by burning coal.

co·a·li·tion (kō′ə·lish′ən), *n.* 1. union; combination. 2. a temporary alliance of statesmen, political parties, etc., for some special purpose. [< Med.L *coalitio* < L *coalescere.* See COALESCE.]

coal oil, *Am.* 1. kerosene. 2. petroleum.

coal tar, a black, sticky residue left after soft coal has been distilled to make coal gas. Coal tar is distilled to make aniline dyes, flavorings, perfumes, benzene, etc.

coam·ing (kōm′ing), *n.* a raised edge around a hatch in the deck of a ship, a skylight, etc., to prevent water from running down below.

coarse (kôrs; kōrs), *adj.,* **coars·er, coars·est.** 1. made up of fairly large parts; not fine: *coarse sand.* 2. rough: *coarse cloth.* 3. common; poor; inferior: *coarse food.* 4. not delicate or refined; crude; vulgar: *coarse manners.* [adjectival use of *course, n.,* meaning "ordinary"] —**coarse′ly**, *adv.* —**coarse′ness**, *n.* —Syn. 4. gross, low.

coarse-grained (kôrs′grānd′; kōrs′-), *adj.* 1. having a coarse texture. 2. crude.

coars·en (kôr′sən; kōr′-), *v.* make or become coarse.

coast (kōst), *n.* 1. land along the sea; seashore. 2. region near a coast. 3. the Coast, *U.S.* the region along the Pacific. 4. *Am.* ride or slide down a hill without using power. —*v.* 1. go along or near the coast of. 2. sail along a coast. 3. sail from port to port of a coast. 4. *Am.* ride or slide down a hill without using power. [< OF < L *costa* side] —**coast′al**, *adj.* —Syn. *n.* 1. seaboard, shore, strand.

coast·er (kōs′tər), *n.* 1. person or thing that coasts. 2. ship trading along a coast. 3. *Am.* sled to coast on. 4. a little tray to hold a glass or bottle.

coaster brake, *Am.* brake on the rear wheel of a bicycle, worked by pushing back on the pedals.

coast guard, 1. group of men whose work is saving lives and preventing smuggling along the coast of a country. 2. member of this group.

coast·land (kōst′land′), *n.* land along a coast.

coast·line (kōst′līn′), *n.* outline of a coast.

coast·ward (kōst′wərd), *adv., adj.* toward the coast.

coast·ways (kōst′wāz′), *adv.* coastwise.

coast·wise (kōst′wīz′), *adv., adj.* along the coast.

coat (kōt), *n.* 1. an outer garment with sleeves. 2. an outer covering: *a dog's coat of hair.* 3. layer covering a surface: *a coat of paint.* —*v.*

1. provide with a coat. 2. cover with a layer. [< OF *cote* < Gmc.] —coat′less, *adj.*

co·a·ti (kō·ä′ti), *n.*, *pl.* –tis. a small animal somewhat like a raccoon, living in Central and South America. [< Brazilian (Tupi)]

coat·ing (kōt′ing), *n.* 1. layer covering a surface. 2. cloth for making coats.

coat of arms, shield, or drawing of a shield, with pictures and designs on it. Each family of noble rank has its own special coat of arms.

coat of mail, *pl.* coats of mail. garment made of metal rings or plates, worn as armor.

co·au·thor (kō·ô′thər), *n.* a joint author.

coax (kōks), *v.* 1. persuade by soft words; influence by pleasant ways. 2. get by coaxing. [< obs. *cokes* a fool] —coax′er, *n.* —coax′ing·ly, *adv.* —Syn. 1. wheedle, cajole, beguile, inveigle.

co·ax·i·al (kō·ak′si·əl), co·ax·al (–ak′səl), *adj.* having a common axis.

coaxial cable, an insulated connecting cable containing conducting materials surrounding a central conductor, used for transmitting telegraph, telephone, and television impulses.

cob (kob), *n.* 1. *Am.* the center part of an ear of corn, on which the kernels grow. 2. a strong horse with short legs. [ME]

co·balt (kō′bôlt), *n.* 1. *Chem.* a silver-white metallic element, Co, with a pinkish tint, used in making steel, paints, etc. 2. dark-blue coloring matter made from cobalt. 3. dark blue. —*adj.* dark-blue. [< G *kobalt*, var. of *kobold* goblin] —co·bal′tic, *adj.* —co·bal′tous, *adj.*

cobalt bomb, 1. a hydrogen bomb encased in a shell of cobalt instead of steel. It is potentially, because of the wide dispersal of radioactive cobalt dust, the most dangerous atomic weapon thus far conceived. 2. cobalt-60 bomb, radioactive cobalt (cobalt 60) enclosed in a lead case, used in the treatment of cancer.

cob·ble¹ (kob′əl), *v.*, –bled, –bling. 1. mend (shoes, etc.). 2. put together clumsily.

cob·ble² (kob′əl), *n.* cobblestone.

cob·bler (kob′lər), *n.* 1. man whose work is mending shoes. 2. *Am.* a fruit pie baked in a deep dish.

cob·ble·stone (kob′əl·stōn′), *n.* a rounded stone that was formerly much used in paving.

co·bel·lig·er·ent (kō′bə·lij′ər·ənt), *n.* nation that helps another nation carry on a war.

co·bra (kō′brə), *n.* a very poisonous snake of southern Asia and Africa. [short for Pg. *cobra de capello* snake with a hood]

cob·web (kob′web′), *n.* 1. a spider's web or the stuff it is made of. 2. anything thin and slight or entangling like a spider's web. [OE (*ātor*)*coppe* spider + *web*] —cob′web′by, *adj.*

co·ca (kō′kə), *n.* 1. a small tropical shrub growing in South America whose dried leaves are used to make cocaine and other alkaloids. 2. its dried leaves. [< Peruvian *cuca*]

co·caine, co·cain (kō·kān′; kō′kān), *n.* drug used to deaden pain and as a stimulant.

coc·cus (kok′əs), *n.*, *pl.* coc·ci (kok′sī). bacterium shaped like a sphere. [< NL < Gk. *kokkos* seed]

coc·cyx (kok′siks), *n.*, *pl.* coc·cy·ges (kok·sī′jēz). a small triangular bone at the lower end of the spinal column. [< L < Gk. *kokkyx*, orig., cuckoo; because shaped like cuckoo's bill]

coch·i·neal (koch′ə·nēl′; koch′ə·nēl), *n.* a bright-red dye made from the dried bodies of the females of a scale insect that lives on cactus plants of tropical America. [< F < Sp. *cochinilla*, ult. < L *coccinus* scarlet < Gk.]

coch·le·a (kok′li·ə), *n.*, *pl.* –le·ae (–li·ē). a spiral-shaped cavity of the inner ear, containing the sensory ends of the auditory nerve. [< L < Gk. *kochlias* snail] —coch′le·ar, *adj.*

cock¹ (kok), *n.* 1. a male chicken; rooster. 2. the male of other birds. 3. faucet used to turn the flow of a liquid or gas on or off. 4. hammer of a gun. 5. position of the hammer of a gun when it is pulled back, ready to fire. 6. weathercock. —*v.* pull back the hammer of (a gun), ready to fire. [OE *cocc*]

cock² (kok), *v.* turn up jauntily; stick up defiantly. —*n.* an upward turn, as of the brim of a hat. [appar. < *cock*¹]

cock³ (kok), *n.* a small, cone-shaped pile of hay in a field. —*v.* pile in cocks. [ME]

cock·ade (kok·ād′), *n.* knot of ribbon or a rosette worn on the hat as a badge. [alter. of *cockard* < F, < *coq* cock] —cock·ad′ed, *adj.*

cock·a·too (kok′ə·tü′; kok′ə·tü), *n.*, *pl.* –toos. a large, brightly colored parrot of Australia, East Indies, etc. [< Du. < Malay *kakatua*]

cock·a·trice (kok′ə·tris), *n.* a fabled serpent whose look was supposed to cause death. [< OF *cocatris* < L *calcare* tread]

cock·boat (kok′bōt′), *n.* a small rowboat.

cock·chaf·er (kok′chāf′ər), *n.* a large European beetle that destroys plants.

cock·crow (kok′krō′), *n.* dawn.

cocked hat, 1. hat with the brim turned up. 2. hat pointed in front and in back.

cock·er·el (kok′ər·əl; kok′rəl), *n.* a young rooster, not more than one year old.

cock·er spaniel (kok′ər), or cocker, *n.* any of a breed of small dogs with long, silky hair and drooping ears.

cock·eyed (kok′īd′), *adj.* 1. cross-eyed. 2. *Slang.* tilted or twisted to one side. 3. *Slang.* foolish; silly.

Cocker spaniel (11 in. tall)

cock·fight (kok′fīt′), *n.* fight between roosters or gamecocks armed with steel spurs. —cock′fight′ing, *n.*

cock·horse (kok′hôrs′), *n.* a child's hobbyhorse.

cock·le (kok′əl), *n.*, *v.*, –led, –ling. —*n.* 1. a salt-water mollusk with two ridged shells that are somewhat heart-shaped. 2. cockleshell. 3. bulge on the surface. 4. cockles of one's heart, the inmost part of one's heart or feelings. —*v.* wrinkle; pucker. [< F *coquille*, blend of F *coque* shell and L *conchylium* < Gk. *konchylion*, dim. of *konche* conch]

cock·le·bur (kok′əl·bėr′), *n. Am.* any of several weeds with spiny burs.

cock·le·shell (kok′əl·shel′), *n.* 1. shell of the cockle. 2. a small, light, shallow boat.

cock·ney (kok′ni), *n.*, *pl.* –neys, *adj.* —*n.* 1. native or inhabitant of the poorer section of London who speaks a particular dialect of English. 2. this dialect. —*adj.* 1. of or like this dialect. 2. of or like cockneys. [ME *cokeney*]

cock·pit (kok′pit′), *n.* 1. a small, open place in an airplane, boat, etc., where the pilot or passengers sit. 2. an enclosed place for cockfights.

cock·roach (kok′rōch′), *n.* any of a family of insects, esp. a small brownish or yellowish species found in kitchens, around water pipes, etc. [alter. of Sp. *cucaracha*]

cocks·comb (koks′kōm′), *n.* 1. the fleshy, red part on the head of a rooster. 2. coxcomb. 3. plant with crested or feathery clusters of red or yellow flowers.

cock·sure (kok′shůr′), *adj.* 1. perfectly sure; absolutely certain. 2. too sure. —*adv.* in a cocksure manner. —cock′sure′ness, *n.*

Cockscomb

cock·swain (kok′sən; –swān′), *n.* coxswain.

cock·tail (kok′tāl′), *n.* 1. *Am.* an iced drink, often composed of gin or whiskey, mixed with bitters, vermouth, fruit juices, etc. 2. appetizer: *a tomato-juice cocktail.* 3. shellfish served in a small glass with a highly seasoned sauce. 4. mixed fruits served in a glass.

cock·y (kok′i), *adj.*, cock·i·er, cock·i·est, *Colloq.* conceited; swaggering. —cock′i·ly, *adv.* —cock′i·ness, *n.*

co·co (kō′kō), *n.*, *pl.* co·cos. 1. a tall palm tree on which coconuts grow. 2. its fruit or seed. Also, cocoa. [< Pg. *coco* grinning face]

co·coa¹ (kō′kō), *n.* 1. powder made by roasting and grinding cacao seeds. 2. drink made of this powder with milk or water and sugar. 3. dull brown. —*adj.* of or having to do with cocoa. [var. of *cacao*]

co·coa² (kō'kō), *n.* coco.

co·co·nut, co·coa·nut (kō'kə·nut'; -nət), *n.* a large, round, brown, hard-shelled fruit of the coco palm. Coconuts have a white, edible lining and a white liquid called coconut milk.

co·coon (kə·kün'), *n.* a silky case spun by the larva of an insect to live in while it is a pupa. [< F cocon < coque shell]

cod (kod), *n., pl.* cods or (*esp. collectively*) cod. an important food fish found in the cold parts of the N Atlantic. [ME]

Cod (kod), *n.* Cape, a hook-shaped peninsula in SE Massachusetts.

C.O.D., c.o.d., *Am.* cash on delivery; collect on delivery.

cod·dle (kod'əl), *v.,* -died, -dling. 1. treat tenderly; pamper. 2. cook in hot water without boiling: *a coddled egg.* [var. of *caudle*, n., gruel < OF < L *calidus* hot] —Syn. 1. humor, indulge.

code (kōd), *n., v.,* cod·ed, cod·ing. —*n.* 1. a collection of the laws of a country arranged in a clear way so that they can be understood and used. 2. any set of rules. 3. system of signals for sending messages by telegraph flags, etc. 4. arrangement of words, figures, etc., to keep a message short or secret. —*v.* 1. change or translate into a code. 2. arrange in a code. [< F < L *codex* CODEX]

co·deine (kō'dēn; -di·ēn), **co·de·in** (kō'di·in), *n.* a white, crystalline drug obtained from opium, used to relieve pain and cause sleep. [< Gk. *kodeia* poppy head]

co·dex (kō'deks), *n., pl.* co·di·ces (kō'də·sēz; kod'ə-). volume of manuscripts, esp. of the Scriptures. [< L, var. of *caudex* tree trunk, book]

cod·fish (kod'fish'), *n., pl.* -fish·es or (*esp. collectively*) -fish. cod.

codg·er (koj'ər), *n. Colloq.* a queer or odd person.

cod·i·cil (kod'ə·səl), *n.* 1. something added to a will to change it, add to it, or explain it. 2. anything added to change or explain something. [< L *codicillus*, dim. of *codex* CODEX]

cod·i·fy (kod'ə·fī; kō'də-), *v.,* -fied, -fy·ing. arrange (laws, etc.) according to a system. —cod'i·fi·ca'tion, *n.* —cod'i·fi'er, *n.*

cod·ling (kod'ling), **cod·lin** (-lin), *n.* an unripe apple.

codling moth, codlin moth, a small moth whose larvae destroy apples, pears, etc.

cod-liv·er oil (kod'liv'ər), oil extracted from the liver of cod, used as a medicine. It is rich in vitamins A and D.

Co·dy (kō'di), *n.* William F. (*"Buffalo Bill"*), 1846-1917, American frontier scout and showman.

co·ed, co·ed (kō'ed'), *n. Am., Colloq.* a girl or woman student at a coeducational college or school.

co·ed·u·ca·tion (kō'ej·ù·kā'shən), *n. Am.* education of boys and girls or men and women together in the same school or classes. —co'ed·u·ca'tion·al, *adj.* —co'ed·u·ca'tion·al·ly, *adv.*

co·ef·fi·cient (kō'ə·fish'ənt), *n.* 1. *Math.* a number or symbol put before and multiplying another. In 3*x*, 3 is the coefficient of *x.* 2. *Physics.* a ratio used as a multiplier to calculate the behavior of a substance under different conditions of heat, light, etc.

coe·la·canth (sē'lə·kanth), *n.* any of a group of fishes having rounded scales and lobed fins, formerly considered extinct. A coelacanth is similar to the primitive sea vertebrates which gave rise to all land vertebrates. [< NL, < Gk. *koilos* hollow + *akantha* thorn, spine]

coe·len·ter·ate (si·len'tər·āt; -it), *Zool.* —*n.* one of a group of salt-water animals with saclike bodies. —*adj.* belonging to this group. Hydras, jellyfish, corals, etc., are coelenterates. [< NL < Gk. *koilos* hollow + *enteron* intestine]

coe·li·ac (sē'li·ak), *adj. Anat.* of or in the abdominal cavity. Also, celiac.

co·e·qual (kō·ē'kwəl), *adj.* equal in rank, degree, etc. —*n.* one that is coequal. —co·e·qual·i·ty (kō'i·kwol'ə·ti), *n.* —co·e'qual·ly, *adv.*

co·erce (kō·ėrs'), *v.,* co·erced, co·erc·ing. 1.

compel; force. 2. control or restrain by force. [< L *coercere* < *co-* together + *arcere* restrain] —co·erc'er, *n.* —co·er'ci·ble, *adj.* —co·er'cive, *adj.* —co·er'cive·ly, *adv.* —co·er'cive·ness, *n.*

co·er·cion (kō·ėr'shən), *n.* 1. use of force; compulsion; constraint. 2. government by force. —co·er'cion·ist, *n.*

co·e·val (kō·ē'vəl), *adj.* 1. of the same age, date, or duration. 2. contemporary. —*n.* a contemporary. [< LL, < *co-* equal + *aevum* age]

co·ex·ec·u·tor (kō'ig·zek'yə·tər), *n.* person who is an executor of a will along with another.

co·ex·ist (kō'ig·zist'), *v.* exist together or at the same time. —co'ex·ist'ence, *n.* —co'ex·ist'ent, *adj.*

co·ex·tend (kō'iks·tend'), *v.* extend equally or to the same limits. —co·ex·ten·sion (kō'iks·ten'shən), *n.* —co'ex·ten'sive, *adj.*

cof·fee (kôf'i), *n.* 1. a dark-brown drink, first used in Europe about 1600. 2. the seeds from which the drink is made. 3. a tall, tropical shrub on which the seeds grow. 4. a social gathering, often in the morning, at which coffee is served. 5. the color of coffee. [< Turk. *qahveh* < Ar. *qahwa*]

coffee break, *Am.* a period during which employees may take time off to have coffee, rest, etc.

cof·fer (kôf'ər; kof'-), *n.* 1. box, chest, or trunk, esp. one used to hold money or other valuable things. 2. coffers, treasury; funds. [< OF < L *cophinus* basket. See COFFIN.]

cof·fin (kôf'in; kof'-), *n.* box into which a dead person is put to be buried. —*v.* put into a coffin. [< OF < L < Gk. *kophinos* basket]

cog (kog), *n.* 1. one of a series of teeth on the edge of a wheel that transfers motion by locking into the teeth of another wheel of the same kind. 2. wheel with such a row of teeth on it. [< Scand. (Sw.) *kugge*] —cogged (kogd), *adj.*

co·gent (kō'jənt), *adj.* forcible; convincing: *cogent arguments.* [< L *cogens*, ult. < *co-* together + *agere* drive] —co'gen·cy, *n.* —co'gent·ly, *adv.* —Syn. potent, compelling.

cog·i·tate (koj'ə·tāt), *v.,* -tat·ed, -tat·ing. think over; consider with care; meditate; ponder. [< L, < *co-* (intensive) + *agitare* consider < *agere* discuss] —cog'i·ta'tion, *n.* —cog'i·ta'tive, *adj.* —cog'i·ta'tive·ly, *adv.* —cog'i·ta'tor, *n.*

co·gnac (kōn'yak; kon'-), *n.* kind of French brandy. [< F]

cog·nate (kog'nāt), *adj.* related by family, origin, nature, or quality: *English, Dutch, and German are cognate languages.* —*n.* person, word, or thing so related to another. German *Wasser* and English *water* are cognates. [< L, < *co-* together + *gnatus* born]

cog·ni·tion (kog·nish'ən), *n.* 1. act of knowing; perception; awareness. 2. thing known, perceived, or recognized. [< L *cognitio*, < *co-* (intensive) + *gnoscere* know] —cog·ni'tion·al, *adj.*

cog·ni·zance (kog'nə·zəns; kon'ə-), *n.* 1. knowledge; perception; awareness. 2. *Law.* a. an official notice. b. right or power to deal with judicially. [< OF *conoissance* < *conoistre* know < L *cognoscere.* See COGNITION.]

cog·ni·zant (kog'nə·zənt; kon'ə-), *adj.* aware.

cog·no·men (kog·nō'mən), *n.* 1. surname; family name; last name. 2. any name. 3. nickname. [< L, < *co-* with + *nomen* name; form infl. by *cognoscere* recognize] —cog·nom·i·nal (kog·nom'ə·nəl; -nō'mə-), *adj.*

cog·wheel (kog'hwēl'), *n.* wheel with teeth projecting from the rim for transmitting or receiving motion.

Cogwheels

co·hab·it (kō·hab'it), *v.* 1. live together as husband and wife and 2. live together. —co·hab'i·tant (kō·hab'ə·tənt), *n.* —co·hab'i·ta'tion, *n.*

co·here (kō·hir'), *v.,* -hered, -her·ing. 1. stick together; hold together. 2. be connected logically; be consistent. [< L, < *co-* together + *haerere* cleave] —Syn. 1. cleave, adhere.

co·her·ence (kō·hir'əns), **co·her·en·cy**

(–ən·si), *n.* **1.** logical connection; consistency. **2.** a sticking together; cohesion. **—Syn. 1.** congruity.

co·her·ent (kō·hir′ənt), *adj.* **1.** sticking together; holding together. **2.** logically connected; consistent. **—co·her′ent·ly,** *adv.*

co·he·sion (kō·hē′zhən), *n.* **1.** a sticking together; tendency to hold together. **2.** *Physics.* attraction between molecules of the same kind. **—co·he′sive,** *adj.* **—co·he′sive·ly,** *adv.* **—co·he′sive·ness,** *n.*

co·hort (kō′hôrt), *n.* **1.** one of the ten infantry divisions of an ancient Roman legion. **2.** group of soldiers. **3.** any group or company. [< L *cohors* court, enclosure. Doublet of COURT.]

coif (koif), *n.* cap or hood that fits closely around the head. *—v.* cover with a coif or something like a coif. [< OF < LL *cofia* < Gmc.]

coif·fure (kwä·fyŭr′), *n.* **1.** style of arranging the hair. **2.** headdress. [< F < *coiffer* COIF, v.]

coign of vantage (koin), good location for watching or doing something.

coil (koil), *v.* **1.** wind around and around in circular or spiral shape. **2.** move in a winding course. *—n.* **1.** anything wound around and around in this way. **2.** one wind or turn of a coil. **3.** series of connected pipes arranged in a coil or row, as in a radiator. **4.** a spiral of wire for conducting electricity. **5.** twist of hair. [< OF < L *colligere* COLLECT] **—coil′er,** *n.*

coin (koin), *n.* **1.** piece of metal stamped by the government for use as money. **2.** metal money. *—v.* **1.** make (money) by stamping metal. **2.** make (metal) into money. **3.** make up; invent: *the word "blurb" was coined by Gelett Burgess.* **4.** coin money, *Colloq.* become rich. [< F, corner, < L *cuneus* wedge] **—coin′er,** *n.*

Coil (def. 1)

coin·age (koin′ij), *n.* **1.** the making of coins. **2.** coins; metal money. **3.** system of coins. **4.** right of coining money. **5.** act or process of making up; inventing. **6.** word, phrase, etc., invented.

co·in·cide (kō′in·sīd′), *v.,* **-cid·ed, -cid·ing. 1.** occupy the same place in space. **2.** occupy the same time. **3.** correspond exactly; agree. [< Med.L *coincidere* < L *co-* together + *in* upon + *cadere* fall] **—Syn.** concur, harmonize, tally.

co·in·ci·dence (kō·in′sə·dəns), *n.* **1.** exact correspondence; agreement, esp. the chance occurrence of two things at such a time as to seem remarkable, fitting, etc. **2.** a coinciding; act or fact of occupying the same time or place.

co·in·ci·dent (kō·in′sə·dənt), *adj.* **1.** happening at the same time. **2.** occupying the same place or position. **—co·in′ci·dent·ly,** *adv.*

co·in·ci·den·tal (kō·in′sə·den′təl), *adj.* **1.** coincident. **2.** showing coincidence. **—co·in′ci·den′tal·ly,** *adv.*

co·i·tion (kō·ish′ən), **co·i·tus** (kō′ə·təs), *n.* sexual intercourse. [< L *co-* together + *ire* go]

coke¹ (kōk), *n., v.,* **coked, cok·ing.** *—n.* fuel made from coal by heating it in a closed oven until the gases have been removed. Coke burns with much heat and little smoke, and is used in furnaces, for melting metal, etc. *—v.* change into coke. [? var. of *colk* core]

Coke² (kōk), *n.* *Trademark.* a dark-colored, carbonated soft drink. [short for *Coca-Cola,* a trademark]

Col., 1. Colonel. **2.** Colorado (officially, Colo.).

col., column.

co·la (kō′lə), *n.* kola.

col·an·der (kul′ən·dər; kol′-), *n.* vessel or dish full of small holes for draining off liquids. [alter. of VL *colator* < L *colare* strain]

cold (kōld), *adj.* **1.** much less warm than the body. **2.** having a relatively low temperature. **3.** not warm enough for comfort. **4.** dead. **5.** unconscious. **6.** lacking in feeling; unfriendly: *a cold greeting.* **7.** lacking in feeling, passion, or enthusiasm; indifferent: *a cold nature.* **8.** failing to excite interest. **9.** depressing. **10.** faint; weak: *a cold scent.* **11.** blue, green, or gray; not red or yellow. *—n.* **1.** lack of heat or warmth; low temperature. **2.** cold weather. **3.** sensation produced by contact with anything cold. **4.** sickness that causes running at the nose, sore throat, sneez-

ing, etc. **5.** catch cold, become sick with a cold. **6.** in the cold, all alone; neglected. [OE *cald*] **—cold′ish,** *adj.* **—cold′ly,** *adv.* **—cold′ness,** *n.* **—Syn.** *adj.* **1.** chill, chilly, frosty, wintry. **2.** cool.

cold-blood·ed (kōld′blud′id), *adj.* **1.** having blood whose temperature varies with that of the surroundings. **2.** feeling the cold because of poor circulation. **3.** lacking in feeling; cruel. **—cold′-blood′ed·ly,** *adv.* **—cold′-blood′ed·ness,** *n.*

cold cream, a creamy, soothing salve for the skin.

cold-heart·ed (kōld′här′tid), *adj.* lacking in feeling; unsympathetic; unkind. **—cold′-heart′ed·ly,** *adv.* **—cold′-heart′ed·ness,** *n.*

cold rubber, a tough synthetic rubber formed at a low temperature.

cold shoulder, *Colloq.* deliberately unfriendly or indifferent treatment; neglect.

cold-shoul·der (kōld′shōl′dər), *v.* *Colloq.* treat in an unfriendly or indifferent way.

cold sore, blister in or on the mouth, often accompanying a cold or a fever.

cold war, a prolonged contest for national advantage, conducted by diplomatic, economic, and psychological rather than military means.

cold wave, 1. a kind of permanent hair waving using a setting solution that does not need to be heated. **2.** period of very cold weather.

cole (kōl), or **cole·wort** (kōl′wėrt′), *n.* any of various plants belonging to the same family as the cabbage, esp. rape. [< L *caulis* cabbage]

co·le·op·ter·ous (kō′li·op′tər·əs; kol′i-), *adj.* belonging to a group of insects including beetles and weevils. [< Gk., < *koleos* sheath + *pteron* wing]

Cole·ridge (kōl′rij), *n.* Samuel Taylor, 1772–1834, English poet, critic, and philosopher.

cole·slaw (kōl′slô′), *n. Am.* salad made of sliced raw cabbage. [< Du. *kool sla* cabbage salad]

col·ic (kol′ik), *n.* severe pains in the abdomen. *—adj.* of or pertaining to the colon. [< LL < Gk. *kolikos* of the COLON²] **—col·ick·y** (kol′ik·i), *adj.*

col·i·se·um (kol′ə·sē′əm), *n.* a large building or stadium for games, contests, etc. [< Med.L var. of *colosseum*]

co·li·tis (kō·lī′tis; kə-), *n.* inflammation of the colon, often causing severe pain in the abdomen.

coll., 1. collect. **2.** college; collegiate.

col·lab·o·rate (kə·lab′ə·rāt), *v.,* **-rat·ed, -rat·ing. 1.** work together. **2.** aid or coöperate traitorously. [< L, < *com-* with + *laborare* work] **—col·lab′o·ra′tion,** *n.* **—col·lab′o·ra′tive,** *adj.* **—col·lab′o·ra′tor, col·lab′o·ra′tion·ist,** *n.*

col·lage (kə·läzh′), *n.* picture made by securing on a background portions of photographs and newspapers, fabric and string, etc. [< MF, a gluing < OF *colle* glue < VL < Gk. *kolla*]

col·lapse (kə·laps′), *v.,* **-lapsed, -laps·ing,** *n.* *—v.* **1.** fall in; shrink together suddenly. **2.** break down; fail suddenly. **3.** *Am.* fold or push together: *collapse a telescope.* **4.** lose courage, strength, etc., suddenly. *—n.* **1.** a falling in; a sudden shrinking together. **2.** breakdown; failure. [< L *collapsus* < *com-* completely + *labi* fall] **—col·laps′i·ble, col·laps′a·ble,** *adj.*

col·lar (kol′ər), *n.* **1.** a straight or turned-over neckband of a coat, a dress, or a shirt. **2.** a separate band of linen, lace, or other material worn around the neck. **3.** a leather or metal band for a dog's neck. **4.** a leather roll for a horse's neck to bear the weight of the loads he pulls. *—v.* **1.** put a collar on. **2.** seize by the collar; capture. **3.** *Colloq.* seize; take. [< L *collare* < *collum* neck]

col·lar·bone (kol′ər·bōn′), *n.* bone connecting the breastbone and the shoulder blade; clavicle.

col·late (kə·lāt′; kol′āt), *v.,* **-lat·ed, -lat·ing. 1.** compare carefully. **2.** check (pages, sheets, etc.) for correct arrangement. [< L, < *com-* together + *latus,* pp. of *ferre* bring] **—col·la′tor,** *n.*

col·lat·er·al (kə·lat′ər·əl), *adj.* **1.** situated at the side. **2.** parallel; side by side. **3.** related but less important; secondary; indirect. **4.** descended from the same ancestors, but in a different line. **5.** additional. **6.** accompanying. **7.** secured by stocks, bonds, etc. *—n.* **1.** a collateral relative. **2.** *Am.* stocks, bonds, etc., pledged as security for a loan. [< Med.L, < *com-* + L *lateralis* lateral] —**col·lat′er·al·ly,** *adv.*

col·la·tion (kə-lā′shən), *n.* **1.** a light meal. **2.** a collating. **3.** a careful comparison.

col·league (kol′ēg), *n.* an associate; fellow worker. [< F < L *collega* < *com-* together + *legare* send or choose as deputy] —**col′leagueship,** *n.*

col·lect (*v., adj., adv.* kə-lekt′; *n.* kol′ekt), *v.* **1.** bring or come together; gather together. **2.** gather together for a set: *collect stamps for a hobby.* **3.** ask and receive pay for (bills, debts, dues, taxes, etc.). **4.** regain control of (oneself). —*n.* a short prayer used in certain church services. —*adj., adv. Am.* to be paid for at the place of delivery: *telephone collect.* [< L *collectus* < *com-* together + *legere* gather] —**collect′a·ble, col·lect′i·ble,** *adj.*

col·lect·ed (kə-lek′tid), *adj.* **1.** brought together; gathered together. **2.** under control; not confused or disturbed; calm. —**col·lect′ed·ly,** *adv.* —**col·lect′ed·ness,** *n.*

col·lec·tion (kə-lek′shən), *n.* **1.** act or practice of collecting. **2.** group of things gathered from many places and belonging together. **3.** money collected. **4.** mass; heap.

col·lec·tive (kə-lek′tiv), *adj.* **1.** of a group; as a group; taken all together. **2.** singular in form, but plural in meaning. *Crowd, people, troop,* and *herd* are collective nouns. **3.** formed by collecting. **4.** forming a collection. —*n.* **1.** noun whose singular form names a group of objects or persons. **2.** farm, factory, or other organization with collectivistic management. ➤ **collective noun.** When a writer means the group as a whole, the noun takes a singular verb and a singular pronoun; when he means the individuals of the group, the noun takes a plural verb or pronoun: *The first couple on the floor was Tom and Janet. We drove near the place where the old couple were living.*
There is often a temptation to use a collective noun and try to keep it singular when the meaning really calls for a plural construction. Often the writer slips unconsciously from singular to plural in such a passage: *Into the church troops the entire town, seats itself on the uncomfortable wooden benches and there remains for a good two hours, while an aged curé preaches to them* [consistency demands *it*] *of their* [its] *wicked lives and awful sins.* [This might better have started *Into the church troop all the people, seat themselves. . . .*] Obviously a collective should not be treated as *both* singular and plural in the same context: *The company was* organized and immediately sent out *its* [not *their*] representatives.

collective bargaining, negotiation about wages, hours, and other working conditions between workers organized as a group and their employer or employers.

col·lec·tive·ly (kə-lek′tiv·li), *adv.* **1.** as a group; all together. **2.** in a singular form, but with a plural meaning.

col·lec·tiv·ism (kə-lek′tiv·iz·əm), *n.* control of the production of goods and services and the distribution of wealth by people as a group or by the government. —**col·lec′tiv·ist,** *n.* —**col·lec′tiv·is′tic,** *adj.*

col·lec·tor (kə-lek′tər), *n.* **1.** person or thing that collects. **2.** person hired to collect money owed. —**col·lec′tor·ship,** *n.*

col·leen (kol′ēn; kə-lēn′), *n. Irish.* girl.

col·lege (kol′ij), *n.* **1.** institution of higher learning that gives degrees. **2.** *Am.* the academic department of a university for general instruction, as distinguished from the special, professional, or graduate schools. **3.** *Am.* school for special or professional instruction, as in medicine, pharmacy, agriculture, or music. **4.** an organized association of persons having certain powers, rights, duties, and purposes. **5.** building or buildings used by a college. [< OF < L *collegium* < *collega* COLLEAGUE]

College of Cardinals, Sacred College.

col·le·gian (kə-lē′jən; -ji·ən), *n.* a college student.

col·le·giate (kə-lē′jit; -ji·it), *adj.* of or like a college or college students.

col·lide (kə-līd′), *v.,* –lid·ed, –lid·ing. **1.** come violently into contact; run into with force; crash. **2.** clash; conflict. [< L *collidere* < *com-* together + *laedere,* orig., to strike]

col·lie (kol′i), *n.* a large, intelligent, long-haired breed of dog used for tending sheep and as a pet.

Collie (ab. 2 ft. high at the shoulder)

col·lier (kol′yər), *n. Esp. Brit.* **1.** ship for carrying coal. **2.** a coal miner. [ME *colier* < *col* COAL]

col·lier·y (kol′yər·i), *n., pl.* –lier·ies. coal mine and its buildings and equipment.

col·li·mate (kol′ə·māt), *v.,* –mat·ed, –mat·ing. **1.** bring into line; make parallel. **2.** adjust accurately the line of sight of (a surveying instrument, telescope, etc.). [< L *collimatus,* misread for *collineatus,* ult. < *com-* together + *linea* line] —**col′li·ma′tion,** *n.*

col·li·sion (kə-lizh′ən), *n.* **1.** a violent rushing against; hitting or striking violently together. **2.** clash; conflict. —**Syn. 1.** impact.

col·lo·cate (kol′ō-kāt), *v.,* –cat·ed, –cat·ing. **1.** place together. **2.** arrange. [< L, < *com-* together + *locare* place] —**col′lo·ca′tion,** *n.*

col·lo·di·on (kə-lō′di·ən), *n.* a gluelike liquid that dries very rapidly and leaves a tough, waterproof, transparent film. [< Gk. *kollodes* gluey < *kolla* glue]

col·loid (kol′oid), *n. Physics, Chem.* substance composed of particles that are extremely small but larger than most molecules. Colloids do not actually dissolve, but remain suspended in a suitable gas, liquid, or solid. —*adj.* colloidal. [< Gk. *kolla* glue]

col·loi·dal (kə-loi′dəl), *adj.* being, containing, or like a colloid. —**col·loid·al·i·ty** (kol′oi·dal′ə·ti), *n.*

col·lop (kol′əp), *n.* **1.** a small slice, esp. of meat. **2.** fold of flesh or skin on the body. [ME *colope*]

colloq., colloquial; colloquialism.

col·lo·qui·al (kə-lō′kwi·əl), *adj.* used in everyday, informal talk, but not in formal speech or writing. —**col·lo′qui·al·ly,** *adv.* —**col·lo′qui·alness,** *n.* —**Syn.** conversational, familiar, informal. ➤ **Colloquial** means conversational, used in speaking. Since the speech of people varies with their education, work, and social status, there are obviously many different types of colloquial English. Since the bulk of conversation is informal, *colloquial* suggests informal rather than formal English. It need not, however, mean the speech of uneducated people, and in this book applies to the language spoken by people of some education and social standing, to language that can be safely used except on decidedly formal occasions.

col·lo·qui·al·ism (kə-lō′kwi·əl·iz′əm), *n.* **1.** a colloquial word or phrase. **2.** a colloquial style or usage.

col·lo·quist (kol′ə-kwist), *n.* interlocutor.

col·lo·quy (kol′ə-kwi), *n., pl.* –quies. **1.** a talking together; conversation. **2.** conference. [< L, < *com-* with + *loqui* speak]

col·lude (kə-lüd′), *v.,* –lud·ed, –lud·ing. act together through a secret understanding; conspire in a fraud. [< L, < *com-* with + *ludere* play]

col·lu·sion (kə-lü′zhən), *n.* a secret agreement for some wrong purpose; conspiracy. —**col·lu′sive,** *adj.* —**col·lu′sive·ly,** *adv.* —**col·lu′siveness,** *n.*

Colo., Colorado (official abbrev.).

co·logne (kə-lōn′), *n. Am.* a fragrant liquid, not so strong as perfume. [for *eau de Cologne,* a trademark meaning water of *Cologne*]

Co·logne (kə-lōn′), *n.* city in W Germany, on the Rhine.

Co·lom·bi·a (kə-lum′bi-ə), *n.* country in NW South America. —**Co·lom′bi·an,** *adj., n.*

Co·lom·bo (kə·lum′bō), *n.* seaport and capital of Ceylon.

co·lon[1] (kō′lən), *n.* mark (:) of punctuation used before a series of items, explanations, long quotations, etc., to set them off from the rest of the sentence. [< L < Gk. *kolon* limb, clause] ➤ The **colon** is a mark of anticipation, directing attention to what follows. (Contrast the semicolon, which is a stop.) The colon is a formal mark and usually emphatic. The principal uses of the colon are:
1. After introductory phrases, as in the preceding line, and after the salutation of formal letters: *Dear Sir:* [contrast the comma in informal letters: *Dear Fritz,*].
2. Between two clauses of a compound sentence when the second is either an illustration of the first, a restatement in different terms, or sometimes an amplification of the first: *They obtained the information by careful digging: they examined old files, read through unpublished manuscripts, and checked thousands of reports.*
3. In a few conventional uses, although even these vary:
(a) Between hours and minutes expressed in figures: *11:42 a.m., 3:28 p.m.* [or: *11.42 a.m., 3.28 p.m.*].
(b) In formal bibliographies and formal citations of books: between author and title—Stuart Chase: *Men and Machines;* between place of publication and publisher—New York: Holt, 1930; between volume and page—*The Atlantic Monthly,* 160: 129–40. In these three positions a comma would often and perhaps usually be found.
4. Followed by either a capital or a small letter. The capital is more usual when the matter following the colon is in the form of a complete sentence, a small letter when it is a phrase.
5. Following an abbreviation. The period of the abbreviation is often omitted (*i.e:* rather than *i.e.:*).

co·lon[2] (kō′lən), *n., pl.* **co·lons, co·la** (kō′lə). *Anat.* the lower part of the large intestine. [< L < Gk. *kolon*] —**co·lon·ic** (kə·lon′ik), *adj.*

Co·lón (kō·lōn′; -lōn′), *n.* seaport in N Panama near the Atlantic end of the Panama Canal.

colo·nel (kér′nəl), *n.* an army officer ranking next below a brigadier general and next above a lieutenant colonel. He usually commands a regiment. [earlier *coronel,* < F *coronel,* now *colonel* < Ital. *colonnello* < *colonna* COLUMN] —**colo′nel·cy, colo′nel·ship,** *n.* ➤ **Colonel** is a good example of a spelling that has survived a change of pronunciation. The word, from the French, had two parallel forms, *colonel, coronel,* each pronounced in three syllables. For 150 years the word has been pronounced (kér′nəl), from the *coronel* form, but spelling has kept *colonel.*

co·lo·ni·al (kə·lō′ni·əl), *adj.* 1. of a colony; having to do with colonies. 2. of or having to do with the thirteen British colonies that became the United States. —*n.* person living in a colony. —**co·lo′ni·al·ism,** *n.* —**co·lo′ni·al·ly,** *adv.*

col·o·nist (kol′ə·nist), *n.* 1. person who helps to found a colony; settler. 2. person living in a colony.

col·o·nize (kol′ə·nīz), *v.,* **–nized, –niz·ing.** 1. establish a colony or colonies in. 2. establish (persons) in a colony; settle in a colony. 3. form a colony. —**col′o·ni·za′tion,** *n.* —**col′o·niz′er,** *n.*

col·on·nade (kol′ə·nād′), *n. Archit.* series of columns set the same distance apart. [< F < Ital. *colonnata* < *colonna* COLUMN] —**col′on·nad′ed,** *adj.*

col·o·ny (kol′ə·ni), *n., pl.* **–nies.** 1. group of people who leave their own country and go to settle in another land, but who still remain citizens of their own country. 2. settlement made by such a group of people. 3. territory distant from the country that governs it. 4. group of people from the same country or with the same occupation, living in a certain part of a city: *a colony of artists.* 5. group of animals or plants of the same kind, living or growing together: *a colony of ants.* 6. an aggregation of bacteria in a culture. 7. **the Colonies,** the

thirteen British colonies that became the United States of America. [< L, < *colonus* cultivator, settler < *colere* cultivate] —**Syn.** 3. possession.

col·o·phon (kol′ə·fon; -fən), *n.* words or inscription placed at the end of a book, telling the name of the publisher, etc. [< LL < Gk. *kolophon* summit, final touch]

col·or (kul′ər), *n.* 1. sensation produced by the effect of waves of light striking the retina of the eye. 2. red, yellow, green, blue, purple, etc., or any combination of these: *she never wears colors, but always dresses in black, white, or gray.* 3. paint; dye; pigment. 4. redness of the face; ruddy complexion. 5. flush caused by blushing. 6. the skin color of any race that is not white. 7. an outward appearance; show: *his lies had some color of truth.* 8. effect of adding realistic details to a description. 9. distinguishing quality; vividness. 10. any hue adopted for distinction, as for a badge. 11. **change color,** a. turn pale. b. blush. 12. **colors,** badge, ribbon, dress, etc., worn to shown allegiance. 13. **give or lend color to,** cause to seem true or likely. 14. **lose color,** turn pale. 15. **show one's colors,** a. show oneself as one really is. b. declare one's opinions or plans. 16. **the colors,** a. the flag of a nation, regiment, etc.: *salute the colors.* b. the ceremony of raising the flag in the morning and lowering it in the evening. c. the army or navy. —*v.* 1. give color to; put color on; change the color of. 2. become red in the face; blush. 3. change to give a wrong idea: *to color a report of a battle.* 4. give a distinguishing quality to. Also, *esp. Brit.* **colour.** [< L] —**col′or·er,** *n.* —**Syn.** *v.* 1. paint, dye, stain, tint, tinge. 2. flush.

col·or·a·ble (kul′ər·ə·bəl), *adj.* 1. capable of being colored. 2. plausible. 3. pretended; deceptive. Also, *esp. Brit.* **colourable.** —**col′or·a·bil′i·ty, col′or·a·ble·ness,** *n.* —**col′or·a·bly,** *adv.*

Col·o·rad·o (kol′ə·rad′ō; -rä′dō), *n.* 1. a Western State of the United States. *Capital:* Denver. *Abbrev.:* Colo. 2. river flowing from N Colorado to the Gulf of California. —**Col′o·rad′an,** *adj., n.*

col·or·a·tion (kul′ər·ā′shən), *n.* coloring. Also, *esp. Brit.* **colouration.**

col·or·a·tu·ra (kul′ə·rə·tur′ə; -tyur′ə), *n.* 1. ornamental passages in music, such as trills, runs, etc. 2. a soprano who sings such passages. —*adj.* fit for singing such passages: *a coloratura soprano.* [< Ital., < L *color* color]

col·or·blind (kul′ər·blīnd′), *adj.* unable to tell certain colors apart; unable to see certain colors. —**color blindness.**

col·or·cast (kul′ər·kast′; -käst′), *n.* television broadcast in color. —*v.* broadcast (a television program) in color.

col·ored (kul′ərd), *adj.* 1. having color; not black or white. 2. having a certain kind of color. 3. of the Negro race or other race than white. 4. influenced; influenced unfairly. Also, *esp. Brit.* **coloured.**

col·or·ful (kul′ər·fəl), *adj.* 1. abounding in color. 2. vivid. Also, *esp. Brit.* **colourful.** —**col′or·ful·ly,** *adv.* —**col′or·ful·ness,** *n.*

col·or·ing (kul′ər·ing), *n.* 1. way in which a person or thing is colored. 2. substance used to color; pigment. 3. false appearance. Also, *esp. Brit.* **colouring.**

col·or·ist (kul′ər·ist), *n.* 1. artist who is skillful in painting with colors. 2. user of color. Also, *esp. Brit.* **colourist.** —**col′or·is′tic,** *adj.*

col·or·less (kul′ər·lis), *adj.* 1. without color. 2. without excitement or variety; uninteresting. Also, *esp. Brit.* **colourless.** —**col′or·less·ly,** *adv.* —**col′or·less·ness,** *n.*

color line, *Am.* difference in social, economic, or political privileges between members of the white race and of the colored races.

co·los·sal (kə·los′əl), *adj.* huge; gigantic; vast. —**co·los′sal·ly,** *adv.*

Col·os·se·um (kol′ə·sē′əm), *n.* a large, outdoor theater at Rome, completed in 80 A.D. The Colosseum was used for games and contests. [< LL, neut. of L *colosseus* gigantic < *colossus* < Gk.]

Co·los·sians (kə·losh′ənz), *n.* book of the New Testament, written by the apostle Paul to the

Christian people of Colossae, an ancient city of Asia Minor.

co·los·sus (kə·los′əs), *n.*, *pl.* **–los·si** (–los′ī), **–los·sus·es. 1.** a huge statue. **2.** anything huge; gigantic person or thing. [< L < Gk. *kolossos*]

Colossus of Rhodes, huge statue of Apollo made at Rhodes about 280 B.C. It was one of the seven wonders of the ancient world.

col·our (kul′ər), *n.*, *v. Esp. Brit.* color. **—col′our·a·ble,** *adj.* **—col′our·a′tion,** *n.* **—col′oured,** *adj.* **—col′our·er,** *n.* **—col′our·ful,** *adj.* **—col′our·ing,** *n.* **—col′our·ist,** *n.* **—col′our·less,** *adj.*

colt (kōlt), *n.* **1.** a young horse, donkey, etc. A male horse until it is four or five years old is a colt. **2.** a young or inexperienced person. [OE]

col·ter (kōl′tər), *n.* a sharp blade or disk on a plow to cut the earth ahead of the plowshare. Also, **coulter.** [< L *culter* knife]

colt·ish (kōl′tish), *adj.* lively and frisky.

colts·foot (kōlts′fut′), *n.* plant of the aster family with yellow flowers and large, heart-shaped leaves which were formerly much used in medicine.

Co·lum·bi·a (kə·lum′bi·ə), *n.* **1.** capital of South Carolina, in the C part. **2.** river flowing from British Columbia through E Washington and Oregon into the Pacific. **3.** *Am.* a name for the United States of America. **—Co·lum′bi·an,** *adj., n.*

col·um·bine (kol′əm·bīn), *n.* plant whose flowers have petals shaped like hollow spurs. [< LL *columbina* < L, fem., dovelike < *columba* dove]

co·lum·bi·um (kə·lum′bi·əm), *n. Chem.* a steel-gray, rare metallic element, Cb, that resembles tantalum in its chemical properties. Also, niobium. [< NL, < *Columbia*]

Co·lum·bus (kə·lum′bəs), *n.* **1.** Christopher, 1446?–1506, Italian navigator in the service of Spain who discovered America in 1492. **2.** capital of Ohio, in the C part.

Columbus Day, *Am.* October 12, the anniversary of Columbus's discovery of America.

col·umn (kol′əm), *n.* **1.** *Archit.* a slender, upright structure, usually used as support or ornament to a building; pillar. **2.** anything that seems slender and upright like a column: *a column of figures; the spinal column is the backbone.* **3.** arrangement of soldiers in several short rows one behind another. **4.** line of ships, one behind another. **5.** a narrow division of a page reading from top to bottom, kept separate by lines or by blank spaces. A newspaper often has eight columns on a page. **6.** part of a newspaper used for a special subject or written by a special writer. [< L *columna*] **—col·umned** (kol′əmd), *adj.*

CAPITAL
SHAFT
BASE
Column

co·lum·nar (kə·lum′nər), *adj.* **1.** like a column. **2.** made of columns. **3.** written or printed in columns.

col·um·nist (kol′əm·nist; –əm·ist), *n. Am.* journalist who comments on people, events, etc., in a special, regular column in a newspaper.

com–, *prefix.* with; together; altogether: *commingle = mingle with one another; compress = press together.* [< L; also by assimilation to the following consonant **col–, con–, cor–**]

Com., 1. Commander. **2.** Committee.

com., commerce.

co·ma¹ (kō′mə), *n., pl.* **co·mas.** a prolonged unconsciousness caused by disease, injury, or poison; stupor. [< Gk. *koma*]

co·ma² (kō′mə), *n., pl.* **co·mae** (kō′mē). *Astron.* a cloudlike mass around the nucleus of a comet. [< L < Gk. *kome* hair] **—co′mal,** *adj.*

Co·man·che (kə·man′chē), *n., pl.* **–ches.** *Am.* member of a tribe of American Indians that formerly roamed from Wyoming to northern Mexico, now living in Oklahoma.

com·a·tose (kom′ə·tōs; kō′mə–), *adj.* **1.** unconscious. **2.** lethargic. **—com′a·tose·ly,** *adv.*

comb (kōm), *n.* **1.** a narrow, short piece of metal, rubber, celluloid, etc., with teeth, used to arrange or clean the hair or to hold it in place. **2.** anything shaped or used like a comb. One kind of comb cleans and takes out the tangles in wool or flax. **3.** currycomb. **4.** the thick, red, fleshy piece on the top of the head in some fowls. **5.** honeycomb. **6.** top of a wave rolling over or breaking. **—v. 1.** arrange, clean, or take out tangles in, with a comb. **2.** *Am.* search through; look everywhere in. **3.** *Am.* (of waves) roll over or break at the top. [OE]

com·bat (*v., n.* kom′bat; *v.* also kəm·bat′), *v.,* **–bat·ed, –bat·ing;** *esp. Brit.* **–bat·ted, –bat·ting,** *n.* **—v. 1.** fight (*with* or *against*); battle; contend. **2.** oppose vigorously. **—n. 1.** a fight, esp. between two. **2.** a struggle; a conflict; a battle. [< F *combattre* < LL < L *com–* (intensive) + *battuere* beat] **—com·bat·a·ble** (kom′bat·ə·bəl; kəm·bat′–), *adj.* **—com′bat·er,** *n.* **—Syn. n. 1.** duel, engagement.

com·bat·ant (kəm·bat′ənt; kom′bə·tənt), *n.* fighter. **—adj. 1.** fighting. **2.** ready to fight.

com·bat·ive (kəm·bat′iv; kom′bə·tiv), *adj.* ready to fight or oppose; fond of fighting. **—com·bat′ive·ly,** *adv.* **—com·bat′ive·ness,** *n.*

combat team, a self-sustaining tactical group combining elements of infantry, artillery, tank, and air forces in the army, and submarines, air forces, etc., as well as surface craft in the navy.

comb·er (kōm′ər), *n.* **1.** one that combs. **2.** *Am.* wave that rolls over or breaks at the top.

com·bi·na·tion (kom′bə·nā′shən), *n.* **1.** a combining or being combined. **2.** thing made by combining. **3.** group of persons or parties joined together for some common purpose. **4.** *Math.* **a.** arrangement of individuals in groups so that each group has a certain number of individuals. **b.** the groups thus formed. **5.** *Am.* series of numbers or letters used in opening or closing a certain kind of lock. **6.** suit of underwear having the shirt and drawers in one piece. **—com′bi·na′tion·al,** *adj.* **—Syn. 3.** league, combine, coöperative.

com·bine (*v.* kəm·bīn′; *n. 1* kom′bīn, kəm·bīn′; *n. 2* kom′bīn), *v.,* **–bined, –bin·ing,** *n.* **—v. 1.** join together; unite. **2.** *Chem.* unite to form a compound. **—n. 1.** *Am., Colloq.* combination (def. 3). **2.** *Am.* machine for harvesting and threshing grain. [< LL *combinare* < *com–* together + *bini* two by two] **—com·bin′a·ble,** *adj.* **—com·bin′er,** *n.* **—Syn. v. 1.** merge, associate. **2.** blend, mix. ► **Combine** is not in good use in the abstract senses of *combination*, but is good colloquial English for a group of people joined together for business or political gain and usually implies either shady or forceful activities.

combining form, a word element.

com·bus·ti·ble (kəm·bus′tə·bəl), *adj.* **1.** capable of taking fire and burning; easy to burn. **2.** easily excited; fiery. **—n.** a combustible substance. **—com·bus′ti·bil′i·ty, com·bus′ti·ble·ness,** *n.* **—com·bus′ti·bly,** *adv.*

com·bus·tion (kəm·bus′chən), *n.* **1.** act or process of burning. **2.** rapid oxidation accompanied by high temperature and usually by light. **3.** slow oxidation not accompanied by high temperature and light. **4.** violent excitement; tumult. [< L *combustio* < *com–* up + *urere* burn] **—com·bus′tive,** *adj.*

come (kum), *v.,* **came, come, com·ing. 1.** move toward the speaker or the place where he is or will be; approach: *come this way.* **2.** arrive: *he came to the city yesterday.* **3.** appear: *light comes and goes.* **4.** reach; extend. **5.** happen; take place; occur: *what will come, let come.* **6.** be caused; result. **7.** be born. **8.** get to be; turn out to be; become. **9.** be brought; pass; enter. **10.** occur to the mind. **11.** be available. **12.** be equal; amount: *the total comes to $100.* **13.** here! look! stop! behave! **14.** come about, a. happen; take place; occur. b. turn around; change direction. **15.** come around, come round, a. return to consciousness or health; recover. b. give in; yield; agree. c. turn around; change direction. **16.** come down, a. lose position, rank, money, etc. b. be handed down or passed along. c. *Am.*, *Colloq.* become ill (*with*). 17. **come out, a.** be revealed or shown. **b.** be offered to the public. **c.** do one's part; leave an activity. **d.** be introduced to society; make a debut. 18. **come to, a.** return to consciousness. **b.** anchor; stop. [OE *cuman*] —**com′er,** *n.*

come·back (kum′bak′), *n.* 1. *Colloq.* return to a former condition or position. 2. *Am.*, *Slang.* clever answer. 3. *Slang.* cause for complaining.

co·me·di·an (kə·mē′di·ən), *n.* 1. actor in comedies. 2. writer of comedies. 3. person who amuses others with his funny talk and actions.

co·me·di·enne (kə·mē′di·en′), *n.* actress in comedies; actress of comic parts.

come·down (kum′doun′), *n.* *Colloq.* loss of position, rank, money, etc.

com·e·dy (kom′ə·di), *n., pl.* **–dies.** 1. amusing play or show having a happy ending. 2. branch of drama concerned with such plays. 3. the comic element of drama, of literature in general, or of life. 4. an amusing happening; funny incident. [< L < Gk., *komoidos* comedian < *komos* merrymaking + *aoidos* singer]

come·ly (kum′li), *adj.*, **–li·er, –li·est.** 1. having a pleasant appearance; attractive. 2. *Archaic.* fitting; suitable; proper. [OE *cymlic*] —**come′li·ness,** *n.* —**Ant.** 1. ugly, homely, plain.

co·mes·ti·ble (kə·mes′tə·bəl), *adj.* eatable. —*n.* Usually, **comestibles.** things to eat.

com·et (kom′it), *n.* a bright heavenly body with a starlike center and often with a cloudy tail of light, moving around the sun in a long, oval course. [< L < Gk. *kometes* wearing long hair < *kome* hair] —**co·met·ic** (kə·met′ik), *adj.*

com·fit (kum′fit; kom′–), *n.* piece of candy. [< OF < L *confectus* prepared < *com–* + *facere* make]

com·fort (kum′fərt), *v.* 1. ease the grief or sorrow of; cheer. 2. give ease to. —*n.* 1. anything that makes trouble or sorrow easier to bear. 2. freedom from pain or hardship; ease. 3. person or thing that makes life easier or takes away hardship. [< OF < LL *confortare* strengthen < *com–* + *fortis* strong] —**com′fort-ing,** *adj.* —**com′fort·ing·ly,** *adv.* —**com′fort-less,** *adj.* —**Syn.** *v.* 1. soothe, solace, console.

com·fort·a·ble (kumf′tə·bəl; kum′fər·tə·bəl), *adj.* 1. giving comfort. 2. in comfort. 3. at ease; contented. 4. *Colloq.* enough for one's needs. —**com′fort·a·ble·ness,** *n.* —**com′fort·a·bly,** *adv.*

com·fort·er (kum′fər·tər), *n.* 1. person or thing that gives comfort. 2. *Am.* a padded or quilted covering for a bed. 3. long woolen scarf.

com·ic (kom′ik), *adj.* 1. of comedy. 2. amusing; funny. —*n.* 1. the amusing or funny side of literature, life, etc. 2. *Colloq.* a comic book. 3. **comics,** *Am.* comic strips. [< L < Gk. *komikos.* See COMEDY.]

com·i·cal (kom′ə·kəl), *adj.* amusing; funny. —**com′i·cal·ly,** *adv.* —**com′i·cal·ness,** *n.*

comic book, *Am.* magazine with comic strips.

comic opera, amusing opera having a happy ending.

comic strip, *Am.* series of drawings, sometimes humorous, presenting an adventure.

Com·in·form (kom′in·fôrm), *n.* an international Communist propaganda organization formed in 1947, and dissolved in 1956.

com·ing (kum′ing), *n.* arrival. —*adj.* 1. next. 2. *Colloq.* on the way to importance or fame.

Com·in·tern (kom′in·tern), *n.* the Third Communist International, an organization founded at Moscow in 1919 to spread communism, and dissolved in 1943.

com·i·ty (kom′ə·ti), *n., pl.* **–ties.** courtesy; civility. [< L, < *comis* friendly]

com·ma (kom′ə), *n.* mark (,) of punctuation, used to show the smallest interruptions in the thought or in the grammatical structure of a sentence. [< L < Gk. *komma* piece cut off < *koptein* to cut] ▶ **comma (,).** As a general thing writers use more commas than are required by the simple material and direct movement of the average sentence. Most textbooks and most teachers have tended to encourage close punctuation, and students for this reason sometimes

give their writing a slow movement that it doesn't deserve. The boy who wrote this sentence was taking no chances: *Naturally, the first thing he does, after his interest is aroused, is to attempt to construct a small receiving set of his own.* No one of those commas is wrong but no one of them is necessary either, and without them the sentence moves more easily—and more appropriately to a simple account of experiences in amateur radio: *Naturally the first thing he does after his interest is aroused is to attempt to construct a small receiving set of his own.* The general advice of this book, then, is to use commas where the reader will expect them, but beyond this to use them only when they actually contribute to the understandability of the sentence. Where choice is possible, the final decision will often depend on fitness to other factors of style: the formal writer will always tend to use more commas than the informal. Partly because the use of commas depends on the movement of a passage, it is better not to pause in writing the first draft to decide about putting in a comma. Commas should be attended to in revision, when the context can help decide questions of appropriateness. The following sections are intended to help you decide how and where to use the comma.

1. Between Clauses. (a) BETWEEN COORDINATE CLAUSES. A comma is used when clauses are long and when it is desirable to emphasize their distinctness from each other: *The frozen steel edges shrieked as they bit into the ice-covered turns, and the driving sleet slashed against their goggles and jackets with such force that it was impossible to keep clear vision, to say nothing of protection for their bodies.*

A comma is generally used between two coördinate locutions joined by *but* or *not*, to emphasize the contrast: *I told him that I was ready to pay my half of the bill, but that didn't satisfy him. The sympathizers with these plans are to be pitied, not blamed.*

A comma is generally used between clauses connected by the conjunction *for*, to avoid confusion with the preposition *for:* Conjunction: *They are obviously mistaken, for all intercollegiate sports are competitive.* Preposition: *The English teacher had assigned us "Treasure Island" [ ] for a book report.*

(b) AFTER A SUBORDINATE CLAUSE (OR LONG PHRASE) THAT PRECEDES THE MAIN CLAUSE OF THE SENTENCE. If a clause or phrase preceding the main clause of the sentence is long or if it is not closely connected with the main clause, it should be followed by a comma: *Although willing to use his athletic ability, he wouldn't study hard enough to become eligible.*

(c) BEFORE A SUBORDINATE CLAUSE THAT FOLLOWS THE MAIN CLAUSE. A comma usually stands before a subordinate clause that follows the main clause if it is not closely related in thought to the main clause. If the subordinate clause is an essential modifier of the main statement, the comma is often omitted. The writer's sense of the closeness of the connection between the two statements should guide him unless actual misunderstanding could arise from omitting the comma: *Last spring the best miler in college failed to run [,] because he was too lazy to practice.*

2. In Lists and Series. The comma is the natural mark to use between the units of:

(a) ENUMERATIONS, LISTS, SERIES: *Among the numerous guests were socialites, artists, chorus girls, and even two university professors.* Usage is divided on the comma before the last member of a series: *celery, onions, and olives* [or] *celery, onions and olives.* Traditional formal usage calls for the comma, but newspaper and business writers quite generally omit it.

(b) ADJECTIVES IN SERIES. In the sentence *When the long, cold, lonesome evenings would come, we gathered about the old wood stove and ate the chestnuts,* there are commas between *long—cold—lonesome* because each stands in the same relation to the noun *evenings.* There is no comma between *old* and *wood* because *old* modifies *wood stove* rather than just *stove.* A comma following *old* would throw more emphasis upon *wood* and might sometimes be wanted.

3. With Nonrestrictive Modifiers. Modifiers which do not limit the meaning of a noun or verb but add a descriptive detail are nonrestrictive and are set off by a comma or commas. The material in italics is nonrestrictive: They had on old tattered overalls, *over which they were wearing a variety of differently colored sweaters.* However, a restrictive modifier, which is essential to a correct understanding of the material it modifies, is not set off by punctuation: Wouldn't it be as just to remove from his suffering a person *who has committed no crime* as to make suffer one *who has committed a crime?*

4. With Interrupting and Parenthetical Words and Phrases. (a) INTERRUPTING CONSTRUCTIONS. A phrase or clause that interrupts the direct movement of the sentence should be set off by commas: *did intelligent people, he asked himself, do things like that?* Usage is divided over setting off short parenthetical words and phrases like *incidentally* and *of course.* Setting them off with commas is more characteristic of formal than of informal writing, though there is often a difference in emphasis according to whether or not commas are used: *These early attempts, of course, brought no results. These early attempts of course brought no results.*

(b) CONNECTIVES. When a conjunctive adverb stands after the first phrase of its clause, as it often does, it is usually set off by commas, and often it is set off when it stands first in the clause: *The next morning, however, they all set out as though nothing had happened. However, the next morning they all set out as though nothing had happened.*

5. For Emphasis and Contrast. (a) The pause indicated by a comma tends to keep distinct the constructions it separates and to emphasize slightly the construction that follows the mark: *Temporarily the wine industry was all but ruined, and farmers turned to dairying, and to coöperation to give them a market.*

(b) This is especially true when a connective is omitted: *And afterwards I told her how I felt, how I kept feeling about her.*

(c) In the idiom *the more ... the greater,* formal usage tends to have a comma, informal not: *The more he pursued the subject [,] the larger its scope seemed to be.*

6. For Clearness. Often a comma can guide a reader in interpreting a sentence and make it unnecessary for him to go back over it for meaning. In material that is likely to be read aloud, the writer should give special heed to this device. Two such constructions are especially helped by commas:

(a) When a word has two possible functions. *For* or *but* may be either a conjunction or a preposition, and confusion may be avoided by using a comma before either when it is used as a conjunction: *The surgeon's face showed no emotion, but anxiety and a little nervousness must be seething behind that impassive mask* [to avoid reading "no emotion but anxiety"].

(b) When a noun might be mistaken for the object of a verb: *When the boll weevil struck, the credit system collapsed and ruined a great part of the landowners and tenants* [not: "When the boll weevil struck the credit system . . ."].

(c) Sometimes a faulty interpretation of word grouping can be prevented: *The only way that you can develop honestly is to discover how you write now, and then write naturally in everything you hand in* [avoiding "now and then"].

(d) Ordinarily when the same word occurs twice consecutively a comma should be used: *What the trouble really is, is of no interest to him.*

7. Conventional Uses. (a) IN DATES, to separate the day of the month from the year: *May 26, 1939.* When the day of the month is not given, a comma may or may not be used: *in May 1939* or *in May, 1939.* The less formal use is without the comma.

(b) IN ADDRESSES, to separate town from state or country when they are written on the same line: *Chicago, Illinois; Berne, Switzerland.*

(c) AFTER SALUTATIONS in informal letters: *Dear Len,*.

(d) IN FIGURES, to separate thousands, millions, etc: *4,672,342.*

(e) TO SEPARATE DEGREES and titles from names: *Elihu Root, Esq.; Charles Evans Hughes, Jr.; Ronald C. MacKenzie, Ph.D.*

com·mand (kə·mand′; –mänd′), *v.* **1.** give an order to; direct. **2.** give orders. **3.** have authority or power over; be in control of. **4.** be commander. **5.** have a position of control over; overlook. **6.** be able to have and use. **7.** deserve and get; force to be given: *command respect.* —*n.* **1.** order; direction. **2.** authority; power; control. **3.** position of a person who has the right to command. **4.** soldiers, ships, district, etc., under a person who has the right to command them. **5.** mastery or control by position. **6.** outlook over. **7.** ability to use; mastery: *he has a good command of French.* [< OF < LL, < L *com-* + *mandare* commit, command] —**Syn.** *v.* **1.** charge, enjoin, instruct. **3.** govern, rule. **7.** exact, secure. —*n.* **1.** charge, injunction, mandate.

com·man·dant (kom′ən·dant′; –dänt′), *n.* officer in command of a fort, navy yard, etc.

com·man·deer (kom′ən·dir′), *v.* **1.** seize (private property) for military or public use. **2.** force (men) into military service. **3.** *Colloq.* take by force. [< Afrikaans < F *commander*]

com·mand·er (kə·man′dər; –män′–), *n.* **1.** person who commands. **2.** officer in charge of an army or a part of an army. **3.** a navy officer ranking next below a captain and next above a lieutenant commander. —**com·mand′er·ship,** *n.*

commander in chief, *pl.* **commanders in chief. 1.** person who has complete command of the army and navy of a country. **2.** officer in command of part of an army or navy.

com·mand·ing (kə·man′ding; –män′–), *adj.* **1.** in command. **2.** controlling; powerful. **3.** authoritative; impressive. **4.** having a position of control. —**com·mand′ing·ly,** *adv.*

com·mand·ment (kə·mand′mənt; –mänd′–), *n.* **1.** order; direction; law. **2.** one of the ten laws that, according to the Bible, God gave to Moses. Exod. 20:2–17; Deut. 5:6–21.

com·man·do (kə·man′dō; –män′–), *n., pl.* **–dos, –does. 1.** Commando, *Esp. Brit.* soldier who makes brief, daring raids upon enemy territory. **2.** an armed force raised for service against marauders, rebellious natives, etc. [< Afrikaans < Pg.]

com·mem·o·rate (kə·mem′ə·rāt), *v.,* **–rat·ed, –rat·ing. 1.** preserve the memory of. **2.** honor the memory of. [< L, < *com-* + *memorare* relate] —**com·mem·o·ra·ble** (kə·mem′ə·rə·bəl), *adj.* —**com·mem′o·ra′tion,** *n.* —**com·mem′o·ra′tive,** *adj.* —**com·mem′o·ra′tive·ly,** *adv.* —**com·mem′o·ra′tor,** *n.* —**com·mem·o·ra·to·ry** (kə·mem′ə·rə·tô′ri; –tō′–), *adj.*

com·mence (kə·mens′), *v.,* **–menced, –menc·ing.** begin; start. [< OF *comencer* < VL < L *com-* + *initiare* begin. See INITIATE.] —**com·menc′er,** *n.*

com·mence·ment (kə·mens′mənt), *n.* **1.** a beginning; start. **2.** day when a school or college gives diplomas or degrees to students who have completed the required course of study; day of graduation. **3.** ceremonies on this day.

com·mend (kə·mend′), *v.* **1.** praise. **2.** mention favorably; recommend. **3.** hand over for safekeeping. [< L *commendare.* See COMMAND.] —**com·mend′a·ble,** *adj.* —**com·mend′a·bly,** *adv.*

com·men·da·tion (kom′ən·dā′shən), *n.* **1.** praise; approval. **2.** favorable mention. **3.** a handing over to another for safekeeping; entrusting.

com·men·da·to·ry (kə·men′də·tô′ri; –tō′–), *adj.* approving; mentioning favorably.

com·men·su·ra·ble (kə·men′shə·rə·bəl; –sə·rə–), *adj.* measurable by the same set of units. —**com·men′su·ra·bil′i·ty, com·men′su·ra·ble·ness,** *n.* —**com·men′su·ra·bly,** *adv.*

com·men·su·rate (kə·men′shə·rit; –sə–), *adj.* **1.** in the proper proportion; proportionate. **2.** of the same size, extent, etc.; equal. **3.** measurable by the same set of units. [< LL *commensuratus.* See COM-, MENSURATION.] —**com·men′su·rate·ly,**

āge, cāre, fär; ēqual, tèrm; īce; ōpen, ôrder; pùt, rüle, ūse; th, then; ə=a in about.

adv. —com·men'su·rate·ness, *n.* —com·men'-su·ra'tion, *n.*

com·ment (kom'ent), *n.* **1.** a short statement, note, or remark that explains, praises, or criticizes something that has been written, said, or done. **2.** remark. **3.** talk; gossip. —*v.* **1.** make a comment or comments. **2.** talk; gossip. [< L *commentum* < *commentus*, pp. of *comminisci* < *com-* up + *-minisci* think]

com·men·tar·y (kom'ən·ter'ĭ), *n., pl.* -tar·ies. **1.** series of notes for explaining the hard parts of a book; explanation. **2.** an explanatory essay or treatise.

com·men·ta·tor (kom'ən·tā'tər), *n.* person who makes comments, as on the radio, explaining or criticizing books, concerts, recent events, etc.

com·merce (kom'ərs; -ərs), *n.* buying and selling in large amounts between different places; trade; business. [< F < L *commercium*, ult. < *com-* with + *merx* wares] —Syn. dealings, traffic.

com·mer·cial (kə·mėr'shəl), *adj.* **1.** having to do with commerce. **2.** made to be sold. **3.** manufactured, or capable of being produced, in sizable quantities. **4.** supported or subsidized by an advertiser: *a commercial radio program.* —*n.* a radio or television program, or the part of a program, that advertises something. —com·mer'cial·ly, *adv.*

com·mer·cial·ism (kə·mėr'shəl·iz·əm), *n.* **1.** methods and spirit of commerce. **2.** business custom; expression used in business.

com·mer·cial·ize (kə·mėr'shəl·īz), *v.,* -ized, -iz·ing. apply the methods and spirit of commerce to; make a matter of business or trade. —com·mer'cial·i·za'tion, *n.*

com·min·gle (kə·ming'gəl), *v.,* -gled, -gling. mingle together; blend.

com·mi·nute (kom'ə·nūt; -nūt), *v.,* -nut·ed, -nut·ing. pulverize. [< L, < *com-* + *minuere* make smaller < *minus* less] —com'mi·nu'tion, *n.*

com·mis·er·ate (kə·miz'ər·āt), *v.,* -at·ed, -at·ing. feel or express sorrow for; sympathize with; pity. —com·mis'er·a'tion, *n.*

com·mis·sar (kom'ə·sär), *n.* head of a government department in Soviet Russia.

com·mis·sar·i·at (kom'ə·sär'ĭ·ət; -at), *n.* **1.** department of an army that supplies food, etc. **2.** a government department in Soviet Russia. [< F, < Med.L *commissarius*. See COMMISSARY.]

com·mis·sar·y (kom'ə·ser'ĭ), *n., pl.* -sar·ies. **1.** *Am.* store handling food and supplies in a mining camp, lumber camp, army camp, etc. **2.** an army officer in charge of food and daily supplies for soldiers. **3.** deputy; representative. [< Med.L *commissarius* < L *commissus*, pp., entrusted. See COMMIT.]

com·mis·sion (kə·mish'ən), *n.* **1.** a written paper giving certain powers, privileges, and duties. **2.** a written order giving military or naval rank and authority. **3.** rank and authority given by such an order. **4.** a giving of authority. **5.** authority, power, or right given. **6.** thing for which authority is given; thing trusted to a person to do. **7.** group of people appointed or elected with authority to do certain things. **8.** doing; performance. **9.** pay based on a percentage of the amount of business done. **10. in commission, a.** in service; in use. **b.** in working order. **11. out of commission, a.** not in service or use. **b.** not in working order. —*v.* **1.** give a commission to. **2.** give authority to; give (a person) the right or power (to do something). **3.** put in service or use; make ready for service or use. —Syn. *n.* **5.** warrant, license. -*v.* **2.** license, authorize, empower.

com·mis·sion·er (kə·mish'ən·ər), *n.* **1.** member of a commission. **2.** official in charge of some department of a government: *police commissioner.* **3.** one of a group of persons elected or appointed to govern a city or a county. —com·mis'sion·er·ship', *n.*

com·mit (kə·mit'), *v.,* -mit·ted, -mit·ting. **1.** hand over for safekeeping; deliver. **2.** confine officially: *commit to prison.* **3.** refer to a committee for consideration. **4.** do or perform (usually something wrong). **5.** involve; pledge. **6.**

commit to memory, learn by heart. [< L < *com-* with + *mittere*, send, put] —com·mit'ta·ble, *adj.* —Syn. **1.** commend, entrust, confide.

com·mit·ment (kə·mit'mənt), **com·mit·tal** (-mit'əl), *n.* **1.** a committing or being committed. **2.** a sending to prison or an asylum. **3.** order sending a person to prison or to an asylum. **4.** pledge; promise.

com·mit·tee (kə·mit'ĭ), *n.* group of persons appointed or elected to do certain things. **▶** Committee is a collective noun, to be construed as singular or plural according as the group or the individuals are meant. The singular would usually be the form desired: *the committee meets today at four; the committee get together with difficulty.* [< AF, committed. See COMMIT.]

com·mit·tee·man (kə·mit'ĭ·mən; -man'), *n., pl.* -men (-mən; -men'). member of a committee.

com·mode (kə·mōd'), *n.* **1.** chest of drawers. **2.** washstand (def. 2). [< F < L *commodus* convenient < *com-* with + *modus* measure]

com·mo·di·ous (kə·mō'di·əs), *adj.* **1.** roomy. **2.** convenient; handy. [< Med.L *commodiosus.* See COMMODE.] —com·mo'di·ous·ly, *adv.*

com·mod·i·ty (kə·mod'ə·ti), *n., pl.* -ties. **1.** anything that is bought and sold. **2.** useful thing.

com·mo·dore (kom'ə·dôr; -dōr), *n.* **1.** an officer in the U.S. Navy ranking next below a rear admiral and next above a captain. **2.** captain in the British navy in temporary command of a squadron. **3.** title of honor given to the president or head of a yacht club. [earlier *commandore;* ? < Du. < F, < *commander* to command]

com·mon (kom'ən), *adj.* **1.** belonging equally to each or all. **2.** of all; from or by all; to all; general: *common knowledge, common nuisance.* **3.** belonging to the community at large; public: *a common council.* **4.** often met with; usual; familiar. **5.** generally known, used, etc. **6.** notorious. **7.** without rank. **8.** below ordinary; inferior; low; vulgar. **9.** applicable to any individual of a class. **10.** belonging equally to two or more quantities: *a common factor.* —*n.* **1.** land owned or used by all the people of a town, village, etc. **2.** in common, equally with another or others; owned, used, done, etc., by both or all. [< OF < L *communis* < *com-* together + *munia* duties] —com'mon·ly, *adv.* —com'mon·ness, *n.* —Syn. *adj.* **1.** joint. **2.** popular, universal. **3.** cheap.

com·mon·al·ty (kom'ən·əl·ti), *n., pl.* -ties. **1.** the common people. **2.** people as a group. **3.** members of a corporation.

common carrier, person or company whose business is conveying goods or people for pay.

com·mon·er (kom'ən·ər), *n.* one of the common people; person who is not a nobleman.

common law, the unwritten law based on custom and usage and confirmed by the decisions of judges, as distinct from statute law.

common noun, name for any one of a class. *Boy, city,* and *dog* are common nouns. *John, Boston,* and *Rover* are proper nouns.

com·mon·place (kom'ən·plās'), *n.* **1.** common or everyday thing. **2.** ordinary or obvious remark. —*adj.* not new or interesting; everyday; ordinary. —com'mon·place'ness, *n.*

com·mons (kom'ənz), *n.pl.* **1.** the common people. **2.** a dining hall or building where food is served to a large group at common tables. **3.** the food served. **4.** food. **5. the Commons,** House of Commons.

common sense, good sense in everyday affairs; practical intelligence. —com'mon·sense', *adj.*

com·mon·weal (kom'ən·wēl'), **common weal,** *n.* general welfare; public good.

com·mon·wealth (kom'ən·welth'), *n.* **1.** group of people who make up a nation; citizens of a state. **2.** a democratic state; republic. **3.** *Am.* one of the States of the United States. **4.** group of persons, nations, etc., united by some common interest.

Commonwealth of Nations, British Commonwealth of Nations.

com·mo·tion (kə·mō'shən), *n.* violent movement; confusion; disturbance; tumult.

com·mu·nal (kom′yə-nəl; kə-mū′nəl), *adj.* **1.** of a community; public. **2.** owned jointly by all; used or participated in by all members of a group or community. **3.** of a commune. —**com′mu·nal·ly,** *adv.*

com·mune¹ (*v.* kə-mūn′; *n.* kom′ūn), *v.,* –muned, –mun·ing, *n.* —*v.* **1.** talk intimately. **2.** receive Holy Communion. —*n.* intimate talk; communion. [< OF, < *comun* COMMON]

com·mune² (kom′ūn), *n.* the smallest division for local government in France, Belgium, and several other European countries. [< F, fem. of *commun* COMMON]

com·mu·ni·ca·ble (kə-mū′nə-kə-bəl), *adj.* that can be communicated. —**com·mu′ni·ca·bil′i·ty, com·mu′ni·ca·ble·ness,** *n.*

com·mu·ni·cant (kə-mū′nə-kənt), *n.* **1.** person who receives Holy Communion. **2.** person who gives information by talking, writing, etc.

com·mu·ni·cate (kə-mū′nə-kāt), *v.,* –cat·ed, –cat·ing. **1.** pass along; transfer: *a stove communicates heat to a room.* **2.** give (information) by talking, writing, etc.; talk, write, telephone, telegraph, etc.; send and receive messages. **3.** be connected. **4.** receive Holy Communion. [< L *communicatus* < *communis* COMMON] —**com·mu′ni·ca′tor,** *n.* —Syn. **1.** convey. **2.** impart.

com·mu·ni·ca·tion (kə-mū′nə-kā′shən), *n.* **1.** act or fact of passing along; transfer. **2.** a giving of information by talking, writing, etc. **3.** information given in this way. **4.** letter, message, etc., that gives information. **5.** means of going from one place to the other; connection; passage. **6.** communications, a system of communicating by telephone, radio, etc.

communications satellite, an artificial satellite that relays radio signals between two points on the earth, as Telstar.

com·mu·ni·ca·tive (kə-mū′nə-kā′tiv; –kə-tiv), *adj.* **1.** ready to give information; talkative. **2.** pertaining to communication. —**com·mu′ni·ca′tive·ly,** *adv.* —**com·mu′ni·ca′tive·ness,** *n.*

com·mun·ion (kə-mūn′yən), *n.* **1.** act of sharing; a having in common. **2.** exchange of thoughts and feelings; intimate talk; fellowship. **3.** close spiritual relationship. **4.** group of people having the same religious beliefs. **5.** Communion, a. act of sharing in the Lord's Supper as a part of church worship. b. celebration of the Lord's Supper. [< L *communio.* See COMMON.]

com·mu·ni·qué (kə-mū′nə-kā′; kə-mū′nə-kā), *n.* an official bulletin, statement, etc.

com·mu·nism (kom′yə-niz-əm), *n.* system by which the means of production and distribution are owned and managed by the government, and the goods produced are shared by all citizens. [< F *communisme* < *commun* COMMON]

com·mu·nist (kom′yə-nist), *n.* **1.** person who favors and supports communism. **2.** Communist, member of a political party advocating communism. —**com′mu·nis′tic, com′mu·nis′ti·cal,** *adj.*

Communist Party, political party that supports communism.

com·mu·ni·ty (kə-mū′nə-ti), *n., pl.* –ties. **1.** a number of people having common ties or interests and living in the same locality. **2.** group of people living together: *a community of monks.* **3.** the public. **4.** ownership together; sharing together. **5.** group of animals or plants living together. **6.** likeness; similarity; identity. [< OF < L *communitas.* See COMMON.]

community center, *Am.* a building where the people of a community meet for recreation, social purposes, etc.

com·mu·tate (kom′yə-tāt), *v.,* –tat·ed, –tat·ing. *Elect.* reverse the direction of (an electric current). —**com′mu·ta′tor,** *n.*

com·mu·ta·tion (kom′yə-tā′shən), *n.* **1.** exchange; substitution. **2.** reduction (of an obligation, penalty, etc.) to a less severe one. **3.** regular, daily travel back and forth to work by train.

commutation ticket, *Am.* ticket sold at a reduced rate, entitling the holder to travel over a given route a certain number of times or during a certain period.

com·mute (kə-mūt′), *v.,* –mut·ed, –mut·ing. **1.** exchange: substitute. **2.** change (an obligation, penalty, etc.) to an easier one. **3.** *Am.* travel regularly back and forth to work by train; use a commutation ticket. [< L, < *com–* + *mutare* change]

com·mut·er (kə-mūt′ər), *n. Am.* person who travels regularly back and forth from his home in a suburb to his work in a city.

com·pact¹ (*adj., v.* kəm-pakt′; *n.* kom′pakt), *adj.* **1.** firmly packed together; closely joined. **2.** composed or made (*of*). **3.** using few words; brief. —*v.* **1.** pack firmly together; join closely. **2.** make by putting together firmly. **3.** condense. —*n.* a small case containing face powder and often rouge. [< L *compactus* < *com–* together + *pangere* fasten] —**com·pact′ly,** *adv.* —**com·pact′ness,** *n.*

com·pact² (kom′pakt), *n.* agreement. [< L *compactum* < *com–* + *pacisci* contract]

com·pan·ion (kəm-pan′yən), *n.* **1.** person who goes along with another; person who shares in what another is doing. **2.** anything that matches or goes with another in kind, size, color, etc. **3.** person paid to live or travel with another as a friend and helper. —*v.* be a companion to; go along with. [< OF < LL *companio* < *com–* together + *panis* bread] —**com·pan′ion·less,** *adj.* —**com·pan′ion·ship,** *n.* —Syn. *n.* **1.** comrade, associate.

com·pan·ion·a·ble (kəm-pan′yən-ə-bəl), *adj.* fitted to be a companion; pleasant; agreeable; sociable. —**com·pan′ion·a·bil′i·ty, com·pan′ion·a·ble·ness,** *n.* —**com·pan′ion·a·bly,** *adv.*

com·pan·ion·ate (kəm-pan′yən-it), *adj.* of companions; of companionship.

com·pan·ion·way (kəm-pan′yən-wā′), *n. Naut.* stairway from the deck of a ship down to the rooms below.

Companionway

com·pa·ny (kum′pə-ni), *n., pl.* –nies, *v.,* –nied, –ny·ing. —*n.* **1.** group of people. **2.** group of people joined together for some purpose: *a business company, a company of actors.* **3.** a gathering of persons for social purposes. **4.** companion or companions. **5.** association as companions. **6.** *Colloq.* guest or guests; visitor or visitors. **7.** *Mil.* part of an army commanded by a captain. **8.** *Naut.* a ship's crew; officers and sailors of a ship. **9.** part company, a. go separate ways. b. end companionship. —*v.* associate. [< OF, < *compagne* COMPANION]

com·par., comparative.

com·pa·ra·ble (kom′pə-rə-bəl), *adj.* **1.** able to be compared. **2.** fit to be compared. —**com′pa·ra·ble·ness,** *n.* —**com′pa·ra·bly,** *adv.*

com·par·a·tive (kəm-par′ə-tiv), *adj.* **1.** that compares. **2.** measured by comparison with something else. **3.** showing the comparative form. —*n.* **1.** the second degree of comparison of an adjective or adverb. **2.** form or combination of words that shows this degree. *Fairer* is the comparative of *fair.* —**com·par′a·tive·ly,** *adv.*

com·pare (kəm-pãr′), *v.,* –pared, –par·ing, *n.* —*v.* **1.** find out or point out the likenesses or differences of. **2.** consider as similar; liken. **3.** bear comparison; be considered like or equal. **4.** change the form of (an adjective or adverb) to show the comparative and superlative degree. —*n.* **1.** comparison. **2.** beyond compare, without an equal. [< F < L, < *com–* with + *par* equal] —**com·par′er,** *n.* —Syn. *v.* **3.** approach, rival, parallel. ▶ compare, contrast. *Compare* is commonly used in two senses: (1) to point out likenesses (used with *to*); (2) to examine two or more objects to find likenesses or differences (used with *with*). *Comparing* in the second sense may discover *differences* as well as *likenesses. Contrast* always means difference: *He compared my stories to Maupassant's* [said they were like his]; *he compared my stories with Maupassant's* [pointed out like and unlike traits]. *He contrasted my work with* (sometimes *to*) *Maupassant's.*

com·par·i·son (kəm·par′ə·sən), *n.* **1.** act or process of comparing; finding the likenesses and differences. **2.** likeness; similarity. **3.** change in an adjective or adverb to show degrees. The three degrees of comparison are positive, comparative, and superlative. *Example:* good, better, best; cold, colder, coldest; helpful, more helpful, most helpful. **4. in comparison with,** compared with. ➤ See adjective and adverb for usage notes.

com·part·ment (kəm·pärt′mənt), *n.* a separate division or section; part of an enclosed space set off by walls or partitions. [< F < Ital. *compartimento* < *compartire* divide < LL, < L *com-* with + *partiri* share]

com·pass (kum′pəs), *n.* **1.** instrument for showing directions, consisting of a needle that points to the N Magnetic Pole. **2.** boundary; circumference. **3.** space within limits; extent; range. **4.** range of a voice or musical instrument. **5.** circuit; going around. **6.** Usually, **compasses.** instrument for drawing circles and measuring distances. —*v.* **1.** make a circuit of; go around. **2.** form a circle around; surround. **3.** do; accomplish; get. [< OF, < *compasser* divide equally < VL, < L *com-* with + *passus* step] —Syn. *n.* **3.** reach, scope.

Compass (def. 6)

com·pas·sion (kəm·pash′ən), *n.* feeling for another's sorrow or hardship that leads to help; sympathy; pity. [< L *compassio* < *com-* with + *pati* suffer]

com·pas·sion·ate (*adj.* kəm·pash′ən·it; *v.* kəm·pash′ən·āt), *adj.*, *v.*, **-at·ed, -at·ing.** —*adj.* desiring to relieve another's suffering; deeply sympathetic. —*v.* take pity on. —**com·pas′sion·ate·ly,** *adv.* —**com·pas′sion·ate·ness,** *n.*

com·pat·i·ble (kəm·pat′ə·bəl), *adj.* **1.** able to exist together; that can get on well together; agreeing; in harmony. **2.** of or having to do with the type of television broadcasting that permits reception either in color on special sets or in black and white on ordinary sets. [< Med.L *compatibilis.* See COMPASSION.] —**com·pat′i·bil′i·ty, com·pat′i·ble·ness,** *n.* —**com·pat′i·bly,** *adv.*

com·pa·tri·ot (kəm·pā′tri·ət; *esp. Brit.* kəm·pat′ri·ət), *n.* a fellow countryman.

com·peer (kəm·pir′; kom′pir), *n.* **1.** equal. **2.** comrade. [< OF < L, < *com-* with + *par* equal]

com·pel (kəm·pel′), *v.*, **-pelled, -pel·ling. 1.** force. **2.** cause or get by force. [< L, < *com-* + *pellere* drive] —**com·pel′la·ble,** *adj.* —**com·pel′ler,** *n.* —Syn. **1.** constrain, oblige.

com·pen·di·ous (kəm·pen′di·əs), *adj.* brief but comprehensive; concise. —**com·pen′di·ous·ly,** *adv.* —**com·pen′di·ous·ness,** *n.*

com·pen·di·um (kəm·pen′di·əm), *n.*, *pl.* **-di·ums, -di·a** (-di·ə). summary that gives much information in little space; concise treatise. [< L, a saving, shortening, < *com-* in addition + *pendere* weigh]

com·pen·sate (kom′pən·sāt), *v.*, **-sat·ed, -sat·ing. 1.** make an equal return to; give an equivalent to. **2.** balance by equal weight, power, etc.; make up (*for*). **3.** *Econ.* stabilize the buying power of (money) to meet varying price levels by changing gold content or backing. **4.** pay. [< L, < *com-* with + *pensare* weigh < *pendere*] —**com′pen·sa′tor,** *n.* —**com·pen·sa·to·ry** (kəm·pen′sə·tô′ri; -tō′-), *adj.* —Syn. **2.** offset.

com·pen·sa·tion (kom′pən·sā′shən), *n.* **1.** something given as an equivalent; something given to make up for a loss, injury, etc. **2.** a balancing by equal power, weight, etc. **3.** *Am.* pay. **4.** increased activity of one part to make up for loss or weakness of another. **5.** any act or instance of compensating. —**com′pen·sa′tion·al,** *adj.*

com·pete (kəm·pēt′), *v.*, **-pet·ed, -pet·ing. 1.** try hard to obtain something wanted by others; be rivals; contend. **2.** take part (in a contest). [< L, < *com-* together + *petere* seek]

com·pe·tence (kom′pə·təns), **com·pe·ten·cy** (-tən·si), *n.* **1.** ability; fitness. **2.** enough money or property to provide a comfortable living.

com·pe·tent (kom′pə·tənt), *adj.* **1.** able; fit. **2.**

legally qualified. [< L, being fit, < *competere* meet. See COMPETE.] —**com′pe·tent·ly,** .*adv.* —Syn. **1.** capable.

com·pe·ti·tion (kom′pə·tish′ən), *n.* **1.** effort to obtain something wanted by others; rivalry. **2.** contest.

com·pet·i·tive (kəm·pet′ə·tiv), *adj.* of or having competition; based on or decided by competition. —**com·pet′i·tive·ly,** *adv.* —**com·pet′i·tive·ness,** *n.*

com·pet·i·tor (kəm·pet′ə·tər), *n.* person who competes; rival.

com·pile (kəm·pīl′), *v.*, **-piled, -pil·ing. 1.** collect and bring together in one list or account. **2.** make (a book, report, etc.) out of various materials. [< F < L *compilare* steal, orig., pile up < *com-* together + *pilare* press] —**com·pi·la·tion** (kom′pə·lā′shən), *n.* —**com·pil′er,** *n.*

com·pla·cen·cy (kəm·plā′sən·si), **com·pla·cence** (-səns), *n.*, *pl.* **-cies; -ces. 1.** being pleased with oneself; self-satisfaction. **2.** contentment.

com·pla·cent (kəm·plā′sənt), *adj.* pleased with oneself; self-satisfied. [< L, < *com-* + *placere* please] —**com·pla′cent·ly,** *adv.*

com·plain (kəm·plān′), *v.* **1.** say that something is wrong; find fault. **2.** talk about one's pains, troubles, etc. **3.** make an accusation or charge. [< OF < VL, bewail, < L *com-* + *plangere* lament] —**com·plain′er,** *n.* —**com·plain′ing·ly,** *adv.* —Syn. **1.** grumble, growl.

com·plain·ant (kəm·plān′ənt), *n.* **1.** person who complains. **2.** plaintiff.

com·plaint (kəm·plānt′), *n.* **1.** a complaining; a finding fault. **2.** a cause for complaining. **3.** accusation; charge. **4.** sickness; ailment.

com·plai·sant (kəm·plā′zənt; kom′plə·zant), *adj.* **1.** obliging; gracious; courteous. **2.** compliant. [< F, < *complaire* acquiesce < L, < *com-* + *placere* please] —**com·plai′sance,** *n.* —**com·plai′sant·ly,** *adv.*

com·ple·ment (*n.* kom′plə·mənt; *v.* kom′plə·ment), *n.* **1.** something that completes or makes perfect. **2.** number required to fill. **3.** either of two parts or things needed to complete each other. **4.** full quantity. **5.** word or group of words completing a predicate. In "The man is good" *good* is a complement. **6.** *Geom.* amount needed to make an angle or an arc equal to 90 degrees. —*v.* supply a lack of any kind; complete. [< L *complementum* < *complere* to COMPLETE] ➤ **complement, compliment.** *Complement* means a number or amount that makes a whole, or an allotment (related to *complete*): *she has her full complement of good looks. Compliment* has to do with politeness and praise: *their progress deserved his compliment.*

The arc BD is the complement of the arc AB and the angle BCD is the complement of the angle ACB.

com·ple·men·tal (kom′plə·men′təl), *adj.* complementary. —**com′ple·men′tal·ly,** *adv.*

com·ple·men·ta·ry (kom′plə·men′tə·ri; -tri), *adj.* forming a complement; completing.

com·plete (kəm·plēt′), *adj.*, *v.*, **-plet·ed, -plet·ing.** —*adj.* **1.** with all the parts; whole; entire. **2.** perfect; thorough. **3.** ended; finished; done. —*v.* **1.** make up all the parts of; make whole or entire. **2.** make perfect or thorough. **3.** get done; end; finish. [< L *completus* < *com-* up + *plere* fill] —**com·plete′ly,** *adv.* —**com·plete′ness,** *n.* —**com·plet′er,** *n.* —**com·ple′tive,** *adj.* —Syn. *adj.* **1.** total, full, intact. —*v.* **1.** complement.

com·ple·tion (kəm·plē′shən), *n.* **1.** act of completing. **2.** condition of being completed.

com·plex (*adj.* kəm·pleks′, kom′pleks; *n.* kom′pleks), *adj.* **1.** made up of a number of parts. **2.** complicated. —*n.* **1.** a complicated whole. **2.** idea or group of ideas associated with emotional disturbance so as to influence a person's behavior to an abnormal degree. **3.** *Colloq.* an unreasonable prejudice; strong dislike. [< L *complexus* embracing < *com-* together + *plecti* twine] —**com·plex′ly,** *adv.* —**com·plex′ness,** *n.* —Syn. *adj.* **1.** composite, compound. **2.** intricate, involved.

com·plex·ion (kəm·plek′shən), *n.* **1.** color, quality, and general appearance of the skin, particularly of the face. **2.** general appearance; nature; character. [< LL *complexio* constitution < L, combination. See COMPLEX.] —**com·plex′ion·al**, *adj.*

com·plex·i·ty (kəm·plek′sə·ti), *n.*, *pl.* **-ties. 1.** a complex quality, condition, or structure. **2.** something complex; complication.

complex sentence, sentence having one main clause and one or more subordinate clauses. ▶ See clause for usage note.

com·pli·a·ble (kəm·plī′ə·bəl), *adj.* complying. —**com·pli′a·ble·ness**, *n.* —**com·pli′a·bly**, *adv.*

com·pli·ance (kəm·plī′əns), **com·pli·an·cy** (-ən·si), *n.* **1.** act of complying; act of doing as another wishes; act of yielding to a request or command. **2.** tendency to yield to others. —*Syn.* **1.** assent, consent, submission.

com·pli·ant (kəm·plī′ənt), *adj.* complying; yielding; obliging. —**com·pli′ant·ly**, *adv.*

com·pli·cate (*v.* kom′plə·kāt; *adj.* kom′plə-kit), *v.*, **-cat·ed, -cat·ing,** *adj.* —*v.* **1.** make hard to understand, settle, cure, etc.; mix up; confuse. **2.** make worse or more mixed up. —*adj.* complex; involved. [< L, *com-* together + *plicare* fold]

com·pli·cat·ed (kom′plə·kāt′id), *adj.* made up of many parts; intricate. —**com′pli·cat′ed·ly**, *adv.* —**com′pli·cat′ed·ness**, *n.*

com·pli·ca·tion (kom′plə·kā′shən), *n.* **1.** a complex or confused state of affairs. **2.** something causing such a state of affairs. **3.** a complicating element in a plot. **4.** act or process of complicating. **5.** *Pathol.* a secondary disease or condition occurring in the course of a primary disease.

com·plic·i·ty (kəm·plis′ə·ti), *n.*, *pl.* **-ties.** partnership in wrongdoing. [< *complice* confederate < L *complex* < *com-* together + *plicare* fold]

com·pli·ment (*n.* kom′plə·mənt; *v.* kom′plə-ment), *n.* something good said about one; something said in praise of one's work. —*v.* pay a compliment to; congratulate. [< F < Ital. < Sp. *cumplimiento*. Var. of COMPLEMENT.] —*Syn. n.* commendation, tribute. —*v.* commend. ▶ See complement for usage note.

com·pli·men·ta·ry (kom′plə·men′tə·ri; -tri), *adj.* **1.** like or containing a compliment; praising. **2.** *U.S.* given free. —**com′pli·men′ta·ri·ly**, *adv.*

com·ply (kəm·plī′), *v.*, **-plied, -ply·ing.** act in agreement with a request or a command. [< Ital. < Sp. < L *complere* complete; infl. by *ply*[1]] —**com·pli′er**, *n.*

com·po·nent (kəm·pō′nənt), *adj.* constituent. —*n.* an essential part; part. [< L, < *com-* together + *ponere* put]

com·port (kəm·pōrt′; -pōrt′), *v.* **1.** behave: *comport oneself with dignity.* **2.** agree; suit. [< F < L, < *com-* together + *portare* carry] —**com·port′ment**, *n.*

com·pose (kəm·pōz′), *v.*, **-posed, -pos·ing. 1.** make up. **2.** make or form by uniting the parts of. **3.** be the parts of. **4.** get (oneself) ready; make up one's mind. **5.** make calm (oneself or one's features). **6.** settle; arrange: *compose a dispute.* **7.** write music, books, etc. [< OF, < *com-* (< L) together + *poser* place (see POSE)]

com·posed (kəm·pōzd′), *adj.* calm; tranquil. —**com·pos·ed·ly** (kəm·pōz′id·li), *adv.*

com·pos·er (kəm·pōz′ər), *n.* person who composes, esp. a writer of music.

com·pos·ite (kəm·poz′it), *adj.* **1.** made up of various parts; compound. **2.** *Bot.* belonging to a group of plants, as the aster, daisy, etc., in which the florets are borne in dense heads. —*n.* **1.** *Bot.* composite plant. **2.** any composite thing. [< L *compositus* < *com-* together + *ponere* put] —**com·pos′ite·ly**, *adv.*

com·po·si·tion (kom′pə·zish′ən), *n.* **1.** make-up of anything; what is in it. **2.** a putting together of a whole. **3.** thing composed. **4.** act or art of composing prose or verse or a musical work. **5.** a short essay written as a school exercise. **6.** *Art* arrangement of parts to produce an esthetically satisfying whole. **7.** mixture of substances. **8.** settlement.

com·pos·i·tor (kəm·poz′ə·tər), *n.* typesetter.

com·post (kom′pōst), *n.* mixture of leaves, manure, etc., for fertilizing land. [< OF. See COMPOSITE.]

com·po·sure (kəm·pō′zhər), *n.* calmness; self-control.

com·pote (kom′pōt), *n.* **1.** *Am.* dish with a supporting stem for fruit, etc. **2.** stewed fruit. [< F. See COMPOSITE.]

com·pound[1] (*adj.* kom′pound, kom·pound′; *n.* kom′pound; *v.* kom·pound′, kəm-), *adj.* having more than one part. *Steamship* is a compound word. [< v.] —*n.* **1.** something made by combining parts. **2.** compound word. **3.** *Chem.* substance formed by chemical combination of two or more substances. [< adj.] —*v.* **1.** mix; combine. **2.** make by combining parts. **3.** settle (a quarrel or a debt) by a yielding on both sides. **4.** **compound a felony,** accept money not to prosecute a crime, etc. [< OF < L, < *com-* together + *ponere* put] —**com·pound′a·ble**, *adj.* —**com·pound′er**, *n.*

com·pound[2] (kom′pound), *n.* an enclosed yard with buildings in it, occupied by foreigners. [prob. < Malay *kampong*]

Compound E, cortisone.

Compound F, hydrocortisone.

compound interest, interest paid on both the original sum of money borrowed and on the unpaid interest added to it.

compound sentence, sentence made up of coördinate independent clauses. *Example:* He went out but she came. ▶ See clause for usage note.

com·pre·hend (kom′pri·hend′), *v.* **1.** understand. **2.** include; contain. [< L, < *com-* + *prehendere* seize] —**com′pre·hend′i·ble**, *adj.* —**com′pre·hend′ing·ly**, *adv.* —*Syn.* **1.** apprehend, grasp, perceive. **2.** comprise, embrace.

com·pre·hen·si·ble (kom′pri·hen′sə·bəl), *adj.* understandable. —**com′pre·hen′si·bil′i·ty**, **com′pre·hen′si·ble·ness**, *n.* —**com′pre·hen′si·bly**, *adv.*

com·pre·hen·sion (kom′pri·hen′shən), *n.* **1.** act or power of understanding; ability to get the meaning. **2.** act or fact of including. **3.** comprehensiveness.

com·pre·hen·sive (kom′pri·hen′siv), *adj.* **1.** including; including much. **2.** comprehending. —**com′pre·hen′sive·ly**, *adv.* —**com′pre·hen′sive·ness**, *n.* —*Syn.* **1.** inclusive, broad, wide, extensive. **2.** understanding.

com·press (*v.* kəm·pres′; *n.* kom′pres), *v.* squeeze together; make smaller by pressure. —*n.* pad of wet cloth applied to some part of the body to create pressure or to reduce inflammation. [< L *compressare*, ult. < *com-* together + *premere* press] —**com·pressed′**, *adj.* —**com·pres′sion**, *n.* —**com·pres′sive**, *adj.*

com·press·i·ble (kəm·pres′ə·bəl), *adj.* that can be compressed. —**com·press′i·bil′i·ty**, *n.*

com·pres·sor (kəm·pres′ər), *n.* **1.** one that compresses. **2.** in surgery, an instrument for compressing a part of the body. **3.** machine for compressing air, gas, etc.

com·pris·al, com·priz·al (kəm·prīz′əl), *n.* comprehension; inclusion.

com·prise, com·prize (kəm·prīz′), *v.*, **-prised, -pris·ing; -prized, -priz·ing.** consist of; include. [< F *compris*, pp. of *comprendre* < L *comprehendere*. See COMPREHEND.] —**com·pris′a·ble, com·priz′a·ble**, *adj.* —*Syn.* embrace.

com·pro·mise (kom′prə·mīz), *v.*, **-mised, -mis·ing.** —*v.* **1.** settle (a dispute) by agreeing that each will give up a part of what he demands. **2.** put under suspicion; put in danger. —*n.* **1.** settlement of a dispute by a partial yielding on both sides. **2.** result of such a settlement. **3.** anything halfway between two different things. **4.** a putting under suspicion. [< F < L *compromissum*. See COM-, PROMISE.] —**com′pro·mis′er**, *n.*

comp·trol·ler (kən·trōl′ər), *n.* controller (def. 1). —**comp·trol′ler·ship**, *n.*

com·pul·sion (kəm·pul′shən), *n.* **1.** act of compelling; use of force; force. **2.** state of being compelled. —**com·pul′sive**, *adj.* —**com·pul′sive·ly**, *adv.* —*Syn.* **1.** coercion. **2.** obligation

com·pul·so·ry (kəm·pul′sə·ri), adj. 1. required. 2. using force. —**com·pul′so·ri·ly**, adv. —**com·pul′so·ri·ness**, n.

com·punc·tion (kəm·pungk′shən), n. the pricking of conscience; regret; remorse. [< LL *compunctio* < L, < *com*- + *pungere* prick]

com·pute (kəm·pūt′), v., -put·ed, -put·ing. do by arithmetical work; reckon; calculate. [< L, < *com*- up + *putare* reckon. Doublet of COUNT¹.] —**com·put′a·ble**, adj. —**com·put′a·bil′i·ty**, n. —**com·pu·ta·tion** (kom′pyə·tā′shən), n.

com·put·er (kəm·pūt′ər), n. person or thing that computes, esp. a calculating machine which solves problems, either directly (if measurable quantities) by means of electrical impulses (ana-logue computer) or by having them coded mathematically (digital computer).

com·rade (kom′rad), n. 1. companion and friend; partner. 2. a fellow member of a union, political party, etc. [< F < Sp. *camarada* room-mate, ult. < L *camera* CHAMBER] —**com′rade-ship**, n. —Syn. 1. chum, pal.

con¹ (kon), adv. against a proposition, opinion, etc. —n. reason, person, etc., against. [short for L *contra* against]

con² (kon), v., conned, con·ning. learn well enough to remember; study. [var. of *can*¹]

con³ (kon), adj., v., conned, con·ning. Am., Slang. —adj. confidence, as in *con game, con man*. —v. to swindle. [short for *confidence*]

Con·a·kry (kon′ə·kri), n. seaport and capital of Guinea, in the W part.

con·cave (adj., v. kon·kāv′, kon′kāv, kong′-; n. kon′kāv, kong′-), adj., n., v., -caved, -cav·ing. —adj. hollow and curved like the inside of a circle or sphere. —n. a concave surface or thing. —v. make concave. [< L, < *com*- + *cavus* hollow] —**con·cave′ly**, adv. —**con·cave′ness**, n.

con·cav·i·ty (kon·kav′ə·ti), n., pl. -ties. 1. a concave condition or quality. 2. a concave surface or thing.

Concave lenses

con·ceal (kən·sēl′), v. 1. hide. 2. keep secret. [< OF < L, < *com*- + *celare* hide] —**con·ceal′-a·ble**, adj. —**con·ceal′er**, n. —**con·ceal′ment**, n. —Syn. 2. shroud, veil, cloak, mask.

con·cede (kən·sēd′), v., -ced·ed, -ced·ing. 1. admit as true; admit. 2. give (what is asked or claimed); grant; yield. [< L, < *com*- + *cedere* yield] —**con·ced′ed·ly**, adv. —**con·ced′er**, n.

con·ceit (kən·sēt′), n. 1. too high an opinion of oneself or of one's ability, importance, etc. 2. a fanciful notion; witty thought or expression. 3. a personal opinion. 4. a favorable opinion. 5. imagination; fancy. 6. thought. —v. 1. flatter. 2. imagine.

con·ceit·ed (kən·sēt′id), adj. having too high an opinion of oneself or one's ability, importance, etc.; vain. —**con·ceit′ed·ly**, adv. —**con·ceit′ed·ness**, n. —Syn. egotistical, proud.

con·ceiv·a·ble (kən·sēv′ə·bəl), adj. that can be conceived or thought of; imaginable. —**con·ceiv·a·bil′i·ty**, **con·ceiv′a·ble·ness**, n. —**con·ceiv′a·bly**, adv.

con·ceive (kən·sēv′), v., -ceived, -ceiv·ing. 1. form in the mind; think up; imagine. 2. have an idea or feeling; think. 3. put in words; express. 4. become pregnant. 5. become pregnant with. [< OF < L *concipere* take in < *com*- + *capere* take] —**con·ceiv′er**, n.

con·cen·trate (kon′sən·trāt), v., -trat·ed, -trat·ing, n. —v. 1. bring or come together to one place. 2. pay close attention; focus the mind. 3. make stronger, purer, or more intense; condense. —n. something that has been concentrated. [< L *com*- + *centrum* CENTER] —**con′cen·tra′tor**, n. —Syn. v. 1. gather, collect, assemble, focus. 3. intensify. —Ant. v. 1. disperse. 3. dilute.

con·cen·tra·tion (kon′sən·trā′shən), n. 1. a concentrating or being concentrated. 2. close attention. 3. something that has been concentrated. —Syn. 1. collection, gathering.

concentration camp, camp where political enemies, prisoners of war, and interned foreigners are held.

con·cen·tric (kən·sen′trik), adj. having the same center. —**con·cen′tri·cal**, adj. —**con·cen′-tri·cal·ly**, adv. —**con·cen·tric·i·ty** (kon′sən·tris′ə·ti), n.

Concentric circles

con·cept (kon′sept), n. general notion; idea of a class of objects; idea. [< L *conceptus*, pp. of *concipere* CONCEIVE]

con·cep·tion (kən·sep′shən), n. 1. act or power of conceiving. 2. a being conceived. 3. a becoming pregnant. 4. idea; impression. 5. design; plan. —**con·cep′tive**, adj.

con·cep·tu·al (kən·sep′chü·əl), adj. having to do with concepts or general ideas. —**con·cep′tu·al·ly**, adv.

con·cern (kən·sérn′), v. 1. have to do with; have an interest for; be the business or affair of. 2. concern oneself, a. take an interest; be busy. b. be troubled or worried; be anxious or uneasy. —n. 1. whatever has to do with a person or thing; important matter; business affair. 2. interest. 3. a troubled state of mind; worry; anxiety; uneasiness. 4. a business company; firm. 5. relation; reference. [< Med.L, relate to, < L *com*- together + *cernere* sift] —Syn. v. 1. affect, touch.

con·cern·ing (kən·sér′ning), prep. having to do with; regarding; relating to; about.

con·cern·ment (kən·sérn′mənt), n. 1. importance. 2. worry; anxiety. 3. affair.

con·cert (n., adj. kon′sərt, -sərt; v. kən·sért′), n. 1. a musical performance in which several musicians or singers take part. 2. agreement; harmony; union. 3. **in concert**, all together. —adj. used in concerts; for concerts. —v. arrange by agreement; plan or make together. [< F < Ital. *concerto* CONCERTO]

con·cert·ed (kən·sér′tid), adj. arranged by agreement; planned or made together; combined.

con·cer·ti·na (kon′sər·tē′nə), n. a small musical instrument somewhat like an accordion.

con·cer·to (kən·cher′tō), n., pl. -tos. a long musical composition for one or more principal instruments, such as a violin, piano, etc., accompanied by an orchestra. [< Ital. < L *concentus* symphony, harmony, ult. < *com*- together + *canere* sing]

con·ces·sion (kən·sesh′ən), n. 1. a conceding. 2. anything conceded or yielded; admission; acknowledgment. 3. something conceded or granted by a government or controlling authority; grant. 4. Am. place rented for a small business, as a newsstand, etc. —Syn. 4. franchise.

conch (kongk; konch), n., pl. conchs (kongks), con·ches (kon′chiz). a large, spiral sea shell. [< L < Gk. *konche*]

con·ci·erge (kon′si·ērzh′; Fr. kôN·syerzh′), n. 1. doorkeeper. 2. janitor. [< F]

con·cil·i·ate (kən·sil′i·āt), v., -at·ed, -at·ing. 1. win over; soothe. 2. gain (good will, regard, favor, etc.) by friendly acts. 3. reconcile; bring into harmony. [< L *conciliatus* < *concilium* COUN-CIL] —**con·cil′i·a′tion**, n. —**con·cil′i·a′tor**, n.

con·cil·i·a·to·ry (kən·sil′i·ə·tô′ri; -tō′-), **con·cil·i·a·tive** (-i·ā′tiv), adj. tending to win over, soothe, or reconcile. —**con·cil′i·a·to′ri·ly**, adv. —**con·cil′i·a·to′ri·ness**, n.

con·cise (kən·sis′), adj. expressing much in few words; brief but full of meaning. [< L *concisus* < *com*- + *caedere* cut] —**con·cise′ly**, adv. —**con·cise′ness**, n.

con·clave (kon′klāv; kong′-), n. 1. a private meeting. 2. a meeting of the cardinals for the election of a pope. 3. rooms where the cardinals meet in private for this purpose. [< L, < *com*- with + *clavis* key]

con·clude (kən·klüd′), v., -clud·ed, -clud·ing. 1. end; finish. 2. say in ending. 3. arrange; settle. 4. find out by thinking; reach (certain facts or opinions) as a result of reasoning; infer. 5. decide; resolve. [< L *concludere* < *com*- up + *claudere* close] —**con·clud′er**, n. —Syn. 1. terminate. 4. deduce.

con·clu·sion (kən·klü′zhən), n. 1. end. 2. the last main division of a speech, essay, etc. 3. a final result; outcome. 4. arrangement; settlement. **5.** decision, judgment, or opinion reached by reasoning. **6. in conclusion,** finally; lastly; to conclude. **—Syn. 1.** termination. **5.** inference.

con·clu·sive (kən-klü′siv), *adj.* decisive; convincing; final. **—con·clu′sive·ness,** *n.*

con·coct (kon-kokt′; kən-), *v.* prepare; make up. [< L *concoctus* < *com–* together + *coquere* cook] **—con·coct′er,** *n.* **—con·coc′tion,** *n.*

con·com·i·tant (kon-kom′ə-tənt; kən-), *adj.* accompanying; attending. **—n.** an accompanying thing, quality, or circumstance; accompaniment. [< L, < *com–* + *comitari* accompany]

con·cord (kon′kôrd; kong′-), *n.* **1.** agreement; harmony; peace. **2.** a harmonious combination of tones sounded together. **3.** treaty. **4.** *Gram.* agreement in number, person, case, or gender of a word or element with another word or element, usually within the same sentence. In "he walk," the elements are not in concord; in "he walks," the elements are in concord. [< F < L *concordia,* ult. < *com–* together + *cor* heart]

Con·cord (kong′kərd), *n.* **1.** town in E Massachusetts; the second battle of the American Revolution, April 19, 1775. **2.** capital of New Hampshire, in the S part.

con·cord·ance (kon-kôr′dəns; kən-), *n.* **1.** agreement; harmony. **2.** an alphabetical list of the principal words of a book with references to the passages in which they occur.

con·cord·ant (kon-kôr′dənt; kən-), *adj.* agreeing; harmonious. **—con·cord′ant·ly,** *adv.*

con·cor·dat (kon-kôr′dat), *n.* **1.** agreement; compact. **2.** a formal agreement between the pope and a government about church affairs. [< F < LL *concordatum,* pp. of *concordare* make harmonious]

con·course (kon′kôrs; kong′-; -kōrs), *n.* **1.** a running, flowing, or coming together. **2.** crowd. **3.** *Am.* place where crowds come. **4.** *Am.* an open space in a railroad station. **5.** driveway; boulevard. [< OF < L *concursus* < *com–* together + *currere* run]

con·crete (*adj., n., and v. 1* kon′krēt, kon-krēt′; *v. 2* kon·krēt′), *adj., n., v.,* –**cret·ed,** –**creting.** **—adj. 1.** existing of itself in the material world, not merely in idea or as a quality; real. **2.** not abstract or general; specific; particular. **3.** naming a thing, esp. something perceived by the senses. *Sugar* is a concrete noun; *sweetness* is an abstract noun. **4.** made of concrete. **5.** formed into a mass; solid; hardened. **—n.** mixture of crushed stone or gravel, sand, cement, and water that hardens as it dries. **—v. 1.** cover with concrete. **2.** form or mix into a mass; harden into a mass. [< L *concretus* < *com–* together + *crescere* grow] **—con·crete′ness,** *n.*

con·cre·tion (kon-krē′shən), *n.* **1.** a forming into a mass; a solidifying. **2.** a solidified mass; hard formation.

con·cu·bine (kong′kyə-bīn; kon′-), *n.* **1.** woman who lives with a man without being legally married to him. **2.** wife who has an inferior rank, rights, etc. [< L, < *com–* with + *cubare* lie] **—con·cu·bi·nage** (kon·kū′bə·nij), *n.*

con·cu·pis·cent (kon-kū′pə-sənt), *adj.* **1.** eagerly desirous. **2.** lustful; sensual. [< L *concupiscens,* ult. < *com–* (intensive) + *cupere* desire] **—con·cu′pis·cence,** *n.*

con·cur (kən-kér′), *v.,* –**curred,** –**cur·ring. 1.** be of the same opinion; agree. **2.** work together. **3.** come together; happen at the same time. [< L, < *com–* together + *currere* run]

con·cur·rence (kən-kér′əns), **con·cur·ren·cy** (-ən·si), *n.* **1.** having the same opinion; agreement. **2.** a working together. **3.** a happening at the same time. **4.** a coming together.

con·cur·rent (kən-kér′ənt), *adj.* **1.** existing side by side; happening at the same time. **2.** coöperating. **3.** having equal authority or jurisdiction; coördinate. **4.** agreeing; consistent; harmonious. **5.** coming together; meeting in a point. **—con·cur′rent·ly,** *adv.*

con·cus·sion (kən-kush′ən), *n.* **1.** a sudden, violent shaking; shock. **2.** injury to the brain, spine, etc., caused by a blow, fall, or other shock. [< L *concussio* < *concutere* shake violently

< *com–* (intensive) + *quatere* shake]

con·demn (kən-dem′), *v.* **1.** express strong disapproval of. **2.** pronounce guilty of a crime or wrong. **3.** doom: *condemned to death.* **4.** declare not sound or suitable for use. **5.** *Am.* take for public use under special provision of the law. [< OF < L, < *com–* + *damnare* cause loss to, condemn] **—con·dem·na·ble** (kən-dem′nə-bəl), *adj.* **—con·dem·na·to·ry** (kən-dem′nə-tô′ri; -tō′-), *adj.* **—con·demn·er** (kən-dem′ər), *n.* **—con·demn′ing·ly,** *adv.* **—Syn. 1.** denounce, damn. **2.** convict. **—Ant. 1.** commend. **2.** acquit.

con·dem·na·tion (kon′dem-nā′shən; -dəm-), *n.* **1.** a condemning or being condemned. **2.** cause or reason for condemning.

con·den·sa·tion (kon′den-sā′shən), *n.* **1.** a condensing or being condensed. **2.** something condensed; condensed mass. **3.** act of changing a gas or vapor to a liquid.

con·dense (kən-dens′), *v.,* –**densed,** –**dens·ing. 1.** make or become denser or more compact. **2.** make stronger; concentrate. **3.** change from a gas or vapor to a liquid. **4.** put into fewer words; express briefly. [< L, < *com–* + *densus* thick] **—con·den′sa·ble, con·den′si·ble,** *adj.* **—con·den′sa·bil′i·ty, con·den′si·bil′i·ty,** *n.* **—Syn. 1.** compress. **4.** reduce, contract, shorten.

con·dens·er (kən-den′sər), *n.* **1.** person or thing that condenses something. **2.** *Elect.* device for receiving and holding a charge of electricity. **3.** apparatus for changing gas or vapor into a liquid. **4.** strong lens or lenses for concentrating light upon a small area.

con·de·scend (kon′di-send′), *v.* come down willingly or graciously to the level of one's inferiors in rank. [< LL *condescendere.* See COM–, DESCEND.] **—con′de·scen′sion, con′de·scend′ence,** *n.* **—Syn.** deign, stoop, vouchsafe.

con·dign (kən-dīn′), *adj.* deserved; adequate; fitting: *condign punishment.* [< F < L *condignus* very worthy < *com–* completely + *dignus* worthy]
➤ Because **condign** is so often coupled with *punishment,* it is sometimes misunderstood and used as a synonym for *severe.*

con·di·ment (kon′də-mənt), *n.* something used to give flavor and relish to food, such as pepper and spices. [< L *condimentum* spice < *condire* put up, preserve]

con·di·tion (kən-dish′ən), *n.* **1.** state in which a person or thing is. **2.** good condition: *keep in condition.* **3.** rank; social position. **4.** thing on which something else depends. **5.** something demanded as an essential part of an agreement. **6.** a restricting or limiting circumstance. **7. on condition that, if. —v. 1.** put in good condition. **2.** be a condition of. **3.** subject to a condition. **4.** make conditions; make it a condition. **5.** adapt or modify by shifting a response to a different stimulus. [< L *condicio* agreement < *com–* together + *dicere* say] **—con·di′tion·er,** *n.*

con·di·tion·al (kən-dish′ən-əl), *adj.* **1.** depending on something else; not absolute; limited. **2.** expressing or containing a condition. **—con·di′tion·al′i·ty,** *n.* **—con·di′tion·al·ly,** *adv.*

con·dole (kən-dōl′), *v.,* –**doled,** –**dol·ing.** express sympathy; sympathize. [< L, < *com–* with + *dolere* grieve, suffer] **—con·do′lence, con·dole′ment,** *n.* **—con·dol′ing·ly,** *adv.*

con·done (kən-dōn′), *v.,* –**doned,** –**don·ing.** forgive; overlook. [< L, < *com–* up + *donare* give] **—con·do·na·tion** (kon′dō-nā′shən), *n.* **—con·don′er,** *n.*

con·dor (kon′dər), *n.* a large American vulture with a bare neck and head. [< Sp. < Peruvian *cuntur*]

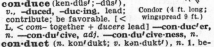

Condor (4 ft. long; wingspread 9 ft.).

con·duce (kən-düs′; -dūs′), *v.,* –**duced,** –**duc·ing.** lead; contribute; be favorable. [< L, < *com–* together + *ducere* lead] **—con·duc′er,** *n.* **—con·du′cive,** *adj.* **—con·du′cive·ness,** *n.*

con·duct (*n.* kon′dukt; *v.* kən-dukt′), *n.* **1.** behavior; way of acting. **2.** direction; management.

3. leading; guidance. [< *v.*] —*v.* 1. act in a certain way; behave: *she always conducts herself like a lady.* 2. direct; manage. 3. direct (an orchestra, etc.) as leader. 4. lead; guide. 5. transmit (heat, electricity, etc.); be a channel for. [< L *conductus* < *com*– together + *ducere* lead] —con·duct′i·ble, *adj.* —con·duct′i·bil′i·ty, *n.* —con·duc′tive, *adj.* —Syn. *n.* 1. deportment.

con·duct·ance (kən·duk′təns), *n. Elect.* power of conducting electricity as affected by the shape, length, etc., of the conductor.

con·duc·tion (kən·duk′shən), *n.* 1. transmission of heat, electricity, etc., by the transferring of energy from one particle to another. 2. a conveying: *conduction of water in a pipe.*

con·duc·tiv·i·ty (kon′duk·tiv′ə·ti), *n.* power of conducting heat, electricity, etc.

con·duc·tor (kən·duk′tər), *n.* 1. person who conducts; director; manager; leader; guide. 2. director of an orchestra, chorus, etc. 3. person in charge of a streetcar, bus, railroad train, etc. 4. thing that transmits heat, electricity, light, sound, etc. 5. *Am.* a lightning rod.

con·duit (kon′dit; -dū·it), *n.* 1. channel or pipe for carrying liquids long distances. 2. tube or underground passage for electric wires. [< OF < Med.L *conductus* a leading, a pipe < L, contraction < *com*– together + *ducere* draw]

cone (kōn), *n., v.,* coned, con·ing. —*n.* 1. solid with a flat, round base that tapers evenly to a point at the top. 2. *Geom.* surface traced by a moving straight line, one point of which is fixed, that constantly touches a fixed curve. 3. anything shaped like a cone. 4. *Am.* a cone-shaped, edible shell filled with ice cream. 5. *Bot.* part that bears the seeds on pine, cedar, fir, and other evergreen trees. 6. in machines, a cone-shaped part. —*v.* shape like a cone. [< L < Gk. *konos* pine cone, cone]

Cone

Con·el·rad (kon′əl·rad), *n.* a system for broadcasting instructions, etc., over radio stations by shifting frequencies, going on and off the air irregularly, etc., while keeping enemy airplanes from utilizing the beams of the station for navigation. [short for *Con(trol) (of) El(ectromagnetic) Rad(iation)*]

co·ney (kō′ni), *n., pl.* co·neys. cony.

con·fab·u·late (kon·fab′yə·lāt), *v.,* –lat·ed, –lat·ing. talk together informally and intimately; chat. [< L, ult. < *com*– together + *fabula* fable] —con·fab′u·la′tion, *n.*

con·fec·tion (kən·fek′shən), *n.* piece of candy, candied fruit, sugared nut, jam, etc. [< L *confectio* < *com*– up + *facere* make]

con·fec·tion·er (kən·fek′shən·ər), *n.* person who makes and sells candies, ice cream, etc.

con·fec·tion·er·y (kən·fek′shən·er′i), *n., pl.* –er·ies. 1. candies, sweets, etc.; confections. 2. business of making or selling confections. 3. *Am.* place where confections, ice cream, etc., are made or sold; candy shop.

con·fed·er·a·cy (kən·fed′ər·ə·si), *n., pl.* –cies. 1. union of countries or states; group of people joined together for a special purpose. 2. league; alliance. 3. conspiracy. 4. **the Confederacy,** *Am.* group of eleven Southern States that seceded from the United States in 1860 and 1861. —Syn. 1. confederation, federation.

con·fed·er·ate (*adj., n.* kən·fed′ər·it; *v.* kən·fed′ər·āt), *adj., n., v.,* –at·ed, –at·ing. —*adj.* 1. joined together for a special purpose; allied. 2. **Confederate,** of or belonging to the Confederacy. —*n.* 1. country, person, etc., joined with another for a special purpose; ally; companion. 2. accomplice; partner in crime. 3. **Confederate,** *Am.* person who lived in and supported the Confederacy. —*v.* join (countries, people, etc.) together for a special purpose; ally. [< L, < *com*– together + *foedus* league] —Syn. *n.* 2. accessory.

con·fed·er·a·tion (kən·fed′ər·ā′shən), *n.* 1. a joining or being together in a league; federation. 2. group of countries, states, etc., joined together for a special purpose; league. 3. **the Confederation,** *Am.* the confederation of the American States from 1781 to 1789.

con·fer (kən·fér′), *v.,* –ferred, –fer·ring. 1. consult together; exchange ideas; talk things over. 2. give; bestow: *confer a medal.* [< L, < *com*– together + *ferre* bring] —con·fer′ment, *n.*

con·fer·ee (kon′fər·ē′), *n. Am.* person who takes part in a conference.

con·fer·ence (kon′fər·əns), *n.* 1. a meeting of interested persons to discuss a particular subject. 2. consultation with a person or a group of persons. 3. association of schools, churches, etc., joined together for some special purpose. 4. act of bestowing; conferment.

con·fess (kən·fes′), *v.* 1. acknowledge; admit; own up. 2. admit one's guilt. 3. tell (one's sins) to a priest in order to obtain forgiveness. 4. acknowledge one's belief in or adherence to. [< LL *confessare,* ult. < *com*– + *fateri* confess] —con·fess′ed·ly, *adv.* —con·fess′er, *n.*

con·fes·sion (kən·fesh′ən), *n.* 1. acknowledgment; admission; owning up. 2. admission of guilt. 3. the telling of one's sins to a priest in order to obtain forgiveness. 4. thing confessed. 5. acknowledgment of belief; profession of faith. 6. belief acknowledged; creed.

con·fes·sion·al (kən·fesh′ən·əl), *n.* a small booth where a priest hears confessions. —*adj.* of or having to do with confession.

con·fes·sor (kən·fes′ər), *n.* 1. person who confesses. 2. priest who has the authority to hear confessions.

con·fet·ti (kən·fet′i), *n.* 1. bits of colored paper thrown about at carnivals, weddings, etc. 2. candies. [< Ital., pl., comfits. See CONFECTION.]

con·fi·dant (kon′fə·dant′; kon′fə·dant), *n.* person trusted with one's secrets, private affairs, etc.; close friend.

con·fi·dante (kon′fə·dant′; kon′fə·dant), *n.* a woman confidant.

con·fide (kən·fīd′), *v.,* –fid·ed, –fid·ing. 1. tell as a secret. 2. entrust secrets, private affairs, etc. 3. hand over (a task, person, etc.) in trust; give to another for safekeeping. 4. put trust; have faith. [< L, < *com*– completely + *fidere* trust]

con·fi·dence (kon′fə·dəns), *n.* 1. firm belief; trust. 2. firm belief in oneself and one's abilities. 3. boldness; too much boldness. 4. a feeling of trust; assurance that a person will not tell others what is said. 5. thing told as a secret. —*adj. Am.* having to do with swindling that takes advantage of the victim's confidence. —Syn. *n.* 1. conviction. 2. assurance, self-reliance. 3. presumption.

confidence game, *Am.* fraud in which the swindler persuades his victim to trust him.

confidence man, *Am.* swindler who persuades his victim to trust him.

con·fi·dent (kon′fə·dənt), *adj.* 1. firmly believing; certain; sure. 2. sure of oneself and one's abilities. 3. too bold; too sure. —*n.* close, trusted friend; confidant. —con′fi·dent·ly, *adv.*

con·fi·den·tial (kon′fə·den′shəl), *adj.* 1. told or written as a secret. 2. showing confidence. 3. trusted with secrets, private affairs, etc. —con′fi·den′tial·ly, *adv.* —con′fi·den′tial·ness, *n.*

con·fig·u·ra·tion (kən·fig′yə·rā′shən), *n.* 1. the relative position of parts; manner of arrangement. 2. form; shape; outline. —con·fig′u·ra′tion·al, *adj.*

con·fine (*v.* kən·fīn′; *n.* kon′fīn), *v.,* –fined, –fin·ing. —*v.* 1. keep within limits; restrict. 2. keep indoors; shut in. 3. imprison. 4. **be confined,** give birth to a child. —*n.* Usually, confines. boundary; border; limit. [< F, < *confins,* pl., bounds < L *confinium,* ult. < *com*– together + *finis* end, border] —con·fine′ment, *n.*

con·firm (kən·férm′), *v.* 1. prove to be true or correct; make certain. 2. approve by formal consent; approve; consent to. 3. strengthen; make firmer. 4. admit to full membership in a church after required study and preparation. [< OF < L, < *com*– + *firmus* firm] —con·firm′a·ble, *adj.* —Syn. 1. verify. 2. ratify.

con·fir·ma·tion (kon′fər·mā′shən), *n.* 1. a confirming. 2. thing that confirms; proof. 3. ceremony of admitting a person to full membership in a church after required study and preparation.

con·firm·a·to·ry (kən·fér′mə·tô′ri; -tō′-), **con·firm·a·tive** (-mə·tiv), *adj.* confirming.

con·firmed (kən·férmd′), *adj.* 1. firmly established; proved. 2. habitual; constant; chronic: *a confirmed invalid.* —**con·firm·ed·ly** (kən·fér′mid·li), *adv.* —**con·firm′ed·ness,** *n.*

con·fis·cate (kon′fis·kāt), *v.,* -cat·ed, -cat·ing. 1. seize for the public treasury. 2. seize by authority; take and keep. [< L, orig., lay away in a chest, < *com-* + *fiscus* chest, public treasury] —**con′fis·ca′tion,** *n.* —**con′fis·ca′tor,** *n.* —Syn. 1, 2. appropriate.

con·fis·ca·to·ry (kən·fis′kə·tô′ri; -tō′-), *adj.* 1. of or like confiscation; tending to confiscate. 2. confiscating.

con·fla·gra·tion (kon′flə·grā′shən), *n.* a big fire. [< L *conflagratio* < *com-* up + *flagrare* burn]

con·flict (*v.* kən·flikt′; *n.* kon′flikt), *v.* 1. fight; struggle. 2. be directly opposed; disagree; clash. —*n.* 1. fight; struggle. 2. direct opposition; disagreement; clash. [< L *conflictus* < *com-* together + *fligere* strike] —**con·flic′tion,** *n.* —**con·flic′tive,** *adj.* —Syn. *n.* 1. strife. 2. collision.

con·flu·ence (kon′flü·əns), *n.* 1. a flowing together, as of two rivers. 2. a coming together of people or things; throng. [< L, < *com-* together + *fluere* flow] —**con′flu·ent,** *adj.*

con·flux (kon′fluks), *n.* confluence.

con·form (kən·fôrm′), *v.* 1. act according to law or rule; be in agreement with generally accepted standards of business, law, conduct, or worship. 2. become the same in form; correspond in form or character. 3. make similar. 4. adapt. [< OF < L, < *com-* + *formare* shape < *forma* a shape] —**con·form′er,** *n.* —Syn. 4. adjust, accommodate, suit.

con·form·a·ble (kən·fôr′mə·bəl), *adj.* 1. similar. 2. adapted; suited. 3. in agreement; agreeable; harmonious. 4. obedient; submissive. —**con·form′a·ble·ness,** *n.* —**con·form′a·bly,** *adv.*

con·form·ance (kən·fôr′məns), *n.* conformity.

con·for·ma·tion (kon′fôr·mā′shən), *n.* 1. structure; shape; form of a thing resulting from the arrangement of its parts. 2. a symmetrical arrangement of the parts of a thing. 3. a conforming; adaptation.

con·form·ist (kən·fôr′mist), *n.* person who conforms.

con·form·i·ty (kən·fôr′mə·ti), *n., pl.* -ties. 1. similarity; corresponding; agreement. 2. action in agreement with generally accepted standards of business, law, conduct, or worship; fitting oneself and one's actions to the ideas of others; compliance. 3. submission.

con·found (kon·found′, kən- *for* 1-3; kon′-found′ *for* 4), *v.* 1. confuse; mix up. 2. be unable to tell apart. 3. surprise and puzzle. 4. damn. *Confound* is used as a mild oath. [< OF < L, < *com-* together + *fundere* pour] —**con·found′er,** *n.*

con·found·ed (kon′foun′did; kən-), *adj.* 1. damned. *Confounded* is used as a mild oath. 2. hateful; detestable. —**con·found′ed·ly,** *adv.*

con·front (kən·frunt′), *v.* 1. meet face to face; stand facing. 2. face boldly; oppose. 3. bring face to face; place before. [< F < Med.L, < L *com-* together + *frons* forehead] —**con·fron·ta·tion** (kon′frun·tā′shən), **con·front′ment,** *n.*

Con·fu·cius (kən·fū′shəs), *n.* 551?-478 B.C., Chinese philosopher and moral teacher. He taught that the chief virtues are respect for parents and ancestors, kindliness, faithfulness, intelligence, and proper behavior. —**Con·fu′cian,** *adj., n.* —**Con·fu′cian·ism,** *n.* —**Con·fu′cian·ist,** *n.*

con·fuse (kən·fūz′), *v.,* -fused, -fus·ing. 1. mix up; throw into disorder. 2. bewilder. 3. be unable to tell apart; mistake (one thing for another). 4. make uneasy and ashamed; embarrass. [< F < L *confusus,* pp. of *confundere.* See CONFOUND.] —**con·fus·ed·ly** (kən·fūz′id·li; -fūzd′li), *adv.* —**con·fus′ed·ness,** *n.* —**con·fus′ing·ly,** *adv.* —Syn. 2. puzzle, perplex. 3. confound. 4. disconcert. —Ant. 3. distinguish.

con·fu·sion (kən·fū′zhən), *n.* 1. act or fact of confusing. 2. confused condition; disorder. 3. failure to distinguish clearly. 4. bewilderment. 5. uneasiness and shame. —**con·fu′sion·al,** *adj.* —Syn. 4. perplexity. 5. embarrassment.

con·fute (kən·fūt′), *v.,* -fut·ed, -fut·ing. 1. prove (an argument, testimony, etc.) to be false or incorrect. 2. prove (a person) to be wrong; overcome by argument. 3. make useless. [< L *confutare*] —**con·fu·ta·tion** (kon′fyü·tā′shən), *n.* —**con·fut′er,** *n.*

Cong., Congress; Congressional.

con·ga (kong′gə), *n.* a Cuban dance.

con·geal (kən·jēl′), *v.* 1. freeze. 2. thicken; stiffen. [< OF < L, < *com-* up + *gelare* freeze] —**con·geal′a·ble,** *adj.* —**con·geal′er,** *n.* —**con·geal′ment,** *n.*

con·gen·ial (kən·jēn′yəl), *adj.* 1. having similar tastes and interests; getting on well together. 2. agreeable; suitable: *he seeks more congenial work.* [< L, < *com-* together + *genialis* < *genius* spirit] —**con·ge·ni·al·i·ty** (kən·jē′ni·al′ə·ti), **con·gen′ial·ness,** *n.* —**con·gen′ial·ly,** *adv.*

con·gen·i·tal (kən·jen′ə·təl), *adj.* present at birth. [< L *congenitus* born with. See GENITAL.] —**con·gen′i·tal·ly,** *adv.*

con·ger (kong′gər), or **conger eel,** *n.* a large ocean eel that is caught for food along the coasts of Europe. [< OF < L < Gk. *gongros*]

con·gest (kən·jest′), *v.* 1. fill too full; overcrowd. 2. *Pathol.* cause too much blood to gather in (one part of the body). 3. become too full of blood. [< L *congestus* < *com-* together + *gerere* carry] —**con·ges′tion,** *n.* —**con·ges′tive,** *adj.*

con·glom·er·ate (*v.* kən·glom′ər·āt; *adj., n.* kən·glom′ər·it), *v.,* -at·ed, -at·ing, *adj., n.* —*v.* gather in a rounded mass. —*adj.* 1. gathered into a rounded mass; clustered. 2. made up of miscellaneous materials gathered from various sources. —*n.* 1. mass formed of fragments. 2. rock consisting of pebbles, gravel, etc., held together by a cementing material. [< L, < *com-* + *glomus* ball] —**con·glom′er·a′tion,** *n.*

Con·go (kong′gō), *n.* 1. the, republic in C Africa, formerly the Belgian Congo. 2. river in C Africa, flowing from SE Belgian Congo to the Atlantic.

Congo Republic, republic in C Africa on the Atlantic, formerly part of French Equatorial Africa.

congo snake or **eel,** *Am.* an eellike amphibian that has very small, weak legs.

con·grat·u·late (kən·grach′ə·lāt), *v.,* -lat·ed, -lat·ing. express one's pleasure at the happiness or good fortune of. [< L, < *com-* + *gratulari* show joy] —**con·grat′u·la′tor,** *n.* —**con·grat·u·la·to·ry** (kən·grach′ə·lə·tô′ri; -tō′-), *adj.*

con·grat·u·la·tion (kən·grach′ə·lā′shən), *n.* 1. act of congratulating. 2. Usually, **congratulations.** expression of pleasure at another's happiness or good fortune.

con·gre·gate (kong′grə·gāt), *v.,* -gat·ed, -gating, *adj.* —*v.* come together into a crowd or mass. —*adj.* assembled; collected. [< L *congregatus* < *com-* together + *grex* flock]

con·gre·ga·tion (kong′grə·gā′shən), *n.* 1. act of congregating. 2. a gathering of people or things; assembly. 3. group of people gathered together for religious worship. 4. a religious community or order with a common rule but not under solemn vows.

con·gre·ga·tion·al (kong′grə·gā′shən·əl), *adj.* 1. of a congregation; done by a congregation. 2. **Congregational,** of or belonging to Congregationalism or Congregationalists.

con·gre·ga·tion·al·ism (kong′grə·gā′shən·əl·iz′əm), *n.* 1. system of church government in which each individual church governs itself. 2. **Congregationalism,** principles and system of organization of a Protestant denomination in which each individual church governs itself. —**con′gre·ga′tion·al·ist, Con′gre·ga′tion·al·ist,** *n., adj.*

con·gress (kong′gris), *n.* 1. the lawmaking body of a nation, esp. of a republic. 2. **Congress,** *Am.* a. the national lawmaking body of the United States, consisting of the Senate and

House of Representatives. **b.** the body of senators and representatives for each term of two years for which representatives are elected. **3.** a formal meeting of representatives to discuss some subject. —*v.* meet in congress. [< L *congressus* < *com*- together + *gradi* go]

con·gres·sion·al (kən-gresh′ən-əl), *adj. Am.* **1.** of a congress. **2.** Congressional, of Congress.

con·gress·man (kong′gris·mən), *n., pl.* -men. Often, Congressman. *Am.* **1.** member of Congress. **2.** member of the House of Representatives.

con·gress·wom·an (kong′gris·wŭm′ən), *n., pl.* -wom·en. *Am.* a woman congressman.

con·gru·ent (kong′grŭ·ənt), *adj.* **1.** agreeing; harmonious. **2.** *Geom.* exactly coinciding. [< L, < *congruere* agree] —**con′gru·ence, con′gru·en·cy,** *n.* —**con′gru·ent·ly,** *adv.*

con·gru·i·ty (kən-grū′ə·ti), *n., pl.* -ties. **1.** agreement; harmony. **2.** *Geom.* the exact coincidence of lines, angles, figures, etc. **3.** point of agreement.

con·gru·ous (kong′grŭ·əs), *adj.* **1.** agreeing; harmonious. **2.** fitting; appropriate. **3.** *Geom.* exactly coinciding. —**con′gru·ous·ly,** *adv.* —**con′gru·ous·ness,** *n.* —Ant. **1.** disagreeing.

con·ic (kon′ik), **con·i·cal** (-ə·kəl), *adj.* **1.** cone-shaped; like a cone. **2.** of a cone. —**con′i·cal·ly,** *adv.*

co·ni·fer (kō′nə·fər; kon′ə-), *n.* any of a large group of trees and shrubs, most of which are evergreen and bear cones. [< L, < *conus* cone (< Gk. *konos*) + *ferre* to bear] —**co·nif·er·ous** (kō·nif′ər·əs), *adj.*

conj., **1.** conjugation. **2.** conjunction.

con·jec·tur·al (kən-jek′chər·əl), *adj.* **1.** involving conjecture. **2.** inclined to conjecture. —**con·jec′tur·al·ly,** *adv.*

con·jec·ture (kən-jek′chər), *n., v.,* -tured, -tur·ing. —*n.* **1.** formation of an opinion without sufficient evidence for proof; guessing. **2.** a guess. —*v.* guess. [< L *conjectura* < *com*- together + *jacere* throw] —**con·jec′tur·a·ble,** *adj.* —**con·jec′tur·a·bly,** *adv.* —**con·jec′tur·er,** *n.* —Syn. *n.* **2.** supposition. —*v.* suppose.

con·join (kən-join′), *v.* unite. —**con·join′er,** *n.*

con·joint (kən-joint′; kon′joint), *adj.* **1.** joined together; united. **2.** joint. —**con·joint′ly,** *adv.*

con·ju·gal (kon′jə·gəl), *adj.* of marriage; having to do with marriage. [< L *conjugalis* < *com*- with + *jugum* yoke] —**con′ju·gal·ly,** *adv.*

con·ju·gate (*v.* kon′jə·gāt; *adj., n.* kon′jə·git, -gāt), *v.,* -gat·ed, -gat·ing, *adj., n.* —*v.* **1.** give the forms of (a verb) according to a systematic arrangement. **2.** join together; couple. —*adj.* joined together; coupled. —*n.* word derived from the same root as another. [< L, < *com*- with + *jugum* yoke] —**con′ju·ga′tive,** *adj.* —**con′ju·ga′tor,** *n.*

con·ju·ga·tion (kon′jə·gā′shən), *n.* **1.** systematic arrangement of the forms of a verb. **2.** group of verbs having similar forms in such an arrangement. **3.** act of giving the forms of a verb according to such an arrangement. **4.** a joining together; a coupling.

con·junc·tion (kən-jungk′shən), *n.* **1.** act of joining together; union; combination. **2.** word that connects words, phrases, clauses, or sentences. **3.** *Astron.* the apparent nearness of two or more heavenly bodies. [< L *conjunctio* < *com*- with + *jungere* join] ➤ **Conjunctions** introduce and tie clauses together and tie together series of words and phrases. **1.** ACCURATE CONJUNCTIONS. The fitting together of clauses by an exact use of conjunctions is a mark of mature, practiced writing. In everyday speech we get along with a relatively small number of conjunctions—*and, as, but, so, when, while,* and a few others. We don't bother to emphasize shades of meaning and exact relationships, which are suggested by pauses, tones of voice, gestures. In writing, accurate connectives go a long way toward making up for the loss of these oral means of holding ideas together. Some conjunctions vary in definiteness of meaning: *as* means *because,* but means it very weakly; *while* may mean *although* or *whereas,* but the core of its meaning relates to time, and careful writers restrict it to that. **2.**

WEIGHT. It is important for the conjunctions to be appropriate to other traits of style. Their weight should fit with the weight of other words and with the formality or informality of constructions. The chief fault in weight of conjunctions has to do with the conjunctive adverbs (*however, therefore, consequently* . . .) in ordinary, informal writing. These words are heavy and fit best in rather formal writing. *But* and *however,* for example, both connect statements in opposition, but one cannot always be substituted for the other. *But* fits in all levels, but *however* is often too formal or too heavy for informal writing: *The entrance and registration desk didn't strike me as beautiful. From here, however, I went upstairs and then I could see what they meant* [but from here . . .]. English has a number of long connecting phrases that are often used in place of shorter conjunctions: Football was distinctively a military pastime in Rome *in the same manner in which* [as] polo is among the soldiers today.

con·junc·ti·va (kon′jungk·tī′və), *n., pl.* -vas, -vae (-vē). *Anat.* the mucous membrane that covers the inner surface of the eyelids.

con·junc·tive (kən-jungk′tiv), *adj.* **1.** joining together. **2.** joined together; joint. **3.** like a conjunction. *When* is a conjunctive adverb. —*n.* a conjunctive word; conjunction. —**con·junc′tive·ly,** *adv.* ➤ **conjunctive adverbs. 1.** A number of words which are primarily adverbs are used also as connectives. They are called conjunctive adverbs (or relative adverbs). Their adverbial meaning remains rather prominent, so that they are relatively weak connectives and need special discussion. Except for *when* and *where* and *so* they are coördinating conjunctions and make compound sentences. The most common are: *accordingly, also, anyhow, anyway* (colloquial), *besides, consequently, furthermore, hence, however, indeed, likewise, moreover, namely, nevertheless, so, still, then, therefore, when, where, yet.* However [adverb] *the election goes, the public will lose. The results were disappointing; however* [conjunction], *we were not surprised. The lights were not yet* [adverb] *turned on. He had been appointed by the governor, yet* [conjunction] *he did not support him.* **2. Weight and Use.** The important fact about the conjunctive adverbs is that most of them are relatively heavy connectives. Except for *so, when,* and *where* they are most appropriate in formal writing.

3. Position. Conjunctive adverbs are often placed within their clauses instead of at the beginning. This helps take the initial stress from them and gives it to more important words. When they are so placed, they are usually set off by commas as in the sentences in paragraph 1 above.

4. Punctuation. The conventional rule is that a clause introduced by a conjunctive adverb is preceded by a semicolon. This is generally true but the semicolon is used not because of the conjunctive adverb but because the clauses are rather heavy and the connecting force of the conjunctive adverb relatively weak. With the lighter conjunctive adverbs, especially with *so, then,* and *yet,* a comma is often sufficient: *The morning had been a bore, so we wanted to make sure that we had a good time after lunch.*

con·junc·ti·vi·tis (kən-jungk′tə·vī′tis), *n. Pathol.* inflammation of the conjunctiva.

con·ju·ra·tion (kon′jŭ·rā′shən), *n.* **1.** act of invoking by a sacred name. **2.** magic form of words used in conjuring; magic spell.

con·jure (kun′jər; kon′-), *v.,* -jured, -jur·ing. **1.** compel (a spirit, devil, etc.) to appear or disappear by magic words. **2.** summon a devil, spirit, etc. **3.** cause to be or happen by magic. **4.** practice magic. **5. conjure up,** a. cause to appear in a magic way. b. cause to appear in the mind. [< OF < L *conjurare* make a compact < *com*- together + *jurare* swear] —**con′jur·er, con′jur·or,** *n.*

conk (kongk), *Slang.* —*n.* hit. —*v.* **1.** hit. **2. conk out,** break down. [dial. < *conk*(er) a blow on the nose < *conk* nose < *conch* shell]

Conn., Connecticut.

con·nect (kə·nekt′), *v.* **1.** join (one thing to

another); link (two things together). 2. join in some business or interest. 3. associate in the mind. 4. *Am.* run so that passengers can change from one train, bus, etc., to another without delay. [< L, < *com*— together + *nectere* tie] —con·nect′ed·ly, *adv.* —con·nect′er, con·nec′tor, *n.* ❯ Connected with and in connection with are wordy locutions, usually for *in* or *with: the environment in connection with a fraternity* (in a fraternity).

Con·nect·i·cut (kə·net′ə·kət), *n.* one of the New England States in NE United States. *Capital:* Hartford. *Abbrev.:* Conn.

con·nec·tion, *esp. Brit.* **con·nex·ion** (kə·nek′shən), *n.* 1. act of connecting. 2. condition of being joined together or connected; union. 3. thing that connects. 4. any kind of practical relation with another thing. 5. group of people associated in some way. 6. thinking of persons or things together. 7. *Am.* meeting of trains, ships, etc., so that passengers can change from one to the other without delay. 8. a relative. —con·nec′tion·al, *esp. Brit.* con·nex′ion·al, *adj.* —Syn. 2. junction. 3. bond, tie, link. 8. kin, kinsman.

con·nec·tive (kə·nek′tiv), *adj.* that connects. —*n.* 1. thing that connects. 2. word used to connect words, phrases, and clauses. Conjunctions and relative pronouns are connectives. —con·nec′tive·ly, *adv.* —con·nec·tiv·i·ty (kon′ek·tiv′ə·ti), *n.*

conn·ing tower (kon′ing), 1. an armored shelter on the deck of a warship. 2. a small tower on the deck of a submarine, used as an entrance and as a place for observation.

con·niv·ance (kə·nīv′əns), **con·niv·an·cy** (—ən·si), *n.* 1. act of conniving. 2. *Law.* pretended ignorance or secret encouragement of wrongdoing.

con·nive (kə·nīv′), *v.,* -nived, -niv·ing. 1. give aid to wrongdoing by not telling of it, or by helping it secretly. 2. coöperate secretly. [< L *connivere* shut the eyes, wink < *com*— together + *niv*— press] —con·niv′er, *n.*

con·nois·seur (kon′ə·sér′), *n.* expert; critical judge. [< F, ult. < L, < *co*— + *gnoscere* recognize]

con·no·ta·tion (kon′ə·tā′shən), *n.* 1. a connoting. 2. what is suggested in addition to the simple meaning. —con·no·ta·tive (kon′ə·tā′tiv; kə·nō′tə·-), *adj.* —con′no·ta′tive·ly, *adv.*

con·note (kə·nōt′), *v.,* -not·ed, -not·ing. suggest in addition to the literal meaning; imply. [< Med.L, < L *com*— with + *notare* to NOTE]

con·nu·bi·al (kə·nü′bi·əl; -nū′-), *adj.* of or having to do with marriage. [< L, < *com*— + *nubere* marry] —con·nu′bi·al′i·ty, *n.* —con·nu′bi·al·ly, *adv.*

con·quer (kong′kər), *v.* 1. get by fighting; win in war. 2. overcome by force; defeat. 3. be victorious. [< OF < L, < *com*— + *quaerere* seek] —con′quer·a·ble, *adj.* —con′quer·ing, *adj.* —con′quer·ing·ly, *adv.* —con′quer·or, *n.* —Syn. 2. vanquish, subdue.

con·quest (kon′kwest; kong′-), *n.* 1. act of conquering. 2. thing conquered; land, people, etc., conquered. 3. person whose love or favor has been won. [< OF, < *conquerre* CONQUER] —Syn. 1. victory, triumph. —Ant. 1. defeat.

con·quis·ta·dor (kon·kwis′tə·dôr), *n., pl.* -dors, -dores. 1. a Spanish conqueror in North or South America during the 16th century. 2. conqueror. [< Sp., < *conquistar* CONQUER]

Con·rad (kon′rad), *n.* Joseph, 1857–1924, English novelist, born in Poland.

con·san·guin·e·ous (kon′sang·gwin′i·əs), *adj.* descended from the same parent or ancestor. [< L, < *com*— together + *sanguis* blood] —con′san·guin′e·ous·ly, *adv.* —con′san·guin′i·ty, *n.*

con·science (kon′shəns), *n.* 1. ideas and feelings within a person that warn him of what is wrong. 2. conscientiousness. [< OF < L *conscientia* < *com*— + *scire* know] —con′science·less, *adj.*

con·sci·en·tious (kon′shi·en′shəs), *adj.* 1.

careful to do what one knows is right; controlled by conscience. 2. done with care to make it right. —con′sci·en′tious·ly, *adv.* —con′sci·en′tious·ness, *n.* —Syn. 1. upright, honorable. 2. particular, painstaking. —Ant. 1. unscrupulous. 2. careless, negligent.

conscientious objector, person whose beliefs forbid him to take an active part in warfare.

con·scion·a·ble (kon′shən·ə·bəl), *adj.* according to conscience; just. —con′scion·a·bly, *adv.*

con·scious (kon′shəs), *adj.* 1. aware; knowing. 2. able to feel. 3. known to oneself; felt: *conscious guilt.* 4. meant; intended: *a conscious lie.* 5. self-conscious; shy; embarrassed. [< L *conscius* < *com*— + *scire* know] —con′scious·ly, *adv.* —Syn. 4. deliberate.

con·scious·ness (kon′shəs·nis), *n.* 1. state of being conscious; awareness. 2. all the thoughts and feelings of a person. 3. awareness of what is going on about one.

con·script (*v.* kən·skript′; *adj., n.* kon′skript), *v.* 1. *Am.* compel by law to enlist in the army or navy; draft. 2. take for government use. —*adj.* conscripted; drafted. —*n.* a conscripted soldier or sailor. [< L *conscriptus* < *com*— down + *scribere* write] —con·scrip′tion, *n.*

con·se·crate (kon′sə·krāt), *v.,* -crat·ed, -crat·ing, *adj.* —*v.* 1. set apart as sacred; make holy: *a church is consecrated to worship.* 2. devote to a purpose. —*adj. Archaic.* consecrated. [< L *consecratus* < *com*— + *sacer* sacred] —con′se·cra′tion, *n.* —con′se·cra′tor, *n.* —Syn. *v.* 1. sanctify. 2. dedicate.

con·sec·u·tive (kən·sek′yə·tiv), *adj.* 1. following without interruption; successive. 2. made up of parts that follow each other in logical order. [< F, < L *consecutus* following closely < *com*— up + *sequi* follow] —con·sec′u·tive·ly, *adv.* —con·sec′u·tive·ness, *n.*

con·sen·sus (kən·sen′səs), *n.* general agreement. [< L, < *consentire* CONSENT]

con·sent (kən·sent′), *v.* agree; give approval or permission. —*n.* 1. agreement; permission. 2. harmony; accord. [< OF < L, < *com*— together + *sentire* feel, think] —con·sent′er, *n.* —Syn. *v.* assent, comply. —*n.* 1. approval, assent. —Ant. *v.* refuse, disapprove.

con·se·quence (kon′sə·kwens; -kwəns), *n.* 1. act or fact of following something as its effect. 2. result; effect. 3. a logical result; deduction; inference. 4. importance. —Syn. 2. outcome, issue.

con·se·quent (kon′sə·kwent; -kwənt), *adj.* 1. following as an effect; resulting. 2. following as a logical conclusion. 3. logically consistent. —*n.* thing that follows something else; result; effect. [< L *consequens,* ppr. of *consequi.* See CONSECUTIVE.]

con·se·quen·tial (kon′sə·kwen′shəl), *adj.* 1. following as an effect; resulting. 2. important. 3. self-important; pompous. —con·se·quen·ti·al·i·ty (kon′sə·kwen′shi·al′ə·ti), *n.* —con′se·quen′tial·ly, *adv.* —con′se·quen′tial·ness, *n.*

con·se·quent·ly (kon′sə·kwent′li; -kwənt-), *adv.* as a result; therefore.

con·ser·va·tion (kon′sér·vā′shən), *n.* 1. a protecting from harm, loss, or from being used up. 2. the official protection and care of forests, rivers, etc. 3. forest, etc., under official protection and care. —con′ser·va′tion·al, *adj.* —con′ser·va′tion·ist, *n.*

conservation of energy, principle that the total amount of energy in the universe does not vary.

con·serv·a·tive (kən·sér′və·tiv), *adj.* 1. inclined to keep things as they are; opposed to change. 2. Often, Conservative. of or belonging to a political party that opposes changes in national institutions. 3. cautious; moderate. —*n.* 1. a conservative person. 2. Often, Conservative. member of a conservative political party. 3. means of preserving. —con·serv′a·tism, *n.* —con·serv′a·tive·ness, *n.* —con·serv′a·tive·ly, *adv.*

con·serv·a·to·ry (kən·sér′və·tô′ri; -tō′-), *n.,*

pl. **–ries. 1.** greenhouse or glass-enclosed room for growing and displaying plants and flowers. **2.** U.S. school for instruction in music, art, or oratory. **3.** preservative.

con·serve (v. kən·sérv′; n. kon′sérv, kən·sérv′), v., **–served, –serv·ing,** n. —v. **1.** protect from harm, loss, or from being used up. **2.** preserve (fruit) with sugar. [< L, < com– + servare preserve] —n. Often, **conserves.** fruit preserved in sugar; jam. [< F, < conserver. See v.] —con·serv′a·ble, adj. —con·serv′er, n.

con·sid·er (kən·sid′ər), v. **1.** think about in order to decide. **2.** think to be; think of as. **3.** allow for; take into account. **4.** be thoughtful of (others and their feelings). **5.** think carefully; reflect. [< L considerare, orig., examine the stars, < com– + sidus star] —Syn. **1.** study, weigh, contemplate. **2.** deem, judge. **4.** respect, regard. **5.** deliberate, ponder.

con·sid·er·a·ble (kən·sid′ər·ə·bəl), adj. **1.** worth thinking about; important. **2.** not a little; much. —n. U.S. Colloq. not a little; much. —con·sid′er·a·bly, adv. **➤** considerable, considerably. In speech there is a tendency to use considerable as an adverb as well as an adjective: the night crew was considerable help (adj.); the night crew helped considerably or in informal speech the night crew helped considerable (adv.).

con·sid·er·ate (kən·sid′ər·it), adj. **1.** thoughtful of others′ feelings. **2.** deliberate. —con·sid′er·ate·ly, adv. —con·sid′er·ate·ness, n.

con·sid·er·a·tion (kən·sid′ər·ā′shən), n. **1.** act of thinking about in order to decide. **2.** something thought of as a reason. **3.** money or other payment. **4.** thoughtfulness for others and their feelings. **5.** sympathetic regard or respect. **6.** importance. —Syn. **1.** attention, deliberation. **3.** compensation, recompense. **5.** esteem.

con·sid·er·ing (kən·sid′ər·ing), prep. taking into account; making allowance for. —adv. taking everything into account: he does very well, considering.

con·sign (kən·sīn′), v. **1.** hand over; deliver. **2.** transmit; send. **3.** set apart; assign. **4.** Com. transmit, as by public carrier, esp. for safekeeping or sale. [< F < L consignare furnish with a seal < com– + signum seal] —con·sign′a·ble, adj. —con·sign·ee (kon′sī·nē′; –sī·nē′), n. —con·sign·or (kən·sīn′ər; kon′sī·nôr′; kon′si–), con·sign·er (kən·sīn′ər), n.

con·sign·ment (kən·sīn′mənt), n. **1.** act of consigning. **2.** shipment sent to a person or company for safekeeping or sale.

con·sist (kən·sist′), v. **1.** be made up; be formed. **2.** agree; be in harmony. **3.** consist in, be contained in; be made up of. [< L, come to a stand, exist, consist, < com– + sistere stand] —Syn. **1.** comprise.

con·sist·en·cy (kən·sis′tən·si), **con·sist·ence** (–təns), n., pl. **–cies; –ces. 1.** firmness; stiffness. **2.** degree of firmness or stiffness. **3.** a keeping to the same principles, course of action, etc. **4.** harmony; agreement.

con·sist·ent (kən·sis′tənt), adj. **1.** keeping or inclined to keep to the same principles, course of action, etc. **2.** in agreement; in accord. **3.** cohering. —con·sist′ent·ly, adv.

con·sis·to·ry (kən·sis′tə·ri), n., pl. **–ries. 1.** a church council or court. **2.** place where it meets.

con·so·la·tion (kon′sə·lā′shən), n. **1.** comfort. **2.** a comforting person, thing, or event. —con·sol·a·to·ry (kən·sol′ə·tô′ri; –tō′–), adj.

con·sole[1] (kən·sōl′), v., **–soled, –sol·ing.** comfort. [< L, < com– + solari soothe] —con·sol′a·ble, adj. —con·sol′er, n.

con·sole[2] (kon′sōl), n. **1.** the desk-like part of an organ containing the keyboard, stops, and pedals. **2.** a radio, television, or phonograph cabinet made to stand on the floor. **3.** a heavy, ornamental bracket. **4.** console table. [< F]

Console (def. 3)

con·sole table (kon′sōl), a narrow table, usually placed against a wall.

con·sol·i·date (kən·sol′ə·dāt), v., **–dat·ed, –dat·ing. 1.** unite; combine; merge. **2.** make or

become solid. **3.** Mil. organize and strengthen (a newly captured position) so that it can be used against the enemy. [< L, < com– + solidus solid] —con·sol′i·da′tion, n.

con·sol·ing (kən·sōl′ing), adj. that consoles. —con·sol′ing·ly, adv.

con·som·mé (kon′sə·mā′), n. a clear soup made by boiling meat in water. [< F, pp. of consommer CONSUMMATE]

con·so·nant (kon′sə·nənt), n. **1.** Phonet. a sound during the articulation of which the breath stream is impeded to a greater or lesser degree, as the sound of b in boy or the sound of f in fast. **2.** a letter representing such a sound. —adj. **1.** harmonious; in agreement; in accord. **2.** agreeing in sound. **3.** consonantal. [< L, < com– + together + sonare sound] —con′so·nance, n. —con′so·nant·ly, adv.

con·so·nan·tal (kon′sə·nan′təl), adj. having to do with a consonant or its sound.

con·sort (n. kon′sôrt; v. kən·sôrt′), n. **1.** husband or wife. **2.** an associate. **3.** ship accompanying another. —v. **1.** associate. **2.** agree; accord. [< F < L, sharer, < com– with + sors lot]

con·sor·ti·um (kən·sôr′shi·əm), n., pl. **–ti·a** (–shi·ə). an agreement among bankers of several nations to give financial aid to another nation. [< L, partnership]

con·spic·u·ous (kən·spik′yū·əs), adj. **1.** easily seen. **2.** worthy of notice; remarkable. [< L conspicuus visible < com– + specere look at] —con·spic′u·ous·ly, adv. —con·spic′u·ous·ness, n. —Syn. **1.** prominent, noticeable. **2.** notable, noteworthy. —Ant. **1.** obscure.

con·spir·a·cy (kən·spir′ə·si), n., pl. **–cies. 1.** secret planning with others to do something wrong. **2.** plot. —con·spir′a·tor, n. —Syn. **1.** intrigue.

con·spire (kən·spīr′), v., **–spired, –spir·ing. 1.** plan secretly with others to do something wrong; plot. **2.** act together. [< L, < com– + together + spirare breathe] —con·spir·a·to·ri·al (kən·spir′ə·tô′ri·əl; –tō′–), adj. —con·spir′er, n.

con·sta·ble (kon′stə·bəl; kun′–), n. a police officer; policeman. [< OF < LL comes stabuli count of the stable; later, chief household officer] —con′sta·ble·ship′, n.

con·stab·u·lar·y (kən·stab′yə·ler′i), n., pl. **–lar·ies. 1.** constables of a district. **2.** police force organized like an army; state police.

con·stant (kon′stənt), adj. **1.** always the same; not changing. **2.** never stopping. **3.** happening often or again and again. **4.** faithful; loyal; steadfast. —n. **1.** thing that is always the same. **2.** Math. quantity assumed to be invariable throughout a given discussion. [< L, < com– (intensive) + stare stand] —con′stan·cy, n. —Syn. adj. **1.** unchanged, steady. **2.** ceaseless, continuous. **4.** true, stanch. —Ant. adj. **1.** variable, varying. **4.** false, fickle.

Con·stan·tine the Great (kon′stən·tīn; –tēn), or **Constantine I,** 288?–337 A.D., Roman emperor from 324 to 337 A.D., who established the city of Constantinople.

Con·stan·ti·no·ple (kon′stan·tə·nō′pəl), n. former name of Istanbul.

con·stant·ly (kon′stənt·li), adv. **1.** without change. **2.** without stopping. **3.** often.

con·stel·la·tion (kon′stə·lā′shən), n. **1.** a group of stars: the Big Dipper is the easiest constellation to locate. **2.** division of the heavens occupied by such a group. [< LL, < L com– together + stella star]

con·ster·na·tion (kon′stər·nā′shən), n. great dismay; paralyzing terror. [< L, < consternare terrify, var. of consternere lay low < com– + sternere strew]

con·sti·pate (kon′stə·pāt), v., **–pat·ed, –pat·ing.** cause constipation in. [< L, < com– together + stipare press] —con′sti·pat′ed, adj.

con·sti·pa·tion (kon′stə·pā′shən), n. sluggish condition of the bowels.

con·stit·u·en·cy (kən·stich′ū·ən·si), n., pl. **–cies. 1.** voters in a district. **2.** the district; the people living there.

con·stit·u·ent (kən·stich′ū·ənt), adj. **1.** forming a necessary part; that composes. **2.** appointing; electing. **3.** having the power to make or change a political constitution. —*n.* **1.** a necessary part of a whole; component. **2.** person who votes or appoints; voter.

con·sti·tute (kon′stə·tūt; –tūt), *v.,* **–tut·ed, –tut·ing. 1.** make up; form. **2.** appoint; elect. **3.** set up; establish. **4.** give legal form to. [< L *constitutus* < *com–* + *statuere* set up] —**Syn. 1.** compose, comprise.

con·sti·tu·tion (kon′stə·tü′shən; –tū′–), *n.* **1.** way in which a person or thing is organized; nature; make-up: *a healthy constitution.* **2.** system of fundamental principles according to which a nation, state, or group is governed. **3.** document stating these principles. **4.** appointing; making. **5. Constitution,** *Am.* the constitution by which the United States is governed. It was drawn up in 1787 and became effective in 1788. Since then 24 amendments have been added to it.

con·sti·tu·tion·al (kon′stə·tü′shən·əl; –tū′–), *adj.* **1.** of or in the constitution of a person or thing. **2.** of, in, or according to the constitution of a nation, state, or group. **3.** for one's health. —*n. Colloq.* walk or other exercise taken for one's health. —**con′sti·tu′tion·al·ly,** *adv.* —**Syn.** *adj.* **1.** inherent.

con·sti·tu·tion·al·i·ty (kon′stə·tü′shən·al′ə·ti; –tū′–), *n.* quality of being constitutional.

con·strain (kən·strān′), *v.* **1.** force; compel. **2.** confine; imprison. **3.** repress; restrain. [< OF *constreindre* < L, < *com–* together + *stringere* pull tightly] —**con·strain′a·ble,** *adj.* —**con·strain′er,** *n.*

con·strained (kən·strānd′), *adj.* forced. —**con·strain·ed·ly** (kən·strān′id·li), *adv.*

con·straint (kən·strānt′), *n.* **1.** confinement. **2.** restraint. **3.** forced or unnatural manner. **4.** force; compulsion. [< OF, < *constreindre* CONSTRAIN]

con·strict (kən·strikt′), *v.* draw together; contract; compress. [< L *constrictus,* pp. of *constringere* CONSTRAIN] —**con·stric′tion,** *n.* —**con·stric′tive,** *adj.*

con·stric·tor (kən·strik′tər), *n.* **1.** snake that kills its prey by squeezing it with its coils. **2.** person or thing that constricts.

con·struct (*v.* kən·strukt′; *n.* kon′strukt), *v.* **1.** put together; build. **2.** *Geom.* draw (a figure, etc.) so as to fulfill given conditions. —*n.* thing constructed. [< L *constructus* < *com–* up + *struere* pile] —**con·struc′tor, con·struct′er,** *n.*

con·struc·tion (kən·struk′shən), *n.* **1.** act of constructing. **2.** way in which a thing is constructed. **3.** thing constructed; a building. **4.** meaning; explanation; interpretation. **5.** arrangement of words in a sentence, clause, phrase, etc. —**con·struc′tion·al,** *adj.*

con·struc·tive (kən·struk′tiv), *adj.* **1.** tending to construct; building up; helpful. **2.** structural. **3.** not directly expressed; inferred. —**con·struc′tive·ly,** *adv.* —**con·struc′tive·ness,** *n.*

con·strue (kən·strü′), *v.,* **–strued, –stru·ing. 1.** show the meaning of; explain; interpret. **2.** translate. **3.** analyze the arrangement and connection of words in (a sentence, clause, phrase, etc.). [< L *construere* CONSTRUCT] —**con·stru′a·ble,** *adj.* —**con·stru′er,** *n.*

con·sul (kon′səl), *n.* **1.** official appointed by a government to live in a foreign city to look after the business interests of his own country and to protect citizens of his country who are traveling or living there. **2.** either of the two chief magistrates of the ancient Roman republic. [< L, prob. orig., one who consults the senate] —**con′su·lar,** *adj.* —**con′sul·ship,** *n.*

con·su·late (kon′sə·lit), *n.* **1.** the duties, authority, and position of a consul. **2.** a consul's term of office. **3.** an official residence or offices of a consul.

consul general, *pl.* **consuls general,** consul of the highest rank.

con·sult (kən·sult′), *v.* **1.** seek information or advice from; refer to. **2.** exchange ideas; talk things over. **3.** take into consideration; have regard for. [< L, < *consulere* take counsel, consult] —**con·sult′a·ble,** *adj.* —**Syn. 2.** confer.

con·sult·ant (kən·sul′tənt), *n.* **1.** person who consults another. **2.** person who gives professional or technical advice.

con·sul·ta·tion (kon′səl·tā′shən), *n.* **1.** act of consulting. **2.** a meeting to exchange ideas or talk things over.

con·sume (kən·süm′), *v.,* **–sumed, –sum·ing. 1.** use up. **2.** eat or drink up. **3.** destroy; burn up. **4.** waste away; be destroyed. **5.** spend; waste (time, money, etc.). [< L, < *com–* + *sumere* take up] —**con·sum′a·ble,** *adj.* —**Syn. 1.** expend, exhaust. **5.** squander. —**Ant. 1.** conserve.

con·sum·er (kən·süm′ər), *n.* **1.** person or thing that consumes. **2.** person who uses food, clothing, or anything grown or made by producers.

con·sum·mate (*v.* kon′sə·māt; *adj.* kən·sum′it), *v.,* **–mat·ed, –mat·ing,** *adj.* —*v.* **1.** complete; fulfill. **2.** complete (a marriage) by sexual intercourse. —*adj.* complete; perfect; in the highest degree. [< L, < *consummare* bring to a peak < *com–* + *summa* highest degree] —**con·sum′mate·ly,** *adv.* —**con′sum·ma′tor,** *n.*

con·sum·ma·tion (kon′sə·mā′shən), *n.* completion; fulfillment.

con·sump·tion (kən·sump′shən), *n.* **1.** act of using up; use. **2.** amount used up. **3.** destruction. **4.** a wasting disease of the lungs or of some other part of the body; tuberculosis of the lungs.

con·sump·tive (kən·sump′tiv), *adj.* **1.** having or likely to have tuberculosis of the lungs. **2.** of tuberculosis of the lungs. **3.** tending to consume; destructive; wasteful. —*n.* person who has tuberculosis of the lungs. —**con·sump′tive·ly,** *adv.* —**con·sump′tive·ness,** *n.*

cont., **1.** containing. **2.** continued.

con·tact (kon′takt), *n.* **1.** condition of touching; touch. **2.** connection. **3.** *Elect.* connection between two conductors of electricity through which a current passes. **4.** device for producing such a connection. —*adj. Am.* in aeronautics, within sight of the ground: *contact flying.* —*v. Am., Colloq.* get in touch with; make a connection with. [< L *contactus* a touching < *com–* + *tangere* touch] ➤ **Contact** as a verb meaning "to get in touch with a person" is a use of the word by salesmen, and many people have unpleasant associations with being "contacted." Others object to using business terms in other contexts. The word in this sense is primarily commercial and familiar and should therefore be used infrequently in other circumstances.

contact lens, a plastic lens which covers the front of the eyeball by fitting under the eyelids and corrects defects in vision.

con·ta·gion (kən·tā′jən), *n.* **1.** the spreading of disease by contact. **2.** disease spread in this way; contagious disease. **3.** means by which disease is spread. **4.** the spreading of any influence from one person to another. [< L *contagio* touching. See CONTACT.]

con·ta·gious (kən·tā′jəs), *adj.* **1.** spread by contact: *scarlet fever is a contagious disease.* **2.** causing contagious diseases. —**con·ta′gious·ly,** *adv.* —**con·ta′gious·ness,** *n.*

con·tain (kən·tān′), *v.* **1.** have within itself; hold as contents; include. **2.** be capable of holding. **3.** be equal to: *a pound contains 16 ounces.* **4.** control; hold back; restrain: *the Western powers hope to contain Russian military strength.* **5.** *Math.* be divisible by without a remainder: *12 contains 2, 3, 4, and 6.* [< OF < L, < *com–* in + *tenere* hold] —**con·tain′a·ble,** *adj.* —**Syn. 1.** enclose. **2.** accommodate. **3.** comprise. **4.** repress.

con·tain·er (kən·tān′ər), *n.* box, can, jar, etc., used to hold something.

con·tain·ment (kən·tān′mənt), *n. International Relations,* the confinement of a hostile or potentially hostile political or military force within existing geographical boundaries.

con·tam·i·nate (kən·tam′ə·nāt), *v.,* **–nat·ed, –nat·ing.** make impure by contact. [< L *contaminatus* < *com–* + *tag–* touch. See CONTACT.] —**con·tam′i·na′tion,** *n.* —**con·tam′i·na′tive,** *adj.* —**con·tam′i·na′tor,** *n.* —**Syn.** taint, corrupt.

contd., continued.

con·temn (kən·tem′), v. treat with contempt; despise; scorn. [< L, < com– + temnere disdain, orig., cut] —**con·temn·er** (kən·tem′ər), **con·tem·nor** (kən·tem′nər), n.

con·tem·plate (kon′təm·plāt), v., –plat·ed, –plat·ing. 1. look at for a long time; gaze at. 2. think about for a long time; study carefully. 3. meditate. 4. expect; intend. [< L, < contemplari survey < com– + templum restricted area marked off for the taking of auguries] —**con·tem·pla·tive** (kon′təm·plā′tiv; kən·tem′plə–), adj. —**con′tem·pla′tor**, n. —Syn. 1. survey, regard.

con·tem·pla·tion (kon′təm·plā′shən), n. 1. act of looking at or thinking about something for a long time. 2. deep thought; meditation. 3. expectation; intention.

con·tem·po·ra·ne·ous (kən·tem′pə·rā′ni·əs), adj. belonging to the same period of time. —**con·tem′po·ra′ne·ous·ly**, adv. —**con·tem′po·ra′ne·ous·ness**, n.

con·tem·po·rar·y (kən·tem′pə·rer′i), adj., n., pl. –rar·ies. —adj. 1. belonging to or living in the same period of time. 2. of the same age or date. —n. 1. person who belongs to the same period of time as another or others. 2. person, magazine, etc., of the same age or date. [< L com– + temporarius < tempus time]

con·tempt (kən·tempt′), n. 1. the feeling that a person, act, or thing is mean, low, or worthless; scorn; a despising. 2. condition of being scorned or despised; disgrace. 3. Law. disobedience to or open disrespect for the rules or decisions of a law court, a lawmaking body, etc. [< L contemptus. See CONTEMN.] —Syn. 1. disdain.

con·tempt·i·ble (kən·tempt′tə·bəl), adj. deserving contempt or scorn. —**con·tempt′i·bil′i·ty, con·tempt′i·ble·ness**, n. —**con·tempt′i·bly**, adv.

con·temp·tu·ous (kən·temp′chú·əs), adj. showing contempt; scornful. —**con·temp′tu·ous·ly**, adv. —**con·temp′tu·ous·ness**, n.

con·tend (kən·tend′), v. 1. fight; struggle. 2. take part in a contest; compete. 3. argue; dispute. 4. declare to be a fact; maintain as true. [< L, < com– (intensive) + tendere stretch] —**con·tend′er**, n. —Syn. 1. cope, wrestle, combat, battle. 3. wrangle. 4. affirm, assert.

con·tent¹ (kon′tent), n. 1. Usually, contents. what is contained. 2. facts and ideas stated, as in a book or speech. 3. power of containing; capacity. 4. amount contained; volume. [< L contentum, pp. of continere CONTAIN] —Syn. 1. substance, matter. ≻ content, contents. Content is used more as an abstract term (the content of the course) and in amounts (the moisture content); contents is rather more concrete (the contents of the box).

con·tent² (kən·tent′), v. satisfy; please; make easy in mind. —adj. 1. satisfied; pleased. 2. easy in mind. 3. willing; ready. —n. contentment. [< F < L contentus, pp., restrained. See CONTAIN.] —Syn. v. gratify, appease. —n. satisfaction, gratification.

con·tent·ed (kən·ten′tid), adj. satisfied; pleased; easy in mind. —**con·tent′ed·ly**, adv. —**con·tent′ed·ness**, n.

con·ten·tion (kən·ten′shən), n. 1. argument; dispute; quarrel. 2. statement or point that one has argued for. 3. an arguing; disputing; quarreling. 4. struggle; contest. —Syn. 3. dissension.

con·ten·tious (kən·ten′shəs), adj. 1. quarrelsome. 2. characterized by contention. —**con·ten′tious·ly**, adv. —**con·ten′tious·ness**, n.

con·tent·ment (kən·tent′mənt), n. satisfaction; being pleased; ease of mind.

con·ter·mi·nous (kən·tér′mə·nəs), adj. 1. having a common boundary; bordering; meeting at their ends. 2. having the same boundaries or limits; coextensive. Also, coterminous.

con·test (n. kon′test; v. kən·test′), n. 1. trial to see which can win; competition. 2. fight; struggle. 3. argument; dispute. [< v.] —v. 1. try to win. 2. fight for; struggle for. 3. argue against; dispute. 4. take part in a contest. [< F < L contestari call to witness < com– + testis witness] —**con·test′a·ble**, adj. —**con·test′er**, n. —Syn. 1. match. –v. 4. compete.

con·test·ant (kən·tes′tənt), n. 1. person who takes part in a contest. 2. person who contests, as election returns, etc.

con·text (kon′tekst), n. parts directly before and after a word, sentence, etc., that influence its meaning. [< L, < com– + texere weave] —**con·tex·tu·al** (kən·teks′chú·əl), adj. —**con·tex′tu·al·ly**, adv.

con·ti·gu·i·ty (kon′tə·gū′ə·ti), n., pl. –ties. condition of being contiguous.

con·tig·u·ous (kən·tig′ū·əs), adj. 1. in actual contact; touching. 2. adjoining; near. [< L contiguus < com– + tag– touch. See CONTACT.] —**con·tig′u·ous·ly**, adv. —**con·tig′u·ous·ness**, n.

con·ti·nence (kon′tə·nəns), **con·ti·nen·cy** (–nən·si), n., pl. –ces; –cies. 1. self-control; self-restraint; moderation. 2. chastity.

con·ti·nent¹ (kon′tə·nənt), n. 1. one of the seven great masses of land on the earth; North America, South America, Europe, Africa, Asia, Australia, or Antarctica. 2. mainland. 3. the Continent, the mainland of Europe. [< L, < continere CONTAIN]

con·ti·nent² (kon′tə·nənt), adj. 1. showing restraint with regard to the desires or passions. 2. chaste. [see CONTINENT¹] —**con′ti·nent·ly**, adv.

con·ti·nen·tal (kon′tə·nen′təl), adj. 1. of or characteristic of a continent. 2. Usually, Continental. belonging to or characteristic of the mainland of Europe. 3. Continental, of or having to do with the American colonies at the time of the American Revolution. —n. 1. Continental, Am. soldier of the American army during the American Revolution. 2. Am. piece of American paper money issued during the American Revolution. 3. Usually, Continental. person living on the Continent.

Continental Congress, Am. either of two legislative assemblies representing the American colonies from 1774 to 1781. The Second Continental Congress adopted the Declaration of Independence in 1776.

con·tin·gen·cy (kən·tin′jən·si), n., pl. –cies. 1. uncertainty of occurrence; dependence on chance. 2. an accidental happening; unexpected event; chance. 3. a happening or event depending on something that is uncertain; possibility.

con·tin·gent (kən·tin′jənt), adj. 1. conditional; depending on something not certain. 2. liable to happen or not to happen; possible; uncertain. 3. happening by chance; accidental; unexpected. —n. 1. share of soldiers, laborers, etc., furnished as an addition to a large force from other sources. 2. group that is part of a larger group. 3. accidental or unexpected event. [< L contingens touching < com– + tangere to touch] —**con·tin′gent·ly**, adv.

con·tin·u·al (kən·tin′ū·əl), adj. 1. never stopping. 2. repeated many times; very frequent. —**con·tin′u·al·ly**, adv. ≻ continual, continuous. Continual means "frequently or closely repeated": Dancing requires continual practice. Continuous means "without interruption": a continuous procession of cars.

con·tin·u·ance (kən·tin′ū·əns), n. 1. continuation. 2. Law. adjournment or postponement until a future time.

con·tin·u·a·tion (kən·tin′ū·ā′shən), n. 1. act of going on with a thing after stopping. 2. a being continued. 3. anything by which a thing is continued; added part. 4. act or fact of not stopping.

con·tin·ue (kən·tin′ū), v., –tin·ued, –tin·u·ing. 1. keep up; keep on; go on; go on with. 2. go on or go on with after stopping; begin again. 3. last; endure. 4. cause to last. 5. stay. 6. cause to stay. 7. put off until a later time; postpone; adjourn. [< L continuare < continere hold together. See CONTAIN.] —**con·tin′u·a·ble**, adj. —**con·tin′u·er**, n. —Syn. 1. prolong, extend.

con·ti·nu·i·ty (kon′tə·nū′ə·ti; –nū′–), n., pl. –ties. 1. state or quality of being continuous. 2. a continuous or connected whole. 3. Am. the detailed plan of a motion picture. 4. connecting comments or announcements between the parts of a radio program.

con·tin·u·ous (kən·tin′ū·əs), adj. without a

stop or break; connected; unbroken. —con·tin'-
u·ous·ly, adv. —con·tin'u·ous·ness, n. —Syn.
ceaseless, incessant, perpetual. ≯ See continual
for usage note.

con·tin·u·um (kən·tin'yū-əm), n., pl. -tin·u·a
(-tin'yū-ə). continuous quantity, series, etc. [< L]

con·tort (kən·tôrt'), v. twist or bend out of
shape; distort. [< L contortus < com- + torquere
twist] —con·tor'tion, n. —con·tor'tive, adj.

con·tor·tion·ist (kən·tôr'shən·ist), n. person
who can twist or bend his body into odd and
unnatural positions.

con·tour (kon'tûr), n. outline of a figure. —v.
mark with lines showing the contour of. —adj. 1.
showing topographical outlines, as hills, valleys,
etc.: a contour map. 2. following natural ridges
and furrows or general contour to avoid erosion:
contour planting. [< F < Ital. contorno, ult. < L
com- + tornus turning lathe < Gk. tornos]

contra-, prefix. in opposition; against, as in
contradistinction. [< L contra]

con·tra·band (kon'trə·band), adj. against the
law; prohibited: contraband trade. —n. 1. goods
imported or exported contrary to law; smuggled
goods. 2. trading contrary to law; smuggling. 3.
contraband of war (see below). [< Sp. < Ital.,
< contra- against (< L) + bando < LL bandum
ban < Gmc.]

contraband of war, goods supplied by
neutral nations to any country at war with
another, that either warring country has a right
to seize.

con·tra·bass (kon'trə·bās'), Music. —n. 1. the
lowest bass voice or instrument. 2. large stringed
instrument shaped like a cello and having a very
low bass tone; double bass. —adj. having to do
with such instruments.

con·tra·cep·tion (kon'trə·sep'shən), n. prevention of conception. [< contra- + (con)cep-
tion] —con'tra·cep'tive, adj., n.

con·tract (v. kən·trakt' for 1-3, kon'trakt,
kən·trakt' for 4; n. kon'trakt), v. 1. draw together; shrink. 2. shorten (a word, etc.) by
omitting some of the letters or sounds. 3. get;
acquire. 4. make a contract; agree by contract.
—n. 1. agreement. 2. a written agreement that
can be enforced by law. 3. a formal agreement of
marriage. [< L contractus < com- together +
trahere draw] —con·tract'ed, adj. —con·tract'-
i·ble, adj. —con·trac'tive, adj.

con·tract bridge (kon'trakt), a card game
played by four people divided into two opposing
pairs. The highest bidder can score toward a
game only as many points as he promised to
make in his bid.

con·trac·tile (kən·trak'təl), adj. 1. capable
of contracting. 2. producing contraction. —con-
trac·til·i·ty (kon'trak·til'ə·ti), n.

con·trac·tion (kən·trak'shən), n. 1. process
of contracting. 2. state of being contracted. 3.
something contracted; shortened form. Can't is
a contraction of cannot.

con·trac·tor (kon'trak·tər; kən·trak'tər), n.
person who agrees to furnish materials or to do
a piece of work for a certain price.

con·trac·tu·al (kən·trak'chū-əl), adj. of, or
having the nature of, a contract.

con·tra·dict (kon'trə·dikt'), v. 1. deny (a
statement, rumor, etc.). 2. deny the words of
(a person). 3. be contrary to; disagree with.
[< L contradictus < contra in opposition +
dicere say] —con'tra·dict'a·ble, adj. —con'tra-
dict'er, con'tra·dic'tor, n.

con·tra·dic·tion (kon'trə·dik'shən), n. 1. act
of denying what has been said. 2. statement
that contradicts another; denial. 3. disagreement; opposition. 4. inconsistency.

con·tra·dic·to·ry (kon'trə·dik'tə·ri), adj. 1.
contradicting; contrary; in disagreement. 2. inclined to contradict.

con·tra·dis·tinc·tion (kon'trə·dis·tingk'-
shən), n. distinction by opposition or contrast.

con·trail (kon'trāl), n. vapor trail left by a
plane flying at a high altitude.

con·tral·to (kən·tral'tō), n., pl. -tos, adj.
Music. —n. 1. the lowest woman's voice. 2. part

to be sung by the lowest woman's voice. 3. person who sings this part. 4. formerly, the highest
male voice. —adj. of or for a contralto. [< Ital.,
< contra- counter to (< L) + alto high < L altus]

con·trap·tion (kən·trap'shən), n. Colloq. contrivance; device; gadget.

con·tra·pun·tal (kon'trə·pun'təl), adj. 1. of
or having to do with counterpoint. 2. according
to the rules of counterpoint. [< Ital. contra-
punto COUNTERPOINT]

con·tra·ri·wise (kon'trer·i·wīz'; for 3, also
kən·trār'i·wīz'), adv. 1. in the opposite way or
direction. 2. on the contrary. 3. perversely.

con·tra·ry (kon'trer·i; for adj. 4, also kən-
trār'i), adj., n., pl. -ries, adv. —adj. 1. opposed;
opposite; completely different. 2. opposite in
direction, position, etc. 3. unfavorable: a contrary wind. 4. opposing others; stubborn; perverse. —n. fact or quality that is the opposite of
something else; the opposite. —adv. in opposition. [< AF < L contrarius < contra against]
—con'tra·ri·ly, adv. —con'tra·ri·ness, n. —Syn.
adj. 2. counter. 4. obstinate.

con·trast (n. kon'trast; v. kən·trast'), n. 1.
a striking difference. 2. person, thing, event,
etc., that shows differences when put side by
side with another. —v. 1. compare (two things)
so as to show their differences. 2. show differences when compared or put side by side. 3.
form a contrast to; set off. 4. put close together
to heighten an effect by emphasizing differences.
[< F < Ital. < LL, < L contra- against + stare
stand] —con·trast'a·ble, adj. —Syn. n. 1. distinction. ≯ See compare for usage note.

con·tra·vene (kon'trə·vēn'), v., -vened, -ven-
ing. 1. conflict with; oppose. 2. violate; infringe.
[< LL, < L contra- against + venire come]
—con'tra·ven'er, n. —con·tra·ven·tion (kon'-
trə·ven'shən), n.

con·trib·ute (kən·trib'yūt), v., -ut·ed, -ut-
ing. 1. give (money, help, etc.) along with others.
2. write (articles, stories, etc.) for a newspaper
or magazine. 3. contribute to, help bring about.
[< L, bring together, collect, < com- together +
tribuere bestow] —con·trib'ut·a·ble, adj. —con-
trib'u·tive, con·trib·u·to·ry (kən·trib'yə·tô'ri;
-tō'-), adj. —con·trib'u·tive·ly, adv. —con-
trib'u·tor, n.

con·tri·bu·tion (kon'trə·bū'shən), n. 1. act
of giving money, help, etc., along with others.
2. money, help, etc., given; gift. 3. article, story,
etc., written for a newspaper or magazine. 4.
tax; levy.

con·trite (kən·trīt'; kon'trīt), adj. 1. broken
in spirit by a sense of guilt; penitent. 2. showing
deep regret and sorrow. [< L contritus crushed
< com- (intensive) + terere rub, grind] —con-
trite'ly, adv. —con·trite'ness, con·tri·tion
(kən·trish'ən), n.

con·triv·ance (kən·trīv'əns), n. 1. thing invented; mechanical device. 2. act or manner of
contriving. 3. power or ability of contriving.

con·trive (kən·trīv'), v., -trived, -triv·ing. 1.
invent; design. 2. plan; scheme; plot. 3. manage.
4. bring about. [< OF, < con- (< L com-) +
trover find < VL, start, rouse, < L turbare stir
up < turba commotion] —con·triv'er, n. —Syn.
1. devise.

con·trol (kən·trōl'), n., v., -trolled, -trol·ling.
—n. 1. power; authority; direction. 2. a holding
back; a keeping down; restraint: he lost control
of his temper. 3. means of restraint; check. 4.
device that controls a machine. 5. standard of
comparison for testing the results of scientific
experiments. —v. 1. have power or authority
over; direct. 2. hold back; keep down; restrain.
3. regulate. [< F contrôler, ult. < OF contrerolle
register < contre against (< L contra) + rôle
ROLL] —con·trol'la·ble, adj. —con·trol'la·bil'-
i·ty, n. —con·trol'ment, n. —Syn. n. 1. regulation, management.

con·trol·ler (kən·trōl'ər), n. 1. Also, comp-
troller. person employed to supervise expenditures, etc. 2. person who controls. 3. device that
controls or regulates. —con·trol'ler·ship, n.

con·tro·ver·sial (kon'trə·vėr'shəl), adj. 1.

āge, cãre, fär; ēqual, tėrm; īce; ōpen, ôrder; pùt, rüle, ūse; th, then; ə=a in about.

of controversy. 2. open to controversy; debatable. 3. fond of controversy. —**con'tro·ver'sial·ist**, *n.* —**con'tro·ver'sial·ly**, *adv.*

con·tro·ver·sy (kon'trə·vér'sĭ), *n., pl.* **-sies.** 1. debate; dispute. 2. quarrel; wrangle. [< L, < *contro-* against + *versus*, pp. of *vertere* turn]

con·tro·vert (kon'trə·vért; kon'trə·vért'), *v.* 1. dispute; deny. 2. discuss; debate.

con·tu·ma·cious (kon'tū·mā'shəs; -tyū-), *adj.* stubbornly rebellious; obstinately disobedient. [< L, < *contumax* insolent < *tumere* swell up] —**con'tu·ma'cious·ly**, *adv.* —**con'tu·ma'cious·ness**, **con·tu·ma·cy** (kon'tū·mə·si, -tyū-; kən·tū'mə·si, -tyū'-), *n.*

con·tu·me·ly (kon'tū·mə·li, -tyū-; kən·tū'mə·li, -tū'-), *n., pl.* **-lies.** 1. insulting words or actions; humiliating treatment. 2. a humiliating insult. [< L *contumelia*, orig., insolent action < *tumere* swell up]

con·tuse (kən·tūz'; -tūz'), *v.,* **-tused, -tus·ing.** bruise. [< L *contusus* < *com-* (intensive) + *tundere* to pound]

con·tu·sion (kən·tū'zhən; -tū'-), *n.* a bruise.

co·nun·drum (kə·nun'drəm), *n.* 1. riddle whose answer involves a pun or play on words. 2. any puzzling problem.

con·va·lesce (kon'və·les'), *v.,* **-lesced, -lesc·ing.** make progress toward health. [< L *con-valescere* < *com-* + *valere* be strong]

con·va·les·cence (kon'və·les'əns), *n.* 1. a gradual recovery of health and strength after illness. 2. time during which one is convalescing. —**con'va·les'cent**, *adj., n.*

con·vec·tion (kən·vek'shən), *n.* 1. act of conveying. 2. *Physics.* the transfer of heat from one place to another by the circulation of heated particles of a gas or liquid. [< L *convectio* < *com-* together + *vehere* carry] —**con·vec'tion·al**, *adj.* —**con·vec'tive**, *adj.*

con·vene (kən·vēn'), *v.,* **-vened, -ven·ing.** meet for some purpose; assemble. [< L, < *com-* together + *venire* come] —**con·ven'er**, *n.*

con·ven·ience (kən·vēn'yəns), *n.* 1. fact or quality of being convenient. 2. a convenient condition or time. 3. comfort; advantage. 4. anything handy or easy to use; thing that saves trouble or work.

con·ven·ient (kən·vēn'yənt), *adj.* 1. saving trouble; well arranged; easy to reach or use; handy. 2. easily done; not troublesome. 3. convenient to, *Colloq.* near. [< L *conveniens*, ppr. of *convenire* meet, agree, be suitable. See CONVENE.] —**con·ven'ient·ly**, *adv.*

con·vent (kon'vent), *n.* 1. community of nuns; group of women living together who devote their lives to religion. 2. building or buildings in which they live. [< AF < L *conventus* assembly < *con-venire* CONVENE] —**Syn.** 2. cloister, abbey.

con·ven·ti·cle (kən·ven'tə·kəl), *n.* 1. a secret meeting, esp. for religious reasons. 2. place of such a meeting. [< L *conventiculum*, dim. of *conventus* meeting. See CONVENT.]

con·ven·tion (kən·ven'shən), *n.* 1. a meeting for some purpose; gathering; assembly. 2. delegates to a meeting or assembly. 3. agreement. 4. general agreement; common consent; custom. 5. custom approved by general agreement; rule based on common consent. [< L *conventio* < *con-venire* CONVENE] —**Syn.** 1. conference. 3. compact. 5. usage, etiquette.

con·ven·tion·al (kən·ven'shən·əl), *adj.* 1. depending on conventions; customary. 2. established by general consent. 3. formal; not natural; not original. 4. *Art.* following custom rather than nature. —**con·ven'tion·al·ism**, *n.* —**con·ven'tion·al·ly**, *adv.*

con·ven·tion·al·i·ty (kən·ven'shən·al'ə·ti), *n., pl.* **-ties.** 1. conventional quality or character. 2. conventional behavior; adherence to custom. 3. a conventional custom or rule.

con·ven·tion·al·ize (kən·ven'shən·əl·īz), *v.,* **-ized, -iz·ing.** 1. make conventional. 2. draw in a conventional manner. —**con·ven'tion·al·i·za'tion**, *n.*

con·verge (kən·vérj'), *v.,* **-verged, -verg·ing.** 1. tend to meet in a point. 2. cause to converge. [< LL, < L *com-* together + *vergere* incline]

con·ver·gence (kən·vér'jəns), **con·ver·gen·cy** (-jən·si), *n., pl.,* **-ces; -cies.** 1. act, process, or fact of converging. 2. tendency to meet in a point. 3. point of meeting. —**con·ver'gent**, *adj.*

con·ver·sant (kən·vér'sənt; kon'vər-), *adj.* 1. familiar by use or study. 2. intimately associated. —**con·ver'sant·ly**, *adv.*

con·ver·sa·tion (kon'vər·sā'shən), *n.* exchange of thoughts by talking informally.

con·ver·sa·tion·al (kon'vər·sā'shən·əl), *adj.* 1. of or having to do with conversation. 2. fond of conversation; good at conversation. —**con'ver·sa'tion·al·ly**, *adv.*

con·ver·sa·tion·al·ist (kon'vər·sā'shən·əl·ist), *n.* person who is fond of or good at conversation.

con·verse¹ (*v.* kən·vérs'; *n.* kon'vérs), *v.,* **-versed, -vers·ing,** *n.* —*v.* talk informally together. —*n.* conversation. [< OF < L, live with < *com-* with + *versari* live, be busy < *verti* turn] —**con·vers'er**, *n.* —**Syn.** *v.* chat.

con·verse² (*adj.* kən·vérs', kon'vérs; *n.* kon'vérs), *adj.* 1. opposite; contrary. 2. reversed in order; turned about. —*n.* 1. thing that is opposite or contrary. 2. thing that is turned around. [< L *conversus* turned around, pp. of *convertere* CONVERT] —**con·verse'ly**, *adv.*

con·ver·sion (kən·vér'zhən; -shən), *n.* act of converting. —**con·ver'sion·al**, *adj.*

con·vert (*v.* kən·vért'; *n.* kon'vért), *v.* 1. change; turn. 2. change from unbelief to faith; change from one religion, party, etc., to another. 3. take and use unlawfully. 4. turn the other way around; invert; transpose. 5. exchange for an equivalent: *convert bank notes into gold.* —*n.* person who has been converted. [< L, < *com-* around + *vertere* turn] —**Syn.** *v.* transform.

con·vert·er, **con·ver·tor** (kən·vér'tər), *n.* 1. person or thing that converts. 2. machine for changing the form of an electric current. 3. furnace in which pig iron is changed into steel.

con·vert·i·ble (kən·vér'tə·bəl), *adj.* 1. capable of being converted. 2. of an automobile, having a top that may be folded down. —*n.* automobile with a folding top. —**con·vert'i·bil'i·ty**, *n.* —**con·vert'i·bly**, *adv.*

con·vert·i·plane (kən·vér'tə·plān'), *n.* an aircraft that operates like a conventional airplane in level flight, but which takes off and lands like a helicopter. [< *converti(ble)* + (*air*) *plane*]

con·vex (*adj.* kon·veks', kən-, kon'veks; *n.* kon'veks), *adj.* curved out. —*n.* a convex surface, part, or thing. [< L *convexus* vaulted, prob. < *com-* around + *vac-* bend] —**con·vex'i·ty**, *n.* —**con·vex'ly**, *adv.*

con·vey (kən·vā'), *v.* 1. carry; transport. 2. transmit; conduct. 3. express; make known; communicate. 4. *Law.* transfer the ownership of (property) from one person to another. [< OF *conveier* < VL, set on the road, accompany < L *com-* with + *via* road. Doublet of CONVOY.] —**con·vey'a·ble**, *adj.*

Convex lenses

con·vey·ance (kən·vā'əns), *n.* 1. act of carrying. 2. thing that carries people and goods; vehicle. 3. *Law.* transfer of the ownership of property from one person to another.

con·vey·er, **con·vey·or** (kən·vā'ər), *n.* 1. person or thing that conveys. 2. device that carries things from one place to another.

con·vict (*v.* kən·vikt'; *n.* kon'vikt), *v.* 1. prove guilty. 2. declare guilty. —*n.* 1. person convicted by a court. 2. person serving a prison sentence. [< L *convictus*, pp. of *convincere*. See CONVINCE.]

con·vic·tion (kən·vik'shən), *n.* 1. act of proving or declaring guilty. 2. state of being proved or declared guilty. 3. act of convincing (a person). 4. a being convinced. 5. firm belief. —**con·vic'tion·al**, *adj.* —**Syn.** 1, 2. condemnation.

con·vince (kən·vins'), *v.,* **-vinced, -vinc·ing.** persuade by argument or proof. [< L, < *com-* + *vincere* overcome] —**con·vinc'er**, *n.* —**con·vin'ci·ble**, *adj.*

con·vinc·ing (kən·vin'sing), *adj.* that convinces. —**con·vinc'ing·ly**, *adv.* —**con·vinc'ing·ness**, *n.* —**Syn.** persuasive, cogent.

con·viv·i·al (kən·viv′i·əl), *adj.* **1.** fond of eating and drinking with friends. **2.** of or suitable for a feast or banquet. [< LL, < *convivium* feast < *com-* with + *vivere* live] —**con·viv′i·al′i·ty**, *n.* —**con·viv′i·al·ly**, *adv.*

con·vo·ca·tion (kon′və·kā′shən), *n.* **1.** a calling together. **2.** an assembly. —**con′vo·ca′tion·al**, *adj.*

con·voke (kən·vōk′), *v.,* **-voked, -vok·ing.** call together; summon to assemble. [< L, < *com-* together + *vocare* call] —**con·vok′er**, *n.*

con·vo·lute (kon′və·lüt), *adj.,* **-lut·ed, -lut·ing.** —*adj.* coiled. —*v.* to coil. [< L *convolutus* < *com-* up + *volvere* roll] —**con′vo·lute′ly**, *adv.*

con·vo·lu·tion (kon′və·lü′shən), *n.* **1.** a coiling, winding, or twisting together. **2.** coil; winding; twist. **3.** an irregular fold or ridge on the surface of the brain.

con·voy (*v.* kən·voi′, kon′voi; *n.* kon′voi), *v.* accompany in order to protect. —*n.* **1.** act of convoying. **2.** an escort; protection. **3.** warships, soldiers, etc., that convoy; protecting escort. **4.** fleet, supplies, etc., accompanied by a protecting escort. [< F *convoyer.* Doublet of CONVEY.]

con·vulse (kən·vuls′), *v.,* **-vulsed, -vuls·ing. 1.** shake violently. **2.** throw into a fit of laughter; cause to shake with laughter. [< L *convulsus* < *com-* (intensive) + *vellere* tear]

con·vul·sion (kən·vul′shən), *n.* **1.** a violent, involuntary contracting and relaxing of the muscles; spasm. **2.** fit of laughter. **3.** a violent disturbance. —**con·vul′sive,** *adj.* —**con·vul′sive·ly,** *adv.*

co·ny (kō′ni), *n., pl.* **-nies. 1.** rabbit fur. **2.** *Archaic.* rabbit. Also, **coney.** [< OF *conil* < L *cuniculus* rabbit < Iberian]

coo (kü), *n., v.,* **cooed, coo·ing.** —*n.* a soft, murmuring sound made by doves or pigeons. —*v.* **1.** make this sound. **2.** murmur softly; speak in a soft, loving manner. [imit.] —**coo′er,** *n.*

coo·ee, coo·ey (kü′i; kü′ē), *n., pl.* **-ees, -eys;** *interj., v.,* **-eed, -ee·ing; -eyed, -ey·ing.** —*n., interj.* long, shrill cry or call. —*v.* utter "cooee."

cook (kük), *v.* **1.** prepare (food) by using heat. **2.** undergo cooking; be cooked. **3.** act as cook; work as cook. **4.** subject (anything) to the action of heat. **5.** *Colloq.* tamper with. [< *n.*] —*n.* person who cooks. [< LL *cocus* < L *coquus*]

cook·book (kük′bük′), *n. Am.* book of recipes containing directions for cooking.

cook·er (kük′ər), *n.* apparatus or container to cook things in.

cook·er·y (kük′ər·i), *n., pl.* **-er·ies. 1.** art of cooking. **2.** room or place for cooking.

cook·out (kük′out′), *n.* cooking and eating of a meal out-of-doors.

cook·y, cook·ie (kük′i), *n., pl.* **-ies.** *Am.* small, flat cake. [< Du. *koekje* little cake]

cool (kül), *adj.* **1.** somewhat cold; more cold than hot. **2.** allowing or giving a cool feeling: *cool clothes.* **3.** not excited; calm. **4.** having little enthusiasm or interest. **5.** bold; impudent. **6.** *Colloq.* without exaggeration or qualification: *a cool million dollars.* —*n.* something cool; cool part, place, or time: *the cool of the evening.* —*v.* **1.** become cool. **2.** make cool. **3.** cool one's heels, *Colloq.* be kept waiting for a long time. [OE *cōl*] —**cool′ish,** *adj.* —**cool′ly,** *adv.* —**cool′ness,** *n.* —**Syn.** *adj.* **1.** unmoved, composed. **3.** indifferent. —**Ant.** *adj.* **1.** warm. **3.** excited, disturbed.

cool·ant (kül′ənt), *n.* a cooling medium, used for machinery, etc.

cool·er (kül′ər), *n.* **1.** apparatus or container that cools foods or drinks, or keeps them cool. **2.** anything that cools. **3.** *Am., Slang.* jail.

Cool·idge (kül′ij), *n.* Calvin, 1872–1933, the 30th president of the United States, 1923–1929.

coo·lie, coo·ly (kül′i), *n., pl.* **-lies.** an unskilled, native laborer in China, India, etc. [prob. < Tamil *kuli* hire, hired servant]

coon (kün), *n. Colloq.* raccoon.

coop (küp; kup), *n.* **1.** a small cage or pen for chickens, rabbits, etc. **2.** any small confining structure. **3.** *Slang.* jail. —*v.* **1.** keep or put in a coop. **2.** confine in a very small space. [ME *coupe* basket < L *cupa* cask]

co·öp (kō′op; kō·op′), *n. Colloq.* a coöperative store.

coop·er (küp′ər; kup′-), *n.* man who makes or repairs barrels, casks, etc. —*v.* make or repair (barrels, casks, etc.). [? < MDu., MLG *kuper* < L *cuparius* < *cupa* cask]

Coop·er (kü′pər; kup′ər), *n.* James Fenimore, 1789–1851, American novelist.

coop·er·age (küp′ər·ij; kup′-), *n.* **1.** work done by a cooper. **2.** shop of a cooper.

co·öp·er·ate, co·op·er·ate, or **co-op·er·ate** (kō·op′ər·āt), *v.,* **-at·ed, -at·ing.** work together. [< LL, < *co-* together + *operari* to work] —**co·öp′er·a′tor,** *n.*

co·öp·er·a·tion, co·op·er·a·tion, or **co-op·er·a·tion** (kō·op′ər·ā′shən), *n.* **1.** act of working together; united effort or labor. **2.** combination of persons for purposes of production, purchase, or distribution for their joint benefit.

co·öp·er·a·tive, co·op·er·a·tive, or **co-op·er·a·tive** (kō·op′ər·ā′tiv; -op′rə·tiv), *adj.* **1.** wanting or willing to work together with others. **2.** of, having to do with, or being a coöperative. —*n.* organization in which the profits and losses are shared by all members. —**co·öp′er·a′tive·ly,** *adv.* —**co·öp′er·a′tive·ness,** *n.*

coöperative store, store managed by an organization whose members share in the profits and losses according to the amount they buy.

co·ör·di·nate, co·or·di·nate, or **co-or·di·nate** (*adj., n.* kō-ôr′də·nit, -nāt; *v.* kō-ôr′də·nāt), *adj., n., v.,* **-nat·ed, -nat·ing.** —*adj.* **1.** equal in importance; of equal rank. **2.** made up of coördinate parts. **3.** joining words, phrases, or clauses of equal grammatical importance. *And* and *but* are coördinate conjunctions. —*n.* **1.** a coördinate person or thing. **2.** *Math.* any of two or more magnitudes that define the position of a point, line, or plane by reference to a fixed figure, system of lines, etc. —*v.* **1.** make coördinate; make equal in importance. **2.** arrange in proper order or relation; harmonize; adjust [< L *co-* with + *ordinatus,* pp. of *ordinare* regulate] —**co·ör′di·nate·ly,** *adv.* —**co·ör′di·nate·ness,** *n.* —**co·ör′di·na′tive,** *adj.* —**co·ör′di·na′tor,** *n.*

co·ör·di·na·tion (kō-ôr′də·nā′shən), *n.* act of coördinating.

European coot
(18 in. long)

coot (küt), *n.* **1.** a wading and swimming bird with short wings and lobate toes. **2.** *Colloq.* fool; simpleton. [? < Du. *koet*]

coot·ie (küt′i), *n. Slang.* louse.

cop (kop), *n., v.,* **copped, cop·ping.** —*n. Colloq.* policeman. —*v. Slang.* steal. [OE *coppian*]

co·part·ner (kō-pärt′nər), *n.* a fellow partner; associate. —**co·part′ner·ship,** *n.*

cope¹ (kōp), *v.,* **coped, cop·ing.** struggle or contend (with), esp. on even terms or successfully. [< F *couper* strike < *coup* COUP]

cope² (kōp), *n., v.,* **coped, cop·ing.** —*n.* **1.** a long cape worn by priests during certain religious rites. **2.** anything like a cope, such as a canopy, the sky, etc. —*v.* cover with a cope. [< Med.L *capa* cloak, var. of LL *cappa* hood]

co·peck (kō′pek), *n.* kopeck.

Co·pen·ha·gen (kō′pən·hā′gən; -hä′-), *n.* capital of Denmark.

Co·per·ni·cus (kə·pér′nə·kəs), *n.* Nikolaus, 1473–1543, Polish astronomer. —**Co·per′ni·can,** *adj.*

cope·stone (kōp′stōn′), *n.* **1.** the top stone of a wall. **2.** a finishing touch. [< *cope²* + *stone*]

cop·i·er (kop′i·ər), *n.* **1.** imitator. **2.** copyist.

co·pi·lot (kō′pī′lət), *n.* the assistant or second pilot in an aircraft.

cop·ing (kōp′ing), *n.* the top layer of a brick or stone wall, usually sloping. [< *cope²*]

coping saw, a narrow saw in a U-shaped frame, used to cut curves.

co·pi·ous (kō′pi·əs), *adj.* **1.** plentiful; abundant. **2.** containing much matter. **3.** containing

many words. [< L, < *copia* plenty] —co'pi-
ous·ly, *adv.* —co'pi·ous·ness, *n.* —Syn. 1. ample.

cop·per (kop'ər), *n.* 1. *Chem.* a tough, reddish-
brown metallic element, Cu, that is easily shaped
into thin sheets or fine wire and resists rust.
2. thing made of copper. 3. *Am.* coin made of
copper or bronze; penny. 4. a reddish brown. —*v.*
cover with copper. —*adj.* 1. of copper. 2. reddish-
brown. [< L *cuprum*, for earlier *aes Cyprium*
metal of Cyprus] —cop'per·y, *adj.*

cop·per·as (kop'ər·əs), *n.* ferrous sulfate,
FeSO₄7H₂O, used in dyeing, inkmaking, medicine, and photography. [< F < Med.L (*aqua*)
cuprosa (water) of copper]

cop·per·head (kop'ər·hed'), *n.* *Am.* 1. a
poisonous North American snake related to the
water moccasin and the rattlesnake. 2. Copper-
head, *Am.* a Northerner sympathetic with the
South during the Civil War.

cop·per·plate (kop'ər·plāt'), *n.* 1. a thin, flat
piece of copper on which a design, writing, etc.,
is engraved or etched. 2. an engraving, picture,
or print made from a copperplate. 3. copperplate
printing or engraving.

cop·ra (kop'rə), *n.* the dried meat of coconuts.
[< Pg. < Malayalam *koppara*]

copse (kops), **cop·pice** (kop'is), *n.* a thicket
of small trees, bushes, etc. [< OF *coupeiz* a cut-
over forest < *couper* cut. See COUP.]

Copt (kopt), *n.* native of Egypt, descended from
the ancient Egyptians.

Cop·tic (kop'tik), *n.* the former language of
the Copts. —*adj.* of or by the Copts.

cop·u·la (kop'yə·lə), *n., pl.* –las, –lae (-lē).
1. verb that connects the subject and the predicate, usually some form of *be.* 2. something that
connects. [< L, bond, < *co*- together + *apere*
fasten. Doublet of COUPLE.] —cop'u·lar, *adj.*

cop·u·late (kop'yə·lāt), *v.,* –lat·ed, –lat·ing.
have sexual intercourse. [< L *copulatus*, pp. of
copulare. See COPULA.] —cop'u·la'tion, *n.*

cop·u·la·tive (kop'yə·lā'tiv; –lə-), *n.* copulative word. —*adj.* 1. connecting. *Be* is a copulative
verb; *and* is a copulative conjunction. 2. pertaining to copulation. —cop'u·la'tive·ly, *adv.*

cop·y (kop'i), *n., pl.* cop·ies, *v.,* cop·ied, cop·y-
ing. —*n.* 1. thing made like another. 2. thing
made to be followed as a pattern or model. 3.
one of a number of books, newspapers, magazines, pictures, etc., made at the same printing.
4. material ready to be set in type. —*v.* follow
as a pattern or model; imitate. [< F < Med.L
copia transcript < L, plenty] —Syn. *n.* 1. duplicate, transcript, reproduction, imitation. —*v.*
duplicate, reproduce. —Ant. *n.* 1. original.

cop·y·book (kop'i·bùk'), *n.* book with models
of handwriting to be copied. —*adj.* commonplace; conventional; ordinary.

copy desk, a central desk in a newspaper
office, where stories, etc., undergo final preparation for publication.

cop·y·ist (kop'i·ist), *n.* 1. person who makes
written copies. 2. imitator.

cop·y·right (kop'i·rīt'), *n.* the exclusive right
to make and sell a certain book, picture, etc.
—*adj.* protected by copyright. —*v.* protect by
getting a copyright. —cop'y·right'a·ble, *adj.*
—cop'y·right'er, *n.*

co·quet (kō·ket'), *v.,* –quet·ted, –quet·ting. 1.
flirt. 2. trifle. [< F, < *coquet,* dim. of *coq* cock]
—co·quet·ry (kō'kə·tri; kō·ket'ri), *n.*

co·quette (kō·ket'), *n.* woman who tries to
attract men merely to please her vanity; flirt.
[< F. See COQUET.] —co·quet'tish, *adj.* —coquet'tish·ly, *adv.* —co·quet'tish·ness, *n.*

cor·a·cle (kôr'ə·kəl; kor'-), *n.* a small, light
boat made by covering a wooden frame with
waterproof material. [< Welsh < *corwg*]

cor·al (kôr'əl; kor'-), *n.* 1. a stony substance
consisting of the skeletons of very small sea
animals called polyps. 2. polyp that secretes
a skeleton of coral and forms large, branching
colonies by budding. 3. a deep pink; red. —*adj.*
1. made of coral. 2. deep-pink; red. [< OF < L
< Gk. *koral(l)ion*]

coral reef, reef consisting mainly of coral.

Coral Sea, part of the Pacific at the NE
Australian coast.

coral snake, *Am.* any of several species of
small, poisonous American snakes, most of which
are banded with alternating rings of red, yellow,
and black.

cor·bel (kôr'bəl), *n., v.,* –beled,
–bel·ing; *esp. Brit.* –belled, –bel-
ling. —*n.* bracket of stone, etc.,
on a wall. —*v.* furnish with corbels; support by corbels. [< OF,
dim. of *corp* raven < L *corvus*]

cord (kôrd), *n.* 1. a thick string; very thin rope.
2. influence that binds or restrains. 3. *Elect.*
a pair of covered wires with fittings to connect
an iron, lamp, etc., with a socket. 4. Also, chord.
Anat. structure in an animal body that is somewhat like a cord: *the spinal cord.* 5. ridge on
cloth. 6. cloth with ridges on it; corduroy. 7.
cords, corduroy breeches or trousers. 8. measure
of cut wood; 128 cubic feet. —*v.* 1. fasten or tie
with a cord. 2. pile (wood) in cords. [< OF < L
< Gk. *chorde* gut. Doublet of CHORD².] —cord'ed,
adj. —cord'er, *n.*

cord·age (kôr'dij), *n.* 1. cords; ropes. The
cordage of a ship is its rigging. 2. quantity of
wood measured in cords.

cor·date (kôr'dāt), *adj.* heart-shaped. [< NL,
< L *cor* heart] —cor'date·ly, *adv.*

cor·dial (kôr'jəl), *n.* 1. food, drink, or medicine that makes the heart beat faster. 2. liqueur.
—*adj.* 1. sincere; hearty; warm; friendly. 2.
stimulating. [< Med.L, < L *cor* heart] —cor'-
dial·ly, *adv.* —cor'dial·ness, *n.*

cor·dial·i·ty (kôr·jal'ə·ti; –ji·al'–), *n., pl.*
–ties. cordial quality or feeling; heartiness;
friendliness.

cor·dil·le·ra (kôr·dəl·yâr'ə; kôr·dil'ər·ə), *n.*
Am., W. a long mountain range. [< Sp., ult.
< L *chorda* rope, CORD] —cor'dil·le'ran, *adj.*

cor·dite (kôr'dīt), *n.* a smokeless gunpowder
composed chiefly of nitroglycerin and guncotton.
[< cord, n. + -*ite²*]

cor·don (kôr'dən), *n.* 1. line or circle of people
or things placed at intervals as a guard. 2.
cord, braid, or ribbon worn as an ornament or
badge of honor. [< F, < *corde* CORD]

cor·do·van (kôr'də·vən; kôr·dō'vən), *n.* kind
of soft, fine-grained leather. —*adj.* of or having
to do with this leather.

cor·du·roy (kôr'də·roi; kôr'də·roi'), *n.* 1. a
thick cotton cloth with close, velvetlike ridges.
2. corduroys, corduroy trousers. —*adj.* 1. made
of corduroy. 2. *Am.* pertaining to a road, etc.,
made of logs or poles placed crosswise, as across
muddy or swampy sections. [appar. < F *corde
du roi* king's cord]

cord·wood (kôrd'wùd'), *n.* 1. wood sold or
piled in cords. 2. wood cut in 4-foot lengths.

core (kôr; kōr), *n., v.,* cored, cor·ing. —*n.* 1.
the central part, containing the seeds, of fruits
like apples and pears. 2. the central or most important part: *the core of an argument.* 3. *Elect.*
bar of soft iron forming the center of an electromagnet or of an induction coil. —*v.* take out the
core. [ME] —Syn. *n.* 2. heart, nucleus.

co·re·op·sis (kō'ri·op'sis; kō'-), *n.* *Am.* plant
with yellow, red-and-yellow, or reddish flowers
shaped like daisies. [< NL, < Gk. *koris* bedbug
+ *opsis* appearance; from the shape of the seed]

co·re·spond·ent (kō'ri·spon'dənt; kôr'i-;
kor'-), *n.* *Law.* person accused of adultery with
a husband or wife being sued for divorce.

co·ri·an·der (kô'ri·an'dər; kō'-), *n.* 1. plant
whose aromatic, seedlike fruits are used in cooking and in medicine. 2. the fruit.
[< F < L < Gk. *koriandron,* var. of
koriannon]

Cor·inth (kôr'inth; kor'-), *n.*
seaport in S Greece. In ancient
times, Corinth was a center of commerce, art, and luxury.

Co·rin·thi·an (kə·rin'thi·ən), *adj.*
1. of or having to do with Corinth
or its people. 2. noting or pertaining
to the most elaborate of the three types of
Greek architecture. The capital of a Corinthian

Corinthian
capital

column is adorned with acanthus leaves. **3.** luxurious. —*n.* **1.** native or inhabitant of Corinth. **2. Corinthians,** either of two books of the New Testament, written by the Apostle Paul to the Christians of Corinth.

cork (kôrk), *n.* **1. a** light, thick, outer bark of a kind of oak, used for bottle stoppers, floats for fishing lines, etc. **2.** Also, **cork oak.** the tree. **3.** shaped piece of cork. **4.** any stopper for a bottle, etc. **5.** *Bot.* the protective outer bark of woody plants. —*v.* **1.** stop up with a cork. **2.** restrain. **3.** blacken with burnt cork. —*adj.* of cork. [< Sp. *alcorque* < Ar. < L *quercus* oak] —**cork′y,** *adj.*

Cork (kôrk), *n.* seaport in S Eire.

cork·screw (kôrk′skrü′), *n.* tool for removing corks from bottles. —*v.* move or advance in a spiral or zigzag course. —*adj.* spiral.

corm (kôrm), *n.* a bulblike underground stem. [< NL < Gk. *kormos* stripped tree trunk < *keirein* shear]

Cork-screw

cor·mo·rant (kôr′mǝ·rǝnt), *n.* **1. a** large, greedy sea bird with a pouch under its beak. **2.** a greedy person. —*adj.* greedy. [< OF *cormareng* < *corp* raven (< L *corvus*) + *marenc* of the sea < L *mare*]

corn¹ (kôrn), *n.* **1.** *Am.* kind of grain that grows on large ears; maize; Indian corn. **2.** plant that it grows on. **3.** in England, grain in general, esp. wheat. **4.** in Scotland and Ireland, oats. **5.** Also, **corn whiskey,** *Am., Colloq.* whiskey made from corn. —*v.* preserve (meat) with strong salt water or by dry salt. [OE] —**corned** (kôrnd), *adj.*

corn² (kôrn), *n.* a hardening of the skin, usually on a toe. [< OF, horn, < L *cornu*]

corn bread, *Am.* bread made of corn meal.

corn·cob (kôrn′kob′), *n.* *Am.* **1.** the central, woody part of an ear of corn. **2.** *Colloq.* a tobacco pipe with a bowl hollowed out of a piece of dried corncob.

cor·ne·a (kôr′ni·ǝ), *n.* *Anat.* the transparent part of the outer coat of the eyeball. The cornea covers the iris and the pupil. [< Med.L *cornea* (*tela*) horny (web) < L *cornu* horn] —**cor′ne·al,** *adj.*

cor·nel (kôr′nǝl), *n.* **1.** in Europe, a shrub or small tree with yellow flowers. **2.** in the United States, the flowering dogwood. [< G < Med.L *cornolius* < L *cornus*]

cor·nel·ian (kôr·nēl′yǝn), *n.* carnelian.

cor·ner (kôr′nǝr), *n.* **1.** the point or place where lines or surfaces meet. **2.** space between two lines or surfaces near where they meet; angle. **3.** the place where two streets meet. **4.** piece to protect or decorate a corner. **5.** place away from crowds. **6.** place that is far away; region. **7.** an awkward or difficult position; place from which escape is impossible. **8.** *Am.* a buying up of the available supply of some stock or article to raise its price. **9.** cut corners, a. *Am.* shorten the way by going across corners. b. save money, effort, time, etc., by cutting down. —*adj.* **1.** at a corner. **2.** for a corner. —*v.* **1.** *Am.* put or drive into a corner. **2.** *Am., Colloq.* force into a difficult position. **3.** *Am.* buy up all or nearly all that can be had of (something) to raise its price. **4.** *Am.* meet at a corner. **5.** *Slang.* (of an automobile) round sharp curves at relatively high speeds without sway, etc. [< AF var. of OF *cornere* < L *cornu* horn, tip] —Syn. *n.* **5.** nook.

cor·ner·stone (kôr′nǝr·stōn′), *n.* **1.** stone at the corner of two walls that holds them together. **2.** main part on which something rests; basis.

cor·ner·wise (kôr′nǝr·wīz′), **cor·ner·ways** (-wāz′), *adv.* **1.** with the corner in front; forming a corner. **2.** diagonally.

cor·net (kôr·net′ *for* 1; kôr′nit, kôr·net′ *for* 2), *n.* **1.** *Music.* a wind instrument somewhat like a trumpet, usually made of brass. **2.** piece of paper rolled into a cone and twisted at one end, used to hold candy, nuts, etc. [< OF, < L *cornu* horn] —**cor·net′tist, cor·net′ist,** *n.*

corn·flow·er (kôrn′flou′ǝr), *n.* plant with blue, pink, white, or purple flowers; bachelor's-button.

corn·husk (kôrn′husk′), *n.* *Am.* husk of an ear of corn. —**corn′husk′ing,** *n. Am.*

cor·nice (kôr′nis), *n., v.* **-niced, -nic·ing.** —*n.* a projecting ornamental molding along the top of a wall, pillar, building, etc. See the diagram under **entablature.** —*v.* furnish or finish with a cornice. [< F < Ital. < Med.Gk. *koronis* copestone < Gk., something bent]

Cor·nish (kôr′nish), *adj.* of or having to do with Cornwall, its people, or their former language. —*n.* the ancient Celtic language of Cornwall. —**Cor·nish·man** (kôr′nish·mǝn), *n.*

corn meal, *Am.* meal made from Indian corn ground up.

corn pone, *Am., S.* a flat, usually rectangular loaf of corn meal shaped by hand.

corn silk, *Am.* the glossy threads or styles at the end of an ear of corn.

corn·stalk (kôrn′stôk′), *n. Am.* stalk of Indian corn.

corn·starch (kôrn′stärch′), *n. Am.* a starchy flour made from Indian corn, used to thicken puddings, etc.

cor·nu·co·pi·a (kôr′nǝ·kō′pi·ǝ), *n.* **1.** a horn-shaped container or ornament. **2.** horn of plenty, overflowing with fruits and flowers. [< LL, for L *cornu copiae* horn of plenty]

Corn·wall (kôrn′wôl; -wǝl), *n.* county in SW England.

Corn·wal·lis (kôrn·wôl′is; -wol′is), *n.* **Charles,** 1738–1805, British general who surrendered to Washington at Yorktown, 1781.

corn·y (kôr′ni), *adj.,* **corn·i·er, corn·i·est.** *Am., Slang.* **1.** trite; of poor quality. **2.** of music, having an unsophisticated or overly sentimental style.

co·rol·la (kǝ·rol′ǝ), *n. Bot.* the internal envelope or floral leaves of a flower; the petals. [< L, garland, dim. of *corona* crown]

cor·ol·lar·y (kôr′ǝ·ler′i; kor′-), *n., pl.* **-lar·ies.** **1.** an additional proposition that can be easily inferred from a proved proposition. **2.** inference. **3.** a natural consequence or result. [< LL *corollarium* < L, gift, < *corolla* garland. See COROLLA.]

co·ro·na (kǝ·rō′nǝ), *n., pl.* **-nas, -nae** (-nē). **1.** ring of light or halo seen around the sun or moon. **2.** *Anat.* the top of the head. **3.** *Bot.* the appendage on the inner side of the corolla of some plants. **4.** *Elect.* discharge on the surface of a conductor. [< L, crown. Doublet of CROWN.] —**co·ro·nal** (kǝ·rō′nǝl; kôr′ǝ·nǝl; kor′-), *adj.*

Co·ro·na·do (kôr′ǝ·nä′dō; kor′-), *n.* **Francisco Vásquez de,** 1500?–1554?, Spanish soldier and explorer.

cor·o·nar·y (kôr′ǝ·ner′i; kor′-), *adj.* **1.** pertaining to or resembling a crown. **2.** *Anat.* of or designating either or both of the two arteries that supply blood to the muscular tissue of the heart. [< L *coronarius* encircling < *corona* crown]

coronary thrombosis, thrombosis of the heart, involving a coronary artery.

cor·o·na·tion (kôr′ǝ·nā′shǝn; kor′-), *n.* ceremony of crowning a king, emperor, etc.

cor·o·ner (kôr′ǝ·nǝr; kor′-), *n.* **1.** a local official who investigates before a jury any unnatural death. **2.** coroner's jury, group of persons chosen to witness the investigation. [< AF *corouner* officer of the crown < *coroune* CROWN] —**cor′o·ner·ship′,** *n.*

cor·o·net (kôr′ǝ·nit; -net; kor′-), *n.* **1.** a small crown worn as a mark of high rank. **2.** circlet of anything worn around the head as an ornament. [< OF *coronet*, dim. of *corone* CROWN] —**cor′o·net·ed,** *adj.*

Co·rot (kō·rō′), *n.* **Jean Baptiste Camille,** 1796–1875, French landscape painter.

Corp., corp., **1.** Corporal. **2.** Corporation.

cor·po·ral¹ (kôr′pǝ·rǝl), *adj.* of the body: *corporal punishment.* [< L *corporalis* < *corpus* body] —**cor′po·ral′i·ty,** *n.* —**cor′po·ral·ly,** *adv.*

cor·po·ral² (kôr′pǝ·rǝl), *n.* the lowest noncommissioned army officer, next below a sergeant and next above a private. [< F < Ital. *caporale* < *capo* head < L *caput*] —**cor′po·ral·ship′,** *n.*

āge, câre, fär; ēqual, tėrm; īce; ōpen, ôrder; pùt, rüle, ūse; th, then; ǝ=a in about.

cor·po·rate (kôr'pə·rit), *adj.* **1.** of or forming a corporation; incorporated. **2.** combined. [< L, < *corporare* form into a body < *corpus* body] —cor'po·rate·ly, *adv.*

cor·po·ra·tion (kôr'pə·rā'shən), *n.* **1.** group of persons who obtain a charter giving them as a group certain legal rights and privileges distinct from those of the individual members of the group. **2.** group of persons with authority to act as a single person. **3.** *Colloq.* prominent abdomen.

cor·po·re·al (kôr·pô'ri·əl; -pō'-), *adj.* **1.** of or for the body; bodily. **2.** material; tangible. [< L *corporeus* < *corpus* body] —cor·po're·al'i·ty, cor·po're·al·ness, *n.* —cor·po're·al·ly, *adv.*

corps (kôr; kōr), *n., pl.* **corps** (kôrz; kōrz). **1.** branch of specialized military service, such as the Signal Corps. **2.** *Mil.* a tactical unit usually consisting of two or more divisions, and smaller than an army. **3.** group of people organized for working together. [< F. See CORPSE.]

corpse (kôrps), *n.* a dead human body. [< OF < L *corpus* body]

cor·pu·lence (kôr'pyə·ləns), **cor·pu·len·cy** (-lən·si), *n.* fatness. —cor'pu·lent, *adj.* —cor'pu·lent·ly, *adv.* [< L, < *corpus* body]

cor·pus (kôr'pəs), *n., pl.* **-po·ra** (-pə·rə). **1.** a body. **2.** a complete collection of writings, laws, etc. [< L, body]

Cor·pus Chris·ti (kôr'pəs kris'tī; kris'tī), feast in honor of the Eucharist, held on the first Thursday after Trinity Sunday.

cor·pus·cle (kôr'pəs·əl; -pus-), *n.* any of the cells that float in the blood, lymph, etc., carrying oxygen and carbon dioxide or destroying disease germs. [< L *corpusculum*, dim. of *corpus* body] —cor·pus·cu·lar (kôr·pus'kyə·lər), *adj.*

cor·pus de·lic·ti (kôr'pəs di·lik'tī), *Law.* a. the actual facts that prove a crime or offense has been committed. **b.** body of a murdered person. [< L, body of the crime]

cor·ral (kə·ral'), *n., v.,* **-ralled, -ral·ling.** *Am.* —*n.* an enclosed space for keeping or for capturing horses, cattle, etc. —*v.* **1.** drive into or keep in a corral. **2.** surround; capture. [< Sp., < *corro* ring]

cor·rect (kə·rekt'), *adj.* **1.** free from mistakes or faults; right. **2.** in good taste; proper. —*v.* **1.** change to what is right; remove mistakes from. **2.** alter to agree with some standard: *correct the reading of a barometer.* **3.** mark the errors of. **4.** find fault with to improve; punish. **5.** counteract (something hurtful); cure. [< L *correctus,* pp. of *corrigere* make straight < *com-* + *regere* direct] —cor·rect'ly, *adv.* —cor·rect'ness, *n.* —cor·rec'tor, *n.* —Syn. *adj.* **1.** accurate, exact, precise. —*v.* **1.** amend. **4.** admonish, discipline. **5.** remedy. —Ant. *adj.* **1.** erroneous.

cor·rec·tion (kə·rek'shən), *n.* **1.** act of correcting. **2.** thing put in place of an error or mistake. **3.** punishment; rebuke; scolding. —cor·rec'tion·al, *adj.*

cor·rec·tive (kə·rek'tiv), *adj.* tending to correct; making better. —*n.* something that tends to correct anything that is wrong or hurtful. —cor·rec'tive·ly, *adv.*

Cor·reg·i·dor (kə·reg'ə·dôr), *n.* a fortified island at the entrance to Manila Bay, Philippines; surrendered to the Japanese in 1942.

cor·re·late (kôr'ə·lāt; kor'-), *v.,* **-lat·ed, -lat·ing,** *adj., n.* —*v.* **1.** have a mutual relation. **2.** bring into proper relation with one another. —*adj.* correlated. —*n.* either of two related things. [< *com-* + *relate*]

cor·re·la·tion (kôr'ə·lā'shən; kor'-), *n.* **1.** the mutual relation of two or more things. **2.** a correlating or being correlated.

cor·rel·a·tive (kə·rel'ə·tiv), *adj.* **1.** mutually dependent; each implying the other. **2.** having a mutual relation and commonly used together. Conjunctions used in pairs, such as *either . . . or* and *both . . . and,* are correlative words. —*n.* either of two closely related things. —correl'a·tiv'i·ty, *n.* —cor·rel'a·tive·ly, *adv.*

cor·re·spond (kôr'ə·spond'; kor'-), *v.* **1.** be in harmony; agree. **2.** be similar: *the arms of a man correspond to the wings of a bird.* **3.** ex-change letters. [< Med.L, < L *com-* together, with + *respondere* answer] —cor're·spond'ing, *adj.* —cor're·spond'ing·ly, *adv.* —Syn. **1.** harmonize, match. **2.** parallel.

cor·re·spond·ence (kôr'ə·spon'dəns; kor'-), *n.* **1.** agreement; harmony. **2.** similarity in structure or function. **3.** exchange of letters; letter writing. **4.** letters.

correspondence school, school that gives lessons by mail.

cor·re·spond·ent (kôr'ə·spon'dənt; kor'-), *n.* **1.** person who exchanges letters with another. **2.** person employed by a newspaper or magazine to send news from a distant place. **3.** thing that corresponds to something else. —*adj.* corresponding; in agreement. —cor're·spond'ent·ly, *adv.*

cor·ri·dor (kôr'ə·dər; -dôr; kor'-), *n.* **1.** a long hallway. **2.** a narrow strip of land connecting two parts of a country or an inland country with a seaport. [< F < Pr. *corredor* < *correr* run < L *currere*] —Syn. **1.** passageway, hall.

cor·ri·gi·ble (kôr'ə·jə·bəl; kor'-), *adj.* **1.** that can be corrected. **2.** open to correction. [< LL, < L *corrigere* CORRECT] —cor'ri·gi·bil'i·ty, *n.* —cor'ri·gi·bly, *adv.*

cor·rob·o·rate (kə·rob'ə·rāt), *v.,* **-rat·ed, -rat·ing.** make more certain; confirm. [< L, < *corroborare* strengthen < *com-* + *robur* oak] —cor·rob'o·ra'tion, *n.* —cor·rob'o·ra'tor, *n.*

cor·rob·o·ra·tive (kə·rob'ə·rā'tiv; -rə·tiv), *adj.* **cor·rob·o·ra·to·ry** (-rə·tô'ri; -tō'-), *adj.* confirming. —cor·rob'o·ra'tive·ly, *adv.*

cor·rode (kə·rōd'), *v.,* **-rod·ed, -rod·ing. 1.** eat away gradually. **2.** become corroded. [< L, < *com-* + *rodere* gnaw] —cor·rod'i·ble, *adj.*

cor·ro·sion (kə·rō'zhən), *n.* **1.** act or process of corroding. **2.** a corroded condition. **3.** product of corroding.

cor·ro·sive (kə·rō'siv), *adj.* producing corrosion; corroding; eating away. —*n.* substance that corrodes. —cor·ro'sive·ly, *adv.* —cor·ro'sive·ness, *n.*

corrosive sublimate, bichloride of mercury, $HgCl_2$, a poisonous, white crystalline substance.

cor·ru·gate (*v.* kôr'ə·gāt, kor'-; *adj.* kôr'ə·git, -gāt, kor'-), *v.,* **-gat·ed, -gat·ing,** *adj.* —*v.* **1.** bend or shape into a row of wavelike folds. **2.** wrinkle; furrow. —*adj.* wrinkled; furrowed. [< L, < *com-* + *ruga* wrinkle]

cor·ru·ga·tion (kôr'ə·gā'shən; kor'-), *n.* **1.** a corrugating. **2.** a being corrugated. **3.** one of a series of wavelike ridges.

cor·rupt (kə·rupt'), *adj.* **1.** evil; wicked. **2.** influenced by bribes; dishonest. **3. a.** incorrect because of alterations, as a text. **b.** considered inferior by some because of change in meaning or form, or deviation from standard usage, as a language, dialect, form, etc. **4.** rotten; decayed. —*v.* **1.** make evil or wicked. **2.** bribe. **3. a.** make incorrect by changing, as a text. **b.** cause to differ from standard usage, as a form, meaning, dialect, etc. **4.** rot; decay. **5.** become corrupt. [< L *corruptus* < *com-* + *rumpere* break] —cor·rupt'er, *n.* —cor·rupt'ing·ly, *adv.* —cor·rupt'ly, *adv.* —cor·rupt'ness, *n.* —Syn. *v.* **1.** pervert; deprave. **4.** taint, spoil.

cor·rupt·i·ble (kə·rup'tə·bəl), *adj.* **1.** that can be corrupted; that can be bribed. **2.** liable to be corrupted; perishable. —cor·rupt'i·bil'i·ty, cor·rupt'i·ble·ness, *n.* —cor·rupt'i·bly, *adv.*

cor·rup·tion (kə·rup'shən), *n.* **1.** a making or being made evil or wicked. **2.** evil conduct; wickedness. **3.** bribery; dishonesty. **4. a.** a making incorrect by changing, as a text. **b.** a causing to differ from standard usage, as a form, meaning, dialect, etc. **c.** an instance of this: a corrupt form of a word. **5.** rot; decay. **6.** thing that causes corruption.

cor·sage (kôr·säzh'), *n.* **1.** *Am.* bouquet to be worn at a woman's waist or her shoulder, etc. **2.** the upper part of a woman's dress. [< F, < OF *cors* body < L *corpus*]

cor·sair (kôr'sãr), *n.* **1.** pirate. **2.** a pirate ship. **3.** privateer. [< F < Ital. < VL *cursarius* runner < L *cursus* a run]

corse·let (kôrs'lit *for* 1; kôr'sə·let' *for* 2), *n.* **1.**

Also, **cors'let.** armor for the body. 2. a woman's undergarment somewhat like a corset. [< F, double dim. of OF *cors* body < L *corpus*]

cor·set (kôr'sit), *n.* Often, **corsets. a** woman's stiff, close-fitting undergarment, worn about the waist and hips to support or shape the body. [< F, dim. of OF *cors* body < L *corpus*]

Cor·si·ca (kôr'sə·kə), *n.* French island in the Mediterranean, SE of France. —**Cor'si·can,** *adj., n.*

cor·tege, cor·tège (kôr·tāzh'; -tezh'), *n.* 1. procession. 2. group of followers, attendants, etc.; retinue. [< F < Ital. *corteggio* < *corte* COURT]

Cor·tés, Cor·tez (kôr·tez'), *n.* Hernando, 1485–1547, Spanish soldier who conquered Mexico.

cor·tex (kôr'teks), *n., pl.* **-ti·ces** (-tə·sēz). 1. *Bot.* bark. 2. *Anat., Zool.* a. the outer layers of an internal organ, as of the kidney. b. layer of gray matter that covers most of the surface of the brain. [< L, bark] —**cor·ti·cal** (kôr'tə·kəl), *adj.* —**cor'ti·cal·ly,** *adv.*

cor·ti·sone (kôr'tə·zōn), *n.* hormone derived from the cortex of the adrenal gland, used experimentally in controlling arthritis. Also, **Compound E.**

co·run·dum (kə·run'dəm), *n.* an extremely hard mineral consisting of aluminum oxide, Al_2O_3, used as an abrasive. [< Tamil *kurundam.* Cf. Skt. *kuruvinda* ruby.]

cor·us·cate (kôr'əs·kāt; kor'-), *v.,* **-cat·ed, -cat·ing.** give off flashes of light; sparkle. [< L, < *coruscus* flashing] —**cor'us·ca'tion,** *n.*

cor·vette, cor·vet (kôr·vet'), *n.* 1. warship with sails and only one tier of guns. 2. gunboat used in antisubmarine convoy work. [prob. < MDu. *korf* a kind of ship < *corbis* basket]

cor·ymb (kôr'imb; -im; kor'-), *n. Bot.* a flat cluster of flowers in which the outer flowers blossom first. [< L < Gk. *korymbos* top, cluster] —**co·rym·bose** (kə·rim'bōs), *adj.* —**co·rym'bose·ly,** *adv.*

Corymb

cor·y·phée (kôr'ə·fā'; kor'-), *n.* 1. dancer who leads a ballet. 2. a ballet dancer. [< F < L < Gk. *koryphaios* chief < *koryphe* head]

co·ry·za (kə·rī'zə), *n. Med.* cold in the head. [< L < Gk. *koryza* catarrh]

cos (kos; kôs), *n.* kind of lettuce. [from the island of *Cos* in the Aegean]

co·se·cant (kō·sē'kənt; -kant), *n. Trigon.* the secant of the complement of a given angle or arc.

co·sig·na·to·ry (kō·sig'nə·tô'ri; -tō'-), *adj., n., pl.* **-ries.** —*adj.* signing along with another or others. —*n.* one who so signs.

co·sine (kō'sīn), *n. Trigon.* sine of the complement of a given angle or arc.

cos·met·ic (koz·met'ik), *n.* preparation for beautifying the skin, etc. —*adj.* beautifying. [< Gk. *kosmetikos* of order, adornment < *kosmos* order]

cos·mic (koz'mik), *adj.* 1. of or belonging to the cosmos; having to do with the whole universe. 2. vast. [< Gk. *kosmikos* < *kosmos* order, world] —**cos'mi·cal·ly,** *adv.*

cosmic dust, fine particles of matter falling upon the earth from outer space.

cosmic rays, *Am.* rays of very short wave lengths and very great penetration, coming to the earth from interstellar space.

cos·mog·o·ny (koz·mog'ə·ni), *n., pl.* **-nies.** 1. origin of the universe. 2. theory of its origin. [< Gk. *kosmogonia* < *kosmos* world + *gignesthai* be born]

cos·mog·ra·phy (koz·mog'rə·fi), *n., pl.* **-phies.** science that deals with the general appearance and structure of the universe. [< Gk., < *kosmos* world + *graphein* write]

cos·mol·o·gy (koz·mol'ə·ji), *n.* science or theory of the universe, its parts, and laws. —**cos·mo·log·i·cal** (koz'mə·loj'ə·kəl), *adj.*

cos·mo·naut (koz'mə·nôt), *n.* astronaut.

cos·mo·pol·i·tan (koz'mə·pol'ə·tən), *adj.* 1. belonging to all parts of the world; widely spread. 2. free from national or local prejudices; feeling at home in any part of the world. —*n.* a cosmopolitan person or thing.

cos·mop·o·lite (koz·mop'ə·līt), *n.* 1. a cosmopolitan person. 2. animal or plant found in all or many parts of the world. [< Gk., < *kosmos* world + *polites* citizen < *polis* city]

cos·mos (koz'məs; -mos), *n.* 1. the universe thought of as an orderly, harmonious system. 2. any complete system that is orderly and harmonious. 3. plant with white, pink, or purple flowers, that blooms in the fall. [< NL < Gk. *kosmos* order, world] —**Ant.** 1. chaos.

cos·mo·tron (koz'mə·tron), *n.* an atomic accelerator at Brookhaven National Laboratory, Upton, N.Y., designed to produce particles with energy of over two billion electron volts. [appar. < *cosm*(ic) + (cycl)*otron*]

Cos·sack (kos'ak; -ək), *n.* one of a people living in S Russia, noted as horsemen.

cos·set (kos'it), *n.* a pet lamb; a pet. [< *v.*] —*v.* treat as a pet; pamper. [< unrecorded OE *cossettan* to kiss < *coss* a kiss]

cost (kôst; kost), *n., v.,* **cost, cost·ing.** —*n.* 1. price paid. 2. loss; sacrifice. 3. **at all costs** or **at any cost,** by all means; no matter what must be done. 4. **costs,** *Law.* expenses of a lawsuit or case in court. —*v.* be obtained at the price of; require. [< OF, < *coster* < L, < *com-* + *stare* stand] —**Syn.** *n.* 1. charge, expense, outlay.

cos·tal (kos'təl), *adj.* 1. of or pertaining to a rib or ribs. 2. bearing ribs. [< Med.L, < L *costa* rib]

Cos·ta Ri·ca (kos'tə rē'kə; kôs'-; kōs'-), country in Central America. —**Costa Rican.**

cos·ter (kos'tər; kôs'-), or **cos·ter·mon·ger** (-mung'gər; -mong'-), *n. Esp. Brit.* person who sells fruit, vegetables, fish, etc., in the street. [< *costard* a kind of English apple]

cos·tive (kos'tiv; kôs'-), *adj.* constipated. [< OF < L *constipatus,* pp. See CONSTIPATE.] —**cos'tive·ly,** *adv.* —**cos'tive·ness,** *n.*

cost·ly (kôst'li; kost'-), *adj.,* **-li·er, -li·est.** 1. of great value. 2. costing much. 3. *Archaic.* costing too much. —**cost'li·ness,** *n.* —**Syn.** 1. precious, valuable, sumptuous, rich. 2. expensive, dear. —**Ant.** 1. cheap. 2. inexpensive.

cos·tume (*n.* kos'tüm, -tüm; *v.* kos·tüm', -tüm'), *n., v.,* **-tumed, -tum·ing.** —*n.* 1. style of dress, etc., including the way the hair is worn, kind of jewelry, etc. 2. dress belonging to another time or place, worn on the stage, etc. 3. a complete set of outer garments. —*v.* provide a costume for; dress. [< F < Ital. < VL *consuetumen* custom. Doublet of CUSTOM.]

cos·tum·er (kos·tüm'ər; -tūm'-), **cos·tum·i·er** (-tüm'i·ər; -tūm'-), *n.* person who makes, sells, or rents costumes or dresses.

co·sy (kō'zi), *adj.,* **co·si·er, co·si·est,** *n., pl.* **co·sies.** cozy. —**co'si·ly,** *adv.* —**co'si·ness,** *n.*

cot¹ (kot), *n.* 1. a narrow, portable bed, esp. one made of canvas. 2. *Brit.* crib. [< Anglo-Ind. < Hind. *khāt.* Cf. Skt, *khatvā.*]

cot² (kot), *n.* 1. cottage. 2. something small built for cover or protection. [OE]

co·tan·gent (kō·tan'jənt), *n. Trigon.* tangent of the complement of a given angle or arc. —**cotan·gen·tial** (kō'tan·jen'shəl), *adj.*

cote (kōt), *n.* 1. shelter or shed for small animals, etc. 2. *Brit.* cottage. [OE. See COT².]

co·te·rie (kō'tə·ri), *n.* set or circle of acquaintances; group of people who often meet socially. [< F, association for holding land, < *cotier* COTTER²] —**Syn.** clique, ring.

co·ter·mi·nous (kō·tér'mə·nəs), *adj.* conterminous.

co·til·lion (kə·til'yən), *n. Esp. U.S.* a dance with complicated steps and much changing of partners. It is led by one couple. [< F, orig., petticoat, dim. of *cotte* COAT]

cot·tage (kot'ij), *n.* 1. a small house. 2. *Am.* house at a summer resort. [see COT², -AGE]

cottage cheese, *Am.* a soft, white cheese made from the curds of sour milk.

cot·tag·er (kot′ij·ər), *n.* person who lives in a cottage.

cot·ter[1] (kot′ər), *n.* **1.** pin that is inserted through a slot to hold small parts of machinery, etc., together. **2.** cotter pin.

cot·ter[2], **cot·tar** (kot′ər), *n.* a Scottish peasant who works for a farmer and is allowed to use a small cottage and a plot of land. [< Med.L *cotarius* < *cota* < OE *cot* COT[2]]

cotter pin, a metal pin, usually split at one end, inserted through a hole or slot to hold parts of machinery together.

cot·ton (kot′ən), *n.* **1.** soft, white fibers in a fluffy mass around the seeds of a plant of the mallow family. **2.** plant or plants that produce these fibers. **3.** thread of cotton fibers. **4.** cloth made of cotton thread. —*adj.* made of cotton. —*v. Colloq.* take a liking. [< OF < Ital. < Ar. *quṭn*] —cot′ton·y, *adj.*

cotton batting, soft, fluffy cotton pressed into thin layers.

cotton gin, *Am.* machine for separating the fibers of cotton from the seeds.

cot·ton·mouth (kot′ən·mouth′), *n. Am.* water moccasin.

cot·ton·seed (kot′ən·sēd′), *n., pl.* **–seeds** or (*esp.* collectively) **–seed.** seed of cotton, used for making cottonseed oil, fertilizer, cattle food, etc.

cottonseed oil, *Am.* oil pressed from cottonseed, used for cooking, for making soap, etc.

cot·ton·tail (kot′ən·tāl′), *n. Am.* a common American wild rabbit.

cot·ton·wood (kot′ən·wůd′), *n.* **1.** an American poplar tree having cottonlike tufts on the seeds. **2.** its soft wood.

cotton wool, **1.** raw cotton, before or after picking. **2.** cotton batting.

cot·y·le·don (kot′ə·lē′dən), *n. Bot.* an embryo leaf in the seed of a plant; the first leaf, or one of the first pair of leaves, growing from a seed. [< L < Gk. *kotylēdōn* cup-shaped hollow < *kotylē* small vessel] —cot′y·le′·don·al, *adj.* —cot′y·le′don·ous, *adj.*

C, cotyledon.

couch (kouch), *n.* **1.** thing made to sleep or rest on. **2.** place to sleep or rest in: *a grassy couch.* —*v.* **1.** lay on a couch. **2.** lie down on a couch. **3.** put in words; express. **4.** lower; bring down. **5.** put in a level position ready to attack. **6.** lie hidden ready to attack. **7.** crouch; cower; stoop. [< OF, < *coucher* lay in place < L, < *com-* + *locare* place < *locus* a place] —couch′er, *n.*

couch·ant (kouch′ənt), *adj.* lying down, but with the head raised. [< F, ppr. See COUCH.]

cou·gar (kü′gər), *n.* a large, tawny American wildcat; puma; mountain lion. [< F < NL < Tupi-Guarani]

cough (kôf; kof), *v.* **1.** force air from the lungs with sudden effort and noise.

Cougar (total length 8 ft.)

2. cough up, a. expel from the throat by coughing. **b.** *Am., Slang.* give; bring out; produce. —*n.* **1.** act of coughing. **2.** repeated acts of coughing. **3.** a diseased condition of the lungs, etc., that causes coughing. [ME *coghen* < OE *cohhetan*]

could (kůd), *v.* pt. of *can.* ➤ **could, might.** *Could,* the past of *can,* and *might,* originally the past of *may,* are now used chiefly to convey a shade of doubt, or a smaller degree of possibility: *it might be all right for her, but it wasn't for me; perhaps I could write a poem, but I doubt it.*

cou·lee (kü′li), *n.* **1.** *Am.* a deep ravine or gulch. A coulee is usually dry in summer. **2.** stream of lava. [< F, < *couler* flow < L *colare* strain]

cou·lomb (kü·lom′), *n.* quantity of electricity furnished by a current of one ampere in one second. [for C. A. de *Coulomb,* French physicist]

coul·ter (kōl′tər), *n.* colter.

coun·cil (koun′səl), *n.* **1.** group of people called together to give advice, talk things over, or settle questions. **2.** a small group of people

elected by citizens to make laws for and govern a city or town. **3.** an ecclesiastical assembly for deciding matters of doctrine or discipline. [< OF < L *concilium* < *com-* together + *calare* call]

coun·cil·man (koun′səl·mən), *n., pl.* **-men.** member of the council of a city or town.

council of war, conference to talk over and decide on matters of importance.

coun·ci·lor, *esp. Brit.* **coun·cil·lor** (koun′sə·lər), *n.* a council member. —coun′ci·lor·ship′, *esp. Brit.* coun′cil·lor·ship′, *n.*

coun·sel (koun′səl), *n., v.,* **-seled, -sel·ing;** *esp. Brit.* **-selled, -sel·ling.** —*n.* **1.** act of exchanging ideas; act of talking things over. **2.** advice. **3.** lawyer or group of lawyers. **4.** design; plan. —*v.* **1.** give advice to; advise. **2.** recommend. **3.** exchange ideas; consult together; deliberate. [< OF < L *consilium* < *consulere* consult, orig., convoke < *com-* together + *sel-* take] —**Syn.** *n.* **1.** consultation, deliberation. **2.** recommendation. **3.** counselor. —*v.* **1.** admonish.

coun·se·lor, *esp. Brit.* **coun·sel·lor** (koun′sə·lər), *n.* **1.** person who gives advice; adviser. **2.** lawyer. —coun′se·lor·ship′, *esp. Brit.* coun′sel·lor·ship′, *n.*

count[1] (kount), *v.* **1.** name numbers in order; name the numbers up to: *wait till I count ten.* **2.** add; find how many. **3.** include in counting; take into account. **4.** depend; rely. **5. count out,** *Am.* **a.** fail to consider or include. **b.** defeat by counting ballots wrongly. **c.** declare (a fallen boxer) the loser when he fails to rise after 10 seconds. **6.** be included in counting. **7.** have an influence; be of value. **8.** consider. —*n.* **1.** an adding up; a finding out how many. **2.** the total number; amount. **3.** an accounting. **4.** ten seconds counted to give a fallen boxer time to rise. **5.** *Law.* each charge in a formal accusation. [< OF < L < *com-* up + *putare* reckon. Doublet of COMPUTE.] —count′a·ble, *adj.*

count[2] (kount), *n.* a European nobleman having a rank about the same as that of an English earl. [< OF < L *comes* companion < *com-* with + *ire* go]

count·down (kount′doun′), *n.* **1.** period of time preceding the firing of a missile, rocket, etc. **2.** the calling out of the passing minutes (and seconds, in the last stage) of this period.

coun·te·nance (koun′tə·nəns), *n., v.,* **-nanced, -nanc·ing.** —*n.* **1.** expression of the face. **2.** face; features. **3.** approval; encouragement. **4.** calmness; composure. **5.** put out of countenance, embarrass and confuse; make uneasy and ashamed. —*v.* approve; encourage. [< OF < Med.L *continentia* demeanor < L, self-control. See CONTINENT[2].] —**Syn.** *n.* **2.** visage. **3.** support.

count·er[1] (koun′tər), *n.* **1.** a piece of wood, metal, etc., used to count, as in card games. **2.** an imitation coin. **3.** *Esp. U.S.* a long table in a store, restaurant, etc. [< OF, < *conter* COUNT[1]]

count·er[2] (koun′tər), *n.* **1.** person who counts. **2.** a machine for counting.

count·er[3] (koun′tər), *adv.* in the opposite direction; opposed; contrary. —*adj.* opposite; contrary. —*v.* **1.** go or act counter to; oppose. **2.** give a blow in boxing in return for another. —*n.* **1.** that which is opposite or contrary to something else. **2.** blow given in boxing in return for another. **3.** a stiff piece inside the back of a shoe around the heel. **4.** part of a ship's stern from the water line to the end of the curved part. [< F < L *contra* against]

counter-, *word element.* **1.** against; in opposition to, as in *counteract.* **2.** in return, as in *counterattack.* **3.** that corresponds; so as to correspond, as in *counterpart.* [see COUNTER[3]]

coun·ter·act (koun′tər·akt′), *v.* act against; neutralize the action or effect of; hinder. —coun′ter·ac′tion, *n.* —coun′ter·ac′tive, *adj., n.*

coun·ter·at·tack (*n.* koun′tər·ə·tak′; *v.* koun′tər·ə·tak′), *n.* attack made to counteract an attack. —*v.* attack in return.

coun·ter·bal·ance (*n.* koun′tər·bal′əns; *v.* koun′tər·bal′əns), *n., v.,* **-anced, -anc·ing.** —*n.* **1.** weight balancing another weight. **2.** influence, power, etc., balancing another. —*v.* act as a counterbalance to; offset.

coun·ter·claim (*n.* koun′tər·klām′; *v.* koun′-

tər·klām′), *n.* an opposing claim; claim made by a person to offset a claim made against him. —*v.* make a counterclaim.

coun·ter·clock·wise (koun′tər·klok′wīz′), *adv., adj.* in the direction opposite to that in which the hands of a clock go.

coun·ter·es·pi·o·nage (koun′tər·es′pī·ə·nij; -näzh′), *n.* measures taken to prevent or confuse enemy espionage.

coun·ter·feit (koun′tər·fit), *v.* 1. copy (money, handwriting, pictures, etc.) in order to deceive or defraud. 2. resemble closely. 3. pretend; dissemble. —*n.* copy made to deceive or defraud and passed as genuine. —*adj.* made to deceive or defraud. [< OF *contrefait* imitated < *contre-* against (< L *contra-*) + *faire* make < L *facere*] —**coun′ter·feit′er,** *n.* —Syn. *adj.* forged, fraudulent. —Ant. *adj.* genuine, real.

coun·ter·ir·ri·tant (koun′tər·ir′ə·tənt), *n.* something used to produce irritation in one place in order to relieve irritation elsewhere.

coun·ter·mand (*v.* koun′tər·mand′, -mänd′; *n.* koun′tər·mand, -mänd), *v.* 1. withdraw or cancel (an order, command, etc.). 2. recall or stop by a contrary order. —*n.* command, etc., that revokes a previous one. [< OF, < L *contra-* against + *mandare* order]

coun·ter·of·fen·sive (koun′tər·ə·fen′siv), *n. Mil.* aggressive action on a large scale undertaken by a defending force to seize the initiative from the attacking force.

coun·ter·pane (koun′tər·pān′), *n.* quilt; coverlet. [alter. of *counterpoint* quilt < OF]

coun·ter·part (koun′tər·pärt′), *n.* 1. copy; duplicate. 2. person or thing closely resembling another. 3. person or thing that complements another.

coun·ter·plot (*n., v.* koun′tər·plot′; *v. also* koun′tər·plot′), *n., v.,* -plot·ted, -plot·ting. —*n.* plot to defeat another plot. —*v.* devise a counterplot.

coun·ter·point (koun′tər·point′), *n. Music.* 1. melody added to another as an accompaniment. 2. art of adding melodies to a given melody according to fixed rules.

coun·ter·poise (koun′tər·poiz′), *n., v.,* -poised, -pois·ing. —*n.* 1. weight balancing another weight. 2. influence, power, etc., balancing or offsetting another. —*v.* act as a counterpoise to; offset. [< OF *countrepeis* < *contre-* against (< L *contra-*) + *peis* weight < L *pensum*]

coun·ter·rev·o·lu·tion (koun′tər·rev′ə·lü′shən), *n.* revolution against a government established by a previous revolution. —**coun′ter·rev·o·lu·tion·ar·y** (koun′tər·rev′ə·lü′shən·er′i), *adj., n.* —**coun′ter·rev′o·lu′tion·ist,** *n.*

coun·ter·shaft (koun′tər·shaft′; -shäft′), *n.* shaft that transmits motion from the main shaft to the working part of a machine.

coun·ter·sign (*n., v.* koun′tər·sīn′; *v. also* koun′tər·sīn′), *n.* 1. *Mil.* password given in answer to the challenge of a sentinel. 2. signature added to another signature to confirm it. —*v.* sign (something already signed by another) to confirm it.

coun·ter·sink (*v., n.* koun′tər·singk′; *v. also* koun′tər·singk′), *v.,* -sunk, -sink·ing, *n.* —*v.* 1. enlarge the upper part of (a hole) to make room for the head of a screw, bolt, etc. 2. sink the head of (a screw, bolt, etc.) into such a hole so that it is even with or below the surface. —*n.* 1. a countersunk hole. 2. tool for countersinking holes.

coun·ter·weight (koun′tər·wāt′), *n.* weight that balances another weight.

counter word, word that is used more frequently than its exact meaning warrants. In "we had a lousy time at the party," *lousy* is a counter word meaning "unpleasant."

count·ess (koun′tis), *n.* 1. wife or widow of an earl or a count. 2. woman whose rank is equal to that of an earl or a count.

counting house or **room,** building or office used for keeping accounts and doing business.

count·less (kount′lis), *adj.* too many to count; very many; innumerable.

coun·tri·fied, coun·try·fied (kun′tri·fīd), *adj.* like the country; rural.

coun·try (kun′tri), *n., pl.* -tries, *adj.* —*n.* 1. land; region; district. 2. all the land of a nation. 3. people of a nation. 4. land where a person was born or is a citizen. 5. land without many houses; rural district. —*adj.* 1. of the country; rural. 2. rustic. [< OF < VL *contr*[ə]ta what lies opposite < L *contra* against]

country club, *Am.* club in the country near a city.

coun·try·dance (kun′tri·dans′; -däns′), *n.* dance in which partners face each other in two long lines.

coun·try·man (kun′tri·mən), *n., pl.* -men. 1. man of one's own country. 2. man who lives in the country.

coun·try·seat (kun′tri·sēt′), *n.* residence or estate in the country.

coun·try·side (kun′tri·sīd′), *n.* 1. rural district; country. 2. certain section of the country. 3. its people.

coun·try·wom·an (kun′tri·wùm′ən), *n., pl.* -wom·en. 1. woman of one's own country. 2. woman living in the country.

coun·ty (koun′ti), *n., pl.* -ties. 1. *Am.* in the United States, the political unit next below the State. 2. one of the chief districts into which a state or country, as Great Britain and Ireland, is divided. 3. people of a county. [< AF *counté* < *counte* COUNT²]

county seat, *Am.* town or city where the county government is located.

coup (kü), *n., pl.* coups (küz). a sudden, brilliant action. [< F < L *colpus* < Gk. *kolaphos*]

coup de grâce (kü′ də gräs′), 1. action that gives a merciful death to a suffering animal or person. 2. the finishing stroke. [< F, lit., stroke of grace]

coup d'é·tat (kü′ dā·tä′), a sudden and decisive measure in politics, esp. one affecting a change of government illegally or by force. [< F, lit., stroke of state]

cou·pé (kü·pā′; *for 1, also* küp), *n.* 1. a closed, two-door automobile seating two to five people. 2. a closed carriage with a seat for the driver outside. [< F, pp. of *couper* cut. See COUP.]

cou·ple (kup′əl), *n., v.,* -pled, -pling. —*n.* 1. two things of the same kind that go together; pair. 2. man and woman who are married, engaged, or partners in a dance. —*v.* join together; join together in pairs. [< OF *cople* < L *copula* bond. Doublet of COPULA.] —**cou′pler,** *n.* —Syn. *n.* 1. mates. —*v.* unite.

cou·plet (kup′lit), *n.* 1. two successive lines of poetry, esp. two that rhyme and are equally long. 2. couple; pair.

cou·pling (kup′ling), *n.* 1. act or process of joining together. 2. device for joining together parts of machinery. 3. device used to join together two railroad cars. 4. *Elect.* device or arrangement for transferring electrical energy from one circuit to another.

cou·pon (kü′pon; kū′-), *n.* 1. a printed statement of interest due on a bond, which can be cut from the bond and presented for payment. 2. part of a ticket, advertisement, ration book, etc., that gives the person who holds it certain rights. [< F, < *couper* cut. See COUP.]

cour·age (kėr′ij), *n.* bravery; fearlessness. [< OF *corage* < *cuer* heart < L *cor*] —Syn. valor, pluck, heroism, daring.

cou·ra·geous (kə·rā′jəs), *adj.* full of courage; brave; fearless. —**cou·ra′geous·ly,** *adv.* —**cou·ra′geous·ness,** *n.*

cou·ri·er (kėr′i·ər; kùr′-), *n.* 1. messenger sent in haste. 2. person who goes with travelers and takes care of hotel reservations, tickets, etc. [< F *courrier* < Ital. < L *currere* run]

course (kôrs; kōrs), *n., v.,* coursed, cours·ing. —*n.* 1. onward movement. 2. direction taken. 3. line of action; way of doing. 4. way; path; track; channel. 5. group of similar things arranged in some regular order. 6. regular order. 7. series of studies in a school, college, or university. 8. one of the studies. 9. part of a meal served at one time. 10. place for races or games. 11. layer of bricks, stones, shingles, etc.; row. 12. in due course, at the proper or usual time; after a while. 13. in the course of, during; in the process of. 14. of course, a. surely; certainly. b. naturally; as should be expected. —v. 1. race; run. 2. hunt with dogs. 3. cause (dogs) to pursue game. [< F *cours* < L *cursus*, a running and < F *course* < Ital. *corsa* a running < L *currere* run] —Syn. n. 1. progress, career. 3. process, method, manner, mode, procedure. 4. road, passage. 6. sequence, succession.

cours·er (kôr′sər; kōr′-), n. Poetic. a swift horse.

court (kôrt; kōrt), n. 1. space partly or wholly enclosed by walls or buildings. 2. a short street. 3. area marked off for a game, as for tennis. 4. one of the divisions of such an area. 5. building or buildings surrounded by a clear space; a stately dwelling. 6. residence where a king, queen, or other sovereign lives; royal palace. 7. family, household, or followers of a sovereign. 8. sovereign and his advisers as a ruling power. 9. a formal assembly held by a sovereign. 10. Law. a. place where justice is administered. b. persons who are chosen to administer justice; judge or judges. c. assembly of such persons to administer justice. 11. attention paid to get favor; effort to please. 12. act of making love; act of wooing. —v. 1. pay attention to (a person) to get his favor; try to please. 2. make love to; woo. 3. try to get; act so as to get; seek: *court danger.* [< OF < L *cohors* enclosure, retinue. Doublet of COHORT.] —Syn. n. 1. yard. -v. 3. invite, solicit.

cour·te·ous (kėr′ti·əs), adj. polite; thoughtful of others. [< OF *corteis* < court COURT] —cour′te·ous·ly, adv. —cour′te·ous·ness, n. —Syn. civil, attentive.

cour·te·san, cour·te·zan (kôr′tə·zən; kôr′-; kėr′-), n. a prostitute. [< F < Ital. *cortigiana* woman of the court < *corte* COURT]

cour·te·sy (kėr′tə·si), n., pl. -sies. 1. polite behavior; thoughtfulness for others. 2. polite act; thoughtful act; favor. 3. curtsy. [< OF *cortesie* < *corteis* COURTEOUS] —Syn. 1. politeness, civility.

court·house (kôrt′hous′; kōrt′-), n. 1. a building where law courts are held. 2. Am. a building used for the government of a county.

cour·ti·er (kôr′ti·ər; kōrt′-), n. 1. person often present at the court of a king, prince, etc. 2. person who tries to win the favor of another.

court·ly (kôrt′li; kōrt′-), adj., -li·er, -li·est. 1. suitable for a king's court; elegant. 2. trying hard to please one's superior; flattering. —court′li·ness, n.

court-mar·tial (kôrt′mär′shəl; kōrt′-), n., pl. courts-mar·tial, v., -tialed, -tial·ing; esp. Brit. -tialled, -tial·ling. —n. 1. court of army or navy officers for trying offenders against military or naval laws. 2. trial by such a court. —v. try by such a court.

Court of St. James's, court of the British sovereign.

court·room (kôrt′rüm′; -rum′; kōrt′-), n. room where a law court is held.

court·ship (kôrt′ship; kōrt′-), n. making love; wooing.

court·yard (kôrt′yärd′; kōrt′-), n. space enclosed by walls, in or near a large building.

cous·in (kuz′ən), n. 1. son or daughter of one's uncle or aunt. 2. a distant relative. 3. term used by one sovereign in speaking to another sovereign or to a great nobleman. [< F < L *consobrinus* mother's sister's child < *com-* together + *soror* sister] —cous′in·ly, adj., adv. —cous′in·ship, n.

cous·in-ger·man (kuz′ən·jėr′mən), n., pl. cous·ins-ger·man. son or daughter of one's uncle or aunt; first cousin.

cou·tu·ri·er (kü·tür′i·ər; Fr. kü·tụ·ryā′), n. a man dressmaker. [< F]

cove (kōv), n., v., coved, cov·ing. —n. 1. a small, sheltered bay; inlet on the shore. 2. sheltered nook. —v. arch; arch over. [OE *cofa* chamber]

cov·e·nant (kuv′ə·nənt), n. 1. a solemn agreement between two or more persons or groups to do or not to do a certain thing; compact. 2. in the Bible, the solemn promises of God to man. 3. Law. a legal contract; formal agreement that is legal. —v. solemnly agree. [< OF, < *covenir* < L *convenire*. See CONVENE.] —cov′e·nant·er, n.

Cov·en·try (kuv′ən·tri; kov′-), n. city in C England.

cov·er (kuv′ər), v. 1. put something over. 2. be over; occupy the surface of; spread over. 3. clothe; wrap up. 4. be thick over. 5. hide; conceal. 6. protect; shelter. 7. go over; travel. 8. include; make up. 9. be enough for; provide for. 10. aim straight at. 11. have within range. 12. put one's hand or cap on. 13. Am. act as a reporter or photographer of: *to cover a fire for a newspaper.* 14. deposit the equivalent of (money deposited in betting); accept the conditions of (a bet). 15. Am. buy (commodities, securities, etc.) for future delivery as a protection against loss. 16. brood or sit on (eggs or chicks). —n. 1. thing that covers. 2. protection; shelter. 3. place for one person at a table, set with a plate, knife, fork, spoon, napkin, etc. 4. break cover, come out in the open. 5. under cover, a. hidden; secret; disguised. b. secretly. [< OF < L, < *co-* up + *operire* cover] —cov′er·er, n. —cov′er·less, adj. —Syn. v. 3. envelop. 5. screen, cloak, shroud. -n. 1. lid, top, case, envelope, wrapping. 2. refuge, retreat.

cov·er·age (kuv′ər·ij), n. 1. amount covered by something. 2. Am. risks covered by an insurance policy.

cover charge, Am. in some restaurants, a charge made for service, music, etc.

covered wagon, Am. a wagon having a removable canvas cover.

cov·er·ing (kuv′ər·ing), n. thing that covers.

cov·er·let (kuv′ər·lit), **cov·er·lid** (-lid), n. 1. an outer covering for a bed; bedspread. 2. any covering.

cov·ert (kuv′ərt; for 4 kō′vərt, kuv′ərt), adj. 1. covered; sheltered. 2. secret; hidden; disguised: *covert glances.* —n. 1. shelter; hiding place. 2. thicket in which animals hide. 3. coverts, the smaller and weaker feathers that cover the bases of the large feathers of a bird's wings and tail. 4. covert cloth. [< OF, pp. of *covrir* COVER] —cov′ert·ly, adv. —cov′ert·ness, n.

co·vert cloth (kō′vərt; kuv′ərt), cloth, of wool, silk and wool, or rayon, usually brownish, used for coats.

cov·et (kuv′it), v. desire eagerly (esp. something that belongs to another). [< OF *coveitier*, ult. < L *cupere* desire] —cov′et·a·ble, adj. —cov′et·er, n.

cov·et·ous (kuv′ə·təs), adj. overly desirous (esp. of things that belong to others). —cov′et·ous·ly, adv. —cov′et·ous·ness, n. —Syn. greedy, avaricious.

cov·ey (kuv′i), n., pl. -eys. 1. brood of partridges, quail, etc. 2. small flock; group. [< OF, < *cover* incubate < L *cubare* lie]

cow¹ (kou), n., pl. cows, (Archaic or Dial.) kine (kīn). 1. female of a bovine family, esp. of the domestic species that furnishes milk. 2. female of various other large animals: *an elephant cow.* [OE *cū*]

cow² (kou), v. make afraid; frighten. [< Scand. *kūga*] —Syn. scare, bully.

cow·ard (kou′ərd), n. person who lacks courage or is afraid. —adj. 1. lacking courage; cowardly. 2. showing fear. [< OF *coart* < *coe* tail < L *cauda*]

cow·ard·ice (kou′ər·dis), n. lack of courage; being easily made afraid.

cow·ard·ly (kou′ərd·li), adj. 1. lacking courage. 2. of a coward. —adv. fit for a coward. —cow′ard·li·ness, n.

cow·boy (kou′boi′), n. Am. man who looks after cattle on a ranch and rides horseback to do most of his work.

cow·catch·er (kou′kach′ər), n. Am. a metal frame on the front of a locomotive, streetcar, etc., for clearing the tracks.

cow·er (kou′ər), v. 1. crouch in fear or shame.

2. draw back tremblingly from another's threats, blows, etc. [< Scand. *kūra* sit moping]

cow·girl (kou'gẽrl'), *n. Am.* woman who works on a ranch, at rodeos, etc.

cow hand, *Am.* person who works on a cattle ranch.

cow·herd (kou'hẽrd'), *n.* person whose work is looking after cattle.

cow·hide (kou'hīd'), *n., v.,* **-hid·ed, -hid·ing.** —*n.* **1.** hide of a cow. **2.** leather made from it. **3.** *Am.* strong leather whip. —*v. Am.* whip with a cowhide; flog.

cowl (koul), *n.* **1.** a monk's cloak with a hood. **2.** the hood itself. **3.** anything shaped like a cowl. **4.** the narrow part of an automobile body that includes the windshield and the dashboard. **5.** metal covering over an airplane engine. **6.** a covering for the top of a chimney to increase the draft. —*v.* **1.** put a monk's cowl on. **2.** cover with a cowl or something resembling a cowl. [< LL *cuculla,* var. of L *cucullus* hood] —**cowled** (kould), *adj.*

Cowl

cow·lick (kou'lik'), *n.* a small tuft of hair that will not lie flat.

cowl·ing (koul'ing), *n.* metal covering over the engine of an airplane.

cow·man (kou'mən), *n., pl.* **-men.** *Am.* an owner of cattle; ranchman.

co·work·er (kō·wẽr'kər), *n.* person who works with another.

cow·pea (kou'pē'), *n. Am.* **1.** plant that has very long pods, used as food for cattle, fertilizer, etc. **2.** seed of this plant.

cow·pox (kou'poks'), *n.* disease of cows causing small pustules on cows' udders. Vaccine for smallpox is obtained from cows that have cowpox.

cow·punch·er (kou'pun'chər), *n. Am., Colloq.* cowboy.

cow·rie, cow·ry (kou'ri), *n., pl.* **-ries.** a yellow shell used as money in some parts of Africa and Asia. [< Hind. *kaurī*]

cow·slip (kou'slip), *n.* **1.** *Am.* a wild plant with yellow flowers; marsh marigold. **2.** an English primrose. [OE, < *cū* cow + *slyppe* slime]

cox (koks), *n. Colloq.* coxswain.

cox·comb (koks'kōm'), *n.* **1.** a vain, empty-headed man; conceited dandy. **2.** *Bot.* cockscomb. **3.** a cap resembling a cock's comb, worn by clowns or jesters. [var. of *cock's comb*]

cox·swain (kok'sən; -swān'), *n.* person who steers a boat, racing shell, etc. Also, **cockswain.**

coy (koi), *adj.* **1.** shy; modest; bashful. **2.** pretending to be shy. [< F *coi* < L *quietus* at rest. Doublet of QUIET[1] and QUIT, adj.] —**coy'ly,** *adv.* —**coy'ness,** *n.*

coy·o·te (kī·ō'tē; kī'ōt), *n., pl.* **-tes** or (*esp. collectively*) **-te.** *Am.* a prairie wolf of W North America. [< Mex.Sp. < Nahuatl *koyotl*]

coy·pu (koi'pū), *n., pl.* **-pus** or (*esp. collectively*) **-pu.** a large ratlike water animal of South America. Its fur is called nutria. [< Sp. < Araucanian (S Am. Ind. linguistic stock) *koypu*]

coz·en (kuz'ən), *v.* cheat. —**coz'en·er,** *n.*

co·zy (kō'zi), *adj.,* **co·zi·er, co·zi·est,** *n., pl.* **co·zies.** —*adj.* warm and comfortable; snug. —*n.* padded cloth cover to keep a teapot warm. Also, **cosy.** [< Scand. (Norw.) *koselig*] —**co'zi·ly,** *adv.* —**co'zi·ness,** *n.*

cp., **1.** compare. **2.** coupon.

C.P.A., *Am.* Certified Public Accountant.

Cpl., cpl., Corporal.

Cr, *Chem.* chromium.

cr., credit; creditor.

crab[1] (krab), *n., v.,* **crabbed, crab·bing.** —*n.* **1.** a shellfish that has a short, broad body with the abdomen or tail folded under, four pairs of legs, and one pair of pincers. **2.** machine for raising heavy weights. **3.** a cross, ill-natured person. **4.** Crab, Cancer, a constellation of the zodiac. —*v.* catch crabs for eating. [OE *crabba*] —**crab'ber,** *n.*

crab[2] (krab), *n.* crab apple.

crab[3] (krab), *v.,* **crabbed, crab·bing.** *Colloq.* find fault (with); criticize. [cf. MDu. *krabben* scratch, quarrel]

crab apple, 1. any of various small, very sour apples, used for making jelly. **2.** tree that bears crab apples.

crab·bed (krab'id), *adj.* **1.** Also, **crab'by.** peevish; ill-natured; cross. **2.** hard to understand. **3.** hard to read or decipher. [< *crab*[1]]

crab grass, *Am.* a coarse grass that spreads rapidly and spoils lawns, etc.

crack (krak), *n.* **1.** place, line, surface, or opening made by breaking without separating into parts. **2.** a sudden, sharp noise, as of a whip. **3.** *Colloq.* blow that makes a sudden, sharp noise. **4.** a narrow opening. **5.** instant; moment. **6.** *Slang.* try; effort. **7.** *Am., Slang.* joke. —*v.* **1.** break without separating into parts. **2.** break with a sudden, sharp noise. **3.** make or cause to make a sudden, sharp noise. **4.** *Colloq.* hit with a sudden, sharp noise. **5.** make or become harsh and shrill: *his voice cracked.* **6.** *Slang.* give way; break down. **7.** tell (a joke, etc.). **8.** break into: *crack a safe.* **9.** crack down, *Am., Slang.* take stern measures. **10.** crack up, **a.** suffer a mental collapse. **b.** crash; go to pieces. **c.** *Colloq.* praise. [OE *cracian*] —**Syn.** *n.* **1.** cleft, fissure, crevice. **2.** clap, report. **4.** chink. —*v.* **1.** split, fracture. **3.** snap, pop.

crack-brained (krak'brānd'), *adj.* crazy; insane.

crack·down (krak'doun'), *n. Am.* taking sudden and stern measures to end a practice, activity, etc.

cracked (krakt), *adj.* **1.** broken without separating into parts. **2.** harsh and shrill. **3.** *Colloq.* crazy; insane.

crack·er (krak'ər), *n.* **1.** a thin, crisp biscuit. **2.** firecracker. **3.** a small, paper roll used as a party favor, containing candy, a motto, a paper cap, etc. It explodes when it is pulled at both ends. **4.** *Am.* a poor white person living in the hills and backwoods regions of Georgia, Florida, etc. **5.** person or instrument that cracks.

crack·er·jack (krak'ər·jak'), *Am.* —*n.* **1.** *Colloq.* person or thing especially fine of its kind. **2. Crackerjack,** *Trademark.* a kind of candied popcorn. —*adj. Colloq.* of superior ability or quality.

crack·ing (krak'ing), *n.* process of changing certain hydrocarbons in petroleum and other oils into lighter hydrocarbons by heat and pressure.

crack·le (krak'əl), *v.,* **-led, -ling,** *n.* —*v.* make slight, sharp sounds. —*n.* **1.** a slight, sharp sound, such as paper makes when crushed. **2.** surface containing very small cracks on some kinds of china, glass, etc. [< *crack*]

crack·ling (krak'ling), *n.* **1.** the crisp, browned skin of roasted pork. **2.** Usually, **cracklings.** *Dial.* crisp part left after lard has been fried out of hog's fat.

crack-up (krak'up'), *n.* **1.** crash; smash. **2.** *Colloq.* mental or physical collapse.

Crac·ow (krak'ou; krä'kō), *n.* city in S Poland.

cra·dle (krā'dəl), *n., v.,* **-dled, -dling.** —*n.* **1.** a baby's little bed, usually on rockers. **2.** place where a thing begins its growth. **3.** frame to support a ship, aircraft, or other large object while it is being built, repaired, lifted, etc. **4.** *Am.* box on rockers to wash gold from earth. **5.** frame attached to a scythe for laying grain evenly as it is cut. —*v.* **1.** put or rock in a cradle; hold as in a cradle. **2.** shelter or train in early life. **3.** support in a cradle. **4.** *Am.* wash in a cradle. **5.** cut with a cradle scythe. [OE *cradol*]

craft (kraft; kräft), *n.* **1.** special skill. **2.** trade or work requiring special skill. **3.** members of a trade requiring special skill. Carpenters are a craft. **4.** skill in deceiving others; slyness; trickiness. **5.** (*pl. in use*) boats, ships, or aircraft. **6.** a boat, ship, or aircraft. [OE *cræft*] —**Syn. 4.** cunning, guile, wile.

crafts·man (krafts'mən; kräfts'-), *n., pl.* **-men. 1.** a skilled workman. **2.** artist. —**crafts'man·ship,** *n.*

craft·y (kraf'ti; kräf'-), adj., craft·i·er, craft-i·est. skillful in deceiving others; sly; tricky. —craft'i·ly, adv. —craft'i·ness, n. —Syn. cunning.

crag (krag), n. a steep, rugged rock rising above others. [< Celtic] —crag'gy, crag·ged (krag'id), adj. —crag'gi·ness, n.

cram (kram), v., crammed, cram·ming. 1. force; stuff. 2. fill too full. 3. eat too fast or too much. 4. Colloq. stuff with knowledge or information, esp. for an examination. 5. Slang. tell lies or exaggerated stories to. 6. Colloq. learn hurriedly. [OE crammian < crimman insert] —cram'mer, n.

cramp¹ (kramp), n. 1. a metal bar bent at both ends, used for holding together blocks of stone, timbers, etc. 2. clamp. 3. something that confines or hinders; limitation; restriction. —v. 1. fasten together with a cramp. 2. confine in a small space; limit; restrict. —adj. 1. confined; limited; restricted. 2. hard to read; difficult to understand. [< MDu. cramp(e), MLG krampe]

cramp² (kramp), n. 1. a sudden, painful contracting of muscles from chill, strain, etc. 2. a paralytic affection of particular muscles. 3. cramps, very sharp pains in the abdomen. —v. cause to have a cramp. [< MDu. See CRAMP¹.]

cran·ber·ry (kran'ber'i; -ber·i), n., pl. -ries. Am. 1. a firm, sour, dark-red berry, used for jelly, sauce, etc. 2. a small shrub that the berries grow on. [< LG kraanbere]

crane (krān), n., v., craned, cran·ing. —n. 1. machine with a long, swinging arm, for lifting and moving heavy weights. 2. a swinging metal arm in a fireplace, used to hold a kettle over the fire. 3. a large wading bird with very long legs and a long neck. 4. any of various herons, esp. the great blue heron. —v. 1. move by, or as if by, a crane. 2. stretch out (one's neck). [OE cran]

crane fly, any of several insects which have long legs; the daddy-longlegs of Great Britain.

cra·ni·ol·o·gy (krā'ni·ol'ə·ji), n. science that deals with the size, shape, and other characteristics of skulls. —cra·ni·o·log·i·cal (krā'ni·ə·loj'ə·kəl), adj. —cra'ni·o·log'i·cal·ly, adv. —cra'ni·ol'o·gist, n.

cra·ni·om·e·try (krā'ni·om'ə·tri), n. science of measuring skulls; measurement of skulls. —cra·ni·o·met·ric (krā'ni·ə·met'rik), adj. —cra'ni·o·met'ri·cal·ly, adv. —cra'ni·om'e·trist, n.

cra·ni·um (krā'ni·əm), n., pl. -ni·ums, -ni·a (-ni·ə). the skull. [< LL < Gk. kranion] —cra'ni·al, adj.

crank (krangk). n. 1. part or handle of a machine connected at right angles to another part to transmit motion. 2. turn of speech or thought. 3. a queer notion or act. 4. Am., Colloq. person with queer notions or habits. 5. Colloq. a cross or ill-tempered person. —v. 1. work or start by means of a crank. 2. bend into the shape of a crank. [OE cranc]

crank·case (krangk'kās'), n. a heavy, metal case enclosing the crankshaft, connecting rods, etc., of an internal-combustion engine.

crank·shaft (krangk'shaft'; -shäft'), n. shaft turned by cranks operated by the movement of the pistons in a gasoline engine.

crank·y (krang'ki), adj., crank·i·er, crank·i·est. 1. cross; irritable; ill-natured. 2. odd; queer. 3. liable to capsize; loose; shaky. —crank'i·ly, adv. —crank'i·ness, n.

cran·ny (kran'i), n., pl. -nies. a small, narrow opening; crack; crevice. [< F cran fissure < Med.L crena notch] —cran'nied, adj.

crape (krāp), n. crepe.

crap·pie (krap'i), n. Am. a small fresh-water fish, used for food.

craps (kraps), n. Am. a gambling game played with two dice.

crap·shoot·er (krap'shüt'ər), n. Am. person who plays craps.

crash¹ (krash), n. 1. a sudden, loud noise. 2. a falling, hitting, or breaking with force and a loud noise. 3. sudden ruin; serious failure in business. 4. of an airplane, a fall to the earth or a bad landing. —v. 1. make a sudden, loud noise. 2. fall, hit, or break with force and a loud noise. 3. move or go with force and a loud noise. 4. be suddenly ruined; fail in business. 5. land in such a way as to damage or wreck an aircraft; make a very bad landing. 6. cause (an aircraft) to land in such a way. 7. Am., Slang. go to (a party, etc.) although not invited. —adj. of or naming something which protects from a crash or is used to rescue persons involved in a crash: a crash boat. [blend of craze shatter and mash] —crash'er, n. —Syn. n. 2. smash. 3. collapse, bankruptcy. —v. 2. smash.

crash² (krash), n. a coarse linen cloth, used for towels, curtains, upholstering, etc. [prob. < Russ.; cf Russ. krashenina colored linen]

crash program, plan of action involving maximum effort and speed.

crass (kras), adj. 1. gross; stupid. 2. thick; coarse. [< L crassus thick] —crass'ly, adv. —crass'ness, n.

crate (krāt), n., v., crat·ed, crat·ing. —n. a large frame, box, basket, etc., used to pack glass, fruit, etc., for shipping or storage. —v. Am. pack in a crate. [< L cratis wickerwork] —crat'er, n.

cra·ter (krā'tər), n. 1. depression around the opening of a volcano. 2. a bowl-shaped hole. [< L < Gk. krater bowl < kra- mix]

cra·vat (krə·vat'), n. 1. necktie. 2. neckcloth; scarf. [< F cravate, special use of Cravate Croat]

crave (krāv), v., craved, crav·ing. 1. long for; yearn for; desire strongly. 2. ask earnestly; beg. [OE crafian demand]

cra·ven (krā'vən), adj. cowardly. —n. coward. —cra'ven·ly, adv. —cra'ven·ness, n.

crav·ing (krāv'ing), n. strong desire; longing.

craw (krô), n. 1. crop of a bird or insect. 2. stomach of any animal. [ME crawe]

craw·fish (krô'fish'), n., pl. -fish·es or (esp. collectively) -fish, v. Am. —n. Also, esp. Brit. crayfish. any of numerous crustaceans much like small lobsters. —v. Colloq. back out of something; retreat. [var. of crayfish]

crawl (krôl), v. 1. move slowly, pulling the body along the ground: worms and snakes crawl. 2. move slowly on hands and knees. 3. move slowly. 4. swarm with crawling things. 5. feel creepy. —n. 1. a crawling; slow movement. 2. a fast way of swimming by overarm strokes. [appar. < Scand. (Dan.) kravle] —crawl'er, n. —crawl'ing·ly, adv.

crawl·y (krôl'i), adj. Colloq. creepy.

cray·fish (krā'fish'), n., pl. -fish·es or (esp. collectively) -fish. Esp. Brit. crawfish. [< OF crevice < Gmc.; akin to CRAB¹]

cray·on (krā'on; -ən), n., v., -oned, -on·ing. —n. 1. stick of white or colored chalk or wax or charcoal used for drawing or writing. 2. drawing made with crayons. —v. draw with a crayon or crayons. [< F, < craie chalk < L creta]

craze (krāz), n., v., crazed, craz·ing. —n. 1. something everybody is very much interested in for a short time; fad. 2. a tiny crack in the glaze of pottery, etc. —v. 1. make or become crazy. 2. make tiny cracks all over the surface of (a dish, etc.). 3. become minutely cracked. [appar. < Scand. (Sw.) krasa break in pieces] —crazed, adj.

cra·zy (krā'zi), adj., -zi·er, -zi·est. 1. having a diseased mind; insane. 2. showing insanity. 3. Colloq. unreasonably eager or enthusiastic. 4. not strong or sound; frail. —cra'zi·ly, adv. —cra'zi·ness, n. —Syn. 1. mad, lunatic. —Ant. 1. sane.

crazy quilt, Am. patchwork quilt.

creak (krēk), v. squeak loudly. —n. a creaking noise. [ME creken < OE cræcettan croak]

creak·y (krēk'i), adj., creak·i·er, creak·i·est. likely to creak; creaking. —creak'i·ly, adv. —creak'i·ness, n.

cream (krēm), n. 1. the oily, yellowish part of milk. 2. food made of cream; food like cream. 3. an oily preparation put on the skin to make it smooth and soft. 4. a yellowish white. 5. the best part. —v. 1. put cream in. 2. take cream from. 3. form like cream on the top; foam; froth. 4. cook with cream. 5. make into a smooth mix-

Crawfish
(3 to 6 in. long)

ture like cream. —*adj.* **1.** containing cream: *cream soup.* **2.** yellowish-white. [< OF *cresme* < LL *crama* cream < Gaulish, and < Eccl.L *chrisma* ointment < Gk., < *chriein* anoint]

cream cheese, a soft, bland, white cheese.

cream·er (krēm′ər), *n.* **1.** *Am.* a small pitcher. **2.** apparatus for separating cream from milk.

cream·er·y (krēm′ər·i), *n., pl.* -er·ies. **1.** *Am.* place where butter and cheese are made. **2.** place where cream, milk, and butter are sold or bought.

cream of tartar, a very sour, white powder, $KHC_4H_4O_6$, used in cooking and in medicine.

crease[1] (krēs), *n., v.*, creased, creas·ing. —*n.* line or mark made by folding; fold; wrinkle. —*v.* **1.** make a crease or creases in. **2.** become creased. —creas′er, *n.*

crease[2] (krēs), *n.* creese.

cre·ate (krē·āt′), *v.*, -at·ed, -at·ing. **1.** cause to be; bring into being; make. **2.** make by giving a new character, function, or status to. **3.** be the first to represent (a role in a play, or the like). **4.** give rise to; cause. [< L, < *creare*] —Syn. **1.** originate, produce, invent. **4.** occasion.

cre·a·tion (krē·ā′shən), *n.* **1.** a creating or being created. **2.** all things created; the universe. **3.** thing created. **4.** an artistic product. **5.** the Creation, the creating of the universe by God. —cre·a′tion·al, *adj.*

cre·a·tive (krē·ā′tiv), *adj.* having the power to create; inventive; productive. —cre·a′tive·ly, *adv.* —cre·a′tive·ness, *n.*

cre·a·tor (krē·ā′tər), *n.* **1.** person who creates. **2.** the Creator, God. —cre·a′tor·ship, *n.*

crea·ture (krē′chər), *n.* **1.** a living being. **2.** a farm animal. **3.** person who is completely under the influence of another. **4.** result; product. [< L *creatura.* See CREATE.]

crèche (kresh; krāsh), *n.* **1.** place where children are taken care of while their mothers are at work. **2.** model of the Christ child in the manger with attendant figures, often displayed at Christmas.

cre·dence (krē′dəns), *n.* belief. [< Med.L, < L *credere* believe]

cre·den·tial (kri·den′shəl), *n.* **1.** that which gives a title to credit or confidence. **2.** Usually, credentials. letters of introduction; references.

cred·i·ble (kred′ə·bəl), *adj.* believable; reliable; trustworthy. [< L, < *credere* believe] —cred′i·bil′i·ty, cred′i·ble·ness, *n.* —cred′i·bly, *adv.*

cred·it (kred′it), *n.* **1.** belief; faith; trust. **2.** trust in a person's ability and intention to pay. **3.** money in a person's bank account, etc. **4.** entry of money paid on account. **5.** the right-hand side of an account where such entries are made. **6.** delayed payment; time allowed for delayed payment. **7.** *Am.* unit of academic work counting toward graduation. **8.** reputation in money matters. **9.** good reputation. **10.** honor; praise. **11.** person or thing that brings honor or praise. —*v.* **1.** believe; have faith in; trust. **2.** give credit in a bank account, etc. **3.** enter on the credit side of an account. **4.** put an academic credit on the record of. [< F < Ital. < *creditum* a loan < *credere* trust, entrust] —Syn. *n.* **9.** repute, standing.

cred·it·a·ble (kred′it·ə·bəl), *adj.* bringing honor or praise. —cred′it·a·ble·ness, cred′it·a·bil′i·ty, *n.* —cred′it·a·bly, *adv.*

cred·i·tor (kred′it·ər), *n.* **1.** person who gives credit. **2.** person to whom a debt is owed.

cre·do (krē′dō; krā′dō), *n., pl.* -dos. creed. [< L, I believe]

cre·du·li·ty (krə·dū′lə·ti; -dū′-), *n.* a too great readiness to believe.

cred·u·lous (krej′ə·ləs), *adj.* **1.** too ready to believe; easily deceived. **2.** characterized by credulity. **3.** caused by credulity. —cred′u·lous·ly, *adv.* —cred′u·lous·ness, *n.*

creed (krēd), *n.* **1.** a brief statement of the essential points of religious belief as approved by some church. **2.** any statement of faith, principles, opinions, etc. [< L *credo* I believe]

creek (krēk; krik), *n.* **1.** *Am.* a small stream. **2.** *Esp. Brit.* a narrow bay, running inland. [appar. < MDu. *crēke,* and/or Scand. *kriki* nook]

creel (krēl), *n.* basket for holding fish. [? < F *creil,* ult. < L *cratis* wickerwork]

creep (krēp), *v.*, crept, creep·ing, *n.* —*v.* **1.** move with the body close to the ground or floor. **2.** move slowly. **3.** grow along the ground or over a wall by means of clinging stems, as ivy. **4.** feel as if things were creeping over the skin. **5.** move in a timid, stealthy, or servile manner. **6.** slip slightly out of place. —*n.* **1.** a creeping. **2.** the creeps, *Colloq.* a feeling as if things were creeping over one's skin. [OE *crēopan*]

creep·er (krēp′ər), *n.* **1.** person or thing that creeps. **2.** *Bot.* any plant that grows along a surface, sending out rootlets from the stem. **3.** creepers, garment combining waist and pants, worn by babies.

creep·ie-peep·ie (krēp′i·pēp′i), *n.* a portable television camera weighing about four pounds. It is powered by batteries. [< *creep* + *peep*[1], modeled on *walkie-talkie*]

creep·y (krēp′i), *adj.*, creep·i·er, creep·i·est. **1.** having a feeling as if things were creeping over one's skin; frightened. **2.** causing such a feeling.

creese (krēs), *n.* dagger with a wavy blade, used by the Malays. Also, crease, kris. [< Malay *kris*]

cre·mate (krē′māt; kri·māt′), *v.*, -mat·ed, -mat·ing. burn (a dead body) to ashes. [< L, < *cremare* burn] —cre·ma′tion, *n.* —cre′ma·tor, *n.*

cre·ma·to·ry (krē′mə·tô′ri; -tō′-; krem′ə-), *n., pl.* -ries, *adj.* —*n.* **1.** furnace for cremating. **2.** building that has a furnace for cremating. —*adj.* of or having to do with cremating.

cre·nate (krē′nāt), *adj.* with a scalloped edge. [< NL, < Med.L *crena* notch] —cre′nate·ly, *adv.*

cren·el·ate, *esp. Brit.* **cren·el·late** (kren′əl·āt), *v.*, -at·ed, -at·ing; *esp. Brit.* -lat·ed, -lat·ing. furnish with battlements. [< F *créneler* < *crenel* notch, ult. < Med.L *crena*]

Cre·ole (krē′ōl), *n.* **1.** *Am.* a white person who is a descendant of the French who settled in Louisiana. **2.** a French or Spanish person born in Spanish America or the West Indies. —*adj.* of or having to do with the Creoles. [< F < Sp. < Pg. *crioulo* < *criar* bring up < L *creare* create]

cre·o·sote (krē′ə·sōt), *n., v.*, -sot·ed, -sot·ing. —*n.* **1.** an oily liquid with a penetrating odor, obtained by distilling wood tar, used as a preservative, etc. **2.** a similar substance obtained from coal tar. —*v.* treat with creosote. [orig., meat preservative < Gk. *kreo-* (for *kreas* flesh) + *soter* savior < *sozein* save]

crepe, crêpe (krāp), *n.* **1.** a thin silk, cotton, rayon, or woolen cloth with a crinkled surface. **2.** Also, crepe paper. tissue paper that looks like crepe. **3.** piece of black crepe worn as a sign of mourning. Also, crape. [< F < L *crispa* curled]

crep·i·tate (krep′ə·tāt), *v.*, -tat·ed, -tat·ing. crackle; rattle. [< L, < *crepitare* crackle < *crepare* crack] —crep·i·ta′tion, *n.*

crept (krept), *v.* pt. and pp. of creep.

cre·pus·cu·lar (kri·pus′kyə·lər), *adj.* **1.** of twilight; resembling twilight; dim; indistinct. **2.** *Zool.* appearing or flying by twilight. [< L *crepusculum* twilight]

cre·scen·do (krə·shen′dō), *n., pl.* -dos, *adj., adv.* —*n.* a gradual increase in force or loudness. —*adj., adv.* gradually increasing in force or loudness. [< Ital., ppr. of *crescere* increase < L]

cres·cent (kres′ənt), *n.* **1.** shape of the moon in its first or last quarter. **2.** anything having this or a similar shape. —*adj.* **1.** shaped like the moon in its first or last quarter. **2.** growing; increasing. [< L, ppr. of *crescere* grow]

cre·sol (krē′sōl; -sol), *n.* oily liquid, C_7H_8O, obtained from tar, used as a disinfectant.

cress (kres), *n.* plant whose leaves have a peppery taste. [OE *cresse*]

cres·set (kres′it), *n.* a metal container for burning oil, wood, etc., to give light. [< OF]

crest (krest), *n.* **1.** comb, tuft, etc., on the head of a bird or animal. **2.** decoration, plumes, etc., on the top of a helmet. **3.** decoration at the top of a coat of arms. **4.** an ornamental part which surmounts a wall, the ridge of

Crest
(def. 2)

a roof, etc. **5.** the top part; top of a hill, wave, etc.; ridge; peak; summit. **6.** the highest or best of its kind. —*v.* **1.** furnish with a crest. **2.** form into a crest. [< OF < L *crista* tuft] —crest′ed, *adj.* —crest′less, *adj.*

crest·fall·en (krest′fôl′ən), *adj.* with bowed head; dejected; discouraged. —crest′fall′en·ly, *adv.* —crest′fall′en·ness, *n.*

cre·ta·ceous (kri·tā′shəs), *adj.* like chalk; containing chalk. [< L, < *creta* chalk]

Crete (krēt), *n.* a Greek island in the Mediterranean, SE of Greece. —Cre′tan, *adj.*, *n.*

cre·tin (krē′tən), *n.* a deformed idiot. [< F < Swiss dial. < L *Christianus* Christian; came to mean "man," then "fellow," then "poor fellow"]

cre·tin·ism (krē′tən·iz·əm), *n.* a chronic, congenital disease due to a deficiency in the thyroid gland, often resulting in deformity and idiocy.

cre·tonne (kri·ton′; krē′ton), *n.* a strong cotton cloth with printed designs, used for curtains, etc. [< F, prob. < *Creton*, village in Normandy]

cre·vasse (krə·vas′), *n.*, *v.*, -vassed, -vass·ing. —*n.* **1.** a deep crack or crevice in the ice of a glacier. **2.** *Am.* break in a levee. —*v.* fissure with crevasses. [< F, CREVICE]

crev·ice (krev′is), *n.* a narrow split or crack. [< OF *crevace* < VL *crepacia* < L *crepare* crack] —crev′iced, *adj.*

crew[1] (krü), *n.* **1.** men needed to do work on a ship, or to row a boat. **2.** group of people working or acting together. **3.** crowd; gang. [< OF *creüe* increase, recruit < *creistre* grow < L *crescere*]

crew[2] (krü), *v.* pt. of **crow**[1].

crew cut, a kind of very short haircut.

crib (krib), *n.*, *v.*, cribbed, crib·bing. —*n.* **1.** a small bed with high sides to keep a baby from falling out. **2.** rack or manger for horses and cows to eat from. **3.** building or box for storing grain, salt, etc. **4.** framework of logs or timbers used in building. **5.** *Colloq.* use of another's words or ideas as one's own. **6.** *Slang.* notes or helps that are unfair to use in doing schoolwork. **7.** a small room or house. —*v.* **1.** provide with a crib. **2.** *Colloq.* use (another's words or ideas) as one's own. **3.** *Slang.* use notes unfairly in doing schoolwork. **4.** shut up in a small space. [OE *cribb*] —crib′ber, *n.*

crib·bage (krib′ij), *n.* a card game for two, three, or four people.

crick (krik), *n.* a sudden, painful muscular cramp. —*v.* cause a crick in.

Cricket (1 in. long)

crick·et[1] (krik′it), *n.* a black insect of the grasshopper family. [< OF *criquet*; imit.]

crick·et[2] (krik′it), *n.* **1.** an outdoor game played by two teams of eleven players each, with ball, bats, and wickets. **2.** *Colloq.* fair play; good sportsmanship. —*v.* play this game. [< OF *criquet* goal post, stick, prob. < MDu. *cricke* stick to lean on] —crick′et·er, *n.*

crick·et[3] (krik′it), *n.* a small stool.

cri·er (krī′ər), *n.* **1.** official who shouts out public announcements. **2.** person who shouts out announcements of goods for sale. **3.** person who cries.

crime (krīm), *n.* **1.** a wrong act that is against the law. **2.** violation of law. **3.** a wrong act; sin. [< OF < L *crimen* < *cernere* judge, decide] —Syn. **1.** offense, trespass.

Cri·me·a (krī·mē′ə; kri-), *n.* peninsula in SW Soviet Union, on the N coast of the Black Sea. Cri·me′an, *adj.*

crim·i·nal (krim′ə·nəl), *n.* person guilty of a crime. —*adj.* **1.** guilty of crime. **2.** having to do with crime. **3.** like crime; wrong; sinful. —crim′i·nal′i·ty, *n.* —crim′i·nal·ly, *adv.*

crim·i·nol·o·gy (krim′ə·nol′ə·ji), *n.* study of crimes and criminals. —crim·i·no·log·ic (krim′-ə·nə·loj′ik), crim′i·no·log′i·cal, *adj.* —crim′i·nol′o·gist, *n.*

crimp (krimp), *v.* press into small, narrow folds; make wavy. —*n.* **1.** a crimping. **2.** something crimped; fold; wave. **3.** a waved or curled lock of hair. **4.** put a crimp in, *Slang.* hinder. [OE *gecrympan*] —crimp′er, *n.* —crimp′y, *adj.*

crim·son (krim′zən), *n.* a deep red. —*adj.* deep-red. —*v.* turn deep red. [< Ital. or Sp. < Ar. *qirmizi* < Skt. *kṛmi-* insect]

cringe (krinj), *v.*, cringed, cring·ing, *n.* —*v.* **1.** shrink or crouch in fear. **2.** try to get favor or attention by servile behavior. —*n.* a cringing. [ME *crengen* < OE *cringan* give way] —cring′er, *n.*

crin·kle (kring′kəl), *v.*, -kled, -kling, *n.* —*v.* **1.** wrinkle; ripple. **2.** rustle: *paper crinkles when it is crushed.* —*n.* **1.** wrinkle; ripple. **2.** rustle. [ME *crenkle(n)* < OE *crincan* bend] —crin′kly, *adv.*

cri·noid (krī′noid; krin′oid), *n.* a flower-shaped sea animal, usually anchored by a stalk. —*adj.* of or like a crinoid. [< Gk., < *krinon* lily]

crin·o·line (krin′ə·lēn), *n.* **1.** a stiff cloth used as a lining. **2.** petticoat of crinoline to hold a skirt out. **3.** a hoop skirt. [< F < Ital., < *crino* horsehair (< L *crinis* hair) + *lino* thread (< L *linum*)]

crip·ple (krip′əl), *n.*, *v.*, -pled, -pling. —*n.* a lame person or animal; one that cannot use his legs, arms, or body properly. —*v.* **1.** make a cripple of. **2.** damage; disable; weaken. [OE *crypel*; akin to CREEP] —crip′pler, *n.* —Syn. *v.* **1.** lame, maim. **2.** impair.

cri·sis (krī′sis), *n.*, *pl.* -ses (-sēz). **1.** the turning point in a disease, toward life or death. **2.** the deciding event in the course of anything. **3.** time of danger or anxious waiting. [< L < Gk., < *krinein* decide]

crisp (krisp), *adj.* **1.** hard and thin; breaking easily with a snap. **2.** fresh; sharp and clear; bracing: *crisp winter air.* **3.** clear-cut; decisive. —*v.* make or become crisp. [< L *crispus* curled] —crisp′ly, *adv.* —crisp′ness, *n.* —Syn. *adj.* **1.** brittle. **2.** brisk.

crisp·y (kris′pi), *adj.*, crisp·i·er, crisp·i·est. crisp.

criss·cross (kris′krôs′; -kros′), *adj.* made or marked with crossed lines; crossed. —*adv.* crosswise. —*v.* mark or cover with crossed lines. —*n.* mark or pattern made of crossed lines. [alter. of *Christ's cross*]

Cris·tó·bal (kris·tō′bəl), *n.* seaport in the Canal Zone, at the Atlantic end of the Panama Canal, near Colón.

cri·te·ri·on (krī·tir′i·ən), *n.*, *pl.* -te·ri·a (-tir′-i·ə), -te·ri·ons. rule or standard for making a judgment; test. [< Gk., < *krinein* judge]

crit·ic (krit′ik), *n.* **1.** person who makes judgments of the merits and faults of books, music, plays, etc. **2.** person whose profession is writing such judgments for a newspaper, etc. **3.** person who finds fault. [< L < Gk. *kritikos* critical < *krinein* judge]

crit·i·cal (krit′ə·kəl), *adj.* **1.** inclined to find fault or disapprove. **2.** skilled as a critic. **3.** coming from one who is skilled as a critic: *a critical judgment.* **4.** belonging to the work of a critic. **5.** of a crisis: *the critical moment.* **6.** full of danger or difficulty. **7.** of supplies, labor, or resources, essential for the work or project but existing in inadequate supply. —crit′i·cal·ly, *adv.* —crit′i·cal·ness, *n.*

crit·i·cism (krit′ə·siz·əm), *n.* **1.** disapproval; faultfinding. **2.** the making of judgments; analysis of merits and faults. **3.** a critical comment, essay, review, etc.

crit·i·cize (krit′ə·sīz), *esp. Brit.* **crit·i·cise** (krit′ə·sīz), *v.*, -cized, -ciz·ing; *esp. Brit.* -cised, -cis·ing. **1.** disapprove; find fault with. **2.** judge or speak as a critic. —crit′i·ciz′a·ble, *esp. Brit.* crit′i·cis′-a·ble, *adj.* —crit′i·ciz′er, *esp. Brit.* crit′i·cis′-er, *n.*

cri·tique (kri·tēk′), *n.* **1.** art of criticism. **2.** a critical essay or review. [< F < Gk. *kritike* (*techne*) the critical art. See CRITIC.]

croak (krōk), *n.* a deep, hoarse cry, as of a frog, crow, or raven. —*v.* **1.** make such a sound. **2.** utter in a deep, hoarse voice. **3.** be always prophesying misfortune; grumble. **4.** *Slang.* die. [< OE *cräcettan*]

croak·er (krōk′ər), *n.* **1.** one that croaks. **2.** *Am.* any of various fishes that make a croaking or grunting noise.

Cro·a·tia (krō-ā′shə), *n.* district in NW Yugoslavia. —**Cro·at** (krō′at), *n.* —**Cro·a′tian**, *adj.*, *n.*

cro·chet (krō-shā′), *v.*, –**cheted** (–shād′), –**chet·ing** (–shā′ing), *n.* —*v.* knit (sweaters, lace, etc.) with a single needle having a hook at one end. —*n.* knitting done in this way. [< F, dim. of *croc* hook < Gmc.]

crock (krok), *n.* pot or jar made of baked clay. [OE *crocc*(*a*)]

crock·er·y (krok′-ər-i), *n.* dishes, jars, etc., made of baked clay; earthenware.

Crock·ett (krok′it), *n.* David, 1786–1836, American pioneer, killed at the Alamo.

Crocodile (14 ft. long)

croc·o·dile (krok′ə-dīl), *n.* a large, lizardlike reptile with a thick skin, long narrow head, and webbed feet. [< OF < L < Gk. *krokodeilos*, earlier, lizard]

crocodile tears, false or insincere grief.

croc·o·dil·i·an (krok′ə-dil′i-ən), *adj.* of or like a crocodile. —*n.* any of a group of reptiles that includes crocodiles, alligators, etc.

cro·cus (krō′kəs), *n.*, *pl.* **cro·cus·es**, **cro·ci** (–sī). 1. a small flowering plant that grows from a bulblike stem, usually blooming very early in the spring. 2. the flower. [< L < Gk. *krokos* < Semitic]

Croe·sus (krē′səs), *n.* 1. a very rich king of Lydia from 560 to 546 B.C. 2. a very rich person.

croft (krôft; kroft), *n.* 1. *Brit.* a small enclosed field. 2. a very small rented farm. [OE] —**croft′er**, *n.*

croix de guerre (krwä′ də gâr′), a French medal given to soldiers for bravery under fire.

Cro-Mag·non (krō-mag′non), *adj.* belonging to a group of prehistoric people who lived in SW Europe.

crom·lech (krom′lek), *n.* 1. circle of upright stones built in prehistoric times. 2. a dolmen. [< Welsh, < *crom* bent + *llech* flat stone]

Crom·well (krom′wel; –wəl), *n.* Oliver, 1599–1658, English general, Puritan leader, and lord protector of the Commonwealth, 1653–1658.

crone (krōn), *n.* a shrunken old woman. [< MDu. < F *carogne* carcass, hag. See CARRION.]

cro·ny (krō′ni), *n.*, *pl.* –**nies.** a very close friend; chum.

crook (krůk), *v.* hook; bend; curve. —*n.* 1. hook; bend; curve. 2. a hooked, curved, or bent part. 3. a shepherd's staff. 4. *Am.*, *Colloq.* a dishonest person; thief; swindler. [appar. < Scand. *krōkr*]

crook·ed (krůk′id *for 1 and 2*; krůkt *for 3*), *adj.* 1. not straight; bent; curved; twisted. 2. *Am.*, *Colloq.* dishonest. 3. having a crook. —**crook′-ed·ly**, *adv.* —**crook′ed·ness**, *n.*

croon (krün), *v.* 1. hum, sing, or murmur in a low tone. 2. sing in a low voice with exaggerated emotion. —*n.* low humming, singing, or murmuring. [< Scand. *krauna* murmur] —**croon′er**, *n.*

crop (krop), *n.*, *v.*, **cropped**, **crop·ping.** —*n.* 1. product grown or gathered for use, esp. for use as food. 2. the whole amount (of the produce of any plant or tree) that is borne in one season. 3. the yield of any product in a season: *a large ice crop*. 4. group; collection. 5. clipped hair; a short haircut. 6. mark produced by clipping the ears. 7. a baglike swelling of a bird's food passage where food is prepared for digestion. 8. a short whip with a loop instead of a lash. 9. handle of a whip. —*v.* 1. plant and cultivate a crop. 2. cut or bite off the top of. 3. clip; cut short. 4. **crop out** or **up**, a. appear; come to the surface. b. be shown unexpectedly. [OE *cropp* sprout, craw]

crop·per (krop′ər), *n.* 1. person or thing that crops. 2. one who raises a crop, esp. on shares. 3. *Colloq.* a heavy fall. 4. *Colloq.* failure; collapse.

cro·quet (krō-kā′), *n.* an outdoor game played by knocking wooden balls through small wire arches with mallets. [< F, dial. var. of *crochet*. See CROCHET.]

cro·quette (krō-ket′), *n.* a small mass of chopped meat, fish, etc., coated with crumbs and fried. [< F, < *croquer* crunch]

cro·sier (krō′zhər), *n.* an ornamental staff carried by or before bishops or certain abbots. Also, **crozier.** [< F, crook bearer, < VL *croccia* crook < Gmc.]

cross (krôs; kros), *n.* 1. stick or post with another across it. 2. **the Cross**, a. the cross on which Christ died. b. Christ's sufferings and death; the Atonement. c. the Christian religion. 3. the symbol (†) of the Christian religion. 4. two intersecting lines (× +). A person who cannot sign his name makes a cross instead. 5. thing, design, or mark shaped like a cross. 6. burden of duty; suffering; trouble. 7. a mixing of kins, breeds, or races. 8. result of such mixing. —*v.* 1. mark with a cross. 2. draw a line across. 3. put or lay across. 4. lie across; be in the form of a cross. 5. go across; move across. 6. meet and pass: *my letter to her and hers to me crossed*. 7. make the sign of the cross on or over. 8. oppose; hinder. 9. cause (different kinds, breeds, races, etc.) to interbreed. —*adj.* 1. crossing; lying or going across. 2. opposing; counter. 3. in a bad temper. 4. mixed in kind, breed, or race. [< OIrish *cros* < L *crux*. Doublet of CRUX.] —**cross′ly**, *adv.* —**cross′ness**, *n.* —Syn. *n.* 6. trial, affliction. 8. hybrid. —*v.* 2. cancel. 8. thwart, frustrate. —*adj.* 3. irritable. 4. hybrid.

cross·bar (krôs′bär′; kros′–), *n.* bar, line, or stripe going crosswise.

cross·beam (krôs′bēm′; kros′–), *n.* a large beam that crosses another or extends from wall to wall.

cross·bones (krôs′bōnz′; kros′–), *n.pl.* two large bones placed crosswise, symbolizing death.

cross·bow (krôs′bō′; kros′–), *n.* a medieval weapon with a bow and a grooved stock in the middle to direct the arrows, stones, etc. —**cross′-bow′man**, *n.*

cross·bred (krôs′bred′; kros′–), *adj.* produced by crossbreeding. —*n.* a crossbreed.

cross·breed (krôs′brēd′; kros′–), *v.*, –**bred**, –**breed·ing**, *n.* —*v.* breed by mixing kinds, breeds, or races. —*n.* individual or breed produced by crossbreeding.

cross bun, bun marked with a cross on the top, often eaten on Good Friday.

cross·coun·try (krôs′kun′tri; kros′–), *adj.* across open country instead of by road.

cross·cut (krôs′kut′; kros′–), *adj.*, *n.*, *v.*, –**cut**, –**cut·ting**. —*adj.* 1. used or made for cutting across. 2. cut across. —*n.* 1. a cut across. 2. short cut. —*v.* cut across.

cross·ex·am·ine (krôs′ig-zam′ən; kros′–), *v.*, –**ined**, –**in·ing**. 1. *Law.* question (a witness for the opposing side) closely to test the truth of his evidence. 2. examine closely or severely. —**cross′-ex·am′i·na′tion**, *n.* —**cross′-ex·am′in·er**, *n.*

cross·eye (krôs′ī′; kros′–), *n.* strabismus, esp. the form in which both eyes turn toward the nose. —**cross′-eyed′**, *adj.*

cross·fer·ti·li·za·tion (krôs′fér′tə-lə-zā′shən; kros′–), *n. Bot.* fertilization of one flower by pollen from another.

cross·fer·ti·lize (krôs′fér′tə-līz; kros′–), *v.*, –**lized**, –**liz·ing**. cause the cross-fertilization of.

cross·grained (krôs′grānd′; kros′–), *adj.* having the grain running across the regular grain.

cross·hatch (krôs′hach′; kros′–), *v.* mark or shade with two sets of parallel lines crossing each other.

cross·ing (krôs′ing; kros′–), *n.* 1. place where things cross each other. 2. place at which a street, river, etc., may be crossed. 3. act of crossing. 4. voyage across water.

cross·patch (krôs′pach′; kros′–), *n. Colloq.* a cross, bad-tempered person.

cross·piece (krôs′pēs′; kros′–), *n.* piece that is placed across something.

cross·pol·li·nate (krôs′pol′ə-nāt; kros′–), *v.*, –**nated**, –**nat·ing**. cause cross-fertilization in. —**cross′-pol′li·na′tion**, *n.*

cross-pur·pose (krôs'pėr'pəs; kros'-), *n.* **1.** opposing or contrary purpose. **2.** at cross-purposes, a. misunderstanding each other's purpose. **b.** acting under such a misunderstanding.

cross-ques·tion (krôs'kwes'chən; kros'-), *v.* cross-examine.

cross-re·fer (krôs'ri·fėr'; kros'-), *v.*, **-ferred**, **-fer·ring. 1.** refer from one part to another. **2.** make a cross reference.

cross reference, reference from one part of a book, index, etc., to another.

cross·road (krôs'rōd'; kros'-), *n.* **1.** road that crosses another. **2.** road connecting main roads. **3.** Often, crossroads (*sing. in use*). a. place where roads cross. **b.** a meeting place, esp. for people living far apart.

cross section, 1. act of cutting anything across. **2.** piece cut in this way. **3.** a representative sample.

cross-stitch (krôs'stich'; kros'-), *n.* **1.** one stitch crossed over another, forming an X. **2.** embroidery made with this stitch. —*v.* embroider or sew with this stitch.

cross trees, *Naut.* two horizontal bars of wood near the top of a mast.

cross·wise (krôs'wīz'; kros'-), **cross·ways** (-wāz'), *adv.* **1.** so as to cross; across. **2.** in the form of a cross. **3.** opposite to what is required; wrongly.

C, cross trees.

cross·word puzzle (krôs'wėrd'; kros'-), puzzle with sets of squares to be filled in with words, one letter to each square. Synonyms or definitions of the words are given with numbers corresponding to numbers in the squares.

crotch (kroch), *n.* **1.** a forked piece or part. **2.** place where the body divides into the two legs. [var. of *crutch*] —**crotched** (krocht), *adj.*

crotch·et (kroch'it), *n.* **1.** an odd notion; unreasonable whim. **2.** a small hook or hooklike part. **3.** *Esp. Brit., Music.* a quarter note. [< OF *crochet.* See CROCHET.]

crotch·et·y (kroch'ə·ti), *adj.* **1.** full of odd notions or unreasonable whims. **2.** of the nature of a crotchet. —**crotch'et·i·ness,** *n.*

cro·ton (krō'tən), *n.* a tropical shrub or tree of Asia with a strong odor. The seeds of a croton tree yield an oil (**croton oil**) used in medicine. [< NL < Gk. *kroton* tick?]

croton bug, *Am.* a small cockroach.

crouch (krouch), *v.* **1.** stoop low with bent legs like an animal ready to spring, or in hiding, or shrinking in fear. **2.** bow down in a timid or slavish manner. **3.** bend low. —*n.* **1.** act or state of crouching. **2.** a crouching position. [< OF *crochir* < *croc* hook < Gmc.]

croup¹ (krüp), *n.* inflammation or diseased condition of the throat and windpipe characterized by a hoarse cough and difficult breathing. [? < *croup, v.*, blend of *croak* and *whoop*] —**croup'y,** *adj.*

croup² (krüp), *n.* rump of a horse, etc. [< F *croupe* < Gmc.]

crou·pi·er (krü'pi·ər), *n.* attendant at a gambling table who rakes in the money and pays the winners. [< F, < *croupe* CROUP²; orig., one who rides behind]

crou·ton (krü'ton), *n.* a small piece of toasted or fried bread, often served in soup. [< F, < *croûte* CRUST]

crow¹ (krō), *n., v.,* **crowed** (or **crew** for **2**), **crowed, crow·ing.** —*n.* **1.** a loud cry made by a rooster. **2.** a happy sound made by a baby. —*v.* **1.** make the happy sound of a baby. **2.** make the cry of a cock. **3.** show happiness and pride; boast. [OE *crāwan;* imit.]

crow² (krō), *n.* **1.** a large, glossyblack bird that has a harsh cry or caw. **2.** any similar bird, such as ravens, magpies, jays, etc. **3.** crowbar. **4.** as the crow flies, in a straight line; in or by the shortest way. **5.** eat crow, *Am., Colloq.* be forced to do something very disagreeable and humiliating. [OE *crāwe*]

Man using a crowbar

Crow (krō), *n. Am.* member of a tribe of American Indians living in Montana.

crow·bar (krō'bär'), *n. Am.* a strong iron or steel bar, used as a lever.

crowd (kroud), *n.* **1.** a large number of people together. **2.** people in general; the masses. **3.** *Am., Colloq.* group; set. **4.** large numbers of things together. [< v.] —*v.* **1.** collect in large numbers. **2.** fill; fill too full. **3.** push; shove. **4.** press forward; force one's way. **5.** force into a small space. **6.** *Am., Colloq.* press; urge; dun. [OE *crūdan* press] —**crowd'ed,** *adj.* —Syn. *n.* **1.** throng, multitude, host, horde, swarm, mob, crush. –*v.* **1.** throng, swarm. **2.** cram, pack.

crow·foot (krō'fût'), *n., pl.* **-foots.** buttercup or other plant with leaves shaped somewhat like a crow's foot.

crown (kroun), *n.* **1.** head covering for a king, queen, etc. **2.** power and authority of a king, queen, etc.; royal power. **3.** a king, queen, etc. **4.** design or thing shaped like a crown. **5.** wreath for the head. **6.** honor; reward. **7.** head. **8.** the highest part; top. **9.** the highest state or quality of anything. **10.** part of a tooth above the gum. **11.** an artificial substitute for this part. **12.** a British silver coin, worth 5 shillings or about $.70 (1950). **13.** *Naut.* end of an anchor between the arms. **14.** the Crown, royal power. —*v.* **1.** make king, queen, etc. **2.** honor; reward. **3.** be on top of; cover the highest part of: *a fort crowns the hill.* **4.** make perfect or complete; add the finishing touch to. **5.** put a crown on. **6.** make a king of (a checker that has been moved across the checkerboard). [< AF < L *corona* garland, wreath. Doublet of CORONA.] —**crown'er,** *n.*

crown glass, very clear glass used in optical instruments.

crown prince, the oldest living son of a king, queen, etc.; heir apparent to a kingdom.

crown princess, 1. wife of a crown prince. **2.** girl or woman who is heir apparent to a kingdom.

crow's-foot (krōz'fût'), *n., pl.* **-feet.** Usually, **crow's-feet.** wrinkle at the outer corner of the eye.

crow's-nest (krōz'nest'), *n. Naut.* **1.** a small, enclosed platform near the top of a mast, used by the lookout. **2.** any similar platform ashore.

Croy·don (kroi'dən), *n.* city in SE England, near London, containing a great airport.

cro·zier (krō'zhər), *n.* crosier.

cru·cial (krü'shəl), *adj.* **1.** very important; critical; decisive. **2.** very trying; severe. [< NL (medical) < L *crux* cross] —**cru'cial·ly,** *adv.*

cru·ci·ble (krü'sə·bəl), *n.* **1.** container in which metals, ores, etc., can be melted. **2.** a severe test or trial. [< Med.L *crucibulum*, orig., night lamp]

cru·ci·fix (krü'sə·fiks), *n.* **1.** a cross with the figure of Christ crucified on it. **2.** a cross. [< LL *crucifixus* fixed to a cross < *crux* cross + *fixus*, pp. of *figere* fasten]

cru·ci·fix·ion (krü'sə·fik'shən), *n.* **1.** act of crucifying. **2.** Crucifixion, a. the putting to death of Christ on the cross. **b.** picture, statue, etc., of this.

cru·ci·form (krü'sə·fôrm), *adj.* shaped like a cross. —**cru'ci·form'ly,** *adv.*

cru·ci·fy (krü'sə·fī), *v.*, **-fied, -fy·ing. 1.** put to death by nailing or binding the hands and feet to a cross. **2.** treat severely; torture. [< OF < L *crucifigere.* See CRUCIFIX.] —**cru'ci·fi'er,** *n.*

crude (krüd), *adj.*, **crud·er, crud·est. 1.** in a natural or raw state; unrefined. **2.** not mature; unripe. **3.** rough; coarse: *a crude log cabin.* **4.** lacking finish, grace, taste, or refinement: *crude manners.* [< L *crudus* raw] —**crude'ly,** *adv.* —**crude'ness, cru'di·ty,** *n.* —Syn. **1.** unfinished. **2.** green. **4.** rude. —Ant. **4.** cultivated, refined.

cru·el (krü'əl), *adj.* **1.** fond of causing pain to others and delighting in their suffering. **2.** showing a cruel nature: *cruel acts.* **3.** causing pain and suffering: *a cruel war.* [< F < L *crudelis* rough. See CRUDE.] —**cru'el·ly,** *adv.* —**cru'el·ness,** *n.* —Syn. **1.** brutal, savage, barbarous, ruthless, pitiless, merciless. —Ant. **1.** kindly.

cru·el·ty (krü'əl·ti), *n., pl.* **-ties. 1.** readiness to give pain to others or to delight in their suffering. **2.** a cruel act.

cru·et (krü′it), *n.* a glass bottle to hold vinegar, oil, etc., for the table. [< OF, dim. of *cruie* pot < Gmc.]

cruise (krüz), *v.,* **cruised, cruis·ing,** *n.* —*v.* 1. sail about from place to place on pleasure or business; sail over or about. 2. journey or travel from place to place. 3. fly in an airplane at the speed of maximum efficiency. —*n.* a cruising voyage. [< Du. *kruisen* < *kruis* < L *crux* cross]

cruis·er (krüz′ər), *n.* 1. warship with less armor and more speed than a battleship. 2. airplane, taxi, etc., that cruises. 3. *Am.* a police car connected with headquarters by radio.

crul·ler (krul′ər), *n. Am.* a twisted doughnut. [appar. < Du., < *krullen* curl]

crumb (krum), *n.* 1. a very small piece of bread, cake, etc., broken from a larger piece. 2. the soft inside part of bread. 3. a little bit: *a crumb of comfort.* —*v.* 1. break into crumbs. 2. cover with crumbs for frying or baking. 3. *Colloq.* brush or wipe the crumbs from (a tablecloth, etc.). [OE *cruma*] —**crumb′y,** *adj.*

crum·ble (krum′bəl), *v.,* **–bled, –bling.** 1. break into very small pieces or crumbs. 2. fall into pieces; decay. [earlier *crimble* < OE *gecrymman* < *cruma* crumb]

crum·bly (krum′bli), *adj.,* **–bli·er, –bli·est.** easily crumbled. —**crum′bli·ness,** *n.*

crum·pet (krum′pit), *n. Esp. Brit.* cake baked on a griddle, that is thicker than a pancake and is usually toasted after being baked. [OE *crompeht* a cake]

crum·ple (krum′pəl), *v.,* **–pled, –pling,** *n.* —*v.* 1. crush together; wrinkle. 2. *Colloq.* collapse. —*n.* wrinkle made by crushing something together. [< OE *crump* bent]

crunch (krunch), *v.* 1. crush noisily with the teeth. 2. crush or grind noisily. —*n.* act or sound of crunching.

crup·per (krup′ər), *n.* strap attached to the back of a harness and passing under a horse's tail. [< OF *cropiere* < *crope* CROUP²]

cru·sade (krü·sād′), *n., v.,* **–sad·ed, –sad·ing.** —*n.* 1. Often, Crusade. any one of the Christian military expeditions between the years 1096 and 1272 to recover the Holy Land from the Mohammedans. 2. war having a religious purpose and approved by the church. 3. a vigorous campaign against a public evil or in favor of some new idea. —*v.* take part in a crusade. [blend of earlier *crusado* (< Sp. *cruzada*) and *croisade* (< F < Pr., from a verb meaning "take the cross"). See CROSS.] —**cru·sad′er,** *n.*

cruse (krüz; krüs), *n.* jug, pot, or bottle made of earthenware. [< MDu. *croes*]

crush (krush), *v.* 1. squeeze together violently so as to break or bruise. 2. wrinkle or crease by wear or rough handling. 3. break into fine pieces by grinding or pounding or pressing. 4. flatten by heavy pressure. 5. subdue; conquer. 6. drink: *to crush a goblet of wine.* —*n.* 1. a violent pressure like grinding or pounding. 2. *Am.* mass of people crowded close together. 3. *Am., Slang.* a. a sudden or ardent infatuation. b. object of a sudden or ardent infatuation. [appar. < OF *croissir* < Gmc.] —**crush′er,** *n.*

Cru·soe (krü′sō), *n.* **Robinson,** shipwrecked hero of a book of the same name by Daniel Defoe.

crust (krust), *n.* 1. the hard, outside part of bread. 2. piece of this; any hard, dry piece of bread. 3. the baked outside covering of a pie. 4. any hard outside covering. 5. the solid outside part of the earth. —*v.* 1. cover or become covered with a crust. 2. form or collect into a crust. [< L *crusta* rind]

crus·ta·cean (krus·tā′shən), *n.* any of a group of water animals with hard shells, jointed bodies and appendages, and gills for breathing, including crabs, lobsters, shrimps, etc. —*adj.* of or belonging to this group. [< NL, < L *crusta* shell, rind]

crust·y (krus′ti), *adj.,* **crust·i·er, crust·i·est.** 1. having a crust; hard; crustlike. 2. harsh in manner, speech, etc.—**crust′i·ly,** *adv.*—**crust′i·ness,** *n.*

crutch (kruch), *n.* 1. stick with a crosspiece at the top that fits under a lame person's arm and supports part of his weight in walking. 2. a forked support or part. 3. anything like a crutch in shape or use; support; prop. —*v.* support with or as with a crutch; prop or sustain. [OE *crycc*]

crux (kruks), *n.* 1. the essential part; the most important point. 2. a puzzling or perplexing question. [< L, cross. Doublet of CROSS.]

cry (krī), *v.,* **cried, cry·ing,** *n., pl.* **cries.** —*v.* 1. make sounds showing pain, fear, sorrow, etc. 2. shed tears; weep. 3. (of animals) give forth characteristic calls. 4. call loudly; shout. 5. **cry down,** make little of; speak of as unimportant or less valuable; deprecate. 6. announce in public. 7. **cry for,** a. ask earnestly for; beg for. b. need very much. —*n.* 1. sound made by a person or animal that shows some strong feeling, such as pain, fear, anger, or sorrow. 2. fit of weeping. 3. noise or call of an animal: *the cry of the crow.* 4. the yelping of hounds in the chase. 5. a loud call; shout: *a cry for help.* 6. general opinion; public report. 7. call to action; slogan. 8. **a far cry,** a. a long way. b. a great difference. [< OF < L *quiritare*]

cry·ing (krī′ing), *adj.* 1. that cries. 2. demanding attention; very bad.

crypt (kript), *n.* an underground room or vault. The crypt beneath the main floor of a church was formerly often used as a burial place. [< L < Gk. *kryptos* hidden. Doublet of GROTTO.]

cryp·tic (krip′tik), **cryp·ti·cal** (–tə·kəl), *adj.* having a hidden meaning; secret; mysterious. [< LL < Gk., < *kryptos* hidden] —**cryp′ti·cal·ly,** *adv.*

cryp·to·gam (krip′tə·gam), *n. Bot.* plant having no stamens and pistils, and therefore no flowers and seeds, as ferns and mosses. [< NL < Gk. *kryptos* hidden + *gamos* marriage] —**cryp′to·gam′ic,** **cryp·tog·a·mous** (krip·tog′ə·məs), *adj.*

cryp·to·gram (krip′tə·gram), *n.* something written in secret code or cipher.

cryp·to·graph (krip′tə·graf; –gräf), *n.* 1. cryptogram. 2. a system of secret writing. —**cryp′to·graph′ic,** **cryp·to·graph′i·cal,** *adj.*

cryp·tog·ra·phy (krip·tog′rə·fi), *n.* process of or writing in secret characters. —**cryp·tog′ra·pher,** *n.*

crys·tal (kris′təl), *n.* 1. a clear, transparent mineral, a kind of quartz, that looks like ice. 2. piece of crystal cut to form an ornament. 3. very transparent glass. 4. glass over the face of a watch. 5. a regularly shaped piece with angles and flat surfaces into which a substance solidifies. 6. *Radio.* piece of quartz used in radio. —*adj.* 1. made of crystal. 2. clear and transparent like crystal. [< OF < L < Gk. *krystallos* clear ice]

Crystal shapes

crystal detector, device consisting of a crystal embedded in soft metal, sometimes used in a radio instead of vacuum tubes.

crys·tal·line (kris′təl·in; –ēn; –īn), *adj.* 1. consisting of crystals; solidified in the form of crystals. 2. made of crystal. 3. clear and transparent like crystal.

crys·tal·lize (kris′təl·īz), *v.,* **–lized, –liz·ing.** 1. form into crystals; solidify into crystals. 2. form into definite shape. 3. coat with sugar. —**crys′tal·liz′a·ble,** *adj.* —**crys′tal·li·za′tion,** *n.*

crys·tal·log·ra·phy (kris′tə·log′rə·fi), *n.* science that deals with the form, structure, and properties of crystals. —**crys′tal·log′ra·pher,** *n.*

crys·tal·loid (kris′təl·oid), *adj.* like crystal. —*n.* substance (usually capable of crystallization) that, when dissolved in a liquid, will diffuse readily through vegetable or animal membranes. —**crys′tal·loi′dal,** *adj.*

crystal set, radio that uses a crystal detector instead of vacuum tubes.

Cs, *Chem.* cesium.

C.S.T., CST, or **c.s.t.,** *Am.* Central Standard Time.

Cu, *Chem.* copper.

cu., cubic.

cub (kub), *n.* **1.** a young bear, fox, lion, etc. **2.** an inexperienced or awkward boy.

Cu·ba (kū′bə), *n.* country on the largest island in the West Indies, S of Florida. —**Cu′ban**, *adj.*, *n.*

cub·by (kub′ĭ), or **cub·by·hole** (–hōl′), *n.* a small, enclosed space.

cube (kūb), *n.*, *v.*, **cubed, cub·ing.** —*n.* **1.** solid with six equal, square sides. **2.** product obtained when a number is cubed: *the cube of 4 is 64.* —*v.* **1.** make or form into the shape of a cube. **2.** use (a number) three times as a factor: *5 cubed is 125.* [< L < Gk. *kybos* cube, die]

cu·beb (kū′beb), *n.* a dried, unripe berry of a tropical shrub, used in medicine. [< F < Ar. *kabāba*]

cube root, number used as the factor of a cube: *the cube root of 125 is 5.*

cu·bic (kū′bĭk), **cu·bi·cal** (–bə·kəl), *adj.* **1.** shaped like a cube. **2.** having length, breadth, and thickness. **3.** having to do with or involving the cubes of numbers. —**cu′bi·cal·ly,** *adv.*

cu·bi·cle (kū′bə·kəl), *n.* a very small room or compartment. [< L *cubiculum* bedroom < *cubare* lie]

cubic measure, system of measurement of volume in cubic units. 1728 cubic inches = 1 cubic foot.

cub·ism (kūb′iz·əm), *n.* method of painting, drawing, and sculpture in which objects are represented by cubes and other geometrical figures rather than by realistic details. —**cub′ist,** *n.* —**cu·bis′tic,** *adj.*

cu·bit (kū′bit), *n.* an ancient measure of length, about 18 to 22 inches. [< L *cubitum* elbow, cubit]

cub reporter, *Am.* a young, inexperienced newspaper reporter.

cuck·old (kuk′əld), *n.* husband of an unfaithful wife. —*v.* make a cuckold of. [< OF *cucuault* < *coucou* cuckoo]

cuck·oo (kŭk′ü; *esp. for adj.* kü′kü), *n.*, *pl.* –oos, *adj.* —*n.* **1.** bird whose call sounds much like its name. The common European cuckoo lays its eggs in the nests of other birds instead of hatching them itself. **2.** *Am.* the American cuckoo, which builds its own nest. **3.** call of the cuckoo. —*adj. U.S. Slang.* crazy; silly. [imit.]

cu·cum·ber (kū′kum·bər), *n.* **1.** vegetable that has a green skin with firm flesh inside, used in salads and for pickles. **2.** vine that it grows on. [< OF < L *cucumis*]

cud (kud), *n.* mouthful of food that cattle and similar animals bring back into the mouth from the first stomach for a slow, second chewing. [OE *cudu*, var. of *cwidu*]

cud·dle (kud′əl), *v.*, **–dled, –dling,** *n.* —*v.* **1.** hold closely and lovingly in one's arms or lap. **2.** lie close and snug; curl up. **3.** hug. —*n.* hug. —**cud′dly,** *adj.*

cudg·el (kuj′əl), *n.*, *v.*, **–eled, –el·ing;** *esp. Brit.* **–elled, –el·ling.** —*n.* **1.** a short, thick stick used as a weapon; club. **2.** take up the cudgels for, defend strongly. —*v.* **1.** beat with a cudgel. **2.** cudgel one's brains, try very hard to think. [OE *cycgel*]

cue¹ (kū), *n.* **1.** hint or suggestion as to what to do or when to act. **2.** in a play, the last word or words of one actor's speech that is the signal for another to come on the stage, begin speaking, etc. **3.** part one is to play; course of action. **4.** frame of mind; mood. [prob. < F *queue* tail, end; with ref. to the end of a preceding actor's speech. See QUEUE.]

cue² (kū), *n.* **1.** queue. **2.** a long, tapering stick used for striking the ball in billiards, pool, etc. [var. of *queue*]

cuff¹ (kuf), *n.* **1.** band around the wrist, either attached to a sleeve or separate. **2.** turned-up fold around the bottom of the legs of trousers. **3.** handcuff. [ME *cuffe* glove]

cuff² (kuf), *v.*, *n.* hit with the hand; slap. [cf. Sw. *kuffa* push]

cui bo·no (kwē′ bō′nō; kī′), *Latin.* **1.** for whose benefit? **2.** of what good?

cui·rass (kwi·ras′), *n.* **1.** piece of armor for the body made of a breastplate and a plate for the back fastened together. **2.** the breastplate alone. [< F *cuirasse* < Ital. < VL < LL *coriacea (vestis)* (garment) of leather < *corium* leather; form infl. by F *cuir* leather < L *corium*]

cui·sine (kwi·zēn′), *n.* **1.** style of cooking or preparing food. **2.** food. **3.** kitchen. [< F < L *cocina,* var. of *coquina* < *coquus* a cook]

cuisse (kwis), *n.* piece of armor to protect the thigh. [< F, thigh, < L *coxa* hip]

cul-de-sac (kul′də·sak′; kŭl′–), *n.* street or passage open at only one end; blind alley. [< F, bottom of the sack]

cu·lex (kū′leks), *n.*, *pl.* **–li·ces** (–lə·sēz). the most common mosquito of North America and Europe. [< L, gnat]

cu·li·nar·y (kū′lə·ner′ĭ; kul′ə–), *adj.* **1.** having to do with cooking. **2.** used in cooking. [< L, < *culina* kitchen]

cull (kul), *v.* **1.** pick out; select. **2.** pick over; make selections from. —*n.* something picked out as being inferior or worthless. [< OF < L *colligere* COLLECT]

culm¹ (kulm), *n.* **1.** coal dust. **2.** hard coal of poor quality. [? akin to COAL]

culm² (kulm), *n.* the jointed stem of grasses, usually hollow. [< L *culmus* stalk]

cul·mi·nate (kul′mə·nāt), *v.*, **–nat·ed, –nat·ing.** reach its highest point; reach a climax. [< LL *culminatus* < L *culmen,* earlier *columen* top]

cul·mi·na·tion (kul′mə·nā′shən), *n.* **1.** the highest point; climax. **2.** a reaching the highest point. —Syn. **1.** acme, zenith, peak.

cul·pa·ble (kul′pə·bəl), *adj.* deserving blame. [< F < L, < *culpa* fault] —**cul′pa·bil′i·ty, cul′pa·ble·ness,** *n.* —**cul′pa·bly,** *adv.*

cul·prit (kul′prit), *n.* **1.** person guilty of a fault or crime; offender. **2.** prisoner in court accused of a crime.

cult (kult), *n.* **1.** system of religious worship. **2.** great admiration for a person, thing, idea, etc.; worship. **3.** group showing such admiration; worshipers. [< L *cultus* worship < *colere* cultivate]

cul·ti·va·ble (kul′tə·və·bəl), **cul·ti·vat·a·ble** (–vāt′ə·bəl), *adj.* that can be cultivated. —**cul′ti·va·bil′i·ty,** *n.*

cul·ti·vate (kul′tə·vāt), *v.*, **–vat·ed, –vat·ing.** **1.** prepare and use (land) to raise crops by plowing it, planting seeds, and taking care of the growing plants. **2.** loosen the ground around (growing plants) to kill weeds, etc. **3.** improve; develop, as by education. **4.** give time, thought, and effort to. **5.** seek better acquaintance with. [< Med.L, < *cultivare* < *cultivus* under cultivation < L *cultus* pp. of *colere* till] —**cul′ti·vat′ed,** *adj.*

cul·ti·va·tion (kul′tə·vā′shən), *n.* **1.** act of cultivating. **2.** improvement; development. **3.** the giving of time and thought to improving and developing (the body, mind, or manners). **4.** culture. —Syn. **4.** refinement, enlightenment.

cul·ti·va·tor (kul′tə·vā′tər), *n.* **1.** person or thing that cultivates. **2.** a tool or machine used to loosen the ground and destroy weeds.

cul·tur·al (kul′chər·əl), *adj.* of or having to do with culture. —**cul′tur·al·ly,** *adv.*

cul·ture (kul′chər), *n.*, *v.*, **–tured, –tur·ing.** —*n.* **1.** fineness of feelings, thoughts, tastes, manners, etc. **2.** civilization of a given race or nation at a given time. **3.** development of the mind or body by education, training, etc. **4.** preparation of land to raise crops by plowing, planting, and necessary care; cultivation. **5.** proper care given to the raising of animals or plants. **6.** *Biol.* colony or growth of germs of a given kind that has been carefully made for a special purpose. —*v.* cultivate. [< F < L *cultura* a tending. See CULT.] —Syn. *n.* **1.** breeding, refinement.

cul·tured (kul′chərd), *adj.* **1.** having or showing culture; refined. **2.** produced or raised by culture.

cul·vert (kul′vərt), *n.* a small channel for water crossing under a road, railroad, canal, etc.

cum·ber (kum′bər), *v.* **1.** burden; trouble. **2.** hinder; hamper. —*n.* hindrance. [prob. < OF *combrer* impede < *combre* barrier < Celtic]

Cum·ber·land (kum′bər-lənd), *n.* river flowing through Kentucky and Tennessee into the Ohio River.

cum·ber·some (kum′bər-səm), **cum·brous** (–brəs), *adj.* 1. clumsy; unwieldy. 2. burdensome. —**cum′ber·some·ly, cum′brous·ly,** *adv.* —**cum′ber·some·ness, cum′brous·ness,** *n.*

cum lau·de (kům lou′dē; kum lô′dē), *Am.* with praise or honor. [< L]

cum·quat (kum′kwot), *n.* kumquat.

cu·mu·late (*v.* kū′myə-lāt; *adj.* kū′myə-lit, –lāt), *v.,* –lat·ed, –lat·ing, *adj.* —*v.* heap up; accumulate. —*adj.* heaped up. [< L, < *cumulus* heap] —**cu′mu·la′tion,** *n.*

cu·mu·la·tive (kū′myə-lā′tiv; –lə-tiv), *adj.* 1. increasing or growing in amount, force, etc., by additions. 2. of a dividend that must be added to future dividends if not paid when due. —**cu′mu·la′tive·ly,** *adv.* —**cu′mu·la′tive·ness,** *n.*

cu·mu·lus (kū′myə-ləs), *n., pl.* –li (–lī). 1. cloud made up of rounded heaps with a flat bottom. 2. heap. [< L, heap] —**cu′mu·lous,** *adj.*

cu·ne·ate (kū′ni-it; –āt), *adj.* wedge-shaped. [< L, < *cuneus* wedge]

cu·ne·i·form (kū-nē′ə-fôrm; kū′ni-ə-fôrm′), **cu·ni·form** (kū′nə-fôrm), *adj.* wedge-shaped. —*n.* cuneiform writing of ancient Babylonia, Assyria, Persia, etc. [< L *cuneus* wedge + –FORM]

▼	**NUMERAL 1**
◀	**10**
⊢	**TAP**
⋈	**BE**
Ⱶ	**ME**

Cuneiform characters

cun·ning (kun′ing), *adj.* 1. clever in deceiving; sly. 2. skillful; clever. 3. *Am., Colloq.* pretty and dear; attractive. —*n.* 1. slyness in getting what one wants. 2. skill; cleverness. [OE *cunning* < *cunnan* know (how). See CAN¹.] —**cun′ning·ly,** *adv.* —**cun′ning·ness,** *n.* —**Syn.** *n.* 1. shrewdness. 2. expertness, ability.

cup (kup), *n., v.,* **cupped, cup·ping.** —*n.* 1. dish to drink from. 2. as much as a cup holds; cupful. 3. a cup with its contents. 4. in cooking, a half pint. 5. thing shaped like a cup. The petals of some flowers form a cup. 6. ornamental cup, vase, etc., given to the winner of a contest. 7. the containing part of a goblet or wineglass. 8. drink; mixture: *a claret cup.* 9. cup used in Communion. 10. wine used in Communion. 11. thing to be endured or experienced; fate. 12. in golf, the hole. 13. **in one's cups,** drunk. —*v.* 1. shape like a cup. 2. take or put in a cup. [< LL *cuppa;* cf. L *cupa* tub]

cup·bear·er (kup′bâr′ər), *n.* person who fills and passes around the cups in which drinks are served.

cup·board (kub′ərd), *n.* 1. closet or cabinet with shelves for dishes, food, etc. 2. *Esp. Brit.* any small closet.

cup·cake (kup′kāk′), *n. Am.* a small cake baked in a cup-shaped tin.

cup·ful (kup′fůl), *n., pl.* –fuls. as much as a cup holds.

Cu·pid (kū′pid), *n.* 1. the Roman god of love, son of Venus, identified with the Greek god Eros. 2. cupid, a winged baby used as a symbol of love.

cu·pid·i·ty (kū-pid′ə-ti), *n.* eager desire; greed. [< L, < *cupidus* desirous < *cupere* long for, desire] —**Syn.** avarice.

cu·po·la (kū′pə-lə), *n.* 1. a rounded roof; dome. 2. a small dome or tower on a roof. [< Ital. < LL *cupula,* dim. of L *cupa* tub]

cup·ping (kup′ing), *n.* use of a glass cup to create a partial vacuum to draw blood to or through the skin.

cu·pre·ous (kū′pri-əs), *adj.* 1. of or containing copper. 2. copper-colored.

cu·pric (kū′prik), *adj. Chem.* of or containing divalent copper.

cu·prous (kū′prəs), *adj. Chem.* of or containing monovalent copper.

cu·prum (kū′prəm), *n.* copper. [< L. See COPPER.]

cur (kėr), *n.* 1. a worthless dog; mongrel. 2. an ill-bred, worthless person. [ME *curre*]

cur·a·ble (kyûr′ə-bəl), *adj.* that can be cured.

—cur′a·bil′i·ty, cur′a·ble·ness, *n.* —**cur′a·bly,** *adv.*

Cu·ra·çao (kyûr′ə-sō′; kū′rä-sou′), *n.* 1. group of Dutch islands in the West Indies. 2. the largest island of this group. 3. curaçao, liqueur or cordial flavored with orange peel.

cu·ra·cy (kyûr′ə-si), *n., pl.* –cies. the position, rank, or work of a curate.

cu·ra·re, cu·ra·ri (kyů-rä′rē), *n.* a poisonous, resinlike substance obtained from a tropical vine. [< Carib *kurare*]

cu·rate (kyûr′it), *n. Esp. Brit.* clergyman who is an assistant to a pastor, rector, or vicar. [< Med.L, < *cura* cure (def. 5) < L, care]

cur·a·tive (kyûr′ə-tiv), *adj.* having the power to cure; curing; tending to cure. —*n.* means of curing.

cu·ra·tor (kyů-rā′tər), *n.* person in charge of all or part of a museum, library, etc. [< L, < *curare* care for < *cura* care] —**cu·ra·to·ri·al** (kyûr′ə-tô′ri·al; –tō′–), *adj.* —**cu·ra′tor·ship,** *n.*

curb (kėrb), *n.* 1. chain or strap fastened to a horse's bit and passing under its lower jaw, used to restrain the horse. 2. check; restraint. 3. a raised border of concrete, stone, or wood along the edge of a pavement, etc. 4. *Am.* market that deals in stocks and bonds not listed on the regular stock exchange. —*v.* 1. hold in check; restrain. 2. provide with a curb. [< F < L *curvus* bent]

curb bit, a horse's bit having a curb.

curb·ing (kėr′bing), *n.* 1. material for making a curb. 2. a raised border of concrete, etc.; curb.

curb·stone (kėrb′stōn′), *n.* stone or stones forming a curb.

cur·cu·li·o (kėr-kū′li-ō), *n., pl.* –li·os. a snout beetle, esp. one that destroys fruit. [< L]

curd (kėrd), *n.* Often, **curds.** the thick part of milk that separates from the watery part when milk sours. —*v.* form into curds; curdle. [ME *curd, crud*] —**curd′y,** *adj.*

cur·dle (kėr′dəl), *v.,* –dled, –dling. 1. form into curds. 2. thicken. 3. curdle the blood, horrify; terrify. [< *curd*]

cure (kyûr), *v.,* **cured, cur·ing,** *n.* —*v.* 1. make well; bring back to health. 2. get rid of. 3. preserve (meat) by drying and salting. —*n.* 1. act or fact of curing. 2. means of curing; treatment that brings a person back to health. 3. medicine that is a means of curing; remedy. 4. way of curing meat. 5. spiritual charge; religious care. [< F < L *cura* care, concern] —**cure′less,** *adj.* —**cur′er,** *n.* —**Syn.** *v.* 1. heal, restore. 2. relieve.

cu·ré (kyů-rā′), *n.* a parish priest. [< F. See CURATE.]

cure-all (kyûr′ôl′), *n. Am.* remedy supposed to cure all diseases or evils.

cur·few (kėr′fū), *n.* 1. a ringing of a bell at a fixed time every evening as a signal, as for children to come off the streets. 2. bell ringing such a signal: *"the curfew tolls the knell of parting day."* 3. time when it is rung. 4. in the Middle Ages, a signal to put out lights and cover fires. [< AF, < *covrir* cover + *feu* fire < L *focus* hearth]

cu·ri·a (kyûr′i·ə), *n., pl.* **cu·ri·ae** (kyûr′i·ē). group of high officials who assist the Pope in the government and administration of the Roman Catholic Church.

Cu·rie (kyûr′ē; kyů-rē′), *n.* 1. **Marie,** 1867–1934, French physicist and chemist, born in Poland. She and her husband, Pierre, discovered radium in 1898. 2. **Pierre,** 1859–1906, French physicist and chemist.

cu·rie (kyûr′ē; kyů-rē′), *n. Chem., Physics.* unit of radioactivity. [for Mme. *Curie*]

cu·ri·o (kyûr′i-ō), *n., pl.* **cu·ri·os.** object valued as a curiosity. [short for *curiosity*]

cu·ri·os·i·ty (kyûr′i-os′ə-ti), *n., pl.* –ties. 1. an eager desire to know. 2. a strange, rare, or novel object. 3. an interesting quality, as from strangeness.

cu·ri·ous (kyûr′i-əs), *adj.* 1. eager to know. 2. too eager to know; prying. 3. interesting because strange, unusual, etc. 4. very careful; exact. 5. *Colloq.* very odd; eccentric. [< OF < L *curiosus* inquisitive, full of care, ult. < *cura* care] —cu'ri·ous·ly, *adv.* —cu'ri·ous·ness, *n.* —Syn. 1. inquisitive. 3. singular, rare, novel.

cu·ri·um (kyŭr'i·əm), *n. Chem.* an element, Cm, produced by bombardment of plutonium and uranium by helium ions. [for Mme. *Curie*]

curl (kérl), *v.* 1. twist into rings; roll into coils. 2. twist out of shape; bend into a curve. —*n.* 1. a curled lock of hair. 2. anything like it. 3. a curling or being curled. [ME *curle(n)*, *crulle(n)* < *crul* curly]

curl·er (kér'lər), *n.* 1. person or thing that curls. 2. a device on which hair is twisted to make it curl.

cur·lew (kér'lū), *n., pl.* -lews or (*esp. collectively*) -lew. a wading bird with a long, thin bill. [< OF *courlieu;* imit.]

Curlew (from 1 to 2 ft. long)

curl·i·cue (kér'li·kū), *n.* a fancy twist, curl, flourish, etc.

curl·ing (kér'ling), *n.* game played on the ice in which large, smooth stones are slid at a target.

curl·y (kér'li), *adj.*, curl·i·er, curl·i·est. 1. curling; wavy. 2. having curls. —curl'i·ly, *adv.* —curl'i·ness, *n.*

cur·mudg·eon (kər·muj'ən), *n.* a rude, stingy, bad-tempered person; miser. —cur·mudg'eon·ly, *adv.*

cur·rant (kér'ənt), *n.* 1. a small, seedless raisin, used in cakes, etc. 2. a small, sour, edible berry that grows in bunches on certain shrubs. 3. bush that bears currants. [< AF (*raisins de*) *Corauntz* raisins of Corinth]

cur·ren·cy (kér'ən·si), *n., pl.* -cies. 1. *Am.* money in actual use in a country. 2. a passing from person to person; circulation: *people who spread a rumor give it currency.* 3. general use or acceptance; common occurrence.

cur·rent (kér'ənt), *n.* 1. a flow. 2. flow of electricity along a wire, etc. 3. course; movement; general direction. —*adj.* 1. going around; passing from person to person. 2. generally used or accepted; commonly occurring. 3. of the present time: *the current issue of a magazine.* [< L *currens,* ppr. of *currere* run] —cur'rent·ly, *adv.* —Syn. *adj.* 2. prevalent, widespread.

cur·ric·u·lar (kə·rik'yə·lər), *adj.* having to do with a curriculum.

cur·ric·u·lum (kə·rik'yə·ləm), *n., pl.* -lums, -la (-lə). course of study or set of courses of study in a school, college, etc. [< L, race course, chariot, dim. of *currus* chariot < *currere* run]

cur·ry¹ (kér'i), *v.*, -ried, -ry·ing. 1. rub and clean (a horse, etc.) with a brush or currycomb. 2. prepare (tanned leather) for use by soaking, scraping, beating, coloring, etc. 3. curry favor, seek a person's favor by insincere flattery, constant attentions, etc. [< OF *correier* put in order < *con-* (< L *com-*) + *reiier* arrange < Gmc.] —cur'ri·er, *n.*

cur·ry², **cur·rie** (kér'i), *n., pl.* -ries, *v.*, -ried, -ry·ing. —*n.* 1. a peppery sauce or powder containing a mixture of spices, seeds, vegetables, etc., much used in India. 2. stew flavored with curry. —*v.* prepare or flavor with curry. [< Tamil *kari*]

cur·ry·comb (kér'i·kōm'), *n.* brush with metal teeth for rubbing and cleaning a horse. —*v.* use a currycomb on.

curse (kérs), *v.*, cursed or curst, curs·ing, *n.* —*v.* 1. ask God to bring evil or harm on. 2. bring evil or harm on. 3. swear; swear at; blaspheme. —*n.* 1. the words that a person says when he asks God to curse someone or something. 2. something that is cursed. 3. harm or evil that comes as if in answer to a curse. 4. cause of evil or harm. 5. word or words used in swearing. [OE *cūrs,* n., *cūrsian,* v.] —curs'er, *n.* —Syn. *v.* 3. damn. —*n.* 5. oath.

curs·ed (kér'sid; kérst), *adj.* 1. under a curse. 2. deserving a curse; evil; hateful; damnable. —curs'ed·ly, *adv.* —curs'ed·ness, *n.*

cur·sive (kér'siv), *adj.* written with the letters joined together: *ordinary handwriting is cursive.* —*n.* 1. letter made to join other letters. 2. type imitating handwriting. [< Med.L, < *cursus,* pp. of L *currere* run] —cur'sive·ly, *adv.*

cur·so·ry (kér'sə·ri), *adj.* hasty and superficial; without attention to details. [< LL *cursorius* of a race < *currere* run] —cur'so·ri·ly, *adv.* —cur'so·ri·ness, *n.* —Syn. rapid, careless.

curt (kért), *adj.* 1. short; brief. 2. rudely brief; abrupt: *a curt way of talking.* [< L *curtus* cut short] —curt'ly, *adv.* —curt'ness, *n.*

cur·tail (kér·tāl'), *v.* cut short; cut off part of; reduce; lessen. [< *curtal,* adj., cut short (esp. of tails) < OF < L *curtus;* infl. by *tail*] —cur·tail'er, *n.* —cur·tail'ment, *n.*

cur·tain (kér'tən), *n.* 1. piece of material hung to shut off, cover, hide, or decorate something. 2. thing that covers or hides. —*v.* 1. provide with a curtain; shut off with a curtain; decorate with a curtain. 2. cover; hide. [< OF < LL *cortina*] —Syn. *n.* 1. hanging, drapery.

curtain call, call for an actor, musician, etc., to return to the stage and acknowledge the applause of the audience.

curt·sy, curt·sey (kért'si), *n., pl.* -sies; -seys; *v.,* -sied, -sy·ing; -seyed, -sey·ing. —*n.* bow of respect or greeting by women, consisting of bending the knees and lowering the body slightly. —*v.* make a curtsy. [var. of *courtesy*]

cur·va·ture (kér'və·chər; -chúr), *n.* 1. a curving. 2. a curved piece or part; curve.

curve (kérv), *n., v.,* curved, curv·ing, *adj.* —*n.* 1. line that has no straight part. 2. something having the shape of a curve; bend: *curves in a road.* 3. *Am.* baseball thrown so as to curve just before it reaches the batter. 4. *Math.* a line or lines that can be defined by an equation or equations. —*v.* 1. bend so as to form a curve. 2. move in the course of a curve. —*adj.* curved. [< L *curvus* bending]

cur·vet (*n.* kér'vit; *v.* kér·vet', kér'vit), *n., v.,* -vet·ed, -vet·ing; -vet·ted, -vet·ting. —*n.* leap in the air made by a horse, in which all the legs are off the ground for a second. —*v.* 1. make such a leap. 2. make (a horse) leap in this way. [< Ital. *corvetta,* dim. of *corvo* CURVE]

cur·vi·lin·e·ar (kér'və·lin'i·ər), **cur·vi·lin·e·al** (-i·əl), *adj.* consisting of or enclosed by curved lines.

cush·ion (kůsh'ən), *n.* 1. a soft pillow or pad used to sit, lie, or kneel on. 2. anything used or shaped like a cushion. 3. the elastic lining of the sides of a billiard table. 4. something to counteract a sudden shock, jar, or jolt. —*v.* 1. put or seat on a cushion; support with cushions. 2. supply with a cushion. 3. protect from sudden shocks or jars with a cushion, esp. a cushion of steam. [< OF *coussin,* prob. < VL *coxinum* < L *coxa* hip]

cusp (kusp), *n.* 1. a pointed end; point. A crescent has two cusps. 2. a blunt or pointed protuberance of the crown of a tooth. [< L *cuspis*]

cus·pid (kus'pid), *n.* tooth having one cusp; canine tooth. —cus'pi·dal, *adj.*

cus·pi·date (kus'pə·dāt), **cus·pi·dat·ed** (-dāt'id), *adj.* having a sharp, pointed end.

cus·pi·dor (kus'pə·dôr), *n. Am.* container to spit into; spittoon. [< Pg., spitter, < *cuspir* spit < L *conspuere*]

cuss (kus), *Colloq.* —*n.* 1. curse. 2. *Am.* an insignificant or troublesome person or animal. —*v.* curse. [var. of *curse*]

cus·tard (kus'tərd), *n.* a baked or boiled pudding made of eggs, sugar, milk, etc. [var. of *crustade* < F < Pr. *croustado* pasty < L *crustare* encrust < *crusta* crust]

Cus·ter (kus'tər), *n.* George Armstrong, 1839–1876, American general in many Indian wars.

cus·to·di·an (kus·tō'di·ən), *n.* person in charge; caretaker: *the custodian of a museum.* —cus·to'di·an·ship', *n.*

cus·to·dy (kus'tə·di), *n., pl.* -dies. 1. keeping; care. 2. a being confined or detained; imprisonment. 3. in custody, in the care of the police; in prison. 4. take into custody, arrest. [< L, < *custos* guardian] —cus·to·di·al (kus·tō'di·əl), *adj.*

cus·tom (kus′təm), *n.* 1. a usual action; habit. 2. habit maintained for so long that it has almost the force of law. 3. habits or usages collectively. 4. the regular business given by a customer. 5. tax or service regularly due from feudal tenants to their lord. 6. **customs,** a. taxes paid to the government on things brought in from a foreign country. b. department of the government that collects these taxes. —*adj.* 1. made specially for individuals; made to order; not ready-made. 2. making things to order. [< OF < VL *consuetumen* < L *com-* + *suescere* accustom. Doublet of CUSTUME.] —**Syn.** *n.* 1. usage.

cus·tom·ar·y (kus′təm·er′i), *adj., n., pl.* **-ar·ies.** —*adj.* 1. according to custom; as a habit; usual. 2. holding or held by custom; pertaining to or established by custom, as distinguished from law. —*n.* 1. **customaries,** a body of legal customs, or customary laws of a manor, city, province, etc. 2. book or document containing them. —**cus·tom·ar·i·ly** (kus′təm·er′ə·li; *emphatic* kus′təm·âr′ə·li), *adv.* —**cus′tom·ar′i·ness,** *n.* —**Syn.** *adj.* 1. habitual, accustomed.

cus·tom-built (kus′təm·bilt′), *adj.* built to order; not ready-made.

cus·tom·er (kus′təm·ər), *n.* 1. person who buys. 2. *Colloq.* person; fellow.

custom house, a building where taxes on things brought into a country are collected.

cus·tom-made (kus′təm·mād′), *adj. Am.* made to order; not ready-made.

cut (kut), *v.,* **cut, cut·ting,** *adj., n.* —*v.* 1. separate, open, or remove with something sharp: *cut meat, timber, grass, one′s nails, etc.* 2. make by cutting. 3. be cut; admit of being cut. 4. wound with a knife, saw, etc. 5. reduce; decrease. 6. pass; go; come: *he cut through the woods to get home.* 7. go across; divide by crossing: *a brook cuts that field.* 8. hit or strike sharply. 9. *Sports.* hit with a slicing stroke: *he cut the ball so that it bounded almost backward.* 10. hurt the feelings of. 11. *Colloq.* refuse to recognize socially. 12. *Colloq.* be absent from (a class, lecture, etc.). 13. make less sticky or stiff; dissolve: *gasoline cuts grease and tar.* 14. divide (a pack of cards) at random. 15. *Colloq.* do; perform; make. 16. **cut across,** go straight across or through. 17. **cut back,** a. *Football.* go back suddenly. b. shorten by cutting off the end. 18. **cut in,** a. go in suddenly. b. break in; interrupt and replace. c. *Am.* interrupt a dancing couple to take the place of one of them. 19. **cut off,** a. remove by cutting. b. shut off. c. stop suddenly. d. break; interrupt. 20. **cut out,** a. remove by cutting. b. take out; leave out. c. take the place of; get the better of. d. make by cutting; make; form. e. *Am., Slang.* stop doing something. 21. **cut teeth,** have teeth grow through the gums. 22. **cut up,** a. cut to pieces. b. *Colloq.* hurt. c. *Am., Slang.* show off; play tricks. —*adj.* 1. that has been cut. 2. shaped or formed by cutting. 3. reduced: *cut prices.* 4. wound or opening made by cutting. 2. passage, channel, etc., made by cutting or digging. 3. piece cut off or cut out. 4. way in which a thing is cut; style; fashion. 5. *Am.* a decrease; reduction. 6. way straight across or through; short cut. 7. a sharp blow or stroke. 8. a slicing stroke. 9. action or speech that hurts the feelings. 10. *Colloq.* refusal to recognize socially. 11. *Am., Colloq.* absence from a class, lecture, etc. 12. block or plate with a picture engraved on it, used in printing. 13. picture made from such a block or plate. 14. *Am., Slang.* share of booty, etc. [ME *cutte(n)*] —**Syn.** *v.* 1. chop, hew, slash.

cu·ta·ne·ous (kū·tā′ni·əs), *adj.* of or having to do with the skin. [< Med.L, < L *cutis* skin]

cut·a·way (kut′ə·wā′), *n.* coat having the lower part cut back in a curve from the waist.

cut·back (kut′bak′), *n. Colloq.* 1. a scheduled slowing down of any industrial operation: *a cutback in steel production.* 2. reduction: *a cutback in the defense budget.*

cute (kūt), *adj.,* **cut·er, cut·est.** *Colloq.* 1. *Am.* pleasing or attractive because pretty, dear, dainty, etc. 2. clever; shrewd. [var. of *acute*] —**cute′ly,** *adv.* —**cute′ness,** *n.*

cut glass, glass shaped or decorated by grinding and polishing. —**cut′-glass′,** *adj.*

cu·ti·cle (kū′tə·kəl), *n.* 1. outer skin. 2. the hardened skin around the edges of the fingernail or toenail. [< L *cuticula,* dim. of *cutis* skin]

cut·lass, cut·las (kut′ləs), *n.* a short, heavy, slightly curved sword. [< F *coutelas* < L *culter* knife]

←CUTLASS

cut·ler (kut′lər), *n.* person who makes, sells, or repairs knives, scissors, and other cutting instruments. [< F, < *coutel* small knife < L *cultellus,* dim. of *culter* knife]

cut·ler·y (kut′lər·i), *n.* 1. knives, scissors, and other cutting instruments. 2. knives, forks, spoons, etc., for table use. 3. business of a cutler.

cut·let (kut′lit), *n.* 1. slice of meat for broiling or frying. 2. a flat, fried cake of chopped meat or fish. [< F *côtelette,* ult. < L *costa* rib]

cut·off (kut′ôf′; -of′), *n.* 1. a short way across or through. 2. a stopping of the passage of steam or working fluid to the cylinder of an engine. 3. mechanism or device that does this.

cut·out (kut′out′), *n.* 1. *Am.* shape or design to be cut out: *some books have cutouts.* 2. device for disconnecting an engine from its muffler. 3. device for breaking an electric current.

cut·purse (kut′pėrs′), *n.* pickpocket.

cut rate, price lower than the usual price: *buy appliances at a cut rate.*

cut·ter (kut′ər), *n.* 1. person who cuts. 2. tool or machine for cutting: *a meat cutter.* 3. *Am.* a small, light sleigh, usually pulled by one horse. 4. a small sailboat with one mast. 5. boat belonging to a warship, used to carry people and supplies to and from the ship. 6. a small, armed ship used by the coast guard.

cut·throat (kut′thrōt′), *n.* murderer. —*adj.* 1. murderous. 2. *Am.* relentless; merciless; severe.

cut·ting (kut′ing), *n.* 1. thing cut off or cut out. 2. a small shoot cut from a plant to grow a new plant. 3. a newspaper or magazine clipping. 4. act of one that cuts. —*adj.* 1. that cuts; sharp. 2. hurting the feelings; sarcastic. —**cut′ting·ly,** *adv.*

cut·tle·fish (kut′əl·fish′), or **cut·tle** (kut′əl), *n., pl.* **-fish·es** or (*esp. collectively*) **-fish; -tles.** a saltwater mollusk with ten sucker-bearing arms and a hard, internal shell. One kind of cuttlefish squirts out an inky fluid when frightened. [OE *cudele* cuttlefish]

Cuttlefish (8 in. long)

cut·up (kut′up′), *n. Am., Slang.* person who shows off or plays tricks.

cut·wa·ter (kut′wô′tər; -wot′ər), *n.* the front part of a ship′s prow.

cut·worm (kut′wėrm′), *n.* caterpillar that cuts off the stalks of young plants near the ground.

cwt., hundredweight.

-cy, *suffix.* 1. office, position, or rank of, as in *captaincy.* 2. quality, state, condition, or fact of being, as in *bankruptcy.* [< F *-cie,* < L *-cia,* Gk. *-kia*]

cy·an·ic (sī·an′ik), *adj.* 1. of cyanogen; containing cyanogen. 2. blue.

cyanic acid, *Chem.* a colorless, poisonous liquid, HOCN.

cy·a·nide (sī′ə·nīd; -nid), **cy·a·nid** (-nid), *n.* 1. salt of hydrocyanic acid. 2. potassium cyanide, KCN, a powerful poison.

cy·an·o·gen (sī·an′ə·jən), *n.* 1. a colorless, poisonous, inflammable gas, C_2N_2, with the odor of bitter almonds. 2. a univalent radical, CN, consisting of one atom of carbon and one of nitrogen.

cy·a·no·sis (sī′ə·nō′sis), *n. Pathol.* blueness or lividness of the skin, caused by lack of oxygen in the blood. [< NL < Gk. *kyanosis* dark-blue color] —**cy·a·not·ic** (sī′ə·not′ik), *adj.*

cy·ber·na·tion (sī′bər·nā′shən), *n.* automation. [< *cybern*(etics) + *-ation*]

cy·ber·net·ics (sī′bər·net′iks), *n. Am.* comparative study of complex calculating machines and the human nervous system in order to understand better the functioning of the brain. —cy·ber·net·ic (sī′bər·net′ik), *adj.*

cy·cad (sī′kad), *n.* a large, tropical, palmlike plant with a cluster of long, fernlike leaves at the top. [< NL < Gk. *kykas*]

cyc·la·men (sik′lə·mən; -men), *n.* plant of the same family as the primrose, with heart-shaped leaves and snowy white, purple, pink, or crimson flowers, whose five petals bend backwards. [< NL < L < Gk. *kyklaminos*]

cy·cle (sī′kəl), *n., v.,* -cled, -cling. —*n.* 1. period of time or complete process of growth or action that repeats itself in the same order. Spring, summer, autumn, and winter make a cycle. 2. a complete set or series. 3. all the stories, poems, legends, etc., about a great hero or event. 4. a very long period of time; age. 5. bicycle, tricycle, etc. 6. *Physics.* a complete or double alteration or reversal of an alternating electric current. —*v.* 1. pass through a cycle; occur over and over again in the same order. 2. ride a bicycle, tricycle, etc. [< LL < Gk. *kyklos*] —cy′cler, *n.*

cy·clic (sī′klik; sik′lik), **cy·cli·cal** (sī′klə·kəl; sik′lə-), *adj.* 1. of a cycle. 2. moving or occurring in cycles. 3. arranged in a ring. 4. containing a ring of atoms. 5. of or pertaining to an arrangement of atoms in a ring or closed chain.

cy·clist (sī′klist), *n. Esp. Brit.* rider of a bicycle, tricycle, etc.

cy·clom·e·ter (sī·klom′ə·tər), *n.* instrument that measures the distance that a wheel travels by recording the revolutions that it makes.

cy·clone (sī′klōn), *n.* 1. a very violent windstorm; tornado. 2. storm moving around and toward a calm center of low pressure, which also moves. [< Gk. *kyklon*, pr. of *kyklōein* move around in a circle] —cy·clon·ic (sī·klon′ik), cy·clon′i·cal, *adj.* —cy·clon′i·cal·ly, *adv.*

cy·clo·pe·di·a, cy·clo·pae·di·a (sī′klə·pē′di·ə), *n.* an encyclopedia. [shortened form of *encyclopedia*] —cy′clo·pe′dic, cy′clo·pae′dic, *adj.* —cy′clo·pe′dist, cy′clo·pae′dist, *n.*

Cy·clops (sī′klops), *n., pl.* Cy·clo·pes (sī·klō′pēz). *Gk. Legend.* one of a group of one-eyed giants. [< L < Gk., < *kyklos* circle + *ops* eye] —Cy·clo·pe·an (sī′klə·pē′ən; sī·klō′pi·ən), *adj.*

cy·clo·ram·a (sī′klə·ram′ə; -rä′mə), *n.* a large picture of a landscape, battle, etc., on the wall of a circular room. [< Gk. *kyklos* circle + *horama* spectacle] —cy′clo·ram′ic, *adj.*

cy·clo·tron (sī′klə·tron), *n. Physics.* a powerful apparatus that sends out electrons at very high velocities, and so can disintegrate atoms and cause radioactivity. [< Gk. *kyklos* circle + E *-tron* (as in *neutron*)]

cyg·net (sig′nit), *n.* a young swan.

cyl·in·der (sil′ən·dər), *n.* 1. *Geom.* a solid bounded by two equal, parallel circles and a curved surface formed by moving a straight line of fixed length so that its ends always lie on the two parallel circles. 2. volume of such a solid. 3. any long, round object, solid or hollow, with flat ends. 4. *Am.* part of a revolver that contains chambers for cartridges. 5. the piston chamber of an engine. [< L < Gk., < *kylindein* to roll]

Cylinder

cy·lin·dri·cal (sə·lin′drə·kəl), **cy·lin·dric** (-drik), *adj.* shaped like a cylinder; having the form of a cylinder. —cy·lin′dri·cal·i·ty, *n.* —cy·lin′dri·cal·ly, *adv.*

cym·bal (sim′bəl), *n.* one of a pair of brass plates, used as a musical instrument. When cymbals are struck together, they make a loud, ringing sound. [< L < Gk., < *kymbe* hollow of a vessel] —cym′bal·ist, *n.*

cyme (sīm), *n.* a flower cluster in which there is a flower at the top of the main stem and of each branch of the cluster. [< L < Gk. *kyma* something swollen, sprout] —cy·mose (sī′mōs; sī·mōs′), *adj.*

Cym·ry (kim′ri), *n.* the Welsh people. —Cymric (kim′rik; sim′-), *adj., n.*

cyn·ic (sin′ik), *n.* 1. person inclined to believe that the motives for people's actions are insincere and selfish. 2. a sneering, sarcastic person. 3. Cynic, member of a group of ancient Greek philosophers who taught that self-control is the essential part of virtue, and despised pleasure, money, and personal comfort. —*adj.* 1. cynical. 2. Cynic, of or having to do with the Cynics or their doctrines. [< L < Gk. *kynikos* doglike < *kyon* dog]

cyn·i·cal (sin′ə·kəl), *adj.* 1. doubting the worth of life. 2. sneering; sarcastic. —cyn′i·cal·ly, *adv.* —cyn′i·cal·ness, *n.*

cyn·i·cism (sin′ə·siz·əm), *n.* 1. cynical quality or disposition. 2. a cynical remark.

cy·no·sure (sī′nə·shùr; sin′ə-), *n.* 1. center of attraction, interest, or attention. 2. something used for guidance or direction. [< L < Gk. *kynosoura* dog's tail < *kyon* dog + *oura* tail]

cy·pher (sī′fər), *n., v.* cipher.

cy·press (sī′prəs), *n.* 1. an evergreen tree of the South, with hard wood and dark leaves. 2. its wood. 3. any of various similar plants such as the European "true" cypress, and the "standing cypress" of the United States. [< OF < L *cypressus* < Gk. *kyparissos*]

cyp·ri·noid (sip′rə·noid), *n.* any of a large group of fresh-water fishes, including the carps, suckers, goldfishes, breams, most fresh-water minnows, etc. —*adj.* of or belonging to this group. [< L *cyprinus* carp (< Gk.) + -OID]

Cyp·ri·ot (sip′ri·ət), *adj.* of Cyprus. —*n.* a native or inhabitant of Cyprus.

Cy·prus (sī′prəs), *n.* an island and republic in E Mediterranean, S of Turkey.

Cy·rus (sī′rəs), *n.* died 529 B.C., king of Persia from 558? to 529 B.C.

cyst (sist), *n.* 1. an abnormal, saclike growth in animals or plants. Cysts usually contain liquid and diseased matter. 2. a saclike structure in animals or plants. [< NL < Gk. *kystis* pouch, bladder] —cyst′ic, *adj.*

Cyth·er·e·a (sith′ər·ē′ə), *n. Gk. Myth.* Aphrodite. —Cyth′er·e′an, *adj.*

cy·tol·o·gy (sī·tol′ə·ji), *n.* branch of biology that deals with the formation, structure, and function of the cells of animals and plants. [< Gk. *kytos* receptacle, cell + -LOGY] —cy·tol′o·gist, *n.*

cy·to·plasm (sī′tə·plaz·əm), **cy·to·plast** (-plast), *n. Biol.* the living substance or protoplasm of a cell, exclusive of the nucleus. —cy′to·plas′mic, *adj.*

C.Z., Canal Zone.

czar (zär), *n.* 1. emperor. It was the title of the emperors of Russia. 2. autocrat; person with absolute power. Also, tsar, tzar. [< Russ. *tsar* < Old Church Slavic < Gothic < L *Caesar* Caesar]

czar·e·vitch (zär′ə·vich), *n.* 1. the eldest son of a Russian czar. 2. son of a Russian czar. Also, tsarevitch, tzarevitch.

cza·ri·na (zä·rē′nə), *n.* wife of a czar; Russian empress. Also, tsarina, tzarina.

Czech (chek), *n.* 1. member of the most westerly branch of the Slavs. Bohemians, Moravians, and Silesians are Czechs. 2. their language; Bohemian. —*adj.* of or having to do with Czechoslovakia, its language, or its people. —Czech′ic, Czech′ish, *adj.*

Czech·o·slo·vak, Czech·o·Slo·vak (chek′ə·slō′vak; -väk), *adj.* of Czechoslovakia, its people, or their language. —*n.* 1. native or inhabitant of Czechoslovakia. 2. their language.

Czech·o·slo·va·ki·a, Czech·o·Slo·va·ki·a (chek′ə·slō·vä′ki·ə; -vak′i·ə), *n.* country in C Europe. —Czech′o·slo·va′ki·an, Czech′o·Slo·va′ki·an, *adj., n.*

D

D, d (dē), *n.*, *pl.* **D's**; **d's**. 1. the fourth letter of the alphabet. 2. the second note or tone of the musical scale of C major. 3. the Roman numeral for 500.

D, *Chem.* deuterium.

D., 1. December. 2. Democrat; Democratic. 3. Dutch.

d., 1. day. 2. dead. 3. degree. 4. delete. 5. died. 6. dollar. 7. dose. 8. English penny; pence.

D.A., District Attorney.

dab (dab), *v.*, **dabbed, dab·bing**, *n.* —*v.* 1. touch lightly; pat with something soft or moist; tap. 2. put on with light strokes. —*n.* 1. a quick, light touch or blow; a pat; a tap. 2. a small, soft or moist mass. 3. a little bit. [ME] —**dab′ber**, *n.*

dab·ble (dab′əl), *v.*, **-bled, -bling.** 1. dip (hands, feet, etc.) in and out of water; splash. 2. do superficially; work a little: *dabble at painting.* [< Flem. *dabbelen*] —**dab′bler**, *n.*

dace (dās), *n.*, *pl.* **dac·es** or (*esp. collectively*) **dace.** *Am.* any of several small fresh-water fish. [ME *darse* < OF *dars* DART]

Dach·au (däH′ou), *n.* a former Nazi concentration camp located in S Germany.

dachs·hund (däks′hund′; -hunt′; daks′-; dash′-), *n.* dog of a German breed that is small, with a long body and very short legs. [< G, < *dachs* badger + *hund* dog]

Da·cron (dā′kron), *n.* *Trademark.* a synthetic wrinkle- and abrasion-resistant fiber used for shirts, suits, etc.

dac·tyl (dak′təl), *n.* a metrical foot of three syllables (— ◡ ◡), one accented followed by two unaccented, or, in classical verse, one long followed by two short. [< L < Gk. *daktylos* finger] —**dac·tyl·ic** (dak·til′ik), *adj.*, *n.*

dad (dad), *n.* *Colloq.* father.

dad·dy (dad′i), *n.*, *pl.* **-dies.** *Colloq.* father.

dad·dy-long·legs (dad′i-lông′legz′; -long′-), *n.*, *pl.* **-legs.** *U.S.* 1. animal similar to a spider, with a small body and very long, thin legs. 2. crane fly.

Daddy-longlegs

da·do (dā′dō), *n.*, *pl.* **-does, -dos.** 1. the lower part of the wall of a room when it is decorated differently from the upper part. 2. part of a pedestal between the base and the cap. [< Ital., DIE²]

Daed·a·lus (ded′ə·ləs), *n. Gk. Legend.* a skillful worker who made wings for flying and built the labyrinth in Crete.

dae·mon (dē′mən), *n.* 1. *Gk. Myth.* **a.** a supernatural being. **b.** an inferior deity. 2. demon. [< L < Gk. *daimon*] —**dae·mon·ic** (dē·mon′ik), *adj.*

daf·fo·dil (daf′ə·dil), *n.* 1. narcissus with yellow flowers and long, slender leaves. 2. the flower. 3. yellow. [var. of *affodill* < VL < L < Gk. *asphodelos*]

daf·fy (daf′i), *adj.*, **daff·i·er, daff·i·est.** *Colloq.* foolish; silly; crazy.

daft (daft; däft), *adj.* 1. silly; foolish. 2. crazy. [cf. OE *gedœfte* gentle] —**daft′ness**, *n.*

da Gam·a (də gam′ə), Vasco, 1469?–1524, Portuguese navigator.

dag·ger (dag′ər), *n.* 1. a small weapon with a short, pointed blade, used for stabbing. 2. sign (†) used in printing to refer the reader to a footnote, etc. [prob. < obs. *dag* slash]

da·guerre·o·type (də·ger′ə·tīp; -i·ə·tīp), *n.*, *v.*, **-typed, -typ·ing.** —*n.* 1. an early method of photography in which the pictures were made on silvered metal plates. 2. picture made in this way. —*v.* photograph by this process. [for L. J. M. *Daguerre*, inventor]

dahl·ia (dal′yə; däl′-; *esp. Brit.* dāl′yə), *n.* 1. a tall plant of the aster family that has large, showy flowers in the autumn. 2. the flower. [< NL; named for A. *Dahl*, botanist]

Da·ho·mey (də·hō′mi), *n.* republic in W Africa on the Atlantic, formerly part of French West Africa.

Dail Eir·eann (dôl âr′ən; doil), or **Dail**, *n.* the lower house of parliament of the Irish Republic.

dai·ly (dā′li), *adj.*, *n.*, *pl.* **-lies**, *adv.* —*adj.* done, happening, or appearing every day, or every day but Sunday. —*n. Am.* newspaper appearing every day, or every day but Sunday. —*adv.* every day; day by day.

dain·ty (dān′ti), *adj.*, **-ti·er, -ti·est**, *n.*, *pl.* **-ties.** —*adj.* 1. having delicate beauty; fresh and pretty. 2. having or showing delicate tastes and feeling; particular. 3. good to eat; delicious. 4. too particular; overnice. [< n.] —*n.* something very good to eat; a delicious bit of food. [< OF < L *dignitas* worthiness < *dignus* worthy] —**dain′ti·ly**, *adv.* —**dain′ti·ness**, *n.*

dair·y (dâr′i), *n.*, *pl.* **dair·ies.** 1. room or building where milk and cream are kept and made into butter and cheese. 2. farm where milk and cream are produced and butter and cheese made. 3. store or company that sells milk, butter, etc. 4. business of producing milk, butter, etc. [ME *deierie* < *deie* maid (OE *dǣge* breadmaker)]

dair·y·man (dâr′i·mən), *n.*, *pl.* **-men.** 1. man who works in a dairy. 2. man who owns or manages a dairy. 3. man who sells milk, butter, etc.

da·is (dā′is; dās), *n.* a raised platform in a hall or large room for a throne, seats of honor, etc. [< OF < L *discus* quoit, DISH]

dai·sy (dā′zi), *n.*, *pl.* **-sies**, *adj.* —*n.* 1. plant of the aster family whose flowers or petals are usually white or pink around a yellow center. 2. *Am.* a tall plant of the same family whose flower heads have a yellow disk and white rays; the common "white daisy" of the U.S. 3. *Slang.* something fine or first-rate. —*adj. Slang.* first-rate. [OE *dǣges edge* day's eye] —**dai′sied**, *adj.*

Da·kar (dä·kär′), *n.* seaport and capital of Senegal.

Da·lai La·ma (dä·lī′ lä′mə), the chief priest of the religion of Lamaism in Tibet and Mongolia. Also, **Grand Lama.**

dale (dāl), *n.* valley. [OE *dœl*]

Da·li (dä′lē), *n.* Salvador, born 1904, Spanish surrealist painter.

Dal·las (dal′əs), *n.* city in NE Texas.

dal·li·ance (dal′i·əns), *n.* 1. flirtation. 2. a playing; trifling.

dal·ly (dal′i), *v.*, **-lied, -ly·ing.** 1. act in a playful manner. 2. flirt (with danger, temptation, a person, etc.); trifle. 3. be idle; loiter. 4. waste (time). [< OF *dalier* chat] —**dal′li·er**, *n.*

Dal·ma·tian (dal·mā′shən), *n.* a large, short-haired dog, usually white with black spots; coach dog.

dam¹ (dam), *n.*, *v.*, **dammed, dam·ming.** —*n.* 1. wall built to hold back flowing water. 2. water held back by a dam. 3. anything resembling a dam. —*v.* 1. provide with a dam; hold back (water, etc.) by means of a dam. 2. hold back; block up. [ME]

Dalmatian (20 in. high at the shoulder)

dam² (dam), *n.* 1. the female parent of four-footed animals. 2. mother. [var. of *dame*]

dam·age (dam′ij), *n.*, *v.*, **-aged, -ag·ing.** —*n.* 1. harm or injury that lessens value or usefulness. 2. *Slang.* cost; price. 3. damages, money necessary to make up for some harm done to a person or his property. —*v.* harm or injure so as to lessen value or usefulness; to harm; to hurt. [< OF, < *dam* < L *damnum* loss, hurt] —**dam′age·a·ble**, *adj.* —**dam′ag·ing·ly**, *adv.* —Syn. *n.* 1. detriment, impairment. —*v.* impair, disfigure.

dam·a·scene (dam′ə·sēn; dam′ə·sēn′), v., -scened, -scen·ing, adj., n. —v. ornament (metal) with inlaid gold or silver or with a wavy design. —adj. of or like such an ornament. —n. the ornament or design itself. [< L < Gk. Damaskenos of Damascus]

Da·mas·cus (də·mas′kəs), n. capital of Syria, a very ancient trading center.

dam·ask (dam′əsk), n. 1. silk woven with an elaborate pattern. 2. linen with woven designs. 3. damascened metal. 4. a rose color; pink. —v. make damask. —adj. 1. of or named after the city of Damascus. 2. made of damask. 3. pink; rose-colored. [< L < Gk. Damaskos Damascus]

damask steel, Damascus steel, ornamented steel, used in making swords, etc.

dame (dām), n. 1. an elderly woman. 2. Slang. woman. 3. in Great Britain, a. title given to a woman who has received an honorable rank corresponding to that of a knight. b. the legal title of the wife or widow of a knight or baronet (in ordinary use, Lady). [< OF < L domina mistress]

damn (dam), v. 1. declare (something) to be bad or inferior; condemn. 2. cause to fail; ruin. 3. doom to eternal punishment; condemn to hell. 4. swear or swear at by saying "damn"; curse. —n. a saying of "damn"; curse. [< OF < L damnare condemn < damnum loss] —damn′er, n. —Syn. v. 1. denounce, proscribe, execrate.

dam·na·ble (dam′nə·bəl), adj. 1. abominable; outrageous; detestable. 2. deserving damnation. —dam′na·ble·ness, n. —dam′na·bly, adv.

dam·na·tion (dam·nā′shən), n. 1. a damning or being damned; condemnation. 2. condemnation to eternal punishment. 3. curse. —dam·na·to·ry (dam′nə·tô′ri, -tō′-), adj.

damned (damd), adj. 1. condemned as bad or inferior. 2. doomed to eternal punishment. 3. cursed; abominable. —n. the damned, the souls in hell. —adv. very.

Dam·o·cles (dam′ə·klēz), n. flatterer and courtier of Dionysius, king of Syracuse, who enjoyed a banquet given by Dionysius until he saw a sword hung by a single hair above his head.

Da·mon (dā′mən), n. Rom. Legend. a man who pledged his life for his friend Pythias, who was sentenced to death.

damp (damp), adj. slightly wet; moist. —n. 1. moisture. 2. thing that checks or deadens. 3. dejection; discouragement. 4. any harmful gas that collects in mines, such as chokedamp or firedamp. —v. 1. make moist or slightly wet. 2. check; deaden. 3. stifle; suffocate. 4. extinguish. [< MDu. or MLG] —damp′ly, adv. —damp′ness, n.

damp·en (dam′pən), v. 1. moisten. 2. depress; discourage. 3. Radio. eliminate extraneous sounds or echoes in a studio by using special wall coverings. —damp′en·er, n.

damp·er (dam′pər), n. 1. person or thing that depresses. 2. a movable plate to control the draft in a stove or furnace. 3. device for checking vibration, as of piano strings.

dam·sel (dam′zəl), n. girl; maiden. [< OF dameisele, ult. < L domina DAME]

dam·son (dam′zən), n. 1. a small, dark-purple plum. 2. tree that it grows on. [< L (prunum) damascenum (plum) of Damascus]

Dan (dan), n. 1. a Hebrew tribe that migrated to N Palestine. 2. city in N Palestine. 3. from Dan to Beersheba, from one end of a place to the other.

Dan., Danish.

Da·na·ï·des (də·nā′ə·dēz), n.pl. Gk. Legend. the fifty daughters of Danaüs (dan′i·əs), a Greek king. All but one killed their husbands on their wedding night, and were condemned to draw water with a sieve forever in Hades.

dance (dans; däns), v., danced, danc·ing, n., adj. —v. 1. move in rhythm, usually in time with music. 2. do or take part in (a dance). 3. jump up and down; move in a lively way. 4. bob up and down. —n. 1. movement in rhythm, usually in time with music. 2. some special group of steps, etc. 3. one round of dancing. 4. piece of music for dancing. 5. party where people dance. 6. movement up and down; lively move-

ment. —adj. of or for dancing. [< OF danser, prob. < Gmc.] —danc′er, n. —danc′ing·ly, adv.

dance hall, Am. a public hall or room in which dances are held.

dan·de·li·on (dan′də·lī′ən), n. weed with deeply notched leaves and bright-yellow flowers. [< F dent de lion lion's tooth; from toothed leaves]

dan·der (dan′dər), n. Colloq. 1. temper; anger. 2. get one's dander up, get angry.

dan·di·fy (dan′də·fī), v., -fied, -fy·ing. make dandylike or foppish. —dan′di·fi·ca′tion, n.

dan·dle (dan′dəl), v., -dled, -dling. 1. move (a child) up and down on one's knees or in one's arms. 2. pet; pamper. —dan′dler, n.

dan·druff (dan′drəf), n. small, whitish scales that form on the scalp.

dan·dy (dan′di), n., pl. -dies, adj., -di·er, -di·est. —n. 1. man who is too careful of his dress and appearance. 2. Slang. an excellent or first-rate thing. —adj. 1. of a dandy; too carefully dressed. 2. Slang. excellent; first-rate. —dan′dy·ism, n. —Syn. n. 1. fop. —adj. 1. foppish.

Dane (dān), n. 1. native or inhabitant of Denmark. 2. person of Danish descent.

Dane·law (dān′lô′), n. 1. set of laws enforced by the Danes when they held NE England in the 9th and 10th centuries A.D. 2. part of England under these laws.

dan·ger (dān′jər), n. 1. chance of harm; nearness to harm; risk; peril. 2. thing that may cause harm. [< OF dangier < L dominium sovereignty < dominus master] —Syn. 1. hazard, jeopardy. 2. menace, threat. —Ant. 1. safety.

dan·ger·ous (dān′jər·əs), adj. likely to cause harm; not safe; risky. —dan′ger·ous·ly, adv. —dan′ger·ous·ness, n. —Syn. perilous, precarious, unsafe.

dan·gle (dang′gəl), v., -gled, -gling, n. —v. 1. hang and swing loosely. 2. hold or carry (a thing) so that it swings loosely. 3. hang about; follow. 4. cause to dangle. —n. 1. act or fact of dangling. 2. something that dangles. [< Scand. (Dan.)] —dan′gler, n.

Dan·iel (dan′yəl), n. 1. Bible. a Hebrew prophet. 2. book of the Bible that tells about him.

Dan·ish (dān′ish), adj. of or having to do with the Danes, their language, or Denmark. —n. language of the Danes.

dank (dangk), adj. unpleasantly damp; moist; wet. —dank′ly, adv. —dank′ness, n.

dan·seuse (dän·sœz′), n., pl. -seuses (-sœz′). a woman dancer in a ballet. [< F]

Dan·te (dan′tē; dän′tä), n. 1265-1321, Italian poet, author of the Divine Comedy.

Dan·ube (dan′ūb), n. river flowing from SW Germany into the Black Sea. —Dan·u·bi·an (dan·ū′bi·ən), adj.

Dan·zig (dant′sig; dänt′-; dan′zig), n. 1. seaport in N Poland, on the Baltic Sea. 2. Bay of, an inlet of the Baltic Sea.

Daph·ne (daf′nē), n. Gk. Legend. nymph pursued by Apollo, whom she escaped by being changed into a laurel tree.

dap·per (dap′ər), adj. 1. neat; trim; spruce. 2. small and active. [cf. MDu. dapper agile, strong] —dap′per·ly, adv. —dap′per·ness, n.

dap·ple (dap′əl), adj., n., v., -pled, -pling. —adj. spotted: a dapple horse. —n. 1. a spotted appearance or condition. 2. animal with a spotted or mottled skin. —v. mark or become marked with spots. [cf. Scand. depill spot]

D.A.R., Am. Daughters of the American Revolution.

Dar·da·nelles (där′də·nelz′), n. strait between Europe and Asia, connecting the Sea of Marmara with the Aegean Sea. In ancient times it was called the Hellespont.

dare (dār), v., dared or durst, dared, dar·ing, n. —v. 1. have courage; be bold; be bold enough. 2. have courage for; not be afraid of; be bold enough for. 3. meet and resist; face and defy. 4. challenge. —n. a challenge. [OE dearr (inf., durran)] —dar′er, n. —Syn. v. 2. venture. 3. brave.

dare·dev·il (dār′dev′əl), n. a reckless person. —adj. reckless.

Dar·i·en (dãr′i·en; dâr′i·en′), *n.* **1.** Isthmus of, a former name of the Isthmus of Panama. **2.** Gulf of, gulf of the Caribbean Sea, between Panama and Colombia.

dar·ing (dãr′ing), *n.* courage to take risks; boldness. —*adj.* courageous; bold. —dar′ing·ly, *adv.* —dar′ing·ness, *n.*

Da·ri·us I (də·rī′əs), 558?–486? B.C., king of Persia from 521 to 486? B.C.

dark (därk), *adj.* **1.** without light; with very little light. **2.** not light-colored: *a dark complexion.* **3.** nearly black. **4.** hard to understand or explain. **5.** secret; hidden. **6.** ignorant. **7.** evil; wicked. **8.** gloomy; dull; dismal. **9.** sad; sullen; frowning. **10.** of radio stations, not broadcasting. **11.** keep dark, keep silent; not tell about. —*n.* **1.** absence of light. **2.** night; nightfall. **3.** a dark color. **4.** obscurity. **5.** secrecy. **6.** ignorance. **7.** in the dark, without knowledge or information. [OE *deorc*] —dark′ish, *adj.* —dark′ish·ness, *n.* —dark′ly, *adv.* —dark′ness, *n.*

Dark Ages, the early part of the Middle Ages, from about 500 A.D. to about 1000 A.D.

dark·en (där′kən), *v.* make or become dark or darker. —dark′en·er, *n.*

dark horse, an unexpected winner that little is known about.

dark lantern, lantern whose light can be hidden by a cover or dark glass.

dark·ling (därk′ling), *adv., adj.* in the dark.

dark·room (därk′rüm′; -rum′), *n.* room arranged for developing photographs.

dar·ling (där′ling), *n.* person very dear to another; person much loved. —*adj.* very dear; much loved. [OE *deorling* < *deore* DEAR]

darn[1] (därn), *v.* mend by making rows of stitches back and forth across a hole, torn place, etc. —*n.* **1.** act of darning. **2.** place so mended. [< dial. F *darner* mend < *darne* piece < Breton *darn*] —darn′er, *n.*

darn[2] (därn), *v. Colloq.* damn; curse. —*n.* not give a darn, be completely indifferent. [< *damn*; infl. by *tarnal* (colloq. for *eternal*)] —darned, *adj., adv.*

dart (därt), *n.* **1.** a slender, pointed weapon to be thrown or shot. **2.** a sudden, swift movement. **3.** stinger of an insect. **4.** seam to make a garment fit better. —*v.i.* **1.** throw or shoot suddenly and swiftly. **2.** move suddenly and swiftly. **3.** send suddenly. [< OF < Gmc.] —Syn. *n.* **2.** dash. -*v.* **1.** hurl, launch. **2.** dash, bolt.

Dart

dart·er (där′tər), *n.* **1.** animal or person that moves suddenly and swiftly. **2.** *Am.* a small fresh-water fish, somewhat like a perch, that darts away very rapidly. **3.** *Am.* a swimming bird that has a long neck and darts at its prey.

Dar·win (där′wən), *n.* Charles, 1809–1882, English scientist, famous for his theory of evolution. —**Dar·win·i·an** (där·win′i·ən), *adj., n.*

Dar·win·ism (där′wən·iz·əm), *n.* doctrine maintained by Charles Darwin respecting the origin of species as derived by descent, with variation, from parent forms through the natural selection of those best adapted to survive in the struggle for existence. —**Dar′win·ist,** *n., adj.*

dash (dash), *v.* **1.** throw. **2.** splash. **3.** apply roughly as by splashing. **4.** rush. **5.** strike violently against something. **6.** smash. **7.** ruin: *our hopes were dashed.* **8.** depress; discourage; abash. **9.** adulterate; dilute. **10.** mix with a small amount of something else. **11.** dash off, do, make, write, etc., quickly. —*n.* **1.** a splash. **2.** a rush. **3.** a smash. **4.** thing that depresses or discourages; check. **5.** a small amount. **6.** *Am.* a short race. **7.** a blow; a stroke. **8.** mark (—) used in writing or printing to show a break in sense, parenthetical material, omitted letters or words, etc. **9.** a long sound used in sending messages by telegraph or radiotelegraph. **10.** energy; spirit; liveliness. **11.** showy appearance or behavior. **12.** dashboard. [ME *dasche(n)*] —dash′er, *n.* —Syn. *n.* **5.** spot, touch, tinge, smack, trace. ≻ dash (-, —, ——). Three dashes of varying lengths are used in printing: – (en dash), — (em dash, the usual mark), and —— (2-em dash). On the typewriter use a hyphen for the first, two hyphens not spaced away from the neighboring words for the usual dash, and four hyphens for the long dash. The em dash, the one we have in mind when we say just *dash*, has aroused more discussion and more violent feeling than punctuation seems to deserve. Some textbooks and some publishers forbid its use generally, while others specify minute shades of meaning which they believe it indicates. Some writers rarely use it. Others, especially in matter not intended for publication, use it at the expense of other marks. A dash is roughly equivalent to a comma, that is, it separates small units within a sentence, but if used sparingly it suggests a definite tone, usually a note of surprise, an emotional emphasis. From a strictly logical point of view some other mark could always be substituted for a dash, but there would be a difference in movement and suggestiveness in the sentence. At its best it is a rather abrupt and emphatic mark.
1. The most typical use of the dash is to mark a sharp turn in the thought or construction of a sentence: *Of course, there is one place safe from salesmen—in heaven.*
2. A dash is often used before an interpolated or added phrase, usually either one that summarizes what has just been said or that gives contrasting or emphasizing details of what has been said, or often a striking apposition. This dash has the force of a more vigorous comma: *The waiting, the watching, the hundreds of small necessary acts about the sickroom—all this was past.*
3. A dash is often used between two compound clauses of a sentence, for abrupt separation: *Ideally, the student listens carefully, the teacher provides many examples—comprehension is at a maximum, not thwarted by professorial vagueness.*
4. A dash is sometimes used to enclose parenthetical statements that are more informal than a parenthesis would be, separating the expression from the context more than a comma and less definitely than parentheses would: *The general feeling among the men—most of them union members—was that the speaker avoided the central issue.*
5. Formerly a dash was often combined with other marks, especially with a comma or a colon, but recently this use has declined. The dash adds nothing in the salutation of a letter (*Dear Sir:—* means no more than *Dear Sir:*) and adds a displeasing mark to the page. Within sentences the old comma-dash combination has very generally disappeared also, so that now we find either a comma, or if emphasis makes it useful, a dash alone.

dash·board (dash′bôrd′; -bōrd′), *n.* **1.** the panel with instruments and gauges in an automobile, airplane, etc. **2.** protection on the front of a boat, etc., that prevents mud or water from being splashed into it.

dash·ing (dash′ing), *adj.* **1.** full of energy and spirit; lively. **2.** stylish; showy. —dash′ing·ly, *adv.*

dash·y (dash′i), *adj.,* dash·i·er, dash·i·est. dashing.

das·tard (das′tərd), *n.* a mean coward; sneak. —*adj.* mean and cowardly; sneaking. [ME, orig., a dullard, appar. < *dased,* pp. of DAZE] —das′tard·ly, *adj.* —das′tard·li·ness, *n.*

dat., dative.

da·ta (dā′tə; dat′ə; dä′tə), *n.* **1.** pl. of da·tum. **2.** *Am.* things known or granted; facts. ≻ data. **1.** pronounced dā′tə, sometimes dat′ə, or (affecting Latin) dä′tə. **2.** Strictly, data is a plural, with a little-used singular *datum.* Its meaning is actually collective and may sometimes stress a group of facts as a unit and so be used with a singular verb. Sometimes, referring to individual facts, *data* is used with a plural: *The actual* *data of history consists of contemporary facts* (sing.). *Our task is to analyze when the data have been secured* (pl.). The singular verb can be safely used in any but the most formal writing.

date[1] (dāt), *n.*, *v.*, **dat·ed, dat·ing.** —*n.* 1. time when something happens. 2. statement of time. 3. period of time. 4. *Am.*, *Colloq.* appointment for a certain time. 5. *Am.*, *Colloq.* person of the opposite sex with whom an appointment is made. 6. **to date,** till now; yet. —*v.* 1. mark with a date; put a date on. 2. find out the date of; give a date to. 3. be dated; have a date on it. 4. belong to a certain period of time; have its origin: *that house dates from the 18th century.* 5. *Am.*, *Colloq.* make a social appointment with (a person of the opposite sex). [< F < Med.L *data*, pp. fem. of L *dare* give] ➤ **dates.** Unless you have good reason for some other form, write dates in the common method: *November 27, 1938; June 16, 1940.* If saving space is important, as in business or reference writing, months having more than four letters should be abbreviated: *Jan., Feb., Mar., Apr., Aug., Sept., Oct., Nov., Dec.* In familiar and informal writing, figures are convenient: *11/27/38, 6/16/40.* In England and other countries the day of the month is usually put first, but that is confusing in the United States, unless Roman numerals are used for the month: *8-vii-38 (July 8, 1938).* Better style now usually omits the *st, nd, th* from the day of the month: *May 1* rather than *May 1st, September 17* rather than *September 17th.* In rather formal style the day of the month may be written in words when the year is not given: *September seventeen* or *September seventeenth.*

date[2] (dāt), *n.* 1. the sweet fruit of a kind of palm tree. 2. date palm. [(< OF < L < Gk. *daktylos* date, finger]

dat·ed (dāt′id), *adj.* 1. marked with a date; showing a date on it. 2. out-of-date.

date·less (dāt′lis), *adj.* 1. without a date; not dated. 2. endless. 3. so old that it cannot be given a date. 4. old but still interesting.

date line, 1. an imaginary line agreed upon as the place where each calendar day first begins. It runs north and south through the Pacific, mostly along the 180th meridian. 2. *Am.* line in a letter, newspaper, etc., giving the date when it was written or issued.

date palm, a palm tree on which dates grow.

da·tive (dā′tiv), *adj.* showing the indirect object of a verb. In "Give me the book," *me* is in the dative case. In Latin *Puero librum dedit,* "He gave the boy a book," *puero* is in the dative case. —*n.* 1. the dative case. 2. word in this case. [< L *dativus* of giving < *datus,* pp. of *dare* give] —**da′tive·ly,** *adv.* ➤ dative case. A noun or pronoun in the dative case either has the same form as the accusative or appears in a phrase made with *to* or *for* or *on.* If both a dative and accusative object are used with the same verb, the dative usually precedes if it is the simple form and follows if it is the prepositional form: *They gave him three dollars. They gave the man three dollars. They gave three dollars to him [to the man].* The dative indicates that the action is for the advantage or disadvantage of the person or object it names or that the act in some way refers to the person or object. Such a noun or pronoun is called an "indirect object."

da·tum (dā′təm; dat′əm; dä′təm), *n.*, *pl.* **da·ta.** fact from which conclusions can be drawn. [< L, (thing) given, pp. of *dare*]

daub (dôb), *v.* 1. coat or cover with plaster, clay, mud, etc. 2. make dirty; soil; stain. 3. paint unskilfully. —*n.* 1. anything daubed on. 2. act of daubing. 3. a badly painted picture. [< F < L, < *de-* + *albus* white] —**daub′er,** *n.*

daugh·ter (dô′tər), *n.* 1. a female child. 2. a female descendant. 3. girl or woman related in the same way that a child is related to its parents. 4. anything thought of as a daughter in relation to its origin. [OE *dohtor*] —**daugh′ter·ly,** *adj.*

daughter element, *Nuclear Physics.* element produced by the decay of a radioactive element.

daugh·ter-in-law (dô′tər·in·lô′), *n.*, *pl.* **daugh·ters-in-law.** wife of one's son.

daunt (dônt; dänt), *v.* 1. frighten. 2. discourage. [< OF *danter* < L *domitare* < *domare* tame] —**Syn.** 1. intimidate, scare. 2. dismay, dishearten.

daunt·less (dônt′lis; dänt′-), *adj.* not to be frightened or discouraged; brave. —**daunt′-less·ly,** *adv.* —**daunt′less·ness,** *n.*

dau·phin (dô′fən), *n.* title of the oldest son of the king of France, from 1349 to 1830. [< F, orig. a family name]

dav·en·port (dav′ən·pôrt; -pōrt), *n.* *Am.* a long couch with back and ends. Some davenports can be made into beds. [prob. from the maker's name]

Da·vid (dā′vid), *n.* the second king of Israel.

da Vin·ci (də vin′chi), **Leonardo,** 1452–1519, Italian painter, architect, and scientist.

Da·vis (dā′vis), *n.* **Jefferson,** 1808–1889, president of the Confederate States, 1861 to 1865.

dav·it (dav′it; dā′vit), *n.* a curved arm at the side of a ship, used to hold or lower a small boat, anchor, etc. [< AF *daviot*]

Da·vy (dā′vi), *n.* **Sir Humphry,** 1778–1829, English Chemist.

Da·vy Jones (dā′vi jōnz′), *Naut.* the sailor's devil.

Da·vy Jones's locker, grave of those who die at sea; bottom of the ocean.

daw (dô), *n.* a jackdaw. [ME *dawe*]

daw·dle (dô′dəl), *v.* —**dled, –dling.** waste time; idle; loiter. —**daw′dler,** *n.*

dawn (dôn), *n.* 1. the first light in the east; daybreak. 2. beginning. —*v.* 1. grow bright or clear. 2. grow clear to the eye or mind. 3. begin; appear: *a new era is dawning.* [< *dawning,* prob. < Scand. (Dan.) *dagning*]

Daw·son (dô′sən), *n.* city in NW Canada, in Yukon Territory.

day (dā), *n.* 1. time between sunrise and sunset. 2. light of day; daylight. 3. the 24 hours of day and night (called a **mean solar day**). 4. a certain day set aside for a particular purpose or for celebration, as Christmas Day. 5. hours for work: *an eight-hour day.* 6. *Astron.* time taken by some specified heavenly body to make one complete turn on its axis: *the moon's day.* 7. time; period: *in days of old.* 8. period of life, activity, power, or influence: *he has had his day.* 9. conflict; contest. 10. victory. [OE *dæg*]

day bed, day·bed (dā′bed′), *n.* *Esp. U.S.* bed, usually narrow, with low head and foot boards of equal height, used as a couch by day.

day book, *Bookkeeping.* book in which a record is kept of each day's business.

day·break (dā′brāk′), *n.* time when it first begins to get light in the morning.

day coach, *Am.* an ordinary passenger car of a railroad train.

day·dream (dā′drēm′), *n.* 1. dreamy thought about pleasant things. 2. a pleasant plan or fancy, unlikely to come true. —*v.* think dreamily about pleasant things. —**day′dream′er,** *n.*

day laborer, an unskilled or manual worker who is paid by the day.

day letter, *Esp. U.S.* telegram sent during the day, usually slower and cheaper than a regular telegram.

day·light (dā′līt′), *n.* 1. light of day. 2. daytime. 3. dawn; daybreak. 4. publicity; openness.

day·light-sav·ing time (dā′līt′sāv′ing), time that is one hour faster than standard time, usually used during the summer to give more daylight after working hours.

day nursery, *Am.* nursery for the care of small children during the day.

Day of Atonement, Yom Kippur.

day school, 1. school held in the daytime. 2. a private school for students who live at home.

day·time (dā′tīm′), *n.* time when it is day.

Day·ton (dā′tən), *n.* city in SW Ohio.

daze (dāz), *v.*, **dazed, daz·ing,** —*v.* 1. confuse and bewilder; cause to feel stupid; stun. 2. dazzle. —*n.* a dazed condition; bewilderment;

stupor. [ME *dase(n)*. Cf. Scand. *dasa* make tired.] —**daz′ed·ly**, *adv.*

daz·zle (daz′əl), *v.*, **-zled, -zling**, *n.* —*v.* **1.** hurt (the eyes) with too bright light or with quick-moving lights. **2.** overcome (the sight or the mind) by brightness, display, etc. —*n.* act or fact of dazzling; bewildering brightness. [< *daze*] —**daz′zler**, *n.* —**daz′zling·ly**, *adv.*

D.C., 1. Also, **d.c.** direct current. **2.** District of Columbia.

D-day (dē′dā′), *n. Mil.* day on which a previously planned attack is to be made, or on which an operation is to be started.

DDT, D.D.T., the symbol for a kind of odorless and very powerful insecticide.

de-, *prefix.* **1.** do the opposite of, as in *decentralize, demobilize.* **2.** down, as in *depress, descend.* **3.** away; off, as in *deport.* **4.** entirely; completely, as in *despoil.* [< L *de* from, away]

dea·con (dē′kən), *n.* **1.** officer of a church who helps the minister in church duties not connected with the preaching. **2.** member of the clergy next below a priest in rank. [< L < Gk. *diakonos* servant] —**dea′con·ry, dea′con·ship,** *n.*

dea·con·ess (dē′kən·is), *n.* **1.** woman who is an official assistant in church service, esp. in caring for the sick and poor. **2.** a female deacon.

dead (ded), *adj.* **1.** no longer living; that has died. **2.** without life. **3.** like death. **4.** not active; dull; quiet. **5.** without force, power, spirit, or feeling. **6.** lacking its characteristic quality: *a dead electric circuit.* **7.** not productive: *dead capital.* **8.** no longer in use. **9.** not to be used as it is. **10.** out of play; not in the game. **11.** *Colloq.* very tired; worn-out. **12.** sure; certain. **13.** complete; absolute. —*adv.* **1.** completely; absolutely. **2.** directly; straight. **3.** precisely; exactly. —*n.* **1.** dead person or persons. **2.** time of greatest darkness, cold, etc.: *the dead of night.* [OE *dēad*] —**dead′ness,** *n.* —**Syn.** *adj.* **1.** deceased, defunct, late. **2.** lifeless, inanimate, inert. —**Ant.** *adj.* **1.** alive, living.

dead beat, *Am., Slang.* **1.** person who avoids paying for what he gets. **2.** loafer.

dead center, position of the crank and connecting rod in an engine, at which the connecting rod has no power to turn the crank.

dead·en (ded′ən), *v.* **1.** make dull or weak; lessen the intenseness or force of: *some drugs deaden pain.* **2.** make soundproof. —**dead′en·er,** *n.*

dead end, street, passage, etc., closed at one end. —**dead′-end′,** *adj.*

dead·head (ded′hed′), *n. Am., Colloq.* person who rides on a bus, sees a game, etc., without paying.

dead letter, 1. an unclaimed letter; letter that cannot be delivered. **2.** law, rule, etc., that is not enforced.

dead·line (ded′līn′), *n. Am.* **1.** the latest possible time to do something. **2.** line or boundary that must not be crossed.

dead·lock (ded′lok′), *n.* a complete standstill. —*v.* bring or come to a deadlock.

dead·ly (ded′li), *adj.*, **-li·er, -li·est,** *adv.* —*adj.* **1.** causing death; liable to cause death; fatal. **2.** like death. **3.** like death's. **4.** until death: *deadly enemies.* **5.** causing death of the spirit: *deadly sin.* **6.** *Colloq.* extreme; intense. —*adv.* **1.** *Colloq.* deathly. **2.** like death. **3.** as if dead. —**dead′li·ness,** *n.* —**Syn.** *adj.* **1.** mortal, lethal.

dead pan, *Am., Slang.* an expressionless face.

dead reckoning, finding one's position by means of a compass and calculations based on speed, time elapsed, and direction from a known position.

Dead Sea, a salt lake on the E boundary of Palestine.

dead·wood (ded′wud′), *n.* **1.** dead branches or trees. **2.** *Am.* useless people or things. **3.** a conventional word or phrase that adds nothing to the meaning of a sentence.

deaf (def), *adj.* **1.** not able to hear. **2.** not able to hear well. **3.** not willing to hear; heedless: *deaf to all requests.* **4.** deaf and dumb, unable

to hear and speak. [OE *dēaf*] —**deaf′ly,** *adv.* —**deaf′ness,** *n.*

deaf·en (def′ən), *v.* **1.** make deaf. **2.** stun with noise. **3.** drown out by a louder sound. **4.** make soundproof. —**deaf′en·ing·ly,** *adv.*

deaf-mute (def′mūt′), *n.* person who is deaf and dumb.

deal¹ (dēl), *v.*, **dealt** (delt), **deal·ing,** *n.* —*v.* **1.** have to do: *arithmetic deals with numbers.* **2.** occupy oneself; take action. **3.** act; behave. **4.** do business; buy and sell: *a butcher deals in meat.* **5.** give: *one fighter dealt the other a blow.* **6.** give a share to each; distribute. **7.** distribute (playing cards). —*n.* **1.** *Am., Colloq.* a business arrangement. **2.** *Colloq.* distribution; arrangement; plan. **3.** in cardplaying, the distribution of cards. **4.** a player's turn to deal. **5.** time during which one deal of cards is being played. **6.** quantity; amount. [OE *dǣlan*] —**deal′er,** *n.*

deal² (dēl), *n.* board of pine or fir wood. [< MLG or MDu. *dele*]

deal·ing (dēl′ing), *n.* Usually, **dealings. a.** business relations. **b.** friendly relations.

dean (dēn), *n.* **1.** *Am.* member of the faculty of a college or university who has charge of the studies of the students. **2.** head of a division or school in a college or university. **3.** a high official of a church, often one in charge of a cathedral. **4.** member who has belonged to a group longest. [< OF < LL *decanus* master of ten < *decem* ten] —**dean′ship,** *n.*

dean·er·y (dēn′ər·i), *n.*, *pl.* **-er·ies. 1.** position or authority of a dean. **2.** residence of a dean.

dear (dir), *adj.* **1.** much loved; precious. **2.** (as a form of address at the beginning of letters) much valued; highly esteemed. **3.** high-priced; costly. —*n.* a dear one. —*adv.* **1.** with affection; fondly. **2.** at a high price. —*interj.* exclamation of surprise. [OE *dēore*] —**dear′ly,** *adv.* —**dear′ness,** *n.* —**Syn.** *adj.* **1.** beloved. **3.** expensive.

dearth (dėrth), *n.* **1.** scarcity; lack. **2.** scarcity of food; famine. [ME *derthe* < *dere* hard]

death (deth), *n.* **1.** the ending of any form of life. **2.** Often, **Death.** power that destroys life, often represented as a skeleton. **3.** any ending that is like dying. **4.** being dead. **5.** any condition like being dead. **6.** cause of death. **7.** bloodshed; murder. [OE *dēath*] —**death′like′,** *adj.*

death·bed (deth′bed′), *n.* **1.** bed on which a person dies. **2.** the last hours of life. —*adj.* during the last hours of life: *a deathbed confession.*

death-blow (deth′blō′), *n.* **1.** blow that kills. **2.** thing that puts an end (to something).

death cup, a poisonous mushroom that has a cuplike enlargement at the base of the stem.

death house, *U.S.* place where condemned prisoners are kept until put to death.

death·less (deth′lis), *adj.* never dying; living forever; immortal; eternal. —**death′less·ly,** *adv.* —**death′less·ness,** *n.*

death·ly (deth′li), *adj.* **1.** like that of death. **2.** causing death; deadly. **3.** *Poetic.* of death. —*adv.* **1.** as if dead. **2.** extremely.

death rate, proportion of the number of deaths per year to the total population or to some other stated number.

death sand, *Mil.* radioactive dust that may be scattered over vast areas. It would kill all, or most, of the life it touched.

death's-head (deths′hed′), *n.* a human skull used as a symbol of death.

death-trap (deth′trap′), *n. Am.* an unsafe building or structure where the fire risk is great.

Death Valley, valley in E California; the lowest land in the Western Hemisphere, 276 ft. below sea level.

death·watch (deth′woch′; -wôch′), *n.* **1.** watch kept beside a dying or dead person. **2.** guard for a person about to be put to death.

de·ba·cle (dā·bä′kəl; di-; -bak′əl), *n.* **1.** disaster; overthrow; downfall. **2.** the breaking up of ice in a river. **3.** a violent rush of waters carrying debris. [< F, < *dé-* + *bâcler* to bar]

de·bar (di·bär′), *v.*, **-barred, -bar·ring.** bar out; shut out; prevent. —**de·bar′ment,** *n.*

āge, cāre, fär; ēqual, tėrm; īce; ōpen, ôrder; pùt, rüle, ūse; th, then; ə=a in about.

de·bark (di·bärk′), *v.* go or put ashore from a ship or aircraft; disembark. [< F, < *dé-* + *barque* BARK³] —**de·bar·ka·tion** (dē′bär·kā′- shən), *n.*

de·base (di·bās′), *v.*, –**based**, –**bas·ing**. make low or lower; lessen the value of. [< *de-* + (a) *base*] —**de·base′ment**, *n.* —**de·bas′er**, *n.*

de·bate (di·bāt′), *v.*, –**bat·ed**, –**bat·ing**, *n.* —*v.* 1. discuss reasons for and against (something); consider. 2. argue about (a question, topic, etc.) in a public meeting. 3. *Obs.* quarrel. —*n.* 1. discussion of reasons for and against. 2. a public argument for and against a question in a meeting. [< OF, < *batre* BEAT] —**de·bat′a·ble**, *adj.* —**de·bat′er**, *n.* —**Syn.** v. 1. deliberate.

de·bauch (di·bôch′), *v.* 1. corrupt morally; seduce. 2. corrupt; pervert; deprave. —*n.* excessive indulgence in sensual pleasures. [< F *débaucher* entice from duty] —**de·bauch′ed·ly**, *adv.* —**de·bauch′er**, *n.* —**de·bauch′ment**, *n.*

deb·au·chee (deb′ô·chē′; –shē′), *n.* a corrupt, dissipated, or depraved person.

de·bauch·er·y (di·bôch′ər·i), *n.*, *pl.* –**er·ies.** 1. excessive indulgence in sensual pleasures. 2. seduction from duty, virtue, or morality.

de·ben·ture (di·ben′chər), *n.* a written acknowledgment of a debt. [< L *debentur* there are owing. See DEBIT.]

de·bil·i·tate (di·bil′ə·tāt), *v.*, –**tat·ed**, –**tat·ing.** weaken. —**de·bil′i·tat′ed**, *adj.* —**de·bil′i·ta′tion**, *n.* —**de·bil′i·ta′tive**, *adj.*

de·bil·i·ty (di·bil′ə·ti), *n.*, *pl.* –**ties.** weakness. [< L, < *debilis* weak]

deb·it (deb′it), *n.* 1. entry of something owed in an account. 2. the left-hand side of an account where such entries are made. —*v.* 1. enter on the debit side of an account. 2. charge with a debt. [< L *debitum* (thing) owed, pp. of *debere*]

deb·o·nair, deb·o·naire, or **deb·on·naire** (deb′ə·nār′), *adj.* 1. gay; cheerful. 2. pleasant; courteous. [< OF, < *de bon aire* of good disposition] —**deb′o·nair′ness**, *n.*

de·bouch (di·büsh′), *v.* come out from a narrow or confined place into open country. [< F, < *dé-* + *bouche* mouth < L *bucca*] —**de·bouch′- ment**, *n.*

de·bris, dé·bris (də·brē′; dā′brē; *esp. Brit.* deb′rē), *n.* 1. scattered fragments; ruins; rubbish. 2. mass of stones, fragments of rocks, etc. [< F, < OF, < *de-* + *brisier* break]

Debs (debz), *n.* Eugene Victor, 1855–1926, American Socialist and labor leader.

debt (det), *n.* 1. something owed to another. 2. liability or obligation to pay or render something. 3. sin. [< OF *dete* < L *debitum* (thing) owed, pp. of *debere*] —**Syn.** 2. indebtedness.

debt·or (det′ər), *n.* person who is in debt.

de·bunk (di·bungk′), *v.* *Am., Slang.* remove nonsense or sentimentality from. —**de·bunk′er**, *n.*

De·bus·sy (də·bü′si; *Fr.* də·by·sē′), *n.* Claude A., 1862–1918, French composer.

de·but, dé·but (dā′bü; dā·bü′; di–), *n.* 1. a first public appearance, as on the stage. 2. a first formal appearance in society. [< F *débuter* make the first stroke < *dé-* + *but* goal]

deb·u·tante, dé·bu·tante (deb′yə·tänt; –tant; deb′yə·tänt′), *n.* 1. girl during her first season in society. 2. woman making a debut.

Dec., December.

dec., 1. deceased. 2. decimeter.

deca–, *prefix.* ten, as in decagram. [< Gk. *deka*]

dec·ade (dek′ād), *n.* 1. ten years. 2. group of ten. [< F < LL < Gk. *dekas* group of ten < *deka* ten]

de·ca·dence (di·kā′dəns; dek′ə·dəns), **de·ca·den·cy** (–dən·si), *n.* a falling off; decline; decay. [< F < Med.L, < L *de-* + *cadere* fall]

dec·a·dent (di·kā′dənt; dek′ə·dənt), *adj.* falling off; declining; growing worse. —*n.* a decadent person. —**dec·a′dent·ly**, *adv.*

dec·a·gon (dek′ə·gon), *n.* *Geom.* a plane figure having 10 angles and 10 sides. —**de·cag·o·nal** (di·kag′ə·nəl), *adj.*

dec·a·gram, *esp. Brit.* **dec·a·gramme** (dek′ə·gram), *n.* weight equal to 10 grams.

dec·a·he·dron (dek′ə·hē′drən), *n.*, *pl.* –**drons,** –**dra** (–drə). *Geom.* a solid figure having 10 surfaces. —**dec·a·he·dral** (dek′ə·hē′drəl), *adj.*

de·cal·co·ma·ni·a (di·kal′kə·mā′ni·ə), or **de·cal** (dē′kal; di·kal′), *n.* 1. design or picture treated so that it will stick fast to glass, wood, etc. 2. process of applying these designs or pictures. [< F *décalcomanie*, < *décalquer* transfer a tracing + *manie* MANIA]

dec·a·li·ter, *esp. Brit.* **dec·a·li·tre** (dek′ə·lē′tər), *n.* measure of volume equal to 10 liters.

Dec·a·logue, Dec·a·log (dek′ə·lôg; –log), *n.* 1. the Ten Commandments. Exod. 20:2–17. 2. decalogue, decalog, any set of ten commandments.

dec·a·me·ter, *esp. Brit.* **dec·a·me·tre** (dek′ə·mē′tər), *n.* measure of length equal to 10 meters.

de·camp (di·kamp′), *v.* 1. depart quickly or secretly. 2. leave a camp. —**de·camp′ment**, *n.*

de·cant (di·kant′), *v.* pour off (liquor or a solution) gently without disturbing the sediment. [< Med.L, < *de-* + *canthus* lip < Gk. *kanthos* corner of the eye] —**de·can·ta·tion** (dē′kan·tā′shən), *n.*

de·cant·er (di·kan′tər), *n.* 1. a bottle used to decant. 2. a glass bottle used for serving wine or liquor.

de·cap·i·tate (di·kap′ə·tāt), *v.*, –**tat·ed**, –**tat·ing.** behead. [< LL < *de-* + L *caput* head] —**de·cap′i·ta′tion**, *n.*

dec·a·pod (dek′ə·pod), *n.* 1. crustacean having ten legs or arms, such as lobsters and crabs. 2. mollusk having ten legs or arms, such as squid. —*adj.* having ten legs or arms.

Decanter

dec·a·syl·la·ble (dek′ə·sil′ə·bəl), *n.* line of poetry having ten syllables. —**dec·a·syl·lab·ic** (dek′ə·sə·lab′ik), *adj.*

de·cath·lon (di·kath′lon), *n.* an athletic contest having ten parts, such as racing, jumping, etc., won by the person having the highest total score. [< DECA– + Gk. *athlon* contest]

de·cay (di·kā′), *v.* 1. rot. 2. grow less in power, strength, beauty, etc. —*n.* 1. process of rotting. 2. loss of power, strength, beauty, etc. 3. *Nuclear Physics.* loss in quantity of a radioactive substance through disintegration of its component nuclei. [< OF, < *de-* + *cair* < L *cadere* fall] —**Syn.** v. 1. decompose, putrefy. 2. deteriorate, decline.

Dec·can (dek′ən; de·kan′), *n.* peninsula in S India.

de·cease (di·sēs′), *n.*, *v.*, –**ceased,** –**ceas·ing.** —*n.* death. —*v.* die. [< F < L *decessus* < *de-* + *cedere* go]

de·ceased (di·sēst′), *adj.* dead. —*n.* the deceased, a dead person.

de·ce·dent (di·sē′dənt), *n. Law.* a dead person.

de·ceit (di·sēt′), *n.* 1. act or fact of deceiving, lying, or cheating. 2. a dishonest trick. 3. deceitful quality; deceitfulness. —**Syn.** 1. hypocrisy, guile. 2. deception, fraud.

de·ceit·ful (di·sēt′fəl), *adj.* 1. ready or willing to deceive or lie. 2. deceiving; fraudulent. —**de·ceit′ful·ly**, *adv.* —**de·ceit′ful·ness**, *n.*

de·ceive (di·sēv′), *v.*, –**ceived,** –**ceiv·ing.** 1. make (a person) believe as true something that is false; mislead. 2. use dishonest tricks. [< OF *deceveir* < L, < *de-* + *capere* take] —**de·ceiv′er**, *n.* —**de·ceiv′ing·ly**, *adv.* —**Syn.** 1. delude, beguile.

de·cel·er·ate (dē·sel′ər·āt), *v.*, –**at·ed**, –**at·ing.** decrease the velocity of; slow down. [< *de-* + (ac)*celerate*] —**de·cel′er·a′tion**, *n.* —**de·cel′er·a′tor**, *n.*

De·cem·ber (di·sem′bər), *n.* the 12th and last month of the year. It has 31 days. [< L, < *decem* ten; from the order of the early Roman calendar]

de·cen·cy (dē′sən·si), *n.*, *pl.* –**cies.** 1. state or quality of being decent. 2. propriety of behavior. 3. a proper regard for modesty or delicacy. 4. decencies, a. suitable acts. b. things required for a proper standard of living.

de·cen·ni·al (di·sen′i·əl), *adj.* 1. of or for ten years. 2. happening every ten years. —*n. Am.* tenth anniversary. [< L *decennium* decade < *decem* ten + *annus* year] —de·cen′ni·al·ly, *adv.*

de·cent (dē′sənt), *adj.* 1. proper and right. 2. conforming to the standard of good taste. 3. respectable. 4. good enough; fairly good. 5. suitable to one's position; adequate. 6. not severe; rather kind. [< L *decens* becoming, fitting, ppr. of *decere*] —de′cent·ly, *adv.* —de′cent·ness, *n.* —Syn. 1. suitable, appropriate. 4. tolerable.

de·cen·tral·ize (dē·sen′trəl·īz), *v.,* -ized, -iz·ing. spread or distribute (authority, power, etc.).

de·cep·tion (di·sep′shən), *n.* 1. act of deceiving. 2. state of being deceived. 3. thing that deceives; illusion. 4. fraud; sham. —Syn. 3. imposture, subterfuge, trickery. 4. hoax, ruse.

de·cep·tive (di·sep′tiv), *adj.* apt or tending to deceive. —de·cep′tive·ly, *adv.* —de·cep′tive·ness, *n.*

deci-, *prefix.* one tenth of, as in *decigram.* [< L *decem* ten, *decimus* tenth]

dec·i·bel (des′ə·bel), *n.* unit for measuring the loudness of sounds.

de·cide (di·sīd′), *v.,* -cid·ed, -cid·ing. 1. settle (a question, dispute, etc.) by giving victory to one side. 2. make up one's mind; resolve. 3. cause (a person) to reach a decision. [< L *decidere* cut off < *de-* + *caedere* cut] —Syn. 2. determine.

de·cid·ed (di·sīd′id), *adj.* 1. clear; definite; unquestionable. 2. firm; determined. —de·cid′ed·ly, *adv.* —de·cid′ed·ness, *n.*

de·cid·u·ous (di·sij′ū·əs), *adj.* 1. falling off at a particular season or stage of growth, as horns. 2. shedding leaves annually. [< L, < *de-* + *cadere* fall] —de·cid′u·ous·ly, *adv.* —de·cid′u·ous·ness, *n.*

dec·i·gram, *esp. Brit.* **dec·i·gramme** (des′ə·gram), *n.* weight equal to ¹⁄₁₀ of a gram.

dec·i·li·ter, *esp. Brit.* **dec·i·li·tre** (des′ə·lē′tər), *n.* measure of volume equal to ¹⁄₁₀ of a liter.

dec·i·mal (des′ə·məl), *adj.* based upon tens or tenths; increasing by tens, as the metric system. —*n.* a decimal fraction. [< L *decimus* tenth] —dec′i·mal·ly, *adv.*

decimal fraction, fraction whose denominator is ten or some power of ten.

decimal point, period placed before a fraction expressed in decimal figures, as in 2.03, .623.

dec·i·mate (des′ə·māt), *v.,* -mat·ed, -mat·ing. 1. destroy much of; kill a large part of. 2. select by lot and execute every tenth man of. [< L *decimatus,* pp. of *decimare* take a tenth, ult. < *decem* ten] —dec′i·ma′tion, *n.* —dec′i·ma′tor, *n.*

dec·i·me·ter, *esp. Brit.* **dec·i·me·tre** (des′ə·mē′tər), *n.* measure of length equal to ¹⁄₁₀ of a meter.

de·ci·pher (di·sī′fər), *v.* 1. make out the meaning of (bad writing, an unknown language, or anything puzzling). 2. translate (a message in code) into plain language by using a key. —de·ci′pher·a·ble, *adj.* —de·ci′pher·ment, *n.*

de·ci·sion (di·sizh′ən), *n.* 1. the deciding or settling of a question, dispute, etc. 2. judgment reached or given, as by a court. 3. a making up of one's mind. 4. firmness; determination. —Syn. 2. verdict, decree.

de·ci·sive (di·sī′siv), *adj.* 1. having or giving a clear result. 2. having or showing decision. —de·ci′sive·ly, *adv.* —de·ci′sive·ness, *n.*

deck (dek), *n.* 1. floor or platform extending from side to side of a ship. 2. part or floor resembling it: *the deck of an airplane.* 3. pack of playing cards. 4. **on deck**, *Am., Colloq.* present; on hand. —*v.* cover; dress. [< MDu. *dec* roof]

deck hand, *Am.* sailor who works on deck.

deck·le edge (dek′əl), 1. the rough edge of untrimmed paper. 2. an imitation of it. [< G *deckel,* dim. of *decke* cover]

de·claim (di·klām′), *v.* 1. recite in public; make a formal speech. 2. speak or write for effect. [< L, < *de-* + *clamare* cry]

dec·la·ma·tion (dek′lə·mā′shən), *n.* 1. act or art of reciting in public. 2. selection of poetry, prose, etc., for reciting. 3. a speaking or writing for effect. —de·clam·a·to·ry (di·klam′ə·tô′ri; -tō′-), *adj.*

dec·la·ra·tion (dek′lə·rā′shən), *n.* 1. act of declaring. 2. thing declared. 3. statement of goods, etc., for taxation. 4. a formal announcement. 5. *Bridge.* a bid, esp. the winning bid.

Declaration of Independence, *Am.* a public statement adopted by the Continental Congress on July 4, 1776, in which the American colonies were declared free and independent of Great Britain.

de·clare (di·klār′), *v.,* -clared, -clar·ing. 1. announce publicly or formally; make known; proclaim: *declare a dividend.* 2. say openly or strongly. 3. make a declaration; proclaim oneself. 4. make a statement of (goods, etc.) for taxation. 5. in bridge, announce (what suit) will be played as trumps. [< L, < *de-* + *clarus* clear] —de·clar·a·tive (di·klar′ə·tiv), de·clar·a·to·ry (di·klar′ə·tô′ri; -tō′-), *adj.* —de·clar′er, *n.*

de·clas·si·fy (dē′klas′ə·fī), *v.,* -fied, -fy·ing. remove (documents, codes, etc.) from the list of restricted, confidential, or secret information.

de·clen·sion (di·klen′shən), *n.* 1. the giving of the different endings to nouns, pronouns, and adjectives according to their case. 2. group of words whose endings for the different cases are alike. 3. a downward movement, bend, or slope. 4. a sinking into a lower or inferior condition; decline. 5. deviation from a standard. 6. a polite refusal. —de·clen′sion·al, *adj.*

dec·li·na·tion (dek′lə·nā′shən), *n.* 1. a downward bend or slope. 2. decline; deterioration. 3. a polite refusal. 4. difference in direction between true north and magnetic north at any given point. 5. the angular distance of a star, planet, etc., from the celestial equator.

CP, celestial poles; CE, celestial equator; DS, declination of the star S.

de·cline (di·klīn′), *v.,* -clined, -clin·ing. —*v.* 1. refuse. 2. refuse politely. 3. bend or slope down. 4. grow less in strength, power, value, etc.; grow worse; decay. 5. give the different cases or case endings of (a noun, pronoun, or adjective). —*n.* 1. a falling; a sinking: *a decline in prices.* 2. a downward slope. 3. a losing of strength, power, value, etc.; a growing worse. 4. the last part of anything. [< L, < *de-* + *clinare* bend] —de·clin′a·ble, *adj.* —de·clin′er, *n.* —Syn. *v.* 1. reject. 4. deteriorate. —*n.* 3. decay.

de·cliv·i·ty (di·kliv′ə·ti), *n., pl.* -ties. a downward slope. [< L, < *de-* + *clivus* slope]

de·coct (di·kokt′), *v.* extract desired substances from (herbs, etc.) by boiling. [< L *decoctus* < *de-* + *coquere* cook] —de·coc·tion (di·kok′shən), *n.*

de·code (dē·kōd′), *v.,* -cod·ed, -cod·ing. translate (secret writing) from code into ordinary language. —de·cod′er, *n.*

dé·col·le·té (dā′kol·tā′; -kol·ə·tā′), *adj.* 1. low-necked. 2. wearing a low-necked gown. [< F]

de·com·pose (dē′kəm·pōz′), *v.,* -posed, -pos·ing. 1. decay; rot. 2. separate (a substance) into what it is made of. —de′com·pos′a·ble, *adj.* —de·com·po·si·tion (dē′kom·pə·zish′ən), *n.*

de·con·tam·i·nate (dē′kən·tam′ə·nāt), *v.,* -nat·ed, -nat·ing. 1. free from poison gas or harmful radioactive agents. 2. free from any sort of contamination. —de′con·tam′i·na′tion, *n.*

de·con·trol (dē′kən·trōl′), *v.,* -trolled, -trol·ling, *n.* —*v.* remove controls from: *decontrol prices.* —*n.* removing of controls.

dé·cor (dā·kôr′), *n.* 1. decoration. 2. scenery on a stage. [< F, < *décorer* DECORATE]

dec·o·rate (dek′ə·rāt), *v.,* -rat·ed, -rat·ing. 1. make beautiful; adorn. 2. paint or paper (a room, etc.). 3. give a medal, ribbon, etc., to (a person) as an honor. [< L *decoratus* < *decus* adornment] —dec·o·ra·tive (dek′ə·rā′tiv; -rə-tiv), *adj.* —dec′o·ra′tive·ly, *adv.* —dec′o·ra′tive·ness, *n.* —dec′o·ra′tor, *n.*

dec·o·ra·tion (dek'ə·rā'shən), *n.* **1.** act of decorating. **2.** thing used to decorate; ornament. **3.** medal, ribbon, etc., given as an honor.

Decoration Day, *Am.* Memorial Day.

dec·o·rous (dek'ə·rəs; di·kô'rəs; –kō'–), *adj.* well-behaved; acting properly. —**dec'o·rous·ly,** *adv.* —**dec'o·rous·ness,** *n.*

de·co·rum (di·kô'rəm; –kō'–), *n.* **1.** propriety of action, speech, dress, etc. **2.** observance or requirement of polite society. [< L, (that which is) seemly]

de·coy (*v.* di·koi'; *n.* dē'koi, di·koi'), *v.* **1.** lure (wild birds, animals, etc.) into a trap or within gunshot. **2.** lead or tempt into danger. —*n.* **1.** an artificial bird used to lure birds into a trap or within gunshot. **2.** place into which wild birds or animals are lured. **3.** any person or thing used to lead or tempt into danger. [< Du. *de kooi* the cage < L *cavea* cave] —**de·coy'er,** *n.*

de·crease (*v.* di·krēs'; *n.* dē'krēs, di·krēs'), *v.,* –creased, –creas·ing, *n.* —*v.* become or make less. —*n.* **1.** a becoming less. **2.** amount by which a thing becomes or is made less. [< OF < L, < *de– + crescere* grow] —**de·creas'ing·ly,** *adv.* —**Syn.** *v.* diminish, dwindle, abate, wane, shrink, reduce. —**Ant.** *v.* increase, expand.

de·cree (di·krē'), *n., v.,* –creed, –cree·ing. —*n.* something ordered or settled by authority. —*v.* order or settle by authority. [< OF < L *decretum < de– + cernere* decide] —**de·cre'er,** *n.*

dec·re·pit (di·krep'it), *adj.* broken down or weakened by old age. [< L *decrepitus* broken down < *de– + crepare* creak] —**de·crep'it·ly,** *adv.*

de·crep·i·tude (di·krep'ə·tüd; –tūd), *n.* feebleness, usually from old age; decrepit condition.

de·cre·scen·do (dē'krə·shen'dō; dā'–), *n., pl.* –dos, *adj., adv.* —*n.* a gradual decrease in force or loudness; diminuendo. —*adj., adv.* with a gradual decrease in force or loudness. [< Ital.]

de·cre·tal (di·krē'təl), *n.* decree or reply by the pope settling some question of doctrine or ecclesiastical law.

de·cry (di·krī'), *v.,* –cried, –cry·ing. **1.** condemn. **2.** make little of; try to lower the value of. [< OF *décrier.* See DE–, CRY.] —**de·cri'al,** *n.* —**de·cri'er,** *n.*

de·cum·bent (di·kum'bənt), *adj.* **1.** reclining. **2.** *Bot.* lying or trailing on the ground with the end tending to climb. [< L *decumbens,* ppr. of *decumbere* lie down]

ded·i·cate (ded'ə·kāt), *v.,* –cat·ed, –cat·ing. **1.** set apart for a sacred or solemn purpose. **2.** give up wholly or earnestly, as to some person or end. **3.** address (a book, poem, etc.) to a friend or patron as a mark of affection, gratitude, etc. [< L, < *de– + dicare* proclaim] —**ded'i·ca'tive,** **ded·i·ca·to·ry** (ded'ə·kə·tô'ri; –tō'–), *adj.*

ded·i·ca·tion (ded'ə·kā'shən), *n.* **1.** a setting apart or being set apart for a sacred or solemn purpose. **2.** words dedicating a book.

de·duce (di·düs'; –dūs'), *v.,* –duced, –duc·ing. **1.** infer from a general rule or principle. **2.** trace the course, descent, or origin of. [< L, < *de– + ducere* lead] —**de·duc'i·ble,** *adj.*

de·duct (di·dukt'), *v.* take away; subtract. [< L *deductus,* pp. See DEDUCE.] —**de·duct'i·ble,** *adj.*

de·duc·tion (di·duk'shən), *n.* **1.** act of taking away; subtraction. **2.** amount deducted. **3.** a logical inference from a general rule or principle. —**de·duc'tive,** *adj.* —**de·duc'tive·ly,** *adv.*

deed (dēd), *n.* **1.** thing done; act. **2.** a brave, skillful, or unusual act. **3.** action; doing; performance. **4.** *Law.* a written or printed agreement legally transferring ownership, esp. of real estate. —*v. Am.* transfer by a deed. [OE *dēd*] —**Syn.** *n.* **2.** feat, exploit.

deem (dēm), *v.* think; believe; consider. [OE *dēman < dōm* judgment]

deep (dēp), *adj.* **1.** going far down or back. **2.** from far down or back. **3.** far down or back. **4.** far on. **5.** in depth. **6.** low in pitch. **7.** strong and dark in color. **8.** strong; great; intense; extreme. **9.** going below the surface. **10.** hard to understand. **11.** with the mind fully taken up. **12.**

wise; shrewd. **13.** sly; crafty. —*adv.* **1.** far down or back. **2.** of time, far on. —*n.* **1.** a deep place. **2.** the most intense part: *the deep of winter.* **3.** the deep, the sea. [OE *dēop*] —**deep'ly,** *adv.* —**deep'ness,** *n.* —**Syn.** *adj.* **8.** heartfelt, profound. **10.** abstruse. **11.** absorbed. **12.** astute.

deep·en (dēp'ən), *v.* make or become deeper.

deep-freeze (dēp'frēz'), *n., v.,* –froze or –freezed, –fro·zen or –freezed, –freez·ing. —*n.* Deep-freeze, *Trademark.* container for freezing and storing food. —*v.* use a Deep-freeze.

deep-root·ed (dēp'rüt'id; –rut'–), *adj.* **1.** deeply rooted. **2.** firmly fixed.

deep-seat·ed (dēp'sēt'id), *adj.* **1.** far below the surface. **2.** firmly fixed.

deep-set (dēp'set'), *adj.* **1.** set deeply. **2.** firmly fixed.

deer (dir), *n., pl.* **deer, deers. 1.** a swift, graceful animal of a group that have hoofs and chew the cud. A male deer has horns or antlers, which are shed and grow again every year. **2.** any of a group of animals including deer, elk, moose, and caribou. [OE *dēor* animal]

deer·hound (dir'hound'), *n.* hound with a shaggy coat, related to the greyhound.

deer·skin (dir'skin'), *n.* **1.** skin of a deer. **2.** leather made from it.

def., definition.

de·face (di·fās'), *v.,* –faced, –fac·ing. spoil the appearance of; mar. [< obs. F *defacer.* See DIS–, FACE.] —**de·face'a·ble,** *adj.* —**de·face'ment,** *n.* —**de·fac'er,** *n.*

de fac·to (dē fak'tō), in fact; in reality. [< L, from the fact]

de·fal·cate (di·fal'kāt; –fôl'–), *v.,* –cat·ed, –cat·ing. steal or misuse money trusted to one's care. [< L *defalcatus < de– + falx* sickle] —**de·fal·ca·tion** (dē'fal·kā'shən; –fôl–), *n.* —**de·fal'ca·tor,** *n.*

de·fame (di·fām'), *v.,* –famed, –fam·ing. attack the good name of; harm the reputation of; speak evil of; slander. [< OF < L, < *de– + fama* rumor] —**def·a·ma·tion** (def'ə·mā'shən; dē'fə–), *n.* —**de·fam·a·to·ry** (di·fam'ə·tô'ri; –tō'–), *adj.* —**de·fam'er,** *n.*

de·fault (di·fôlt'), *n.* **1.** failure to do something or to appear somewhere when due; neglect. **2.** in sports, failure to compete in a scheduled match. **3.** failure to pay when due. —*v.* **1.** fail to do something or appear somewhere when due. **2.** fail to pay when due. [< OF *defaute < defaillir.* See FAULT.] —**de·fault'er,** *n.*

de·feat (di·fēt'), *v.* **1.** win a victory over; overcome. **2.** frustrate; thwart. **3.** make useless. —*n.* a defeating or being defeated. [< OF < LL, < L *dis– un– + facere* undo] —**de·feat'er,** *n.* —**Syn.** *v.* **1.** vanquish, conquer, beat. **2.** foil, outwit, baffle.

de·feat·ism (di·fēt'iz·əm), *n.* attitude or behavior of a person who expects, wishes for, or admits the defeat of his country, cause, party, etc. —**de·feat'ist,** *n.*

def·e·cate (def'ə·kāt), *v.,* –cat·ed, –cat·ing. have a movement of the bowels. [< L, < *de–* from + *faeces,* pl., dregs] —**def'e·ca'tion,** *n.*

de·fect (di·fekt'; dē'fekt), *n.* **1.** fault; blemish; imperfection. **2.** lack of something essential to completeness; a falling short. —*v.* forsake one's own country, group, etc. for another, esp. another that is opposed to it in political or social doctrine. [< L *defectus* want < *deficere* fail. See DEFICIENT.] —**de·fec'tor,** *n.* —**Syn.** *n.* **1.** flaw. **2.** want, deficiency.

de·fec·tion (di·fek'shən), *n.* **1.** a falling away from loyalty, duty, religion, etc.; desertion. **2.** failure.

de·fec·tive (di·fek'tiv), *adj.* **1.** having a flaw or blemish; not perfect. **2.** *Psychol.* subnormal in behavior or intelligence. **3.** *Gram.* lacking one or more of the usual forms of grammatical inflection. —*n.* person who has some defect of body or mind. —**de·fec'tive·ly,** *adv.* —**de·fec'tive·ness,** *n.* —**Syn.** *adj.* **1.** faulty, imperfect.

de·fence (di·fens'), *n. Brit.* defense. —**de·fence'less,** *adj.* —**de·fence'less·ly,** *adv.* —**de·fence'less·ness,** *n.*

de·fend (di·fend'), *v.* **1.** guard from attack or harm. **2.** act, speak, or write in favor of. **3.** contest (a lawsuit). 4. *Law.* make a defense. [< OF < L *defendere* ward off] —de·fend′a·ble, *adj.* —defend′er, *n.* —Syn. 1. protect. 2. uphold.

de·fend·ant (di·fen′dənt), *n. Law.* person accused or sued in a law court.

de·fense (di·fens′), *n.* 1. act of defending or protecting. 2. thing that defends or protects. 3. act of defending oneself, as in boxing or fencing. 4. team or players defending a goal in a game. 5. action, speech, or writing in favor of something. 6. answer of a defendant to an accusation or lawsuit against him. 7. a defendant and his lawyers. Also, *Brit.* defence. [< OF < L *defensa* < *defendere* DEFEND] —de·fense′less, *adj.* —de·fense′less·ly, *adv.* —de·fense′less·ness, *n.* —de·fen′si·ble, *adj.* —de·fen′si·bil′i·ty, de·fen′si·ble·ness, *n.* —de·fen′si·bly, *adv.*

defense in depth, *Mil.* system of mutually supporting positions designed to break up and absorb an attack.

de·fen·sive (di·fen′siv), *adj.* 1. ready to defend; defending. 2. for defense. 3. of defense. —*n.* 1. position or attitude of defense. 2. thing that defends. —de·fen′sive·ly, *adv.* —de·fen′sive·ness, *n.*

de·fer[1] (di·fėr′), *v.,* —ferred, —fer·ring. put off; delay. [< L *differre.* See DIFFER.] —de·fer′ment, *n.* —de·fer′rer, *n.* —Syn. postpone.

de·fer[2] (di·fėr′), *v.,* —ferred, —fer·ring. yield in judgment or opinion; submit courteously. [< F < L, < *de-* down + *ferre* carry] —de·fer′rer, *n.*

def·er·ence (def′ər·əns), *n.* 1. a yielding to the judgment or opinion of another; courteous submission. 2. great respect.

def·er·en·tial (def′ər·en′shəl), *adj.* showing deference; respectful. —def′er·en′tial·ly, *adv.*

de·fi·ance (di·fī′əns), *n.* 1. a standing up against authority and refusing to recognize or obey it; open resistance. 2. challenge to meet in a contest, to do something, or to prove something. [< OF. See DEFY.]

de·fi·ant (di·fī′ənt), *adj.* showing defiance; challenging; openly resisting. —de·fi′ant·ly, *adv.* —de·fi′ant·ness, *n.*

de·fi·cien·cy (di·fish′ən·si), *n., pl.* —cies. 1. lack or absence of something needed or required; incompleteness. 2. amount by which something falls short or is too small.

de·fi·cient (di·fish′ənt), *adj.* 1. incomplete; defective. 2. not sufficient in quantity, force, etc. [< L *deficiens* failing < *de-* + *facere* do] —de·fi′cient·ly, *adv.*

def·i·cit (def′ə·sit), *n.* amount by which a sum of money falls short; shortage. [< L, it is wanting. See DEFICIENT.]

de·fi·er (di·fī′ər), *n.* person who defies.

de·file[1] (di·fīl′), *v.,* —filed, —fil·ing. 1. make filthy or dirty; make disgusting in any way. 2. destroy the purity or cleanness of; corrupt. [alter. of *defoul* < OF *defouler* trample down, violate) after obs. *file befoul* < OE *fȳlan* < *fūl* foul] —de·file′ment, *n.* —de·fil′er, *n.*

de·file[2] (di·fīl′; dē′fīl), *v.,* —filed, —fil·ing, *n.* —*v.* march in a line. —*n.* a narrow way or passage, esp. a steep and narrow valley. [< F, special use of pp. of *défiler* march by files < *dé-* off + *file* FILE[1]]

de·fine (di·fīn′), *v.,* —fined, —fin·ing. 1. make clear the meaning of; explain. 2. make clear; make distinct. 3. fix; settle. 4. settle the limits of. [< F < L *definire* to limit < *de-* + *finis* end] —de·fin′a·ble, *adj.* —de·fin′a·bly, *adv.* —de·fin′er, *n.*

def·i·nite (def′ə·nit), *adj.* 1. clear; exact; not vague. 2. limited; restricted. 3. limiting; restricting. The English definite article is *the.* —def′i·nite·ness, *n.*

def·i·nite·ly (def′ə·nit·li), *adv.* 1. in a definite manner. 2. certainly. ➤ **Definitely** is one of the most frequently misspelled words. Remember there is no *a* in it and associate def *i ni* tion with def i *nite* and def i *nite* ly. At present *definitely* is overused as a counter word to give emphasis or in the sense of "certainly, quite" (*I will not do it, definitely; he was definitely worse than usual; she definitely disapproves of those methods*) in-

stead of in its exact sense of "in a definite manner."

def·i·ni·tion (def′ə·nish′ən), *n.* 1. act of defining. 2. statement that makes clear the meaning of a word; explanation. 3. capacity of a lens to give a clear, distinct image. 4. *Radio.* accuracy with which sound is reproduced by a receiver. 5. clearness.

de·fin·i·tive (di·fin′ə·tiv), *adj.* 1. conclusive; final. 2. limiting; defining. —*n.* word that limits or defines a noun. *The, this, all, none,* etc., are definitives. —de·fin′i·tive·ly, *adv.* —de·fin′i·tive·ness, *n.*

de·flate (di·flāt′), *v.,* —flat·ed, —flat·ing. 1. let air or gas out of (a balloon, tire, football, etc.). 2. reduce the amount of; reduce. [< L, < *de-* off + *flare* blow] —de·fla′tor, *n.*

de·fla·tion (di·flā′shən), *n.* 1. act of letting the air or gas out: *the deflation of a tire.* 2. reduction. 3. reduction of the amount of available money in circulation. 4. increase in the value of money so that prices go down. —de·fla·tion·ar·y (di·flā′shən·er′i), *adj.*

de·flect (di·flekt′), *v.* bend or turn aside; change the direction of. [< L, < *de-* away + *flectere* bend] —de·flec′tion, *n.* —de·flec′tive, *adj.* —de·flec′tor, *n.*

de·flow·er (dē·flou′ər), *v.* 1. strip flowers from. 2. deprive of virginity; ravish. 3. spoil; ruin.

De·foe (di·fō′), *n.* Daniel, 1661?–1731, English author.

de·for·est (dē·fôr′ist; -for′-), *v.* clear of trees. —de·for′est·a′tion, *n.* —de·for′est·er, *n.*

de·form (di·fôrm′), *v.* 1. spoil the form or shape of. 2. make ugly. 3. change the form of; transform. —de·for·ma·tion (dē′fôr·mā′shən; def′ər-), *n.* —de·formed′, *adj.*

de·form·i·ty (di·fôr′mə·ti), *n., pl.* —ties. 1. part that is not properly formed. 2. condition of being improperly formed. 3. an improperly formed person or thing. 4. ugliness.

de·fraud (di·frôd′), *v.* take money, rights, etc., away from by fraud; cheat. [< L *defraudare.* See DE-, FRAUD.]

de·fray (di·frā′), *v.* pay (costs or expenses). [< F, < *dé-* + *frai* cost] —de·fray′a·ble, *adj.* —de·fray′al, de·fray′ment, *n.* —de·fray′er, *n.*

de·frost (dē·frôst′; -frost′), *v.* remove frost or ice from. —de·frost′er, *n.*

deft (deft), *adj.* skillful; nimble. [var. of *daft*] —deft′ly, *adv.* —deft′ness, *n.*

de·funct (di·fungkt′), *adj.* dead; extinct. [< L *defunctus* finished < *de-* + *fungi* perform] —de·funct′ness, *n.*

de·fy (di·fī′), *v.,* —fied, —fy·ing. 1. resist boldly or openly. 2. withstand; resist. 3. challenge (a person) to do or prove something. [< OF *desfier* < VL, < L *dis-* + *fidus* faithful] —Syn. 1. brave.

De·gas (dā·gä′; də-; -gäs′), *n.* Hilaire Germaine Edgard, 1834–1917, French painter.

De Gaulle (də gōl′), Charles, born 1890, French army officer and political leader, President of France since 1959.

de·gauss (di·gous′; -gōs′), *v.* equip (a steel ship) with a device preventing the explosion of magnetic mines. [< Karl F. *Gauss* (1777–1855), German mathematician]

de·gen·er·a·cy (di·jen′ər·ə·si), *n.* degenerate condition.

de·gen·er·ate (*v.* di·jen′ər·āt; *adj., n.* di·jen′ər·it), *v.,* —at·ed, —at·ing, *adj., n.* —*v.* 1. decline in physical, mental, or moral qualities; grow worse. 2. *Biol.* sink to a lower or less organized type. —*adj.* showing a decline in physical, mental, or moral qualities. —*n.* person having an evil and unwholesome character. [< L, ult. < *de-* + *genus* race, kind] —de·gen′er·ate·ly, *adv.* —de·gen′er·ate·ness, *n.* —de·gen′er·a′tion, *n.* —de·gen′er·a′tive, *adj.*

de·grade (di·grād′), *v.,* —grad·ed, —grad·ing. 1. reduce to a lower rank; take away a position, an honor, etc., from. 2. make worse; debase. 3. wear down by erosion. [< Eccl.L < L *de-* + *gradus* step, grade] —deg·ra·da·tion (deg′rə·dā′shən), *n.* —de·grad′er, *n.*

de·gree (di·grē′), *n.* 1. stage or step in a scale

or process. 2. step in direct line of descent. 3. amount; extent. 4. unit for measuring temperature. 5. unit for measuring angles or arcs. A degree is ⅟₃₆₀ of the circumference of a circle. 6. rank. 7. rank or title given by a college or university to a student whose work fulfills certain requirements, or to a person as an honor: *an A.B. degree.* 8. one of the three stages in the comparison of adjectives or adverbs. *Fastest* is the superlative degree of *fast.* 9. *Algebra.* rank as determined by an exponent or sum of exponents. 10. relative condition, manner, way, or respect. 11. *Law.* the relative measure of guilt: *murder in the first degree.* 12. interval between any note of the scale and the next note. 13. by degrees, gradually. 14. to a degree, a. to a large amount; to a great extent. b. somewhat; rather. [< OF *degre* < VL, < *degradare* divide into steps < LL, DEGRADE] **>** degrees. Ordinarily a person's academic degrees are not given with his name except in college publications, reference works, etc. When used, they are separated from the name by a comma, and in campus publications are often followed by the year of granting: *Harvey J. Preble, A.B.; James T. Thomson, M.A.; Harvey J. Preble, A.B. '08; James T. Thomson, A.B. '21, A.M. '24; James T. Thomson, Ph.D., M.D.* As a rule, except in reference lists, only a person's highest degree in each academic or professional field need be mentioned. If the institution granting the degree is named, the following forms are usual: *George H. Cook, A.B.* (*Grinnell*), *A.M.* (*Indiana*), *Ph.D.* (*Chicago*).

Degrees (def. 5)

de·his·cence (di·his′əns), *n.* a bursting open, esp. of seed capsules, etc., to scatter the seeds. [< L *dehiscens,* ult. < *de-* + *hiare* gape] —**de·his′cent,** *adj.*

de·hy·drate (dē·hī′drāt), *v.,* —**drat·ed,** —**drat·ing.** 1. deprive (a chemical compound) of water or the elements of water. 2. take moisture from. 3. lose water or moisture. —**de′hy·dra′tion,** *n.*

de·ic·er (dē·īs′ər), *n.* device to prevent or remove ice formation.

de·i·fy (dē′ə·fī), *v.,* —**fied,** —**fy·ing.** 1. make a god of. 2. worship or regard as a god. [< OF < LL *deificare* < *deus* god + *facere* make] —**de·i·fi·ca·tion** (dē′ə·fə·kā′shən), *n.* —**de·i′fi·er,** *n.*

deign (dān), *v.* 1. condescend. 2. condescend to give (an answer, a reply, etc.). [< OF < L, < *dignus* worthy]

de·ism (dē′iz·əm), *n.* 1. belief that God exists entirely apart from our world and does not influence the lives of human beings. 2. belief in God without accepting any particular religion. [< L *deus* god] —**de′ist,** *n.* —**de·is′tic, de·is′ti·cal,** *adj.* —**de·is′ti·cal·ly,** *adv.*

de·i·ty (dē′ə·ti), *n., pl.* —**ties.** 1. god or goddess. 2. divine nature; being a god. 3. the Deity, God. [< F < L *deitas* < *deus* god]

de·ject·ed (di·jek′tid), *adj.* in low spirits; sad; discouraged. —**de·ject′ed·ly,** *adv.* —**de·ject′ed·ness,** *n.*

de·jec·tion (di·jek′shən), *n.* lowness of spirits; sadness; discouragement. [< L *dejectio* < *dedown* + *jacere* throw]

de ju·re (dē jur′ē), *Latin.* by right.

Del., Delaware.

Del·a·ware (del′ə·wâr), *n.* 1. an Eastern State of the United States. *Capital:* Dover. *Abbrev.:* Del. 2. river flowing from 8 New York State between Pennsylvania and New Jersey into the Atlantic. —**Del·a·war·e·an** (del′ə·wâr′1·ən), *adj.,* *n.*

de·lay (di·lā′), *v.* 1. put off till a later time. 2. make late; keep waiting; hinder. 3. be late; wait; go slowly. —*n.* 1. act of delaying. 2. fact of being delayed. [< OF, < *de-* + *laier* leave, let, prob. < Celtic] —**de·lay′er,** *n.* —**Syn.** *v.* 1. postpone, defer. 2. retard.

de·le (dē′lē), *v.,* —**led,** —**le·ing.** cross out; delete. [< L, imperative of *delere* delete]

de·lec·ta·ble (di·lek′tə·bəl), *adj.* very pleasing; delightful. [< OF < L, < *delectare* DELIGHT] —**de·lec′ta·ble·ness,** *n.* —**de·lec′ta·bly,** *adv.*

de·lec·ta·tion (dē′lek·tā′shən), *n.* delight.

del·e·gate (*n.* del′ə·gāt, -git; *v.* del′ə·gāt), *n., v.,* —**gat·ed,** —**gat·ing.** —*n.* 1. person given power or authority to act for others; representative. 2. representative of a Territory in the United States House of Representatives. 3. member of the lower branch of the legislature in Maryland, Virginia, and West Virginia. —*v.* 1. appoint or send (a person) as a delegate. 2. give over (one's power or authority) to another as agent or deputy. [< L, < *de-* + *legare* send with a commission]

del·e·ga·tion (del′ə·gā′shən), *n.* 1. act of delegating. 2. fact of being delegated. 3. group of delegates.

de·lete (di·lēt′), *v.,* —**let·ed,** —**let·ing.** strike out or take out (anything written or printed). [< L, pp. of *delere* destroy] —**de·le′tion,** *n.*

del·e·te·ri·ous (del′ə·tir′1·əs), *adj.* harmful; injurious. [< NL < Gk. *deleterios,* ult. < *deleesthai* hurt] —**del′e·te′ri·ous·ly,** *adv.*

delft (delft), **delf** (delf), or **delft·ware** (delft′wâr′), *n.* kind of glazed earthenware made in Holland, often decorated in blue.

Del·hi (del′i), *n.* 1. city in N India, a former capital of the Mogul empire. 2. New Delhi.

Delft

de·lib·er·ate (*adj.* di·lib′ər·it; *v.* di·lib′ər·āt), *adj., v.,* —**at·ed,** —**at·ing.** —*adj.* 1. carefully thought out; made or done on purpose. 2. slow and careful in deciding what to do. 3. not hurried; slow. —*v.* 1. think over carefully; consider. 2. discuss reasons for and against something; debate. [< L, < *de-* + *librare* weigh] —**de·lib′er·ate·ly,** *adv.* —**de·lib′er·ate·ness,** *n.* —**de·lib′er·a′tor,** *n.* —**Syn.** *adj.* 1. premeditated, intentional. 2. thoughtful, cautious. 3. unhurried. —*v.* 1. ponder.

de·lib·er·a·tion (di·lib′ər·ā′shən), *n.* 1. careful thought. 2. discussion of reasons for and against something; debate: *the deliberations of Congress.* 3. slowness and care.

de·lib·er·a·tive (di·lib′ər·ā′tiv), *adj.* 1. for deliberation; having to do with deliberation: *Congress is a deliberative body.* 2. characterized by deliberation. —**de·lib′er·a′tive·ly,** *adv.* —**de·lib′er·a′tive·ness,** *n.*

del·i·ca·cy (del′ə·kə·si), *n., pl.* —**cies.** 1. delicate quality or nature; slightness and grace. 2. subtle quality. 3. fineness of feeling for small differences; sensitiveness. 4. need of care, skill, or tact. 5. thought or regard for the feelings of others. 6. a shrinking from what is offensive or not modest. 7. susceptibility to illness; weakness. 8. a choice kind of food; a dainty.

del·i·cate (del′ə·kit), *adj.* 1. pleasing to the taste; lightly flavored; mild; soft: *delicate foods.* 2. of fine weave, quality, or make; easily torn; thin. 3. requiring careful handling: *a delicate situation.* 4. very rapidly responding to slight changes of condition: *delicate instruments.* 5. easily hurt or made ill: *a delicate child.* 6. hard to appreciate. 7. subtle. 8. careful of the feelings of others; considerate. 9. avoiding anything that is offensive or immodest. [< L *delicatus* pampered] —**del′i·cate·ly,** *adv.* —**del′i·cate·ness,** *n.* —**Syn.** 1. exquisite, dainty. 2. fragile. 3. critical. 5. frail, weakly, sickly. 8. tactful.

del·i·ca·tes·sen (del′ə·kə·tes′ən), *n. Am.* 1. (*sing. in use*) store that sells prepared foods, such as cooked meats, salads, relishes, etc. 2. (*pl. in use*) the foods. [< G, pl. of *delikatesse* delicacy < F]

de·li·cious (di·lish′əs), *adj.* 1. very pleasing to taste or smell. 2. very pleasing; delightful. [< OF < LL, < *deliciae* a delight < *delicere* entice. See DELIGHT.] —**de·li′cious·ly,** *adv.* —**de·li′cious·ness,** *n.* —**Syn.** 1. luscious.

de·light (di·līt′), *n.* 1. great pleasure; joy. 2. thing that gives great pleasure. —*v.* 1. please greatly. 2. have great pleasure. [< OF *delit,* ult. < L *delectare* to charm < *delicere* entice < *de-* + *lacere* entice] —**de·light′ed,** *adj.* —**de·light′ed·ly,** *adv.* —**de·light′ed·ness,** *n.* —**de·light′er,** *n.* —**Syn.** *n.* 1. ecstasy, rapture. —*v.* 1. gladden. —**Ant.** *v.* 1. grieve, depress.

de·light·ful (di·līt′fəl), *adj.* very pleasing; giving joy. —**de·light′ful·ly,** *adv.* —**de·light′ful·ness,** *n.* —Syn. enjoyable, pleasurable.

De·li·lah (di·lī′lə), *n.* **1.** woman who betrayed Samson, her lover, to the Philistines. Judges 16. **2.** a false, treacherous woman; temptress.

de·lim·it (di·lim′it), *v.* fix the limits of; mark the boundaries of. —**de·lim′i·ta′tion,** *n.* —**de·lim′i·ta′tive,** *adj.*

de·lin·e·ate (di·lin′i·āt), *v.,* -at·ed, -at·ing. **1.** trace the outline of. **2.** draw; sketch. **3.** describe in words. [< L, < *de-* + *linea* line] —**de·lin′e·a′tion,** *n.* —**de·lin′e·a′tor,** *n.*

de·lin·quen·cy (di·ling′kwən·si), *n., pl.* -cies. **1.** failure to do what is required by law or duty; guilt. **2.** fault; offense.

de·lin·quent (di·ling′kwənt), *adj.* **1.** failing to do what is required by law or duty. **2.** having to do with delinquents. —*n.* a delinquent person; offender; criminal. [< L, < *de-* + *linquere* leave] —**de·lin′quent·ly,** *adv.*

del·i·quesce (del′ə·kwes′), *v.,* -quesced, -quesc·ing. become liquid by absorbing moisture from the air. [< L, < *de-* + *liquere* be liquid] —**del′i·ques′cence,** *n.* —**del′i·ques′cent,** *adj.*

de·lir·i·ous (di·lir′i·əs), *adj.* **1.** temporarily out of one's senses. **2.** wildly excited. **3.** caused by delirium. —**de·lir′i·ous·ly,** *adv.* —**de·lir′i·ous·ness,** *n.*

de·lir·i·um (di·lir′i·əm), *n., pl.* -lir·i·ums, -lir·i·a (-lir′i·ə). **1.** a temporary disorder of the mind, as during fevers, characterized by wild excitement, irrational talk, and hallucinations. **2.** any wild excitement that cannot be controlled. [< L, < *delirare* rave, be crazy < *de lira (ire)* (go) out of the furrow (in plowing)]

delirium tre·mens (trē′mənz), delirium caused by excessive drinking of alcoholic liquor. [< NL, trembling delirium]

de·liv·er (di·liv′ər), *v.* **1.** carry and give out; distribute: *the postman delivers letters.* **2.** give up; hand over. **3.** give forth in words: *the jury delivered its verdict.* **4.** strike; throw: *deliver a blow.* **5.** set free; rescue. **6.** help (a woman) give birth to a child. **7.** deliver oneself of, speak; give out. [< F < L *deliberare* set free < *de-* + *liber* free] —**de·liv′er·a·ble,** *adj.* —**de·liv′er·er,** *n.* —Syn. **2.** cede, surrender. **3.** utter. **5.** liberate.

de·liv·er·ance (di·liv′ər·əns), *n.* **1.** act of setting free or state of being set free. **2.** a formal expression of opinion or judgment.

de·liv·er·y (di·liv′ər·i; -liv′ri), *n., pl.* -er·ies. **1.** act or fact of delivering or distributing: *parcel-post delivery.* **2.** a giving up; handing over. **3.** way of giving a speech, lecture, etc. **4.** act or way of striking, throwing, etc. **5.** rescue; release. **6.** giving birth to a child; childbirth. **7.** anything that is delivered. —Syn. **2.** surrender.

dell (del), *n.* a small, sheltered glen or valley, usually with trees in it. [OE]

de·louse (dē·lous′; -louz′), *v.,* -loused, -lous·ing. remove lice from.

Del·phi (del′fī), *n.* town in ancient Greece where an oracle of Apollo was located. —**Del·phic** (del′fik), **Del·phi·an** (del′fi·ən), *adj.*

Delphic oracle, oracle of Apollo at Delphi.

del·phin·i·um (del·fin′i·əm), *n.* larkspur. [< NL < Gk., < *delphin* dolphin; from shape of nectar gland]

del·ta (del′tə), *n.* **1.** deposit of earth and sand that collects at the mouths of some rivers and is usually three-sided. **2.** the fourth letter of the Greek alphabet (Δ or δ).

Delta of the Mississippi River

Del·ta-wing (del′tə·wing′), *adj.* of a jet plane, having wings in the shape of a Greek delta or triangle.

del·toid (del′toid), *adj.* triangular. —*n.* a large, triangular muscle of the shoulder.

de·lude (di·lüd′), *v.,* -lud·ed, -lud·ing. mislead; deceive. [< L, < *de-* (to the detriment of) + *ludere* play] —**de·lud′er,** *n.*

del·uge (del′ūj), *n., v.,* -uged, -ug·ing. —*n.* **1.** a great flood. **2.** a heavy fall of rain. **3.** any overwhelming rush. **4. the Deluge,** *Bible.* the great flood in the days of Noah. Gen. 7. —*v.* **1.** to flood. **2.** overwhelm. [< OF < L *diluvium* < *dis-* away + *luere* wash]

de·lu·sion (di·lü′zhən), *n.* **1.** a deluding or being deluded. **2.** a false notion or belief. **3.** *Psychiatry.* a fixed belief maintained in the face of indisputable evidence to the contrary.

de·lu·sive (di·lü′siv), *adj.* deceptive; false; unreal. —**de·lu′sive·ly,** *adv.* —**de·lu′sive·ness,** *n.*

de·lu·so·ry (di·lü′sə·ri), *adj.* delusive; deceptive.

de luxe, de·luxe (də·lùks′; -lüks′), *adj.* of exceptionally good quality; elegant. [< F]

delve (delv), *v.,* delved, delv·ing. **1.** *Archaic* or *Dial.* dig. **2.** search carefully for information. [OE *delfan*] —**delv′er,** *n.*

Dem., Democrat; Democratic.

de·mag·net·ize (dē·mag′nə·tīz), *v.,* -ized, -iz·ing. deprive of magnetism. —**de′mag·net·i·za′tion,** *n.* —**de·mag′net·iz′er,** *n.*

dem·a·gog·ic (dem′ə·goj′ik; -gog′ik), **dem·a·gog·i·cal** (-ə·kəl), *adj.* of or like a demagogue. —**dem′a·gog′i·cal·ly,** *adv.*

dem·a·gogue, dem·a·gog (dem′ə·gôg; -gog), *n.* a popular leader who stirs up the people in order to get something for himself. [< Gk., < *demos* people + *agogos* leader < *agein* lead]

dem·a·gog·uer·y (dem′ə·gôg′ər·i; -gog′-), *n.* Am. methods or principles of a demagogue.

dem·a·go·gy (dem′ə·gō′ji; -gôg′i; -gog′i), *n.* Esp. Brit. **1.** demagoguery. **2.** character of a demagogue.

de·mand (di·mand′; -mänd′), *v.* **1.** ask for as a right. **2.** ask for with authority. **3.** ask to know or be told. **4.** call for; require; need. **5.** summon (to court). —*n.* **1.** act of demanding. **2.** thing demanded. **3.** claim; requirement. **4.** desire and ability to buy. **5.** inquiry. [< L, < *de-* + *mandare* to order] —**de·mand′a·ble,** *adj.* —**de·mand′er,** *n.* —Syn. *v.* **1.** claim. **2.** requisition.

de·mar·ca·tion, de·mar·ka·tion (dē′mär·kā′shən), *n.* **1.** act of setting and marking the limits. **2.** separation; distinction. [< Sp., < *de-* off + *marcar* mark]

de·mean[1] (di·mēn′), *v.* lower in dignity or standing; humble. [< *de-* + *mean*[2]; formed after *debase*]

de·mean[2] (di·mēn′), *v.* behave or conduct (oneself). [< OF, < *de-* + *mener* lead < L *minare* drive]

de·mean·or, *esp. Brit.* **de·mean·our** (di·mēn′ər), *n.* way a person looks and acts; behavior. [ME *demenure* < *demenen* behave]

de·ment·ed (di·men′tid), *adj.* insane; crazy. [< L, < *de-* out of + *mens* mind] —**de·ment′ed·ly,** *adv.* —**de·ment′ed·ness,** *n.*

de·men·tia (di·men′shə), *n.* a partial or complete loss of mind.

dementia prae·cox (prē′koks), insanity that usually occurs or begins in late adolescence. [< L, precocious insanity]

de·mer·it (dē·mer′it), *n.* **1.** fault; defect. **2.** mark against a person's record for poor work or unsatisfactory behavior.

de·mesne (di·mān′; -mēn′), *n.* **1.** *Law.* the possession of land as one's own. **2.** land or land and buildings possessed as one's own. **3.** house and land belonging to a lord and used by him. **4.** domain; realm. **5.** region. [< AF *demeyne* DOMAIN]

De·me·ter (di·mē′tər), *n. Gk. Myth.* the Greek goddess of agriculture and of the fruitful earth, identified with the Roman goddess Ceres.

demi-, *prefix.* half, as in *demigod.* [< F *demi* half < VL < L, < *dis-* apart + *medius* middle]

dem·i·god (dem′i·god′), *n.* **1.** god that is partly human. **2.** a minor or lesser god.

dem·i·god·dess (dem′i·god′is), *n.* a female demigod.

dem·i·john (dem′i·jon), *n.* a large bottle of earthenware enclosed in wicker.

Demijohn

de·mil·i·tar·ize (dē·mil′ə·tə·rīz), v., -rized, -riz·ing. free from miltary control. —de·mil′i·ta·ri·za′tion, n.

dem·i·monde (dem′i·mond; dem′i·mond′), n. class of women whose reputation and morals are doubtful. [< F, half-world]

de·mise (di·mīz′), n., v., -mised, -mis·ing. —n. 1. death. 2. Law. transfer of an estate by a will or lease. 3. transfer of royal power by death or abdication. —v. 1. Law. transfer (an estate) by a will or lease. 2. transfer (royal power) by death or abdication. [appar. < AF, pp. of desmettre put away < des- away (< L dis-) + mettre put (< L mittere let go, send] —de·mis′a·ble, adj.

dem·i·sem·i·qua·ver (dem′i·sem′i·kwā′vər), n. Music. a thirty-second note.

dem·i·tasse (dem′i·tas′; -täs′), n. a very small cup of coffee. [< F, half-cup]

de·mo·bi·lize (dē·mō′bə·līz), v., -lized, -liz·ing. disband (troops, etc.). —de·mo′bi·li·za′tion, n.

de·moc·ra·cy (di·mok′rə·si), n., pl. -cies. 1. government that is run directly or indirectly by the people who live under it. 2. country, state, or community having such a government. 3. treatment of others as one's equals. 4. Democracy, Am. a. the principles of the Democratic Party. b. its members collectively. [< F < Gk., < demos people + kratos rule]

dem·o·crat (dem′ə·krat), n. 1. person who believes that a government should be run by the people who live under it. 2. person who holds or acts on the belief that all people are his equals. 3. Democrat, Am. member of the Democratic Party.

dem·o·crat·ic (dem′ə·krat′ik), **dem·o·crat·i·cal** (-ə·kəl), adj. 1. of a democracy; like a democracy. 2. treating all classes of people as one's equals. 3. Democratic, Am. of the Democratic Party.

Democratic Party, Am. one of the two main political parties in the United States.

de·moc·ra·tize (di·mok′rə·tīz), v., -tized, -tiz·ing. make or become democratic. —de·moc′ra·ti·za′tion, n.

de·mog·ra·phy (di·mog′rə·fi), n. science dealing with statistics of births, deaths, diseases, etc., of a community. —de·mog′ra·pher, n.

de·mol·ish (di·mol′ish), v. pull or tear down; destroy. [< F < L demoliri tear down < de- + moles mass] —de·mol′ish·er, n. —de·mol′ish·ment, n.

dem·o·li·tion (dem′ə·lish′ən; dē′mə-), n. destruction; ruin.

demolition bomb, Mil. a bomb with a relatively large explosive charge designed to destroy buildings, etc.

de·mon (dē′mən), n. 1. an evil spirit; devil; fiend. 2. a very wicked or cruel person. 3. an evil influence. 4. person who has great energy or vigor. 5. an attendant or guiding spirit. 6. daemon. [(defs. 1-5) < L < Gk. daimonion divine (thing), in Christian writings, evil spirit; (def. 6) see DAEMON]

de·mon·e·tize (dē·mon′ə·tīz; -mun′-), v., -tized, -tiz·ing. deprive of its standard value as money. —de·mon′e·ti·za′tion, n.

de·mo·ni·ac (di·mō′ni·ak), adj. Also, de·mo·ni·a·cal (dē′mə·nī′ə·kəl). 1. of demons. 2. devilish; fiendish; frantic. —n. person supposed to be possessed by an evil spirit. —de·mo·ni·a·cal·ly (dē′mə·nī′ik·li), adv.

de·mon·ic (di·mon′ik), adj. 1. of or caused by evil spirits. 2. influenced by a guiding spirit.

de·mon·ol·o·gy (dē′mən·ol′ə·ji), n. study of demons or of beliefs about demons. —de′mon·ol′o·gist, n.

de·mon·stra·ble (di·mon′strə·bəl; dem′ən-), adj. capable of being proved. —de·mon′stra·bil′i·ty, n. —de·mon′stra·bly, adv.

dem·on·strate (dem′ən·strāt), v., -strat·ed, -strat·ing. 1. establish the truth of; prove. 2. explain by using examples, experiments, etc. 3. show or advertise the merits of (a thing for sale). 4. show openly; exhibit. 5. show feeling by a parade, meeting, etc. 6. display military

strength to frighten or deceive an enemy. [< L, < de- + monstrare show] —dem′on·stra′tor, n. —Syn. 1. attest.

dem·on·stra·tion (dem′ən·strā′shən), n. 1. clear proof. 2. explanation with the use of examples, experiments, etc. 3. a showing of the merits of a thing for sale; advertising or making known some new product or process in a public place. 4. an open show or exhibition, as of feeling, ability, etc. 5. show of feeling by a parade, meeting, etc. 6. display of military strength to frighten or deceive an enemy.

de·mon·stra·tive (di·mon′strə·tiv), adj. 1. expressing one's affections freely and openly. 2. showing clearly; explanatory. 3. giving proof; conclusive. 4. pointing out. This and that are demonstrative pronouns and also demonstrative adjectives. —n. pronoun or adjective that points out. —de·mon′stra·tive·ly, adv. —de·mon′stra·tive·ness, n. ▶ This, that, these, those are called demonstrative adjectives or pronouns according to their use in a sentence: This car we bought in May (adj.). This costs a good bit more than those (pron.).

de·mor·al·ize (di·môr′əl·īz; -mor′-), v., -ized, iz·ing. Am. 1. corrupt the morals of. 2. weaken the spirit, courage, or discipline of; dishearten. 3. throw into confusion or disorder. —de·mor′al·i·za′tion, n. —de·mor′al·iz′er, n. Am.

De·mos·the·nes (di·mos′thə·nēz), n. 384?-322 B.C., the most famous orator of ancient Greece.

de·mote (di·mōt′), v., -mot·ed, -mot·ing. Am. put back to a lower grade; reduce in rank. [< de- + (pro) mote] —de·mo′tion, n. Am.

de·mul·cent (di·mul′sənt), adj. soothing. —n. a soothing ointment or medicine. [< L, < de- + mulcere soothe]

de·mur (di·mėr′), v., -murred, -mur·ring, n. —v. 1. object. 2. Law. interpose a demurrer. —n. an objection. [< OF < L, < de- + morari delay]

de·mure (di·myúr′), adj., -mur·er, -mur·est. 1. falsely proper; unnaturally modest; coy. 2. serious; sober. [< obs. mure, adj., demure < OF < L maturus mature] —de·mure′ly, adv.

de·mur·rage (di·mėr′ij), n. 1. failure to load or unload a ship, railroad car, etc., within the time specified. 2. payment made for this.

de·mur·rer (di·mėr′ər), n. 1. person who objects. 2. objection. 3. Law. a legal plea that a lawsuit be dismissed, even if the facts are as alleged by the opposite party, because the facts do not sustain his claim.

den (den), n., v., denned, den·ning. —n. 1. place where a wild animal lives. 2. place where thieves or the like have their headquarters. 3. a small and cozy private room. —v. inhabit a den. [OE denn]

de·nar·i·us (di·nâr′i·əs), n., pl. -nar·i·i (-nâr′i·ī). 1. an ancient Roman silver coin. 2. an ancient Roman gold coin. [< L, containing ten (here, ten times the value of an as²) < deni ten at a time]

de·na·tion·al·ize (dē·nash′ən·əl·īz; -nash′nəl-), v., -ized, -iz·ing. deprive of national rights, scope, etc. —de·na′tion·al·i·za′tion, n.

de·nat·u·ral·ize (dē·nach′ə·rəl·īz; -nach′rəl-), v., -ized, -iz·ing. make unnatural. —de·nat′u·ral·i·za′tion, n.

de·na·ture (dē·nā′chər), v., -tured, -tur·ing. 1. change the nature of. 2. make (alcohol, food, etc.) unfit for drinking or eating without destroying for other purposes. —de·na′tur·a′tion, n.

de·na·zi·fy (dē·nät′sə·fī; -nat′-), v., -fied, -fy·ing. get rid of Nazi doctrines or Nazi influences. —de·na′zi·fi·ca′tion, n. Am.

den·drite (den′drīt), n. Anat. the branching part at the receiving end of a nerve cell. [< Gk., < dendron tree]

de·neu·tral·ize (dē·nū′trəl·īz; -nū′-), v., -ized, -iz·ing. abolish the neutral status of (a country, territory, etc.). —de·neu′tral·i·za′tion, n.

den·gue (deng′gā; -gi), n. Am. an infectious fever with skin rash and severe pain in the joints and muscles. [< Sp., < Swahili (lang. of C Africa) kidinga popo]

de·ni·al (di·nī′əl), n. 1. act of saying that something is not true. 2. act of saying that one does not hold to or accept: *a public denial of communism.* 3. a refusing. 4. a refusing to acknowledge. 5. self-denial.

de·ni·er[1] (di·nī′ər), *n.* person who denies.

den·ier[2] (den′yər; də·nir′), *n.* unit of weight used to express the fineness of silk, rayon, or nylon yarn. [< OF < L *denarius* DENARIUS]

den·im (den′əm), *n. Am.* a heavy, coarse cotton cloth for overalls, etc. [short for F *serge de Nîmes* serge of Nîmes]

den·i·zen (den′ə·zən), *n.* 1. inhabitant; occupant. 2. a foreign word, plant, animal, etc., that has been adopted. —*v.* make (one) a denizen; naturalize. [< OF *denzein* < *denz* within < LL < L *de* from + *intus* within]

Den·mark (den′märk), *n.* a small country in N Europe.

de·nom·i·nate (*v.* di·nom′ə·nāt; *adj.* di·nom′ə·nit, -nāt), *v.,* -nat·ed, -nat·ing, *adj.* —*v.* give a name to; name. —*adj.* called by a specific name. [< L, < *de-* + *nomen* name]

de·nom·i·na·tion (di·nom′ə·nā′shən), *n.* 1. name for a group or class of things. 2. a religious group or sect. 3. class or kind of units: *a coin of low denomination.*

de·nom·i·na·tion·al (di·nom′ə·nā′shən·əl; -nāsh′nəl), *adj.* having to do with some religious denomination or denominations; controlled by a religious denomination. —**de·nom′i·na′tion·al·ly,** *adv.*

de·nom·i·na·tion·al·ism (di·nom′ə·nā′shən·əl·iz′əm; -nāsh′nəl-), *n.* 1. denominational principles. 2. division into denominations.

de·nom·i·na·tive (di·nom′ə·nā′tiv; -nə·tiv), *adj.* 1. giving a distinctive name; naming. 2. formed from a noun or an adjective. *To center* is a denominative verb. —*n.* a denominative word. —**de·nom′i·na′tive·ly,** *adv.*

de·nom·i·na·tor (di·nom′ə·nā′tər), *n.* 1. number below the line in a fraction, stating the size of the parts in their relation to the whole. 2. person or thing that names.

de·no·ta·tion (dē′nō·tā′shən), *n.* 1. meaning, esp. the exact, literal meaning. The denotation of *home* is "place where one lives," but it has many connotations. 2. indication; denoting.

de·note (di·nōt′), *v.,* -not·ed, -not·ing. 1. be the sign of; indicate. 2. be a name for; mean. [< F < L, < *de-* + *notare* note < *nota* mark]

de·noue·ment, **dé·noue·ment** (dā′nü·mäN′), *n.* solution of a plot in a play, a story, etc.; outcome; end. [< F, < *dénouer* untie < L *dis-* + *nodus* knot]

de·nounce (di·nouns′), *v.,* -nounced, -nouncing. 1. condemn publicly; express strong disapproval of. 2. inform against; accuse. 3. give formal notice of the termination of (a treaty, etc.). [< OF < L, < *de-* + *nuntiare* announce < *nuntius* messenger] —**de·nounce′ment,** *n.*

de no·vo (dē nō′vō), *Latin.* anew; afresh.

dense (dens), *adj.,* dens·er, dens·est. 1. closely packed together; thick. 2. stupid. [< L *densus*] —**dense′ly,** *adv.* —**dense′ness,** *n.* —Syn. 1. compact.

den·si·ty (den′sə·ti), *n., pl.* -ties. 1. dense condition or quality; compactness; thickness. 2. stupidity. 3. *Physics.* quantity of matter in a unit of volume. 4. specific gravity.

dent (dent), *n.* hollow made by a blow or pressure. —*v.* 1. make a dent in. 2. become dented. [ME *dente,* var. of *dint*]

den·tal (den′təl), *adj.* 1. of or for the teeth. 2. of or for a dentist's work. 3. *Phonet.* produced by placing the tip of the tongue against or near the upper front teeth. —*n.* a dental sound. [< L *dens* tooth]

den·tate (den′tāt), *adj. Bot., Zool.* having toothlike projections; toothed; notched. —**den′tate·ly,** *adv.*

den·ti·frice (den′tə·fris), *n.* paste, powder, or liquid for cleaning the teeth. [< F < L, < *dens* tooth + *fricare* rub] Dentate leaf

den·tine (den′tēn; -tin), **den·tin** (-tin), *n.* the hard, bony material that forms the main part of a tooth.

den·tist (den′tist) *n.* doctor who cleans and extracts teeth, fills cavities in them, and supplies artificial teeth.

den·tist·ry (den′tis·tri), *n.* work, art, or occupation of a dentist.

den·ti·tion (den·tish′ən), *n.* 1. growth of teeth; teething. 2. kind, number, and arrangement of the teeth.

den·ture (den′chər), *n.* 1. set of artificial teeth. 2. set of teeth.

de·nude (di·nüd′; -nūd′), *v.,* -nud·ed, -nuding. 1. make bare; strip. 2. lay (a rock, etc.) bare by removing what lies above. —**de·nu·da·tion** (dē′nü·dā′shən; -nū-; den′yü-), *n.*

de·nun·ci·a·tion (di·nun′si·ā′shən; -shi-), *n.* 1. strong, public disapproval. 2. act of informing against; accusation. 3. formal notice of the intention to end a treaty, etc. 4. a warning; threat.

de·nun·ci·a·to·ry (di·nun′si·ə·tô′ri; -shi-, -tō′-), *adj.* condemning; accusing.

Den·ver (den′vər), *n.* capital of Colorado, in the central part.

de·ny (di·nī′), *v.,* -nied, -ny·ing. 1. declare (something) is not true. 2. say that one does not hold to or accept. 3. refuse. 4. refuse to acknowledge; disown. 5. deny oneself, do without the things one wants. [< F < L, < *de-* + *negare* say no] —Syn. 1. contradict, dispute. 4. repudiate, disclaim. —Ant. 1. admit, concede.

de·o·dor·ant (dē·ō′dər·ənt), *n.* preparation that destroys odors. —*adj.* that destroys odors.

de·o·dor·ize (dē·ō′dər·īz), *v.,* -ized, -iz·ing. destroy the odor of. —**de·o′dor·i·za′tion,** *n.* —**de·o′dor·iz′er,** *n.*

dep., 1. department. 2. deputy.

de·part (di·pärt′), *v.* 1. go away; leave. 2. turn away; change (*from*). 3. die. [< OF, < LL *departire* divide < L *de-* + *partire* < *pars* part] —Syn. 1. quit, retire. 2. diverge, deviate. —Ant. 1. arrive, come.

de·part·ed (di·pär′tid), *n.* dead person or persons. —*adj.* 1. dead. 2. gone; past.

de·part·ment (di·pärt′mənt), *n.* 1. separate part; division: *the fire department.* 2. one of the administrative districts into which France is divided. 3. a chief division of governmental administration. —**de·part·men·tal** (dē′pärt·men′təl), *adj.* —**de′part·men′tal·ly,** *adv.*

department store, *Am.* store that sells many kinds of articles arranged in separate departments.

de·par·ture (di·pär′chər), *n.* 1. act of going away; act of leaving. 2. a turning away; change. 3. *Archaic.* death.

de·pend (di·pend′), *v.* 1. rely; trust. 2. rely for support or help. 3. be controlled or influenced by something else. 4. depend on, be controlled or influenced by. [< OF < L, < *de-* from + *pendere* hang]

de·pend·a·ble (di·pen′də·bəl), *adj.* reliable; trustworthy. —**de·pend′a·bil′i·ty,** **de·pend′a·ble·ness,** *n.* —**de·pend′a·bly,** *adv.*

de·pend·ence (di·pen′dəns), *n.* 1. reliance on another for support or help. 2. reliance; trust. 3. fact of being controlled or influenced by something else: *the dependence of crops on the weather.* 4. person or thing relied on.

de·pend·en·cy (di·pen′dən·si), *n., pl.* -cies. 1. country or territory controlled by another country. 2. dependence. 3. thing that depends on another for existence, support, or help.

de·pend·ent (di·pen′dənt), *adj.* 1. relying on another for support or help. 2. controlled or influenced by something else. 3. hanging down. —*n.* person who relies on another for support or help. —Syn. *adj.* 2. contingent, conditional. ▶A dependent clause modifies or supports in some way a word or sentence element: The house *that stood on the other side* was more dilapidated. [Clause modifies *house.*] Ordinarily a dependent clause does not stand by itself but is part of a complex sentence.

de·pict (di·pikt′), *v.* represent by drawing, painting, or describing; show; picture; portray. [< L *depictus* < *de-* + *pingere* paint] —**de·pict′er,** *n.* —**de·pic′tion,** *n.*

de·pil·a·to·ry (di·pil′ə·tô′ri; -tō′-), *adj.*, *n.*, *pl.* -ries. —*adj.* capable of removing hair. —*n.* paste, liquid, or other preparation for removing hair. [< L, < *de-* + *pilus* hair]

de·plete (di·plēt′), *v.*, -plet·ed, -plet·ing. empty; exhaust. [< L *depletus* empty < *de-* + *-plere* fill] —de·ple′tion, *n.* —de·ple′tive, *adj.*

de·plor·a·ble (di·plôr′ə·bəl; -plōr′-), *adj.* 1. to be deplored; lamentable. 2. wretched; miserable. —de·plor′a·bly, *adv.*

de·plore (di·plôr′; -plōr′), *v.*, -plored, -plor·ing. be very sorry about; lament. [< L, < *de-* + *plorare* weep] —Syn. bewail, bemoan.

de·ploy (di·ploi′), *v.* *Mil.* spread out from a column into a long battle line. [< F, < *dé-* (< L *dis-*) + *ployer* < L *plicare* fold] —de·ploy′ment, *n.*

de·po·nent (di·pō′nənt), *n.* 1. *Law.* person who testifies in writing under oath. 2. in Greek and Latin grammar, verb passive in form but active in meaning. —*adj.* having passive form but active meaning. [< L, < *de-* away, down + *ponere* put]

de·pop·u·late (dē·pop′yə·lāt), *v.*, -lat·ed, -lat·ing. deprive of inhabitants. —de′pop·u·la′tion, .*n.* —de·pop′u·la′tor, *n.*

de·port (di·pôrt′; -pōrt′), *v.* 1. banish; expel; remove. 2. behave or conduct (oneself) in a particular manner. [< F < L, < *de-* away + *portare* carry]

de·por·ta·tion (dē′pôr·tā′shən; -pōr-), *n.* expulsion, as of undesirable aliens; banishment.

de·port·ment (di·pôrt′mənt; -pōrt′-), *n.* way a person acts; behavior; conduct.

de·pose (di·pōz′), *v.*, -posed, -pos·ing. 1. put out of office or a position of authority: *depose a government.* 2. declare under oath; testify. [< OF, < *de-* down + *poser* POSE] —de·pos′a·ble, *adj.* —de·pos′al, *n.*

de·pos·it (di·poz′it), *v.* 1. put down; lay down; leave lying. 2. put in a place for safekeeping. 3. pay as a pledge to do something or to pay more later. —*n.* 1. something laid down or left lying. 2. thing put in a place for safekeeping. 3. money put in a bank. 4. money paid as a pledge to do something or to pay more later. 5. mass of some mineral in rock or in the ground. [< L *depositus* < *de-* away + *ponere* put]

de·pos·i·tar·y (di·poz′ə·ter′i), *n.*, *pl.* -tar·ies. 1. person or company that receives something for safekeeping; trustee. 2. depository.

dep·o·si·tion (dep′ə·zish′ən; dē′pə-), *n.* 1. act of deposing. 2. *Law.* a. testimony. b. a sworn statement in writing. 3. act of depositing. 4. thing deposited; deposit.

de·pos·i·tor (di·poz′ə·tər), *n.* 1. person who deposits. 2. person who deposits money in a bank.

de·pos·i·to·ry (di·poz′ə·tô′ri; -tō′-), *n.*, *pl.* -ries. 1. place where a thing is put for safekeeping; storehouse. 2. trustee.

de·pot (dē′pō; *Mil.* and *Brit.* dep′ō), *n.* 1. *Am.* a railroad station. 2. storehouse; warehouse. 3. place where military supplies are stored. 4. place where recruits are brought together and trained. [< F < L *depositum.* See DEPOSIT.]

de·prave (di·prāv′), *v.*, -praved, -prav·ing. make bad; corrupt. [< L, < *de-* + *pravus* crooked, wrong] —de·prav′er, *n.*

de·praved (di·prāvd′), *adj.* corrupt; perverted.

de·prav·i·ty (di·prav′ə·ti), *n.*, *pl.* -ties. 1. wickedness; corruption. 2. a corrupt act; bad practice.

dep·re·cate (dep′rə·kāt), *v.*, -cat·ed, -cat·ing. express strong disapproval of; protest against. [< L, plead in excuse, avert by prayer < *de-* + *precari* pray] —dep′re·cat′ing·ly, *adv.* —dep′re·ca′tion, *n.* —dep′re·ca′tor, *n.*

dep·re·ca·to·ry (dep′rə·kə·tô′ri; -tō′-), *adj.* 1. deprecating. 2. apologetic. —dep′re·ca·to′ri·ly, *adv.* —dep′re·ca·to′ri·ness, *n.*

de·pre·ci·ate (di·prē′shi·āt), *v.*, -at·ed, -at·ing. 1. lessen the value or price of. 2. *Am.* lessen in value, as money. 3. speak slightingly of; belittle. [< L, < *de-* + *pretium* price] —de·pre′ci·a′tor, *n.*

de·pre·ci·a·tion (di·prē′shi·ā′shən), *n.* 1. *Am.* a lessening or lowering in value. 2. a speaking slightingly of; a belittling.

de·pre·ci·a·to·ry (di·prē′shi·ə·tô′ri; -tō′-), *adj.* tending to depreciate, disparage, or undervalue.

dep·re·da·tion (dep′rə·dā′shən), *n.* act of plundering; robbery; a ravaging. [< L, < *de-* + *praeda* booty]

de·press (di·pres′), *v.* 1. press down; push down; lower. 2. lower in pitch. 3. lower in amount or value. 4. reduce the activity of; weaken. 5. make sad or gloomy; cause to have low spirits. [< OF, < L *depressus* < *de-* + *premere* press] —de·press′ing·ly, *adv.* —Syn. 5. deject, sadden.

de·pres·sant (di·pres′ənt), *Med.* —*adj.* decreasing the rate of vital activities. —*n.* medicine that lessens pain or excitement; sedative.

de·pressed (di·prest′), *adj.* 1. sad; gloomy; low-spirited. 2. pressed down; lowered. 3. *Bot.*, *Zool.* flattened down; broader than high.

de·pres·sion (di·presh′ən), *n.* 1. act of pressing down. 2. depressed condition. 3. a low place; hollow. 4. sadness; gloominess; low spirits. 5. reduction of activity; dullness of trade. 6. the angular distance of an object below the horizon. —de·pres′sive, *adj.* —de·pres′sive·ly, *adv.* —Syn. 4. dejection, melancholy.

dep·ri·va·tion (dep′rə·vā′shən), *n.* act of depriving; state of being deprived.

de·prive (di·prīv′), *v.*, -prived, -priv·ing. 1. take away from by force. 2. keep from having or doing. [< OF, < *de-* (< L *de-*) + *priver* deprive < L, orig., exempt] —Syn. 1. dispossess, divest. 2. debar.

dept., 1. department. 2. deputy.

depth (depth), *n.* 1. quality of being deep; deepness. 2. distance from top to bottom. 3. distance from front to back. 4. a deep place. 5. the deepest part: *in the depths of the earth.* 6. the most central part: *in the depth of the forest.* 7. profound penetration: *depth of mind.* 8. deep tone; intensity. [ME, < OE *dēop* deep]

depth charge or **bomb**, an explosive charge dropped from a ship or airplane and arranged to explode at a certain depth under water.

dep·u·ta·tion (dep′yə·tā′shən), *n.* 1. act of deputing. 2. group of persons appointed to act for others.

de·pute (di·pūt′), *v.*, -put·ed, -put·ing. 1. appoint to do one's work or to act in one's place. 2. give (work, power, etc.) to another. [< F < LL, assign < L, consider as < *de-* + *putare* think, count]

dep·u·tize (dep′yə·tīz), *v.*, -tized, -tiz·ing. 1. appoint as deputy. 2. act as deputy.

dep·u·ty (dep′yə·ti), *n.*, *pl.* -ties, *adj.* —*n.* 1. person appointed to do the work or to act in the place of another: *a sheriff's deputy.* 2. representative in certain lawmaking assemblies. —*adj.* acting as a deputy. —Syn. *n.* 1. proxy, delegate.

De Quin·cey (di kwin′si), Thomas, 1785–1859, English essayist.

der., derivation; derivative; derived.

de·rail (dē·rāl′), *v.* 1. cause (a train, etc.) to run off the rails. 2. run off the rails. —de·rail′ment, *n.*

de·range (di·rānj′), *v.*, -ranged, -rang·ing. 1. disturb the order or arrangement of. 2. make insane. [< F *déranger.* See DE-, RANGE.] —de·ranged′, *adj.* —de·range′ment, *n.*

Der·by (dér′bi; *Brit.* där′bi), *n.*, *pl.* -bies. 1. a horse race in England run every year at Epsom Downs. 2. a horse race of similar importance: *the Kentucky Derby.* 3. an important race, as of automobiles or airplanes. 4. **derby**, *Am.* a stiff hat with a rounded crown and narrow brim.

der·e·lict (der′ə·likt), *adj.* 1. abandoned; deserted; forsaken. 2. *Am.* failing in one's duty; negligent. —*n.* 1. ship abandoned at sea. 2. any worthless, deserted person or thing. [< L *derelictus* < *de-* wholly + *re-* behind + *linquere* leave]

der·e·lic·tion (der′ə·lik′shən), *n.* 1. failure in one's duty; negligence. 2. abandonment; desertion; forsaking.

de·ride (di·rīd′), *v.*, -rid·ed, -rid·ing. laugh at in scorn; ridicule. [< L, < *de-* at + *ridere* laugh] —de·rid′er, *n.* —de·rid′ing·ly, *adv.* —Syn. jeer, scoff, mock.

de ri·gueur (də rē·gœr′), *French.* required by etiquette; according to custom; proper.

de·ri·sion (di·rizh′ən), *n.* 1. scornful laughter; ridicule; contempt. 2. an object of ridicule.

de·ri·sive (di·rī′siv), **de·ri·so·ry** (-sə·ri), *adj.* mocking; ridiculing. —**de·ri′sive·ly,** *adv.*

deriv., derivation; derivative.

der·i·va·tion (der′ə·vā′shən), *n.* 1. act or fact of deriving. 2. state of being derived. 3. source; origin. 4. theory of the development or origin of a word. —**der′i·va′tion·al,** *adj.*

de·riv·a·tive (di·riv′ə·tiv), *adj.* derived; not original. —*n.* 1. something derived. 2. a word formed by adding a prefix or suffix to another word. 3. *Chem.* substance obtained from another by substituting a different element.

de·rive (di·rīv′), *v.,* –rived, –riv·ing. 1. get; receive; obtain. 2. obtain from a source or origin. 3. come from a source or origin; originate. 4. trace (a word, custom, etc.) from or to a source or origin. 5. obtain by reasoning. 6. *Chem.* obtain (a compound) from another by substituting a different element. [< F < L *derivare* lead off, draw off < *de-* + *rivus* stream] —**de·riv′a·ble,** *adj.* —**de·riv′er,** *n.*

der·ma (dėr′mə), *n.* 1. the sensitive layer of skin beneath the epidermis. 2. skin. [< Gk., skin] —**der′mal,** *adj.*

der·ma·tol·o·gy (dėr′mə·tol′ə·ji), *n.* science that deals with the skin and its diseases. —**der·ma·to·log·i·cal** (dėr′mə·tə·loj′ə·kəl), *adj.* —**der′·ma·tol′o·gist,** *n.*

der·mis (dėr′mis), *n.* derma. —**der′mic,** *adj.*

der·o·gate (der′ə·gāt), *v.,* –gat·ed, –gat·ing. 1. take away; detract. 2. become worse; degenerate. [< L, < *de-* away from + *rogare* ask] —**der′o·ga′tion,** *n.*

de·rog·a·to·ry (di·rog′ə·tô′ri; –tō′-), **de·rog·a·tive** (-ə·tiv), *adj.* 1. disparaging; belittling. 2. lessening the value; detracting. —**de·rog′a·to′ri·ly, de·rog′a·tive·ly,** *adv.*

der·rick (der′ik), *n.* 1. machine with a long arm for lifting and moving heavy objects. 2. *Am.* a towerlike framework over an oil well, gas well, etc. [for *Derrick,* a hangman at Tyburn, London]

der·ring-do (der′ing·dü′), *n. Archaic.* daring deeds. [alter. of ME *dorryng don* daring to do]

der·rin·ger (der′ən·jər), *n. Am.* a short pistol that has a large caliber. [for the inventor]

der·vish (dėr′vish), *n.* a member of any of various Mohammedan orders. [< Turk. < Pers. *darvish*]

des·cant (*v.* des·kant′, dis–; *n.* des′kant), *v.* 1. talk at great length; discourse. 2. *Music.* sing or play a melody with another melody. —*n. Music.* a. part music. b. melody to be played or sung with another melody. [< OF < Med.L, < L *dis-* + *cantus* song < *canere* sing]

Des·cartes (dā·kärt′), *n.* René, 1596–1650, French philosopher and mathematician.

de·scend (di·send′), *v.* 1. go or come down from a higher place to a lower place. 2. go from earlier to later time. 3. go from greater to less. 4. go from more important to less important matters. 5. go from general to particular matters. 6. go from higher to lower standards; lower oneself; stoop. 7. slope downward. 8. be handed down from parent to child. 9. make a sudden attack. 10. *Astron.* move toward the horizon. [< OF < L, < *de-* + *scandere* climb] —**de·scend′a·ble,** *adj.*

de·scend·ant (di·sen′dənt), *n.* 1. person born of a certain family or group. 2. offspring; child. —*adj.* Also, **de·scend′ent.** descending. ➤ De·scendant is used both as adjective and noun; de·scendent, only as adjective. Obviously, to be on the safe side, use descendant: Noun: *He claims to be a descendant of Benjamin Franklin.* Adjective: *Nearly all the people of the town are descendant from* [more usual, *descended from*] *these first settlers.*

de·scent (di·sent′), *n.* 1. a coming down or going down from a higher to a lower place. 2. a downward slope. 3. way or passage down; means of descending. 4. family line; ancestry. 5. a lowering of oneself. 6. a sudden attack.

de·scribe (di·skrīb′), *v.,* –scribed, –scrib·ing. 1. tell or write about. 2. give a picture or account of in words. 3. draw the outline of; trace. [< L, < *de-* + *scribere* write] —**de·scrib′a·ble,** *adj.* —**de·scrib′er,** *n.* —*Syn.* 1. recount, relate. 2. depict.

de·scrip·tion (di·skrip′shən), *n.* 1. act of describing. 2. composition or account that describes or gives a picture in words. 3. kind; sort: *people of every description.* 4. act of drawing in outline.

de·scrip·tive (di·skrip′tiv), *adj.* describing; using description. —**de·scrip′tive·ly,** *adv.* —**de·scrip′tive·ness,** *n.*

de·scry (di·skrī′), *v.,* –scried, –scry·ing. catch sight of; be able to see; make out. [< OF *des-crier* proclaim. See DIS–, CRY.]

des·e·crate (des′ə·krāt), *v.,* –crat·ed, –crat·ing. disregard the sacredness of. [< de- + (con)*secrate*] —**des′e·crat′er, des′e·cra′tor,** *n.* —**des′e·cra′tion,** *n.*

de·seg·re·gate (dē·seg′rə·gāt), *v.,* –gat·ed, –gat·ing. 1. abolish segregation in. 2. of a place or institution, become desegregated.

de·seg·re·ga·tion (dē·seg′rə·gā′shən), *n.* abolishment of the practice of segregating Negroes from whites, esp. in the U.S. public schools.

de·sen·si·tize (dē·sen′sə·tīz), *v.,* –tized, –tiz·ing. make less sensitive. —**de·sen′si·ti·za′tion,** *n.* —**de·sen′si·tiz′er,** *n.*

des·ert¹ (dez′ərt), *n.* 1. a dry, barren region, usually sandy and without trees. 2. region that is not inhabited or cultivated; wilderness. —*adj.* 1. dry; barren. 2. not inhabited or cultivated; wild. [< OF < Eccl.L *desertum,* (thing) abandoned, pp. See DESERT².]

de·sert² (di·zėrt′), *v.* 1. go away and leave; abandon; forsake. 2. run away from duty. 3. leave military service without permission. [< F < LL *desertare* < L *deserere* abandon < *de-* DIS- + *serere* join] —**de·sert′er,** *n.*

de·sert³ (di·zėrt′), *n.* what is deserved; suitable reward or punishment: *the robber got his just deserts; he was sentenced to five years in prison.* [< OF *deserte,* pp. of *deservir* DESERVE] —*Syn.* merit, due, meed.

de·ser·tion (di·zėr′shən), *n.* 1. a deserting, esp. in violation of duty or obligation. 2. state of being deserted.

de·serve (di·zėrv′), *v.,* –served, –serv·ing. have a claim or right to; be worthy of. [< F < L *deservire* serve well < *de-* + *servire* serve] —**de·serv′er,** *n.* —*Syn.* merit.

de·serv·ed·ly (di·zėr′vid·li), *adv.* justly.

de·serv·ing (di·zėr′ving), *adj.* 1. that deserves; worthy (of something). 2. worth helping.

des·ha·bille (dez′ə·bēl′), *n.* dishabille.

des·ic·cate (des′ə·kāt), *v.,* –cat·ed, –cat·ing. 1. dry thoroughly. 2. preserve by drying thoroughly. [< L, < *de-* + *siccus* dry] —**des′ic·ca′tion,** *n.* —**des′ic·ca′tive,** *adj.*

de·sid·er·a·tum (di·sid′ər·ā′təm; –ä′təm), *n.,* *pl.* –ta (–tə). something desired or needed. [< L, pp. of *desiderare* long for]

de·sign (di·zīn′), *n.* 1. a drawing, plan, or sketch made to serve as a pattern from which to work: *design for a machine.* 2. arrangement of detail, form, and color in painting, etc.: *a wallpaper design.* 3. art of making designs: *school of design.* 4. piece of artistic work. 5. a plan in mind to be carried out. 6. scheme of attack; evil plan. 7. intention. —*v.* 1. make a first sketch of; plan out. 2. make drawings, sketches, plans, etc. 3. form in the mind; contrive. 4. have in mind to do. [< F < L, < *de-* + *signum* mark]

des·ig·nate (*v.* dez′ig·nāt; *adj.* dez′ig·nit, –nāt), *v.,* –nat·ed, –nat·ing, *adj.* —*v.* 1. point out; indicate definitely. 2. name; entitle. 3. select for duty, office, etc.; appoint. —*adj.* appointed; selected. [< L *designatus,* pp. See DESIGN.] —**des′ig·na′tive,** *adj.* —**des′ig·na′tor,** *n.*

des·ig·na·tion (dez′ig·nā′shən), *n.* 1. act of designating. 2. a descriptive title; name. 3. appointment; selection.

de·sign·ed·ly (di·zīn′id·li), *adv.* purposely.

de·sign·er (di·zīn′ər), *n.* 1. person who designs: *a dress designer.* 2. plotter; schemer.

de·sign·ing (di·zīn′ing), *adj.* 1. scheming; plotting. 2. showing plan or forethought. —*n.* art of making designs. —**de·sign′ing·ly**, *adv.*

de·sir·a·ble (di·zīr′ə·bəl), *adj.* worth wishing for; worth having. —**de·sir′a·bil′i·ty, de·sir′a·ble·ness**, *n.* —**de·sir′a·bly**, *adv.*

de·sire (di·zīr′), *v.,* –sired, –sir·ing, *n.* —*v.* 1. wish for; wish strongly for. 2. express a wish for; ask for. 3. crave sexually. —*n.* 1. wish; strong wish. 2. an expressed wish; request. 3. thing desired. 4. sexual craving; lust. [< OF < L *desiderare* long for] —Syn. *v.* 1. long, yearn, crave. —*n.* 1. longing, yearning.

de·sir·ous (di·zīr′əs), *adj.* having or showing desire; full of desire; desiring.

de·sist (di·zist′), *v.* stop; cease. [< OF < L *de-* + *sistere* stop]

desk (desk), *n.* 1. piece of furniture with a flat or sloping top on which to write or to rest books for reading. 2. lectern; pulpit. [< Med.L *desca* < Ital. *desco* < L *discus* quoit, DISH < Gk. *diskos*]

Des Moines (də moin′), capital of Iowa, in the central part.

des·o·late (*adj.* des′ə·lit; *v.* des′ə·lāt), *adj., v.,* –lat·ed, –lat·ing. —*adj.* 1. laid waste; devastated; barren. 2. not lived in; deserted. 3. left alone; solitary; lonely. 4. unhappy; wretched; forlorn. 5. dreary; dismal. —*v.* 1. make unfit to live in; lay waste. 2. deprive of inhabitants. 3. make lonely, unhappy, or forlorn. [< L, < *de-* + *solus* alone] —**des′o·late·ly**, *adv.* —**des′o·late·ness**, *n.* —**des′o·lat′er, des′o·la′tor**, *n.* —Syn. *adj.* 1. ravaged. 3. forsaken.

des·o·la·tion (des′ə·lā′shən), *n.* 1. act of making desolate. 2. a lonely or deserted condition. 3. desolate place. 4. sadness; sorrow.

De So·to (di sō′tō), Hernando, 1500?–1542, Spanish explorer in America.

de·spair (di·spār′), *n.* 1. loss of hope; hopelessness. 2. person or thing that causes despair. —*v.* lose hope; be without hope. [< OF < L, < *de-* + *sperare* to hope] —**de·spair′ing**, *adj.* —**de·spair′ing·ly**, *adv.* —**de·spair′ing·ness**, *n.*

des·patch (dis·pach′), *v., n.* dispatch.

des·per·a·do (des′pər·ä′dō; –ä′dō), *n., pl.* –does, –dos. a bold, reckless criminal. [< OSp. See DESPERATE.]

des·per·ate (des′pər·it), *adj.* 1. reckless because of despair. 2. showing recklessness caused by despair. 3. with little or no hope of improvement; very serious. 4. hopeless. [< L *desperatus*, pp. See DESPAIR.] —**des′per·ate·ly**, *adv.* —**des′per·ate·ness**, *n.*

des·per·a·tion (des′pər·ā′shən), *n.* act or fact of despairing; despair.

des·pi·ca·ble (des′pi·kə·bəl; des·pik′ə·bəl), *adj.* to be despised; contemptible. —**des′pi·ca·ble·ness**, *n.* —**des′pi·ca·bly**, *adv.*

de·spise (di·spīz′), *v.,* –spised, –spis·ing. look down on; feel contempt for. [< OF < L, < *de-* down + *specere* look at] —**de·spis′er**, *n.* —Syn. scorn. —Ant. admire.

de·spite (di·spīt′), *n., v.,* –spit·ed, –spit·ing, *prep.* —*n.* 1. malice; spite. 2. contempt; scorn. 3. insult; injury. 4. in despite of, in spite of. —*v.* treat with contempt. —*prep.* in spite of. [< OF < L *despectus* a looking down upon < *de-* + *specere* look at]

de·spoil (di·spoil′), *v.* rob; plunder. [< OF < L, < *de-* + *spoliare* strip < *spolium* armor, booty] —**de·spoil′er**, *n.* —**de·spoil′ment, de·spo·li·a·tion** (di·spō′li·ā′shən), *n.*

de·spond (di·spond′), *v.* lose heart, courage, or hope. —*n. Archaic.* despondency. [< L, < *de-* + *spondere* lose heart] —**de·spond′ing**, *adj.* —**de·spond′ing·ly**, *adv.*

de·spond·en·cy (di·spon′dən·si), **de·spond·ence** (–dəns), *n., pl.* –cies; –ces. loss of courage or hope. —**de·spond′ent**, *adj.*

des·pot (des′pət; –pot), *n.* 1. tyrant; oppressor. 2. monarch having unlimited power; absolute ruler. [< OF < Med.Gk. *despotes* master < Gk.]

des·pot·ic (des·pot′ik), *adj.* of a despot; tyrannical. —**des·pot′i·cal·ly**, *adv.*

des·pot·ism (des′pət·iz·əm), *n.* 1. tyranny; oppression. 2. government by a monarch having unlimited power.

des·sert (di·zért′), *n.* a course served at the end of a meal, such as pie, cake, ice cream, etc. [< F, < *desservir* clear the table < *des-* (< L *dis-*) + *servir* serve < L]

de·sta·lin·i·za·tion (dē·stä′lin·ə·zā′shən), *n.* elimination or alteration by a Communist government of policies, doctrines, etc. originated by or associated with Stalin.

des·ti·na·tion (des′tə·nā′shən), *n.* 1. place to which a person or thing is going or is being sent. 2. a setting apart for a particular purpose.

des·tine (des′tən), *v.,* –tined, –tin·ing. 1. set apart for a particular purpose or use; intend. 2. cause by fate. 3. destined for, a. intended for. b. bound for: *ships destined for England.* [< OF < L *destinare* make fast, < *de-* + *stare* stand]

des·ti·ny (des′tə·ni), *n., pl.* –nies. 1. what becomes of a person or thing in the end; one's lot or fortune. 2. what will happen in spite of all efforts to change or prevent it. 3. fate.

des·ti·tute (des′tə·tüt; –tūt), *adj.* 1. lacking necessary things such as food, clothing, and shelter. 2. destitute of, having no; without [< L, < *destituere* forsake < *de-* away + *statuere* put, place] —Syn. 1. needy, indigent. 2. deprived.

des·ti·tu·tion (des′tə·tü′shən; –tū′–), *n.* 1. destitute condition; extreme poverty. 2. lack.

de·stroy (di·stroi′), *v.* 1. break to pieces; make useless; ruin; spoil. 2. put an end to; do away with. 3. deprive of life; kill. 4. counteract the effect of; make void. [< OF < VL < L, < *de-* un- + *struere* pile, build] —**de·stroy′a·ble**, *adj.* —Syn. 1. demolish, raze. 2. abolish, extinguish.

de·stroy·er (di·stroi′ər), *n.* 1. person or thing that destroys. 2. a relatively small, very fast warship used to attack submarines, for escort duty, etc.

destroyer escort, a warship which is smaller and slower than a destroyer, but larger than a corvette (def.2).

de·struct·i·ble (di·struk′tə·bəl), *adj.* capable of being destroyed. —**de·struct′i·bil′i·ty**, *n.*

de·struc·tion (di·struk′shən), *n.* 1. act of destroying. 2. state of being destroyed. 3. cause or means of destroying.

de·struc·tive (di·struk′tiv), *adj.* 1. tending to destroy. 2. causing destruction. 3. tearing down; not helpful. —**de·struc′tive·ly**, *adv.* —**de·struc′tive·ness**, *n.* —Syn. 1. ruinous.

des·ue·tude (des′wə·tüd; –tūd), *n.* disuse. [< F < L *desuetudo* < *de-* dis- + *suescere* accustom]

des·ul·to·ry (des′əl·tô′ri; –tō′–), *adj.* 1. jumping from one thing to another; unconnected. 2. without aim or method. [< L *desultorius* of a leaper, ult. < *de-* down + *salire* leap] —**des′ul·to′ri·ly**, *adv.* —**des′ul·to′ri·ness**, *n.*

de·tach (di·tach′), *v.* 1. loosen and remove; unfasten; separate. 2. send away on special duty. [< F, formed with *dé-* (< L *dis-*) after *attacher* ATTACH] —**de·tach′a·ble**, *adj.* —**de·tach′er**, *n.*

de·tached (di·tacht′), *adj.* 1. separate from others; isolated. 2. not influenced by others or by one's own interests and prejudices.

de·tach·ment (di·tach′mənt), *n.* 1. separation. 2. group of soldiers or ships sent on some special duty. 3. a standing apart; aloofness. 4. freedom from prejudice or bias; impartiality.

de·tail (*n.* di·tāl′, dē′tāl; *v.* di·tāl′), *n.* 1. a small or unimportant part. 2. a dealing with small things one by one. 3. a minute account. 4. a minor decoration or subordinate part in a building, picture, machine, etc. 5. a small group selected for or sent on some special duty. 6. in detail, part by part. —*v.* 1. tell fully; give the particulars of. 2. select for or send on special duty. [< F, < *détaillir* cut in pieces < *de-* + *tailler* cut] —Syn. *n.* 1. item, trifle. 5. squad, detachment, party. ► detail, *n.* The formal pronunciation is di·tāl′; informal usage is divided but the pronunciation is likely to be dē′tāl.

de·tain (di·tān′), *v.* 1. hold back; keep from going; delay. 2. keep in custody; confine. 3. withhold. [< OF < L, < *de-* + *tenere* hold] —**de·tain′er**, *n.* —**de·tain′ment**, *n.* —Syn. 1. retard.

de·tect (di·tekt′), *v.* **1.** find out; discover. **2.** discover the existence of. **3.** change (the alternating currents in a radio set) by a detector. [< L *detectus* < *de-* un- + *tegere* cover] —detect′a·ble, de·tect′i·ble, *adj.*

de·tec·tion (di·tek′shən), *n.* **1.** a finding out; discovery. **2.** a being found out or discovered. **3.** change of alternating currents in a radio set.

de·tec·tive (di·tek′tiv), *n.* policeman or other person whose work is finding information secretly, discovering who committed a crime, etc. —*adj.* pertaining to detectives and their work.

de·tec·tor (di·tek′tər), *n.* **1.** person or thing that detects. **2.** a vacuum tube or crystal in a radio that helps in the change of radio waves into sound waves.

de·ten·tion (di·ten′shən), *n.* **1.** act of detaining. **2.** state of being detained; delay. **3.** confinement.

de·ter (di·tér′), *v.,* -terred, -ter·ring. discourage; keep back; hinder. [< L, < *de-* from + *terrere* frighten] —de·ter′ment, *n.*

de·ter·gent (di·tér′jənt), *adj.* cleansing. —*n.* a detergent substance. [< L, < *de-* off + *tergere* wipe]

de·te·ri·o·rate (di·tir′i·ə·rāt), *v.,* -rat·ed, -rat·ing. make or become worse; depreciate. [< L, < *deterior* worse] —de·te′ri·o·ra′tion, *n.* —de·te′ri·o·ra′tive, *adj.*

de·ter·mi·na·ble (di·tér′mə·nə·bəl), *adj.* capable of being settled or decided.

de·ter·mi·nant (di·tér′mə·nənt), *n.* thing that determines. —*adj.* determining.

de·ter·mi·nate (di·tér′mə·nit), *adj.* **1.** with exact limits; fixed; definite. **2.** settled; positive. **3.** determined; resolute. **4.** *Bot.* having the primary and each secondary axis ending in a flower or bud. —de·ter′mi·nate·ly, *adv.* —de·ter′mi·nate·ness, *n.*

de·ter·mi·na·tion (di·tér′mə·nā′shən), *n.* **1.** act of settling beforehand. **2.** finding out the exact amount or kind, by weighing, measuring, or calculating. **3.** result of finding out exactly; conclusion. **4.** state of being determined; settlement; decision. **5.** great firmness in carrying out a purpose. **6.** a fixed direction or tendency.

de·ter·mi·na·tive (di·tér′mə·nā′tiv; -nə·tiv), *adj.* determining. —*n.* thing that determines. —de·ter′mi·na′tive·ly, *adv.* —de·ter′mi·na′tive·ness, *n.*

de·ter·mine (di·tér′mən), *v.,* -mined, -min·ing. **1.** make up one's mind firmly; resolve. **2.** settle; decide. **3.** find out exactly; fix. **4.** fix the geometrical position of. **5.** be the deciding factor in reaching a certain result. **6.** fix or settle beforehand. **7.** give an aim to; direct; impel. **8.** limit; define. [< OF < L *determinare* set limits to < *de-* + *terminus* end] —de·ter′min·er, *n.* —Syn. **3.** ascertain, establish. **5.** influence.

de·ter·mined (di·tér′mənd), *adj.* firm; resolute. —de·ter′mined·ly, *adv.* —de·ter′mined·ness, *n.*

de·ter·min·ism (di·tér′mən·iz·əm), *n.* doctrine that human actions and all events are the necessary results of antecedent causes. —de·ter′min·ist, *n., adj.*

de·ter·rent (di·tér′ənt; -ter′-), *adj.* deterring; restraining. —*n.* something that deters. —de·ter′rence, *n.*

de·test (di·test′), *v.* dislike very much; hate. [< F < L *detestari* curse while calling the gods to witness < *de-* + *testis* witness] —de·test′a·ble, *adj.* —de·test′a·bil′i·ty, de·test′a·ble·ness, *n.* —de·test′a·bly, *adv.* —de·test′er, *n.* —Syn. abhor, loathe. —Ant. love.

de·tes·ta·tion (dē′tes·tā′shən), *n.* **1.** very strong dislike; hatred. **2.** a detested person or thing.

de·throne (dē·thrōn′), *v.,* -throned, -thron·ing. deprive of the power to rule; remove from a throne; depose. —de·throne′ment, *n.* —de·thron′er, *n.*

det·o·nate (det′ə·nāt), *v.,* -nat·ed, -nat·ing. explode with a loud noise. [< L, < *de-* (intensive) + *tonare* thunder] —det′o·na′tion, *n.* —det′o·na′tor, *n.*

de·tour (dē′tur; di·tur′), *n.* **1.** road that is used when the main or direct road cannot be traveled. **2.** a roundabout way. —*v.* **1.** use a detour. **2.** cause to use a detour. [< F, < *détourner* turn aside < *dé-* (< L *dis-*) + *tourner* turn]

de·tract (di·trakt′), *v.* take away. [< L *detractus* < *de-* away + *trahere* draw] —de·trac′tion, *n.* —de·trac′tive, *adj.* —de·trac′tor, *n.*

det·ri·ment (det′rə·mənt), *n.* **1.** damage; injury; harm. **2.** something that causes damage or harm. [< L *detrimentum* < *de-* away + *terere* wear]

det·ri·men·tal (det′rə·men′təl), *adj.* damaging; injurious; harmful. —det′ri·men′tal·ly, *adv.*

de·tri·tus (di·trī′təs), *n. Geol.* particles of rock or other material worn away from a mass. [< L, a rubbing away]

De·troit (di·troit′), *n.* city in SE Michigan.

deuce¹ (düs; dūs), *n.* **1.** in a game of cards or dice, two. **2.** a playing card marked with a 2. **3.** the side with two spots in dice. **4.** *Tennis.* a tie score at 40 each in a game, or 5 games each in a set. [< OF *deus* two < L *duos,* accus. of *duo* two]

deuce² (düs; dūs), *interj. Colloq.* exclamation of annoyance meaning "bad luck," "the mischief," "the devil." [prob. < LG *duus* DEUCE¹, an unlucky throw at dice]

deu·ced (dü′sid, dū′-; düst, dūst), *adj. Colloq.* devilish; excessive. —*adv.* devilishly; excessively. —deu′ced·ly, *adv.*

Deut., Deuteronomy.

deu·te·ri·um (dü·tir′i·əm; dū-), *n. Chem.* an isotope of hydrogen, D, whose molecules weigh twice as much as those of ordinary hydrogen; heavy hydrogen. [< NL < Gk. *deuteroin,* neut., having second place < *deuteros* second]

deu·ter·on (dü′tər·on; dū′-), *n. Physics.* the nucleus of deuterium, consisting of one proton and one neutron that have parallel spins. [< Gk. *deuteron,* neut. of *deuteros* second (with ref. to deuterium as H²)]

Deu·ter·on·o·my (dü′tər·on′ə·mi; dū′-), *n.* the fifth book of the Old Testament. [< L < Gk., < *deuteros* second + *nomos* law]

De Va·le·ra (dā′ və·lâr′ə; dev′ə-; -lir′ə), Eamon, born 1882, Irish statesman.

de·val·u·ate (dē·val′yū·āt), *v.,* -at·ed, -at·ing. lessen the value of. —de·val′u·a′tion, *n.*

dev·as·tate (dev′əs·tāt), *v.,* -tat·ed, -tat·ing. make desolate; destroy; ravage. [< L, < *de-* + *vastus* waste] —dev′as·tat′ing·ly, *adv.* —dev′as·ta′tion, *n.* —dev′as·ta′tor, *n.*

de·vel·op (di·vel′əp), *v.* **1.** bring or come into being or activity; grow. **2.** make or become bigger, better, fuller, more useful, etc. **3.** *Music.* elaborate (a theme) by changes of rhythm, melody, or harmony. **4.** display; show. **5.** make or become known; reveal. **6.** treat or be treated with chemicals to bring out an image, as a photograph. [< F *développer* unwrap] —de·vel′op·a·ble, *adj.* —Syn. **1.** generate, evolve, unfold. **2.** mature, expand. **5.** disclose.

de·vel·op·er (di·vel′əp·ər), *n.* **1.** person or thing that develops. **2.** a chemical used to bring out the picture on a photographic film, plate, print, etc.

de·vel·op·ment (di·vel′əp·mənt), *n.* **1.** a developing. **2.** a developed stage, state, or result. —de·vel′op·men′tal, *adj.*

de·vi·ate (dē′vi·āt), *v.,* -at·ed, -at·ing. turn aside (from a way, course, rule, truth, etc.); diverge. [< LL, < *de-* aside + *via* way] —de′vi·a′tion, *n.* —de′vi·a′tor, *n.*

de·vice (di·vīs′), *n.* **1.** a mechanical invention used for a special purpose; machine; apparatus. **2.** plan; scheme; trick. **3.** a drawing or figure used in a pattern or as an ornament. **4.** picture or design on a coat of arms, often accompanied by a motto. **5.** motto. **6.** leave to one's own devices, leave to do as one thinks best. [fusion of ME *devis* separation, talk + *devise* design, emblem, plan; both < OF < L *divisus,* pp. of *dividere* DIVIDE] —Syn. **1.** contrivance. **2.** ruse, wile.

dev·il (dev′əl), *n., v.,* -iled, -il·ing; *esp. Brit.*

-illed, -il·ling, interj. —n. 1. a. an evil spirit; fiend; demon. b. the Devil, Satan. 2. a wicked or cruel person. 3. a very clever, energetic, or reckless person. 4. an unfortunate or wretched person. 5. an evil influence or power. 6. the errand boy in a printing office; printer's apprentice. 7. the devil to pay, much trouble ahead. —v. 1. Am., Colloq. bother; tease; torment. 2. prepare (food) with hot seasoning. —interj. exclamation of disgust, anger, etc. [< L < Gk. diabolos slanderer < dia– across, against + ballein throw]

dev·iled, esp. Brit. **dev·illed** (dev′əld), adj. highly seasoned: deviled ham.

dev·il·fish (dev′əl·fish′), n., pl. -fish·es or (esp. collectively) -fish. 1. a large, odd-shaped fish related to the shark; giant ray. 2. octopus.

Devilfish (ab. 20 ft. across)

dev·il·ish (dev′əl·ish; dev′lish), adj. 1. like a devil. 2. mischievous; daring. 3. Colloq. very great; extreme. —adv. Colloq. extremely. —dev′il·ish·ly, adv. —dev′il·ish·ness, n.

dev·il·ment (dev′əl·mənt), n. devilish behavior.

dev·il·try (dev′əl·tri), n., pl. -tries. U.S. 1. wicked behavior. 2. daring behavior; mischief. 3. great cruelty or wickedness.

de·vi·ous (dē′vi·əs), adj. 1. winding; twisting. 2. straying from the right course; not straightforward. [< L, < de– out of + via way] —de′vi·ous·ly, adv. —de′vi·ous·ness, n.

de·vise (di·vīz′), v., -vised, -vis·ing, n. —v. 1. think out; plan; contrive; invent. 2. Law. give or leave (land, buildings, etc.) by a will. —n. Law. a. a giving or leaving of land, buildings, etc., by a will. b. a will or part of a will doing this. c. land, buildings, etc., given or left in this way. [< OF deviser dispose in portions, arrange, ult. < L dividere DIVIDE] —de·vis′a·ble, adj. —de·vis′er, esp. Law. de·vi′sor, n.

de·vis·ee (di·vīz′ē′; dev′ə·zē′), n. Law. person to whom land, etc., is devised.

de·vi·tal·ize (dē·vī′təl·īz), v., -ized, -iz·ing. take the life or vitality of. —de·vi′tal·i·za′tion, n.

de·void (di·void′), adj. lacking (of): devoid of sense. [< OF, < des– (< L dis–) + voidier VOID]

de·voir (də·vwär′; dev′wär), n. 1. act of courtesy or respect. 2. duty. [< F < L debere owe]

de·volve (di·volv′), v., -volved, -volv·ing. 1. transfer (duty, work, etc.) to someone else. 2. be handed down to someone else; be transferred. [< L, < de– down + volvere roll] —dev·o·lu·tion (dev′ə·lü′shən), de·volve′ment, n.

Dev·on (dev′ən), or **Dev·on·shire** (-shir; -shər), n. county in SW England.

de·vote (di·vōt′), v., -vot·ed, -vot·ing. 1. give up (oneself, one's money, time, or efforts) to some person, purpose, or service. 2. dedicate; consecrate. [< L devotus < de– entirely + vovere vow] —de·vote′ment, n. —Syn. 1. apply, appropriate, assign.

de·vot·ed (di·vōt′id), adj. 1. loyal; faithful. 2. dedicated; consecrated. —de·vot′ed·ly, adv. —de·vot′ed·ness, n.

dev·o·tee (dev′ə·tē′), n. person deeply devoted to something, such as a religion.

de·vo·tion (di·vō′shən), n. 1. deep, steady affection; loyalty; faithfulness. 2. act of devoting or state of being devoted. 3. earnestness in religion; devoutness. 4. a religious observance. 5. devotions, religious worship; prayers. —de·vo′tion·al, adj. —de·vo′tion·al·ly, adv.

de·vour (di·vour′), v. 1. eat (usually said of animals). 2. eat like an animal; eat hungrily. 3. consume; waste; destroy: a devouring disease. 4. swallow up; engulf. 5. take in with eyes or ears in a hungry, greedy way: devour a book. [< OF < L, < de– down + vorare gulp] —de·vour′er, n. —de·vour′ing·ly, adv.

de·vout (di·vout′), adj. 1. active in worship and prayer; religious. 2. devoted; earnest; sincere. [< OF < L devotus, pp. See DEVOTE.] —de·vout′ly, adv. —de·vout′ness, n. —Syn. 1. pious.

dew (dū; dū), n. 1. moisture from the air that condenses and collects in small drops on cool surfaces during the night. 2. moisture in small drops, as perspiration. 3. anything fresh or refreshing like dew. —v. wet with dew; moisten. [OE dēaw] —dew′less, adj.

dew·ber·ry (dū′ber′i; dū′–), n., pl. -ries. 1. a blackberry vine that grows along the ground. 2. fruit of one of these vines.

dew·drop (dū′drop′; dū′–), n. a drop of dew.

Dew·ey (dū′i; dū′–), n. 1. George, 1837–1917, American admiral. 2. John, 1859–1952, American philosopher and educator. 3. Thomas Edmund, born 1902, American lawyer and political leader.

dew·lap (dū′lap′; dū′–), n. a loose fold of skin under the throat of cattle and some other animals. [< dew (orig. and meaning uncert.) + lap < OE læppa pendulous piece]

DEW line, D.E.W. line, the Distant Early Warning line, a chain of radar stations stretching across northern Canada, north of the Arctic Circle, designed to give the earliest possible warning of an attack on the United States or Canada by bombing planes over the north polar region.

dew point, temperature of the air at which dew begins to form.

dew·y (dū′i; dū′i), adj., dew·i·er, dew·i·est. 1. wet with dew. 2. of dew. 3. like dew; refreshing. —dew′i·ness, n.

Dex·e·drine (deks′ə·drēn; -drin), n. Trademark. drug, ($C_9H_{13}N$)$_2H_2SO_4$, that causes wakefulness and loss of appetite.

dex·ter (deks′tər), adj. of or on the right-hand side. [< L, right]

dex·ter·i·ty (deks·ter′ə·ti), n. 1. skill in using the hands. 2. skill in using the mind; cleverness.

dex·ter·ous (deks′tər·əs; -trəs), adj. 1. having or showing skill in using the hands. 2. having or showing skill in using the mind. Also, **dextrous.** —dex′ter·ous·ly, adv. —dex′ter·ous·ness, n.

dex·tral (deks′trəl), adj. right; right-hand. —dex·tral′i·ty, n. —dex′tral·ly, adv.

dex·trin (deks′trin), **dex·trine** (-trin; -trēn), n. a gummy substance obtained from starch, used as an adhesive, for sizing paper, etc. [< F dextrine]

dex·trose (deks′trōs), n. a sugar, $C_6H_{12}O_6$, less sweet than cane sugar; a form of glucose.

dex·trous (deks′trəs), adj. dexterous. —dex′trous·ly, adv. —dex′trous·ness, n.

di (dē), n. tone of the musical scale, intermediate between do and re.

di–, prefix. twice; double; twofold, as in dioxide. [< Gk. dis]

di·a·be·tes (dī′ə·bē′tis; -tēz), n. disease in which the digestive system is unable to absorb normal amounts of sugar and starch. [< NL < Gk., a passer-through < dia– through + bainein go] —di·a·bet·ic (dī′ə·bet′ik; -bē′tik), adj., n.

di·a·bol·ic (dī′ə·bol′ik), **di·a·bol·i·cal** (-ə·kəl), adj. 1. like the Devil; very cruel or wicked. 2. having to do with the Devil or devils. [< LL < Gk. diabolikos. See DEVIL.] —di′a·bol′i·cal·ly, adv.

di·a·crit·ic (dī′ə·krit′ik), adj. diacritical. —n. a diacritical mark. [< Gk. diakritikos < dia– apart + krinein separate]

di·a·crit·i·cal (dī′ə·krit′ə·kəl), adj. used to distinguish. —di′a·crit′i·cal·ly, adv.

diacritical mark, mark like – ·· ^ / or ˎ placed over or under a letter to indicate pronunciation, etc.

di·a·dem (dī′ə·dem), n. crown. [< L < Gk. diadema < dia– across + deein bind]

di·aer·e·sis (dī·er′ə·sis), n., pl. -ses (-sēz). dieresis.

di·ag·nose (dī′əg·nōs′; -nōz′), v., -nosed, -nos·ing. make a diagnosis of.

di·ag·no·sis (dī′əg·nō′sis), n., pl. -ses (-sēz). 1. act or process of finding out what disease a person or animal has by examination and careful study of the symptoms. X rays and blood tests are used in diagnosis. 2. careful study of the facts about something to find out its essential features, faults, etc. 3. decision reached after a careful study of symptoms or facts. [< NL < Gk., < *dia-* apart + *gignoskein* learn to know] **—di·ag·nos·tic** (dī′əg-nos′tik), *adj.* **—di·ag·nos·ti·cian** (dī′əg-nos-tish′ən), *n.*

di·ag·o·nal (dī-ag′ə-nəl), *n.* 1. a straight line that cuts across in a slanting direction, often from corner to corner. 2. any slanting line, row, course, etc. *—adj.* 1. taking the direction of a diagonal; slanting; oblique. 2. having slanting lines, ridges, etc. 3. connecting two corners that are not next to each other. [< L, < Gk. *diagonios* from angle to angle < *dia-* across + *gonia* angle] **—di·ag′o·nal·ly**, *adv.*

Line AB is a diagonal.

di·a·gram (dī′ə-gram), *n.*, *v.*, **-gramed**, **-gram·ing**; *esp. Brit.* **-grammed**, **-gram·ming**. *—n.* an outline, a plan, a drawing, a figure, a chart, or a combination of any of these made to show clearly what a thing is or how it works. *—v.* make a diagram of. [< L < Gk. *diagramma* < *dia-* apart, out + *graphein* mark] **—di·a·gram·mat·ic** (dī′ə-grə-mat′ik), **di·a·gram·mat′i·cal**, *adj.* **—di′a·gram·mat′i·cal·ly**, *adv.*

di·al (dī′əl), *n.*, *v.*, **-aled**, **-al·ing**; *esp. Brit.* **-alled**, **-al·ling**. *—n.* 1. a marked surface on which time is shown by a moving pointer or shadows. 2. disk with numbers, etc., on which the amount of water, pressure, etc., is shown by a pointer. 3. plate, disk, etc., of a radio with numbers, letters, etc., on it for tuning in to a radio station. 4. part of an automatic telephone used in making telephone calls. *—v.* 1. show on a telephone dial. 2. call by means of a telephone dial. [appar. < Med.L (*rota*) *dialis* daily (wheel) < L *dies* day]

di·al., dialect; dialectal.

di·a·lect (dī′ə·lekt), *n.* 1. form of speech characteristic of a fairly definite region: *the Scottish dialect.* 2. words and pronunciations used by certain professions, classes of people, etc. 3. one of a group of closely related languages. Some of the dialects descended from the Latin language are French, Italian, Spanish, and Portuguese. [< L < Gk. *dialektos*, ult. < *dia-* between + *legein* speak] ▶ A dialect is the speech (words, sounds, stress, phrasing, grammatical habits) that does not attract attention to itself among the residents of a region. Dialects exist because of the separation of groups of speakers and are not peculiar to backward regions, for the "Oxford accent" forms a minor dialect, and the people of Boston and of New York speak differently from their neighbors. Nor do dialects depend upon education or social standing. An educated, as well as an uneducated, westerner will speak somewhat differently from a southerner or New Englander of a similar degree and quality of education. Regional differences in the United States are not so conspicuous as are the differences between other kinds of usage (between formal and informal English, for example), but characteristic differences in vocabulary and, even more noticeably, in pronunciation are found.

di·a·lec·tal (dī′ə·lek′təl), *adj.* of a dialect; like that of a dialect. **—di′a·lec′tal·ly**, *adv.*

di·a·lec·tic (dī′ə·lek′tik), *n.* 1. art or practice of logical discussion. 2. Also, **dialectics**. the principles of logic. *—adj.* 1. pertaining to logical discussion. 2. dialectal.

di·a·lec·ti·cian (dī′ə·lek·tish′ən), *n.* person skilled in dialectic or dialectics; logician.

di·a·logue, di·a·log (dī′ə·lôg; -log), *n.* 1. conversation. 2. a literary work in the form of a conversation. 3. conversation in a play, story, etc. [< L < Gk. < *dia-* between + *logos* speech] **—di′a·logu′er**, *n.*

di·al·y·sis (dī·al′ə·sis), *n.*, *pl.* **-ses** (-sēz). separation of crystalloids from colloids in solution by diffusion through a membrane. [< Gk., < *dia-* apart + *lyein* loose] **—di·a·lyt·ic** (dī′ə·lit′ik), *adj.*

diam., diameter.

di·a·mag·net·ic (dī′ə·mag·net′ik), *adj.* re-

pelled by a magnet. **—di′a·mag·net′i·cal·ly**, *adv.* **—di·a·mag·net·ism** (dī′ə·mag′nə·tiz·əm), *n.*

di·am·e·ter (dī·am′ə·tər), *n.* 1. a straight line passing from one side to the other through the center of a circle, sphere, etc. 2. the length of such a line; width; thickness. [< OF < L < Gk., < *dia-* across + *metron* measure]

Line AB is a diameter.

di·a·met·ric (dī′ə·met′rik), **di·a·met·ri·cal** (-rə·kəl), *adj.* 1. of or along a diameter. 2. exactly opposite. **—di′a·met′ri·cal·ly**, *adv.*

dia·mond (dī′mənd; dī′ə-), *n.* 1. a form of pure carbon in crystals, the hardest known substance, used as a precious stone. 2. tool having a diamond tip for cutting glass. 3. a plane figure shaped like this ◊. 4. a playing card with one or more red designs like a diamond on it. 5. diamonds, the complete suit. 6. *Am.* space inside the lines that connect the bases in baseball. 7. a very small size of type; 4½ point. *—adj.* made of diamonds. *—v.* adorn with diamonds or as with diamonds. [< OF < Med.L *diamas*, alter. of L *adamas* ADAMANT]

dia·mond·back (dī′mənd·bak′; dī′ə-), *n. Am.* 1. any rattlesnake with diamond-shaped markings on its back. 2. Also, **diamondback terrapin**. turtle that has diamond-shaped markings on its shell.

Di·an·a (dī·an′ə), *n.* the Roman goddess of the hunt and of the moon and protectress of women, identified with the Greek goddess Artemis.

di·a·net·ics (dī′ə·net′iks), *n.* system of mental treatment that seeks to alleviate certain apparently physical ailments that are supposedly caused primarily by a mental attitude, etc.

di·a·pa·son (dī′ə·pā′zən; -sən), *n. Music.* 1. melody; strain. 2. the whole range of a voice or instrument. 3. either of two principal stops in an organ: **a. open diapason**, a stop giving full, majestic tones. **b. stopped diapason**, a stop giving powerful flutelike tones. [< L < Gk., < *dia pason* (*chordon*) across all (the notes of the scale)]

di·a·per (dī′ə·pər; dī′pər), *n.* a small piece of cloth used as part of a baby's underclothing. *—v.* put a diaper on. [< OF < Med.Gk. *diaspros* < *dia-* (intensive) + *aspros* white]

di·aph·a·nous (dī·af′ə·nəs), *adj.* transparent. [< Med.L < Gk., < *dia-* through + *phainein* show] **—di·aph′a·nous·ly**, *adv.*

di·a·phragm (dī′ə·fram), *n.* 1. *Anat.* a partition of muscles and tendons separating the cavity of the chest from the cavity of the abdomen. 2. a vibrating disk in a telephone. 3. device for controlling the light entering a camera, microscope, etc. *—v.* 1. furnish with a diaphragm. 2. act upon by a diaphragm. [< LL < Gk. *diaphragma* < *dia-* across + *phrassein* fence] **—di·a·phrag·mat·ic** (dī′ə·frag·mat′ik), *adj.*

di·ar·rhe·a, di·ar·rhoe·a (dī′ə·rē′ə), *n.* too many and too loose movements of the bowels. [< L < Gk., < *dia-* through + *rheein* flow]

di·a·ry (dī′ə·ri), *n.*, *pl.* **-ries**. 1. account written down each day, of what one has done, thought, etc. 2. book for keeping such an account, with a blank space for each day of the year. [< L *diarium* < *dies* day] **—di·a·rist** (dī′ə·rist), *n.*

di·a·stase (dī′ə·stās), *n.* enzyme that changes starch into dextrin and maltose during digestion, germination of seeds, etc. [< F < Gk. *diastasis* separation < *dia-* apart + *sta-* stand] **—di·a·stat·ic** (dī′ə·stat′ik), *adj.*

di·as·to·le (dī·as′tə·lē), *n.* 1. the normal, rhythmical dilation of the heart, esp. that of the ventricles. 2. the lengthening of a syllable which is regularly short. [< LL < Gk., expansion < *dia-* apart + *stellein* send] **—di·as·tol·ic** (dī′əs·tol′-ik), *adj.*

di·as·tro·phism (dī·as′trə·fiz·əm), *n. Geol.* action of the forces which have caused the deformation of the earth's crust, producing continents, mountains, etc. [< Gk. *diastrophe* distortion < *dia-* apart + *strephein* twist] **—di·a·stroph·ic** (dī′ə·strof′ik), *adj.*

di·a·ther·my (dī′ə·thėr′mi), *n.* 1. method of treating diseases by heating the tissues beneath the skin with an electric current. 2. apparatus for doing this. [< F < Gk. *dia-* through + *therme* heat] —**di'a·ther'mic,** *adj.*

di·a·ton·ic (dī'ə·ton'ik), *adj. Music.* of or using the tones of a standard major or minor scale. [< L < Gk., < *dia–* through + *tonos* tone]

di·a·tribe (dī'ə·trīb), *n.* a bitter and violent denunciation of some person or thing. [< L < Gk. *diatribe* pastime, study, discourse < *dia-* away + *tribein* wear]

Dí·az, Di·az (dē'äs), *n.* Porfirio, 1830–1915, president of Mexico, 1877–1880, 1884–1911.

di·ba·sic (dī·bā'sik), *adj. Chem.* having two hydrogen atoms that can be replaced by two atoms or radicals of a base in forming salts.

dib·ble (dib'əl), *n., v.,* –bled, –bling. —*n.* a pointed tool for making holes in the ground for seeds, young plants, etc. —*v.* make a hole in (the ground) with or as with a dibble. —**dib'bler,** *n.*

dice (dīs), *n.pl., sing.* **die,** *v.,* **diced, dic·ing.** —*n.* 1. small cubes with a different number of spots (one to six) on each side, used in playing games and gambling. 2. game played with dice. 3. small cubes. —*v.* 1. play dice. 2. cut into small cubes. —**dic'er,** *n.*

di·chot·o·my (dī·kot'ə·mi), *n., pl.* –mies. 1. division into two parts. 2. branching by repeated divisions into two parts. [< L < Gk. *dichotomos* cut in half < *dicha* in two + *temnein* cut] —**di·chot'o·mous, di·chot·om·ic** (dī'kō·tom'ik), *adj.*

Dichotomy (def. 2)

di·chro·mat·ic (dī'krō·mat'ik), *adj.* 1. having two colors. 2. *Zool.* showing two color phases.

Dick·ens (dik'ənz), *n.* Charles, 1812–1870, English novelist.

dick·ens (dik'ənz), *n., interj.* devil.

dick·er (dik'ər), *Am.* —*v.* trade by barter or by petty bargaining; haggle. —*n.* a petty bargain. [< *dicker,* n., a lot of ten hides]

dick·ey, dick·y, or **dick·ie** (dik'i), *n., pl.* **dick·eys; dick·ies; dick·ies.** a shirt front that can be detached.

Dick·in·son (dik'ən·sən), *n.* Emily, 1830–1886, American poet.

di·cot·y·le·don (dī·kot'ə·lē'dən; dī'kot–), *n.* a flowering plant that has two seed leaves. —**di·cot'y·le'don·ous,** *adj.*

dict., 1. dictator. 2. dictionary.

dic·ta (dik'tə), *n.* pl. of dictum.

Dic·ta·phone (dik'tə·fōn), *n.* Trademark. instrument that records and reproduces words that are spoken into it. [< *dicta(te)* + *–phone*]

dic·tate (*v.* dik'tāt, dik·tāt'; *n.* dik'tāt), *v.,* –tat·ed, –tat·ing, *n.* —*v.* 1. say or read (something) aloud for another person or other persons to write down. 2. command with authority; give orders that must be obeyed. —*n.* direction or order that is to be carried out or obeyed. [< L *dictatus,* pp. of *dictare* say often < *dicere* tell, say] —Syn. *v.* 2. order, decree. —*n.* command.

dic·ta·tion (dik·tā'shən), *n.* 1. act of saying or reading (something) aloud for another person or persons to write down. 2. words said or read aloud to be written down. 3. act of commanding with authority. —**dic·ta'tion·al,** *adj.*

dic·ta·tor (dik'tā·tər; dik·tā'–), *n.* 1. person exercising absolute authority, esp. over a country. 2. one who dictates. —**dic'ta·tor·ship',** *n.*

dic·ta·to·ri·al (dik'tə·tô'ri·əl; –tō'–), *adj.* 1. of or like that of a dictator. 2. imperious; domineering; overbearing. —**dic'ta·to'ri·al·ly,** *adv.*

dic·tion (dik'shən), *n.* 1. manner of expressing ideas in words; style of speaking or writing. 2. manner of using the voice in speaking; the utterance or enunciation of words. ➤ Good diction means that the words of an article, book, speech, etc., seem to the reader or listener well chosen to convey the meanings or attitudes the writer or speaker wishes; faulty diction, that the words either fail to convey the meaning fully or accurately or do not satisfy the reader's or listener's expectation in some other way.

dic·tion·ar·y (dik'shən·er'i), *n., pl.* –ar·ies. book containing a selection of the words of a language or of some special subject, arranged alphabetically, with explanations of their meanings and other information about them. ➤ dictionaries. The most useful tool for a writer, in or out of a composition course, is a good dictionary. Nowhere else can he find so much information about words and their use and nowhere else, if he is really interested in his language, can he find so much curious, incidental, and even amusing information about words. The more he refers to his dictionary and browses in it, the more his powers of communication can grow. But dictionaries are primarily for reference. They answer questions about the meaning of words so that the student can read with more understanding. They settle doubts (or arguments) over single words. And they help a writer decide on the most accurate and effective word or phrase to use. A writer will use his dictionary most in the revision state and should get the habit of turning to it frequently while revising a paper and preparing the final copy. Obviously to get the most out of a dictionary, its owner needs to know what various matters it includes. He should look through its table of contents to see what units of material there are besides the main alphabetical list of words. He should read a page or two consecutively to see how words and phrases are handled, and he should try pronouncing some familiar words to see how the pronunciation key works. A few pains taken to learn a particular dictionary will be more than repaid by its increased usefulness.

Dic·to·graph (dik'tə·graf; –gräf), *n.* Trademark. telephone with a transmitter so sensitive that no mouthpiece is needed, used in secretly listening to or recording conversation.

dic·tum (dik'təm), *n., pl.* –tums, –ta (–tə). 1. a formal comment; authoritative opinion. 2. maxim; saying. [< L, (thing) said, pp. of *dicere* say]

did (did), *v.* pt. of do[1].

di·dac·tic (dī·dak'tik; di–), **di·dac·ti·cal** (–tə·kəl), *adj.* 1. intended to instruct. 2. inclined to instruct others; teacherlike. [< Gk. *didaktikos* < *didaskein* teach] —**di·dac'ti·cal·ly,** *adv.* —**di·dac'ti·cism,** *n.*

did·dle (did'əl), *v.,* –dled, –dling. *Colloq.* waste (time). —**did'dler,** *n.*

did·n't (did'ənt), did not.

Di·do (dī'dō), *n.* the legendary founder and queen of Carthage who killed herself when Aeneas left her.

di·do (dī'dō), *n., pl.* –dos, –does. *U.S. Colloq.* prank; trick.

didst (didst), *v. Archaic or Poetic.* did. "Thou didst" means "You did."

die[1] (dī), *v.,* **died, dy·ing.** 1. cease to live; stop living; become dead. 2. come to an end; lose force or strength; stop. 3. lose spiritual life. 4. suffer as if dying. 5. want very much; be very desirous. 6. die away or down, stop or end little by little; lose force or strength gradually. 7. die out, a. lose force or strength gradually. b. cease or end completely. [OE *diegan*]

die[2] (dī), *n., pl.* **dice** *for 1,* **dies** *for 2, v.,* **died, die·ing.** —*n.* 1. one of a set of dice. 2. any tool or apparatus for shaping, cutting, or stamping things. —*v.* to shape with a die. [< OF < L *datum* (thing) given (i.e., by fortune), pp. of *dare* give]

di·e·cious (dī·ē'shəs), *adj.* dioecious. —**di·e'cious·ly,** *adv.*

die-hard, die·hard (dī'härd'), *adj.* resisting to the very end; refusing to give in. —*n.* person who resists vigorously to the end.

di·e·lec·tric (dī'i·lek'trik), *adj.* conveying electricity otherwise than by conduction; nonconducting: *dry air is dielectric.* —*n.* a dielectric substance, such as glass, rubber, or wood. —**di'e·lec'tri·cal·ly,** *adv.*

Dien·bien·phu, Dien Bien Phu (dyen'byen'fü'), *n.* a fortified town in E Indo-China, in N Viet-Nam, taken by Communist Viet Minh soldiers in May, 1954 from the French.

di·er·e·sis (dī·er'ə·sis), *n., pl.* –ses (–sēz). two dots (··) placed over the second of two consecutive vowels to indicate that the second vowel is to be pronounced in a separate syllable, as in coöperate. Also, diaeresis. [< LL < Gk. *diairesis* separation, division < *dia-* apart + *haireein* take] —di·e·ret·ic (dī'ə·ret'ik), adj. > dieresis. A hyphen is often used instead of a dieresis to indicate that the vowels are to be kept separate, especially in words with *re-* (*re-enlist*). There is a tendency now not to use either dieresis or hyphen in the more commonly used words, so that *cooperation, zoology* are now common.

Die·sel engine or **motor** (dē'zəl; -səl), an internal-combustion engine that burns oil with heat caused by the compression of air.

die·sink·er (dī'singk'ər), n. person who makes dies for shaping or stamping. —die'-sink'ing, n.

Di·es I·rae (dī'ēz ī'rē; dē'ās ē'rī), a medieval Latin hymn describing the judgment day. [< L, day of wrath]

di·et¹ (dī'ət), n., v., -et·ed, -et·ing. —n. 1. the usual food and drink for a person or animal. 2. a special selection of food and drink eaten during sickness, or to gain or lose weight. —v. keep to a diet. [< OF < L < Gk. *diaita* way of life] —di'et·er, n.

di·et² (dī'ət), n. 1. a formal assembly. 2. the national lawmaking body in certain countries. [< Med.L *dieta* day's work, session of councilors, ult. identical with *diet¹* but infl. by L *dies* day]

di·e·tar·y (dī'ə·ter'i), adj., n., pl. -tar·ies. —adj. having to do with diet. —n. system of diet.

di·e·tet·ic (dī'ə·tet'ik), **di·e·tet·i·cal** (-ə·kəl), adj. having to do with diet. —di'e·tet'i·cal·ly, adv.

di·e·tet·ics (dī'ə·tet'iks), n. science that deals with the amount and kinds of food needed by the body.

di·e·ti·tian, di·e·ti·cian (dī'ə·tish'ən), n. person trained to plan meals that have the proper proportion of various kinds of food.

dif·fer (dif'ər), v. 1. be unlike; be different. 2. have or express a different opinion; disagree. 3. differ from, a. be unlike; disagree. b. vary. [< F < L *differre* set apart, differ < *dis-* apart + *ferre* carry] —Syn. 2. dissent. —Ant. 2. agree, concur.

dif·fer·ence (dif'ər·əns; dif'rəns), n., v., -enced, -enc·ing. —n. 1. condition of being different. 2. way of being different; point in which people or things are different. 3. amount by which one quantity is different from another. 4. condition of having a different opinion; disagreement. 5. dispute. —v. make different. —Syn. n. 1. variance, disparity, distinction.

dif·fer·ent (dif'ər·ənt; dif'rənt), adj. 1. not alike; not like. 2. not the same; separate; distinct. 3. not like others or most others; unusual. —dif'fer·ent·ly, adv. —Syn. 1. dissimilar, unlike. > different. The formal American idiom with *different* is *from: His second book was entirely different from his first.* Informal usage is divided, using *from* occasionally, sometimes *to* (which is the common British idiom), and more often *than: She was different than any other girl he had ever known. Different than* is becoming more common when the object is a clause.

dif·fer·en·tial (dif'ər·en'shəl), adj. 1. of a difference; showing a difference; depending on a difference. 2. distinguishing; distinctive. 3. pertaining to distinguishing characteristics or specific differences. 4. *Math.* pertaining to or involving differentials: *differential calculus.* 5. *Physics.* concerning the difference of two or more motions, pressures, etc. —n. 1. a differential duty or rate; the difference involved. 2. *Math.* an infinitesimal difference between consecutive values of a variable quantity. 3. arrangement of gears in an automobile that allows one of the rear wheels to turn faster than the other in going round a corner or curve. —dif'fer·en'tial·ly, adv.

dif·fer·en·ti·ate (dif'ər·en'shi·āt), v., -at·ed, -at·ing. 1. make different. 2. become different. 3. perceive the difference in; make a distinction between. 4. note differences. 5. *Math.* obtain the differential of. —dif'fer·en'ti·a'tion, n. —dif'fer·en'ti·a'tor, n.

dif·fi·cult (dif'ə·kult; -kəlt), adj. 1. hard to understand. 2. hard to deal with, get along with, or please. —dif'fi·cult·ly, adv. —Syn. 1. arduous. 2. trying. —Ant. 1. easy, simple.

dif·fi·cul·ty (dif'ə·kul'ti; -kəl·ti), n., pl. -ties. 1. fact or condition of being difficult. 2. hard work; much effort. 3. trouble. 4. financial trouble. 5. thing that is difficult; thing in the way; obstacle. 6. disagreement; quarrel. [< L *difficultas < difficilis* hard < *dis-* + *facilis* easy] —Syn. 3. hardship, dilemma, predicament. 5. hindrance. 6. controversy.

dif·fi·dent (dif'ə·dənt), adj. lacking in self-confidence; shy. —dif'fi·dence, n. —dif'fi·dent·ly, adv. [< L, ult. < *dis-* + *fidere* trust]

dif·fract (di·frakt'), v. break up by diffraction. [< L *diffractus < dis-* up + *frangere* break]

dif·frac·tion (di·frak'shən), n. *Physics.* 1. a breaking up of a ray of light into a series of light and dark bands or into colored bands of the spectrum. 2. a similar breaking up of sound waves, electricity, etc.

dif·frac·tive (di·frak'tiv), adj. causing or pertaining to diffraction. —dif·frac'tive·ly, adv. —dif·frac'tive·ness, n.

dif·fuse (v. di·fūz'; adj. di·fūs'), v., -fused, -fus·ing, adj. —v. 1. spread out so as to cover a larger space or surface; scatter widely. 2. mix together by spreading into one another, as gases and liquids do. —adj. 1. not drawn together at a single point; spread out. 2. using many words where a few would do. [< L *diffusus < dis-* in every direction + *fundere* pour] —dif·fuse·ly (di·fūs'li), adv. —dif·fuse'ness, n. —dif·fus·er, dif·fu·sor (di·fūz'ər), n. —Syn. v. 1. disseminate, disperse. —adj. 1. widespread, scattered, dispersed. 2. wordy. —Ant. adj. 1. compact.

dif·fu·sion (di·fū'zhən), n. 1. act or fact of diffusing. 2. a being widely spread or scattered; diffused condition. 3. a mixing together of the molecules of gases, etc. by spreading into one another. 4. use of too many words; wordiness.

dif·fu·sive (di·fū'siv), adj. 1. tending to diffuse. 2. showing diffusion. 3. using too many words; wordy. —dif·fu'sive·ly, adv. —dif·fu'sive·ness, n.

dig (dig), v., dug or (*Archaic*) digged, dig·ging, n. —v. 1. use a shovel, spade, hands, claws, or snout in making a hole or in turning over the ground. 2. break up and turn over (ground) with a spade, etc. 3. make (a hole, cellar, etc.) by moving material. 4. make a way by digging. 5. get by digging: *dig clams.* 6. make a careful search or inquiry (for information or into some author). 7. *Am., Colloq.* study hard. 8. *Am., Slang.* understand; comprehend. 9. dig in, *Colloq.* a. dig trenches for protection. b. *Am.* work hard. 10. dig into, *Colloq.* work hard at. 11. dig up, a. *Am., Colloq.* bring to light; produce. b. excavate. —n. 1. act of digging. 2. *Colloq.* a thrust or poke; a sarcastic remark. [ME *dygge(n)*, prob. < F *diguer* < Gmc.] —Syn. v. 1. delve, spade, grub.

di·gest (v. də·jest', dī-; n. dī'jest), v. 1. change (food) in the stomach and intestines so that the body can absorb it. 2. undergo this process. 3. promote such change in (food). 4. understand and absorb mentally; make part of one's thoughts. 5. condense and arrange according to some system; summarize. 6. *Chem.* soften by heat or moisture; dissolve. —n. information condensed and arranged according to some system; summary: *a digest of law.* [< L *digestus*, pp. of *digerere* separate, dissolve < *dis-* apart + *gerere* carry] —di·gest'er, n. —Syn. v. 4. assimilate.

di·gest·i·ble (də·jes'tə·bəl; dī-), adj. capable of being digested; easily digested. —di·gest'i·bil'i·ty, n.

di·ges·tion (də·jes'chən; dī-), n. 1. the digesting of food. 2. ability to digest. 3. act of digesting.

di·ges·tive (də·jes'tiv; dī-), adj. 1. of or for digestion. 2. helping digestion. —n. something that aids digestion.

dig·ger (dig'ər), n. 1. person that digs. 2. the part of a machine that turns up the ground. 3. any tool for digging.

dig·gings (dig′ingz), n.pl. **1.** mine or place where digging is being done. **2.** Esp. Brit. Colloq. place to live.

dig·it (dij′it), n. **1.** finger or toe. **2.** any of the figures 0, 1, 2, 3, 4, 5, 6, 7, 8, 9. Sometimes 0 is not called a digit. [< L digitus finger]

dig·it·al (dij′ə-təl), adj. of a digit or digits. —n. key of an organ, piano, etc., played with the fingers. —dig′it·al·ly, adv.

digital computer, a calculating machine which uses numbers, esp. simple numbers on a binary basis, to solve problems capable of expression in mathematical terms.

dig·i·tal·is (dij′ə-tal′is; -tā′lis), n. **1.** medicine used for stimulating the heart, obtained from the leaves and seeds of the foxglove. **2.** foxglove. [< L, < digitus finger; from shape of corolla]

dig·i·tate (dij′ə-tāt), **dig·i·tat·ed** (-tāt′id), adj. **1.** having fingers or toes. **2.** having radiating divisions like fingers. —dig′i·tate·ly, adv.

dig·ni·fied (dig′nə-fīd), adj. having dignity; noble; stately. —dig′ni·fied′ly, adv.

dig·ni·fy (dig′nə-fī), v., -fied, -fy·ing. **1.** give dignity to; make noble, worth-while, or worthy. **2.** give a high-sounding name to. [< OF < L, < dignus worthy + facere make]

dig·ni·tar·y (dig′nə-ter′i), n., pl. -tar·ies. person who has a position of honor.

dig·ni·ty (dig′nə-ti), n., pl. -ties. **1.** proud and self-respecting character or manner; stateliness. **2.** degree of worth, honor, or importance. **3.** a high office, rank, or title. **4.** person of high office, rank, or title. **5.** such persons as a group. **6.** worth; nobleness. [< OF < L, < dignus worthy]

dig·raph (dī′graf; -gräf), n. two letters used together to spell a single sound, as ea in each or head. —di·graph′ic, adj.

di·gress (də-gres′; dī-), v. turn aside; get off the main subject in talking or writing. [< L digressus < dis- aside + gradi to step]

di·gres·sion (də-gresh′ən; dī-), n. a turning aside; a getting off the main subject in talking or writing. —di·gres′sion·al, adj.

di·gres·sive (də-gres′iv; dī-), adj. tending to digress; digressing. —di·gres′sive·ly, adv. —di·gres′sive·ness, n.

di·he·dral (dī·hē′drəl), adj. **1.** having two plane surfaces. **2.** formed by two plane surfaces. **3.** making a dihedral angle. **4.** of an airplane, having important nonhorizontal surfaces. —n. the figure formed by two intersecting plane surfaces. [< Gk. di- two + hedra seat] —di·he′dral·ly, adv.

A dihedral angle is included between the planes ABCD and ABMN.

dike (dīk), n., v., diked, dik·ing. —n. **1.** a bank of earth or a dam built as a defense against flooding by a river or the sea. **2.** ditch or channel for water. **3.** bank of earth thrown up in digging. **4.** a low wall of earth or stone; causeway. **5.** Geol. a fissure in a stratum filled with deposited matter. —v. **1.** provide with dikes. **2.** drain with a ditch or channel for water. Also, dyke. [< Scand. dīk; akin to DITCH] —dik′er, n.

Di·lan·tin (dī·lan′tin), n. Trademark. a white, powdery drug, $C_{15}H_{11}N_2O_2Na$, used in controlling epilepsy.

di·lap·i·dat·ed (də·lap′ə·dāt′id), adj. falling to pieces; partly ruined or decayed through neglect. [< L dilapidatus, pp. of dilapidare lay low (with stones) < dis- (intensive) + lapidare to stone < lapis stone]

di·lap·i·da·tion (də·lap′ə·dā′shən), n. a falling to pieces; decayed condition.

dil·a·ta·tion (dil′ə·tā′shən; dī′lə-), n. dilation.

di·late (dī·lāt′; də-), v., -lat·ed, -lat·ing. **1.** make or become larger or wider. **2.** speak or write in a very complete or detailed manner. **3.** set forth at length. [< L, < dis- apart + latus wide] —di·lat′a·ble, adj. —di·la′tor, n.

di·la·tion (dī·lā′shən; də-), n. **1.** act of dilating; enlargement; widening. **2.** dilated condition. **3.** a dilated part.

dil·a·to·ry (dil′ə·tô′ri; -tō′-), adj. **1.** tending to delay; not prompt. **2.** causing delay. —dil′a·to′ri·ly, adv. —dil′a·to′ri·ness, n.

di·lem·ma (də-lem′ə; dī-), n. **1.** situation requiring a choice between two evils. **2.** any perplexing situation; a difficult choice. **3.** argument forcing an opponent to choose one of two alternatives equally unfavorable to him. [< LL < Gk., < di- two + lemma premise]

dil·et·tan·te (dil′ə·tan′tē; -tänt′), n., pl. -tes, -ti (-tē), adj. —n. **1.** lover of the fine arts. **2.** person who follows some art or science as an amusement or in a trifling way. **3.** trifler. —adj. having to do with dilettantes. [< Ital., < dilettare DELIGHT] —dil′et·tant′ish, adj. —dil′et·tant′ism, n.

dil·i·gence[1] (dil′ə·jəns), n. a working hard; careful effort; being diligent; industry. [< F < L diligentia, from DILIGENT.]

dil·i·gence[2] (dil′ə·jəns), n. a public stage-coach formerly used in some parts of Europe. [special use of diligence[1]]

dil·i·gent (dil′ə·jənt), adj. **1.** hard-working; industrious. **2.** careful and steady. [< L diligens, ppr. of diligere value highly, love < dis- apart + legere choose] —dil′i·gent·ly, adv.

dill (dil), n. **1.** spicy seeds or leaves used to flavor pickles. **2.** plant that they grow on. [OE dile]

dill pickle, Am. a cucumber pickle flavored with dill.

dil·ly-dal·ly (dil′i·dal′i), v., -lied, -ly·ing. waste time; loiter; trifle.

di·lute (də·lüt′; dī-), v., -lut·ed, -lut·ing, adj. —v. **1.** make weaker or thinner by adding water or some other liquid. **2.** weaken; lessen. **3.** become diluted. —adj. weakened or thinned by the addition of water or other liquid. [< L, < dis- apart + luere wash] —di·lute′ness, n.

di·lu·tion (də·lü′shən; dī-), n. **1.** act of diluting. **2.** fact or state of being diluted. **3.** something diluted.

di·lu·vi·al (də·lü′vi·əl; dī-), **di·lu·vi·an** (-ən), adj. of, having to do with, or caused by a flood. [< L, < diluvium DELUGE]

dim (dim), adj., dim·mer, dim·mest, v., dimmed, dim·ming. —adj. **1.** not bright; not clear; not distinct. **2.** not clearly seen, heard, or understood. **3.** not seeing, hearing, or understanding clearly. —v. make or become dim. [OE dimm] —dim′ly, adv. —dim′ness, n.

dim., dimin., 1. diminuendo. **2.** diminutive.

dime (dīm), n. Am. a silver coin of the United States and of Canada, worth 10 cents. [< OF < L decima (pars) tenth (part) < decem ten]

dime novel, Am. a sensational story that has no literary merit.

di·men·sion (də·men′shən), n. **1.** measurement of length, breadth, or thickness. **2.** size; extent. [< F < L dimensio < dis- out + metiri measure] —di·men′sion·al, adj. —di·men′sion·less, adj.

dime store, Am. store handling a large variety of low-priced commodities.

di·min·ish (də·min′ish), v. **1.** make or become smaller in size, amount, or importance; lessen; reduce. **2.** lessen in esteem; degrade. **3.** cause to taper. **4.** Music. lessen (an interval) by a half step. [blend of diminue (< L, < dis- (intensive) + minuere lessen) and minish (< OF < VL minutiare, ult. < L minutus small)] —di·min′ish·a·ble, adj.

di·min·u·en·do (də·min′yù·en′dō), n., pl. -dos, adj., adv. Music. —n. **1.** a gradual lessening of loudness. **2.** passage to be played or sung with a diminuendo. —adj., adv. with a diminuendo. [< Ital., ppr. of diminuire diminish]

dim·i·nu·tion (dim′ə·nü′shən; -nū′-), n. a diminishing; a lessening; decrease.

di·min·u·tive (də·min′yə·tiv), adj. **1.** small; tiny. **2.** Gram. expressing smallness or affection. —n. **1.** a small person or thing. **2.** Gram. word or part of a word expressing smallness. The suffixes -let and -kin are diminutives. —di·min′u·tive·ly, adv. —di·min′u·tive·ness, n.

dim·i·ty (dim′ə·ti), n., pl. -ties. a thin cotton cloth woven with heavy threads at intervals in striped or crossbarred arrangement, used for dresses, curtains, etc. [< Ital. < Gk. *dimitos* of double thread < *di-* double + *mitos* warp thread]

dim·mer (dim′ər), *n.* **1.** person or thing that dims. **2.** device that dims an electric light or automobile headlight.

dim·out (dim′out′), *n.* a lessening or concealment of light at night.

dim·ple (dim′pəl), *n., v.,* -pled, -pling. —*n.* **1.** a small hollow, usually in the cheek or chin. **2.** any small, hollow place. —*v.* **1.** make or show dimples in. **2.** form dimples. [ME *dympull*]

din (din), *n., v.,* dinned, din·ning. —*n.* a loud, confused noise that lasts. —*v.* **1.** make a din. **2.** strike with din. **3.** say over and over. [OE *dynn*]

dine (dīn), *v.,* dined, din·ing. **1.** eat dinner. **2.** give a dinner to or for. **3.** dine out, eat dinner away from home. [< F *dîner* < VL *disjejunare* to breakfast < *dis-* + *jejunium* fast]

din·er (dīn′ər), *n.* **1.** person who is eating dinner. **2.** *Am.* a railroad car in which meals are served. **3.** *Am.* restaurant shaped like such a car.

di·nette (dī-net′), *n. Am.* a small dining room.

ding (ding), *v.* **1.** make a sound like a bell; ring continuously. **2.** *Colloq.* say over and over. —*n.* sound made by a bell. [imit.]

ding-dong (ding′dông′; -dong′), *n.* sound made by a bell or anything like a bell; continuous ringing. [imit.]

din·ghy, din·gey, or **din·gy** (ding′gi), *n., pl.* -ghies; -geys; -gies. **1.** a small rowboat. **2.** a small boat used as a tender by a large boat. [< Hind. *dingī*]

din·gy (din′ji), *adj.,* -gi·er, -gi·est. dirty-looking; not bright and fresh; dull. —din′gi·ly, *adv.* —din′gi·ness, *n.*

dining car, *Am.* a railroad car in which meals are served.

dining room, room in which meals are served.

dink·ey (dingk′i), *n., pl.* dink·eys. *Am.* a small locomotive, used for pulling freight cars, hauling logs, etc.

dink·y (dingk′i), *adj.,* dink·i·er, dink·i·est. *Slang.* small; insignificant.

din·ner (din′ər), *n.* **1.** the main meal of the day. **2.** a formal meal in honor of some person or occasion. [< F *dîner* dine; inf. used as n.]

di·no·saur (dī′nə·sôr), *n.* any of a group of extinct reptiles. [< NL < Gk. *deinos* terrible + *sauros* lizard]

dint (dint), *n.* **1.** force. **2.** dent. —*v.* dent. [OE *dynt*] —dint′less, *adj.*

di·oc·e·san (dī-os′ə·sən; dī′ə·sē′sən), *adj.* of or having to do with a diocese. —*n.* bishop of a diocese.

di·o·cese (dī′ə·sis; -sēs), *n.* district over which a bishop has authority. [< OF < LL < L < Gk. *dioikesis* province, diocese]

di·oe·cious (dī-ē′shəs), *adj. Biol.* having male and female flowers in separate plants. Also, **diecious.** [< NL *dioecia* < Gk. *di-* double + *oikos* house] —di·oe′cious·ly, *adv.*

Di·og·e·nes (dī-oj′ə·nēz), *n.* 412?-323 B.C., Greek Cynic philosopher.

Di·o·ny·si·us (dī′ə·nish′i·əs; -nis′i-), *n.* 430?-367 B.C., ruler of the ancient Greek city of Syracuse.

Di·o·ny·sus, Di·o·ny·sos (dī′ə·nī′səs), *n.* Greek god of wine; Bacchus. —Di·o·ny·sian (dī′ə·nish′ən; -nis′i·ən), *adj.*

di·o·ram·a (dī′ə·ram′ə; -rä′mə), *n.* picture that is usually looked at through a small opening. It is lighted in such a way as to be very realistic. [< F < Gk. *dia-* through + *horama* sight]

di·ox·ide (dī-ok′sīd; -sid), **di·ox·id** (-sid), *n. Chem.* oxide containing two atoms of oxygen and one of a metal or other element.

dip (dip), *v.,* dipped or dipt, dip·ping, *n.* —*v.* **1.** put under water or any liquid and lift quickly out again. **2.** go under water and come quickly out again. **3.** dye in a liquid. **4.** make wet; immerse. **5.** make (a candle) by putting a wick into hot tallow or wax. **6.** take up in the hollow

of the hand or with a pail, pan, or other container. **7.** put (one's hand, a spoon, etc.) into to take out something. **8.** lower and raise again quickly: *the flag is dipped as a kind of salute.* **9.** make a curtsy. **10.** sink or drop down: *a bird dips in its flight.* **11.** sink or drop down but rise again soon. **12.** slope downward. **13.** dip into, read or look at for a short time; glance at. —*n.* **1.** a dipping of any kind, esp. a plunge into and out of a tub of water, the sea, etc. **2.** mixture in which to dip something. **3.** candle made by dipping. **4.** that which is taken out or up by dipping. **5.** a sudden drop. **6.** a sudden drop followed by a rise. **7.** amount of slope down; angle made with a horizontal plane. **8.** *Slang.* pickpocket. [OE *dyppan*]

diph·the·ri·a (dif-thir′i·ə; dip-), *n.* a dangerous, infectious disease of the throat, usually accompanied by a high fever and formation of membranes that hinder breathing. [< F < Gk. *diphthera* hide]

diph·the·rit·ic (dif′thə·rit′ik; dip′-), **diph·the·ri·al** (-thir′i·əl), *adj.* **1.** of diphtheria; like diphtheria. **2.** suffering from diphtheria.

diph·thong (dif′thông; -thong; dip′-), *n.* a vowel sound made up of two identifiable vowel sounds in immediate sequence and pronounced in one syllable, as *oi* in *point*. [< F < LL < Gk., < *di-* double + *phthongos* sound] —diph·thong′-al, *adj.* ➤ Sometimes a diphthong is represented by only one letter, as *i* in *ice.* The commonest English diphthongs are: ī (ä + ĭ), oi (ō + ĭ), ou (ä + ŭ), and ū (ĭ[y] + ŭ).

di·plo·ma (di·plō′mə), *n., pl.* -mas, -ma·ta (-mə·tə). **1.** certificate given by a school, college, or university to its graduating students. **2.** any certificate that bestows certain rights, privileges, honors, etc. [< L < Gk., paper folded double, ult. < *diploos* double]

di·plo·ma·cy (di·plō′mə·si), *n., pl.* -cies. **1.** management of relations between nations. **2.** skill in managing such relations. **3.** skill in dealing with others; tact. [< F, < *diplomate* diplomat]

dip·lo·mat (dip′lə·mat), *esp. Brit.* **di·plo·ma·tist** (di·plō′mə·tist), *n.* **1.** representative of a nation who is located in a foreign country to look after the interests of his own nation in the foreign country. **2.** a tactful person.

dip·lo·mat·ic (dip′lə·mat′ik), *adj.* **1.** of or having to do with diplomacy. **2.** skillful in dealing with others; tactful. —dip′lo·mat′i·cal·ly, *adv.*

dip·per (dip′ər), *n.* **1.** person or thing that dips. **2.** *Am.* a long-handled cup or larger vessel for dipping water or other liquids. **3. Dipper,** *Am.* either of two groups of stars in the northern sky somewhat resembling the shape of a dipper; Big Dipper or Little Dipper.

dip·so·ma·ni·a (dip′sə·mā′ni·ə), *n.* an abnormal, uncontrollable craving for alcoholic liquor. [< NL < Gk. *dipsa* thirst + *mania* mania]

dip·so·ma·ni·ac (dip′sə·mā′ni·ak), *n.* person who has dipsomania.

dipt (dipt), *v.* pt. and pp. of dip.

dip·ter·ous (dip′tər·əs), *adj.* **1.** *Bot.* having two winglike parts. **2.** belonging to the order including mosquitoes, gnats, and houseflies, characterized by one pair of membranous wings. [< L < Gk., < *di-* two + *pteron* wing]

dire (dīr), *adj.,* dir·er, dir·est. causing great fear or suffering; dreadful. [< L *dirus*] —dire′ly, *adv.* —dire′ness, *n.*

di·rect (də·rekt′; dī-), *v.* **1.** manage; control; guide. **2.** give orders; order; command. **3.** tell or show the way; give information about where to go, what to do, etc. **4.** point (to); aim (at). **5.** put the address on (a letter, package, etc.). **6.** address (words, etc.) to a person. **7.** turn (a thing) straight to. —*adj.* **1.** proceeding in a straight line; straight. **2.** in an unbroken line of descent. **3.** immediate. **4.** without anyone or anything in between; not through others: *a direct tax.* **5.** straightforward; frank; plain; truthful. **6.** exact; absolute: *the direct opposite.* —*adv.* directly. [< L *directus,* pp. of *dirigere* set straight < *dis-* apart + *regere* guide] —di·rect′-

ness, *n.* ❭ **direct address.** The name or descriptive term by which a person or persons are addressed in speaking, reading, or writing: *My friends, I wish you would forget this night. That's all right, Mrs. Williams, you may come in.* As these examples show, the person or persons addressed are separated from the rest of the sentence by a comma or commas.

direct current, *Elect.* a steady current that flows in one direction.

di·rec·tion (də·rek'shən; dī–), *n.* **1.** guidance; management; control: *the direction of a play or movie.* **2.** order; command. **3.** a knowing or telling what to do, how to do, where to go, etc.; instruction. **4.** address on a letter or package. **5.** course taken by a moving body, such as a ball or a bullet. **6.** any way in which one may face or point. **7.** line of action; tendency.

di·rec·tion·al (də·rek'shən·əl; dī–), *adj.* **1.** of or having to do with direction in space. **2.** fitted for determining the direction from which signals come, or for signaling in one direction only.

di·rect·ly (də·rekt'li; dī–), *adv.* **1.** in a direct line or manner; straight. **2.** *Esp. Brit.* immediately; at once.

direct object, a grammatical term denoting the person or thing upon which the verb directly acts.

di·rec·tor (də·rek'tər; dī–), *n.* **1.** person who directs, esp. one who directs the production of a play or motion picture. **2.** one of the persons chosen to direct the affairs of a company or institution. —**di·rec·to·ri·al** (di·rek'tô'ri·əl; -tō'-; dī'rek-), *adj.* —**di·rec'tor·ship,** *n.*

di·rec·tor·ate (də·rek'tər·it; dī–), *n.* **1.** position of a director. **2.** group of directors.

di·rec·to·ry (də·rek'tə·ri; -tri; dī–), *n., pl.* -ries, *adj.* —*n.* **1.** book of names and addresses. **2.** book of rules or instructions. **3.** group of directors; directorate. —*adj.* directing; advisory.

direct primary, election in which the voters of a political party choose the candidates of their party for office.

direct tax, tax demanded of the very persons who must pay it, as a poll tax, income tax, etc.

dire·ful (dīr'fəl), *adj.* dire; dreadful; terrible. —**dire'ful·ly,** *adv.* —**dire'ful·ness,** *n.*

dirge (dérj), *n.* a funeral song or tune. [contraction of L *dirige* DIRECT (imperative of *dirigere*), first word in office for the dead]

dir·i·gi·ble (dir'ə·jə·bəl; də·rij'ə-), *n.* balloon that can be steered. —*adj.* capable of being directed. [< L *dirigere* to DIRECT] —**dir'i·gi·bil'i·ty,** *n.*

dirk (dérk), *n.* dagger. —*v.* stab with a dirk.

dirn·dl (dérn'dəl), *n.* **1.** an Alpine peasant girl's costume consisting of a blouse, a tight bodice, and a full skirt. **2.** dress imitating it. [< South G dial., girl, dim. of *dirne* maid]

dirt (dért), *n.* **1.** mud, dust, earth, or anything like them. **2.** loose earth; soil. **3.** *Mining.* earth, gravel, or other refuse. **4.** unclean action, thought, or speech. **5.** uncleanness; meanness. [ME *drit,* ? short for OE *dríting* excrement]

dirt-cheap (dért'chēp'), *adj.* very cheap.

dirt farmer, *Am., Colloq.* person who has practical experience in doing his own farming.

dirt·y (dér'ti), *adj.* dirt·i·er, dirt·i·est, *v.,* dirt·ied, dirt·y·ing. —*adj.* **1.** soiled by dirt; unclean. **2.** not clear or pure in color; clouded. **3.** low; mean; vile. **4.** unclean in action, thought, or speech. **5.** causing a great amount of radioactive fall-out: *dirty bombs.* **6.** stormy; windy. —*v.* make dirty; soil. —**dirt'i·ly,** *adv.* —**dirt'i·ness,** *n.*

Dis (dis), *n. Roman Myth.* **1.** god of the lower world, identified with the Greek god Pluto. **2.** the lower world; Hades.

dis-, *prefix.* **1.** opposite of, as in *discontent.* **2.** reverse of, as in *disentangle.* **3.** apart; away, as in *dispel.* [< L; also, *di-, dif-*]

dis·a·bil·i·ty (dis'ə·bil'ə·ti), *n., pl.* -ties. **1.** a disabled condition. **2.** something that disables. **3.** something that disqualifies.

dis·a·ble (dis·ā'bəl), *v.,* -bled, -bling. **1.** deprive of ability or power; make useless; cripple. **2.** disqualify legally. —**dis·a'ble·ment,** *n.*

dis·a·buse (dis'ə·būz'), *v.,* -bused, -bus·ing. free from deception or error.

dis·ad·van·tage (dis'əd·van'tij; -vän'-), *n., v.,* -taged, -tag·ing. —*n.* **1.** lack of advantage; unfavorable condition: *a deaf person is at a disadvantage in school.* **2.** loss; injury. —*v.* subject to a disadvantage.

dis·ad·van·ta·geous (dis·ad'vən·tā'jəs; dis'ad-), *adj.* causing disadvantage; unfavorable. —**dis·ad'van·ta'geous·ly,** *adv.* —**dis·ad'van·ta'geous·ness,** *n.*

dis·af·fect (dis'ə·fekt'), *v.* make unfriendly, disloyal, or discontented. —**dis'af·fec'tion,** *n.*

dis·af·fect·ed (dis'ə·fek'tid), *adj.* unfriendly; disloyal; discontented.

dis·a·gree (dis'ə·grē'), *v.,* -greed, -gree·ing. **1.** fail to agree; differ. **2.** quarrel; dispute. **3.** have a bad effect; be harmful.

dis·a·gree·a·ble (dis'ə·grē'ə·bəl), *adj.* **1.** not to one's liking; unpleasant. **2.** bad-tempered; cross. —**dis'a·gree'a·ble·ness,** *n.* —**dis'a·gree'a·bly,** *adv.*

dis·a·gree·ment (dis'ə·grē'mənt), *n.* **1.** failure to agree; difference of opinion. **2.** quarrel; dispute. **3.** difference; unlikeness.

dis·al·low (dis'ə·lou'), *v.* refuse to allow; deny the truth or value of; reject. —**dis'al·low'ance,** *n.*

dis·ap·pear (dis'ə·pir'), *v.* **1.** pass from sight. **2.** pass from existence; be lost. —**dis'ap·pear'ance,** *n.*

dis·ap·point (dis'ə·point'), *v.* **1.** fail to satisfy or please; leave (one) wanting or expecting something. **2.** fail to keep a promise to. **3.** keep from happening; oppose and defeat.

dis·ap·point·ment (dis'ə·point'mənt), *n.* **1.** state of being or feeling disappointed. **2.** person or thing that causes disappointment. **3.** act or fact of disappointing.

dis·ap·pro·ba·tion (dis'ap·rə·bā'shən), *n.* disapproval.

dis·ap·prov·al (dis'ə·prüv'əl), *n.* **1.** opinion or feeling against; expression of an opinion against; dislike. **2.** refusal to consent; rejection.

dis·ap·prove (dis'ə·prüv'), *v.,* -proved, -proving. **1.** have or express an opinion against. **2.** show dislike (of). **3.** refuse consent to; reject. —**dis'ap·prov'ing·ly,** *adv.*

dis·arm (dis·ärm'), *v.* **1.** take weapons away from. **2.** stop having an army and navy; reduce or limit the size of an army, navy, etc. **3.** remove suspicion from; make friendly; calm the anger of. **4.** make harmless.

dis·ar·ma·ment (dis·är'mə·mənt), *n.* **1.** act of disarming. **2.** reduction or limitation of armies, navies, and their equipment.

dis·ar·range (dis'ə·rānj'), *v.,* -ranged, -ranging. disturb the arrangement of; put out of order. —**dis'ar·range'ment,** *n.*

dis·ar·ray (dis'ə·rā'), *n.* **1.** disorder; confusion. **2.** disorder of clothing. —*v.* **1.** put into disorder or confusion. **2.** undress; strip.

dis·as·sem·ble (dis'ə·sem'bəl), *v.,* -bled, -bling. take apart. —**dis'as·sem'bly,** *n.*

dis·as·ter (di·zas'tər; -zäs'-), *n.* event that causes much suffering or loss; great misfortune. [< F < Ital. < L *dis-* without + *astrum* star < Gk. *astron*]

dis·as·trous (di·zas'trəs; -zäs'-), *adj.* bringing disaster; causing great danger, suffering, loss, etc. —**dis·as'trous·ly,** *adv.*

dis·a·vow (dis'ə·vou'), *v.* deny that one knows about, approves of, or is responsible for; disclaim. —**dis'a·vow'al,** *n.* —**dis'a·vow'er,** *n.*

dis·band (dis·band'), *v.* **1.** disperse; scatter. **2.** dismiss from service. —**dis·band'ment,** *n.*

dis·bar (dis·bär'), *v.,* -barred, -bar·ring. *Law.* deprive (a lawyer) of the right to practice law. —**dis·bar'ment,** *n.*

dis·be·lief (dis'bi·lēf'), *n.* lack of belief; refusal to believe.

dis·be·lieve (dis'bi·lēv'), *v.,* -lieved, -liev·ing. have no belief in. —**dis'be·liev'er,** *n.*

dis·bur·den (dis·bér'dən), *v.* **1.** relieve of a burden. **2.** get rid of (a burden). —**dis·bur'den·ment,** *n.*

dis·burse (dis·bérs'), *v.,* -bursed, -burs·ing. pay out; expend. [< OF, < *des-* (< L *dis-*) +

bourse purse < LL *bursa* < Gk. *byrsa* leather, wineskin] —dis·burs′a·ble, *adj.* —dis·burse′-ment, *n.* —dis·burs′er, *n.*

disc (disk), *n.* disk.

dis·card (*v.* dis·kärd′; *n.* dis′kärd), *v.* **1.** give up as useless or worn out; throw aside. **2.** get rid of (useless or unwanted playing cards) by throwing them aside or playing them. **3.** throw out an unwanted card. —*n.* **1.** act of throwing aside as useless. **2.** thing thrown aside as useless or not wanted. **3.** unwanted cards thrown aside; card played as useless. [see DIS-, CARD]

dis·cern (di·zėrn′; -sėrn′), *v.* **1.** perceive; see clearly. **2.** recognize as distinct or different; distinguish. [< F < L, < *dis-* off + *cernere* separate] —dis·cern′er, *n.* —dis·cern′i·ble, *adj.* —dis·cern′i·bly, *adv.*

dis·cern·ing (di·zėr′ning; -sėr′-), *adj.* shrewd; acute; discriminating. —dis·cern′ing·ly, *adv.*

dis·cern·ment (di·zėrn′mənt; -sėrn′-), *n.* **1.** keenness in perceiving and understanding; good judgment; shrewdness. **2.** act of discerning.

dis·charge (*v.* dis·chärj′; *n. also* dis′chärj), *v.,* -charged, -charg·ing, *n.* —*v.* **1.** unload (a ship); unload (cargo) from a ship; unload. **2.** fire; shoot: *discharge a gun.* **3.** release; let go; dismiss; get rid of: *discharge a servant.* **4.** come or pour forth. **5.** rid of an electric charge; withdraw electricity from. **6.** pay (a debt, etc.). **7.** perform (a duty). **8.** *Law.* cancel or set aside (a court order). —*n.* **1.** an unloading. **2.** a firing off of a gun, a blast, etc. **3.** a release; a letting go; a dismissing. **4.** writing that shows a person's release or dismissal; certificate of release: *a soldier's discharge.* **5.** a giving off; a letting out. **6.** thing given off or let out. **7.** rate of flow. **8.** transference of electricity between two charged bodies when placed in contact or near each other. **9.** payment. **10.** performance. [see DIS-, CHARGE] —dis·charge′a·ble, *adj.* —dis·charg′er, *n.*

dis·ci·ple (di·sī′pəl), *n., v.,* -pled, -pling. —*n.* **1.** believer in the thought and teaching of a leader; follower. **2.** one of the followers of Jesus. —*v.* cause to become a follower. [< L *discipulus* pupil < unrecorded *discipere* grasp, apprehend] —dis·ci′ple·ship, *n.*

dis·ci·pli·nar·i·an (dis′ə·plə·nãr′i·ən), *n.* person who enforces discipline or who believes in strict discipline. —*adj.* disciplinary.

dis·ci·pli·nar·y (dis′ə·plə·ner′i), *adj.* **1.** having to do with discipline. **2.** for discipline.

dis·ci·pline (dis′ə·plin), *n., v.,* -plined, -plin·ing. —*n.* **1.** training, esp. training of the mind or character. **2.** the training effect of experience, adversity, etc. **3.** trained condition of order and obedience. **4.** order among school pupils, soldiers, or members of any group. **5.** a particular system of rules for conduct. **6.** methods or rules for regulating the conduct of members of a church. **7.** punishment; chastisement. **8.** branch of instruction or education. —*v.* **1.** train; bring to a condition of order and obedience; bring under control. **2.** punish. [< L *disciplina.* See DISCIPLE.] —dis′ci·plin·er, *n.*

dis·claim (dis·klām′), *v.* **1.** refuse to recognize as one's own; deny connection with. **2.** give up all claim to.

dis·claim·er (dis·klām′ər), *n.* **1.** a disclaiming. **2.** person who disclaims.

dis·close (dis·klōz′), *v.,* -closed, -clos·ing. **1.** open to view; uncover. **2.** make known; reveal. —dis·clos′er, *n.*

dis·clo·sure (dis·klō′zhər), *n.* **1.** act of disclosing. **2.** thing disclosed.

dis·coid (dis′koid), *adj.* flat and circular; disklike.

dis·col·or, *esp. Brit.* **dis·col·our** (dis·kul′ər), *v.* **1.** change or spoil the color of; stain. **2.** become changed in color. —dis′col·or·a′tion, dis·col′or·ment; *esp. Brit.* dis′col·our·a′tion, dis·col′our·ment, *n.*

dis·com·fit (dis·kum′fit), *v.* **1.** overthrow completely; defeat; rout. **2.** defeat the plans or hopes of; frustrate. **3.** embarrass greatly; confuse; disconcert. [< OF, ult. < L *dis-* + *conficere* accomplish] —Syn. **1.** vanquish. **3.** baffle, abash.

dis·com·fi·ture (dis·kum′fi·chər), *n.* **1.** a complete overthrow; defeat; rout. **2.** defeat of plans or hopes; frustration. **3.** confusion.

dis·com·fort (dis·kum′fərt), *v.* **1.** disturb the comfort of. **2.** distress; sadden. **3.** make uncomfortable or uneasy. —*n.* **1.** thing that causes discomfort. **2.** lack of comfort; uneasiness.

dis·com·mode (dis′kə·mōd′), *v.,* -mod·ed, -mod·ing. disturb; trouble; inconvenience.

dis·com·pose (dis′kəm·pōz′), *v.,* -posed, -pos·ing. disturb the self-possession of; make uneasy; bring into disorder. —dis′com·pos′ed·ly, *adv.* —dis′com·pos′ing·ly, *adv.*

dis·com·po·sure (dis′kəm·pō′zhər), *n.* state of being disturbed; uneasiness; embarrassment.

dis·con·cert (dis′kən·sėrt′), *v.* **1.** disturb the self-possession of; confuse. **2.** upset; disorder. —dis′con·cert′ing·ly, *adv.* —dis′con·cer′tion, *n.* —Syn. **1.** embarrass.

dis·con·cert·ed (dis′kən·sėrt′id), *adj.* disturbed; confused. —dis′con·cert′ed·ly, *adv.*

dis·con·nect (dis′kə·nekt′), *v.* undo or break the connection of; unfasten. —dis′con·nec′tion, *esp. Brit.* dis′con·nex′ion, *n.* —Syn. separate.

dis·con·nect·ed (dis′kə·nek′tid), *adj.* **1.** not connected; separate. **2.** incoherent; broken. —dis′con·nect′ed·ly, *adv.* —dis′con·nect′ed·ness, *n.*

dis·con·so·late (dis·kon′sə·lit), *adj.* **1.** without hope; forlorn. **2.** unhappy; cheerless. [< Med.L, < L *dis-* + *consolatus,* pp. of *consolari* CONSOLE[1]] —dis·con′so·late·ly, *adv.* —dis·con·so·la′tion (dis′kon·sə·lā′shən), dis·con′so·late·ness, *n.* —Syn. **2.** dejected, sad.

dis·con·tent (dis′kən·tent′), *adj.* not content; dissatisfied. —*n.* Also, dis′con·tent′ment. dislike of what one has and a desire for something different; feeling not satisfied; uneasiness; restlessness. —*v.* dissatisfy; displease.

dis·con·tent·ed (dis′kən·ten′tid), *adj.* not contented; not satisfied. —dis′con·tent′ed·ly, *adv.* —dis′con·tent′ed·ness, *n.* —Syn. dissatisfied, displeased.

dis·con·tin·ue (dis′kən·tin′ū), *v.,* -tin·ued, -tin·u·ing. **1.** cause to cease; put an end to or stop to. **2.** cease from; cease to take, use, etc. **3.** *Law.* terminate (a suit) by request of the plaintiff or by his failing to continue it. —dis′con·tin′u·ance, dis′con·tin′u·a′tion, *n.* —dis′con·tin′u·er, *n.* —Syn. **2.** stop, quit.

dis·con·tin·u·ous (dis′kən·tin′yū·əs), *adj.* not continuous; broken; interrupted. —dis·con·ti·nu·i·ty (dis′kon·tə·nü′ə·ti; -nū′-), dis′con·tin′u·ous·ness, *n.* —dis′con·tin′u·ous·ly, *adv.*

dis·cord (*n.* dis′kôrd; *v.* dis·kôrd′), *n.* **1.** difference of opinion; disagreement. **2.** *Music.* a lack of harmony in notes sounded at the same time. **3.** harsh, clashing sounds. —*v.* be out of harmony; disagree. [< OF < *discors* discordant < *dis-* apart + *cor* heart] —Syn. *n.* **1.** dissension.

dis·cord·ant (dis·kôr′dənt), *adj.* **1.** not in harmony: *a discordant note in music.* **2.** not in agreement; not fitting together. **3.** harsh; clashing. —dis·cord′ance, dis·cord′an·cy, *n.*

dis·co·thèque (dis′kə·tāk′; *French* dēs·kô·tek′), *n.* night club where phonograph records are played for dancing. [< F, lit., disk collection]

dis·count (*v.* dis′kount, dis·kount′; *n.* dis′kount), *v.* **1.** deduct (a certain percentage) of the amount or cost. **2.** allow for exaggeration, prejudice, or inaccuracy in; believe only part of. **3.** leave out of account; disregard. **4.** make less effective by anticipation. **5.** buy, sell, or lend money on (a note, bill of exchange, etc.), deducting a certain percentage to allow for unpaid interest. **6.** lend money, deducting the interest in advance. —*n.* **1.** deduction from the amount or cost. **2.** percentage charged for doing this. **3.** interest deducted in advance. [< OF, < *des-* (< L *dis-*) + *conter* COUNT[1]] —dis′count·a·ble, *adj.* —dis′count·er, *n.*

dis·coun·te·nance (dis·koun′tə·nəns), *v.,* -nanced, -nanc·ing. **1.** refuse to approve; discourage. **2.** abash.

dis·cour·age (dis·kėr′ij), *v.,* -aged, -ag·ing. **1.** take away the courage of; lessen the hope or confidence of. 2. try to prevent by disapproving; frown upon. 3. prevent; hinder. [< OF, < *des-* (< L *dis-*) + *corage* COURAGE] —dis·cour'age·ment, *n.* —dis·cour'ag·er, *n.* —dis·cour'ag·ing·ly, *adv.* —Syn. 1. dishearten, depress, daunt.

dis·course (*n.* dis'kôrs, -kōrs, dis·kôrs', -kōrs'; *v.* dis·kôrs', -kōrs'), *n., v.,* -coursed, -cours·ing. —*n.* 1. a formal speech or writing: *a lecture is a discourse.* 2. conversation; talk. —*v.* 1. speak or write formally. 2. converse; talk. [< F < Med.L, < L, < *dis-* in different directions + *currere* run] —dis·cours'er, *n.*

dis·cour·te·ous (dis·kér'ti·əs), *adj.* not courteous; rude; impolite. —dis·cour'te·ous·ly, *adv.* —dis·cour'te·ous·ness, *n.* —Syn. uncivil, disrespectful.

dis·cour·te·sy (dis·kér'tə·si), *n., pl.* -sies. 1. lack of courtesy; rudeness; impoliteness. 2. a rude or impolite act.

dis·cov·er (dis·kuv'ər), *v.* 1. see or learn of for the first time; find out. 2. *Archaic.* make known; reveal. [< OF < *des-* (< L *dis-*) + *covrir* COVER] —dis·cov'er·a·ble, *adj.* —dis·cov'er·er, *n.*

dis·cov·er·y (dis·kuv'ər·i; -kuv'ri), *n., pl.* -er·ies. 1. act of discovering. 2. thing discovered.

dis·cred·it (dis·kred'it), *v.* 1. cast doubt on; destroy belief, faith, or trust in. 2. refuse to believe; decline to trust or have faith in. —*n.* 1. loss of belief, faith, or trust; doubt. 2. loss of good name or standing; disgrace. 3. thing that causes loss of good name or standing; disgrace. —Syn. *v.* 2. dishonor.

dis·cred·it·a·ble (dis·kred'it·ə·bəl), *adj.* bringing discredit. —dis·cred'it·a·bly, *adv.* —Syn. disgraceful, dishonorable.

dis·creet (dis·krēt'), *adj.* careful and sensible in speech and action; wisely cautious. [< OF < Med.L < L *discretus,* pp., separated. See DISCERN.] —dis·creet'ly, *adv.* —dis·creet'ness, *n.* —Syn. prudent, wary.

dis·crep·an·cy (dis·krep'ən·si), *n., pl.* -cies. 1. lack of consistency; difference; disagreement. 2. an example of inconsistency.

dis·crep·ant (dis·krep'ənt), *adj.* disagreeing; different; inconsistent. [< L, < *dis-* differently + *crepare* sound] —dis·crep'ant·ly, *adv.*

dis·crete (dis·krēt'), *adj.* 1. separate; distinct. 2. consisting of distinct parts. [< L *discretus,* separated, pp. See DISCERN.] —dis·crete'ly, *adv.* —dis·crete'ness, *n.*

dis·cre·tion (dis·kresh'ən), *n.* 1. freedom to judge or choose. 2. good judgment; carefulness in speech or action; wise caution. —Syn. 1. choice, liberty.

dis·cre·tion·ar·y (dis·kresh'ən·er'i), *adj.* left to one's own judgment.

dis·crim·i·nate (*v.* dis·krim'ə·nāt; *adj.* dis·krim'ə·nit), *v.,* -nat·ed, -nat·ing, *adj.* —*v.* 1. make or see a difference. 2. make a distinction. 3. make or see a difference between; distinguish. 4. constitute a distinction in or between; differentiate. —*adj.* having discrimination; making nice distinctions. [< L *discriminatus* distinguished < *discrimen* separation < *discernere* DISCERN] —dis·crim'i·nate·ly, *adv.* —dis·crim'i·nat'ing, *adj.* —dis·crim'i·nat'ing·ly, *adv.* —dis·crim'i·na'tor, *n.*

dis·crim·i·na·tion (dis·krim'ə·nā'shən), *n.* 1. act of making or recognizing differences and distinctions. 2. ability to make fine distinctions. 3. the making of a difference in favor of or against. —Syn. 2. discernment, insight, acumen.

dis·crim·i·na·tive (dis·krim'ə·nā'tiv), **dis·crim·i·na·to·ry** (-ə·nə·tô'ri; -tō'-), *adj.* 1. discriminating. 2. showing discrimination. —dis·crim'i·na'tive·ly, *adv.*

dis·cur·sive (dis·kér'siv), *adj.* wandering or shifting from one subject to another; rambling. —dis·cur'sive·ly, *adv.* —dis·cur'sive·ness, *n.*

dis·cus (dis'kəs), *n.* a heavy, circular plate of stone or metal, used in athletic games as a test of skill and strength in throwing. [< L < Gk. *diskos*]

dis·cuss (dis·kus'), *v.* consider from various points of view; talk over. [< L *discussus* < *dis-* apart + *quatere* shake] —Syn. argue, debate.

dis·cus·sion (dis·kush'ən), *n.* a going over the reasons for and against; discussing things.

dis·dain (dis·dān'), *v.* look down on; consider beneath oneself; scorn. —*n.* act of disdaining; feeling of scorn. [< OF, < *des-* (< L *dis-*) + *deignier* DEIGN] —Syn. *v.* despise, spurn.

dis·dain·ful (dis·dān'fəl), *adj.* feeling or showing disdain. —dis·dain'ful·ly, *adv.* —dis·dain'ful·ness, *n.* —Syn. contemptuous, scornful.

dis·ease (di·zēz'), *n., v.,* -eased, -eas·ing. —*n.* 1. sickness; illness. 2. any particular illness. 3. unhealthy condition of a plant or a product: *the diseases of grains.* 4. disordered or bad condition of mind, morals, public affairs, etc. —*v.* 1. affect with disease. 2. disorder. [< OF, < *des-* (< L *dis-*) + *aise* EASE] —dis·eased', *adj.* —Syn. *n.* 1. malady, ailment.

dis·em·bark (dis'em·bärk'), *v.* go or put ashore from a ship; land from a ship. —dis·em·bar·ka·tion (dis'em·bär·kā'shən), dis·em·bark'ment, *n.*

dis·em·bar·rass (dis'em·bar'əs), *v.* 1. disengage. 2. free from embarrassment or uneasiness.

dis·em·bod·y (dis'em·bod'i), *v.,* -bod·ied, -bod·y·ing. separate (a soul, spirit, etc.) from the body. —dis'em·bod'i·ment, *n.*

dis·em·bow·el (dis'em·bou'əl), *v.,* -eled, -el·ing; *esp. Brit.* -elled, -el·ling. take or rip out the bowels of. —dis'em·bow'el·ment, *n.*

dis·en·chant (dis'en·chant'; -chänt'), *v.* free from a magic spell or illusion. —dis'en·chant'er, *n.* —dis'en·chant'ment, *n.*

dis·en·cum·ber (dis'en·kum'bər), *v.* free from a burden, annoyance, or trouble.

dis·en·fran·chise (dis'en·fran'chīz), *v.,* -chised, -chis·ing. disfranchise. —dis·en·fran·chise·ment (dis'en·fran'chiz·mənt), *n.*

dis·en·gage (dis'en·gāj'), *v.,* -gaged, -gag·ing. 1. free from an engagement, pledge, obligation, etc. 2. detach; loosen. —dis'en·gage'ment, *n.* —Syn. 1. release, liberate.

dis·en·tan·gle (dis'en·tang'gəl), *v.,* -tan·gled, -tan·gling. free from tangles or complications; untangle. —dis'en·tan'gle·ment, *n.*

dis·es·tab·lish (dis'es·tab'lish), *v.* deprive of the character of being established, esp. to withdraw state recognition or support from (a church). —dis'es·tab'lish·ment, *n.*

dis·es·teem (dis'es·tēm'), *v., n.* scorn; dislike.

dis·fa·vor (dis·fā'vər), *n.* 1. dislike; disapproval. 2. state of being regarded with dislike or disapproval. —*v.* regard with dislike; disapprove. —Syn. *n.* 2. disgrace.

dis·fig·ure (dis·fig'yər), *v.,* -ured, -ur·ing. spoil the appearance of; hurt the beauty of. —dis·fig'ure·ment, *n.* —dis·fig'ur·er, *n.* —Syn. deface.

dis·fran·chise (dis·fran'chīz), *v.,* -chised, -chis·ing. 1. take the rights of citizenship away from. 2. take a right or privilege from. —dis·fran·chise·ment (dis·fran'chiz·mənt), *n.* —dis·fran·chis·er (dis·fran'chīz·ər), *n.*

dis·gorge (dis·gôrj'), *v.,* -gorged, -gorg·ing. 1. throw up what has been swallowed. 2. pour forth; discharge. 3. give up unwillingly.

dis·grace (dis·grās'), *n., v.,* -graced, -grac·ing. —*n.* 1. loss of honor or respect; shame. 2. cause of disgrace. 3. loss of favor or trust. —*v.* 1. cause disgrace to. 2. dismiss in disgrace. [< F < Ital. *disgrazia.* See DIS-, GRACE.] —dis·grac'er, *n.* —Syn. *n.* 1. dishonor, disrepute, discredit.

dis·grace·ful (dis·grās'fəl), *adj.* causing loss of honor or respect; shameful. —dis·grace'ful·ly, *adv.* —dis·grace'ful·ness, *n.*

dis·grun·tle (dis·grun'təl), *v.,* -tled, -tling. fill with bad humor or discontent. [< *dis-* + obs. *gruntle* to grunt, grumble] —dis·grun'tle·ment, *n.* —Syn. disgust, displease.

dis·guise (dis·gīz'), *v.,* -guised, -guis·ing. —*v.* 1. make a change in clothes and appearance to hide who one really is or to look like someone else. 2. hide what (a thing) really is; make (a thing) seem like something else. —*n.* 1. use of a changed or unusual dress and appearance in order not to be known. 2. clothes, actions, etc., used to hide who one really is or to make a person look like someone else. 3. a false or misleading appearance; deception; conceal-

ment. [< OF, < des- (< L dis-) + guise GUISE]
—dis·guis'er, n.

dis·gust (dis·gust'), n. strong dislike; sickening dislike. —v. arouse disgust in. [< early modern F, < des- (< L dis-) + goust taste < L gustus] —dis·gust'ing·ly, adv. —Syn. n. distaste, loathing, repugnance.

dis·gust·ed (dis·gus'tid), adj. filled with disgust. —dis·gust'ed·ly, adv. —dis·gust'ed·ness, n.

dish (dish), n. 1. anything to serve food in, such as a plate, platter, bowl, cup, or saucer. 2. amount of food served in a dish. 3. the food served. 4. thing shaped like a dish. —v. 1. serve (food) by putting it in a dish. 2. make concave. [< L discus dish, DISCUS]

dis·ha·bille (dis'ə·bēl'), n. 1. informal, careless dress. 2. garment or costume worn in dishabille; negligee. 3. condition of being only partly dressed. Also, deshabille. [< F déshabillé, pp. < dés- (< L dis-) + habiller dress]

dis·har·mo·ny (dis·här'mə·ni), n., pl. -nies. lack of harmony; discord.

dish·cloth (dish'klôth'; -kloth'), n. cloth to wash dishes with.

dis·heart·en (dis·här'tən), v. discourage; depress. —dis·heart'en·ing·ly, adv. —dis·heart'en·ment, n.

di·shev·eled, esp. Brit. **di·shev·elled** (dishev'əld), adj. 1. rumpled; mussed; disordered; untidy. 2. hanging loosely or in disorder: disheveled hair.

dis·hon·est (dis·on'ist), adj. not honest: lying, stealing, and cheating are dishonest acts. —dishon'est·ly, adv. —Syn. corrupt, fraudulent.

dis·hon·es·ty (dis·on'əs·ti), n., pl. -ties. 1. lack of honesty. 2. a dishonest act.

dis·hon·or, esp. Brit. **dis·hon·our** (dis·hon'ər), n. 1. loss of honor or reputation; shame; disgrace. 2. cause of dishonor. 3. refusal or failure to pay a check, bill, etc. —v. 1. cause or bring dishonor to. 2. refuse or fail to pay (a check, bill, etc.).

dis·hon·or·a·ble, esp. Brit. **dis·hon·our·a·ble** (dis·on'ər·ə·bəl), adj. 1. causing loss of honor; shameful; disgraceful. 2. without honor. —dis·hon'or·a·ble·ness, esp. Brit. dis·hon'our·a·ble·ness, n. —dis·hon'or·a·bly, esp. Brit. dis·hon'our·a·bly, adv.

dish·pan (dish'pan'), n. Am. pan in which to wash dishes.

dis·il·lu·sion (dis'i·lü'zhən), v. free from illusion. —n. a freeing or being freed from illusion. —dis·il·lu'sion·ment, n. —dis·il·lusive (dis'i·lü'siv), adj.

dis·in·cli·na·tion (dis·in·klə·nā'shən), n. unwillingness.

dis·in·cline (dis'in·klīn'), v., -clined, -clining. make or be unwilling.

dis·in·fect (dis'in·fekt'), v. destroy the disease germs in. —dis'in·fec'tion, n. —dis'in·fec'tor, n.

dis·in·fect·ant (dis'in·fek'tənt), n. means for destroying disease germs. Alcohol, iodine, and carbolic acid are disinfectants. —adj. destroying disease germs.

dis·in·gen·u·ous (dis'in·jen'yü·əs), adj. not frank; insincere. —dis'in·gen'u·ous·ly, adv. —dis'in·gen'u·ous·ness, n.

dis·in·her·it (dis'in·her'it), v. prevent from inheriting; deprive of an inheritance. —dis'inher'it·ance, n.

dis·in·te·grate (dis·in'tə·grāt), v., -grat·ed, -grat·ing. 1. separate into small parts or bits. 2. Physics. change in nuclear structure through bombardment by charged particles. —dis·in·tegra·ble (dis·in'tə·grə·bəl), adj. —dis'in·te·gra'tion, n. —dis·in'te·gra'tor, n.

dis·in·ter (dis'in·tér'), v., -terred, -ter·ring. 1. take out of a grave or tomb; dig up. 2. discover and reveal. —dis'in·ter'ment, n.

dis·in·ter·est (dis·in'tər·ist; -trist), n. lack of interest; indifference.

dis·in·ter·est·ed (dis·in'tər·is·tid; -tər·es'tid), adj. 1. free from selfish motives; impartial; fair. 2. U.S. Colloq. not interested.

—dis·in'ter·est·ed·ly, adv. —dis·in'ter·est·edness, n. ⯈ See interested for usage note.

dis·join (dis·join'), v. separate.

dis·joint (dis·joint'), v. 1. take apart at the joints. 2. break up; disconnect; put out of order. 3. put out of joint; dislocate. 4. come apart; be put out of joint. —dis·joint'ed, adj. —dis·joint'ed·ly, adv. —dis·joint'ed·ness, n.

dis·junc·tion (dis·jungk'shən), n. a disjoining or being disjoined; separation.

dis·junc·tive (dis·jungk'tiv), adj. 1. causing separation; separating. 2. showing a choice or contrast between two ideas, words, etc. But, yet, either . . . or, etc., are disjunctive conjunctions. Otherwise, else, etc., are disjunctive adverbs. 3. involving alternatives. A disjunctive proposition asserts that one or the other of two things is true. —n. 1. statement involving alternatives. 2. a disjunctive conjunction. —dis·junc'tive·ly, adv.

disk (disk), n. 1. a round, flat, thin object. 2. a round, flat surface, or an apparently round, flat surface: the sun's disk. 3. Bot., Zool. a roundish, flat part in a plant or animal. 4. anything resembling a disk. 5. a phonograph record. 6. discus. Also, disc. [< L discus DISCUS] —disk'like', adj.

Disk

disk harrow, Am. harrow with a row of sharp, revolving disks used in preparing ground for planting or sowing.

disk jockey, Slang. announcer for a radio program consisting chiefly of recorded music.

dis·like (dis·līk'), n., v., -liked, -lik·ing. —n. a feeling of not liking; a feeling against. —v. not like; object to; have a feeling against. —dislik'a·ble, adj. —Syn. n. distaste, aversion.

dis·lo·cate (dis'lō·kāt), v., -cat·ed, -cat·ing. 1. put out of joint. 2. put out of order; disturb; upset. —dis'lo·ca'tion, n.

dis·lodge (dis·loj'), v., -lodged, -lodg·ing. drive or force out of a place, position, etc. —dislodg'ment, n.

dis·loy·al (dis·loi'əl), adj. not loyal; unfaithful. —dis·loy'al·ly, adv. —Syn. false, traitorous.

dis·loy·al·ty (dis·loi'əl·ti), n., pl. -ties. 1. lack of loyalty. 2. a disloyal act.

dis·mal (diz'məl), adj. 1. dark; gloomy. 2. dreary; miserable. —dis'mal·ly, adv. —dis'malness, n. —Syn. 1. somber. 2. cheerless, sad.

dis·man·tle (dis·man'təl), v., -tled, -tling. 1. strip of covering, equipment, furniture, guns, rigging, etc. 2. pull down; take apart. [< OF desmanteler. See DIS-, MANTLE.] —dis·man'tlement, n.

dis·may (dis·mā'), n. loss of courage because of fear of what is about to happen. —v. trouble greatly; make afraid. [ME desmayen < AF < VL, deprive of strength < L ex- + unrecorded Frankish magan have strength] —Syn. n. consternation, fear, apprehension.

dis·mem·ber (dis·mem'bər), v. 1. separate or divide into parts. 2. cut or tear the limbs from. —dis·mem'ber·ment, n.

dis·miss (dis·mis'), v. 1. send away; allow to go. 2. remove from office or service. 3. put out of mind; stop thinking about. 4. refuse to consider (a complaint, plea, etc.) in a law court. [< L dismissus, var. of dimissus < dis- away + mittere send] —dis·miss'al, n. —Syn. 2. discharge, oust.

dis·mount (dis·mount'), v. 1. get off a horse, bicycle, etc. 2. throw or bring down from a horse; unhorse. 3. take (a thing) from its setting or support. 4. take apart; take to pieces. —dismount'a·ble, adj.

dis·o·be·di·ent (dis'ə·bē'di·ənt), adj. refusing or failing to obey. —dis'o·be'di·ence, n. —dis'o·be'di·ent·ly, adv.

dis·o·bey (dis'ə·bā'), v. refuse or fail to obey. —dis'o·bey'er, n. —Syn. defy.

dis·o·blige (dis'ə·blīj'), v., -bliged, -blig·ing. 1. refuse or fail to oblige. 2. give offense to. —dis'o·blig'ing, adj. —dis'o·blig'ing·ly, adv.

dis·or·der (dis·ôr'dər), n. 1. lack of order; confusion. 2. public disturbance; riot. 3. sickness; disease. —v. 1. destroy the order of; throw into confusion. 2. cause sickness in. —Syn. n. 1. jumble. 2. commotion, tumult.

dis·or·der·ly (dis-ôr′dər-li), adj. 1. not orderly; in confusion. 2. causing disorder; unruly. 3. Law. contrary to good morals or decency. —adv. in a disorderly manner. —**dis·or′der·li·ness,** n.

dis·or·gan·ize (dis-ôr′gən-īz), v., -ized, -iz·ing. throw into confusion and disorder. —**dis·or′gan·i·za′tion,** n. —**dis·or′gan·iz′er,** n.

dis·own (dis-ōn′), v. refuse to recognize as one's own.

+ **dis·par·age** (dis-par′ij), v., -aged, -ag·ing. 1. speak slightingly of; belittle. 2. lower the reputation of; discredit. [< OF *desparagier* match unequally < *des-* (< L *dis-*) + *parage* rank, lineage < L *par* equal. See PEER¹.] —**dis·par′age·ment,** n. —**dis·par′ag·er,** n. —**dis·par′ag·ing·ly,** adv. —Syn. 1. depreciate.

dis·pa·rate (dis′pə·rit), adj. essentially different; unlike. [< L, < *dis-* apart + *parare* get] —**dis′pa·rate·ly,** adv. —**dis′pa·rate·ness,** n.

dis·par·i·ty (dis-par′ə·ti), n., pl. -ties. inequality; difference.

dis·pas·sion (dis-pash′ən), n. freedom from emotion or prejudice; impartiality.

dis·pas·sion·ate (dis-pash′ən·it), adj. free from emotion or prejudice; calm; impartial. —**dis·pas′sion·ate·ly,** adv. —**dis·pas′sion·ate·ness,** n.

dis·patch (dis-pach′), v. 1. send off to some place or for some purpose. 2. get (something) done promptly or speedily. 3. give the death blow to; kill. —n. 1. a sending off (of a letter, a messenger, etc.). 2. a written message, such as special news or government business. 3. promptness; speed. 4. a putting to death; a killing. Also, despatch. [< Ital. *dispacciare* hasten or Sp. *despachar*] —**dis·patch′er,** n.

dis·pel (dis-pel′), v., -pelled, -pel·ling. drive away and scatter; disperse. [< L, < *dis-* away + *pellere* drive] —**dis·pel′ler,** n.

dis·pen·sa·ble (dis-pen′sə·bəl), adj. 1. that may be done without; unimportant. 2. that may be forgiven, condoned, or declared not binding. 3. capable of being dispensed or administered. —**dis·pen′sa·bil′i·ty, dis·pen′sa·ble·ness,** n.

dis·pen·sa·ry (dis-pen′sə·ri), n., pl. -ries. place where medicines and medical advice are given free or for a very small charge.

dis·pen·sa·tion (dis′pən·sā′shən; -pen-), n. 1. act of distributing: *the dispensation of charity to the poor.* 2. thing given out or distributed: *the dispensations of Providence.* 3. rule; management: *England under the dispensation of Elizabeth.* 4. management or ordering of the affairs of the world by Providence or Nature. 5. a religious system: *the Christian dispensation, the Jewish dispensation.* 6. official permission to disregard a rule. —**dis′pen·sa′tion·al,** adj. —**dis′pen·sa′tor,** n.

dis·pen·sa·to·ry (dis-pen′sə·tô′ri; -tō′-), n., pl. -ries. 1. book that tells how to prepare and use medicines. 2. dispensary.

dis·pense (dis-pens′), v., -pensed, -pens·ing. 1. give out; distribute. 2. carry out; put in force; apply. 3. prepare and give out: *a druggist dispenses medicines.* 4. release; excuse. 5. **dispense with,** a. do away with. b. get along without. [< OF < L *dispensare* weigh out < *dis-* out + *pendere* weigh] —**dis·pens′er,** n. —Syn. 1. allot, apportion.

dis·perse (dis-pèrs′), v., -persed, -pers·ing. 1. spread in different directions; scatter. 2. distribute; diffuse; disseminate. 3. dispel; dissipate. 4. be dispelled; disappear. 5. divide (white light) into its colored rays. [< F < L *dispersus* < *dis-* in every direction + *spargere* scatter] —**dis·pers′ed·ly,** adv. —**dis·pers′er,** n. —**dis·pers′i·ble,** adj. —**dis·pers′ive,** adj.

dis·per·sion (dis-pèr′zhən; -shən), n. 1. Also, **dis·per′sal.** a. a dispersing. b. a being dispersed. 2. the separation of light into its different colors, as by a prism.

dis·pir·it (dis-pir′it), v. depress; discourage. —**dis·pir′it·ed,** adj. —**dis·pir′it·ed·ly,** adv.

dis·place (dis-plās′), v., -placed, -plac·ing. 1. put something else in the place of. 2. remove from a position of authority. 3. move from its usual place or position.

displaced person, a European or other person forced out of his native country by war or threat of captivity.

dis·place·ment (dis-plās′mənt), n. 1. act of displacing. 2. a being displaced. 3. weight of the volume of water displaced by a ship or other floating object.

dis·play (dis-plā′), v. 1. expose to view; show. 2. show in a special way, so as to attract attention. 3. let appear; reveal. 4. spread out; unfold. —n. 1. a displaying; exhibition. 2. *Printing.* the choice and arrangement of type so as to make certain words, etc., prominent. 3. printed matter so chosen and arranged. 4. a showing off; ostentation. [< OF < L *displicare* scatter. See DEPLOY.] —**dis·play′er,** n. —Syn. n. 1. show, exhibit.

dis·please (dis-plēz′), v., -pleased, -pleas·ing. not please; offend; annoy. —Syn. anger.

dis·pleas·ure (dis-plezh′ər), n. 1. the feeling of being displeased; slight anger; annoyance. 2. Archaic. discomfort. 3. Archaic. offense.

dis·port (dis-pôrt′; -pōrt′), v. amuse (oneself); sport; play. —n. Archaic. pastime; amusement. [< OF, < *des-* (< L *dis-*) away from + *porter* carry < L *portare*]

dis·pos·a·ble (dis-pōz′ə·bəl), adj. 1. capable of being disposed of. 2. at one's disposal.

dis·pos·al (dis-pōz′əl), n. 1. act of getting rid (of something). 2. act of giving away. 3. sale. 4. an arranging of matters; a settling of affairs. 5. act of putting in a certain order or position; arrangement. 6. at or in one's disposal, ready for one's use or service at any time.

dis·pose (dis-pōz′), v., -posed, -pos·ing, n. —v. 1. put in a certain order or position; arrange. 2. arrange (matters). 3. make ready or willing. 4. make liable or subject. 5. arrange or decide matters; make terms. 6. **dispose of,** a. get rid of. b. give away. c. sell. —n. Archaic. disposition. [< OF, < *dis-* (< L) variously + *poser* place (see POSE)] —**dis·pos′er,** n.

dis·po·si·tion (dis′pə·zish′ən), n. 1. one's natural way of acting toward others or of thinking about things; nature: *a cheerful disposition.* 2. tendency; inclination: *a disposition to argue.* 3. act of putting in order or position; arrangement: *the disposition of soldiers in battle.* 4. management; settlement. 5. disposal.

dis·pos·sess (dis′pə·zes′), v. force to give up the possession of a house, land, etc.; oust. —**dis′pos·ses′sion,** n. —**dis′pos·ses′sor,** n. —Syn. evict, remove.

dis·praise (dis-prāz′), v., -praised, -prais·ing, n. —v. express disapproval of; blame. —n. expression of disapproval; blame.

dis·proof (dis-prüf′), n. 1. a disproving; refutation. 2. fact, reason, etc., that disproves something.

dis·pro·por·tion (dis′prə·pôr′shən; -pōr′-), n. lack of proper proportion; lack of symmetry. —v. make disproportionate.

dis·pro·por·tion·al (dis′prə·pôr′shən·əl; -pōr′-), adj. disproportionate. —**dis′pro·por′tion·al·ly,** adv.

dis·pro·por·tion·ate (dis′prə·pôr′shən·it; -pōr′-), adj. out of proportion; lacking in proper proportion. —**dis′pro·por′tion·ate·ly,** adv. —**dis′pro·por′tion·ate·ness,** n.

dis·prove (dis-prüv′), v., -proved, -prov·ing. prove false or incorrect; refute. —**dis·prov′a·ble,** adj.

dis·put·a·ble (dis-pūt′ə·bəl; dis′pyū·tə·bəl), adj. liable to be disputed; uncertain. —**dis·put′a·bil′i·ty,** n. —**dis·put′a·bly,** adv.

dis·pu·tant (dis′pyū·tənt; dis-pū′-), adj. engaged in argument or controversy. —n. person who takes part in a dispute or debate.

dis·pu·ta·tion (dis′pyū·tā′shən), n. 1. debate; controversy. 2. dispute.

dis·pu·ta·tious (dis′pyū·tā′shəs), **dis·put·a·tive** (dis-pūt′ə·tiv), adj. fond of disputing; inclined to argue. —**dis′pu·ta′tious·ly,** adv. —**dis′pu·ta′tious·ness,** n. —Syn. quarrelsome.

dis·pute (dis·pūt′), *v.*, -put·ed, -put·ing, *n.*
—*v.* 1. discuss; argue; debate. 2. quarrel. 3. disagree with (a statement); declare not true; call in question. 4. fight against; oppose; resist. 5. fight for; fight over. 6. contend for; try to win. —*n.* 1. argument; debate. 2. a quarrel. [< L, ex-amine, discuss, argue < *dis-* item by item + *putare* calculate] —dis·put′er, *n.*

dis·qual·i·fi·ca·tion (dis′kwol·ə·fə·kā′shən), *n.* 1. a disqualifying. 2. a being disqualified. 3. something that disqualifies.

dis·qual·i·fy (dis·kwol′ə·fī), *v.*, -fied, -fy·ing. 1. make unable to do something. 2. declare unfit or unable to do something.

dis·qui·et (dis·kwī′ət), *v.* make uneasy or anxious; disturb. —*n.* uneasiness; anxiety.

dis·qui·e·tude (dis·kwī′ə·tüd; -tūd), *n.* anxiety.

dis·qui·si·tion (dis′kwə·zish′ən), *n.* a long or formal speech or writing about a subject. [< L *disquisitio*, ult. < *dis-* (intensive) + *quaerere* seek]

Dis·rae·li (diz·rā′li), *n.* Benjamin (*Earl of Beaconsfield*), 1804–1881, English statesman and novelist.

dis·re·gard (dis′ri·gärd′), *v.* 1. pay no attention to; take no notice of. 2. treat without proper regard or respect; slight. —*n.* 1. lack of attention; neglect. 2. lack of proper regard or respect. —dis′re·gard′ful, *adj.* —Syn. *v.* 1. ignore, overlook, neglect.

dis·re·pair (dis′ri·pãr′), *n.* bad condition.

dis·rep·u·ta·ble (dis·rep′yə·tə·bəl), *adj.* 1. having a bad reputation. 2. not respectable. —dis·rep′u·ta·bil′i·ty, *n.* —dis·rep′u·ta·bly, *adv.*

dis·re·pute (dis′ri·pūt′), *n.* disgrace; discredit; disfavor.

dis·re·spect (dis′ri·spekt′), *n.* lack of respect. —*v.* treat or consider with a lack of respect. —dis′re·spect′ful, *adj.* —dis′re·spect′ful·ly, *adv.* —dis′re·spect′ful·ness, *n.* —Syn. discourtesy, impoliteness, rudeness.

dis·robe (dis·rōb′), *v.*, -robed, -rob·ing. undress. —dis·robe′ment, *n.* —dis·rob′er, *n.*

dis·rupt (dis·rupt′), *v.* break up; split. [< L *disruptus* < *dis-* apart + *rumpere* break] —dis·rupt′er, *n.* —dis·rup′tion, *n.* —dis·rup′tive, *adj.*

dis·sat·is·fac·tion (dis′sat·is·fak′shən), *n.* discontent; displeasure.

dis·sat·is·fac·to·ry (dis′sat·is·fak′tə·ri), *adj.* causing discontent; unsatisfactory.

dis·sat·is·fy (dis·sat′is·fī), *v.*, -fied, -fy·ing. fail to satisfy; displease.

dis·sect (di·sekt′; dī–), *v.* 1. separate or divide the parts of (an animal, plant, etc.) in order to examine or study the structure. 2. examine carefully part by part; analyze. [< L, < *dis-* apart + *secare* cut] —dis·sec′tion, *n.* —dis·sec′tor, *n.*

dis·sect·ed (di·sek′tid; dī–), *adj.* 1. cut or divided into many parts. 2. *Bot.* deeply cut into numerous segments. 3. *Geol.* cut up by irregular valleys.

dis·sem·ble (di·sem′bəl), *v.*, -bled, -bling. 1. disguise or hide (one's real feelings, thoughts, plans, etc.). 2. conceal one's motives, etc.; be a hypocrite. 3. pretend; feign. 4. disregard; ignore. [alter., after *resemble*, of obs. *dissimule* dissimulate] —dis·sem′bler, *n.*

dis·sem·i·nate (di·sem′ə·nāt), *v.*, -nat·ed, -nat·ing. scatter widely; spread abroad. [< L, < *dis-* in every direction + *semen* seed] —dis·sem′i·na′tion, *n.* —dis·sem′i·na′tive, *adj.* —dis·sem′i·na′tor, *n.*

dis·sen·sion (di·sen′shən), *n.* 1. a disputing; a quarreling. 2. hard feeling caused by a difference in opinion. —Syn. 1. disagreement, contention.

dis·sent (di·sent′), *v.* 1. differ in opinion; disagree. 2. refuse to conform to the rules and beliefs of an established church. —*n.* 1. difference of opinion; disagreement. 2. refusal to conform to the rules and beliefs of an established church. [< L, < *dis-* differently + *sentire* think, feel] —dis·sent′er, *n.*

dis·sen·tient (di·sen′shənt), *adj.* dissenting. —*n.* person who dissents. —dis·sen′tience, *n.*

dis·ser·ta·tion (dis′ər·tā′shən), *n.* a formal discussion of a subject; treatise. [< L *dissertatio* < *dis-* + *serere* join words]

dis·serv·ice (dis·sėr′vis), *n.* harm; injury.

dis·sev·er (di·sev′ər), *v.* sever; separate. —dis·sev′er·ance, *n.*

dis·si·dent (dis′ə·dənt), *adj.* disagreeing; dissenting. —*n.* person who disagrees or dissents. —dis′si·dence, *n.*

dis·sim·i·lar (di·sim′ə·lər), *adj.* not similar; unlike; different. —dis·sim·i·lar·i·ty (di·sim′ə·lar′ə·ti), *n.* —dis·sim′i·lar·ly, *adv.*

dis·si·mil·i·tude (dis′si·mil′ə·tüd; -tūd), *n.* unlikeness; difference.

dis·sim·u·late (di·sim′yə·lāt), *v.*, -lat·ed, -lat·ing. disguise; dissemble. —dis·sim′u·la′tion, *n.* —dis·sim′u·la′tor, *n.*

dis·si·pate (dis′ə·pāt), *v.*, -pat·ed, -pat·ing. 1. spread in different directions; scatter. 2. disappear or cause to disappear; dispel. 3. spend foolishly. 4. indulge too much in evil or foolish pleasures. [< L, < *dis-* in different directions + *sipare* throw] —dis′si·pat′er, dis′si·pa′tor, *n.* —dis′si·pa′tive, *adj.* —Syn. 3. squander, waste.

dis·si·pat·ed (dis′ə·pāt′id), *adj.* 1. indulging too much in evil or foolish pleasures; dissolute. 2. scattered. 3. wasted. —dis′si·pat′ed·ly, *adv.* —dis′si·pat′ed·ness, *n.*

dis·si·pa·tion (dis′ə·pā′shən), *n.* 1. a dissipating or being dissipated. 2. amusement; diversion, esp. harmful amusements. 3. too much indulgence in evil or foolish pleasures.

dis·so·ci·ate (di·sō′shi·āt), *v.*, -at·ed, -at·ing. 1. break the connection or association with; separate. 2. *Chem.* separate or decompose by dissociation. [< L, < *dis-* apart + *socius* ally]

dis·so·ci·a·tion (di·sō′si·ā′shən; –shi·ā′–), *n.* 1. act of dissociating or state of being dissociated. 2. *Chem.* separation or decomposition of a substance into simpler constituents. —dis·so·ci·a·tive (di·sō′shi·ā′tiv), *adj.*

dis·sol·u·ble (di·sol′yə·bəl), *adj.* capable of being dissolved. —dis·sol′u·bil′i·ty, dis·sol′u·ble·ness, *n.*

dis·so·lute (dis′ə·lüt), *adj.* living an evil life; very wicked; lewd; immoral. [< L *dissolutus*, pp. of *dissolvere* DISSOLVE] —dis′so·lute·ly, *adv.* —dis′so·lute·ness, *n.* —Syn. dissipated.

dis·so·lu·tion (dis′ə·lü′shən), *n.* 1. a breaking up into parts. 2. the ending of a business partnership. 3. the breaking up of an assembly by ending its session. 4. ruin; destruction. 5. death.

dis·solve (di·zolv′), *v.*, -solved, -solv·ing. —*v.* 1. make or become liquid, esp. by putting or being put into a liquid. 2. break up; end: *dissolve a partnership.* 3. fade away. 4. separate into parts; decompose. —*n. Am.* in movies and television, the gradual disappearing of the figures of a scene while those of a succeeding scene slowly take their place. [< L, < *dis-* (intensive) + *solvere* loose] —dis·solv′a·ble, *adj.* —dis·solv′er, *n.* —Syn. *v.* 1. melt, thaw.

dis·so·nance (dis′ə·nəns), **dis·so·nan·cy** (-nən·si), *n., pl.* -nanc·es; -cies. 1. combination of sounds that is not harmonious; discord. 2. *Music.* a chord in a state of unrest and needing completion. [< L, < *dis-* differently + *sonare* to sound]

dis·so·nant (dis′ə·nənt), *adj.* 1. harsh in sound. 2. out of harmony. —dis′so·nant·ly, *adv.*

dis·suade (di·swād′), *v.*, -suad·ed, -suad·ing. persuade not to do something. [< L, < *dis-* against + *suadere* to urge] —dis·suad′er, *n.* —dis·sua·sion (di·swā′zhən), *n.* —dis·sua·sive (di·swā′siv), *adj.*

dis·syl·la·ble (dis′sil′ə·bəl; di·sil′–), *n.* word having two syllables. [< F < L < Gk., < *di-* two + *syllabe* SYLLABLE] —dis·syl·lab·ic (dis′si·lab′-ik; dis′i–), *adj.*

dist., 1. distance. 2. district.

dis·taff (dis′taf; –tãf), *n.* 1. a split stick that holds the wool, flax, etc., for spinning. See the picture on the next page. 2. woman's work or affairs. **3.** the female sex; woman or women. [OE, < *dis-* (see DIZEN) + *stœf* staff]

distaff side, the mother's side of a family.

dis·tance (dis′tⱥns), *n.,* *v.,* **-tanced, -tanc·ing.** —*n.* **1.** space in between. **2.** a being far away. **3.** place far away. **4.** time in between; interval. **5.** *Music.* the interval or difference between two tones. **6.** lack of friendliness or familiarity; reserve. —*v.* leave far behind; do much better than.

dis·tant (dis′tⱥnt), *adj.* **1.** far away in space. **2.** away. **3.** far apart in time, relationship, likeness, etc.; not close. **4.** not friendly. [< F < L *distans* < *dis-* off + *stare* stand] —**dis′tant·ly,** *adv.* —Syn. **1.** remote, far. **4.** aloof, reserved.

dis·taste (dis·tāst′), *n.* dislike.

dis·taste·ful (dis·tāst′fⱥl), *adj.* unpleasant; disagreeable; offensive. —**dis·taste′ful·ly,** *adv.* —**dis·taste′ful·ness,** *n.*

dis·tem·per¹ (dis·tem′pⱥr), *n.* **1.** an infectious disease of dogs and other animals, accompanied by a short, dry cough and a loss of strength. **2.** sickness of the mind or body; disorder; disease. **3.** disturbance. [< v.] —*v.* **1.** disturb; disorder. **2.** *Archaic.* trouble. [< LL *distemperare* mix improperly. See DIS-, TEMPER.]

dis·tem·per² (dis·tem′pⱥr), *n.* **1.** paint made by mixing the colors with eggs or glue instead of oil. **2.** method of painting with such a mixture. —*v.* paint with such a mixture. [< OF *destemprer* < Med.L, soak, < LL, mix thoroughly. See DIS-, TEMPER.]

dis·tend (dis·tend′), *v.* stretch out; expand. [< L, < *dis-* apart + *tendere* stretch] —**dis·ten·si·ble** (dis·ten′sⱥ·bⱥl), *adj.* —**dis·ten′si·bil′i·ty,** *n.* —**dis·ten′tion,** *n.*

dis·tich (dis′tik), *n., pl.* **-tichs.** two lines of verse together that make complete sense; couplet. [< L < Gk., < *di-* two + *stichos* line]

dis·til, *esp. Brit.* **dis·till** (dis·til′), *v.,* **-tilled, -till·ing. 1.** heat a (liquid, or other substance) and condense the vapor given off. **2.** obtain by distilling. **3.** extract; refine. **4.** fall or let fall in drops; drip. [< L, < *de-* down + *stillare* to drop < *stilla* drop] —**dis·till′a·ble,** *adj.*

dis·til·late (dis′tⱥ·lit; -lāt), *n.* a distilled liquid; something obtained from distilling.

dis·til·la·tion (dis′tⱥ·lā′shⱥn), *n.* **1.** a distilling. **2.** something distilled; extract; essence.

dis·till·er (dis·til′ⱥr), *n.* **1.** person or thing that distills. **2.** person or corporation that makes whiskey, rum, brandy, etc.

dis·till·er·y (dis·til′ⱥr·ĭ), *n., pl.* **-er·ies.** place where distilling is done.

dis·tinct (dis·tingkt′), *adj.* **1.** not the same; separate. **2.** not alike; not like; different. **3.** clear; plain. **4.** unmistakable; definite; decided. [< L *distinctus,* pp. of *distinguere* DISTINGUISH] —**dis·tinct′ness,** *n.* —Syn. **1.** different, dissimilar. **3.** obvious.

dis·tinc·tion (dis·tingk′shⱥn), *n.* **1.** act of distinguishing; making a difference: *he gave every servant 10 dollars without distinction.* **2.** difference. **3.** point of difference; special quality or feature. **4.** honor: *the soldier served with distinction.* **5.** mark or sign of honor. **6.** excellence; superiority.

dis·tinc·tive (dis·tingk′tiv), *adj.* distinguishing from others; special; characteristic. —**dis·tinc′tive·ly,** *adv.* —**dis·tinc′tive·ness,** *n.*

dis·tinct·ly (dis·tingkt′li), *adv.* **1.** clearly; plainly. **2.** unmistakably; decidedly.

dis·tin·gué (dis′tang·gā′; dis·tang′gā), *adj.* looking important or superior; distinguished.

dis·tin·guish (dis·ting′gwish), *v.* **1.** tell apart; see or show the difference in. **2.** see or show the difference. **3.** see or hear clearly. **4.** be a special quality or feature of. **5.** make famous or well-known. **6.** separate into different groups. [< L, < *dis-* between + *stinguere* to prick] —**dis·tin′guish·a·ble,** *adj.* —**dis·tin′guish·a·bly,** *adv.*

dis·tin·guished (dis·ting′gwisht), *adj.* **1.** famous; well-known. **2.** having the appearance of an important person.

dis·tort (dis·tôrt′), *v.* **1.** pull or twist out of shape. **2.** change from the truth. [< L *distortus* < *dis-* (intensive) + *torquere* twist] —**dis·tort′ed, *adj.* —**dis·tort′ed·ly,** *adv.* —**dis·tort′ed·ness,** *n.* —**dis·tort′er,** *n.* —**dis·tor′tion,** *n.* —**dis·tor′tion·al,** *adj.* —Syn. **1.** contort. **2.** misrepresent, falsify.

dis·tract (dis·trakt′), *v.* **1.** draw away (the mind, attention, etc.). **2.** confuse; disturb; bewilder. **3.** put out of one's mind; make insane. [< L *distractus* < *dis-* away + *trahere* draw] —**dis·tract′ed,** *adj.* —**dis·tract′ed·ly,** *adv.* —**dis·tract′er,** *n.* —**dis·tract′ing,** *adj.* —**dis·tract′ing·ly,** *adv.* —**dis·trac′tive,** *adj.*

dis·trac·tion (dis·trak′shⱥn), *n.* **1.** act of distracting. **2.** thing that distracts. **3.** confusion of mind; disturbance of thought. **4.** insanity; madness. **5.** confusion; perplexity. **6.** relief from continued thought, grief, or effort.

dis·train (dis·trān′), *v.* seize (goods) for unpaid rent or other debts. [< OF < L, < *dis-* apart + *stringere* draw] —**dis·train′a·ble,** *adj.* —**dis·train′er, dis·train′or,** *n.* —**dis·train′ment,** *n.*

dis·trait (dis·trā′), *adj.* not paying attention; absent-minded. [< F, pp. of *distraire* DISTRACT]

dis·traught (dis·trôt′), *adj.* **1.** distracted. **2.** crazed. [var. of obs. *distract,* adj. See DISTRACT.]

dis·tress (dis·tres′), *n.* **1.** great pain or sorrow; anxiety; trouble. **2.** something that causes distress; misfortune. **3.** dangerous condition; difficult situation: *ship in distress.* **4.** a legal seizure of the goods of another as security or satisfaction for debt, etc. **5.** the thing so seized. —*v.* cause pain, grief, or suffering to. [< OF *distrece,* ult. < L *districtus* < *dis-* apart + *stringere* draw] —**dis·tress′ful,** *adj.* —**dis·tress′ful·ly,** *adv.* —**dis·tress′ing,** *adj.* —**dis·tress′ing·ly,** *adv.* —Syn. *n.* **1.** grief, agony, anguish.

dis·trib·ute (dis·trib′yūt), *v.,* **-ut·ed, -ut·ing. 1.** divide and give out in shares. **2.** spread; scatter. **3.** divide into parts. **4.** arrange; classify. [< L, < *dis-* individually + *tribuere* assign] —**dis·trib′ut·a·ble,** *adj.* —Syn. **1.** deal, dispense, allot. **4.** sort, group.

dis·tri·bu·tion (dis′trⱥ·bū′shⱥn), *n.* **1.** act of distributing. **2.** way of being distributed. **3.** thing distributed. **4.** the distributing to consumers of goods grown or made by producers. —**dis′tri·bu′tion·al,** *adj.*

dis·trib·u·tive (dis·trib′yⱥ·tiv), *adj.* **1.** of or having to do with distribution; distributing. **2.** referring to each individual of a group considered separately. *Each, every, either,* and *neither* are distributive words. —*n.* a distributive word. —**dis·trib′u·tive·ly,** *adv.* —**dis·trib′u·tive·ness,** *n.*

dis·trib·u·tor, dis·trib·ut·er (dis·trib′yⱥ·tⱥr), *n.* **1.** person or thing that distributes. **2.** person or company that distributes to consumers the goods grown or made by producers. **3.** part of a gasoline engine that distributes electric current to the spark plugs.

dis·trict (dis′trikt), *n.* **1.** portion of a country; region. **2.** portion of a country, state, or city serving as a unit for policing, fire prevention, political representation, etc. —*v. Am.* divide into districts. [< LL *districtus* district < L *distringere.* See DISTRESS.]

district attorney, *Am.* lawyer who handles cases for the government for a certain district.

District of Columbia, *Am.* district in the E United States belonging to the federal government. It is entirely occupied by the capital, Washington, and is governed by Congress. *Abbrev.:* D.C.

dis·trust (dis·trust′), *v.* have no confidence in; be suspicious of. —*n.* lack of trust or confidence; suspicion. —**dis·trust′ful,** *adj.* —**dis·trust′ful·ly,** *adv.* —Syn. *n.* doubt, mistrust.

dis·turb (dis·tėrb′), *v.* **1.** destroy the peace, quiet, or rest of. **2.** break in upon with noise or change. **3.** put out of order. **4.** make uneasy; trouble. [< L < *dis-* (intensive) + *turbare* agitate < *turba* commotion] —**dis·turb′er,** *n.* —**dis·turb′ing·ly,** *adv.* —Syn. **1.** agitate, perturb.

dis·turb·ance (dis·tėr′bⱥns), *n.* **1.** a disturbing or being disturbed. **2.** thing that disturbs. **3.** confusion; disorder.

di·sul·fide, di·sul·phide (dī·sul′fīd; –fīd),
di·sul·fid, or **di·sul·phid** (–fĭd), *n.* compound consisting of two atoms of sulfur combined with another element or radical; bisulfide.

dis·un·ion (dis·ūn′yən), *n.* **1.** separation; division. **2.** lack of unity; disagreement.

dis·u·nite (dis′yů·nīt′), *v.,* –nit·ed, –nit·ing. **1.** separate; divide. **2.** destroy the unity of. —**dis·u·ni·ty** (dis·ū′nə·ti), *n.*

dis·use (*n.* dis·ūs′; *v.* dis·ūz′), *n., v.,* –used, –us·ing. —*n.* lack of use. —*v.* stop using.

ditch (dich), *n.* a long, narrow place dug in the earth, usually used to carry off water. —*v.* dig a ditch in. **2.** *Slang.* get rid of. [OE *dic*] —**ditch′er,** *n.*

dith·er (dith′ər), *n.* **1.** a tremble; shiver; quiver. **2.** *Colloq.* a confused, excited condition.

dith·y·ramb (dith′ə·ram; –ramb), *n.* **1.** a Greek choral song in honor of Dionysus. **2.** poem that is full of wild emotion, enthusiasm, etc. **3.** any speech or writing like this. [< L < Gk. *dithyrambos*] —**dith·y·ram·bic** (dith′ə·ram′bik), *adj.*

dit·to (dit′ō), *n., pl.* –tos, *v.,* –toed, –to·ing, *adv.* —*n.* **1.** the same as was said before; the same. **2.** mark (″) or abbreviation (do.) that stands for ditto. **3.** a copy; duplicate. —*v.* copy; duplicate. —*adv.* as said before; likewise. [< Ital., said, < L *dictus,* pp. of *dicere* say] ➤ Ditto marks are used with lists and tabulations in reference works instead of repeating words that fall directly underneath. Ditto marks are not used in consecutive writing, nor are they used now in footnotes and bibliographies. In general they are much less used than formerly.

dit·ty (dit′i), *n., pl.* –ties. a short, simple song or poem. [< OF *ditié* < L *dictatum* (thing) dictated, pp. of *dictare* DICTATE]

ditty bag, a small bag used by sailors to hold needles, thread, buttons, etc.

di·u·ret·ic (dī′yů·ret′ik), *Med.* —*adj.* causing an increase in the flow of urine. —*n.* drug that does this. [< LL < Gk., < *dia–* through + *oureein* urinate]

di·ur·nal (dī·ėr′nəl), *adj.* **1.** occurring every day; daily. **2.** of or belonging to the daytime. **3.** lasting a day. [< LL *diurnalis* < L *dies* day. Doublet of JOURNAL.] —**di·ur′nal·ly,** *adv.*

div., **1.** divide; divided. **2.** dividend. **3.** division.

di·va (dē′və), *n., pl.* –vas. a prima donna. [< Ital. < L, goddess]

di·va·lent (dī·vā′lənt), *adj. Chem.* having a valence of two.

di·van (dī′van, di·van′), *n.* a long, low, soft couch or sofa. [< Turk. < Pers. *dēvān*]

dive (dīv), *v.,* dived or (*U.S. Colloq. and Brit. Dial.*) dove, dived, div·ing, *n.* —*v.* **1.** plunge head first into water. **2.** go down or out of sight suddenly. **3.** (of an airplane) plunge downward at a steep angle. —*n.* **1.** act of diving. **2.** the downward plunge of an airplane. **3.** *Am., Colloq.* a low, cheap place for drinking and gambling. [OE *dȳfan*] —**div′er,** *n.*

dive bomber, airplane used to bomb a target by making an almost vertical dive straight at it. —**dive bombing.**

di·verge (də·vėrj′; dī–), *v.,* –verged, –verg·ing. **1.** move or lie in different directions from the same point. **2.** differ; vary; deviate. [< LL, < *dis–* in different directions + *vergere* slope] —**di·ver′gence, di·ver′gen·cy,** *n.* —**di·ver′gent,** *adj.* —**di·ver′gent·ly,** *adv.*

di·vers (dī′vėrz), *adj.* **1.** several different; various. **2.** *Obs.* diverse. [< OF < L *diversus,* pp. of *divertere* DIVERT]

di·verse (də·vėrs′; dī–), *adj.* **1.** different; unlike. **2.** varied: *a person of diverse interests.* [var. of *divers;* now regarded as immediately from L] —**di·verse′ly,** *adv.* —**di·verse′ness,** *n.*

di·ver·si·fy (də·vėr′sə·fī; dī–), *v.,* –fied, –fy·ing. give variety to; vary. —**di·ver′si·fi·ca′tion,** *n.* —**di·ver′si·fi′er,** *n.*

di·ver·sion (də·vėr′zhən; –shən; dī–), *n.* **1.** a turning aside. **2.** amusement; entertainment; pastime. —**Syn. 1.** deviation. **2.** sport, recreation.

di·ver·sion·ar·y (də·vėr′zhən·er′i; –shən–; dī–), *adj. Esp. Brit.* of or like a diversion or feint, esp. in military tactics.

di·ver·si·ty (də·vėr′sə·ti; dī–), *n., pl.* –ties. **1.** complete difference. **2.** variety.

di·vert (də·vėrt′; dī–), *v.* **1.** turn aside. **2.** amuse; entertain. [< F < L, < *dis–* aside + *vertere* turn] —**di·vert′er,** *n.* —**di·vert′ive,** *adj.*

di·ver·tisse·ment (dē·ver·tēs·män′), *n.* amusement; entertainment. [< F]

di·vest (də·vest′; dī–), *v.* **1.** strip; rid; free. **2.** force to give up; deprive. [< Med.L *divestire* < OF, < *des–* away < L *dis–*) + *vestir* < L *vestire* clothe]

di·vide (də·vīd′), *v.,* –vid·ed, –vid·ing, *n.* —*v.* **1.** separate into parts: *a brook divides the field.* **2.** separate into equal parts: *divide 8 by 2, and you get 4.* **3.** mark off or arrange regular steps, stages, or degrees on. **4.** find a quotient by mathematical procedures. **5.** give some of to each; share: *the children divided the candy among them.* **6.** disagree or cause to disagree; differ or cause to differ in feeling, opinion, etc.: *the school divided on the choice of a motto; jealousy divided us.* **7.** separate into two groups in voting. —*n. Am.* ridge of land between two regions drained by different river systems. [< L *dividere*] —**di·vid′a·ble,** *adj.* —**di·vid′er,** *n.* —**Syn. v. 1.** sever, split, part.

di·vid·ed (də·vīd′id), *adj.* **1.** separated. **2.** *Bot.* (of a leaf) cut to the base so as to form distinct portions. ➤ **divided usage.** Usage is said to be *divided* when two or more forms exist in the language, both in reputable use in the same dialect or style. *Divided usage* is not applied, for example, to localisms, like *sack, bag, poke,* or to differences like *ain't* and *isn't* which belong to separate styles of the language. It applies to spellings, pronunciations, or constructions on which speakers and writers of similar education might differ. The two pronunciations of *either* (ē′thər and ī′thər), the two spellings of *catalogue* (catalog and catalogue), and the two past tenses of *sing* (sang and sung) are examples of divided usage.

div·i·dend (div′ə·dend), *n.* **1.** number or quantity to be divided by another: *in 8 ÷ 2, 8 is the dividend.* **2.** money to be shared by those to whom it belongs. If a company makes a profit, it declares a dividend to the owners of the company. **3.** share of anything that is divided. [< L, (thing) to be divided]

di·vid·er (də·vīd′ər), *n.* **1.** person or thing that divides. **2.** Usually, **dividers.** instrument for dividing lines, etc.; compasses.

div·i·na·tion (div′ə·nā′shən), *n.* **1.** act of foreseeing the future or foretelling the unknown. **2.** a skillful guess or prediction. —**di·vin·a·to·ry** (də·vin′ə·tô′ri; –tō′–), *adj.*

di·vine (də·vīn′), *adj., n., v.,* –vined, –vin·ing. —*adj.* **1.** of God or a god. **2.** by or from God. **3.** to or for God; sacred; holy. **4.** like God or a god; heavenly. **5.** very excellent. —*n.* clergyman; minister; priest. —*v.* find out or foretell. [< OF < L *divinus* of a deity < *divus* deity] —**di·vine′ly,** *adv.* —**di·vine′ness,** *n.* —**di·vin′er,** *n.*

diving bell, a large, hollow container filled with air. People can work in it under water.

divining rod, a forked stick supposed to be useful in locating water, oil, metal, and other things underground.

Diving bell

di·vin·i·ty (də·vin′ə·ti), *n., pl.* –ties. **1.** a divine being; a god. **2.** the **Divinity,** God; the Deity. **3.** divine nature or quality. **4.** study of God, religion, and divine things; theology. **5.** godlike character or attribute. **6.** creamy fudge.

di·vis·i·ble (də·viz′ə·bəl), *adj.* **1.** capable of being divided. **2.** capable of being divided without leaving a remainder: *any even number is divisible by 2.* —**di·vis′i·bil′i·ty,** *n.* —**di·vis′i·bly,** *adv.*

di·vi·sion (də·vizh′ən), *n.* **1.** a dividing or being divided. **2.** act of giving some to each; a sharing. **3.** process of dividing one number by another. **4.** thing that divides. **5.** part; group; section. **6.** part of an army consisting of two or three brigades of infantry and a certain amount of cavalry, artillery, etc., usually commanded by a major general. **7.** difference of opinion, thought, or feeling; disagreement. **8.** separation of a legislature, parliament, etc., into two groups in taking a vote. —di·vi′sion·al, *adj.* —Syn. **2.** allotment, distribution, apportionment. ➤ division of words. When necessary in manuscript or print, a word is divided at the end of a line by a hyphen ("division hyphen"). In preparing manuscript if you will leave a reasonable right-hand margin, you will not be forced to divide so many words as you will if you crowd to the end of the line. A good habit is not to divide words unless the lines will be conspicuously uneven if the last word is completely written or completely carried over to the next line. In manuscript for publication most publishers prefer an uneven right margin to divided words. When it is necessary to divide a word, break it between syllables. Both the divided parts should be pronounceable; that is, words of one syllable, like *matched, said, thought,* should not be divided at all. English syllables are difficult to determine but in general they follow pronunciation groups: *auto-cratic* would be divided into syllables *au to crat ic,* but *autocracy* is *au toc ra cy.* The following words are divided to show typical syllables: *mar gin, hi lar i ous, hy phen, ac com-plished, long ing, pitch er.* Double consonants are usually separable: *ef fi cient, com mit tee, bat ted.* A single letter is not allowed to stand by itself; that is, do not divide at the end of lines words like *enough* (which would leave a lone *e* at the end of a line) or *many* (which would put a lone *y* at the beginning of a line). Words spelled with a hyphen (*half-hearted, well-disposed*) should be divided only at the point of the hyphen to avoid the awkwardness of two hyphens in the same word.

division of labor, a dividing up of work so that each person has a certain part to do.

di·vi·sor (də·vī′zər), *n.* number or quantity by which another is divided: *in 8 + 2, 2 is the divisor.*

di·vorce (də·vôrs′; -vōrs′), *n., v.,* -vorced, -vorc·ing. —*n.* **1.** the legal ending of a marriage. **2.** a complete separation. —*v.* **1.** end legally a marriage between. **2.** separate from by divorce: *Mrs. Smith divorced her husband.* **3.** separate. [< OF < L *divortium* separation < *divertere* DIVERT]

di·vor·cee (də·vôr′sē′; -vōr′-), *n.* a divorced woman.

div·ot (div′ət), *n.* a small piece of turf or earth dug up by a golf club in making a stroke.

di·vulge (də·vulj′), *v.,* -vulged, -vulg·ing. make known; make public; tell; reveal: *the traitor divulged secret plans to the enemy.* [< L *divulgare* make common < *dis-* + *vulgus* common people] —di·vulge′ment, —di·vulg′er, *n.* —Syn. disclose.

Dix·ie (dik′si), or **Dixie Land,** *n. Am.* the Southern States of the United States.

Dix·ie·crat (dik′si·krat), *n. Am.* one of those Democrats who opposed first the civil rights program of the Truman Administration and later the civil rights plank of the 1948 platform of the Democratic Party. Also, States' Rights Democrat. [< *Dixie* + (*demo*)*crat*]

diz·en (diz′ən; dī′zən), *v.* dress gaudily. [cf. MDu. *disen* wind up flax, MLG *dise* bunch of flax on distaff]

diz·zy (diz′i), *adj.,* -zi·er, -zi·est, *v.,* -zied, -zy·ing. —*adj.* **1.** disposed to fall, stagger, or spin around; not steady. **2.** confused; bewildered. **3.** causing dizziness: *a dizzy height.* **4.** *Colloq.* foolish; stupid. —*v.* make dizzy. [OE *dysig* foolish] —diz′zi·ly, —diz′zi·ness, *n.*

Dja·kar·ta (jə·kär′tə), *n.* seaport and capital of Indonesia, in NW Java. Also, **Jakarta.**

DNB, D.N.B., a German news agency.

Dnie·per (nē′pər), *n.* river flowing from W Soviet Union into the Black Sea.

do¹ (dü), *v., pres. sing.* 1 do, 2 (*Archaic*) do·est or dost, 3 does or (*Archaic*) do·eth or doth; *pl.* do; *pt.* did; *pp.* done; *ppr.* do·ing; *n.* —*v.* **1.** carry out; perform: *do your work.* **2.** act; work: *do or die.* **3.** complete; finish; end: *that's done!* **4.** make; produce: *Walt Disney did a movie about the seven dwarfs.* **5.** be the cause of; bring about: *your work does you credit.* **6.** act; behave: *do wisely.* **7.** render: *do homage.* **8.** deal with as the case may require; put in order: *do the dishes.* **9.** get along; manage; fare: *how do you do?* **10.** be satisfactory; be enough; serve: *this hat will do.* **11.** work out. **12.** cook: *the roast will be done in an hour.* **13.** cover; traverse: *we did 80 miles in an hour.* **14.** *Colloq.* cheat; trick. **15.** *Do* has special uses where it has no definite meaning: **a.** in asking questions: *do you like milk?* **b.** in emphasizing a verb: *I do want to go.* **c.** in standing for a verb already used: *my dog goes where I do.* **d.** in expressions that contain *not: people talk; animals do not.* **e.** in inverted constructions after the adverbs *rarely, hardly, little,* etc.: *rarely did she laugh.* **16.** do away with, **a.** abolish. **b.** kill. **17.** do by, act or behave toward; treat. **18.** do in, **a.** cheat. **b.** ruin. **c.** *Slang.* kill. **19.** do up, **a.** wrap up. **b.** clean and get ready for use. **c.** comb (one's hair). **d.** *Colloq.* wear out; exhaust. —*n. Colloq.* a festive party. [OE *dōn*] —Syn. *v.* **1.** execute, effect. **9.** prosper. **10.** suffice, answer.

do² (dō), *n.* the first and last of a series of syllables that are used for the eight tones of a musical scale. [substituted for *ut.* See GAMUT.]

do., ditto.

do·a·ble (dü′ə·bəl), *adj.* that can be done.

dob·bin (dob′ən), *n.* a slow, gentle horse.

Do·ber·man pin·scher (dō′bər·mən pin′shər), a medium-sized dog with short, dark hair.

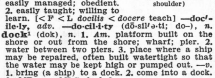

Doberman pinscher (ab. 2 ft. high at the shoulder)

doc·ile (dos′əl), *adj.* **1.** easily managed; obedient. **2.** easily taught; willing to learn. [< F < L *docilis* < *docere* teach] —doc′ile·ly, *adv.* —do·cil·i·ty (dō·sil′ə·ti; do-), *n.*

dock¹ (dok), *n.* **1.** *Am.* platform built on the shore or out from the shore; wharf; pier. **2.** water between two piers. **3.** place where a ship may be repaired, often built watertight so that the water may be kept high or pumped out. —*v.* **1.** bring (a ship) to a dock. **2.** come into a dock. [< MDu. or MLG *docke*]

dock² (dok), *n.* the solid, fleshy part of an animal's tail. —*v.* **1.** cut short; cut the end off. **2.** cut down; reduce: *dock wages for lateness.* [OE *-docca,* as in *finger-docca* finger muscle]

dock³ (dok), *n.* place where an accused person stands in a law court. [cf. Flem. *dok* pen]

dock⁴ (dok), *n.* a large weed with sour or bitter leaves. [OE *docce*]

dock·age (dok′ij), *n.* **1.** place to dock ship. **2.** charge for using a dock. **3.** the docking of ships.

dock·et (dok′it), *n., v.,* -et·ed, -et·ing. —*n.* **1.** *Am.* list of lawsuits to be tried by a court. **2.** *U.S.* any list of matters to be considered by some group of people. **3.** label or ticket giving the contents of a package, document, etc. —*v.* **1.** *Am.* enter on a docket. **2.** make a summary or list of. **3.** mark with a docket.

dock·yard (dok′yärd′), *n.* place where ships are built, equipped, and repaired.

doc·tor (dok′tər), *n.* **1.** person licensed to treat diseases or physical disorders; physician or surgeon. **2.** any person who treats diseases: *a witch doctor.* **3.** person who has received one of the highest degrees given by a university: *a Doctor of Philosophy.* **4.** the academic degree held by such a person. **5.** *Archaic.* a learned man; teacher. —*v.* **1.** *Colloq.* be a doctor; practice medicine. **2.** treat diseases in (a person, animal, etc.). **3.** take medicine. **4.** repair; mend. **5.** *Colloq.* tamper with. [< OF < L, teacher, < *docere* teach] —doc′tor·al, *adj.*

doc·tor·ate (dok′tər·it), *n.* degree of doctor given by a university.

doc·tri·naire (dok'trə·nãr'), **doc·tri·nar·i·an** (-nãr'ĭ·ən), *n.* an impractical theorist; person who tries to apply a theory without considering the actual circumstances.

doc·trine (dok'trən), *n.* 1. what is taught as the belief of a church, nation, etc. 2. what is taught; teachings. [< F < L *doctrina* < *doctor* DOCTOR] —**doc'tri·nal,** *adj.* —**doc'tri·nal·ly,** *adv.*

doc·u·ment (*n.* dok'yə·mənt; *v.* dok'yə·ment), *n.* 1. something written, printed, etc., that gives information or proof of some fact. 2. a printed or woven material or wallpaper. —*v.* 1. provide with documents. 2. prove or support by means of documents. [< L *documentum* example, proof <*docere* show] —**doc'u·men·ta'tion,** *n.*

doc·u·men·ta·ry (dok'yə·men'tə·ri), *adj., n., pl.* -ries. —*adj.* 1. of, pertaining to, or like a document or documents. 2. verified in writing. 3. presenting or recording factual information in an artistic fashion: *a documentary film.* —*n.* a documentary motion picture.

dod·der (dod'ər), *v.* shake; tremble; totter.

Do·dec·a·nese Islands (dō'dek·ə·nēs'; -nēz'; dō·dek'ə-), group of Greek islands in the Aegean Sea, off SW Turkey.

dodge (doj), *v.,* **dodged, dodg·ing,** *n.* —*v.* 1. move quickly to one side. 2. move quickly in order to get away from (a person, a blow, or something thrown). 3. get away from by some trick. —*n.* 1. sudden movement to one side. 2. *Colloq.* a clever trick or ruse. —**Syn.** *v.* 3. evade, equivocate.

dodg·er (doj'ər), *n.* 1. person who dodges. 2. a shifty or dishonest person. 3. *Am.* a small handbill. 4. *Am.* kind of corn bread.

Dodg·son (doj'sən), *n.* Charles L., 1832–1898, English mathematician who wrote *Alice in Wonderland.* His pen name was Lewis Carroll.

do·do (dō'dō), *n., pl.* **-dos, -does.** a large, clumsy bird unable to fly. Dodoes are now extinct. [< Pg. *doudo* fool]

Dodo (4 ft. long)

doe (dō), *n.* a female deer, antelope, rabbit, or hare. [OE *dā*]

Doe (dō), *n.* John, name used in legal documents, etc., to mean anyone.

do·er (dü'ər), *n.* person who does something.

does (duz), *v.* third pers. sing., pres. indic. of do[1].

doe·skin (dō'skin'), *n.* 1. skin of a female deer. 2. leather made from it. 3. a smooth, soft woolen cloth.

does·n't (duz'ənt), does not.

do·est (dü'ist), *v. Archaic.* do.

do·eth (dü'ith), *v. Archaic.* does.

doff (dof; dôf), *v.* take off; remove, as a hat. [contraction of *do off*]

dog (dôg; dog), *n., v.,* **dogged, dog·ging.** —*n.* 1. a domesticated carnivorous animal (of the genus *Canis*), kept as a pet, for hunting, etc. Two varieties are the cocker spaniel and the greyhound. 2. any animal of the family that includes wolves, foxes, and jackals. 3. a male dog, fox, wolf, etc. 4. any of various animals somewhat like a dog, such as the prairie dog. 5. a low, worthless man. 6. man; fellow. 7. *Am., Slang.* outward show. 8. thing that holds or grips. 9. andiron. 10. go to the dogs, be ruined. —*v.* hunt or follow like a dog. [OE *docga*]

dog·cart (dôg'kärt'; dog'-), *n.* 1. a small cart pulled by dogs. 2. a small, open carriage with two seats that are back to back.

dog days, period of very hot and uncomfortable weather during July and August.

doge (dōj), *n.* the chief magistrate of Venice or Genoa when they were republics. [< Venetian Ital. < L *dux* leader. Doublet of DUCE, DUKE.]

dog-ear (dôg'ir'; dog'-), *n.* a folded-down corner of a page in a book. —*v.* fold down the corner of (the page or pages of a book). Also, **dog's-ear.** —**dog'-eared',** *adj.*

dog·fight (dôg'fīt'; dog'-), *n. Colloq.* an engagement of fighter planes at close quarters with the enemy. —**dog'fight',** *v.*

dog·fish (dôg'fish'; dog'-), *n., pl.* **-fish·es** or (*esp. collectively*) **-fish.** any of several kinds of small shark, as the spiny dogfish of the North Atlantic coast.

dog·ged (dôg'id; dog'-), *adj.* stubborn: *dogged determination.* —**dog'ged·ly,** *adv.* —**dog'ged·ness,** *n.* —**Syn.** obstinate, headstrong.

dog·ger·el (dôg'ər·əl; dog'-), **dog·grel** (dôg'rəl; dog'-), *n.* very poor poetry that is not artistic in form or meaning. —*adj.* of or like doggerel; not artistic; poor.

dog·gy (dôg'i), *adj.,* -gi·er, -gi·est. 1. like a dog. 2. *Am., Colloq.* outwardly showy.

dog·house (dôg'hous'; dog'-), *n.* 1. a small house or shelter for a dog. 2. in the doghouse, *Am., Slang.* out of favor.

do·gie (dō'gi), *n. Am., W.* a motherless calf on the range or in a range herd.

dog·ma (dôg'mə; dog'-), *n., pl.* **-mas, -ma·ta** (-mə·tə). 1. belief taught or held as true, esp. by a church. 2. doctrine. 3. opinion asserted in a positive manner as if it were authoritative. [< L < Gk. opinion, < *dokeein* think]

dog·mat·ic (dôg·mat'ik; dog-), **dog·mat·i·cal** (-ə·kəl), *adj.* 1. having to do with dogma. 2. asserting opinions as if one were the highest authority; positive; overbearing. 3. asserted without proof. —**dog·mat'i·cal·ly,** *adv.* —**dog·mat'i·cal·ness,** *n.*

dog·ma·tism (dôg'mə·tiz·əm; dog'-), *n.* positive or authoritative assertion of opinion. —**dog'ma·tist,** *n.*

dog·ma·tize (dôg'mə·tīz; dog'-), *v.,* **-tized, -tiz·ing.** speak or write in a dogmatic way. —**dog'ma·ti·za'tion,** *n.* —**dog'ma·tiz'er,** *n.*

do-good·er (dü'gŏŏd'ər), *n.* a person who is overly eager to correct or set things right.

dog's-ear (dôgz'ir'; dogz'-), *n., v.* dog-ear.

Dog Star, 1. Sirius. 2. Procyon.

dogtooth violet, dog's-tooth violet, a small plant of the lily family that has yellow, white, or purple flowers; adder's-tongue.

dog·trot (dôg'trot'; dog'-), *n.* a gentle trot.

dog·watch (dôg'woch'; -wŏch'; dog'-), *n.* one of the two two-hour periods of work on a ship, from 4 to 6 P.M. and from 6 to 8 P.M.

Dogtooth violet

dog·wood (dôg'wŏŏd'; dog'-), *n.* 1. tree with pink or white flowers that bloom in the spring. 2. its hard wood.

doi·ly (doi'li), *n., pl.* **-lies.** a small piece of linen, lace, paper, etc., used under plates, vases, etc. [after a London dry-goods dealer]

do·ing (dü'ing), *n.* 1. action. 2. doings, *Am.* a. things done; actions. b. behavior; conduct.

dol·drum (dol'drəm; dōl'-), *n.* 1. a calm, windless region of the ocean near the equator. 2. doldrums, dullness; low spirits.

dole[1] (dōl), *n., v.,* **doled, dol·ing.** —*n.* 1. portion of money, food, etc., given in charity. 2. a small portion. 3. relief money given by a government to unemployed workers. —*v.* 1. deal out in portions to the poor. 2. give in small portions. [OE *dāl* part; akin to DEAL[1]]

dole[2] (dōl), *n. Archaic.* sorrow; grief. [< OF *doel* < VL *dolus* grief, < L *dolere* grieve]

dole·ful (dōl'fəl), *adj.* sad; mournful; dreary; dismal. —**dole'ful·ly,** *adv.* —**dole'ful·ness,** *n.* —**Syn.** sorrowful, woeful, plaintive.

doll (dol), *n.* 1. a child's plaything made to look like a baby, child, or grown person. 2. a pretty girl or woman without much intelligence. —*v. Slang.* dress (*up* or *out*) in a stylish or showy way. [pet name for *Dorothy*]

dol·lar (dol'ər), *n.* 1. *Am.* a unit of money in the United States, equivalent to 100 cents. 2. a similar unit of money in Canada, Mexico, etc.

3. *Am.* a silver coin or piece of paper money worth one dollar. [earlier *daler* < LG; corresponds to HG *Joachimsthaler* coin of St. Joachim's valley (in Bohemia)]

dollar crisis, condition resulting when a country reduces its supply of dollars through failure to balance its imports from the United States by its exports.

dollar gap, the shortage of dollars (for exchange) in a country suffering from a dollar crisis.

dollar imperialism, the extending of control and authority into foreign countries through the buying power of the dollar. —**dollar imperialist.**

doll·y (dol′ĭ), *n.*, *pl.* **doll·ies.** **1.** a child's name for a doll. **2.** a small, low frame with wheels, used to move heavy things.

dol·man (dol′mən), *n.*, *pl.* **-mans.** a woman's coat with capelike flaps instead of sleeves. [ult. < Turk. *dōlāmān*]

dol·men (dol′mən), *n.* a prehistoric tomb made by laying a large, flat stone across several upright stones. [< F]

dol·o·mite (dol′ə·mīt), *n.* a rock consisting of calcium and magnesium carbonate. [for M. *Dolomieu*, geologist]

do·lor, *Brit.* **do·lour** (dō′lər), *n. Poetic.* sorrow; grief. [< OF < L *dolor*]

dol·or·ous (dol′ər·əs; dō′lər-), *adj.* **1.** mournful; sorrowful. **2.** grievous; painful. —**dol′orous·ly,** *adv.* —**dol′orous·ness,** *n.*

dol·phin (dol′fən), *n.* **1.** a small whale that has a beaklike snout. **2.** post or buoy to which to moor a vessel. [< OF *daulphin* < L < Gk. *delphis*]

Dolphin (6 to 10 ft. long)

dolt (dōlt), *n.* a dull, stupid person.

dolt·ish (dōl′tish), *adj.* dull and stupid. —**dolt′ish·ly,** *adv.* —**dolt′ish·ness,** *n.*

-dom, *suffix.* **1.** position, rank, or realm of a ——, as in *kingdom.* **2.** condition of being ——, as in *martyrdom.* **3.** all those who are ——, as in *heathendom.* [OE *-dōm*]

do·main (dō·mān′), *n.* **1.** territory under the control of one ruler or government. **2.** land owned by one person; estate. **3.** field of thought, action, etc. [< F *domaine* < L, < *dominus* lord, master]

dome (dōm), *n.*, *v.*, **domed, dom·ing.** —*n.* **1.** a large, rounded roof on a circular or many-sided base. **2.** something high and rounded: *the dome of the sky.* —*v.* **1.** cover with a dome. **2.** shape like a dome. **3.** rise or swell as a dome does. [< F < Pr. < LL, roof, house, < Gk. *doma*]

do·mes·tic (də·mes′tik), *adj.* **1.** of the home, household, or family affairs. **2.** fond of home and family life. **3.** not wild; tame. **4.** of one's own country; not foreign. **5.** made in one's own country; native. —*n.* servant in a household. [< L, ult. < *domus* house] —**do·mes′ti·cal·ly,** *adv.*

do·mes·ti·cate (də·mes′tə·kāt), *v.*, **-cat·ed, -cat·ing.** **1.** change (animals, savages, or plants) from a wild to a tame state; tame. **2.** make fond of home and family life. **3.** naturalize. —**do·mes′ti·ca′tion,** *n.*

do·mes·tic·i·ty (dō′mes·tis′ə·ti), *n.*, *pl.* **-ties.** **1.** home and family life. **2.** fondness for home and family life.

dom·i·cile (dom′ə·səl; -sīl), *n.*, *v.*, **-ciled, -cil·ing.** —*n.* **1.** house; home; residence. **2.** place of permanent residence. —*v.* **1.** settle in a domicile. **2.** dwell; reside. [< F < L *domicilium* < *domus* house + *colere* dwell] —**dom·i·cil·i·ar·y** (dom′ə·sil′i·er′ĭ), *adj.*

dom·i·cil·i·ate (dom′ə·sil′i·āt), *v.*, **-at·ed, -at·ing.** domicile. —**dom′i·cil′i·a′tion,** *n.*

dom·i·nance (dom′ə·nəns), **dom·i·nan·cy** (-nən·si), *n.*, *pl.* **-ces, -cies.** a being dominant; rule; control.

dom·i·nant (dom′ə·nənt), *adj.* **1.** most influential; ruling. **2.** occupying a commanding position. **3.** *Music.* based on or pertaining to the dominant. **4.** *Biol.* of a characteristic that reappears in a larger number of offspring than a contrasting characteristic. —*n. Music.* the fifth

note in a scale. —**dom′i·nant·ly,** *adv.* —**Syn.** *adj.* **1.** governing, controlling.

dom·i·nate (dom′ə·nāt), *v.*, **-nat·ed, -nat·ing.** **1.** control or rule by strength or power. **2.** rise high above; hold a commanding position over. [< L, < *dominus* lord, master] —**dom′i·na′tive,** *adj.* —**dom′i·na′tor,** *n.*

dom·i·na·tion (dom′ə·nā′shən), *n.* act or fact of dominating; control; rule.

dom·i·neer (dom′ə·nir′), *v.* rule (over) at one's own will; tyrannize. [< Du. < F < L *dominari.* See DOMINATE.]

dom·i·neer·ing (dom′ə·nir′ing), *adj.* inclined to domineer; arrogant. —**dom′i·neer′ing·ly,** *adv.* —**dom′i·neer′ing·ness,** *n.*

Dom·i·nic (dom′ə·nik), *n.* Saint, 1170–1221, Spanish priest who founded an order called the Dominican order.

Do·min·i·can (də·min′ə·kən), *adj.* **1.** of Saint Dominic or the religious order founded by him. **2.** of the Dominican Republic. —*n.* **1.** friar or nun belonging to the Dominican order. **2.** native or inhabitant of the Dominican Republic.

Dominican Republic, republic in the E part of the island of Hispaniola (Haiti), in the West Indies. Also, Santo Domingo.

dom·i·nie (dom′ə·ni; *for 2, also* dō′mə·ni), *n.* **1.** *Esp. Scot.* schoolmaster. **2.** clergyman. [< L *domine* (vocative) lord, master]

do·min·ion (də·min′yən), *n.* **1.** supreme authority; rule; control. **2.** territory under the control of one ruler or government. **3.** a self-governing territory. [< obs. F < Med.L *dominio,* alter. of L *dominium* ownership]

Dominion Day, July 1, a national holiday in Canada in honor of the establishment of the Dominion of Canada in 1867.

dom·i·no¹ (dom′ə·nō), *n.*, *pl.* **-noes, -nos.** a loose cloak with a small mask covering the upper part of the face, worn esp. at masquerades. [< F < L *dominus* lord, master]

dom·i·no² (dom′ə·nō), *n.*, *pl.* **-noes.** **1.** dominoes (*sing. in use*), game played with flat, oblong pieces having dots marked on one side. **2.** one of these pieces.

don¹ (don), *n.* **1.** Don, Mr.; Sir (a Spanish title). **2.** a Spanish lord or gentleman. **3.** a distinguished person. **4.** *Colloq.* head, fellow, or tutor of a college at Oxford or Cambridge University. [< Sp. < L *dominus* lord, master]

don² (don), *v.*, **donned, don·ning.** put on (clothing, etc.). [contraction of *do on*]

Don (don), *n.* river flowing from C Soviet Union into the Sea of Azov.

Do·ña (dō′nyä), *n.* **1.** Lady; Madam (a Spanish title). **2.** doña, a Spanish lady. [< Sp. < L *domina* mistress]

do·nate (dō′nāt), *v.*, **-nat·ed, -nat·ing.** *Am.* give; contribute. [< L, < *donum* gift]

do·na·tion (dō·nā′shən), *n.* **1.** act of giving or contributing. **2.** gift; contribution.

done (dun), *adj.* **1.** completed; finished; ended. **2.** *Colloq.* worn out; exhausted. **3.** cooked enough. —*v.* pp. of do¹.

Do·nets (dō·nets′), *n.* river in S Soviet Union that flows into the Don.

don·jon (dun′jən; don′-), *n.* a large, strongly fortified tower of a castle. [var. of *dungeon*]

Don Juan (don′ wän′; jü′ən), **1.** a legendary Spanish nobleman who led a dissolute life. **2.** person leading an immoral life.

don·key (dong′ki; dung′-), *n.*, *pl.* **-keys. 1.** a small animal somewhat like a horse but with longer ears, a shorter mane, and a tuft of hair on the end of its tail. **2.** a stubborn person. **3.** a silly or stupid person.

donkey engine, a small steam engine.

don·na (don′ə), *n.* **1.** a lady. **2.** Donna, title of respect; Madam. [< Ital. < L *domina* mistress]

Donne (dun), *n.* John, 1573–1631, English poet.

do·nor (dō′nər), *n.* person who contributes; giver. [< AF < L *donator* < *donare* DONATE] —**do′nor·ship,** *n.*

Don Qui·xo·te (don′ ki·hō′tē; kwik′sət), **1.** story by Cervantes that satirized chivalric romances. It was published in two parts in 1605 and 1615. **2.** its hero.

don't (dōnt), do not. ❯ Don't is universally used in conversation and often in informal writing when *do not* would seem too emphatic or when rhythm seems more comfortable with the shorter form. In substandard usage *don't = doesn't*, and the usage often finds its way into familiar speech and even into casual writing: *he don't look as well as he used to.* Educated speakers and writers avoid it.

doo·dad (dü′dad), *n. Am., Colloq.* a fancy, trifling ornament.

doo·dle (dü′dəl), *v.,* –**dled,** –**dling,** *n. Am.* —*v.* make drawings, etc., while talking or thinking. —*n.* 1. a meaningless drawing or mark. 2. a silly person; simpleton.

doo·dle·bug[1] (dü′dəl·bug′), *n. Am.* larva of the ant lion.

doo·dle·bug[2] (dü′dəl·bug′), *n.* 1. *Am., Colloq.* any of various devices with which it is claimed mineral and oil deposits can be located. 2. *Colloq.* buzz bomb.

doom (düm), *n.* 1. fate. 2. an unhappy or terrible fate; ruin; death. 3. judgment; sentence. —*v.* 1. fate. 2. destine to an unhappy or terrible fate. 3. ordain or fix as a sentence or fate: *the emperor will doom her death.* [OE *dōm* law, judgment] —**Syn.** *n.* 1. destiny, lot, portion.

dooms·day (dümz′dā′), *n.* end of the world; day of God's final judgment of mankind.

door (dôr; dōr), *n.* 1. a movable part to close an opening in a wall. A door turns on hinges or slides open and shut. 2. any movable part that suggests a door. 3. an opening where a door is; doorway. 4. room, house, or building to which a door belongs: *his house is three doors down the street.* 5. way to get something. [OE *duru*]

door·bell (dôr′bel′; dōr′–), *n.* bell to be rung on the outside of a door as a signal that someone wishes to have the door opened.

door·jamb (dôr′jam′; dōr′–), **door·post** (–pōst′), *n.* the upright piece forming the side of a doorway.

door·keep·er (dôr′kēp′ər; dōr′–), *n.* 1. person who guards a door or entrance. 2. doorman.

door·knob (dôr′nob′; dōr′–), *n.* handle on a door.

door·man (dôr′mən; –man′; dōr′–), *n., pl.* –**men.** 1. man whose work is opening the door of a hotel, store, apartment house, etc., for people going in or out. 2. man who guards a door.

door·nail (dôr′nāl′; dōr′–), *n.* 1. nail with a large head. 2. **dead as a doornail,** entirely dead.

door·sill (dôr′sil′; dōr′–), *n.* threshold.

door·step (dôr′step′; dōr′–), *n.* step leading from an outside door to the ground.

door·way (dôr′wā′; dōr′–), *n.* an opening in a wall where a door is.

door·yard (dôr′yärd′; dōr′–), *n. Am.* yard near the door of a house; yard around a house.

dope (dōp), *n., v.,* **doped, dop·ing.** —*n.* 1. *Am., Slang.* a. a harmful, narcotic drug, such as opium, morphine, etc. b. a drug addict. 2. oil, grease, etc., used to make machinery run smoothly. 3. varnish put on the cloth parts of an airplane to make them stronger, waterproof, and airtight. 4. *Racing Slang.* drug, e.g. Adrenalin, given to a horse to stimulate it. 5. *Am., Slang.* information; forecast; prediction. 6. *U.S. Slang.* a very stupid person. —*v.* 1. *Am., Slang.* apply or give dope to. 2. use dope. 3. *Am., Slang.* work out; forecast; predict. [< Du. *doop* dipping sauce < *doopen* dip] —*dop′er, n. Slang.*

Do·ré (dō·rā′), *n.* **Paul Gustave,** 1832?–1883, French illustrator, painter, and sculptor.

Dor·ic (dôr′ik; dor′–), *adj.* of or having to do with the oldest and simplest of the Greek kinds of architecture.

Doric capital

dorm (dôrm), *n. Am., Colloq.* dormitory.

dor·man·cy (dôr′mən·si), *n.* dormant state.

dor·mant (dôr′mənt), *adj.* 1. sleeping. 2. quiet as if asleep. 3. inactive. Plant bulbs stay dormant during the cold of winter. [< OF, ppr. of *dormir* sleep < L *dormire*]

dor·mer (dôr′mər), *n.* 1. Also, **dormer window.** an upright window that projects from a sloping roof. 2. the projecting part of a roof that contains such a window. [< OF < L *dormitorium* DORMITORY]

dor·mi·to·ry (dôr′mə·tô′ri; –tō′–), *n., pl.* –**ries.** 1. *U.S.* a building with many sleeping rooms. 2. a sleeping room containing several beds. [< L, < *dormire* sleep]

dor·mouse (dôr′mous′), *n., pl.* –**mice.** a small animal that looks somewhat like a squirrel and sleeps all winter.

dor·sal (dôr′səl), *adj.* of, on, or near the back. [< LL < L *dorsum* back] —*dor′sal·ly, adv.*

Dor·set (dôr′sit), or **Dor·set·shire** (–shir; –shər), *n.* county in S England.

Dort·mund (dôrt′mūnt), *n.* city in W Germany.

do·ry (dô′ri; dō′–), *n., pl.* –**ries.** *Am.* rowboat with a flat bottom and high sides. [< Central Am. Ind.]

dos·age (dōs′ij), *n.* 1. amount of a medicine to be taken at one time. 2. the giving of medicine in doses.

dose (dōs), *n., v.,* **dosed, dos·ing.** —*n.* 1. amount of a medicine to be given or taken at one time. 2. amount of anything given at one time as a remedy, treatment, etc. —*v.* give medicine to in doses; treat with medicine. [< F < LL < Gk. *dosis* a giving < *didonai* give] —*dos′er, n.*

dos·si·er (dos′i·ā; –i·ər), *n.* collection of documents about some subject. [< F]

dost (dust), *v. Archaic.* dost.

Dos·to·ev·ski (dos′tə·yef′ski), *n.* **Feodor,** 1821–1881, Russian novelist.

dot[1] (dot), *n., v.,* **dot·ted, dot·ting.** —*n.* 1. a tiny round mark; very small spot; point. 2. a small spot. 3. *Music.* a point after a note or rest that makes it half again as long. 4. a short sound used in sending messages by telegraph or radio. 5. **on the dot,** *Colloq.* at exactly the right time. —*v.* 1. mark with a dot or dots. 2. be here and there in. [OE *dott* head of a boil] —*dot′ter, n.*

dot[2] (dot), *n. Law.* dowry. [< F < L *dos*] —*do·tal* (dō′təl), *adj.*

dot·age (dō′tij), *n.* weak-minded and childish condition caused by old age. [< *dote*]

do·tard (dō′tərd), *n.* person who is weak-minded and childish because of old age. [< *dote*]

dote (dōt), *v.,* **dot·ed, dot·ing.** 1. be weak-minded and childish because of old age. 2. **dote on** or **upon,** be foolishly fond of. [ME *doten*] —*dot′er, n.* —*dot′ing, adj.* —*dot′ing·ly, adv.*

doth (duth), *v. Archaic.* does.

dot·ty (dot′i), *adj.,* –**ti·er,** –**ti·est.** 1. *Esp. Brit. Colloq.* half-witted; partly insane. 2. *Colloq.* unsteady; shaky; feeble. 3. full of dots.

Dou·ai, Dou·ay (dü·ā′), *n.* town in N France.

Douay Bible or **Version,** an English translation of the Latin Vulgate Bible, made by a group of Roman Catholics. The New Testament was published at Reims in 1582, the Old Testament at Douai in 1609–1610.

dou·ble (dub′əl), *adj., adv., n., v.,* –**bled,** –**bling.** —*adj.* 1. twice as much, as many, as large, as strong, etc. 2. for two. 3. made of two like parts: *double doors.* 4. *Music.* having two beats (or some multiple of two) to the measure. 5. made of two unlike parts; combining two in one. Bear has a double meaning: *carry* and *animal.* 6. insincere; deceitful; false. 7. *Bot.* having more than one set of petals. —*adv.* 1. twice. 2. two together. —*n.* 1. number or amount that is twice as much. 2. person or thing just like another. 3. in motion pictures, a person who acts in the place of a leading actor or actress. 4. a fold; bend. 5. a sharp backward bend or turn; shift. 6. the next quickest step to a run. 7. *Am.* hit by which a batter gets to second base in baseball. 8. act of doubling a bid in bridge. 9. **doubles,** game with two players on each side. 10. **on the double,** a. quickly. b. *Mil.* in double time. —*v.* 1. make twice as much or twice as many. 2. become twice as much or as many. 3. be used for another; be the double of. 4. serve two purposes; play two parts: *the maid doubled as cook.* 5. fold; bend:

he doubled his fists in anger. 6. bend or turn sharply backward. 7. go around: *the ship doubled the Cape.* 8. increase the points or penalties of (an opponent's bid) in bridge. [< OF < L *duplus*] —**dou′ble·ness,** *n.* —**dou′bler,** *n.* —Syn. *adj.* 3. paired.

double bass, a musical instrument shaped like a cello but much larger, with a very low bass tone; bass viol.

double bassoon, a large bassoon, an octave lower in pitch than the ordinary bassoon.

double boiler, *Am.* pair of cooking pans, one of which fits down into the other.

dou·ble-breast·ed (dub′əl·bres′tid), *adj.* overlapping enough to make two layers across the breast and having two rows of buttons.

dou·ble-cross (dub′əl·krôs′; -kros′), *v. Slang.* promise to do one thing and then do another; be treacherous to. —**dou′ble-cross′er,** *n.*

double cross, act of treachery.

double dagger, mark (‡) used to refer the reader to another section or to a note in a book.

dou·ble-deal·ing (dub′əl·dēl′ing), *n., adj.* pretending to do one thing and then doing another; deceiving. —**dou′ble-deal′er,** *n.*

dou·ble-dome (dub′əl·dōm′), *n. Am., Slang.* person of advanced intellect and refined taste; highbrow.

dou·ble-en·ten·dre (dü·blän·tän′drə), *n.* word or expression with two meanings. One meaning is often improper. [< obs. F, lit., to be taken two ways]

double entry, system of bookkeeping in which each transaction is written down twice, once on the credit side of the account and once on the debit side.

dou·ble-faced (dub′əl·fāst′), *adj.* 1. pretending to be what one is not; hypocritical; deceitful. 2. having two faces or aspects.

dou·ble-head·er (dub′əl·hed′ər), *n. Am.* in baseball, two games on the same day in immediate succession.

dou·ble-park (dub′əl·pärk′), *v. Am.* park (a car, etc.) beside another car which is occupying the area specified for parking. —**dou′ble-park′ing,** *n. Am.*

dou·ble-quick (dub′əl·kwik′), *n.* the next quickest step to a run in marching. —*adj.* very quick. —*adv.* in double-quick time. —*v.* march in double-quick step.

dou·blet (dub′lit), *n.* 1. a man's close-fitting jacket. 2. pair of two similar or equal things. 3. one of a pair. 4. one of two words in a language, derived from the same original but coming by different routes, as *guard* and *ward.*

Doublet

double talk, speech that is purposely incoherent, but that is made to seem serious by mixing in normal words, intonations, etc.

double time, 1. in the U.S. army, a rate of marching in which 180 paces, each of 3 feet, are taken in a minute. 2. double-quick.

dou·ble-tree (dub′əl·trē′), *n.* crossbar on a carriage, wagon, plow, etc.

dou·bloon (dub·lün′), *n.* a former Spanish gold coin. [< Sp. *doblón* < *doble* DOUBLE]

dou·bly (dub′li), *adv.* 1. twice; twice as. 2. two at a time.

doubt (dout), *v.* 1. not believe; not be sure of; feel uncertain about. 2. be uncertain. 3. *Archaic.* be afraid; fear. —*n.* 1. lack of belief or sureness; uncertainty. 2. *Obs.* fear; apprehension. 3. no doubt, a. surely; certainly. b. probably. [< OF *douter* < L *dubitare*] —**doubt′a·ble,** *adj.* —**doubt′er,** *n.* —**doubt′ing·ly,** *adv.* —Syn. *v.* 1. mistrust, question. —*n.* 1. misgiving, mistrust. ▶ **doubt.** The idioms with *doubt* are: 1. negative (where there is no real doubt), *doubt that: I do not doubt that he means well.* 2. positive (when doubt exists), *doubt that, whether* (in formal use): *I doubt whether he meant it that way; I doubt that he meant it that way* (indicating unbelief really more than doubt); *if* (in informal use): *I doubt if he meant it that way.*

doubt·ful (dout′fəl), *adj.* 1. in doubt; not sure; uncertain. 2. causing doubt; open to question or suspicion. —**doubt′ful·ly,** *adv.* —**doubt′ful-**

ness, *n.* —Syn. 1. indefinite. 2. questionable.

doubt·less (dout′lis), *adv.* 1. surely; certainly. 2. probably. —*adj.* sure; certain. —**doubt′less·ly,** *adv.* —**doubt′less·ness,** *n.*

douche (düsh), *n., v.,* douched, douch·ing. —*n.* 1. jet of water applied on or into any part of the body. 2. application of a douche. 3. spray, syringe, or other device for applying a douche. —*v.* 1. apply a douche to. 2. take a douche. [< F < Ital. *doccia,* ult. < L *ducere* lead]

dough (dō), *n.* 1. a mixture of flour, liquid, and other materials for baking. 2. any soft, thick mass like this. 3. *Am., Slang.* money. [OE *dāg*]

dough·boy (dō′boi′), *n. Am., Colloq.* an infantryman in the U.S. army during World War I.

dough·nut (dō′nut′), *n.* a small, brown cake, usually ring-shaped, cooked in deep fat.

dough·ty (dou′ti), *adj.,* -ti·er, -ti·est. *Archaic or Humorous.* brave; valiant; strong. [OE *dohtig* < *dugan* be good] —**dough′ti·ly,** *adv.* —**dough′ti·ness,** *n.*

dough·y (dō′i), *adj.,* dough·i·er, dough·i·est. of or like dough.

Doug·las (dug′ləs), *n.* 1. Stephen A., 1813-1861, American statesman and political leader. 2. William Orville, born 1898, associate justice of the United States Supreme Court from 1939.

Douglas fir, *Am.* a very tall evergreen tree common in the western United States.

Doug·las-Home (dug′ləs hūm), *n.* Sir Alec, born 1903, British prime minister, 1963-1964.

Doug·lass (dug′ləs), *n.* Frederick, 1817-1895, American Negro leader who opposed slavery.

dour (dur; dour), *adj.* 1. gloomy; sullen. 2. stern; severe. 3. stubborn. [< L *durus* hard, stern]

douse (dous), *v.,* doused, dous·ing. 1. plunge into water or any other liquid. 2. throw water over; extinguish. 3. *Colloq.* put out (a light); extinguish. 4. *Colloq.* take off; doff. 5. lower or slacken (a sail) in haste. 6. close (a porthole). —**dous′er,** *n.*

dove[1] (duv), *n.* 1. bird with a thick body, short legs, and a beak enlarged at the tip; pigeon. 2. Dove, the Holy Ghost. 3. an innocent, gentle, or loving person. 4. person who is eager for peace. [OE *dufe-;* akin to DIVE]

dove[2] (dōv), *v. U.S. Colloq. and Brit. Dial.* pt. of dive.

dove·cote (duv′kōt′), **dove·cot** (-kot′), *n.* a small shelter for doves or pigeons.

Do·ver (dō′vər), *n.* 1. seaport in SE England, the nearest English port to France. 2. Strait of, a narrow channel or strait between N France and SE England. 3. capital of Delaware.

dove·tail (duv′tāl′), *n.* 1. projection at the end of a piece of wood, metal, etc., that can be fitted into a corresponding opening at the end of another piece to form a joint. 2. the joint formed in this way. —*v.* 1. fasten, join, or fit together with projections that fit into openings. 2. fit together exactly.

dow·a·ger (dou′ə·jər), *n.* 1. widow who holds some title or property from her dead husband. 2. *Colloq.* a dignified, elderly lady. [< OF *douagere* (def. 1) < *douage* DOWER]

dow·dy (dou′di), *adj.,* -di·er, -di·est, *n., pl.* -dies. —*adj.* poorly dressed; not neat; not stylish; shabby. —*n.* woman whose clothes are dowdy. —**dow′di·ly,** *adv.* —**dow′di·ness,** *n.*

DOWEL

dow·el (dou′əl), *n., v.,* -eled, -el·ing; *esp. Brit.* -elled, -el·ling. —*n.* peg on a piece of wood, metal, etc., to fit into a corresponding hole on another piece, and so form a joint. —*v.* fasten with dowels.

dow·er (dou′ər), *n.* 1. a widow's share for life of her dead husband's property. 2. dowry. 3. a natural gift, talent, or quality; endowment. —*v.* provide with a dower; endow. [< OF < Med.L *dotarium,* < LL *dotare* endow < L *dos* dowry]

down[1] (doun), *adv.* 1. from a higher to a lower place or condition. 2. in a lower place or condition. 3. to a place or condition thought of as lower: *down South.* 4. to a position or condition that is difficult, dangerous, etc.: *the dogs ran down the fox.* 5. from an earlier to a later time or person: *hand down a house.* 6. from a larger to a smaller amount, degree, etc. **7.** actually; really: *get down to work.* **8.** on paper; in writing: *take down what I say.* **9.** when bought: *you can pay part of the price down and the rest later.* —*prep.* down along, through, or into: *walk down a street.* —*adj.* **1.** in a lower place or condition. **2.** going or pointed down. **3.** sick; ill: *she is down with a cold.* **4.** sad; discouraged: *he felt down about his failure.* **5.** of a football; no longer in play. **6.** behind an opponent by a certain number. —*v.* **1.** put down; get down: *he downed the medicine at one swallow.* **2.** lie down: *down, Fido!* —*n.* **1.** a downward movement. **2.** piece of bad luck. **3.** chance to move a football forward: *a team has four downs to make ten yards.* [var. of *adown*]

down² (doun), *n.* soft feathers or hair; fluff. [< Scand. *dūnn*]

down³ (doun), *n.* **1.** mound or ridge of sand heaped up by the wind; dune. **2.** Usually, **downs.** rolling, grassy land. [OE *dūn* hill]

down·cast (doun′kast′; -käst′), *adj.* **1.** directed downward. **2.** dejected; sad; discouraged. —*n.* **1.** a downcast look. **2.** a casting down; overthrow; ruin. **3. a.** a drawing or forcing down, esp. of air for ventilation in a mine or the like. **b.** shaft used for this.

down·fall (doun′fôl′), *n.* **1.** overthrow; ruin. **2.** a heavy rain or snow. **3.** a kind of trap in which a weight or missile falls upon the prey. —**down′fall′en,** *adj.*

down·grade (doun′grād′), *n., adj., adv., v.,* -grad·ed, -grad·ing. —*n. Am.* a downward slope. —*adj., adv.* downward. —*v. Am.* move to a lower position with a smaller salary. —**down′grad′ing,** *adj., n. Am.*

down·heart·ed (doun′här′tid), *adj.* dejected. —**down′heart′ed·ly,** *adv.* —**down′heart′ed·ness,** *n.*

down·hill (doun′hil′), *adv.* down the slope of a hill; downward. —*adj.* **1.** sloping downward; tending downward. **2.** worse.

Down·ing Street (doun′ing). **1.** street in London where several important offices of the British government are located. **2.** the British government.

down·pour (doun′pôr′; -pōr′), *n.* a heavy rain.

down·right (doun′rīt′), *adj.* **1.** thorough; complete. **2.** plain; positive. **3.** directed straight downward. —*adv.* **1.** thoroughly; completely. **2.** straight down. —**down′right′ly,** *adv.* —**down′-right′ness,** *n.*

down·stairs (doun′stärz′), *adv.* **1.** down the stairs. **2.** on a lower floor. —*adj.* on a lower floor. —*n.* lower floor or floors.

down·stream (doun′strēm′), *adv., adj.* with the current of a stream; down a stream.

down town, *Am.* the commercial section or main district of a town.

down·town (doun′toun′), *adv., adj.* **1.** to, toward, or in the lower part of a town. **2.** *Am.* to or in the main part of a town.

down·trod·den (doun′trod′ən), **down·trod** (-trod′), *adj.* **1.** oppressed. **2.** trodden down.

down·ward (doun′wərd), *adv.* Also, **down′-wards.** toward a lower place or condition. —*adj.* moving or tending toward a lower place or condition. —**down′ward·ly,** *adv.* —**down′ward·ness,** *n.*

down·y (doun′i), *adj.,* **down·i·er, down·i·est. 1.** of soft feathers or hair. **2.** covered with soft feathers or hair. **3.** like down; soft; fluffy. —**down′i·ness,** *n.*

dow·ry (dou′ri), *n., pl.* -ries. **1.** money, property, etc., that a woman brings to her husband when she marries him. **2.** a natural gift, talent, or quality. Also, **dower.** [< AF *dowarie*]

dowse (douz), *v.,* dowsed, dows·ing. use a divining rod to locate water, etc. —**dows′er,** *n.*

dox·ol·o·gy (doks·ol′ə·ji), *n., pl.* -gies. hymn or statement praising God. Three of the best-known doxologies begin: "Glory to God in the highest," "Glory be to the Father and to the Son and to the Holy Ghost," and "Praise God from whom all blessings flow." [< Med.L. < Gk., <

doxa glory, praise + -*logos* speaking] —**dox-o·log·i·cal** (dok′sə·loj′ə·kəl), *adj.* —**dox′o·log′i-cal·ly,** *adv.*

Doyle (doil), *n.* Sir Arthur Conan, 1859–1930, English writer of detective stories.

doz., dozen; dozens.

doze (dōz), *v.,* dozed, doz·ing, *n.* —*v.* **1.** sleep lightly; be half asleep. **2.** doze off, fall into a doze. —*n.* a light sleep; a nap. [cf. Dan. *döse* make dull] —**doz′er,** *n.*

doz·en (duz′ən), *n., pl.* -ens or (*after a number*) -en. group of 12. [< OF *dozeine* < *douse* twelve < L *duodecim*] —**doz′enth,** *adj.*

Dr., Dr, Doctor.

dr., **1.** debtor. **2.** dram; drams.

drab¹ (drab), *n., adj.* drab·ber, drab·best. —*n.* a dull, brownish gray. —*adj.* **1.** dull; monotonous; unattractive. **2.** dull brownish-gray. [appar. var. of *drap* cloth < F. See DRAPE.] —**drab′ly,** *adv.* —**drab′ness,** *n.*

drab² (drab), *n., v.,* drabbed, drab·bing. —*n.* **1.** a dirty, untidy woman. **2.** prostitute. —*v.* keep company with drabs. [cf. Irish *drabog* slattern]

drachm (dram), *n.* **1.** *Brit.* dram. **2.** drachma.

drach·ma (drak′mə), *n., pl.* -mas, -mae (-mē). **1.** a unit of Greek money. **2.** an ancient Greek silver coin, varying in value. [< L < Gk. *drachme* handful < *drassesthai* grasp]

draft (draft; dräft), *n.* **1.** current of air. **2.** device for regulating a current of air: *the draft of a furnace.* **3.** a plan; a sketch. **4.** a rough copy: *a draft of a speech.* **5.** selection of persons for some special purpose: *in time of war men are often supplied to the army and navy by draft.* **6.** persons selected for some special purpose. **7.** act of pulling loads. **8.** the quantity pulled. **9.** Usually, **draught.** **a.** the pulling in of a net to catch fish. **b.** quantity of fish caught in a net. **10.** a written order from one person or bank to another, requiring the payment of a stated amount of money. **11.** a heavy demand or drain on anything. **12.** Usually, **draught.** depth of water that a ship needs for floating. **13.** Usually, **draught. a.** act of drinking: *he emptied the glass at one draft.* **b.** amount taken in one drink. **c.** breathing in of air, smoke, etc. **d.** air, smoke, etc., breathed in. **e.** drawing beer, ale, etc., from a barrel when ordered. —*v.* **1.** make a plan or sketch of. **2.** write out a rough copy of. **3.** select for some special purpose. —*adj.* **1.** for pulling loads: *a big, strong horse or ox is a draft animal.* **2.** Usually, **draught.** drawn from a barrel when ordered. [var. of *.draught*] —**draft′er,** *n.* ❯ See **draught** for usage note.

draft·ee (draf·tē′; dräf-), *n. Am.* person who is drafted for military service.

drafts (drafts; dräfts), *n.pl.* U.S. spelling of **draughts.**

drafts·man (drafts′mən; dräfts′-), *n., pl.* -men. **1.** person who makes plans or sketches, as of buildings and machines. **2.** person who writes out rough copies of documents, speeches, etc. Also, **draughtsman.** —**drafts′man·ship,** *n.*

draft·y (draf′ti; dräf′-), *adj.,* draft·i·er, draft·i·est. **1.** in a current of air. **2.** having many currents of air. **3.** causing a current of air. —**draft′-i·ly,** *adv.* —**draft′i·ness,** *n.*

drag (drag), *v.,* dragged, drag·ging, *n.* —*v.* **1.** pull or move along heavily or slowly. **2.** go too slowly. **3.** pull a net, hook, harrow, etc., over or along for some purpose. **4.** be drawn or hauled along; trail on the ground. —*n.* **1.** net, hook, etc., used in dragging. **2.** act of dragging. **3.** thing dragged. **4.** anything that holds back; hindrance. **5.** a low, strong sled for carrying heavy loads. **6.** a heavy harrow to break up ground. **7.** *Am., Slang.* influence. [ME *dragge(n)*] —**Syn.** *v.* **1.** haul, tug, trail. —*n.* **4.** impediment, obstruction.

drag·gle (drag′əl), *v.,* -gled, -gling. make or become wet or dirty by dragging through mud, water, dust, etc.

drag·net (drag′net′), *n.* **1.** net pulled over the bottom of a river, pond, etc., or along the ground. **2.** means of catching criminals.

drag·o·man (drag′ə·mən), *n., pl.* -mans,

–men. in the Orient, an interpreter. [< F < Ital. < Med.Gk. < Ar. < Aram. < Assyrian-Babylonian *targumānu*]

drag·on (drag′ən), n. 1. a huge, fierce animal supposed to look like a snake with wings and claws, often breathing out fire and smoke. 2. a very strict and watchful woman, esp. a stern chaperon. [< OF < L < Gk. *drakon*]

drag·on·fly (drag′ən·flī′), n., pl. –flies. a large, harmless insect, with a long, slender body and two pairs of gauzy wings, that catches flies, mosquitoes, etc.

Dragonfly (½ to 4 in. long)

dra·goon (drə·gün′), n. soldier who fights on horseback. —v. 1. oppress or persecute by dragoons. 2. compel by oppression or persecution. [< F *dragon* DRAGON, pistol, (later) soldier]

drag race, Am., Slang. a race to test acceleration, in which two cars compete over a measured distance (**drag strip**), usually a quarter of a mile. —drag′·rac′er, n.

drain (drān), v. 1. draw off or flow off slowly. 2. empty or dry by draining. 3. use up little by little; deprive. —n. 1. channel or pipe for carrying off water or other liquid. 2. anything that drains. 3. a slow taking away. [OE *drēahnian*; akin to DRY] —drain′a·ble, adj. —drain′er, n.

drain·age (drān′ij), n. 1. act or process of draining. 2. system of channels or pipes for carrying off water or waste of any kind. 3. what is drained off. 4. area that is drained.

drainage basin, Am. area that is drained by a river and its tributaries.

drain·pipe (drān′pīp′), n. pipe for carrying off water or other liquid.

drake (drāk), n. a male duck. [ME]

Drake (drāk), n. Sir Francis, 1540?–1596, English admiral.

dram (dram), n. 1. a small weight. In apothecaries' weight, 8 drams make one ounce; in avoirdupois weight, 16 drams make one ounce. 2. a fluid dram. 3. Esp. Brit. a small drink of intoxicating liquor. 4. Esp. Brit. a small amount of anything. Also, Brit. **drachm.** [< OF < L *drachma* DRACHMA]

dra·ma (drä′mə; dram′ə), n. 1. story written to be acted out by actors on a stage. 2. series of happenings that seem like those of a play. 3. the drama, the art of writing, acting, or producing plays. [< LL < Gk., play, deed < *draein* do]

Dram·a·mine (dram′ə·mēn), n. Trademark. drug used as a remedy for seasickness, etc.

dra·mat·ic (drə·mat′ik), adj. 1. of drama; having to do with plays. 2. seeming like a drama or play; exciting. —dra·mat′i·cal·ly, adv.

dra·mat·ics (drə·mat′iks), n. 1. (sing. or pl. in use) art of acting or producing plays. 2. (pl. in use) plays given by amateurs.

dram·a·tis per·so·nae (dram′ə·tis pər·sō′nē), characters or actors in a play. [< L]

dram·a·tist (dram′ə·tist), n. writer of plays; playwright.

dram·a·tize (dram′ə·tīz), v., –tized, –tiz·ing. 1. make a drama of; arrange in the form of a play. 2. show or express in a dramatic way. —dram′a·ti·za′tion, n. —dram′a·tiz′er, n.

dram·a·tur·gy (dram′ə·tėr′ji), n. art of writing or producing dramas. [< Gk. *dramatourgia* < *drama* DRAMA + –*ourgos* making < *ergon* work] —dram′a·tur′gic, dram′a·tur′gi·cal, adj. —dram′a·tur′gist, n.

dram·shop (dram′shop′), n. Esp. Brit. place where intoxicating liquor is sold; saloon.

drank (drangk), v. pt. of drink.

drape (drāp), v., draped, drap·ing, n. —v. 1. cover or hang with cloth falling loosely in folds. 2. arrange (clothes, hangings, etc.) in graceful folds. 3. fall in folds. —n. cloth hung in graceful folds; hanging. [< F < *drap* cloth < LL *drappus*]

drap·er (drāp′ər), n. 1. Esp Brit. dealer in cloth or dry goods. 2. person that drapes.

dra·per·y (drā′pər·i), n., pl. –per·ies. 1. clothing or hangings arranged in graceful folds. 2. graceful arrangement of hangings or clothing. 3. cloth or fabric.

dras·tic (dras′tik), adj. acting with force or violence; extreme. [< Gk. *drastikos* effective < *draein* do] —dras′ti·cal·ly, adv.

draught (draft; dräft), n., v., adj. draft. [ME *draht* < OE *dragan* draw] —draught′er, n.

draft, draught. The spelling of *draught* (from the Old English *dragan*, to draw) has gradually come to represent its pronunciation (draft). *Draft* is always the spelling for a *bank draft*, the *military draft*, a *draft of a composition*, a *draft of air*; usage is divided on the word in the sense of a maker of drawings — *draftsman* or *draughtsman*; *draught* is more common for a *ship's draught*, a *draught of fish*, and for a *draught of ale* or *beer on draught* — though *draft* is rapidly gaining in this last sense.

draughts (drafts; dräfts), n.pl. Brit. (sing. in use) game of checkers.

draughts·man (drafts′mən; dräfts′–), n., pl. –men. draftsman. —draughts′man·ship, n.

drave (drāv), v. Archaic. pt. of drive.

Dra·vid·i·an (drə·vid′i·ən), adj. of or having to do with the non-Aryan races in southern India and in Ceylon. —n. 1. member of any of these races. 2. languages spoken by them.

draw (drô), v., drew, drawn, draw·ing, n. —v. 1. pull; drag: a horse draws a wagon. 2. pull out; pull up; pull back: he drew his hand from his pocket. 3. bring out; take out; get out: draw a pail of water from the well. 4. take out a pistol, sword, etc., for action. 5. take; get; receive: I drew another idea from the story. 6. make; cause; bring: your actions draw praise or blame on yourself. 7. move; come; go: we drew near the fire to get warm. 8. attract: a parade draws a crowd. 9. make a picture or likeness of with pencil, pen, chalk, crayon, etc.; represent by lines. 10. write out in proper form; frame; draft. 11. write (an order to pay money). 12. make a demand; be a drain. 13. make a current of air to carry off smoke: a chimney draws. 14. breathe in; inhale; take in. 15. utter: draw a sigh. 16. make the same score in; finish with neither side winning. 17. make or become longer; stretch. 18. make or become smaller; shrink. 19. make (wire) by pulling a rod of metal through a succession of holes of decreasing diameter. 20. (of a ship) need for floating; sink to a depth of. 21. take out the insides of. 22. make (tea) by extracting the essence. 23. steep: the tea is drawing. 24. draw up, a. arrange in order. b. write out. c. stop. —n. 1. act of drawing. 2. thing that attracts. 3. a tie in a game. 4. Am. part of a drawbridge that can be moved. 5. a drawing of lots. 6. the lot drawn. 7. a land basin into or through which water drains; valley. [OE *dragan*] —Syn. v. 1. haul, tug. 3. extract. 5. obtain, derive, infer. 8. entice, allure. 9. trace, sketch, depict. 10. formulate. 17. lengthen, prolong.

draw·back (drô′bak′), n. 1. something unfavorable or unpleasant; disadvantage; hindrance. 2. Am. money paid back from a charge made.

draw·bridge (drô′brij′), n. bridge that can be wholly or partly lifted, lowered, or moved to one side.

draw·ee (drô·ē′), n. person for whom an order to pay money is written.

draw·er (drôr for 1; drô′ər for 2 and 3), n. 1. box that slides in and out of a chest, desk, table, etc. 2. person or thing that draws. 3. person who writes an order to pay money. 4. drawers (drôrz), undergarment fitting over the legs and around the waist.

draw·ing (drô′ing), n. 1. picture or likeness made with pencil, pen, chalk, crayon, etc.; lines representing a person or thing. 2. the making of such pictures or likenesses. 3. act of a person or thing that draws anything.

drawing room, 1. room for receiving or entertaining guests; parlor. 2. Am. a private compartment in a Pullman car. [for *withdrawing room*]

draw·knife (drô′nīf′), or **drawing knife,** n., pl. –knives. blade with a handle at each end, used to shave off surfaces. Also, **drawshave.**

drawl (drôl), v. talk in a slow, lazy way. —n. a slow, lazy way of talking. [appar. akin to DRAW] —drawl′er, n. —drawl′ing·ly, adv.

drawn (drôn), *v.* pp. of draw.

drawn work, ornamental work done by drawing threads from a fabric, the remaining portions usually being formed into patterns by needlework.

draw·shave (drô'shāv'), *n.* drawknife.

dray (drā), *n.* a low, strong cart for hauling heavy loads. —*v.* transport or carry on a cart. [OE *dræg*– drag < *dragan* draw]

dray·age (drā'ij), *n.* 1. act of hauling a load on a dray. 2. *Am.* charge for hauling a load on a dray.

dray·man (drā'mən), *n.*, *pl.* **-men.** man who drives a dray.

dread (dred), *v.* look forward to with fear. —*n.* 1. fear, esp. fear of something that will happen or may happen. 2. person or thing inspiring fear. 3. awe. —*adj.* 1. dreaded; dreadful. 2. held in awe; awe-inspiring. [OE *drǣdan*] —Syn. *v.* apprehend.

dread·ful (dred'fəl), *adj.* 1. causing dread; awe-inspiring. 2. *Colloq.* very bad; very unpleasant. —**dread'ful·ly,** *adv.* —**dread'ful·ness,** *n.* —Syn. 1. fearful, terrible, dire.

dread·nought, dread·naught (dred'-nôt'), *n.* a big, powerful battleship with heavy armor and large guns.

dream (drēm), *n.*, *v.*, **dreamed** or **dreamt** (dremt), **dream·ing.** —*n.* 1. something thought, felt, seen, or heard during sleep. 2. something as unreal as a dream. 3. state in which a person has dreams. 4. something having great beauty or charm. —*v.* 1. have dreams. 2. think of (something) as possible; imagine. 3. spend in dreaming. 4. **dream up,** *Colloq.* create (an invention, etc.) mentally. [OE *drēam* joy, music] —**dream'-er,** *n.* —**dream'ing·ly,** *adv.* —**dream'less,** *adj.* —Syn. *n.* vision, fantasy.

dream·y (drēm'ĭ), *adj.*, **dream·i·er, dream·i·est.** 1. full of dreams. 2. like a dream; vague; dim: *a dreamy recollection.* 3. impractical: *a dreamy person.* 4. causing dreams; soothing. —**dream'i·ly,** *adv.* —**dream'i·ness,** *n.*

drear (drir), *adj. Poetic.* dreary.

drear·y (drir'ĭ), *adj.*, **drear·i·er, drear·i·est.** 1. dull; gloomy; cheerless; depressing. 2. *Archaic.* sad; sorrowful. [OE *drēorig*] —**drear'i·ly,** *adv.* —**drear'i·ness,** *n.* —Syn. 1. tedious, tiresome, dismal.

dredge[1] (drej), *n.*, *v.*, **dredged, dredg·ing.** —*n.* 1. machine with a scoop or series of buckets for removing mud, sand, or other materials from the bottom of a river, harbor, etc. 2. apparatus with a net, used for gathering oysters, etc. —*v.* 1. clean out or deepen (a channel, harbor, etc.) with a dredge. 2. bring up or gather with a dredge. [ME *dreg;* akin to DRAG] —**dredg'er,** *n.*

dredge[2] (drej), *v.*, **dredged, dredg·ing.** sprinkle: *dredge meat with flour.* [appar. < *dredge,* *n.,* grain mixture] —**dredg'er,** *n.*

dreg (dreg), *n.* Usually, **dregs.** 1. solid bits of matter that settle to the bottom of a liquid. 2. the most worthless part. [< Scand. *dreggjar*] —**dreg'gy,** *adj.*

Drei·ser (drī'sər; -zər), *n.* Theodore, 1871-1945, American novelist.

drench (drench), *v.* wet thoroughly; soak. —*n.* 1. a thorough wetting; a soaking. 2. something that drenches. 3. solution for soaking. [OE *drencan* < *drincan* drink] —**drench'er,** *n.*

Dres·den (drez'dən), *n.* city in C Germany, on the Elbe River.

dress (dres), *n.*, *adj.*, *v.*, **dressed** or **drest, dress·ing.** —*n.* 1. the outer garment worn by women, girls, and babies. 2. an outer covering. 3. clothes. 4. formal clothes. [< v.] —*adj.* 1. of or for a dress. 2. of formal dress; characterized by formal dress. [< v.] 1. put clothes on. 2. put formal clothes on. 3. decorate; trim; adorn. 4. make ready for use; prepare. 5. cultivate (land). 6. comb, brush, and arrange (hair). 7. put a medicine, bandage, etc., on (a wound or sore). 8. form in a straight line: *the captain ordered the soldiers to dress their ranks.* 9. smooth; finish: *dress leather.* 10. dress down, a. scold; rebuke. b. beat; thrash. 11. **dress up, a.** put best

clothes on. **b.** put formal clothes on. [< OF *dresser* arrange, ult. < L *directus* straight. See DIRECT.] —Syn. *n.* 1. frock, gown. 3. clothing, attire, apparel, garments, garb, raiment. —*v.* 1. attire, garb, clothe.

dress·er[1] (dres'ər), *n.* person who dresses (himself, another person, a shop window, or a wound).

dress·er[2] (dres'ər), *n.* 1. *Am.* piece of furniture with a mirror and drawers for clothes; bureau. 2. piece of furniture with shelves for dishes. 3. table on which to get food ready for serving. [< early F *dresseur.* See DRESS.]

dress·ing (dres'ing), *n.* 1. what is put on or in something to get it ready for use. 2. sauce for salads, fish, meat, etc. 3. a stuffing of bread crumbs, seasoning, etc., for chicken, turkey, etc. 4. medicine, bandage, etc., put on a wound or sore. 5. fertilizer. 6. *Colloq.* a scolding or beating. 7. any act or process of dressing.

dress·ing-down (dres'ing-doun'), *n. Colloq.* 1. a scolding; rebuke. 2. a beating; a thrashing.

dressing gown, a loose robe worn while dressing or resting.

dress·mak·er (dres'māk'ər), *n.* person whose work is making dresses, etc. —*adj.* of women's apparel, characterized by delicate or flowing lines and decoration. —**dress'mak'ing,** *n.*

dress parade, a formal parade of soldiers or sailors in dress uniform.

dress rehearsal, rehearsal of a play with costumes and scenery just as for a regular performance.

dress suit, a formal suit worn by men in the evening.

dress·y (dres'ĭ), *adj.*, **dress·i·er, dress·i·est.** *Colloq.* 1. fond of wearing showy clothes. 2. stylish; fashionable. —**dress'i·ness,** *n.*

drest (drest), *v.* pt. and pp. of dress.

drew (drü), *v.* pt. of draw.

Drey·fus (drā'fəs; drī'–), *n.* Alfred, 1859-1935, French army officer of Jewish birth who was convicted of treason in 1894 but was proved innocent in 1906.

drib·ble (drib'əl), *v.*, **-bled, -bling,** *n.* —*v.* 1. flow or let flow in drops, small amounts, etc. 2. trickle. 2. let saliva run from the mouth. 3. move (a ball) along by bouncing it or giving it short kicks. —*n.* 1. a dropping; dripping; trickle. 2. a very light rain. 3. act of dribbling a ball. [< *drib,* var. of *drip*] —**drib'bler,** *n.*

drib·let, drib·blet (drib'lit), *n.* a small amount.

dried (drīd), *v.* pt. and pp. of dry.

dri·er (drī'ər), *adj.* comparative of dry. —*n.* 1. person or thing that dries. 2. Also, **dryer.** a. device or machine that removes water by heat, air, etc. b. substance put in paint, varnish, etc., to make it dry more quickly.

drift (drift), *v.* 1. carry or be carried along, as by currents of water or air: *the wind drifted the boat onto the rocks.* 2. go along without knowing or caring where one is going. 3. heap or be heaped up, as by the wind: *the snow is drifting badly, the wind is so strong it's drifting the snow.* [< n.] —*n.* 1. a drifting. 2. direction of drifting. 3. tendency; trend. 4. direction of thought; meaning. 5. snow, sand, etc., heaped up by the wind. 6. current of water or air caused by the wind. 7. a driving movement or force. 8. current; flow. 9. distance that a ship or aircraft is off its course because of currents. 10. sand, gravel, rocks, etc., moved from one place and left in another by a river, glacier, etc. 11. an almost horizontal passageway in a mine along a vein of ore, coal, etc. [ME, a driving, < OE *drīfan* DRIVE] —**drift'er,** *n.* —Syn. *v.* 1. float. –*n.* 4. intent. 7. impulse, impetus, pressure.

drift·age (drif'tij), *n.* 1. a drifting. 2. the distance drifted. 3. what has drifted.

Drill
(def. 1)

drift·wood (drift'wùd'), *n.* wood drifting in the water or washed ashore by water.

drill¹ (dril), *n.* **1.** tool or machine for boring holes. See picture on p. 253. **2.** method of teaching or training by having the learners do a thing over and over again. **3.** group instruction and training in physical exercises or in marching, handling a gun, etc. **4.** *Am.* snail that bores into and destroys oysters. —*v.* **1.** bore a hole in; pierce with a drill. **2.** teach by having learners do a thing over and over again. **3.** do or cause to do military or physical exercises. [< Du. *dril* < *drillen* to bore] —**drill′er,** *n.* —**Syn.** *n.* **2.** exercise, practice.

drill² (dril), *n.* **1.** machine for planting seeds in rows. **2.** a small furrow to plant seeds in. **3.** row of planted seeds. —*v.* plant in small furrows. —**drill′er,** *n.*

drill³ (dril), *n.* a strong, twilled cotton or linen cloth, used for overalls, linings, etc. [short for *drilling* < G *drillich* < L *trilix* of three threads < *tri-* three + *licium* thread]

drill⁴ (dril), *n.* baboon of western Africa, smaller than the mandrill. [prob. < African name]

drill·mas·ter (dril′mas′tər; -mäs′-), *n.* **1.** officer who drills soldiers in marching, handling guns, etc. **2.** person who drills others in anything.

dri·ly (dri′li), *adv.* dryly.

drink (dringk), *v.*, **drank** or (*formerly*) **drunk;** **drunk** or (*formerly as pred. adj.*) **drunk·en; drink·ing;** *n.* —*v.* **1.** swallow (liquid). **2.** take and hold; absorb: *the dry ground drank up the rain.* **3.** drink alcoholic liquor. **4.** drink in honor of. **5.** drink to, drink in honor of. —*n.* **1.** liquid swallowed or to be swallowed. **2.** alcoholic liquor. **3.** too much drinking of alcoholic liquor. [OE *drincan*] —**drink′a·ble,** *adj., n.* —**drink′er,** *n.*

Drink·wa·ter (dringk′wô′tər; -wot′ər), *n.* **John,** 1882–1937, English dramatist and critic.

drip (drip), *v.*, **dripped** or **dript** (dript), **drip·ping,** *n.* —*v.* **1.** fall or let fall in drops. **2.** be so wet that drops fall. —*n.* **1.** a falling in drops. **2.** liquid that falls in drops. **3.** part that projects to keep water off the parts below. [OE *dryppan* < *dropa* a drop]

drip·ping (drip′ing), *n.* **1.** function of a thing which drips. **2. drippings, a.** liquids that have dripped down. **b.** melted fat and juices that drip down from meat while roasting.

drive (driv), *v.*, **drove** or (*Archaic*) **drave, driv·en, driv·ing,** *n.* —*v.* **1.** make go: *grief drove her insane.* **2.** force (into or out of some place, condition, act, etc.): *hunger drove him to steal.* **3.** direct the movement of (an automobile, vehicle drawn by a horse, etc.). **4.** go or carry in an automobile, carriage, etc. **5.** work hard or compel to work hard. **6.** dash or rush with force. **7.** carry out with vigor; bring about: *drive a bargain.* **8.** hit very hard and fast: *drive a golf ball.* **9.** aim; strike. **10.** get or make by drilling, boring, etc.: *drive a well.* **11.** drive at, mean; intend. —*n.* **1.** trip in an automobile, carriage, etc. **2.** road to drive on. **3.** vigor; energy. **4.** an impelling force; pressure: *the craving for approval is a strong drive in mankind.* **5.** a special effort of a group for some purpose: *the town had a drive to get money for charity.* **6.** a very hard, fast hit. **7.** *Mil.* an attack. **8.** a driving. **9.** thing or things driven: *a drive of logs.* **10.** the driving mechanism for an automobile, machine, etc. [OE *drifan*] —**Syn.** *v.* **2.** impel, push, compel. **3.** steer.

drive-in (driv′in′), *n. Am.* place where customers may make purchases, eat, attend movies, etc., while seated in their cars.

driv·el (driv′əl), *v.*, **-eled, -el·ing;** *esp. Brit.* **-elled, -el·ling,** *n.* —*v.* **1.** let saliva run from the mouth. **2.** flow like saliva running from the mouth. **3.** talk or say in a stupid, foolish manner; talk silly nonsense. **4.** waste (time, energy, etc.) in a stupid, foolish way. —*n.* **1.** saliva running from the mouth. **2.** stupid, foolish talk; silly nonsense. [OE *dreflian*] —**driv′el·er,** *esp. Brit.* **driv′el·ler,** *n.*

driv·en (driv′ən), *v.* pp. of **drive.** —*adj.* carried along and gathered into heaps by the wind.

driv·er (driv′ər), *n.* **1.** person or thing that drives. **2.** person who directs the movement of an engine, automobile, horses, etc. **3.** person who

makes the people under him work very hard. **4.** a golf club with a wooden head, used in hitting the ball from the tee. **5.** any of several tools used in forcing things in, on, out, or through. **6.** in machinery, a part that transmits force or motion.

drive·way (driv′wā′), *n.* a private road that leads from a house to the street.

driz·zle (driz′əl), *v.*, **-zled, -zling.** *n.* rain in very small drops like mist. [? < ME *drese* to fall < OE *drēosan* to fall] —**driz′zly,** *adj.*

drogue (drōg), *n.* a device shaped like a large funnel at the end of the hose used to refuel planes in flight. The pilot of the plane being refueled guides the nose of his plane into the drogue. [appar. < F, card game in which the loser wears clothespins on his nose; orig., a drug]

droll (drōl), *adj.* amusingly odd; humorously quaint. [< F *drôle* (orig. n.) good fellow < Du. *drol* little fat fellow]

droll·er·y (drōl′ər·i), *n., pl.* **-er·ies. 1.** laughable trick. **2.** quaint humor. **3.** jesting.

drom·e·dar·y (drom′ə·der′i; drum′-), *n., pl.* **-dar·ies.** a swift camel for riding, usually the one-humped camel of Arabia. [< LL *dromedarius* < Gk. *dromas kamēlos* running camel < *dromos* a running]

drone¹ (drōn), *n.* **1.** a male honeybee. **2.** person not willing to work; idler; loafer. [OE *drān*]

drone² (drōn), *v.*, **droned, dron·ing,** *n.* —*v.* **1.** make a deep, continuous, humming sound. **2.** talk or say in a monotonous voice. —*n.* **1.** a deep, continuous, humming sound: *the drone of airplane motors.* **2.** the bass pipe of a bagpipe. [akin to DRONE¹]

Drone (life size)

drool (drül), *v.* **1.** let saliva run from the mouth as a baby does. **2.** *Slang.* talk or say foolishly. —*n.* **1.** saliva running from the mouth. **2.** *Am., Slang.* foolish talk. [contraction of DRIVEL]

droop (drüp), *v.* **1.** hang down; bend down. **2.** become weak; lose strength and energy. **3.** become discouraged or depressed; be sad and gloomy. —*n.* a bending position; hanging down. [< Scand. *drūpa*] —**droop′ing·ly,** *adv.* —**droop′y,** *adj.* —**Syn.** *v.* **2.** fade, wilt, flag, fail.

drop (drop), *n., v.*, **dropped** or **dropt, drop·ping.** —*n.* **1.** a small amount of liquid in a roundish shape. **2.** a very small amount of liquid. **3.** anything roundish like a drop. **4.** a sudden fall. **5.** distance down; length of a fall: *from the top of the cliff to the water is a drop of 200 feet.* **6.** anything arranged to fall, as a trapdoor, curtain, etc. **7.** a drop kick. **8.** drops, liquid medicine given in drops. —*v.* **1.** fall or let fall in drops. **2.** fall suddenly; let fall suddenly. **3.** fall or cause to fall. **4.** fall dead, wounded, or tired out. **5.** cause to fall dead; kill. **6.** go or make lower; sink. **7.** pass into a less active or a worse condition: *she finally dropped off to sleep.* **8.** *U.S.* let go; dismiss. **9.** leave behind: *our fast car soon dropped its pursuers.* **10.** leave out; omit. **11.** stop; end: *let a matter drop.* **12.** send (a letter, etc.). **13.** come casually or unexpectedly. **14.** give or express casually: *drop a hint.* **15.** go along gently with the current or tide. **16.** in cooking, poach. **17.** set down from a ship, automobile, carriage, etc. **18.** of animals: **a.** give birth to. **b.** be born. **19.** drop off, **a.** go away; disappear. **b.** go to sleep. [OE *dropa*]

drop-forge (drop′fôrj′; -fōrj′), *v.*, **-forged, -forg·ing.** beat (hot metal) into shape with a very heavy hammer or weight. —**drop′-forg′er,** *n.* —**drop forging.**

drop hammer, a very heavy weight lifted by machinery and then dropped on the metal to be beaten into shape.

drop kick, kick given to a football as it touches the ground after being dropped.

drop-kick (drop′kik′), *v.* give (a football) a drop kick. —**drop′-kick′er,** *n.*

drop·let (drop′lit), *n.* a tiny drop.

drop·per (drop′ər), *n.* **1.** person or thing that drops. **2.** a glass tube with a hollow rubber cap at one end and a small opening at the other end from which a liquid can be made to fall in drops.

drop·si·cal (drop′sə·kəl), *adj.* **1.** of or like dropsy. **2.** having dropsy. —**drop′si·cal·ly,** *adv.*

drop·sy (drop′si), *n. Pathol.* an abnormal accumulation of watery fluid in certain tissues or cavities of the body. [var. of *hydropsy* < OF < L *hydropisis*, ult. < Gk. *hydrops* < *hydor* water]

dropt (dropt), *v.* pt. and pp. of **drop**.

drosh·ky (drosh′ki), **dros·ki**, **dros·ky** (dros′ki), *n., pl.* **-kies.** a low, four-wheeled, open carriage used in Russia. [< Russ. *drozhki*, dim. of *drogi* wagon]

dro·soph·i·la (drō·sof′ə·lə), *n., pl.* **-lae** (-lē). a small fly whose larvae feed on fruit and decaying plants; fruit fly. [< NL < Gk. *drosos* dew + *philos* loving]

dross (drôs; dros), *n.* 1. waste or scum that comes to the surface of melting metals. 2. waste material; rubbish. [OE *drōs*]

drought (drout), **drouth** (drouth), *n.* 1. a long period of dry weather; continued lack of rain. 2. lack of moisture; dryness. [OE *drūgath;* akin to DRY] **—drought′y, drouth′y,** *adj.* ➤ **drought, drouth.** Both forms are in good use, *drought* probably more common in formal English, *drouth* in informal and colloquial. Newspaper accounts of the unusually dry seasons of the mid-1930's did much to give *drouth* increased currency.

drove¹ (drōv), *v.* pt. of **drive.**

drove² (drōv), *n., v.,* **droved, drov·ing.** *—n.* 1. group of cattle, sheep, hogs, etc., moving or driven along together; herd; flock. 2. many people moving along together; crowd. *—v.* 1. drive (cattle) to market. 2. deal in (cattle). [OE *drāf*]

dro·ver (drō′vər), *n.* 1. man who drives cattle, sheep, hogs, etc., to market. 2. dealer in cattle.

drown (droun), *v.* 1. die under water or other liquid because of lack of air to breathe. 2. kill by keeping under water or other liquid. 3. cover with water; flood. 4. be stronger or louder than. 5. get rid of; suppress. [OE *druncnian;* akin to DRINK] **—drown′er,** *n.*

drowse (drouz), *v.,* **drowsed, drows·ing,** *n.* *—v.* 1. be sleepy; be half asleep. 2. make sleepy. 3. pass (time) in drowsing. *—n.* being half asleep; sleepiness. [OE *drūs(i)an* sink, become slow]

drow·sy (drou′zi), *adj.,* **-si·er, -si·est.** 1. half asleep; sleepy. 2. causing sleepiness; lulling. 3. caused by sleepiness. **—drow′si·ly,** *adv.* **—drow′si·ness,** *n.*

drub (drub), *v.,* **drubbed, drub·bing,** *n.* *—v.* 1. beat with a stick; whip soundly. 2. defeat by a large margin in fight, game, contest, etc. 3. stamp (the feet). *—n.* a blow; thump; knock. [? < Ar. *ḍaraba* beat] **—drub′ber,** *n.* **—Syn.** *v.* 1. thrash, cudgel.

drub·bing (drub′ing), *n.* 1. a beating. 2. a thorough defeat.

drudge (druj), *n., v.,* **drudged, drudg·ing.** *—n.* person who does hard, tiresome, or disagreeable work. *—v.* do such work. [ME *drugge(n);* cf. OE *drēogan* work, suffer] **—drudg′er,** *n.*

drudg·er·y (druj′ər·i), *n., pl.* **-er·ies.** hard, uninteresting, or disagreeable work.

drug (drug), *n., v.,* **drugged, drug·ging.** *—n.* 1. substance (other than food) that, when taken into the body, produces a change in it. If the change helps the body, the drug is a medicine; if the change harms the body, the drug is a poison. 2. **drug on the market,** article that is too abundant, is no longer in demand, or has too slow a sale. *—v.* 1. give harmful drugs to. 2. put a harmful or poisonous drug in (food or drink). 3. affect or overcome (the body or senses) in a way not natural: *the wine had drugged him.* [< OF *drogue,* ? < Du. *drog,* akin to E DRY] **—drug′less,** *adj.*

drug·gist (drug′ist), *n.* 1. person who sells drugs, medicines, etc. 2. *U.S.* person licensed to fill prescriptions; pharmacist.

drug·store (drug′stôr′; -stōr′), *n. Am.* pharmacy, often also selling soft drinks, cosmetics, magazines, etc., as well as drugs.

Dru·id (drü′id), *n.* Often, **druid.** member of a religious order of priests, prophets, poets, etc., among the ancient Celts of Britain, Ireland, and France. **—dru·id′ic, dru·id′i·cal,** *adj.* **—dru′idism,** *n.*

drum (drum), *n., v.,* **drummed, drum·ming.** *—n.* 1. a musical instrument that makes a sound when it is beaten. A drum is hollow with a covering stretched tightly over the ends. 2. sound made when a drum is beaten; sound like this. 3. anything shaped somewhat like a drum. 4. part around which something is wound in a machine. 5. drum-shaped container to hold oil, food, etc. 6. membrane covering the hollow part of the ear. 7. the hollow part of the middle ear. *—v.* 1. beat or play a drum. 2. beat, tap, or strike again and again. 3. force into one's mind by repeating over and over. [< *drumslade* drummer < Du. or LG *trommelslag* drumbeat]

drum·beat (drum′bēt′), *n.* sound made when a drum is beaten.

drum·head (drum′hed′), *n.* 1. parchment or membrane stretched tightly over the end of a drum. 2. eardrum. 3. the top part of a capstan.

drum·lin (drum′lən), *n. Geol.* ridge or oval hill formed by deposit from a glacier. [for *drumling,* dim. of *drum* ridge < Scotch Gaelic and Irish *druim* ridge]

drum major, leader or director of a marching band.

drum·mer (drum′ər), *n.* 1. person who plays a drum. 2. *U.S. Colloq.* a traveling salesman.

drum·stick (drum′stik′), *n.* 1. stick for beating a drum. 2. the lower half of the leg of a cooked chicken, turkey, etc.

drunk (drungk), *adj.* 1. overcome with alcoholic liquor; intoxicated. 2. very much excited or affected. *—n. Colloq.* 1. person who is drunk. 2. spell of drinking alcoholic liquor. *—v.* 1. pp. of **drink.** 2. *Archaic.* pt. of **drink.** ➤ **drunk.** It seems to take courage to use this natural word. We either go formal—*intoxicated;* or grasp at respectability through euphemisms—*under the influence of liquor* or *indulged to excess;* or make a weak attempt at humor with one of the dozen slang phrases like *get plastered.* But *drunk* is the word.

drunk·ard (drungk′ərd), *n.* person who is often drunk.

drunk·en (drungk′ən), *adj.* 1. drunk. 2. caused by or resulting from being drunk. 3. often drinking too much alcoholic liquor. *—v. Archaic.* pp. of **drink.** **—drunk′en·ly,** *adv.* **—drunk′en·ness,** *n.* **—Syn.** *adj.* 1. intoxicated.

dru·pa·ceous (drü·pā′shəs), *adj. Bot.* 1. like a drupe. 2. producing drupes.

drupe (drüp), *n. Bot.* fruit whose seed is contained in a hard pit or stone surrounded by soft, pulpy flesh, as cherries, peaches, etc. [< NL < L *druppa* very ripe olive < Gk. *drypepa,* accus. of *drypeps* ripening on the tree]

drupe·let (drüp′lit), *n. Bot.* a small drupe. A raspberry or blackberry is a mass of drupelets.

dry (drī), *adj.,* **dri·er, dri·est,** *v.,* **dried, dry·ing,** *n., pl.* **drys.** *—adj.* 1. not wet; not moist. 2. having little or no rain. 3. not giving milk. 4. having no water in it. 5. not shedding tears; not accompanied by tears. 6. wanting a drink; thirsty. 7. causing thirst: *dry work.* 8. not liquid; solid: *dry measure.* 9. showing no feeling: *dry humor.* 10. not interesting; dull. 11. without butter: *dry toast.* 12. without mucus: *a dry cough.* 13. without bloodshed: *a dry fight.* 14. not using live ammunition: *dry fire.* 15. free from sweetness or fruity flavor: *dry wine.* 16. *Am., Colloq.* having or favoring laws against making and selling alcoholic drinks. 17. not covered with water: *dry land.* *—v.* 1. make or become dry. 2. **dry up,** *Slang.* a. make or become completely dry. b. *Am.* stop talking. *—n. Am., Colloq.* person who favors laws against making and selling alcoholic drinks. [OE *drýge*] **—Syn.** *adj.* 1. arid. 2. droughty. *-v.* 1. evaporate.

dry·ad, Dry·ad (drī′əd; -ad), *n., pl.* **-ads, -a·des** (-ə·dēz). *Gk. Myth.* nymph that lives in a tree; wood nymph. [< L < Gk. *Dryades,* pl., < *drys* tree] **—dry·ad·ic** (drī·ad′ik), *adj.*

dry battery, *Elect.* a. set of dry cells connected to produce electric current. b. dry cell.

dry cell, a small, portable device that produces electric current. It is an electric cell made with

dry-clean (drī′klēn′), v. clean (clothes, etc.) with naphtha, benzine, etc., instead of water. —dry cleaner. —dry cleaning.

Dry·den (drī′dən), n. John, 1631–1700, English poet, dramatist, and critic.

dry dock, dock from which the water can be pumped out. Dry docks are used for building or repairing ships.

dry-dock (drī′dok′), v. 1. place in a dry dock. 2. go into dry dock.

dry·er (drī′ər), n. drier (def. 2).

dry farming, way of farming land in regions where there is no irrigation and little rain.

dry goods, cloth, ribbon, lace, etc.

Dry Ice, Trademark. a very cold, white solid formed when carbon dioxide is greatly compressed and then cooled, used as a refrigerant.

dry law, law prohibiting the making and selling of alcoholic liquor.

dry·ly (drī′li), adv. in a dry manner. Also, drily.

dry measure, 1. system for measuring such things as grain, vegetables, or fruit. In the United States: 2 pints = 1 quart; 8 quarts = 1 peck; 4 pecks = 1 bushel. 2. measurement of dry things.

dry·ness (drī′nis), n. a being dry; dry quality.

dry nurse, nurse who takes care of a baby, but does not suckle it.

dry-nurse (drī′nėrs′), v., -nursed, -nurs·ing. act as dry nurse to.

dry point, 1. picture made from a copper plate into which lines have been engraved with a hard needle without using acid. 2. the needle used. 3. this method of engraving.

dry rot, decay of seasoned wood, causing it to crumble to a dry powder, due to various fungi.

dry run, 1. a practice test or session. 2. Mil. simulated firing practice, bombing approach, etc., without use of ammunition.

Ds, Chem. dysprosium. Also, **Dy.**

D.S., D. Sc., Doctor of Science.

d.s., daylight saving.

D.S.C., Distinguished Service Cross.

D.S.T., Daylight Saving Time.

d.t., **d.t.'s**, Colloq. delirium tremens.

du·al (dū′əl; dū′-), adj. 1. of two; showing two. 2. consisting of two parts; double; twofold. 3. Gram. signifying or implying two persons or things. —n. the dual number. [< L dualis < duo two] —du′al·ly, adv.

du·al·ism (dū′əl·iz·əm; dū′-), n. 1. dual condition. 2. Philos. doctrine that all the phenomena of the universe can be explained by two separate and distinct substances or principles, such as mind and matter. —du′al·ist, n. —du′al·is′tic, adj.

du·al·i·ty (dū·al′ə·ti; dū–), n., pl. -ties. dual condition or quality.

dub[1] (dub), v., dubbed, dub·bing. 1. make (a man) a knight by striking his shoulder lightly with a sword. 2. give a title to; call; name. 3. smooth by cutting, rubbing, scraping, etc. [OE dubbian]

dub[2] (dub), n. Slang. an awkward, clumsy player. [? akin to DUB[1]]

dub[3] (dub), v., dubbed, dub·bing. —v. add or alter sounds on a motion-picture film. —n. the sounds thus added or altered. [short for double]

Du Bar·ry (dū bar′i; dū), Comtesse, 1746?–1793, mistress of Louis XV of France who had great political influence.

du·bi·e·ty (dū·bī′ə·ti; dū–), n., pl. -ties. 1. doubtfulness; uncertainty. 2. something which is doubtful.

du·bi·ous (dū′bi·əs; dū′-), adj. 1. doubtful; uncertain. 2. of questionable character; probably bad. [< L dubiosus < dubius doubtful < du– two] —du′bi·ous·ly, adv. —du′bi·ous·ness, n.

Dub·lin (dub′lən), n. capital of the Republic of Ireland.

du·cal (dū′kəl; dū′-), adj. of a duke or dukedom. —du′cal·ly, adv.

duc·at (duk′ət), n. 1. a gold or silver coin

formerly used in some European countries. Its value varied, being at most about $2.30. 2. Slang. a ticket. [< F < Ital. ducato < Med.L < L dux leader]

du·ce (dū′chā), n. Italian. 1. leader. 2. il Duce, title given to Mussolini. [< Ital. < L dux leader. Doublet of DOGE, DUKE.]

duch·ess (duch′is), n. 1. wife or widow of a duke. 2. lady with a rank equal to a duke's.

duch·y (duch′i), n., pl. duch·ies. territory under the rule of a duke or duchess; dukedom.

Pintail duck (2 ft. long)

duck[1] (duk), n. 1. a wild or tame swimming bird with a short neck, short legs, and webbed feet. Most ducks have broad, flat bills. 2. the female duck. 3. flesh of a duck used for food. 4. Colloq. darling; pet. 5. Am., Slang. a fellow; chap. 6. play ducks and drakes with, handle recklessly; squander foolishly. [OE dūce; akin to DUCK[2]]

duck[2] (duk), v. 1. dip or plunge suddenly under water and out again. 2. lower the head or bend the body suddenly to keep from being hit, seen, etc. 3. lower (the head) or bend (the body) suddenly. 4. Am., Colloq. get or keep away from by ducking; avoid. —n. 1. a sudden dip or plunge under water and out again. 2. a sudden lowering of the head or bending of the body to keep from being hit, seen, etc. [ME duke(n)]

duck[3] (duk), n. 1. a strong, cotton or linen cloth with a lighter and finer weave than canvas, used for sails, tents, etc. 2. ducks, trousers made of duck. [< Du. doek cloth]

duck[4] (duk), n. an amphibious army truck of World War II, used to carry supplies or troops over water. [for DUKW, code name]

duck·bill (duk′-bil′), or **duck-billed platypus**, n. a small water mammal that lays eggs and has webbed feet and a beak like a duck. Also, **platypus**.

Duckbill (ab. 1½ ft. long)

duck·ling (duk′ling), n. a young duck.

duck·weed (duk′wēd′), n. a very small flowering plant that grows in water.

duct (dukt), n. 1. tube, pipe, or channel for carrying liquid, air, wires, etc. 2. tube in the body for carrying a bodily fluid: tear ducts. [< L, < ducere lead] —duct′less, adj.

duc·tile (duk′təl), adj. 1. capable of being hammered out thin or drawn out into a wire, as gold or copper. 2. easily molded or shaped, as wax. 3. easily managed or influenced; docile. —duc·til′i·ty, n.

ductless gland, Anat., Zool. gland without a duct whose secretion passes directly into the blood or lymph circulating through it. The thyroid and the spleen are ductless glands.

dud (dud), n. Colloq. 1. an article of clothing. 2. duds, a. clothes. b. belongings. 3. Mil. shell or bomb that did not explode. 4. Slang. failure.

dude (dūd; dūd), n. Am. 1. man who pays too much attention to his clothes; dandy. 2. W. an Easterner or city-bred person, esp. one who vacations on a ranch. —dud′ish, adj.

dude ranch, Am. ranch that is run as a tourist resort.

dudg·eon (duj′ən), n. 1. anger; resentment. 2. in high dudgeon, very angry; resentful.

due (dū; dū), adj. 1. owed as a debt; to be paid as a right. 2. proper; suitable; rightful: due reward. 3. as much as needed; enough. 4. promised to come; be ready, be paid, etc.; expected. 5. due to, caused by. —n. 1. thing owed as a debt or to be paid as a right. 2. dues, a. amount of money owed or to be paid. b. amount of money owed or to be paid to a club, etc., by a member. —adv. straight; directly; exactly: the wind is due east. [< OF deü, pp. of devoir owe < L debere] —Syn. adj. 1. payable. 2. appropriate, fitting. 3. adequate, sufficient. -n. 2 a, b. fee. ▶ Due in the sense of because of has long been used popularly as a preposition. Advocates of strict usage have set themselves sternly against it. *Due* was originally an adjective and is still most strictly used as one: *the epidemic was due to the brown rat*, in which *due* modifies *epidemic*. But the prepositional use is convenient and has been increasingly common in print: *due to the danger of war, we have had to increase military expenditures*. Opinion of *due* as a preposition is then divided. A writer should consider whether or not it is appropriate to his style: if he is rather formal, he should not use *due to* as a preposition; if he is less formal he doesn't need to worry—except perhaps in writing for readers known to be formal. A person may not care to use *due* to himself, but in view of actual usage today he hardly has the right to deny it to others.

du·el (dü′əl; dü′-), *n., v.,* −eled, −el·ing; *esp. Brit.* −elled, −el·ling. —*n.* 1. a formal fight between two people armed with swords or firearms, arranged to settle a quarrel, etc. 2. any fight or contest between two opponents: *duel of wits.* —*v.* fight a duel. [< F < Med.L *duellum* < L (archaistic for *bellum*) war] —**du′el·er,** *esp. Brit.* **du′el·ler,** *n.* —**du′el·ist,** *esp. Brit.* **du′el·list,** *n.*

du·en·na (dü·en′ə; dü–), *n.* 1. (in Spain and Portugal) an elderly woman who is the governess and chaperon of a young girl. 2. governess; chaperon. [< Sp. < L *domina* mistress. See DOMINATE.]

du·et (dü·et′; dü–), *n.* 1. piece of music to be sung or played by two people. 2. two singers or players performing together. [< Ital. *duetto,* dim. of *duo* DUO]

duff (duf), *n.* a flour pudding boiled in a cloth bag. [var. of *dough*]

duf·fel (duf′əl), *n. Am.* camping equipment. [< Du.; named for town near Antwerp]

duffel bag, duffle bag, 1. a bag of stout material. 2. a small canvas bag used by soldiers for carrying personal effects.

duff·er (duf′ər), *n. Brit. Colloq.* a useless, clumsy, or stupid person.

dug[1] (dug), *v.* pt. and pp. of **dig.**

dug[2] (dug), *n.* nipple; teat. [< Scand. Cf. Dan. *dægge,* Sw. *dägga* suckle.]

du·gong (dü′gong), *n.* a large, fish-shaped mammal of tropical seas with flipperlike forelimbs and a crescent-shaped tail. [< Malay *düyong*]

dug·out (dug′out′), *n. Am.* 1. a rough shelter made by digging into the side of a hill, trench, etc. 2. *Baseball.* a small shelter at the side of a field, used by players who are not at bat or not in the game. 3. boat made by hollowing out a large log.

Dugong (10 ft. long)

Duis·burg-Ham·born (dɪs′bürk-häm′-bôrn), *n.* city in W Germany, on the Rhine River.

duke (dük; dük), *n.* 1. nobleman ranking next below a prince. 2. prince who rules a small state or country called a duchy. 3. dukes, *Slang.* fists. [< OF < L *dux* leader. Doublet of DOGE, DUCE.] —**duke′dom,** *n.*

dul·cet (dul′sit), *adj.* soothing, esp. to the ear; sweet; pleasing. [< F *doucet,* dim. of *doux* sweet < L *dulcis*]

dul·ci·mer (dul′sə·mər), *n. Music.* instrument with strings, played by striking the strings with two hammers. [< OF < L *dulcis* sweet + *melos* song (< Gk.)]

dull (dul), *adj.* 1. not sharp or pointed. 2. not bright or clear. 3. slow in understanding; stupid. 4. having little feeling; insensitive. 5. not interesting; tiresome; boring. 6. having little life, energy, or spirit; not active. 7. not felt sharply: *a dull pain.* —*v.* 1. make dull. 2. become dull. [ME *dul*] —**dull′ness, dul′ness,** *n.* —**dul′ly,** *adv.* —**Syn. *adj.*** 1. blunt. 2. dim, clouded, dingy. 3. dense, slow. 5. uninteresting, colorless. 6. lifeless, sluggish. —**Ant.** *adj.* 1. sharp. 2. acute, quick, smart. 6. keen, eager.

dull·ard (dul′ərd), *n.* a stupid person who learns very slowly.

dull·ish (dul′ish), *adj.* somewhat dull.

dulse (duls), *n.* any of several coarse, edible seaweeds that have red fronds. [< Irish and Scotch Gaelic *duileasg*]

Du·luth (də·lüth′; dü–), *n.* city in E Minnesota, on Lake Superior.

du·ly (dü′li; dü′-), *adv.* 1. according to what is due; as due; properly; suitably; rightfully. 2. as much as is needed; enough. 3. when due; at the proper time.

Du·mas (dü·mä′, dü– ; dü′mä, dü′-), *n.* 1. Alexandre, 1802–1870, French novelist and dramatist. 2. his son, Alexandre, 1824–1895, French dramatist and novelist.

dumb (dum), *adj.* 1. not able to speak: *dumb animals.* 2. silenced for the moment by fear, surprise, shyness, etc. 3. that does not speak; silent. 4. *Am., Colloq.* stupid; dull. 5. lacking some usual property or characteristic. [(defs. 1–3, 5) OE; (def. 4) < G *dumm* stupid] —**dumb′ly,** *adv.* —**dumb′ness,** *n.* —**Syn.** 1. mute. 2. speechless.

dumb·bell (dum′bel′), *n.* 1. a short bar of wood or iron with large, heavy, round ends, used to exercise the muscles of the arms, back, etc. 2. *Am., Slang.* a very stupid person.

dumb show, gestures without words; pantomime.

dumb·wait·er (dum′wāt′ər), *n.* 1. *Am.* a small box with shelves, pulled up and down a shaft to send dishes, food, rubbish, etc., from one floor to another. 2. a small stand placed near a dining table, for holding dishes, etc.

dum·dum (dum′dum), or **dumdum bullet,** *n.* bullet that spreads out when it strikes, causing a serious wound. [after *Dum Dum,* India]

dum·found, dumb·found (dum′found′), *v.* amaze and make unable to speak; bewilder; confuse. [< *dumb* + (con)*found*] —**dum′found′er, dumb′found′er,** *n.*

dum·my (dum′i), *n., pl.* −mies, *adj.* —*n.* 1. figure of a person, used to display clothing in store windows, to shoot at in rifle practice, to tackle in football, etc. 2. *Am., Colloq.* a stupid person; blockhead. 3. an imitation; counterfeit. 4. person supposedly acting for himself, but really acting for another. 5. in card games, a. player whose cards are laid face up on the table and played by his partner. b. hand of cards played in this way. 6. *Am.* a kind of locomotive with a silent exhaust. —*adj.* 1. imitation; counterfeit; sham. 2. acting for another while supposedly acting for oneself.

dump (dump), *v.* 1. empty out; throw down; unload in a mass. 2. unload rubbish. 3. *Am.* put (goods) on the market in large quantities and at a low price. —*n.* 1. *Am.* place for unloading rubbish. 2. heap of rubbish. 3. *Mil.* place for storing ammunition or other supplies. [? < Scand. (Dan.) *dumpe* fall with a thud] —**dump′er,** *n.*

dump·ling (dump′ling), *n.* 1. a rounded piece of dough, boiled or steamed and served with meat. 2. a small pudding made by enclosing fruit in a piece of dough and baking or steaming it.

dumps (dumps), *n.pl. Colloq.* low spirits.

dump·y (dump′i), *adj.,* **dump·i·er, dump·i·est.** short and fat. —**dump′i·ly,** *adv.* —**dump′i·ness,** *n.*

dun[1] (dun), *v.,* dunned, dun·ning. —*v.* demand payment of a debt from, again and again. —*n.* 1. demand for payment of a debt. 2. person constantly demanding payment of a debt. [appar. < obs. *dun* make a DIN < Scand. *duna* to thunder]

dun[2] (dun), *n.* a dull, grayish brown. —*adj.* dull grayish-brown. [OE *dunn,* ? < Celtic]

dunce (duns), *n.* 1. child slow at learning his lessons in school. 2. a stupid person. [< *Duns(man),* name applied by attackers to any follower of *Duns Scotus,* theologian]

dunce cap, dunce's cap, a tall, cone-shaped cap formerly worn as a punishment by a child who was slow in learning his lessons in school.

Dun·dee (dun·dē′), *n.* seaport in E Scotland.

dun·der·head (dun′dər·hed′), *n.* a stupid, foolish person; dunce; blockhead.

dune (dūn; dŭn), *n.* mound or ridge of loose sand heaped up by the wind. [< F < MDu. *düne*; akin to DOWN³]

dung (dung), *n.* waste matter from animals; manure. —*v.* put dung on as a fertilizer. [OE] —**dung′y**, *adj.*

dun·ga·ree (dung′gə·rē′), *n.* 1. a coarse cotton cloth, used for work clothes, sails, etc. 2. dungarees, trousers or clothing made of this cloth. [< Hind. *dungrī*]

dun·geon (dun′jən), *n.* 1. a dark underground room to keep prisoners in. 2. donjon. —*v.* confine in a dungeon; imprison. [< OF *donjon* < Gmc.]

dung·hill (dung′hil′), *n.* 1. heap of dung. 2. a vile place or person.

dunk (dungk), *v. Am., Colloq.* dip (something to eat) into a liquid: *dunk doughnuts into coffee.* [< LG *dunken* dip] —**dunk′er**, *n.*

Dun·kirk (dun′kėrk; dun·kėrk′), *n.* seaport in N France; evacuation of British forces, 1940.

dun·lin (dun′lən), *n., pl.* -lins or (*esp. collectively*) -lin. a small wading bird that has a broad black stripe across the abdomen during the breeding season. [dim. of *dun*²]

Dunlin (8 to 9 in. long)

dun·nage (dun′ij), *n.* 1. baggage or clothes. 2. *Naut.* branches, mats, etc., placed around a cargo to protect it from damage by water or chafing.

du·o (dū′ō; dŭ′ō), *n.* duet. [< Ital. < L, two]

du·o·dec·i·mal (dū′ō·des′ə·məl; dŭ′-), *adj.* pertaining to twelfths or to twelve; proceeding by twelves. —*n.* 1. one twelfth. 2. one of a system of numerals, the base of which is twelve instead of ten. 3. duodecimals, system of counting by twelves.

du·o·dec·i·mo (dū′ō·des′ə·mō; dŭ′-), *n., pl.* -mos. 1. the page size of a book in which each leaf is one twelfth of a whole sheet of paper, or about 5 by 7½ inches. 2. book having pages of this size. [< L *in duodecimo* in a twelfth]

du·o·de·num (dū′ō·dē′nəm; dŭ′-), *n., pl.* -na (-nə). *Anat., Zool.* the first part of the small intestine, just below the stomach. [< Med.L < L *duodeni* twelve each; with ref. to its length, about twelve finger breadths] —**du′o·de′nal**, *adj.*

dup., duplicate.

dupe (dūp, dŭp), *n., v.,* duped, dup·ing. —*n.* person easily deceived or tricked. —*v.* deceive; trick. [< F < L *upupa* hoopoe (a bird)] —**dup′er**, *n.*

du·ple (dū′pəl; dŭ′-), *adj.* 1. double. 2. *Music.* having two or a multiple of two beats to the measure. [< L *duplus* double]

du·plet (dū′plit; dŭ′-), *n.* 1. *Nuclear Physics.* pair of charged particles. 2. *Chem.* pair of electrons which is shared by two atoms.

duple time, *Music.* two-part time.

du·plex (dū′pleks; dŭ′-), *adj.* double; twofold. —*n.* a duplex house or duplex apartment. [< L, < *du*- two + *plicare* fold] —**du·plex′i·ty**, *n.*

duplex apartment, an apartment having rooms on two floors.

duplex house, *Am.* a house accommodating two families.

du·pli·cate (*adj., n.* dū′plə·kit, dū′-; *v.* dū′plə·kāt, dū′-), *adj., n., v.,* -cat·ed, -cat·ing. —*adj.* 1. exactly like something else; corresponding to something else. 2. double. 3. having two corresponding parts; twofold. 4. of card games, so arranged that the same hands are played by different players. —*n.* 1. one of two things exactly alike; an exact copy. 2. in duplicate, in two forms exactly alike. —*v.* make an exact copy of; repeat exactly. [< L < *duplicare* double. See DUPLEX.] —**du′pli·ca′tion,** *n.*

du·pli·ca·tor (dū′plə·kā′tər; dū′-), *n.* ma-

chine for making many exact copies of anything written or typed.

du·plic·i·ty (dū·plis′ə·ti; dū-), *n., pl.* -ties. deceitfulness in speech or action; treachery.

du·ra·ble (dūr′ə·bəl; dyūr′-), *adj.* lasting a long time; not soon injured or worn out. [< F < L, < *durare* to last, harden < *durus* hard] —**du′ra·bil′i·ty, du′ra·ble·ness,** *n.* —**du′ra·bly,** *adv.* —Syn. permanent, stable, enduring, strong. —Ant. fragile, frail, weak.

Du·ral·u·min (dū·ral′yə·min; dyū-), *n. Trademark.* a light, strong, hard metal that is an alloy of aluminum, containing copper, manganese, and sometimes magnesium. [< *dur(able)* + *alumin(um)*]

du·rance (dūr′əns; dyūr′-), *n.* imprisonment.

du·ra·tion (dū·rā′shən; dyū-), *n.* 1. length of time; time during which anything continues. 2. for the duration, until the end, esp. of a war.

Dur·ban (dėr′bən; dėr·ban′), *n.* seaport in the SE part of the Republic of South Africa.

dur·bar (dėr′bär), *n.* 1. an official court or reception held by a native prince of India or by a British king, viceroy, governor, etc., in India. 2. hall where a durbar is held.

Dü·rer (dy′rər), *n.* Albrecht, 1471–1528, German artist noted for his engravings.

du·ress (dū·res′, dyū-; dūr′es, dyūr′-), *n.* 1. compulsion. 2. imprisonment. [< OF < L *duritia* hardness < *durus* hard]

dur·ing (dūr′ing; dyūr′-), *prep.* 1. through the whole time of. 2. at some time in; in the course of. [ppr. of obs. *dure* ENDURE]

dur·ra (dûr′ə), *n.* kind of sorghum with slender stalks that produces grain. [< Ar. *dhura*]

durst (dėrst), *v.* pt. of dare.

du·rum (dûr′əm; dyûr′-), or **durum wheat,** *n.* a hard wheat from which the flour used in macaroni, spaghetti, etc., is made.

Du·se (dū′zā), *n.* Eleonora, 1859–1924, Italian actress.

dusk (dusk), *n.* 1. time just before dark. 2. shade; gloom. —*adj.* dark-colored; dusky. —*v.* make or become dusky. [var. of OE *dux* dark] —Syn. *n.* 1. twilight.

dusk·y (dus′ki), *adj.,* dusk·i·er, dusk·i·est. 1. somewhat dark; dark-colored. 2. dim; obscure. 3. sad; gloomy. —**dusk′i·ly,** *adv.* —**dusk′i·ness,** *n.* —Syn. 1. swarthy.

Düs·sel·dorf (düs′əl·dôrf, dûs′-; *Ger.* dYs′-), *n.* city in W Germany, on the Rhine River.

dust (dust), *n.* 1. fine, dry earth; any fine powder. 2. earth; ground. 3. what is left of a dead body after decay. 4. cloud of dust in the air. 5. turmoil; disturbance. 6. low or humble condition. 7. a worthless thing. 8. *Am.* gold dust. 9. *Slang.* money. —*v.* 1. brush or wipe the dust from; get dust off. 2. get dust on; soil with dust. 3. sprinkle (with dust, powder, etc.). [OE *dūst*] —**dust′less,** *adj.*

dust bowl, *Am.* area, esp. in the W part of the United States, where dust storms are frequent and violent.

dust·er (dus′tər), *n.* 1. person or thing that dusts. 2. cloth, brush, etc., used to get dust off things. 3. *Am.* a long, lightweight coat worn over the clothes to keep dust off them. 4. *Am., Colloq.* a dust storm.

dust jacket, *Am.* the jacket of a book.

dust·pan (dust′pan′), *n.* a flat, broad pan to sweep dust into from the floor.

dust storm, a strong wind carrying clouds of dust across or from a dry region.

dust·y (dus′ti), *adj.,* dust·i·er, dust·i·est. 1. covered with dust; filled with dust. 2. like dust; dry and powdery. 3. having the color of dust; grayish. —**dust′i·ly,** *adv.* —**dust′i·ness,** *n.*

Dutch (duch), *adj.* 1. of or having to do with the Netherlands, its people, or their language. 2. *Slang.* German. 3. go Dutch, *Colloq.* have each person pay for himself. —*n.* 1. the Dutch, a. the people of the Netherlands. b. *Slang.* the people of Germany. The ancestors of the Pennsylvania Dutch came from Germany, not from the Netherlands. 2. language of the Netherlands. 3. *Slang.* the German language. 4. in Dutch, *Am., Slang.* a. in disgrace. b. in trouble.

Dutch East Indies, islands in the East Indies formerly belonging to the Netherlands, now mostly in Indonesia. Also, **Netherlands Indies.**

Dutch Guiana, Surinam.

Dutch Harbor, a U.S. naval station in the Aleutian Islands.

Dutch·man (duch′mən), *n., pl.* **-men. 1.** native or inhabitant of the Netherlands. **2.** *Slang.* German.

Dutch·man's-breech·es (duch′mənz-brich′iz), *n. sing. and pl. Am.* **1.** a spring wild flower shaped somewhat like breeches. **2.** the plant that bears it.

Dutch oven, 1. a metal box that opens in front, used for roasting meat, etc., before an open fire or on top of a stove. **2.** a heavy iron kettle with a close-fitting cover.

Dutch treat, *Am., Colloq.* meal or entertainment in which each person pays for himself.

Dutch uncle, *Colloq.* person who sternly or severely criticizes or scolds another.

Dutch West Indies, Surinam and six islands off South America belonging to the Netherlands. Also, **Netherlands West Indies.**

du·te·ous (dü′ti·əs; dü′-), *adj.* dutiful; obedient. **—du′te·ous·ly,** *adv.* **—du′te·ous·ness,** *n.*

du·ti·a·ble (dü′ti·ə·bəl; dü′-), *adj.* on which a duty or tax must be paid.

du·ti·ful (dü′tə·fəl; dü′-), *adj.* **1.** performing the duties one owes; obedient. **2.** required by duty; proceeding from or expressing a sense of duty. **—du′ti·ful·ly,** *adv.* **—du′ti·ful·ness,** *n.*

du·ty (dü′ti; dü′-), *n., pl.* **-ties. 1.** thing that a person ought to do; thing that is right to do. **2.** the binding force of what is right: *sense of duty.* **3.** thing that a person has to do in his work; action required by one's occupation or position. **4.** proper behavior owed to an older or superior person; obedience; respect. **5.** tax on articles brought into or taken out of a country, made, sold, etc. **6. off duty,** not at one's work. **7. on duty,** at one's work. [< AF *dueté < du* DUE] **—Syn. 1, 2.** obligation. **3.** responsibility, office, function. **4.** deference, homage. **5.** customs.

du·ve·tyn, du·ve·tyne, or **du·ve·tine** (dü′və·tēn), *n.* a soft, closely woven cloth having a velvety finish. [< *duvet* down quilt < F]

D.V., God willing. [< L *Deo volente*]

Dvo·řák (dvôr′zhäk), *n.* Anton, 1841–1904, Czech composer.

dwarf (dwôrf), *n.* **1.** person, animal, or plant much smaller than the usual size for its kind. **2.** in fairy tales, an ugly little man with magic power. **—adj.** much smaller than the usual size of its kind; checked in growth. **—v. 1.** keep from growing large; check in growth. **2.** cause to seem small by contrast or by distance: *that tall building dwarfs the other.* [OE *dweorg*] **—dwarf′ness,** *n.* **—Syn. v. 1.** stunt.

dwarf·ish (dwôr′fish), *adj.* like a dwarf; smaller than usual. **—dwarf′ish·ly,** *adv.* **—dwarf′ish·ness,** *n.*

dwell (dwel), *v.,* **dwelt** (dwelt) or **dwelled, dwell·ing. 1.** make one's home; live. **2.** dwell on, a. think, write, or speak about for a long time. b. put stress on. [OE *dwellan* delay] **—dwell′er,** *n.* **—Syn. 1.** reside, abide.

dwell·ing (dwel′ing), or **dwelling place,** *n.* house to live in; place in which one lives. **—Syn.** residence, abode, habitation.

dwin·dle (dwin′dəl), *v.,* **-dled, -dling.** become smaller and smaller; shrink; diminish. [dim. of obs. *dwine* < OE *dwīnan* waste away] **—Syn.** lessen, decrease, decline, wane.

dwt., pennyweight; pennyweights.

Dy, *Chem.* dysprosium. Also, **Ds.**

dye (dī), *n., v.,* **dyed, dye·ing. —n. 1.** a coloring matter used to color cloth, hair, etc.; liquid containing this. **2.** color produced by such coloring matter; tint; hue. **—v. 1.** color (cloth, hair, etc.) by putting in a liquid containing coloring matter. **2.** color; stain. [OE *dēag*]

dyed-in-the-wool (dīd′in·tħə·wůl′), *adj.* **1.** dyed before being woven into cloth. **2.** *Am.* thoroughgoing, esp. in a political sense; complete.

dye·ing (dī′ing), *n.* the coloring of fabrics with dye.

dy·er (dī′ər), *n.* person whose business is dyeing fabrics.

dye·stuff (dī′stuf′), *n.* substance yielding a dye or used as a dye, as indigo.

dy·ing (dī′ing), *adj.* **1.** about to die. **2.** coming to an end. **3.** of death; at death. **—n.** death.

dyke (dīk), *n., v.,* **dyked, dyk·ing.** dike.

dy·nam·ic (dī·nam′ik), **dy·nam·i·cal** (-ə-kəl), *adj.* **1.** having to do with energy or force in motion. **2.** having to do with dynamics. **3.** active; energetic; forceful. [< Gk. *dynamikos < dynamis* power < *dynasthai* be powerful] **—dy·nam′i·cal·ly,** *adv.*

dy·nam·ics (dī·nam′iks), *n.* **1.** (*sing. in use*) branch of physics dealing with the action of force on bodies either at motion or at rest. Dynamics includes kinematics, kinetics, and statics. **2.** (*pl. in use*) forces, physical or moral, at work in any field.

dy·na·mite (dī′nə·mīt), *n., v.,* **-mit·ed, -mit·ing. —n.** a powerful explosive used in blasting rock, tree stumps, etc. **—v.** blow up or destroy with dynamite. **—dy′na·mit′er,** *n.*

dy·na·mo (dī′nə·mō), *n., pl.* **-mos.** machine that changes mechanical energy into electric energy and produces electric current.

dy·na·mo·e·lec·tric (dī′nə·mō·i·lek′trik), *adj.* pertaining to the transformation of mechanical energy into electric energy, or vice versa.

dy·na·mom·e·ter (dī′nə·mom′ə·tər), *n.* apparatus to measure force.

dy·na·mo·tor (dī′nə·mō′tər), *n.* a combined electric motor and dynamo for changing the voltage of an electric current.

dy·nast (dī′nast; -nəst), *n.* **1.** member of a dynasty; hereditary ruler. **2.** any ruler. [< L < Gk., < *dynasthai* be powerful]

dy·nas·ty (dī′nəs·ti; *esp. Brit.* din′əs-), *n., pl.* **-ties. 1.** series of rulers who belong to the same family. **2.** period of time during which a dynasty rules. **—dy·nas·tic** (dī·nas′tik; dī-), **dy·nas′ti·cal,** *adj.* **—dy·nas′ti·cal·ly,** *adv.*

dyne (dīn), *n. Physics.* amount of force that, acting on a mass of one gram for one second, gives it a velocity of one centimeter per second. [< F < Gk. *dynamis* power < *dynasthai* be powerful]

Dy·nel (dī·nel′), *n. Trademark.* a synthetic fiber resembling wool, resistant to fire, mildew, etc.

dys·en·ter·y (dis′ən·ter′i), *n.* a painful disease of the intestines, producing diarrhea with blood and mucus. [< OF < L < Gk., < *dys-* bad + *entera* intestines] **—dys′en·ter′ic,** *adj.*

dys·pep·si·a (dis·pep′si·ə; -shə), *n.* poor digestion; indigestion. [< L < Gk., < *dys-* bad + *pep-* cook, digest]

dys·pep·tic (dis·pep′tik), **dys·pep·ti·cal** (-tə·kəl), *adj.* **1.** pertaining to dyspepsia. **2.** suffering from dyspepsia. **3.** gloomy; pessimistic. **—n.** person who has dyspepsia. **—dys·pep′ti·cal·ly,** *adv.*

dys·pro·si·um (dis·prō′si·əm; -shi-), *n. Chem.* a rare element, Dy or Ds, the most magnetic substance known. [< NL < Gk. *dysprositos* hard to get at]

dz., dozen; dozens.

E

E, e (ē), *n., pl.* **E's; e's. 1.** the fifth letter of the alphabet. **2.** *Music.* the third tone of the scale of C major.

E, E., **1.** East; east; Eastern; eastern. **2.** English.

ea., each.

each (ēch), *adj.* every one of two or more considered separately or one by one: *each dog has a name.* —*pron.* each one: *each went his way.* —*adv.* for each; to each; apiece: *these pencils are a penny each.* [OE *ǣlc* < *ā* ever + *gelīc* alike]

➤ **each.** 1. As a pronoun, *each* is singular: *Each of the three has a different instructor.* 2. As an adjective, *each* does not affect the number of a verb; when the subject modified by *each* is plural, the verb is plural: *Each applicant has to fill out the blanks* (sing.). *Three students, also from this country, each receive a scholarship* (pl.).

each other, 1. each the other: *they struck each other,* that is, they struck, *each striking the other.* 2. one another: *they struck at each other.* ➤ **each other, one another.** By some grammarians *each other* is restricted to cases in which only two are concerned, *one another* being used of the greater number.

ea·ger (ē'gər), *adj.* 1. wanting very much; desiring strongly; anxious to do or get something. 2. ardent in desire or feeling. 3. characterized by intensity of desire or feeling: *eager looks, an eager contest.* [< OF < L *acer* keen] —**ea'ger·ly,** *adv.* —**ea'ger·ness,** *n.* —Syn. 2. keen, fervent.

ea·gle (ē'gəl), *n.* 1. a large bird of prey that has keen eyes and powerful wings. 2. picture of an eagle, or object shaped like an eagle, used as an emblem on a flag, stamp, etc. 3. standard bearing the figure of an eagle as an emblem. 4. *Am.* a former gold coin of the United States, worth $10. 5. *Golf.* two strokes less than par for any hole. [< OF < L *aquila*]

Eagle (3 ft. from head to tail)

ea·gle-eyed (ē'gəl·īd'), *adj.* able to see far and clearly.

ea·glet (ē'glit), *n.* a young eagle.

ear¹ (ir), *n.* 1. part of the body by which human beings and animals hear; organ of hearing. 2. the external ear; visible part of the ear. 3. sense of hearing. 4. ability to distinguish small differences in sounds. 5. favorable attention; listening. 6. thing shaped like the external part of an ear. 7. **be all ears,** *Colloq.* listen eagerly; pay careful attention. 8. **fall on deaf ears,** not be listened to; receive no attention. 9. **have or keep an ear to the ground,** *Am.* pay attention to what people are thinking and saying so that one can act accordingly. 10. **up to the ears,** *Colloq.* thoroughly involved; almost overcome. [OE *ēare*]

ear² (ir), *n.* part of certain plants, such as corn, wheat, etc., that contains the grains. —*v.* grow ears; form ears. [OE *ēar*]

ear·ache (ir'āk'), *n.* pain in the ear.

ear·drum (ir'drum'), *n.* a thin membrane across the middle ear that vibrates when sound waves strike it; tympanic membrane.

earl (érl), *n.* a British nobleman ranking below a marquis and above a viscount. [OE *eorl*] —**earl'dom, earl'ship,** *n.*

ear·ly (ér'li), *adj., adv.,* –li·er, –li·est. —*adv.* 1. in the first part. 2. before the usual time: *call me early.* 3. long ago; in ancient times. 4. before very long; soon. —*adj.* 1. of or occurring in the first part: *in early life.* 2. occurring before the usual or expected time: *have an early dinner.* 3. occurring far back in time: *in early times.* 4. occurring in the near future: *an early reply.* [OE, < *ǣr* ere + –*līce* -LY¹] —**earl'li·ness,** *n.*

early bird, person who gets up or arrives early; one who gains by acting promptly.

ear·mark (ir'märk'), *n.* 1. mark made on the ear of an animal to show who owns it. 2. a special mark, quality, or feature that gives information about a person or thing; sign. —*v.* 1. make an earmark on; identify or give information about. 2. set aside for some special purpose.

ear·muffs (ir'mufs'), *n.pl. Am.* pair of coverings to put over the ears to keep them warm.

earn (érn), *v.* 1. receive for work or service; be paid. 2. do enough work for; deserve; be worth. 3. bring or get as deserved. [OE *earnian*] —**earn'er,** *n.*

ear·nest¹ (ér'nist), *adj.* 1. sincerely zealous; firm in purpose; serious. 2. important: *"Life is*

real, life is earnest." —*n.* in earnest, sincerely zealous; serious. [OE *eornost*] —**ear'nest·ly,** *adv.* —**ear'nest·ness,** *n.* —Syn. *adj.* 1. sincere, diligent, eager.

ear·nest² (ér'nist), *n.* part given or done in advance as a pledge for the rest, or to bind a bargain. [ME *ernes,* appar. alter. (by assoc. with –NESS) of *erres* < OF, pl. < L *arra* < Gk. *arrhabon* < Heb. '*ērābôn*]

earn·ing (ér'ing), *n.* 1. act of gaining. 2. earnings, money earned; wages; profits.

ear·phone (ir'fōn'), *n.* receiver that is fastened over the ear; headphone.

ear·ring (ir'ring'), *n.* ornament for the ear.

ear·shot (ir'shot'), *n.* distance a sound can be heard; range of hearing: *he was out of earshot and could not hear our shouts.*

earth (érth), *n.* 1. planet on which we live; the third planet from the sun, and the fifth in size. 2. inhabitants of this planet. 3. this world (often in contrast to heaven and hell). 4. dry land. 5. ground; soil; dirt. 6. hole of a fox or other burrowing animal. 7. worldly matters. 8. *Chem.* a metallic oxide from which it is hard to remove the oxygen, such as alumina. 9. connection of an electrical conductor with the earth. 10. **come back to earth,** stop dreaming and get back to practical matters. 11. **run to earth,** hunt until found. —*v.* 1. of an animal, hide underground. 2. drive (a fox, etc.) to its hole. 3. cover with earth. [OE *eorthe*]

earth·en (ér'thən), *adj.* 1. made of earth. 2. made of baked clay.

earth·en·ware (ér'thən·wār'), *n.* 1. coarse baked clay dishes, containers, etc. 2. baked clay.

earth·ly (érth'li), *adj.,* –li·er, –li·est. 1. having to do with the earth, not with heaven. 2. possible; conceivable. —**earth'li·ness,** *n.*

earth·nut (érth'nut'), *n.* an underground part of certain plants, such as a root, tuber, etc.

earth·quake (érth'kwāk'), *n.* a shaking of the earth, caused by the sudden movement of rock masses or by changes beneath the surface.

earth satellite, a satellite of the earth, esp. a metal sphere or other structure launched by rockets into an orbit around the earth.

earth science, any science dealing with the earth, as geology, meteorology, or oceanography.

earth·ward (érth'wərd), *adv.* Also, **earth'wards.** toward the earth. —*adj.* at or toward the earth.

earth·work (érth'wérk'), *n.* 1. bank of earth piled up for a fortification. 2. a moving of earth in engineering operations.

earth·worm (érth'wérm'), *n.* a reddish-brown worm that lives in the soil; angleworm.

earth·y (ér'thi), *adj.,* earth·i·er, earth·i·est. 1. of or like earth or soil. 2. not spiritual; worldly. 3. not refined; coarse. —**earth'i·ness,** *n.*

ear trumpet, a trumpet-shaped instrument held to the ear as an aid in hearing.

ear·wax (ir'waks'), *n.* the sticky, yellowish substance in the canal of the outer ear.

ear·wig (ir'wig'), *n., v.,* –wigged, –wig·ging. —*n.* a beetlelike insect. Supposedly it creeps into the ear. —*v.* make private insinuations to. [OE, < *ēare* ear + *wicga* beetle, worm]

ease (ēz), *n., v.,* eased, eas·ing. —*n.* 1. freedom from pain or trouble; comfort. 2. freedom from trying hard; lack of effort; readiness: *he writes with ease.* 3. freedom from constraint; natural or easy manner. 4. **at ease,** a. free from pain or trouble; comfortable. b. *Mil.* with the body relaxed and the feet apart but quiet and stationary in position. —*v.* 1. make free from pain or trouble; give relief or comfort to. 2. lessen; lighten: *some medicines ease pain.* 3. release from tension; make easy; loosen: *ease a rudder, rope,* or *sail.* 4. move slowly and carefully: *he eased the big box through the narrow door.* 5. **ease off** or **up,** a. lessen; lighten. b. loosen. [< OF *aise* comfort, opportunity < VL *adjaces* neighborhood < L, ADJACENT] —**eas'er,** *n.* —Syn. *n.* 1. tranquility, rest. —*v.* 1. relieve, soothe.

ea·sel (ē'zəl), *n.* a support or upright frame for a picture, blackboard, etc. [< Du. *ezel* easel, lit., ass < L *asinus*]

ease·ment (ēz'mənt), *n. Law.* a right held by one person in land owned by another.

eas·i·ly (ēz'ə·li), *adv.* in an easy manner; with little effort.

eas·i·ness (ēz'i·nis), *n.* **1.** quality, condition, or state of being easy. **2.** carelessness; indifference.

east (ēst), *n.* **1.** direction of the sunrise; direction just opposite west. **2.** Also, **East.** part of any country toward the east. **3. the East,** the Orient. **4. East, a.** *Am.* region from Maine through Maryland in the United States. **b.** the Communist nations, especially the Soviet Union and its satellites in Eastern Europe. **5. down East,** *Am.* **a.** New England. **b.** the E part of New England. —*adj.* **1.** lying toward or situated in the east. **2.** originating in or coming from the east: *an east wind.* —*adv.* **1.** toward the east. **2.** in the east. [OE *ēast*]

East China Sea. See China Sea.

East·er (ēs'tər), *n.* day for celebrating Christ's rising from the dead, observed on the first Sunday after the first full moon after March 21. [OE *ēastre*, orig., name of dawn goddess < *ēast* EAST]

Easter Island, island in the S Pacific, 2000 miles W of Chile, and belonging to it.

east·er·ly (ēs'tər·li), *adj., adv.* **1.** toward the east. **2.** from the east. —*east'er·li·ness,* *n.*

east·ern (ēs'tərn), *adj.* **1.** toward the east. **2.** from the east. **3.** of or in the east. **4. Eastern,** *Am.* of or in the E part of the United States. **5.** Usually, **Eastern.** of or in the countries in Asia; Oriental. —**east·ern·most** (ēs'tərn·mōst), *adj.*

Eastern Church, 1. group of Christian churches in E Europe, W Asia, and Egypt that do not recognize the Pope as spiritual leader but follow the ceremonies used by the patriarch of Constantinople. **2.** the Orthodox Church.

east·ern·er (ēs'tər·nər), *n.* **1.** native or inhabitant of the east. **2. Easterner,** *Am.* native or inhabitant of the E part of the United States.

Eastern Hemisphere, the half of the world that includes Europe, Asia, Africa, and Australia.

East·er·tide (ēs'tər·tīd'), *n.* Easter time.

East Germany, area of Germany, including part of Berlin, under Communist control since World War II; the East Zone.

East Indies, 1. the collective name given to India, Indo-China, and the Malay Archipelago. **2.** the islands of the Malay Archipelago. —**East Indian.**

East Prussia, region on the SE Baltic coast, divided after World War II between Poland and Russia.

east·ward (ēst'wərd), *adv.* Also, **east'wards.** toward the east. —*adj.* **1.** toward the east. **2.** east.

East Zone, Eastern Zone, East Germany.

eas·y (ēz'i), *adj.,* **eas·i·er, eas·i·est,** *adv.* —*adj.* **1.** requiring little effort; not hard: *easy work.* **2.** free from pain, discomfort, trouble, or worry: *easy circumstances.* **3.** giving comfort or rest: *an easy chair.* **4.** fond of comfort or rest; lazy. **5.** not harsh; not severe; not strict: *easy terms, an easy master.* **6.** not hard to influence; ready to agree with, believe in, or help anyone. **7.** smooth and pleasant: *an easy literary style.* **8.** not tight; loose: *an easy fit.* **9.** not fast; slow: *an easy pace.* **10.** not much in demand; not hard to get. **11. on easy street,** *Am.* in comfortable circumstances. —*adv.* **1.** with little effort. **2.** *Colloq.* easily. [< OF *aisié,* pp. of *aaisier* set at ease < *a—* (< L *ad—*) + *aise* at EASE] —Syn. *adj.* **2.** tranquil, comfortable, contented.

eas·y·go·ing (ēz'i·gō'ing), *adj.* taking matters easily; not worrying.

easy mark, *Am., Colloq.* person who is easily imposed on.

eat (ēt), *v.,* **ate, eat·en** (ēt'ən), **eat·ing** (see usage note below). **1.** chew and swallow (food). **2.** have a meal. **3.** bite into and destroy: *acid eats metal.* **4.** destroy as if by eating; use up; wear away; waste away. **5.** make by eating. **6. eat one's words,** take back what one has said; retract. **7. eat out, a.** eat away from home. **b.** *Colloq.* admonish; castigate. **8. eat up, a.** eat all of. **b.** use up; waste away: *extravagance ate up*

his inheritance. [OE *etan*] —*eat'er, n.* —Syn. **4.** consume, waste. ≥ **eat.** The principal parts of *eat* are: in formal and informal usage, *eat* (ēt), *ate, eaten, eating;* in local and substandard usage, *eat, eat* (et or ēt), *eat* (ēt or et), *eating. Eat* is more common as the past tense in British than in American speech and writing and is pronounced et.

eat·a·ble (ēt'ə·bəl), *adj.* fit to eat. —*n.* Usually, **eatables.** things fit to eat; edibles.

eau de Co·logne (ō' də kə·lōn'), *Trademark.* cologne. [< F, water of Cologne]

eaves (ēvz), *n.pl.* the lower edge of a roof that projects beyond a wall. [OE *efes*]

eaves·drop (ēvz'drop'), *v.,* **-dropped, -dropping.** listen to what one is not supposed to hear; listen secretly to private conversation. —*eaves'drop'per, n.* —*eaves'drop'ping, n.*

ebb (eb), *n.* **1.** a flowing of the tide away from the shore; fall of the tide. **2.** a growing less or weaker; decline. **3.** point of decline. —*v.* **1.** flow out; fall. **2.** grow less or weaker; decline. [OE *ebba*] —Syn. *v.* **2.** wane, decrease.

eb·on (eb'ən), *n.* ebony. —*adj. Poetic.* **1.** made of ebony. **2.** dark; black.

eb·on·ite (eb'ən·īt), *n.* vulcanite.

eb·on·y (eb'ən·i), *n., pl.* **-on·ies,** *adj.* —*n.* **1.** a hard, heavy, durable wood, used for the black keys of a piano, the backs and handles of brushes, ornamental woodwork, etc. **2.** a tropical tree that yields this wood. —*adj.* **1.** made of ebony. **2.** like ebony; black; dark. [< L < Gk., < *ebenos* ebony < Egypt. *hebni*]

e·bul·lient (i·bul'yənt), *adj.* **1.** overflowing with enthusiasm, liveliness, etc. **2.** boiling; bubbling. [< L, < *ex—* out + *bullire* boil] —*e·bul'lience, e·bul'lien·cy, n.* —*e·bul'lient·ly, adv.*

eb·ul·li·tion (eb'ə·lish'ən), *n.* **1.** a boiling; a bubbling up. **2.** outburst (of feeling, etc.).

ECA, E.C.A., Economic Coöperation Administration.

é·car·té (ā'kär·tā'), *n.* a card game for two people, played with 32 cards. [< F, pp. of *écarter* discard < *é—* (< L *ex—*) out + *carte* CARD]

ec·ce ho·mo (ek'sē hō'mō; ek'e), *Latin.* behold the man.

ec·cen·tric (ik·sen'trik), *adj.* **1.** out of the ordinary; odd; peculiar. **2.** not having the same center. **3.** not moving in a circle. **4.** off center; having its axis set off center. **5.** *Astron.* not circular in form. —*n.* **1.** an eccentric person. **2.** disk or wheel set off center so that it can change circular motion into back-and-forth motion. [< Med.L < L *eccentrus* < Gk., < *ex—* out + *kentron* center] —*ec·cen'tri·cal·ly, adv.* —Syn. *adj.* **1.** irregular, queer, strange.

ec·cen·tric·i·ty (ek'sən·tris'ə·ti; -sen–), *n., pl.* **-ties.** **1.** eccentric quality or condition. **2.** something queer or out of the ordinary; oddity; peculiarity.

eccl., ecclesiastical.

Ec·cle·si·as·tes (i·klē'zi·as'tēz), *n.* book of the Old Testament. [< LL < Gk. *ekklēsiastes* preacher, ult. < *ex—* out + *kaleein* call]

ec·cle·si·as·tic (i·klē'zi·as'tik), *n.* clergyman. —*adj.* ecclesiastical.

ec·cle·si·as·ti·cal (i·klē'zi·as'tə·kəl), *adj.* of or having to do with the church or the clergy. —*ec·cle'si·as'ti·cal·ly, adv.*

ech·e·lon (esh'ə·lon), *n.* **1.** a steplike arrangement of troops, ships, etc. **2.** *Mil.* level of command. —*v.* form into a steplike arrangement. [< F, round of a ladder < *échelle* ladder < L *scala*]

e·chid·na (i·kid'nə), *n., pl.* **-nas, -nae** (-nē). a small, egg-laying, ant-eating animal of Australia with a covering of spines and a long, slender snout. [< L < Gk., viper]

e·chi·no·derm (i·kī'nə·dėrm; ek'i·nə-), *n.* starfish, sea urchin, or other similar small sea animal with a stony shell and a body whose parts are arranged radially. [< NL, < Gk. *echinos,* sea urchin, orig., hedgehog + *derma* skin]

ech·o (ek'ō), *n., pl.* **ech·oes,** *v.,* **ech·oed, echo·ing.** —*n.* **1.** a sounding again; a repeating of a sound. **2.** person who repeats the words or imitates the feelings, acts, etc., of another. **3.**

imitation of the feelings, acts, etc., of another. 4. a sympathetic response. —*v.* 1. sound again; repeat or be repeated in sound; reflect sounds. 2. repeat (the words) or imitate (the feelings, acts, etc.) of another. [< L < Gk.] —ech'o·er, *n.* —Syn. *v.* 1. resound.

Ech·o (ek'ō), *n.* Gk. *Legend.* a nymph who pined away with love for Narcissus until only her voice was left.

é·clair (ā·klãr'), *n.* an oblong puff or piece of pastry filled with whipped cream or custard and covered with icing. [< F, lightning, ult. < L *ex- clarare* lighten < *ex-* out + *clarus* clear]

é·clat (ā·klä'), *n.* 1. a brilliant success. 2. fame; glory. 3. burst of applause or approval. [< F]

ec·lec·tic (ek·lek'tik), *adj.* 1. selecting and using what seems best from various sources. 2. from various sources. —*n.* follower of an eclectic method. [< Gk. *eklektikos* < *ex-* out + *legein* pick] —ec·lec'ti·cism, *n.*

e·clipse (i·klips'), *n., v.*, e·clipsed, e·clips·ing. —*n.* 1. a darkening of the sun, moon, etc., when some other heavenly body is in a position that cuts off its light. A solar eclipse occurs when the moon is between the sun and the earth. 2. loss of importance or reputation; failure for a time. —*v.* 1. cut off or obscure the light from; darken. 2. cut off or obscure the importance of; make less outstanding by comparison; surpass. [< OF < L < Gk. *ekleipsis* < *ex-* out + *leipein* leave] —Syn. *v.* 2. out- shine, excel.

e·clip·tic (i·klip'tik), *n.* path that the sun appears to travel in one year. It is the great circle of the celestial sphere, cut by the plane containing the orbit of the earth. —*adj.* Also, e·clip'- ti·cal. 1. of this circle. 2. having to do with eclipses.

ABCD, orbit of the earth; A₁B₁C₁D₁, ecliptic; S, sun.

ec·logue (ek'lôg; -log), *n.* a short poem about country life, esp. a dialogue between shepherds. [< L < Gk. *ekloge* a selection. See ECLECTIC.]

e·col·o·gy (ē·kol'ə·ji), *n.* branch of biology that deals with the relation of living things to their environment and to each other. [< Gk. *oikos* house + -LOGY] —e·co·log·ic (ek'ə·loj'ik; ē'kə-), ec'o·log'i·cal, *adj.* —ec'o·log'i·cal·ly, *adv.* —e·col'o·gist, *n.*

econ., economic; economics; economy.

e·co·nom·ic (ē'kə·nom'ik; ek'ə-), *adj.* 1. of or pertaining to economics. Economic problems have to do with the production, distribution, and consumption of wealth. 2. having to do with the management of the income, supplies, and ex- penses of a household, community, government, etc.

e·co·nom·i·cal (ē'kə·nom'ə·kəl; ek'ə-), *adj.* 1. avoiding waste; saving: *an efficient engine is economical of fuel.* 2. having to do with econom- ics. —e'co·nom'i·cal·ly, *adv.* —Syn. 1. frugal, thrifty.

Economic Coöperation Administra- tion, governmental agency of the United States in charge of economic aid granted to foreign nations, abolished in December, 1951.

e·co·nom·ics (ē'kə·nom'iks; ek'ə-), *n.* science of the production, distribution, and consump- tion of wealth. Economics deals with the ma- terial welfare of mankind and the problems of capital, labor, wages, prices, tariffs, taxes, etc.

e·con·o·mist (i·kon'ə·mist), *n.* 1. an expert in economics. 2. person who is economical.

e·con·o·mize (i·kon'ə·mīz), *v.*, -mized, -miz- ing. 1. manage so as to avoid waste; use to the best advantage. 2. cut down expenses. —e·con'o- miz'er, *n.* —Syn. 2. retrench.

e·con·o·my (i·kon'ə·mi), *n., pl.* -mies. 1. a making the most of what one has; freedom from waste in the use of anything; thrift. 2. instance of this. 3. managing affairs and resources so as to avoid waste; management. 4. efficient ar- rangement of parts; organization; system. 5. system of managing the production, distribution, and consumption of goods: *feudal economy.* [< L < Gk. *oikonomia* < *oikos* house + *nemein* manage]

ec·ru, é·cru (ek'rü; ā'krü), *n., adj.* pale

brown; light tan. [< F, raw, unbleached, var. of *cru* raw < L *crudus*]

ec·sta·sy (ek'stə·si), *n., pl.* -sies. 1. state of great joy; thrilling or overwhelming delight; rapture. 2. any strong feeling that completely absorbs the mind; uncontrollable emotion. 3. trance. [< L < Gk. *ekstasis* trance, distraction < *ex-* out + *histanai* to place]

ec·stat·ic (ik·stat'ik), *adj.* Also, ec·stat'i·cal. 1. full of or tending to show ecstasy. 2. caused by ecstasy. —*n.* 1. one subject to fits of ecstasy. 2. ecstatics, fits of ecstasy. —ec·stat'i·cal·ly, *adv.*

ec·to·derm (ek'tə·dėrm), *n.* the outer layer of cells formed during the development of the em- bryos of animals. —ec'to·der'mal, *adj.*

ec·to·plasm (ek'tə·plaz·əm), *n.* 1. the outer portion of the cytoplasm of a cell. 2. an alleged emanation from the body of a medium in a trance. —ec'to·plas'mic, *adj.*

Ec·ua·dor (ek'wə·dôr), *n.* country in NW South America. —Ec·ua·do'ri·an, *adj., n.*

ec·u·men·i·cal (ek'yu̇·men'ə·kəl), **ec·u- men·ic** (-men'ik), *adj.* 1. general; universal. 2. of or representing the whole Christian Church. Also, *Brit.* oecumenical, oecumenic. [< L *oecu- menicus* < Gk., < *oikoumene* (ge) inhabited (world), ult. < *oikos* dwelling] —ec'u·men'i- cal·ly, *adv.*

ec·u·men·ism (ek'yu̇·mə·niz·əm), *n.* prin- ciple of world-wide Christian harmony and unity, especially in the Protestant church. Also, *Brit.* oecumenism.

ec·ze·ma (ek'sə·mə; ig·zē'-), *n.* a skin inflam- mation characterized by itching and the forma- tion of patches of red scales. [< NL < Gk. *ekzema* < *ex-* out + *zeein* boil]

-ed, *suffix.* 1. forming the past tense. 2. forming the past participle. 3. with various meanings: a. having; supplied with, as in *bearded, long- legged, pale-faced, tender-hearted.* b. having the characteristics of, as in *honeyed.* [OE]

ed., 1. edited; edition; editor. 2. educated.

E·dam cheese (ē'dam; ē'dəm), or **Edam,** *n.* a round, yellow cheese made in Holland, usu- ally colored red on the outside. [after village in Holland]

Ed·da (ed'ə), *n., pl.* Ed·das. either of two books written in Old Icelandic.

Ed·ding·ton (ed'ing·tən), *n.* Sir Arthur Stanley, 1882–1944, English astronomer and physicist.

ed·dy (ed'i), *n., pl.* -dies, *v.*, -died, -dy·ing. —*n.* water, air, etc., moving against the main current and having a whirling motion; small whirlpool or whirlwind. —*v.* 1. move against the main current in a whirling motion; whirl. 2. move in circles. [? < OE *ed-* turning + *ēa* stream]

Ed·dy (ed'i), *n.* Mary Baker, 1821–1910, founder of the Christian Science Church.

e·del·weiss (ā'dəl·vīs), *n.* a small Alpine plant having yellow flowers covered with white fuzz. [< G, < *edel* noble + *weiss* white]

e·de·ma (i·dē'mə), *n., pl.* -ma·ta (-mə·tə). a watery swelling in the tissues of the body. [< NL < Gk., < *oidos* tumor]

E·den (ē'dən), *n.* 1. garden where Adam and Eve lived at first. 2. a delightful spot; paradise.

E·den (ē'dən), *n.* Anthony, born 1897, English statesman, prime minister, 1955 to 1957.

e·den·tate (ē·den'tāt), *adj.* toothless. —*n.* one of a group of animals that are toothless or lack front teeth, as anteaters, armadillos, and sloths. [< L, < *ex-* without + *dens* tooth]

edge (ej), *n., v.*, edged, edg·ing. —*n.* 1. line or place where something ends; part farthest from the middle; side. 2. brink; verge. 3. a thin, sharp side that cuts. 4. sharpness; keenness. 5. *Colloq.* advantage. 6. **on edge**, a. disturbed; excited; un- comfortable. b. eager; anxious; impatient. 7. **take the edge off**, deprive of force, strength, or enjoyment. —*v.* 1. put an edge on; form an edge on. 2. move in a sidewise manner or little by little. 3. border. 4. edge in, manage to get in. [OE *ecg*] —edged, *adj.* —Syn. *n.* 1. margin, border. 2. rim.

edge·ways (ej'wāz'), **edge·wise** (-wīz'), *adv.* 1. with the edge forward; in the direction of the edge. 2. get a word in edgeways, manage to say a few words.

edg·ing (ej′ing), *n.* border or trimming on or for an edge.

edg·y (ej′i), *adj.*, edg·i·er, edg·i·est. 1. having a sharp edge. 2. impatient; irritable.

ed·i·ble (ed′ə·bəl), *adj.* fit to eat. —*n.* Usually, edibles. things fit or intended for eating. [< LL, < L *edere* eat] —ed′i·bil′i·ty, ed′i·ble·ness, *n.*

e·dict (ē′dikt), *n.* a public order or command by some authority; decree. [< L, < *ex-* out + *dicere* say] —e·dic′tal, *adj.* —Syn. proclamation.

ed·i·fi·ca·tion (ed′ə·fə·kā′shən), *n.* moral improvement; spiritual benefit; instruction.

ed·i·fice (ed′ə·fis), *n.* a building, esp. a large or imposing building. [< F < L *aedificium* < *aedis* temple (pl., house) + *facere* make]

ed·i·fy (ed′ə·fī), *v.*, -fied, -fy·ing. 1. improve morally; benefit spiritually; instruct. 2. build; construct. [< F < L *aedificare* build (up). See EDIFICE.] —ed′i·fi′er, *n.*

e·dile (ē′dīl), *n.* aedile.

Ed·in·burgh (ed′ən·bér′ō; *Brit.* ed′ən·brə, -bə·rə), *n.* capital of Scotland.

Ed·i·son (ed′ə·sən), *n.* Thomas Alva, 1847–1931, American inventor.

ed·it (ed′it), *v.* 1. prepare (another person's writings) for publication. 2. have charge of (a newspaper, magazine, etc.) and decide what shall be printed. [< L *editus* < *ex-* out + *dare* give; partly < *editor*]

edit., edited; edition; editor.

e·di·tion (i·dish′ən), *n.* 1. all the copies of a book, newspaper, etc., issued about the same time. 2. form in which a book is printed or published: *a three-volume edition.*

ed·i·tor (ed′ə·tər), *n.* 1. person who edits. 2. person who writes editorials. [< L. See EDIT.] —ed′i·tor·ship′, *n.*

ed·i·to·ri·al (ed′ə·tô′ri·əl; -tō′-), *adj.* of or having to do with an editor; by an editor. —*n.* *Am.* article in a newspaper or magazine written by the editor or under his direction, giving an opinion or attitude of the paper. —ed′i·to′ri·al·ly, *adv.*

ed·i·to·ri·al·ize (ed′ə·tô′ri·əl·īz; -tō′-), *v.*, -ized, -iz·ing. 1. write an editorial. 2. express one's opinions publicly, esp. in a newspaper. 3. *Am.* write news articles as if they were editorials.

Ed·mon·ton (ed′mən·tən), *n.* city in SW Canada; the capital of Alberta.

E·dom (ē′dəm), *n.* region in Palestine S of the Dead Sea. —**E·dom·ite** (ē′dəm·īt), *n.*

E.D.T., e.d.t., Eastern daylight time.

ed·u·ca·ble (ed′ù·kə·bəl), *adj. Am.* capable of being educated.

ed·u·cate (ej′ù·kāt), *v.*, -cat·ed, -cat·ing. 1. develop in knowledge, skill, ability, or character by training, study, etc. 2. send to school. [< L *educatus*, pp. of *educare* bring up, raise, akin to *educere* EDUCE] —Syn. 1. train, teach, instruct.

ed·u·ca·tion (ej′ù·kā′shən), *n.* 1. development in knowledge, skill, ability, or character by teaching, training, study, or experience. 2. knowledge, skill, ability, or character developed by teaching, training, study, or experience. 3. science or art that deals with the principles, problems, etc., of teaching and learning. —ed′u·ca′tor, *n.*

ed·u·ca·tion·al (ej′ù·kā′shən·əl), *adj.* 1. of or having to do with education. 2. giving education; tending to educate. —ed′u·ca′tion·al·ist, ed′u·ca′tion·ist, *n.* —ed′u·ca′tion·al·ly, *adv.*

ed·u·ca·tive (ej′ù·kā′tiv), *adj.* that educates.

e·duce (i·düs′; i·dūs′), *v.*, e·duced, e·duc·ing. bring out; draw forth; elicit; develop. [< L, < *ex-* out + *ducere* lead] —e·duc′i·ble, *adj.* —e·duc·tion (i·duk′shən), *n.*

Ed·ward (ed′wərd), *n.* 1. VI, 1537–1553, king of England 1547–1553, son of Henry VIII. 2. VII, 1841–1910, king of England 1901–1910, son of Queen Victoria. 3. VIII, born 1894, king of England in 1936, son of George V. He abdicated and received the title of Duke of Windsor.

Ed·wards (ed′wərdz), *n.* Jonathan, 1703–1758, American theologian and metaphysician.

Edward the Confessor, 1004?–1066, king of England from 1042 to 1066.

-ee, *suffix.* 1. person who is ——, as in *absentee.* 2. person who is ——ed, as in *appointee.* 3. person to whom something is ——ed, as in *mortgagee.* [< F *-é*, masc. pp. ending]

E.E., Electrical Engineer.

eel (ēl), *n.* a long, slippery fish shaped like a snake and lacking ventral fins. [OE *ēl*] —eel′-like′, *adj.*

eel·grass (ēl′gräs′; -gras′), *n. Am.* a North Atlantic sea plant with long, narrow leaves.

eel·pout (ēl′pout′), *n.* 1. a small, eellike saltwater fish. 2. the burbot.

e·en (ēn), *adv. Poetic.* even.

e·er (ãr), *adv. Poetic.* ever.

-eer, *suffix.* 1. one who is concerned or deals with, as in *auctioneer, charioteer.* 2. person who produces, as in *pamphleteer, sonneteer.* 3. be concerned or deal with, as in *electioneer.* [< F *-ier*]

ee·rie, ee·ry (ir′i), *adj.*, -ri·er, -ri·est. 1. causing fear; strange; weird. 2. timid because of superstition. [ME *eri*, var. of *erg*, OE *earg* cowardly] —ee′ri·ly, *adv.* —ee′ri·ness, *n.*

ef·face (i·fās′), *v.*, -faced, -fac·ing. 1. rub out; blot out; do away with; destroy; wipe out. 2. keep (oneself) from being noticed; make inconspicuous. [< F, < *es-* (< L *ex-*) away + *face* FACE] —ef·face′a·ble, *adj.* —ef·face′ment, *n.* —ef·fac′er, *n.*

ef·fect (i·fekt′), *n.* 1. whatever is produced by a cause; something made to happen by a person or thing; result. 2. power to produce results; force; validity. 3. influence. 4. impression produced. 5. combination of color or form in a picture, etc. 6. purport; intent; meaning. 7. effects, a. personal property; belongings; goods. b. *Brit.* imitation: *tweed effects.* 8. for effect, for show; to impress or influence others. 9. in effect, a. in result; in fact; really. b. in operation; active. 10. into effect, in operation; in action; in force. 11. take effect, begin to operate; become active. 12. to the effect, with the meaning or purpose. —*v.* produce as a result; make happen; get done; bring about. [< L *effectus* < *ex-* + *facere* make] —ef·fect′er, *n.* —ef·fect′i·ble, *adj.* —Syn. *n.* 1. outcome, consequence. —*v.* accomplish, achieve, realize. ▶ See affect for usage note.

ef·fec·tive (i·fek′tiv), *adj.* 1. producing the desired effect. 2. in operation; active. 3. striking; impressive. —*n. Mil.* soldier or sailor equipped and available for fighting. —ef·fec′tive·ly, *adv.* —ef·fec′tive·ness, *n.*

ef·fec·tu·al (i·fek′chu·əl), *adj.* 1. producing the effect desired; capable of producing the effect desired: *quinine is an effectual preventive for malaria.* 2. valid. —ef·fec′tu·al′i·ty, —ef·fec′tu·al·ly, *adv.*

ef·fec·tu·ate (i·fek′chu·āt), *v.*, -at·ed, -at·ing. cause; make happen; bring about; accomplish. —ef·fec′tu·a′tion, *n.*

ef·fem·i·nate (i·fem′ə·nit), *adj.* lacking in manly qualities; showing unmanly weakness or delicacy; womanish. [< L, < *ex-* + *femina* woman] —ef·fem′i·na·cy (i·fem′ə·nə·si), *n.* —ef·fem′i·nate·ly, *adv.* —ef·fem′i·nate·ness, *n.*

ef·fen·di (i·fen′di), *n.*, pl. -dis. 1. a former Turkish title of respect equivalent to "Sir" or "Master." 2. person having this title; Turkish doctor, official, scholar, etc. [< Turk. < Gk. *authentes* master, doer. See AUTHENTIC.]

ef·fer·ent (ef′ər·ənt), *adj.* conveying outward from a central organ or point. Efferent nerves carry impulses from the brain to the muscles. —*n.* an efferent nerve or blood vessel. [< L, < *ex-* out + *ferre* carry]

ef·fer·vesce (ef′ər·ves′), *v.*, -vesced, -vesc·ing. 1. give off bubbles of gas; bubble. 2. be lively and gay; be excited. [< L *effervescere* boil up < *ex-* out + *fervere* be hot] —ef′fer·ves′cence, ef′fer·ves′cen·cy, *n.* —ef′fer·ves′cent, *adj.*

ef·fete (i·fēt′), *adj.* unable to produce; worn out; exhausted. [< L *effetus* worn out by bearing < *ex-* out + *fe-* breed, bear] —ef·fete′ness, *n.*

ef·fi·ca·cious (ef′ə·kā′shəs), *adj.* producing

the desired results; effective. —**ef·fi·ca'cious·ly,** *adv.* —**ef'fi·ca'cious·ness,** *n.*

ef·fi·ca·cy (ef'ə·kə·si), *n., pl.* **–cies.** power to produce a desired effect or result; effectiveness. [< L, < *efficere* accomplish. See EFFICIENT.]

ef·fi·cien·cy (i·fish'ən·si), *n., pl.* **–cies. 1.** ability to produce the effect wanted without waste of time, energy, etc. **2.** efficient operation.

efficiency expert, *Am.* person whose profession is to devise more effective, economical methods of doing things.

ef·fi·cient (i·fish'ənt), *adj.* **1.** able to produce the effect wanted without waste of time, energy, etc. **2.** producing an effect. [< L *efficiens* < *ex–* + *facere* do, make] —**ef·fi'cient·ly,** *adv.* —**Syn. 1.** competent, capable.

ef·fi·gy (ef'ə·ji), *n., pl.* **–gies. 1.** statue, etc., of a person; image. **2. burn or hang in effigy,** burn or hang a stuffed image of a person to show hatred or contempt. [< F < L *effigies* < *ex–* out + *fingere* form] —**ef·fi·gi·al** (e·fij'i·əl), *adj.*

ef·flo·resce (ef'lō·res', –lō–), *v.,* **–resced, –resc·ing. 1.** burst into bloom. **2.** change from crystals to powder by loss of water. **3.** become covered with a crusty deposit when water evaporates. [< L *efflorescere* < *ex–* out + *flos* flower]

ef·flo·res·cence (ef'lō·res'əns; –lō–), **ef·flo·res·cen·cy** (–ən·si), *n., pl.* **–cen·ces, –cies. 1.** a blooming; a flowering. **2.** mass of flowers or anything resembling it. **3.** a change in which crystals lose water and become powder. **4.** powder formed in this way. **5.** eruption on the skin; rash. **6.** a crusty deposit formed when water evaporates from a solution. —**ef·flo·res'cent,** *adj.*

ef·flu·ent (ef'lū·ənt), *adj.* flowing out or forth. —*n.* Often, **ef'flu·ence. 1.** that which flows out or forth; outflow. **2.** stream flowing out of another stream, lake, etc. [< L, < *ex–* out + *fluere* flow]

ef·flu·vi·um (i·flū'vi·əm), *n., pl.* **–vi·a** (–vi·ə), **–vi·ums,** vapor or odor. [< L. See EFFLUENT.] —**ef·flu'vi·al,** *adj.*

ef·fort (ef'ərt), *n.* **1.** exertion of power, physical or mental; use of energy and strength to do something; trying hard. **2.** hard try; strong attempt. **3.** result of effort; thing done with effort; achievement. [< F < OF, < *esforcier* force, exert < L *ex–* out + *fortis* strong] —**ef'fort·less,** *adj.* —**ef'fort·less·ly,** *adv.* —**ef'fort·less·ness,** *n.*

ef·fron·ter·y (i·frun'tər·i), *n., pl.* **–ter·ies.** shameless boldness; impudence. [< F < OF *esfront* shameless < L *ex–* out + *frons* brow] —**Syn.** presumption, insolence.

ef·ful·gent (i·ful'jənt), *adj.* shining brightly; radiant. [< L, < *ex* forth + *fulgere* shine] —**ef·ful'gence,** *n.* —**ef·ful'gent·ly,** *adv.*

ef·fuse (i·fūz'; *adj.* i·fūs'), *v.,* **–fused, –fus·ing,** *adj.* —*v.* pour out; spill; shed. —*adj.* **1.** *Bot.* spread out. **2.** profuse. [< L *effusus* < *ex–* out + *fundere* pour]

ef·fu·sion (i·fū'zhən), *n.* **1.** a pouring out. **2.** unrestrained expression of feeling, etc., in talking or writing.

ef·fu·sive (i·fū'siv), *adj.* showing too much feeling; too emotional. —**ef·fu'sive·ly,** *adv.* —**ef·fu'sive·ness,** *n.*

eft[1] (eft), *n. U.S.* a small newt. [OE *efete.* See NEWT.]

eft[2] (eft), *adv. Obs.* again.

eft·soon (eft·sün'), **eft·soons** (–sünz'), *adv. Archaic.* **1.** soon afterward. **2.** again. [OE, < *eft* again + *sōna* at once]

e.g., for example. [< L *exempli gratia*] ⟩ **E.g.** is not usually italicized. In formal style or in a long, rather complicated sentence, it would usually be preceded by a semicolon.

egg[1] (eg), *n.* **1.** a roundish body covered with a shell or membrane that is laid by the female of birds, reptiles, and fishes. Their offspring come from these eggs. **2.** anything shaped like a hen's egg. **3.** a female germ cell. —*v.* **1.** prepare (food) with eggs. **2.** *Colloq.* pelt with eggs. [< Scand.]

egg[2] (eg), *v.* urge; encourage: *the boys egged him on to fight.* [< Scand. *eggja < egg* edge]

egg cell, the reproductive cell produced by a female plant or animal.

egg·head (eg'hed'), *n. Am. Colloq.* an intellectual.

egg·nog (eg'nog'), *n. Am.* drink made of eggs,

milk, and sugar, often containing whiskey, brandy, or wine. [< *egg*[1] + *nog* strong ale]

egg·plant (eg'plant'; –plänt'), *n.* **1.** plant with a large, oval, purple-skinned fruit. **2.** the fruit, used as a vegetable.

egg·shell (eg'shel'), *n.* shell covering an egg. —*adj.* like an eggshell; very thin and delicate.

e·gis (ē'jis), *n.* aegis.

eg·lan·tine (eg'lən·tīn; –tēn), *n.* a wild rose with pink flowers; sweetbrier. [< F, dim. of OF *aiglent* < VL *aculentus* < L *acus* needle]

e·go (ē'gō; eg'ō), *n., pl.* **e·gos. 1.** the individual as a whole in his capacity to think, feel, and act; self. **2.** *Colloq.* conceit. [< L, I]

e·go·ism (ē'gō·iz·əm; eg'ō–), *n.* **1.** seeking the welfare of oneself only; selfishness. **2.** talking too much about oneself; conceit. —**e'go·ist,** *n.*

e·go·is·tic (ē'gō·is'tik; eg'ō–), **e·go·is·ti·cal** (–tə·kəl), *adj.* **1.** seeking the welfare of oneself only; selfish. **2.** talking too much about oneself; conceited. —**e'go·is'ti·cal·ly,** *adv.*

e·go·tism (ē'gə·tiz·əm; eg'ə–), *n.* **1.** excessive use of *I, my,* and *me;* habit of thinking, talking or writing too much of oneself. **2.** selfishness. —**e'go·tist,** *n.* —**Syn. 1.** self-conceit, vanity.

e·go·tis·tic (ē'gə·tis'tik; eg'ə–), **e·go·tis·ti·cal** (–tə·kəl), *adj.* **1.** characterized by egotism; conceited. **2.** selfish. —**e'go·tis'ti·cal·ly,** *adv.*

e·gre·gious (i·grē'jəs), *adj.* **1.** outrageous; flagrant. **2.** remarkable; extraordinary. [< L *egregius* < *ex–* out + *grex* herd, flock] —**e·gre'gious·ly,** *adv.* —**e·gre'gious·ness,** *n.*

e·gress (ē'gres), *n.* **1.** a going out. **2.** way out; exit. **3.** right to go out. [< L *egressus* < *ex–* out + *gradi* step, go]

e·gret (ē'gret; eg'ret), *n.* **1.** heron with tufts of beautiful, long plumes. **2.** one of its plumes; aigrette. **3. snowy egret,** the North American egret. [< F *aigrette*]

E·gypt (ē'jipt), *n.* country in NE Africa. It joined with Syria from 1958 to 1961 to form the United Arab Republic.

Egypt., Egyptian.

E·gyp·tian (i·jip'shən), *adj.* **1.** of or having to do with Egypt or its people. **2.** Gypsy. —*n.* **1.** native or inhabitant of Egypt. **2.** language of the ancient Egyptians. **3.** Gypsy.

E·gyp·tol·o·gy (ē'jip·tol'ə·ji), *n.* science or study of the history, language, etc., of ancient Egypt. —**E·gyp·to·log·i·cal** (i·jip'tə·loj'ə·kəl), *adj.* —**E'gyp·tol'o·gist,** *n.*

ei·der (ī'dər), *n.* **1.** eider duck. **2.** its down. [< Scand. *æthr*]

eider down, 1. the soft feathers of the eider duck, used as stuffing. **2.** quilt stuffed with these feathers. [< Scand. *æthar-dūn*]

eider duck, a large, northern sea duck with very soft feathers on its breast.

Eider duck (2 ft. long)

Eif·fel Tower (ī'fəl), a lofty tower in Paris.

eight (āt), *n.* **1.** a cardinal number, one more than seven. **2.** symbol of this number; 8. **3.** crew of eight rowers. —*adj.* one more than seven; 8. [OE *eahta*]

eight ball, 1. *Pool.* a black-colored ball carrying the number 8. **2. behind the eight ball,** *Am.* in a difficult situation.

eight·een (ā'tēn'), *n.* **1.** a cardinal number, eight more than ten. **2.** symbol of this number; 18. —*adj.* eight more than ten; 18. —**eight·eenth** (ā'tēnth'), *adj., n.*

eight·fold (āt'fōld'), *adj.* **1.** eight times as much or as many. **2.** having eight parts. —*adv.* eight times as much or as many.

eighth (ātth), *adj.* **1.** next after the seventh; last in a series of 8. **2.** being one of 8 equal parts. —*n.* **1.** next after the seventh; last in a series of 8. **2.** one of 8 equal parts. **3.** *Music.* one octave.

eighth note, *Music.* a short note; one eighth of a whole note; quaver. See picture on next page.

eight·y (ā/ti), *n., pl.* **eight·ies,** *adj.* —*n.* 1. a cardinal number, eight times ten. 2. symbol of this number; 80. —*adj.* eight times ten; 80. —**eight·i·eth** (ā/ti·ith), *adj., n.*

ei·kon (ī/kon), *n.* icon.

Ein·stein (īn/stīn), *n.* Albert, 1879–1955, American physicist, born in Germany, who developed the theory of relativity.

Eighth note

ein·stein·i·um (īn·stīn/i·əm), *n.* a rare, radioactive, artificial element, E, produced as a by-product of nuclear fission. [named for Albert *Einstein*]

Eir·e (ār/ə), *n.* the Republic of Ireland.

Ei·sen·how·er (ī/zən·hou/ər), *n.* Dwight D., born 1890, American general, the 34th president of the United States, 1953–1961.

ei·ther (ē/thər; ī/–), *adj.* 1. one or the other of two: *either hat is becoming.* 2. each of two: *take seats on either side.* —*pron.* one or the other of two: *either of the hats is becoming.* —*adv.* any more than another: *if you do not go, I shall not go either.* —*conj.* one or the other of two: *either come in or go out.* [OE *ǣgther* < *ǣghwæther* each of two < *ā* always + *gehwæther* each of two. See WHETHER.] ➤ **either.** 1. The pronunciation ī′thər has not made so much progress in the United States as in England, and outside some communities in New England and a few families or circles that radiate from New England it is usually an affectation. 2. *Either* means primarily "one or the other of two," as adjective (*either way you look at it*), or pronoun (*bring me either*). For emphasis the pronoun is usually supported by one (*bring me either one*). Used of three or more objects (*either of the corners*) it is loose and rare; *any one of the corners* is the more usual idiom. *Either* is construed as singular. 3. *Either* meaning "each" is definitely formal: *broil the fish on either side. Each* or *both* would be more common in such expressions.

e·jac·u·late (i·jak/yə·lāt), *v.,* -lat·ed, -lat·ing. 1. say suddenly and briefly; exclaim. 2. eject; discharge. [< L, < *ex-* out + *jaculum* javelin < *jacere* throw] —**e·jac/u·la/tive,** *adj.* —**e·jac/u·la/tor,** *n.*

e·jac·u·la·tion (i·jak/yə·lā/shən), *n.* 1. something said suddenly and briefly; exclamation. 2. ejection; discharge.

e·jac·u·la·to·ry (i·jak/yə·lə·tô/ri; -tō/–), *adj.* 1. said suddenly and briefly; containing exclamations. 2. ejecting; discharging.

e·ject (i·jekt/), *v.* throw out; force out; expel. [< L *ejectare,* ult. < *ex-* out + *jacere* throw] —**e·jec/tion,** **e·ject/ment,** *n.* —**e·jec/tive,** *adj.* —**e·jec/tor,** *n.*

eke (ēk), *v.,* eked, ek·ing. 1. *Archaic and Dial.* increase; enlarge; lengthen. 2. eke out, a. supply what is lacking to; supplement. b. barely make (a living). [dial. var. of obs. *eche* to augment < OE *ēacan* < *ēaca* addition]

eke² (ēk), *adv., conj. Archaic.* also. [OE *ēac*]

el (el), *n.* 1. ell¹. 2. ell². 3. *Colloq.* an elevated railroad.

e·lab·o·rate (*adj.* i·lab/ə·rit; *v.* i·lab/ə·rāt), *adj., v.,* -rat·ed, -rat·ing. —*adj.* 1. worked out with great care; having many details; complicated. —*v.* 1. work out with great care; add details to. 2. talk, write, etc., in great detail; give added details. 3. make with labor; produce. [< L, < *ex-* out + *labor* work] —**e·lab/o·rate·ly,** *adv.* —**e·lab/o·rate·ness,** *n.* —**e·lab/o·ra/tive,** *adj.* —**e·lab/o·ra/tor,** *n.* —Syn. *adj.* detailed, minute.

e·lab·o·ra·tion (i·lab/ə·rā/shən), *n.* 1. an elaborating. 2. a being elaborated. 3. something elaborated.

El A·la·mein (el ä/lə·mān/; al/ə–), a coastal town in N Egypt; scene of a decisive British victory over the Germans in 1942.

E·lam (ē/ləm), *n.* an ancient country in what is now W Iran, E of ancient Babylonia. —**E·lam·ite** (ē/ləm·īt), *n.* —**E·lam·it·ic** (ē/ləm·it/ik), *adj.*

é·lan (ā·län/), *n.* enthusiasm; liveliness. [< F, < *élancer* to dart]

e·land (ē/lənd), *n.* a large African antelope with twisted horns. [< Du., elk]

e·lapse (i·laps/), *v.,* e·lapsed, e·laps·ing. slip away; glide by; pass. [< L *elapsus* < *ex-* away + *labi* glide]

e·las·mo·branch (i·las/mə·brangk; i·laz/–), *n.* fish whose skeleton is formed of cartilage and whose gills are thin and platelike. [< NL < Gk. *elasmos* metal plate + *branchia* gills]

e·las·tic (i·las/tik), *adj.* 1. having the quality of springing back to its original size, shape, or position after being stretched, squeezed, etc. 2. springing back; springy: *an elastic step.* 3. recovering quickly from low spirits, etc.; buoyant. 4. easily altered to suit changed conditions; flexible; adaptable. —*n.* 1. tape, cloth, etc., woven partly of rubber. 2. a rubber band. [< NL < Gk. *elastikos* driving, propulsive < *elaunein* drive] —**e·las/ti·cal·ly,** *adv.* —**e·las·tic·i·ty** (i·las/tis/ə·ti; ē/las–), *n.* —Syn. *adj.* 2. rebounding, flexible.

e·late (i·lāt/), *v.,* e·lat·ed, e·lat·ing. put in high spirits; make joyful or proud. [< L, < *ex-* out, away + *latus,* pp. to *ferre* carry] —**e·lat/er,** *n.*

e·lat·ed (i·lāt/id), *adj.* in high spirits; joyful; proud. —**e·lat/ed·ly,** *adv.*

e·la·tion (i·lā/shən), *n.* high spirits; joyous pride; exultant gladness.

El·ba (el/bə), *n.* an Italian island between Italy and Corsica. Napoleon I was in exile there from 1814 to 1815.

El·be (el/bə), *n.* river flowing from Czechoslovakia through C Germany into the North Sea.

el·bow (el/bō), *n.* 1. joint between the upper and lower arm. 2. anything resembling a bent elbow. 3. up to the elbows, a. very busy. b. deeply involved. —*v.* push with the elbow or elbows. [OE *elnboga.* See ELL¹, BOW².]

elbow room, el·bow·room (el/bō·rüm/, -rüm/), *n. Am.* plenty of room; enough space to move or work in.

El·brus, El·bruz (el/brüs; -brüz; āl/–), *n.* Mount, the highest mountain in Europe, located in S Russia, in the Caucasus Mountains.

El Cha·co (el chä/kō), region divided between Bolivia and Paraguay in 1938.

eld (eld), *n. Archaic.* 1. old age. 2. old times; former times. [OE *eldu* < *ald* old]

eld·er¹ (el/dər), *adj.* 1. born, produced, or formed before something else; older; senior: *my elder brother.* 2. prior in rank, validity, etc.: *an elder title to an estate.* 3. earlier; former: *in elder times.* —*n.* 1. an older person. 2. an aged person. 3. ancestor. 4. one of the older and more influential men of a tribe or community; chief, ruler, etc. 5. any of various important officers in certain churches. [OE *eldra,* comp. of *ald* old] ➤ **elder, eldest.** These archaic forms of *old* survive in formal English and they are used, when speaking of persons, only of members of the same family: *the elder brother; our eldest daughter.*

eld·er² (el/dər), *n.* elderberry. [OE *ellærn*]

el·der·ber·ry (el/dər·ber/i), *n., pl.* -ries. 1. shrub or tree with black or red berries, sometimes used in making wine. 2. berry of this plant.

eld·er·ly (el/dər·li), *adj.* somewhat old; beyond middle age; near old age. —**eld/er·li·ness,** *n.*

eld·er·ship (el/dər·ship), *n.* 1. office or position of an elder in a church. 2. group or court of elders; presbytery.

eld·est (el/dist), *adj.* oldest (of brothers and sisters or of a group). [OE, superl. of *ald* old] ➤ See elder for usage note.

El Do·ra·do (el/də·rä/dō; -rä/–), El Do·ra·do, *n., pl.* -dos. 1. a legendary city of great wealth. 2. any fabulously wealthy place.

e·lect (i·lekt/), *v.* 1. choose or select for an office by voting. 2. choose. —*adj.* 1. elected but not yet in office. 2. chosen; selected. 3. chosen by God for salvation and eternal life. —*n.* the elect, a. people selected or chosen by God for salvation and eternal life. b. people who belong to a group with special rights and privileges. [< L *electus* < *ex-* out + *legere* choose] —Syn. *v.* 2. select, pick.

elect., elec., electric; electrical; electricity.

e·lec·tion (i·lek/shən), *n.* 1. choice. 2. a choosing by vote. **3.** selection by God for salvation. —**Syn. 1.** selection, preference.

e·lec·tion·eer (i·lek′shən·ir′), v. Am. work for the success of a candidate or party in an election. —n. Esp. Brit. a political campaigner. —**e·lec′tion·eer′er,** n. —**e·lec′tion·eer′ing,** n.

e·lec·tive (i·lek′tiv), adj. **1.** chosen by an election: elective officials. **2.** filled by an election: an elective office. **3.** having the right to vote in an election. **4.** open to choice; not required. —n. course of study that may be taken, but is not required. —**e·lec′tive·ly,** adv. —**e·lec′tive·ness,** n.

e·lec·tor (i·lek′tər), n. **1.** one having the right to vote in an election. **2.** Am. member of the electoral college. **3.** one of the princes who had the right to elect the emperor of the Holy Roman Empire. —**e·lec′tor·al,** adj.

electoral college, Am. group of people chosen by the voters to elect the president and vice-president of the United States.

e·lec·tor·ate (i·lek′tər·it), n. **1.** the persons having the right to vote in an election. **2.** territory under the rule of an elector of the Holy Roman Empire.

E·lec·tra (i·lek′trə), n. Gk. Legend. daughter of Agamemnon and Clytemnestra.

e·lec·tric (i·lek′trik), adj. Also, **e·lec′tri·cal. 1.** of electricity; having to do with electricity. **2.** charged with electricity. **3.** producing electricity. **4.** run by electricity. **5.** exciting; thrilling. —n. Am., Colloq. car or railroad run by electricity. [< NL electricus < L < Gk. elektron amber (which, under friction, has the property of attracting)] —**e·lec′tri·cal·ly,** adv. —**Syn.** adj. **5.** stimulating, stirring.

electrical transcription, 1. radio broadcasting from a special phonograph record. **2.** a special phonograph record used in radio broadcasting.

electric brain, electronic brain.

electric chair, Am. chair used in electrocuting criminals.

electric eel, a large, eellike fish of South America that can give strong electric shocks.

electric eye, a photoelectric cell. An electric eye can operate a mechanism so as to open a door when its invisible beam is interrupted.

electric heater, 1. a portable device furnishing heat by means of small electric coils. **2.** in England, a radiator.

e·lec·tri·cian (i·lek′trish′ən; ē′lek-), n. Am. person whose work is installing or repairing electric wires, lights, motors, etc.

e·lec·tric·i·ty (i·lek′tris′ə·ti; ē′lek-), n. **1.** form of energy that can produce light, heat, magnetism, and chemical changes, and which can be generated by friction, induction, or chemical changes. **2.** an electric current; flow of electrons. **3.** branch of physics that deals with electricity.

e·lec·tri·fy (i·lek′trə·fī), v., -fied, -fy·ing. **1.** charge with electricity. **2.** equip to use electricity. **3.** give an electric shock to. **4.** excite; thrill. —**e·lec′tri·fi·ca′tion,** n. —**e·lec′tri·fi′er,** n.

electro-, word element. **1.** electric, as in electromagnet. **2.** electrically, as in electropositive. **3.** electricity. [< Gk. elektron amber]

e·lec·tro·chem·is·try (i·lek′trō·kem′is·tri), n. branch of chemistry that deals with chemical changes produced by electricity and the production of electricity by chemical changes. —**e·lec·tro·chem·i·cal** (i·lek′trō·kem′ə·kəl), adj.

e·lec·tro·cute (i·lek′trə·kūt), v., -cut·ed, -cut·ing. Am. kill by electricity. [< electro- + (exe) cute] —**e·lec′tro·cu′tion,** n., Am.

e·lec·trode (i·lek′trōd), n. either of the two terminals of a battery or any other source of electricity. [< electro- + Gk. hodos way]

e·lec·tro·dy·nam·ics (i·lek′trō·dī·nam′iks), n. branch of physics that deals with the action of electricity or with electric currents. —**e·lec′tro·dy·nam′ic, e·lec′tro·dy·nam′i·cal,** adj.

e·lec·tro·lier (i·lek′trə·lir′), n. chandelier or other support for electric lights. [< electro- + (chande) lier]

e·lec·trol·y·sis (i·lek′trol′ə·sis; ē′lek-), n. **1.** decomposition of a chemical compound into ions

by the passage of an electric current through a solution of it. **2.** removal of excess hair, moles, etc., by destruction with an electrified needle.

e·lec·tro·lyte (i·lek′trə·līt), n. **1.** Elect. solution that will conduct a current. **2.** Chem. compound whose solution is a conductor. [< electro- + Gk. lytos dissoluble < lyein loose] —**e·lec·tro·lyt·ic** (i·lek′trə·lit′ik), **e·lec′tro·lyt′i·cal,** adj. —**e·lec′tro·lyt′i·cal·ly,** adv.

e·lec·tro·lyze (i·lek′trə·līz), v., -lyzed, -lyz·ing. decompose by electrolysis. —**e·lec′tro·ly·za′tion,** n. —**e·lec′tro·lyz′er,** n.

e·lec·tro·mag·net (i·lek′trō·mag′nit), n. piece of iron that becomes a strong magnet when electricity passes through wire coiled around it. —**e·lec·tro·mag·net·ic** (i·lek′trō·mag·net′ik), adj.

e·lec·tro·mag·net·ism (i·lek′trō·mag′nə·tiz·əm), n. **1.** magnetism as produced by electric currents. **2.** branch of physics that deals with this.

e·lec·trom·e·ter (i·lek′trom′ə·tər; ē′lek-), n. instrument for measuring differences in electrical charge or potential.

e·lec·tro·mo·tive (i·lek′trə·mō′tiv), adj. of or producing a flow of electricity.

electromotive force, force that causes an electric current to flow, produced by differences in electrical charge or potential.

e·lec·tro·mo·tor (i·lek′trə·mō′tər), n. **1.** machine producing electric current. **2.** motor run by electricity.

e·lec·tron (i·lek′tron), n. unit charge of negative electricity. All atoms are composed of electrons and protons. [< electric + -on (as in ion, etc.)] —**e·lec·tron·ic** (i·lek′tron′ik; ē′lek-), adj.

e·lec·tro·neg·a·tive (i·lek′trō·neg′ə·tiv), adj. **1.** charged with negative electricity. **2.** assuming negative potential in contacting a dissimilar substance. **3.** nonmetallic; acid.

electron gun, device that guides the flow and greatly increases the speed of atomic particles. Electron guns are being developed for use in oil refining and various other industries.

electronic brain, a complex electric calculating machine, as UNIVAC. Also, **electric brain.**

e·lec·tron·ics (i·lek′tron′iks; ē′lek-), n. branch of physics that treats of electrons.

electron microscope, microscope that uses beams of electrons instead of beams of light, and has much higher power than any ordinary microscope.

electron tube, Electronics. vacuum tube.

e·lec·troph·o·rus (i·lek′trof′ə·rəs; ē′lek-), n., pl. -ri (-rī). a simple device for producing charges of electricity by means of induction. [< NL, < electro- + Gk. -phoros bearing]

e·lec·tro·plate (i·lek′trə·plāt′), v., -plat·ed, -plat·ing, n. —v. cover with a coating of metal by means of electrolysis. —n. silverware, etc., covered in this way. —**e·lec′tro·plat′er,** n.

e·lec·tro·pos·i·tive (i·lek′trō·poz′ə·tiv), adj. **1.** charged with positive electricity. **2.** assuming positive potential when contacting another substance. **3.** metallic; basic.

e·lec·tro·scope (i·lek′trə·skōp), n. device that indicates the presence of minute charges of electricity and shows whether they are positive or negative. —**e·lec·tro·scop·ic** (i·lek′trə·skop′ik), adj.

e·lec·tro·stat·ics (i·lek′trə·stat′iks), n. branch of physics dealing with objects charged with electricity. —**e·lec′tro·stat′ic,** adj.

Electroscope

e·lec·tro·ther·a·py (i·lek′trō·ther′ə·pi), n. treatment of disease by electricity. —**e·lec′tro·ther′a·pist,** n.

e·lec·tro·type (i·lek′trə·tīp), n., v., -typed, -typ·ing. —n. a copy of a page of type, an engraving, etc., used in printing, consisting of a thin shell of metal deposited by electrolytic action in a wax mold of the original and backed with type metal. —v. make such a plate or plates of. —**e·lec′tro·typ′er,** n.

e·lec·trum (i·lek′trəm), n. a pale-yellow alloy of gold and silver, used by the ancients. [< L < Gk. elektron]

el·ee·mos·y·nar·y (el'ə·mos'ə·ner'i; el'i·ə-), *adj.* **1.** of or for charity; charitable. **2.** provided by charity; free. **3.** dependent on charity; supported by charity. [< LL, < L *eleemosyna* ALMS]

el·e·gance (el'ə·gəns), **el·e·gan·cy** (-gən-si), *n., pl.* **-gan·ces; -cies. 1.** refined grace and richness; luxury free from showiness. **2.** something elegant. **—Syn. 1.** fineness, choiceness.

el·e·gant (el'ə·gənt), *adj.* **1.** having or showing good taste; gracefully and richly refined. **2.** expressed with taste; correct and polished in expression or arrangement. **3.** *Colloq.* fine; excellent; superior. [< L *elegans*] **—el'e·gant·ly,** *adv.*

el·e·gi·ac (el'ə·jī'ak; -ək; i·lē'ji·ak), *adj.* Also, **el'e·gi'a·cal. 1.** of or suitable for an elegy. **2.** sad; mournful; melancholy. **3.** written in elegiacs. **—n.** a dactylic hexameter couplet, the second line having only an accented syllable in the third and sixth feet.

el·e·gize (el'ə·jīz), *v.,* **-gized, -giz·ing. 1.** compose an elegy. **2.** lament in an elegy.

el·e·gy (el'ə·ji), *n. pl.* **-gies. 1.** a mournful or melancholy poem; poem that is a lament for the dead. **2.** poem written in elegiac verses. [< F < L < Gk. *elegeia,* ult. < *elegos* mournful poem]

elem., element; elementary; elements.

el·e·ment (el'ə·mənt), *n.* **1.** one of the simple substances, such as gold, hydrogen, etc., that cannot as yet be separated into simpler parts by ordinary means; substance composed of atoms that are chemically alike. **2.** one of the parts of which anything is made up. **3.** one of the four substances—earth, water, air, and fire—that were once thought to make up all other things. **4.** natural or suitable surroundings. **5.** *Mil.* any unit or part of a larger group, formation, or maneuver. **6.** *U.S. Air Force.* group of two or three fighter planes flying in formation. **7. the elements, a.** the simple, necessary parts to be learned first; the first principles. **b.** the atmospheric forces: *the storm seemed a war of the elements.* **c.** bread and wine used in the Eucharist. [< L *elementum* rudiment, first principle]

el·e·men·tal (el'ə·men'təl), *adj.* **1.** of the four elements—earth, water, air, and fire. **2.** of the forces of nature. **3.** as found in nature; simple but powerful: *hunger is an elemental feeling.* **4.** being a necessary or essential part. **5.** elementary. **—el'e·men'tal·ly,** *adv.*

el·e·men·ta·ry (el'ə·men'tə·ri; -tri), *adj.* **1.** of or dealing with the simple, necessary parts to be learned first; introductory. **2.** made up of only one chemical element; not a compound. **3.** having to do with a chemical element or elements. **4.** elemental. **—el'e·men'ta·ri·ly,** *adv.* **—el'e·men'ta·ri·ness,** *n.* **—Syn. 1.** rudimentary.

elementary school, 1. school of six grades followed by junior high school. **2.** school of eight grades, followed by a four-year high school.

el·e·phant (el'ə·fənt), *n., pl.* **-phants** or (*esp. collectively*) **-phant.** a huge, heavy mammal, with a long trunk and ivory tusks, that is the largest four-footed animal now living. [< OF < L < Gk. *elephas* elephant, ivory, prob. < Egypt.]

el·e·phan·ti·a·sis (el'ə·fən·tī'ə·sis; -fan-), *n.* disease in which parts of the body, usually the legs, become greatly enlarged, caused by parasitic worms that block the flow of lymph.

el·e·phan·tine (el'ə·fan'tin; -tīn; -tēn), *adj.* **1.** like an elephant; huge; heavy; clumsy; slow. **2.** of elephants.

E·leu·sis (i·lü'sis), *n.* city in ancient Greece, near Athens, site of yearly secret religious ceremonies in honor of the goddesses Demeter and Persephone. **—El·eu·sin·i·an** (el'yū·sin'i·ən), *adj.*

el·e·vate (el'ə·vāt), *v.,* **-vat·ed, -vat·ing. 1.** lift up; raise. **2.** raise in rank or station. **3.** raise in quality. **4.** put in high spirits; make joyful or proud. [< L, < *ex-* out + *levare* lighten, raise] **—Syn. 1.** hoist. **2.** promote, advance. **4.** cheer.

el·e·vat·ed (el'ə·vāt'id), *adj.* **1.** lifted up; raised; high. **2.** dignified; lofty; noble. **3.** in high spirits; joyful; proud. **—n.** *Am., Colloq.* a street railway raised above the ground.

el·e·va·tion (el'ə·vā'shən), *n.* **1.** a raised place; high place. **2.** height above the earth's surface or above sea level. **3.** a raising or being raised. **4.** loftiness; nobility. **5.** a drawing showing how the front, rear, or side of something looks from the outside.

el·e·va·tor (el'ə·vā'tər), *n.* **1.** thing that raises or lifts up. **2.** *Am.* a moving platform or cage to carry people and things up and down in a building, mine, etc. **3.** *Am.* a building for storing grain. **4.** an adjustable surface that causes an airplane to go up or down.

elevator shaft, *Am.* a verticle chute or passageway for an elevator.

e·lev·en (i·lev'ən), *n.* **1.** a cardinal number, one more than ten. **2.** symbol of this number; 11. **3.** team of eleven players. **—adj.** one more than ten; 11. [OE *endleofan* one left (over ten)] **—e·lev'enth,** *adj., n.*

eleventh hour, the latest possible moment.

elf (elf), *n., pl.* **elves. 1.** a tiny, mischievous fairy. **2.** a small, mischievous person. [OE *œlf*] **—elf'like',** *adj.*

elf·in (el'fən), *adj.* of or suitable for elves; like an elf's. **—n.** elf.

elf·ish (el'fish), *adj.* elflike; elfin; mischievous. **—elf'ish·ly,** *adv.* **—elf'ish·ness,** *n.*

elf·lock (elf'lok'), *n.* a tangled lock of hair.

El Gre·co (el grek'ō; grä'kō), 1548?-1614, painter of religious pictures in Spain and Italy, who was born in Crete.

E·li·a (ē'li·ə), *n.* pen name of Charles Lamb.

e·lic·it (i·lis'it), *v.* draw forth: *elicit a reply, elicit applause.* [< L *elicitus* < *ex-* out + *lacere* entice] **—e·lic'i·ta'tion,** *n.* **—e·lic'i·tor,** *n.*

e·lide (i·līd'), *v.,* **e·lid·ed, e·lid·ing. 1.** omit or slur over in pronunciation. The *e* in *the* is elided in "th" inevitable hour." **2.** *Law.* annul. [< L, < *ex-* out + *laedere* dash] **—e·lid'i·ble,** *adj.*

el·i·gi·bil·i·ty (el'ə·jə·bil'ə·ti), *n., pl.* **-ties.** fitness; qualification; desirability.

el·i·gi·ble (el'ə·jə·bəl), *adj.* fit to be chosen; properly qualified; desirable. **—n.** an eligible person. [< F < LL < L *eligere* pick out, choose. See ELECT.] **—el'i·gi·bly,** *adv.*

E·li·jah (i·lī'jə), *n.* a great Hebrew prophet who lived in the ninth century B.C. I Kings 17-19; II Kings 2:1-11.

e·lim·i·nate (i·lim'ə·nāt), *v.,* **-nat·ed, -nat·ing. 1.** get rid of; remove. **2.** pay no attention to; leave out of consideration; omit. **3.** *Math.* get rid of (an unknown quantity) by combining algebraic equations. **4.** *Physiol.* to void. **5.** execute. [< L, < *ex-* off + *limen* threshold] **—e·lim'i·na'tion,** *n.* **—e·lim'i·na'tive,** *adj.* **—e·lim'i·na'tor,** *n.* **—Syn. 2.** exclude, except.

El·i·ot (el'i·ət; el'yət), *n.* **1.** Charles W., 1834-1926, American educator, president of Harvard University from 1869 to 1909. **2.** George, 1819-1880, pen name of Mary Ann Evans, an English novelist. **3.** T(homas) S(tearns), 1888-1965, British poet, essayist, and critic, born in the United States.

E·lis (ē'lis), *n.* an ancient division of W Greece. Olympic games were held on the plains of Olympia in Elis.

E·li·sha (i·lī'shə), *n.* Hebrew prophet who was taught by Elijah. II Kings 2.

e·li·sion (i·lizh'ən), *n.* suppression of a vowel or a syllable. In poetry it generally consists in omitting a final vowel when the next word has an initial vowel.

e·lite, é·lite (i·lēt'; ā-), *n.* the choice or distinguished part; the best people. **—adj.** distinguished: *an elite group.* [< F, fem. pp. of *élire* pick out < L *eligere.* See ELECT.]

e·lix·ir (i·lik'sər), *n.* **1.** substance allegedly having the power of changing lead, iron, etc., into gold or of lengthening life indefinitely. **2.** a universal remedy; cure-all. **3.** medicine made of more than one base, usually of drugs or herbs mixed with alcohol and syrup. [< Med.L < Ar. *al-iksir* (def. 1), prob. < Gk. *xerion* drying powder used on wounds < *xeros* dry]

E·liz·a·beth (i·liz'ə·bəth), *n.* **1.** 1533-1603, Queen Elizabeth, ruler of England from 1558 to

1603, daughter of Henry VIII. 2. born 1926, queen of Great Britain and Northern Ireland, and head of the British Commonwealth of Nations, daughter of George VI. 3. *Bible.* cousin of the Virgin Mary. 4. city in NE New Jersey.

E·liz·a·be·than (i·liz′ə·bē′thən; –beth′ən), *adj.* of the time of Queen Elizabeth. —*n.* person, esp. a writer, of the time of Queen Elizabeth.

Elizabethan sonnet, type of sonnet written by Shakespeare and many other Elizabethans. It has the rhyme scheme *abab cdcd efef gg.*

elk (elk), *n., pl.* **elks** or (*esp. collectively*) **elk.** 1. a large deer of N Europe and Asia. It has antlers like a moose. 2. a large, reddish deer of North America; wapiti. [appar. < AF form of OE *eolh*]

ell¹ (el), *n.* an old measure of length, chiefly used in measuring cloth. In England it was equal to 45 inches. Also, **el.** [OE *eln* length of lower arm]

ell² (el), *n.* 1. something shaped like an L. 2. an extension of a building at right angles to it. Also, **el.**

el·lipse (i·lips′), *n. Geom.* a plane curve, the path of a point that moves so that the sum of its distances from two fixed points remains the same. [< L *ellipsis* ELLIPSIS]

el·lip·sis (i·lip′sis), *n., pl.* **–ses** (–sēz) 1. omission of a word or words needed to complete the grammatical construction of a sentence. *Example:* She is as tall as her brother (is tall), if not taller (than her brother is tall). 2. marks (. . . or ***) used to show an omission in writing or printing. [< L < Gk., < *elleipein* come short, leave out]

el·lip·ti·cal (i·lip′tə·kəl), **el·lip·tic** (–tik), *adj.* 1. like an ellipse; of an ellipse. 2. showing ellipsis; having a word or words omitted. —**el·lip′ti·cal·ly,** *adv.*

El·lis Is·land (el′is), a small island in New York harbor where immigrants were examined, until 1954, before entering the United States.

elm (elm), *n.* 1. a tall, graceful shade tree. 2. its hard, heavy wood. [OE]

el·o·cu·tion (el′ə·kū′shən), *n.* 1. art of speaking or reading clearly and effectively in public; art of public speaking. 2. manner of speaking or reading in public. [< L *elocutio* < *ex*– out + *loqui* speak] —**el·o·cu·tion·ar·y** (el′ə·kū′shən·er′i), *adj.* —**el′o·cu′tion·ist,** *n.*

e·lon·gate (i·lông′gāt; i·long′–), *v.,* –gat·ed, –gat·ing, *adj.* —*v.* lengthen; extend; stretch. —*adj.* 1. lengthened. 2. long and thin: *the elongate leaf of the willow.* [< L, < *ex*– out + *longus* long] —**e·lon·ga·tion** (i·lông′gā′shən, i·long′–; ē′lông–), *n.*

e·lope (i·lōp′), *v.,* e·loped, e·lop·ing. 1. run away with a lover. 2. run away; escape. [< AF *aloper* < ME *lope*(*n*) run. See LOPE.] —**e·lope′ment,** *n.* —**e·lop′er,** *n.*

el·o·quence (el′ə·kwens), *n.* 1. flow of speech that has grace and force. 2. power to win by speaking; art of speaking so as to stir the feelings. [< L *eloquentia* < *ex*– out + *loqui* speak] —**Syn.** 1. elocution. 2. oratory, rhetoric.

el·o·quent (el′ə·kwənt), *adj.* 1. having eloquence. 2. very expressive. —**el′o·quent·ly,** *adv.* —**Syn.** 1. voluble, fluent, glib. 2. significant.

El Pas·o (el pas′ō), city in W Texas, on the Rio Grande.

El Sal·va·dor (el sal′və·dôr), country in W Central America.

else (els), *adj.* 1. other; different. 2. in addition. —*adv.* 1. instead. 2. differently. 3. otherwise; if not. [OE *elles*] ► Because else follows the word (usually a pronoun) it modifies, it takes the sign of the possessive: *he finally decided the book was somebody else's.*

else·where (els′hwâr; –hwĕr), *adv.* somewhere else; in or to some other place.

el·u·ci·date (i·lū′sə·dāt), *v.,* –dat·ed, –dat·ing. make clear; explain. [< LL, < L *ex*– out + *lucidus* bright] —**e·lu′ci·da′tion,** *n.* —**e·lu′ci·da′tive,** *adj.* —**e·lu′ci·da′tor,** *n.*

e·lude (i·lūd′), *v.,* e·lud·ed, e·lud·ing. 1. slip away from; escape by cleverness, quickness, etc. 2. escape discovery by; baffle. [< L, < *ex*– out + *ludere* play] —**e·lud′er,** *n.* —**e·lu·sion** (i·lū′zhən), *n.* —**Syn.** 1. avoid, evade, shun. 2. foil, frustrate.

e·lu·sive (i·lū′siv), **e·lu·so·ry** (–sə·ri), *adj.* 1. hard to describe or understand; baffling. 2. tending to elude. —**e·lu′sive·ly,** *adv.* —**e·lu′sive·ness,** *n.*

elves (elvz), *n. pl.* of elf.

elv·ish (el′vish), *adj.* elfish; elflike. —**elv′ish·ly,** *adv.*

E·ly·si·um (i·lizh′i·əm; i·liz′–; i·lizh′əm), *n.* 1. *Gk. Myth.* place where heroes and virtuous people lived after death. 2. any place or condition of perfect happiness; paradise. —**E·ly·sian** (i·lizh′ən), *adj.*

em (em), *n., pl.* **ems.** 1. the letter M, m. 2. unit for measuring the amount of print in a line, page, etc.

e·ma·ci·ate (i·mā′shi·āt), *v.,* –at·ed, –at·ing. make unnaturally thin; cause to lose flesh or waste away. [< L, ult. < *ex*– + *macies* leanness] —**e·ma·ci·a·tion** (i·mā′shi·ā′shən; –si–), *n.*

em·a·nate (em′ə·nāt), *v.,* –nat·ed, –nat·ing. come forth. [< L, < *ex*– out + *manare* flow] —**em′a·na′tion,** *n.* —**em′a·na′tive,** *adj.*

e·man·ci·pate (i·man′sə·pāt), *v.,* –pat·ed, –pat·ing. release from slavery or restraint; set free. [< L *emancipatus* < *ex*– away + *manceps* purchaser < *manus* hand + *capere* take] —**e·man′ci·pa′tion,** *n.* —**e·man′ci·pa′tive,** *adj.* —**e·man′ci·pa′tor,** *n.*

e·mas·cu·late (*v.* i·mas′kyə·lāt; *adj.* i·mas′-kyə·lit; –lāt), *v.,* –lat·ed, –lat·ing, *adj.* —*v.* 1. remove the male glands of; castrate. 2. destroy the force of; weaken. —*adj.* deprived of vigor; weakened; effeminate. [< L *emasculatus* < *ex*– away + *masculus* male] —**e·mas′cu·la′tion,** *n.* —**e·mas′cu·la′tor,** *n.*

em·balm (em·bäm′), *v.* 1. treat (a dead body) with drugs, chemicals, etc., to keep it from decaying. 2. keep in memory; preserve. 3. fill with sweet scent; perfume. —**em·balm′er,** *n.* —**em·balm′ment,** *n.*

em·bank (em·bangk′), *v.* protect, enclose, or confine with a raised bank of earth, stones, etc.

em·bank·ment (em·bangk′mənt), *n.* 1. a raised bank of earth, stones, etc., used to hold back water, support a roadway, etc. 2. an embanking.

em·bar·go (em·bär′gō), *n., pl.* **–goes,** *v.,* –goed, –go·ing. —*n.* 1. order of a government forbidding ships to enter or leave its ports. 2. any restriction put on commerce by law. 3. restriction; restraint; hindrance. —*v.* lay an embargo on; forbid to enter or leave port. [< Sp., < *embargar* restrain < VL *in*– in + *barra* BAR]

em·bark (em·bärk′), *v.* 1. go on board ship. 2. put on board ship. 3. set out; start. 4. involve (a person) in an enterprise; invest (money) in an enterprise. [< F *embarquer.* See EN–, BARK³.] —**em′bar·ka′tion,** **em′bar·ca′tion,** *n.* —**em·bark′ment,** *n.*

em·bar·rass (em·bar′əs), *v.* 1. disturb (a person); make self-conscious. 2. complicate; mix up. 3. involve in difficulties; hinder. 4. burden with debt; involve in financial difficulties. [< F, lit., to block < Ital., < *imbarrare* to bar < VL *barra* BAR] —**em·bar′rass·ing,** *adj.* —**em·bar′-rass·ing·ly,** *adv.* —**em·bar′rass·ment,** *n.* —**Syn.** 1. discomfit, disconcert, abash, confuse. 3. hamper, impede, obstruct.

em·bas·sa·dor (em·bas′ə·dər; –dôr), *n.* ambassador.

em·bas·sy (em′bə·si), *n., pl.* **–sies.** 1. ambassador and his staff of assistants. 2. the official residence, offices, etc., of an ambassador in a foreign country. 3. position or duties of an ambassador. 4. person or group officially sent as ambassadors. 5. a special errand; important mission; official message. [< OF < Ital. < Pr. < Gothic *andbahti* service, ult. < Gaulish *ambactus*]

em·bat·tle¹ (em·bat′əl), *v.,* –tled, –tling. prepare for battle; form into battle order. [see EN–, BATTLE]

em·bat·tle² (em·bat′əl), v., -tled, -tling. provide with battlements; fortify. [< en- + obs. battle, v., furnish with battlements]

em·bed (em·bed′), v., -bed·ded, -bed·ding. 1. put in a bed. 2. fix or enclose in a surrounding mass. Also, imbed.

em·bel·lish (em·bel′ish), v. 1. decorate; adorn; ornament. 2. make more interesting by adding real or imaginary details; elaborate. [< OF embellir < en- in (< L in-) + bel handsome < L bellus] —em·bel′lish·er, n. —em·bel′lish·ment, n. —Syn. 1. beautify.

em·ber (em′bər), n. piece of wood or coal still glowing in the ashes of a fire. [OE æmerge]

Ember days, three days set apart in each season for fasting and prayer by the Roman Catholic, Anglican, and some other churches.

em·bez·zle (em·bez′əl), v., -zled, -zling. steal (money, securities, etc., entrusted to one's care). [< AF enbesiler < en- + beseler destroy] —em·bez′zle·ment, n. —em·bez′zler, n.

em·bit·ter (em·bit′ər), v. make bitter; make more bitter.

em·bla·zon (em·blā′zən), v. 1. display conspicuously; picture in bright colors. 2. decorate; adorn. 3. praise highly; honor publicly; make known the fame of. —em·bla′zon·er, n. —em·bla′zon·ment, em·bla′zon·ry, n.

em·blem (em′bləm), n. 1. representation of an invisible quality, idea, etc., by some connection of thought; symbol. The dove is an emblem of peace. 2. a heraldic device. [< L, inlaid work < Gk. emblema insertion < en- in + ballein throw] —Syn. 1. token, sign, badge.

em·blem·at·ic (em′blə·mat′ik), **em·blem·at·i·cal** (-ə·kəl), adj. used as an emblem; symbolical. The Cross is emblematic of Christianity. —em′blem·at′i·cal·ly, adv.

em·bod·y (em·bod′i), v., -bod·ied, -bod·y·ing. 1. put into visible form; express in definite form. 2. bring together and include in a book, system, etc.; organize. 3. make part of an organized book, law, system, etc.; incorporate. —em·bod′i·ment, n. —Syn. 1. incarnate, materialize, externalize. 3. include, combine.

em·bold·en (em·bōl′dən), v. make bold; encourage.

em·bo·lism (em′bə·liz·əm), n. Med. obstruction of a blood vessel by a clot, a bit of fat, or other obstacle. [< L < Gk. embolismos. See EMBLEM.] —em′bo·lis′mic, adj.

em·bo·lus (em′bə·ləs), n., pl. -li (-lī). a solid material in the vascular system.

em·bos·om (em·būz′əm; -bü′zəm), v. 1. surround; enclose; envelop. 2. embrace; cherish.

em·boss (em·bôs′; -bos′), v. decorate with a design, pattern, etc., that stands out from the surface. [see EN-, BOSS²] —em·boss′er, n. —em·boss′ment, n.

em·bou·chure (äm′bù·shùr′), n. 1. mouth of a river or valley. 2. mouthpiece of a wind instrument. [< F, < emboucher put into or discharge from a mouth < en- in (< L in-) + bouche mouth < L bucca]

em·bow·er (em·bou′ər), v. enclose in a shelter of leafy branches.

em·brace (em·brās′), v., -braced, -brac·ing. n. —v. 1. clasp or hold in the arms to show love or friendship; hug. 2. hug one another. 3. take up; take for oneself; accept: embrace the Christian religion. 4. include; contain. 5. surround; enclose. —n. an embracing; a hug. [< OF < VL, < L in- in + brachium arm] —em·brace′a·ble, adj. —em·brace′ment, n. —em·brac′er, n. —Syn. v. 3. adopt, espouse. 4. comprise. —Ant. v. 3. spurn, reject. 4. exclude, eliminate.

em·bra·sure (em·brā′zhər), n. 1. an opening in a wall for a gun, with sides that spread outward. 2. a slanting off of the wall at an oblique angle on the inner sides of a window or door. [< F, < embraser widen an opening]

em·bro·cate (em′brō·kāt), v., -cat·ed, -cat·ing. bathe and rub with liniment or lotion. [< LL embrocatus < embroch(a)a < Gk. embroche lotion] —em′bro·ca′tion, n.

em·broi·der (em·broi′dər), v. 1. ornament (cloth, leather, etc.) with a design, pattern, etc., of stitches. 2. make or put (a design, pattern, etc.) on cloth, leather, etc., with stitches. 3. do embroidery. 4. add imaginary details to; exaggerate. [see EN-, BROIDER] —em·broi′der·er, n. —Syn. 1. embellish, beautify, decorate.

em·broi·der·y (em·broi′dər·i), n., pl. -der·ies. 1. art of working raised and ornamental designs in cloth, leather, etc., with a needle; embroidering. 2. embroidered work or material.

em·broil (em·broil′), v. 1. involve (a person, country, etc.) in a quarrel. 2. throw (affairs, etc.) into a state of confusion. —em·broil′er, n. —em·broil′ment, n.

em·brown (em·broun′), v. tan; darken.

em·bry·o (em′bri·ō), n., pl. -bry·os, adj. —n. 1. animal during the period of its growth from the fertilized egg until its organs have developed so that it can live independently. 2. Bot. an undeveloped plant within a seed. —adj. embryonic; undeveloped; not mature. [< Med.L < Gk. embryon, < en- in + bryein swell]

embryol., embryology.

em·bry·ol·o·gy (em′bri·ol′ə·ji), n. Biol. study of the formation and development of embryos. —em·bry·o·log·i·cal (em′bri·ə·loj′ə·kəl), em′bry·o·log′ic, adj. —em′bry·ol′o·gist, n.

em·bry·on·ic (em′bri·on′ik), adj. 1. of the embryo. 2. undeveloped; not mature.

em·cee (em′sē′), n., v., -ceed, -cee·ing. U.S. —n. master of ceremonies. —v. act as master of ceremonies of. Also, M.C.

e·meer (ə·mir′), n. emir.

e·mend (i·mend′), v., **e·men·date** (ē′men·dāt), v., e·mend·ed, e·mend·ing; e·men·dat·ed, e·men·dat·ing. suggest changes to free (a faulty text, document, etc.) from errors; correct; improve. [< L, < ex- away + menda fault] —e·mend′a·ble, adj. —e·men·da·tion (ē′men·dā′shən; em′en-), n. —e·men·da·to·ry (i·men′də·tô′ri; -tō′-), adj.

em·er·ald (em′ər·əld; em′rəld), n. a bright-green precious stone; transparent green beryl. —adj. bright-green. [< OF esmeralde < L < Gk. smaragdos]

e·merge (i·mérj′), v., e·merged, e·merg·ing. come out; come into view. [< L, < ex- out + mergere dip] —e·mer′gence, n. —e·mer′gent, adj.

e·mer·gen·cy (i·mér′jən·si), n., pl. -cies, adj. —n. a sudden need for immediate action. —adj. for use in time of sudden need. —Syn. n. crisis.

e·mer·i·tus (i·mer′ə·təs), adj. honorably discharged; retired from active service, but still holding one's rank and title. [< L, < ex- to the end + merere serve]

e·mer·sion (i·mér′zhən; -shən), n. an emerging.

Em·er·son (em′ər·sən), n. Ralph Waldo, 1803–1882, American essayist, poet, and philosopher.

em·er·y (em′ər·i), n. a hard, dark mineral, an impure corundum, used for grinding, smoothing, and polishing. [< F < Ital. < VL smericulum < Med.Gk. smeris < Gk. smyris abrasive powder]

e·met·ic (i·met′ik), adj. causing vomiting. —n. medicine or treatment that causes vomiting. [< L < Gk. emetikos < emeein vomit]

E.M.F., e.m.f., or **emf**, electromotive force.

em·i·grant (em′ə·grənt), n. person who leaves his own country or region to settle in another. —adj. leaving one's own country or region to settle in another.

em·i·grate (em′ə·grāt), v., -grat·ed, -grat·ing. leave one's own country or region to settle in another. [< L, < ex- out + migrare to move. See MIGRATE.] —em′i·gra′tion, n. ▶ emigrate, immigrate. Emigrate means to move out of a country or region, immigrate to move into a country. An emigrant from Norway would be an immigrant to the United States.

é·mi·gré (em'ə·grā), n., pl. **-grés** (-grāz). 1. emigrant. 2. member of a refugee group. [< F]

em·i·nence (em'ə·nəns), n. 1. rank or position above all or most others; high standing; fame. 2. a high place; lofty hill. 3. **Eminence**, title of honor given to a cardinal in the Roman Catholic Church. [< L eminentia < ex- out + minere jut] —Syn. 1. distinction, prominence, renown.

em·i·nent (em'ə·nənt), adj. 1. distinguished; exalted. 2. conspicuous; noteworthy. 3. high; lofty. 4. projecting. —em'i·nent·ly, adv.

eminent domain, right of government to take private property for public use. The owner must be paid for the property taken.

e·mir (ə·mir'), n. 1. an Arabian chief, prince, or military leader. 2. title of the descendants of Mohammed. 3. title of certain Turkish officials. Also, emeer. [< Ar. amir commander]

em·is·sar·y (em'ə·ser'i), n., pl. **-sar·ies**, adj. —n. 1. person sent on a mission or errand. 2. a secret agent; spy. —adj. of, or acting as, an emissary. [< L emissarius. See EMIT.]

e·mis·sion (i·mish'ən), n. 1. act or fact of emitting. 2. thing emitted. —e·mis'sive, adj.

e·mit (i·mit'), v., e·mit·ted, e·mit·ting. 1. give off; send out. 2. put into circulation; issue. 3. utter; voice. [< L, < ex- out + mittere send] —e·mit'ter, n. —Syn. 1. exude, expel, eject.

Em·man·u·el (i·man'yū·əl), n. Immanuel.

Em·my (em'i), n., pl. **-mies**. Am. a small statuette awarded annually by the Academy of Television Arts and Sciences for achievements of outstanding excellence in television.

e·mol·lient (i·mol'yənt), adj. softening; soothing. —n. something that softens and soothes. [< L < emollire soften < ex- + mollis soft]

e·mol·u·ment (i·mol'yə·mənt), n. profit from an office or position; fee [< L, profit, ult. < ex- out + molere grind]

e·mote (i·mōt'), v., e·mot·ed, e·mot·ing. Am. 1. act, esp. in an exaggerated manner. 2. show emotion. —e·mo'tive, adj. —e·mo·tiv·i·ty (ē'mō·tiv'ə·ti), n.

e·mo·tion (i·mō'shən), n. a strong feeling, as of fear, anger, love, joy, etc. [< F, (after motion) < émouvoir stir up < L, < ex- out + movere move] —e·mo'tion·al, adj. —e·mo'tion·al·i·ty, n. —e·mo·tion·al·ly, adv. —e·mo'tion·less, adj. —Syn. sentiment, sensation, passion.

e·mo·tion·al·ism (i·mō'shən·əl·iz'əm), n. 1. emotional quality or character. 2. an appealing to the emotions. 3. tendency to display emotion too easily.

em·pan·el (em·pan'əl), v., -eled, -el·ing; esp. Brit. -elled, -el·ling. impanel.

em·pa·thy (em'pə·thi), n. the complete understanding of another's feelings, motives, etc. [< Gk., < en- in + pathos feeling] —em·path·ic (em·path'ik), adj.

em·per·or (em'pər·ər), n. man who is the ruler of an empire. [< OF < L imperator commander < in- in + parare to order] —em'per·or·ship', n. —Syn. kaiser, czar.

em·pha·sis (em'fə·sis), n., pl. **-ses** (-sēz). 1. special force; stress; importance. 2. special force given to particular syllables, words, or phrases. [< L < Gk., < emphainein indicate < en- in + phainein show] —Syn. 2. accent, accentuation.

em·pha·size (em'fə·sīz), v., -sized, -siz·ing. give special force to; stress.

em·phat·ic (em·fat'ik), adj. 1. spoken or done with force or stress; strongly expressed. 2. speaking with force or stress; expressing oneself strongly. 3. attracting attention; striking. —em·phat'i·cal·ly, adv. —Syn. 1. forcible.

em·pire (em'pīr), n. 1. group of countries or states under the same ruler or government: the British Empire. 2. country ruled by an emperor or empress: the Japanese Empire. 3. absolute power; supreme authority. [< OF < L imperium. See EMPEROR.] —Syn. 1. realm.

em·pir·ic (em·pir'ik), n. 1. person who lacks theoretical or scientific knowledge and relies entirely on practical experience. 2. person without regular or proper training; quack. —adj. empirical. [< L < Gk. empeirikos < en- in + peira experience, experiment]

em·pir·i·cal (em·pir'ə·kəl), adj. 1. based on experiment and observation. 2. based entirely on practical experience. —em·pir'i·cal·ly, adv.

em·pir·i·cism (em·pir'ə·siz·əm), n. 1. use of methods based on experiment and observation. 2. undue reliance upon experience; unscientific practice; quackery. —em·pir'i·cist, n.

em·place·ment (em·plās'mənt), n. 1. space or platform for a heavy gun or guns. 2. an assigning to a place; locating.

em·ploy (em·ploi'), v. 1. use the services of; give work and pay to. 2. use. 3. engage the attention of; keep busy; occupy. —n. a being employed; service for pay; employment. [< F < L, < in- in + plicare fold] —em·ploy'a·ble, adj. —Syn. v. 1. engage, hire.

em·ploy·ee, **em·ploy·e**, or **em·ploy·é** (em·ploi'ē; em'ploi·ē'), n. person who works for some person or firm for pay.

em·ploy·er (em·ploi'ər), n. 1. person or firm that employs one or more persons. 2. user.

em·ploy·ment (em·ploi'mənt), n. 1. an employing or being employed. 2. what a person is doing; business. 3. use. —Syn. 2. occupation, work, trade, profession, vocation.

em·po·ri·um (em·pô'ri·əm; -pō'-), n., pl. **-po·ri·ums, -po·ri·a** (-pô'ri·ə; -pō'-), 1. center of trade; market place. 2. a large store selling many different things. [< L < Gk. emporion < emporos merchant, traveler < en- on + poros voyage]

em·pow·er (em·pou'ər), v. 1. give power to. 2. enable; permit. Also, impower. —em·pow'er·ment, n. —Syn. 1. authorize, commission.

em·press (em'pris), n. 1. wife of an emperor. 2. woman who is the ruler of an empire.

emp·ty (emp'ti), adj., -ti·er, -ti·est, v., -tied, -ty·ing, n., pl. -ties. —adj. 1. with nothing or no one in it. 2. not real; meaningless: an empty threat has no force. 3. Colloq. hungry. 4. empty of, having no. —v. 1. pour out or take out the contents of; make empty. 2. become empty. 3. flow out; discharge. —n. Colloq. something with nothing or no one in it. [OE ǣmtig < ǣmetta leisure] —emp'ti·ly, adv. —emp'ti·ness, n. —Syn. adj. 1. vacant, unoccupied, unfilled. 2. hollow, unsubstantial. —v. 1. unload, unburden, evacuate.

em·pur·pled (em·pér'pəld), adj. made purple; colored with purple.

em·pyr·e·al (em·pir'i·əl; em'pə·rē'əl, -pī-), adj. 1. of the empyrean; celestial; heavenly. 2. formed of pure fire or light.

em·py·re·an (em'pə·rē'ən; -pī-), n. 1. the highest heaven; region of pure light. 2. sky; firmament. —adj. empyreal. [< LL < Gk. empyrios, empyros < en- in + pyr fire]

e·mu (ē'mū), n. a large, flightless Australian bird resembling an ostrich but smaller. [< Moluccan emeu]

em·u·late (em'yə·lāt), v., -lat·ed, -lat·ing. try to equal or excel. [< L, < aemulus striving to equal] —em'u·la'tion, n. —em'u·la'tive, adj.

em·u·lous (em'yə·ləs), adj. 1. wishing to equal or excel. 2. arising from or pertaining to emulation. —em'u·lous·ly, adv. —em'u·lous·ness, n.

e·mul·si·fy (i·mul'sə·fī), v., -fied, -fy·ing. make into an emulsion. —e·mul'si·fi·ca'tion, n. —e·mul'si·fi'er, n.

e·mul·sion (i·mul'shən), n. 1. liquid that is a mixture of liquids that do not dissolve in each other. 2. a coating on a camera film, plate, etc., that is sensitive to light. [< NL emulsio < L ex- out + mulgere milk]

en (en), n. 1. the letter N, n. 2. half the width of an em in printing.

en-, prefix. 1. cause to be; make, as in enable, enfeeble. 2. put in; put on, as in encircle, enthrone. 3. other meanings, as in enact, encourage, entwine. En- often changes the meaning of a verb little or not at all. [< OF < L in-; before b, p, or m the form becomes em-] ▸ en-, in-. In- is either a native English prefix or a prefix of Latin origin; en- is the same Latin prefix modified in French. (Em- and im- are variant forms.) In several common words, usage is divided, though usually one form is more common. We tend to use in- more than the British do but en- is often preferred in formal usage.

In the following examples of divided usage, the preferred form is put first: enclose—inclose (gaining); endorse—indorse; ensure—insure (but insure is preferred in the financial sense).

–en, suffix. 1. cause to be; make, as in blacken, sharpen. 2. cause to have, as in heighten, strengthen. 3. become, as in sicken, soften. 4. come to have; gain, as in lengthen. 5. made of, as in silken, wooden. 6. –en is used to form past participles of strong verbs, as in fallen, shaken. 7. –en is used to form the plural of a few nouns, as in children, oxen. [OE]

en·a·ble (en·ā′bəl), v., –bled, –bling. give ability, power, or means to; make able. —Syn. empower, permit, authorize, warrant.

en·act (en·akt′), v. 1. pass (a bill) giving it validity as law; make into a law. 2. decree; order. 3. play the part of; act out; play. —Syn. 2. ordain, adjudge.

en·act·ment (en·akt′mənt), n. 1. an enacting. 2. a being enacted. 3. law.

e·nam·el (i·nam′əl), n., v., –eled, –el·ing; esp. Brit. –elled, –el·ling. —n. 1. a glasslike substance melted and then cooled to make a smooth, hard surface. 2. paint or varnish used to make a smooth, hard, glossy surface. 3. a coating applied to the skin to simulate a beautiful complexion. 4. the smooth, hard, glossy outer layer of the teeth. 5. thing covered or decorated with enamel. 6. any smooth, hard coating or surface that shines. [< v.] —v. cover or decorate with enamel. [< AF enamayller < en– on (< L in–) + amayl (OF esmail) enamel < Gmc.] —e·nam′el·er, esp. Brit. e·nam′el·ler, n. —e·nam′el·work′, n.

en·am·or, esp. Brit. **en·am·our** (en·am′ər), v. arouse to love; charm: her beauty enamored the prince. [< OF enamourer < en– in (< L in–) + amour love < L amor] —en·am′ored, esp. Brit. en·am′oured, adj.

en bloc (en blok′; än), all together; in one lump. [< F]

en·camp (en·kamp′), v. 1. make a camp. 2. stay in a camp. 3. put in a camp. —en·camp′ment, n.

en·case (en·kās′), v., –cased, –cas·ing. incase.

–ence, suffix. 1. act, fact, quality, or state of —ing, as in abhorrence, indulgence. 2. quality or state of being ——ent, as in absence, confidence, competence, prudence. [< L –entia]

en·ceph·a·li·tis (en·sef′ə·lī′tis), n. inflammation of the brain caused by injury, infection, poison, etc. —en·ceph·a·lit·ic (en·sef′ə·lit′ik), adj.

en·ceph·a·lon (en·sef′ə·lon), n. the brain. [< NL < Gk., < en– in + kephale head] —en·ce·phal·ic (en′sə·fal′ik), adj.

en·chain (en·chān′), v. 1. put in chains; fetter. 2. attract and fix firmly; hold fast. —en·chain′ment, n.

en·chant (en·chant′; –chänt′), v. 1. use magic on; put under a spell. 2. delight greatly; charm. [< F < L < in– against + cantare chant] —Syn. 2. fascinate, captivate, enrapture.

en·chant·er (en·chan′tər; –chän′–), n. one that enchants.

en·chant·ing (en·chan′ting; –chän′–), adj. 1. very delightful; charming. 2. bewitching. —en·chant′ing·ly, adv.

en·chant·ment (en·chant′mənt; –chänt′–), n. 1. an enchanting or being enchanted. 2. something that enchants.

en·chan·tress (en·chan′tris; –chän′–), n. woman who enchants.

en·cir·cle (en·sér′kəl), v., –cled, –cling. 1. form a circle around; surround. 2. go in a circle around. —en·cir′cle·ment, n. —Syn. 1. encompass, gird, circumscribe.

en·clave (en′klāv), n. country or district surrounded by a foreign territory. [< F, < enclaver enclose]

en·close (en·klōz′), v., –closed, –clos·ing. 1. shut in on all sides; surround. 2. put a wall or fence around. 3. put in an envelope along with a letter, etc. 4. contain. Also, inclose.

en·clo·sure (en·klō′zhər), n. 1. an enclosing

or being enclosed. 2. an enclosed place. 3. thing that encloses. 4. thing enclosed. Also, inclosure.

en·co·mi·ast (en·kō′mi·ast), n. writer or speaker of encomiums; eulogist.

en·co·mi·um (en·kō′mi·əm), n., pl. –mi·ums, –mi·a (–mi·ə). an elaborate expression of praise; high praise; eulogy. [< LL < Gk. enkomion, neut., laudatory < en– in + komos revelry]

en·com·pass (en·kum′pəs), v. 1. surround completely; shut in on all sides; encircle. 2. enclose; contain. —en·com′pass·ment, n.

en·core (äng′kôr; –kôr; än′–), interj., n., v., –cored, –cor·ing. —interj. once more; again. —n. 1. demand by the audience for the repetition of a song, etc., or for another appearance of the performer or performers. 2. repetition of a song, etc., in response to such a demand. 3. an additional song, etc., given in response to such a demand. —v. make such a demand for (a performer, etc.) by applauding. [< F]

en·coun·ter (en·koun′tər), v. 1. meet unexpectedly. 2. meet with (difficulties, opposition, etc.). 3. meet as an enemy; meet in a fight or battle. —n. 1. a meeting, esp. an unexpected one. 2. a meeting of enemies; fight; battle. [< OF < VL, < L in– in + contra against] —Syn. n. 2. conflict, combat, skirmish.

en·cour·age (en·kér′ij), v., –aged, –ag·ing. 1. give courage to; increase the hope or confidence of; urge on. 2. be favorable to; help; support. [< OF, < en– in + corage COURAGE] —en·cour′ag·er, n. —en·cour′ag·ing·ly, adv. —Syn. 1. hearten, inspirit, animate. 2. promote, advance.

en·cour·age·ment (en·kér′ij·mənt), n. 1. an encouraging. 2. a being encouraged. 3. thing that encourages.

en·croach (en·krōch′), v. 1. go beyond proper or usual limits. 2. trespass upon the property or rights of another; intrude. [< OF, < en– in (< L in–) + croc hook < Gmc.] —en·croach′er, n. —en·croach′ment, n.

en·crust (en·krust′), v. incrust. —en′crus·ta′tion, n.

en·cum·ber (en·kum′bər), v. 1. hold back (from running, doing, etc.); hinder; hamper. 2. make difficult to use; fill; obstruct. 3. weigh down; burden. Also, incumber. [< OF, < en in + combre barrier, prob. < Celtic]

en·cum·brance (en·kum′brəns), n. 1. anything that encumbers; hindrance; obstruction; burden. 2. a dependent person; child. 3. claim, mortgage, etc., on property. Also, incumbrance.

–ency, suffix. 1. act, fact, quality, or state of —ing, as in dependency. 2. quality or state of being ——ent, as in frequency. 3. other meanings, as in agency, currency. [< L –entia]

en·cyc·li·cal (en·sik′lə·kəl; –sī′klə–), **en·cyc·lic** (–lik), n. letter about the general welfare of the church from the pope to his clergy. —adj. intended for wide circulation. [< LL encyclicus < Gk., < en– in + kyklos circle]

en·cy·clo·pe·di·a, en·cy·clo·pae·di·a (en·sī′klə·pē′di·ə), n. book or series of books giving information, arranged alphabetically, on all branches of knowledge. [< LL < Gk. enkyklopaideia, for enkyklios paideia well-rounded education] —en·cy′clo·pe′dic, en·cy′clo·pae′dic, adj. —en·cy′clo·pe′dist, en·cy′clo·pae′dist, n.

en·cyst (en·sist′), v. enclose or become enclosed in a cyst or sac. —en·cyst′ment, n.

end (end), n. 1. the last part; conclusion. 2. place where a thing stops. 3. purpose; object. 4. result; outcome. 5. death; destruction. 6. part left over; remnant; fragment. 7. Am. player at either end of the line in football. —v. 1. bring or come to an end; stop; finish. 2. destroy; kill. 3. form the end of; be the end of. [OE ende] —end′er, n. —Syn. n. 1. termination, close, finish, expiration. 3. intention, design, goal, aim. 4. issue, consequence. 5. extermination, annihilation. 6. remainder. —v. 1. conclude, terminate, cease.

en·dan·ger (en·dān′jər), v. cause danger to; expose to loss or injury. —en·dan′ger·ment, n.

en·dear (en·dir′), v. make dear. —en·dear′ing·ly, adv.

en·dear·ment (en·dir′mənt), n. 1. an endearing. **2.** thing that endears. **3.** act or word showing love or affection; caress.

en·deav·or, *esp. Brit.* **en·deav·our** (en-dev′ər), *v.* try hard; attempt earnestly; make an effort; strive. —*n.* an earnest attempt; effort. [< *en-* + F *devoir* duty] —en·deav′or·er, *esp. Brit.* en·deav′our·er, *n.* —Syn. *v.* struggle, labor, essay. —*n.* exertion, struggle.

en·dem·ic (en-dem′ik), *adj.* Also, **en·dem′i·cal.** regularly found in a particular people or locality. —*n.* an endemic disease. [< Gk. *endemos* native < *en-* in + *demos* people] —en·dem′i·cal·ly, *adv.*

end·ing (en′ding), *n.* **1.** the last part; end. **2.** death. **3.** letter or syllable added to a word or stem to change its meaning or to show its relationship to other words; inflection. The common plural ending in English is *s* or *es.*

en·dive (en′dīv; än′dēv), *n. U.S.* **1.** kind of chicory with finely divided, curly leaves, used for salads. **2.** kind of chicory that looks like very smooth white celery, also used for salads. [< OF < Med.L < Med.Gk. < L *intibum*]

end·less (end′lis), *adj.* **1.** having no end; never stopping; lasting or going on forever. **2.** with the ends joined for continuous action: *an endless chain.* —end′less·ly, *adv.* —end′less·ness, *n.* —Syn. **1.** boundless, limitless, immeasurable, interminable, incessant, unceasing, continual, perpetual, eternal. —Ant. **1.** limited, finite, brief, transient, temporary.

end·most (end′mōst), *adj.* nearest to the end; last; farthest.

endo-, *word element.* within; inside; inner, as in *endocarp, endoplasm.* [< Gk.]

en·do·carp (en′dō-kärp), *n. Bot.* the inner layer of a ripened ovary of a plant.

en·do·crine (en′dō-krīn; -krin), *adj.* of or having to do with the endocrine glands. —*n.* **1.** an endocrine gland. **2.** its secretion. [< *endo-* + Gk. *krinein* separate]

E, endocarp of a peach.

endocrine gland, any of various glands that produce secretions that pass directly into the blood stream instead of into a duct, as the thyroid gland.

en·dog·e·nous (en·doj′ə-nəs), *adj.* growing from the inside; originating within. —en·dog′e·nous·ly, *adv.*

en·do·plasm (en′dō-plaz-əm), *n. Biol.* the inner portion of the cytoplasm of a cell. —en′do·plas′mic, *adj.*

en·dorse (en·dôrs′), *v.,* -dorsed, -dors·ing. **1.** write one's name, comment, etc., on the back of (a check or other document). **2.** approve; support. Also, **indorse.** [alter. of ME *endosse(n)* < OF, < *en-* on + *dos* back < L *dorsum*] —en·dors′a·ble, *adj.* —en·dor·see (en·dôr′sē′; en′dôr-), *n.* —en·dorse′ment, *n.* —en·dors′er, *n.*

en·do·sperm (en′dō-spérm), *n.* nourishment for the embryo enclosed with it in the seed of a plant. See the picture under embryo.

en·dow (en·dou′), *v.* **1.** give money or property to provide an income for. **2.** provide with some ability, quality, or talent: *nature endowed her with both beauty and brains.* **3.** *Archaic.* provide with a dower. [< OF, < *en-* (< L *in-*) + *douer* endow < L *dotare*] —en·dow′er, *n.* —Syn. **2.** furnish, equip, invest.

en·dow·ment (en·dou′mənt), *n.* **1.** an endowing. **2.** money or property given to provide an income. **3.** Usually, **endowments.** talent, esp. a natural, inborn talent; ability.

end product, 1. portion remaining after something is processed; the result of a processing. **2.** *Nuclear Physics.* the last stable member of a series of isotopes, each produced by the radioactive decay of the preceding isotope.

end stop, a mark of punctuation used at the end of a sentence, usually a period, exclamation mark, or question mark.

en·due (en·dū′; -dū′), *v.,* -dued, -du·ing. provide with a quality or power. Also, **indue.**

en·dur·ance (en·dûr′əns; -dyûr′-), *n.* **1.** power to last or keep on. **2.** power to put up with, bear, or stand. **3.** act or instance of enduring pain, hardship, etc. **4.** duration. —Syn. **2.** fortitude, patience, forbearance, tolerance.

en·dure (en·dûr′; -dyûr′), *v.,* -dured, -dur·ing. **1.** keep on; last. **2.** undergo; bear; tolerate. [< OF < LL < L, make hard < *in-* + *durus* hard] —en·dur′a·ble, *adj.* —en·dur′a·bly, *adv.* —Syn. **1.** continue, remain. **2.** suffer, stand, experience.

en·dur·ing (en·dûr′ing; -dyûr′-), *adj.* lasting; permanent. —en·dur′ing·ly, *adv.* —en·dur′ing·ness, *n.* —Syn. abiding, unchangeable.

end use, the particular function which a manufactured product serves or is limited to.

end·ways (end′wāz′), **end·wise** (-wīz′), *adv.* **1.** on end; upright. **2.** with the end forward; in the direction of the end. **3.** lengthwise. **4.** end to end.

en·e·ma (en′ə-mə), *n., pl.* **en·e·mas, e·nem·a·ta** (i-nem′ə-tə). injection of liquid into the rectum to flush the bowels. [< Gk., < *en-* in + *hienai* send]

en·e·my (en′ə-mi), *n., pl.* -mies, *adj.* —*n.* **1.** person or group that hates and tries to harm another. **2.** a hostile force, nation, army, fleet, or air force; person, ship, etc., of a hostile nation. **3.** anything harmful: *frost is an enemy of plants.* —*adj.* of an enemy. [< OF < L, < *in-* not + *amicus* friendly] —Syn. *n.* **1, 2.** adversary, opponent, foe.

en·er·get·ic (en′ər-jet′ik), *adj.* full of energy; eager to work; full of force; active. —en′er·get′i·cal·ly, *adv.* —Syn. vigorous, strenuous, forcible.

en·er·gize (en′ər-jīz), *v.,* -gized, -giz·ing. give energy to. —en′er·giz′er, *n.*

en·er·gy (en′ər-ji), *n., pl.* -gies. **1.** active strength or force; healthy power; vigor. **2.** strength; force; power. **3.** *Physics.* capacity for doing work. [< LL < Gk., < *energos* active < *en-* in + *ergon* work] —Syn. **1.** potency, push, zeal.

en·er·vate (en′ər-vāt), *v.,* -vat·ed, -vat·ing. lessen the vigor or strength of; weaken. [< L, < *ex-* away + *nervus* sinew, nerve] —en′er·va′tion, *n.* —en′er·va′tor, *n.*

en fa·mille (än fä·mē′yə), *French.* with one's family; at home; informally.

en·fant ter·ri·ble (än·fän te·rē′blə), *French.* **1.** child whose behavior, questions, remarks, etc., embarrass older people. **2.** person who is indiscreet or lacks a sense of responsibility.

en·fee·ble (en·fē′bəl), *v.,* -bled, -bling. make feeble; weaken. —en·fee′ble·ment, *n.* —en·fee′bler, *n.*

en·fi·lade (en′fə·lād′), *n., v.,* -lad·ed, -lad·ing. *Am.* —*n.* **1.** gunfire directed from the side at a line of troops or a position held by them. **2.** situation exposed to such raking gunfire. —*v.* fire guns at (a line of troops or the position held by them) from the side. [< F, < *enfiler* thread, pierce < *en-* on (< L *in-*) + *fil* thread < L *filum*] —en·fi·lad′er, *n.*

en·fold (en·fōld′), *v.* infold. —en·fold′er, *n.* —en·fold′ment, *n.*

en·force (en·fôrs′; -fōrs′), *v.,* -forced, -forc·ing. **1.** force obedience to; put into force: *policemen and judges enforce the laws.* **2.** force; compel: *the bandits enforced obedience to their demand by threats of violence.* **3.** urge with force: *the teacher enforced the principle by examples.* **4.** produce or effect by force. **5.** obtain (payment, obedience, etc.) by force. **6.** use force upon. [< OF, ult. < L *in-* + *fortis* strong] —en·force′a·ble, *adj.* —en·for·ced·ly (en·fôr′sid·li; -fōr′-), *adv.* —en·force′ment, *n.* —en·forc′er, *n.* —Syn. **1.** execute, administer.

en·fran·chise (en·fran′chīz), *v.,* -chised, -chis·ing. **1.** give the right to vote. **2.** set free; release from slavery or restraint. —en·fran·chise·ment (en·fran′chiz·mənt), *n.* —en·fran′chis·er, *n.*

Eng., England; English.

eng., **1.** engineer; engineering. **2.** engraved; engraving.

en·gage (en·gāj′), *v.,* -gaged, -gag·ing. **1.** bind by a pledge; bind oneself; promise; pledge. **2.** promise or pledge to marry. **3.** keep busy; occupy. **4.** keep oneself busy; be occupied; be active. **5.** hire; employ; take for use or work; reserve (seats, rooms, a cab, etc.). **6.** catch and hold; attract. **7.** fit into; lock together: *gears that engage.* **8.** start a battle with; attack. [< F, < *en gage* under pledge] —en·gag′er, *n.*

en·gaged (en·gājd′), *adj.* **1.** promised or

pledged to marry. 2. busy; occupied. 3. taken for use or work; hired. 4. fitted together. 5. involved in a fight or battle. —**Syn.** 1. betrothed, affianced.

en·gage·ment (en·gāj′mənt), *n.* 1. act of engaging. 2. fact or condition of being engaged. 3. promise; pledge. 4. promise to marry. 5. a meeting with someone at a certain time; appointment. 6. period of being hired; time of use or work. 7. fight; battle. 8. the interlocking of mechanical parts. —**Syn.** 3. contract, agreement. 4. betrothal. 7. encounter, combat, conflict.

en·gag·ing (en·gāj′ing), *adj.* attractive; pleasing; charming. —**en·gag′ing·ly,** *adv.* —**en·gag′-ing·ness,** *n.*

En·gels (eng′gəlz; *Ger.* eng′əls), *n.* Friedrich, 1820–1895, German socialist writer in England, collaborator with Karl Marx.

en·gen·der (en·jen′dər), *v.* bring into existence; produce; cause. [< OF < L, < *in-* in + *generare* create] —**en·gen′der·er,** *n.* —**en·gen′-der·ment,** *n.*

en·gine (en′jən), *n.* 1. machine that applies power to some work, esp. a machine that can start others moving. 2. machine that pulls a railroad train. 3. machine; device; instrument: *big guns are engines of war.* [< OF < L *ingenium* inborn qualities, talent < *in-* in + *gen-* create]

en·gi·neer (en′jə·nir′), *n.* 1. man who runs an engine. 2. person who plans, builds, or manages engines, machines, roads, bridges, canals, railroads, forts, etc.; expert in engineering. 3. member of a group of men who do engineering work in the army or navy. —*v.* 1. plan, build, direct, or work as an engineer. 2. *Am.* manage cleverly; guide skillfully.

en·gi·neer·ing (en′jə·nir′ing), *n.* science, work, or profession of an engineer; planning, building, or managing engines, machines, roads, bridges, canals, railroads, forts, etc.

Eng·land (ing′glənd), *n.* the largest division of Great Britain, in the S part.

Eng·lish (ing′glish), *adj.* of or having to do with England, its people, or their language. —*n.* 1. the people of England collectively. 2. the English language, including Old English or Anglo-Saxon (before 1100), Middle English (about 1100–1500), and Modern English (from about 1500). 3. the English used in a certain locality or by a certain group. 4. Sometimes, **english,** *Am., Sports.* a spinning motion imparted to a ball. —*v.* translate into English; express in plain English. [OE *Englisc* < *Engle* the English people]

➤ **English** is a member of the Germanic branch of Indo-European languages, which also includes the Scandinavian languages, German, and Dutch. The Germanic branch comprises the following:

	North (Scandinavian)	Swedish Danish Norwegian Icelandic
Germanic	East (Gothic—extinct)	
	West	German Dutch Flemish Frisian English

A brief selection of facts about the different periods of our language will show some of the roots of the richness—and confusion—of modern English.

1. Old English, Before 1100. The Angles, Saxons, and Jutes brought to England from their old homes in northwestern Europe somewhat differing Germanic dialects. They pushed back the native Celts from the parts of the island they conquered, so that Celtic speech contributed almost nothing to English, but survived in Welsh, Cornish, and Highland Scotch. The conquerors' languages developed into several main dialects—Northumbrian, Mercian, Kentish, West Saxon—which together were known as Old English (or Anglo-Saxon). These dialects still leave their marks in the substandard speech of various parts of England. They had many points in common, and were gradually brought

together, each making some contribution, but East Midland, a descendant of Mercian, contributed the most to what now after seven or eight hundred years we know as English. Somewhat less than a quarter of the present English vocabulary goes back to the words of Old English. The modern descendants of Old English words are often changed in meaning and almost always in pronunciation—according to regular processes: Old English *stān* becomes Modern English *stone,* *bān* becomes *bone,* etc. Our common verbs (*go, sit, eat, fight, whistle*), many of our most common nouns (*meat, house, breakfast, land, water*), and adjectives like *fast, slow, high* go back to Old English words, so that though less than a fourth of the dictionary words are of this "native" origin, they play a part in our speech out of proportion to their number.

Furthermore, most of the machinery of our language is from Old English: the articles *a, an, the,* most of the connecting words (*at, by, for, from, in, out, under . . . as, like, since, when*); most of the pronouns (*I, we, us . . .*); the inflectional endings of nouns (*house—houses, boy—boys—boy's*) and of adjectives and adverbs (*merry—merrier—merriest* or *more merry—most merry;* *harshly, kindly*); the forms of verbs (*pass, passes, passed, passing*). These endings are applied to words borrowed from other languages (*indict-ed, political-ly*), so that although three quarters of the vocabulary may come from Romance or other languages the borrowed words are built into an English pattern. And when we consider word order we see that the texture of English is Germanic and it must be regarded as a Germanic language.

Within the Old English period the practice of absorbing words from other languages was already strong. A number of other Latin words, some of them originally Greek, were taken in, most of them pertaining to the church (*abbot, priest, school*), though there was still a tendency to translate the elements of the Latin words into Old English elements, so that we have *gospel* from *gōd spel,* "good tidings," which is a translation of the Greek-Latin *evangelium.*

In the ninth century the east and north of England was conquered by the Danes, whose language left a large number of words and forms, partly because it was a closely related language, partly because of the intimacy between the two peoples. The *sk* words are likely to date from this mixture (*sky, skin, scream, skirt*—a cousin of the Old English *shirt,* both related to *short*), place names ending in *–by* and *–thorp,* and a number of common words like *odd, anger, egg.* Nearly five per cent of our words are Scandinavian.

A number of the most conspicuous irregularities of Modern English existed already in Old English: *be, is, are, was, were* as forms of the verb "to be"; *may, might, shall, should, ought,* and the other "auxiliaries"; the pronouns *I, my, me, we, our, us, he, she, it.* These words are in such common use that they have never been brought into any consistent grammatical pattern. Here and there we have remnants of Old English forms that generally lost out in the development of the language, as the plurals *children, oxen, men, geese,* instead of the regular plural in *–s.* There is a considerable body of writing from the Old English period. It includes poems, sermons, riddles, history, translations from Latin, and most conspicuously the *Anglo-Saxon Chronicles,* *Beowulf,* and the large group of writings and translations in West Saxon made by or at the court of Alfred the Great, King of the West Saxons, 871–899. Some 30,000 different words are found in this literature.

2. Middle English, 1100–1500. The conquest of England by the Normans in 1066 was the most far-reaching single historical event influencing our language. The speakers of Old English in the main became serfs, servants, everything but leaders in affairs. Their language was seldom used in official proceedings and rarely written. One result was the loss of the more elevated

āge, câre, fär; ēqual, tèrm; īce; ōpen, ôrder; pût, rüle, ûse; ŧħ, then; ə=a in about.

Old English words that had been used in poetry and that would correspond to the rather archaic vocabulary of our formal literature.

A far-reaching development of this period was the decline and in some instances complete loss of the inflectional endings that Old English had used. The definite article was no longer declined (our *the* is the sole descendant of eight forms in Old English); *-n* disappeared from the infinitive of most verbs, and other endings, since they were in unstressed syllables and did not receive full pronunciation, dropped away. This process went far to make English one of the least inflected languages.

On the other hand the language of the invaders was making its way. The words for the acts of the ruling class—war, government, law, social activity—were Anglo-French (a dialect of Old French) and they have generally come down to Modern English: *siege, soldier, judge, jury, suit, servant.* Over a fourth of our current English words are from Anglo-French. The majority of the Anglo-French words were ultimately from Latin, though considerably changed in form. For many notions Modern English has two roughly synonymous words, one Anglo-French, one Old English: *dress—clothes, aid—help, royal —kingly.* Some French spellings made their way into English, like *gu* for hard *g* (*guest, guess*) and *qu* for *cw* (*queen* for Old English *cwēn*).

In 1362 English was restored as the language of the law courts, an official recognition that it was reasserting itself again after conquest. The speech of the region around London was now the basis for future development. How far the fusion of Old English and Anglo-French resources had gone can be seen from a few lines by Chaucer, written in the 1380's. The Anglo-French words are in italics:

"What folk ben ye, that at myn hoomcominge
Perturben so my *feste* with *crynge?*"
Quod Theseus, "have ye so greet *envye*
Of myn *honour,* that thus *compleyne* and *crye?*
Or who hath yow misboden, or *offended?*
And telleth me if it may been *amended;*
And why that ye ben clothed thus in blak?"
      Geoffrey Chaucer, "The Knightes Tale"

Except for the Old English *misboden* ("insulted"), all of these words, both native and French, are in use today, and in spite of some differences in spelling, the passage can be read by anyone. Many of the words show inflectional endings that have since been dropped or changed: *ben* for *are* or *be,* perturb*en,* tell*eth,* and the final *e* of nouns.

3. Early Modern English, 1500–1700. In this period we have the beginnings of conscious concern for the language and actual or attempted "improvement" by manipulation of words and constructions, "school-mastering the speech." The early printers, from 1476 on, felt the need for uniformity, especially in spelling and choice of word forms, and began the domination of these traits that ever since in the written language has been exercised by publishers. Translators and writers believed the language was rough, unpolished, incapable of doing what Latin and Greek had done and what Italian could do. They set about enlarging the vocabulary, chiefly by transliterating words from Greek and Latin. More than twenty-five per cent of modern English words are pretty directly from classical languages and very often we have two words that go back to the same Latin original, one brought in by the Normans and one taken in directly later: *paint—picture, certainty—certitude.* Latin was the language of the Church at the beginning of this period, though after the Reformation the Book of Common Prayer and the King James translation of the Bible became tremendous forces for elevated English. Most books of the learned world were in Latin—and college classes were conducted in Latin, even in the United States, until a century and a half ago.

The spoken language was vigorous and was written down in some popular literature but most literature that has survived was from the hands of university men and conscious stylists. Shakespeare shows the complete range, from formal,

Latinized lines to rough and tumble lines, often combining the elevated and the simple in a single speech.

Prose style lagged behind poetic, especially in sentence sense, producing "sentence heaps" running to hundreds of words. In the sixteen hundreds the wealth of experiment of the preceding century was analyzed and many words and phrases were disposed of. The less useful and more ponderous of the Latin importations were dropped, and interest in native words increased the proportion of Saxon words in use. Prose style especially developed in directness and sureness until in Dryden modern English prose is usually said to be established.

4. Modern English, 1700–. By 1700 English had become substantially the language we now know and use. The vocabulary has been enlarged in the last two centuries chiefly from two sources: borrowings from India and America and from all peoples touched by British and American traders; and through scientific coinages, chiefly from Greek and Latin roots. There has been, especially in recent years, a tendency toward shorter and more direct sentences. The paragraph has become a more distinct unit in written expression. The most important point for study in this period has probably been the different levels of usage, and different traditions of style, especially formal and informal style and the relations between them. Today the language of England and the British Empire and of the United States is spoken by considerably over 200,000,000 people—perhaps the largest group of people who can easily understand each other. The result of this varied history is a language full of anomalies, with exceptions to every rule, but of unusual range.

English Channel, strait between England and France.

English horn, a wooden musical instrument resembling an oboe, but larger and having a lower tone.

English ivy, ivy (def. 1).

Eng·lish·man (ing′glish·mən), *n., pl.* **-men.** 1. native or inhabitant of England. 2. one whose ancestry is English. Canadians and Australians sometimes call themselves Englishmen.

English sparrow, a small, brownish-gray bird, now very common in America.

Eng·lish·wom·an (ing′glish·wům′ən), *n., pl.* **-wom·en.** 1. woman who is a native or inhabitant of England. 2. woman whose ancestry is English.

engr., 1. engineer. 2. engraved; engraver.

en·graft (en·graft′; -gräft′), *v.* insert or graft (a shoot from one tree or plant) into or on another. Also, **ingraft.**

en·grave (en·grāv′), *v.,* **-graved, -grav·ing.** 1. carve artistically; decorate by engraving. 2. cut in lines on a metal plate, block of wood, etc., for printing. 3. print from such a plate, block, etc. 4. impress deeply. [< *en-* + *grave*[3]] —**en·grav′er,** *n.* —**Syn.** 1. chisel, carve, cut.

en·grav·ing (en·grāv′ing), *n.* 1. art of an engraver; cutting lines in metal plates, blocks of wood, etc., for printing. 2. picture printed from an engraved plate, block, etc. 3. an engraved plate, block, etc.; engraved design or pattern.

en·gross (en·grōs′), *v.* 1. occupy wholly; take up all the attention of. 2. copy or write in large letters; write a beautiful copy of. 3. write out in formal style; express in legal form. 4. buy all or much of (the supply of some commodity) so as to control prices. [(defs. 1, 4) < *in gross* < F *en gros* in a lump; (defs. 2, 3) < AF, < *en-* in + *grosse* large writing, document. See GROSS.] —**en·gross′er,** *n.* —**en·gross′ing,** *adj.* —**en·gross′ment,** *n.*

en·gulf (en·gulf′), *v.* swallow up; overwhelm; submerge. Also, **ingulf.**

en·hance (en·hans′; -häns′), *v.,* **-hanced, -hanc·ing.** make greater; add to; heighten. [< AF var. of OF *enhaucier* < *en-* on, up + *haucier* raise. See HAWSER.] —**en·hance′ment,** *n.* —**en·hanc′er,** *n.* —**Syn.** increase, intensify, augment.

EN·I·AC (en′i·ak), *n. Am., Trademark.* an electronic brain used by the U.S. Army. [< *E* (*lec-*

tronic) *N(umerical)* *I(ntegrator)* *A(nd)* *C(om-puter)*]

e·nig·ma (i·nig′mə), *n.* **1.** a puzzling statement; riddle. **2.** a baffling or puzzling problem, situation, person, etc. [< L < Gk. *ainissesthai* speak darkly < *ainos* fable] —en·ig·mat·i·cal (en′ig·mat′ə·kəl; ē′nig-), en′ig·mat′ic, *adj.* —en′ig·mat′i·cal·ly, *adv.*

En·i·we·tok (en′i·wē′tok), *n.* atoll in the Marshall Islands, site of U.S. atomic bomb tests which started in 1948.

en·join (en·join′), *v.* **1.** order; direct; urge. **2.** forbid; prohibit: *the judge enjoined him from infringing on the rights of his neighbors.* [< OF *enjoindre* < L, attack, charge < *in–* on + *jungere* join] —en·join′er, *n.* —Syn. **1.** prescribe, command, charge, bid.

en·joy (en·joi′), *v.* **1.** have or use with joy; be happy with; take pleasure in. **2.** have as an advantage or benefit. [< OF, < *en–* + *joir* enjoy < L *gaudere*] —en·joy′a·ble, *adj.* —en·joy′a·ble·ness, *n.* —en·joy′a·bly, *adv.* —en·joy′er, *n.*

en·joy·ment (en·joi′mənt), *n.* **1.** an enjoying. **2.** thing enjoyed. **3.** joy; happiness; pleasure. —Syn. **3.** delight, felicity, satisfaction.

en·kin·dle (en·kin′dəl), *v.*, -dled, -dling. light up; brighten. —en·kin′dler, *n.*

en·lace (en·lās′), *v.*, -laced, -lac·ing. **1.** wind about; encircle; infold. **2.** twine together; interlace. —en·lace′ment, *n.*

en·large (en·lärj′), *v.*, -larged, -larg·ing. make or become larger; increase in size. —en·larg′er, *n.* —Syn. augment, broaden, extend, expand.

en·large·ment (en·lärj′mənt), *n.* **1.** an enlarging or being enlarged. **2.** anything that is an enlarged form of something else. An enlargement is often made from a small photograph. **3.** thing that enlarges something else; addition.

en·light·en (en·līt′ən), *v.* give the light of truth and knowledge to; free from prejudice, ignorance, etc. —en·light′en·er, *n.* —en·light′en·ment, *n.* —Syn. instruct, teach, inform, edify.

en·list (en·list′), *v.* **1.** enroll in some branch of the military service. **2.** induce to join in some cause or undertaking; secure the help or support of. —en·list′er, *n.* —Syn. **1.** register.

en·list·ed man, *Esp. U.S.* member of the armed forces who is not a commissioned officer or cadet.

en·list·ment (en·list′mənt), *n.* **1.** an enlisting. **2.** a being enlisted. **3.** time for which a person enlists.

en·liv·en (en·līv′ən), *v.* make lively, active, gay, or cheerful. —en·liv′en·er, *n.* —en·liv′en·ment, *n.*

en masse (en mas′; än mäs′), in a group; all together. [< F]

en·mesh (en·mesh′), *v.* catch in a net; enclose in meshes; entangle.

en·mi·ty (en′mə·ti), *n.*, *pl.* -ties. the feeling that enemies have for each other; hate. [< OF *ennemistie* < VL < L *inimicus* ENEMY] —Syn. hostility, hatred, animosity, ill-will, antipathy.

en·no·ble (en·nō′bəl), *v.*, -bled, -bling. **1.** give a title or rank of nobility to. **2.** raise in the respect of others; dignify; exalt. —en·no′ble·ment, *n.* —en·no′bler, *n.* —Syn. **2.** elevate.

en·nui (än′wē), *n.* a feeling of weariness and discontent from lack of occupation or interest; boredom. [< F. See ANNOY.]

e·nor·mi·ty (i·nôr′mə·ti), *n.*, *pl.* -ties. **1.** extreme wickedness; outrageousness. **2.** an extremely wicked crime; outrageous offense.

e·nor·mous (i·nôr′məs), *adj.* **1.** extremely large; huge. **2.** extremely wicked; outrageous. [< L, < *ex–* out of + *norma* pattern] —e·nor′mous·ly, *adv.* —e·nor′mous·ness, *n.* —Syn. **1.** immense, colossal, gigantic, vast, mammoth, prodigious, stupendous. **2.** abominable, atrocious.

e·nough (i·nuf′), *adj.* adequate for the need or want. —*n.* an adequate quantity or number. —*adv.* **1.** sufficiently; adequately. **2.** quite; fully: *he is willing enough to take a tip.* —*interj.* stop! no more! [OE *genōg*] —Syn. *adj.* sufficient, ample. —*n.* sufficiency, plenty.

en·quire (en·kwīr′), *v.*, -quired, -quir·ing. inquire. —en·quir·y (en·kwīr′i; en′kwə·ri), *n.*

en·rage (en·rāj′), *v.*, -raged, -rag·ing. put into a rage; make very angry. —en·rage′ment, *n.* —Syn. infuriate, exasperate, incense, anger.

en rap·port (än rä·pôr′), *French.* in sympathy; in agreement.

en·rap·ture (en·rap′chər), *v.*, -tured, -tur·ing. fill with great delight; entrance.

en·rich (en·rich′), *v.* **1.** make rich or richer: *an education enriches your mind, fertilizer enriches soil.* **2.** raise the nutritive value of (a food) by adding vitamins and minerals in processing. —en·riched′, *adj.*

en·roll, en·rol (en·rōl′), *v.*, -rolled, -roll·ing. **1.** write in a list. **2.** have one's name written in a list. **3.** make a member. **4.** become a member. **5.** enlist. —en·roll′er, *n.* —Syn. **1.** register, record. **4.** enter.

en·roll·ment, en·rol·ment (en·rōl′mənt), *n.* **1.** an enrolling. **2.** number enrolled.

en route (än rüt′), on the way. [< F]

Ens., Ensign.

en·sconce (en·skons′), *v.*, -sconced, -sconc·ing. **1.** shelter safely; hide. **2.** settle comfortably and firmly. [< *en–* + *sconce* fortification, prob. < Du. *schans*]

en·sem·ble (än·säm′bəl), *n.* **1.** all the parts of a thing considered together; general effect. **2.** a united performance of the full number of singers, musicians, etc. **3.** group of musicians or the musical instruments used in taking part in such a performance. **4.** a complete, harmonious costume. [< F, < VL < L *in–* + *simul* at the same time]

en·shrine (en·shrīn′), *v.*, -shrined, -shrin·ing. **1.** enclose in a shrine. **2.** keep sacred; cherish. —en·shrine′ment, *n.*

en·shroud (en·shroud′), *v.* cover with, or as with, a shroud; hide; veil: *fog enshrouded the ship.*

en·sign (en′sən; en′sīn, *esp. for 1, 3, and 4*), *n.* **1.** flag; banner: *the ensign of the United States is the Stars and Stripes.* **2.** *Am.* the lowest commissioned officer in the navy. **3.** a former British army officer whose duty was carrying the flag. **4.** sign of one's rank, position, or power; symbol of authority. [< OF < L *insignia* INSIGNIA] —en′sign·ship, en′sign·cy, *n.*

en·si·lage (en′sə·lij), *n.*, *v.*, -laged, -lag·ing. —*n.* **1.** preservation of green fodder by packing it in a silo or pit. **2.** fodder preserved in this way. Ensilage is used to feed cattle in winter. —*v.* preserve in a silo. [< F]

en·slave (en·slāv′), *v.*, -slaved, -slav·ing. make a slave or slaves of; take away freedom from. —en·slave′ment, *n.* —en·slav′er, *n.*

en·snare (en·snār′), *v.*, -snared, -snar·ing. catch in a snare; trap. Also, insnare. —en·snare′ment, *n.* —en·snar′er, *n.*

en·sue (en·sü′), *v.*, -sued, -su·ing. come after; happen as a result; follow. The ensuing year means the next year. [< OF *ensivre* < L, < *in–* upon + *sequi* follow] —Syn. succeed, result.

en·sure (en·shúr′), *v.*, -sured, -sur·ing. **1.** make sure or certain. **2.** make sure of getting; secure. **3.** make safe; protect. **4.** *Obs.* assure; convince. [< AF, < *en–* (< L *in–*) + *seür* SURE]

-ent, *suffix.* **1.** ——ing, as in *absorbent, indulgent, coincident.* **2.** one that ——s, as in *correspondent, president, superintendent.* **3.** other meanings, as in *competent, confident.* [< L *-ens (-ent-)*]

en·tab·la·ture (en·tab′lə·chər), *n.* part of a building resting on the top of columns. [< Ital. *intavolatura* < *in–* on (< L *in-*) + *tavola* board, tablet < L *tabula*]

en·tail (en·tāl′), *v.* **1.** impose; require. **2.** limit the inheritance of (property, etc.) to a specified line of heirs so that it cannot be left to anyone else. —*n.* **1.** an entailing. **2.** an entailed inheritance. **3.** order of descent specified for an entailed estate. —en·tail′ment, *n.*

en·tan·gle (en·tang′gəl), *v.*, -gled, -gling. **1.**

get twisted up and caught; tangle. 2. get into difficulty; involve. 3. perplex; confuse. —en·tan'·gle·ment, n. —Syn. 1. snarl, knot, mat. 2. implicate, ensnare. 3. bewilder, embarrass.

en·tente (än·tänt'), n. 1. an understanding; agreement between two or more governments. 2. parties to an understanding; governments that have made an agreement. [< F]

en·tente cor·diale (än·tänt' kôr·dyäl'), French. a friendly understanding or agreement.

en·ter (en'tər), v. 1. go into; come into. 2. go in; come in. 3. become a part or member of; join. 4. cause to join or enter; obtain admission for. 5. begin; start. 6. write or put in a book, list, etc. 7. put in regular form; record: *the injured man entered a complaint in court.* 8. report (a ship or its cargoes) at the custom house. [< OF < L *intrare* < *intro* inwards, *intra* within] —en'·ter·a·ble, adj.

en·ter·ic (en·ter'ik), adj. intestinal. [< Gk., < *entera* intestines]

en·ter·prise (en'tər·prīz), n. 1. an important, difficult, or dangerous undertaking. 2. an undertaking; project: *a business enterprise.* 3. readiness to start projects; courage and energy in starting projects. [< OF, < *entre*- between < L *inter*-) + *prendre* take < L *prehendere*] —Syn. 2. plan, venture. 3. boldness.

en·ter·pris·ing (en'tər·prīz'ing), adj. courageous and energetic in starting projects. —en'·ter·pris'ing·ly, adv. —Syn. bold, venturesome.

en·ter·tain (en'tər·tān'), v. 1. interest; please; amuse. 2. have as a guest. 3. have guests; provide entertainment for guests. 4. take into the mind; consider. [< F, < *entre*- among (< L *inter*-) + *tenir* hold < L *tenere*] —en'ter·tain'·er, n. —Syn. 1. divert, beguile, delight. 4. harbor.

en·ter·tain·ing (en'tər·tān'ing), adj. interesting; pleasing; amusing. —en'ter·tain'ing·ly, adv. —en'ter·tain'ing·ness, n.

en·ter·tain·ment (en'tər·tān'mənt), n. 1. an entertaining. 2. a being entertained. 3. thing that interests, pleases, or amuses. —Syn. 3. amusement, diversion, recreation, pastime.

en·thrall, en·thral (en·thrôl'), v., -thralled, -thrall·ing. 1. captivate; fascinate; charm. 2. make a slave of; enslave. Also, inthrall, inthral. —en·thrall'er, n. —en·thrall'·ing, adj. —en·thrall'ing·ly, adv. —en·thrall'·ment, en·thral'ment, n.

en·throne (en·thrōn'), v., -throned, -thron·ing. 1. set on a throne. 2. invest with authority, esp. as a sovereign or as a bishop. Also, inthrone. —en·throne'ment, n.

en·thuse (en·thüz'), v., -thused, -thus·ing. Am. 1. become enthusiastic; show enthusiasm. 2. fill with enthusiasm. [< *enthusiasm*] ≫ Many people object to enthuse and most dictionaries label it colloquial, but *enthuse* seems to be an improvement over the only locution we have for the idea, the clumsy *be enthusiastic over* or *about.* It is now in fairly general use.

en·thu·si·asm (en·thü'zi·az·əm), n. 1. eager interest; zeal. 2. extreme religious emotion; ecstasy. [< LL < Gk., < *entheos* god-possessed < *en*- in + *theos* god] —Syn. 1. eagerness, warmth, ardor, fervor. —Ant. 1. indifference, apathy.

en·thu·si·ast (en·thü'zi·ast), n. 1. person who is filled with enthusiasm. 2. person who is carried away by his feelings for a cause. —Syn. 2. zealot, fanatic, devotee.

en·thu·si·as·tic (en·thü'zi·as'tik), adj. full of enthusiasm; eagerly interested. —en·thu'si·as'ti·cal·ly, adv. —Syn. zealous, eager, ardent.

en·tice (en·tīs'), v., -ticed, -tic·ing. tempt by arousing hopes or desires; attract by offering some pleasure or reward. [< OF *enticier* stir up, incite < *en*- in (< L *in*-) + L *titio* firebrand] —en·tice'ment, n. —en·tic'er, n. —en·tic'ing·ly, adv. —Syn. lure, inveigle, decoy.

en·tire (en·tīr'), adj. 1. having all the parts or elements; whole; complete. 2. not broken; having an unbroken outline. 3. *Bot.* of leaves, not indented. 4. of animals, not gelded. [< OF < L *integer* < *in*- not + *tag*- touch] —en·tire'ly, adv. —en·tire'ness, n. —Syn. 1. total, full. 2. intact, unimpaired.

en·tire·ty (en·tīr'ti), n., pl. -ties. 1. whole-

ness; completeness. 2. a complete thing; the whole. 3. in its entirety, wholly; completely.

en·ti·tle (en·tī'təl), v., -tled, -tling. 1. give the title of; call by the name of. 2. give a claim or right to. Also, intitle. —Syn. 1. name, denominate, designate. 2. empower, qualify, enable.

en·ti·ty (en'tə·ti), n., pl. -ties. 1. something that has a real and separate existence either actually or in the mind. 2. being; existence. [< LL *entitas* < L *ens*, ppr. of *esse* be]

en·tomb (en·tüm'), v. place in a tomb; bury. Also, intomb. —en·tomb'ment, n.

en·to·mo·log·i·cal (en'tə·mə·loj'ə·kəl), **en·to·mo·log·ic** (-loj'ik), adj. of or pertaining to entomology. —en'to·mo·log'i·cal·ly, adv.

en·to·mol·o·gy (en'tə·mol'ə·ji), n. branch of zoölogy that deals with insects. [< Gk. *entomon* insect + -LOGY] —en'to·mol'o·gist, n.

en·tou·rage (än'tu·räzh'), n. 1. environment, esp. social environment. 2. family, servants, attendants, and others accompanying a person. [< F, < *entourer* surround]

en·tr'acte (än·trakt'), n. 1. interval between two acts of a play. 2. music, dancing, or any entertainment performed during this interval. [< F, between-act]

en·trails (en'trālz; -trəlz), n.pl. 1. the inner parts of a man or animal. 2. intestines; bowels. 3. any inner parts. [< OF < LL *intralia* < L *interanea* < *inter* within]

en·train (en·trān'), v. 1. get on a train. 2. put on a train. —en·train'ment, n.

en·trance¹ (en'trəns), n. 1. act of entering. 2. place by which to enter; door, passageway, etc. 3. freedom or right to enter; permission to enter. [< OF, < *entrer* ENTER] —Syn. 1. entry, ingress. 2. opening, inlet, gate, portal.

en·trance² (en·trans'; -träns'), v., -tranced, -tranc·ing. 1. put into a trance. 2. fill with joy; delight; charm. —en·trance'ment, n. —en·tranc'ing, adj. —en·tranc'ing·ly, adv.

en·trant (en'trənt), n. person who enters.

en·trap (en·trap'), v., -trapped, -trap·ping. 1. catch in a trap. 2. bring into difficulty or danger; deceive; trick. —en·trap'ment, n.

en·treat (en·trēt'), v. ask earnestly; beg and pray; implore. Also, intreat. [< OF, < *en*- (< L *in*-) + *traitier* TREAT] —en·treat'ing·ly, adv. —en·treat'ment, n. —Syn. beseech, supplicate.

en·treat·y (en·trēt'i), n., pl. -treat·ies. an earnest request; prayer. —Syn. supplication, appeal, solicitation, suit, petition.

en·tree, en·trée (än'trā), n. 1. freedom or right to enter; access. 2. *U.S.* the main dish of food at dinner or lunch. 3. dish of food served before the roast or between the main courses at dinner. [< F, fem. pp. of *entrer* ENTER]

en·trench (en·trench'), v. 1. surround with a trench; fortify with trenches. 2. establish firmly. 3. trespass; encroach; infringe. Also, intrench. —en·trench'ment, n.

en·tre nous (än'trə nü'), French. between ourselves; confidentially.

en·tre·pre·neur (än'trə·prə·nėr'), n. person who organizes and manages a business or industrial enterprise, taking the risk of loss and getting the profit when there is one. [< F, < *entreprendre* undertake. See ENTERPRISE.]

en·trust (en·trust'), v. 1. charge with a trust; trust. 2. give the care of; hand over for safekeeping. Also, intrust.

en·try (en'tri), n., pl. -tries. 1. act of entering. 2. place by which to enter; way to enter: *a vestibule is an entry.* 3. thing written or printed in a book, list, etc. Each word explained in a dictionary is an entry. 4. person or thing that takes part in a contest. 5. *Law.* the act of taking possession of lands or buildings by entering or setting foot on them. [< OF, < *entrer* ENTER]

en·twine (en·twīn'), v., -twined, -twin·ing. 1. twine together. 2. twine around. —en·twine'ment, n.

e·nu·mer·ate (i·nü'mər·āt; -nü'-), v., -at·ed, -at·ing. 1. name one by one; give a list of. 2. count. —e·nu'mer·a'tion, n. —e·nu'mer·a'tive, adj. —e·nu'mer·a'tor, n. —Syn. 1. recapitulate, recount, rehearse, detail.

e·nun·ci·ate (i·nun′si·āt; -shi-), v., -at·ed, -at·ing. 1. pronounce (words): *a well-trained actor enunciates very distinctly.* 2. state definitely; announce: *after many experiments the scientist enunciated a new theory.* [< L, < *ex*-out + *nuntius* messenger] —e·nun′ci·a′tion, n. —e·nun′ci·a′tive, adj. —e·nun′ci·a′tor, n.

en·vel·op (en·vel′əp), v., -oped, -op·ing, n. —v. 1. wrap; cover. 2. surround: *our soldiers enveloped the enemy.* 3. hide; conceal: *fog enveloped the village.* —n. envelope. [< OF, < en- in (< L *in*-) + *voloper* wrap] —en·vel′op·er, n. —Syn. v. 1. infold. 2. encompass, encircle.

en·ve·lope (en′və·lōp; än′-), n. 1. a folded and gummed paper cover in which a letter or anything flat can be mailed. 2. a covering; wrapper. 3. bag that holds the gas in a balloon. [< F *enveloppe* < *envelopper* ENVELOP]

en·vel·op·ment (en·vel′əp·mənt), n. 1. an enveloping. 2. a being enveloped. 3. thing that envelops; wrapping; covering.

en·ven·om (en·ven′əm), v. 1. make poisonous. 2. fill with bitterness, hate, etc.

en·vi·a·ble (en′vi·ə·bəl), adj. to be envied; desirable; worth having. —en′vi·a·ble·ness, n. —en′vi·a·bly, adv.

en·vi·ous (en′vi·əs), adj. full of envy; feeling or showing envy. —en′vi·ous·ly, adv. —en′vi·ous·ness, n.

en·vi·ron (en·vī′rən), v. surround; enclose. [< OF *environner* < *environ* around < *en*- in (< L *in*-) + *viron* circle]

en·vi·ron·ment (en·vī′rən·mənt), n. 1. act or fact of surrounding. 2. surroundings. 3. all of the surrounding conditions and influences that affect the development of a living thing. —en·vi′ron·men′tal, adj.

en·vi·rons (en·vī′rənz), n.pl. surrounding districts; suburbs.

en·vis·age (en·viz′ij), v., -aged, -ag·ing. 1. look in the face of. 2. contemplate. 3. form a mental picture of. [< F *envisager.* See EN-, VISAGE.]

en·voy (en′voi), n. 1. messenger. 2. diplomat ranking next below an ambassador and next above a minister. [< OF, < *envoier* send < VL, < L *in via* on the way]

en·vy (en′vi), n., pl. -vies, v., -vied, -vy·ing. —n. 1. discontent or ill will at another's good fortune because one wishes it had been his. 2. the object of such feeling. —v. feel envy for or because of. [< OF *envie* < L *invidia*, ult. < *invidere* look with enmity at < *in*- against + *videre* see] —en′vi·er, n. —en′vy·ing·ly, adv.

en·wrap (en·rap′), v., -wrapped, -wrap·ping. wrap. Also, inwrap.

en·wrought (en·rôt′), adj. inwrought.

en·zyme (en′zīm; -zim), n. a chemical substance, produced in living cells, that can cause changes in other substances without being changed itself. Pepsin is an enzyme. [< Med.Gk. *enzymos* leavened < en- in + *zyme* leaven] —en·zy·mat·ic (en·zi·mat′ik; -zī-), adj.

E·O·K·A (ē·ō′kä′ä; ē·ō′kə), n. the anti-British terrorist organization on the island of Cyprus.

E·o·li·an (ē·ō′li·ən), adj. Aeolian.

e·o·lith·ic (ē′ə·lith′ik), adj. pertaining to an early stage of human culture, characterized by the use of very primitive stone instruments. [< Gk. *eos* dawn + *lithos* stone]

e·on (ē′ən; ē′on), n. aeon.

E·os (ē′os), n. the Greek goddess of the dawn, identified with the Roman goddess Aurora.

E·pam·i·non·das (i·pam′ə·non′dəs), n. 418?-362 B.C., Greek general and statesman.

Eph., Ephesians.

e·phah (ē′fə), n. a Hebrew dry measure equal to a little more than a bushel. [< Heb.]

e·phed·rine (i·fed′rin; Chem., also ef′ə·drēn,

-drin), **e·phed·rin** (i·fed′rin; Chem., also ef′ə·drin), n. drug, $C_{10}H_{15}ON$, used to relieve hay fever, asthma, head colds, etc. [< NL *ephedra* < L, horsetail (a plant) < Gk.]

e·phem·er·al (i·fem′ər·əl), adj. lasting for only a day; lasting for only a very short time; very short-lived. [< Gk. *ephemeros* liable to be cut short < *epi*- subject to + *hemera* the day (of destiny)] —e·phem′er·al·ly, adv.

e·phem·er·id (i·fem′ər·id), n. May fly.

E·phe·sian (i·fē′zhən), adj. of Ephesus or its people. —n. 1. native or inhabitant of Ephesus. 2. Ephesians, book of the New Testament written in the name of the Apostle Paul to the Christians at Ephesus.

Eph·e·sus (ef′ə·səs), n. an ancient Greek city in W Asia Minor.

eph·od (ef′od; ē′fod), n. an official vestment worn by Hebrew priests in ancient times. [< Heb.]

E·phra·im (ē′fri·əm), n. 1. in the Bible, the younger son of Joseph. 2. tribe of Hebrews descended from him. 3. kingdom of Israel.

ep·ic (ep′ik), n. a long poem that tells of the adventures of one or more great heroes. An epic is written in a dignified, majestic style, and often gives expression to the ideals of a nation or race. The *Iliad*, the *Aeneid*, and *Paradise Lost* are epics. —adj. Also, ep′i·cal. 1. of or having to do with an epic. 2. like an epic; grand in style; heroic. [< L < Gk. *epikos* < *epos* word, story] —ep′i·cal·ly, adv.

ep·i·ca·lyx (ep′ə·kā′liks; -kal′iks), n. Bot. ring of bracts at the base of a flower that looks like an outer calyx.

ep·i·carp (ep′ə·kärp), n. the outer layer of a fruit or ripened ovary of a plant. The skin of a pear is its epicarp.

ep·i·cen·ter (ep′ə·sen′tər), n. Geol. point of focus for the vibrations of an earthquake.

ep·i·cure (ep′ə·kyûr), n. person who has a refined taste in eating and drinking and cares much about foods and drinks. [Anglicized var. of *Epicurus*] —Syn. gourmet.

ep·i·cu·re·an (ep′ə·kyū·rē′ən), adj. 1. like an epicure; fond of pleasure and luxury. 2. fit for an epicure. 3. Epicurean, of Epicurus or his philosophy. —n. 1. person fond of pleasure and luxury; epicure. 2. believer in the philosophy of Epicurus.

Ep·i·cu·re·an·ism (ep′ə·kyū·rē′ən·iz·əm), n. 1. philosophy or principles of Epicurus or his followers. 2. Also, epicureanism, belief or practice of this philosophy.

Ep·i·cu·rus (ep′ə·kyûr′əs), n. 342?-270 B.C., Greek philosopher who taught that happiness is the highest good and that virtue alone produces happiness.

ep·i·dem·ic (ep′ə·dem′ik), n. 1. the rapid spreading of a disease so that many people have it at the same time. 2. the rapid spread of an idea, fashion, etc. —adj. Also, ep′i·dem′i·cal. affecting many people at the same time; widespread. [< F *épidémie* < Med.L < Gk., < *epi*- among + *demos* people] —ep′i·dem′i·cal·ly, adv. —ep·i·de·mic·i·ty (ep′ə·də·mis′ə·ti), n.

ep·i·der·mis (ep′ə·dér′mis), n. 1. the outer layer of the skin. 2. the outer covering on the shells of many mollusks. 3. any of various other outer layers of invertebrates. 4. a skinlike layer of cells in seed plants and ferns. [< LL < Gk., < *epi*- on + *derma* skin] —ep′i·der′mal, ep′i·der′mic, adj.

ep·i·der·moid (ep′ə·dér′moid), **ep·i·der·moi·dal** (-dér·moi′dəl), adj. resembling epidermis.

ep·i·glot·tis (ep′ə·glot′is), n. a thin, triangular plate of cartilage that covers the entrance to the windpipe during swallowing, so that food, etc., does not get into the lungs. [< LL < Gk., < *epi*- on + *glotta* tongue]

ep·i·gram (ep′ə·gram), n. 1. a short, pointed

Epaulet

OPENING OF / PORE —HAIR

—EPIDERMIS

—DERMIS

—MUSCLE

or witty saying. 2. a short poem ending in a witty or clever turn of thought. [< L < Gk., < *epi*– on + *graphein* write] —**ep·i·gram·mat·ic** (ep′ə·grə·mat′ik), **ep′i·gram·mat′i·cal**, *adj.* —**ep′i·gram·mat′i·cal·ly**, *adv.* ▶ Epigrams. An *epigram* is a short, pithy statement, usually with a touch of wit, in either verse or prose. In prose this means really a detached or detachable and "quotable" sentence. *Epigrams* are the chief stock in trade of columnists and newspaper "paragraphers" (writers of the one- or two-sentence remarks that come at the end of the editorial columns in some dailies). In consecutive prose, *epigrams* sometimes become too prominent, attract too much attention to themselves, or suggest straining for effect. But they can be really useful for focusing attention or for putting a fact or opinion so that a reader can remember (and perhaps repeat) it. Example: *It's no disgrace to be poor, but it might as well be.* A special type of epigram is the *paradox*, which makes a statement that as it stands contradicts fact or common sense or itself, and yet suggests a truth or at least a half truth: *All generalizations are false, including this one.*

ep·i·gram·ma·tize (ep′ə·gram′ə·tīz), *v.*, **-tized, -tiz·ing.** 1. express by epigrams. 2. make epigrams.

e·pig·ra·phy (i·pig′rə·fi), *n.* 1. inscriptions. 2. branch of knowledge that deals with the deciphering and interpretation of inscriptions. —**e·pig′ra·phist, e·pig′ra·pher,** *n.*

ep·i·lep·sy (ep′ə·lep′si), *n.* a chronic nervous disease whose attacks cause convulsions and unconsciousness. [< LL < Gk. *epilepsia* seizure, ult. < *epi*– on + *lambanein* take]

ep·i·lep·tic (ep′ə·lep′tik), *adj.* 1. of or having to do with epilepsy. 2. having epilepsy. —*n.* person who has epilepsy.

ep·i·logue, ep·i·log (ep′ə·lôg; –log), *n.* 1. the concluding part of a novel, poem, etc. 2. speech or poem after the end of a play. It is addressed to the audience and is spoken by one of the actors. [< F < L < Gk., ult. < *epi*– in addition + *legein* speak]

E·piph·a·ny (i·pif′ə·ni), *n.* January 6, the anniversary of the coming of the Wise Men to Christ at Bethlehem.

ep·i·phyte (ep′ə·fīt), *n.* plant that grows on another plant for support, but not for nourishment. Many mosses, lichens, and orchids are epiphytes. [< Gk. *epi*– on + *phyton* plant] —**ep·i·phyt·ic** (ep′ə·fit′ik), **ep′i·phyt′i·cal,** *adj.* —**ep′i·phyt′i·cal·ly,** *adv.*

e·pis·co·pa·cy (i·pis′kə·pə·si), *n., pl.* **-cies.** 1. government of a church by bishops. 2. bishops as a group. 3. position, rank, or term of office of a bishop; episcopate.

e·pis·co·pal (i·pis′kə·pəl), *adj.* 1. of or having to do with bishops. 2. governed by bishops. 3. Episcopal, of or having to do with the Church of England, or certain Protestant churches of the United States, such as the Protestant Episcopal Church. [< LL, < L *episcopus* BISHOP] —**e·pis′co·pal·ly,** *adv.*

E·pis·co·pa·lian (i·pis′kə·pāl′yən; –pāl′li·ən), *n.* member of the Protestant Episcopal church. —*adj.* Episcopal.

e·pis·co·pate (i·pis′kə·pit; –pāt), *n.* 1. position, rank, or term of office of a bishop. 2. district under the charge of a bishop; bishopric. 3. bishops as a group.

ep·i·sode (ep′ə·sōd), *n.* a single happening or group of happenings in real life or a story. [< Gk. *epeisodion,* neut., coming in besides, ult. < *epi*– on + *eis* into + *hodos* way] —**ep·i·sod·ic** (ep′ə·sod′ik), **ep′i·sod′i·cal,** *adj.* —**ep′i·sod′i·cal·ly,** *adv.*

e·pis·te·mol·o·gy (i·pis′tə·mol′ə·ji), *n.* part of philosophy that deals with the origin, nature, and limits of knowledge. [< Gk. *episteme,* knowledge + –LOGY] —**e·pis·te·mo·log·i·cal** (i·pis′tə·mə·loj′ə·kəl), *adj.* —**e·pis′te·mo·log′i·cal·ly,** *adv.* —**e·pis′te·mol′o·gist,** *n.*

e·pis·tle (i·pis′əl), *n.* 1. letter, usually a long, instructive letter written in formal or elegant language. 2. Epistle, a. letter written by one of Christ's Apostles. The Epistles make up 21 books

of the New Testament. **b.** selection from one of these, read as part of Mass or of the Anglican service of Holy Communion. [< L < Gk. *epistole,* ult. < *epi*– to + *stellein* send]

e·pis·to·lar·y (i·pis′tə·ler′i), *adj.* 1. carried on by letters; contained in letters. 2. of letters; suitable for writing letters.

ep·i·taph (ep′ə·taf; –täf), *n.* a short statement in memory of a dead person, usually put on his tombstone. [< L < Gk. *epitaphion* funeral oration < *epi*– at + *taphos* tomb] —**ep′i·taph′ic,** *adj.* —**ep′i·taph′ist,** *n.*

ep·i·the·li·um (ep′ə·thē′li·əm), *n., pl.* **-li·ums, -li·a** (–li·ə). *Biol.* a thin layer of cells forming a tissue that covers surfaces and lines hollow organs. [< NL, < Gk. *epi*– on + *thele* nipple] —**ep′i·the′li·al,** *adj.*

ep·i·thet (ep′ə·thet), *n.* a descriptive expression; adjective or noun expressing some quality or attribute, as in "Richard the Lion-Hearted." [< L < Gk. *epitheton* added < *epi*– on + *tithenai* place] —**ep·i·thet′ic, ep′i·thet′i·cal,** *adj.*

e·pit·o·me (i·pit′ə·mē), *n.* 1. a condensed account; summary. 2. a condensed representation of something; some thing or part that is typical or representative of the whole. [< L < Gk., < *epi*– into + *temnein* cut] —**e·pit·o·mist** (i·pit′ə·mist), *n.*

e·pit·o·mize (i·pit′ə·mīz), *v.,* **-mized, -miz·ing.** make an epitome of; summarize. —**e·pit′o·miz′er,** *n.* —**Syn.** abridge, condense, reduce.

ep·i·zo·ot·ic (ep′ə·zō·ot′ik), *adj.* temporarily prevalent among animals. —*n.* an epizoötic disease. [< Gk. *epi*– among + *zoion* animal]

e plu·ri·bus u·num (ē plŭr′ə·bəs ū′nəm), *Latin.* out of many, one; the motto on the official seal of the United States. It was once the official motto of the United States, but since 1956 the official motto has been "In God We Trust."

ep·och (ep′ək; *esp. Brit.* ē′pok), *n.* 1. period of time; era. 2. period of time in which striking things happened. 3. the starting point of such a period. 4. *Astron.* an arbitrarily fixed instant of time used as a reference point. 5. the dividing line between geological periods. [< Med.L < Gk. *epoche* a stopping, fixed point in time < *epi*– up + *echein* hold] —**ep′och·al,** *adj.* —**Syn.** 1. age.

ep·ode (ep′ōd), *n.* 1. a lyric poem in which a long line is followed by a shorter one. 2. part of a lyric ode following the strophe and antistrophe. [< F < L < Gk. *epoidos* < *epi*– after + *aidein* sing]

ep·on·y·mous (ep·on′ə·məs), *adj.* giving one's name to a nation, tribe, place, etc. Romulus is the eponymous hero of Rome. [< Gk., < *epi*– to + *onyma* (dial.) name]

ep·si·lon (ep′sə·lon; –lən), *n.* the fifth letter of the Greek alphabet (E, ε).

Ep·som (ep′səm), *n.* 1. town in SE England, near London. 2. Epsom Downs, track where England's famous horse race, the Derby, is run.

Epsom salt or **salts,** hydrated magnesium sulfate, $MgSO_4·7H_2O$, a bitter, white, crystalline powder taken in water to move the bowels.

E.P.T., EPT, excess-profits tax.

eq., 1. equal. 2. equation. 3. equivalent.

e·qua·ble (ek′wə·bəl; ē′kwə–), *adj.* changing little; uniform; even; tranquil. [< L, < *aequare* make uniform < *aequus* even, just] —**eq′ua·bil′i·ty, eq′ua·ble·ness,** *n.* —**eq′ua·bly,** *adv.* —**Syn.** unvarying, steady, smooth.

e·qual (ē′kwəl), *adj., n., v.* **e·qualed, e·qual·ing;** *esp. Brit.* **e·qualled, e·qual·ling.** —*adj.* 1. the same in amount, size, number, value, degree, rank, etc.; as much; neither more nor less. 2. the same throughout; even; uniform. 3. equal to, able to; strong enough for; brave enough for; etc. —*n.* person or thing that is equal. —*v.* 1. be equal to. 2. make or do something equal to. [< L, < *aequus* even, just] —**Syn.** *adj.* 1. equivalent. —*n.* peer, equivalent, match.

e·qual·i·ty (i·kwol′ə·ti), *n., pl.* **-ties.** a being equal; sameness in amount, size, number, value, degree, rank, etc.

e·qual·ize (ē′kwəl·īz), *v.,* **-ized, -iz·ing.** 1. make equal. 2. make even or uniform. —**e′qual·i·za′tion,** *n.* —**e′qual·iz′er,** *n.*

e·qual·ly (ē′kwəl·i), *adv.* in an equal manner; in or to an equal degree; so as to be equal.

e·qua·nim·i·ty (ē′kwə·nim′ə·ti; ek′wə-), *n.* evenness of mind or temper; calmness. [< L, < *aequus* even + *animus* mind, temper] —**Syn.** composure.

e·quate (i·kwāt′), *v.,* e·quat·ed, e·quat·ing. 1. state to be equal; put in the form of an equation. 2. consider, treat, or represent as equal. 3. make equal. [< L *aequatus* made equal < *aequus* equal]

e·qua·tion (i·kwā′zhən; -shən), *n.* 1. statement of equality between two quantities. *Examples:* (4×8) + 12 = 44. C = 2πr. 2. expression using chemical formulas and symbols showing the substances used and produced in a chemical change. *Example:* HCl + NaOH = NaCl + H_2O. 3. an equating or being equated.

e·qua·tor (i·kwā′tər), *n.* 1. an imaginary circle around the middle of the earth, halfway between the North Pole and the South Pole. 2. a similarly situated circle on any heavenly or spherical body. 3. an imaginary circle in the sky corresponding to that of the earth. [< LL *aequator* (*diei et noctis*) equalizer (of day and night). See **EQUAL.**] —**e·qua·to·ri·al** (ē′kwə·tô′ri·əl; -tō′-; ek′wə-), *adj.* —**e′qua·to′ri·al·ly,** *adv.*

eq·uer·ry (ek′wər·i), *n., pl.* -ries. 1. officer of a household who has charge of the horses or who accompanies his master's carriage. 2. attendant on a royal or noble person. [< F *écurie* stable < Gmc.; infl. by L *equus* horse]

e·ques·tri·an (i·kwes′tri·ən), *adj.* 1. of horsemen or horsemanship; having to do with horseback riding. 2. on horseback; mounted on horseback. —*n.* rider or performer on horseback. [< L *equestris* of a horseman < *equus* horse]

e·ques·tri·enne (i·kwes′tri·en′), *n.* a woman rider or performer on horseback. [< F]

equi-, *word element.* 1. equal, as in *equivalence.* 2. equally, as in *equidistant.* [< L *aequus* equal]

e·qui·an·gu·lar (ē′kwi·ang′gyə·lər), *adj.* having all angles equal, as a square.

e·qui·dis·tant (ē′kwə·dis′tənt), *adj.* equally distant. —**e′qui·dis′tance,** *n.* —**e′qui·dis′tant·ly,** *adv.*

e·qui·lat·er·al (ē′kwə·lat′ər·əl), *adj.* having all sides equal. —*n.* figure having all sides equal. —**e′qui·lat′er·al·ly,** *adv.*

e·quil·i·brant (i·kwil′ə·brənt), *n.* force able to balance a specified force or set of forces.

Equilateral triangle

e·qui·li·brate (ē′kwə·lī′brāt; i·kwil′ə-), *v.,* -brat·ed, -brat·ing. balance. —**e·qui·li·bra·tion** (ē′kwə·lə·brā′shən; i·kwil′ə-), *n.*

e·qui·lib·ri·um (ē′kwə·lib′ri·əm), *n.* 1. state of balance; condition in which opposing forces exactly balance or equal each other. 2. mental poise. [< L, ult. < *aequus* equal + *libra* balance]

e·quine (ē′kwīn), *adj.* of horses; like a horse; like that of a horse. —*n.* a horse. [< L, < *equus* horse]

e·qui·noc·tial (ē′kwə·nok′shəl), *adj.* 1. having to do with either equinox. 2. occurring at or near the equinox: *equinoctial gales.* 3. at or near the earth's equator. —*n.* the equinoctial line.

equinoctial line, an imaginary circle in the sky corresponding to the earth's equator.

e·qui·nox (ē′kwə·noks), *n.* either of the two times in the year when the center of the sun crosses the celestial equator, and day and night are of equal length all over the earth, occurring about March 21 (vernal equinox) and Sept. 22 (autumnal equinox). [< Med.L < L, < *aequus* equal + *nox* night]

e·quip (i·kwip′), *v.,* e·quipped, e·quip·ping. 1. furnish with all that is needed; fit out; provide. 2. fit up; array. [< F *équipper* < OF *esquiper* < Scand. *skipa* to man (a ship)]

eq·ui·page (ek′wə·pij), *n.* 1. carriage. 2. carriage with its horses, driver, and servants. 3. equipment; outfit.

e·quip·ment (i·kwip′mənt), *n.* 1. act of equipping. 2. state of being equipped. 3. anything used in or provided for equipping; outfit. 4. knowledge or skill; ability.

e·qui·poise (ē′kwə·poiz; ek′wə-), *n.* 1. state of balance. 2. a balancing force; counterbalance.

eq·ui·se·tum (ek′wə·sē′təm), *n., pl.* -tums, -ta (-tə). 1. genus of plants with hard, rough, unbranched stems. 2. horsetail. [< NL < L, < *equus* horse + *saeta* (coarse) hair]

eq·ui·ta·ble (ek′wə·tə·bəl), *adj.* 1. fair; just. 2. *Law.* pertaining to or dependent upon equity; valid in equity, as distinguished from common law and statute law. —**eq′ui·ta·ble·ness,** *n.* —**eq′ui·ta·bly,** *adv.*

eq·ui·ty (ek′wə·ti), *n., pl.* -ties. 1. fairness; justice. 2. what is fair and just. 3. system of rules and principles based on fairness and justice. Equity supplements common law and statute law by covering cases in which fairness and justice require a settlement not covered by law. In the U.S., law and equity are usually administered by the same court. 4. interest of a shareholder. 5. amount that a property is worth beyond what is owed on it. [< L, < *aequus* even, just]

e·quiv·a·lence (i·kwiv′ə·ləns), **e·quiv·a·len·cy** (-lən·si), *n., pl.* -len·ces; -cies. a being equivalent; equality in value, force, significance, etc.

e·quiv·a·lent (i·kwiv′ə·lənt), *adj.* 1. equal in value, area, force, effect, meaning, etc. 2. having the same extent. A triangle and a square of equal area are equivalent. —*n.* 1. something equivalent. 2. *Chem.* the number of parts by weight in which an element will combine with or displace 8 parts of oxygen or 1 part of hydrogen. [< LL, < L *aequus* equal + *valere* be worth] —**e·quiv′a·lent·ly,** *adv.*

e·quiv·o·cal (i·kwiv′ə·kəl), *adj.* 1. having two or more meanings; intentionally vague or ambiguous. 2. undecided; uncertain. 3. questionable; suspicious. [< LL *aequivocus* ambiguous < L *aequus* equal + *vocare* call] —**e·quiv′o·cal·ly,** *adv.* —**e·quiv′o·cal·ness,** *n.* —**Syn.** 1. doubtful. —**Ant.** 1. certain, evident, definite.

e·quiv·o·cate (i·kwiv′ə·kāt), *v.,* -cat·ed, -cat·ing. use expressions of double meaning in order to mislead. —**e·quiv′o·ca′tion,** *n.* —**e·quiv′o·ca′tor,** *n.*

-er¹, *suffix.* 1. person or thing that ——s, as in *admirer, burner.* 2. person living in ——, as in *New Yorker, villager.* 3. person that makes or works with ——, as in *hatter, tiler, tinner.* 4. person or thing that is or has ——, as in *six-footer, three-master, fiver.* [OE *-ere*] ▶ *-er,* or *-or.* Names of persons performing an act (nouns of agent) and some other nouns are freely formed in English by adding *-er* to a verb (*doer, killer, painter, thinker*), but many, chiefly nouns taken in from Latin or French (*assessor, prevaricator*), end in *-or.* Since the two endings are pronounced the same (ər), it is hard to tell whether *-er* or *-or* should be written. Here are a few as samples; a dictionary will have to settle most questions. With *-er: advertiser, adviser* (now shifting to *advisor*), *debater, manufacturer, subscriber.* With *-or: administrator, competitor, conductor, distributor, inventor* (or sometimes *inventer*), *objector, supervisor.*

-er², *suffix* forming the comparative degree. 1. of adjectives, as in *softer, smoother.* 2. of adverbs, as in *slower.* [OE *-ra, -re*]

Er, *Chem.* erbium.

e·ra (ir′ə; ē′rə), *n.* 1. a historical period distinguished by certain important or significant happenings. 2. period of time starting from some important or significant happening, date, etc. 3. system of reckoning time from some important or significant happening, given date, etc. The Christian era is the period of time reckoned from about four years after the birth of Christ. 4. a point of time from which succeeding years are numbered. 5. one of five very extensive periods of time in geological history. [< LL, var. of *aera* number, epoch, prob. same word as L *aera* counters (for reckoning), pl. of *aes* brass]

ERA, E.R.A., Emergency Relief Administration.

e·rad·i·ca·ble (i·rad′ə·kə·bəl), *adj.* that can be eradicated.

e·rad·i·cate (i·rad′ə·kāt), v., -cat·ed, -cat·ing. 1. get entirely rid of; destroy completely. 2. pull out by the roots. [< L, < ex- out + radix root] —e·rad′i·ca′tion, n. —e·rad′i·ca′tive, adj. —e·rad′i·ca′tor, n.

e·rase (i·rās′), v., e·rased, e·ras·ing. 1. rub out; scrape out. 2. remove all trace of; blot out. [< L erasus < ex- out + radere scrape] —e·ras′a·ble, adj. —Syn. 2. efface, obliterate, delete.

e·ras·er (i·rās′ər), n. thing for erasing marks made with pencil, ink, chalk, etc.

E·ras·mus (i·raz′məs), n. 1466?–1536, Dutch scholar and humanist, a leader of the Renaissance movement.

e·ra·sure (i·rā′shər; -zhər), n. 1. an erasing. 2. an erased word, letter, etc. 3. place where a word, letter, etc., has been erased.

er·bi·um (ẽr′bi·əm), n. Chem. a rare metallic element, Er, of the yttrium group. [< NL, < (Ytt)erb(y), Swedish place name]

ere (ãr), prep. before. —conj. 1. sooner than; rather than. 2. before. [OE ǣr]

e·rect (i·rekt′), adj. 1. straight up; upright. 2. raised; bristling. —v. 1. put straight up; set upright. 2. build; form. 3. in geometry, draw; construct. 4. put together; set up. 5. Archaic. establish. [< L erectus < ex- up + regere direct] —e·rect′er, e·rec′tor, n. —e·rec′tion, n. —e·rect′ly, adv. —e·rect′ness, n. —Syn. adj. 1. perpendicular, vertical, standing.

e·rec·tile (i·rek′təl), adj. 1. capable of being erected. 2. that can become distended and rigid: erectile tissues in animals. —e·rec·til·i·ty (i·rek′til′ə·ti; ē′rek-), n.

ere·long (ãr′lông′; -long′), adv. before long; soon.

er·e·mite (er′ə·mīt), n. hermit. [< L < Gk. eremites < eremos uninhabited] —er·e·mit·ic (er′ə·mit′ik), er′e·mit′i·cal, adj.

erg (ẽrg), n. unit for measuring work or energy. It is the amount of work done by one dyne acting through a distance of one centimeter. [< Gk. ergon work]

er·go (ẽr′gō), adv., conj. therefore. [< L]

er·got (ẽr′gət; -got), n. 1. disease of rye caused by a fungus. 2. a hard, dark body produced by this disease. 3. medicine made from this body, used to stop bleeding and to contract unstriped muscles. [< F < OF argot cock's spur]

er·i·ca·ceous (er′ə·kā′shəs), adj. belonging to the heath family. Heather, azalea, and rhododendron are ericaceous plants.

Er·ic·son (er′ik·sən), n. Leif, Viking chieftain and son of Eric the Red. He probably discovered North America about 1000 A.D.

Er·ic the Red (er′ik), born 950? A.D., Viking chief who discovered Greenland about 982 A.D.

E·rie (ir′i), n. 1. Lake, one of the five Great Lakes, between the United States and Canada. 2. city in NW Pennsylvania on Lake Erie. 3. Am. member of a tribe of American Indians formerly living along the S and E shores of Lake Erie.

Erie Canal, Am. canal in New York State between Buffalo and Albany. Parts of it are now abandoned, but most of it is included in the New York State Barge Canal system.

Er·in (er′ən; ir′-), n. Poetic. Ireland.

E·ris (ir′is; er′-), n. the Greek goddess of strife and discord.

E·ri·tre·a (er′ə·trē′ə), n. a former Italian colony on the Red Sea in NE Africa, now federated with Ethiopia.

erl·king (ẽrl′king′), n. in Teutonic legend, spirit or personification of a natural force, such as cold, storm, etc., that does harm, esp. to children. [< G erlkönig alder-king, a mistrans. of Dan. ellerkonge king of the elves]

er·mine (ẽr′mən), n., pl. -mines or (esp. collectively) -mine. 1. weasel of northern climates. It is brown in summer, but white with a black-tipped tail in winter. 2. its soft, white fur, used for women's coats, trimming, etc. The official robes of English judges are trimmed with ermine as a symbol of purity and fairness. 3. position, rank, or duties of a judge. [< OF < Gmc.]

erne, ern (ẽrn), n. eagle that lives near the sea. [OE earn]

e·rode (i·rōd′), v., e·rod·ed, e·rod·ing. 1. eat into; eat or wear away gradually. 2. form by a gradual eating or wearing away. [< L, < ex- away + rodere gnaw]

E·ros (ir′os; er′-), n. the Greek god of love, the son of Aphrodite, identified by the Romans with Cupid.

e·rose (i·rōs′), adj. 1. shaped unevenly. 2. Bot. having an irregularly incised margin.

e·ro·sion (i·rō′zhən), n. 1. a gradual eating or wearing away. 2. a being eaten or worn away. —e·ro′sive, adj.

e·rot·ic (i·rot′ik), **e·rot·i·cal** (-ə·kəl), adj. of or having to do with sexual love. [< Gk. erotikos of Eros] —e·rot′i·cal·ly, adv. —e·rot′i·cism, n.

ERP, E.R.P., European Recovery Program.

err (ẽr; er), v. 1. go wrong; make mistakes. 2. be wrong; be mistaken or incorrect. 3. do wrong; sin. [< OF < L errare wander] —err′ing, adj. —err′ing·ly, adv. —Syn. 1. stray, deviate, blunder. ➤ err. Usually pronounced ẽr; but there is a growing tendency to pronounce it er, from analogy with error (er′ər).

er·rand (er′ənd), n. 1. a trip to do something. 2. what one is sent to do. 3. purpose or object of a trip. [OE ǣrende]

er·rant (er′ənt), adj. 1. traveling in search of adventure; wandering; roving. 2. wrong; mistaken; incorrect. [< F, ppr. of OF errer travel (< VL iterare < L iter journey), blended with F errant, ppr. of errer ERR] —er′rant·ly, adv. —er′rant·ry (er′ənt·ri), n., pl. -ries. conduct or action of a knight-errant.

er·rat·ic (i·rat′ik), adj. 1. not steady; uncertain; irregular. 2. queer; odd: erratic behavior. [< L, < errare err] —er·rat′i·cal·ly, adv. —Syn. 2. eccentric.

er·ra·tum (i·rā′təm; i·rä′-), n., pl. -ta (-tə). error or mistake in writing or printing. [< L, neut. pp. of errare err]

er·ro·ne·ous (ə·rō′ni·əs; e–), adj. incorrect. —er·ro′ne·ous·ly, adv. —er·ro′ne·ous·ness, n.

er·ror (er′ər), n. 1. something wrong; what is incorrect; mistake. 2. condition of being wrong, mistaken, or incorrect. 3. wrongdoing; sin. 4. Am., Baseball. a faulty play that gives the side at bat some added advantage. [< OF < L. See ERR.] —Syn. 1. blunder, slip, inaccuracy.

er·satz (er′zäts), adj., n. substitute: ersatz rubber. [< G]

Erse (ẽrs), n. 1. Scotch Gaelic. 2. the Celtic language of Ireland. —adj. of either of these languages. [Scot. var. of Irish]

erst (ẽrst), adv. Archaic. formerly; long ago. [OE ǣrst, superl. of ǣr ere]

erst·while (ẽrst′hwīl′), adv. some time ago; in time past; formerly. —adj. former; past. ➤ Erstwhile is often only affected for former.

e·ruct (i·rukt′), v. belch. [< L, < ex- out + ructare belch]

e·ruc·tate (i·ruk′tāt), v., -tat·ed, -tat·ing. belch. —e·ruc·ta·tion (i·ruk′tā′shən; ē′ruk-), n. —e·ruc′ta·tive, adj.

er·u·dite (er′ū·dīt; er′yū-), adj. scholarly; learned. [< L eruditus instructed < ex- away + rudis rude] —er′u·dite′ly, adv. —er′u·dite′ness, n.

er·u·di·tion (er′ū·dish′ən; er′yū-), n. acquired knowledge; scholarship; learning. —er′u·di′tion·al, adj.

e·rupt (i·rupt′), v. 1. burst forth. 2. throw forth. 3. break out in a rash. The skin erupts during measles. [< L eruptus < ex- out + rumpere burst]

e·rup·tion (i·rup′shən), n. 1. a bursting forth. 2. a throwing forth of lava, etc., from a volcano or of hot water from a geyser. 3. a breaking out in a rash. 4. red spots on the skin; rash. —e·rup′tive, adj.

-ery, suffix. 1. place for ——ing, as in cannery, hatchery. 2. place for ——s, as in nunnery. 3. occupation or business of a ——, as in cookery. 4. state or condition of a ——, as in slavery. 5. qualities, actions, etc., of a ——, as in knavery. 6. ——s as a group, as in machinery. [< OF -erie]

er·y·sip·e·las (er'ə·sip'ə·ləs; ir'ə-), *n.* an acute infectious disease caused by streptococcus bacteria and characterized by a high fever and a deep-red inflammation of the skin. [< Gk.]

e·ryth·ro·my·cin (i·rith'rō·mī'sin), *n.* drug related to streptomycin. [< Gk. *erythros* red + *mykes* fungus]

E·sau (ē'sô), *n. Bible.* older son of Isaac and Rebecca, who sold his birthright to his brother Jacob. Gen. 25:21-34.

es·ca·drille (es'kə·dril'), *n.* a small fleet of airplanes. [< F, dim. of *escadre* SQUADRON; form infl. by Sp. *escuadrilla*, dim. of *escuadra*]

es·ca·lade (es'kə·lād'), *n., v.,* -lad·ed, -lad·ing. —*n.* climbing the walls of a fortified place by ladders. —*v.* climb thus. [< F < Ital. *scalata*, ult. < L *scala* ladder]

es·ca·la·tor (es'kə·lā'tər), *n. Am.* 1. a moving stairway. 2. Escalator, *Trademark.* a moving stairway built by the Otis Elevator Company. [blend of *escalade* and *elevator*]

escalator clause, provision in a contract allowing an increase or decrease in wages under specified conditions.

es·cal·lop, es·cal·op (es·kol'əp; -kal'-), *v.* bake in a cream sauce or with bread crumbs. —*n.* scallop. [(orig. n.) < OF *escalope* shell < Gmc.] —es·cal'loped, *adj. Am.*

es·ca·pade (es'kə·pād; es'kə·pād'), *n.* a breaking loose from rules or restraint; wild adventure or prank. [< F < Ital., < *scappare* ESCAPE]

es·cape (es·kāp'), *v.,* -caped, -cap·ing, *n., adj.* —*v.* 1. get free; get out and away. 2. get free from. 3. keep free or safe from; avoid. 4. avoid capture, trouble, etc. 5. come out of without being intended: *a cry escaped her lips.* 6. fail to be noticed or remembered by: *his name escapes me.* —*n.* 1. an escaping. 2. way of escaping. 3. *Psychol.* an avoiding of reality. 4. outflow or leakage of gas, water, etc. —*adj.* providing a way of escape or avoidance. [< OF *escaper*, ult. < L *ex-* out of + *cappa* cloak] —es·cap'er, *n.* —Syn. *v.* 1. flee, abscond. 3. evade, elude, shun.

escape clause, clause that frees a signer of a contract from certain responsibilities under specified circumstances.

es·ca·pee (es'kə·pē'; es·kāp'ē), *n.* person who has escaped, esp. one who has escaped from an area under Communist control.

es·cape·ment (es·kāp'mənt), *n.* 1. device in a timepiece by which the motion of the wheels and of the pendulum or balance wheel are accommodated to each other. 2. mechanism that controls the movement of a typewriter carriage.

Two forms of escapement

es·cap·ism (es·kāp'iz·əm), *n.* a habitual avoidance of unpleasant realities by recourse to imagination and fiction. —es·cap'ist, *n.*

es·ca·role (es'kə·rōl), *n.* a broad-leaved kind of endive, used for salads.

es·carp·ment (es·kärp'mənt), *n.* 1. a steep slope; cliff. 2. ground made into a steep slope in a fortification. [< F < Ital. *scarpa* < Gmc.]

es·cheat (es·chēt'), *Law.* —*n.* 1. a reverting of the ownership of property to the legal state or the lord of a manor when there are no legal heirs. 2. property whose ownership has so reverted. —*v.* revert thus. [< OF *eschete*, ult. < L *ex-* out + *cadere* fall] —es·cheat'a·ble, *adj.*

es·chew (es·chü'), *v.* avoid as bad or harmful; shun. [< OF *eschiver* < Gmc.]

es·cort (*n.* es'kôrt; *v.* es·kôrt'), *n.* 1. one or a group going with another to give protection, show honor, etc. 2. act of going with another as an escort. —*v.* go with as an escort. [< F < Ital. *scorta* < *scorgere* guide < L *ex-* + *corrigere* CORRECT] —Syn. *v.* accompany, conduct, attend.

es·cri·toire (es'kri·twär'), *n.* a writing desk. [< F < LL *scriptorium* < L *scribere* write]

es·crow (es'krō; es·krō'), *n.* deed, bond, or other written agreement put in charge of a third person until certain conditions are fulfilled. [< AF var. of OF *escroue* scrap, scroll < Gmc.]

es·cu·do (es·kü'dō), *n., pl.* -dos. 1. a unit of

Portuguese gold money. 2. a former gold or silver coin of Spain, Portugal, etc. [< Sp., Pg. < L *scutum* shield]

es·cu·lent (es'kyə·lənt), *adj.* suitable for food; edible. [< L, < *esca* food]

es·cutch·eon (es·kuch'ən), *n.* shield or shield-shaped surface on which a coat of arms is put. [< OF *escuchon*, < L *scutum* shield]

Es·dras (ez'drəs), *n.* 1. either of the first two books of the Protestant Apocrypha. 2. two books in the Douay Bible, called Ezra and Nehemiah in the Protestant and Jewish Bibles.

-ese, *suffix.* 1. of or pertaining to, as in *Japanese* art. 2. native or inhabitant of, as in *Portuguese.* 3. language of, as in *Chinese.* [< OF *-eis* < L *-ensis*]

Es·ki·mo (es'kə·mō), *n., pl.* -mos, -mo, *adj.* —*n.* member of a race living on the arctic shores of North America and NE Asia. Eskimos are short and stocky, and have broad, flat faces, yellowish skin, and black hair. —*adj.* of or having to do with the Eskimos or their language. [< Dan. < F < Algonquian *eskimantsis* raw-flesh-eaters]

Eskimo dog, a strong dog used by the Eskimos to pull sledges.

e·soph·a·gus (ē·sof'ə·gəs), *n., pl.* -gi (-jī). passage for food from the mouth to the stomach; gullet. Also, oesophagus. [< NL < Gk., < *oiso-* carry + *phagein* eat]

es·o·ter·ic (es'ə·ter'ik), *adj.* 1. understood only by the select few; intended for an inner circle of disciples, scholars, etc. 2. secret; confidential. [< Gk. *esoterikos*, ult. < *eso* within] —es'o·ter'i·cal·ly, *adv.*

ESP, extrasensory perception.

esp., especially.

es·pal·ier (es·pal'yər), *n.* 1. framework upon which trees and shrubs grow. 2. tree or shrub trained to grow this way.

es·pe·cial (es·pesh'əl), *adj.* 1. special; particular. 2. exceptional in amount or degree. [< OF < L *specialis* SPECIAL]

es·pe·cial·ly (es·pesh'əl·i), *adv.* particularly; chiefly. —Syn. mostly, principally, primarily.

Es·pe·ran·to (es'pə·rän'tō; -ran'-), *n.* a simple artificial language for international use.

es·pi·al (es·pī'əl), *n.* 1. act of spying. 2. act of watching. 3. discovery.

es·pi·o·nage (es'pi·ə·nij; es'pi·ə·näzh), *n.* use of spies; spying. [< F, < *espion* spy < Ital. *spione* < *spia* spy]

es·pla·nade (es'plə·nād'; -näd'), *n.* 1. an open, level space used for public walks or drives. 2. an open space between a fortress and a town. [< F < Sp., ult. < L *ex-* out + *planus* level]

es·pous·al (es·pouz'əl), *n.* 1. an espousing; adoption of a cause, etc.). 2. ceremony of becoming engaged or married.

es·pouse (es·pouz'), *v.,* -poused, -pous·ing. 1. marry. 2. take up or make one's own: *espouse a cause.* [< OF < L *sponsare* < *sponsus* betrothed, pp. of *spondere* betroth] —es·pous'er, *n.*

es·pres·so (es·pres'ō), *n.* strong, dark-roasted coffee brewed in a special machine by an infusion of steam and usually served black. [< Ital.]

es·prit (es·prē'), *n.* lively wit; spirit. [< F < L *spiritus* SPIRIT]

es·prit de corps (es·prē' də kôr'), *French.* a sense of union and of common interests and responsibilities to some group.

es·py (es·pī'), *v.,* -pied, -py·ing. see; spy. [< OF *espier* < Gmc.] ▶ Usually *espy* suggests that a thing is hard to see because it is far away, etc.

Esq., Esqr., Esquire. ▶ Esq., Esquire. Written following a man's name in the inside and outside address of a letter, *Esq.* or *Esquire* is formal, with archaic or British suggestion, and in the United States is not often except used to professional men, chiefly to lawyers. No other title (such as *Mr., Dr., Hon.*) should be used with the word: *Harry A. Kinne, Esq.*

-esque, *suffix.* 1. in the —— style; resembling the —— style, as in *Romanesque.* 2. like a ——, as in *statuesque.* [< F < Ital. *-esco*]

es·quire (es·kwīr'; es'kwīr), *n., v.,* -quired,

–quir·ing. —n. 1. in the Middle Ages, a young man of noble family who attended a knight until he himself was made a knight. **2.** Englishman ranking next below a knight. **3. Esquire,** title of respect placed after a man's last name. **—v. 1.** raise to the rank of esquire. **2.** address as esquire. **3.** escort (a lady). [< OF < L *scutarius* shieldbearer < *scutum* shield] ➤ See Esq. for usage note.

-ess, *suffix.* female, as in *heiress, hostess, lioness.* [< F *-esse* < L *-issa* < Gk.]

es·say (n. 1 es′ā; n. 2 es′ā, e·sā′; v. e·sā′), n. **1.** a literary composition on a certain subject. An essay is usually shorter and less methodical than a treatise. **2.** try; attempt. **—v.** try; attempt. [< OF < L *exagium* a weighing] **—es·say′er,** *n.* **—Syn.** *n.* **2.** effort, endeavor.

es·say·ist (es′ā·ist), *n.* writer of essays.

Es·sen (es′ən), *n.* city in W Germany.

es·sence (es′əns), *n.* **1.** that which makes a thing what it is; necessary part or parts; important feature or features. **2.** substance. **3.** entity, esp. a spiritual entity. **4.** any concentrated substance that has the characteristic flavor, fragrance, or effect of the plant, fruit, etc., from which it is obtained. **5.** solution of such a substance in alcohol. **6.** perfume. [< L, < *esse* be]

es·sen·tial (ə·sen′shəl), *adj.* **1.** needed to make a thing what it is; necessary; very important. **2.** of, like, or constituting the essence of a substance. **3.** of the highest sort; in the highest sense: *essential happiness.* **—n.** an absolutely necessary element or quality; fundamental feature. [< Med.L *essentialis.* See ESSENCE.] **—es·sen′tial·ly,** *adv.* **—es·sen′tial·ness,** *n.* **—Syn.** *adj.* **1.** indispensable, requisite, vital.

essential oil, a volatile oil that gives a plant, fruit, etc., its characteristic flavor, fragrance, or effect.

-est, *suffix* forming the superlative degree. **1.** of adjectives, as in *warmest.* **2.** of adverbs, as in *slowest.*

E.S.T., EST, or **e.s.t.,** *Am.* Eastern Standard Time.

es·tab·lish (es·tab′lish), *v.* **1.** set up permanently: *establish a business.* **2.** settle in a position; set up in business. **3.** bring about permanently; cause to be accepted: *establish a custom.* **4.** show beyond dispute; prove: *establish a fact.* **5.** make (a church) a national institution recognized and supported by the government. [< OF *establir* < L *stabilire* make STABLE²] **—es·tab′lish·er,** *n.* **—Syn.** **4.** verify, substantiate.

established church, church that is a national institution recognized and supported by the government.

es·tab·lish·ment (es·tab′lish·mənt), *n.* **1.** an establishing. **2.** a being established. **3.** thing established. **4.** recognition by the state of a church as the official church. **5.** an institution. A household, business, church, or army is an establishment.

es·tate (es·tāt′), *n.* **1.** a large piece of land belonging to a person; landed property. **2.** that which a person owns; property; possessions. **3.** interest, ownership, or property in land or other things. **4.** condition or stage in life. **5.** social status or rank; high rank. **6.** class or group of people in a nation. [< OF < L *status* state]

es·teem (es·tēm′), *v.* **1.** have a favorable opinion of; regard highly. **2.** value; rate. **3.** think; consider. **—n.** a very favorable opinion; high regard. [< OF < L *aestimare* value] **—Syn.** *n.* estimation, favor, respect. **—Ant.** *n.* contempt.

es·ter (es′tər), *n.* **1.** *Chem.* compound in which the acid hydrogen of an acid is replaced by the organic radical of an alcohol. Animal and vegetable fats and oils are esters. **2.** any salt containing a hydrocarbon radical.

Es·ther (es′tər), *n.* **1.** the Jewish wife of a Persian king, who saved her people from massacre. **2.** book of the Old Testament that tells her story.

es·thete (es′thēt), *n.* aesthete. **—es·thet·ic** (es·thet′ik), *adj.* **—es·thet′i·cal,** *adj.* **—es·thet′i·cal·ly,** *adv.*

es·thet·ics (es·thet′iks), *n.* aesthetics.

Es·tho·ni·a (es·thō′ni·ə; -tō′-), *n.* Estonia. **—Es·tho′ni·an,** *adj., n.*

es·ti·ma·ble (es′tə·mə·bəl), *adj.* **1.** worthy of esteem; deserving high regard. **2.** capable of being estimated or calculated. **—es′ti·ma·ble·ness,** *n.* **—es′ti·ma·bly,** *adv.*

es·ti·mate (*n.* es′tə·mit; -māt; *v.* es′tə·māt), *n., v.,* **-mat·ed, -mat·ing. —n. 1.** judgment or opinion about how much, how many, how good, etc. **2.** statement of what certain work will cost, made by one willing to do the work. **—v. 1.** have an opinion of. **2.** fix the worth, size, amount, etc., esp. in a rough way; calculate approximately. [< L. *aestimatus,* pp. of *aestimare* value] **—es′ti·ma′tive,** *adj.* **—es′ti·ma′tor,** *n.* **—Syn.** *v.* **1.** judge. **2.** reckon, gauge.

es·ti·ma·tion (es′tə·mā′shən), *n.* **1.** judgment; opinion. **2.** esteem; respect. **3.** act or process of estimating.

Es·to·ni·a (es·tō′ni·ə), *n.* a small country in N Europe, on the Baltic Sea, now under Soviet control. Also, **Esthonia. —Es·to′ni·an,** *adj., n.*

es·top (es·top′), *v.,* **-topped, -top·ping. 1.** *Law.* prevent from asserting or doing something contrary to a previous assertion or act. **2.** stop; bar; obstruct. [< OF, < *estoupe* tow < L *stuppa*]

es·trange (es·trānj′), *v.,* **-tranged, -trang·ing. 1.** turn (a person) from affection to indifference, dislike, or hatred; make unfriendly; separate: *a quarrel had estranged him from his family.* **2.** keep apart; keep away. [< OF < L, < *extraneus* STRANGE] **—es·trange′ment,** *n.* **—es·trang′er,** *n.* **—Syn. 1.** alienate.

es·tro·gen (es′trə·jən), *n.* any of various hormones which induce a series of physiological changes in females, esp. in the reproductive or sexual organs. **—es·tro·gen·ic** (es′trə·jen′ik), *adj.*

es·tu·ar·y (es′chū·er′i), *n., pl.* **-ar·ies. 1.** a broad mouth of a river into which the tide flows. **2.** inlet of the sea. [< L, < *aestus* tide] **—es·tu·ar′i·al** (es′chū·ār′i·əl), *adj.*

-et, *suffix.* little, as in *owlet, islet.* This meaning has disappeared in most words formed by adding *-et.* [< OF]

e·ta (ā′tə; ē′tə), *n.* the seventh letter of the Greek alphabet (H, η).

et al., **1.** and elsewhere. **2.** and others. [(def.1) < L *et alibi;* (def. 2) < L *et alii*]

etc., et cetera. ➤ **etc., et cetera.** *Etc.,* usually read *and so forth,* is sometimes a convenient way to end a series that samples rather than completes an enumeration, but it belongs primarily to reference and business usage: *The case is suitable for prints, maps, blueprints, etc.* Its inappropriateness can be seen in a sentence like this: *A student's professors can be of immense aid to him because of their knowledge of boys and their habits, customs, needs, ideals, etc.* Writing out *et cetera* now seems an affectation. In consecutive writing most people would probably use the English "and so forth." It is better to avoid these end tags (which really take away from emphasis by putting a catchall at the end of a clause or sentence) by rephrasing the list, preceding it by *such as* or some other warning that the list you have given is not exhaustive. *And etc.* shows the writer doesn't realize that the *et* of *etc.* means *and,* so that he is really writing *and and so forth.*

et cet·er·a (et set′ər·ə; set′rə), and others; and the rest; and so forth; and so on; and the like. [< L] ➤ See etc. for usage note.

etch (ech), *v.* **1.** engrave (a drawing or design) on metal, glass, etc., by means of acid. When filled with ink, the lines of the design will reproduce a copy on paper. **2.** engrave a drawing or design on by means of acid. **3.** make drawings or designs by this method. [< Du. < G *ätzen;* akin to EAT] **—etch′er,** *n.*

etch·ing (ech′ing), *n.* **1.** picture or design printed from an etched plate. **2.** an etched plate; etched drawing or design. **3.** art of an etcher; process of engraving a drawing or design on metal, glass, etc., by means of acid.

e·ter·nal (i·tér′nəl), *adj.* **1.** without beginning or ending; lasting throughout all time. **2.** always and forever the same. **3.** seeming to go on forever; occurring very frequently. —*n.* the Eternal, God. [< L *aeternalis,* ult. < *aevum* age] —e·ter'nal·ly, *adv.* —e·ter'nal·ness, *n.* —Syn. *adj.* 1. everlasting, perpetual, immortal.

Eternal City, the, Rome.

e·ter·ni·ty (i·tẽr'nə·ti), *n., pl.* –ties. 1. time without beginning or ending; all time. 2. eternal quality; endlessness. 3. the endless period after death; future life. 4. a seemingly endless period of time.

e·ter·nize (i·tẽr'nīz), *v.,* –nized, –niz·ing. make eternal; perpetuate; immortalize.

eth·ane (eth'ān), *n. Chem.* a colorless, odorless, inflammable gas, C_2H_6. It is a hydrocarbon present in natural gas and illuminating gas.

e·ther (ē'thər), *n.* 1. *Chem.* a colorless, strong-smelling liquid, $(C_2H_5)_2O$, that burns and evaporates readily. Its fumes cause unconsciousness when deeply inhaled. Ether is used as a solvent for fats and resins. 2. Also, **aether.** a. the upper regions of space beyond the earth's atmosphere; clear sky. b. the invisible, elastic substance supposed to be distributed evenly through all space and to conduct light waves, electric waves, etc. [< L < Gk. *aither* upper air]

e·the·re·al (i·thir'i·əl), *adj.* 1. light; airy; delicate: *ethereal beauty.* 2. not of the earth; heavenly. 3. of or pertaining to the upper regions of space. 4. of or pertaining to the ether diffused through space. Also, **aethereal.** —e·the're·al·i·ty, *n.* —e·the're·al·ly, *adv.* —e·the're·al·ness, *n.* —Syn. 1. intangible, tenuous.

e·the·re·al·ize (i·thir'i·əl·īz), *v.,* –ized, –iz·ing. make ethereal. —e·the're·al·i·za'tion, *n.*

e·ther·ize (ē'thər·īz), *v.,* –ized, –iz·ing. *Am.* 1. make unconscious with ether fumes. 2. change into ether. —e'ther·i·za'tion, *n.* —e'ther·iz'er, *n.*

eth·ic (eth'ik), *adj.* ethical. —*n.* ethics; system of ethics. [< L < Gk., < *ethos* moral character]

eth·i·cal (eth'ə·kəl), *adj.* 1. having to do with standards of right and wrong; of ethics or morality. 2. in accordance with formal or professional rules of right and wrong. —eth'i·cal'i·ty, *n.* —eth'i·cal·ly, *adv.* —eth'i·cal·ness, *n.*

eth·ics (eth'iks), *n.* 1. (*sing. in use*) study of standards of right and wrong; that part of science and philosophy dealing with moral conduct, duty, and judgment. 2. (*sing. in use*) book about ethics. 3. (*pl. in use*) formal or professional rules of right and wrong; system of conduct or behavior.

E·thi·o·pi·a (ē'thi·ō'pi·ə), *n.* 1. an ancient region in NE Africa, S of Egypt. 2. country in E Africa; Abyssinia.

E·thi·o·pi·an (ē'thi·ō'pi·ən), **E·thi·op** (ē'thi·op), *adj.* 1. of or having to do with Ethiopia or its people. 2. Negro. —*n.* 1. native or inhabitant of Ethiopia. 2. Negro.

E·thi·op·ic (ē'thi·op'ik; –ō'pik), *adj.* of or having to do with the ancient language of Ethiopia or the church using this language. —*n.* the ancient language of Ethiopia.

eth·nic (eth'nik), **eth·ni·cal** (–nə·kəl), *adj.* 1. having to do with the various races of people and the characteristics and customs they have in common; racial. 2. heathen; pagan; not Christian; not Jewish. [< L < Gk., < *ethnos* nation] —eth'ni·cal·ly, *adv.*

eth·nog·ra·phy (eth·nog'rə·fi), *n.* the scientific description and classification of the various races of people. —eth·nog'ra·pher, *n.* —eth·no·graph·ic (eth'nə·graf'ik), eth'no·graph'i·cal, *adj.* —eth'no·graph'i·cal·ly, *adv.*

eth·nol·o·gy (eth·nol'ə·ji), *n.* science that deals with the various races of people, their origin, distribution, characteristics, customs, institutions, and culture. —eth·no·log·ic (eth'nə·loj'ik), eth'no·log'i·cal, *adj.* —eth'no·log'i·cal·ly, *adv.* —eth·nol'o·gist, *n.*

eth·yl (eth'əl), *n.* 1. *Chem.* a univalent radical, –C_2H_5, in many organic compounds. Ordinary alcohol contains ethyl. 2. Ethyl, *Trademark.* a poisonous, colorless lead compound, Pb $(C_2H_5)_4$, used in gasoline to reduce knocking.

ethyl alcohol, ordinary alcohol, C_2H_5OH, made by the fermentation of grain, sugar, etc.

eth·yl·ene (eth'ə·lēn), *n.* a colorless, inflammable gas, C_2H_4, with an unpleasant odor, used as a fuel and anesthetic, and for coloring and ripening citrus fruits.

e·ti·ol·o·gy (ē'ti·ol'ə·ji), *n.* 1. an assigning of a cause. 2. science that deals with origins or causes. 3. theory of the causes of disease. Also, **aetiology.** [< L < Gk., < *aitia* cause + *-logos* treating of] —e·ti·o·log·i·cal (ē'ti·ə·loj'ə·kəl), *adj.* —e'ti·o·log'i·cal·ly, *adv.* —e'ti·ol'o·gist, *n.*

et·i·quette (et'ə·ket), *n.* 1. conventional rules for conduct or behavior in polite society. 2. formal rules or conventions governing conduct in a profession, official ceremony, etc.: *medical etiquette.* [< F < Gmc.]

Et·na (et'nə), *n.* Mount, volcano in NE Sicily. Also, **Aetna, Mount.**

E·tru·ri·a (i·trur'i·ə), *n.* an ancient country in W Italy.

E·trus·can (i·trus'kən), **E·tru·ri·an** (i·trur'i·ən), *adj.* of or having to do with Etruria, its people, their language, art, or customs. —*n.* 1. native or inhabitant of Etruria. 2. language of Etruria.

et seq., and the following; and that which follows. [< L *et sequens*]

-ette, *suffix.* 1. little, as in *kitchenette, statuette.* 2. female, as in *farmerette, suffragette.* 3. substitute for, as in *leatherette.* [< F, fem. of –*et* –ET]

é·tude (ā·tüd'; ā·tūd'), *n.* 1. study. 2. piece of music intended to develop skill in technique. [< F, study]

et·y·mol·o·gy (et'ə·mol'ə·ji), *n., pl.* –gies. 1. account or explanation of the origin and history of a word. 2. a historical study dealing with linguistic changes, esp. a study dealing with individual word origins. [< L < Gk., < *etymon* the original sense or form of a word (neut. of *etymos* true, real) + *-logos* treating of] —et·y·mo·log·i·cal (et'ə·mə·loj'ə·kəl), *adj.* —et'y·mo·log'i·cal·ly, *adv.* —et'y·mol'o·gist, *n.*

eu-, *prefix.* good; well, as in *eulogy, euphony.* [< Gk.]

Eu, *Chem.* europium.

Eu·boe·a (ū·bē'ə), *n.* the largest island in the Aegean Sea, near Greece and belonging to it. —Eu·boe'an, *n., adj.*

eu·ca·lyp·tus (ū'kə·lip'təs), *n., pl.* –tus·es, –ti (–tī). a very tall tree that originated in Australia. It is valued for its timber and for an oil made from its leaves. [< NL, < Gk. *eu-* well + *kalyptos* covered; with ref. to bud covering]

Eu·cha·rist (ū'kə·rist), *n.* 1. sacrament of the Lord's Supper; Holy Communion. 2. the consecrated bread and wine used in this sacrament. [< LL < Gk. *eucharistia* thankfulness, the Eucharist] —Eu'cha·ris'tic, Eu'cha·ris'ti·cal, *adj.*

eu·chre (ū'kər), *n., v.,* –chred, –chring. —*n. Am.* a simple card game for two, three, or four players, using the 32 (or 28, or 24) highest cards. —*v.* 1. defeat (the side that declared the trump) at euchre. 2. *Am., Colloq.* outwit.

Eu·clid (ū'klid), *n.* Greek mathematician who wrote a book on geometry about 300 B.C.

Eu·clid·e·an, Eu·clid·i·an (ū·klid'i·ən), *adj.* of Euclid or his principles of geometry.

eu·gen·ic (ū·jen'ik), **eu·gen·i·cal** (–ə·kəl), *adj.* 1. having to do with improvement of the race; improving the offspring produced; improving the race. 2. possessing good inherited characteristics. [< Gk. *eugenes* well-born < *eu-* well + *genos* birth] —eu·gen'i·cal·ly, *adv.*

eu·gen·ics (ū·jen'iks), *n.* science of improving the human race. Eugenics would apply the same principles to human beings that have long been applied to animals and plants, and develop healthier, more intelligent, and better children.

Eu·gé·nie (œ·zhā·nē'), *n.* 1826–1920, wife of Napoleon III and empress of the French.

eu·lo·gist (ū'lə·jist), *n.* person who eulogizes.

eu·lo·gis·tic (ū'lə·jis'tik), **eu·lo·gis·ti·cal** (–tə·kəl), *adj.* praising highly. —eu'lo·gis'ti·cal·ly, *adv.*

eu·lo·gi·um (ū·lō'ji·əm), *n., pl.* –gi·ums, –gi·a (–ji·ə). eulogy; praise.

āge, cāre, fär; ēqual, tẽrm; īce; ōpen, ôrder; put, rüle, ūse; th, then; ə=a in about.

eu·lo·gize (ū′lə·jīz), v., -gized, -giz·ing. praise very highly. —eu′lo·giz′er, n.

eu·lo·gy (ū′lə·ji), n., pl. -gies. speech or writing in praise of a person, action, etc.; high praise. [< Gk. eulogia < eu- well + legein speak]

eu·nuch (ū′nək), n. 1. a castrated man. 2. a castrated man in charge of a harem or the household of an Oriental ruler. [< L < Gk., < eune bed + echein keep]

eu·pep·sia (ū·pep′shə; -si·ə), n. good digestion. [< NL < Gk. See EU-, DYSPEPSIA.] —eu·pep·tic (ū·pep′tik), adj.

eu·phe·mism (ū′fə·miz·əm), n. 1. use of a mild or indirect expression instead of one that is harsh or unpleasantly direct. 2. a mild or indirect expression used in this way. "Pass away" is a common euphemism for "die." [< Gk., < eu- good + pheme speaking] —eu′phe·mist, n. —eu′phe·mis′tic, adj. —eu′phe·mis′ti·cal·ly, adv. ▶ The most excusable euphemisms are those intended to soften the misfortunes of life, as laid to rest for buried. The largest group of euphemisms consists of substitutes for many short abrupt words, the names of physical functions and social unpleasantness. For years sweat was taboo and was replaced by perspire and perspiration.

eu·phe·mize (ū′fə·mīz), v., -mized, -miz·ing. 1. employ euphemism. 2. express by euphemism. —eu′phe·miz′er, n.

eu·phon·ic (ū·fon′ik), **eu·phon·i·cal** (-ə·kəl), adj. 1. having to do with euphony. 2. euphonious. —eu·phon′i·cal·ly, adv. —eu·phon′i·cal·ness, n.

eu·pho·ni·ous (ū·fō′ni·əs), adj. sounding well; pleasing to the ear; harmonious. —eu·pho′ni·ous·ly, adv. —eu·pho′ni·ous·ness, n.

eu·pho·ni·um (ū·fō′ni·əm), n. a brass musical instrument like a tuba, having a loud, deep tone.

eu·pho·ny (ū′fə·ni), n., pl. -nies. 1. agreeableness of sound; pleasing effect to the ear; agreeableness of speech sounds as uttered or combined in utterance. 2. tendency to change sounds so as to favor ease of utterance. [< LL < Gk., < eu- good + phone sound]

eu·phor·bi·a (ū·fôr′bi·ə), n. any of a genus of plants with acrid, milky juice and small, inconspicuous flowers; spurge. Some euphorbias resemble cacti. [< L, < Euphorbus, a Greek physician]

eu·pho·ri·a (ū·fō′ri·ə; -fô′-), n. 1. Psychol. sense of well-being and expansiveness. 2. Med. physical soundness; good health. [< NL < Gk., < eu well + pherein to bear]

Eu·phra·tes (ū·frā′tēz), n. river in SW Asia, flowing from E Turkey into the Persian Gulf. It joins the Tigris River in Iraq.

eu·phu·ism (ū′fū·iz·əm), n. 1. an affected style of speaking and writing English that was fashionable around 1600, characterized by long series of antitheses, frequent similes, and alliteration. 2. any affected, elegant style of writing; flowery, artificial language. [< Euphues, main character in two works of John Lyly, English dramatist]

eu·phu·is·tic (ū′fū·is′tik), **eu·phu·is·ti·cal** (-tə·kəl), adj. using or containing euphuism; like euphuism. —eu′phu·is′ti·cal·ly, adv.

Eur., Europe; European.

Eur·a·sia (yūr·ā′zhə; -shə), n. Europe and Asia. —Eur·a′sian, adj., n.

Eur·at·om (yūr·at′əm), n. a group of six European countries (France, West Germany, Italy, Belgium, the Netherlands, and Luxemburg) organized for atomic research on a coöperative basis.

eu·re·ka (yū·rē′kə), interj. I have found it! (the motto of California). [< Gk.]

Eu·rip·i·des (yū·rip′ə·dēz), n. 480?–406? B.C., Greek tragic poet.

Eu·rope (yūr′əp), n. continent W of Asia.

Eu·ro·pe·an (yūr′ə·pē′ən), adj. of or having to do with Europe or its people. —n. native or inhabitant of Europe.

Eu·ro·pe·an·ize (yūr′ə·pē′ən·īz), v., -ized, -iz·ing. make European in appearance, habit, way of life, etc.

European plan, Am. system of charges to guests in a hotel by which the price covers the room, but not the meals (distinguished from American plan).

European Recovery Program, plan adopted by the United States for giving financial aid to European nations after World War II.

eu·ro·pi·um (yū·rō′pi·əm), n. Chem. a rare metallic element, Eu, of the same group as cerium. [< NL, < L Europa Europe < Gk.]

Eu·ryd·i·ce (yū·rid′ə·sē), n. Gk. Myth. the wife of Orpheus, who freed her from Hades by the charm of his music, but lost her again because he disobeyed orders and turned back to see whether she was following.

Eu·sta·chi·an tube (ū·stā′ki·ən; -stā′shən), Anat. a slender canal between the pharynx and the middle ear. It equalizes the air pressure on the two sides of the eardrum.

Eu·ter·pe (ū·tér′pē), n. the Greek Muse of music and lyric song.

eu·tha·na·sia (ū′thə·nā′zhə), n. 1. easy, painless death. 2. a painless killing, esp. to end a painful and incurable disease. [< Gk., < eu- easy + thanatos death]

eu·then·ics (ū·then′iks), n. Am. science or art of improving living conditions. [< Gk. euthenia well-being] —eu·then·ist (ū′thən·ist), n. Am.

Euxine Sea (ūk′sin), an ancient name for the Black Sea.

e·vac·u·ate (i·vak′yū·āt), v., -at·ed, -at·ing. 1. leave empty; withdraw from: after surrendering, the soldiers evacuated the fort. 2. withdraw; remove: efforts were made to evacuate all foreign residents from the war zone. 3. make empty: evacuate the bowels. [< L, < ex- out + vacuus empty] —e·vac′u·a′tion, n. —e·vac′u·a′tor, n.

e·vac·u·ee (i·vak′yū·ē; i·vak′yū·ē′), n. one who is removed to a place of greater safety.

e·vade (i·vād′), v., e·vad·ed, e·vad·ing. 1. get away from by trickery; avoid by cleverness. 2. elude. [< L, < ex- away + vadere go] —e·vad′a·ble, e·vad′i·ble, adj. —e·vad′er, n. —e·vad′ing·ly, adv. —Syn. 2. avoid, escape, dodge.

e·val·u·ate (i·val′yū·āt), v., -at·ed, -at·ing. find the value or the amount of; fix the value of. —e·val′u·a′tion, n.

ev·a·nesce (ev′ə·nes′), v., -nesced, -nes·cing. disappear; fade away; vanish. [< L evanescere < ex- out + vanus insubstantial] —ev′a·nes′cence, n.

ev·a·nes·cent (ev′ə·nes′ənt), adj. tending to disappear or fade away; able to last only a short time. —ev′a·nes′cent·ly, adv. —Syn. fleeting.

e·van·gel (i·van′jəl), n. 1. good news of the saving of mankind through Christ. 2. good news. 3. evangelist. 4. Evangel, one of the four gospels; Matthew, Mark, Luke, or John. [< LL < Gk. euangelion good tidings, ult. < eu- good + angellein announce]

e·van·gel·i·cal (ē′van·jel′ə·kəl; ev′ən-), adj. Also, e′van·gel′ic. 1. of, concerning, or according to the four Gospels or the New Testament. 2. of or having to do with the Protestant churches that emphasize Christ's atonement and salvation by faith as the most important parts of Christianity, as the Methodists and Baptists. 3. evangelistic. —n. 1. an adherent of evangelical doctrines. 2. member of an evangelical church. —e′van·gel′i·cal·ism, n. —e′van·gel′i·cal·ly, adv.

e·van·ge·lism (i·van′jə·liz·əm), n. 1. a preaching of the Gospel; earnest effort for the spread of the Gospel. 2. work of an evangelist. 3. belief in the doctrines of an evangelical church or party.

e·van·ge·list (i·van′jə·list), n. 1. preacher of the Gospel. 2. a traveling preacher who stirs up religious feeling in revival services or camp meetings. 3. Evangelist, any of the writers of the four Gospels; Matthew, Mark, Luke, or John. —e·van′ge·lis′tic, e·van·ge·lis′ti·cal, adj. —e·van′ge·lis′ti·cal·ly, adv.

e·van·ge·lize (i·van′jə·līz), v., -lized, -liz·ing. 1. preach the Gospel to. 2. convert to Christianity by preaching. —e·van′ge·li·za′tion, n. —e·van′ge·liz′er, n.

Ev·ans (ev′ənz), n. Mary Ann, 1819–1880, English novelist whose pen name was George Eliot.

Ev·ans·ville (ev′ənz·vil), n. city in SW Indiana, on the Ohio River.

e·vap·o·rate (i·vap'ə·rāt), v., –rat·ed, –rating. 1. change from a liquid or solid into a vapor.
2. remove water or other liquid from: *heat is
used to evaporate milk.* 3. give off moisture. 4.
vanish; disappear. [< L, < *ex*– out + *vapor*
VAPOR] —e·vap'o·ra'tion, n. —e·vap'o·ra'tive,
adj. —e·vap'o·ra'tor, n.

evaporated milk, *Am.* a thick, unsweetened,
canned milk, prepared by evaporating some of
the water from ordinary milk.

e·va·sion (i·vā'zhən), n. 1. a getting away from
something by trickery; an avoiding by cleverness. 2. an attempt to escape an argument, a
charge, a question, etc. 3. means of evading;
trick or excuse used to avoid something.

e·va·sive (i·vā'siv; –ziv), *adj.* tending or trying
to evade. "Perhaps" is an evasive answer.
—e·va'sive·ly, *adv.* —e·va'sive·ness, n. —Syn.
shifty, misleading.

eve (ēv), n. 1. evening or day before a holiday
or some other special day: *Christmas Eve.* 2.
time just before. 3. *Poetic.* evening. [var. of
*even*²]

Eve (ēv), n. *Bible.* the first woman, Adam's wife.

e·ven¹ (ē'vən), *adj.* 1. level; flat; smooth. 2. at
the same level; in the same plane or line. 3. always the same; regular; uniform. 4. equal. 5.
leaving no remainder when divided by 2. 6.
neither more nor less; exact. 7. owing nothing.
8. not easily disturbed or angered; calm. 9. not
favoring one more than another; fair. —v. make
even; make level; make equal. —*adv.* 1. evenly.
2. just; exactly. 3. indeed. 4. fully; quite: *he was
faithful even unto death.* 5. though one would
not expect it; as one would not expect: *even the
least noise disturbs her.* 6. still; yet. 7. break
even, have equal gains and losses. 8. get even,
a. owe nothing. b. *Am.* have revenge. [OE *efen*]
—e'ven·er, n. —e'ven·ly, *adv.* —e'ven·ness, n.
—Syn. *adj.* 1. plane. 8. equable, unruffled.

e·ven² (ē'vən), n. *Poetic.* evening. [OE *ǣfen*]

e·ven-hand·ed (ē'vən·han'did), *adj.* impartial; fair; just.

eve·ning (ēv'ning), n. 1. the last part of day
and early part of night; time between sunset
and bedtime. 2. *Southern U.S.* afternoon. 3. the
last part: *old age is the evening of life.* —*adj.*
in the evening; of the evening; for the evening.
[OE *ǣfnung* < *ǣfnian* become evening < *ǣfen*
evening]

evening dress, formal clothes for evening.

evening primrose, a tall plant with spikes
of fragrant yellow or white flowers that open in
the evening.

evening star, a bright planet seen in the
western sky after sunset.

e·ven·song (ē'vən·sông'; –song'), n. a church
service said or sung in the late afternoon or
early evening; vespers.

e·vent (i·vent'), n. 1. a happening. 2. result;
outcome. 3. item or contest in a program of
sports. [< L, < *ex*– out + *venire* come] —Syn. 1.
occurrence, episode, affair. 2. consequence.

e·ven-tem·pered (ē'vən·tem'pərd), *adj.* not
easily disturbed or angered; calm.

e·vent·ful (i·vent'fəl), *adj.* 1. full of events;
having many unusual events. 2. having important results; important. —e·vent'ful·ly, *adv.*
—e·vent'ful·ness, n.

e·ven·tide (ē'vən·tīd'), n. *Poetic.* evening.

e·ven·tu·al (i·ven'chü·əl), *adj.* 1. coming in
the end; final. 2. depending on uncertain events;
possible. —e·ven'tu·al·ly, *adv.*

e·ven·tu·al·i·ty (i·ven'chü·al'ə·ti), n., pl.
–ties. a possible occurrence or condition; possibility.

e·ven·tu·ate (i·ven'chü·āt), v., –at·ed, –at-
ing. come out in the end; happen finally; result.

ev·er (ev'ər), *adv.* 1. at any time: *was there
ever a man with such bad luck.* 2. at all times:
ever at your service. 3. continuously: *ever since.*
4. at all; by any chance; in any case. [OE *ǣfre*]
—Syn. 2. always, forever. 3. constantly.

Ev·er·est (ev'ər·ist), n. Mount, peak in the
Himalayas in S Tibet, the highest in the world.

ev·er·glade (ev'ər·glād'), n. *Am.* 1. a large

tract of low, wet ground partly covered with tall
grass; large swamp or marsh. 2. Everglades, a
swampy region in S Florida.

ev·er·green (ev'ər·grēn'), *adj.* having green
leaves all the year. —n. 1. an evergreen plant, as
pine, spruce, cedar, ivy, etc. 2. evergreens, evergreen twigs or branches used for decoration, esp.
at Christmas.

ev·er·last·ing (ev'ər·las'ting; –läs'–), *adj.* 1.
lasting forever; never ending or stopping. 2.
lasting a long time. 3. lasting too long; repeated
too often; tiresome. —n. 1. eternity. 2. flower
that keeps its shape and color when dried. 3.
the Everlasting, God. —ev'er·last'ing·ly, *adv.*
—ev'er·last'ing·ness, n.

ev·er·more (ev'ər·môr'; –mōr'), *adv.*, n. always; forever.

e·ver·sion (i·vér'zhən; –shən), n. a turning of
an organ, structure, etc., inside out. —ev·er·si·ble (i·vér'sə·bəl),
turned inside out. *adj.*

e·vert (i·vért'), v. turn inside out. [< L, < *ex*–
out + *vertere* turn]

ev·er·y (ev'ri), *adj.* 1. all, regarded singly or
separately; each and all. 2. all possible: *we
showed him every consideration.* 3. every other,
each first, third, fifth, etc., or second, fourth,
sixth, etc. [< OE *ǣfre* ever + *ǣlc* each]

ev·er·y·bod·y (ev'ri·bod'i), *pron.* every person;
everyone: *everybody likes the new minister.*

ev·er·y·day (ev'ri·dā'), *adj.* 1. of every day;
daily. 2. for every ordinary day; not for Sundays
or holidays. 3. not exciting; usual.

ev·er·y·one (ev'ri·wun; –wən), **every one,**
pron. every person; everybody: *everyone took
his purchases home.*

ev·er·y·thing (ev'ri·thing), *pron.* every thing;
all things. —n. something extremely important;
very important thing.

ev·er·y·where (ev'ri·hwâr), *adv.* in every
place; in all places.

e·vict (i·vikt'), v. expel by a legal process from
land, a building, etc.; eject (a tenant). [< L
evictus < *ex*– out + *vincere* conquer] —e·vic'-
tion, n. —e·vic'tor, n.

ev·i·dence (ev'ə·dəns), n., v., –denced, –denc-
ing. —n. 1. whatever makes clear the truth or
falsehood of something. 2. *Law.* facts established
and accepted in a court of law. 3. person who
gives testimony in a court of law; witness:
state's evidence. 4. indication; sign. 5. in evidence, easily seen or noticed. —v. make easy to
see or understand; show clearly; prove. [< L,
< *ex*– out + *videns*, ppr. of *videre* to see] —Syn.
n. 1. proof. 2. testimony.

ev·i·dent (ev'ə·dənt), *adj.* easy to see or understand; clear; plain. —ev·i·den·tial (ev'ə·den'-
shəl), *adj.* —ev·i·dent·ly (ev'ə·dənt·li; –dent'–),
adv. —Syn. obvious, manifest, apparent.

e·vil (ē'vəl), *adj.* 1. bad; wrong; sinful; wicked.
2. causing harm or injury. 3. unfortunate. 4. due
to bad character or conduct: *an evil reputation.*
—n. 1. something bad; sin; wickedness. 2. thing
that causes harm or injury. —*adv.* badly. [OE
yfel] —e'vil·ly, *adv.* —e'vil·ness, n. —Syn. *adj.*
1. depraved, vicious, corrupt. 2. harmful, pernicious.

e·vil·do·er (ē'vəl·dü'ər), n. person who does
evil. —e'vil·do'ing, n.

evil eye, the supposed power of causing harm
or bringing bad luck to others by looking at
them.

e·vil-mind·ed (ē'vəl·mīn'did), *adj.* having an
evil mind; wicked; malicious.

e·vince (i·vins'), v., e·vinced, e·vinc·ing. 1.
show clearly; reveal. 2. show that one has (a
quality, trait, etc.). [< L, < *ex*– out + *vincere*
conquer] —e·vin'ci·ble, e·vin'cive, *adj.*

e·vis·cer·ate (i·vis'ər·āt), v., –at·ed, –at·ing.
1. remove the bowels from; disembowel. 2. deprive of something essential. [< L, < *ex*– out +
viscera VISCERA] —e·vis'cer·a'tion, n.

e·voke (i·vōk'), v., e·voked, e·vok·ing. call
forth; bring out. [< L, < *ex*– out + *vocare* call]
—ev·o·ca·tion (ev'ō·kā'shən), n. —e·vok'er, n.

ev·o·lu·tion (ev'ə·lü'shən), n. 1. any process

of formation or growth; gradual development: *the evolution of the modern steamship from the first boat.* 2. something evolved; product of development; not a sudden discovery or creation. 3. *Biol.* theory that all living things developed from a few simple forms of life. 4. movement of ships or soldiers, planned beforehand. 5. movement that is a part of a definite plan, design, or series. 6. a releasing; giving off; setting free: *the evolution of heat from burning coal.* —e·vo·lu·tion·ar·y (ev′ə·lū′shən·er′i), ev′o·lu′tion·al, *adj.* —ev′o·lu′tion·al·ly, *adv.*

e·vo·lu·tion·ist (ev′ə·lū′shən·ist), *n.* student of, or believer in, the theory of evolution.

e·volve (i·volv′), *v.*, e·volved, e·volv·ing. 1. develop gradually; work out. 2. *Biol.* develop by a process of growth and change to a more highly organized condition. 3. release; give off; set free. [< L, < *ex-* out + *volvere* roll] —e·volv′er, *n.*

ewe (ū), *n.* a female sheep. [OE *ēowu*]

ew·er (ū′ər), *n.* a wide-mouthed water pitcher. [< AF < L *aquaria* < L *aquarius* for drawing water < *aqua* water]

Ewer and basin

ex (eks), *prep.* 1. out of. "Ex elevator" means free of charges until the time of removal out of the elevator. 2. without; not including. Ex-dividend stocks are stocks on which the purchaser will not receive the next dividend to be paid. [< L]

ex-, *prefix.* 1. out of; from; out, as in *exclude, exit, export.* 2. utterly; thoroughly, as in *excruciating, exasperate.* 3. former; formerly, as in *ex-member, ex-president, ex-soldier.* [< L *ex-* out of, without; also, *e-* (before *b, d, g, h, l, m, n, r, v*), and *ef-* (before *f*)]

Ex., Exodus.

ex., 1. example. 2. except.

ex·act (ig·zakt′), *adj.* 1. without any error or mistake; strictly correct. 2. strict; severe; rigorous. 3. characterized by or using strict accuracy. —*v.* 1. demand and get; force to be paid. 2. call for; need; require. [< L *exactus,* pp. of *exigere* weigh accurately < *ex-* out + *agere* weigh] —ex·act′a·ble, *adj.* —ex·act′er, ex·ac′tor, *n.* —ex·act′ness, *n.* —Syn. *adj.* 1. accurate, precise.

ex·act·ing (ig·zak′ting), *adj.* 1. requiring much; making severe demands; hard to please. 2. requiring effort, care, or attention. —ex·act′ing·ly, *adv.* —ex·act′ing·ness, *n.*

ex·ac·tion (ig·zak′shən), *n.* 1. an exacting. 2. thing exacted, as taxes, fees, etc.

ex·act·i·tude (ig·zak′tə·tūd; -tūd), *n.* exactness.

ex·act·ly (ig·zakt′li), *adv.* 1. in an exact manner; accurately; precisely. 2. just so; quite right.

ex·ag·ger·ate (ig·zaj′ər·āt), *v.*, -at·ed, -at·ing. 1. make (something) greater than it is; overstate: *exaggerate a misfortune.* 2. increase or enlarge abnormally. 3. say or think something is greater than it is. [< L, < *ex-* out, up + *agger* heap] —ex·ag′ger·at′ed, *adj.* —ex·ag′ger·a′tion, *n.* —ex·ag′ger·a′tor, *n.* —Syn. 1. stretch, magnify.

ex·alt (ig·zôlt′), *v.* 1. raise in rank, honor, power, character, quality, etc. 2. fill with pride, joy, or noble feeling. 3. praise; honor; glorify. 4. intensify; heighten. [< L, < *ex-* out, up + *altus* high] —ex·alt′ed·ly, *adv.* —ex·alt′er, *n.* —Syn. 1. elevate, promote, ennoble.

ex·al·ta·tion (eg′zôl·tā′shən), *n.* 1. an exalting. 2. a being exalted. 3. lofty emotion; rapture.

ex·am (ig·zam′), *n. Colloq.* examination.

ex·am·i·na·tion (ig·zam′ə·nā′shən), *n.* 1. an examining or being examined. 2. test of knowledge or qualifications; list of questions. 3. answers given in such a test. 4. *Law.* a formal interrogation.

ex·am·ine (ig·zam′ən), *v.*, -ined, -in·ing. 1. look at closely and carefully. 2. test the knowledge or qualifications of; ask questions of. [< F < L *examinare* < *examen* a weighing. See EXACT.] —ex·am′in·a·ble, *adj.* —ex·am′in·er, *n.* —Syn. 1. scrutinize, investigate. 2. interrogate.

ex·am·i·nee (ig·zam′ə·nē′), *n.* person who is being examined.

ex·am·ple (ig·zam′pəl; -zäm′-), *n., v.,* -pled, -pling. —*n.* 1. one taken to show what others are like; case that shows something; sample. 2. a parallel case; precedent. 3. person or thing to be imitated; model; pattern. 4. problem in arithmetic, etc. 5. warning to others: *the captain made an example of the soldiers who shirked by making them clean up the camp.* —*v.* 1. be an example of; exemplify. 2. set an example to. [< OF < L *exemplum.* See EXEMPT.] —Syn. *n.* 1. specimen. 3. paragon, ideal.

ex·as·per·ate (ig·zas′pər·āt; -zäs′-), *v.*, -at·ed, -at·ing. 1. irritate very much; annoy extremely; make angry. 2. increase the intensity or violence of. [< L, < *ex-* thoroughly + *asper* rough] —ex·as′per·at′er, *n.* —ex·as′per·at′ing·ly, *adv.* —Syn. 1. incense, anger, nettle, vex, provoke.

ex·as·per·a·tion (ig·zas′pər·ā′shən; -zäs′-), *n.* extreme annoyance; irritation; anger.

Exc., Excellency.

Ex·cal·i·bur (eks·kal′ə·bər), *n.* the magic sword of King Arthur.

ex ca·the·dra (eks kə·thē′drə; kath′ə-), *Latin.* with authority; from the seat of authority.

ex·ca·vate (eks′kə·vāt), *v.*, -vat·ed, -vat·ing. 1. make hollow; hollow out. 2. make by digging; dig. 3. dig out; scoop out. 4. get or uncover by digging. [< L, < *ex-* out + *cavus* hollow] —ex′ca·va′tion, *n.* —ex′ca·va′tor, *n.*

ex·ceed (ik·sēd′), *v.* 1. go beyond; overstep. 2. be more or greater than others; surpass. [< F < L, < *ex-* out + *cedere* go] —ex·ceed′er, *n.* —Syn. 1. transcend. 2. excel.

ex·ceed·ing (ik·sēd′ing), *adj.* surpassing; very great; unusual; extreme.

ex·cel (ik·sel′), *v.*, -celled, -cel·ling. 1. be better than; do better than. 2. be better than others; do better than others. [< F < L *excellere*] —Syn. 1. surpass, outstrip, eclipse.

ex·cel·lence (ek′sə·ləns), *n.* 1. a being better than others; superiority. 2. an excellent quality or feature. —Syn. 1. preëminence, transcendence. 2. merit, worth, virtue.

ex·cel·len·cy (ek′sə·lən·si), *n., pl.* -cies. 1. excellence. 2. Excellency, title of honor used in speaking to or of a president, governor, ambassador, bishop, etc.

ex·cel·lent (ek′sə·lənt), *adj.* unusually good; better than others. —ex′cel·lent·ly, *adv.* —Syn. superior, meritorious, worthy, estimable, choice.

ex·cel·si·or (*adj.* ik·sel′si·ôr; *n.* ik·sel′si·ər), *Am., adj.* ever upward; higher. —*n.* short, thin, curled shavings of soft wood. [< L, comparative of *excelsus* high, pp. of *excellere* excel]

ex·cept (ik·sept′), *prep.* Also, ex·cept′ing. leaving out; other than. —*v.* 1. take out; leave out; exclude: *present company excepted.* 2. make objection. —*conj. Archaic.* unless. [< L *exceptus* < *ex-* out + *capere* take] ► except, accept. *Except,* as a verb, means to "leave out, exclude": *He excepted those who had done the assignment from the extra reading.* It is decidedly formal, and *excused* or even *exempted* would be more natural in the sentence given. *Accept* means to *get* or *receive* and is slightly formal: *I accept with pleasure. He accepted the position.* Confusing the two words in writing, practically always due to carelessness rather than to ignorance, comes from the fact that we see and write the preposition *except* (*everyone except you*) so much oftener than we do either of the verbs.

ex·cep·tion (ik·sep′shən), *n.* 1. a leaving out. 2. person or thing left out. 3. an unusual instance; case that does not follow the rule. 4. objection. ► exception. "And this was no exception" is a colorless and often wordy way of combining a particular and a general statement: *Most young actors experience numerous difficulties in their early appearances. I was no exception.* Better: *Like most young actors, I experienced. . . .*

ex·cep·tion·a·ble (ik·sep′shən·ə·bəl), *adj.* objectionable. —ex·cep′tion·a·bly, *adv.*

ex·cep·tion·al (ik·sep′shən·əl), *adj.* out of the ordinary; unusual. —ex·cep′tion·al·ly, *adv.* —Syn. uncommon, singular, extraordinary.

ex·cerpt (*n.* ek′sėrpt; *v.* ik·sėrpt′), *n.* a selected passage; quotation. —v. take out; select (a passage) from; quote. [< L *excerptum* < *ex*- out + *carpere* pluck]

ex·cess (n. ik·ses′; adj. ek′ses, ik·ses′), n. **1.** more than enough; part that is too much. **2.** amount or degree by which one thing is more than another. **3.** action that goes beyond what is necessary or just. **4.** eating or drinking too much; overindulgence; intemperance. —adj. extra: *excess baggage*. [< L *excessus* < *ex*- out + *cedere* go; akin to EXCEED] —Syn. n. **1.** surplus, superfluity. **4.** dissipation, immoderation. —Ant. n. **1.** dearth, deficiency, lack.

ex·ces·sive (ik·ses′iv), adj. too much; too great; going beyond what is necessary or right. —ex·ces′sive·ly, adv. —ex·ces′sive·ness, n. —Syn. superfluous, immoderate, inordinate, extreme.

ex·change (iks·chānj′), v., -changed, -changing, n. —v. **1.** give (for something else). **2.** give and take (one thing in return for another); change for another. **3.** be taken in a trade. —n. **1.** an exchanging. **2.** what is exchanged. **3.** place where things are exchanged. Stocks are bought, sold, and traded in a stock exchange. **4.** a central office. A telephone exchange handles telephone calls. **5.** system of settling accounts in different places by exchanging bills of exchange that represent money instead of exchanging money itself. **6.** changing the money of one country into the money of another. **7.** fee charged for settling accounts or changing money. **8.** rate of exchange; varying rate or sum in one currency given for a fixed sum in another currency. [< OF < VL, < *ex*- out + *cambiare* change < Celtic] —ex·change′a·ble, adj. —ex·change′a·bil′i·ty, n. —ex·chang′er, n. —Syn. v. **2.** interchange, trade.

exchange reaction, *Nuclear Physics.* ejection of a subatomic particle by a nucleus when penetrated by another such particle.

ex·cheq·uer (iks·chek′ər; eks′chek·ər), n. **1.** treasury of a state or nation. **2.** treasury. **3.** *Colloq.* finances; funds. **4.** Exchequer, department of the British government in charge of its finances and the public revenues. [< OF *eschequier* chessboard; because accounts were kept on a table marked in squares]

ex·cise¹ (ek′sīz; -sīs; ik·sīz′), n. tax on the manufacture, sale, or use of certain articles made, sold, or used within a country. [appar. < MDu. < OF *acceis* tax, ult. < L *ad*- to + *census* tax]

ex·cise² (ik·sīz′), v., -cised, -cis·ing. cut out; remove. [< L *excisus* < *ex*- out + *caedere* cut] —ex·cis′a·ble, adj. —ex·ci·sion (ik·sizh′ən), n.

ex·cit·a·ble (ik·sīt′ə·bəl), adj. capable of being excited; easily excited. —ex·cit′a·bil′i·ty, ex·cit′a·ble·ness, n. —ex·cit′a·bly, adv. —Syn. emotional. —Ant. impassive, imperturbable.

ex·ci·ta·tion (ek′sī·tā′shən), n. **1.** an exciting. **2.** a being excited.

ex·cite (ik·sīt′), v., -cit·ed, -cit·ing. **1.** stir up the feelings of. **2.** arouse. **3.** stir to action; stimulate. [< L *excitare*, ult. < *ex*- out + *ciere* set in motion] —ex·cit′ed, adj. —ex·cit′ed·ly, adv. —ex·cit′er, n. —Syn. **1.** rouse, animate, kindle.

excited atom, *Nuclear Physics.* atom having a higher energy level than is normal.

ex·cite·ment (ik·sīt′mənt), n. **1.** an exciting; arousing. **2.** state of being excited. **3.** thing that excites. —Syn. **2.** agitation, perturbation, commotion, ado, tumult.

ex·cit·ing (ik·sīt′ing), adj. arousing; stirring. —ex·cit′ing·ly, adv.

ex·claim (iks·klām′), v. say or speak suddenly in surprise or strong feeling; cry out. [< F < L, < *ex*- + *clamare* cry out] —ex·claim′er, n. —Syn. shout, ejaculate.

ex·cla·ma·tion (eks′klə·mā′shən), n. **1.** an exclaiming. **2.** thing exclaimed. *Ah!* and *oh!* are exclamations. —ex·clam·a·to·ry (iks·klam′ə·tô′rĭ; -tō′-), adj. ➤ **exclamation mark** (!). An *exclamation mark* (or *point*) is used after an emphatic interjection and after a phrase, clause, or sentence that is genuinely exclamatory. Clear-cut exclamations offer no problem: *Oh! Ouch!*

No, no, no! But many interjections are weak and deserve no more than a comma: *Well, well, so you're in college now.*

ex·clude (iks·klüd′), v., -clud·ed, -clud·ing. **1.** shut out; keep out. **2.** drive out and keep out; expel. [< L *excludere* < *ex*- out + *claudere* shut] —ex·clud′a·ble, adj. —ex·clud′er, n. —ex·clusion (iks·klü′zhən), n. —Syn. **1.** eliminate, reject. **2.** eject, exile.

ex·clu·sive (iks·klü′siv; -ziv), adj. **1.** shutting out all others. **2.** shutting out all or most: *an exclusive school.* **3.** each shutting out the other: *exclusive terms.* **4.** not divided or shared with others; single; sole: *an exclusive right.* **5.** very particular about choosing friends, members, patrons, etc.: *an exclusive club.* —ex·clu′sive·ly, adv. —ex·clu′sive·ness, n. —Syn. **4.** undivided. **5.** select, clannish, snobbish.

ex·com·mu·ni·cate (eks′kə·mū′nə·kāt), v., -cat·ed, -cat·ing. cut off from membership in a church; expel formally from the fellowship of a church; prohibit from participating in any of the rites of a church. —ex′com·mu′ni·ca′tion, n. —ex′com·mu′ni·ca′tor, n.

ex·co·ri·ate (iks·kô′ri·āt; -kō′-), v., -at·ed, -at·ing. **1.** strip or rub off the skin of; make raw and sore. **2.** denounce violently. [< LL, < *ex*- off + *corium* hide, skin] —ex·co′ri·a′tion, n.

ex·cre·ment (eks′krə·mənt), n. waste matter discharged from the bowels. [< L *excrementum*, ult. < *ex*- out + *cernere* sift] —ex′cre·men′tal, adj.

ex·cres·cence (iks·kres′əns), **ex·cres·cen·cy** (-ən·si), n., pl. -cen·ces; -cies. **1.** an unnatural growth; disfiguring addition, as a wart. **2.** a natural outgrowth, as a fingernail. [< L, < *ex*- out + *crescere* grow] —ex·cres′cent, adj.

ex·cre·ta (iks·krē′tə), n.pl. waste matter discharged from the body. —ex·cre′tal, adj.

ex·crete (iks·krēt′), v., -cret·ed, -cret·ing. discharge (waste matter) from the body; separate (waste matter) from the blood or tissues. [< L *excretus*, pp. See EXCREMENT.] —ex·cre′tion, n. —ex·cre′tive, ex·cre·to·ry (eks′krə·tô′ri; -tō′-), adj.

ex·cru·ci·ate (iks·krü′shi·āt), v., -at·ed, -ating. crucify; torture. [< L *excruciatus* < *ex*- utterly + *cruciare* to torture < *crux* cross] —ex·cru′ci·at′ing, adj. —ex·cru′ci·at′ing·ly, adv.

ex·cul·pate (eks′kul·pāt; iks·kul′-), v., -pated, -pat·ing. free from blame; prove innocent. [< L *ex*- out + *culpa* guilt] —ex′cul·pa′tion, n.

ex·cur·sion (iks·kér′zhən; -shən), n. **1.** a short journey made with the intention of returning; pleasure trip. **2.** trip on a train, ship, etc., at lower fares than are usually charged. **3.** group of people who go on an excursion. **4.** sally; raid. **5.** a wandering from the subject; deviation; digression. [< L *excursio* < *ex*- out + *currere* run] —ex·cur′sion·ist, n. —Syn. **1.** expedition, tour, jaunt.

ex·cur·sive (iks·kér′siv), adj. off the subject; wandering; rambling. —ex·cur′sive·ly, adv. —ex·cur′sive·ness, n.

ex·cuse (v. iks·kūz′; n. iks·kūs′), v., -cused, -cus·ing, n. —v. **1.** overlook (a fault, etc.); pardon; forgive. **2.** give a reason or apology for; try to clear of blame. **3.** be a reason or explanation for; clear of blame. **4.** free from duty or obligation; let off. **5.** seek exemption or release for. —n. **1.** a real or pretended reason or explanation. **2.** apology. **3.** act of excusing. [< OF < L *excusare* < *ex*- away + *causa* cause] —ex·cus′a·ble, adj. —ex·cus′a·bly, adv. —ex·cus′er, n. —Syn. v. **1.** condone, absolve, exculpate. **3.** justify, extenuate. —n. **1.** justification. ➤ **excuse, pardon.** Small slips are *excused*, more considerable faults (and crimes) are *pardoned*. "Pardon me" is sometimes incorrectly considered more elegant than "Excuse me" in upper-class social situations. *Excuse* has also the special meaning of "give permission to leave."

exec., executive; executor.

ex·e·cra·ble (ek′sə·krə·bəl), adj. abominable; detestable. —ex′e·cra·bly, adv.

ex·e·crate (ek′sə·krāt), v., -crat·ed, -crat·ing. **1.** abhor; loathe; detest. **2.** curse. [< L *execratus*, ult. < *ex-* completely + *sacer* accursed] —ex'e-cra'tion, *n.* —ex'e-cra'tive, *adj.* —ex'e-cra'tor, *n.*

ex·e·cute (ek'sə·kūt), *v.,* -cut·ed, -cut·ing. 1. carry out; do. 2. put into effect; enforce. 3. put to death according to law. 4. make according to a plan or design. 5. *Law.* make (a deed, contract, etc.) legal by signing, sealing, or doing whatever is necessary. [< Med.L *executare,* ult. < L *ex-* out + *sequi* follow] —ex'e·cut'a·ble, *adj.* —ex'e·cut'er, *n.* —**Syn.** 1. perform, accomplish, fulfill, complete. 3. kill, hang, electrocute.

ex·e·cu·tion (ek'sə·kū'shən), *n.* 1. an executing. 2. a being executed. 3. mode or style of performance. 4. infliction of capital punishment. 5. effective action.

ex·e·cu·tion·er (ek'sə·kū'shən·ər), *n.* person who puts criminals to death according to law.

ex·ec·u·tive (ig·zek'yə·tiv), *adj.* 1. having to do with carrying out or managing affairs. 2. having the duty and power of putting the laws into effect. —*n.* 1. person who carries out or manages affairs. 2. person, group, or branch of government that has the duty and power of putting the laws into effect. 3. Usually, **Executive.** *Am.* the President of the United States. —ex·ec'u·tive·ly, *adv.*

Executive Mansion, *Am.* 1. the official residence of the President of the United States; the White House in Washington, D.C. 2. the official residence of the governor of a State.

ex·ec·u·tor (ig·zek'yə·tər *for 1*; ek'sə·kū'tər *for 2*), *n.* 1. *Law.* person named in a will to carry out the provisions of the will. 2. person who executes plans, laws, etc. —ex·ec·u·to·ri·al (ig·zek'-yə·tô'ri·əl; -tō'-), *adj.*

ex·ec·u·trix (ig·zek'yə·triks), *n., pl.* **ex·ec·u·tri·ces** (ig·zek'yə·trī'sēz), **ex·ec·u·trix·es.** a woman executor.

ex·e·ge·sis (ek'sə·jē'sis), *n., pl.* -ses (-sēz). 1. a scholarly explanation or interpretation of the Bible. 2. an explanatory note. [< Gk., < *ex-* out + *hegeesthai* lead, guide] —ex·e·get·ic (ek'sə·jet'ik), ex'e·get'i·cal, *adj.* —ex'e·get'i·cal·ly, *adv.*

ex·em·plar (ig·zem'plər; -plär), *n.* 1. model; pattern. 2. a typical case; example.

ex·em·pla·ry (ig·zem'plə·ri; eg'zəm·pler'i), *adj.* 1. worth imitating; being a good model or pattern: *exemplary conduct.* 2. serving as a warning to others: *exemplary punishment.* 3. serving as an example; typical. [< L *exemplaris.* See EXAMPLE.] —ex·em'pla·ri·ly, *adv.* —ex·em'pla·ri·ness, *n.*

ex·em·pli·fy (ig·zem'plə·fī), *v.,* -fied, -fy·ing. 1. show by example; be an example of. 2. make an attested copy of under seal. —ex·em'pli·fi·ca'tion, *n.*

ex·em·pli gra·ti·a (ig·zem'plī grā'shi·ə), *Latin.* for example; for instance.

ex·empt (ig·zempt'), *v.* free from a duty, obligation, rule, etc., to which others are subject; release. —*adj.* freed from a duty, obligation, rule, etc.; released. —*n.* an exempt person. [< L *exemptus* < *ex-* out + *emere* take] —ex·empt'i·ble, *adj.* —ex·emp'tion, *n.*

ex·er·cise (ek'sər·sīz), *n., v.,* -cised, -cis·ing. —*n.* 1. active use to give practice and training or to cause improvement. 2. thing that gives practice and training or causes improvement. 3. active use. 4. Often, **exercises.** *Am.* ceremony. —*v.* 1. give exercise to; train. 2. take exercise. 3. use actively. 4. carry out in action; perform. 5. have as an effect. 6. occupy the attention of. 7. make uneasy; worry; trouble; annoy. [< OF < L *exercitium* < *exercere* not allow to rest < *ex-* + *arcere* keep away] —ex'er·cis'a·ble, *adj.* —ex'er·cis'er, *n.* —**Syn.** *n.* 1. discipline, drilling, drill. 3. employment, application. —*v.* 1. discipline, drill. 3. employ, apply.

ex·ert (ig·zért'), *v.* use actively; put into action. [< L, thrust out, < *ex-* out + *serere* attach] —ex·er'tive, *n.*

ex·er·tion (ig·zér'shən), *n.* 1. effort. 2. a putting into action; active use; use. —**Syn.** 1. endeavor, struggle, attempt.

Ex·e·ter (ek'sə·tər), *n.* city in SW England.

ex·e·unt (ek'si·ənt), *v. Latin.* they go out (stage direction for actors to leave the stage).

ex·hale (eks·hāl'), *v.,* -haled, -hal·ing. 1. breathe out. 2. give off (air, vapor, smoke, odor, etc.). 3. pass off as vapor; rise like vapor. 4. change into vapor. [< F < L, < *ex-* out + *halare* breathe] —ex·ha·la·tion (eks'hə·lā'shən), *n.*

ex·haust (ig·zôst'), *v.* 1. empty completely. 2. use up. 3. tire very much. 4. drain of strength, resources, etc. 5. draw off: *exhaust the air in a jar.* 6. create a vacuum in. 7. leave nothing important to be found out or said about; study or treat thoroughly. 8. be discharged; go forth. —*n.* 1. the escape of used steam, gasoline, etc., from a machine. 2. means or way for used steam, gasoline, etc., to escape from an engine. 3. the used steam, gasoline, etc., that escapes. [< L *exhaustus* < *ex-* out, off + *haurire* draw] —ex·haust'er, *n.* —ex·haust'i·ble, *adj.* —ex·haust'i·bil'i·ty, *n.* —**Syn.** *v.* 1. drain, deplete. 2. consume. 3. fatigue, enervate.

ex·haus·tion (ig·zôs'chən), *n.* 1. an exhausting. 2. a being exhausted. 3. extreme fatigue. —**Syn.** 3. weariness, lassitude, languor.

ex·haus·tive (ig·zôs'tiv), *adj.* leaving out nothing important; thorough; comprehensive. —ex·haus'tive·ly, *adv.* —ex·haus'tive·ness, *n.*

ex·hib·it (ig·zib'it), *v.* 1. show; display. 2. show publicly. 3. *Law.* show in court as evidence; submit for consideration or inspection. —*n.* 1. show; display. 2. thing or things shown publicly. 3. a public show. 4. *Law.* thing shown in court as evidence. [< L *exhibitus* < *ex-* out + *habere* hold] —ex·hib'i·tor, ex·hib'it·er, *n.* —**Syn.** *v.* 1. manifest, evince, reveal, disclose.

ex·hi·bi·tion (ek'sə·bish'ən), *n.* 1. a showing; display: *an exhibition of bad manners.* 2. a public show. 3. thing or things shown publicly; exhibit. —**Syn.** 2. exposition.

ex·hi·bi·tion·ism (ek'sə·bish'ən·iz·əm), *n.* 1. an excessive tendency to show off one's abilities. 2. tendency to show what should not be shown. —ex·hi·bi'tion·ist, *n.*

ex·hil·a·rate (ig·zil'ə·rāt), *v.,* -rat·ed, -rat·ing. make merry or lively; put into high spirits; stimulate. [< L, < *ex-* thoroughly + *hilaris* merry] —ex·hil'a·rat'ing, *adj.* —ex·hil'a·rat'ing·ly, *adv.* —ex·hil'a·ra'tion, *n.*

ex·hort (ig·zôrt'), *v.* urge strongly; advise or warn earnestly. [< L, < *ex-* + *hortari* urge strongly] —ex·hor·ta·tion (eg'zôr·tā'shən; ek'-sôr-), *n.* —ex·hor'ta·tive, ex·hor·ta·to·ry (ig-zôr'tə·tô'ri; -tō'-), *adj.* —ex·hort'er, *n.*

ex·hume (eks·hūm'; ig·zūm'), *v.,* -humed, -hum·ing. 1. take out of a grave or the ground; dig up. 2. reveal. [< Med.L, < L *ex-* out of + *humus* ground] —ex·hu·ma·tion (eks'hyū·mā'-shən), *n.*

ex·i·gen·cy (ek'sə·jən·si), **ex·i·gence** (-jəns), *n., pl.* -cies; -gen·ces. 1. Usually, **exigencies.** an urgent need; demand for immediate action or attention. 2. situation demanding immediate action or attention; emergency.

ex·i·gent (ek'sə·jənt), *adj.* 1. demanding immediate action or attention; urgent. 2. demanding a great deal; exacting. [< L *exigens,* ppr. of *exigere* EXACT]

ex·ig·u·ous (ig·zig'yū·əs; ik·sig'-), *adj.* scanty; small. —ex·i·gu·i·ty (ek'sə·gū'ə·ti), *n.*

ex·ile (eg'zīl; ek'sīl), *v.,* -iled, -il·ing, *n.* —*v.* force (a person) to leave his country or home; banish. —*n.* 1. a being exiled; banishment. 2. an exiled person. 3. any prolonged absence from one's own country. [< OF < L *exilium*] —ex·il·ic (eg·zil'ik; ek·sil'-), *adj.* —**Syn.** *v.* expel, expatriate. *n.* 1. expulsion, expatriation.

ex·ist (ig·zist'), *v.* 1. have actual existence; be; be real. 2. continue to be; live; have life. 3. be present; occur. [< F < L, < *ex-* forth + *sistere* stand] —ex·ist'ent, *adj.*

ex·ist·ence (ig·zis'təns), *n.* 1. real or actual being; being. 2. continued being; living; life. 3. occurrence; presence. 4. all that exists. 5. thing that exists.

ex·is·ten·tial·ism (eg'zis·ten'shəl·iz·əm; ek'-sis-), *n.* philosophy stressing the need for personal decision in a world lacking purpose. —ex'is·ten'tial·ist, *n.*

ex·it (eg'zit; ek'sit), *n.* 1. way out. 2. a going out; departure. 3. act of leaving the stage. —*v.* goes out; departs; leaves (stage direction for an actor to leave the stage). [< L, goes out; also < L *exitus* a going out < *ex-* out + *ire* go]

ex li·bris (eks lī′bris; lē′-), *Latin.* from the library (of).

ex·o·bi·ol·o·gy (ek′sō·bī·ol′ə·ji), *n.* study of life on other planets or celestial bodies. —**ex′·o·bi·ol′o·gist,** *n.*

Exod., Exodus.

ex·o·dus (ek′sə·dəs), *n.* 1. a going out; departure. 2. Often, Exodus. departure of the Israelites from Egypt. 3. Exodus, second book of the Old Testament. [< L < Gk., < *ex-* out + *hodos* way]

ex of·fi·ci·o (eks ə·fish′i·ō), because of one's office. [< L] —ex′-of·fi′ci·o, *adj.*

ex·og·e·nous (eks·oj′ə·nəs), *adj.* 1. *Bot.* having stems that grow by the addition of layers of wood on the outside under the bark. 2. originating from the outside. [< NL *exogenus* growing on the outside < Gk. *exo-* outside + *gen-* bear, produce] —ex·og′e·nous·ly, *adv.*

ex·on·er·ate (ig·zon′ər·āt), *v.,* -at·ed, -at·ing. free from blame. [< L, < *ex-* off + *onus* burden] —ex·on′er·a′tion, *n.* —ex·on′er·a′tive, *adj.*

ex·or·bi·tant (ig·zôr′bə·tənt), *adj.* exceeding what is customary, proper, or reasonable; very excessive. [< L, < *ex-* out of + *orbita* track. See ORBIT.] —ex·or′bi·tance, ex·or′bi·tan·cy, *n.* —ex·or′bi·tant·ly, *adv.*

ex·or·cise, ex·or·cize (ek′sôr·sīz), *v.,* -cised, -cis·ing; -cized, -ciz·ing. 1. drive out (an evil spirit) by prayers, ceremonies, etc. 2. free (a person or place) from an evil spirit. [< LL < Gk. *exorkizein* bind by oath < *ex-* + *horkos* oath] —ex′or·cis·er, ex′or·ciz′er, *n.*

ex·or·cism (ek′sôr·siz·əm), *n.* 1. an exorcising. 2. prayers, ceremonies, etc., used in exorcising. —ex′or·cist, *n.*

ex·or·di·um (ig·zôr′di·əm; ik·sôr′-), *n., pl.* -di·ums, -di·a (-di·ə). 1. the beginning. 2. the introductory part of a speech, treatise, etc. [< L, < *ex-* + *ordiri* begin, orig., begin a web] —ex·or′di·al, *adj.*

ex·o·sphere (ek′sə·sfir), *n.* the atmospheric layer in which the ionosphere begins to merge with interplanetary space.

ex·ot·ic (ig·zot′ik), *adj.* foreign; strange; rare. —*n.* anything exotic. [< L < Gk. *exotikos* < *exo* outside < *ex-* out of] —ex·ot′i·cal·ly, *adv.*

ex·pand (iks·pand′), *v.* 1. increase in size; enlarge; swell. 2. spread out; open out; unfold; extend. 3. express in fuller form or greater detail. [< L, < *ex-* out + *pandere* spread. Doublet of SPAWN.] —ex·pand′er, *n.* —Syn. 1. dilate.

ex·panse (iks·pans′), *n.* a large, unbroken space or stretch; wide, spreading surface.

ex·pan·si·ble (iks·pan′sə·bəl), *adj.* capable of being expanded. —ex·pan′si·bil′i·ty, *n.*

ex·pan·sion (iks·pan′shən), *n.* 1. an expanding. 2. a being expanded; increase in size, volume, etc. 3. amount or degree of expansion. 4. an expanded part or form.

ex·pan·sive (iks·pan′siv), *adj.* 1. capable of expanding; tending to expand. 2. wide; spreading. 3. taking in much or many things; broad; extensive. 4. showing one's feelings freely and openly; effusive. —ex·pan′sive·ly, *adv.* —ex·pan′sive·ness, *n.*

ex·pa·ti·ate (iks·pā′shi·āt), *v.,* -at·ed, -at·ing. write or talk much. [< L, < *exspatiari* walk about < *ex-* out + *spatium* space] —ex·pa′ti·a′tion, *n.* —ex·pa′ti·a′tor, *n.*

ex·pa·tri·ate (*v.* eks·pā′tri·āt; *adj., n.* eks·pā′tri·it, -āt), *v.,* -at·ed, -at·ing, *adj., n.* —*v.* banish; exile. —*adj.* expatriated. —*n.* an expatriated person; exile. [< LL, < *ex-* out of + *patria* fatherland] —ex·pa′tri·a′tion, *n.*

ex·pect (iks·pekt′), *v.* 1. look forward to; think likely to come or happen. 2. look forward to with reason or confidence; desire and feel sure of getting. 3. *Colloq.* think; suppose; guess. [< L, < *ex-* out + *specere* look] —Syn. 1. anticipate.

ex·pect·an·cy (iks·pek′tən·si), **ex·pect·ance** (-təns), *n., pl.* -cies; -anc·es. expectation.

ex·pect·ant (iks·pek′tənt), *adj.* 1. having expectations; expecting. 2. showing expectation.

3. pregnant. —*n.* person who expects something. —ex·pect′ant·ly, *adv.*

ex·pec·ta·tion (eks′pek·tā′shən), *n.* 1. an expecting or being expected; anticipation. 2. thing expected. 3. ground for expecting something; prospect. —Syn. 1. expectancy, hope.

ex·pec·to·rant (iks·pek′tə·rənt), *Med.* —*adj.* causing or helping the discharge of phlegm, etc. —*n.* an expectorant medicine.

ex·pec·to·rate (iks·pek′tə·rāt), *v.,* -rat·ed, -rat·ing. cough up and spit out (phlegm, etc.); spit. [< L, < *ex-* out of + *pectus* breast] —ex·pec′to·ra′tion, *n.*

ex·pe·di·en·cy (iks·pē′di·ən·si), **ex·pe·di·ence** (-əns), *n., pl.* -cies; -enc·es. 1. suitability for bringing about a desired result; desirability or fitness under the circumstances. 2. personal advantage; self-interest.

ex·pe·di·ent (iks·pē′di·ənt), *adj.* 1. fit for bringing about a desired result; desirable or suitable under the circumstances. 2. giving or seeking personal advantage; based on self-interest. —*n.* a useful means of bringing about a desired result. [< L *expediens,* ppr. of *expedire* to free from a net, set right < *ex-* out + *pes* foot] —ex·pe′di·ent·ly, *adv.* —Syn. *adj.* 1. advantageous, profitable, advisable, wise. —*n.* resort, resource, shift, device.

ex·pe·dite (eks′pə·dīt), *v.,* -dit·ed, -dit·ing. 1. make easy and quick; speed up. 2. do quickly. 3. issue officially. [< L *expeditus.* See EXPEDITE.]

ex·pe·dit·er (eks′pə·dīt′ər), *n.* 1. person who is responsible for supplying raw materials or delivering finished products on schedule. 2. person who issues official statements and decisions. 3. any person who supplies something.

ex·pe·di·tion (eks′pə·dish′ən), *n.* 1. journey for some special purpose. 2. group of people, ships, etc., that make such a journey. 3. efficient and prompt action. —Syn. 1. voyage, trip, excursion. 3. promptness, haste, quickness, speed.

ex·pe·di·tion·ar·y (eks′pə·dish′ən·er′i), *adj.* of or making up an expedition.

ex·pe·di·tious (eks′pə·dish′əs), *adj.* efficient and prompt. —ex′pe·di′tious·ly, *adv.*

ex·pel (iks·pel′), *v.,* -pelled, -pel·ling. 1. force out; force to leave. 2. put out; dismiss permanently. [< L, < *ex-* out + *pellere* drive] —ex·pel′la·ble, *adj.* —ex·pel′ler, *n.* —Syn. 1. banish.

ex·pend (iks·pend′), *v.* spend; use up. [< L, < *ex-* out + *pendere* weigh, pay. Doublet of SPEND.] —ex·pend′er, *n.* —Syn. disburse, consume.

ex·pend·a·ble (iks·pen′də·bəl), *adj.* 1. that can be expended. 2. *Mil.* worth giving up or sacrificing to the enemy or to destruction for strategic reasons. —*n.* Usually, expendables. expendable persons or things.

ex·pen·di·ture (iks·pen′di·chər; -chūr), *n.* 1. act of expending. 2. cost; expense.

ex·pense (iks·pens′), *n.* 1. an expending; paying out money; outlay. 2. cost; charge. 3. cause of spending. 4. loss; sacrifice. [< AF < LL *expensa.* See EXPEND.] —Syn. 1. expenditure, disbursement. 2. price.

ex·pen·sive (iks·pen′siv), *adj.* costly; high-priced. —ex·pen′sive·ly, *adv.* —ex·pen′sive·ness, *n.* —Syn. dear.

ex·pe·ri·ence (iks·pir′i·əns), *n., v.,* -enced, -enc·ing. —*n.* 1. what has happened to one; anything or everything observed, done, or lived through. 2. an observing, doing, or living through things: *people learn by experience.* 3. skill, practical knowledge, or wisdom gained by observing, doing, or living through things. —*v.* have happen to one. [< OF < L, < *experiri* test < *ex-* out + *peri-* try] —Syn. *v.* undergo, endure, suffer, bear.

ex·pe·ri·enced (iks·pir′i·ənst), *adj.* 1. having had experience. 2. taught by experience. 3. skillful or wise because of experience. —Syn. 3. skilled, expert, practiced, veteran.

ex·per·i·ment (*v.* iks·per′ə·ment; *n.* iks·per′ə·mənt), *v.* try in order to find out; make trials or tests: *that man is experimenting with dyes to get the color he wants.* —*n.* 1. test or trial to find out something: *a cooking experiment.* 2. a conducting of such tests or trials: *scientists test out theories by experiments.* [< L *experimentum.* See EXPERIENCE.] —ex·per'i·ment'er, n. —Syn. n. 1. examination.

ex·per·i·men·tal (iks·per'ə·men'təl), adj. 1. based on experiments: *chemistry is an experimental science.* 2. used for experiments. 3. based on experience, not on theory or authority. —per'i·men'tal·ly, adv.

ex·per·i·men·ta·tion (iks·per'ə·men·tā'shən), n. an experimenting.

ex·pert (n. eks'pėrt; adj. iks·pėrt', eks'pėrt), n. person who knows a great deal about some special thing. —adj. 1. very skillful; knowing a great deal about some special thing. 2. from an expert; requiring or showing knowledge about some special thing. [< L *expertus,* pp. of *experiri* test. See EXPERIENCE.] —ex·pert'ly, adv. —ex·pert'ness, n. —Syn. n. authority, specialist. —adj. 1. experienced, practiced, skilled. —Ant. novice, beginner, amateur.

ex·pi·ate (eks'pi·āt), v., -at·ed, -at·ing. make amends for (a wrong, sin, etc.); atone for. [< L, < *ex-* completely + *piare* appease < *pius* devout] —ex·pi·a·ble (eks'pi·ə·bəl), adj. —ex'pi·a'tion, n. —ex'pi·a'tor, n.

ex·pi·a·to·ry (eks'pi·ə·tô'ri; -tō'-), adj. intended to expiate; expiating; atoning.

ex·pi·ra·tion (ek'spə·rā'shən), n. 1. a coming to an end. 2. a breathing out. —ex·pir·a·to·ry (ik·spīr'ə·tô'ri; -tō'-), adj.

ex·pire (ik·spīr'), v., -pired, -pir·ing. 1. come to an end. 2. die. 3. breathe out: *used air is expired from the lungs.* 4. Obs. emit. [< L, < *ex-* out + *spirare* breathe] —ex·pir'er, n. —Syn. 2. perish, decease.

ex·plain (iks·plān'), v. 1. make plain or clear; tell how to do. 2. tell the meaning of; interpret. 3. give reasons for; account for. [< L, < *ex-* out +*planus* flat] —ex·plain'a·ble, adj. —ex·plain'er, n. —ex·plan·a·to·ry (iks·plan'ə·tô'ri; -tō'-), adj. —ex·plan'a·to'ri·ly, adv. —Syn. 1. elucidate, expound.

ex·pla·na·tion (eks'plə·nā'shən), n. 1. an explaining. 2. thing that explains. 3. interpretation. —Syn. 1. elucidation, exposition, definition.

ex·ple·tive (eks'plə·tiv), adj. filling out a sentence or line; completing. —n. 1. something that fills out a sentence or line. 2. oath or meaningless exclamation. [< LL *expletivus* < *ex-* out + *plere* fill] —ex'ple·tive·ly, adv.

ex·pli·ca·ble (eks'pli·kə·bəl; iks·plik'ə-), adj. capable of being explained.

ex·pli·cate (eks'plə·kāt), v., -cat·ed, -cat·ing. 1. develop (a principle, doctrine, etc.). 2. explain. —ex'pli·ca'tion, n.

ex·plic·it (iks·plis'it), adj. 1. clearly expressed; distinctly stated; definite. 2. not reserved; frank; outspoken. [< L, < *ex-* un- + *plicare* fold] —ex·plic'it·ly, adv. —ex·plic'it·ness, n. —Syn. 1. precise, exact, unequivocal. —Ant. 1. vague, indefinite, ambiguous.

ex·plode (iks·plōd'), v., -plod·ed, -plod·ing. 1. blow up; burst with a loud noise. 2. cause to explode. 3. burst forth noisily: *explode with laughter.* 4. cause to be rejected; destroy belief in. [< L *explodere* drive out by clapping < *ex-* out + *plaudere* clap] —ex·plod'er, n. —Syn. 1. detonate. 4. discredit, disprove.

ex·ploit (n. eks'ploit, iks·ploit'; v. iks·ploit'), n. a bold, unusual act; daring deed. —v. 1. make use of; turn to practical account. 2. make unfair use of; use selfishly for one's own advantage. [< OF < VL *explicitum* achievement < L, pp. neut. of *explicare* unfold, settle. See EXPLICIT.] —ex·ploit'a·ble, adj. —ex'ploi·ta'tion, n. —ex·ploit'a·tive (iks·ploit'ə·tiv), adj. —ex·ploit'er, n. —Syn. n. feat, achievement.

ex·plore (iks·plôr'; -plōr'), v., -plored, -plor·ing. 1. travel in (little known lands or seas) for the purpose of discovery. 2. go over carefully; look into closely; examine. [< L *explorare* spy out, orig. cry out (at sight of game or enemy) < *ex-* out + *plorare* weep] —ex'plo·ra'tion, n. —ex·plor·a·to·ry (iks·plôr'ə·tô'ri; iks·plōr'ə·tō'-ri), ex·plor'a·tive, adj. —ex·plor'er, n. —Syn. 2. search, investigate, scrutinize.

ex·plo·sion (iks·plō'zhən), n. 1. a blowing up;

a bursting with a loud noise. 2. loud noise caused by this. 3. a noisy bursting forth; outbreak: *explosions of anger.*

ex·plo·sive (iks·plō'siv; -ziv), adj. 1. of or for explosion; tending to explode. 2. tending to burst forth noisily. —n. an explosive substance. —ex·plo'sive·ly, adv. —ex·plo'sive·ness, n.

ex·po·nent (iks·pō'nənt), n. 1. person or thing that explains, interprets, etc. 2. person or thing that stands as an example, type or symbol of something: *Lincoln is a famous exponent of self-education.* 3. index or small number written above and to the right of an algebraic symbol or a quantity to show how many times the symbol or quantity is to be used as a factor, as in a^3. [< L *exponens.* See EXPOUND.] —ex·po·nen·tial (eks'pō·nen'shəl), adj. —ex'po·nen'tial·ly, adv.

ex·port (v. iks·pôrt', -pōrt', eks'pôrt, -pōrt; n. eks'pôrt, -pōrt), v. send (goods) out of one country for sale and use in another. —n. 1. article exported. 2. an exporting; exportation. [< L, < *ex-* away + *portare* carry] —ex·port'a·ble, adj. —ex'por·ta'tion, n. —ex·port'er, n.

ex·pose (iks·pōz'), v., -posed, -pos·ing. 1. lay open; leave unprotected; uncover. 2. show openly; display: *goods are exposed for sale in a store.* 3. make known; show up; reveal: *he exposed the plot.* 4. allow light to reach and act on (a photographic film or plate). [< OF, < *ex-* forth + *poser* put, POSE] —ex·pos'er, n. —Syn. 2. exhibit. 3. disclose.

ex·po·sé (eks'pō·zā'), n. a showing up of crime, dishonesty, etc. [< F. See EXPOSE.]

ex·po·si·tion (eks'pə·zish'ən), n. 1. a public show or exhibition. 2. a detailed explanation. 3. speech or writing explaining a process or idea. —Syn. 1. display, fair. 2. elucidation.

ex·pos·i·tor (iks·poz'ə·tər), n. person or thing that explains; expounder, interpreter.

ex·pos·i·to·ry (iks·poz'ə·tô'ri; -tō'-), ex·pos·i·tive (-ə·tiv), adj. explaining; serving or helping to explain.

ex post fac·to (eks' pōst' fak'tō), made or done after something, but applying to it. [< Med.L *ex postfacto* from what is done afterward]

ex·pos·tu·late (iks·pos'chə·lāt), v., -lat·ed, -lat·ing. reason earnestly with a person, protesting against something he means to do or has done; remonstrate. [< L, < *ex-* (intensive) + *postulare* demand] —ex·pos'tu·la'tion, n. —ex·pos'tu·la'tor, n. —ex·pos·tu·la·to·ry (iks·pos'chə·lə·tô'ri; -tō'-), adj.

ex·po·sure (iks·pō'zhər), n. 1. an exposing. 2. a being exposed. 3. position in relation to the sun and wind: *a southern exposure.* 4. time during which light reaches and acts on a photographic film or plate. 5. a putting off without shelter; abandoning.

ex·pound (iks·pound'), v. 1. make clear; explain; interpret. 2. set forth or state in detail. [< OF < L, < *ex-* forth + *ponere* put] —ex·pound'er, n.

ex·press (iks·pres'), v. 1. put into words: *your thoughts are well expressed.* 2. show by look, voice, or action; reveal: *express feeling in one's tone.* 3. show by a sign, figure, etc.; indicate. 4. *Am.* send by express. 5. press out; squeeze out: *express the juice of grapes.* —adj. 1. clear; definite. 2. for a particular purpose; special. 3. exact. 4. having to do with express. 5. traveling fast and making few stops: *an express train.* 6. for fast traveling: *an express highway.* —n. 1. message sent for a particular purpose. 2. a quick or direct means of sending things. 3. *Am.* system or company for sending parcels, money, etc. 4. *Am.* things sent by express. 5. train, bus, elevator, etc., traveling fast and making few stops. —adv. by express; directly. [< L *expressus* < *ex-* out + *premere* press] —ex·press'er, n. —ex·press'i·ble, adj. —Syn. v. 1. utter, declare, state, say. 3. signify.

ex·press·age (iks·pres'ij), n. *Am.* 1. business of carrying parcels, money, etc., by express. 2. charge for carrying parcels, etc., by express.

ex·pres·sion (iks·presh'ən), n. 1. a putting into words. 2. word or group of words used as a unit. 3. a showing by look, voice, or action. 4.

indication of feeling, spirit, etc.; look that shows feeling. **5.** a bringing out the meaning or beauty of something read, sung, etc. **6.** a showing or expressing by a sign, figure, etc. **7.** symbol or group of symbols expressing some mathematical fact. **8.** a pressing out. —**ex·pres′sion·less**, *adj.* —**expres′sion·less·ness**, *n.* —Syn. **1.** utterance, declaration. **4.** sign, token.

ex·pres·sive (iks·pres′ĭv), *adj.* **1.** serving as a sign or indication; expressing. **2.** full of expression; having much feeling, meaning, etc. —**ex·pres′sive·ly**, *adv.* —**ex·pres′sive·ness**, *n.* —Syn. **1.** indicative, significant.

ex·press·ly (iks·pres′lĭ), *adv.* **1.** clearly; plainly; definitely. **2.** on purpose.

ex·press·man (iks·pres′mən), *n.*, *pl.* —**men**. *Am.* person who works in the express business.

ex·press·way (iks·pres′wā′), *n.* an express highway.

ex·pro·pri·ate (eks·prō′prĭ·āt), *v.*, —**at·ed**, —**at·ing**. **1.** take (land, etc.) out of the owner's possession, esp. for public use. **2.** put (a person) out of possession; dispossess. [< Med.L, < *ex-* away from + *proprius* one's own] —**ex·pro′pri·a′tion**, *n.* —**ex·pro′pri·a′tor**, *n.*

ex·pul·sion (iks·pul′shən), *n.* **1.** an expelling; forcing out. **2.** a being expelled or forced out: *expulsion from school.* —**ex·pul′sive**, *adj.*

ex·punge (iks·punj′), *v.*, —**punged**, —**pung·ing.** remove completely; blot out; erase. [< L, < *ex-* out + *pungere* prick] —**ex·pung′er**, *n.*

ex·pur·gate (eks′pər·gāt), *v.*, —**gat·ed**, —**gat·ing.** remove objectionable passages or words from (a book, letter, etc.); purify. [< L, < *ex-* out + *purgare* purge] —**ex′pur·ga′tion**, *n.* —**ex′pur·ga′tor**, *n.*

ex·qui·site (eks′kwĭ·zĭt; iks·kwiz′ĭt), *adj.* **1.** very lovely; delicate. **2.** sharp; intense. **3.** of highest excellence; most admirable: *exquisite taste and manners.* **4.** keenly sensitive. —*n.* person who is overnice in dress; a dandy. [< L *exquisitus* < *ex-* out + *quaerere* seek] —**ex′qui·site·ly**, *adv.* —**ex′qui·site·ness**, *n.* —Syn. *adj.* **1.** dainty, fine, beautiful. **2.** acute, keen.

ex·tant (eks′tənt; iks·tant′), *adj.* still in existence. [< L *exstans* < *ex-* out, forth + *stare* stand]

ex·tem·po·ra·ne·ous (iks·tem′pə·rā′nĭ·əs), **ex·tem·po·ra·ry** (—tem′pə·rer′ĭ), *adj.* **1.** spoken or done without preparation; offhand: *an extemporaneous speech.* **2.** made for the occasion: *an extemporaneous shelter against a storm.* [< LL, < L *ex tempore* according to the moment] —**ex·tem′po·ra′ne·ous·ly**, **ex·tem·po·rar·i·ly** (iks·tem′pə·rer′ə·lĭ; *emphatic* iks·tem′-pə·rãr′ə·lĭ), *adv.* —**ex·tem′po·ra′ne·ous·ness**, **ex·tem′po·rar′i·ness**, *n.*

ex·tem·po·re (iks·tem′pə·rē), *adv.* on the spur of the moment; without preparation; offhand. —*adj.* extemporaneous. [< L]

ex·tem·po·rize (iks·tem′pə·rīz), *v.*, —**rized**, —**riz·ing**. **1.** speak, play, sing, or dance, composing as one proceeds. **2.** compose offhand; make for the occasion. —**ex·tem′po·ri·za′tion**, *n.* —**ex·tem′po·riz′er**, *n.*

ex·tend (iks·tend′), *v.* **1.** stretch out. **2.** straighten out. **3.** lengthen. **4.** widen; enlarge. **5.** give; grant. [< L, < *ex-* out + *tendere* stretch] —**ex·tend′ed**, *adj.* —**ex·tend′ed·ly**, *adv.* —**ex·tend′i·ble**, *adj.* —Syn. **3.** prolong, protract.

ex·ten·si·ble (iks·ten′sə·bəl), *adj.* capable of being extended. —**ex·ten′si·bil′i·ty**, **ex·ten′si·ble·ness**, *n.*

ex·ten·sion (iks·ten′shən), *n.* **1.** an extending. **2.** a being extended. **3.** an extended part; addition. **4.** range; extent. **5.** *Physics.* that property of a body by which it occupies a portion of space. —**ex·ten′sion·al**, *adj.* —Syn. **1.** stretching, expansion, enlargement. **3.** projection.

ex·ten·sive (iks·ten′sĭv), *adj.* **1.** of great extent. **2.** affecting many things; comprehensive. **3.** depending on the use of large areas: *extensive agriculture.* —**ex·ten′sive·ly**, *adv.* —**ex·ten′sive·ness**, *n.* —Syn. **1.** extended, broad, large, ample.

ex·ten·sor (iks·ten′sər; —sôr), *n.* muscle that extends or straightens out a limb or other part of the body.

ex·tent (iks·tent′), *n.* **1.** size, space, length, amount, or degree to which a thing extends. **2.** something extended; extended space. —Syn. **1.** magnitude, area, scope, compass, range.

ex·ten·u·ate (iks·ten′yū·āt), *v.*, —**at·ed**, —**at·ing**. **1.** make (guilt, a fault, offense, etc.) seem less; excuse in part. **2.** make thin or weak; diminish. [< L, < *ex-* out + *tenuis* thin] —**ex·ten′u·a′tion**, *n.* —**ex·ten′u·a′tive**, *adj.* —**ex·ten′u·a′tor**, *n.*

ex·te·ri·or (iks·tir′ĭ·ər), *n.* **1.** an outer surface or part; outward appearance; outside: *a harsh exterior but a kind heart.* **2.** exteriors, externals. —*adj.* **1.** on the outside; outer. **2.** coming from without; happening outside. [< L, < *exterus* outside < *ex* out of] —**ex·te′ri·or·ly**, *adv.* —Syn. **1.** outward, outlying, external.

ex·ter·mi·nate (iks·tér′mə·nāt), *v.*, —**nat·ed**, —**nat·ing**. destroy completely. [< LL, < L, drive out < *ex-* out of + *terminus* boundary] —**ex·ter′mi·na′tion**, *n.* —**ex·ter′mi·na′tor**, *n.*

ex·ter·nal (iks·tér′nəl), *adj.* **1.** on the outside; outer. **2.** to be used on the outside of the body. **3.** entirely outside; coming from without. **4.** having existence outside one's mind. **5.** having to do with outward appearance or show; superficial. **6.** having to do with international affairs; foreign. —*n.* **1.** an outer surface or part; outside. **2.** externals, clothing, manners, outward acts, or appearances. [< L *externus* outside < *exterus* outside < *ex* out of] —**ex·ter′nal·ly**, *adv.* —Syn. *adj.* **1.** outward, exterior.

ex·tinct (iks·tĭngkt′), *adj.* **1.** no longer in existence. **2.** no longer active; extinguished: *an extinct volcano.* [< L *exstinctus*, pp. of *exstinguere*. See EXTINGUISH.] —Syn. **1.** dead.

ex·tinc·tion (iks·tĭngk′shən), *n.* **1.** an extinguishing. **2.** a being extinguished; extinct condition. **3.** a doing away with completely; wiping out; destruction.

ex·tin·guish (iks·tĭng′gwĭsh), *v.* **1.** put out; quench. **2.** put an end to; do away with; wipe out; destroy. **3.** eclipse or obscure by superior brilliancy. [< L, < *ex-* out + *stinguere* quench] —**ex·tin′guish·a·ble**, *adj.* —**ex·tin′guish·a·bly**, *adv.* —**ex·tin′guish·er**, *n.* —**ex·tin′guish·ment**, *n.*

ex·tir·pate (eks′tər·pāt; iks·tér′pāt), *v.*, —**pat·ed**, —**pat·ing**. **1.** remove completely; destroy totally. **2.** tear up by the roots. [< L, < *ex-* out + *stirps* root] —**ex′tir·pa′tion**, *n.* —**ex′tir·pa′-tive**, *adj.* —**ex′tir·pa′tor**, *n.*

ex·tol, **ex·toll** (iks·tōl′; —tol′), *v.*, —**tolled**, —**tol·ling**. praise highly. [< L, < *ex-* up + *tollere* raise] —**ex·tol′ler**, *n.* —**ex·tol′ment**, **ex·toll′-ment**, *n.* —Syn. commend, laud, eulogize.

ex·tort (iks·tôrt′), *v.* obtain (money, a promise, etc.) by threats, force, fraud, or illegal use of authority. [< L *extortus* < *ex-* out + *torquere* twist] —**ex·tort′er**, *n.* —**ex·tor′tive**, *adj.*

ex·tor·tion (iks·tôr′shən), *n.* **1.** act of extorting. **2.** anything obtained by extorting.

ex·tor·tion·ar·y (iks·tôr′shən·er′ĭ), *adj.* characterized by or given to extortion.

ex·tor·tion·ate (iks·tôr′shən·ĭt), *adj.* characterized by extortion. —**ex·tor′tion·ate·ly**, *adv.*

ex·tor·tion·er (iks·tôr′shən·ər), **ex·tor·tion·ist** (—ĭst), *n.* person who is guilty of extortion.

ex·tra (eks′trə), *adj.* more, greater, or better than what is usual, expected, or needed. —*n.* **1.** something in addition to what is usual, expected, or needed. **2.** an additional charge. **3.** *Am.* a special edition of a newspaper. **4.** *Am.* person who is employed by the day to play minor parts in motion pictures. **5.** an additional worker. —*adv.* more than usually. [prob. short for *extraordinary*] —Syn. *adj.* additional, supplemental, supplementary.

extra-, *prefix.* outside; beyond; besides, as in *extraordinary.* [< L]

ex·tra·bold (eks′trə·bōld′), *n.* a very heavy boldface.

ex·tract (*v.* iks·trakt′; *n.* eks′trakt), *v.* **1.** pull out or draw out, usually with some effort: *extract a tooth, extract a confession.* **2.** obtain by pressure, suction, etc.: *oil is extracted from* olives. 3. deduce: *extract a principle from a collection of facts.* 4. derive: *extract pleasure from a situation.* 5. take out; select (a passage) from a book, speech, etc. 6. calculate or find (the root of a number). —*n.* 1. something drawn out or taken out; passage taken from a book, speech, etc. 2. a concentrated preparation of a substance: *vanilla extract.* [< L *extractus* < *ex-* out + *trahere* draw] —**ex·tract′a·ble, ex·tract′i·ble,** *adj.* —**ex·trac′tive,** *adj., n.* —**ex·trac′tor,** *n.* —**Syn.** *v.* 1. elicit, exact, extort, wrest, separate. —*n.* 1. excerpt, citation, quotation, selection.

ex·trac·tion (iks·trak′shən), *n.* 1. an extracting. 2. a being extracted. 3. descent; origin.

ex·tra·cur·ric·u·lar (eks′trə·kə·rik′yə·lər), *adj.* outside the regular course of study: *football is an extracurricular activity.*

ex·tra·dite (eks′trə·dīt), *v.,* **-dit·ed, -dit·ing.** 1. give up or deliver (a fugitive or prisoner) to another nation or legal authority for trial or punishment. 2. obtain the extradition of (such a person). [< *extradition*] —**ex′tra·dit′a·ble,** *adj.*

ex·tra·di·tion (eks′trə·dish′ən), *n.* surrender of a fugitive or prisoner by one state, nation, or legal authority to another for trial or punishment. [< L, < *ex-* out + *tradere* trade]

ex·tra·ne·ous (iks·trā′ni·əs), *adj.* from outside; not belonging; foreign. [< L, < *extra* outside < *ex-* out of. Doublet of STRANGE.] —**ex·tra′ne·ous·ly,** *adv.* —**ex·tra′ne·ous·ness,** *n.*

ex·traor·di·nar·y (iks·trôr′də·ner′i; *esp. for* 2 eks′trə·ôr′-), *adj.* 1. beyond what is ordinary; most unusual; very remarkable. 2. outside of, additional to, or ranking below the regular class of officials; special. [< L, < *extra ordinem* out of the (usual) order] —**ex·traor′di·nar′i·ly,** *adv.* —**ex·traor′di·nar′i·ness,** *n.* —**Syn.** 1. uncommon, exceptional, singular.

ex·tra·sen·so·ry (eks′trə·sen′sə·ri), *adj.* not within ordinary sense perception.

extrasensory perception, the perceiving of thoughts, actions, etc., in other than a normal fashion; mental telepathy.

ex·tra·ter·ri·to·ri·al (eks′trə·ter′ə·tô′ri·əl; -tō′-), *adj.* beyond territorial limits or jurisdiction, as persons resident in a country but not subject to its laws. Any ambassador to the United States has certain extraterritorial privileges. —**ex′tra·ter′ri·to′ri·al′i·ty,** *n.* —**ex′tra·ter′ri·to′ri·al·ly,** *adv.*

ex·trav·a·gance (iks·trav′ə·gəns), *n.* 1. careless and lavish spending; wastefulness. 2. a going beyond the bounds of reason; excess. —**Syn.** 1. dissipation, profusion. —**Ant.** 1. thrift.

ex·trav·a·gant (iks·trav′ə·gənt), *adj.* 1. spending carelessly and lavishly; wasteful. 2. beyond the bounds of reason; excessive; exorbitant. [< Med.L, < L *extra-* outside + *vagari* wander] —**ex·trav′a·gant·ly,** *adv.* —**Syn.** 1. prodigal, lavish. 2. immoderate, inordinate.

ex·trav·a·gan·za (iks·trav′ə·gan′zə), *n.* a fantastic play, piece of music, etc. [blend of Ital. *stravaganza* peculiar behavior, and E *extra*]

ex·treme (iks·trēm′), *adj.,* **-trem·er, -trem·est.** *n.* —*adj.* 1. much more than usual; very great; very strong. 2. very severe; very violent. 3. at the very end; farthest possible; last. —*n.* 1. something extreme; one of two things as far or as different as possible from each other. 2. an extreme degree. 3. *Math.* the first or last term in a proportion or series. 4. **go to extremes,** do or say too much. [< L *extremus,* superl. of *exterus* outer] —**ex·treme′ly,** *adv.* —**ex·treme′ness,** *n.* —**Syn.** *adj.* 1. immoderate, excessive, radical, fanatical. 3. outermost, utmost, final.

extreme unction, sacrament of the Roman Catholic Church, given by a priest to a dying person or one in danger of death.

ex·trem·ist (iks·trēm′ist), *n.* 1. person who goes to extremes. 2. person who has extreme ideas or favors extreme measures.

ex·trem·i·ty (iks·trem′ə·ti), *n., pl.* **-ties.** 1. the very end; farthest possible place; last part or point. 2. extreme need, danger, suffering, etc. 3. an extreme degree. 4. an extreme action. 5. extremities, hands and feet. —**Syn.** 1. termination, verge, limit.

ex·tri·cate (eks′trə·kāt), *v.,* **-cat·ed, -cat·ing.** set free (from entanglements, difficulties, embarrassing situations, etc.); release. [< L, < *ex-* out of + *tricae* perplexities] —**ex·tri·ca·ble** (eks′trə·kə·bəl), *adj.* —**ex′tri·ca·bil′i·ty,** *n.* —**ex′·tri·ca·bly,** *adv.* —**ex′tri·ca′tion,** *n.*

ex·trin·sic (eks·trin′sik), *adj.* 1. not essential or inherent; caused by external circumstances. 2. being outside of a thing; coming from without; external. [< later L *extrinsecus* outer < earlier L, from outside, < unrecorded OL *extrim* from outside + *secus* toward] —**ex·trin′si·cal·ly,** *adv.*

ex·tro·vert (eks′trə·vėrt), *n.* person more interested in what is going on around him than in his own thoughts and feelings. [< *extro-* (var. of *extra-* outside) + L *vertere* turn]

ex·trude (iks·trüd′), *v.,* **-trud·ed, -trud·ing.** 1. thrust out; push out. 2. stick out; protrude. [< L, < *ex-* out + *trudere* thrust] —**ex·tru·sion** (iks·trü′zhən), *n.* —**ex·tru·sive** (iks·trü′siv), *adj.*

ex·u·ber·ance (ig·zü′bər·əns), **ex·u·ber·an·cy** (-ən·si), *n.* fact, quality, state, or condition of being exuberant. [< L, < *exuberare* grow luxuriantly < *ex-* thoroughly + *uber* fertile]

ex·u·ber·ant (ig·zü′bər·ənt), *adj.* 1. very abundant; overflowing; lavish. 2. profuse in growth; luxuriant. —**ex·u′ber·ant·ly,** *adv.*

ex·ude (ig·züd′; ik·süd′), *v.,* **-ud·ed, -ud·ing.** 1. ooze. 2. give forth. [< L, < *ex-* out + *sudare* to sweat] —**ex·u·da·tion** (eks′yu·dā′shən), *n.*

ex·ult (ig·zult′), *v.* 1. be very glad; rejoice greatly. 2. *Obs.* leap for joy. [< L *exsultare* < *ex-* forth + *salire* leap] —**ex·ul·ta·tion** (eg′zul·tā′shən; ek′sul-), *n.* —**ex·ult′ing·ly,** *adv.*

ex·ult·ant (ig·zul′tənt), *adj.* rejoicing greatly; exulting. —**ex·ult′ant·ly,** *adv.*

ex·ur·ban·ite (eks′ėr′bən·īt), *n.* person who lives in the exurbs. [< *ex-* (def. 1, ? also def. 3) + (sub)*urbanite*]

ex·ur·bi·a (eks′ėr′bi·ə), *n.* the exurbs.

ex·urbs (eks′ėrbz), *n.pl.* region outside a large city, between the suburbs and the country, inhabited largely by people who have moved out from the city and whose way of life is a mixture of urban and rural elements. [< *ex-* + (sub)*urbs*]

-ey, *suffix.* full of; containing; like, as in *clayey, skyey.* [var. of *-y*¹]

eye (ī), *n., v.,* **eyed, ey·ing** or **eye·ing.** —*n.* 1. organ of the body by which people and animals see; organ of sight. 2. the colored part of the eye; iris. 3. region surrounding the eye: *the blow gave him a black eye.* 4. any organ that is sensitive to light. 5. sense of seeing; vision; sight. 6. ability to see small differences in things: *an eye for color.* 7. look; glance. 8. a watchful look. 9. way of thinking or considering; view; opinion: *in the eye of the law.* 10. thing shaped like, resembling, or suggesting an eye. —*v.* 1. look at; watch: *the dog eyed the stranger.* [OE *ēage*]

eye·ball (ī′bôl′), *n.* the ball-shaped part of the eye, without the lids and bony socket.

eye·brow (ī′brou′), *n.* 1. arch of hair above the eye. 2. the bony ridge that it grows on.

eye·glass (ī′glas′; ī′gläs′), *n.* 1. a glass lens to aid poor vision. 2. eyepiece. 3. eyeglasses, pair of glass lenses to help vision.

eye·hole (ī′hōl′), *n.* 1. the bony socket for the eyeball. 2. hole to look through. 3. a round opening for a pin, hook, rope, etc., to go through.

eye·lash (ī′lash′), *n.* one of the hairs on the edge of the eyelid.

eye·less (ī′lis), *adj.* without eyes; blind.

eye·let (ī′lit), *n.* 1. a small, round hole for a lace or cord to go through. 2. a metal ring around such a hole to strengthen it.

eye·lid (ī′lid′), *n.* the movable fold of skin over the eye.

eye·piece (ī′pēs′), *n.* lens nearest to the eye of the user in a telescope, microscope, etc.

eye·shot (ī′shot′), *n.* range of vision.

eye·sight (ī′sīt′), *n.* 1. power of seeing; sight. 2. range of vision; view.

eye·sore (ī′sôr′; ī′sōr′), *n.* thing unpleasant to look at.

eye·strain (ī′strān′), *n.* a tired or weak condition of the eyes caused by using them too much, reading in a dim light, etc.

eye·tooth (ī'tüth'), *n., pl.* -teeth. an upper canine tooth.

eye·wash (ī'wosh'; ī'wôsh'), *n.* a liquid preparation to clean or heal the eyes.

eye·wink·er (ī'wingk'ər), *n.* eyelash.

eye·wit·ness (ī'wit'nis), *n.* person who actually sees or has seen some act or happening.

ey·rie, ey·ry (âr'i; ir'i), *n., pl.* -ries. aerie.

E·ze·ki·el (i·zē'ki·əl; i·zēk'yəl), *n.* **1.** a Hebrew prophet in the sixth century B.C. **2.** book of the Old Testament.

Ez·ra (ez'rə), *n.* **1.** a Hebrew scribe who led a revival of the religion of Judaism. **2.** a book of chronicles in the Old Testament.

F

F, f (ef), *n., pl.* F's; f's. **1.** the sixth letter of the alphabet. **2.** *Music.* the fourth note of the scale of C major.

F, **1.** *Chem.* fluorine. Also, Fl. **2.** French.

F., **1.** Fahrenheit. **2.** February. **3.** Friday.

f., **1.** feminine. **2.** folio. **3.** following.

fa (fä), *n. Music.* the fourth note of the scale. [see GAMUT]

Fa·bi·an (fā'bi·ən), *adj.* using stratagem and delay to wear out an opponent; cautious; slow.

fa·ble (fā'bəl), *n., v.,* -bled, -bling. —*n.* **1.** story made up to teach a lesson. **2.** an untrue story; falsehood. **3.** legend; myth. —*v.* **1.** tell or write fables. **2.** lie. [< OF < L *fabula* < *fari* speak] —fa'bled, *adj.* —fa'bler, *n.*

fab·ric (fab'rik), *n.* **1.** woven or knitted material; cloth. **2.** construction; texture. **3.** thing constructed of combined parts; framework. [< F < L *fabrica* workshop. Doublet of FORGE¹.]

fab·ri·cate (fab'rə·kāt), *v.,* -cat·ed, -cat·ing. **1.** build; construct; manufacture. **2.** make by fitting together standardized parts. **3.** make up; invent (stories, lies, excuses, etc.). —fab'ri·ca'tion, *n.* —fab'ri·ca'tor, *n.*

fab·u·list (fab'yə·list), *n.* **1.** person who tells, writes, or makes up fables. **2.** liar.

fab·u·lous (fab'yə·ləs), *adj.* **1.** like a fable. **2.** not believable; amazing. **3.** of or belonging to a fable; imaginary. [< L *fabulosus* < *fabula* FABLE] —fab'u·lous·ly, *adv.* —fab'u·lous·ness, *n.* —Syn. **2.** incredible, astonishing. **3.** legendary, mythical.

fa·cade (fə·säd'), *n.* the front part or principal side of a building. [< F, < *face* FACE]

face (fās), *n., v.,* faced, fac·ing. —*n.* **1.** the front part of the head. **2.** look; expression. **3.** an ugly or peculiar look made by distorting the face. **4.** outward appearance. **5.** show; pretense. **6.** the front part; right side; surface: *the face of a clock.* **7.** the working surface of an implement. **8.** the principal side of a building; front. **9.** the printing side of a plate or piece of type. **10.** *Colloq.* boldness; impudence. **11.** personal importance; dignity; self-respect: *face is very important to Oriental peoples.* **12.** the stated value. **13.** face to face, a. with faces toward each other. b. in the actual presence. **14.** in the face of, a. in the presence of. b. in spite of. —*v.* **1.** have the face (toward); be opposite (to). **2.** turn the face (toward). **3.** cause to face. **4.** meet face to face; stand before. **5.** meet bravely or boldly; oppose and resist. **6.** present itself to: *a crisis faced us.* **7.** cover or line with a different material. **8.** smooth the surface of (stone, etc.). **9.** turn face up: *face a card.* [< F, ult. < L *facies* form] —face'a·ble, *adj.* —face'less, *adj.* —Syn. *n.* **1.** visage, countenance, physiognomy, features. **3.** grimace. **10.** assurance, effrontery, audacity. —*v.* **4.** front, confront. **5.** brave, defy, oppose.

face card, *Cards.* king, queen, or jack.

fac·et (fas'it), *n., v.,* -et·ed, -et·ing; *esp. Brit.* -et·ted, -et·ting. —*n.* **1.** any one of the small, polished surfaces of a cut gem. **2.** thing like the facet of a gem. —*v.* cut facets on. [< F *facette,* dim. of *face* FACE]

Cut gem showing facets

fa·ce·tious (fə·sē'shəs), *adj.* **1.** having the habit of joking. **2.** said in fun; not to be taken seriously. [< L *facetious* jest < *facetus* witty] —fa·ce'tious·ly, *adv.* —fa·ce'tious·ness, *n.*

face value, **1.** value stated on a bond, check, note, etc. **2.** apparent worth, meaning, etc.

fa·cial (fā'shəl), *adj.* **1.** of the face. **2.** for the face. —*n. Colloq.* massage or treatment of the face. —fa'cial·ly, *adv.*

fac·ile (fas'əl), *adj.* **1.** easily done, used, etc.: *a facile task.* **2.** moving, acting, working, etc., with ease: *a facile pen.* **3.** of easy manners or temper; agreeable; yielding: *a facile nature.* [< L *facilis* easy < *facere* do] —fac'ile·ly, *adv.* —fac'ile·ness, *n.*

fa·cil·i·tate (fə·sil'ə·tāt), *v.,* -tat·ed, -tat·ing. make easy; lessen the labor of; assist. —fa·cil'i·ta'tion, *n.* —Syn. help, expedite, promote.

fa·cil·i·ty (fə·sil'ə·ti), *n., pl.* -ties. **1.** absence of difficulty; ease. **2.** power to do anything easily, quickly, and smoothly. **3.** something that makes an action easy; aid; convenience. **4.** easy-going quality; tendency to yield to others. —Syn. **1.** easiness. **2.** knack, readiness.

fac·ing (fās'ing), *n.* **1.** a covering of different material for ornament, protection, etc. **2.** material put around the edge of cloth to protect or trim it.

fac·sim·i·le (fak·sim'ə·lē), *n., v.,* -led, -le·ing, *adj.* —*n.* **1.** an exact copy or likeness; perfect reproduction. **2.** process for transmitting printed matter and photographs by radio and reproducing them on paper at the receiving set. —*v.* make a facsimile of. —*adj.* of a facsimile. [< L *fac* make! + *simile* like]

fact (fakt), *n.* **1.** thing known to be true or to have really happened. **2.** what is true or has really happened; truth; reality. **3.** thing said or supposed to be true or to have really happened: *we doubted his facts.* **4.** deed; act. [< L *factum* (thing) done, pp. of *facere* do. Doublet of FEAT.] —Syn. **2.** actuality. ▶ **fact (the fact that).** *The fact that* is very often a circumlocution for which *that* alone would do as well: *He was quite conscious [of the fact] that his visitor had some other reason for coming.*

fac·tion (fak'shən), *n.* **1.** group of people in a political party, church, club, etc., acting together or having a common end in view. **2.** strife among the members of a political party, church, club, etc.; discord. [< L *factio* party, orig., a doing < *facere* do. Doublet of FASHION.] —fac'tion·al, *adj.* —fac'tion·al·ism, *n.* —Syn. **1.** party, group, clique, cabal. **2.** dissension, division.

fac·tious (fak'shəs), *adj.* **1.** fond of causing faction. **2.** of or caused by faction. —fac'tious·ly, *adv.* —fac'tious·ness, *n.*

fac·ti·tious (fak·tish'əs), *adj.* developed by effort; not natural; forced; artificial. [< L *facticius* artificial] —fac·ti'tious·ly, *adv.* —fac·ti'tious·ness, *n.*

fac·tor (fak'tər), *n.* **1.** element, condition, quality, etc., that helps to bring about a result. **2.** *Math.* any of the numbers, algebraic expressions, etc., that form a product when multiplied together. **3.** person who does business for another; agent. —*v. Math.* separate into factors. —fac'tor·ship, *n.*

fac·to·ry (fak'tə·ri, -tri), *n., pl.* -ries. a building or group of buildings where things are manufactured. —fac'to·ry·like', *adj.* —Syn. mill, shop.

fac·to·tum (fak·tō'təm), *n.* person employed to do all kinds of work. [< Med.L, < L *fac* do! + *totum* the whole]

fac·tu·al (fak'chū·əl), *adj.* concerned with fact; consisting of facts. —fac'tu·al·ly, *adv.*

fac·ul·ty (fak'əl·ti), *n., pl.* -ties. **1.** power of the mind or body; ability. **2.** power to do some special thing, esp. a power of the mind. **3.** power or privilege conferred; license; authorization. 4. a. *Am.* teachers of a school, college, or university. b. department of learning: *faculty of theology.* 5. members of a profession. [< L *facultas* < *facilis* FACILE] —Syn. 1. capacity, capability.

fad (făd), *n.* 1. something everybody is very much interested in for a short time; craze; rage. 2. hobby. —**fad′dish,** *adj.* —**fad′dist,** *n.*

fade (fād), *v.,* **fad·ed, fad·ing.** 1. lose color or brightness. 2. lose freshness or strength; wither. 3. die away; disappear. 4. cause to fade. 5. *Am.* in motion pictures and television: a. **fade in,** appear slowly. b. **fade out,** disappear slowly. [< OF, < *fade* VAPID] —Syn. 1. blanch, bleach, pale. 2. droop, languish.

fade-out (fād′out′), *n.* 1. *Am.* scene in a motion picture that slowly disappears. 2. a gradual disappearance.

fae·ces (fē′sēz), *n.pl.* feces. —**fae·cal** (fē′kəl), *adj.*

fa·ër·ie, fa·ër·y (fā′ər·i; fâr′i), *n., pl.* **-ër·ies,** *adj. Archaic.* —*n.* 1. fairyland. 2. fairy. —*adj.* fairy.

fag¹ (fag), *v.,* **fagged, fag·ging,** *n.* —*v.* 1. work hard or until wearied. 2. tire by work. —*n.* 1. *Brit.* hard, uninteresting work. 2. person who does hard work; drudge.

fag² (fag), *n. Esp. Brit. Slang.* cigarette.

fag end, 1. the last and poorest part of anything; remnant. 2. an untwisted end of rope.

fag·ot, *esp. Brit.* **fag·got** (fag′ət), *n.* bundle of sticks or twigs tied together. —*v.* tie or fasten together into bundles; make into a fagot. [< OF]

fag·ot·ing, *esp. Brit.* **fag·got·ing** (fag′ət·ing), *n.* an ornamental stitch made with the threads of a piece of cloth.

Fagoting

Fahr·en·heit (far′ən·hīt), *adj.* of, based on, or according to a scale for measuring temperature on which 32 degrees marks the freezing point of water and 212 degrees the boiling point. [after G. D. *Fahrenheit,* physicist]

fail (fāl), *v.* 1. not succeed; be unable to do or become; come out badly. 2. not do; neglect. 3. be of no use or help to. 4. be lacking or absent; be not enough. 5. lose strength; become weak; die away. 6. be unable to pay what one owes. 7. be unsuccessful in an examination, etc.; receive a mark of failure. 8. *Colloq.* give the mark of failure to (a student). —*n.* failure. [< OF *faillir,* ult. < L *fallere* deceive] —Syn. *v.* 5. decline, sink, wane, dwindle, deteriorate.

fail·ing (fāl′ing), *n.* 1. failure. 2. fault; defect. —*prep.* in the absence of; lacking. —*adj.* that fails. —**fail′ing·ly,** *adv.*

faille (fīl; fāl), *n.* a soft, ribbed silk or rayon cloth. [< F]

fail·ure (fāl′yər), *n.* 1. a being unable to do or become; failing. 2. a not doing; neglecting. 3. a being lacking or absent; being not enough; falling short. 4. losing strength; becoming weak; dying away. 5. a being unable to pay what one owes. 6. person or thing that has failed. —Syn. 4. decline, decay, deterioration. 5. bankruptcy.

fain (fān), *Archaic and Poetic.* —*adv.* by choice; gladly; willingly. —*adj.* 1. willing, but not eager; forced by circumstances. 2. glad; willing. 3. eager; desirous. [OE *fægen*]

faint (fānt), *adj.* 1. not clear or plain; dim. 2. weak; feeble. 3. timid. 4. done feebly or without zest. 5. ready to faint; about to faint. —*v.* lose consciousness temporarily. —*n.* condition in which a person lies for a time as if asleep and does not know what is going on around him. [< OF, pp. of *faindre* FEIGN] —**faint′er,** *n.* —**faint′ish,** *adj.* —**faint′ly,** *adv.* —**faint′ness,** *n.* —Syn. *adj.* 1. indistinct, faded, dull. 2. faltering, languid, wearied. 3. irresolute.

faint-heart·ed (fānt′här′tid), *adj.* lacking courage; cowardly; timid. —**faint′-heart′ed·ly,** *adv.* —**faint′-heart′ed·ness,** *n.*

fair¹ (fâr), *adj.* 1. not favoring one more than the other or others; just; honest. 2. according to the rules. 3. pretty good; average. 4. favorable; promising. 5. not dark; light. 6. not cloudy or stormy; clear; sunny. 7. pleasing to see; beauti-

ful. 8. civil; courteous. 9. without spots or stains; clean: *a person's fair name.* 10. easily read; plain. 11. not blocked up; open. —*adv.* 1. in a fair manner. 2. directly; straight: *the stone hit him fair in the head.* —*n. Archaic.* woman; sweetheart. [OE *fæger*] —**fair′ish,** *adj.* —**fair′ness,** *n.* —Syn. *adj.* 1. impartial, unprejudiced, unbiased. 3. middling, passable, tolerable. 4. propitious, likely. 5. blond, white. 7. pretty, comely, attractive. 9. spotless, untarnished, pure.

fair² (fâr), *n.* 1. display of goods, products, etc. 2. a gathering of people to buy and sell, often held in a certain place at regular times during the year: *a county fair.* 3. *Am.* a combined entertainment and sale of articles for charity, a church, etc. [< OF < LL *feria* holiday]

fair ball, *Am., Baseball.* ball hit to or over the legal playing area.

fair·ly (fâr′li), *adv.* 1. in a fair manner. 2. to a fair degree. 3. justly; honestly. 4. rather; somewhat. 5. actually. 6. clearly. —Syn. 2. tolerably. 3. impartially. 5. positively, absolutely. 6. legibly, distinctly, plainly.

fair-mind·ed (fâr′mīn′did), *adj.* not prejudiced; just; impartial. —**fair′-mind′ed·ness,** *n.*

fair-spo·ken (fâr′spō′kən), *adj.* speaking smoothly and pleasantly; courteous.

fair trade agreement, agreement which permits U.S. manufacturers to set minimum price levels on products, to which retailers must adhere in States that have legalized the practice.

fair·way (fâr′wā′), *n.* 1. an unobstructed passage or way. 2. *Golf.* the mowed and tended area between the tee and putting green.

fair-weath·er (fâr′weth′ər), *adj.* of or fitted for fair weather; weakening or failing in time of need.

fair·y (fâr′i), *n., pl.* **fair·ies,** *adj.* —*n.* a tiny supernatural being, very lovely and delicate, supposed to help or harm human beings. —*adj.* 1. of fairies. 2. like a fairy; lovely; delicate. [< OF *faerie* < *fae* FAY] —**fair′y·like′,** *adj.* —Syn. *n.* elf, fay, sprite, brownie.

fair·y·land (fâr′i·land′), *n.* 1. the imaginary place where the fairies live. 2. an enchanting and pleasant place.

fait ac·com·pli (fe·tä·kôn·plē′), *French.* thing done and no longer worth opposing.

faith (fāth), *n.* 1. a believing without proof; trust. 2. belief in God, religion, or spiritual things. 3. what is believed. 4. religion. 5. a being faithful; loyalty. —*interj.* truly; indeed. [< OF *feit* < L *fides*] —Syn. 1. confidence, reliance. 3. doctrine, tenet, creed, belief. 5. fidelity, constancy, faithfulness. —Ant. *n.* 1. doubt.

faith·ful (fāth′fəl), *adj.* 1. worthy of trust; doing one's duty; keeping one's promise; loyal. 2. true; accurate. 3. full of faith. —*n.* the faithful, a. the true believers. b. loyal followers or supporters. —**faith′ful·ly,** *adv.* —**faith′ful·ness,** *n.* —Syn. *adj.* 1. devoted, constant. 2. precise, exact.

faith·less (fāth′lis), *adj.* 1. unworthy of trust; failing in one's duty; breaking one's promise; not loyal. 2. not reliable. 3. without faith; unbelieving. —**faith′less·ly,** *adv.* —**faith′less·ness,** *n.* —Syn. 1. disloyal, false, inconstant, fickle. 3. doubting, skeptical.

fake (fāk), *v.,* **faked, fak·ing,** *n., adj.* —*v.* make to seem satisfactory; falsify; counterfeit. —*n.* 1. fraud; deception. 2. *Am.* one who fakes. —*adj. Am.* intended to deceive; false. —*v.* make.

fa·kir, fa·keer (fə·kir′; fā′kər), *n.* 1. a Mohammedan holy man who lives by begging. 2. a Hindu ascetic. [< Ar. *faqir* poor]

Fa·lan·gist (fə·lan′jist), *n.* member of the Falange, a Spanish fascist group. —**Fa·lan′gism,** *n.*

fal·cate (fal′kāt), *adj.* curved like a sickle; hooked. [< L, < *falx* sickle]

fal·chion (fôl′chən), *n.* 1. a broad, short sword with an edge that curves to a point. 2. *Poetic.* any sword. [< OF < Ital. *falcione,* ult. < L *falx* sickle]

fal·con (fôl′kən; fô′kən), *n.* 1. hawk trained to hunt and kill birds and small game. 2. a swift-flying hawk having a short, curved, notched bill. See picture on next page. [< OF < LL *falco*]

fal·con·ry (fôl′kən·rĭ; fô′kən-), *n.* 1. sport of hunting with falcons. 2. the training of falcons to hunt. —fal′con·er, *n.*

fal·de·ral (fal′də·ral), **fal·de·rol** (-rol), *n.* 1. a flimsy thing; trifle. 2. nonsense. 3. a meaningless refrain in songs. Also, **folderol.**

Falk·land Islands (fôk′lənd), group of islands in the S Atlantic, E of the Strait of Magellan, administered by Great Britain but claimed also by Argentina.

fall (fôl), *v.,* **fell, fall·en, fall·ing,** *n.* —*v.* 1. drop or come down from a higher place: *the snow falls fast.* 2. come down suddenly from an erect position. 3. hang down: *her curls fell upon her shoulders.* 4. droop: *she blushed and her eyes fell.* 5. become bad or worse: *he was tempted and fell.* 6. lose position, dignity, etc.; be taken by any evil. 7. be captured or destroyed. 8. drop wounded or dead; be killed. 9. pass into a certain condition: *he fell asleep.* 10. come as if by dropping: *when night falls, the stars appear.* 11. come by chance or lot: *our choice fell on him.* 12. come to pass; happen; occur: *Christmas falls on Sunday this year.* 13. come by right: *the money fell to the only son.* 14. be put properly: *the accent of "farmer" falls on the first syllable.* 15. become lower or less: *prices fell sharply.* 16. be divided: *the story falls into five parts.* 17. look sad or disappointed: *his face fell at the bad news.* 18. slope downward: *the land falls gradually to the beach.* 19. be directed: *the light falls on my book.* 20. fall away, a. withdraw support or allegiance. b. become bad or worse. c. be overthrown or destroyed. d. become thin. 21. fall back, go toward the rear; retreat. 22. fall in, a. *Mil.* take a place in a formation and come to a position of attention. b. meet. c. agree. 23. fall on, attack. 24. fall out, a. *Mil.* leave a place in a formation. b. stop being friends; quarrel. c. turn out; happen. 25. fall through, fail. 26. fall under, belong under; be classified as. —*n.* 1. a dropping from a higher place. 2. amount that falls: *a heavy fall of snow.* 3. distance that anything falls. 4. a coming down suddenly from an erect position. 5. a hanging down; dropping. 6. a becoming bad or worse. 7. capture; destruction. 8. a lowering; becoming less. 9. a downward slope. 10. *Esp. U.S.* season of the year between summer and winter; autumn. 11. in wrestling, a being thrown on one's back. 12. Usually, **falls.** waterfall; cataract; cascade. 13. the Fall, the sin of Adam and Eve in yielding to temptation and eating the forbidden fruit. [OE *feallan*] —Syn. *v.* 1. descend, sink. —*n.* 1. drop, descent. ➤ Falls is plural in form but really singular (or collective) in meaning. In informal and colloquial usage people speak of *a falls;* formal usage keeps *falls* strictly plural.

fal·la·cious (fə·lā′shəs), *adj.* 1. deceptive; misleading. 2. logically unsound; erroneous. —fal·la′cious·ly, *adv.* —fal·la′cious·ness, *n.*

fal·la·cy (fal′ə·sĭ), *n., pl.* **-cies.** 1. a false idea; mistaken belief; error. 2. mistake in reasoning; misleading or unsound argument. [< L, ult. < *fallere* deceive]

fall·en (fôl′ən), *v.* pp. of **fall.** —*adj.* 1. dropped. 2. on the ground; down flat. 3. degraded. 4. overthrown; destroyed. 5. dead. —Syn. *adj.* 1. decreased, depreciated. 2. debased. 4. ruined.

fall guy, *Am., Slang.* person left in a difficult situation.

fal·li·ble (fal′ə·bəl), *adj.* 1. liable to be deceived or mistaken; liable to err. 2. liable to be erroneous, inaccurate, or false. [< Med.L, < L *fallere* deceive] —fal′li·bil′i·ty, fal′li·ble·ness, *n.* —fal′li·bly, *adv.*

falling sickness, epilepsy.

falling star, meteor.

Fal·lo·pi·an tubes (fə·lō′pĭ·ən), *Anat., Zool.* pair of slender tubes through which ova from the ovaries pass to the uterus.

fall·out (fôl′out′), *n.* the radioactive particles or dust that fall to the earth after an atomic explosion.

fal·low[1] (fal′ō), *adj.* plowed and left unseeded for a season or more; uncultivated; inactive. —*n.* 1. land plowed and left unseeded for a season or more. 2. the plowing of land without seeding it for a season in order to destroy weeds, improve the soil, etc. —*v.* plow and harrow (land) without seeding. [OE *fealg*]

fal·low[2] (fal′ō), *adj.* pale yellowish-brown. [OE *fealu*]

fallow deer, a small European deer with a yellowish coat that is spotted with white in the summer.

Fall River, city in SE Massachusetts.

false (fôls), *adj.,* **fals·er, fals·est,** *adv.* —*adj.* 1. not true; not correct; wrong. 2. not truthful; lying. 3. not loyal; not faithful. 4. used to deceive; deceiving: *false weights.* 5. substitute; supplementary. 6. not true in pitch. 7. not real; artificial. 8. *Biol.* improperly called or named. The false acacia is really a locust tree. —*adv.* in a false manner. [< L *falsus* < *fallere* deceive] —false′ly, *adv.* —false′ness, *n.* —Syn. *adj.* 1. erroneous, mistaken, incorrect. 2. untruthful, mendacious. 3. disloyal, unfaithful, inconstant, treacherous, traitorous. 4. misleading, deceptive, fallacious. 7. spurious, bogus, counterfeit, sham.

false·hood (fôls′hŭd), *n.* 1. quality of being false. 2. something false. 3. a making of false statements; lying. 4. a false statement; lie. —Syn. 1. falseness, untruthfulness, mendacity. 4. untruth, fib.

fal·set·to (fôl·set′ō), *n., pl.* **-tos,** *adj.,* *adv.* —*n.* an unnaturally high-pitched voice, esp. in a man. —*adj.* that sings in a falsetto. —*adv.* in a falsetto. [< Ital., dim. of *falso* FALSE]

fal·si·fy (fôl′sə·fī), *v.,* **-fied, -fy·ing.** 1. make false; change in order to deceive; misrepresent. 2. make false statements; lie. 3. prove to be false; disprove. —fal′si·fi·ca′tion, *n.* —fal′si·fi′er, *n.*

fal·si·ty (fôl′sə·tĭ), *n., pl.* **-ties.** 1. a being false; incorrectness. 2. untruthfulness; deceitfulness. 3. that which is false.

Fal·staff (fôl′staf; -stäf), *n.* a fat, jolly, swaggering soldier, brazen and without scruples, in three of Shakespeare's plays. —Fal·staff·i·an (fôl·staf′i·ən; -stäf′-), *adj.*

fal·ter (fôl′tər), *v.* 1. lose courage; draw back; hesitate; waver. 2. move unsteadily; stumble; totter. 3. speak in hesitating, broken words; stammer. 4. come forth in hesitating, broken sounds. —*n.* act of faltering; faltering sound. [cf. Scand. *faltrask* be cumbered] —fal′ter·er, *n.* —fal′ter·ing·ly, *adv.* —Syn. *v.* 1. vacillate. 2. stagger, tremble. 3. stutter.

fame (fām), *n., v.,* **famed, fam·ing.** —*n.* 1. a being very well known; having much said or written about one. 2. what is said about one; reputation. 3. *Archaic.* rumor. —*v.* make famous. [< obs. F < L *fama* < *fari* speak] —Syn. *n.* 1. notoriety, celebrity, renown, eminence.

famed (fāmd), *adj.* made famous; celebrated; well-known. ➤ famed. When *famed* is used for *famous* or *well-known,* it usually suggests a journalese style, or a staccato one: *famed Nobel prize winner.* It is often a sign of amateur writing to label as *famed* (or as *famous,* for that matter) really well-known people.

fa·mil·iar (fə·mil′yər), *adj.* 1. well-known. 2. widely used. 3. well-acquainted. 4. close; personal; intimate. 5. not formal; friendly. 6. too friendly; presuming; forward. —*n.* 1. a familiar friend or acquaintance. 2. spirit or demon supposed to serve a particular person. [< OF < L *familiaris.* See FAMILY.] —fa·mil′iar·ly, *adv.* —Syn. *adj.* 3. conversant, versed. 4. confidential. 5. unceremonious, informal.

Falcon (17 in. long)

Fallow deer
(3 ft. high at the shoulder)

➤ **Familiar English** is the way we speak and write for ourselves—as in diaries and notes for future work—and with or for our friends. In such informal circumstances we know that we are not going to be judged by our language, as in part we are when we speak or write for strangers, and we can therefore use our natural, easy speech—with contractions, clipped words and abbreviated sentences, and allusions to our common background that might puzzle an outsider. In more formal circumstances we have to approach the standards set for the language used in carrying on public affairs.

fa·mil·iar·i·ty (fə·mil′yar′ə·ti), n., pl. **-ties.** 1. close acquaintance. 2. freedom of behavior suitable only to friends; lack of formality or ceremony. 3. instance of such behavior. —Syn. 1. intimacy, friendship, fellowship. 2. informality, unconstraint.

fa·mil·iar·ize (fə·mil′yər·īz), v., **-ized, -iz·ing.** 1. make well acquainted. 2. make well known. —**fa·mil′iar·i·za′tion,** n.

fam·i·ly (fam′ə·li; fam′li), n., pl. **-lies.** 1. father, mother, and their children. 2. children of a father and mother. 3. group of people living in the same house. 4. all of a person's relatives. 5. group of related people; tribe. 6. Esp. Brit. good or noble descent. 7. group of related or similar things. 8. Biol. group of related animals or plants ranking below an order and above a genus. [< L familia household < famulus servant] —Syn. 5. clan, race. 6. ancestry, stock, lineage.

family name, the last name of all the members of a certain family; surname.

fam·ine (fam′ən), n. 1. starvation. 2. lack of food in a place; time of starving. 3. a very great lack of anything. [< F, ult. < L fames hunger] —Syn. 3. scarcity, insufficiency, deficiency.

fam·ish (fam′ish), v. be or make extremely hungry; starve. —**fam′ish·ment,** n.

fa·mous (fā′məs), adj. 1. very well known; noted. 2. Colloq. first-rate; excellent. [< AF < L fama FAME] —**fa′mous·ly,** adv. —**fa′mous·ness,** n. —Syn. 1. celebrated, renowned, distinguished, illustrious, eminent. —Ant. 1. obscure, unknown. ➤ See **notorious** for usage note.

fan¹ (fan), n., v., **fanned, fan·ning.** —n. 1. instrument or device to make a current of air. It causes a cooling breeze, blows dust away, etc. 2. thing spread out like an open fan. 3. a winnowing machine. 4. Baseball. a striking out. —v. 1. make a current of (air) with a fan, etc. 2. direct a current of air toward with a fan, etc. 3. drive away with a fan, etc. 4. stir up; arouse: bad treatment fanned their dislike into hate. 5. spread out like an open fan. 6. winnow. 7. Am., Baseball. strike out. [< L vannus fan for winnowing grain] —**fan′ner,** n.

fan² (fan), n. Am., Colloq. 1. an enthusiastic devotee or follower of a sport, hobby, etc.: a baseball fan. 2. admirer of an actor, writer, etc. [short for fanatic]

fa·nat·ic (fə·nat′ik), n. person who is carried away beyond reason by his beliefs. —adj. enthusiastic or zealous beyond reason. [< L, < fanum temple] —**fa·nat′i·cism,** n.

fa·nat·i·cal (fə·nat′ə·kəl), adj. unreasonably enthusiastic; extremely zealous. —**fa·nat′i·cal·ly,** adv.

fan·cied (fan′sid), adj. imagined; imaginary.

fan·ci·er (fan′si·ər), n. person who is especially interested in something, as dogs, etc.

fan·ci·ful (fan′si·fəl), adj. 1. showing fancy; quaint; odd. 2. influenced by fancy; imaginative. 3. suggested by fancy; imaginary; unreal. —**fan′ci·ful·ly,** adv. —**fan′ci·ful·ness,** n.

fan·cy (fan′si), n., pl. **-cies,** v., **-cied, -cy·ing,** adj., **-ci·er, -ci·est.** —n. 1. power to imagine; imagination. 2. thing imagined. 3. thing supposed; idea; notion. 4. a personal taste or judgment. 5. a liking; fondness. —v. 1. imagine. 2. have an idea or belief; suppose. 3. be fond of; like. —adj. 1. made or arranged specially to please; valued for beauty rather than use. 2. decorated; ornamental. 3. requiring much skill: fancy skating. 4. costing extra to please the fancy or one's special taste, etc.: fancy fruit. 5. bred for special excellence. [contraction of fan-

tasy] —Syn. n. 1. fantasy. 3. conception, whim, caprice. -v. 1. conceive, picture. 2. presume, conjecture. -adj. 1. fine, elegant.

fan·cy-free (fan′si·frē′), adj. free from influence; not in love.

fan·cy·work (fan′si·wėrk′), n. ornamental needlework; embroidery, crocheting, etc.

fan·dan·go (fan·dang′gō), n., pl. **-gos.** a lively Spanish dance in three-quarter time. [< Sp.]

fane (fān), n. Archaic and Poetic. temple; church. [< L fanum temple]

fan·fare (fan′fãr), n. 1. a short tune or call sounded by trumpets, bugles, etc. 2. a loud show of activity, talk, etc.; showy flourish. [< F, < fanfarer, v., < Sp. < Ar.]

fang (fang), n. 1. a long, pointed tooth of a dog, wolf, snake, etc. 2. a long, slender, tapering part of anything. [OE] —**fanged** (fangd), adj. —**fang′less,** adj. —**fang′like′,** adj.

Fangs of a snake

fan-jet (fan′jet′), n. a turbofan engine.

fan·light (fan′līt′), n. 1. a semicircular window with bars spread out like an open fan. 2. any semicircular or other window over a door.

fan·tail (fan′tāl′), n. 1. tail, end, or part spread out like an open fan. 2. pigeon whose tail spreads out like an open fan.

fan-tan (fan′tan′), n. 1. a Chinese gambling game. 2. Cards. game in which the player who gets rid of his cards first wins the game. [< Chinese fan t'an repeated divisions]

fan·ta·si·a (fan·tā′zhi·ə; -zhə; -zi·ə), n. Music. 1. composition following no fixed form or style. 2. medley of well-known airs. [< Ital. See FANTASY.]

fan·tas·tic (fan·tas′tik), **fan·tas·ti·cal** (-tə·kəl), adj. 1. very odd or queer; wild and strange in shape; showing unrestrained fancy: weird, fantastic shadows. 2. very fanciful; capricious; eccentric; irrational: a fantastic idea. 3. existing only in the imagination; unreal: superstition causes fantastic fears. —**fan·tas′ti·cal·ly,** adv. —**fan·tas′ti·cal·ness, fan·tas′ti·cal′i·ty,** n. —Syn. 1. freakish, bizarre, grotesque.

fan·ta·sy (fan′tə·si; -zi), n., pl. **-sies.** 1. play of the mind; imagination; fancy. 2. a wild, strange fancy. 3. caprice; whim. 4. daydream. 5. Music. fantasia. Also, **phantasy.** [< OF < L < Gk. phantasia appearance, image, ult. < phainein show] —Syn. 2. illusion, hallucination.

far (fär), adj., **far·ther, far·thest,** adv. —adj. 1. distant; not near: a far country. 2. more distant: the far side of the hill. —adv. 1. a long way off in time or space. 2. very much. 3. as far as, to the distance, point, or degree that. 4. by far, very much. 5. far and away, very much. 6. far and near, everywhere. 7. far and wide, everywhere; even in distant parts. 8. far be it from me, I do not dare or want. 9. go far, a. last long. b. tend very much. c. get ahead. 10. how far, to what distance, point, or degree. 11. in so far as, to the extent that. 12. so far, a. to this or that point. b. until now or then. 13. so far as, to the extent that. 14. so far so good, until now everything has been safe or satisfactory. [OE feorr]

far·ad (far′əd), n. Elect. a unit of capacity. It is the capacity of a condenser that, when charged with one coulomb, gives a pressure of one volt. [for Michael Faraday]

Far·a·day (far′ə·dā; -di), n. Michael, 1791–1867, English physicist and chemist.

far·a·way (fär′ə·wā′), adj. 1. distant. 2. dreamy.

farce (färs), n., v., **farced, farc·ing.** —n. 1. play intended merely to make people laugh, full of ridiculous happenings, absurd actions, etc. 2. kind of humor found in such plays; broad humor. 3. ridiculous mockery; absurd pretense. —v. season (a speech or writing), as with jokes and allusions. [< F, lit., stuffing, ult. < L farcire stuff] —**far·cial** (fär′shəl), adj.

far·ci·cal (fär′sə·kəl), adj. of or like a farce; absurd; improbable. —**far′ci·cal′i·ty, far′ci·cal·ness,** n. —**far′ci·cal·ly,** adv.

fare (fãr), n., v., **fared, far·ing.** —n. 1. sum

of money paid to ride in a train, car, bus, etc.
2. passenger on a train, car, bus, etc. 3. food.
[blend of OE *faer* and *faru*] —*v.* 1. eat food; be
fed. 2. get along; do. 3. turn out; happen. 4. go;
travel. [OE *faran*] —**far′er,** *n.*

Far East, China, Japan, and other parts of E
Asia. —**Far Eastern.**

fare·well (fâr′wel′), *interj.* good-by; good
luck. —*n.* 1. expression of good wishes at parting;
good-by. 2. departure; leave-taking. —*adj.* of
farewell; parting; last.

far-fetched (fär′fecht′), *adj.* not coming
naturally; forced; strained.

far-flung (fär′flung′), *adj.* widely spread; covering a large area.

fa·ri·na (fə·rē′nə), *n.* flour or meal made from
grain, potatoes, beans, nuts, etc. [< L, < *far*
grits]

far·i·na·ceous (far′ə·nā′shəs), *adj.* consisting of flour or meal; starchy; mealy.

far·kle·ber·ry (fär′kəl·ber′i), *n., pl.* -ries.
Am. shrub or small tree that has small black
berries.

farm (färm), *n.* 1. piece of land used to raise
crops or animals. 2. thing like a farm. A sheet of
water for cultivating oysters is an oyster farm.
3. *Am., Baseball.* a minor-league team belonging
to or associated with a major-league club.
—*v.* 1. raise crops or animals on a farm. 2. cultivate (land). 3. take proceeds or profits of (a tax,
undertaking, etc.) on paying a fixed sum. 4. let
out (taxes, revenues, an enterprise, etc.) to another for a fixed sum or percentage. 5. let the
labor or services of (a person) for hire. 6. be a
farmer. 7. **farm out,** *Baseball.* assign to a minor-
league team. [< F, ult. < L *firmus* firm]

farm·er (fär′mər), *n.* 1. person who raises
crops or animals on a farm; person who runs a
farm. 2. person who takes a contract for the
collection of taxes by agreeing to pay a certain
sum to the government. —**Syn.** 1. agriculturist,
husbandman, granger.

farm hand, man who works on a farm.

farm·house (färm′hous′), *n.* house on a farm.

farm·ing (fär′ming), *n.* 1. business of raising
crops or animals on a farm; agriculture. 2. practice of letting out the collection of public revenue. 3. condition of being let out at a fixed sum.
—*adj.* of or pertaining to farms. —**Syn.** *n.* 1.
husbandry, tillage, agronomy.

farm·stead (färm′sted), **farm·stead·ing**
(-sted·ing), *n. Esp. Brit.* farm with its buildings.

farm·yard (färm′yärd′), *n.* yard connected
with the farm buildings or enclosed by them.

far·o (fâr′ō), *n.* a gambling game played by betting on the order in which certain cards will
appear. [appar. alter. of *Pharaoh*]

far-off (fär′ôf′; -of′), *adj.* distant.

Fa·rouk I (fä·rük′), 1920–1965, king of Egypt
1936–1952.

far·ra·go (fə·rā′gō; -rä′-), *n., pl.* -goes. a confused mixture; hodgepodge; jumble. [< L, mixed
fodder, ult. < *far* grits]

far-reach·ing (fär′rēch′ing), *adj.* having a
wide influence or effect; extending far.

far·ri·er (far′i·ər), *n. Esp. Brit.* 1. blacksmith
who shoes horses. 2. a horse doctor; veterinarian.
[< OF < L, < *ferrum* iron]

far·ri·er·y (far′i·ər·i), *n., pl.* -er·ies. *Esp. Brit.*
1. work of a farrier. 2. place where a farrier
works.

far·row (far′ō), *n.* litter of pigs. —*v.* 1. give
birth to a litter of pigs. 2. give birth to (pigs).
[OE *fearh*]

far-see·ing (fär′sē′ing), *adj.* 1. able to see
far. 2. looking ahead; planning wisely for the
future.

far-sight·ed (fär′sīt′id), *adj.* 1. able to see
far. 2. seeing distant things more clearly than
near ones. 3. looking ahead; planning wisely for
the future. —**far′-sight′ed·ly,** *adv.* —**far′-
sight′ed·ness,** *n.*

far·ther (fär′thər), *comparative* of far. —*adj.*
1. more distant. 2. more; additional: *do you need
farther help?* —*adv.* 1. at or to a greater distance. 2. at or to a more advanced point. 3. in

addition; also. [ME *ferther*] ➤ **farther, further.**
In formal English some people make a distinction between *farther* and *further,* confining the
first to expression of physical distance and the
second to abstract relationships of degree or
quantity: *We went on twenty miles farther. He
went farther than I but neither of us reached
the town. He carries that sort of thing further
than I would. He went further into his family
history. He got further and further into debt.* In
colloquial and informal English the distinction
is not kept and there seems to be a rather definite tendency for *further* to be used in all senses.

far·ther·most (fär′thər·mōst), *adj.* most distant; farthest.

far·thest (fär′thist), *superlative* of far. —*adj.*
1. most distant. 2. longest. —*adv.* 1. to or at the
greatest distance. 2. most. [ME *ferthest*]

far·thing (fär′thing), *n.* a British coin, worth
a fourth of a British penny. [OE
feorthung < *feortha* fourth]

far·thin·gale (fär′thing·gāl), *n.*
a hoop skirt worn in England from
about 1550 to about 1650. [< F <
Sp., < *verdugo* rod]

fas·ces (fas′ēz), *n.pl., sing.* fascis (fas′is). bundle of rods or sticks
containing an ax with the blade
projecting, carried before a Roman
magistrate as a symbol of authority. [< L, pl. of *fascis* bundle]

fas·ci·cle (fas′ə·kəl), *n.* 1. a small
bundle. 2. *Bot.* a close cluster of
flowers, leaves, etc. 3. a single part
of a printed work issued in sections.
[< L *fasciculus,* dim. of *fascis* bundle] —**fas′ci-
cled,** *adj.*

Ancient Ro-
man holding
fasces

fas·ci·nate (fas′ə·nāt), *v.,* -nat·ed, -nat·ing.
1. attract very strongly; enchant by charming
qualities. 2. hold motionless by strange power,
terror, etc. Snakes are said to fascinate small
birds. 3. *Obs.* bewitch. [< L, < *fascinum* spell]
—**fas′ci·nat′ed·ly,** *adv.* —**fas′ci·nat′ing,** *adj.*
—**fas′ci·nat′ing·ly,** *adv.* —**fas′ci·na′tor,** *n.*
—**Syn.** 1. charm, entrance, enrapture, captivate.

fas·ci·na·tion (fas′ə·nā′shən), *n.* 1. a fascinating or being fascinated. 2. very strong attraction; charm; enchantment.

fas·cism (fash′iz·əm), *n.* 1. Fascism, a strongly
nationalistic movement in favor of government
control of business. Fascism seized control of the
Italian government in 1922 under the leadership
of Mussolini. 2. any system of government
in which property is privately owned, but all
industry and business is regulated by a strong
national government. [< Ital., < *fascio* bundle
(as political emblem) < L *fascis*] ➤ **fascism,**
fascist. Pronounced fash′iz·əm, fash′ist; rarely
fas′iz·əm, fas′ist. *Fascism, Fascist* are capitalized when they refer to Italian politics, as
we capitalize *Republican* and *Democrat* in this
country. When the word refers to a movement in
another country in which the party has a different name, it need not be capitalized but often is.
When it refers to the general idea of fascist politics, or an unorganized tendency, as in the
United States, it is not capitalized. *Fascisti*
(singular, *Fascista*) has also been Anglicized in
pronunciation: fə·shis′ti; Italian pronunciation
fä·shē′stē. *Fascismo* (fä·shēz′mō) is rarely used
in English, *Fascism* being the translation. Compare Nazi.

fas·cist (fash′ist), *n.* 1. person who favors and
supports fascism. 2. Fascist, person who favored
and supported Fascism in Italy. —*adj.* of or
having to do with fascism or fascists. ➤ See
fascism for usage note.

fash·ion (fash′ən), *n.* 1. manner; way. 2. the
prevailing style; current use in clothes, manners,
speech, etc. 3. a particular make; kind; sort;
form; shape. 4. polite society; fashionable people. 5. after or in a fashion, in some way or
other; not very well. —*v.* make; shape; form.
[< OF < L *factio* a doing or making. Doublet of
FACTION.] —**fash′ion·er,** *n.* —**Syn.** *n.* 1. mode,
practice, custom. 2. vogue, fad, rage. —*v.* frame,
construct.

fash·ion·a·ble (fash'ən-ə-bəl; fash'nə-bəl), *adj.* 1. following the fashion; in fashion; stylish. 2. of, like, or used by people of fashion. —**fash'·ion·a·ble·ness**, *n.* —**fash'ion·a·bly**, *adv.* —Syn. 1. modish, smart.

fast[1] (fast; fäst), *adj.* 1. quick; rapid; swift. 2. facilitating the rapid motion of something: *a fast race track*. 3. indicating a time ahead of the correct time. 4. not restrained in pleasures; too gay; wild. 5. firm; secure; tight: *a fast hold on a rope, roots fast in the ground*. 6. loyal; faithful. 7. that will not fade easily. —*adv.* 1. quickly; rapidly; swiftly. 2. firmly; securely; tightly. 3. thoroughly; completely; soundly: *he was fast asleep*. 4. **play fast and loose**, say one thing and do another; be tricky, insincere, or unreliable. [OE *fæst*] —Syn. *adj.* 1. fleet, speedy, hasty. 4. dissipated, dissolute, profligate, immoral. 5. fixed, immovable, tenacious, adhesive.

fast[2] (fast; fäst), *v.* go without food; eat little or nothing; go without certain kinds of food. —*n.* 1. a fasting. 2. day or time of fasting. [OE *fæstan*]

fast day, day observed by fasting, esp. a day regularly set apart by a church.

fas·ten (fas'ən; fäs'-), *v.* 1. fix firmly in place; tie; lock; shut. 2. attach; connect: *he tried to fasten the blame upon his companions*. 3. direct; fix: *the dog fastened his eyes on the stranger*. 4. become fast. 5. become fastened. [OE *fæstnian* < *fæst* fast[1]] —**fas'ten·er**, *n.* —Syn. 1. link, hook, clasp, clamp, secure, bind, moor, latch.

fas·ten·ing (fas'ən·ing; fas'ning; fäs'-), *n.* thing used to fasten something, as a lock, bolt, clasp, hook, button, etc.

fas·tid·i·ous (fas·tid'i·əs), *adj.* hard to please; extremely refined or critical; easily disgusted. [< L, < *fastidium* loathing] —**fas·tid'i·ous·ly**, *adv.* —**fas·tid'i·ous·ness**, *n.*

fast·ness (fast'nis; fäst'-), *n.* 1. a strong, safe place; stronghold. 2. a being fast.

fat (fat), *n.*, *adj.*, **fat·ter**, **fat·test**, *v.*, **fat·ted**, **fat·ting**. —*n.* 1. a white or yellow, oily substance formed in the bodies of animals. 2. animal tissue containing this substance. 3. *Chem.* any of a class of organic compounds of which the natural fats are usually mixtures. 4. the richest or best part. —*adj.* 1. consisting of or containing fat; oily: *fat meat*. 2. abounding in some element; fertile: *fat land*. 3. yielding much money; profitable: *a fat office*. 4. affording good opportunities. 5. plentifully supplied; plentiful. 6. fleshy; plump; well-fed. 7. thick; broad. 8. dull; stupid. 9. too fat; corpulent; obese. —*v.* make fat; become fat. [OE *fætt*, orig. pp., fatted] —**fat'ly**, *adv.* —**fat'ness**, *n.* —Syn. *adj.* 1. greasy, unctuous. 3. lucrative, remunerative. 9. stout.

fa·tal (fā'təl), *adj.* 1. causing death. 2. causing destruction or ruin. 3. important; decisive; fateful. [< L, < *fatum* FATE] —**fa'tal·ly**, *adv.* —**fa'tal·ness**, *n.* —Syn. 1. mortal, deadly. 2. destructive, disastrous, ruinous.

fa·tal·ism (fā'təl·iz·əm), *n.* 1. belief that fate controls everything that happens. 2. submission to everything that happens as inevitable. —**fa'tal·ist**, *n.* —**fa'tal·is'tic**, *adj.* —**fa'tal·is'ti·cal·ly**, *adv.*

fa·tal·i·ty (fā·tal'ə·ti; fə-), *n.*, *pl.* **-ties**. 1. a fatal accident or happening; death. 2. a fatal influence or effect. 3. liability to disaster. 4. a being controlled by fate; inevitable necessity: *doctrine of fatality*.

fate (fāt), *n.*, *v.*, **fat·ed**, **fat·ing**. —*n.* 1. power supposed to fix beforehand and control everything that happens. 2. what is caused by fate. 3. what becomes of a person or thing. 4. death; ruin. —*v.* destine. [< L *fatum* (thing) spoken (i.e., by the gods), pp. of *fari* speak] —Syn. *n.* 1. destiny, lot, fortune, doom.

fat·ed (fāt'id), *adj.* determined by fate.

fate·ful (fāt'fəl), *adj.* 1. controlled by fate. 2. determining what is to happen; important; decisive. 3. showing what fate decrees; prophetic. 4. causing death, destruction, or ruin; disastrous. —**fate'ful·ly**, *adv.* —**fate'ful·ness**, *n.*

Fates (fāts), *n.pl. Gk.* and *Roman Myth.* the three goddesses supposed to control human life.

fa·ther (fä'thər), *n.* 1. a male parent. 2. person

who is like a father. 3. a male ancestor; forefather. 4. person who helped to make something; founder; inventor; author. 5. title of respect used in addressing priests or other clergymen. 6. clergyman having this title. 7. senator of ancient Rome. 8. **the Father**, God. 9. **the fathers**, the Christian writers and teachers of the Christian Church during the first six centuries A.D. —*v.* 1. be the father of. 2. take care of as a father does; act as a father to. 3. make; originate. [OE *fæder*] —**fa'ther·hood**, *n.* —**fa'ther·less**, *adj.* —**fa'ther·less·ness**, *n.*

fa·ther-in-law (fä'thər·in·lô'), *n.*, *pl.* **fathers-in-law**. 1. father of one's husband or wife. 2. *Colloq.* stepfather.

fa·ther·land (fä'thər·land'), *n.* one's native country; land of one's ancestors.

fa·ther·ly (fä'thər·li), *adj.* 1. of a father. 2. like a father; kindly. —*adv.* in the manner of a father. —**fa'ther·li·ness**, *n.*

fath·om (fath'əm), *n.*, *pl.* **fath·oms** or (*esp. collectively*) **fath·om**, *v.* —*n.* a unit of measure equal to 6 feet, used mostly in measuring the depth of water and the length of ships' ropes, cables, etc. —*v.* 1. measure the depth of. 2. get to the bottom of; understand fully. [OE *fæthm* width of the outstretched arms] —**fath'om·a·ble**, *adj.* —**fath'om·er**, *n.* —**fath'om·less**, *adj.* —**fath'om·less·ly**, *adv.*

fa·tigue (fə·tēg'), *n.*, *v.*, **-tigued**, **-ti·guing**, *adj.* —*n.* 1. weariness. 2. hard work; effort. 3. a weakening (of metal) caused by long-continued use or strain. 4. *Mil.* fatigue duty. 5. **fatigues**, *Mil.* work clothes. —*v.* 1. cause fatigue in; weary. 2. weaken by much use or strain. —*adj.* pertaining to fatigue. [< F, ult. < L *fatigare* tire] —**fa·tigue'less**, *adj.* —Syn. 1. lassitude, languor, exhaustion. —*v.* 1. tire, exhaust.

fatigue duty, *Mil.* nonmilitary work done by soldiers, as cleaning up the camp, etc.

Fa·ti·ma (fə·tē'mə; fat'i·mə), *n.* 606?–632 A.D., only daughter of Mohammed.

fat·ling (fat'ling), *n.* calf, lamb, kid, or pig fattened to be killed for food.

fat·ten (fat'ən), *v.* make fat; become fat. —**fat'ten·er**, *n.*

fat·tish (fat'ish), *adj.* somewhat fat. —**fat'tish·ness**, *n.*

fat·ty (fat'i), *adj.*, **-ti·er**, **-ti·est**. 1. of fat; containing fat. 2. like fat; oily; greasy. —**fat'ti·ly**, *adv.* —**fat'ti·ness**, *n.*

fa·tu·i·ty (fə·tū'ə·ti; -tü'-), *n.*, *pl.* **-ties**. self-satisfied stupidity; silliness.

fat·u·ous (fach'ū·əs), *adj.* 1. stupid but self-satisfied; foolish; silly. 2. unreal; illusory. [< L *fatuus* foolish] —**fat'u·ous·ly**, *adv.* —**fat'u·ous·ness**, *n.*

fau·ces (fô'sēz), *n.pl. Anat.* cavity at the back of the mouth, leading into the pharynx. [< L] —**fau·cal** (fô'kəl), **fau·cial** (fô'shəl), *adj.*

fau·cet (fô'sit), *n.* device containing a valve for controlling the flow of water or other liquid from a pipe, tank, barrel, etc. [< F *fausset* < *fausser* bore through]

fault (fôlt), *n.* 1. something that is not as it should be. 2. mistake. 3. cause for blame. 4. *Geol.* a break in a rock or vein with part pushed up or down. 5. failure to serve the ball into the right place in tennis and similar games. 6. **at fault**, a deserving blame; wrong. b. puzzled; perplexed. 7. **find fault with**, object to; criticize. 8. **find fault**, find something wrong; complain. 9. **in fault**, deserving blame; wrong. 10. **to a fault**, too much; very. —*v. Geol.* suffer or cause a fault. [< OF *faute*, ult. < L *fallere* deceive] —Syn. *n.* 1. defect, flaw, imperfection. 2. error, slip, lapse.

fault·find·ing (fôlt'fīn'ding), *n.*, *adj.* finding fault; complaining; pointing out faults. —**fault'find'er**, *n.*

fault·less (fôlt'lis), *adj.* without a single fault; free from blemish or error; perfect. —**fault'less·ly**, *adv.* —**fault'less·ness**, *n.*

fault·y (fôl'ti), *adj.*, **fault·i·er**, **fault·i·est**. 1. having faults; containing blemishes or errors; wrong; imperfect. 2. blamable. —**fault'i·ly**, *adv.* —**fault'i·ness**, *n.* —Syn. 1. defective, incomplete. 2. culpable, reprehensible.

faun (fôn), *n. Roman Myth.* deity that helped

farmers and shepherds, represented as looking like a man, but with the ears, horns, tail, and sometimes the legs, of a goat. [< L *Faunus* a pastoral deity]

fau·na (fô′nə), *n.* animals of a given region or time. [< NL, orig. (in LL) name of a rural goddess]

Faust (foust), *n.* man who sold his soul to the devil in return for having everything that he wanted on earth.

faux pas (fō′ pä′), *pl.* **faux pas** (fō′ päz′), slip in speech, conduct, manners, etc.; breach of etiquette; blunder. [< F]

Faun

fa·vor, *esp. Brit.* **fa·vour** (fā′vər), *n.* **1.** kindness. **2.** liking; approval. **3.** condition of being liked or approved: *in favor, out of favor.* **4.** indulgence. **5.** pardon. **6.** permission. **7.** more than fair treatment; too great kindness. **8.** gift; token. **9. in favor of, a.** on the side of; supporting. **b.** to the advantage of; helping. **c.** to be paid to: *write a check in favor of the bank.* —*v.* **1.** show kindness to. **2.** like; approve. **3.** give more than fair treatment to. **4.** be on the side of; support. **5.** be to the advantage of; help. **6.** treat gently: *the dog favors his sore foot.* **7.** look like: *the girl favors her mother.* [< OF < L, < *favere* show kindness to] —fa′vored, *esp. Brit.* fa′voured, *adj.* —fa′vor·er, *esp. Brit.* fa′vour·er, *n.* —fa′vor·ing·ly, *esp. Brit.* fa′vour·ing·ly, *adv.* —Syn. *n.* **2.** good will, grace, countenance, patronage. —*v.* **1.** patronize, befriend.

fa·vor·a·ble, *esp. Brit.* **fa·vour·a·ble** (fā′vər·ə·bəl; fāv′rə-), *adj.* **1.** favoring; approving. **2.** being to one's advantage; helping: *a favorable wind.* **3.** granting what is desired. **4.** boding well; promising. —fa′vor·a·ble·ness, *esp. Brit.* fa′vour·a·ble·ness, *n.* —fa′vor·a·bly, *esp. Brit.* fa′vour·a·bly, *adv.* —Syn. **1.** well-disposed, commendatory, friendly. **2.** advantageous, helpful.

fa·vor·ite, *esp. Brit.* **fa·vour·ite** (fā′vər·it; fāv′rit), *adj.* liked better than others; liked very much. —*n.* **1.** one liked better than others; person or thing liked very much. **2.** person treated with special favor. **3.** one expected to win a contest.

fa·vor·it·ism, *esp. Brit.* **fa·vour·it·ism** (fā′vər·ə·tiz′əm; fāv′rə-), *n.* **1.** a favoring of one or some more than others; having favorites. **2.** state of being a favorite.

fawn[1] (fôn), *n.* **1.** deer less than a year old. **2.** a light, yellowish brown. —*adj.* light yellowish-brown. [< OF *faon*, ult. < L *fetus* fetus]

fawn[2] (fôn), *v.* **1.** cringe and bow; act slavishly. **2.** (of dogs, etc.) show fondness by crouching, wagging the tail, licking the hand, etc. [OE *fagnian* < *fægen* fain] —fawn′er, *n.* —fawn′ing·ly, *adv.* —Syn. **1.** shrink, cower, truckle.

fay (fā), *n.* fairy. [< OF, ult. < L *fatum* FATE]

faze (fāz), *v.*, **fazed, faz·ing.** *U.S. Colloq.* disturb; worry; bother. [var. of *feeze,* OE *fēsian* drive] ➤ *Faze* is a word which has worked its way from dialect to good American colloquial and informal usage. It is almost always used negatively (*the rebuke did not faze him*). Do not confuse this word with *phase,* meaning "aspect."

FBI, *Am.* Federal Bureau of Investigation.

F.C.C., FCC, Federal Communications Commission.

F clef, the bass clef in music.

Fe, *Chem.* iron. [< L *ferrum*]

fe·al·ty (fē′əl·ti), *n., pl.* **-ties. 1.** loyalty and duty owed by a vassal to his feudal lord. **2.** loyalty; faithfulness; allegiance. [< OF < L *fidelitas.* Doublet of FIDELITY.]

fear (fir), *n.* **1.** a being afraid; feeling that danger or evil is near; dread. **2.** cause for fear; danger: *there is no fear of our losing.* **3.** an uneasy feeling; anxious thought. **4.** awe; reverence. **5. for fear of** (a thing), in order to prevent (that thing) from occurring. **6. without fear or favor,** impartially; justly. —*v.* **1.** feel fear. **2.** feel fear of **3.** have an uneasy feeling or anxious thought; feel concern. **4.** have awe or reverence for. [OE *fǣr* peril] —fear′er, *n.* —fear′less, *adj.* —fear′-

less·ly, *adv.* —fear′less·ness, *n.* —Syn. *n.* **1.** terror, fright, alarm. —*v.* **2.** dread, apprehend.

fear·ful (fir′fəl), *adj.* **1.** causing fear; terrible; dreadful. **2.** full of fear; afraid. **3.** showing fear; caused by fear. **4.** *Colloq.* very bad, unpleasant, ugly, etc. —fear′ful·ly, *adv.* —fear′ful·ness, *n.* —Syn. **1.** awful, frightful, horrible, appalling, dire. **2.** frightened, alarmed.

fear·some (fir′səm), *adj.* **1.** causing fear; frightful. **2.** timid; afraid. —fear′some·ly, *adv.* —fear′some·ness, *n.*

fea·si·ble (fē′zə·bəl), *adj.* **1.** capable of being done or carried out easily. **2.** likely; probable. **3.** suitable; convenient. [< OF *faisable,* ult. < L *facere* do] —fea′si·bil′i·ty, fea′si·ble·ness, *n.* —fea′si·bly, *adv.*

feast (fēst), *n.* **1.** an elaborate meal prepared for some special occasion and for a number of guests. **2.** an unusually delicious or abundant meal. **3.** thing that gives pleasure or joy. **4.** a religious festival or celebration. —*v.* **1.** have a feast. **2.** provide with a feast. **3.** give pleasure or joy to. [< OF < L *festa* festal ceremonies] —feast′er, *n.* —Syn. *n.* **1.** banquet.

feat (fēt), *n.* a great or unusual deed; act showing great skill, strength, etc. [< OF < L *factum* (thing) done. Doublet of FACT.] —Syn. achievement, exploit, stunt.

feath·er (feth′ər), *n.* **1.** one of the light, thin growths that cover a bird's skin. **2.** something like a feather in shape or lightness. **3.** feather in one's cap, thing to be proud of. **4.** in fine, good, or high feather, in good health, high spirits, etc. —*v.* **1.** supply or cover with feathers. **2.** grow like feathers. **3.** move like feathers. **4.** join by a tongue and groove. **5.** turn the edge of a blade in the direction of movement. **6. feather one's nest,** take advantage of chances to get rich. [OE *fether*] —feath′ered, *adj.* —feath′er·less, *adj.* —feath′er·like′, *adj.*

feath·er·bed·ding (feth′ər·bed′ing), *n. Am.* the practice on the part of unions of forcing employers to hire more men than are needed for a particular job.

feath·er·brain (feth′ər·brān′), *n.* a silly, foolish, weak-minded person. —feath′er·brained′, *adj.*

feath·er·edge (feth′ər·ej′), *n.* a very thin edge. —feath′er·edged′, *adj.*

feath·er·weight (feth′ər·wāt′), *n.* **1.** a very light thing or person. **2.** boxer who weighs less than 126 pounds and more than 118 pounds. —*adj.* very light.

feath·er·y (feth′ər·i), *adj.* **1.** having feathers; covered with feathers. **2.** like feathers. **3.** light; flimsy. —feath′er·i·ness, *n.*

fea·ture (fē′chər), *n., v.,* **-tured, -tur·ing.** —*n.* **1.** part of the face. The nose, mouth, chin, and forehead are features. **2.** features, the face. **3.** a distinct part or quality; thing that stands out and attracts attention. **4.** a long motion picture. **5.** a special article, comic strip, etc., in a newspaper. —*v.* **1.** be a feature of. **2.** make a feature of. **3.** show the features of. [< OF < L *factura* < *facere* do] —fea′ture·less, *adj.* —Syn. *n.* **3.** characteristic, attribute, property, mark, trait.

fea·tured (fē′chərd), *adj.* **1.** made a feature of; given prominence to. **2.** having a certain kind of features: *hard-featured.*

Feb., February.

feb·ri·fuge (feb′rə·fūj), *adj.* that cures or lessens fever. —*n.* medicine to reduce fever. [< F < L < *febris* fever + *fugare* drive away] —fe·brif·u·gal (fi·brif′yə·gəl; feb′rə·fū′gəl), *adj.*

fe·brile (fē′brəl; feb′rəl), *adj.* **1.** of fever; feverish. **2.** caused by fever. [< Med.L *febrilis.* See FEVER.]

Feb·ru·ar·y (feb′rü·er′i; feb′yü-), *n., pl.* **-ar·ies.** the second month of the year. It has 28 days except in leap years, when it has 29. [< L, < *februa,* pl., the feast of purification celebrated on Feb. 15]

fe·ces (fē′sēz), *n.pl.* **1.** waste matter discharged from the intestines. **2.** dregs; sediment. Also, **faeces.** [< L *faeces,* pl., dregs] —fe·cal (fē′kəl), *adj.*

feck·less (fek′lis), *adj.* 1. futile; ineffective. 2. weak; helpless. [< *feck* vigor, var. of *fect* < *effect*] —**feck′less·ly,** *adv.* —**feck′less·ness,** *n.*

fe·cund (fē′kənd; fek′ənd), *adj.* fruitful; productive; fertile. [< F < L *fecundus*] —**fe·cun·di·ty** (fi·kun′də·ti), *n.*

fed (fed), *v.* pt. and pp. of feed.

fed·er·al (fed′ər·əl; fed′rəl), *adj.* 1. formed by an agreement between groups establishing a central organization. 2. of or having to do with such a central organization. 3. Federal, a. of or having to do with the central government of the United States. b. supporting the Constitution. c. supporting the central government of the United States during the Civil War. —*n.* Federal, *Am.* supporter or soldier of the central government of the United States during the Civil War. [< L *foedus* compact] —**fed′er·al·ly,** *adv.*

Federal Bureau of Investigation, *Am.* bureau of the Department of Justice established to investigate violations of Federal laws and safeguard national security.

fed·er·al·ism (fed′ər·əl·iz′əm; fed′rəl-), *n.* 1. federal principles of government. 2. Federalism, principles of the Federalist Party.

fed·er·al·ist (fed′ər·əl·ist; fed′rəl-), *n.* 1. Federalist, *Am.* member of the Federalist Party in the United States. 2. *Am.* advocate of a federal union among the colonies during and after the War of Independence. 3. federalist, person who favors the federal principle of government. —*adj. Am.* of federalism or the Federalists. —**fed′er·al·is′tic,** *adj.*

Federalist Party, *Am.* a political party in the United States that favored the adoption of the Constitution and a strong central government. It existed from about 1791 to about 1816.

fed·er·al·ize (fed′ər·əl·īz; fed′rəl-), *v.,* **-ized, -iz·ing.** 1. unite into a federal union. 2. bring under control of the federal government. —**fed′er·al·i·za′tion,** *n.*

fed·er·ate (*v.* fed′ər·āt; *adj.* fed′ər·it, fed′rit), *v.,* **-at·ed, -at·ing,** *adj.* —*v.* form into a federation. —*adj.* federated. [< L *foederatus* leagued together. See FEDERAL.]

fed·er·a·tion (fed′ər·ā′shən), *n.* 1. formation of a political unity out of a number of separate states, etc. 2. union by agreement, often a union of states or nations. —**fed′er·a′tive,** *adj.* —**fed′er·a′tive·ly,** *adv.*

fe·do·ra (fi·dô′rə; -dō′-), *n. Am.* a man's soft felt hat with a curved brim.

fee (fē), *n., v.,* **feed, fee·ing.** —*n.* 1. sum of money asked or paid for a service or privilege; charge. Doctors and lawyers get fees for their services. 2. a small present of money; tip. 3. right to keep and use land; fief. 4. *Law.* an inherited estate in land. 5. ownership. —*v.* give a fee to. [< AF *fleu* < Gmc.] —**Syn.** *n.* 1. pay, compensation, payment, recompense.

fee·ble (fē′bəl), *adj.,* **-bler, -blest.** weak; ineffective: *a feeble old man, a feeble mind, a feeble attempt.* [< OF < L *flebilis* lamentable < *flere* weep] —**fee′ble·ness,** *n.* —**fee′blish,** *adj.* —**fee′bly,** *adv.* —**Syn.** infirm, frail, sickly.

fee·ble-mind·ed (fē′bəl·mīn′did), *adj.* weak in mind; lacking normal intelligence. —**fee′ble·mind′ed·ly,** *adv.* —**fee′ble·mind′ed·ness,** *n.*

feed (fēd), *v.,* **fed, feed·ing,** *n.* —*v.* 1. give food to. 2. eat. 3. supply with material: *feed a machine.* 4. satisfy; gratify: *praise fed his vanity.* 5. nourish: *he fed his anger with thoughts of revenge.* —*n.* 1. food for animals; allowance of food for an animal. 2. *Am., Colloq.* meal for a person. 3. a supplying with material. 4. the material supplied. 5. part of a machine that supplies material. [OE *fēdan* < *fōda* food] —**feed′er,** *n.* —**Syn.** *v.* 5. sustain. —*n.* 1. fodder.

feed·back (fēd′bak′), *n.* 1. the return of the results of a process, or a part of them, to the same or an earlier stage of the process, as a self-criticizing or regulating mechanism. 2. the return of part of the energy in an electronic circuit from the output to the input, either in positive phase to amplify or in negative phase to control the output.

feel (fēl), *v.,* **felt, feel·ing,** *n.* —*v.* 1. touch: *feel this cloth.* 2. try to touch; try to find by touch-ing: *feel in all your pockets.* 3. find out from touching: *feel how cold my hands are.* 4. be aware of: *feel the cool breeze.* 5. have the feeling of being; be: *she feels sure.* 6. give the feeling of being; seem: *the air feels cold.* 7. have in one's mind; experience. 8. have pity or sympathy: *she feels for all who suffer.* 9. think; believe; consider: *I feel that we shall win.* —*n.* 1. touch: *the feel of silk.* 2. a feeling: *a feel of frost in the air.* 3. the sense of touch. [OE *fēlan*]

feel·er (fēl′ər), *n.* 1. person or thing that feels. 2. *Zool.* a special part of an animal's body for touching, as an insect's antenna. 3. suggestion, remark, hint, question, etc., made to find out what others are thinking or planning.

FEELERS

LEGS

feel·ing (fēl′ing), *n.* 1. act or condition of one that feels. 2. sense of touch. 3. a being conscious; awareness. 4. emotion. 5. pity; sympathy. 6. opinion; sentiment. 7. quality felt to belong to something. 8. impression made by a work of art. 9. emotional insight. 10. feelings, sympathies; susceptibilities: *hurt one's feelings.* —*adj.* 1. sensitive; emotional. 2. showing emotion. —**feel′ing·ly,** *adv.* —**Syn.** 3. sensation, impression. 4. passion.

feet (fēt), *n.* pl. of foot.

feign (fān), *v.* 1. put on a false appearance of; make believe; pretend. 2. make up to deceive; invent falsely: *feign an excuse.* [< OF *feindre* (*feign-*) < L *fingere* form] —**feigned,** *adj.* —**feign·ed·ly** (fān′id·li), *adv.* —**feign′er,** *n.* —**feign′ing·ly,** *adv.* —**Syn.** 1. assume, affect, simulate.

feint (fānt), *n.* 1. false appearance; pretense. 2. movement intended to deceive; pretended blow; sham attack. —*v.* make a pretended blow or sham attack. [< F, < *feindre* FEIGN]

feld·spar (feld′spär′; fel′-), *n.* any of several crystalline minerals composed mostly of aluminum silicates. Also, felspar. [< *feld-* (< G *feldspat,* lit. field spar) + *spar*[3]] —**feld·spath·ic** (feld·spath′ik; fel-), *adj.*

fe·lic·i·tate (fə·lis′ə·tāt), *v.,* **-tat·ed, -tat·ing.** formally express good wishes to; congratulate. [< LL, < *felix* happy] —**fe·lic′i·ta′tion,** *n.*

fe·lic·i·tous (fə·lis′ə·təs), *adj.* 1. well chosen for the occasion; unusually appropriate. 2. having a gift for apt speech. —**fe·lic′i·tous·ly,** *adv.* —**fe·lic′i·tous·ness,** *n.*

fe·lic·i·ty (fə·lis′ə·ti), *n., pl.* **-ties.** 1. happiness. 2. good fortune; blessing. 3. a pleasing aptness in expression; appropriateness; grace. 4. a happy turn of thought; well-chosen phrase.

fe·line (fē′līn), *adj.* 1. of or belonging to the cat family. 2. catlike; stealthy. —*n.* any animal belonging to the cat family, such as lions, tigers, and panthers. [< L *felis* cat] —**fe′line·ly,** *adv.* —**fe′line·ness, fe·lin·i·ty** (fi·lin′ə·ti), *n.*

fell[1] (fel), *v.* pt. of fall.

fell[2] (fel), *v.* 1. cause to fall; knock down. 2. cut down (a tree). 3. turn down and stitch one edge of (a seam) over the other. —*n.* 1. all the trees cut down in one season. 2. seam made by felling. [OE *fellan* < *feallan* fall] —**fell′a·ble,** *adj.* —**fell′er,** *n.*

fell[3] (fel), *adj.* 1. cruel; fierce; terrible: *a fell blow.* 2. deadly; destructive: *a fell disease.* [< OF < VL *fello.* See FELON[1].] —**fell′ness,** *n.*

fell[4] (fel), *n.* skin or hide of an animal. [OE; akin to FILM.]

fel·loe (fel′ō), *n.* the circular rim of a wheel into which the outer ends of the spokes are inserted. Also, felly. [var. of *felly*]

SPOKE

HUB

AXLE

RIM

FELLOE

fel·low (fel′ō), *n.* 1. man; boy. 2. *Colloq.* a young man courting a young woman; beau. 3. companion; comrade; associate. 4. *Colloq.* person. 5. one of the same class or rank; equal: *the world has not his fellow.* 6. the other one of a pair; mate. 7. a graduate student who has a fellowship in a university or college. **8.** an honored member of a learned society. —*adj.* belonging to the same class; united by the same work, aims, etc.; being in the same or a like condition: *fellow citizens, fellow workers.* —*v.* produce an equal to; match. [< Scand. *fēlagi* partner (lit., fee-layer)] ▶ **Fellow** is colloquial and informal when used to mean "person"; formal in sense of "associate." Most commonly used in writing as adjective: *his fellow sufferers, a fellow feeling.*

fel·low·ship (fel′ō·ship), *n., v.,* **-shiped, -ship·ing;** *esp. Brit.* **-shipped, -ship·ping.** —*n.* **1.** condition or relation of being a fellow. **2.** companionship. **3.** a taking part with others; sharing. **4.** group of people having similar tastes, interests, etc.; brotherhood. **5.** position or sum of money given to a graduate student in a university or college to enable him to go on with his studies. —*v.* **1.** admit to fellowship. **2.** join in fellowship. —**Syn.** *n.* **2.** comradeship, friendship.

fellow traveler, one sympathizing with a political movement or party but who is a nonmember.

fel·ly (fel′i), *n., pl.* **-lies. felloe.** [OE *felg*]

fel·on[1] (fel′ən), *n. Law.* person who has committed a serious crime. —*adj.* wicked; cruel. [< OF, ult. < L *fellare* suck (obscene)]

fel·on[2] (fel′ən), *n. Pathol.* a very painful infection on a finger or toe, usually near the nail.

fe·lo·ni·ous (fə·lō′ni·əs), *adj. Law.* that is a felony; criminal. **2.** very wicked; villainous. —**fe·lo′ni·ous·ly,** *adv.* —**fe·lo′ni·ous·ness,** *n.*

fel·o·ny (fel′ə·ni), *n., pl.* **-nies.** *Law.* crime more serious than a misdemeanor. Murder and burglary are felonies.

fel·spar (fel′spär′), *n.* feldspar.

felt[1] (felt), *v.* pt. and pp. of feel.

felt[2] (felt), *n.* cloth made by rolling and pressing together wool, hair, or fur, used to make hats, slippers, etc. —*adj.* made of felt. —*v.* **1.** make into felt. **2.** cover with felt. [OE]

fem., feminine.

fe·male (fē′māl), *n.* **1.** woman or girl. **2.** animal belonging to the sex that brings forth young. **3.** *Bot.* plant having a pistil and no stamens. —*adj.* **1.** of or pertaining to women or girls. **2.** belonging to the sex that brings forth young. **3.** *Bot.* having pistils. **4.** designating some part of a machine, connection, etc., into which a corresponding part fits. [< OF < L < *femella,* dim. of *femina* woman; form infl. by *male*] —**fe·mal·i·ty** (fi·mal′ə·ti), *n.* ▶ **female.** Usage now restricts *female* to designations of sex, usually in scientific contexts, leaving English without a single word for female-human-being-regardless-of-sex.

fem·i·nine (fem′ə·nin), *adj.* **1.** of women or girls. **2.** like a woman; womanly. **3.** like that of a woman; not suited to a man. **4.** of or belonging to the female sex. **5.** *Gram.* of the gender to which names of females belong. *Actress, queen,* and *cow* are feminine nouns. —*n. Gram.* **a.** the feminine gender. **b.** word or form in the feminine gender. [< OF < L, < *femina* woman] —**fem′i·nine·ly,** *adv.* —**fem·i·nin·i·ty** (fem′ə·nin′ə·ti), **fem′i·nine·ness,** *n.*

fem·i·nism (fem′ə·niz·əm), *n.* **1.** doctrine that favors more rights and activities for women. **2.** feminine nature or character. —**fem′i·nist,** *n.* —**fem′i·nis·tic,** *adj.*

femme fa·tale (fam fä·täl′), French. a dangerously fascinating or alluring woman; siren.

fe·mur (fē′mər), *n., pl.* **fe·murs, fem·o·ra** (fem′ə·rə). *Anat.* the thighbone. [< L, thigh] —**fem·o·ral** (fem′ə·rəl), *adj.*

fen (fen), *n. Brit.* marsh; swamp; bog. [OE *fenn*]

fence (fens), *n., v.,* **fenced, fenc·ing.** —*n.* **1.** railing, wall, or other means of enclosing a yard, garden, field, farm, etc., to show where it ends or to keep people or animals out or in. **2.** skill or adroitness in argument or repartee. **3.** person who buys and sells stolen goods. **4.** place where stolen goods are bought and sold. **5. on the fence,** *Am., Colloq.* not having made up one's mind which side to take; doubtful; hesitating.

—*v.* **1.** put a fence around; enclose. **2.** fight with swords or foils. **3.** parry; evade. **4.** defend. [var. of *defence*] —**fence′less,** *adj.* —**fence′less·ness,** *n.* —**fenc′er·like′,** *adj.* —**fenc′er,** *n.*

fenc·ing (fen′sing), *n.* **1.** art of fighting with swords or foils. **2.** *Am.* material for fences.

fend (fend), *v.* **1.** defend; resist. **2. fend for oneself,** *Colloq.* provide for oneself; get along by one's own efforts. [var. of *defend*]

fend·er (fen′dər), *n.* **1.** anything that keeps or wards something off. **2.** *Am.* guard or protection over the wheel of an automobile, motorcycle, etc.; mudguard. **3.** *Am.* a metal frame on the front of a locomotive, streetcar, etc., to catch or thrust aside anything in the way; cowcatcher. **4.** *Am.* a metal guard, frame, or screen in front of a fireplace to keep hot coals and sparks from the room. [var. of *defender*]

Fe·ni·an (fē′ni·ən; fēn′yən), *Am.* —*n.* member of an Irish secret organization founded in the United States about 1858 for the purpose of overthrowing English rule in Ireland. —*adj.* of or having to do with the Fenians. —**Fe′ni·an·ism,** *n.*

fen·nel (fen′əl), *n. Bot.* a tall plant with yellow flowers, used in medicine and cooking. [< VL *fenuclum,* ult. < L *fenum* hay]

fen·ny (fen′i), *adj. Brit.* marshy; swampy.

feoff (*n.* fēf; *v.* fef, fēf), *n.* fief. —*v.* invest with a fief. —**feoff·ment** (fef′mənt; fēf′-), *n.* —**feof′for, feof′fer,** *n.*

FEPC, Fair Employment Practices Committee.

fe·ral (fir′əl), *adj.* **1.** wild; untamed. **2.** brutal; savage. [< L *fera* beast]

fer-de-lance (fer·də·läns′), *n.* a large, poisonous snake of tropical America. [< F, iron (tip) of a lance]

Fer·di·nand V of Castile (fér′də·nand), 1452–1516, Spanish king 1474–1516. His queen, Isabella, encouraged Christopher Columbus in his voyages.

fer·ment (*v.* fər·ment′; *n.* fér′ment), *v.* **1.** undergo a gradual chemical change, becoming sour or alcoholic and giving off bubbles of gas. **2.** cause this chemical change in. **3.** cause unrest in; excite; agitate. **4.** be excited; seethe with agitation or unrest. —*n.* **1.** substance causing fermentation: *yeast is a ferment.* **2.** excitement; agitation; unrest: *national ferment.* [< L *fermentum* < *fervere* boil] —**fer·ment′a·ble,** *adj.*

fer·men·ta·tion (fér′men·tā′shən), *n.* **1.** act or process of fermenting. **2.** excitement; agitation; unrest. **3.** *Chem.* a change, as becoming sour or alcoholic and giving off bubbles of gas, caused by a ferment.

Fer·mi (fér′mē), *n.* Enrico, 1901–1954, American physicist, born in Italy, director of first nuclear reactor.

fer·mi·um (fer′mi·əm), *n.* a rare, radioactive, artificial element, Fm, produced as a by-product of nuclear fission. [named for Enrico *Fermi*]

fern (fern), *n. Bot.* plant that has roots, stems, and leaves, but no flowers, and reproduces by spores instead of seeds. [OE *fearn*] —**fern′like′,** *adj.* —**fern′y,** *adj.*

Fern

fern·er·y (fér′nər·i), *n., pl.* **-er·ies.** **1.** place where ferns grow. **2.** container in which ferns are grown.

fe·ro·cious (fə·rō′shəs), *adj.* savagely cruel; fierce. [< L, < *ferox* fierce] —**fe·ro′cious·ly,** *adv.* —**fe·roc·i·ty** (fə·ros′ə·ti), **fe·ro′cious·ness,** *n.* —**Syn.** ruthless, brutal, murderous.

fer·ret (fer′it), *n.* a white or yellowish-white weasel used for killing rats, hunting rabbits, etc. —*v.* **1.** hunt with ferrets. **2.** hunt; search. [< OF *furet,* ult. < L *fur* thief] —**fer′ret·er,** *n.*

Ferret (total length ab. 1½ ft.)

fer·ric (fer'ik), *adj. Chem.* a. of or containing iron. b. containing trivalent iron. [< L *ferrum* iron]

Fer·ris wheel (fer'is), *Am.* a large, revolving wheel with seats hanging from its rim, used in carnivals, amusement parks, etc. [for G. W. G. Ferris, its inventor]

fer·rous (fer'əs), *adj. Chem.* a. of or containing iron. b. containing divalent iron.

fer·ru·gi·nous (fə·rü'jə·nəs), *adj.* 1. of or containing iron; like that of iron. 2. reddish-brown like rust. [< L, < *ferrugo* iron rust < *ferrum* iron]

fer·rule (fer'əl; -ül), *n., v.,* -ruled, -rul·ing. —*n.* 1. a metal ring or cap put around the end of a cane, umbrella, etc. 2. a metal ring or short tube. —*v.* supply with a ferrule. Also, **ferule.** [< OF, ult. < L *viriola,* dim. of *viriae* bracelets]

fer·ry (fer'i), *n., pl.* -ries, *v.,* -ried, -ry·ing. —*n.* 1. place where boats carry people and goods across a river or narrow stretch of water. 2. the boat used; ferryboat. 3. system for flying airplanes to a destination for delivery. [< v.] —*v.* 1. carry (people and goods) back and forth across a river or narrow stretch of water. 2. go across in a ferryboat. 3. carry back and forth across a wide stretch of water in an airplane. 4. fly an airplane to a destination for delivery. [OE *ferian* < *fœr* fare]

fer·ry·boat (fer'i·bōt'), *n.* boat used for ferrying.

fer·ry·man (fer'i·mən), *n., pl.* -men. man who owns or has charge of a ferry.

fer·tile (fer'təl), *adj.* 1. able to produce much; rich in things that aid growth, development, etc. 2. *Obs.* abundant. 3. capable of reproduction; able to produce seeds, fruit, young, etc. 4. *Biol.* capable of developing into a new individual; fertilized. [< L *fertilis* < *ferre* bear] —**fer'tile·ly,** *adv.* —**fer'tile·ness,** *n.*

fer·til·i·ty (fer·til'ə·ti), *n.* a being fertile.

fer·ti·lize (fer'tə·liz), *v.,* -lized, -liz·ing. 1. make fertile; make able to produce much. 2. put fertilizer on. 3. *Biol.* unite with (an egg cell) in fertilization; impregnate. —**fer'ti·liz·a·ble,** *adj.* —**fer'ti·li·za'tion,** *n.*

fer·ti·liz·er (fer'tə·liz'ər), *n.* substance put on land to make it able to produce more, as manure.

fer·ule¹ (fer'əl; -ül), *n., v.,* -uled, -ul·ing. —*n.* stick or ruler used for punishing children by striking them on the hand. —*v.* punish with a stick or ruler. [< L *ferula* rod]

fer·ule² (fer'əl; -ül), *n., v.,* -uled, -ul·ing. ferrule.

fer·vent (fer'vənt), *adj.* 1. showing warmth of feeling; very earnest. 2. hot; glowing. [< F < L *fervens* boiling] —**fer'ven·cy, fer'vent·ness,** *n.* —**fer'vent·ly,** *adv.* —**Syn.** 1. ardent, zealous, passionate.

fer·vid (fer'vid), *adj.* 1. showing great warmth of feeling; intensely emotional. 2. intensely hot. [< L, < *fervere* boil] —**fer'vid·ly,** *adv.* —**fer'vid·ness,** *n.*

fer·vor, *esp. Brit.* **fer·vour** (fer'vər), *n.* 1. great warmth of feeling; intense emotion. 2. intense heat. [< OF < L. See **FERVENT.**] —**Syn.** 1. zeal, ardor.

fes·cue (fes'kū), *n.* a tough grass used for pasture. [< OF, ult. < L *festuca*]

fess, fesse (fes), *n.* in heraldry, a wide, horizontal band across the middle of a shield. [< OF < L *fascia* band]

fes·tal (fes'təl), *adj.* of a feast, festival, or holiday; gay; joyous; festive. [< OF < LL < L *festum* feast] —**fes'tal·ly,** *adv.*

fes·ter (fes'tər), *v.* 1. form pus. 2. cause pus to form. 3. cause soreness or pain; rankle. 4. decay; rot. [< n.] —*n.* sore that forms pus; small ulcer. [< OF < L *fistula* pipe, ulcer]

fes·ti·val (fes'tə·vəl), *n.* 1. day or special time of rejoicing or feasting, often in memory of some great happening. 2. celebration; entertainment: *a music festival.* 3. merrymaking; revelry. —*adj.* having to do with a festival. [< Med.L, ult. < L *festum* feast]

fes·tive (fes'tiv), *adj.* of or for a feast, festi-val, or holiday; joyous; merry. —**fes'tive·ly,** *adv.* —**fes'tive·ness,** *n.*

fes·tiv·i·ty (fes·tiv'ə·ti), *n., pl.* -ties. 1. festive activity; thing done to celebrate. 2. gaiety; merriment. 3. festivities, festive proceedings.

fes·toon (fes·tün'), *n.* a hanging curve of flowers, leaves, ribbons, etc. —*v.* 1. decorate with festoons. 2. form into festoons; hang in curves. [< F < Ital. *festone* < *festa* festival, feast]

Festoon

fe·tal (fē'təl), *adj.* 1. of a fetus. 2. like that of a fetus. Also, **foetal.**

fetch (fech), *v.* 1. go and get; bring. 2. cause to come; succeed in bringing. 3. be sold for. 4. *Colloq.* attract; charm. 5. *Colloq.* hit; strike. 6. give (a groan, sigh, etc.). 7. take a course (said chiefly of ships); move; go. —*n.* act of fetching. [OE *feccan*] —**fetch'er,** *n.*

fetch·ing (fech'ing), *adj. Colloq.* attractive; charming. —**fetch'ing·ly,** *adv.*

fete, fête (fāt), *n., v.,* fet·ed, fet·ing; fêt·ed, fêt·ing. —*n.* festival; entertainment; party. —*v.* honor with a fete; entertain: *the engaged couple were feted by their friends.* [< F, feast]

fet·id (fet'id; fē'tid), *adj.* smelling very bad; stinking. [< L *foetidus* < *foetere* to smell] —**fet'id·ly,** *adv.* —**fet'id·ness, fe·tid'i·ty,** *n.*

fet·ish, fe·tich (fē'tish; fet'ish), *n.* 1. any material thing supposed to have magic power. 2. anything regarded with unreasoning reverence or devotion. [< F < Pg. *feitiço* charm < L *facticius* artificial] —**fe'tish·like', fe'tich·like',** *adj.*

fe·tish·ism, fe·tich·ism (fē'tish·iz·əm; fet'ish-), *n.* 1. belief in fetishes; worship of fetishes. 2. *Psychiatry.* an abnormal attachment of erotic feeling to some inanimate object. —**fe'tish·ist, fe'tich·ist,** *n.* —**fe'tish·is'tic, fe'tich·is'tic,** *adj.*

fet·lock (fet'lok), *n.* 1. tuft of hair above a horse's hoof on the back part of the leg. See the picture under **cannon bone.** 2. part of a horse's leg where this tuft grows. [ME *fetlok*]

fet·ter (fet'ər), *n.* 1. chain or shackle for the feet to prevent escape. 2. Usually, **fetters.** anything that shackles or binds; restraint. —*v.* 1. bind with fetters; chain the feet of. 2. bind; restrain. [OE *feter;* akin to **FOOT**] —**Syn.** *v.* 2. confine, hamper, impede.

fet·tle (fet'əl), *n.* condition; trim: *the horse is in fine fettle.* [? < ME *fettel(en)* gird up, < OE *fetel* belt]

fe·tus (fē'təs), *n.* an animal embryo during the later stages of its development. Also, **foetus.** [< L]

feud¹ (fūd), *n.* 1. a long and deadly quarrel between families, often passed down from generation to generation. 2. bitter hatred between two persons, groups, etc. 3. quarrel. [var. of ME *fede* < OF < OHG *fehida* enmity] —**feu'dal,** *adj.* —**Syn.** 2. hostility, enmity.

feud² (fūd), *n.* a feudal estate; fief. [< Med.L *feudum* < Gmc.]

feu·dal (fū'dəl), *adj.* 1. of or having to do with feudalism. 2. of or having to do with feuds or fiefs. [< Med.L *feudalis.* See **FEUD².**] —**feu'dal·ly,** *adv.*

feu·dal·ism (fū'dəl·iz·əm), *n.* the feudal system or its principles and practices. —**feu'dal·ist,** *n.* —**feu'dal·is'tic,** *adj.*

feudal system, the social, economic, and political system of Europe in the Middle Ages, under which vassals held land on condition of giving military and other services to the lord owning it in return for the protection and the use of the land.

feu·da·to·ry (fū'də·tô'ri; -tō'-), *adj., n., pl.* -ries. —*adj.* 1. owing feudal services to a lord. 2. holding or held as a feudal estate or fief. —*n.* 1. a feudal vassal: *the duke summoned his feudatories to aid him in war.* 2. a feudal estate; fief.

feud·ist (fūd'ist), *n. Am.* person engaging in a feud.

fe·ver (fē'vər), *n.* 1. an unhealthy condition of

the body in which the temperature is higher than normal. 2. any of various diseases that cause fever, such as scarlet fever and typhoid fever. 3. an excited, restless condition. —*v.* 1. affect with fever; heat. 2. become feverish. [< L *febris*] —**fe′vered,** *adj.* —**fe′ver·less,** *adj.*

fe·ver·few (fē′vər·fū), *n.* a perennial plant of the aster family with small, white, daisylike flowers. [< LL *febrifug(i)a* FEBRIFUGE]

fe·ver·ish (fē′vər·ish), *adj.* 1. having fever. 2. having a slight degree of fever. 3. causing fever. 4. infested with fever. 5. excited; restless. —**fe′ver·ish·ly,** *adv.* —**fe′ver·ish·ness,** *n.*

fe·ver·ous (fē′vər·əs), *adj.* feverish. —**fe′ver·ous·ly,** *adv.*

fe·ver·root (fē′vər·rüt′; -rüt′), *n.* *Am.* a coarse plant sometimes used for medicine.

fever sore, a cold sore.

few (fū), *adj.* not many. —*n.* 1. a small number. 2. the few, the minority. 3. quite a few, *Colloq.* a good many. [OE *fēawe*] —**few′ness,** *n.* **>** **fewer,** less. *Fewer* refers only to number and things that are counted: *Fewer cars were on the road. There were fewer than sixty present.* In formal usage *less* refers only to amount or quantity and things measured: *There was a good deal less tardiness in the second term* [amount]. *There was even less hay than the summer before.* In general usage it refers also to number: *In the making of the present book no less than 100,000 words were critically examined.*

fez (fez), *n.*, *pl.* **fez·zes.** a felt cap, usually red, ornamented with a long, black tassel, formerly worn by Turkish men. [< Turk.; named after *Fez,* Morocco]

ff., and the following; and what follows.

fi·an·cé (fē′än·sā′; fē′än·sā), *n.* man engaged to be married. [< F, betrothed] **>** **fiancé, fiancée.** About a century ago the simple English *betrothed* was replaced by the French word (probably by "society" journalists), and now we are cursed not only with accent marks but with separate forms for the man (*fiancé*) and the woman (*fiancée*). Pronunciation for both is fē′än·sā′, with a strong informal tendency to fē′än·sā. The plurals are *fiancés, fiancées.* In newspapers and much informal writing the accent mark is dropped and probably it will soon disappear generally.

fi·an·cée (fē′än·sā′; fē′än·sā), *n.* woman engaged to be married. [< F]

fi·as·co (fi·as′kō), *n.*, *pl.* **-cos, -coes.** failure; breakdown. [< F < Ital., flask]

fi·at (fī′ət; -at), *n.* 1. an authoritative order or command; decree. 2. sanction. [< L, let it be done]

fiat money, *Am.* paper currency made legal tender by the decree of the government, but not based on or convertible into coin.

fib (fib), *n.*, *v.*, **fibbed, fib·bing.** lie about some small matter. [? < *fibble-fable* < *fable*] —**fib′ber,** *n.*

fi·ber, fi·bre (fī′bər), *n.* 1. a threadlike part; thread: *a muscle is made up of many fibers.* 2. substance made up of threads or threadlike parts. Hemp fiber can be spun into rope or woven into a coarse cloth. 3. texture: *cloth of coarse fiber.* 4. character; nature. 5. a threadlike root of a plant. [< F < L *fibra*]

fi·ber·board (fī′bər·bôrd′; -bōrd′), *n.* a building material made by compressing fibers, esp. of wood, into flat sheets.

Fi·ber·glas (fī′bər·glas′; -gläs′), *n.* *Trademark.* a very fine, flexible glass fiber that can be made into insulating material or even into fabrics.

fi·bril (fī′brəl), *n.* a small fiber.

fi·brin (fī′brən), *n.* 1. a tough, elastic, yellowish protein formed when blood clots. 2. *Bot.* gluten in plants. —**fi·brin·ous** (fī′brə·nəs), *adj.*

fi·broid (fī′broid), *adj.* composed of fibers. —*n.* *Pathol.* tumor composed of fibers or fibrous tissue.

fi·brous (fī′brəs), *adj.* composed of fibers; having fibers; like fiber.

fib·u·la (fib′yə·lə), *n.*, *pl.* **-lae** (-lē), **-las.** 1. *Anat.* the outer and thinner of the two bones in the human lower leg. It extends from knee to ankle. 2. *Zool.* a similar bone in the hind leg of animals. [< L, clasp, brooch] —**fib′u·lar,** *adj.*

fich·u (fish′ü), *n.* a three-cornered piece of muslin, lace, or other soft material worn by women about the neck, with the ends drawn together or crossed on the breast. [< F]

Fichu

fick·le (fik′əl), *adj.* likely to change without reason; changing; not constant. [OE *ficol*] —**Syn.** unstable, unsteady. —**Ant.** constant, steadfast, unchanging.

fic·tion (fik′shən), *n.* 1. novels, short stories, and other prose writings that tell about imaginary people and happenings. 2. what is imagined or made up. 3. an imaginary account or statement; made-up story. 4. an inventing of imaginary accounts, stories, etc. 5. thing acted upon as a fact, in spite of its possible falsity. It is a legal fiction that a corporation is a person. [< L *fictio* < *fingere* to form, fashion] —**fic′tion·al,** *adj.* —**fic′tion·al·ly,** *adv.*

fic·ti·tious (fik·tish′əs), *adj.* 1. not real; imaginary; made-up: *characters in novels are usually fictitious.* 2. assumed in order to deceive; false: *the criminal used a fictitious name.* —**fic·ti′tious·ly,** *adv.* —**fic·ti′tious·ness,** *n.* —**Syn.** 2. counterfeit, sham, feigned.

fid·dle (fid′əl), *n.*, *v.*, **-dled, -dling.** —*n.* 1. *Colloq.* violin. 2. **play second fiddle,** take a secondary part. —*v.* 1. *Colloq.* play on a violin. 2. make aimless movements; play nervously. 3. trifle: *he fiddled away the whole day doing absolutely nothing.* [OE *fithele* (recorded in *fithelere* fiddler; prob. akin to *viol*] —**fid′dler,** *n.*

fid·dle·stick (fid′əl·stik′), *n.* 1. a violin bow. 2. a mere nothing; trifle.

fid·dle·sticks (fid′əl·stiks′), *interj.* nonsense! rubbish!

fi·del·i·ty (fi·del′ə·ti; fə-), *n.*, *pl.* **-ties.** 1. faithfulness to a trust or vow; steadfast faithfulness. 2. accuracy; exactness. [< L *fidelitas,* ult. < *fides* faith. Doublet of FEALTY.] —**Syn.** 1. constancy, loyalty.

fidg·et (fij′it), *v.* 1. move about restlessly; be uneasy: *a child fidgets if he has to sit still a long time.* 2. make uneasy. —*n.* 1. condition of being restless or uneasy. 2. person who moves about restlessly. 3. the fidgets, fit of restlessness or uneasiness. [< obs. *fidge* move restlessly] —**fidg′et·y,** *adj.* —**fidg′et·i·ness,** *n.*

fi·du·ci·ar·y (fi·dū′shi·er′i; -dū′-), *adj.*, *n.*, *pl.* **-ar·ies.** —*adj.* 1. held in trust: *fiduciary estates.* 2. *Law.* holding in trust. A fiduciary possessor is legally responsible for what belongs to another. 3. of a trustee; of trust and confidence. 4. depending upon public trust and confidence for its value. Paper money that cannot be redeemed in gold or silver is fiduciary currency. —*n.* *Law.* trustee. [< L, < *fiducia* trust]

fie (fī), *interj.* for shame! shame! [< OF]

fief (fēf), *n.* 1. piece of land held on condition of giving military and other services to the lord owning it in return for protection and the use of the land; feudal estate. 2. the land or territory so held. Also, **feoff.** [< F < Gmc.]

field (fēld), *n.* 1. land with few or no trees. 2. piece of land used for crops or pasture. 3. piece of land used for some special purpose, esp. one used for sports or contests. 4. land yielding some product: *a coal field.* 5. place where a battle is or has been fought. 6. battle. 7. region where military or other operations are carried on. 8. a flat space; broad surface: *a field of ice.* 9. surface on which something is pictured or painted: *the field of a coat of arms.* 10. range of opportunity or interest; sphere of activity or operation. 11. *Physics.* space throughout which a force operates. A magnet has a magnetic field around it. 12. *Television.* the entire screen area occupied by an image. 13. all those in a game, contest, or outdoor sport. **14. take the field,** begin a battle, campaign, game, etc. —*v.* **1.** stop or catch and return (a ball) in baseball, cricket, etc. **2.** act as a fielder in baseball, cricket, etc. —*adj.* **1.** of or pertaining to fields. **2.** growing or living in fields. **3.** performed on a field, not on a track. [OE *feld*]

field·er (fēl′dər), *n.* **1.** *Baseball.* player who is stationed around or outside the diamond to stop the ball and throw it in. **2.** a similar player in a game of cricket.

field glass, a small binocular telescope.

field goal, *Am.* **1.** *Football.* a goal counting 3 points made by a drop kick. **2.** *Basketball.* a toss into the basket made during regular play, not as a result of a foul.

field grade, *Mil.* classification of officers above captain and below brigadier general.

Field·ing (fēl′ding), *n.* Henry, 1707–1754, English novelist, author of the novel *Tom Jones.*

field marshal, an army officer ranking next to the commander in chief in the British, German, and some other armies.

field of fire, *Mil.* area that a gun or battery covers effectively.

field·piece (fēld′pēs′), *n. Mil.* cannon mounted on a carriage for use in the field.

field work, scientific or technical work done in the field by surveyors, geologists, etc. —**field′-work′er,** *n.*

field·work (fēld′wėrk′), *n.* a temporary fortification for defense made by soldiers in the field.

fiend (fēnd), *n.* **1.** an evil spirit; devil. **2.** a very wicked or cruel person. **3.** *Colloq.* person who gives himself up to some habit, practice, game, etc.; devotee. **4. the Fiend,** the Devil. [OE *fēond*] —**fiend′like′,** *adj.*

fiend·ish (fēn′dish), *adj.* very cruel or wicked; devilish. —**fiend′ish·ly,** *adv.* —**fiend′ish·ness,** *n.*

fierce (firs), *adj.,* **fierc·er, fierc·est. 1.** savage; wild: *a fierce lion.* **2.** raging; violent: *a fierce wind.* **3.** very eager or active; ardent: *fierce efforts.* **4.** *Slang.* very bad, unpleasant, etc. [< OF < L *ferus* wild] —**fierce′ly,** *adv.* —**fierce′ness,** *n.* —Syn. **1.** cruel, ferocious. —Ant. **1.** tame, gentle.

fier·y (fir′i; fī′ər·i), *adj.,* **fier·i·er, fier·i·est. 1.** containing fire; burning; flaming. **2.** like fire; very hot; flashing; glowing. **3.** full of feeling or spirit; ardent: *a fiery speech.* **4.** easily aroused or excited: *a fiery temper.* **5.** inflamed: *a fiery sore.* —**fier′i·ly,** *adv.* —**fier′i·ness,** *n.* —Syn. **3.** fervent, fervid, spirited.

fi·es·ta (fi·es′tə), *n.* **1.** a religious festival; saint's day. **2.** holiday; festivity. [< Sp., FEAST]

fife (fīf), *n., v.,* **fifed, fif·ing.** —*n.* a small, shrill musical instrument like a flute. —*v.* play on a fife. [< G *pfeife* pipe] —**fif′er,** *n.*

fif·teen (fif′tēn′), *n.* **1.** a cardinal number, five more than ten. **2.** symbol of this number; 15. —*adj.* five more than ten; 15. —**fif·teenth** (fif′tēnth′), *adj., n.*

fifth (fifth), *adj.* **1.** next after the fourth; last in a series of 5. **2.** being one of 5 equal parts. —*n.* **1.** next after the fourth; last in a series of 5. **2.** one of 5 equal parts. **3. a.** one fifth of a gallon (U.S.), a measure used for alcoholic beverages. **b.** bottle or container holding a fifth. —**fifth′ly,** *adv.*

fifth column, persons within a country who secretly aid its enemies. —**fifth columnist.**

fif·ty (fif′ti), *n., pl.* **-ties,** *adj.* —*n.* **1.** a cardinal number, five times ten. **2.** symbol of this number; 50. —*adj.* five times ten; 50. —**fif′ti·eth,** *adj., n.*

fif·ty-fif·ty (fif′ti-fif′ti), *adv., adj. Slang.* in or with equal shares.

fig (fig), *n.* **1.** a small, soft, sweet fruit that grows in warm regions, eaten fresh or dried like dates and raisins. **2.** tree that figs grow on. **3.** very small amount: *I don't care a fig for your opinion.* [< OF < Pr., ult. < L *ficus* fig tree]

Figs

fig., **1.** figurative; figuratively. **2.** figure; figures.

fig·eat·er (fig′ēt′ər), *n. Am., S.* a large, green-

and-red beetle that feeds on ripe fruit; southern June bug.

fight (fīt), *n., v.,* **fought, fight·ing.** —*n.* **1.** struggle; battle; conflict. **2.** an angry dispute. **3.** power or will to fight. [< v.] —*v.* **1.** take part in a fight. **2.** take part in a fight against; war against. **3.** carry on (a fight, conflict, etc.). **4.** get or make by fighting. **5.** cause to fight. **6.** maneuver (ships, guns, etc.) in battle. **7.** fight shy of, keep away from; avoid. [OE *feohtan*] —**fight′a·ble,** *adj.* —Syn. *n.* **1.** combat, contest, engagement.

fight·er (fīt′ər), *n.* **1.** one who or that which fights. **2.** a professional boxer. **3.** Also, **fighter plane.** *Mil.* a highly maneuverable and heavily armed airplane used mainly for attacking enemy airplanes or strafing ground forces.

fig·ment (fig′mənt), *n.* something imagined; made-up story. [< L *figmentum* < *fingere* to form, fashion]

fig·u·ra·tion (fig′yər·ā′shən), *n.* **1.** form; shape. **2.** a forming; shaping. **3.** representation by a likeness or symbol.

fig·ur·a·tive (fig′yər·ə·tiv), *adj.* **1.** using words out of their literal meaning to add beauty or force. **2.** having many figures of speech. **3.** representing by a likeness or symbol. —**fig′ur·a·tive·ly,** *adv.* —**fig′ur·a·tive·ness,** *n.*

fig·ure (fig′yər), *n., v.,* **-ured, -ur·ing.** —*n.* **1.** symbol for a number, as 1, 2, 3, 4, etc. **2.** figures, arithmetic. **3.** amount or value given in figures. **4.** form; shape: *she saw dim figures moving.* **5.** form enclosing a surface or space. Circles, triangles, squares, cubes, and spheres are geometrical figures. **6.** person; character: *a great figure in history.* **7.** human form. **8.** way in which a person looks or appears: *the poor old woman was a figure of distress.* **9.** image; likeness. **10.** emblem; type. **11.** picture; drawing; diagram; illustration. **12.** design; pattern. **13.** outline traced by movements: *figures made by an airplane.* **14.** set of movements in dancing or skating. **15.** expression in which words are used out of their ordinary meaning to add beauty or force; figure of speech. **16.** *Music.* a brief succession of notes which produces a single, complete, and distinct impression. —*v.* **1.** use figures to find the answer to a problem; reckon; compute. **2.** *Colloq.* conclude; judge. **3.** show by a figure; represent in a diagram. **4.** make; shape. **5.** decorate with a figure or pattern. **6.** be conspicuous; appear: *the names of great leaders figure in the story of human progress.* **7. figure on,** *Am., Colloq.* **a.** depend on; rely on. **b.** consider as part of a plan or undertaking. [< F < L *figura* < *fingere* form] —**fig′ur·er,** *n.* —Syn. *n.* **4.** conformation, outline. **9.** effigy, statue. **10.** symbol. —*v.* **1.** calculate, cipher.

fig·ured (fig′yərd), *adj.* **1.** decorated with a design or pattern; not plain. **2.** formed; shaped.

fig·ure·head (fig′yər·hed′), *n.* **1.** statue or carving put on the front of a ship to decorate it. **2.** person who is the head in name only, and has no real authority or responsibility.

figure of speech, expression in which words are used out of their literal meaning or out of their ordinary use to add beauty or force. Similes and metaphors are figures of speech.

fig·ur·ine (fig′yər·ēn′), *n.* a small ornamental figure made of stone, pottery, metal, etc.; statuette. [< F < Ital. *figurina*]

fig·wort (fig′wėrt′), *n.* **1.** a tall, coarse plant with small, greenish-purple or yellow flowers that have a disagreeable odor. **2.** any similar plant.

Fi·ji (fē′jē), *n.* **1.** Fiji Islands. **2.** native of these islands. **3.** a British colony including these islands. —**Fi·ji·an** (fē′ji·ən; fi·jē′ən), *adj., n.*

Fiji Islands, group of British islands in the S Pacific, N of New Zealand.

fil·a·gree (fil′ə·grē), *n., v., -greed, -gree·ing, adj.* filigree.

fil·a·ment (fil′ə·mənt), *n.* **1.** a very fine thread; very slender, threadlike part. **2.** *Elect.* wire that gives off light in an electric-light bulb. **3.** *Bot.* the stalklike part of a stamen that supports the anther. [< LL, < L *filum* thread] —**fil·a·men-**

FILAMENT

ta·ry (fĭl′ə·mĕn′tə·rĭ), **fil·a·men·tous** (fĭl′ə-mĕn′təs), *adj.*

fil·bert (fĭl′bərt), *n.* a cultivated hazelnut. [for St. *Philibert*, because the nuts ripen about the time of his day]

filch (fĭlch), *v.* steal in small quantities; pilfer. —**filch′er,** *n.*

file¹ (fīl), *n., v.,* **filed, fil·ing.** —*n.* 1. place for keeping papers in order. 2. set of papers kept in order. 3. line of people or things one behind another. 4. *Mil.* a small detachment of soldiers. 5. on file, in a file; put away and kept in order. —*v.* 1. put away in order. 2. march or move in a file. 3. make application. [< F *fil* thread (< L *filum*) and F *file* row (ult. < LL *filare* spin a thread)] —**fil′er,** *n.*

file² (fīl), *n., v.,* **filed, fil·ing.** —*n.* a steel tool with many small ridges or teeth on it. Its rough surface is used to smooth or wear away hard substances. —*v.* smooth or wear away with a file. [OE *fíl*] —**fil′er,** *n.*

file-fish (fīl′fĭsh′), *n., pl.* **-fish·es** or (*esp. collectively*) **-fish.** fish whose skin is covered with many very small spines instead of scales.

fi·let (fĭ·lā′; fĭl′ā), *n.* 1. net or lace having a square mesh. 2. fillet (def. 3). —*v.* fillet (def. 2). [< F. See FILLET.]

fil·i·al (fĭl′ĭ·əl), *adj.* 1. of a son or daughter; due from a son or daughter. 2. *Genetics.* of any generation following that of the parents. [< LL, < L *filius* son, *filia* daughter] —**fil′i·al·ly,** *adv.*

fil·i·bus·ter (fĭl′ə·bŭs′tər), *n.* 1. *Am.* a. member of a legislature who deliberately hinders the passage of a bill by long speeches or other means of delay. b. the deliberate hindering of the passage of a bill by such means. 2. person who fights against another country without the authorization of his government; pirate. —*v.* 1. *Am.* deliberately hinder the passage of a bill by long speeches or other means of delay. 2. fight against another country without the authorization of one's government; act as a pirate. [< Sp. < Du. *vrijbuiter* freebooter] —**fil′i·bus′ter·er,** *n.*

fil·i·gree (fĭl′ə·grē), *n., v.,* **-greed, -gree·ing.** —*n.* 1. very delicate, lacelike ornamental work of gold or silver wire. 2. anything very delicate or fanciful. —*v.* ornament with filigree. —*adj.* Also, fil′i-greed′. ornamented with filigree; made into filigree. Also, **filagree, fillagree.** [for *filigrane* < F < Ital. < L *filum* thread + *granum* grain]

Filigree around a gem

fil·ings (fīl′ĭngz), *n.pl.* small pieces removed by a file.

Fil·i·pine (fĭl′ə·pēn), *adj.* Philippine.

Fil·i·pi·no (fĭl′ə·pē′nō), *n., pl.* **-nos.** native of the Philippines. —*adj.* Philippine.

fill (fĭl), *v.* 1. put into until there is room for no more; make full: *fill a cup.* 2. become full: *the hall filled rapidly.* 3. take up all the space in: *the crowd filled the hall.* 4. satisfy hunger or appetite. 5. supply what is needed for: *a store fills orders, prescriptions, etc.* 6. stop up or close by putting something in: *a dentist fills decayed teeth.* 7. hold and do the duties of (a position, office, etc.). 8. supply a person for or appoint a person to (a position, office, etc.). 9. fill in, a. fill with something; put in. b. complete by filling. c. put in to complete something. 10. fill out, a. make larger; grow larger; swell. b. make rounder; grow rounder. c. complete by filling. 11. fill up, fill; fill completely. —*n.* 1. enough to fill something. 2. all that is needed or wanted. 3. something that fills. [OE *fyllan* < *full* full] —Syn. *v.* 3. pervade, permeate. 7. occupy. 10a. inflate, expand, distend.

fil·la·gree (fĭl′ə·grē), *n., v.,* **-greed, -gree·ing,** *adj.* filigree.

fill·er (fĭl′ər), *n.* 1. person or thing that fills. 2. thing put in to fill space.

fil·let (fĭl′ĭt; *n.* 3 *and v.* 2, *usually* fĭ·lā′, fĭl′ā), *n.* 1. a narrow band, ribbon, etc., put around the head to keep the hair in place or as an ornament. 2. a narrow band or strip of any material.

3. Also, **filet.** slice of fish, meat, etc., without bones or fat. 4. *Bookbinding.* line impressed upon the cover of a book as a decoration. —*v.* 1. bind or decorate with a narrow band, ribbon, strip, etc. 2. Also, **filet.** cut (fish, meat, etc.) into fillets. [< F, dim. of *fil* < L *filum* thread]

fill·ing (fĭl′ĭng), *n.* thing put in to fill something.

filling station, *Am.* place where gasoline and oil for automobiles are sold.

fil·lip (fĭl′əp), *v.* 1. strike with the fingernail as it is snapped quickly from the end of the thumb. 2. toss or cause to move by striking in this way. 3. rouse; revive; stimulate. —*n.* 1. act of filliping. 2. thing that rouses, revives, or stimulates. [prob. imit.]

Fill·more (fĭl′môr; -mōr), *n.* Millard, 1800–74, the 13th president of the United States, 1850–53.

fil·ly (fĭl′ĭ), *n., pl.* **-lies.** 1. a female colt; young mare. 2. *Slang.* a lively girl. [? < Scand. *fylja*; akin to FOAL]

film (fĭlm), *n.* 1. a very thin layer, sheet, surface, or coating. 2. roll or sheet of thin, flexible material, such as cellulose nitrate or cellulose acetate, used in making photographs. This roll or sheet is coated with an emulsion that is sensitive to light. 3. a motion picture. 4. a delicate web of fine threads; a single fine thread. —*v.* 1. cover or become covered with a film: *her eyes filmed with tears.* 2. make a motion picture of. 3. photograph or be photographed for motion pictures. [OE *filmen*; akin to FELL⁴]

film·y (fĭl′mĭ), *adj.,* **film·i·er, film·i·est.** 1. of or like a film; very thin. 2. covered with a film. —**film′i·ly,** *adv.* —**film′i·ness,** *n.*

fil·ter (fĭl′tər), *n.* 1. device for straining out substances from a liquid or gas by passing it slowly through felt, paper, sand, charcoal, etc. 2. felt, paper, sand, charcoal, or other porous material used in such a device. 3. device for controlling certain light rays, electric currents, etc. —*v.* 1. pass through a filter; strain. 2. act as a filter for. 3. pass or flow very slowly. 4. remove or control by a filter. [< Med.L *filtrum* felt < Gmc.] —**fil′ter·er,** *n.*

fil·ter·a·ble (fĭl′tər·ə·bəl), **fil·tra·ble** (-trə-bəl), *adj.* 1. that can be filtered. 2. that passes through a filter. —**fil′ter·a·bil′i·ty, fil′ter·a·ble·ness; fil′tra·bil′i·ty, fil′tra·ble·ness,** *n.*

filth (fĭlth), *n.* 1. foul, disgusting dirt. 2. obscene words or thoughts; vileness; moral corruption. [OE *fylth* < *fúl* foul]

filth·y (fĭl′thĭ), *adj.,* **filth·i·er, filth·i·est.** 1. disgustingly dirty; foul. 2. vile. —**filth′i·ly,** *adv.* —**filth′i·ness,** *n.* —Syn. 1. squalid, nasty. 2. obscene, corrupt, indecent.

fil·trate (fĭl′trāt), *n., v.,* **-trat·ed, -trat·ing.** —*n.* liquid that has been passed through a filter. —*v.* pass through a filter. —fil·tra′tion, *n.*

fin (fĭn), *n., v.,* **finned, fin·ning.** —*n.* 1. A movable winglike part of a fish's body. 2. thing shaped or used like a fin. —*v.* 1. cut off the fins from. 2. move the fins. 3. lash the water with the fins. [OE *finn*] —**fin′less,** *adj.* —**fin′like′,** *adj.*

fi·na·gle (fə·nā′gəl), *v.,* **-gled, -gling.** 1. manage craftily or cleverly. 2. cheat. —**fi·na′gler,** *n.*

fi·nal (fī′nəl), *adj.* 1. at the end; last; with no more after it. 2. settling the question; not to be changed: *a decision of the Supreme Court is final.* 3. having to do with purpose. —*n.* 1. something final. 2. finals, the last or deciding set in a series of contests, examinations, etc. [< L, < *finis* end] —Syn. *adj.* 1. ultimate, eventual, terminal. 2. definitive.

fi·na·le (fĭ·nä′lē), *n.* 1. the last part of a piece of music or a play. 2. the last part; end. [< Ital., < FINAL]

fi·nal·ist (fī′nəl·ĭst), *n.* person who takes part in the deciding set in a series of contests, etc.

fi·nal·i·ty (fī·năl′ə·tĭ), *n., pl.* **-ties.** 1. a being final, finished, or settled. 2. something final; final act, speech, etc.

fi·nal·ize (fī′nəl·īz), *v.,* **-ized, -iz·ing.** *Am., Colloq.* make final or definite.

fi·nal·ly (fī′nəl·ĭ), *adv.* 1. at the end; at last. 2. so as to decide or settle the question.

fi·nance (fə·nans′; fī–; fī′nans), n., v., **-nanced,** **-nanc·ing.** —n. 1. money matters. 2. management of large sums of government revenue and expenditure. 3. finances, money matters; money; funds; revenues. —v. 1. provide money for. 2. manage the finances of. [< OF, ending, settlement of a debt, ult. < fin end < L finis; akin to FINE²]

fi·nan·cial (fə·nan′shəl; fī–), adj. 1. having to do with money matters. 2. having to do with the management of large sums of money. —fi·nan′cial·ly, adv.

fin·an·cier (fin′ən·sir′; fī′-nən–), n. 1. person skilled in finance. 2. person who is active in matters involving large sums of money.

fin·back (fin′bak′), n. kind of whale having a fin on its back.

finch (finch), n. a small song-bird having a cone-shaped bill, as sparrows, buntings, and canaries. [OE finc]

House finch
(6 in. long)

find (find), v., **found, find-ing,** n. —v. 1. come upon; happen on; meet with: find a splinter in the sugar. 2. look for and get; obtain: find favor with the public. 3. discover: an astronomer finds a new star, find conditions satisfactory. 4. see; know; feel; perceive: he found himself growing sleepy. 5. perceive by trial to be: we found him honest. 6. get the use of: can you find time to do this? 7. arrive at; reach: water finds its level. 8. decide and declare: the jury found the accused man guilty. 9. provide; supply: find food and lodging for a friend. 10. find oneself, learn one's abilities and how to make good use of them. 11. find out, learn about; come to know; discover. —n. 1. a finding. 2. thing found. [OE findan] —find′-a·ble, adj.

find·er (fīn′dər), n. 1. person or thing that finds. 2. a small extra lens on the outside of a camera that shows what is being photographed. 3. Astron. a small telescope attached to a larger one to help find objects more easily.

fin de siè·cle (fan də syä′klə), French. end of the century.

find·ing (fīn′ding), n. 1. discovery. 2. thing found. 3. Law. decision reached after an examination or inquiry; the verdict of a jury.

fine¹ (fīn), adj., **fin·er, fin·est,** adv. —adj. 1. of very high quality; very good; excellent: a fine sermon, a fine view, a fine scholar. 2. very small or thin: fine wire. 3. sharp: a tool with a fine edge. 4. not coarse or heavy; delicate: fine linen. 5. refined; elegant: fine manners. 6. subtle: the law makes fine distinctions. 7. too highly decorated; showy: fine language or writing. 8. good-looking. 9. clear; bright: fine weather. 10. without impurities. 11. having a stated proportion of gold or silver in it. —adv. Colloq. very well; excellently. [< OF fin, ult. < L finire finish] —fine′ly, adv. —fine′ness, n. —Syn. adj. 1. choice, rare, splendid. 2. slender, minute. 4. dainty. 8. handsome. ➤ Fine is a counter word of general approval, slightly more vigorous than nice, but of little value in writing and better omitted: Spring football practice has one aim: to weld eleven men into a [fine, coördinated team.

fine² (fīn), n., v., **fined, fin·ing.** —n. 1. sum of money paid as a punishment. 2. in fine, a. finally. b. in a few words; briefly. —v. cause to pay a fine. [< OF < L finis end; in Med.L, settlement, payment]

fine arts, arts depending upon taste and appealing to the sense of beauty; painting, drawing, sculpture, and architecture. Literature, music, dancing, and acting are also often included in the fine arts.

fine-drawn (fīn′drôn′), adj. 1. drawn out until very small or thin. 2. very subtle.

fine-grained (fīn′grānd′), adj. having a fine, close grain.

fin·er·y (fīn′ər·i), n., pl. **-er·ies.** showy clothes, ornaments, etc.

fine-spun (fīn′spun′), adj. 1. spun or drawn out until very small or thin. 2. very subtle.

fi·nesse (fə·nes′), n., v., **-nessed, -ness·ing.** —n. 1. delicacy of execution; skill. 2. the skillful handling of a delicate situation to one's advantage; craft; stratagem. 3. Cards. attempt to take a trick in bridge, whist, etc., with a low card while holding a higher card in the same hand. —v. 1. use finesse. 2. bring or change by finesse. 3. make a finesse with (a card). [< F, < fin FINE¹] —Syn. n. 2. artifice, subterfuge, strategy.

fin·ger (fing′gər), n. 1. one of the five end parts of the hand, esp. the four besides the thumb. 2. part of a glove that covers a finger. 3. anything shaped or used like a finger. 4. breadth of a finger; ¾ inch. 5. length of a finger; 4½ inches. 6. put one's finger on, point out exactly. —v. touch or handle with the fingers; use the fingers on. [OE] —fin′ger·er, n. —fin′ger·less, adj.

finger bowl, a small bowl to hold water for rinsing the fingers after or during a meal.

fin·ger·ing (fing′gər·ing), n. 1. a touching or handling with the fingers; using the fingers. 2. Music. signs marked on a piece to show how the fingers are to be used in playing it.

fin·ger·nail (fing′gər·nāl′), n. a hard layer of horn at the end of a finger.

fin·ger·print (fing′gər·print′), n. impression of the markings on the inner surface of the last joint of a finger or thumb. —v. take the fingerprints of.

fin·i·al (fin′i·əl; fī′ni–), n. Archit. ornament on top of a roof or lamp, end of a pew in church, etc. [< Med.L finium final settlement (prob. orig., end) < L finis]

fin·i·cal (fin′ə·kəl), **fin·ick·y** (-ə·ki), adj. too dainty or particular; too precise; fussy. [appar. < fine²] —fin′i·cal·i·ty, fin′i·cal·ness, n. —fin′i·cal·ly, adv. —Syn. overnice, fastidious, squeamish.

fi·nis (fī′nis; fin′is), n. end. [< L]

fin·ish (fin′ish), v. 1. bring (action, speech, etc.) to an end; end. 2. bring (work, affairs, etc.) to completion; complete: he started the race but did not finish it. 3. use up completely: finish a spool of thread. 4. overcome completely: my answer finished him. 5. destroy; kill: finish a wounded animal. 6. perfect; polish. 7. prepare the surface of in some way: finish cloth with nap. —n. 1. end. 2. polished condition or quality; perfection. 3. way in which the surface is prepared. 4. thing used to finish something. [< OF fenir < L finire] —fin′ished, adj. —fin′ish·er, n.

finishing school, a private school that prepares young women for social life rather than for business or a profession.

fi·nite (fī′nīt), adj. 1. having limits or bounds; not infinite: death ends man's finite existence. 2. having definite grammatical person and number; not an infinitive or participle. —n. what is finite; something finite. [< L finitus finished] —fi′nite·ly, adv. —fi′nite·ness, n. ➤ finite verbs. A finite verb form is one that indicates person (by one of the pronouns or by a subject), or time (by a tense form: had gone), or number (singular or plural). These are contrasted with the "infinite" forms, the infinitives (go, to go, to have gone), participles (going, gone), and verbal nouns (going) which do not indicate person or number. Finite verbs can be main verbs in clauses and sentences (I had gone before he came); infinite forms ordinarily cannot (before coming, gone with the wind).

fink (fingk), n. 1. Slang. informer. 2. Am. Slang. strikebreaker. 3. Colloq. an undesirable person.

Fin·land (fin′lənd), n. 1. country in N Europe. 2. Gulf of, part of the Baltic Sea, south of Finland. —Fin′land·er, Finn (fin), n.

fin·nan had·die (fin′ən had′i) or **had·dock** (had′ək), smoked haddock. [for Findhorn haddock; from name of town in Scotland]

Finn·ish (fin′ish), adj. of or having to do with Finland, its people, or their language. —n. language of Finland.

fiord (fyôrd; fyōrd), n. a long, narrow bay of the sea between high banks or cliffs. Also, fjord. [< Norw., earlier fjorthr; akin to FIRTH]

fir (fèr), n. 1. tree somewhat like a pine. 2. its wood. [OE fyrh]

fire (fīr), *n.*, *v.*, **fired, fir·ing.** —*n.* **1.** flame, heat, and light caused by burning. **2.** something burning. **3.** destruction by burning. **4.** preparation that will burn: *red fire is used in signaling.* **5.** fuel burning or arranged so that it will burn quickly. **6.** something that suggests a fire because it is hot, glowing, brilliant, or light: *the fire in a diamond.* **7.** any feeling that suggests fire; passion, fervor, excitement, etc. **8.** burning pain; fever; inflammation: *the fire of a wound.* **9.** severe trial or trouble. **10.** the shooting or discharge of guns, etc. **11. on fire,** a. burning. b. full of a feeling or spirit like fire. **12. under fire,** a. exposed to shooting from the enemy's guns. b. attacked; blamed. —*v.* **1.** cause to burn. **2.** begin to burn; burst into flame. **3.** supply with fuel; tend the fire of: *fire a furnace.* **4.** dry with heat; bake. Bricks are fired to make them hard. **5.** grow or make hot, red, glowing, etc. **6.** arouse; excite; inflame. **7.** become inflamed, excited, or aroused. **8.** discharge (gun, bomb, gas mine, etc.). **9.** shoot. **10.** *Colloq.* throw. **11.** *Am.*, *Colloq.* dismiss from a job, etc. [OE *fȳr*] —**fir′er,** *n.* —**Syn.** *n.* **1.** blaze, combustion, conflagration. **7.** ardor, enthusiasm, vehemence.

fire·arm (fīr′ärm′), *n.* gun, pistol, or other weapon to shoot with.

fire·ball (fīr′bôl′), *n.* **1.** the great billowing mass of fire produced by an atomic explosion. **2.** a very fast pitch to the batter in baseball.

fire·box (fīr′boks′), *n.* place for the fire in a furnace, boiler, etc.

fire·brand (fīr′brand′), *n.* **1.** piece of burning wood. **2.** person who arouses strife or angry feeling in others.

fire·brick (fīr′brik′), *n.* brick that can stand great heat, used to line furnaces and fireplaces.

fire·bug (fīr′bug′), *n.* *Am.*, *Colloq.* person who purposely sets houses or property on fire.

fire clay, clay capable of resisting high temperatures, used for making firebricks, etc.

fire·crack·er (fīr′krak′ər), *n.* *Am.* a paper roll containing gunpowder and a fuse.

fire·damp (fīr′damp′), *n.* metnane, a gas formed in coal mines, dangerously explosive when mixed with certain proportions of air.

fire·dog (fīr′dôg′, -dog′), *n.* andiron.

fire engine, machine for throwing water, chemicals, etc., to put out fires.

fire escape, stairway, ladder, etc., in or on a building, to use in case of fire.

fire extinguisher, container filled with chemicals which, when sprayed upon the fire, extinguish it.

fire·fly (fīr′flī′), *n.*, *pl.* **-flies.** a small beetle that gives off flashes of light when it flies at night; lightning bug.

Firefly
(½ in. long)

fire·man (fīr′mən), *n.*, *pl.* **-men.** **1.** man whose work is putting out fires. **2.** man whose work is taking care of the fire in a furnace, boiler, locomotive, etc.

fire·place (fīr′plās′), *n.* place built in the wall of a room or outdoors to hold a fire.

fire·pow·er (fīr′pou′ər), *n.* the total number of bullets, directed missiles, etc., that can be fired at an enemy or target in a given instant.

fire·proof (fīr′prüf′), *adj.* that will not burn; almost impossible to burn. —*v.* make fireproof.

fire·side (fīr′sīd′), *n.* **1.** space around a fireplace or hearth. **2.** home. **3.** home life. —*adj.* beside the fire: *fireside comfort.*

fire·trap (fīr′trap′), *n.* **1.** a building hard to get out of when it is on fire. **2.** a building that will burn very easily.

fire·wa·ter (fīr′wô′tər, -wot′-), *n.* *Am.* strong alcoholic drink. The American Indians called whiskey, gin, rum, etc., firewater.

fire·weed (fīr′wēd′), *n.* any of various weeds which grow on land that has been burned over.

fire·wood (fīr′wùd′), *n.* wood to make a fire.

fire·works (fīr′wėrks′), *n.pl.* **1.** firecrackers, bombs, rockets, etc., that make a loud noise or a beautiful, fiery display at night. **2.** display of these.

fir·kin (fėr′kən), *n.* **1.** quarter of a barrel, used as a measure of capacity. **2.** a small wooden cask for butter, etc. [ME *ferdekyn* < MDu. *verdelkijn,* dim. of *verdel,* lit., fourth part]

firm[1] (fėrm), *adj.* **1.** not yielding easily to pressure or force; solid; hard: *firm ground.* **2.** not easily moved or shaken; tightly fastened or fixed: *a candle firm in its socket.* **3.** not easily changed; determined; resolute; positive: *a firm purpose.* **4.** not changing; staying the same; steady: *a firm price.* —*v.* **1.** make or become firm. **2.** *Archaic.* establish; confirm. [< L *firmus*] —**firm′ly,** *adv.* —**firm′ness,** *n.* —**Syn.** *adj.* **1.** compact, impenetrable, rigid. **2.** fast, secure, immovable. **4.** enduring, constant, steadfast.

firm[2] (fėrm), *n.* a business company or partnership. [< Ital. < Sp., Pg. *firma* signature, ult. < L *firmus* firm[1]]

fir·ma·ment (fėr′mə·mənt), *n.* arch of the heavens; sky. [< L, ult. < *firmus* firm[1]]

first (fėrst), *adj.* **1.** before all others; before anything else. **2.** most important. **3.** *Music.* a. highest in pitch. b. playing or singing the part highest in pitch. —*adv.* **1.** before all others; before anything else: *the good die first.* **2.** in the first place. **3.** before some other thing or event: *first bring me the chalk.* **4.** for the first time. **5.** rather; sooner: *I'll go to jail first.* —*n.* **1.** person, thing, place, etc., that is first. **2.** *Sports.* the winning position in a race, etc. **3.** beginning. [OE *fyrst*] —**Syn.** *adj.* **1.** earliest, original, initial. **2.** chief, foremost, principal, leading. ➤ **first, last, latest.** *First, last* refer to items in a series, usually of more than two: *The first president had set up a very informal organization. His last act was to advise his family on their future. Latest* refers to the current item of a series that is still continuing (*the latest fashions*). *Last* refers either to the final item of a completed series (*their last attempt was successful*) or to the most recently completed or past item of a continuing series (*the last election, last week*).

first aid, emergency treatment given to an injured person before a doctor comes. —**first′-aid′,** *adj.*

first base, *Am.*, *Baseball.* **1.** the first of the bases from the home plate. **2.** player stationed there.

first-born (fėrst′bôrn′), *adj.* born first; oldest. —*n.* the first-born child.

first-class (fėrst′klas′; -kläs′), *adj.* of the highest class or best quality; excellent. —*adv.* on a first-class ship, train, etc.

first-hand (fėrst′hand′), *adj.*, *adv.* from the original source; direct.

first lady, *Am.* the wife of the president of the United States.

first lieutenant, *U.S. Army.* officer ranking below a captain and above a second lieutenant.

first·ling (fėrst′ling), *n.* **1.** the first of its kind. **2.** the first product or result. **3.** the first offspring of an animal.

first·ly (fėrst′li), *adv.* in the first place; first.

first person, *Gram.* form of a pronoun or verb used to refer to the speaker. *I, me, my,* and *we, us, our* are pronouns of the first person.

first-rate (fėrst′rāt′), *adj.* **1.** of the highest class. **2.** excellent; very good. —*adv. Colloq.* excellently; very well.

first sergeant, *U.S. Army.* a master sergeant in direct charge of a company or similar unit under the commissioned officer in command.

firth (fėrth), *n. Esp. Scot.* a narrow arm of the sea; estuary of a river. [< Scand. *firthir,* pl. of *fjǫrthr;* akin to FIORD]

fis·cal (fis′kəl), *adj.* **1.** financial. **2.** having to do with a treasury or exchequer. [< L, < *fiscus* purse] —**fis′cal·ly,** *adv.*

fish (fish), *n.*, *pl.* **fish·es** or (*esp. collectively*) **fish,** *v.*, *adj.* —*n.* **1.** a vertebrate animal that lives in water and has gills instead of lungs for breathing. Fish are usually covered with scales

---

and have fins for swimming. In popular use, whales and dolphins are called fish, and certain invertebrates are called shellfish. 2. flesh of fish used for food. 3. *Colloq.* person; fellow. 4. Fishes, Pisces. —v. 1. catch fish; try to catch fish. 2. try to catch fish in. 3. search. 4. find and pull: *he fished the map from the back of the drawer.* —adj. of or pertaining to fishes, fishing, or the sale of fish. [OE *fisc*] —**fish′a·ble**, adj. —**fish′less**, adj. —**fish′like′**, adj.

fish·er (fish′ər), n. 1. fisherman. 2. *Am.* a slender animal like a weasel but larger.

fish·er·man (fish′ər·mən), n., pl. -men. 1. man who fishes for a living or for pleasure. 2. ship used in fishing.

fish·er·y (fish′ər·i), n., pl. -er·ies. 1. business or industry of catching fish. 2. place for catching fish. 3. right of fishing in certain waters in certain ways.

fish hawk, large bird that feeds on fish; osprey.

fish·hook (fish′hůk′), n. hook used for catching fish.

fish·ing (fish′ing), n. the catching of fish for a living or for pleasure.

fishing rod, a long pole with a line attached to it, used in catching fish.

fish·mon·ger (fish′mung′gər; -mong′-), n. *Esp. Brit.* dealer in fish.

fish·wife (fish′wīf′), n., pl. -wives. woman who sells fish.

fish·y (fish′i), adj., fish·i·er, fish·i·est. 1. like a fish in smell, taste, or shape. 2. of fish. 3. full of fish. 4. *Colloq.* doubtful; unlikely; suspicious. 5. dull. —**fish′i·ly,** adv. —**fish′i·ness,** n.

fis·sile (fis′əl), adj. 1. easily split. 2. capable of nuclear fission. [< L *fissilis* < *findere* cleave]

fis·sion (fish′ən), n. 1. a splitting apart; division into parts. 2. *Biol.* method of reproduction in which the body of the parent divides to form two or more independent individuals. 3. *Physics, Chem.* the splitting that occurs when the nucleus of an atom under bombardment absorbs a neutron. Nuclear fission releases tremendous amounts of energy when heavy elements, esp. plutonium and uranium, are involved. [< L *fissio.* See FISSILE.]

fis·sion·a·ble (fish′ən·ə·bəl), adj. capable of nuclear fission: *fissionable material.*

fission bomb, atomic bomb that derives its force solely from the splitting of atoms. The original atomic bombs were fission bombs; the newer hydrogen bombs are fusion bombs.

fis·sure (fish′ər), n., v., -sured, -sur·ing. —n. 1. split or crack; long, narrow opening. 2. a splitting apart; division into parts. —v. split apart; divide into parts.

fist (fist), n. 1. hand closed tightly. 2. *Colloq.* hand. 3. *Colloq.* handwriting. 4. symbol (☞) used in printing. [OE *fȳst*]

fist·ic (fis′tik), adj. having to do with fighting with the fists; done with the fists.

fist·i·cuff (fis′tə·kuf′), n. 1. blow with the fist. 2. fisticuffs, a fight with the fists. b. blows with the fists. —**fist′i·cuff′er,** n.

fis·tu·la (fis′chů·lə), n., pl. -las, -lae (-lē). 1. tube or pipe. 2. *Pathol.* a tubelike sore. [< L, pipe, ulcer] —**fis·tu·lous** (fis′chů·ləs), **fis′tu·lar,** adj.

fit¹ (fit), adj., fit·ter, fit·test, v., fit·ted, fit·ting, n. —adj. 1. having the necessary qualities; suitable. 2. right; proper. 3. ready; prepared: *fit for active service.* 4. in good health; in good physical condition. —v. 1. be fit; be fit for. 2. have the right size or shape; have the right size or shape for. 3. cause to fit; make fit. 4. make ready; prepare. 5. supply with what is needed; equip. —n. 1. manner in which one thing fits another: *a tight fit.* 2. process of fitting. 3. thing that fits: *this coat is a good fit.* [ME *fyt*] —**fit′ly,** adv. —**fit′ness,** n. —**fit′ter,** n. —Syn. adj. 1. appropriate, qualified. 2. seemly. —v. 5. furnish.

fit² (fit), n. 1. a sudden, sharp attack of disease: *a fit of colic.* 2. a sudden attack characterized by loss of consciousness or by convulsions: *a fainting fit, fit of epilepsy.* 3. a sudden, sharp attack: *in a fit of anger he hit his friend.* 4. a short period of doing one thing. [OE *fitt* conflict]

fitch (fich), **fitch·et** (fich′it), or **fitch·ew** (fich′ü), n. 1. polecat of Europe. 2. its fur, yellowish with dark markings. [? < MDu. *vitsche*]

fit·ful (fit′fəl), adj. going on and then stopping awhile; irregular. —**fit′ful·ly,** adv. —**fit′ful·ness,** n. —Syn. spasmodic, variable, intermittent.

fit·ting (fit′ing), adj. right; proper; suitable. —n. 1. a making fit. 2. a trying on unfinished clothes to see if they will fit. 3. fittings, furnishings; fixtures. —**fit′ting·ly,** adv. —**fit′ting·ness,** n.

Fitch (body ab. 17 in. long)

Fiu·me (fü′mā), n. the Italian name of Rieka, a seaport in NW Yugoslavia.

five (fīv), n. 1. a cardinal number, one more than four. 2. symbol for this number; 5. 3. *Sports.* team of five players. —adj. one more than four; 5. [OE *fīf*]

five·fold (fīv′fōld′), adj. 1. five times as much or as many. 2. having five parts. —adv. five times as much or as many.

Five Nations, *Am.* confederacy of Iroquois Indian tribes, consisting of the Mohawks, Oneidas, Onondagas, Cayugas, and Senecas.

five percenter, person who obtains government contracts for others in return for a 5% fee.

fix (fiks), v., fixed or fixt, fix·ing, n. —v. 1. make firm; become firm; fasten tightly; be fastened tightly: *fix a post in the ground.* 2. settle; set: *fix the price at one dollar.* 3. direct or hold (eyes, attention, etc.) steadily; be directed or held steadily. 4. make or become rigid. 5. put definitely: *fix the blame on the leader.* 6. treat to keep from changing or fading. 7. treat (organisms or parts of organisms) to preserve them for future study. 8. mend; repair. 9. *U.S. Colloq.* put in order; arrange; prepare. 10. *Colloq.* put in a condition or position favorable to oneself or unfavorable to one's opponents. 11. *Colloq.* get revenge upon; get even with; punish. 12. *Chem.* make (nitrogen) into a compound that can be used. 13. **fix up,** *Esp. U.S. Colloq.* a. mend; repair. b. put in order; arrange. —n. 1. *Colloq.* position hard to get out of; awkward state of affairs. 2. point on a map or chart at which two lines of position cross one another. [< F, ult. < L *fixus* fixed] —**fix′a·ble,** adj. —**fix′er,** n. —Syn. v. 2. determine, confirm.

fix·a·tion (fiks·ā′shən), n. 1. act of fixing or condition of being fixed. 2. treatment to keep something from changing or fading: *fixation of a photographic film.* 3. *Chem.* process of combining nitrogen with hydrogen under high pressure to form ammonia, used in making fertilizers and explosives. 4. *Psychol.* a morbid attachment or prejudice.

fix·a·tive (fiks′ə·tiv), adj. that prevents fading or change. —n. substance used to keep something from fading or changing.

fixed (fikst), adj. 1. not movable; firm. 2. settled; set; definite. 3. steady; not moving. 4. made stiff or rigid. 5. not volatile; permanent. 6. put into order. 7. *Colloq.* prearranged privately or dishonestly. —**fix·ed·ly** (fik′sid·li), adv. —**fix′ed·ness,** n. —Syn. 1. stationary. 2. established.

fixed star, *Astron.* star whose position in relation to other stars appears not to change.

fix·ing (fik′sing), n. 1. act of one who or that which fixes. 2. fixings, *Am., Colloq.* trimmings.

fix·i·ty (fik′sə·ti), n., pl. -ties. 1. fixed condition or quality; permanence; steadiness; firmness. 2. something fixed.

fixt (fikst), v. pt. and pp. of fix.

fix·ture (fiks′chər), n. 1. thing put in place to stay: *electric-light fixtures.* 2. person or thing that stays in one place, job, etc.

fiz (fiz), v., fizzed, fiz·zing, n. fizz.

fizz (fiz), n. 1. a hissing sound. —n. 1. a hissing sound. 2. a bubbling drink, such as champagne, soda water, etc. —**fizz′er,** n.

fiz·zle (fiz′əl), v., -zled, -zling, n. —v. 1. hiss or sputter weakly. 2. *Colloq.* fail. —n. 1. a hissing; sputtering. 2. *Colloq.* failure.

fizz·y (fiz′i), adj., fizz·i·er, fizz·i·est. that fizzes.

fjord (fyôrd; fyord), *n.* fiord.

Fl, *Chem.* fluorine. Also, **F.**

fl., 1. flourished. 2. fluid.

Fla., Florida.

flab·ber·gast (flab'ər·gast), *v. Colloq.* make speechless with surprise; astonish greatly; amaze. [? blend of *flap* or *flabby* + *aghast*]

flab·by (flab'i), *adj.,* **-bi·er, -bi·est.** lacking firmness or force; soft. [var. of earlier *flappy* < *flap*] **—flab'bi·ly,** *adv.* **—flab'bi·ness,** *n.*

flac·cid (flak'sid), *adj.* limp; weak: *flaccid muscles, a flaccid will.* [< L, < *flaccus* flabby] **—flac·cid'i·ty, flac'cid·ness,** *n.* **—flac'cid·ly,** *adv.*

fla·con (flä·kôn'), *n.* a small bottle with a stopper, used for perfume, smelling salts, etc. [< F. See FLAGON.]

flag¹ (flag), *n., v.,* **flagged, flag·ging. —n.** 1. piece of cloth with a color or pattern that stands for some country, city, party, club, etc., or which gives some information or signal. 2. something that suggests a flag. 3. flags, a. feathers on the second joint of a bird's wing. b. long feathers on the lower parts of certain birds' legs. **—v.** 1. put a flag or flags over or on; decorate with flags. 2. stop or signal by a flag: *flag a train.* 3. communicate by a flag: *flag a message.* [? < *flag*³] **—Syn.** *n.* 1. ensign, standard, banner.

flag² (flag), *n.* 1. iris with blue, purple, yellow, or white flowers and sword-shaped leaves. 2. the sweet flag. [cf. Dan. *flœg*]

flag³ (flag), *v.,* **flagged, flag·ging.** get tired; grow weak; droop. [cf. earlier Du. *vlaggheren* flutter] **—Syn.** decline, languish, fail.

flag⁴ (flag), *n., v.,* **flagged, flag·ging. —n.** flagstone. **—v.** pave with flagstones. [var. of *flake*]

Flag Day, *Am.* June 14, the anniversary of the day in 1777 when the flag of the United States was adopted.

flag·el·lant (flaj'ə·lənt; flə·jel'ənt), *n.* 1. person who whips. 2. a religious fanatic who whips himself for religious discipline or for penance. **—adj.** having the habit of whipping.

flag·el·late (flaj'ə·lāt), *v.,* **-lat·ed, -lat·ing,** *adj.* **—v.** whip; flog. **—adj.** Also, flag'el·lat'ed. 1. shaped like a whiplash. 2. having flagella. [< L, *flagellum* whip] **—flag'el·la'tion,** *n.* **—flag'el·la'tor,** *n.*

fla·gel·lum (flə·jel'əm), *n., pl.* **-la** (-lə), **-lums.** 1. *Biol.* a long, whiplike tail or part, which is an organ of locomotion in certain cells, bacteria, protozoa, etc. 2. whip. 3. *Bot.* runner of a plant. [< L, whip]

flag·eo·let (flaj'ə·let'), *n.* a wind instrument somewhat like a flute, with a mouthpiece at one end, six main finger holes, and sometimes keys. [< F, dim. of OF *flajol* flute, ult. < L *flare* blow]

flag·ging¹ (flag'ing), *adj.* drooping; tired; weak. **—flag'ging·ly,** *adv.*

flag·ging² (flag'ing), *n.* 1. flagstones. 2. pavement made of flagstones.

fla·gi·tious (flə·jish'əs), *adj.* scandalously wicked; shamefully vile. [< L, ult. < *flagitium* shame] **—fla·gi'tious·ly,** *adv.* **—fla·gi'tious·ness,** *n.*

flag·on (flag'ən), *n.* 1. container for liquids, usually having a handle and a spout, and often a cover. 2. a large bottle, holding about two quarts. 3. contents of a flagon. [< OF *flascon*. Cf. FLASK.]

flag·pole (flag'pōl'), **flag·staff** Flagon (-staf'; -stäf'), *n.* pole from which a flag is flown.

fla·gran·cy (flā'grən·si), **fla·grance** (-grəns), *n.* flagrant nature or quality.

fla·grant (flā'grənt), *adj.* 1. notorious; outrageous; scandalous. 2. *Archaic.* blazing; burning; glowing. [< L *flagrans* burning] **—fla'grant·ly,** *adv.* **—Syn.** 1. glaring.

flag·ship (flag'ship'), *n.* ship that carries the officer in command of a fleet or squadron and displays his flag.

flag·stone (flag'stōn'), *n.* a large, flat stone, used for paving walks, etc.

flail (flāl), *n.* instrument for threshing grain by hand. **—v.** 1. strike with a flail. 2. beat; thrash. [< LL *flagellum* < L, whip]

flair (flār), *n.* 1. keen perception: *a flair for bargains.* 2. talent: *a flair for making clever rhymes.* [< F, scent < *flairer* smell < L *fragrare*]

flak (flak), *n.* fire from anti-aircraft guns. [for *Fl.A.K.,* G abbrev. of *flieger-abwehrkanone* antiaircraft cannon]

flake (flāk), *n., v.,* **flaked, flak·ing. —n.** 1. a small, light mass; soft, loose bit: *a flake of snow.* 2. a thin, flat piece or layer: *flakes of rust.* **—v.** 1. come off in flakes; take off, chip, or peel in flakes. 2. break or separate into flakes. 3. cover or mark with flakes; spot. 4. form into flakes. [? < Scand. (Dan.) (*sne*) *flage* (*snow*) flake]

flak·y (flāk'i), *adj.,* **flak·i·er, flak·i·est.** 1. consisting of flakes. 2. easily broken or separated into flakes. **—flak'i·ly,** *adv.* **—flak'i·ness,** *n.*

flam·beau (flam'bō), *n., pl.* **-beaux** (-bōz), **-beaus.** a flaming torch. [< F, < OF *flambe* flame, ult. < L *flamma*]

flam·boy·ant (flam·boi'ənt), *adj.* 1. gorgeously brilliant; flaming. 2. very ornate. 3. having wavy lines or flamelike curves. [< F, flaming. See FLAMBEAU.] **—flam·boy'ance, flam·boy'an·cy,** *n.* **—flam·boy'ant·ly,** *adv.*

flame (flām), *n. v.,* **flamed, flam·ing. —n.** 1. one of the glowing, red or yellow tongues of light that shoot out from a blazing fire. 2. a burning gas or vapor. 3. a burning with flames; blaze. 4. thing or condition that suggests flame. 5. a bright light. 6. a burning feeling. 7. *Slang.* sweetheart. **—v.** 1. burn with flame; blaze. 2. grow hot, red, etc. 3. shine brightly; give out a bright light. 4. have or show a burning feeling. 5. burst out quickly and hotly; be or act like a flame. [< OF < L *flamma*] **—flame'less,** *adj.* **—flam'er,** *n.* **—Syn.** *v.* 1. flare, glow, flash.

fla·men·co (flə·meng'kō), *n.* gypsy dancing, music, etc. of a style characteristic of Andalusia. [< Sp.]

flame·out (flām'out'), *n.* the sudden failure of a jet engine to function, esp. while the aircraft containing it is in flight.

flame thrower, *Mil.* weapon that throws a spray of oil that ignites in the air.

flam·ing (flām'ing), *adj.* 1. burning with flames. 2. like a flame; very bright; brilliant. 3. violent; vehement. **—flam'ing·ly,** *adv.*

fla·min·go (flə·ming'gō), *n., pl.* **-gos, -goes.** a tropical wading bird with very long legs and feathers that vary from pink to scarlet. [< Pg. < Sp. < Pr. *flamenc* < *flama* FLAME]

flam·ma·ble (flam'ə·bəl), *adj.* inflammable.

Flan·ders (flan'dərz; flän'-), *n.* district in W Belgium, N France, and SW Netherlands.

flange (flanj), *n., v.,* **flanged, flang·ing. —n.** a projecting edge, rim, collar, Flanges etc., on an object for keeping it in place, attaching it to another object, strengthening it, etc. **—v.** provide with a flange. [var. of *flanch,* n., < *flanch,* v., < OF *flanchir* bend; akin to *flank*]

flank (flangk), *n.* 1. side of an animal or person between the ribs and the hip. 2. piece of beef cut from this part. 3. side. 4. *Mil.* a. the far right or left side of an army, fleet, etc. b. part of a fortification that defends another part by gunfire along the outside of the latter's parapet. **—v.** 1. be at the side of: *high buildings flanked the dark, narrow alley.* 2. get around the far right or left side of. 3. attack from or on the side. [< OF *flanc* <Gmc.] **—flank'er,** *n.*

flan·nel (flan'əl), *n.* 1. a soft, warm woolen cloth. 2. flannelet. 3. flannels, a. clothes made of flannel. b. woolen underwear.

flan·nel·et, flan·nel·ette (flan'əl·et'), *n.* a soft, warm cotton cloth with a fuzzy nap.

flap (flap), *v.,* **flapped, flap·ping,** *n.* **—v.** 1. swing or sway about loosely and with more or less noise: *curtains flapped in the open windows* 2. move (wings, arms, etc.) up and down. 3. fly by moving wings up and down: *the large bird flapped away.* 4. strike noisily with something broad and flat. —*n.* 1. a flapping motion. 2. noise caused by flapping. 3. blow from something broad and flat. 4. a broad, flat piece, usually hanging or fastened at one edge only. 5. an extra hinged section on an airfoil of an airplane, esp. a wing, which can be moved to assist a take-off or a landing. [prob. imit.]

flap·jack (flap′jak′), *n.* a griddlecake.

flap·per (flap′ər), *n.* 1. a flap (def. 4). 2. *Colloq.* a young girl who is rather forward and unconventional.

flare (flâr), *v.,* flared, flar·ing, *n.* —*v.* 1. flame up briefly or unsteadily, sometimes with smoke. 2. spread out in the shape of a bell: *the sides of a ship flare from the keel to the deck.* 3. flare up or out, flame up; burst into anger, violence, etc. —*n.* 1. a bright, unsteady light or blaze that lasts only a short time. 2. a dazzling light that burns for a short time, used for signaling. 3. a sudden outburst. 4. a spreading out into a bell shape. 5. part that spreads out. [cf. Norw. *flara* blaze]

flare-up (flâr′up′), *n.* 1. outburst of flame. 2. *Colloq.* a sudden outburst of anger, violence, etc.

flar·ing (flâr′ing), *adj.* 1. flaming. 2. gaudy. 3. spreading gradually outward in form.

flash (flash), *n.* 1. a sudden, brief light or flame: *a flash of lightning.* 2. a sudden, brief feeling or display: *a flash of hope, a flash of wit.* 3. a very brief time; instant. 4. *Am.* a brief news report, usually received by telegraph or teletype. 5. a showy display. —*v.* 1. give out a sudden, brief light or flame. 2. come suddenly; pass quickly. 3. cause to flash. 4. give out or send out like a flash. 5. communicate by flashes; send by telegraph, radio, etc. 6. *Colloq.* show off. [appar. imit.] —flash′er, *n.* —flash′ing·ly, *adv.*

flash burn, a severe burn caused by instantaneous thermal radiation, as from an atomic bomb.

flash flood, a very sudden, violent flooding of a river, stream, etc.

flash gun, bulb, or **lamp,** a portable electric device used to make bright flashes for taking photographs indoors or at night.

flash·light (flash′līt′), *n.* 1. light that flashes, used in a lighthouse or for signaling. 2. *Am.* a portable electric light, operated by batteries. 3. a flash gun.

flash·y (flash′i), *adj.,* flash·i·er, flash·i·est. 1. very bright for a short time; flashing. 2. showy; gaudy. —flash′i·ly, *adv.* —flash′i·ness, *n.* —Syn. 1. glittering, dazzling. 2. tawdry.

flask (flask; fläsk), *n.* 1. any bottle-shaped container. 2. a small bottle with flat sides, made to be carried in the pocket. [OE *flasce.* Cf. LL *flasca* < Gmc.]

Flask

flat¹ (flat), *adj.,* flat·ter, flat·test, *n., adv., v.,* flat·ted, flat·ting. —*adj.* 1. smooth and level; even: *flat land.* 2. spread out; at full length. 3. not very deep or thick: *a plate is flat.* 4. with little air in it: *a flat tire.* 5. not to be changed; positive: *a flat refusal.* 6. without much life, interest, flavor, etc.: *flat food.* 7. not shiny or glossy: *a flat yellow.* 8. not clear or sharp in sound. 9. *Music.* a. below the true pitch. b. one half step or half note below natural pitch. 10. *Phonet.* having the sound of *a* in *hat.* 11. *Gram.* not having a characteristic ending or sign. 12. *Am.* of times, exact or within a fifth of a second. —*n.* 1. something flat. 2. a flat part. 3. *Am.* flat land. 4. land covered with shallow water; marsh; swamp. 5. *Music.* sign (♭) that lowers a tone or note one half step below natural pitch. 6. *Colloq.* tire with little air in it. —*adv.* 1. *Music.* below the true pitch. 2. in a flat manner. 3. in a flat position. 4. fall flat, fail completely; have no effect or interest. —*v.* make or become flat. [< Scand. *flatr*] —flat′ly, *adv.* —flat′ness, *n.* —flat′tish, *adj.* —Syn. *adj.* 1. plane. 2. prostrate, prone, supine. 5. downright, absolute. 6. dull, monotonous.

flat² (flat), *n.* apartment or set of rooms on one floor. [alter. of *flet,* OE *flett*]

flat·boat (flat′bōt′), *n.* a large boat with a flat bottom, often used on a river or canal.

flat·car (flat′kär′), *n. Am., Colloq.* a railroad freight car without a roof or sides.

flat·fish (flat′fish′), *n., pl.* –fish·es or (*esp. collectively*) –fish. fish with a flat body, and with both eyes on the side kept uppermost when lying flat.

flat·foot (flat′fut′), *n., pl.* –feet. 1. *Pathol.* a. foot with a flattened arch. b. condition in which the feet have flattened arches. 2. *Slang.* policeman.

flat·foot·ed (flat′fut′id), *adj.* 1. having feet with flattened arches. 2. *Am.* not to be changed or influenced; firm; uncompromising. —flat′-foot′ed·ly, *adv.* —flat′-foot′ed·ness, *n.*

flat·i·ron (flat′ī′ərn), *n.* iron with a flat surface, used for pressing cloth.

flat silver, *Am.* silver knives, forks, etc.

flat·ten (flat′ən), *v.* make or become flat. —flat′ten·er, *n.*

flat·ter (flat′ər), *v.* 1. praise too much or beyond what is true; praise insincerely. 2. show to be better looking than what is true: *this picture flatters her.* 3. try to please or win over by flattering. 4. cause to be pleased or feel honored. 5. flatter oneself, be pleased to know or think. [? extended use of ME *flateren* float, FLUTTER] —flat′ter·er, *n.* —flat′ter·ing·ly, *adv.* —Syn. 1. compliment. 3. cajole, blandish.

flat·ter·y (flat′ər·i), *n., pl.* –ter·ies. 1. act of flattering. 2. words of praise, usually untrue or overstated.

flat·top (flat′top′), *n. U.S.* an aircraft carrier.

flat·u·lent (flach′ə·lənt), *adj.* 1. having gas in the stomach or intestines. 2. causing gas in the stomach or intestines. 3. pompous in speech or behavior; vain; empty. [< F < L *flatus* a blowing] —flat′u·lence, flat′u·len·cy, *n.* —flat′u·lent·ly, *adv.*

flat·worm (flat′wėrm′), *n.* worm with a flat body, that lives in water or as a parasite on some animal.

Flau·bert (flō·bâr′), *n.* Gustave, 1821–1880, French novelist.

flaunt (flônt; flänt), *v.* 1. show off: *the ill-bred woman flaunted her riches in public.* 2. wave proudly: *banners flaunting in the breeze.* —*n.* a flaunting. [? < Scand. (Norw.) *flanta* gad about] —flaunt′er, *n.* —flaunt′ing·ly, *adv.* —flaunt′y, *adj.* ➤ **flaunt, flout.** *Flaunt* (flônt; flänt), to "show off," and *flout* (flout), to "treat with contempt or scorn," are sometimes confused.

flau·tist (flô′tist), *n.* flutist.

fla·vor, *esp. Brit.* **fla·vour** (flā′vər), *n.* 1. taste, esp. a characteristic taste: *chocolate and vanilla have different flavors.* 2. thing used to give a certain taste to food or drink; flavoring. 3. a characteristic quality: *stories that have a flavor of the sea.* 4. aroma; odor. —*v.* 1. give an added taste to; season. 2. give a characteristic quality to. [< OF *flaur,* ult. < L *fragrare* emit odor] —fla′vor·er, *esp. Brit.* fla′vour·er, *n.* —fla′vor·less, *esp. Brit.* fla′vour·less, *adj.* —Syn. *n.* 1. savor, smack, tang, relish.

fla·vor·ing, *esp. Brit.* **fla·vour·ing** (flā′vər·ing; flā′vring), *n.* thing used to give a certain taste to food or drink.

flaw¹ (flô), *n.* 1. a defective place; crack. 2. fault; defect. —*v.* make or become defective; crack. [< Scand. (Sw.) *flaga*] —Syn. *n.* 1. chink, rent, breach. 2. imperfection, blemish.

flaw² (flô), *n.* 1. a sudden gust; brief windstorm. 2. a short period of rough weather. [cf. Scand. (Sw.) *flaga* gust]

flaw·less (flô′lis), *adj.* without a flaw. —flaw′less·ly, *adv.* —flaw′less·ness, *n.*

flax (flaks), *n.* 1. plant with small, narrow leaves, blue flowers, and slender stems about two feet tall. Linseed oil is made from its seeds. 2. the threadlike fibers of this plant, spun into linen thread. [OE *fleax*]

flax·en (flak′sən), **flax·y** (flak′si), *adj.* 1. made of flax. 2. like the color of flax; pale-yellow: *flaxen hair.*

flax·seed (flaks′sēd′), *n.* seeds of flax.

flay (flā), *v.* 1. strip off the skin or outer covering of. 2. scold severely; criticize without pity or mercy. 3. rob; cheat. [OE *flēan*] —flay′er,

flea (flē), *n.* a small, wingless, jumping insect that lives as a parasite on animals, sucking their blood. [OE *flēah*]

flea·bane (flē′bān′), *n.* plant supposed to drive away fleas.

fleck (flek), *n.* 1. spot or patch of color, light, etc. 2. a small particle; flake. —*v.* sprinkle with spots or patches of color, light, etc.; speckle. [? < Scand. *flekkr*] —**flecked** (flekt), *adj.*

Flea.
Line shows actual length.

flec·tion (flek′shən), *n.* 1. a bending. 2. a bent part; bend. Also, *esp. Brit.* **flexion.** [< L *flexio* < *flectere* bend] —**flec′tion·al,** *adj.*

fledge (flej), *v.,* **fledged, fledg·ing.** 1. grow the feathers needed for flying. 2. bring up (a young bird) until it is able to fly. 3. provide or cover with feathers. [cf. OE *unflicge* unfledged, unfit to fly]

fledg·ling, *esp. Brit.* **fledge·ling** (flej′ling), *n.* 1. a young bird just able to fly. 2. a young, inexperienced person.

flee (flē), *v.,* **fled** (fled), **flee·ing.** 1. run away; try to get away by running. 2. run away from. 3. go quickly; move swiftly. 4. pass away; cease; vanish. [OE *flēon*] —**fle′er,** *n.* —Syn. 2. escape.

fleece (flēs), *n., v.,* **fleeced, fleec·ing.** —*n.* 1. wool that covers a sheep or similar animal. 2. quantity of wool cut from a sheep at one time. 3. something like a fleece. 4. cloth having a soft nap or pile. —*v.* 1. cut the fleece from. 2. strip of money or belongings; rob; cheat; swindle. [OE *flēos*] —**fleeced** (flēst), *adj.* —**fleece′less,** *adj.* —**fleec′er,** *n.*

fleec·y (flē′si), *adj.,* **fleec·i·er, fleec·i·est.** 1. like a fleece; soft and white. 2. covered with fleece. 3. made of fleece. —**fleec′i·ly,** *adv.* —**fleec′i·ness,** *n.*

fleer (flir), *v., n.* sneer; gibe. —**fleer′ing·ly,** *adv.*

fleet[1] (flēt), *n.* 1. group of warships under one command; navy. 2. any group of boats sailing together. 3. group of airplanes, automobiles, etc., moving or working together. [OE *flēot* < *flēotan* float]

fleet[2] (flēt), *adj.* swift; rapid. [< v.] —*v.* pass swiftly; move rapidly. [OE *flēotan* float] —**fleet′-ly,** *adv.* —**fleet′ness,** *n.*

fleet·ing (flēt′ing), *adj.* passing swiftly; moving rapidly; soon gone. —**fleet′ing·ly,** *adv.* —**fleet′ing·ness,** *n.* —Syn. transitory, momentary, temporary.

Flem., Flemish.

Flem·ing (flem′ing), *n.* 1. native of Flanders. 2. a Belgian whose native language is Flemish.

Flem·ish (flem′ish), *adj.* of or having to do with Flanders, its people, or their language. —*n.* 1. the people of Flanders. 2. their language.

flesh (flesh), *n.* 1. a soft substance of the body that covers the bones and is covered by skin. Flesh consists mostly of muscles and fat. 2. tissue of muscles. 3. fatness. 4. meat. 5. body, not the soul or spirit. 6. the bad side of human nature. 7. the human race; people as a group. 8. all living creatures. 9. family or relatives by birth. 10. *Bot.* the soft part of fruits or vegetables; the part of fruits that can be eaten. 11. a pinkish white with a little yellow. 12. in the flesh, a. alive. b. in person. [OE *flǣsc*] —**flesh′-less,** *adj.*

flesh-col·ored (flesh′kul′ərd), *adj.* pinkish-white with a tinge of yellow.

flesh·ly (flesh′li), *adj.,* **-li·er, -li·est.** 1. of the flesh; bodily. 2. sensual. —**flesh′li·ness,** *n.*

flesh·y (flesh′i), *adj.,* **flesh·i·er, flesh·i·est.** 1. having much flesh; fat. 2. of or like flesh. 3. *Bot.* pulpy. —**flesh′i·ness,** *n.*

fleur-de-lis (flér′də·lē′; -lēs′), *n., pl.* **fleurs-de-lis** (flér′də·lēz′). 1. design or device used in heraldry. See the picture in the next column. 2. the royal coat of arms of France. 3. the iris flower or plant. [< F, lily flower]

flew (flü), *v.* pt. of **fly**[2].

flex (fleks), *v.* bend. [< L *flexus* bent]

flex·i·ble (flek′sə·bəl), *adj.* 1. easily bent; not stiff; bending without breaking. Leather, rubber, and wire are flexible. 2. easily adapted to fit various uses, purposes, etc.: *the actor's flexible voice.* 3. easily managed; willing to yield to influence or persuasion. [< F < L *flexibilis*. See **flex.**] —**flex′i·bil′i·ty, flex′i·ble·ness,** *n.* —**flex′i·bly,** *adv.* —Syn. 1. pliable, pliant, supple, limber. 3. compliant, yielding, tractable.

Fleur-de-lis design

flex·ion (flek′shən), *n. Esp. Brit.* flection. [var. of *flection*] —**flex′ion·al,** *adj.*

flex·or (flek′sər), *n. Anat.* any muscle that bends some part of the body.

flex·ure (flek′shər), *n.* 1. a bending; curving. 2. bend; curve. —**flex′ur·al,** *adj.*

flib·ber·ti·gib·bet (flib′ər·ti·jib′it), *n.* 1. a frivolous, flighty person. 2. a chatterbox.

flic (flik; *Fr.* flēk), *n. French Slang.* policeman.

flick (flik), *n.* 1. a quick, light blow; sudden, snapping stroke. 2. the light, snapping sound of such a blow or stroke. 3. streak; splash; fleck. —*v.* 1. strike lightly with a quick, snapping blow. 2. make a sudden, snapping stroke with: *the boys flicked wet towels at each other.* 3. flutter; move quickly and lightly. [prob. imit.] —**flick′er,** *n.*

flick·er[1] (flik′ər), *v.* 1. shine with a wavering light; burn with an unsteady flame. 2. move quickly and lightly in and out or back and forth: *the tongue of a snake flickers.* —*n.* 1. a wavering, unsteady light or flame. 2. a brief flame; spark. 3. a quick, light movement. [OE *flicorian*] —**flick′er·ing·ly,** *adv.*

flick·er[2] (flik′ər), *n. Am.* woodpecker of North America with golden-yellow feathers on the underside of the wings. [? imit. of its note]

fli·er (flī′ər), *n.* 1. person or thing that flies. 2. an aviator. 3. a very fast train, ship, bus, etc. 4. *Am., Colloq.* a risky financial venture. Also, **flyer.**

Flicker
(ab. 12 in. long)

flight[1] (flīt), *n.* 1. act or manner of flying. 2. distance a bird, bullet, airplane, etc., can fly. 3. group of things flying through the air together. 4. *U.S. Air Force.* a tactical unit consisting of two or more airplanes, but frequently two or three elements flying together. 5. trip in an airplane or airship. 6. a swift movement. 7. a soaring above or beyond what is ordinary. 8. set of stairs or steps between landings or stories of a building. [OE *flyht*; akin to **fly**[2]]

flight[2] (flīt), *n.* act of fleeing; running away. [ME *fliht* < OE *flēon* flee]

flight·less (flīt′lis), *adj.* unable to fly.

flight·y (flīt′i), *adj.,* **flight·i·er, flight·i·est.** 1. likely to have sudden fancies; full of whims; frivolous. 2. slightly crazy; light-headed. —**flight′i·ly,** *adv.* —**flight′i·ness,** *n.*

flim·sy (flim′zi), *adj.,* **-si·er, -si·est,** *n.* —*adj.* 1. light and thin; frail. 2. lacking seriousness or sense; trivial: *a flimsy excuse.* —*n.* 1. a thin paper used by reporters. 2. a newspaper report on this paper. [? < alter. of *film*] —**flim′si·ly,** *adv.* —**flim′si·ness,** *n.* —Syn. *adj.* 2. shallow, feeble, weak.

flinch (flinch), *v.* draw back from difficulty, danger, or pain; shrink. —*n.* 1. a drawing back. 2. game played with cards bearing numbers from 1 to 14. [prob. < OF *flenchir* < unrecorded Frankish *hlankjan* bend. Cf. G *lenken.*] —**flinch′er,** *n.* —**flinch′ing·ly,** *adv.* —Syn. *v.* wince, quail, recoil.

flin·der (flin′dər), *n.* a small piece; fragment; splinter: *smashed to flinders.* [cf. Norw. *flindra*]

fling (fling), *v.,* **flung, fling·ing.** —*v.* 1. throw with force; throw: *fling a stone.* 2. rush; dash. 3. plunge; kick. 4. put suddenly or violently:

fling him **into** jail. —n. 1. a sudden throw. 2. plunge; kick. 3. time of doing as one pleases. 4. a lively Scottish dance. 5. have a fling at, a. try; attempt. b. make scornful remarks about. [? akin to Scand. *flengja* flog] —fling′er, n.

flint (flint), n. 1. a very hard, gray or brown stone that makes a spark when struck against steel. 2. piece of this used with steel to light fires, explode gunpowder, etc. 3. anything very hard or unyielding. [OE]

Flint (flint), n. city in SE Michigan.

flint glass, a brilliant glass containing lead, potassium or sodium, and silicon.

FLINT STEEL

TRIGGER PRIMING-PAN

Gun showing flintlock

flint-lock (flint′lok′), n. 1. gunlock in which a flint striking against steel makes sparks that explode the gunpowder. 2. an old-fashioned gun with such a gunlock.

flint-y (flin′ti), adj., flint-i-er, flint-i-est. 1. consisting of flint; containing flint. 2. like flint; very hard; unyielding. —flint′i-ly, adv. —flint′i-ness, n.

flip¹ (flip), v., flipped, flip-ping, n., adj., flip-per, flip-pest. —v. 1. toss or move with a snap of a finger and thumb. 2. jerk: *the branch flipped back.* 3. flick. —n. 1. a smart tap; snap. 2. a sudden jerk. —adj. Colloq. flippant. [prob. imit.]

flip² (flip), n. a hot drink containing beer, ale, cider, or the like, with sugar and spice. [n. use of flip¹, v.]

flip-pan-cy (flip′ən-si), n., pl. -cies. a being flippant.

flip-pant (flip′ənt), adj. smart or pert in speech; not respectful. [cf. Scand. *fleipa* babble] —flip′pant-ly, adv. —flip′pant-ness, n. —Syn. impertinent, saucy.

flip-per (flip′ər), n. a broad, flat limb esp. adapted for swimming. Seals have flippers.

flirt (flėrt), v. 1. make love without meaning it. 2. trifle; toy: *he flirted with the idea of going to Europe.* 3. move quickly; flutter. 4. toss; jerk. —n. 1. person who makes love without meaning it. 2. a quick movement or flutter. 3. toss; jerk. [imit.] —flirt′er, n. —flirt′ing-ly, adv.

flir-ta-tion (flėr-tā′shən), n. 1. a making love without meaning it. 2. a love affair that is not serious. —flir-ta′tious, adj. —flir-ta′tious-ly, adv. —flir-ta′tious-ness, n. —Syn. 1. dalliance.

flit (flit), v., flit-ted, flit-ting, n. —v. 1. fly lightly and quickly; flutter. 2. pass quickly. —n. a light, quick movement. [? < Scand. *flytjask*] —flit′ter, n.

flitch (flich), n. side of a hog salted and cured; side of bacon. [OE *flicce*]

flit-ter (flit′ər), v., n. flutter.

fliv-ver (fliv′ər), n. Am., Slang. a small, cheap automobile.

float (flōt), v. 1. stay on top of or be held up by air, water, or other liquid. 2. move with a moving liquid; drift: *the boat floated out to sea.* 3. rest or move in a liquid, the air, etc. 4. move around gently. 5. be unattached; be unstable. 6. cause to float. 7. cover with liquid; flood. 8. set going as a company. 9. sell (securities): *float an issue of stock.* —n. 1. anything that stays up or holds up something else in water. 2. a raft. 3. a cork on a fish line. 4. a low, flat car that carries something to be shown in a parade. [OE *flotian*] —float′a-ble, adj.

float-a-tion (flō-tā′shən), n. Brit. flotation.

float-er (flōt′ər), n. 1. person or thing that floats. 2. Am., Colloq. person who often changes his place of living, working, etc. 3. Am. person who votes illegally in several places.

float-ing (flōt′ing), adj. 1. that floats. 2. not fixed; not staying in one place; moving around. 3. in use or circulation; not permanently invested. 4. Com. not funded; changing. —float′ing-ly, adv.

floating ribs, Anat. ribs not attached to the breastbone; last two pairs of ribs.

floc-cu-lent (flok′yə-lənt), adj. 1. like bits of wool. 2. made up of soft, woolly masses. [< L *floccus* tuft of wool] —floc′cu-lence, n. —floc′cu-lent-ly, adv.

flock¹ (flok), n. 1. group of animals of one kind keeping, feeding, or herded together, esp. of sheep, goats, or birds. 2. a large group; crowd. 3. people of the same church group. —v. go gather in a flock; come crowding. [OE *flocc*] —Syn. n. 1. herd, drove. 2. throng, multitude.

flock² (flok), n. 1. tuft of wool. 2. waste wool or cotton used for stuffing furniture, etc. 3. a tiny woolly flake. [< OF < L *floccus*]

floe (flō), n. 1. field or sheet of floating ice. 2. a floating piece broken off from such a field or sheet. [< Scand. (Norw.) *flo*]

flog (flog; flôg), v., flogged, flog-ging. whip very hard; beat with a whip, stick, etc. —flog′ger, n.

flood (flud), n. 1. flow of water over what is usually dry land. 2. a large amount of water; ocean, lake, etc. 3. a great outpouring of anything: *flood of light, flood of words.* 4. a flowing of the tide toward the shore; rise of the tide. 5. the Flood, the water that covered the earth in the time of Noah. Gen. 7. —v. 1. flow over. 2. fill much fuller than usual. 3. put much water on. 4. pour out or stream like a flood. 5. fill, cover, or overcome like a flood. 6. flow like a flood. [OE *flōd*] —flood′a-ble, adj. —flood′er, n. —flood′less, adj.

flood control, control of rivers that tend to overflow by the use of dams, levees, dikes, extra outlets, reforestation, etc.

flood-gate (flud′gāt′), n. 1. gate in a canal, river, stream, etc., to control the flow of water. 2. thing that controls any flow or passage.

flood-light (flud′līt′), n. 1. lamp that gives a broad beam of light. 2. a broad beam of light from such a lamp. —v. illuminate by such a lamp.

floor (flōr; flôr), n. 1. the inside bottom covering of a room. 2. story of a building. 3. a flat surface at the bottom. 4. part of a room or hall where members of a lawmaking body, etc., sit and from which they speak. 5. right or privilege to speak in a lawmaking body, etc. The chairman decides who has the floor. 6. the main part of an exchange, where buying and selling of stocks, bonds, etc., is done. 7. Colloq. of prices, amounts, etc., the lowest level. —v. 1. put a floor in or over. 2. knock down. 3. Colloq. defeat. 4. Colloq. confuse; puzzle. [OE *flōr*] —floor′less, adj.

floor-ing (flōr′ing; flôr′-), n. 1. floor. 2. floors. 3. material for making floors.

floor leader, Am. member of a lawmaking body chosen to direct the members who belong to his political party.

floor show, Am. an entertainment presented at a night club.

floor-walk-er (flōr′wôk′ər; flôr′-), n. Am. person employed in a large store to oversee sales, direct customers, etc.

flop (flop), v., flopped, flop-ping, n. —v. 1. move loosely or heavily; flap around clumsily. 2. fall, throw, or move heavily. 3. change or turn suddenly. 4. fail. —n. 1. a flopping. 2. sound made by flopping. 3. failure. [imit. var. of *flap*] —flop′per, n.

flop-py (flop′i), adj., -pi-er, -pi-est. Colloq. flopping; tending to flop. —flop′pi-ly, adv. —flop′pi-ness, n.

flo-ra (flō′rə; flô′-), n. plants of a particular region or time. [< L]

flo-ral (flō′rəl; flô′-), adj. 1. of flowers; having to do with flowers. 2. resembling flowers. —flo′ral-ly, adv.

Flor-ence (flôr′əns; flor′-), n. city in C Italy. —Flor-en-tine (flôr′ən-tēn; flor′-), adj., n.

flo-res-cence (flō-res′əns; flô-), n. 1. act of blossoming. 2. condition of blossoming. 3. period of blossoming. [< NL *florescentia*, ult. < L *florere* flourish] —flo-res′cent, adj.

flo-ret (flō′rit; flô′-), n. 1. a small flower. 2. Bot. one of the small flowers in a flower head of a composite plant.

flo-ri-cul-ture (flō′rə-kul′chər; flô′-), n. cultivation of flowers. —flo′ri-cul′tur-al, adj. —flo′ri-cul′tur-al-ist, n. —flo′ri-cul′tur-al-ly, adv.

flor·id (flôr′id; flor′-), *adj.* 1. highly colored; ruddy: *a florid complexion.* 2. elaborately ornamented; flowery; showy; ornate. [< L *floridus* < *flos* flower] —**flo·rid·i·ty** (flô-rid′ə·ti; flō-) flo-), **flor′id·ness,** *n.* —**flor′id·ly,** *adv.*

Flor·i·da (flôr′ə·də; flor′-), *n.* a State in the extreme SE part of the United States. *Capital:* Tallahassee. *Abbrev.:* Fla. —**Flo·rid·i·an** (flô-rid′i·ən; fiō-; flo-), **Flor′i·dan,** *adj., n. Am.*

flor·in (flôr′ən; flor′-), *n.* 1. an English silver coin worth 2 shillings. 2. a gold coin issued at Florence in 1252. 3. any of various gold or silver coins used in different countries of Europe since then. [< F < Ital. *florino* Florentine coin marked with a lily, ult. < L *flos*]

flo·rist (flō′rist; flō′-; flor′ist), *n.* person who raises or sells flowers.

floss (flôs; flos), or **floss silk,** *n.* 1. short loose silk fibers. 2. a shiny, untwisted silk thread made from such fibers. 3. soft, silky fluff or fibers.

floss·y (flôs′i; flos′i), *adj.,* floss·i·er, floss·i·est. 1. of floss. 2. like floss.

flo·ta·tion (flō-tā′shən), *n.* 1. a floating or launching. 2. a selling or putting on sale. Also, *Brit.* **floatation.**

flo·til·la (flō-til′ə), *n.* 1. a small fleet. 2. fleet of small ships. [< Sp., dim. of *flota* fleet]

flot·sam (flot′səm), *n.* 1. wreckage of a ship or its cargo found floating on the sea. 2. person or thing that is adrift. [< AF *floteson* < *floter* float < OE]

flounce[1] (flouns), *v.,* flounced, flounc·ing, *n.* —*v.* 1. go with an angry or impatient fling of the body: *she flounced out of the room in a rage.* 2. twist; turn; jerk. —*n.* 1. an angry or impatient fling of the body. 2. twist; turn; jerk. [< Scand. (Sw.) *flunsa* plunge]

flounce[2] (flouns), *n., v.,* flounced, flounc·ing. —*n.* a wide ruffle used to trim a dress, skirt, etc. —*v.* trim with a flounce or flounces. [var. of *frounce* < OF *fronce* wrinkle]

floun·der[1] (floun′dər), *v.* 1. struggle awkwardly without making much progress; plunge about. 2. be clumsy or confused and make mistakes. —*n.* a floundering. —**floun′der·ing·ly,** *adv.*

Dress with flounces

floun·der[2] (floun′dər), *n., pl.* -ders or (*esp. collectively*) -der. flatfish that has a large mouth. [< AF *flo(u)ndre* < Scand. (Norw.) *flundra*]

flour (flour), *n.* 1. a fine, powdery substance made by grinding and sifting wheat or other grain. 2. any fine, soft powder. —*v.* 1. cover with flour. 2. make (grain) into flour. [special use of *flower* (i.e., the flower of the meal)] —**flour′-less,** *adj.* —**flour′y,** *adj.*

flour·ish (flér′ish), *v.* 1. grow or develop with vigor; thrive; do well. 2. be in the best time of life or activity. 3. wave (a sword, arm, etc.) in the air. 4. make a showy display. 5. make fanciful strokes with a pen; embellish by such strokes. 6. parade, flaunt, or display ostentatiously. —*n.* 1. a waving in the air. 2. a showy decoration in writing. 3. *Music.* a showy trill or passage. 4. a showy display. [< OF *florir,* ult. < L *flos* flower] —**flour′ish·er,** *n.* —**flour′ish·ing,** *adj.* —**flour′ish·ing·ly,** *adv.* —Syn. *v.* 1. succeed, prosper. 3. brandish.

R.E. Avery

Flourishes in handwriting

flout (flout), *v.* 1. treat with contempt or scorn; mock; scoff at. 2. show contempt or scorn; scoff. —*n.* contemptuous speech or act; insult; mockery; scoffing. [var. of *flute,* v.] —**flout′er,** *n.* —**flout′ing·ly,** *adv.* —Syn. *v.* 1. jeer, taunt. ➤ See flaunt for usage note.

flow (flō), *v.* 1. run like water; circulate. 2. pour out; pour along. 3. move easily or smoothly; glide. 4. hang loose and waving. 5. be plentiful; be full and overflowing. 6. flow in; rise. 7. flood.

—*n.* 1. act of flowing. 2. any continuous movement like that of water in a river. 3. way of flowing. 4. rate of flowing. 5. thing that flows; current; stream. 6. the flowing of the tide toward the shore; rise of the tide. [OE *flōwan*]

flow·er (flou′ər), *n.* 1. part of a plant that produces the seed; blossom; bloom. 2. plant grown for its blossoms. 3. *Bot.* any of several kinds of reproductive structures in lower plants, such as the mosses. 4. the finest part. 5. time of being at one's best. 6. **flowers,** *Chem.* substance in the form of a fine powder. 7. in flower, flowering. —*v.* 1. have flowers; produce flowers. 2. cover or decorate with flowers. 3. be at one's best. [< OF < L *flos*]

flow·ered (flou′ərd), *adj.* 1. having flowers. 2. covered or decorated with flowers.

flow·er·et (flou′ər·it), *n.* a small flower; floret.

flow·er·ing (flou′ər·ing), *adj.* having flowers.

flow·er·pot (flou′ər·pot′), *n.* pot to hold dirt for a plant to grow in.

flow·er·y (flou′ər·i), *adj.,* -er·i·er, -er·i·est. 1. having many flowers. 2. containing many fine words and fanciful expressions. —**flow′er·i·ly,** *adv.* —**flow′er·i·ness,** *n.* ➤ Flowery language originally meant too figurative language, but is now loosely used for any high-flown writing.

flown (flōn), *v.* pp. of **fly**[2].

flu (flü), *n. Colloq.* influenza.

flub (flub), *v.,* flubbed, flub·bing. *Colloq.* do (something) very clumsily; make a mess of.

fluc·tu·ate (fluk′chů·āt), *v.,* -at·ed, -at·ing. 1. rise and fall; change continually; vary irregularly. 2. move in waves. [< L, < *fluctus* wave] —**fluc′tu·a′tion,** *n.* —Syn. 1. oscillate, vacillate.

flue (flü), *n.* 1. tube, pipe, or other enclosed passage for conveying smoke, hot air, etc. 2. a flue pipe in an organ. 3. the air passage in such a pipe.

flu·ent (flü′ənt), *adj.* 1. flowing. 2. flowing smoothly or easily: *speak fluent French.* 3. speaking or writing easily and rapidly. [< L *fluens* flowing] —**flu′en·cy,** **flu′ent·ness,** *n.* —**flu′ent·ly,** *adv.* —Syn. 3. voluble, glib.

flue pipe, an organ pipe in which the sound is made by a current of air striking the mouth or opening in the pipe.

fluff (fluf), *n.* 1. soft, light, downy particles. 2. a downy mass: *a fluff of fur.* —*v.* 1. shake or puff out (hair, feathers, etc.) into a soft, light mass. 2. become fluffy. —**fluff′er,** *n.*

fluff·y (fluf′i), *adj.,* fluff·i·er, fluff·i·est. 1. soft and light like fluff: *whipped cream is fluffy.* 2. covered with fluff; downy: *fluffy baby chicks.* —**fluff′i·ly,** *adv.* —**fluff′i·ness,** *n.*

flu·id (flü′id), *n.* any liquid or gas; any substance that flows. Water, mercury, air, and oxygen are fluids. —*adj.* 1. in the state of a fluid; like a fluid; flowing. 2. of or having to do with fluids. 3. changing easily; not fixed. [< L, < *fluere* flow] —**flu·id′ic,** *adj.* —**flu·id′i·ty,** **flu′id·ness,** *n.* **flu′id·ly,** *adv.*

fluid dram, one eighth of a fluid ounce.

fluid ounce, measure for liquids. In the United States, 16 fluid ounces = 1 pint.

fluke[1] (flük), *n.* 1. either of the two points of an anchor. 2. *Am.* the barbed head or barb of an arrow, harpoon, etc. [? special use of *fluke*[3]]

fluke[2] (flük), *n.* 1. a lucky shot in billiards or pool. 2. a lucky chance; fortunate accident.

fluke[3] (flük), *n.* flatfish. [OE *flōc*]

fluk·y, **fluk·ey** (flük′i), *adj.,* fluk·i·er, fluk·i·est. *Colloq.* obtained by chance rather than by skill.

flume (flüm), *n.* 1. a deep, narrow valley with a stream running through it. 2. a large, inclined trough or chute for carrying water. [< OF < L *flumen* river < *fluere* flow]

flum·mer·y (flum′ər·i), *n., pl.* -mer·ies. 1. oatmeal or flour boiled with water, etc., until thick. 2. silly talk; nonsense. [< Welsh *llymru*]

flung (flung), *v.* pt. and pp. of **fling.**

flunk (flungk), *Am., Colloq.* —*v.* 1. fail in school work. 2. cause to fail. 3. mark or grade as having failed. 4. give up; back out. —*n.* failure.

flunk·y, **flunk·ey** (flungk′i), *n., pl.* **flunk·ies.**

flunk·eys. 1. a man servant who wears livery; footman. **2.** a flattering, fawning person.

flu·o·resce (flü´ə·res´), *v.*, -resced, -resc·ing. give off light by fluorescence.

flu·o·res·cence (flü´ə·res´əns), *n. Physics, Chem.* **1.** a giving off of light by a substance when it is exposed to certain rays (X rays and ultraviolet rays). **2.** property of a substance that causes this. **3.** light given off in this way. —**flu´o·res´cent,** *adj.*

fluorescent lamp, an electric lamp usually comprised of a cathode-ray tube containing a gas or vapor which produces light (fluorescent light) when electric current is introduced. —**fluorescent lighting.**

fluor·i·date (flür´ə·dāt; flü´ə·rə-), *v.*, -dat·ed, -dat·ing. add small amounts of fluorine to drinking water, esp. to decrease tooth decay in children. [< *fluoridation*]

fluor·i·da·tion (flür´ə·dā´shən; flü´ə·rə-), *n.* act or process of fluoridating. [< *fluoride*]

flu·o·ride (flü´ə·rīd; -rid), *n. Chem.* compound of fluorine and another element or radical.

flu·o·rine (flü´ə·rēn; -rin), **flu·o·rin** (-rin), *n. Chem.* a poisonous, greenish-yellow gas, F or Fl, that is a very active element similar to chlorine. —**flu·or·ic** (flü·ôr´ik; -ôr´-), *adj.*

flu·o·rite (flü´ə·rīt), **flu·or·spar** (flü´ôr·spär´; -ər-), *n.* calcium fluoride, CaF₂, a transparent, crystalline mineral that occurs in many colors.

fluor·o·scope (flür´ə·skōp; flü´ə·rə-), *n. Am.* device containing a fluorescent screen for examining objects exposed to X rays, etc.

flur·ry (flér´i), *n., pl.* -ries, *v.*, -ried, -ry·ing. —*n.* **1.** a sudden gust. **2.** *Am.* a sudden, gusty shower or snowfall. **3.** sudden excitement, confusion, or commotion. —*v.* excite; confuse; disturb.

flush¹ (flush), *v.* **1.** blush; glow. **2.** cause to blush or glow. **3.** rush suddenly; flow rapidly: *embarrassment caused the blood to flush to her cheeks.* **4.** wash or cleanse with a rapid flow of water. **5.** make joyful and proud; excite. —*n.* **1.** blush; glow. **2.** a sudden rush; rapid flow. **3.** an excited condition or feeling; sudden rush of joyous pride, etc. **4.** a sudden, fresh growth. **5.** glowing vigor; freshness: *the first flush of youth.* **6.** fit of feeling very hot. [? connected with *flash, blush*]

flush² (flush), *adj.* **1.** even; level. **2.** well supplied; having plenty: *flush with money.* **3.** abundant; plentiful. **4.** glowing; ruddy. **5.** vigorous. —*adv.* **1.** so as to be level; evenly. **2.** directly; squarely. —*v.* make even; level. [? extended use of *flush¹*]

flush³ (flush), *v.* **1.** fly or start up suddenly, as a bird. **2.** cause to fly or start up suddenly.

flush⁴ (flush), *n. Cards.* a hand all of one suit. [cf. F *flus, fluz* < L *fluxus* flow]

flus·ter (flus´tər), *v.* make or become nervous and excited; confuse. —*n.* nervous excitement; confusion. [cf. Scand. *flaustr* bustle and *flaustra* be flustered] —**flus´ter·a´tion,** **flus·tra´tion,** *n.* —**Syn.** *v.* agitate, embarrass, disconcert.

flute (flüt), *n., v.,* flut·ed, flut·ing. —*n.* **1.** *Music.* a long, slender, pipelike instrument with a series of finger holes or keys along the side. It is played by blowing across a hole near one end. **2.** a long, round groove, as in cloth, a column, etc. —*v.* **1.** play on a flute. **2.** sing or whistle so as to sound like a flute. **3.** make long, round grooves in. [< OF < Pr. *flauta*, ult. < L *flatus* blown] —**flut´ed,** *adj.* —**flute´like´,** *adj.*

flut·ing (flüt´ing), *n.* **1.** decoration made of flutes. **2.** act of playing a flute.

flut·ist (flüt´ist), *n.* person who plays a flute. Also, **flautist.**

flut·ter (flut´ər), *v.* **1.** wave back and forth quickly and lightly. **2.** flap the wings; flap. **3.** come or go with a fluttering motion. **4.** move restlessly. **5.** move quickly and unevenly; tremble: *her heart fluttered.* **6.** beat feebly and irregularly: *her pulse fluttered.* **7.** confuse; excite. —*n.* **1.** a fluttering. **2.** confused or excited condition. Also, **flitter.** [OE *flotorian* < *fléotan* float] —**flut´-**

Fluting

ter·er, *n.* —**flut´ter·ing·ly,** *adv.* —**Syn.** *v.* **3.** hover, flicker, flit.

flux (fluks), *n.* **1.** a flow; flowing. **2.** a flowing in of the tide. **3.** continuous change. **4.** *Physiol.* an unnatural discharge of blood or liquid matter from the body. **5.** substance used to help metals or minerals melt together. **6.** rate of flow of a fluid, heat, etc., across a certain surface or area. —*v.* **1.** cause a discharge in; purge. **2.** melt together. [< L *fluxus* < *fluere* flow]

flux·ion (fluk´shən), *n.* **1.** a flowing; flow. **2.** discharge.

fly¹ (flī), *n., pl.* flies. **1.** a housefly. **2.** any of a large group of insects that have two wings, including houseflies, mosquitoes, gnats, etc. **3.** any insect with transparent wings, such as a May fly. **4.** fishhook with feathers, silk, tinsel, etc., on it to make it look like an insect. [OE *fléoge*]

fly² (flī), *v.,* flew, flown, **fly·ing** *for 1-9;* flied, fly·ing *for 10; n., pl.* flies. —*v.* **1.** move through the air with wings. **2.** float or wave in the air. **3.** cause to fly. **4.** travel through the air in an airplane or airship. **5.** travel over in an airplane or airship. **6.** manage (an airplane or airship). **7.** carry in an airplane or airship. **8.** move swiftly; go rapidly; flee; flee from; shun. **10.** *Am., Baseball.* hit a ball high in the air. —*n.* **1.** flap to cover buttons on clothing. **2.** flap forming the door of a tent. **3.** a light, public carriage for passengers. **4.** *Am., Baseball.* ball hit high in the air with a bat. [OE *fléogan*] —**Syn.** *v.* **9.** abscond, decamp.

fly·blown (flī´blōn´), *adj.* **1.** tainted by the eggs or larvae of flies. **2.** spoiled.

fly-by-night (flī´bī·nīt´), *adj.* not reliable; not to be trusted.

fly·catch·er (flī´kach´ər), *n.* any of a family of songless, perching birds having small, weak feet, short necks, and large heads with broad, flattened bills hooked at the tip.

fly·er (flī´ər), *n.* flier.

fly-fish (flī´fish´), *v.* fish with flies as bait. —**fly´-fish´er,** *n.* —**fly´-fish´ing,** *n.*

fly·ing (flī´ing), *adj.* **1.** that flies; moving through the air. **2.** floating or waving in the air. **3.** swift. **4.** short and quick; hasty.

flying boat, airplane that can float on water; seaplane.

flying buttress, *Archit.* an arched support or brace built against the wall of a building to resist outward pressure.

flying colors, success; victory.

flying fish, a tropical fish that has winglike fins and can leap through the air.

flying jib, *Naut.* a small, triangular sail set in front of the regular jib.

flying machine, 1. airplane. **2.** airship.

flying saucer or disk, any of various mysterious disklike objects reportedly seen flying over the United States and Mexico, since 1947.

flying spot, *Television.* a moving beam of light which produces a succession of thin lines against a surface containing an image.

fly·leaf (flī´lēf´), *n., pl.* -leaves. a blank sheet of paper at the beginning or end of a book, pamphlet, etc.

fly·o·ver (flī´ō´vər), *n.* a mass flight of aircraft over a city, reviewing stand, etc., usually as a display of air power.

fly·past (flī´past´; -päst´), *n. Brit.* flyover.

fly·speck (flī´spek´), *n.* a tiny spot left by a fly. —*v.* make flyspecks on.

fly·weight (flī´wāt´), *n.* boxer who weighs not more than 112 pounds.

fly·wheel (flī´hwēl´), *n.* a heavy wheel attached to machinery to keep the speed even.

Fm, fermium.

FM, F.M., frequency modulation.

foal (fōl), *n.* a young horse, donkey, etc.; colt or filly. —*v.* give birth to (a foal). [OE *fola*]

foam (fōm), *n.* mass of very small bubbles. —*v.* **1.** form or gather foam. **2.** cause to foam. **3.** break into foam. [OE *fám*] —**foam´less,** *adj.*

foam rubber, rubber processed so that it is soft and porous, used for cushions, etc.

foam·y (fōm′i), *adj.*, **foam·i·er, foam·i·est. 1.** covered with foam; foaming. **2.** made of foam. **3.** like foam. **—foam′i·ly,** *adv.* **—foam′i·ness,** *n.*

fob (fob), *n.* **1.** a small pocket in trousers or breeches to hold a watch, etc. **2.** *Am. a.* a short watch chain, ribbon, etc., that hangs out of a watch pocket. **b.** ornament worn at the end of such a chain, ribbon, etc. [cf. dial. HG *fuppe* pocket]

f.o.b., F.O.B., free on board. The price $850, f.o.b. Detroit, means that the $850 does not pay for freight or other expenses after the article has been put on board a freight car at Detroit.

fo·cal (fō′kəl), *adj.* of a focus; having to do with a focus. **—fo′cal·ly,** *adv.*

focal distance or **length,** distance of the focus from the optical center of a lens.

fo·cal·ize (fō′kəl·īz), *v.*, **-ized, -iz·ing. 1.** focus. **2.** bring into focus. **—fo′cal·i·za′tion,** *n.*

fo·cus (fō′kəs), *n.*, *pl.* **-cus·es, -ci** (-sī), *v.*, **-cused, -cus·ing;** *esp. Brit.* **-cussed, -cus·sing.** **—n. 1.** point where rays of light, heat, etc., meet, appear to meet, or should meet after being bent by a lens, curved mirror, etc. **2.** distance of this point from the lens, curved mirror, etc.; focal distance. **3.** correct adjustment of a lens, the eye, etc., to make a clear image. **4.** the central point of attention, activity, disturbance, etc. **5. in focus,** clear; distinct. **6. out of focus,** blurred; indistinct. **—v. 1.** bring (rays of light, heat, etc.) to a point. **2.** adjust (a lens, the eye, etc.) to make a clear image. **3.** make (an image, etc.) clear by adjusting a lens, the eye, etc. **4.** concentrate: *when studying, he focused his mind on his lessons.* [< L, hearth] **—fo′cus·er,** *n.*

Rays of light brought to a focus at F by the lens, L.

fod·der (fod′ər), *n.* coarse food for horses, cattle, etc. [OE *fōdor* < *fōda* food]

foe (fō), *n.* enemy. [OE *fāh* hostile]

foe·man (fō′mən), *n.*, *pl.* **-men.** *Archaic.* enemy.

foe·tus (fē′təs), *n.* fetus. **—foe′tal,** *adj.*

fog (fog; fôg), *n.*, *v.*, **fogged, fog·ging. —n. 1.** cloud of fine drops of water just above the earth's surface; thick mist. **2.** a darkened condition; dim, blurred state. **3.** a confused or puzzled condition. **—v. 1.** cover with fog. **2.** darken; dim; blur. **3.** confuse; puzzle. [< *foggy*]

fog bank, a dense mass of fog.

fog·gy (fog′i; fôg′i), *adj.*, **-gi·er, -gi·est. 1.** having much fog; misty. **2.** not clear; dim; blurred. **3.** confused; puzzled. [< *fog* long grass; orig., marshy] **—fog′gi·ly,** *adv.* **—fog′gi·ness,** *n.*

fog·horn (fog′hôrn′; fôg′-), *n.* horn that warns ships in foggy weather.

fo·gy, fo·gey (fō′gi), *n.*, *pl.* **-gies, -geys. 1.** person who lacks enterprise. **2.** person who is behind the times. **—fo′gy·ish, fo′gey·ish,** *adj.*

foi·ble (foi′bəl), *n.* a weak point; weakness. [< F, older form of modern *faible* FEEBLE] **—Syn.** failing, fault, frailty.

foil[1] (foil), *v.* prevent from carrying out (plans, attempts, etc.); turn aside or hinder. [< OF *fuler* trample, full (cloth). See FULLER.]

foil[2] (foil), *n.* **1.** metal beaten, hammered, or rolled into a very thin sheet. **2.** anything that makes something else look or seem better by contrast. **3.** a very thin layer of polished metal, placed under a gem to give it more color or sparkle. **4.** *Archit.* a leaflike ornament. **—v. 1.** cover or back with metal foil. **2.** set off by contrast. **3.** ornament with foils. [< F < L *folia* leaves]

foil[3] (foil), *n.* a long, narrow sword with a knob or button on the point to prevent injury, used in fencing.

foist (foist), *v.* **1.** palm off as genuine; impose slyly. **2.** insert secretly or slyly. [prob. < dial. Du. *vuisten* take in hand < *vuist* fist]

fold[1] (fōld), *v.* **1.** bend or double over on itself. **2.** bring together with the parts in or around one another. **3.** bring close to the body. **4.** put the arms around and hold tenderly. **5.** wrap;

enclose. **6.** fail. **—n. 1.** layer of something folded. **2.** a hollow place made by folding. **3.** a doubling; bending. **4.** *Geol.* bend in rock after its stratification. [OE *fealdan*]

fold[2] (fōld), *n.* **1.** pen to keep sheep in. **2.** sheep kept in a pen. **3.** church group; church. **—v.** put or keep (sheep) in a pen. [OE *falod*]

-fold, *suffix.* **1.** times as many; times as great, as in *tenfold.* **2.** formed or divided into ——parts, as in *manifold.* [OE *-feald*]

fold·er (fōl′dər), *n.* **1.** person or thing that folds. **2.** holder for papers, made by folding a piece of stiff paper. **3.** a small book made of one or more folded sheets.

fol·de·rol (fol′də·rol), *n.* falderal.

fo·li·a·ceous (fō′li·ā′shəs), *adj.* **1.** leaflike; leafy. **2.** made of leaflike plates or thin layers. [< L, < *folia* leaves]

fo·li·age (fō′li·ij), *n.* **1.** leaves. **2.** decoration made of carved or painted leaves, flowers, etc. [alter. of F *feuillage,* ult. < L *folia* leaves]

fo·li·ate (*adj.* fō′li·it, -āt; *v.* fō′li·āt) *adj.*, *v.*, **-at·ed, -at·ing. —adj.** having leaves; covered with leaves. **—v.** put forth leaves.

fo·li·a·tion (fō′li·ā′shən), *n.* **1.** a growing of leaves; putting forth of leaves. **2.** a being in leaf. **3.** decoration with leaflike ornaments. **4.** the arrangement of leaves within the bud. **5.** the consecutive numbering of leaves of a book.

fo·li·o (fō′li·ō), *n.*, *pl.* **-li·os,** *adj.*, *v.*, **-li·oed, -li·o·ing. —n. 1.** a large sheet of paper folded once to make two leaves, or four pages, of a book, etc. **2.** book of the largest size, having pages made by folding large sheets of paper once. **3.** any book more than 11 inches in height. **4.** in printing, a page number of a book, etc. **5.** leaf of a book, manuscript, etc., numbered on the front side only. **6. in folio,** of folio size or form. **—adj.** of the largest size; made of large sheets of paper folded once. **—v.** number the leaves of a book, pamphlet, etc. [< L, abl. of *folium* leaf]

folk (fōk), *n.*, *pl.* **folk, folks,** *adj.* **—n. 1.** people. **2.** tribe; nation. **3. folks,** a people. **b.** members of one's own family. **—adj.** of or having to do with the common people, their beliefs, legends, customs, etc. [OE *folc*] ▶ *folk, folks.* Formal English, and some local speech, uses *folk* as the plural; informal usually has *folks,* esp. in the sense of "members of one's family."

folk dance. 1. dance originating and handed down among the common people. **2.** music for it.

folk·lore (fōk′lôr′; -lōr′), *n.* beliefs, legends, customs, etc., of a people, tribe, etc. **—folk′lor′ist,** *n.* **—folk′lor·is′tic,** *adj.*

folk music, music originating and handed down among the common people.

folk song, folk·song (fōk′sông′; -song′), *n.* **1.** song originating and handed down among the common people. **2.** song imitating this.

folk·sy (fōk′si), *adj.*, **-si·er, -si·est.** *Colloq.* **1.** appealing to ordinary people; informal. **2.** sociable.

folk tale or **story,** story or legend originating and handed down among the common people.

folk·way (fōk′wā′), *n.* custom or habit that has grown up within a social group and is common among the members of this group.

fol·li·cle (fol′ə·kəl), *n.* **1.** *Anat.* a small cavity, sac, or gland. Hair grows from follicles. **2.** *Bot.* a dry, one-celled seed vessel. Milkweed pods are follicles. [< L *folliculus,* dim. of *follis* bellows] **—fol·lic·u·lar** (fə·lik′yə·lər), *adj.*

fol·low (fol′ō), *v.* **1.** go or come after. **2.** result from; result. **3.** go along. **4.** go (def. 2) along with; accompany. **5.** pursue. **6.** act according to; take as a guide; use; obey. **7.** keep the eyes or attention on. **8.** keep the mind on; keep up with and understand. **9.** take as one's work; be concerned with. **10. follow out,** carry out to the end. **11. follow through,** continue a stroke or motion through to the end. **12. follow up, a.** follow closely and steadily. **b.** carry out to the end. **c.** increase the effect of by further action. **—n.** act of following. [OE *folgian*] **—fol′low·a·ble,** *adj.* **—Syn.** *v.* **2.** ensue. **4.** attend.

Follicles (def. 2)

fol·low·er (fol′ō·ər), *n.* 1. person or thing that follows. 2. person who follows the ideas or beliefs of another. 3. attendant; servant. 4. a male admirer; beau. —*Syn.* 2. adherent, disciple.

fol·low·ing (fol′ō·ing), *n.* 1. followers; attendants. 2. the following, persons, things, items, etc., now to be named, related, described, etc. —*adj.* that follows; next after.

fol·ly (fol′i), *n., pl.* –lies. 1. being foolish; lack of sense; unwise conduct. 2. a foolish act, practice, or idea; something silly. 3. a costly but foolish undertaking. [< OF, < *fol* foolish. See FOOL.]

fo·ment (fō·ment′), *v.* 1. promote; foster (trouble, rebellion, etc.). 2. apply warm water, hot cloths, etc., to (a hurt or pain). [< LL *fomentare*, ult. < L *fovere* to warm] —fo′men·ta′tion, *n.* —fo·ment′er, *n.*

fond (fond), *adj.* 1. liking: *fond of children.* 2. loving: *a fond look.* 3. loving foolishly or too much. 4. cherished. 5. *Archaic.* foolish. [ME *fonned,* pp. of *fonne(n)* be foolish] —fond′ly, *adv.* —fond′ness, *n.* —*Syn.* 2. affectionate, amorous.

fon·dant (fon′dənt), *n.* a creamy sugar candy used as a filling or coating of other candies. [< F, lit., melting]

fon·dle (fon′dəl), *v.,* –dled, –dling. pet; caress. [< *fond,* v., special use of *fond,* adj.] —fon′dler, *n.*

fon·due (fon′dü; fon·dü′), *n.* a combination of melted cheese, eggs, and butter. [< F, fem. pp. of *fondre* melt]

font¹ (font), *n.* 1. basin holding water for baptism. 2. basin for holy water. 3. fountain; source. [< L *fons* spring]

font² (font), *n.* in printing, a complete set of type of one size and style. Also, *esp. Brit.* fount. [< F *fonte* < *fondre* melt]

Fon·taine·bleau (fon′tən·blō; fon′tən·blō′), *n.* town, in a forest of the same name, near Paris, France. It contains a palace long used by the rulers of France.

Foo·chow (fü′chou′), *n.* seaport in SE China.

food (füd), *n.* 1. what an animal or plant takes in to enable it to live and grow. 2. what is eaten: *give food to the hungry.* 3. a particular kind or article of food. 4. what sustains or serves for consumption in any way: *food for thought.* [OE *fōda*] —food′less, *adj.* —*Syn.* 1. nourishment, sustenance, aliment.

food·stuff (füd′stuf′), *n.* material for food.

fool (fül), *n.* 1. person without sense; unwise or silly person. 2. clown formerly kept by a king or lord to amuse people; jester. 3. person who has been deceived or tricked; dupe. —*v.* 1. act like a fool for fun; play; joke. 2. make a fool of; deceive; trick. 3. fool around, *Am., Colloq.* waste time foolishly. 4. fool away, *Colloq.* waste foolishly. 5. fool with, *Colloq.* meddle foolishly with. [< OF *fol* madman, prob. < LL *follis* empty-headed < L, bag, bellows] —*Syn. n.* 1. simpleton, dunce.

fool·er·y (fül′ər·i), *n., pl.* –er·ies. foolish action or behavior.

fool·har·dy (fül′här′di), *adj.,* –di·er, –di·est. foolishly bold; rash. —fool′har′di·ly, *adv.* —fool′har′di·ness, *n.*

fool·ish (fül′ish), *adj.* 1. like a fool; without sense; unwise; silly. 2. ridiculous. 3. trifling. —fool′ish·ly, *adv.* —fool′ish·ness, *n.*

fool·proof (fül′prüf′), *adj. Am., Colloq.* so safe or simple that even a fool can use or do it.

fools·cap (fülz′kap′), *n.* writing paper in sheets from 12 to 13½ inches wide and 15 to 17 inches long. [from the watermark]

fool's gold, mineral that looks like gold; iron pyrites or copper pyrites.

foot (füt), *n., pl.* feet, *v.* —*n.* 1. the end part of a leg; part that a person, animal, or thing stands on. 2. part near the feet; end toward which the feet are put. 3. the lowest part; bottom; base. 4. part that covers the foot. 5. soldiers that go on foot; infantry. 6. measure of length, twelve inches. 7. one of the parts into which a line of poetry is divided. This line has four feet: "The boy|stood on|the burn|ing deck." —*v.* 1. make or

renew the foot of (a stocking, etc.). 2. walk; step; pace. 3. dance. 4. add. 5. *Colloq.* pay (a bill, etc.). [OE *fōt*]

foot·age (füt′ij), *n.* length in feet.

foot-and-mouth disease, a dangerous, contagious disease of cattle and some other animals, characterized by blisters in the mouth and around the hoofs.

foot·ball (füt′bôl′), *n.* 1. game played with a large, inflated leather ball by two teams of eleven players each on a field with a goal at each end. 2. ball used in this game. 3. any game or ball like this.

foot·board (füt′bôrd′; –bōrd′), *n.* 1. board or small platform to be used as a support for the feet. 2. an upright piece across the foot of a bed.

foot·bridge (füt′brij′), *n.* bridge for people on foot only.

foot·can·dle (füt′kan′dəl), *n.* unit for measuring illumination. It is the amount of light produced by a standard candle at a distance of one foot.

foot·ed (füt′id), *adj.* having a certain kind or number of feet: *a four-footed animal.*

foot·fall (füt′fôl′), *n.* sound of steps coming or going; footstep.

foot·hill (füt′hil′), *n.* a low hill at the base of a mountain or mountain range.

foot·hold (füt′hōld′), *n.* 1. place to put the feet; support for the feet; surface to stand on. 2. a firm footing or position.

foot·ing (füt′ing), *n.* 1. a firm placing or position of the feet. 2. place to put the feet; support for the feet; surface to stand on. 3. a firm place or position. 4. condition; position; relationship: *the United States and Canada are on a friendly footing.* 5. an adding.

foot·lights (füt′līts′), *n.pl.* 1. row of lights at the front of a stage. 2. profession of acting; stage; theater.

foot·loose (füt′lüs′), *adj. Colloq.* free to go anywhere or do anything.

foot·man (füt′mən), *n., pl.* –men. a male servant who answers the bell, waits on the table, etc.

foot·note (füt′nōt′), *n.* note at the bottom of a page about something on the page.

foot·pad (füt′pad′), *n.* a highway robber who goes on foot only.

foot·path (füt′path′; –päth′), *n.* path for people on foot only.

foot·pound (füt′pound′), *n.* quantity of energy needed to raise a weight of one pound to a height of one foot.

foot·print (füt′print′), *n.* mark made by a foot.

foot soldier, soldier who fights on foot; infantryman.

foot·sore (füt′sôr′; –sōr′), *adj.* having sore feet from much walking.

foot·step (füt′step′), *n.* 1. sound of steps coming or going. 2. mark made by a foot; footprint. 3. distance covered in one step. 4. step on which to go up or down.

foot·stool (füt′stül′), *n.* a low stool to put the feet on when sitting.

foot·wear (füt′wār′), *n.* shoes, slippers, stockings, gaiters, etc.

foot·work (füt′wėrk′), *n. Sports, etc.* way of using the feet.

foo·zle (fü′zəl), *v.,* –zled, –zling, *n.* —*v.* do clumsily; bungle (a stroke in golf, etc.). —*n.* a foozling.

fop (fop), *n.* a vain man who is very fond of fine clothes and has affected manners; empty-headed dandy. —fop′per·y, *n.* —fop′pish, *adj.* —fop′pish·ly, *adv.* —fop′pish·ness, *n.*

for (fôr; *unstressed* fər), *prep.* 1. in place of: *we used boxes for chairs.* 2. in support of; in favor of: *he voted for Roosevelt.* 3. representing: in the interest of: *a lawyer acts for his client.* 4. in consideration of: *these apples are twelve for a dollar.* 5. with the object or purpose of: *he went for a walk.* 6. in order to become, have, keep, etc.: *the navy trains men for sailors, he ran for his life.* 7. in search of: *she is hunting for her cat.* 8. in order to get to: *he has just left for New York.* 9. meant to belong to or be used with;

suited to: *books for children.* **10.** because of; by reason of: *he was punished for stealing.* **11.** in honor of: *a party was given for her.* **12.** with a feeling toward: *we longed for home.* **13.** with respect or regard to: *eating too much is bad for one's health.* **14.** as far or as long as; throughout; during: *we worked for an hour.* **15.** as being: *they know it for a fact.* **16.** in spite of: *for all his faults, we like him still.* **17.** in proportion to: *for one poisonous snake there are many harmless ones.* **18.** to the amount of: *his father gave him a check for $20.* —*conj.* because: *we can't go, for it is raining.* [OE] ➤ **for.** See the usage note under **because.** A comma is usually needed between two coördinate clauses joined by *for;* without it the *for* might be read as a preposition: *He was glad to go, for Mrs. Crane had been especially good to him.* [Not: *He was glad to go for Mrs. Crane.* . . .]

for·age (fôr′ij; for′-), *n., v.,* **-aged, -ag·ing.** —*n.* **1.** food for horses, cattle, etc. **2.** a hunting or searching for food. —*v.* **1.** supply with food; feed. **2.** hunt or search for food. **3.** get by hunting or searching about. **4.** hunt; search about. **5.** get or take food from. **6.** plunder. [< F, < OF *fuerre* fodder < Gmc.] —**for′ag·er,** *n.*

fo·ram·i·nif·er·a (fō·ram′ə·nif′ər·ə; fō-), *n.pl.* group of tiny, one-celled sea animals, most of which have shells with tiny holes in them. [< NL, < L *foramen* a small opening + *ferre* to bear] —**fo·ram′i·nif′er·al, fo·ram′i·nif′er·ous,** *adj.*

for·as·much as (fôr′əz·much′ az), in view of the fact that; since; because.

for·ay (fôr′ā; for′ā), *n.* a raid for plunder. —*v.* plunder; lay waste; pillage. [akin to FORAGE. Cf. OF *forrer* forage.] —**for′ay·er,** *n.*

for·bear¹ (fôr·bãr′), *v.,* **-bore, -borne, -bear·ing. 1.** hold back; keep from doing, saying, using, etc. **2.** be patient; control oneself. [OE *forberan*] —**for·bear′er,** *n.* —**for·bear′ing·ly,** *adv.* —Syn. **1.** refrain, abstain.

for·bear² (fôr′bãr), *n.* forebear; ancestor.

for·bear·ance (fôr·bãr′əns), *n.* **1.** act of forbearing. **2.** patience; self-control.

for·bid (fər·bid′), *v.,* **-bade** (-bad′) or **-bad** (-bad′), **-bid·den** or **-bid, -bid·ding. 1.** order (one) not to do something; make a rule against; prohibit. **2.** rule against the appearance or use of; exclude. **3.** keep from happening; prevent: *God forbid!* **4.** command to keep away from; exclude from: *I forbid you the house.* [OE *forbēodan*] —**for·bid′der,** *n.* —Syn. **1.** interdict, proscribe.

for·bid·ding (fər·bid′ing), *adj.* causing fear or dislike; looking dangerous or unpleasant. —**for·bid′ding·ly,** *adv.* —**for·bid′ding·ness,** *n.* —Syn. disagreeable, displeasing, grim.

force (fôrs; fōrs), *n., v.,* **forced, forc·ing.** —*n.* **1.** strength; power. **2.** strength used against a person or thing; violence. **3.** power to control, influence, persuade, convince, etc.; effectiveness. **4.** *Am.* group of people working or acting together: *our office force.* **5.** group of soldiers, sailors, policemen, etc. **6.** *Physics.* cause that produces, changes, or stops the motion of a body. **7.** meaning. **8.** forces, army, navy, etc. **9.** in force, **a.** in effect or operation; binding; valid. **b.** with full strength. —*v.* **1.** use force on. **2.** compel. **3.** *Cards.* **a.** compel (an opponent) to play a trump or to indicate the strength of his hand. **b.** compel to play (a particular card). **4.** *Am., Baseball.* compel a player to leave one base and try in vain to reach the next. **5.** make or drive by force. **6.** get or take by force. **7.** put by force. **8.** break open or through by force. **9.** ravish; violate. **10.** urge to violent effort. **11.** make by an unusual or unnatural effort; strain. **12.** hurry the growth or development of. [< F, ult. < L *fortis* strong] —**force′a·ble,** *adj.* —**force′less,** *adj.* —**forc′er,** *n.* —Syn. *n.* **1.** might, vigor, energy. **2.** coercion, compulsion, constraint. **7.** significance, import.

forced (fôrst; fōrst), *adj.* **1.** made, compelled, or driven by force: *forced labor.* **2.** made by an unusual or unnatural effort: *a forced smile.* —Syn. **1.** compulsory, enforced. **2.** strained.

forced march, an unusually long, fast march.

force·ful (fôrs′fəl; fōrs′-), *adj.* full of force; strong; powerful; vigorous; effective. —**force′ful·ly,** *adv.* —**force′ful·ness,** *n.*

force·meat (fôrs′mēt′; fōrs′-), *n.* chopped and seasoned meat, used for stuffing, etc.

for·ceps (fôr′seps; -səps), *n.* small pincers or tongs used by surgeons, dentists, etc., for seizing, holding, and pulling. [< L, < *formus* hot + *capere* take]

force pump, pump with a valveless piston whose action forces liquid through a pipe; any pump which delivers liquid under pressure.

for·ci·ble (fôr′sə·bəl; fōr′-), *adj.* **1.** made or done by force; using force: *a forcible entrance into a house.* **2.** having or showing force; strong; powerful; effective; convincing: *a forcible speaker.* —**for′ci·ble·ness,** *n.* —**for′ci·bly,** *adv.*

ford (fôrd; fōrd), *n.* place where a river or other body of water is not too deep to cross by walking through the water. —*v.* cross by a ford. [OE] —**ford′a·ble,** *adj.* —**ford′less,** *adj.*

fore (fôr; fōr), *adj., adv.* at the front; toward the beginning or front; forward. [adj. use of *fore-*] —*n.* the forward part; front. [< adj.] —*interj. Golf.* shout of warning to persons ahead who are liable to be struck by the ball.

fore-, *prefix.* **1.** front; in front; at or near the front, as in *foredeck, foremast.* **2.** before; beforehand, as in *foreknow, foresee.* [OE *for(e)*]

fore-and-aft (fôr′ənd·aft′; fōr′-; -äft′), *adj. Naut.* lengthwise on a ship; from bow to stern; placed lengthwise.

fore and aft, *Naut.* **1.** at or toward both bow and stern of a ship. **2.** lengthwise on a ship; from bow to stern; placed lengthwise.

fore·arm¹ (fôr′ärm′; fōr′-), *n.* that part of the arm between the elbow and wrist.

fore·arm² (fôr·ärm′; fōr-), *v.* prepare for trouble ahead of time; arm beforehand.

fore·bear (fôr′bãr; fōr′-), *n.* ancestor; forefather. Also, **forbear.**

fore·bode (fôr·bōd′; fōr-), *v.,* **-bod·ed, -bod·ing. 1.** give warning of; predict. **2.** have a feeling that something bad is going to happen. —**fore·bod′er,** *n.* —**fore·bod′ing,** *n., adj.* —**fore·bod′ing·ly,** *adv.* —Syn. **1.** foretell.

fore·brain (fôr′brān′; fōr′-), *n.* the front section of the brain.

fore·cast (fôr′kast′; fōr′-; -käst′), *v.,* **-cast** or **-cast·ed, -cast·ing.** —*n.* **1.** prophesy; predict. **2.** be a prophecy or pre-diction of. **3.** foresee; plan ahead. —*n.* **1.** prophecy; prediction. **2.** a planning ahead; foresight. —**fore′cast′er,** *n.*

fore·cas·tle (fōk′səl; fôr′kas′əl; fōr′-; -käs′-), *n. Naut.* **1.** the upper deck in front of the foremast. **2.** sailors' quarters in a merchant ship, formerly in the forward part of the ship.

fore·close (fôr·klōz′; fōr-), *v.,* **-closed, -closing. 1.** shut out; prevent; exclude. **2.** *Law.* take away the right to redeem (a mortgage). [< OF *forclos* excluded < *for-* out (< Frankish *for-* and L *foris*) + *clore* shut < L *claudere*] —**fore·clos′a·ble,** *adj.*

fore·clo·sure (fôr·klō′zhər; fōr-), *n.* the foreclosing of a mortgage.

fore·done (fôr·dun′; fōr-), *adj., v. Archaic.* exhausted.

fore·doom (fôr·düm′; fōr-), *v.* doom beforehand.

fore·fa·ther (fôr′fä′t͟hər; fōr′-), *n.* ancestor.

fore·fin·ger (fôr′fing′gər; fōr′-), *n.* finger next to the thumb; first finger; index finger.

fore·foot (fôr′fut′; fōr′-), *n., pl.* **-feet. 1.** one of the front feet of an animal having four or more feet. **2.** *Naut.* the forward end of a ship's keel.

fore·front (fôr′frunt′; fōr′-), *n.* place of greatest importance, activity, etc.; foremost part.

fore·gath·er (fôr·gat͟h′ər; fōr-), *v.* forgather.

fore·go[1] (fôr·gō′; fôr′-), v., **-went, -gone, -going.** forgo. —**fore·go′er,** n.

fore·go[2] (fôr·gō′; fôr′-), v., **-went, -gone, -going.** precede; go before. —**fore·go′er,** n.

fore·go·ing (fôr′gō′ing, fôr′-; fôr′gō′ing, fôr′-), adj. preceding; previous.

fore·gone (fôr·gôn′, fôr-, -gon′; fôr′gôn, fôr′-, -gon), adj. that has gone before; previous.

foregone conclusion, fact that was almost surely known beforehand.

fore·ground (fôr′ground′; fôr′-), n. part of a picture or scene nearest the observer; part toward the front.

fore·hand (fôr′hand′; fôr′-), adj. **1.** foremost. **2.** Tennis, etc. made with the palm of the hand turned forward. —n. **1.** Tennis, etc. a forehand stroke. **2.** position in front or above; advantage.

fore·hand·ed (fôr′han′did; fôr′-), adj. **1.** providing for the future; prudent; thrifty. **2.** done beforehand; early. —**fore′hand′ed·ness,** n.

fore·head (fôr′id; fôr′id; fôr′hed′), n. **1.** part of the face above the eyes. **2.** a front part.

for·eign (fôr′ən; fôr′-), adj. **1.** outside one's own country. **2.** of, characteristic of, or coming from outside one's own country: foreign money. **3.** having to do with other countries; carried on or dealing with other countries: foreign trade. **4.** not belonging; not related: sitting still is foreign to a boy's nature. **5.** not belonging naturally to the place where found: a foreign substance in the blood. [< OF forain, ult. < L foras outside] —**for′eign·ness,** n. —**Syn. 4.** unfamiliar, strange.

foreign affairs, a country's relations with other countries.

for·eign-born (fôr′ən-bôrn′; fôr′-), adj. born in another country.

for·eign·er (fôr′ən·ər; fôr′-), n. person from another country; alien.

foreign office, Brit. the government department in charge of foreign affairs.

fore·judge (fôr·juj′; fôr′-), v., **-judged, -judging.** judge beforehand.

fore·know (fôr·nō′; fôr′-), v., **-knew, -known, -know·ing.** know beforehand. —**fore′know′a·ble,** adj. —**fore·knowl·edge** (fôr′nol′ij, fôr′-; fôr·nol′ij, fôr-), n.

fore·land (fôr′land′; fôr′-), n. cape; headland; promontory.

fore·leg (fôr′leg′; fôr′-), n. one of the front legs of an animal having four or more legs.

fore·lock (fôr′lok′; fôr′-), n. lock of hair that grows just above the forehead.

fore·man (fôr′mən; fôr′-), n., pl. **-men. 1.** man in charge of a group of workers or of some part of a factory. **2.** Law. chairman of a jury.

fore·mast (fôr′mast′; fôr′-; -mäst′; Naut. -məst), n. Naut. mast nearest the bow of a ship.

fore·most (fôr′mōst; fôr′-), adj. first in rank, order, place, etc. —adv. first: he stumbled and fell head foremost.

fore·noon (fôr·nūn′; fôr′-), n. time between early morning and noon.

fo·ren·sic (fə·ren′sik), adj. of or suitable for a law court or public debate. —n. a spoken or written exercise in argumentation, as in a college or high-school class in speech or rhetoric. [< L forensis < forum forum]

fore·or·dain (fôr′ôr·dān′; fôr′-), v. ordain beforehand; predestine. —**fore′or·dain′ment, fore·or·di·na·tion** (fôr′ôr·də·nā′shən; fôr′-), n. —Syn. predetermine.

fore·paw (fôr′pô′; fôr′-), n. a front paw.

fore·quar·ter (fôr′kwôr′tər; fôr′-), n. a front leg, shoulder, and nearby ribs of beef, lamb, pork, etc.; front quarter.

fore·run (fôr·run′; fôr′-), v., **-ran, -run, -running. 1.** precede. **2.** be a sign or warning of (something to come). **3.** forestall.

fore·run·ner (fôr′run′ər, fôr′-; fôr·run′ər, fôr′-), n. **1.** person that goes before or is sent before; herald. **2.** sign or warning of something to come. **3.** predecessor; ancestor. —**Syn. 2.** harbinger.

fore·sail (fôr′sāl′; fôr′-; Naut. -səl), n. **1.** the principal sail on the foremast of a schooner. **2.**

the lowest sail on the foremast of a square-rigged ship.

fore·see (fôr·sē′; fôr′-), v., **-saw, -seen, -see·ing.** see or know beforehand. —**fore·see′a·ble,** adj. —**fore·se′er,** n. —Syn. anticipate, divine.

fore·shad·ow (fôr·shad′ō; fôr-), v. indicate beforehand; be a warning of. —**fore·shad′ow·er,** n.

fore·sheet (fôr′shēt′; fôr′-), n. one of the ropes used to hold a foresail in place.

fore·shore (fôr′shôr′; fôr′shôr′), n. part of the shore between the high-water mark and low-water mark.

fore·short·en (fôr·shôr′tən; fôr-), v. represent (lines, etc.) as of less than true length in order to give the proper impression to the eye.

Fore-shortening of lines in a cube

fore·show (fôr·shō′; fôr′-), v., **-showed, -shown, -show·ing.** show beforehand; foreshadow.

fore·sight (fôr′sīt′; fôr′-), n. **1.** power to see or realize beforehand what is likely to happen. **2.** careful thought for the future; prudence. **3.** a looking ahead; view into the future. —**fore′sight′ed,** adj. —**fore′sight′ed·ness,** n.

fore·skin (fôr′skin′; fôr′-), n. Anat. fold of skin that covers the end of the penis; prepuce.

for·est (fôr′ist; fôr′-), n. **1.** a large area of land covered with trees; thick woods; woodland. **2.** the trees themselves. —v. plant with trees; change into a forest. [< OF, ult. < L foris out of doors] —**for′est·ed,** adj. —**for′est·less,** adj. —**for′est-like′,** adj.

fore·stall (fôr·stôl′; fôr′-), v. **1.** prevent by acting first. **2.** deal with (a thing) in advance; anticipate; be ahead of. [ME forstalle(n) < OE foresteall prevention] —**fore·stall′er,** n. —**fore·stall′ment, fore·stal′ment,** n.

for·est·a·tion (fôr′is·tā′shən; fôr′-), n. the planting or taking care of forests.

fore·stay (fôr′stā′; fôr′-), n. Naut. rope or cable reaching from the foremast to the bowsprit.

for·est·er (fôr′is·tər; fôr′-), n. **1.** person in charge of a forest who looks after the trees and guards against fires. **2.** person who lives in a forest.

forest preserve, forest protected by the government from wasteful cutting, fires, etc.

for·est·ry (fôr′is·tri; fôr′-), n. **1.** science of planting and taking care of forests. **2.** art of making and managing forests. **3.** forest land.

fore·taste (n. fôr′tāst′, fôr′-; v. fôr·tāst′, fôr′-), n., v., **-tast·ed, -tast·ing.** —n. a preliminary taste; anticipation. —v. taste beforehand; anticipate.

fore·tell (fôr·tel′; fôr′-), v., **-told, -tell·ing.** tell or show beforehand; predict; prophesy. —**fore·tell′er,** n. —Syn. forecast.

fore·thought (fôr′thôt′; fôr′-), n. **1.** previous thought or consideration; planning. **2.** careful thought for the future; prudence.

fore·to·ken (v. fôr·tō′kən, fôr′-; n. fôr′tō′kən, fôr′-), v. indicate beforehand; be an omen of. —n. indication of something to come; omen.

fore·top (fôr′top′; fôr′-; Naut. -təp), n. Naut. platform at the top of the foremast.

fore·top·gal·lant (fôr′top·gal′ənt; fôr′-; Naut. -tə·gal′ənt), adj. Naut. next above the fore-topmast.

fore·top·mast (fôr′top′mast′; fôr′-; -mäst′; Naut. -məst), n. Naut. mast next above the foremast.

fore·top·sail (fôr′top′sāl′; fôr′-; Naut. -səl), n. Naut. sail set on the fore-topmast and next above the foresail.

for·ev·er (fər·ev′ər), adv. **1.** for always; without ever coming to an end. **2.** all the time; always. —Syn. **1.** ever, evermore, eternally, everlastingly. **2.** continually.

for·ev·er·more (fər·ev′ər·môr′; -mōr′), adv. forever.

fore·warn (fôr·wôrn′; fôr′-), v. warn beforehand.

fore·went (fôr·went′; fôr′-), v. pt. of forego.

fore·word (fôr′werd′; fôr′-), n. introduction; preface.

for·feit (fôr′fĭt), v. lose or have to give up as a penalty for some act, neglect, fault, etc. —n. 1. thing lost or given up because of some act, neglect, or fault; penalty; fine. 2. loss or giving up of something as a penalty. —adj. lost or given up as a penalty. [< OF *forfait* < *forfaire* transgress < *for*- wrongly (< Frankish *for*- and L *foris* outside) + *faire* do < L *facere*] —**for′feit·a·ble,** adj. —**for′feit·er,** n.

for·fei·ture (fôr′fĭ·chər), n. 1. a forfeiting. 2. thing forfeited; penalty; fine.

for·gat (fər·gat′), v. Archaic. pt. of forget.

for·gath·er (fôr·gath′ər), v. 1. gather together; assemble; meet. 2. meet by accident. 3. be friendly; associate. Also, **foregather.**

for·gave (fər·gāv′), v. pt. of forgive.

forge[1] (fôrj; fôrj), n., v., **forged, forg·ing.** —n. 1. place with fire where metal is heated very hot and then hammered into shape. 2. a blacksmith's shop; smithy. 3. place where iron or other metal is melted and refined. —v. 1. heat (metal) very hot and then hammer into shape. 2. make; shape; form. 3. make or write (something false). 4. sign (another's name) falsely to deceive. [< OF, ult. < L *fabrica* workshop. Doublet of FABRIC.] —**forge′a·ble,** adj. —**forg′er,** n. —Syn. v. 3. counterfeit, falsify.

forge[2] (fôrj; fôrj), v., **forged, forg·ing.** move forward slowly but steadily.

for·ger·y (fôr′jər·ĭ; fôr′-), n., pl. -ger·ies. 1. act of forging a signature, etc. 2. something made or written falsely to deceive.

for·get (fər·get′), v., -got or (Archaic) -gat, -got·ten or -got, -get·ting. 1. let go out of the mind; fail to remember; be unable to remember. 2. omit or neglect without meaning to. [OE *forgietan*]

for·get·ful (fər·get′fəl), adj. 1. apt to forget; having a poor memory. 2. heedless. 3. causing to forget. —**for·get′ful·ly,** adv. —**for·get′ful·ness,** n.

for·get-me-not (fər·get′mē-not′), n. any of several small plants with hairy leaves and clusters of small blue or white flowers.

for·give (fər·giv′), v., -gave, -giv·en, -giv·ing. 1. give up the wish to punish or get even with; pardon; excuse. 2. give up all claim to; not demand payment for: *forgive a debt.* [OE *forgiefan*] —**for·giv′a·ble,** adj. —**for·giv′er,** n. —Syn. 1. absolve.

for·give·ness (fər·giv′nĭs), n. 1. act of forgiving; pardon. 2. willingness to forgive.

for·giv·ing (fər·giv′ĭng), adj. that forgives; willing to forgive. —**for·giv′ing·ly,** adv. —**for·giv′ing·ness,** n.

for·go (fôr·gō′), v., -went, -gone, -go·ing. 1. do without; give up. 2. refrain; forbear. Also, **forego.** [OE *forgān*] —**for·go′er,** n. —Syn. surrender, relinquish, yield.

for·got (fər·got′), v. pt. and pp. of forget.

for·got·ten (fər·got′ən), v. pp. of forget.

fork (fôrk), n. 1. instrument with a handle and two or more long, pointed parts at one end. 2. anything shaped like a fork, as the place where a tree, road, or stream divides into branches. 3. one of the branches into which anything is divided. —v. 1. lift, throw, or dig with a fork. 2. make in the shape or form of a fork. 3. have a fork or forks; divide into branches. 4. fork over, Am., Slang. hand over; pay out. [< L *furca*] —**fork′less,** adj. —**fork′like′,** adj.

forked (fôrkt; Archaic and Poetic fôr′kĭd), adj. 1. having a fork or forks. 2. zigzag: *forked lightning.* —**fork·ed·ly** (fôr′kĭd·lĭ), adv. —**fork′ed·ness,** n.

for·lorn (fôr·lôrn′), adj. 1. left alone; neglected; deserted. 2. wretched in feeling or looks; unhappy. 3. hopeless; desperate. 4. bereft (of). [OE *forloren* lost, pp. of *forlēosan*] —**for·lorn′ly,** adv. —**for·lorn′ness,** n. —Syn. 1. abandoned, forsaken. 2. miserable.

form (fôrm), n. 1. appearance apart from color or materials; shape. 2. shape of body; body of a person or animal. 3. thing that gives shape to something. A mold is a form. 4. an orderly arrangement of parts. The effect of a work of literature, art, or music comes from its form as well as its content. 5. way of doing something; manner; method: *he is a fast runner, but his form in running is bad.* 6. a set way of doing something; set way of behaving according to custom or rule; formality; ceremony. 7. a set order of words; formula. 8. document with printing or writing on it and blank spaces to be filled in. 9. way in which a thing exists, takes shape, or shows itself; condition; character. 10. kind; sort; variety: *heat, light, and electricity are forms of energy.* 11. Philos. that which determines the mode in which a thing exists or is perceived. 12. good condition of body or mind: *athletes exercise to keep in form.* 13. Gram. any of the various shapes a word has to express different relationships, etc. *Boys* is the plural form of *boy, saw* is the past form of *see.* 14. Brit. class in school. 15. in printing, type fastened in a frame ready for printing or making plates. —v. 1. give shape to; make. 2. be formed; take shape: *clouds form in the sky.* 3. become: *water forms ice when it freezes.* 4. make up; compose. 5. organize; establish: *we formed a club.* 6. develop: *form good habits while you are young.* 7. arrange in some order: *the soldiers formed themselves into lines.* [< OF < L *forma* form, mold] —Syn. n. 1. contour, outline. 6. conventionality. —v. 1. fashion, shape, mold.

-form, suffix. 1. shaped, as in *cruciform.* 2. (number of) forms, as in *multiform.* [< L *-formis*]

for·mal (fôr′məl), adj. 1. with strict attention to outward forms and ceremonies; not familiar and homelike. 2. according to set customs or rules; conventional. 3. done with the proper forms; clear and definite: *a contract is a formal agreement.* 4. very regular; symmetrical; rigorously methodical; orderly. 5. of language, conforming to established convention in grammar, syntax, and pronunciation. 6. Philos. having to do with the form, not the content. 7. observant of forms; devoted to ceremony. [< L *formalis.* See FORM.] —**for′mal·ly,** adv. —**for′mal·ness,** n. —Syn. 1. stiff, ceremonious. 4. systematic.

form·al·de·hyde (fôr·mal′də·hīd), n. Chem. a colorless gas, CH_2O, with a sharp, irritating odor. It is used in solution as a disinfectant and preservative.

for·mal·ism (fôr′məl·iz·əm), n. strict attention to outward forms and ceremonies. —**for′mal·ist,** n. —**for′mal·is′tic,** adj.

for·mal·i·ty (fôr·mal′ə·tĭ), n., pl. -ties. 1. procedure required by custom or rule; outward form; ceremony. 2. attention to forms and customs. 3. stiffness of manner, behavior, or arrangement. 4. something done merely for form's sake.

for·mal·ize (fôr′məl·īz), v., -ized, -iz·ing. 1. make formal. 2. give a definite form to. —**for′mal·i·za′tion,** n. —**for′mal·iz′er,** n.

for·mat (fôr′mat), n. shape, size, and general arrangement of a book, magazine, etc. [< F < L (liber) *formatus* (book) formed (in a special way)]

for·ma·tion (fôr·mā′shən), n. 1. a forming or being formed. 2. way in which a thing is arranged; arrangement; order: *troops in battle formation.* 3. thing formed. 4. Geol. series of layers or deposits of the same kind of rock or mineral.

form·a·tive (fôr′mə·tĭv), adj. 1. having to do with formation or development; forming; molding. 2. Gram. used to form words. The suffixes *-ly* and *-ness* are formative endings. —n. Gram. a formative element. —**form′a·tive·ly,** adv. —**form′a·tive·ness,** n.

for·mer[1] (fôr′mər), adj. 1. first of two. 2. earlier; past; long past. [ME *formere,* a comparative patterned after *formest* foremost] —Syn. 2. prior, bygone.

form·er[2] (fôr′mər), n. person or thing that forms.

for·mer·ly (fôr′mər·lĭ), adv. in the past; some time ago. —Syn. previously, once.

for·mic acid (fôr′mĭk), Chem. a colorless liquid, CH_2O_2, that is irritating to the skin. It occurs in ants, spiders, nettles, etc. [< L *formica* ant]

for·mi·da·ble (fôr′mə·də·bəl), *adj.* hard to overcome; hard to deal with; to be dreaded. [< L, < *formidare* dread] —**for′mi·da·ble·ness,** **for′mi·da·bil′i·ty,** *n.* —**for′mi·da·bly,** *adv.* —Syn. dread, appalling, fearful.

form·less (fôrm′lis), *adj.* without definite or regular form; shapeless. —**form′less·ly,** *adv.* —**form′less·ness,** *n.*

form letter, *Am.* letter so phrased that it may be sent to many different people.

For·mo·sa (fôr·mō′sə), *n.* Taiwan.

for·mu·la (fôr′myə·lə), *n.*, *pl.* **-las, -lae** (-lē). 1. a set form of words, esp. one which by much use has partly lost its meaning. "How do you do?" is a polite formula. 2. statement of religious belief or doctrine. 3. rule for doing something, esp. as used by those who do not know the reason on which it is based. 4. recipe; prescription: *formula for making soap.* 5. *Chem.* expression showing by chemical symbols the composition of a compound. The formula for water is H_2O. 6. *Math.* expression showing by algebraic symbols a rule, principle, etc. [< L, dim. of *forma* form]

for·mu·lar·y (fôr′myə·ler′i), *n.*, *pl.* **-lar·ies,** *adj.* —*n.* 1. collection of formulas. 2. a set form of words; formula. —*adj.* having to do with formulas.

for·mu·late (fôr′myə·lāt), *v.*, **-lat·ed, -lat·ing.** 1. state definitely; express in systematic form. 2. express in a formula; reduce to a formula. —**for′mu·la′tion,** *n.* —**for′mu·la′tor,** *n.*

for·ni·cate (fôr′nə·kāt), *v.*, **-cat·ed, -cat·ing.** commit fornication. [< Eccl.L, < *fornix* brothel] —**for′ni·ca′tor,** *n.*

for·ni·ca·tion (fôr′nə·kā′shən), *n.* a sexual act between unmarried persons.

for·sake (fôr·sāk′), *v.*, **-sook** (-sůk′), **-sak·en, -sak·ing.** give up; leave alone; leave. [OE, < *for-* + *sacan* dispute, deny] —Syn. abandon, desert.

for·sak·en (fôr·sāk′ən), *v.* pp. of forsake. —*adj.* deserted; abandoned; forlorn. —**for·sak′en·ly,** *adv.*

for·sooth (fôr·sūth′), *adv. Archaic.* in truth; indeed. [OE *forsōth*]

for·spent (fôr·spent′), *adj. Archaic.* worn out or exhausted with effort, work, etc.

for·swear (fôr·swâr′), *v.*, **-swore, -sworn, -swear·ing.** 1. renounce on oath; swear or promise solemnly to give up. 2. deny solemnly or on oath. 3. be untrue to one's sworn word or promise; perjure (oneself). —**for·swear′er,** *n.*

for·syth·i·a (fôr·sith′i·ə; -sī′thi·ə), *n. Am.* shrub having many bell-shaped, yellow flowers in early spring before its leaves come out. [< NL; named for W. *Forsyth,* horticulturist]

fort (fôrt; fôrt), *n.* a strong building or place that can be defended against an enemy. [< F < L *fortis* strong]

forte[1] (fôrt; fôrt), *n.* something a person does very well; strong point. [< F *fort* < L *fortis* strong]

for·te[2] (fôr′tā), *adj.*, *adv. Music.* loud. [< Ital., strong, < L *fortis*]

forth (fôrth; fôrth), *adv.* 1. forward; onward. 2. into view or consideration; out. 3. away. [OE]

Forth (fôrth; fôrth), *n.* river in S Scotland.

forth·com·ing (fôrth′kum′ing; fôrth′-), *adj.* 1. about to appear; approaching. 2. ready when wanted: *she needed help, but none was forthcoming.* —*n.* appearance; approach.

forth·right (fôrth′rīt′, fôrth′-; fôrth′rīt′, fôrth′-), *adj.* frank and outspoken; straightforward; direct: *forthright criticism.* —*adv.* 1. straight ahead; directly forward. 2. at once; immediately. —**forth′right′ness,** *n.*

forth·with (fôrth′with′; fôrth′-; -with′), *adv.* at once; immediately.

for·ti·fi·ca·tion (fôr′tə·fə·kā′shən), *n.* 1. a fortifying. 2. fort, wall, ditch, etc., used in fortifying. 3. a fortified place. 4. the enriching of foods, as with vitamins.

for·ti·fy (fôr′tə·fī), *v.*, **-fied, -fy·ing.** 1. build forts, walls, etc.; strengthen against attack; provide with forts, walls, etc. 2. give support to;

strengthen. 3. strengthen with alcohol. 4. enrich (def. 2). 5. confirm: *a claim fortified by facts.* [< F < LL, ult. < L *fortis* strong + *facere* make] —**for′ti·fi′a·ble,** *adj.* —**for′ti·fi′er,** *n.*

for·tis·si·mo (fôr·tis′ə·mō), *adj.*, *adv. Music.* very loud. [< Ital., superlative of *forte* strong]

for·ti·tude (fôr′tə·tūd; -tůd), *n.* courage in facing pain, danger, or trouble; firmness of spirit. [< L, < *fortis* strong] —Syn. endurance, bravery, resolution.

Fort La·my (lä·mē′), capital of Chad, in the S part.

fort·night (fôrt′nīt; -nit), *n.* two weeks.

fort·night·ly (fôrt′nīt·li), *adv.*, *adj.*, *n.*, *pl.* **-lies.** —*adv.* once in every two weeks. —*adj.* appearing or happening once in every two weeks. —*n.* periodical published every two weeks.

for·tress (fôr′tris), *n.* a fortified place; fort. —Syn. citadel, stronghold.

for·tu·i·tous (fôr·tū′ə·təs; -tū′-), *adj.* happening by chance; accidental: *a fortuitous meeting.* [< L *fortuitus,* ult. < *fors* chance] —**for·tu′i·tous·ly,** *adv.* —**for·tu′i·tous·ness,** *n.*

for·tu·i·ty (fôr·tū′ə·ti; -tū′-), *n.*, *pl.* **-ties.** chance; accident.

for·tu·nate (fôr′chə·nit), *adj.* 1. having good luck; lucky. 2. bringing good luck; having favorable results. [< L, < *fortuna* fortune] —**for′tu·nate·ly,** *adv.* —**for′tu·nate·ness,** *n.*

for·tune (fôr′chən), *n.*, *v.*, **-tuned, -tun·ing.** —*n.* 1. good luck; prosperity. 2. what is going to happen to a person; fate. 3. what happens; luck; chance. 4. a great deal of money or property; riches; wealth. 5. amount of wealth. 6. position in life. —*v.* happen; chance. [< OF < L *fortuna*] —**for′tune·less,** *adj.* —Syn. *n.* 1. success. 2. destiny, lot.

for·tune-tell·er (fôr′chən·tel′ər), *n.* person who claims to be able to tell what will happen to people. —**for′tune-tell′ing,** *adj.*, *n.*

Fort Wayne (wān), city in NE Indiana.

Fort Worth (wėrth), city in N Texas.

for·ty (fôr′ti), *n.*, *pl.* **-ties,** *adj.* —*n.* 1. a cardinal number, four times ten. 2. symbol of this number; 40. —*adj.* four times ten; 40. [OE *fēowertig*] —**for′ti·eth,** *adj.*, *n.*

for·ty-nin·er (fôr′ti·nīn′ər), *n. Am.* person who went to California to seek gold in 1849, soon after its discovery there in 1848.

fo·rum (fô′rəm; fō′-), *n.*, *pl.* **fo·rums, fo·ra** (fô′rə; fō′-). 1. the public square or market place of an ancient Roman town. 2. assembly for discussing questions of public interest. 3. a law court; tribunal. [< L]

for·ward (fôr′wərd), *adv.* Also, **for′wards.** 1. ahead; onward: *run forward.* 2. toward the front. —*adj.* 1. toward the front: *the forward part of a ship.* 2. of or pertaining to the future: *forward buying.* 3. far ahead; advanced: *a child of four years that can read is forward for his age.* 4. radical; extreme. 5. ready; eager: *he knew his lesson and was forward with his answers.* 6. pert; bold. —*v.* 1. send on further: *please forward my mail to my new address.* 2. help along. —*n. Sports.* a player whose position is in the front line in certain games. b. a forward pass. [OE *foreweard*] —**for′ward·er,** *n.* —**for′ward·ly,** *adv.* —**for′ward·ness,** *n.* —Syn. *adj.* 3. precocious. 6. impertinent, presumptuous.

forward pass, *Am.* in football, a pass in the direction of the opponents' goal.

for·went (fôr·went′), *v.* pt. of forgo.

fos·sa (fos′ə), *n.*, *pl.* **fos·sae** (fos′ē). *Anat.* a shallow depression or pit in a bone, etc. [< L, ditch]

fosse, foss (fôs; fos), *n.* ditch; trench; canal; moat. [< F < L *fossa* ditch]

fos·sil (fos′əl), *n.* 1. the hardened remains or traces of animals or plants. 2. a very old-fashioned person, set in his ways. —*adj.* 1. forming a fossil; of the nature of a fossil. 2. belonging to the outworn past: *fossil ideas.* [< F < L *fossilis* dug up < *fodere* dig] —**fos′sil·like,** *adj.*

Fossil arthropod

fos·sil·if·er·ous (fos′ə·lif′ər·əs), *adj.* containing fossils.

fos·sil·ize (fos′ə·līz), v., –ized, –iz·ing. 1. change into a fossil; turn into stone. 2. make or become antiquated, set, stiff, or rigid. 3. search for fossils. —fos′sil·i·za′tion, n.

fos·ter (fôs′tər; fos′–), v. 1. help the growth or development of. 2. care for fondly; cherish. 3. bring up; rear. —adj. in the same family, but not related by birth: a foster brother. [OE fōstrian nourish, fōster nourishment; akin to FOOD] —fos′ter·er, n. —Syn. v. 1. promote, further. 3. nourish, support.

Fos·ter (fôs′tər; fos′–), n. Stephen Collins, 1826–1864, American composer.

fought (fôt), v. pt. and pp. of **fight**.

foul (foul), adj. 1. containing filth; covered with filth; very dirty; nasty; smelly. 2. very wicked; vile. 3. against the rules; unfair. 4. hitting against: one boat was foul of the other. 5. tangled up; caught: the sailor cut the foul rope. 6. clogged up: the fire will not burn because the chimney is foul. 7. unfavorable; stormy: foul weather delayed the ship. 8. contrary: a foul wind. 9. very unpleasant or objectionable. 10. Am., Baseball. pertaining to a ball not hit within the legal playing area: a foul ball. —v. 1. make or become dirty; soil; defile; disgrace. 2. make a foul; make a foul against. 3. Am., Baseball. hit a ball so that it falls outside the base lines. 4. Naut. hit against: one boat fouled the other. 5. get tangled up with; catch: the rope fouled the anchor chain. 6. clog up. 7. Naut. cover (a ship's bottom) with seaweed, barnacles, etc. —n. 1. thing done contrary to the rules; unfair play. 2. Am., Baseball. ball hit so that it falls outside the base lines. —adv. go, fall, or run foul of, a. hit against and get tangled up with. b. get into trouble or difficulties with. [OE fūl] —foul′ly, adv. —foul′ness, n. —Syn. adj. 1. soiled, polluted, unclean.

fou·lard (fū·lärd′; fə–), n. a soft, thin fabric made of silk, rayon, or cotton, used for neckties, dresses, etc. [< F < Swiss F foulat cloth that has been cleansed and thickened]

foul line, Am., Baseball. either the line from home to first base, or from home to third base, with their unmarked continuations.

found¹ (found), v. pt. and pp. of **find**.

found² (found), v. 1. establish; set up: the Pilgrims founded a colony at Plymouth. 2. rest or support; base: he founded his claim on facts. 3. be founded or based. [< OF < L, < fundus bottom] —Syn. 1. settle, plant.

found³ (found), v. melt and mold (metal); make of molten metal; cast. [< F < L fundere pour]

foun·da·tion (foun·dā′shən), n. 1. part on which the other parts rest for support; base. 2. basis; ground. 3. a founding or establishing. 4. a being founded or established. 5. institution founded and endowed. 6. fund given to support an institution. —foun·da′tion·al, adj.

foun·der¹ (foun′dər), v. 1. fill with water and sink. 2. break down; go lame; stumble. 3. become worn out; fail. 4. cause (a horse) to break down, fall lame, etc. [< OF foundrer, ult. < L fundus bottom]

found·er² (foun′dər), n. person who founds or establishes something.

found·er³ (foun′dər), n. person who casts metals.

found·ling (found′ling), n. baby or child found deserted. [ME fundeling; akin to FIND]

found·ry (foun′dri), n., pl. –ries. 1. place where metal is melted and molded; place where things are made of molten metal. 2. the melting and molding of metal; making things of molten metal.

fount¹ (fount), n. 1. fountain. 2. source. [< L fons spring]

fount² (fount; font), n. Esp. Brit. font².

foun·tain (foun′tən), n. 1. stream of water rising into the air. 2. pipes through which the water is forced and the basin that receives it. 3. spring of water. 4. place to get a drink. 5. source; origin. 6. container to hold a steady supply of ink, oil, etc. [< OF < LL fontana of a

spring < L fons spring] —foun′tain·less, adj. —foun′tain·like′, adj.

foun·tain·head (foun′tən·hed′), n. 1. source of a stream. 2. original source.

fountain pen, pen for writing that has a reservoir to give a steady supply of ink.

four (fôr; fōr), n. 1. a cardinal number, one more than three. 2. symbol for this number; 4. —adj. one more than three; 4. [OE fēower]

four-flush·er (fôr′flush′ər; fōr′–), n. Am., Slang. person who pretends to be more or other than he really is; bluffer.

four·fold (fôr′fōld′; fōr′–), adj. 1. four times as much or as many. 2. having four parts. —adv. four times as much or as many.

four-foot·ed (fôr′fut′id; fōr′–), adj. having four feet.

four freedoms, freedom of speech, freedom of worship, freedom from want, and freedom from fear; set forth by Franklin D. Roosevelt in 1941.

four hundred, the most fashionable or exclusive social set.

four-in-hand (fôr′in·hand′; fōr′–), n. 1. necktie tied in a slip knot with the ends left hanging. 2. Am. carriage pulled by four horses driven by one person. 3. team of four horses. —adj. 1. tied in a slip knot. 2. pulled by four horses.

four·pence (fôr′pəns; fōr′–), n. 1. four British pennies. 2. a former British silver coin worth four British pennies.

four·pen·ny (fôr′pen′i; fōr′–; –pən·i), n., pl. –nies, adj. 1. fourpence. —adj. worth fourpence; costing fourpence.

four-post·er (fôr′pōs′tər; fōr′–), n. bed with four tall corner posts for supporting curtains.

four·score (fôr′skôr′; fōr′skōr′), adj., n. four times twenty; 80.

four·some (fôr′səm; fōr′–), n. 1. in golf, a game played by four people, two on each side. 2. the players. 3. group of four people.

four·square (adj. fôr′skwâr′, fōr′–; n. fôr′-skwâr′, fōr′–), adj. 1. square. 2. frank; outspoken. 3. not yielding; firm. —n. a square. —four′square′ly, adv. —four′square′ness, n.

four·teen (fôr′tēn′; fōr′–), n. 1. a cardinal number, four more than ten. 2. symbol of this number; 14. —adj. four more than ten; 14. —four′teenth′, adj., n.

fourth (fôrth; fōrth), adj. 1. next after the third; last in a series of 4. 2. being one of 4 equal parts. —n. 1. next after the third; last in a series of 4. 2. one of 4 equal parts. 3. Music. a. tone on the 4th degree from a given tone that is counted as the 1st. b. interval between such tones. c. combination of such tones. —fourth′ly, adv.

fourth dimension, dimension in addition to length, width, and thickness. Time can be thought of as a fourth dimension. —fourth′-di·men′sion·al, adj.

fourth estate, newspapers or newspaper workers; journalism or journalists.

Fourth of July, Am. holiday in honor of the adoption of the Declaration of Independence on July 4, 1776; Independence Day.

fowl (foul), n., pl. **fowls** or (esp. collectively) **fowl**, v. —n. 1. any bird. 2. any of several kinds of large birds used for food, such as the hen, rooster, and turkey. 3. flesh of a fowl used for food. —v. hunt wild fowl. [OE fugol] —fowl′er, n.

fowling piece, a light gun for shooting wild birds.

fox (foks), n. 1. a wild animal somewhat like a dog. 2. its fur. 3. a sly, crafty person. —v. 1. Colloq. trick by being sly and crafty. 2. become discolored; cause to become discolored. [OE] —fox′like′, adj.

Red fox
(total length ab. 3½ ft.)

fox·glove (foks′gluv′), n. plant with tall stalks having many bell-shaped flowers.

fox·hole (foks′hōl′), *n. Mil.* hole in the ground for protection against enemy fire.

fox·hound (foks′hound′), *n.* hound with a keen sense of smell, bred and trained to hunt foxes.

fox·tail (foks′tāl′), *n.* 1. tail of a fox. 2. grass with brushlike spikes of flowers.

fox terrier, a small, active dog of a breed once trained to drive foxes from their holes.

fox trot, *Am.* 1. dance with short, quick steps. 2. music for it. 3. pace of a horse between a walk and a trot.

fox-trot (foks′trot′), *v.,* **-trot·ted, -trot·ting.** 1. *Am.* dance the fox trot. 2. (of a horse) go at a pace between a walk and a trot.

fox·y (fok′si), *adj.,* **fox·i·er, fox·i·est.** 1. like a fox; sly; crafty. 2. discolored; stained. **—fox′i·ly,** *adv.* **—fox′i·ness,** *n.*

foy·er (foi′ər; foi′ā), *n.* 1. an entrance hall used as a lounging room in a theater or hotel; lobby. 2. an entrance hall. [< F, ult. < L *focus* hearth]

Fr, *Chem.* francium.

Fr., 1. Father. 2. French. 3. Friday.

fr., 1. fragment. 2. *pl.* **fr., frs.** franc. 3. from.

Fra (frä), *n.* Brother. It is used as the title of a monk or friar.

fra·cas (frā′kəs), *n.* a noisy quarrel or fight; disturbance; brawl. [< F < Ital. *fracasso* < *fracassare* smash]

frac·tion (frak′shən), *n.* 1. *Math.* one or more of the equal parts of a whole. 2. a part: *he got only a fraction of what he wanted.* 3. a very small part, amount, etc.; fragment. [< LL *fractio* < L *frangere* break] **—frac′tion·al,** *adj.* **—frac′tion·al·ly,** *adv.*

frac·tious (frak′shəs), *adj.* 1. cross; fretful; peevish. 2. hard to manage; unruly. **—frac′tious·ly,** *adv.* **—frac′tious·ness,** *n.* **—Syn.** 1. irritable, snappish. 2. refractory, intractable.

frac·ture (frak′chər), *v.,* **-tured, -tur·ing,** *n.* **—v.** break; crack. **—n.** 1. break; crack. 2. a breaking or being broken. 3. a breaking of a bone or cartilage. 4. *Geol.* surface of a freshly broken mineral. [< F < L *fractura* < *frangere* break] **—frac′tur·al,** *adj.*

frae (frā), *Scot.* **—prep.** from. **—adv.** fro.

frag·ile (fraj′əl), *adj.* easily broken, damaged, or destroyed; delicate; frail. [< L *fragilis;* akin to *frangere* break. Doublet of FRAIL.] **—frag′ile·ly,** *adv.* **—fra·gil·i·ty** (frə·jil′ə·ti), **frag′ile·ness,** *n.* **—Syn.** breakable, weak. **—Ant.** tough, strong, elastic.

frag·ment (frag′mənt), *n.* 1. a broken piece; part broken off. 2. an incomplete or disconnected part. 3. part of an incomplete or unfinished work. [< L *fragmentum* < *frangere* break] **—frag·men′tal,** *adj.* **—Syn.** chip, scrap, bit.

frag·men·tar·y (frag′mən·ter′i), *adj.* made up of fragments; incomplete; disconnected. **—frag′men·tar′i·ly,** *adv.* **—frag′men·tar′i·ness,** *n.*

frag·men·ta·tion (frag′mən·tā′shən), *adj.* denoting a bomb, grenade, etc., that scatters pieces of its casing or contents widely upon explosion.

fra·grance (frā′grəns), **fra·gran·cy** (-grən·si), *n., pl.* **-granc·es; -cies.** a sweet smell; pleasing odor.

fra·grant (frā′grənt), *adj.* having a pleasing odor; sweet-smelling. [< L *fragrans* smelling, emitting odor] **—fra′grant·ly,** *adv.*

frail (frāl), *adj.* 1. slender and not very strong; weak. 2. easily broken, damaged, or destroyed. 3. morally weak; liable to yield to temptation. [< OF < L *fragilis.* Doublet of FRAGILE.] **—frail′ly,** *adv.* **—frail′ness,** *n.* **—Syn.** 1. delicate. 2. brittle, fragile.

frail·ty (frāl′ti), *n., pl.* **-ties.** 1. a being frail. 2. moral weakness; liability to yield to temptation. 3. fault or sin caused by moral weakness.

frame (frām), *n., v.,* **framed, fram·ing.** **—n.** 1. support over which something is stretched or built: *frame of a house.* 2. framework. 3. body. 4. skeleton. 5. way in which a thing is put together. 6. an established order; plan; system. 7. shape; form. 8. border in which a thing is set:

a picture frame. 9. one of the individual pictures on a strip of motion-picture film. 10. a triangular form used to set up the balls in the game of pool. 11. one turn at bowling. [< v.] **—v.** 1. shape; form. 2. take shape. 3. put together; plan; make. 4. put a border around. 5. be a border for. 6. *Am., Slang.* prearrange falsely; make seem guilty. [OE *framian* to profit < *fram* forth] **—frame′less —fram′er,** *n.* **—Syn. v.** 1. fashion. 3. devise, fabricate, concoct.

frame of mind, way of thinking or feeling; disposition; mood.

frame-up (frām′up′), *n. Am., Slang.* 1. a secret and dishonest arrangement made beforehand. 2. arrangement made to have a person falsely accused.

Part of the frame of a house

frame·work (frām′wérk′), *n.* 1. support over which a thing is stretched or built; stiff part that gives shape to a thing. 2. way in which a thing is put together; structure.

franc (frangk), *n.* 1. unit of money in France, Belgium, and Switzerland. 2. coin worth one franc. [< OF < *Francorum Rex* king of the Franks, on early coins]

France (frans; fräns), *n.* country in W Europe.

fran·chise (fran′chiz), *n.* 1. privilege or right granted by a government: *a franchise to operate buses on the city streets.* 2. right to vote. [< OF, < *franc* free; akin to FRANK] **—fran′chised,** *adj.* **—fran·chise·ment** (fran′chiz·mənt), *n.*

Fran·cis (fran′sis; frän′-), *n.* **Saint,** 1181?-1226, the Italian founder of the Franciscan order.

Fran·cis·can (fran·sis′kən), *n.* member of a religious order founded by Saint Francis in 1209. **—adj.** of this religious order.

fran·ci·um (fran′si·əm), *n. Chem.* a rare radioactive element, Fr.

Franck (frängk), *n.* **César,** 1822-1890, French composer, born in Belgium.

Fran·co (frang′kō), *n.* **Francisco,** born 1892, Spanish military leader and politician.

fran·gi·ble (fran′jə·bəl), *adj.* breakable. [< OF < L *frangere* break] **—fran′gi·bil′i·ty, fran′gi·ble·ness,** *n.*

frank (frangk), *adj.* 1. free in expressing one's real thoughts, opinions, and feelings; not afraid to say what one thinks. 2. clearly manifest; undisguised; plain: *frank mutiny.* **—v.** send (a letter, package, etc.) without charge. **—n.** 1. mark to show that a letter, package, etc., is to be sent without charge. 2. right to send letters, packages, etc., without charge. 3. letter, package, etc., sent without charge. [< OF, free, sincere (orig., a Frank) < Gmc.] **—frank′a·ble,** *adj.* **—frank′er,** *n.* **—frank′ly,** *adv.* **—frank′ness,** *n.* **—Syn. adj.** 1. open, sincere, straightforward, outspoken. **—Ant. adj.** 1. insincere, hypocritical, deceitful.

Frank (frangk), *n.* 1. member of a group of German tribes that conquered northern Gaul in the sixth century A.D. 2. a Greek or Mohammedan name for any European.

Frank·en·stein (frangk′ən·stīn), *n.* 1. man in a story, who creates a monster that he cannot control. 2. thing that causes the ruin of its creator. [from novel by Mary Shelley]

Frank·fort (frangk′fərt), *n.* capital of Kentucky, in the N part.

Frankfort on the Main (mān), city in W Germany, on the Main River, headquarters of the American occupation forces after World War II.

Frankfort on the O·der (ō′dər), city in E Germany, on the Oder River.

frank·furt·er (frangk′fər·tər), **frank·furt** (-fərt), *n. Am.* a reddish sausage made of beef and pork. [< G, of Frankfort]

frank·in·cense (frangk′in·sens), *n.* a fragrant resin from certain Asiatic or African trees. [< OF *franc encens* pure incense]

Frank·ish (frangk′ish), *adj.* of or having to do with the Franks. **—n.** the language of the Franks (def. 1).

Frank·lin (frangk′lən), *n.* Benjamin, 1706–1790, American statesman, author, and scientist.

frank·lin (frangk′lən), *n.* in the 14th and 15th centuries, an English landowner of free birth who ranked next below the gentry. [ME *francoleyn*, ult. < Med.L *francus* free. See FRANK.]

fran·tic (fran′tik), *adj.* **1.** very much excited. **2.** *Archaic.* insane. [< OF < L < Gk. *phrenitikos* < *phrenitis* FRENZY. Doublet of PHRENETIC.] —**fran′ti·cal·ly, fran′tic·ly,** *adv.* —**fran′tic·ness,** *n.* —**Syn. 1.** mad, distracted, raving, raging.

frap·pé (fra-pā′), *Am.* —*adj.* iced; cooled. —*n.* **1.** fruit juice sweetened and frozen. **2.** any frozen or iced food or drink. [< F, chilled, beaten]

fra·ter·nal (frə-tér′nəl), *adj.* **1.** brotherly. **2.** having to do with a fraternal order. [< L *fraternus* brotherly < *frater* brother] —**fra·ter′nal·ism,** *n.* —**fra·ter′nal·ly,** *adv.*

fraternal order, group organized for mutual aid and fellowship; secret society.

fra·ter·ni·ty (frə-tér′nə-ti), *n., pl.* **-ties. 1.** *Am.* group of men or boys joined together for fellowship or for some other purpose. **2.** group having the same interests, kind of work, etc. **3.** a fraternal feeling; brotherhood.

frat·er·nize (frat′ər-nīz), *v.,* **-nized, -niz·ing. 1.** associate in a brotherly way; be friendly. **2.** associate intimately with the citizens of a hostile nation during occupation of their territory. —**frat′er·ni·za′tion,** *n.* —**frat′er·niz′er,** *n.*

frat·ri·cide[1] (frat′rə-sīd; frā′trə-), *n.* act of killing one's brother or sister. [< L, < *frater* brother + *cidium* a killing] —**frat′ri·cid′al,** *adj.*

frat·ri·cide[2] (frat′rə-sīd; frā′trə-), *n.* person who kills his own brother or sister. [< L, < *frater* brother + *-cida* killer]

Frau (frou), *n., pl.* **Fraus** (frouz), *Ger.* **Frau-en** (frou′ən). *German.* **1.** Mrs. **2.** wife.

fraud (frôd), *n.* **1.** deceit; cheating; dishonesty. **2.** a dishonest act, statement, etc.; something done to deceive or cheat; trick. **3.** *Esp. U.S. Colloq.* person who is not what he pretends to be. [< OF < L *fraus* cheating] —**Syn. 2.** dodge, sham, fake. **3.** cheat, impostor, humbug.

fraud·u·lent (frôj′ə-lənt; frôd′yù–), *adj.* **1.** deceitful; cheating; dishonest. **2.** intended to deceive. **3.** done by fraud. —**fraud′u·lence, fraud′u·len·cy,** *n.* —**fraud′u·lent·ly,** *adv.*

fraught (frôt), *adj.* loaded; filled. [< MDu. or MLG *vracht* freight]

Fräu·lein (froi′līn), *n., pl.* **Fräu·leins,** *Ger.* **Fräu·lein.** *German.* **1.** Miss. **2.** an unmarried woman; young lady.

fray[1] (frā), *n.* a noisy quarrel; fight. [var. of *affray*]

fray[2] (frā), *v.* **1.** separate into threads; make or become ragged or worn along the edge. **2.** wear away; rub. [< F *frayer* < L *fricare* rub]

fraz·zle (fraz′əl), *v.,* **-zled, -zling,** *n. Esp. U.S.* —*v.* **1.** tear to shreds; fray; wear out. **2.** tire out; weary. —*n. Colloq.* frazzled condition.

F.R.B., FRB, Federal Reserve Board.

freak (frēk), *n.* **1.** something very queer or unusual. **2.** a sudden change of mind without reason; odd notion or fancy. —*adj.* very queer or unusual. [cf. OE *frician* dance] —**freak′ish,** *adj.* —**freak′ish·ly,** *adv.* —**freak′ish·ness,** *n.* —**Syn.** *n.* **2.** whim, vagary, caprice.

freck·le (frek′əl), *n., v.,* **-led, -ling.** —*n.* a small, light-brown spot on the skin. —*v.* **1.** cover with freckles. **2.** become marked or spotted with freckles. [prob. alter. of *frecken* < Scand. *freknur, pl.*] —**freck′led, freck′ly,** *adj.*

Fred·er·ick the Great (fred′rik; fred′ər-ik), (*Frederick II*), 1712–1786, second king of Prussia, from 1740 to 1786.

Fred·er·ic·ton (fred′rik-tən; fred′ər-ik–), *n.* capital of New Brunswick, Canada.

free (frē), *adj., adv., fre-est, adv., v., freed, free-ing.* —*adj.* **1.** not under another's control; having liberty; able to do, act, or think as one pleases. **2.** showing liberty; caused by liberty. **3.** not held back, fastened, or shut up; released; loose. **4.** not hindered. **5.** clear; open. **6.** open to all: *a free port.* **7.** without cost, payment, or return. **8.** without paying a tax or duty. **9.** giving

or using much. **10.** abundant. **11.** not following rules, forms, or words exactly; not strict. **12.** saying what one thinks; frank. **13.** not restrained enough by manners or morals. **14.** not combined with something else: *oxygen exists free in air.* —*adv.* **1.** without cost, payment, or return. **2.** freely. —*v.* **1.** relieve from any kind of burden, bondage, or slavery; make free. **2.** let loose; release. **3.** clear [OE *frēo, frīo*] —**free′ly,** *adv.* —**free′ness,** *n.* —**Syn.** *adj.* **1.** independent. **3.** movable, unfastened. **9.** generous, liberal, lavish. —*v.* **1.** liberate, emancipate. —**Ant.** *adj.* **1.** subject, bound, restrained. **3.** firm, fastened, tied.

free·board (frē′bôrd′; –bōrd′), *n. Naut.* part of a ship's side between the water line and the deck or gunwale.

free·boot·er (frē′büt′ər), *n.* pirate; buccaneer. [< Du. *vrijbuiter* < *vrij* free + *buit* booty]

free·born (frē′bôrn′), *adj.* **1.** born free, not in slavery. **2.** of or suitable for people born free.

free city, city forming an independent state.

freed·man (frēd′mən), *n., pl.* **-men.** man freed from slavery.

free·dom (frē′dəm), *n.* **1.** state or condition of being free. **2.** not being under another's control; power to do, say, or think as one pleases; liberty. **3.** right of enjoying all privileges accompanying citizenship, membership, etc. **4.** release from ties, obligations, control, etc. **5.** exemption; immunity. **6.** free use: *we give a guest the freedom of our home.* **7.** frankness. **8.** undue familiarity. **9.** ease of movement or action.

freed·wom·an (frēd′wùm′ən), *n., pl.* **-wom·en.** woman freed from slavery.

free enterprise, right of private business to organize and operate under open competition with a minimum of government regulation.

free·hand (frē′hand′), *adj.* done by hand without using instruments, measurements, etc.

free·hand·ed (frē′han′did), *adj.* **1.** generous; liberal. **2.** having the hands free.

free·hold (frē′hōld′), *n. Law.* **1.** piece of land held for life or with the right to transfer it to one's heirs. **2.** the holding of land in this way. —**free′hold′er,** *n.*

free lance, 1. writer, artist, etc., who sells his work to anyone who will buy it. **2.** soldier in the Middle Ages who fought for any person, group, or state that would pay him. **3.** person who fights or works for any cause that he chooses.

free-lance (frē′lans′; –läns′), *v.,* **-lanced, -lanc·ing.** work as a free lance.

free·man (frē′mən), *n., pl.* **-men. 1.** person who is not a slave or a serf. **2.** person who has civil or political freedom; citizen.

Free·ma·son (frē′mā′sən), *n.* member of a world-wide secret society; Mason. The purpose of the society of Freemasons is mutual aid and fellowship. —**free·ma·son·ic** (frē′mə-son′ik), *adj.*

Free·ma·son·ry (frē′mā′sən-ri), *n.* **1.** principles or doctrines of the society of Freemasons. **2.** freemasonry, natural fellowship.

free on board, *Com.* delivered free of charge on a train, ship, etc.

free-piston engine, an internal-combustion engine in which each cylinder contains two opposed pistons which are driven apart by the explosion of the fuel so as to force air out of the cylinder and against the blades of a turbine.

free press, *Am.* a press not censored or controlled by the government.

free silver, *Am.* the free coinage of silver; making silver into coins for anybody who brings it to the mint.

free-soil (frē′soil′), *adj. Am., Hist.* pertaining to or in favor of the nonextension of slavery into those parts of the country not yet erected into States. —**free′-soil′er,** *n. Am.*

free-spo·ken (frē′spō′kən), *adj.* speaking freely; saying what one thinks; frank. —**free′-spo′ken·ly,** *adv.* —**free′-spo′ken·ness,** *n.*

free·stone (frē′stōn′), *n.* **1.** stone, such as limestone or sandstone, that can easily be cut without splitting. **2.** fruit having a stone that is easily separated from the pulp. —*adj.* having a fruit stone that is easily separated from the pulp.

free·think·er (frē'thingk'ər), *n.* person who forms his religious opinions independently of authority or tradition. —**free'think'ing,** *n., adj.* —free thought.

free trade, trade unrestricted by taxes, imposts, or differences of treatment; esp. international trade free from protective duties, subject only to tariff for revenue. —**free' trad'er,** *n.*

free verse, poetry not restricted by the usual rules about meter, rhyme, etc.

free·way (frē'wā'), *n.* a high-speed highway for which no tolls are charged.

free·will (frē'wil'), *adj.* of one's own accord; voluntary: *a freewill offering.*

free will, will free from outside restraints; voluntary choice; freedom of decision.

free world, Free World, the non-Communist nations. —**free' world',** *adj.*

freeze (frēz), *v.,* froze, fro·zen, freez·ing, *n.* —*v.* **1.** turn into ice; harden by cold. **2.** make very cold. **3.** become very cold. **4.** kill or injure by frost. **5.** be killed or injured by frost. **6.** cover or become covered with ice; clog with ice. **7.** fix or become fixed to something by freezing. **8.** make or become stiff and unfriendly. **9.** chill or be chilled with fear, etc. **10.** become motionless. **11.** *Am.* fix a price at a definite amount, usually by governmental decree. **12.** *Finance.* make (funds, bank balances, etc.) unusable and inaccessible by governmental decree. **13.** freeze out, *Am., Colloq.* force out; get rid of. —*n.* **1.** a freezing or being frozen. **2.** period during which there is freezing weather. [OE *frēosan*]

freez·er (frēz'ər), *n.* **1.** machine to freeze ice cream. **2.** a refrigerator cabinet (for frozen foods, ice cream, etc.) within which a temperature below the freezing point is maintained.

freezing point, temperature at which a liquid freezes. The freezing point of water is 32 degrees F. or 0 degrees C.

freight (frāt), *n.* **1.** load of goods carried on a train, ship, etc. **2.** the carrying of goods on a train, ship, etc. **3.** charge for this. **4.** train for carrying goods. **5.** load; burden. —*v.* **1.** load with freight. **2.** carry as freight. **3.** send as freight. **4.** load; burden. [< MDu. or MLG *vrecht*] —**freight'less,** *adj.*

freight·age (frāt'ij), *n.* **1.** the carrying of goods on a train, ship, etc. **2.** charge for this. **3.** freight; cargo.

freight·er (frāt'ər), *n. Am.* ship for carrying freight.

French (french), *adj.* of or having to do with France, its people, or their language. —*n.* **1.** people of France. **2.** their language. —**French'-man,** *n.*

French chalk, talc used for marking lines on cloth or removing grease.

French Community, France, its overseas departments and territories, and six of its former African colonies.

French Guiana, a French colony in N South America.

French Guinea, a former French colony in W Africa.

French horn, a brass wind instrument that has a mellow tone.

Man playing a French horn

French·i·fy (fren'chə·fī), *v.,* -fied, -fy·ing. make French or like the French.

French Indo-China, territory in SE Asia, S of China, formerly a French colonial possession but since 1949 divided into separate states.

French leave, act of leaving without ceremony, permission, or notice.

French Revolution, revolution in France from 1789 to 1799, which changed France from a monarchy to a republic.

French toast, slices of bread dipped in a mixture of egg and milk and then fried.

French West Africa, former group of French colonies in W Africa, including Guinea and seven members of the French Community.

fre·net·ic (frə·net'ik), *adj.* frantic; frenzied. Also, **phrenetic.** [var. of *phrenetic*] —**fre·net'i·cal·ly,** *adv.*

fren·zy (fren'zi), *n., pl.* -zies, *v.,* -zied, -zy·ing. —*n.* brief fury; near madness; very great excitement. —*v.* make frantic. [< OF < L *phrenesis,* ult. < Gk. *phren* mind] —**fren'zied,** *adj.* —*Syn. n.* rage, raving.

fre·quen·cy (frē'kwən·si), *n., pl.* -cies. **1.** Also, **frequence.** a frequent occurrence. **2.** rate of occurrence. **3.** *Physics.* number of complete cycles per second of an alternating current.

frequency modulation, *Electronics.* **1.** a deliberate modulation of the frequency of the transmitting wave in broadcasting. **2.** a broadcasting system, relatively free of static, using this method of modulation. Cf. **amplitude modulation.**

fre·quent (*adj.* frē'kwənt; *v.* fri·kwent'), *adj.* **1.** occurring often, near together, or every little while. **2.** doing (the act specified) often; regular; habitual. —*v.* go often to; be often in. [< L *frequens* crowded] —**fre·quent'er,** *n.* —**fre'quent·ly,** *adv.* —*Syn. v.* haunt, infest.

fre·quen·ta·tive (fri·kwen'tə·tiv), *Gram.* —*adj.* expressing frequent repetition of an action. —*n.* a frequentative verb.

fres·co (fres'kō), *n., pl.* -coes, -cos, *v.,* -coed, -co·ing. —*n.* **1.** act or art of painting with water colors on damp, fresh plaster. **2.** picture or design so painted. **3.** in fresco, with water colors on damp, fresh plaster. —*v.* paint in fresco. [< Ital., cool, fresh] —**fres'co·er,** *n.*

fresh (fresh), *adj.* **1.** newly made, arrived, or obtained: *fresh footprints.* **2.** not known, seen, or used before; new; recent. **3.** additional; further; another: *a fresh start.* **4.** not salty. **5.** not spoiled; not stale. **6.** not artificially preserved. **7.** not wearied; vigorous; lively. **8.** not faded or worn; bright. **9.** looking healthy or young. **10.** pure; cool; refreshing: *a fresh breeze.* **11.** *Meteorol.* fairly strong; brisk: *a fresh wind.* **12.** not experienced. **13.** *Am., Slang.* too bold; impudent. —*n.* **1.** the early part. **2.** spring, pool, or stream of fresh water. **3.** flood. —*adv.* freshly. [OE *fersc;* but infl. in form by OF *freis,* fem. *fresche* < Gmc.] —**fresh'ness,** *n.* —*Syn. adj.* **2.** novel. **12.** untrained.

fresh·en (fresh'ən), *v.* make fresh; become fresh. —**fresh'en·er,** *n.*

fresh·et (fresh'it), *n.* **1.** flood caused by heavy rains or melted snow. **2.** rush of fresh water flowing into the sea.

fresh·ly (fresh'li), *adv.* in a fresh manner.

fresh·man (fresh'mən), *n., pl.* -men, *adj.* —*n.* **1.** *Am.* student in the first year of high school or college. **2.** beginner. —*adj.* of these students.

fresh·wa·ter (fresh'wô'tər; -wot'ər), *adj.* of or living in water that is not salty.

fret¹ (fret), *v.,* fret·ted, fret·ting, *n.* —*v.* **1.** be peevish, unhappy, discontented, or worried. **2.** make peevish, unhappy, discontented, or worried. **3.** eat away; wear; rub. **4.** roughen; disturb. —*n.* peevish complaining; worry; discontented condition. [OE *fretan* eat] —**fret'ter,** *n.* —*Syn. v.* **2.** harass, vex, provoke, irritate.

fret² (fret), *n., v.,* fret·ted, fret·ting. —*n.* an ornamental pattern made of straight lines bent or combined at angles. —*v.* decorate with fretwork. [? < OF *frete*]

fret³ (fret), *n., v.,* fret·ted, fret·ting. —*n.* any of a series of ridges of wood, ivory, or metal on a guitar, banjo, etc., to show where to put the fingers in order to produce certain tones. —*v.* provide with frets. —**fret'ted,** *adj.*

fret·ful (fret'fəl), *adj.* apt to fret; peevish. —**fret'ful·ly,** *adv.* —**fret'ful·ness,** *n.*

fret·work (fret'wėrk'), *n.* **1.** ornamental openwork or carving. **2.** anything patterned like fretwork.

Fretwork

Freud (froid), *n.* Sigmund, 1856–1939, Austrian physician who developed a theory and technique of psychoanalysis. —**Freud·i·an** (froid'i·ən), *adj., n.* —**Freud'i·an·ism,** *n.*

Fri., Friday.

fri·a·ble (frī'ə·bəl), *adj.* easily crumbled. [< L

< *friare* crumble] —fri′a·bil′i·ty, fri′a·ble·ness, *n.*

fri·ar (frī′ər), *n.* member of certain religious orders of the Roman Catholic Church. [< OF < L *frater* brother]

fri·ar·y (frī′ər·i), *n., pl.* -ar·ies. 1. a building or buildings where friars live; monastery. 2. brotherhood of friars.

fric·as·see (frik′ə·sē′), *n., v.,* -seed, -see·ing. —*n.* meat cut up, stewed, and served in a sauce made with its own gravy. —*v.* prepare (meat) in this way. [< F, < *fricasser* mince and cook in sauce]

fric·a·tive (frik′ə·tiv), *Phonet.* —*adj.* pronounced by forcing the breath through a narrow opening formed by placing the tongue or lips near or against the palate, teeth, etc.; spirant. *F, v, s,* and *z* are fricative consonants. —*n.* a fricative consonant.

fric·tion (frik′shən), *n.* 1. a rubbing of one object against another; rubbing. 2. resistance to motion of surfaces that touch. 3. conflict of differing ideas, opinions, etc.; disagreement. [< L, < *fricare* rub] —fric′tion·al, *adj.* —fric′-tion·al·ly, *adv.* —fric′tion·less, *adj.*

Fri·day (frī′di; -dā), *n.* 1. the sixth day of the week, following Thursday. 2. servant of Robinson Crusoe. 3. any faithful servant or devoted follower.

fried (frīd), *adj.* cooked in hot fat. —*v.* pt. and pp. of fry[1].

friend (frend), *n.* 1. person who knows and likes another. 2. person who favors and supports. 3. person who belongs to the same side or group. 4. Friend, member of the Society of Friends, a religious group opposed to war and to taking oaths; Quaker. [OE *frēond*] —friend′ed, *adj.* —friend′less, *adj.* —friend′less·ness, *n.* —Syn. 1. comrade, chum, crony, companion. 2. favorer, supporter, patron, advocate.

friend at court, person who can help one with others; influential friend.

friend·ly (frend′li), *adj.,* -li·er, -li·est, *adv.* —*adj.* 1. of a friend; having the attitude of a friend. 2. like a friend; like a friend's. 3. on good terms; not hostile. 4. wanting to be a friend: *a friendly dog.* 5. favoring and supporting; favorable. —*adv.* in a friendly manner; as a friend. —friend′li·ly, *adv.* —friend′li·ness, *n.*

friend·ship (frend′ship), *n.* 1. state of being friends. 2. the liking between friends. 3. friendly feeling or behavior.

Fries·land (frēz′lənd), *n.* district in N Netherlands.

frieze[1] (frēz), *n. Archit.* 1. a horizontal band of decoration around a room, building, mantel, etc. 2. a horizontal band, often ornamented with sculpture, between the cornice and architrave of a building. See the diagram under *entablature.* [< F *frise*]

frieze[2] (frēz), *n.* a thick woolen cloth with a shaggy nap on one side. [< F < MDu.]

frig·ate (frig′it), *n.* a three-masted, sailing warship of medium size. [< F < Ital. *fregata*]

frigate bird, a strong-flying, tropical sea bird that steals other birds' food.

fright (frīt), *n.* 1. sudden fear; sudden terror. 2. *Colloq.* person or thing that is ugly, shocking, or ridiculous. —*v. Poetic.* frighten. [OE *fryhto*] —Syn. 1. dismay, consternation, alarm.

fright·en (frīt′ən), *v.* 1. fill with fright; make afraid; scare. 2. become afraid. 3. drive (away, off, etc.) by scaring. —fright′en·er, *n.* —fright′en·ing·ly, *adv.* —Syn. 1. alarm, dismay, terrify

fright·ful (frīt′fəl), *adj.* 1. that should caus fright; dreadful; terrible. 2. ugly; shocking. ? *Colloq.* disagreeable; unpleasant. 4. *Colloq.* ver. great. —fright′ful·ly, *adv.* —fright′ful·ness, *n.*

frig·id (frij′id), *adj.* 1. very cold: *a frigid climate.* 2. cold in feeling or manner; stiff; chilling: *a frigid bow.* [< L, ult. < *frigus* cold] —fri-gid′i·ty, frig′id·ness, *n.* —frig′id·ly, *adv.*

Frigid Zone, region within the Arctic or the Antarctic Circle.

fri·jol (frē′hōl), **fri·jole** (frē′hōl; frē·hō′lē), *n., pl.* fri·joles (frē′hōlz; frē·hō′lēz; Sp. frē·hō′-

lās). *Am.* kind of bean much used for food in Mexico and SW United States. [< Sp.]

frill (fril), *n.* 1. a ruffle. 2. *Am.* thing added merely for show; useless ornament; affectation of dress, manner, speech, etc. 3. fringe of feathers, hair, etc., around the neck of a bird or animal. —*v.* decorate with a ruffle; adorn with ruffles. —frill′er, *n.* —frill′y, *adj.*

fringe (frinj), *n., v.,* fringed, fring·ing. —*n.* 1. border or trimming made of threads, cords, etc., either loose or tied together in small bunches. 2. anything like this; border: *a fringe of hair hung over her forehead.* —*v.* 1. make a fringe for. 2. be a fringe for: *bushes fringed the road.* [< OF < L *fimbria*] —fringe′less, *adj.* —fringe′like′, *adj.* —fring′y, *adj.*

Fringes

fringe benefit, compensation other than wages, as insurance, pensions, etc., or privileges, received by an employee from the company.

frip·per·y (frip′ər·i), *n., pl.* -per·ies. 1. cheap, showy clothes; gaudy ornaments. 2. a showing off; foolish display; pretended refinement. [< F *friperie,* ult. < *frepe* rag]

Fris., Frisian.

Fri·sian (frizh′ən), *adj.* of or having to do with Friesland, its people, or their language. —*n.* 1. native or inhabitant of Friesland or certain nearby islands. 2. language spoken in Friesland and certain nearby islands, a West Germanic dialect.

frisk (frisk), *v.* 1. run and jump about playfully; skip and dance joyously; frolic. 2. *Slang.* search (a person) for concealed weapons, stolen goods, etc., by running a hand quickly over his clothes. 3. *Slang.* steal from (a person) in this way. —*n.* a frolic. —*adj.* frisky. [orig. *adj.,* < F *frisque*] —frisk′er, *n.*

frisk·y (fris′ki), *adj.,* frisk·i·er, frisk·i·est. playful; lively. —frisk′i·ly, *adv.* —frisk′i·ness, *n.*

frit·ter[1] (frit′ər), *v.* 1. waste little by little. 2. cut or tear in small pieces; break into fragments. —*n.* a small piece; fragment. [< *fritters* small pieces, ? alter. of *fitters*] —frit′ter·er, *n.*

frit·ter[2] (frit′ər), *n.* a small cake of batter, sometimes containing fruit or other food, fried in fat. [< F *friture,* ult. < L *frigere* fry]

fri·vol·i·ty (fri·vol′ə·ti), *n., pl.* -ties. 1. a being frivolous. 2. a frivolous act or thing.

friv·o·lous (friv′ə·ləs), *adj.* 1. lacking in seriousness or sense; silly. 2. of little worth or importance; trivial. [< L *frivolus*] —friv′o·lous·ly, *adv.* —friv′o·lous·ness, *n.* —Syn. 1. foolish. 2. trifling, unimportant, petty.

friz, frizz (friz), *v.,* frizzed, friz·zing, *n., pl.* friz·zes. —*v.* 1. form into small, crisp curls; curl. 2. form into little tufts: *cloth with a frizzed nap.* —*n.* hair curled in small, crisp curls or a very close crimp. [appar. < F *friser*]

friz·zle[1] (friz′əl), *v.,* -zled, -zling. form into small, crisp curls; curl. [? akin to OE *fris* curly] —friz′zler, *n.*

friz·zle[2] (friz′əl), *v.,* -zled, -zling. make a hissing, sputtering noise when cooking; sizzle.

friz·zly (friz′li), *adj.* full of small, crisp curls; curly.

friz·zy (friz′i), *adj.* frizzly. —friz′zi·ly, *adv.* —friz′zi·ness, *n.*

fro (frō), *adv.* 1. from; back. 2. to and fro, first one way and then back again; back and forth. [< Scand. *frā;* akin to FROM]

frock (frok), *n.* 1. gown; dress. 2. a loose outer garment. 3. robe worn by a clergyman. —*v.* clothe in a frock. [< OF *froc*] —frock′less, *adj.*

frock coat, a man's coat reaching about to the knees, and equally long in front and in back.

Froe·bel (frœ′bəl), *n.* Friedrich, 1782–1852, German educator who originated the kindergarten.

frog[1] (frog; frôg), *n., v.,* frogged, frog·ging. —*n.* 1. a small, leaping animal with webbed feet, that lives in or near water. 2. animal like this. 3. *Am.* arrangement of a rail where a railroad track crosses or branches from another. 4. pad of horny substance in the middle of the bottom of a foot of a horse, donkey, etc. —v. hunt frogs. [OE *frogga*] —frog'-like', *adj.*

frog² (frog; frôg), *n.* an ornamental fastening for a coat or dress. [? < Pg. *froco* < L *floccus* flock²]

frog·man (frog'man), *n., pl.* -men. person trained and equipped with aqualungs for underwater operations of various kinds. Most of the world's navies now have frogmen.

F, frogs on a cloak.

Frois·sart (froi'särt; *French* frwä·sär'), *n.* Jean, 1337?–1410?, French chronicler and poet.

frol·ic (frol'ik), *n., v.,* -icked, -ick·ing, *adj.* —*n.* 1. a gay prank; fun. 2. a merry game or party. [< v. or adj.] —v. play; have fun; make merry. [< adj.] —*adj.* full of fun; gay; merry. [< Du. *vrolijk* < MDu. *vro* glad] —frol'ick·er, *n.*

frol·ic·some (frol'ik·səm), *adj.* full of fun; gay; merry; playful. —frol'ic·some·ly, *adv.* —frol'ic·some·ness, *n.*

from (from; frum; *unstressed* frəm), *prep.* 1. out of: *a train from New York.* 2. out of the control or possession of: *take the book from her.* 3. starting at; beginning with: *from that time forward.* 4. caused by; because of; by reason of: *act from a sense of duty.* 5. as being unlike: *tell one tree from another.* [OE *from*]

frond (frond), *n.* Bot. 1. a divided leaf of a fern, palm, etc. 2. a leaflike part of a seaweed, lichen, etc. [< L *frons* leaf] —frond'ed, *adj.*

front (trunt), *n.* 1. the first part; foremost part. 2. part that faces forward. 3. part that faces a street or road: *the front of a house.* 4. part containing the main entrance. 5. thing fastened or worn on the front. 6. place where fighting is going on; line of battle. 7. the forces fighting for some political or social aim. 8. the united forces of a political or ideological movement, usually having diverse internal groups and elements. 9. land facing a street, river, etc. 10. manner of looking or behaving. 11. *Colloq.* an outward appearance of wealth, importance, etc. 12. *Am., Colloq.* person appointed to add respectability or prestige to an enterprise. 13. *Am., Colloq.* person or thing that serves as a cover for illicit or illegal activities. 14. *Meteorol.* the dividing surface between two dissimilar air masses. —*adj.* of, on, in, or at the front. —v. 1. have the front toward; face. 2. be in front of. 3. meet face to face; defy; oppose. [< L *frons*, lit., forehead]

front·age (frun'tij), *n.* 1. front of a building or of a lot. 2. length of this front. 3. direction that the front of a building or lot faces. 4. land facing a street, river, etc. 5. land between a building and a street, river, etc.

fron·tal (frun'təl), *adj.* 1. of, on, in, or at the front. 2. of the forehead. —*n.* bone of the forehead. —fron'tal·ly, *adv.*

fron·tier (frun·tir'; frun'tir; fron'tir), *n.* 1. *U.S.* the farthest part of a settled country, where the wilds begin. 2. *Esp. Brit.* part of a country next to another country. 3. an uncertain or undeveloped region: *the frontiers of science.* —*adj.* of or on the frontier. [< OF < *front* FRONT]

fron·tiers·man (frun·tirz'mən), *n., pl.* -men. man who lives on the frontier.

fron·tis·piece (frun'tis·pēs; fron'-), *n.* 1. a front part. 2. *Archit.* pediment over a door, gate, etc. 3. picture facing the title page of a book or of a division of a book. [< F < LL *frontispicium*, lit., looking at the forehead < L *frons* forehead + *specere* look]

front-page (frunt'pāj'), *adj.* suitable for the front page of a newspaper; important.

frost (frost; frôst), *n.* 1. freezing condition; act or process of freezing. 2. temperature below the point at which water freezes. 3. ice crystals formed when water vapor in the air condenses at a temperature below freezing. 4. coldness of manner or feeling. 5. *Slang.* failure. —v. 1. cover with frost. 2. cover with anything that suggests frost. 3. kill or injure by frost. [OE] —frost'less, *adj.* —frost'like', *adj.*

Frost (frôst; frost), *n.* Robert, 1875–1963, American poet.

frost-bite (frôst'bīt'; frost'-), *n., v.,* -bit, -bit·ten, -bit·ing. —*n.* injury to the body caused by severe cold. —v. injure by severe cold. —frost-bit·ten (frôst'bit'ən; frost'-), *adj.*

frost·ing (frôs'ting; fros'-), *n.* 1. mixture of sugar, eggs, water, etc., for covering a cake. 2. a dull finish on glass, metal, etc.

frost·y (frôs'ti; fros'-), *adj.,* frost·i·er, frost·i·est. 1. cold enough for frost. 2. covered with frost. 3. covered with anything like frost. 4. cold in manner or feeling; unfriendly. —frost'i·ly, *adv.* —frost'i·ness, *n.* —frost'less, *adj.*

froth (frôth; froth), *n.* 1. foam. 2. trivial talk, etc. —v. 1. give out frost; foam. 2. cover with foam. 3. cause to foam. [ME *frothe*; ? < Scand. *frotha*; but cf. OE *āfrēothan*, v.] —froth'er, *n.* —Syn. *n.* 1. spume, lather, scum, suds.

froth·y (frôth'i; froth'i), *adj.,* froth·i·er, froth·i·est. 1. foamy. 2. trifling; unimportant. —froth'i·ly, *adv.* —froth'i·ness, *n.*

frou-frou (frü'frü'), *n.* a rustling. [< F]

fro·ward (frō'wərd; frō'ərd), *adj.* not easily managed; willful; contrary. [< *fro* + *-ward*] —fro'ward·ly, *adv.* —fro'ward·ness, *n.* —Syn. perverse, obstinate, refractory, untoward.

frown (froun), *n.* 1. a drawing together of the brows, usually in deep thought or in strong feeling. 2. any expression or show of disapproval. —v. 1. wrinkle the forehead in annoyance or disapproval. 2. look displeased or angry. 3. express by frowning. [< OF *froignier* < Celtic] —frown'er, *n.* —frown'ing·ly, *adv.* —Syn. v. 1, 2. scowl, lower, glower.

frowz·y, frows·y (frouz'i), *adj.,* frowz·i·er, frowz·i·est; frows·i·er, frows·i·est. 1. slovenly; untidy. 2. smelling bad. —frowz'i·ly, frows'i·ly, *adv.* —frowz'i·ness, frows'i·ness, *n.*

froze (trōz), v. pt. of freeze.

fro·zen (frō'zən), *adj.* 1. turned into ice; hardened by cold. 2. very cold. 3. killed or injured by frost. 4. covered or clogged with ice. 5. cold and unfeeling. 6. too frightened or stiff to move. 7. made temporarily impossible to sell or exchange: *frozen assets.* —v. pp. of freeze. —fro'zen·ly, *adv.* —fro'zen·ness, *n.*

fruc·ti·fy (fruk'tə·fī), v., -fied, -fy·ing. 1. bear fruit. 2. make fruitful; fertilize. [< F < L, < *fructus* fruit + *facere* make] —fruc'ti·fi·ca'tion, *n.*

fruc·tose (fruk'tōs), *n.* fruit sugar, $C_6H_{12}O_6$, a carbohydrate found in all sweet fruits and in honey.

fru·gal (frü'gəl), *adj.* 1. avoiding waste; saving: *a frugal housekeeper.* 2. costing little; barely sufficient: *a frugal meal.* [< L, < *frugi* economical] —fru·gal'i·ty, fru'gal·ness, *n.* —fru'gal·ly, *adv.* —Syn. 1. economical, sparing, thrifty.

fruit (früt), *n.* 1. product of a tree, bush, shrub, or vine that is good to eat. 2. *Bot.* part of a plant that contains the seeds. A fruit is the ripened ovary of a flower and the tissues connected with it. Pea pods, acorns, grains of wheat, etc., are fruits. 3. the useful product of plants: *the fruits of the earth.* 4. offspring. 5. product; result. —v. 1. have or produce fruit. 2. cause to produce fruit. [< OF < L *fructus*] —fruit'like', *adj.*

fruit·er·er (früt'ər·ər), *n.* dealer in fruit.

fruit fly, a small fly whose larvae feed on decaying fruits and vegetables.

fruit·ful (früt'fəl), *adj.* 1. producing much fruit. 2. producing much of anything. 3. having good results; bringing benefit or profit. —fruit'ful·ly, *adv.* —fruit'ful·ness, *n.* —Syn. 2. productive, prolific, fertile.

fru·i·tion (frü·ish'ən), *n.* 1. condition of having results; fulfillment; attainment. 2. pleasure that comes from possession or use. 3. condition of producing fruit. [< LL, < *frui* enjoy]

fruit·less (früt'lis), *adj.* 1. having no results; useless; unsuccessful. 2. producing no fruit; barren. —fruit'less·ly, *adv.* —fruit'less·ness, *n.* —Syn. 1. ineffective, abortive, futile.

fruit sugar, fructose.

fruit·y (früt'i), *adj.,* fruit·i·er, fruit·i·est. tasting or smelling like fruit. —fruit'i·ness, *n.*

frump (frump), *n.* woman who is frumpish.

frump·ish (frump'ish), *adj.* shabby and out of style in dress.

frump·y (frump'i), *adj.*, **frump·i·er**, **frump·i·est.** frumpish. —**frump'i·ly**, *adv.* —**frump'i·ness**, *n.*

frus·trate (frus'trāt), *v.*, **-trat·ed**, **-trat·ing.** 1. bring to nothing; make useless or worthless; foil; defeat. 2. thwart; baffle. [< L, < *frustra* in vain] —**frus'trat·er**, *n.* —**frus·tra'tion**, *n.* —**frus·tra·tive** (frus'trə·tiv), *adj.* —Syn. 1. circumvent, outwit.

frus·tum (frus'təm), *n.*, *pl.* **-tums**, **-ta** (-tə). *Geom.* part of a conical solid left after the top has been cut off by a plane parallel to the base. [< L, piece]

fry[1] (frī), *v.*, **fried**, **fry·ing**, *n.*, *pl.* **fries.** —*v.* cook in hot fat. —*n.* 1. fried food; dish of fried meat, fish, etc. 2. *Am.* an outdoor social gathering at which food, usually fish, is fried and eaten. [< F < L *frigere*]

fry[2] (frī), *n.*, *pl.* **fry.** 1. a young fish. 2. small adult fish living together in large groups. 3. young creatures; offspring; children. [cf. Scand. *frjō seed*]

fry·er (frī'ər), *n.* 1. one who fries. 2. fowl (chicken, duck, etc.) intended for frying.

ft., 1. foot; feet. 2. fort.

fuch·sia (fū'shə), *n.* shrub with handsome pink, red, or purple flowers that droop from the stems. [< NL; named for L. *Fuchs*, botanist]

fud·dle (fud'əl), *v.*, **-dled**, **-dling.** 1. make stupid with drink; intoxicate. 2. confuse.

fudge (fuj), *n.*, *interj.*, *v.*, **fudged**, **fudg·ing.** —*n.* 1. a soft candy made of sugar, milk, butter, etc. 2. nonsense. —*interj.* nonsense! bosh! —*v.* 1. do or make in a perfunctory way. 2. talk nonsense. 3. fake.

fu·el (fū'əl), *n.*, *v.*, **-eled**, **-el·ing**; *esp. Brit.* **-elled**, **-el·ling.** —*n.* 1. thing that can be burned to make a fire. Coal and oil are fuels. 2. thing that keeps up or increases a feeling. —*v.* 1. supply with fuel. 2. get fuel. [< OF *feuaile*, ult. < L *focus* hearth] —**fu'el·er**, *esp. Brit.* **fu'el·ler**, *n.*

fuel injection, the spraying of gasoline or other fuel directly into the combustion chamber of an internal-combustion engine, without prior vaporization and mixing with air in a carburetor.

fu·gi·tive (fū'jə·tiv), *n.* person who is fleeing or who has fled. —*adj.* 1. fleeing; having fled; runaway. 2. lasting only a very short time; passing swiftly. 3. dealing with subjects of temporary interest. 4. roving; shifting. [< F < L < *fugere* flee] —**fu'gi·tive·ly**, *adv.* —**fu'gi·tive·ness**, *n.*

fugue (fūg), *n. Music.* composition based on one or more short themes in which different voices or instruments repeat the same melody with slight variations. [< F < Ital. < L *fuga* flight] —**fugue'like'**, *adj.*

Füh·rer, Fueh·rer (fy'rər), *n.* German. 1. leader. 2. der Führer, Adolf Hitler.

Fu·ji·ya·ma (fū'ji·yä'mə), or **Fu·ji** (fū'ji), *n.* a beautiful mountain in S Japan, near Tokyo.

-ful, *suffix.* 1. full of, as in *cheerful.* 2. having; characterized by, as in *careful, thoughtful.* 3. having a tendency to, as in *harmful, mournful.* 4. enough to fill, as in *cupful, handful.* 5. other meanings, as in *manful, useful.* [see FULL, adj.]

ful·crum (ful'krəm), *n.*, *pl.* **-crums**, **-cra** (-krə). 1. support on which a lever turns or is supported. See the picture under lever. 2. a prop. [< L, bedpost, < *fulcire* to support]

ful·fill, ful·fil (ful·fil'), *v.*, **-filled**, **-fill·ing.** 1. carry out (a promise, prophecy, etc.); cause to happen or take place. 2. do or perform (a duty); obey (a command, etc.). 3. satisfy (a requirement, condition, etc.); serve (a purpose). 4. finish; complete. [OE *fullfyllan*] —**ful·fill'er**, *n.* —**ful·fill'ment, ful·fil'ment**, *n.* —Syn. 1. accomplish, realize. 2. execute, discharge.

full (fŭl), *n.* 1. the greatest size, amount, extent, volume, etc. 2. **in full**, a. to or for the complete amount. b. written or said with all the words; not abbreviated or shortened. —*v.* make or become full. —*adj.* 1. able to hold no more; filled: *a full cup.* 2. complete; entire: *a full supply.* 3. of the greatest size, amount, extent, volume, etc.: *a full mile.* 4. more than enough to satisfy; well supplied; abundant. 5. well filled out; plump; round. 6. strong, sonorous, and distinct: *a full voice.* 7. made with wide folds or much cloth. —*adv.* 1. completely; entirely. 2. straight; directly: *the blow hit him full in the face.* [OE] —**full'ness**, *n.* —**ful'ly**, *adv.* —Syn. *adj.* 1. replete, sated. 2. whole. 4. ample, plentiful, copious.

full·back (fŭl'bak'), *n.* Football, *etc.* player whose position is farthest behind the front line.

full-blood·ed (fŭl'blud'id), *adj. Am.* 1. of pure race, breed, etc. 2. vigorous; hearty.

full dress, formal clothes worn in the evening or on important occasions.

full-dress (fŭl'dres'), *adj.* 1. pertaining to full dress: *a full-dress dinner.* 2. complete; formal: *a full-dress conference, debate, etc.*

full·er (fŭl'ər), *n.* person whose work is cleaning and thickening cloth. [< L *fullo* fuller]

fuller's earth, a claylike mixture used for removing grease from cloth and for purifying oil.

full-fash·ioned (fŭl'fash'ənd), *adj.* knitted to fit the shape of the foot or leg.

full-grown (fŭl'grōn'), *adj.* mature.

full house, a poker hand made up of three cards of one kind and two of another.

full moon, the moon seen as a whole circle.

ful·mi·nate (ful'mə·nāt), *v.*, **-nat·ed**, **-nat·ing**, *n.* —*v.* 1. lighten and thunder. 2. thunder forth in speech or writing. 3. denounce violently; censure strongly. 4. explode violently. —*n. Chem.* an unstable, explosive salt. [< L, < *fulmen* lightning] —**ful'mi·na'tion**, *n.* —**ful'mi·na'tor**, *n.*

ful·ness (fŭl'nis), *n.* fullness.

ful·some (fŭl'səm; ful'-), *adj.* so much as to be disgusting; offensive. [< *full* + *-some*; infl. in meaning by *foul*] —**ful'some·ly**, *adv.* —**ful'some·ness**, *n.* —Syn. excessive, immoderate.

Ful·ton (fŭl'tən), *n.* Robert, 1765-1815, American inventor.

fu·ma·gil·lin (fū'mə·gil'in), *n.* an antibiotic derived from a fungus, used esp. against amoebic infections.

fum·ble (fum'bəl), *v.*, **-bled**, **-bling.** —*v.* 1. grope awkwardly. 2. handle awkwardly. 3. *Sports.* fail to hold (a ball). —*n.* 1. an awkward groping or handling. 2. *Sports.* failure to hold a ball. [cf. LG *fummeln*] —**fum'bler**, *n.* —**fum'bling**, *adj.*, *n.* —**fum'bling·ly**, *adv.*

fume (fūm), *v.*, **fumed**, **fum·ing**, *n.* —*v.* 1. give off fumes. 2. pass off in fumes. 3. make angry complaints; show anger or irritation. 4. treat with fumes. —*n.* 1. Often, **fumes.** vapor, gas, or smoke, esp. if harmful, strong, or odorous. 2. any smokelike or odorous exhalation. 3. fit of anger; angry or irritable mood. [< OF < L *fumus* smoke] —**fume'less**, *adj.* —**fum'er**, *n.* —**fum'ing·ly**, *adv.* —Syn. *v.* 1. smoke. 3. chafe, fret.

fu·mi·gate (fū'mə·gāt), *v.*, **-gat·ed**, **-gat·ing.** disinfect with fumes; expose to fumes. [< L *fumigatus* < *fumus* fume] —**fu'mi·ga'tion**, *n.* —**fu'mi·ga'tor**, *n.*, *Am.*

fun (fun), *n.*, *v.*, **funned**, **fun·ning.** —*n.* 1. playfulness; merry play; amusement; joking. 2. **for** or **in fun**, playfully; as a joke. 3. **make fun of** or **poke fun at**, laugh at; ridicule. —*v. Colloq.* make fun; joke. [? orig. *v.*, var. of obs. *fon* befool]

func·tion (fungk'shən), *n.* 1. proper work; normal action or use; purpose. 2. a formal public or social gathering for some purpose. 3. *Math.* quantity whose value depends on, or varies with, the value given to one or more related quantities. 4. thing, quality, or feature which depends on and varies with something else: *longevity is in part a function of health.* 5. *Gram.* role a linguistic form plays in communication. —*v.* work; be used; act. [< L *functio* < *fungi* perform] —**func'tion·less**, *adj.* —Syn. *n.* 1. capacity.

func·tion·al (fungk'shən·əl), *adj.* 1. having to do with a function or functions. 2. having a function; working; acting. 3. useful in many ways; adaptable. —**func'tion·al·ly**, *adv.*

func·tion·ar·y (fungk'shən·er'i), *n.*, *pl.* **-ar·ies.** person charged with a function or office.

function word, *Gram.* word whose function in a sentence is mainly to express relationships between other elements or to express grammatical meanings. Prepositions, conjunctions, and auxiliary verbs are considered the most important subgroups of function words.

fund (fund), *n.* **1.** sum of money set aside for a special purpose. **2.** stock or store ready for use; supply: *a fund of information.* **3. funds,** a. money ready to use. b. money. —*v.* **1.** set aside a sum of money to pay the interest on (a debt). **2.** change (a debt) from a short term to a long term. [< L *fundus* bottom, piece of land]

fun·da·men·tal (fun′də·men′təl), *adj.* **1.** of the foundation or basis; forming a foundation or basis; essential. **2.** *Music.* having to do with the lowest note of a chord. —*n.* **1.** principle, rule, law, etc., that forms a foundation or basis; essential part. **2.** *Music.* the lowest note of a chord. **3.** *Physics.* that component of a wave which has the greatest wave length. [< NL, < L *fundamentum* foundation, ult. < *fundus* bottom] —fun′da·men·tal′i·ty, *n.* —fun′da·men′tal·ly, *adv.* —Syn. *adj.* 1. basic, indispensable.

fun·da·men·tal·ism (fun′də·men′təl·iz·əm), *n. Am.* **1.** the belief that the words of the Bible were inspired by God and should be believed and followed literally. **2.** movement in certain Protestant churches upholding this belief. —fun′da·men′tal·ist, *n., adj. Am.*

Fun·dy (fun′di), *n.* Bay of, a deep inlet of the Atlantic in SE Canada.

fu·ner·al (fū′nər·əl; fūn′rəl), *n.* **1.** ceremonies performed when a dead person's body is buried or burned. **2.** procession taking a dead person's body to the place where it is buried or burned. —*adj.* of or suitable for a funeral. [< LL *funeralis* < L *funus* funeral, death]

fu·ne·re·al (fū·nir′i·əl), *adj.* **1.** of or suitable for a funeral. **2.** gloomy; dismal. —fu·ne′re·al·ly, *adv.* —Syn. 2. solemn, sad, mournful.

fun·gi·cide (fun′jə·sīd), *n.* any substance that destroys fungi. [< L *fungus* + *–cida* killer] —fun′gi·cid′al, *adj.*

fun·gous (fung′gəs), *adj.* **1.** of a fungus or fungi; like a fungus; spongy. **2.** caused by a fungus.

fun·gus (fung′gəs), *n., pl.* **fun·gi** (fun′jī), **fun·gus·es,** *adj.* —*n.* **1.** plant without flowers, leaves, or green coloring matter. Mushrooms, toadstools, molds, smuts, and mildews are fungi. **2.** something that grows or springs up rapidly like a mushroom. **3.** a diseased, spongy growth on the skin. —*adj.* fungous. [< L; prob. akin to Gk. *sphongos* sponge] —fun′gus·like′, *adj.*

Fungi growing on a tree

funk (fungk), *Colloq.* —*n.* **1.** fear; panic. **2.** coward. —*v.* **1.** be afraid of. **2.** frighten. **3.** shrink from; shirk.

fun·nel (fun′əl), *n., v.,* -neled or -nelled; -nel·ing; *esp. Brit.* -nelled, -nel·ling. —*n.* **1.** a small, tapering tube with a wide, cone-shaped mouth. **2.** anything shaped like a funnel. **3.** a round, metal chimney; smokestack. **4.** flue. —*v.* **1.** pass or feed through a funnel. **2.** converge. [< OF < LL < L, < in- in + *fundere* pour] —fun′nel·like′, *adj.*

fun·ny (fun′i), *adj.,* -ni·er, -ni·est, *n., pl.* -nies. —*adj.* **1.** causing laughter; amusing. **2.** strange; queer; odd. **3.** *Am.* of or pertaining to the part of a newspaper containing comic strips. —*n.* funnies, *Am.* a. comic strips. b. section of a newspaper devoted to them. —fun′ni·ly, *adv.* —fun′ni·ness, *n.* —Syn. *adj.* 1. comic, droll, witty, facetious.

funny bone, part of the elbow over which a nerve passes.

fur (fėr), *n., v.,* furred, fur·ring. —*n.* **1.** the soft hair covering the skin of certain animals. **2.** skin with such hair on it. **3.** Usually, **furs.** garment made of fur. **4.** a coating of foul or waste matter like fur. [< v.] —*v.* **1.** make, cover, trim, or line with fur. **2.** coat with foul or waste matter like fur. **3.** put furring on. [< OF *forrer* line, encase < *forre* sheath < Gmc.] —fur′less, *adj.*

fur·be·low (fėr′bə·lō), *n.* bit of elaborate trimming. —*v.* trim in an elaborate way. [alter. of *falbala* < Rom.]

fur·bish (fėr′bish), *v.* **1.** brighten by rubbing or scouring; polish. **2.** restore to good condition; make usable again. [< OF *forbir* polish < Gmc.] —fur′bish·er, *n.*

Fu·ries (fyūr′iz), *n.pl. Gk. and Roman Myth.* the three spirits of revenge.

fu·ri·ous (fyūr′i·əs), *adj.* **1.** intensely violent; raging. **2.** full of wild, fierce anger. **3.** of unrestrained energy, speed, etc.: *furious activity.* [< L, < *furia* fury] —fu′ri·ous·ly, *adv.* —fu′ri·ous·ness, *n.*

furl (fėrl), *v.* roll up; fold up: *furl a flag.* —*n.* **1.** act of furling. **2.** roll or coil of something furled. [< F *ferler* < AF *ferlier* < *fer* firm (< L *firmus*) + *lier* bind < L *ligare*] —furl′er, *n.*

fur·long (fėr′lông; -long), *n.* measure of distance equal to one eighth of a mile. [OE *furlang* < *furh* furrow + *lang* long]

fur·lough (fėr′lō), *n.* leave of absence, esp. for a soldier. —*v. Am.* give leave of absence to. [< Du. *verlof*]

fur·nace (fėr′nis), *n.* **1.** an enclosed structure to make a very hot fire in. Furnaces are used to heat buildings. **2.** a very hot place. [< OF < L *fornax* < *fornus* oven] —fur′nace·like′, *adj.*

fur·nish (fėr′nish), *v.* **1.** supply; provide. The sun furnishes heat. **2.** supply (a room, house, etc.) with furniture, equipment, etc. [< OF *furnir* accomplish < Gmc.] —fur′nish·er, *n.*

fur·nish·ings (fėr′nish·ingz), *n.pl.* **1.** furniture or equipment for a room, house, etc. **2.** accessories of dress; articles of clothing.

fur·ni·ture (fėr′nə·chər), *n.* **1.** movable articles needed in a room, house, etc. **2.** articles needed; equipment. [< F *fourniture.* See FUR-NISH.]

fu·ror (fyūr′ôr), *n.* **1.** outburst of wild enthusiasm or excitement. **2.** craze; mania. **3.** madness; frenzy. [< F *fureur* < L, < *furere* rage]

furred (fėrd), *adj.* **1.** having fur. **2.** made, covered, trimmed, or lined with fur. **3.** wearing fur. **4.** with furring on it.

fur·ri·er (fėr′i·ər), *n.* **1.** dealer in furs. **2.** person whose work is preparing furs or making and repairing fur coats, etc.

fur·ring (fėr′ing), *n.* **1.** act of covering, trimming, or lining with fur. **2.** the fur used. **3.** a coating of foul or waste matter like fur. **4.** the nailing of thin strips of wood to beams, walls, etc. **5.** the strips so used.

fur·row (fėr′ō), *n.* **1.** a long, narrow groove or track cut in the ground by a plow. **2.** any long, narrow groove or track. **3.** wrinkle. —*v.* **1.** plow. **2.** make furrows in. **3.** wrinkle. [OE *furh*] —fur′row·er, *n.* —fur′row·less, *adj.* —fur′row·like′, *adj.* —fur′row·y, *adj.*

fur·ry (fėr′i), *adj.,* -ri·er, -ri·est. **1.** of fur. **2.** covered with fur. **3.** looking or feeling like fur. —fur′ri·ness, *n.*

fur·ther (fėr′thėr), *compar. adj.* and *adv., superl.* fur·thest (fėr′thist), *v.* —*adj.* **1.** farther; more distant: *on the further side.* **2.** more: *have you any further need of me?* —*adv.* **1.** at or to a greater distance: *seek no further for happiness.* **2.** to a greater extent: *inquire further into the matter.* **3.** also; besides: *say further.* —*v.* help forward; promote. [OE *furthra,* adj., *further,* adv., < *forth* forth] —fur′ther·er, *n.* ▶ See farther for usage note.

fur·ther·ance (fėr′thėr·əns), *n.* act of furthering; helping forward; promotion.

fur·ther·more (fėr′thėr·môr; -mōr), *adv.* moreover; also; besides.

fur·ther·most (fėr′thėr·mōst), *adj.* furthest.

fur·tive (fėr′tiv), *adj.* **1.** done stealthily; secret: *a furtive glance.* **2.** sly; stealthy; shifty: *a furtive manner.* [< L, < *fur* thief] —fur′tive·ly, *adv.* —fur′tive·ness, *n.*

fu·ry (fyūr′i), *n., pl.* -ries. **1.** wild, fierce anger; rage. **2.** violence; fierceness. **3.** a raging or violent person. **4.** like fury, *Colloq.* violently; very rapidly. [< L *furia*] —Syn. 1. frenzy, ire, wrath. 2. vehemence.

furze (fėrz), *n.* a low, prickly, evergreen shrub

with yellow flowers, common on waste lands in Europe; gorse. [OE *fyrs*] —**furz′y,** *adj.*

fuse¹ (fūz), *n.* **1.** *Elect.* part of a circuit that melts and breaks the connection when the current becomes dangerously strong. **2.** a fuze (def. 1). [< Ital. < L *fusus* spindle] —**fuse′less,** *adj.* —**fuse′-like′,** *adj.*

fuse² (fūz), *v.,* **fused, fus·ing. 1.** melt; melt together. Copper and zinc are fused to make brass. **2.** blend; unite. [< L *fusus* poured, melted]

fu·see (fū·zē′), *n.* **1.** a large-headed match that will burn in a wind. **2.** a signal flare. Also, **fuzee.** [< F, spindleful, < unrecorded OF *fus* spindle < L *fusus*]

fu·se·lage (fū′zə·läzh; -lij; -sə-), *n.* framework of the body of an airplane that holds passengers, cargo, etc. [< F, < *fuselé* spindle-shaped. See FUSE¹.]

fu·sel oil (fū′zəl; -səl), an acrid, oily liquid that occurs in alcoholic liquors when they are not distilled enough.

fu·si·ble (fū′zə·bəl), *adj.* that can be fused or melted. —**fu′si·bil′i·ty, fu′si·ble·ness,** *n.* —**fu′si·bly,** *adv.*

fu·sil·ier, fu·sil·eer (fū′zə·lir′), *n.* formerly, a soldier armed with a light flintlock musket. [< F, < *fusil* musket]

fu·sil·lade (fū′zə·lād′), *n., v.,* **-lad·ed, -lad·ing.** —*n.* **1.** discharge of many firearms. **2.** something that resembles a fusillade: *a fusillade of questions.* —*v.* attack or shoot down by a fusillade. [< F, < *fusiller* shoot < *fusil* musket]

fu·sion (fū′zhən), *n.* **1.** a melting; melting together; fusing. **2.** a blending; union. **3.** a fused mass. **4.** *Nuclear Physics.* the combining of two nuclei to create a nucleus of greater mass. The fusion of atomic nuclei releases tremendous amounts of energy which can be used, as in the hydrogen or fusion bomb.

fusion bomb, hydrogen bomb.

fu·sion·ist (fū′zhən·ist), *n.* person taking part in a union of political parties or factions. —**fu′sion·ism,** *n.*

fuss (fus), *n.* **1.** much bother about small matters; useless talk and worry. **2.** person who fusses too much. —*v.* **1.** make a fuss. **2.** make nervous or worried; bother. —**fuss′er,** *n.* —Syn. *n.* **1.** bustle, ado, commotion.

fuss·y (fus′i), *adj.,* **fuss·i·er, fuss·i·est. 1.** inclined to fuss; hard to please; very particular. **2.** much trimmed; elaborately made. **3.** full of details; requiring much care. —**fuss′i·ly,** *adv.* —**fuss′i·ness,** *n.*

fus·tian (fus′chən), *n.* **1.** a coarse, heavy cloth made of cotton and flax. **2.** a thick cotton cloth like corduroy. **3.** pompous, high-sounding language; would-be eloquence. —*adj.* **1.** made of fustian. **2.** pompous and high-sounding but cheap. [< OF < Med.L < L *fustis* stick of wood]

fust·y (fus′ti), *adj.,* **fust·i·er, fust·i·est. 1.** having a stale smell; musty; moldy; stuffy. **2.** old-fashioned; out-of-date. [< *fust,* n., < OF. wine cask, < L *fustis* cudgel] —**fust′i·ly,** *adv.* —**fust′i·ness,** *n.*

fu·tile (fū′təl), *adj.* **1.** not successful; useless. **2.** not important; trifling. [< L *futilis* pouring easily, worthless < *fundere* pour] —**fu′tile·ly,** *adv.* —**fu·til′i·ty, fu′tile·ness,** *n.* —Syn. **1.** ineffectual, profitless, vain. **2.** frivolous, idle, trivial.

fu·ture (fū′chər), *n.* **1.** time to come; what is to come; what will be. **2.** chance of success or prosperity. **3.** *Gram.* a future tense or verb form. **4.** **futures,** things bought or sold to be received or delivered at a future date. —*adj.* **1.** that is to come; that will be; coming. **2.** *Gram.* expressing or indicating time to come. *Shall go* or *will go* is the future tense of *go.* [< L *futurus,* future participle of *esse* be] —**fu′ture·less,** *adj.*

fu·tur·ism (fū′chər·iz·əm), *n.* movement in art, literature, music, etc., that opposes traditional methods and tries to express the life of the present and future in new ways. —**fu′tur·ist,** *n.*

fu·tu·ri·ty (fū·tūr′ə·ti; -tyur′-), *n., pl.* **-ties. 1.** future. **2.** a future state or event. **3.** quality of being future.

fuze (fūz), *n.* **1.** *Military.* a slow-burning wick or other device to detonate a shell, bomb, etc. **2.** fuse¹.

fu·zee (fū·zē′), *n.* fusee.

fuzz (fuz), *n.* loose, light fibers or hairs; down. —*v.* **1.** make fuzzy. **2.** become fuzzy. **3.** fly out in fuzz. [cf. Du. *voos* spongy]

fuzz·y (fuz′i), *adj.,* **fuzz·i·er, fuzz·i·est. 1.** of fuzz. **2.** like fuzz. **3.** covered with fuzz. **4.** blurred; indistinct. —**fuzz′i·ly,** *adv.* —**fuzz′i·ness,** *n.*

-fy, *suffix.* **1.** make; cause to be; change into, as in *simplify, intensify.* **2.** become, as in *solidify.* **3.** other meanings, as in *modify, qualify.* [< F *-fier* < L *-ficare* < *facere* do, make]

G

G, g (jē), *n., pl.* **G's; g's. 1.** the seventh letter of the alphabet. **2.** *Music.* the fifth note in the scale of C major.

G, German. Also, **Ger.**

g., **1.** *Elect.* conductance. **2.** gram.

Ga, *Chem.* gallium.

Ga., Georgia.

gab (gab), *n., v.,* **gabbed, gab·bing.** *Colloq.* chatter; gabble.

gab·ar·dine (gab′ər·dēn; gab′ər·dēn′), *n.* a closely woven woolen or cotton cloth having small, diagonal ribs on its surface, used for raincoats, suits, etc. [< Sp. *gabardina*]

gab·ble (gab′əl), *v.,* **-bled, -bling,** *n.* —*v.* **1.** talk rapidly with little or no meaning; jabber. **2.** make rapid, meaningless sounds: *the geese gabbled.* —*n.* rapid talk with little or no meaning. [< *gab,* var. of *gob* < Scotch Gaelic, mouth] —**gab′bler,** *n.*

gab·by (gab′i), *adj.,* **-bi·er, -bi·est.** loquacious.

ga·bi·on (gā′bi·ən), *n.* **1.** cylinder of wicker filled with earth, used as a military defense. **2.** a similar cylinder made of metal, etc., and filled with stones, used in building dams, supporting bridge foundations, etc. [< F < Ital. *gabbione,* ult. < L *cavea* cage] —**ga′bi·oned,** *adj.*

ga·ble (gā′bəl), *n., v.,* **-bled, -bling.** *Archit.*
—*n.* **1.** end of a ridged roof, with the three-cornered piece of wall that it covers. **2.** an end wall with a gable. **3.** a triangular ornament or canopy over a door, window, etc. —*v.* build or form as a gable. [< OF *gable* < Scand. *gafl*] —**ga′bled,** *adj.* —**ga′ble·like′,** *adj.*

gable roof, roof that forms a gable at one or both ends.

Ga·bon (gä·bôn′), *n.* republic in C Africa on the Atlantic, formerly part of French Equatorial Africa.

Ga·bri·el (gā′bri·əl), *n.* archangel who acts as God's messenger.

gad¹ (gad), *v.,* **gad·ded, gad·ding,** *n.* —*v.* move about restlessly; go about looking for pleasure or excitement. —*n.* a gadding. [? extended use of *gad²*] —**gad′der,** *n.*

gad² (gad), *n.* goad. [< Scand. *gaddr*]

Gad, gad (gad), *n., interj. Archaic.* word used as a mild oath, exclamation of surprise, etc.

gad·a·bout (gad′ə·bout′), *n. Colloq.* person who wanders about looking for pleasure or excitement.

gad·fly (gad′flī′), *n., pl.* **-flies. 1.** fly that stings cattle, horses, etc. 2. an irritating or annoying person. [< *gad²* + *fly*]

gadg·et (gaj'it), *n. Colloq.* a small mechanical device or contrivance; any ingenious device.

gad·o·lin·i·um (gad'ə·lin'i·əm), *n. Chem.* a rare metallic element, Gd.

Gael (gāl), *n.* 1. a Scottish Highlander. 2. Celt born or living in Scotland or the Isle of Man, or, occasionally, in Ireland.

Gael·ic (gā'lik), *adj.* of or having to do with the Gaels or their language. —*n.* language of the Gaels.

gaff (gaf), *n.* 1. a strong hook or barbed spear for pulling large fish out of the water. 2. a sharp metal spur fastened to the leg of a gamecock. 3. *Naut.* spar or pole extending along the upper edge of a fore-and-aft sail. 4. **stand the gaff,** *Am., Slang.* hold up well under strain or punishment of any kind. —*v.* hook or pull (a fish) out of the water with a gaff. [< OF *gaffe* < Celtic]

gaf·fer (gaf'ər), *n.* an old man. [alter. of *godfather*]

gag (gag), *n., v.,* **gagged, gag·ging.** —*n.* 1. something thrust into a person's mouth to keep him from talking, crying out, etc. 2. anything used to silence a person; restraint or hindrance to free speech. 3. *Slang.* an amusing remark or trick; joke. —*v.* 1. put a gag into; keep from talking, crying out, etc., with a gag. 2. force to keep silent; restrain or hinder from free speech. 3. choke or strain in an effort to vomit. 4. cause to choke or strain in an effort to vomit. [prob. imit.] —**gag'ger,** *n.* —**Syn.** 2. silence, suppress.

gage¹ (gāj), *n.* 1. pledge to fight; challenge: *the knight threw down his gauntlet as a gage of battle.* 2. pledge; security. [< OF < Gmc. Doublet of WAGE.]

gage² (gāj), *n., v.,* **gaged, gag·ing. gauge.** —**gag'er,** *n.*

gai·e·ty (gā'ə·ti), *n., pl.* **-ties.** 1. cheerful liveliness; merriment. 2. gay entertainment. 3. bright appearance. Also, **gayety.**

gai·ly (gā'li), *adv.* 1. as if gay; happily; merrily. 2. brightly; showily. Also, **gayly.**

gain (gān), *v.* 1. get; obtain; secure. 2. get as an increase, addition, advantage, or profit; make a profit; benefit. 3. make progress; advance; improve. 4. be the victor in; win. 5. get to; arrive at. 6. **gain on,** come closer to; get nearer to. 7. **gain over,** persuade to join one's side. —*n.* 1. act of gaining or getting anything. 2. what is gained; increase; addition; advantage; profit. 3. getting wealth. 4. **gains,** profits; earnings; winnings. [< OF *gaaigner* < Gmc.] —**gain'a·ble,** *adj.* —**Syn.** *v.* 1. acquire, attain. —*n.* 2. benefit, acquisition.

gain·er (gān'ər), *n.* 1. person or thing that gains. 2. a fancy dive in which the diver turns a back somersault in the air.

gain·ful (gān'fəl), *adj.* bringing in money or advantage; profitable. —**gain'ful·ly,** *adv.* —**gain'ful·ness,** *n.*

gain·say (*v.* gān·sā'; *n.* gān'sā'), *v.,* **-said, -say·ing,** *n.* —*v.* deny; contradict; dispute. —*n.* contradiction. [< *gain-* against + *say*] —**gain·say'er,** *n.* —**Syn.** *v.* oppose. —**Ant.** *v.* affirm, assert, aver.

Gains·bor·ough (gānz'bér'ō; *Brit.* gānz'bər·ə, -brə), *n.* Thomas, 1727–1788, English painter.

gainst, 'gainst (genst; *esp. Brit.* gänst), *prep., conj. Poetic.* against.

gait (gāt), *n.* kind of steps used in going along; way of walking or running. [< Scand. *gata* way] —**gait'ed,** *adj.*

gai·ter (gā'tər), *n.* 1. a covering for the lower leg or ankle, made of cloth, leather, etc. 2. shoe with an elastic strip in each side. [< F *guêtre*]

gal., gallon; gallons.

ga·la (gā'lə; gal'ə), *n.* a festive occasion; festival. —*adj.* of festivity; for a festive occasion; with festivities. [< F < Ital. < OF *gale* merriment]

ga·lac·tic (gə·lak'tik), *adj.* 1. *Astron.* of or having to do with the Milky Way. 2. of milk; obtained from milk. [< Gk. *galaktikos* < *gala* milk]

Gal·a·had (gal'ə·had), *n.* Sir, noblest and purest knight of the Round Table, who found the Holy Grail.

gal·an·tine (gal'ən·tēn), *n.* veal, chicken, or other white meat boned, tied up, boiled, and then served cold with its own jelly. [< F]

Ga·lá·pa·gos Islands (gə·lä'pə·gōs; -gōs), group of islands in the Pacific, 600 miles west of and belonging to Ecuador.

Ga·la·tia (gə·lā'shə), *n.* an ancient country in C Asia Minor that later became a Roman province. —**Ga·la'tian,** *adj., n.*

Ga·la·tians (gə·lā'shənz), *n.pl.* book of the New Testament, written by the Apostle Paul.

gal·ax·y (gal'ək·si), *n., pl.* **-ax·ies.** 1. a brilliant or splendid group. 2. *Astron.* a so-called island universe, a portion of space in which stars are clustered relatively thickly. Our Milky Way is only one of over a million such galaxies. 3. **Galaxy,** Milky Way. [< LL *galaxias* < Gk., < *gala* milk]

gale¹ (gāl), *n.* 1. a very strong wind. 2. *Meteorol.* wind with a velocity of 25 to 75 miles per hour. 3. a noisy outburst: *gales of laughter.*

gale² (gāl), *n.* shrub with fragrant leaves that grows in marshy places. [OE *gagel*]

Ga·len (gā'lən), *n.* Claudius, 130?–200? A.D., famous Greek physician and medical writer.

ga·le·na (gə·lē'nə), *n.* a metallic, gray ore containing much lead sulfide, PbS. It is the most important source of lead. [< L]

Ga·li·cia (gə·lish'ə), *n.* region in C Europe, now divided between Poland and the Soviet Union.

Gal·i·le·an (gal'ə·lē'ən), *adj.* of or having to do with Galilee or its people. —*n.* 1. native or inhabitant of Galilee. 2. **the Galilean,** Jesus.

Gal·i·le·an (gal'ə·lē'ən), *adj.* of or having to do with Galileo.

Gal·i·lee (gal'ə·lē), *n.* 1. region in N Palestine that was a Roman province in the time of Christ. 2. **Sea of,** a small, fresh-water lake in NE Palestine.

Gal·i·le·o (gal'ə·lē'ō; -lā'ō), *n.* 1564–1642, Italian astronomer who was the first to use the telescope and prove that the earth goes round the sun. His full name was Galileo Galilei.

gal·i·ot (gal'i·ət), *n.* 1. a small, fast galley moved with oars and sails. 2. a single-masted Dutch cargo or fishing boat. [< OF *galiote,* dim. of *galie,* ult. < Med.Gk. *galea*]

gall¹ (gôl), *n.* 1. a bitter, yellow, brown, or greenish liquid secreted by the liver and stored in the gall bladder; bile of animals. 2. gall bladder. 3. anything very bitter or harsh. 4. bitterness; hate. 5. *U.S. Slang.* too great boldness; impudence. [OE *galla*]

gall² (gôl), *v.* 1. make or become sore by rubbing: *the rough strap galled the horse's skin.* 2. annoy; irritate. —*n.* 1. a sore spot on the skin caused by rubbing. 2. cause of annoyance or irritation. [extended use of *gall¹*]

gall³ (gôl), *n.* lump or ball that forms on the leaves, stems, or roots of plants where they have been injured by insects or fungi. [< F < L *galla*]

gal·lant (*adj.* 1–3 gal'ənt; *adj.* 4 gə·lant', gal'ənt; *n.* gal'ənt, gə·lant'), *adj.* 1. noble; brave; daring. 2. grand; fine; stately. 3. gay; showy. 4. very polite and attentive to women. —*n.* 1. a spirited or courageous man. 2. man who is gay or wears showy clothes; man of fashion. 3. man who is very polite and attentive to women. [< OF *galant,* ppr. of *galer* make a show. See GALA.] —**gal'lant·ly,** *adv.* —**gal'lant·ness,** *n.* —**Syn.** *adj.* 1. valiant, heroic. 4. chivalrous, courtly.

gal·lant·ry (gal'ən·tri), *n., pl.* **-ries.** 1. the conduct of a gallant. 2. noble spirit or conduct; dashing courage. 3. great politeness and attention to women. 4. a gallant act or speech. 5. gay appearance; showy display.

gall bladder, *Anat.* sac attached to the liver, in which excess gall or bile is stored until needed.

gal·le·on (gal'i·ən; gal'yən), *n. Naut.* a large, high ship, usually with three or four decks. [< Sp. *geleón* < *galea* GALLEY]

Galls on a leaf

gal·ler·y (gal′ər·ĭ; gal′rĭ), *n., pl.* **-ler·ies.** **1.** a long, narrow platform or passage projecting from the wall of a building. **2.** a projecting upper floor in a church, theater, or hall with seats or room for part of the audience; a balcony. **3.** the highest floor of this kind in a theater. **4.** people who sit there. **5.** group of people watching or listening. **6.** a long, narrow room or passage; hall. **7.** *U.S., S.* veranda. **8.** room or building where works of art are shown. **9.** collection of works of art. **10.** room or building where photographs are taken, shooting is practiced, etc. **11.** *Naut.* a balconylike platform or structure at the stern or quarters of old-time ships. [< Ital. *galleria*]

gal·ley (gal′ĭ), *n., pl.* **-leys.** **1.** a long, narrow ship of former times having oars and sails. **2.** a large rowboat. **3.** kitchen of a ship. **4.** *Printing.* a long, narrow tray for holding type that has been set. **5.** galley proof. [< OF *galee*, ult. < Med.Gk. *galea*]

galley proof, *Printing.* proof printed from type in a galley.

galley slave, **1.** person compelled or condemned to row a galley. **2.** drudge.

gall·fly (gôl′flī′), *n., pl.* **-flies.** insect that causes galls on plants.

Gal·lic (gal′ĭk), *adj.* **1.** of or having to do with Gaul or its people. **2.** French.

gal·lic acid (gal′ĭk), *Chem.* acid obtained esp. from galls on plants, $C_7H_6O_5H_2O$.

Gal·li·cism, gal·li·cism (gal′ə·siz·əm), *n.* a French idiom or expression.

gal·li·na·ceous (gal′ə·nā′shəs), *adj.* belonging to a large group of birds that nest on the ground and fly only short distances. [< L, *gallina* hen]

gall·ing (gôl′ing), *adj.* that galls; chafing.

gal·li·nule (gal′ə·nūl; -nūl), *n.* any of certain long-toed wading birds of the rail family, as the moor hen of Europe.

Gal·lip·o·li (gə·lip′ə·lĭ), *n.* peninsula in NW Turkey, forming the N shore of the Dardanelles.

gal·li·pot (gal′ə·pot), *n.* **1.** a small pot or jar of glazed earthenware used esp. by druggists to hold medicine, salve, etc. **2.** *Colloq.* druggist. [< *galley* + *pot*]

gal·li·um (gal′ĭ·əm), *n. Chem.* a shining, white metal, Ga, with a low melting point. It is an element similar to mercury. [< NL, ? < L *gallus* cock, trans of Lecoq (de Boisbaudran), the discoverer]

gal·li·vant (gal′ə·vant), *v.* go about seeking pleasure; gad about. [? < *gallant*]

gall·nut (gôl′nut′), *n.* a nutlike gall on plants.

gal·lon (gal′ən), *n.* a measure for liquids, equal to 4 quarts. The U.S. gallon equals 231 cubic inches. The British gallon equals 277.274 cubic inches. [< OF *galon*]

gal·loon (gə·lün′), *n.* a narrow braid of gold, silver, or silk thread used in trimming uniforms, furniture, etc. [< F, < *galonner* dress the hair with ribbons]

gal·lop (gal′əp), *n.* **1.** the fastest gait of a horse or other four-footed animal. In a gallop, all four feet are off the ground together once in each stride. **2.** a ride at a gallop. **3.** rapid motion; rapid progress. —*v.* **1.** ride at a gallop. **2.** go at a gallop. **3.** cause to gallop. **4.** go very fast; hurry. [< F *galoper* < Gmc.] —**gal′lop·er,** *n.*

gal·lows (gal′ōz), *n., pl.* **-lows·es** or **-lows.** **1.** a wooden frame made of a crossbar on two upright posts, used for hanging criminals. **2.** any similar structure. **3.** hanging as a punishment. [OE *galga*]

gallows bird, *Colloq.* person who deserves to be hanged.

gall·stone (gôl′stōn′), *n.* a pebblelike mass that sometimes forms in the gall bladder or its duct.

ga·lore (gə·lôr′; -lōr′), *adv.* in abundance. [< Irish *go leór*]

ga·losh (gə·losh′), *n.* Usually, **galoshes.** a rubber overshoe covering the ankle, worn in wet or snowy weather. Also, **golosh.** [< F *galoche*]

gals., gallons.

Gals·wor·thy (gôlz′wêr′thĭ), *n.* John, 1867–1933, English author.

Gal·ton (gôl′tən), *n.* Sir Francis, 1822–1911, English scientist who studied heredity.

Gal·va·ni (gäl·vä′nē), *n.* Luigi, 1737–1798, Italian physicist.

gal·van·ic (gal·van′ik), *adj.* **1.** producing an electric current by chemical action. **2.** of or caused by an electric current. **3.** affecting or affected as if by galvanism; startling.

gal·va·nism (gal′və·niz·əm), *n.* **1.** electricity produced by chemical action. **2.** branch of physics dealing with this. **3.** use of such electricity for medical purposes. [for Luigi *Galvani*]

gal·va·nize (gal′və·nīz), *v.,* **-nized, -niz·ing.** **1.** apply an electric current to. **2.** arouse suddenly; startle. **3.** cover (iron or steel) with a thin coating of zinc to prevent rust. —**gal′va·ni·za′tion,** *n.* —**gal′va·niz′er,** *n.*

galvanized iron, iron covered with a thin coating of zinc, which resists rust.

gal·va·nom·e·ter (gal′və·nom′ə·tər), *n.* instrument for measuring and determining the direction of an electric current. —**gal·va·no·met·ric** (gal′və·nə·met′rik; gal·van′ə-), *adj.* —**gal′va·nom′e·try,** *n.*

gal·va·no·scope (gal′və·nə·skōp; gal·van′ə-), *n.* instrument for detecting very small electric currents and showing their direction. —**gal·va·no·scop·ic** (gal′və·nə·skop′ik; gal·van′ə-), *adj.*

Gam·bi·a (gam′bi·ə), *n.* republic in W Africa.

gam·bit (gam′bit), *n.* **1.** way of opening a game of chess by purposely sacrificing a pawn or a piece to gain some advantage. [< F < Pr. *cambi* an exchange]

gam·ble (gam′bəl), *v.,* **-bled, -bling,** *n.* —*v.* **1.** play games of chance for money. **2.** take a risk; take great risks in business, speculation, etc. **3.** bet; wager. **4.** lose or squander by gambling. —*n.* *Colloq.* a risky venture or undertaking. [prob. akin to *game*, v.] —**gam′bler,** *n.* —**gam′bling,** *n.*

gam·boge (gam·bōj′; -büzh′), *n.* gum resin from certain tropical trees, used as a yellow pigment and as a cathartic. [< NL *gambogium* < *Cambodia,* a district in Indo-China]

gam·bol (gam′bəl), *n., v.,* **-boled, -bol·ing;** *esp. Brit.* **-bolled, -bol·ling.** —*n.* a running and jumping about in play; caper; frolic. —*v.* frisk about; run and jump about in play. [< F *gambade* < Ital., ult. < *gamba* leg]

gam·brel (gam′brəl), *n.* **1.** hock of a horse or other animal. **2.** *Am.* gambrel roof. [< OF *gam·berel* < *gambe* leg < LL *gamba*]

Gambrel roof

gambrel roof, *Am.* roof having two slopes on each side. The lower slope is usually steeper than the upper one.

game¹ (gām), *n., adj.,* **gam·er, gam·est,** *v.,* **gamed, gam·ing.** —*n.* **1.** way of playing; pastime; amusement. **2.** things needed to play a game: *this store sells games.* **3.** contest with certain rules. **4.** a single round in a game: *the winner won three games out of five.* **5.** number of points required to win. **6.** a particular manner of playing: *a betting game.* **7.** activity or undertaking that is carried on like a game: *the game of diplomacy.* **8.** plan; scheme: *we discovered his game.* **9.** what is hunted or pursued. **10.** wild animals, birds, or fish hunted or caught for sport or for food. **11.** flesh of wild animals or birds used for food. **12.** make game of, make fun of; laugh at; ridicule. **13.** play the game, *Colloq.* follow the rules; be a good sport. **14.** the game is up, the plan or scheme has failed. —*adj.* **1.** having to do with game, hunting, or fishing: *game laws protect wild life.* **2.** brave; plucky: *the losing team put up a game fight.* **3.** having spirit or will enough: *the explorer was game for any adventure.* —*v.* gamble. [OE *gamen* joy] —**game′ly,** *adv.* —**game′ness,** *n.*

game² (gām), *adj. Colloq.* lame; crippled.

game bird, bird hunted for sport or food.

game·cock (gām′kok′), *n.* rooster bred and trained for fighting.

game fish, fish that fights to get away when hooked.

game of chance, game that depends on luck, not skill.

game·some (gām′səm), *adj.* full of play; sportive; ready to play. —**game′some·ly,** *adv.*

game·ster (gām′stər), *n.* gambler.

gam·ete (gam′ēt; gə·mēt′), *n. Biol.* a reproductive cell capable of uniting with another to form a fertilized cell that can develop into a new plant or animal. [< NL < Gk. *gamete* wife, *gametes* husband, ult. < *gamos* marriage] —**ga·met·ic** (gə·met′ik), *adj.*

ga·me·to·phyte (gə·mē′tə·fīt), *n.* part or structure producing gametes.

game warden, official whose duty it is to enforce the game laws in a certain district.

gam·in (gam′ən), *n.* a neglected boy left to roam about the streets. [< F]

gam·ing (gām′ing), *n.* the playing of games of chance for money; gambling.

gam·ma (gam′ə), *n.* 1. the third letter of the Greek alphabet (Γ, γ). 2. the third in any series or group.

gamma glob·u·lin (glob′yə·lin), a constituent of the human blood. Gamma globulin contains antibodies which are used against infantile paralysis and other diseases.

gamma rays, *Nuclear Physics.* penetrating electromagnetic radiations of very high frequency given off by radium and other radioactive substances, that are like X rays, but have a shorter wave length. Lethal gamma rays are emitted by the nuclei of excited atoms in atomic explosions.

gam·mer (gam′ər), *n. Dial.* an old woman. [alter. of *godmother*]

gam·mon¹ (gam′ən), *n. Brit. Colloq.* nonsense; humbug. [< ME *gamen* game¹]

gam·mon² (gam′ən), *n.* 1. the lower end of a side of bacon. 2. smoked or cured ham. [< OF *gambon* < *gambe* leg < LL *gamba*]

gam·mon³ (gam′ən), *n.* 1. the game of backgammon. 2. in this game, a victory by throwing off all of one's men before the opponent throws off any.

gam·o·pet·al·ous (gam′ə·pet′əl·əs), *adj. Bot.* having the petals joined to form a tube-shaped corolla. [< Gk. *gamos* marriage + E *petal*]

gam·o·sep·al·ous (gam′ə·sep′əl·əs), *adj. Bot.* having the sepals joined together.

gam·ut (gam′ət), *n.* 1. *Music.* a. the whole series of recognized musical notes. b. the major scale. 2. the entire range of anything: *the gamut of feeling from hope to despair.* [contraction of Med.L *gamma ut* < *gamma* G, the lowest tone, + *ut,* later *do;* notes of the scale were named from syllables in a Latin hymn: *Ut queant laxis resonare fibris, Mira gestorum famuli tuorum, Solve polluti labi reatum, Sancte Iohannes*]

gam·y (gām′i), *adj.,* **gam·i·er, gam·i·est.** 1. having a strong taste or smell like the flesh of wild animals or birds; slightly tainted. 2. abounding in game. 3. brave; plucky. —**gam′i·ly,** *adv.* —**gam′i·ness,** *n.*

gan, ’gan (gan), *v. Archaic and Poetic.* pt. of **gin¹.**

gan·der (gan′dər), *n.* a male goose. [OE *gandra*]

Gan·dhi (gän′di; gan′-), *n.* 1. Mohandas K., 1869–1948, Hindu political, social, and religious leader. 2. Indira, born 1917, prime minister of India from 1965.

gang (gang), *n.* 1. group of people acting or going around together. 2. group of people working together under one foreman. 3. set of similar tools or machines arranged to work together. —*v.* 1. *Colloq.* a. form a gang. b. *Am.* attack in a gang. 2. *Scot.* go; walk. [OE, a going]

Gan·ges (gan′jēz), *n.* river flowing across N India and E Pakistan into the Bay of Bengal. It is regarded as sacred by the Hindus.

gan·gling (gang′gling), *adj.* awkwardly tall and slender; lank and loosely built. [appar. ult. < *gang,* v.]

gan·gli·on (gang′gli·ən), *n., pl.* **-gli·a** (-gli·ə), **-gli·ons.** 1. *Anat.* group of nerve cells forming

a nerve center, esp. outside of the brain or spinal cord. 2. center of activity, etc. [< LL < Gk.]

gang·plank (gang′plangk′), *n.* a movable bridge used in getting on and off a ship, etc.

gan·grene (gang′grēn; gang·grēn′), *n., v.,* **-grened, -gren·ing.** —*n.* decay of a part of a living person or animal when the blood supply is interfered with by injury, infection, freezing, etc. —*v.* cause or have gangrene in; decay. [< L < Gk. *gangraina*] —**gan·gre·nous** (gang′grə·nəs), *adj.*

gang·ster (gang′stər), *n. Am., Colloq.* member of a gang of criminals, roughs, etc.

gang·way (gang′wā′), *n.* 1. passageway. 2. passageway on a ship. 3. gangplank. 4. *Brit.* aisle in a theater, auditorium, etc. —*interj.* get out of the way! stand aside and make room!

gan·net (gan′it), *n.* a large, fish-eating sea bird somewhat like a pelican, but with long, pointed wings and a shorter tail. [OE *ganot*]

gan·oid (gan′oid), *adj.* of fishes, having hard scales of bone overlaid with enamel. —*n.* a ganoid fish. [< Gk. *ganos* brightness]

gant·let¹ (gônt′lit; gant′-; gänt′-), *n.* a former military punishment in which the offender had to run between two rows of men who struck him with clubs or other weapons as he passed. Also, **gauntlet.** [< Sw. *gatlopp* < *gata* lane + *lopp* course]

gant·let² (gônt′lit; gant′-; gänt′-), *n.* **gauntlet¹.**

Gan·y·mede (gan′ə·mēd), *n. Class. Myth.* a beautiful youth, cupbearer to the gods of Olympus.

gaol (jāl), *n. Brit.* jail. —**gaol′er,** *n.*

gap (gap), *n., v.,* **gapped, gap·ping.** —*n.* 1. a broken place; opening. 2. an empty part; unfilled space; blank. 3. a wide difference of opinion, character, etc. 4. a pass through mountains. —*v.* make a gap. [< Scand.; akin to GAPE]

gape (gāp; gap), *v.,* **gaped, gap·ing,** *n.* —*v.* 1. open wide. 2. open the mouth wide; yawn. 3. stare with the mouth open. —*n.* 1. a wide opening. 2. act of opening the mouth wide; yawning. 3. an open-mouthed stare. [< Scand. *gapa*]

gapes (gāps), *n.pl.* 1. fit of yawning. 2. disease of birds and poultry.

gar (gär), *n., pl.* **gars** or (*esp. collectively*) **gar.** *Am.* garfish. [for *garfish*]

G.A.R., Grand Army of the Republic.

ga·rage (gə·räzh′; -räj′), *n., v.,* **-raged, -rag·ing.** —*n.* place where automobiles are kept; shop for repairing automobiles. —*v.* put or keep in a garage. [< F, < *garer* put in shelter]

Gar·and rifle (gar′ənd), a semiautomatic rifle used by the U.S. Army from 1936 to 1958. [after J. C. *Garand,* the inventor]

garb (gärb), *n.* 1. way one is dressed. 2. clothing. 3. outward covering, form, or appearance. —*v.* clothe. [< F < Ital. *garbo* grace]

gar·bage (gär′bij), *n.* waste animal or vegetable matter from a kitchen, store, etc.; scraps of food to be thrown away.

gar·ble (gär′bəl), *v.,* **-bled, -bling.** make unfair or misleading selections from (facts, statements, writings, etc.); omit parts of in order to misrepresent. [< Ital. < Ar. *gharbala* sift, prob. < LL *cribellare,* ult. < *cribrum* sieve] —**gar′bler,** *n.* —**Syn.** falsify, distort, misquote.

gar·çon (gär·sôN′), *n., pl.* **-çons** (-sôN′). *French.* 1. a young man; boy. 2. servant. 3. waiter.

gar·den (gär′dən), *n.* 1. piece of ground used for growing vegetables, herbs, flowers, or fruits. 2. park or place where people go for amusement or to see things that are displayed. 3. a fertile and delightful spot; well-cultivated region. —*v.* take care of a garden; make a garden; work in a garden. —*adj.* 1. growing or grown in a garden; for a garden. 2. common; ordinary. [< OF *gardin* < Gmc.] —**gar′den·er,** *n.* —**gar′den·like′,** *adj.*

gar·de·nia (gär·dē′nyə; -ni·ə), *n. Am.* 1. a fragrant, roselike, white flower with waxy petals. 2. shrub having these flowers. [< NL; named for A. *Garden,* botanist]

Gar·field (gär′fēld), *n.* James, 1831–1881, the 20th president of the United States, in 1881.

gar·fish (gär′fish′), *n.*, *pl.* **–fish·es** or (*esp. collectively*) **–fish**. fish with a long, slender body and long, narrow jaws. [< *gar* (OE *gār* spear) + *fish*]

Gar·gan·tu·a (gär·gan′chů·ə), *n.* a good-natured giant in a satire by Rabelais. —**Gar·gan′tu·an**, *adj.*

gar·gle (gär′gəl), *v.*, **–gled, –gling**, *n.* —*v.* wash or rinse (the throat) with a liquid kept in motion by the breath. —*n.* liquid used for gargling. [prob. imit.]

gar·goyle (gär′goil), *n.* spout for carrying off rain water, ending in a grotesque head that projects from the gutter of a building. [< OF *gargouille*. Cf. L *gargulio* gullet.] —**gar′goyled**, *adj.*

Gargoyle

Gar·i·bal·di (gar′ə·bôl′di), *n.* Giuseppe, 1807–1882, Italian patriot and general. —**Gar′i·bal′di·an**, *adj.*, *n.*

gar·ish (gär′ish), *adj.* unpleasantly bright; glaring; showy; gaudy. [ult. < obs. *gaure* stare] —**gar′ish·ly**, *adv.* —**gar′ish·ness**, *n.*

gar·land (gär′lənd), *n.* **1.** wreath of flowers, leaves, etc. **2.** book of short literary selections, esp. poems. —*v.* decorate with garlands. [< OF *garlande*]

gar·lic (gär′lik), *n.* **1.** plant like an onion whose strong-smelling bulb is composed of small sections called cloves. **2.** bulb or clove of this plant, used to season meats, salads, etc. [OE *gārlēac* < *gār* spear + *lēac* leek] —**gar′lick·y**, *adj.*

gar·ment (gär′mənt), *n.* **1.** article of clothing. **2.** an outer covering. —*v.* clothe. [< OF *garnement* < *garnir* fit out. See GARNISH.] —**gar′ment·less**, *adj.*

gar·ner (gär′nər), *v.* gather and store away. [< n.] —*n.* **1.** storehouse for grain. **2.** a store of anything. [< OF < L *granarium* < *granum* grain]

gar·net (gär′nit), *n.* **1.** a hard, vitreous silicate mineral occurring in a number of varieties. A common deep-red, transparent variety is used as a gem. **2.** a deep red. —*adj.* deep-red. [< OF *grenat* < Med.L *granatum* < L, pomegranate] —**gar′net·like′**, *adj.*

gar·nish (gär′nish), *n.* **1.** something laid on or around food as a decoration. **2.** decoration; trimming. —*v.* **1.** decorate (food). **2.** decorate; trim. **3.** *Law.* warn or notify by a garnishment. [< OF *garnir* provide, defend < Gmc.] —**gar′nish·er**, *n.* —Syn. *v.* **2.** adorn.

gar·nish·ee (gär′nish·ē′), *v.*, **–nish·eed, –nish·ee·ing**, *n. Law.* —*v.* **1.** attach (money or property) by legal authority in payment of a debt. **2.** notify (a person) not to hand over money or property belonging to the defendant in a lawsuit until the plaintiff's claims have been settled. —*n.* person served with a notice of garnishment.

gar·nish·ment (gär′nish·mənt), *n.* **1.** decoration; trimming. **2.** *Law.* a. a legal notice warning a person to hold in his possession property that belongs to the defendant in a lawsuit until the plaintiff's claims have been settled. b. summons to a third person to appear in court while a lawsuit between others is being heard.

gar·ni·ture (gär′nə·chər), *n.* decoration; trimming; garnish.

gar·ret (gar′it), *n.* space in a house just below a sloping roof; attic. [< OF *garite* < *garir* defend < Gmc.]

gar·ri·son (gar′ə·sən), *n.* **1.** soldiers stationed in a fort, town, etc., to defend it. **2.** place that has a garrison. —*v.* **1.** station soldiers in (a fort, town, etc.) to defend it. **2.** occupy (a fort, town, etc.) as a garrison. [< OF *garison* < *garir*. See GARRET.]

Gar·ri·son (gar′ə·sən), *n.* William Lloyd, 1805–1879, American editor and abolitionist.

gar·rote, gar·rotte, ga·rotte (gə·rōt′; –rot′), *n.*, *v.*, **–rot·ed, –rot·ing; –rot·ted, –rot·ting**. —*n.* **1.** a Spanish method of executing a person by strangling him with an iron collar. **2.** the iron collar used for this. **3.** a strangling and robbery; strangling. —*v.* **1.** execute by garroting.

2. strangle and rob; strangle. [< Sp., stick for twisting cord] —**gar·rot′er, gar·rot′ter, ga·rot′ter**, *n.*

gar·ru·lous (gar′ə·ləs; –yə–), *adj.* **1.** talking too much about trifles. **2.** wordy. [< L, < *garrire* chatter] —**gar·ru·li·ty** (gə·rü′lə·ti), **gar′ru·lous·ness**, *n.* —**gar′ru·lous·ly**, *adv.* —Syn. **1.** talkative, loquacious, prattling, babbling.

gar·ter (gär′tər), *n.* band or strap to hold up a stocking or sock. —*v.* fasten with a garter. [< OF *gartier* < *garet* bend of the knee]

garter snake, *Am.* a small, harmless, brownish or greenish snake with long yellow stripes.

Gar·y (gãr′i), *n.* city in NW Indiana, on Lake Michigan.

gas (gas), *n.*, *pl.* **gas·es**, *v.*, **gassed, gas·sing.** —*n.* **1.** *Physics.* any fluid substance that can expand without limit; not a solid or liquid. **2.** any gas or mixture of gases except air. **3.** any mixture of gases that can be burned, obtained from coal and other substances. **4.** any gas used as an anesthetic. **5.** an explosive mixture of firedamp with air. **6.** substance used in warfare that poisons, suffocates, etc. **7.** *Am., Colloq.* gasoline. **8.** *Am., Slang.* empty or boasting talk. —*v.* **1.** supply with gas. **2.** treat with gas; use gas on. **3.** give off gas. **4.** attack with gas in warfare. **5.** *Colloq.* supply with gasoline. **6.** *Am., Slang.* talk idly. [alter. of Gk. *chaos* chaos; coined by J. B. van Helmont, physicist] —**gas′less**, *adj.*

Gas·con (gas′kən), *n.* **1.** native of Gascony. Gascons were noted for their boastfulness. **2.** gascon, boaster. —*adj.* **1.** of Gascony or its people. **2.** gascon, boastful.

gas·con·ade (gas′kən·ād′), *n.*, *v.*, **–ad·ed, –ad·ing.** —*n.* extravagant boasting. —*v.* boast extravagantly.

Gas·co·ny (gas′kə·ni), *n.* region in SW France.

gas·e·ous (gas′i·əs), *adj.* in the form of gas; of or like a gas. —**gas′e·ous·ness**, *n.*

gas fitter, person whose work is putting in and repairing gas pipes.

gash (gash), *n.* a long, deep cut or wound. [< v.] —*v.* make a long, deep cut or wound in. [earlier *garsh* < OF *garser* scarify]

gas·i·fy (gas′ə·fī), *v.*, **–fied, –fy·ing.** change into a gas. —**gas′i·fi′a·ble**, *adj.* —**gas′i·fi·ca′tion**, *n.* —**gas′i·fi′er**, *n.*

gas jet, **1.** a small nozzle of a gas fixture where gas comes out and is burned. **2.** flame of gas.

gas·ket (gas′kit), *n.* **1.** ring or strip of rubber, metal, plaited hemp, etc., packed around a piston, pipe joint, etc., to keep steam, gas, etc., from escaping. **2.** *Naut.* cord or small rope used to secure a furled sail on a yard.

Gasket (def. 2)

gas mantle, a lacelike tube around a gas flame that glows and gives off light when heated.

gas mask, helmet or mask supplied with a filter containing chemicals to neutralize poisonous gases, etc.

gas·o·line, gas·o·lene (gas′ə·lēn; gas′ə·lēn′), *n. Am.* a colorless liquid that evaporates and burns very easily, made by distilling petroleum, used as a fuel, solvent, and cleansing agent.

gas·om·e·ter (gas·om′ə·tər), *n.* **1.** container for holding and measuring gas. **2.** tank in which gas is stored.

gasp (gasp; gäsp), *n.* a catching of the breath with open mouth, as if out of breath or surprised. —*v.* **1.** catch the breath with difficulty; breathe with gasps. **2.** utter with gasps. [< Scand. *geispa* yawn] —Syn. *v.* **1.** pant, blow, puff.

gas station, place that sells gasoline and oil.

gas·sy (gas′i), *adj.*, **–si·er, –si·est. 1.** full of gas; containing gas. **2.** like gas.

gas·tric (gas′trik), *adj.* of or near the stomach. [< Gk. *gaster* stomach]

gastric juice, the digestive fluid secreted by glands in the lining of the stomach. It contains pepsin and other enzymes and hydrochloric acid.

gas·tri·tis (gas·trī′tis), *n.* inflammation of the stomach, esp. of its mucous membrane. —**gas·trit·ic** (gas·trit′ik), *adj.*

gas·tron·o·my (gas·tron′ə·mi), *n.* art or science of good eating. [< F < Gk., < *gaster* stomach + *nomos* law] —**gas·tro·nom·ic** (gas′trə·nom′ik), **gas′tro·nom′i·cal,** *adj.* —**gas′tro·nom′i·cal·ly,** *adv.* —**gas·tron′o·mist,** *n.*

gas·tro·pod (gas′trə·pod), *n.* mollusk with a disklike organ of locomotion on the ventral surface of its body. —*adj.* of such mollusks. [< NL, < Gk. *gaster* stomach + *-podos* footed < *pous* foot]

gas·tru·la (gas′trŭ·lə), *n., pl.* **-lae** (-lē). state in the development of all many-celled animals, when the embryo is usually saclike and composed of two layers of cells. [< NL, dim. of Gk. *gaster* stomach] —**gas′tru·lar,** *adj.*

gat[1] (gat), *v.* Archaic. pt. of get.

gat[2] (gat), *n. Am., Slang.* a revolver or pistol. [for *Gatling gun*]

gate (gāt), *n., v.,* **gat·ed, gat·ing.** —*n.* 1. a movable part or frame to close an opening in a wall or fence. 2. a movable barrier to close a road, bridge, etc. 3. fort or other structure at a gate. 4. an opening in a wall or fence where a gate is; gateway. 5. way to go in or out; way to get something. 6. door, valve, etc., to stop or control the flow of water in a pipe, dam, lock, etc. 7. number of people who pay to see a contest, exhibition, etc. 8. the total amount of money received from them. —*v. Brit.* punish by confinement to the grounds of a school. [OE *gatu*, pl. of *geat*] —**gate′less,** *adj.* —**gate′like′,** *adj.* —**gate′-man,** *n.*

gate crasher, person who attends parties, gatherings, etc., without an invitation; uninvited guest.

gate·way (gāt′wā′), *n.* 1. an opening in a wall or fence where a gate is. 2. way to go in or out; way to get to something.

gath·er (gaᵗʰ′ər), *v.* 1. bring into one place or group. 2. come together; assemble. 3. get together from various places or sources, or gradually: *gather sticks for a fire.* 4. form a mass; collect: *tears gathered in her eyes.* 5. pick and collect; take: *farmers gather their crops.* 6. get or gain little by little: *the train gathered speed.* 7. collect (oneself, one's strength, energies, thoughts, etc.) for an effort. 8. put together in the mind; conclude; infer. 9. pull together in folds; wrinkle: *she gathered her brows in a frown.* 10. pull together in little folds and stitch. 11. come to a head and form pus. —*n.* one of the little folds between stitches when cloth is gathered. [OE *gaderian* < *geador* together] —**gath′er·a·ble,** *adj.* —**gath′er·er,** *n.* —**Syn.** *v.* 1. muster. 4. accumulate. 5. harvest, garner. 8. deduce. —**Ant.** *v.* 1. scatter, separate.

gath·er·ing (gaᵗʰ′ər·ing), *n.* 1. act of one that gathers. 2. that which is gathered. 3. meeting; assembly; party; crowd. 4. *Med.* swelling that comes to a head and forms pus.

Gat·ling gun (gat′ling), *Am.* an early type of machine gun consisting of a revolving cluster of barrels. [for R. J. *Gatling,* the inventor]

gauche (gōsh), *adj.* awkward; clumsy; tactless. [< F, left] —**gauche′ly,** *adv.* —**gauche′ness,** *n.*

gau·che·rie (gō′shə·rē′), *n.* 1. awkwardness; tactlessness. 2. an awkward or tactless movement, act, etc.

gau·cho (gou′chō), *n., pl.* **-chos.** cowboy of mixed Spanish and Indian descent in the southern plains of South America. [< Sp.]

gaud (gôd), *n.* a cheap, showy ornament. [appar. < AF, < *gaudir* rejoice < L *gaudere*]

gaud·y (gôd′i), *adj.,* **gaud·i·er, gaud·i·est.** too bright and gay to be in good taste; showy but cheap. —**gaud′i·ly,** *adv.* —**gaud′i·ness,** *n.* —**Syn.** flashy, tawdry, garish.

gauge (gāj), *n., v.,* **gauged, gaug·ing.** —*n.* 1. standard measure; scale of standard measurements; measure. 2. instrument for measuring. 3. means of estimating or judging. 4. size; capacity; extent. 5. distance between railroad rails or between the right and left wheels of a wagon, automobile, etc. —*v.* 1. measure accurately; find the size of with a gauge. 2. estimate; judge. Also, **gage.** [< OF *gauger*] —**gauge′a·ble,** *adj.*

gaug·er (gāj′ər), *n.* 1. person or thing that gauges. 2. official who measures the contents of barrels of taxable liquor. 3. collector of excise taxes. Also, **gager.**

Gau·guin (gō·gaⁿ′), *n.* Paul, 1848–1903, French painter.

Gaul (gôl), *n.* 1. an ancient country in W Europe. It included France, Belgium, the Netherlands, and parts of Switzerland, Germany, and N Italy. 2. one of the Celtic inhabitants of ancient Gaul. 3. a Frenchman.

gaunt (gônt; gänt), *adj.* 1. very thin and bony; with hollow eyes and a starved look. 2. looking bare and gloomy; desolate; grim. —**gaunt′ly,** *adv.* —**gaunt′ness,** *n.* —**Syn.** 1. lean, spare, lank.

gaunt·let[1] (gônt′lit; gänt′-), *n.* 1. a stout, heavy glove, usually of leather covered with plates of iron or steel, that was part of a knight's armor. 2. a stout, heavy glove with a wide, flaring cuff. 3. the wide, flaring cuff. 4. throw down the gauntlet, challenge. Also, **gantlet.** [< OF *gantelet,* dim. of *gant* glove < Gmc.] —**gaunt′let·ed,** *adj.*

gaunt·let[2] (gônt′lit; gänt′-), *n.* gantlet[1].

Iron gauntlet

Gau·ta·ma (gō′tə·mə; gou′-), *n.* Buddha.

gauze (gôz), *n.* 1. a very thin, light cloth, easily seen through. 2. a thin haze. [< F *gaze;* named for *Gaza,* Palestine] —**gauze′like′,** *adj.*

gauz·y (gôz′i), *adj.,* **gauz·i·er, gauz·i·est.** like gauze; thin and light as gauze. —**gauz′i·ly,** *adv.* —**gauz′i·ness,** *n.*

gave (gāv), *v.* pt. of give.

gav·el (gav′əl), *n.* a small mallet used by a presiding officer to signal for attention or order. [OE *gafeluc* spear < Welsh]

ga·vi·al (gā′vi·əl), *n.* a large crocodile of India that has a long, slender snout. [< F < Hind. *ghariyāl*]

ga·votte, ga·vot (gə·vot′), *n.* 1. dance like a minuet but much more lively. 2. music for it. [< F < Pr. *gavoto* < *Gavots* Alpine people]

G.A.W., GAW, guaranteed annual wage.

Ga·wain (gä′win; -wān), *n.* knight of the Round Table and nephew of King Arthur.

gawk (gôk), *n.* an awkward person; clumsy fool. —*v. Colloq.* stare rudely or stupidly. [? < dial. *gaulick(-handed)* left(-handed)]

gawk·y (gôk′i), *adj.,* **gawk·i·er, gawk·i·est.** awkward; clumsy. —**gawk′i·ly,** *adv.* —**gawk′i·ness,** *n.*

gay (gā), *adj.,* **gay·er, gay·est.** 1. happy and full of fun; merry. 2. bright-colored; showy. 3. fond of pleasures. 4. dissipated; immoral. [< F *gai*] —**gay′ness,** *n.* —**Syn.** 1. blithe, jolly, jovial. 2. bright, brilliant, gaudy.

gay·e·ty (gā′ə·ti), *n., pl.* **-ties.** gaiety.

gay·ly (gā′li), *adv.* gaily.

gaze (gāz), *v.,* **gazed, gaz·ing,** *n.* —*v.* look long and steadily. —*n.* a long, steady look. [cf. Scand. (dial. Norw.) *gasa*] —**gaz′er,** *n.*

ga·zelle (gə·zel′), *n.* a small, graceful antelope of Africa and Asia that has soft, lustrous eyes. [< F < Ar. *ghazāl*] —**ga·zelle′like′,** *adj.*

ga·zette (gə·zet′), *n., v.,* **-zet·ted, -zet·ting.** —*n.* 1. a newspaper. 2. an official government journal containing lists of appointments, promotions, etc. —*v.* publish, list, or announce in a gazette. [< F < Ital. *gazzetta,* orig., coin; from price of paper]

gaz·et·teer (gaz′ə·tir′), *n.* 1. dictionary of geographical names. 2. writer for a gazette. 3. official appointed to publish a gazette.

G clef, *Music.* the treble clef.

Gd, *Chem.* gadolinium.

Gdy·nia (gdēn′yä), *n.* seaport in N Poland.

Ge, *Chem.* germanium.

gear (gir), *n.* 1. wheel having teeth that fit into the teeth of another wheel of the same kind. 2. arrangement of fixed and moving parts for transmitting or changing motion; mechanism; machinery. 3. working order; adjustment: *his watch got out of gear and would not run.* 4. equipment needed for some purpose. 5. movable property; goods. —*v.* 1. connect by gears. 2. fit or work together; mesh. 3. provide with gear; equip. 4. provide with gearings. 5. connect by gearing. 6. put into gear. [appar. < Scand. *gervi*, *görvi*] —**gear'less**, *adj.*

gear·ing (gir'ing), *n.* set of gears, chains, etc., for transmitting motion or power; gears.

gear·shift (gir'shift'), *n.* device for connecting a motor, etc., to any of several sets of gears.

gear·wheel (gir'hwēl'), *n.* wheel having teeth that fit into the teeth of another wheel of the same kind; cogwheel.

geck·o (gek'ō), *n.*, *pl.* **geck·os**, **geck·oes**. a small, harmless, insect-eating lizard with suction pads on its feet so that it can walk on ceilings, walls, etc. [< Malay *gēkoq;* imit.]

Gecko (ab. 1 ft. long)

gee (jē), *interj.*, *v.*, **geed**, **gee·ing.** —*interj.* 1. command to horses, oxen, etc., directing them to turn to the right. 2. exclamation or mild oath. —*v.* turn to the right.

geese (gēs), *n.* pl. of **goose**.

Ge·hen·na (gə·hen'ə), *n.* 1. *New Test.* hell. 2. *Old Test.* place of torment or misery.

Gei·ger counter (gī'gər), **Geiger-Müller counter** (mul'ər; *Ger.* —mYl'ər), device which detects and counts ionizing particles. It is used to measure radioactivity, test cosmic-ray particles, etc. [after H. *Geiger*, physicist]

Gei·gers (gī'gərz), *n.* *Colloq.* radioactive particles and radiation collectively.

gei·sha (gā'shə; gē'-), *n.*, *pl.* **-sha**, **-shas.** a Japanese singing and dancing girl. [< *Jap.*]

gel (jel), *n.*, *v.*, **gelled**, **gel·ling.** —*n.* a jellylike or solid material formed from a colloidal solution. —*v.* form a gel. Egg white gels when it is cooked. [for *gelatin*]

gel·a·tin (jel'ə·tən), **gel·a·tine** (-tən; -tēn), *n.* 1. an odorless, tasteless substance obtained by boiling animal tissues, bones, hoofs, etc. It dissolves easily in hot water and is used in making jellied desserts, camera film, glue, etc. 2. any of various vegetable substances having similar properties. 3. preparation or product in which gelatin is the essential constituent. [< F < Ital., < *gelata* jelly < L *gelare* freeze] —**gel'a·tin·like'**, *adj.*

ge·lat·i·nous (jə·lat'ə·nəs), *adj.* 1. jellylike. 2. of or containing gelatin. —**ge·lat'i·nous·ly**, *adv.* —**ge·lat'i·nous·ness**, *n.*

geld (geld), *v.*, **geld·ed** or **gelt**, **geld·ing.** remove the male glands of (a horse or other animal); castrate. [< Scand. *gelda* castrate]

geld·ing (gel'ding), *n.* a gelded horse or other animal.

gel·id (jel'id), *adj.* cold as ice; frosty. [< L, < *gelum* cold] —**ge·lid'i·ty**, **gel'id·ness**, *n.* —**gel'id·ly**, *adv.*

gem (jem), *n.*, *v.*, **gemmed**, **gem·ming.** —*n.* 1. a precious stone; jewel. 2. person or thing that is very precious, beautiful, etc. 3. *Am.* a kind of muffin. 4. in printing, a very small size of type (4 point). —*v.* set or adorn with gems, or as if with gems. [< F < L *gemma* gem, bud] —**gem'·like'**, *adj.*

gem·i·nate (jem'ə·nāt), *v.*, **-nat·ed**, **-nat·ing**, *adj.* —*v.* make or become double; combine in pairs. —*adj.* combined in a pair or pairs; coupled. [< L, < *geminus* twin] —**gem'i·nate·ly**, *adv.* —**gem'i·na'tion**, *n.*

Gem·i·ni (jem'ə·nī), *n.pl.*, *gen.* **Gem·i·no·rum** (jem'ə·nô'rəm; -nō'-). 1. *Astron.* a northern constellation in the zodiac containing two bright stars. 2. the third sign of the zodiac; the Twins. 3. Castor and Pollux, the twin sons of Zeus.

gem·ma (jem'ə), *n.*, *pl.* **-mae** (-mē). *Biol.* 1. a bud. 2. a budlike growth that can develop into a new plant or animal. [< L, bud]

gem·mate (jem'āt), *v.*, **-mat·ed**, **-mat·ing.** put forth buds; reproduce by budding.

gems·bok (gemz'bok'), *n.* a large antelope of South Africa, having long, straight horns and a long, tufted tail. [< Afrikaans < G, < *gemse* chamois + *bock* buck]

Gen., 1. General. 2. Genesis.

gen., 1. gender. 2. general. 3. genitive.

gen·darme (zhän'därm), *n.*, *pl.* **-darmes** (-därmz). policeman with military training. [< F, < *gens d'armes* men of arms]

gen·der (jen'dər), *n.* 1. *Gram.* a. in many languages, the grouping of nouns into a series of classes, such as masculine, feminine, and neuter. b. one of such classes. 2. *Colloq.* sex. [< OF < L *genus* kind, sort]

gene (jēn), *n.* *Biol.* element of a germ cell transmitted from parent to offspring. Genes are carriers of hereditary traits. [< Gk. *genea* breed, kind]

ge·ne·al·o·gy (jē'ni·al'ə·ji; jen'i-; -ol'-), *n.*, *pl.* **-gies.** 1. account of the descent of a person or family from an ancestor or ancestors. 2. descent of a person or family from an ancestor; pedigree; lineage. 3. the making or investigation of such accounts; study of pedigrees. [< L < Gk., ult. < *genea* generation + *-logos* treating of] —**ge·ne·a·log·i·cal** (jē'ni·ə·loj'ə·kəl; jen'i-), **ge'·ne·a·log'ic**, *adj.* —**ge'ne·a·log'i·cal·ly**, *adv.* —**ge'ne·al'o·gist**, *n.*

gen·er·a (jen'ər·ə), *n.* pl. of **genus**.

gen·er·al (jen'ər·əl; jen'rəl), *adj.* 1. of all; for all; from all: *a government takes care of the general welfare.* 2. common to many or most; widespread: *there is a general interest in sports.* 3. not special; not limited to one kind, class, department, or use: *a general reader reads different kinds of books.* 4. not detailed; sufficient for practical purposes: *general instructions.* 5. indefinite; vague: *she referred to her trip in a general way.* 6. of or for all those forming a group: *"cat" is a general term for cats, lions, and tigers.* 7. in chief; of highest rank: *the postmaster general.* —*n.* 1. a general fact, idea, principle, or statement. 2. in the U.S. Army: a. officer ranking next below General of the Army and next above lieutenant general. b. any officer of the six highest ranks; officer ranking above a colonel. 3. head of a religious order. 4. in general, usually; for the most part. [< L *generalis* of a (whole) class < *genus* class, race] —**gen'er·al·ness**, *n.* —**Syn.** *adj.* 2. prevalent, ordinary, universal. —**Ant.** *adj.* 2. exceptional, rare. 5. specific, definite.

General Assembly, 1. *Am.* legislature of certain States of the United States. 2. the legislative body of the United Nations.

gen·er·al·is·si·mo (jen'ər·əl·is'ə·mō; jen'rəl-), *n.*, *pl.* **-mos.** commander in chief of all or several armies in the field. [< Ital., superlative of *generale* general]

gen·er·al·i·ty (jen'ər·al'ə·ti), *n.*, *pl.* **-ties.** 1. general quality or condition. 2. a general principle or rule. 3. the greater part; main body; mass. 4. a general statement; word or phrase not definite enough to have much meaning or value.

gen·er·al·ize (jen'ər·əl·īz; jen'rəl-), *v.*, **-ized**, **-iz·ing.** 1. make into one general statement; bring under a common heading, class, or law. 2. infer (a general rule) from particular facts. 3. state in a more general form; extend in application. 4. talk indefinitely or vaguely; use generalities. 5. make general; bring into general use or knowledge. 6. make general inferences. —**gen'er·al·i·za'tion**, *n.* —**gen'er·al·iz'er**, *n.*

gen·er·al·ly (jen'ər·əl·i; jen'rəl·i), *adv.* 1. in most cases; usually. 2. for the most part; widely. 3. in a general way; without giving details.

General of the Army, *U.S.* general of the highest rank.

gen·er·al·ship (jen'ər·əl·ship'; jen'rəl-), *n.* 1. ability as a general; skill in commanding an army. 2. skillful management; leadership. 3. rank, commission, authority, or term of office of a general.

general staff, *Mil.* group of high army officers who make plans for war or national defense.

gen·er·ate (jen'ər·āt), *v.*, **-at·ed**, **-at·ing.** 1. produce; cause to be: *friction generates heat.* 2.

āge, câre, fär; ēqual, tėrm; īce; ōpen, ôrder; pùt, rūle, ūse; th, then; ə=a in about.

produce (offspring). 3. *Math.* form (a line, surface, figure, or solid) by moving a point, line, etc. [< L, < *genus* race]

gen·er·a·tion (jen'ər·ā'shən), *n.* 1. all the people born about the same time. 2. time from the birth of one generation to the birth of the next generation; about 30 years. 3. one step or degree in the descent of a family. 4. production of offspring. 5. production: *generation of electricity.* 6. *Math.* the formation of a line, surface, or solid by moving a point, line, etc. 7. descent; genealogy. —**gen'er·a'tive**, *adj.*

gen·er·a·tor (jen'ər·ā'tər), *n.* 1. machine that changes mechanical energy into electrical energy; dynamo. 2. *Chem.* apparatus for producing gas or steam. 3. person or thing that generates.

gen·er·a·trix (jen'ər·ā'triks), *n., pl.* **gen·er·a·tri·ces** (jen'ər·ə·trī'sēz). *Math.* point, line, etc., whose motion produces a line, surface, figure, or solid.

ge·ner·ic (jə·ner'ik), *adj.* 1. having to do with or characteristic of a genus of plants or animals. 2. having to do with a class or group of similar things; inclusive. 3. applied to, or referring to, a group or class; general. —**ge·ner'i·cal·ly**, *adv.*

gen·er·os·i·ty (jen'ər·os'ə·ti), *n., pl.* —**ties**. 1. a being generous; willingness to share with others; unselfishness. 2. nobleness of mind; absence of meanness. 3. a generous act.

gen·er·ous (jen'ər·əs), *adj.* 1. willing to share with others; unselfish. 2. having or showing a noble mind; willing to forgive; not mean. 3. large; plentiful. 4. fertile: *generous fields.* 5. rich and strong: *a generous wine.* 6. *Archaic.* born of a good family. [< L *generosus* of noble birth < *genus* race, stock] —**gen'er·ous·ly**, *adv.* —**gen'er·ous·ness**, *n.* —Syn. 1. liberal, bountiful, lavish. 2. high-minded, magnanimous. 3. ample.

Gen·e·sis (jen'ə·sis), *n.* 1. the first book of the Old Testament, that gives an account of the creation of the world. 2. **genesis**, origin; creation. [< L < Gk.]

gen·et (jen'it), *n.* jennet.

ge·net·ic (jə·net'ik), *adj.* 1. having to do with origin and natural growth. 2. of or having to do with genetics. [< Gk. *genetikos* < *genesis* origin, creation] —**ge·net'i·cal·ly**, *adv.*

ge·net·ics (jə·net'iks), *n. Biol.* science dealing with the principles of heredity and variation in animals and plants. —**ge·net·i·cist** (jə·net'ə·sist), *n.*

Ge·ne·va (jə·nē'və), *n.* 1. city in SW Switzerland. 2. Lake of. Also, Lake Leman. a long, narrow lake in SW Switzerland. —**Ge·ne'van, Gen·e·vese** (jen'ə·vēz'; -vēs'), *adj., n.*

Geneva Convention, agreement between nations providing for the neutrality of the members and buildings of the medical departments on battlefields. It was first formulated at Geneva, Switzerland, in 1864.

Gen·ghis Khan (jeng'gis kän'), 1162-1227, Mongol conqueror of central Asia. Also, **Jenghis Khan, Jenghiz Khan**.

gen·ial (jēn'yəl), *adj.* 1. smiling and pleasant; cheerful and friendly: *a genial welcome.* 2. helping growth; pleasantly warming; comforting: *genial sunshine.* 3. pertaining to the production of offspring. [< L *genialis*, lit., belonging to the GENIUS] —**ge·ni·al·i·ty** (jē'ni·al'ə·ti), **gen'ial·ness**, *n.* —**gen'ial·ly**, *adv.* —Syn. 1. bland, cordial.

ge·nie (jē'ni), *n.* spirit; jinni. [< F *génie*]

gen·i·tal (jen'ə·təl), *adj.* having to do with reproduction or the sex organs. [< L *genitalis*, ult. < *gignere* beget]

gen·i·tals (jen'ə·təlz), *n.pl.* the external sex organs.

gen·i·tive (jen'ə·tiv), *Gram.* —*n.* 1. case in certain languages showing possession, source, origin, etc. 2. word or construction in this case. —*adj.* of this case; in this case; having to do with its forms or constructions. [< L *genitivus* of origin] —**gen·i·ti·val** (jen'ə·tī'vəl), *adj.* —**gen'i·ti'val·ly**, *adv.*

gen·ius (jēn'yəs; jē'ni·əs), *n., pl.* **gen·ius·es** *for 1-4, 7,* **ge·ni·i** (jē'ni·ī) *for 5, 6, 8.* 1. very great natural power of mind. 2. person having

such power. 3. great natural ability of some special kind: *genius for acting.* 4. the special character or spirit of a person, nation, age, language, etc. 5. guardian spirit of a person, place, etc. 6. either of two spirits, one good and one evil, supposed to influence a person's fate. 7. person who powerfully influences another. 8. spirit; jinn. [< L, tutelary spirit, male generative power]

Gen·o·a (jen'ō·ə), *n.* seaport in NW Italy. —**Gen·o·ese** (jen'ō·ēz'; -ēs'), *adj., n.*

gen·o·cide (jen'ə·sīd), *n. Am.* systematic measures for the extermination of a cultural or racial group. [< Gk. *genos* race + E *–cide* killing < L *caedere* to kill; coined by R. Lemkin in 1944] —**gen'o·cid'al**, *adj.*

gen·re (zhän're), *n.* 1. kind; sort; style. 2. style or kind of painting, etc., that shows scenes from ordinary life. [< F < L *genus* kind]

gens (jenz), *n., pl.* **gen·tes** (jen'tēz). group of families in ancient Rome that claimed the same ancestor. [< L]

gen·teel (jen·tēl'), *adj.* 1. belonging or suited to polite society. 2. polite; well-bred; fashionable. [< F *gentil* < L *gentilis*. Doublet of GENTILE, GENTLE.] —**gen·teel'ly**, *adv.* —**gen·teel'ness**, *n.* —Syn. 2. refined, polished.

gen·tian (jen'shən), *n.* plant with funnelshaped, usually blue flowers, stemless leaves, and bitter juice. [< L *gentiana*; said to be named for *Gentius*, king of Illyria (ancient country on the Adriatic)]

gen·tile, Gen·tile (jen'tīl), *n.* 1. person who is not a Jew. 2. heathen; pagan. 3. among Mormons, a person who is not a Mormon. —*adj.* 1. not Jewish. 2. heathen; pagan. 3. *Am.* among Mormons, of or having to do with those outside of the Mormon community. [< LL *gentilis* foreign < L, of a people, national. Doublet of GENTEEL, GENTLE.]

gen·til·i·ty (jen·til'ə·ti), *n., pl.* —**ties**. 1. gentle birth; membership in the aristocracy or upper class. 2. good manners. 3. refinement. 4. Usually, **gentilities**. pretended refinements.

gen·tle (jen'təl), *adj.,* -**tler**, -**tlest**, *n., v.,* -**tled**, -**tling**. —*adj.* 1. not severe, rough, or violent; mild: *a gentle tap.* 2. soft; low: *a gentle sound.* 3. moderate: *a gentle wind.* 4. kindly; friendly: *a gentle disposition.* 5. easily handled or managed: *a gentle dog.* 6. of good family and social position; wellborn. 7. honorable; good; superior. 8. noble; gallant: *a gentle knight.* 9. refined; polite. —*n. Archaic.* person of good family. —*v. Colloq.* make mild or moderate; tame (a horse). [< OF < L *gentilis* of the (same) family, national < *gens* family, nation. Doublet of GENTEEL, GENTILE.] —**gen'tle·ness**, *n.* —**gen'tly**, *adv.* —Syn. *adj.* 4. tender, humane. 5. docile, tame. —Ant. *adj.* 1. rough, severe. 4. cruel, brutal. 5. wild.

gen·tle·folk (jen'təl·fōk'), **gen·tle·folks** (-fōks'), *n.pl.* people of good family and social position.

gen·tle·man (jen'təl·mən), *n., pl.* -**men**. 1. man of good family and social position. 2. man who is honorable and well-bred. 3. (as a polite term) any man. 4. valet or personal male servant: *a gentleman's gentleman.* —**gen'tle·man·like'**, *adj.* ► See man for usage note.

gen·tle·man·ly (jen'təl·mən·li), *adj.* like a gentleman; suitable for a gentleman; polite; well-bred. —**gen'tle·man·li·ness**, *n.*

gentleman's agreement, gentlemen's agreement, *Am.* agreement binding as a matter of honor, not legally.

gen·tle·wom·an (jen'təl·wùm'ən), *n., pl.* -**wom·en**. 1. woman of good family and social position. 2. a well-bred woman; lady. 3. formerly, a woman attendant of a lady of rank. —**gen'tle·wom'an·ly**, *adj.* —**gen'tle·wom'an·li·ness**, *n.*

gen·try (jen'tri), *n.* 1. people of good family and social position. The English gentry are next below the nobility. 2. people of any particular class. [alter. of *gentrice* < OF *genterise*, ult. < *gentil* GENTLE]

gen·u·flect (jen'yù·flekt), *v.* bend the knee as an act of reverence or worship. [< Med.L < L *genu* knee + *flectere* bend] —**gen'u·flec'tor**, *n.*

gen·u·flec·tion, *esp. Brit.* **gen·u·flex·ion**

(jen'yụ·flek'shən), *n.* a bending of the knee as an act of reverence or worship.

gen·u·ine (jen'yụ-ən), *adj.* **1.** actually being what it seems or is claimed to be; real; true. **2.** without pretense; sincere; frank. [< L *genuinus*, native, ult. < *gignere* beget] —**gen'u·ine·ly,** *adv.* —**gen'u·ine·ness,** *n.* —**Syn. 1.** authentic. **2.** unaffected. —**Ant. 1.** false, sham, counterfeit.

ge·nus (jē'nəs), *n., pl.* **gen·er·a** (jen'ər·ə), **ge·nus·es. 1.** kind; sort; class. **2.** *Biol.* group of related animals or plants ranking below a family and above a species. The scientific name of an animal or plant consists of the genus written with a capital letter and the species written with a small letter. **3.** *Logic.* class or group of individuals divided into subordinate groups called species. [< L]

ge·o·cen·tric (jē'ō·sen'trik), **ge·o·cen·tri·cal** (-trə·kəl), *adj. Astron.* **1.** as viewed or measured from the earth's center. **2.** having or representing the earth as a center. [< *geo-* earth (< Gk. *gē*) + Gk. *kentron* center] —**ge'o·cen'tri·cal·ly,** *adv.*

ge·od·e·sy (ji·od'ə·si), **ge·o·det·ics** (jē'ə·det'iks), *n.* branch of applied mathematics dealing with the shape and dimensions of the earth, the determination of the shape and area of large tracts on its surface, variations in terrestrial gravity, and the exact position of geographical points. [< NL < Gk. *geōdaisia* < *gē* earth + *daiein* divide] —**ge·o·des·ic** (jē'ə·des'ik; -dē'sik), **ge'o·des'i·cal,** *adj.* —**ge·od'e·sist,** *n.*

ge·o·det·ic (jē'ə·det'ik), *adj.* having to do with geodesy. —**ge'o·det'i·cal·ly,** *adv.*

ge·og·ra·phy (ji·og'rə·fi), *n., pl.* **-phies. 1.** study of the earth's surface, climate, continents, countries, peoples, industries, and products. **2.** the surface features of a place or region. **3.** textbook or treatise on geography. [< L < Gk., < *gē* earth + *graphein* describe] —**ge·og'ra·pher,** *n.* —**ge·o·graph·i·cal** (jē'ə·graf'ə·kəl), **ge'o·graph·ic,** *adj.* —**ge'o·graph'i·cal·ly,** *adv.*

geol., geology; geologic.

ge·ol·o·gy (ji·ol'ə·ji), *n., pl.* **-gies. 1.** science that deals with the earth's crust, the layers of which it is composed, and their history. **2.** features of the earth's crust in a place or region; rocks, rock formation, etc., of a particular area. [< NL, < Gk. *gē* earth + *-logos* treating of] —**ge·o·log·ic** (jē'ə·loj'ik), **ge'o·log'i·cal,** *adj.* —**ge'o·log'i·cal·ly,** *adv.* —**ge·ol'o·gist,** *n.*

geom., geometry; geometric.

geometrical progression, progression (def. 2).

ge·om·e·tri·cian (ji·om'ə·trish'ən; jē'əm·ə-), **ge·om·e·ter** (ji·om'ə·tər), *n.* person trained in geometry.

ge·om·e·trid (ji·om'ə·trid), *n.* any of a group of gray or greenish moths with slender bodies, whose larvae are called measuring worms or inchworms.

ge·om·e·try (ji·om'ə·tri), *n.* branch of mathematics that deals with lines, angles, surfaces, and solids. Geometry includes the definition, comparison, and measurement of squares, triangles, circles, cubes, cones, spheres, etc. [< L < Gk., < *gē* earth + *-metres* measurer] —**ge·o·met·ric** (jē'ə·met'rik), **ge'o·met'ri·cal,** *adj.* —**ge'o·met'ri·cal·ly,** *adv.*

ge·o·phys·ics (jē'ō·fiz'iks), *n.* science dealing with the relations between the features of the earth and the forces that produce them. —**ge·o·phys·i·cist** (jē'ō·fiz'ə·sist), *n.*

ge·o·po·lit·i·cal (jē'ō·pə·lit'ə·kəl), **ge·o·pol·i·tic** (-pol'ə·tik), *adj.* pertaining to or involved in geopolitics. —**ge'o·po·lit'i·cal·ly,** *adv.* —**ge·o·pol·i·ti·cian** (jē'ō·pol'ə·tish'ən), *n.*

ge·o·pol·i·tics (jē'ō·pol'ə·tiks), *n.* study of government and its policies as affected by physical geography.

George (jôrj), *n.* **1.** Saint, died 303? A.D., Christian martyr, the patron saint of England. **2.** III, 1738–1820, king of England 1760–1820. **3.** V, 1865–1936, king of England 1910–1936. **4.** VI, 1895–1952, king of England 1936–1952.

Geor·gette (jôr·jet'), or **Georgette crepe,**

n. a thin, fine, transparent silk cloth with a slightly wavy surface, used for dresses, etc. [from name of French modiste]

Geor·gia (jôr'jə), *n.* **1.** a Southern State of the U.S. *Capital:* Atlanta. *Abbrev.:* Ga. **2.** a Soviet republic in SE European Russia, between the Black and Caspian seas. —**Geor'gian,** *adj., n.*

ge·ot·ro·pism (ji·ot'rə·piz·əm), *n. Biol.* response to gravity. Positive geotropism is a tendency to move down into the earth. Negative geotropism is a tendency to move upward. [< *geo-* earth (< Gk. *gē*) + Gk. *tropikos* < *trope* turning] —**ge·o·trop·ic** (jē'ə·trop'ik), *adj.* —**ge'o·trop'i·cal·ly,** *adv.*

Ger., 1. Also, **G.** German. **2.** Germany. **3.** Also, **Gmc.** Germanic.

ger., gerund.

ge·ra·ni·um (jə·rā'ni·əm), *n.* **1.** a cultivated plant having large clusters of showy flowers or fragrant leaves. **2.** a wild plant having pink or purple flowers, deeply notched leaves, and long, pointed pods. [< L < Gk., < *geranos* crane; from resemblance of seed pod to crane's bill]

ger·fal·con (jėr'fôl'kən; -fô'-), *n.* a large falcon of the arctic. Also, **gyrfalcon.** [< OF *gerfaucon* < Gmc.]

ger·i·at·rics (jer'i·at'riks), *n. Med.* science dealing with the study of old age and its diseases. [< Gk. *geras* old age + *iatreia* healing]

germ (jėrm), *n.* **1.** a microscopic animal or plant that causes disease. **2.** the earliest form of a living thing; seed; bud. **3.** origin. [< F < L *germen* sprout] —**germ'less,** *adj.*

Ger·man (jėr'mən), *n.* **1.** native or inhabitant of Germany. **2.** language of Germany, esp. that used in literature, on the radio, etc. See also **High German** and **Low German.** —*adj.* of Germany, its people, or their language.

ger·man (jėr'mən), *adj.* **1.** having the same parents. Children of the same father and mother are brothers-german or sisters-german. **2.** related as a child of one's uncle or aunt. A cousin-german is a first cousin. [< OF < L *germanus*]

ger·mane (jėr·mān'), *adj.* closely connected; to the point; pertinent. [var. of *german*]

Ger·man·ic (jėr·man'ik), *adj.* **1.** German. **2.** Teutonic. —*n.* a branch of the Indo-European language family, customarily divided into East Germanic (Gothic), North Germanic (the Scandinavian languages), and West Germanic (English, Frisian, Dutch, German).

ger·ma·ni·um (jėr·mā'ni·əm), *n. Chem.* a rare metallic element, Ge, with a grayish-white color. Its compounds resemble those of tin.

German measles, a contagious disease resembling measles, but much less serious.

German shepherd dog, police dog.

German silver, a white alloy of copper, zinc, and nickel, used for ornaments, utensils, etc.

Ger·ma·ny (jėr'mə·ni), *n.* country in C Europe. Germany was divided in 1949 into West Germany (Federal Republic of Germany) and East Germany (German Democratic Republic).

germ cell, *Biol.* cell that can produce a new individual; egg or sperm cell.

ger·mi·cide (jėr'mə·sīd), *n.* any substance that kills germs, esp. disease germs. [< *germ* + *-cide* < L *-cida* killer < *caedere* to kill] —**ger'mi·cid'al,** *adj.*

ger·mi·nal (jėr'mə·nəl), *adj.* **1.** of germs or germ cells. **2.** like that of germs or germ cells. **3.** in the earliest stage of development.

ger·mi·nant (jėr'mə·nənt), *adj.* germinating.

ger·mi·nate (jėr'mə·nāt), *v.,* **-nat·ed, -nat·ing.** start growing or developing; sprout. —**ger'mi·na'tion,** *n.* —**ger'mi·na'tor,** *n.*

germ warfare, the spreading of germs to produce disease among the enemy in time of war.

ger·on·tol·o·gy (jer'ən·tol'ə·ji), *n.* branch of science dealing with the phenomena and problems of old age. —**ger·on·to·log·i·cal** (jer'ən·tə·loj'ə·kəl), *adj.* —**ger·on·tol'o·gist,** *n.*

ger·ry·man·der (ger'i·man'dər; jer'-), *Am.* —*n.* arrangement of the political divisions of a State, county, etc., made to give one political party an unfair advantage in elections. —*v.* 1. arrange the political divisions of (a State, county, etc.) to give one political party an unfair advantage in elections. 2. manipulate unfairly. [< *Gerry* + (*sala*) *mander;* Gov. Gerry's party redistricted Mass. in 1812, and Essex Co. became roughly salamander-shaped]

ger·und (jer′ənd), *n. Gram.* a verb form used as a noun; verbal noun. [< LL *gerundium,* ult. < L *gerere* bear] —**ge·run·di·al** (jə·run′di·əl), *adj.* ⯈ The English gerund ends in -*ing.* It has the same form as the present participle but differs in use. In "Watching him carefully was a job," *watching* is a gerund used as the subject of *was;* like a verb it can take an object (*him*) and can be modified by an adverb (*carefully*).

ge·run·dive (jə·run′div), *n. Gram.* 1. a Latin verb form used as an adjective, frequently expressing the idea of necessity or duty. 2. an analogous verbal adjective in other languages. —**ger·un·di·val** (jer′ən·dī′vəl), *adj.* —**ge·run′dive·ly,** *adv.*

gest, geste (jest), *n. Archaic.* 1. story or romance in verse. 2. story; tale. 3. deed; exploit. [< OF < L *gesta* deeds < *gerere* carry on, accomplish]

Ge·stalt psychology (gə·shtält′), psychology that emphasizes the fact that a whole may be something more than the sum of its parts, and that the parts of a whole are often modified by their relationships to it and to one another. [< G, configuration]

Ge·sta·po (gə·stä′pō; -shtä′-), *n.* an offical organization of secret police and detectives in Germany under Hitler. [< G *ge(heime) sta(ats) po(lizei)* secret state police]

ges·tate (jes′tāt), *v.,* -tat·ed, -tat·ing. 1. carry (young) in the uterus from conception to birth. 2. form and develop (a project, idea, etc.). [< L *gestatus* carried < *gestare* carry] —**ges·ta′tion,** *n.*

ges·tic·u·late (jes·tik′yə·lāt), *v.,* -lat·ed, -lat·ing. 1. make or use gestures. 2. make or use many vehement gestures. [< L *gesticulatus,* ult. < *gestus* gesture] —**ges·tic′u·la′tor,** *n.* —**ges·tic·u·la·to·ry** (jes·tik′yə·lə·tô′ri; -tō′-), **ges·tic′u·la′tive,** *adj.*

ges·tic·u·la·tion (jes·tik′yə·lā′shən), *n.* 1. act of gesticulating. 2. gesture.

ges·ture (jes′chər), *n., v.,* -tured, -tur·ing. —*n.* 1. movement of the hands, arms, or any parts of the body, used instead of words or with words to help express an idea or feeling. 2. the use of such movements. 3. any action for effect or to impress others: *her refusal was merely a gesture; she really wanted to go.* —*v.* make or use gestures. [< Med.L *gestura* < L *gerere* to bear, conduct] —**ges′tur·er,** *n.* —Syn. *n.* 1. gesticulation, flourish.

get (get), *v.,* got or (*Archaic*) gat, got or (*esp. U.S.*) got·ten, get·ting, *n.* —*v.* 1. obtain by effort; gain; win: *get first prize.* 2. attain; achieve: *get a reputation.* 3. come (followed by an infinitive): *they never got to be good friends.* 4. come to be; become: *get sick.* 5. commit to memory; learn: *get one's lessons.* 6. obtain by entreaty, insistence, etc.: *get permission.* 7. receive: *get a gift.* 8. receive as punishment or penalty: *get ten days in jail.* 9. come to have; acquire: *get skill through practice.* 10. catch or contract (a disease or illness). 11. seek out and obtain or secure (something required). 12. succeed in finding (a thing or a person). 13. *U.S. Slang.* get into one's power. 14. bring into a particular position, situation, or condition: *get a fire under control.* 15. cause (a person or thing) to be (as specified): *get one's hair cut.* 16. induce or cause to do something; persuade: *we got him to speak.* 17. *Am.* succeed in making: *he got me nervous.* 18. beget (now usually of animals). 19. *Colloq.* with *have* and *had,* be obliged to: *we have got to die sometime.* 20. come to or arrive in a place specified or implied: *his boat got in yesterday.* 21. *Slang.* hit; strike. 22. *Am., Colloq.* kill. 23. puzzle; annoy. 24. *Am., Slang.* understand (a person or idea). 25. *Am., Slang.* —a. make clear or convincing. b. succeed. 26. **get along,** a. go away. b. advance. c. *Am.* manage. d. *Am.* suc-

ceed; prosper. e. agree. 27. **get around,** a. go from place to place. b. become widely known; spread. c. overcome. d. *Am.* deceive; trick. 28. **get away,** a. go away. b. escape. c. start. 29. **get away with,** *Am., Colloq.* a. get the advantage of. b. succeed in taking or doing something and getting off safely. c. eat. 30. **get back at,** *Am., Slang.* get revenge. 31. **get behind,** *Am.* support; endorse. 32. **get by,** *Colloq.* a. pass. b. *Am.* not be noticed or caught. 33. **get down on,** *Am.* develop a dislike for. 34. **get even,** *Am.* retaliate. 35. **get into,** *Am.* a. find out about. b. get control of. 36. **get off,** a. *Am.* come down from or out of. b. take off. c. escape. d. help to escape. e. start. f. *Am.* put out; issue. g. *Am.* say or express (a joke or witticism). h. deliver (a speech). 37. **get on,** a. go up on or into. b. put on. c. advance. d. manage. e. succeed. f. agree. 38. **get out,** a. go out. b. take out. c. go away. d. escape. e. help to escape. f. *Am.* become known. g. publish. h. find out. 39. **get over,** a. recover from. b. overcome. c. *Am., Colloq.* make clear or convincing. d. *Am., Colloq.* succeed. 40. **get there,** *Am.* succeed. 41. **get through,** *Am.* secure favorable action on. 42. **get together,** *Colloq.* a. bring or come together; meet; assemble. b. *Am.* come to an agreement. 43. **get up,** a. get out of bed, etc. b. stand up. c. prepare; arrange. d. dress up. e. *Am.* go ahead. —*n.* 1. a getting. 2. offspring of an animal. [< Scand. *geta*] —**get′ta·ble, get′a·ble,** *adj.* —**get′-ter,** *n.* ⯈ Get is increasingly used as an emphatic passive auxiliary: *He got thrown out.*

get·a·way (get′ə·wā′), *n., Colloq.* 1. act of getting away; escape. 2. start of a race.

Geth·sem·a·ne (geth·sem′ə·nē), *n.* garden near Jerusalem, the scene of Jesus's agony, betrayal, and arrest. Matt. 26:36.

get-to·geth·er (get′tŏŏ·gethʹər), *n., Am., Colloq.* an informal social gathering or party.

Get·tys·burg (get′iz·bèrg), *n.* town in S Pennsylvania; Civil War battle, July 1, 2, and 3, 1863.

get-up (get′up′), *n. Colloq.* 1. way a thing is put together; arrangement. 2. dress; costume. 3. *Am.* initiative; energy; ambition.

gew·gaw (gū′gô), *n.* a showy trifle; bauble.

gey·ser (gī′zər), *n.* spring that sends a column of hot water and steam into the air at intervals. [< Icelandic *Geysir,* name of a spring in Iceland, < *geysa* gush]

G.G., GG, *Colloq.* gamma globulin.

Gha·na (gä′nə), *n.* country in W Africa, member of the British Commonwealth of Nations. It includes most of the former British colony of the Gold Coast.

ghast·ly (gast′li; gäst′-), *adj.,* -li·er, -li·est, *adv.* —*adj.* 1. horrible: *a ghastly wound.* 2. like a dead person or ghost; deathly pale. 3. *Colloq.* shocking: *a ghastly failure.* —*adv.* in a ghastly manner; deathly. [OE *gāstlīc* < *gāst* ghost] —**ghast′li·ness,** *n.* —Syn. *adj.* 1. frightful, hideous, grisly, gruesome. 2. deathlike, pallid.

ghat (gôt), *n.* in India: 1. a landing place. 2. a mountain pass. [< Hind.]

Ghent (gent), *n.* city in NW Belgium.

gher·kin (gèr′kən), *n.* 1. a small, prickly cucumber often used for pickles. 2. a young, green cucumber used for pickles. [< earlier Du. *agurkje,* dim. of *agurk* < G < Slavic < Med.Gk., ult. < Pers. *angorah* watermelon]

ghet·to (get′ō), *n., pl.* -tos. 1. part of a city where Jews are required to live. 2. part of a city where many Jews live. [< Ital.]

ghost (gōst), *n.* 1. spirit of a dead person. It is supposed to live in another world and appear to living people as a pale, dim, shadowy form. 2. a faint image; slightest suggestion: *not a ghost of a chance.* 3. give up the ghost, die. 4. a ghost writer. 5. *Television.* a secondary image resulting from the reflection of a transmitted signal. —*v. Am., Colloq.* be a ghost writer for. —*adj. Am.* designating a habitation, town, etc., that is deserted: *a ghost town.* [OE *gāst*] —**ghost′like′,** *adj.* —**ghost′y,** *adj.* 1. specter.

ghost·ly (gōst′li), *adj.,* -li·er, -li·est. 1. like a ghost; pale, dim, and shadowy. 2. spiritual; religious. —**ghost′li·ness,** *n.*

ghost-write (gōst′rīt′), *v.,* -wrote, -writ·ten,

-writ·ing. *Am.* **1.** write (something) for an employer who is the ostensible author. **2.** write (a supposedly factual account) entirely from imagination.

ghost writer, *Am.* person who writes something for another who takes the credit.

ghoul (gül), *n.* **1.** a horrible demon in Oriental stories, believed to feed on corpses. **2.** person who robs graves or corpses. **3.** person who enjoys what is revolting, brutal, and horrible. [< Ar. *ghūl*] **—ghoul′ish,** *adj.* **—ghoul′ish·ly,** *adv.* **—ghoul′ish·ness,** *n.*

G.H.Q., *Mil.* General Headquarters.

G.I., GI (jē′ī′), *adj., n., pl.* **G.I.'s; GI's or GIs** (jē′īz′). **—adj. 1.** from government issue; from general issue; designating anything issued by the U.S. Army Quartermaster: *G.I. equipment.* **2.** *Colloq.* conforming to regulations; standard: *G.I. dress.* **3.** *Colloq.* of, characteristic of, or for enlisted army personnel: *a G.I. story, a G.I. obstacle course.* **—n.** *Colloq.* an enlisted soldier; serviceman. [< the initial letters of the phrase "Government Issue"]

gi·ant (jī′ənt), *n.* **1.** an imaginary being having human form, but larger and more powerful than a man. **2.** person or thing of unusual size, strength, importance, etc. **—adj.** like a giant; unusually big and strong; huge. [< OF < L < Gk. *gigas*]

gi·ant·ess (jī′ən·tis), *n.* a woman giant.

giaour (jour), *n.* in Mohammedan usage, a person who does not believe in the Mohammedan religion. [< Turk. < Pers. *gaur*]

gib·ber (jib′ər; gib′-), *v.* chatter senselessly; talk rapidly and indistinctly. **—n.** senseless chattering. **—Syn.** *v.* babble, prattle.

gib·ber·ish (jib′ər·ish; gib′-), *n.* senseless chatter; rapid, indistinct talk; jargon.

gib·bet (jib′it), *n., v., -bet·ed, -bet·ing. —n.* **1.** an upright post with a projecting arm at the top, from which the bodies of criminals were hung after execution. **2.** gallows. **—v. 1.** hang on a gibbet. **2.** hold up to public scorn or ridicule. **3.** put to death by hanging. [< OF *gibet,* dim. of *gibe* club]

gib·bon (gib′ən), *n.* a small, long-armed ape of SE Asia and the East Indies, that lives in trees. [< F]

Gib·bon (gib′ən), *n.* Edward, 1737–1794, English historian.

gib·bous (gib′əs), *adj.* **1.** curved out; humped. A gibbous moon is more than half full but less than full. **2.** hunchbacked. [< L *gibbus* a hump]

Gibbon
(ab. 30 in. tall)

gibe (jīb), *v.,* **gibed, gib·ing,** *n.* **—v.** jeer; scoff; sneer. **—n.** a sneering or sarcastic remark. Also, **jibe.** [? < OF *giber* handle roughly < *gibe* staff] **—gib′er,** *n.* **—Syn.** *v.* mock, taunt, ridicule.

gib·let (jib′lit), *n.* Usually, **giblets.** the heart, liver, or gizzard of a fowl. [< OF *gibelet* stew of game]

Gi·bral·tar (jə·brôl′tər), *n.* **1.** seaport and fortress on a high rock at the S tip of Spain. It is a British colony. **2.** Rock of, the large rock on which this fortress stands. **3.** Strait of, strait between Africa and Europe, connecting the Mediterranean Sea with the Atlantic.

gid·dy (gid′ī), *adj.,* **-di·er, -di·est,** *v.,* **-died, -dy·ing.** **—adj. 1.** having a confused, whirling feeling in one's head; dizzy. **2.** likely to make dizzy; causing dizziness. **3.** rarely or never serious; flighty. **—v.** make or become giddy. [OE *gydig* mad, possessed (by an evil spirit) < *god* a god] **—gid′di·ly,** *adv.* **—gid′di·ness,** *n.* **—Syn.** *adj.* **1.** light-headed. **3.** frivolous, unstable.

Gid·e·on (gid′i·ən), *n.* **1.** hero of Israel who defeated the Midianites. Judges 6 and 7. **2.** *Am.* member of a Christian organization of American commercial travelers, founded in 1899.

gift (gift), *n.* **1.** thing given; present. **2.** act of

giving: *get a thing by gift.* **3.** power or right of giving: *the office is within his gift.* **4.** natural ability; special talent. **—v.** present with a gift or gifts; endow. [< Scand.; akin to *give*] **—Syn.** *n.* **1.** donation, contribution, offering. **4.** aptitude.

gift·ed (gif′tid), *adj.* having natural ability or special talent: *a gifted musician.*

gig (gig), *n.* **1.** a light, two-wheeled carriage drawn by one horse. **2.** a long, light ship's boat moved by oars or sails.

gi·gan·tic (jī·gan′tik), *adj.* like a giant; unusually big; huge; enormous. **—gi·gan′ti·cal·ly,** *adv.* **—gi·gan′tic·ness,** *n.* **—Syn.** immense, colossal, herculean.

gig·gle (gig′əl), *v.,* **-gled, -gling,** *n.* **—v.** laugh in a silly or undignified way. **—n.** a silly or undignified laugh. [< *giglet* laughing girl] **—gig′gler,** *n.* **—gig′gling·ly,** *adv.* **—gig′gly,** *adj.*

gig·o·lo (jig′ə·lō), *n., pl.* **-los.** man who is paid for being a dancing partner or escort for a woman. [< F]

Gi·la monster (hē′lə), *Am.* a large, poisonous lizard of Arizona and New Mexico, covered with beadlike, orange-and-black scales. [after *Gila* River, Arizona]

Gila monster (1½ ft. long)

Gil·bert (gil′bərt), *n.* Sir William Schwenck, 1836–1911, English humorist who wrote the words for most of the operas for which Sir Arthur Sullivan wrote the music. **—Gil·bert′i·an,** *adj.*

Gilbert and El·lice Islands (el′is), a British colony in the C Pacific which includes a large number of small islands near the equator.

gild[1] (gild), *v.,* **gild·ed** or **gilt, gild·ing. 1.** cover with a thin layer of gold or similar material; make golden. **2.** make (a thing) look bright and pleasing. **3.** make (a thing) seem better than it is. [OE *gyldan* < *gold*] **—gild′a·ble,** *adj.* **—gild′-ed,** *adj.* **—gild′er,** *n.* **—gild′ing,** *n.*

gild[2] (gild), *n.* guild. **—gilds·man** (gildz′mən), *n.*

gild·hall (gild′hôl′), *n.* guildhall.

gill[1] (gil), *n.* part of the body of a fish, tadpole, crab, etc., arranged for breathing in water. [< Scand. (Sw.) *gäl*] **—gilled,** *adj.* **—gill′-like′,** *adj.*

gill[2] (jil), *n.* measure for liquids; one fourth of a pint. [< OF *gille* wine measure]

gil·lie (gil′i), *n. Scot.* **1.** attendant of a hunter or fisherman. **2.** follower; servant. [< Scotch Gaelic *gille* lad]

gil·ly·flow·er (jil′i·flou′ər), *n.* any of various flowers that have a spicy fragrance. [< OF < L < Gk. *karyophyllon* clove tree < *karyon* clove + *phyllon* leaf]

gilt (gilt), *v.* pt. and pp. of **gild**[1]. **—n.** a thin layer of gold or similar material with which a thing is gilded. **—adj.** gilded.

gilt-edged (gilt′ejd′), *adj.* **1.** having gilded edges. **2.** of the very best quality.

gim·bals (jim′bəlz; gim′-), *n.pl. Naut.* arrangement for keeping an object horizontal. A ship's compass is supported on gimbals. [ult. < OF *gemel* twin < L *gemellus*]

gim·crack (jim′krak′), *n.* a showy, useless trifle. **—adj.** showy but useless.

gim·let (gim′lit), *n.* a small tool with a screw point, for boring holes. [< OF *guimbelet*]

gim·let-eyed (gim′lit·īd′), *adj.* having eyes that are sharp and piercing.

gim·mick (gim′ik), *n. U.S. Slang.* **1.** a secret device by which a magician is able to perform a trick. **2.** any tricky device.

Gimlet

gimp (gimp), *n.* a braidlike trimming made of silk, worsted, or cotton, sometimes stiffened with wire, used on garments, curtains, furniture, etc. [< F *guimpe* < Gmc. Doublet of GUIMPE.]

gin¹ (jin), *n.* a strong alcoholic drink, usually flavored with juniper berries. [short for *geneva* liquor]

gin² (jin), *n., v.,* **ginned, gin·ning.** —*n.* 1. *Am.* machine for separating cotton from its seeds. 2. trap; snare. —*v.* 1. separate (cotton) from its seeds. 2. catch in a gin. [< OF *engin* ENGINE]

gin³ (jin), *n. Cards.* gin rummy.

gin⁴ (gin), *v.,* **gan, gun, gin·ning.** *Archaic and Poetic.* begin. [OE *onginnan*]

gin·ger (jin′jər), *n.* 1. spice made from the root of a tropical plant, used for flavoring and in medicine. 2. the root, often preserved in syrup or candied. 3. the plant. 4. *Am., Colloq.* liveliness; energy. [< LL < L < Gk. < Prakrit (an ancient lang. of India) *singabēra*] —gin′ger·y, *adj.*

ginger ale, a nonalcoholic, bubbling drink flavored with ginger.

ginger beer, an English drink similar to ginger ale, but made with fermenting ginger.

gin·ger·bread (jin′jər·bred′), *n.* 1. cake flavored with ginger and sweetened with molasses. 2. something showy and elaborate, but not in good taste. —*adj.* gaudy.

gin·ger·ly (jin′jər·li), *adv.* with extreme care or caution. —*adj.* extremely cautious. —gin′ger·li·ness, *n.*

gin·ger·snap (jin′jər·snap′), *n.* a thin, crisp cooky flavored with ginger.

ging·ham (ging′əm), *n.* a cotton cloth made from colored threads, usually in stripes, plaids, or checks. [< F < Malay *ginggang*, orig., striped]

gink·go (ging′kō; jing′kō), **ging·ko** (ging′kō), *n., pl.* **-goes; -koes.** a large, ornamental tree of China and Japan with fan-shaped leaves and edible nuts. [< Jap.]

gin rummy (jin), *Am., Cards.* a kind of rummy in which players form sequences and matching combinations and lay down their hands when having ten or less points.

gin·seng (jin′seng), *n.* 1. a low plant with a thick, branched root. 2. this root, much used in medicine by the Chinese. [< Chinese *jên shēn; jên = man*]

Giot·to (jot′ō), *n.* 1266?-1337?, the greatest Italian painter before the Renaissance.

Gip·sy, gip·sy (jip′si), *n., pl.* **-sies,** *adj. Esp. Brit.* Gypsy. —gip′sy·like′, *adj.*

gipsy moth, gypsy moth.

gi·raffe (jə·raf′; -räf′), *n.* a large African mammal with a very long neck and legs and a spotted skin, the tallest of living animals. [< F < Ar. *zarāfah*]

gird (gèrd), *v.,* **girt** or **gird·ed, gird·ing.** 1. put a belt or girdle around. 2. fasten with a belt or girdle. 3. surround; enclose. 4. get ready for action. 5. clothe; furnish. [OE *gyrdan*]

gird·er (gèr′dər), *n.* a main supporting beam. A tall building or big bridge often has steel girders for its frame. [< *gird*]

gir·dle (gèr′dəl), *n., v.,* **-dled, -dling.** —*n.* 1. belt, sash, cord, etc., worn around the waist. 2. anything that surrounds or encloses. 3. support like a corset worn about the hips or waist. —*v.* 1. form a girdle around; encircle. 2. *Am.* kill (a tree) by cutting a ring around its trunk. 3. put a girdle on or around. [OE *gyrdel.* See GIRD.] —gir′dle·like′, *adj.* —gir′dler, *n.*

girl (gèrl), *n.* 1. a female child. 2. a young, unmarried woman. 3. a female servant. 4. *Colloq.* sweetheart. 5. *Colloq.* woman of any age. [OE *gyrl-* in *gyrlgyden* virgin goddess] —girl′ish, *adj.* —girl′ish·ly, *adv.* —girl′ish·ness, *n.*

girl·hood (gèrl′hud), *n.* 1. time or condition of being a girl. 2. girls as a group.

girl·ie (gèr′li), *n. Colloq.* a little girl.

girl scout, *Am.* member of the Girl Scouts.

Girl Scouts, *Am.* organization for girls that seeks to develop health, character, and a knowledge of homemaking.

girt (gèrt), *v.* 1. pt. and pp. of **gird.** 2. put a girth around. 3. fasten with a girth.

girth (gèrth), *n.* 1. the measure around anything: *man of large girth.* 2. strap or band that keeps a saddle, pack, etc., in place on a horse's back. 3. girdle. —*v.* 1. measure in girth. 2. fasten with a strap or band. 3. girdle. [< Scand. *gjörth* girdle; akin to GIRD]

gist (jist), *n.* the essential part; main idea; substance of a longer statement. [< OF, (it) consists (in), depends (on) < L *jacet* it lies] —Syn. essence, pith.

git·tern (git′ərn), *n.* an old musical instrument with wire strings, somewhat like a guitar. [< OF *guiterne*]

give (giv), *v.,* **gave, giv·en, giv·ing,** *n.* —*v.* 1. hand over as a present: *my brother gave me his watch.* 2. hand over; deliver: *please give me a drink, give a person into custody, give one's word.* 3. hand over in exchange for something: *I gave it to him for $5.* 4. let have; cause to have: *give me permission.* 5. propose; offer: *give a toast.* 6. furnish; provide: *give aid to the enemy.* 7. set forth; show: *the newspaper gave a long account.* 8. deal; administer: *give one a blow.* 9. communicate: *give advice.* 10. allot; award: *give a contract to a person.* 11. assign as a basis: *given these premises.* 12. attribute: *give credit to another.* 13. produce; deliver: *give a lecture, a play, etc.* 14. put forth; utter: *give a cry.* 15. cause; occasion: *give trouble.* 16. do; perform: *give battle.* 17. afford a passage or view: *a window that gives upon a court.* 18. make a gift. 19. yield to force or pressure. 20. **give away,** *Colloq.* a. give as a present. b. hand over (a bride) to a bridegroom. c. *Am.* betray a secret, esp. unintentionally; expose (a person). 21. **give back,** return. 22. **give out,** a. send out; put forth. b. distribute. c. make known. d. become used up or worn out. 23. **give up,** a. hand over; deliver; surrender. b. stop having or doing. c. stop trying. d. have no more hope for. e. devote entirely. —*n.* a yielding to force or pressure; elasticity. [< Scand. (Dan.) *give*] —giv′er, *n.*

give-and-take (giv′ən·tāk′), *n.* 1. an even or fair exchange; mutual concession. 2. good-natured banter; exchange of talk.

give·a·way (giv′ə·wā′), *n. Am., Colloq.* 1. an unintentional revelation; exposure; betrayal. 2. Also, **giveaway show** or **program.** a radio or television show in which contestants participate and receive prizes.

giv·en (giv′ən), *adj.* 1. stated; fixed; specified. 2. inclined; disposed. 3. assigned as a basis of calculating, reasoning, etc. 4. *Math.* known. —*v.* pp. of **give.**

given name, name given to a person in addition to his family name. *John* is the given name of John Smith.

giz·zard (giz′ərd), *n.* a bird's second stomach, where the food from the first stomach is ground up fine. [< OF, ult. < L *gigeria* cooked entrails of a fowl]

Gk., Greek. Also, **Gr.**

Gl, *Chem.* glucinum.

gla·brous (glā′brəs), *adj. Bot., Zool.* without hair or down; smooth. [< L *glaber* smooth]

gla·cé (gla·sā′), *adj.* 1. covered with sugar, frosting, or icing. 2. frozen. 3. finished with a glossy surface. [< F, pp. of *glacer* impart a gloss to]

gla·cial (glā′shəl), *adj.* 1. of ice or glaciers; having much ice or many glaciers. 2. relating to a glacial epoch or period. 3. made by the action of ice or glaciers. 4. very cold; icy. [< L, < *glacies* ice] —gla′cial·ly, *adv.*

gla·ci·ate (glā′shi·āt), *v.,* **-at·ed, -at·ing.** 1. cover with ice or glaciers. 2. act on by ice or glaciers. —gla·ci·a·tion (glā′si·ā′shən; -shi-), *n.*

gla·cier (glā′shər), *n.* a large mass of ice formed from snow on high ground wherever winter snowfall exceeds summer melting, which moves very slowly down a mountain or along a valley. [< F, ult. < L *glacies* ice] —gla′ciered, *adj.*

glad (glad), *adj.,* **glad·der, glad·dest.** 1. happy; pleased. 2. bringing joy; pleasant. 3. bright; gay. [OE *glad* bright, shining] —glad′ly, *adv.* —glad′ness, *n.* —Syn. 1. delighted, gratified. 3. joyful, joyous, cheerful, merry. —Ant. 1. sad.

Giraffe
(ab. 18 ft. tall)

glad·den (glad′ən), v. make or become glad. —glad′den·er, n. —Syn. cheer, enliven, delight.

glade (glād), n. 1. an open space in a wood or forest. 2. Am. a marshy tract of low ground covered with grass. [prob. akin to glad]

glad hand, Am., Colloq. the hand extended in cordial greeting.

glad-hand·er (glad′hand′ər), n. Am., Colloq. person who makes a show of being friendly to all.

glad·i·a·tor (glad′i·ā′tər), n. 1. in ancient Rome, a slave, captive, or paid fighter who fought at the public shows. 2. a skilled contender in any field or cause. [< L, < gladius sword] —glad·i·a·to·ri·al (glad′i·ə·tô′ri·əl; -tō′-), adj.

glad·i·o·lus (glad′i·ō′ləs; glə·dī′-ə-), **glad·i·o·la** (-lə), n., pl. -li (-lī), -lus·es; -las. kind of iris with spikes of large, handsome flowers in various colors. [< L, dim. of gladius sword]

glad·some (glad′səm), adj. 1. glad; joyful; cheerful. 2. causing gladness. —glad′some·ly, adv. —glad′some·ness, n.

Glad·stone (glad′stōn; -stən), n. 1. William Ewart, 1809–1898, British statesman. 2. Gladstone bag.

Gladstone bag, a traveling bag that opens flat into two equal compartments. [so named in compliment to W. E. Gladstone]

glair (glãr), n. 1. the raw white of an egg or any similar viscous substance. 2. glaze or size made from it. [< OF glaire, ult. < L clarus clear] —glair′y, adj.

glaive (glāv), n. Archaic. sword; broadsword. [< OF < L gladius sword]

glam·or·ize (glam′ər·īz), v., -ized, -iz·ing. make (someone or something) glamorous.

glam·or·ous (glam′ər·əs), adj. full of glamour; fascinating. —glam′or·ous·ly, adv.

glam·our, glam·or (glam′ər), n. 1. mysterious fascination; alluring charm. 2. a magic spell or influence; enchantment. [alter. of grammar or its var. gramarye occult learning; orig., a spell] ▶ Glamor is rapidly gaining ground. The adjective should always be glamorous.

glance (glans; gläns), n., v., glanced, glanc·ing. —n. 1. a quick look. 2. flash of light; gleam. 3. a glancing off; deflected motion; swift, oblique movement. 4. a passing reference. —v. 1. direct in a quick look. 2. flash with light; gleam. 3. direct obliquely. 4. hit and go off at a slant. 5. make a short reference and go on to something else. [var. of ME glace(n) strike a glancing blow < OF glacier to slip] —Syn. n. 1. glimpse.

gland (gland), n. Anat. organ in the body by which certain substances are separated from the blood and changed into some secretion for use in the body, such as bile, or into a product to be discharged from the body, such as sweat. [< F glande, ult. < L glandula, dim. of glans acorn] —gland′less, adj. —gland′like′, adj.

glan·ders (glan′dərz), n. a serious contagious disease of horses, mules, etc., accompanied by swellings beneath the lower jaw and a profuse discharge from the nostrils. [< OF glandre GLAND] —glan′der·ous, adj.

glan·du·lar (glan′jə·lər), **glan·du·lous** (-ləs), adj. of or like a gland; having glands.

glare¹ (glãr), n., v., glared, glar·ing. —n. 1. a strong, bright light; light that shines so brightly that it hurts the eyes. 2. a fierce, angry stare. 3. too great brightness and showiness. —v. 1. give off a strong, bright light; shine so brightly as to hurt the eyes. 2. stare fiercely and angrily. 3. express by a fierce, angry stare. 4. be too bright and showy. [ME glaren. Cf. OE glæren glassy.]

glare² (glãr), Am. a bright, smooth surface. —adj. bright and smooth. [extended use of glare¹]

glar·ing (glãr′ing), adj. 1. very bright; dazzling. 2. staring fiercely and angrily. 3. too bright and showy. 4. conspicuous. —glar′ing·ly, adv. —glar′ing·ness, n. —Syn. 1. brilliant.

glar·y (glãr′i), adj. glaring.

Glas·gow (glas′gō; -kō; gläs′-), n. the largest city and chief seaport in Scotland.

glass (glas; gläs), n. 1. a hard, brittle substance that is usually transparent, made by melting sand with soda, potash, lime, or other substances. 2. thing to drink from made of glass. 3. as much as a glass holds. 4. something made of glass. A windowpane, a mirror, a watch crystal, a telescope, or an hourglass is a glass. 5. things made of glass. 6. glasses, a. pair of lenses to correct defective eyesight; eyeglasses; spectacles. b. field glasses; binoculars. —v. 1. put glass in; cover or protect with glass. 2. reflect. —adj. made of glass. [OE glæs]

glass blowing, art or process of shaping glass by blowing while it is still hot and soft. —glass blower.

glass·ful (glas′ful; gläs′-), n., pl. -fuls. as much as a glass holds.

glass snake, Am. a legless, snakelike lizard of the 8 United States, whose tail breaks off very easily.

glass·ware (glas′wãr; gläs′-), n. articles made of glass.

glass·y (glas′i; gläs′i), adj., glass·i·er, glass·i·est. 1. like glass; smooth; easily seen through. 2. having a fixed, stupid stare. —glass′i·ly, adv. —glass′i·ness, n.

glau·co·ma (glô·kō′mə), n. disease of the eye, characterized by hardening of the eyeball and gradual loss of sight. [< Gk. glaukoma. See GLAUCOUS.] —glau·co·ma·tous (glô·kō′mə·təs; -kom′ə-), adj.

glau·cous (glô′kəs), adj. 1. light bluish-green. 2. Bot. covered with whitish powder as plums and grapes are. [< L < Gk. glaukos gray]

glaze (glāz), v., glazed, glaz·ing, n. —v. 1. put glass in; cover with glass. 2. make a smooth, glassy surface or glossy coating on (china, food, etc.). 3. become smooth, glassy, or glossy. —n. 1. a smooth, glassy surface or glossy coating: the glaze on a china cup. 2. Am. a. a coating of smooth ice. b. an area covered with such a coating. [ME glase(n) < glas GLASS] —glaz′er, n. —glaz′ing, n. —glaz′y, adj. —glaz′i·ness, n.

gla·zier (glā′zhər), n. person whose work is putting glass in windows, picture frames, etc.

gleam (glēm), n. 1. flash or beam of light. 2. a short or faint light. 3. a faint show: a gleam of hope. —v. 1. flash or beam with light. 2. shine with a short or faint light. 3. appear suddenly. [OE glǣm]

glean (glēn), v. 1. gather (grain) left on a field by reapers. 2. gather little by little or slowly. [< OF < LL glennare < Celtic] —glean′er, n.

glebe (glēb), n. 1. Poetic. soil; earth; field. 2. portion of land assigned to a parish church or clergyman. [< L gleba]

glee (glē), n. 1. joy; delight; mirth. 2. song for three or more voices singing different parts, usually without instrumental accompaniment. [OE glēo] —Syn. 1. merriment, gaiety, jollity.

glee club, group organized for singing songs.

glee·ful (glē′fəl), adj. filled with glee; merry; joyous. —glee′ful·ly, adv. —glee′ful·ness, n. —Syn. gay, jolly, mirthful.

glee·man (glē′mən), n., pl. -men. Archaic. singer; ministrel.

glee·some (glē′səm), adj. gleeful. —glee′some·ness, n.

glen (glen), n. a small, narrow valley. [< Scotch Gaelic gle(a) nn] —glen′like′, adj.

glen·gar·ry (glen·gar′i), n., pl. -ries. a Scottish cap with straight sides and a creased top, often having short ribbons at the back. [after Glengarry, valley in Scotland]

glib (glib), adj., glib·ber, glib·best. 1. speaking or spoken smoothly and easily. 2. speaking or spoken too smoothly and easily to be sincere: a glib excuse.

Gladiolus

Glengarry

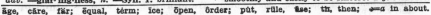

3. acting smoothly and easily. [short for *glibbery* slippery. Cf. Du. *glibberig*.] —**glib′ly**, *adv.* —**glib′ness**, *n.* —Syn. 1. fluent, voluble, smooth-tongued.

glide (glīd), *v.*, **glid·ed**, **glid·ing**, *n.* —*v.* 1. move along smoothly, evenly, and easily. 2. pass gradually, quietly, or imperceptibly. 3. of an airplane, come down slowly at a slant without using a motor. —*n.* 1. a smooth, even, easy movement. 2. of an airplane, act of gliding. 3. *Music.* a slur. 4. *Phonet.* sound made in passing from one speech sound to another. [OE *glīdan*] —**glid′ing·ly**, *adv.*

glid·er (glīd′ər), *n.* 1. aircraft resembling an airplane without a motor. Rising air currents keep it in the air. 2. person or thing that glides.

glim·mer (glim′ər), *n.* 1. a faint, unsteady light. 2. a vague idea; dim notion; faint glimpse. —*v.* 1. shine with a faint, unsteady light. 2. appear faintly or dimly. [cf. OE *gleomu* splendor] —**glim′mer·ing**, *n.* —**glim′mer·ing·ly**, *adv.*

glimpse (glimps), *n.*, *v.*, **glimpsed**, **glimps·ing**. —*n.* 1. a short, quick view. 2. a short, faint appearance. —*v.* 1. catch a short, quick view of. 2. look quickly; glance. [akin to *glimmer*] —**glimps′er**, *n.*

glint (glint), *v.*, *n.* gleam; flash. [cf. dial. Sw. *glinta*]

glis·ten (glis′ən), *v.*, *n.* sparkle; glitter; shine. [OE *glisnian*] —**glis′ten·ing·ly**, *adv.*

glis·ter (glis′tər), *v.*, *n.* *Archaic.* glisten; glitter; sparkle. [? < *glisten*]

glit·ter (glit′ər), *v.* 1. shine with a bright, sparkling light. 2. be bright and showy. —*n.* 1. a bright, sparkling light. 2. brightness; showiness. [cf. Scand. *glitra*] —**glit′ter·ing**, **glit′ter·y**, *adj.* —**glit′ter·ing·ly**, *adv.*

gloam·ing (glōm′ing), *n.* *Poetic.* evening twilight; dusk. [OE *glōmung* < *glōm* twilight]

gloat (glōt), *v.* gaze intently; ponder with pleasure; stare: *the miser gloated over his gold.* [cf. Scand. *glotta* smile scornfully] —**gloat′er**, *n.* —**gloat′ing·ly**, *adv.*

glob·al (glōb′əl), *adj.* 1. shaped like a globe. 2. world-wide. —**glob′al·ly**, *adv.*

globe (glōb), *n.*, *v.*, **globed**, **glob·ing**. —*n.* 1. anything round like a ball; sphere. 2. earth; world. 3. sphere with a map of the earth or sky on it. 4. planet, eyeball, or anything rounded like a globe. —*v.* gather or form into a globe. [< F < L *globus*]

globe·fish (glōb′fish′), *n.*, *pl.* **-fish·es** or (*esp. collectively*) **-fish**. fish that can make itself nearly ball-shaped by drawing in air.

globe·trot·ter (glōb′trot′ər), *n.* person who travels widely over the world for sightseeing. —**globe′trot′ting**, *n.*, *adj.*

glo·bose (glō′bōs), *adj.* globular. —**glo′bose·ly**, *adv.* —**glo·bos·i·ty** (glō·bos′ə·ti), *n.*

glob·u·lar (glob′yə·lər), *adj.* 1. shaped like a globe or globule; spherical. 2. consisting of globules. —**glob·u·lar·i·ty** (glob′yə·lar′ə·ti), *n.* —**glob′u·lar·ly**, *adv.*

glob·ule (glob′ūl), *n.* a very small ball; tiny drop.

glock·en·spiel (glok′ən·spēl′), *n.* *Music.* instrument consisting of a series of small, tuned bells, metal bars, or tubes mounted in a frame and struck by two little hammers. [< G, < *glocke* bell + *spiel* play]

glom·er·ate (glom′ər·it), *adj.* clustered together; collected into a rounded mass. [< L, < *glomus* ball] —**glom·er·a·tion** (glom′ər·ā′shən), *n.*

gloom (glüm), *n.* 1. deep shadow; darkness; dimness. 2. low spirits; sadness. 3. a dejected or sad look. —*v.* 1. be or become dark, dim, or dismal. 2. be in low spirits; feel miserable. 3. look sad or dismal. [OE *glōm* twilight] —Syn. *n.* 1. obscurity, shade. 2. despondency, dejection, depression, melancholy.

gloom·y (glüm′i), *adj.*, **gloom·i·er**, **gloom·i·est**. 1. dark; dim. 2. in low spirits; sad; melancholy. 3. causing low spirits; discouraging; dismal. —**gloom′i·ly**, *adv.* —**gloom′i·ness**, *n.* —Syn. 1. shadowy, somber. 2. dejected, downhearted. —Ant. 2. happy.

glo·ri·a (glô′ri·ə; glō′-), *n.* 1. song of praise to God, or its musical setting. 2. Gloria, one of three songs of praise to God, beginning "Glory be to God on high," "Glory be to the Father," and "Glory be to Thee, O Lord." 3. halo. [< L]

glo·ri·fy (glô′rə·fī; glō′-), *v.*, **-fied**, **-fy·ing**. 1. give glory to; make glorious. 2. praise; honor; worship. 3. make more beautiful or splendid. 4. exalt to the glory of heaven. [< OF < L, < *gloria* glory + *facere* make] —**glo′ri·fi′a·ble**, *adj.* —**glo′ri·fi·ca′tion**, *n.* —**glo′ri·fi′er**, *n.*

glo·ri·ous (glô′ri·əs; glō′-), *adj.* 1. having or deserving glory; illustrious. 2. giving glory. 3. magnificent; splendid. —**glo′ri·ous·ly**, *adv.* —**glo′ri·ous·ness**, *n.* —Syn. 1. famous, renowned. 3. grand, brilliant.

glo·ry (glô′ri; glō′-), *n.*, *pl.* **-ries**, *v.*, **-ried**, **-ry·ing**. —*n.* 1. great praise and honor; fame; renown. 2. that which brings praise and honor; source of pride and joy. 3. adoring praise and thanksgiving. 4. radiant beauty; brightness; magnificence; splendor. 5. condition of magnificence, splendor, or greatest prosperity. 6. splendor and bliss of heaven; heaven. 7. halo. —*v.* be proud; rejoice. [< OF < L *gloria*] —Syn. *n.* 1. distinction, eminence. —Ant. *n.* 1. dishonor.

gloss¹ (glôs; glos), *n.* 1. a smooth, shiny surface; luster. 2. an outward appearance or surface that covers wrong underneath. —*v.* 1. put a smooth, shiny surface on. 2. smooth over; make seem right: *gloss over a mistake.* [cf. Scand. *glossi* flame] —**gloss′er**, *n.* —Syn. *n.* 1. sheen, polish.

gloss² (glôs; glos), *n.* 1. explanation; interpretation; comment. 2. glossary. 3. translation inserted between the lines of a text printed in a foreign language. —*v.* 1. comment on; explain; annotate. 2. explain away. 3. make glosses. [< L < Gk. *glossa*, lit., tongue] —**gloss′er**, *n.*

glos·sar·i·al (glo·sâr′i·əl; glō-), *adj.* of or like a glossary. —**glos·sar′i·al·ly**, *adv.*

glos·sa·ry (glos′ə·ri; glôs′-), *n.*, *pl.* **-ries.** list of special, technical, or difficult words with explanations or comments: *glossary of Shakespeare's plays.* [< L, < *glossa* GLOSS²] —**glos′sa·rist**, *n.*

gloss·y (glôs′i; glos′i), *adj.*, **gloss·i·er**, **gloss·i·est.** smooth and shiny. —**gloss′i·ly**, *adv.* —**gloss′i·ness**, *n.* —Syn. lustrous, polished, sleek.

glot·tal (glot′əl), *adj.* 1. of the glottis. 2. *Phonet.* produced in the glottis. H in *hope* is a glottal sound.

glot·tis (glot′is), *n.* an opening at the upper part of the windpipe, between the vocal cords. [< NL < Gk., ult. < *glotta* tongue]

Glouces·ter·shire (glos′tər·shir; glôs′-), *n.* county in SW England.

glove (gluv), *n.*, *v.*, **gloved**, **glov·ing.** —*n.* 1. a covering for the hand, usually with separate places for each of the four fingers and the thumb. 2. a boxing glove. 3. handle with gloves, treat gently. —*v.* 1. cover with a glove; provide with gloves. 2. serve as a glove for. [OE *glōf*] —**glove′less**, *adj.* —**glove′like′**, *adj.*

glov·er (gluv′ər), *n.* person who makes or sells gloves.

glow (glō), *n.* 1. shine from something that is red-hot or white-hot; similar shine. 2. brightness: *the glow of sunset.* 3. a warm feeling or color of the body: *the glow of health on his cheeks.* 4. an eager look on the face: *glow of interest or excitement.* —*v.* 1. shine as if red-hot or white-hot. 2. show a warm color; be red or bright. 3. be hot; burn. 4. be eager or animated. [OE *glōwan*] —**glow′ing**, *adj.* —**glow′ing·ly**, *adv.*

glow·er (glou′ər), *v.* 1. stare angrily; scowl. 2. *Scot.* gaze intently; stare. —*n.* an angry or sullen look. [? < obs. *glow*, *v.*, stare] —**glow′er·ing·ly**, *adv.*

glow·worm (glō′wėrm′), *n.* any insect larva or wormlike insect that glows in the dark.

gloze (glōz), *v.*, **glozed**, **gloz·ing.** 1. smooth over; explain away. 2. talk flatteringly. [< F *gloser* < OF *glose* GLOSS²]

glu·ci·num (glü·sī′nəm), **glu·cin·i·um** (-sin′i·əm), *n.* *Chem.* beryllium.

glu·cose (glü′kōs), *n.* 1. *Chem.* kind of sugar, $C_6H_{12}O_6$, occurring in fruits. 2. syrup made from starch.

glue (glü), *n., v.,* glued, glu·ing. —*n.* 1. substance used to stick things together, often made by boiling the hoofs, skins, and bones of animals in water. 2. any similar sticky substance. —*v.* 1. stick together with glue. 2. fasten tightly; attach firmly. [< OF *gluz* < LL *glutis*] —glue′like′, *adj.* —glu′er, *n.*

glue·y (glü′ĭ), *adj.,* glu·i·er, glu·i·est. 1. like glue; sticky. 2. smeared with glue.

glum (glum), *adj.,* glum·mer, glum·mest. gloomy; dismal; sullen. —glum′ly, *adv.* —glum′ness, *n.*

glut (glut), *v.,* glut·ted, glut·ting, *n.* —*v.* 1. fill full; feed or satisfy fully. 2. fill too full; supply too much for. —*n.* 1. a full supply; great quantity. 2. too great a supply. [< obs. *glut*, *n.,* GLUTTON < OF]

glu·ten (glü′tən), *n.* a tough, sticky substance that remains in flour when the starch is taken out. [< L, glue] —glu·te·nous (glü′tə·nəs), *adj.*

glu·ti·nous (glü′tə·nəs), *adj.* sticky. —glu′ti·nous·ly, *adv.* —glu′ti·nous·ness, glu·ti·nos·i·ty (glü′tə·nos′ə·tĭ), *n.*

glut·ton (glut′ən), *n.* 1. a greedy eater; person who eats too much. 2. person who never seems to have enough of something. 3. wolverine. [< OF < L *gluto*]

glut·ton·ous (glut′ən·əs), *adj.* greedy about food; having the habit of eating too much. —glut′ton·ous·ly, *adv.* —glut′ton·ous·ness, *n.*

glut·ton·y (glut′ən·ĭ), *n., pl.* -ton·ies. excess in eating.

glyc·er·in (glis′ər·ĭn), **glyc·er·ine** (-ĭn; -ēn), *n.* a colorless, syrupy, sweet liquid, $C_3H_8O_3$, obtained from fats and oils, used in ointments, lotions, antifreeze solutions, and explosives.

glyc·er·ol (glis′ər·ōl; -ol), *n.* glycerin.

gly·co·gen (glī′kə·jən), *n.* a starchlike substance in the liver and other animal tissues that is changed into sugar as needed.

gm., gram; grams.

G-man (jē′man′), *n., pl.* -men. *Am., Colloq.* a special agent of the U.S. Department of Justice; agent of the FBI.

Gmc., Germanic. Also, Ger.

gnarl (närl), *n.* knot in wood; hard, rough lump. —gnarled, gnarl′y, *adj.*

gnash (nash), *v.* 1. strike or grind (the teeth) together; grind together. 2. bite by gnashing the teeth. [var. of *gnast*, appar. < Scand. *gnastan* gnashing]

gnat (nat), *n.* 1. any of various small, two-winged insects or flies. Most gnats are bloodsucking and make bites that itch. 2. *Brit.* mosquito. [OE *gnœtt*] —gnat′like′, *adj.*

gnaw (nô), *v.,* gnawed, gnawed or gnawn (nôn), gnaw·ing. 1. bite at and wear away. 2. make by biting. 3. wear away; consume; corrode. 4. torment. [OE *gnagan*] —gnaw′er, *n.* —gnaw′ing, *adj.* —gnaw′ing·ly, *adv.*

gneiss (nīs), *n. Geol.* rock like granite, but with flatter crystals in more nearly parallel layers. [< G] —gneiss′ic, *adj.*

gnome (nōm), *n.* dwarf supposed to live in the earth and guard precious treasures. [< F < NL *gnomus*] —gnom′ish, *adj.*

gno·mic (nō′mik; nom′ik), *adj.* aphoristic; sententious. —gno′mi·cal·ly, *adv.*

gno·mon (nō′mon), *n.* rod, pointer, or triangular piece on a sundial, etc., that shows the time of day by the length of its shadow. [< Gk., indicator, < *gignoskein* know]

Gnos·tic (nos′tik), *n.* believer in Gnosticism. —*adj.* Also, Gnos′ti·cal. of Gnosticism or Gnostics. [< Gk. *gnostikos* of knowledge < *gignoskein* know]

Gnos·ti·cism (nos′tə·siz·əm), *n.* the mystical religious and philosophical doctrine of pre-Christian and early Christian times.

gnu (nü; nū), *n., pl.* gnus or (*esp. collectively*) gnu. an African antelope with an oxlike head and a long tail; wildebeest. [< Kaffir *nqu*]

go (gō), *v.,* went, gone, go·ing, *n., pl.* goes. —*v.* 1. move along: *go straight home.* 2. move away; leave (opposed to *come* or *arrive*). 3. be in motion; act; work; run: *the clock goes.* 4. get to be; become: *go mad.* 5. be habitually; be: *go hungry.* 6. proceed; advance: *go to New York.* 7. be current, as coin or notes. 8. be known: *go under an alias.* 9. put oneself: *don't go to any trouble for me.* 10. extend; reach: *his memory does not go back that far.* 11. pass: *time goes.* 12. be given: *first prize goes to you.* 13. be sold. 14. tend; lead: *this goes to show.* 15. turn out; have a certain result: *how did the game go?* 16. have its place; belong: *this book goes on the top shelf.* 17. harmonize: *these colors go well together.* 18. have certain words; be said. 19. explode. 20. refer; appeal: *go to court.* 21. *Am., Colloq. or Dial.* yield or produce (a certain amount). 22. *Am., Colloq. or Dial.* put up with: *I can't go tea.* 23. *Am., Colloq.* carry authority; be done without any question: *what he says goes.* 24. stop being; be given up, used up, or lost: *his eyesight is going.* 25. die: *his wife went first.* 26. break down; give way. 27. as people or things go, considering how others are. 28. **go about,** a. be busy at; work on. b. move from place to place. c. turn around; change direction. 29. **go around,** a. move from place to place. b. be enough to give some to all. 30. **go at,** attack. 31. **go back of,** *Am., Colloq.* investigate. 32. **go back on,** *Am., Colloq.* fail (one); break (one's word). 33. **go behind,** investigate the real or hidden reasons for. 34. **go by,** a. pass. b. be guided by; follow. c. be controlled by. d. be known by. 35. **go down,** a. descend; decline; sink. b. be defeated; lose. c. *Am.* decline in health. 36. **go for,** *Colloq.* a. try to get. b. favor; support. c. be taken or considered as. d. attack. 37. **go in for,** *Am., Colloq.* try to do; take part in; spend time and energy at. 38. **go into,** a. be contained in. b. investigate. 39. **go off,** a. leave; depart. b. be fired; explode. c. take place; happen. 40. **go on,** a. go ahead; go forward. b. manage. c. behave. 41. **go out,** a. stop being; end. b. go to parties, etc. c. give sympathy. d. go on strike. 42. **go over,** *Colloq.* a. look at carefully. b. do again. c. read again. d. succeed. 43. **go through,** a. go to the end of; do all of. b. undergo; experience. c. search. d. *Am.* be accepted or approved. 44. **go together,** *Am.* keep steady company as lovers. 45. **go under,** a. be overwhelmed or sunk. b. *Am.* be ruined; fail. c. *Am.* die. 46. **go up,** a. ascend. b. increase. 47. **go with,** a. accompany. b. be in harmony with. 48. **let go,** a. allow to escape. b. give up one's hold. c. give up. d. fail to keep in good condition. 49. **let oneself go,** a. give way to one's feelings or desires. b. fail to keep oneself in good condition. —*n.* 1. act of going. 2. *Colloq.* spirit; energy. 3. *Colloq.* state of affairs; way that things are. 4. *Colloq.* fashion; style. 5. *Colloq.* try; attempt; chance. 6. something successful. 7. **on the go,** *Colloq.* always moving or acting. [OE *gān*] —go′er, *n.*

Go·a (gō′ə), *n.* a former Portuguese colony in India, S of Bombay, now a part of India.

goad (gōd), *n.* 1. Also, gad. a sharp-pointed stick for driving cattle, etc. 2. anything that drives or urges one on. —*v.* drive on; urge on; act as a goad to. [OE *gād*] —goad′like′, *adj.*

go-a·head (gō′ə·hed′), *Am., Colloq.* —*n.* action of going forward; ambition; spirit; authority to proceed. —*adj.* disposed to push ahead.

goal (gōl), *n.* 1. place where a race ends. 2. place to which players try to advance a ball, etc., in certain games. 3. act of advancing a ball, etc., to this place. 4. score or points won by advancing a ball, etc., to this place. 5. goalkeeper. 6. thing wanted. [ME *gol*] —goal′less, *adj.*

goal·keep·er (gōl′kēp′ər), **goal·ie** (gōl′ĭ), *n.* player who tries to prevent the ball, etc., from reaching the goal in certain games.

goat (gōt), *n., pl.* goats or (*esp. collectively*) goat. 1. a cud-chewing mammal with hollow horns and long, usually straight hair, closely related to the sheep, but stronger, less timid, and more active. 2. *Am.* the Rocky Mountain goat. 3. Goat, *Astron.* Capricorn. 4. *U.S. Slang.*

āge, cāre, fär; ēqual, tėrm; īce; ōpen, ôrder; put, rūle, ūse; th, then; ə=a in about.

person made to suffer for the mistakes of others; scapegoat. **5. get one's goat,** *Am., Slang.* make a person angry or annoyed; tease him. [OE *gāt*] **—goat′like′,** *adj.*

goat·ee (gō·tē′), *n. Am.* a pointed beard on a man's chin.

goat·herd (gōt′hėrd′), *n.* person who tends goats.

goat·skin (gōt′skin′), *n.* **1.** skin of a goat. **2.** leather made from it.

goat·suck·er (gōt′suk′ər), *n.* bird with a flat head, wide mouth, and long wings that flies at night and feeds on flying insects.

Goatee

gob[1] (gob), *n. Am., Slang.* sailor in the navy.

gob[2] (gob), *n. Colloq.* lump; mass. [appar. < OF *gobe*]

gob·bet (gob′it), *n.* lump; mass. [< OF *gobet*, dim. of *gobe* gob[2]]

gob·ble[1] (gob′əl), *v.,* **–bled, –bling. 1.** eat fast and greedily; swallow quickly in big pieces. **2.** gobble up, *Am., Colloq.* seize upon eagerly. [< gob[2]] **—gob′bler,** *n.* **—Syn. 1.** gulp, bolt, devour.

gob·ble[2] (gob′əl), *v.,* **–bled, –bling,** *n.* **—v.** make the throaty sound that a turkey does. **—n.** this sound. [imit.]

gob·ble·dy·gook, gob·ble·de·gook (gob′-əl·di·gŭk′), *n. Am., Colloq.* speech or exposition that is obscured by excessive use of technical terminology, involved sentences, and big words.

gob·bler (gob′lər), *n.* a male turkey.

go-be·tween (gō′bi·twēn′), *n.* person who goes back and forth between others with messages, proposals, etc.; intermediary.

Go·bi (gō′bi), *n.* desert in E Asia.

gob·let (gob′lit), *n.* a drinking glass with a base and stem. [< OF *gobelet*, dim. of *gobel* cup]

gob·lin (gob′lən), *n.* a mischievous sprite or elf in the form of an ugly-looking dwarf. [< F *gobelin* < MHG *kobold* demon]

go-by (gō′bī′), *n. Colloq.* a going by; casting off; intentional neglect.

go·cart (gō′kärt′), *n.* **1.** a low seat on wheels to take a small child around on. **2.** a light carriage.

God (god), *n.* **1.** the maker and ruler of the world; Supreme Being. **2. god,** *n.* a being thought of as superior to nature and to human beings and considered worthy of worship. **b.** a male god. **c.** image of a god; idol. **d.** person or thing worshiped like a god; person intensely admired and respected. [OE]

god·child (god′chīld′), *n., pl.* **–chil·dren.** child for whom a grown-up person takes vows at its baptism.

god·daugh·ter (god′dô′tər), *n.* a female godchild.

god·dess (god′is), *n.* **1.** a female god. **2.** a very beautiful or charming woman. **—god′dess·hood,** *god′dess-ship,* *n.*

god·fa·ther (god′fä′tʜər), *n.* man who takes vows for a child when it is baptized.

God-giv·en (god′giv′ən), *adj.* **1.** given by God. **2.** very welcome and suitable.

God·head (god′hed), *n.* **1.** God. **2.** divine nature; divinity.

god·hood (god′hůd), *n.* divine character; divinity.

Go·di·va (gə·dī′və), *n.* in English legend, the wife of an English nobleman, who rode naked through the town of Coventry to win relief for the people from a burdensome tax.

god·less (god′lis), *adj.* **1.** not believing in God; not religious. **2.** wicked; evil. **—god′less·ly,** *adv.* **—god′less·ness,** *n.* **—Syn. 1.** ungodly, impious.

god·like (god′līk′), *adj.* **1.** like God or a god; divine. **2.** suitable for God or a god. **—god′like′-ness,** *n.*

god·ly (god′li), *adj.,* **–li·er, –li·est.** obeying God's laws; religious; pious; devout. **—god′li·ly,** *adv.* **—god′li·ness,** *n.*

god·moth·er (god′muʜ′ər), *n.* woman who takes vows for a child when it is baptized.

god·par·ent (god′pâr′ənt), *n.* godfather or godmother.

God's acre, a burial ground; cemetery.

god·send (god′send′), *n.* something unexpected and very welcome, as if sent from God.

god·ship (god′ship), *n.* character of a god; divinity.

god·son (god′sun′), *n.* a male godchild.

God·speed (god′spēd′), *n.* wish of success to a person starting on a journey.

Goeb·bels (gœb′əls), *n.* **Paul Joseph,** 1897–1945, propaganda leader of Nazi Germany.

Goe·ring (gœ′ring), *n.* **Hermann,** 1893–1946, German field marshal and a Nazi leader.

Goe·the (gœ′tə), *n.* **Johann Wolfgang von,** 1749–1832, German poet, prose writer, and dramatist.

go-get·ter (gō′get′ər), *n. Am., Slang.* an energetic person who gets what he seeks.

gog·gle (gog′əl), *n., v.,* **–gled, –gling,** *adj.* **—n.** Usually, **goggles.** large, close-fitting spectacles to protect the eyes from light, dust, etc. **—v. 1.** roll one's eyes; stare with bulging eyes. **2.** roll; bulge. **—adj.** rolling; bulging: *a frog has goggle eyes.* [ME *gogel(en)*] **—gog′gle-eyed′,** *adj.*

Gogh (gō; gôk), *n.* **Vincent van,** 1853–1890, Dutch painter.

go·ing (gō′ing), *n.* **1.** a going away. **2.** condition of the ground or road for walking, riding, etc. **—adj. 1.** moving; acting; working; running. **2.** that goes; that can or will go.

going concern, *U.S.* company, store, etc., that is doing business.

goi·ter, goi·tre (goi′tər), *n.* **1.** disease of the thyroid gland, that often causes a large swelling in the neck. **2.** the swelling. [< F *goitre,* ult. < L *guttur* throat]

gold (gōld), *n.* **1.** a shiny, bright-yellow, precious metal, used for making coins and jewelry. Gold is a chemical element. *Symbol:* Au. **2.** coins made of gold. **3.** money in large sums; wealth; riches. **4.** a bright, beautiful, or precious thing or material: *a heart of gold.* **—adj. 1.** made of gold. **2.** of or like gold. **3.** bright-yellow. [OE]

gold brick, *Am., Colloq.* anything that looks good at first, but turns out to be worthless.

gold-brick (gōld′brik′), *Am., Colloq.* **—v. 1.** pretend illness to avoid duties. **2.** swindle. **—n.** Also, **gold′-brick′er.** person, esp. in the army or navy, who avoids duty or shirks work.

Gold Coast, region in W Africa, former British colony, now largely included in Ghana.

gold digger, *Am., Slang.* woman who tries by various schemes to get money from men.

gold dust, gold in a fine powder.

gold·en (gōl′dən), *adj.* **1.** made or consisting of gold. **2.** containing or yielding gold. **3.** shining like gold; bright-yellow. **4.** very good; most excellent; extremely favorable, valuable, or important. **5.** very happy and prosperous; flourishing. **6.** pertaining to the fiftieth year or event in a series: *a golden wedding anniversary.* **—gold′en·ly,** *adv.* **—gold′en·ness,** *n.*

Golden Fleece, *Gk. Legend.* a fleece of gold taken from a ram. It was guarded by a dragon until Jason and the Argonauts carried it away.

Golden Gate, entrance to San Francisco Bay.

golden mean, avoidance of extremes; safe, sensible way of doing things; moderation.

gold·en·rod (gōl′dən·rod′), *n.* plant that blooms in the autumn and has many small yellow flowers on tall, branching stalks.

golden rule, rule of conduct set forth by Jesus: "All things whatsoever ye would that men should do to you, do ye even so to them." Matt. 7:12.

gold-filled (gōld′fild′), *adj.* made of cheap metal covered with a layer of gold.

gold·finch (gōld′finch′), *n.* **1.** a small American songbird. The male is yellow marked with black. **2.** a European songbird with yellow on its wings.

gold·fish (gōld′fish′), *n., pl.* **-fish·es** or (*esp. collectively*) **-fish.** a small, reddish-golden fish. Goldfish are often kept in garden pools or glass bowls.

American goldfinch (5 in. long)

gold leaf, gold beaten into very thin sheets.

gold rush, *Am.* a sudden rush of people to a place where gold has just been found.

gold·smith (gōld′smith′), *n.* man whose work is making articles of gold.

Gold·smith (gōld′smith′), *n.* Oliver, 1728–1774, British poet, novelist, and dramatist.

gold standard, *Am.* use of gold as the standard of value for the money of a country. A nation's unit of money value is declared by the government to be equal and exchangeable for a certain amount of gold.

golf (golf; gôlf), *n.* an outdoor game played with a small, hard ball and a set of long-handled clubs having wooden or iron heads. The player tries to hit the ball into a series of holes with as few strokes as possible. —*v.* play this game. —**golf′er,** *n.*

Gol·go·tha (gol′gə·thə), *n.* 1. place of Christ's crucifixion; Calvary. 2. place of burial.

Go·li·ath (gə·lī′əth), *n.* in the Bible, a giant whom David killed with a stone from a sling.

go·losh (gə·losh′), *n.* galosh.

Go·mor·rah, Go·mor·rha (gə·môr′ə; -mor′-), *n.* in the Bible, a wicked city destroyed, together with Sodom, by fire from heaven. Gen. 18 and 19.

Gom·pers (gom′pərz), *n.* Samuel, 1850–1924, American labor leader.

gon·ad (gon′ad; gō′nad), *n. Anat.* organ in which reproductive cells develop. Ovaries and testes are gonads. [< NL < Gk. *gone* seed] —**gon′ad·al, go·na·di·al** (gō·nā′di·əl), **go·nad·ic** (gō·nad′ik), *adj.*

gon·do·la (gon′də·lə), *n.* 1. a long, narrow boat with a high peak at each end, used on the canals of Venice. 2. *Am.* a large, flat-bottomed river boat with pointed ends. 3. car that hangs under a dirigible and holds the motors, passengers, etc. [< dial. Ital., < *gondolar* rock]

gondola car, *Am.* a freight car that has low sides and no top.

gon·do·lier (gon′də·lir′), *n.* man who rows or poles a gondola.

gone (gôn; gon), *adj.* 1. moved away; left. 2. lost: *a gone case.* 3. dead. 4. *Am.* used up. 5. failed; ruined. 6. weak; faint: *a gone feeling.* 7. far gone, much advanced; deeply involved. 8. gone on, *Colloq.* in love with. —*v.* pp. of go.

gon·er (gôn′ər; gon′-), *n. Colloq.* person or thing that is dead, ruined, past help, etc.

gon·fa·lon (gon′fə·lən), *n.* flag or banner hung from a crossbar instead of a pole, often having several streamers. [< Ital., ult. < OHG *gundfano,* lit., war banner]

gong (gông; gong), *n.* 1. a metal disk with a turned-up rim, that makes a loud noise when struck. 2. bell shaped like a shallow bowl or saucer. [< Malay] —**gong′like′,** *adj.*

gon·or·rhe·a, gon·or·rhoe·a (gon′ə·rē′ə), *n. Pathol.* a contagious venereal disease that causes inflammation of the genital and urinary organs. [< LL < Gk. < *gonos* seed + *rhoia* flow] —**gon′or·rhe′al, gon′or·rhoe′al,** *adj.*

goo·ber (gü′bər), *n. Am., S., Colloq.* peanut. [< Bantu]

good (gůd), *adj.,* **bet·ter, best,** *n., interj.* —*adj.* 1. having the right qualities; admirable; desirable: *a good book, a good game.* 2. as it ought to be; right; proper: *do what seems good to you.* 3. well-behaved: *a good boy.* 4. kind; friendly: *say a good word for me.* 5. doing right. 6. honorable; worthy: *my good friend.* 7. reliable; dependable: *good judgment.* 8. real; genuine. 9. agreeable; pleasant: *have a good time.* 10. beneficial; advantageous; useful: *drugs good for a fever.* 11. satisfying; full: *a good day.* 12. sufficient; thorough: *a good whipping.* 13. skillful; clever: *a good manager, be good at arithmetic.* 14. fairly great; more than a little: *a good while.* 15. as good as, almost the same as; almost; practically. 16. feel good, *Am., Colloq.* feel well or elated. 17. good for, a. able to do, live, or last. b. able to pay. c. worth. —*n.* 1. benefit; advantage; use: *work for the common good.* 2. that which is good: *find the good in people.* 3. a good

thing. 4. good people. 5. for good or for good and all, forever; finally; permanently. 6. make good, a. make up for; give or do in place of; pay for. b. carry out; fulfill. c. succeed in doing. d. *Am.* succeed. e. prove. —*interj.* that is good! [OE *gōd*] ➤ good, well. *Good* is an adjective, *well* is either an adjective or an adverb: *I feel good* and *I feel well* (adjectives) are both usual but have different connotations (*good* implying actual bodily sensation, *well* referring merely to a state, "not ill"). In uneducated usage *well* is rarely used, *good* taking its place (*he rowed good for he rowed well*).

Good Book, Bible.

good-by, good-bye (gůd′bī′), *interj., n., pl.* **-bys; -byes.** farewell. [contraction of *God be with ye*] ➤ good-by, good-bye. Both are in use—and the hyphen is dropping out in informal use: *goodby, goodbye.*

good English, language that is effective for a particular communication, that is appropriate to the subject and situation, to the listener or reader, and to the speaker or writer.

good-for-noth·ing (gůd′fər·nuth′ing), *adj.* worthless; useless. —*n.* person who is worthless or useless.

Good Friday, Friday before Easter, observed in commemoration of Christ's crucifixion.

good-heart·ed (gůd′här′tid), *adj.* kind and generous. —**good′-heart′ed·ly,** *adv.* —**good′-heart′ed·ness,** *n.*

Good Hope, Cape of, cape near the SW tip of Africa.

good humor, a cheerful, pleasant disposition or mood.

good-hu·mored (gůd′hū′mərd; -ū′-), *adj.* cheerful; pleasant. —**good′-hu′mored·ly,** *adv.* —**good′-hu′mored·ness,** *n.*

good·ish (gůd′ish), *adj.* 1. pretty good. 2. *Esp. Brit.* fairly great; considerable.

good-look·ing (gůd′lůk′ing), *adj.* having a pleasing appearance; handsome.

good·ly (gůd′li), *adj.,* **-li·er, -li·est.** 1. pleasant; excellent: *a goodly land.* 2. good-looking: *a goodly youth.* 3. considerable: *a goodly quantity.* —**good′li·ness,** *n.*

good·man (gůd′mən), *n., pl.* **-men.** *Archaic.* 1. master of a household; husband. 2. title for a man ranking below a gentleman: *Goodman Brown.*

good nature, a pleasant or kindly disposition; cheerfulness; agreeableness.

good-na·tured (gůd′nā′chərd), *adj.* pleasant; kindly; cheerful; agreeable. —**good′-na′tured·ly,** *adv.* —**good′-na′tured·ness,** *n.*

Good Neighbor Policy, a diplomatic policy, first sponsored by the United States in 1933, to encourage friendly relations and mutual defense among the nations of the Western Hemisphere.

good·ness (gůd′nis), *n.* 1. quality or state of being good. 2. excellence; virtue. 3. kindness; friendliness. 4. valuable quality; best part. —*interj.* exclamation of surprise.

good night, form of farewell said at night.

goods (gůdz), *n.pl.* 1. personal property; belongings. 2. thing or things for sale; wares. 3. *Am.* material for clothing; cloth. 4. *Am., Slang.* what is needed to do something. 5. *Brit.* freight.

Good Samaritan, person who is unselfish in helping others.

Good Shepherd, Jesus. John 10:11.

good-tem·pered (gůd′tem′pərd), *adj.* easy to get along with. —**good′-tem′pered·ly,** *adv.*

good·wife (gůd′wīf′), *n., pl.* **-wives.** *Archaic.* 1. mistress of a household. 2. title for a woman ranking below a lady: *Goodwife Brown.*

good will, 1. kindly or friendly feeling. 2. cheerful consent; willingness. 3. reputation and steady trade that a business has with its customers.

good·y¹ (gůd′i), *n., pl.* **good·ies,** *adj., interj. Colloq.* —*n.* something very good to eat; piece of candy or cake. —*adj.* making too much of being good; weakly good. —*interj.* exclamation of pleasure. [< *good*]

good·y² (gŭd'ĭ), *n.*, *pl.* **good·ies. 1.** an old woman of humble station. **2.** Goody, term of address for such a woman. [var. of *goodwife*]

goon (gün), *n. Am.*, *Slang.* **1.** thug hired to disrupt labor disputes. **2.** a stupid person. [from semihuman characters in a comic strip of the 1930's]

goose (güs), *n.*, *pl.* **geese** *for 1–4,* **goos·es** *for 5.* **1.** a wild or tame web-footed swimming bird, like a duck but larger and having a longer neck. **2.** a female goose. **3.** flesh of a goose used for food. **4.** a silly person. **5.** a tailor's smoothing iron that has a long, curved handle like a goose's neck. **6. the goose hangs high,** *Am.* all is well; prospects are good. [OE *gōs*] **—goose'like',** *adj.*

Goose Bay, air base in Labrador, built in World War II and subsequently important in transatlantic air service.

goose·ber·ry (güs'ber'ĭ; güz'–), *n.*, *pl.* **–ries. 1.** a small, sour berry somewhat like a currant but larger, used to make pies, tarts, jam, etc. **2.** the thorny bush that it grows on.

goose flesh or **pimples,** a rough condition of the skin caused by cold or fear.

goose·neck (güs'nek'), *n.* anything long and curved like a goose's neck, such as an iron hook, or a movable support for a lamp.

goose step, a marching step in which the leg is swung high with a straight, stiff knee.

goose-step (güs'step'), *v.*, **–stepped,** **–stepping.** march with a goose step.

G.O.P., *Am.* the "Grand Old Party" (the Republican Party in the United States).

go·pher (gō'fer), *n. Am.* **1.** *S., W.* a burrowing, ratlike rodent with large cheek pouches. **2.** ground squirrel. [? < early United States F, *gaufre,* lit., honeycomb; with ref. to burrowing]

Gopher
(total length ab. 9 in.)

Gor·di·an knot (gôr'dĭ·ən). cut the Gordian knot, find and use a quick, easy way out of a difficulty. [with ref. to the knot tied by *Gordius,* king of Phrygia, and cut by Alexander the Great]

gore¹ (gôr; gōr), *n.* blood that is shed; thick blood; clotted blood. [OE *gor* dirt, dung]

gore² (gôr; gōr), *v.*, **gored, gor·ing.** wound with a horn or tusk: *the savage bull gored the farmer to death.* [ME *gorre*(n)]

gore³ (gôr; gōr), *n.*, *v.*, **gored, gor·ing. —n.** a long, triangular piece of cloth put or made in a skirt, sail, etc., to give greater width or change the shape. **—v.** put or make a gore in. [OE *gāra* point < *gār* spear] **—gored,** *adj.* **—gor'ing,** *n.*

gorge (gôrj), *n.*, *v.*, **gorged, gorg·ing. —n. 1.** a deep, narrow valley, usually steep and rocky. **2.** mass stopping up a narrow passage: *an ice gorge blocked the river.* **3.** *Archaic.* throat; gullet. **—v. 1.** eat greedily until full; stuff with food. **2.** fill full; stuff. [< OF, ult. < LL *gurges* throat, jaws < L, abyss, whirlpool] **—gorg'er,** *n.*

gor·geous (gôr'jəs), *adj.* richly colored; splendid: *a gorgeous sunset.* [< OF *gorgias* fashionable] **—gor'geous·ly,** *adv.* **—gor'geous·ness,** *n.* **—Syn.** magnificent.

gor·get (gôr'jĭt), *n.* piece of armor for the throat. [< OF *gorgete,* dim. of *gorge* GORGE]

Gor·gon (gôr'gən), *n.* **1.** *Gk. Legend.* any of three horrible sisters who had snakes for hair and whose look turned the beholder to stone. **2.** gorgon, a very ugly or terrible woman. [< L < Gk., < *gorgos* terrible]

G, gorget.

Gor·gon·zo·la (gôr'gən·zō'lə), *n.* a strong, white Italian cheese that looks and tastes much like Roquefort cheese.

go·ril·la (gə·ril'ə), *n. Am.* **1.** a very large manlike ape of Africa. **2.** *Slang.* a strong and brutal man. [< NL < Gk. < an African lang.] **—go·ril'la·like',** *adj.*

Gor·ki (gôr'kĭ), *n.* **1.** Maxim (*A. M. Pyeshkov*), 1868–1936, Russian writer. **2.** city in C European Russia, on the Volga River.

gor·mand (gôr'mənd), *n.* gourmand.

gor·mand·ize (gôr'mən·dīz), *v.*, **–ized, –iz·ing.** stuff oneself with food; eat very greedily; gorge. [orig. n., < F *gourmandise* gluttony] **—gor'mand·iz'er,** *n.*

gorse (gôrs), *n. Esp. Brit.* furze. [OE *gorst*] **—gors'y,** *adj.*

gor·y (gôr'ĭ; gōr'ĭ), *adj.*, **gor·i·er, gor·i·est.** bloody. **—gor'i·ly,** *adv.* **—gor'i·ness,** *n.*

gosh (gosh), *interj.* exclamation or mild oath.

gos·hawk (gos'hôk'), *n.* a powerful, short-winged hawk, formerly much used in falconry. [OE *gōshafoc* < *gōs* goose + *hafoc* hawk]

Go·shen (gō'shən), *n.* **1.** *Bible.* a fertile part of Egypt where the Israelites were permitted to live. **2.** land of plenty and comfort.

gos·ling (goz'ling), *n.* a young goose.

gos·pel (gos'pəl), *n.* **1.** the teachings of Jesus and the Apostles. **2.** Usually, Gospel. any one of the first four books of the New Testament, by Matthew, Mark, Luke, and John. **3.** Often, Gospel. part of one of these books read during a religious service. **4.** *Colloq.* anything earnestly believed or taken as a guide for action. **5.** the absolute truth. **—adj. 1.** evangelical. **2.** of or pertaining to the gospel. [OE *gōdspel* good tidings (i.e., of the Nativity) < *gōd* good + *spel* spell²]

gos·sa·mer (gos'ə·mər), *n.* **1.** film or thread of cobweb. **2.** a very thin, light cloth. **3.** *Am.* a thin, light, waterproof cloth or coat. **4.** anything very light and thin. **—adj.** very light and thin; filmy. [ME *gossomer* goose summer, name for "Indian summer," the season for goose and cobwebs]

gos·sip (gos'ip), *n.*, *v.*, **–siped, –sip·ing. —n. 1.** idle talk, not always true, about other people and their affairs. **2.** person who gossips a good deal. **—v.** repeat what one knows, or the idle talk that one hears, about other people and their affairs. [OE *godsibb,* orig., godparent < *god* God + *sibb* relative] **—gos'sip·er,** *n.* **—gos'sip·ing,** *n.* **—gos'sip·ing·ly,** *adv.* **—gos'sip·y,** *adj.* **—Syn.** **1.** tattle, scandal.

gos·soon (go·sün'), *n.* **1.** boy. **2.** a male servant. [alter. of *garçon*]

got (got), *v.* pt. and pp. of get. ➤ Got is often redundant—and so is generally confined to colloquial usage—in expressions like *have you got a pencil?* and *I've got to study now. Have you a pencil?* and *I have to study now* mean just as much and sound more formal—but in free and easy speech the *got* adds a little emphasis, being more vigorous than *have.* Ordinarily, in writing, these constructions are confined to dialogue. See also gotten.

Gö·te·borg (yœ'tə·bôr'ĭ), **Goth·en·burg** (got'ən·bérg), *n.* seaport in SW Sweden.

Goth (goth), *n.* **1.** member of a Teutonic tribe that overran the Roman Empire in the third, fourth, and fifth centuries A.D. The Goths settled in S and E Europe. **2.** an uncivilized person; barbarian.

Goth·am (goth'əm; gō'thəm), *n. Am.* New York City.

Goth·ic (goth'ik), *n.* **1.** style of architecture using pointed arches and high, steep roofs, developed in W Europe during the Middle Ages from about 1150 to 1550. **2.** language of the Goths. **3.** *Am.* kind of type used in printing. **—adj. 1.** of Gothic architecture. **2.** of the Goths or their language. **3.** uncivilized; crude; barbarous. **4.** medieval. **—Goth'i·cal·ly,** *adv.*

Got·land (got'lənd), *n.* a Swedish island in the Baltic between Sweden and Latvia.

got·ten (got'ən), *v.* pp. of get. ➤ Gotten was brought to America by the colonists of the seventeenth century, when it was the usual English form, and has remained in general American usage ever since, while in England the form has given way to *got.* Today both forms are used by Americans as the past participle, the choice between them depending largely on the meaning: *I've gotten* = I've acquired, I've become. *I've got* = I have.

gouge (gouj), *n.*, *v.*, **gouged, goug·ing. —n. 1.** chisel with a curved blade. **2.** groove or hole made by gouging. **3.** *Am.*, *Colloq.* trick; cheat;

swindle. —v. 1. cut with a gouge. 2. dig out; force out. 3. Am., Colloq. trick; cheat. [< F < LL gulbia] —goug′er, n.

gou·lash (gū′läsh), n. stew made out of beef or veal and vegetables, usually highly seasoned. [< Hung. gulyás (hús) herdsman's (meat)]

Gou·nod (gū′nō), n. Charles François, 1818–1893, French composer.

gourd (gōrd; gôrd; gůrd), n. 1. the hard-shelled fruit of certain vines. 2. cup, bowl, bottle, rattle, etc., made from a dried shell of this fruit. 3. vine that gourds grow on. 4. any plant of the family to which cucumbers, pumpkins, and muskmelons belong. [< F < OF cohorde < L cucurbita] —gourd′like′, adj. —gourd-shaped (gōrd′-shåpt′; gōrd′-; gůrd′-), adj.

gour·mand (gůr′mənd), n. person who is fond of good eating. Also, gormand. [< F, gluttonous < gourmet gourmet]

gour·met (gůr′mā), n. person who is expert in judging and choosing fine foods, wines, etc.; epicure. [< F < OF groumet wine tester]

gout (gout), n. 1. a painful disease of the joints, often characterized by a painful swelling of the big toe. 2. drop; splash; clot. [< OF < L gutta a drop, in Med.L, gout]

goût (gū), n. French. taste.

gout·y (gout′i), adj., gout·i·er, gout·i·est. 1. diseased or swollen with gout. 2. of gout; caused by gout. 3. causing gout. 4. like gout. —gout′i·ly, adv. —gout′i·ness, n.

Gov., Governor.

gov., 1. government. 2. governor.

gov·ern (guv′ərn), v. 1. rule; control; manage. 2. exercise a directing or restraining influence over; determine: motives governing a person's decision. 3. hold back; restrain; check. 4. be a rule or law for: principles governing a case. 5. Gram. require (a word) to be in a certain case or mood; require (a certain case or mood). [< OF < L < Gk. kybernaein steer] —gov′ern·a·ble, adj. —Syn. 1. direct, conduct. 3. curb, bridle.

gov·ern·ance (guv′ər·nəns), n. rule; control.

gov·ern·ess (guv′ər·nis), n. woman who teaches children in a private house.

gov·ern·ment (guv′ərn·mənt; —ər-), n. 1. act or fact of governing; rule; control. 2. rule or authority over a country, state, district, etc.; direction of the affairs of state. 3. person or persons ruling a country, state, district, etc.; administration. 4. system of ruling: republican government. 5. country, state, district, etc., ruled. 6. Gram. the influence of one word in determining the case or mood of another. —gov·ern·men·tal (guv′ərn·men′təl; —ər-), adj. Am. —gov′ern·men′tal·ly, adv.

gov·er·nor (guv′ər·nər; guv′nər), n. 1. Am. official elected as the executive head of a State of the United States. 2. official appointed to govern a province, city, fort, etc. 3. Esp. Brit. person who manages or directs a club, society, institution, etc. 4. an automatic device that controls the supply of steam, gas, etc., and keeps a machine going at a certain speed. 5. Esp. Brit. Slang. one's father, guardian, or employer.

governor general, pl. governors general. governor who has subordinate or deputy governors under him. —gov′er·nor-gen′er·al·ship′, n.

gov·er·nor·ship (guv′ər·nər·ship′; guv′nər-), n. Am. position or term of office of governor.

govt., Govt., government.

gown (goun), n. 1. a woman's dress. 2. a loose outer garment worn to show position, profession, etc., as that of a judge. 3. nightgown or dressing gown. —v. put a gown on; dress in a gown. [< OF < LL gunna]

gowns·man (gounz′mən), n., pl. -men. person who wears a gown to show his position, profession, etc.; judge, lawyer, clergyman, or member of a university.

Go·ya (gō′yə), n. Francisco, 1746–1828, Spanish painter and etcher.

Gr., 1. Grecian. 2. Greece. 3. Also, Gk. Greek.

gr., 1. grain. 2. gram. 3. gross.

grab (grab), v., grabbed, grab·bing, n. —v. 1.

seize suddenly; snatch. 2. seize unscrupulously. —n. 1. a snatching; a sudden seizing. 2. that which is grabbed. 3. a mechanical device for firmly holding something that is to be lifted. [cf. MDu. grabben] —grab′ber, n.

grace (grās), n., v., graced, grac·ing. —n. 1. beauty of form, movement, or manner; pleasing or agreeable quality. 2. good will; favor. 3. mercy; pardon. 4. God's free and undeserved favor to and love for mankind. 5. the condition of being influenced and favored by God. 6. a short prayer of thanks before or after a meal. 7. favor shown by granting a delay. 8. allowance of time. 9. virtue; merit; excellence. 10. Usually, Grace. title used in speaking to or of a duke, duchess, or archbishop. 11. Music. grace note. 12. Grace, Class. Myth. one of the three sister goddesses controlling beauty and charm in people and in nature. —v. 1. give or add grace to; set off with grace. 2. do a favor or honor to. 3. Music. add grace notes to. [< F < L gratia < gratus pleasing] —Syn. n. 1. charm, ease, elegance. 2. kindness. —v. 1. adorn, decorate. 2. honor.

grace·ful (grās′fəl), adj. having or showing grace; beautiful in form, movement, or manner. —grace′ful·ly, adv. —grace′ful·ness, n.

grace·less (grās′lis), adj. 1. without grace. 2. not caring for what is right or proper. —grace′less·ly, adv. —grace′less·ness, n.

grace note, Music. note not essential to the harmony or melody, added for embellishment.

gra·cious (grā′shəs), adj. 1. pleasant; kindly; courteous. 2. pleasant, kindly, and courteous to people of lower social position. 3. merciful; kindly. —interj. exclamation of surprise. [< OF < L gratiosus] —gra′cious·ly, adv. —gra′cious·ness, gra·ci·os·i·ty (grā′shi·os′ə·ti), n.

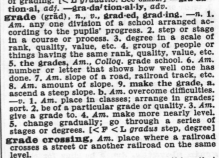
Grackle (1 ft. long)

grack·le (grak′əl), n. Am. kind of blackbird. [< L graculus jackdaw]

grad., graduate; graduated.

gra·da·tion (grā·dā′shən), n. 1. a change by steps or stages; gradual change. 2. Usually, gradations. step, stage, or degree in a series. 3. act or process of grading. [< L gradatio. See GRADE.] —gra·da′tion·al, adj. —gra·da′tion·al·ly, adv.

grade (grād), n., v., grad·ed, grad·ing. —n. 1. Am. any one division of a school arranged according to the pupils' progress. 2. step or stage in a course or process. 3. degree in a scale of rank, quality, value, etc. 4. group of people or things having the same rank, quality, value, etc. 5. the grades, Am., Colloq. grade school. 6. Am. number or letter that shows how well one has done. 7. Am. slope of a road, railroad track, etc. 8. Am. amount of slope. 9. make the grade, a. ascend a steep slope. b. Am. overcome difficulties. —v. 1. Am. place in classes; arrange in grades; sort. 2. be of a particular grade or quality. 3. Am. give a grade to. 4. Am. make more nearly level. 5. change gradually; go through a series of stages or degrees. [< F < L gradus step, degree]

grade crossing, Am. place where a railroad crosses a street or another railroad on the same level.

grad·er (grād′ər), n. 1. person or thing that grades. 2. Am. person who is in a certain grade at school.

grade school, graded school, Am. elementary school; grammar school.

gra·di·ent (grā′di·ənt), n. 1. rate at which a road, railroad track, etc., rises. 2. the sloping part of a road, etc. 3. rate at which temperature or pressure changes. 4. rate of change of any variable. —adj. 1. going up or down gradually. 2. moving by taking steps; walking. 3. adapted to walking. [< L gradiens walking. See GRADE.]

grad·u·al (graj′u·əl), adj. by degrees too small to be separately noticed; little by little. —grad′u·al·ly, adv. —grad′u·al·ness, n.

grad·u·ate (*v.* graj′ů·āt; *n., adj.* graj′ů·ĭt), *v.*, **-at·ed, -at·ing,** *n., adj.* —*v.* **1.** finish a course of study at a school, college, or university and receive a diploma or other document saying so. **2.** give a diploma to for finishing a course of study. **3.** mark with degrees for measuring. A thermometer is graduated. **4.** arrange (anything) in regular steps, stages, or degrees. **5.** change gradually. —*n.* **1.** person who has graduated. **2.** container marked with degrees for measuring. —*adj.* **1.** that is a graduate: *a graduate student.* **2.** of or for graduates. [< Med.L *graduatus.* See GRADE.] —**grad′u·a′tor,** *n.* ▶ **graduate.** The idiom *to be graduated from* an institution has generally gone out of use except in formal and somewhat archaic writing, replaced by *graduated from: He graduated from Yale in 1902.*

grad·u·a·tion (graj′ů·ā′shən), *n.* **1.** a graduating from a school, college, or university. **2.** graduating exercises. **3.** a marking with degrees for measuring. **4.** mark or set of marks to show degrees for measuring. **5.** arrangement in regular steps, stages, or degrees.

graft[1] (graft; gräft), *v.* **1.** insert (a shoot, bud, etc.) from one tree or plant into a slit in another so that it will grow there permanently. **2.** produce or improve (fruit, flower, etc.) by grafting. **3.** do grafting on. **4.** transfer (a piece of skin, bone, etc.) from one part of the body to another so that it will grow there permanently. —*n.* **1.** shoot, bud, etc., used in grafting. **2.** place on a tree or plant where the shoot, bud, etc., is grafted. **3.** tree or plant that has had a shoot, bud, etc., grafted on it. **4.** act of grafting. **5.** piece of skin, bone, etc., transferred in grafting. [earlier *graff* < OF < L < Gk. *grapheion* stylus < *graphein* write; from similarity of shape] —**graft′er,** *n.* —**graft′ing,** *n.*

graft[2] (graft; gräft), *Am.* —*n.* **1.** the taking of money dishonestly in connection with public business. **2.** method of getting money dishonestly. **3.** money dishonestly taken or obtained. —*v.* *Colloq.* make money dishonestly through one's job, esp. in political positions. —**graft′er,** *n.*

gra·ham (grā′əm), *adj. Am.* made from unsifted whole wheat or whole-wheat flour. [for S. *Graham,* reformer of dietetics]

Grail (grāl), *n.* the Holy Grail. [< OF < Med.L *gradale* plate, or < VL *cratale* < *crater* bowl < Gk.]

grain (grān), *n.* **1.** a single seed or seedlike fruit of wheat, oats, and similar cereal grasses. **2.** seeds or seedlike fruits of such plants in the mass. **3.** plants that these seeds or seedlike fruits grow on. **4.** a tiny, hard particle of sand, salt, sugar, etc. **5.** the smallest unit of weight. One pound avoirdupois equals 7000 grains; one pound troy equals 5760 grains. **6.** the smallest possible amount; tiniest bit: *grain of truth.* **7.** arrangement or direction of fibers in wood, layers in stone, etc. **8.** little lines and other markings in wood, marble, etc. **9.** the rough surface of leather. **10.** texture. **11.** natural character; disposition. —*v.* **1.** form into grains. **2.** paint in imitation of the grain in wood, marble, etc. **3.** roughen the surface of (leather). **4.** give a granular surface to. [< OF < L *granum* grain, seed] —**grained** (grānd), *adj.* —**grain′er,** *n.* —**grain′less,** *adj.* —**grain′y,** *adj.*

grain alcohol, ethyl alcohol, often made from grain.

grain elevator, *Am.* a building for storing grain.

gram, *esp. Brit.* **gramme** (gram), *n.* unit of weight in the metric system. Twenty-eight grams weigh about one ounce avoirdupois. [< F < LL < Gk. *gramma* small weight < *graphein* write]

—**gram,** *word element.* **1.** something written; message, as in *cablegram, telegram, monogram.* [< Gk. –*gramma* something written, writing < *graphein* write] **2.** grams; of a gram, as in *kilogram, milligram.* [< Gk., < *gramma* small weight, ult. < *graphein* write]

gram., grammar; grammatical.

gram·mar (gram′ər), *n.* **1.** scientific study and classification of the classes, forms, sounds, and uses of words of a particular language. **2.** systematic study comparing the forms and con-

structions of two or more languages. **3.** systematic study comparing present with past forms and usage. **4.** a treatise or book on one of these subjects. **5.** manner of speech or writing with reference to conformity to established usage. **6.** statements about the use of words. **7.** the elements of any subject: *grammar of painting.* [< OF < L < Gk. *grammatike* (*techne*) (art) of letters, ult. < *graphein* write]

gram·mar·i·an (grə·mãr′i·ən), *n.* expert in grammar.

grammar school, 1. *Am.* a public school in the United States having the grades between primary school and high school. **2.** *Brit.* a secondary school.

gram·mat·i·cal (grə·mat′ə·kəl), *adj.* **1.** according to correct use of words. **2.** of grammar. —**gram·mat′i·cal·ly,** *adv.* —**gram·mat′i·cal·ness,** *n.*

gram·mo·lec·u·lar (gram′mə·lek′yə·lər), *adj.* of or having to do with a gram molecule.

gram molecule, gram-molecular weight, *Chem.* amount of an element or compound that equals its molecular weight expressed in grams.

gram·o·phone (gram′ə·fōn), *n. Am.* **1.** phonograph. **2.** Gramophone, *Trademark.* type of sound-recording machine. [inversion of *phonogram* < Gk. *phone* speech + *gramma* a writing < *graphein* write]

gram·pus (gram′pəs), *n.* **1.** a large, fierce dolphin; killer whale. **2.** a small, toothed whale. [earlier *grapays* < OF < Med.L *crassus piscis* fat fish]

Grampus (15 to 20 ft. long)

Gra·na·da (grə·nä′də), *n.* city in S Spain.

gran·a·ry (gran′ə·ri; grān′–), *n., pl.* **–ries. 1.** place where grain is stored. **2.** region having much grain. [< L, < *granum* grain]

grand (grand), *adj.* **1.** large and of fine appearance: *grand mountains.* **2.** fine; noble; dignified; stately; splendid: *grand music, a grand old man.* **3.** highest or very high in rank; chief: *grand jury.* **4.** great; important; main: *the grand staircase.* **5.** complete; comprehensive: *grand total.* **6.** *Colloq.* very satisfactory. **7.** in names of relationship, in the second degree of ascent or descent: *grandmother, grandson.* —*n. Am., Slang.* a thousand dollars. [< OF < L *grandis* big] —**grand′ly,** *adv.* —**grand′ness,** *n.* —Syn. *adj.* **1.** great, lofty. **2.** majestic, imposing.

gran·dam (gran′dam), **gran·dame** (–dām), *n.* **1.** grandmother. **2.** old woman. [< AF *graund dame.* See GRAND, DAME.]

grand·aunt (grand′ant′; –änt′), *n.* greataunt.

Grand Bank, shoal off SE Newfoundland. It is important for cod fishing.

Grand Canyon, *Am.* a deep gorge of the Colorado River, in N Arizona.

grand·child (grand′chīld′), *n., pl.* **–chil·dren.** child of one's son or daughter.

Grand Cou·lee Dam (kü′lē), a large dam on the Columbia River, in E Washington.

grand·daugh·ter (grand′dô′tər), *n.* daughter of one's son or daughter.

grand duchess, 1. wife or widow of a grand duke. **2.** lady equal in rank to a grand duke. **3.** princess of the ruling house of Russia before it became a republic in 1917.

grand duchy, territory under the rule of a grand duke or grand duchess.

grand duke, 1. prince who ranks just below a king. **2.** prince of the ruling house of Russia before it became a republic in 1917.

gran·dee (gran·dē′), *n.* **1.** a Spanish or Portuguese nobleman of the highest rank. **2.** person of high rank or great importance. [< Sp., Pg. *grande.* See GRAND.]

gran·deur (gran′jər; –jůr), *n.* greatness; majesty; nobility; dignity; splendor.

grand·fa·ther (grand′fä′tƷər), *n.* **1.** father of one's father or mother. **2.** forefather. —**grand′fa′ther·ly,** *adj.*

gran·dil·o·quent (gran·dil′ə·kwənt), *adj.* using lofty or pompous words. [< L, < *grandis* grand + *loquens* speaking] —**gran·dil′o·quence**, *n.* —**gran·dil′o·quent·ly**, *adv.*

gran·di·ose (gran′di·ōs), *adj.* 1. grand in an imposing or impressive way. 2. grand in an affected or pompous way; trying to seem magnificent. [< F < Ital. *grandioso*] —**gran′di·ose·ly**, *adv.* —**gran·di·os·i·ty** (gran′di·os′ə·ti), *n.*

grand jury, jury chosen to investigate accusations and bring an indictment against the accused if there is enough evidence for trial before an ordinary jury.

Grand Lama, Dalai Lama.

grand·ma (grand′mä′; gram′mä′; gram′ə), *n. Colloq.* grandmother.

grand·moth·er (grand′muth′ər), *n.* 1. mother of one's father or mother. 2. ancestress. —**grand′moth′er·ly**, *adj.*

grand·neph·ew (grand′nef′ū; –nev′ū), *n.* son of one's nephew or niece.

grand·niece (grand′nēs′), *n.* daughter of one's nephew or niece.

Grand Old Party, *Am.* the Republican Party.

grand opera, a musical drama in which all the speeches are sung to the accompaniment of an orchestra.

grand·pa (grand′pä′; gram′pä′; gram′pə), *n. Colloq.* grandfather.

grand·par·ent (grand′pâr′ənt), *n.* grandfather or grandmother.

Grand Rapids, city in SW Michigan.

grand·sire (grand′sīr′), *n. Archaic.* 1. grandfather. 2. forefather. 3. an old man.

grand·son (grand′sun′), *n.* son of one's son or daughter.

grand·stand (grand′stand′), *n.* the principal seating place for people at an athletic field, race track, etc.

grand·un·cle (grand′ung′kəl), *n.* great-uncle.

grange (grānj), *n.* 1. farm. 2. *Esp. Brit.* farmhouse with barns, etc. 3. Grange, *Am.* a. organization of farmers for the improvement of their welfare. b. a local branch of this organization. [< OF *granica* < L *granum* grain]

grang·er (grān′jər), *n.* 1. farmer. 2. Granger, *Am.* member of the Grange.

gran·ite (gran′it), *n.* a hard igneous rock made of grains of other rocks, chiefly quartz and feldspar. [< Ital. *granito* grained, ult. < L *granum* grain] —**gran′ite·like′**, *adj.* —**gra·nit·ic** (grə·nit′ik), *adj.*

gran·ny, gran·nie (gran′i), *n., pl.* -**nies**. *Colloq.* 1. grandmother. 2. an old woman. 3. a fussy person.

granny knot, knot differing from a square knot in having the ends crossed the wrong way.

grant (grant; gränt), *v.* 1. give what is asked; allow. 2. admit to be true; accept without proof; concede. 3. bestow or confer (a right, etc.) by formal act; transfer or convey (the ownership of property), esp. by deed or writing. —*n.* 1. thing granted, such as a privilege, right, sum of money, or tract of land. 2. act of granting. 3. take for granted, assume to be true; use as proved or agreed to. [< OF *granter*, var. of *creanter*, promise, authorize, ult. < L *credens* trusting] —**grant′a·ble**, *adj.* —**gran·tee′**, *n.* —**grant′er,** *Law* **grant·or** (gran′tər; gran·tôr′; grän–), *n.* —**Syn.** *n.* 1. gift, present, allowance.

Grant (grant), *n.* Ulysses Simpson, 1822–1885, American general, 18th president of the United States, 1869–1877.

gran·u·lar (gran′yə·lər), *adj.* 1. consisting of or containing grains or granules. 2. resembling grains or granules. —**gran·u·lar·i·ty** (gran′yə·lar′ə·ti), *n.* —**gran′u·lar·ly**, *adv.*

granular eyelids, eyelids roughened inside by disease.

gran·u·late (gran′yə·lāt), *v.*, -**lat·ed**, -**lat·ing**. 1. form into grains or granules. 2. roughen on the surface. 3. become granular; develop granulations. —**gran′u·lat′ed**, *adj.* —**gran′u·lat′er, gran′u·la′tor,** *n.* —**gran′u·la′tion,** *n.* —**gran′u·la′tive**, *adj.*

gran·ule (gran′ūl), *n.* 1. a small grain. 2. a small bit or spot like a grain. [< LL *granulum*, dim. of *granum* grain]

grape (grāp), *n.* 1. a small, round fruit that grows in bunches on a vine. 2. grapevine. 3. a dark, purplish red. 4. grapeshot. [< OF, bunch of grapes, < *graper* pick grapes < *grape* hook < Gmc.] —**grape′less**, *adj.* —**grape′like′**, *adj.*

grape·fruit (grāp′früt′), *n.* a pale-yellow citrus fruit like an orange, but larger and sourer.

grape·shot (grāp′shot′), *n.* cluster of small iron balls used as a charge for cannon.

grape sugar, sugar formed in all green plants, but esp. in grapes; dextrose.

grape·vine (grāp′vīn′), *n.* 1. vine that bears grapes. 2. *Am., Colloq.* a. way by which reports are mysteriously spread. b. a baseless report.

graph (graf; gräf), *n.* 1. line or diagram showing how one quantity depends on or changes with another. 2. any line or lines representing a series of relations. —*v.* draw (such a line or diagram); draw a line representing some change, equation, or function. [for *graphic formula*. See GRAPHIC.]

-graph, *word element.* 1. make a picture, draw, or write, as in *photograph*. 2. machine that makes a picture, draws, or writes, as in *seismograph*. 3. drawn or written, as in *autograph*. 4. something drawn or written, as in *lithograph*. [< Gk. *graphein* write]

graph·ic (graf′ik), **graph·i·cal** (–ə·kəl), *adj.* 1. lifelike; vivid. 2. of or about diagrams and their use. 3. shown by a graph. 4. of or about drawing, painting, engraving, or etching: *the graphic arts.* 5. of or used in handwriting: *graphic symbols.* 6. written; inscribed. [< L < Gk., < *graphein* write] —**graph′i·cal·ly, graph′ic·ly**, *adv.* —**graph′i·cal·ness**, *n.*

graph·ite (graf′īt), *n.* a soft, black form of carbon with a metallic luster, used for lead in pencils and for lubricating machinery. [< G *graphit* < Gk. *graphein* write] —**gra·phit·ic** (grə·fit′ik), *adj.*

grap·nel (grap′nəl), *n.* 1. instrument with one or more hooks for seizing and holding. 2. a small anchor with three or more hooks. [< OF *grapin* hook, dim. of *grape* hook]

grap·ple (grap′əl), *v.*, -**pled**, -**pling**, *n.* —*v.* 1. seize and hold fast; grip or hold firmly. 2. struggle; fight. 3. use a grapnel; search for with a grapnel. [< n.] —*n.* 1. a seizing and holding fast; firm grip or hold. 2. grapnel. [< OF *grapil* hook] —**grap′pler,** *n.* —**Syn.** *v.* 1. grasp, clinch. 2. wrestle, contend.

grappling iron, grapnel.

grasp (grasp; gräsp), *v.* 1. seize and hold fast by closing the fingers around. 2. understand. 3. grasp at, a. try to take hold of. b. accept eagerly. —*n.* 1. a seizing and holding tightly; clasp of the hand. 2. power of seizing and holding. 3. control; possession. 4. understanding. [ME *graspe(n)*; akin to GROPE] —**grasp′a·ble**, *adj.* —**grasp′er,** *n.* —**Syn.** *v.* 1. grip, clutch, grab, snatch. 2. comprehend.

grasp·ing (gras′ping; gräs′–), *adj.* 1. eager to get all that one can; greedy. 2. that grasps. —**grasp′ing·ly**, *adv.* —**grasp′ing·ness**, *n.*

grass (gras; gräs), *n.* 1. any of various plants that cover fields, lawns, and pastures, and are eaten by horses, cows, and sheep. 2. such plants collectively. 3. land covered with grass; pasture. 4. plant that has jointed stems and long, narrow leaves. Wheat, corn, sugar cane, and bamboo are grasses. —*v.* 1. cover with grass. 2. feed on growing grass; graze. 3. lay on grass to bleach. [OE *græs*; akin to GREEN, GROW] —**grass′less**, *adj.* —**grass′like′**, *adj.*

grass·hop·per (gras′hop′ər; gräs′–), *n.* 1. insect with strong legs and wings for jumping. 2. *Mil.* a small airplane used for scouting and for directing fire from artillery units.

Grasshopper
(2 to 3 in. long)

grass·land (gras′land′; gräs′–), *n.* land with grass on it, used for pasture.

grass roots, the ordinary citizens of a region or State taken all together: *Senator Tompkins is sure he will get support from the grass roots.*

grass widow, woman divorced or separated from her husband.

grass·y (gras′ĭ; gräs′ĭ), *adj.,* **grass·i·er, grass·i·est.** 1. covered with grass. 2. of or like grass. **—grass′i·ness,** *n.*

grate¹ (grāt), *n., v.,* **grat·ed, grat·ing. —n.** 1. framework of iron bars to hold a fire. 2. framework of bars over a window or opening; grating. —*v.* furnish with a grate or grating. [< Med.L < Ital. < LL *cratis,* L, hurdle] **—grate′less,** *adj.* **—grate′like′,** *adj.*

grate² (grāt), *v.,* **grat·ed, grat·ing.** 1. make (a grinding sound); sound harshly. 2. rub with a harsh sound: *the door grated on its old, rusty hinges.* 3. have an annoying or unpleasant effect: *his rude manners grate on me.* 4. wear down or grind off in small pieces: *grate cheese.* [< OF *grater* < Gmc.] **—grat′er,** *n.*

grate·ful (grāt′fəl), *adj.* 1. feeling gratitude; thankful. 2. pleasing; welcome. [< obs. *grate* agreeable (< L *gratus*) + *full*] **—grate′ful·ly,** *adv.* **—grate′ful·ness,** *n.*

grat·i·fy (grat′ə·fī), *v.,* **-fied, -fy·ing.** 1. give pleasure or satisfaction to; please. 2. satisfy; indulge. [< F < L, *gratus* pleasing + *facere* make, do] **—grat′i·fi·ca′tion,** *n.* **—grat′i·fi′er,** *n.* **—grat′i·fy′ing·ly,** *adv.* **—Syn.** 1. delight.

grat·ing¹ (grāt′ing), *n.* framework of bars over a window or opening.

grat·ing² (grāt′ing), *adj.* harsh or unpleasant. **—grat′ing·ly,** *adv.*

grat·is (grat′is; grā′tis), *adv., adj.* free of charge. [< L, ult. < *gratia* favor]

grat·i·tude (grat′ə·tūd; -tūd), *n.* kindly feeling because of a favor received; thankfulness. [< LL, < *gratus* thankful]

gra·tu·i·tous (grə·tū′ə·təs; -tū′-), *adj.* 1. freely given or obtained; free. 2. without reason or cause. **—gra·tu′i·tous·ly,** *adv.* **—gra·tu′i·tous·ness,** *n.* **—Syn.** 2. unwarranted.

gra·tu·i·ty (grə·tū′ə·tĭ; -tū′-), *n., pl.* **-ties.** 1. present of money in return for service; tip. 2. present; gift. [< Med.L, gift, appar. < L *gratuitus* free]

gra·va·men (grə·vā′mən), *n., pl.* **-vam·i·na** (-vam′ə·nə). 1. grievance. 2. part of an accusation that weighs most heavily against the accused. [< L, ult. < *gravis* heavy]

grave¹ (grāv), *n.* 1. hole dug in the ground where a dead body is to be buried. 2. mound or monument over it. 3. any place that becomes the receptacle of what is dead: *a watery grave.* [OE *græf.* See GRAVE³.]

grave² (grāv), *adj., v.,* **grav·er, grav·est,** *n.* **—adj.** 1. important; weighty; momentous. 2. serious; threatening. 3. dignified; sober; solemn. 4. somber. 5. *Phonet.* a. low in pitch; not acute. b. having a particular accent (ˋ) that may indicate pitch, quality of sound (as in French *père*), or syllabic value (as in *belovèd*). **—n.** the grave accent. [< F < L *gravis* serious] **—grave′ly,** *adv.* **—grave′ness,** *n.* **—Syn.** *adj.* 3. staid, sedate. **—Ant.** *adj.* 1. unimportant, trivial. 3. lively.

grave³ (grāv), *v.,* **graved, graved** or **grav·en, grav·ing.** 1. engrave; carve. 2. impress deeply; fix firmly. [OE *grafan*] **—grav′er,** *n.*

grave⁴ (grāv), *v.,* **graved, grav·ing.** clean (a ship's bottom) and cover with tar.

grave-clothes (grāv′klōz′; -klōᵗʜz′), *n.pl.* clothes in which a dead body is buried.

grav·el (grav′əl), *n., v.,* **-eled, -el·ing;** *esp.* *Brit.* **-elled, -el·ling. —n.** 1. pebbles and rock fragments coarser than sand. 2. *Pathol.* a. small, hard substances formed in the bladder and kidneys. b. disease causing them. **—v.** 1. lay or cover with gravel. 2. puzzle; perplex. [< OF *gravele,* dim. of *grave* sand, seashore < Celtic] **—grav′el·ly,** *adj.*

grav·en (grāv′ən), *adj.* 1. engraved; carved; sculptured. 2. deeply impressed; firmly fixed. **—v.** pp. of GRAVE³.

graven image, 1. statue. 2. idol.

grave-stone (grāv′stōn′), *n.* stone that marks a grave.

grave·yard (grāv′yärd′), *n.* place for burying the dead; cemetery; burial ground.

graveyard shift, *Am., Colloq.* working hours between midnight and the morning shift.

grav·i·tate (grav′ə·tāt), *v.,* **-tat·ed, -tat·ing.** 1. move or tend to move by gravitation. 2. settle down; sink. 3. tend to go; be strongly attracted. [< NL, ult. < L *gravis* heavy]

grav·i·ta·tion (grav′ə·tā′shən), *n.* 1. *Physics.* a. force that attracts bodies toward one another. b. a moving or tendency to move caused by this force. 2. a natural tendency toward some point or object of influence: *gravitation of population to the cities.* **—grav′i·ta′tion·al,** *adj.* **—grav′i·ta′tion·al·ly,** *adv.*

grav·i·ty (grav′ə·tĭ), *n., pl.* **-ties.** 1. the natural force that causes objects to move or tend to move toward the center of the earth. Gravity causes objects to have weight. 2. the natural force that makes objects move or tend to move toward each other; gravitation. 3. heaviness; weight. 4. seriousness; solemnity; earnestness. 5. serious or critical character; importance. 6. lowness of pitch. [< L, < *gravis* heavy]

gra·vure (grə·vyûr′; grā′vyər), *n.* 1. photogravure. 2. plate or print produced by photogravure. [< F, < *graver* engrave < Gmc.]

gra·vy (grā′vĭ), *n., pl.* **-vies.** 1. juice that comes out of meat in cooking. 2. sauce for meat, potatoes, etc., made from this juice. [ME *grave,* a mistaken writing of OF *grané* properly grained, seasoned, ult. < L *granum* grain]

gray (grā), *n.* 1. color made by mixing black and white. 2. gray cloth or clothing. 3. person dressed in gray. **—adj.** 1. having a color between black and white. 2. having gray hair. 3. old; ancient. 4. dark; gloomy; dismal. **—v.** make or become gray. Also, *esp. Brit.* **grey.** [OE *grǣg*] **—gray′ly,** *adv.* **—gray′ness,** *n.*

Gray (grā), *n.* Thomas, 1716–1771, English poet.

gray·beard (grā′bird′), *n.* old man. Also, *esp. Brit.* **greybeard.**

gray·hound (grā′hound′), *n.* greyhound.

gray·ish (grā′ish), *adj.* somewhat gray. Also, *esp. Brit.* **greyish.**

gray·lag (grā′lag′), *n.* a wild, gray goose that is common in Europe. Also, *esp. Brit.* **greylag.** [< *gray* + *lag;* because these birds migrate south at a very late date]

gray·ling (grā′ling), *n.* a fresh-water fish somewhat like a trout.

gray market, the buying and selling of products at prices considered exorbitant.

gray mar·ket·eer (mär′kə·tir′), one who deals in the gray market.

gray matter, 1. *Anat.* grayish tissue in the brain and spinal cord that contains nerve cells and some nerve fibers. 2. *Colloq.* intelligence; brains.

graze¹ (grāz), *v.,* **grazed, graz·ing.** 1. feed on growing grass. 2. put (cattle, sheep, etc.) to feed on growing grass or a pasture. 3. tend or look after (cattle, sheep, etc.) while they are grazing. [OE *grasian* < *græs* grass] **—graz′er,** *n.*

graze² (grāz), *v.,* **grazed, graz·ing,** *n.* **—v.** 1. touch lightly in passing; rub lightly (against). 2. scrape the skin from. **—n.** 1. a grazing. 2. a slight wound made by grazing. **—graz′ing·ly,** *adv.*

graz·ing (grāz′ing), *n.* growing grass that cattle, sheep, etc., feed on; pasture.

grease (*n.* grēs; *v.* grēs, grēz), *n., v.,* **greased, greas·ing. —n.** 1. soft animal fat. 2. any thick, oily substance. **—v.** 1. smear with grease; put grease on. 2. cause to run smoothly by greasing. 3. *Slang.* give money as a bribe or tip. [< OF, ult. < L *crassus* fat] **—grease′less,** *adj.* **—greas′er,** *n.*

grease·wood (grēs′wŭd′), *n. Am.* a stiff, prickly shrub with narrow leaves, growing in alkaline regions in the western United States.

greas·y (grēs′ĭ; grēz′ĭ), *adj.,* **greas·i·er, greas·i·est.** 1. smeared with grease; having grease on it. 2. containing much grease. 3. like grease; smooth; slippery. **—greas′i·ly,** *adv.* **—greas′i·ness,** *n.*

great (grāt), *adj.* 1. big; large: *a great house,*

a great crowd. 2. more than usual; much: *great ignorance.* 3. important; remarkable; famous: *a great composer.* 4. most important; main; chief: *the great seal.* 5. noble; generous. 6. much in use; favorite: *that is a great habit of his.* 7. very much of a: *a great talker.* 8. *Am., Colloq.* very good; fine: *we had a great time at the party.* 9. of the next generation before or after. 10. *Archaic.* pregnant. [OE *grēat*] —**great′ly,** *adv.* —**great′ness,** *n.* —Syn. 1. immense, enormous. 3. renowned, eminent, distinguished. 5. magnanimous. 8. first-rate, excellent. —Ant. 1. small. 3. insignificant, obscure.

great-aunt (grāt′ant′; -änt′), *n.* aunt of one's father or mother; grandaunt.

Great Barrier Reef, reef in the S Pacific, off NE Australia.

Great Bear, *Astron.* the constellation Ursa Major.

Great Britain, England, Scotland, and Wales. It is the largest island of Europe.

great circle, any circle on the surface of a sphere having its plane passing through the center of the sphere.

great-coat (grāt′kōt′), *n. Esp. Brit.* a heavy overcoat.

Great Dane, one of a breed of large, powerful, short-haired dogs.

Great Divide, *Am.* the Rocky Mountains of N America.

Greater Antilles, Cuba, Haiti, Puerto Rico, and Jamaica, the largest islands in the West Indies.

great-heart-ed (grāt′här′tid), *adj.* 1. noble; generous. 2. brave; fearless. —**great′-heart′ed-ness,** *n.*

Great Lakes, *Am.* series of lakes between the United States and Canada; Lakes Ontario, Erie, Huron, Michigan, and Superior.

Great Plains, *Am.* a semiarid region just east of the Rocky Mountains in the United States and SW Canada.

great seal, the most important seal of a country or state, stamped on official documents as proof of approval by the government.

Great Slave Lake, lake in Northwest Territories, in NW Canada.

Great Smoky Mountains, or **Great Smokies,** part of the Appalachian Mountains in Tennessee and North Carolina.

great-un-cle (grāt′ung′kəl), *n.* uncle of one's father or mother; granduncle.

Great White Way, *Am.* brightly lighted theater district along Broadway, a street in New York City.

greave (grēv), *n.* armor for the leg below the knee. [< OF]

grebe (grēb), *n.* a diving bird like a loon, having feet not completely webbed and a pointed bill. [< F]

Gre-cian (grē′shən), *adj., n.* Greek.

Gre-co - Ro-man (grē′kō-rō′mən), *adj.* Greek and Roman.

Grebe (ab. 19 in. long)

Greece (grēs), *n.* country in S Europe, on the Mediterranean Sea.

greed (grēd), *n.* extreme or excessive desire, esp. for money. [OE *grǣd*] —**greed′less,** *adj.* —Syn. avidity, avarice, cupidity, covetousness.

greed-y (grēd′i), *adj.*, **greed-i-er, greed-i-est.** 1. wanting to get more than one's share; having a very great desire to possess something. 2. wanting to eat or drink a great deal in a hurry; piggish. [OE *grǣdig*] —**greed′i-ly,** *adv.* —**greed′i-ness,** *n.*

Greek (grēk), *adj.* of Greece, its people, or their language. —*n.* 1. native or inhabitant of Greece. 2. language of Greece. Ancient or classical Greek was the language until about 200 A.D.; modern Greek is the language since about 1500.

Greek Orthodox Church, 1. Christian church of the countries in communion or doctrinal agreement with the patriarch of Constantinople. 2. Also, **Greek Church.** part of this church that constitutes the established church in Greece.

Gree-ley (grē′li), *n.* Horace, 1811-1872, American journalist and politician.

green (grēn), *n.* 1. color of most growing plants, grass, and leaves. 2. green coloring matter, dye, paint, etc. 3. grassy land or a plot of grassy ground. 4. *Golf.* a putting green. 5. a grassy plot, as a town common. 6. **greens,** a. green leaves and branches used for decoration. b. leaves and stems of plants used for food. —*adj.* 1. having the color green. 2. covered with growing plants, grass, leaves, etc.: *green fields.* 3. characterized by growing grass, etc.: *a green Christmas.* 4. not dried, cured, seasoned, or otherwise prepared for use. 5. not ripe; not fully grown. 6. not trained or experienced; not mature in age, judgment, etc. 7. easily fooled; easy to trick or cheat. 8. having a pale, sickly color because of fear, jealousy, or sickness. —*v.* make or become green. [OE *grēne*; akin to GRASS, GROW] —**green′ish,** *adj.* —**green′ness,** *n.* —Syn. *adj.* 5. immature, unripe. 6. inexperienced, untrained, unsophisticated, callow. 7. gullible, ignorant. —Ant. *adj.* 2. sear, parched. 6. experienced. 7. clever, shrewd, astute.

green-back (grēn′bak′), *n. Am.* paper money having the back printed in green.

green-bri-er (grēn′brī′ər), *n.* a climbing smilax with prickly stems and green leaves.

green corn, *Am.* fresh, tender corn.

green-er-y (grēn′ər-i), *n., pl.* **-er-ies.** 1. green plants, grass, or leaves; verdure. 2. place where green plants are grown or kept.

green-eyed (grēn′īd′), *adj.* 1. having green eyes. 2. jealous.

green-gage (grēn′gāj′), *n.* a large plum with a light-green skin and pulp. [after Sir Wm. *Gage,* who introduced it into England]

green-gro-cer (grēn′grō′sər), *n. Brit.* person who sells fresh vegetables and fruit. —**green′gro′cer-y,** *n.*

green-horn (grēn′hôrn′), *n. Colloq.* person without experience. [with ref. to the green horns of young oxen]

green-house (grēn′hous′), *n.* a building with a glass roof and glass sides kept warm for growing plants; hothouse.

green-ing (grēn′ing), *n.* apple with a yellowish-green skin when ripe.

Green-land (grēn′lənd), *n.* the largest island in the world, belonging to Denmark. It lies northeast of North America.

green light, *Am., Colloq.* official permission to proceed on a particular task or undertaking.

Green Mountains, part of the Appalachian Mountains extending through Vermont.

green-room (grēn′rüm′; -rüm′), *n.* room in old theaters for the use of actors and actresses when they are not on the stage.

green-sward (grēn′swôrd′), *n.* green grass.

green tea, tea whose leaves have been withered by steam.

green thumb, a remarkable ability to grow flowers, vegetables, etc., esp. as a hobby.

Green-wich (grin′ij; gren′-; -ich), *n.* borough in SE London, England. Longitude is measured east and west of Greenwich.

Green-wich Village (gren′ich), section of New York City, famous as a district where artists and writers live.

green-wood (grēn′wúd′), *n.* forest in spring and summer when the trees are green.

greet (grēt), *v.* 1. speak or write to in a friendly, polite way; address in welcome. 2. address; salute. 3. interchange greetings. 4. receive: *his speech was greeted with cheers.* 5. present itself to; meet. [OE *grētan*] —**greet′er,** *n.* —Syn. 1. welcome. 2. hail, accost.

greet-ing (grēt′ing), *n.* 1. act or words of a person who greets another; welcome. 2. **greetings,** friendly wishes, as on a special occasion.

gre-gar-i-ous (grə-gãr′i-əs), *adj.* 1. living in

flocks, herds, or other groups. 2. fond of being with others. 3. of or having to do with a flock or crowd. 4. *Bot.* growing in open clusters. [< L *gregarius* < *grex* flock] —**gre·gar'i·ous·ly,** *adv.* —**gre·gar'i·ous·ness,** *n.*

Gre·go·ri·an calendar (grə·gô'ri·ən; -gō'-), calendar now in use in the United States and most other countries, introduced by Pope Gregory XIII in 1582. It is a correction of the calendar of Julius Caesar.

Gregorian chant, vocal music having free rhythm and a limited scale, used in the Roman Catholic Church.

Greg·o·ry I (greg'ə·ri), Saint, 540?–604 A.D., pope 590–604 A.D.

Gregory XIII, 1502–1585, pope 1572–1585.

grem·lin (grem'lən), *n.* an imaginary elf that troubles the pilots of airplanes.

gre·nade (grə·nād'), *n.* 1. *Mil.* a small bomb, usually hurled by hand. 2. a round, glass bottle filled with chemicals that scatter as the glass breaks. Fire grenades are thrown on fires to put them out. [< F < Sp. *granada* pomegranate (lit., having grains) < L *granatus.* See GARNET.]

gren·a·dier (gren'ə·dir'), *n.* 1. originally, a soldier who threw grenades. 2. later, a very tall foot soldier. 3. now, a member of a special regiment of guards in the British army. [< F, < *grenade* GRENADE] —**gren·a·dier'i·al,** *adj.* —**gren·a·dier'ly,** *adv.*

gren·a·dine¹ (gren'ə·dēn; gren'ə·dēn'), *n.* thin, openwork fabric used for women's dresses. [< F, ? named for *Granada,* Spain]

gren·a·dine² (gren'ə·dēn'; gren'ə·dēn), *n.* syrup made from pomegranate or currant juice. [< F *grenade.* See GRENADE.]

Gret·na Green (gret'nə), village in S Scotland where many runaway couples from England were married.

grew (grü), *v.* pt. of *grow.*

grew·some (grü'səm), *adj.* gruesome. —**grew'-some·ness,** *n.*

grey (grā), *n., adj., v. Esp. Brit.* gray. —**grey'-ly,** *adv.* —**grey'ness,** *n.*

grey·beard (grā'bird'), *n. Esp. Brit.* gray-beard.

grey·hound (grā'hound'), *n.* one of a breed of tall, slender, swift dogs. Also, **grayhound.** [prob. < Scand. *greyhundr* < *grey* bitch + *hundr* dog]

grey·ish (grā'ish), *adj. Esp. Brit.* grayish.

grey·lag (grā'lag'), *n. Esp. Brit.* graylag.

grid (grid), *n.* 1. framework of parallel iron bars; grating; gridiron. 2. the lead plate in a storage battery. 3. *Radio.* electrode in a vacuum tube that controls the flow of current between the filament and the plate. [short for *gridiron*]

grid·dle (grid'əl), *n., v.,* –**dled,** –**dling.** —*n.* a heavy, flat plate of metal or soapstone, used for cooking griddlecakes, etc. —*v.* cook by means of a griddle. [< unrecorded OF *gredil*; cf. OF *grediller* singe. See GRILL.]

grid·dle·cake (grid'əl·kāk'), *n.* thin, flat cake of batter cooked on a griddle; pancake; flapjack.

grid·i·ron (grid'ī'ərn), *n.* 1. a cooking utensil consisting of a framework of parallel iron bars or wires, usually with a handle. 2. any framework or network that looks like a gridiron. 3. *Am.* a football field. [ME *gredire* GRIDDLE; final element assimilated to *iron*]

grid leak, *Radio.* a very high resistance placed in a vacuum tube to prevent the accumulation of electrons on the grid.

grief (grēf), *n.* 1. deep sadness caused by trouble or loss; heavy sorrow. 2. come to grief, have trouble; fail. 3. cause of sadness or sorrow. [< OF, < *grever* GRIEVE] —**grief'less,** *adj.* —**Syn.** 1. anguish, heartache, distress, melancholy.

Grieg (grēg), *n.* Edvard, 1843–1907, Norwegian musical composer.

griev·ance (grēv'əns), *n.* a real or imagined wrong; reason for being angry or annoyed; cause for complaint. —**Syn.** injustice, injury.

grieve (grēv), *v.,* **grieved, griev·ing.** 1. feel grief; be very sad. 2. cause to feel grief; make very sad; afflict. [< OF *grever,* ult. < L *gravis* heavy] —**griev'er,** *n.* —**griev'ing·ly,** *adv.*

griev·ous (grēv'əs), *adj.* 1. hard to bear; causing great pain or suffering. 2. flagrant; atrocious. 3. causing grief. 4. full of grief; showing grief: *a grievous cry.* —**griev'ous·ly,** *adv.* —**griev'ous·ness,** *n.* —**Syn.** 1. distressing, oppressive, severe.

grif·fin, grif·fon (grif'ən), *n. Gk. Myth.* creature with the head and wings of an eagle, and the body of a lion. Also, **gryphon.** [< OF *grifon* < L *gryphus,* var. of *gryps* < Gk.]

grig (grig), *n. Dial.* 1. a small or young eel. 2. a cricket. 3. a grasshopper.

grill (gril), *n.* 1. a cooking utensil consisting of a framework of parallel iron bars for broiling meat, fish, etc.; gridiron. 2. dish of broiled meat, fish, etc. 3. restaurant or dining room that specializes in serving broiled meat and fish. —*v.* 1. broil. 2. torture with heat. 3. *Am.* question severely and persistently: *the detectives grilled the prisoner until he finally confessed.* [< F *gril,* ult. < LL *cratis* grate < L *cratis,* hurdle] —**grill'er,** *n.*

grille (gril), *n.* an openwork metal structure or screen, used as a gate, door, or window. [< F < L *craticula* < *cratis* hurdle] —**grilled,** *adj.*

grill·room (gril'rüm'; -rüm'), *n.* restaurant or dining room that specializes in serving broiled meat, fish, etc.

grilse (grils), *n., pl.* **grilse.** a young salmon that has returned from the sea to the river for the first time.

grim (grim), *adj.,* **grim·mer, grim·mest.** 1. without mercy; stern; harsh; fierce. 2. not yielding; not relenting. 3. looking stern, fierce, or harsh. 4. horrible; ghastly. [OE *grimm* fierce] —**grim'ly,** *adv.* —**grim'ness,** *n.* —**Syn.** 1. cruel, merciless. 2. relentless, unyielding. 3. hard, forbidding, severe. —**Ant.** 1. kind, tender.

gri·mace (grə·mās'; grim'is), *n., v.,* –**maced,** –**mac·ing.** —*n.* twisting of the face; ugly or funny smile. —*v.* make grimaces. [< F < Sp. *grimazo* panic] —**gri·mac'er,** *n.*

gri·mal·kin (grə·mal'kən; –môl'–), *n.* 1. cat. 2. an old female cat. 3. a spiteful old woman. [prob. < *gray* + *Malkin,* dim. of *Maud,* proper name]

grime (grīm), *n., v.,* **grimed, grim·ing.** —*n.* dirt rubbed deeply and firmly into a surface. —*v.* cover with grime; make very dirty. [? OE *grīma* mask]

Grimm (grim), *n.* 1. Jakob, 1785–1863, German philologist and collector of fairy tales. 2. his brother, Wilhelm, 1786–1859, German philologist and collector of fairy tales.

grim·y (grīm'i), *adj.,* **grim·i·er, grim·i·est.** covered with grime; very dirty. —**grim'i·ly,** *adv.* —**grim'i·ness,** *n.*

grin (grin), *v.,* **grinned, grin·ning,** *n.* —*v.* 1. smile broadly. 2. show, make, or express by smiling broadly: *he grinned approval.* —*n.* a broad smile. [OE *grennian*] —**grin'ner,** *n.* —**grin'ning·ly,** *adv.*

grind (grīnd), *v.,* **ground** or (*Rare*) **grind·ed, grind·ing,** *n.* —*v.* 1. crush into bits or into powder. 2. crush by harshness or cruelty. 3. sharpen, smooth, or wear by rubbing on something rough. 4. rub harshly (on, into, against, or together): *grind one's heel into the earth,* or *grind one's teeth in anger.* 5. work by turning a crank; produce by turning a crank: *grind a hand organ.* 6. *Colloq.* work or study long and hard. —*n.* 1. act of grinding. 2. *Colloq.* long, hard work or study. 3. *Am., Colloq.* person who works long and hard at his studies. [OE *grindan*] —**grind'ing·ly,** *adv.* —**Syn.** *v.* 1. pulverize, powder. 2. oppress, persecute. 4. grit, grate.

grind·er (grīn'dər), *n.* 1. person or thing that grinds. 2. man or machine that sharpens tools. 3. a back tooth for grinding food; molar.

grind·stone (grīnd'stōn'), *n.* 1. a flat, round stone set in a frame and turned by a crank, treadle, etc., used to sharpen tools, such as axes and knives, or to smooth and polish things. 2. have, keep, or put one's nose to the grindstone, work long and hard.

Grindstone

grin·go (gring′gō), *n., pl.*, **-gos.** *Am.* among Spanish-Americans, an unfriendly term for a foreigner, esp. for an American or Englishman. [< Mex. Sp. < Sp., gibberish]

grip (grip), *n., v.,* **gripped** (gript) or **gript** (gript), **grip·ping.** —*n.* **1.** a firm hold; seizing and holding tight; tight grasp. **2.** power of gripping. **3.** thing for gripping something. **4.** part to take hold of; handle. **5.** special way of shaking hands. **6.** *Am.* a small suitcase; handbag. **7.** firm control. **8.** mental grasp. **9.** a sudden, sharp pain. **10.** *Am.* grippe; influenza. **11.** *Am.* in the theater, a stagehand. —*v.* **1.** take a firm hold on; seize and hold tight. **2.** get and keep the interest and attention of: *an exciting story grips you.* [OE *gripe* < *gripan* to grasp] —**grip′per,** *n.* —**grip′ping·ly,** *adv.*

gripe (grīp), *v.,* **griped, grip·ing,** *n.* —*v.* **1.** clutch; pinch. **2.** oppress; distress. **3.** cause pain in the bowels. **4.** *U.S. Colloq.* complain. **5.** *U.S. Colloq.* bother; annoy. —*n.* **1.** fast hold; gripping; clutch. **2.** grasp; control. **3.** *U.S. Colloq.* complaint. **4.** gripes, pain in the bowels; colic. [OE *grīpan*]

grippe (grip), *n.* a contagious disease like a very severe cold with fever; influenza. [< F < Russ. *khrip* hoarseness] —**grippe′like′,** *adj.*

grip·sack (grip′sak′), *n. Am.* valise.

Gri·sel·da (gra·zel′da), *n.* heroine of an old romance famed for her patience.

gri·sette (gra·zet′), *n.* a French working girl. [< F, < *gris* gray; from usual color of their dresses]

gris·ly (griz′li), *adj.,* **-li·er, -li·est.** frightful; horrible; ghastly. [OE *grislic*] —**gris′li·ness,** *n.*

grist (grist), *n.* **1.** grain to be ground. **2.** grain that has been ground; meal or flour. [OE *grist* < *grindan* grind]

gris·tle (gris′al), *n.* cartilage. [OE]

gris·tly (gris′li), *adj.,* **-tli·er, -tli·est.** of, containing, or like gristle.

grist mill, mill for grinding grain.

grit (grit), *n., v.,* **grit·ted, grit·ting.** —*n.* **1.** very fine gravel or sand. **2.** a coarse sandstone. **3.** *Am.,* *Slang.* courage; pluck. —*v.* grate; grind: *he gritted his teeth and plunged into the cold water.* [OE *grēot*] —**grit′less,** *adj.*

grits (grits), *n.pl.* **1.** coarsely ground corn, oats, etc., with the husks removed. **2.** *Am.* coarse hominy. [OE *gryttan,* pl.]

grit·ty (grit′i), *adj.,* **-ti·er, -ti·est.** **1.** of or containing grit; like grit; sandy. **2.** *Am.,* *Slang.* courageous; plucky. —**grit′ti·ly,** *adv.* —**grit′ti·ness,** *n.*

griz·zled (griz′ald), *adj.* **1.** grayish; gray. **2.** gray-haired. [< *grizzle* gray hair, (adj.) gray < OF *grisel,* dim. of *gris* gray < Gmc.]

griz·zly (griz′li), *adj.,* **-zli·er, -zli·est,** *n., pl.* **-zlies.** —*adj.* **1.** grayish; gray. **2.** gray-haired. —*n. Am.* grizzly bear.

grizzly bear, *Am.* a large, fierce, gray or brownish-gray bear of western North America.

groan (grōn), *n.* a deep-throated sound expressing grief, pain, or disapproval; short moan. —*v.* **1.** give a groan or groans. **2.** be loaded or overburdened. **3.** express by groaning. **4.** suffer greatly. [OE *grānian*] —**groan′er,** *n.* —**groan′ing,** *n., adj.* —**groan′ing·ly,** *adv.*

groat (grōt), *n.* **1.** an old English silver coin worth fourpence. **2.** a very small sum. [< MDu. *groot,* lit., thick (coin)]

groats (grōts), *n.pl.* hulled grain; hulled and crushed grain. [OE *grotan,* pl.]

gro·cer (grō′sər), *n.* person who sells food and household supplies. [< OF *grossier,* ult. < L *grossus* thick]

gro·cer·y (grō′sər·i; grōs′ri), *n., pl.* **-cer·ies.** **1.** *Am.* store that sells food and household supplies. **2.** groceries, food and household supplies sold by a grocer. **3.** business of a grocer.

grog (grog), *n. Esp. Brit.* **1.** drink made of rum or any other strong alcoholic liquor, diluted with water. **2.** any strong alcoholic liquor. [short for *grogram,* nickname of Brit. Admiral Vernon, from his *grogram* cloak]

grog·ger·y (grog′ər·i), *n., pl.* **-ger·ies.** *Esp. Brit.* saloon.

grog·gy (grog′i), *adj.,* **-gi·er, -gi·est.** **1.** shaky; unsteady. **2.** drunk; intoxicated. —**grog′gi·ly,** *adv.* —**grog′gi·ness,** *n.*

grog·ram (grog′rəm), *n.* a coarse cloth made of silk, wool, or combinations of these with mohair. [< F *gros grain* coarse grain]

grog·shop (grog′shop′), *n. Esp. Brit.* place where strong alcoholic drinks are sold.

groin (groin), *n.* **1.** *Anat.* part of the body where the thigh joins the abdomen. **2.** *Archit.* a curved line where two vaults of a roof cross. —*v. Archit.* build with groins. [ME *grynde,* infl. by *loin*]

grom·met (grom′it), *n.* **1.** a metal eyelet. **2.** *Naut.* ring of rope, used as an oarlock, to hold a sail on its stays, etc. [< obs. F *gromette* curb of bridle < *gourmer* curb]

Gro·my·ko (grō·mē′kō), *n.* Andrei Andreievich, born 1909, Russian diplomat.

groom (grüm), *n.* **1.** man or boy who has charge of horses. **2.** bridegroom. **3.** any of several officers of the English royal household. **4.** *Archaic.* manservant. —*v.* **1.** feed and take care of (horses); rub down and brush. **2.** take care of the appearance of; make neat and tidy. **3.** *Am.* prepare (a person) to run for a position or political office. [ME *grom(e)* boy] —**groom′er,** *n.*

grooms·man (grümz′mən), *n., pl.* **-men.** man who attends the bridegroom at a wedding.

groove (grüv), *n., v.,* **grooved, groov·ing.** —*n.* **1.** a long, narrow channel or furrow, esp. one cut by a tool. **2.** a fixed way of doing things. **3.** **in the groove.** *Slang.* a. *Music.* playing or played smoothly and with great skill. b. in best form. —*v.* make a groove in. [OE *grōf* ditch] —**groove′-less,** *adj.* —**groove′like′,** *adj.* —**groov′er,** *n.*

grope (grōp), *v.,* **groped, grop·ing.** **1.** feel about with the hands. **2.** search blindly and uncertainly. **3.** find by feeling about with the hands. [OE *grāpian,* akin to *gripan* to grasp] —**grop′er,** *n.* —**grop′ing·ly,** *adv.*

gros·beak (grōs′bēk′), *n.* finch with a cone-shaped bill. [< F, < *gros* large + *bec* beak]

gros·grain (grō′grān′), *n.* a closely woven silk or rayon cloth with heavy cross threads and a dull finish. —*adj.* having heavy cross threads and a dull finish. [var. of *grogram*]

Red-breasted grosbeak (ab. 8 in. long)

gross (grōs), *adj., n., pl.* **gross·es** *for 1,* **gross** *for 2.* —*adj.* **1.** with nothing taken out; whole; entire: *gross receipts.* **2.** very bad: *gross errors.* **3.** coarse; vulgar. **4.** too big and fat; overfed. **5.** thick; heavy; dense: *the gross growth of a jungle.* —*n.* **1.** whole sum; total amount. **2.** unit consisting of twelve dozen; 144. [< OF < L *grossus* thick] —**gross′ly,** *adv.* —**gross′ness,** *n.* —Syn. *adj.* **1.** aggregate, total. **2.** shameful, outrageous, glaring. **3.** broad, indecent, low. **5.** rank.

gross ton, 2240 pounds.

gro·tesque (grō·tesk′), *adj.* **1.** odd or unnatural in shape, appearance, manner, etc.; fantastic; queer. **2.** ridiculous; absurd. —*n.* **1.** painting, sculpture, etc., combining designs, ornaments, figures of persons or animals, etc., in a fantastic or unnatural way. **2.** any piece of such work. [< F < Ital. *grottesco* < *grotta* grotto] —**gro·tesque′ly,** *adv.* —**gro·tesque′ness,** *n.* —Syn. *adj.* **1.** bizarre, strange.

grot·to (grot′ō), *n., pl.* **-toes, -tos.** **1.** cave. **2.** an artificial cave made for coolness or pleasure. [< Ital. *grotta* < L < Gk. *krypte.* vault. Doublet of CRYPT.]

grouch (grouch), *Am., Colloq.* —*v.* be sulky or ill-tempered; complain. —*n.* **1.** a sulky person. **2.** a sulky, discontented feeling. [var. of obs. *grutch* < OF *groucher* murmur]

grouch·y (grouch′i), *adj.,* **grouch·i·er, grouch·i·est.** *Am., Colloq.* sulky; sullen; discontented. —**grouch′i·ly,** *adv.* —**grouch′i·ness,** *n.*

ground[1] (ground), *n.* **1.** the solid part of the earth's surface. **2.** soil; dirt. **3.** particular piece of land; land for some special purpose. **4.** foundation for what is said, thought, claimed, or done; basis; reason. 5. underlying surface; background: *a blue pattern on a white ground.* 6. Often, **grounds.** land or area for some purpose or special use. 7. **grounds,** land, lawns, and gardens around a house. 8. **grounds,** small bits that sink to the bottom of a drink such as coffee or tea; dregs; sediment. 9. **grounds,** foundation; basis. 10. connection of an electrical conductor with the earth. 11. connection in a radio for the conductor that leads to the ground. 12. bottom (of an ocean, lake, etc.). 13. cover ground, a. go over a certain distance or area. b. travel. c. do a certain amount of work, etc. 14. **gain ground, a.** go forward; advance; progress. **b.** become more common or widespread. 15. **give ground,** retreat; yield. 16. **hold one's ground,** keep one's position; not retreat or yield. 17. **lose ground, a.** go backward; retreat; yield. **b.** become less common or widespread. 18. **shift one's ground,** change one's position; use a different defense or argument. 19. **stand one's ground,** keep one's position; refuse to retreat or yield. —*v.* 1. put on the ground; cause to touch the ground. 2. *Naut.* run aground; hit the bottom or shore. 3. put on a firm foundation or basis; establish firmly. 4. have a foundation or basis. 5. instruct in the first principles or elements: *well grounded in grammar.* 6. furnish with a background. 7. connect (an electric wire or other conductor) with the earth. [OE *grund* bottom] —Syn. *n.* 2. loam, mold. 4. premise, motive.

ground² (ground), *v.* pt. and pp. of **grind.**

ground crew, *U.S. Air Force.* the nonflying personnel responsible for conditioning and maintenance of airplanes.

ground·er (groun′dər), *n.* baseball hit or thrown so as to bound or roll along the ground.

ground floor, *Am.* the most advantageous position in relation to a business deal, etc.

ground hog, *Am.* the woodchuck.

ground·less (ground′lis), *adj.* without foundation, basis, or reason. —**ground′less·ly,** *adv.* —**ground′less·ness,** *n.* —Syn. baseless.

ground·ling (ground′ling), *n.* 1. plant or animal that lives close to the ground. 2. fish that lives at the bottom of the water. 3. spectator or reader who has poor taste.

ground·nut (ground′nut′), *n. Am.* 1. any of various plants having edible underground parts, such as the peanut. 2. the edible tuber, pod, or the like, of such a plant.

ground pine, *Am.* a low, creeping evergreen, a kind of club moss, used for Christmas decorations and the like.

ground plan, 1. plan of a floor of a building. 2. first or fundamental plan.

ground·sel (ground′səl), *n.* plant with small heads of yellow flowers. [OE *g(r)undeswelge < grund* ground or *gund* pus + *swelgan* swallow¹]

ground·sill (ground′sil′), *n.* a horizontal timber used as a foundation; lowest part of a wooden framework; sill. [ME *gronsel.* See GROUND¹, SILL.]

ground squirrel, *Am.* any one of various burrowing rodents belonging to the squirrel family, esp. the chipmunk.

ground swell, broad, deep waves caused by a distant storm, earthquake, etc.

ground water, water from a spring or well.

ground wire, wire connecting electric wiring, a radio, etc., with the ground.

ground·work (ground′werk′), *n.* foundation; basis.

ground zero, *Mil.* the exact point where a bomb strikes the ground or, in an atomic explosion, the area directly beneath the core of radiation.

group (grüp), *n.* 1. number of persons or things together. 2. number of persons or things belonging or classed together. 3. number of persons or things that act as a unit. 4. *Chem.* a radical. 5. *Mil.* an air-force unit smaller than a wing and larger than a squadron, corresponding to an infantry regiment. —*v.* 1. form into a group. 2.

put in a group. 3. arrange in groups. [< F < Ital. *gruppo*] —Syn. *n.* 1. cluster, aggregation, assemblage, crowd.

group·er (grüp′ər), *n., pl.* **-ers** or (*esp. collectively*) **-er.** a large food fish of warm seas. [< Pg. *garupa*]

grouse¹ (grous), *n., pl.* **grouse.** a game bird with feathered legs. The prairie chicken, sage hen, and ruffed grouse of the United States are different kinds. —**grouse′like′,** *adj.*

Ruffed grouse (ab. 17 in. long)

grouse² (grous), *v.,* **groused, grous·ing,** *n. Slang.* —*v.* grumble; complain. —*n.* complaint. —**grous′er,** *n.*

grove (grōv), *n.* group of trees standing together; orchard. [OE *grāf*]

grov·el (gruv′əl; grov′-), *v.,* **-eled, -el·ing;** *esp. Brit.* **-elled, -el·ling.** 1. lie face downward; crawl at someone's feet; humble oneself. 2. enjoy low, mean, or contemptible things. [< *groveling,* orig. adv., < phrase *on gruʃe* prone < Scand. *ā grūʃu*] —**grov′el·er,** *esp. Brit.* **grov′el·ler,** *n.* —**grov′el·ing·ly,** *esp. Brit.* **grov′el·ling·ly,** *adv.* —Syn. 1. creep, cringe, fawn.

grow (grō), *v.,* **grew, grown, grow·ing.** 1. become bigger by taking in food, as plants and animals do: *a tree growing only in the tropics.* 2. germinate; sprout. 3. exist; spring; arise: *the affair grew out of an indiscreet letter.* 4. become greater; increase: *his fame grew.* 5. **grow on** or **upon,** have an increasing effect or influence on: *the habit grew on me.* 6. become gradually attached or united by growth: *grow fast to the wall.* 7. become: *grow cold, grow rich.* 8. **grow up, a.** advance to or arrive at full growth. **b.** come into being; be produced; develop. 9. cause to grow; produce; raise: *grow corn.* 10. allow to grow: *grow a beard.* [OE *grōwan;* akin to GRASS, GREEN] —**grow′er,** *n.* —Syn. 4. expand, develop, flourish. 9. cultivate.

growl (groul), *v.* 1. make a deep, low, angry sound. 2. express by growling. —*n.* a deep, low, angry sound; deep, warning snarl. [prob. imit.] —**growl′er,** *n.* —**growl′ing·ly,** *adv.* —Syn. *v.* 1, 2. grumble.

grown (grōn), *adj.* 1. arrived at full growth. 2. covered with a growth. —*v.* pp. of **grow.**

grown-up (*adj.* grōn′up′; *n.* grōn′up′), *adj.* 1. adult. 2. characteristic of or for adults. —*n.* adult.

growth (grōth), *n.* 1. process of growing; development. 2. amount of growing or developing; increase. 3. what has grown or is growing: *a thick growth of bushes covered the ground.* 4. an unhealthy mass of tissue formed in or on the body, as a tumor. —Syn. 2. expansion, enlargement.

grub (grub), *n., v.,* **grubbed, grub·bing.** —*n.* 1. a wormlike form or larva of an insect, esp. the smooth, thick larva of a beetle. 2. drudge. 3. *Slang.* food. [< v.] —*v.* 1. dig. 2. root out of the ground; dig up. 3. drudge. [ME *grubbe(n)*] —**grub′ber,** *n.*

grub·by (grub′i), *adj.,* **-bi·er, -bi·est.** 1. dirty; grimy. 2. infested with grubs. —**grub′bi·ly,** *adv.* —**grub′bi·ness,** *n.*

grub·stake (grub′stāk′), *n., v.,* **-staked, -stak·ing.** *Am., W., Colloq.* —*n.* food, outfit, money, etc., supplied to a prospector on the condition of sharing in whatever he finds. —*v.* supply with a grubstake. —**grub′stak′er,** *n. Am., W., Colloq.*

grudge (gruj), *n., v.,* **grudged, grudg·ing.** —*n.* ill will; sullen feeling against; dislike of long standing. —*v.* 1. feel anger or dislike toward (a person) because of (something); envy the possession of. 2. give or let have unwillingly. [var. of obs. *grutch* < OF *groucher*] —**grudg′er,** *n.* —**grudg′ing·ly,** *adv.* —Syn. *n.* resentment, spite. —*v.* 1. envy, begrudge.

gru·el (grü′əl), *n., v.,* **-eled, -el·ing;** *esp. Brit.* **-elled, -el·ling.** —*n.* a thin, almost liquid food made by boiling oatmeal, etc., in water or milk. —*v.* subject to an exhausting or tiring experience. [< OF, ult. < Gmc.] —gru·el·ing, esp. Brit. gru·el·ling (grü′əl·ing), adj.

grue·some (grü′səm), adj. revolting in a ghastly way; horrible. Also, **grewsome**. [< grue to shudder. Cf. MDu., MLG gruwen.] —grue′some·ly, adv. —grue′some·ness, n.

gruff (gruf), adj. 1. deep and harsh; hoarse. 2. rough; rude; unfriendly; bad-tempered. [< Du. grof] —gruff′ly, adv. —gruff′ness, n. —Syn. 2. grumpy, brusque, impolite. —Ant. 2. courteous.

grum·ble (grum′bəl), v., -bled, -bling, n. —v. 1. mutter in discontent; complain in a bad-tempered way. 2. express by grumbling. 3. rumble. —n. 1. mutter of discontent; bad-tempered complaint. 2. rumble. [akin to OE grymettan roar, and GRIM] —grum′bler, n. —grum′bling·ly, adv. —Syn. v. 1, 2. growl, murmur.

grump·y (grump′i), adj., grump·i·er, grump·i·est. surly; ill-humored; gruff. —grump′i·ly, adv. —grump′i·ness, n.

grunt (grunt), n. 1. the deep, hoarse sound that a hog makes. 2. sound like this. 3. an edible sea fish that grunts when taken out of the water. —v. 1. make this sound. 2. say with this sound. [OE grunnettan < grunian grunt] —grunt′er, n. —grunt′ing·ly, adv.

Gru·yère (grī·yâr′; grü-), n. variety of firm, light-yellow cheese made from whole milk. [after Gruyère, district in Switzerland]

gryph·on (grif′ən), n. griffin.

Gua·dal·ca·nal (gwä′dəl·kə·nal′), n. one of the Solomon Islands in the Pacific. The Japanese were defeated here by U.S. armed forces, 1942–43.

Gua·de·loupe (gwä′də·lüp′), n. island in the West Indies, an overseas department of France.

Guam (gwäm), n. a U.S. island in the W Pacific, east of the Philippines.

gua·no (gwä′nō), n., pl. -nos. 1. manure of sea birds, found esp. on islands near Peru, used for fertilizing. 2. Am. fertilizer made from fish. [< Sp. < Kechua (Ind. lang. of Peru) huanu]

guar·an·tee (gar′ən·tē′), n., v., -teed, -tee·ing. —n. 1. a promise to pay or do something if another fails; pledge to replace goods if they are not as represented. 2. person who so promises. 3. one to whom such a pledge is made. —v. 1. stand back of; give a guarantee for; assure genuineness or permanence of. 2. undertake to secure for another. 3. make secure (against or from). 4. engage to do (something). [prob. var. of guaranty] —Syn. n. 1. warrant, security, surety.

guar·an·tor (gar′ən·tôr; -tər), n. person who makes or gives a guarantee.

guar·an·ty (gar′ən·ti), n., pl. -ties, v., -tied, -ty·ing. —n. 1. act or fact of giving security. 2. pledge or promise given as security; security. 3. person who acts as guarantee. —v. guarantee. [< OF guarantie < guarant warrant < Gmc. Doublet of WARRANTY.]

guard (gärd), v. 1. keep safe; watch over carefully; defend; protect. 2. keep in check; prevent from getting out; hold back. 3. act as a guard; take precautions (against); watch. —n. 1. somebody or something that guards. 2. anything that gives protection; contrivance or appliance to protect against injury, loss, etc. 3. careful watch. 4. defense; protection. 5. position of defense in boxing, fencing, or cricket. 6. person who opens and closes the doors or gates on a train. 7. Football. player at either side of the center. 8. Basketball. either of two players defending the goal. 9. guards, certain groups of soldiers in the British army. [< F garder, v., guarde, n. < Gmc. Doublet of WARD.] —guard′er, n. —Syn. v. 1. shield. 3. safeguard, preserve. —n. 1. defender, protector, sentry, sentinel. 4. bulwark, shield.

guard·ed (gär′did), adj. 1. kept safe; carefully watched over; protected. 2. careful; cautious. —guard′ed·ly, adv. —guard′ed·ness, n. —Syn. 1. defended. 2. circumspect, reserved.

guard·house (gärd′hous′), n. Am., Mil. 1. a building used as a jail for soldiers. 2. a building occupied by soldiers on guard.

guard·i·an (gär′di·ən), n. 1. person appointed by law to take care of the affairs of someone who

cannot take care of them himself. 2. any person who takes care of somebody or something. —adj. protecting: a guardian angel. —guard′i·an·ship′, n. —Syn. n. 1. trustee, warden, keeper.

guards·man (gärdz′mən), n., pl. -men. 1. guard. 2. U.S. soldier who belongs to the National Guard.

Gua·te·ma·la (gwä′tə·mä′lə), n. 1. country in NW Central America. 2. Also, Guatemala City. its capital. —Gua′te·ma′lan, adj., n.

gua·va (gwä′və), n. 1. a tropical American tree or shrub with a yellowish, pear-shaped fruit. 2. the fruit, used for jelly, jam, etc. [< Sp. guayaba]

Guay·a·quil (gwī′ə·kēl′), n. seaport in W Ecuador.

gua·yu·le (gwä·ü′lā), n. Am. a small shrub growing in Mexico and Texas. Rubber is obtained from its juice. [< a Mexican lang.]

gu·ber·na·to·ri·al (gü′bər·nə·tô′ri·əl; -tō′-; gü′-), adj. Am. of or having to do with a governor. [< L gubernator, orig., pilot. See GOVERN.]

gudg·eon (guj′ən), n. 1. a small European fresh-water fish. It is easily caught and often used for bait. 2. minnow. 3. person easily fooled or cheated. —v. dupe; cheat. [< OF goujon, ult. < L gobius, a kind of fish < Gk. kobios]

guer·don (gér′dən), n., v. Poetic. reward. [< OF, var. of werdon < Med.L < OHG widarlōn, infl. by L donum gift] —guer′don·er, n.

Guern·sey (gérn′zi), n., pl. -seys. 1. any of a breed of dairy cattle resembling the Jersey, but somewhat larger. 2. a British island in the English Channel.

guer·ril·la, gue·ril·la (gə·ril′ə), n. fighter in a war carried on by independent bands which harass the enemy by sudden raids, plundering supplies, etc. —adj. of or by guerrillas. [< Sp., dim. of guerra war]

guess (ges), v. 1. form an opinion without really knowing: guess the height of a building. 2. get right by guessing: guess a riddle. 3. Esp. U.S. think; believe; suppose: I guess I can get there. —n. opinion formed without really knowing. [prob. < Scand. (Sw.) gissa] —guess′er, n. —guess′ing·ly, adv. —Syn. v. 1. estimate, suppose, surmise, conjecture. —n. estimate, supposition, surmise, conjecture. ≽ See calculate for usage note.

guess·work (ges′wérk′), n. work, action, or results based on guessing; guessing.

guest (gest), n. 1. person who is received and entertained at one's home, club, etc.; person who is not a regular member; visitor. 2. person staying at a hotel, boarding house, etc. [< Scand. gestr. Cf. OE giest.] —guest′less, adj.

guf·faw (gu·fô′), n. a loud, coarse burst of laughter. —v. laugh loudly and coarsely.

Gui·a·na (gē·ä′nə; -an′ə), n. region in N South America, divided into French Guiana, Guyana, and Surinam (Dutch Guiana).

guid·ance (gīd′əns), n. 1. a guiding; leadership; direction. 2. thing that guides.

guide (gīd), v., guid·ed, guid·ing. —v. 1. show the way; lead; conduct; direct. 2. manage; control. —n. 1. person who shows the way; leads, conducts, or directs. 2. mark, sign, etc., to direct the eye or mind. 3. guidebook. [< OF guider < Gmc.] —guid′a·ble, adj. —guide′less, adj. —guid′er, n. —Syn. v. 1. pilot, steer. 2. regulate, govern. —n. 1. leader, conductor, director, pilot.

guide·book (gīd′bŭk′), n. book of directions and information, esp. one for travelers.

guided missile, Mil. projectile that can be guided accurately often for great distances and usually by means of transmitted electronic impulses.

guide·post (gīd′pōst′), n. post with signs and directions on it for travelers.

gui·don (gī′dən), n. 1. a small flag or streamer carried as a guide by soldiers, or used for signaling. 2. U.S. Army. flag, streamer, or pennant of a company, regiment, etc. 3. soldier who carries the guidon. [< F < Ital. guidone]

guild (gild), n. 1. society for mutual aid or for

some common purpose: *the Ladies' Auxiliary Guild of the church.* 2. in the Middle Ages, a union of the men in one trade to keep standards high and to look out for the interests of their trade. Also, **gild.** [< Scand. *gildi*]

guil·der (gil′dər), *n.* 1. a silver coin or unit of money in the Netherlands. 2. coin formerly used in the Netherlands, Germany, or Austria. Also, **gulden.** [alter. of *gulden*]

guild·hall (gild′hôl′), *n.* 1. hall in which a guild meets. 2. Brit. a town hall; city hall. Also, **gildhall.**

guilds·man (gildz′mən), *n., pl.* **-men.** member of a guild. Also, **gildsman.**

guile (gīl), *n.* crafty deceit; craftiness; sly tricks. [< OF < Gmc. Doublet of WILE.] —Syn. cunning, wiliness, trickery. —Ant. honesty.

guile·ful (gīl′fəl), *adj.* crafty and deceitful; sly and tricky. —**guile′ful·ly,** *adv.* —**guile′ful·ness,** *n.* —Syn. cunning, wily, artful.

guile·less (gīl′lis), *adj.* without guile. —**guile′less·ly,** *adv.* —**guile′less·ness,** *n.* —Syn. sincere, honest, frank, candid.

guil·le·mot (gil′ə·mot), *n.* any of several arctic diving birds of the auk family with narrow bills. [< F, prob. < *Guillaume* William]

guil·lo·tine (*n.* gil′ə·tēn; *v.* gil′ə·tēn′), *n., v.,* **-tined, -tin·ing.** —*n.* machine for beheading persons by means of a heavy blade that slides down between two grooved posts. —*v.* behead with this machine. [< F; named for J. I. *Guillotin,* physician and advocate of its use]

guilt (gilt), *n.* 1. fact or state of having done wrong; being guilty; being to blame. 2. guilty action or conduct. [OE *gylt* offense] —Syn. 1. guiltiness, culpability. 2. crime, wrongdoing.

guilt·less (gilt′lis), *adj.* not guilty; free from guilt; innocent. —**guilt′less·ly,** *adv.* —**guilt′less·ness,** *n.*

guilt·y (gil′ti), *adj.,* **guilt·i·er, guilt·i·est.** 1. having done wrong; deserving to be blamed and punished: *the jury pronounced the prisoner guilty of murder.* 2. knowing or showing that one has done wrong: *a guilty conscience.* 3. *Obs.* conscious. —**guilt′i·ly,** *adv.* —**guilt′i·ness,** *n.* —Syn. 1. culpable, sinful, criminal.

guimpe (gimp; gamp), *n.* blouse worn under a dress and showing at the neck or at the neck and arms. [< F < Gmc. Doublet of GIMP.]

guin·ea (gin′i), *n.* 1. amount equal to 21 shillings, used in England in stating prices, fees, etc. 2. a former English gold coin worth 21 shillings. 3. guinea fowl.

Guin·ea (gin′i), *n.* 1. republic in W Africa on the Atlantic, formerly including French, Portuguese, and Spanish colonies. 2. Gulf of, a large gulf of the Atlantic in W Africa.

guinea fowl, a domestic fowl somewhat like a pheasant, having dark-gray feathers with small, white spots.

guinea hen, 1. guinea fowl. 2. a female guinea fowl.

guinea pig, 1. a short-eared, tailless animal like a big, fat, harmless rat, often used for laboratory experiments. 2. any person or thing serving as a subject for experiment or observation.

Guinea pig (ab. 6 in. long)

Guin·e·vere (gwin′ə·vir), **Guin·e·ver** (-vər), *n.* King Arthur's queen.

guise (gīz), *n.* 1. style of dress; garb: *the soldier went in the guise of a monk.* 2. external appearance; aspect; semblance. 3. assumed appearance; pretense: *under the guise of friendship.* [< OF < Gmc.]

gui·tar (gə·tär′), *n.* a musical instrument having six strings, played with the fingers. [< Sp. *guitarra* < Gk. *kithara* cithara. Doublet of CITHARA and ZITHER.] —**gui·tar′ist,** *n.* —**gui·tar′like′,** *adj.*

gulch (gulch), *n. Am.* a deep, narrow ravine with steep sides, esp. one marking the course of a stream or torrent.

gul·den (gùl′dən), *n., pl.* **-dens, -den.** guilder. [< Du., G, lit., golden (coin)]

gules (gūlz), *n., adj.* Heraldry. red. [< OF *gueules* red fur neckpiece, ult. < *gole* throat < L *gula*]

gulf (gulf), *n.* 1. a large bay; arm of an ocean or sea extending into the land. 2. a very deep break or cut in the earth. 3. any wide separation: *a gulf between old friends.* 4. the Gulf, *Am.* the Gulf of Mexico. —*v.* engulf. [< F < Ital., ult. < Gk. *kolpos,* orig., bosom] —**gulf′like′,** *adj.*

Gulf Stream, *Am.* current of warm water flowing north from the Gulf of Mexico along the Atlantic coast to Newfoundland, where it turns northeast toward the British Isles.

gull[1] (gul), *n.* a graceful, gray-and-white bird with long wings, webbed feet, and a thick, strong beak, living on or near large bodies of water. [? < Welsh *gwylan*]

Gull (ab. 18 in. long)

gull[2] (gul), *v.* deceive; cheat. —*n.* person who is easily deceived or cheated.

Gul·lah (gul′ə), *n. Am.* 1. one of a group of Negroes living along the coast of South Carolina and Georgia and on the islands off the coast. 2. dialect of English spoken by the Gullahs.

gul·let (gul′it), *n.* 1. passage for food from the mouth to the stomach; esophagus. 2. throat. [< OF, ult. < L *gula* throat]

gul·li·ble (gul′ə·bəl), *adj.* easily deceived. —**gul′li·bil′i·ty,** *n.* —**gul′li·bly,** *adv.*

gul·ly (gul′i), *n., pl.* **-lies,** *v.,* **-lied, -ly·ing.** —*n.* a narrow gorge; ditch made by running water. —*v. Am.* erode (land) so as to form gullies. [? var. of *gullet*]

gulp (gulp), *v.* 1. swallow eagerly or greedily. 2. keep in; choke back. 3. gasp; choke. —*n.* 1. act of swallowing. 2. amount swallowed at one time; mouthful. [imit.] —**gulp′er,** *n.* —**gulp′ing·ly,** *adv.*

gum[1] (gum), *n., v.,* **gummed, gum·ming.** —*n.* 1. a sticky juice, obtained from or given off by certain trees and plants, that hardens in the air and dissolves in water. Gum is used to make candy, medicine, and mucilage. 2. any similar secretion, such as resin. 3. preparation of such a substance for use in industry or the arts. 4. *Am.* chewing gum. 5. substance on the back of a stamp, the flap of an envelope, etc.; mucilage; glue. —*v.* 1. smear, stick together, or stiffen with gum. 2. give off gum; form gum. 3. *Am.* make or become sticky; clog with something sticky. [< OF < L < Gk. *kommi*] —**gum′like′,** *adj.* —**gum′mer,** *n.*

gum[2] (gum), *n.* Often, **gums.** flesh around the teeth. [OE *gōma* palate]

gum ammoniac, a natural mixture of gum and resin, used in medicine; ammoniac.

gum arabic, gum obtained from acacia trees, used in making candy, medicine, mucilage, etc.

gum·bo (gum′bō), *n., pl.* **-bos.** *Am.* 1. the okra plant. 2. its sticky pods. 3. soup thickened with okra pods. 4. *W.* soil that contains much silt and becomes very sticky when wet. [of African origin]

gum·boil (gum′boil′), *n.* a small abscess on the gums.

gum·drop (gum′drop′), *n. Am.* a stiff, jellylike piece of candy made of gum arabic, gelatin, etc., sweetened and flavored.

gum·my (gum′i), *adj.,* **-mi·er, -mi·est.** 1. sticky like gum. 2. covered with gum. 3. giving off gum. —**gum′mi·ness,** *n.*

gump·tion (gump′shən), *n. Colloq.* 1. initiative; energy. 2. good judgment.

gum·shoe (gum′shü′), *n., v.,* **-shoed, -shoe·ing.** *Am.* —*n.* 1. a rubber overshoe. 2. gumshoes, sneakers. 3. *Slang.* detective. —*v. Slang.* go around quietly and secretly.

gum tree, a sweet gum, tupelo, eucalyptus, or other tree that yields gum.

gun[1] (gun), *n., v.,* **gunned, gun·ning.** —*n.* 1. rifle, cannon, or other weapon with a long metal tube for shooting bullets, shot, etc. 2. *Am.* pistol or revolver. **3.** anything resembling a gun in use or shape. **4.** the shooting of a gun as a signal or salute. —*v.* **1.** *Am.* shoot with a gun; hunt with a gun. **2.** *Slang.* open the throttle of (an airplane) wide; accelerate rapidly. [< OF *engan* engine, trap, snare, ult. < L *canna* reed] —**gun′less,** *adj.*

gun² (gun), *v., Archaic* and *Poetic.* pp. of **gin⁴.**

gun·boat (gun′bōt′), *n. Am.* a small warship that can be used in shallow water.

gun·cot·ton (gun′kot′ən), *n.* explosive made by treating cotton with nitric and sulfuric acids.

gun·fire (gun′fīr′), *n.* the shooting of a gun or guns.

gun·lock (gun′lok′), *n.* part of a gun by which the charge is fired.

gun·man (gun′mən), *n., pl.* -men. *Am.* man who uses a gun to rob, kill, etc.

gun metal, 1. a dark-gray alloy used for chains, buckles, handles, etc. **2.** dark gray. **3.** kind of bronze formerly used for making guns. —**gun′-met′al,** *adj.*

gun·nel¹ (gun′əl), *n.* gunwale.

gun·nel² (gun′əl), *n.* a small N Atlantic fish resembling a perch.

gun·ner (gun′ər), *n.* **1.** man trained to fire artillery; soldier who handles and fires cannon. **2.** a navy officer in charge of a ship's guns. **3.** person who hunts with a gun.

gun·ner·y (gun′ər·i), *n.* **1.** art and science of constructing and managing big guns. **2.** use of guns; shooting of guns. **3.** guns collectively.

gun·ning (gun′ing), *n.* hunting with a gun.

gun·ny (gun′i), *n., pl.* -nies. **1.** a strong, coarse fabric used for sacks, bags, etc. **2.** Also, **gunny sack.** sack, etc., made of this. [< Hind. *goni*]

gun·pow·der (gun′pou′dər), *n.* powder that explodes with force when brought into contact with fire, used esp. in gunnery.

gun·run·ning (gun′run′ing), *n.* the bringing of guns and ammunition into a country illegally. —**gun′run′ner,** *n.*

gun·shot (gun′shot′), *n.* **1.** shot fired from a gun. **2.** the shooting of a gun. **3.** distance that a gun will shoot.

gun·smith (gun′smith′), *n.* person whose work is making or repairing small guns.

gun·stock (gun′stok′), *n.* the wooden support to which the barrel of a gun is fastened.

Gun·ther (gŭn′tər), *n.* a Burgundian king, husband of Brunhild.

gun·wale (gun′əl), *n.* the upper edge of a ship's or boat's side. Also, **gunnel.**

gup·py (gup′i), *n., pl.* -pies. a very small, brightly colored, viviparous fish of tropical fresh water. [for R. J. L. *Guppy*]

gur·gle (gẽr′gəl), *v.,* -gled, -gling, *n.* —*v.* **1.** flow or run with a bubbling sound. **2.** make a bubbling sound. —*n.* a bubbling sound. [? imit.]

gush (gush), *v.* **1.** rush out suddenly; pour out. **2.** *Colloq.* talk in a silly way about one's affections or enthusiasms. **3.** give forth suddenly or very freely. —*n.* **1.** rush of water or other liquid from an enclosed place. **2.** *Colloq.* silly, emotional talk. [prob. imit.] —**gush′ing,** *adj.* —**gush′ing·ly,** *adv.* —**Syn.** *v.* **1.** spurt, spout.

gush·er (gush′ər), *n.* **1.** *Esp. U.S.* an oil well that gives oil in large quantities without pumping. **2.** a gushy person.

gush·y (gush′i), *adj.,* **gush·i·er, gush·i·est.** showing silly feeling; effusive; sentimental.

gus·set (gus′it), *n.* a triangular piece of material inserted to give greater strength or more room. [< OF *gousset* < *gousse* husk]

gust (gust), *n.* **1.** a sudden, violent rush of wind. **2.** a sudden burst of rain, smoke, sound, etc. **3.** outburst of anger, enthusiasm, etc. [< Scand. *gustr*]

gus·ta·to·ry (gus′tə·tô′ri, -tō′-), *adj.* of the sense of taste; having to do with tasting. [< L *gustatus,* pp. of *gustare* taste]

Gus·ta·vus VI (gus·tā′vəs; -tä′-), born 1882, king of Sweden since 1950.

gus·to (gus′tō), *n., pl.* -tos. **1.** keen relish; hearty enjoyment. **2.** liking or taste. [< Ital., orig., taste < L *gustus*]

gust·y (gus′ti), *adj.,* **gust·i·er, gust·i·est. 1.** coming in gusts; windy; stormy. **2.** marked by outbursts: *gusty laughter.* —**gust′i·ly,** *adv.* —**gust′i·ness,** *n.*

gut (gut), *n., v.,* **gut·ted, gut·ting.** —*n.* **1.** intestine. **2. guts, a.** *Slang.* pluck; courage; endurance. **b.** entrails; bowels. **3.** a tough string made from the intestines of a sheep, cat, etc., used for violin strings, tennis rackets, etc. —*v.* **1.** remove the entrails of; disembowel. **2.** plunder or destroy the inside of. [OE *guttas,* pl.] —**gut′ter,** *n.*

Gu·ten·berg (gü′tən·bẽrg), *n.* Johann, 1398?-1468, German printer, supposedly the first European to print from movable type.

gut·ta-per·cha (gut′ə·pẽr′chə), *n.* substance resembling rubber, obtained from the thick, milky juice of certain tropical trees, used in dentistry, etc. [< Malay]

gut·ter (gut′ər), *n.* **1.** channel along the side of a street or road to carry off water; low part of a street beside the sidewalk. **2.** channel or trough along the lower edge of a roof to carry off rain water. **3.** channel; groove. —*v.* **1.** form gutters in. **2.** flow or melt in streams. **3.** become channeled. [< OF *goutiere,* ult. < L *gutta* drop] —**gut′ter·like′,** *adj.* —**gut′ter·y,** *adj.*

gut·ter·snipe (gut′ər·snīp′), *n. Colloq.* **1.** gamin who lives in the streets. **2.** person without breeding or decency; mucker.

gut·tur·al (gut′ər·əl), *adj.* **1.** of the throat. **2.** formed in the throat; harsh. **3.** *Phonet.* formed between the back of the tongue and soft palate. The *g* in *go* is a guttural sound. —*n.* sound formed in this way. [< NL, < L *guttur* throat] —**gut′tur·al′i·ty,** *n.* —**gut′tur·al·ly,** *adv.* —**gut′tur·al·ness,** *n.*

guy¹ (gī), *n., v.,* **guyed, guy·ing.** —*n.* rope, chain, wire, etc., attached to something to steady or secure it. —*v.* steady or secure with a guy or guys. [< OF *guie* a guide, ult. < Gmc.]

guy² (gī), *n., v.,* **guyed, guy·ing.** —*n.* **1.** *Slang.* fellow; chap. **2.** a queer-looking person. —*v. Colloq.* make fun of; tease. [for *Guy* Fawkes]

Guy·a·na (gē·ä′nə; -an′ə), *n.* republic in NE South America; formerly the British colony of British Guiana.

guz·zle (guz′əl), *v.,* -zled, -zling. drink greedily; drink too much. —**guz′zler,** *n.*

gym (jim), *n.* gymnasium.

gym·na·si·um (jim·nā′zi·əm), *n., pl.* -si·ums, -si·a (-zi·ə). room, building, etc., fitted up for physical exercise or training and for indoor athletic sports. [< L < Gk. *gymnasion,* ult. < *gymnos* naked]

Gym·na·si·um (jim·nā′zi·əm; *Ger.* gim·nä′-zi·ùm), *n.* a German secondary school that prepares students for the universities.

gym·nast (jim′nast), *n.* expert in gymnastics. [< Gk., < *gymnazein* exercise. See GYMNASIUM.]

gym·nas·tic (jim·nas′tik), *adj.* having to do with bodily exercise or activities. —**gym·nas′ti·cal·ly,** *adv.*

gym·nas·tics (jim·nas′tiks), *n.* physical exercises for developing the muscles.

gym·no·sperm (jim′nə·spẽrm), *n. Bot.* any of a large group of plants having the seeds exposed, not enclosed in ovaries. The pine, fir, and spruce, which bear seeds on the surface of cone scales instead of in pods, are gymnosperms. [< NL < Gk., < *gymnos* naked + *sperma* seed] —**gym′no·sper′mous,** *adj.*

gy·ne·col·o·gy (gī′nə·kol′ə·ji; jī′nə-; jin′ə-), *n.* branch of medical science that deals with the functions and diseases peculiar to women. [< Gk. *gyne* woman + -LOGY] —**gy′ne·co·log′ic** (gī′nə·kə·loj′ik; jī′nə-; jin′ə-), **gy′ne·co·log′i·cal,** *adj.* —**gy′ne·co·log′i·cal·ly,** *adv.* —**gy′ne·col′o·gist,** *n.*

gy·noe·ci·um (jī·nē′si·əm; jī-), *n., pl.* -ci·a (-si·ə). *Bot.* pistil or pistils of a flower. [< NL, < Gk. *gyne* woman + *oikion* house]

gyp (jip), *v.,* **gypped, gyp·ping,** *n. U.S. Slang.* —*v.* defraud or rob by some sharp practice; cheat; swindle. —*n.* **1.** a cheat or swindle. **2.** a swindler. [shortened from *gypsy*] —**gyp′per,** *n.*

āge, cãre, fär; ēqual, tẽrm; īce; ōpen, ôrder; pùt, rüle, ūse; th, then; ə=a in about.

gyp·soph·i·la (jip·sof′ə·lə), *n.* plant with many small, fragrant, white or pink flowers on delicate, branching stalks with few leaves.

gyp·sum (jip′səm), *n.* a hydrated calcium sulfate, CaSO₄·2H₂O, a mineral used for making plaster of Paris, fertilizer, etc. [< L < Gk. *gypsos*]

Gyp·sy (jip′si), *n., pl.* **-sies,** *adj.* —*n.* **1.** person belonging to a wandering group of people having dark eyes and black hair, who probably came from India originally. **2.** language of the Gypsies. **3.** *gypsy, U.S.* person who looks or lives like a Gypsy. —*adj.* **gypsy,** a. of the Gypsies. b. resembling a Gypsy or gypsy. Also, *esp. Brit.* **Gipsy, gipsy.** [ult. < *Egyptian*] —**gyp′sy·like′,** *adj.*

gypsy moth, a brownish or white moth whose larvae eat the leaves of trees. Also, **gipsy moth.**

gy·rate (jī′rāt; jī·rāt′), *v.,* **-rat·ed, -rat·ing. 1.** move in a circle or spiral. **2.** whirl; rotate. [< L, < *gyrus* circle < Gk. *gyros*] —**gy·ra′tion,** *n.*

—**gy·ra′tor,** *n.* —**gy·ra·to·ry** (jī′rə·tô′ri; -tō′-), *adj.*

gyr·fal·con (jėr′fôl′kən; -fô′-), *n.* gerfalcon.

gy·ro·com·pass (jī′rō·kum′pəs), *n.* compass using a motor-driven gyroscope instead of a magnetic needle to point to the north. It points to the geographic North Pole instead of to the magnetic pole.

gy·ro·scope (jī′rə·skōp), *n.* a heavy wheel or disk mounted so that its axis can turn freely in one or more directions. A spinning gyroscope tends to resist change in the direction of its axis. —**gy·ro·scop·ic** (jī′rə·skop′ik), *adj.* —**gy′·ro·scop′i·cal·ly,** *adv.*

gy·ro·sta·bi·liz·er (jī′rō·stā′bə·līz′ər), *n.* device for stabilizing a seagoing vessel by counteracting its rolling motion.

gyve (jīv), *n., v.,* **gyved, gyv·ing.** —*n.* Usually, **gyves.** shackle, esp. for the leg; fetter. —*v.* fetter; shackle.

H

H, h (āch), *n., pl.* **H's;** h's. the eighth letter of the alphabet.

H, 1. *Elect.* henry (unit of inductance). **2.** *Chem.* hydrogen.

h., H., 1. high. **2.** *Baseball.* hits. **3.** hour.

ha (hä), *interj.* **1.** exclamation of surprise, joy, triumph, etc. **2.** sound of a laugh.

Haa·kon VII (hô′kůn), 1872–1957, king of Norway from 1905 to 1957.

Haar·lem (här′ləm), *n.* city in W Netherlands.

Hab·ak·kuk (hab′ə·kuk; hə·bak′ək), *n.* **1.** a Hebrew prophet. **2.** book of the Old Testament.

Ha·ba·na (ä·vä′nä), *n.* Spanish name of Havana.

ha·be·as cor·pus (hā′bi·əs kôr′pəs), *Law.* writ requiring that a prisoner be brought before a judge or into court to decide whether he is being held lawfully. [L, you may have the person]

hab·er·dash·er (hab′ər·dash′ər), *n.* **1.** *Am.* dealer in men's wear. **2.** dealer in small articles, such as needles, trimmings, etc.

hab·er·dash·er·y (hab′ər·dash′ər·i; -dash′ri), *n., pl.* **-er·ies. 1.** articles sold by a haberdasher. **2.** shop of a haberdasher.

hab·er·geon (hab′ər·jən), *n.* **1.** a short hauberk. **2.** any hauberk. Also, **haubergeon.** [< OF *haubergeon,* dim. of *hauberc* HAUBERK]

ha·bil·i·ment (hə·bil′ə·mənt), *n.* **1.** habiliments, articles of clothing. **2.** dress; attire. [< OF, < *abiller* prepare, fit out, orig., reduce (a tree) to a trunk by stripping off the branches < *a-* (< L *ad*) + *bille* long stick < Celtic]

hab·it (hab′it), *n.* **1.** tendency to act in a certain way or to do a certain thing; usual way of acting: *habit of smoking.* **2.** the distinctive dress or costume worn by members of a religious order. **3.** a woman's riding suit. **4.** condition of body or mind. **5.** the characteristic form, mode of growth, etc., of an animal or plant. —*v.* put a habit on; dress. [< OF < L *habitus* < *habere* hold, live in, stay] —Syn. *n.* **1.** custom, practice, usage, use, wont.

hab·it·a·ble (hab′ə·tə·bəl), *adj.* fit to live in. —**hab′it·a·bil′i·ty, hab′it·a·ble·ness,** *n.* —**hab′it·a·bly,** *adv.*

hab·it·ant (hab′ə·tənt), *n.* inhabitant. [< F < L, ppr. of *habitare* live in]

hab·i·tat (hab′ə·tat), *n.* **1.** place where an animal or plant naturally lives or grows. **2.** a dwelling place.

hab·i·ta·tion (hab′ə·tā′shən), *n.* **1.** place to live in. **2.** an inhabiting. —Syn. **1.** home, dwelling, residence.

ha·bit·u·al (hə·bich′ů·əl), *adj.* **1.** done by habit; caused by habit: *a habitual smile.* **2.** being or doing something by habit: *a habitual reader.* **3.** often done, seen, or used: *ice and snow are a habitual sight in arctic regions.* —**ha·bit′u·al·ly,** *adv.* —**ha·bit′u·al·ness,** *n.* —Syn. **2.** regu-

lar, steady. **3.** customary, ordinary. ➤ **habitual action.** *Would* is the typical auxiliary verb for habitual action in the past, especially in formal English: *He would always go by the longer way.* Habitual action is also expressed by *used to* or by an adverb: *He used to go by the longer way. He usually went by the longer way.*

ha·bit·u·ate (hə·bich′ů·āt), *v.,* **-at·ed, -at·ing.** make used (to); accustom. —**ha·bit′u·a′tion,** *n.* —Syn. familiarize, naturalize, acclimate.

hab·i·tude (hab′ə·tūd; -tūd), *n.* **1.** characteristic condition of body or mind. **2.** custom.

ha·bit·u·é (hə·bich′ů·ā′), *n.* person who has the habit of going to any place frequently. [< F]

ha·ci·en·da (hä′si·en′də), *n. Am.* a large ranch; landed estate; country house. [< Sp. < L *facienda* (things) to be done < *facere* do]

hack¹ (hak), *v.* **1.** cut roughly or unevenly; deal cutting blows. **2.** give short, dry coughs. —*n.* **1.** a rough cut. **2.** tool or instrument for hacking, such as an ax, pick, hoe, etc. **3.** a short, dry cough. [OE *-haccian*] —**hack′er,** *n.*

hack² (hak), *n.* **1.** *U.S.* carriage for hire. **2.** *Colloq.* taxi. **3.** *Brit.* horse for hire. **4.** an old or worn-out horse. **5.** horse for ordinary riding. **6.** person hired to do routine literary work; drudge. —*v.* **1.** ride on horseback over roads. **2.** *Colloq.* drive a taxi. —*adj.* working or done merely for money. [short for *hackney*] —Syn. *adj.* hired, drudging.

hack·a·more (hak′ə·môr; -mōr), *n. Am.* a halter (def. 1).

hack·ber·ry (hak′ber′i), *n., pl.* **-ries.** *Am.* **1.** tree related to the elm that has small, cherrylike fruit. **2.** the fruit.

hack·le¹ (hak′əl), *n., v.,* **-led, -ling.** —*n.* **1.** comb used in dressing flax, hemp, etc. **2.** one of the long, slender feathers on the neck of certain birds. **3.** the neck plumage of certain birds. **4.** a wingless artificial fly, used by fishermen. —*v.* comb (flax, hemp, etc.) with a hackle. [ME *hakell;* akin to HECKLE] —**hack′ler,** *n.*

hack·le² (hak′əl), *v.,* **-led, -ling.** cut roughly; hack; mangle. [< *hack¹*]

hack·ney (hak′ni), *n., pl.* **-neys,** *adj., v.,* **-neyed, -ney·ing.** —*n.* **1.** horse for ordinary riding. **2.** carriage for hire. —*adj.* hired. —*v.* use too often; make commonplace. [< OF *haquenee*]

hack·neyed (hak′nid), *adj.* used too often; commonplace. —Syn. trite, stale, banal.

hack·saw (hak′sô′), *n.* saw for cutting metal, consisting of a narrow, fine-toothed blade fixed in a frame.

had (had), *v.* pt. and pp. of **have.** ➤ **had better, had rather.** *Had better* is the usual idiom for giving advice or making an indirect command: *you had better take care of that cold. You'd better go. Had rather* and *would rather* are both used to express preference: *He would rather ski than eat. He had rather ski than eat.*

had·dock (had′ək), *n., pl.* **-docks** or (*esp. col-*

lectively) —**dock.** a food fish of the N Atlantic, somewhat like a cod, but smaller. [ME *haddok*]

Ha·des (hā′dēz), *n.* 1. *Gk. Myth.* a. home of the dead, below the earth. b. Pluto. 2. hades, *Colloq.* hell. [< Gk. *Haides*]

had·n't (had′ənt), had not.

Ha·dri·an (hā′dri-ən), *n.* 76–138 A.D., Roman emperor 117–138 A.D.

hadst (hadst), *v. Archaic.* 2nd pers. sing. pt. of have.

haem·a·tite (hem′ə-tīt; hē′mə-), *n.* hematite.

hae·mo·glo·bin (hē′mə-glō′bən; hem′ə-), *n.* hemoglobin.

hae·mo·phil·i·a (hē′mə-fil′i-ə; hem′ə-), *n.* hemophilia. —**hae·mo·phil·i·ac** (hē′mə-fil′i-ak; hem′ə-), *n.*

haem·or·rhage (hem′ə-rij; hem′rij), *n.* hemorrhage. —**haem·or·rhag·ic** (hem′ə-raj′ik), *adj.*

haem·or·rhoids (hem′ə-roidz), *n.pl.* hemorrhoids.

haf·ni·um (haf′ni-əm; häf′-), *n. Chem.* a rare metallic element, Hf, somewhat like zirconium. [< *Hafnia*, L name for Copenhagen]

haft (haft; häft), *n.* handle (of a knife, sword, dagger, etc.). —*v.* furnish with a handle or hilt; set in a haft. [OE *hæft*]

hag (hag), *n.* 1. a very ugly old woman, esp. one who is vicious or malicious. 2. witch. [ME *hagge*, akin to OE *hægtesse* witch, fury] —**hag′gish,** *adj.* —**hag′like′,** *adj.*

Ha·gar (hā′gär; -gər), *n. Bible.* slave of Abraham's wife Sarah. Gen. 16.

hag·fish (hag′fish′), *n., pl.* **-fish·es** or (*esp. collectively*) **-fish.** a small salt-water fish shaped like an eel, that attaches itself to other fish by its round mouth and bores into them with its horny teeth.

Hag·ga·dah, Hag·ga·da (hə-gä′də), *n., pl.* **-doth** (-dōth). 1. story or legend in the Talmud that explains the law. 2. the legendary part of the Talmud. 3. religious rites for the first two nights of the Jewish Passover. —**hag·gad·ic** (hə-gad′ik; -gä′dik), **hag·gad′i·cal,** *adj.*

Hag·ga·i (hag′i-ī; hag′ī; -ā-ī), *n.* 1. a Hebrew prophet. 2. book of the Old Testament.

hag·gard (hag′ərd), *adj.* wild-looking from pain, fatigue, worry, hunger, etc. —**hag′gard·ly,** *adv.* —**hag′gard·ness,** *n.* —**Syn.** gaunt, careworn, emaciated.

hag·gis (hag′is), *n. Scot.* heart, lungs, and liver of a sheep mixed with suet and oatmeal and boiled in the stomach of the animal.

hag·gle (hag′əl), *v.,* **-gled, -gling.** 1. dispute about a price or the terms of a bargain; wrangle. 2. mangle in cutting; hack. [< *hag* chop < Scand. *höggva*] —**hag′gler,** *n.*

hag·i·ol·o·gy (hag′i-ol′ə-ji; hā′ji-), *n., pl.* **-gies.** 1. literature that deals with the lives and legends of saints. 2. list of saints. [< Gk. *hagios* holy + -LOGY] —**hag·i·o·log·ic** (hag′i-ə-loj′ik; hā′ji-), **hag′i·o·log′i·cal,** *adj.* —**hag′i·ol′o·gist,** *n.*

hag·rid·den (hag′rid′ən), *adj.* worried or tormented, as if by witches.

Hague (hāg), *n.* The, city in SW Netherlands; site of the World Court.

Hai·fa (hī′fə), *n.* seaport in NW Israel.

hail¹ (hāl), *v.* 1. shout in welcome to; greet; cheer. 2. greet as: *they hailed him leader.* 3. call loudly to; shout to. 4. **hail from,** come from. [< n.] —*n.* 1. greeting; cheer. 2. a loud call; shout. 3. **within hail,** near enough to hear a call or shout. —*interj. Poetic.* greetings! welcome! [< Scand. *heill* health] —**hail′er,** *n.* —**Syn.** *v.* 1. address, salute.

hail² (hāl), *n.* 1. small, roundish pieces of ice coming down from the clouds in a shower; frozen rain. 2. shower like hail: *a hail of bullets.* —*v.* 1. come down in hail. 2. pour down or upon in a shower like hail. [OE *hægel*]

hail·stone (hāl′stōn′), *n.* a small, roundish piece of ice coming down from the clouds.

hail·storm (hāl′stôrm′), *n.* storm with hail.

hair (hār), *n.* 1. a fine, threadlike growth from the skin of people and animals. 2. mass of such

growths. 3. a fine, threadlike growth from the outer layer of plants. 4. a very narrow space; something very small; least degree. 5. split hairs, make too fine distinctions. [OE *hǣr*] —**hair′less, ** *adj.* —**hair′less·ness,** *n.* —**hair′like′,** *adj.*

hair·breadth (hār′bredth′), *n., adj.* hair's-breadth.

hair·cloth (hār′klôth′; -kloth′), *n.* cloth made of horsehair or camel's hair, used to cover furniture, stiffen garments, etc.

hair·cut (hār′kut′), *n.* act or manner of cutting the hair. —**hair′cut′ter,** *n.*

hair·do (hār′dü′), *n., pl.* **-dos.** way of arranging the hair.

hair·dress·er (hār′dres′ər), *n.* person whose work is taking care of people's hair or cutting it. —**hair′dress′ing,** *n., adj.*

hair·line (hār′līn′), *n.* very thin line.

hair·pin (hār′pin′), *n.* pin, usually a U-shaped piece of wire, shell, or celluloid, used by women to keep the hair in place.

hair-rais·ing (hār′rāz′ing), *adj. Colloq.* making the hair stand on end; terrifying.

hair's-breadth, hairs-breadth (hārz′- bredth′), *n.* a very small space or distance. —*adj.* extremely narrow or close. Also, **hair′breadth′.**

hair shirt, a rough shirt or girdle made of horsehair, worn as a penance.

hair·split·ting (hār′split′ing), *n., adj.* making too fine distinctions. —**hair′split′ter,** *n.*

hair·spring (hār′spring′), *n.* a fine, hairlike spring that regulates the motion of the balance wheel in a watch or clock.

hair trigger, trigger that operates by very slight pressure.

hair·y (hār′i), *adj.,* **hair·i·er, hair·i·est.** 1. covered with hair; having much hair. 2. of or like hair. —**hair′i·ness,** *n.* —**Syn.** 1. shaggy, hirsute.

Hai·ti (hā′ti), *n.* 1. former name of Hispaniola. 2. republic in the western part of this island. —**Hai·ti·an** (hā′ti·ən; hā′shən), *adj., n.*

hake (hāk), *n., pl.* **hakes** or (*esp. collectively*) **hake,** a sea fish related to the cod. [? < Scand. (Norw.) *hakefisk,* lit., hook fish; from the hooklike growth under the lower jaw]

ha·kim¹ (hə-kēm′), *n.* in Moslem use, a physician. [< Ar. *ḥakīm* wise man]

ha·kim² (hä′kim), *n.* in Moslem use, a ruler or judge. [< Ar. *ḥākim*]

hal·berd (hal′bərd), **hal·bert** (-bərt), *n.* weapon that is both a spear and a battle-ax, used in warfare in the 15th and 16th centuries. [< F *hallebarde* < Ital. *alabarda*]

hal·berd·ier (hal′bər-dir′), *n.* soldier armed with a halberd.

hal·cy·on (hal′si-ən), *adj.* calm; peaceful; happy. —*n. Archaic or Poetic.* bird that was supposed to calm the waves; kingfisher. [< L < Gk., var. of *alkyon* kingfisher]

hale¹ (hāl), *adj.,* **hal·er, hal·est.** strong and well; healthy. [OE *hāl*] —**hale′ness,** *n.* —**Syn.** sound, robust. —**Ant.** sickly.

hale² (hāl), *v.,* **haled, hal·ing.** 1. drag by force. 2. compel to go. [< OF *haler* < Gmc. Doublet of HAUL.]

Hale (hāl), *n.* Nathan, 1755–1776, American patriot hanged as a spy by the British.

Halberdier

half (haf; häf), *n., pl.* **halves,** *adj., adv.* —*n.* 1. one of two equal (or approximately equal) parts. 2. one of two equal periods in certain games. 3. a half-hour: *half past ten.* —*adj.* 1. forming a half; being or making half of. 2. not complete; being only part of: *a half truth.* —*adv.* 1. to half of the full amount or degree: *a glass half full of milk.* 2. partly: *half aloud.* 3. almost: *half dead from hunger.* 4. not half bad, fairly good. [OE] ≯ **half.** The more formal idiom is *a half,* the informal *half a: He ran half a mile, half an hour* (informal). *He ran a half mile, a half hour* (formal).

half-and-half (haf′ənd-haf′; häf′ənd-häf′),

adj. **1.** half one thing and half another. **2.** not clearly one thing or the other. —*adv.* in two equal parts. —*n.* **1.** *U.S.* mixture of milk and cream. **2.** *Brit.* beverage of two mixed liquors.

half-back (haf′bak′; häf′-), *n. Football.* player whose position is behind the forward line.

half-baked (haf′bākt′; häf′-), *adj.* **1.** not cooked enough. **2.** *Colloq.* not fully worked out; incomplete. **3.** *Colloq.* not experienced; showing poor judgment.

half-blood (haf′blud′; häf′-), *n.* **1.** half-breed. **2.** person related to another person through one parent only. —**half′-blood′ed,** *adj.*

half blood, relationship between persons who are related through one parent only.

half-breed (haf′brēd′; häf′-), *n.* person whose parents are of different races.

half brother, brother related through one parent only.

half-caste (haf′kast′; häf′käst′), *n.* half-breed.

half cock, 1. position of the hammer of a gun when it is pulled back halfway and locked. **2.** **go off at half cock, a.** fire too soon. **b.** act or speak without sufficient thought or preparation.

half dollar, *Am.* a silver coin of the United States and Canada, worth 50 cents.

half eagle, *Am.* a former gold coin of the United States, worth $5.00.

half-heart-ed (haf′här′tid; häf′-), *adj.* lacking courage, interest, or enthusiasm. —**half′-heart′ed-ly,** *adv.* —**half′-heart′ed-ness,** *n.* —**Syn.** indifferent, perfunctory, lukewarm.

half hitch, an easily unfastened knot, formed by passing the end of a rope under and over its standing part and then inside the loop.

half-hour (haf′our′; häf′-), *n.* **1.** thirty minutes. **2.** the halfway point in an hour. —*adj.* of or lasting a half-hour. —**half′-hour′ly,** *adv.*

Half hitch

half-life (haf′līf′; häf′-), *n.* time in which half of the original radiant energy of an element is given off, used to measure radioactivity.

half-mast (haf′mast′; häf′mäst′), *n.* position halfway down from the top of a mast, staff, etc. —*v.* hang at half-mast.

half moon, 1. moon when only half of its surface appears bright. **2.** something shaped like a half moon or crescent.

half nelson, *Wrestling.* hold accomplished by hooking one arm around an opponent's armpit and putting the hand on the back of his neck.

half note, *Music.* note held half as long as a whole note; minim.

Half note

half-pen-ny (hā′pə-ni; hāp′ni), *n.,* *pl.* **half-pen-nies** (hā′pə-niz; hāp′niz), **half-pence** (hā′pəns), *adj.* —*n. Brit.* a bronze coin worth half a British penny. —*adj.* **1.** worth only a halfpenny. **2.** having little value.

half sister, sister related through one parent only.

half sole, sole of a shoe or boot from the toe to the instep.

half-sole (haf′sōl′; häf′-), *v.,* **-soled, -soling.** put a new half sole or half soles on (shoes, etc.).

half step, 1. *Music.* difference in pitch between two adjacent keys on a piano. **2.** *U.S. Army.* a marching step of 15 inches in quick time, or of 18 inches in double time.

half-tone (haf′tōn′; häf′-), *n.* **1.** process in photoengraving for making pictures for books and magazines. **2.** picture made by this process. **3.** *Painting.* tone between the highlight and deep shades.

half tone, *Music.* half step (def. 1).

half-track, half track (haf′trak′; häf′-), *n.* **1.** an endless-track mechanism for vehicles, driven by revolving inside wheels. **2.** *U.S. Army.* a motor vehicle that has wheels in front and short tracks in the rear for driving, used to carry personnel and weapons.

half-way (haf′wā′; häf′-), *adv.* **1.** half the way: *halfway home.* **2.** go or meet halfway, do

one's share to agree or be friendly (with). —*adj.* **1.** midway: *a halfway house between two towns.* **2.** not going far enough; incomplete.

half-wit (haf′wit′; häf′-), *n.* **1.** a feeble-minded person. **2.** a stupid, foolish person.

half-wit-ted (haf′wit′id; häf′-), *adj.* **1.** feeble-minded. **2.** very stupid; foolish. —**half′-wit′ted-ly,** *adv.* —**half′-wit′ted-ness,** *n.*

hal-i-but (hal′ə-bət; hol′-), *n.,* *pl.* **-buts** or (*esp. collectively*) **-but.** a large flatfish much used for food, often weighing several hundred pounds. [ME *halybutte* < *haly* holy + *butte* flatfish; eaten on holy days]

hal-i-dom (hal′ə-dəm), **hal-i-dome** (-dōm), *n. Archaic.* **1.** sanctuary. **2.** a holy relic. [OE *hāligdōm.* See HOLY, -DOM.]

Hal-i-fax (hal′ə-faks), *n.* seaport in SE Canada, the capital of Nova Scotia.

hal-ite (hal′īt; hā′līt), *n.* a native rock salt. [< NL, < Gk. *hals* salt]

hal-i-to-sis (hal′ə-tō′sis), *n.* bad or offensive breath. [< NL, < L *halitus* breath]

hall (hôl), *n.* **1.** *U.S.* way to go through a building; passageway. **2.** passageway or room at the entrance of a building. **3.** a large room for holding meetings, parties, banquets, etc. **4.** a building for public business: *the town hall.* **5.** a building of a school, college, or university. **6.** *Brit.* residence of a landowner. [OE *heall*]

Hal-le (häl′ə), *n.* city in C Germany.

hal-le-lu-jah, hal-le-lu-iah (hal′ə-lū′yə), *interj.* praise ye the Lord! —*n.* a rendering of this. Also, **alleluia, alleluiah.** [< Heb. *hallēlū-yāh* praise ye Yah (Jehovah)]

hal-liard (hal′yərd), *n. Naut.* halyard.

hall-mark (hôl′märk′), *n.* **1.** an official mark indicating standard of purity, put on gold and silver articles. **2.** mark or sign of genuineness or good quality. —*v.* put a hallmark on. [from Goldsmiths' *Hall* in London, the seat of the Goldsmiths' Company, by whom the stamping was legally regulated]

hal-loo (hə-lū′), *interj., n., pl.* **-loos,** *v.,* **-looed, -loo-ing.** —*interj.* **1.** shout to make hounds run faster. **2.** call or shout to attract attention. —*n., v.* shout; call.

hal-low[1] (hal′ō), *v.* **1.** make holy; make sacred. **2.** honor as holy or sacred. [OE *hālgian* < *hālig* holy] —**Syn.** **1.** consecrate, sanctify.

hal-low[2] (hal′ō), *interj., n., v.* halloo.

hal-lowed (hal′ōd; *in worship, often* hal′ō-id), *adj.* **1.** made holy; sacred; consecrated. **2.** honored or observed as holy. —**hal′lowed-ness,** *n.*

Hal-low-een, Hal-low-e'en (hal′ō-ēn′; hol′-), *n.* evening of October 31, preceding All Saints' Day. [for *Allhallow-even*]

Hal-low-mas (hal′ō-məs; -mas), *n.* a former name of All Saints' Day.

hal-lu-ci-na-tion (hə-lū′sə-nā′shən), *n.* **1.** apparent perception of an object or sound that is not really present. **2.** the object or sound apparently perceived; illusion. [< LL, < *alucinari* wander (of the mind)]

hall-way (hôl′wā′), *n.* **1.** *Am.* way to go through a building. **2.** passageway or room at the entrance of a building. —**Syn.** **1.** corridor, passage. **2.** hall.

ha-lo (hā′lō), *n., pl.* **-los, -loes,** *v.,* **-loed, -loing.** —*n.* **1.** ring of light around the sun, moon, or other shining body. **2.** a golden circle of light represented about the head of a saint, etc. **3.** glory or glamour that surrounds an idealized person or thing: *a halo of romance surrounds King Arthur and his knights.* —*v.* surround with a halo. [< L (def. 1) < Gk. *halos* disk, threshing floor (with ref. to circular path of the oxen)] —**ha′lo-like′,** *adj.*

Halo about the head of Joan of Arc

hal-o-gen (hal′ə-jən), *n. Chem.* any one of the elements iodine, bromine, chlorine, and fluorine, that combine directly with metals to form salts. [< Gk. *hals* salt + *gennaein* to produce]

Hals (häls), *n. Frans,* 1580?-1666, Dutch painter of portraits and everyday scenes.

halt[1] (hôlt), *v.* stop for a time, as in marching.

[< n.] —n. **1.** a temporary stop. **2.** call a halt, order a stop. [< F *halte* < G *halt* < *halten* to stop]

halt² (hôlt), v. **1.** be in doubt; hesitate; waver: *speak in a halting manner.* **2.** be faulty or imperfect: *a halting line of verse.* **3.** Archaic. lame. —adj. Archaic. lame. —n. Archaic. lameness. [OE *healt*, adj.] —**halt′ing·ly,** adv. —**halt′ing·ness,** n.

hal·ter (hôl′tər), n. **1.** rope, strap, etc., for leading or tying an animal. **2.** rope for hanging a person; noose. **3.** death by hanging. **4.** an abbreviated shirt for women which fastens behind the neck and across the back. —v. put a halter on; tie with a halter. [OE *hælftre*]

halve (hav; häv), v., **halved, halv·ing. 1.** share equally: *halve expenses on a trip.* **2.** reduce to half: *halve the time of doing the work.* [< *half*]

halves (havz; hävz), n. **1.** pl. of **half. 2.** by **halves,** a. partly. b. in a half-hearted way. **3. go halves,** share equally.

hal·yard (hal′yərd), n. Naut. rope or tackle used on a ship to raise or lower a sail, yard, flag, etc. Also, **halliard.** [ME *hallyer* < HALE²]

ham (ham), n. **1.** salted and smoked meat from the upper part of a hog's hind leg. **2.** the upper part of an animal's hind leg, used for food. **3.** Often, **hams.** back of the thigh; thigh and buttock. **4.** part of the leg back of the knee. **5.** Am., Slang. a poor actor or performer. **6.** Am., Slang. an amateur radio operator. [OE *hamm*]

Ham (ham), n. Bible. the second son of Noah.

ham·a·dry·ad (ham′ə·drī′əd; -ad), n. Gk. Myth. a wood nymph supposed to live and die with the tree she dwelt in; dryad. [< L < Gk. *Hamadryas* < *hama* together (with) + *drys* tree]

ham·burg (ham′bèrg), n. Am. hamburger.

Ham·burg (ham′bèrg), n. city in NW Germany, on the Elbe River.

ham·burg·er (ham′bèr·gər), n. Am. **1.** ground beef, usually shaped into round, flat cakes and fried or broiled. **2.** Colloq. sandwich made with this meat. [< G, pertaining to *Hamburg*]

Hamburg steak, hamburg steak, Am. hamburger (def. 1).

Ham·il·ton (ham′əl·tən), n. **1.** Alexander, 1757–1804, American statesman, the first secretary of the treasury. **2.** city in SE Canada. **3.** capital of Bermuda.

Ham·it·ic (ham·it′ik; hə·mit′-), adj. of or having to do with a group of languages in N and E Africa, including ancient Egyptian, Berber, Ethiopian, etc.

ham·let (ham′lit), n. a small village. [< OF *hamelet,* dim. of *hamel* village < Gmc.; akin to HOME]

Ham·let (ham′lit), n. **1.** one of Shakespeare's greatest tragedies, first printed in 1603. **2.** the principal character in this play.

Ham·mar·skjöld (ham′ər·shèld′), n. Dag, 1905–1961, Swedish statesman; Secretary General of the United Nations, 1953–1961.

ham·mer (ham′ər), n. **1.** tool with a metal head and a handle, used to drive nails and beat metal into shape. **2.** anything shaped or used like a hammer: a. mallet or gavel used by an auctioneer. b. cock of a gun or pistol. —v. **1.** drive, hit, or work with a hammer. **2.** beat into shape with a hammer. **3.** fasten by using a hammer. **4.** hit again and again. **5.** force by many efforts. **6.** work out with much effort. [OE *hamor*] —**ham′mer·er,** n. —**ham′mer·less,** adj. —**ham′mer·like′,** adj.

hammer and sickle, symbol of a sickle and hammer crossed, used on the flag of the Soviet Union since 1923. The two elements represent the farmer and the laborer.

ham·mer·head (ham′ər·hed′), n. a fierce shark whose wide head looks somewhat like a double-headed hammer.

hammer lock, Wrestling. a hold in which an opponent's arm is twisted and held behind his back.

ham·mock (ham′ək), n. a hanging bed or couch made of canvas, netted cord, etc. [< Sp. *hamaca* < Carib] —**ham′mock·like′,** adj.

ham·per¹ (ham′pər), v. hold back; hinder. [ME *hampre(n)*] —Syn. restrain, restrict.

ham·per² (ham′pər), n. a large basket, usually with a cover. [var. of *hanaper* < OF, < *hanap* cup < Gmc.]

Hamp·ton Roads (hamp′tən), a southern extension of Chesapeake Bay.

ham·string (ham′string′), n., v., -**strung** or (Rare) -**stringed, -string·ing.** —n. **1.** one of the tendons at the back of the knee in man. **2.** the great tendon at the back of the hock of a four-footed animal. —v. **1.** cripple by cutting the hamstring. **2.** destroy activity, efficiency, etc., of.

Han·cock (han′kok), n. John, 1737–1793, American statesman, the first signer of the Declaration of Independence.

hand (hand), n. **1.** the end part of an arm; part that a person grasps and holds things with. **2.** anything resembling a hand in shape, appearance, or use. **3.** a hired worker who uses his hands: *a farm hand.* **4.** Often, **hands.** possession; control: *this is no longer in my hands.* **5.** part or share in doing something: *he had no hand in the matter.* **6.** side: *at her left hand stood two men.* **7.** source: *she heard the story at second hand.* **8.** style of handwriting: *he writes in a clear hand.* **9.** a person's signature. **10.** skill; ability. **11.** person, with reference to action, skill, or ability: *she is a great hand at thinking up new games.* **12.** round of applause or clapping: *the crowd gave the winner a big hand.* **13.** promise of marriage. **14.** measure used in giving the height of horses, etc.; breadth of a hand; 4 inches. **15.** cards held by a player in one round of a card game. **16.** one round in a card game. **17.** player in a card game. **18.** at hand, a. within reach; near; close. b. ready. **19.** bear or give a hand, help. **20.** by hand, by using the hands, not machinery. **21.** change hands, pass from one person to another. **22.** hand in hand, a. holding hands. b. together. **23.** in hand, a. under control. b. in possession. c. going along; being done. **24.** lay hands on, a. seize; take; get. b. arrest. c. attack; harm. d. bless by touching with the hands. **25.** on hand, a. within reach; near; close. b. ready. c. Am. present. **26.** on the other hand, considering the other side; from the opposite point of view. **27.** out of hand, a. beyond control. b. at once. c. finished; done with. —v. **1.** give with the hand; pass; pass along: *please hand me the butter.* **2.** help with the hand: *the polite boy handed the lady into her car.* —adj. of, for, by, or in the hand. [OE] —**hand′less,** adj.

hand·bag (hand′bag′), n. **1.** a woman's small bag for money, keys, cosmetics, etc. **2.** a small traveling bag to hold clothes, etc.

hand·ball (hand′bôl′), n. **1.** game played by hitting a small ball against a wall with the hand. **2.** ball used in this game.

hand·bar·row (hand′bar′ō), n. frame with two handles at each end by which it is carried.

hand·bill (hand′bil′), n. a printed announcement to be handed out to people.

hand·book (hand′bûk′), n. **1.** a small book of reference; manual. **2.** guidebook for tourists. **3.** book for recording bets.

hand·breadth (hand′bredth′), n. breadth of a hand, used as a measure. It varies from 2½ to 4 inches. Also, **hand's-breadth.**

hand·cart (hand′kärt′), n. a small cart pulled or pushed by hand.

hand·cuff (hand′kuf′), n. Usually, **handcuffs.** device to keep a person from using his hands, usually one of a pair of metal clasps joined by a short chain and fastened around the wrists. —v. put handcuffs on.

Handcuffs and key

-**handed,** suffix. **1.** having a hand or hands. **2.** having a certain kind or number of hands, as in *left-handed.* **3.** using a certain number of hands: *a two-handed stroke.*

Han·del (han′dəl), n. George Frederick, 1685–1759, German musical composer.

hand·ful (hand′fûl), n., pl. -**fuls. 1.** as much

age, câre, fär; ēqual, tèrm; īce; ōpen, ôrder; pút, rüle, ûse; th, then; ə=a in about.

or as many as the hand can hold. 2. a small number or quantity. 3. *Colloq.* person or thing that is hard to manage.

hand·i·cap (han'di·kap), *n., v.,* -capped, -cap·ping. —*n.* 1. race, contest, game, etc., in which the better contestants are given certain disadvantages, or the poorer ones certain advantages, so that all have an equal chance to win. 2. disadvantage or advantage given. 3. something that puts a person at a disadvantage; hindrance. —*v.* 1. give a handicap to. 2. put at a disadvantage; hinder. [for *hand in cap;* appar. with ref. to an old game] —hand'i·cap'per, *n.*

hand·i·craft (han'di·kraft; -kräft), *n.* 1. skill with the hands. 2. trade or art requiring skill with the hands. [alter. of *handcraft,* patterned after *handiwork*] —hand'i·crafts'man, *n.* —hand'i·crafts'man·ship, *n.*

hand·i·work (han'di·wėrk'), *n.* 1. work done with the hands. 2. work that a person has done himself. 3. result of a person's action. [OE *handgeweorc* handwork]

hand·ker·chief (hang'kər·chif), *n.* 1. a soft, square piece of cloth used for wiping the nose, face, eyes, etc. 2. piece of cloth worn over the head or around the neck; kerchief.

han·dle (han'dəl), *n., v.,* -dled, -dling. —*n.* 1. part of a thing made to be held or grasped by the hand. 2. chance; opportunity; occasion: *a handle for gossip.* —*v.* 1. touch, feel, hold, or move with the hand; use the hands on. 2. manage; direct; control. 3. behave or act when handled: *this car handles easily.* 4. deal with; treat. 5. *Am.* deal in; trade in: *that store handles meat and groceries.* [OE, < *hand*] —han'dled, *adj.* —han'dle·less, *adj.*

handle bar. Often, **handle bars.** the bar, usually curved, in front of the rider, by which a bicycle, etc., is guided.

han·dler (han'dlər), *n.* 1. person or thing that handles. 2. person who helps to train a boxer or who acts as his second.

hand·made (hand'mād'), *adj.* made by hand, not by machinery; not machine-made.

hand·maid (hand'mād'), **hand·maid·en** (-mād'ən), *n.* 1. a female servant. 2. a female attendant.

hand organ, a large music box that is made to play tunes by turning a crank.

hand·out (hand'out'), *n. Am., Slang.* 1. portion of food, money, etc. handed out: *to give a handout to a beggar.* 2. money given out, as by the government, with little or nothing expected in return. 3. written material given to reporters as news, but often contrived to serve some purpose of publicity, propaganda, etc.

hand·picked (hand'pikt'), *adj.* 1. picked by hand. 2. carefully selected. 3. unfairly selected.

hand·rail (hand'rāl'), *n.* railing used as a guard or support on a stairway, platform, etc.

hand's-breadth (handz'bredth'), *n.* handbreadth.

hand·sel (han'səl), *n.* gift made at New Year's or on entering a new job, house, etc. Also, hansel. [OE *handselen* giving of the hand (i.e., to confirm a bargain)]

hand·shake (hand'shāk'), *n.* a clasping and shaking each other's hands in friendship.

hand·some (han'səm), *adj.,* -som·er, -som·est. 1. good-looking; pleasing in appearance. We usually say that a man is handsome, but that a woman is pretty or beautiful. 2. fairly large; considerable: *a handsome sum of money.* 3. generous: *a handsome gift.* [ME, easy to handle, ready at hand < *hand* + -*some*[1]] —hand'some·ly, *adv.* —hand'some·ness, *n.*

hand·spike (hand'spīk'), *n.* bar used as a lever, esp. on a ship.

hand·spring (hand'spring'), *n.* spring or leap in which a person turns his heels over his head while balancing on one or both hands.

hand-to-hand (hand'tə·hand'), *adj.* close together; at close quarters.

hand-to-mouth (hand'tə·mouth'), *adj.* not providing for the future; not thrifty.

hand·work (hand'wėrk'), *n.* work done by hand, not by machinery.

hand·writ·ing (hand'rīt'ing), *n.* 1. writing by hand; writing with pen, pencil, etc. 2. manner or style of writing.

hand·y (han'di), *adj.,* hand·i·er, hand·i·est. 1. easy to reach or use; saving work; convenient. 2. skillful with the hands. 3. easy to handle or manage. —hand'i·ly, *adv.* —hand'i·ness, *n.*

handy man, man who does odd jobs.

Han·ford (han'fərd), *n.* community in S Washington, important industrial center for atomic research.

hang (hang), *v.,* hung or (*esp. for execution or suicide*) hanged, hang·ing. —*v.* 1. fasten or be fastened to something above. 2. fasten or be fastened so as to swing or turn freely: *hang a door on its hinges.* 3. put to death by hanging with a rope around the neck. 4. die by hanging. 5. cover or decorate with things that hang: *hang a window with curtains.* 6. bend down; droop: *he hung his head in shame.* 7. fasten in position. 8. attach (paper, etc.) to walls. 9. depend. 10. hold fast; cling. 11. be doubtful or undecided; hesitate; waver. 12. *Am.* keep (a jury) from making a decision or reaching a verdict. One member can hang a jury by refusing to agree with the others. 13. loiter; linger. 14. hover. 15. hang on. a. hold tightly (to). b. be unwilling to let go, stop, or leave. c. depend on. d. consider or listen to very carefully. 16. hang up, a. put on a hook, peg, etc. b. put a telephone receiver back in place. —*n.* 1. way that a thing hangs. 2. *Am., Colloq.* way of using or doing; idea. 3. a trifle: *not care a hang.* [OE *hangian*] —hang'a·ble, *adj.* ➤ hanged, hung. In formal English the principal parts of *hang* when referring to the death penalty are *hang, hanged, hanged,* archaic forms kept alive by legal phrases; in other senses they are *hang, hung, hung:* murderers are *hanged,* pictures are *hung.* Informal usage does not keep this distinction.

hang·ar (hang'ər), *n.* 1. shed for airplanes or airships. 2. shed. [< F, ? < Gmc.]

hang·bird (hang'bėrd'), *n. Am.* any bird that builds a hanging nest, esp. the Baltimore oriole.

Hang·chow (hang'chou'), *n.* seaport in E China.

hang·dog (hang'dôg'; -dog'), *adj.* ashamed; sneaking; degraded.

hang·er (hang'ər), *n.* 1. person who hangs things: *a paper hanger.* 2. tool or machine that hangs things. 3. thing on which something else is hung: *a coat hanger.* 4. kind of short sword.

hang·er-on (hang'ər·on'; -ôn'), *n., pl.* hang·ers-on. 1. follower; dependent. 2. an undesirable follower. 3. person who often goes to a place.

hang·ing (hang'ing), *n.* 1. death by hanging with a rope around the neck. 2. Often, hangings. thing that hangs from a wall, bed, etc. —*adj.* 1. deserving to be punished by hanging. 2. fastened to something above. 3. leaning over or down. 4. located on a height or steep slope. 5. directed downward; downcast.

hang·man (hang'mən), *n., pl.* -men. man who puts criminals to death by hanging them.

hang·nail (hang'nāl'), *n.* bit of skin that hangs partly loose near a fingernail.

hang·out (hang'out'), *n. Slang.* 1. place where one lives. 2. a rendezvous, esp. for criminals.

hang·o·ver (hang'ō'vər), *n. Am.* 1. *Colloq.* something that remains from an earlier time or condition. 2. *Slang.* condition the morning after drinking too much alcoholic liquor.

hank (hangk), *n.* 1. coil; loop. 2. skein. [appar. < Scand. *hǫnk*]

han·ker (hang'kər), *v.* wish; crave. —hank'er·er, *n.* —han'ker·ing, *n.*

han·kie (hang'ki), *n. Colloq.* handkerchief.

Han·kow (han'kou'), *n.* city in E China, on the Yangtze River.

Han·ni·bal (han'ə·bəl), *n.* 247–183? B.C., a Carthaginian general who invaded Italy.

Ha·noi (hä·noi'), *n.* capital of North Vietnam; formerly the capital of French Indo-China.

Han·o·ver (han'ō·vər; han'ə-), *n.* 1. city in NW Germany. 2. the English royal house from 1714 to 1901. —Han·o·ve·ri·an (han'ō·vir'i·ən; han'ə-), *adj., n.*

hanse (hans), *n.* medieval guild of a town. [< OF < OHG *hansa* band, MHG *hanse* merchants' guild]

Han·se·at·ic League (han'si·at'ik), a medieval league of towns in Germany and nearby countries for the promotion and protection of commerce.

han·sel (han'sǝl), *n.* handsel.

han·som (han'sǝm), *n.* a two-wheeled cab for two passengers, drawn by one horse, with the driver on a seat high up behind the cab. [from name of early designer of such cabs]

hap (hap), *n., v.,* **happed, hap·ping.** *Archaic.* —*n.* chance; luck. —*v.* happen. [< Scand. *happ*]

hap·haz·ard (*n.* hap'haz'ǝrd; *adj., adv.* hap'haz'ǝrd), *n.* chance. —*adj.* random; not planned: *haphazard answers.* —*adv.* by chance; at random. —**hap'haz'ard·ly,** *adv.* —**hap'haz'ard·ness,** *n.*

hap·less (hap'lis), *adj.* unlucky; unfortunate. —**hap'less·ly,** *adv.* —**hap'less·ness,** *n.*

hap·ly (hap'li), *adv. Archaic.* by chance.

hap·pen (hap'ǝn), *v.* 1. take place; occur: *nothing happens here.* 2. be or take place by chance: *accidents will happen.* 3. have the fortune; chance: *I happened to sit by Mary.* 4. be done (to): *something has happened to this lock.* 5. happen on, a. meet. b. find. [ME *happene(n)* < HAP]

hap·pen·ing (hap'ǝn·ing), *n.* thing that happens; event; occurrence.

hap·py (hap'i), *adj.,* **-pi·er, -pi·est.** 1. feeling or showing pleasure and joy; glad. 2. lucky; fortunate: *by a happy chance, I found the money.* 3. clever and fitting; apt; successful and suitable. [ME, < HAP] —**hap'pi·ly,** *adv.* —**hap'pi·ness,** *n.* —**Syn.** 1. pleased, contented, joyful, delighted. 2. favorable. 3. appropriate, felicitous.

hap·py-go-luck·y (hap'i·gō·luk'i), *adj.* taking things easily; trusting to luck. —*adv.* by mere chance.

Haps·burg (haps'bérg), *n.* a German princely family, prominent since about 1100.

har·a·ki·ri (har'ǝ·kir'i; hä'rǝ-), **har·a·kar·i** (-kar'i; -kä'ri), *n.* suicide by ripping open the abdomen with a knife, the national form of honorable suicide in Japan. Also, **hari-kari.** [< Jap., belly cut]

ha·rangue (hǝ·rang'), *n., v.,* **-rangued, -rangu·ing.** —*n.* a noisy speech. 2. a long, pompous speech. —*v.* 1. address in a harangue. 2. deliver a harangue. [< OF *arenge* < Gmc.] —**ha·rangu'er,** *n.*

har·ass (har'ǝs; hǝ·ras'), *v.* 1. trouble by repeated attacks; harry. 2. disturb; worry; torment. [< F *harasser* < OF *harer* set a dog on] —**har'ass·er,** *n.* —**har'ass·ing·ly,** *adv.* —**har'ass·ment,** *n.* —**Syn.** 2. plague, bother, pester.

Har·bin (här'bēn'; -bin), *n.* city in C Manchuria.

har·bin·ger (här'bin·jǝr), *n.* one that goes ahead to announce another's coming; forerunner. —*v.* announce beforehand; announce. [< OF *herbergere* provider of shelter (hence, one who goes ahead), ult. < *herberge* lodging < Gmc.]

har·bor, *esp. Brit.* **har·bour** (här'bǝr), *n.* 1. place of shelter for ships and boats. 2. any place of shelter. —*v.* 1. give shelter to; give a place to hide: *a dog that harbors fleas.* 2. keep or nourish in the mind: *harbor unkind thoughts.* [OE *hereberg* lodgings < *here* army + *beorg* shelter] —**har'bor·er,** *esp. Brit.* **har'bour·er,** *n.* —**har'bor·less,** *esp. Brit.* **har'bour·less,** *adj.* —**Syn.** *n.* 2. refuge, retreat.

har·bor·age, *esp. Brit.* **har·bour·age** (här'bǝr·ij), *n.* 1. shelter for ships and boats. 2. any shelter.

harbor master, officer who has charge of a port and enforces the rules respecting it.

hard (härd), *adj.* 1. solid and firm to the touch; not soft. 2. firmly formed; tight: *a hard knot.* 3. needing much ability, effort, or time; difficult: *a hard problem.* 4. causing much pain, trouble, care, etc.; severe: *a hard illness.* 5. stern; unfeeling: *be hard on a person.* 6. not pleasant; harsh: *a hard face.* 7. *Am., Colloq.* bad; dis-

reputable. 8. stingy. 9. acting or done with energy, persistence, etc.: *a hard worker.* 10. containing mineral salts that interfere with the action of soap: *hard water.* 11. *U.S.* containing much alcohol: *hard liquor.* 12. *Phonet.* pronounced as an explosive sound, not as a fricative or an affricate. The *c* and *g* in *corn* and *get* are "hard"; in *city* and *gem* they are "soft." 13. hard of hearing, somewhat deaf. 14. hard up, *Colloq.* needing money or anything very badly. —*adv.* 1. so as to be hard, solid, or firm: *frozen hard.* 2. firmly; tightly: *hold hard.* 3. with difficulty: *breathe hard.* 4. so as to cause trouble, pain, care, etc.; harshly; severely: *taxes that bear hard upon us.* 5. with effort or energy: *try hard.* 6. close; near: *the house stands hard by the bridge.* 7. *Naut.* to the extreme limit; fully. [OE *heard*] —**hard'ness,** *n.* —**Syn.** *adj.* 1. rigid. 3. arduous, laborious, burdensome. 5. strict.

hard-bit·ten (härd'bit'ǝn), *adj.* stubborn; unyielding; dogged.

hard-boiled (härd'boild'), *adj.* 1. boiled until hard. 2. *Colloq.* not easily influenced by the feelings. 3. *Slang.* hard; rough; tough.

hard coal, anthracite.

hard core, the permanent or most persistent part of any thing or group; central or vital part. —**hard-core** (härd'kôr'; -kōr'), *adj.*

hard·en (här'dǝn), *v.* 1. make or become hard. 2. make or become capable of endurance. 3. make or become unfeeling or pitiless. 4. strengthen. —**hard'en·er,** *n.* —**Syn.** 1. solidify. 2. discipline.

hard goods, machinery, vehicles, and other heavy goods. —**hard-goods** (härd'gŭdz), *adj.*

hard-head·ed (härd'hed'id), *adj.* 1. not easily excited or deceived. 2. stubborn; obstinate. —**hard'-head'ed·ly,** *adv.* —**hard'-head'ed·ness,** *n.* —**Syn.** 1. practical, shrewd.

hard-heart·ed (härd'här'tid), *adj.* without pity; cruel; unfeeling. —**hard'-heart'ed·ly,** *adv.* —**hard'-heart'ed·ness,** *n.*

hard-hit·ting (härd'hit'ing), *adj. Colloq.* vigorous; aggressive; powerful.

har·di·hood (här'di·hůd), *n.* boldness; daring.

Har·ding (här'ding), *n.* Warren Gamaliel, 1865–1923, the 29th president of the United States, 1921–1923.

hard·ly (härd'li), *adv.* 1. only just; barely: *he had hardly reached there, when it began to snow.* 2. not quite: *hardly strong enough.* 3. almost not: *hardly ever.* 4. probably not: *he will hardly come now.* 5. with trouble or effort: *money hardly earned.* 6. harshly; severely: *deal hardly with a person.* ► **hardly.** In writing there is danger of falling into a concealed double negative when using *hardly.* In formal and informal English a sentence like "For the most part our college paper contains hardly nothing" should read "For the most part our college paper contains *hardly anything.*"

hard palate, the front, bony part of the roof of the mouth.

hard·pan (härd'pan'), *n.* 1. hard, firm, underlying earth. 2. *Am.* a solid foundation; hard, underlying reality.

hard-pressed (härd'prest'), *adj. Colloq.* under severe pressure; in difficulty.

hard·ship (härd'ship), *n.* something hard to bear; hard condition of living.

hard·tack (härd'tak'), *n.* a very hard, dry biscuit, eaten by sailors.

hard·top (härd'top'), *adj.* of a passenger car, having a nonfolding top but maximum window space. —*n.* a passenger car of this design.

hard·ware (härd'wâr'), *n.* 1. articles made from metal, as locks, screws, etc. 2. *Am., Colloq.* military equipment, as tanks, guns, etc., as distinguished from manpower.

hard·wood (härd'wůd'), *n.* 1. any hard, compact wood. 2. in forestry, any tree that has broad leaves or does not have needles. 3. wood of such a tree, as the oak or maple.

har·dy (här'di), *adj.,* **-di·er, -di·est.** 1. able to bear hard treatment, fatigue, etc.; strong; robust. 2. able to withstand the cold of winter in the open air: *hardy plants.* 3. bold; daring. 4. too bold; rash. [< OF *hardi,* pp. of *hardir* harden

< Gmc.] —har'di·ly, adv. —har'di·ness, n.
—Syn. 1. hale, hearty. 3. courageous, intrepid.
Har·dy (här'di), n. Thomas, 1840-1928, English novelist and poet.
hare (hãr), n., pl. **hares** or (esp. collectively) **hare.** 1. a gnawing animal very much like a rabbit but larger, having long ears, long hind legs, a short tail, and a divided upper lip. 2. a rabbit. [OE hara] —hare'like', adj.
hare·bell (hãr'bel'), n. a slender plant with blue, bell-shaped flowers; bluebell.
hare·brained (hãr'brãnd'), adj. giddy; heedless; reckless.
hare·lip (hãr'lip'), n. a congenital deformity caused when parts of the lip fail to grow together before birth. —hare'lipped', adj.
har·em (hãr'əm), n. 1. part of a Mohammedan house where the women live. 2. its occupants; the wives, female relatives, female servants, etc., of a Mohammedan household. [< Ar. ḥarim forbidden]
har·i·cot (har'ə·kō), n. string bean. [< Mex. (Nahuatl) ayecotli]
har·i·ka·ri (har'i·kar'i); hä'ri·kä'ri), n. harakiri.
hark (härk), v. 1. listen. 2. hark back, go back; turn back. [ME herkien]
hark·en (här'kən), v. hearken. [OE heorcnian] —hark'en·er, n.
Har·lem (här'ləm), n. part of New York City where many Negroes live.
har·le·quin (här'lə·kwin; -kin), n. 1. Often, Harlequin. character in comedy and pantomime who is usually masked, has a costume of varied colors, and carries a wooden sword. 2. a mischievous person; buffoon. —adj. varied in color; many-colored. [< F; OF var. of Herlequin < ME Herle King King Herla (mythical figure); modern meaning in French is from Ital. arlecchino < F Harlequin]
har·lot (här'lət), n. prostitute. [< OF, vagabond]
har·lot·ry (här'lət·ri), n. prostitution.
harm (härm), n. 1. hurt; damage. 2. evil; wrong. —v. damage; injure; hurt. [OE hearm] —harm'er, n.
harm·ful (härm'fəl), adj. causing harm; injurious; hurtful. —harm'ful·ly, adv. —harm'ful·ness, n. —Syn. detrimental, deleterious, pernicious.
harm·less (härm'lis), adj. causing no harm; that would not harm anyone or anything. —harm'less·ly, adv. —harm'less·ness, n. —Syn. innocuous, inoffensive.
har·mon·ic (här·mon'ik), adj. 1. Music. having to do with harmony. 2. musical. 3. Physics. indicating a series of oscillations accompanying a fundamental frequency. —n. a fainter and higher tone heard along with the main tone; overtone. [< L < Gk. har-monikos harmonic, musical. See HARMONY.] —har·mon'i·cal·ly, adv.
har·mon·i·ca (här·mon'ə-kə), n. Am. a small, oblong musical instrument with metal reeds, played by the mouth; mouth organ.
har·mon·ics (här·mon'iks), n. science of musical sounds.
har·mo·ni·ous (här·mō'ni·əs), adj. 1. agreeing in feelings, ideas, or actions; getting along well together: play together in a harmonious group. 2. arranged so that the parts are orderly or pleasing; going well together: harmonious colors. 3. sweet-sounding; musical. —har·mo'ni·ous·ly, adv. —har·mo'ni·ous·ness, n. —Syn. 1. peaceable, cordial, amicable. 2. congruous, consonant, consistent. 3. melodious. —Ant. 1. antagonistic, unfriendly, hostile.
har·mo·ni·um (här·mō'ni·əm), n. a small organ with metal reeds.
har·mo·nize (här'mə·nīz), v. -nized, -niz·ing. 1. bring into harmony or agreement. 2. be in harmony or agreement: the colors in the room harmonized. 3. Music. add tones to (a melody) to make successive chords. —har'mo·ni·za'tion, n. —har'mo·niz'er, n.

har·mo·ny (här'mə·ni), n., pl. -nies. 1. agreement of feeling, ideas, or actions; getting along well together: work in perfect harmony. 2. an orderly or pleasing arrangement of parts; going well together: harmony of colors in a picture. 3. Music. a. sounding together of notes in a chord. b. study of chords and of relating them to successive chords. [< F < L < Gk. harmonia concord, a joining < harmos joint] —Syn. 1. unity, friendship, peace. 2. congruity.
har·ness (här'nis), n. 1. combination of leather straps, bands, and other pieces used to connect a horse or other animal to a carriage, wagon, plow, etc. 2. Archaic. armor for a knight, soldier, or horse. 3. in harness, in or at one's regular work. —v. 1. put harness on. 2. cause to produce power. 3. Archaic. put armor on. [< OF harneis < Scand.] —har'ness·er, n. —har'ness·less, adj. —har'ness·like', adj.
Har·old II (har'əld), 1022?-1066, the last Saxon king of England, defeated by William the Conqueror in 1066.
harp (härp), n. Music. instrument with strings set in a triangular frame, played by plucking the strings with the fingers. —v. 1. Music. play on a harp. 2. harp on, keep on tiresomely talking or writing about; refer continually to. [OE hearpe] —harp'er, n. —harp'ist, n. —harp'like', adj.
har·poon (här·pün'), n. a barbed spear with a rope tied to it, used for catching whales and other sea animals. —v. strike, catch, or kill with a harpoon. [(? < Du.) < F harpon < L harpe sickle, hook < Gk.] —har·poon'er, n. —har·poon'like', adj.
harp·si·chord (härp'sə·kôrd), n. Music. a stringed instrument like a piano, used from about 1550 to 1750. [< obs. F. harpechorde < harpe harp (< Gmc.) + chorde CHORD²]
Har·py (här'pi), n., pl. -pies. 1. Gk. Legend. any of several filthy, greedy monsters having women's heads and birds' bodies, wings, and claws. 2. harpy, a very greedy person; person who preys upon others. [< L < Gk. harpyia, prob. akin to harpazein snatch]
har·que·bus (här'kwə·bəs), n. an old form of portable gun, used before muskets. Also, arquebus. [< F < Ital. < Du. haakbus, lit., hook gun]
har·ri·dan (har'ə·dən), n. a bad-tempered, disreputable old woman.
har·ri·er¹ (har'i·ər), n. 1. a small hound of the kind used to hunt hares. 2. a cross-country runner. [appar. < hare]
har·ri·er² (har'i·ər), n. 1. person who harries. 2. Am. hawk that preys on small animals.
Har·ri·man (har'ə·mən), n. W(illiam) Averell, born 1891, American political leader, governor of New York from 1954 to 1958.
Har·ris (har'is), n. Joel Chandler, 1848-1908, American author.
Har·ris·burg (har'is·bėrg), n. capital of Pennsylvania, in the S part.
Har·ri·son (har'ə·sən), n. 1. Benjamin, 1833-1901, the 23rd president of the United States, 1889-1893. 2. his grandfather, William Henry, 1773-1841, American general and ninth president of the United States, in 1841.
har·row (har'ō), n. a heavy frame with iron teeth or upright disks, used on plowed fields for breaking up clods, covering seeds, etc. —v. 1. draw a harrow over (land, etc.). 2. hurt; wound. 3. arouse uncomfortable feelings in; distress; torment. [ME harwe] —har'row·er, n. —har'row·ing, adj. —har'row·ing·ly, adv.
har·ry (har'i), v., -ried, -ry·ing. 1. raid and rob with violence. 2. keep troubling; worry; torment. [OE hergian < here army]
harsh (härsh), adj. 1. rough to the touch, taste, eye, or ear; sharp and unpleasant. 2. without pity; cruel; severe. 3. rugged; bleak. [var. of ME harsk < Scand. (Dan.) harsk rancid] —harsh'ly, adv. —harsh'ness, n. —Syn. 1. grating, rasping, acrid, sour, inharmonious, discordant, strident, raucous. 2. unfeeling, unkind.
hart (härt), n., pl. **harts** or (esp. collectively) **hart.** 1. a male red deer after its fifth year. 2. a male deer; stag. [OE heorot]
Harte (härt), n. (Francis) Bret, 1839-1902, American writer of short stories.

har·te·beest (här′tə·bēst; härt′bēst′), n., pl.
-beests or (esp. collectively) **-beest**. a large,
swift African antelope with ringed, curved horns
bent backward at the tips. [< Afrikaans, hart
beast]

Hart·ford (härt′fərd), n. capital of Connecticut, in the C part.

harts·horn (härts′hôrn′), n. 1. ammonia dissolved in water. 2. smelling salts.

har·um-scar·um (hār′əm·skār′əm), adj. reckless; rash. —adv. recklessly; wildly. —n. 1. a
reckless person. 2. reckless behavior. [appar. <
hare frighten + scare]

har·vest (här′vist), n. 1. a reaping and gathering in of grain and other food crops, usually
in the late summer or early autumn. 2. time or
season when grain, fruit, etc., are gathered in.
3. one season's yield of any natural product;
crop. 4. result; consequences. —v. gather in and
bring home for use. [OE hærfest]

har·vest·er (här′vis·tər), n. 1. person who
works in a harvest field; reaper. 2. Am. machine
for harvesting crops, esp. grain.

har·vest·man (här′vist·mən), n., pl. -men.
1. man who harvests. 2. daddy-longlegs.

harvest moon, full moon at harvest time or
about September 23.

Har·vey (här′vi), n. William, 1578–1657, English physician who discovered the circulation of
the blood.

has (haz), v. 3rd pers. sing. pres. indic. of have.

has-been (haz′bin′), n. Colloq. person or thing
whose best days are past.

hash (hash), n. 1. mixture of cooked meat,
potatoes, etc., chopped into small pieces and
fried or baked. 2. mixture; jumble. 3. mess;
muddle. 4. Am., Colloq. meal or meals. [< v.]
—v. 1. chop into small pieces. 2. mess; muddle.
[< F hacher < hache hatchet]

hash·ish, hash·eesh (hash′ēsh), n. the dried
flowers, top leaves, and tender parts of Indian
hemp, used in the Orient for its narcotic effect.
[< Ar. ḥashīsh dried hemp leaves]

has·n't (haz′ənt), has not.

hasp (hasp; häsp), n. clasp or fastening for a
door, window, trunk, box, etc., esp. one that fits
over a staple or into a hole and is fastened by
a peg, padlock, etc. [var. of OE hæpse]

has·sle (has′əl), n. struggle; contest. [appar.
< Southern U.S. dial. hassle pant, breathe noisily
(cf. E dial. hussle, same meaning), frequentative
of E dial. hoose cough, wheeze; related to
wheeze]

has·sock (has′ək), n. 1. a thick cushion to rest
the feet on, sit on, or kneel on. 2. tuft or bunch
of coarse grass. [OE hassuc coarse grass]

hast (hast), v. Archaic. 2nd pers. sing. pres.
indic. of have.

haste (hāst), n., v., hast·ed, hast·ing. —n. 1. a
trying to be quick; hurrying: the king's business
required haste. 2. quickness without thought or
care: haste makes waste. 3. in haste, a. in a
hurry; quickly. b. without careful thought;
rashly. 4. make haste, hurry; be quick. —v.
Poetic. hasten. [< OF < Gmc.] —Syn. n. 1. speed.

has·ten (hās′ən), v. 1. cause to be quick; speed;
hurry: hasten everyone off to bed. 2. be quick;
go fast: hasten to explain, hasten to a place.
—has′ten·er, n. —Syn. 1. quicken, accelerate.

hast·y (hās′ti), adj., hast·i·er, hast·i·est. 1.
hurried; quick: a hasty visit. 2. not well thought
out; rash: a hasty decision. 3. easily angered;
quick-tempered. —hast′i·ly, adv. —hast′i·ness,
n.

hasty pudding, 1. Am. mush made of corn
meal. 2. Brit. mush made of flour or oatmeal.

hat (hat), n., v., hat·ted, hat·ting. —n. 1. a
covering for the head, usually with a brim. 2.
pass the hat, ask for contributions; take up a
collection. —v. cover or furnish with a hat. [OE
hætt] —hat′less, adj. —hat′like′, adj.

hat·band (hat′band′), n. band around the
crown of a hat, just above the brim.

hatch¹ (hach), v. 1. bring forth (young) from
an egg or eggs. 2. keep (an egg or eggs) warm

until the young come out. 3. come out from the
egg: three chickens hatched today. 4. arrange;
plan. 5. plan secretly; plot. —n. 1. act of hatching. 2. the brood hatched. [ME hacche(n)]
—hatch′er, n. —Syn. v. 5. scheme, contrive.

hatch² (hach), n. 1. an opening in a ship's
deck through which the cargo is put in. 2. an
opening in the floor or roof of a building, etc.
3. a trap door covering such an opening. [OE
hæcc]

hatch³ (hach), v. draw, cut, or engrave fine
parallel lines on. [< F hacher chop, hatch. See
HASH.]

hatch·er·y (hach′ər·i; hach′ri), n., pl. -er·ies.
place for hatching eggs of fish, hens, etc.

hatch·et (hach′it), n. 1. a small ax with a short
handle, for use with one hand. 2. tomahawk. 3.
bury the hatchet, Am. make peace. [< OF
hachette, dim. of hache ax. See HASH.] —hatch′-
et·like′, adj.

hatch·ing (hach′ing), n. fine, parallel lines
drawn, cut, or engraved close together.

hatch·ment (hach′mənt), n. in heraldry, a
square tablet bearing the coat of arms of a dead
person, usually placed diagonally.

hatch·way (hach′wā′), n. 1. an opening in the
deck of a ship to the lower part. 2. a similar
opening in a floor, roof, etc.

hate (hāt), v., hat·ed, hat·ing, n. —v. 1. dislike
very strongly: do good to them that hate you.
2. dislike: I hate to study. —n. 1. a strong dislike. 2. object of hatred. [OE hatian] —hat′-
a·ble, hate′a·ble, adj. —hat′er, n. —Syn. v. 1.
detest, abhor, loathe, despise.

hate·ful (hāt′fəl), adj. 1. causing hate; to be
hated. 2. feeling hate; showing hate. —hate′ful-
ly, adv. —hate′ful·ness, n. —Syn. detestable,
odious.

hath (hath), v. Archaic. 3rd pers. sing. pres.
indic. of have.

ha·tred (hā′trid), n. very strong dislike; hate.
—Syn. loathing, aversion, animosity, ill will.

hat·ter (hat′ər), n. person who makes or sells
hats.

hau·ber·geon (hô′bər·jən), n. hab-
ergeon.

hau·berk (hô′bērk), n. a long coat of
mail. [< OF hauberc < Gmc., lit., neck
cover]

haugh·ty (hô′ti), adj., -ti·er, -ti·est.
1. too proud of oneself and too scornful of others: a haughty man. 2. showing pride and scorn: a haughty smile.
3. Archaic. exalted; noble. [< haut or
haught < F haut < L altus high; form
infl. by OG hauh high] —haugh′ti·ly,
adv. —haugh′ti·ness, n. —Syn. 1. arrogant, disdainful, contemptuous.

Hauberk

haul (hôl), v. 1. pull or drag with
force: haul logs to a mill with horses. 2. haul
up, Naut. a. turn a ship nearer to the direction of the wind. b. change the course of (a
ship). 3. change; shift: the wind hauled around
to the east. —n. 1. act of hauling; hard pull. 2.
load hauled. 3. Am. distance that a load is
hauled. 4. amount won, taken, etc., at one
time; catch: a good haul of fish. [< F haler
< Gmc. Doublet of HALE².] —haul′er, n.

haul·age (hôl′ij), n. 1. act of hauling. 2. force
used in hauling. 3. charge made for hauling.

haunch (hônch; hänch), n. 1. part of the body
around the hip; the hip. 2. a hind quarter of an
animal. 3. leg and loin of a deer, sheep, etc.,
used for food. [< OF hanche < Gmc.]

haunt (hônt; hänt), v. 1. go often to; visit frequently: ghosts were supposed to haunt the old
house. 2. be often with; come often to: memories of his youth haunted the old man. 3. stay
habitually. —n. 1. Often, haunts. place frequently gone to or often visited: a swimming
pool is a favorite haunt of boys in summer. 2.
Dial. ghost. [< OF hanter < OE hāmettan shelter (cf. HOME).] —haunt′er, n. —haunt′ing·ly,
adv.

haunt·ed (hôn′tid; hän′-), adj. visited or frequented by ghosts.

haut·boy (hō′boi; ō′–), *n.* oboe. [< F, < *haut* high + *bois* wood; with ref. to its high notes]

hau·teur (hō·tėr′; ō–), *n.* haughtiness; haughty manner or spirit. [< F, < *haut* high < L *altus*]

Ha·van·a (hə·van′ə), *n.* 1. capital of Cuba, on the NW coast. Also, *Spanish* Habana. 2. cigar made from Cuban tobacco.

have (hav; *unstressed* həv, əv), *v., pres. 1* have, *2* have or (*Archaic*) hast, *3* has or (*Archaic*) hath, *pl.* have; *pt. and pp.* had; *ppr.* hav·ing. 1. hold; possess; own: *I have a house in the country.* 2. cause to: *have him shut the door.* 3. be obliged: *men have to eat.* 4. obtain; receive; take; get: *have a seat.* 5. show by action: *have the courage to.* 6. experience: *have fun.* 7. engage in; carry on; perform: *have a talk with him.* 8. allow; permit: *he won't have any noise while he is reading.* 9. maintain; assert: *they will have it so.* 10. keep; retain: *he has the directions in mind.* 11. know; understand: *he has no Latin.* 12. hold in the mind: *have an idea.* 13. be in a certain relation to: *she has three brothers.* 14. *Colloq.* hold an advantage over: *you have him there.* 15. become the father or mother of. 16. *Have* is used with past participles to express completed action (the perfect tense): *they have come.* 17. have it in for, *Colloq.* have a grudge against; try to get revenge on. 18. have it out, fight or argue until a question is settled. 19. have on, wear. 20. have to do with, a. be connected with; be related to. b. be a companion, partner, or friend of. [OE *habban*]

ha·ven (hā′vən), *n.* 1. harbor; port. 2. place of shelter and safety. —*v.* shelter in a haven. [OE *hæfen*] —**ha′ven·less,** *adj.*

have-not (hav′not′), *n. Colloq.* person or country that has little or no property or wealth.

have·n't (hav′ənt), have not.

hav·er·sack (hav′ər·sak), *n.* bag used by soldiers and hikers to carry food. [< F < LG *habersack* oat sack]

hav·oc (hav′ək), *n., v.,* –ocked, –ock·ing. —*n.* 1. very great destruction or injury. 2. play havoc with, injure severely; ruin; destroy. —*v.* devastate. [< AF var. of OF *havot* plundering, devastation] —**hav′ock·er,** *n.* —**Syn.** *n.* 1. wreck, ruin.

Ha·vre (hä′vər; –vrə), *n.* Le Havre.

haw[1] (hô), *n.* 1. the red berry of the hawthorn. 2. the hawthorn. [OE *haga*]

haw[2] (hô), *interj.* a stammering sound between words. —*v.* make this sound; stammer.

haw[3] (hô), *interj.* word of command to horses, oxen, etc., directing them to turn to the left. —*v.* turn to the left.

Ha·wai·i (hə·wī′ē; –wä′yə), *n.* 1. a group of islands in the N Pacific, the 50th state of the United States. *Capital:* Honolulu. 2. the largest of the Hawaiian Islands. —**Ha·wai′ian,** *adj., n.*

Hawaiian Islands, an island group in the N Pacific, a State of the United States.

hawk[1] (hôk), *n.* 1. bird of prey with a strong hooked beak, large curved claws, short rounded wings, and a long tail. 2. bird of prey like a hawk; buzzard or kite. 3. person who is eager for war. —*v.* hunt with trained hawks. [OE *hafoc*] —**hawk′er,** *n.* —**hawk′ing,** *n.* —**hawk′ish, hawk′like′,** *adj.*

Red-tailed hawk (ab. 2 ft. long)

hawk[2] (hôk), *v.* 1. carry (goods) about for sale as a street peddler does. 2. spread (a report) around. [< *hawker* peddler, prob. < MLG *hoker*. See HUCKSTER.] —**hawk′er,** *n.*

hawk[3] (hôk), *v.* clear the throat noisily. —*n.* a noisy effort to clear the throat. [prob. imit.]

hawk-eyed (hôk′īd′), *adj.* having sharp eyes like a hawk.

hawk moth, a large moth with a long body and narrow wings.

hawks·bill turtle (hôks′bil′), **hawk′s-bill,** or **hawksbill,** *n.* a sea turtle whose mouth is shaped like a hawk's beak and whose horny plates furnish tortoise shell.

hawse (hôz; hôs), *n.* 1. part of a ship's bow having holes for hawsers or cables to pass through. 2. one of these holes. 3. space between the bow of a ship at anchor and her anchors. [< Scand. *hāls*]

hawse·hole (hôz′hōl′; hôs′–), *n.* hole in a ship's bow for a hawser to pass through.

haw·ser (hô′zər; –sər), *n.* a large rope or small cable, esp. one used for mooring or towing ships. [appar. < AF *hauceour* < OF *haucier* hoist, ult. < L *altus* high]

haw·thorn (hô′thôrn), *n.* a thorny shrub or tree with clusters of white, red, or pink blossoms and small, red berries called haws.

Haw·thorne (hô′thôrn), *n.* Nathaniel, 1804–1864, American author of novels and stories.

hay (hā), *n.* grass, alfalfa, clover, etc., cut and dried for use as food for cattle, horses, etc. —*v.* cut and dry grass, alfalfa, clover, etc., for hay. [OE *hēg;* akin to HEW]

hay·cock (hā′kok′), *n. Esp. Brit.* a small pile of hay in a field.

Hay·dn (hī′dən; hā′–), *n.* Franz Joseph, 1732–1809, Austrian composer.

Hayes (hāz), *n.* Rutherford B., 1822–1893, the 19th president of the United States, 1877–1881.

hay fever, disease like a cold, caused by the pollen of ragweed and other plants.

hay·field (hā′fēld′), *n.* field where grass, alfalfa, clover, etc., is grown or cut for hay.

hay·loft (hā′lôft′; –loft′), *n.* place in a stable or barn where hay is stored.

hay·mak·er (hā′māk′ər), *n.* 1. one who makes hay, esp. one who tosses and spreads hay to dry. 2. apparatus for drying and curing hay. 3. *Am.* a swinging, upward blow in a fight with fists, often wild but usually of considerable force.

hay·mow (hā′mou′), *n.* 1. hayloft. 2. heap of hay stored in a barn.

hay·seed (hā′sēd′), *n.* 1. seed shaken out of hay. 2. *U.S. Slang.* person from the country; farmer.

hay·stack (hā′stak′), *esp. Brit.* **hay·rick** (–rik′), *n.* a large pile of hay outdoors.

hay·wire (hā′wīr′), *n. Am.* wire used to tie up bales of hay. —*adj. Slang.* 1. in a mess; in utter confusion. 2. crazy; insane.

haz·ard (haz′ərd), *n.* 1. risk; danger; peril: *at all hazards.* 2. chance. 3. any obstruction on a golf course. 4. a dice game. —*v.* 1. take a chance with; risk; venture. 2. expose to risk. [< OF *hasard* < Ar. *az-zahr* the die] —**haz′ard·a·ble,** *adj.* —**haz′ard·er,** *n.* —**haz′ard·less,** *adj.* —**Syn.** *n.* 1. jeopardy. —**Ant.** *n.* 1. security, safety.

haz·ard·ous (haz′ər·dəs), *adj.* dangerous; risky; perilous. —**haz′ard·ous·ly,** *adv.* —**haz′ard·ous·ness,** *n.*

haze[1] (hāz), *n.* 1. a small amount of mist, smoke, dust, etc., in the air. 2. vagueness of the mind; slight confusion. [cf. E dial. *haze* to drizzle, be foggy]

haze[2] (hāz), *v.,* hazed, haz·ing. *Am.* in schools, universities, etc., force (a fellow student, esp. a freshman) to do unnecessary or ridiculous tasks; bully. [< OF *haser* irritate, annoy] —**haz′er,** *n.* —**haz′ing,** *n.*

ha·zel (hā′zəl), *n.* 1. shrub or small tree whose light-brown nuts are good to eat. 2. a light brown. —*adj.* 1. light-brown. 2. of or pertaining to the hazel. [OE *hæsel*]

ha·zel·nut (hā′zəl·nut′), *n.* nut of the hazel.

Haz·litt (haz′lit), *n.* William, 1778–1830, English critic and essayist.

ha·zy (hā′zi), *adj.,* –zi·er, –zi·est. 1. full of haze; misty; smoky: *hazy air.* 2. rather confused; vague; obscure: *hazy ideas.* —**ha′zi·ly,** *adv.* —**ha′zi·ness,** *n.*

H-bomb (āch′bom′), *n.* the hydrogen bomb.

he (hē; *unstressed* ē, i), *pron., nom.,* he; *poss.,* his, of him, of his; *obj.,* him; *pl.nom.,* they; *poss.,* theirs, their, of them, of theirs; *obj.,* them; *n., pl.* he's. —*pron.* 1. boy, man, or male animal spoken about or mentioned before. 2. anyone: *he who hesitates is lost.* —*n.* boy; man; male animal. [OE *hē*]

He, *Chem.* helium.

head (hed), *n., pl.* **heads** (*1–7, 9–28*), **head** (*def. 8*), *adj., v.* —*n.* **1.** the top part of the human body where the eyes, ears, and mouth are. **2.** the corresponding part of an animal's body. **3.** the top part of anything: *head of a pin.* **4.** the foremost part or end of anything; the front: *the head of a column of troops.* **5.** chief person; leader. **6.** position of head; chief authority; leadership. **7.** person: *the crowned heads of England.* **8.** one or ones; individual or individuals: *ten head of cattle.* **9.** anything rounded like a head: *head of lettuce.* **10.** hair covering the head. **11.** *Bot.* cluster of flowers in which the flowers or florets grow close together from the main stem. **12.** part of a boil or pimple where pus is about to break through the skin. **13.** the striking part of a tool or implement. **14.** *Music.* piece of skin stretched tightly over the end of a drum, tambourine, etc. **15.** either end of a barrel. **16.** the side of a coin that bears the more important figure. **17.** the higher or more important end of anything: *head of a lake.* **18.** headland. **19.** mind; understanding; intelligence; intellect: *have a good head for mathematics.* **20.** topic; point: *he arranged his speech under four main heads.* **21.** a decisive point; crisis; conclusion: *his sudden refusal brought matters to a head.* **22.** heading. **23.** strength or force gained little by little: *the movement for old-age pensions has gathered head.* **24.** *Mach.* part containing or holding one or more cutting implements. **25.** pressure of water, steam, etc. **26.** body of water at a height above a particular level. **27.** source of a river or stream. **28.** foam; froth. **29.** go to one's head, a. affect one's mind. b. make one dizzy. c. make one conceited. **30.** lose one's head, get excited; lose one's self-control. **31.** off or out of one's head, *Colloq.* crazy; insane. **32.** over one's head, a. beyond one's power to understand. b. to a person higher in authority. **33.** turn one's head, a. affect the mind. b. make one dizzy. c. make one conceited. —*adj.* **1.** at the head, top, or front: *the head division of a parade.* **2.** coming from in front: *a head wind.* **3.** chief; leading; commanding; directing. —*v.* **1.** be or go at the head, top, or front of: *head a parade.* **2.** move or face (toward): *head a boat toward shore.* **3.** be the head or chief of: *head a business.* **4.** put a head on; furnish with a head. **5.** form a head; come to a head. **6.** head off, get in front of and turn back or aside. [OE *hēafod*] —Syn. *n.* **5.** commander, director. **6.** command, direction. —*v.* **3.** lead, command, direct.

head·ache (hed′āk′), *n.* **1.** pain in the head. **2.** *Am., Slang.* thing, situation, etc., that is the cause of great bother, vexation, etc.

head·cheese (hed′chēz′), *n. Am.* a jellied loaf formed of parts of the head and feet of hogs cut up, cooked, and seasoned.

head·dress (hed′dres′), *n.* **1.** a covering or decoration for the head. **2.** way of wearing or arranging the hair.

head·ed (hed′id), *adj.* **1.** having a head. **2.** having a heading. **3.** shaped into a head.

–headed, *suffix.* **1.** having a certain kind of head, as in *long-headed.* **2.** having a specified number of heads, as in *two-headed.*

head·er (hed′ər), *n.* **1.** person, tool, or machine that puts on or takes off heads of grain, barrels, pins, nails, etc. **2.** *Am.* machine that harvests heads of grain. **3.** *Colloq.* a plunge or dive headfirst.

head·first (hed′fėrst′), *adv.* **1.** with the head first. **2.** hastily; rashly.

head·fore·most (hed′fôr′mōst; –fōr′–), *adv.* headfirst.

head·gear (hed′gir′), *n.* **1.** a covering for the head; hat, cap, etc. **2.** harness for an animal's head.

head·hunt·ing (hed′hun′ting), *n.* practice among some savage tribes of taking the heads of enemies as signs of victory, manhood, etc. —head′hunt′er, *n.*

head·ing (hed′ing), *n.* **1.** part forming the head, top, or front. **2.** something written or printed at the top of a page. **3.** title of a page, chapter, etc.; topic.

head·land (hed′lənd), *n.* point of land jutting out into water; cape.

head·less (hed′lis), *adj.* **1.** having no head. **2.** without a leader. **3.** without brains; stupid.

head·light (hed′līt′), *n.* **1.** *Am.* a bright light at the front of an automobile, streetcar, locomotive, etc. **2.** light at a masthead.

head·line (hed′līn′), *n., v.,* –**lined**, –**lin·ing.** —*n.* **1.** *Am.* words printed at the top of an article in a newspaper, indicating what it is about. **2.** line at the top of a page giving the running title, page number, etc. —*v.* furnish with a headline.

head·long (hed′lông; –long), *adv., adj.* **1.** headfirst. **2.** with great haste and force. **3.** in too great a rush; without stopping to think. **4.** rash; rashly.

head·man (hed′man′; –mən), *n., pl.* –**men.** chief; leader.

head·mas·ter (hed′mas′tər; –mäs′–), *n.* person in charge of a school, esp. of a private school; principal. —head′mas′ter·ship, *n.*

head·mis·tress (hed′mis′tris), *n.* a woman headmaster.

head·most (hed′mōst), *adj.* first; foremost.

head·on (hed′on′; –ôn′), *adj.* with the head or front first.

head·phone (hed′fōn′), *n.* a telephone or radio receiver held on the head, against the ears.

head·piece (hed′pēs′), *n.* **1.** piece of armor for the head; helmet. **2.** hat, cap, or other covering for the head. **3.** headphone. **4.** head; mind; intellect.

head·quar·ters (hed′kwôr′tərz), *n. pl. or sing.* **1.** place from which the chief or commanding officer of an army, police force, etc., sends out orders. **2.** center from which any organization is controlled and directed; main office.

head·set (hed′set′), *n.* headphone.

head·ship (hed′ship), *n.* position of head; chief authority. —Syn. leadership, command, direction.

Headstall

heads·man (hedz′mən), *n., pl.* –**men.** man who beheads condemned persons.

head·stall (hed′stôl′), *n.* part of a bridle or halter that fits around a horse's head.

head·stock (hed′stok′), *n.* part of a machine that contains the revolving or working parts.

head·stone (hed′stōn′), *n.* **1.** stone set at the head of a grave. **2.** cornerstone.

head·stream (hed′strēm′), *n.* stream that is the source of a larger stream.

head·strong (hed′strông; –strong′), *adj.* **1.** rashly or foolishly determined to have one's own way; hard to control or manage; obstinate. **2.** showing rash or foolish determination to have one's own way. —head′strong′ness, *n.* —Syn. **1.** willful, perverse, stubborn.

head·wait·er (hed′wāt′ər), *n.* man in charge of the waiters in a restaurant, hotel, etc.

head·wa·ters (hed′wô′tərz; –wot′ərz), *n.pl.* sources or upper parts of a river.

head·way (hed′wā′), *n.* **1.** motion forward: *the ship made headway against the tide.* **2.** progress with work, etc. **3.** a clear space overhead in a doorway or under an arch, bridge, etc.; clearance.

head wind, wind blowing straight against the front of a ship, etc.

head·work (hed′wėrk′), *n.* mental work; thought. —head′work′er, *n.*

head·y (hed′i), *adj.,* head·i·er, head·i·est. **1.** hasty; rash. **2.** apt to affect the head and make one dizzy; intoxicating. —head′i·ly, *adv.* —head′i·ness, *n.*

heal (hēl), *v.* **1.** make whole, sound, or well; bring back to health; cure (a disease or wound). **2.** become whole or sound; get well. **3.** get rid of (anything bad). [OE *hǣlan* < *hāl* whole] —heal′er, *n.* —heal′ing, *n.* —heal′ing·ly, *adv.*

health (helth), *n.* **1.** a being well; freedom from sickness. **2.** condition of body or mind: *in poor health.* **3.** a drink in honor of a person, with a wish for health and happiness: *drink a health to the bride.* [OE *hǣlth* < *hāl* whole]

health·ful (helth'fəl), *adj.* giving health; good for the health. —**health'ful·ly,** *adv.* —**health'ful·ness,** *n.* **>** healthful, healthy. *Healthful* means "giving health"; *healthy* carries the same meaning in informal English but formal usage restricts it to "having health."

health·y (hel'thi), *adj.,* health·i·er, health·i·est. 1. having good health. 2. showing good health: *a healthy appearance.* 3. healthful. —**health'i·ly,** *adv.* —**health'i·ness,** *n.* —Syn. 1. hale, hearty, robust, strong, sound. 3. nourishing, salutary.

heap (hēp), *n.* 1. pile of many things thrown or lying together: *a heap of sand.* 2. *Colloq.* a large amount. —*v.* 1. form into a heap; gather in heaps. 2. give generously or in large amounts. 3. fill full or more than full: *heap a plate with food.* [OE *hēap*] —**heap'er,** *n.* —Syn. *n.* 1. mass, stack, accumulation.

hear (hir), *v.,* heard (hėrd), hear·ing, *interj.* —*v.* 1. perceive by the ear: *hear sounds.* 2. be able to perceive by the ear: *he cannot hear well.* 3. listen (often in the imperative). 4. listen to: *hear a person's explanation.* 5. listen to with favor: *hear my prayer.* 6. give a chance to be heard; give a formal hearing to, as a judge, teacher, etc., does. 7. find out by hearing: *hear .news.* 8. be told; receive news or information: *hear from a friend.* 9. will not hear of it, will not listen to, think of, agree to, or allow it. —*interj.* hear! hear! *Esp. Brit.* shouts of approval; cheering. [OE *hēran*] —**hear'er,** *n.*

hear·ing (hir'ing), *n.* 1. sense by which sound is perceived: *the old man's hearing is poor.* 2. act or process of perceiving sound. 3. a formal or official listening: *the judge gave both sides a hearing in court.* 4. chance to be heard: *give us a hearing.* 5. distance that a sound can be heard: *be within hearing.*

heark·en (här'kən), *v.* 1. listen; listen attentively. 2. *Poetic.* listen to; give heed to; hear. Also, **harken.** [OE *hercnian, heorcnian*] —**heark'en·er,** *n.*

hear·say (hir'sā'), *n.* common talk; gossip.

hearse (hėrs), *n.* 1. automobile, carriage, etc., for carrying a dead person to his grave. 2. *Archaic.* bier; coffin; tomb. [< OF < L *hirpex* harrow; orig., a frame like a harrow]

heart (härt), *n.* 1. a hollow, muscular organ that pumps the blood throughout the body by contracting and dilating. 2. feelings; mind; soul: *a kind heart.* 3. source of the emotions, esp. of love: *give one's heart.* 4. person loved or praised: *group of stout hearts.* 5. kindness; sympathy: *have no heart.* 6. spirit; courage; enthusiasm: *take heart.* 7. the innermost part; middle; center: *heart of the forest.* 8. the main part; vital or most important part: *the very heart of the matter.* 9. figure shaped somewhat like this ♥. 10. *Cards.* a. a playing card with one or more red, heart-shaped figures. b. **hearts,** suit of playing cards with red designs like hearts on them. c. **hearts** (*sing. in use*), game in which the players try to get rid of cards of this suit. 11. **after one's own heart,** just as one likes it; pleasing one perfectly. 12. **at heart,** in one's deepest thoughts or feelings. 13. **by heart,** a. by memory. b. from memory. 14. **with all one's heart,** a. sincerely. b. gladly. [OE *heorte*]

heart·ache (härt'āk'), *n.* sorrow; grief.

heart·beat (härt'bēt'), *n.* pulsation of the heart, including one complete contraction and dilation.

heart·break (härt'brāk'), *n.* a crushing sorrow or grief. —**heart'break'er,** *n.* —**heart'break'ing,** *adj.* —**heart'break'ing·ly,** *adv.*

heart·bro·ken (härt'brō'kən), *adj.* crushed with sorrow or grief. —**heart'bro'ken·ly,** *adv.* —**heart'bro'ken·ness,** *n.*

heart·burn (härt'bėrn'), *n.* 1. a burning feeling in the stomach, often rising to the chest and throat. 2. Also, **heart'burn'ing.** envy; jealousy.

heart·ed (här'tid), *adj.* having a heart (of the kind mentioned): *good-hearted.*

heart·en (här'tən), *v.* encourage; cheer up.

heart·felt (härt'felt'), *adj.* sincere; genuine.

hearth (härth), *n.* 1. floor of a fireplace. 2. home; fireside. 3. the lowest part of a blast furnace. [OE *heorth*]

hearth·stone (härth'stōn'), *n.* 1. stone forming a hearth. 2. home; fireside.

heart·i·ly (här'tə·li), *adv.* 1. sincerely; genuinely. 2. with enthusiasm; vigorously. 3. with a good appetite. 4. very; completely; thoroughly.

heart·less (härt'lis), *adj.* 1. without kindness or sympathy. 2. without courage, spirit, or enthusiasm. —**heart'less·ly,** *adv.* —**heart'less·ness,** *n.* —Syn. 1. unfeeling, cruel.

heart·rend·ing (härt'ren'ding), *adj.* causing mental anguish; very distressing. —**heart'rend'ing·ly,** *adv.*

heart·sick (härt'sik'), *adj.* sick at heart; very much depressed; very unhappy. —**heart'sick'ness,** *n.*

heart·sore (härt'sôr'; -sōr'), *adj.* feeling or showing grief; grieved.

heart·strik·en (härt'strik'ən), *adj.* struck to the heart with grief; shocked with fear; dismayed.

heart·strings (härt'stringz'), *n.pl.* deepest feelings; strongest affections.

heart·throb (härt'throb'), *n. Colloq.* 1. a pleasant emotion. 2. person who is the object of passionate affection.

heart-to-heart (härt'tə·härt'), *adj. Am.* without reserve; frank; sincere.

heart·wood (härt'wùd'), *n.* the hard, central wood of a tree.

heart·y (här'ti), *adj.* heart·i·er, heart·i·est, *n., pl.* heart·ies. —*adj.* 1. warm and friendly; genuine; sincere: *a hearty welcome.* 2. strong and well; vigorous: *the old man was still hale and hearty.* 3. full of energy and enthusiasm; not restrained: *a loud, hearty laugh.* 4. with plenty to eat; nourishing: *a hearty meal.* 5. requiring or using much food: *a hearty eater.* 6. fertile. —*n.* 1. a fellow sailor; brave and good comrade. 2. sailor. [< *heart*] —**heart'i·ness,** *n.* —Syn. *adj.* 1. cordial, genial. 2. hale, healthy, robust.

heat (hēt), *n.* 1. hotness; high temperature. 2. degree of hotness; temperature. 3. sensation or perception of hotness or warmth. 4. *Physics.* form of energy that consists of the motion of the molecules of a substance. The rate of motion determines the temperature. 5. hot weather. 6. warmth or intensity of feeling. 7. the hottest point; most violent or active state. 8. *Slang.* pressure; coercion; torture. 9. *Slang.* a trailing or hunting down and investigating. 10. *Sports.* one trial in a race. 11. one operation of heating in a furnace or a forge. 12. *Zool.* sexual excitement in female animals. —*v.* 1. make hot or warm; become hot or warm. 2. fill with strong feeling; excite; become excited. [OE *hǣtu*; akin to HOT] —**heat'ed,** *adj.* —**heat'less,** *adj.* —Syn. *n.* 6. anger, violence, excitement, eagerness, ardor.

heat barrier, point of speed beyond which the wings and fuselage of a plane are made dangerously hot by friction with the atmosphere.

heat·ed·ly (hēt'id·li), *adv.* in a vigorous, angry, or excited manner.

heat·er (hēt'ər), *n.* stove, furnace, or other apparatus that gives heat or warmth.

heat exchanger, device by means of which heat is transferred from one medium to another in order that it may be utilized as a source of power, as in an atomic power plant, gas turbine, etc.

heath (hēth), *n.* 1. *Brit.* open, waste land with heather or low bushes growing on it, but few or no trees. 2. a low bush growing on such land. Heather is one kind of heath. 3. one's native heath, place where one was born or brought up. [OE *hǣth*] —**heath'like',** *adj.* —**heath'y,** *adj.*

hea·then (hē'thən), *n., pl.* -thens, -then, *adj.* —*n.* 1. person who does not believe in the God of the Bible; person who is not a Christian, Jew, or Mohammedan. 2. an irreligious or unenlightened person. —*adj.* 1. of or having to do with the heathen. 2. irreligious; unenlightened. [OE *hǣthen* < *hǣth* heath] —**hea'then·dom,** *n.* —**hea'then·ish,** *adj.* —**hea'then·ish·ly,** *adv.* —**hea'then·ish·ness,** *n.* —**hea'then·ism,** *n.* —**hea'then·ness,** *n.*

heath·er (heth′ər), *n.* a low, evergreen shrub with stalks of small, rosy-pink, bell-shaped flowers, covering many heaths of Scotland and N England. [? < *heath*] —**heath′er·y**, *adj.*

heat lightning, *Am.* flashes of light without any thunder, seen near the horizon, esp. on hot summer evenings.

heat·stroke (hēt′strōk′), *n.* collapse or sudden illness caused by too much heat.

heat wave, a long period of very hot weather.

heave (hēv), *v.,* heaved or (*esp. Naut.*) hove, heav·ing, *n.* —*v.* 1. lift with force or effort: *heave a heavy box into a wagon.* 2. lift and throw: *heave the anchor overboard.* 3. pull with force or effort; haul: *they heaved on the rope.* 4. give (a sigh, groan, etc.) with a deep, heavy breath. 5. rise and fall alternately: *waves heave in a storm.* 6. breathe hard; pant. 7. try to vomit; vomit. 8. rise; swell; bulge. 9. heave in sight, come into view. 10. heave to, stop a ship; stop. —*n.* 1. act or fact of heaving. 2. heaves (*sing. in use*), *Am.* disease of horses characterized by difficult breathing, coughing, and heaving of the flanks. [OE *hebban*] —**heav′er,** *n.*

heav·en (hev′ən), *n.* 1. in Christian use, the place where God and the angels live. 2. Heaven, God; Providence: *the will of Heaven.* 3. place or condition of greatest happiness. 4. Usually, **heavens.** the upper air; sky. [OE *heofon*]

heav·en·ly (hev′ən·li), *adj.* 1. of or in heaven; divine; holy: *our heavenly Father.* 2. like heaven; suitable for heaven: *a heavenly spot.* 3. of or in the heavens: *the moon and other heavenly bodies.* —**heav′en·li·ness,** *n.* —**Syn.** 2. blissful, beautiful, excellent.

heav·en·ward (hev′ən·wərd), *adv.* Also, **heav′en·wards.** toward heaven. —*adj.* directed toward heaven.

Heav·i·side layer (hev′i·sīd), the ionosphere's second layer, which reflects radio waves of frequencies produced in short-wave broadcasting.

heav·y (hev′i), *adj.,* heav·i·er, heav·i·est, *n., pl.* heav·ies, *adv.* —*adj.* 1. hard to lift or carry; of great weight. 2. having much weight for its size or kind: *heavy metal, heavy silk.* 3. of great amount, force, or intensity; greater than usual; large: *a heavy vote, heavy sleep, heavy rain.* 4. being such in an unusual degree: *a heavy buyer, heavy smoker.* 5. hard to bear or endure: *heavy taxes.* 6. hard to deal with; trying or difficult in any way: *a heavy road, heavy slope, heavy food.* 7. weighted down; laden: *air heavy with moisture, eyes heavy with sleep.* 8. weary; sorrowful; gloomy. 9. grave; serious; sober; somber: *a heavy part in a play.* 10. cloudy: *a heavy sky.* 11. broad; thick; coarse: *a heavy line, heavy features.* 12. clumsy; sluggish; slow: *a heavy walk.* 13. ponderous; dull: *heavy reading.* 14. loud and deep: *the heavy roar of cannon.* 15. *Mil.* a. heavily armed or equipped. b. of large size: *heavy artillery.* 16. not risen enough: *heavy bread.* 17. not easily digested: *heavy food.* 18. *Chem.* among isotopes, indicating one possessing a greater atomic weight. 19. pregnant. —*n.* 1. a heavy person or thing. 2. *Colloq.* villain in a play. —*adv.* 1. in a heavy manner; heavily. 2. hang heavy, pass slowly and uninterestingly. [OE *hefig* < *hebban* heave] —**heav′i·ly,** *adv.* —**heav′i·ness,** *n.* —**Syn.** *adj.* 1. massive, ponderous. 6. hard. 8. depressed, sad. 12. lumbering.

heav·y-heart·ed (hev′i·här′tid), *adj.* sad; gloomy. —**heav′y-heart′ed·ness,** *n.*

heavy hydrogen, *Chem.* deuterium, D.

heavy water, water formed of oxygen and heavy hydrogen, D_2O, similar to ordinary water, but 1.1 times as heavy.

heav·y·weight (hev′i·wāt′), *n.* 1. person or thing of much more than average weight. 2. boxer or wrestler who weighs 175 pounds or more. 3. *Am., Colloq.* person who has much intelligence or importance.

Heb., 1. Hebrew. 2. Hebrews.

heb·dom·a·dal (heb·dom′ə·dəl), *adj.* weekly. [< LL, < L *hebdomas* seven, seven days < Gk.] —**heb·dom′a·dal·ly,** *adv.*

He·be (hē′bē), *n.* the Greek goddess of youth, the cupbearer to the gods before Ganymede was given that duty.

He·bra·ic (hi·brā′ik), *adj.* of or having to do with the Hebrews or their language or culture; Hebrew. —**He·bra′i·cal·ly,** *adv.*

He·bra·ism (hē′brā·iz·əm), *n.* 1. Hebrew usage or idiom. 2. Hebrew character, spirit, thought, or practice. —**He′bra·ist,** *n.* —**He′bra·is′tic,** *adj.*

He·brew (hē′brū), *n.* 1. Jew; Israelite. 2. the ancient language of the Jews, in which the Old Testament was recorded. 3. the present-day language of Israel. —*adj.* Jewish.

He·brews (hē′brūz), *n.* book of the New Testament.

Heb·ri·des (heb′rə·dēz), *n.pl.* group of Scotch islands off NW Scotland. —**Heb′ri·de′an,** *adj.*

Hec·a·te (hek′ə·tē), *n. Gk. Myth.* the goddess of the moon, earth, and infernal regions, later associated with magic and witchcraft. Also, **Hekate.**

hec·a·tomb (hek′ə·tōm; –tūm; –tom), *n.* 1. sacrifice of 100 oxen at one time. 2. any great slaughter. [< L < Gk. *hekatombe* sacrifice of 100 oxen < *hekaton* hundred + *bous* ox]

heck·le (hek′əl), *v.,* –led, –ling. harass and annoy by asking many bothersome questions, etc. Also, **hatchel.** [< *heckle,* n., ME *hekele;* akin to HACKLE¹] —**heck′ler,** *n.* —**heck′ling,** *n.*

hec·tare (hek′tār), *n.* measure of area in the metric system, equal to 100 ares, 10,000 square meters, or 2.471 acres. [< F < Gk. *hekaton* hundred + F *are* ARE²]

hec·tic (hek′tik), *adj.* 1. flushed. 2. feverish. 3. *Colloq.* very excited or exciting. 4. showing the signs of tuberculosis; consumptive. [< L < Gk. *hektikos* habitual, consumptive] —**hec′ti·cal·ly,** *adv.*

hecto-, *prefix.* hundred, as in *hectogram, hectoliter, hectometer.* [< Gk. *hekaton*]

hec·to·graph (hek′tə·graf; –gräf), *n.* 1. machine for making copies of a page of writing, a drawing, etc., in which the original is transferred to a gelatinous surface, and reproductions are made from this. 2. this process. —*v.* make copies of with a hectograph. [< *hecto-* hundred (< Gk. *hekaton*) + -GRAPH] —**hec′to·graph′ic,** *adj.*

Hec·tor (hek′tər), *n. Gk. Legend.* in the *Iliad,* a son of Priam, the bravest of the Trojans, who was killed by Achilles.

hec·tor (hek′tər), *n.* a bragging, bullying fellow. —*v.* 1. bluster; bully. 2. tease.

Hec·u·ba (hek′yu·bə), *n. Gk. Legend.* in the *Iliad,* the wife of Priam and mother of Hector.

he'd (hēd; *unstressed* ēd, id, hid), 1. he had. 2. he would.

hedge (hej), *n., v.,* hedged, hedg·ing. —*n.* 1. Also, **hedge·row** (hej′rō′). a thick row of bushes or small trees, planted as a fence or boundary. 2. any barrier or boundary. 3. act of hedging. —*v.* 1. put a hedge around. 2. enclose or separate with a hedge. 3. avoid giving a direct answer or taking a definite stand. 4. protect (a bet, etc.) by leaving some offsetting risk. 5. hedge in, a. hem in; surround on all sides. b. keep from getting away or moving freely. [OE *hecg*] —**hedg′er,** *n.*

hedge·hog (hej′hog′; –hôg′), *n.* 1. *Am.* the porcupine. 2. any of a group of small European mammals that have spines on the back. 3. *Mil.* a. an X-shaped portable obstacle, usually laced with barbed wire. b. an area defended by pillboxes, mines, and lanes for machine-gun fire.

hedge·hop (hej′hop′), *v.,* –hopped, –hop·ping. fly an airplane very low. —**hedge′-hop′per,** *n.* —**hedge′-hop′ping,** *adj., n.*

He·djaz (he·jaz′; –jäz′), *n.* Hejaz.

he·don·ism (hē′dən·iz·əm), *n.* doctrine that pleasure or happiness is the highest good. [< Gk. *hedone* pleasure] —**he′don·ist,** *n., adj.* —**he′do·nis′tic,** *adj.* —**he′do·nis′ti·cal·ly,** *adv.*

heed (hēd), *v.* give careful attention to; take notice of. —*n.* careful attention. [OE *hēdan*] —**heed′er,** *n.* —**heed′ing·ly,** *adv.* —**Syn.** *v.* regard, note, consider, mind. —n. notice, regard.

heed·ful (hēd′fəl), adj. careful; attentive. —heed′ful·ly, adv. —heed′ful·ness, n. —Syn. mindful, watchful. —Ant. neglectful.

heed·less (hēd′lis), adj. careless; thoughtless. —heed′less·ly, adv. —heed′less·ness, n.

heel¹ (hēl), n. 1. the back part of a person's foot, below the ankle. 2. part of a stocking or shoe that covers the heel. 3. part of a shoe or boot that is under the heel or raises the heel. 4. part of the hind leg of an animal that corresponds to a person's heel. 5. anything shaped, used, or placed at an end like a heel, such as an end crust of bread, etc. 6. down at the heel or heels, a. with the heel of the shoe worn down. b. shabby. c. slovenly. 7. out at the heels, a. with the heel of the stocking or shoe worn through. b. shabby. c. slovenly. —v. 1. follow closely. 2. put a heel or heels on. [OE hēla] —heel′less, adj.

heel² (hēl), v. lean over to one side; tilt: *the ship heeled as it turned.* —n. act of heeling. [alter. of earlier *heeld* < OE h(i)eldan < heald inclined]

heel³ (hēl), n. U.S. Colloq. a hateful or odious person. [special use of heel¹]

heeled (hēld), adj. Am., Slang. provided with money.

heel·er (hēl′ər), n. 1. person who puts heels on shoes. 2. Am., Slang. follower or hanger-on of a political boss.

heft (heft), n. 1. Colloq. weight; heaviness. 2. Am., Colloq. the greater part; bulk. —v. 1. judge the weight or heaviness of by lifting. 2. lift; heave. [< heave]

heft·y (hef′ti), adj., heft·i·er, heft·i·est. Colloq. 1. weighty; heavy. 2. big and strong.

He·gel (hā′gəl), n. Georg Wilhelm Friedrich, 1770–1831, German philosopher. —He·ge·li·an (hā·gē′li·ən; hi·jē′-), adj.

he·gem·o·ny (hi·jem′ə·ni; hej′ə·mō′ni), n., pl. -nies. political domination, esp. the leadership or domination of one state in a group; leadership. [< Gk., < hegemon leader] —heg·e·mon·ic (hej′ə·mon′ik; hē′jə-), adj.

He·gi·ra (hi·jī′rə; hej′ə-), n. 1. flight of Mohammed from Mecca to Medina in 622 A.D. 2. hegira, departure; flight. Also, Hejira.

Hei·del·berg (hī′dəl·bérg), n. city in SW Germany.

heif·er (hef′ər), n. a young cow that has not had a calf. [OE hēahfore]

heigh (hā; hī), interj. sound used to attract attention, give encouragement, express surprise, etc.

height (hīt), n. 1. measurement from top to bottom; how high a thing is; elevation above ground, sea level, etc. 2. a fairly great distance up. 3. a high point or place; hill. 4. the highest part; top. 5. the highest point; greatest degree: *the height of folly.* [OE hiehthu < hēah high] ➤ **height, heighth.** Uneducated English usually has heighth, like width and breadth (and the original Old English form had th), but height is the only form current in formal and informal English.

height·en (hīt′ən), v. 1. make or become higher. 2. make or become stronger or greater; increase. —height′en·er, n.

heil (hīl), interj. German. hail!

Hei·ne (hī′nə), n. Heinrich, 1797–1856, German poet and prose writer.

hei·nous (hā′nəs), adj. very wicked; extremely offensive; hateful. [< OF hainos, ult. < OF hair hate < Gmc.] —hei′nous·ly, adv. —hei′nous·ness, n. —Syn. odious, infamous, atrocious.

heir (âr), n. 1. person who receives, or has the right to receive, someone's property or title after the death of its owner. 2. person who inherits anything. —v. inherit. [< OF < L heres heir] —heir′dom, heir′ship, n. —heir′less, adj.

heir apparent, pl. heirs apparent. person who will be heir if he lives longer than the one holding the property or title.

heir·ess (âr′is), n. 1. a female heir. 2. woman or girl inheriting great wealth.

heir·loom (âr′lüm′), n. possession handed down from generation to generation. [< heir + loom, orig., implement]

heir presumptive, pl. heirs presumptive. person who will be heir unless a nearer relative is born.

He·jaz (he·jaz′; -jäz′), n. a former country in NW Arabia, now part of Saudi Arabia. Also, Hedjaz.

He·ji·ra (hi·jī′rə; hej′ə-), n. Hegira.

Hek·a·te (hek′ə·tē), n. Hecate.

held (held), v. pt. and pp. of hold¹.

Hel·e·na (hel′ə·nə), n. capital of Montana, in the W part.

Helen of Troy (hel′ən), Gk. Legend. the beautiful wife of King Menelaus of Sparta. Her abduction by Paris led to the Trojan War.

hel·i·cal (hel′ə·kəl), adj. having to do with, or having the form of, a helix; spiral. —hel′i·cal·ly, adv.

hel·i·ces (hel′ə·sēz), n. pl. of helix.

Hel·i·con (hel′ə·kon; -kən), n. Mount, Gk. Myth. mountain in S Greece, considered by ancient Greeks as sacred to the Muses. —Hel·i·co·ni·an (hel′ə·kō′ni·ən), adj.

hel·i·cop·ter (hel′ə·kop′tər; hē′lə-), n. a flying machine lifted from the ground and kept in the air by horizontal propellers. [< F, < Gk. helix spiral + pteron wing]

he·li·o·cen·tric (hē′li·ō·sen′trik), adj. 1. viewed or measured from the sun's center. 2. having or representing the sun as a center. [< Gk. helios sun + kentron center]

he·li·o·graph (hē′li·ə·graf′; -gräf′), n. device for signaling by means of a movable mirror that flashes beams of light to a distance. —v. communicate or signal by heliograph. —he·li·og·ra·pher (hē′li·og′rə·fər), n. —he′li·o·graph′ic, adj. —he′li·og′ra·phy, n.

He·li·os (hē′li·os), n. Gk. Myth. the sun god.

he·li·o·scope (hē′li·ə·skōp′), n. device for looking at the sun without injury to the eye. [< Gk. helios sun + -skopion means of viewing < skopos watcher]

he·li·o·trope (hē′li·ə·trōp′; hēl′yə-), n. 1. plant with clusters of small, fragrant purple or white flowers. 2. a pinkish purple. 3. bloodstone. —adj. pinkish-purple. [< L < Gk., < helios sun + -tropos turning]

he·li·ot·ro·pism (hē′li·ot′rə·piz·əm), n. an involuntary response to the sun's rays; tendency that makes a plant turn itself toward the light.

hel·i·port (hel′ə·pōrt; hēl′ə-; -pōrt), n. airport designed esp. for helicopters.

he·li·um (hē′li·əm), n. Chem. a rare, very light, inert gaseous element, He, that will not burn, much used in balloons and dirigibles. [< NL, < Gk. helios sun]

he·lix (hē′liks), n., pl. hel·i·ces (hel′ə·sēz), he·lix·es. 1. spiral, as a screw thread or a watch spring. 2. a spiral ornament. 3. Anat. rim of the outer ear. [< L < Gk., spiral]

Helixes as used for ornament

hell (hel), n. 1. in Christian use, a place where wicked persons are punished after death. 2. the powers of evil. 3. the persons in hell. 4. abode of the dead; Hades. 5. any place or state of wickedness, torment, or misery. [OE]

he'll (hēl), 1. he will. 2. he shall.

Hel·las (hel′əs), n. Greece.

hell·bend·er (hel′ben′dər), n. Am. a large salamander that is common in the Ohio River and its tributaries.

hell·bent (hel′bent′), adj. Am., Slang. recklessly determined.

hell·cat (hel′kat′), n. 1. a mean, spiteful woman. 2. witch.

hel·le·bore (hel′ə·bōr; -bôr), n. 1. any of several plants of the buttercup family with showy flowers that bloom before spring. 2. any of several tall plants of the lily family. [< L < Gk. helleboros]

Hel·lene (hel′ēn), n. Greek.

Hel·len·ic (he·len′ik; -lē′nik), adj. 1. Greek. 2. of Greek history, language, or culture from 776 B.C. to the death of Alexander the Great in 323 B.C.

Hel·len·ism (hel′ən·iz·əm), *n.* **1.** ancient Greek culture or ideals. **2.** adoption or imitation of Greek speech, ideals, or customs. **3.** idiom or expression peculiar to the Greek language. —**Hel′len·ist**, *n.* —**Hel′len·is′tic**, **Hel′len·is′ti·cal**, *adj.*

Hel·len·ize (hel′ən·īz), *v.*, –ized, –iz·ing. **1.** make Greek in character. **2.** use or imitate the Greek language, ideals, or customs. —**Hel′len·i·za′tion**, *n.* —**Hel′len·iz′er**, *n.*

Hel·les·pont (hel′əs·pont), *n.* an ancient name of the Dardanelles.

hell·fire (hel′fīr′), *n.* fire of hell; punishment in hell.

hel·lion (hel′yən), *n. Colloq.* a mischievous, troublesome person.

hell·ish (hel′ish), *adj.* **1.** fit to have come from hell; devilish; fiendish. **2.** of hell. —**hell′ish·ly**, *adv.* —**hell′ish·ness**, *n.* —**Syn. 1.** diabolical, infernal, wicked.

hel·lo (he·lō′; hə–), *interj., n., pl.* –los, *v.*, –loed, –lo·ing. —*interj.* **1.** exclamation to attract attention or express greeting (much used over the telephone). **2.** exclamation of surprise. —*n.* **1.** call of greeting or surprise. **2.** call to attract attention. —*v.* shout or call to attract attention or in greeting or surprise.

helm[1] (helm), *n.* **1.** handle or wheel by which a ship is steered. **2.** the entire steering apparatus. **3.** position of control or guidance. —*v.* steer. [OE *helma*] —**helm′less**, *adj.*

helm[2] (helm), *Archaic.* —*n.* helmet. —*v.* put a helmet on. [OE. See HELMET.]

hel·met (hel′mit), *n.* a covering, usually metal, which protects the head. [< OF, dim. of *helme* helm[2] < Gmc.] —**hel′met·ed**, *adj.*

hel·minth (hel′minth), *n.* an intestinal worm, such as the tapeworm, etc. [< Gk. *helmins*]

helms·man (helmz′mən), *n., pl.* –men. man who steers a ship.

Hel·ot, hel·ot (hel′ət; hē′lət), *n.* **1.** slave or serf in ancient Sparta. **2.** slave; serf. [< L < Gk. *Heilos*, prob. akin to Gk. *haliskesthai* be captured] —**hel′ot·ism**, *n.* —**hel′ot·ry**, *n.*

help (help), *v.*, helped or (*Archaic*) holp, helped or (*Archaic*) holp·en, help·ing, *n.* —*v.* **1.** provide with what is needed or useful: *help a person with one's strength.* **2.** aid; assist: *help someone with his work.* **3.** make better; relieve: *this will help your cough.* **4.** prevent; stop: *it can't be helped.* **5.** avoid; keep from: *he can't help yawning.* **6.** give food to; serve with food: *help her to some cake.* —*n.* **1.** thing done or given in helping; aid; assistance. **2.** person or thing that helps. **3.** *Am.* a hired helper or group of hired helpers. **4.** means of making better; remedy. **5.** means of preventing or stopping. **6.** portion of food served to a person at one time. [OE *helpan*] —**help′a·ble**, *adj.* —**help′er**, *n.* —**Syn.** *v.* **1.** support, uphold, back, abet. **3.** remedy, heal, alleviate, mitigate. ➤ See can't for usage note.

help·ful (help′fəl), *adj.* giving help; useful. —**help′ful·ly**, *adv.* —**help′ful·ness**, *n.* —**Syn.** serviceable, beneficial.

help·ing (help′ing), *n.* portion of food served to a person at one time.

help·less (help′lis), *adj.* **1.** not able to help oneself; weak. **2.** without help, protection, etc. —**help′less·ly**, *adv.* —**help′less·ness**, *n.*

help·mate (help′māt′), **help·meet** (–mēt′), *n.* companion and helper; wife or husband.

Hel·sin·ki (hel′sing·ki), *Swedish* **Hel·sing·fors** (hel′sing·fôrz; –fôrs), *n.* seaport and capital of Finland.

hel·ter-skel·ter (hel′tər·skel′tər), *adv.* with headlong, disorderly haste. —*n.* noisy and disorderly haste, confusion, etc. —*adj.* carelessly hurried; confused.

helve (helv), *n. Esp. Brit.* handle of an ax, hammer, etc. [OE *hielfe*]

Hel·ve·tia (hel·vē′shə), *n. Poetic.* Switzerland.

hem[1] (hem), *n., v.*, hemmed, hem·ming. —*n.* **1.** border or edge on a garment; edge made by folding over the cloth and sewing it down. **2.** border; edge. —*v.* **1.** fold over and sew down the edge of (cloth). **2.** hem in, around, or about, a. surround on all sides. b. keep from getting away or moving freely. [OE *hemm*] —**hem′mer**, *n.*

hem[2] (hem), *interj., n., v.*, hemmed, hem·ming. —*interj., n.* sound like clearing the throat, used to attract attention or show doubt or hesitation. —*v.* **1.** make this sound. **2.** hesitate in speaking. [imit.]

hem·a·tite (hem′ə·tīt; hē′mə–), *n.* an important iron ore, Fe_2O_3, that is reddish-brown when powdered. Also, **haematite**. [< L < Gk. *haimatites* bloodlike < *haima* blood] —**hem·a·tit·ic** (hem′ə·tit′ik; hē′mə–), *adj.*

hemi-, *prefix.* half, as in *hemisphere*. [< Gk.]

Hem·ing·way (hem′ing·wā), Ernest, 1898–1961, American novelist and short-story writer.

he·mip·ter·ous (hi·mip′tər·əs), *adj.* belonging to a large group of insects including bedbugs, chinch bugs, lice, and aphids. [< Gk. *hemi-* half + *pteron* wing]

hem·i·sphere (hem′ə·sfir), *n.* **1.** half of a sphere or globe. **2.** half of the earth's surface. [< F < L < Gk., < *hemi-* half + *sphaira* sphere] —**hem·i·spher·i·cal** (hem′ə·sfer′ə·kəl), *adj.* —**hem′i·spher′i·cal·ly**, *adv.*

hem·i·stich (hem′ə·stik), *n.* **1.** half a line of verse. **2.** an incomplete line of verse. [< L < Gk., < *hemi-* half + *stichos* row] —**he·mis·ti·chal** (hi·mis′tə·kəl; hem′ə·stik·əl), *adj.*

hem·lock (hem′lok), *n.* **1.** *Esp. Brit.* a poisonous plant of the carrot family, with spotted stems, finely divided leaves, and small white flowers. **2.** poison made from it. **3.** *Am.* an evergreen tree of the pine family with small cones and drooping branches, whose bark is used in tanning. **4.** its wood. [OE *hymlice*]

he·mo·glo·bin (hē′mə·glō′bən; hem′ə–), *n.* the protein matter in the red corpuscles of the blood that carries oxygen from the lungs to the tissues, and carbon dioxide from the tissues to the lungs. Also, **haemoglobin**. [for *hematoglobulin*, ult. < Gk. *haima* blood + L *globulus*, dim. of *globus* globe]

he·mo·phil·i·a (hē′mə·fil′i·ə; hem′ə–), *n. Pathol.* an inherited condition in which the blood does not clot normally, resulting in excessive bleeding from the slightest cut. Also, **haemophilia**. [< NL, < Gk. *haima* blood + *philia* affection, tendency] —**he·mo·phil·i·ac** (hē′mə·fil′i·ak; hem′ə–), *n.*

hem·or·rhage (hem′ə·rij; hem′rij), *n.* discharge of blood, as a nosebleed. Also, **haemorrhage**. [< L < Gk. *haimorrhagia*, ult. < *haima* blood + *rhegnynai* break, burst] —**hem·or·rhag·ic** (hem′ə·raj′ik), *adj.*

hem·or·rhoids (hem′ə·roidz), *n.pl.* painful swellings formed by the dilation of blood vessels near the anus; piles. Also, **haemorrhoids**. [< L < Gk., ult. < *haima* blood + *-rhoos* flowing] —**hem′or·rhoi′dal**, *adj.*

hemp (hemp), *n.* **1.** a tall Asiatic plant whose tough fibers are made into heavy string, rope, coarse cloth, etc. **2.** the tough fibers of this plant. **3.** a hangman's rope. **4.** hashish or other drug obtained from some kinds of hemp. [OE *henep*] —**hemp′en**, *adj.*

hem·stitch (hem′stich′), *v.* hem along a line from which threads have been drawn out, gathering the cross threads into a series of little groups. —*n.* **1.** the stitch used. **2.** ornamental needlework made by hemstitching. —**hem′stitch′er**, *n.*

hen (hen), *n.* **1.** a female domestic fowl. **2.** female of other birds. [OE *henn*]

hen·bane (hen′bān′), *n.* a coarse, bad-smelling plant with sticky, hairy leaves and clusters of yellowish-brown flowers, poisonous to fowls.

hence (hens), *adv.* **1.** as a result of this; therefore: *it is very late, hence you must go to bed.* **2.** from now; from this time onward: *years hence.* **3.** from this source or origin. **4.** from here: *a mile hence.* —*interj.* go away! [ME *hennes* < OE *heonan* + *-s*, adv. ending] ➤ **Hence** is a formal word for the less formal *conse-*

age, cāre, fär; ēqual, térm; īce; ōpen, ôrder; pŭt, rüle, ūse; th, then; ə=a in about.

quently, therefore; rare in current informal writing.

hence·forth (hens'fôrth'; -fôrth'), **hence·for·ward** (-fôr'wərd), *adv.* from this time on.

hench·man (hench'mən), *n., pl. -men.* a trusted attendant or follower. [ME *henxstman* < OE *hengest* horse + MAN; orig., a groom]

hen·e·quen, hen·e·quin (hen'ə·kin), *n.* 1. a yellow fiber from leaves of an agave of Yucatán, used for making binder twine, ropes, coarse fabrics, etc. 2. plant that yields this fiber. [< Sp. < native Yucatán word]

hen·house (hen'hous'), *n.* house for poultry.

hen·na (hen'ə), *n., adj., v., -naed, -na·ing.* —*n.* 1. a dark, reddish-orange dye used on the hair. 2. tree of Asia and Africa from whose leaves this dye is made. —*adj.* reddish-brown. —*v.* dye or color with henna. [< Ar. *ḥinnā'*]

hen·ner·y (hen'ər·i), *n., pl. -ner·ies.* place where fowls are kept.

hen·peck (hen'pek'), *v.* domineer over: *he was henpecked by his wife.* —hen'pecked', *adj.*

Hen·ry (hen'ri), *n.* 1. O., 1862–1910, American writer of short stories. His real name was William Sydney Porter. 2. Patrick, 1736–1799, American patriot, orator, and statesman. 3. II, 1519–1559, king of France 1547–1559. 4. VII, 1457–1509, king of England 1485–1509. 5. VIII, 1491–1547, king of England 1509–1547. He made himself head of the Church of England.

hen·ry (hen'ri), *n., pl. -ries, -rys. Elect.* unit of inductance. When a current varying at the rate of one ampere per second induces an electromotive force of one volt, the circuit has an inductance of one henry. [after J. *Henry*, physicist]

hep (hep), *adj. Am., Slang.* having intimate knowledge; informed.

he·pat·ic (hi·pat'ik), *adj.* 1. of or having to do with the liver. 2. acting on the liver as a medicine. [< L < Gk., < *hepar* liver]

he·pat·i·ca (hi·pat'ə·kə), *n.* a low plant with delicate purple, pink, or white flowers that bloom early in the spring. [< NL, ult. < Gk. *hepar* liver; leaf thought to resemble the liver in shape]

hep·cat (hep'kat'), *n. Slang.* 1. performer in a swing band. 2. an informed admirer of swing music.

hep·ta·gon (hep'tə·gon), *n.* a plane figure having seven angles and seven sides. [< LL < Gk., < *hepta* seven + *gonia* angle] —**hep·tag·o·nal** (hep·tag'ə·nəl), *adj.*

Heptagon

hep·tam·e·ter (hep·tam'ə·tər), *n.* line of verse having seven feet. [< LL < Gk., < *hepta* seven + *metron* measure] —hep·ta·met·ri·cal (hep'tə·met'rə·kəl), *adj.*

her (hėr; *unstressed* hər, ėr), *pron.* the objective case of she: *I like her.* —*adj.* the possessive form of she: *of her; belonging to her; done by her: her look, her book, her work.* [OE *hire*]

her., heraldic; heraldry.

He·ra (hir'ə), *n. Gk. Myth.* goddess, wife of Zeus and queen of gods and men, identified by the Romans with Juno. Also, Here.

Her·a·cles, Her·a·kles (her'ə·klēz), *n.* Hercules. —Her'a·cle'an, Her'a·kle'an, *adj.*

her·ald (her'əld), *n.* 1. formerly, an officer who carried messages, made announcements, arranged and supervised tourneys and other public ceremonies, and regulated the use of armorial bearings. 2. person who carries messages and makes announcements; messenger. 3. forerunner; harbinger: *dawn is the herald of day.* —*v.* 1. bring news of; announce. 2. go before and announce the coming of. [< Med.L *heraldus* < Rom. < Gmc.] —Syn. *n.* 3. precursor.

he·ral·dic (he·ral'dik), *adj.* of or having to do with heraldry or heralds. —he·ral'di·cal·ly, *adv.*

her·ald·ry (her'əld·ri), *n., pl. -ries.* 1. science or art dealing with coats of arms; science of settling a person's right to use a coat of arms, of tracing family descent, of making up a coat of arms for a new country, etc. 2. a heraldic device. 3. coat of arms.

herb (ėrb; hėrb), *n.* 1. plant whose leaves or stems are used for medicine, seasoning, food, or perfume. Sage, mint, and lavender are herbs. 2. a flowering plant whose stems live only one season. Herbs do not form woody tissue as shrubs and trees do, though their roots may live many years. Peonies, buttercups, corn, wheat, cabbage, lettuce, etc., are herbs. 3. herbage. [< OF < L *herba*] —herb'less, *adj.* —herb'like', *adj.*

her·ba·ceous (hėr·bā'shəs), *adj.* 1. of an herb; like an herb; having stems that are soft and not woody. 2. like a leaf; green.

herb·age (ėr'bij; hėr'-), *n.* 1. herbs. 2. grass. 3. the green leaves and soft stems of plants.

herb·al (hėr'bəl; ėr'-), *adj.* of herbs. —*n.* book about herbs.

herb·al·ist (hėr'bəl·ist; ėr'-), *n.* 1. person who gathers or deals in herbs. 2. formerly, a botanist.

her·bar·i·um (hėr·bār'i·əm), *n., pl. -bar·i·ums, -bar·i·a** (-bār'i·ə). 1. collection of dried plants systematically arranged. 2. room or building where such a collection is kept.

Her·bert (hėr'bərt), *n.* Victor, 1859–1924, American composer of operettas, born in Ireland.

her·biv·o·rous (hėr·biv'ə·rəs), *adj.* feeding on grass or other plants. [< NL, < L *herba* herb + *vorare* devour]

her·cu·le·an, Her·cu·le·an (hėr·kū'li·ən; hėr'kyə·lē'ən), *adj.* 1. of great strength, courage, or size; very powerful. 2. requiring great strength, courage, or size; hard to do.

Her·cu·les (hėr'kyə·lēz), *n.* 1. *Class. Legend.* hero famous for his great strength. 2. a northern constellation. Also, Heracles, Herakles.

herd (hėrd), *n.* 1. number of animals together, esp. large animals: *a herd of cows, a herd of elephants.* 2. a large number of people. 3. the common people; rabble. —*v.* 1. join together; flock together. 2. form into a flock, herd, or group. 3. tend or take care of (cattle, sheep, etc.). [OE *heord*] —herd'er, *n.*

herds·man (hėrdz'mən), *n., pl. -men.* man who takes care of a herd.

here (hir), *adv.* 1. in this place; at this place: *place it here, here the speaker paused.* 2. to this place: *come here.* 3. at this time; now. 4. in this life. 5. (often used to call attention to some person or thing): *my friend here can help you.* 6. here and there, in this place and that; at intervals. 7. here's to!, a wish of health, happiness, or success to. 8. neither here nor there, off the subject; unimportant. —*n.* 1. this place. 2. this life. —*interj.* answer showing that one is present when the roll is called. [OE *hēr*]

He·re (hir'ē), *n.* Hera.

here·a·bout (hir'ə·bout'), **here·a·bouts** (-bouts'), *adv.* about this place; around here; near here.

here·af·ter (hir·af'tər; -äf'-), *adv.* 1. after this; in the future. 2. in life after death. —*n.* 1. the future. 2. life after death.

here·at (hir·at'), *adv.* 1. when this happened; at this time. 2. because of this.

here·by (hir·bī'), *adv.* by this means; in this way.

he·red·i·ta·ble (hə·red'ə·tə·bəl), *adj.* that can be inherited. —he·red'i·ta·bil'i·ty, *n.* —he·red'i·ta·bly, *adv.*

he·red·i·tar·y (hə·red'ə·ter'i), *adj.* 1. coming by inheritance: *a hereditary title.* 2. holding a position by inheritance: *a hereditary ruler.* 3. transmitted or caused by heredity: *hereditary color blindness.* 4. having to do with inheritance or heredity. —he·red'i·tar'i·ly, *adv.* —he·red'i·tar'i·ness, *n.* —Syn. 3. inherited.

he·red·i·ty (hə·red'ə·ti), *n., pl. -ties. Biol.* 1. the fact that one generation of plants and animals produces the next. 2. the transmission of genetic physical or mental characteristics from parent to offspring. 3. qualities that have come to offspring from parents. 4. tendency of offspring to be like the parents. [< L *hereditas* < *heres* heir]

Her·e·ford (hėr'fərd; hėr'ə·fərd), *n.* one of a breed of beef cattle having a red body, white face, and white markings under the body.

here·in (hir·in′), adv. 1. in this place. 2. in this matter; in view of this.

here·in·af·ter (hir′in·af′tər; -äf′-), adv. afterward in this document, statement, etc.

here·in·be·fore (hir·in′bi·fôr′; -fōr′), adv. before in this document, statement, etc.

here·in·to (hir·in′tü), adv. 1. into this place. 2. into this matter.

here·of (hir·ov′; -uv′), adv. of this; about this.

here·on (hir·on′; -ôn′), adv. 1. on this. 2. immediately after this.

her·e·sy (her′ə·si), n., pl. -sies. 1. belief different from the accepted belief of a church, school, profession, etc. 2. the holding of such a belief. [< OF < L < Gk. *hairesis* a taking, choosing < *haireein* take]

her·e·tic (her′ə·tik), n. person who holds a belief that is different from the accepted belief of his church, school, profession, etc. —adj. holding such a belief. —Syn. n. dissenter.

he·ret·i·cal (hə·ret′ə·kəl), adj. 1. of or having to do with heresy or heretics. 2. containing heresy; characterized by heresy. —he·ret′i·cal·ly, adv.

here·to (hir·tü′), adv. to this place, thing, etc.

here·to·fore (hir′tə·fôr′; -fōr′), adv. before this time; until now.

here·un·to (hir′un·tü′), adv. 1. unto this. 2. until this time.

here·up·on (hir′ə·pon′; -pôn′), adv. 1. upon this. 2. immediately after this.

here·with (hir·with′; -with′), adv. 1. with this. 2. by this means; in this way.

her·it·a·ble (her′ə·tə·bəl), adj. 1. capable of being inherited. 2. capable of inheriting. —her′·it·a·bil′i·ty, n. —her′it·a·bly, adv.

her·it·age (her′ə·tij), n. what is or may be handed on to a person from his ancestors; inheritance. [< OF, < *heriter* inherit < LL, ult. < L *heres* heir]

her·maph·ro·dite (hèr·maf′rə·dīt), n. 1. animal or plant having the reproductive organs of both sexes. 2. person or thing that combines two opposite qualities. 3. *Naut.* a hermaphrodite brig. —adj. of or like a hermaphrodite. [< L < Gk. *Hermaphroditos* Hermaphroditus, son of Hermes and Aphrodite, who became united in body with a nymph] —her·maph·ro·dit·ic (hèr·maf′rə·dit′ik), adj. —her·maph′ro·dit′i·cal·ly, adv.

hermaphrodite brig, a two-masted ship, square-rigged forward and schooner-rigged aft.

Her·mes (hèr′mēz), n. *Gk. Myth.* god who was the messenger of Zeus and the other gods, identified by the Romans with Mercury.

her·met·ic (hèr·met′ik), adj. airtight. [< Med.L *hermeticus* < *Hermes* Hermes] —her·met′i·cal·ly, adv.

Her·mi·o·ne (hèr·mī′ə·nē), n. *Gk. Myth.* daughter of Menelaus and Helen of Troy.

her·mit (hèr′mit), n. person who goes away from other people and lives by himself, esp. one who does so for religious reasons; anchorite. [< OF < LL < Gk. *eremites* < *eremia* desert < *eremos* solitary] —her·mit′ic, her·mit′i·cal, adj. —her·mit′i·cal·ly, adv. —her′mit·like′, adj.

her·mit·age (hèr′mə·tij), n. 1. home of a hermit. 2. place to live away from other people.

hermit crab, a soft-bodied crab that lives in the empty shells of snails, whelks, etc.

her·ni·a (hèr′ni·ə), n., pl. -ni·as, -ni·ae (-ni·ē). protrusion of a part of the intestine or some other organ through a break in its surrounding walls; rupture. [< L] —her′ni·al, adj.

he·ro (hir′ō), n., pl. -roes. 1. man or boy admired for his bravery, great deeds, or noble qualities. 2. the most important male person in a story, play, poem, etc. [ult. < L < Gk. *heros*]

Her·od (her′əd), n. 1. (*"the Great"*) 73?–4 B.C., king of the Jews from 37? to 4 B.C. 2. his son, Herod An·ti·pas (an′tə·pas), ruler of Galilee from 4 B.C. to 39 A.D.

He·rod·o·tus (hə·rod′ə·təs), n. 484?–425 B.C., Greek historian, called "the father of history."

he·ro·ic (hi·rō′ik), adj. Also, **he·ro′i·cal.** 1. like a hero, his deeds, or his qualities. 2. of or about heroes and their deeds: *heroic poetry.* 3. noble. 4. unusually daring or bold. 5. magniloquent; grand. 6. unusually large; larger than life size. —n. 1. a heroic poem. 2. heroics, high-sounding language. 3. heroics, words, feelings, or actions that seem grand or noble but are only for effect. 4. Usually, heroics. heroic verse. —he·ro′i·cal·ly, adv. —he·ro′i·cal·ness, he·ro′ic·ness, n. —Syn. adj. 1. brave, great.

heroic couplet, two successive lines of poetry in iambic pentameter that rhyme.

heroic verse, iambic pentameter couplets.

her·o·in (her′ō·in), n. 1. a poisonous, habit-forming drug made from morphine. 2. **Heroin,** a trademark for this drug.

her·o·ine (her′ō·in), n. 1. woman or girl admired for her great deeds or noble qualities. 2. the most important female person in a story, play, poem, etc. [< L < Gk., fem. of *heros* hero]

her·o·ism (her′ō·iz·əm), n. 1. actions and qualities of a hero or heroine; great bravery; daring courage. 2. a very brave act or quality. —Syn. 1. valor, gallantry, intrepidity.

her·on (her′ən), n. a wading bird with a long neck, long bill, and long legs. [< OF *hairon* < Gmc.]

her·on·ry (her′ən·ri), n., pl. -ries. place where many herons come in the breeding season.

her·pes (hèr′pēz), n. 1. disease of the skin or mucous membrane characterized by clusters of blisters. 2. shingles (the disease). [< L < Gk., shingles, < *herpein* creep] —her·pet·ic (hèr·pet′ik), adj.

her·pe·tol·o·gy (hèr′pə·tol′ə·ji), n. branch of zoölogy dealing with reptiles. [< Gk. *herpeton* reptile (< *herpein* creep) + -LOGY] —her·pe·to·log·i·cal (hèr′pə·tə·loj′ə·kəl), adj. —her′pe·tol′o·gist, n.

Herr (her), n., pl. Her·ren (her′ən). *German.* 1. Mr.; Sir. 2. gentleman.

Her·rick (her′ik), n. Robert, 1591–1674, English lyric poet.

her·ring (her′ing), n., pl. -rings or (esp. collectively) -ring. a small food fish of the N Atlantic. [OE *hēring*]

her·ring·bone (her′ing·bōn′), adj. having a zigzag pattern or arrangement. —n. a zigzag pattern or arrangement.

hers (hèrz), pron. 1. of her; belonging to her. 2. the one or ones belonging to her.

her·self (hèr·self′), pron. 1. the emphatic form of she or her: *she herself did it.* 2. the reflexive form of her: *she hurt herself.* 3. her real self: *in those fits she is not herself.*

hertz·i·an wave (hert′si·ən), an electromagnetic radiation, such as the wave used in communicating by radio, produced by irregular fluctuation of electricity in a conductor. [first investigated by H. R. Hertz, physicist]

Her·ze·go·vi·na (her′tsə·gō·vē′nə), n. region in W Yugoslavia, formerly a part of Austria-Hungary.

he's (hēz; *unstressed* ēz, iz, hiz), 1. he is. 2. he has.

hes·i·tan·cy (hez′ə·tən·si), **hes·i·tance** (hez′ə·təns), n., pl. -cies; -tanc·es. hesitation; doubt; indecision.

hes·i·tant (hez′ə·tənt), adj. hesitating; doubtful; undecided. —hes′i·tant·ly, adv.

hes·i·tate (hez′ə·tāt), v., -tat·ed, -tat·ing. 1. fail to act promptly; hold back because one feels doubtful; be undecided; show that one has not yet made up one's mind. 2. feel that perhaps one should not; not want: *I hesitated to ask you, because you were so busy.* 3. stop for an instant; pause. 4. speak with stops or pauses. [< L *haesitare* < *haerere* stick fast] —hes′i·tat′er, hes′i·ta′tor, n. —hes′i·tat′ing, adj. —hes′i·tat′ing·ly, adv. —Syn. 1. doubt, waver, vacillate, falter. 4. stammer, stutter.

hes·i·ta·tion (hez′ə·tā′shən), n. 1. a hesitating; doubt; indecision; unwillingness; delay. 2. a speaking with short stops or pauses.

āge, cāre, fär; ēqual, tèrm; īce; ōpen, ôrder; pùt, rüle, ūse; th, then; ə=a in about.

Hes·per·i·des (hes·per′ə·dēz), *n.pl. Gk. Myth.* 1. the four nymphs who guarded the golden apples of Hera. 2. garden where these apples were kept.

Hes·per·us (hes′pər·əs), **Hes·per** (hes′pər), *n.* the evening star.

Hesse (hes; *Ger.* hes′ə), *n.* district in W Germany.

Hes·sian (hesh′ən), *adj.* of Hesse or its people. —*n.* 1. native or inhabitant of Hesse. 2. *U.S.* a German soldier hired by England to fight against the Americans during the American Revolution. 3. hireling; ruffian.

Hessian fly, *Am.* a small, two-winged insect whose larvae are very destructive to wheat.

hest (hest), *n. Archaic.* behest; command. [alter. of OE *hǣs*]

he·tae·ra (hi·tir′ə), *n.*, *pl.* **-tae·rae** (-tir′ē). courtesan of ancient Greece. [< Gk. *hetaira*, fem., companion]

heter-, hetero-, *word element.* other; different, as in *hetero*geneous. [< Gk., < *heteros*]

het·er·o·dox (het′ər·ə·doks), *adj.* rejecting the regularly accepted beliefs or doctrines; differing from an acknowledged standard; not orthodox. [< LL < Gk., < *heteros* other + *doxa* opinion]

het·er·o·dox·y (het′ər·ə·dok′si), *n.*, *pl.* **-dox·ies.** 1. rejection of regularly accepted beliefs or doctrines; departure from an acknowledged standard; opposite of orthodoxy. 2. belief, doctrine, or opinion not in agreement with what is regularly accepted.

het·er·o·dyne (het′ər·ə·dīn′), *adj.* having to do with the production of sounds by combining radio oscillations of slightly different frequencies.

het·er·o·ge·ne·ous (het′ər·ə·jē′ni·əs; -jēn′yəs), *adj.* 1. different in kind; unlike; not at all similar; varied. 2. made up of unlike elements or parts; miscellaneous. [< Med.L *heterogeneus*, ult. < Gk. *heteros* other + *genos* kind] —het·er·o·ge·ne·i·ty (het′ər·ə·jə·nē′ə·ti), het′er·o·ge′ne·ous·ness, *n.* —het′er·o·ge′ne·ous·ly, *adv.*

hew (hū), *v.*, **hewed, hewed** or **hewn** (hūn), **hew·ing.** 1. cut with an ax, sword, etc. 2. cut into shape; form by cutting: *hew stone for building.* 3. cut down; fell with cutting blows. [OE *hēawan*] —hew′er, *n.*

hex (heks), *Am., Colloq.* —*v.* practice witchcraft on; bewitch. [< n.] —*n.* 1. witch. 2. a magic spell. [< G *hexe* witch]

hex·a·gon (hek′sə·gon), *n.* a plane figure having six angles and six sides. [< LL < Gk., ult. < *hex* six + *gonia* angle] —hex·ag·o·nal (heks·ag′ə·nəl), *adj.* —hex·ag′o·nal·ly, *adv.*

Hexagons

hex·a·gram (hek′sə·gram), *n.* a six-pointed star formed of two equilateral triangles.

hex·a·he·dron (hek′sə·hē′drən), *n.*, *pl.* **-drons, -dra** (-drə). a solid figure having six faces. [< Gk., < *hex* six + *hedra* surface] —hex′a·he′dral, *adj.*

hex·am·e·ter (heks·am′ə·tər), *adj.* of poetry, consisting of six feet or measures. —*n.* poetry having six feet or measures in each line. [< Gk., < *hex* six + *metron* measure] —hex·a·met·ric (hek′sə·met′rik), hex′a·met′ri·cal, *adj.*

hex·a·pod (hek′sə·pod), *n.* a true insect; arthropod having six feet. —*adj.* having six feet. [< Gk., < *hex* six + *pous* foot] —hex·ap·o·dous (heks·ap′ə·dəs), *adj.*

hey (hā), *interj.* sound made to attract attention, to express surprise or other feeling, or to ask a question.

hey·day (hā′dā′), *n.* period of greatest strength, vigor, spirits, prosperity, etc.

Hez·e·ki·ah (hez′ə·kī′ə), *n.* king of Judah. II Kings 18–20.

Hf, *Chem.* hafnium.

HG, High German.

Hg, *Chem.* mercury.

hhd., hogshead.

hi (hī), *interj. Colloq.* hello! how are you?

H.I., Hawaiian Islands.

hi·a·tus (hī·ā′təs), *n.*, *pl.* **-tus·es, -tus.** 1. an empty space; gap. 2. interruption of continuity:

several hiatuses in the testimony. 3. a slight pause between two vowels that come together in successive syllables or words, as between the *e*'s in pre**ēm**inent. [< L, gap, < *hiare* gape]

hi·ber·nal (hī·bėr′nəl), *adj.* of winter; wintry.

hi·ber·nate (hī′bər·nāt), *v.*, **-nat·ed, -nat·ing.** spend the winter in sleep or in an inactive condition, as bears and woodchucks do. [< L, < *hibernus* wintry] —hi′ber·na′tion, *n.*

Hi·ber·ni·a (hī·bėr′ni·ə), *n. Poetic.* Ireland. —Hi·ber′ni·an, *n., adj.*

hi·bis·cus (hə·bis′kəs; hī-), *n.* plant, shrub, or tree with large, showy, bell-shaped flowers. [< L]

hic·cup, hic·cough (hik′up; -əp), *n.* an involuntary catching of the breath. —*v.* catch the breath in this way.

hick (hik), *Slang.* —*n.* 1. farmer. 2. an unsophisticated person. —*adj.* of or like hicks.

hick·o·ry (hik′ə·ri; hik′ri), *n., pl.* **-ries.** *Am.* 1. a North American tree whose nuts are good to eat. 2. its tough, hard wood. [< Am.Ind.]

hi·dal·go (hi·dal′gō), *n., pl.* **-gos.** a Spanish nobleman of the second class, not so high in rank as a grandee. [< Sp., < OSp. *hijo de algo* son of property (orig., son of something)]

hid·den (hid′ən), *adj.* concealed; secret; mysterious; obscure. —*v.* pp. of hide[1]. —Syn. *adj.* covert, clandestine, occult, esoteric, latent.

hide[1] (hīd), *v.*, **hid** (hid), **hid·den** or **hid, hid·ing.** 1. put or keep out of sight; conceal. 2. cover up; shut off from sight. 3. keep secret. 4. conceal oneself. 5. turn away in displeasure. [OE *hȳdan*] —hid′er, *n.* —Syn. 1. secrete. —Ant. 1. uncover.

hide[2] (hīd), *n., v.*, **hid·ed, hid·ing.** —*n.* skin of an animal, either raw or tanned. —*v. Colloq.* beat; thrash. [OE *hȳd*]

hide-and-seek (hīd′ənd·sēk′), *n.* children's game in which some hide and others try to find them.

hide·bound (hīd′bound′), *adj.* 1. with the skin sticking close to the bones. 2. narrow-minded and stubborn.

hid·e·ous (hid′i·əs), *adj.* 1. very ugly; frightful: *a hideous monster.* 2. revolting to the moral sense: *a hideous crime.* [< OF *hide* fear, horror] —hid′e·ous·ly, *adv.* —hid′e·ous·ness, *n.* —Syn. 2. detestable, odious.

hide-out (hīd′out′), *n. Am.* place for hiding or being alone.

hid·ing[1] (hīd′ing), *n.* 1. concealment. 2. place to hide.

hid·ing[2] (hīd′ing), *n. Colloq.* a beating.

hie (hī), *v.*, **hied, hie·ing** or **hy·ing.** hasten; go quickly. [OE *hīgian*]

hi·er·ar·chy (hī′ər·är′ki), *n., pl.* **-chies.** 1. government by priests. 2. body of church officials of different ranks, as archbishops, bishops, priests, etc. 3. any system of persons, etc., which has higher and lower ranks. [< Med.L < Gk., < *hieros* sacred + *archos* ruler] —hi′er·ar′chic, hi′er·ar′chi·cal, *adj.* —hi′er·ar′chi·cal·ly, *adv.*

hi·er·at·ic (hī′ər·at′ik), **hi·er·at·i·cal** (-ə·kəl), *adj.* 1. having to do with the priestly caste; used by the priestly class; priestly. 2. designating or having to do with a form of Egyptian writing used by the early priests in their records. Hieratic writing is a simplified form of hieroglyphics. [< L < Gk., ult. < *hieros* sacred] —hi′er·at′i·cal·ly, *adv.*

hier·o·glyph·ic (hir′ə·glif′ik), *n.* 1. picture or symbol of an object standing for a word, idea, or sound, used by ancient Egyptians, etc. 2. any writing that uses hieroglyphics. 3. a secret symbol. 4. hieroglyphics, letter or word that is hard to read. —*adj.* Also, hier′o·glyph′i·cal. 1. of or written in hieroglyphics. 2. symbolical. 3. hard to read. [< LL < Gk., < *hieros* sacred + *glyphe* carving] —hier′o·glyph′i·cal·ly, *adv.*

hi-fi (*adj.* hī′fī′; *n.* hī′fī′), *Colloq.* —*adj.* high-fidelity. —*n.* high-fidelity reproduction, as of music, or the equipment for this.

hig·gle (hig′əl), *v.*, **-gled, -gling.** dispute about prices in a petty way; haggle. [? akin to HAGGLE] —hig′gler, *n.*

hig·gle·dy-pig·gle·dy (hig′əl·di·pig′əl·di), *adv.* in jumbled confusion. —*adj.* jumbled; confused. —*n.* a jumble; confusion.

high (hī), *adj.* **1.** of more than usual height; tall: *a high building.* **2.** rising to a specified extent: *the mountain is 20,000 feet high.* **3.** far above the ground or some base: *an airplane high in the air.* **4.** extending to or down from a height: *a high leap.* **5.** above others in rank, quality, character, etc.: *high office.* **6.** greater, stronger, or better than average: *high temperature.* **7.** most important; chief; main: *the high altar.* **8.** extreme of its kind: *high crimes.* **9.** costly: *strawberries are high in winter.* **10.** not low in pitch; shrill; sharp: *a high voice.* **11.** advanced to its peak: *high summer.* **12.** slightly tainted: *game is often eaten after it has become high.* **13.** haughty: *a high manner.* **14.** Colloq. excited by alcoholic drinks. —*adv.* at or to a high point, place, rank, amount, degree, price, pitch, etc.: *the eagle flies high.* —*n.* **1.** something that is high. **2.** arrangement of gears to give the greatest speed. **3.** *Am., Meteorol.* region or area of high barometric pressure. **4.** on high, a. high above; up in the air. b. in heaven. [OE *hēah*] —Syn. *adj.* **1.** lofty, towering. **5.** eminent, elevated, exalted, noble.

high·ball (hī′bôl′), *n. Am.* whiskey, brandy, etc., mixed with soda water or ginger ale and served with ice in a tall glass.

high·born (hī′bôrn′), *adj.* of noble birth.

high·boy (hī′boi′), *n. Am.* a tall chest of drawers on legs.

high·bred (hī′bred′), *adj.* **1.** of superior breeding or stock. **2.** well-mannered; refined.

high·brow (hī′brou′), *Am., Colloq.* —*n.* person who claims to care a great deal about knowledge and culture. —*adj.* of or suitable for a highbrow.

High Church, in the Anglican Church, a party which lays great stress on church authority and ceremonial observances. —**High′-Church′,** *adj.* —**High Churchman.**

high comedy, comedy dealing with polite society and depending more on witty dialogue and well-drawn characters than on comic situations.

high·er-up (hī′ər·up′), *n. Am., Colloq.* one occupying a superior position.

high·fa·lu·tin, high·fa·lu·ting (hī′fə·lü′tən), *adj. Am., Slang.* pompous; bombastic.

high-fi·del·i·ty (hī′fə·del′ə·ti; -fī-), *adj. Electronics.* indicating reproduction of the full audio range of a transmitted signal with a minimum of distortion.

high·fli·er, high·fly·er (hī′flī′ər), *n.* **1.** person or thing that flies high. **2.** person who is extravagant or has pretentious ideas.

high-flown (hī′flōn′), *adj.* **1.** aspiring; extravagant. **2.** attempting to be elegant or eloquent: *high-flown compliments.*

high-fre·quen·cy (hī′frē′kwən·si), *adj. Electronics.* of a frequency having from 1.5 to 30 megacycles per second.

High German, the literary and official language of Germany, a development of the dialects of the highlands in C and S Germany.

high-grade (hī′grād′), *adj.* superior.

high-hand·ed (hī′han′did), *adj.* bold; arbitrary; domineering; overbearing. —**high′-hand′-ed·ly,** *adv.* —**high′-hand′ed·ness,** *n.* —Syn. tyrannical, autocratic.

high-hat (v. hī′hat′; *adj.* hī′hat′), *v.,* —**hatted, –hat·ting,** *adj. U.S. Slang* —*v.* treat as inferior; snub. —*adj.* **1.** stylish; grand. **2.** snobbish.

high jump, *Athletics.* contest or event in which the contestants try to jump as high as possible.

high·land (hī′lənd), *n.* **1.** country or region that is higher and hillier than the neighboring country. **2.** a mountain region.

High·land·er (hī′lən·dər), *n.* native or inhabitant of the Highlands of Scotland.

Highland fling, a lively dance of the Highlands of Scotland.

High·lands (hī′ləndz), *n.pl.* a mountainous region in N and W Scotland.

high·light (hī′līt′), *n., v.,* –light·ed, –light·ing. —*n.* Also, high light. **1.** effect or representation of bright light. **2.** part of a painting, photograph, etc., in which light is represented

as falling with full force. **3.** the most conspicuous or interesting part, event, scene, etc. —*v.* **1.** cast a bright light on. **2.** make prominent.

high·ly (hī′li), *adv.* **1.** in a high degree; very. **2.** favorably. **3.** at a high price.

High Mass, a complete ritual of Mass with music. The priest chants the service, assisted by a deacon and subdeacon.

high-mind·ed (hī′mīn′did), *adj.* **1.** having or showing high principles and feelings. **2.** proud. —**high′-mind′ed·ly,** *adv.* —**high′-mind′ed·ness,** *n.* —Syn. **1.** noble.

high·ness (hī′nis), *n.* **1.** a being high; height. **2.** Highness, title of honor given to members of royal families.

high-pitched (hī′picht′), *adj.* **1.** of high tone or sound; shrill. **2.** having a steep slope.

high-pres·sure (hī′presh′ər), *adj., v.,* –sured, –sur·ing. *Am.* —*adj.* **1.** having or using more than the usual pressure. **2.** *Colloq.* using strong, vigorous methods. —*v. Colloq.* use strong, vigorous methods in selling, etc.

high priest, 1. a chief priest. **2.** head of the ancient Jewish priesthood.

high-rise (hī′rīz′), *adj.* of or having to do with a tall apartment building, usually providing luxury or status at high prices.

high-road (hī′rōd′), *n.* **1.** a main road; highway. **2.** a direct and easy way.

high school, *Am.* school attended after the elementary school. —**high′-school′,** *adj.* > high school. Capitalize only when referring to a particular school (some newspaper styles do not use capitals even then): *I graduated from high school at seventeen; I graduated from the Lincoln High School in 1951.*

high seas, the open ocean, outside the authority of any country.

high-sound·ing (hī′soun′ding), *adj.* having an imposing or pretentious sound.

high-spir·it·ed (hī′spir′it·id), *adj.* **1.** proud. **2.** courageous. **3.** spirited; fiery.

high spot, *Am.* **1.** an outstanding part or feature. **2.** hit the high spots, *Colloq.* go with great speed; mention briefly.

high-strung (hī′strung′), *adj.* very sensitive; easily excited; nervous.

hight (hīt), *v.* pp. of an archaic verb hight; named; called. [OE *heht,* preterit of *hātan* be called]

high-test (hī′test′), *adj.* **1.** passing very difficult requirements and tests. **2.** having a very low boiling point.

high tide, 1. the highest level of the tide. **2.** time when the tide is highest. **3.** highest point.

high time, 1. time just before it is too late. **2.** *Am., Colloq.* a gay, jolly time at a party, etc.

high-toned (hī′tōnd′), *adj.* **1.** high in tone or pitch. **2.** *Am.* dignified. **3.** *Colloq.* fashionable.

high treason, treason against one's sovereign, state, or government.

high water, 1. highest level of water. **2.** high tide.

high-wa·ter mark (hī′wô′tər; –wot′ər), **1.** the highest level reached by a body of water. **2.** any highest point.

high·way (hī′wā′), *n.* **1.** a public road. **2.** a main road or route. **3.** a direct line or way to some end.

high·way·man (hī′wā′mən), *n., pl.* –men. man who robs travelers on the public road.

hi·jack (hī′jak′), *v. Am., Colloq.* rob or take by force, esp. goods, liquor, etc., being transported illegally. —**hi′jack′er,** *n. Am.*

hike (hīk), *v.,* hiked, hik·ing, *n. Colloq.* —*v.* **1.** take a long walk; tramp; march. **2.** move, draw, or raise with a jerk. —*n. Am.* **1.** a march or tramp. **2.** increase. —**hik′er,** *n.*

hi·lar·i·ous (hə·lâr′i·əs; hī-), *adj.* very merry; noisily gay. —**hi·lar′i·ous·ly,** *adv.* —**hi·lar′i·ous·ness,** *n.* —Syn. rollicking, boisterous.

hi·lar·i·ty (hə·lar′ə·ti; hī-), *n.* great mirth; noisy gaiety. [< L, < *hilaris, hilarus* gay < Gk. *hilaros*]

hill (hil), *n.* **1.** a raised part on the earth's

surface, not so big as a mountain. **2.** a little heap or pile: *an ant hill.* **3.** a little heap of soil put over and around the roots of a plant or cluster of plants. **4.** the plant or plants so surrounded. —*v.* **1.** cover with soil in this way. **2.** form into a heap. [OE *hyll*] —**hill′er,** *n.*

hill·bil·ly (hil′bil′i), *n., pl.* -**lies.** *Am., Colloq.* person who lives in the backwoods or a mountain region, esp. in the South.

hill·ock (hil′ək), *n.* a little hill. —**hill′ock·y,** *adj.*

hill·side (hil′sīd′), *n.* side of a hill.

hill·top (hil′top′), *n.* top of a hill.

hill·y (hil′i), *adj.,* hill·i·er, hill·i·est. **1.** having many hills. **2.** like a hill; steep. —**hill′i·ness,** *n.*

hilt (hilt), *n.* **1.** handle of a sword, dagger, etc. **2.** up to the hilt, completely. [OE] —**hilt′ed,** *adj.*

hi·lum (hī′ləm), *n., pl.* -**la** (-lə). *Bot.* mark or scar on a seed at the point of attachment to the seed vessel. [< L, *trifle*]

him (him; *unstressed* im), *pron.* the objective case of he: *take him home.*

Him·a·la·yas (him′ə-lā′əz; hə-mäl′yəz), or **Himalaya Mountains,** *n.pl.* a mountain range extending for 1600 miles along the N border of India. —**Him′a·la′yan,** *adj.*

Himm·ler (him′lər), *n.* **Heinrich,** 1900–1945, head of the Gestapo in Nazi Germany.

him·self (him·self′; *unstressed* im·self′), *pron.* **1.** the emphatic form of he or him: *he himself did it.* **2.** the reflexive form of him: *he hurt himself.* **3.** his real self: *he feels like himself again.*

hind¹ (hīnd), *adj.,* hind·er, hind·most or hind·er·most. back; rear. [see HINDER², BEHIND]

hind² (hīnd), *n., pl.* hinds or (*esp. collectively*) hind. a female deer, usually a female red deer after its third year. [OE]

hind³ (hīnd), *n. Archaic* or *Brit. Dial.* **1.** a farm worker. **2.** peasant. [OE *hīne,* pl.]

Hind., Hindustani.

hind·brain (hīnd′brān′), *n. Anat.* the back part of the brain.

Hin·den·burg (hin′dən·bérg), *n.* **Paul von,** 1847–1934, German general and field marshal, president of Germany, 1925–1934.

hin·der¹ (hin′dər), *v.* keep back; hold back; get in the way of; make difficult; stop; prevent. [OE *hindrian*] —**hin′der·er,** *n.* —**hin′der·ing·ly,** *adv.* —**Syn.** impede, encumber, retard, hamper.

hind·er² (hīn′dər), *adj.* hind; back; rear. [cf. OE *hinder* and *hindan* in back, behind]

Hin·di (hin′di), *n.* **1.** an Indo-European vernacular language of N India. **2.** form of Hindustani.

hind·most (hīnd′mōst), **hind·er·most** (hīn′dər·mōst), *adj.* furthest behind; last.

hind·quar·ter (hīnd′kwôr′tər), *n.* the hind leg and loin of a carcass of beef, lamb, etc.

hin·drance (hin′drəns), *n.* **1.** person or thing that hinders; obstacle. **2.** act of hindering.

hind·sight (hīnd′sīt′), *n. Am.* ability to see, too late, what should have been done.

Hin·du, Hin·doo (hin′dü), *n., pl.* -**dus; -doos;** *adj.* —*n.* **1.** member of a native race of India. **2.** person who believes in Hinduism. —*adj.* having to do with the Hindus, their languages, or their religion.

Hin·du·ism, Hin·doo·ism (hin′dü·iz·əm), *n.* the religious and social system of the Hindus.

Hin·du·stan (hin′dü·stän′; -stan′), *n.* **1.** India. **2.** part of India north of the Deccan.

Hin·du·sta·ni, Hin·doo·sta·ni (hin′dü·stä′ni; -stan′i), *adj.* having to do with India, its people, or their languages. —*n.* the commonest language of India.

hinge (hinj), *n., v.,* hinged, hing·ing. —*n.* **1.** joint on which a door, gate, cover, lid, etc., moves back and forth. **2.** a natural joint doing similar work: *hinge of the knee.* **3.** a critical point. —*v.* **1.** furnish with hinges; attach by hinges. **2.** hang or turn on a hinge. **3.** depend. [OE *henge-;* akin to HANG] —**hinged,** *adj.*

hin·ny (hin′i), *n., pl.* -**nies.** a mulelike animal that is the offspring of a male horse and a female donkey. [< L *hinnus* < Gk. *innos*]

hint (hint), *n.* a slight sign; indirect suggestion. —*v.* **1.** give a slight sign of; suggest indirectly. **2.** hint at, give a hint of; suggest. [appar. < *hent,* v., seize, OE *hentan*] —**hint′er,** *n.* —**hint′ing·ly,** *adv.* —**Syn.** *n.* intimation, allusion, inkling, innuendo, insinuation.

hin·ter·land (hin′tər·land′), *n.* **1.** land or district behind a coast; back country. **2.** remote parts; background. [< G]

hip¹ (hip), *n.* **1.** the projecting part on a person where the leg joins the body; joint formed by the upper thighbone and pelvis. **2.** on the hip, at a disadvantage. [OE *hype*] —**hip′like′,** *adj.*

hip² (hip), *n.* pod containing the ripe seed of a rose bush. [OE *hēope*]

hipped (hipt), *adj. Am., Slang.* obsessed. [var. of *hypt* < *hyp,* n., for *hypochondria*]

Hip·poc·ra·tes (hi·pok′rə·tēz), *n.* 460?–357? B.C., Greek physician, called "the father of medicine." —**Hip·po·crat·ic** (hip′ə·krat′ik), *adj.*

Hippocratic oath, a famous oath describing the duties and obligations of a physician.

Hip·po·crene (hip′ə·krēn; hip′ə·krē′nē), *n. Gk. Myth.* fountain sacred to the Muses and regarded as a source of poetic inspiration.

hip·po·drome (hip′ə·drōm), *n.* **1.** in ancient Greece and Rome, an oval track for horse races and chariot races, surrounded by tiers of seats for spectators. **2.** arena or building for a circus, rodeo, etc. [< L < Gk., < *hippos* horse + *dromos* course]

hip·po·pot·a·mus (hip′ə·pot′ə·məs), *n., pl.* -**mus·es, -mi** (-mī). a huge, thick-skinned, hairless mammal found in and near the rivers of Africa. [< L < Gk., < *hippos* horse + *potamos* river]

Hippopotamus
(ab. 13 ft. long)

hir·cine (hér′sīn; -sin), *adj.* of goats; resembling a goat. [< L, < *hircus* goat]

hire (hīr), *v.,* hired, hir·ing, *n.* —*v.* **1.** pay for the use of (a thing) or the work or services of (a person). **2.** give the use of (a thing) or the work or services of (a person) in return for payment. [OE *hyrian,* < n.] —*n.* **1.** payment for such use or work. **2.** a hiring. [OE *hyr*] —**hir′a·ble, hire′a·ble,** *adj.* —**hir′er,** *n.* —**Syn.** *v.* **1, 2.** lease, rent.

hire·ling (hīr′ling), *n.* person who works only for money, without interest or pride in the task. —*adj.* to be had for hire; mercenary.

Hir·o·hi·to (hir′ō·hē′tō), *n.* born 1901, emperor of Japan since 1926.

Hir·o·shi·ma (hir′ə·shē′mə), *n.* seaport in W Japan, largely destroyed by the first military use of the atomic bomb, Aug. 6, 1945.

hir·sute (hér′süt), *adj.* hairy. [< L *hirsutus*] —**hir′sute·ness,** *n.*

his (hiz; *unstressed* iz), *pron.* **1.** of him; belonging to him: *this is his.* **2.** the one or ones belonging to him: *the others are not his.* —*adj.* of him; belonging to him: *this is his book.* [OE, gen. of *hē* he]

His·pa·ni·a (his·pā′ni·ə; -nyə), *n. Poetic.* Spain. —**His·pan·ic** (his·pan′ik), *adj.*

His·pan·io·la (his′pən·yō′lə), *n.* the second largest island in the West Indies, divided into the Dominican Republic and the republic of Haiti. Former name, Haiti.

hiss (his), *v.* **1.** make a sound like *ss.* Geese and snakes hiss. **2.** show disapproval of or scorn for by hissing: *hiss poor acting.* **3.** force or drive by hissing: *hiss him off the stage.* **4.** say or show by hissing. —*n.* a sound like *ss.* [imit.] —**hiss′er,** *n.*

hist (hist), *interj.* be still! listen!

hist., historian; historical; history.

his·ta·mine (his′tə·mēn; -min), *n.* an amine, $C_5H_9N_3$, released by the body in allergic reactions. It lowers the blood pressure, stimulates contraction of the uterus, etc.

his·tol·o·gy (his·tol′ə·ji), *n.* science of the tissues of animals and plants; study of the structure, esp. the microscopic structure, of

organic tissues. [< Gk. *histos* web + –LOGY]
—**his·to·log·i·cal** (his′tə·loj′ə·kəl), his′to·log′ic,
adj. —**his·tol′o·gist,** *n.*
his·to·ri·an (his·tô′ri·ən; –tō′–), *n.* 1. person
who writes about history. 2. scholar who is an
authority on history.
his·tor·ic (his·tôr′ik; –tor′–), *adj.* 1. famous
or important in history. 2. historical.
his·tor·i·cal (his·tôr′ə·kəl; –tor′–), *adj.* 1. of
or having to do with history. 2. according to
history; based on history. 3. known to be real or
true; in history, not in legend. 4. historic. —**his·**
tor′i·cal·ly, *adv.* —**his·tor′i·cal·ness,** *n.*
historical present, *Gram.* the present tense
used in describing past events.
his·to·ri·og·ra·pher (his·tô′ri·og′rə·fər;
–tō′–), *n.* 1. historian. 2. the official historian of
a court, public institution, etc. —**his·to′ri·og′·**
ra·phy, *n.*
his·to·ry (his′tə·ri; his′tri), *n., pl.* –ries. 1.
statement of what has happened. 2. story of a
man or a nation; systematic written account. 3.
a known past: *this ship has a history.* 4. all past
events considered together; course of human
affairs. 5. a recording and explaining of past
events; study of such records. [< L < Gk. *his·*
toria inquiry, record, history. Doublet of STORY¹.]
his·tri·on·ic (his′tri·on′ik), *adj.* 1. having to
do with actors or acting. 2. theatrical; insincere.
[< L, < *histrio* actor < Etruscan (*h*)*ister*] —**his′·**
tri·on′i·cal·ly, *adv.*
his·tri·on·ics (his′tri·on′iks), *n.pl.* 1. dramatic representation; theatricals; dramatics. 2.
a theatrical or insincere manner, expression, etc.
hit (hit), *v.,* hit, hit·ting, *n.* —*v.* 1. come against
with force; give a blow to; strike; knock. 2. propel by a stroke: *hit the ball over the fence.* 3.
Am., Colloq. arrive at: *hit town.* 4. have a painful effect on; affect severely. 5. attack or criticize.
6. *Colloq.* of an engine, ignite the mixture in a
cylinder: *the car hits on all eight cylinders.* 7.
agree with; suit exactly. 8. **hit it off,** *Colloq.* get
along well together; agree. 9. **hit on** or **upon,** a.
come on; meet with; get to. b. find, esp. by accident; guess correctly. 10. **hit or miss,** by chance;
at random. —*n.* 1. a blow; stroke. 2. a getting
to what is aimed at. 3. attack or criticism. 4.
a successful attempt, performance, or production: *the song was a hit.* 5. *Baseball.* ball so
struck that the batter can get to first base
safely, and perhaps further. [< Scand. *hitta*]
—**hit′ter,** *n.*
hitch (hich), *v.* 1. move or pull with a jerk;
move jerkily. 2. limp; hobble. 3. harness to a
cart or conveyance. 4. fasten with a hook, ring,
rope, strap, etc. 5. become fastened or caught;
catch. —*n.* 1. a short, sudden pull or jerk; jerky
movement. 2. limp; hobble. 3. a making fast;
catching hold. 4. a fastening; catch. 5. obstacle;
hindrance. 6. *Naut.* kind of knot used for temporary fastening. [ME *hyche*(*n*)] —**hitch′er,** *n.*
—Syn. *v.* 4. attach, tie, hook, tether, harness.
hitch·hike (hich′hīk′), *v.,* –hiked, –hik·ing.
Am., Slang. travel by getting free rides from
passing automobiles. —**hitch′hik′er,** *n. Am.*
hith·er (hith′ər), *adv.* to this place; toward
this place; here: *come hither.* —*adj.* on this side;
nearer. [OE *hider*; akin to HERE]
hith·er·to (hith′ər·tü′), *adv.* up to this time;
until now.
hith·er·ward (hith′ər·wərd), **hith·er·**
wards (–wərdz), *adv.* toward this place; hither.
Hit·ler (hit′lər), *n.* Adolf, 1889–1945, German
dictator, born in Austria, chancellor of Germany from 1933 to 1945.
Hit·ler·ism (hit′lər·iz·əm), *n.* program and
teachings of the political party founded in Germany by Hitler and others in 1919 and 1920.
—Hit·ler·ite (hit′lər·īt), *n.*
Hit·tite (hit′īt), *n.* 1. member of an ancient
people in Asia Minor and Syria, existing from
about 2000 B.C. until about 1200 B.C. 2. language
of the Hittites. —*adj.* of or having to do with the
Hittites or their language.
hive (hīv), *n., v.,* hived, hiv·ing. —*n.* 1. house
or box for bees to live in. 2. a large number of
bees living together. 3. a busy, swarming place

full of people or animals. 4. a swarming crowd.
—*v.* put (bees) in a hive. [OE *hȳf*]
hives (hīvz), *n.* any of various diseases in which
the skin itches and shows patches of red.
H.M., His Majesty; Her Majesty.
H.M.S., His (Her) Majesty's Service; His (Her)
Majesty's Ship.
ho (hō), *interj.* 1. exclamation of scornful
laughter, joy, or surprise. 2. exclamation to attract attention.
Ho, *Chem.* holmium.
hoar (hôr; hōr), *adj.* hoary. —*n.* 1. hoariness.
2. hoarfrost. [OE *hār*]
hoard (hôrd; hōrd), *n.* what is saved and stored
away; things stored. —*v.* save and store away.
[OE *hord*] —**hoard′er,** *n.* —Syn. *v.* treasure,
amass, accumulate.
hoard·ing (hôr′ding; hōr′–), *n. Brit.* 1. a temporary board fence around a building that is
being put up or repaired. 2. billboard. [< *hoard*
fence, appar. < AF *hurdis,* ult. < Gmc.]
hoar·frost (hôr′frôst′; hōr′–; –frost′), *n.*
white frost.
hoar·hound (hôr′hound′; hōr′–), *n.* hore-
hound.
hoarse (hôrs; hōrs), *adj.,* hoars·er, hoars·est.
1. sounding rough and deep. 2. having a rough
voice. [OE *hās*; infl. by Scand. *hāss*] —**hoarse′·**
ly, *adv.* —**hoarse′ness,** *n.* —Syn. 1. harsh, husky.
hoar·y (hôr′i; hōr′i), *adj.,* hoar·i·er, hoar·i·est.
1. white or gray. 2. white or gray with age. 3.
old; ancient. —**hoar′i·ness,** *n.*
hoax (hōks), *n.* a mischievous trick, esp. a
made-up story. —*v.* play a mischievous trick on;
deceive in fun or to injure. (prob. alter. of *hocus*]
—**hoax′er,** *n.*
hob¹ (hob), *n.* 1. shelf at the back or side of a
fireplace. 2. peg at which quoits, etc., are thrown.
hob² (hob), *n.* 1. hobgoblin; elf. 2. *Am., Colloq.*
play hob or **raise hob,** cause trouble. [ME, for
Rob (*Robert* or *Robin*)]
Ho·bart (hō′bärt; –bərt), *n.* capital of Tasmania.
hob·ble (hob′əl), *v.,* –bled, –bling, *n.* —*v.* 1.
walk awkwardly; limp. 2. cause to walk awkwardly or limp. 3. move unsteadily. 4. tie the legs
of (a horse, etc.) together. 5. hinder. —*n.* 1. an
awkward walk; limp. 2. rope or strap used to
hobble a horse, etc. [ME *hobelen.* Cf. Du. *hob-*
belen to rock.] —**hob′bler,** *n.* —**hob′bling,** *adj.*
hob·ble·de·hoy (hob′əl·di·hoi′), *n.* 1. youth
between boyhood and manhood. 2. an awkward,
clumsy boy.
hob·by (hob′i), *n., pl.* –bies. 1. something a
person especially likes to work at or study apart
from his main business; any favorite pastime,
topic of conversation, etc. 2. hobbyhorse. [ME
hobyn small horse]
hob·by·horse (hob′i·hôrs′), *n.* 1. stick with a
horse's head, used as a toy horse by
children. 2. a rocking horse.
hob·gob·lin (hob′gob′lən), *n.* 1. goblin; elf. 2. bogy. [< *hob²* + *goblin*]
hob·nail (hob′nāl′), *n.* a short nail
with a large head to protect the soles of Hobnails
heavy shoes. [< *hob* peg + *nail*] —**hob′nailed′,**
adj.
hob·nob (hob′nob′), *v.,* –nobbed, –nob·bing.
1. associate intimately; talk together on familiar
terms. 2. drink together. [from drinking phrase
hob or *nob* give or take, ult. < OE *hæbbe* have +
næbbe not have]
ho·bo (hō′bō), *n., pl.* –bos, –boes. *Am.* a tramp
or vagrant.
Hob·son's choice (hob′sənz), choice of taking the thing offered or nothing. [from T. *Hob-*
son, who rented the horse nearest his stable door
or none]
Ho Chi Minh (hō′ chē′ min′), born 1892,
Indo-Chinese politician, president of North Vietnam since 1954.
hock¹ (hok), *n.* joint in the hind leg of a horse,
cow, etc., above the fetlock joint. See the picture
under cannon bone. Also, hough. [OE *hōh*]

hock[2] (hok), *n. Esp. Brit.* kind of white Rhine wine. [for *Hockamore*, alter. of *Hochheimer*]

hock[3] (hok), *v., n. Am., Slang.* pawn. [orig. n. Cf. Du. *hok* pen, jail.]

hock·ey (hok′i), *n.* game played by two teams on ice or on a field, where players hit a rubber disk or ball with curved sticks to drive it across a goal.

ho·cus (hō′kəs), *v.,* -cused, -cus·ing; *esp. Brit.* -cussed, -cus·sing. 1. play a trick on; hoax; cheat. 2. stupefy with drugs. 3. put drugs in (alcoholic drink). [short for *hocus-pocus*]

ho·cus-po·cus (hō′kəs-pō′kəs), *n., v.,* -cused, -cus·ing; *esp. Brit.* -cussed, -cus·sing. —*n.* 1. form of words used in conjuring. 2. sleight of hand; magic. 3. trickery; deception. —*v.* play tricks on; deceive. [sham Latin used by jugglers, etc.]

hod (hod), *n.* 1. trough or tray with a long handle, used for carrying bricks, mortar, etc., on the shoulder. 2. a coal scuttle. [cf. MDu. *hodde*]

hodge-podge (hoj′poj′), *n.* a disorderly mixture; mess; jumble. [var. of *hotchpot* < OF *hochepot* ragout]

hoe (hō), *n., v.,* hoed, hoe·ing. —*n.* tool with a small blade set across the end of a long handle, used to loosen soil and cut weeds. —*v.* 1. loosen, dig, or cut with a hoe. 2. use a hoe. [< OF *houe* < Gmc.] —hoe′like′, *adj.*

hoe·cake (hō′kāk′), *n. Am., S.* kind of bread made of corn meal.

hog (hog; hôg), *n., v.,* hogged, hog·ging. —*n.* 1. pig. 2. a full-grown pig, raised for food. 3. *Colloq.* a selfish, greedy, or dirty person. —*v. Am., Slang.* take more than one's share of. [OE *hogg*]

Ho·garth (hō′gärth), *n.* William, 1697–1764, English painter and engraver.

hog·gish (hog′ish; hôg′-), *adj.* 1. like a hog; very selfish; greedy. 2. dirty; filthy. —hog′gish·ly, *adv.* —hog′gish·ness, *n.*

hog·nose snake (hog′nōz′; hôg′-), *Am.* a harmless North American snake with an upturned snout.

hogs·head (hogz′hed; hôgz′-), *n.* 1. a large barrel that contains from 63 to 140 gallons. 2. a liquid measure, usually equal to 63 gallons.

hog-tie (hog′tī′; hôg′-), *v.,* -tied, -ty·ing. tie all four feet together.

hog·wash (hog′wosh′; -wôsh′; hôg′-), *n.* 1. swill. 2. worthless stuff; nonsense.

Hoh·en·zol·lern (hō′ən·zol′ərn), *n.* the family that included the kings of Prussia, 1701–1918, and the emperors of Germany, 1871–1918.

hoi·den (hoi′dən), *n., adj.* hoyden.

hoi pol·loi (hoi′ pə·loi′), the masses. [< Gk.]

hoist (hoist), *v.* raise on high; lift up, often with ropes and pulleys. —*n.* 1. a hoisting; lift. 2. elevator or other apparatus for hoisting heavy loads. [earlier *hoise* < Du. *hijschen*] —hoist′er, *n.*

hoi·ty-toi·ty (hoi′ti·toi′ti), *interj.* exclamation showing surprise and some contempt. —*adj.* 1. giddy; flighty. 2. inclined to put on airs; haughty. —*n.* 1. flightiness. 2. haughtiness.

Hok·kai·do (hō′ki′dō), *n.* the second largest island in Japan.

ho·kum (hō′kəm), *n. Slang.* 1. sentimental matter introduced merely for effect. 2. humbug; nonsense; bunk. [? < *hocus*]

hold[1] (hōld), *v.,* held, held or (Archaic) hold·en, hold·ing, *n.* —*v.* 1. take in the hands or arms and keep: *hold a child.* 2. not let go. 3. keep from getting away. 4. keep a grasp. 5. keep in some position or condition: *please hold still.* 6. keep from falling; support. 7. keep from acting; keep back: *hold your breath.* 8. keep by force against an enemy; defend: *hold the fort.* 9. keep or have within itself; contain: *this theater holds 500 people.* 10. have and keep as one's own. 11. possess; occupy: *hold an office.* 12. have a property, right, title, etc.: *the vassal held directly from the king.* 13. have and take part in; carry on together. 14. keep or have in mind: *hold a belief.* 15. think; consider: *hold human life cheap.* 16. remain firm; adhere; cling: *hold to one's purpose.* 17. be true; be in force or effect: *the rule holds in all cases.* 18. keep on; continue:

the weather held warm. 19. decide legally: *the court holds him guilty.* 20. hold back, keep back; keep from acting. 21. hold down, a. keep down; keep under control. b. *Am., Slang.* have and keep: *hold down a job.* 22. hold forth, a. talk; preach. b. offer. 23. hold off, keep at a distance; keep from acting or attacking. 24. hold on, *Colloq.* a. keep one's hold. b. keep on; continue. c. stop! wait a minute! 25. hold out, a. continue; last. b. extend. c. keep resisting; not give in. d. offer. e. keep back; restrain. 26. hold over, a. keep for future action or consideration. b. *Am.* stay in office beyond the regular term. 27. hold up, a. keep from falling; support. b. show; display. c. continue; last; endure. d. stop. e. *Am.* stop by force and rob. —*n.* 1. act of holding: *release one's hold.* 2. thing to hold by, as a handle. 3. thing to hold something else with. 4. a controlling force or influence: *have a secret hold on a person.* 5. *Wrestling, etc.* way of holding one's opponent; grasp or grip. 6. sign for a pause in music. 7. *Archaic.* fort; stronghold. 8. prison. [OE *healdan*] —**Syn.** *v.* 6. bear. 15. regard.

hold[2] (hōld), *n.* interior of a ship below the deck. [var. of *hole*]

hold·back (hōld′bak′), *n.* 1. thing that holds back; restraint; hindrance. 2. device that enables a horse to hold back or to back a vehicle.

hold·er (hōl′dər), *n.* 1. person who holds something. 2. thing to hold something else with. 3. *Law.* one legally entitled to receive payment on, or negotiate, a note, bill, etc.

hold·fast (hōld′fast′; -fäst′), *n.* device used to hold things in place, as a catch, hook, etc.

hold·ing (hōl′ding), *n.* 1. land; piece of land. 2. Often, **holdings.** property in stocks or bonds.

holding action, 1. a military operation that seeks merely to prevent an enemy advance. 2. any undertaking that resembles this: *a holding action against inflation.*

holding company, company that owns stocks or bonds of other companies and often controls them.

hold·out (hōld′out′), *n.* refusal to compromise or come to an agreement on something, esp. in order to exact a higher price, better terms, etc.

hold·up (hōld′up′), *n.* 1. *Am., Colloq.* act of stopping by force and robbing. 2. a stopping. ➤ **holdup.** The verb is written as two words. See definition 27e of **hold**.

hole (hōl), *n., v.,* holed, hol·ing. —*n.* 1. an open place. 2. a hollow place. 3. place dug by an animal to live in. 4. a small, dark, dirty place. 5. dungeon. 6. *Colloq.* flaw; defect. 7. *Colloq.* position hard to get out of; embarrassing position. 8. *Sports.* a small place into which a ball, marble, or the like, is to be hit, rolled, or tossed. 9. *Golf.* part of a course leading from a tee to such a place. 10. pick holes, find fault with; criticize. —*v.* 1. make holes in. 2. hit or drive (a golf ball) into a hole. 3. hole out, hit a golf ball into a hole. 4. hole up, go into a hole for the winter. [OE *hol*] —hole′less, *adj.* —hol′ey, *adj.*

hol·i·day (hol′ə·dā), *n.* 1. day when one does not work; day for pleasure and enjoyment. 2. Often, **holidays,** *Esp. Brit.* vacation. 3. Now usually, **holy day,** a religious festival. —*adj.* suited to a holiday; gay. [OE *hāligdœg* holy day]

ho·li·ness (hō′li·nis), *n.* 1. a being holy. 2. **Holiness,** title used in speaking to or of the Pope.

Hol·land (hol′ənd), *n.* the Netherlands, a small country in N Europe. —Hol′land·er, *n.*

Hol·lands (hol′əndz), or **Holland gin,** *n.* a strong gin made in Holland.

hol·low (hol′ō), *adj.* 1. having nothing, or only air, inside; empty; with a hole inside; not solid. A tube or pipe is hollow. 2. bowl-shaped; cupshaped: *a hollow dish for vegetables.* 3. as if coming from something hollow; dull: *a hollow voice.* 4. not real or sincere; false; worthless: *hollow promises, hollow praise.* 5. deep and sunken: *hollow eyes and cheeks.* 6. hungry. —*n.* 1. a hollow place; hole: *a hollow in the road.* 2. valley: *Sleepy Hollow.* —*v.* 1. make hollow; bend or dig out to a hollow shape. 2. become hollow. —*adv. Colloq.* thoroughly. [OE *holh,* n.] —hol′low·ly, *adv.* —hol′low·ness, *n.* —**Syn.** *adj.* 1.

void, unfilled, vacant. 4. hypocritical, insincere. 5. concave, depressed. —**Ant.** *adj.* 1. filled, full, solid. 4. sincere, straightforward.

hol·ly (hol′ĭ), *n.*, *pl.* –lies. 1. tree or shrub with shiny, sharp-pointed, green leaves and bright-red berries. 2. the leaves and berries used as Christmas decorations. [OE *holegn*]

hol·ly·hock (hol′ĭ·hok), *n.* a tall plant with clusters of large, showy flowers of various colors. [ME *holihoc* < *holi* holy + *hoc* mallow (OE *hocc*)]

Hol·ly·wood (hol′ĭ·wůd′), *n.* section of Los Angeles where many motion pictures are made.

Holmes (hōmz), *n.* 1. Oliver Wendell, 1809–1894, American author, humorist, and physician. 2. his son, Oliver Wendell, 1841–1935, an associate justice of the U.S. Supreme Court from 1902 to 1932. 3. Sherlock, detective in stories by A. Conan Doyle.

hol·mi·um (hōl′mi·əm), *n. Chem.* a rare metallic element, Ho, belonging to the yttrium group. [< NL; named for *Stockholm*]

holm oak (hōm), an evergreen oak of S Europe with leaves like those of the holly. [OE *holegn* holly + *āc* oak]

hol·o·caust (hol′ə·kôst), *n.* 1. an offering all of which is burned. 2. complete destruction by fire, esp. of animals or human beings. 3. great or wholesale destruction. [< L < Gk., < *holos* whole + *kaustos* burned] —**hol′o·caus′tal, hol′o·caus′tic,** *adj.*

hol·o·graph (hol′ə·graf; –gräf), *adj.* wholly written in the handwriting of the person in whose name it appears: *a holograph will.* —*n.* a holograph manuscript, letter, document, etc. [< LL < Gk., < *holos* whole + *graphe* writing] —**hol′o·graph′ic,** *adj.*

holp (hōlp), *v. Archaic.* pt. of help.

hol·pen (hōl′pən), *v. Archaic.* pp. of help.

Hol·stein (hōl′stīn; –stēn), **Holstein-Friesian** (–frē′zhən), *n.* any of a breed of large, black-and-white dairy cattle.

hol·ster (hōl′stər), *n.* a leather case for a pistol, attached to a belt or a horseman's saddle. [cf. Du. *holster*] —**hol′stered,** *adj.*

ho·ly (hō′lĭ), *adj.*, –li·er, –li·est, *n.*, *pl.* –lies. —*adj.* 1. set apart or devoted to the service of God, the church, or religion: *a holy man.* 2. declared sacred by religious use and authority: *a holy day.* 3. like a saint; spiritually perfect; very good; pure in heart. 4. worthy of reverence. 5. religious: *holy rites.* —*n.* a holy place. [OE *hālig*] —**Syn.** *adj.* 2. hallowed, blessed. 3. devout, pious, pure, saintly.

Holy City, 1. city considered sacred by the adherents of any religion: Jerusalem, Rome, and Mecca are Holy Cities. 2. heaven.

Holy Communion, 1. a sharing in the Lord's Supper as a part of church worship; a receiving of the Holy Eucharist. 2. celebration of the Lord's Supper.

holy day, a religious festival, esp. one not occurring on Sunday, as Ash Wednesday, Good Friday, etc.

Holy Father, *Rom. Cath. Church.* a title of the Pope.

Holy Ghost, spirit of God; third person of the Trinity.

Holy Grail, cup or dish supposed to have been used by Christ at the Last Supper, in which one of His followers received the last drops of blood from Christ's body on the cross.

Holy Land, Palestine.

holy of holies, 1. the holiest place. 2. the inner shrine of the Jewish tabernacle and temple.

holy orders, 1. the rite or sacrament of ordination. 2. the rank or position of an ordained Christian minister or priest. 3. the three higher ranks or positions in the Roman Catholic and Anglican churches. Bishops, priests, and deacons are members of holy orders.

Holy Roman Empire, empire in western and central Europe regarded both as the continuation of the Roman Empire and as the temporal form of a universal dominion whose spiritual head was the Pope, begun in 962 A.D., or, according to some, in 800 A.D., and ended in 1806.

Holy Scriptures, the Bible; scripture (def. 2).

Holy See, 1. position or authority of the Pope. 2. the Pope's court.

Holy Spirit, Holy Ghost.

ho·ly·stone (hō′li·stōn′), *n.*, *v.*, –stoned, –ston·ing. —*n.* piece of soft sandstone used for scrubbing the wooden decks of ships. —*v.* scrub with a holystone.

Holy Week, week before Easter.

Holy Writ, the Bible; the Scriptures.

hom·age (hom′ĭj; om′–), *n.* 1. respect; reverence: *pay homage to a great leader.* 2. a formal acknowledgment by a vassal that he owed loyalty and service to his lord. 3. thing done or given to show such acknowledgment. [< OF, < *hom* man, vassal < L *homo*] —**Syn.** 1. deference.

hom·bre (ôm′brā), *n. Spanish.* man.

hom·burg (hom′bėrg), *n.* a man's soft felt hat with the crown dented in at the top.

home (hōm), *n.*, *adj.*, *adv.*, *v.*, homed, hom·ing. —*n.* 1. place where a person or family lives; one's own house. 2. place where a person was born or brought up; one's own town or country. 3. place where an animal or plant lives; habitat. 4. place where a person can rest and be safe. 5. place where people who are homeless, poor, old, sick, blind, etc., may live. 6. place of existence near death. 7. family life. 8. *Sports, etc.* point to be hit; goal. 9. *Baseball.* home plate. 10. **at home, a.** in one's own home or country. **b.** in a friendly place or familiar condition; at ease; comfortable. **c.** ready to receive visitors. —*adj.* 1. having to do with one's own home or country. 2. reaching its goal; effective: *a home thrust.* —*adv.* 1. at, to, or toward one's own home or country: *go home.* 2. to the place where it belongs; to the thing aimed at: *strike home.* 3. to the heart or center; deep in: *drive a nail home.* 4. bring home, make clear, emphatic, or realistic. —*v.* 1. go home. 2. send or bring home. 3. have a home. 4. furnish with a home. [OE *hām*] 5. home (in) on, of a guided missile, reach the target. —**home′like′,** *adj.* —**Syn.** *n.* 1. residence, dwelling, abode.

home·bred (hōm′bred′), *adj.* 1. native; domestic. 2. crude; unsophisticated.

home-brew (hōm′brü′), *n.* beer or other alcoholic liquor made at home.

home economics, *Am.* science and art that deals with the management of a household.

home·land (hōm′land′), *n.* one's native land.

home·less (hōm′lis), *adj.* having no home. —**home′less·ly,** *adv.* —**home′less·ness,** *n.*

home·ly (hōm′lĭ), *adj.*, –li·er, –li·est. 1. suited to home life; simple; everyday: *homely pleasures.* 2. of plain manners; unpretending. 3. lacking cultivation; rude. 4. *U.S.* not good-looking; ugly; plain. —**home′li·ness,** *n.*

home·made (hōm′mād′), *adj.* made at home.

ho·me·op·a·thy (hō′mi·op′ə·thĭ; hom′ĭ–), *n.* method of treating disease by drugs, given in very small doses, which would in large doses produce in a healthy person symptoms similar to those of the disease. Also, homoeopathy. [< Gk. *homoios* similar + –PATHY] —**ho·me·o·path** (hō′mi·ə·path; hom′ĭ–), **ho′me·op′a·thist,** *n.* —**ho′me·o·path′ic, ho′me·o·path′i·cal·ly,** *adv.*

home plate, *Am., Baseball.* block or slab beside which a player stands to bat the ball, and to which he must return, after hitting the ball and rounding the bases, in order to score.

hom·er (hōm′ər), *n.* 1. *Am., Baseball.* a home run. 2. a homing pigeon.

Ho·mer (hō′mər), *n.* about the 10th cent. B.C., the great epic poet of ancient Greece; author of the *Iliad* and the *Odyssey.*

Ho·mer·ic (hō·mer′ik), *adj.* 1. by Homer. 2. of or pertaining to Homer or his poems. 3. in the style of Homer. 4. of the time when Homer lived.

Homeric laughter, loud, hearty laughter.

home rule, local self-government.

āge, cāre, fär; ēqual, tėrm; īce; ōpen, ôrder; půt, rüle, ūse; tл, then; ə=a in about.

home run, *Am., Baseball.* run made by a player on a hit that enables him, without aid from fielding errors of the opponents, to make the entire circuit of the bases without a stop.

home·sick (hōm′sĭk′), *adj.* longing for home. —**home′sick′ness,** *n.*

home·spun (hōm′spun′), *adj.* **1.** spun or made at home. **2.** not polished; plain; simple. —*n.* **1.** cloth made of yarn spun at home. **2.** a strong, loosely woven cloth similar to it.

home·stead (hōm′sted), *n. Am.* **1.** house with its land and other buildings; farm with its buildings. **2.** parcel of 160 acres of public land granted to a settler under certain conditions by the U.S. government. —**home′stead·er,** *n. Am.*

home stretch, 1. *Am.* part of a track over which the last part of a race is run. **2.** the last part.

home·ward (hōm′wərd), *adv.* Also, **home′-wards.** toward home. —*adj.* being in the direction of home.

home·work (hōm′wêrk′), *n.* **1.** work done at home. **2.** lesson to be studied or prepared outside the classroom.

hom·ey (hōm′ĭ), *adj.,* **hom·i·er, hom·i·est.** *Colloq.* like home; cozy and comfortable.

hom·i·cide[1] (hom′ə·sīd; hō′mə-), *n.* the killing of one human being by another. Intentional homicide is murder. [< OF < L, < *homo* man + *-cidium* act of killing] —**hom′i·cid′al,** *adj.* —**hom′i·cid′al·ly,** *adv.*

hom·i·cide[2] (hom′ə·sīd; hō′mə-), *n.* person who kills a human being. [< OF < L, < *homo* man + *-cida* killer]

hom·i·let·ics (hom′ə·let′ĭks), *n.* art of composing and preaching sermons. [< LL < Gk., affable, ult. < *homileein* associate with. See HOMILY.] —**hom′i·let′ic,** *adj.* —**hom′i·let′i·cal·ly,** *adv.*

hom·i·ly (hom′ə·lĭ), *n., pl.* **–lies. 1.** sermon, usually on some part of the Bible. **2.** a serious moral talk or writing. [< OF < LL < Gk. *homilia* < *homilos* throng < *homou* together]

homing pigeon, pigeon trained to fly home from great distances carrying written messages.

hom·i·ny (hom′ə·ni), *n. Am.* corn hulled and coarsely ground or crushed, usually eaten boiled. [< Algonquian]

ho·mo (hō′mō), *n., pl.* **hom·i·nes** (hom′ə·nēz). man. [< L]

ho·moe·op·a·thy (hō′mĭ·op′ə·thĭ; hom′ĭ-), *n.* homeopathy. —**ho·moe·o·path** (hō′mĭ·ə·path; hom′ĭ-), **ho′moe·op′a·thist,** *n.* —**ho·moe·o·path′ic,** *adj.* —**ho′moe·o·path′i·cal·ly,** *adv.*

ho·mo·ge·ne·ous (hō′mə·jē′ni·əs; -jēn′yəs; hom′ə-), *adj.* **1.** of the same kind; similar. **2.** composed of similar elements or parts. [< Med.L < Gk., < *homos* the same + *genos* kind] —**ho·mo·ge·ne·i·ty** (hō′mə·jə·nē′ə·tĭ; hom′ə-), **ho′mo·ge′ne·ous·ness,** *n.* —**ho′mo·ge′ne·ous·ly,** *adv.*

ho·mog·e·nize (hə·moj′ə·nīz), *v.,* **–nized, –niz·ing.** make homogeneous. In homogenized milk the fat is distributed evenly throughout and does not rise in the form of cream.

hom·o·graph (hom′ə·graf; -grȧf; hō′mə-), *n.* word having the same spelling as another, but a different origin and meaning. *Mail,* meaning "letters," and *mail,* meaning "armor," are homographs. [< Gk., < *homos* the same + *graphe* writing] —**hom′o·graph′ic,** *adj.*

ho·mol·o·gous (hō·mol′ə·gəs), *adj.* **1.** corresponding in position, value, etc. **2.** *Biol.* corresponding in type of structure and in origin. The wing of a bird and the foreleg of a horse are homologous. [< Gk., agreeing, < *homos* same + *logos* reasoning, relation]

ho·mol·o·gy (hō·mol′ə·ji), *n., pl.* **–gies.** correspondence in position, proportion, structure, origin, etc.

hom·o·nym (hom′ə·nim), *n.* word having the same pronunciation as another, but a different meaning. *Meat* and *meet* are homonyms. [< L < Gk., < *homos* same + *onyma* (dial.) name] —**hom′o·nym′ic,** *adj.*

hom·o·phone (hom′ə·fōn; hō′mə-), *n.* **1.** letter or symbol having the same sound as another.

The letters *c* and *k* are homophones in the word *cork.* **2.** homonym. [< Gk., < *homos* same + *phone* sound]

ho·moph·o·ny (hō·mof′ə·ni; hom′ə·fō′ni), *n.* **1.** sameness of sound. **2.** music having one part or melody predominating. —**hom·o·phon·ic** (hom′ə·fon′ik; hō′mə-), **ho·moph·o·nous** (hō·mof′ə·nəs), *adj.*

ho·mop·ter·ous (hō·mop′tər·əs), *adj. Zool.* belonging to a group of insects (including the aphids and cicadas) with mouth parts adapted to sucking and wings of the same texture throughout. [< Gk. *homos* same + *pteron* wing]

Ho·mo sa·pi·ens (hō′mō sā′pi·enz), man; human being; the species including all existing races of mankind. [L, lit., man having sense]

ho·mo·sex·u·al (hō′mə·sek′shu̇·əl), *adj.* pertaining to or manifesting sexual feelings for one of the same sex. —*n.* a homosexual person. [< Gk. *homos* same + L *sexus* sex] —**ho′mo·sex′u·al′i·ty,** *n.*

ho·mun·cu·lus (hō·mung′kyə·ləs), *n., pl.* **–li** (-lī). a little man. [< L, dim. of *homo* man]

Hon., Honorable; Honorary.

Hon·du·ras (hon·dûr′əs; -dyur′əs), *n.* country in N Central America. —**Hon·du′ran,** *adj., n.*

hone (hōn), *n., v.,* **honed, hon·ing.** —*n.* a fine-grained whetstone on which to sharpen cutting tools, esp. razors. —*v.* sharpen on a hone. [OE *hān* a stone]

hon·est (on′ist), *adj.* **1.** not lying, cheating, or stealing; fair and upright; truthful: *an honest man.* **2.** obtained by fair and upright means: *honest profits.* **3.** not hiding one's real nature; frank; open: *honest opposition.* **4.** not mixed with something of less value; genuine; pure: *honest goods.* **5.** *Archaic.* chaste; virtuous. [< OF < L *honestus* < *honos* honor] —**hon′est·ly,** *adv.* —**Syn. 1.** just, incorruptible. **3.** sincere, candid.

hon·es·ty (on′is·ti), *n.* **1.** fairness and uprightness. **2.** truthfulness. **3.** freedom from deceit or fraud. **4.** *Archaic.* chastity.

hon·ey (hun′ĭ), *n., pl.* **hon·eys,** *adj., v.,* **honeyed** or **hon·ied, hon·ey·ing.** —*n.* **1.** a thick, sweet, yellow liquid, good to eat, that bees make out of the drops they collect from flowers. **2.** drop of sweet liquid, found in many flowers, that draws bees to them. **3.** sweetness. **4.** darling; dear. —*adj.* of or like honey; sweet; dear. —*v.* **1.** sweeten with or as with honey. **2.** talk sweetly; flatter. [OE *hunig*] —**hon′ey·like′,** *adj.*

hon·ey·bee (hun′ĭ·bē′), *n.* bee that makes honey.

hon·ey·comb (hun′ĭ·kōm′), *n.* **1.** structure of wax containing rows of six-sided cells formed by bees, in which to store honey, pollen, and their eggs. **2.** anything like this. —*adj.* like a honeycomb: *a honeycomb pattern.* —*v.* **1.** make like a honeycomb. **2.** pierce with many holes. **3.** permeate: *the city is honeycombed with crime.*

Honeycomb

hon·ey·dew (hun′ĭ·dū′; -dū′), *n.* **1.** a sweet substance on the leaves of certain plants in hot weather. **2.** a sweet substance on leaves and stems, secreted by tiny insects called aphids. **3.** a honeydew melon.

honeydew melon, a variety of melon with sweet, green flesh and a smooth, whitish skin.

hon·eyed (hun′ĭd), *adj.* **1.** sweetened with honey. **2.** laden with honey. **3.** sweet as honey.

honey locust, *Am.* a thorny North American tree with long, divided leaves and large, flat pods containing sweet pulp.

hon·ey·moon (hun′ĭ·mün′), *n.* **1.** vacation spent together by a newly married couple. **2.** the first month of marriage. —*v.* spend or have a honeymoon. —**hon′ey·moon′er,** *n.*

hon·ey·suck·le (hun′ĭ·suk′əl), *n.* **1.** shrub or vine with small, fragrant flowers. **2.** any of various similar plants. —**hon′ey·suck′led,** *adj.*

Hong Kong, Hong·kong (hong′ kong′; hŏng′ kŏng′), *n.* a British colony in SE China.

honk (hongk; hôngk), *n. Am.* **1.** cry of the wild goose. **2.** any similar sound: *honk of a taxi.* —*v.* make such a sound. [imit.] —**honk′er,** *n.*

honk·y-tonk (hong′ki·tongk′; hông′ki·tôngk′), *n. Am., Slang.* a cheap saloon, cabaret, etc.

Hon·o·lu·lu (hon′ə·lū′lū), *n.* seaport and capital of Hawaii.

hon·or (on′ər), *n.* **1.** glory; fame; renown. **2.** credit for acting well; good name. **3.** source of credit; cause of honor. **4.** a nice sense of what is right or proper; sticking to action that is right or that is usual and expected. **5.** great respect; high regard: *hold in honor.* **6.** act of respect: *funeral honors.* **7.** rank; dignity; distinction: *knighthood is an honor.* **8.** chastity; virtue. **9.** Honor, title used in speaking to or of a judge, mayor, etc. **10.** honors, a. special favors or courtesies. b. special mention, grade, or credit given to a student. c. ace, king, queen, jack, and ten of trumps, or the four aces in no-trump in the game of bridge. **11.** do the honors, act as host or hostess. —*v.* **1.** respect greatly; regard highly. **2.** show respect to. **3.** worship. **4.** confer dignity upon; be an honor to; favor: *be honored by a royal visit.* **5.** accept and pay (a bill, draft, note, etc.) when due. Also, *esp. Brit.* honour. [< OF < L *honos, honor*] —**hon′or·er,** *n.* —**Syn.** *n.* **4.** integrity, uprightness. **5.** deference, veneration, reverence. **7.** eminence, position.

hon·or·a·ble (on′ər·ə·bəl), *adj.* **1.** having or showing a sense of what is right and proper; honest; upright. **2.** causing honor; bringing honor to the one that has it. **3.** worthy of honor; to be respected; noble. **4.** Honorable, in the U.S., a widely used, but vague, title of respect before the names of certain officials and many others: *the Honorable Robert M. La Follette.* Also, *esp. Brit.* honourable. —**hon′or·a·ble·ness,** *n.* —**hon′or·a·bly,** *adv.*

hon·o·rar·i·um (on′ə·rãr′i·əm), *n., pl.* **-rar·i·ums, -rar·i·a** (-rãr′i·ə). fee for professional services on which no fixed price is set.

hon·or·ar·y (on′ər·er′i), *adj.* **1.** given or done as an honor. **2.** as an honor only; without pay or regular duties: *an honorary secretary.*

hon·or·if·ic (on′ər·if′ik), *adj.* **1.** doing or giving honor. **2.** showing respect or deference. —*n.* an honorific word or phrase. —**hon′or·if′i·cal·ly,** *adv.*

honor system, *Am.* system of trusting people in schools and other institutions to obey the rules and do their work without being watched or forced.

hon·our (on′ər), *n., v. Esp. Brit.* honor. —**hon′our·a·ble,** *adj.* —**hon′our·a·ble·ness,** *n.* —**hon′our·a·bly,** *adv.* —**hon′our·er,** *n.*

Hon·shu (hon′shū), *n.* the main island of Japan.

hooch (hūch), *n. Am., Slang.* alcoholic drink, esp. that which is made illegally. [for *hoochinoo,* alter. of *Hutsnuwa,* Alaskan Indians who made liquor]

hood (hud), *n.* **1.** a soft covering for the head and neck, either separate or as part of a cloak. **2.** anything like a hood in shape or use. **3.** *Am.* a metal covering over the engine of an automobile. **4.** in falconry, a cover for the head of a hawk. **5.** *Slang.* hoodlum. —*v.* cover with a hood. [OE *hōd*] —**hood′ed,** *adj.* —**hood′less,** *adj.* —**hood′like′,** *adj.*

Hood (hud), *n.* **1.** Mount, mountain in N Oregon. **2.** Robin, a legendary English outlaw.

-hood, *suffix.* **1.** state or condition of being, as in *boyhood, likelihood.* **2.** character or nature of, as in *manhood, sainthood.* **3.** group, body of, as in *priesthood, sisterhood.* [OE *-hād*]

hood·lum (hūd′ləm), *n. Am., Colloq.* a young rowdy; street ruffian. —**hood′lum·ism,** *n. Am.*

hoo·doo (hū′dū), *n., pl.* **-doos,** *v.* **-dooed, -doo·ing.** *Am.* —*n.* **1.** voodoo. **2.** person or thing that brings bad luck. **3.** bad luck. —*v.* bring or cause bad luck to. [? var. of *voodoo*]

hood·wink (hud′wingk), *v.* **1.** mislead by a trick; deceive. **2.** blindfold. —**hood′wink·er,** *n.*

hoo·ey (hū′i), *Am., Slang.* —*n.* nonsense. —*interj.* exclamation of disgust or disapproval.

hoof (huf; hūf), *n., pl.* **hoofs** or (*Rare*) **hooves,** *v.* —*n.* **1.** a hard, horny covering on the feet of horses, cattle, sheep, pigs, and some other animals. **2.** the whole foot of such animals. **3.** on the hoof, alive; not killed and butchered. —*v. Colloq.* **1.** walk. **2.** dance. [OE *hōf*] —**hoofed,** *adj.* —**hoof′er,** *n.* —**hoof′like′,** *adj.*

hoof·beat (huf′bēt′; hūf′-), *n.* sound made by an animal's hoof.

hook (huk), *n.* **1.** piece of metal, wood, or other stiff material, curved or having a sharp angle for catching hold of something or for hanging things on. **2.** a curved piece of wire, usually with a barb at the end, for catching fish. **3.** trap; snare. **4.** anything curved or bent like a hook. **5.** a sharp bend. **6.** point of land. **7.** act of hooking. **8.** *Baseball.* a curve. **9.** *Golf.* a ball's path of flight curving to the left away from a right-handed player. **10.** *Boxing.* a short, swinging blow. **11.** *Music.* line on the stem of certain notes. **12.** by hook or by crook, in any way at all; by fair means or foul. **13.** on one's own hook, *Slang.* independently. —*v.* **1.** attach or fasten with a hook or hooks: *please hook my dress for me.* **2.** join; fit; be fastened: *this dress hooks up the back.* **3.** catch or take hold of with a hook. **4.** catch (fish) with a hook. **5.** give the form of a hook to. **6.** be curved or bent like a hook. **7.** catch by a trick. **8.** *Colloq.* steal. **9.** throw (a ball) so that it curves. **10.** *Golf.* hit a hook. **11.** *Boxing.* hit with a hook. **12.** hook up, a. attach or fasten with a hook or hooks. b. arrange and connect the parts of (a radio set, telephone, etc.). [OE *hōc*] —**hook′less,** *adj.* —**hook′like′,** *adj.*

hook·ah, hook·a (huk′ə), *n.* a tobacco pipe with a long tube by which the smoke is drawn through water. [< Ar. *ḥuqqa* vase, pipe]

hooked (hukt), *adj.* **1.** curved or bent like a hook. **2.** having hooks. **3.** made with a hook. —**hook·ed·ness** (huk′id·nis), *n.*

Man smoking a hookah

hooked rug, *Am.* rug made by pulling yarn or strips of cloth through a piece of canvas, burlap, etc.

hook·up (huk′up′), *n.* **1.** arrangement and connection of the parts of a radio set, telephone, radio-broadcasting facilities, etc. **2.** an effecting of relationships: *a hookup between nations.*

hook·worm (huk′werm′), *n. Am.* **1.** worm that gets into the intestines and causes a disease characterized by weakness and apparent laziness. **2.** the disease.

hook·y (huk′i), *n.* **play hooky,** *Am.* run away; be absent without reason.

hoo·li·gan (hū′lə·gən), *n. Slang.* a street ruffian; hoodlum. —**hoo′li·gan·ism,** *n.*

hoop (hūp; hup), *n.* **1.** ring or flat band in the form of a circle: *hoop for holding the staves of a barrel.* **2.** a circular frame formerly used to expand a woman's skirt. **3.** *Croquet.* arch or wicket. **4.** anything shaped like a hoop. —*v.* fasten together with hoops. [OE *hōp*] —**hooped,** *adj.* —**hoop′er,** *n.* —**hoop′like′,** *adj.*

hoop·la (hūp′lä′), *n., Am., Slang.* any meaningless, showy, or overexuberant activity to gain publicity, promote a product, etc.; ballyhoo.

hoo·poe (hū′pū), *n.* a bright-colored bird with a long, sharp bill and a fanlike crest on its head. [earlier *hoop* < F < L *upupa* (imit.)]

hoop skirt, a woman's skirt worn over a flexible hoop.

hoo·ray (hù·rā′), *interj., n., v.* hurrah.

hoose·gow (hūs′gou), *n. Am., Slang.* jail. [? < Sp. *juzgado* a court, in Mex.Sp., jail]

Hoop skirt

Hoo·sier (hū′zhər), *n. Am.* native or inhabitant of Indiana.

hoot (hüt), *n.* **1.** sound that an owl makes. **2.** any similar sound. **3.** shout to show disapproval or scorn. **4.** thing of little value. —*v.* **1.** make the sound that an owl makes or one like it. **2.** make a shout to show disapproval or scorn. **3.** show disapproval of, or scorn for, by hooting. **4.** force or drive by hooting. **5.** say or show by hooting. [ME *hute(n)*; ? imit.] —**hoot′er,** *n.*

Hoo·ver (hü′vər), *n.* Herbert Clark, 1874–1964, the 31st president of the United States, 1929–1933.

Hoover Dam, dam on the Colorado River between Arizona and Nevada. Also, Boulder Dam.

hooves (hüvz; hüvz), *n. Rare.* pl. of hoof.

hop¹ (hop), *v.,* hopped, hop·ping, *n.* —*v.* **1.** spring, or move by springing, on one foot. **2.** spring, or move by springing, with all feet at once: *many birds hop.* **3.** jump over: *hop a ditch.* **4.** *Colloq.* jump on (a train, car, etc.). **5.** *Colloq.* fly across in an airplane; make a flight. **6.** dance. **7.** hop off, *Colloq.* rise from the ground in an airplane. —*n.* **1.** a hopping; spring. **2.** *Colloq.* flight in an airplane. **3.** *Colloq.* a dancing party. **4.** *Colloq.* dance. [OE *hoppian*]

hop² (hop), *n., v.,* hopped, hop·ping. —*n.* **1.** vine having flower clusters that look like small, yellow pine cones. **2.** hops, dried flower clusters of the hop vine, used to flavor beer and other malt drinks. —*v.* **1.** pick hops. **2.** flavor with hops. [< MDu. *hoppe*]

hope (hōp), *n., v.,* hoped, hop·ing. —*n.* **1.** a feeling that what one desires will happen. **2.** instance of such a desire. **3.** person or thing that expectation centers in: *he is the hope of the family.* **4.** thing hoped for. **5.** ground for expectation: *no hope of recovery.* **6.** *Archaic.* trust; reliance. —*v.* **1.** wish and expect. **2.** *Archaic.* trust; rely. [OE *hopa*] —**Syn.** *n.* **1.** expectation, anticipation, optimism.

hope chest, *Am.* chest in which a young woman collects articles that will be useful after she marries.

hope·ful (hōp′fəl), *adj.* **1.** feeling or showing hope. **2.** causing hope; giving hope; likely to succeed. —*n.* boy or girl thought likely to succeed. —**hope′ful·ly,** *adv.* —**hope′ful·ness,** *n.*

hope·less (hōp′lis), *adj.* **1.** feeling no hope. **2.** giving no hope: *a hopeless illness.* —**hope′less·ly,** *adv.* —**hope′less·ness,** *n.*

Ho·pi (hō′pi), *n., pl.* -pis. *Am.* member of a tribe of Pueblo Indians living largely in stone-built towns in N Arizona.

hop·lite (hop′līt), *n.* a heavily armed foot soldier of ancient Greece. [< Gk., < *hopla* arms]

hop·per (hop′ər), *n.* **1.** person or thing that hops. **2.** grasshopper or other hopping insect. **3.** container to hold something and feed it into another part, usually larger at the top than at the bottom.

hop·scotch (hop′skoch′), *n.* a children's game in which the players hop over the lines of a figure drawn on the ground.

Hor·ace (hôr′is; hor′-), *n.* 65–8 B.C., Roman poet and satirist. —**Ho·ra·tian** (hə·rā′shən; hō-), *adj.*

horde (hôrd; hōrd), *n., v.,* hord·ed, hord·ing. —*n.* **1.** crowd; swarm. **2.** a wandering tribe or troop. —*v.* gather in a horde. [< F < G < Polish < Turk. *urdū* camp]

hore·hound (hôr′hound′; hōr′-), *n.* **1.** plant with woolly, whitish leaves and clusters of small, whitish flowers. **2.** a bitter extract made from the leaves of this plant. **3.** candy or cough medicine flavored with it. Also, hoarhound. [OE *hārhūne* < *hār* hoar + *hūne* name of a plant]

ho·ri·zon (hə·rī′zən), *n.* **1.** line where the earth and sky seem to meet. **2.** limit of one's thinking, experience, interest, or outlook. [< OF < L < Gk. *horizon (kyklos)* bounding (circle), ult. < *horos* limit]

hor·i·zon·tal (hôr′ə·zon′təl; hor′-), *adj.* **1.** parallel to the horizon; at right angles to a vertical line. **2.** flat; level. **3.** placed, acting, or working wholly or mainly in a horizontal direction. **4.** in commercial fields, etc., so organized as to include only one stage in production or one group of people or crafts: *a horizontal union, horizontal trusts.* —*n.* a horizontal line, plane, direction, position, etc. —**hor′i·zon·tal′i·ty,** *n.* —**hor′i·zon′tal·ly,** *adv.*

hor·mone (hôr′mōn), *n.* **1.** *Physiol.* substance formed in certain parts of the body that enters the blood stream and influences the activity of some organ, as adrenalin and insulin. **2.** *Bot.* any similar substance produced in plants. [< Gk. *hormon* setting in motion] —**hor·mo′nal,** **hor·mon·ic** (hôr·mon′ik), *adj.*

horn (hôrn), *n.* **1.** a hard growth, usually curved and pointed, on the heads of cattle, sheep, goats, and some other animals. **2.** anything that sticks up on the head of an animal: *a snail's horns, an insect's horns.* **3.** the substance or material of horns. **4.** thing made, or formerly made, of horn. **5.** container made by hollowing out a horn: *a drinking horn, a powder horn.* **6.** *Music.* instrument sounded by blowing into the smaller end. **7.** device sounded as a warning signal: *a foghorn.* **8.** anything that projects like a horn or is shaped like a horn: *a saddle horn, the horn of an anvil.* **9.** either pointed tip of a new or old moon, or of a crescent. **10.** horns of a dilemma, two unpleasant choices, one of which must be taken. —*adj.* made of horn. —*v.* **1.** hit or wound with horns; gore. **2.** furnish with horns. **3.** horn in, *U.S. Slang.* meddle; intrude. [OE] —**horned,** *adj.* —**horn′less,** *adj.* —**horn′like′,** *adj.*

Horn (hôrn), *n.* Cape, cape on an island at the southern tip of South America.

horn·bill (hôrn′bil′), *n.* a large bird having a very large bill with a horn or horny lump on it.

horn·blende (hôrn′blend′), *n.* a common black, dark-green, or brown mineral found in granite and other rocks. [< G] —**horn·blen′dic,** *adj.*

horn·book (hôrn′bůk′), *n.* **1.** page with the alphabet, etc., on it, covered with a sheet of transparent horn and fastened in a frame with a handle, formerly used in teaching children to read. **2.** a primer.

horned toad, *Am.* a small lizard with a broad, flat body, short tail, and many spines.

hor·net (hôr′nit), *n.* a large wasp that can give a very painful sting. [OE *hyrnet(u)*]

horn of plenty, cornucopia.

horn·pipe (hôrn′pip′), *n.* **1.** a lively dance done by one person, formerly popular among sailors. **2.** music for it. **3.** a musical wind instrument of olden times, consisting of a wooden pipe with a bell-shaped end.

Hornet
(ab. 1 in. long)

horn·swog·gle (hôrn′swog′əl), *v.,* -gled, -gling. *Am., Slang.* hoax; cheat.

horn·y (hôr′ni), *adj.,* horn·i·er, horn·i·est. **1.** made of horn or a substance like it. **2.** hard like a horn: *hands horny from work.* **3.** having a horn or horns. —**horn′i·ness,** *n.*

hor·o·loge (hôr′ə·lōj; -loj; hor′-), *n.* timepiece, as a clock, sundial, hourglass, etc. [< OF < L < Gk. *horologion* < *hora* hour + *-logos* telling]

ho·rol·o·ger (hō·rol′ə·jər), **ho·rol·o·gist** (-jist), *n.* expert in horology.

ho·rol·o·gy (hō·rol′ə·ji), *n.* **1.** science of measuring time. **2.** art of making timepieces. —**ho·ro·log·ic** (hôr′ə·loj′ik; hor′-), **hor′o·log′i·cal,** *adj.*

hor·o·scope (hôr′ə·skōp; hor′-), *n.* **1.** appearance of the heavens with the relative position of the planets at the hour of a person's birth, regarded as influencing his life. **2.** diagram of the heavens at given times, used in telling fortunes by the planets and the stars. [< F < L < Gk., < *hora* hour + *skopos* watcher]

hor·ren·dous (hô·ren′dəs; ho-), *adj.* horrible; terrible; frightful. —**hor·ren′dous·ly,** *adv.*

hor·ri·ble (hôr′ə·bəl; hor′-), *adj.* **1.** causing horror; terrible; dreadful; frightful; shocking. **2.** *Colloq.* extremely unpleasant or amazing. [< OF < L, < *horrere* bristle] —**hor′ri·ble·ness,** *n.* —**hor′ri·bly,** *adv.* —**Syn. 1.** hideous, grim, horrid.

hor·rid (hôr′id; hor′-), *adj.* 1. terrible; frightful. 2. *Colloq.* very unpleasant. —**hor′rid·ly,** *adv.* —**hor′rid·ness,** *n.*

hor·ri·fy (hôr′ə·fī; hor′-), *v.,* **-fied, -fy·ing.** 1. cause to feel horror. 2. *Colloq.* shock very much. —**hor′ri·fi·ca′tion,** *n.*

hor·ror (hôr′ər; hor′-), *n.* 1. a shivering, shaking fear and dislike; terror and disgust caused by something frightful or shocking. 2. a very strong dislike; very great disgust. 3. quality of causing horror. 4. cause of horror. [< L, < *horrere* bristle] —**Syn.** 1. dread. 2. loathing, abhorrence, aversion.

hor·ror-strick·en (hôr′ər·strik′ən; hor′-), **hor·ror-struck** (-struk′), *adj.* horrified.

hors d'oeu·vre (ôr′dėrv′; *Fr.* ôr dœ′vrə), *pl.* **d'oeu·vres** (dėrvz′; *Fr.* dœ′vrə). relish or light food served before the regular courses of a meal, as olives, celery, anchovies, etc. [F, apart from (the main) work]

horse (hôrs), *n., pl.* **hors·es** or (*esp. collectively*) **horse,** *v.,* **horsed, hors·ing,** *adj.* —*n.* 1. a four-legged animal with solid hoofs and flowing mane and tail, used from very early times to draw loads, carry riders, etc. 2. a full-grown male horse. 3. soldiers on horses; cavalry. 4. piece of gymnasium apparatus to jump or vault over. 5. frame with legs to support something. —*v.* 1. provide with a horse or horses. 2. put or go on horseback. 3. set or carry on a person's back; carry on one's own back. 4. *Colloq.* tease in a rough way. 5. *Colloq.* act boisterously. —*adj.* 1. having to do with horses. 2. on horses. [OE *hors*]

horse·back (hôrs′bak′), *n.* the back of a horse. —*adv.* on the back of a horse.

horse·car (hôrs′kär′), *n. Am.* 1. streetcar pulled by a horse or horses. 2. car used for transporting horses.

horse chestnut, 1. a shade tree with spreading branches, large leaves, clusters of showy white flowers, and glossy brown nuts. 2. the nut. 3. any tree or shrub of the same family as the horse chestnut.

horse·flesh (hôrs′flesh′), *n.* 1. horses. 2. meat from horses.

horse·fly (hôrs′flī′), *n., pl.* **-flies.** fly that bites horses.

horse·hair (hôrs′hãr′), *n.* 1. hair from the mane or tail of a horse. 2. a stiff fabric made of this hair.

Horsefly (somewhat over life size)

horse·hide (hôrs′hīd′), *n.* 1. hide of a horse. 2. leather made from this hide.

horse latitudes, two regions where there is often very calm weather, extending around the world at about 30° north and 30° south of the equator.

horse laugh, a loud, boisterous laugh.

horse·less (hôrs′lis), *adj.* 1. without a horse. 2. not requiring a horse; self-propelled: *automobiles were called horseless carriages.*

horse·man (hôrs′mən), *n., pl.* **-men.** 1. man who rides on horseback. 2. man skilled in riding or managing horses. —**horse′man·ship,** *n.*

horse pistol, a large pistol that used to be carried by horsemen.

horse·play (hôrs′plā′), *n.* rough, boisterous fun.

horse·pow·er (hôrs′pou′ər), *n.* unit for measuring the power of engines, motors, etc.; 1 horsepower = 550 foot-pounds per second.

horse·rad·ish (hôrs′rad′ish), *n.* 1. a tall plant with a white, hot-tasting root that is ground up and used as a relish with meat, oysters, etc. 2. relish made of this root.

horse sense, *Am., Colloq.* common sense; plain, practical good sense.

horse·shoe (hôrsh′shü′; hôrs′-), *n., v.,* **-shoed, -shoe·ing.** —*n.* 1. a U-shaped metal plate nailed to a horse's hoof to protect it. 2. thing shaped like a horseshoe. 3. **horseshoes** (*sing. in use*), game in which the players try to

throw horseshoes over or near a stake. —*v.* put a horseshoe or horseshoes on. —**horse′sho′er,** *n.*

horseshoe crab, *Am.* a crablike sea animal with a body shaped like a horseshoe and a long, spiny tail; king crab.

horse·tail (hôrs′tāl′), *n.* a flowerless plant with hollow, jointed stems and scalelike leaves at each joint.

horse·whip (hôrs′hwip′), *n., v.,* **-whipped, -whip·ping.** —*n.* whip for driving or controlling horses. —*v.* beat with a horsewhip.

horse·wom·an (hôrs′wüm′ən), *n., pl.* **-wom·en.** 1. woman who rides on horseback. 2. woman skilled in riding or managing horses.

hors·y (hôr′si), *adj.,* **hors·i·er, hors·i·est.** 1. having to do with horses. 2. fond of horses or horse racing. 3. dressing or talking like people who spend much time with horses. 4. *Slang.* large and awkward in appearance. —**hors′i·ness,** *n.*

hort., horticultural; horticulture.

hor·ta·tive (hôr′tə·tiv), *adj.* hortatory. —**hor′ta·tive·ly,** *adv.*

hor·ta·to·ry (hôr′tə·tô′ri; -tō′-), *adj.* serving to urge or encourage; giving advice; exhorting. [< LL, < L *hortari* exhort]

hor·ti·cul·ture (hôr′tə·kul′chər), *n.* 1. science of growing flowers, fruits, vegetables, etc. 2. cultivation of a garden. [< L *hortus* garden + *cultura* cultivation] —**hor′ti·cul′tur·al,** *adj.* —**hor′ti·cul′tur·ist,** *n.*

ho·san·na (hō·zan′ə), *interj.* shout of praise to the Lord. —*n.* a shout of "hosanna." [< LL < Gk. < Heb. *hōshī′āh nnā* save now, we pray]

hose (hōz), *n., pl.* **hose** or (*Archaic*) **ho·sen** (hō′zən), *v.,* **hosed, hos·ing.** —*n.* 1. stockings. 2. a close-fitting outer garment extending from the waist to the toes, formerly worn by men. 3. tube made of rubber, canvas, or other flexible material, used to carry water or other liquids for short distances. —*v.* put water on with a hose. [OE *hosa*]

Ho·se·a (hō·zē′ə; -zā′ə), *n.* 1. book of the Old Testament. 2. its author, a Hebrew prophet who lived in the eighth century B.C.

ho·sier (hō′zhər), *n.* person who makes or sells hosiery.

ho·sier·y (hō′zhər·i), *n.* 1. hose; stockings. 2. business of a hosier.

hos·pice (hos′pis), *n.* house where travelers can lodge. [< F < L *hospitium* < *hospes* guest, host]

hos·pi·ta·ble (hos′pi·tə·bəl; hos·pit′ə-), *adj.* 1. giving or liking to give a welcome, food and shelter, and friendly treatment to guests or strangers: *a hospitable family.* 2. willing and ready to entertain; favorably receptive: *hospitable to new ideas.* —**hos′pi·ta·ble·ness,** *n.* —**hos′pi·ta·bly,** *adv.*

hos·pi·tal (hos′pi·təl), *n.* 1. place where sick or injured people are cared for. 2. similar place for animals. [< OF < Med.L *hospitale* inn. See HOST¹.]

hos·pi·tal·i·ty (hos′pə·tal′ə·ti), *n., pl.* **-ties.** friendly, generous reception and treatment of guests or strangers. [< L *hospitalitas.* See HOST¹.]

hos·pi·tal·ize (hos′pi·təl·īz), *v.,* **-ized, -iz·ing.** put in a hospital. —**hos′pi·tal·i·za′tion,** *n.*

host¹ (hōst), *n.* 1. person who receives another at his house as his guest. 2. keeper of an inn or hotel. 3. plant or animal in or on which a parasite lives. [< OF < L *hospes* guest, host]

host² (hōst), *n.* 1. a large number; multitude. 2. army. [< OF < LL *hostis* army < L, enemy (*orig.,* stranger)]

Host (hōst), *n. Eccles.* bread or wafer used in the Eucharist. [< OF *oiste* < L *hostia* animal sacrificed]

hos·tage (hos′tij), *n.* 1. person given up to another or held by an enemy as a pledge that certain promises, agreements, etc., will be carried out. 2. pledge; security. [< OF, ult. < L *hospes* guest] —**hos′tage·ship,** *n.*

hos·tel (hos′təl), *n.* a lodging place, esp. a supervised lodging place for young people on bicycle trips, hikes, etc.; inn; hotel. [< OF, < *oste* HOST¹. Doublet of HOTEL.] —hos′tel·er, *n.*

hos·tel·ry (hos′təl·ri), *n., pl.* –ries. inn; hotel.

host·ess (hōs′tis), *n.* 1. woman who receives another person as her guest. 2. woman paid to entertain or dance with guests, travelers, etc.

hos·tile (hos′təl; *sometimes* hos′tīl), *adj.* 1. of an enemy or enemies. 2. opposed; unfriendly; unfavorable. [< L, < *hostis* enemy] —hos′tile·ly, *adv.* —Syn. 2. inimical, antagonistic.

hos·til·i·ty (hos·til′ə·ti), *n., pl.* –ties. 1. feeling as an enemy does; being an enemy; unfriendliness. 2. state of being at war. 3. opposition; resistance. 4. hostilities, acts of war; warfare; fighting.

hos·tler (os′lər; hos′-), *n.* person who takes care of horses at an inn or stable. Also, ostler.

hot (hot), *adj.,* hot·ter, hot·test, *adv.* —*adj.* 1. much warmer than the body; having much heat: *a fire is hot.* 2. having a relatively high temperature: *the food is too hot to eat.* 3. having a sensation of great bodily heat: *a person hot with fever.* 4. having a sharp, burning taste: *pepper and mustard are hot.* 5. *Elect.* actively conducting current: *a hot wire.* 6. *Nuclear Physics.* charged (with radioactivity); radioactive: *the hot debris left by an atomic explosion.* 7. full of any strong feeling: *hot with rage.* 8. thrilling; exciting: *a hot singer.* 9. *Colloq.* good; excellent: *he's not so hot.* 10. full of great interest or enthusiasm; very eager. 11. new; fresh: *a hot scent.* 12. following closely: *in hot pursuit.* 13. of swing music or jazz, played with variations from the score. 14. *Slang.* obtained illegally. —*adv.* in a hot manner. [OE *hāt*] —hot′ly, *adv.* —hot′ness, *n.* —Syn. *adj.* 1. scorching, scalding. 4. pungent, peppery. 7. passionate, violent, vehement, fiery. 10. ardent, fervent, fervid.

hot air, *Am., Slang.* empty talk or writing.

hot atom, *Nuclear Physics.* atom whose nucleus is radioactive.

hot·bed (hot′bed′), *n.* 1. bed of earth covered with glass and kept warm for growing plants. 2. place favorable to rapid growth.

hot·blood·ed (hot′blud′id), *adj.* 1. easily excited or angered. 2. rash; reckless. 3. passionate.

hot·box (hot′boks′), *n. Am.* an overheated bearing on a shaft or axle.

hot cake, *Am.* a griddle cake.

hot cross bun, bun marked with a cross, usually eaten during Lent or on Good Friday.

hot dog, *Am., Slang.* a hot frankfurter enclosed in a roll.

hos·tel (hō·tel′), *n.* house or large building that provides lodging, food, etc., to travelers and others. [< F *hôtel* < OF *hostel.* Doublet of HOS-TEL.]

hot·foot (hot′fut′), *Colloq.* —*adv.* in great haste. —*v.* go in great haste; hurry.

hot·head (hot′hed′), *n.* a hot-headed person.

hot·head·ed (hot′hed′id), *adj.* 1. having a fiery temper. 2. impetuous; rash. —hot′-head′-ed·ly, *adv.* —hot′head′ed·ness, *n.*

hot·house (hot′hous′), *n.* greenhouse.

hot laboratory or **lab,** *Nuclear Physics, Chem.* laboratory exposed to radiations of more than one curie.

hot rod, *Am., Slang.* 1. a stripped-down flivver with a supercharged motor. 2. person, esp. an adolescent boy, who drives such an automobile.

hot-tem·pered (hot′tem′pərd), *adj.* easily angered.

Hot·ten·tot (hot′ən·tot), *n.* 1. member of a South African race having a dark, yellowish-brown complexion. 2. their language.

hot war, war involving actual fighting.

hou·dah (hou′də), *n.* howdah.

hough (hok), *n.* hock¹.

hound (hound), *n.* 1. dog of any of various breeds, most of which hunt by scent and have large, drooping ears and short hair. 2. any dog. 3. a contemptible person. 4. *Slang.* person who is very fond of something. 5. follow the hounds or ride to hounds, go hunting on horseback with hounds. —*v.* 1. hunt; chase. 2. urge (on). [OE *hund*]

hour (our), *n.* 1. 60 minutes; ¹⁄₂₄ of a day. 2. one of the 12 points that measure time from noon to midnight and from midnight to noon. 3. time of day. Some clocks strike the hours and half-hours. 4. a particular or fixed time: *the breakfast hour.* 5. period in a classroom, often less than a full hour. 6. the present time: *the man of the hour.* 7. 15 degrees of longitude. 8. hours, a. seven special times of the day set aside for prayer and worship, as in a monastery. b. prayers or services for these times. c. time for work, study, etc. d. usual time for going to bed and getting up. [< OF < L < Gk. *hora* season, time, hour]

hour·glass (our′glas′; –gläs′), *n.* device for measuring time, requiring just an hour for its contents (sand or mercury) to go from the container on top to one on the bottom.

Hourglass

hou·ri (hůr′i; hou′ri), *n., pl.* –ris. a young, eternally beautiful girl of the Mohammedan paradise. [< F < Pers. *hūrī* < Ar. *hūr* black-eyed]

hour·ly (our′li), *adj.* 1. done, happening, or counted every hour. 2. coming very often; frequent. —*adv.* 1. every hour; hour by hour. 2. very often; frequently.

house (*n.* hous; *v.* houz), *n., pl.* hous·es (houz′-iz), *v.,* housed, hous·ing. —*n.* 1. a building in which people live. 2. people living in a house; household. 3. abode; habitation. 4. a building to hold anything: *greenhouse, warehouse.* 5. assembly for making laws and considering questions of government; lawmaking body: *the House of Representatives.* 6. the building in which such an assembly meets. 7. place of business. 8. *Am.* a business firm. 9. place of entertainment; theater. 10. audience. 11. family regarded as consisting of ancestors, descendants, and kindred, esp. a noble or royal family. 12. bring down the house, *Colloq.* be loudly applauded. 13. keep house, manage a home and its affairs; do housework. 14. on the house, paid for by the owner of the business; free. —*v.* 1. put or receive into a house; provide with a house. 2. give shelter to; harbor; lodge. 3. place in a secure or protected position. [OE *hūs*] —house′-less, *adj.*

house·boat (hous′bōt′), *n.* boat that can be used as a place to live in.

house·break·er (hous′brāk′ər), *n.* person who breaks into a house to steal or commit some other crime. —house′break′ing, *n.*

house·bro·ken (hous′brō′kən), **house-broke** (–brōk′), *adj.* of a dog, cat, etc., trained to live indoors.

house·coat (hous′kōt′), **house coat,** *n.* a light dresslike garment with a long skirt, for casual wear in one's home.

house·fly (hous′flī′), *n., pl.* –flies. a two-winged fly that lives around and in houses, feeding on food, garbage, and filth.

house·hold (hous′hōld), *n.* 1. all the people living in a house; family; family and servants. 2. home and its affairs. 3. a royal household. —*adj.* of a household; having to do with a household; domestic: *household expenses.*

house·hold·er (hous′hōl′dər), *n.* 1. person who owns or lives in a house. 2. head of a family.

household word, very familiar word or phrase.

house·keep·er (hous′kēp′ər), *n.* 1. woman who manages a home and its affairs and does the housework. 2. woman who directs the servants that do the housework. —house′keep′ing, *n.*

house·maid (hous′mād′), *n.* woman servant who does housework.

House of Burgesses, *Am.* the lower house of the colonial legislature in Virginia or Maryland.

House of Commons, the lower, elective branch of the lawmaking body of Great Britain and Northern Ireland, or of Canada.

house of correction, place of confinement and reform for persons convicted of minor offenses and not regarded as confirmed criminals.

House of Delegates, *Am.* the lower branch of the legislature in Maryland, Virginia, and West Virginia.

House of Lords, the upper, nonelective branch of the lawmaking body of Great Britain and Northern Ireland, composed of nobles and clergymen of high rank.

House of Representatives, 1. *Am.* the lower branch of the lawmaking body of the United States. **2.** *Am.* the lower branch of the lawmaking body of certain States of the United States. **3.** the lower branch of the Parliament of Australia, or of the general assembly of New Zealand.

house party, entertainment of guests in a home for a few days.

house·top (hous′top′), *n.* top of a house; roof.

house·warm·ing (hous′wôr′ming), *n.* party given when a family moves into a house for the first time.

house·wife (hous′wīf′ *for 1;* huz′if *for 2*), *n., pl.* **-wives. 1.** woman who is the head of a household. **2.** a small case for needles, thread, etc. —**house′wife′ly,** *adj.* —**house′wife′li·ness,** *n.*

house·wif·er·y (hous′wīf′ər·i; -wīf′ri), *n.* work of a housewife; housekeeping.

house·work (hous′wėrk′), *n.* work to be done in housekeeping, such as washing, ironing, cleaning, sweeping, or cooking.

hous·ing[1] (houz′ing), *n.* **1.** act of sheltering; provision of houses as homes. **2.** houses. **3.** shelter; covering. **4.** frame or plate to hold part of a machine in place.

hous·ing[2] (houz′ing), *n.* an ornamental covering for a horse. [< *house* covering < OF *huche*]

Hous·ton (hūs′tən), *n.* **1.** Samuel, 1793–1863, American frontier soldier and hero, twice president of Texas before it became a State in 1845. **2.** city in SE Texas.

hove (hōv), *v. Esp. Naut.* pt. and pp. of **heave.**

hov·el (huv′əl; hov′-), *n., v.,* **-eled, -el·ing;** *esp. Brit.* **-elled, -el·ling.** —*n.* **1.** house that is small, mean, and unpleasant to live in. **2.** an open shed for sheltering cattle, tools, etc. —*v.* lodge in a hovel. [ME]

hov·er (huv′ər; hov′-), *v.* **1.** stay in or near one place in the air: *the two birds hovered over their nest.* **2.** wait near at hand. **3.** be in an uncertain condition; waver: *the sick man hovered between life and death.* —*n.* **1.** act of hovering. **2.** state of hovering. [ME *hover(en)* < *hoven* hover] —**hov′er·er,** *n.* —**hov′er·ing·ly,** *adv.*

hov·er·craft (huv′ər·kraft; hov′-; -kräft), *n.* vehicle which travels just above the ground on a cushion of air created by a system of fans.

how (hou), *adv.* **1.** in what way; by what means: *tell her how to do it.* **2.** to what degree, extent, etc.: *how long?* **3.** at what price: *how do you sell these apples?* **4.** in what state or condition: *tell me how Mrs. Jones is.* **5.** for what reason; why: *how is it you are late?* **6.** to what effect; with what meaning; by what name: *how do you mean?* **7.** what? —*n.* **1.** question beginning with "how." **2.** way or manner of doing: *she considered all the hows and wherefores.* [OE *hū*]

how·be·it (hou·bē′it), *adv.* nevertheless.

how·dah (hou′də), *n.* seat for persons riding on the back of an elephant. Also, **houdah.** [< Hind. < Ar. *haudaj*]

how·e′er (hou·âr′), *conj., adv.* however.

How·ells (hou′əlz), *n.* William Dean, 1837–1920, American novelist and writer.

how·ev·er (hou·ev′ər), *adv.* **1.** to whatever degree or amount; no matter how. **2.** in whatever way; by whatever means. —*conj.* nevertheless; yet. **►however. 1.** As a connective, *however* is more apppropriate to the fully developed sentences of formal style, and is especially useful as a connective between sentences. We can read many pages of informal English without encountering *however*, its place being taken by the lighter *but*, even as a connective between sentences. **2.** As a simple adverb, *however* modifies an adjective or other adverb: *However hard we tried, the current swept us back.*

how·itz·er (hou′it·sər), *n.* a short cannon for firing shells in a high curve. [earlier *howitz* < Du. < G < Czech *houfnice* catapult]

howl (houl), *v.* **1.** give a long, loud, mournful cry. Dogs and wolves howl. **2.** give a long, loud cry of pain, rage, scorn, etc. **3.** yell; shout: *howl with laughter.* **4.** force or drive by howling. —*n.* **1.** a long, loud, mournful cry. **2.** a loud cry of pain, rage, etc. **3.** yell of scorn, amusement, etc. **4.** yell; shout. [ME *houle(n)*]

howl·er (houl′ər), *n.* **1.** person or thing that howls. **2.** *Colloq.* a ridiculous mistake; stupid blunder.

how·so·ev·er (hou′sō·ev′ər), *adv.* **1.** to whatever degree or amount. **2.** in whatever way.

hoy·den (hoi′dən), *n.* a boisterous, romping girl; tomboy. —*adj.* boisterous; rude. Also, **hoiden.** —**hoy′den·ish,** *adj.* —**hoy′den·ish·ly,** *adv.* —**hoy′den·ish·ness,** *n.*

Hoyle (hoil), *n.* **1.** book of rules and instructions for playing card games. **2.** according to Hoyle, according to the rules or customs; fair.

HP, H.P., hp., or **h.p.,** horsepower.

H.Q., h.q., headquarters.

hr., pl. **hrs.** hour.

H.R., House of Representatives.

H.R.H., His (Her) Royal Highness.

ht., height.

hub (hub), *n.* **1.** the central part of a wheel. **2.** any center of interest, importance, activity, etc.

hub·bub (hub′ub), *n.* a noisy tumult; uproar.

huck·a·back (huk′ə·bak), *n.* a heavy, coarse, linen or cotton cloth with a rough surface, used for towels.

huck·le·ber·ry (huk′əl·ber′i), *n., pl.* **-ries.** *Am.* **1.** a small berry like a blueberry, but darker. **2.** shrub that it grows on.

huck·ster (huk′stər), *n.* Also, **huck·ster·er** (-stər·ər). **1.** peddler. **2.** person who sells small articles. **3.** *U.S. Colloq.* person who is in the advertising business. **4.** mean and unfair trader. —*v.* sell; peddle; haggle. [cf. MDu. *hokester.* See HAWK[2].]

hud·dle (hud′əl), *v.,* **-dled, -dling,** *n.* —*v.* **1.** crowd close: *the sheep huddled together in a corner.* **2.** nestle in a heap: *the cat huddled itself on the cushion.* **3.** *Football.* group together behind the line of scrimmage to receive signals. —*n.* **1.** a confused heap, mass, or crowd. **2.** slovenly hurry; confusion. **3.** *Football.* a grouping of players behind the line of scrimmage to receive signals. **4.** go into a huddle, *Colloq.* confer secretly.

Hud·son (hud′sən), *n.* **1.** Henry, died 1611, English navigator and explorer in America. **2.** river in E New York State, flowing into New York Bay.

Hudson Bay, a large bay in C Canada.

Hudson seal, a muskrat fur that is dyed and plucked to look like seal.

hue[1] (hū), *n.* **1.** color. **2.** that quality whereby one color (as red) differs from other colors (as blue, green, etc.). **3.** a particular color: *a greenish hue.* [OE *hīw*] —**hued,** *adj.*

hue[2] (hū), *n.* **1.** a shouting. **2.** hue and cry, shouts of alarm or protest. [< F *hu* < *huer* shout]

huff (huf), *n.* fit of anger or peevishness. —*v.* **1.** make angry; offend. **2.** *Dial.* puff; blow.

huff·y (huf′i), *adj.,* **huff·i·er, huff·i·est. 1.** offended. **2.** easily offended; touchy. —**huff′i·ly,** *adv.* —**huff′i·ness,** *n.*

hug (hug), *v.,* **hugged, hug·ging,** *n.* —*v.* **1.** put the arms around and hold close, esp. in affection. **2.** squeeze tightly with the arms, as a bear does. **3.** cling firmly or fondly to: *hug an opinion.* **4.** keep close to: *the boat hugged the shore.* —*n.* **1.** a tight clasp with the arms. **2.** a tight squeeze with the arms; grip in wrestling. [cf. Scand. *hugga* comfort]

huge (hūj), *adj.,* **hug·er, hug·est.** extremely large. [< OF *ahuge*] —**huge′ly,** *adv.* —**huge′ness,** *n.* —**Syn.** enormous, immense, gigantic.

hug·ger-mug·ger (hug′ər·mug′ər), *n.* confusion; disorder. —*adj.* **1.** confused; disorderly. **2.** secret. —*v.* **1.** keep secret. **2.** act secretly. —*adv.* in a confused, disorderly manner.

āge, cãre, fär; ēqual, tėrm; ice; ōpen, ôrder; pút, rūle, ūse; tʜ, then; ə=a in about.

Hughes (hūz), *n*. Charles Evans, 1862-1948, American statesman, chief justice of the U.S. Supreme Court, 1930-1941.

Hu·go (hū′gō), *n*. Victor, 1802-1885, French poet, novelist, and dramatist.

Hu·gue·not (hū′gə·not), *n*. a French Protestant of the 16th and 17th centuries.

Huk (huk), *n*. one of a Communist group in the Philippines engaged in military and other violent activities against the government.

hu·la-hu·la (hū′lə·hū′lə), or **hula**, *n*. a native Hawaiian dance. [< Hawaiian]

hulk (hulk), *n*. 1. body of an old or worn-out ship. 2. ship used as a prison. 3. a big, clumsy ship. 4. a big, clumsy person or thing. [OE *hulc*, ? < Med.L < Gk. *holkas* merchant ship]

hulk·ing (hul′king), *adj*. big and clumsy.

hull[1] (hul), *n*. 1. the outer covering of a seed. 2. calyx of some fruits, such as the green frill of a strawberry. 3. any outer covering. —*v*. remove the hull or hulls from. [OE *hulu*] —**hull′er**, *n*.

hull[2] (hul), *n*. 1. body or frame of a ship, exclusive of masts, sails, or rigging. 2. the main body or frame of a seaplane, airship, etc. —*v*. strike or pierce the hull of (a ship) with a shell, torpedo, etc. [? same word as *hull*[1]]

hul·la·ba·loo (hul′ə·bə·lū′), *n*. uproar.

hul·lo (hə·lō′), *interj., n., pl.* -los, *v.,* -loed, -lo·ing. hello.

hum (hum), *v.*, **hummed, hum·ming,** *n., interj.* —*v*. 1. make a continuous murmuring sound like that of a bee or of a spinning top: *the sewing machine hums busily*. 2. make a low sound like the letter *m*, in hesitation, embarrassment, dissatisfaction, etc. 3. sing with closed lips, not sounding words. 4. put or bring by humming: *hum a baby to sleep*. 5. *Colloq*. be busy and active: *make things hum.* —*n*. 1. a continuous murmuring sound: *the hum of the city street*. 2. a low sound like that of the letter *m*, used to express hesitation, disagreement, etc. 3. a singing with closed lips, not sounding words. —*interj*. a low sound like that of the letter *m*, used to express hesitation, disagreement, etc. [imit.] —**hum′mer**, *n*. —**Syn.** *v*. 1. drone, buzz, murmur.

hu·man (hū′mən), *adj*. 1. of a person; that a person has: *selfishness is a human weakness*. 2. being a person or persons; having the form or qualities of people: *men, women, and children are human beings*. 3. having or showing qualities (good or bad) natural to people: *he is more human than his brother*. 4. of people; having to do with people: *human affairs*. 5. having to do with people and what they can or cannot do: *beyond human power.* —*n*. a human being; person. [< OF < L *humanus*] —**hu′man·ness,** *n*.

hu·mane (hū·mān′), *adj*. 1. kind; merciful; not cruel or brutal. 2. tending to humanize and refine: *humane studies*. [var. of *human*] —**humane′ly**, *adv*. —**hu·mane′ness**, *n*. —**Syn.** 1. tender, compassionate. —**Ant.** 1. brutal, cruel.

hu·man·ism (hū′mən·iz·əm), *n*. 1. any system of thought or action concerned with human interests. 2. study of the humanities. 3. Sometimes, **Humanism,** the principles or culture of the scholars of the Renaissance who pursued and spread the study, and a truer understanding of the literature, ideas, etc., of ancient Rome and Greece. —**hu′man·ist,** *n*. —**hu′man·is′tic,** *adj*.

hu·man·i·tar·i·an (hū·man′ə·tãr′i·ən), *adj*. helpful to humanity; philanthropic. —*n*. person who is devoted to the welfare of all human beings. [< *humanity*; patterned after *unitarian*, etc.] —**hu·man′i·tar′i·an·ism,** *n*.

hu·man·i·ty (hū·man′ə·ti), *n., pl.* -ties. 1. human beings taken as a group; people: *advances in science help all humanity*. 2. fact of being human; human character or quality. 3. fact of being humane; humane treatment; kindness: *treat animals with humanity.* 4. the humanities, a. the Latin and Greek languages and literatures. b. languages, literatures, art, etc. c. branches of learning concerned with man.

hu·man·ize (hū′mən·īz), *v.,* -ized, -iz·ing. 1. make human; give a human character or quality to. 2. make humane; cause to be kind or merciful. —**hu′man·i·za′tion,** *n*. —**hu′man·iz′er,** *n*.

hu·man·kind (hū′mən·kīnd′), *n*. human beings; people; human race; mankind.

hu·man·ly (hū′mən·li), *adv*. 1. in a human manner; by human means. 2. according to the feelings, knowledge, or experience of people.

hum·ble (hum′bəl), *adj.,* -bler, -blest, *v.,* -bled, -bling. —*adj*. 1. low in position or condition; not important or grand: *a humble place to live*. 2. having or showing a feeling that one is unimportant, weak, poor, etc.; modest in spirit. 3. deeply or courteously respectful: *in my humble opinion*. —*v*. make humble; make lower in position, condition, or pride. [< OF < L *humilis* low < *humus* earth] —**hum′ble·ness,** *n*. —**hum′bler,** *n*. —**hum′bly,** *adv*. —**Syn.** *adj*. 1. unpretentious.

hum·ble·bee (hum′bəl·bē′), *n*. bumblebee. [ME *humbalbee,* ult. < *hum*]

humble pie. eat humble pie, be forced to do something very disagreeable and humiliating.

hum·bug (hum′bug′), *n., v.,* -bugged, -bugging. —*n*. 1. a cheat; sham. 2. quality of falseness, deception, etc. —*v*. deceive with a sham; cheat. —**hum′bug′ger,** *n*.

hum·bug·ger·y (hum′bug′ər·i), *n*. sham.

hum·drum (hum′drum′), *adj*. without variety; commonplace; dull. —*n*. humdrum routine.

hu·mer·us (hū′mər·əs), *n., pl.* -mer·i (-mər·ī). 1. *Anat*. the long bone in the upper part of the forelimb or arm, from the shoulder to the elbow. 2. the upper part of the forelimb or arm. [< L *umerus*] —**hu′mer·al,** *adj*.

hu·mid (hū′mid), *adj*. 1. moist; damp, esp. moist with aqueous vapor: *humid air*. 2. characterized by much moisture in the air: *a humid region*. [< L *umidus* < *umere* be moist] —**hu′mid·ly,** *adv*. —**hu′mid·ness,** *n*.

hu·mid·i·fy (hū·mid′ə·fī), *v.,* -fied, -fy·ing. make humid, moist, or damp. —**hu·mid′i·fi·ca′tion,** *n*. —**hu·mid′i·fi′er,** *n*.

hu·mid·i·ty (hū·mid′ə·ti), *n*. 1. moistness; dampness. 2. amount of moisture in the air.

hu·mi·dor (hū′mə·dôr), *n*. box, jar, etc., for keeping things, esp. tobacco, moist.

hu·mil·i·ate (hū·mil′i·āt), *v.,* -at·ed, -at·ing. lower the pride, dignity, or self-respect of: *John felt humiliated by his failure*. [< L, < *humilis* HUMBLE] —**hu·mil′i·at′ing·ly,** *adv*. —**hu·mil′i·a′tion,** *n*. —**Syn.** humble, mortify, chagrin.

hu·mil·i·ty (hū·mil′ə·ti), *n., pl.* -ties. 1. humbleness of mind; meekness. 2. Usually, humilities. act that shows a humble spirit. —**Syn.** 1. lowliness, modesty.

hu·mit (hū′mit), *n*. unit of measurement used in expressing humiture. If the temperature is 80° and relative humidity is 60%, the humiture is 70 humits. [< *humiture*]

hu·mi·ture (hū′mə·chər), *n*. a combined measurement of temperature and humidity, arrived at by adding degrees of temperature to percentage of relative humidity and dividing by two. [< *humi-.(dity)* + *(tempera)ture*; coined by O. F. Hevener of New York in 1937]

hum·ming·bird (hum′ing·bėrd′), *n. Am.* a very small, brightly colored American bird with a long, narrow bill and narrow wings that make a humming sound.

Hummingbird (ab. 3 ¾ in. long)

hum·mock (hum′ək), *n*. 1. a very small, rounded hill; knoll; hillock. 2. bump or ridge in a field of ice. —**hum′mock·y,** *adj*.

hu·mor, *esp. Brit.* **hu·mour** (hū′mər; ū′-), *n*. 1. funny or amusing quality: *I see no humor in your tricks*. 2. ability to see or show the funny or amusing side of things. 3. speech, writing, etc., showing this ability. 4. state of mind; mood; disposition: *success puts you in good humor.* 5. fancy; whim. 6. in old physiology, any of various body fluids supposed to determine a person's health and disposition; blood, phlegm, choler (yellow bile), and melancholy (black bile). —*v*. 1. give in to the fancies or whims of (a person); indulge: *a sick person has to be humored.* 2. adapt oneself to; act so as to agree

with. [< L *umor* fluid] —**hu′mor·less**, *esp. Brit.*
hu′mour·less, *adj.*

hu·mor·esque (hū′mər·esk′), *n.* a light, playful, or humorous piece of music.

hu·mor·ist (hū′-
mər·ist; *ū′-*), *n.* **1.** person with a strong sense of
humor. **2.** a humorous talker; writer of jokes
and funny stories. —**hu′mor·is′tic**, *esp. Brit.*
hu′mour·is′tic, *adj.*

hu·mor·ous, *esp. Brit.* **hu·mour·ous** (hū′-
mər·əs; *ū′-*), *adj.* full of humor; funny; amusing.
—**hu′mor·ous·ly**, *esp. Brit.* **hu′mour·ous·ly**,
adv. —**hu′mor·ous·ness**, *esp. Brit.* **hu′mour·
ous·ness**, *n.*

hump (hump), *n.* **1.** a rounded lump that sticks
out. **2.** mound. —*v.* **1.** raise or bend up into a
lump: *the cat humped her back when she saw
the dog.* **2.** *U.S. Slang.* exert (oneself). [cf. Du.
homp lump] —**humped**, *adj.* —**hump′less**, *adj.*

hump·back (hump′bak′), *n.* **1.** hunchback.
2. back having a hump on it. **3.** *Am.* a large
whale that has a humplike dorsal fin. —**hump′-
backed′**, *adj.*

humph (humf), *interj., n.* exclamation expressing doubt, disgust, contempt, etc.

Hum·phrey (hum′fri), *n.* Hubert H., born
1911, vice-president of the United States since
1965.

hump·y (hump′i), *adj.*, **hump·i·er, hump·i·est.**
1. full of humps. **2.** humplike.

hu·mus (hū′məs), *n.* soil made from decayed
leaves and other vegetable matter, containing
valuable plant foods. [< L, earth]

Hun (hun), *n.* **1.** member of a warlike, brutal
Asiatic people who overran eastern and central
Europe between about 375 and 453 A.D. **2.** a bar-
barous, destructive person; vandal.

hunch (hunch), *v.* **1.** hump. **2.** draw, bend, or
form into a hump: *he sat hunched up with his
chin between his knees.* **3.** move, push, or shove
by jerks. —*n.* **1.** a hump. **2.** *Am., Colloq.* a vague
feeling or suspicion: *he had a hunch that it
would rain.* **3.** a thick slice or piece; chunk.

hunch·back (hunch′bak′), *n.* **1.** person with
a hump on his back; humpback. **2.** back having
a hump on it. —**hunch′backed′**, *adj.*

hun·dred (hun′drəd), *n., pl.* **-dreds** or (*as
after a numeral*) **-dred**, *adj.* —*n.* **1.** a cardinal
number, ten times ten. **2.** symbol of this number,
100. **3.** set of one hundred persons or things.
4. *Brit.* division of a county. —*adj.* ten times
ten; 100. [OE] —**hun′dredth** (hun′drədth), *adj.*

hun·dred·fold (hun′drəd·fōld′), *adj.* **1.** a
hundred times as much or as many. **2.** having
one hundred parts. —*adv.* a hundred times as
much or as many.

hun·dred·weight (hun′drəd·wāt′), *n., pl.*
-weights or (*as after a numeral*) **-weight.** measure of weight, equal to 100 pounds in the United
States or 112 pounds in England.

hung (hung), *v.* pt. and pp. of **hang.** ➤ See
hang for usage note.

Hung., **1.** Hungarian. **2.** Hungary.

Hun·gar·i·an (hung·gãr′i·ən), *adj.* of Hungary, its people, or their language. —*n.* **1.** native
or inhabitant of Hungary. **2.** language of Hungary.

Hun·ga·ry (hung′gə·ri), *n.* country in C
Europe, formerly a part of Austria-Hungary.

hun·ger (hung′gər), *n.* **1.** an uncomfortable or
painful feeling or weak condition caused by lack
of food. **2.** desire or need for food. **3.** a strong
desire: *a hunger for kindness.* —*v.* **1.** feel hunger; be hungry. **2.** starve. **3.** have a strong desire. [OE *hungor*] —**hun′ger·ing·ly**, *adv.*

hunger strike, refusal to eat until certain
demands are granted.

hun·gry (hung′gri), *adj.*, **-gri·er, -gri·est. 1.**
feeling a desire or need for food. **2.** showing
hunger: *a hungry look.* **3.** causing hunger. **4.**
having a strong desire or craving; eager: *hungry for books.* **5.** not rich or fertile: *hungry soil.*
—**hun′gri·ly**, *adv.* —**hun′gri·ness**, *n.* —**Syn. 1.**
ravenous, famished, starved.

hunk (hungk), *n. Colloq.* a big lump or piece.

hunt (hunt), *v.* **1.** chase or go after (wild animals, game birds, etc.) for food or sport. **2.**
search through (a region) in pursuit of game. **3.**
use (horses or dogs) in the chase. **4.** drive (out,
away); pursue. **5.** try to find: *hunt a clue.*
6. look thoroughly; search carefully: *hunt
through drawers.* —*n.* **1.** act of hunting. **2.** group
of persons hunting together. **3.** region hunted
over with hounds. **4.** attempt to find something;
thorough look; careful search. [OE *huntian*]
—**Syn.** *v.* **4.** harry, persecute. **6.** ransack.

hunt·er (hun′tər), *n.* **1.** person who hunts. **2.**
horse or dog for hunting.

hunting ground, place or region for hunting.

hunting horn, horn used in a hunt.

hunt·ress (hun′tris), *n.* woman who hunts.

hunts·man (hunts′mən), *n., pl.* **-men.** *Esp.
Brit.* **1.** hunter. **2.** manager of a hunt.

hur·dle (hér′dəl), *n., v.*, **-dled, -dling.** —*n.* **1.**
barrier for people or horses to jump over in a
race. **2.** hurdles, hurdle race, race in which the
runners jump over hurdles. **3.** obstacle; difficulty. **4.** frame made of sticks used as a temporary fence. —*v.* **1.** jump over. **2.** overcome (an
obstacle, difficulty, etc.). **3.** enclose with a hurdle.
[OE *hyrdel*] —**hur′dler**, *n.*

hur·dy-gur·dy (hér′di·gér′di), *n., pl.* **-dies.**
a barrel organ or street piano played by turning a handle. [? imit.]

hurl (hérl), *v.* **1.** throw with much force. **2.**
fling forth (words, cries, etc.) violently; utter
with vehemence. —*n.* a forcible or violent throw.
[cf. LG *hurreln*] —**hurl′er**, *n.*

hurl·y-burl·y (hér′li·bér′li), *n., pl.* **-burl·ies.**
disorder and noise; tumult.

Hu·ron (hyūr′ən), *n. Am.* **1.** Lake, the second
largest of the five Great Lakes, between the
United States and Canada. **2.** member of a tribe
of Iroquois Indians. —*adj.* of this tribe.

hur·rah (hə·rä′; -rô′), **hur·ray** (hə·rā′),
interj., n. shout of joy, approval, etc. —*v.* shout
hurrahs; cheer. Also, **hooray.**

hur·ri·cane (hér′i·kān), *n.* **1.** a tropical cyclone; storm with violent wind and, usually,
very heavy rain. **2.** a sudden, violent outburst.
[< Sp. *huracán* < Carib]

hurricane deck, an upper deck on a ship.

hur·ried (hér′id), *adj.* **1.** forced to hurry. **2.**
done or made in a hurry; hasty. —**hur′ried·ly**,
adv. —**hur′ried·ness**, *n.*

hur·ry (hér′i), *v.*, **-ried, -ry·ing,** *n., pl.* **-ries.**
—*v.* **1.** drive, carry, send, or move quickly. **2.**
move or act with more than an easy or natural
speed. **3.** urge to act soon or too soon. **4.** urge to
great speed or to too great speed. **5.** cause to go
on or occur more quickly; hasten. —*n.* **1.** a hurried movement or action. **2.** eagerness to have
quickly or do quickly. —**hur′ry·ing·ly**, *adv.*
—**Syn.** *v.* **3.** quicken, accelerate, expedite.

hur·ry-scur·ry, hur·ry-skur·ry (hér′i·
skér′i), *n., pl.* **-ries,** *adj., adv.* —*n.* a hurrying
and confusion. —*adj.* hurried and confused.
—*adv.* with hurrying and confusion.

hurt (hért), *v.*, **hurt, hurt·ing,** *n.* —*v.* **1.** cause
pain, harm, or damage. **2.** cause pain to; give a
wound to; injure. **3.** suffer pain. **4.** have a bad
effect on. —*n.* **1.** pain; injury; wound. **2.** a bad
effect; damage; harm. [appar. < OF *hurter*
strike < Gmc.] —**hurt′er**, *n.* —**hurt′less**, *adj.*

hurt·ful (hért′fəl), *adj.* causing hurt, harm,
or damage; injurious. —**hurt′ful·ly**, *adv.*
—**hurt′ful·ness**, *n.* —**Syn.** harmful, pernicious.
—**Ant.** helpful, beneficial, salutary.

hur·tle (hér′təl), *v.*, **-tled, -tling. 1.** dash or
drive violently; rush suddenly; come with a
crash: *spears hurtled against shields.* **2.** move
with a clatter; rush noisily or violently: *the
train hurtled past.* **3.** dash or drive violently;
fling. **4.** dash against; collide with. [? < *hurt*]

hus·band (huz′bənd), *n.* man who has a wife;
married man. —*v.* **1.** marry. **2.** manage carefully; be saving of: *husband one's resources.*
[OE *hūsbōnda* < *hūs* house + *bōnda* head of
family < Scand. *bōndi*] —**hus′band·less**, *adj.*

hus·band·man (huz′bənd·mən), *n., pl.* **-men.**
farmer.

hus·band·ry (huz′bənd·ri), *n.* 1. farming. 2. management of one's affairs or resources. 3. careful management.

hush (hush), *v.* 1. stop making a noise; make or become silent or quiet. 2. soothe; calm. 3. hush up, keep from being told; stop discussion of. —*n.* a stopping of noise; silence; quiet. —*interj.* stop the noise! be silent! keep quiet! [< ME *hussht* silent]

hush money, money paid to keep a person from telling something.

husk (husk), *n.* 1. the dry outer covering of certain seeds or fruits. An ear of corn has a husk. 2. the dry or worthless outer covering of anything. —*v.* remove the husk from. [ME *huske*] —husk′er, *n.*

husking bee, *Am.* a gathering of neighbors and friends to husk corn.

husk·y¹ (hus′ki), *adj.,* husk·i·er, husk·i·est, *n., pl.* husk·ies. —*adj.* 1. dry in the throat; hoarse; rough of voice. 2. of, like, or having husks. 3. *Am., Colloq.* big and strong. —*n. Am., Colloq.* a big, strong person. —husk′i·ly, *adv.* —husk′i·ness, *n.*

Husk·y, husk·y² (hus′ki), *n., pl.* Husk·ies, husk·ies. *Am.* an Eskimo dog.

Huss (hus), *n.* John, 1369?–1415, Bohemian religious reformer. —**Huss·ite** (hus′īt), *n.*

hus·sar (hú·zär′), *n.* a European light-armed cavalry soldier. [< Hung. < OSerbian < Ital. *corsaro* runner. See CORSAIR.]

hus·sy (huz′i; hus′-), *n., pl.* -sies. 1. a bad-mannered or pert girl. 2. a worthless woman.

hus·tings (hus′tingz), *n. pl.* or *sing.* platform from which speeches are made in a political campaign. [< Scand. *hūsthing* council < *hūs* house + *thing* assembly]

hus·tle (hus′əl), *v.,* -tled, -tling, *n.* —*v.* 1. hurry. 2. force hurriedly or roughly. 3. push or shove roughly; jostle rudely. 4. *Am., Colloq.* work with tireless energy. —*n.* 1. a hurry. 2. a rough pushing; rude jostling. 3. *Am., Colloq.* tireless energy. [< Du. *hutselen* shake] —hus′tler, *n.*

hut (hut), *n.* a small, roughly built house; small cabin. [< F < G *hütte*] —hut′like′, *adj.*

hutch (huch), *n.* 1. pen for rabbits, etc. 2. hut. 3. box; chest; bin. —*v.* put in a hutch; hoard. [< OF < Med.L *hutica* chest]

Hux·ley (huks′li), *n.* Thomas Henry, 1825-1895, English biologist.

huz·za (hə·zä′), *interj., n., pl.* -zas, *v.,* -zaed, -za·ing. —*interj., n.* a loud shout of joy, encouragement, or applause; hurrah. —*v.* shout huzzas; cheer.

Hwang Ho, Hwang·ho (hwäng′hō′), *n.* river in China flowing from E Tibet into the Yellow Sea. Also, Yellow River.

hy·a·cinth (hī′ə·sinth), *n.* 1. plant of the lily family that grows from a bulb and has a spike of small, fragrant, bell-shaped flowers. 2. a reddish-orange gem, a variety of zircon. [< L < Gk. *hyakinthos* kind of flower]

hy·ae·na (hī·ē′nə), *n.* hyena.

hy·a·lu·ron·i·dase (hī′ə·lú·ron′ə·dās), *n.* enzyme that aids the circulation of body fluids.

hy·brid (hī′brid), *n.* 1. offspring of two animals or plants of different species, varieties, etc. A loganberry is a hybrid between a raspberry and blackberry. 2. anything of mixed origin. A word formed of parts from different languages is a hybrid. —*adj.* 1. bred from two different species, varieties, etc. A mule is a hybrid animal. 2. of mixed origin. [< L *hybrida,* var. of *ibrida* mongrel, hybrid] —hy′brid·ism, *n.*

hy·brid·ize (hī′brid·īz), *v.,* -ized, -iz·ing. 1. cause to produce hybrids. Botanists hybridize different kinds of plants to get new varieties. 2. produce hybrids. —hy′brid·i·za′tion, *n.*

Hyde Park (hīd), 1. park in London, England. 2. village in SE New York State, birthplace of Franklin D. Roosevelt.

Hy·der·a·bad (hī′dər·ə·bad′; -bäd′; hī′drə-), *n.* 1. city in S India. 2. city in W Pakistan, on the Indus River.

hy·dra (hī′drə), *n., pl.* -dras, -drae (-drē). 1. any persistent evil. 2. *Zool.* kind of fresh-water polyp, so called because when the body is cut into pieces, each piece forms a new individual. 3. Hydra, *Gk. Legend.* a monstrous serpent having nine heads. [< L < Gk., water serpent]

hy·dran·gea (hī·drān′jə), *n.* shrub with opposite leaves and large, showy clusters of small white, pink, or blue flowers. [< NL, < Gk. *hydor* water + *angeion* vessel, capsule]

hy·drant (hī′drənt), *n. Am.* an upright street fixture from which water may be drawn to fight fires, wash the streets, etc. [< Gk. *hydor* water]

hy·drate (hī′drāt), *n., v.,* -drat·ed, -drat·ing. *Chem.* —*n.* compound produced when certain substances unite with water, represented in formulas as containing molecules of water. Washing soda ($Na_2CO_3 \cdot 10H_2O$) is a hydrate. —*v.* become or cause to become a hydrate; combine with water to form a hydrate. [< Gk. *hydor* water] —hy·dra′tion, *n.* —hy′dra·tor, *n.*

hy·drau·lic (hī·drô′lik), *adj.* 1. having to do with water in motion. 2. operated by water: *a hydraulic press.* 3. hardening under water: *hydraulic cement.* [< L < Gk., ult. < *hydor* water + *aulos* pipe] —hy·drau′li·cal·ly, *adv.*

hy·drau·lics (hī·drô′liks), *n.* science treating of water and other liquids in motion, their uses in engineering, the laws of their actions, etc.

hy·dride (hī′drīd; -drid), **hy·drid** (-drid), *n. Chem.* compound of hydrogen with another element or radical.

hydro-, hydr-, *word element.* 1. of or having to do with water, as in *hydrometer, hydrostatics.* 2. combined with hydrogen, as in *hydrochloric, hydrosulfuric.* [< Gk., < *hydor* water]

hy·dro·car·bon (hī′drō·kär′bən), *n. Chem.* any of a class of compounds containing only hydrogen and carbon, as methane, benzene, and acetylene. Gasoline is a mixture of hydrocarbons.

hy·dro·chlo·ric acid (hī′drō·klô′rik; -klō′-), *Chem.* a. a colorless gas, HCl, with a strong, sharp odor. b. an aqueous solution of this.

hy·dro·cor·ti·sone (hī′drō·kôr′tə·zōn), *n.* an adrenal hormone similar to cortisone, used experimentally in treating arthritis. Also, Compound F.

hy·dro·cy·an·ic acid (hī′drō·sī·an′ik), prussic acid.

hy·dro·dy·nam·ics (hī′drō·dī·nam′iks; -dī-), *n.* branch of physics dealing with the forces that water and other liquids exert, often called hydraulics. —hy′dro·dy·nam′ic, *adj.*

hy·dro·e·lec·tric (hī′drō·i·lek′trik), *adj.* of or pertaining to the production of electricity by water power. —hy·dro·e·lec·tric·i·ty (hī′drō·i·lek′tris′ə·ti), *n.*

hy·dro·flu·or·ic acid (hī′drō·flú·ôr′ik; -or′-), *Chem.* a colorless, corrosive, volatile liquid, HF, used for etching glass.

hy·dro·gen (hī′drə·jən), *n. Chem.* a very light, colorless gas, H, that burns easily and weighs less than any other known element. [< F, ult. < Gk. *hydor* water + *geinasthai* produce; form infl. by *-genes* born] —hy·drog·e·nous (hī·droj′ə·nəs), *adj.*

hy·dro·gen·ate (hī′drə·jən·āt; hī·droj′ən-), *v.,* -at·ed, -at·ing. combine with hydrogen; treat with hydrogen.

hy·dro·gen·a·tion (hī′drə·jən·ā′shən), *n.* 1. combination with hydrogen. 2. a method of producing hydrocarbons by pulverizing coal and combining it with hydrogen under very high pressure.

hydrogen bomb, bomb that uses the fusion of atoms to cause an explosion of tremendous force; fusion bomb; superatomic bomb. It will, supposedly, be many times more powerful than the atomic bomb. Also, H-bomb.

hy·dro·gen·ize (hī′drə·jən·īz; hī·droj′ən-), *v.,* -ized, -iz·ing. hydrogenate.

hydrogen peroxide, a colorless, unstable liquid, H_2O_2, often used in dilute solution as an antiseptic, bleaching agent, etc.

hy·drog·ra·phy (hī·drog′rə·fi), *n.* science of the measurement and description of seas, lakes, rivers, etc., with special reference to their use for navigation and commerce. —hy·drog′ra·pher, *n.* —hy·dro·graph·ic (hī′drə·graf′ik), *adj.*

hy·droid (hī′droid), *n. Zool.* a very simple form

Husk on an ear of corn

of hydrozoan that grows into branching colonies by budding; polyp. —*adj.* like a polyp.

hy·drol·y·sis (hī·drol′ə·sis), *n., pl.* -ses (-sēz). *Chem.* decomposition that changes a compound into other compounds by taking up the elements of water. —**hy·dro·lyt·ic** (hī′drə·lit′ik), *adj.*

hy·dro·lyze (hī′drə·līz), *v.,* -lyzed, -lyz·ing. decompose by hydrolysis. —**hy′dro·lyz′a·ble,** *adj.* —**hy′dro·ly·za′tion,** *n.*

hy·drom·e·ter (hī·drom′ə·tər), *n. Physics.* a graduated instrument for finding the specific gravity of liquids. It is used to test automobile batteries. —**hy·dro·met·ric** (hī′drə·met′rik), **hy′dro·met′ri·cal,** *adj.* —**hy·drom′e·try,** *n.*

hy·drop·a·thy (hī·drop′ə·thi), *n.* treatment of disease by external or internal use of water; hydrotherapy; hydrotherapeutics. —**hy·dro·path·ic** (hī′drə·path′ik), **hy′dro·path′i·cal,** *adj.* —**hy·drop′a·thist,** *n.*

hy·dro·pho·bi·a (hī′drə·fō′bi·ə), *n.* **1.** an infectious disease of dogs and other flesh-eating mammals that causes convulsions, frothing at the mouth, and madness; rabies. **2.** a morbid dread of water. —**hy·dro·pho·bic** (hī′drə·fō′bik), *adj.*

hy·dro·phyte (hī′drə·fīt), *n.* any plant that can grow only in water or very wet soil.

hy·dro·plane (hī′drə·plān), *n., v.,* -planed, -plan·ing. —*n.* **1.** motorboat that glides on the surface of water. **2.** airplane provided with floats or with a boatlike underpart, enabling it to alight upon and ascend from water; seaplane. —*v.* ride in a hydroplane.

hy·dro·pon·ics (hī′drə·pon′iks), *n.* the growing of plants without soil. [< HYDRO- + L *ponere* to place] —**hy′dro·pon′ic,** *adj.*

hy·dro·sphere (hī′drə·sfir), *n.* **1.** water on the surface of the globe. **2.** water vapor in the atmosphere.

hy·dro·stat (hī′drə·stat), *n.* **1.** device for preventing injury to a steam boiler from low water. **2.** device for detecting the presence of water.

hy·dro·stat·ics (hī′drə·stat′iks), *n.* branch of physics that deals with the equilibrium and pressure of liquids. —**hy′dro·stat′ic, hy′dro·stat′i·cal,** *adj.* —**hy′dro·stat′i·cal·ly,** *adv.*

hy·dro·ther·a·peu·tics (hī′drō·ther′ə·pū′tiks), *n.* hydropathy. —**hy′dro·ther′a·peu′tic,** *adj.*

hy·dro·ther·a·py (hī′drō·ther′ə·pi), *n.* hydropathy. —**hy·dro·the·rap·ic** (hī′drō·thə·rap′ik), *adj.*

hy·drot·ro·pism (hī·drot′rə·piz·əm), *n.* tropism in response to water.

hy·drous (hī′drəs), *adj.* **1.** containing water. **2.** *Chem.* containing water or its elements in some kind of union, as in hydrates or in hydroxides.

hy·drox·ide (hī·drok′sīd; -sid), **hy·drox·id** (-sid), *n. Chem.* any compound consisting of an element or radical combined with one or more hydroxyl radicals.

hy·drox·yl radical (hī·drok′səl), *Chem.* a univalent radical, OH, in all hydroxides.

hy·dro·zo·an (hī′drə·zō′ən), *n.* any of a group of invertebrate water animals including hydras, polyps, many jellyfishes, etc. [< NL *Hydrozoa,* genus name < Gk. *hydor* water + *zoion* animal]

hy·e·na (hī·ē′nə), *n.* a wolflike, flesh-eating mammal of Africa and Asia. Most hyenas are cowardly, but utter blood-curdling yells. Also, **hyaena.** [< L < Gk. *hyaina* < *hys* pig]

Hy·ge·ia (hī·jē′ə), *n.* Gk. *Myth.* goddess of health.

hy·giene (hī′jēn; -ji·ēn), *n.* rules of health; science of keeping well. [< NL (*ars*) *hygieina* the healthful art < Gk., ult. < *hygies* healthy] —**hy·gien·ist** (hī′jēn·ist; -ji·en-), *n.*

Striped hyena (ab. 2 ft. high at the shoulder)

hy·gi·en·ic (hī′ji·en′ik; -jē′nik), *adj.* **1.** healthful; sanitary. **2.** having to do with health or hygiene. —**hy′gi·en′i·cal·ly,** *adv.*

hy·grom·e·ter (hī·grom′ə·tər), *n.* instrument for determining the amount of moisture in the air. [< Gk. *hygron* moisture (neut. of *hygros* wet) + -METER]

hy·grom·e·try (hī·grom′ə·tri), *n.* science of determining the amount of moisture in the air. —**hy·gro·met·ric** (hī′grə·met′rik), *adj.*

hy·gro·scope (hī′grə·skōp), *n.* instrument that shows the variations in the humidity of the air.

hy·gro·scop·ic (hī′grə·skop′ik), *adj.* **1.** pertaining to or perceptible by the hygroscope. **2.** absorbing or attracting moisture from the air. —**hy′gro·scop′i·cal·ly,** *adv.*

hy·ing (hī′ing), *v.* ppr. of hie.

hy·la (hī′lə), *n.* a tree toad. [< NL < Gk. *hyle* woods]

Hy·men (hī′mən), *n.* Gk. *Myth.* god of marriage.

hy·men (hī′mən), *n. Anat.* a fold of mucous membrane extending partly across the opening into the vagina. [< LL < Gk.]

hy·me·ne·al (hī′mə·nē′əl), *adj.* having to do with marriage. —*n.* a wedding song.

hy·me·nop·ter·ous (hī′mə·nop′tər·əs), *adj.* belonging to a group of insects including ants, bees, and wasps. [< Gk., < *hymen* membrane + *pteron* wing]

hymn (him), *n.* **1.** song in praise of God. **2.** any similar song. —*v.* praise or honor with a hymn. [< L < Gk. *hymnos*] —**hymn′like′,** *adj.*

hym·nal (him′nəl), *n.* Also, **hymn′book′.** book of hymns. —*adj.* of hymns.

hym·nol·o·gy (him·nol′ə·ji), *n.* **1.** study of hymns, their history, classification, etc. **2.** hymns. —**hym·no·log·ic** (him′nə·loj′ik), **hym′no·log′i·cal,** *adj.* —**hym·nol′o·gist,** *n.*

hy·oid (hī′oid), *n. Anat.* the U-shaped bone at the root of the tongue. [< NL < Gk. *hyoeides* U-shaped < T (upsilon) + *eidos* form]

hyper-, *prefix.* over; above; beyond; exceedingly; to excess, as in *hyperacidity, hypersensitive, hypertension.* [< Gk. *hyper*]

hy·per·a·cid·i·ty (hī′pər·ə·sid′ə·ti), *n.* excessive acidity. —**hy·per·ac·id** (hī′pər·as′id), *adj.*

hy·per·bo·la (hī·pér′bə·lə), *n., pl.* -las. *Geom.* a curve formed when a cone is cut by a plane making a larger angle with the base than the side of the cone makes. [< NL < Gk. *hyperbole,* ult. < *hyper-* beyond + *ballein* throw]

Hyperbola

hy·per·bo·le (hī·pér′bə·lē), *n.* exaggeration for effect. [< L < Gk. See HYPERBOLA.]

hy·per·bol·ic (hī′pər·bol′ik), *adj.* **1.** of, like, or using hyperbole; exaggerated; exaggerating. **2.** of hyperbolas. —**hy′per·bol′i·cal·ly,** *adv.*

Hy·per·bo·re·an (hī′pər·bō′ri·ən; -bō′-), *n.* Gk. *Legend.* one of a group of people described as living in a land of perpetual sunshine and plenty beyond the north wind. —*adj.* **hyperborean,** of the far north; arctic; frigid.

hy·per·crit·i·cal (hī′pər·krit′ə·kəl), *adj.* too critical. —**hy′per·crit′i·cal·ly,** *adv.*

hy·per·on (hī′pər·on), *n. Physics.* a very short-lived, unstable particle with a mass between that of the neutron and the deuteron.

hy·per·sen·si·tive (hī′pər·sen′sə·tiv), *adj.* excessively sensitive. —**hy′per·sen′si·tive·ness, hy′per·sen′si·tiv′i·ty,** *n.*

hy·per·son·ic (hī′pər·son′ik), *adj.* having to do with or operating at or above a speed five times the speed of sound. See supersonic.

hy·per·ten·sion (hī′pər·ten′shən), *n. Med.* an abnormally high blood pressure.

hy·per·ten·sive (hī′pər·ten′siv), *Med.* —*adj.* having or marked by rising, or unusually high, blood pressure. —*n.* a hypertensive person.

hy·per·tro·phy (hī·pér′trə·fi), *n., pl.* -phies, *v.,* -phied, -phy·ing. *Pathol., Bot.* —*n.* enlargement of a part or organ. —*v.* grow too big. [< NL, < Gk. *hyper-* over + *trophe* nourishment] —**hy·per·troph·ic** (hī′pər·trof′ik), *adj.*

hy·phen (hī′fən), *n.* mark (-) used to connect the parts of a compound word, or the parts of a word divided at the end of a line, etc. —*v*. hy·phenate. [< LL < Gk., in one, hyphen, < *upo*-under + *hen* one] ❯ **hyphen.** The conclusion one comes to after serious consideration of current habits in the use of hyphens is well put by John Benbow in *Manuscript and Proof*, the stylebook of the Oxford University Press of New York: "If you take hyphens seriously you will surely go mad." The only consolation is that hyphening is more a publisher's worry than a writer's. A publisher may wish for uniformity in principle and may struggle to get it in printing particular words, though absolute consistency is impossible. But in a person's ordinary writing, he does not need to be too particular. For words in common use he can consult this dictionary.

It is obvious that use of hyphens should be appropriate to other traits of style, esp. to punctuation. In general, formal and conservative writers tend to use more hyphens, informal writers tend to use fewer, and those who follow an open punctuation often get along with almost no hyphens. The present style is to use rather few, writing the word pairs as two separate words or joined as one.

The following rules may help:

1. In certain types of compounds of a preposition and a root word a hyphen is necessary to avoid confusion, or for emphasis or appearance:

a. between a prefix ending with a vowel and a root word beginning with the same vowel; as in *re-enter.* Usage is divided on words made with *co-*, the more common ones now generally being written solid or with a dieresis, as in *coöperate, cooperate,* or *co-operate.*

b. to avoid confusion with another word; as in *re-cover—recover.*

c. between a prefix and a proper name; as in *anti-Nazi.*

d. when the prefix is stressed; as in *ex-husband, ex-wife, anti-aircraft.*

2. With modifiers preceding a noun:

a. occasionally some pairs of modifiers might be ambiguous without a hyphen: *a light yellow scarf* might be either a light scarf that was yellow or a scarf that was light yellow, so that *light-yellow* is safest for the latter meaning, and conservative writers would put *light, yellow scarf* for the first.

b. Usage is divided on hyphening noun phrases when used as modifiers, as in *seventeenth century philosophy.* Formal writers would usually write *seventeenth-century,* informal *seventeenth century.* This division applies to such expressions as the following: *a Seventh Avenue shop, summer vacation freedom.*

c. A hyphen is used to carry the force of a modifier over to a later noun ("suspension hyphen"): *The third-, fourth-, and fifth-grade rooms have been redecorated.*

3. A hyphen is conventionally used in certain group words:

a. in the compound numerals from twenty-one to ninety-nine, and in fractions: *one hundred sixty-two, three-sixteenths.*

b. in names of family relationships: (hyphened) *father-in-law, daughter-in-law, etc.;* (one word) *stepson, stepdaughter, stepmother;* (two words) *half brother, half sister.*

c. in compounds with *self-,* which are usually hyphened in dictionaries but are often found in print as two words: *self-government—self government. Selfhood, selfless* are written as one word. If words of this sort raise any question, consult this dictionary.

4. The question of compound and occasionally compounded words is more complex. Many compound words will be found written as two words, hyphened, or as one word. As a rule the form does not affect meaning: *tax payers, tax-payers,* and *taxpayers* all pay taxes. In the past, words that were becoming fused into compounds were required to pass through a probationary period with hyphens before being admitted as single words. *Baseball,* for instance, was hyphened for a time, and *football* and *basketball* until quite recently. There is less tendency to use hyphens now, except in quite formal writing, and compounds are now made immediately without hy-

phens if the word is really needed. A hyphen is less likely to be used when one of the elements has two or more syllables, as in *tenement house. Schoolbook* is usually written solid, *pocket book* is written solid, hyphened, or as two words; *reference book* would almost always be found as two separate words. ❯ See **division** for another usage note.

hy·phen·ate (hī′fən·āt), *v.,* -at·ed, -at·ing. connect by a hyphen; write or print with a hyphen. —hy′**phen·a′tion,** *n.*

hyp·no·sis (hip·nō′sis), *n., pl.* -ses (-sēz). state resembling deep sleep, but more active, in which a person has little will of his own and little feeling, and acts according to the suggestions of the person who brought about the hypnosis.

hyp·not·ic (hip·not′ik), *adj.* **1.** of hypnosis. **2.** easily hypnotized. **3.** causing sleep. —*n.* **1.** person who is hypnotized or easily hypnotized. **2.** drug or other means of causing sleep. [< LL < Gk. *hypnotikos* putting to sleep < *hypnoein* put to sleep < *hypnos* sleep] —hyp·not′i·cal·ly, *adv.*

hyp·no·tism (hip′nə·tiz·əm), *n.* **1.** the inducing of hypnosis. **2.** science dealing with hypnosis. —hyp′no·tist, *n.*

hyp·no·tize (hip′nə·tīz), *v.,* -tized, -tiz·ing. **1.** put into a hypnotic state; cause hypnosis. **2.** *Colloq.* dominate the mind by suggestion. —hyp′no·tiz′a·ble, *adj.* —hyp′no·ti·za′tion, *n.* —hyp′no·tiz′er, *n.*

hy·po¹ (hī′pō), *n. Chem.* a colorless, crystalline salt used as a fixing agent in photography.

hy·po² (hī′pō), *n., pl.* -pos. *Colloq.* a hypodermic.

hypo-, *prefix.* under; beneath; below; less than; slightly; somewhat, as in *hypodermic.* [< Gk., < *hypo*]

hy·po·chlo·rite (hī′pə·klō′rīt; -klō′-), *n.* salt of hypochlorous acid.

hy·po·chlo·rous acid (hī′pə·klō′rəs; -klō′-), *Chem.* an acid, HClO, used as a bleach, disinfectant, etc.

hy·po·chon·dri·a (hī′pə·kon′dri·ə), *n.* **1.** unnatural anxiety about one's health; imaginary illness. **2.** low spirits without any real reason. [< LL, abdomen, < Gk., < *hypo*- under + *chondros* cartilage (of the breastbone); from the supposed seat of melancholy]

hy·po·chon·dri·ac (hī′pə·kon′dri·ak), *n.* person suffering from hypochondria. —*adj.* Also, **hy·po·chon·dri·a·cal** (hī′pō·kon·drī′ə·kəl). suffering from hypochondria. —hy′po·chon·dri′a·cal·ly, *adv.*

hy·po·cot·yl (hī′pə·kot′əl), *n. Bot.* part of the stem below the cotyledons in the embryo of a plant. —hy′po·cot′y·lous, *adj.*

hy·poc·ri·sy (hi·pok′rə·si), *n., pl.* -sies. **1.** act or fact of putting on a false appearance of goodness or religion. **2.** pretending to be what one is not. [< OF < LL < Gk. *hypokrisis* acting, dissimulation, ult. < *hypo*- under + *krinein* judge]

hyp·o·crite (hip′ə·krit), *n.* **1.** person who puts on a false appearance of goodness or religion. **2.** person who pretends to be what he is not. [< OF < L < Gk. *hypokrites* actor. See HYPOCRISY.] —hyp′o·crit′i·cal, *adj.* —hyp′o·crit′i·cal·ly, *adv.*

hy·po·der·mic (hī′pə·dėr′mik), *adj.* **1.** under the skin. **2.** injected under the skin: *a hypodermic needle.* —*n.* **1.** dose of medicine injected under the skin. **2.** syringe used to inject a dose of medicine under the skin. [< NL, < Gk. *hypo*-under + *derma* skin] —hy′po·der′mi·cal·ly, *adv.*

hy·po·phos·phite (hī′pə·fos′fīt), *n. Chem.* a salt of hypophosphorous acid.

hy·po·phos·phor·ic acid (hī′pō·fos·fôr′ik; -fōr′-), an acid, $H_4P_2O_6$, produced by the slow oxidation of phosphorus in moist air.

hy·po·phos·pho·rous acid (hī′pə·fos′fə·rəs), *adj. Chem.* an acid of phosphorus, H_3PO_2.

hy·po·sul·fite (hī′pə·sul′fīt), *n. Chem.* salt of hyposulfurous acid.

hy·po·sul·fur·ous acid (hī′pō·sul′fər·əs; -fyər-; -sul·fyūr′əs), acid, $H_2S_2O_4$, used as a reducing and bleaching agent.

hy·pot·e·nuse, hy·poth·e·nuse (hī·pot′ənūs; –nŭs), *n. Geom.* side of a right-angled triangle opposite the right angle. [< LL < Gk. *hypoteinousa* subtending < *hypo–* under + *teinein* stretch]

hy·poth·e·cate (hī-pŏth′ə-kāt), *v.*, –cat·ed, –cat·ing. pledge to a creditor as security; mortgage. [< Med.L *hypothecatus* < L < Gk. *hypotheke* pledge < *hypo–* under + *tithenai* place] —hy·poth′e·ca′tion, *n.* —hy·poth′e·ca′tor, *n.*

hy·poth·e·sis (hī-pŏth′ə-sĭs), *n., pl.* –ses (–sēz). 1. something assumed because it seems likely to be a true explanation; theory. 2. proposition assumed as a basis for reasoning. 3. a mere guess. [< NL < Gk., < *hypo–* under + *thesis* a placing]

hy·poth·e·size (hī-pŏth′ə-sīz), *v.*, –sized, –siz·ing. 1. make a hypothesis. 2. assume; suppose.

hy·po·thet·i·cal (hī′pə-thĕt′ə-kəl), **hy·po·thet·ic** (–ĭk), *adj.* 1. of or based on a hypothesis; assumed; supposed. 2. fond of making hypotheses: *a hypothetical scientist.* 3. in logic, conditional: *a hypothetical proposition.* 4. of a syllogism, having a hypothetical proposition for one of its premises. —hy′po·thet′i·cal·ly, *adv.*

hy·son (hī′sən), *n.* a Chinese green tea. [< Chinese *hsi-ch′un* blooming spring]

hys·sop (hĭs′əp), *n.* 1. *Am.* a fragrant, bushy plant of the same family as mint, used for medicine, flavoring, etc. 2. *Bible.* a plant whose twigs were used in certain Jewish ceremonies. Psalms 51:7. [< L < Gk. *hyssopos* < Semitic]

hys·ter·ec·to·my (hĭs′tər-ĕk′tə-mĭ), *n., pl.* –mies. removal of the uterus or a portion of it. [< Gk. *hystera* uterus + *ex–* out + *tomos* cutting]

hys·te·ri·a (hĭs-tĭr′ĭ-ə; –tĕr′–), *n.* 1. a nervous disorder that causes violent fits of laughing and crying, imaginary illnesses, or general lack of self-control. 2. senseless excitement. [< NL, < Gk. *hystera* uterus; because women are thought to be more often affected than men]

hys·ter·ic (hĭs-tĕr′ĭk), *adj.* hysterical. —*n.* Usually, **hysterics.** fit of hysterical laughing and crying.

hys·ter·i·cal (hĭs-tĕr′ə-kəl), *adj.* 1. unnaturally excited; showing an unnatural lack of control; unable to stop laughing, crying, etc. 2. suffering from hysteria. 3. of, characteristic of, or pertaining to hysteria. —hys·ter′i·cal·ly, *adv.*

I, i (ī), *n., pl.* **I's; i's.** 1. the ninth letter of the alphabet. 2. the Roman numeral for 1.

I (ī), *pron., nom.* I, *poss.* my or mine, *obj.* me; *pl. nom.* we, *poss.* ours or our, *obj.* us; *n., pl.* **I's.** —*pron.* the nominative case singular of the pronoun of the first person, used by a speaker or writer to denote himself. —*n.* the pronoun I used as a noun. [OE *ic*] ➤ The pronoun *I* is written with a capital simply because in the old manuscript hands a small *i* was likely to get lost or to get attached to a neighboring word, and a capital helped keep it a distinct word. There is no conceit implied. The widely circulated theory that *I* should not be the first word in a letter (sometimes even that it should not be the first word of a sentence) is unfounded. The best way to avoid conspicuous use of *I* is to keep it out of emphatic sentence positions, especially from the stressed beginning of a sentence. A subordinate clause or longish phrase put first will throw the stress off the *I: After a long struggle I decided to go.*

I, *Chem.* iodine.

I., 1. Island; Islands. 2. Isle; Isles.

Ia., Iowa.

–ial, *suffix.* form of –al, as in *adverbial, facial,* etc.

i·amb (ī′amb), *n.* an iambic foot or measure. [< L < Gk. *iambos*]

i·am·bic (ī-am′bĭk), *n.* 1. measure in poetry consisting of two syllables, an unaccented followed by an accented as in English poetry, or a short by a long (◡ —) as in Latin and Greek poetry. 2. Usually, **iambics.** verse of iambics. —*adj.* of or containing such measures. Much English poetry is iambic.

–ian, *suffix.* form of –an, as in *Bostonian, Episcopalian,* etc.

I·be·ri·a (ī-bĭr′ĭ-ə), or **Iberian Peninsula,** *n.* peninsula in SW Europe, occupied by Spain and Portugal. —I·be′ri·an (ī-bĭr′ĭ-ən), *adj., n.*

i·bex (ī′bĕks), *n., pl.* **i·bex·es,** **ib·i·ces** (ĭb′ə-sēz; ī′bə–), or (*esp. collectively*) **i·bex.** a wild goat of Europe, Asia, or Africa, the male of which has very large horns. [< L]

ibid., ib., ibidem. ➤ **ibid.** is used in a footnote to refer to the work mentioned in the immediately preceding footnote.

Ibis (ab. 3½ ft. long)

i·bi·dem (ĭ-bī′dem), *adv. Latin.* in the same place; in the same book, chapter, page, etc.

i·bis (ī′bĭs), *n., pl.* **i·bis·es** or (*esp. collectively*)

i·bis. a long-legged wading bird like a heron, regarded by ancient Egyptians as sacred. [< L < Gk. < Egyptian]

–ible, *suffix.* that can be ——ed, as in *impressible, perfectible, reducible.* [< OF < L *–ibilis*] ➤ See –able for usage note.

Ib·sen (ĭb′sən), *n.* Henrik, 1828–1906, Norwegian dramatist and poet.

–ic, *suffix.* 1. of or pertaining to, as in *atmospheric, Icelandic.* 2. having the nature of, as in *artistic, heroic.* 3. constituting or being, as in *bombastic, monolithic.* 4. characterized by; containing; made up of, as in *alcoholic, iambic.* 5. made by; caused by, as in *phonographic.* 6. like; like that of; characteristic of, as in *meteoric, sophomoric.* 7. *Chem.* –ic implies a smaller proportion of the element than –ous implies, as in *sulfuric.* [< F *–ique* or L *–icus* or Gk. *–ikos*]

–ical, *suffix.* 1. –ic, as in *geometrical, parasitical, hysterical.* 2. –ic specialized or differentiated in meaning, as in *economical.* 3. –ical sometimes equals –al added to nouns ending in –ic, as in *critical, musical.*

Ic·a·rus (ĭk′ə-rəs; ī′kə–), *n. Gk. Legend.* the son of Daedalus. Icarus and his father escaped from Crete by using wings that Daedalus had made. Icarus flew so high that the sun melted the wax by which his wings were attached. —I·car·i·an (ī-kâr′ĭ-ən; ī–), *adj.*

ICBM, Intercontinental Ballistic Missile, a ballistic missile of great range (up to 5000 miles).

I.C.C., ICC, Interstate Commerce Commission.

ice (īs), *n., v.,* **iced, ic·ing,** *adj.* —*n.* 1. water made solid by cold; frozen water. 2. layer or surface of ice. 3. something that looks or feels like ice. 4. a frozen dessert usually made of sweetened fruit juice. 5. icing. 6. *Slang.* diamonds. 7. **break the ice, a.** make a beginning. **b.** overcome first difficulties in talking or getting acquainted. 8. **on thin ice,** in a dangerous or difficult position. —*v.* 1. cool with ice; put ice in or around. 2. cover with ice. 3. turn to ice; freeze. 4. cover (cake) with icing. —*adj.* of ice; having to do with ice. [OE *īs*] —ice′less, *adj.* —ice′like′, *adj.*

ice age, *Geol.* the glacial epoch.

ice·berg (īs′bûrg′), *n.* a large mass of ice floating in the sea. [< Dan. *isberg,* or Swed. *isberg,* or Du. *ijsberg,* lit., ice mountain]

ice·boat (īs′bōt′), *n.* 1. a triangular frame on runners, fitted with sails for sailing on ice. 2. icebreaker (def. 1).

ice·bound (īs′bound′), *adj.* 1. held fast by ice. 2. shut in or obstructed by ice.

ice·box (īs′bŏks′), *n. Am.* an insulated box in which to keep food, liquids, etc., cool with ice, etc.

āge, câre, fär; ēqual, tèrm; īce; ōpen, ôrder; pŭt, rūle, ūse; th, then; ə=a in about.

ice·break·er (īs′brāk′ər), n. Am. 1. a strong boat used to break a channel through ice. 2. machine or tool for cutting ice into small pieces.

ice·cap (īs′kap′), n. a permanent covering of ice over an area, sloping down on all sides from an elevated center.

ice cream, a frozen dessert made of cream or custard sweetened and flavored.

iced (īst), adj. 1. cooled with ice; with ice in or around it. 2. covered with icing.

ice field, a large sheet of ice floating in the sea.

Ice·land (īs′lənd), n. a large island in the N Atlantic, formerly a Danish possession, an independent republic since 1944. —Ice·land·er (īs′lan′dər; -lən·dər), n.

Ice·lan·dic (īs·lan′dik), adj. of or having to do with Iceland, its people, or their language. —n. the language of Iceland.

ice·man (īs′man′), n., pl. -men (-men′). Am. man who sells, delivers, or handles ice.

ice pack, 1. large area of masses of ice floating in the sea. 2. bag containing ice for application to the body.

ice sheet, a broad, thick sheet of ice covering a very large area for a long time.

ice·skate (īs′skāt′), v., -skat·ed, -skat·ing. skate on ice.

ice skates, a pair of metal runners, usually attached to shoes, for skating.

ich·neu·mon (ik·nū′mən; -nū′-), n. 1. a small brown, weasellike animal of Egypt. 2. the ichneumon fly. [< L < Gk., lit., searcher (supposedly for crocodile's eggs), ult. < ichnos track]

ichneumon fly, insect that looks like a wasp but does not sting. Its larvae live as parasites in or on other insects, usually killing them.

ich·thy·ol·o·gy (ik′thi·ol′ə·ji), n. branch of zoölogy dealing with fishes. [< Gk. ichthys fish + -LOGY] —ich·thy·o·log·ic (ik′thi·ə·loj′ik), ich·thy·o·log′i·cal, adj. —ich·thy·ol′o·gist, n.

ich·thy·o·saur (ik′thi·ə·sôr′), **ich·thy·o·sau·rus** (ik′thi·ə·sô′rəs), n., pl. -saurs; -sau·ri (-sô′rī). an extinct fishlike marine reptile with four paddlelike flippers. [< NL, < Gk. ichthys fish + sauros lizard]

Ichthyosaur (from 4 to 40 ft. long)

i·ci·cle (ī′si·kəl), n. a pointed, hanging stick of ice formed by the freezing of dripping water. [ME isykle < OE is ice + gicel icicle] —i′ci·cled, adj.

ic·ing (īs′ing), n. mixture of sugar with white of egg or other things, used to cover cakes.

i·con (ī′kon), n., pl. i·cons, i·co·nes (ī′kə·nēz). 1. in the Eastern Church, a sacred picture or image of Christ, an angel, a saint, etc. 2. picture; image. Also, ikon, eikon. [< L < Gk. eikon]

i·con·o·clast (ī·kon′ə·klast), n. 1. person opposed to worshiping images. 2. person who attacks cherished beliefs or institutions as wrong or foolish. [< Med.L < Gk. eikonoklastes < Gk. eikon image + klaein to break] —i·con′o·clas′tic, adj. —i·con′o·clas′ti·cal·ly, adv.

-ics, suffix. 1. facts, principles, science, as in physics. 2. methods, system, activities, as in athletics, politics, tactics. ➤ Nouns formed with -ics were originally plural, denoting things pertaining to a particular subject, but are now chiefly singular in use (without dropping the -s), denoting the body of knowledge, facts, principles, etc., pertaining to a subject, and being a science, study, or art, as economics, linguistics, physics. Some are singular or plural according to the context, as acoustics, athletics, ethics: Ethics is a new course in the philosophy department. The young lawyer's ethics are above reproach. Others can be construed either way. See the usage note under politics.

ic·tus (ik′təs), n., pl. -tus·es, -tus. 1. rhythmical or metrical stress. 2. beat of the pulse. [< L, < icere to hit]

i·cy (ī′si), adj., i·ci·er, i·ci·est. 1. like ice; very cold; slippery. 2. having much ice; covered with ice. 3. of ice. 4. without warm feeling; cold and unfriendly. —i′ci·ly, adv. —i′ci·ness, n. —Syn. 1. frosty, frigid.

id (id), n. Psychoanalysis. the preformed, primitive psychic force in the unconscious, which is the source of instinctive energy essential for propagation and self-preservation. [< G use of L id it]

I'd (īd), 1. I should. 2. I would. 3. I had.

id., idem.

Ida., Id., Idaho.

I·da·ho (ī′də·hō), n. a Western State of the United States. Capital: Boise. Abbrev.: Ida. or Id. —I′da·ho′an, adj., n.

-ide, -id, suffix. compound of, as in chloride, sulfide. [< oxide]

i·de·a (ī·dē′ə), n. 1. plan, picture, or belief of the mind. 2. thought; fancy; opinion. ➤ Idea strictly means a "concept," something thought about something. It is frequently used as a substitute for intention and similar words in constructions that are usually wordy: I got the idea that [I thought] every policeman was my enemy. [< L < Gk., < idein see] —i·de′a·less, adj. —Syn. 1. conception, concept. 2. notion.

i·de·al (ī·dē′əl; ī·dēl′), n. perfect type; model to be imitated; what one would wish to be: religion holds up high ideals for us to follow. —adj. 1. just as one would wish; perfect: an ideal day for a picnic. 2. existing only in thought. A point without length, breadth, or thickness is an ideal object. 3. not practical; visionary. 4. having to do with ideas; representing an idea. —i·de′al·ness, n. —Syn. adj. 3. unreal, fanciful. —Ant. adj. 1. imperfect, faulty. 3. practical, real, actual.

i·de·al·ism (ī·dē′əl·iz·əm), n. 1. an acting according to one's ideals of what ought to be, regardless of circumstances or of the approval or disapproval of others. 2. the cherishing of fine ideals. 3. in art or literature, representing imagined types rather than an exact copy of any one person, instance, or situation. 4. in philosophy, belief that all our knowledge is a knowledge of ideas and that it is impossible to know whether there really is a world of objects on which our ideas are based.

i·de·al·ist (ī·dē′əl·ist), n. 1. person who acts according to his ideals; person who has fine ideals. 2. person who neglects practical matters in following ideals. 3. adherent of idealism in art or philosophy.

i·de·al·is·tic (ī·dē′əl·is′tik), adj. 1. having high ideals and acting according to them. 2. forgetting or neglecting practical matters in trying to follow out one's ideals; not practical. 3. of idealism or idealists. —i·de′al·is′ti·cal·ly, adv.

i·de·al·ize (ī·dē′əl·īz), v., -ized, -iz·ing. make ideal; think of or represent as perfect rather than as is actually the case: Mary idealized her older sister and thought that everything she did was right. —i·de′al·i·za′tion, n. —i·de′al·iz′er, n.

i·de·al·ly (ī·dē′əl·i), adv. 1. according to an ideal; perfectly. 2. in idea or theory.

i·dem (ī′dem; id′em), pron., adj. Latin. the same as previously given or mentioned.

i·den·ti·cal (ī·den′tə·kəl), adj. 1. the same: both events happened on the identical day. 2. exactly alike: identical houses. [< Med.L identicus < L idem same] —i·den′ti·cal·ly, adv. —i·den′ti·cal·ness, n.

identical twin, one of twins, of the same sex, developing from a single fertilized ovum.

i·den·ti·fi·ca·tion (ī·den′tə·fə·kā′shən), n. 1. an identifying or being identified. 2. something used to identify a person or thing.

i·den·ti·fy (ī·den′tə·fī), v., -fied, -fy·ing. 1. recognize as being, or show to be, a certain person or thing; prove to be the same: identify handwriting. 2. make the same; treat as the same. 3. connect closely; link; associate (with). —i·den′ti·fi′a·ble, adj. —i·den′ti·fi′er, n.

i·den·ti·ty (ī·den′tə·ti), n., pl. -ties. 1. individuality; who a person is; what a thing is: the writer concealed his identity under an assumed name. 2. exact likeness; sameness: the identity of the two crimes. 3. state or fact of being the same one: establish the identity of a person seen today with one seen yesterday.

id·e·o·graph (id′i·ə·graf′; -gräf′; ī′di-), id-

e·o·gram (-gram'), *n.* a graphic symbol that represents a thing or an idea without indicating a word for the thing or the idea, as Egyptian hieroglyphics and Chinese characters. [< Gk. *idea* idea + -GRAPH] —**id'e·o·graph'ic, id'e·o·graph'i·cal,** *adj.* —**id'e·o·graph'i·cal·ly,** *adv.*

i·de·ol·o·gy (i'di·ol'ə·ji; id'i-), *n., pl.* **-gies. 1.** set of doctrines; body of opinions. **2.** fundamental doctrines and point of view. **3.** the combined doctrines, assertions, and intentions of a social or political movement. —**i·de·o·log·ic** (i'di·ə·loj'ik; id'i-), **i'de·o·log'i·cal,** *adj.* —**i'de·o·log'i·cal·ly,** *adv.* —**i'de·ol'o·gist,** *n.*

ides (idz), *n.pl.* in the ancient Roman calendar, the 15th day of March, May, July, and October, and the 13th day of the other months. [< F < L *idus* < Etruscan]

id·i·o·cy (id'i·ə·si), *n., pl.* **-cies. 1.** being an idiot. **2.** very great stupidity or folly.

id·i·om (id'i·əm), *n.* **1.** phrase or expression whose meaning cannot be understood from the ordinary meanings of the words in it. "How do you do?" and "I have caught cold" are English idioms. **2.** dialect. **3.** a people's way of expressing themselves. **4.** individual manner of expression in music, art, etc. [< LL < Gk. *idioma,* ult. < *idios* one's own]

id·i·o·mat·ic (id'i·ə·mat'ik), **id·i·o·mat·i·cal** (-ə·kal), *adj.* **1.** using an idiom or idioms. **2.** of or concerning idioms. **3.** characteristic of a particular language. —**id'i·o·mat'i·cal·ly,** *adv.*

id·i·o·syn·cra·sy (id'i·ō·sing'krə·si; -sin'-), *n., pl.* **-sies.** personal peculiarity. [< Gk., < *idios* one's own + *synkrasis* temperament < *syn* together + *kerannymi* mix] —**id·i·o·syn·crat·ic** (id'i·ō·sin·krat'ik), *adj.*

id·i·ot (id'i·ət), *n.* **1.** person born with such slight mental capacities that he can never learn to read or count. **2.** a very stupid or foolish person. **3.** *Psychol.* the lowest grade of feeblemindedness, ranging in IQ from 0 to 25. [< L < Gk. *idiotes,* orig., private person < *idios* one's own]

id·i·ot·ic (id'i·ot'ik), *adj.* of or like an idiot; very stupid or foolish. —**id'i·ot'i·cal·ly,** *adv.*

i·dle (i'dəl), *adj.,* **i·dler, i·dlest,** *v.,* **i·dled, i·dling.** —*adj.* **1.** doing nothing; not busy; not working: *idle hands, money lying idle.* **2.** not willing to do things; lazy. **3.** useless; worthless: *idle pleasures.* **4.** without any good reason, cause, or foundation: *idle fears.* —*v.* **1.** be idle; do nothing. **2.** waste (time); spend. **3.** *Mach.* run slowly without transmitting power. [OE *idel*] —**i'dle·ness,** *n.* —**i'dler,** *n.* —**i'dly,** *adv.* —**Syn.** *adj.* **1.** inactive, unemployed. **2.** indolent.

I·dle·wild (i'dəl·wild), *n.* a major international airport, in New York City. Also called **Kennedy International Airport.**

Idol

i·dol (i'dəl), *n.* **1.** image or other object worshiped as a god. **2.** *Bible.* a false god. **3.** object of extreme devotion. **4.** a fallacy. [< OF < L < Gk. *eidolon* image < *eidos* form]

i·dol·a·ter (i·dol'ə·tər), *n.* **1.** person who worships idols. **2.** admirer; adorer; devotee.

i·dol·a·trous (i·dol'ə·trəs), *adj.* **1.** worshiping idols. **2.** having to do with idolatry. **3.** blindly adoring. —**i·dol'a·trous·ly,** *adv.* —**i·dol'a·trous·ness,** *n.*

i·dol·a·try (i·dol'ə·tri), *n., pl.* **-tries. 1.** worship of idols. **2.** worship of a person or thing; extreme devotion. [< OF < L < Gk., < *eidolon* image + *latreia* service]

i·dol·ize (i'dəl·iz), *v.,* **-ized, -iz·ing. 1.** worship as an idol. **2.** love or admire very much; be extremely devoted to. —**i'dol·i·za'tion,** *n.*

i·dyl, i·dyll (i'dəl), *n.* **1.** a short description in poetry or prose of a simple and charming scene or event, esp. one connected with country life. **2.** scene or event suitable for such a description. [< L < Gk. *eidyllion,* dim. of *eidos* form]

i·dyl·lic (i·dil'ik), *adj.* suitable for an idyl; simple and charming. —**i·dyl'li·cal·ly,** *adv.*

i.e., that is; that is to say. ≯ *i.e.* is the abbreviation for Latin *id est,* "that is." It is not common now outside rather routine reference exposition, *that is* being ordinarily written.

if (if), *conj.* **1.** supposing that; on condition that; in case that: *if you are going, leave now.* **2.** whether: *I wonder if he will go.* **3.** *Colloq.* although; even though: *if he is little, he is strong.* **4.** as if, as it would be if. —*n.* condition; supposition. [OE *gif*] ≯ **if. 1.** *If* is a subordinating conjunction introducing a condition: *If the weather holds good, we shall stay another week.* **2.** if and whether. In formal usage, *if* is used for conditions, and *whether,* usually with *or,* is used, though not consistently, in indirect questions (*He asked whether the mail had come*), in conditions, and in expressions of doubt (*We could not be sure whether the State was Republican or Democratic*).

if·fy (if'i), *adj. Colloq.* **1.** full of ifs. **2.** doubtful.

ig·loo, ig·lu (ig'lü), *n., pl.* **-loos; -lus.** a dome-shaped hut used by Eskimos, often built of blocks of hard snow. [< Eskimo, house]

Ig·na·tius Loy·o·la (ig·nā'shəs loi·ō'lə), Saint, 1491–1556, Spanish monk who founded the Jesuit order.

ig·ne·ous (ig'ni·əs), *adj.* **1.** of fire; pertaining to fire. **2.** *Geol.* produced by fire, intense heat, or volcanic action. [< L, < *ignis* fire]

ig·nis fat·u·us (ig'nis fach'ü·əs), *pl.* **ig·nes fat·u·i** (ig'nēz fach'ü·i). **1.** a flitting phosphorescent light seen at night chiefly over marshy ground; will-o'-the-wisp. **2.** something deluding or misleading.

ig·nite (ig·nit'), *v.,* **-nit·ed, -nit·ing. 1.** set on fire. **2.** *Chem.* make intensely hot; cause to glow with heat. **3.** take fire; begin to burn. [< L, < *ignis* fire] —**ig·nit'a·ble, ig·nit'i·ble,** *adj.* —**ig·nit'a·bil'i·ty, ig·nit'i·bil'i·ty,** *n.* —**ig·nit'er, ig·ni'tor,** *n.*

ig·ni·tion (ig·nish'ən), *n.* **1.** a setting on fire. **2.** a catching on fire. **3.** apparatus for igniting the explosive vapor in the cylinders of an internal-combustion engine.

ig·no·ble (ig·nō'bəl), *adj.* **1.** mean; base; without honor. **2.** of low birth. [< L, < *in-* not + Old L *gnobilis* noble] —**ig'no·bil'i·ty, ig·no'ble·ness,** *n.* —**ig·no'bly,** *adv.* —**Syn. 1.** degraded, dishonorable, contemptible. —**Ant. 1.** noble.

ig·no·min·i·ous (ig'nə·min'i·əs), *adj.* **1.** shameful; disgraceful; humiliating. **2.** contemptible. —**ig'no·min'i·ous·ly,** *adv.* —**ig'no·min'i·ous·ness,** *n.*

ig·no·min·y (ig'nə·min'i), *n., pl.* **-min·ies. 1.** loss of one's good name; public shame and disgrace; dishonor. **2.** shameful action or conduct. [< L *ignominia* < *in-* not + *nomen* name]

ig·no·ra·mus (ig'nə·rā'məs; -ram'əs), *n., pl.* **-mus·es.** an ignorant person. [< L, we do not know]

ig·no·rance (ig'nə·rəns), *n.* lack of knowledge; quality or condition of being ignorant.

ig·no·rant (ig'nə·rənt), *adj.* **1.** knowing little or nothing; without knowledge. A person who has not had much chance to learn may be ignorant but not stupid. **2.** uninformed; unaware: *he was ignorant of the fact that the town had been destroyed.* **3.** showing lack of knowledge: *an ignorant remark.* [< L *ignorans* not knowing] —**ig'no·rant·ly,** *adv.* —**Syn. 1.** untaught, uneducated. **2.** unknowing. —**Ant. 1.** learned.

ig·nore (ig·nôr'; -nor'), *v.,* **-nored, -nor·ing.** pay no attention to; disregard. [< L *ignorare* not know] —**ig·nor'er,** *n.* —**Syn.** overlook.

Ig·o·rot (ig'ə·rōt'), **Ig·or·ro·te** (-rō'tē), *n., pl.* **-rot, -rots; -ro·te, -ro·tes. 1.** member of a Malay tribe of the Philippine Islands. **2.** their language.

i·gua·na (i·gwä'nə), *n.* a large climbing lizard found in tropical America. See picture on next page. [< Sp. < Carib] —**i·gua·ni·an** (i·gwä'ni·ən), *adj., n.*

IGY, International Geophysical Year.

IHS, first three letters of the name of Jesus in Greek.

i·kon (ī′kon), *n*. icon.

Il, *Chem*. illinium.

Il Du·ce (ēl dū′chā). See duce (def. 2).

il·e·i·tis (il′i·ī′tis), *n*. inflammation of the ileum, due to infection, a tumor, or other cause and involving partial or complete blocking of the passage of food through the small intestine.

il·e·um (il′i·əm), *n. Anat*. the lowest part of the small intestine. [< LL, var. of *ilium*, sing. to L *ilia* loins, entrails] —**il·e·ac** (il′i·ak), *adj*.

i·lex (ī′leks), *n*. 1. holm oak. 2. holly. [< L]

il·i·ac (il′i·ak), *adj. Anat*. of or having to do with the ilium; near the ilium.

Il·i·ad (il′i·əd), *n*. a long Greek epic poem

Iguana (ab. 5 ft. long)

about the siege of Ilium, or Troy, supposedly written by Homer. —**Il·i·ad·ic** (il′i·ad′ik), *adj*.

il·i·um (il′i·əm), *n., pl*. il·i·a (il′i·ə). *Anat*. the broad upper portion of the hipbone. [< NL < LL, sing. to L *ilia* flank, groin]

Il·i·um (il′i·əm), *n*. ancient Troy.

ilk (ilk), *adj*. Archaic. same. —*n*. 1. *Colloq*. family; kind; sort. 2. of that ilk, *Colloq*. a. of the same place or name. b. of that kind or sort. [OE *ilca* same]

ill (il), *adj*., worse, worst, *n., adv*. —*adj*. 1. having some disease; not well; sick. 2. bad; evil; harmful: *an ill deed*. 3. unfavorable; unfortunate: *an ill wind*. 4. unkind; harsh; cruel. 5. ill at ease, uncomfortable. —*n*. 1. sickness; disease. 2. an evil; a harm; a trouble. —*adv*. 1. badly; harmfully. 2. unfavorably; unfortunately. 3. in an unkind manner; harshly; cruelly. 4. with trouble or difficulty; scarcely. [< Scand. *illr*] ➤ **ill**. See sick for usage note.

I'll (īl), 1. I shall. 2. I will.

Ill., Illinois.

ill., illustrated; illustration.

ill-ad·vised (il′əd·vīzd′), *adj*. acting or done without enough consideration; unwise. —**ill-ad·vis·ed·ly** (il′əd·vīz′id·li), *adv*.

ill-bred (il′bred′), *adj*. badly brought up; rude.

ill breeding, bad manners; rudeness.

ill-con·sid·ered (il′kən·sid′ərd), *adj*. unwise.

ill-dis·posed (il′dis·pōzd′), *adj*. unfriendly.

il·le·gal (i·lē′gəl), *adj*. not lawful; against the law; forbidden by law. —**il·le′gal·ly**, *adv*. —**il·le′gal·ness**, *n*. —Syn. unlawful, illicit.

il·le·gal·i·ty (il′ē·gal′ə·ti), *n., pl*. **-ties**. 1. unlawfulness. 2. an illegal act.

il·leg·i·ble (i·lej′ə·bəl), *adj*. very hard or impossible to read. —**il·leg′i·bil′i·ty, il·leg′i·ble·ness**, *n*. —**il·leg′i·bly**, *adv*.

il·le·git·i·mate (il′ə·jit′ə·mit), *adj*. 1. born of parents who are not married to each other. 2. not according to the law or the rules. —**il′le·git′i·ma·cy, il′le·git′i·mate·ness**, *n*. —**il′le·git′i·mate·ly**, *adv*.

ill-fat·ed (il′fāt′id), *adj*. 1. sure to have a bad fate or end. 2. unlucky.

ill-fa·vored, *esp. Brit*. **ill-fa·voured** (il′fā′vərd), *adj*. 1. ugly. 2. offensive. —**ill′-fa′vored·ly**, *esp. Brit*. **ill′-fa′voured·ly**, *adv*. —**ill′-fa′vored·ness**, *esp. Brit*. **ill′-fa′voured·ness**, *n*.

ill-found·ed (il′foun′did), *adj*. without a good reason or sound basis.

ill-got·ten (il′got′ən), *adj*. acquired by evil or unfair means; dishonestly obtained.

ill health, poor health.

ill humor, *esp. Brit*. **ill humour,** cross, unpleasant temper or mood.

ill-hu·mored, *esp. Brit*. **ill-hu·moured** (il′hū′mərd; -ū′-), *adj*. cross; unpleasant. —**ill′-hu′mored·ly**, *esp. Brit*. **ill′-hu′moured·ly**, *adv*. —**ill′-hu′mored·ness**, *esp. Brit*. **ill′-hu′moured·ness**, *n*.

il·lib·er·al (i·lib′ər·əl), *adj*. 1. not liberal; narrow-minded; prejudiced. 2. stingy; miserly. 3. without liberal culture. —**il·lib′er·al′i·ty, il·lib′er·al·ness**, *n*. —**il·lib′er·al·ly**, *adv*.

il·lic·it (i·lis′it), *adj*. not permitted by law; forbidden. —**il·lic′it·ly**, *adv*. —**il·lic′it·ness**, *n*.

il·lim·it·a·ble (i·lim′it·ə·bəl), *adj*. limitless; boundless; infinite. —**il·lim′it·a·bil′i·ty, il·lim′it·a·ble·ness**, *n*. —**il·lim′it·a·bly**, *adv*.

il·lin·i·um (i·lin′i·əm), *n. Chem*. promethium. [< NL; named after *Illinois*]

Il·li·nois (il′ə·noi′; -noiz′), *n*. 1. a Middle Western State of the United States. *Capital*: Springfield. *Abbrev*.: Ill. 2. *Am*. member of an American Indian tribe formerly living between the Mississippi and Wabash rivers. —*adj*. of this tribe. —**Il′li·nois′an**, *adj., n. Am*.

il·lit·er·a·cy (i·lit′ər·ə·si), *n., pl*. **-cies**. 1. inability to read or write. 2. lack of education. 3. error in speaking or writing, caused by ignorance.

il·lit·er·ate (i·lit′ər·it), *adj*. 1. unable to read or write. 2. lacking in education. 3. showing lack of culture. —*n*. an illiterate person. —**il·lit′er·ate·ly**, *adv*. —**il·lit′er·ate·ness**, *n*.

ill-judged (il′jujd′), *adj*. unwise; rash.

ill-man·nered (il′man′ərd), *adj*. having or showing bad manners; impolite; rude. —**ill′-man′nered·ly**, *adv*. —**ill′-man′nered·ness**, *n*.

ill nature, crossness; disagreeableness; spite. —**ill-na·tured** (il′nā′chərd), *adj*. —**ill′-na′tured·ly**, *adv*. —**ill′-na′tured·ness**, *n*.

ill·ness (il′nis), *n*. sickness; disease.

il·log·i·cal (i·loj′ə·kəl), *adj*. not logical; not reasonable. —**il·log′i·cal′i·ty, il·log′i·cal·ness**, *n*. —**il·log′i·cal·ly**, *adv*. —Syn. unreasonable, irrational, unsound, fallacious.

ill-spent (il′spent′), *adj*. spent badly; wasted.

ill-starred (il′stärd′), *adj*. unlucky; disastrous.

ill-suit·ed (il′süt′id; -sūt′-), *adj*. unsuitable.

ill temper, bad temper or disposition; crossness. —**ill-tem·pered** (il′tem′pərd), *adj*. —**ill′-tem′pered·ly**, *adv*. —**ill′-tem′pered·ness**, *n*.

ill-timed (il′tīmd′), *adj*. inappropriate.

ill-treat (il′trēt′), *v*. treat badly or cruelly; do harm to; abuse. —**ill′-treat′ment**, *n*.

il·lu·mi·nant (i·lü′mə·nənt), *adj*. giving light. —*n*. something that gives light.

il·lu·mi·nate (i·lü′mə·nāt), *v*., **-nat·ed, -nat·ing**. 1. light up; make bright. 2. make clear; explain. 3. decorate with lights. 4. decorate with gold, colors, pictures, and designs: *some old books and manuscripts were illuminated*. 5. enlighten; inform; instruct. 6. make illustrious. [< L *illuminatus*, ult. < *in-* in + *lumen* light] —**il·lu′mi·nat′ing, il·lu′mi·na′tive**, *adj*. —**il·lu′mi·nat′ing·ly**, *adv*. —**il·lu′mi·na′tor**, *n*.

il·lu·mi·na·tion (i·lü′mə·nā′shən), *n*. 1. a lighting up; a making bright. 2. amount of light; light. 3. a making clear; explanation. 4. decoration with lights. 5. decoration of books and letters with gold, colors, pictures, and designs. 6. enlightenment.

il·lu·mine (i·lü′mən), *v*., **-mined, -min·ing**. make or become bright; illuminate; light up. —**il·lu′mi·na·ble**, *adj*.

illus., illust., illustrated; illustration.

ill-use (*v*. il′ūz′; *n*. il′ūs′), *v*., **-used, -us·ing**, *n*. —*v*. treat badly, cruelly, or unfairly. —*n*. Also, ill′-us′age. bad, cruel, or unfair treatment.

il·lu·sion (i·lü′zhən), *n*. 1. appearance which is not real; misleading appearance. 2. a false impression or perception. 3. a false idea, notion, or belief. 4. thing that deceives by giving a false impression or idea: *an optical illusion*. [< L *illusio* < *illudere* mock] —**il·lu′sion·al**, *adj*. ➤ **Illusion, allusion** are sometimes confused. *Illusion* is "a misleading appearance," as in *an illusion of wealth*; *allusion* is a reference to something written or to someone or something: *He made allusions to recent events without recounting them*.

Optical illusion.
The verticals appear to converge and diverge under the influence of the crosspieces.

il·lu·sive (i·lü′siv), *adj*. due to an illusion;

unreal; misleading; deceptive. —il·lu′sive·ly, *adv.* —il·lu′sive·ness, *n.* —Syn. delusive.

il·lu·so·ry (i·lü′sə·ri), *adj.* illusive. —il·lu′so·ri·ly, *adv.* —il·lu′so·ri·ness, *n.*

il·lus·trate (il′əs·trāt; i·lus′-), *v.,* -trat·ed, -trat·ing. 1. make clear or explain by stories, examples, comparisons, etc. 2. provide with pictures, diagrams, maps, etc., that explain or decorate. [< L *illustratus* lighted up, ult. < *in*- in + *lustrum* purification] —il′lus·tra′tor, *n.* —Syn. 1. demonstrate, elucidate, exemplify.

il·lus·tra·tion (il′əs·trā′shən), *n.* 1. picture, diagram, map, etc., used to explain or decorate something. 2. story, example, comparison, etc., used to make clear or explain something. 3. act or process of illustrating.

il·lus·tra·tive (i·lus′trə·tiv; il′əs·trā′-), *adj.* illustrating; used to illustrate; helping to explain. —il·lus′tra·tive·ly, *adv.*

il·lus·tri·ous (i·lus′tri·əs), *adj.* very famous; outstanding. [< L *illustris* lighted up, bright] —il·lus′tri·ous·ly, *adv.* —il·lus′tri·ous·ness, *n.* —Syn. distinguished, renowned, eminent.

ill will, unkind or unfriendly feeling; dislike; hate. —ill′-willed′, *adj.*

I'm (īm), I am.

im·age (im′ij), *n., v.,* -aged, -ag·ing. —*n.* 1. likeness; picture; copy. 2. likeness made of stone, wood, etc.; statue. 3. picture in the mind; idea. Your memory or imagination forms images of people and things that you do not actually see. 4. description or figure of speech that helps the mind to form forceful or beautiful pictures. Poetry often contains images. 5. *Physics.* picture of an object produced by a mirror, lens, etc. 6. the impression that a person, company, etc., makes or wishes to make upon the public or a segment of it. —*v.* 1. form an image of. 2. reflect as a mirror does. 3. picture in one's mind; imagine. 4. symbolize. [< OF < L *imago*]

im·age·ry (im′ij·ri), *n., pl.* -ries. 1. pictures in the mind; things imagined. 2. descriptions and figures of speech that help the mind to form forceful or beautiful pictures. 3. images; statues. —im·a·ge·ri·al (im′ə·jir′i·əl), *adj.*

i·mag·i·na·ble (i·maj′ə·nə·bəl), *adj.* that can be imagined. —i·mag′i·na·ble·ness, *n.* —i·mag′i·na·bly, *adv.*

i·mag·i·nar·y (i·maj′ə·ner′i), *adj.* existing only in the imagination; not real: *the equator is an imaginary line.* —i·mag′i·nar′i·ly, *adv.*

i·mag·i·na·tion (i·maj′ə·nā′shən), *n.* 1. an imagining; power of forming pictures in the mind of things not present to the senses. 2. ability to create new things or ideas or to combine old ones in new forms. 3. creation of the mind; fancy. —i·mag′i·na′tion·al, *adj.*

i·mag·i·na·tive (i·maj′ə·nā′tiv; -nə·tiv), *adj.* 1. showing imagination. 2. able to imagine well; fond of imagining. 3. of imagination. 4. fanciful. —i·mag′i·na′tive·ly, *adv.* —i·mag′i·na′tive·ness, *n.* —Syn. 1, 2. inventive, creative.

i·mag·ine (i·maj′ən), *v.,* -ined, -in·ing. 1. picture in one's mind; have an idea: *we can hardly imagine life without electricity.* 2. suppose: *imagine this to be the case.* 3. guess: *I cannot imagine what you mean.* 4. think; believe: *she imagined someone was watching her.* [< F < L, < *imago* image] —Syn. 2. assume, surmise. 3. conjecture. 4. fancy.

im·ag·ism (im′ij·iz·əm), *n.* theory or practice of the imagists.

im·ag·ist (im′ij·ist), *n.* poet who expresses his ideas and feelings by images or word pictures. Most imagists use free verse. —im′ag·is′tic, *adj.*

i·ma·go (i·mā′gō), *n., pl.* i·ma·gos, i·mag·i·nes (i·maj′ə·nēz). *Zool.* insect in the final adult, esp. winged, stage. [< L, image]

im·be·cile (im′bə·səl), *n.* 1. person of very weak mind: *an imbecile is almost an idiot.* 2. a very stupid or foolish person. —*adj.* 1. very weak in mind. 2. very stupid or foolish. [< F < L *imbecillus* weak < *in*- without + *bacillus* staff] —im′be·cile·ly, *adv.* —im′be·cil′i·ty, *n.*

im·bed (im·bed′), *v.,* -bed·ded, -bed·ding. embed.

im·bibe (im·bīb′), *v.,* -bibed, -bib·ing. 1. drink; drink in. 2. absorb. 3. take into one's mind. [< L, < *in*- in + *bibere* drink] —im·bib′er, *n.*

im·bri·cate (*v.* im′brə·kāt; *adj.* im′brə·kit, -kāt), *v.,* -cat·ed, -cat·ing, *adj.* —*v.* overlap. —*adj.* overlapping. [< L *imbricatus* < *imbrex* hollow tile] —im′bri·cate·ly, *adv.* —im′bri·ca′tion, *n.* —im′bri·ca′tive, *adj.*

im·bro·glio (im·brōl′yō), *n., pl.* -glios. 1. a difficult situation. 2. a complicated disagreement. [< Ital.]

im·brue (im·brü′), *v.,* -brued, -bru·ing. wet; stain, esp. with blood. [< OF *embreuver* give to drink, ult. < L *bibere* drink] —im·brue′ment, *n.*

im·bue (im·bū′), *v.,* -bued, -bu·ing. 1. fill; inspire: *he imbued his son's mind with the ambition to succeed.* 2. fill with moisture or color. [< L *imbuere*] —im·bue′ment, *n.*

imit., imitative (def. 2).

im·i·ta·ble (im′ə·tə·bəl), *adj.* that can be imitated. —im′i·ta·bil′i·ty, *n.*

im·i·tate (im′ə·tāt), *v.,* -tat·ed, -tat·ing. 1. try to be like; follow the example of: *the little boy imitated his father.* 2. make or do something like; copy: *a parrot imitates the sounds it hears.* 3. act like: *John imitated a bear.* 4. be like; look like; resemble: *wood painted to imitate stone.* [< L *imitatus*] —im′i·ta′tor, *n.* —Syn. 2. reproduce. 3. mimic, ape.

im·i·ta·tion (im′ə·tā′shən), *n.* 1. an imitating: *we learn many things by imitation.* 2. a copy: *give us an imitation of a rooster crowing.* —*adj.* not real: *imitation pearls.* —im′i·ta′tion·al, *adj.*

im·i·ta·tive (im′ə·tā′tiv), *adj.* 1. likely or inclined to imitate others: *monkeys are imitative.* 2. imitating; showing imitation. *Bang* and *whiz* are imitative words. 3. not real. —im′i·ta′tive·ly, *adv.* —im′i·ta′tive·ness, *n.*

im·mac·u·late (i·mak′yə·lit), *adj.* 1. without a spot or stain; absolutely clean. 2. without sin; pure. 3. having no faults, flaws, or errors. [< L, < *in*- not + *macula* spot] —im·mac′u·la·cy, im·mac′u·late·ness, *n.* —im·mac′u·late·ly, *adv.* —Syn. 1. spotless, stainless.

Immaculate Conception, *Rom. Cath. Ch.* doctrine that the Virgin Mary was conceived free of original sin.

im·ma·nence (im′ə·nəns), im·ma·nen·cy (-nən·si), *n.* state of being immanent.

im·ma·nent (im′ə·nənt), *adj.* dwelling within. [< L, < *in*- in + *manere* stay] —im′ma·nent·ly, *adv.*

Im·man·u·el (i·man′yū·əl), *n.* Christ. Also, Emmanuel.

im·ma·te·ri·al (im′ə·tir′i·əl), *adj.* 1. not important; insignificant. 2. not material; spiritual. —im′ma·te′ri·al·ly, *adv.* —im′ma·te′ri·al·ness, *n.* —Syn. 1. unimportant, unessential.

im·ma·ture (im′ə·chúr′; -túr′; -tyúr′), *adj.* not mature; not ripe; not full-grown; not fully developed. —im′ma·ture′ly, *adv.* —im′ma·tur′i·ty, im′ma·ture′ness, *n.*

im·meas·ur·a·ble (i·mezh′ər·ə·bəl), *adj.* too vast to be measured; boundless; without limits. —im·meas′ur·a·bil′i·ty, im·meas′ur·a·ble·ness, *n.* —im·meas′ur·a·bly, *adv.*

im·me·di·a·cy (i·mē′di·ə·si), *n.* a being immediate.

im·me·di·ate (i·mē′di·it), *adj.* 1. coming at once; without delay: *an immediate reply.* 2. with nothing between: *in immediate contact.* 3. direct: *the immediate result.* 4. closest; nearest: *my immediate neighbor.* 5. close; near: *the immediate neighborhood.* 6. pertaining to the present: *our immediate plans.* [< LL *immediatus,* ult. < L *in*- not + *medius* in the middle] —im′me′di·ate·ness, *n.*

im·me·di·ate·ly (i·mē′di·it·li), *adv.* 1. at once; without delay. 2. with nothing between. 3. next. 4. directly.

im·me·mo·ri·al (im′ə·mô′ri·əl; -mō′-), *adj.* extending back beyond the bounds of memory; extremely old. —im′me·mo′ri·al·ly, *adv.*

im·mense (i·mens′), *adj.* 1. very big; huge; vast. 2. *Slang.* very good. [< L, < *in-* not + *mensus* measured] —**im·mense′ly**, *adv.* —**im·mense′ness**, *n.* —Syn. 1. enormous.

im·men·si·ty (i·men′sə·ti), *n., pl.* **-ties.** 1. very great or boundless extent; vastness. 2. infinite space or existence.

im·merse (i·mèrs′), *v.,* **-mersed, -mers·ing.** 1. plunge (something) into a liquid. 2. baptize by dipping (a person) under water. 3. involve deeply; absorb: *immersed in business affairs.* [< L *immersus* < *in-* in + *mergere* plunge] —**im·mer′sion** (i·mèr′shən; -zhən), *n.* —Syn. 1. submerge, duck, dip. 3. engross, occupy.

im·mi·grant (im′ə·grənt), *n.* person who comes into a foreign country or region to live: *Canada has many immigrants from Europe.* —*adj.* immigrating.

im·mi·grate (im′ə·grāt), *v.,* **-grat·ed, -grat·ing.** come into a foreign country or region to live. [< L, < *in-* into + *migrare* move] —**im′mi·gra′tor,** *n.* ► See emigrate for usage note.

im·mi·gra·tion (im′ə·grā′shən), *n.* 1. a coming into a foreign country or region to live. 2. immigrants: *the immigration of 1918.*

im·mi·nence (im′ə·nəns), **im·mi·nen·cy** (-nən·si), *n.* 1. state or fact of being imminent. 2. thing that is imminent; evil or danger about to occur.

im·mi·nent (im′ə·nənt), *adj.* 1. likely to happen soon; about to occur. 2. overhanging. [< L *imminens* overhanging] —**im′mi·nent·ly**, *adv.* —Syn. 1. impending.

im·mis·ci·ble (i·mis′ə·bəl), *adj.* incapable of being mixed. —**im·mis′ci·bil′i·ty**, *n.* —**im·mis′ci·bly**, *adv.*

im·mo·bile (i·mō′bəl; -bēl), *adj.* 1. not movable; firmly fixed. 2. not moving; not changing; motionless. —**im·mo·bil·i·ty** (im′ō·bil′ə·ti), *n.*

im·mo·bi·lize (i·mō′bə·līz), *v.,* **-lized, -liz·ing.** make immobile. —**im·mo′bi·li·za′tion**, *n.*

im·mod·er·ate (i·mod′ər·it), *adj.* not moderate; too much; going too far; extreme; more than is right or proper. —**im·mod′er·ate·ly**, *adv.* —**im·mod′er·ate·ness**, *n.* —Syn. excessive, intemperate, exorbitant, inordinate.

im·mod·est (i·mod′ist), *adj.* 1. bold and rude. 2. indecent; improper. —**im·mod′est·ly**, *adv.* —Syn. 1. forward, impudent. 2. lewd, obscene.

im·mod·es·ty (i·mod′is·ti), *n.* 1. lack of modesty; boldness and rudeness. 2. lack of decency; improper behavior.

im·mo·late (im′ə·lāt), *v.,* **-lat·ed, -lat·ing.** 1. kill as a sacrifice. 2. sacrifice. [< L *immolatus* sacrificed, orig., sprinkled with sacrificial meal < *in-* on + *mola* sacrificial meal] —**im′mo·la′tion**, *n.* —**im′mo·la′tor**, *n.*

im·mor·al (i·môr′əl; i·mor′-), *adj.* 1. morally wrong; wicked. Lying and stealing are immoral. 2. lewd; unchaste. —**im·mor′al·ly**, *adv.*

im·mo·ral·i·ty (im′ə·ral′ə·ti), *n., pl.* **-ties.** 1. wickedness; wrongdoing; vice. 2. lewdness; unchastity. 3. an immoral act.

im·mor·tal (i·môr′təl), *adj.* 1. living forever; never dying; everlasting. 2. perpetual; lasting; constant. 3. remembered or famous forever. 4. heavenly; divine. —*n.* 1. an immortal being. 2. Usually, immortals. one of the gods of ancient Greek and Roman mythology. 3. person remembered or famous forever: *Shakespeare is one of the immortals.* —**im·mor′tal·ly**, *adv.* —Syn. *adj.* 1. eternal, endless.

im·mor·tal·i·ty (im′ôr·tal′ə·ti), *n.* 1. endless life; living forever. 2. fame that lasts forever.

im·mor·tal·ize (i·môr′təl·īz), *v.,* **-ized, -iz·ing.** 1. make immortal. 2. give everlasting fame to. —**im·mor′tal·i·za′tion**, *n.* —**im·mor′tal·iz′er**, *n.*

im·mov·a·ble (i·müv′ə·bəl), *adj.* 1. that cannot be moved; firmly fixed. 2. not moving; not changing position; motionless. 3. firm; steadfast; unyielding. 4. unfeeling; impassive. —*n.* **immovables**, *Law.* land, buildings, and other property that cannot be carried from one place to another. —**im·mov′a·bil′i·ty**, **im·mov′a·ble·ness**, *n.* —**im·mov′a·bly**, *adv.* —Syn. *adj.* 1. stationary. 3. resolute.

im·mune (i·mūn′), *adj.* having immunity: **a.** exempt, as from taxes, laws, etc. **b.** protected against disease, as by inoculation. [< L *immunis*, orig., free from obligation]

im·mu·ni·ty (i·mū′nə·ti), *n., pl.* **-ties.** 1. resistance to disease, poison, etc. 2. freedom or protection from obligation, service, or duty.

im·mu·nize (im′yů·nīz), *v.,* **-nized, -niz·ing.** give immunity to; make immune. —**im′mu·ni·za′tion**, *n.*

im·mu·nol·o·gy (im′yů·nol′ə·ji), *n.* science of the nature and causation of immunity from diseases. —**im·mu·no·log·ic** (i·mū′nə·loj′ik), **im·mu′no·log′i·cal**, *adj.* —**im′mu·nol′o·gist**, *n.*

im·mure (i·myůr′), *v.,* **-mured, -mur·ing.** 1. imprison. 2. confine closely. [< L *in-* in + *murus* wall] —**im·mure′ment**, *n.*

im·mu·ta·ble (i·mū′tə·bəl), *adj.* never changing; unchangeable. —**im·mu′ta·bil′i·ty**, **im·mu′ta·ble·ness**, *n.* —**im·mu′ta·bly**, *adv.* —Syn. unalterable, permanent.

imp (imp), *n.* 1. a young or small devil or demon. 2. a mischievous child. [OE *impe* a shoot, graft, ult. < VL *imputus* < Gk. *emphytos* engrafted]

imp., 1. imperative. 2. imperfect. 3. imperial. 4. import.

im·pact (im′pakt), *n.* the striking (of one thing against another): *the impact of the two swords broke both of them.* [< L *impactus* struck against. See IMPINGE.] —**im·pac′tion**, *n.*

im·pact·ed (im·pak′tid), *adj.* of a tooth, pressed between the jawbone and another tooth.

im·pair (im·pār′), *v.* make worse; damage; weaken. [< OF *empeirer*, ult. < L *in-* + *pejor* worse] —**im·pair′er**, *n.* —**im·pair′ment**, *n.* —Syn. harm, hurt, injure.

im·pale (im·pāl′), *v.,* **-paled, -pal·ing.** 1. pierce through with anything pointed; fasten upon anything pointed. 2. torture or punish by thrusting upon a pointed stake. [< F, ult. < L *in-* on + *palus* stake] —**im·pale′ment**, *n.* —**im·pal′er**, *n.*

im·pal·pa·ble (im·pal′pə·bəl), *adj.* 1. that cannot be perceived by the sense of touch: *sunbeams are impalpable.* 2. very hard for the mind to grasp: *impalpable distinctions.* —**im·pal′pa·bil′i·ty**, *n.* —**im·pal′pa·bly**, *adv.*

im·pan·el (im·pan′əl), *v.,* **-eled, -el·ing;** *esp.* *Brit.* **-elled, -el·ling.** 1. put on a list for duty on a jury. 2. select a (jury) from the list. Also, **empanel.** —**im·pan′el·ment**, *n.*

im·part (im·pärt′), *v.* 1. give a share in; give: *rich furnishings that impart elegance to a room.* 2. communicate; tell: *impart a secret.* [< L, < *in-* in + *pars* part] —**im′par·ta′tion, im·part′ment**, *n.* —**im·part′er**, *n.* —**im·part′i·ble**, *adj.* —Syn. 1. bestow, convey. 2. relate, reveal.

im·par·tial (im·pär′shəl), *adj.* showing no more favor to one side than to the other; fair; just. —**im·par′tial·ly**, *adv.* —**im·par′tial·ness**, *n.* —Syn. unbiased, unprejudiced.

im·par·ti·al·i·ty (im′pär·shi·al′ə·ti), *n.* fairness; justice.

im·pass·a·ble (im·pas′ə·bəl; -päs′-), *adj.* not passable; so that one cannot go through or across. —**im·pass′a·bil′i·ty**, **im·pass′a·ble·ness**, *n.* —**im·pass′a·bly**, *adv.*

im·passe (im·pas′, -päs′; im′pas, -päs), *n.* 1. position from which there is no escape; deadlock. 2. road or way closed at one end. [< F]

im·pas·si·ble (im·pas′ə·bəl), *adj.* 1. unable to suffer or feel pain. 2. that cannot be harmed. 3. without feeling; impassive. [< L *impassibilis*, ult. < *in-* not + *pati* suffer] —**im·pas′si·ble·ness**, *n.* —**im·pas′si·bly**, *adv.*

im·pas·sioned (im·pash′ənd), *adj.* full of strong feeling; ardent; emotional. —**im·pas′sioned·ly**, *adv.* —**im·pas′sioned·ness**, *n.*

im·pas·sive (im·pas′iv), *adj.* 1. without feeling or emotion; unmoved; indifferent. 2. calm; serene. —**im·pas′sive·ly**, *adv.* —**im·pas′sive·ness**, *n.* —Syn. 1. apathetic, passive.

im·pas·siv·i·ty (im′pa·siv′ə·ti), *n.* state of being impassive.

im·pa·tience (im·pā′shəns), *n.* 1. lack of patience; being impatient. 2. uneasiness and eagerness. 3. unwillingness to bear delay, opposition, pain, bother, etc., calmly.

im·pa·tient (im·pā′shənt), *adj.* **1.** not patient; not willing to bear delay, opposition, pain, bother, etc., calmly. **2.** restless: *the horses were impatient to start in the race.* **3.** showing lack of patience: *an impatient answer.* —**im·pa′tient·ly,** *adv.* —**im·pa′tient·ness,** *n.*

im·peach (im·pēch′), *v.* **1.** call in question: *to impeach a person's honor or accuracy.* **2.** charge with wrongdoing; accuse. **3.** accuse (a public officer) of wrong conduct during office before a competent tribunal: *a judge may be impeached for taking a bribe.* [< OF *empechier* hinder, < L *in-* on + *pedica* shackle] —**im·peach′a·ble,** *adj.* —**im·peach′a·bil′i·ty,** *n.* —**im·peach′er,** *n.* —**im·peach′ment,** *n.*

im·pec·ca·ble (im·pek′ə·bəl), *adj.* **1.** faultless. **2.** sinless. [< LL, < *in-* not + *peccare* sin] —**im·pec′ca·bil′i·ty,** *n.* —**im·pec′ca·bly,** *adv.*

im·pe·cu·ni·os·i·ty (im′pi·kū′ni·os′ə·ti), *n.* lack of money; pennilessness.

im·pe·cu·ni·ous (im′pi·kū′ni·əs), *adj.* having little or no money; penniless; poor. [< L, < *in-* not + *pecunia* money] —**im′pe·cu′ni·ous·ly,** *adv.* —**im′pe·cu′ni·ous·ness,** *n.*

im·ped·ance (im·pēd′əns), *n. Elect.* the apparent resistance in an alternating-current circuit, made up of two components, reactance and true or ohmic resistance.

im·pede (im·pēd′), *v.,* -**ped·ed,** -**ped·ing.** hinder; obstruct. [< L *impedire* < *in-* on + *pes* foot] —**im·ped′er,** *n.* —**im·ped′ing·ly,** *adv.* —**Syn.** hamper, retard.

im·ped·i·ment (im·ped′ə·mənt), *n.* **1.** hindrance. **2.** defect in speech. —**im·ped′i·men′tal,** **im·ped·i·men′ta·ry** (im·ped′ə·men′tə·ri), *adj.*

im·ped·i·men·ta (im·ped′ə·men′tə), *n.pl.* **1.** traveling equipment; baggage. **2.** military supplies carried along with an army. **3.** *Law.* obstacles; hindrances. [< L]

im·pel (im·pel′), *v.,* -**pelled,** -**pel·ling.** **1.** cause to move; drive forward; push along: *the wind impelled the boat to shore.* **2.** drive; force; cause: *hunger impelled the lazy man to work.* [< L, < *in-* on + *pellere* push] —**im·pel′ler,** *n.*

im·pend (im·pend′), *v.* **1.** be likely to happen soon; be near: *when war impends, wise men try to prevent it.* **2.** hang; hang threateningly. [< L, < *in-* over + *pendere* hang]

im·pend·ing (im·pen′ding), *adj.* **1.** likely to happen soon. **2.** overhanging. —**Syn.** **1.** imminent.

im·pen·e·tra·ble (im·pen′ə·trə·bəl), *adj.* **1.** that cannot be entered, pierced, or passed. **2.** not open to ideas, influences, etc. **3.** impossible for the mind to understand; inscrutable. —**im·pen′e·tra·bil′i·ty,** **im·pen′e·tra·ble·ness,** *n.* —**im·pen′e·tra·bly,** *adv.*

im·pen·i·tent (im·pen′ə·tənt), *adj.* not penitent; feeling no sorrow or regret for having done wrong. —**im·pen′i·tence,** **im·pen′i·ten·cy,** **im·pen′i·tent·ness,** *n.* —**im·pen′i·tent·ly,** *adv.*

imper., imperative.

im·per·a·tive (im·per′ə·tiv), *adj.* **1.** not to be avoided; urgent; necessary. **2.** expressing a command; peremptory: *an imperative tone.* **3.** *Gram.* expressing command: *the imperative mood.* —*n.* **1.** a command. **2.** *Gram.* **a.** the imperative mood. **b.** a verb form in this mood. [< L, < *imperare* order] —**im·per′a·ti·val** (im·per′ə·tī′vəl), *adj.* —**im·per′a·tive·ly,** *adv.* —**im·per′a·tive·ness,** *n.* ➤ **imperative.** The imperative has the form of the infinitive: *Go! Please shut the door.*

im·per·a·tor (im′pə·rā′tər), *n.* **1.** an absolute or supreme ruler. **2.** emperor; commander. [< L, < *imperare* command] —**im·per·a·to′ri·al** (im·per′ə·tô′ri·əl; -tō′-), *adj.* —**im·per·a·to′ri·al·ly,** *adv.*

im·per·cep·ti·ble (im′pər·sep′tə·bəl), *adj.* **1.** that cannot be perceived or felt. **2.** very slight; gradual. —**im′per·cep′ti·bil′i·ty,** **im′per·cep′ti·ble·ness,** *n.* —**im′per·cep′ti·bly,** *adv.*

imperf., imperfect.

im·per·fect (im·pér′fikt), *adj.* **1.** not perfect; having some defect or fault. **2.** not complete; lacking some part. **3.** *Gram.* expressing continued or customary action in the past. **4.** *Music.* di-

minished. —*n. Gram.* the imperfect tense or verb form. English has no imperfect, but such forms as *was studying* and *used to study* are like the imperfect in other languages. —**im·per′fect·ly,** *adv.* —**im·per′fect·ness,** *n.*

im·per·fec·tion (im′pər·fek′shən), *n.* **1.** lack of perfection. **2.** fault; defect.

im·per·fo·rate (im·pér′fə·rit; -rāt), **im·per·fo·rat·ed** (-rāt′id), *adj.* **1.** not pierced through with holes. **2.** not separated from other stamps by perforations. —**im·per′fo·ra′tion,** *n.*

im·pe·ri·al (im·pir′i·əl), *adj.* **1.** of or pertaining to an empire or its ruler. **2.** of or having to do with the rule or authority of one country over other countries and colonies. **3.** supreme; majestic; magnificent. **4.** imperious; domineering. **5.** of larger size or better quality. **6.** according to the British standard of weights and measures. —*n.* **1.** a small beard left growing beneath the lower lip. **2.** size of paper, 23 by 31 inches (in England 22 by 30 inches). [< L, < *imperium* empire] —**im·pe′ri·al·ly,** *adv.* —**im·pe′ri·al·ness,** *n.*

imperial gallon, British gallon, equal to about 1¼ U.S. gallons.

im·pe·ri·al·ism (im·pir′i·əl·iz′əm), *n.* **1.** policy of extending the rule or authority of one country over other countries and colonies. **2.** an imperial system of government. —**im·pe′ri·al·ist,** *n.* —**im·pe′ri·al·is′tic,** *adj.* —**im·pe′ri·al·is′ti·cal·ly,** *adv.*

Man wearing an imperial

Imperial Valley, a flat irrigated region in S California.

im·per·il (im·per′əl), *v.,* -**iled,** -**il·ing;** *esp. Brit.* -**illed,** -**il·ling.** put in danger. —**im·per′il·ment,** *n.* —**Syn.** endanger, jeopardize.

im·pe·ri·ous (im·pir′i·əs), *adj.* **1.** haughty; domineering. **2.** imperative; urgent. [< L *imperiosus* commanding. See IMPERATIVE.] —**im·pe′ri·ous·ly,** *adv.* —**im·pe′ri·ous·ness,** *n.* —**Syn. 1.** dictatorial, arrogant, overbearing.

im·per·ish·a·ble (im·per′ish·ə·bəl), *adj.* everlasting; not perishable; indestructible. —**im·per′ish·a·bil′i·ty,** **im·per′ish·a·ble·ness,** *n.* —**im·per′ish·a·bly,** *adv.*

im·per·ma·nent (im·pér′mə·nənt), *adj.* temporary. —**im·per′ma·nence,** **im·per′ma·nen·cy,** *n.* —**im·per′ma·nent·ly,** *adv.*

im·per·me·a·ble (im·pér′mi·ə·bəl), *adj.* **1.** impassable. **2.** impervious. —**im·per′me·a·bil′i·ty,** **im·per′me·a·ble·ness,** *n.* —**im·per′me·a·bly,** *adv.*

impers., impersonal.

im·per·son·al (im·pér′sən·əl; -pérs′nəl), *adj.* **1.** referring to all or any persons, not to any special one: *"first come, first served" is an impersonal remark.* **2.** having no existence as a person: *electricity is an impersonal force.* **3.** *Gram.* of a verb, having nothing but an indefinite *it* for a subject. Example: *rained* in "It rained yesterday."

im·per·son·al·i·ty (im·pér′sən·al′ə·ti), *n., pl.* -**ties. 1.** impersonal character. **2.** impersonal thing, force, etc.

im·per·son·al·ly (im·pér′sən·əl·i; -pérs′nəl·i), *adv.* in an impersonal manner; without personal reference or connection.

im·per·son·ate (im·pér′sən·āt), *v.,* -**at·ed,** -**at·ing. 1.** act the part of: *impersonate Hamlet on the stage.* **2.** pretend to be; mimic the voice, appearance, and manners of: *impersonate a well-known news commentator.* **3.** personify; typify. —**im·per′son·a′tion,** *n.* —**im·per′son·a′tor,** *n.*

im·per·ti·nence (im·pér′tə·nəns), **im·per·ti·nen·cy** (-nən·si), *n., pl.* -**nenc·es;** -**cies. 1.** impertinent quality. **2.** impertinent act or speech. **3.** lack of pertinence; irrelevance. —**Syn. 1.** impudence, insolence.

im·per·ti·nent (im·pér′tə·nənt), *adj.* **1.** saucy; impudent; insolent. **2.** not pertinent; not to the point; out of place. —**im·per′ti·nent·ly,** *adv.* —**Syn. 1.** officious, presumptuous, uncivil. pert. **2.** inappropriate, incongruous, irrelevant.

im·per·turb·a·ble (im′pər·tér′bə·bəl), *adj.*

unexcitable; not easily excited; calm. **—im′per·turb′a·bil′i·ty, im′per·turb′a·ble·ness,** *n.* **—im′per·turb′a·bly,** *adv.*

im·per·vi·ous (im·pér′vi·əs), *adj.* **1.** not letting things pass through; not allowing passage. **2.** not open to argument, suggestions, etc. **—im·per′vi·ous·ly,** *adv.* **—im·per′vi·ous·ness,** *n.*

im·pe·ti·go (im′pə·tī′gō), *n.* an infectious skin disease causing pimples filled with pus. [< L, < *impetere* attack < *in-* + *petere* aim for]

im·pet·u·os·i·ty (im·pech′ú·os′ə·ti), *n.,* *pl.* **-ties.** sudden or rash energy; ardor.

im·pet·u·ous (im·pech′ú·əs), *adj.* **1.** moving with great force or speed. **2.** acting hastily, rashly, or with sudden feeling. **—im·pet′u·ous·ly,** *adv.* **—im·pet′u·ous·ness,** *n.*

im·pe·tus (im′pə·təs), *n.* **1.** force with which a moving body tends to maintain its velocity and overcome resistance. **2.** a driving force; incentive. [< L, attack] **—Syn. 1.** momentum. **2.** stimulus, impulse.

im·pi·e·ty (im·pī′ə·ti), *n.,* *pl.* **-ties. 1.** lack of piety or reverence for God. **2.** lack of respect. **3.** an impious act.

im·pinge (im·pinj′), *v.,* **-pinged, -ping·ing. 1.** hit; strike: *rays of light impinge on the eye.* **2.** encroach; infringe. [< L *impingere* < *in-* on + *pangere* strike] **—im·pinge′ment,** *n.* **—im·ping′er,** *n.*

im·pi·ous (im′pi·əs), *adj.* not pious; not having or not showing reverence for God; wicked; profane. **—im′pi·ous·ly,** *adv.* **—im′pi·ous·ness,** *n.*

imp·ish (imp′ish), *adj.* **1.** of or like an imp. **2.** mischievous. **—imp′ish·ly,** *adv.* **—imp′ish·ness,** *n.*

im·pla·ca·ble (im·plā′kə·bəl; -plak′ə-), *adj.* that cannot be placated, pacified, or appeased. **—im·pla′ca·bil′i·ty, im·pla′ca·ble·ness,** *n.* **—im·pla′ca·bly,** *adv.* **—Syn.** unforgiving, relentless, inexorable.

im·plant (im·plant′; -plänt′), *v.* **1.** instill or fix deeply (a desire, opinion, etc.): *a good teacher implants high ideals in children.* **2.** plant in something. **—im′plan·ta′tion,** *n.* **—im·plant′er,** *n.*

im·ple·ment (*n.* im′plə·mənt; *v.* im′plə·ment), *n.* a useful article of equipment; tool; instrument; utensil, such as a plow, ax, shovel, broom, etc. **—v. 1.** provide with implements or other means. **2.** provide the power and authority necessary to accomplish or put (something) into effect: *implement a directive or policy.* **3.** carry out; get done. [< LL *implementum*, lit., that which fills a need, ult. < *in-* in + *-plere* fill] **—im′ple·men′tal,** *adj.*

im·pli·cate (im′plə·kāt), *v.,* **-cat·ed, -cat·ing. 1.** show to have a part to or be connected; involve: *the thief's confession implicated two other men.* **2.** imply. **3.** entangle. [< L, < *in-* in + *plicare* fold]

im·pli·ca·tion (im′plə·kā′shən), *n.* **1.** an implying or being implied: *admit a thing by implication.* **2.** indirect suggestion; hint: *no implication of dishonesty.* **—im′pli·ca′tion·al,** *adj.*

im·plic·it (im·plis′it), *adj.* **1.** without doubting, hesitating, or asking questions; absolute: *implicit obedience.* **2.** meant, but not clearly expressed or distinctly stated; implied: *implicit consent.* **3.** involved as a necessary part or condition. [< L *implicitus,* pp. of *implicare* IMPLICATE] **—im·plic′it·ly,** *adv.* **—im·plic′it·ness,** *n.* **—Syn. 1.** unquestioning, unreserved. **2.** tacit.

im·plied (im·plīd′), *adj.* involved, indicated, suggested, or understood without express statement. **—im·pli·ed·ly** (im·plī′id·li), *adv.*

im·plore (im·plôr′; -plōr′), *v.,* **-plored, -plor·ing. 1.** beg earnestly for. **2.** beg (a person to do some act). [< L, < *in-* toward + *plorare* cry] **—im′plo·ra′tion,** *n.* **—im·plor·a·to·ry** (im·plôr′ə·tô′ri; im·plōr′ə·tō′ri), *adj.* **—im·plor′er,** *n.* **—im·plor′ing·ly,** *adv.* **—im·plor′ing·ness,** *n.* **—Syn. 1.** beseech, entreat.

im·ply (im·plī′), *v.,* **-plied, -ply·ing. 1.** indicate without saying outright; express indirectly; suggest: *her smile implied that she had forgiven us.* **2.** involve as a necessary part or condition: *speech implies a speaker.* **3.** signify; mean. [< OF *emplier* involve, put (in). See IMPLICATE.] **—Syn.**

1. insinuate. **>** imply, infer. Strictly, a writer or speaker *implies* something in his words or manner; a reader or listener *infers* something from what he reads or hears.

im·po·lite (im′pə·līt′), *adj.* not polite; having or showing bad manners; rude; discourteous. **—im′po·lite′ly,** *adv.* **—im′po·lite′ness,** *n.* **—Syn.** disrespectful, uncivil.

im·pol·i·tic (im·pol′ə·tik), *adj.* not politic; not expedient; unwise. **—im·pol′i·tic·ly,** *adv.* **—im·pol′i·tic·ness,** *n.*

im·pon·der·a·ble (im·pon′dər·ə·bəl), *adj.* without weight that can be felt or measured. **—n.** something imponderable. **—im·pon′der·a·bil′i·ty, im·pon′der·a·ble·ness,** *n.* **—im·pon′der·a·bly,** *adv.*

im·port (*v.* im·pôrt′, -pōrt′, im′pôrt, -pōrt; *n.* im′pôrt, -pōrt), *v.* **1.** bring in from a foreign country for sale or use: *we import coffee from Brazil.* **2.** mean; signify: *tell me what your remark imports.* **3.** be of importance or consequence. **—n. 1.** thing imported: *rubber is a useful import.* **2.** an importing; importation. **3.** meaning: *what is the import of your remark?* **4.** importance. [< L, < *in-* in + *portare* carry] **—im·port′a·ble,** *adj.* **—im·port′a·bil′i·ty,** *n.* **—im·port′er,** *n.*

im·por·tance (im·pôr′təns), *n.* quality or fact of being important; consequence; significance.

im·por·tant (im·pôr′tənt), *adj.* **1.** meaning much; worth noticing or considering; having value or significance. **2.** having social position or influence. **3.** acting or seeming important. [< F < Med.L *importans* being significant < L, bringing on or in. See IMPORT.] **—im·por′tant·ly,** *adv.* **—Syn.** significant, momentous, weighty.

im·por·ta·tion (im′pôr·tā′shən; -pōr-), *n.* **1.** act of importing. **2.** something imported.

im·por·tu·nate (im·pôr′chə·nit), *adj.* asking repeatedly; annoyingly persistent. **—im·por′tu·nate·ly,** *adv.* **—im·por′tu·nate·ness,** *n.*

im·por·tune (im′pôr·tün′; -tün′; im·pôr′chən), *v.,* **-tuned, -tun·ing.** ask urgently or repeatedly; trouble with demands. [< MF < L *importunus* inconvenient] **—im′por·tune′ly,** *adv.* **—im′por·tun′er,** *n.*

im·por·tu·ni·ty (im′pôr·tü′nə·ti; -tū′-), *n.,* *pl.* **-ties.** persistence in asking; act of demanding again and again.

im·pose (im·pōz′), *v.,* **-posed, -pos·ing. 1.** put (a burden, tax, punishment, etc.) on. **2.** force or thrust one's or its authority or influence on another or others. **3.** force or thrust (oneself or one's company) on another or others. **4.** pass off (a thing upon a person) to deceive. **5.** arrange (pages of type) for printing. [< F, < *in-* on + *poser* put, place, POSE] **—im·pos′a·ble,** *adj.* **—im·pos′er,** *n.* **—Syn. 3.** obtrude, presume.

im·pos·ing (im·pōz′ing), *adj.* impressive because of size, appearance, dignity, etc.: *the Capitol is an imposing building.* **—im·pos′ing·ly,** *adv.* **—im·pos′ing·ness,** *n.* **—Syn.** commanding, stately, majestic.

im·po·si·tion (im′pə·zish′ən), *n.* **1.** act or fact of imposing. **2.** tax, duty, task, burden, etc. **3.** an unfair tax, etc. **4.** an imposing upon a person by taking advantage of his good nature. **5.** deception; fraud; trick.

im·pos·si·bil·i·ty (im·pos′ə·bil′ə·ti; im′pos-), *n.,* *pl.* **-ties. 1.** quality of being impossible. **2.** something impossible.

im·pos·si·ble (im·pos′ə·bəl), *adj.* **1.** that cannot be or happen: *the accident seemed impossible.* **2.** not possible to use; not to be done: *few things are impossible.* **3.** that cannot be true: *an impossible rumor.* **4.** not endurable; very objectionable: *an impossible person.* **—im·pos′si·ble·ness,** *n.* **—im·pos′si·bly,** *adv.* **—Syn. 2.** impracticable, unfeasible.

im·post (im′pōst), *n.* **1.** tax on goods brought into a country. **2.** tax; tribute. **—v.** fix duties on. [< OF, ult. < L *in-* on + *ponere* place, put]

im·pos·tor (im·pos′tər), *n.* **1.** person who assumes a false name or character. **2.** deceiver; cheat. [< LL, < L *imponere* impose. See IMPOST.]

im·pos·ture (im·pos′chər), *n.* deception; fraud.

im·po·tence (im′pə·təns), *n.* lack of power; condition or quality of being impotent.

im·po·tent (im′pə·tənt), *adj.* 1. not having power; helpless. 2. lacking in sexual power. —im′po·tent·ly, *adv.* —im′po·tent·ness, *n.* —Syn. 1. weak, feeble, infirm.

im·pound (im·pound′), *v.* 1. shut up in a pen or pound. 2. shut up; enclose; confine. 3. put in the custody of a law court: *the court impounded the documents to use as evidence.* —im·pound′age, *n.* —im·pound′er, *n.*

im·pov·er·ish (im·pov′ər·ish; –pov′rish), *v.* 1. make very poor. 2. exhaust the strength, richness, or resources of. [< OF *empoveriss–*, ult. < L *in–* + *pauper* poor] —im·pov′er·ish·er, *n.* —im·pov′er·ish·ment, *n.*

im·pow·er (im·pou′ər), *v.* empower. —im·pow′er·ment, *n.*

im·prac·ti·ca·ble (im·prak′tə·kə·bəl), *adj.* 1. not working well in practice: *impracticable suggestions.* 2. that cannot be used: *an impracticable road.* —im·prac′ti·ca·bil′i·ty, im·prac′ti·ca·ble·ness, *n.* —im·prac′ti·ca·bly, *adv.*

im·prac·ti·cal (im·prak′tə·kəl), *adj.* not practical. —im·prac·ti·cal·i·ty (im·prak′tə·kal′ə·ti), *n.*

im·pre·cate (im′prə·kāt), *v.*, –cat·ed, –cat·ing. call down (curses, evil, etc.). [< L *imprecatus*, ult. < *in–* on + *prex* prayer] —im′pre·ca′tion, *n.* —im′pre·ca′tor, *n.* —im·pre·ca·to·ry (im′prə·kə·tô′ri; –tō′–), *adj.*

im·preg·na·ble (im·preg′nə·bəl), *adj.* that cannot be overthrown by force; able to resist attack: *an impregnable fortress, an impregnable argument.* [< F, < *in–* not + *prenable* pregnable] —im·preg′na·bil′i·ty, im·preg′na·ble·ness, *n.* —im·preg′na·bly, *adv.*

im·preg·nate (im·preg′nāt), *v.*, –nat·ed, –nat·ing. 1. make pregnant; fertilize. 2. fill (with); saturate. 3. inspire; imbue. [< LL *impraegnatus* made pregnant] —im′preg·na′tion, *n.* —im·preg′na·tor, *n.*

im·pre·sa·ri·o (im′prə·sä′ri·ō), *n.*, *pl.* –sa·ri·os, *Ital.* –sa·ri (–sä′rē). organizer or manager of an opera or concert company. [< Ital., < *impresa* undertaking, ult. < L *in–* on + *prehendere* take] —im′pre·sa′ri·o·ship′, *n.*

im·pre·scrip·ti·ble (im′pri·skrip′tə·bəl), *adj.* existing independently of law or custom; not justly to be taken away or violated. —im′pre·scrip′ti·bil′i·ty, *n.* —im′pre·scrip′ti·bly, *adv.*

im·press[1] (*v.* im·pres′; *n.* im′pres), *v.*, –pressed or (*Archaic*) –prest (–prest), –press·ing, *n.* –*v.* 1. have a strong effect on the mind or feelings of: *a hero impresses us with his courage.* 2. fix in the mind: *she impressed the words to impress them in her memory.* 3. mark by pressing or stamping; imprint. —*n.* 1. impression; mark; stamp. 2. act of impressing. [< L *impressus* < *in–* in + *premere* press] —im·press′er, *n.* —im·press′i·ble, *adj.* —im·press′i·bil′i·ty, *n.*

im·press[2] (im·pres′), *v.*, –pressed or (*Archaic*) –prest, –press·ing. 1. seize by force for public use. 2. force (men) to serve in the navy or army. 3. bring in and use. [< *in–*[2] + *press*[2]] —im·press′ment, *n.*

im·pres·sion (im·presh′ən), *n.* 1. effect produced on a person: *make a bad impression.* 2. idea; notion: *a vague impression.* 3. something produced by pressure; mark, stamp, print, etc.: *impression of a rabbit's feet in the snow.* 4. the total number of copies of a book made at one time. 5. a printed copy.

im·pres·sion·a·ble (im·presh′ən·ə·bəl), *adj.* sensitive to impressions; easily impressed or influenced. —im·pres′sion·a·bil′i·ty, im·pres′sion·a·ble·ness, *n.*

im·pres·sion·ism (im·presh′ən·iz·əm), *n.* 1. method of painting or writing that gives general impressions without much attention to details. 2. method of composing music that expresses impressions and feelings by new and unusual means. —im·pres′sion·ist, *n.* —im·pres′sion·is′tic, *adj.*

im·pres·sive (im·pres′iv), *adj.* able to impress the mind, feelings, conscience, etc.: *an impressive sermon.* —im·pres′sive·ly, *adv.* —im·pres′sive·ness, *n.* —Syn. imposing, commanding, striking.

im·pri·ma·tur (im′pri·mā′tər; –prī–), *n.* 1. an official license to print or publish a book, etc., now usually works sanctioned by the Roman Catholic Church. 2. sanction; approval. [< NL, let it be printed. See IMPRESS[1].]

im·print (*n.* im′print; *v.* im·print′), *n.* 1. mark made by pressure; print: *the imprint of a foot in the sand.* 2. impression; mark: *suffering left its imprint on her face.* 3. a publisher's name, with the place and date of publication, on the title page or at the end of a book. —*v.* 1. mark by pressing or stamping; print: *imprint a postmark on an envelope.* 2. press or impress: *scene imprinted on my memory.* —im·print′er, *n.*

im·pris·on (im·priz′ən), *v.* 1. put in prison; keep in prison. 2. confine closely; restrain. —im·pris′on·ment, *n.*

im·prob·a·ble (im·prob′ə·bəl), *adj.* not probable; not likely to happen; not likely to be true. —im·prob′a·bil′i·ty, im·prob′a·ble·ness, *n.* —im·prob′a·bly, *adv.*

im·promp·tu (im·promp′tü; –tū), *adv.*, *adj.* without previous thought or preparation; offhand. —*n.* improvisation. [< L *in promptu* in readiness] —Syn. *adj.* extempore, improvised.

im·prop·er (im·prop′ər), *adj.* 1. not correct. 2. not suitable. 3. not decent. —im·prop′er·ly, *adv.* —im·prop′er·ness, *n.* —Syn. 2. inappropriate, unfit. 3. indecent, indecorous, unseemly.

improper fraction, fraction greater than 1. *Examples:* ½, ⅘.

im·pro·pri·e·ty (im′prə·prī′ə·ti), *n.*, *pl.* –ties. 1. lack of propriety; quality of being improper. 2. improper conduct. 3. improper act, expression, etc.

im·prove (im·prüv′), *v.*, –proved, –prov·ing. 1. make better. 2. become better: *his health is improving.* 3. *Am.* increase the value of (land or property). 4. use well; make good use of: *improve your time by studying.* 5. improve on, make better; do better than. [< AF *emprouer* < OF *en–* in + *prou* profit] —im·prov′a·ble, *adj.* —im·prov′a·bil′i·ty, im·prov′a·ble·ness, *n.* —im·prov′a·bly, *adv.* —im·prov′er, *n.* —im·prov′ing·ly, *adv.* —Syn. 1. ameliorate, promote. 3. develop. 4. utilize.

im·prove·ment (im·prüv′mənt), *n.* 1. a making better or becoming better. 2. increase in value. 3. change or addition that increases value: *a house with all the modern improvements.* 4. better condition; thing that is better than another; advance. 5. good use.

im·prov·i·dent (im·prov′ə·dənt), *adj.* lacking foresight; not looking ahead; not careful in providing for the future; not thrifty. —im·prov′i·dence, *n.* —im·prov′i·dent·ly, *adv.* —Syn. shiftless, imprudent, wasteful.

im·pro·vise (im′prə·vīz), *v.*, –vised, –vis·ing. 1. compose or utter (verse, music, etc.) without preparation. 2. prepare or provide offhand; extemporize. [< F < Ital. *improvvisare*, ult. < L *in–* not + *pro–* beforehand + *videre* see] —im·prov·i·sa·tion (im′prə·vi·sā′shən; im′prov·ə–), *n.* —im′pro·vi·sa′tion·al, *adj.* —im′pro·vis′er, *n.*

im·pru·dence (im·prü′dəns), *n.* lack of prudence; imprudent behavior.

im·pru·dent (im·prü′dənt), *adj.* not prudent; rash; not discreet. —im·pru′dent·ly, *adv.* —im·pru′dent·ness, *n.* —Syn. indiscreet, ill-advised, heedless.

im·pu·dence (im′pyə·dəns), *n.* lack of shame or modesty; rude boldness.

im·pu·dent (im′pyə·dənt), *adj.* without shame or modesty; offensively impertinent; rudely bold. [< L, < *in–* not + *pudere* be modest] —im′pu·dent·ly, *adv.* —im′pu·dent·ness, *n.* —Syn. insolent, presumptuous. —Ant. modest, meek.

im·pugn (im·pūn′), *v.* call in question; attack by words or arguments; challenge as false. [< OF < L *impugnare* assault < *in–* against + *pugnare* fight] —im·pugn′a·ble, *adj.* —im·pug·na–

tion (im'pug·nā'shən), im·pugn'ment, n. —im·pugn'er, n.

im·pulse (im'puls), n. 1. a sudden, driving force or influence; push: *the impulse of hunger.* 2. effect of a sudden, driving force or influence. 3. a sudden inclination or tendency to act. 4. the stimulating force of desire or emotion: *an angry mob is influenced more by impulse than by reason.* 5. Physiol. a change in living matter that is transmitted, esp. by nerve cells, and influences action in the muscle, gland, or other nerve cells that it reaches. [< L *impulsus* < *impellere* IMPEL] —Syn. 1. thrust, impetus, drive.

im·pul·sion (im·pul'shən), n. 1. an impelling; driving force. 2. impulse. 3. impetus.

im·pul·sive (im·pul'siv), adj. 1. acting upon impulse; easily moved. 2. driving onward; impelling; pushing. —im·pul'sive·ly, adv. —im·pul'sive·ness, n. —Syn. 1. rash, hasty, impetuous.

im·pu·ni·ty (im·pū'nə·ti), n. freedom from punishment, injury, or other bad consequences. [< L *impunitas*, ult. < *in-* without + *poena* punishment]

im·pure (im·pyùr'), adj. 1. not pure; dirty. 2. immoral; corrupt. 3. mixed with something of lower value; adulterated. 4. not of one color, style, etc.; mixed. 5. forbidden by religion as unclean. —im·pure'ly, adv. —im·pure'ness, n. —Syn. 1. filthy, unclean.

im·pu·ri·ty (im·pyùr'ə·ti), n., pl. -ties. 1. lack of purity; being impure. 2. Often, impurities. impure thing or element; thing that makes something else impure.

im·pute (im·pūt'), v., -put·ed, -put·ing. consider as belonging; attribute; charge (a fault, etc.) to a person; blame. [< L, < *in-* in + *putare* reckon] —im·put'a·ble, adj. —im·pu·ta·tion (im'pyù·tā'shən), n. —im·put·a·tive (im·pūt'ə·tiv), adj. —im·put'a·tive·ly, adv. —im·put'a·tive·ness, n. —im·put'er, n.

in (in), prep. In expresses inclusion, situation, presence, existence, position, and action within limits of space, time, state, circumstances, etc. 1. inside; within: *in the box.* 2. into: *go in the house.* 3. with; by: *cover in an envelope.* 4. of; made of; using: *a dress in silk.* 5. from among; out of: *one in a hundred.* 6. because of; for: *act in self-defense.* 7. about; concerning: *a book in American history.* 8. at; during: *in the present time.* 9. while; when: *in crossing the street.* 10. **in that,** because. —adv. 1. in or into some place, position, condition, etc.: *come in.* 2. present, esp. in one's home or office: *he is not in today.* 3. **in for,** unable to avoid; sure to get or have. 4. **in with,** a. friendly with. b. partners with. —adj. that is in; being in. —n. 1. **ins,** people in office; political party in power. 2. **ins and outs,** a. turns and twists; nooks and corners. b. different parts; details. [OE] ➤ **in, into, in to.** *In* generally shows location (literal or figurative); *into* generally shows direction: *He was in the house. He came into the house.* However, *in* is often used for *into:* *He fell in the brook. In to* is the adverb *in* followed by the preposition *to:* *They went into the dining room. They went in to dinner.*

In, Chem. indium.

in-¹, prefix. not; the opposite of; the absence of, as in *inexpensive, inattention.* [< L; *in-* becomes *il-* before *l, im-* before *b, m,* and *p,* and *ir-* before *r*] ➤ *in-* or *un-* prefixed to many words gives them a negative meaning: *inconsiderate, incapable, uneven, unloved.* American and British usage differs in many words. If you are not sure whether a word takes *in-* or *un-* consult this dictionary.

in-², prefix. in; within; into; toward, as in *inborn, indoors, inland.* [OE]

in., inch; inches.

in·a·bil·i·ty (in'ə·bil'ə·ti), n. lack of ability, power, or means; fact or state of being unable.

in ab·sen·tia (in ab·sen'shə), *Latin.* while absent.

in·ac·ces·si·ble (in'ək·ses'ə·bəl), adj. 1. not accessible; that cannot be reached or entered. 2. hard to get at; hard to reach or enter. 3. that cannot be obtained. —in'ac·ces'si·bil'i·ty, in'ac·ces'si·bly, adv.

in·ac·cu·ra·cy (in·ak'yə·rə·si), n., pl. -cies. 1. lack of accuracy. 2. error; mistake.

in·ac·cu·rate (in·ak'yə·rit), adj. not exact; containing mistakes. —in·ac'cu·rate·ly, adv. —in·ac'cu·rate·ness, n. —Syn. inexact, erroneous, faulty.

in·ac·tion (in·ak'shən), n. absence of action; idleness.

in·ac·ti·vate (in·ak'tə·vāt), v., -vat·ed, -vat·ing. make inactive. —in·ac·ti·va·tion (in'ak·tə·vā'shən; in·ak'-), n.

in·ac·tive (in·ak'tiv), adj. not active; idle; sluggish. —in·ac'tive·ly, adv. —in·ac'tiv'i·ty, in·ac'tive·ness, n. —Syn. inert, passive, motionless.

in·ad·e·quate (in·ad'ə·kwit), adj. not adequate; not enough; not as much as is required. —in·ad'e·qua·cy, in·ad'e·quate·ness, n. —in·ad'e·quate·ly, adv.

in·ad·mis·si·ble (in'əd·mis'ə·bəl), adj. 1. not allowable. 2. not to be admitted. —in'ad·mis'si·bil'i·ty, n. —in'ad·mis'si·bly, adv.

in·ad·vert·ence (in'əd·vėr'təns), **in·ad·vert·en·cy** (-tən·si), n., pl. -enc·es, -cies. 1. lack of attention; carelessness. 2. oversight; mistake.

in·ad·vert·ent (in'əd·vėr'tənt), adj. 1. not attentive; heedless; negligent. 2. not done on purpose; caused by oversight. —in'ad·vert'ent·ly, adv. —Syn. 1. thoughtless. 2. unintentional, accidental.

in·ad·vis·a·ble (in'əd·vīz'ə·bəl), adj. not advisable; unwise; not prudent. —in'ad·vis'a·bil'i·ty, in'ad·vis'a·ble·ness, n. —in'ad·vis'a·bly, adv.

in·a·lien·a·ble (in·āl'yən·ə·bəl; -ā'li·ən-), adj. that cannot be given away or taken away. —in·al'ien·a·bil'i·ty, n. —in·al'ien·a·bly, adv.

in·am·o·ra·ta (in·am'ə·rä'tə), n., pl. -tas. girl or woman with whom one is in love; sweetheart. [< Ital., ult. < L *in-* in + *amor* love]

in·ane (in·ān'), adj. 1. silly; senseless. 2. empty. [< L *inanis*] —in·ane'ly, adv. —in·ane'ness, n. —Syn. 1. foolish. 2. void.

in·an·i·mate (in·an'ə·mit), adj. 1. lifeless. 2. dull. —in·an'i·mate·ly, adv. —in·an'i·mate·ness, n.

in·a·ni·tion (in'ə·nish'ən), n. 1. emptiness. 2. weakness from lack of food. [< LL, < *inanire* to empty]

in·an·i·ty (in·an'ə·ti), n., pl. -ties. 1. silliness; lack of sense. 2. a silly or senseless act, practice, remark, etc. 3. emptiness.

in·ap·pli·ca·ble (in·ap'lə·kə·bəl; in'ə·plik'ə·bəl), adj. not applicable; not appropriate; not suitable. —in·ap'pli·ca·bil'i·ty, in·ap'pli·ca·ble·ness, n. —in·ap'pli·ca·bly, adv. —Syn. unbecoming, unfitting.

in·ap·po·site (in·ap'ə·zit), adj. not pertinent; inappropriate. —in·ap'po·site·ly, adv.

in·ap·pre·ci·a·ble (in'ə·prē'shi·ə·bəl; -shə·bəl), adj. too small to be noticed or felt; very slight. —in'ap·pre'ci·a·bly, adv.

in·ap·pro·pri·ate (in'ə·prō'pri·it), adj. not suitable; not fitting. —in'ap·pro'pri·ate·ly, adv. —in'ap·pro'pri·ate·ness, n.

in·apt (in·apt'), adj. 1. not apt; not suitable; unfit. 2. unskillful; awkward. —in·apt'ly, adv. —in·apt'ness, n. —Syn. 1. inappropriate. 2. unhandy.

in·ap·ti·tude (in·ap'tə·tūd; -tūd), n. 1. unfitness. 2. lack of skill.

in·ar·tic·u·late (in'är·tik'yə·lit), adj. 1. not distinct; not like regular speech: *an inarticulate mutter or groan.* 2. unable to speak in words; dumb. 3. Zool. not jointed. 4. not hinged. —in'ar·tic'u·late·ly, adv. —in'ar·tic'u·late·ness, n.

in·ar·tis·tic (in'är·tis'tik), adj. not artistic; lacking good taste. —in'ar·tis'ti·cal·ly, adv.

in·as·much as (in'əz·much'), 1. because. 2. in so far as.

in·at·ten·tion (in'ə·ten'shən), n. lack of attention; negligence. —Syn. heedlessness, disregard.

in·at·ten·tive (in′ə·ten′tiv), *adj.* not attentive; careless; negligent. —**in′at·ten′tive·ly**, *adv.* —**in′at·ten′tive·ness**, *n.* —**Syn.** heedless, unmindful, preoccupied.

in·au·di·ble (in·ô′də·bəl), *adj.* that cannot be heard. —**in·au′di·bil′i·ty**, **in·au′di·ble·ness**, *n.* —**in·au′di·bly**, *adv.*

in·au·gu·ral (in·ô′gyə·rəl), *adj.* of or for an inauguration. —*n.* 1. *Am.* inaugural address. 2. inaugural ceremonies.

inaugural address, *Am.* speech made by a president of the United States, or a governor of a State, when he is inaugurated.

in·au·gu·rate (in·ô′gyə·rāt), *v.,* -rat·ed, -rat·ing. 1. install in office with a ceremony. 2. make a formal beginning of; begin. [< L, ult. < *in-* + *augur* taker of omens] —**in·au′gu·ra′tor**, *n.*

in·au·gu·ra·tion (in·ô′gyə·rā′shən), *n.* 1. act or ceremony of installing a person in office. 2. formal beginning; beginning. 3. opening for public use with a ceremony or celebration.

in·aus·pi·cious (in′ôs·pish′əs), *adj.* unfavorable; unlucky. —**in′aus·pi′cious·ly**, *adv.* —**in′·aus·pi′cious·ness**, *n.* —**Syn.** unpromising.

in·board (in′bôrd′; -bōrd′), *adv., adj.* inside the hull of a ship.

in·born (in′bôrn′), *adj.* born in a person; instinctive; natural. —**Syn.** innate, inbred, native.

in·bound (in′bound′), *adj.* inward bound.

in·bred (in′bred′), *adj.* 1. inborn; natural: *an inbred courtesy.* 2. bred for generations from ancestors closely related.

in·breed (in′brēd′), *v.,* -bred, -breed·ing. 1. breed from closely related animals or plants. 2. produce or develop within.

in·breed·ing (in′brēd′ing), *n.* breeding from closely related persons, animals, or plants.

inc., 1. inclosure. 2. including. 3. inclusive. 4. Also, **Inc.** incorporated. 5. increase.

In·ca (ing′kə), *n.* member of the race of South American Indians who ruled Peru before the Spanish conquest. —**In′can**, *n., adj.*

in·cal·cu·la·ble (in·kal′kyə·lə·bəl), *adj.* 1. too great in number to be counted; numerous. 2. not to be reckoned beforehand. 3. not to be relied on; uncertain. —**in·cal′cu·la·bil′i·ty**, **in·cal′cu·la·ble·ness**, *n.* —**in·cal′cu·la·bly**, *adv.*

in·can·desce (in′kən·des′), *v.,* -desced, -desc·ing. glow or cause to glow.

in·can·des·cence (in′kən·des′əns), *n.* red-hot or white-hot condition.

in·can·des·cent (in′kən·des′ənt), *adj.* 1. glowing with heat; red-hot or white-hot. 2. intensely bright; brilliant. 3. pertaining to or containing a material that gives light by incandescence: *an incandescent filament or lamp.* [< L *incandescens* beginning to glow < *in-* + *candere* be gleaming white] —**in′can·des′cent·ly**, *adv.*

in·can·ta·tion (in′kan·tā′shən), *n.* 1. set of words spoken as a magic charm or to cast a magic spell. 2. use of such words. [< L, ult. < *in-* against + *cantare* chant]

in·ca·pa·ble (in·kā′pə·bəl), *adj.* 1. without ordinary ability; not efficient; not competent: *incapable workers.* 2. incapable of, a. without the ability, power, or fitness for: *incapable of work.* b. not legally qualified for: *a foreigner is incapable of becoming president of the United States.* c. not susceptible to; not capable of receiving or admitting: *incapable of exact measurement.* —**in·ca′pa·bil′i·ty**, **in·ca′pa·ble·ness**, *n.* —**in·ca′pa·bly**, *adv.*

in·ca·pac·i·tate (in′kə·pas′ə·tāt), *v.,* -tat·ed, -tat·ing. 1. deprive of ability, power, or fitness; disable. 2. legally disqualify. —**in′ca·pac′i·ta′tion**, *n.*

in·ca·pac·i·ty (in′kə·pas′ə·ti), *n., pl.* -ties. 1. lack of ability, power, or fitness; disability. 2. legal disqualification. —**Syn.** 1. unfitness, inability.

in·car·cer·ate (in·kär′sər·āt), *v.,* -at·ed, -at·ing. imprison. [< LL, < L *in-* in + *carcer* jail] —**in·car′cer·a′tion**, *n.* —**in·car′cer·a′tor**, *n.*

in·car·na·dine (in·kär′nə·din; -dīn; -dēn),

adj., v., -dined, -din·ing, *n.* —*adj.* 1. blood-red. 2. flesh-colored. —*v.* make incarnadine. —*n.* a blood-red color. [< F < Ital. *incarnadino.* See INCARNATE.]

in·car·nate (*adj.* in·kär′nit, -nāt; *v.* in·kär′-nāt), *adj., v.,* -nat·ed, -nat·ing. —*adj.* embodied in flesh, esp. in human form. —*v.* 1. make incarnate; embody. 2. put into an actual form; realize. 3. be the living embodiment of. [< L, < *in-* + *caro* flesh]

in·car·na·tion (in′kär·nā′shən), *n.* 1. a taking on of human form by a divine being. 2. embodiment. 3. person or thing that represents some quality or idea. 4. **the Incarnation**, *Theol.* the union of divine nature and human nature in the person of Jesus Christ.

in·case (in·kās′), *v.,* -cased, -cas·ing. 1. put into a case. 2. cover completely; enclose. Also, **encase.** —**in·case′ment**, *n.*

in·cau·tious (in·kô′shəs), *adj.* not cautious; heedless; reckless; rash. —**in·cau′tious·ly**, *adv.* —**in·cau′tious·ness**, *n.* —**Syn.** imprudent, unwary.

in·cen·di·ar·y (in·sen′di·er′i), *adj., n., pl.* -ar·ies. —*adj.* 1. having to do with the setting of property on fire maliciously. 2. causing fires; used to start a fire: *incendiary bombs.* 3. deliberately stirring up strife or rebellion: *incendiary speeches.* —*n.* 1. person who maliciously sets fire to property. 2. person who deliberately stirs up strife or rebellion. 3. *Mil.* shell or bomb containing chemical agents which cause fire. [< L, < *incendium* fire] —**in·cen·di·a·rism** (in·sen′di·ə·riz′əm), *n.*

in·cense¹ (in′sens), *n., v.,* -censed, -cens·ing. —*n.* 1. substance giving off a sweet smell when burned. 2. perfume or smoke from it. 3. something sweet like incense, such as the perfume of flowers, flattery, or praise. —*v.* burn or offer as incense. [< LL *incensus* < L *incendere* burn] —**in′cense·less**, *adj.*

in·cense² (in·sens′), *v.,* -censed, -cens·ing. make very angry; fill with rage. [< L *incensus* kindled] —**in·cense′ment**, *n.* —**Syn.** enrage, madden, provoke.

in·cen·tive (in·sen′tiv), *n.* motive; stimulus. —*adj.* inciting; encouraging. [< L *incentivus* striking up the tune < *in-* + *canere* sing] —**Syn.** *n.* spur, incitement.

in·cep·tion (in·sep′shən), *n.* a beginning; commencement. [< L *inceptio* < *incipere* begin < *in-* on + *capere* take] —**in·cep′tive**, *adj.* —**Syn.** origin.

in·cer·ti·tude (in·sér′tə·tüd; -tūd), *n.* uncertainty; doubt.

in·ces·sant (in·ses′ənt), *adj.* never stopping; continued or repeated without interruption. [< LL, < L *in-* not + *cessare* cease] —**in·ces′san·cy**, **in·ces′sant·ness**, *n.* —**in·ces′sant·ly**, *adv.* —**Syn.** ceaseless, continual, constant.

in·cest (in′sest), *n.* crime of sexual intercourse between persons so closely related that their marriage is prohibited by law. [< L *incestum* < *in-* not + *castus* chaste]

in·ces·tu·ous (in·ses′chü·əs), *adj.* 1. involving incest. 2. guilty of incest. —**in·ces′tu·ous·ly**, *adv.* —**in·ces′tu·ous·ness**, *n.*

inch (inch), *n.* 1. measure of length, ¹⁄₁₂ of a foot. 2. the amount of rainfall, etc., that would cover a surface to the depth of one inch. 3. the smallest part, amount, or degree; very little bit. 4. **by inches** or **inch by inch**, slowly; little by little. —*v.* move slowly or little by little: *a worm inches along.* [< L *uncia*, orig., a twelfth. Doublet of OUNCE¹]

inch·meal (inch′mēl′), *adv.* little by little; slowly. —*n.* **by inchmeal,** little by little; slowly.

in·cho·ate (in·kō′it), *adj.* just begun; in an early stage; incomplete; undeveloped. [< L *inchoatus* begun] —**in·cho′ate·ly**, *adv.* —**in·cho′-ate·ness**, *n.*

inch·worm (inch′wėrm′), *n. Am.* a measuring worm.

in·ci·dence (in′sə·dəns), *n.* 1. range of occurrence or influence; extent of effects; way of falling on or affecting: *in an epidemic the incidence* *of a disease is widespread.* **2.** a falling on; a striking. **3.** direction in which one thing falls on or strikes,another, esp. the angle **(angle of incidence)** that a line or ray of light falling upon a surface makes with a line perpendicular to that surface.

in·ci·dent (in′sə·dənt), *n.* **1.** a happening; event. **2.** event that helps or adds to something else. **3.** a distinct piece of action in a story, play, or poem. —*adj.* **1.** liable to happen; belonging: *hardships incident to the life of an explorer.* **2.** falling or striking (upon): *rays of light incident upon a mirror.* [< L *incidens* happening < *in*- on + *cadere* to fall] —**Syn.** *n.* **1.** occurrence, episode. —*adj.* **1.** relating, accessory.

Angle of incidence.
Ray IC impinges on surface AB at point C, CD being the perpendicular and angle ICD the angle of incidence. The angle DCR is the angle of reflection.

in·ci·den·tal (in′sə·den′təl), *adj.* **1.** happening or likely to happen along with something else more important: *discomforts incidental to camping out.* **2.** occurring by chance. **3.** secondary. —*n.* something incidental. —**Syn.** *adj.* **2.** occasional, casual.

in·ci·den·tal·ly (in′sə·den′təl·i; -dent′li), *adv.* as an incident along with something else; accidentally.

in·cin·er·ate (in·sin′ər·āt), *v.,* -at·ed, -at·ing. burn to ashes. [< Med.L, < L *in*- into + *cinis* ashes] —**in·cin′er·a′tion,** *n.*

in·cin·er·a·tor (in·sin′ər·ā′tər), *n.* furnace or other arrangement for burning things.

in·cip·i·ent (in·sip′i·ənt), *adj.* just beginning; in an early stage. [< L *incipiens* beginning < *in*- on + *capere* take] —**in·cip′i·ence,** *n.* **in·cip′i·en·cy,** *n.* —**in·cip′i·ent·ly,** *adv.*

in·cise (in·sīz′), *v.,* -cised, -cis·ing. **1.** cut into. **2.** carve; engrave. [< F *inciser,* ult. < *in*- into + *caedere* cut] —**in·cised′,** *adj.*

in·ci·sion (in·sizh′ən), *n.* **1.** cut made in something; gash. **2.** act of incising. **3.** incisive quality.

in·ci·sive (in·sī′siv), *adj.* sharp; penetrating; piercing; keen: *an incisive criticism.* [< Med.L *incisivus* < L *incidere* INCISE] —**in·ci′sive·ly,** *adv.* —**in·ci′sive·ness,** *n.*

in·ci·sor (in·sī′zər), *n.* tooth adapted for cutting; one of the front teeth.

in·ci·ta·tion (in′sī·tā′shən; -si-), *n.* an inciting.

in·cite (in·sīt′), *v.,* -cit·ed, -cit·ing. move to action; urge on; stir up; rouse. [< L *incitare,* ult. < *in*- on + *citare* cause to move] —**in·cite′ment,** *n.* —**in·cit′er,** *n.* —**in·cit′ing·ly,** *adv.* —**Syn.** impel, instigate, provoke, goad, spur.

in·ci·vil·i·ty (in′sə·vil′ə·ti), *n., pl.* -ties. **1.** rudeness; lack of courtesy; impoliteness. **2.** a rude or impolite act. —**Syn. 1.** discourtesy, disrespect.

incl., 1. inclosure. **2.** including. **3.** inclusive.

in·clem·en·cy (in·klem′ən·si), *n., pl.* -cies. severity; harshness: *the inclemency of the weather kept us at home.*

in·clem·ent (in·klem′ənt), *adj.* **1.** rough; stormy. **2.** severe; harsh. —**in·clem′ent·ly,** *adv.* —**Syn. 1.** rigorous, boisterous. **2.** cruel.

in·cli·na·tion (in′klə·nā′shən), *n.* **1.** tendency: *an inclination to become fat.* **2.** preference; liking: *a strong inclination for sports.* **3.** a leaning; a bending; a bowing: *a nod is an inclination of the head.* **4.** slope; slant: *the inclination of a roof.* **5.** *Geom.* the angle between two lines or planes. —**in′cli·na′tion·al,** *adj.* —**Syn. 1.** proneness. **2.** bias, predilection. **4.** declivity.

in·cline (*v.* in·klīn′; *n.* in′klīn, in·klīn′), *v.,* -clined, -clin·ing, *n.* —*v.* **1.** be favorable; be disposed; tend: *dogs incline toward meat as a food.* **2.** make favorable or willing; influence: *incline your hearts to obey God's laws.* **3.** slope; slant. **4.** lean; bend; bow. **5.** incline one's ear, listen favorably. —*n.* **1.** slope; slant. **2.** a sloping surface. [< L, < *in*- + *-clinare* bend] —**in·clined′,** *adj.* —**in·clin′er,** *n.*

inclined plane, plank or other plane surface put at an oblique angle with a horizontal surface.

in·cli·nom·e·ter (in′klə·nom′ə·tər), *n.* instrument for measuring the angle that an aircraft makes with the horizontal.

in·close (in·klōz′), *v.,* -closed, -clos·ing. enclose. —**in·clos′er,** *n.*

in·clo·sure (in·klō′zhər), *n.* enclosure.

in·clude (in·klüd′), *v.,* -clud·ed, -clud·ing. **1.** put, hold, or enclose within limits. **2.** contain; comprise: *the farm includes 160 acres.* **3.** put in a total, a class, or the like; reckon in a count: *all on board the ship were lost, including the captain.* [< L *includere* < *in*- in + *claudere* shut] —**in·clud′i·ble,** **in·clud′a·ble,** *adj.* —**Syn.** comprehend, embrace.

in·clu·sion (in·klü′zhən), *n.* **1.** an including or being included. **2.** thing included.

in·clu·sive (in·klü′siv), *adj.* **1.** including in consideration; including; comprising: *read pages 10 to 20 inclusive.* **2.** including much; including everything concerned: *an inclusive list of expenses.* —**in·clu′sive·ly,** *adv.* —**in·clu′sive·ness,** *n.*

in·cog·ni·to (in·kog′nə·tō; in′kog·nē′tō), *adj., adv., n., pl.* -tos. —*adj., adv.* with one's name, character and rank, etc., concealed. —*n.* **1.** person who is incognito. **2.** a disguised state or condition. [< Ital. < L *incognitus* unknown, ult. < *in*- not + *cognoscere* come to know]

in·co·her·ence (in′kō·hir′əns), **in·co·her·en·cy** (-ən·si), *n., pl.* -enc·es; -cies. **1.** failure to stick together; looseness. **2.** lack of logical connection. **3.** disconnected thought or speech.

in·co·her·ent (in′kō·hir′ənt), *adj.* **1.** not sticking together. **2.** disconnected; confused. —**in′co·her′ent·ly,** *adv.* —**Syn. 2.** inconsistent.

in·com·bus·ti·ble (in′kəm·bus′tə·bəl), *adj.* that cannot be burned; fireproof. —*n.* an incombustible substance. —**in′com·bus′ti·bil′i·ty,** **in′com·bus′ti·ble·ness,** *n.* —**in′com·bus′ti·bly,** *adv.*

in·come (in′kum), *n.* what comes in from property, business, labor, etc.; receipts. —**Syn.** revenue, proceeds, profit, salary.

income tax, government tax on a person's income.

in·com·ing (in′kum′ing), *adj.* coming in.

in·com·men·su·ra·ble (in′kə·men′shə·rə·bəl; -sə·rə-), *adj.* **1.** that cannot be compared because not measurable in the same units or by the same scale. **2.** having no common integral divisor except 1, as 8, 17, and 11. **3.** utterly disproportionate. —**in′com·men′su·ra·bil′i·ty,** **in′com·men′su·ra·ble·ness,** *n.* —**in′com·men′su·ra·bly,** *adv.*

in·com·men·su·rate (in′kə·men′shə·rit; -sə·rit), *adj.* **1.** not in proportion; not adequate. **2.** incommensurable. —**in′com·men′su·rate·ly,** *adv.* —**in′com·men′su·rate·ness,** *n.*

in·com·mode (in′kə·mōd′), *v.,* -mod·ed, -mod·ing. inconvenience; trouble. [< L, ult. < *in*- not + *commodus* convenient] —**Syn.** annoy.

in·com·mo·di·ous (in′kə·mō′di·əs), *adj.* **1.** not roomy enough. **2.** inconvenient; uncomfortable. —**in′com·mo′di·ous·ly,** *adv.* —**in′com·mo′di·ous·ness,** *n.*

in·com·mu·ni·ca·ble (in′kə·mū′nə·kə·bəl), *adj.* not capable of being communicated or told. —**in′com·mu′ni·ca·bil′i·ty,** **in′com·mu′ni·ca·ble·ness,** *n.* —**in′com·mu′ni·ca·bly,** *adv.*

in·com·mu·ni·ca·do (in′kə·mū′nə·kä′dō), *adj. Am.* deprived of communication with others. [< Sp.]

in·com·pa·ra·ble (in·kom′pə·rə·bəl; -prə·bəl), *adj.* **1.** without equal; matchless: *incomparable beauty.* **2.** not to be compared; unsuitable for comparison. —**in·com′pa·ra·bil′i·ty,** **in·com′pa·ra·ble·ness,** *n.* —**in·com′pa·ra·bly,** *adv.* —**Syn. 1.** peerless, unequaled, unrivaled.

in·com·pat·i·bil·i·ty (in′kəm·pat′ə·bil′ə·ti), *n., pl.* -ties. **1.** lack of harmony. **2.** incompatible thing, quality, etc.

in·com·pat·i·ble (in′kəm·pat′ə·bəl), *adj.* **1.** not able to live or act together peaceably; opposed in character. **2.** inconsistent: *late hours* *are incompatible with health.* —**in′com·pat′i·ble·ness,** *n.* —**in′com·pat′i·bly,** *adv.*

in·com·pe·tence (in·kom′pə·təns), **in·com·pe·ten·cy** (-tən·si), *n.* **1.** lack of ability, power, or fitness. **2.** lack of legal qualification.

in·com·pe·tent (in·kom′pə·tənt), *adj.* **1.** not competent; lacking ability, power, or fitness. **2.** not legally qualified. —*n.* an incompetent person. —**in·com′pe·tent·ly,** *adv.* —Syn. *adj.* **1.** incapable, unfit.

in·com·plete (in′kəm·plēt′), *adj.* not complete; lacking some part; unfinished. —**in′com·plete′ly,** *adv.* —**in′com·plete′ness,** **in′com·ple′tion,** *n.* —Syn. imperfect, deficient.

in·com·pre·hen·si·ble (in′kom·pri·hen′sə·bəl), *adj.* **1.** impossible to understand. **2.** *Archaic.* illimitable. —**in′com·pre·hen′si·bil′i·ty,** **in′·com·pre·hen′si·ble·ness,** *n.* —**in′com·pre·hen′si·bly,** *adv.*

in·com·press·i·ble (in′kəm·pres′ə·bəl), *adj.* not capable of being squeezed into a smaller size. —**in′com·press′i·bil′i·ty,** *n.*

in·con·ceiv·a·ble (in′kən·sēv′ə·bəl), *adj.* impossible to imagine; unthinkable; incredible. —**in′con·ceiv′a·bil′i·ty,** **in′con·ceiv′a·ble·ness,** *n.* —**in′con·ceiv′a·bly,** *adv.*

in·con·clu·sive (in′kən·klü′siv), *adj.* not decisive; not effective. —**in′con·clu′sive·ly,** *adv.* —**in′con·clu′sive·ness,** *n.*

in·con·gru·i·ty (in′kong·grü′ə·ti; -kon-; -kən-), *n.*, *pl.* **-ties. 1.** unfitness; inappropriateness; being out of place. **2.** lack of agreement or harmony; inconsistency. **3.** something that is incongruous.

in·con·gru·ous (in·kong′grü·əs), *adj.* **1.** out of keeping; not appropriate; out of place. **2.** lacking in agreement or harmony; not consistent. —**in·con′gru·ous·ly,** *adv.* —**in·con′gru·ous·ness,** *n.* —Syn. **1.** inappropriate, unsuited. **2.** inharmonious, inconsistent.

in·con·se·quent (in·kon′sə·kwent; -kwənt), *adj.* **1.** not logical; not logically connected. **2.** not to the point; off the subject. **3.** apt to think or talk without logical connection. —**in·con′se·quence,** *n.* —**in·con′se·quent·ly,** *adv.*

in·con·se·quen·tial (in′kon·sə·kwen′shəl), *adj.* **1.** unimportant; trifling. **2.** inconsequent. —**in·con′se·quen′ti·al′i·ty,** *n.* —**in·con′se·quen′tial·ly,** *adv.*

in·con·sid·er·a·ble (in′kən·sid′ər·ə·bəl), *adj.* not worthy of consideration; not important. —**in′con·sid′er·a·ble·ness,** *n.* —**in′con·sid′er·a·bly,** *adv.* —Syn. unimportant, insignificant, petty.

in·con·sid·er·ate (in′kən·sid′ər·it), *adj.* **1.** not thoughtful of the rights and feelings of others. **2.** thoughtless; heedless. —**in′con·sid′er·ate·ly,** *adv.* —**in′con·sid′er·ate·ness,** **in′con·sid′er·a′tion,** *n.*

in·con·sist·en·cy (in′kən·sis′tən·si), *n.*, *pl.* **-cies. 1.** lack of agreement or harmony; variance. **2.** failure to keep to the same principles, course of action, etc.; changeableness. **3.** thing, act, etc., that is inconsistent.

in·con·sist·ent (in′kən·sis′tənt), *adj.* **1.** lacking in agreement or harmony; at variance. **2.** lacking harmony between its different parts; not uniform. **3.** failing to keep to the same principles, course of action, etc.; changeable. —**in′con·sist′ent·ly,** *adv.* —Syn. **1.** discrepant, incongruous.

in·con·sol·a·ble (in′kən·sōl′ə·bəl), *adj.* not to be comforted. —**in′con·sol′a·bil′i·ty,** **in′con·sol′a·ble·ness,** *n.* —**in′con·sol′a·bly,** *adv.*

in·con·so·nant (in·kon′sə·nənt), *adj.* not harmonious; not in agreement or accord. —**in·con′so·nance,** *n.* —**in·con′so·nant·ly,** *adv.*

in·con·spic·u·ous (in′kən·spik′yü·əs), *adj.* attracting little or no attention. —**in′con·spic′u·ous·ly,** *adv.* —**in′con·spic′u·ous·ness,** *n.*

in·con·stan·cy (in·kon′stən·si), *n.* fickleness.

in·con·stant (in·kon′stənt), *adj.* not constant; changeable; fickle. —**in·con′stant·ly,** *adv.* —Syn. variable, capricious.

in·con·test·a·ble (in′kən·tes′tə·bəl), *adj.* not to be disputed; unquestionable. —**in′con·test′-**

a·bil′i·ty, **in′con·test′a·ble·ness,** *n.* —**in′con·test′a·bly,** *adv.* —Syn. indisputable, undeniable, certain.

in·con·ti·nence (in·kon′tə·nəns), *n.* **1.** lack of self-restraint. **2.** lack of chastity.

in·con·ti·nent (in·kon′tə·nənt), *adj.* **1.** without self-restraint. **2.** not chaste; licentious. —**in·con′ti·nent·ly,** *adv.*

in·con·tro·vert·i·ble (in′kon·trə·vér′tə·bəl), *adj.* that cannot be disputed; unquestionable. —**in′con·tro·vert′i·bil′i·ty,** **in′con·tro·vert′i·ble·ness,** *n.* —**in′con·tro·vert′i·bly,** *adv.*

in·con·ven·ience (in′kən·vēn′yəns), *n.*, *v.*, **-ienced, -ienc·ing.** —*n.* **1.** lack of convenience or ease; trouble; bother. **2.** cause of trouble, difficulty, or bother. —*v.* cause trouble, difficulty, etc., to.

in·con·ven·ient (in′kən·vēn′yənt), *adj.* not convenient; troublesome; causing bother or discomfort. —**in′con·ven′ient·ly,** *adv.* —Syn. embarrassing, awkward.

in·con·vert·i·ble (in′kən·vér′tə·bəl), *adj.* incapable of being converted or exchanged. —**in′con·vert′i·bil′i·ty,** **in′con·vert′i·ble·ness,** *n.* —**in′con·vert′i·bly,** *adv.*

in·cor·po·rate (*v.* in·kôr′pə·rāt; *adj.* in·kôr′pə·rit), *v.*, **-rat·ed, -rat·ing,** *adj.* —*v.* **1.** make (something) a part of something else; join or combine (something) with something else: *we will incorporate your suggestion in this new plan.* **2.** form into a corporation: *incorporate a business.* **3.** form a corporation. **4.** unite or combine so as to form one body. **5.** embody; give material form to: *incorporate one's thoughts in an article.* —*adj.* united; combined; incorporated. [< L, < *in-* into + *corpus* body] —**in·cor′po·ra′tive,** *adj.* —**in·cor′po·ra′tor,** *n.* —Syn. *v.* **1.** merge, unite.

in·cor·po·ra·tion (in·kôr′pə·rā′shən), *n.* **1.** an incorporating: *the incorporation of air bubbles in the glass spoiled it.* **2.** a being incorporated: *incorporation gives a company the power to act as one person.*

in·cor·po·re·al (in′kôr·pô′ri·əl; -pō′-), *adj.* not made of any material substance; spiritual. —**in′cor·po′re·al·ly,** *adv.* —Syn. immaterial, disembodied.

in·cor·rect (in′kə·rekt′), *adj.* **1.** not correct; wrong; faulty. **2.** not proper. —**in′cor·rect′ly,** *adv.* —**in′cor·rect′ness,** *n.* —Syn. **1.** erroneous, inaccurate.

in·cor·ri·gi·ble (in·kôr′ə·jə·bəl; in·kor′-), *adj.* **1.** so firmly fixed (in bad ways, a bad habit, etc.) that nothing else can be expected: *an incorrigible liar.* **2.** so fixed that it cannot be changed or cured. —*n.* an incorrigible person. —**in·cor′ri·gi·bil′i·ty,** **in·cor′ri·gi·ble·ness,** *n.* —**in·cor′ri·gi·bly,** *adv.* —Syn. *adj.* **1.** hardened.

in·cor·rupt·i·ble (in′kə·rup′tə·bəl), *adj.* **1.** not to be corrupted; honest. **2.** not capable of decay. —**in′cor·rupt′i·bil′i·ty,** **in′cor·rupt′i·ble·ness,** *n.* —**in′cor·rupt′i·bly,** *adv.*

in·crease (*v.* in·krēs′; *n.* in′krēs), *v.*, **-creased, -creas·ing,** *n.* —*v.* **1.** make greater or more numerous; make richer, more prosperous, or more powerful. **2.** become greater; grow in numbers, esp. by propagation; advance in quality, success, power, etc. —*n.* **1.** gain in size, numbers, etc.; growth; multiplication by propagation. **2.** addition; result of increasing; increased product. **3.** on the increase, increasing. **4.** offspring. [< AF var. of OF *encreistre* < L, < *in-* in + *crescere* grow] —**in·creas′a·ble,** *adj.* —**in·creas′er,** *n.* —Syn. *v.* **1.** enlarge, extend, augment. —*n.* **1, 2.** enlargement, extension.

in·creas·ing·ly (in·krēs′ing·li), *adv.* more and more.

in·cred·i·ble (in·kred′ə·bəl), *adj.* seeming too extraordinary to be possible; unbelievable: *incredible bravery.* —**in·cred′i·bil′i·ty,** **in·cred′i·ble·ness,** *n.* —**in·cred′i·bly,** *adv.* ▶ **incredible, incredulous.** A story or situation is *incredible* (unbelievable); a person is *incredulous* (unbelieving).

in·cre·du·li·ty (in′krə·dü′lə·ti; -dū′-), *n.* lack of belief; doubt. —Syn. unbelief, distrust.

in·cred·u·lous (in·krej′ə·ləs), *adj.* **1.** not ready to believe; not credulous; doubting. **2.** showing a lack of belief. —**in·cred′u·lous·ly,** *adv.* —**in·cred′u·lous·ness,** *n.* ⟩ See incredible for usage note.

in·cre·ment (in′krə·mənt; ing′-), *n.* **1.** increase; growth. **2.** amount by which something increases. [< L *incrementum* < *increscere* IN-CREASE] —**in′cre·men′tal,** *adj.*

in·crim·i·nate (in·krim′ə·nāt), *v.,* —**nat·ed,** —**nat·ing.** accuse of a crime; show to be guilty: *in his confession the thief incriminated two others who helped him steal.* [< LL, < L *in-* against + *crimen* charge] —**in·crim′i·na′tion,** *n.* —**in·crim′i·na′tor,** *n.* —**in·crim·i·na·to·ry** (in·krim′ə·nə·tô′ri; -tō′-), *adj.*

in·crust (in·krust′), *v.* **1.** cover with a crust or hard coating. **2.** form a crust; form into a crust. Also, **encrust.** —**in′crus·ta′tion,** *n.*

in·cu·bate (in′kyə·bāt; ing′-), *v.,* —**bat·ed,** —**bat·ing.** **1.** sit on (eggs) in order to hatch them. **2.** brood. **3.** keep (eggs, etc.) warm so that they will hatch or grow. [< L, < *in-* on + *cubare* lie] —**in′cu·ba′tive,** *adj.*

in·cu·ba·tion (in′kyə·bā′shən; ing′-), *n.* **1.** an incubating or being incubated. **2.** stage of a disease from the time of infection until the appearance of the first symptoms. —**in′cu·ba′tion·al,** *adj.*

in·cu·ba·tor (in′kyə·bā′tər; ing′-), *n.* **1.** apparatus having a box or chamber for keeping eggs at a specific temperature so that they will hatch. **2.** a similar apparatus for rearing children born prematurely. **3.** apparatus in which bacterial cultures are developed.

in·cu·bus (in′kyə·bəs; ing′-), *n., pl.* —**bi** (-bī), —**bus·es.** **1.** an evil spirit supposed to descend upon sleeping persons. **2.** nightmare. **3.** an oppressive or burdensome thing. [< Med.L (def. 1), LL (def. 2), < L, < *in-* on + *cubare* lie]

in·cul·cate (in·kul′kāt; in′kul·kāt), *v.,* —**cat·ed,** —**cat·ing.** impress by repetition; teach persistently. [< L *inculcatus,* orig., trampled in, ult. < *in-* in + *calx* heel] —**in′cul·ca′tion,** *n.* —**in·cul′ca·tor,** *n.*

in·cul·pate (in·kul′pāt; in′kul·pāt), *v.,* —**pat·ed,** —**pat·ing.** **1.** blame; accuse. **2.** involve in responsibility for wrongdoing; incriminate. [< LL, < L *in-* in + *culpa* blame] —**in′cul·pa′tion,** *n.*

in·cum·ben·cy (in·kum′bən·si), *n., pl.* —**cies.** a holding of an office, position, etc., and performance of its duties; term of office.

in·cum·bent (in·kum′bənt), *adj.* **1.** lying, leaning, or pressing (on). **2.** resting (on a person) as a duty: *it is incumbent on a judge to be just.* —*n.* person holding an office, position, church living, etc. [< L *incumbens* lying down on] —**in·cum′bent·ly,** *adv.*

in·cum·ber (in·kum′bər), *v.* encumber.

in·cum·brance (in·kum′brəns), *n.* encumbrance.

in·cu·nab·u·la (in′kyu·nab′yə·lə), *n.pl., sing.* —**lum** (-ləm). **1.** earliest stages or first traces of anything; beginnings. **2.** books printed before the year 1500. [< L, cradle] —**in′cu·nab′u·lar,** *adj.*

in·cur (in·kėr′), *v.,* —**curred,** —**cur·ring.** run or fall into (something unpleasant); bring (blame, punishment, danger, etc.) on oneself: *the hunter incurred great danger in killing the tiger.* [< L, < *in-* upon + *currere* run]

in·cur·a·ble (in·kyur′ə·bəl), *adj.* not capable of being cured or remedied. —*n.* person having an incurable disease. —**in·cur′a·bil′i·ty, in·cur′a·ble·ness,** *n.* —**in·cur′a·bly,** *adv.* —**Syn.** *adj.* fatal, hopeless.

in·cu·ri·ous (in·kyur′i·əs), *adj.* not curious; without curiosity. —**in·cu·ri·os·i·ty** (in′kyur·i·os′ə·ti), **in·cu′ri·ous·ness,** *n.* —**in·cu′ri·ous·ly,** *adv.*

in·cur·sion (in·kėr′zhən; -shən), *n.* invasion; raid; sudden attack. [< L *incursio* < *incurrere.* See INCUR.]

in·cur·sive (in·kėr′siv), *adj.* making incursions.

in·curve (*v.* in·kėrv′; *n.* in′kėrv′), *v.,* —**curved,** —**curv·ing,** *n.* —*v.* curve inward. —*n.* Baseball.

pitch that curves toward the batter. —**in′cur·va′tion,** *n.*

in·cus (ing′kəs), *n.* the middle one of a chain of three small bones in the middle ear of man and other animals. [< L, anvil]

Ind., **1.** India. **2.** Indian. **3.** Indiana.

ind., **1.** independent. **2.** index. **3.** indicative.

in·debt·ed (in·det′id), *adj.* in debt; obliged; owing money or gratitude. —**in·debt′ed·ness,** *n.*

in·de·cen·cy (in·dē′sən·si), *n., pl.* —**cies.** **1.** lack of decency. **2.** an indecent act or word.

in·de·cent (in·dē′sənt), *adj.* **1.** not decent; in very bad taste; improper: *an indecent lack of gratitude to the man who saved his life.* **2.** modest; morally bad; obscene. —**in·de′cent·ly,** *adv.* —**Syn. 1.** unbecoming, unseemly. **2.** coarse, disgusting.

in·de·ci·pher·a·ble (in′di·sī′fər·ə·bəl), *adj.* incapable of being deciphered; illegible. —**in′de·ci′pher·a·bil′i·ty,** *n.*

in·de·ci·sion (in′di·sizh′ən), *n.* lack of decision; tendency to delay or to hesitate. —**Syn.** hesitation, uncertainty.

in·de·ci·sive (in′di·sī′siv), *adj.* **1.** having the habit of hesitating and putting off decisions. **2.** not deciding or settling the matter. —**in′de·ci′sive·ly,** *adv.* —**in′de·ci′sive·ness,** *n.*

in·de·clin·a·ble (in′di·klīn′ə·bəl), *adj.* not changing its form for changes in grammatical use. *None* is an indeclinable pronoun. —**in′de·clin′a·bly,** *adv.*

in·dec·o·rous (in·dek′ə·rəs; in′di·kô′rəs, -kō′-), *adj.* not suitable; improper. —**in·dec′o·rous·ly,** *adv.* —**in·dec′o·rous·ness,** *n.* —**Syn.** unseemly, rude.

in·de·co·rum (in′di·kô′rəm; -kō′-), *n.* **1.** lack of decorum. **2.** improper behavior, dress, etc.

in·deed (in·dēd′), *adv.* in fact; really; truly; surely. —*interj.* expression of surprise, incredulity, irony, or contempt.

indef., indefinite.

in·de·fat·i·ga·ble (in′di·fat′ə·gə·bəl), *adj.* tireless; untiring. —**in′de·fat′i·ga·bil′i·ty, in′de·fat′i·ga·ble·ness,** *n.* —**in′de·fat′i·ga·bly,** *adv.* —**Syn.** unflagging, unwearying, persistent.

in·de·fea·si·ble (in′di·fē′zə·bəl), *adj.* not to be annulled or made void. —**in′de·fea′si·bil′i·ty,** *n.* —**in′de·fea′si·bly,** *adv.*

in·de·fen·si·ble (in′di·fen′sə·bəl), *adj.* **1.** that cannot be defended. **2.** not justifiable. —**in′de·fen′si·bil′i·ty, in′de·fen′si·ble·ness,** *n.* —**in′de·fen′si·bly,** *adv.*

in·de·fin·a·ble (in′di·fīn′ə·bəl), *adj.* that cannot be defined. —**in′de·fin′a·ble·ness,** *n.* —**in′de·fin′a·bly,** *adv.*

in·def·i·nite (in·def′ə·nit), *adj.* **1.** not clearly defined; not precise; vague. **2.** not limited. **3.** *Gram.* not specifying (person, time, etc.) precisely. *Some, many,* and *few* are often indefinite pronouns. —**in·def′i·nite·ly,** *adv.* —**in·def′i·nite·ness,** *n.* —**Syn. 1.** obscure, ambiguous, equivocal, inexact.

indefinite article, *Gram. a* or *an.*

in·de·his·cent (in′di·his′ənt), *adj. Bot.* not opening at maturity. —**in′de·his′cence,** *n.*

in·del·i·ble (in·del′ə·bəl), *adj.* **1.** that cannot be erased or removed; permanent: *indelible ink, an indelible disgrace.* **2.** making an indelible mark: *an indelible pencil.* [< L, < *in-* not + *delere* destroy] —**in·del′i·bil′i·ty, in·del′i·ble·ness,** *n.* —**in·del′i·bly,** *adv.* —**Syn. 1.** fixed, fast, ineffaceable.

in·del·i·ca·cy (in·del′ə·kə·si), *n., pl.* —**cies.** lack of delicacy; being indelicate.

in·del·i·cate (in·del′ə·kit), *adj.* **1.** not delicate; coarse; crude. **2.** improper; immodest. —**in·del′i·cate·ly,** *adv.* —**in·del′i·cate·ness,** *n.* —**Syn. 2.** vulgar.

in·dem·ni·fi·ca·tion (in·dem′nə·fə·kā′shən), *n.* **1.** an indemnifying or being indemnified. **2.** compensation; recompense.

in·dem·ni·fy (in·dem′nə·fī), *v.,* —**fied,** —**fy·ing.** **1.** repay; make good; compensate for damage, loss, or expense incurred. **2.** secure against damage or loss; insure. —**in·dem′ni·fi′er,** *n.* —**Syn. 1.** recompense, reimburse.

in·dem·ni·ty (in·dem'nə·ti), *n., pl.* **-ties. 1.** payment for damage, loss, or expense incurred: *money demanded by a victorious nation at the end of a war as a condition of peace is an indemnity.* **2.** security against damage or loss; insurance. [< LL, < L *indemnis* unhurt < *in-* not + *damnum* damage]

in·dent¹ (*v.* in·dent'; *n.* in'·dent, in·dent'), *v.* **1.** cut (an edge) so that it looks like a row of teeth; notch. **2.** form deep notches or bays in. **3.** form a notch or recess. **4.** begin (a line) farther from the edge than the other lines. —*n.* **1.** a notch. **2.** an indenting. **3.** an indenture. [< OF *endenter*, ult. < L *in-* in + *dens* tooth] —**in·dent'er,** *n.*

Indented molding

in·dent² (in·dent'), *v.* **1.** make a dent in. **2.** press in; stamp. [< *in-²* + *dent*]

in·den·ta·tion (in'den·tā'shən), *n.* **1.** an indenting or being indented. **2.** dent; notch; cut. **3.** indention.

in·den·tion (in·den'shən), *n.* **1.** a beginning of a line farther from the edge than the other lines. **2.** blank space left by doing this. **3.** indentation.

in·den·ture (in·den'chər), *n., v.,* **-tured, -turing.** —*n.* **1.** written agreement. **2.** contract by which a person is bound to serve someone else. **3.** indentation. —*v.* bind by a contract for service. [< OF *endenteure* indentation]

in·de·pend·ence (in'di·pen'dəns), *n.* **1.** freedom from the control, influence, support, or help of another. **2.** enough to live on.

In·de·pend·ence (in'di·pen'dəns), *n.* city in W Missouri. It was one of the terminals of the Santa Fé Trail.

Independence Day, *Am.* the Fourth of July.

in·de·pend·en·cy (in'di·pen'dən·si), *n., pl.* **-cies. 1.** independence. **2.** an independent country.

in·de·pend·ent (in'di·pen'dənt), *adj.* **1.** needing, wishing, or getting no help from others: *independent thinking.* **2.** acting, working, or esp. voting by one's own ideas, not as the crowd does. **3.** guiding, ruling, or governing oneself; not under another's rule. **4.** not depending on others. **5.** having an adequate private income. **6.** not resulting from another thing; not controlled or influenced by something else; separate; distinct. —*n.* **1.** person who is independent in thought or behavior. **2.** person who votes without regard to party. —**in'de·pend'ent·ly,** *adv.* —**Syn.** *adj.* **6.** free, uncontrolled.

in·de·scrib·a·ble (in'di·skrīb'ə·bəl), *adj.* that cannot be described; beyond description. —**in'de·scrib'a·bil'i·ty,** **in'de·scrib'a·ble·ness,** *n.* —**in'de·scrib'a·bly,** *adv.*

in·de·struct·i·ble (in'di·struk'tə·bəl), *adj.* that cannot be destroyed. —**in'de·struct'i·bil'i·ty,** **in'de·struct'i·ble·ness,** *n.* —**in'de·struct'i·bly,** *adv.*

in·de·ter·mi·na·ble (in'di·tér'mə·nə·bəl), *adj.* **1.** not capable of being settled or decided. **2.** not capable of being ascertained. —**in'de·ter'mi·na·bly,** *adv.*

in·de·ter·mi·nate (in'di·tér'mə·nit), *adj.* not determined; indefinite; vague. —**in'de·ter'mi·nate·ly,** *adv.* —**in'de·ter'mi·nate·ness,** *n.*

in·de·ter·mi·na·tion (in'di·tér'mə·nā'shən), *n.* **1.** lack of determination. **2.** an unsettled state.

in·dex (in'deks), *n., pl.* **-dex·es, -di·ces** (-də·sēz), *v.* —*n.* **1.** list of what is in a book, telling on what pages to find topics, names, etc., usually put at the end of the book and arranged in alphabetical order. **2.** thing that points out or shows; sign. **3.** Also, **index finger.** finger next to the thumb; forefinger. **4.** pointer: *a dial or scale usually has an index.* **5.** in printing, a sign (☞) used to point out a particular note, paragraph, etc. **6.** number or formula expressing some property, ratio, etc., in science. **7.** *Math.* an exponent. **8.** Index, list of books that the Roman Catholic Church forbids its members to read. —*v.* **1.** provide with an index; make an index of. **2.** enter in an index. [< L, orig., that which points out]

In·di·a (in'di·ə), *n.* **1.** a peninsular subcontinent and former country in Asia, S of the Himalayas, between the Bay of Bengal and the Arabian Sea, projecting into the Indian Ocean. Until Aug. 15, 1947, largely under British rule; now chiefly divided between the republic of India and Pakistan, both self-governing affiliated units of the British Commonwealth of Nations. **2.** a republic in S Asia, independent since 1950.

India ink, 1. a black pigment consisting of lampblack mixed with a binding material. **2.** liquid ink prepared from this pigment.

In·di·a·man (in'di·ə·mən), *n., pl.* **-men.** a ship in the trade with India.

In·di·an (in'di·ən), *n.* **1.** *Am.* member of the so-called red race living in America before the Europeans came; an American Indian. **2.** *Am.* any one of the languages of the American Indians. **3.** native of India or the East Indies. —*adj.* **1.** *Am.* of or having to do with American Indians. **2.** of, living in, or belonging to India or the East Indies.

In·di·an·a (in'di·an'ə), *n.* a Middle Western State of the United States. *Capital:* Indianapolis. *Abbrev.:* Ind. —**In·di·an·i·an** (in'di·an'i·ən), *adj., n.*

In·di·an·ap·o·lis (in'di·ən·ap'ə·lis), *n.* capital of Indiana, near the center of the State.

Indian club, a bottle-shaped wooden club swung for exercise.

Indian corn, *Am.* **1.** grain that grows on large ears; maize. **2.** plant that it grows on.

Indian file, *Am.* single file.

Indian giver, *Am., Colloq.* person who takes back a gift after having bestowed it.

In·di·an·ize (in'di·ən·īz), *v.,* **-ized, -iz·ing. 1.** *Am., Colloq.* make Indian in form, shape, or manner. **2.** in India, replace British officials and personnel by Indians. —**In'di·an·iz·a'tion,** *n.*

Indian corn
(ears vary in length from 1 to 20 in.)

Indian Ocean, ocean S of Asia, E of Africa, and W of Australia.

Indian pipe, *Am.* a leafless plant with a solitary flower that looks like a tobacco pipe.

Indian pudding, *Am.* a baked pudding made with corn meal, molasses, milk, and suet.

Indian summer, *Am.* time of mild, dry, hazy weather in late autumn.

India paper, a thin, tough paper, used for Bibles, prayer books, etc.

India rubber, india rubber, substance of great elasticity derived from the coagulated, milky juice of various tropical plants; rubber.

indic., indicative.

in·di·cate (in'də·kāt), *v.,* **-cat·ed, -cat·ing. 1.** point out; point to: *the arrow on a sign indicates the right way to go.* **2.** show; make known: *a thermometer indicates temperature.* **3.** be a sign or hint of: *fever indicates sickness.* **4.** give a sign or hint of. **5.** state; express: *indicate one's intention.* **6.** show to be needed as a remedy or treatment. [< L, < *in-* in + *dicare* proclaim] —**Syn. 1.** designate. **2.** reveal, disclose. **3.** signify.

in·di·ca·tion (in'də·kā'shən), *n.* **1.** an indicating. **2.** thing that indicates; sign. **3.** amount or degree indicated.

in·dic·a·tive (in·dik'ə·tiv), *adj.* **1.** pointing out; showing; being a sign (of); suggestive. **2.** *Gram.* expressing or denoting a state, act, or happening as actual; asking a question of simple fact. In "I go" and "Did I go?" the verbs are in the indicative mood. —*n. Gram.* **a.** the indicative mood. **b.** a verb form in this mood. —**in·dic'a·tive·ly,** *adv.*

in·di·ca·tor (in'də·kā'tər), *n.* **1.** person or thing that indicates. **2.** pointer on the dial of an instrument that measures something. **3.** a measuring or recording instrument. **4.** *Chem.* substance used to indicate chemical conditions or changes, as litmus. —**in·di·ca·to·ry** (in'də·kə·tô'ri, -tō'-), *adj.*

in·di·ces (in'də·sēz), *n. pl.* of **index.**

---

in·dict (in·dīt′), v. 1. charge with an offense or crime; accuse. 2. find enough evidence against (an accused person) so that a trial is necessary. [< AF *enditer* INDITE] —**in·dict′a·ble**, adj. —**in·dict′er, in·dict′or**, n.

in·dict·ment (in·dīt′mənt), n. 1. Law. a formal accusation, esp. the legal accusation presented by a grand jury. 2. accusation.

In·dies (in′dēz), n.pl. 1. East Indies, India, and Indochina. 2. the East Indies. 3. the West Indies.

in·dif·fer·ence (in·dif′ər·əns; -dif′rəns), n. 1. lack of interest or attention. 2. lack of importance: *where we ate was a matter of indifference.* —**Syn.** 1. apathy, unconcern. 2. insignificance.

in·dif·fer·ent (in·dif′ər·ənt; -dif′rənt), adj. 1. having no feeling for or against: *indifferent to an admirer.* 2. impartial; neutral; without preference: *an indifferent decision.* 3. unimportant; not mattering much: *the time for starting is indifferent to me.* 4. neither good nor bad; just fair. 5. rather bad. 6. neutral in chemical, electrical, or magnetic quality. —**Syn.** 1. apathetic, unconcerned. 2. unbiased, disinterested, fair.

in·dif·fer·ent·ly (in·dif′ər·ənt·li; -dif′rənt-), adv. 1. with indifference. 2. without distinction; equally. 3. moderately; tolerably; passably. 4. poorly; badly.

in·di·gence (in′də·jəns), n. poverty.

in·dig·e·nous (in·dij′ə·nəs), adj. 1. originating in the region or country where found; native. 2. innate; inherent. [< L *indigena* native] —**in·dig′e·nous·ly**, adv. —**in·dig′e·nous·ness**, n. **in·di·gen·i·ty** (in′də·jen′ə·ti), n.

in·di·gent (in′də·jənt), adj. poor; needy. [< L *indigens* needing] —**in′di·gent·ly**, adv.

in·di·gest·i·ble (in′də·jes′tə·bəl; -dī-), adj. that cannot be digested; hard to digest. —**in′di·gest′i·bil′i·ty, in′di·gest′i·ble·ness**, n. —**in′di·gest′i·bly**, adv.

in·di·ges·tion (in′də·jes′chən; -dī-), n. inability to digest food; difficulty in digesting food.

in·dig·nant (in·dig′nənt), adj. angry at something unworthy, unjust, or mean. —**in·dig′nant·ly**, adv. —**Syn.** incensed, provoked.

in·dig·na·tion (in′dig·nā′shən), n. anger at something unworthy, unjust, or mean; righteous anger. [< L, ult. < *in-* not + *dignus* worthy]

in·dig·ni·ty (in·dig′nə·ti), n., pl. -ties. injury to dignity; an insult; a slight.

in·di·go (in′də·gō), n., pl. -gos, -goes, adj. —n. 1. blue dyestuff that can be obtained from certain plants, but is now usually made artificially. 2. plant from which indigo is obtained. 3. a deep violet blue. —adj. deep violet-blue. [< Sp. < L < Gk. *indikon*, orig. adj., Indian]

indigo bunting or **bird,** Am. a small American finch, the male of which is a deep violet-blue.

in·di·rect (in′də·rekt′; -dī-), adj. 1. not direct; not straight: *an indirect route.* 2. not directly connected; secondary: *an indirect consequence.* 3. not straightforward and to the point: *an indirect reply.* 4. dishonest, deceitful: *indirect methods.* —**in′di·rect′ly**, adv. —**in′di·rect′ness**, n. —**Syn.** 1. circuitous, roundabout. 2. incidental.

indirect discourse, repetition of the substance of a person's speech without directly quoting it. *Example:* "He said that he would come," instead of "He said, 'I will come.'"

indirect object, Gram. person or thing that is indirectly affected by the action of the verb. The indirect object usually comes before the direct object and shows to whom or for whom something is done. In "I gave John a book," *John* is the indirect object and *book* is the direct object.

indirect tax, tax paid by the consumer in the form of higher prices for the taxed goods.

in·dis·cern·i·ble (in′di·zér′nə·bəl; -sèr′-), adj. imperceptible. —**in′dis·cern′i·ble·ness**, n. —**in′dis·cern′i·bly**, adv.

in·dis·creet (in′dis·krēt′), adj. not discreet; not wise and judicious; imprudent. —**in′dis·creet′ly**, adv. —**in′dis·creet′ness**, n. —**Syn.** unwise, foolish, rash.

in·dis·cre·tion (in′dis·kresh′ən), n. 1. lack of good judgment. 2. an indiscreet act.

in·dis·crim·i·nate (in′dis·krim′ə·nit), adj. 1. with no feeling for differences: *an indiscriminate reader.* 2. confused: *an indiscriminate mass.* —**in′dis·crim′i·nate·ly**, adv. —**in′dis·crim′i·nate·ness**, n.

in·dis·pen·sa·ble (in′dis·pen′sə·bəl), adj. absolutely necessary: *air is indispensable to life.* —n. an indispensable person or thing. —**in′dis·pen′sa·bil′i·ty, in′dis·pen′sa·ble·ness**, n. —**in′dis·pen′sa·bly**, adv.

in·dis·pose (in′dis·pōz′), v., -posed, -pos·ing. 1. make unwilling; make averse. 2. make slightly ill. 3. make unfit or unable.

in·dis·posed (in′dis·pōzd′), adj. 1. slightly ill. 2. unwilling; without inclination; averse. —**Syn.** 1. sick. 2. disinclined.

in·dis·po·si·tion (in′dis·pə·zish′ən), n. 1. disturbance of health; slight illness. 2. unwillingness; disinclination; aversion.

in·dis·put·a·ble (in′dis·pūt′ə·bəl; in·dis′pyə·tə-), adj. not to be disputed; undoubtedly true; unquestionable. —**in′dis·put′a·bil′i·ty, in′dis·put′a·ble·ness**, n. —**in′dis·put′a·bly, in·dis′put·a·bly**, adv. —**Syn.** undeniable, certain, positive.

in·dis·sol·u·ble (in′di·sol′yə·bəl), adj. not capable of being dissolved, undone, or destroyed; lasting; firm. —**in′dis·sol′u·bil′i·ty, in′dis·sol′u·ble·ness**, n. —**in′dis·sol′u·bly**, adv.

in·dis·tinct (in′dis·tingkt′), adj. not distinct; not clear to the eye, ear, or mind. —**in′dis·tinct′ly**, adv. —**in′dis·tinct′ness**, n. —**Syn.** undefined, confused, vague, obscure.

in·dis·tin·guish·a·ble (in′dis·ting′gwish·ə·bəl), adj. that cannot be distinguished. —**in′dis·tin′guish·a·ble·ness**, n. —**in′dis·tin′guish·a·bly**, adv.

in·dite (in·dīt′), v., -dit·ed, -dit·ing. put in words or writing; compose, as a letter, poem, etc. [< OF *enditer* < L *in-* in + *dictare* DICTATE, express in writing] —**in·dite′ment**, n. —**in·dit′er**, n.

in·di·um (in′di·əm), n. Chem. a metallic element, In, that is soft, white, malleable, and easily fusible. [< NL, < L *indicum* INDIGO]

in·di·vid·u·al (in′də·vij′ū·əl), n. 1. person. 2. one person, animal, or thing. —adj. 1. single; particular; separate: *an individual question.* 2. for one person only: *individual saltcellars.* 3. pertaining or peculiar to one person or thing: *individual tastes.* 4. marking off one person or thing specially: *an individual style.* [< Med.L, ult. < L *in-* not + *dividuus* divisible] ▶ See person for usage note.

in·di·vid·u·al·ism (in′də·vij′ū·əl·iz′əm), n. 1. theory that individual freedom is as important as the welfare of the community or group as a whole. 2. any ethical, economic, or political theory that emphasizes the importance of individuals. 3. each for himself; selfishness. 4. individuality.

in·di·vid·u·al·ist (in′də·vij′ū·əl·ist), n. 1. one who lives his own life for himself and does not try to coöperate with others. 2. supporter of individualism. —**in′di·vid′u·al·is′tic**, adj.

in·di·vid·u·al·i·ty (in′də·vij′ū·al′ə·ti), n., pl. -ties. 1. individual character; sum of the qualities that make a person himself, not someone else. 2. state of being individual; existence as an individual. 3. an individual person or thing.

in·di·vid·u·al·ize (in′də·vij′ū·əl·īz), v., -ized, -iz·ing. 1. make individual; give a distinctive character to. 2. consider as individuals; list one by one; specify. —**in′di·vid′u·al·i·za′tion**, n. —**in′di·vid′u·al·iz′er**, n.

in·di·vid·u·al·ly (in′də·vij′ū·əl·i), adv. 1. personally; one at a time; as individuals: *the teacher helps us individually.* 2. each from the others: *people differ individually.*

in·di·vis·i·ble (in′də·viz′ə·bəl), adj. 1. not capable of being divided. 2. not capable of being divided without a remainder. —**in′di·vis′i·bil′i·ty, in′di·vis′i·ble·ness**, n. —**in′di·vis′i·bly**, adv.

In·do·chi·na or **In·do·Chi·na** (in′dō·chī′nə), n. 1. the southeastern peninsula of Asia, comprising E Burma, the Malay Peninsula, Thailand, and the area which formerly constituted French Indo-China. 2. countries in the E part of this peninsula; Cambodia, Laos and Vietnam.

In·do-Chi·nese (in'dō-chī-nēz'; –nēs'), *adj.* 1. of or having to do with Indochina, the Mongoloid peoples living there, or their languages. 2. of or having to do with the family of languages comprising these languages and the Tibetan and Chinese groups of languages.

Indochina (def. 1)

in·doc·tri·nate (in·dok'tre·nāt), *v.,* –nat·ed, –nat·ing. 1. teach a doctrine, belief, or principle to. 2. inculcate. [prob. < Med.L, < *in–* in + *doctrinare* teach <L *doctrina* DOCTRINE] —**in·doc'tri·na'tion,** *n.* —**in·doc'tri·na'tor,** *n.*

In·do-Eu·ro·pe·an (in'dō·yur'ə·pē'ən), *adj.* 1. of India and Europe. 2. of or having to do with a group of related languages spoken in India, western Asia, and Europe. English, German, Latin, Greek, Persian, and Sanskrit are some of the Indo-European languages. —*n.* this group of languages.

In·do-Ger·man·ic (in'dō·jér·man'ik), *adj.* Indo-European.

in·do·lence (in'də·ləns), *n.* laziness; dislike of work; idleness.

in·do·lent (in'də·lənt), *adj.* lazy; disliking work. [< LL, < *in–* not + *dolere* be in pain] —**in'do·lent·ly,** *adv.* —Syn. idle, slothful, sluggish.

in·dom·i·ta·ble (in·dom'ə·tə·bəl), *adj.* unconquerable; unyielding. [< LL *indomitabilis,* ult. < L *in–* not + *domare* tame] —**in·dom'i·ta·ble·ness,** *n.* —**in·dom'i·ta·bly,** *adv.*

In·do·ne·sia (in'dō·nē'shə; –zhə), *n.* 1. Republic of, an autonomous republic in the Malay Archipelago, including Java, Sumatra, Madura, Borneo, Celebes, Bali, and other islands. It formerly belonged to the Netherlands, and was technically a member of the Netherlands Union from 1949 to 1954. 2. Malay Archipelago. —**In'do·ne'sian,** *adj., n.*

in·door (in'dôr'; –dōr'), *adj.* done, used, etc., in a house or building: *indoor tennis.*

in·doors (in'dôrz'; –dōrz'), *adv.* in or into a house or building.

in·dorse (in·dôrs'), *v.,* –dorsed, –dors·ing. endorse. —**in·dors'a·ble,** *adj.* —**in'dor·see',** *n.* —**in·dorse'ment,** *n.* —**in·dors'er, in·dor'sor,** *n.*

in·du·bi·ta·ble (in·dū'bə·tə·bəl; –dū'–), *adj.* not to be doubted; certain. —**in·du'bi·ta·ble·ness,** *n.* —**in·du'bi·ta·bly,** *adv.*

in·duce (in·dūs'; –dūs'), *v.,* –duced, –duc·ing. 1. lead on; influence; persuade: *advertising induces people to buy.* 2. cause; bring about: *some drugs induce sleep.* 3. produce (an electric current, electric charge, or magnetic change) without contact. 4. infer by reasoning from particular facts to a general rule or principle. [< L, < *in–* in + *ducere* lead] —**in·duc'er,** *n.* —**in·duc'i·ble,** *adj.* —Syn. 1. incite, impel.

in·duce·ment (in·dūs'mənt; –dūs'–), *n.* something that influences or persuades; incentive.

in·duct (in·dukt'), *v.* 1. bring in; introduce (into a place, seat, position, office, benefice, etc.). 2. put formally in possession of (an office, etc.): *Mr. Gage was inducted into the office of governor.* 3. *U.S.* enroll in military service: *I expect to be inducted next month.* 4. initiate. [< L *inductus,* pp. of *inducere.* See INDUCE.]

in·duct·ance (in·duk'təns), *adj.* property of an electrical conductor or circuit that makes induction possible.

in·duc·tee (in·duk'tē), *n.* 1. person who is soon to be inducted. 2. person who is inducted, esp. one who is inducted into military service.

in·duc·tile (in·duk'təl), *adj.* not ductile. —**in'·duc·til'i·ty,** *n.*

in·duc·tion (in·duk'shən), *n.* 1. process by which an object having electrical or magnetic properties produces similar properties in a nearby object, usually without direct contact. 2. reasoning from particular facts to a general rule or principle. 3. conclusion reached in this way. 4. act of inducting; act or ceremony of installing a person in office.

induction coil, *Elect.* device in which an interrupted direct current in one coil produces an alternating current in a surrounding coil.

Magnetic induction

in·duc·tive (in·duk'tiv), *adj.* 1. of or using induction; reasoning by induction. 2. having to do with electrical or magnetic induction. —**in·duc'tive·ly,** *adv.* —**in·duc'tive·ness,** *n.*

in·duc·tiv·i·ty (in'duk·tiv'ə·ti), *n., pl.* –ties. *Elect.* inductive property; capacity for induction.

in·duc·tor (in·duk'tər), *n.* part of an electrical apparatus that works or is worked by induction.

in·due (in·dū'; –dū'), *v.,* –dued, –du·ing. endue.

in·dulge (in·dulj'), *v.,* –dulged, –dulg·ing. 1. yield to the wishes of; humor: *indulge a sick person.* 2. give way to: *indulge our desires.* 3. give way to one's pleasures; give oneself up to; allow oneself something desired: *indulge in tobacco.* [< L *indulgere*] —**in·dulg'er,** *n.* —**in·dulg'ing·ly,** *adv.* —Syn. 1. gratify, satisfy, pamper.

in·dul·gence (in·dul'jəns), *n.* 1. an indulging: *indulgence in rich food.* 2. thing indulged in. 3. favor; privilege. 4. in the Roman Catholic Church, remission of the punishment still due to sin after the guilt has been forgiven.

in·dul·gent (in·dul'jənt), *adj.* indulging; kind; almost too kind: *the indulgent mother bought her boy everything he wanted.* —**in·dul'gent·ly,** *adv.*

in·du·rate (*v.* in'dú·rāt, –dyu–; *adj.* in'dú·rit, –dyu–), *v.,* –rat·ed, –rat·ing, *adj.* —*v.* 1. harden. 2. make or become unfeeling. —*adj.* hardened; unfeeling. [< L, < *in–* + *durus* hard] —**in'du·ra'tion,** *n.* —**in'du·ra'tive,** *adj.*

In·dus (in'dəs), *n.* river flowing from NW India through Pakistan into the Arabian Sea.

in·dus·tri·al (in·dus'tri·əl), *adj.* 1. of or resulting from industry or productive labor. 2. having to do with or connected with the industries, trades, or manufactures: *industrial workers.* 3. manufacturing rather than agricultural or commercial: *an industrial community.* 4. of or having to do with the workers in industries: *industrial insurance.* —**in·dus'tri·al·ly,** *adv.*

in·dus·tri·al·ism (in·dus'tri·əl·iz'əm), *n.* system of social and economic organization in which large industries are very important and industrial activities or interests prevail.

in·dus·tri·al·ist (in·dus'tri·əl·ist), *n.* person who conducts or owns an industrial enterprise.

in·dus·tri·al·i·za·tion (in·dus'tri·əl·ə·zā'shən), *n.* development of large industries as an important feature in a country or a social or economic system.

in·dus·tri·al·ize (in·dus'tri·əl·īz), *v.,* –ized, –iz·ing. 1. make industrial. 2. organize as an industry.

in·dus·tri·ous (in·dus'tri·əs), *adj.* hardworking. —**in·dus'tri·ous·ly,** *adv.* —**in·dus'tri·ous·ness,** *n.* —Syn. diligent, busy.

in·dus·try (in'dəs·tri), *n., pl.* –tries. 1. systematic work or labor. 2. steady effort. 3. any branch of business, trade, or manufacture: *the automobile industry.* 4. management and ownership of factories, mills, etc. [< L *industria*] —Syn. 2. diligence.

in·dwell (in·dwel'), *v.,* –dwelt, –dwell·ing. dwell in; dwelling within. —**in'dwell'er,** *n.*

-ine[1], *suffix.* of; like; like that of; characteristic of; having the nature of; being, as in *crystalline*, *elephantine*. [< L *-inus*]

-ine², *suffix*. used esp. in the names of chemicals, as in *chlorine, aniline*. [< F < L *-ina*]

in·e·bri·ate (*v*. in·ē′brī·āt; *n., adj*. in·ē′brī·it), *v*., -at·ed, -at·ing, *n., adj*. —*v*. 1. make drunk; intoxicate. 2. intoxicate mentally; excite. —*n*. habitual drunkard; intoxicated person. —*adj*. intoxicated; drunk. [< L, < *in-* + *ebrius* drunk] —in·e′bri·a′tion, *n*.

in·e·bri·e·ty (in′i·brī′ə·ti), *n*. drunkenness.

in·ed·i·ble (in·ed′ə·bəl), *adj*. not fit to eat. —in·ed′i·bil′i·ty, *n*.

in·ef·fa·ble (in·ef′ə·bəl), *adj*. 1. not to be expressed in words; too great to be described in words. 2. that must not be spoken. [< L *ineffabilis*, ult. < *in-* not + *ex-* out + *fari* speak] —in·ef′fa·bil′i·ty, in·ef′fa·ble·ness, *n*. —in·ef′fa·bly, *adv*.

in·ef·face·a·ble (in′ə·fās′ə·bəl), *adj*. that cannot be rubbed out or wiped out. —in′ef·face′a·bil′i·ty, *n*. —in′ef·face′a·bly, *adv*.

in·ef·fec·tive (in′ə·fek′tiv), *adj*. 1. not effective; of little use. 2. unfit for work; incapable. —in′ef·fec′tive·ly, *adv*. —in′ef·fec′tive·ness, *n*.

in·ef·fec·tu·al (in′ə·fek′chü·əl), *adj*. 1. without effect; useless. 2. not able to produce the effect wanted. —in′ef·fec′tu·al′i·ty, in′ef·fec′tu·al·ness, *n*. —in′ef·fec′tu·al·ly, *adv*. —Syn. 1. ineffective, futile, vain.

in·ef·fi·ca·cious (in′ef·ə·kā′shəs), *adj*. not efficacious; not able to produce the effect wanted. —in′ef·fi·ca′cious·ly, *adv*. —in′ef·fi·ca′cious·ness, in·ef·fi·cac·i·ty (in′ef·ə·kas′ə·ti), *n*.

in·ef·fi·ca·cy (in·ef′ə·kə·si), *n*. lack of efficacy; inability to produce the effect wanted.

in·ef·fi·cien·cy (in′ə·fish′ən·si), *n*. lack of efficiency; inability to get things done.

in·ef·fi·cient (in′ə·fish′ənt), *adj*. 1. not efficient; not able to produce, accomplish, or effect anything without waste of time, energy, etc. 2. incapable; not able to get things done. —in′ef·fi′cient·ly, *adv*. —Syn. 1. incompetent, ineffective.

in·e·las·tic (in′i·las′tik), *adj*. not elastic; stiff; inflexible; unyielding.

in·e·las·tic·i·ty (in′i·las·tis′ə·ti), *n*. lack of elasticity.

in·el·e·gance (in·el′ə·gəns), **in·el·e·gan·cy** (-gən·si), *n., pl*. -ganc·es; -cies. 1. lack of elegance; lack of good taste. 2. something that is not elegant or graceful.

in·el·e·gant (in·el′ə·gənt), *adj*. not elegant; not in good taste; crude; vulgar. —in·el′e·gant·ly, *adv*. —Syn. rough, unrefined.

in·el·i·gi·ble (in·el′ə·jə·bəl), *adj*. not suitable; not qualified. —*n*. person who is not suitable or not qualified. —in·el′i·gi·bil′i·ty, *n*. —in·el′i·gi·bly, *adv*.

in·e·luc·ta·ble (in′i·luk′tə·bəl), *adj*. that cannot be escaped. [< L *ineluctabilis* < *in-* not + *ex-* out of + *luctari* to struggle] —in′e·luc′ta·bil′i·ty, *n*. —in′e·luc′ta·bly, *adv*.

in·ept (in·ept′), *adj*. 1. not suitable; out of place. 2. absurd; foolish. [< L *ineptus* < *in-* not + *aptus* apt] —in·ept′ly, *adv*. —in·ept′ness, *n*.

in·ept·i·tude (in·ept′ə·tüd; -tūd), *n*. 1. unfitness; foolishness. 2. a silly or inappropriate act or remark.

in·e·qual·i·ty (in′i·kwol′ə·ti), *n., pl*. -ties. 1. lack of equality; a being unequal in amount, size, value, rank, etc. 2. lack of evenness, regularity, or uniformity. 3. *Math*. expression showing that two quantities are unequal, like *a* > *b* or *c* < *d*. —Syn. 1. disparity. 2. unevenness, variableness.

in·eq·ui·ta·ble (in·ek′wə·tə·bəl), *adj*. unfair; unjust. —in·eq′ui·ta·bly, *adv*.

in·eq·ui·ty (in·ek′wə·ti), *n., pl*. -ties. unfairness; injustice.

in·e·rad·i·ca·ble (in′i·rad′ə·kə·bəl), *adj*. that cannot be rooted out or got rid of. —in′e·rad′i·ca·ble·ness, *n*. —in′e·rad′i·ca·bly, *adv*.

in·ert (in·ert′), *adj*. 1. having no power to move or act; lifeless. 2. inactive; slow; sluggish. 3. with few or no active properties. Helium and neon are inert gases. [< L *iners* idle, unskilled

< *in-* without + *ars* art, skill] —in·ert′ly, *adv*. —in·ert′ness, *n*.

in·er·tia (in·ėr′shə), *n*. 1. tendency to remain in the state one is in and not start changes. 2. *Physics*. tendency of all objects and matter to stay still if still, or if moving, to go on moving in the same direction unless acted on by some outside force. [< L, < *iners* INERT] —in·er′tial, *adj*.

inertial guidance, a complex, essentially gyroscopic navigational system which keeps an airplane, missile, submarine, etc. on a predetermined course or enables it to navigate without recourse to radio, the stars, etc.

in·es·cap·a·ble (in′əs·kāp′ə·bəl), *adj*. that cannot be escaped or avoided.

in·es·ti·ma·ble (in·es′tə·mə·bəl), *adj*. too good, great, valuable, etc., to be measured or estimated. —in·es′ti·ma·bly, *adv*. —Syn. invaluable, priceless.

in·ev·i·ta·ble (in·ev′ə·tə·bəl), *adj*. not avoidable; sure to happen; certain to come. —*n*. that which is inevitable. —in·ev′i·ta·bil′i·ty, in·ev′i·ta·ble·ness, *n*. —in·ev′i·ta·bly, *adv*.

in·ex·act (in′ig·zakt′), *adj*. not exact; not accurate. —in′ex·act′ly, *adv*. —in′ex·act′ness, *n*.

in·ex·cus·a·ble (in′iks·kūz′ə·bəl), *adj*. that ought not to be excused; that cannot be justified. —in′ex·cus′a·bil′i·ty, in′ex·cus′a·ble·ness, *n*. —in′ex·cus′a·bly, *adv*. —Syn. unpardonable.

in·ex·haust·i·ble (in′ig·zôs′tə·bəl), *adj*. 1. that cannot be exhausted; very abundant. 2. tireless. —in′ex·haust′i·bil′i·ty, in′ex·haust′i·ble·ness, *n*. —in′ex·haust′i·bly, *adv*.

in·ex·o·ra·ble (in·ek′sə·rə·bəl), *adj*. relentless; unyielding; not influenced by prayers or entreaties. [< L, < *in-* not + *ex-* successfully + *orare* entreat] —in·ex′o·ra·bil′i·ty, in·ex′o·ra·ble·ness, *n*. —in·ex′o·ra·bly, *adv*. —Syn. unrelenting, implacable, immovable.

in·ex·pe·di·en·cy (in′iks·pē′di·ən·si), *n*. lack of expediency; being inexpedient.

in·ex·pe·di·ent (in′iks·pē′di·ənt), *adj*. not expedient; not practicable, suitable, or wise —in′ex·pe′di·ent·ly, *adv*. —Syn. inadvisable, unwise, unprofitable.

in·ex·pen·sive (in′iks·pen′siv), *adj*. not expensive; cheap; low-priced. —in′ex·pen′sive·ly, *adv*. —in′ex·pen′sive·ness, *n*.

in·ex·pe·ri·ence (in′iks·pir′i·əns), *n*. lack of experience; lack of skill or wisdom gained from experience. —in′ex·pe′ri·enced, *adj*.

in·ex·pert (in·eks′pėrt; in′iks·pėrt′), *adj*. unskilled. —in′ex·pert′ly, *adv*. —in′ex·pert′ness, *n*.

in·ex·pi·a·ble (in·eks′pi·ə·bəl), *adj*. that cannot be atoned for: *an inexpiable crime*. —in·ex′pi·a·ble·ness, *n*. —in·ex′pi·a·bly, *adv*.

in·ex·pli·ca·ble (in·eks′pli·kə·bəl; in′iks·plik′ə·bəl), *adj*. impossible to explain or understand; mysterious. —in·ex′pli·ca·bil′i·ty, in·ex′pli·ca·ble·ness, *n*. —in·ex′pli·ca·bly, *adv*. —Syn. unaccountable.

in·ex·press·i·ble (in′iks·pres′ə·bəl), *adj*. that cannot be expressed; beyond expression. —in′ex·press′i·bil′i·ty, in′ex·press′i·ble·ness, *n*. —in′ex·press′i·bly, *adv*. —Syn. unutterable.

in·ex·pres·sive (in′iks·pres′iv), *adj*. not expressive; lacking in expression. —in′ex·pres′sive·ly, *adv*. —in′ex·pres′sive·ness, *n*.

in·ex·tin·guish·a·ble (in′iks·ting′gwish·ə·bəl), *adj*. that cannot be put out or stopped. —in′ex·tin′guish·a·bly, *adv*.

in ex·tre·mis (in iks·trē′mis), at the point of death. [< L, lit., amid the final things]

in·ex·tri·ca·ble (in·eks′tri·kə·bəl), *adj*. 1. that one cannot get out of. 2. that cannot be disentangled or solved. —in·ex′tri·ca·bil′i·ty, in·ex′tri·ca·ble·ness, *n*. —in·ex′tri·ca·bly, *adv*.

inf., 1. Also, **Inf.** infantry. 2. infinitive. 3. information. 4. infra (below).

in·fal·li·bil·i·ty (in·fal′ə·bil′ə·ti), *n*. absolute freedom from error.

in·fal·li·ble (in·fal′ə·bəl), *adj*. 1. free from error; that cannot be mistaken. 2. absolutely reliable; sure. 3. in the Roman Catholic Church, incapable of error in explaining matters pertaining to faith or morals. —in·fal′li·ble·ness, *n*. —in·fal′li·bly, *adv*.

in·fa·mous (in′fə·məs), *adj.* **1.** shamefully bad; extremely wicked. **2.** having a very bad reputation; in public disgrace. —**in′fa·mous·ly**, *adv.* —**in′fa·mous·ness**, *n.* —**Syn. 1.** odious. **2.** notorious, disreputable.

in·fa·my (in′fə·mi), *n.*, *pl.* **-mies. 1.** very bad reputation; public disgrace. **2.** shameful badness; extreme wickedness. [< L, < *in-* without + *fama* (good) reputation]

in·fan·cy (in′fən·si), *n.*, *pl.* **-cies. 1.** condition or time of being an infant; babyhood. **2.** early stage; beginning of development. **3.** condition of being under legal age of responsibility (in common law, under 21).

in·fant (in′fənt), *n.* **1.** baby; very young child. **2.** person under the legal age of responsibility; a minor. **3.** beginner. —*adj.* **1.** of or for an infant. **2.** in an early stage; just beginning to develop. [< L *infans*, orig., not speaking < *in-* not + *fari* speak] —**in′fant·hood**, *n.*

in·fan·ta (in·fan′tə), *n.* royal princess of Spain or Portugal. [< Sp., Pg., fem.]

in·fan·te (in·fan′tā), *n.* royal prince of Spain or Portugal, but not the heir to the throne. [< Sp., Pg.]

in·fan·ti·cide (in·fan′tə·sīd), *n.* the killing of a baby. [< L, < *infans* INFANT + *-cidium* act of killing < *caedere* kill] —**in·fan′ti·cid′al**, *n.*

in·fan·tile (in′fən·tīl; -til), *adj.* **1.** of an infant or infants; having to do with infants. **2.** like an infant; babyish; childish. **3.** in an early stage; just beginning to develop.

infantile paralysis, an acute infectious disease that destroys tissue in the brain and spinal cord, causing fever, paralysis of various muscles, and often death; poliomyelitis.

in·fan·ti·lism (in·fan′tə·liz·əm), *n.* abnormal persistence or appearance of childish traits in adults.

in·fan·tine (in′fən·tīn; -tin), *adj.* infantile; babyish; childish.

in·fan·try (in′fən·tri), *n.*, *pl.* **-tries.** soldiers who fight on foot. [< F < Ital., < *infante, fante* foot soldier, orig., a youth. See INFANT.]

in·fan·try·man (in′fən·tri·mən), *n.*, *pl.* **-men.** soldier who fights on foot.

in·fat·u·ate (*v.* in·fach′ú·āt; *adj., n.* in·fach′ú·it, -āt), *v.*, **-at·ed**, **-at·ing**, *adj., n.* —*v.* **1.** make foolish. **2.** inspire with a foolish or extreme passion. —*adj.* infatuated. —*n.* an infatuated person. [< L, < *in-* + *fatuus* foolish]

in·fat·u·at·ed (in·fach′ú·āt′id), *adj.* extremely adoring; foolishly in love. —**in·fat′u·at′ed·ly**, *adv.*

in·fat·u·a·tion (in·fach′ú·ā′shən), *n.* **1.** an infatuating or being infatuated. **2.** foolish love; unreasoning fondness.

in·fect (in·fekt′), *v.* **1.** cause disease in by introducing germs: *dirt infects an open cut.* **2.** influence in a bad way; contaminate: *one bad companion can infect a whole group of boys.* **3.** influence by spreading from one to another: *the captain's courage infected his soldiers.* [< L *infectus* dyed, orig., put in < *in-* in + *facere* make] —**in·fec′tor**, *n.* —**Syn.** pollute.

in·fec·tion (in·fek′shən), *n.* **1.** causing of disease in people, animals, and plants by the introduction of germs. **2.** disease caused in this way. **3.** influence, feeling, or idea spreading from one to another. **4.** fact or state of being infected.

in·fec·tious (in·fek′shəs), *adj.* **1.** spread by infection: *measles is an infectious disease.* **2.** causing infection. **3.** apt to spread. —**in·fec′tious·ly**, *adv.* —**in·fec′tious·ness**, *n.* —**Syn. 3.** contagious, catching.

in·fec·tive (in·fek′tiv), *adj.* infectious. —**in·fec′tive·ness**, **in′fec·tiv′i·ty**, *n.*

in·fe·lic·i·tous (in′fə·lis′ə·təs), *adj.* **1.** unsuitable; not appropriate. **2.** unfortunate; unhappy. —**in′fe·lic′i·tous·ly**, *adv.*

in·fe·lic·i·ty (in′fə·lis′ə·ti), *n.*, *pl.* **-ties. 1.** unsuitability; inappropriateness. **2.** misfortune; unhappiness. **3.** something unsuitable; inappropriate word, remark, etc.

in·fer (in·fėr′), *v.*, **-ferred**, **-fer·ring. 1.** find out by reasoning; conclude: *from the facts*

known we infer his innocence. **2.** indicate; imply: *ragged clothing infers poverty.* **3.** draw inferences. [< L, < *in-* in + *ferre* bring] —**in·fer·a·ble** (in·fėr′ə·bəl; in′fər-), *adj.* —**in·fer′a·bly**, *adv.* —**in·fer′rer**, *n.* —**Syn. 1.** deduce. ➤ See imply for usage note.

in·fer·ence (in′fər·əns), *n.* **1.** process of inferring. **2.** that which is inferred; conclusion.

in·fer·en·tial (in′fər·en′shəl), *adj.* having to do with inference; depending on inference. —**in′fer·en′tial·ly**, *adv.*

in·fe·ri·or (in·fir′i·ər), *adj.* **1.** lower in position or rank: *a lieutenant is inferior to a captain.* **2.** not so good; lower in quality; worse. **3.** below average: *an inferior mind.* **4.** inferior to, **a.** below; lower than. **b.** not so good or so great as; worse than. —*n.* **1.** person who is lower in rank or station. **2.** an inferior thing. [< L, compar. of *inferus*, adj., situated below] —**in·fe′ri·or·ly**, *adv.*

in·fe·ri·or·i·ty (in·fir′i·ôr′ə·ti; -or′-), *n.* inferior condition or quality.

inferiority complex, an abnormal or morbid feeling of being inferior to other people.

in·fer·nal (in·fėr′nəl), *adj.* **1.** of hell; having to do with the lower world. **2.** hellish; diabolical. **3.** *Colloq.* abominable; outrageous. **4.** of the lower world which the ancient Greeks and Romans thought was the abode of the dead. [< LL *infernalis*, ult. < L *inferus* below] —**in·fer′nal·i·ty**, *n.* —**in·fer′nal·ly**, *adv.*

infernal machine, an explosive apparatus for maliciously destroying life and property.

in·fer·no (in·fėr′nō), *n.*, *pl.* **-nos. 1.** hell. **2.** a hell-like place or thing. [< Ital.]

in·fer·tile (in·fėr′təl), *adj.* not fertile; sterile. —**in·fer·til·i·ty** (in′fėr·til′ə·ti), *n.*

in·fest (in·fest′), *v.* trouble or disturb frequently or in large numbers: *mosquitoes infest swamps.* [< L, attack, < *infestus* hostile] —**in′fes·ta′tion**, *n.* —**in·fest′er**, *n.* —**Syn.** overrun.

in·fi·del (in′fə·dəl), *n.* **1.** person who does not believe in religion. **2.** person who does not accept a particular faith: *Mohammedans call Christians infidels.* **3.** person who does not accept Christianity. —*adj.* **1.** not believing in religion. **2.** not accepting a particular faith, esp. Christianity or Mohammedanism. [< L, < *in-* not + *fides* faith]

in·fi·del·i·ty (in′fə·del′ə·ti), *n.*, *pl.* **-ties. 1.** lack of religious faith. **2.** unbelief in Christianity. **3.** unfaithfulness, esp. of husband or wife; disloyalty. **4.** an unfaithful or disloyal act.

in·field (in′fēld′), *n. Am.* **1.** a baseball diamond. **2.** first, second, and third basemen and shortstop of a baseball team.

in·field·er (in′fēl′dər), *n. Am., Baseball.* an infield player.

in·fil·trate (in·fil′trāt), *v.*, **-trat·ed**, **-trat·ing**, *n.* —*v.* **1.** pass into or through by, or as by, filtering: *enemy troops infiltrated the front lines.* **2.** filter into or through; permeate. —*n.* that which infiltrates. —**in′fil·tra′tion**, *n.* —**in·fil′tra·tive**, *adj.*

infin., infinitive.

in·fi·nite (in′fə·nit), *adj.* **1.** without limits or bounds; endless: *the infinite power of God.* **2.** extremely great. —*n.* **1.** that which is infinite. **2.** the Infinite, God. [< L, < *in-* not + *finis* boundary] —**in′fi·nite·ly**, *adv.* —**in′fi·nite·ness**, *n.* —**Syn.** *adj.* **1.** boundless, unlimited. **2.** immeasurable, immense.

in·fin·i·tes·i·mal (in′fin·ə·tes′ə·məl), *adj.* so small as to be almost nothing. —*n.* an infinitesimal amount. [< NL *infinitesimus* the "nth" < L *infinitus* INFINITE] —**in′fin·i·tes′i·mal·ly**, *adv.*

in·fin·i·tive (in·fin′ə·tiv), *n. Gram.* a form of a verb not limited by person and number. *Examples:* Let him go. We want to go now. [< LL, < L *infinitus* unrestricted, INFINITE] —**in·fin′i·tive·ly**, *adv.* ➤ *to* and the infinitive *To* is the "sign of the infinitive" when the infinitive is used as a noun (Just *to hear* him talk is an inspiration) and usually when it is used to complete the meaning of a verb (They all tried *to get in* first). After some verbs (can, may, shall, *will, do, dare, make, help, need,* . . .) no *to* is used (Do not make him *stop*). In short, clear, unemphatic series of infinitives in parallel constructions, the *to* is not repeated (*To sit* and *smoke* and *think* and *dream* was his idea of pleasure). The infinitive may be used as a subject (*To err* is human), object (he wanted *to go* fishing), adjective modifier (money *to burn*), adverbial modifier (They came *to play*), and with auxiliaries (He will *pass* this time). See also usage note under **split infinitive**.

in·fin·i·tude (in-fin′ə-tüd; -tūd), *n.* 1. a being infinite. 2. an infinite extent, amount, or number. 3. infinity.

in·fin·i·ty (in-fin′ə-ti), *n., pl.* –ties. 1. state of being infinite. 2. an infinite distance, space, time, or quantity. 3. an infinite extent, amount, or number.

in·firm (in-fêrm′), *adj.* 1. weak; feeble. 2. weak in will or character; not steadfast. 3. not firm; not stable. —in·firm′ly, *adv.* —in·firm′ness, *n.* —Syn. 1. shaky, decrepit.

in·fir·ma·ry (in-fêr′mə-ri), *n., pl.* –ries. 1. place for the care of the infirm, sick, or injured; hospital in a school or institution. 2. a hospital.

in·fir·mi·ty (in-fêr′mə-ti), *n., pl.* –ties. 1. weakness; feebleness. 2. sickness; illness. 3. moral weakness or failing.

in·fix (*v.* in-fiks′; *n.* in′fiks′), *v.* 1. fix in; drive in. 2. fix in the mind or memory; impress. 3. *Gram.* insert an infix. —*n.* *Gram.* a formative element inserted within the body of a word.

infl., influenced.

in·flame (in-flām′), *v.,* –flamed, –flam·ing. 1. excite; make more violent. 2. become excited with intense feeling. 3. make unnaturally hot, red, sore, or swollen. 4. become red or hot from disease, etc. 5. set ablaze; set on fire. [< OF *enflamer* < L, ult. < *in–* in + *flamma* flame] —in·flam′er, *n.* —in·flam′ing·ly, *adv.* —Syn. 1. arouse, fire. 5. kindle.

in·flam·ma·ble (in-flam′ə-bəl), *adj.* 1. easily set on fire. 2. easily excited or aroused. —*n.* something inflammable. —in·flam′ma·bil′i·ty, in·flam′ma·ble·ness, *n.* —in·flam′ma·bly, *adv.*

in·flam·ma·tion (in′flə-mā′shən), *n.* 1. a diseased condition of some part of the body, marked by heat, redness, swelling, and pain. 2. an inflaming or being inflamed.

in·flam·ma·to·ry (in-flam′ə-tô′ri; -tō′-), *adj.* 1. tending to excite or arouse. 2. of, causing, or accompanied by inflammation.

in·flate (in-flāt′), *v.,* –flat·ed, –flat·ing. 1. blow out or swell with air or gas: *inflate a balloon.* 2. swell or puff out: *inflate with pride.* 3. increase (prices or currency) beyond the normal amount. [< L, < *in–* into + *flare* blow] —in·flat′a·ble, *adj.* —in·flat′er, in·fla′tor, *n.* —Syn. 1. distend, expand.

in·fla·tion (in-flā′shən), *n.* 1. a swelling (with air, gas, pride, etc.). 2. swollen state; too great expansion. 3. increase of the currency of a country by issuing much paper money. 4. a sharp and sudden rise of prices resulting from a too great expansion in paper money or bank credit.

in·fla·tion·ar·y (in-flā′shən·er′i), *adj.* of or having to do with inflation; tending to inflate.

in·fla·tion·ist (in-flā′shən·ist), *n. Am.* person who favors inflation.

in·flect (in-flekt′), *v.* 1. change the tone or pitch of (the voice). 2. *Gram.* vary the form of (a word) to show case, number, gender, person, tense, mood, comparison, etc. 3. bend; curve. [< L, < *in–* in + *flectere* bend] —in·flec′tive, *adj.* —in·flec′tor, *n.*

in·flec·tion, *esp. Brit.* **in·flex·ion** (in-flek′shən), *n.* 1. change in the tone or pitch of the voice. We usually end questions with a rising inflection. 2. *Gram.* variation in the form of a word to show case, number, gender, person, tense, mood, comparison, etc. 3. bend; curve. —in·flec′tion·al·ly, *esp. Brit.* in·flex′ion·al·ly, *adv.* —Syn. 1. modulation, intonation, accent.

in·flec·tion·al, *esp. Brit.* **in·flex·ion·al** (in-flek′shən·əl), *adj.* of, pertaining to, or exhibiting grammatical inflection.

in·flex·i·ble (in-flek′sə-bəl), *adj.* 1. firm; un-

yielding; steadfast. 2. that cannot be changed; unalterable. 3. not easily bent; stiff; rigid. —in·flex′i·bil′i·ty, in·flex′i·ble·ness, *n.* —in·flex′i·bly, *adv.* —Syn. 1. dogged, stubborn, obstinate. 3. unbending, firm.

in·flict (in-flikt′), *v.* 1. give or cause, as a blow, wound, pain, etc. 2. impose, as a burden, suffering, anything unwelcome, etc. [< L *inflictus* < *in–* on + *fligere* dash] —in·flict′er, in·flic′tor, *n.* —in·flic′tive, *adj.*

in·flic·tion (in-flik′shən), *n.* 1. act of inflicting. 2. something inflicted; pain; suffering; burden; punishment.

in·flo·res·cence (in′flō-res′əns; -flō–), *n.* 1. flowering stage. 2. *Bot.* a. arrangement of flowers on the stem or axis. b. a flower cluster. c. flowers collectively. [< NL *inflorescentia* < L *in–* in + *flos* flower] —in′flo·res′cent, *adj.*

in·flow (in′flō′), *n.* 1. a flowing in or into. 2. that which flows in.

in·flu·ence (in′flü-əns), *n., v.,* –enced, –encing. —*n.* 1. power of persons or things to act on others. 2. power to produce an effect without using coercion: *a person may have influence by his ability, personality, position, or wealth.* 3. person or thing that has such power. —*v.* have power over; change the nature or behavior of: *the moon influences the tides.* [< Med.L *influentia,* orig., a flowing in, ult. < L *in–* in + *fluere* to flow] —in′flu·enc·er, *n.* —Syn. *v.* move, stir, sway, persuade.

in·flu·en·tial (in′flü·en′shəl), *adj.* 1. having much influence; having influence. 2. using influence; producing results. —in′flu·en′tial·ly, *adv.*

in·flu·en·za (in′flü·en′zə), *n.* an acute contagious disease, like a very bad cold in its symptoms, but much more dangerous and exhausting; flu. [< Ital., INFLUENCE] —in′flu·en′zal, *adj.*

in·flux (in′fluks), *n.* 1. a flowing in; steady flow. 2. the mouth of a stream. [< LL *influxus,* ult. < L *in–* in + *fluere* flow]

in·fold (in-fōld′), *v.* 1. fold in; wrap up: *infolded in a shawl.* 2. embrace; clasp. Also, **enfold.** —in·fold′er, *n.* —in·fold′ment, *n.*

in·form (in-fôrm′), *v.* 1. supply with knowledge, facts, or news; tell. 2. instruct; train. 3. make an accusation or complaint: *one thief informed against the others.* 4. animate. [< L, < *in–* + *forma* form] —in·form′ing·ly, *adv.* —Syn. 1. notify, acquaint.

in·for·mal (in-fôr′məl), *adj.* 1. not in the regular or prescribed manner. 2. done without ceremony. 3. used in everyday, common talk, but not used in formal talking or writing. —in·for′mal·ly, *adv.* —Syn. 2. unconventional, easy. ▶ **Informal English** is the typical language of an educated person going about his everyday affairs. It lies between the uncultivated level on one side and the more restricted formal level on the other. It is used not only for personal affairs, but for most public affairs—of business and politics, for example, except in strictly legal matters—for most newspaper and magazine articles, for the bulk of fiction and drama, for a good deal of poetry. In the last generation or so it has come to dominate English writing, partly in reaction against the more elaborate style of the nineteenth century. It has a long and honorable tradition. Informal usage is characteristic of the pamphleteers and popular storytellers of Elizabethan literature; of the plainer portions of the English Bible, especially of the direct narratives; of the works of such writers as Defoe and Fielding and to a large degree of Swift. Formal English is passed on chiefly through reading and so represents in many respects the usage and style of the preceding generation of writers; informal English lies closer to speech.

in·for·mal·i·ty (in′fôr·mal′ə-ti), *n., pl.* –ties. 1. lack of ceremony. 2. an informal act.

in·form·ant (in-fôr′mənt), *n.* 1. person who gives information to another. 2. person who speaks in his native language or dialect for the benefit of persons studying that language or dialect, or for purposes of transcription.

in·for·ma·tion (in′fər·mā′shən), *n.* 1. knowledge; facts; news: *a dictionary gives informa-*

tion *about words.* **2.** an informing: *a guidebook is for the information of travelers.* **3.** person or office whose duty it is to answer questions. **4.** accusation or complaint against a person. —**in′for·ma′tion·al,** *adj.*

in·form·a·tive (in·fôr′mə·tiv), *adj.* giving information; instructive.

in·form·er (in·fôr′mər), *n.* **1.** person who makes an accusation or complaint against others: *an informer told the police that the store was selling stolen goods.* **2.** informant.

in·frac·tion (in·frak′shən), *n.* a breaking of a law or obligation; violation. [< L *infractio* < *in*- in + *frangere* to break]

in·fra·red (in′frə·red′), *n.* the invisible part of the spectrum whose rays have wave lengths longer than those of the red part of the visible spectrum. —*adj.* pertaining to the infrared.

in·fre·quen·cy (in·frē′kwən·si), **in·fre·quence** (-kwəns), *n.* a being infrequent; scarcity; rarity.

in·fre·quent (in·frē′kwənt), *adj.* not frequent; occurring seldom or far apart. —**in·fre′quent·ly,** *adv.* —Syn. scarce, rare.

in·fringe (in·frinj′), *v.,* –fringed, –fring·ing. **1.** violate: *infringe the food and drug law.* **2.** trespass; encroach: *infringe upon rights.* [< L, < *in*- in + *frangere* break] —**in·fringe′ment,** *n.* —**in·fring′er,** *n.* —Syn. **1.** break. **2.** intrude.

in·fu·ri·ate (in·fyùr′i·āt), *v.,* –at·ed, –at·ing. put into a fury; make furious; enrage. [< Med. L, < L *in*- into + *furia* fury] —**in·fu·ri·ate·ly** (in·fyùr′i·it·li), *adv.* —**in·fu′ri·at′ing·ly,** *adv.* —**in·fu′ri·a′tion,** *n.*

in·fuse (in·fūz′), *v.,* –fused, –fus·ing. **1.** introduce as by pouring: *the captain infused his own courage into his soldiers.* **2.** inspire: *infuse with courage.* **3.** steep or soak in a liquid to get something out. [< L *infusus* < *in*- in + *fundere* pour] —**in·fus′er,** *n.*

in·fu·si·ble (in·fū′zə·bəl), *adj.* that cannot be fused or melted. —**in·fu′si·bil′i·ty, in·fu′si·ble·ness,** *n.*

in·fu·sion (in·fū′zhən), *n.* **1.** act or process of infusing. **2.** something poured in or mingled; infused element. **3.** a liquid extract obtained by steeping or soaking.

in·fu·so·ri·an (in′fyù·sô′ri·ən; –sō′-), *n.* one of a group of one-celled animals that move by vibrating filaments.

–ing¹, *suffix.* **1.** action, result, product, material, etc., of some verb, as in *hard thinking, the art of painting.* **2.** action, result, product, material, etc., of some other part of speech, as in *lobstering, offing, shirting.* **3.** of one that ——; of those that ——, as in *smoking habit, printing trade, drinking song.* [ME *–ing,* OE *–ing, –ung*]

–ing², *suffix.* **1.** element forming the present participle. **2.** that ——s, as in *seeing eye, lasting happiness, growing child.* [ME *–ing, –inge*]

in·gen·ious (in·jēn′yəs), *adj.* **1.** skillful in making; good at inventing. **2.** cleverly planned and made. [< L *ingenium* natural talent] —**in·gen′ious·ly,** *adv.* —**in·gen′ious·ness,** *n.* —Syn. **1.** clever, inventive, resourceful.

in·gé·nue (an′zhə·nü), *n., pl.* –nues. **1.** a simple, innocent girl or young woman, esp. as represented on the stage. **2.** actress who plays such a part. [< F, orig. adj., ingenuous]

in·ge·nu·i·ty (in′jə·nü′ə·ti; –nū′-), *n., pl.* –ties. skill in planning, inventing, etc.; cleverness. [< L *ingenuitas* frankness < *ingenuus* ingenuous; infl. by association with *ingenious*]

in·gen·u·ous (in·jen′yù·əs), *adj.* **1.** frank; open; sincere. **2.** simple; natural; innocent. [< L *ingenuus,* orig., native, free born] —**in·gen′u·ous·ly,** *adv.* —**in·gen′u·ous·ness,** *n.* —Syn. **1.** candid. **2.** naïve, guileless.

in·gest (in·jest′), *v.* take (food, etc.) into the body for digestion. [< L *ingestus* < *in*- in + *gerere* carry] —**in·ges′tion,** *n.* —**in·ges′tive,** *adj.*

in·gle·nook (ing′gəl·nùk′), *n.* corner by the fire.

in·glo·ri·ous (in·glô′ri·əs; –glō′-), *adj.* **1.** bringing no glory; shameful; disgraceful. **2.**

having no glory; not famous. —**in·glo′ri·ous·ly,** *adv.* —**in·glo′ri·ous·ness,** *n.* —Syn. **1.** ignoble. **2.** humble, obscure.

in·go·ing (in′gō′ing), *adj.* entering.

in·got (ing′gət), *n.* mass of metal, such as gold, silver, or steel, cast into a convenient shape in a mold. [< OE *in-* in + *goten* poured]

in·graft (in·graft′; –gräft′), *v.* engraft. —**in·graft′ment,** *n.*

in·grained (in·grānd′; in′grānd′), *adj.* **1.** deeply and firmly fixed; thoroughly imbued: *ingrained honesty.* **2.** thorough; inveterate.

in·grate (in′grāt), *n.* an ungrateful person. [< L, *in*- not + *gratus* thankful]

in·gra·ti·ate (in·grā′shi·āt), *v.,* –at·ed, –at·ing. bring (oneself) into favor: *ingratiate oneself by giving presents.* [< *in*-² + L *gratia* favor] —**in·gra′ti·at′ing·ly,** *adv.* —**in·gra′ti·a′tion,** *n.*

in·grat·i·tude (in·grat′ə·tüd; –tūd), *n.* lack of gratitude; being ungrateful.

in·gre·di·ent (in·grē′di·ənt), *n.* one of the parts of a mixture: *the ingredients of a cake.* [< L *ingrediens* entering < *in*- in + *gradi* go] —Syn. constituent, component.

In·gres (aN′grə), *n.* Jean Auguste Dominique, 1780–1867, French painter.

in·gress (in′gres), *n.* **1.** a going in: *ingress to a field.* **2.** way in; entrance. **3.** right to go in. [< L *ingressus* < *ingredi.* See INGREDIENT.] —**in·gres′sion,** *n.* —**in·gres′sive,** *adj.* —**in·gres′sive·ness,** *n.*

in·grow·ing (in′grō′ing), *adj.* **1.** growing inward. **2.** growing into the flesh.

in·grown (in′grōn′), *adj.* **1.** grown within; grown inward. **2.** grown into the flesh.

in·gui·nal (ing′gwə·nəl), *adj.* of the groin; in or near the groin. [< L, < *inguen* groin]

in·gulf (in·gulf′), *v.* engulf.

in·hab·it (in·hab′it), *v.* live in (a place, region, house, cave, tree, etc.). [< L, < *in*- in + *habitare* dwell < *habere* have, dwell] —**in·hab′it·a·ble,** *adj.* —**in·hab′it·a·bil′i·ty,** *n.* —**in′hab·i·ta′tion,** *n.* —**in·hab′it·er,** *n.*

in·hab·it·ant (in·hab′ə·tənt), *n.* person or animal that lives in a place. —Syn. dweller.

in·hal·ant (in·hāl′ənt), *n.* **1.** medicine to be inhaled. **2.** apparatus for inhaling it.

in·hale (in·hāl′), *v.,* –haled, –hal·ing. draw into the lungs; breathe in (air, gas, fragrance, tobacco smoke, etc.). [< L, < *in*- in + *halare* breathe] —**in·ha·la·tion** (in′hə·lā′shən), *n.*

in·hal·er (in·hāl′ər), *n.* **1.** apparatus used in inhaling medicine. **2.** person who inhales.

in·har·mon·ic (in′här·mon′ik), **in·har·mon·i·cal** (–ə·kəl), *adj.* not harmonic; not musical.

in·har·mo·ni·ous (in′här·mō′ni·əs), *adj.* discordant; disagreeing. —**in′har·mo′ni·ous·ly,** *adv.* —**in′har·mo′ni·ous·ness,** *n.*

in·here (in·hir′), *v.,* –hered, –her·ing. exist; belong to as a quality or attribute: *greed inheres in human nature, power inheres in a ruler.* [< L, < *in*- in + *haerere* to stick]

in·her·ent (in·hir′ənt; –her′-), *adj.* belonging to (a person or thing) as a quality or attribute: *inherent modesty, inherent probability.* —**in·her′ence,** *n.* —**in·her′ent·ly,** *adv.* —Syn. intrinsic, existing, abiding.

in·her·it (in·her′it), *v.* **1.** receive as an heir: *the widow inherited the farm.* **2.** get or possess from one's ancestors: *she inherits her father's blue eyes.* [< OF *enheriter,* ult. < L *in*- + *heres* heir] —**in·her′i·tor,** *n.*

in·her·it·a·ble (in·her′ə·tə·bəl), *adj.* **1.** capable of being inherited. **2.** capable of inheriting; qualified to inherit. —**in·her′it·a·bil′i·ty, in·her′it·a·ble·ness,** *n.*

in·her·it·ance (in·her′ə·təns), *n.* **1.** act or process of inheriting: *he obtained his house by inheritance from an aunt.* **2.** right of inheriting. **3.** anything inherited: *good health is a fine inheritance.* —Syn. **3.** heritage, legacy.

inheritance tax, *U.S., Law.* tax on inherited property.

in·hib·it (in·hib′it), *v.* **1.** hinder by obstruction or restriction; restrain: *the soldier's sense of duty inhibited his impulse to run away.* 2. prohibit; forbid. [< L *inhibitus* < *in–* in + *habere* hold] **—in·hib·it·a·ble,** *adj.* **—in·hib·it·er, in·hib·i·tor,** *n.* **—in·hib·i·tive,** *adj.* **—Syn.** 1. check, repress, stop. 2. interdict.

in·hi·bi·tion (in′i·bish′ən; in′hi–), *n.* 1. an inhibiting or being inhibited. 2. *Psychol.* idea, emotion, habit, or other inner force that restrains natural impulses. **—in·hib·i·tive** (in·hib′ə·tiv), **in·hib·i·to·ry** (in·hib′ə·tô′ri; –tō′–), *adj.*

in hoc sig·no vin·ces (in hok sig′nō vin′sēz), *Latin.* in this sign shalt thou conquer.

in·hos·pi·ta·ble (in·hos′pi·tə·bəl; in′hos·pit′ə·bəl), *adj.* 1. not hospitable. 2. providing no shelter; barren: *an inhospitable shore.* **—in·hos′pi·ta·ble·ness,** *n.* **—in·hos′pi·ta·bly,** *adv.* **—Syn.** 2. cheerless, uninviting.

in·hos·pi·tal·i·ty (in·hos′pə·tal′ə·ti), *n.* lack of hospitality; inhospitable behavior.

in·hu·man (in·hū′mən), *adj.* not human; not having the qualities natural to a human being. **—in·hu′man·ly,** *adv.* **—in·hu′man·ness,** *n.* **—Syn.** unfeeling, hardhearted, brutal, cruel, pitiless, merciless.

in·hu·mane (in′hū·mān′), *adj.* lacking in compassion, humanity, or kindness. **—in′hu·mane′ly,** *adv.* **—Syn.** cruel, brutal.

in·hu·man·i·ty (in′hū·man′ə·ti), *n., pl.* **–ties.** 1. inhuman quality; lack of feeling; cruelty; brutality. 2. an inhuman, cruel, or brutal act.

in·im·i·cal (in·im′ə·kəl), *adj.* 1. unfriendly; hostile. 2. adverse; unfavorable; harmful. [< LL, < L *inimicus* < *in–* not + *amicus* friendly] **—in·im′i·cal′i·ty,** *n.* **—in·im′i·cal·ly,** *adv.* **—Syn.** 1. antagonistic.

in·im·i·ta·ble (in·im′ə·tə·bəl), *adj.* that cannot be imitated or copied; matchless. **—in·im′i·ta·bil′i·ty, in·im′i·ta·ble·ness,** *n.* **—in·im′i·ta·bly,** *adv.*

in·iq·ui·tous (in·ik′wə·təs), *adj.* 1. very unjust. 2. wicked. **—in·iq′ui·tous·ly,** *adv.* **—in·iq′ui·tous·ness,** *n.*

in·iq·ui·ty (in·ik′wə·ti), *n., pl.* **–ties.** 1. very great injustice. 2. wickedness. 3. a wicked or unjust act. [< L *iniquitas,* ult. < *in–* not + *aequus* just]

i·ni·tial (i·nish′əl), *adj., n., v.,* **–tialed, –tialing;** *esp. Brit.* **–tialled, –tial·ling.** **—***adj.* occurring at the beginning; first; earliest. **—***n.* the first letter of a word. **—***v.* mark or sign with initials. [< L *initialis,* ult. < *inire* begin < *in–* in + *ire* go]

i·ni·tial·ly (i·nish′əl·i), *adv.* at the beginning.

i·ni·ti·ate (*v.* i·nish′i·āt; *n., adj.* i·nish′i·it, –āt), *v.,* **–at·ed, –at·ing,** *n., adj.* **—***v.* 1. be the first one to start; begin. 2. admit (a person) by special forms or ceremonies (into mysteries, secret knowledge, or a society). 3. introduce into the knowledge of some art or subject. **—***n.* person who is initiated. **—***adj.* initiated. [< L *initiatus,* ult. < *inire* begin. See INITIAL.] **—Syn.** *v.* 1. commence, originate. 2. install, induct. **—i·ni′ti·a′tor,** *n.*

i·ni·ti·a·tion (i·nish′i·ā′shən), *n.* 1. an initiating or being initiated. 2. formal admission into a group or society. 3. ceremonies by which one is admitted to a group or society.

initiation fee, *Am.* fee one pays upon being initiated into a society, club, etc.

i·ni·ti·a·tive (i·nish′i·ə·tiv; –i·ā′tiv), *n.* 1. active part in taking the first steps in any undertaking; the lead: *take the initiative in making acquaintances.* 2. readiness and ability to be the one to start a course of action: *a leader must have initiative.* 3. right to be the first to act, legislate, etc. 4. right of citizens outside the legislature to introduce or enact a new law by vote. **—***adj.* that initiates; introductory. **—i·ni′ti·a·tive·ly,** *adv.*

i·ni·ti·a·to·ry (i·nish′i·ə·tô′ri; –tō′–), *adj.* 1. first; beginning; introductory. 2. of initiation. **—i·ni′ti·a·to′ri·ly,** *adv.*

in·ject (in·jekt′), *v.* 1. force (liquid) into a passage, cavity, or tissue). 2. throw in: *inject a remark into the conversation.* [< L *injectus* < *in–* + *jacere* to throw] **—in·jec′tion,** *n.* **—in·jec′tor,** *n.*

in·ju·di·cious (in′jü·dish′əs), *adj.* showing lack of judgment; unwise; not prudent. **—in′ju·di′cious·ly,** *adv.* **—in′ju·di′cious·ness,** *n.*

in·junc·tion (in·jungk′shən), *n.* 1. command; order. 2. a formal order issued by a law court ordering a person or group to do, or refrain from doing, something. [< LL *injunctio* < L *injungere* ENJOIN]

in·jure (in′jər), *v.,* **–jured, –jur·ing.** 1. do damage to; harm; hurt. 2. do wrong to; be unfair to. [< *injury*] **—in′jur·er,** *n.*

in·ju·ri·ous (in·jür′i·əs), *adj.* 1. causing injury; harmful. 2. wrongful; unfair; unjust. **—in·ju′ri·ous·ly,** *adv.* **—in·ju′ri·ous·ness,** *n.*

in·ju·ry (in′jər·i), *n., pl.* **–ju·ries.** 1. damage; harm; hurt. 2. wrong; unfairness. [< L *injuria* < *in–* not + *jus* right] **—Syn.** 2. injustice.

in·jus·tice (in·jus′tis), *n.* 1. lack of justice; being unjust. 2. an unjust act.

ink (ingk), *n.* liquid used for writing or printing. **—***v.* put ink on; mark or stain with ink. [< OF *enque* < LL < Gk. *enkauston* < *en* in + *kaiein* burn] **—ink′er,** *n.* **—ink′less,** *adj.* **—ink′like′,** *adj.*

ink·horn (ingk′hôrn′), *n.* a small container formerly used to hold ink, often made of horn. **—***adj.* bookish; pedantic.

Inkhorn

ink·ling (ingk′ling), *n.* slight suggestion; vague notion; hint. [< OE *inca* doubt]

ink·stand (ingk′stand′), *n.* 1. stand to hold ink and pens. 2. container used to hold ink.

ink·well (ingk′wel′), *n.* container used to hold ink on a desk or table.

ink·y (ingk′i), *adj.,* **ink·i·er, ink·i·est.** 1. like ink; dark; black. 2. covered with ink; marked or stained with ink. 3. of ink. **—ink′i·ness,** *n.*

in·laid (in′lād′), *adj.* 1. set in the surface as a decoration or design. 2. decorated with a design or material set in the surface.

in·land (*adj.* in′lənd; *n., adv., also* in′land′), *adj.* 1. away from the coast or the border; situated in the interior: *an inland sea.* 2. domestic; not foreign: *inland trade.* **—***n.* interior of a country; land away from the border or the coast. **—***adv.* in or toward the interior.

in-law (in′lô′), *n. Colloq.* relative by marriage.

in·lay (in′lā′), *v.,* **–laid, –lay·ing,** *n.* **—***v.* 1. set in the surface as a decoration or design: *inlay strips of gold.* 2. decorate with something set in the surface: *inlay a wooden box with silver.* **—***n.* 1. an inlaid decoration, design, or material. 2. a shaped piece of gold, porcelain, etc., cemented in a tooth as a filling. **—in′lay′er,** *n.*

in·let (in′let), *n.* 1. a narrow strip of water extending from a larger body of water into the land or between islands. 2. entrance.

in lo·co pa·ren·tis (in lō′kō pə·ren′tis), *Latin.* in the place of a parent; as a parent.

in·ly (in′li), *adv. Poetic.* 1. inwardly. 2. thoroughly.

in·mate (in′māt), *n.* 1. person confined in a prison, asylum, hospital, etc. 2. occupant; inhabitant.

in me·di·as res (in mā′di·ās rās′; in mē′di·əs rēz′), *Latin.* into the midst of things.

in me·mo·ri·am (in mə·mô′ri·əm; –mō′–), in memory (of); to the memory (of). [< L]

in·most (in′mōst), *adj.* 1. farthest in; deepest within: *inmost depths.* 2. most private; most secret: *inmost desire.*

inn (in), *n.* 1. a public house for lodging and caring for travelers, now largely superseded by hotels. 2. tavern. [OE, lodging] **—inn′less,** *adj.*

in·nate (i·nāt′; in′āt), *adj.* natural; inborn: *an innate talent for drawing.* [< L *innatus* < *in–* + *nasci* be born] **—in·nate′ly,** *adv.* **—in·nate′ness,** *n.*

in·ner (in′ər), *adj.* 1. farther in; inside. 2. more private; more secret: *inner thoughts.* 3. of the mind or soul: *a person's inner life.* —**in′ner·ly,** *adv.* —**in′ner·ness,** *n.*

in·ner·most (in′ər·mōst), *adj.* farthest in; inmost: *the innermost parts.*

in·ning (in′ing), *n.* 1. turn of one side in a game; chance to play. 2. time a person or party is in power. [OE *innung* a taking in]

in·nings (in′ingz), *n. Esp. Brit.* an inning.

inn·keep·er (in′kēp′ər), *n.* person who owns, manages, or keeps an inn.

in·no·cence (in′ə·səns), **in·no·cen·cy** (-sən-si), *n.* 1. freedom from sin, wrong, or guilt. 2. simplicity.

in·no·cent (in′ə·sənt), *adj.* 1. doing no wrong; free from sin or wrong; not guilty. 2. without knowledge of evil: *a baby is innocent.* 3. without evil effects; harmless: *innocent amusements.* 4. simple; artless. —*n.* an innocent person. [< L, < *in*- not + *nocere* to harm] —**in′no·cent·ly,** *adv.* —Syn. *adj.* 1. pure, clean, guiltless. 4. naïve, guileless.

in·noc·u·ous (i·nok′yü·əs), *adj.* harmless. [< L, < *in*- not + *nocuus* hurtful < *nocere* to harm] —**in·noc′u·ous·ly,** *adv.* —**in·noc′u·ous·ness,** *n.*

in·no·vate (in′ə·vāt), *v.,* **-vat·ed, -vat·ing.** make changes; bring in something new or new ways of doing things. [< L, < *in*- + *novus* new] —**in′no·va′tive,** *adj.* —**in′no·va′tor,** *n.*

in·no·va·tion (in′ə·vā′shən), *n.* 1. change made in the established way of doing things. 2. making changes; bringing in new things or new ways of doing things. —**in′no·va′tion·al,** *adj.* —**in′no·va′tion·ist,** *n.*

in·nox·ious (i·nok′shəs), *adj.* harmless.

in·nu·en·do (in′yü·en′dō), *n., pl.* **-does.** 1. indirect hint or reference. 2. indirect suggestion against somebody: *spread scandal by innuendo.* [< L, lit., by giving a nod to, < *in*- in + *-nuere* nod] —Syn. 1. insinuation.

in·nu·mer·a·ble (i·nü′mər·ə·bəl, -nū′-), *adj.* too many to count; very many. —**in·nu′mer·a·ble·ness,** *n.* —**in·nu′mer·a·bly,** *adv.* —Syn. countless, myriad.

in·oc·u·late (in·ok′yə·lāt), *v.,* **-lat·ed, -lat·ing.** 1. infect (a person or animal) with germs that will cause a very mild form of a disease so that thereafter the individual will not take that disease. 2. use disease germs to prevent or cure diseases. 3. put bacteria, serums, etc., into: *inoculate soil with bacteria.* 4. fill (a person's mind). [< L *inoculatus* engrafted < *in*- in + *oculus* bud, eye] —**in·oc′u·la′tion,** *n.* —**in·oc′u·la′tive,** *adj.* —**in·oc′u·la′tor,** *n.*

in·of·fen·sive (in′ə·fen′siv), *adj.* harmless; not arousing objections. —**in′of·fen′sive·ly,** *adv.* —**in′of·fen′sive·ness,** *n.*

in·op·er·a·tive (in·op′ər·ā′tiv; -op′rə·tiv), *adj.* without effect. —**in·op′er·a·tive·ness,** *n.*

in·op·por·tune (in′op·ər·tün′; -tūn′), *adj.* not opportune; coming at a bad time; unsuitable. —**in′op·por·tune′ly,** *adv.* —**in′op·por·tune′ness,** *n.* —Syn. untimely, unseasonable.

in·or·di·nate (in·ôr′də·nit), *adj.* much too great; excessive; unrestrained. [< L *in*- not + *ordo* order] —**in·or·di·na·cy** (in·ôr′də·nə·si), **in·or′di·nate·ness,** *n.* —**in·or′di·nate·ly,** *adv.*

in·or·gan·ic (in′ôr·gan′ik), *adj.* 1. not having the organized physical structure of animals and plants: *minerals are inorganic.* 2. not produced by animal or plant activities. —**in′or·gan′i·cal·ly,** *adv.*

inorganic chemistry, branch of chemistry dealing with all compounds except the organic compounds.

in·put (in′put′), *n.* 1. what is put in or taken in. 2. power supplied to a machine.

in·quest (in′kwest), *n.* a legal inquiry, esp. before a jury, to determine the cause of a death that may possibly have been the result of a crime. [< OF *enqueste,* ult. < L *inquirere* IN-QUIRE]

in·qui·e·tude (in·kwī′ə·tüd; -tūd), *n.* restlessness; uneasiness.

in·quire (in·kwīr′), *v.,* **-quired, -quir·ing.** 1. try to find out by questions; ask. 2. make a

search for information, knowledge, or truth; make an examination of facts or principles. Also, **enquire.** [< L *inquirere* < *in*- into + *quaerere* ask] —**in·quir′er,** *n.* —**in·quir′ing·ly,** *adv.*

in·quir·y (in·kwīr′i; in′kwə·ri), *n., pl.* **-quir·ies.** 1. an inquiring; an asking. 2. question. 3. search for information, knowledge, or truth; examination of facts or principles.

in·qui·si·tion (in′kwə·zish′ən), *n.* 1. a thorough investigation; searching inquiry. 2. official investigation; judicial inquiry. 3. **the Inquisition, a.** court appointed by the Roman Catholic Church to discover and suppress heresy and to punish heretics. **b.** activities of this court. —**in′qui·si′tion·al,** *adj.*

in·quis·i·tive (in·kwiz′ə·tiv), *adj.* 1. asking many questions. 2. too curious; prying into other people's affairs. —**in·quis′i·tive·ly,** *adv.* —**in·quis′i·tive·ness,** *n.* —Syn. 1. curious. —Ant. 1. uninterested.

in·quis·i·tor (in·kwiz′ə·tər), *n.* 1. person who makes an inquisition; official investigator; judicial inquirer. 2. **Inquisitor,** member of the Inquisition.

in·quis·i·to·ri·al (in·kwiz′ə·tô′ri·əl; -tō′-), *adj.* 1. of or pertaining to an inquisitor or inquisition. 2. making searching inquiry; thorough. 3. unduly curious. —**in·quis′i·to′ri·al·ly,** *adv.* —**in·quis′i·to′ri·al·ness,** *n.*

in re (in rē′; rā′), *Latin.* concerning; in the matter of.

I.N.R.I., Jesus of Nazareth, King of the Jews. [for Latin *Iesus Nazarenus, Rex Iudaeorum*]

in·road (in′rōd′), *n.* 1. attack; raid. 2. forcible encroachment: *inroads upon savings.*

in·rush (in′rush′), *n.* rushing in; inflow. —**in′rush′ing,** *n., adj.*

ins., inst. 1. inches. 2. inspector. 3. insurance.

in·sane (in·sān′), *adj.* 1. not sane; mentally deranged. 2. for insane people: *an insane asylum.* 3. characteristic of an insane person. 4. extremely foolish. —**in·sane′ly,** *adv.* —**in·sane′ness,** *n.* —Syn. 1. demented, lunatic, mad. 4. senseless, wild.

in·san·i·tar·y (in·san′ə·ter′i), *adj.* unhealthful. —**in·san′i·tar′i·ness,** *n.*

in·san·i·ty (in·san′ə·ti), *n., pl.* **-ties.** 1. state of being insane. 2. extreme folly.

in·sa·tia·ble (in·sā′shə·bəl), *adj.* that cannot be satisfied. —**in·sa′tia·bil′i·ty, in·sa′tia·ble·ness,** *n.* —**in·sa′tia·bly,** *adv.* —Syn. unquenchable.

in·sa·ti·ate (in·sā′shi·it), *adj.* never satisfied. —**in·sa′ti·ate·ly,** *adv.* —**in·sa′ti·ate·ness,** *n.*

in·scribe (in·skrīb′), *v.,* **-scribed, -scrib·ing.** 1. write, engrave, or mark (words, letters, etc.) on paper, metal, stone, etc. 2. mark or engrave (with words, letters, etc.). 3. address or dedicate (a book, etc.) informally to a person. 4. impress deeply: *my father's words are inscribed in my memory.* 5. put in a list; enroll. 6. *Geom.* draw (one figure) within another figure so that the inner touches the outer at as many points as possible. [< L, < *in*- on + *scribere* write] —**in·scrib′a·ble,** *adj.* —**in·scrib′er,** *n.*

in·scrip·tion (in·skrip′shən), *n.* 1. something inscribed, as by writing or engraving. A monument or a coin has an inscription on it. 2. informal dedication in a book, on a picture, etc. —**in·scrip′tion·al,** *adj.*

in·scru·ta·ble (in·skrü′tə·bəl), *adj.* that cannot be understood; so mysterious or obscure that one cannot make out its meaning. [< LL, < L *in*- not + *scrutari* examine, ransack < *scruta* trash] —**in·scru′ta·bil′i·ty, in·scru′ta·ble·ness,** *n.* —**in·scru′ta·bly,** *adv.* —Syn. unfathomable, incomprehensible.

FEELERS

HEAD

THORAX

WINGS

LEG

ABDOMEN

Parts of an insect

in·sect (in′sekt), *n.* 1. *Zool.* a small invertebrate animal with its body divided into three parts (head, thorax, and abdomen), with three pairs of legs, and usually two pairs of wings, as flies, mosquitoes, and beetles. 2. any similar small animal with its body divided into several parts, with several pairs of legs, as spiders, centipedes, etc. [< L *insectum*, lit., divided < *in*- into + *secare* to cut] —in′sect·like′, *adj.*

in·sec·ti·cide (in·sek′tə·sīd), *n.* substance for killing insects. —in·sec′ti·cid′al, *adj.*

in·sec·tiv·o·rous (in′sek·tiv′ə·rəs), *adj.* 1. insect-eating; feeding mainly on insects. 2. of or belonging to a group of small mammals including moles, hedgehogs, etc. —in·sec·ti·vore (in·sek′tə·vôr), *n.*

in·se·cure (in′si·kyŭr′), *adj.* 1. not secure; unsafe. 2. liable to give way; not firm: *an insecure lock.* —in′se·cure′ly, *adv.* —Syn. 1. uncertain. 2. unstable, shaky.

in·se·cu·ri·ty (in′si·kyŭr′ə·ti), *n.*, *pl.* -ties. 1. lack of security. 2. something insecure.

in·sem·i·nate (in·sem′ə·nāt), *v.*, -nat·ed, -nat·ing. 1. sow; implant. 2. impregnate. —in·sem′i·na′tion, *n.*

in·sen·sate (in·sen′sāt; -sit), *adj.* 1. without sensation. 2. unfeeling: *insensate cruelty.* 3. senseless; stupid: *insensate folly.* —in·sen′sate·ly, *adv.* —in·sen′sate·ness, *n.*

in·sen·si·bil·i·ty (in·sen′sə·bil′ə·ti), *n.*, *pl.* -ties. 1. lack of feeling. 2. lack of consciousness.

in·sen·si·ble (in·sen′sə·bəl), *adj.* 1. not sensitive; not able to feel or observe: *a blind man is insensible to colors.* 2. not aware: *insensible of the danger.* 3. not able to feel anything; unconscious: *the man hit by the truck was insensible for hours.* 4. not easily felt: *the room grew cold by insensible degrees.* —in·sen′si·bly, *adv.*

in·sen·si·tive (in·sen′sə·tiv), *adj.* 1. not sensitive. 2. slow to feel or notice. —in·sen′si·tive·ness, in·sen′si·tiv′i·ty, *n.*

in·sen·ti·ent (in·sen′shi·ənt; -shənt), *adj.* unable to feel; lifeless.

in·sep·a·ra·ble (in·sep′ə·rə·bəl; -sep′rə·bəl), *adj.* that cannot be separated. —*n.* inseparables, inseparable persons or things. —in·sep′a·ra·bil′i·ty, in·sep′a·ra·ble·ness, *n.* —in·sep′a·ra·bly, *adv.*

in·sert (*v.* in·sėrt′; *n.* in′sėrt), *v.* put in; set in: *insert a key into a lock or a letter into a word.* —*n.* something set in or to be set in: *an insert of several pages.* [< L, < *in*- in + *serere* entwine] —in·sert′er, *n.*

in·ser·tion (in·sėr′shən), *n.* 1. an inserting: *the insertion of pictures in a book.* 2. thing inserted. 3. band of lace or embroidery to be sewed at each edge between parts of other material.

in·set (*v.* in·set′, in′set′; *n.* in′set′), *v.*, -set, -set·ting, *n.* —*v.* set in; insert. —*n.* 1. something inserted. 2. influx.

in·shore (in′shôr′; -shōr′), *adj.* near the shore. —*adv.* in toward the shore.

in·side (*n.*, *adj.* in′sīd′; *adv.*, *prep.* in′sīd′), *n.* 1. side or surface that is within; inner part: *the inside of a house.* 2. inward nature. 3. Often, **insides.** *Colloq.* parts inside the body; stomach and bowels. —*adj.* 1. being on the inside: *an inside seat.* 2. *Slang.* done or known by those inside; private; secret: *the theft was an inside job.* 3. *Slang.* working within a group or company as an emissary or spy: *an inside man.* —*adv.* 1. on or to the inside; within. 2. indoors: *go inside.* 3. inside out, so that what should be inside is outside; with the inside showing. —*prep.* Often, **inside of.** in; within the limits of. —Syn. *adj.* 1. internal, interior.

in·sid·er (in′sīd′ər), *n.* 1. person who is inside some place, society, organizaton, etc. 2. *Am.*, *Colloq.* person who is so situated as to understand the actual conditions or facts of a case.

in·sid·i·ous (in·sid′i·əs), *adj.* 1. crafty; tricky; treacherous. 2. working secretly or subtly: *an insidious disease.* < *in*- in + *sedere* sit] —in·sid′i·ous·ly, *adv.* —Syn. 1. wily, sly.

in·sight (in′sīt′), *n.* 1. a viewing of the inside or inner parts of (something) with understanding. 2. wisdom and understanding in dealing with people or with facts.

in·sig·ni·a (in·sig′ni·ə), *n.pl.*, *sing.* **in·sig·ne** (in·sig′nē). emblems, badges, or other distinguishing marks of a high position, military order, etc. [< L, pl. of *insigne* badge < *in*- on + *signum* mark]

in·sig·nif·i·cance (in′sig·nif′ə·kəns), *n.* 1. unimportance. 2. meaninglessness.

in·sig·nif·i·cant (in′sig·nif′ə·kənt), *adj.* 1. having little use or importance. 2. meaningless. —in′sig·nif′i·cant·ly, *adv.* —Syn. 1. petty, trifling.

in·sin·cere (in′sin·sir′), *adj.* not sincere; not honest or candid; deceitful. —in′sin·cere′ly, *adv.* —Syn. hypocritical.

in·sin·cer·i·ty (in′sin·ser′ə·ti), *n.*, *pl.* -ties. lack of sincerity; hypocrisy.

in·sin·u·ate (in·sin′yŭ·āt), *v.*, -at·ed, -at·ing. 1. push in or get in by an indirect, twisting way: *the spy insinuated himself into the confidence of important army officers.* 2. suggest indirectly; hint. [< L, < *in*- in + *sinus* a curve] —in·sin′u·at′ing·ly, *adv.* —in·sin′u·a′tive, *adj.* —in·sin′u·a′tor, *n.*

in·sin·u·a·tion (in·sin′yŭ·ā′shən), *n.* 1. an insinuating. 2. indirect suggestion against someone. 3. hint; suggestion. 4. act or speech to gain favor.

in·sip·id (in·sip′id), *adj.* 1. without much taste. 2. uninteresting; colorless; weak. [< LL *insipidus* < L *in*- not + *sapidus* tasty] —in·sip′id·ly, *adv.* —in·sip′id·ness, *n.* —Syn. 1. flat. 2. stupid, dull, vapid.

in·si·pid·i·ty (in′si·pid′ə·ti), *n.*, *pl.* -ties. 1. lack of flavor; lack of interest. 2. something insipid.

in·sist (in·sist′), *v.* keep firmly to some demand, some statement, or some position. [< L, < *in*- on + *sistere* take a stand] —in·sist′er, *n.* —Syn. urge, persist, press.

in·sist·ent (in·sis′tənt), *adj.* 1. insisting; continuing to make a strong, firm demand or statement. 2. compelling attention or notice; pressing; urgent. —in·sist′ence, in·sist′en·cy, *n.* —in·sist′ent·ly, *adv.*

in·snare (in·snâr′), *v.*, -snared, -snar·ing. ensnare.

in·so·bri·e·ty (in′sə·brī′ə·ti), *n.* intemperance.

in·sole (in′sōl′), *n.* the inner sole of a shoe or boot.

in·so·lence (in′sə·ləns), *n.* bold rudeness; insulting behavior or speech.

in·so·lent (in′sə·lənt), *adj.* boldly rude; insulting. [< L *insolens*, orig., unusual < *in*- not + *solere* be wont] —in′so·lent·ly, *adv.* —Syn. arrogant, impudent.

in·sol·u·ble (in·sol′yə·bəl), *adj.* 1. that cannot be dissolved. 2. that cannot be solved. —in·sol′u·bil′i·ty, in·sol′u·ble·ness, *n.* —in·sol′u·bly, *adv.*

in·solv·a·ble (in·sol′və·bəl), *adj.* that cannot be solved.

in·sol·vent (in·sol′vənt), *adj.* 1. not able to pay one's debts; bankrupt. 2. pertaining to bankrupts. —*n.* an insolvent person. —in·sol′ven·cy, *n.*

in·som·ni·a (in·som′ni·ə), *n.* inability to sleep; sleeplessness. [< L, < *in*- not + *somnus* sleep] —in·som′ni·ous, *adj.*

in·so·much (in′sō·much′), *adv.* 1. to such an extent or degree; so. 2. inasmuch.

in·sou·ci·ance (in·sü′si·əns), *n.* freedom from care or anxiety; carefree feeling.

in·sou·ci·ant (in·sü′si·ənt), *adj.* free from care or anxiety. [< F] —in·sou′ci·ant·ly, *adv.*

in·spect (in·spekt′), *v.* 1. look over carefully; examine. 2. examine officially. [< L *inspectus* < *in*- upon + *specere* look]

in·spec·tion (in·spek′shən), *n.* 1. an inspecting. 2. formal or official examination. —in·spec′tion·al, *adj.*

in·spec·tor (in·spek′tər), *n.* 1. person who inspects. 2. police officer ranking next below a superintendent. —in·spec′to·ral, in·spec·to·ri·al (in′spek·tô′ri·əl; -tō′-), in·spec′tor·ship, *n.*

in·spi·ra·tion (in′spə·rā′shən), *n.* 1. influence of thought and strong feelings on actions, esp. on good actions: *get inspiration from a sermon*. 2. any influence that arouses effort to do well: *the captain was an inspiration to his men*. 3. idea that is inspired. 4. suggestion to another; act of causing something to be told or written by another. 5. divine influence directly and immediately exerted upon the mind or soul of man. 6. a breathing in; a drawing air into the lungs. —**in'spi·ra'tion·al,** *adj.* —**in'spi·ra'tion·al·ly,** *adv.*

in·spire (in·spīr'), *v.,* **-spired, -spir·ing.** 1. put thought, feeling, life, force, into: *the speaker inspired the crowd*. 2. cause (thought or feeling): *the leader's courage inspired confidence in others*. 3. affect; influence: *his sly ways inspire me with distrust*. 4. arouse or influence by a divine force. 5. suggest; cause to be told or written: *his enemies inspired false stories about him*. 6. breathe in; breathe in air. [< L, < *in-* in + *spirare* breathe] —**in·spir'a·ble,** *adj.* —**in·spir'er,** *n.* —**in·spir'ing·ly,** *adv.*

in·spir·it (in·spir'it), *v.* put spirit into; encourage; hearten. —**in·spir'it·ing·ly,** *adv.*

inst., 1. installment. 2. instant. 3. Also, **Inst.** institute; institution. ▶ **inst.** Abbreviations such as *inst.* (of the current month: "Yours of the 18th *inst.* duly rec'd and contents noted") are not now used by businessmen who pay attention to the impression their correspondence will make on readers.

in·sta·bil·i·ty (in'stə·bil'ə·ti), *n.* lack of firmness; liability to give way or change.

in·stall (in·stôl'), *v.* 1. place (a person) in office with ceremonies. 2. establish in a place: *install oneself in an easy chair*. 3. put in position for use: *install a telephone*. [< Med.L, < *in-* in (< L) + *stallum* STALL¹ (< Gmc.)] —**in·stal·la·tion** (in'stə·lā'shən), *n.* —**in·stall'er,** *n.*

in·stall·ment¹, in·stal·ment¹ (in·stôl'mənt), *n.* 1. part of a sum of money or of a debt to be paid at certain regular times. 2. any of several parts furnished or issued at successive times: *a serial story in a magazine in six installments*. [prob. < *install* pay periodically]

in·stall·ment², in·stal·ment² (in·stôl'mənt), *n.* installation.

installment plan, *Am.* system of paying for goods in installments.

in·stance (in'stəns), *n., v.,* **-stanced, -stanc·ing.** —*n.* 1. example; case: *an instance of neglect*. 2. stage or step in an action; occasion: *in the first instance*. 3. request; suggestion; urging: *he came at our instance*. 4. for instance, for example. —*v.* 1. refer to as an example. 2. exemplify. [< OF < L *instantia* insistence < *instans* insistent. See INSTANT.]

in·stant (in'stənt), *n.* 1. particular moment: *stop talking this instant*. 2. moment of time: *he paused for an instant*. —*adj.* 1. immediate; without delay: *instant relief*. 2. pressing; urgent: *an instant need for action*. 3. of the present month; present. —*adv.* Poetic. at once. [< L *instans* insisting, standing near < *in-* in + *stare* stand]

in·stan·ta·ne·ous (in'stən·tā'ni·əs), *adj.* occurring, done, or made in an instant. —**in'stan·ta'ne·ous·ly,** *adv.* —**in'stan·ta'ne·ous·ness,** *n.*

instant coffee, powdered coffee which may be mixed with water and drunk without being brewed.

in·stan·ter (in·stan'tər), *adv.* immediately. [< L, insistently]

in·stant·ly (in'stənt·li), *adv.* 1. in an instant; at once; immediately. 2. urgently.

in·state (in·stāt'), *v.,* **-stat·ed, -stat·ing.** install. —**in·state'ment,** *n.*

in·stead (in·sted'), *adv.* 1. in place (of): *instead of studying, she read a book*. 2. in one's or its place: *let him go instead*.

in·step (in'step), *n.* 1. the upper surface of the human foot between the toes and the ankle. 2. part of a shoe, stocking, etc., over the instep.

in·sti·gate (in'stə·gāt), *v.,* **-gat·ed, -gat·ing.** urge on; stir up: *foreign agents instigated a rebellion*. [< L *instigatus*] —**in'sti·ga'tion,** *n.* —**in'sti·ga'tive,** *adj.* —**in'sti·ga'tor,** *n.*

in·still, in·stil (in·stil'), *v.,* **-stilled, -stilling.** 1. put in little by little; impart gradually: *reading good books instills a love of literature*. 2. put in drop by drop. [< L, < *in-* in + *stilla* a drop] —**in·stil·la·tion** (in'stə·lā'shən), *n.* —**in·still'er,** *n.* —**in·still'ment,** *n.* —**in·stil'ment,** *n.*

in·stinct¹ (in'stingkt), *n.* 1. natural feeling, knowledge, or power, such as guides animals; unlearned tendency: *an instinct leads birds to fly.* 2. a natural bent, tendency, or gift; talent: *an instinct to govern.* [< L *instinctus,* n. < *instinguere* impel]

in·stinct² (in·stingkt'), *adj.* charged or filled with something: *the picture is instinct with life and beauty.* [< L *instinctus,* pp. See INSTINCT¹.]

in·stinc·tive (in·stingk'tiv), *adj.* of, caused, or done by instinct; born in an animal or person, not learned. —**in·stinc'tive·ly,** *adv.* —Syn. intuitive, natural, innate, inherent.

in·sti·tute (in'stə·tüt; -tūt), *v.,* **-tut·ed, -tut·ing,** *n.* —*v.* 1. set up; establish; begin: *the Pilgrims instituted Thanksgiving.* 2. set in operation; initiate: *the police instituted an inquiry into the causes of the accident.* 3. establish in a position; inaugurate. —*n.* 1. an established principle, law, custom, organization, or society. 2. organization or society for some special purpose, as an art institute. [< L *institutus* < *in-* in + *statuere* establish] —**in'sti·tut'er, in'sti·tu'tor,** *n.* —Syn. *v.* 1. found, organize.

in·sti·tu·tion (in'stə·tü'shən; -tū'-), *n.* 1. organization or society for some public or social purpose, as a church, school, hospital, etc. 2. established law, custom, organization, or society: *giving presents on Christmas is an institution.* 3. setting up; establishing; beginning: *the institution of a savings bank in our city.* 4. Colloq. a familiar person or thing.

in·sti·tu·tion·al (in'stə·tü'shən·əl; -tū'-), *adj.* 1. of, like, or established by an institution. 2. *Advertising.* promoting reputation and establishing good will for a business rather than aiming at immediate sales. —**in'sti·tu'tion·al·ly,** *adv.*

in·struct (in·strukt'), *v.* 1. teach. 2. give directions or orders to. 3. inform. [< L *instructus* < *in-* on + *struere* to pile] —Syn. 1. train, educate, tutor, coach. 2. direct, order, command.

in·struc·tion (in·struk'shən), *n.* 1. a teaching; knowledge; education. 2. instructions, directions; orders. —**in·struc'tion·al,** *adj.*

in·struc·tive (in·struk'tiv), *adj.* useful for instruction; instructing: *an instructive experience.* —**in·struc'tive·ly,** *adv.* —**in·struc'tive·ness,** *n.*

in·struc·tor (in·struk'tər), *n.* 1. teacher. 2. *Am.* teacher ranking below an assistant professor in American colleges and universities. —**in·struc'tor·less,** *adj.* —**in·struc'tor·ship,** *n.*

in·stru·ment (in'strə·mənt), *n.* 1. thing with or by which something is done; a person so made use of; means. 2. tool or mechanical device: *a dentist's instruments.* 3. device for producing musical sounds: *stringed instruments.* 4. a formal legal document, such as a contract. [< L *instrumentum* < *instruere* arrange, INSTRUCT]

in·stru·men·tal (in'strə·men'təl), *adj.* 1. acting or serving as a means; useful; helpful. 2. *Music.* played on or written for instruments. 3. of an instrument; made by a device or tool. —**in'stru·men'tal·ly,** *adv.*

in·stru·men·tal·ist (in'strə·men'təl·ist), *n. Music.* person who plays on an instrument. —**in'stru·men'tal·is'tic,** *adj.*

in·stru·men·tal·i·ty (in'strə·men·tal'ə·ti), *n., pl.* **-ties.** helpfulness as an instrument; agency; means.

in·stru·men·ta·tion (in'strə·men·tā'shən), *n.* 1. *Music.* arrangement or composition for instruments. 2. use of instruments.

in·stru·ment·ed (in'strə·ment'id), *adj.* equipped with electronic or other devices necessary for guidance: *a fully instrumented missile.*

instrument flying, directing an airplane by instruments only.

in·sub·or·di·nate (in'sə·bôr'də·nit), *adj.* resisting authority; disobedient; unruly. —*n.* one who is insubordinate. —in'sub·or'di·nate·ly, adv. —Syn. adj. mutinous.

in·sub·or·di·na·tion (in'sə·bôr'də·nā'shən), n. resistance to authority; disobedience.

in·sub·stan·tial (in'səb·stan'shəl), adj. **1.** frail; flimsy; weak: a cobweb is very insubstantial. **2.** unreal; not actual; imaginary: ghosts are insubstantial. —in'sub·stan'ti·al'i·ty, n.

in·suf·fer·a·ble (in·suf'ər·ə·bəl; -suf'rə·bəl), adj. intolerable; unbearable: insufferable insolence. —in·suf'fer·a·ble·ness, n. —in·suf'fer·a·bly, adv.

in·suf·fi·cien·cy (in'sə·fish'ən·si), n. too small an amount; lack; deficiency.

in·suf·fi·cient (in'sə·fish'ənt), adj. not enough. —in'suf·fi'cient·ly, adv.

in·su·lar (in'sə·lər), adj. **1.** of or having to do with islands or islanders. **2.** living or situated on an island. **3.** forming an island. **4.** narrow-minded; prejudiced. [< LL, < L insula island] —in'su·lar·ism, in·su·lar·i·ty (in'sə·lar'ə·ti), n. —in'su·lar·ly, adv.

in·su·late (in'sə·lāt), v., -lat·ed, -lat·ing. **1.** Physics. keep from losing or transferring electricity, heat, sound, etc. **2.** cover or surround (electric wire, etc.) with nonconducting material. **3.** set apart; separate from others; isolate. [< L insulatus formed into an island < insula island]

in·su·la·tion (in'sə·lā'shən), n. **1.** an insulating or being insulated. **2.** material used in insulating.

in·su·la·tor (in'sə·lā'tər), n. that which insulates; nonconductor.

in·su·lin (in'sə·lin), n. **1.** hormone secreted by the pancreas that enables the body to use sugar and other carbohydrates. **2.** Insulin, Trademark. extract containing this hormone, obtained from the pancreas of slaughtered animals, used in treating diabetes. [< L insula island (i.e., of the pancreas)]

Glass insulator for electric wires

in·sult (v. in·sult'; n. in'sult), v. treat with scorn, abuse, or great rudeness: the rebels insulted the flag by throwing mud on it. —n. an insulting speech or action. [< L insultare < in- on, at + salire to leap] —in·sult'er, n. —in·sult'ing, adj. —in·sult'ing·ly, adv.

in·su·per·a·ble (in·sü'pər·ə·bəl), adj. that cannot be passed over or overcome: an insuperable barrier. —in·su'per·a·bil'i·ty, in·su'per·a·ble·ness, n. —in·su'per·a·bly, adv. —Syn. insurmountable, impassable.

in·sup·port·a·ble (in'sə·pôr'tə·bəl; -pōr'-), adj. unbearable; unendurable; intolerable. —in'sup·port'a·ble·ness, n. —in'sup·port'a·bly, adv.

in·sur·a·ble (in·shur'ə·bəl), adj. capable of being insured; fit to be insured. —in·sur'a·bil'i·ty, n.

in·sur·ance (in·shur'əns), n. **1.** an insuring of property, person, or life: fire insurance, life insurance. **2.** the business of insuring property, life, etc. **3.** amount of money for which a person or thing is insured: he has $10,000 insurance, which his wife will receive when he dies. **4.** amount of money paid for insurance; premium: his insurance is $300 a year. Also, Brit. assurance.

in·sure (in·shur'), v., -sured, -sur·ing. **1.** make sure; ensure: check your work to insure its accuracy. **2.** make safe; protect; ensure: more care will insure you against making so many mistakes. **3.** arrange for money payment in case of loss (of property, profit, etc.) or accident or death to (a person): an insurance company will insure your life. **4.** make safe from financial loss by accident, death, etc., by paying money to an insurance company: was he insured at the time of the accident? **5.** issue an insurance policy. [var. of ensure < AF, < en- in + OF seur SURE]

in·sured (in·shurd'), n. person whose property, life, etc., are insured.

in·sur·er (in·shur'ər), n. **1.** person who insures. **2.** something that insures or protects.

in·sur·gence (in·sér'jəns), **in·sur·gen·cy** (-jən·si), n. a rising in revolt; rebellion.

in·sur·gent (in·sér'jənt), n. **1.** person who rises in revolt; rebel. **2.** U.S. rebel within a political party. —adj. rising in revolt; rebellious. [< L, < in- against + surgere rise]

in·sur·mount·a·ble (in'sər·moun'tə·bəl), adj. that cannot be overcome. —in'sur·mount'a·bly, adv.

in·sur·rec·tion (in'sə·rek'shən), n. an uprising against established authority; revolt. [< LL insurrectio < L insurgere. See INSURGENT.] —in'sur·rec'tion·al, adj. —in'sur·rec'tion·al·ly, adv. —in·sur·rec·tion·ar·y (in'sə·rek'shən·er'i), adj., n. —in'sur·rec'tion·ism, n. —in'sur·rec'tion·ist, n. —Syn. rebellion, revolution, riot.

in·sus·cep·ti·ble (in'sə·sep'tə·bəl), adj. not susceptible; not easily influenced. —in'sus·cep'ti·bil'i·ty, n. —in'sus·cep'ti·bly, adv.

int., 1. interest. **2.** international. **3.** intransitive.

in·tact (in·takt'), adj. with no part missing; untouched; uninjured; whole: dishes left intact after a fall. [< L intactus, ult. < in- not + tangere touch] —in·tact'ness, n.

in·tag·lio (in·tal'yō; -täl'-), n., pl. in·tag·lios, Ital. in·ta·gli (ēn·tä'lyē), v., -ioed, -io·ing. —n. **1.** process of engraving by making cuts in a surface. **2.** design engraved in this way. **3.** gem ornamented in this way. —v. engrave in intaglio. [< Ital., ult. < in- into + tagliare to cut]

in·take (in'tāk'), n. **1.** place where water, gas, etc., enters a channel, pipe, or other narrow opening. **2.** a taking in. **3.** amount or thing taken in.

in·tan·gi·ble (in·tan'jə·bəl), adj. **1.** not capable of being touched. **2.** not easily grasped by the mind. —n. something intangible. —in·tan'gi·bil'i·ty, in·tan'gi·ble·ness, n. —in·tan'gi·bly, adv. —Syn. adj. **1.** insubstantial.

in·te·ger (in'tə·jər), n. **1.** a whole number as distinguished from a fraction or mixed number. 1, 2, 3, 15, 106, etc., are integers. **2.** thing complete in itself; something whole. [< L, whole]

in·te·gral (in'tə·grəl), adj. **1.** necessary to the completeness of the whole; essential. **2.** entire; complete. **3.** having to do with whole numbers; not fractional. —n. a whole; a whole number. [< LL, < L integer whole] —in'te·gral'i·ty, n. —in'te·gral·ly, adv.

in·te·grate (in'tə·grāt), v., -grat·ed, -grat·ing. **1.** make into a whole; complete. **2.** bring together (parts) into a whole. **3.** indicate the total amount or mean value of. **4.** U.S. make all schools, parks, etc. available to white and Negro citizens on an equal basis. [< L, < integer whole] —in'te·gra'tion, n. —in'te·gra'tive, adj. —in'te·gra'tor, n.

in·teg·ri·ty (in·teg'rə·ti), n. **1.** honesty; sincerity; uprightness: a man of integrity. **2.** wholeness; completeness: defend the integrity of one's country. **3.** perfect condition; soundness. [< L integritas. See INTEGER.]

in·teg·u·ment (in·teg'yü·mənt), n. an outer covering, as a skin or a shell. [< L integumentum < in- on + tegere to cover]

in·tel·lect (in'tə·lekt), n. **1.** power of knowing; understanding. **2.** great intelligence; high mental ability: a man of intellect. **3.** person having high mental ability. [< L intellectus < intelligere. See INTELLIGENT.]

in·tel·lec·tu·al (in'tə·lek'chü·əl), adj. **1.** of the intellect: intellectual power. **2.** needing or using intelligence: an intellectual process. **3.** possessing or showing intelligence: an intellectual type of mind. **4.** directed or inclined toward things that involve the intellect: intellectual tastes. —n. person who is well informed, or chiefly concerned with things that involve the intellect. —in'tel·lec'tu·al'i·ty, in'tel·lec'tu·al·ness, n. —in'tel·lec'tu·al·ly, adv.

in·tel·lec·tu·al·ism (in'tə·lek'chü·əl·iz'əm), n. **1.** exercise of the intellect; devotion to intellectual pursuits. —in'tel·lec'tu·al·ist, n. —in'tel·lec'tu·al·is'tic, adj.

in·tel·li·gence (in·tel'ə·jəns), n. **1.** ability to learn and know; understanding; mind. **2.** knowledge; news; information. **3.** the obtaining or distributing of information, esp. secret information. **4.** group of persons engaged in obtaining secret information. **5.** Often, Intelligence. intelligent being or spirit. **—Syn. 1.** intellect, discernment, insight. **2.** tidings, notice.

intelligence quotient, number used to measure a child's intelligence, obtained by dividing the mental age by the chronological age (up to 16 years).

intelligence test, test used to measure mental development.

in·tel·li·gent (in·tel′ə·jənt), *adj.* having or showing intelligence; able to learn and know; quick at learning. [< L *intelligens* understanding < *inter-* between + *legere* choose] **—in·tel′li·gent·ly,** *adv.* **—Syn.** bright, clever.

in·tel·li·gent·si·a (in·tel′ə·jent′si·ə; -gent′-), *n.pl.* persons representing, or claiming to represent, the superior intelligence or enlightened opinion of a country; the intellectuals. [< Russ. < L *intelligentia.* See INTELLIGENT.] ▶ **Intelligentsia** often carries the suggestion of too great preoccupation with intellectual matters.

in·tel·li·gi·ble (in·tel′ə·jə·bəl), *adj.* capable of being understood; comprehensible. [< L, < *intelligere.* See INTELLIGENT.] **—in·tel′li·gi·bil′i·ty, in·tel′li·gi·ble·ness,** *n.* **—in·tel′li·gi·bly,** *adv.* **—Syn.** understandable, plain, clear.

in·tem·per·ance (in·tem′pər·əns; -prəns), *n.* **1.** lack of moderation or self-control; excess. **2.** the excessive use of intoxicating liquor.

in·tem·per·ate (in·tem′pər·it; -prit), *adj.* **1.** not moderate; lacking in self-control; excessive. **2.** drinking too much intoxicating liquor. **3.** not temperate; severe: *an intemperate winter.* **—in·tem′per·ate·ly,** *adv.* **—in·tem′per·ate·ness,** *n.* **—Syn. 1.** extreme, inordinate.

in·tend (in·tend′), *v.* **1.** have in mind as a purpose; mean; plan: *we intend to go home soon.* **2.** design; destine: *a book intended for beginners.* [< L, < *in-* toward + *tendere* stretch] **—in·tend′er,** *n.* **—Syn. 1.** contemplate, propose.

in·tend·an·cy (in·ten′dən·si), *n., pl.* **-cies.** position or work of an intendant.

in·tend·ant (in·ten′dənt), *n.* person in charge; director. [< F, ult. < L *intendere* attend to. See INTEND.]

in·tend·ed (in·ten′did), *adj.* **1.** meant; planned. **2.** prospective: *a woman's intended husband.* **—n.** *Colloq.* a prospective husband or wife.

in·tense (in·tens′), *adj.* **1.** very much; very great; very strong: *intense pain.* **2.** full of vigorous activity, strong feelings, etc.: *an intense life.* **3.** having or showing strong feelings: *an intense person.* [< L *intensus,* pp. of *intendere* strain. See INTEND.] **—in·tense′ly,** *adv.* **—in·tense′ness,** *n.*

in·ten·si·fy (in·ten′sə·fī), *v.,* **-fied, -fy·ing.** make or become intense or more intense; strengthen: *blowing on a fire intensifies the heat.* **—in·ten′si·fi·ca′tion,** *n.* **—in·ten′si·fi′er,** *n.* **—Syn.** heighten, aggravate, increase.

in·ten·si·ty (in·ten′sə·ti), *n., pl.* **-ties. 1.** a being intense; great strength; extreme degree. **2.** great strength or violence of feeling. **3.** amount or degree of strength of electricity, heat, light, sound, etc., per unit of area, volume, etc.

in·ten·sive (in·ten′siv), *adj.* **1.** deep and thorough: *an intensive study.* **2.** *Gram.* giving force or emphasis; expressing intensity. In "He himself said it," *himself* is an intensive pronoun. **3.** increasing in intensity. **—n. 1.** something that makes intense. **2.** *Gram.* intensive word, prefix, etc. **—in·ten′sive·ly,** *adv.* **—in·ten′sive·ness,** *n.*

in·tent¹ (in·tent′), *n.* **1.** purpose; intention. **2.** meaning; significance. **3.** to all intents and purposes, in almost every way; practically. [< OF *entent, entente* < L *intendere* INTEND]

in·tent² (in·tent′), *adj.* **1.** very attentive; having the eyes or thoughts earnestly fixed on something; earnest. **2.** earnestly engaged; much interested. [< L *intentus,* pp. of *intendere* to strain. See INTEND.] **—in·tent′ly,** *adv.* **—in·tent′ness,** *n.*

in·ten·tion (in·ten′shən), *n.* **1.** purpose; design; plan: *our intention is to travel next summer.* **2.** meaning. **3.** intentions, *Colloq.* purposes with respect to marrying. **—Syn. 1.** intent.

in·ten·tion·al (in·ten′shən·əl), *adj.* done on purpose; meant; intended. **—in·ten′tion·al·ly,** *adv.* **—Syn.** deliberate, premeditated, designed.

in·ter (in·tėr′), *v.,* **-terred, -ter·ring.** put (a dead body) into a grave or tomb; bury. [< OF *enterrer,* ult. < L *in-* in + *terra* earth]

inter-, *prefix.* **1.** together; one with the other, as in *intercommunicate, intermixture.* **2.** between, as in *interpose, interlay, interlude.* **3.** among a group, as in *interscholastic.* [< L, as in *inter,* prep., adv., among, between, during]

in·ter·act (in′tər·akt′), *v.* act on each other. **—in′ter·ac′tion,** *n.* **—in′ter·ac′tive,** *adj.*

in·ter a·li·a (in′tər ā′li·ə), *Latin.* among other things.

in·ter·breed (in′tər·brēd′), *v.,* **-bred, -breed·ing.** breed by the mating of different kinds; breed by using different varieties or species of animals or plants.

in·ter·ca·lar·y (in·tėr′kə·ler′i), *adj.* inserted in a calendar: *February 29 is an intercalary day.*

in·ter·ca·late (in·tėr′kə·lāt), *v.,* **-lat·ed, -lat·ing. 1.** put into the calendar. **2.** put in between; interpolate. [< L, < *inter-* between + *calare* proclaim] **—in·ter′ca·la′tion,** *n.*

in·ter·cede (in′tər·sēd′), *v.,* **-ced·ed, -ced·ing. 1.** plead or beg in another's behalf: *Will interceded with the teacher for Dan.* **2.** interfere in order to bring about an agreement. [< L, < *inter-* between + *cedere* go] **—in′ter·ced′er,** *n.*

in·ter·cel·lu·lar (in′tər·sel′yə·lər), *adj.* situated between or among cells.

in·ter·cept (in′tər·sept′), *v.* **1.** take or seize on the way from one place to another; intercept *a letter.* **2.** cut off (light, water, etc.). **3.** check; stop: *intercept the flight of a criminal.* **4.** *Math.,* etc. mark off between two points or lines. [< L *interceptus* < *inter- between + capere* catch] **—in′ter·cep′tion,** *n.* **—in′ter·cep′tive, adj.** **—in′ter·cep′tor,** *n.*

The line intercepts the circle at A and B.

in·ter·ces·sion (in′tər·sesh′-ən), *n.* act or fact of interceding. **—in′ter·ces′sion·al,** *adj.* **—in·ter·ces·sor** (in′tər·ses′ər; in′tər·ses′ər), *n.* **—in′ter·ces′so·ry,** *adj.*

in·ter·change (*v.* in′tər·chānj′; *n.* in′tər·chānj′), *v.,* **-changed, -chang·ing,** *n.* **—v. 1.** put each of (two or more persons or things) in the place of the other. **2.** give and take; exchange: *interchange gifts.* **3.** cause to happen by turns; alternate: *interchange severity with indulgence.* **4.** change places. **—n. 1.** a putting each of two or more persons or things in the other's place. **2.** a giving and taking; exchanging. **3.** alternate succession; alternation. **4.** point at which an express highway connects with another road.

in·ter·change·a·ble (in′tər·chān′jə·bəl), *adj.* **1.** capable of being used in place of each other. **2.** able to change places. **—in′ter·change′·a·bil′i·ty, in′ter·change′a·ble·ness,** *n.* **—in′ter·change′a·bly,** *adv.*

in·ter·col·le·giate (in′tər·kə·lē′jit; -ji·it), *adj.* between colleges or universities.

in·ter·com (in′tər·kom′), *n. Slang.* telephone apparatus with which members of the crew of an airplane, tank, ship, etc., can talk to each other.

in·ter·com·mu·ni·cate (in′tər·kə·mū′nə·kāt), *v.,* **-cat·ed, -cat·ing.** communicate with each other. **—in′ter·com·mu′ni·ca′tion,** *n.*

in·ter·con·nect (in′tər·kə·nekt′), *v.* connect with each other. **—in′ter·con·nec′tion,** *n.*

in·ter·con·ti·nen·tal (in′tər·kon′tə·nen′təl), *adj.* **1.** for use between continents. **2.** of more than one continent.

in·ter·cos·tal (in′tər·kos′təl; -kôs′-), *adj.* between the ribs. [< NL, < L *inter-* between + *costa* rib] **—in′ter·cos′tal·ly,** *adv.*

in·ter·course (in′tər·kôrs; -kōrs), *n.* **1.** communication; dealings between people; exchange of thoughts, services, feelings, etc. **2.** sexual connection.

in·ter·de·nom·i·na·tion·al (in′tər·di·nom′-ə·nā′shən·əl; -nāsh′nəl), *adj.* between or involving different religious denominations.

in·ter·de·pend·ence (in′tər·di·pen′dəns), *n.* **in·ter·de·pend·en·cy** (-dən·si), *n.* dependence on each other; mutual dependence.

āge, cāre, fär; ēqual, tėrm; īce; ŏpen, ôrder; pŭt, rūle, ūse; th, then; ə=a in about.

in·ter·de·pend·ent (in'tər·di·pen'dənt), *adj.* dependent each upon the other. —**in'ter·de·pend'ent·ly**, *adv.*

in·ter·dict (*v.* in'tər·dikt'; *n.* in'tər·dikt), *v.* 1. prohibit; forbid. 2. restrain. 3. cut off from certain church privileges. —*n.* 1. prohibition based on authority; formal order forbidding something. 2. a cutting off from certain church privileges. [< L, < *inter*- between + *dicere* speak] —**in'ter·dic'tion**, *n.* —**in'ter·dic'tive**, *adj.* —**in'ter·dic'tor**, *n.* —**in'ter·dic'to·ry**, *adj.*

in·ter·est (in'tər·ist; -trist), *n.* 1. a feeling of wanting to know, see, do, own, share in, or take part in: *an interest in sports*. 2. power of arousing such a feeling: *a dull book lacks interest*. 3. share; part; portion: *buy a half interest in a business*. 4. thing in which a person has an interest, share, or part, as a business, pastime, etc. 5. group of people having the same business, activity, etc. 6. advantage; benefit. 7. regard for one's own advantage; self-interest. 8. power of influencing action. 9. **in the interest of**, for; to help. 10. money paid for the use of money: *the interest on the loan was 5 per cent*. 11. something extra given in return. —*v.* 1. arouse the attention, curiosity, concern, etc., of: *an exciting story interests you*. 2. cause (a person) to take a share or interest in: *the agent tried to interest us in buying a car*. [< L, it is of importance, it makes a difference < *inter*- between + *esse* be] —Syn. *v.* 1. engage, occupy, entertain. ➤ The noun **interest** has no antonym made from itself (*disinterest* not being a word in general use). It is necessary to resort to specific words like *boredom* or phrases like *lack of interest*.

in·ter·est·ed (in'tər·is·tid; -tris·tid; -tər·es'-tid), *adj.* 1. feeling or showing interest. 2. having an interest or share. 3. influenced by personal considerations; prejudiced. —**in'ter·est·ed·ly**, *adv.* —**in'ter·est·ed·ness**, *n.* ➤ **interested**. The adjective *interested* has two opposites: *uninterested*, which is merely its negative, and *disinterested*, which means "not motivated by personal interest, impartial," though informally the latter is sometimes used in the sense of *uninterested*.

in·ter·est·ing (in'tər·is·ting; -tris·ting; -tər·es'ting), *adj.* arousing interest; holding one's attention. —**in'ter·est·ing·ly**, *adv.* —**in'ter·est·ing·ness**, *n.*

in·ter·fere (in'tər·fir'), *v.*, **-fered, -fer·ing.** 1. come into opposition; clash: *come on Saturday if nothing interferes*. 2. disturb the affairs of others; meddle. 3. take part for a purpose: *the police interfered to stop the riot*. 4. interfere with, hinder. 5. *Am., Football*. obstruct the action of an opposing player who is trying to tackle. 6. *Physics*. of waves, act one upon another. [< OF, < L *inter*- between + *ferire* to strike] —**in'ter·fer'er**, *n.* —**in'ter·fer'ing·ly**, *adv.* —Syn. 1. conflict. 3. intervene.

in·ter·fer·ence (in'tər·fir'əns), *n.* 1. an interfering. 2. *Physics*. the reciprocal action of waves by which they reinforce or neutralize one another. 3. *Radio*. a. interruption or scrambling of a desired signal by other signals. b. signals thus interfering. 4. *Am., Football*. act of interfering with a player who is trying to tackle.

in·ter·fold (in'tər·fōld'), *v.* fold one within another; fold together.

in·ter·fuse (in'tər·fūz'), *v.*, **-fused, -fus·ing.** 1. be diffused through; permeate. 2. fuse together; blend. [< L *interfusus* < *inter*- between + *fundere* pour] —**in'ter·fu'sion**, *n.*

in·ter·im (in'tər·im), *n.* meantime; time between. —*adj.* for the meantime; temporary. [< L, in the meantime < *inter* between]

in·te·ri·or (in·tir'i·ər), *n.* 1. inside; inner surface or part. 2. part of a region or country away from the coast or border. 3. affairs within a country: *Department of the Interior*. —*adj.* 1. on the inside; inner. 2. away from the coast or border. 3. domestic. 4. private; secret. [< L, inner] —**in·te·ri·or·i·ty** (in·tir'i·ôr'ə·ti; -or'-), *n.* —**in·te'ri·or·ly**, *adv.*

interj., interjection.

in·ter·ject (in'tər·jekt'), *v.* throw in between other things; insert abruptly: *interject a witty remark*. [< L *interjectus* < *inter*- between + *jacere* throw] —**in'ter·jec'tor**, *n.*

in·ter·jec·tion (in'tər·jek'shən), *n.* 1. *Gram.* an exclamation regarded as a part of speech, as *oh!, hurrah!* 2. an interjecting. 3. something interjected; remark; exclamation. —**in'ter·jec'tion·al**, *adj.* —**in'ter·jec'tion·al·ly**, *adv.*

in·ter·lace (in'tər·lās'), *v.*, **-laced, -lac·ing.** 1. cross over and under each other; weave together; intertwine. 2. cross in an intricate manner. —**in'ter·lace'ment**, *n.*

in·ter·lard (in'tər·lärd'), *v.* give variety to; mix; intersperse. [< F, < L *inter*- between + *lardum* fat] —**in'ter·lard'ment**, *n.*

in·ter·lay (in'tər·lā'), *v.*, **-laid, -lay·ing.** 1. lay between. 2. diversify with something laid between.

in·ter·leave (in'tər·lēv'), *v.*, **-leaved, -leaving.** insert a leaf or leaves of paper between the pages.

in·ter·line¹ (in'tər·līn'), *v.*, **-lined, -lin·ing.** insert an extra lining between the outer cloth and the ordinary lining of (a garment).

in·ter·line² (in'tər·līn'), *v.*, **-lined, -lin·ing.** write, print, or mark between the lines.

in·ter·lin·e·ar (in'tər·lin'i·ər), *adj.* 1. inserted between the lines. 2. containing two different languages or versions in alternate lines.

in·ter·lin·ing (in'tər·līn'ing), *n.* an extra lining inserted between the outer cloth and the ordinary lining of a garment.

in·ter·link (in'tər·lingk'), *v.* link together.

in·ter·lock (in'tər·lok'), *v.* lock or join with one another. —**in'ter·lock'er**, *n.*

in·ter·loc·u·tor (in'tər·lok'yə·tər), *n.* 1. person who takes part in a conversation or dialogue. 2. *Am.* man in a minstrel show who asks the end man questions. [< L *interlocutus* < *inter*- between + *loqui* speak]

in·ter·loc·u·to·ry (in'tər·lok'yə·tô'ri; -tō'-), *adj.* 1. of or in conversation or dialogue. 2. made during a lawsuit or other action; not final.

in·ter·lop·er (in'tər·lōp'ər), *n.* intruder.

in·ter·lude (in'tər·lüd), *n.* 1. anything thought of as filling the time between two things; interval. 2. piece of music played between the parts of a song, church service, play, etc. 3. entertainment between the acts of a play. [< Med.L, < L *inter*- between + *ludus* play]

in·ter·mar·ry (in'tər·mar'i), *v.*, **-ried, -rying.** 1. become connected by marriage. 2. marry within the family. —**in'ter·mar'riage**, *n.*

in·ter·med·dle (in'tər·med'əl), *v.*, **-dled, -dling.** meddle; interfere. —**in'ter·med'dler**, *n.*

in·ter·me·di·ar·y (in'tər·mē'di·er'i), *n., pl.* **-ar·ies**, *adj.* —*n.* person who acts for one person with another; go-between. —*adj.* 1. acting between. 2. being between; intermediate.

in·ter·me·di·ate (in'tər·mē'di·it), *adj.* being or occurring between; gray is intermediate between black and white. —*n.* 1. something in between. 2. mediator. [< Med.L, ult. < L *inter*- between + *medius* in the middle] —**in'ter·me'di·ate·ly**, *adv.* —**in'ter·me'di·ate·ness**, *n.* —Syn. *adj.* intervening.

in·ter·ment (in·tėr'mənt), *n.* burial.

in·ter·mez·zo (in'tər·met'sō; -med'zō), *n., pl.* **-zos, -zi** (-sē; -zē). 1. a short dramatic or musical entertainment between the acts of a play. 2. a short musical composition between the main divisions of an extended musical work. 3. an independent musical composition of similar character. [< Ital.]

in·ter·mi·na·ble (in·tėr'mə·nə·bəl), *adj.* endless; so long as to seem endless. —**in·tėr'mi·na·bly**, *adv.* —Syn. unending, limitless.

in·ter·min·gle (in'tər·ming'gəl), *v.*, **-gled, -gling.** mix together; mingle. —**in'ter·min'gle·ment**, *n.*

in·ter·mis·sion (in'tər·mish'ən), *n.* 1. time between periods of activity; pause. 2. stopping for a time; interruption: *rain without intermission*. —Syn. 1. interval.

in·ter·mit (in'tər·mit'), *v.*, **-mit·ted, -mit·ting.** stop for a time. [< L, < *inter*- between + *mittere* to leave] —**in'ter·mit'ter**, *n.* —**in'ter·mit'ting·ly**, *adv.*

in·ter·mit·tent (in'tər·mit'ənt), *adj.* 1. stopping and beginning again. 2. pausing at intervals. —**in'ter·mit'tence, in'ter·mit'ten·cy,** *n.* —**in'ter·mit'tent·ly,** *adv.*

in·ter·mix (in'tər·miks'), *v.* mix together; blend. —**in'ter·mix'ture,** *n.*

in·tern[1] (in·tûrn'), *v.* 1. confine within a country; *intern soldiers in a neutral country.* 2. force to stay in a certain place. [< F *interner* < L *internus* within] —**in·tern'ment,** *n.*

in·tern[2] (in'tûrn), *n.* Also, **interne.** *Am.* doctor acting as a resident assistant in a hospital. —*v.* act as an intern. [< F *interne.* See INTERN[1].] —**in'tern·ship,** *n. Am.*

in·ter·nal (in·tûr'nəl), *adj.* 1. inner; on the inside: *internal injuries.* 2. to be taken inside the body: *internal remedies.* 3. entirely inside; coming from within: *internal evidence.* 4. having to do with affairs within a country; domestic: *internal disturbances.* 5. of the mind; subjective: *thoughts are internal.* —*n.* 1. inner nature. 2. **internals,** inner organs. [< Med.L *internalis.* See INTERN[1].] —**in·ter'nal·ly,** *adv.*

internal-combustion engine, engine in which the pressure is produced by gas or vapor exploding inside the cylinder and against the piston.

in·ter·na·tion·al (in'tər·nash'ən·əl; -nash'-nəl), *adj.* 1. between or among nations: *an international agreement.* 2. of or pertaining to different nations or their citizens. 3. having to do with the relations between nations: *international law.* —*n.* **International,** one of several international socialist or communist organizations. —**in'ter·na'tion·al'i·ty,** *n.* —**in'ter·na'tion·al·ly,** *adv.*

International Date Line, date line (def. 1).

International Geophysical Year, an eighteen-month study of the features of the earth and the forces that produce them by the scientists of many countries working together. It lasted from July 1, 1957 to December 31, 1958. *Abbrev.:* IGY.

in·ter·na·tion·al·ism (in'tər·nash'ən·əl·iz'-əm; -nash'nəl-), *n.* principle of international coöperation for the good of all nations. —**in'ter·na'tion·al·ist,** *n.*

in·ter·na·tion·al·ize (in'tər·nash'ən·əl·īz; -nash'nəl-), *v.,* **-ized, -iz·ing.** make international; bring (territory) under the control of several nations. —**in'ter·na'tion·al·i·za'tion,** *n.*

in·terne (in'tûrn), *n. Am.* intern[2].

in·ter·ne·cine (in'tər·nē'sin; -sīn), *adj.* 1. destructive to both sides. 2. deadly; destructive. [< L *internecinus,* ult. < *inter-* between + *nex* slaughter]

in·tern·ee (in'tûr·nē'), *n.* person interned, as a prisoner of war, enemy alien, etc.

in·ter·pel·late (in'tər·pel'āt; in·tûr'pə·lāt), *v.,* **-lat·ed, -lat·ing.** ask formally in a legislature for an explanation of official action or government policy. [< L *interpellatus* interrupted] —**in·ter·pel·la·tion** (in'tər·pe·lā'shən; in·tûr'pə-), *n.*

in·ter·pen·e·trate (in'tər·pen'ə·trāt), *v.,* **-trat·ed, -trat·ing.** 1. penetrate thoroughly; permeate. 2. penetrate each into the other. —**in'ter·pen'e·tra'tion,** *n.* —**in'ter·pen'e·tra'tive,** *adj.*

in·ter·phone (in'tər·fōn'), *n.* intercom.

in·ter·plan·e·tar·y (in'tər·plan'ə·ter'i), *adj. Astron.* within the solar system, but not within the atmosphere of the sun or any planet.

in·ter·play (in'tər·plā'), *n.* action or influence on each other: *interplay of light and shadow.*

in·ter·po·late (in·tûr'pə·lāt), *v.,* **-lat·ed, -lat·ing.** 1. alter (a book, passage, etc.) by putting in new words or groups of words. 2. put in (new words, passages, etc.). 3. *Math.* insert (intermediate terms) in a series. [< L *interpolatus* refurbished] —**in·ter'po·lat'er, in·ter'po·la'tor,** *n.* —**in·ter'po·la'tion,** *n.* —**in·ter'po·la'tive,** *adj.*

in·ter·pose (in'tər·pōz'), *v.,* **-posed, -pos·ing.** 1. put between; insert. 2. come between; be between. 3. interrupt. 4. interfere in order to help; intervene: *mother interposed in the dispute.* 5.

put in as an interference or interruption. [< F, < *inter-* between + *poser* place, POSE] —**in'ter·pos'er,** *n.* —**in'ter·pos'ing·ly,** *adv.* —**in·ter·po·si·tion** (in'tər·pə·zish'ən), *n.*

in·ter·pret (in·tûr'prit), *v.* 1. explain the meaning of: *interpret a dream.* 2. bring out the meaning of: *interpret a part in a play.* 3. understand in a certain way: *interpret silence as consent.* 4. serve as an interpreter; translate. [< L *interpretari* < *interpres* mediary] —**in·ter'pret·a·ble,** *adj.* —**in·ter'pret·a·bil'i·ty,** *n.* —**in·ter'pre·tive,** *adj.* —**in·ter'pre·tive·ly,** *adv.*

in·ter·pre·ta·tion (in·tûr'prə·tā'shən), *n.* 1. an interpreting; explanation: *different interpretations of the same facts.* 2. bringing out the meaning of a dramatic part, music, etc. 3. translation. —**in·ter'pre·ta'tion·al, in·ter'pre·ta'-tive,** *adj.* —**in·ter'pre·ta'tive·ly,** *adv.*

in·ter·pret·er (in·tûr'prə·tər), *n.* 1. person who interprets. 2. person whose business is translating from a foreign language.

in·ter·ra·cial (in'tər·rā'shəl), *adj.* between or involving different races.

in·ter·reg·num (in'tər·reg'nəm), *n., pl.* **-nums, -na** (-nə). 1. time between the end of one ruler's reign and the beginning of the next one. 2. any time during which a nation is without its usual ruler. 3. period of inactivity; pause. [< L, < *inter-* between + *regnum* reign] —**in'ter·reg'nal,** *adj.*

in·ter·re·late (in'tər·ri·lāt'), *v.,* **-lat·ed, -lat·ing.** connect closely with each other; bring into mutual relation. —**in'ter·re·lat'ed,** *adj.* —**in'ter·re·la'tion,** *n.* —**in'ter·re·la'tion·ship,** *n.*

in·ter·ro·gate (in·ter'ə·gāt), *v.,* **-gat·ed, -gat·ing.** 1. question thoroughly; examine by asking questions: *interrogate a witness.* 2. ask a series of questions. [< L, < *inter-* between + *rogare* ask] —**in·ter'ro·gat'ing·ly,** *adv.* —**in·ter'ro·ga'tor,** *n.*

in·ter·ro·ga·tion (in·ter'ə·gā'shən), *n.* 1. a questioning. The formal examination of a witness by asking questions is interrogation. 2. a question. —**in·ter'ro·ga'tion·al,** *adj.*

interrogation mark or **point,** question mark (?).

in·ter·rog·a·tive (in'tə·rog'ə·tiv), *adj.* asking a question; having the form of a question. —*n. Gram.* a word used in asking a question. —**in'ter·rog'a·tive·ly,** *adv.*

in·ter·rog·a·to·ry (in'tə·rog'ə·tô'ri; -tō'-), *adj., n., pl.* **-ries.** —*adj.* questioning. —*n.* a formal question. —**in·ter·rog'a·to'ri·ly,** *adv.*

in·ter·rupt (in'tə·rupt'), *v.* 1. break in upon (talk, work, rest, a person speaking, etc.); hinder; stop. 2. make a break in: *interrupt the view.* 3. cause a break; break in: *do not interrupt the speech.* [< L *interruptus* < *inter-* between + *rumpere* break] —**in'ter·rupt'er,** *n.*

in·ter·rup·tion (in'tə·rup'shən), *n.* 1. an interrupting. 2. a being interrupted. 3. thing that interrupts. 4. intermission.

in·ter·scho·las·tic (in'tər·skə·las'tik), *adj.* between schools: *interscholastic competition.*

in·ter·sect (in'tər·sekt'), *v.* 1. cut or divide by passing through or crossing. 2. cross each other. [< L, < *inter-* between + *secare* cut]

in·ter·sec·tion (in'tər·sek'shən), *n.* 1. an intersecting. 2. point or line where one thing crosses another. In the diagram there are two intersections where the line AB crosses the parallel lines. —**in'ter·sec'tion·al,** *adj.*

The line AB intersects the parallel lines.

in·ter·sperse (in'tər·spûrs'), *v.,* **-spersed, -spers·ing.** 1. vary with something put here and there: *grass interspersed with beds of flowers.* 2. scatter here and there among other things: *bushes were interspersed among trees.* [< L *interspersus* < *inter-* between + *spargere* scatter] —**in'ter·sper'sion** (in'tər·spûr'zhən; -shən), *n.*

in·ter·state (in'tər·stāt'; in'tər·stāt'), *adj.* between states: *interstate commerce.*

in·ter·stel·lar (in'tər·stel'ər; in'tər·stel'ər), *adj.* among or between the stars.

in·ter·stice (in·tûr'stis), *n.* a small or narrow space between things or parts; chink. [< LL *interstitium* < L *inter–* between + *stare* to stand] —**in·ter·sti·tial** (in′tər·stish′əl), *adj.* —**in′ter·sti′tial·ly**, *adv.*

in·ter·twine (in′tər·twīn′), *v.*, –twined, –twin·ing. twine, one with another. —**in′ter·twine′ment**, *n.* —**in′ter·twin′ing·ly**, *adv.*

in·ter·twist (in′tər·twist′), *v.* twist, one with another. —**in′ter·twist′ing·ly**, *adv.*

in·ter·ur·ban (in′tər·ér′bən; in′tər·ér′bən), *Am.* —*adj.* between cities or towns. —*n.* an interurban railroad.

in·ter·val (in′tər·vəl), *n.* 1. time or space between: *an interval of a week.* 2. at intervals, a. now and then. b. here and there. 3. *Music.* the difference in pitch between two tones. [< L *intervallum*, orig., space between palisades < *inter–* between + *vallum* wall]

in·ter·vene (in′tər·vēn′), *v.*, –vened, –ven·ing. 1. come between; be between: *a week intervenes between Christmas and New Year's.* 2. come in to help settle a dispute: *the President intervened in the strike.* [< L, < *inter–* between + *venire* come] —**in′ter·ven′er**, **in′ter·ve′nor**, *n.* —Syn. 2. mediate, intercede.

in·ter·ven·tion (in′tər·ven′shən), *n.* 1. an intervening. 2. interference by one nation in the affairs of another. —**in′ter·ven′tion·al**, *adj.* —**in′ter·ven′tion·ist**, *n.*

in·ter·view (in′tər·vū), *n.* 1. a meeting to talk over something special: *an interview with a manager for a job.* 2. *Am.* a. a meeting between a reporter and a person from whom information is sought for publication. b. newspaper or magazine article resulting from such a meeting. —*v.* have an interview with; meet and talk with. [< F *entrevue*, ult. < L *inter–* between + *videre* see] —**in′ter·view′er**, *n.*

in·ter·weave (in′tər·wēv′), *v.*, –wove or –weaved, –wo·ven or –wove or –weaved, –weav·ing. 1. weave together. 2. intermingle; connect closely. —**in′ter·weave′ment**, *n.* —**in′ter·weav′er**, *n.* —**in′ter·wo′ven**, *adj.*

in·tes·tate (in·tes′tāt; –tit), *adj.* 1. having made no will. 2. not disposed of by a will. —*n.* person who has died without making a will. [< L, < *in–* not + *testari* make a will < *testis* witness] —**in·tes·ta·cy** (in·tes′tə·si), *n.*

in·tes·ti·nal (in·tes′tə·nəl), *adj.* of or in the intestines. —**in·tes′ti·nal·ly**, *adv.*

in·tes·tine (in·tes′tən), *n. Anat.* 1. part of the alimentary canal that extends from the stomach to the anus. 2. a portion of this. The first, narrower and longer portion is the small intestine and the other the large intestine. —*adj.* within a country; internal: *intestine strife.* [< L *intestina*, neut. pl., internal, ult. < *in* in]

in·thrall, in·thral (in·thrôl′), *v.* enthrall. —**in·thrall′ment, in·thral′ment**, *n.*

in·throne (in·thrōn′), *v.*, –throned, –thron·ing. enthrone.

in·ti·ma·cy (in′tə·mə·si), *n., pl.* –cies. 1. a being intimate; close acquaintance. 2. a familiar or intimate act. 3. sexual relations. —Syn. 1. closeness. 2. familiarity.

in·ti·mate¹ (in′tə·mit), *adj.* 1. very familiar; known very well; closely acquainted. 2. close; thorough: *intimate knowledge of a matter.* 3. very personal; most private. 4. far within; inmost. 5. maintaining illicit sexual relations. —*n.* a close friend. [< L *intimatus* (see INTIMATE²), confused with *intimus* inmost] —**in′ti·mate·ly**, *adv.* —**in′ti·mate·ness**, *n.*

in·ti·mate² (in′tə·māt), *v.*, –mat·ed, –mat·ing. 1. suggest indirectly; hint. 2. announce; notify. [< L *intimatus*, orig., made to sink in, ult. < L *intimus* inmost] —**in′ti·mat′er**, *n.*

in·ti·ma·tion (in′tə·mā′shən), *n.* 1. indirect suggestion; hint. 2. announcement; notice.

in·tim·i·date (in·tim′ə·dāt), *v.*, –dat·ed, –dat·ing. 1. frighten; make afraid. 2. influence or force by fear. [< Med.L, < L *in–* + *timidus* fearful] —**in·tim′i·da′tion**, *n.* —**in·tim′i·da′tor**, *n.*

in·ti·tle (in·tī′təl), *v.*, –tled, –tling. entitle.

in·to (in′tü; *unstressed* in′tû, –tə), *prep.* 1. to the inside of; toward the inside; within: *go into*

the house. 2. to the condition of; to the form of: *divided into ten rooms.* ➤ See in for usage note.

in·tol·er·a·ble (in·tol′ər·ə·bəl), *adj.* unbearable; too much, too painful, etc., to be endured. —**in·tol′er·a·bil′i·ty**, **in·tol′er·a·ble·ness**, *n.* —Syn. unendurable, insufferable.

in·tol·er·a·bly (in·tol′ər·ə·bli), *adv.* unbearably; beyond endurance.

in·tol·er·ance (in·tol′ər·əns), *n.* 1. lack of tolerance; unwillingness to let others do and think as they choose, esp. in matters of religion. 2. inability to endure; unwillingness to endure.

in·tol·er·ant (in·tol′ər·ənt), *adj.* 1. not tolerant; unwilling to let others do and think as they choose, esp. in matters of religion. 2. intolerant of, not able to endure; unwilling to endure. —**in·tol′er·ant·ly**, *adv.* —Syn. 1. bigoted, narrow, dogmatic.

in·tomb (in·tüm′), *v.* entomb. —**in·tomb′ment**, *n.*

in·to·na·tion (in′tō·nā′shən; –tə–), *n.* 1. act of intoning. 2. pattern of modulation and inflection in connected speech.

in·tone (in·tōn′), *v.*, –toned, –ton·ing. 1. read or recite in a singing voice; chant. 2. utter with a particular tone. [< Med.L, ult. < L *in–* in + *tonus* tone] —**in·ton′er**, *n.*

in to·to (in tō′tō), *Latin.* completely.

in·tox·i·cant (in·tok′sə·kənt), *n.* any intoxicating agent, esp. alcoholic liquor. —*adj.* intoxicating.

in·tox·i·cate (in·tok′sə·kāt), *v.*, –cat·ed, –cat·ing. 1. make drunk. 2. excite beyond self-control. [< Med.L, ult. < L *in–* in + *toxicum* poison. See TOXIC.] —**in·tox′i·cat′ed**, *adj.* —**in·tox′i·cat′ing·ly**, *adv.* —**in·tox′i·ca′tive**, *adj.* —**in·tox′i·ca′tor**, *n.*

in·tox·i·ca·tion (in·tok′sə·kā′shən), *n.* 1. drunkenness. 2. great emotional excitement. 3. *Pathol.* poisoning.

intra–, *prefix.* within; inside; on the inside. [< L *intra*, prep., adv.]

in·trac·ta·ble (in·trak′tə·bəl), *adj.* hard to manage; stubborn. —**in·trac′ta·bil′i·ty**, **in·trac′ta·ble·ness**, *n.* —**in·trac′ta·bly**, *adv.* —Syn. unruly, perverse, headstrong.

in·tra·dos (in·trā′dos), *n. Archit.* the interior curve or surface of an arch or vault. [< F, < L *intra–* within + F *dos* back]

in·tra·mu·ral (in′trə·myûr′əl), *adj.* within the walls; inside. ➤ intramural. No hyphen. It means "within the walls," referring specifically to college activities carried on by groups from the same college; the opposite of *intercollegiate.*

intrans., intr., intransitive.

in·tran·si·gence (in·tran′sə·jəns), **in·tran·si·gen·cy** (–jən·si), *n.* uncompromising hostility.

in·tran·si·gent (in·tran′sə·jənt), *adj.* unwilling to agree or compromise; irreconcilable. —*n.* person who is unwilling to agree or compromise. [< F < Sp., ult. < L *in–* not + *transigere* come to an agreement < *trans–* through + *agere* to drive] —**in·tran′si·gent·ly**, *adv.*

in·tran·si·tive (in·tran′sə·tiv), *Gram.* —*adj.* of verbs, not taking a direct object. —*n.* an intransitive verb. —**in·tran′si·tive·ly**, *adv.* —**in·tran′si·tive·ness**, *n.* ➤ See verb for usage note.

in·tra·state (in′trə·stāt′), *adj. Am.* within a state.

in·tra·ve·nous (in′trə·vē′nəs), *adj.* 1. within a vein or the veins. 2. into a vein. [< INTRA– + L *vena* vein] —**in′tra·ve′nous·ly**, *adv.*

in·treat (in·trēt′), *v.* entreat.

in·trench (in·trench′), *v.* entrench. —**in·trench′er**, *n.* —**in·trench′ment**, *n.*

in·trep·id (in·trep′id), *adj.* fearless; dauntless; very brave. [< L, < *in–* not + *trepidus* alarmed] —**in′tre·pid′i·ty**, *n.* —**in·trep′id·ly**, *adv.* —Syn. bold, courageous, daring, valiant.

in·tri·ca·cy (in′trə·kə·si), *n., pl.* –cies. 1. a being intricate; complexity. 2. complication; something involved; intricate proceeding.

in·tri·cate (in′trə·kit), *adj.* 1. with many twists and turns; entangled; complicated. 2. very hard to understand; *per–*

plexing: *an intricate piece of machinery.* [< L *intricatus* entangled, ult. < *in-* in + *tricae* hindrances] —in′tri·cate·ly, *adv.* —in′tri·cate·ness, *n.* —Syn. 1. involved, complex.

in·trigue (*n.* in·trēg′, in′trēg; *v.* in·trēg′), *n.*, *v.*, -trigued, -tri·guing. —*n.* 1. underhand planning; plotting; secret scheming. 2. a crafty plot; secret scheme. 3. a secret love affair. —*v.* 1. carry on an underhand plan; scheme secretly; plot. 2. excite the curiosity and interest of. 3. have a secret love affair. [< F < Ital. < L *intricare* entangle. See INTRICATE.] —in·tri′guer, *n.* —in·tri′guing·ly, *adv.* —Syn. *n.* 1. conspiracy.

in·trin·sic (in·trin′sik), in·trin·si·cal (-sə-kəl), *adj.* belonging to a thing by its very nature; essential; inherent: *the intrinsic value of a dollar bill is only that of a piece of paper.* [< Med.L *intrinsecus* internal < L, inwardly] —in·trin′si·cal·ly, *adv.* —Syn. genuine.

intro., introd., introduction; introductory.

in·tro·duce (in′trə·düs′; -dūs′), *v.*, -duced, -duc·ing. 1. bring in: *introduce a story into the conversation.* 2. put in; insert: *introduce a tube into the throat.* 3. bring into use, notice, knowledge, etc.: *introduce a new word.* 4. make known: *introduce a speaker.* 5. present formally: *introduce (one) to society.* 6. give an introduction to: *this book introduces us to biochemistry.* 7. bring forward: *introduce a question for debate.* 8. begin: *relative pronouns introduce adjective clauses.* [< L, < *intro-* in + *ducere* lead] —in′tro·duc′er, *n.* —in′tro·duc′i·ble, *adj.*

in·tro·duc·tion (in′trə·duk′shən), *n.* 1. an introducing: *the introduction of steel made tall buildings easy to build.* 2. a being introduced: *introduction to strangers.* 3. thing that introduces; first part of a book, speech, piece of music, etc., leading up to the main part. 4. first book for beginners. 5. thing introduced.

in·tro·duc·to·ry (in′trə·duk′tə·ri), in·tro·duc·tive (-tiv), *adj.* used to introduce; serving as an introduction; preliminary. —in′tro·duc′to·ri·ly, in′tro·duc′tive·ly, *adv.*

in·tro·spec·tion (in′trə·spek′shən), *n.* examination of one's own thoughts and feelings. [< L, < *intro-* into + *specere* to look] —in′tro·spec′tive, *adj.* —in′tro·spec′tive·ly, *adv.*

in·tro·ver·sion (in′trə·vér′zhən; -shən), *n.* tendency to be more interested in one's own thoughts and feelings than in what is going on around one. —in·tro·ver·sive (in′trə·vér′siv), *adj.*

in·tro·vert (*v.* in′trə·vért′; *n.*, *adj.* in′trə·vért′), *v.* 1. turn (one's thoughts, etc.) upon oneself. 2. turn or bend inward. —*n.* person interested in his own thoughts and feelings than in what is going on around him; person tending to think rather than act. —*adj.* characterized by introversion. [< L *intro-* within + *vertere* to turn]

in·trude (in·trüd′), *v.*, -trud·ed, -trud·ing. 1. thrust oneself in; come unasked and unwanted. 2. Geol. thrust in; force in. [< L, < *in-* in + *trudere* to thrust] —in·trud′er, *n.* —in·trud′ing·ly, *adv.* —Syn. 1. trespass.

in·tru·sion (in·trü′zhən), *n.* act of intruding.

in·tru·sive (in·trü′siv), *adj.* intruding. —in·tru′sive·ly, *adv.* —in·tru′sive·ness, *n.*

in·trust (in·trust′), *v.* entrust.

in·tu·i·tion (in′tü·ish′ən; -tyü-), *n.* 1. perception of truths, facts, etc., without reasoning. 2. something so perceived. [< LL *intuitio* a gazing at, ult. < *in-* at + *tueri* to look] —in′tu·i′tion·al, *adj.* —in′tu·i′tion·al·ly, *adv.*

in·tu·i·tive (in·tü′ə·tiv; -tyü′-), *adj.* 1. perceiving by intuition. 2. acquired by intuition: *intuitive knowledge.* —in·tu′i·tive·ly, *adv.* —in·tu′i·tive·ness, *n.*

in·un·date (in′un·dāt; in·un′dāt), *v.*, -dat·ed, -dat·ing. overflow; flood. [< L, < *in-* onto + *undare* flow] —in′un·da′tion, *n.* —in′un·da′tor, *n.*

in·ure (in·yūr′), *v.*, -ured, -ur·ing. 1. toughen or harden; accustom; habituate. 2. have effect; be useful. [< *in* + obs. *ure* use, n. < AF < L *opera* work] —in·ure′ment, *n.*

inv., 1. inventor; invented. 2. invoice.

in·vade (in·vād′), *v.*, -vad·ed, -vad·ing. 1. enter with force or as an enemy; attack: *soldiers invaded the country.* 2. enter as if to take possession: *tourists invaded the city.* 3. interfere with; encroach upon; violate: *invade the rights of others.* [< L, < *in-* in + *vadere* go, walk] —in·vad′er, *n.*

in·va·lid¹ (in′və·lid), *n.* a sick, weak person not able to get about and do things. —*adj.* 1. not well; weak and sick. 2. of or for an invalid or invalids. —*v.* 1. make weak or sick; disable. 2. remove from active service because of sickness or injury. [< L, < *in-* not + *validus* strong]

in·val·id² (in·val′id), *adj.* not valid; without force or effect. —in·va·lid·i·ty (in′və·lid′ə·ti), *n.* —in·val′id·ly, *adv.* —Syn. worthless.

in·val·i·date (in·val′ə·dāt), *v.*, -dat·ed, -dat·ing. make valueless; deprive of force or effect. —in·val′i·da′tion, *n.* —in·val′i·da′tor, *n.*

in·va·lid·ism (in′və·lid·iz′əm), *n.* condition of being an invalid; prolonged ill health.

in·val·u·a·ble (in·val′yü·ə·bəl; -yə·bəl), *adj.* very precious; valuable beyond measure. —in·val′u·a·ble·ness, *n.* —in·val′u·a·bly, *adv.* —Syn. priceless.

in·var·i·a·ble (in·vãr′i·ə·bəl), *adj.* always the same; unchangeable; unchanging. —in·var′i·a·bil′i·ty, in·var′i·a·ble·ness, *n.* —in·var′i·a·bly, *adv.* —Syn. uniform, constant.

in·va·sion (in·vā′zhən), *n.* 1. an invading; an attack. 2. interference; encroachment; violation. —in·va·sive (in·vā′siv), *adj.*

in·vec·tive (in·vek′tiv), *n.* violent attack in words; abusive language. —*adj.* inveighing; denouncing. [< LL *invectivus.* See INVEIGH.] —in·vec′tive·ly, *adv.* —in·vec′tive·ness, *n.*

in·veigh (in·vā′), *v.* make a violent attack in words. [< L, < *in-* against + *vehere* carry] —in·veigh′er, *n.*

in·vei·gle (in·vē′gəl; -vā′-), *v.*, -gled, -gling. lead by trickery; entice; allure. [ult. < F *aveugler* make blind < *aveugle* blind, ult. < L *ab-* away + *oculus* eye] —in·vei′gle·ment, *n.* —in·vei′gler, *n.* —Syn. ensnare, beguile, dupe.

in·vent (in·vent′), *v.* 1. make or think out (something new): *Bell invented the telephone.* 2. make up; think up: *invent an excuse.* [< L, < *in-* in + *venire* come] —in·vent′i·ble, *adj.* —in·ven′tor, in·vent′er, *n.*

in·ven·tion (in·ven′shən), *n.* 1. a making something new: *the invention of gunpowder.* 2. thing invented. 3. power of inventing. 4. a made-up story; false statement. —in·ven′tion·al, *adj.*

in·ven·tive (in·ven′tiv), *adj.* 1. good at inventing. 2. of invention. 3. showing power of inventing. —in·ven′tive·ly, *adv.* —in·ven′tive·ness, *n.*

in·ven·to·ry (in′vən·tō′ri; -tô′-), *n.*, *pl.* -to·ries, *v.*, -to·ried, -to·ry·ing. —*n.* 1. a detailed list of articles with their estimated value. 2. collection of articles that are or may be so listed; stock. —*v.* make a detailed list of; enter in a list. [< Med.L *inventorium.* See INVENT.] —in′ven·to′ri·al, *adj.* —in′ven·to′ri·al·ly, *adv.*

In·ver·ness (in′vər·nes′), or **Inverness cape**, *n.* overcoat with a long removable cape.

in·verse (*adj.*, *n.* in·vérs′; *v.* in·vérs′), *adj.*, *n.*, *v.*, -versed, -vers·ing. —*adj.* reversed in position, direction, or tendency; inverted: *DCBA is the inverse order of ABCD.* —*n.* 1. an inverted condition. 2. something reversed. 3. direct opposite: *evil is the inverse of good.* —*v.* invert. [< L *inversus*, pp. of *invertere* INVERT] —in·verse′ly, *adv.*

Inverness

in·ver·sion (in·vér′zhən; -shən), *n.* 1. an inverting or being inverted. 2. something inverted.

in·vert (*v.* in·vért′; *n.* in′vért), *v.* 1. turn upside down. 2. turn around or reverse in position, direction, order, etc. 3. *Music.* change by making the lower or lowest note an octave higher or the higher or highest note an octave lower. —*n.* one that is inverted. [< L, < *in-* + *vertere* to turn] —in·vert′er, *n.* —in·vert′i·ble, *adj.*

in·ver·te·brate (in·vėr′tə·brit; -brāt), *adj.* 1. *Zool.* without a backbone. 2. of or having to do with invertebrates. —*n.* animal without a backbone. All animals except fishes, amphibians, reptiles, birds, and mammals are invertebrates. —in·ver·te·bra·cy (in·vėr′tə·brə·si), in·ver′te·brate·ness, *n.*

in·vest (in·vest′), *v.* 1. use (money) to buy something that is expected to produce a profit, or income, or both: *people invest their money in stocks, bonds, lands, etc.* 2. invest money: *learn to invest wisely.* 3. loosely, lay out; spend: *invest large sums in books.* 4. clothe; cover; surround: *darkness invests the earth at night.* 5. give power, authority, or right to: *he invested his lawyer with complete power to act for him.* 6. install in office with a ceremony: *a king is invested in office by crowning him.* 7. *Mil.* surround with soldiers or ships; besiege: *the enemy invested the city and cut it off from our army.* [< L, < *in-* in + *vestis* clothing] —in·ves′tor, *n.*

in·ves·ti·gate (in·ves′tə·gāt), *v.* -gat·ed, -gat·ing. search into; examine closely: *scientists investigate nature.* [< L, < *in-* in + *vestigare* to track, trace] —in·ves′ti·ga·tive, in·ves·ti·ga·to·ry (in·ves′tə·gə·tô′ri, -tō′-), *adj.* —in·ves′ti·ga′tor, *n.* —Syn. explore, scrutinize.

in·ves·ti·ga·tion (in·ves′tə·gā′shən), *n.* careful search; detailed or careful examination.

in·ves·ti·ture (in·ves′tə·chər), *n.* 1. a formal investing of a person with an office, dignity, power, right, etc. 2. clothing; covering.

in·vest·ment (in·vest′mənt), *n.* 1. an investing; a laying out of money. 2. amount of money invested. 3. something that is expected to yield money as income or profit or both. 4. a surrounding with soldiers or ships; siege. 5. investiture.

in·vet·er·a·cy (in·vet′ər·ə·si), *n.* settled, fixed condition; habitualness.

in·vet·er·ate (in·vet′ər·it), *adj.* 1. confirmed in a habit, practice, feeling, etc.; habitual: *an inveterate smoker.* 2. long and firmly established. [< L, < *in-* + *veterascere* grow old < *vetus* old] —in·vet′er·ate·ly, *adv.* —in·vet′er·ate·ness, *n.* —Syn. 1. hardened, chronic.

in·vid·i·ous (in·vid′i·əs), *adj.* likely to arouse ill will or resentment; giving offense because unfair or unjust. [< L, < *invidia* envy] —in·vid′i·ous·ly, *adv.* —in·vid′i·ous·ness, *n.* —Syn. hateful, odious, offensive.

in·vig·or·ate (in·vig′ər·āt), *v.* -at·ed, -at·ing. give vigor to; fill with life and energy. [< *vigor*] —in·vig′or·at′ing·ly, *adv.* —in·vig′or·a′tion, *n.* —in·vig′or·a·tive, *adj.* —in·vig′or·a·tive·ly, *adv.* —in·vig′or·a′tor, *n.* —Syn. brace, refresh, stimulate, animate.

in·vin·ci·ble (in·vin′sə·bəl), *adj.* not to be overcome; unconquerable. [< L, < *in-* not + *vincere* conquer] —in·vin′ci·bil′i·ty, in·vin′ci·ble·ness, *n.* —in·vin′ci·bly, *adv.*

in·vi·o·la·ble (in·vī′ə·lə·bəl), *adj.* 1. that must not be violated or injured; sacred. 2. that cannot be violated or injured. —in·vi′o·la·bil′i·ty, in·vi′o·la·ble·ness, *n.* —in·vi′o·la·bly, *adv.*

in·vi·o·late (in·vī′ə·lit; -lāt), *adj.* not violated; uninjured; unbroken; not profaned. —in·vi·o·la·cy (in·vī′ə·lə·si), in·vi′o·late·ness, *n.* —in·vi′o·late·ly, *adv.*

in·vis·i·ble (in·viz′ə·bəl), *adj.* 1. not visible; not capable of being seen: *germs are invisible to the naked eye.* 2. out of sight. 3. hidden: *invisible assets.* —*n.* 1. an invisible being or thing. 2. the invisible, the unseen world. —in·vis′i·bil′i·ty, in·vis′i·ble·ness, *n.* —in·vis′i·bly, *adv.*

in·vi·ta·tion (in′və·tā′shən), *n.* 1. request to come to some place or to do something. 2. act of inviting. 3. attraction; inducement. —in′vi·ta′tion·al, *adj.*

in·vite (*v.* in·vīt′; *n.* in′vīt), *v.* -vit·ed, -vit·ing, *n.* —*v.* 1. ask (someone) politely to come to some place or to do something. 2. make a polite request for: *he invited our opinion of his work.* 3. give occasion for: *the letter invites some question.* 4. attract; tempt. —*n. Colloq.* invitation.

[< L *invitare*] —in·vit′er, *n.* —Syn. *v.* 1. bid, request. 4. encourage, incite. ❭ Invite is ordinarily a verb. Its use as a noun (in′vīt) is colloquial or would-be humorous: *Did you get an invite?*

in·vit·ing (in·vīt′ing), *adj.* attractive; tempting. —in·vit′ing·ly, *adv.* —in·vit′ing·ness, *n.*

in·vo·ca·tion (in′və·kā′shən), *n.* act of calling upon in prayer; appeal for help or protection.

in·voice (in′vois), *n.*, *v.*, -voiced, -voic·ing. —*n.* list of goods sent to a purchaser showing prices, amounts, shipping charges, etc. —*v.* make an invoice of; enter on an invoice. [earlier *invoyes*, pl. of *invoy*, var. of ENVOY]

in·voke (in·vōk′), *v.*, -voked, -vok·ing. 1. call on in prayer; appeal to for help or protection. 2. ask earnestly for; beg for. 3. call forth by magic. [< L, < *in-* on + *vocare* call] —in·vok′er, *n.*

in·vo·lu·cre (in′və·lū′kər), *n.* circle of bracts around a flower cluster. [< F < L *involucrum* a cover < *involvere*. See INVOLVE.] —in′vo·lu′cral, *adj.*

INVOLUCRE

in·vol·un·tar·y (in·vol′ən·ter′i), *adj.* 1. not voluntary; not done of one's own free will; unwilling: *an involuntary witness.* 2. not done on purpose; not intended: *an involuntary injury.* 3. not controlled by the will: *breathing is mainly involuntary.* —in·vol′un·tar′i·ly, *adv.* —in·vol′un·tar′i·ness, *n.* —Syn. 1. compulsory, forced. 2. unintentional, inadvertent. 3. automatic, instinctive.

in·vo·lute (in′və·lūt), *adj.* 1. involved; intricate. 2. rolled up on itself; curved spirally. 3. *Bot.* rolled inward from the edge. 4. *Zool.* having the whorls closely wound, as a spiral shell. —*n.* something involved. [< L *involutus*, pp. of *involvere* INVOLVE] —in′vo·lut′ed·ly, *adv.*

in·vo·lu·tion (in′və·lū′shən), *n.* 1. an involving. 2. a being involved; entanglement; complexity. 3. something involved; complication. —in′vo·lu′tion·al, *n.*

in·volve (in·volv′), *v.*, -volved, -volv·ing. 1. have as a necessary part, condition, or result; affect; take in; include. 2. cause to be unpleasantly concerned; implicate; bring (into difficulty, danger, etc.). 3. entangle; complicate: *involved sentences are hard to understand.* 4. take up the attention of; occupy: *involved in working out a puzzle.* 5. wrap; infold; envelop: *the outcome of the war is involved in doubt.* [< L, < *in-* + *volvere* to roll] —in·volve′ment, *n.* —in·volv′er, *n.* —Syn. 1. entail. 4. absorb. 5. surround.

in·vul·ner·a·ble (in·vul′nər·ə·bəl), *adj.* that cannot be wounded or injured; proof against attack. —in·vul′ner·a·bil′i·ty, in·vul′ner·a·ble·ness, *n.* —in·vul′ner·a·bly, *adv.*

in·ward (in′wərd), *adv.* Also, in′wards. 1. toward the inside: *a passage leading inward.* 2. into the mind or soul: *turn your thoughts inward.* —*adj.* 1. placed within; internal: *the inward parts of the body.* 2. inland: *inward Australia.* 3. directed toward the inside: *an inward slant of the eyes.* 4. in the mind or soul: *inward peace.* —*n.* in·wards (in′ərdz). parts inside the body.

in·ward·ly (in′wərd·li), *adv.* 1. on the inside; within. 2. toward the inside. 3. in the mind or soul. 4. not aloud or openly.

in·ward·ness (in′wərd·nis), *n.* 1. inner nature or meaning. 2. spirituality. 3. earnestness.

in·weave (in·wēv′), *v.*, -wove or -weaved, -wov·en or -wove or -weaved, -weav·ing. weave in.

in·wrap (in·rap′), *v.*, -wrapped, -wrap·ping. enwrap.

in·wrought (in·rôt′), *adj.* 1. having a decoration worked in. 2. worked in. 3. mixed together; closely blended. Also, enwrought.

I·o (ī′ō), *n. Gk. Myth.* maiden loved by Zeus, changed into a white heifer by Hera.

Io, *Chem.* ionium.

i·o·dide (ī′ə·dīd; -did), **i·o·did** (-did), *n. Chem.* compound of iodine with another element or radical.

i·o·dine (ī′ə·dīn, -din; *Chem.* ī′ə·dēn), **i·o·din**

(–din), *n. Chem.* **1.** a nonmetallic element, I, consisting of blackish crystals that give off a dense, violet-colored vapor with an irritating odor, used in medicine, in making dyes, in photography, etc. **2.** a brown liquid, tincture of iodine, used as an antiseptic. [< F *iode* iodine < Gk. *iodes* rust-colored < *ios* rust]

i·o·do·form (ī-ō′də-fôrm; ī′od′ə-), *n. Chem.* a crystalline compound of iodine, CHI₃, used as an antiseptic.

i·on (ī′ən; ī′on), *n. Physics, Chem.* **1.** either of the two substances into which a compound is broken up by an electric current. **2.** an electrified atom or group of atoms. **3.** an electrically charged particle formed in a gas. [< Gk., neut. ppr. of *ienai* go] —**i·on·ic** (ī-on′ik), *adj.*

-ion, *suffx.* **1.** act of ——ing, as in *attraction.* **2.** condition or state of being ——ed, as in *adoption.* **3.** result of ——ing, as in *abbreviation.* [< F < L –*io,* –*ionis*]

I·o·ni·a (ī-ō′ni-ə), *n.* an ancient region on the W coast of Asia Minor, with nearby islands, colonized by the Greeks in very early times. —**I·o′ni·an,** *adj., n.*

Ionian Sea, part of the Mediterranean Sea between Greece and S Italy.

I·on·ic (ī-on′ik), *adj.* **1.** noting or pertaining to the order of Greek architecture having scrolls in the capitals of the columns. **2.** of Ionia or its people.

i·o·ni·um (ī-ō′ni-əm), *n. Chem.* a radioactive element, Io, formed from disintegrating uranium.

i·on·ize (ī′ən-īz), *v.,* –**ized,** –**iz**ing. separate into ions; produce ions in. Acids, bases, and salts ionize in solution. —**i′on·i·za′tion,** *n.* —**i′on·iz′er,** *n.*

Ionic capital

i·on·o·sphere (ī-on′ə-sfir), *n.* a region of ionized layers of air beginning 18 to 28 miles above the earth's surface.

i·o·ta (ī-ō′tə), *n.* **1.** the ninth letter of the Greek alphabet (I, ι). **2.** a very small quantity. —Syn. **2.** bit, jot.

I.O.U., I O U (ī′ō′ū′), **1.** I owe you. **2.** informal note showing a debt.

I·o·wa (ī′ə-wə), *n.* a Middle Western State of the United States. *Capital:* Des Moines. *Abbrev.:* I·a. —**I·o′wan,** *n.*

ip·e·cac (ip′ə-kak), **ip·e·cac·u·an·ha** (ip′ə-kak′yū-an′ə), *n. Am.* **1.** medicine made from the dried roots of a South American vine, used as an emetic or purgative. **2.** the dried roots. **3.** the vine. [< Pg. < Tupi *ipe-kaa-guéne* creeping plant causing nausea]

Iph·i·ge·ni·a (if′ə-jə-nī′ə), *n. Gk. Legend.* daughter of Agamemnon and Clytemnestra.

ip·se dix·it (ip′sē dik′sit), a dogmatic assertion. [< L, he himself said (it)]

ip·so fac·to (ip′sō fak′tō), *Latin.* by that very fact; by the fact itself.

IQ, I.Q., intelligence quotient.

Ir, *Chem.* iridium.

Ir., Ireland; Irish.

I·ran (i-ran′; ī–; ē-rän′), *n.* kingdom in SW Asia. Formerly called Persia. —**I·ra·ni·an** (i-rā′ni·ən; ī–), *adj., n.*

I·raq, I·rak (i-rak′; ē-räk′), *n.* country in SW Asia, N of Arabia. Formerly called Mesopotamia. —**I·ra·qi** (ē-rä′kē; i-rak′i), *n., pl.* –**qis,** *adj.* —*n.* native of Iraq. —*adj.* of or having to do with Iraq or its inhabitants.

i·ras·ci·ble (i-ras′ə-bəl), *adj.* **1.** easily made angry; irritable. **2.** showing anger. [< LL, < L *irasci* grow angry < *ira* anger] —**i·ras′ci·bil′i·ty,** i·ras′ci·ble·ness, *n.* —**i·ras′ci·bly,** *adv.*

i·rate (ī′rāt; ī·rāt′), *adj.* angry. [< L, < *ira* anger] —**i′rate·ly,** *adv.*

IRBM, Intermediate Range Ballistic Missile, a ballistic missile of great range (up to 1500 miles) but less than that of the ICBM.

ire (ir), *n.* anger; wrath. [< OF < L *ira*] —**ire**′ful, *adj.* —**ire′ful·ly,** *adv.* —**ire′ful·ness,** *n.* —**ire′less,** *adj.*

Ire., Ireland.

Ire·land (īr′lənd), *n.* **1.** one of the British Isles divided into the Republic of Ireland and Northern Ireland. **2.** Republic of, the Irish Republic.

ir·i·des·cence (ir′ə-des′əns), *n.* changing or play of colors, as in mother-of-pearl, opals, a peacock's feathers, etc. [< L *iris* rainbow < Gk.] —**ir′i·des′cent,** *adj.* —**ir′i·des′cent·ly,** *adv.*

i·rid·i·um (i-rid′i-əm), *n. Chem.* a rare metallic element, Ir, that resembles platinum and is twice as heavy as lead, used for the points of gold pens.

i·ris (ī′ris), *n., pl.* **i·ris·es,** **ir·i·des** (ir′ə-dēz; ī′rə-). **1.** *Bot.* **a.** plant with sword-shaped leaves and large flowers with three upright petals and three drooping petallike sepals. **b.** the flower. **2.** *Anat.* the colored part around the pupil of the eye. **3.** *Iris, Gk. Myth.* goddess of the rainbow and messenger of the gods. **4.** rainbow. [< L < Gk., rainbow]

I·rish (ī′rish), *adj.* of or having to do with Ireland, its people, or their language. —*n.* **1.** (*pl. in use*) people of Ireland. **2.** the Celtic language spoken in part of Ireland; Gaelic. **3.** English as spoken by the Irish.

Irish Free State, former name of the Irish Republic.

I·rish·man (ī′rish-mən), *n., pl.* –**men.** man of Irish birth.

Irish potato, the common white potato.

Irish Republic, an independent republic in C and S Ireland. *Capital:* Dublin.

Irish Sea, part of the Atlantic between Ireland and England.

Irish setter, a hunting dog with long, silky, reddish-brown hair.

Irish stew, stew made of meat, potatoes, and onions.

Irish terrier, a small dog with brown wiry hair, somewhat like a small Airedale.

I·rish·wom·an (ī′rish-wûm′ən), *n., pl.* –**wom**·en. woman of Irish birth or Irish descent.

irk (ėrk), *v.* weary; disgust; annoy; trouble. [ME *irke(n)*]

irk·some (ėrk′səm), *adj.* tiresome; tedious. —**irk′some·ly,** *adv.* —**irk′some·ness,** *n.* —Syn. annoying.

Irish terrier (ab. 18 in. high at the shoulder)

Ir·kutsk (ir-kŭtsk′), *n.* city in S Soviet Union in Asia.

i·ron (ī′ərn), *n.* **1.** the commonest and most useful metal, from which tools, machinery, etc., are made. It is a chemical element, Fe. **2.** tool, instrument, or weapon made from this metal. **3.** great hardness and strength; firmness: *men of iron.* **4.** tool with a flat surface for smoothing cloth or pressing clothes. **5.** golf club with an iron or steel head. **6.** irons, chains or bands of iron; handcuffs; shackles. —*adj.* **1.** made of iron; pertaining to iron. **2.** like iron; hard or strong; unyielding: *an iron will.* **3.** harsh or cruel: *the iron hand of fate.* —*v.* **1.** smooth or press (cloth, etc.) with a heated iron. **2.** furnish or cover with iron. [OE *īren,* ? < Celtic] —**i′ron·like′,** *adj.*

i·ron·bound (ī′ərn-bound′), *adj.* **1.** bound with iron. **2.** hard; firm; rigid; unyielding. **3.** rocky.

i·ron·clad (ī′ərn-klad′), *adj.* **1.** protected with iron plates. **2.** very hard to change or get out of: *an ironclad agreement.* —*n.* warship protected with iron plates.

Iron Curtain, an imaginary wall separating Russia and the nations under Russian control or influence from the rest of the world, behind which strict censorship and secrecy are enforced.

i·ron·i·cal (ī-ron′ə-kəl), **i·ron·ic** (–ik), *adj.* **1.** expressing one thing and meaning the opposite: *"Speedy" would be an ironical name for a snail.* **2.** contrary to what would naturally be expected. —**i·ron′i·cal·ly,** *adv.* —**i·ron′i·cal·ness,** *n.*

ironing board, board covered with a smooth cloth, used for ironing clothes.

iron lung, device to give artificial respiration.

i·ron·mon·ger (ī′ərn-mung′gər; –mong′–), *n.*

Esp. Brit. dealer in ironware or hardware. —**i'ron·mon'ger·y,** *n.*

iron pyrites, mineral, FeS₂, that looks somewhat like gold; fool's gold.

i·ron·sides (ī'ərn·sīdz'), *n.pl.* (*sing. in use*) an armor-clad warship.

i·ron·ware (ī'ərn·wār'), *n.* articles made of iron, such as pots, kettles, tools, etc.; hardware.

i·ron·wood (ī'ərn·wůd'), *n.* **Am.** 1. any of various trees with hard heavy wood. 2. the wood itself.

i·ron·work (ī'ərn·wérk'), *n.* 1. things made of iron. 2. work in iron. —**i'ron·work'er,** *n.*

i·ron·works (ī'ərn·wérks'), *n. pl. or sing.* place where iron is made or worked into iron articles.

i·ro·ny (ī'rə·ni), *n., pl.* —**nies.** 1. method of expression in which the ordinary meaning of the words is the opposite of the thought in the speaker's mind: *the boys called the very thin boy "Fatty" in irony.* 2. event contrary to what would naturally be expected. [< L < Gk. *eironeia* dissimulation < *eiron* dissembler] —**Syn.** 1. sarcasm, satire.

Ir·o·quois (ir'ə·kwoi), *n. sing. and pl.* **Am.** member of a powerful group of American Indian tribes called the Five Nations, formerly living mostly in New York State. —**Ir·o·quoi·an** (ir'ə·kwoi'ən), *adj.* **Am.**

ir·ra·di·ate (i·rā'di·āt), *v.,* —**at·ed,** —**at·ing,** *adj.* —*v.* 1. shine upon; make bright; illuminate. 2. shine. 3. radiate; give out. 4. treat with ultraviolet rays. —*adj.* bright. [< L, < *in* + *radius* ray] —**ir·ra'di·a'tion,** *n.* —**ir·ra'di·a'tive,** *adj.* —**ir·ra'di·a'tor,** *n.*

ir·ra·tion·al (i·rash'ən·əl; i·rash'nəl), *adj.* 1. not rational; unreasonable: *it is irrational to be afraid of the number 13.* 2. unable to think and reason clearly. 3. **Math.** that cannot be expressed by a whole number or a common fraction. √3 is an irrational number. —**ir·ra'tion·al'i·ty,** **ir·ra'tion·al·ness,** *n.* —**ir·ra'tion·al·ly,** *adv.* —**Syn.** 1. illogical, unsound.

Ir·ra·wad·dy (ir'ə·wod'i), *n.* river in E Asia, flowing through Burma into the Bay of Bengal.

ir·re·claim·a·ble (ir'i·klām'ə·bəl), *adj.* that cannot be reclaimed. —**ir're·claim'a·bil'i·ty,** **ir're·claim'a·ble·ness,** *n.* —**ir're·claim'a·bly,** *adv.*

ir·re·con·cil·a·ble (i·rek'ən·sīl'ə·bəl; i·rek'-ən·sīl'-), *adj.* that cannot be reconciled; that cannot be made to agree; opposed. —*n.* person who persists in opposing. —**ir·rec'on·cil'a·bil'i-ty,** **ir·rec'on·cil'a·ble·ness,** *n.* —**ir·rec'on·cil'-a·bly,** *adv.*

ir·re·cov·er·a·ble (ir'i·kuv'ər·ə·bəl), *adj.* 1. that cannot be regained or got back: *wasted time is irrecoverable.* 2. that cannot be remedied: *irrecoverable sorrow.* —**ir're·cov'er·a·ble·ness,** *n.* —**ir're·cov'er·a·bly,** *adv.* —**Syn.** 1. irretrievable.

ir·re·deem·a·ble (ir'i·dēm'ə·bəl), *adj.* 1. that cannot be bought back. 2. that cannot be exchanged for coin: *irredeemable paper money.* 3. beyond remedy; hopeless. —**ir're·deem'a·bly,** *adv.*

ir·re·duc·i·ble (ir'i·dūs'ə·bəl; —dūs'-), *adj.* that cannot be reduced. —**ir're·duc'i·bil'i·ty,** **ir're·duc'i·ble·ness,** *n.* —**ir're·duc'i·bly,** *adv.*

ir·ref·ra·ga·ble (i·ref'rə·gə·bəl), *adj.* that cannot be refuted; unanswerable; undeniable. [< LL, < L *in-* not + *refragari* oppose] —**ir·ref'ra·ga·bil'i·ty,** *n.* —**ir·ref'ra·ga·bly,** *adv.*

ir·ref·u·ta·ble (i·ref'yə·tə·bəl; ir'i·fūt'ə·bəl), *adj.* that cannot be refuted or disproved. —**ir·ref'u·ta·bil'i·ty,** *n.* —**ir·ref'u·ta·bly,** *adv.* —**Syn.** undeniable, unanswerable.

irreg., 1. irregular. 2. irregularly.

ir·reg·u·lar (i·reg'yə·lər), *adj.* 1. not regular; not according to rule; out of the usual order or natural way: *irregular breathing.* 2. not even; not smooth; not straight; without symmetry: *an irregular pattern.* 3. not according to law or morals: *irregular behavior.* 4. **Mil.** not in the regular army. 5. not accepted as a member of some established group: *an irregular doctor.* 6. **Gram.** not inflected in the usual way. *Come* is an irregular verb. —*n.* one that is irregular.

—**ir·reg'u·lar·ly,** *adv.* —**Syn.** *adj.* 1. unnatural, abnormal, erratic. 2. uneven, variable. 3. lawless.

ir·reg·u·lar·i·ty (i·reg'yə·lar'ə·ti), *n., pl.* —**ties.** 1. lack of regularity. 2. something irregular.

ir·rel·e·vant (i·rel'ə·vənt), *adj.* not to the point; off the subject. —**ir·rel'e·vance, ir·rel'e·van·cy,** *n.* —**ir·rel'e·vant·ly,** *adv.*

ir·re·li·gion (ir'i·lij'ən), *n.* 1. lack of religion. 2. hostility to religion; disregard of religion. —**ir're·li'gion·ist,** *n.*

ir·re·li·gious (ir'i·lij'əs), *adj.* 1. not religious; indifferent to religion. 2. contrary to religious principles; impious. —**ir're·li'gious·ly,** *adv.* —**ir're·li'gious·ness,** *n.*

ir·re·me·di·a·ble (ir'i·mē'di·ə·bəl), *adj.* that cannot be remedied; incurable. —**ir're·me'di·a·ble·ness,** *n.* —**ir're·me'di·a·bly,** *adv.*

ir·re·mov·a·ble (ir'i·müv'ə·bəl), *adj.* that cannot be removed. —**ir're·mov'a·bil'i·ty,** *n.* —**ir're·mov'a·bly,** *adv.*

ir·rep·a·ra·ble (i·rep'ə·rə·bəl), *adj.* that cannot be repaired or made good. —**ir·rep'a·ra·bil'i·ty, ir·rep'a·ra·ble·ness,** *n.* —**ir·rep'a·ra·bly,** *adv.*

ir·re·place·a·ble (ir'i·plās'ə·bəl), *adj.* not replaceable; impossible to replace with another.

ir·re·press·i·ble (ir'i·pres'ə·bəl), *adj.* that cannot be repressed or restrained. —**ir're·press'-i·bil'i·ty, ir're·press'i·ble·ness,** *n.* —**ir're·press'i·bly,** *adv.*

ir·re·proach·a·ble (ir'i·prōch'ə·bəl), *adj.* free from blame; faultless. —**ir're·proach'a·ble·ness,** *n.* —**ir're·proach'a·bly,** *adv.* —**Syn.** blameless.

ir·re·sist·i·ble (ir'i·zis'tə·bəl), *adj.* that cannot be resisted; too great to be withstood. —**ir're·sist'i·bil'i·ty, ir're·sist'i·ble·ness,** *n.* —**ir're·sist'i·bly,** *adv.*

ir·res·o·lute (i·rez'ə·lüt), *adj.* not resolute; unable to make up one's mind. —**ir·res'o·lute·ly,** *adv.* —**ir·res'o·lute·ness, ir·res'o·lu'tion,** *n.* —**Syn.** hesitating, doubtful, vacillating.

ir·re·spec·tive (ir'i·spek'tiv), *adj.* regardless: *any person, irrespective of age, may join the club.* —**ir're·spec'tive·ly,** *adv.*

ir·re·spon·si·ble (ir'i·spon'sə·bəl), *adj.* 1. not responsible; that cannot be called to account: *a dictator is an irresponsible ruler.* 2. without a sense of responsibility. —*n.* an irresponsible person. —**ir're·spon'si·bil'i·ty, ir're·spon'si·ble·ness,** *n.* —**ir're·spon'si·bly,** *adv.*

ir·re·triev·a·ble (ir'i·trēv'ə·bəl), *adj.* that cannot be retrieved or recovered; that cannot be recalled or restored to its former condition. —**ir're·triev'a·bil'i·ty, ir're·triev'a·ble·ness,** *n.* —**ir're·triev'a·bly,** *adv.*

ir·rev·er·ence (i·rev'ər·əns), *n.* 1. lack of reverence; disrespect. 2. act of showing irreverence.

ir·rev·er·ent (i·rev'ər·ənt), *adj.* not reverent; disrespectful. —**ir·rev'er·ent·ly,** *adv.*

ir·re·vers·i·ble (ir'i·vér'sə·bəl), *adj.* not capable of being reversed. —**ir're·vers'i·bil'i·ty, ir're·vers'i·ble·ness,** *n.* —**ir're·vers'i·bly,** *adv.*

ir·rev·o·ca·ble (i·rev'ə·kə·bəl), *adj.* not to be recalled, withdrawn, or annulled: *an irrevocable decision.* —**ir·rev'o·ca·bil'i·ty, ir·rev'o·ca·ble·ness,** *n.* —**ir·rev'o·ca·bly,** *adv.*

ir·ri·ga·ble (ir'i·gə·bəl), *adj.* that can be irrigated.

ir·ri·gate (ir'ə·gāt), *v.,* —**gat·ed,** —**gat·ing.** 1. supply (land) with water by using ditches. 2. **Med.** supply (a wound, cavity in the body, etc.) with a continuous flow of some liquid. 3. supply land, wounds, etc., thus. [< L, < *in* + *rigare* wet] —**ir'ri·ga'tion,** *n.* —**ir'ri·ga'tion·al,** *adj.* —**ir'ri·ga'tor,** *n.*

ir·ri·ta·bil·i·ty (ir'ə·tə·bil'ə·ti), *n., pl.* —**ties.** 1. a being irritable; impatience. 2. unnatural sensitiveness (of an organ or part of the body). 3. **Biol.** property that living plant or animal tissue has of responding to a stimulus.

ir·ri·ta·ble (ir'ə·tə·bəl), *adj.* 1. easily made angry; impatient. 2. unnaturally sensitive or sore. 3. **Biol.** able to respond to stimuli. —**ir'ri·ta·ble·ness,** *n.* —**ir'ri·ta·bly,** *adv.* —**Syn.** 1. touchy, testy.

ir·ri·tant (ir'ə·tənt), *n.* thing that causes irritation. —*adj.* causing irritation. —**ir'ri·tan·cy,** *n.*

ir·ri·tate (ir'ə·tāt), *v.,* -tat·ed, -tat·ing. 1. arouse to impatience or anger; provoke: *his foolish questions irritated me.* 2. make unnaturally sensitive or sore: *sunburn irritates the skin.* 3. *Biol.* stimulate (an organ, muscle, tissue, etc.) to perform some characteristic action or function. [< L *irritatus* enraged, provoked] —**ir'ri·tat'ing,** **ir'ri·ta'tive,** *adj.* —**ir'ri·tat'ing·ly,** *adv.* —**ir'ri·ta'tion,** *n.* —**ir'ri·ta'tor,** *n.* —Syn. 1. vex, annoy, exasperate.

ir·rup·tion (i·rup'shən), *n.* a breaking or bursting in; violent invasion. [< L *irruptio,* ult. < *in-* in + *rumpere* break] —**ir·rup'tive,** *adj.*

Ir·ving (ėr'ving), *n.* Washington, 1783–1859, American writer, author of *Rip Van Winkle.*

is (iz), *v.* 1. 3rd pers. sing. pres. indic. of *be.* He is, she is, it is. 2. as is, as it is now; in its present condition. [OE]

is., Is., 1. island. 2. isle.

Isa., Is., Isaiah.

I·saac (ī'zək), *n.* son of Abraham and Sarah, and father of Jacob and Esau. Gen. 21:3.

Is·a·bel·la I (iz'ə·bel'ə), 1451–1504, queen of Castile and León, patron of Columbus.

I·sai·ah (ī·zā'ə; ī·zī'ə), **I·sai·as** (—əs), *n.* 1. the greatest of the Hebrew prophets. 2. book of the Old Testament.

Is·car·i·ot (is·kar'i·ət), *n.* 1. surname of Judas, who betrayed Christ for money. 2. a traitor.

-ise, *suffix.* variant of *-ize.* **>** See *-ize* for usage note.

I·seult (i·sült'), *n. Arthurian Legend.* 1. the daughter of the King of Ireland and the wife of King Mark of Cornwall, loved by Tristram. 2. daughter of the ruler of Brittany, and Tristram's wife. Also, Isolde.

-ish, *suffix.* 1. somewhat, as in *oldish, sweetish.* 2. resembling; like, as in *a childish man.* 3. like that of; having the characteristics of, as in *a childish idea.* 4. of or pertaining to; belonging to, as in *British, Turkish.* 5. tending to; inclined to, as in *bookish, thievish.* 6. near, but usually somewhat past, as in *fortyish.* [OE –*isc*]

Ish·ma·el (ish'mi·əl), *n.* 1. son of Abraham and Hagar, driven into the wilderness by Sarah. Gen. 16. 2. outcast.

Ish·ma·el·ite (ish'mi·əl·īt), *n.* 1. descendant of Ishmael. 2. outcast. —**Ish'ma·el·it'ish,** *adj.*

i·sin·glass (ī'zing·glas'; -gläs'), *n.* 1. kind of gelatin obtained from air bladders of sturgeon, cod, and similar fishes, used for making glue, clearing liquors, etc. 2. mica, esp. in thin semi-transparent layers. [alter. of MDu. *huysenblas* sturgeon bladder; infl. by *glass*]

I·sis (ī'sis), *n.* the Egyptian goddess of fertility.

isl., 1. *pl.* isls. island. 2. isle.

Is·lam (is'ləm; is·läm'), *n.* 1. the Mohammedan religion. 2. Mohammedans as a group. 3. the countries under Mohammedan rule. —**Is·lam·ic** (is·lam'ik; -lä'mik), **Is·lam·it·ic** (is'ləm·it'ik), *adj.* —**Is·lam·ism** (is'ləm·iz·əm), *n.* —**Is·lam·ite** (is'ləm·īt), *n., adj.*

is·land (ī'lənd), *n.* 1. body of land surrounded by water. 2. something resembling this. 3. a safety platform in the middle of a busy street. 4. *Physiol., Anat.* a group of cells distinct from its neighbors in structure or function. 5. *Naut.* superstructure, esp. of a battleship or aircraft carrier. —*v.* make into an island. [OE *igland* < *ig* island + *land* land; spelling infl. by *isle*] —**is'land·less,** *adj.* —**is'land·like',** *adj.*

is·land·er (ī'lən·dər), *n.* native or inhabitant of an island.

isle (īl), **is·let** (ī'lit), *n.* a small island. [< OF < L *insula*]

ism (iz'əm), *n.* distinctive doctrine, theory, system, or practice. [see –ISM]

-ism, *suffix.* 1. action; practice, as in *baptism, criticism.* 2. doctrine; system; principle, as in *communism, socialism.* 3. quality; characteristic; state; condition, as in *heroism, paganism, Americanism.* 4. illustration; case; instance, as in *colloquialism, witticism.* 5. *Med.* unhealthy con-

dition caused by, as in *alcoholism, morphinism.* [< Gk. *-ismos, -isma*]

is·n't (iz'ənt), is not.

iso-, is-, *word element.* equal; alike, as in *isometric, isotope.* [< Gk., < *isos* equal]

i·so·bar (ī'sə·bär), *n.* 1. line on a weather map connecting places having the same average atmospheric pressure. 2. *Physics, Chem.* one of two or more kinds of atoms that have the same atomic weight, but in most cases different atomic numbers. [< Gk., < *isos* equal + *baros* weight] —**i·so·bar·ic** (ī'sə·bar'ik), *adj.*

i·soch·ro·nous (ī·sok'rə·nəs), *adj.* 1. equal in time. 2. performed in equal times.

i·so·gon·ic (ī'sə·gon'ik), *adj.* 1. having equal angles; having to do with equal angles. 2. having equal deviations of the magnetic needle from the true north. —*n.* line connecting points that have such equal deviations.

i·so·late (ī'sə·lāt; is'ə-), *v.,* -lat·ed, -lat·ing. 1. place apart; separate from others. 2. *Chem.* obtain (a substance) in a pure or uncombined form. 3. *Med.* keep apart or separate (an infected person) from other noninfected persons. [< *isolated* < F < Ital. *isolato* < L *insulatus,* ult. < *insula* island] —**i'so·la'tion,** *n.* —**i'so·la'tor,** *n.*

i·so·la·tion·ist (ī'sə·lā'shən·ist), *n. Am.* one who objects to his country's participation in international affairs. —**i'so·la'tion·ism,** *n.*

I·sol·de (i·sōl'də; i·sōld'; i·zōl'də), *n.* Iseult.

i·so·mer (ī'sə·mər), *n. Chem.* an isomeric compound.

i·so·mer·ic (ī'sə·mer'ik), *adj. Chem.* composed of the same elements in the same proportions by weight, but differing in one or more properties because of the difference in arrangement of atoms. [< Gk., < *isos* equal + *meros* part] —**i·som·er·ism** (ī·som'ər·iz·əm), *n.*

i·som·er·ous (ī·som'ər·əs), *adj. Bot.* of a flower, having the same number of members in each whorl.

i·so·met·ric (ī'sə·met'rik), **i·so·met·ri·cal** (-rə·kəl), *adj.* pertaining to equality of measure; having equality of measure. —**i'so·met'ri·cal·ly,** *adv.*

isometric exercises, exercises which are intended to strengthen muscles by pushing against an immovable object, as a wall.

i·so·mor·phic (ī'sə·môr'fik), *adj.* having similar appearance or structure, but different ancestry. —**i'so·mor'phism,** *n.*

i·so·ni·a·zid (ī'sō·nī'ə·zid), *n.* drug chemically related to nicotinic acid, used in the treatment of tuberculosis.

i·sos·ce·les (ī·sos'ə·lēz), *adj. Geom.* having two sides equal.

Isosceles triangles

[< LL < Gk., < *isos* equal + *skelos* leg]

i·so·therm (ī'sə·thėrm), *n.* line connecting places having the same average temperature. [< iso- + Gk. *therme* heat] —**i'so·ther'mal,** *adj.* —**i'so·ther'mal·ly,** *adv.*

i·so·tope (ī'sə·tōp), *n. Chem.* any of two or more elements that have the same chemical properties and the same atomic number, but different atomic weights or radioactive behavior. Hydrogen and heavy hydrogen are isotopes. [< iso- + Gk. *topos* place] —**i·so·top·ic** (ī'sə·top'ik), *adj.*

i·so·trop·ic (ī'sə·trop'ik), **i·sot·ro·pous** (ī·sot'rə·pəs), *adj. Physics.* having the same properties, such as conduction, in all directions.

Is·ra·el (iz'ri·əl), *n.* 1. name given to Jacob after he had wrestled with the angel. Gen. 32:28. 2. name given to his descendants; the Jews; the Hebrews. 3. ancient kingdom in N Palestine. 4. republic comprising a portion of Palestine, declared a Jewish state May 15, 1948. 5. the Christian church.

Is·rae·li (iz·rā'li), *n., pl.* -lis, *adj.* —*n.* citizen or inhabitant of Israel. —*adj.* of or pertaining to Israel.

Is·ra·el·ite (iz'ri·əl·īt), *n.* 1. Jew; Hebrew; descendant of Israel. —*adj.* of or pertaining to Israel or the Jews. —**Is·ra·el·it·ic** (iz'ri·əl·it'ik), **Is·ra·el·it·ish** (iz'ri·əl·īt'ish), *adj.*

āge, cāre, fär; ēqual, tėrm; īce; ōpen, ôrder; půt, rüle, ūse; th, then; ə=a in about.

Is·sei (ēs′sā′), *n., pl.* **–sei.** a first-generation Japanese living in the United States. [< Jap., first generation]

is·su·ance (ish′ů·əns), *n.* an issuing; issue.

is·sue (ish′ů), *v.,* **–sued, –su·ing,** *n.* —*v.* **1.** send out; put forth: *the government issues stamps.* **2.** come out; go out; proceed: *smoke issues from the chimney.* **3.** put into public circulation; publish: *issue a bulletin.* **4.** emerge. **5.** result or end (in): *the game issued in a tie.* **6.** result (from). **7.** be born; be descended; be derived. —*n.* **1.** something sent out; quantity (of bonds, stamps, copies of a magazine, etc.) sent out at one time. **2.** a sending out; a putting forth: *issue of an order.* **3.** a coming forth; a flowing out; a discharge: *an issue of blood.* **4.** way out; outlet; exit. **5.** that which comes out. **6.** result; outcome: *the issue of the battle.* **7.** point to be debated; problem: *the issues of a political campaign.* **8.** child or children; offspring. **9.** at issue, in question; to be considered or decided. **10.** take issue, disagree. [< OF, ult. < L *ex*- out + *ire* go] —**is′su·a·ble,** *adj.* —**is′su·er,** *n.* —**Syn.** *v.* **2.** emanate. **3.** print. —*n.* **3.** outflow. **6.** conclusion, upshot.

–ist, *suffix.* **1.** a person who does or makes, as in *theorist, tourist.* **2.** one who knows about or has skill with, as in *biologist, flutist.* **3.** one engaged in or busy with, as in *horticulturist, machinist.* **4.** one who believes in; adherent of, as in *abolitionist, idealist.* [< Gk. *–istes*]

Is·tan·bul (is′tän·bůl′; –tan–), *n.* a city in European Turkey. Formerly called **Constantinople.**

isth·mi·an (is′mi·ən), *adj.* **1.** of or having to do with an isthmus. **2. Isthmian,** a. of or having to do with the Isthmus of Panama. b. of or having to do with the Isthmus of Corinth in Greece.

isth·mus (is′məs), *n., pl.* **–mus·es, –mi** (–mī). **1.** a narrow strip of land, having water on either side, connecting two larger bodies of land. **2. Isthmus,** the Isthmus of Panama. [< L < Gk. *isthmos*]

it (it), *pron., nom.* **it,** *poss.* **its** or (*Obs. or Dial.*) **it,** *obj.* **it;** *pl. nom.* **they,** *poss.* **their** or **theirs,** *obj.* **them;** —*pron.* **1.** thing, part, animal, or person spoken about. **2.** subject of an impersonal verb: *it rains.* **3.** apparent subject of a clause when the logical subject comes later: *it is hard to believe that he is dead.* **4.** antecedent to any relative pronoun when separated by the predicate: *it was a blue car that passed.* **5.** object without definite force: *he lorded it over us.* —*n. Games.* player who must perform a given task. [OE *hit*]

Ital., It., Italian; Italy.

ital., italic.

I·tal·ian (i·tal′yən), *adj.* of Italy, its people, or their language. —*n.* **1.** native or inhabitant of Italy. **2.** language of Italy.

i·tal·ic (i·tal′ik), *adj.* **1.** of or in type whose letters slant to the right: *these words are in italic type.* —*n.* **1.** an italic type, letter, or number. **2.** Often, **italics.** type whose letters slant to the right. [< L, < *Italia* Italy < Gk.] ▶ In manuscript, both longhand and typewritten, italics are shown by underlining.

i·tal·i·cize (i·tal′ə·sīz), *v.,* **–cized, –ciz·ing. 1.** print in type in which the letters slant to the right. **2.** underline with a single line to indicate italics. **3.** use italics.

It·a·ly (it′ə·li), *n.* country in S Europe on the Mediterranean, including Sicily and Sardinia.

itch (ich), *n.* **1.** a tickly, prickling feeling in the skin that makes one want to scratch. **2. the itch,** contagious disease of the skin caused by a tiny mite, accompanied by this feeling. **3.** a restless, uneasy feeling, longing, or desire for anything. —*v.* **1.** cause an itching feeling. **2.** have an itching feeling. **3.** have an uneasy desire. [OE *gyccan*] —**itch′y,** *adj.* —**itch′i·ness,** *n.*

–ite[1], *suffix.* person associated with, as in *Israelite, Canaanite, laborite.* [< Gk. *–ites*]

–ite[2], *suffix.* **1.** salt of, as in *phosphite, sulfite, nitrite.* **2.** new substances often receive names ending in *–ite,* as in *bakelite, dynamite.* [< Gk. *–ites*]

i·tem (ī′təm), *n.* **1.** a separate thing or article:

the list contains twelve items. **2.** piece of news; bit of information: *the interesting items in today's paper.* —*adv.* also; likewise. [< L, adv., likewise]

i·tem·ize (ī′təm·īz), *v.,* **–ized, –iz·ing.** *Am.* give each item of; list by items: *itemize the cost of a house.* —**i′tem·i·za′tion,** *n.* —**i′tem·iz′er,** *n.*

it·er·ate (it′ər·āt), *v.,* **–at·ed, –at·ing.** repeat. [< L, < *iterum* again] —**it′er·a′tion,** *n.*

it·er·a·tive (it′ər·ā′tiv), *adj.* repeating; full of repetitions.

Ith·a·ca (ith′ə·kə), *n.* **1.** a small island west of Greece, the home of Odysseus. **2.** city in S New York.

i·tin·er·ant (ī·tin′ər·ənt; i·tin′–), *adj.* traveling from place to place. —*n.* person who travels from place to place. [< LL *itinerans* traveling < L *iter* journey] —**i·tin′er·an·cy, i·tin′er·a·cy,** *n.* —**i·tin′er·ant·ly,** *adv.*

i·tin·er·ar·y (ī·tin′ər·er′i; i·tin′–), *n., pl.* **–ar·ies,** *adj.* —*n.* **1.** route of travel; plan of travel. **2.** record of travel. **3.** guidebook for travelers. —*adj.* **1.** of traveling or routes of travel. **2.** itinerant.

i·tin·er·ate (ī·tin′ər·āt; i·tin′–), *v.,* **–at·ed, –at·ing.** travel from place to place. —**i·tin′er·a′tion,** *n.*

–itis, *suffix.* inflammation of; inflammatory disease of, as in *appendicitis, bronchitis, tonsillitis.* [< Gk. *–itis,* fem. of *–ites*]

its (its), *pron., adj.* of it; belonging to it: *the dog wagged its tail.*

it's (its), **1.** it is: *it's going to rain.* **2.** it has: *it's rained over a week.*

it·self (it·self′), *pron.* **1.** emphatic form of it: *the land itself is worth more.* **2.** reflexive form of it: *the horse tripped and hurt itself.*

–ity, *suffix.* condition or quality of being; —ness, as in *absurdity, brutality, cordiality, activity, hostility, sincerity.* [< F *–ité*]

I·van III (ī′vən; i·vän′), ("the Great") 1440–1505, grand duke of Muscovy, 1462–1505.

Ivan IV, ("the Terrible") 1530–1584, grand duke of Muscovy from 1533 to 1547, and czar of Russia, 1547–1584.

I've (īv), I have.

–ive, *suffix.* **1.** of or pertaining to, as in *interrogative, inductive.* **2.** tending to; likely to, as in *active, appreciative, imitative.* [< L *–ivus*]

i·vied (ī′vid), *adj.* overgrown with ivy.

i·vo·ry (ī′və·ri; īv′ri), *n., pl.* **–ries,** *adj.* —*n.* **1.** a hard white substance composing the tusks of elephants, walruses, etc. **2.** substance like ivory. **3.** any article made of ivory. **4.** creamy white. **5. ivories,** *Slang.* a. piano keys. b. dice. —*adj.* **1.** made of ivory. **2.** of or like ivory. **3.** creamy-white. [< AF < L *eboreus* of ivory < *ebur* ivory < Egyptian] —**i′vo·ry·like′,** *adj.*

Ivory Coast, republic in W Africa on the Atlantic, formerly part of French West Africa.

ivory tower, *Am.* place or condition of withdrawal from the world of action into a world of ideas and dreams.

i·vy (ī′vi), *n., pl.* **i·vies. 1.** Also, **English ivy.** a climbing plant with smooth, shiny, evergreen leaves. **2.** any of various other climbing plants that resemble this plant, as *American ivy, poison ivy,* etc. [OE *īfig*] —**i′vy·like′,** *adj.*

Ivy:
A, English ivy;
B, poison ivy

I·wo Ji·ma (ē′wō jē′mə), a small island in the N Pacific, formerly held by the Japanese; captured by U.S. forces Feb.–Mar., 1945.

I.W.W., Industrial Workers of the World.

–ize, *suffix.* **1.** make, as in *legalize, centralize.* **2.** become, as in *crystallize, materialize.* **3.** engage in; be busy with; use, as in *apologize, theorize.* **4.** treat with, as in *circularize, macadamize.* **5.** other meanings, as in *alphabetize, criticize, memorize.* Also, **–ise.** [< Gk. *–izein*] ▶ –ize, –ise. English has many words ending in the sound of iz, some of which are spelled *–ise* and some *–ize*, and on many usage is divided. American usage, differing somewhat from British, prefers *–ize*, as in the following common verbs of this class: *apologize, characterize, realize, revolutionize, visualize; –ise* is the usual spelling in the following: *advertise, chastise, devise, exercise, supervise, surmise.* In general, follow American usage, and when that is divided, use whichever you are accustomed to.

Iz·mir (iz′mir; iz·mir′), *n.* seaport in W Turkey, on the Aegean Sea. Formerly, Smyrna.

iz·zard (iz′ərd), *n. Colloq.* the letter Z. [< F *isard*]

J

J, j (jā), *n., pl.* **J's; j's.** the tenth letter of the alphabet.

j., *Physics.* joule.

Ja., January. Also, **Jan.**

jab (jab), *v.,* **jabbed, jab·bing,** *n.* —*v.* thrust with something pointed; poke. —*n.* a sharp thrust or poke. [ME *jobbe(n)*; prob. imit.]

jab·ber (jab′ər), *v.* talk very fast in a confused, senseless way; chatter. —*n.* rapid, unintelligible talk; chatter. [prob. imit.] —**jab′ber·er,** *n.* —**Jab′ber·ing·ly,** *adv.* —**Syn.** *v.* babble.

ja·bot (zha·bō′; zhab′ō; jab′ō), *n.* ruffle or frill of lace, worn at the throat or down the front of a woman's dress or, formerly, on a man's shirt. [< F, orig., maw of a bird]

ja·cinth (jā′sinth; jas′inth), *n.* a reddish-orange gem. [< OF < L *hyacinthus* hyacinth]

jack (jak), *n.* **1.** man; boy; fellow. **2.** Jack or jack, sailor. **3.** tool or machine for lifting or pushing up heavy weights a short distance. **4.** *U.S.* playing card with a picture of a court page on it; knave. **5.** a jackstone. **6.** jacks, jackstones. **7.** a small flag used on a ship to show nationality or as a signal. **8.** *Am.* a male donkey. **9.** *Am.* jack rabbit. **10.** *Elect.* device to receive a plug. **11.** *Naut.* a horizontal bar of iron at the head of a topgallant mast. —*v.* **1.** lift or push up with a jack. **2.** jack up, *Colloq.* **a.** raise (prices, wages, etc.). **b.** remind of one's duty. [orig. proper name < *Jackie,* var. of *Jankin,* dim. of *John*]

jack·al (jak′ôl; –əl), *n.* **1.** a wild dog of Asia and Africa. **2.** person who does drudgery for another. [< Turk. < Pers. *shaghāl*]

jack·a·napes (jak′ə-nāps), *n.* **1.** a pert, presuming fellow. **2.** monkey.

jack·ass (jak′as′; –äs′), *n.* **1.** a male donkey. **2.** a very stupid person; fool.

jack·boot (jak′büt′), *n.* a large strong boot reaching above the knee.

Jackal (ab. 15 in. high at the shoulder)

jack·daw (jak′dô′), *n.* **1.** a European crow. **2.** *Am.* one of several kinds of American grackle.

jack·et (jak′it), *n.* **1.** a short coat. **2.** an outer covering, as the paper cover for a book or the skin of a potato. —*v.* put a jacket on; cover with a jacket. [< OF *jaquet,* dim. of *jaque* tunic < Sp. *jaco* < Ar.] —**jack′et·ed,** *adj.* —**jack′et·less,** *adj.* —**jack′et·like′,** *adj.*

jack-in-the-box (jak′in·thə·boks′), **jack-in-a-box** (–ə·boks′), *n.* a toy figure that springs up from a box when the lid is unfastened.

jack-in-the-pul·pit (jak′in·thə·pul′pit), *n. Am.* a plant with a greenish, petallike sheath arched over the flower stalk.

jack·knife (jak′nīf′), *n., pl.* **–knives.** *Am.* **1.** a large strong pocketknife. **2.** kind of dive in which the diver touches his feet with his hands before entering the water.

jack of all trades, person who can do many different kinds of work fairly well.

jack-o'-lan·tern (jak′ə·lan′tərn), *n.* **1.** pumpkin hollowed out and cut to look like a face, used as a lantern at Halloween. **2.** will-o'-the-wisp (def. 1).

jack pot, *Am.* stakes that accumulate in a poker game until some player wins with a pair of jacks or something better.

jack rabbit, *Am.* a large hare of W North America, having very long legs and ears.

jack·screw (jak′skrü′), *n.* tool or machine for lifting heavy weights short distances, operated by a screw.

Jack·son (jak′sən), *n.* **1.** Andrew, 1767–1845, the seventh president of the United States, 1829–1837. **2.** Thomas Jonathan ("Stonewall Jackson") 1824–1863, American Confederate general. **3.** capital of Mississippi, in the C part.

Jack·so·ni·an (jak·sō′ni·ən), *Am.* —*adj.* of or like Andrew Jackson or his principles. —*n.* follower of Andrew Jackson.

Jack·son·ville (jak′sən·vil), *n.* city in NE Florida.

jack·stone (jak′stōn′), *n.* **1.** pebble or piece of metal tossed up and caught in a child's game. **2.** jackstones (*sing. in use*), game played with a set of these; jacks.

jack·straw (jak′strô′), *n.* **1.** straw, strip of wood, bone, etc., used in a game. **2.** jackstraws (*sing. in use*), game played with a set of these thrown down in a confused pile and picked up one at a time without moving any of the rest of the pile.

Ja·cob (jā′kəb), *n.* son of Isaac, and younger twin brother of Esau. Gen. 25–50.

Jac·o·be·an (jak′ə·bē′ən), *adj.* of King James I of England or the period of his reign, 1603–1625.

Jac·o·bin (jak′ə·bin), *n.* **1.** member of a radical political club organized in 1789 during the French Revolution. **2.** an extreme radical in politics. —**Jac′o·bin′ic, Jac′o·bin′i·cal,** *adj.* —**Jac′o·bin′i·cal·ly,** *adv.* —**Jac′o·bin·ism,** *n.*

Jac·o·bite (jak′ə·bīt), *n.* supporter of James II and his descendants in their claims to the English throne after the English Revolution in 1688. —**Jac·o·bit·ic** (jak′ə·bit′ik), **Jac′o·bit′i·cal,** *adj.*

Jacob's ladder, *Naut.* a rope ladder used on ships.

jade¹ (jād), *n.* **1.** a hard stone, usually green, used for jewels and ornaments. **2.** Also, jade green. sea green. [< F < Sp. (*piedra de*) *ijada* (stone of) colic (jade being supposed to cure this), ult. < L *ilia* flanks] —**jade′like′,** *adj.*

jade² (jād), *n., v.,* **jad·ed, jad·ing.** —*n.* **1.** an inferior or worn-out horse. **2.** (*used opprobriously or playfully*) woman. —*v.* **1.** wear out; tire; weary. **2.** dull by continual use; surfeit; satiate. —**jad′ish,** *adj.* —**Syn.** *v.* **1.** exhaust, fatigue.

jad·ed (jād′id), *adj.* **1.** weary. **2.** satiated. —**jad′ed·ly,** *adv.* —**jad′ed·ness,** *n.*

jae·ger, jä·ger (yā′gər; jā′–), *n.* a sea bird like a gull, that pursues weaker birds and makes them disgorge their prey.

Jaf·fa (jaf′ə), *n.* seaport in W Israel.

jag¹ (jag), *n., v.,* **jagged, jag·ging.** —*n.* a sharp point sticking out; pointed projection. —*v.* **1.** make notches in. **2.** cut or tear unevenly.

jag² (jag), *n. U.S. Slang.* a fit of drunkenness.

jag·ged (jag′id), *adj.* with sharp points sticking out. —**jag′ged·ly,** *adv.* —**jag′ged·ness,** *n.* —**Syn.** notched, craggy.

Jaguar (total length ab. 6 ft.)

jag·uar (jag′wär; –yù·är′), *n.* a fierce animal of tropical America, much like a leopard, but larger. [< Tupi-Guarani]

Jah·ve, Jah·veh (yä'vä), *n.* Yahweh.
jail (jāl), *n.* **1.** Also, *Brit.* **gaol.** prison for people awaiting trial or being punished for minor offenses. **2.** break jail, escape from jail. —*v.* put in jail; keep in jail. [< OF *jaiole*, ult. < L *cavea* coop] —**jail'less**, *adj.* —**jail'like'**, *adj.*
jail·bird (jāl'bėrd'), *n.* **1.** prisoner in jail. **2.** person who has been in jail many times.
jail·break (jāl'brāk'), *n. Colloq.* escape from prison.
jail·er, jail·or (jāl'ər), *n.* keeper of a jail. Also, *Brit.* **gaoler.**
Ja·kar·ta (jə·kär'tə), *n.* Djakarta. Formerly, Batavia.
ja·lop·y (jə·lop'i), *n., pl.* **-lop·ies.** *Am., Colloq.* an old automobile or airplane in bad repair.
jam¹ (jam), *v.*, **jammed, jam·ming.** —*v.* **1.** press tightly; squeeze. **2.** crush; bruise. **3.** push; shove. **4.** fill up; block up. **5.** stick or catch so that it cannot be worked. **6.** cause to stick or catch. **7.** make (radio signals, etc.) unintelligible by sending out others of approximately the same frequency. **8.** *Slang.* make a musical composition more lively by improvisations, etc. —*n.* **1.** mass of people or things crowded together so that they cannot move freely: *a traffic jam.* **2.** a jamming or being jammed. **3.** *Am., Colloq.* a difficulty or tight spot. [? imit.] —**Syn.** *v.* **1.** wedge, pack. **3.** force, thrust, ram. **4.** obstruct.
jam² (jam), *n.* fruit boiled with sugar until thick. [? special use of *jam¹*] —**jam'like'**, *adj.*
Ja·mai·ca (jə·mā'kə), *n.* **1.** an island country in the West Indies, S of Cuba, a member of the British Commonwealth. **2.** kind of rum made there. —**Ja·mai'can**, *adj., n.*
jamb, jambe (jam), *n.* the upright piece forming the side of a doorway, window, fireplace, etc. [< F *jambe*, orig., leg < LL *gamba*]
jam·bo·ree (jam'bə·rē'), *n. Am., Slang.* a noisy party; lively entertainment.
James (jāmz), *n.* **1.** the name of two of Christ's disciples. **2.** book of the New Testament. **3.** Henry, 1843–1916, American novelist who lived in England. **4.** Jesse, 1847–1882, American bandit and outlaw. **5.** William, 1842–1910, American psychologist and philosopher, brother of Henry James. **6.** river flowing from western Virginia into Chesapeake Bay.
James I, 1566–1625, king of England, 1603–1625.
James II, 1633–1701, king of England, 1685–1688. He was deposed by Parliament.
James·town (jāmz'toun'), *n.* a ruined village in SE Virginia; site of the first successful English settlement in North America, in 1607.
jam-packed, jam-packed (jam'pakt'), *adj. Am., Colloq.* filled to absolute capacity.
jam session, *Slang.* gathering at which musicians play music enlivened by improvisation.
Jan., January. Also, **Ja.**
jan·gle (jang'gəl), *v.*, **-gled, -gling,** *n.* —*v.* **1.** sound harshly. **2.** cause to sound harshly. **3.** quarrel; dispute. —*n.* **1.** harsh sound. **2.** quarrel; dispute. [< OF *jangler*] —**jan'gler**, *n.*
jan·i·tor (jan'ə·tər), *n.* **1.** person hired to take care of a building, offices, etc. **2.** doorkeeper. [< L, doorkeeper]
Jan·u·ar·y (jan'yū·er'i), *n., pl.* **-ar·ies.** the first month of the year. It has 31 days. [< L, < *Janus* Janus]
Ja·nus (jā'nəs), *n.* Roman god of gates and doors, and of beginnings and endings. He is represented with two faces, one looking forward and the other looking backward.
Jap (jap), *adj., n. Contemptuous.* Japanese.
Jap., Japan; Japanese.
Ja·pan (jə·pan'), *n.* an island nation in the Pacific, east of Asia. Also, *Japanese* Nippon.
ja·pan (jə·pan'), *n., v.*, **-panned, -pan·ning.** —*n.* **1.** a hard, glossy varnish, used on wood or metal. **2.** articles varnished and decorated in the Japanese manner. **3.** liquid used to make paint dry faster. —*v.* put japan on.
Jap·a·nese (jap'ə·nēz'), *adj., n., pl.* **-nese.** —*adj.* of Japan, its people, or their language. —*n.* **1.** native of Japan. **2.** language of Japan.

Japanese beetle, a small green-and-brown beetle that eats fruits, leaves, and grasses.
jape (jāp), *n., v.*, **japed, jap·ing. 1.** joke; jest. **2.** trick. —**jap'er**, *n.*
ja·pon·i·ca (jə·pon'ə·kə), *n.* **1.** camellia. **2.** shrub with showy red, pink, or white flowers. [< NL, orig. fem. adj., Japanese]
jar¹ (jär), *n.* **1.** a deep container made of glass, earthenware, etc., with a wide mouth. **2.** amount that it holds. [< F *jarre*, ult. < Ar. *jarrah*]
jar² (jär), *n., v.*, **jarred, jar·ring.** —*n.* **1.** shake; rattle. **2.** a harsh, grating noise. **3.** a harsh, unpleasant effect; shock. **4.** clash; quarrel. —*v.* **1.** shake; rattle. **2.** make a harsh, grating noise. **3.** have a harsh, unpleasant effect on; shock. **4.** clash; quarrel. [OE *ceorran* creak] —**Syn.** *n.* **3.** jolt. —*v.* **2.** scrape, grate, grind.
jar·di·niere (jär'də·nir'), *n.* an ornamental pot or stand for flowers or plants. [< F, < *jardin* garden]
jar·gon (jär'gən; -gon), *n.* **1.** confused, meaningless talk or writing. **2.** language that is not understood. **3.** language of a special group, profession, etc. Doctors, actors, and sailors have jargons. **4.** mixture of languages. **5.** chatter. —*v.* **1.** talk jargon. **2.** chatter. [< OF, prob. ult. imit.] —**Syn.** *n.* **3.** lingo, cant, argot, slang. ➤ **jargon.** **1.** Applied to style, *jargon* is the name for verbal fuzziness of various sorts—wordiness, abstract for concrete words, big words, and the use of words that add nothing to the meaning of a statement. **2.** In a linguistic sense, *jargon* means a dialect composed of two or more languages. *Jargons* involving English are used by non-English-speaking peoples in doing business with the English, as the Chinook jargon of the Pacific Northwest and the Chinese-English jargon, pidgin English.
jas·mine, jas·min (jas'mən; jaz'-), *n.* shrub or vine with clusters of fragrant flowers. There are yellow, white, and red jasmines. Also, **jessamine.** [< F *jasmin* < Ar. < Pers. *yāsmīn*]
Ja·son (jā'sən), *n. Gk. Legend.* Greek hero who led the expedition of the Argonauts and secured the Golden Fleece.
jas·per (jas'pər), *n.* **1.** a colored quartz, usually red or brown. **2.** a green precious stone of ancient times. [< OF *jaspre*, ult. < L < Gk. *iaspis* < Phoenician]
ja·to (jā'tō), *n. Aeron.* a unit consisting of one or more jet engines, used to provide auxiliary propulsion for speeding up the take-off of an airplane. [< *j*(et) + *a*(ssisted) + *t*(ake)-o(ff).]
jaun·dice (jôn'dis; jän'-), *n., v.*, **-diced, -dic·ing.** —*n.* **1.** disease that causes yellowness of the skin, eyes, and body fluids, and disturbed vision. **2.** a disturbed or unnaturally sour mental outlook, due to envy, jealousy, etc. —*v.* **1.** cause jaundice in. **2.** prejudice the mind and judgment of, by envy, discontent, or jealousy; sour the temper of. [< OF *jaunisse*, ult. < L *galbinus* greenish-yellow]
jaunt (jônt; jänt), *n.* a short pleasure trip or excursion. —*v.* take such a trip.
jaun·ty (jôn'ti; jän'-), *adj.*, **-ti·er, -ti·est. 1.** easy and lively; sprightly; carefree: *jaunty steps.* **2.** smart; stylish: *a jaunty little hat.* [< F *gentil* GENTLE] —**jaun'ti·ly**, *adv.* —**jaun'ti·ness**, *n.* —**Syn. 1.** airy, gay.
Ja·va (jä'və; jav'ə), *n.* **1.** a large island southeast of Asia. **2.** *Am.* kind of coffee obtained from Java and nearby islands. **3.** *Am., Colloq.* coffee.
Jav·a·nese (jav'ə·nēz'; -nēs'), *adj., n., pl.* **-nese.** —*adj.* of Java, its people, or their language. —*n.* **1.** native of Java. **2.** language of Java.
jave·lin (jav'lin; -ə·lin), *n.* a light spear thrown by hand. [< F *javeline*]
jaw (jô), *n.* **1.** either of the two bones, or sets of bones, that form the framework of the mouth. **2.** jaws, a. mouth with its jawbones and teeth. b. narrow entrance to a valley, mountain pass, channel, etc. **3.** either of the parts in a tool or machine that grip and hold. **4.** *Slang.* talk; gossip. —*v. Slang.* **1.** talk; gossip. **2.** find fault; scold. [? akin to *chew*; infl. by F *joue* cheek]

jaw·bone (jô'bōn'), *n.* **1.** bone of either jaw. **2.** bone of the lower jaw.

jay (jā), *n.* **1.** a noisy American bird with blue feathers; bluejay. **2.** a noisy European bird with a crest. **3.** any of various birds of the same family as these two. **4.** *Slang.* a silly, stupid person. [< OF]

Jay (jā), *n.* John, 1745–1829, the first chief justice of the U.S. Supreme Court, 1789–1795.

Jay·hawk·er (jā'hôk'ər), *n. Am.* native or inhabitant of Kansas.

European jay
(ab. 1 ft. long)

jay·walk (jā'wôk'), *v. Am., Colloq.* walk across a street without paying attention to traffic rules. —jay'walk'er, *n.* —jay'walk'ing, *n.*

jazz (jaz), *n.* **1.** *Am.* music with the accents falling at unusual places; syncopated music. **2.** *Slang.* liveliness. —*adj.* of or like jazz: *a jazz band.* —*v.* **1.** *Am.* play (music) as jazz. **2.** *Slang.* make lively. [of American Negro orig.]

JCS, J.C.S., Joint Chiefs of Staff.

Je., June. Also, **Jun.**

jeal·ous (jel'əs), *adj.* **1.** fearful that a person one loves may love someone else better or may prefer someone else. One may be jealous of the person loved or of the rival. **2.** full of envy; envious: *he is jealous of John or of John's marks.* **3.** requiring complete loyalty or faithfulness: *"The Lord thy God is a jealous God."* **4.** watchful in keeping or guarding something; careful: *a city jealous of its rights.* **5.** close; watchful; suspicious: *the dog was a jealous guardian of the child.* [< OF *gelos,* ult. < L *zelus* ZEAL] —jeal'ous·ly, *adv.* —jeal'ous·ness, *n.* —Syn. **2.** grudging, resentful.

jeal·ous·y (jel'əs·i), *n., pl.* -ous·ies. jealous condition or feeling.

Jean (jēn), *n.* **1.** a strong twilled cotton cloth, used for overalls, etc. **2.** jeans, overalls; trousers. [prob. < F *Gênes* Genoa]

Jeanne d'Arc (zhän därk'), *French.* Joan of Arc.

jeep (jēp), *n.* a small, but powerful, army general-purpose automobile with a four-wheel drive and a quarter-ton capacity. [back formation from *"Jeepers creepers!"* (the exclamation of Major General George Lynch, Chief of Infantry, U.S. Army, upon the occasion of his first ride in the prototype model of the vehicle, in November, 1939, at Fort Myers, Virginia; coined at the time by Mr. Charles H. Payne, his companion in, and designer of, the vehicle)]

jeer (jir), *v.* make fun rudely or unkindly; mock; scoff. —*n.* a jeering remark; rude, sarcastic comment. —jeer'er, *n.* —jeer'ing·ly, *adv.*

Jef·fer·son (jef'ər·sən), *n.* Thomas, 1743–1826, American statesman, third president of the United States, 1801–1809. He drafted the Declaration of Independence. —Jef·fer·so·ni·an (jef'ər·sō'ni·ən), *adj., n. Am.*

Jefferson City, capital of Missouri.

Je·hol (jē'hōl; rä'hō'), *n.* part of NE China.

Je·ho·vah (ji·hō'və), *n.* one of the names of God in the Old Testament.

Je·hu (jē'hū), *n. Colloq.* **1.** a fast driver. **2.** coachman.

Je·june (ji·jün'), *adj.* **1.** lacking nourishing qualities. **2.** flat and uninteresting; unsatisfying. [< L *jejunus,* orig., hungry] —je·june'ly, *adv.*

Je·ju·num (ji·jü'nəm), *n. Anat.* the middle portion of the small intestine, between the duodenum and the ileum. [< NL < L, neut., empty]

jell (jel), *v. Colloq.* become jelly. [< *jelly*]

jel·lied (jel'id), *adj.* **1.** turned into jelly; having the consistency of jelly. **2.** spread with jelly.

jel·ly (jel'i), *n., pl.* -lies, *v.,* -lied, -ly·ing. —*n.* **1.** a food, soft when hot, but somewhat firm and partly transparent when cold, made by boiling fruit juice and sugar together, cooking bones and meat juice, using gelatin, etc. **2.** a jellylike

substance. —*v.* become jelly; turn into jelly. [< OF *gelee,* orig., frost, ult. < L *gelare* congeal]

jel·ly·fish (jel'i·fish'), *n., pl.* -fish·es or (*esp. collectively*) -fish. any of a group of invertebrate sea animals with a body formed of a mass of jellylike tissue that is often transparent. Most jellyfish have long trailing tentacles that may bear stinging hairs or feelers.

Jen·ghis Khan, Jen·ghiz Khan (jeng'gis kän'; jen'-), Genghis Khan. Also, **genet.**

jen·net (jen'it), *n.* a small Spanish horse. Also, **genet.**

jen·ny (jen'i), *n., pl.* -nies. **1.** spinning jenny. **2.** female of certain animals. [orig. proper name, dim. of *Jane,* fem. of *John*]

jeop·ard·ize (jep'ər·dīz), **jeop·ard** (-ərd), *v.,* -ized, -iz·ing; -ard·ed, -ard·ing. risk; endanger; imperil: *soldiers jeopardize their lives in war.* —Syn. hazard.

jeop·ard·y (jep'ər·di), *n.* **1.** risk; danger; peril: *his life was in jeopardy when the tree fell.* **2.** *Law.* condition of a person on trial for a criminal offense. [< OF *jeu parti* an even or divided game, ult. < L *jocus* play + *pars* part]

Jer., **1.** Jeremiah. **2.** Jersey.

jer·bo·a (jər·bō'ə), *n.* a small, jumping, mouse-like mammal of Asia and northern Africa. [< NL < Ar. *yarbū'*]

Jer·e·mi·ad (jer'ə·mī'ad), *n.* a mournful complaint; lamentation. [< F, < *Jérémie* Jeremiah (reputed author of *Lamentations* in the Bible)]

Jer·e·mi·ah (jer'ə·mī'ə), **Jer·e·mi·as** (-əs), *n.* **1.** a Hebrew prophet who denounced and lamented the evils of his time. **2.** book of the Old Testament.

Jerboa
(total length ab. 15 in.)

Jer·i·cho (jer'ə·kō), *n., pl.* -chos. **1.** an ancient city in Palestine. **2.** an out-of-the-way place.

jerk[1] (jėrk), *n.* **1.** a sudden, sharp pull, twist, or start: *get up with a jerk.* **2.** pull or twist of the muscles that one cannot control; twitch. **3.** *Slang.* an unsophisticated or stupid person. —*v.* **1.** pull or twist suddenly: *jerk one's hand out of hot water.* **2.** throw with a movement that stops suddenly. **3.** move with a jerk: *the old wagon jerked along.* **4.** speak or say abruptly. [prob. imit.]

jerk[2] (jėrk), *v.* preserve (meat) by cutting it into long thin slices and drying it in the sun. [< Am. Sp. *charquear,* v., < *charqui* < Kechua (Ind. lang. of Peru)]

jer·kin (jėr'kən), *n.* a short coat or jacket, with or without sleeves.

jerk·wa·ter (jėrk'wô'tər; -wot'ər), *Am., Colloq.* —*n.* train on a branch railway. —*adj.* **1.** not on the main line. **2.** insignificant.

jerk·y (jėr'ki), *adj.,* jerk·i·er, jerk·i·est. with sudden starts and stops; with jerks. —jerk'i·ly, *adv.* —jerk'i·ness, *n.*

Je·rome (jə·rōm'; *esp. Brit.* jer'əm), *n.* Saint, 340?–420 A.D., monk and scholar, author of the Latin translation of the Bible, the Vulgate.

jer·ry-build (jer'i·bild'), *v.,* -built, -build-ing. build quickly and cheaply of poor materials.

Jer·sey (jėr'zi), *n., pl.* -seys. **1.** one of a group of British islands, near the coast of France. **2.** one of a breed of small, fawn-colored cattle that came from this island. **3.** New Jersey.

jer·sey (jėr'zi), *n., pl.* -seys. **1.** a close-fitting sweater that is pulled on over the head. **2.** a woman's close-fitting knitted undergarment. **3.** a machine-knitted cloth.

Jersey City, seaport in NE New Jersey, across the Hudson River from New York City.

Je·ru·sa·lem (jə·rü'sə·ləm), *n.* city on the Israel-Jordan border, capital of Israel. It is a holy city to Jews, Christians, and Moslems. —Je·ru'sa·lem·ite', *adj., n.*

Je·ru·sa·lem ar·ti·choke, 1. kind of sunflower whose root is edible. 2. its root.

jess (jes), *n.* a short strap fastened around a falcon's leg. [< OF *ges*, ult. < L *jacere* to throw]

jes·sa·mine (jes′ə·min), *n.* jasmine.

jest (jest), *n.* 1. joke. 2. act of poking fun; mockery. 3. thing to be mocked or laughed at. 4. **in jest,** in fun; not seriously. —*v.* 1. joke. 2. poke fun (at); make fun. 3. deride; banter. [< OF *geste,* orig., story, exploit, ult. < L *gerere* accomplish] —**jest′ing·ly,** *adv.*

jest·er (jes′tər), *n.* 1. person who jests. 2. in the Middle Ages, a professional clown.

Je·su (jē′zü; -zü), *n. Poetic.* Jesus.

Jes·u·it (jezh′ü·it; jez′yü-), *n.* member of a Roman Catholic religious order called the Society of Jesus, founded by Saint Ignatius Loyola in 1534. —**Jes′u·it′ic, Jes′u·it′i·cal,** *adj.* —**Jes′u·it′i·cal·ly,** *adv.*

Je·sus (jē′zəs), or **Jesus Christ,** *n.* founder of the Christian religion.

jet¹ (jet), *n., v.,* **jet·ted, jet·ting.** —*n.* 1. a stream of water, steam, etc., sent with force, esp. from a small opening. 2. liquid or gas that comes forth. 3. a spout or nozzle for sending out a jet. 4. a jet plane. —*v.* 1. gush out; shoot forth in a jet or forceful stream. 2. fly by jet. [< F, < *jeter* to throw]

jet² (jet), *n.* 1. a hard black mineral, glossy when polished, used for making beads, buttons, etc. 2. a deep glossy black. —*adj.* 1. made of jet. 2. deep glossy black. [< OF < L < Gk. *gagates* < *Gagai,* in Lycia]

jet-black (jet′blak′), *adj.* very black.

jet·lin·er (jet′lin′ər), *n.* a transport airplane driven by jet propulsion.

jet pilot, one who operates a jet plane.

jet plane, airplane driven by jet propulsion.

jet·port (jet′pôrt′; -pōrt′), *n.* airport designed for use by jet planes.

jet propulsion, propulsion in one direction by a jet of air, gas, etc., forced in the opposite direction. —**jet-pro·pelled** (jet′prə·peld′), *adj.*

jet·sam (jet′səm), *n.* 1. goods thrown overboard to lighten a ship in distress and often afterward washed ashore. 2. thing tossed aside as useless.

jet stream, a high-speed air current (up to 250 miles per hour or more) traveling from west to east at high altitudes (six to ten miles).

jet·ti·son (jet′ə·sən; -zən), *v.* 1. throw (goods) overboard to lighten ship in distress. 2. throw away; discard. —*n.* 1. act of doing this. 2. goods thrown overboard; jetsam. [< AF *getteson,* ult. < L *jacere* throw]

jet·ty (jet′i), *n., pl.* **-ties.** 1. structure built out into the water to protect a harbor or influence the current; breakwater. 2. a landing place; pier. [< OF, < *jeter* throw, ult. < L *jacere*]

Jew (jü), *n.* 1. member of a people that formerly lived in Palestine, but now live in many countries. 2. person whose religion is Judaism; Hebrew. —*adj.* Jewish.

jew·el (jü′əl), *n., v.,* **-eled, -el·ing;** *esp. Brit.* **-elled, -el·ling.** —*n.* 1. a precious stone; gem. 2. a valuable ornament to be worn, set with precious stones. 3. person or thing that is very precious. 4. gem or some substitute used as a bearing in a watch. —*v.* set or adorn with jewels or with things like jewels. [< OF *juel,* ult. < L *jocus* joke, game] —**jew′el·like′,** *adj.*

jew·el·er, *esp. Brit.* **jew·el·ler** (jü′əl·ər), *n.* person who makes, sells, or repairs jewels, jeweled ornaments, watches, etc.

jew·el·ry, *esp. Brit.* **jew·el·ler·y** (jü′əl·ri), *n.* jewels.

jew·fish (jü′fish′), *n., pl.* **-fish·es** or (*esp. collectively*) **-fish.** 1. giant sea bass. 2. any of various other large fishes of warm seas.

Jew·ish (jü′ish), *adj.* of, belonging to, or characteristic of the Jews. —*n.* Yiddish.

Jew·ry (jü′ri), *n., pl.* **-ries.** 1. Jews as a group; Jewish people. 2. ghetto. 3. Judea.

jews'-harp, jew's-harp (jüz′härp′), *n.* a simple musical instrument, held between the teeth and played by striking the

free end of a piece of metal with a finger.

Jez·e·bel (jez′ə·bəl; -bel) *n.* 1. the wicked wife of Ahab, king of Israel. II Kings 9:7-10, 30-37. 2. a shameless, immoral woman.

jg, j.g., junior grade.

jib¹ (jib), *n.* 1. *Naut.* a triangular sail in front of the foremast. 2. cut of one's jib, *Colloq.* one's outward appearance. [? < *jib*²]

jib² (jib), *v.,* **jibbed, jib·bing.** jibe¹.

jib³ (jib), *v.,* **jibbed, jib·bing.** *Esp. Brit.* move sidewise or backward instead of forward; refuse to go ahead. —**jib′ber,** *n.*

jib boom, *Naut.* spar extending out from a ship's bowsprit.

jibe¹ (jib), *v.,* **jibed, jib·ing.** 1. shift (a sail) from one side of a ship to the other when sailing before the wind. 2. of a sail or boom, shift thus. 3. change the course of a ship so that the sails shift in this way. Also, jib. [< Du. *gijben*]

jibe² (jib), *v.,* **jibed, jib·ing,** *n.* gibe. —jib′er, *n.*

jibe³ (jib), *v.,* **jibed, jib·ing.** *U.S. Colloq.* be in harmony; agree.

jif·fy (jif′i), **jiff** (jif), *n., pl.* **jif·fies; jiffs.** *Colloq.* a very short time; moment.

jig¹ (jig), *n., v.,* **jigged, jig·ging.** —*n.* 1. a lively dance, often in triple time. 2. music for it. 3. **the jig is up,** *Slang.* there's no more chance. —*v.* 1. dance a jig. 2. move jerkily; jerk up and down or back and forth. [< OF *giguer* dance < *gigue* fiddle] —**jig′like′,** *adj.*

jig² (jig), *n.* 1. fishhook, or set of fishhooks, loaded with a bright metal or having a spoon-shaped piece of bone attached, for drawing through the water. 2. any of various mechanical contrivances or devices, esp. a guide in using a drill, file, etc. [var. of *gauge*]

jig·ger¹ (jig′ər), *n.* 1. *Naut.* a. a small set of ropes and pulleys used on a ship. b. a small sail. c. a jigger mast. 2. machine with a jerky motion. 3. *Colloq.* some device, article, or part that one cannot name more precisely; gadget; contraption. 4. jig used in fishing. 5. *Am.* a. a small glass used to measure liquor. b. the quantity it holds, usually 1½ oz. [< *jig*²]

jig·ger² (jig′ər), *n.* 1. a small flea; chigoe. 2. *Am.* chigger. [alter. of *chigoe*]

jigger mast, mast in the stern of a ship.

jig·gle (jig′əl), *v.,* **-gled, -gling,** *n.* —*v.* shake or jerk slightly. —*n.* a slight shake; light jerk; rocky motion. [< *jig*¹]

jig·saw (jig′sô′), *n.* a narrow saw mounted in a frame and worked with an up-and-down motion, used to cut curves or irregular lines. —*v.* cut with a jigsaw.

jigsaw puzzle, picture sawed into irregular pieces that can be fitted together again.

jill, Jill (jil), *n.* 1. woman; girl. 2. sweetheart.

jilt (jilt), *v.* cast off (a lover or sweetheart) after giving encouragement. —*n.* woman who casts off a lover after encouraging him. —**jilt′er,** *n.*

Jim Crow (jim′ krō′), **Jim Crow·ism** (krō′iz·əm), *Am., Slang.* discrimination against Negroes.

jim·my (jim′i), *n., pl.* **-mies,** *v.,* **-mied, -my·ing.** —*n.* a short crowbar used esp. by burglars to force windows, doors, etc., open. —*v.* force open with a jimmy.

jim·son weed, Jim·son weed (jim′sən), *Am.* a coarse, bad-smelling weed with white flowers and poisonous, narcotic leaves. [alter. of *Jamestown* (Va.)]

jin·gle (jing′gəl), *n., v.,* **-gled, -gling.** —*n.* 1. sound like that of little bells, or of coins or keys striking together. 2. verse or music that has a jingling sound. —*v.* 1. make a jingling sound: *the sleigh bells jingle as we ride.* 2. cause to jingle: *jingle one's money.* 3. make jingling verse. [imit.] —**jin′gling·ly,** *adv.* —**jin′gly,** *adj.*

jin·go (jing′gō), *n., pl.* **-goes,** *adj.* —*n.* person who favors an aggressive foreign policy that might lead to war with other nations. —*adj.* of jingoes; like that of jingoes. —**jin′go·ism,** *n.* —**jin′go·ist,** *n.* —**jin′go·is′tic,** *adj.*

jinn (jin), *n.pl., sing.* **jin·ni** (ji·nē′). *Mohammedan Myth.* 1. spirits that can appear in human or animal form and do good or harm to people. 2.

(*sing.* in use with *pl.* **jinns**) one of these spirits; jinni. [< Ar.]

jin·rik·i·sha, jin·rick·sha (jin·rik′shə; -shō), *n.* a small, two-wheeled, hooded carriage pulled by one or more men, used in Japan, China, etc. Also, **rickshaw, ricksha.** [< Jap. < *jin* man + *riki* strength + *sha* vehicle]

Jinrikisha

jinx (jingks), *Am., Slang.* —*n.* person or thing that brings bad luck. —*v.* bring bad luck to. [< L *iynx* bird used in charms < Gk.]

jit·ney (jit′ni), *n., pl.* **-neys,** *v.* **-neyed, -ney·ing.** *Am., Slang.* —*n.* **1.** automobile that carries passengers for a small fare. **2.** a five-cent piece; nickel. —*v.* travel in or carry in a jitney.

jit·ter (jit′ər), *Am., Slang.* —*n.* jitters, extreme nervousness. —*v.* act nervous.

jit·ter·bug (jit′ər·bug′), *n., v.,* **-bugged, -bug·ging.** *Colloq.* —*n.* person who is extremely fond of swing music and excited by it to queer dance movements and gesticulations. —*v.* dance in such a way.

jit·ter·y (jit′ər·i), *adj. U.S. Slang.* nervous.

jiu·jit·su, jiu·jut·su (jü·jit′sü), *n.* jujitsu.

jive (jīv), *n., v.,* **jived, jiv·ing.** *Slang.* —*n.* **1.** swing music. **2.** the jargon of technical terms associated with it. **3.** the latest slang. —*v.* perform swing music.

Jo (jō), *n., pl.* **joes.** *Scot.* sweetheart. [var. of JOY]

Joan of Arc (jōn′ əv ärk′), 1412–1431, French heroine who led armies against the invading English and saved the city of Orléans. She was condemned as a witch and burned to death. In 1920 she was made a saint. *French,* Jeanne d'Arc.

Job (job), *n., adj., v.,* **jobbed, job·bing.** —*n.* **1.** piece of work. **2.** definite piece of work done regularly for pay. **3.** *Am., Colloq.* work; employment. **4.** anything one has to do. **5.** *Colloq.* affair; matter. **6. on the job,** *Slang.* tending to one's work or duty. —*adj.* done by the job; hired for a particular piece of work. —*v.* **1.** buy (goods) from manufacturers in large quantities and sell to dealers in smaller lots. **2.** let out (work) to different contractors, workmen, etc. —*job′less, adj.* —**job′less·ness,** *n.* ≫ Job is informal and colloquial for the formal *position: He got a job at Baker's.* It is shoptalk for something made, as an automobile, refrigerator, etc.: *a nice little job.*

Job (jōb), *n.* **1.** a very patient man in the Bible who kept his faith in God in spite of many troubles. **2.** book of the Old Testament.

job·ber (job′ər), *n.* **1.** person who buys goods from manufacturers in large quantities and sells to retailers in smaller quantities. **2.** person who works by the job; pieceworker.

job·ber·y (job′ər·i), *n.* dishonest management of public business for private gain.

job·hold·er (job′hōl′dər), *n.* **1.** person regularly employed. **2.** employee of the U.S. government.

job lot, quantity of goods bought or sold together, often containing several different kinds of things usually of inferior quality.

Jo·cas·ta (jō·kas′tə), *n. Gk. Legend.* mother of Oedipus, who married him without knowing who he was.

jock·ey (jok′i), *n., pl.* **-eys,** *v.,* **-eyed, -ey·ing.** —*n.* boy or man whose occupation is riding horses in races. —*v.* **1.** ride (a horse) in a race. **2.** trick; cheat. **3.** maneuver to get advantage: *the crews were jockeying their boats to get into the best position for the race.* [orig. proper name, < *Jack*] —**jock′ey·ship,** *n.*

jo·cose (jō·kōs′), *adj.* jesting; humorous; playful. [< L, < *jocus* jest] —**jo·cose′ly,** *adv.* —**jo·cose′ness,** **jo·cos·i·ty** (jō·kos′ə·ti), *n.*

joc·u·lar (jok′yə·lər), *adj.* funny; joking. [< L, ult. < *jocus* jest] —**joc·u·lar·i·ty** (jok′yə·lar′ə·ti), *n.* —**joc′u·lar·ly,** *adv.*

joc·und (jok′ənd; jō′kənd), *adj.* cheerful; merry; gay. [< var. of L *jucundus* pleasant < *juvare* please] —**jo·cun·di·ty** (jō·kun′də·ti), *n.*

jodh·purs (jod′pərz), *n.pl.* breeches for horseback riding, loose above the knees and fitting closely below. [< *Jodhpur,* India]

Jo·el (jō′əl), *n.* **1.** a Hebrew prophet of the fifth century B.C. **2.** book of the Old Testament.

jog[1] (jog), *v.,* **jogged, jog·ging,** *n.* —*v.* **1.** shake with a push or jerk: *jog a person's elbow to get his attention.* **2.** stir up (one's own or another person's memory). **3.** move up and down with a jerking or shaking motion: *the old horse jogged along.* **4.** go forward heavily and slowly. —*n.* **1.** a shake, push, or nudge. **2.** a hint or reminder: *give one's memory a jog.* **3.** a slow walk or trot. [blend of *jot* jolt and *shog* shake] —**jog′ger,** *n.*

jog[2] (jog), *n. Am., Colloq.* part that sticks out or in; unevenness in a line or a surface: *a jog in a wall.* [var. of JAG[1]]

jog·gle[1] (jog′əl), *v.,* **-gled, -gling,** *n.* —*v.* **1.** shake slightly. **2.** move with a jerk. —*n.* a slight shake. [< *jog*[1]]

jog·gle[2] (jog′əl), *n., v.,* **-gled, -gling.** —*n.* projection on one of two joining surfaces, or notch on the other, to prevent slipping. —*v.* join or fasten with a joggle. [? < *jog*[2]]

jog trot, a slow, regular trot.

Jo·han·nes·burg (jō·han′is·bėrg; yō·hän′-), *n.* largest city in the Republic of South Africa, noted for its gold mines.

John (jon), *n.* **1.** one of Christ's Apostles who may be the author of the Gospel of Saint John, the three epistles of John, and Revelation. **2.** the fourth book of the New Testament. **3.** John the Baptist. **4.** 1167?–1216, king of England, 1199–1216. He signed the Magna Charta in 1215.

John XXIII, 1881–1963, Pope from 1958 to 1963.

John Bull, 1. the typical Englishman. **2.** the English nation.

John Doe, a fictitious name used in legal forms or proceedings for the name of an unknown person.

John Hancock, *Am.* a person's signature.

john·ny·cake (jon′i·kāk′), *n. Am.* kind of corn bread.

John·ny-jump-up (jon′i·jump′up′), *n. Am.* **1.** a wild pansy. **2.** violet.

John·son (jon′sən), *n.* **1.** Andrew, 1808–1875, the 17th president of the United States, from 1865 to 1869. **2.** Lyndon B., born 1908, the 36th president of the United States, since 1963. **3.** Samuel, 1709–1784, English author, dictionary maker, and literary leader.

John·so·ni·an (jon·sō′ni·ən), *adj.* having a literary style like that of Samuel Johnson; pompous and ponderous.

Johns·town (jonz′toun), *n.* city in SW Pennsylvania. A serious flood occurred there in 1889.

John the Baptist, *Bible.* man who foretold the coming of Christ and baptized him. Matt. 3.

Jo·hore (jō·hôr′; -hōr′), *n.* a native state at the southern end of the Malay Peninsula.

joie de vi·vre (zhwä də vē′vrə), *French.* joy of living; enjoyment of life.

join (join), *v.* **1.** bring or put together; connect; fasten: *join hands.* **2.** come together; meet: *the two roads join here.* **3.** meet and unite with: *the brook joins the river.* **4.** make or become one; combine; unite: *join in marriage.* **5.** take part with others: *join in a song.* **6.** become a member of: *join a club.* **7.** come into the company of: *I'll join you later.* **8.** take or return to one's place in: *after a few days on shore the sailor joined his ship.* **9.** adjoin: *his farm joins mine.* **10.** join battle, begin to fight. —*n.* **1.** place or line of joining; seam. **2.** act or fact of joining. [< OF *joindre* < L *jungere*] —*Syn. v.* **1.** link, couple.

join·er (join′ər), *n.* **1.** person or thing that joins. **2.** a skilled workman who makes woodwork and furniture. **3.** *Am., Colloq.* person who joins many clubs, societies, etc.

join·er·y (join′ər·i), *n.* **1.** skill or trade of a joiner. **2.** things made by a joiner.

joint (joint), *n.* **1.** place at which two things or

āge, cãre, fär; ēqual, tėrm; īce; ōpen, ôrder; put, rüle, ūse; th, then; ə=a in about.

parts are joined together. 2. the way parts are joined: *a perfect joint*. 3. in an animal, the parts where two bones move on one another. 4. one of the parts of which a jointed thing is made up: *the middle joint of the finger*. 5. *Zool., Bot.* part between two articulations or nodes. 6. **out of joint**, a. out of place at the joint. b. out of order; in bad condition. 7. *Bot.* part of the stem from which a leaf or branch grows. 8. piece of meat cut for cooking. 9. *Am., Slang.* a. a cheap, low place, often for the illegal sale of liquor. b. any place or establishment. —*v.* 1. connect by a joint or joints. 2. divide at the joints. —*adj.* 1. owned together; owned by, held by, or done by two or more persons: *joint efforts.* 2. sharing: *joint owners.* [< OF, < *joindre* JOIN] —**joint′less,** *adj.*

joint·ly (joint′li), *adv.* together; in common: *the two boys owned the newsstand jointly.*

joint-stock company, company or firm whose capital is owned in shares by stockholders, any of whom can sell some or all of his shares without the consent of the others.

join·ture (join′chər), *n. Law.* property given to a woman at the time of her marriage. [< F < L *junctura* a joining < *jungere* join. Doublet of JUNCTURE.]

joist (joist), *n.* one of the parallel pieces of timber to which the boards of a floor or ceiling are fastened. —*v.* provide with joists. [< OF *giste*, ult. < L *jacere* lie] —**joist′less,** *adj.*

joke (jōk), *n., v.,* **joked, jok·ing.** —*n.* 1. something said or done to make somebody laugh; something amusing: *this was a good joke on me.* 2. person or thing laughed at. —*v.* 1. make a joke; say or do something as a joke. 2. laugh at; make fun of; tease. [< L *jocus*] —**jok′ing·ly,** *adv.* —Syn. *n.* 1. jest, witticism.

jok·er (jōk′ər), *n.* 1. person who jokes. 2. *Am.* phrase or sentence hidden away in a law, contract, etc., to defeat its apparent purpose. 3. an extra playing card used in some games.

jol·li·fi·ca·tion (jol′ə·fə·kā′shən), *n.* gay entertainment; merrymaking.

jol·li·ty (jol′ə·ti), *n., pl.* **-ties.** fun; merriment; festivity; gaiety.

jol·ly (jol′i), *adj.,* **-li·er, -li·est,** *adv., v.,* **-lied, -ly·ing.** —*adj.* 1. full of fun; merry: *a jolly disposition.* 2. *Esp. Brit. Colloq.* pleasant; agreeable; delightful. 3. *Esp. Brit. Colloq.* big; large. —*adv. Esp. Brit. Colloq.* extremely; very. —*v.* 1. *Am.* flatter (a person) to make him feel good or agreeable. 2. *Colloq.* make fun of; kid. [< OF *joli,* ? < Gmc.] —**jol′li·ly,** *adv.* —**jol′li·ness,** *n.* —Syn. *adj.* 1. gay, joyful, mirthful, jovial.

jolly boat, a small boat carried on a ship.

Jolly Rog·er (roj′ər), a pirates' black flag with a skull and crossbones on it.

jolt (jōlt), *v.* move with a shock or jerk; jar; shake up: *the wagon jolted us when the wheel went over a rock.* —*n.* jar; shock; jerk: *stop with a jolt.* —**jolt′er,** *n.* —**jolt′y,** *adj.*

Jo·nah (jō′nə), **Jo·nas** (-nəs), *n.* 1. *Bible.* a Hebrew prophet who was thrown overboard during a storm, swallowed by a large fish, and later cast up on land. 2. book of the Old Testament. 3. person whose presence is supposed to bring bad luck.

Jon·a·than (jon′ə·thən), *n.* son of Saul, and a devoted friend of David. I Sam. 19:1–10.

Jones (jōnz), *n.* John Paul, 1747–1792, American naval commander in the American Revolution.

jon·gleur (jong′glər; Fr. zhôn·glœr′), *n.* a wandering minstrel or entertainer in the Middle Ages. [< F < OF *jogleor* juggler. See JUGGLE.]

jon·quil (jong′kwəl; jon′-), *n.* 1. plant of the narcissus family with yellow or white flowers and long slender leaves. 2. the flower. [< F < Sp. *junquillo,* ult. < L *juncus* reed]

Jon·son (jon′sən), *n.* Ben, 1573?–1637, English dramatist and poet.

Jor·dan (jôr′dən), *n.* 1. river in Palestine, flowing into the Dead Sea. 2. country in SW Asia, officially called the Hashemite Kingdom of Jordan. Formerly, **Transjordan.**

Jo·seph (jō′zəf), *n.* 1. the favorite son of Jacob. His jealous brothers sold him into slavery in Egypt, where he finally became governor. Gen. 37, 39–41. 2. the husband of Mary, the mother of Jesus.

Jo·se·phine (jō′zə·fēn), *n.* 1763–1814, first wife of Napoleon Bonaparte.

Joseph of Ar·i·ma·the·a (ar′ə·mə·thē′ə), a rich man who put the body of Jesus in his own tomb. Matt. 27:57–60.

Josh (josh), *v. Am., Slang.* make good-natured fun of; tease playfully; banter. —*n.* a bantering remark. —**josh′er,** *n.*

Josh·u·a (josh′ū·ə), *n.* 1. successor of Moses. He led the children of Israel into the Promised Land. 2. book of the Old Testament.

joss (jos), *n.* image of a Chinese god; Chinese idol. [pidgin Eng. form of Pg. *deos* god < L *deus*]

joss house, a Chinese temple.

joss stick, a slender stick of dried fragrant paste, burned by the Chinese as incense.

jos·tle (jos′əl), *v.,* **-tled, -tling.** *n.* —*v.* crowd, strike, or push against; elbow roughly: *we were jostled by the big crowd at the entrance.* —*n.* a jostling; push; knock. Also, **justle.** [< *joust*] —**jos′tle·ment,** *n.* —**jos′tler,** *n.*

jot (jot), *n., v.,* **jot·ted, jot·ting.** —*n.* little bit; very small amount: *not care a jot.* —*v.* write briefly or in haste: *jot down the order.* [< L < Gk. *iota* iota] —**jot′ter,** *n.*

Jo·tun, Jo·tunn, Jö·tunn (yō′tún), *n. Norse Myth.* giant.

Jo·tun·heim, Jo·tunn·heim, Jö·tunn·heim (yō′tún·hām), *n. Norse Myth.* home of the giants.

joule (joul; jūl), *n. Physics.* a unit of work or energy, equal to ten million ergs. [for J. P. *Joule,* scientist]

jounce (jouns), *v.,* **jounced, jounc·ing,** *n.* —*v.* bounce; bump; jolt. —*n.* a jolting movement.

jour·nal (jėr′nəl), *n.* 1. a daily record. 2. account of what happens or of what one thinks or notices, as a diary. 3. a ship's log. 4. newspaper; magazine. 5. *Bookkeeping.* book in which every item of business is written down so that the item can be entered under the proper account. 6. *Mach.* part of a shaft or axle that turns on a bearing. [< OF < LL *diurnalis.* Doublet of DIURNAL.]

jour·nal·ese (jėr′nəl·ēz′; -ēs′), *n.* careless style of writing such as is sometimes used in newspapers.

jour·nal·ism (jėr′nəl·iz·əm), *n.* 1. work of writing for, editing, managing, or producing a newspaper or magazine. 2. newspapers and magazines as a group.

jour·nal·ist (jėr′nəl·ist), *n.* person engaged in journalism, as an editor or reporter. —**jour′nal·is′tic,** *adj.* —**jour′nal·is′ti·cal·ly,** *adv.*

jour·ney (jėr′ni), *n., pl.* **-neys,** *v.,* **-neyed, -ney·ing.** —*n.* 1. travel; trip: *a journey around the world.* 2. distance traveled or that one can travel in a certain time. —*v.* take a trip; travel. [< OF *journee,* orig., a day, ult. < L *diurnus* of one day] —Syn. *n.* 1. excursion, tour, voyage.

jour·ney·man (jėr′ni·mən), *n., pl.* **-men.** a qualified workman who has completed his apprenticeship, but has not become an employer or master workman.

joust (just; joust; jũst), *n.* 1. combat between two knights on horseback, armed with lances. 2. **jousts,** a tournament. —*v.* fight with lances on horseback. [< OF *jouster,* ult. < L *juxta* beside] —**joust′er,** *n.*

Jove (jōv), *n.* 1. the Roman god Jupiter. 2. **by Jove,** exclamation of surprise, pleasure, etc. —**Jo′vi·an,** *adj.*

jo·vi·al (jō′vi·əl), *adj.* good-hearted and full of fun; good-humored and merry. [< L *Jovialis* pertaining to Jupiter (those born under the planet's sign being supposedly cheerful)] —**jo′vi·al·ly,** *adv.* —**jo′vi·al·ness, jo·vi·al·i·ty** (jō′vi·al′ə·ti), *n.*

jowl[1] (joul; jōl), *n.* 1. part under the jaw; jaw. 2. cheek. [OE *ceafl*]

jowl[2] (joul; jōl), *n.* fold of flesh hanging from the jaw. [akin to OE *ceole* throat]

joy (joi), *n.* 1. a strong feeling of pleasure; gladness; happiness. 2. something that causes gladness or happiness: *"a thing of beauty is a joy forever."* 3. expression of happiness; outward rejoicing. —*v.* be joyful. [< OF *joie* < L *gaudia* joys] —Syn. *n.* 1. delight, rapture, bliss.

Joyce (jois), *n.* **James,** 1882–1941, Irish writer.

joy·ful (joi′fəl), *adj.* 1. glad; happy: *a joyful heart.* 2. causing joy: *joyful news.* 3. showing joy: *a joyful look.* —**joy′ful·ly,** *adv.* —**joy′ful·ness,** *n.*

joy·less (joi′lis), *adj.* 1. without joy; sad; dismal. 2. not causing joy: *a joyless prospect.* —**joy′less·ly,** *adv.* —**joy′less·ness,** *n.*

joy·ous (joi′əs), *adj.* joyful; glad; gay. —**joy′ous·ly,** *adv.* —**joy′ous·ness,** *n.*

joy ride, *Am., Colloq.* ride in an automobile for pleasure, esp. when the car is driven recklessly or used without the owner's permission. —**joy rider,** *Am.* —**joy riding,** *Am.*

joy-ride (joi′rīd′), *v.,* **-rode, -rid·den, -rid·ing.** *Am., Colloq.* take a joy ride.

J.P., Justice of the Peace.

Jr., jr., Junior. Also, **Jun.**

ju·bi·lance (jü′bə-ləns), *n.* a rejoicing.

ju·bi·lant (jü′bə-lənt), *adj.* 1. rejoicing; exulting. 2. expressing or showing joy. [< L *jubilans* shouting with joy < *jubilum* wild shout] —**ju′bi·lant·ly,** *adv.* —Syn. 1. joyful, exultant.

ju·bi·la·tion (jü′bə-lā′shən), *n.* 1. a rejoicing. 2. a joyful celebration.

ju·bi·lee (jü′bə-lē), *n.* 1. time of rejoicing or great joy: *hold a jubilee over a victory.* 2. rejoicing; great joy: *a day of jubilee.* 3. 25th or 50th anniversary. [< OF < LL < Gk. *iobelaios* < Heb. *yōbēl,* orig., trumpet, ram('s horn)]

Ju·dah (jü′də), *n.* 1. son of Jacob and ancestor of the tribe of Judah. 2. the most powerful of the twelve tribes of Israel. 3. an ancient Hebrew kingdom in S Palestine, consisting of the tribes of Judah and Benjamin.

Ju·da·ic (jü·dā′ik), **Ju·da·i·cal** (-ə·kəl), *adj.* of the Jews; Jewish.

Ju·da·ism (jü′dē·iz·əm; -dā–), *n.* 1. the religion of the Jews. 2. the following of Jewish rules and customs.

Ju·das (jü′dəs), *n.* 1. the disciple who betrayed Christ for money. 2. an utter traitor; person treacherous enough to betray a friend. —**Ju′das-like′,** *adj.*

Judas tree, tree that has red, pink, or purplish flowers before the leaves come out.

Jude (jüd), *n.* 1. one of the twelve disciples chosen by Jesus as his Apostles. 2. book of the New Testament. 3. its author.

Ju·de·a, Ju·dae·a (jü·dē′ə), *n.* the southern part of Palestine when it was a province of the Roman Empire.

Ju·de·an, Ju·dae·an (jü·dē′ən), *adj.* 1. of Judea. 2. of the Jews. —*n.* a Jew.

judge (juj), *n., v.,* **judged, judg·ing.** —*n.* 1. a government official appointed or elected to hear and decide cases in a law court. 2. person chosen to settle a dispute or decide who wins. 3. person qualified to form an opinion: *a good judge of cattle.* 4. person who decides: *let me be the judge of that.* 5. ruler in ancient Israel before the time of the kings. —*v.* 1. hear and decide in a law court. 2. settle (a dispute); decide who wins (a race, contest, etc.). 3. form an opinion or estimate (of): *judge the merits of a book.* 4. think; suppose; consider: *I judged the slight to be intentional.* 5. criticize; condemn: *who can judge another?* [< OF < L *judex* < *ius* law + root of *dicere* say] —**judge′less,** *adj.* —**judge′like′,** *adj.* —**judg′er,** *n.* —Syn. *v.* 4. deem, regard.

judge advocate, officer who acts as a prosecutor at a court-martial.

Judg·es (juj′iz), *n.* book of the Old Testament dealing with the period in Hebrew history between Joshua and the birth of Samuel.

judge·ship (juj′ship), *n.* position, duties, or term of office of a judge.

judg·ment, *esp. Brit.* **judge·ment** (juj′-mənt), *n.* 1. act of judging: *hall of judgment.* 2.

decision, decree, or sentence given by a judge or court. 3. certificate embodying such a decision. 4. debt arising from a judge's decision. 5. opinion: *it was a bad plan in his judgment.* 6. ability to form opinions; good sense. 7. criticism; condemnation. 8. **the Judgment,** judgment day. —Syn. 5. estimation, belief.

judgment day, day of God's final judgment of mankind at the end of the world.

ju·di·ca·to·ry (jü′də·kə·tô′rī; -tō′-), *adj., n., pl.* **-to·ries.** —*adj.* of the administration of justice: *a judicatory tribunal.* —*n.* 1. administration of justice. 2. court of justice. [< LL *judicatorius,* ult. < L *judex* judge]

ju·di·ca·ture (jü′də·kə·chər), *n.* 1. administration of justice. 2. position, duties, or authority of a judge. 3. extent of jurisdiction of a judge or court. 4. group of judges. 5. court of justice.

ju·di·cial (jü·dish′əl), *adj.* 1. of or having to do with courts, judges, or the administration of justice: *judicial proceedings.* 2. ordered, permitted, or enforced by a judge or a court: *a judicial separation.* 3. of or suitable for a judge: *a judicial mind considers both sides of a question.* [< L *judicialis,* ult. < *judex* judge] —**ju·di′cial·ly,** *adv.* —Syn. 3. impartial, fair.

ju·di·ci·ar·y (jü·dish′i·er′i), *n., pl.* **-ar·ies,** *adj.* —*n.* 1. branch of government that administers justice; system of courts of justice of a country. 2. judges of a country, state, or city. —*adj.* of or having to do with courts, judges, or the administration of justice.

ju·di·cious (jü·dish′əs), *adj.* having, using, or showing good judgment; wise; sensible: *a judicious historian selects and considers facts carefully and critically.* [< F *judicieux,* ult. < L *judex* judge] —**ju·di′cious·ly,** *adv.* —**ju·di′cious·ness,** *n.* —Syn. discreet, prudent, astute.

Ju·dith (jü′dith), *n.* 1. a Hebrew woman who saved her countrymen by killing an Assyrian general. 2. book of the Apocrypha and of the Douay Version of the Bible that relates her story.

ju·do (jü′dō), *n.* jujitsu.

jug (jug), *n., v.,* **jugged, jug·ging.** —*n.* 1. container for liquids, usually one with a spout or a narrow neck and a handle. 2. *Slang.* jail. —*v.* 1. put in a jug. 2. *Slang.* jail. [prob. orig. proper name, alter. of *Joan,* fem. of *John*]

Jug·ger·naut (jug′ər·nôt), *n.* 1. idol of the Hindu god Krishna, pulled around on a huge car. Devotees of the god are said to have thrown themselves under the wheels to be crushed to death. 2. something to which a person blindly devotes himself or is cruelly sacrificed.

jug·gle (jug′əl), *v.,* **-gled, -gling,** *n.* —*v.* 1. do tricks that require skill of hand or eye. 2. do such tricks with: *juggle three balls in the air.* 3. change by trickery: *juggle accounts to hide thefts.* —*n.* 1. a juggling. 2. trick; deception; fraud. [< OF *jogler* < L *joculari* to joke, ult. < *jocus* jest] —**jug′gler,** *n.*

jug·gler·y (jug′lər·i), *n., pl.* **-gler·ies.** 1. sleight of hand. 2. trickery; fraud.

Ju·go·slav, Ju·go·Slav (ü′gō·släv′; -släv′), *n., adj.* Yugoslav. —**Ju′go·slav′ic, Ju′go·Slav′ic,** *adj.*

Ju·go·sla·vi·a, Ju·go·Sla·vi·a (ü′gō·slä′-vi-ə), *n.* Yugoslavia. —**Ju′go·sla′vi·an, Ju′go·Sla′vi·an,** *adj., n.*

jug·u·lar (jug′yə·lər; jü′gyə–), *Anat.* —*adj.* 1. of the neck or throat. 2. of the jugular vein. —*n.* jugular vein. [< NL, < L *jugulum* collarbone, dim. of *jugum* yoke]

jugular vein, one of the two large veins in the neck that return blood from the head to the heart.

juice (jüs), *n.* 1. liquid in fruits, vegetables, and meats. 2. liquid in the body. The gastric juices of the stomach help to digest food. 3. *Am., Slang.* electricity. 4. *Slang.* gasoline. [< OF < L *jus* broth] —**juice′less,** *adj.*

juic·y (jüs′i), *adj.,* **juic·i·er, juic·i·est.** 1. full of juice; having much juice. 2. full of interest; lively. —**juic′i·ly,** *adv.* —**juic′i·ness,** *n.*

ju·jit·su, ju·jut·su (jü·jit′sü), *n.* Japanese method of wrestling or fighting without weapons that uses the strength and weight of an opponent to his disadvantage. Also, **jiujitsu, jiu-jutsu, judo.** [< Jap., < *jū* soft + *jutsu* art]

ju·jube (jü′jüb), *n.* **1.** lozenge or small tablet of gummy candy. **2.** an edible datelike fruit of a shrub or tree, used to flavor this candy. [< F or < Med.L *jujuba,* ult. < Gk. *zizyphon*]

juke box (jük), *Am., Slang.* an automatic phonograph that plays one record for each nickel deposited in the slot.

juke joint (jük), *Am., Slang.* **1.** tavern, roadhouse, etc., where music is furnished by a juke box. **2.** any small building where liquor is sold.

Jul., July. Also, **Jy.**

ju·lep (jü′ləp), *n. Am.* drink made of whiskey or brandy, sugar, crushed ice, and fresh mint. [< F < Ar. < Pers. *gulāb,* orig., rose water]

Jul·ian (jül′yən), *adj.* of Julius Caesar.

Ju·li·an·a (jü′li·an′ə; -ä′nə), *n.* (in full, *Juliana Louise Emma Marie Wilhelmina*) born 1909, queen of the Netherlands since 1948.

Julian calendar, calendar in which the average length of a year was 365¼ days. It was introduced by Julius Caesar in 46 B.C.

ju·li·enne (jü′li·en′), *adj.* cut in thin strips or small pieces, as potatoes. —*n.* a clear soup containing vegetables cut into thin strips or small pieces.

Ju·li·et (jü′li·et; -ət), *n.* the young heroine of Shakespeare's play *Romeo and Juliet.*

Jul·ius Cae·sar (jül′yəs sē′zər). See Caesar.

Ju·ly (jü·lī′), *n., pl.* -lies. the seventh month of the year. It has 31 days. [after *Julius* Caesar]

jum·ble (jum′bəl), *v.* —bled, —bling, *n.* —*v.* mix; confuse: *things strangely jumbled together.* —*n.* a confused mixture. [? imit.] —**Syn.** *n.* medley, hodgepodge, muddle, mess.

jum·bo (jum′bō), *n., pl.* -bos, *adj. Am., Colloq.* —*n.* a big, clumsy person, animal, or thing. —*adj.* very big.

jump (jump), *v.* **1.** spring from the ground; leap; bound: *jump up and down.* **2.** leap over; skip; pass over: *jump a stream.* **3.** cause to jump: *jump a horse over a fence.* **4.** move suddenly and quickly: *I jumped from my bed.* **5.** give a sudden start or jerk: *you made me jump.* **6.** rise suddenly: *prices jumped.* **7.** *Am.* in checkers, pass over and capture (an opponent's piece). **8.** in contract bridge, raise (a partner's bid) by more than one trick. **9.** *Slang.* evade by running away: *jump bail.* **10.** *Am., Slang.* get aboard (a train) by jumping. **11.** jump a claim, seize a piece of land claimed by another. **12.** jump at, accept eagerly and quickly. **13.** jump off, *Mil.* leave one's lines for an attack on the enemy. **14.** jump on, *Slang.* blame; scold; criticize. **15.** jump the track, leave the rails suddenly. —*n.* **1.** spring from the ground; leap; bound. **2.** thing to be jumped over. **3.** distance jumped. **4.** contest in jumping. **5.** a sudden nervous start or jerk. **6.** a sudden rise. **7.** in checkers, move made to capture an opponent's piece. **8.** get or have the jump on, *Am., Slang.* get or have an advantage over. [prob. imit.] —**Syn.** *v.* **2.** vault, hop.

jump area, *Mil.* locality assigned for the landing of parachute troops, usually behind enemy lines.

jump·er[1] (jump′ər), *n.* one that jumps.

jump·er[2] (jump′ər), *n.* **1.** a loose jacket. **2.** a loose blouse reaching to the hips. **3.** a one-piece dress without sleeves, worn over a blouse. **4.** jumpers, rompers. [< *jump* short coat, ? alter. of F *juppe,* ult. < Ar. *jubbah* long open coat]

jumping bean, *Am.* seed of a Mexican plant containing a larva whose movements cause the seed to jump.

jumping jack, toy man or animal that can be made to jump by pulling a string.

jump·mas·ter (jump′mas′tər; -mäs′-), *n. Mil.* officer who controls the dropping of parachute troops and their equipment from an aircraft.

jump·y (jump′i), *adj.,* jump·i·er, jump·i·est. **1.** moving by jumps; making sudden, sharp jerks. **2.** easily excited or frightened; nervous. —**jump′i·ness,** *n.*

Jun., **1.** June. Also, **Je. 2.** Also, **Jr.** Junior.

Junc., Junction.

jun·co (jung′kō), *n., pl.* -cos. *Am.* any of several small North American finches often seen in flocks during the winter. [< Sp. < L *juncus* reed]

junc·tion (jungk′-shən), *n.* **1.** a joining or being joined: *the junction of two armies.* **2.** place where things join. **3.** place where railroad lines meet or cross.

Junco (ab. 6 in. long)

junc·ture (jungk′chər), *n.* **1.** point of time. **2.** state of affairs. **3.** crisis. **4.** joint. **5.** a joining or being joined; junction. [< L *junctura.* Doublet of JOINTURE.]

June (jün), *n.* the sixth month of the year. It has 30 days. [< L *Junius,* a Roman gens]

Ju·neau (jü′nō), *n.* capital of Alaska, in the SE part.

June bug or **beetle,** *Am.* **1.** a large brown beetle of the N United States that appears in June. **2.** figeater.

Jung·frau (yung′frou′), *n.* mountain in the Alps of S Switzerland.

jun·gle (jung′gəl), *n.* **1.** a wild land thickly overgrown with bushes, vines, trees, etc. **2.** a tangled mass. **3.** *U.S. Slang.* camp for tramps. [< Hind. *jangal* < Skt. *jangala* desert]

jun·ior (jün′yər), *adj.* **1.** the younger: *John Parker, Junior, is the son of John Parker, Senior.* **2.** of lower position, rank, or standing; of more recent appointment: *a junior officer, a junior partner.* **3.** of or having to do with juniors in high school or college. **4.** of later date: subsequent (to). —*n.* **1.** a younger person. **2.** person of lower position, rank, or standing; person of more recent appointment. **3.** *Am.* student in the third year of high school or college. [< L, compar. of *juvenis* young]

junior college, school giving only the first two years of a regular four-year college course.

junior high school, *Am.* school consisting of grades 7, 8, and 9.

ju·ni·per (jü′nə·pər), *n. Am.* an evergreen shrub or tree with small berrylike cones. [< L *juniperus*]

junk[1] (jungk), *n.* **1.** *Am.* old metal, paper, rags, etc. **2.** *Slang.* rubbish; trash. —*v. Colloq.* throw away or discard as junk.

junk[2] (jungk), *n.* a Chinese sailing ship. [< Pg. *junco,* prob. ult. < Javanese *jong*]

Jun·ker, jun·ker (yung′kər), *n.* member of the aristocratic, formerly privileged class in Prussia. [< G]

jun·ket (jung′kit), *n.* **1.** curdled milk, sweetened and flavored. **2.** feast; picnic. **3.** pleasure trip. **4.** *Am.* trip taken by an American official at the expense of the government. —*v.* go on a junket. [prob. < dial. OF *jonquette* basket < *jonc* reed < L *juncus*] —**jun′ket·er,** *n. Am.*

junk·man (jungk′man′), *n., pl.* -men. *Am.* man who buys and sells old metal, paper, rags, etc.

Ju·no (jü′nō), *n., pl.* -nos. **1.** *Roman Myth.* goddess of marriage, wife of Jupiter and queen of the gods, identified with the Greek goddess Hera. **2.** a stately, majestic woman.

jun·ta (jun′tə), *n.* **1.** a Spanish council for deliberation or administration. **2.** junto. [< Sp., ult. < L *jungere* join]

jun·to (jun′tō), *n., pl.* -tos. a political faction; group of plotters or partisans. [alter. of *junta*]

Ju·pi·ter (jü′pə·tər), *n.* **1.** *Roman Myth.* the ruler of the gods and men, identified with the Greek god Zeus. **2.** the largest planet.

Ju·ra Mountains (jur′ə), mountain range in France and Switzerland.

Ju·ras·sic (jü·ras′ik), *n.* **1.** geological period when birds first appeared. **2.** rocks of this period. —*adj.* of this period.

ju·rid·i·cal (jü·rid′ə·kəl), **ju·rid·ic** (-ik), *adj.* **1.** having to do with the administration of justice. **2.** of law; legal. [< L, ult. < *jus* law + *dicere* say] —**ju·rid′i·cal·ly,** *adv.*

ju·ris·dic·tion (jŭr´is·dĭk´shən), n. 1. right or power of administering law or justice. 2. authority; power; control. 3. extent of authority: *the judge ruled that the case was not within his jurisdiction.* [< L, ult. < *jus* law + *dicere* say] —**ju´ris·dic´tion·al,** adj. —**ju´ris·dic´tion·al·ly,** adv.

ju·ris·pru·dence (jŭr´is·prū´dəns), n. 1. science or philosophy of law. 2. system of laws. 3. branch of law: *medical jurisprudence.* [< L, < *jus* law + *prudentia* prudence] —**ju·ris·pru·den·tial** (jŭr´is·prū·den´shəl), adj.

ju·rist (jŭr´ist), n. 1. expert in law. 2. a learned writer on law. [< Med.L *jurista* < L *jus* law]

ju·ris·tic (jū·ris´tik), **ju·ris·ti·cal** (-tə·kəl), adj. of or having to do with jurists or jurisprudence; relating to law. —**ju·ris´ti·cal·ly,** adv.

ju·ror (jŭr´ər), n. member of a jury.

ju·ry[1] (jŭr´i), n., pl. **ju·ries.** 1. group of persons selected to hear evidence in a law court and sworn to give a decision in accordance with the evidence presented to them. See also **grand jury** and **petty jury.** 2. group of persons chosen to give a judgment or to decide a contest and award prizes. [< AF *jurie*, ult. < L *jurare* swear] —**ju´ry·less,** adj.

ju·ry[2] (jŭr´i), adj. Naut. for temporary use on a ship; makeshift. [prob. ult. < OF *ajurie* help, ult. < L *ad-* + *juvare* aid]

ju·ry·man (jŭr´i·mən), n., pl. **-men.** juror.

just (just), adj. 1. right; fair. 2. righteous. 3. deserved; merited: *a just reward.* 4. having good grounds; well-founded: *just anger.* 5. lawful: *a just claim.* 6. in accordance with standards or requirements; proper: *just proportions.* 7. true; correct: *a just description.* 8. exact: *just weights.* —adv. 1. exactly: *just a pound.* 2. almost exactly: *I saw him just now.* 3. a very little while ago: *he has just gone.* 4. barely: *it just missed the mark.* 5. only; merely: *just an ordinary man.* 6. Colloq. quite; truly; positively: *the weather is just glorious.* [< L *justus* upright < *jus* right] —**just´ly,** adv. —**just´ness,** n. —Syn. adj. 1. impartial, equitable. 2. upright, honest. 3. due, rightful. 6. fitting. 8. precise.

jus·tice (jus´tis), n. 1. just conduct; fair dealing: *have a sense of justice.* 2. a being just; fairness; rightness; correctness: *uphold the justice of our cause.* 3. rightfulness; lawfulness; well-founded reason: *complain with justice.* 4. just treatment; deserved reward or punishment. 5. exercise of power and authority to maintain what is just and right. 6. administration of law; trial and judgment by process of law: *a court of justice.* 7. judge: *the justices of the U.S. Supreme Court.* 8. justice of the peace. 9. **bring a person to justice,** do what is necessary in order that a

person shall be legally punished for his crime or crimes. 10. **do justice to,** a. treat fairly. b. show proper appreciation for. 11. **do oneself justice,** do as well as one really can do. [< OF < L *justitia*] —**jus´tice·ship,** n.

justice of the peace, a local magistrate who tries minor cases, administers oaths, performs civil marriages, etc.

jus·ti·fi·a·ble (jus´tə·fī´ə·bəl), adj. capable of being justified; that can be shown to be just and right; defensible. —**jus´ti·fi´a·bil´i·ty, jus´-ti·fi´a·ble·ness,** n. —**jus´ti·fi´a·bly,** adv.

jus·ti·fi·ca·tion (jus´tə·fə·kā´shən), n. 1. a justifying or being justified. 2. fact or circumstance that justifies; good reason. 3. Theol. a freeing or being freed from the guilt or penalty of sin.

jus·ti·fy (jus´tə·fī), v., **-fied, -fy·ing.** 1. show to be just or right; give a good reason for: *the fine quality of the cloth justifies its high price.* 2. clear of blame or guilt. 3. make (lines of type) the right length by proper spacing. 4. Law. show a satisfactory reason or excuse for something done. —**jus´ti·fi´er,** n. —Syn. 1. uphold, defend. 2. exonerate.

Jus·tin·i·an (jus·tin´i·ən), n. 483–565 A.D., emperor of the Eastern Roman Empire, 527–565 A.D.

jus·tle (jus´əl), v., **-tled, -tling,** n. jostle.

jut (jut), v., **jut·ted, jut·ting,** n. —v. stick out; project: *the pier juts out from the shore into the water.* —n. part that sticks out; projection. [var. of *jet*[1]]

jute (jūt), n. strong fiber used for making coarse sacks, burlap, rope, etc., obtained from two tropical plants. [< Bengali (lang. of Bengal) *jhōto* < Skt. *jūta* mat of hair] —**jute´like´,** adj.

Jute (jūt), n. member of a Germanic tribe. Some of the Jutes invaded and settled in SE Britain in the fifth century A.D. —**Jut´ish,** adj.

Jut·land (jut´lənd), n. peninsula of Denmark.

Ju·ve·nal (jū´və·nəl), n. 60–140? A.D., Roman satirical poet.

ju·ve·nile (jū´və·nəl, -nīl), adj. 1. young; youthful; childish. 2. of or for young people: *juvenile books.* —n. 1. a young person. 2. book for young people. 3. in the theater, a. a youthful male part. b. actor who plays youthful parts. [< L, < *juvenis* young] —**ju´ve·nile·ly,** adv. —**ju´ve·nile·ness, ju·ve·nil·i·ty** (jū´və·nil´ə·ti), n. —Syn. adj. 1. immature, undeveloped.

juvenile court, Am. law court where cases involving boys and girls are heard.

jux·ta·pose (juks´tə·pōz´), v., **-posed, -posing.** put close together; place side by side. [< F, < L *juxta* beside + F *poser* place, POSE] —**jux·ta·po·si·tion** (juks´tə·pə·zish´ən), n.

Jy., July. Also, **Jul.**

K

K, k (kā), n., pl. **K's; k's.** the 11th letter of the alphabet.

K, Chem. potassium.

K., 1. King; Kings. 2. Knight.

k., 1. karat. 2. kilogram. 3. knot.

Kaa·ba (kä´bə), n. the sacred shrine of the Mohammedans, a small structure, containing a black stone, in the great mosque at Mecca. Also, **Caaba.**

Ka·bul (kä´bŭl), n. capital of Afghanistan.

ka·di (kä´di; kä´-), n., pl. **-dis.** cadi.

Kaf·fir, Kaf·ir (kaf´ər), n. 1. member of a Negroid race in South Africa. 2. their language. 3. kaffir, kafir, kaffir corn.

kaffir corn, kafir corn, a sorghum grown for grain and forage in dry regions.

kaf·tan (kaf´tən; käf·tän´), n. caftan.

kai·ak (kī´ak), n. kayak.

Kai·ser, kai·ser (kī´zər), n. 1. title of the rulers of Germany from 1871 to 1918. 2. title of the rulers of Austria from 1804 to 1918. 3. title of the rulers of the Holy Roman Empire from 962

A.D. to 1806. [< G, < Julius *Caesar*] —**Kai´ser·ship, kai´ser·ship,** n.

kale, kail (kāl), n. 1. any of various kinds of cabbage that have loose leaves instead of a compact head. Kale looks somewhat like spinach. 2. Am., Slang. money; cash. [var. of *cole*]

ka·lei·do·scope (kə·lī´də·skōp), n. 1. tube containing bits of colored glass and two mirrors. As it is turned, it reflects continually changing patterns. 2. anything that changes continually; a continually changing pattern. [< Gk. *kalos* pretty + *eidos* shape + E -*scope* instrument of viewing < Gk. *skopein* look at] —**ka·lei·do·scop·ic** (kə·lī´də·skop´ik), **ka·lei´do·scop´i·cal,** adj. —**ka·lei´do·scop´i·cal·ly,** adv.

kal·ends (kal´əndz), n.pl. calends.

Ka·le·va·la (kä´lā·vä´lä), n. the national epic poem of Finland.

Ka·li·nin (kä·lē´nin), n. Mikhail Ivanovich, 1875–1946, Russian political leader.

Ka·li·nin·grad (kə·lē´nin·grad), n. city in W Soviet Union, in East Prussia. Formerly, Königsberg.

Kal·muck, Kal·muk (kal′muk), *n.* 1. member of a group of Mongol tribes living in W China and SE Soviet Union. 2. their language.

kal·so·mine (kal′sə·mīn; –min), *n., v.,* –mined, –min·ing. calcimine.

Kam·chat·ka (kam·chat′kə), *n.* peninsula of NE Asia between the Sea of Okhotsk and Bering Sea.

Ka·nak·a (kə·nak′ə; kan′ə·kə), *n. Am.* 1. native of Hawaii. 2. native of any island in the S Pacific; South Sea islander. [< Hawaiian, man]

kan·ga·roo (kang′gə·rū′), *n., pl.* –roos or (*esp. collectively*) –roo. mammal of Australia and New Guinea having small forelegs and very strong hind legs, which give it great leaping power. The female kangaroo has a pouch in front in which she carries her young. [prob. < Australian lang.] —**kan′ga·roo′like′**, *adj.*

kangaroo rat, *Am.* a small, mouselike animal of the desert regions of the U.S. and Mexico.

Kans., Kan., Kansas.

Kan·sas (kan′zəs), *n.* 1. a Middle Western State of the United States. *Capital:* Topeka. *Abbrev.:* Kans. or Kan. 2. river flowing from NE Kansas into the Missouri. —**Kan′san,** *adj., n. Am.*

Kansas City, 1. city in W Missouri, on the Missouri River. 2. city in NE Kansas near it.

Kant (kant; *Ger.* känt), *n.* Immanuel, 1724–1804, German philosopher. —**Kant·i·an** (kan′ti·ən), *adj., n.*

ka·o·lin, ka·o·line (kā′ə·lin), *n.* a fine white clay, used in making porcelain. [< F < Chinese *Kao-ling,* mountain in China]

ka·pok (kā′pok; kap′ək), *n.* the silky fibers around the seeds of a tropical tree, used for stuffing pillows and mattresses. [< Malay *kapoq*]

kap·pa (kap′ə), *n.* the tenth letter (K, κ) of the Greek alphabet.

Ka·ra·chi (kə·rä′chi), *n.* former capital of Pakistan, in the W part.

kar·a·kul (kar′ə·kəl), *n.* 1. variety of Russian or Asiatic sheep. 2. caracul. [< *Kara Kul,* lake in Turkestan]

kar·at (kar′ət), *n.* carat.

ka·ra·te (kä·rä′tä, –ti), *n.* Japanese method of fighting without weapons by striking certain vulnerable parts of the opponent's body. [< Jap.]

Ka·re·li·a (kə·rē′li·ə; –rēl′yə), *n.* Soviet republic in NW Russia, next to Finland.

Kar·nak (kär′nak), *n.* village in Egypt on the Nile River. The N part of ancient Thebes was located there.

Ka·sa·vu·bu (kas′ə·vü′bü), *n.* Joseph, born 1917, Congo statesman and political leader, President of the Congo since 1960.

Kash·mir (kash·mir′; kash′mir), *n.* district in N India. Also, Cashmere.

Kat·man·du (kät′män·dü′), *n.* capital of Nepal.

Kat·te·gat (kat′ə·gat), *n.* arm of the North Sea between Denmark and Sweden.

ka·ty·did (kā′ti·did), *n. Am.* a large green insect somewhat like a grasshopper. The male makes a shrill noise sounding like "Katy did, Katy didn't."

Katydid (ab. 1¾ in. long from forehead to tips of folded wings)

Kau·ai (kou·ī′), *n.* the fourth largest island of Hawaii.

Kau·nas (kou′näs), *n.* capital of Lithuania.

kau·ri, kau·ry (kou′ri), *n., pl.* –ris, –ries. 1. a tall pine tree that grows in New Zealand. 2. its wood. 3. a resin obtained from it that is used in varnish. [< Maori]

kay·ak (kī′ak), *n.* an Eskimo canoe made of skins stretched over a light frame of wood or bone with an opening in the middle for a person. Also, **kaiak.** [< Eskimo]

Ka·zakh (kə·zäk′), *n.* a Soviet republic in C Asia.

Ka·zan (kä·zän′), *n.* city in E European Russia, near the Volga River.

kc., kilocycle; kilocycles.

K.C., 1. King's Counsel. 2. Knights of Columbus.

ke·a (kā′ə; kē′ə), *n.* a large, greenish parrot of New Zealand, that kills sheep to feed upon their fat. [< Maori]

Keats (kēts), *n.* John, 1795–1821, English poet.

kedge (kej), *v.,* kedged, kedg·ing, *n.* —*v.* move (a ship, etc.) by pulling on a rope attached to an anchor that has been dropped some distance away. —*n.* Also, **kedge anchor.** a small anchor used in kedging a boat, etc.

keel (kēl), *n.* 1. the main timber or steel piece that extends the whole length of the bottom of a ship or boat. 2. *Poetic.* ship. 3. part in an airplane or airship resembling a ship's keel. 4. on an even keel, horizontal. —*v.* 1. turn upside down; upset. 2. **keel over, a.** turn over or upside down; upset. **b.** fall over suddenly. **c.** *Am., Colloq.* faint. [< Scand. *kjölr*]

keel·haul (kēl′hôl′), *v. Naut.* haul (a person) under the keel of a ship for punishment.

keel·son (kel′sən; kēl′–), *n.* beam or line of timbers or iron plates fastened along the top of a ship's keel to strengthen it. Also, **kelson.**

keen[1] (kēn), *adj.* 1. so shaped as to cut well: *a keen blade.* 2. sharp; piercing; cutting: *keen wind, keen hunger, keen wit, keen pain.* 3. strong; vivid. 4. able to do its work quickly and accurately: *a keen mind, a keen sense of smell.* 5. *Colloq.* full of enthusiasm; eager: *keen to go, keen about sailing.* [OE *cēne*] —**keen′ly,** *adv.* —**keen′ness,** *n.* —Syn. 2. acute, penetrating, biting, bitter. 4. acute, penetrating. 5. ardent.

keen[2] (kēn), *n.* a wailing lament for the dead. —*v.* wail; lament. [< Irish *caoine*] —**keen′er,** *n.*

keep (kēp), *v.,* kept, keep·ing, *n.* —*v.* 1. have for a long time or forever: *keep a job.* 2. have and not let go: *keep the interest of the public.* 3. have and let nobody else have: *keep a secret.* 4. have and take care of: *keep chickens.* 5. take care of and protect: *may God keep you.* 6. have; hold: *keep a thing in mind.* 7. have in one's service: *keep servants.* 8. hold back; prevent: *what is keeping her from coming?* 9. hold oneself back; refrain: *she could not keep from laughing.* 10. maintain in good condition; maintain: *keep a garden.* 11. stay in good condition: *the butter kept in the icebox.* 12. continue; remain; stay: *he kept indoors all day.* 13. cause to continue in some stated place, condition, etc.: *keep a light burning.* 14. do the right thing with; celebrate: *keep Christmas.* 15. be faithful to: *keep a promise.* 16. provide for; support: *he is not able to keep himself, much less a family.* 17. have habitually for sale: *that store keeps canned goods.* 18. **keep books,** make a record of all money received or spent. 19. *Am.* of school, be in session. 20. **keep company, a.** together. **b.** *Colloq.* be sweethearts. —*n.* 1. food and a place to sleep: *he works for his keep.* 2. the strongest part of a castle or fort. 3. **for keeps, a.** for the winner to keep his winnings. **b.** *Am., Colloq.* forever. [OE *cēpan* observe] —Syn. *v.* 2. retain. 3. withhold, repress. 4. raise. 5. shield, guard. 8. detain, restrain. 14. observe, commemorate. 15. fulfill. 17. stock. —*n.* 1. maintenance, support. 2. stronghold.

keep·er (kēp′ər), *n.* 1. person or thing that keeps: *a keeper of promises.* 2. guard; watchman. 3. guardian; protector. —**keep′er·less,** *adj.*

keep·ing (kēp′ing), *n.* 1. care; charge; maintenance: *the keeping of the orphaned children was paid for by their uncle.* 2. celebration; observance: *the keeping of Thanksgiving Day is an old American custom.* 3. agreement; harmony: *a good man's actions are in keeping with his promises.* 4. being kept for future use; preservation. —Syn. 1. support. 2. commemoration.

keep·sake (kēp′sāk′), *n.* thing kept in memory of the giver. —Syn. remembrance, souvenir.

keg (keg), *n.* 1. a small barrel, usually holding less than 10 gallons. 2. 100 pounds of nails. [< Scand. *kaggi*]

Kei·jo (kā′jō), *n.* Japanese name of Seoul.

Kel·ler (kel′ər), *n.* Helen, born 1880, American writer. She was deaf, dumb, and blind from babyhood, but was taught to read and speak, and graduated from college.

kelp (kelp), *n.* 1. a large, tough, brown seaweed that contains iodine. 2. ashes of seaweed.

kel·pie, kel·py (kel'pi), *n., pl.* **–pies.** a water spirit, usually in the form of a horse, supposed to drown people or warn them of drowning.

kel·son (kel'sən), *n.* keelson.

Kelt (kelt), *n.* Celt. **—Kelt'ic,** *adj., n.*

kel·ter (kel'tər), *n. Brit. Dial.* kilter.

Ke·mal A·ta·türk (kə·mäl' ä'tä·tyrk'; at'-ə·térk'), Mustafa, 1878–1938, president of Turkey, 1923–1938.

ken (ken), *n., v.,* **kenned** or **kent** (kent), **ken·ning. —n. 1.** range of sight. **2.** range of knowledge: *what happens on Mars is beyond our ken.* [< v.] **—v.** *Scot.* know. [OE *cennan* make declaration < *cann* know, can[1]]

Ken., Kentucky.

Ken·ne·dy (ken'ə·di), *n.* John F., 1917–1963, the 35th president of the United States, 1961–1963.

Kennedy International Airport, a major airport in New York City. Also called Idlewild.

ken·nel (ken'əl), *n., v.,* **–neled, –nel·ing;** *esp. Brit.* **–nelled, –nel·ling. —n. 1.** house for a dog or dogs. **2.** Often, **kennels.** place where dogs are bred. **3.** pack of dogs. **—v. 1.** put or keep in a kennel. **2.** take shelter or lodge in a kennel. [< OF *kenel*, ult. < L *canis* dog]

ke·no (kē'nō), *n. Am.* a gambling game somewhat like lotto.

Kent (kent), *n.* **1.** county in SE England. **2.** an early English kingdom.

Kent·ish (ken'tish), *adj.* of Kent or its people. **—n.** an Anglo-Saxon dialect spoken in the kingdom of Kent.

Ken·tuck·y (kən·tuk'i), *n.* **1.** a Southern State of the United States. *Capital:* Frankfort. *Abbrev.:* Ky. or Ken. **2.** river flowing from E Kentucky into the Ohio River. **—Ken·tuck'i·an,** *adj., n. Am.*

Ken·ya (ken'yə; kēn'yə), *n.* country in E Africa; formerly a British colony and protectorate.

kep·i (kep'i), *n., pl.* **kep·is.** cap with a round flat top, worn by French soldiers. [< F, ult. < G *kappe* cap]

Kep·ler (kep'lər), *n.* Johann, 1571–1630, German astronomer.

kept (kept), *v.* pt. and pp. of **keep.**

ker·a·tin (ker'ə·tin), *n.* a complex protein, the chief constituent of horn, nails, hair, feathers, etc. [< Gk. *keras* horn]

kerb (kérb), *n. Brit.* curb of a pavement.

ker·chief (kér'chif), *n.* **1.** piece of cloth worn over the head or around the neck. **2.** handkerchief. [< OF, < *couvrir* COVER + *chief* head (< L *caput*)]

kerf (kérf), *n.* **1.** cut made by saw, axe, etc. **2.** something cut off. [OE *cyrf* < *ceorfan* carve]

ker·mis, ker·mess (kér'mis), *n.* **1.** fair with games and merrymaking, held in Holland, Belgium, and adjacent regions. **2.** any fair or entertainment, usually to raise money for charity. Also, **kirmess.** [< Du., < *kerk* church + *mis* Mass]

ker·nel (kér'nəl), *n.* **1.** the softer part inside the hard shell of a nut or inside the stone of a fruit. **2.** grain or seed like wheat or corn. **3.** the central or most important part. [OE *cyrnel* < *corn* seed, grain] **—ker'nel·less,** *adj.*

ker·o·sene (ker'ə·sēn; ker'ə·sēn'), *n. Am.* a thin oil produced by distilling petroleum; coal oil. It is used in lamps and stoves. [< Gk. *keros* wax]

kes·trel (kes'trəl), *n.* a small European falcon. [prob. < OF *cresserelle,* ult. < L *crista* crest]

ketch (kech), *n.* **1.** a fore-and-aft-rigged sailing ship with a large mainmast toward the bow and a smaller mast toward the stern. **2.** formerly, a sturdy sailing vessel with two masts. [? < *catch*]

Kestrel (ab. 1 ft. long)

ketch·up (kech'əp), *n.* catchup.

ket·tle (ket'əl), *n.* **1.** a metal container for boiling liquids, cooking fruit, etc. **2.** teakettle. **3.** kettle of fish, awkward state of affairs; mess; muddle. [< L *catillus,* dim. of *catinus* vessel]

ket·tle·drum (ket'əl·drum'), *n.* drum consisting of a hollow brass or copper hemisphere and a parchment top.

key[1] (kē), *n., pl.* **keys,** *adj., v.,* **keyed, key·ing. —n. 1.** instrument that locks and unlocks; thing that turns or opens: *key to a door.* **2.** thing that explains or answers: *key to a puzzle.* **3.** a book, etc., giving the answers to problems. **4.** place that commands or gives control of a sea, a district, etc., because of its position: *Gibraltar is the key to the Mediterranean.* **5.** an important or essential person, thing, etc. **6.** pin, bolt, wedge, or other piece put in a hole or space to hold parts together. **7.** device to turn a bolt or nut, as a key for a roller skate. **8.** one of a set of parts pressed in playing a piano, in typewriting, and in operating other instruments. **9.** scale or system of notes in music related to one another in a special way and based on a particular note: *key of B flat.* **10.** tone of voice; style of thought or expression: *write in a melancholy key.* **—adj.** controlling; very important: *the key industries of a nation.* **—v. 1.** regulate the pitch of: *key a piano up to concert pitch.* **2.** adjust; attune: *key a speech to an audience.* **3.** fasten or adjust with a key. **4.** lock. **5. key up,** raise the courage or nerve of (to the point of doing something): *the coach keyed up the team for the big game.* [OE *cǣg*]

key[2] (kē), *n., pl.* **keys.** a low island; reef. [< Sp. < F *quai* < Celtic]

Key (kē), *n.* Francis Scott, 1779–1843, American lawyer, author of "The Star-Spangled Banner."

key·board (kē'bôrd'; –bōrd'), *n.* set of keys in a piano, organ, typewriter, etc.

keyed (kēd), *adj.* **1.** having keys: *a keyed flute.* **2.** set or pitched in a particular key. **3.** fastened or strengthened with a key.

key·hole (kē'hōl'), *n.* opening in a lock through which a key is inserted to turn the lock.

key·note (kē'nōt'), *n., v.,* **–not·ed, –not·ing. —n. 1.** note on which a scale or system of tones in music is based. **2.** main idea; guiding principle. **—v.** give the keynote speech of.

keynote speech, *Am.* speech, usually at a political gathering, that presents the principal issues in which those present are interested.

key signature, sharps or flats placed after the clef at the beginning of a staff of music to indicate the key.

key·stone (kē'stōn'), *n.* **1.** middle stone at the top of an arch, holding the other stones or pieces in place. **2.** part on which other associated parts depend; essential principle.

KEYSTONE

Key West, **1.** island off the coast of SW Florida. **2.** seaport on this island.

kg., kilogram; kilograms.

khak·i (kak'i; kä'ki), *adj., n., pl.* **khak·is. —adj.** dull yellowish-brown. **—n. 1.** a dull, yellowish brown. **2.** a stout twilled cloth of this color, used for soldiers' uniforms. **3.** uniform or uniforms made of this cloth. [< Pers., orig., dusty < *khāk* dust]

kha·lif (kā'lif; kal'if), *n.* caliph.

khan[1] (kän; kan), *n.* **1.** title of a ruler among Tartar or Mongol tribes, or of the emperor of China during the Middle Ages. **2.** title of dignity in Iran, Afghanistan, India, etc. [< Turk.]

khan[2] (kän; kan), *n.* in Turkey and nearby countries, an inn without furnishings. [< Pers.]

Khar·kov (kär'kof; –kôf), *n.* city in the S Soviet Union.

Khar·toum, Khar·tum (kär·tüm'), *n.* capital of Sudan, on the Nile.

khe·dive (kə·dēv'), *n.* title of the Turkish viceroys who ruled Egypt between 1867 and 1914.

[< Turk. < Pers. *khidīv* \ ruler] **—khe·di′val,** khe·di·vi·al (kə-dē′vi·əl), *adj.*

Khru·shchev (krü′shef, krü′shof), *n.* Nikita S., born 1894, Russian statesman, head of the Soviet government, 1958–1964.

Khu·fu (kü′fü), *n.* Cheops.

Khy·ber Pass (kī′bər), a mountain pass between Pakistan and Afghanistan.

kibe (kīb), *n.* a chapped or ulcerated sore, inflammation, or swelling on the heel caused by exposure to cold.

kib·butz (ki·bùts′), *n., pl.* **kib·butz·im.** Hebrew. a collective farm in Israel.

kib·itz (kib′its), *v. Am., Slang.* look on as an outsider and offer unwanted advice. [< Yiddish < colloq. G *kiebitzen* look on at cards < *kiebitz* an annoying onlooker < *kiebetz* plover]

kib·itz·er (kib′it·sər), *n. Am., Colloq.* **1.** person watching a card game. **2.** person watching a card game who insists on making suggestions to the players. **3.** meddler. [< *kibitz*]

kick (kik), *v.* **1.** strike out with the foot: *that horse kicks when anyone comes near him.* **2.** strike with the foot: *the horse kicked the boy.* **3.** drive, force, or move by kicking: *kick a ball.* **4.** win by a kick: *kick a goal in football.* **5.** spring back when fired: *this shotgun kicks.* **6.** *Colloq.* complain; object; grumble. **7. kick back,** *Colloq.* **a.** recoil suddenly and unexpectedly. **b.** return (a stolen item) to its owner. **c.** return a portion of money received as a fee. **8. kick in,** *Slang.* **a.** die. **b.** *Am.* pay what is due or expected. **9. kick off,** **a.** *Am.* put a football in play with a kick. **b.** *Slang.* die. **10. kick up,** *Slang.* start; cause. **—n.** **1.** act of kicking. **2.** recoil of a gun. **3.** *Am., Slang.* complaint. **4.** *Am., Slang.* thrill, excitement. **—kick′er,** *n.*

kick·back (kik′bak′), *n. Am., Colloq.* **1.** a restoring of stolen goods. **2.** amount or portion returned, esp. as a fee.

kick·off (kik′ôf′; -of′), *n. Am.* kick that puts a football in play.

kid¹ (kid), *n.* **1.** a young goat. **2.** its flesh, used as food. **3.** its skin, used as fur. **4.** leather made from the skin of young goats, used for gloves and shoes. **5.** *Colloq.* child. [< Scand. (Dan.)]

kid² (kid), *v.*, **kid·ded, kid·ding.** *Slang.* **1.** tease playfully; talk jokingly. **2.** humbug; fool. [? < *kid¹* in sense of "treat as a child"] **—kid′der,** *n.*

Kidd (kid), *n.* William, 1645?–1701, British privateer and pirate, known as "Captain Kidd."

kid·nap (kid′nap), *v.,* **-naped,** *esp.* *Brit.* **-napped, -nap·ping.** steal (a child); carry off by force; seize and hold against the will by force or fraud. [< *kid¹* child + *nap* snatch away] **—kid′nap·er,** *esp. Brit.* **kid′nap·per,** *n.*

kid·ney (kid′ni), *n., pl.* **-neys. 1.** one of the pair of organs in the body that separate waste matter and water from the blood and pass them off through the bladder as urine. **2.** kidney or kidneys of an animal, cooked for food. **3.** nature; disposition. **4.** kind; sort. [? < *kiden–,* of uncert. meaning + *ey* egg] **—kid′ney·like′,** *adj.*

kidney bean, **1.** a kidney-shaped bean. **2.** plant that it grows on. **3.** the scarlet runner.

Kiel (kēl), *n.* seaport in NW Germany.

Kiel Canal, ship canal from the North Sea to the Baltic Sea.

Ki·ev (kē′ef), *n.* capital of the Ukraine, in the SW Soviet Union.

Ki·ku·yu (kik′ə·yü; ki·kü′-), *n.* one of the principal Negro tribes in Kenya.

Ki·lau·e·a (kē′lou·ä′ä), *n.* crater on the volcano Mauna Loa, in Hawaii.

Kil·i·man·ja·ro (kil′i·män·jä′rō), *n.* Mount, the highest mountain in Africa.

kill¹ (kil), *v.* **1.** put to death; cause the death of: *the blow killed him.* **2.** cause death: *"Thou shalt not kill."* **3.** put an end to; destroy: *kill odors, kill faith.* **4.** *Am.* cancel (a word, paragraph, item, etc.). **5.** defeat or veto (a legislative bill). **6.** destroy or neutralize the active qualities of: *kill the law by overusing it.* **7.** spoil the effect of: *one color may kill another near it.* **8.** use up (time). **9.** overcome completely. **—n.** **1.** act of killing. **2.** animal killed. [ME *kyllen, cullen;* prob. akin to QUELL] **—Syn.** *v.* **1.** assassinate, slay.

kill² (kil), *n. Am., Dial.* stream. [< Du. *kil*]

Kil·lar·ney (ki-lär′ni), *n.* **1.** town in SW Republic of Ireland. **2.** Lakes of, three beautiful lakes near there.

kill·deer (kil′dir′), **kill·dee** (-dē′), *n., pl.* **-deers** or (*esp. collectively*) **-deer; -dees** or (*esp. collectively*) **-dee.** *Am.* a small wading bird that has a loud, shrill cry, the commonest plover of North America. [imit. of its call]

kill·er (kil′ər), *n.* **1.** person, animal, or thing that kills. **2.** *Am., Slang.* criminal who recklessly or wantonly kills others.

killer whale, dolphin that kills and eats large fish, seals, and even whales.

kill·ing (kil′ing), *adj.* **1.** deadly; destructive; fatal: *a killing frost.* **2.** overpowering; exhausting. **3.** *Colloq.* irresistibly funny. **—n.** *Am., Colloq.* a sudden great financial success.

kill·joy (kil′joi′), *n.* person who spoils other people's fun.

kiln (kil; kiln), *n.* furnace or oven for burning, baking, or drying something. **—v.** burn, bake, or dry in a kiln. [< L *culina* kitchen]

ki·lo (kē′lō; kil′ō), *n., pl.* **ki·los. 1.** kilogram. **2.** kilometer.

kilo–, *prefix.* one thousand, as in *kilogram, kilometer, kilowatt.* [< F]

kil·o·cal·o·rie (kil′ə·kal′ə·ri), *n. Physics.* a large calorie. See calorie.

kil·o·cy·cle (kil′ə·sī′kəl), *n.* **1.** 1000 cycles. **2.** 1000 cycles per second.

kil·o·gram, *esp. Brit.* **kil·o·gramme** (kil′ə·gram), *n.* unit of mass and weight equal to 1000 grams, or 2.2046 pounds avoirdupois.

kil·o·gram-me·ter, *esp. Brit.* **kil·o·gram-me·tre** (kil′ə·gram·mē′tər), *n.* unit used in measuring work, equal to 7.2334 foot-pounds.

kil·o·li·ter, *esp. Brit.* **kil·o·li·tre** (kil′ə·lē′tər), *n.* unit of capacity equal to 1000 liters, or one cubic meter; 264.17 U.S. gallons, or 1.308 cubic yards.

kil·o·me·ter, *esp. Brit.* **kil·o·me·tre** (kil′ə·mē′tər, kə·lom′ə·tər), *n.* distance equal to 1000 meters, or 3280.8 feet. **—kil·o·met·ric** (kil′ə·met′rik), **kil′o·met′ri·cal,** *adj.*

kil·o·ton (kil′ə·tun′), *n.* a measure of atomic power equivalent to the energy released by one thousand tons of high explosive, specifically TNT. [< *kilo–* + *ton* (of explosive energy)]

kil·o·watt (kil′ə·wot′), *n. Elect.* unit of power equal to 1000 watts.

kil·o·watt-hour (kil′ə·wot′our′), *n. Elect.* unit of energy equal to the work done by one kilowatt acting for one hour.

kilt (kilt), *n.* a pleated skirt reaching to the knees, worn by men in the Scottish Highlands. **—v.** *Scot.* tuck up; fasten up. [prob. < Scand. (Dan.)] *kilte* tuck up] **—kilt′like′,** *adj.*

kil·ter (kil′tər), *n. Colloq.* good condition; order: *our radio is out of kilter.* Also, *Brit. Dial.* **kelter.**

Kim·ber·ley (kim′bər·li), *n.* city in the C part of the Republic of South Africa. The world's largest diamond mines are near it.

ki·mo·no (kə·mō′nə), *n., pl.* **-nos. 1.** a loose outer garment held in place by a sash, worn by Japanese men and women. **2.** a woman's loose dressing gown. [< Jap.]

Man wearing a kilt

kin (kin), *n.* **1.** family or relatives; kindred. **2.** family relationship; connection by birth or marriage: *what kin is she to you?* **3.** of kin, related. **—adj.** related. [OE *cynn*] **—kin′less,** *adj.*

-kin, *suffix.* little, as in *lambkin.* [ME]

kind¹ (kīnd), *adj.* **1.** friendly; doing good: *kind words.* **2.** gentle: *be kind to animals.* **3.** showing or characterized by kindness: *a kind master.* [OE *(ge) cynde* natural < *(ge) cynd* kind²] **—Syn. 1.** benevolent, charitable. **2.** tender.

kind² (kīnd), *n.* **1.** class; sort; variety: *many kinds of candy.* **2.** natural group; race: *snakes belong to the serpent kind.* **3. in kind, a.** in goods or produce, not in money. **b.** in something of the same sort. **c.** in characteristic quality: *difference in kind not merely in degree.* **4. kind of,** *Colloq.*

nearly; almost; somewhat; rather. 5. of a kind, a. of the same kind; alike. b. of a poor or mediocre quality: *two boxes and a plank make a table of a kind.* [OE *(ge) cynd*] —Syn. 1. type, description. 2. species, genus. ➤ **kind, sort.** *Kind* and *sort* are both singular nouns in form: *This kind of a person is a menace. This sort of thing shouldn't be allowed.* But *kind* and *sort* are so closely associated with the noun they stand before that they seem like adjectives, and colloquially the demonstrative adjectives used with them usually agree with the principal noun of the construction: *those sort of ideas; that sort of life.*

kin·der·gar·ten (kin′dər·gär′tən), *n.* school that educates children from 3 to 6 years old by games, toys, and pleasant occupations. [< G, < *kinder* children + *garten* garden] — Kindergarten preserves the spelling of its German origin and is pronounced and spelled with *t*.

kin·der·gart·ner, kin·der·gar·ten·er (kin′dər·gärt′nər), *n.* 1. child who goes to kindergarten. 2. teacher in a kindergarten.

kind-heart·ed (kīnd′här′tid), *adj.* having or showing a kind heart; kindly; sympathetic. —**kind′-heart′ed·ly,** *adv.*

kin·dle (kin′dəl), *v.,* —dled, —dling. 1. set on fire; light. 2. catch fire; begin to burn. 3. arouse; stir up: *kindle suspicion.* 4. become stirred up or aroused. 5. light up; brighten: *the boy's face kindled as he told about the circus.* [prob. ult. < Scand. *kynda* kindle] —kin′dler, *n.* —Syn. 1, 2. ignite. 3. excite, awaken, stimulate.

kin·dling (kin′dling), *n.* small pieces of wood for starting a fire.

kind·ly (kīnd′li), *adj.,* —li·er, —li·est, *adv.* —*adj.* 1. kind; friendly: *kindly faces.* 2. pleasant; agreeable: *a kindly shower.* —*adv.* 1. in a kind or friendly way. 2. pleasantly; agreeably: *he does not take kindly to criticism.* 3. cordially; heartily: *thank you kindly.* —**kind′li·ness,** *n.*

kind·ness (kīnd′nis), *n.* 1. quality of being kind; kind nature. 2. kind treatment. 3. a kind act.

kin·dred (kin′drid), *n.* 1. family or relatives. 2. family relationship; connection by birth or marriage. 3. likeness; resemblance. —*adj.* 1. related: *kindred tribes.* 2. like; similar: *we are studying about dew, frost, and kindred facts of nature.* [< *kin*] —Syn. *adj.* 1. cognate, allied.

kine (kīn), *n.pl. Archaic* or *Dial.* cows; cattle.

kin·e·mat·ics (kin′ə·mat′iks), *n.* branch of physics that deals with the characteristics of different kinds of pure motion, that is, without reference to mass or to the causes of the motion. [< Gk. *kinema* motion < *kineein* move] —kin′e·mat′ic, kin′e·mat′i·cal, *adj.*

kin·e·mat·o·graph (kin′ə·mat′ə·graf; -gräf), *n.* cinematograph.

kin·e·scope (kin′ə·skōp), *n.* 1. record on film of a television show or other entertainment that may be rebroadcast. 2. **Kinescope,** *Trademark.* a cathode-ray tube that has a screen at one end on which images are reproduced.

kin·es·thet·ic (kin′əs·thet′ik), *adj.* of or having to do with muscular movement.

ki·net·ic (ki·net′ik), *adj.* 1. of motion. 2. caused by motion. [< Gk., < *kineein* move]

kinetic art, 1. form of abstract art representing or suggesting movement. 2. optical art.

ki·net·ics (ki·net′iks), *n.* branch of physics that deals with the effects of forces in causing or changing the motion of objects.

kin·folk (kin′fōk′), **kin·folks** (-fōks′), *n.pl. Dial.* kinsfolk.

king (king), *n.* 1. the male ruler of a nation; male sovereign, either with absolute or limited power. 2. *Am., Colloq.* man supreme in a certain sphere: *a baseball king.* 3. something best in its class. 4. the chief piece in chess. 5. piece that has moved entirely across the board in checkers. 6. a playing card bearing a picture of a king. [OE *cyning*] —**king′less,** *adj.*

King (king), *n.* **(William Lyon) McKenzie,** 1874–1950, Canadian statesman and prime minister, 1921–1926, 1926–1930, and 1935–1948.

King Arthur, hero in a group of legends about the knights of the Round Table.

king·bird (king′bėrd′), *n. Am.* a quarrelsome bird that catches and eats insects as it flies.

king·bolt (king′bōlt′), *n.* a vertical bolt connecting the body of a wagon, etc., with the front axle, or the body of a railroad car with a set of wheels.

king crab, *Am.* horseshoe crab.

king·dom (king′dəm), *n.* 1. country that is governed by a king or a queen. 2. realm; domain; province: *the mind is the kingdom of thought.* 3. one of the three divisions of the natural world; the animal kingdom, the vegetable kingdom, or the mineral kingdom.

king·fish (king′fish′), *n., pl.* -fish·es or *(esp. collectively)* -fish. 1. *Am.* any of several large food fishes of the Atlantic or Pacific coast. 2. *Colloq.* person having uncontested control in a group or community.

king·fish·er (king′fish′ər), *n.* a bright-colored bird with a large head and a strong beak. The American kingfishers eat fish; some of the European kinds eat insects.

King James Version, English translation of the Bible published in 1611, still widely used by English-speaking Protestants.

king·ly (king′li), *adj.,* -li·er, -li·est, *adv.* —*adj.* 1. of a king or kings; of royal rank. 2. fit for a king: *a kingly crown.* 3. like a king; royal; noble. —*adv.* as a king does. —**king′li·ness,** *n.* —Syn. *adj.* 3. regal, majestic, august.

king·pin (king′pin′), *n.* 1. pin in front or in the center in bowling games. 2. *Am., Colloq.* the most important person or thing. 3. kingbolt.

king post, a vertical post between the apex of a triangular roof truss and a tie beam.

Kings (kingz), *n.pl.* 1. in the Protestant Old Testament, either of two books (I Kings or II Kings) containing the history of the reigns of the Hebrew kings after David. 2. in the Roman Catholic Old Testament, one of four books that include I and II Samuel and I and II Kings.

king's English, correct English.

king's evil, scrofula, a disease that was supposed to be cured by the touch of a king.

king·ship (king′ship), *n.* 1. position, rank, or dignity of a king. 2. rule of a king; government by a king.

king-size (king′sīz′), *adj. Colloq.* large or long for its kind: *a king-size cigarette.*

king snake, *Am.* a large, harmless snake that lives in the southern United States. It eats mice and rats and is supposed to kill other snakes.

king's ransom, very large amount of money.

Kings·ton (king′stən), *n.* capital and chief seaport of Jamaica.

kink (kingk), *n.* 1. a twist or curl in thread, rope, hair, etc. 2. pain or stiffness in the muscles of the neck, back, etc.; crick. 3. *Am., Colloq.* mental twist; queer idea; odd notion; eccentricity; whim. —*v.* form a kink; make kinks in. [prob. < Du., twist]

Kinkajou
(total length ab. 2½ ft.)

kin·ka·jou (king′kə·jü), *n.* a yellowish-brown mammal of Central and South America. It resembles a raccoon, but has a long prehensile tail. [< F *quincajou* < Tupi]

kink·y (kingk′i), *adj.,* kink·i·er, kink·i·est. full of kinks; twisted; curly. —**kink′i·ly,** *adv.* —**kink′i·ness,** *n.*

kins·folk (kinz′fōk′), **kins·folks** (-fōks′), *n.pl.* family; relatives; kin. Also, *Dial.* kinfolks.

Kin·sha·sa (kēn·shä′sä), *n.* capital of the Congo. Formerly, Leopoldville.

kin·ship (kin′ship), *n.* 1. family relationship. 2. relationship. 3. resemblance.

kins·man (kinz′mən), *n., pl.* -men. a male relative.

kins·wom·an (kinz'wûm'ən), *n.*, *pl.* -wom·en. a female relative.

ki·osk (kē·osk'; kē'osk), *n.* a small building with one or more sides open, used as a newsstand, a bandstand, or an opening to a subway. [< F < Turk. *kiushk* pavilion]

Kio·to (kyō'tō), *n.* Kyoto.

kip (kip), *n.* hide of a young or undersized animal.

Kip·ling (kip'ling), *n.* Rudyard, 1865–1936, English writer of stories, novels, and poems.

kip·per (kip'ər), *v.* salt and dry or smoke (herring, salmon, etc.). —*n.* 1. herring, salmon, etc., that has been kippered. 2. male salmon or sea trout during or after the spawning season. [OE *cypera* (def. 2)]

Kir·ghiz (kir·gēz'), *n.*, *pl.* -ghiz, -ghiz·es. 1. a member of a Mongolian people widely scattered over the western part of central Asia. 2. their language.

kirk (kérk), *n. Scot.* church.

kir·mess (kér'mis), *n.* kermis.

kir·tle (kér'təl), *n. Archaic.* 1. skirt or dress. 2. a man's short coat. [OE *cyrtel*, prob. ult. < L *curtus* short] —**kir'tled**, *adj.*

kis·met (kiz'met; kis'-), *n.* fate; destiny. [< Turk. < Ar. *qismat*]

kiss (kis), *v.* 1. touch with the lips as a sign of love, greeting, or respect. 2. touch gently: *a soft wind kissed the treetops.* 3. put, bring, take, etc., by kissing: *kiss away tears.* —*n.* 1. a touch with the lips. 2. a gentle touch. 3. a fancy cake made of white of egg and powdered sugar. 4. a piece of candy of certain sorts. [OE *cyssan*] —**kiss'a·ble**, *adj.* —**kiss'er**, *n.*

kit (kit), *n.* 1. equipment that a soldier carries with him. 2. any person's equipment packed for traveling. 3. outfit of tools: *a shoemaker's kit.* 4. bag, case, knapsack, etc., for carrying such equipment or such an outfit. 5. *Colloq.* lot; set; collection. 6. a small wooden tub or pail. [prob. < MDu. *kitte*]

kitch·en (kich'ən), *n.* 1. room where food is cooked. 2. cooking department. [ult. < L *coquina* < *coquus* a cook]

kitch·en·ette, kitch·en·et (kich'ə·net'), *n. Am.* a very small, compactly arranged kitchen.

kitchen garden, garden where vegetables and fruit for a family are grown. —**kitchen gardener.**

kitchen police, 1. army duty of helping the cook prepare and serve the food, wash the dishes, and clean up the kitchen. 2. soldiers assigned to this duty.

kitch·en·ware (kich'ən·wãr'), *n.* kitchen utensils.

kite (kīt), *n.*, *v.*, **kit·ed, kit·ing.** —*n.* 1. a light wooden frame covered with paper or cloth, flown in the air on the end of a long string. 2. hawk with long pointed wings. 3. any of the very high and light sails of a ship. 4. *Com.* a fictitious certificate, check, contract, etc., not representing any actual transaction, used for raising money or sustaining credit. —*v.* 1. *Colloq.* fly like a kite; move rapidly and easily. 2. *Com.* obtain money or credit through kites. [OE *cȳta*]

kith and kin (kith), 1. friends and relatives. 2. kin. [OE *cȳthth* acquaintance, ult. < *cunnan* know]

kit·ten (kit'ən), *n.* a young cat. [< var. of OF *cheton,* ult. < LL *cattus* cat]

kit·ten·ish (kit'ən·ish), *adj.* 1. like a kitten; playful. 2. coquettish. —**kit'ten·ish·ly,** *adv.* —**kit'ten·ish·ness,** *n.*

kit·ti·wake (kit'i·wāk), *n.* kind of sea gull. [imit. of its call]

kit·ty[1] (kit'i), *n.*, *pl.* -ties. 1. kitten. 2. pet name for a cat. [ult. < *kitten*]

kit·ty[2] (kit'i), *n.*, *pl.* -ties. 1. stakes in a poker game. 2. money pooled by the players in other games for some special purpose.

Kiu·shu (kyü'shü), *n.* Kyushu.

Ki·wa·nis (ki·wä'nis), *n. Am.* an international group of clubs of business and professional men, organized for civic service and higher ideals in business and professional life. —**Ki·wa·ni·an** (ki·wä'ni·ən), *n., adj.*

ki·wi (kē'wi), *n., pl.* -wis. apteryx. [< Maori]

K.K.K., KKK, Ku Klux Klan.

kl., kiloliter.

Klan (klan), *n. Am.* Ku Klux Klan.

Klans·man (klanz'mən), *n., pl.* -men. *Am.* member of the Ku Klux Klan.

klep·to·ma·ni·a (klep'tə·mā'ni·ə), *n.* an insane impulse to steal. [< NL, < Gk. *kleptes* thief + *mania* madness] —**klep'to·ma'ni·ac,** *n.*

klieg light (klēg), *Am.* a bright, hot arc light used in taking motion pictures. [after *Kliegl* brothers, the inventors]

Klon·dike (klon'dīk), *n.* region in NW Canada, along the Yukon River, famous for its gold fields.

km., 1. kilometer; kilometers. 2. kingdom.

knack (nak), *n.* 1. special skill; power to do something easily. 2. trick; habit. —**Syn.** 1. aptitude, facility.

knap·sack (nap'sak'), *n.* a canvas or leather bag for carrying clothes, equipment, etc., on the back. [< LG, < *knappen* eat + *sack* sack]

Knapsack

knave (nāv), *n.* 1. a tricky, dishonest person; rogue; rascal. 2. the jack, a playing card with a picture of a servant or soldier on it. 3. *Archaic.* a male servant; man of humble birth or position. [OE *cnafa* boy] —**Syn.** 1. scoundrel.

knav·er·y (nāv'ər·i), *n., pl.* -er·ies. 1. behavior characteristic of a knave. 2. a tricky, dishonest act. 3. *Obs.* mischief.

knav·ish (nāv'ish), *adj.* tricky; dishonest. —**knav'ish·ly,** *adv.* —**knav'ish·ness,** *n.* —**Syn.** rascally, villainous, fraudulent.

knead (nēd), *v.* 1. mix (dough, clay, etc.) by pressing and squeezing, usually with one's hands: *a baker kneads dough.* 2. press and squeeze with the hands; massage. 3. make or shape by kneading. [OE *cnedan*] —**knead'er,** *n.*

knee (nē), *n., v.,* **kneed, knee·ing.** —*n.* 1. the joint between the thigh and the lower leg. 2. any joint corresponding to the human knee or elbow. 3. anything like a bent knee in shape or position. 4. part of a garment covering the knee. 5. bring to one's knees, force to yield. —*v.* strike or touch with the knee. [OE *cnēo*]

knee·cap (nē'kap'), *n.* a flat, movable bone at the front of the knee; patella; kneepan.

knee-deep (nē'dēp'), *adj.* so deep as to reach the knees.

kneel (nēl), *v.,* **knelt** (nelt) or **kneeled, kneel·ing.** 1. go down on one's knee or knees. 2. remain in this position. [OE *cnēowlian* < *cnēo* knee] —**kneel'er,** *n.*

knee·pad (nē'pad'), *n.* pad worn around the knee for protection.

knee·pan (nē'pan'), *n.* kneecap; the patella.

knell (nel), *n.* 1. sound of a bell rung slowly after a death or at a funeral. 2. warning sign of death, failure, etc. 3. a mournful sound. —*v.* 1. ring slowly. 2. give a warning sign of death, failure, etc. 3. make a mournful sound. [OE *cnyllan*]

knew (nü; nū), *v.* pt. of know.

Knick·er·bock·er (nik'ər·bok'ər), *n.* descendant of the early Dutch settlers of New York.

knick·ers (nik'ərz), or **knick·er·bock·ers** (nik'ər·bok'ərz), *n.pl.* short loose-fitting trousers gathered in at or just below the knee.

knick·knack (nik'nak'), *n.* a pleasing trifle; ornament; trinket. Also, **nicknack.**

knife (nīf), *n., pl.* **knives,** *v.,* **knifed, knif·ing.** —*n.* 1. a cutting tool with a sharp-edged blade and handle. 2. a cutting blade in a tool or machine: *the knives of a lawn mower.* 3. under the knife, *Colloq.* undergoing a surgical operation. —*v.* 1. cut or stab with a knife. 2. *Am., Slang.* try to defeat in an underhand way. [OE *cnif*] —**knife'less,** *adj.* —**knife'like',** *adj.*

knight (nīt), *n.* 1. in the Middle Ages, a man raised to an honorable military rank and pledged to do good deeds. After serving as a page and squire, a man was made a knight by the king or a lord. 2. in modern times, a man raised to an honorable rank because of personal achievement or because he has won distinction in some way. A knight has the title *Sir* before his name. 3. man devoted to the service or protection of a lady. 4. *Am.* member of the Knights of Columbus, the Knights Templar, etc. 5. piece in the game of chess. —*v.* raise to the rank of knight. [OE *cniht* boy] —**knight′less,** *adj.*

knight-er·rant (nīt′er′ənt), *n., pl.* **knights-er·rant.** knight traveling in search of adventure.

knight-er·rant·ry (nīt′er′ən-tri), *n., pl.* **knight-er·rant·ries.** 1. conduct or action characteristic of a knight-errant. 2. quixotic conduct or action.

knight·hood (nīt′hůd), *n.* 1. rank or dignity of a knight. 2. profession or occupation of a knight. 3. character or qualities of a knight. 4. knights as a group or class.

knight·ly (nīt′li), *adj.* of a knight; brave; generous; courteous; chivalrous. —*adv.* as a knight should do; bravely; generously; courteously. —**knight′li·ness,** *n.*

Knights of Columbus, a fraternal society of Roman Catholic men, founded in 1882.

Knight Templar, *pl.* **Knights Templars** *for* 1; **Knights Templar** *for* 2. 1. Templar (def. 1). 2. member of an order of Masons in the United States.

knit (nit), *v.,* **knit·ted** or **knit, knit·ting.** 1. make (cloth or article of clothing) by looping yarn or thread together with long needles: *mother is knitting a sweater.* 2. make an article or fabric by looping yarn or thread together: *she knits all day.* 3. form into cloth by looping stitches, not by weaving: *jersey is cloth knitted by machine.* 4. join closely and firmly together. 5. grow together; be joined closely and firmly: *a broken bone knits.* 6. draw (the brows) together in wrinkles. [OE *cnyttan < cnotta* knot] —**knit′ter,** *n.*

knit·ting (nit′ing), *n.* knitted work.

knitting needle, one of a pair of long needles used in knitting.

knives (nīvz), *n. pl.* of knife.

knob (nob), *n.* 1. a rounded lump. 2. handle of a door, drawer, etc. 3. a rounded hill or mountain. [cf. MLG *knobbe*] —**knobbed,** *adj.* —**knob′like′,** *adj.* —Syn. 1. knot, protuberance.

knob·by (nob′i), *adj.,* **-bi·er, -bi·est.** 1. covered with knobs. 2. rounded like a knob. —**knob′bi·ness,** *n.*

knock (nok), *v.* 1. hit: *he knocked him on the head.* 2. hit each other: *his knees knocked with fright.* 3. hit and cause to fall. 4. hit with a noise: *knock on a door.* 5. make a noise, esp. a rattling or pounding noise: *the engine is knocking.* 6. *Am., Slang.* criticise; find fault. 7. **knock about,** *Colloq.* wander from place to place. 8. **knock down, a.** sell (an article) to the highest bidder at an auction. **b.** take apart. **c.** strike down. 9. **knock off,** *Colloq.* **a.** take off; deduct. **b.** stop work. **c.** make quickly; do quickly. 10. **knock out,** hit so hard as to make helpless or unconscious. 11. **knock together,** make or put together hastily. —*n.* 1. hit. 2. hit with a noise. 3. act of knocking. 4. sound of knocking: *she did not hear the knock at the door.* 5. sound caused by loose parts: *a knock in the engine.* [OE *cnocian*] —Syn. *v.* 1. strike, rap, beat. 4. rap.

knock·a·bout (nok′ə-bout′), *n. Am.* a small, easily handled sailboat having one mast, a mainsail, and a jib, but no bowsprit. —*adj.* 1. suitable for rough use. 2. noisy; boisterous.

knock·er (nok′ər), *n.* 1. person or thing that knocks. 2. knob, ring, etc., fastened on a door for use in knocking.

knock-kneed (nok′nēd′), *adj.* having legs bent inward at the knees.

knock·out (nok′out′), *n.* 1. act of knocking out. 2. condition of being knocked out. 3. blow that knocks out. 4. *Am., Slang.* a very attractive person; overwhelming or striking thing. —*adj. Slang.* that knocks out: *a knockout blow.*

knoll (nōl), *n.* a small rounded hill; mound. [OE *cnoll*]

Knos·sos (nos′əs), *n.* the ancient capital of Crete. Also, **Cnossus.**

knot (not), *n., v.,* **knot·ted, knot·ting.** —*n.* 1. a fastening made by tying or twining together pieces of rope, cord, string, etc. 2. bow of ribbon, etc., worn as an ornament. 3. group; cluster: *a knot of people.* 4. a hard mass of wood formed where a branch grows out from a tree, which shows as a roundish, cross-grained piece in a board. 5. a hard lump: *a knot sometimes forms in a tired muscle.* 6. joint where leaves grow out on the stem of a plant. 7. *Naut.* **a.** unit of speed used on ships; one nautical mile per hour: *the ship averaged 12 knots.* **b.** nautical mile, 6080.27 feet. 8. difficulty; problem. 9. thing that unites closely or intricately. —*v.* 1. tie or twine together in a knot. 2. tangle in knots. 3. form (a fringe) by making knots. 4. form or knit knots in making fringes. 5. form into a hard lump. 6. unite closely or intricately. [OE *cnotta*] —**knot′less,** *adj.* —**knot′ted,** *adj.* —Syn. *n.* 3. company. 5. knob. 8. puzzle, perplexity. 9. bond, tie, link. —*v.* 2. snarl. 6. bind.

Knots: A, overhand; B, figure of eight; C, square; D, slip.

knot·hole (not′hōl′), *n.* hole in a board where a knot has fallen out.

knot·ty (not′i), *adj.,* **-ti·er, -ti·est.** 1. full of knots: *knotty wood.* 2. difficult; puzzling: *a knotty problem.* —**knot′ti·ness,** *n.*

knout (nout), *n.* whip formerly used in Russia to inflict punishment. —*v.* flog with a knout. [< F < Russ. *knut*]

know (nō), *v.,* **knew, known, know·ing,** *n.* —*v.* 1. be sure of; have true information about: *he knows the facts of the case.* 2. have firmly in the mind or memory: *know a lesson.* 3. be aware of; have seen or heard; have information about: *know a person's name.* 4. be sure; have information: *he does not have to guess, he knows.* 5. be acquainted with; be familiar with: *I know her.* 6. have an understanding of; have experience with; be skilled in: *he knows that subject.* 7. recognize; identify: *you would hardly know him nowadays.* 8. be able to tell apart from others; distinguish: *you will know his house by the red roof.* —*n.* **in the know,** *Colloq.* having inside information. [OE *cnāwan*] —**know′er,** *n.*

know·a·ble (nō′ə-bəl), *adj.* capable of being known. —**know′a·ble·ness,** *n.*

know-how (nō′hou′), *n. Am., Colloq.* ability to do something.

know·ing (nō′ing), *adj.* 1. having knowledge; well-informed. 2. clever; shrewd. 3. suggesting shrewd or secret understanding of matters: *a knowing look.* —**know′ing·ly,** *adv.* —**know′ing·ness,** *n.* —Syn. 2. sharp, cunning.

knowl·edge (nol′ij), *n.* 1. what one knows: *his knowledge of the subject is limited.* 2. all that is known or can be learned. 3. fact of knowing: *the knowledge of our victory caused great joy.* 4. act of knowing. 5. practical understanding. 6. a branch of learning: *all the knowledges and skills.*

knowl·edge·a·ble (nol′ij·ə-bəl), *adj. Colloq.* intelligent.

know-noth·ing (nō′nuth′ing), *n.* 1. an ignorant person. 2. **Know-Nothing,** *Am.* **a.** American political party prominent from 1853 to 1856. It aimed to keep control of the government in the hands of native-born citizens. **b.** member of this party.

Knox (noks), *n.* **John,** 1505?–1572, Scottish preacher and religious reformer.

Knox·ville (noks′vil), *n.* city in E Tennessee, on the Tennessee River.

knuck·le (nuk′əl), *n., v.,* **-led, -ling.** —*n.* 1. finger joint; joint between a finger and the rest of the hand. 2. knee or hock joint of an animal used as food: *boiled pigs′ knuckles.* 3. knuckles, pieces of metal worn over the knuckles as a weapon. —*v.* 1. put the knuckles on the ground in playing marbles. 2. **knuckle down, a.** submit; yield. **b.** *Am., Colloq.* apply oneself earnestly; work hard. 3. **knuckle under,** submit; yield. [cf. Du. *kneukel* < *knok* bone]

knurl (nérl), *n.* 1. knot; knob. 2. a small ridge, as on the edge of a coin or round nut. [? < *knur* knot. Cf. MDu. *knorre.*] —**knurled** (nérld), *adj.*

knurl·y (nér′li), *adj.*, **knurl·i·er, knurl·i·est.** gnarled.

k.o., K.O., knockout.

ko·a·la (kō·ä′lə), *n.* a gray, furry animal of Australia that carries its young in a pouch. [< Australian lang.]

Koala
(2 ft. long)

Ko·be (kō′bē; -bā), *n.* seaport in W Japan.

ko·dak (kō′dak), *n., v.,* **–daked, –dak·ing.** *Am.* —*n.* Kodak, *Trademark.* a small camera with rolls of film on which photographs are taken, made by the Eastman Kodak Company. —*v.* take photographs with a kodak. —**ko′dak·er,** *n.*

Ko·di·ak (kō′di·ak), *n.* island in the N Pacific near Alaska.

Koh·i·noor (kō′ə·nûr), *n.* a very large and famous diamond that is now one of the British crown jewels.

kohl·ra·bi (kōl′rä′bi), *n., pl.* **–bies.** vegetable that looks somewhat like a turnip, but is a kind of cabbage. [< G < Ital. *cavoli rape*, ult. < L *caulis* cabbage + *rapa* turnip]

ko·la (kō′lə), *n.* 1. kola nut. 2. stimulant or tonic made from kola nuts. Also, **cola.** [< African lang.]

kola nut, a bitter brownish nut of a tropical tree. It contains about 3 per cent of caffein.

ko·lin·sky (kə·lin′ski), *n.* 1. mink that lives in Asia. 2. its tawny fur. [< Russ. *kolinski,* adj., from *Kola,* section of Russia]

Kö·nigs·berg (kœ′niks·berk), *n.* Kaliningrad.

koo·doo (kü′dü), *n., pl.* **–doos.** kudu.

ko·peck, ko·pek (kō′pek), *n.* a Russian copper or bronze coin. 100 kopeks = 1 ruble. Also, **copek.** [< Russ. *kopeika*]

Ko·ran (kō·rän′; -ran′; kō–), *n.* the sacred book of the Mohemmedans. It consists of reports of revelations to the prophet Mohammed. [< Ar. *qur′ān* a reading < *qara′a* to read]

Ko·re·a (kō·rē′ə; kō–), *n.* a country on a peninsula in E Asia. After World War II it was divided into two republics, North Korea and South Korea. In 1950 war broke out between North and South Korea; a cease-fire agreement was signed in 1953. Also, *Japanese* **Chosen.** —**Ko·re′an,** *adj., n.*

Kos·ci·us·ko (kos′i·us′kō), *n.* Thaddeus, 1746–1817, Polish general who served in the American army during the American Revolution.

ko·sher (kō′shər), *adj.* 1. right or clean according to Jewish ritualistic law. 2. *Am., Slang.* all right; fine; legitimate. —*v.* prepare (food) according to the Jewish law. —*n. Colloq.* food thus prepared. [< Heb. *kāshēr* proper]

Ko·sy·gin (kō·sē′gin), *n.* Aleksei N., Soviet premier since October, 1964.

kou·mis, kou·miss, kou·myss (kü′mis), *n.* kumiss.

kow·tow (kou′tou′), *n.* **ko·tow** (kō′–), *v.* 1. kneel and touch the ground with the forehead to show deep respect, submission, or worship. 2. show slavish respect or obedience. —*n.* act of kowtowing. [< Chinese *k′o-t′ou*, lit., knock (the) head] —**kow′tow′er, ko′tow′er,** *n.*

K.P., kitchen police.

Kr, *Chem.* krypton.

kraal (kräl), *n.* 1. village of South African natives, protected by a fence. 2. pen for cattle or sheep in South Africa. [< Afrikaans < Pg. *curral* corral]

K-ra·tion (kā′rash′ən; –rā′shən), *n. U.S. Army.* one of the emergency field rations used when other rations are not available.

Kreis·ler (krīs′lər), *n.* Fritz, 1875–1962, Austrian violinist and composer, in the U.S.

Krem·lin (krem′lin), *n.* citadel of Moscow.

The chief offices of the Soviet government are in the Kremlin. [< F < Russ. *kreml* < Tatar]

Kril·i·um (kril′i·əm), *n. Trademark.* a soil conditioner obtainable in liquid, powder, or flake form, made by Monsanto Chemical Company. [< (sodium salt of hydrolyzed *polya*) *cryl-(onitrile)*]

krim·mer (krim′ər), *n.* a gray fur resembling Persian lamb, made from lambskins from the Crimea. [< G, < *Krim* Crimea]

kris (krēs), *n.* creese.

Krish·na (krish′nə), *n.* one of the most important Hindu gods, one of the incarnations of Vishnu.

Kriss Krin·gle (kris′ kring′gəl), *Am.* Santa Claus. [< G *Christkindl, –del* Christ child, Christmas gift]

kro·na (krō′nə), *n., pl.* **–nor** (–nôr). a Swedish or Icelandic silver coin. [< Swed., lit., crown]

kro·ne¹ (krō′ne), *n., pl.* **–ner** (–ner). a Danish or Norwegian silver coin. [< Dan., Norw., crown]

kro·ne² (krō′nə), *n., pl.* **–nen** (–nən). 1. former German gold coin, worth about $2.38. 2. former Austrian silver coin, worth about 20 cents. [< G, crown]

Kron·stadt (krōn′shtät), *n.* fortress and naval station in NW Soviet Union, near Leningrad.

Krupp (krup; *Ger.* krūp), *n.* Alfred, 1812–1887, German manufacturer of artillery, munitions, etc.

kryp·ton (krip′ton), *n. Chem.* a rare inert gas, Kr, one of the chemical elements. [< NL < Gk., neut. adj., hidden]

Kt., 1. Also, **kt.** karat. 2. Knight.

Kua·la Lum·pur (kwä′lə lŭm′pûr′), capital of Malaysia.

Ku·blai Khan (kü′blī kän′), 1216?–1294, Mongol emperor from 1259 to 1294. He was the first of the Mongol rulers of China.

ku·dos (kü′dos; kü′–), *n. Colloq.* glory; fame. [< Gk. *kydos*]

ku·du (kü′dü), *n.* a large, grayish-brown African antelope with white stripes. Also, **koodoo.**

Ku Klux Klan (kü′ kluks′ klan′; kü′), or **Ku-Klux, Ku·klux,** *n. Am.* 1. a secret society of white people in the southern United States formed after the Civil War to regain and maintain their control. 2. a secret society founded in 1915, opposed to Negroes, Jews, Catholics, and foreigners.

ku·lak (kü·läk′), *n.* a Russian farmer who had poorer peasants working for him or who opposed the Soviet government. [< Russ., lit., fist]

ku·miss (kü′mis), *n.* fermented mare's or camel's milk used as a drink by Asiatic nomads. Also, **koumis, koumiss,** or **koumyss.** [< Russ. < Tatar *kumiz*]

küm·mel (kim′əl), *n.* liqueur flavored with caraway seeds, anise, etc. [< G]

kum·quat (kum′kwot), *n.* 1. a yellow fruit somewhat like a small orange. It has a sour pulp and a sweet rind, and is used in preserves and candy. 2. tree that it grows on. Also, **cumquat.** [< Chinese (Cantonese dial.)]

Kun·ming (kün′ming′), *n.* city in S China.

Kuo·min·tang (kwō′min·tang′; –täng′), *n.* a Chinese nationalist party organized by Sun Yat-sen.

Kurd (kérd; kûrd), *n.* member of a nomadic and warlike Mohammedan people living chiefly in Kurdistan. —**Kurd′ish,** *adj.*

Kur·di·stan (kér′də·stan; kûr′di·stän′), *n.* an extensive plateau and mountainous region in SW Asia now divided between Turkey, Iran, and Iraq.

Ku·rile Islands, Ku·ril Islands (kûr′il; kü·rēl′), chain of 31 small islands N of Japan, returned to Russia after World War II.

Ku·wait (kü·wit′), *n.* 1. a country in NE Arabia. 2. its capital.

kw., kilowatt.

K.W.H., kw-hr., kilowatt-hour.

Ky., Kentucky.

Kyo·to (kyō′tō), *n.* city in C Japan. It was formerly the capital. Also, **Kioto.**

Kyu·shu (kyü′shü), *n.* a large island at the SW end of the Japanese empire. Also, **Kiushu.**

L

Ľ¹, 1 (el), *n.*, *pl.* **Ľ's; l's.** 1. the 12th letter of the alphabet. 2. Roman numeral for 50.

Ľ² (el), *n.*, *pl.* **Ľ's.** thing shaped like an L; extension to a building at right angles with the main part.

L, 1. Latin. 2. *Physics.* length. 3. Libra.

Ľ., 1. Lake. 2. Late. 3. Latin. 4. Liberal.

l., 1. book. [< L *liber*] 2. latitude. 3. law. 4. leaf. 5. league. 6. left. 7. length. 8. *pl.* **ll.** line. 9. liter; liters. 10. pound; pounds. [< L *libra; libras*]

la¹ (lä), *n.* the sixth tone of the musical scale. [see GAMUT]

la² (lä; lô), *interj.* exclamation of surprise.

La, *Chem.* lanthanum.

La., Louisiana.

lab (lab), *n. Colloq.* laboratory.

Lab., 1. Laborite. 2. Labrador.

la·bel (lā′bəl), *n.*, *v.*, **-beled, -bel·ing;** *esp. Brit.* **-belled, -bel·ling.** —*n.* 1. slip of paper or other material attached to anything and marked to show what or whose it is, or where it is to go. 2. a short phrase used to describe some person, thing, or idea. —*v.* 1. put or write a label on: *the bottle is labeled poison.* 2. put in a class; call; name: *label a man a liar.* [< OF, ? < Gmc.] —**la′bel·er,** *esp. Brit.* **la′bel·ler,** *n.*

la·bi·al (lā′bi·əl), *adj.* 1. of the lips. 2. *Phonet.* made by closing, nearly closing, or rounding the lips. —*n. Phonet.* sound made in this way. *B, p, m,* and *w* are labials. [< Med.L, < L *labium* lip] —**la′bi·al·ly,** *adv.*

la·bi·ate (lā′bi·āt; -it), *adj.* having one or more liplike parts.

la·bi·o·den·tal (lā′bi·ō·den′təl), *Phonet.* —*adj.* made with the lower lip and upper teeth; made with the lips and teeth. —*n.* sound made in this way. *F* and *v* are labiodentals.

Labiate corolla

la·bi·um (lā′bi·əm), *n.*, *pl.* **-bi·a** (-bi·ə). *Anat., Zool., Bot.* lip or liplike part. [< L]

la·bor, *esp. Brit.* **la·bour** (lā′bər), *n.* 1. work; toil. 2. piece of work; task. 3. work done by skilled and unskilled workers who are not clerks, managers, professional workers, or owners. 4. skilled and unskilled workers as a group. 5. childbirth. —*v.* 1. work; toil. 2. do work; work hard. 3. elaborate with effort or in detail: *the speaker labored the point.* 4. move slowly and heavily: *the ship labored in the high waves.* 5. be burdened, troubled, or distressed: *labor under a mistake.* 6. be in childbirth. [< OF < L] —**la′bor·ing·ly,** *esp. Brit.* **la′bour·ing·ly,** *adv.*

lab·o·ra·to·ry (lab′rə·tô′ri; -tō′-; lab′ə·rə-; *Brit.* lə·bor′ə·tə·ri), *n.*, *pl.* **-ries.** 1. place where scientific work is done; room or building fitted with apparatus for conducting scientific investigations, experiments, tests, etc.: *a chemical laboratory.* 2. place fitted up for manufacturing chemicals, medicines, explosives, etc. 3. workshop. —**lab′o·ra·to′ri·al,** *adj.*

Labor Day, *Am.* the first Monday in September, a legal holiday in most States of the United States in honor of labor and laborers.

la·bored, *esp. Brit.* **la·boured** (lā′bərd), *adj.* done with effort; forced; not easy or natural: *labored politeness.*

la·bor·er, *esp. Brit.* **la·bour·er** (lā′bər·ər), *n.* 1. worker. 2. person who does work requiring strength rather than skill or training.

la·bo·ri·ous (lə·bô′ri·əs; -bō′-), *adj.* 1. requiring much work; requiring hard work: *climbing a mountain is laborious.* 2. hard-working; industrious: *bees are laborious insects.* 3. labored. —**la·bo′ri·ous·ly,** *adv.* —**la·bo′ri·ous·ness,** *n.*

Labor Party, a political party organized to protect and promote the interests of workers.

la·bor-sav·ing (lā′bər·sāv′ing), *adj.* that

takes the place of or lessens labor: *a labor-saving device.*

labor turnover, 1. number of new workers hired by an employer in place of workers who have quit. 2. proportion of new workers hired (per year, month, etc.) in place of others, to the average number of workers an employer has working for him.

labor union, *Am.* association of workers to protect and promote their interests, and for dealing collectively with employers.

Labour Party, British political party that claims esp. to protect and advance the interests of working people. It was founded by the trade unions. —**La′bour·ite,** *n.*

Lab·ra·dor (lab′rə·dôr), *n.* 1. peninsula in NE North America, between Hudson Bay and the Atlantic. 2. the eastern part of this peninsula, belonging to Newfoundland.

la·bur·num (lə·bėr′nəm), *n.* a small tree or shrub with hanging clusters of yellow flowers. [< L]

lab·y·rinth (lab′ə·rinth), *n.* 1. place through which it is hard to find one's way; maze. 2. a confusing, complicated arrangement. 3. a confusing, complicated state of affairs. 4. Labyrinth, *Gk. Myth.* maze built by Daedalus for King Minos of Crete. 5. *Anat.* the internal ear. [< L < Gk. *labyrinthos*]

lab·y·rin·thine (lab′ə·rin′thin; -thēn), **lab·y·rin·thi·an** (-thi·ən), *adj.* 1. of a labyrinth; forming a labyrinth. 2. intricate; confusing.

lac¹ (lak), *n.* a resinous substance deposited on trees in S Asia by certain insects, used in making sealing wax, varnish, etc. [< Hind. < Skt. *lākshā*]

lac² (lak), *n.* in India: a. 100,000. b. any large number; great amount. Also, **lakh.** [< Hind. < Skt. *laksha* 100,000]

lace (lās), *n.*, *v.*, **laced, lac·ing.** —*n.* 1. an open weaving or net of fine thread in an ornamental pattern. 2. cord, string, leather strip, etc., for pulling or holding together. 3. gold or silver braid used for trimming: *some uniforms have lace on them.* —*v.* 1. trim with lace. 2. put laces through; pull or hold together with a lace or laces. 3. be laced: *these shoes lace easily.* 4. adorn or trim with narrow braid: *his uniform was laced with gold.* 5. interlace; intertwine. 6. mark with streaks; streak: *a white petunia laced with purple.* 7. *Colloq.* lash; beat; thrash. 8. mix (coffee, etc.) with liquor. 9. squeeze in the waist by a tight corset. [< OF *laz* < L *laqueus* noose. Doublet of LASSO.] —**lace′like′,** *adj.*

lac·er·ate (las′ər·āt), *v.*, **-at·ed, -at·ing,** *adj.* —*v.* 1. tear roughly; mangle. 2. wound; hurt (the feelings, etc.). —*adj.* 1. torn; jagged. 2. deeply and irregularly indented: *lacerate leaves.* [< L, < *lacer* mangled]

lac·er·a·tion (las′ər·ā′shən), *n.* 1. a lacerating. 2. rough tear; mangled place; wound.

lace·wing (lās′wing′), *n.* insect that has four lacelike wings.

lace·work (lās′wèrk′), *n.* 1. lace. 2. openwork like lace.

lach·es (lach′iz), *n. Law.* failure to do a thing at the right time; inexcusable negligence. [< AF < OF, ult. < L *laxus* loose]

lach·ry·mal (lak′rə·məl), *adj.* 1. of tears; producing tears. 2. *Anat.* noting, pertaining to, or situated near the lachrymals. —*n.* lachrymals, glands that produce tears. Also, **lacrimal, lacry-mal.** [< Med.L, < L *lacrima* tear]

lach·ry·ma·to·ry (lak′rə·mə·tô′ri; -tō′-), *adj.*, *n.*, *pl.* **-ries.** —*adj.* 1. of tears; producing tears. 2. for tears. —*n.* a small vase with a narrow neck.

lach·ry·mose (lak′rə·mōs), *adj.* tearful; mournful. [< L, < *lacrima* tear] —**lach′ry-mose·ly,** *adv.*

lac·ing (lās'ing), *n.* 1. cord, string, etc., for pulling or holding something together. 2. gold or silver braid used for trimming. 3. lashing; beating; thrashing. 4. act of one that laces.

lack (lak), *v.* 1. have not enough; need: *a desert lacks water.* 2. be without; have no: *a homeless person lacks a home.* 3. be absent or missing, as something needed or desirable. 4. supply the lack, supply what is needed. —*n.* 1. shortage; not having enough: *lack of rest made her tired.* 2. fact or condition of being without: *lack of a fire made him cold.* 3. thing needed: *if you are cold, your lack is heat.* [cf. MDu. *lac*, MLG *lak*] —Syn. *n.* 1. want, deficiency. 2. absence.

lack·a·dai·si·cal (lak'ə·dā'zə·kəl), *adj.* languid; listless; dreamy; weakly sentimental. —**lack'a·dai'si·cal·ly**, *adv.* —**lack'a·dai'si·cal·ness**, *n.*

lack·er (lak'ər), *n., v.* lacquer. —**lack'er·er**, *n.*

lack·ey (lak'i), *n., pl.* **-eys**, *v.,* **-eyed, -ey·ing.** —*n.* 1. a male servant; footman. 2. a slavish follower. —*v.* 1. wait on. 2. be slavish to. Also, **lacquey.** [< F < Sp. *lacayo* footsoldier]

lack·ing (lak'ing), *adj.* 1. not having enough; deficient. 2. absent; not here. —*prep.* without; not having: *lacking anything better we must use what we have.*

lack·lus·ter, *esp. Brit.* **lack·lus·tre** (lak'·lus'tər), *adj.* not shining or bright; dull. —*n.* a lack of luster.

la·con·ic (lə·kon'ik), **la·con·i·cal** (-ə·kəl), *adj.* using few words; brief in speech or expression; concise. [< L < Gk. *lakonikos* Spartan; Spartans were noted for pithy speech] —**la·con'i·cal·ly**, *adv.*

lac·quer (lak'ər), *n.* 1. varnish consisting of shellac dissolved in alcohol, used for coating brass. 2. varnish made from the resin of a sumac tree of SE Asia. 3. articles coated with such varnish. —*v.* coat with lacquer. Also, **lacker.** [< F < Pg. *laca* lac[1]] —**lac'quer·er**, *n.*

lac·quey (lak'i), *n., pl.* **-queys**, *v.,* **-queyed, -quey·ing.** lackey.

lac·ri·mal, lac·ry·mal (lak'rə·məl), *adj., n.* lachrymal.

la·crosse (lə·krôs'; -kros'), *n. Am.* game played with a ball and long-handled rackets by two teams of 10 players each. The players try to send the ball through a goal. [< F]

lac·tate (lak'tāt), *n., v.,* **-tat·ed, -tat·ing.** —*n. Chem.* any salt of lactic acid. —*v.* produce milk.

lac·ta·tion (lak·tā'shən), *n.* 1. act of suckling a baby. 2. time during which a mother gives milk. 3. secretion or formation of milk.

lac·te·al (lak'ti·əl), *adj.* 1. of or like milk; milky. 2. *Anat.* carrying chyle, a milky liquid formed from digested food. —*n. Anat.* any of the tiny vessels that carry this liquid to be mixed with the blood. [< L, < *lac* milk] —**lac'te·al·ly**, *adv.*

lac·tic (lak'tik), *adj.* of or from milk. [< L *lac* milk]

lactic acid, *Chem.* a colorless, odorless acid, $C_3H_6O_3$, formed in sour milk.

lac·to·fla·vin (lak'tō·flā'vin), *n.* riboflavin.

lac·tom·e·ter (lak·tom'ə·tər), *n.* instrument for testing the purity or richness of milk.

lac·tose (lak'tōs), *n. Chem.* a crystalline sugar, $C_{12}H_{22}O_{11}$, present in milk; milk sugar.

la·cu·na (lə·kū'nə), *n., pl.* **-nae** (-nē), **-nas.** 1. an empty space; gap; blank: *lacunae in an old manuscript.* 2. *Anat.* a tiny cavity in bones or tissues. [< L, hole]

lac·y (lās'i), *adj.,* **lac·i·er, lac·i·est.** 1. of lace. 2. like lace; having an open pattern. —**lac'i·ly**, *adv.* —**lac'i·ness**, *n.*

lad (lad), *n.* 1. youth. 2. *Colloq.* man. [ME *ladde*]

lad·der (lad'ər), *n.* 1. set of rungs or steps fastened to two long sidepieces, for use in climbing. 2. means of climbing higher. [OE *hlǣder*]

lad·die (lad'i), *n. Esp. Scot.* 1. young boy. 2. man.

lade (lād), *v.,* **lad·ed, lad·en** or **lad·ed, lad·ing.** 1. put a burden on; load. 2. dip; scoop; ladle. 3. take on cargo. [OE *hladan*]

lad·en (lād'ən), *adj.* loaded; burdened. —*v.* pp. of lade.

lad·ing (lād'ing), *n.* 1. act of loading. 2. load.

la·dle (lā'dəl), *n., v.,* **-dled, -dling.** —*n.* a large cup-shaped spoon with a long handle, for dipping out liquids. —*v.* 1. dip out. 2. carry in a ladle. [OE *hlædel* < *hladan* lade] —**la'dle·ful'**, *n.* —**la'dler**, *n.*

Ladle

La·do·ga (lä'dō·gə), *n.* Lake, lake in NW Soviet Union, the largest lake in Europe.

La·drone Islands (lə·drōn'), or **La·drones** (lə·drōnz'), *n.pl.* Marianas Islands.

la·dy (lā'di), *n., pl.* **-dies.** 1. woman who has the rights or authority of a lord; mistress of a household. 2. noblewoman; woman who has the title of Lady. 3. a well-bred woman; woman of high social position. 4. Lady, title given to women of certain ranks in the British Empire. 5. any woman. 6. woman whom a man loves or is devoted to. 7. wife. [OE *hlǣfdīge*, lit., loafkneader] ➤ See man for usage note.

la·dy·bug (lā'di·bug'), **la·dy·bird** (-bėrd'), or **lady beetle**, *n.* a small round beetle with black spots, that eats other insects.

Lady Day, March 25, the day when the angel told Mary that she would be the mother of Jesus; Annunciation Day.

la·dy·fin·ger (lā'di·fing'gər), *n. Am.* a small sponge cake shaped somewhat like a finger.

lady in waiting, lady who is an attendant of a queen or princess.

la·dy·kill·er (lā'di·kil'ər), *n. Slang.* man supposed to be dangerously fascinating to women.

la·dy·like (lā'di·līk'), *adj.* 1. like a lady. 2. suitable for a lady. —**la'dy·like'ness**, *n.* —Syn. 1. refined, well-bred.

la·dy·love (lā'di·luv'), *n.* woman who is loved by a man; sweetheart.

la·dy·ship (lā'di·ship), *n.* 1. rank or position of a lady. 2. Often, Ladyship. *Brit.* title used by or to an inferior in speaking to or of a woman having the rank of Lady: *your Ladyship, her Ladyship.*

la·dy's-slip·per (lā'diz·slip'ər), **la·dy's-slip·per** (lā'di-), *n.* wild orchid whose flower looks somewhat like a slipper.

La·fa·yette (laf'i·et'; lä'fi-), *n.* Marquis de, 1757–1834, French general and statesman who helped the Americans during the American Revolution.

Lady's-slipper

La Fol·lette (lə fol'it), Robert Marion, 1855–1925, American statesman and political leader.

La Fon·taine (lä fôn·ten'), Jean de, 1621–1695, French poet and writer of fables.

lag (lag), *v.,* **lagged, lag·ging,** *n.* —*v.* move too slowly; fall behind. —*n.* 1. a lagging. 2. amount by which a person or thing lags.

la·ger (lä'gər), or **lager beer**, *n. Am.* beer stored from six weeks to six months before being used. [short for G *lagerbier*]

lag·gard (lag'ərd), *n.* Also, **lag'ger.** person who moves too slowly or falls behind; backward person. —*adj.* slow; falling behind; backward.

la·gniappe, la·gnappe (lan·yap'; lan'yap), *n. Am.* something given to a customer with a purchase. [< Louisiana F < Sp. *la ñapa* the gift]

la·goon, la·gune (lə·gün'), *n.* 1. pond or small lake connected with a larger body of water. 2. shallow water separated from the sea by low sandbanks. 3. water within a ring-shaped coral island. [< Ital. *laguna* < L *lacuna* pond]

La·gos (lā'gos; lä'gōs), *n.* capital of Nigeria.

La Guar·di·a Airport (lə gwär'di·ə; gär'-), a major domestic and international airport, in New York City.

La·hore (lə·hôr'; -hōr'), *n.* city in W Pakistan.

la·ic (lā'ik), *adj.* Also, **la'i·cal**, lay; secular. —*n.* layman. [< L *laicus* < Gk., < *laos* people. Doublet of LAY[2].] —**la'i·cal·ly**, *adv.*

laid (lād), *v.* pt. and pp. of lay[1]. —*adj.* **laid up, a.** stored up; put away for future use. **b.** forced to stay indoors or in bed by illness. **c.** dismantled and put in dock.

lain (lān), v. pp. of lie².

lair (lâr), n. den or resting place of a wild animal. [OE leger < licgan lie²]

laird (lârd), n. Scot. owner of land. [Scot. var. of lord] —laird'ly, adj. —laird'ship, n.

lais·sez faire, lais·ser faire (les'ā·fâr'), 1. principle of letting people do as they please. 2. absence of regulation and interference by government. [< F, allow to do] —lais'sez-faire', lais'ser-faire', adj.

la·i·ty (lā'ə·ti), n., pl. -ties. laymen; the people as distinguished from the clergy or from a professional class. [< lay³]

lake¹ (lāk), n. 1. a large body of water entirely or nearly surrounded by land. 2. a wide place in a river. [< L lacus]

lake² (lāk), n. 1. a deep-red or purplish-red coloring matter. 2. an insoluble colored compound formed from organic coloring matter and metallic oxides. [< F < Pers. lāk]

Lake District, region of mountains and lakes in NW England, associated with Wordsworth, Coleridge, and other English poets.

lake dwelling, house built on piles over a lake in prehistoric times. —lake dweller.

lake trout, a gray trout of the lakes of North America.

lakh (lak), n. lac².

Lam., Lamentations.

lam¹ (lam), v., lammed, lam·ming. Slang. beat; thrash. [cf. Scand. lemja and E LAME]

lam² (lam), v., lammed, lam·ming, n. Slang. —v. run off; run away from arrest, etc. —n. 1. a running away. 2. on the lam, a. escaping. b. in hiding. [special use of lam¹]

la·ma (lä'mə), n. a Buddhist priest or monk in Tibet and Mongolia. [< Tibetan blama]

La·ma·ism (lä'mə·iz·əm), n. the religious system of the lamas, a form of Buddhism. —La'ma·ist, n. —La'ma·is'tic, adj.

La·marck (lə·märk'), n. Jean de, 1744–1829, French biologist who evolved the theory of organic evolution. —La·marck·i·an (lə·mär'ki·ən), adj., n.

la·ma·ser·y (lä'mə·ser'i), n., pl. -ser·ies. monastery of lamas.

lamb (lam), n. 1. a young sheep. 2. meat from a lamb. 3. the Lamb, Christ. John 1:29 and 36. 4. a young, dear, or innocent person. 5. Slang. an inexperienced speculator. 6. like a lamb, a. meekly; timidly. b. easily fooled. —v. give birth to a lamb or lambs. [OE] —lamb'like', adj.

Lamb (lam), n. Charles, 1775–1834, English writer. His pen name was Elia.

lam·baste (lam·bāst'), v., -bast·ed, -bast·ing. Slang. 1. beat; thrash. 2. scold roughly. [? < lam¹ + baste³]

lamb·da (lam'də), n. the 11th letter of the Greek alphabet. (Λ, λ).

lam·bent (lam'bənt), adj. 1. moving lightly over a surface: a lambent flame. 2. playing lightly and brilliantly over a subject: a lambent wit. 3. softly bright: moonlight is lambent. [< L lambens licking] —lam'ben·cy, n. —lam'bent·ly, adv.

lamb·kin (lam'kin), n. 1. a little lamb. 2. a young or dear person.

Lamb of God, Christ. John 1:29 and 36.

lam·bre·quin (lam'brə·kin; lam'bər-), n. 1. Am. drapery covering the top of a window or door, or hanging from a shelf. 2. scarf worn over a helmet. [< F]

lamb·skin (lam'skin'), n. 1. skin of a lamb, esp. with the wool on it. 2. leather made from the skin of a lamb. 3. parchment.

lame (lām), adj., lam·er, lam·est, v., lamed, lam·ing. —adj. 1. not able to walk properly; having an injured leg or foot; crippled. 2. stiff and sore. 3. poor; weak; unsatisfactory: a lame excuse. —v. 1. make lame; cripple. 2. become lame; go lame. [OE lama] —lame'ly, adv. —lame'ness, n. —Syn. adj. 1. disabled, halt.

la·mé (la·mā'; lä-), n. a rich fabric made, wholly or partly, of metal threads. [< F, lit., laminated, < lame metal leaf]

lame duck, 1. Am. Congressman who has been defeated for reëlection and is serving the last part of his term. 2. a disabled or helpless person or thing.

la·mel·la (lə·mel'ə), n., pl. -mel·lae (-mel'ē), -mel·las. a thin plate, scale, or layer, esp. of flesh or bone. [< L, dim. of lamina thin plate] —la·mel·lar (lə·mel'ər; lam'ə·lər), lam·el·late (lam'ə·lāt, -lit; lə·mel'āt, -it), adj.

la·mel·li·branch (lə·mel'ə·brangk), n. Zool. any of a class of bivalve mollusks including oysters, mussels, etc. [< lamella + branchia]

la·ment (lə·ment'), v. 1. express grief for; mourn for: lament the dead. 2. express grief; mourn; weep: why does she lament? 3. regret: we lamented his absence. —n. 1. expression of grief; wail. 2. poem, song, or tune that expresses grief. [< L, < lamentum a wailing] —la·ment'er, n. —la·ment'ing, adj. —la·ment'ing·ly, adv. —Syn. v. 1. bewail, deplore. 2. grieve, wail.

lam·en·ta·ble (lam'ən·tə·bəl), adj. 1. to be regretted or pitied: a lamentable accident, a lamentable failure. 2. sorrowful; mournful. —lam'en·ta·ble·ness, n. —lam'en·ta·bly, adv.

lam·en·ta·tion (lam'ən·tā'shən), n. 1. loud grief; mourning; wailing; cries of sorrow. 2. Lamentations, book of the Old Testament ascribed by tradition to Jeremiah.

lam·i·na (lam'ə·nə), n., pl. -nae (-nē), -nas. 1. a thin plate, scale, or layer. 2. Bot. the flat wide part of a leaf. [< L] —lam'i·nar, adj.

lam·i·nate (v. lam'ə·nāt; adj., n. lam'ə·nāt, -nit), v., -nat·ed, -nat·ing, adj., n. —v. 1. split into thin layers. 2. make by putting layer on layer. 3. beat or roll (metal) into a thin plate. 4. cover with thin plates. —adj. Also, lam'i·nat'ed. having, or composed of, thin layers, plates, etc. —n. a laminated plastic. —lam'i·na'tion, n.

lamp (lamp), n. 1. thing that gives light, as oil lamps, gas lamps, and electric lamps. 2. something that suggests the light of a lamp. [< OF < L < Gk. lampas < lampein shine]

lamp·black (lamp'blak'), n. a fine black soot consisting of almost pure carbon that is deposited when oil, gas, etc., burn incompletely, used as a coloring matter in paint and ink.

lam·poon (lam·pün'), n. piece of malicious or virulent writing that attacks and ridicules a person. —v. attack in a lampoon. [< F lampon drinking-song < lampons let us drink] —lampoon'er, lam·poon'ist, n.

lam·prey (lam'pri), n., pl. -preys. a water animal having a body like an eel, gill slits like a fish, no jaws, and a large, round mouth. Some species live on the blood of fish they attach themselves to. [< OF < Med.L lampreda. Doublet of LIMPET.]

Lan·ca·shire (lang'kə·shir; -shər), n. county in NW England.

Lan·cas·ter (lang'kəs·tər), n. the English royal house from 1399 to 1461. —Lan·cas·tri·an (lang·kas'tri·ən), adj., n.

lance (lans; läns), n., v., lanced, lanc·ing. —n. 1. a long wooden spear with a sharp iron or steel head: knights carried lances. 2. soldier armed with a lance. 3. any instrument like a soldier's lance. 4. lancet. —v. 1. pierce with a lance. 2. cut open with a lancet: the dentist lanced the gum. [< F < L lancea light Spanish spear]

lance corporal, in the British army, a private acting as a corporal, without increase of pay.

Lan·ce·lot (lan'sə·lot; -lət; län'-), n. bravest of King Arthur's knights of the Round Table.

lan·ce·o·late (lan'si·ə·lāt; -lit), adj. shaped like the head of a lance. [< L, < lanceola small LANCE]

lanc·er (lan'sər; län'-), n. a mounted soldier armed with a lance.

lance sergeant, in the British army, a corporal appointed to act as sergeant.

lan·cet (lan'sit; län'-), n. a small, sharp-pointed surgical knife, usually having two sharp edges. [< OF lancette small LANCE]

Lanceolate leaves

lance·wood (lans′wud′; läns′–), *n*. 1. a tough, straight-grained, springy wood, used for fishing rods, carriage shafts, cabinetwork, etc. 2. the tropical American tree that yields it.

Lan·chow (län′jō′), *n*. city in N China.

land (land), *n*. 1. the solid part of the earth's surface: *dry land*. 2. ground; soil: *arable land*. 3. landed property; real estate: *the company's land, common land.* 4. country; region: *mountainous land.* 5. people of a country; nation. —*v*. 1. come to land; bring to land: *the ship landed at the pier, the pilot landed the airplane.* 2. put on land; set ashore: *the ship landed its passengers.* 3. go ashore: *the passengers landed.* 4. arrive; cause to arrive: *the thief landed in jail.* 5. *Colloq.* catch; get: *land a job.* [OE] —Syn. *n*. 2. earth.

lan·dau (lan′dô; –dou), *n*. 1. a four-wheeled carriage with two seats and a top made in two parts that can be folded back. 2. automobile with a similar top. [from name of German town]

land·ed (lan′did), *adj.* 1. owning land: *landed nobles.* 2. consisting of land: *landed property.*

land·fall (land′fôl′), *n*. 1. approach to land from the sea or air; landing. 2. sighting land. 3. land sighted or reached.

land grant, *Am.* grant of land; gift of land by the government for colleges, railroads, etc.

land·hold·er (land′hōl′dər), *n*. person who owns or occupies land. —**land′hold′ing,** *adj.*, *n*.

land·ing (lan′ding), *n*. 1. a coming to land: *the landing of the Pilgrims.* 2. place where persons or goods are landed from a ship: *the steamboat landing.* 3. platform between flights of stairs.

landing craft, *U.S. Navy.* any of various kinds of boats or ships used for landing troops or equipment on a shore, esp. during an assault.

landing gear, wheels, pontoons, etc., under an airplane.

landing mat, *Am.* a 12-by-3-foot mat of meshed steel which can be joined to others to furnish a landing surface for airplanes.

landing strip, a long, narrow runway for airplanes to take off from and land on.

land·la·dy (land′lā′di), *n*., *pl.* –dies. 1. woman who owns buildings or land that she rents to others. 2. mistress of an inn, boarding house, etc.

land·less (land′lis), *adj.* without land; owning no land.

land·locked (land′lokt′), *adj.* 1. shut in, or nearly shut in, by land. 2. living in waters shut off from the sea: *landlocked salmon.*

land·lord (land′lôrd′), *n*. 1. person who owns buildings or land that he rents to others. 2. keeper of an inn, lodging house, or boarding house.

land·lub·ber (land′lub′ər), *n*. person not used to being on ships; person clumsy on ships. Sailors call landsmen landlubbers in scorn.

land·mark (land′märk′), *n*. 1. something familiar or easily seen, used as a guide. 2. an important fact or event; happening that stands out above others: *invention of the printing press was a landmark in the progress of communication.* 3. stone or other object that marks the boundary of a piece of land.

land mine, container filled with explosives or chemicals, placed on the ground or lightly covered.

land office, government office that takes care of the business connected with public lands, and records sales, transfers, etc.

Land of Promise, country promised by God to Abraham and his descendants; Canaan. Gen. 15:18; 17:8.

land·own·er (land′ōn′ər), *n*. person who owns land. —**land′own′er·ship,** *n*. —**land′own′ing,** *n*.

land·scape (land′skāp), *n*., *v*., –scaped, –scaping. —*n*. 1. view of scenery on land. 2. picture flowers, etc.: *the park is landscaped.* [< Du., < showing a land scene. —*v*. make (land) more pleasant to look at by arranging trees, shrubs, *land* land + –*schap* –ship]

landscape gardening, arrangement of trees, shrubs, flowers, etc., to give a pleasing ap-

pearance to grounds, parks, etc. —**landscape gardener.**

land·slide (land′slīd′), *n*. *Am.* 1. a. a sliding down of a mass of soil or rock on a steep slope. b. mass that slides down. 2. overwhelming majority of votes for one political party or candidate.

land·slip (land′slip′), *n*. *Esp. Brit.* landslide (def. 1).

lands·man (landz′mən), *n*., *pl.* –men. 1. man who lives or works on land. 2. an inexperienced seaman.

land·ward (land′wərd), *adv.* Also, land′wards. toward the land. —*adj.* directed toward the land.

lane (lān), *n*. 1. a narrow way between hedges, walls, houses, or fences; narrow country road. 2. *Am.* portion of a highway used by traffic going in one direction only. 3. any narrow way: *a lane on a running track for sprinters.* 4. alley between buildings. 5. course or route used by ships or airplanes going in the same direction. [OE]

lang., language.

Lang·ley (lang′li), *n*. Samuel Pierpont, 1834–1906, American astronomer and physicist. In 1896 he constructed and flew successfully a model airplane driven by an engine.

lang·syne (lang′sīn′; –zīn′), *Scot.* —*adv.* long since; long ago. —*n*. time long ago. [see LONG, SINCE]

lan·guage (lang′gwij), *n*. 1. human speech, spoken or written. 2. speech of one nation or race: *the French language.* 3. form, style, or kind of language: *bad language, Shakespeare's language, the language of chemistry.* 4. wording; words: *the language of the Lord's Prayer.* 5. any means of expressing thoughts or feelings: *dogs' language.* 6. study of language; linguistics. [< OF *langage* < *langue* tongue < L *lingua*]

lan·guid (lang′gwid), *adj.* 1. drooping; weak; weary; without energy: *people feel languid in hot weather.* 2. without interest or enthusiasm; indifferent: *he is too languid to go anywhere.* 3. sluggish; dull; not brisk or lively: *a languid market.* [< L, < *languere* be faint] —**lan′guid·ly,** *adv.* —**lan′guid·ness,** *n*. —Syn. 1. feeble, fatigued, exhausted. 2. apathetic, listless.

lan·guish (lang′gwish), *v*. 1. become weak or weary; lose energy; droop: *flowers languish from lack of water.* 2. suffer under any unfavorable conditions: *languish in prison.* 3. grow dull, slack, or less intense: *his vigilance never languished.* 4. long; pine: *she languished for home.* 5. assume a soft, tender look for effect: *she smiles and languishes prettily.* [< F *languir* < L *languere*] —**lan′guish·er,** *n*. —**lan′guish·ment,** *n*. —Syn. 1. wither, fade.

lan·guish·ing (lang′gwish·ing), *adj.* 1. drooping; pining; longing. 2. tender; sentimental; loving. 3. lasting; lingering. —**lan′guish·ing·ly,** *adv.*

lan·guor (lang′gər), *n*. 1. lack of energy; weakness; weariness: *long illness causes languor.* 2. lack of interest or enthusiasm; indifference. 3. softness or tenderness of mood. 4. quietness; stillness: *the languor of a summer afternoon.* 5. lack of activity; sluggishness. [< L] —**lan′guor·ous,** *adj.* —**lan′guor·ous·ly,** *adv.* —Syn. 1. feebleness, fatigue. 2. apathy.

lan·iard (lan′yərd), *n*. lanyard.

La·nier (lə·nir′), *n*. Sidney, 1842–1881, American poet and musician.

lank (langk), *adj.* 1. long and thin; slender; lean. 2. straight and flat; not curly or wavy. [OE *hlanc*] —**lank′ly,** *adv.* —**lank′ness,** *n*.

lank·y (langk′i), *adj.* lank·i·er, lank·i·est. awkwardly long and thin; tall and ungraceful. —**lank′i·ly,** *adv.* —**lank′i·ness,** *n*.

lan·o·lin (lan′ə·lin), **lan·o·line** (–lin; –lēn), *n*. fat or grease obtained from wool, used in ointments. [< L *lana* wool]

Lan·sing (lan′sing), *n*. capital of Michigan, in the S part.

lan·tern (lan′tərn), *n*. 1. case to protect a light from wind, rain, etc., having sides of glass or some other material through which the light can shine. 2. room at the top of a lighthouse where the light is. 3. an upright structure on a roof or dome, for letting in light and air or for decoration. 4. a magic lantern. [< F < L < Gk. *lampter* torch < *lampein* to shine]

lan·tern-jawed (lan'tərn-jôd'), *adj.* having long thin jaws and hollow cheeks.

lantern slide, small thin sheet of glass with a picture on it that is projected on a screen by a magic lantern or stereopticon.

lan·tha·num (lan'thə·nəm), *n. Chem.* a rare metallic element, La, belonging to the same group of chemical elements as cerium.

lan·yard (lan'yərd), *n.* 1. *Naut.* a short rope or cord used on ships to fasten rigging. Sailors sometimes use lanyards to hang knives around their necks. 2. *Mil.* cord with a small hook at one end, used in firing certain kinds of cannon. Also, **laniard.** [blend of *lanyer* (< F *lanière* thong) and *yard²*]

La·os (lä'ŏs), *n.* country in SE Asia, formerly part of French Indo-China.

La·o·tian (lā·ō'shən), *adj.* of or having to do with Laos, its people, or their language. —*n.* native or inhabitant of Laos.

Lao-tse, Lao-tsze, or **Lao-tzu** (lou'dzu'), *n.* born 604? B.C., Chinese philosopher who is supposed to have founded Taoism.

lap¹ (lap), *n.* 1. the front part from the waist to the knees of a person sitting down. 2. clothing that covers it. 3. place where anything rests or is cared for. 4. loosely hanging edge of clothing; flap. [OE *læppa*]

lap² (lap), *v.,* **lapped, lap·ping,** *n.* —*v.* 1. lay or lie together, one partly over or beside another: *shingles on a roof lap.* 2. extend out beyond: *lap from Christmas into next year.* 3. wind or wrap (around); fold (over or about): *he lapped himself in a warm blanket.* 4. surround; envelop: *joy lapped over him.* 5. nurse; fondle; cherish. 6. in a race, get a lap or more ahead of (other racers). —*n.* 1. lapping over. 2. amount of lapping over. 3. part that laps over. 4. one time around a race track. [< *lap¹*] —**lap'per,** *n.*

lap³ (lap), *v.,* **lapped, lap·ping,** *n.* —*v.* 1. drink by lifting up with the tongue: *cats and dogs lap up water.* 2. move or beat gently with a lapping sound; splash gently: *little waves lapped against the boat.* —*n.* 1. act of lapping. 2. sound of lapping. [OE *lapian*] —**lap'per,** *n.*

La Paz (lä päs'), one of the two capitals of Bolivia (Sucre is the other), in the W part.

lap dog, a small pet dog.

la·pel (lə·pel'), *n.* part of the front of a coat folded back just below the collar. [< *lap¹*]

lap·ful (lap'fúl), *n., pl.* **-fuls.** as much as a lap can hold.

lap·i·dar·y (lap'ə·der'i), *n., pl.* **-dar·ies.** person who cuts, polishes, or engraves precious stones. [< L *lapidarius* < *lapis* stone]

lap·in (lap'ən), *n.* 1. rabbit. 2. rabbit fur. [< F]

lap·is laz·u·li (lap'is laz'yū·lī), a deep-blue, opaque semiprecious stone used for an ornament. [< Med.L, < L *lapis* stone + Med.L *lazuli,* gen. of *lazulum* lapis lazuli < Ar.]

La·place (lä·pläs'), *n.* Pierre de, 1749–1827, French astronomer and mathematician.

Lap·land (lap'land), *n.* region in N Norway, Sweden, Finland, and NW Soviet Union. —**Lap'-land·er,** *n.*

La Pla·ta (lä plä'tə), seaport in E Argentina.

Lapp (lap), *n.* 1. member of a Mongoloid race living in Lapland. The Lapps are small and have short, broad heads. 2. language of the Lapps.

lap·pet (lap'it), *n.* 1. a small flap or fold. 2. a loose fold of flesh or membrane. 3. lobe of the ear. [< *lap¹*]

lap robe, *Am.* blanket, fur robe, etc., used to keep the lap and legs warm when riding in an automobile, carriage, etc.

Cap with lappets over the ears

lapse (laps), *n., v.,* **lapsed, laps·ing.** —*n.* 1. a slight mistake or error: *a lapse of memory.* 2. a slipping or falling away from what is right: *a moral lapse.* 3. a slipping back; sinking down; slipping into a lower condition: *a lapse into savage ways.* 4. a slipping by; a passing away: *a minute is a short lapse of time.* 5. *Law.* ending of a right or privilege because it was not renewed, not used, or otherwise neglected. —*v.* 1. make a slight mistake or error. 2. slip or fall away from what is right. 3. slip back; sink down: *the house lapsed into ruin.* 4. slip by; pass away: *the boy's interest soon lapsed.* 5. *Law.* terminate a right or privilege because it was not renewed, not used, etc. [< L *lapsus* slip < *labi* to slip] —**laps'er,** *n.* —**Syn.** *n.* 1. slip, fault.

lap·wing (lap'wing'), *n.* a crested plover of Europe, Asia, and N Africa that has a slow, irregular flight and a peculiar wailing cry.

Lar·a·mie (lar'ə·mi), *n.* city in SE Wyoming.

lar·board (lär'bərd; -bôrd; -bōrd), *Naut.* —*n.* side of a ship to the left of a person looking from the stern toward the bow; port. —*adj.* on this side of a ship. [ME *laddeborde*]

lar·ce·ny (lär'sə·ni), *n., pl.* **-nies.** 1. theft. 2. *Law.* unlawful taking, carrying away, and using of the personal property belonging to another person without his consent. [< AF < L *latrocinium* < *latro* bandit] —**lar'ce·nous,** *adj.*

larch (lärch), *n.* 1. tree of the pine family with small woody cones and needles that fall off in the autumn. 2. its strong, tough wood. [< G, ult. < L *larix*]

lard (lärd), *n.* fat of pigs and hogs, melted down and made clear, used in cooking. —*v.* 1. insert strips of bacon or salt pork in (meat) before cooking. 2. give variety to; enrich: *lard a long speech with stories.* 3. cover or smear with lard or grease. [< OF < L *lardum*] —**lard'like',** *adj.*

lard·er (lär'dər), *n.* 1. pantry; place where food is kept. 2. stock of food. [< OF < L *lardum* lard]

lar·es and pe·na·tes (lär'ēz; pə·nā'tēz), 1. household gods of the ancient Romans. 2. cherished possessions of a family or household.

large (lärj), *adj.,* **larg·er, larg·est.** —*adj.* 1. of great size, amount, or number; big; huge: *a large crowd.* 2. big compared with others of the same sort: *a large apple.* 3. of great scope or range; extensive; broad: *a man of large experience.* 4. on a great scale: *a large employer of labor.* —*n.* **at large,** *a.* at liberty; free. *b.* fully; in detail. *c.* as a whole; altogether. *d. Am.* representing the whole of a State or district, not merely one division of it: *a congressman at large.* [< OF < L *largus* copious] —**large'ness,** *n.* —**Syn.** *adj.* 1. great, vast, enormous, massive.

large·ly (lärj'li), *adv.* 1. in great quantity; much: *drink largely.* 2. to a great extent; mainly: *largely a matter of conjecture.*

large-scale (lärj'skāl'), *adj.* 1. wide; extensive; involving many persons or things: *a large-scale disaster.* 2. made or drawn to a large scale.

lar·gess, lar·gesse (lär'jis), *n.* 1. generous giving. 2. a generous gift or gifts. [< OF, < *large* LARGE]

lar·ghet·to (lär·get'ō), *adj., n., pl.* **-ghet·tos.** *Music.* —*adj.* rather slow. —*n.* passage or piece of music in rather slow time. [< Ital., dim. of *largo* LARGO]

larg·ish (lär'jish), *adj.* rather large.

lar·go (lär'gō), *adj., n., pl.* **-gos.** *Music.* —*adj.* slow and dignified; stately. —*n.* a slow, stately passage or piece of music. [< Ital. < L *largus*]

lar·i·at (lar'i·ət), *n. Am.* lasso. [< Sp. *la reata* the rope]

lark¹ (lärk), *n.* 1. a small songbird of Europe, Asia, and N Africa with brown feathers and long hind claws, esp. the skylark. 2. any of several similar songbirds, as the meadow lark. [OE *lāwerce*]

lark² (lärk), *Colloq.* —*n.* a merry adventure; frolic; prank. —*v.* have fun; play pranks. —**lark'er,** *n.* —**lark'some,** *adj.*

lark·spur (lärk'spėr), *n.* plant whose flowers have a petallike sepal shaped like a spur. Most larkspurs have clusters of blue flowers on tall stalks.

lar·rup (lar′əp), v., -ruped, -rup·ing. Colloq. beat; thrash. —lar′rup·er, n.

lar·va (lär′və), n., pl. -vae (-vē). 1. early form of an insect from the time it leaves the egg until it becomes a pupa, as caterpillars, grubs, and maggots. 2. immature form of certain animals that is different in structure from the adult form, as a tadpole. [< L, ghost] —lar′val, adj.

la·ryn·ge·al (lə·rin′ji·əl), adj. 1. produced or influenced by the larynx. 2. in the larynx. 3. used on the larynx.

lar·yn·gi·tis (lar′ən·jī′tis), n. inflammation of the larynx. —lar·yn·git·ic (lar′ən·jit′ik), adj.

lar·ynx (lar′ingks), n., pl. la·ryn·ges (lə·rin′jēz), lar·ynx·es. 1. Anat. cavity at the upper end of the windpipe, containing the vocal cords and acting as an organ of voice. 2. Zool. similar organ in other mammals, or corresponding structure in other animals. [< Gk.]

La Salle (lə sal′), René Robert Cavelier, Sieur de, 1643–1687, Frenchman who explored the Mississippi and Ohio rivers.

las·car (las′kər), n. a native sailor of the East Indies. [< Pg., prob. < Urdu (lang. derived from Hindustani) lashkarī soldier]

las·civ·i·ous (lə·siv′i·əs), adj. 1. feeling lust. 2. showing lust. 3. causing lust. [< LL, < L lascivia playfulness] —las·civ′i·ous·ly, adv. —las·civ′i·ous·ness, n.

la·ser (lā′zər), n. Electronics. a device which generates and amplifies light waves of a pure color in a narrow and extremely intense beam of light. [< l(ight) a(mplification by) s(timulated) e(mission of) r(adiation)]

lash¹ (lash), n. 1. the part of a whip that is not the handle. 2. stroke or blow with a whip, etc. 3. a sudden, swift movement. 4. anything that hurts as a blow from a whip does: the lash of the wind on one's face. 5. eyelash. —v. 1. beat or drive with a whip, etc.: he lashed his horse. 2. wave or beat back and forth: the wind lashes the sails. 3. rush violently; pour: the rain lashed against the windows. 4. attack severely in words; hurt severely. 5. lash out, a. hit; attack; strike. b. attack severely in words; scold vigorously. c. break forth into violent action, excess, or extravagance. [ME lassh] —Syn. v. 1. flog.

lash² (lash), v. bind with a rope, cord, etc. [? ult. < OF lache LACE]

lash·ing¹ (lash′ing), n. 1. act of one that lashes. 2. severe attack in words; sharp scolding.

lash·ing² (lash′ing), n. rope, cord, etc., used in tying or fastening. [ME lasse]

lass (las), n. 1. girl; young woman. 2. sweetheart.

las·sie (las′i), n. 1. girl. 2. sweetheart.

las·si·tude (las′ə·tüd; -tūd), n. lack of energy; weakness; weariness. [< L, < lassus tired]

las·so (las′ō; las′ü; la·sü′), n., pl. -sos, -soes, v., -soed, -so·ing. Am. —n. a long rope with a running noose at one end; lariat. —v. catch with a lasso. [< Sp. lazo < L laqueus noose. Doublet of LACE.] —las′so·er, n.

last¹ (last; läst), adj. 1. coming after all others; being at the end; final: the last page of the book. 2. latest; most recent: I saw him last week. 3. most unlikely; least suitable: that is the last thing one would expect. 4. very great; extreme. 5. that remains: his last dollar. 6. conclusive: say the last word on a subject. —adv. 1. after all others; at the end; finally: he arrived last. 2. on the latest or most recent occasion: when did you last see him? —n. 1. person or thing that is last: the last in the row. 2. end: faithful to the last. 3. at last, at the end; after a long time; finally. 4. breathe one's last, die. 5. see the last of, not see again. [OE latost, lætest, superl. of læt late] —Syn. adj. 1. ultimate, concluding, closing. ➤ At long last is an individual idiom recently revived. It is slightly more emphatic than at last, at least when it is spoken, but usually the phrase has a British or

Cowboy using a lasso

formal connotation. ➤ last, latest. In the following illustration, last implies the final member of a series; latest, the most recent in time (of a series which may or may not be continued): the scholar's latest (we hope it won't be his last) biography. See first for another usage note.

last² (last; läst), v. 1. go on; hold out; continue to be; endure: the storm lasted three days. 2. continue in good condition, force, etc.: cloth too flimsy to last. 3. be enough (for): while our money lasts. [OE læstan < läst track; akin to LAST³] —last′er, n. —Syn. 1. persist, abide.

last³ (last; läst), n. 1. block shaped like a person's foot, on which shoes and boots are formed or repaired. 2. stick to one's last, pay attention to one's own work; mind one's own business. —v. form (shoes and boots) on a last. [OE læste < läst track] —last′er, n.

last·ing (las′ting; läs′-), adj. that lasts a long time; permanent. —last′ing·ly, adv.

Last Judgment, God's final judgment of all mankind at the end of the world.

last·ly (last′li; läst′-), adv. finally; in the last place; in conclusion.

last offices, prayers for a dead person.

last straw, last of a series of troublesome things that finally causes a collapse, outburst, etc.

Last Supper, supper of Jesus and His disciples on the evening before He was crucified.

last word, 1. last thing said. 2. Colloq. the latest thing; most up-to-date style. 3. Colloq. thing that cannot be improved.

Lat., Latin.

lat., latitude.

latch (lach), n. catch for fastening a door, gate, or window, consisting of a movable piece of metal or wood that fits into a notch, opening, etc. [< v.] —v. fasten with a latch. [OE læccan grasp]

Latch

latch·key (lach′kē′), n. key used to draw back or unfasten the latch of a door.

latch·string (lach′string′), n. string used to unfasten the latch of a door.

late (lāt), adj., lat·er or lat·ter, lat·est or last, adv., lat·er, lat·est or last. —adj. 1. happening, coming, etc., after the usual or proper time: too late for the train. 2. happening, coming, etc., at an advanced time: success late in life. 3. recent: the late war. 4. recently dead or gone out of office: the late professor. 5. of late, lately; a short time ago; recently. —adv. 1. after the usual or proper time: he worked late. 2. at an advanced time: late in the afternoon. 3. recently. 4. recently but no longer. [OE læt] —late′ness, n. —Syn. adj. 1. tardy, delayed. ➤ See first, last, and latter for usage notes.

la·teen (la·tēn′; lə-), adj. Naut. having a lateen sail. [< F voile latine Latin sail]

lateen sail, Naut. a triangular sail held up by a long yard on a short mast.

Late Latin, the Latin language from about 300–700 A.D.

late·ly (lāt′li), adv. a short time ago; recently.

la·ten·cy (lā′tən·si), n. latent condition or quality.

la·tent (lā′tənt), adj. present but not active; hidden; concealed: latent germs. [< L latens lying hidden] —Syn. dormant, potential.

lat·er·al (lat′ər·əl), adj. of the side; at the side; from the side; toward the side: a lateral branch of a family is a branch not in the direct line of descent. —n. 1. a lateral part or outgrowth. 2. Football. a lateral pass. [< L, < latus side] —lat′er·al·ly, adv.

lateral pass, Football. a short throw of the ball from one player to another in a direction almost parallel with the goal line.

Lat·er·an (lat′ər·ən), n. church of Saint John Lateran, the official church of the Pope.

la·tex (lā′teks), n., pl. lat·i·ces (lat′ə·sēz), la·tex·es (lā′tek·siz). 1. a milky liquid found in the rubber tree, dandelion, milkweed, etc. 2. any of various thermoplastics produced as an aqueous dispersion of a high molecular weight polymer prepared by emulsion polymerization, used in paints, adhesives, etc. [< L, liquid]

lath (lath; läth), *n., pl.* **laths** (lathz; laths; läthz; läths), *v.* —*n.* **1.** one of the thin narrow strips of wood used to form a support for plaster or to make a lattice. **2.** a wire cloth or sheet metal with holes in it, used in place of laths. **3.** lining made of laths; lathwork; lathing. —*v.* cover or line with laths. [ME *laththe*]

lathe (lāth), *n.* machine for holding articles of wood, metal, etc., and turning them against a cutting tool used to shape them. [< Scand. (Dan.) *(dreje)lad* (turning) lathe]

lath·er¹ (lath′ər), *n.* **1.** foam made from soap and water. **2.** foam formed in sweating. —*v.* **1.** put lather on. **2.** form a lather. **3.** become covered with foam. **4.** *Colloq.* beat; flog. [OE *lēathor*] —**lath′er·er,** *n.* —**lath′er·y,** *adj.*

lath·er² (lath′ər; läth′-), *n.* workman who puts laths on walls, ceilings, etc. [< *lath*]

lath·ing (lath′ing; läth′-), **lath·work** (-wérk′), *n.* **1.** laths. **2.** work of putting laths on walls, etc.

Lat·in (lat′ən), *n.* **1.** language of the ancient Romans, considered classical in the form acquired during the 2nd and 1st centuries B.C. **2.** member of any of the peoples whose languages came from Latin, as the Italians, French, Spanish, Portuguese, Rumanians, etc. **3.** native or inhabitant of Latium or of ancient Rome. —*adj.* **1.** of Latin; in Latin. **2.** of the Latin peoples. **3.** of Latium or its people. ▶ **Latin and English. 1.** Latin words. Many Latin words came into English in early periods of the language, either direct or through French, and cannot now be told from other English words: *patience, candle, receive* . . . . Most borrowings from Latin are subject to the same process of anglicizing as other foreign words in English, and in general they are pronounced like English words—*agenda* (ə·jen′də); *erratum* (i·rā′təm; i·rä′təm)—instead of according to the system of sounds now taught in Latin classes. **2.** Latin and English grammar. The first and a number of other English grammars were composed by men thoroughly familiar with Latin, who believed that English was or at any rate should be a language like Latin. As a result, English, which was a Germanic language in structure, was described in terms of Latin grammar, and rules were devised for making the language fit the picture. This is one reason for the conventional taboo of the split infinitive (which would be impossible in Latin because the infinitive is one word, as in *laborare* where English has *to work*) and of putting a preposition at the end of a sentence, which is impossible in Latin but is a characteristic English idiom. Only recently has English grammar been based squarely on a study of the English language and freed from the categories and some of the rules of Latin grammar.

Latin America, South America, Central America, Mexico, and most of the West Indies. —**Lat′in-A·mer′i·can,** *adj., n.*

Latin Church, that part of the Catholic Church which follows the Latin Rite.

Lat·in·ism (lat′ən·iz·əm), *n.* **1.** Latin idiom or expression. **2.** use of Latin idioms or expressions. **3.** conformity to Latin models.

Lat·in·ist (lat′ən·ist), *n.* person with much knowledge of the Latin language; Latin scholar.

Lat·in·ize (lat′ən·īz), *v.,* **-ized, -iz·ing. 1.** translate into Latin. **2.** make like Latin. —**Lat′-in·i·za′tion,** *n.*

Latin Quarter, district in Paris, S of the Seine River. Many students and artists live there.

Latin Rite, church ceremonies as used in the Diocese of Rome.

lat·ish (lāt′ish), *adj., adv.* rather late.

lat·i·tude (lat′ə·tüd; -tūd), *n.* **1.** distance north or south of the equator, measured in degrees. **2.** place or region having a certain latitude: *the cold latitudes.* **3.** room to act; scope; freedom from narrow rules: *you are allowed much latitude in this work; use your own judgment.* [< L, < *latus* wide] —**lat′i·tu′di·nal,** *adj.*

lat·i·tu·di·nar·i·an (lat′ə·tü′də·nãr′i·ən; -tū′-), *adj.* allowing others their own beliefs; not insisting on strict adherence to established principles, esp. in religious views. —*n.* person who is latitudinarian in outlook or action. —**lat′-i·tu′di·nar′i·an·ism,** *n.*

La·ti·um (lā′shi·əm), *n.* ancient country in Italy, SE of Rome.

la·trine (lə·trēn′), *n.* toilet in a camp, barracks, factory, etc.; privy. [< F < L *latrina*]

lat·ter (lat′ər), *adj.* **1.** second of two: *Canada and the United States are in North America; the former lies N of the latter.* **2.** later; more recent; nearer the end: *Friday comes in the latter part of the week.* [OE *lætra* later] ▶ **Latter** (lat′ər) and **later** (lā′tər) are often carelessly confused. The habit of reading your copy aloud to yourself should catch this type of error.

Latter-day Saint, *Am.* Mormon.

lat·ter·ly (lat′ər·li), *adv.* lately; recently.

lat·tice (lat′is), *n., v.,* **-ticed, -tic·ing.** —*n.* **1.** structure of crossed wooden or metal strips with open spaces between them. **2.** window, gate, etc., having a lattice. —*v.* **1.** form into a lattice; make like a lattice. **2.** furnish with a lattice. [< OF *lattis* < *latte* lath < Gmc.]

Lattice

lat·tice·work (lat′is·wérk′), *n.* **1.** lattice. **2.** lattices.

Lat·vi·a (lat′vi·ə), *n.* a small country in N Europe, on the Baltic Sea, now under Soviet control. —**Lat′vi·an,** *adj., n.*

laud (lôd), *v.* praise. —*n.* **1.** praise. **2.** song or hymn of praise. **3.** lauds, **Lauds, a.** morning church service with psalms of praise to God. **b.** in Roman Catholic use, a prescribed devotional service for priests and religious, forming, with matins, the first of the seven canonical hours. [ult. < L *laus* praise] —**laud′er,** *n.*

laud·a·ble (lôd′ə·bəl), *adj.* worthy of praise; commendable. —**laud′a·bil′i·ty, laud′a·ble·ness,** *n.* —**laud′a·bly,** *adv.*

lau·da·num (lô′də·nəm), *n.* solution of opium in alcohol, used to lessen pain. [< NL; coined by Paracelsus]

lau·da·tion (lô·dā′shən), *n.* praise.

laud·a·to·ry (lôd′ə·tô′ri; -tō′-), **laud·a·tive** (-tiv), *adj.* expressing praise.

laugh (laf; läf), *v.* **1.** make the sounds and movements of the face and body that show mirth, amusement, scorn, etc. **2.** express with laughter: *laugh a reply.* **3. laugh at,** make fun of. **4. laugh off,** pass off or dismiss with a laugh; get out of by laughing. **5.** drive, put, bring, etc., by or with laughing: *laugh one's tears away.* **6.** suggest the feeling of joy; be lively. —*n.* act or sound of laughing. [OE *hliehhan*] —**laugh′er,** *n.* —**Syn. v. 1.** chuckle, chortle, giggle, guffaw, titter.

laugh·a·ble (laf′ə·bəl; läf′-), *adj.* such as to cause laughter; amusing; funny. —**laugh′a·ble·ness,** *n.* —**laugh′a·bly,** *adv.* —**Syn.** comic, comical, humorous, ridiculous.

laugh·ing (laf′ing; läf′-), *adj.* **1.** that laughs or seems to laugh: *the laughing brook.* **2.** accompanied by laughter. **3. no laughing matter,** matter that is serious. —*n.* laughter. —**laugh′ing·ly,** *adv.*

laughing gas, nitrous oxide, N_2O, a colorless gas that makes one insensible to pain.

laughing jackass, an Australian bird with a harsh cackling voice.

laugh·ing·stock (laf′ing·stok′; läf′-), *n.* object of ridicule; person or thing that is made fun of.

laugh·ter (laf′tər; läf′-), *n.* **1.** action of laughing. **2.** sound of laughing.

launch¹ (lônch; länch), *n.* **1.** the largest boat carried by a warship. **2.** more or less open motorboat used for pleasure trips, etc. [< Sp., Pg. *lancha* < *lanchar* LAUNCH²]

launch² (lônch; länch), *v.* **1.** cause to slide into the water; set afloat: *launch a ship.* **2.** push out or put forth on the water or into the air. 3. start; set going; set out: *launch a new business.* 4. throw; hurl; send out: *launch threats against enemies.* 5. burst; plunge: *launch into a violent attack on the government.* 6. **launch out,** begin; start. —*n.* movement of a boat or ship from the land into the water. [ult. < OF *lancer* < *lance* LANCE] —**launch′er,** *n.*

launching pad, the raised surface on which a rocket or missile is prepared for launching and from which it is shot into the air.

laun·der (lôn′dər; län′-), *v.* 1. wash and iron (clothes, etc.). 2. be able to be washed; stand washing: *some shirts launder well.* [< OF, ult. < L *lavanda* (things) to be washed < *lavare* wash] —**laun′der·er,** *n.*

laun·dress (lôn′dris; län′-), *n.* woman whose work is washing and ironing clothes, etc.

laun·dry (lôn′dri; län′-), *n., pl.* -**dries.** 1. room or building where clothes, etc., are washed and ironed. 2. clothes, etc., washed or to be washed.

laun·dry·man (lôn′dri·mən; län′-), *n., pl.* -**men.** 1. man who works in a laundry. 2. man who collects and delivers laundry.

laun·dry·wom·an (lôn′dri·wum′ən; län′-), *n., pl.* -**wom·en.** laundress.

lau·re·ate (lô′ri·it), *adj.* 1. crowned with a laurel wreath as a mark of honor. 2. honored; distinguished. —*n.* poet laureate. [< L, ult. < *laurus* laurel] —**lau′re·ate·ship′,** *n.*

lau·rel (lô′rəl; lor′əl), *n.* 1. a small evergreen tree with smooth, shiny leaves; bay tree. 2. the leaves. The ancient Greeks and Romans crowned victors with wreaths of laurel. 3. any tree or shrub of the same family as the bay tree. 4. *Am.* American evergreen shrub, the mountain laurel. 5. Usually, **laurels.** a. honor; fame. b. victory. [< OF, ult. < L *laurus*] —**lau′reled,** *esp. Brit.* **lau′relled,** *adj.*

Lau·ren·tian Mountains (lô·ren′shən), low mountain range in Canada, between Hudson Bay and the St. Lawrence River.

Lau·sanne (lō·zan′), *n.* city in W Switzerland, on Lake Geneva.

la·va (lä′və; lav′ə), *n.* 1. molten rock flowing from a volcano or fissure in the earth. 2. rock formed by the cooling of this molten rock. Some lavas are hard and glassy; others are light and porous. [< dial. Ital., stream, ult. < L *lavare* wash]

lava bed, layer or surface of lava.

lav·a·liere, lav·a·lier, or **lav·al·lière** (lav′ə·lir′), *n.* ornament hanging from a small chain, worn around the neck by women. [< F]

lav·a·to·ry (lav′ə·tô′ri; -tō′-), *n., pl.* -**ries.** 1. room where a person can wash his hands and face. 2. bowl or basin to wash in. 3. bathroom; toilet. [< LL, < L *lavare* wash]

lave (lāv), *v.,* **laved, lav·ing.** *Poetic.* 1. wash; bathe. 2. wash or flow against. [< L *lavare*]

lav·en·der (lav′ən·dər), *n.* 1. a pale purple. 2. a small shrub with spikes of fragrant pale-purple flowers, yielding an oil much used in perfumes. 3. its dried flowers, leaves, and stalks, used to perfume or preserve linens, clothes, etc. —*adj.* pale-purple. [< AF < Med.L *lavendula*]

la·ver (lā′vər), *n.* *Archaic.* bowl to wash in.

lav·ish (lav′ish), *adj.* 1. very free or too free in giving, using, or spending; prodigal: *lavish with money.* 2. very abundant; more than enough; given or spent too freely: *lavish gifts.* —*v.* give or spend very freely or too freely: *she lavished kindness on her guest.* [ult. < OF *lavasse* flood < *laver* wash < L *lavare*] —**lav′ish·er,** *n.* —**lav′ish·ly,** *adv.* —**lav′ish·ness,** *n.*

law (lô), *n.* 1. body of rules recognized by a state or a community as binding on its members: *English law is different from French law.* 2. one of these rules: *there is a law against spitting in streetcars.* 3. controlling influence of these rules, or the condition of society brought about by their observance: *maintain law and order.* 4. law as a system: *courts of law.* 5. department of knowledge or study concerned with these rules; jurisprudence: *study law.* 6. body of such rules concerned with a particular subject or

derived from a particular source: *commercial law, criminal law.* 7. legal profession: *enter the law.* 8. legal action: *go to law.* 9. any act passed upon by the highest legislative body of a state or nation: *a congressional law.* 10. any rule or principle that must be obeyed: *a law of the school.* 11. statement of a relation or sequence of phenomena invariable under the same conditions: *the law of gravitation.* 12. divine rule or commandment. 13. *Math.* rule on which the construction of a curve, a series, etc., depends. 14. **go to law,** appeal to law courts; take legal action. 15. **lay down the law.** a. give orders that must be obeyed. b. give a scolding. 16. **read law,** study to be a lawyer. 17. **the Law,** a. the books of the Old Testament that contain the Mosaic law. b. the Old Testament. [OE *lagu* < Scand.] —**Syn.** 2. regulation, statute, ordinance.

law-a·bid·ing (lô′ə·bīd′ing), *adj.* obedient to the law; peaceful and orderly.

law·break·er (lô′brāk′ər), *n.* person who breaks the law. —**law′break′ing,** *n., adj.*

law court, place where justice is administered; court of law.

law·ful (lô′fəl), *adj.* 1. according to law; done as the law directs: *lawful arrest.* 2. allowed by law; rightful: *lawful demands.* —**law′ful·ly,** *adv.* —**law′ful·ness,** *n.* —**Syn.** 1. legitimate. 2. legal.

law·giv·er (lô′giv′ər), *n.* man who prepares and puts into effect a system of laws for a people; lawmaker; legislator. —**law′giv′ing,** *n., adj.*

law·less (lô′lis), *adj.* 1. paying no attention to the law; breaking the law: *lawless criminal.* 2. hard to control; unruly: *lawless passions.* 3. having no laws: *lawless wilderness.* —**law′less·ly,** *adv.* —**law′less·ness,** *n.* —**Syn.** 2. uncontrolled, ungovernable, unbridled.

law·mak·er (lô′māk′ər), *n.* person who helps to make laws; member of a legislature, congress, or parliament; legislator.

law·mak·ing (lô′māk′ing), *adj.* that makes laws; legislative. —*n.* making the laws; legislation.

lawn[1] (lôn), *n.* land covered with grass kept closely cut, esp. near or around a house. [< OF *launde* wooded ground < Celtic] —**lawn′y,** *adj.*

lawn[2] (lôn), *n.* a thin, sheer linen or cotton cloth. [? ult. < *Laon,* French city] —**lawn′y,** *adj.*

lawn mower, machine with revolving blades for cutting the grass on a lawn.

lawn tennis, game in which a ball is hit back and forth over a low net; tennis.

law of Moses, first five books of the Old Testament; Genesis, Exodus, Leviticus, Numbers, and Deuteronomy.

Law·rence (lô′rəns; lor′-), *n.* D(avid) H(erbert), 1885-1930, English novelist and poet.

law·suit (lô′süt′), *n.* case in a law court; application to a court for justice.

law·yer (lô′yər), *n.* person whose profession is giving advice about the laws or acting for others in a law court. —**Syn.** attorney, counselor.

lax (laks), *adj.* 1. not firm or tight; loose; slack: *lax cord.* 2. not strict; careless: *lax mental powers.* 3. loose in morals: *lax scruples.* 4. not exact; vague: *lax description.* [< L *laxus*] —**lax′ly,** *adv.* —**lax′ness,** *n.* —**Syn.** 1. relaxed, flabby. 2. negligent, remiss.

lax·a·tive (lak′sə·tiv), *n. Med.* medicine that makes the bowels move. —*adj.* making the bowels move. [< L *laxativus* loosening, ult. < *laxus* loose]

lax·i·ty (lak′sə·ti), *n.* lax condition or quality.

lay[1] (lā), *v.,* **laid, lay·ing,** *n.* —*v.* 1. bring down; beat down: *a storm laid the crops low.* 2. put down; keep down: *lay your hat on the table.* 3. make quiet or make disappear: *lay a ghost.* 4. smooth down: *lay the nap of cloth.* 5. place in a lying-down position or a position of rest: *lay the baby down gently.* 6. place, set, or cause to be in a particular situation or condition: *lay great emphasis on good manners, the scene of the story is laid in New York.* 7. place in proper position or in orderly fashion: *lay bricks.* 7.

place on or over a surface. **9.** put cloth, dishes, etc., on (a table). **10.** devise; arrange: *lay plans.* **11.** put down as a bet; wager: *lay five dollars on a horse.* **12.** impose a burden, penalty, etc.: *lay a tax on tea.* **13.** present; bring forward: *lay claim to an estate.* **14.** impute; attribute: *the theft was laid to him.* **15.** of a hen, to produce (an egg or eggs). **16.** lay eggs. **17.** apply oneself vigorously: *the men laid to their oars.* **18.** deal blows; aim blows. **19.** lay aside, away, or by, put away for future use; save. **20.** lay down, **a.** declare; state. **b.** give; sacrifice. **c.** *Slang.* quit; resign. **d.** store away for future use. **e.** bet. **21.** lay for, *Colloq.* lie in wait for. **22.** lay hold of or on, grasp, seize. **23.** lay in, provide; save; put aside for the future. **24.** lay into, **a.** beat; thrash. **b.** *Slang.* scold. **25.** lay off, **a.** put aside. **b.** *Am.*, *Slang.* stop for a time. **c.** put out of work. **d.** mark off. **26.** lay on, **a.** apply. **b.** supply. **c.** strike; inflict. **27.** lay out, **a.** spread out. **b.** prepare (a dead body) for burial. **c.** arrange; plan. **d.** *Slang.* spend. **28.** lay up, **a.** put away for future use; save. **b.** cause to stay in bed or indoors because of illness or injury. **c.** put (a ship) in dock. —*n.* way or position in which a thing is laid or lies: *the lay of the land.* [OE *lecgan* < *licgan* lie²] —Syn. v. **9.** set. **11.** stake, bet. **14.** ascribe, charge. ➤ lay, lie. In uneducated English the work of these two verbs is generally done by one (*lay*, *lay* or *laid*, *laid*). Formal and careful informal writing use them as follows: *lie* ("to recline," intransitive), *lay*, *lain*; *lay* ("to place," transitive), *laid*, *laid. You lie down for a rest or lie down on the job; a farm lies in a valley. You lay a floor, lay a book on the table, lay a bet, lay out clothes.* For egglaying use *lay*, *laid*, *laid.*

lay² (lā), v. pt. of lie².

lay³ (lā), *adj.* **1.** of ordinary people; not of the clergy. **2.** of ordinary people; not of lawyers, doctors, or those learned in the profession in question. [< OF < L *laicus.* Doublet of LAIC.]

lay⁴ (lā), *n.* **1.** a short poem to be sung; poem. **2.** song; tune. [< OF *lai,* ? < Celtic]

lay·er (lā′ər), *n.* **1.** person or thing that lays. **2.** one thickness or fold: *a cake made of layers.* **3.** branch of a plant bent down and covered with earth so that it will take root and form a new plant. —*v.* form (new plants) in this way; spread thus.

layer cake, *Am.* cake made of two or more layers put together with frosting, jelly, etc., between.

lay·ette (lā·et′), *n.* set of clothes, bedding, etc., for a newborn baby. [< F, < *laie* chest]

lay figure, 1. jointed model of a human body, used by artists and in shop windows. **2.** an unimportant person; puppet. [earlier *layman* < Du., < *lee* limb + *man* man]

lay·man (lā′mən), *n., pl.* -**men.** person outside of any particular profession, esp. one not belonging to the clergy.

lay·off (lā′ôf′, -of′), *n.* **1.** a dismissing of workmen temporarily. **2.** time during which the workmen are out of work.

lay of the land, 1. way in which the land lies. **2.** condition of things; state of affairs.

lay·out (lā′out′), *n.* **1.** act of laying out. **2.** *Am.* arrangement; plan: *the layout of a house.* **3.** plan or design for an advertisement, book, etc. **4.** thing laid or spread out; display. **5.** outfit; supply; set.

lay·o·ver (lā′ō′vər), *n.* a stopping for a time in a place.

laz·ar (laz′ər), *n. Archaic.* **1.** leper. **2.** a poor, sick person. [< Med.L, < *Lazarus*] —**laz′ar·like′,** *adj.*

laz·a·ret·to (laz′ə·ret′ō), **laz·a·ret,** or **laz·a·rette** (-ret′), *n., pl.* -**tos;** -**rets;** -**rettes.** **1.** hospital for people having contagious or loathsome diseases. **2.** building or ship used for quarantine purposes. **3.** *Naut.* place in some merchant ships, near the stern, in which supplies are kept. [< Ital. *lazzaretto,* blend of *lazzaro* LAZAR and name of hospital, Santa Maria di *Nazaret*]

Laz·a·rus (laz′ə·rəs), *n.* **1.** brother of Mary and Martha, whom Jesus raised from the dead.

John 11:1–44. **2.** beggar in the parable who suffered on earth but went to heaven. Luke 16:19–25.

laze (lāz), *v.,* lazed, laz·ing. be lazy or idle.

la·zy (lā′zi), *adj.,* la·zi·er, la·zi·est. **1.** not willing to work or be active: *a lazy student.* **2.** moving slowly; not very active: *a lazy walk.* —**la′zi·ly,** *adv.* —**la′zi·ness,** *n.*

la·zy·bones (lā′zi·bōnz′), *n. Colloq.* a lazy person.

lb., *pl.* **lbs., lb.** pound; pounds.

LC, *U.S. Navy.* landing craft.

l.c., 1. in the place cited. [< L *loco citato*] **2.** *Printing.* lower case; in small letters, not capital letters.

lea (lē), *n.* a grassy field; meadow. [OE *lēah*]

leach (lēch), *v.* **1.** dissolve out soluble parts from (ashes, etc.) by running water through slowly. **2.** lose soluble parts when water passes through. —*n.* **1.** solution obtained by leaching. **2.** container for use in leaching. [OE *leccan* to wet] —**leach′er,** *n.*

lead¹ (lēd), *v.,* led, lead·ing, *n.* —*v.* **1.** show the way by going along with or in front of; guide: *the star led the three wise men to Bethlehem.* **2.** conduct by the hand, a rope, etc.: *lead a horse.* **3.** act as guide: *lead, I will follow.* **4.** bring to a place, condition, etc.: *hard work leads to success.* **5.** conduct or bring (water, steam, a rope, a wire, etc.) in a particular channel or course. **6.** pass or spend (life, time, etc.): *lead an idle life.* **7.** afford passage or way to: *this road leads to the city.* **8.** influence; induce: *she is too easily led.* **9.** be a means of: *one word led to another.* **10.** be led; submit to being led: *this horse leads easily.* **11.** take or bring: *we led them away prisoners.* **12.** go or be at the head of: *lead a parade.* **13.** go or be first; have first place: *he leads his class.* **14.** be chief of; command; direct: *lead an army.* **15.** be chief; direct; act as leader. **16.** begin or open: *she led the dance.* **17.** begin with (card or suit named). **18.** make first play at cards. **19.** *Am.* in boxing, direct a blow at an opponent. —*n.* **1.** guidance; direction; example; precedence. **2.** first or foremost place; position in advance: *take the lead.* **3.** extent of advance. **4.** in cardplaying, the right of playing first or the card or suit so played. **5.** something that leads. **6.** in theatrical use: **a.** the principal part in a play. **b.** the person who plays it. **7.** string, strap, etc., for leading a dog or other animal. **8.** a guiding indication. **9.** *Am.* in mining, a lode. **10.** conductor conveying electricity. **11.** in boxing, blow directed at an opponent. **12.** the opening paragraph in a newspaper article. [OE *lædan*] —Syn. v. **1.** conduct. **8.** persuade, entice. **14.** head. ➤ lead, led. Lead and *led* show the confusion that English suffers because of representing one sound by different symbols. *Lead* (lēd), the present tense of the verb, gives no trouble; but *led,* the past tense, is often confused with *lead* (led), the metal, and misspelled: *Please lead the horse away. The culprit was led into the office. Lead is known as a base metal.*

lead² (led), *n.* **1.** a heavy, easily melted, bluish-gray metal, used to make pipe, etc. Lead is a chemical element. *Symbol:* Pb. **2.** something made of this metal or an alloy of it. **3.** weight on a line used to find out the depth of water; plummet. **4.** bullets; shot. **5.** a long, thin piece of graphite as used in pencils. **6.** metal strip for widening the space between lines in printing. —*v.* **1.** insert leads between lines of (print). **2.** cover, frame, or weight with lead. —*adj.* made of lead. [OE *lēad*]

lead·en (led′ən), *adj.* **1.** made of lead. **2.** like lead in any way: **a.** heavy. **b.** slow and heavy. **c.** dull; gloomy. **d.** bluish-gray: *leaden clouds.* —**lead′en·ly,** *adv* —**lead′en·ness,** *n.*

lead·er (lēd′ər), *n.* **1.** person or thing that leads. **2.** *Music.* conductor or principal performer. **3.** person who is well fitted to lead. **4.** *Am.* an important or leading article or editorial in a newspaper. **5.** *Am.* a short length of transparent material attaching the lure to a fish line. **6.** article offered at a low price to attract customers. **7.** leaders, row of dots or dashes to guide

āge, cāre, fär; ēqual, tėrm; īce; ōpen, ôrder; pùt, rüle, ūse; тн, then; ə=*a* in about.

the eye across a printed page. —**lead′er·less**, *adj.*
—**lead′er·ship**, *n.*

lead·ing[1] (lēd′ing), *n.* guidance; direction.
—*adj.* 1. guiding; directing. 2. most important;
chief: *the leading lady in a play.* —**lead′ing·ly**,
adv. —Syn. *adj.* 2. principal, main, foremost.

lead·ing[2] (led′ing), *n.* 1. covering or frame of
lead. 2. metal strips for widening the space between lines of type.

lead·ing question (lēd′ing), question so
worded that it suggests the answer desired.

lead pencil (led), pencil having a graphite
lead; ordinary pencil.

leaf (lēf), *n., pl.* **leaves,** *v.* —*n.* 1. one of the thin,
flat, green parts that grow on the stem of a tree
or other plant. 2. the leaves of some plant, such
as tobacco, as a commercial product. 3. foliage.
4. petal of a flower. 5. a sheet of paper. Each side
of a leaf is called a page. 6. something resembling
a leaf of a plant. 7. a very thin sheet of metal,
etc. 8. a flat movable piece in the top of a table.
9. the sliding, hinged, or movable part of a door,
shutter, etc. 10. **turn over a new leaf,** try to do
or be better in the future. —*v.* 1. put forth
leaves: *the trees leaf out in the spring.* 2. turn
the pages of. [OE *lēaf*] —**leaf′like′**, *adj.*

leaf·age (lēf′ij), *n.* leaves; foliage.

leaf bud, a bud producing a stem with leaves
only.

leaf·less (lēf′lis), *adj.* having no leaves.

leaf·let (lēf′lit), *n.* 1. a small or young leaf. 2.
one of the separate blades or divisions of a compound leaf. 3. a small, flat or folded sheet of
printed matter: *advertising leaflets.*

leaf·stalk (lēf′stôk′), *n.* a petiole.

leaf·y (lēf′i), *adj.,* **leaf·i·er, leaf·i·est.** having
many leaves; covered with leaves. —**leaf′i·ness,** *n.*

league[1] (lēg), *n., v.,* **leagued, lea·guing.** —*n.* 1.
association of persons, parties, or countries
formed to help one another. 2. persons, parties,
or countries associated in a league. 3. *Am.* an
association of baseball clubs. 4. **in league,** associated by agreement; associated. 5. **the League,**
the League of Nations. —*v.* associate in a league;
form a league. [< OF < Ital., ult. < L *ligare* bind]
—**lea′guer,** *n.* —Syn. *n.* 1. union, federation,
society, alliance.

league[2] (lēg), *n.* measure of distance, usually
about 3 miles. [< LL *leuga* < Celtic]

League of Nations, association of many
countries, formed in 1919 and dissolved in April,
1946, to promote peace and coöperation between
nations.

Le·ah (lē′ə), *n.* Jacob's first wife. Gen. 29:16.

leak (lēk), *n.* 1. hole or crack not meant to be
there that lets something in or out: *a leak in the
roof.* 2. leakage. 3. *Elect.* a point where current
escapes from a conductor. 4. means of escape.
—*v.* 1. go in or out through a hole or crack.
2. let something in which should be kept out; let
something out which should be kept in: *his boat
leaks.* 3. let (something) pass in or out: *that pipe
leaks gas.* 4. become known gradually: *the secret
leaked out.* [< Scand. *leka*]

leak·age (lēk′ij), *n.* 1. a leaking; a going in or
out through a leak. 2. that which leaks in or out.
3. amount of leaking.

leak·y (lēk′i), *adj.,* **leak·i·er, leak·i·est.** leaking;
having a leak or leaks. —**leak′i·ness,** *n.*

leal (lēl), *adj. Archaic or Scot.* loyal. —**leal′ly,**
adv.

lean[1] (lēn), *v.,* **leaned** or (*esp. Brit.*) **leant**
(lent), **lean·ing,** *n.* —*v.* 1. stand slanting, not
upright; bend: *a small tree leans over in the
wind.* 2. rest sloping or slanting: *lean against me.*
3. set or put in a leaning position: *lean against
the picture against the wall.* 4. depend; rely: *lean on a
friend's advice.* 5. bend or turn a little: *lean toward mercy.* 6. **lean over backward,** be excessive
in one direction so as to more than balance a
tendency in the opposite direction. —*n.* act of
leaning; inclination. [OE *hleonian*] —Syn. *v.* 1.
slant, incline, slope. 5. tend.

lean[2] (lēn), *adj.* 1. with little or no fat. 2. producing little; scant: *a lean harvest, a lean diet.*
—*n.* meat having little fat. [OE *hlǣne*]
—**lean′ly,** *adv.* —**lean′ness,** *n.* —Syn. *adj.* 1.

thin, spare, skinny, gaunt. 2. meager, barren,
unprofitable. —Ant. *adj.* 1. fat. 2. bountiful,
plentiful.

lean·ing (lēn′ing), *n.* tendency; inclination.
—Syn. proneness, bias, bent.

lean-to (lēn′tü′), *n., pl.* **-tos.** 1. building attached to another, to-
ward which its supports
or roof slants. 2. a crude
shelter built against a
tree or post. It is usually
open on one side.

Lean-to

leap (lēp), *n., v.,* **leaped**
or **leapt** (lept; lēpt),
leap·ing. —*n.* 1. a jump
or spring. 2. thing to be jumped. 3. distance covered by a jump. 4. **by leaps and bounds,** very
fast and very much; swiftly. —*v.* 1. jump: *a frog
leaps.* 2. jump over: *leap a wall.* 3. cause to
jump: *leap a horse over a wall.* 4. move quickly
and lightly: *the flames leaped up.* [OE *hlēapan*]
—**leap′er,** *n.* —Syn. *v.* 1. spring, bound. 2. vault.

leap·frog (lēp′frog′; -frôg′), *n.* game in which
one player jumps over another who is bending
over.

leap year, year having 366 days. The extra day
is February 29. A year is a leap year if its number
can be divided exactly by four, except years at
the end of a century, which must be exactly divisible by 400. The years 1952 and 2000 are leap
years; 1953 and 1900 are not.

learn (lérn), *v.,* **learned** or **learnt** (lérnt),
learn·ing. 1. gain knowledge of (a subject) or
skill in (an art, trade, etc.) by study, instruction,
or experience: *learn French.* 2. acquire knowledge, skill, etc.: *he learns easily.* 3. memorize:
learn a poem by heart. 4. find out; come to know.
5. become informed; hear. [OE *leornian*]
—**learn′er,** *n.* **> learn, teach.** Uneducated English often uses *learn* in the sense of *teach* (*He
learned me how to tie six kinds of knots*). Educated usage keeps the distinction: *He taught me
how to tie six kinds of knots. I learned how to tie
knots from him.*

learn·ed (lér′nid), *adj.* having, showing, or requiring much knowledge; scholarly. —**learn′-
ed·ly,** *adv.* —**learn′ed·ness,** *n.* —Syn. educated,
erudite.

learn·ing (lér′ning), *n.* 1. the gaining of
knowledge or skill. 2. possession of knowledge
gained by study; scholarship. 3. knowledge.
—Syn. 2. education.

lease (lēs), *n., v.,* **leased, leas·ing.** —*n.* 1. contract, usually in the form of a written agree-
ment, giving the right to use property for a
certain length of time, usually by paying rent. 2.
length of time for which such an agreement is
made. —*v.* 1. give a lease on. 2. take a lease on.
3. be leased. [< AF < L *laxare* loosen < *laxus*
loose] —**leas′er,** *n.*

leash (lēsh), *n.* 1. strap, chain, etc., for holding
a dog or other animal in check. 2. **hold in leash,**
control. —*v.* fasten or hold in with a leash; control. [< OF < L *laxa*, fem., loose]

least (lēst), *adj.* less than any other; smallest;
slightest: *the least distance.* —*n.* 1. least amount
or degree: *that is the least you can do.* 2. **at
least** or **at the least,** a. at the lowest estimate.
b. at any rate; in any case. 3. **not in the least,**
not at all. —*adv.* to the least extent, amount, or
degree: *he liked that book least of all.* [OE *lǣst*]

least·wise (lēst′wīz′), **least·ways** (-wāz′),
adv. Colloq. at least; at any rate.

leath·er (leth′ər), *n.* material made from the
skin of animals by removing the hair and then
tanning it. —*adj.* made of leather: *leather
gloves.* —*v.* furnish or cover with leather. [OE
lether]

leath·ern (leth′ərn), *adj.* 1. made of leather.
2. like leather.

leath·er·neck (leth′ər·nek′), *n. Slang.* a U.S.
marine.

leath·er·y (leth′ər·i), *adj.* like leather; tough.
—**leath′er·i·ness,** *n.*

leave[1] (lēv), *v.,* **left, leav·ing.** 1. go away: *he has
just left.* 2. go away from: *he left the house.* 3.
stop living in, belonging to, or working at or for:

leave a club. 4. go without taking; let remain: *the wound left a scar.* 5. forsake; abandon: *he left his wife.* 6. leave off, stop. 7. let remain in a particular condition: *leave a window open.* 8. leave out, fail to do, say, or put in; omit. 9. let remain when one dies; bequeath: *he left a large fortune.* 10. give to be kept; deposit: *leave until called for.* 11. let be; leave (to someone) to do: *leave him alone.* 12. let remain uneaten, unused, unremoved, etc.: *there is some coal left.* [OE *lǣfan*] —**leav′er**, *n.* —Syn. 1. depart. 5. desert. 9. will, devise. ➤ See let for usage note.

leave² (lēv), *n.* 1. permission; consent: *they gave him leave to go.* 2. permission to be absent from duty. 3. length of time that this lasts. 4. on leave, absent from duty with permission. 5. take leave of, say good-by to. [OE *lēaf*] —Syn. 1. authorization, liberty.

leave³ (lēv), *v.,* leaved, leav·ing. put forth leaves: *trees leave in the spring.* [var. of *leaf*]

leav·en (lev′ən), *n.* 1. any substance, such as yeast, that will cause fermentation and raise dough. 2. a small amount of fermenting dough kept for this purpose. 3. influence that, spreading silently and strongly, changes conditions or opinions. —*v.* 1. raise with a leaven; make (dough) light or lighter. 2. spread through and transform. [< OF < L *levamen* a lifting < *levare* raise]

leaves (lēvz), *n.* pl. of leaf.

leave-tak·ing (lēv′tāk′ing), *n.* act of taking leave; saying good-by.

leav·ing (lēv′ing), *n.* 1. thing left over. 2. leavings, leftovers; remnants.

Leb·a·non (leb′ə·nən), *n.* republic at the E end of the Mediterranean, N of Israel. —**Leb·a·nese** (leb′ə·nēz′; -nēs′), *adj., n.*

Le·bens·raum (lā′bəns·roum′), *n.* additional territory that a nation must control in order to expand economically. [< G, lit., living space]

lech·er (lech′ər), *n.* man who indulges in lechery. [< OF *lecheor* licker < *lechier* lick < Gmc.]

lech·er·ous (lech′ər·əs), *adj.* lewd; lustful. —**lech′er·ous·ly,** *adv.* —**lech′er·ous·ness,** *n.*

lech·er·y (lech′ər·i), *n.* lewdness.

lec·tern (lek′tərn), *n.* a reading desk in a church, esp. the desk from which the lessons are read. [< OF < Med.L *lectrum* < L *legere* read]

Lectern

lec·ture (lek′chər), *n., v.,* -tured, -tur·ing. —*n.* 1. speech; planned talk on a chosen subject; such a talk written down or printed. 2. a scolding. —*v.* 1. give a lecture. 2. instruct or entertain by a lecture. 3. scold; reprove. [< L *lectura* < L *legere* read] —**lec′tur·er,** *n.* —**lec′ture·ship,** *n.*

led (led), *v.* pt. and pp. of lead¹. ➤ See lead¹ for usage note.

Le·da (lē′də), *n.* Gk. Myth. the mother of Castor and Pollux, Clytemnestra, and Helen of Troy.

ledge (lej), *n.* 1. a narrow shelf: *a window ledge.* 2. shelf or ridge of rock. [< ME *legge(n)* lay¹] —**ledged,** *adj.*

ledg·er (lej′ər), *n.* book of accounts in which a business keeps a record of all money transactions. [< ME *legge(n)* lay¹]

ledger line, Music. line added above or below the staff for notes that are too high or too low to be put on the staff. Also, leger line.

lee¹ (lē), *n.* 1. shelter. 2. side or part sheltered from the wind. 3. side away from the wind. 4. direction toward which the wind is blowing. —*adj.* 1. sheltered from the wind. 2. on the side away from the wind. 3. in the direction toward which the wind is blowing. [OE *hlēo*]

lee² (lē), *n.* Usually, lees. dregs; sediment, as from wine. [< F *lie* < Celtic]

Lee (lē), *n.* Robert E., 1807–1870, the most famous Confederate general in the Civil War.

leech¹ (lēch), *n.* 1. worm living in ponds and streams that sucks the blood of animals, formerly used to suck blood from sick people. 2. person who tries persistently to get what he can out of others. 3. Archaic. doctor. [OE *lǣce*] —**leech′-like′,** *adj.*

leech² (lēch), *n. Naut.* edge of a sail not fastened to a rope or spar.

Leeds (lēdz), *n.* city in N England.

leek (lēk), *n.* vegetable somewhat like an onion, but with larger leaves, a smaller bulb shaped like a cylinder, and a milder flavor. [OE *lēac*]

leer (lir), *n.* a sly sidelong look; evil glance. —*v.* give a sly sidelong look; glance evilly. [? OE *hlēor* cheek] —**leer′ing·ly,** *adv.*

leer·y (lir′i), *adj. Slang.* 1. sly. 2. wary.

lee·ward (lē′wərd; lū′ərd), *adj.* 1. on the side away from the wind. 2. in the direction toward which the wind is blowing. —*adv.* toward the lee side. —*n.* side away from the wind.

Lee·ward Islands (lē′wərd), 1. the northern part of the Lesser Antilles in the West Indies. 2. part of the Leeward Islands forming a British colony.

lee·way (lē′wā′), *n.* 1. side movement of a ship to leeward, out of its course. 2. extra space at the side; time, money, etc., more than is needed. 3. convenient room or scope for action.

left¹ (left), *adj.* 1. belonging to the side of the less used hand (in most people); having this relation to the front of any object: *the left wing of an army.* 2. situated nearer the observer's or speaker's left hand than his right. —*adv.* on or to the left side: *turn left.* —*n.* 1. the left side or hand. 2. part of a lawmaking body consisting of the more radical groups. [dial. OE *left* (for *lyft*) weak]

left² (left), *v.* pt. and pp. of leave¹.

left-hand (left′hand′), *adj.* 1. on or to the left. 2. of, for, or with the left hand.

left-hand·ed (left′han′did), *adj.* 1. using the left hand more easily and readily than the right. 2. done with the left hand. 3. made to be used with the left hand. 4. turning from right to left. 5. clumsy; awkward. 6. doubtful; insincere. —**left′-hand′ed·ly,** *adv.* —**left′-hand′ed·ness,** *n.*

left·ist (left′tist), *n.* 1. person who has radical ideas. 2. member of a radical or extreme organization. —*adj. Colloq.* having radical ideas.

left·o·ver (left′ō′vər), *n.* thing that is left: *scraps of food from a meal are leftovers.* —*adj.* that is left; remaining.

left wing, the radical members, as of a political party. —**left′-wing′,** *adj.* —**left′-wing′er,** *n.*

leg (leg), *n., v.,* legged, leg·ging. —*n.* 1. one of the limbs on which men and animals support themselves and walk. 2. part of a garment that covers a leg. 3. anything shaped or used like a leg. 4. one of the distinct portions or stages of any course: *last leg of a trip.* 5. course or run made by a sailing vessel on one tack. 6. side of a triangle that is not the base or hypotenuse. 7. pull one's leg, Colloq. fool, trick, or make fun of him. 8. stretch one's legs, take a walk. —*v. Colloq.* walk; run: *we could not get a ride, so we had to leg it.* [< Scand. *leggr*] —**leg′less,** *adj.*

leg., 1. legal. 2. legislative; legislature.

leg·a·cy (leg′ə·si), *n., pl.* -cies. 1. money or other property left to a person by a will. 2. something that has been handed down from an ancestor or predecessor. [< OF < Med.L *legatia* < L *legatum* bequest]

le·gal (lē′gəl), *adj.* 1. of law: *legal knowledge.* 2. of lawyers. 3. according to law; lawful. 4. recognized by law rather than by equity. [< L *legalis* < *lex* law. Doublet of LOYAL.] —**le′gal·ly,** *adv.*

le·gal·ism (lē′gəl·iz·əm), *n.* strict adherence to law or prescription. —**le′gal·ist,** *n.* —**le′gal·is′-tic,** *adj.*

le·gal·i·ty (li·gal′ə·ti), *n., pl.* -ties. accordance with law; lawfulness.

le·gal·ize (lē′gəl·īz), *v.,* -ized, -iz·ing. make legal; authorize by law; sanction. —**le′gal·i·za′-tion,** *n.*

legal tender, money that must, by law, be accepted in payment of debts.

leg·ate (leg′it), *n.* 1. ambassador; representative; messenger. 2. a representative of the Pope. [< L *legatus*, orig., provided with a contract < *lex* contract] —**leg′ate·ship,** *n.*

leg·a·tee (leg′ə·tē′), *n.* person to whom a legacy is left.

le·ga·tion (li·gā′shən), *n.* 1. the diplomatic representative of a country and his staff of assistants. A legation ranks next below an embassy. 2. the official residence, offices, etc., of a diplomatic representative in a foreign country. [< F < L *legatio*] —**le·ga·tion·ar·y** (li·gā′shən·er′i), *adj.*

le·ga·to (li·gä′tō), *adj. Music.* smooth and connected; without breaks between successive tones. [< Ital., bound]

leg·end (lej′ənd), *n.* 1. story coming down from the past, which many people have believed. The stories about King Arthur and his knights are legends, not history. 2. such stories as a group. 3. inscription on a coin or medal. 4. words, etc., accompanying a picture or diagram; caption. [< OF < Med.L, < L *legenda* (things) to be read < *legere* read]

leg·end·ar·y (lej′ən·der′i), *adj.* of a legend or legends; like a legend; not historical.

leg·er·de·main (lej′ər·də·mān′), *n.* 1. sleight of hand; conjuring tricks; jugglery. 2. trickery. [< F, quick of hand] —**leg′er·de·main′ist,** *n.*

leg·er line (lej′ər), *Music.* ledger line.

leg·gings (leg′ingz), *n.pl.* extra outer coverings of cloth or leather for the legs, for use out of doors.

Leg·horn (leg′hôrn *for 1; also* -ərn *for 2, 3*), *n.* 1. seaport in W Italy. 2. a small kind of domestic fowl. 3. leghorn, hat made of flat, yellow, braided straw.

leg·i·ble (lej′ə·bəl), *adj.* 1. that can be read. 2. easy to read; plain and clear. [< LL, < L *legere* read] —**leg′i·bil′i·ty, leg′i·ble·ness,** *n.* —**leg′i·bly,** *adv.*

le·gion (lē′jən), *n.* 1. body of soldiers; army. 2. body of soldiers in the ancient Roman army consisting of 3000 to 6000 foot soldiers and 300 to 700 cavalrymen. 3. great many; very large number. [< OF < L *legio*]

le·gion·ar·y (lē′jən·er′i), *adj., n., pl.* -ar·ies. —*adj.* of or belonging to a legion. —*n.* soldier of a legion.

le·gion·naire (lē′jən·ãr′), *n.* member of a legion.

leg·is·late (lej′is·lāt), *v.,* -lat·ed, -lat·ing. 1. make laws: *Congress legislates for the United States.* 2. force by legislation: *the council legislated him out of office.*

leg·is·la·tion (lej′is·lā′shən), *n.* 1. the making of laws. 2. the laws made.

leg·is·la·tive (lej′is·lā′tiv), *adj.* 1. having to do with making laws. 2. having the duty and power of making laws: *Congress is a legislative body.* 3. ordered by law. —**leg′is·la′tive·ly,** *adv.*

leg·is·la·tor (lej′is·lā′tər), *n.* lawmaker; member of a legislative body. [< L *legis lator* proposer of a law]

leg·is·la·ture (lej′is·lā′chər), *n.* group of persons that has the duty and power of making laws for a state or country.

le·git (lə·jit′), *adj. Slang.* legitimate.

le·git·i·ma·cy (lə·jit′ə·mə·si), *n.* being legitimate or lawful; being recognized as lawful or proper.

le·git·i·mate (*adj.* lə·jit′ə·mit; *v.* lə·jit′ə·māt), *adj., v.,* -mat·ed, -mat·ing. —*adj.* 1. rightful; lawful; allowed: *a legitimate excuse.* 2. conforming to accepted standards. 3. born of parents who are married. 4. resting on, or ruling by, the principle of hereditary right: *the legitimate title to a throne.* 5. logical: *a legitimate conclusion.* —*v.* make or declare lawful. [< Med.L, < L *legitimus* lawful] —**le·git′i·mate·ly,** *adv.* —**le·git′i·mate·ness,** *n.*

legitimate stage, drama acted on the stage as opposed to motion pictures.

le·git·i·mist (lə·jit′ə·mist), *n.* supporter of legitimate authority, esp. of claims to rule based on direct descent. —**le·git′i·mism,** *n.* —**le·git′i·mis′tic,** *adv.*

le·git·i·mize (lə·jit′ə·mīz), *v.,* -mized, -mizing. make or declare to be legitimate. —**le·git′i·mi·za′tion,** *n.*

leg·ume (leg′ūm; li·gūm′), *n.* 1. plant having a number of seeds in a pod, such as beans, peas, etc. Many legumes can absorb nitrogen from the air. 2. seed pod of such a plant. [< F < L *legumen*]

le·gu·mi·nous (li·gū′mə·nəs), *adj.* 1. of or bearing legumes. 2. of the same group of plants as beans and peas.

Le Ha·vre (lə hä′vər; -vrə), seaport in N France. Also, Havre.

lei (lā), *n., pl.* leis. wreath of flowers, leaves, etc. [< Hawaiian]

Leib·nitz (līb′nits), *n.* Gottfried Wilhelm, 1646–1716, German philosopher, mathematician, and writer.

Leices·ter (les′tər), *n.* 1. Earl of (*Robert Dudley*) 1532?–1588, English statesman, favorite of Queen Elizabeth. 2. city in C England.

Lei·den (lī′dən), *n.* city in SW Netherlands. Also, Leyden.

Leip·zig, Leip·sic (līp′sig; -sik), *n.* city in C Germany.

lei·sure (lē′zhər; lezh′ər), *n.* 1. time free from required work in which a person may rest, amuse himself, and do the things he likes to do. 2. at leisure, a. free; not busy. b. without hurry; taking plenty of time. 3. at one's leisure, at one's convenience. —*adj.* 1. free; not busy: *leisure hours.* 2. having leisure: *the leisure class.* [< OF *leisir* < L *licere* be allowed]

lei·sure·ly (lē′zhər·li; lezh′ər-), *adj., adv.* without hurry; taking plenty of time. —**lei′sure·li·ness,** *n.*

leit·mo·tif, leit·mo·tiv (līt′mō·tēf′), *n.* a short passage in a musical composition, associated throughout the work with a certain person, situation, or idea. [< G *leitmotiv* leading motive]

le·man (lem′ən), *n. Archaic.* 1. sweetheart. 2. unlawful lover; mistress. [ME *leofman* < *leof* dear + *man* man]

Le·man (lē′mən), *n.* Lake. See Geneva, Lake of.

Lem·berg (lem′bérg), *n.* German name of Lvov.

lem·ming (lem′ing), *n.* a small, mouselike arctic animal, having a short tail and furry feet. [< Norw.]

lem·on (lem′ən), *n.* 1. a sour, light-yellow citrus fruit growing in warm climates. 2. a thorny tree that bears this fruit. 3. a pale yellow. 4. *Am., Slang.* something disagreeable, unpleasant, or worthless. —*adj.* pale-yellow. [< OF < Ar. < Pers. *līmūn*]

lem·on·ade (lem′ən·ād′), *n.* drink made of lemon juice, sugar, and water.

le·mur (lē′mər), *n.* animal somewhat like a monkey, but having a foxlike face and woolly fur, found mainly in Madagascar. [< L, specter]

Lemur (total length ab. 3 ft.)

lend (lend), *v.,* lent, lend·ing. 1. let another have or use for a time: *lend an umbrella.* 2. give the use of (money) for a fixed or specified amount of payment: *banks lend money and charge interest.* 3. make a loan or loans. 4. give for a time; give: *a becoming dress lends charm to a girl.* 5. lend itself or oneself to, help or be suitable for. [OE *lǣnan* < *lǣn* loan] —**lend′er,** *n.*

Lend-Lease Act (lend′lēs′), an act passed March 11, 1941 enabling the president of the United States to give material aid to any nation whose defense he felt vital to U.S. security.

length (lengkth; length), *n.* 1. how long a thing is; thing's measurement from end to end; longest way a thing can be measured: *the length of a rope.* 2. distance a thing extends. 3. extent in time: *length of an hour.* 4. long stretch or tent. 5. piece or portion of given length: *a length of rope.* 6. at length, a. at last; finally. b. in full; with all the details. 7. go to any length, do everything possible. 8. **keep at arm's length,** keep from being too familiar. [OE, < *lang* long[1]]

length·en (lengk'thən; leng'-), *v.* 1. make longer. 2. become or grow longer. —Syn. 1, 2. stretch.

length·wise (lengkth'wīz'; length'-), *adv.* Also, **length·ways** (lengkth'wāz'; length'-). In the direction of the length. —*adj.* directed toward the length.

length·y (lengk'thi; leng'-), *adj.*, **length·i·er, length·i·est.** Am. long; too long. —**length'i·ly,** *adv.* —**length'i·ness,** *n.* —Syn. extended.

len·ien·cy (lēn'yən·si; lē'ni·ən-), **len·ience** (-yəns; -ni·əns), *n.* mildness; gentleness; mercy.

len·ient (lēn'yənt; lē'ni·ənt), *adj.* mild; gentle; merciful. [< L *leniens* softening < *lenis* mild] —**len'ient·ly,** *adv.* —Syn. compassionate, tolerant.

Len·in (len'in), *n.* Nikolay, 1870–1924, Russian leader, the founder of the Soviet government and its head from 1917 to 1924.

Len·in·grad (len'in·grad; -gräd), *n.* seaport in NW Soviet Union, on the Gulf of Finland. Formerly St. Petersburg or Petrograd.

len·i·tive (len'ə·tiv), *adj.* softening; soothing. —*n.* anything that soothes or softens.

len·i·ty (len'ə·ti), *n.*, *pl.* -**ties.** mildness; gentleness; mercifulness. [< L, < *lenis* mild]

lens (lenz), *n.*, *pl.* **lens·es.** piece of glass, or something like glass, that brings closer together or sends wider apart the rays of light passing through it. The lens of the eye and the lens of a camera form images. The lenses of a telescope make things look larger and nearer. [< L, *lentil* (which has a biconvex shape)]

lent (lent), *v.* pt. and pp. of **lend.**

Lent (lent), *n.* 1. the forty weekdays before Easter, kept as a time for fasting and repenting of sins. 2. any similar period of fasting. [OE *lengten* spring < *lang* long[1] (from lengthening days)]

Lent·en, lent·en (len'tən), *adj.* of or during Lent; suitable for Lent.

len·til (len'təl), *n.* 1. plant whose pods contain two seeds shaped like double-convex lenses. Lentils grow mostly in S Europe and Asia. 2. seed of this plant. Lentils are eaten like peas. [< F < L *lenticula,* dim. of *lens* lentil]

len·to (len'tō), *adj.*, *adv. Music.* slow; slowly. [< Ital., slow]

l'en·voi, l'en·voy (len'voi; len·voi'), *n.* a short stanza ending a poem. [< F, lit., the sending]

Le·o (lē'ō), *n.*, *gen.* **Le·o·nis** (li·ō'nis). 1. a northern constellation that was thought of as arranged in the shape of a lion. 2. the fifth sign of the zodiac; the Lion.

le·o·nine (lē'ə·nīn), *adj.* of or like a lion. [< L, < *leo* LION]

leop·ard (lep'ərd), *n.* 1. a fierce animal of Africa and Asia that has a dull-yellowish skin spotted with black. 2. jaguar or American leopard. [< OF < L < Gk., < *leon* lion + *pardos* leopard]

leop·ard·ess (lep'ər·dis), *n.* a female leopard.

Le·o·pold III (lē'ə·pōld), born 1901, king of Belgium 1934–1950.

Le·o·pold·ville (lē'ə·pōld·vil'), *n.* former name of the capital of the Congo. Now, Kinshasa.

lep·er (lep'ər), *n.* person who has leprosy. [< OF < L < Gk. *lepra* leprosy. See LEPROUS.]

lep·i·dop·ter·ous (lep'ə·dop'tər·əs), *adj.* belonging to the group of insects including butterflies and moths. The larvae are wormlike; the adults have four broad wings. [< NL, < Gk. *lepis* scale + *pteron* wing] —**lep'i·dop'ter·an,** *adj.*, *n.*

lep·re·chaun (lep'rə·kôn), *n.* in Irish folklore, a sprite or goblin resembling a little old man. [< Irish *lupracan*]

lep·ro·sy (lep'rə·si), *n.* an infectious disease, characterized by ulcers and white, scaly scabs. [< *leprous*]

lep·rous (lep'rəs), *adj.* 1. having leprosy. 2. of or like leprosy. [< LL, < *lepra* leprosy < Gk., < *lepein* to peel] —**lep'rous·ly,** *adv.*

Les·bi·an (lez'bi·ən), *adj.* pertaining to Lesbianism. —*n.* **lesbian,** a homosexual woman.

Les·bi·an·ism (lez'bi·ən·iz'əm), *n.* homosexual relations between women.

Les·bos (lez'bos), *n.* former name of Mytilene.

lese-maj·es·ty (lēz'maj'is·ti), *n.* crime or offense against the sovereign power in a state; treason. [< F < L *laesa majestas* insulted sovereignty]

le·sion (lē'zhən), *n.* 1. injury; hurt. 2. a diseased condition. [< L *laesio* injury < *laedere* to strike]

less (les), *adj.* 1. smaller; not so much: *less time.* 2. lower in age, rank, or importance: *no less a person than the President.* —*n.* a smaller amount or quantity. —*adv.* to a smaller extent or degree: *less known.* —*prep.* lacking; without; minus: *a year less two days.* [OE lǣs(sa)] ▶ **less, lesser.** Both are used as comparatives (of *little*), *less* more usually referring to size, or quantity (*less time, less food*), *lesser* a formal word, referring to value or importance (*a lesser writer*). See also *few* for another usage note.

-less, *suffix.* 1. without; that has no, as in *childless, homeless.* 2. that does not, as in *ceaseless, tireless.* 3. that cannot be ——ed, as in *countless.* [OE *-lēas*] ▶ **-less** is freely added to almost any noun to form an adjective with any of the above meanings.

les·see (les·ē'), *n.* person to whom a lease is granted. —**les·see'ship,** *n.*

less·en (les'ən), *v.* 1. grow less. 2. make less; decrease. 3. represent as less; minimize. —Syn. 1, 2. diminish, shrink. 3. belittle.

less·er (les'ər), *adj.* 1. less; smaller: *the lesser evil.* 2. the smaller or less important of two. ▶ See **less** for usage note.

Lesser Antilles, chain of small islands in the West Indies, SE of Puerto Rico.

les·son (les'ən), *n.* 1. something learned or studied. 2. unit of learning or teaching; what is to be studied or practiced at one time: *a music lesson.* 3. an instructive experience, serving to encourage or warn. 4. selection from the Bible, read as part of a church service. 5. rebuke; lecture. [< OF < L *lectio* reading < *legere* read]

les·sor (les'ôr; les·ôr'), *n.* person who grants a lease.

lest (lest), *conj.* 1. for fear that; that ——not; in order that ——not: *be careful lest you fall from that tree.* 2. that: *I was afraid lest he should come too late to save us.* [OE *thȳ lǣs the* whereby less]

let[1] (let), *v.*, **let, let·ting.** 1. allow; permit: *she is letting her hair grow.* 2. allow to pass, go, or come: *let a person on board a ship.* 3. allow to run out: *doctors used to let blood from people to lessen a fever.* 4. rent; hire out: *let a boat by the hour.* 5. be rented: *that house lets for $80 a month.* 6. assign by contract: *let work to a contractor.* 7. *Let* is used in giving suggestions or giving commands. "Let's go home" means "I suggest that we go home." 8. suppose; assume: *let the two lines be parallel.* 9. **let alone, a.** leave alone; not touch or interfere with. **b.** not to mention. 10. **let be, a.** leave alone. **b.** leave off. 11. **let down, a.** lower. **b.** slow up. **c.** disappoint. **d.** humiliate. 12. **let go,** release the hold on. 13. **let in,** admit; permit to enter. 14. **let know,** tell. 15. **let off,** allow to go free. 16. **let on,** *Colloq.* **a.** allow to be known; reveal one's knowledge of. **b.** pretend; make believe. 17. **let out, a.** permit to go out. **b.** make larger. **c.** rent. **d.** *Am., Colloq.* dismiss or be dismissed, as a school or a meeting. **e.** make known; disclose. 18. **let up,** *Colloq.* stop; pause. [OE *lǣtan*] ▶ **let, leave.** A very common uneducated idiom is the use of *leave* where formal and informal English use *let.* Both idioms are shown in this sentence by a writer who was obviously making a transition between the two levels: *By the time I got to high school, I was cured of the practice of leaving* [uneducated] *notebooks go, but I fell immediately into the habit of letting* [informal] *homework slide.* Use *let:* Let it go. Let it lie where it is.

let[2] (let), *v.*, **let·ted** or **let, let·ting,** *n.* —*v.*

Archaic. prevent; hinder. —*n.* **1.** prevention; hindrance; obstruction. **2. without let or hindrance,** with nothing to prevent, hinder, or obstruct. [OE *lettan* < *læt* late]

-let, *suffix.* **1.** little, as in *booklet, streamlet.* **2.** thing worn as a band on, as in *anklet, armlet.* **3.** other meanings, as in *couplet, gauntlet, ringlet.* [< OF *-elet*]

let·down (let′doun′), *n.* **1.** a slowing up. **2.** *Colloq.* disappointment. **3.** humiliation.

le·thal (lē′thəl), *adj.* causing death; deadly: *a lethal dose.* [< L *let(h)alis* < *letum* death]

le·thar·gic (lə·thär′jik), **le·thar·gi·cal** (-jə·kəl), *adj.* **1.** unnaturally drowsy; sluggish; dull: *a hot, humid day produces a lethargic condition.* **2.** producing lethargy. —**le·thar′gi·cal·ly,** *adv.*

leth·ar·gy (leth′ər·ji), *n., pl.* **-gies. 1.** drowsy dullness; lack of energy; sluggish inactivity. **2.** *Pathol.* unnatural sleep. [< L < Gk. *lethargia,* ult. < *lethe* forgetfulness] —**Syn. 1.** torpor, apathy, stupor.

Le·the (lē′thē), *n. Gk. Myth.* **1.** river in Hades. Drinking its water caused forgetfulness of the past. **2.** forgetfulness; oblivion. [< L < Gk., oblivion] —**Le·the·an** (li·thē′ən), *adj.*

let's (lets), let us.

Lett (let), *n.* **1.** member of a group of people living in Latvia. **2.** their language; Lettish.

let·ter (let′ər), *n.* **1.** mark or sign (on paper, etc.) that stands for any one of the sounds that make up words. **2.** written or printed message. **3.** official document granting some right or privilege. **4.** exact wording; actual terms: *he kept the letter of a law but not the spirit.* **5.** letters, **a.** literature. **b.** knowledge of literature; literary culture. **c.** profession of an author. **6. to the letter,** very exactly; just as one has been told. —*v.* **1.** mark with letters. **2.** inscribe (something) in letters. [< OF < L *littera*] —**let′ter·er,** *n.* ► For a guide to letter writing see pp. 28-32.

let·tered (let′ərd), *adj.* **1.** marked with letters. **2.** able to read and write; educated. **3.** knowing literature; having literary culture.

let·ter·head (let′ər·hed′), *n.* **1.** words printed at the top of a sheet of paper, usually a name and address. **2.** sheet of paper so printed.

let·ter·ing (let′ər·ing), *n.* **1.** letters drawn, painted, stamped, etc. **2.** a marking with letters; making letters.

letter of credit, document issued by a bank, allowing the person named in it to draw money up to a certain amount from other specified banks.

let·ter-per·fect (let′ər·pér′fikt), *adj.* correct in every detail.

letter press, machine for making copies of letters.

let·ter·press (let′ər·pres′), *n.* **1.** matter printed from types, rather than from engraved plates. **2.** printed text, as distinguished from illustrations, etc.

letters of marque, or **letters of marque and reprisal,** an official document giving a person permission from a government to capture the merchant ships of an enemy.

letters patent, an official document giving a person authority from a government to do some act or to have some right.

Let·tish (let′ish), *adj.* of the Letts or their language. —*n.* language of the Letts.

let·tuce (let′is), *n.* **1.** the large, crisp, green leaves of a plant much used in salad. **2.** the plant. [< OF < L *lactuca* < *lac* milk]

let·up (let′up′), *n. Colloq.* stop; pause.

leu·co·cyte (lü′kə·sīt), *n. Physiol.* a white blood corpuscle; one of the tiny white cells in the blood that destroy disease germs. [< Gk. *leukos* white + *kytos* hollow body]

leu·ke·mi·a (lü·kē′mi·ə; -kēm′yə), *n.* a rare, and usually fatal, disease characterized by a large excess of white corpuscles in the blood.

Lev., Leviticus.

Le·vant (lə·vant′), *n.* countries on the Mediterranean Sea, E of Italy. —**Le·van·tine** (lə·van′tin; lev′ən·tīn; -tēn), *adj., n.*

lev·ee¹ (lev′i), *n. Am.* **1.** bank built to keep a river from overflowing. **2.** a landing place for boats. [< F, < *lever* raise < L *levare*]

lev·ee², lev·ée (lev′i; le·vē′), *n.* reception. French kings used to hold levees in the morning while they were getting up and dressing. [< F *levé, lever.* See LEVEE¹.]

lev·el (lev′əl), *adj., n., v.,* **-eled, -el·ing;** *esp.* Brit. **-elled, -el·ling.** —*adj.* **1.** having the same height everywhere; flat; even: *a level floor.* **2.** horizontal. **3.** of equal height, importance, etc.: *the table is level with the edge of the window.* **4.** even; uniform; steady: *a calm and level tone.* **5.** one's level best, *Colloq.* one's very best; as well as one can do. **6.** *Am.* well-balanced; sensible. —*n.* **1.** something that is level. **2.** instrument for showing whether a surface is level. **3.** level position or condition. **4.** height: *the flood rose to a level of 60 feet.* **5.** position or standard from a social, moral, or intellectual point of view. **6. find one's** or **its level,** arrive at the natural or proper level. **7. on the level,** *Am., Colloq.* in a fair straightforward manner. —*v.* **1.** make level; put on the same level. **2.** bring to a level. **3.** lay low; bring (something) to the level of the ground. **4.** raise and hold level for shooting; aim. **5.** aim or direct (words, intentions, etc.). **6.** remove or reduce (differences, etc.); make uniform. [< OF, ult. < L *libella,* dim. of *libra* balance] —**lev′el·er,** *esp. Brit.* **lev′el·ler,** *n.* —**lev′el·ly,** *adv.* —**lev′el·ness,** *n.* —**Syn.** *adj.* **1.** smooth, plane. —**Ant.** *adj.* **1.** uneven, rough, undulating.

Level (def. 2)

lev·eled (lev′əld), *adj. Gram.* of words in sentences, phrases, etc., made equal to each other by a word such as *and* or by accent. In "The coat, hat, and cane belong to him," *coat, hat,* and *cane* are leveled.

lev·el-head·ed (lev′əl·hed′id), *adj. Am.* having good common sense and judgment.

lev·er (lev′ər; lē′vər), *n.* **1.** bar for raising or moving a weight at one end by pushing down at the other end. It must be supported at a point in between. **2.** any bar working on an axis or support. —*v.* **1.** move with a lever. **2.** use a lever. [< OF *leveor* < *lever* raise < L *levare*] —**lev′er·like′,** *adj.*

LEVER
FULCRUM

lev·er·age (lev′ər·ij; lē′vər-), *n.* **1.** action of a lever. **2.** advantage or power gained by using a lever. **3.** increased power of action.

lev·er·et (lev′ər·it), *n.* a young hare.

Le·vi (lē′vī), *n. Bible.* a son of Jacob and ancestor of the Levites.

le·vi·a·than (lə·vī′ə·thən), *n.* **1.** *Bible.* a huge sea animal. **2.** a huge ship. **3.** any great and powerful person or thing. [< LL < Heb. *liwyāthān* dragon, crocodile, prob. < *lavāh* twist, wind]

Le·vis (lē′vīz), *n.pl. Am.* **1.** *Trademark.* heavy blue denim trousers reinforced at strain points with copper rivets, as made by Levi Strauss and Company. **2.** bibless overalls.

lev·i·tate (lev′ə·tāt), *v.,* **-tat·ed, -tat·ing. 1.** rise or float in the air. **2.** cause to rise or float in the air. [< L *levitas* lightness (see LEVITY), modeled after *gravitate*] —**lev′i·ta′tion,** *n.* —**lev′i·ta′tor,** *n.*

Le·vite (lē′vīt), *n.* member of the tribe of Levi, from which assistants to the Jewish priests were chosen.

Le·vit·i·cal (lə·vit′ə·kəl), *adj.* **1.** of the Levites. **2.** of Leviticus or the law contained in it.

Le·vit·i·cus (lə·vit′ə·kəs), *n.* the third book of the Old Testament, containing the laws for the priests and Levites and the ritual for Jewish rites and ceremonies.

lev·i·ty (lev′ə·ti), *n., pl.* **-ties.** lightness of mind, character, or behavior; lack of proper seriousness or earnestness: *giggling in church shows levity.* [< L, < *levis* light] —**Syn.** flippancy, frivolity, flightiness.

lev·u·lose (lev′yə-lōs), *n. Chem.* fructose. [< L *laevus* left; under polarized light its plane of polarization is turned to the left]

lev·y (lev′ĭ), *v.*, **lev·ied, lev·y·ing,** *n., pl.* **lev·ies.** —*v.* **1.** order to be paid: *the government levies taxes to pay its expenses.* **2.** collect (men) for an army: *troops are levied in time of war.* **3.** seize by law for unpaid debts: *a court can levy on a person's property for unpaid debts.* **4.** levy war on, make war on; start a war against. —*n.* **1.** money collected. **2.** men collected for an army. **3.** a levying. [< F *levée* < *lever* raise. See LEVEE[1].] —lev·i·er (lev′ĭ-ər), *n.*

lewd (lūd), *adj.* **1.** lustful; lascivious. **2.** indecent; obscene. [OE *lǣwede* laic] —lewd′ly, *adv.* —lewd′ness, *n.* —**Syn. 1.** lecherous, sensual, wanton. —**Ant. 1.** chaste, pure.

Lew·is (lū′ĭs), *n.* **1.** John L(lewellyn), born 1880, American labor leader. **2.** Meriwether, 1774-1809, American explorer. **3.** Sinclair, 1885-1951, American novelist.

lew·is·ite (lū′ĭs-īt), *n.* a colorless, irritating, poisonous gas, used in warfare. [after W. Lee *Lewis,* chemist]

lex (leks), *n., pl.* **le·ges** (lē′jēz). *Latin.* law.

lex·i·cog·ra·pher (lek′sə-kog′rə-fər), *n.* dictionary maker. [< Gk., < *lexikon* wordbook + *graphein* write]

lex·i·cog·ra·phy (lek′sə-kog′rə-fĭ), *n.* dictionary making. —lex·i·co·graph·ic (lek′sə-kə-graf′ĭk), lex′i·co·graph′i·cal, *adj.* —lex′i·co·graph′i·cal·ly, *adv.*

lex·i·con (lek′sə-kən; -kon), *n.* dictionary, esp. of Greek, Latin, or Hebrew. [< Gk. *lexikon (biblion)* wordbook]

Lex·ing·ton (lek′sing-tən), *n.* town in E Massachusetts. The first battle of the American Revolution was fought there on April 19, 1775.

Ley·den (lī′dən), *n.* Leiden.

Leyden jar, device for accumulating frictional electricity, consisting essentially of a glass jar lined inside and outside, for most of its height, with tin foil. [from *Leyden, Leiden,* Holland]

Ley·te (lā′tā), *n.* island in the C Philippine Islands.

LG, Low German.

LGk., Late Greek.

Lha·sa (lä′sə; las′ə), *n.* capital of Tibet.

Li, *Chem.* lithium.

L.I., Long Island.

li·a·bil·i·ty (lī′ə-bil′ə-tĭ), *n., pl.* **-ties. 1.** state of being susceptible: *liability to a disease.* **2.** state of being under obligation: *liability for a debt.* **3.** debt. **4.** thing to one's disadvantage: *poor handwriting is a liability.* —**Syn. 1.** susceptibility, proneness. **2.** responsibility, accountability.

li·a·ble (lī′ə-bəl; lī′bəl), *adj.* **1.** likely; unpleasantly likely: *glass is liable to break.* **2.** in danger of having, doing, etc.: *we are all liable to diseases.* **3.** responsible; bound by law to pay: *liable for damage.* **4.** under obligation; subject: *citizens are liable to jury duty.* [< OF, ult. < L *ligare* bind] —li′a·ble·ness, *n.* —**Syn. 1.** apt. **3.** accountable, answerable. —**Ant. 2.** immune. **3.** exempt. ▶ See **likely** for usage note.

li·ai·son (lē′ā-zon′; lĭ-ā′zon; lē′ə-zon; -zən), *n.* **1.** connection between parts of an army to secure proper coöperation. **2.** unlawful intimacy between a man and a woman. **3.** in speaking French, joining a usually silent final consonant to a following word that begins with a vowel or mute *h.* [< F < L *ligatio* < *ligare* bind]

li·a·na (lĭ-ä′nə; -an′ə), **li·ane** (-än′), *n.* a climbing vine with a woody stem. [< F *liane,* earlier *liorne*]

li·ar (lī′ər), *n.* person who tells lies.

lib., **1.** book. [< L *liber*] **2.** librarian; library.

li·ba·tion (lī-bā′shən), *n.* **1.** a pouring out of wine, water, etc., as an offering to a god. **2.** wine, water, etc., offered in this way. [< L, *libare* pour out]

li·bel (lī′bəl), *n., v.,* **-beled, -bel·ing;** *esp. Brit.* **-belled, -bel·ling.** —*n.* **1.** a written or printed statement tending to damage a person's repu-

tation. **2.** crime of writing or printing a libel. **3.** any false or damaging statement about a person. —*v.* **1.** write or print a libel about. **2.** make false or damaging statements about. **3.** institute suit against by means of a libel. [< L *libellus,* dim. of *liber* book] —li′bel·er, *esp. Brit.* li′bel·ler, *n.*

li·bel·ous, *esp. Brit.* **li·bel·lous** (lī′bəl-əs), *adj.* **1.** containing a libel. **2.** spreading libels: *a libelous tongue.* —li′bel·ous·ly, *esp. Brit.* li′bel·lous·ly, *adv.*

lib·er·al (lib′ər-əl; lib′rəl), *adj.* **1.** generous: *a liberal donation.* **2.** plentiful; abundant: *a liberal amount.* **3.** broad-minded; not narrow in one's ideas: *a liberal thinker.* **4.** favoring progress and reforms: *a liberal party.* **5.** giving the general thought, not a word-for-word rendering: *a liberal translation.* —*n.* **1.** person favorable to progress and reforms. **2.** Liberal, member of a Liberal Party. [< L *liberalis* befitting free men < *liber* free] —lib′er·al·ly, *adv.* —lib′er·al·ness, *n.* —**Syn.** *adj.* **1.** bountiful, unstinted. **2.** ample, large. **3.** tolerant.

liberal arts, subjects studied for culture rather than for immediate practical use, as literature, languages, history, and philosophy.

liberal education, education for culture rather than as a preparation for a profession.

lib·er·al·ism (lib′ər-əl-iz′əm; lib′rəl-), *n.* liberal principles and ideas; belief in progress and reforms. —lib′er·al·ist, *n., adj.* —lib′er·al·is′tic, *adj.*

lib·er·al·i·ty (lib′ər-al′ə-tĭ), *n., pl.* **-ties. 1.** generosity. **2.** a gift. **3.** broad-mindedness.

lib·er·al·ize (lib′ər-əl-īz; lib′rəl-), *v.,* **-ized, -iz·ing.** make or become liberal. —lib′er·al·i·za′tion, *n.* —lib′er·al·iz′er, *n.*

lib·er·al-mind·ed (lib′ər-əl-mīn′did; lib′rəl-), *adj.* broad-minded.

Liberal Party, political party that favors progress and reforms.

lib·er·ate (lib′ər-āt), *v.,* **-at·ed, -at·ing.** set free. [< L, < *liber* free] —lib′er·a′tion, *n.* —lib′er·a′tor, *n.* —**Syn.** emancipate, release. —**Ant.** enslave, subjugate, restrict.

Li·be·ri·a (lī-bir′i-ə), *n.* country in W Africa, founded by freed American Negro slaves in 1847. —Li·be′ri·an, *adj., n.*

lib·er·tine (lib′ər-tēn), *n.* person without moral restraints; man who does not respect women. —*adj.* without moral restraints; dissolute; licentious. [< L *libertinus* freedman, ult. < *liber* free]

lib·er·tin·ism (lib′ər-tēn-iz′əm; -tin-), *n.* behavior of a libertine.

lib·er·ty (lib′ər-tĭ), *n., pl.* **-ties. 1.** freedom: *grant liberty to slaves, land of liberty, the colonies won their liberty.* **2.** right or power to do as one pleases; power or opportunity to do something: *liberty of speech or action.* **3.** power of free choice. **4.** leave granted to a sailor to go ashore. **5.** right of being in, using, etc.: *we give our dog the liberty of the yard.* **6.** privilege or right granted by a government. **7.** too great freedom; setting aside rules and manners. **8. at liberty,** **a.** free. **b.** allowed; permitted. **c.** not busy. **9. take liberties,** be too familiar. [< L, < *liber* free] —**Syn. 1.** emancipation. —**Ant. 1.** slavery, serfdom, bondage, servitude.

Liberty Bell, *Am.* bell in Independence Hall in Philadelphia regarded as a symbol of liberty.

Liberty Ship, a cargo ship carrying about 10,000 gross tons, built in large numbers by the United States during World War II.

li·bid·i·nous (lə-bid′ə-nəs), *adj.* lustful; lewd. —li·bid′i·nous·ly, *adv.* —li·bid′i·nous·ness, *n.*

li·bi·do (lə-bē′dō), *n.* **1.** sexual desire or instinct. **2.** instinct generally; vital impulse; the force motivating mental life. [< L, desire] —li·bid·i·nal (lə-bid′ə-nəl), *adj.*

Li·bra (lī′brə), *n., gen.* **-brae** (-brē). **1.** *Astron.*

a southern constellation that was thought of as arranged in the shape of a pair of scales. 2. the seventh sign of the zodiac; the Scales. [< L, balance]

li·brar·i·an (lī-brâr′i·ən), *n.* 1. person in charge of a library or part of a library. 2. person trained for work in a library.

li·brar·y (lī′brer′i; lī′brər·i), *n., pl.* **-brar·ies.** 1. collection of books. 2. room or building where a collection of books is kept. [< L *librarium* bookcase < *liber* book]

li·bret·tist (lə·bret′ist), *n.* writer of a libretto.

li·bret·to (lə·bret′ō), *n., pl.* **-tos, -ti** (-tē). 1. words of an opera or other long musical composition. 2. book containing the words. [< Ital., dim. of *libro* book]

Lib·y·a (lib′i·ə), *n.* 1. ancient Greek and Roman name for that part of Africa W of Egypt. 2. Also, *Italian* **Libia.** a former Italian colony in N Africa W of Egypt. It was formally declared by the United Nations to be a sovereign kingdom as of Jan. 1, 1952. —**Lib′y·an,** *adj., n.*

lice (līs), *n.* pl. of louse.

li·cense, li·cence (lī′səns), *n., v.,* **-censed, -cens·ing; -cenced, -cenc·ing.** —*n.* 1. permission given by law to do something: *a license to drive a car.* 2. paper, card, plate, etc., showing such permission: *show your driver's license.* 3. freedom of action, speech, thought, etc., that is permitted or conceded: *poetic license.* 4. too much liberty; abuse of liberty. —*v.* give a license to; permit by law: *a doctor is licensed to practice medicine.* [< OF < L *licentia* < *licere* be allowed] —**li′cens·a·ble, li′cence·a·ble,** *adj.* —**li′cens·er, li′cenc·er,** *n.*

li·cen·see, li·cen·cee (lī′sən·sē′), *n.* person to whom a license is given.

li·cen·ti·ate (lī·sen′shi·it; -āt), *n.* 1. person who has a license or permit to practice an art or profession. 2. holder of any of certain European university degrees higher than that of bachelor and lower than that of doctor. —**li·cen′ti·ate·ship′,** *n.*

li·cen·tious (lī·sen′shəs), *adj.* 1. disregarding commonly accepted rules or principles. 2. lawless; immoral. 3. lewd. [< L, < *licentia* LICENSE] —**li·cen′tious·ly,** *adv.* —**li·cen′tious·ness,** *n.* —Syn. 1. lustful, lascivious, sensual, wanton.

li·chee (lē′chē), *n.* litchi.

li·chen (lī′kən), *n.* plant that looks somewhat like moss and grows in patches on trees, rocks, etc., consisting of a fungus and an alga growing together. —*v.* cover with lichens. [< L < Gk. *leichen*] —**li′chen·like′,** *adj.* —**li′chen·ous,** *adj.*

lic·it (lis′it), *adj.* lawful; permitted. [< L *licitus*] —**lic′it·ly,** *adv.*

lick (lik), *v.* 1. pass the tongue over: *lick a stamp.* 2. lap up with the tongue. 3. make or bring by using the tongue: *the cat licked the plate clean.* 4. pass about or play over like a tongue: *the flames were licking the roof.* 5. *Colloq.* beat; thrash; defeat. —*n.* 1. stroke of the tongue over something. 2. *Am.* place where natural salt is found and where animals go to lick it up. 3. *Colloq.* a blow. 4. a small quantity. 5. *Am., Colloq.* brief stroke of activity or effort. 6. *Colloq.* speed. [OE *liccian*] —**lick′er,** *n.*

lick·er·ish (lik′ər·ish), *adj.* 1. fond of choice food. 2. greedy. 3. lecherous. Also, **liquorish.** —**lick′er·ish·ness,** *n.*

lick·spit·tle (lik′spit′əl), *n.* a contemptible flatterer; parasite.

lic·o·rice (lik′ə·ris; lik′ris; -rish), *n.* 1. a sweet, black, gummy extract obtained from the roots of a European plant, used as a flavoring. 2. plant that yields this. 3. its root. 4. candy flavored with this extract. Also, **liquorice.** [< AF < LL < Gk. *glykyrrhiza* < *glykys* sweet + *rhiza* root]

lic·tor (lik′tər), *n.* attendant on a public official in ancient Rome who punished offenders at the official's orders.

lid (lid), *n.* 1. a movable cover; top: *the lid of a box.* 2. cover of skin that is moved in opening and shutting the eye; eyelid. 3. *Slang.* hat; cap. [OE *hlid*] —**lid′ded,** *adj.* —**lid′less,** *adj.*

lie¹ (lī), *n., v.,* **lied, ly·ing.** —*n.* 1. a false statement, esp. one known to be false by the person who makes it. 2. something intended to give a false impression. 3. **give the lie to,** a. call a liar; accuse of lying. b. show to be false. [OE *lyge*] —*v.* 1. tell a lie; tell lies. 2. get, bring, put, etc., by lying: *lie oneself out of a difficulty.* 3. convey a false impression. [OE *lēogan*] —Syn. *n.* 1. falsehood, untruth, fib. —*v.* 1. prevaricate.

lie² (lī), *v.,* **lay, lain, ly·ing,** *n.* —*v.* 1. have one's body in a flat position along the ground or other surface: *lie on the grass.* 2. assume such a position: *lie down on the couch.* 3. be in a horizontal or flat position: *the book was lying on the table.* 4. be kept or stay in a given position, state, etc.: *lie idle.* 5. be; be placed: *the ship lies to the south of us.* 6. exist; be; have its place; belong: *the cure lies in education.* 7. be in the grave; be buried. 8. *Archaic.* spend the night; lodge. 9. lie in, be confined in childbirth. 10. lie low, *Colloq.* a. conceal oneself. b. conceal one's views or intentions. 11. lie off, stay not far from. 12. lie over, be left waiting until a later time. 13. lie to, come almost to a stop, facing the wind. —*n.* manner, position, or direction in which something lies. [OE *licgan*] —**li′er,** *n.* —Syn. *v.* 1. recline, repose. ➤ See lay for usage note.

Lie (lē), *n.* Trygve Halvdan, born 1896, Norwegian lawyer, secretary-general of the United Nations 1946-1953.

Liech·ten·stein (liκ′tən·shtīn), *n.* country between SW Germany and NE Switzerland.

lie·der·kranz (lē′dər·kränts), *n.* 1. a German male singing society. 2. a smooth cheese with a strong odor. 3. Liederkranz, a trademark for this cheese. [< G, garland of songs]

lief (lēf), *adv.* willingly. Also, **lieve.** [OE *lēof* dear]

liege (lēj), *n.* 1. lord having a right to the homage and loyal service of his vassals. 2. vassal obliged to give homage and loyal service to his lord. —*adj.* having the right to, or obliged to give, homage and loyal service to a lord. [< OF < LL *leticus* < *letus* freedman, ult. < Gmc.]

Li·ége (li·āzh′), *n.* city in E Belgium.

lien (lēn), *n.* legal claim on the property of another for payment of a debt: *the garage owner has a lien upon my automobile until I pay his bill.* [< F < L *ligamen* bond < *ligare* bind]

lieu (lū), *n.* 1. place; stead. 2. **in lieu of,** in place of; instead of. [< F < L *locus*]

Lieut., Lieutenant.

lieu·ten·an·cy (lū·ten′ən·si), *n., pl.* **-cies.** rank, commission, or authority of a lieutenant.

lieu·ten·ant (lū·ten′ənt; *in general Brit. usage, except in the navy,* lef·ten′ənt), *n.* 1. person who acts in the place of someone above him in authority. 2. a commissioned army officer ranking next below a captain. 3. a commissioned naval officer ranking next below a lieutenant commander. [< F, < *lieu* a place + *tenant,* ppr. of *tenir* hold < L *tenere*]

lieutenant colonel, a commissioned army officer ranking next below a colonel and next above a major.

lieutenant commander, *Am.* a commissioned naval officer ranking next below a commander and next above a lieutenant.

lieutenant general, a commissioned army officer ranking next below a general and next above a major general.

lieutenant governor, 1. *Am.* an officer next in rank to the governor of a State and taking his place during his absence or in the event of his death. 2. official who acts in place of the governor general in a district or province.

lieve (lēv), *adv.* lief.

life (līf), *n., pl.* **lives.** 1. living; being alive; quality that people, animals, and plants have and that rocks, dirt, and metals lack. 2. time of being alive: *a short life.* 3. time of existence or action of inanimate things, as a machine. 4. living being; person: *five lives were lost.* 5. living beings considered together: *the desert island had almost no animal or vegetable life.* 6. the experiences of a living being. 7. way of living: *a dull life.* 8. account of a person's life: *a* *life* of Lincoln. **9.** spirit; vigor: *put more life into your work.* **10.** source of activity or liveliness. **11.** person or thing necessary to someone; absorbing interest. **12.** existence in the world of affairs or society. **13. for life, a.** during the rest of one's life. **b.** to save one's life. **14. from life,** using a living model. **15. take life,** kill. **16. take one's own life,** kill oneself. **17. to the life,** like the model; exactly; perfectly. [OE *līf*] —Syn. **1.** being, existence. **8.** biography. **9.** animation, liveliness, vivacity.

life assurance, life insurance.

life belt, life preserver made like a belt.

life·blood (līf′blud′), *n.* **1.** blood necessary to life. **2.** source of strength and energy.

life·boat (līf′bōt′), *n.* **1.** strong boat specially built for saving lives at sea or along the coast. **2.** boat carried on a ship for use in emergencies.

life buoy, life preserver; something to keep a person afloat until rescued.

life·guard (līf′gärd′), *n. Am.* man employed on a bathing beach to help in case of accident or danger to bathers.

life insurance, 1. system by which a person pays a small sum regularly to have a large sum paid to his family or heirs at his death. **2.** sum paid by the insurance company at death. **3.** payments made to the insurance company. **4.** a combination of life insurance and endowment insurance. Also, **life assurance.**

life·less (līf′lis), *adj.* **1.** without life: *a lifeless planet.* **2.** dead: *lifeless bodies on the battlefield.* **3.** dull: *a lifeless performance.* —**life′less·ly,** *adv.* —**life′less·ness,** *n.* —Syn. **1.** inanimate. **3.** sluggish, torpid.

life·like (līf′līk′), *adj.* like life; looking as if alive; like the real thing: *a lifelike description.* —**life′like′ness,** *n.*

life line, rope for saving life, such as one thrown to a ship from the shore.

life·long (līf′lông′; -long′), *adj.* lasting all one's life: *a lifelong companion.*

life preserver, a wide belt, jacket, or circular tube, usually made of cloth and cork, to keep a person afloat in the water; something to keep a person afloat until rescued.

lif·er (līf′ər), *n. Slang.* convict in prison for life.

life·sav·er (līf′sāv′ər), *n. Colloq.* **1.** person who saves people from drowning. **2.** lifeguard. **3.** person or thing that saves someone from trouble, discomfort, embarrassment, etc. —**life′sav′ing,** *adj.*, *n.*

Life preserver

life·size (līf′sīz′), *adj.* as big as the living person, animal, etc.: *a life-size statue.*

life·time (līf′tīm′), *n.* time of being alive; time during which a life lasts. —*adj.* for life.

life·work (līf′wėrk′), *n.* work that takes or lasts a whole lifetime; main work in life.

lift (lift), *v.* **1.** raise; take up; raise into a higher position: *lift a chair.* **2.** hold up; display on high. **3.** raise in rank, condition, estimation, etc.; elevate; exalt. **4.** rise and go; go away: *the darkness lifts.* **5.** go up; yield to an effort to raise something: *this window will not lift.* **6.** pull or tug upward. **7.** send up loudly: *lift a voice or cry.* **8.** rise to view above the horizon. **9.** pick or take up. **10.** *Colloq.* steal; plagiarize: *to lift things from a store.* **11.** *Am.* pay off: *to lift a mortgage.* —*n.* **1.** an elevating influence. **2.** act or fact of lifting. **3.** a holding high: *a lift of the head.* **4.** load lifted. **5.** a lifting force. **6.** distance through which a thing is lifted. **7.** a helping hand. **8.** ride in a vehicle given to a traveler on foot; free ride. **9.** *Esp. Brit.* elevator. **10.** one of the layers of leather in the heel of a shoe. **11.** a rise in ground. [< Scand. *lypta* < *lopt* air] —**lift′a·ble,** *adj.* —**lift′er,** *n.*

lig·a·ment (lig′ə-mənt), *n., pl.* **lig·a·ments,** **lig·a·men·ta** (lig′ə-men′tə). **1.** *Anat.* band of strong tissue that connects bones or holds parts

of the body in place. **2.** tie; bond. [< L *ligamentum* < *ligare* bind] —**lig·a·men·tous** (lig′ə-men′təs), *adj.*

lig·a·ture (lig′ə-chər; -chúr), *n., v.,* **-tured, -tur·ing.** —*n.* **1.** anything used to bind or tie up; bandage, cord, etc. **2.** thread, string, etc., used to tie up a bleeding artery or vein. **3.** a binding or tying up. **4.** *Music.* a slur or a group of notes connected by a slur. **5.** two or three letters joined in printing. Æ and ff are ligatures. —*v.* bind or tie up with a ligature. [< LL *ligatura,* ult. < L *ligare* bind]

Ligature (def. 4)

light¹ (līt), *n., adj.* —*v.,* **light·ed** or **lit, lighting.** —*n.* **1.** that by which we see; form of radiant energy that acts on the retina of the eye. **2.** thing that gives light, as the sun, a lamp, etc. **3.** supply of light: *a tall building cuts off our light.* **4.** *Physics.* the radiation of the visible spectrum plus infrared and ultraviolet rays. **5.** brightness; clearness; illumination; particular case of this: *a strong or dim light.* **6.** a bright part: *light and shade.* **7.** daytime. **8.** dawn. **9.** window or other means of letting in light. **10.** thing with which to start something burning. **11.** knowledge; information; illumination of mind. **12.** spiritual guidance and inspiration. **13.** public knowledge; open view: *bring to light.* **14.** aspect in which a thing is viewed: *he put the matter in the right light.* **15.** shining figure; model; example: *George Washington is one of the lights of history.* **16.** favor; approval: *the light of his countenance.* **17.** according to one's lights, following one's own ideas, intelligence, and conscience in the best way that one knows. **18. see the light,** or **see the light of day, a.** be born. **b.** be made public. **c.** get the right idea. —*adj.* **1.** having light. **2.** bright; clear: *it is as light as day.* **3.** pale in color; whitish. —*v.* **1.** cause to give light. **2.** give light to; provide with light. **3.** make or become bright: *her face was lighted by a smile, her face always lights up when he comes in.* **4.** become light: *the sky lights up at sunset.* **5.** set fire to: *she lighted the candles.* **6.** take fire. [OE *lēoht*] —Syn. **5.** radiance, luminosity. ▶ **lighted, lit.** Both forms are in good use as the past tense and past participle of *light.* **Lighted** is probably more common as the adjective and past participle: *a lighted lamp. He had lighted a fire. Lit* is perhaps more common as the past tense: *He lit a cigarette.*

light² (līt), *adj.* **1.** easy to carry; not heavy: *a light load.* **2.** of little weight for its size: *a light chair.* **3.** of less than standard or usual weight: *light clothing.* **4.** less than usual in amount, force, etc.: *a light sleep.* **5.** of a wind, up to 7 miles an hour. **6.** of foods, easy to digest. **7.** of bread and pastry, not dense or soggy. **8.** of a syllable, not stressed. **9.** easy to do or bear; not hard or severe. **10.** not looking heavy; graceful; delicate: *a light bridge, light carving.* **11.** moving easily; nimble: *light on one's feet.* **12.** happy; gay; cheerfully careless. **13.** not serious enough; fickle. **14.** aiming to entertain; not serious: *light reading.* **15.** not important: *light losses.* **16.** careless in morals. **17.** not dense: *a light fog.* **18.** porous; sandy: *a light soil.* **19.** containing little alcohol. **20.** *Mil.* lightly armed or equipped: *light cavalry, in light marching order.* **21. light in the head, a.** dizzy. **b.** silly; foolish. **c.** crazy; out of one's head. **22. make light of,** treat as of little importance. —*adv.* lightly. [OE *lēoht, līht*] —Syn. *adj.* **11.** agile, active. **12.** buoyant. **15.** slight, trivial, unimportant.

light³ (līt), *v.,* **light·ed** or **lit, light·ing. 1.** come down to the ground; alight. **2.** come down from flight: *a bird lighted on the branch.* **3.** come by chance: *his eye lighted upon a sentence.* **4.** fall suddenly: *the blow lit on his head.* **5. light into,** *Am., Slang.* **a.** attack. **b.** scold. **6. light out,** *Am., Slang.* leave suddenly; go away quickly. [OE *līhtan* < *līht* light²]

light-armed (līt′ärmd′), *adj.* equipped with light weapons.

light·en¹ (līt′ən), *v.* **1.** make light; grow light: *the sky lightens before the dawn.* **2.** brighten:

her face lightened. 3. flash with lightning: *it thundered and lightened outside.* [ME, < *light¹*] —**light′en·er,** *n.*

light·en² (līt′ən), *v.* 1. reduce the load of (a ship); have the load reduced. 2. make or become less of a burden: *to lighten taxes.* 3. make or become more cheerful. [ME, < *light²*]

light·er¹ (līt′ər), *n.* thing or person that starts something burning. [ME, < *light¹*]

light·er² (līt′ər), *n.* a flat-bottomed barge used for loading and unloading ships. —*v.* carry (goods) in such a barge. [< *light²* or ? < Du. *lichter*]

light·er·age (līt′ər·ij), *n.* 1. loading, unloading, or carrying of goods in a lighter. 2. charge for this.

light·face (līt′fās′), *Printing.* —*n.* type that has thin, light lines. —*adj.* in or using lightface.

light-fin·gered (līt′fing′gərd), *adj.* thievish; skillful at picking pockets.

light-foot·ed (līt′fut′id), *Poetic.* **lightfoot** (-fut′), *adj.* stepping lightly. —**light′foot′ed·ly,** *adv.* —**light′-foot′ed·ness,** *n.*

light-head·ed (līt′hed′id), *adj.* 1. dizzy. 2. delirious. 3. frivolous; flighty. —**light′-head′ed·ly,** *adv.* —**light′-head′ed·ness,** *n.*

light-heart·ed (līt′här′tid), *adj.* carefree; cheerful; gay. —**light′-heart′ed·ly,** *adv.* —**light′-heart′ed·ness,** *n.*

light heavyweight, boxer who weighs between 161 and 175 pounds.

light·house (līt′hous′), *n.* tower or framework with a bright light that shines far over the water to warn and guide ships.

light·ing (līt′ing), *n.* 1. giving of light; providing with light. 2. way in which lights are arranged. 3. starting to burn.

light·ly (līt′li), *adv.* 1. with little weight, force, etc.: *rest lightly on a thing.* 2. to a small degree or extent: *lightly clad.* 3. in an airy way: *flags floating lightly.* 4. quickly; easily: *to jump lightly aside.* 5. cheerfully: *take bad news lightly.* 6. indifferently; slightingly: *speak lightly of a person.* 7. thoughtlessly; carelessly: *behave lightly.*

light-mind·ed (līt′mīn′did), *adj.* emptyheaded; thoughtless; frivolous. —**light′-mind′ed·ly,** *adv.* —**light′-mind′ed·ness,** *n.*

light·ness¹ (līt′nis), *n.* 1. brightness; clearness. 2. paleness; whiteness. 3. amount of light.

light·ness² (līt′nis), *n.* 1. a being light; not being heavy. 2. not being hard or severe. 3. gracefulness; delicacy. 4. being gay or cheerful. 5. lack of proper seriousness.

light·ning (līt′ning), *n.* discharge or flash of electricity in the sky. [< *lighten¹*]

lightning bug, *Am.* firefly.

lightning rod, *Am.* metal rod fixed on a building or ship to conduct lightning into the earth or water.

light·ship (līt′ship′), *n.* ship with a bright light that shines far over the water, anchored at a dangerous place to warn and guide ships.

light·some (līt′səm), *adj.* 1. nimble; lively. 2. happy; gay; cheerful. 3. frivolous. —**light′some·ly,** *adv.* —**light′some·ness,** *n.*

light·weight (līt′wāt′), *n.* 1. person or thing of less than average weight. 2. boxer who weighs less than 135 pounds. 3. *Colloq.* person who has little intelligence or importance.

light-year (līt′yir′), *n. Astron.* distance that light travels in one year; about 6,000,000,000,000 miles.

lig·ne·ous (lig′ni·əs), *adj.* of or like wood; woody. [< L, < *lignum* wood]

lig·nite (lig′nīt), *n.* a dark-brown kind of coal in which the texture of the wood can be seen. [< F, < L *lignum* wood] —**lig·nit·ic** (lig·nit′ik), *adj.*

lig·num vi·tae (lig′nəm vī′tē), 1. an extremely heavy and hard wood, used for making pulleys, rulers, etc. 2. a tropical tree from which it comes. [< L, wood of life; from its supposed medicinal value]

lik·a·ble, like·a·ble (līk′ə·bəl), *adj.* having

qualities that win good will or friendship; popular. —**lik′a·ble·ness, like′a·ble·ness,** *n.*

like¹ (līk), *adj., Poetic.* **lik·er, lik·est,** *prep., adv., n., conj., v.,* **liked, lik·ing.** —*adj.* 1. similar; similar to; resembling something or each other: *our house is like theirs.* 2. characteristic of: *isn't that just like a boy?* 3. prophetic or indicative of: *it looks like rain.* 4. in the right state or frame of mind for: *I feel like working.* 5. *Archaic.* likely: *the king is sick and like to die.* —*prep.* in like manner with; similarly to: *she works like a beaver.* —*adv.* 1. *Colloq.* probably: *like enough it will rain.* 2. in like manner. 3. *Archaic.* to a like extent or degree. 4. had like, *Dial.* came near; was about. 5. **nothing like,** not nearly. —*n.* 1. person or thing like another; match; counterpart or equal. 2. something of similar nature: *wheat, oats, and the like are cereals.* —*conj. Colloq.* 1. like as; as. 2. as if. —*v.* 1. *Obs.* compare. 2. *Dial.* come near. [OE *gelīc*] —**Syn.** *adj.* 1. corresponding, akin. ➤ **like, as.** 1. In written English *as* and *as if* are used to introduce clauses of comparison: *Habit grips a person as an octopus does. He dives so that it looks as if he would land flat, but he enters the water perfectly.* 2. In colloquial English *like* is often heard in such constructions, instead of *as* or *as if. Like* is less common in the East than in the West and South, but is used more or less throughout the United States and in England also: *He dives so it looks like he would land flat.* In all regions *like* is used (as a preposition) when the comparison resembles a phrase, i.e., does not contain a definite subject or verb: *The description fits him like a glove. She works like a beaver.* 3. In the last few years the colloquial use of *like* as a conjunction has greatly increased. The vogue of fiction, in which it often stands appropriately in the conversation and sometimes in the informal prose surrounding the conversation, as well as the popular radio programs in colloquial or uneducated English are doubtless in part responsible for this increased currency. In fact, if editors and publishers did not enforce the use of *as* instead of *like* according to the rules in their stylebooks, it is possible that *like* would become the dominant form, and it occasionally appears in print even now: *Henry sat nervously, like he was afraid of the job.* This use of *like* in public address is quite common, even among careful people. There is a historical basis for both forms, since both are parts of the older *like as* ("Like as a father pitieth his children . . ."). Some speakers have taken *as,* others *like. Like* is preferable from the standpoint of meaning, because *as* has several different meanings and several functions in the language and so is relatively weak. *Like* is more exact and more emphatic in a comparison than *as* can be.

like² (līk), *v.,* **liked, lik·ing,** *n.* —*v.* 1. be pleased with; be satisfied with. 2. wish for; wish. —*n.* liking; preference. [OE *līcian* to please] —**Syn.** *v.* 1. fancy, enjoy. 2. prefer, choose.

–like, *suffix.* 1. like, as in *wolflike.* 2. like that of; characteristic of, as in *childlike.* 3. suited to; fit or proper for, as in *businesslike.* [< *like¹, adj.*] ➤ –like is a living suffix that can be freely added to nouns to form adjectives.

like·li·hood (līk′li·hud), *n.* probability: *is there any great likelihood of rain this afternoon?*

like·ly (līk′li), *adj.,* **-li·er, -li·est,** *adv.* —*adj.* 1. probable: *one likely result of this heavy rain is the rising of the river.* 2. to be expected: *it is likely to be hot in August.* 3. suitable: *is there a likely place to fish?* 4. showing ability: *a likely boy.* —*adv.* probably: *I shall very likely be at home all day.* [< Scand. *līkligr*] ➤ **likely, apt, liable.** The principal meanings of these words are: *likely:* expected, probably; *liable:* possible [of an unpleasant event], responsible [as for damages]; *apt:* tending toward, naturally fit. *Likely* is the most commonly needed of the three, and colloquially both *apt* and (in some localities) *liable* are used in the ordinary sense of *likely: it is likely to rain when the wind is southwest.* [Or, if the rain is viewed with disfavor] *It is liable to rain when the wind is southwest.* [Or, colloquially] *it is apt to rain when the wind is southwest.*

lik·en (lĭk′ən), *v.* compare; represent as like.

like·ness (līk′nĭs), *n.* 1. a resembling; a being alike: *a boy's likeness to his father.* 2. something that is like; copy; picture: *have one's likeness painted.* 3. appearance; shape: *assume the likeness of a swan.*

like·wise (līk′wīz′), *adv.* 1. the same: *go and do likewise.* 2. also; moreover; too.

lik·ing (līk′ĭng), *n.* 1. preference; fondness; kindly feeling: *a liking for apples.* 2. taste; pleasure: *food to your liking.*

li·lac (lī′lək; -lak), *n.* 1. shrub with clusters of tiny fragrant flowers. 2. the cluster of flowers. 3. a pale pinkish purple. —*adj.* pale pinkish-purple. [< F < Sp. < Ar. < Pers. *līlak* < *nīl* indigo]

lil·i·a·ceous (lĭl′ĭ·ā′shəs), *adj.* 1. of or like the lily. 2. belonging to the lily family.

Li·li·u·o·ka·la·ni (lē·lē′ū·ō·kä·lä′nē), *n.* 1838–1917, the last queen of Hawaii, from 1891 to 1893.

Lille (lēl), *n.* city in N France.

Lil·li·put (lĭl′ə·put; -pət), *n.* an imaginary island inhabited by tiny people, described in Swift's *Gulliver's Travels.*

Lil·li·pu·tian (lĭl′ə·pū′shən), *adj.* 1. of or suitable for Lilliput. 2. very small; tiny; petty. —*n.* 1. inhabitant of Lilliput. 2. a very small person; dwarf.

lilt (lĭlt), *v.* sing or play (a tune) in a light tripping manner. —*n.* 1. lively song or tune with a swing. 2. a lively, springing movement. [ME *lulte*]

lil·y (lĭl′ĭ), *n., pl.* **lil·ies,** *adj.* —*n.* 1. any plant of a family of herbs, shrubs, and trees that grow from a bulb, usually have flowers with six parts, and have stemless leaves. 2. the flower. 3. the bulb. 4. any of various related or similar plants, such as the calla lily or water lily. —*adj.* like a lily; white; pale; pure; lovely; delicate. [< L, akin to Gk. *leirion*] —lil′y·like′, *adj.*

Tiger lily (flower 3 to 5 in. in diam.)

lil·y-liv·ered (lĭl′ĭ·lĭv′ərd), *adj.* cowardly.

lily of the valley, *pl.* **lilies of the valley.** plant having tiny, fragrant, bell-shaped, white flowers arranged up and down a single stem.

Li·ma (lē′mə), *n.* capital of Peru.

Li·ma bean (lī′mə), 1. a broad, flat bean used for food. 2. plant that it grows on.

limb (lĭm), *n.* 1. leg, arm, or wing. 2. a large branch of a tree. 3. part that projects; branch; arm. 4. person or thing thought of as a branch or offshoot. —*v.* dismember. [OE *lim*] —**limbed** (lĭmd), *adj.* —**limb′less,** *adj.*

lim·ber¹ (lĭm′bər), *adj.* bending easily; flexible: *limber fingers.* —*v.* make or become limber: *limber up by exercise.* [? < *limp²* or *limb*] —**lim′ber·ly,** *adv.* —**lim′ber·ness,** *n.*

lim·ber² (lĭm′bər), *n.* the detachable front part of the carriage of a field gun. —*v.* attach the limber. [? < F *limonière*]

lim·bo (lĭm′bō), *n.* 1. Often, **Limbo.** in Catholic theology, a place for those who have not received the grace of Christ while living, and yet have not deserved the punishments of willful and impenitent sinners. 2. place for people and things forgotten, cast aside, or out of date. [< L (*in*) *limbo* on the edge]

Lim·burg·er (lĭm′bėrg·ər), *n.* a soft cheese having a strong smell.

lime¹ (līm), *n., v.* **limed, lim·ing.** —*n.* 1. a white substance obtained by burning limestone, shells, bones, etc.; calcium oxide; quicklime. Lime is used in making mortar and on fields to improve the soil. 2. birdlime. —*v.* put lime on. [OE *līm*]

lime² (līm), *n.* 1. a greenish-yellow fruit much like a lemon, but smaller and sourer. Its juice is used as a flavoring and in medicine. 2. tree that it grows on. [< F < Sp. < Ar. *līma*]

lime³ (līm), *n.* linden tree, often used for shade. [var. of earlier *line* < OE *lind*]

lime·kiln (līm′kĭl′; -kĭln′), *n.* furnace for making lime by burning limestone, shells, etc.

lime·light (līm′līt′), *n.* 1. a strong light thrown upon the stage of a theater to light up certain persons or objects and draw attention to them. 2. center of public attention and interest.

lim·er·ick (lĭm′ər·ĭk; lĭm′rĭk), *n.* kind of nonsense verse of five lines. [appar. from a song about *Limerick,* Ireland]

Lim·er·ick (lĭm′ər·ĭk; lĭm′rĭk), *n.* county in SW Ireland.

lime·stone (līm′stōn′), *n.* rock consisting mostly of calcium carbonate, used for building and for making lime. Marble is a kind of limestone.

lime·wa·ter (līm′wô′tər; -wot′ər), *n.* solution of slaked lime in water. It is used to counteract an acid condition.

lim·it (lĭm′ĭt), *n.* 1. farthest edge or boundary; where something ends or must end: *the limits of the school grounds.* 2. the limit, *Am., Slang.* as much as, or more than, one can stand. —*v.* 1. set a limit to; restrict: *her food was limited to bread and water.* 2. *Law.* assign definitely. [< OF < L *limes* boundary] —**lim′it·a·ble,** *adj.* —**lim′it·er,** *n.* —Syn. *n.* 1. border, bound, terminal. —*v.* 1. restrain, check.

lim·i·ta·tion (lĭm′ə·tā′shən), *n.* 1. a limiting. 2. limited condition. 3. a limiting rule or circumstance; restriction. 4. period of time, set by law, after which a claim cannot be enforced.

lim·i·ta·tive (lĭm′ə·tā′tĭv), *adj.* limiting.

lim·it·ed (lĭm′it·ĭd), *adj.* 1. kept within limits; restricted. 2. *Am.* traveling fast and making only a few stops. —*n. Am.* a limited train, bus, etc. —**lim′it·ed·ly,** *adv.* —**lim′it·ed·ness,** *n.*

limited monarchy, monarchy in which the ruler's powers are limited by law.

lim·it·less (lĭm′it·lĭs), *adj.* without limits; boundless. —Syn. infinite, illimitable.

limn (lĭm), *v.* 1. paint (a picture). 2. portray in words. [< OF, ult. < L *lumen* light]

Li·moges (li·mōzh′), *n.* 1. city in C France. 2. porcelain made at Limoges.

lim·ou·sine (lĭm′ə·zēn′; lĭm′ə·zēn), *n.* a closed automobile, seating up to five passengers in the back, often with a glass panel between them and the driver. [< F, < *Limousin,* former French province]

limp¹ (lĭmp), *n.* a lame step or walk. —*v.* walk with a limp. [cf. OE *lemphealt* lame] —**limp′er,** *n.*

limp² (lĭmp), *adj.* lacking stiffness or firmness: *a starched collar soon gets limp in hot weather.* [akin to Scand. *limpa* indisposition] —**limp′ly,** *adv.* —**limp′ness,** *n.* —Syn. flabby, drooping, flaccid. —Ant. stiff.

lim·pet (lĭm′pĭt), *n.* a small shellfish that sticks to rocks. [< LL *lampreda* lamprey. Doublet of LAMPREY.]

lim·pid (lĭm′pĭd), *adj.* clear; transparent: *limpid water, limpid eyes.* [< L *limpidus*] —**lim·pid′i·ty, lim′pid·ness,** *n.* —**lim′pid·ly,** *adv.*

lim·y (līm′ĭ), *adj.* **lim·i·er, lim·i·est.** 1. of, containing, or resembling lime. 2. smeared with birdlime.

lin·age (līn′ĭj), *n.* 1. alignment. 2. quantity of printed or written matter estimated in lines. 3. rate of payment by the line. ▶ **linage, lineage.** *Linage* (līn′ĭj) is the number of lines of printed matter; *lineage* (lĭn′i·ĭj) is a line of descent.

linch·pin (lĭnch′pĭn′), *n.* pin inserted through a hole in the end of an axle to keep the wheel on.

Lin·coln (lĭng′kən), *n.* 1. Abraham, 1809–1865, the 16th president of the United States, 1861–1865. 2. capital of Nebraska, in the SE part.

Lind (lĭnd), *n.* Jenny, 1820–1887, soprano singer.

lin·dane (lĭn′dān), *n.* a benzene compound used as an insecticide.

Lind·bergh (lĭnd′bėrg), *n.* Charles Augustus, born 1902, American aviator.

lin·den (lĭn′dən), *n.* shade tree with heart-shaped leaves and clusters of small, fragrant, yellowish flowers. [OE, orig. adj., < *lind* linden, lime³]

line¹ (līn), *n., v.,* **lined, lin·ing.** —*n.* **1.** piece of rope, cord, or wire: *a fishing line.* **2.** cord for measuring, making level, etc. **3.** cord with a hook for catching fish. **4.** a long narrow mark: *draw two lines along the margin.* **5.** anything like such a mark, as a band, seam, crease, furrow, wrinkle, etc. **6.** a straight line. **7.** *Math.* path or track a point may be imagined to leave as it moves. **8.** circle of the earth or heavens: *the equinoctial line.* **9.** use of lines in drawing: *clearness of line in an artist's work.* **10.** lines, outline; contour: *a ship of fine lines.* **11.** lines, plan of construction. **12.** edge; limit; boundary: *the line between Texas and Mexico.* **13.** row of persons or things: *a line of trees.* **14.** row of words on a page or in a column: *a column of 40 lines.* **15.** short letter; note: *drop me a line.* **16.** lines, a. words that an actor speaks in a play. b. poetry; verses. c. *Colloq.* marriage certificate. **17.** one's fate; one's lot in life. **18.** connected series of persons or things following one another in time: *the Stuarts were a line of English kings.* **19.** family or lineage: *of noble line.* **20.** course; track; direction: *a line of march.* **21.** course of action, conduct, or thought: *a line of policy.* **22.** *Am.* a. wire or wires connecting points or stations in a telegraph or telephone system. b. the system itself. **23.** any rope, wire, pipe, hose, etc., running from one point to another. **24.** single track of railroad. **25.** *Am.* a. one branch of a system of transportation: *the main line of a railroad.* b. a whole system of transportation or conveyance: *the Grand Trunk Line.* **26.** field of experience or interest: *that's not in my line.* **27.** branch of business; kind or activity: *the dry-goods line.* **28.** kind or branch of goods: *a good line of hardware.* **29.** a single verse of poetry. **30.** one of the horizontal lines that make a staff in music. **31.** *Mil.* a. lines, trenches or other defenses used in war. b. double row (front and rear rank) of soldiers. **32.** troops or ships arranged abreast. **33.** arrangement of an army or a fleet for battle. **34.** fighting forces, as distinguished from staff, supply, etc. **35.** *Am.* in football, the players lined up even with the ball before the action of a down begins. **36.** the line, a. the equator. b. regular forces of army or navy. c. fighting forces, as distinguished from staff, supply, etc. —*v.* **1.** mark with lines on paper, etc. **2.** cover with lines: *a face lined by age.* **3.** arrange in a line. **4.** arrange a line along; form a line along. **5.** sketch; delineate; outline. **6.** take a position in a line; form a line; range. [coalescence of OE *line* line, rope (< *lin* flax) and L *linea* line, linen thread (< *linum* flax)] —Syn. *n.* **1.** thread, string, cable. **4.** stroke, scratch, streak, dash. **13** rank, file. **20.** route, way.

line² (līn), *v.,* **lined, lin·ing. 1.** put a layer inside of. **2.** fill: *line one's pockets with money.* **3.** serve as a lining for. [< OE *lin* flax]

lin·e·age (lin′i·ij), *n.* **1.** descent in a direct line from an ancestor. **2.** family; race. [< OF *lignage* < *ligne* line < L *linea*] —Syn. **1.** ancestry. **2.** stock, extraction. ➤ See **linage** for usage note.

lin·e·al (lin′i·əl), *adj.* **1.** in the direct line of descent: *a lineal descendant.* **2.** hereditary. **3.** linear. —**lin′e·al·ly,** *adv.*

lin·e·a·ment (lin′i·ə·mənt), *n.* part or feature; part or feature of a face with attention to its outline. [< L, < *linea* line¹]

lin·e·ar (lin′i·ər), *adj.* **1.** of or in a line or lines. **2.** made of lines; making use of lines. **3.** long and narrow. [< L, < *linea* line¹] —**lin′e·ar·ly,** *adv.*

linear measure, 1. measure of length. **2.** system for measuring length in which 12 inches = 1 foot.

line·man (līn′mən), *n., pl.* **-men. 1.** man who sets up or repairs telegraph, telephone, or electric wires. **2.** *Football.* center, guard, tackle, or end. **3.** man who inspects railroad tracks.

lin·en (lin′ən), *n.* **1.** cloth or thread made from flax. **2.** articles made of linen or some substitute. [OE *linen,* adj., < *lin* flax]

line of force, *Physics.* line in a field of electrical or magnetic force that indicates the direction in which the force is acting.

lin·er¹ (līn′ər), *n.* **1.** *Am.* ship or airplane belonging to a transportation system. **2.** person or thing that makes lines. **3.** *Am.* a baseball hit so that it travels not far above the ground.

lin·er² (līn′ər), *n.* **1.** one that lines. **2.** a lining.

lines·man (līnz′mən), *n., pl.* **-men. 1.** in certain games, person who watches the lines which mark out the field, court, etc., and assists the umpire. **2.** lineman.

line-up, line up (līn′up′), *n.* **1.** formation of persons or things into a line: *a police line-up.* **2.** *Am.* arrangement of the players in football, baseball, etc., before a play begins.

ling (ling), *n., pl.* **ling, lings.** fish of northern Europe and Greenland, used for food. [ME *lenge* < OE *lang* long¹]

-ling, *suffix.* **1.** little; unimportant, as in *lordling.* **2.** one that is, as in *underling.* **3.** one belonging to or concerned with, as in *earthling, hireling.* [OE]

lin·ger (ling′gər), *v.* **1.** stay on in a place: *linger in the country.* **2.** continue; persist: *traces linger.* **3.** go slowly, as if unwilling to leave; loiter. [frequentative of earlier *leng* delay, OE *lengan* < *lang* long¹] —**lin′ger·er,** *n.* —Syn. **1.** tarry. **3.** dawdle, saunter, delay, lag.

lin·ge·rie (lan′zhə·rē′; län′zhə·rā′), *n.* women's underwear. [< F, ult. < *linge* linen]

lin·go (ling′gō), *n., pl.* **-goes.** *Humorous or Contemptuous.* **1.** language. **2.** any speech regarded as outlandish or queer: *writers about baseball use a strange lingo.* [blend of Pr. *lengo* and Ital. *lingua,* both < L *lingua* tongue]

lin·gua fran·ca (ling′gwə frang′kə), **1.** a hybrid language, consisting largely of Italian, used by the Latin races in dealing with Arabs, Turks, Greeks, etc. **2.** any hybrid language similarly used. [< Ital., Frankish language]

lin·gual (ling′gwəl), *adj.* **1.** of the tongue: *a lingual defect.* **2.** *Phonet.* formed with the aid of the tongue. —*n. Phonet.* sound formed with the aid of the tongue. *D* and *t* are linguals. [< Med.L, < L *lingua* tongue] —**lin′gual·ly,** *adv.*

lin·guist (ling′gwist), *n.* **1.** person skilled in a number of languages besides his own. **2.** scientist who studies the structure of language. [< L *lingua* tongue]

lin·guis·tic (ling·gwis′tik), *adj.* having to do with language or the study of languages. —**lin·guis′ti·cal·ly,** *adv.*

lin·guis·tics (ling·gwis′tiks), *n.* science of language. ➤ Linguistics is a complex science, with numerous subdivisions, each with its technique for observing and considering its material, its hypotheses, laws, and theories, and often forecasts of future trends. The principal subdivisions of linguistics are: a. *Phonetics and phonemics,* the study of sounds. b. *Morphology* (or *accidence*), the forms of words. c. *Syntax,* the study of the use of words in phrases, clauses, sentences. d. *Semantics* (or *semasiology*), study of the meanings of words. e. *Etymology,* the derivation of words and the steps by which they have moved from their early to their current forms. The outstanding trait of a linguist's approach to language is detachment—contrasting with the emotion often shown by nonprofessional users in defending or disapproving matters of speech. A linguist accepts such locutions as "I seen him yesterday," "He ain't got none," "That book is hern" as facts of the language—as well as words like *phagocyte* and *sternutation.* This does not mean that he uses any of these locutions himself or recommends them to others, but he notices that certain people use them and he observes and defines their place in the language. See the articles on **due to, like vs. as,** and other debated locutions.

lin·i·ment (lin′ə·mənt), *n.* liquid for rubbing on the skin to relieve soreness, sprains, bruises, etc. [< LL, < *linere* anoint]

lin·ing (līn′ing), *n.* layer of material covering the inner surface of something: *the lining of a coat, the lining of a stove.*

link¹ (lingk), *n.* **1.** one ring or loop of a chain. **2.** anything that joins as a link joins. **3.** bond or tie. **4.** fact or thought that connects others: *a link in a chain of evidence.* **5.** link of a surveying chain used as a measure; 7.92 inches. —*v.* join as a link does; unite or connect. [< Scand. (Sw.) *länk*] —**linked** (lingkt), *adj.*

link² (lingk), *n.* torch.

link·age (lingk′ij), *n.* **1.** a linking or being linked. **2.** arrangement or system of links.

linking verb, a verb with little or no meaning of its own that connects a subject with a predicate adjective or noun. ≻ **linking verbs.** *Be* is the most common linking verb, since in its ordinary use it has little specific meaning and merely performs the verb functions of tense, person, number: *the man is a carpenter; this bottle was full.* Many other verbs are used as linking verbs—probably about sixty in current English. Instead of having a verb of full meaning like *colden,* English uses the nearly meaningless verb *turn* and the adjective *cold,* which carries the chief part of the meaning, in such a sentence as *The weather turned cold.* Many verbs are used with full meaning of their own (as *fell* in "The tree fell in the water") or as linking verbs (as *fell* in "She fell silent" or "He fell ill"). *Be* and other linking verbs are followed not by adverbs but by adjectives or nouns, known as *predicate adjectives* and *predicate nominatives* respectively.

links (lingks), *n.pl.* golf course. [OE *hlinc* rising ground]

Lin·nae·us (li·nē′əs), *n.* Carolus, 1707–1778, Swedish botanist. —**Lin·ne′an, Lin·nae′an,** *adj.*

lin·net (lin′it), *n.* a small songbird of Europe, Asia, and Africa. [OE *līnēte* flax-eater; flaxseeds form much of its diet]

li·no·le·um (li·nō′li·əm), *n.* **1.** floor covering made by putting a hard surface of ground cork mixed with oxidized linseed oil on a canvas back. **2.** any similar floor covering. [< L *linum* flax + *oleum* oil]

lin·o·type (lin′ə·tip), *n. Am.* **1.** typesetting machine that is operated like a typewriter and that casts each line of type in one piece. **2.** Linotype. trademark for this machine. [orig., *line o′ type* line of type] —**lin′o·typ′er,** *n.Am.*

lin·seed (lin′sēd′), *n.* seed of flax. [OE *līnsǣd* flaxseed]

linseed oil, a yellowish oil pressed from linseed, used in making paints, printing inks, and linoleum.

lin·sey-wool·sey (lin′zi·wúl′zi), or **lin·sey,** *n., pl.* -wool·seys; lin·seys. a strong coarse fabric made of linen and wool or of cotton and wool. [< OE *līn* linen + *wull* wool]

lint (lint), *n.* **1.** a soft down or fleecy material obtained by scraping linen. Lint was formerly much used as a dressing for wounds. **2.** tiny bits of thread. [ME *lynet* < OE *līn* flax] —**lint′y,** *adj.*

lin·tel (lin′təl), *n.* a horizontal beam or stone over a door, window, etc., to support the structure above it. [< OF, ult. < L *limes* boundary]

li·on (li′ən), *n.* **1.** a large, strong, tawny animal of the cat family, found in Africa and S Asia. The male has a full, flowing mane of coarse hair. **2.** a very brave or strong person. **3.** a famous person. **4.** Lion, *Astron.* Leo, a constellation and sign of the zodiac. [< OF < L < Gk. *leon*]

li·on·ess (li′ən·is), *n.* a female lion.

li·on-heart·ed (li′ən·här′tid), *adj.* brave.

li·on·ize (li′ən·iz), *v.,* -ized, -iz·ing. treat as very important. —**li′on·i·za′tion,** *n.*

lion's share, the biggest or best part.

lip (lip), *n., v.,* lipped, lip·ping, *adj.* —*n.* **1.** either of the two fleshy movable edges of the mouth. **2.** lips, mouth. **3.** folding or bent-out edge of any opening: *the lip of a pitcher.* **4.** mouthpiece of a musical instrument. **5.** *Slang.* impudent talk. —*v.* **1.** touch with the lips. **2.** use the lips in playing a wind instrument. **3.** murmur. —*adj.* not heartfelt or deep, but just on the surface: *lip worship.* [OE *lippa*] —**Syn.** *adj.* superficial.

lip reading, understanding of speech by watching the movements of the speaker's lips. —**lip reader.**

lip·stick (lip′stik′), *n. Am.* a small stick of rouge, etc., used for coloring the lips.

liq., **1.** liquid. **2.** liquor.

liq·ue·fac·tion (lik′wə·fak′shən), *n.* **1.** process of changing into a liquid. **2.** liquefied condition.

liq·ue·fy (lik′wə·fi), *v.,* -fied, -fy·ing. change into a liquid. [< L, < *liquere* be fluid + *facere* make] —**liq′ue·fi′a·ble,** *adj.* —**liq′ue·fi′er,** *n.*

li·ques·cent (li·kwes′ənt), *adj.* becoming liquid. —**li·ques′cence, li·ques′cen·cy,** *n.*

li·queur (li·kėr′; -kyūr′), *n.* a strong, sweet, highly flavored alcoholic liquor. [< F. Doublet of LIQUOR.]

liq·uid (lik′wid), *n.* **1.** substance that is neither a solid nor a gas; substance that flows freely like water. **2.** *Phonet.* sound of *l* or *r.* —*adj.* **1.** in the form of a liquid; melted: *liquid soap.* **2.** clear and bright like water. **3.** clear and smooth-flowing in sound: *the liquid notes of a bird.* **4.** easily turned into cash: *a liquid investment.* [< L *liquidus* < *liquere* be fluid] —**liq′uid·ly,** *adv.* —**liq′uid·ness,** *n.* —**Syn.** *n.* **1.** fluid.

liquid air, intensely cold, transparent liquid formed when air is very greatly compressed and then cooled.

liq·ui·date (lik′wə·dāt), *v.,* -dat·ed, -dat·ing. **1.** pay (a debt). **2.** settle the accounts of (a business, etc.); clear up the affairs of (a bankrupt). **3.** get rid of (an undesirable person or thing): *the Russian revolution liquidated the nobility.* **4.** kill ruthlessly; exterminate. **5.** *Law.* determine the amount of (indebtedness or damages). —**liq′ui·da′tion,** *n.* —**liq′ui·da′tor,** *n.* —**li·quid′i·ty,** *n.*

liquid measure, **1.** measurement of liquids. **2.** system for measuring liquids: 2 pints = 1 quart; 4 quarts = 1 gallon.

liq·uor (lik′ər), *n.* **1.** an alcoholic drink, esp. brandy, gin, rum, and whiskey. **2.** any liquid: *pickles are put up in a salty liquor.* —*v.* **1.** *Slang.* furnish with alcoholic liquor. **2.** *Slang.* drink alcoholic liquor. [< L. Doublet of LIQUEUR.]

liq·uo·rice (lik′ə·ris; lik′ris; -rish), *n.* licorice.

liq·uor·ish (lik′ər·ish), *adj.* lickerish.

li·ra (lir′ə), *n., pl.* li·re (lir′ā), li·ras. **1.** unit of money in Italy, formerly worth 19.3 cents. **2.** coin worth a lira. [< Ital. < L *libra* pound]

Lis·bon (liz′bən), *n.* capital of Portugal.

lisle (lil), *n.* a fine, strong, linen or cotton thread, used for making stockings, gloves, etc. [< F *Lisle,* former name of Lille]

lisp (lisp), *v.* **1.** use the sounds of *th,* as in *thin* and *then,* instead of the sound of *s* and the sound of *z* in speaking. **2.** speak imperfectly. —*n.* act, habit, or sound of lisping. [ult. < OE *wlisp,* *adj.,* lisping] —**lisp′er,** *n.* —**lisp′ing·ly,** *adv.*

lis·some, lis·som (lis′əm), *adj.* **1.** lithe; limber; supple. **2.** nimble; active. [var. of *lithesome* < *lithe*] —**lis′some·ly, lis′som·ly,** *adv.* —**lis′some·ness, lis′som·ness,** *n.*

list¹ (list), *n.* series of names, numbers, words, etc.: *a shopping list.* —*v.* **1.** make a list of; enter in a list. **2.** enlist. [< F *liste* < Gmc.] —**Syn.** *n.* roll, register, roster, catalogue, index.

list² (list), *n.* **1.** the edge of cloth, where the material is a little different. **2.** a cheap fabric made out of such edges. **3.** a strip. **4.** a stripe of color. —*v.* **1.** put list around the edges of. **2.** border or edge. **3.** arrange in strips, bands, or stripes. —*adj.* made of list. [OE *līste*]

list³ (list), *n.* a tipping to one side; tilt: *the list of a ship.* —*v.* tip to one side; tilt.

list⁴ (list), *v. Archaic.* **1.** be pleasing to; please: *me lists not to speak.* **2.** like; wish: *the wind bloweth where it listeth.* [OE *lystan* < *lust* pleasure]

list⁵ (list), *v. Archaic and Poetic.* 1. listen. 2. listen to. [OE *hlystan* < *hlyst* hearing; akin to LISTEN]

lis·ten (lis'ən), *v.* 1. try to hear; attend closely for the purpose of hearing: *listen to the radio.* 2. give heed (to advice, temptation, etc.); pay attention. 3. listen in, a. listen to others talking on a telephone. b. listen to the radio. [OE *hlysnan*; akin to LIST⁵] —**lis'ten·er,** *n.* —Syn. 1. hearken.

Lis·ter (lis'tər), *n.* Joseph, 1827–1912, English surgeon, first to use antiseptic methods in performing operations.

list·er (lis'tər), *n.* plow that throws the dirt to both sides of the furrow. [< *list²*]

list·less (list'lis), *adj.* seeming too tired to care about anything; not interested in things; not caring to be active. [< *list⁴*] —**list'less·ly,** *adv.* —**list'less·ness,** *n.* —Syn. indifferent, languid.

list price, price given in a catalogue or list.

lists (lists), *n.pl.* 1. place where knights fought in tournaments. 2. barriers enclosing such a field. 3. any place or scene of combat. 4. enter the lists, join in a contest; take part in a fight, argument, etc. [< *list²*]

Liszt (list), *n.* Franz, 1811–1886, Hungarian composer and pianist.

lit (lit), *v.* pt. and pp. of light¹ and light³.

lit., 1. liter. 2. literal; literally. 3. literature.

lit·a·ny (lit'ə·ni), *n., pl.* **-nies.** 1. series of prayers by the minister with responses by the congregation. 2. a repeated series. [< LL < Gk. *litaneia* litany, an entreating]

li·tchi (lē'chē), *n., pl.* **-chis.** 1. Also, litchi nut, a nut-shaped fruit with a hard, rough skin. 2. the Chinese tree that it grows on. Also, lichee. [< Chinese]

li·ter (lē'tər), *n.* the common measure of capacity in France, Germany, and other countries which use the metric system. One liter equals 1.0567 qt. liquid measure, or .908 qt. dry measure. Also, *esp. Brit.* litre. [< F *litre*, ult. < Gk. *litra* pound]

lit·er·a·cy (lit'ər·ə·si), *n.* ability to read and write.

lit·er·al (lit'ər·əl), *adj.* 1. following the exact words of the original: *a literal translation.* 2. of persons, taking words in their usual meaning, without exaggeration or imagination; matter-of-fact. 3. of meaning, precise; strict: *the literal meaning of a word.* 4. true to fact: *a literal account.* 5. being actually such: *a literal transformation.* [< LL, < L *lit(t)era* letter] —**lit'er·al'i·ty,** *n.* —**lit'er·al·ly,** *adv.* —**lit'er·al·ness,** *n.*

lit·er·al·ism (lit'ər·əl·iz'əm), *n.* 1. exact translation or interpretation. 2. exact portrayal in art or literature. —**lit'er·al·ist,** *n.* —**lit'er·al·is'tic,** *adj.*

lit·er·ar·y (lit'ər·er'i), *adj.* 1. having to do with literature. 2. knowing much about literature. 3. engaged in literature as a profession. —**lit'er·ar'i·ly,** *adv.* —**lit'er·ar'i·ness,** *n.* ▸ Literary, as applied to style, usually means possessing traits that are characteristic of the more conservative tradition of English literature. Its connotation may be "distinguished" or it may be "bookish."

lit·er·ate (lit'ər·it), *adj.* 1. able to read and write. 2. acquainted with literature; educated. —*n.* 1. person who can read and write. 2. educated person.

lit·er·a·ti (lit'ə·rä'ti; -rā'ti), *n.pl.* scholarly or literary people. [< L, pl., lit., lettered]

lit·er·a·tim (lit'ə·rā'tim), *adv.* letter for letter; exactly as written. [< Med.L, < L *lit(t)era* letter]

lit·er·a·ture (lit'ər·ə·chər; -chūr; lit'rə-), *n.* 1. writings of a period or of a country, esp. those kept alive by their beauty or style or thought. Shakespeare is a great name in English literature. 2. all the books and articles on a subject: *the literature of stamp collecting.* 3. profession of a writer. 4. *Colloq.* printed matter of any kind. [< F < L *lit(t)eratura* writing < *lit(t)era* letter] —Syn. 1. belles-lettres.

lith·arge (lith'ärj; li·thärj'), *n. Chem.* a yellow oxide of lead, PbO, used in making glass,

glazes for pottery, and driers for paints and varnishes. [< OF < L < Gk., < *lithos* stone + *argyros* silver]

lithe (līᵺ), **lithe·some** (līᵺ'səm), *adj.* bending easily; supple. [OE *līthe* mild] —**lithe'ly,** *adv.* —**lithe'ness,** *n.*

lith·i·um (lith'i·əm), *n. Chem.* a soft, silver-white metallic element, Li, similar to sodium. Lithium is the lightest of all metals. [< NL, < Gk. *lithos* stone]

lith·o·graph (lith'ə·graf; -gräf), *n.* picture, print, etc., made from a flat, specially prepared stone or a metal plate. —*v.* print from a stone or plate. [< Gk. *lithos* stone + -GRAPH] —**li·thog·ra·pher** (li·thog'rə·fər), *n.*

li·thog·ra·phy (li·thog'rə·fi), *n.* art or process of making lithographs. —**lith·o·graph·ic** (lith'ə·graf'ik), **lith'o·graph'i·cal,** *adj.* —**lith'o·graph'i·cal·ly,** *adv.*

lith·o·sphere (lith'ə·sfir), *n.* crust of the earth.

Lith·u·a·ni·a (lith'ū·ā'ni·ə), *n.* a small country in N Europe, now under Soviet control. —**Lith'u·a'ni·an,** *adj., n.*

lit·i·ga·ble (lit'ə·gə·bəl), *adj.* capable of being made the subject of a suit in a law court.

lit·i·gant (lit'ə·gənt), *n.* person engaged in a lawsuit. —*adj.* 1. engaging in a lawsuit. 2. inclined to go to law.

lit·i·gate (lit'ə·gāt), *v.,* **-gat·ed, -gat·ing.** 1. engage in a lawsuit. 2. contest in a lawsuit. [< L *litigatus* < *lis* lawsuit] —**lit'i·ga'tor,** *n.*

lit·i·ga·tion (lit'ə·gā'shən), *n.* 1. the carrying on of a lawsuit. 2. a going to law.

li·ti·gious (lə·tij'əs), *adj.* 1. having the habit of going to law. 2. that can be disputed in a court of law. 3. of lawsuits. —**li·ti'gious·ly,** *adv.* —**li·ti'gious·ness,** *n.*

lit·mus (lit'məs), *n.* a blue coloring matter, obtained from certain plants. [< Scand. *litmosi* dyer's herbs < *litr* color + *mosi* moss]

litmus paper, paper treated with litmus. It turns red when put into an acid and back to blue when put into an alkali.

li·tre (lē'tər), *n. Esp. Brit.* liter.

lit·ter (lit'ər), *n.* 1. things scattered about or left in disorder. 2. disorder; untidiness. 3. young animals produced at one time: *a litter of puppies.* 4. straw, hay, etc., used as bedding for animals. 5. stretcher for carrying a sick or wounded person. 6. framework to be carried on men's shoulders or by beasts of burden, with a couch usually enclosed by curtains. —*v.* 1. leave odds and ends lying around; scatter things about. 2. make disordered or untidy: *litter a yard with bottles and cans.* 3. give birth to (young animals). [< AF, ult. < L *lectus* bed]

Litter (def. 6)

lit·té·ra·teur, lit·te·ra·teur (lit'ə·rə·tėr'), *n.* literary man; writer or critic of literature.

lit·tle (lit'əl), *adj.,* **less** or **less·er, least;** or **lit·tler, lit·tlest;** *adv.,* **less, least;** *n.* —*adj.* 1. not great or big; small: *a little house.* 2. not much; small in number, amount, degree, or importance: *little discomforts, little hope.* 3. on a small scale: *the little fellows in business.* 4. short; brief: *a little walk.* 5. mean; narrow-minded: *little thoughts.* —*adv.* 1. in a small amount or degree; slightly: *he eats very little.* 2. not at all: *little did I think it would happen.* —*n.* 1. a small amount, quantity, or degree: *add a little.* 2. a short time or distance: *move a little to the left.* 3. **little by little,** slowly; gradually; by a small amount at a time. 4. **make little of,** treat or represent as of little importance. 5. **not a little,** much; very. 6. **think little of,** a. not value much; consider as unimportant or worthless. b. not hesitate about. [OE *lȳtel*] —**lit'tle·ness,** *n.* —Syn. *adj.* 1. minute, tiny, diminutive. 2. trivial, insignificant. 5. petty, illiberal.

Little Assembly, *Colloq.* the interim committee of the United Nations General Assembly.
Little Bear, Ursa Minor.
Little Dipper, group of stars in the constellation of Ursa Minor (the Little Bear).
little magazine or **review,** magazine devoted to printing artistic work and experimental writing not normally handled by popular magazines.
Little Rock, capital of Arkansas, in the C part.
lit·to·ral (lit′ə·stol), *adj.* 1. of a shore. 2. on the shore. —*n.* region along the shore. [ult. < L *litoralis* < *litus* shore]
li·tur·gi·cal (lə·tẽr′jə·kəl), **li·tur·gic** (-jik), *adj.* of or used in liturgies; having to do with liturgies. —**li·tur′gi·cal·ly,** *adv.*
lit·ur·gy (lit′ər·ji), *n.,* *pl.* -gies. 1. form of public worship. Different churches use different liturgies. 2. communion service. [< LL < Gk. *leitourgia* < *leitos* public + *ergon* work]
Lit·vi·nov (lit·vē′nôf; -nof; lit′vi-), *n.* Maksim Maksimovich, 1876–1951, Russian statesman.
liv·a·ble, live·a·ble (liv′ə·bəl), *adj.* 1. fit to live in: *a livable house.* 2. easy to live with. 3. worth living; endurable. —**liv′a·ble·ness, live′a·ble·ness,** *n.*
live¹ (liv), *v.,* **lived, liv·ing.** 1. have life; be alive; exist: *all creatures have an equal right to live.* 2. remain alive; last; endure: *if I live till May.* 3. keep up life: *live on one′s income.* 4. feed or subsist: *the Chinese live largely on rice.* 5. pass (life): *live in peace.* 6. dwell: *live with one′s parents.* 7. carry out or show in life: *live one′s ideals.* 8. have a rich and full life. 9. **live down,** live so worthily that (some fault or sin) is overlooked or forgotten. 10. **live up to,** act according to; do (what is expected or promised). [OE *liflan, libban*] —Syn. 6. reside, sojourn, lodge, abide.
live² (liv), *adj.* 1. having life; alive: *a live animal.* 2. burning or glowing: *live coals.* 3. full of energy or activity: *a live person.* 4. *Colloq.* up-to-date. 5. *Esp. U.S.* of present interest: *a live question.* 6. moving or imparting motion: *live wheels, a live axle.* 7. still in use or to be used: *live steam.* 8. carrying an electric current: *a live wire.* 9. loaded: *a live cartridge.* 10. not recorded on tape or film: *a live television show.* [var. of *alive*]
live·li·hood (līv′li·hûd), *n.* means of keeping alive; support: *Dickens wrote for a livelihood.*
live·long (liv′lông′; -long′), *adj.* whole length of; whole; entire.
live·ly (līv′li), *adj.* -li·er, -li·est, *adv.* —*adj.* 1. full of life; active; vigorous; spirited: *a lively child.* 2. exciting: *a lively time.* 3. bright; vivid: *lively green.* 4. cheerful; gay: *a lively dance or conversation.* 5. bounding back quickly: *a lively baseball.* —*adv.* in a lively manner. —**live′li·ly,** *adv.* —**live′li·ness,** *n.* —Syn. *adj.* 1. brisk, energetic, animated, vivacious. 4. blithe, buoyant.
liv·en (līv′ən), *v.* make or become more lively; brighten; cheer up. —**liv′en·er,** *n.*
live oak (līv), *Am.* 1. an evergreen oak of the S United States. 2. its hard wood.
liv·er¹ (liv′ər), *n.* 1. a large, reddish-brown organ in vertebrate animals that secretes bile and helps in the absorption of food. 2. the liver of an animal used as food. [OE *lifer*]
liv·er² (liv′ər), *n.* person who lives.
liv·er·ied (liv′ər·id; liv′rid), *adj.* clothed in a livery.
Liv·er·pool (liv′ər·pül), *n.* seaport in W England.
liv·er·wort (liv′ər·wẽrt′), *n.* 1. any of various plants somewhat like mosses. 2. hepatica.
liv·er·wurst (liv′ər·wẽrst′; -wûrst′), *n.* *Am.* sausage consisting largely of liver. [< G *leberwurst* liver sausage]
liv·er·y (liv′ər·i; liv′ri), *n.,* *pl.* -er·ies. 1. any special uniform provided for the servants of a household, or adopted by any group or profession. 2. a distinctive dress, badge, or cognizance provided for retainers. 3. any characteristic

dress, garb, or outward appearance. 4. the feeding, stabling, and care of horses for pay; the hiring out of horses and carriages. 5. *U.S.* livery stable. [< OF *livrée* < *livrer* dispense; orig., provisions dispensed to servants]
liv·er·y·man (liv′ər·i·mən; liv′ri-), *n.,* *pl.* -men. person who works in or keeps a livery stable.
livery stable, stable engaged in the livery business.
lives (līvz), *n.* pl. of life.
live·stock (līv′stok′), *n.* farm animals. Cows, horses, sheep, and pigs are livestock.
live wire, 1. wire in which an electric current is flowing. 2. *Colloq.* specially alert and enterprising person.
liv·id (liv′id), *adj.* 1. having a dull-bluish or leaden color. 2. discolored by a bruise. [< L *lividus* < *livere* be bluish] —**liv′id·ly,** *adv.* —**liv′id·ness, li·vid′i·ty,** *n.*
liv·ing (liv′ing), *adj.* 1. having life; being alive: *a living plant.* 2. full of life; strong: *a living faith.* 3. burning; glowing: *a living coal.* 4. in actual existence; still in use: *living language.* 5. of or pertaining to persons who are alive: *within living memory.* 6. true to life; vivid; lifelike: *a living picture.* 7. of life; for living in: *living conditions.* 8. sufficient to live on: *a living wage.* —*n.* 1. act or condition of one that lives. 2. manner of life: *the importance of right living.* 3. means of obtaining what is needed to support life; livelihood. 4. benefice. —**liv′ing·ly,** *adv.* —**liv′ing·ness,** *n.* —Syn. *adj.* 2. lively, active, vigorous. —*n.* 3. subsistence, sustenance, maintenance.
living quarters, place to live.
living room, *Am.* room for general family use.
living wage, sufficient pay to buy the necessities of life.
Liv·y (liv′i), *n.* 59 B.C.–17 A.D., Roman historian.
liz·ard (liz′ərd), *n.* any of a large group of reptiles, most of which are small and have long bodies with four legs and a long tail. Chameleons, horned toads, and glass snakes are lizards. Some lizards without limbs look much like snakes, but have movable eyelids. [< OF < L *lacertus*]
LL, Late Latin.
ll., lines.

lla·ma (lä′mə), *n.,* *pl.* -mas or (*esp. collectively*) -ma. a South American animal somewhat like a camel, but smaller and without a hump. [< Sp. < Kechua (Ind. lang. of Peru)]

Llama (ab. 3 ft. high at the shoulder)

lla·no (lä′nō), *n.,* *pl.* -nos. *Am.* a broad treeless plain. [< Sp. < L *planus* level]
LL.D., Doctor of Laws.
Lloyd George (loid′ jôrj′), David, 1863–1945, British statesman and prime minister, 1916–1922.
lo (lō), *interj.* look! see! behold! [OE *lā*]
loach (lōch), *n.* a small European fresh-water fish. [< OF *loche*]
load (lōd), *n.* 1. what one is carrying; burden. 2. something that oppresses mind or spirit. 3. quantity that can be or usually is carried; such quantity taken as a unit of measure or weight. 4. **loads,** *Colloq.* great quantity or number. 5. in mechanics, weight supported by a structure or part. 6. external resistance overcome by an engine, dynamo, or the like, under a given condition, measured by the power required. 7. one charge of powder and shot for a gun. —*v.* 1. place on or in something for conveyance: *load grain.* 2. heap on; pile on. 3. put a load in or on: *load a wagon.* 4. take on a load. 5. burden; oppress. 6. supply amply or in excess: *they loaded her with compliments.* 7. add weight to: *load dice.* 8. put a charge in (a gun). [OE *lād* course, carrying. See LODE.] —**load′er,** *n.* —Syn. *n.* 1. weight, pack, cargo.

load·star (lōd′stär′), *n.* lodestar.

load·stone (lōd′stōn′), *n.* **1.** stone that attracts iron as a magnet does. **2.** something that attracts. Also, lodestone.

loaf[1] (lōf), *n., pl.* loaves. **1.** bread shaped and baked as one piece. **2.** a rather large cake, often baked in the shape of a loaf of bread. **3.** food shaped like a loaf of bread. **4.** cone-shaped mass of sugar. [OE *hlāf*]

loaf[2] (lōf), *v. Am.* spend time idly; do nothing.

loaf·er (lōf′ər), *n. Am.* **1.** one who loafs. **2.** shoe resembling a moccasin, but with sole and heel stitched to the upper.

loam (lōm), *n.* rich, fertile earth; earth in which much humus is mixed with clay and sand. —*v.* cover or fill with loam. [OE *lām*] —**loam′y**, *adj.*

loan (lōn), *n.* **1.** a lending. **2.** money lent. **3.** anything lent. —*v.* make a loan; lend. [< Scand. *lān*] —**loan′er**, *n.* ➤ **loan as a verb.** In spite of attempts to keep *loan* only as a noun and to make *lend* the corresponding verb, *loan* is also properly a verb, at least in American usage: *I loaned* [or *lent*] *him* $2. *He got a loan of two dollars.*

loan shark, *Colloq.* person who lends money at an extremely high or unlawful rate of interest.

loan word, foreign word that has been anglicized, as *khaki* or *intelligentsia.*

loath (lōth), *adj.* **1.** unwilling; reluctant: *the little girl was loath to leave.* **2.** nothing loath, willing; willingly. Also, **loth.** [OE *lāth* odious]

loathe (lōth), *v.*, loathed, loath·ing. feel strong dislike and disgust for; abhor; hate. [OE *lāthian* be hateful < *lāth* odious] —**loath′er**, *n.* —Syn. abominate, detest.

loath·ing (lōth′ing), *n.* strong dislike and disgust; intense aversion. —**loath′ing·ly**, *adv.*

loath·ly[1] (lōth′li), *adj.* loathsome.

loath·ly[2] (lōth′li; *older* lōth′li), *adv.* unwillingly.

loath·some (lōth′səm), *adj.* disgusting; sickening: *a loathsome stench.* —**loath′some·ly**, *adv.* —**loath′some·ness**, *n.* —Syn. abominable.

loaves (lōvz), *n. pl.* of **loaf**[1].

lob (lob), *n., v.*, lobbed, lob·bing. —*n.* a tennis ball hit high to the back of the opponent's court. —*v.* hit (a ball) thus. —**lob′ber**, *n.*

lo·bar (lō′bər), *adj.* of or having to do with a lobe or lobes.

lo·bate (lō′bāt), **lo·bat·ed** (-id), *adj.* having a lobe or lobes; having the form of a lobe: *the liver is lobate.* —**lo′bate·ly**, *adv.*

lo·ba·tion (lō-bā′shən), *n.* **1.** a lobate formation. **2.** lobe.

lob·by (lob′i), *n., pl.* -bies, *v.*, -bied, -by·ing. —*n.* **1.** entrance hall; passageway: *the lobby of a theater.* A hotel lobby usually has chairs and couches to sit on. **2.** *Am.* person or group that tries to influence legislators. —*v. Am.* **a.** try to influence legislators. **b.** get or try to get (a bill) passed by lobbying. [< Med.L *lobia* < Gmc. Doublet of LODGE, LOGE, LOGGIA.] —**lob′by·ist**, *n. Am.*

lobe (lōb), *n.* a rounded projecting part: *the lobes of an oak leaf.* The lobe of the ear is the lower rounded end. [< F < LL < Gk. *lobos*] —**lobed**, *adj.*

lo·bel·ia (lō-bēl′yə), *n.* plant with blue, red, yellow, or white flowers. [for M. de *Lobel*, botanist]

lob·lol·ly (lob′lol′i), *n., pl.* -lies. *Am.* **1.** Also, loblolly pine. a pine tree of the S United States that has thick bark and long needles. **2.** its coarse, inferior wood.

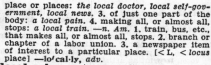

lo·bo (lō′bō), *n., pl.* -bos. *Am.* a large gray wolf. [< Sp. < L *lupus*]

lob·ster (lob′stər), *n.* an edible sea animal with two big claws in front and eight legs. [OE *loppestre,* prob. < *loppe* spider; from the shape]

Lobster (ab. 1 ft. long, including claws)

lob·ule (lob′ūl), *n.* **1.** a small lobe. **2.** part of a lobe. —**lob′u·lar**, *adj.*

lo·cal (lō′kəl), *adj.* **1.** of place: *"a local habitation and a name."* **2.** having to do with a certain place or places: *the local doctor, local self-government, local news.* **3.** of just one part of the body: *a local pain.* **4.** making all, or almost all, stops: *a local train.* —*n. Am.* **1.** train, bus, etc., that makes all, or almost all, stops. **2.** branch or chapter of a labor union. **3.** a newspaper item of interest to a particular place. [< L, < *locus* place] —**lo′cal·ly**, *adv.*

local color, customs, peculiarities, etc., of a certain place or period, used in stories and plays to make them seem more real.

lo·cale (lō-kal′), *n.* place, esp. with reference to events or circumstances connected with it. [< F *local* LOCAL]

lo·cal·ism (lō′kəl-iz-əm), *n.* **1.** a local expression, custom, etc. **2.** provincialism. ➤ **A localism** is a pronunciation, a word or meaning of a word, or an idiom that for natural and usually traceable historical reasons is current in one region and not in others. Wherever people from different parts of the United States are together, different pronunciations are easily noticed. Some New Englanders will use a broad *a* (äsk, gräss, päst) where most Americans have short *a*, as in *hat.* In vocabulary, different words will be found for many common objects. People's attitudes toward the use of localisms vary greatly. Some believe that localisms should be weeded out; others believe that a person should retain as much as possible of the flavor of his native speech. It is a problem each person will have to settle for himself, on the basis of appropriateness. In formal English, however, localisms are avoided.

lo·cal·i·ty (lō-kal′ə-ti), *n., pl* -ties. **1.** the place in which a thing is or occurs, esp. a geographical place or situation: *the locality of a crime.* **2.** state or fact of being local.

lo·cal·ize (lō′kəl-iz), *v.*, -ized, -iz·ing. make local; fix in, assign, or limit to a particular place or locality: *an infection localized in the foot.* —**lo′cal·iz′a·ble**, *adj.* —**lo′cal·i·za′tion**, *n.*

local option, right of choice exercised by a minor political division, such as a county or city, esp. as to whether the sale of liquor shall be permitted within its limits.

lo·cate (lō′kāt; lō-kāt′), *v.*, -cat·ed, -cat·ing. **1.** establish in a place: *he located his new store on Main Street.* **2.** *Am.* establish oneself in a place: *he went to New York and located there.* **3.** find out the exact position of: *the general tried to locate the enemy's camp.* **4.** state or show the position of: *locate Boston.* **5.** be located, be situated: *Rome is located in Italy.* [< L, < *locus* place] —**lo′ca·tor**, *n.*

lo·ca·tion (lō-kā′shən), *n.* **1.** a locating or being located. **2.** position; place. **3.** plot of ground marked out by boundaries; lot. **4.** *Am.* a place outside of the studio used in making all or part of a motion picture. —Syn. **2.** locality. **3.** site.

loc·a·tive (lok′ə-tiv), *Gram.* —*adj.* indicating place. —*n.* **1.** case used to indicate place in which. **2.** word in this case.

loc. cit., in the place cited. [< L *loco citato*]

loch (lok; loH), *n. Scot.* **1.** lake: *Loch Lomond.* **2.** arm of the sea partly shut in by land. [< Scotch Gaelic]

Loch Lomond. See Lomond.

lo·ci (lō′sī), *n. pl.* of **locus.**

lock[1] (lok), *n.* **1.** means of fastening doors, boxes, etc., usually needing a key of special shape to open it. **2.** a locking or being locked. **3.** part of a canal, dock, etc., in which the level of the water can be changed by letting water in or out to raise or lower ships. **4.** part of a gun by which the charge is fired. **5.** a kind of hold in wrestling. —*v.* **1.** fasten with a lock: *lock the door.* **2.** shut (something in or out or up): *lock a prisoner in a cell.* **3.** hold fast: *a ship locked in ice, a secret locked in one's heart.* **4.** join, fit, jam, or link together: *the girls locked arms.* **5.** become locked: *two cars locked together in passing.* **6.** move (a ship) by means of a lock. **7.** lock out, refuse to give work to workers until they accept the employer's terms. [OE *loc*] —Syn. *n.* **1.** bolt, latch, catch.

lock[2] (lok), *n.* **1.** tress of hair. **2.** locks, the hair of the head. **3.** portion of wool, flax, cotton, etc. [OE *locc*]

Locke (lok), *n.* John, 1632–1704, English philosopher.

lock·er (lok′ər), *n.* **1.** one that locks. **2.** chest, drawer, closet, or cupboard that can be locked. **3.** a refrigerated compartment that may be rented for storing frozen foods.

lock·et (lok′it), *n.* a small ornamental case of gold, silver, etc., for holding a picture of someone or a lock of hair. It is usually worn around the neck on a necklace. [< F *loquet* latch, dim. of OF *loc* < Gmc.]

lock·jaw (lok′jô′), *n.* blood poisoning in which the jaws become firmly closed.

lock·out (lok′out′), *n.* refusal to give work to workers until they accept the employer's terms.

lock·smith (lok′smith′), *n.* man who makes or repairs locks and keys.

lock step, way of marching in step very close together.

lock·up (lok′up′), *n.* jail.

lo·co (lō′kō), *n., pl.* -cos, *v.,* -coed, -co·ing, *adj. Am.* —*n.* **1.** locoweed. **2.** disease caused by eating this weed. —*v.* poison with this weed. —*adj. Slang.* crazy. [< Sp., insane]

lo·co·mo·tion (lō′kə·mō′shən), *n.* act or power of moving from place to place. Walking, swimming, and flying are common forms of locomotion. [< L *loco* from a place + *motio* motion]

lo·co·mo·tive (lō′kə·mō′tiv), *n.* **1.** a railroad engine. **2.** any engine that goes from place to place on its own power. —*adj.* **1.** moving from place to place. **2.** having to do with the power to move from place to place.

lo·co·mo·tor (lō′kə·mō′tər), *adj.* of or pertaining to locomotion.

locomotor ataxia, a degenerative disease of the spinal cord, marked by loss of control over walking and certain other movements.

lo·co·weed (lō′kō·wēd′), *n. Am.* plant of W United States that affects the brains of horses, sheep, etc., that eat it. Also, loco.

lo·cus (lō′kəs), *n., pl.* lo·ci (lō′sī), **1.** place. **2.** *Math.* curve, surface, or other figure that contains all the points, and only those points, that satisfy a given condition. [< L]

lo·cust (lō′kəst), *n.* **1.** any of the grasshoppers with short antennae, certain species of which migrate in great swarms, destroying crops. **2.** cicada. **3.** *Am.* a. tree with small rounded leaflets and clusters of sweet-smelling white flowers. b. its wood, hard and resisting decay. **4.** *Am.* any of various other trees, such as the honey locust. [< L *locusta*]

lo·cu·tion (lō·kū′shən), *n.* **1.** style of speech: *childish locution.* **2.** form of expression: *foreign locutions.* [< L *locutio* < *loqui* speak]

lode (lōd), *n.* vein of metal ore. [OE *lād* course, carrying. See LOAD.]

lode·star (lōd′stär′), *n.* **1.** star that shows the way. **2.** polestar; North Star. **3.** guiding principle; center of attraction. Also, loadstar.

lode·stone (lōd′stōn′), *n.* loadstone.

lodge (loj), *v.,* lodged, lodg·ing, *n.* —*v.* **1.** live in a place for a time. **2.** provide with a place to live in or sleep in for a time. **3.** live in a rented room in another's house. **4.** rent a room or rooms to. **5.** get caught or stay in a place:*the kite lodged in the top of a tree.* **6.** put or send into a place: *the hunter lodged a bullet in the lion's heart.* **7.** put for safekeeping. **8.** put before some authority: *lodge a complaint with the police.* **9.** put (power, authority, etc.) in a person or thing. —*n.* **1.** place to live in; small or temporary house; house. **2.** branch of a secret society. **3.** place where it meets. **4.** den of a beaver or otter. [OF *loge* arbor, covered walk < Gmc. Doublet of LOBBY, LOGE, LOGGIA.] —Syn. *v.* **1.** dwell, reside. **6.** deposit, implant.

lodg·er (loj′ər), *n.* person who lives in a rented room in another's house.

lodg·ing (loj′ing), *n.* **1.** place to live in for a time. **2.** lodgings, a rented room or rooms in a house, not in a hotel.

lodging house, house in which rooms are rented.

lodg·ment, *esp. Brit.* **lodge·ment** (loj′mənt), *n.* **1.** a lodging or being lodged. **2.** something lodged or deposited.

Lodz (lŭj), *n.* city in C Poland.

lo·ess (lō′is; lœs), *n.* a yellowish-brown loam, usually deposited by the wind. [< G *löss*]

loft (lôft; loft), *n.* **1.** attic. **2.** room under the roof of a barn. **3.** gallery in a church or hall. **4.** *U.S.* upper floor of a business building or warehouse. **5.** backward slope of the face of a golf club. **6.** stroke that drives a golf ball upward. —*v.* hit (a golf ball) high up. [< Scand. *lopt* air, sky]

loft-bomb·ing (lôft′bom′ing; loft′-), *n.* technique of releasing a bomb as an aircraft goes into a sharp climb at high speed, so that the bomb proceeds toward its target in a long, looping curve while the aircraft speeds to a safe distance from the point of explosion, used esp. with atomic bombs.

loft·y (lôf′ti; lof′-), *adj.,* loft·i·er, loft·i·est. **1.** very high: *lofty mountains.* **2.** exalted; dignified; grand: *lofty aims.* **3.** proud; haughty: *a lofty contempt for others.* —loft′i·ly, *adv.* —loft′i·ness, *n.* —Syn. **1.** tall. **2.** sublime, stately, majestic. **3.** arrogant.

log (lôg; log), *n., v.,* logged, log·ging, *adj.* —*n.* **1.** length of wood just as it comes from the tree. **2.** *Naut.* daily record of a ship's voyage. **3.** record of an airplane trip, performance of an engine, etc. **4.** float for measuring the speed of a ship. —*v.* **1.** cut down trees, cut them into logs, and get them out of the forest. **2.** cut (trees) into logs. **3.** enter in a ship's log. —*adj.* made of logs: *a log house.* [ME *logge*]

log., logarithm.

lo·gan·ber·ry (lō′gən·ber′i), *n., pl.* -ries. *Am.* a large, purplish-red fruit of a bramble developed from a cross between a blackberry and a red raspberry. [after J. H. *Logan,* its first grower]

log·a·rithm (lôg′ə·rith·əm; log′-), *n. Math.* **1.** exponent of the power to which a fixed number (usually 10) must be raised in order to produce a given number. If the fixed number is 10, the logarithm of 1000 is 3; the logarithm of 10,000 is 4. **2.** one of a system of such exponents used to shorten calculations in mathematics. [< NL, < Gk. *logos* proportion + *arithmos* number] —log′a·rith′mic, log′a·rith′mi·cal, *adj.* —log′a·rith′mi·cal·ly, *adv.*

log·book (lôg′bůk′; log′-), *n.* book in which a daily record of a ship's voyage, airplane's trip, etc., is kept.

loge (lōzh), *n.* box in a theater or opera house. [< F < Gmc. Doublet of LOBBY, LODGE, LOGGIA.]

log·ger (lôg′ər; log′-), *n.* **1.** person whose work is logging. **2.** machine for loading or hauling logs.

log·ger·head (lôg′ər·hed′; log′-), *n.* **1.** a stupid person. **2.** Also, loggerhead turtle, *Am.* a large-headed turtle of the Atlantic. **3.** at loggerheads, disputing; at enmity. [< *log* + *head*]

log·gia (loj′ə), *n., pl.* log·gias. gallery or arcade open to the air on at least one side. [< Ital. < Gmc. Doublet of LOBBY, LODGE, LOGE.]

log·ging (lôg′ing; log′-), *n. Am.* work of cutting down trees, cutting them into logs and getting them from the forest.

log·ic (loj′ik), *n.* **1.** science of proof. **2.** science of reasoning. **3.** book on logic. **4.** reasoning; use of argument. **5.** reason; sound sense. [< LL < Gk. *logike* (techne) reasoning (art) < *logos* word]

log·i·cal (loj′ə·kəl), *adj.* **1.** having to do with logic; according to the principles of logic. **2.** reasonable; reasonably expected. **3.** reasoning correctly. —log′i·cal′i·ty, log′i·cal·ness, *n.* —log′i·cal·ly, *adv.* —Syn. **3.** rational, sound.

lo·gi·cian (lō·jish′ən), *n.* expert in logic.

lo·gis·tic (lō·jis′tik), **lo·gis·ti·cal** (-tə·kəl), *adj.* pertaining to logistics.

lo·gis·tics (lō·jis′tiks), *n.* the military science of transportation and supply.

log·roll (lôg′rōl′; log′-), *v. Am., Colloq.* **1.** get (a bill) passed by logrolling. 2. take part in logrolling. —**log′roll′er,** *n. Am.*

log·roll·ing (lôg′rōl′ing; log′–), *n. Am.* giving of political aid in return for a like favor.

log·wood (lôg′wŭd′; log′–), *n.* 1. the heavy brownish-red wood of a tropical American tree, used in dyeing. 2. the tree.

lo·gy (lō′gi), *adj.,* **-gi·er, -gi·est.** *U.S.* heavy; sluggish; dull. [cf. Du. *log*]

–logy, *word element.* 1. account, doctrine, or science of, as in *biology.* 2. speaking; discussion, as in *eulogy.* [< Gk., in a few cases < *logos* word, discourse, but usually < *-logos* treating of]

Lo·hen·grin (lō′ən-grin), *n.* knight in German legend who is the hero of Richard Wagner's opera *Lohengrin.*

loin (loin), *n.* 1. Usually, **loins.** part of the body between the ribs and the hipbones. The loins are on both sides of the backbone. 2. piece of meat from this part. 3. **gird up one's loins,** get ready for action. [< OF *loigne,* ult. < L *lumbus*]

loin·cloth (loin′klôth′; -kloth′), *n.* piece of cloth worn around the loins by natives of warm countries.

Loire (lwär), *n.* river flowing from S France into the Bay of Biscay.

loi·ter (loi′tər), *v.* 1. linger idly; stop and play along the way. 2. spend (time) idly: *loiter the hours away.* [< MDu. *leuteren* be loose] —**loi′ter·er,** *n.* —**loi′ter·ing·ly,** *adv.* —**Syn.** 1. delay, tarry, lag, dawdle.

Lo·ki (lō′ki), *n.* the Norse god of destruction.

loll (lol), *v.* 1. recline or lean in a lazy manner: *loll on a sofa.* 2. hang loosely or droop: *a dog's tongue lolls out in hot weather.* —*n.* a lolling. [ME *lolle(n)*] —**loll′er,** *n.*

Lol·lard (lol′ərd), *n.* one of the followers of John Wycliffe. The Lollards advocated certain religious, political, and economic reforms, and were persecuted as heretics. [< MDu. *lollaerd* mumbler < *lollen* mumble]

lol·li·pop, lol·ly·pop (lol′i-pop), *n.* piece of hard candy, often on the end of a small stick.

Lom·bard (lom′bärd; -bərd; lum′–), *n.* 1. member of a German tribe which in the sixth century A.D. conquered the part of N Italy since known as Lombardy. 2. native or inhabitant of Lombardy. —**Lom·bar′dic,** *adj.*

Lom·bard·y (lom′bər-di; lum′–), *n.* district in N Italy.

Lo·mond (lō′mənd), *n.* **Loch,** lake in W Scotland.

Lon·don (lun′dən), *n.* capital of Great Britain and the British Commonwealth, in SE England on the Thames River. —**Lon′don·er,** *n.*

lone (lōn), *adj.* 1. alone; solitary: *a lone survivor.* 2. lonesome; lonely: *a lone life.* 3. *Humorous.* single or widowed. 4. standing apart; isolated: *a lone house.* [var. of *alone*]

lone·ly (lōn′li), *adj.,* **-li·er, -li·est.** 1. feeling oneself alone and longing for company or friends: *she was lonely when among strangers.* 2. without many people: *a lonely road.* 3. alone: *a lonely tree.* —**lone′li·ly,** *adv.* —**lone′li·ness,** *n.* —**Syn.** 1. lonesome. 2. secluded. 3. solitary.

lon·er (lōn′ər), *n. Colloq.* 1. person who is or prefers to be alone. 2. independent person: *a political loner.*

lone·some (lōn′səm), *adj.* **-som·er, -som·est.** 1. feeling lonely. 2. making one feel lonely. —**lone′some·ly,** *adv.* —**lone′some·ness,** *n.*

long¹ (lông; long), *adj.,* **long·er, long·est,** *adv., n.* —*adj.* 1. measuring much, or more than usual, from end to end in space or time: *a long distance.* 2. having a specified length in space or time: *five feet long.* 3. far-reaching; extending to a great distance in space or time: *a long memory, a long sight.* 4. of vowels or syllables, taking a comparatively long time to speak. 5. well supplied (with some commodity or stock): depending on a rise in prices for profit. —*adv.* 1. throughout the whole length of: *all night long.* 2. for a long time: *a reform long advocated.* 3. at a point of time far distant from the time indicated: *long before, long since.* —*n.* 1. a long time: *for long, before long.* 2. a long sound. 3. as **long as,** provided that. 4. **so long as,** provided

that. [OE *lang*] —**long′ish,** *adj.* —**Syn.** *adj.* 1. extended, prolonged, lengthy.

long² (lông; long), *v.* wish very much; desire greatly. [OE *langian* < *lang* long¹] —**Syn.** yearn.

long., longitude.

Long Beach, seaside resort in SW California.

long·boat (lông′bōt′; long′–), *n.* the largest and strongest boat carried by a sailing ship.

long·bow (lông′bō′; long′–), *n.* bow drawn by hand and discharging a long, feathered arrow (distinguished from *crossbow*).

long-dis·tance (lông′dis′təns; long′–), *Am.* —*adj.* of or having to do with telephone service to another town, city, etc. —*n.* operator or exchange that takes care of long-distance calls.

long-drawn (lông′drôn′; long′–), *adj.* lasting a long time; prolonged to great length.

lon·gev·i·ty (lon-jev′ə-ti), *n.* long life. [< L *longaevitas,* ult. < *longus* long + *aevum* age]

Long·fel·low (lông′fel′ō; long′–), *n.* Henry Wadsworth, 1807–1882, American poet.

long·hair (lông′hãr′), *Am., Colloq.* —*n.* person devoted to the classics, esp. classical music. —*adj.* suitable for a longhair. —**long′haired,** *adj.*

long·hand (lông′hand′; long′–), *n.* ordinary writing, not shorthand or typewriting.

long-head·ed (lông′hed′id; long′–), *adj.* 1. having a long head. 2. shrewd; far-sighted.

long·horn (lông′hôrn′; long′–), *n.* one of a breed of cattle having very long horns.

long·ing (lông′ing; long′–), *n.* earnest desire: *a longing for home.* —*adj.* having or showing earnest desire: *a child's longing look at a window full of toys.* —**long′ing·ly,** *adv.*

Long Island, island S of Connecticut. It is part of New York State.

Long Island Sound, a long narrow strip of water between Connecticut and Long Island.

lon·gi·tude (lon′jə-tūd; -tūd), *n.* 1. distance E or W on the earth's surface, measured in degrees from a certain meridian. Usually the meridian through Greenwich, England, is used. 2. length. [< L *longitudo* length < *longus* long]

lon·gi·tu·di·nal (lon′jə-tū′də-nəl; -tū′–), *adj.* 1. of length; in length. 2. running lengthwise: *our flag has longitudinal stripes.* 3. of longitude. —**lon′gi·tu′di·nal·ly,** *adv.*

long-lived (lông′līvd′; long′–; -livd′), *adj.* living or lasting a long time.

long-play·ing (lông′plā′ing), *adj.* of a phonograph record, playing at a speed slower than 78 r.p.m., especially at 33⅓ r.p.m.

long-range (lông′rānj′; long′–), *adj.* looking ahead; future: *long-range plans.*

long·shore·man (lông′shôr′mən; long′–; -shōr′–), *n., pl.* **-men.** man whose work is loading and unloading ships.

long-sight·ed (lông′sīt′id; long′–), *adj.* 1. farsighted; focusing at more than the right distance. 2. having foresight; wise.

long-stand·ing (lông′stan′ding; long′–), *adj.* having lasted for a long time.

long-suf·fer·ing (lông′suf′ər·ing; long′–; -suf′ring), *adj.* enduring trouble, pain, or injury long and patiently. —*n.* long and patient endurance of trouble, pain, or injury.

long-time, long·time (lông′tīm′; long′–), *adj.* for a long time; of long standing.

long ton, British ton, 2240 pounds.

long-wind·ed (lông′win′did; long′–), *adj.* talking or writing at great lengths; tiresome. —**long′-wind′ed·ly,** *adv.* —**long′-wind′ed·ness,** *n.*

long·wise (lông′wīz′; long′–), **long·ways** (-wāz′), *adv.* lengthwise.

look (lŭk), *v.* 1. see; try to see; direct the eyes: *he looked this way.* 2. direct the mind: *look into the matter.* 3. search: *find without looking.* 4. face; have a view: *our house looks on a garden.* 5. look at: *look a book through hastily.* 6. seem; appear: *she looks pale.* 7. express or suggest by looks: *look daggers at a person.* 8. bring, put, etc., by looks: *look a person down.* 9. **look after,** attend to; take care of. 10. **look down on,** despise; scorn. 11. **look in,** make a short visit. 12. **look on,** a. watch without taking part. b. regard; consider. 13. **look out,** be careful; watch out. 14. **look over,** examine, inspect: *look over*

papers. **15. look to, a.** attend to; take care of.
b. turn to for help. **16. look up, a.** find; refer to.
b. *Colloq.* call on; visit. **c.** *Colloq.* get better; improve. **17. look up to,** respect; admire. —*n.* **1.**
act of looking: *a careful look.* **2.** looks, appearance; aspect. [OE *lōcian*] —**look′er,** *n.* —**Syn.**
v. **1.** gaze, stare, observe, glance. **14.** investigate.
➤ look. When used as a verb of complete meaning, equivalent to *see,* look is modified by an adverb: *look searchingly, look sharp.* As a linking verb, equivalent to *appear,* look is followed by an adjective which modifies the subject: *He looks well,* or *healthy,* or *tired.*

look·er-on (lŭk′ər·on′; -ôn′), *n., pl.* **look·ers-on.** person who watches without taking part; spectator.

looking glass, mirror.

look·out (lŭk′out′), *n.* **1.** a careful watch for someone to come or for something to happen. **2.** person or group that keeps such a watch. **3.** *Am.* place from which to watch. **4.** *Naut.* crow′s-nest. **5.** outlook. **6.** *Colloq.* thing to be cared for or worried about.

loom¹ (lüm), *n.* machine for weaving cloth. [OE *(ge)lōma* implement]

loom² (lüm), *v.* **1.** appear indistinctly: *an iceberg loomed through the thick fog.* **2.** appear in a vague, unusually large, or threatening shape: *war loomed ahead.*

loon¹ (lün), *n.* a large diving bird that has a loud wild cry. [earlier *loom* < Scand. *lōmr*]

loon² (lün), *n.* a worthless or stupid person.

loon·y (lün′i), *adj.,* **loon·i·er, loon·i·est,** *n., pl.* **loon·ies.**
Slang. —*adj.* crazy. —*n.* crazy person; lunatic. —**loon′i·ness,** *n.*

Loon (ab. 32 in. long)

loop (lüp), *n.* **1.** the shape of a curved string, ribbon, bent wire, etc., that crosses itself. In writing, *b* and *g* and *h* and *l* have loops. **2.** thing, bend, course, or motion shaped like this. **3.** a fastening or ornament formed of cord, etc., bent and crossed. **4.** a complete vertical turn or revolution. —*v.* **1.** make a loop of. **2.** make loops in. **3.** fasten with a loop. **4.** form a loop or loops. [ME *loupe,* ? < Celtic] —**loop′er,** *n.*

loop·hole (lüp′hōl′), *n.* **1.** a small opening in a wall to shoot through, look through, or let in light and air. **2.** means of escape: *find a loophole in the law.* [? < MDu. *lupen* peer]

loose (lüs), *adj.,* **loos·er, loos·est,** *v.,* **loosed, loos·ing,** *adv., n.* —*adj.* **1.** not fastened: *a loose thread.* **2.** not tight: *loose clothing.* **3.** not firmly set or fastened in: *a loose tooth.* **4.** not bound together: *loose papers.* **5.** not put up in a box, can, etc.: *loose coffee.* **6.** free; not shut in or up: *we let the dog loose at night.* **7.** not pressed close together: *loose earth, cloth with a loose weave.* **8.** not strict, close, or exact: *a loose translation, loose thinking.* **9.** moving too freely: *a loose tongue, loose bowels.* **10.** careless about morals or conduct: *a loose character.* —*v.* **1.** set free; let go. **2.** discharge (an arrow, gun, etc.); shoot. **3.** make loose; untie; unfasten. **4.** relax. —*adv.* **1.** in a loose manner. **2. cut loose, a.** separate from anything; break a connection or relation. **b.** run away; free oneself. **c.** *Colloq.* go on a spree. —*n.* **on the loose,** *Colloq.* **a.** free; without restraint. **b.** on a spree. [< Scand. *lauss*] —**loose′ly,** *adv.* —**loose′ness,** *n.* —**Syn.** *adj.* **1.** unbound, unfastened, untied. **8.** vague, indefinite, careless. **10.** wanton, immoral.

loose-joint·ed (lüs′join′tid), *adj.* **1.** having loose joints; loosely built. **2.** able to move freely.

loose-leaf (lüs′lēf′), *adj.* having pages or sheets that can be taken out and replaced.

loos·en (lüs′ən), *v.* **1.** make loose or looser; untie; unfasten. **2.** become loose or looser. —**loos′en·er,** *n.*

loot (lüt), *n.* spoils; plunder; booty. —*v.* plunder; rob. [< Hind. *lūt*] —**loot′er,** *n.* —**Syn.** *v.* pillage, sack, rifle.

---

lop¹ (lop), *v.,* **lopped, lop·ping. 1.** cut; cut off. **2.** cut branches, twigs, etc., from. —**lop′per,** *n.*

lop² (lop), *v.,* **lopped, lop·ping. 1.** hang loosely; droop. **2.** flop.

lope (lōp), *v.,* **loped, lop·ing,** *n.* —*v.* run with a long, easy stride. —*n.* a long, easy stride. [ult. < Scand. *hlaupa* leap] —**lop′er,** *n.*

lop-eared (lop′ird′), *adj.* having ears that hang loosely or droop.

lop·sid·ed (lop′sīd′id), *adj.* larger or heavier on one side than the other; unevenly balanced. —**lop′sid′ed·ly,** *adv.* —**lop′sid′ed·ness,** *n.*

lo·qua·cious (lō·kwā′shəs), *adj.* talking much; fond of talking. —**lo·qua′cious·ly,** *adv.*

lo·quac·i·ty (lō·kwas′ə·ti), *n.* inclination to talk a great deal; talkativeness. [< L, < *loquax* talkative] —**Syn.** garrulity, volubility, glibness.

lo·ran (lô′rən; lō′-), *n.* device by which a navigator can determine his geographical position by utilizing signals sent out from two radio stations. [abstracted from *long range navigation*]

lord (lôrd), *n.* **1.** owner, ruler, or master; one who has the power. **2.** a feudal superior. **3. the Lord, a.** God. **b.** Christ. **4. Lord, a.** in Great Britain, a titled nobleman or peer of the realm belonging to the House of Lords, the upper of the two branches of the British Parliament. **b.** title used in speaking to or of noblemen of certain ranks: *Lord Tennyson.* **c.** title given by courtesy to men holding certain positions: *Lord Chief Justice.* **5. the Lords,** the House of Lords; the upper house of the British Parliament. —*v.* **1.** rule; domineer; behave like a lord. **2. lord it over,** domineer over. [OE *hlāford* < *hlāf* loaf + *weard* keeper, ward]

lord·ly (lôrd′li), *adj.,* **-li·er, -li·est,** *adv.* —*adj.* **1.** like a lord; suitable for a lord; grand; magnificent. **2.** haughty; insolent; scornful. —*adv.* in a lordly manner. —**lord′li·ness,** *n.* —**Syn.** *adj.* **1.** noble, aristocratic. **2.** arrogant, proud, overbearing.

Lord's Day, Sunday.

lord·ship (lôrd′ship), *n.* **1.** rank or position of a lord. **2.** Often, **Lordship,** *Brit.* title used by or to an inferior in speaking to or of a lord: *your Lordship, his Lordship.* **3.** rule; ownership.

Lord's Prayer, prayer given by Jesus to His disciples. Matt. 6:9–13.

Lord's Supper, 1. Jesus's last supper with His disciples. **2.** church service in memory of this; Holy Communion.

lore (lôr; lōr), *n.* **1.** facts and stories about a certain subject. **2.** learning; knowledge. [OE *lār;* akin to LEARN]

Lor·e·lei (lôr′ə·lī; lor′-), *n. German Legend.* siren whose beautiful singing distracted sailors and caused them to wreck their ships. [< G]

lor·gnette (lôr·nyet′), *n.* **1.** eyeglasses mounted on a handle. **2.** opera glass. [< F, < *lorgner* look sidelong at, eye < OF *lorgne* squinting]

lorn (lôrn), *adj. Archaic.* **1.** forsaken; forlorn. **2.** lost; ruined. [OE *-loren,* pp. of *-lēosan* lose. See FORLORN.]

Lor·raine (lə·rān′), *n.* region in W Europe, now chiefly in NE France.

Woman using a lorgnette

lor·ry (lôr′i; lor′i), *n., pl.* **-ries. 1.** *Brit.* automobile truck. **2.** a long, flat wagon without sides.

Los Al·a·mos (lôs al′ə·mōs), town in N New Mexico, a center for atomic research.

Los An·ge·les (lôs an′jə·ləs; -lēz; ang′gə·ləs), city in SW California.

lose (lüz), *v.,* **lost, los·ing. 1.** not have any longer; have taken away from one by accident, carelessness, parting, death, etc.: *lose one's life.* **2.** be unable to find: *lose a book.* **3.** fail to keep, preserve, or maintain; cease to have: *lose patience.* **4.** fail to follow with eye, hearing, mind, etc.: *lose words here and there in a speech.* **5.**

leave behind in a race or contest. 6. wander from; become separated from: *lose one's way.* 7. fail to have, get, catch, etc.: *lose a sale.* 8. fail to win: *lose the prize.* 9. be defeated: *our team lost.* 10. bring to destruction; ruin: *the ship and its crew were lost.* 11. let pass without use or profit; waste: *lose time.* 12. suffer loss: *lose on a contract.* 13. cause the loss of: *delay lost the battle.* 14. cause to lose. 15. lose oneself, a. let oneself go astray; become bewildered. b. become absorbed. [OE *-lēosan*, var. of *-lēosan lose*] —los′a·ble, *adj.* —los′er, *n.*

los·ings (lüz′ingz), *n.pl.* losses.

loss (lôs; los), *n.* 1. a losing or being lost: *loss of life.* 2. person or thing lost. 3. amount lost. 4. harm or disadvantage caused by losing something. 5. at a loss, puzzled; uncertain; in difficulty. [OE *los*]

loss leader, in stores, a product sold at a price lower than normal or below cost to attract customers.

lost (lôst; lost), *v.* pt. and pp. of lose. —*adj.* 1. no longer possessed or retained: *lost friends.* 2. no longer to be found; missing: *lost articles.* 3. attended with defeat: *a lost battle.* 4. not used to good purpose; wasted: *lost time.* 5. having gone astray. 6. destroyed or ruined. 7. bewildered. 8. lost in, completely absorbed or interested in. 9. lost to, a. no longer possible or open to. b. no longer belonging to. c. insensible to. —Syn. *adj.* 2. astray. 7. dazed.

lost sheep, person who has strayed from the right sort of conduct or religious belief.

lot (lot), *n., v.* lot·ted, lot·ting, *adv.* —*n.* 1. object used to decide something by chance: *we drew lots to decide who should be captain.* 2. such a method of deciding: *divide property by lot.* 3. choice made in this way: *the lot fell to me.* 4. what one gets by lot; share or portion. 5. fate; fortune: *a happy lot.* 6. plot of ground. 7. Am. place where motion pictures are made. 8. a distinct portion or parcel of anything. 9. number of persons or things considered as a group; a collection: *a fine lot of boys.* 10. Often, lots, *Colloq.* a great many; a great deal: *a lot of books, lots of money.* 11. *Colloq.* person of a certain kind: *he is a bad lot.* 12. cast or draw lots, use lots to decide something. 13. cast or throw in one's lot with, share the fate of; become a partner with. —*v.* 1. draw lots. 2. draw lots for. 3. divide into lots. 4. allot. —*adv.* to a great extent: *a lot better.* [OE *hlot*] —Syn. *n.* 4. allotment, part, parcel. 5. destiny, doom. ▶ lot, lots of. The colloquial uses of these words, appropriate in speech and in some informal writing, are avoided in formal writing: Colloquial: *We tried a lot of different kinds.* Formal: *We tried a good many different kinds.* Colloquial: *He has lots of friends . . . a lot of money.* Formal: *He has many friends . . . a good deal of money.*

Lot (lot), *n. Bible.* a righteous man who was allowed to escape from Sodom before God destroyed it. His wife looked back and was changed into a pillar of salt. Gen. 19:1-26.

loth (lōth), *adj.* loath.

Lo·thar·i·o (lō-thâr′i·ō), *n., pl.* -thar·i·os. man who makes love to many women; libertine.

lo·tion (lō′shən), *n.* liquid containing medicine, used on the skin to soothe, heal, or cleanse. [< L *lotio* a washing, ult. < *lavere* to wash]

lot·ter·y (lot′ər·i), *n., pl.* -ter·ies. scheme for distributing prizes by lot or chance. In a lottery a large number of tickets are sold, some of which draw prizes. [< Ital. *lotteria* < *lotto* lot. See LOTTO.]

lot·to (lot′ō), *n.* game played by drawing numbered disks from a bag or box and covering the corresponding numbers on cards. [< Ital., lot, ult. < Gmc.]

lo·tus, lo·tos (lō′təs), *n.* 1. water lily that grows in Egypt and Asia. 2. plant with red, pink, or white flowers, of the same family as the pea. 3. *Gk. Legend.* plant whose fruit was supposed to cause a dreamy and contented forgetfulness in those who ate it. [< L < Gk. *lotos*]

lo·tus-eat·er, lo·tos-eat·er (lō′təs-ēt′ər), *n.* person who leads a life of dreamy, indolent ease.

loud (loud), *adj.* 1. making a noise; not quiet or soft. 2. resounding; noisy. 3. clamorous; insistent: *be loud in demands.* 4. *Colloq.* showy or flashy: *loud clothes.* 5. *Colloq.* obtrusive; somewhat vulgar. —*adv.* in a loud manner. [OE *hlūd*] —loud′ly, *adv.* —loud′ness, *n.* —Syn. *adj.* 2. deafening. 3. vociferous. 4. gaudy.

loud·ish (loud′ish), *adj.* somewhat loud.

loud-speak·er (loud′spēk′ər), *n.* device for amplifying the sound of a speaker's voice, music, etc., esp. in radio.

Lou·is (lü′is), *n.* Joe, born 1914, American pugilist, world's heavyweight champion, 1937-49.

Lou·is XIV (lü′i), ("Louis the Great") 1638-1715, king of France from 1643 to 1715.

Louis XVI, 1754-1793, king of France from 1774 to 1792, guillotined in the French Revolution.

Lou·ise (lü·ēz′), *n.* Lake, lake in the Canadian Rockies.

Lou·i·si·an·a (lü·ē′zi·an′ə; lü′i-), *n.* a Southern State of the United States. *Capital:* Baton Rouge. *Abbrev.:* La. —Lou·i′si·an′an, *Am.* Lou·i·si·an·i·an (lü·ē′zi·an′i·ən; lü′i-), *adj., n.*

Lou·is·ville (lü′i·vil), *n.* city in N Kentucky, on the Ohio River.

lounge (lounj), *v.,* lounged, loung·ing, *n.* —*v.* stand, stroll, sit, or lie at ease and lazily. —*n.* 1. act or state of lounging. 2. a comfortable and informal room in which one can lounge. 3. couch; sofa. —loung′er, *n.*

lour (lour), *v., n.* lower[2].

Lourdes (lürd), *n.* town in SW France where there is a famous Catholic shrine.

lour·ing (lour′ing), *adj.* lowering. —lour′ing·ly, *adv.*

louse (lous), *n., pl.* lice. 1. a small, wingless insect that infests the hair or skin of people and animals. 2. anything like it. [OE *lūs*]

lous·y (louz′i), *adj.,* lous·i·er, lous·i·est. 1. infested with lice. 2. *Am., Slang.* dirty; disgusting. 3. *Slang.* well supplied: *lousy with money.* —lous′i·ly, *adv.* —lous′i·ness, *n.* ▶ lousy. Except when meaning "infested with lice" (or, figuratively, with something else, which is named) *lousy* is a rather violent slang word of abuse, just now weakened to a counter word of disapproval, expressive if not used too often, but offensive to most ears.

Louse (def. 1)

lout (lout), *n.* an awkward, stupid fellow; boor. [? n. use of v. OE *lūtan* bow or *lūtian* skulk] —lout′ish, *adj.* —lout′ish·ly, *adv.* —lout′ish·ness, *n.* —Syn. lubber, lummox.

lou·ver (lü′vər), *n.* 1. window or other opening covered with louver boards. 2. a ventilating slit. 3. a louver board. [< OF *lover*] —lou′vered, *adj.*

louver boards, horizontal strips of wood set slanting in a window or other opening, so as to keep out rain, but provide ventilation.

Lou·vre (lü′vrə), *n.* a famous museum in Paris, formerly a palace of the kings of France.

lov·a·ble, love·a·ble (luv′ə·bəl), *adj.* deserving love; endearing. —lov′a·bil′i·ty, love′a·bil′i·ty; lov′a·ble·ness, love′a·ble·ness, *n.* —lov′a·bly, love′a·bly, *adv.* —Syn. likable, winning, pleasing, amiable.

love (luv), *n., v.,* loved, lov·ing. —*n.* 1. strong or passionate affection for a person of the opposite sex. 2. instance of such feeling. 3. this feeling as a subject for books, or as a personified influence. 4. Love, a. Venus. b. Cupid. 5. a loved one; sweetheart. 6. a warm liking; fond or tender feeling. 7. a strong liking: *a love of books.* 8. *Colloq.* something charming or delightful. 9. no score in tennis and certain other games. 10. fall in love, begin to love; come to feel love. 11. in love, feeling love. —*v.* 1. be in love with: *he loves his wife.* 2. be in love; fall in love: *she loved much.* 3. caress: *she held the baby and loved him.* 4. like very much; take great pleasure in: *the children love ice cream.* 5. be fond of; hold dear: *love one's associates.* 6. have affection. [OE *lufu, n., lufian, v.*] —Syn. *n.* 6. affection, fondness, regard.

love apple, an old name for the tomato.

love·bird (luv′bėrd′), *n.* a small parrot that shows great affection for its mate.

love knot, an ornamental knot or bow of ribbons as a token of love.

love·less (luv′lis), *adj.* 1. not loving. 2. not loved. —**love′less·ly,** *adv.* —**love′less·ness,** *n.*

love-lies-bleed·ing (luv′līz-blēd′ing), *n.* a kind of amaranth having spikes of crimson flowers.

love·lorn (luv′lôrn′), *adj.* suffering because of love; forsaken by the person whom one loves. —**love′lorn′ness,** *n.*

love·ly (luv′li), *adj.,* **–li·er, –li·est,** *n., pl.* **–lies.** —*adj.* 1. beautiful in mind or character; beautiful: *a lovely woman.* 2. *Colloq.* very pleasing; delightful: *a lovely evening.* —*n. Colloq.* a very pretty girl. —**love′li·ly,** *adv.* —**love′li·ness,** *n.* —Syn. *adj.* 2. charming.

love potion, magic drink supposed to cause love for a certain person.

lov·er (luv′ər), *n.* 1. person who loves. 2. man who is in love with a woman. 3. lovers, man and woman who are in love with each other. 4. person having a strong liking: *a lover of books.* —**lov′er·like′,** *adj.* —Syn. 2. suitor, admirer, beau.

love seat, seat or small sofa for two persons.

love·sick (luv′sik′), *adj.* languishing because of love. —**love′sick′ness,** *n.*

lov·ing (luv′ing), *adj.* feeling or showing love; affectionate; fond. —**lov′ing·ly,** *adv.* —**lov′ing·ness,** *n.*

loving cup, a large cup with handles, passed around for all to drink from.

lov·ing-kind·ness (luv′ing-kīnd′nis), *n.* kindness coming from love.

low¹ (lō), *adj.* 1. not high or tall: *low walls.* 2. rising but slightly from a surface: *low relief.* 3. of less than ordinary height, depth, or quantity: *the well is getting low.* 4. near the ground, floor, or base: *a low shelf.* 5. lying or being below the general level: *low ground.* 6. of a dress, having a low neck. 7. small in amount, degree, force, value, etc.: *a low price.* 8. not loud; soft: *a low whisper.* 9. not advanced in civilization, organization, etc.; inferior: *a low organism.* 10. lacking in dignity or elevation, as thought. 11. humble: *low birth.* 12. affording little strength; feeble; weak: *a low state of health.* 13. unfavorable; poor: *I have a low opinion of his abilities.* 14. depressed or dejected: *low spirits.* 15. mean or base; coarse; vulgar; degraded: *low company.* 16. near the horizon: *a low sun.* 17. near the equator: *low latitudes.* 18. naming or pertaining to regions near the sea or near sea level: *low country.* 19. prostrate or dead: *lay one low.* 20. deep: *a low bow.* 21. of sounds, produced by relatively slow vibrations; at or toward the bottom of a scale for pitch. 22. *Phonet.* pronounced with the tongue far from the palate. 23. relatively recent, as a date. —*n.* 1. that which is low. 2. arrangement of the gears used for the lowest speed in an automobile and similar machines. 3. *Am.* an area of low barometric pressure. —*adv.* 1. near the ground, floor, or base: *fly low.* 2. in, at, or to a low portion, point, degree, condition, price, etc.: *the sun sank low, supplies are running low.* 3. at low pitch; softly: *speak low.* 4. humbly; meanly: *act low.* 5. near the horizon. 6. near the equator. 7. lately. 8. lay low, a. knock down. b. kill. 9. lie low, *Colloq.* stay hidden; keep still. [< Scand. *lāgr*] —**low′ness,** *n.* —Syn. *adj.* 7. moderate. 11. obscure, lowly. 14. dispirited. 15. sordid, ignoble.

low² (lō), *v.* 1. make the sound of a cow; moo. —*n.* sound a cow makes; mooing. [OE *hlōwan*]

low-born (lō′bôrn′), *adj.* of humble birth.

low·boy (lō′boi′), *n. Am.* a low chest of drawers.

low·bred (lō′bred′), *adj.* coarse; vulgar.

low·brow (lō′brou′), *Slang.* —*n. Am.* person who is not or does not claim to be intellectual or elegant. —*adj.* 1. being a lowbrow. 2. fit for lowbrows.

Low Church, in the Episcopalian Church, a party which lays little stress on church authority and ceremonies (opposed to *High Church*). —**Low-Church** (lō′chėrch′), *adj.* —**Low′-Church′man,** *n.*

low comedy, broadly humorous comedy.

Low Countries, Netherlands, Belgium, and Luxemburg. —**low′-coun′try,** *adj.*

low-down (*n.* lō′doun′; *adj.* lō′doun′), *Am.* —*n. Slang.* actual facts or truth. —*adj. Colloq.* low; mean; contemptible.

Low·ell (lō′əl), *n.* 1. James Russell, 1819–1891, American poet, essayist, and diplomat. 2. city in NE Massachusetts.

low·er¹ (lō′ər), *v.* 1. let down or haul down: *lower the flag.* 2. make lower: *lower water in a pool, lower the volume of a radio, lower a soldier's rank.* 3. sink; become lower: *the sun lowered slowly.* —*adj., adv.* comparative of **low.** —Syn. *v.* 2. decrease, diminish. 3. descend, fall.

low·er² (lou′ər), *v.* 1. look dark and threatening. 2. frown; scowl. —*n.* 1. a dark and threatening look. 2. frown; scowl. Also, **lour.** [ME *loure(n)*]

Lower California (lō′ər), narrow peninsula in NW Mexico, S of California.

lower case, small letters, not capital.

low·er-case (lō′ər-kās′), *adj., v.,* **-cased, -casing.** —*adj.* in small letters; not capitals. —*v.* print in small letters.

Lower House, lower house, the more representative branch of a legislature that has two branches.

low·er·ing (lou′ər·ing), *adj.* 1. dark and threatening. 2. frowning; scowling. Also, **louring.** —**low′er·ing·ly,** *adv.*

low·er·most (lō′ər-mōst), *adj.* lowest.

lower world, 1. Also, **lower regions.** hell; Hades. 2. earth.

Low German, the Germanic speech of the Low Countries (Dutch, Flemish, etc.) and esp. of N Germany.

low·land (lō′lənd), *n.* 1. land that is lower and flatter than the neighboring country. 2. **Lowlands,** low flat region in S and E Scotland. —*adj.* of or in the lowlands. —**Low′land·er, Low′land·er,** *n.*

Low Latin, Latin as spoken in the Middle Ages.

low·ly (lō′li), *adj.,* **-li·er, -li·est,** *adv.* —*adj.* 1. low in rank, station, position, or development: *a lowly corporal, a lowly occupation.* 2. modest in feeling, behavior, or condition; humble: *he held a lowly opinion of himself.* —*adv.* humbly; meekly. —**low′li·ness,** *n.* —Syn. *adj.* 1. inferior. 2. meek, submissive, unassuming.

Low Mass, a simplified form of High Mass, conducted by one priest assisted by altar boys. Low Mass is usually read, not sung.

low-mind·ed (lō′mīn′did), *adj.* mean; vulgar. —**low′-mind′ed·ly,** *adv.* —**low′-mind′ed·ness,** *n.*

low-pres·sure (lō′presh′ər), *adj.* having or using less than the usual pressure.

low-spir·it·ed (lō′spir′it·id), *adj.* sad; depressed. —**low′-spir′it·ed·ly,** *adv.* —**low′-spir′it·ed·ness,** *n.*

low tide, 1. lowest level of the tide. 2. time when the tide is lowest. 3. lowest point.

low·water, 1. lowest level of water. 2. low tide.

low-water mark, 1. mark showing low water. 2. lowest point.

loy·al (loi′əl), *adj.* 1. faithful to love, promise, or duty: *a loyal husband.* 2. faithful to one's king, one's government, or one's country: *a loyal citizen.* 3. characterized by or showing faithfulness to obligations, promises, etc.: *loyal devotion.* [< F < L *legalis* < *lex* law. Doublet of LEGAL.] —**loy′al·ly,** *adv.* —Syn. 1, 2. true, devoted, constant. —Ant. 1, 2. disloyal, faithless.

loy·al·ist (loi′əl·ist), *n.* 1. person who is loyal to his government, esp. in time of revolt. 2. Sometimes, **Loyalist,** *Am.* American who favored England at the time of the American Revolution. 3. **Loyalist,** person loyal to the Republic during the civil war in Spain, 1936–1939. —**loy′al·ism, Loy′al·ism,** *n.*

loy·al·ty (loi′əl·ti), n., pl. –ties. loyal feeling or behavior; faithfulness. —Syn. fidelity, allegiance.

Loy·o·la (loi·ō′lə), n. Ignatius, 1491–1556, Spanish soldier, priest, and saint, founder of the Jesuit Order.

loz·enge (loz′inj), n. 1. design or figure shaped like this ◇. 2. a small tablet of medicine or piece of candy. [< OF losenge, ult. < LL lausa slab]

LP, Trademark. identification of the long-playing microgroove records made by Columbia Records, Inc.

Lt., Lieutenant.

Ltd., **ltd.**, Esp. Brit. limited.

Lu, Chem. lutecium.

lu·au (lü′ou), n. a feast, originally in Hawaii, generally held outdoors, with roast pig as the main dish. [< Haw.]

lub·ber (lub′ər), n. 1. a big, clumsy, stupid fellow. 2. a clumsy sailor. —Syn. 1. dolt, bumpkin.

lub·ber·ly (lub′ər·li), adj. 1. loutish; clumsy; stupid. 2. awkward in the work of a sailor. —adv. in a lubberly manner. —lub′ber·li·ness, n.

Lü·beck (ly′bek), n. seaport in NW Germany.

lu·bri·cant (lü′brə·kənt), n. oil, grease, etc., for putting on parts of machines that slide or move against one another, to make them work smoothly and easily. —adj. lubricating.

lu·bri·cate (lü′brə·kāt), v., –cat·ed, –cat·ing. 1. make (machinery) smooth and easy to work by putting on oil, grease, etc. 2. make slippery or smooth. [< L, < lubricus slippery] —lu′bri·ca′tion, n. —lu′bri·ca′tion·al, lu′bri·ca′tive, adj. —lu′bri·ca′tor, n.

lu·bric·i·ty (lü·bris′ə·ti), n., pl. –ties. 1. oily smoothness; slipperiness. 2. shiftiness. 3. lewdness. [< LL, < L lubricus slippery, slimy]

lu·cent (lü′sənt), adj. 1. shining; luminous. 2. letting the light through; clear. [< L lucens shining] —lu′cence, lu′cen·cy, n. —lu′cent·ly, adv.

lu·cerne, lu·cern (lü·sèrn′), n. Esp. Brit. alfalfa. [< F < Pr. luzerno, ult. < L lux light]

Lu·cerne (lü·sèrn′), n. Lake of, lake in C Switzerland.

lu·cid (lü′sid), adj. 1. easy to understand. 2. clear; transparent: a lucid stream. 3. sane: an insane person sometimes has lucid intervals. 4. shining; bright: the lucid stars. [< L lucidus < lux light] —lu·cid′i·ty, lu′cid·ness, n. —lu′cid·ly, adv.

Lu·ci·fer (lü′sə·fər), n. 1. chief rebel angel who was cast out of heaven; Satan; the Devil. 2. planet Venus when it is the morning star. 3. Also, lucifer match. match that lights by friction.

Lu·cite (lü′sīt), n. Trademark. a clear plastic compound used for airplane windows, ornaments, etc.

luck (luk), n. 1. that which seems to happen or come to one by chance; chance. 2. good luck. 3. down on one's luck, Colloq. having bad luck; unlucky. 4. in luck, having good luck; lucky. 5. out of luck, having bad luck; unlucky. 6. try one's luck, see what one can do. 7. worse luck, unfortunately. [< MDu. (ghe)luc, MLG (ge)lucke] —Syn. 1. fortune, hazard.

luck·less (luk′lis), adj. having or bringing bad luck; unlucky. —luck′less·ly, adv.

Luck·now (luk′nou), n. city in central India.

luck·y (luk′i), adj., luck·i·er, luck·i·est. having or bringing good luck. —luck′i·ly, adv. —luck′i·ness, n. —Syn. fortunate, happy.

lu·cra·tive (lü′krə·tiv), adj. bringing in money; profitable. —lu′cra·tive·ly, adv. —lu′cra·tive·ness, n. —Syn. gainful, remunerative.

lu·cre (lü′kər), n. money considered as a bad influence. [< L lucrum gain]

Lu·cre·tius (lü·krē′shəs), n. 99?–55 B.C., Roman poet. —Lu·cre′tian, adj.

lu·cu·bra·tion (lü′kyə·brā′shən), n. 1. study, esp. late at night. 2. laborious study. 3. a learned or carefully written production, esp. one that is labored and dull. [< L, < lucubrare work at night]

lu·di·crous (lü′də·krəs), adj. amusingly absurd; ridiculous. [< L ludicrus < ludus sport] —lu′di·crous·ly, adv. —lu′di·crous·ness, n.

luff (luf), Naut. —v. 1. turn the bow of a ship toward the wind. —n. 1. turning the bow of a ship toward the wind. 2. the forward edge of a fore-and-aft sail. [< Du. loef]

Luft·waf·fe (lůft′väf′ə), n. German. the German air force, esp. under the Nazis in World War II.

lug[1] (lug), v., lugged, lug·ging, —v. pull along or carry with effort; drag. —n. a pull; haul; drag. [< Scand. (Sw.) lugga pull by the hair]

lug[2] (lug), n. a projecting part to hold or grip something.

lug[3] (lug), n. lugsail.

lug·gage (lug′ij), n. Esp. Brit. baggage. [< lug[1]]

lug·ger (lug′ər), n. boat with lugsails.

Lugger

lug·sail (lug′sāl′; –səl), n. Naut. a four-cornered sail held by a yard that slants across the mast.

lu·gu·bri·ous (lù·gü′bri·əs; –gū′–), adj. sad; mournful. [< L lugubris < lugere mourn] —lu·gu′bri·ous·ly, adv. —lu·gu′bri·ous·ness, n. —Syn. dismal, doleful, melancholy.

Luke (lük), n. 1. Bible. a physician who was the companion of the Apostle Paul. 2. the third book of the New Testament.

luke·warm (lük′wôrm′), adj. 1. neither hot nor cold. 2. showing little enthusiasm; half-hearted. [< ME leuk tepid + warm] —luke′warm′ly, adv. —luke′warm′ness, n. —Syn. 1. tepid. 2. indifferent, unconcerned.

lull (lul), v. 1. hush to sleep: the mother lulled the crying baby. 2. quiet: lull one's suspicions. 3. become calm or more nearly calm: the wind lulled. —n. 1. period of less noise or violence; brief calm. 2. a soothing sound. [ME lulle(n)]

lul·la·by (lul′ə·bī), n., pl. –bies, v., –bied, –by·ing. —n. song to put a baby to sleep. —v. lull with or as with a lullaby.

lum·ba·go (lum·bā′gō), n. pain in the muscles of the back and in the loins. [< LL, < L lumbus loin]

lum·bar (lum′bər), adj. of the loin or loins: the lumbar region. —n. a lumbar vertebra, artery, nerve, etc. [< NL, < L lumbus loin]

lum·ber[1] (lum′bər), n. 1. Am. timber, logs, beams, boards, etc., roughly cut and prepared for use. 2. household articles no longer in use, old furniture, etc., that takes up room. —v. Am. 1. cut and prepare lumber. 2. fill up or obstruct by taking space that is wanted for something else. 3. heap together in disorder. —lum′ber·er, n. —lum′ber·ing, n.

lum·ber[2] (lum′bər), v. move along heavily and noisily. —lum′ber·ing, adj.

lum·ber·jack (lum′bər·jak′), n. Am. man whose work is cutting down trees and getting out the logs.

lum·ber·man (lum′bər·mən), n., pl. –men. 1. lumberjack. 2. man whose work is cutting and preparing timber for use. 3. man whose business is buying and selling timber or lumber.

lu·men (lü′mən), n., pl. –mi·na (–mə·nə). unit of light; the light given out by a point source of one candle power. [< L, light]

lu·mi·nar·y (lü′mə·ner′i), n., pl. –nar·ies. 1. the sun, moon, or other light-giving body. 2. a famous person. [< Med.L, < L lumen light]

lu·mi·nes·cence (lü′mə·nes′əns), n. emission of light occurring at a temperature below that of incandescent bodies. Luminescence includes phosphorescence and fluorescence. [< L lumen light + E –escence a beginning to be < L –escere] —lu′mi·nes′cent, adj.

lu·mi·nif·er·ous (lü′mə·nif′ər·əs), adj. producing or transmitting light. [< L lumen light + E –ferous yielding < L ferre to bear]

lu·mi·nous (lü′mə·nəs), adj. 1. shining by its own or reflected light: the sun and stars are luminous bodies. 2. full of light; bright. 3. easily understood; clear; enlightening. —lu·mi·nos·i·ty (lü′mə·nos′ə·ti), lu′mi·nous·ness, n. —lu′mi·nous·ly, adv.

lum·mox (lum′əks), *n. Colloq.* an awkward, stupid person.

lump[1] (lump), *n.* 1. solid mass of no particular shape: *a lump of coal.* 2. swelling; bump: *a lump on the head.* 3. lot; mass. 4. *Colloq.* a stupid person. —*v.* 1. make lumps of, on, or in. 2. form into a lump or lumps. 3. put together; deal with in a mass or as a whole: *we will lump all our expenses.* 4. move heavily. —*adj.* 1. in lumps; in a lump. 2. including a number of items. [ME]

lump[2] (lump), *v. Am., Colloq.* put up with; endure: *if you don't like it, you can lump it.*

lump·ish (lump′ish), *adj.* 1. like a lump; heavy and clumsy. 2. stolid; stupid. —**lump′ish·ly**, *adv.* —**lump′ish·ness**, *n.*

lump·y (lump′i), *adj.*, **lump·i·er, lump·i·est.** 1. full of lumps: *lumpy gravy.* 2. covered with lumps: *lumpy ground.* 3. heavy and clumsy: *a lumpy animal.* —**lump′i·ly**, *adv.* —**lump′i·ness**, *n.*

Lu·na (lü′nə), *n.* 1. Roman goddess of the moon. 2. moon.

lu·na·cy (lü′nə·si), *n., pl.* **-cies.** 1. insanity. 2. extreme folly. [< *lunatic*]

lu·nar (lü′nər), *adj.* 1. of the moon. 2. like the moon. 3. crescent-shaped. [< L, < *luna* moon]

lunar month, interval between one new moon and the next, about 29½ days.

lu·nate (lü′nāt), **lu·nat·ed** (-id), *adj.* crescent-shaped. [< L, < *luna* moon] —**lu′nate·ly**, *adv.*

lu·na·tic (lü′nə·tik), *n.* 1. an insane person. 2. an extremely foolish person. —*adj.* Also, **lu·nat·i·cal** (lü·nat′ə·kəl). 1. insane. 2. for insane people. [< LL, ult. < L *luna* moon] —**lu·nat′i·cal·ly**, *adv.*

lunatic fringe, *Am., Colloq.* those whose zeal in some cause, movement, or ism goes beyond reasonable limits. —**lunatic fringer,** *Am.*

lunch (lunch), *n.* 1. a light meal between breakfast and dinner, or breakfast and supper. 2. a light meal. —*v.* eat lunch. [short for *luncheon*] —**lunch′er**, *n.*

lunch·eon (lun′chən), *n.* 1. lunch. 2. a formal lunch. —*v.* lunch.

lunch·eon·ette (lun′chən·et′), *n.* restaurant that serves lunches.

lung (lung), *n.* one of the pair of breathing organs in vertebrates by means of which the blood receives oxygen and is relieved of carbon dioxide. [OE *lungen*]

lunge (lunj), *n., v.*, **lunged, lung·ing.** —*n.* any sudden forward movement; thrust. —*v.* move suddenly forward; thrust. [ult. < F *allonger*, ult. < L *ad-* toward + *longus* long] —**lung′er**, *n.* —**Syn.** *v.* plunge, lurch.

lung·wort (lung′wėrt′), *n.* plant with blue flowers and spotted leaves.

lu·pine[1] (lü′pən), *n.* 1. any of several plants of the same family as peas and beans, that have long spikes of flowers, radiating clusters of grayish, hairy leaflets, and flat pods with bean-shaped seeds. 2. one of the seeds. [< L *lupinus, lupinum.* See LUPINE[2].]

lu·pine[2] (lü′pīn), *adj.* 1. wolflike; fierce. 2. related to the wolf. [< L *lupinus* < *lupus* wolf]

lurch[1] (lėrch), *n.* sudden leaning or roll to one side: *the car gave a lurch and upset.* —*v.* lean or roll suddenly to one side. —**Syn.** *v.* pitch, stagger, sway, lunge.

lurch[2] (lėrch), *n.* **leave in the lurch,** leave in a helpless condition or difficult situation. [< F *lourche,* name of a game]

lure (lür), *n., v.*, **lured, lur·ing.** —*n.* 1. attraction: *the lure of the sea.* 2. decoy; bait. —*v.* 1. lead away or into something by arousing desire; attract; tempt. 2. attract with a bait. [< OF *leurre* < Gmc.] —**lur′er**, *n.* —**Syn.** *v.* allure, entice, captivate, decoy.

lu·rid (lür′id), *adj.* 1. lighted up with a red or fiery glare: *lurid flashes of lightning.* 2. terrible; sensational; startling: *lurid crimes.* [< L *luridus*] —**lu′rid·ly**, *adv.* —**lu′rid·ness**, *n.*

lurk (lėrk), *v.* 1. stay about without arousing attention; wait out of sight: *a tiger was lurking in the jungle.* 2. be hidden. [appar. < *lour* lower[2]] —**lurk′er**, *n.* —**lurk′ing·ly**, *adv.* —**Syn.** 1. hide, sneak, slink, prowl.

lus·cious (lush′əs), *adj.* 1. delicious; richly sweet: *a luscious peach.* 2. very pleasing to taste, smell, hear, see, or feel. —**lus′cious·ly**, *adv.* —**lus′cious·ness**, *n.* —**Syn.** 2. savory.

lush (lush), *adj.* 1. tender and juicy; growing thick and green. 2. characterized by abundant growth. [? < OF *lasche* LAX] —**lush′ly**, *adv.* —**lush′ness**, *n.*

lust (lust), *n.* 1. strong desire. 2. bad desire or appetite. 3. desire for indulgence of sex. —*v.* have a strong desire: *a miser lusts after gold.* [OE, pleasure]

lus·ter, *esp. Brit.* **lus·tre** (lus′tər), *n.* 1. bright shine on the surface: *the luster of pearls.* 2. brightness: *her eyes lost their luster.* 3. fame; glory; brilliance. 4. a. in ceramics, a metallic, sometimes iridescent, glaze. b. kind of china that has this surface. 5. a thin fabric of cotton and wool that has a lustrous surface. —*v.* put a luster or gloss on. [< F < Ital. *lustro,* ult. < L *lustrare* illuminate] —**Syn.** *n.* 1. sheen, gloss, polish.

lust·ful (lust′fəl), *adj.* desiring indulgence of sex; sensual; lewd. —**lust′ful·ly**, *adv.* —**lust′ful·ness**, *n.* —**Syn.** lecherous, carnal, lascivious.

lus·trate (lus′trāt), *v.*, **-trat·ed, -trat·ing.** purify by a propitiatory offering; purify by any ceremonial method. [< L *lustratus* brightened, cleaned < *lustrum* lustrum] —**lus·tra′tion**, *n.* —**lus·tra·tive** (lus′trə·tiv), *adj.*

lus·trous (lus′trəs), *adj.* having luster; shining; glossy. —**lus′trous·ly**, *adv.* —**lus′trous·ness**, *n.*

lus·trum (lus′trəm), *n., pl.* **-trums, -tra** (-trə). 1. ceremonial purification of the ancient Romans, performed every five years. 2. period of five years. [< L]

lust·y (lus′ti), *adj.*, **lust·i·er, lust·i·est.** strong and healthy; full of vigor. —**lust′i·ly**, *adv.* —**lust′i·ness**, *n.* —**Syn.** robust, sturdy, vigorous, hearty.

lute (lüt), *n.* a stringed musical instrument, formerly much used, having a long neck and a hollow resonant body, played with the fingers of one hand or with a plectrum. [< OF < Pr. < Ar. *al-'ud* the lute]

Lute player

lu·te·ci·um (lü·tē′shi·əm), *n. Chem.* a rare metallic element, Lu. [< NL, < L *Lutetia* Paris]

Lu·ther (lü′thər), *n.* **Martin,** 1483–1546, leader of the Protestant Reformation in Germany.

Lu·ther·an (lü′thər·ən; lüth′rən), *adj.* having to do with Luther or the church that was named for him. —*n.* member of the Lutheran Church. —**Lu′ther·an·ism**, *n.*

Lux·em·burg (luk′səm·bėrg), *n.* 1. a small country between Germany, France, and Belgium. 2. its capital.

Lux·or (luk′sôr), *n.* town in E Egypt on the site of part of ancient Thebes.

lux·u·ri·ance (lug·zhür′i·əns; luk·shür′-), **lux·u·ri·an·cy** (-ən·si), *n.* luxuriant growth or productiveness; rich abundance. —**Syn.** richness, profusion.

lux·u·ri·ant (lug·zhür′i·ənt; luk·shür′-), *adj.* 1. growing thick and green. 2. producing abundantly. 3. rich in ornament. [< L *luxurians* luxuriating. See LUXURIATE.] —**lux·u′ri·ant·ly**, *adv.* —**Syn.** 1. lush, profuse.

lux·u·ri·ate (lug·zhür′i·āt; luk·shür′-), *v.*, **-at·ed, -at·ing.** 1. indulge in luxury. 2. take great delight. 3. grow very abundantly. [< L *luxuriatus,* ult. < *luxus* excess] —**lux·u′ri·a′tion**, *n.*

lux·u·ri·ous (lug·zhür′i·əs; luk·shür′-), *adj.* 1. fond of luxury; tending toward luxury; self-indulgent: *a luxurious age.* 2. giving luxury; very comfortable and beautiful: *a luxurious hotel.* —**lux·u′ri·ous·ly**, *adv.* —**lux·u′ri·ous·ness**, *n.* —**Syn.** 1. voluptuous.

lux·u·ry (luk′shə·ri; lug′zhə-), *n., pl.* **-ries.** 1.

comforts and beauties of life beyond what is really necessary. 2. use of the best and most costly food, clothes, houses, furniture and amusements. 3. thing that one enjoys, usually something choice and costly. 4. thing pleasant but not necessary. [< L *luxuria* < *luxus* excess] —Syn. 1. extravagance.

Lu·zon (lü·zon′), *n.* chief island of the Philippines.

Lvov (lə·vôf′), *Polish* **Lwów** (lə·vüf′), *n.* city in SW Soviet Union. Also, *German* Lemberg.

-ly¹, *suffix forming adverbs.* 1. in a —— manner, as *cheerfully, warmly.* 2. in —— ways or respects, as *financially, medically, physically.* 3. to a —— degree or extent, as *greatly, slightly, moderately.* 4. in, to, or from a —— direction, as *northwardly, laterally.* 5. in a —— place, as *inwardly, thirdly.* 6. at a —— time, as *recently.* [OE *-līce* < *līc*] ❯ **-ly.** A few adjectives end in **-ly** (*comely, kindly, lovely*), but **-ly** is more distinctly an ending for adverbs, representing the Old English adverbial ending *-līce* of adjectives and participles: *brightly, formerly, graciously, frankly. -ly* is a living suffix and is freely added to adjectives to form adverbs.

-ly², *suffix forming adjectives.* 1. like a ——, as *a ghostly form.* 2. like that of a ——; characteristic of a ——, as *a brotherly kiss.* 3. suited to a ——; fit or proper for a ——, as *a manly fight, womanly kindness.* 4. of each or every ——; occurring once per ——, as *hourly, daily, monthly.* 5. being a ——; that is a ——, as *our heavenly home.* [OE *-līc*]

ly·cée (lē·sā′), *n.* a French secondary school maintained by the government. [< F. See LY-CEUM.]

ly·ce·um (lī·sē′əm; lī′si·əm), *n.* 1. lecture hall; place where lectures are given. 2. *Am.* association for instruction and entertainment through lectures, debates, and concerts. 3. **Lyceum,** an ancient outdoor grove and gymnasium near Athens, where Aristotle taught. 4. lycée. [< L < Gk. *Lykeion* (def. 3), from the nearby temple of Apollo, *Lykeios*]

lydd·ite (lid′īt), *n.* a high explosive, consisting chiefly of picric acid. [< *Lydd,* English town]

Lyd·i·a (lid′i·ə), *n.* an ancient country in W Asia Minor, famous for its wealth and luxury. —**Lyd′i·an,** *adj., n.*

lye (lī), *n.* any strong alkaline solution, used in making soap and in cleaning. Sodium hydroxide and potassium hydroxide are kinds of lye. [OE *lēag*]

ly·ing¹ (lī′ing), *n.* telling a lie; habit of telling lies. —*adj.* false; untruthful: *a lying rumor.* —*v.* ppr. of lie¹. —**Syn.** *adj.* deceptive.

ly·ing² (lī′ing), *v.* ppr. of lie²: *a book lying on the table.*

ly·ing-in (lī′ing·in′), *n.* 1. confinement in childbirth. 2. childbirth.

lymph (limf), *n. Anat., Physiol.* a nearly colorless liquid in the tissues of the body, somewhat like blood without the red corpuscles. [< L *lympha* clear water]

lym·phat·ic (lim·fat′ik), *adj.* 1. of lymph; carrying lymph. 2. sluggish; lacking energy. —*n.* vessel that contains or carries lymph.

lymph gland, lymphatic gland, any of the glandlike bodies occurring in the course of the lymphatic vessels, and supposed to be a source of leucocytes.

lym·pho·cyte (lim′fə·sīt), *n.* one of the colorless cells of lymph.

lynch (linch), *v. Am.* put (an accused person) to death without a lawful trial. [see LYNCH LAW] —**lynch′er,** *n. Am.* —**lynch′ing,** *n. Am.*

lynch law, *Am.* putting an accused person to death without a lawful trial. [orig. *Lynch's law,* from Wm. *Lynch* of Va.]

Lynn (lin), *n.* city in E Massachusetts.

lynx (lingks), *n., pl.* **lynx·es** or (*esp. collectively*) **lynx.** wildcat of the Northern Hemisphere that has a short tail and rather long legs. [< L < Gk.] —**lynx′like′,** *adj.*

lynx-eyed (lingks′īd′), *adj.* having sharp eyes.

ly·on·naise (lī′ə·nāz′), *adj.* fried with pieces of onion: *lyonnaise potatoes.* [< F, < *Lyon* Lyons]

Ly·ons (lī′ənz), *n.* city in E France, on the Rhone River.

lyre (līr), *n.* an ancient stringed musical instrument somewhat like a small harp. [< OF < L < Gk. *lyra*]

lyre·bird (līr′bėrd′), *n.* an Australian bird, the male of which has a long tail that is lyre-shaped when spread.

lyr·ic (lir′ik), *n.* 1. a short poem expressing personal emotion, as a love poem, a lament, etc. 2. *Colloq.* words for a song. —*adj.* 1. having to do with lyric poems: *a lyric poet.* 2. characterized by a spontaneous expression of feeling. 3. of or suitable for singing.

lyr·i·cal (lir′ə·kəl), *adj.* 1. emotional; poetic. 2. lyric. —**lyr′i·cal·ly,** *adv.* —**lyr′i·cal·ness,** *n.*

Ly·san·der (lī·san′dər), *n.* died 395 B.C., Spartan naval commander and statesman.

ly·sin (lī′sin), *n. Chem.* any of a class of substances which are developed in blood serum, and which are capable of causing the dissolution or destruction of bacteria, blood corpuscles, and other cellular elements. [< Gk. *lysis* a loosening]

Ly·sol (lī′sōl; -sol), *n. Trademark.* a brown oily liquid containing cresols and soap, used as a disinfectant and antiseptic. [< Gk. *lysis* a loosening]

Lyt·ton (lit′ən), *n.* Edward George Earle Lytton Bulwer-Lytton, Baron, 1803–1873, English novelist and dramatist.

M

M, m (em), *n., pl.* **M's; m's.** 1. the 13th letter of the alphabet. 2. Roman numeral for 1000.

M, Middle (def. 4).

M., 1. Majesty. 2. Monday. 3. *pl.* **MM.** Monsieur. 4. noon. [< L *meridies*]

m., 1. male. 2. married. 3. masculine. 4. *Mech.* mass. 5. meter. 6. mile. 7. minim. 8. minute. 9. month. 10. noon. [< L *meridies*]

ma (mä), *n. Colloq.* mamma; mother.

Ma, *Chem.* masurium.

M.A., Master of Arts. Also, A. M.

ma'am (mam; mäm), *n. Colloq.* madam.

ma·ca·bre (mə·kä′brə; -bər), **ma·ca·ber** (-bər), *adj.* gruesome; horrible; ghastly. [< F]

mac·ad·am (mə·kad′əm), *n.* 1. small, broken stones, rolled until solid and smooth to make roads. 2. *Am.* road made of layers of this. [after J. L. *McAdam,* engineer]

mac·ad·am·ize (mə·kad′əm·īz), *v.,* **-ized, -iz·ing.** make or cover (a road) with macadam.

Ma·cao (mə·kou′), *n.* 1. island near the SE coast of China. 2. a Portuguese colony on this island and two small islands near by.

ma·caque (mə·käk′), *n.* any of several kinds of monkeys of Asia, the East Indies, and Africa. [< F < Pg. < African lang.]

mac·a·ro·ni (mak′ə·rō′ni), *n., pl.* **-nis, -nies.** 1. flour paste dried, usually in the form of hollow tubes, to be cooked for food. 2. an English dandy of the 18th century. [< earlier Ital. *maccaroni,* pl., ult. < LGk. *makaria* barley broth]

mac·a·roon (mak′ə·rün′), *n.* a very sweet cooky made of whites of eggs, sugar, and ground almonds or coconut. [< F < Ital. *maccarone,* sing.; for pl., see MACARONI]

Mac·Ar·thur (mək·är′thər), *n.* Douglas, 1880–1964, American general, head of the occupational forces in Japan and commander-in-chief of United Nations forces in Korea.

Ma·cau·lay (mə·kô′li), *n.* Thomas Babington Macaulay, Baron, 1800–1859, English essayist, historian, poet, and statesman.

ma·caw (mə·kô′), *n.* a large parrot with a long tail, brilliant feathers, and a harsh cry, living in South America and Central America. [< Pg. *macao* < Brazilian]

Mac·beth (mək·beth′; mak–), *n.* 1. play by Shakespeare. 2. its principal character.

Mac·ca·bees (mak′ə·bēz), *n.pl.* 1. family of Jewish patriots who led successful revolts against Syria in the second century B.C. 2. two books of the Old Testament Apocrypha, telling about these revolts. —**Mac′ca·be′an,** *adj.*

mace¹ (mās), *n.* 1. a war club used in the Middle Ages. 2. staff used as a symbol of authority: *a chancellor's mace.* 3. bearer of a mace. [< OF]

mace² (mās), *n.* spice made from the dried outer covering of nutmegs. [< OF *macis*]

Mac·e·do·ni·a (mas′ə·dō′ni·ə), *n.* 1. Also, **Mac·e·don** (mas′ə·don). an ancient country in Europe, N of Greece. 2. region in Europe including parts of Yugoslavia, Bulgaria, and Greece. —**Mac′e·do′ni·an,** *adj., n.*

mac·er·ate (mas′ər·āt), *v.,* –ated, –at·ing. 1. soften by soaking for some time: *macerate flowers to extract their perfume.* 2. cause to grow thin. 3. become thin; waste away. [< L *maceratus,* pp. of *macerare* soften] —**mac′er·at′er, mac′er·a′tor,** *n.* —**mac′er·a′tion,** *n.*

mach., machinery; machines; machinist.

ma·chete (mə·shet′ē; mə·shet′; *Sp.* mä·chā′tā), *n. Am.* a large heavy knife, used as a tool and weapon, esp. in Latin America. [< Sp.]

Machete

Mach·i·a·vel·li (mak′i·ə·vel′i), *n.* 1469–1527, Italian statesman and writer who advised rulers to use craftiness and deceit to maintain their authority. —**Mach′i·a·vel′li·an,** *adj., n.* —**Mach′i·a·vel′li·an·ism,** *n.*

ma·chic·o·lat·ed (mə·chik′ə·lāt′id), *adj.* having machicolations.

ma·chic·o·la·tion (mə·chik′ə·lā′shən), *n.* an opening in the floor of a projecting gallery or parapet, or in the roof of an entrance, through which missiles, hot liquids, etc., might be cast upon attackers, much used in medieval fortified structures. [< Med.L, < OF < Pr. *machacol* projection, balcony]

mach·i·nate (mak′ə·nāt), *v.,* –nat·ed, –nat·ing. contrive or devise artfully or with evil purpose; plot; intrigue. [< L, < *machina* MACHINE] —**mach′i·na′tor,** *n.*

mach·i·na·tion (mak′ə·nā′shən), *n.* 1. evil or artful plotting; scheming against authority. 2. Usually, **machinations.** evil plot; secret or cunning scheme.

ma·chine (mə·shēn′), *n., v.,* –chined, –chin·ing. —*n.* 1. arrangement of fixed and moving parts for doing work, each with some special thing to do: *a washing machine makes housework easier.* 2. device for applying power or changing its direction. Levers and pulleys are simple machines. 3. automobile. 4. airplane. 5. person or group that acts without thinking. 6. *Am.* group of people controlling a political organization. —*v.* make or finish with a machine. [< F < L < Gk. *mechane* device, means]

machine gun, gun for keeping up a rapid fire of bullets.

ma·chine-gun (mə·shēn′gun′), *v.,* –gunned, –gun·ning. fire at with a machine gun.

machine language, information or instructions in the form of numbers, characters, punched tape, etc., that can be processed by an electric computer.

ma·chin·er·y (mə·shēn′ər·i; –shēn′ri), *n., pl.* –er·ies. 1. machines: *a factory contains much machinery.* 2. the parts or works of a machine: *machinery is oiled to keep it running smoothly.* 3. any combination of persons or things by which something is kept going or something is done: *judges and courts are a part of the legal machinery.*

machine shop, *Am.* workshop where men make or repair machines or parts of machines.

machine tool, tool worked by power.

machine translation, translation from one language to another by an electronic computer.

ma·chin·ist (mə·shēn′ist), *n.* 1. a skilled worker with machine tools. 2. person who runs a machine. 3. man who makes and repairs machinery.

mach·me·ter (mäk′mē′tər; mak′–), *n.* device that indicates the speed of an aircraft relative to the speed of sound.

Mach One, in aeronautics, the speed of sound.

Mac·ken·zie (mə·ken′zi), *n.* river flowing from W Canada into the Arctic Ocean.

mack·er·el (mak′ər·əl; mak′rəl), *n., pl.* –el, (occasionally, esp. with reference to different species) –els. a salt-water fish of the northern Atlantic, much used for food. [< OF *maquerel*]

mackerel sky, sky spotted with small, white, fleecy clouds.

Mack·i·nac (mak′ə·nô), *n.* 1. Strait of, strait connecting Lake Michigan and Lake Huron. 2. island in Lake Huron, near this strait.

mack·i·naw (mak′ə·nô), *n. Am.* kind of short coat made of heavy woolen cloth. [after *Mackinac,* Mich.]

mack·in·tosh, mac·in·tosh (mak′ən·tosh), *n.* 1. a waterproof coat; raincoat. 2. waterproof cloth. [after C. *Macintosh,* the inventor]

Mac·mil·lan (mək·mil′ən), *n.* Harold, born 1894, prime minister from 1957 to 1963.

mac·ro·cosm (mak′rə·koz·əm), *n.* the universe. [< F < Med.L, < Gk. *makros* great + *kosmos* world] —**mac′ro·cos′mic,** *adj.*

ma·cron (mā′kron; mak′ron), *n.* a straight, horizontal line (–) placed over a vowel to show its sound. *Examples:* cāme, bē. [< Gk. *makron,* neut. adj., long]

mad (mad), *adj.,* mad·der, mad·dest. 1. out of one's head; crazy; insane. 2. much excited; wild; wildly gay. 3. like mad, furiously; very hard, fast, etc. 4. foolish; unwise: *mad spending.* 5. blindly and unreasonably fond: *mad about going to dances.* 6. furious. 7. *Colloq.* angry. 8. having rabies or hydrophobia: *a mad dog.* [OE *gemǣdd*] —**Syn.** 1. demented, lunatic.

Mad·a·gas·car (mad′ə·gas′kər), *n.* the Malagasy Republic, a large island in the Indian Ocean, SE of Africa; formerly a French colony and now a member of the French Community.

mad·am (mad′əm), *n., pl.* mad·ams, mes·dames (mā·däm′). a polite title used in speaking to or of a lady. [< OF *ma dame* my lady. See DAME.] ➤ As a formula of address *Madam* or *Dear Madam* is used to both married and unmarried women.

ma·dame (mad′əm; *Fr.* mä·däm′), *n., pl.* mes·dames. 1. French title for a married woman. 2. title often used by women singers, artists, etc.

mad·cap (mad′kap′), *n.* a very impulsive person. —*adj.* impulsive; hasty; wild.

mad·den (mad′ən), *v.* 1. make or become crazy; drive insane. 2. make or become very angry or excited; irritate greatly. —**mad′den·ing,** *adj.* —**mad′den·ing·ly,** *adv.*

mad·der (mad′ər), *n.* 1. vine with small yellowish flowers. 2. its red root. 3. a red dye made from these roots. 4. red; crimson. [OE *mædere*]

made (mād), *v.* pt. and pp. of make. —*adj.* 1. built; formed. 2. specially prepared. 3. artificially produced: *made land.* 4. invented: *a made word.* 5. certain of success; successful.

Ma·dei·ra (mə·dir′ə), *n.* 1. group of Portuguese islands NW of Africa. 2. the chief island of this group. 3. Often, **madeira.** wine made there.

mad·e·moi·selle (mad′ə·mə·zel′; *Fr.* mäd·mwä·zel′), *n., pl.* mes·dem·oi·selles (mād·mwä·zel′). French title for an unmarried woman; Miss. [< F, orig. *ma demoiselle* my young lady]

made-up (mād′up′), *adj.* 1. put together. 2. invented; untrue. 3. painted, powdered, etc.

mad·house (mad′hous′), *n.* 1. asylum for insane people. 2. place of uproar and confusion.

Mad·i·son (mad′ə·sən), *n.* 1. James, 1751–1836, the fourth president of the United States, 1809–1817. 2. his wife, Dolley, 1768–1849. 3. capital of Wisconsin, in the S part.

mad·ly (mad'li), *adv.* 1. insanely. 2. furiously. 3. foolishly.

mad·man (mad'man'; -mən), *n., pl.* -men. an insane man; crazy person. —Syn. lunatic.

mad·ness (mad'nis), *n.* 1. being crazy; loss of one's mind. 2. great rage; fury. 3. folly.

Ma·doe·ra (mə·dûr'ə), *n.* Madura.

Ma·don·na (mə·don'ə), *n.* 1. Mary, the mother of Jesus. 2. picture or statue of her. [< Ital., my lady]

mad·ras (mad'rəs; mə·dras'), *n.* a closely woven cotton cloth, used for shirts, dresses, etc. [after *Madras*, India]

Ma·dras (mə·dras'; -dräs'), *n.* seaport in SE India.

mad·re·pore (mad'rə·pôr; -pōr), *n.* kind of coral that forms coral islands and reefs. [< F < Ital. *madrepora*]

Ma·drid (mə·drid'), *n.* capital of Spain, in the C part.

mad·ri·gal (mad'rə·gəl), *n.* 1. a short poem that can be set to music. 2. song with parts for several voices, sung without instrumental accompaniment. 3. any song. [< Ital. < LL *matricale* original, chief < *matrix* womb]

Ma·du·ra (mə·dûr'ə), *n.* island NE of Java, part of the Republic of Indonesia. Also, Madoera.

Mae·ce·nas (mi·sē'nəs), *n.* 1. 74?–8 B.C., Roman patron of literature, and friend of Vergil and Horace. 2. a generous patron of literature or art.

mael·strom (māl'strəm), *n.* 1. a great or violent whirlpool of water. 2. a violent confusion of feelings, ideas, or conditions. 3. Maelstrom, a dangerous whirlpool off NW Norway. [< earlier Du., < *malen* grind + *stroom* stream]

mae·nad (mē'nad), *n.* 1. a woman attendant of Bacchus. 2. woman in a frenzy. [< L < Gk. *mainas*] —**mae·nad'ic**, *adj.*

maes·tro (mīs'trō; *Ital.* mä·es'trō), *n., pl.* -tros, *Ital.* ma·es·tri (mä·es'trē). 1. a great composer, teacher, or conductor of music. 2. master of any art. [< Ital. < L *magister* master]

Mae·ter·linck (mā'tər·lingk), *n.* Maurice, 1862–1949, Belgian poet, dramatist, and essayist.

Maf·fi·a, Ma·fi·a (mä'fi·ä), *n.* a secret society of criminals. [< Ital.]

mag., 1. magazine. 2. magnitude.

mag·a·zine (mag'ə·zēn'; mag'ə·zēn), *n.* 1. publication appearing regularly and containing stories, articles, etc., by various writers, usually published either weekly or monthly. 2. room in a fort or warship for storing gunpowder and other explosives. 3. a building for storing gunpowder, guns, food, or other military supplies. 4. place for cartridges in a repeating gun. 5. place for film in a camera, fuel in a stove, etc.; receptacle. [< F <Ital., ult. < Ar. *makhzan* storehouse]

MAGAZINE

Mag·da·lene (mag'də·lēn), **Mag·da·len** (-lən), *n.* 1. Mary Magdalene. 2. magdalene, magdalen, woman who has reformed from a sinful life; repentant prostitute.

Mag·de·burg (mag'də·bérg), *n.* city in NW Germany, on the Elbe River.

mage (māj), *n. Archaic.* magician. [< F < L *magus*]

Ma·gel·lan (mə·jel'ən), *n.* 1. Ferdinand, 1480?–1521, Portuguese navigator whose ship was the first to sail around the world. 2. **Strait of,** strait at the S tip of South America, discovered by Magellan.

ma·gen·ta (mə·jen'tə), *n.* 1. a purplish-red dye. 2. a purplish red. —*adj.* purplish-red. [after Battle of *Magenta*, 1859, because discovered in that year]

mag·got (mag'ət), *n.* 1. insect in the wormlike stage just after leaving the egg; legless larva of any of various kinds of flies. 2. a queer notion; whim. [ME *magot*] —**mag'got·y**, *adj.*

Ma·gi (mā'jī; maj'ī), *n.pl., sing.* **ma·gus** (mā'gəs). the three "Wise Men" from the East, who brought gifts to the infant Jesus. Matt. 2:1 and 2, 7–13.

mag·ic (maj'ik), *n.* 1. the pretended art of making things happen by secret charms and sayings. 2. something that produces results as if by magic; mysterious influence; unexplained power: *the magic of music.* —*adj.* Also, mag'i·cal. 1. of magic; used by magic; done by magic. 2. like magic; mysterious; unexplained. [< L, ult. < Gk. *magos* astrologer < OPers.] —**mag'i·cal·ly**, *adv.* —Syn. *n.* 1. sorcery, necromancy, witchcraft.

ma·gi·cian (mə·jish'ən), *n.* 1. person skilled in the use of magic. 2. person skilled in sleight of hand. [< OF *magicien*] —Syn. 1. sorcerer, necromancer. 2. conjurer.

magic lantern, device with a lamp and lenses, that throws a magnified image of a picture on a screen. The picture is on a glass slide.

Ma·gi·not line (mazh'ə·nō), an elaborate system of French defenses against Germany constructed after the first World War.

mag·is·te·ri·al (maj'is·tir'i·əl), *adj.* 1. of a magistrate; suited to a magistrate: *a judge has magisterial rank.* 2. showing authority: *the captain's magisterial voice.* 3. imperious; domineering; overbearing. [< LL, < L *magister* master] —**mag'is·te'ri·al·ly**, *adv.* —**mag'is·te'ri·al·ness**, *n.* —Syn. 2. authoritative. 3. dictatorial, haughty, arrogant. —Ant. 3. humble, meek, submissive.

mag·is·tra·cy (maj'is·trə·si), *n., pl.* -cies. 1. position, rank, or duties of a magistrate. 2. magistrates as a group. 3. district under a magistrate.

mag·is·trate (maj'is·trāt; -trit), *n.* 1. officer of the government who has power to apply the law and put it in force. The President is the chief magistrate of the United States. 2. judge. A justice of the peace is a magistrate. [< L *magistratus*, ult. < L *magister* master]

Mag·na Char·ta or **Car·ta** (mag'nə kär'tə), 1. the great charter guaranteeing the personal and political liberties of the people of England, granted by King John as a result of demands by the English barons at Runnymede, June 15, 1215. 2. any fundamental constitution guaranteeing civil and political rights. [< Med.L, great charter]

mag·na cum lau·de (mag'nə kùm lou'də; kum lô'dē), with high honors. [< L]

mag·na·nim·i·ty (mag'nə·nim'ə·ti), *n., pl.* -ties. 1. magnanimous nature or quality. 2. a magnanimous act.

mag·nan·i·mous (mag·nan'ə·məs), *adj.* noble in soul or mind; generous in forgiving; free from mean or petty feelings and acts. [< L, < *magnus* great + *animus* spirit] —**mag·nan'i·mous·ly**, *adv.* —**mag·nan'i·mous·ness**, *n.* —Syn. high-minded, unselfish. —Ant. ignoble, selfish, uncharitable.

mag·nate (mag'nāt), *n.* a great man; important person. [< LL, < L *magnus* great]

mag·ne·sia (mag·nē'shə; -zhə), *n.* 1. magnesium oxide, MgO, a white tasteless powder, used as a laxative. 2. magnesium. [< Med.L < Gk. *he Magnesia lithos* the Magnesian stone (from *Magnesia*, in Thessaly)]

mag·ne·si·um (mag·nē'shi·əm; -zhi-), *n. Chem.* a light, silver-white metallic element, Mg, that burns with a dazzling white light.

mag·net (mag'nit), *n.* 1. piece of iron, steel, etc., that attracts iron or steel. 2. anything that attracts. [< OF < L < Gk. *Magnes (lithos)* Magnesian stone. See MAGNESIA.]

mag·net·ic (mag·net'ik), *adj.* 1. having the properties of a magnet. 2. of magnetism; producing magnetism. 3. of the earth's magnetism: *the magnetic meridian.* 4. capable of being magnetized. 5. attractive: *a magnetic personality.* —**mag·net'i·cal·ly**, *adv.*

Magnet attracting nails

magnetic field, space around a magnet in which it exerts appreciable magnetic force.

magnetic mine, an underwater mine which is exploded by the action of the metal parts of a ship upon a magnetic needle.

mag·net·ic nee·dle, a slender bar of magnetized steel. When mounted so that it turns easily, it points approximately north and south toward the earth's Magnetic Poles.

mag·net·ic pole, 1. one of the two poles of a magnet. 2. Magnetic Pole, point on the earth's surface toward which a magnetic needle points. The earth has a North and a South Magnetic Pole.

mag·net·ism (mag′nə·tiz·əm), n. 1. properties of a magnet; manifestation of magnetic properties. 2. branch of physics dealing with magnets and magnetic properties. 3. power to attract or charm: *a person of great magnetism.*

mag·net·ite (mag′nə·tīt), n. an important iron ore, Fe₃O₄, that is strongly attracted by a magnet; black iron oxide.

mag·net·ize (mag′nə·tīz), v., –ized, –iz·ing. 1. give the properties of a magnet to. 2. become magnetic. 3. attract or influence (a person). —mag′net·iz′a·ble, adj. —mag′net·i·za′tion, n. —mag′net·iz′er, n.

mag·ne·to (mag·nē′tō), n., pl. –tos. a small machine for producing electricity. In some gasoline engines, a magneto supplies an electric spark to explode the vapor.

mag·ne·to·e·lec·tric (mag·nē′tō·i·lek′trik), **mag·ne·to·e·lec·tri·cal** (–trə·kəl), adj. of electricity produced by magnets.

mag·ne·tron (mag′nə·tron), n. a large vacuum tube that comprises the principal means of power modification in a radar set or similar device.

Mag·nif·i·cat (mag·nif′ə·kat), n. hymn of the Virgin Mary beginning "My soul doth magnify the Lord." Luke 1:46–55.

mag·ni·fi·ca·tion (mag′nə·fə·kā′shən), n. 1. act of magnifying. 2. a magnified condition. 3. a magnified copy, model, or picture.

mag·nif·i·cence (mag·nif′ə·səns), n. richness of material, color, and ornament; grand beauty; splendor. [< OF < L *magnificentia* < *magnificus* noble < *magnus* great + *facere* make] —Syn. grandeur, sumptuousness.

mag·nif·i·cent (mag·nif′ə·sənt), adj. richly colored or decorated; splendid; grand; stately. [< OF, < *magnificence* MAGNIFICENCE] —magnif′i·cent·ly, adv. —Syn. sumptuous, superb.

mag·nif·i·co (mag·nif′ə·kō), n., pl. –coes. an important person. [< Ital.]

mag·ni·fy (mag′nə·fī), v., –fied, –fy·ing. 1. cause to be or look larger; increase the real or apparent size of an object. 2. make too much of; go beyond the truth in telling: *magnify the facts.* 3. Archaic. praise highly. [< L *magnificare* esteem greatly, ult. < *magnus* great + *facere* make] —mag′ni·fi′er, n. —Syn. 1. enlarge, amplify. 2. exaggerate, overstate.

mag·nil·o·quence (mag·nil′ə·kwəns), n. 1. high-flown, lofty style of speaking or writing. 2. boastfulness. [< L, < *magnus* great + *loquens*, ppr. of *loqui* speak]

mag·nil·o·quent (mag·nil′ə·kwənt), adj. 1. using big and unusual words; in high-flown language. 2. boastful. [< *magniloquence*] —magnil′o·quent·ly, adv.

Mag·ni·to·gorsk (mag·nē′tō·gôrsk; māg′ni·tō·gôrsk′), n. city in the C Soviet Union, important iron and steel center.

mag·ni·tude (mag′nə·tūd; –tüd), n. 1. size. 2. importance. 3. degree of brightness of a star: *stars of the first magnitude are the brightest.* [< L, < *magnus* large] —Syn. 1. largeness.

mag·no·lia (mag·nōl′yə), n. 1. tree with large white, pink, or purplish flowers. 2. the flower. [< NL, after P. *Magnol*, French botanist.]

mag·num (mag′nəm), n. 1. bottle that holds two quarts of alcoholic liquor. 2. amount that it holds. [< L, neut. adj., great]

Magnolia blossom

mag·num o·pus (mag′nəm ō′pəs), 1. a great work of literature or art. 2. person's greatest work. [< L]

mag·pie (mag′pī), n. 1. a noisy bird, black and white with a long tail and short wings, related to the jays. 2. person who chatters. [< *Mag*, for *Margaret*, + *pie*[2]]

Mag·say·say (mäg·sī′sī), n. Ramón, 1907–1957, president of the Philippines from 1953 to 1957.

mag·uey (mag′wā), n. plant with fleshy leaves, growing in tropical America and SW United States. A century plant or agave is a maguey. [< Sp. < West Ind. lang.]

Mag·yar (mag′yär; Hung. mod′yor), n. 1. member of the chief race living in Hungary. 2. their language; Hungarian. —adj. of the Magyars or their language; Hungarian. [< Hung.]

ma·ha·ra·ja, ma·ha·ra·jah (mä′hə·rä′jə), n. title of certain great ruling princes in India. [< Skt., < *mahā*– great + *rājā* rajah]

ma·ha·ra·nee, ma·ha·ra·ni (mä′hə·rä′nē), n. wife of a maharaja. [< Hind., < Skt. *mahā*– great + *rājñī* rani]

ma·hat·ma (mə·hät′mə; –hat′–), n. in India, a wise and holy person who has extraordinary powers. [< Skt., < *mahā*– great + *ātman* soul]

Ma·hi·can (mə·hē′kən), n. Am. 1. Mohican. 2. Mohican.

mah-jongg, mah-jong (mä′jong′; –zhong′), n. a Chinese game played with 144 dominolike pieces. [< Chinese *ma chiang* name of the game, lit. sparrows]

ma·hog·a·ny (mə·hog′ə·ni), n., pl. –nies, adj. —n. 1. a hard reddish-brown wood of a large evergreen tree that grows in tropical America, much used for furniture. 2. the tree itself. 3. a dark reddish brown. —adj. 1. made of mahogany. 2. dark reddish-brown. [< West Ind. lang.]

Ma·hom·et (mə·hom′it), n. Mohammed. —Ma·hom′et·an, adj., n. —Ma·hom′et·an·ism, n.

ma·hout (mə·hout′), n. in the East Indies, driver of an elephant. [< Hind. *mahāut*]

maid (mād), n. 1. a young unmarried woman; girl. 2. an unmarried woman. 3. virgin. 4. a woman servant. [shortened from *maiden*]

maid·en (mād′ən), n. a young unmarried woman; girl. —adj. 1. of a maiden. 2. unmarried; virgin: *a maiden aunt.* 3. new; fresh; untried; unused: *maiden ground.* 4. first: *a ship's maiden voyage.* [OE *mægden*]

maid·en·hair (mād′ən·hār′), n. a delicate fern with very slender stalks.

maid·en·head (mād′ən·hed), n. 1. maidenhood; virginity. 2. the vaginal membrane.

maid·en·hood (mād′ən·hud), n. 1. condition of being a maiden. 2. time when one is a maiden.

maid·en·ly (mād′ən·li), adj. 1. of a maiden. 2. like a maiden; gentle; modest. 3. suited to a maiden. —maid′en·li·ness, n.

maiden name, a woman's surname before her marriage.

maid of honor, 1. Am. an unmarried woman who is the chief attendant of the bride at a wedding. 2. an unmarried noble lady who attends a queen or princess.

maid·serv·ant (mād′sér′vənt), n. a woman servant.

mail[1] (māl), n. 1. letters, papers, parcels, etc., sent by the postal system. 2. system by which they are sent, managed by the Post Office Department. —v. send by mail; put in a mailbox. —adj. of mail. [< OF *male* wallet < Gmc.] —mail′a·ble, adj. Am. —mail′er, n.

mail[2] (māl), n. 1. armor made of metal rings or small loops of chain. 2. armor; protective covering. —v. cover or protect with mail. [< OF < L *macula* a mesh in network] —mailed, adj.

mail·box (māl′boks′), n. Am. 1. a public box from which mail is collected. 2. a private box to which mail is delivered.

mail·man (māl′man′), n., pl. –men. man who carries or delivers mail; postman.

mail order, Am. order for goods sent by mail.

mail-or·der house (māl′ôr′dər), Am. business that receives orders and sends goods by mail.

maim (mām), v. cut off or make useless some part of; cripple; disable: *automobile accidents* *maim thousands of people each year.* [var. of *mayhem*] —**maim′er**, *n.* —**Syn.** mutilate.

main (mān), *adj.* 1. most important; largest: *the main street of a town.* 2. by main force or strength, by using full strength. —*n.* 1. a large pipe for water, gas, etc. 2. *Poetic.* the open sea; ocean. 3. *Archaic.* mainland. 4. in the main, for the most part; chiefly; mostly. 5. with might and main, with all one's strength. [OE *mægen* power] —**Syn.** *adj.* 1. principal, leading, chief.

Maine (mān), *n.* a New England State of the United States. *Capital:* Augusta. *Abbrev.:* Me.

main·land (mān′land′; –lənd), *n.* the largest part of a continent; land that is not a small island or peninsula.

main·ly (mān′li), *adv.* for the most part; chiefly; mostly.

main·mast (mān′mast′; –mäst′; –məst), *n.* the principal mast of a ship.

main·sail (mān′sāl′; –səl), *n.* the largest sail of a ship.

main·sheet (mān′shēt′), *n.* rope that controls the angle at which the mainsail is set.

main·spring (mān′spring′), *n.* 1. the principal spring in a clock, watch, etc. 2. the main cause, motive, or influence.

main·stay (mān′stā′), *n.* 1. rope supporting the mainmast. 2. main support.

Main Street, the ordinary behavior, point of view, and opinions of an average American community.

main·tain (mān·tān′), *v.* 1. keep; keep up; carry on: *maintain an action, a business, etc.* 2. defend; uphold: *maintain an opinion.* 3. declare to be true: *he maintained his innocence.* 4. provide for: *he maintained his family.* [< F maintenir < L *manu tenere* hold by the hand] —**main·tain′a·ble,** *adj.* —**main·tain′er,** *n.* —**Syn.** 1. continue, preserve. 2. vindicate. 3. assert, affirm, contend. 4. sustain, support.

main·te·nance (mān′tə·nəns), *n.* 1. a maintaining: *maintenance of quiet is necessary in a hospital.* 2. a being maintained; support: *a government collects taxes to pay for its maintenance.* 3. enough to support life; means of living: *his small farm provides only a maintenance.* —**Syn.** 3. sustenance, livelihood.

main·top (mān′top′), *n.* platform on the mainmast.

main·top·mast (mān′top′mast′; –mäst′; –məst), *n.* the second section of the mainmast above the deck.

main·top·sail (mān′top′sāl′; –səl), *n.* sail above the mainsail.

maî·tre d'hô·tel (mā′trə dô·tel′), 1. butler; steward. 2. a hotel manager. 3. headwaiter. 4. with a sauce of softened butter, chopped parsley, and lemon juice. [< F]

maize (māz), *n.* 1. a kind of grain that grows on large ears; corn; Indian corn. 2. plant that it grows on. 3. the color of ripe corn; yellow. [< Sp. *maiz,* of West Ind. orig.]

Maj., Major.

ma·jes·tic (mə·jes′tik), **ma·jes·ti·cal** (–tə·kəl), *adj.* grand; noble; dignified; stately. —**ma·jes′ti·cal·ly,** *adv.* —**Syn.** regal, august, imposing.

maj·es·ty (maj′is·ti), *n., pl.* –ties. 1. grandeur; nobility; dignity; stateliness. 2. supreme power or authority: *the majesty of the law.* 3. Majesty, title used in speaking to or of a king, queen, emperor, etc.: *your Majesty, his Majesty, her Majesty.* [< F < L *majestas*]

ma·jol·i·ca (mə·jol′ə·kə; –yol′–), *n.* kind of enameled Italian pottery richly decorated in colors. [< Ital. *maiolica* Majorca]

ma·jor (mā′jər), *adj.* 1. larger; greater; more important: *take the major share.* 2. elder; senior: *Cato major.* 3. of legal age. —*n.* 1. *Mil.* an army officer ranking next below a lieutenant colonel and next above a captain. 2. person of the legal age of responsibility. 3. *Am.* a. subject or course of study to which a student gives most of his time and attention. b. student who selects or studies a special subject. 4. *Music.* one of two sets of intervals, chords, scales, or keys: *the scale of C major.* —*v. Am.* specialize in a subject

or course of study: *major in mathematics.* [< L, compar. of *magnus* great. Doublet of MAYOR.]

Ma·jor·ca (mə·jôr′kə), *n.* a Spanish island in the W Mediterranean Sea, largest of the Balearic Islands. Also, *Spanish* Mallorca.

ma·jor·do·mo (mā′jər·dō′mō), *n., pl.* –mos. 1. man in charge of a royal or noble household. 2. butler; steward. [< Sp. or Ital. < Med.L *major domus* chief of the household]

major general, an army officer ranking next below a lieutenant general and next above a brigadier general. —**ma′jor·gen′er·al·ship′,** *n.*

ma·jor·i·ty (mə·jôr′ə·ti; –jor′–), *n., pl.* –ties. 1. the larger number; greater part; more than half: *the majority of mankind.* 2. a larger number of votes than all the rest. If Smith received 12,000 votes, Adams 7000, and White 3000, Smith had a majority of 2000 and a plurality of 5000. 3. the legal age of responsibility: *attain one's majority.* 4. rank or position of an army major.

major league, *Am.* either of the two chief leagues in American professional baseball.

major scale, a musical scale having eight notes, with half steps instead of whole steps after the third and seventh notes.

make (māk), *v.,* made, mak·ing, *n.* —*v.* 1. bring into being; put together; build; form; shape: *make a dress.* 2. have the qualities needed for: *wood makes a good fire.* 3. cause; bring about: *make trouble.* 4. cause to; force to: *he made me go.* 5. cause to be or become; cause oneself to be: *make public.* 6. turn out to be; become: *a lawyer makes a good legislator.* 7. get ready for use; arrange: *make a bed.* 8. get; obtain; acquire; earn: *make a fortune, make a reputation.* 9. *Colloq.* get on; get a place on: *he made the team.* 10. do; perform: *make a movement.* 11. increase in depth or force: *the tide is making fast.* 12. amount to; add up to; count as: *two and two make four.* 13. think of as; figure to be: *I make the distance across the room 15 feet.* 14. reach; arrive at: *the ship made port.* 15. go; travel: *make 200 miles an hour in an airplane.* 16. cause the success of: *one big deal made the young businessman.* 17. close (an electric circuit). 18. make away with, a. get rid of. b. kill. c. steal. 19. make believe, pretend. 20. make out, a. write out. b. show to be; prove. c. try to prove; declare to be. d. understand. e. see with difficulty. f. complete; fill out. g. *U.S. Colloq.* get along; manage. 21. make over, a. alter; make different. b. hand over; transfer ownership of. 22. make time, go with speed. 23. make up, a. put together. b. compose. c. invent. d. set right; make satisfactory. e. pay for. f. become friends again after a quarrel. g. put paint, powder, etc., on the face. h. disguise. i. arrange (type, pictures, etc.) in the pages of a book, paper, or magazine. j. decide: *make up one's mind.* 24. make up to, try to get the friendship of; flatter. —*n.* 1. way in which a thing is made; style; fashion. 2. kind; brand. 3. nature; character. 4. act or fact of making. 5. amount made. 6. completing of an electric circuit. 7. on the make, *Am., Colloq.* trying for success, profit, etc. [OE *macian*]

make-be·lieve (māk′bi·lēv′), *n.* 1. pretense. 2. pretender. —*adj.* pretended.

mak·er (māk′ər), *n.* 1. person or thing that makes. 2. Maker, God.

make·shift (māk′shift′), *n.* something used for a time instead of the right thing; temporary substitute: *when the electric lights went out, we used candles as a makeshift.* —*adj.* used for a time instead of the right thing.

make-up (māk′up′), *n.* 1. way of being put together. 2. nature; disposition: *a nervous make-up.* 3. way in which an actor is dressed and painted to look his part. 4. paint, powder, etc., put on the face. 5. arrangement of type, pictures, etc., in a book, paper, or magazine.

mak·ing (māk′ing), *n.* 1. cause of a person's success; means of advancement. 2. material needed. 3. qualities needed. 4. something made. 5. amount made at one time. 6. in the making, in the process of being made; not yet fully developed.

mal–, *word element.* bad or badly; poor or

poorly, as in *malnutrition, maltreat.* [< OF *mal-* < L *male* badly < *malus* bad]

Mal·a·bar Coast (mal′ə·bär), region along the SW coast of India.

Ma·lac·ca (mə·lak′ə), *n.* 1. a settlement in the SW part of the Malay Peninsula. 2. **Strait of,** strait between the Malay Peninsula and Sumatra.

Malacca cane, walking stick made of rattan.

Mal·a·chi (mal′ə·kī), *n.* 1. Hebrew prophet who lived about 450 B.C.; the last of the minor prophets. 2. last book of the Old Testament.

mal·a·chite (mal′ə·kīt), *n.* a green mineral, Cu₂(OH)₂CO₃, used for ornamental articles. [< F < Gk. *malache* mallow (from the similar color)]

mal·ad·just·ed (mal′ə·jus′tid), *adj.* badly adjusted.

mal·ad·just·ment (mal′ə·just′mənt), *n.* bad adjustment.

mal·ad·min·is·ter (mal′əd·min′is·tər), *v.* administer badly; manage inefficiently or dishonestly. —**mal′ad·min′is·tra′tion,** *n.*

mal·a·droit (mal′ə·droit′), *adj.* unskillful; awkward; clumsy. —**mal′a·droit′ness,** *n.*

mal·a·dy (mal′ə·di), *n., pl.* **-dies.** sickness; illness; disease. [< OF, < *malade* ill < L *male habitus* doing poorly]

Mál·a·ga (mal′ə·gə), *n.* seaport in S Spain.

Mal·a·ga (mal′ə·gə), *n.* 1. kind of large, oval, firm, white grape. 2. kind of white wine.

Mal·a·gas·y Republic (mal·ə·gas′i), a republic on the island of Madagascar.

ma·laise (ma·lāz′), *n.* vague bodily discomfort. [< F, < *mal-* imperfect + *aise* ease]

mal·ap·por·tion·ment (mal′ə·pôr′shən·mənt; -pōr′-), *n. Am.* wrong or unfair assignment of representation in a legislature.

mal·a·prop·ism (mal′ə·prop·iz′əm), *n.* 1. a ridiculous misuse of words. 2. a misused word. [after Mrs. *Malaprop,* a character in Sheridan's *Rivals,* who constantly misuses words] ▸ A malapropism is a confusion of two words somewhat similar in sound but different in meaning, as *arduous* love for *ardent* love.

mal·ap·ro·pos (mal′ap·rə·pō′), *adv., adj.* at the wrong time or place. [< F *mal à propos* badly for the purpose]

ma·lar·i·a (mə·lãr′i·ə), *n.* disease characterized by periodic chills followed by fever and sweating. Malaria is transmitted by the bite of certain kinds of mosquito. [< Ital. < *mala aria* bad air] —**ma·lar′i·al, ma·lar′i·ous,** *adj.*

Ma·la·wi (ma·lä′wē), *n.* country in SE Africa; formerly the British protectorate of Nyasaland.

Ma·lay (mā′lā; mə·lā′), **Ma·lay·an** (mə·lā′ən), *n.* 1. member of the brown race living in the Malay Peninsula and nearby islands. 2. their language. —*adj.* of the Malays, their country, or their language.

Ma·lay·a (mə·lā′ə), *n.* 1. the Malay Peninsula. 2. **Federation of,** federation of the Malay States, Malacca, and Penang, part of the Federation of Malaysia since 1963.

Mal·a·ya·lam (mal′ə·yä′ləm), *n.* the Dravidian language spoken on the SW coast of India.

Malay Archipela·go, Malaysia (def. 1).

Malay Peninsula, peninsula in SE Asia.

Ma·lay·sia (mə·lā′zhə; -shə), *n.* 1. group of islands between SE Asia and Australia; East Indies. Also called Malay Archipelago. 2. **Federation of,** association of the Federation of Malaya, Sabah, and Sarawak. —**Ma·lay′sian,** *adj., n.*

Malay States, group of states on the Malay Peninsula, formerly under British control.

mal·con·tent (mal′kən·tent′), *adj.* discontented; rebellious. —*n.* a discontented person.

mal de mer (mäl də mãr′), *French.* seasickness.

male (māl), *n.* man; boy; he-animal. —*adj.* 1. belonging to the sex that includes men, boys, and he-animals. 2. of men, boys, or he-animals: *male love of fighting.* 3. *Bot.* able to fertilize the female. 4. *Mach.* fitting into a corresponding part. [< OF < L *masculus,* dim. of *mas* male]

mal·e·dic·tion (mal′ə·dik′shən), *n.* a curse. [< L, ult. < *male* ill + *dicere* speak]

mal·e·fac·tion (mal′ə·fak′shən), *n.* crime; evil deed.

mal·e·fac·tor (mal′ə·fak′tər), *n.* criminal; evildoer. [< L, ult. < *male* badly + *facere* do]

ma·lef·i·cence (mə·lef′ə·səns), *n.* harm; evil. [< L, < *maleficus* wicked < *male* badly + *facere* do]

ma·lef·i·cent (mə·lef′ə·sənt), *adj.* harmful; evil.

Ma·len·kov (mä·len′kôf), *n.* Georgi Maksimilianovich, born 1901, Soviet premier from March, 1953, to February, 1955.

ma·lev·o·lent (mə·lev′ə·lənt), *adj.* wishing evil to happen to others; showing ill will; spiteful. [< L *malevolens,* ult. < *male* ill + *velle* wish] —**ma·lev′o·lence,** *n.* —**ma·lev′o·lent·ly,** *adv.* —**Syn.** malicious, resentful, hostile, bitter.

mal·fea·sance (mal·fē′zəns), *n.* official misconduct; violation of a public trust or duty. A judge is guilty of malfeasance if he accepts a bribe. [< F *malfaisance,* ult. < *mal-* badly + *faire* do] —**mal·fea′sant,** *adj., n.*

mal·for·ma·tion (mal′fôr·mā′shən), *n.* bad shape; faulty structure.

mal·formed (mal·fôrmd′), *adj.* badly shaped; having a faulty structure.

Ma·li (mä′lī), *n.* **Republic of,** a republic in W Africa S of Algeria, formerly part of French West Africa.

mal·ic acid (mal′ik; mā′lik), an acid, C₄H₆O₅, found in certain fruits.

mal·ice (mal′is), *n.* active ill will; wish to hurt others; spite. [< OF < L, < *malus* evil] —**Syn.** maliciousness, spitefulness, grudge, rancor.

malice aforethought, *Law.* evil intent on the part of one who commits a wrong.

ma·li·cious (mə·lish′əs), *adj.* showing active ill will; wishing to hurt others; spiteful. —**ma·li′cious·ly,** *adv.* —**ma·li′cious·ness,** *n.*

ma·lign (mə·līn′), *v.* speak evil of; slander. —*adj.* 1. evil; injurious. 2. hateful; malicious. 3. very harmful; causing death. [< OF < L *malignus* < *malus* evil + *gen-* birth, nature] —**malign′er,** *n.* —**ma·lign′ly,** *adv.*

ma·lig·nant (mə·lig′nənt), *adj.* 1. very evil; very hateful; very malicious. 2. very harmful. 3. *Pathol.* very infectious; very dangerous; causing death: *a malignant growth.* [< LL *malignans* acting from malice < *malignus* MALIGN] —**ma·lig′nance, ma·lig′nan·cy,** *n.* —**ma·lig′nant·ly,** *adv.*

ma·lig·ni·ty (mə·lig′nə·ti), *n., pl.* **-ties.** 1. great malice; extreme hate. 2. great harmfulness; dangerous quality; deadliness. 3. malignant act. —**Syn.** 1. enmity, animosity.

ma·lin·ger (mə·ling′gər), *v.* pretend to be sick in order to escape work or duty; shirk. [< F *malingre* sickly] —**ma·lin′ger·er,** *n.*

mall (môl; mal), *n.* a shaded walk; public walk or promenade. [< OF < L *malleus* hammer]

mal·lard (mal′ərd), *n., pl.* **-lards** or (*esp. collectively*) **-lard.** kind of wild duck. The male has a green head and a white band around his neck. [< OF *mallart,* prob. < Gmc.]

mal·le·a·ble (mal′i·ə·bəl), *adj.* 1. capable of being hammered or pressed into various shapes without being broken. 2. adaptable; yielding. [< OF, < L *malleare* hammer, v. < *malleus,* n.] —**mal′le·a·bil′i·ty, mal′le·a·ble·ness,** *n.*

mal·let (mal′it), *n.* a wooden hammer. Specially shaped mallets are used to play croquet and polo. [< OF *maillet,* dim. of *mail* < L *malleus* hammer]

mal·le·us (mal′i·əs), *n., pl.* **mal·le·i** (mal′i·ī). the outermost of three small bones in the middle ear, shaped like a hammer. [< L, hammer]

Mal·lor·ca (mä·lyôr′kä; mä·yôr′-), *n.* Spanish name of Majorca.

mal·low (mal′ō), *n.* **1.** an ornamental plant with purple, pink, or white flowers, and downy leaves and stems. **2.** any plant like this. [< L *malva.* Cf. Gk. *malache*.]

malm·sey (mäm′zi), *n.* kind of strong sweet wine. [< Med.L *malmasia*, from Monembasia, Greek town]

mal·nu·tri·tion (mal′nü·trish′ən; -nü-), *n.* poor nourishment; lack of nourishment.

mal·o·dor·ous (mal·ō′dər·əs), *adj.* smelling bad. —**mal·o′dor·ous·ly**, *adv.* —**mal·o′dor·ous·ness**, *n.* —**Syn.** unsavory, fetid, stinking.

Mal·o·ry (mal′ə·ri), *n.* Sir Thomas, English writer who lived about 1470. He collected legends about King Arthur and his knights.

mal·prac·tice (mal·prak′tis), *n.* **1.** criminal neglect or unprofessional treatment of a patient by a doctor. **2.** wrong practice or conduct in any official or professional position. —**mal·prac·ti·tion·er** (mal′prak·tish′ən·ər), *n.*

malt (môlt), *n.* **1.** barley or other grain soaked in water until it sprouts and tastes sweet, used in brewing and distilling alcoholic liquors. **2.** beer or ale. —*v.* **1.** change into malt. **2.** prepare with malt. —*adj.* of malt; containing malt. [OE *mealt*] —**malt′y**, *adj.*

Mal·ta (môl′tə), *n.* island republic in the Mediterranean, S of Sicily, formerly a British colony. —**Mal·tese** (môl·tēz′; -tēs′), *adj.*, *n.*

Maltese cat, kind of bluish-gray cat.

Maltese cross, a kind of cross.

malt extract, a sugary substance obtained by soaking malt in water.

Mal·thus (mal′thəs), *n.* Thomas R., 1766-1834, English economist. —**Mal·thu·sian** (mal·thü′zhən; -zi·ən), *adj.*, *n.*

malt·ose (môl′tōs), *n. Chem.* sugar made by the action of diastase on starch, $C_{12}H_{22}O_{11}\cdot H_2O$.

mal·treat (mal·trēt′), *v.* treat roughly or cruelly; abuse. —**mal·treat′ment**, *n.*

malt·ster (môlt′stər), *n.* one who makes or sells malt.

mam·bo (mam′bō; mäm′-), *n.* **1.** a ballroom dance of Caribbean origin. **2.** the music for it. [< Am. Sp.; ? related to *mambi* a festival and dance of the Antilles]

mam·e·luke (mam′ə·lük), *n.* in Mohammedan countries, a slave. [< Ar. *mamlūk* slave]

mam·ma¹, ma·ma (mä′mə; *esp.* Brit. mə·mä′), *n.* mother. [reduplication of an infantile sound]

mam·ma² (mam′ə), *n., pl.* **mam·mae** (mam′ē). a milk-giving gland in female mammals. [< L, breast]

mam·mal (mam′əl), *n.* a vertebrate animal that gives milk to its young. Human beings, horses, dogs, lions, rats, and whales are all mammals. [< NL, ult. < L *mamma* breast] —**mam·ma·li·an** (ma·mā′li·ən; -lyən), *adj., n.*

mam·ma·ry (mam′ə·ri), *adj.* of the mammae.

Mam·mon, mam·mon (mam′ən), *n.* riches thought of as an evil; greed for wealth. [< L < Gk. < Aram. *māmōn(ā)* riches]

mam·moth (mam′əth), *n.* a very large, extinct kind of elephant with a hairy skin and long, curved tusks. —*adj.* huge; gigantic. [< earlier Russ. *mammot*] —**Syn.** *adj.* colossal.

mam·my (mam′i), *n., pl.* **-mies. 1.** *Am., S.* a Negro woman who takes care of white children. **2.** mamma; mother (used especially in the Appalachians).

man (man), *n., pl.* **men,** *v.,* **manned, man·ning.** —*n.* **1.** an adult male person. **2.** person; human being: *no man knows.* **3.** the human race: *man has existed for thousands of years.* **4.** a male follower, servant, or employee. **5.** *Archaic.* vassal. **6.** husband. **7.** one of the pieces used in games such as chess and checkers. **8.** person characterized by manly qualities: *every inch a man.* **9.** to a man, without an exception; all. —*v.* **1.** supply with men: *man a ship with sailors.* **2.** serve or operate; get ready to operate: *man the guns.* **3.** make strong; brace: *the captive manned himself to endure torture.* [OE *mann*] —**Syn.** *n.* **2.** individual, being, mortal. **3.** humanity, mankind. **4.** valet, attendant. ▶ **man, woman.** These are preferred to the more pretentious

gentleman or *lady*, except when *man* or *woman* would sound conspicuously blunt. In business English the original social distinctions between *woman—lady* and *man—gentleman* have been almost reversed. A salesman faced with a customer who wanted to exchange a purchase, turned to his fellow salesmen and said, "Did any of you gentlemen wait on this man?" And a woman looking for work asked, "Are you the woman who wanted a lady to wash for her?"

Man (man), *n.* **Isle of,** a small island W of northern England, in the Irish Sea, one of the British Isles.

Man., **1.** Manila. **2.** Manitoba.

man·a·cle (man′ə·kəl), *n., v.,* **-cled, -cling.** —*n.* **1.** Usually, **manacles.** handcuff; shackles for the hands. **2.** restraint. —*v.* **1.** put manacles on. **2.** restrain. [< OF < L *manicula*, dim. of *manicae* sleeves, manacles < *manus* hand]

man·age (man′ij), *v.,* **-aged, -ag·ing,** *n.* —*v.* **1.** control; conduct; handle; direct: *manage a business, manage a horse.* **2.** conduct affairs. **3.** succeed in accomplishing; contrive; arrange: *can you manage to keep warm?* **4.** get along: *manage on one's income.* **5.** make use of. **6.** get one's way with (a person) by craft or by flattering. —*n.* manège. [< Ital. *maneggiare* < *mano* hand < L *manus*] —**Syn.** *v.* **1.** guide, manipulate. **2.** administer, supervise. **3.** engineer.

man·age·a·ble (man′ij·ə·bəl), *adj.* that can be managed. —**man′age·a·bil′i·ty, man′age·a·ble·ness,** *n.* —**man′age·a·bly,** *adv.*

managed currency, currency whose purchasing power is regulated by the government.

man·age·ment (man′ij·mənt), *n.* **1.** control; handling; direction. **2.** persons that manage a business or an institution. —**Syn. 1.** guidance, regulation. **2.** administration.

man·ag·er (man′ij·ər), *n.* person who manages. —**man′ag·er·ship′,** *n.* —**Syn.** director, executive, administrator.

man·a·ge·ri·al (man′ə·jir′i·əl), *adj.* of a manager; having to do with management. —**man′a·ge′ri·al·ly,** *adv.*

Ma·na·gua (mə·nä′gwə), *n.* **1.** capital of Nicaragua. **2.** Lake, lake in W Nicaragua.

ma·ña·na (mä·nyä′nä), *n., adv. Am., S.W.* tomorrow; some time. [< Sp.]

Ma·nas·seh (mə·nas′ə), *n.* one of the twelve tribes of Israel.

man-at-arms (man′ət·ärmz′), *n., pl.* **men-at-arms. 1.** soldier. **2.** a heavily armed soldier on horseback.

man·a·tee (man′ə·tē′), *n.* a sea cow, a large sea mammal with flippers and a flat, oval tail. [< Sp. *manatí* < Carib lang.]

Man·ches·ter (man′ches′tər; -chis·tər), *n.* an important textile-manufacturing city in W England.

Man·chu (man′chü), *n.* **1.** member of a Mongolian people living in Manchuria. The Manchus conquered China in 1644 and ruled it until 1912. **2.** their language. —*adj.* of the Manchus, their country, or their language.

Man·chu·kuo, Man·chou·kuo (man′chü′kwō′), *n.* a former country in E Asia, north of China, under Japanese protection, now a part of China.

Man·chu·ri·a (man·chùr′i·ə), *n.* region in E Asia, including several provinces of China. —**Man·chu′ri·an,** *adj., n.*

Man·da·lay (man′də·lā′; man′də·lā), *n.* city in C Burma.

man·da·mus (man·dā′məs), *n.* a written order from a higher court to a lower court, an official, a city, a corporation, etc., directing that a certain thing be done. [< L, we order]

man·da·rin (man′də·rin), *n.* **1.** a Chinese official of high rank. **2. Mandarin,** the main dialect of the Chinese language. Chinese officials and educated people speak Mandarin. **3.** kind of small, sweet orange with a very loose peel; tangerine. [< Chinese pidgin Eng. < Pg. *mandar* to order (< L *mandere*), blended with Malay *man-trī* < Hind. < Skt. *mantrin* advisor]

man·da·tar·y (man′də·ter′i), *n.*, *pl.* **-tar·ies.** nation to which a mandate over another country has been given.

man·date (*n.* man′dāt, -dit; *v.* man′dāt), *n.*, *v.*, **-dat·ed, -dat·ing.** —*n.* **1.** command; order. **2.** order from a higher court or official to a lower one. **3.** the expressed will of voters to their representative. **4.** commission given to one nation by a group of nations to administer the government and affairs of a territory, etc. **5.** mandated territory, etc. —*v.* put (a territory, etc.) under the administration of. [< L *mandatum*, n. use of neut. pp. of *mandare* order] —Syn. *n.* **1.** edict, behest, injunction.

man·da·to·ry (man′də·tô′ri, -tō′-), *adj.*, *n.*, *pl.* **-ries.** —*adj.* **1.** of or like a mandate; giving a command or order. **2.** required by a command or order. —*n.* mandatary.

man·di·ble(man′də·bəl), *n.* **1.** jawbone; jaw, esp. the lower jaw. **2.** either part of a bird's beak. **3.** organ in insects for seizing and biting. See the picture under maxilla. [< L *mandibula* < *mandere* chew]

man·do·lin (man′də·lin; man′də·lin′), *n.* a musical instrument with a pear-shaped body, having four or more strings, played with a plectrum. [< F < Ital. *mandolino*, dim. of *mandola*, ult. < Gk. *pandoura* three-stringed instrument]

Man playing a mandolin

man·drag·o·ra (man·drag′ə·rə), *n. Bot.* a genus of plants belonging to the nightshade family. [< L < Gk. *mandragoras*]

man·drake (man′drāk), *n.* **1.** plant with a very short stem and a thick root, used in medicine. **2.** *Am.* the May apple. [by popular etymology < *mandragora*]

man·drel, man·dril (man′drəl), *n.* spindle or bar of a lathe that supports the material being turned. [< F *mandrin*]

man·drill (man′dril), *n.* a large, fierce baboon of western Africa. [< *man* + *drill* baboon (< African lang.)]

mane (mān), *n.* the long, heavy hair on the back of the neck of a horse, lion, etc. [OE *manu*] —maned, *adj.*

ma·nège, ma·nege (mə·nezh′; -nāzh′), *n.* **1.** art of training or riding horses; horsemanship. **2.** movements of a trained horse. **3.** a riding school. [< F < Ital. *maneggio* < *maneggiare* manage]

ma·nes, Ma·nes (mā′nēz), *n.pl.* among the ancient Romans, the deified souls of dead persons. [< L]

ma·neu·ver (mə·nū′vər), *n.*, *v.*, **-vered, -ver·ing.** —*n.* **1.** a planned movement of troops or warships. **2.** a skillful plan; clever trick. —*v.* **1.** perform maneuvers. **2.** cause to perform maneuvers. **3.** plan skillfully; use clever tricks. **4.** force by skillful plans; get by clever tricks. Also, **ma·noeuvre.** [< F *manoeuvre*, ult. < L *manu operare* work by hand] —ma·neu′ver·a·ble, *adj.* —ma·neu′ver·a·bil′i·ty, *n.* —ma·neu′ver·er, *n.*

man Friday, a faithful servant; servile follower.

man·ful (man′fəl), *adj.* manly; brave; resolute. —man′ful·ly, *adv.* —man′ful·ness, *n.*

man·ga·nese (mang′gə·nēs; -nēz), *n. Chem.* a hard, brittle, grayish-white metallic element, Mn, used in making glass, paints, and medicines. [< F < Ital., alter. of Med.L *magnesia* MAGNESIA]

mange (mānj), *n.* a skin disease of animals that forms scabs and causes loss of hair. [< OF *manjue* itch < *mangier* eat < L *manducare* chew]

man·gel-wur·zel (mang′gəl-wėr′zəl), or **man·gel,** *n.* a large, coarse variety of beet, used as a food for cattle. [< G, var. of *mangold-wurzel* beet root]

man·ger (mān′jər), *n.* box or trough in which hay can be placed for horses or cows to eat. [< OF *mangeoire*, ult. < L *manducare* chew]

man·gle[1] (mang′gəl), *v.*, **-gled, -gling.** **1.** cut or tear (the flesh) roughly. **2.** spoil; ruin. [< AF *mangler*, ? < OF *mahaignier*. See MAYHEM.] —man′gler, *n.* —Syn. **1.** lacerate, mutilate. **2.** disfigure, mar.

man·gle[2] (mang′gəl), *n.*, *v.*, **-gled, -gling.** —*n.* machine with rollers for pressing and smoothing sheets and other flat things. —*v.* make smooth in such a machine. [< Du. *mangel* < MDu. *mange* < LL *manganon* contrivance < Gk.]

man·go (mang′gō), *n.*, *pl.* **-goes, -gos.** **1.** a slightly sour, juicy fruit with a thick, yellowish-red rind. **2.** the tropical tree that it grows on. [< Pg. < Malay < Tamil *mānkāy*]

man·grove (mang′grōv), *n.* a tropical tree that sends down many branches that take root and form new trunks. [< Sp. *mangle* < Malay *manggi-manggi*; infl. by *grove*]

man·gy (mān′ji), *adj.*, **-gi·er, -gi·est.** **1.** having the mange; with the hair falling out. **2.** shabby and dirty. **3.** *Colloq.* mean; contemptible. —man′gi·ly, *adv.* —man′gi·ness, *n.*

man·han·dle (man′han′dəl), *v.*, **-dled, -dling. 1.** treat roughly; pull or push about. **2.** move by human strength without mechanical appliances.

Man·hat·tan (man·hat′ən), *n.* **1.** island on which the chief business section of New York City is located. **2.** borough of New York City that consists of the island of Manhattan. **3.** *Am.* cocktail of whiskey, sweet vermouth, and bitters.

Manhattan District, organization established in 1942 under the U.S. Army to administer the various scientific and industrial groups responsible for atomic research, esp. in connection with the atom bomb. It was dissolved in 1947.

man·hole (man′hōl′), *n.* hole through which a workman can enter a sewer, steam boiler, etc., to inspect or repair it.

man·hood (man′hud), *n.* **1.** condition or time of being a man. **2.** courage; manliness. **3.** men as a group. —Syn. **2.** virility, bravery, fortitude.

man-hour (man′our′), *n.* hour of work by one man, used as a time unit in industry.

ma·ni·a (mā′ni·ə), *n.* **1.** kind of insanity characterized by great excitement and sometimes violence. **2.** unusual fondness; craze. [< L < Gk., madness]

ma·ni·ac (mā′ni·ak), *n.* an insane person; raving lunatic. —*adj.* Also, **ma·ni·a·cal** (mə·nī′ə·kəl). insane; raving. —ma·ni′a·cal·ly, *adv.*

ma·nic (mā′nik; man′ik), *adj.* **1.** of or like mania. **2.** suffering from mania.

man·ic-de·pres·sive (man′ik·di·pres′iv), *adj.* having alternating attacks of mania and depression: *manic-depressive insanity.*

man·i·cure (man′ə·kyūr), *v.*, **-cured, -curing,** *n.* care for (the fingernails and hands); trim, clean, and polish (the fingernails). —*n.* care of the hands; trimming, cleaning, and polishing of fingernails. [< F, < L *manus* hand + *cura* care] —man′i·cur′ist, *n.*

man·i·fest (man′ə·fest), *adj.* apparent to the eye or to the mind; plain; clear. —*v.* **1.** show plainly; reveal; display. **2.** prove; put beyond doubt. —*n.* list of a ship's cargo. [< L *manifestus* palpable < *manus* hand + ? *fers-* seize] —man′i·fest′ly, *adv.* —man′i·fest′ness, *n.* —Syn. *adj.* obvious, evident, unmistakable. -*v.* **1.** exhibit, disclose, evidence.

man·i·fes·ta·tion (man′ə·fes·tā′shən), *n.* **1.** a manifesting or being manifested. **2.** thing that manifests: *diving in to rescue the child was a manifestation of courage.* **3.** public demonstration.

man·i·fes·to (man′ə·fes′tō), *n.*, *pl.* **-toes.** a public declaration of intentions, purposes, or

man·i·fold (man′ə·fōld), *adj.* **1.** of many kinds; many and various: *manifold duties.* **2.** having many parts or forms: *the manifold wisdom of God.* **3.** doing many things at the same time. —*n.* **1.** pipe with several openings. **2.** one of many copies. —*v.* make many copies of. [OE *manigfeald*] —**man′i·fold′ly,** *adv.* —**man′i·fold′ness,** *n.* —Syn. *adj.* **1.** varied, diverse, sundry.

man·i·kin (man′ə·kin), *n.* **1.** a little man; dwarf. **2.** mannequin. Also, **mannikin.** [< Du. *manneken,* dim. of *man* man]

Ma·nil·a (mə·nil′ə), *n.* the largest city and former capital of the Philippine Islands.

ma·nil·a, ma·nil·la (mə·nil′ə), *n.* **1.** Manila hemp. **2.** Manila paper.

Manila hemp, a strong fiber made from the leaves of a Philippine banana plant, used for making ropes and fabrics; abacá.

Manila paper, a strong, brown or brownish-yellow wrapping paper.

man in the street, the average person.

man·i·oc (man′i·ok; mā′ni-), *n.* cassava. [< Sp., Pg., < Tupi *manioca*]

ma·nip·u·late (mə·nip′yə·lāt), *v.,* -lat·ed, -lat·ing. **1.** handle or treat skillfully; handle: *manipulate the gear shift of an automobile.* **2.** manage; deal with: *a mathematician can manipulate equations.* **3.** manage by clever use of influence, esp. unfair influence: *he so manipulated the ball team that he was elected captain.* **4.** change for one's own purpose or advantage: *the bookkeeper manipulated the company's accounts to conceal his theft.* [< F, < L *manipulus* handful] —**ma·nip′u·lat′a·ble,** *adj.* —**ma·nip′u·la′tion,** *n.* —**ma·nip′u·la′tive, ma·nip′u·la·to′ry,** *adj.* —**ma·nip′u·la′tor,** *n.*

man·i·to (man′ə·tō), **man·i·tou** (-tü), *n. Am.* spirit worshiped by Algonquian Indians as a force of nature. [< Algonquian]

Man·i·to·ba (man′ə·tō′bə), *n.* **1.** province in S Canada. **2.** Lake, lake in S Canada.

man·kind (man·kīnd′ *for 1;* man′kīnd′ *for 2*), *n.* **1.** the human race; all human beings. **2.** men; the male sex (as distinguished from women).

man·like (man′līk′), *adj.* **1.** like a man. **2.** suitable for a man; masculine.

man·ly (man′li), *adj.,* -li·er, -li·est. **1.** like a man; as a man should be; strong, frank, brave, noble, independent, and honorable. **2.** suitable for a man; masculine. —**man′li·ness,** *n.*

Mann (man), *n.* Horace, 1796–1859, American educator.

man·na (man′ə), *n.* **1.** food miraculously supplied to the Israelites in the wilderness. Exod. 16:14–36. **2.** food for the soul. **3.** a much needed thing that is unexpectedly supplied. [< LL < Gk. < Heb. *mān*]

man·ne·quin (man′ə·kin), *n.* **1.** woman whose work is wearing new clothes to show them to customers. **2.** figure of a person used by tailors, artists, stores, etc. Also, **manikin.** [< F < Du. See MANIKIN.]

man·ner (man′ər), *n.* **1.** way of doing, being done, or happening: *the trouble arose in this manner.* **2.** way of acting or behaving: *an austere manner.* **3. manners, a.** ways of behaving: *good manners, bad manners.* **b.** polite ways of behaving. **c.** customs; ways of living: *a comedy of manners.* **4.** characteristic style in art or literature: *verses in the manner of Spenser.* **5.** kind or kinds: *all manner of things.* **6. by all manner of means,** most certainly. **7. by no manner of means,** not at all; under no circumstances. **8. in a manner of speaking,** as one might say. **9. to the manner born,** accustomed since birth to some way or condition. [< AF *manere,* ult. < L *manus* hand] —Syn. **1.** mode, method, fashion. **2.** bearing, demeanor, deportment, conduct.

man·nered (man′ərd), *adj.* **1.** having manners of a certain kind, as in *well-mannered.* **2.** affected; artificial; having many mannerisms.

man·ner·ism (man′ər·iz·əm), *n.* **1.** too much

use of some manner in speaking, writing, or behaving. **2.** an odd little trick; queer habit; peculiar way of acting. —Syn. **1.** affectation. **2.** peculiarity.

man·ner·less (man′ər·lis), *adj.* without good manners.

man·ner·ly (man′ər·li), *adj.* having or showing good manners; polite. —*adv.* politely. —**man′ner·li·ness,** *n.* —Syn. *adj.* courteous, civil, well-behaved.

man·ni·kin (man′ə·kin), *n.* manikin.

man·nish (man′ish), *adj.* **1.** characteristic of a man: *a mannish way of holding a baby.* **2.** imitating a man: *a mannish style of dress.* —**man′nish·ly,** *adv.* —**man′nish·ness,** *n.*

ma·noeu·vre (mə·nü′vər), *n., v.,* -vred, -vring. maneuver.

man of letters, 1. writer. **2.** person who has a wide knowledge of literature.

man of the world, man who knows people and customs, and is tolerant of both.

man-of-war (man′əv·wôr′), *n., pl.* men-of-war. warship.

ma·nom·e·ter (mə·nom′ə·tər), *n.* instrument for measuring the pressure of gases or vapors. [< F, < Gk. *manos* thin + *metron* measure]

man·or (man′ər), *n.* a landed estate, part of which was set aside for the lord and the rest divided among his peasants, who paid the owner rent in goods, services, or money. In the Middle Ages, if the lord sold his manor, the peasants or serfs were sold with it. [< OF *manoir,* orig. v., dwell < L *manēre* stay] —**ma·no·ri·al** (mə·nô′ri·əl; -nō′-), *adj.*

manor house, house of the owner of a manor.

man power, man·pow·er (man′pou′ər), *n.* **1.** power supplied by the physical work of men. **2.** strength thought of in terms of the number of men needed or available.

man·sard (man′särd), or **mansard roof,** *n.* roof with two slopes on each side. [after F. *Mansard,* architect]

manse (mans), *n.* a minister's house; parsonage. [< Med.L *mansa* dwelling, n. use of fem. pp. of L *manēre* stay]

man·serv·ant (man′sėr′vənt), *n., pl.* men·serv·ants. a male servant.

man·sion (man′shən), *n.* a large house; stately residence. [< OF < L *mansio* < *manēre* stay]

man·slaugh·ter (man′slô′tər), *n.* **1.** killing a human being. **2.** *Law.* killing a person unlawfully but without malice.

man·tel (man′təl), *n.* **1.** shelf above a fireplace with its supports. **2.** mantelpiece′. the shelf. [var. of *mantle*]

man·til·la (man·til′ə), *n.* a lace or silk veil or scarf covering the hair and falling down over the shoulders, often worn by Spanish and Mexican women. [< Sp., dim. of *manta,* ult. < L *mantellum* mantle]

Mantilla

man·tis (man′tis), *n.* insect that holds its forelegs doubled up as if praying. It eats other insects. [NL use of Gk. *mantis* prophet (from its praying posture)]

man·tle (man′təl), *n., v.,* -tled, -tling. —*n.* **1.** a loose cloak without sleeves; cape. **2.** anything that covers like a mantle. **3.** a lacelike tube around a flame that gets so hot it glows and gives light. —*v.* **1.** cover with a mantle. **2.** cover; conceal. **3.** blush: *her cheek mantled.* **4.** become covered with a coating or scum. [< L *mantellum*]

man·tu·a (man′chü·ə), *n.* a loose gown or cloak formerly worn by women.

man·u·al (man′yü·əl), *adj.* of the hands; done with the hands: *manual labor.* —*n.* **1.** a small book that helps its readers to understand or use something; handbook. A cookbook is a manual. **2.** drill in handling a rifle or other weapons.

3. *Music.* an organ keyboard played with the hands. [< L, < *manus* hand] —man′u·al·ly, *adv.*

manual training, *Am.* training in work done with the hands; practice in various arts and crafts, esp. in making things out of wood.

man·u·fac·to·ry (man′yə·fak′tə·ri), *n., pl.* -ries. factory.

man·u·fac·ture (man′yə·fak′chər), *v.,* -tured, -tur·ing, *n.* —v. 1. make by hand or by machine. A big factory manufactures goods in large quantities by using machines and dividing the work up among many people. 2. make into something useful. 3. invent; make up: *manufacture an excuse.* —n. 1. act or process of manufacturing. 2. thing manufactured. [< F, ult. < L *manu facere* make by hand]

man·u·fac·tur·er (man′yə·fak′chər·ər), *n.* person whose business is manufacturing; owner of a factory.

man·u·mis·sion (man′yə·mish′ən), *n.* a freeing or a being freed from slavery.

man·u·mit (man′yə·mit′), *v.,* -mit·ted, -mitting. set free from slavery. [< L *manu mittere* release from control]

ma·nure (mə·nûr′; -nyûr′), *n., v.,* -nured, -nur·ing. —n. 1. any substance put in or on the soil as fertilizer. 2. refuse from stables, etc. —v. put manure in or on. [< AF *maynoverer* work with the hands. See MANEUVER.] —ma·nur′er, *n.*

man·u·script (man′yə·skript), *n.* book or paper written by hand or with a typewriter. —adj. written by hand or with a typewriter. [< L *manu scriptus* written by hand]

Manx (mangks), *adj.* of the Isle of Man, its people, or their language. —n. 1. (*pl. in use*) people of the Isle of Man. 2. (*sing. in use*) their language.

Manx cat, kind of cat that has no tail.

Manx·man (mangks′mən), *n., pl.* -men. native of the Isle of Man.

man·y (men′i), *adj.,* more, most, *n.* —adj. consisting of a great number; numerous: *many people, many years ago.* —n. 1. a great number: *did many come? Yes, a great many.* 2. many people or things: *there were many at the dance.* [OE *manig*] —Syn. *adj.* innumerable. —Ant. *adj.* few.

man·za·ni·ta (man′zə·nē′tə), *n. Am.* a heathlike evergreen shrub that grows in the W United States. [< Sp., dim. of *manzana* apple]

Ma·o·ri (mä′ō·ri; mou′ri; mä′ri), *n., pl.* -ris, *adj.* —n. 1. member of the native brown race of New Zealand. 2. their language. —adj. of the Maoris or their language.

Mao Tse-tung (mou′tse′tùng′), born 1893, Chinese Communist leader.

map (map), *n., v.,* mapped, map·ping. —n. 1. drawing representing the earth's surface or part of it, usually showing countries, cities, rivers, seas, lakes, and mountains. 2. drawing representing part of the sky, showing the position of the stars. —v. 1. make a map of; show on a map. 2. plan; arrange in detail: *map out the week's work.* [< Med.L *mappa mundi* map of the world (L *mappa* napkin)]

ma·ple (mā′pəl), *n.* 1. tree grown for its shade, its wood, or its sap. There are many kinds of maples, but all have dry fruits with two wings and opposite leaves without stipules. 2. its hard, light-colored wood. 3. flavor of maple sugar or maple syrup. [OE *mapeltrēow* maple tree]

maple sugar, *Am.* sugar made from the sap of one variety of maple.

maple syrup, *Am.* syrup made from the sap of one variety of maple.

mar (mär), *v.,* marred, mar·ring. spoil the beauty of; damage; injure. [OE *merran* waste] —Syn. disfigure, deface.

Mar., March.

mar·a·bou (mar′ə·bü), *n.* 1. kind of large stork common in Africa and the East Indies. 2. a furlike trimming made from its soft, downy feathers. [< F]

mar·a·schi·no (mar′ə·skē′nō), *n.* a strong, sweet alcoholic drink made from a kind of small black cherry. [< Ital., ult. < L *amarus* sour]

maraschino cherries, cherries preserved in a syrup flavored with maraschino.

mar·a·thon (mar′ə·thon), *n.* 1. a foot race of 26 miles, 385 yards. 2. any long race or contest. 3. Marathon, plain in Greece about 20 miles northeast of Athens. After the Athenians defeated the Persians there in 490 B.C., a runner ran all the way to Athens with the news of the victory.

ma·raud (mə·rôd′), *v.* go about in search of plunder; make raids on for booty. —n. a raid for booty. [< F, < *maraud* rascal] —ma·raud′er, *n.* —ma·raud′ing, *adj.*

mar·ble (mär′bəl), *n., adj., v.,* -bled, -bling. —n. 1. a hard limestone, white or colored, capable of taking a beautiful polish. 2. marbles, collection of sculptures. 3. a small ball of clay, glass, stone, etc., used in games. 4. marbles (*sing. in use*), game played with marbles. —adj. 1. made of marble. 2. like marble; white, hard, cold, or unfeeling. —v. color in imitation of the patterns in marble: *binders marble the edges of some books.* [< OF < L < Gk. *marmaros* gleaming stone]

mar·ca·site (mär′kə·sīt), *n.* yellow mineral used for ornaments; iron pyrites. [< Med.L < Ar. *marqashīṭā* < Aram.]

mar·cel (mär·sel′), *n., v.,* -celled, -cel·ling. —n. series of regular waves put in the hair. —v. put such waves in. [after *Marcel*, a French hairdresser]

march[1] (märch), *v.* 1. walk in time and with steps of the same length. 2. walk in a stately manner. 3. walk or proceed steadily. 4. cause to march or go: *the policeman marched the thief off to jail.* —n. 1. act or fact of marching: *a quick march.* 2. music for marching. 3. distance marched. 4. a long, hard walk. 5. advance; progress: *the march of events.* [< F *marcher*, earlier, to trample] —march′er, *n.*

march[2] (märch), *n.* land along the border of a country; frontier. [< OF *marche* < Gmc.]

March (märch), *n.* the third month of the year, having 31 days. [< OF *marche* < L *Martius* (month) of Mars]

mar·chion·ess (mär′shən·is), *n.* 1. wife or widow of a marquis. 2. lady equal in rank to a marquis. [< Med.L *marchionissa* < *marchio* MARQUIS]

march·pane (märch′pān′), *n.* marzipan.

Mar·co·ni (mär·kō′ni), *n.* Guglielmo, 1874–1937, Italian inventor.

Mar·co Po·lo (mär′kō pō′lō), 1254?–1324?, Italian merchant who wrote about his travels in Asia.

Mar·cus Au·re·li·us (mär′kəs ô·rē′li·əs; ô·rēl′yəs), 121–180 A.D., Roman emperor and Stoic philosopher.

Mar·di gras (mär′di grä′), the last day before Lent; Shrove Tuesday. It is celebrated in New Orleans and other cities with parades and festivities. [< F, fat Tuesday]

mare (mār), *n.* a female horse, donkey, etc. [OE *mere*]

mare's-nest (mārz′nest′), *n.* something supposed to be a great discovery that turns out to be a mistake or joke.

mar·ga·rine (mär′jə·rēn; -rin), *n.,* **mar·ga·rin** (-rin), *n.* a substitute for butter consisting mainly of vegetable fat derived from cottonseed and soybean oils and to a lesser extent from corn and peanut oils; oleomargarine. [< F]

marge (märj), *n. Poetic.* edge; border. [< F]

mar·gin (mär′jən), *n.* 1. edge; border: *the margin of a lake.* 2. blank space around the writing or printing on a page. 3. extra amount; amount beyond what is necessary; difference. 4. difference between the cost and selling price of stocks, etc. 5. money or security deposited with a broker to protect him from loss on contracts undertaken for the real buyer or seller. —v. provide with a margin. [< L *margo* edge]

mar·gin·al (mär′jə·nəl), *adj.* 1. written or

printed in a margin. 2. of a margin. 3. on or near the margin. —**mar′gin·al·ly**, *adv.*

mar·grave (mär′grāv), *n.* title of certain German princes. [< MDu. *markgrave* count of the marches]

mar·gue·rite (mär′gə·rēt′), *n.* kind of daisy with white petals and a yellow center. [< F < L < Gk. *margarites* pearl]

Mar·i·an·as Islands (mãr′i·an′əs), group of 15 small islands in the Pacific, east of the Philippine Islands. The largest island, Guam, belongs to the United States; the other 14 islands, formerly under Japanese supervision, are now under U.S. trusteeship. Also, **Ladrone Islands, Ladrones.**

Ma·rie An·toi·nette (mə·rē′ an′twə·net′). See Antoinette, Marie.

mar·i·gold (mar′ə·gōld), *n.* **1.** plant of the aster family with yellow, orange, or red flowers. **2.** the flower. [< (the Virgin) *Mary* + *gold*]

mar·i·jua·na, mar·i·hua·na (mar′ə·wä′nə), *n. Am.* **1.** kind of hemp. **2.** a poisonous drug made from its leaves and flowers. [< Am.Sp.; ? < Am. Ind. word, infl. by name *Maria Juana* Mary Jane]

ma·rim·ba (mə·rim′bə), *n.* a musical instrument somewhat like a xylophone. [< Bantu]

ma·ri·na (mə·rē′nə), *n.* a boat basin, esp. one having full facilities for rest and recreation of the owners and crews as well as for berthing, repairing, and supplying all types of craft.

Marimba

mar·i·nate (mar′ə·nāt), *v.*, **-nat·ed, -nat·ing. 1.** steep in a pickle, usually one of vinegar or wine seasoned with herbs, spices, etc. **2.** soak in oil and vinegar. [< F *mariner*] —**mar′i·na′tion**, *n.*

ma·rine (mə·rēn′), *adj.* **1.** of the sea; found in the sea; produced by the sea: *marine animals.* **2.** of shipping; of the navy; for use at sea. —*n.* **1.** shipping; fleet. **2.** soldier formerly serving only at sea, now also participating in land and air action. [< F < L, < *mare* sea]

Marine Corps, *Am.* a separate branch of the U.S. armed forces independently responsible to the Secretary of the Navy, trained for land, sea, and air action, often used as a landing force.

mar·i·ner (mar′ə·nər), *n.* sailor; seaman. [< AF, < OF *marin* MARINE]

mar·i·o·nette (mar′i·ə·net′), *n.* a small doll moved by strings or the hands. A marionette show is often given on a miniature stage. [< F, ult. < *Marie* Mary]

Mar·i·po·sa lily (mar′ə·pō′sə; -zə), *Am.* **1.** plant with tuliplike flowers that grows in the W United States and Mexico. **2.** the flower. [< Sp. *mariposa* butterfly]

mar·i·tal (mar′ə·təl), *adj.* **1.** of marriage; pertaining to marriage: *marital vows.* **2.** of a husband: *faithfulness is a marital obligation.* [< L, < *maritus* married man] —**mar′i·tal·ly,** *adv.*

mar·i·time (mar′ə·tīm), *adj.* **1.** on or near the sea: *a maritime city.* **2.** living near the sea: *maritime peoples.* **3.** of the sea; having to do with shipping and sailing: *maritime law.* [< L *maritimus* < *mare* sea] —**Syn.** 3. nautical.

Maritime Provinces, New Brunswick, Nova Scotia, and Prince Edward Island.

mar·jo·ram (mär′jə·rəm), *n.* a fragrant plant of the same family as mint. Sweet marjoram is used in cooking. [< OF *majorane*, ? < L *amaracus* < Gk.]

mark¹ (märk), *n.* **1.** trace or impression made by some object on the surface of another. **2.** line, dot, or other object to show position. **3.** line where a race starts. **4.** something that shows what or whose a thing is; sign; indication. **5.** written or printed stroke or sign: *punctuation marks.* **6.** grade or rating. **7.** cross made by a person who cannot write his name. **8.** something to be aimed at; goal. **9.** what is usual, proper, or expected; standard: *a tired person does not*

feel up to the mark. **10.** influence; impression: *a great man leaves his mark on whatever he does.* **11.** of mark, important; famous. **12.** tag, label, stamp, seal, etc., that shows price, quality, etc. —*v.* **1.** give grades to; rate. **2.** make a mark or marks; put a mark or marks on. **3.** trace or form by marks or as if by marks. **4.** show by a mark or marks. **5.** show clearly; manifest: *a frown marked her displeasure.* **6.** distinguish; set off: *many important inventions mark the last 150 years.* **7.** pay attention to; notice; observe: *mark my words.* **8.** keep (the score); record. **9.** put a tag, label, stamp, etc., on. **10.** mark down, **a.** write down; note down. **b.** *Am.* mark for sale at a lower price. **11.** mark time, **a.** *Mil.* move the feet as in marching, but without advancing. **b.** suspend in progress temporarily. **12.** mark up, *Am.* mark for sale at a higher price. [OE *mearc*] —**mark′er**, *n.* —**Syn.** *n.* 4. token, symbol. 8. target. –*v.* 7. note, heed, regard, consider.

mark² (märk), *n.* **1.** a unit of money of Germany, worth 23.8 cents (1950). **2.** coin or paper note equal to the mark. [OE *m(e)arc*]

Mark (märk), *n.* **1.** one of the four Evangelists, a fellow worker with the Apostle Paul and the Apostle Peter. **2.** the second book of the New Testament, telling the story of the life of Christ. **3.** King, *Arthurian Legend.* a treacherous ruler of Cornwall.

marked (märkt), *adj.* **1.** having a mark or marks on it. **2.** very noticeable; easily recognized: *there is a marked difference between grapes and oranges.* —**mark·ed·ly** (mär′kid·li), *adv.* —**mark′ed·ness**, *n.* —**Syn.** 2. prominent, conspicuous, outstanding.

mar·ket (mär′kit), *n.* **1.** a meeting of people for buying and selling. **2.** the people so gathered. **3.** space or building in which provisions, cattle, etc., are shown for sale. **4.** store for the sale of provisions: *a meat market.* **5.** trade, esp. as regards a particular article: *the cotton market.* **6.** opportunity to sell or buy: *lose one's market.* **7.** demand (for something); price offered. **8.** region where goods can be sold: *Africa is a new market for many products.* **9.** play the market, *Am.* speculate on the stock exchange. —*v.* **1.** buy or sell in a market. **2.** sell: *market goods.* **3.** carry or send to market. [< OF < L *mercatus* trade, ult. < *merx* merchandise] —**mar′ket·er,** *n.*

mar·ket·a·ble (mär′kit·ə·bəl), *adj.* that can be sold; salable. —**mar′ket·a·bil′i·ty,** *n.*

market place, place where a market is held.

market price or **value,** the current price.

mark·ing (mär′king), *n.* **1.** mark or marks. **2.** arrangement of marks.

marks·man (märks′mən), *n., pl.* **-men.** person who shoots well. —**marks′man·ship,** *n.*

marl (märl), *n.* soil containing clay and calcium carbonate, used in making cement and as a fertilizer. [< OF < Med.L *margila* < L *marga*, prob. < Celtic] —**marl′y,** *adj.*

Marl·bor·ough (märl′bėr′ə; esp. Brit. môl′bə·rə, -brə), *n.* **John Churchill,** 1st Duke of, 1650–1722, English general.

mar·lin (mär′lən), *n.* a large sea fish like a sailfish. [short for *marlinespike*]

mar·line (mär′lən), *n. Naut.* a small cord wound around the ends of a rope to keep it from fraying. [< Du. *marlijn* < *marren* tie + *lijn* line]

mar·line·spike, mar·lin·spike (mär′lən·spīk′), *n.* a pointed iron implement used by sailors to separate strands of rope in splicing, etc.

Mar·lowe (mär′lō), *n.* **Christopher,** 1564–1593, English dramatist and poet.

mar·ma·lade (mär′mə·lād), *n.* preserve like jam, made of oranges or of other fruit. [< F < Pg., < *marmelo*, quince, ult. < Gk., < *meli* honey + *melon* apple]

Mar·ma·ra, Mar·mo·ra (mär′mə·rə), *n.* **Sea of,** a small sea between Europe and Asia Minor, connected with the Aegean Sea by the Dardanelles and with the Black Sea by the Bosporus.

mar·mo·set (mär′mə·zet), *n.* a very small monkey with a soft thick fur, living in South America and Central America. [< OF *marmouset* grotesque figurine]

mar·mot (mär′mət), *n. Am.* a gnawing animal with a thick body and a bushy tail. Woodchucks and prairie dogs are marmots. [< F *marmotte*]

Marne (märn), *n.* river flowing from NE France into the Seine River near Paris; battles, 1914, 1918, 1944.

ma·roon¹ (mə·rün′), *n., adj.* very dark brownish-red. [< F < Ital. *marrone* chestnut]

ma·roon² (mə·rün′), *v.* 1. put (a person) ashore in a lonely place and leave him there. 2. leave in a lonely, helpless position. [< F *marron*, ? < Sp. *cimarron* wild < *cimarra* bushes]

marque (märk), *n.* official permission from a government to capture enemy merchant ships. [< F < Pr. *marca* reprisal < *marcar* seize as a pledge, ult. < Gmc.]

mar·quee (mär·kē′), *n.* 1. a large tent, often one put up for some outdoor entertainment. 2. a rooflike shelter over an entrance. [< F *marquise* (misunderstood as plural)]

Mar·que·sas Islands (mär·kā′səs), group of thirteen French islands in the S Pacific.

mar·que·try, mar·que·te·rie (mär′kə·tri), *n., pl.* -tries; -te·ries. inlaid decoration in furniture. [< F, < *marqueter* inlay < *marque* mark¹ < Gmc.]

mar·quis, *esp. Brit.* **mar·quess** (mär′kwis), *n.* nobleman ranking below a duke and above an earl or count. [< OF, < *march* < Gmc. See MARCH².] —**mar·quis·ate** (mär′kwiz·it), *n.*

mar·quise (mär·kēz′), *n.* 1. wife or widow of a marquis. 2. woman equal in rank to a marquis. [< F]

mar·qui·sette (mär′ki·zet′; -kwi-), *n.* a very thin fabric with square meshes, made of cotton, silk, or rayon and often used for window draperies. [< F, dim. of *marquise* marquise]

Mar·ra·kech, Mar·ra·kesh, or **Ma·ra·kesh** (mä·rä′kesh), *n.* city in W Morocco. Also, Morocco.

mar·riage (mar′ij), *n.* 1. a living together as husband and wife; married life. 2. ceremony of being married; a marrying. 3. a close union. [< OF, < *marier* MARRY¹] —Syn. 1. matrimony. 2. wedding.

mar·riage·a·ble (mar′ij·ə·bəl), *adj.* fit for marriage; old enough to marry. —**mar′riage·a·bil′i·ty, mar′riage·a·ble·ness,** *n.*

marriage portion, dowry.

mar·ried (mar′id), *adj.* 1. having a husband or wife. 2. of marriage; of husbands and wives.

mar·row (mar′ō), *n.* 1. the soft tissue that fills the cavities of most bones. 2. the inmost or essential part. [OE *mearg*]

mar·ry¹ (mar′i), *v.,* -ried, -ry·ing. 1. join as husband and wife: *the minister married them.* 2. take as husband or wife: *John married Grace.* 3. become married; take a husband or wife: *she married late in life.* 4. give in marriage: *she has married all her daughters.* 5. unite closely. [< OF < L, < *maritus* husband < *mas* male] —**mar′ri·er,** *n.*

mar·ry² (mar′i), *interj. Archaic.* exclamation showing surprise, indignation, etc. [< (the Virgin) *Mary*]

Mars (märz), *n.* 1. *Rom. Myth.* god of war, identified with the Greek god Ares. 2. war. 3. planet next beyond the earth. It is the fourth in order from the sun.

Mar·seil·laise (mär′sə·lāz′), *n.* French national song, written in 1792 during the French Revolution.

Mar·seilles (mär·sā′; -sālz′), *n.* seaport in SE France, on the Mediterranean Sea.

mar·seilles (mär·sālz′), *n.* a thick cotton cloth woven in figures or stripes, used for bedspreads, etc. [< *Marseilles*]

marsh (marsh), *n.* low land covered at times by water; soft wet land; swamp. —*adj.* swampy; marshy. [OE *mersc* < *mere* lake] —**Syn.** *n.* bog, fen.

mar·shal (mär′shəl), *n., v.,* -shaled, -shaling; *esp. Brit.* -shalled, -shal·ling. —*n.* 1. officer of various kinds, esp. a police officer. 2. *Am.* an officer of a U.S. Federal court whose duties are like those of a sheriff. 3. a high officer in an army: *Marshal of France.* 4. person arranging the order of march in a parade. 5. person in charge of events or ceremonies. —*v.* 1. arrange in order: *he marshaled his facts well.* 2. conduct with ceremony: *marshaled into the presence of the king.* [< OF < LL *mariscalcus* groom < Gmc., lit., horse servant]

Mar·shall (mär′shəl), *n.* 1. George Catlett, 1880–1959, American general, secretary of state 1947–49, secretary of defense 1950–51. 2. John, 1755–1835, chief justice of the United States Supreme Court 1801–1835.

Marshall Islands, group of islands in the N Pacific, near the equator, formerly under Japanese supervision, now under U.S. trusteeship.

Marshall Plan, former name of the European Recovery Program.

marsh gas, methane.

marsh·mal·low (marsh′mal′ō; *often* -mel′ō), *n.* a soft, white, spongy candy, covered with powdered sugar. [OE *merscmealwe*; orig. made from the root of the marsh mallow]

marsh mallow, plant with pink flowers that grows in marshy places.

marsh marigold, cowslip.

marsh·y (mär′shi), *adj.,* marsh·i·er, marsh·i·est. 1. soft and wet like a marsh. 2. having many marshes. 3. of marshes. —**marsh′i·ness,** *n.*

mar·su·pi·al (mär·sü′pi·əl), *n.* animal that carries its young in a pouch. Kangaroos and opossums are marsupials. —*adj.* 1. of marsupials. 2. having a pouch for carrying the young.

mar·su·pi·um (mär·sü′pi·əm), *n., pl.* -pi·a (-pi·ə). pouch or fold of skin on the abdomen of a female marsupial for carrying the young. [< L < var. of Gk. *marsippion,* dim. of *marsippos* pouch]

mart (märt), *n.* market; center of trade. [< Du. *markt* MARKET]

mar·ten (mär′tən), *n., pl.* -tens or (*esp. collectively*) -ten. 1. a slender animal like a weasel, but larger. 2. its valuable fur. [< OF *martrine,* ult. < Gmc.]

Mar·tha (mär′thə), *n. Bible.* sister of Lazarus and Mary. Luke 10:38–42.

mar·tial (mär′shəl), *adj.* 1. of war; suitable for war: *martial music.* 2. fond of fighting; warlike; brave: *martial spirit.* [< L *Martialis* < *Mars* Mars] —**mar′tial·ly,** *adv.*

Mar·tial (mär′shəl), *n.* 40?–102? A.D., Roman poet famous for his witty epigrams.

martial law, rule by the army or militia with special military courts instead of by the usual civil authorities, as during war.

Mar·tian (mär′shən), *adj.* of the planet Mars. —*n.* a supposed inhabitant of the planet Mars.

mar·tin (mär′tən), *n.* swallow with a short beak and a forked or square tail. [from the name *Martin*]

mar·ti·net (mär′tə·net′; mär′tə·net), *n.* person who enforces very strict discipline. [after J. Martinet, French general]

Purple martin (ab. 8 in. long)

mar·tin·gale (mär′tən·gāl), *n.* 1. strap of a horse's harness that prevents the horse from rising on its hind legs or throwing back its head. 2. rope or spar that steadies the jib boom on a ship. [< F]

mar·ti·ni (mär·tē′ni), *n., pl.* -nis. *Am.* a cocktail containing gin and dry vermouth.

Mar·ti·nique (mär′tə·nēk′), *n.* island in the West Indies, since 1946 an overseas department of France.

age, cāre, fär; ēqual, tėrm; īce; ōpen, ôrder; pùt, rüle, ūse; th, then; ə=a in about.

mar·tyr (mär′tər), *n.* 1. person who chooses to die or suffer rather than renounce his faith; person who is put to death or made to suffer greatly for his religion or other beliefs. 2. person who suffers great pain or anguish. —*v.* 1. put (a person) to death or torture because of his religion or other beliefs. 2. cause to suffer greatly; torture. [< L < Gk., witness] —**mar′-tyr·dom,** *n.*

mar·vel (mär′vəl), *n., v.,* -veled, -vel·ing; *esp. Brit.* -velled, -vel·ling. —*n.* something wonderful; astonishing thing: *the marvels of science.* —*v.* be filled with wonder. [< OF < VL < L *mirabilia* wonders, ult. < *mirus* strange]

mar·vel·ous, *esp. Brit.* **mar·vel·lous** (mär′vəl·əs), *adj.* 1. wonderful; extraordinary. 2. improbable. —**mar′vel·ous·ly,** *esp. Brit.* **mar′vel·lous·ly,** *adv.* —**mar′vel·ous·ness,** *esp. Brit.* **mar′vel·lous·ness,** *n.* —**Syn.** 1. astonishing, stupendous, amazing.

Marx (märks), *n.* Karl, 1818–1883, German writer on economics and advocate of socialism. —**Marx·i·an** (märk′si·ən), *adj., n.* —**Marx′ism,** *n.* —**Marx′ist,** *n., adj.*

Mar·y (mãr′i), *n. Bible.* mother of Jesus. Matt. 1:18–25.

Mary I, 1516–1558, queen of England 1553–1558 and wife of Philip II of Spain.

Mary II, 1662–1694, queen of England 1689–1694, ruling with her husband William III.

Mar·y·land (mer′ə·lənd), *n.* an Eastern State of the United States. *Capital:* Annapolis. *Abbrev.:* Md. —**Mar′y·land·er,** *n. Am.*

Mary Magdalene, *Bible.* woman from whom Jesus cast out seven devils. Luke 8:2.

Mary, Queen of Scots, or **Mary Stuart,** 1542–1587, queen of Scotland from 1542 to 1567, beheaded by order of her cousin, Queen Elizabeth.

mar·zi·pan (mär′zə·pan), *n.* ground almonds and sugar, molded into various forms. Also, **marchpane.** [< G < Ital. *marzapane* < unrecorded Ar. *marṭabān* porcelain container]

Ma·sa·ryk (mä′sä·rik), *n.* Tomáš, 1850–1937, first president of Czechoslovakia, 1918–1935.

masc., masculine.

mas·car·a (mas·kar′ə), *n.* preparation used for coloring the eyelashes. [< Sp., mask]

mas·cot (mas′kot), *n.* animal, person, or thing supposed to bring good luck. [< F *mascotte,* ult. < Pr. *masco* witch]

mas·cu·line (mas′kyə·lin), *adj.* 1. of men; male. 2. like a man; manly; strong; vigorous. 3. having qualities suited to a man; mannish. 4. *Gram.* of the gender of male names. *Actor, king, ram,* and *bull* are masculine nouns. —*n. Gram.* 1. masculine gender. 2. word or form in the masculine gender. [< L *masculinus,* ult. < *mas* male] —**mas′cu·line·ly,** *adv.* —**mas′cu·lin′i·ty,** **mas′cu·line·ness,** *n.*

Mase·field (mãs′fēld; māz′-), *n.* John, born 1874, English poet, dramatist, and novelist.

mash (mash), *n.* 1. a soft mixture; soft mass. 2. a warm mixture of bran or meal and water for horses and other animals. 3. crushed malt or meal soaked in hot water for making beer. —*v.* 1. beat into a soft mass; crush to a uniform mass. 2. mix crushed malt or meal with hot water in brewing. [OE *māsc-*]

mash·er (mash′ər), *n.* 1. one that mashes. 2. *Am., Slang.* man who makes advances to women.

mash·ie, mash·y (mash′i), *n., pl.* **mash·ies.** *Golf.* club with a short sloping face made of steel.

mask (mask; mäsk), *n.* 1. a covering to hide or protect the face: *the burglar wore a mask.* 2. covering for the face or head of an actor, made to suggest the character he represents. 3. false face worn for amusement. 4. thing that hides or disguises: *he hid his evil plans under a mask of friendship.* 5. clay, wax, or plaster likeness of a person's face. 6. masque. —*v.* 1. cover (the face) with a mask. 2. hide; disguise: *a smile masked his disappointment.* [< F < Ital. *maschera* < Ar. *maskhara* laughingstock < *sakhira* to ridicule] —**mask′er,** *n.* —**Syn. v.** 2. conceal.

mas·och·ism (mas′ək·iz·əm; maz′-), *n.* perversion in which sexual pleasure is derived from the experience of physical pain. [after L. von Sacher *Masoch,* who described it in his novels] —**mas′och·ist,** *n.* —**mas′och·is′tic,** *adj.*

ma·son (mā′sən), *n.* 1. man whose work is building with stone or brick. 2. Often, **Mason.** member of the world-wide secret society of Freemasons. [< OF, ult. < VL *maccare* beat < Gmc.]

Ma·son-Dix·on line (mā′sən·dik′sən), **Mason and Dixon's line,** *Am.* boundary between Pennsylvania and Maryland, as laid out in 1763–67, formerly thought of as separating the North and the South of the United States or the free and slave States.

ma·son·ic, Ma·son·ic (mə·son′ik), *adj.* having to do with the Freemasons or Freemasonry.

ma·son·ry (mā′sən·ri), *n., pl.* -ries. 1. work built by a mason; stonework; brickwork. 2. trade or skill of a mason. 3. Often, **Masonry. a.** principles or doctrines of the society of Freemasons. **b.** members of this society.

masque (mask; mäsk), *n.* 1. a former amateur dramatic entertainment in which fine costumes, scenery, music, and dancing were more important than the story. 2. play written for such an entertainment. 3. a masked ball; masquerade. Also, **mask.** [< F. See MASK.] —**mas′quer,** *n.*

mas·quer·ade (mas′kər·ād′), *n., v.,* -ad·ed, -ad·ing. —*n.* 1. party or dance at which masks and fancy costumes are worn. 2. false pretense; disguise. —*v.* 1. take part in a masquerade. 2. disguise oneself; go about under false pretenses: *the king masqueraded as a beggar.* [< F < Ital. < *maschera* MASK] —**mas′quer·ad′er,** *n.*

mass¹ (mas), *n.* 1. lump: *mass of dough.* 2. large quantity together: *mass of treasure.* 3. majority; greater part: *the mass of the people.* 4. bulk; size. 5. quantity of matter a body contains: *the mass of a piece of lead is not changed by melting it.* 6. the masses, the common people; the working classes; the lower classes. —*v.* form or collect into a mass; assemble: *mass the peonies behind the roses.* [< L *massa* kneaded dough < Gk. *maza* barley bread < *massein* knead] —**Syn.** 2. aggregate, accumulation. —*v.* amass, gather, accumulate.

Mass, mass² (mas), *n.* 1. central service of worship in the Roman Catholic Church and some other churches; Holy Eucharist as a sacrifice. The Mass consists of various prayers and ceremonies. 2. music written for certain parts of it. [< LL *missa* < L *mittere* send away]

Mass., Massachusetts.

Mas·sa·chu·setts (mas′ə·chü′sits; -zits), *n.* a New England State of the United States. *Capital:* Boston. *Abbrev.:* Mass.

mas·sa·cre (mas′ə·kər), *n., v.,* -cred, -cring. —*n.* wholesale, pitiless slaughter of people or animals. —*v.* kill (many people or animals) needlessly or cruelly; slaughter in large numbers. [< F, in OF *macecle* shambles] —**mas·sa·crer** (mas′ə·krər), *n.* —**Syn.** *n.* butchery, carnage.

mas·sage (mə·säzh′), *n., v.,* -saged, -sag·ing. —*n.* a rubbing and kneading of the muscles and joints to make them work better and to increase the circulation of blood. —*v.* give a massage to. [< F, ult. < *masse* mass] —**mas·sag′er, mas·sag′ist,** *n.*

mas·seur (ma·sœr′), *n.* person whose work is massaging people. [< F]

mas·seuse (ma·sœz′), *n.* woman masseur. [< F]

mas·sive (mas′iv), *adj.* 1. big and heavy; large and solid; bulky. 2. imposing; impressive. —**mas′sive·ly,** *adv.* —**mas′sive·ness,** *n.* —**Syn.** 1. weighty, ponderous, huge.

mass meeting, *Am.* a large public gathering of people to hear or discuss some matter of common interest.

mass production, making of goods in large quantities by machinery.

mass·y (mas′i), *adj.,* mass·i·er, mass·i·est. massive. —**mass′i·ness,** *n.*

mast¹ (mast; mäst), *n.* 1. a long pole of wood

or steel set upright on a ship to support the sails and rigging. 2. **before the mast**, as a common sailor. 3. any upright pole. [OE *mæst*]

mast² (mast; mäst), *n.* acorns, chestnuts, beechnuts, etc., esp. as food for pigs. [OE *mæst*]

mas·ter (mas′tər; mäs′–), *n.* 1. person who has power or authority; one in control; employer; owner. 2. man at the head of a household. 3. captain of a merchant ship. 4. *Esp. Brit.* teacher. 5. person whose teachings one follows or accepts. 6. **the Master,** Christ. 7. person with much knowledge; expert. 8. a skilled worker; craftsman in business for himself: *master carpenter.* 9. a great artist. 10. picture or painting by a great artist. 11. title of respect for a boy: *young Master George.* 12. victor. 13. Also, **Master.** a. person who has taken a certain advanced degree at a college or university. b. the degree. 14. a court officer appointed to assist the judge. —*adj.* 1. being master; of a master: *a master key.* 2. main; controlling. —*v.* 1. become master of; conquer; control. 2. become expert in; become skillful at: *master French.* [< L *magister*; cf. *magis* more] —mas′ter·dom, *n.* —mas′ter·less, *adj.* —Syn. *n.* 1. chief, ruler, commander, manager, director. –*v.* 1. overcome, subjugate, subdue.

master builder, 1. architect. 2. contractor.

mas·ter·ful (mas′tər·fəl; mäs′–), *adj.* 1. fond of power or authority; domineering. 2. expert; skillful. —mas′ter·ful·ly, *adv.* —mas′ter·ful·ness, *n.* —Syn. 1. imperious, lordly.

mas·ter·ly (mas′tər·li; mäs′–), *adj.* expert; skillful. —*adv.* expertly; skillfully. —mas′ter·li·ness, *n.* —Syn. *adj.* proficient, finished.

mas·ter·mind (mas′tər·mīnd′, mäs′–), *n.* person who plans and supervises a scheme of action, usually from behind the scenes. —mas′ter·mind, *v.*

master of ceremonies, person in charge of a ceremony or entertainment who makes sure that all its parts occur in the proper order.

mas·ter·piece (mas′tər·pēs′; mäs′–), *n.* 1. anything done or made with wonderful skill. 2. person's greatest work.

Mas·ters (mas′tərz; mäs′–), *n.* Edgar Lee, 1869–1950, American poet.

master sergeant, *U.S. Army.* the highest ranking noncommissioned officer, formerly next above technical sergeant, since 1948 next above sergeant first class.

mas·ter·ship (mas′tər·ship; mäs′–), *n.* 1. position of a master. 2. position of a teacher in a school. 3. power; control. 4. great skill.

master stroke, very skillful act or achievement.

mas·ter·y (mas′tər·i; –tri; mäs′–), *n., pl.* –ter·ies. 1. power such as a master has; control: *the mastery of the seas.* 2. the upper hand; victory. 3. great skill; expert knowledge: *mastery of a foreign language.* —Syn. 1. command, rule, sway. 2. triumph. 3. grasp.

mast·head (mast′hed′; mäst′–), *n.* 1. top of a ship's mast. 2. *Am.* that part of a newspaper or magazine that gives the title, owner, address, rates, etc.

mas·tic (mas′tik), *n.* a yellowish resin used in making varnish, chewing gum, and incense, and as an astringent. [< OF < L < Gk. *mastiche*]

mas·ti·cate (mas′tə·kāt), *v.,* –cat·ed, –cat·ing. 1. chew. 2. reduce to a pulp. [< LL, < *masticare* < Gk. *mastichaein* gnash the teeth] —mas′ti·ca′tion, *n.* —mas′ti·ca′tor, *n.*

mas·ti·ca·to·ry (mas′tə·kə·tô′ri; –tō′–), *adj., n., pl.* –ries. —*adj.* of or used in chewing. —*n.* substance chewed to increase the flow of saliva.

mas·tiff (mas′tif; mäs′–), *n.* a large, strong dog with drooping ears and hanging lips. [< OF *mastin,* ult. < L *mansuetus* tame]

mas·to·don (mas′tə·don), *n.* a very large extinct animal much like an elephant. [< NL, < Gk. *mastos* breast + *odon* tooth]

mas·toid (mas′toid), *n.* Also, **mastoid process.** projection of bone behind the ear. —*adj.* of this bone. [< Gk., < *mastos* breast + *eidos* form]

mas·toid·i·tis (mas′toid·ī′tis), *n.* inflammation of the mastoid.

mas·tur·ba·tion (mas′tər·bā′shən), *n.* sexual self-abuse. [< L *masturbatio,* ult. < *manus* hand + *stuprum* defilement]

ma·su·ri·um (mə·sur′i·əm), *n. Chem.* former name of the element technetium. [from *Masuria,* in Poland]

mat¹ (mat), *n., v.,* mat·ted, mat·ting. —*n.* 1. piece of coarse fabric like a rug, made of woven grass, straw, rope, etc. 2. piece of material to put under a dish, vase, lamp, etc. 3. a large thick pad used to protect wrestlers or gymnasts. 4. anything packed or tangled thickly together: *mat of weeds.* —*v.* 1. cover with mats. 2. pack or tangle thickly together. [< LL *matta*]

mat² (mat), *n.* border or background for a picture, between it and the frame. [< F, orig. adj., dull, dead. See MAT³.]

mat³ (mat), *adj., n., v.,* mat·ted, mat·ting. —*adj.* dull; not shiny. —*n.* a dull surface or finish. —*v.* give a dull finish to. [< F, < *mater* subdue, CHECKMATE]

mat·a·dor (mat′ə·dôr), *n.* man appointed to kill the bull in bullfights. [< Sp., ult. < *mate* dead < Ar. *māt*]

match¹ (mach), *n.* 1. a short, slender piece of wood, pasteboard, etc., tipped with a mixture that takes fire when rubbed on a rough or specially prepared surface. 2. cord prepared to burn at a uniform rate, for firing guns, cannon, etc. [< OF *meiche,* prob. ult. < Gk. *myxa* lamp wick]

Matador

match² (mach), *n.* 1. person or thing equal to another: *a boy is not a match for a man.* 2. person or thing like another. 3. two persons or things that are alike or go well together: *her hat is a match for her coat.* 4. game; contest. 5. marriage. 6. person considered as a possible husband or wife. —*v.* 1. be equal to; be a match for: *no one could match him in singing.* 2. be alike; go well together: *the rugs and the wallpaper match.* 3. be the same as. 4. find one like; get a match for: *match a color.* 5. make like; fit together: *match one's gloves to one's shoes.* 6. put in opposition; oppose: *Tom matched his strength against Bob's.* 7. match coins, toss or reveal coins to decide something. 8. marry. [OE *gemæcca* companion] —match′er, *n.* —Syn. *n.* 4. competition, tournament, tourney.

match·less (mach′lis), *adj.* so great or wonderful that it cannot be equaled. —match′-less·ly, *adv.* —match′-less·ness, *n.* —Syn. unequaled, unparalleled, unrivaled, peerless, incomparable.

match·lock (mach′-lok′), *n.* 1. an old form of gun fired by lighting the powder with a wick or cord. 2. the mechanism for firing it.

Soldier using a matchlock

match·mak·er¹ (mach′māk′ər), *n.* 1. person who arranges, or tries to arrange, marriages for others. 2. person who arranges contests, prize fights, races, etc. —match′mak′ing, *n., adj.*

match·mak·er² (mach′māk′ər), *n.* person who makes matches for burning.

mate¹ (māt), *n., v.,* mat·ed, mat·ing. —*n.* 1. one of a pair: *where is the mate to this glove?* 2. husband or wife. 3. a ship's officer next below the captain. 4. assistant: *gunner's mate.* 5. companion; fellow worker. —*v.* 1. join in a pair: *birds mate in the spring.* 2. marry. [appar. < MLG *mate* messmate; akin to MEAT] —Syn. *n.* 1. match. 5. comrade, crony, colleague.

mate² (māt), *n., v.,* mat·ed, mat·ing. defeat in the game of chess. [< OF *mater* CHECKMATE]

ma·té, ma·te³ (mä′tā; mat′ā), *n.* 1. kind of tea made from the dried leaves of a South American plant. 2. the plant. 3. its leaves. [< Sp., < Kechua (Ind. lang. of Peru) *mati* calabash dish]

ma·ter (mā′tər), *n. Brit. Colloq.* mother. [< L]

ma·te·ri·al (mə·tir′i·əl), *n.* 1. what a thing is made from; matter or articles needed for making or doing something: *dress material, building materials.* 2. fabric: *what is the material of that coat?* —*adj.* 1. having to do with whatever occupies space; physical. 2. of, relating to, or involved with matter: *material laws.* 3. of the body: *material comforts.* 4. caring too much for the things of this world and neglecting spiritual needs. 5. that matters; important: *no material objections to the plan.* [< L, < *materia* timber, matter < *mater* trunk (of a tree). Doublet of MATÉRIEL.] —*Syn. n.* 1. substance. 2. cloth, goods. —*adj.* 1. substantial. 3. bodily. 5. essential, necessary.

ma·te·ri·al·ism (mə·tir′i·əl·iz′əm), *n.* 1. belief that all action, thought, and feeling can be explained by the movements and changes of matter. 2. tendency to care too much for the things of this world and neglect spiritual needs. —ma·te′ri·al·ist, *n.* —ma·te′ri·al·is′tic, *adj.* —ma·te′ri·al·is′ti·cal·ly, *adv.*

ma·te·ri·al·ize (mə·tir′i·əl·īz), *v.*, –ized, –izing. 1. *Am.* become an actual fact; be realized: *our plans did not materialize.* 2. give material form to: *an inventor materializes his ideas by building a model.* 3. *Am.* appear in bodily form: *a spirit materialized from the smoke of the magician's fire.* 4. cause to appear in bodily form. —ma·te′ri·al·i·za′tion, *n.* —ma·te′ri·al·iz′er, *n.*

ma·te·ri·al·ly (mə·tir′i·əl·i), *adv.* 1. physically. 2. considerably; greatly. 3. in matter or substance; not in form.

ma·te·ri·a med·i·ca (mə·tir′i·ə med′ə·kə), 1. drugs or other substances used in medicine. 2. branch of medical science dealing with these drugs and substances. [< NL, healing matter]

ma·té·ri·el (mə·tir′i·el′), *n.* everything used by an army, organization, undertaking, etc.; equipment. [< F, material. Doublet of MATERIAL.]

ma·ter·nal (mə·tėr′nəl), *adj.* 1. of or like a mother; motherly. 2. related on the mother's side of the family: *everyone has two maternal grandparents.* 3. received or inherited from a mother. [< F *maternel*, ult. < L *mater* mother] —ma·ter′nal·ly, *adv.*

ma·ter·ni·ty (mə·tėr′nə·ti), *n.* 1. motherhood; being a mother. 2. motherliness; qualities of a mother. —*adj.* for a woman soon to have a baby: *a maternity hospital.*

math., mathematics.

math·e·mat·i·cal (math′ə·mat′ə·kəl; math·mat′-), **math·e·mat·ic** (–ik), *adj.* 1. of or having to do with mathematics: *mathematical problems.* 2. exact; accurate. —math′e·mat′i·cal·ly, *adv.*

math·e·ma·ti·cian (math′ə·mə·tish′ən; math′mə–), *n.* person skilled in mathematics.

math·e·mat·ics (math′ə·mat′iks; math·mat′-), *n.* science dealing with numbers and the measurement, properties, and relationships of quantities. Mathematics includes arithmetic, algebra, geometry, calculus, etc. [pl. of *mathematic* < L < Gk. *mathematikos*, ult. < *manthanein* learn]

mat·i·née, mat·i·nee (mat′ə·nā′; *esp. Brit.* mat′ə·nā), *n.* a dramatic or musical performance held in the afternoon. [< F, < *matin* morning]

ma·tins (mat′ənz), *n.pl.* 1. first of the seven canonical hours in the breviary. 2. morning prayers in the Church of England. 3. *matin, Poetic.* morning song. [< OF, < LL *matutinus* of or in the morning]

Ma·tisse (mä·tēs′), *n.* Henri, 1869–1954, French painter.

ma·tri·arch (mā′tri·ärk), *n.* 1. mother who is the ruler of a family or tribe. 2. a venerable old woman. [< *matri-* (L *mater* mother) + (*patri*) *arch*] —ma′tri·ar′chal, ma′tri·ar′chic, *adj.*

ma·tri·arch·y (mā′tri·är′ki), *n., pl.* –chies.

form of social organization in which the mother is the ruler of a family or tribe, descent being traced through the mother.

ma·tri·cide¹ (mā′trə·sīd; mat′rə–), *n.* act of killing one's mother. [< L, < *mater* mother + *-cidium* act of killing] —ma′tri·cid′al, *adj.*

ma·tri·cide² (mā′trə·sīd; mat′rə–), *n.* person who kills his mother. [< L, < *mater* mother + *-cida* killer]

ma·tric·u·late (mə·trik′yə·lāt), *v.*, –lat·ed, –lat·ing. enroll as a student in a college or university. [< LL *matricula*, dim. of L *matrix* register] —ma·tric′u·la′tion, *n.*

mat·ri·mo·ny (mat′rə·mō′ni), *n., pl.* –nies. 1. married life. 2. act of marrying; rite or ceremony of marriage. 3. relation between married persons. [< L *matrimonium* < *mater* mother] —mat′ri·mo′ni·al, *adj.* —mat′ri·mo′ni·al·ly, *adv.*

ma·trix (mā′triks; mat′riks), *n., pl.* **ma·tri·ces** (mā′trə·sēz; mat′rə–), **ma·trix·es.** 1. that which gives origin or form to something enclosed within it. A mold for a casting is a matrix. 2. womb. [< L, womb]

ma·tron (mā′trən), *n.* 1. wife or widow, esp. one who is fairly old. 2. woman who manages the household affairs or supervises the inmates of a school, hospital, or other institution: *a police matron.* [< OF < L *matrona* < *mater* mother] —ma·tron·al (mā′trən·əl; mat′rən–), *adj.* —ma′tron·like′, *adj.* —ma′tron·ly, *adv.* —ma′tron·li·ness, *n.*

matron of honor, *Am.* a married woman who is the chief attendant of the bride at a wedding.

Mat·su (mät·st′), *n.* a small island close to the coast of SE China.

Matt., Matthew.

mat·ted (mat′id), *adj.* formed into a mat; entangled in a thick mass.

mat·ter (mat′ər), *n.* 1. what things are made of; material. Matter occupies space. 2. some particular kind of substance: *coloring matter.* 3. words written or printed. 4. what is said or written, thought of apart from the way in which it is said or written: *the matter of a speech.* 5. grounds; occasion; cause: *matter for complaint.* 6. thing; things: *matter of record.* 7. affair: *a matter of life and death.* 8. amount; quantity: *a matter of 20 miles.* 9. importance; significance. 10. difficulty; trouble: *what's the matter?* 11. mail. Letters are first-class matter. 12. pus. —*v.* 1. be of importance. 2. form or discharge pus; suppurate. [< OF < L *materia*, orig., timber] —*Syn. n.* 1. substance, stuff. 4. topic, subject. 9. moment, weight, concern.

Mat·ter·horn (mat′ər·hôrn), *n.* a mountain peak in the Alps, between Switzerland and Italy.

matter of course, something to be expected.

mat·ter-of-fact (mat′ər·əv·fakt′), *adj.* dealing with facts; not fanciful; unimaginative: *a matter-of-fact account of the accident.*

Mat·thew (math′ū), *n.* 1. one of the twelve disciples chosen by Jesus as his Apostles. 2. first book of the New Testament, telling the story of the life of Christ.

mat·ting (mat′ing), *n.* fabric of grass, straw, hemp, or other fiber, for covering floors, etc.

mat·tock (mat′ək), *n.* tool like a pickax, but having a flat blade on one side or flat blades on both sides, used for loosening soil and cutting roots. [OE *mattuc*]

mat·tress (mat′ris), *n.* a covering of strong cloth stuffed with hair, cotton, straw, etc., used on a bed or as a bed. [< OF < Ital. < Ar. *al-matrah* the cushion]

mat·u·rate (mach′ú·rāt), *v.*, –rat·ed, –rating. 1. discharge pus; suppurate. 2. ripen. [< L *maturus* ripe] —mat′u·ra′tion, *n.* —ma·tu·ra·tive (mach′ú·rā′tiv; mə·chúr′ə·tiv), *adj.*

ma·ture (mə·chûr′; –tūr′; –tyūr′), *adj., v.*, –tured, –tur·ing. —*adj.* 1. ripe; full-grown: *fifty is a mature age.* 2. fully worked out; carefully thought out; fully developed: *mature plans.* 3. due; payable: *a mature note.* —*v.* 1. come to full growth; ripen. 2. bring to full growth. 3. work out carefully. 4. fall due. [< L *maturus* ripe]

—ma·ture′ly, adv. —ma·ture′ness, n. —Syn. adj. 2. perfected, thorough.

ma·tu·ri·ty (mə·chŭr′ə·ti; -tûr′-; -tyŭr′-), n. 1. full development; ripeness. 2. a being completed or ready. 3. a falling due; time a debt is payable.

ma·tu·ti·nal (mə·tū′tə·nəl; -tū′-), adj. occurring in the morning; early in the day; having to do with the morning. [< LL, < matutinus of or in the morning] —ma·tu′ti·nal·ly, adv.

matz·oth (mät′sōth), matz·os (mät′sōs; pop. -səz), n.pl. thin pieces of unleavened bread, eaten by Jews during the Passover. [< Heb. matstsōth, pl. of matstsāh, unleavened bread]

maud·lin (môd′lən), adj. 1. sentimental in a weak, silly way: a maudlin sympathy for criminals. 2. sentimental and tearful because of drunkenness or excitement. [alter. of Mary Magdalene, often painted as weeping]

Maugham (môm), n. (William) Somerset, 1874–1965, English author.

mau·gre, mau·ger (mô′gər), prep. Archaic. in spite of. [< OF, orig. n., ill will, spite]

Mau·i (mou′i), n. the second largest island of Hawaii.

maul (môl), n. a very heavy hammer or mallet. —v. beat and pull about; handle roughly: the lion mauled its keeper badly. [var. of mall]

Mau Mau (mou′ mou′), a secret society, active during the 1950's, of (chiefly) Kikuyu tribesmen engaged in activities, generally violent, designed to expel Europeans from Kenya.

Mau·na Lo·a (mou′nə lō′ə), an active volcano in Hawaii.

maun·der (môn′dər), v. 1. talk in a rambling, foolish way. 2. move or act in an aimless, confused manner. —maun′der·er, n.

Maun·dy Thursday (môn′di), the Thursday before Easter. [< OF mande < L mandatum a command]

Mau·ri·ta·ni·a (mô′rə·tā′ni·ə; -tān′yə), n. a republic in W Africa on the Atlantic, formerly part of French West Africa.

Mau·ser (mou′zər), n. Trademark. a kind of powerful repeating rifle or pistol. [after Paul Mauser, inventor]

mau·so·le·um (mô′sə·lē′əm), n., pl. -le·ums, -le·a (-lē′ə), a large, magnificent tomb. [< L < Gk. Mausoleion, tomb of a king, Mausolus]

mauve (mōv), n., adj. delicate, pale purple. [< F < L malva mallow]

mav·er·ick (mav′ər·ik), n. Am. 1. W. calf or other animal not marked with an owner's brand. 2. Colloq. one who does not conform to the policies of his group or refuses to fall in with a regular political party. [prob. after S. Maverick, Texan who did not brand his cattle]

ma·vis (mā′vis), n. a European song thrush. [< OF mauvis < Celtic]

ma·vour·neen, ma·vour·nin (mə·vûr′nēn), n. Irish. my darling. [< Irish mo muirnín]

maw (mô), n. 1. mouth. 2. throat. 3. stomach. [OE maga]

mawk·ish (môk′ish), adj. 1. sickening. 2. sickly sentimental; weakly emotional. [orig., maggoty < mawk maggot < Scand. mathkr] —mawk·ish·ly, adv. —mawk′ish·ness, n.

max., maximum.

max·il·la (mak·sil′ə), n., pl. -il·lae (-sil′ē). 1. jaw; jawbone; upper jawbone. 2. either of a pair of appendages just behind the mandibles of insects, crabs, etc. [< L, jaw] —max·il·lar·y (mak′sə·ler′i), adj.

MANDIBLES
MAXILLAE

max·im (mak′səm), n. a short rule of conduct; proverb; statement of a general truth. [< F < LL maxima (propositio) axiom]

Max·i·mil·ian (mak′sə·mil′yən), n. 1832–1867, archduke of Austria, emperor of Mexico, 1864–1867.

max·i·mize (mak′sə·mīz), v. -mized, -miz·ing. increase to the highest possible amount or degree. —max′i·mi·za′tion, n.

max·i·mum (mak′sə·məm), n., pl. -mums, -ma (-mə), adj. —n. the largest or highest amount; greatest possible amount. —adj. largest; highest; greatest possible: the maximum score on the test is 100. [< L, neut. adj., greatest, superl. of magnus great]

may (mā), auxiliary v., pt. might. 1. possibility, opportunity, or permission: you may enter. 2. wish or prayer: may you be very happy. 3. contingency, esp. in clauses expressing condition, concession, purpose, result, etc: I write that you may know my plans. 4. ability or power (more commonly can). [OE mæg (inf., magan)] ➤ See can for usage note.

May (mā), n. the fifth month of the year, having 31 days. [< L Maius]

Ma·ya (mä′yə), n. 1. member of a race of Indians living in Central America. 2. their language. —adj. of the Mayas or their language. —Ma′yan, adj., n.

May apple, Am. 1. plant with a large, white flower; mandrake. 2. its yellowish, egg-shaped fruit.

may·be (mā′bi), adv. possibly; perhaps. ➤ maybe, may be. Maybe is an adverb meaning "perhaps," a cutting down of it may be; may be is a verb form: Maybe you'll have better luck next time. He may be the next mayor.

May Day, May 1, often celebrated by crowning the May queen and dancing around the Maypole or, in some parts of the world, by labor parades and meetings.

May·flow·er (mā′flou′ər), n. 1. ship on which the Pilgrims came to America in 1620. 2. plant whose flowers blossom in May; trailing arbutus (in the U.S.); hawthorn or cowslip (in England).

May fly, a slender insect, having the forewings much larger than the hind wings, that dies soon after reaching the adult stage; ephemerid.

may·hap (mā′hap′; mā′hap), adv. Archaic. perhaps. [for it may hap]

may·hem (mā′hem; -əm), n. Law. crime of intentionally maiming a person or injuring him so that he is less able to defend himself. [< OF mahaigne]

may·n't (mā′ənt), may not.

may·on·naise (mā′ə·nāz′), n. a salad dressing made of egg yolks, olive oil, vinegar or lemon juice, and seasoning, beaten together until thick. [< F, ult. < Mahon, Minorca]

may·or (mā′ər; mâr), n. the chief official of a city or town. [< OF maire, maor < L major. Doublet of MAJOR.] —may′or·ship, n.

may·or·al·ty (mā′ər·əl·ti; mâr′əl·ti), n., pl. -ties. 1. position of mayor. 2. mayor's term of office.

May·pole, may·pole (mā′pōl′), n. a high pole decorated with flowers or ribbons, around which merrymakers dance on May Day.

mayst (māst), v. Archaic. may. "Thou mayst" means "you may."

Maz·a·rin (maz′ə·rin), n. Jules, 1602–1661, French cardinal and statesman, born in Italy.

maze (māz), n. 1. network of paths through which it is hard to find one's way. 2. state of confusion; muddled condition. [var. of amaze] —Syn. 1. labyrinth. 2. bewilderment, perplexity.

ma·zur·ka, ma·zour·ka (mə·zėr′kə; -zůr′-), n. 1. a lively Polish dance. 2. music for it. [< Polish, woman of Mazovia in Poland]

Maz·zi·ni (mät·sē′ni), n. Giuseppe, 1805–1872, leader in the movement for uniting Italy.

M.C., 1. Master of Ceremonies. 2. Am. Member of Congress.

Mc·Clel·lan (mə·klel′ən), n. George B., 1826–1885, Union general in the U.S. Civil War.

Mc·Cor·mick (mə·kôr′mik), n. Cyrus Hall, 1809–1884, American inventor.

Mc·Coy (mə·koi′), n. the real, Am. a genuine person or thing.

Mc·Kin·ley (mə·kin′li), n. 1. William, 1843–1901, the 25th president of the United States, 1897–1901. 2. Mount, mountain in C Alaska, the highest peak in North America.

Md., Maryland.

M.D., Doctor of Medicine.
M-day (em′dā′), n. mobilization day.
mdse., merchandise.
me (mē; *unstressed* mi), *pron.* the objective, or accusative, case of I: *the dog bit me, give me a bandage.* [OE *mē*]
Me., Maine.
ME, Middle English.
mead[1] (mēd), n. *Poetic.* meadow. [OE *mǣd*]
mead[2] (mēd), n. an alcoholic drink made from fermented honey and water. [OE *medu*]
Mead (mēd), n. Lake, lake formed by Hoover Dam in the Colorado River, the largest artificial lake in the world.
Meade (mēd), n. George Gordon, 1815–1872, Union general in the U.S. Civil War.
mead·ow (med′ō), n. **1.** piece of grassy land; field where hay is grown. **2.** low, grassy land near a stream. [OE *mǣdwe*, oblique case of *mǣd* mead[1]] —**mead′ow·y,** adj.
meadow lark, Am. songbird with a black crescent on a yellow breast.
mea·ger, mea·gre (mē′gər), adj. **1.** poor; scanty: *meager fare.* **2.** thin; lean: *a meager man.* [< F < L *macer* thin] —**mea′ger·ly, mea′gre·ly,** adv. —**mea′ger·ness, mea′gre·ness,** n. —Syn. **1.** sparse, stinted. **2.** spare, lank, gaunt, emaciated.

Meadow lark
(ab. 10 in. long)

meal[1] (mēl), n. **1.** breakfast, lunch, dinner, supper, or tea. **2.** food served or eaten at one time. [OE *mǣl*]
meal[2] (mēl), n. **1.** ground grain, esp. corn meal. **2.** anything ground to a powder. [OE *melu*]
meal·ie (mēl′i), n. *South African.* ear of corn.
meal·time (mēl′tīm′), n. the usual time for eating a meal.
meal·y (mēl′i), adj., **meal·i·er, meal·i·est. 1.** like meal; dry and powdery. **2.** of meal. **3.** containing meal. **4.** pale. —**meal′i·ness,** n.
meal·y-mouthed (mēl′i·mouтнd′; -mouтнt′), adj. unwilling to tell the straight truth in plain words; using soft words insincerely.
mean[1] (mēn), v., **meant, mean·ing. 1.** have as a purpose; have in mind; intend: *I do not mean to go.* **2.** intend for a particular purpose, person, etc.: *we meant the gift for you.* **3.** have intentions: *he means well.* **4.** intend to express or indicate: *keep out; that means you.* **5.** signify; import; denote: *what does this word mean?* [OE *mǣnan*] —Syn. **1.** design, purpose.
mean[2] (mēn), adj. **1.** low in quality or grade; poor. **2.** low in social position or rank; humble. **3.** of little importance or value: *the meanest flower.* **4.** of poor appearance; shabby: *a mean appearance.* **5.** small-minded; ignoble: *mean thoughts.* **6.** stingy: *mean about money.* **7.** *Colloq.* humiliated; ashamed: *feel mean.* **8.** *Colloq.* hard to manage; troublesome; bad-tempered: *a mean horse.* **9.** *Colloq.* in poor physical condition; unwell: *I feel mean today.* [OE *(ge)mǣne* common] —**mean′ly,** adv. —**mean′ness,** n. —Syn. **2.** common, plebeian. **3.** insignificant, obscure, petty. **5.** base, contemptible, despicable.
mean[3] (mēn), adj. **1.** halfway between two extremes. **2.** intermediate in kind, quality, or degree. —n. **1.** means, a. (*sing. or pl. in use*) that which a thing is done by; agency; method: *by fair means.* b. (*pl. in use*) wealth: *man of means.* **2.** condition, quality, or course of action halfway between two extremes: *a happy mean between extravagance and stinginess.* **3.** *Math.* quantity having a value intermediate between the values of other quantities, esp. the average obtained by dividing the sum of several quantities by their number. **4.** *Math.* either the second or third term of a proportion of four terms. **5. by all means,** certainly; without fail. **6. by any means,** at all; in any possible way; at any cost. **7. by means of,** by the use of; through; with. **8. by no means,**

certainly not. [< OF < L *medianus* middle < *medius*] —Syn. adj. **2.** medium, average. —n. **1. a.** device, instrumentality, expedient, shift, way. **b.** resources, funds, income, property.
me·an·der (mi·an′dər), v. **1.** follow a winding course. **2.** wander aimlessly. —n. **1.** a winding course. **2.** aimless wandering. [< L < Gk. *Maiandros,* name of a winding river]
mean·ing (mēn′ing), n. what is meant or intended; significance. —adj. that means something; expressive. —**mean′ing·ful,** adj. —**mean′ing·ful·ly,** adv. —**mean′ing·ly,** adv. —Syn. n. import, sense, gist, explanation, drift.
mean·ing·less (mēn′ing·lis), adj. without meaning; not significant. —**mean′ing·less·ly,** adv. —**mean′ing·less·ness,** n.
mean solar time, a system of reckoning time so that all the days and their like subdivisions are of equal length.
meant (ment), v. pt. and pp. of mean[1].
mean·time (mēn′tīm′), **mean·while** (-hwīl′), n. time between. —adv. in the time between.
mea·sles (mē′zəlz), n. **1.** an infectious disease characterized by a bad cold, fever, and a breaking out of small red spots on the skin. **2.** a similar but much less severe disease; German measles. [ME *maseles;* prob. infl. by ME *mezel* leprous < OF, ult. < L *miser* wretched]
mea·sly (mē′zli), adj., **-sli·er, -sli·est. 1.** of or like measles. **2.** infected with measles. **3.** *Slang.* very unsatisfactory.
meas·ur·a·ble (mezh′ər·ə·bəl; māzh′-), adj. capable of being measured. —**meas′ur·a·bil′i·ty, meas′ur·a·ble·ness,** n. —**meas′ur·a·bly,** adv.
meas·ure (mezh′ər; māzh′-), v., **-ured, -ur·ing,** n. —v. **1.** find out the extent, size, quantity, capacity, etc., of something; estimate by some standard: *measure the room.* **2.** be of specified measure: *this brick measures $2 \times 4 \times 8$ inches.* **3.** get or take by measuring: *measure out a bushel of potatoes.* **4.** take measurements; find out sizes or amounts. **5.** admit of measurement. **6.** serve as a measure of. **7.** compare. **8.** adjust: *measure one's behavior by the company one is in.* **9.** *Poetic.* travel over; traverse. **10.** measure up, Am. have the necessary qualifications. —n. **1.** act or process of finding extent, size, quantity, capacity, etc., of something, esp. by comparison with a standard. **2.** size, dimensions, quantity, etc., thus ascertained: *his waist measure is 30 inches.* **3.** instrument for measuring: *a pint measure.* **4.** system of measuring: *dry measure.* **5.** unit or standard of measuring. Inch, quart, pound, and hour are common measures. **6.** quantity or degree that should not be exceeded; reasonable limit: *angry beyond measure.* **7.** quantity; degree; proportion: *sickness is in great measure preventable.* **8.** rhythm in poetry or music. **9.** a metrical unit; foot of poetry. **10.** bar of music. **11.** dance or dance movement. **12.** course of action; procedure: *take measures to relieve suffering.* **13.** a legislative enactment. **14.** a definite quantity measured out: *drink a measure.* **15. in a measure,** to some degree; partly. **16. take one's measure,** judge one's character. [< OF < L *mensura,* n., < *mensus,* pp. of *metiri,* v., measure] —**meas′ur·er,** n. —Syn. n. **2.** extent, capacity, volume, amount. **12.** step.
meas·ured (mezh′ərd; māzh′-), adj. **1.** regular; uniform: *a measured pace.* **2.** rhythmical. **3.** deliberate and restrained: *measured speech.* —**meas′ured·ly,** adv.
meas·ure·less (mezh′ər·lis; māzh′-), adj. too great to be measured; unlimited; vast.
meas·ure·ment (mezh′ər·mənt; māzh′-), n. **1.** way of measuring: *clocks give us a measurement of time.* **2.** act or fact of measuring: *the measurement of length by a yardstick is easy.* **3.** size or amount found by measuring. **4.** system of measuring.
measuring worm, Am. larva of any geometrid; inchworm.
meat (mēt), n. **1.** animal flesh used as food. Fish and poultry are not usually called meat. **2.** food of any kind: *meat and drink.* **3.** part that can be

eaten: *meat of a nut.* 4. meal: *say grace before meat.* 5. substance; food for thought. [OE *mete*] —meat'less, *adj.*

me·a·tus (mi·ā'təs), *n., pl.* -tus·es, -tus. passage, duct, or opening (in the body). [< L, path, < *meare* pass]

meat·y (mēt'i), *adj.*, meat·i·er, meat·i·est. 1. of meat; having the flavor of meat. 2. like meat. 3. full of meat. 4. *Am.* full of substance; giving food for thought: *a meaty speech.*

Mec·ca (mek'ə), *n.* 1. city in W Saudi Arabia. Because Mohammed was born there, Mohammedans turn toward Mecca when praying and go there on pilgrimages. 2. mecca, any place that a person longs to visit or reach. —Mec'can, *adj., n.*

me·chan·ic (mə·kan'ik), *n.* 1. worker skilled with tools. 2. worker who repairs machinery. [< L < Gk., < *mechane* machine]

me·chan·i·cal (mə·kan'ə·kəl), *adj.* 1. having to do with machinery. 2. made or worked by machinery. 3. like a machine; like that of a machine; automatic; without expression: *her reading is very mechanical.* 4. of, pertaining to, or in accordance with the science of mechanics. —me·chan'i·cal·ly, *adv.*

mechanical drawing, drawing done with the help of rulers, scales, compasses, etc.

mech·a·ni·cian (mek'ə·nish'ən), *n.* worker skilled in making and repairing machines.

me·chan·ics (mə·kan'iks), *n.* 1. branch of physics dealing with the action of forces on bodies and with motion. Mechanics includes kinetics, statics, and kinematics. 2. knowledge dealing with machinery. 3. (*pl. in use*) mechanical part; technique.

mech·a·nism (mek'ə·niz·əm), *n.* 1. means or way by which something is done; machinery. 2. system of parts working together as the parts of a machine do: *the mechanism of the body.* 3. mechanical part; technique. 4. *Psychol.* arrangements in the mind or brain that determine thought, feeling, or action in regular and predictable ways. 5. theory that everything in the universe is produced by mechanical or material forces. —mech'a·nist, *n.* —mech'a·nis'tic, *adj.*

mech·a·nize (mek'ə·nīz), *v.*, -nized, -niz·ing. 1. make mechanical. 2. do by machinery, rather than by hand: *much housework can be mechanized.* 3. replace men or animals by machinery in (a business, etc.). 4. *Mil.* equip a unit with armored vehicles, tanks, and other machines. —mech'a·ni·za'tion, *n.*

Med., Medieval.

med., medical; medicine.

med·al (med'əl), *n.* a flat piece of metal with a design or words stamped on it. Medals are intended to be worn or exhibited, and are often given to persons who have done something great. Sometimes medals are made to celebrate an important event. [< F < Ital. *medaglia*, ult. < L *metallum* metal]

med·al·ist, *esp. Brit.* med·al·list (med'əl·ist), *n.* 1. person who designs or makes medals. 2. person who has won a medal.

me·dal·lion (mə·dal'yən), *n.* 1. a large medal. 2. design, ornament, etc., shaped like a medal.

med·dle (med'əl), *v.*, -dled, -dling. busy oneself with other people's things or affairs without being asked or needed. [< OF *medler*, ult. < L *miscere* mix] —med'dler, *n.* —Syn. interfere.

med·dle·some (med'əl·səm), *adj.* fond of meddling in other people's affairs; meddling. —med'dle·some·ness, *n.* —Syn. interfering, officious, intrusive.

Mede (mēd), *n.* native or inhabitant of Media.

Me·de·a (mi·dē'ə), *n. Gk. Legend.* enchantress who helped Jason get the Golden Fleece.

Med. Gk., Medieval Greek.

me·di·a (mē'di·ə), *n.* pl. of medium.

Me·di·a (mē'di·ə), *n.* ancient country in SW Asia, south of the Caspian Sea. —Me'di·an, *adj., n.*

me·di·ae·val (mē'di·ē'vəl; med'i-), *adj.* medieval. —me'di·ae·val·ly, *adv.* ▶ See medieval for usage note.

me·di·ae·val·ism (mē'di·ē'vəl·iz·əm; med'i-), *n.* medievalism.

me·di·ae·val·ist (mē'di·ē'vəl·ist; med'i-), *n.* medievalist.

me·di·al (mē'di·əl), *adj.* 1. in the middle. 2. average; ordinary. [< LL, < L *medius* middle]

me·di·an (mē'di·ən), *adj.* middle. —*n.* 1. the middle number of a series. The median of 1, 3, 4, 8, 9 is 4. 2. measurement so chosen that half the numbers in the series are above it and half are below it. The median of 1, 3, 4, 8, 9, 10 is 6. 3. line or point in the middle. [< L, < *medius* middle] —me'di·an·ly, *adv.*

me·di·ate (*v.* mē'di·āt; *adj.* mē'di·it), *v.*, -at·ed, -at·ing, *adj.* —*v.* 1. be a connecting link. 2. be a go-between; act in order to bring about an agreement between persons or sides. 3. effect by intervening; settle by intervening. 4. be the medium for effecting (a result), for conveying (a gift), or for communicating knowledge. —*adj.* 1. connected, but not directly; connected through some other person or thing. 2. intermediate. [< LL *mediatus* situated in the middle < L *medius* middle] —me'di·ate·ly, *adv.* —me'di·a'tion, *n.* —me'di·a'tive, *adj.* —me'di·a'tor, *n.*

me·di·a·to·ry (mē'di·ə·tô'ri; -tō'-), me·di·a·to·ri·al (mē'di·ə·tô'ri·əl; -tō'-), *adj.* mediating; having to do with mediation.

med·ic (med'ik), *n.* 1. physician. 2. *Colloq.* medical student. 3. *Colloq.* a member of a medical battalion in the army. [< L *medicus* physician]

med·i·ca·ble (med'ə·kə·bəl), *adj.* capable of being cured or relieved by medical treatment.

med·i·cal (med'ə·kəl), *adj.* of or having to do with the science or practice of medicine. [< F < LL, < L *medicus* doctor] —med'i·cal·ly, *adv.*

me·dic·a·ment (mə·dik'ə·mənt; med'ə·kə-), *n.* substance used to cure or heal; medicine. [< L, ult. < *medicus* healing]

med·i·cate (med'ə·kāt), *v.*, -cat·ed, -cat·ing. 1. treat with medicine. 2. put medicine on or in. [< L, < *medicus* healing] —med'i·ca'tion, *n.*

Med·i·ci (med'ə·chē), *n.* 1. a rich, famous, and powerful family of Florence, Italy, during the 15th and 16th centuries. 2. Catherine de', 1519–1589, queen of Henry II of France, 1547–1559. 3. Lorenzo de', 1449–1492, ruler of Florence, statesman, poet, and patron of art and literature. —Med·i·ce·an (med'ə·sē'ən), *adj.*

me·dic·i·nal (mə·dis'ə·nəl), *adj.* having value as medicine; healing; helping; relieving. —me·dic'i·nal·ly, *adv.*

med·i·cine (med'ə·sən), *n., v.*, -cined, -cin·ing. —*n.* 1. substance, drug, or means used to cure disease or improve health. 2. science of curing disease or improving health; skill in healing; doctor's art; treatment of diseases. 3. magic power that savages believe certain men have over disease, evil spirits, and other things. 4. take one's medicine, do what one must; do something one dislikes to do. —*v.* administer medicine to. [< L, < *medicus* doctor]

medicine ball, a large, heavy leather ball tossed from one person to another for exercise.

medicine man, man believed by North American Indians and other primitive peoples to have magic power over diseases, evil spirits, and other things.

me·di·e·val (mē'di·ē'vəl; med'i-), *adj.* 1. belonging to or having to do with the Middle Ages (the years from about 500 A.D. to about 1450 A.D.). 2. like that of the Middle Ages. Also, mediaeval. [< L *medium* middle + *aevum* age] —me'di·e'val·ly, *adv.* ▶ medieval. A number of years ago the American Historical Association decided to change the spelling from *mediaeval* to *medieval*, which is now the usual form.

Medieval Greek, the Greek language from about 700 to about 1500 A.D.

me·di·e·val·ism (mē'di·ē'vəl·iz·əm; med'i-), *n.* 1. spirit, ideals, and customs of the Middle Ages; medieval thought, religion, and art. 2. devotion to medieval ideals; adoption of medieval customs. 3. a medieval belief or custom. Also, mediaevalism.

me·di·e·val·ist (mē'di·ē'vəl·ist; med'i-), n. 1. person who knows much about the Middle Ages. 2. person who is in sympathy with medieval ideals, customs, etc. Also, mediaevalist.

Medieval Latin, the Latin language from about 700 to about 1500 A.D.

Me·di·na (mə·dē'nə), n. city in W Saudi Arabia. Mohammed's tomb is there.

me·di·o·cre (mē'di·ō'kər; mē'di·ō'kər), adj. neither good nor bad; average; ordinary. [< F < L mediocris, orig., halfway up < medius middle + ocris jagged mountain] —Syn. medium, middling, commonplace, indifferent.

me·di·oc·ri·ty (mē'di·ok'rə·ti), n., pl. -ties. 1. mediocre quality. 2. mediocre ability or accomplishment. 3. mediocre person. [L mediocritas]

Medit., Mediterranean.

med·i·tate (med'ə·tāt), v., -tat·ed, -tat·ing. 1. consider in the mind as something to be done or effected: the king struck a blow that he had meditated for some time. 2. engage in thought or contemplation; reflect: monks meditate on holy things for hours at a time. 3. plan; intend: meditate a visit. [< L meditatus] —med'i·ta'tor, n. —Syn. 1. ponder. 2, 3. contemplate.

med·i·ta·tion (med'ə·tā'shən), n. continued thought; reflection, esp. on sacred or solemn subjects. —Syn. contemplation.

med·i·ta·tive (med'ə·tā'tiv), adj. 1. fond of meditating. 2. expressing meditation. —med'i·ta'tive·ly, adv.

Med·i·ter·ra·ne·an (med'ə·tə·rā'ni·ən; -rān'yən), n. a large sea between Europe and Africa. —adj. of this sea or the lands around it.

me·di·um (mē'di·əm), adj., n., pl. -di·ums, -di·a (-di·ə). —adj. having a middle position; moderate. —n. 1. that which is in the middle; neither one extreme nor the other; middle condition. 2. substance or agent through which anything acts; a means: radio is a medium of communication; billboards and magazines are important media for advertising. 3. substance in which something can live; environment: water is the medium in which fish live. 4. liquid with which paints are mixed. 5. Am. person through whom supposed messages from the world of spirits are sent. [< L, neut. adj., middle]

Med.L, Medieval Latin.

med·lar (med'lər), n. 1. fruit that looks like a small brown apple. 2. the small, bushy tree that it grows on. [< OF meslier (tree) < mesle (fruit), ult. < L < Gk. mespilon]

med·ley (med'li), n., pl. -leys, adj. —n. 1. mixture of things that ordinarily do not belong together. 2. piece of music made up of parts from other pieces. —adj. made up of parts that are not alike; mixed. [< OF meslée < mesler mix, ult. < L miscere. Doublet of MELEE.]

me·dul·la (mi·dul'ə), n., pl. -lae (-ē). 1. Anat. medulla oblongata. 2. Anat. marrow of bones. 3. Anat. the inner substance of an organ or structure. 4. Bot. the pith of plants. [< L, marrow]

me·dul·la ob·lon·ga·ta (mi·dul'ə ob'long-gä'tə; -gā'tə), Anat. the lowest part of the brain, at the top end of the spinal cord. [< NL, prolonged medulla]

med·ul·lar·y (med'ə·ler'i; mi·dul'ər·i), adj. of or like medulla or the medulla oblongata.

Me·du·sa (mə·dū'sə; -zə; -dū'-), n., pl. -sas. Gk. Legend. a horrible monster, one of the three Gorgons. She had snakes for hair, and anyone who looked upon her was turned to stone. [< L < Gk. Medousa]

me·du·sa (mə·dū'sə; -zə; -dū'-), n., pl. -sas, -sae (-sē; -zē). jellyfish. —me·du'san, adj.

meed (mēd), n. Poetic. what one deserves; reward. [OE mēd]

meek (mēk), adj. 1. patient; not easily angered; mild. 2. submitting tamely when ordered about or injured by others. [< Scand. miúkr soft] —meek'ly, adv. —meek'ness, n. —Syn. 1. forbearing. 2. submissive, yielding, docile.

meer·schaum (mir'shəm; -shôm), n. 1. a soft, light stone used to make tobacco pipes. 2. a tobacco pipe made of this material. [< G, sea foam, trans. of Pers. kef-i-daryā]

meet¹ (mēt), v., met, meet·ing, n. —v. 1. come face to face; come face to face with: turn aside to avoid meeting a person. 2. come together; come into contact or connection with: sword met sword in battle. 3. join: where the two streets meet. 4. be united; join in harmony. 5. come into company with: the hosts met their guests at the restaurant. 6. be introduced to; become acquainted with. 7. be present at the arrival of: meet a boat. 8. satisfy: meet obligations, objections, etc. 9. pay: meet bills, debts, etc. 10. fight with; oppose; deal with. 11. come together in conflict; fight. 12. face directly: he met her glance with a smile. 13. come to: strange sights and sounds met our eyes and ears. 14. experience: he met open scorn before he won fame. 15. assemble: Congress will meet next month. 16. meet with, have; get: the plan met with approval. —n. 1. a meeting; a gathering: an athletic meet. 2. people at a meeting. 3. place of meeting. [OE mētan] —Syn. v. 1. confront, encounter. 2. collide. 3. settle, fulfill. 14. undergo, suffer. 15. gather, convene, congregate.

meet² (mēt), adj. suitable; proper; fitting. [OE gemǣte] —meet'ly, adv.

meet·ing (mēt'ing), n. 1. a coming together. 2. assembly. 3. assembly of people for worship. 4. junction. —Syn. 2. gathering, congregation.

meeting house, building used for worship; church.

meg·a·cy·cle (meg'ə·sī'kəl), n. Physics. a million cycles in radio. [< mega- one million times (< Gk. megas great) + cycle < Gk. kyklos circle]

meg·a·lo·ma·ni·a (meg'ə·lō·mā'ni·ə), n. insanity marked by delusions of greatness, wealth, etc. [< Gk. megas (megalo-) great + mania madness] —meg·a·lo·ma·ni·ac (meg'ə·lō·mā'ni·ak), n.

meg·a·lop·o·lis (meg'ə·lop'ə·lis), n. city of enormous size, especially when thought of as the center of power, wealth, etc., in a country or the world. [< Gk. mégas, megálou great + pólis city]

meg·a·phone (meg'ə·fōn), n. Am. a large, funnel-shaped horn used to increase the loudness of the voice or the distance at which it can be heard. [< Gk. megas great + phone sound]

meg·a·ton (meg'ə·tun), n. a measure of atomic power equivalent to the energy released by one million tons of high explosive, specifically TNT. [< mega- one million times + ton]

me·grim (mē'grim), n. 1. migraine. 2. whim; fancy. 3. megrims, morbid low spirits. [var. of migraine; infl. by grim]

mel·an·cho·li·a (mel'ən·kō'li·ə), n. a mental disorder characterized by great depression of spirits and gloomy fears. [< LL < Gk., < melas black + chole bile]

mel·an·chol·y (mel'ən·kol'i), n., pl. -chol·ies, adj. —n. 1. sadness; low spirits; tendency to be sad. 2. sober thoughtfulness; pensiveness. —adj. 1. sad; gloomy. 2. causing sadness; depressing. 3. soberly thoughtful; pensive. —mel'an·chol'ic, adj. —mel'an·chol'i·cal·ly, adv. —Syn. n. 1. depression, dejection. —adj. 1. depressed, despondent, downcast. —Ant. n. 1. cheerfulness.

Mel·a·ne·sia (mel'ə·nē'zhə; -shə), n. group of islands in the Pacific NE of Australia.

Mel·a·ne·sian (mel'ə·nē'zhən; -shən), n. 1. a member of any of the dark-skinned peoples living in Melanesia. 2. the languages of Melanesia. —adj. of or pertaining to Melanesia, its inhabitants, or their languages.

mé·lange (mā·länzh'), n. mixture; medley. [< F, < mêler mix]

Mel·ba toast (mel'bə), very thin, crisp toast.

Mel·bourne (mel'bərn), n. seaport in SE Australia, capital of Victoria.

meld (meld), Am. —n. in canasta, pinochle, etc., the announcement of any counting combination in a hand. —v. make a meld.

me·lee, mê·lée (mā'lā; mā·lā'; mel'ā), n. a confused fight; hand-to-hand fight among a number of fighters. [< F mêlée. Doublet of MEDLEY.]

mel·io·rate (mēl'yə·rāt; mēl'i·ə·rāt), v., -rat·ed, -rat·ing. improve. [< LL, < L melior better]

mel·io·ra′·tion, *n.* —**mel′·io·ra′·tive,** *adj.* —**mel′·io·ra′·tor,** *n.*

mel·lif·lu·ent (mə·lif′lu̇·ənt), *adj.* mellifluous. —**mel·lif′lu·ence,** *n.* —**mel·lif′lu·ent·ly,** *adv.*

mel·lif·lu·ous (mə·lif′lu̇·əs), *adj.* sweetly or smoothly flowing: *the mellifluous speech of the orator.* [< LL, < L *mel* honey + *fluere* to flow] —**mel·lif′lu·ous·ly,** *adv.*

mel·low (mel′ō), *adj.* **1.** soft and full-flavored from ripeness; sweet and juicy: *a mellow apple.* **2.** fully matured: *mellow wine.* **3.** soft and rich: *mellow tones.* **4.** rich; loamy: *mellow soil.* **5.** softened and made wise by age and experience. —*v.* make or become mellow. [var. of OE *mearu* soft, tender] —**mel′low·ly,** *adv.* —**mel′low·ness,** *n.* —**Syn.** *adj.* **2.** ripe, mature.

mel·o·de·on (mə·lō′di·ən), *n. Am.* a small reed organ. [see MELODY]

mel·od·ic (mə·lod′ik), *adj.* **1.** having to do with melody. **2.** melodious. —**me·lod′i·cal·ly,** *adv.*

me·lo·di·ous (mə·lō′di·əs), *adj.* **1.** sweet-sounding; pleasing to the ear; musical. **2.** producing melody. —**me·lo′di·ous·ly,** *adv.* —**me·lo′di·ous·ness,** *n.* —**Syn.** **1.** melodic, tuneful.

mel·o·dra·ma (mel′ə·drä′mə; -dram′ə), *n.* **1.** a sensational drama with exaggerated appeal to the emotions and, usually, a happy ending. **2.** any sensational writing, speech, or action with exaggerated appeal to the emotions. [< F, < Gk. *melos* music + *drama* drama]

mel·o·dra·mat·ic (mel′ə·drə·mat′ik), *adj.* of, like, or suitable for melodrama; sensational and exaggerated. —**mel′o·dra·mat′i·cal·ly,** *adv.* —**mel·o·dram·a·tist** (mel′ə·dram′ə·tist), *n.*

mel·o·dy (mel′ə·di), *n., pl.* -**dies. 1.** sweet music; any sweet sound. **2.** succession of single tones in music; tune. Music has melody, harmony, and rhythm. **3.** the main tune in harmonized music; air. [< L < Gk. *meloidia,* ult. < *melos* song + *oide* song] —**Syn.** **3.** song, theme.

mel·on (mel′ən), *n.* **1.** a large juicy fruit that grows on a vine. Watermelons, cantaloupes or muskmelons, and honeydew melons are different kinds. **2.** cut a melon, *Slang.* divide extra profits. [< F < LL *melo,* short for L *melopepo* < Gk., < *melon* apple + *pepon* gourd]

melt (melt), *v.,* melt·ed, melt·ed or mol·ten, melt·ing, *n.* —*v.* **1.** change from solid to liquid: *great heat melts iron.* **2.** dissolve: *sugar melts in water.* **3.** disappear or cause to disappear gradually: *the clouds melted away.* **4.** change very gradually: *the green of the rainbow melted into the blue.* **5.** soften: *pity melted her heart.* —*n.* act of melting. [OE *meltan*] —**melt′a·ble,** *adj.* —**melt′er,** *n.* —**Syn.** *v.* **1.** liquefy. **5.** mollify. —**Ant.** *v.* **1.** harden, solidify.

melting point, degree of temperature at which a solid substance melts.

mel·ton (mel′tən), *n.* a heavy woolen cloth. [after *Melton Mowbray,* town in C England]

Mel·ville (mel′vil), *n.* Herman, 1819–1891, American author of sea stories.

mem·ber (mem′bər), *n.* **1.** one belonging to a group: *a member of Congress.* **2.** constituent part of a whole: *a member of an equation.* **3.** part of a plant, animal, or human body, esp. a leg or arm. [< OF, < L *membrum* limb, part] —**Syn.** **3.** component. **3.** organ, limb.

mem·ber·ship (mem′bər·ship), *n.* **1.** fact or state of being a member: *membership in the Boy Scouts.* **2.** members. **3.** number of members.

mem·brane (mem′brān), *n.* **1.** a thin, soft sheet or layer of animal tissue lining or covering some part of the body. **2.** a similar layer of vegetable tissue. [< L *membrana* < *membrum* member] —**mem·bra·nous** (mem′brə·nəs), *adj.*

me·men·to (mə·men′tō), *n., pl.* -tos, -toes. thing serving as a reminder, warning, or remembrance. [< L, remember!]

mem·o (mem′ō), *n., pl.* mem·os. *Colloq.* memorandum.

mem·oir (mem′wär; -wôr), *n.* **1.** biography. **2.** report of a scientific or scholarly study. **3.** mem-oirs, **a.** record of facts and events written from personal knowledge or special information. **b.** autobiography. [< F *mémoire* < L *memoria.* Doublet of MEMORY.]

mem·o·ra·bil·i·a (mem′ə·rə·bil′i·ə), *n.pl.* things or events worth remembering. [< L (pl.). See MEMORABLE.]

mem·o·ra·ble (mem′ə·rə·bəl), *adj.* worth remembering; not to be forgotten; notable. [< L, ult. < *memor* mindful] —**mem′o·ra·bil′i·ty,** *n.* —**mem′o·ra·bly,** *adv.* —**Syn.** remarkable.

mem·o·ran·dum (mem′ə·ran′dəm), *n., pl.* -dums, -da (-də). **1.** a short written statement for future use; note to aid one's memory. **2.** an informal letter, note, or report. **3.** a writing containing the terms of a transaction, esp. of a consignment. [< L, (thing) to be remembered]

me·mo·ri·al (mə·mô′ri·əl; -mō′-), *n.* **1.** something that is a reminder of some event or person, such as a statue, an arch or column, a book, or a holiday. **2.** statement sent to a government or person in authority, usually giving facts and asking that some wrong be corrected. —*adj.* helping people to remember: *memorial services.* [< L, < *memoria* MEMORY]

Memorial Day, *Am.* day for honoring dead soldiers and sailors. In most States it falls on May 30.

me·mo·ri·al·ize (mə·mô′ri·əl·īz; -mō′-), *v.,* -ized, -iz·ing. **1.** preserve the memory of; commemorate. **2.** submit a memorial to; petition. —**me·mo′ri·al·i·za′tion,** *n.* —**me·mo′ri·al·iz′-er,** *n.*

mem·o·rize (mem′ə·rīz), *v.,* -rized, -riz·ing. *Am.* commit to memory; learn by heart. —**mem′o·ri·za′tion,** *n.* —**mem′o·riz′er,** *n.*

mem·o·ry (mem′ə·ri; mem′ri), *n., pl.* -ries. **1.** ability to remember. **2.** act or fact of remembering. **3.** all that a person remembers. **4.** person, thing, or event that is remembered. **5.** length of time during which the past is remembered: *this has been the hottest summer within my memory.* **6.** reputation after death. **7.** a system of storing information in an electronic computer on film, plastic cards, magnetic tape, etc. **8.** in memory of, to help in remembering; as a reminder of. [< L *memoria* < *memor* mindful. Doublet of MEMOIR.] —**Syn.** **2.** remembrance, recollection.

Mem·phis (mem′fis), *n.* city in SW Tennessee, on the Mississippi.

mem·sa·hib (mem′sä′ib), *n.* in India, native's term of respect for a European lady.

men (men), *n.pl.* **1.** pl. of man. **2.** human beings; people in general.

men·ace (men′is), *n., v.,* -aced, -ac·ing. —*n.* threat: *forest fires are a menace.* —*v.* threaten: *floods menaced the valley with destruction.* [< F < L *minaciae* (pl.), ult. < *minae* projecting points, threats] —**men′ac·ing·ly,** *adv.*

mé·nage, me·nage (mā·näzh′), *n.* **1.** a household. **2.** housekeeping. [< F]

me·nag·er·ie (mə·naj′ər·i; -nazh′-), *n.* **1.** collection of wild animals kept in cages for exhibition. **2.** place where such animals are kept. [< F, lit. management of a household]

mend (mend), *v.* **1.** put in good condition again; make whole; repair: *mend a road.* **2.** set right; improve: *he should mend his manners.* **3.** get back one's health. —*n.* **1.** place that has been mended. **2.** a mending; improvement. [var. of *amend*] —**mend′a·ble,** *adj.* —**mend′er,** *n.* —**Syn.** *v.* **1.** patch. **2.** correct, rectify, better.

men·da·cious (men·dā′shəs), *adj.* **1.** lying; untruthful. **2.** false; untrue. [< L, < *mendax* lying] —**men·da′cious·ly,** *adv.* —**men·da′cious·ness,** men·dac·i·ty (men·das′ə·ti), *n.*

Men·del (men′dəl), *n.* Gregor, 1822–1884, Austrian biologist. —**Men·de·li·an** (men·dē′li·ən), *adj.* —**Men′del·ism, Men·de′li·an·ism,** *n.*

men·de·le·vi·um (men′də·lā′vi·əm), *n.* a rare, radioactive, artificial element, Mv, produced as a by-product of nuclear fission. [named for D. I. *Mendeleev,* Russian chemist]

Mendel's Law, law describing the inheritance of many characteristics in animals and plants.

Men·dels·sohn (men′dəl·sən; -sōn), *n.* **Felix**, 1809–1847, German composer of music.

men·di·cant (men′də·kənt), *adj.* begging: *mendicant friars ask alms for charity.* —*n.* 1. beggar. 2. a mendicant friar. [< L *mendicans* < *mendicus* beggar] —**men′di·can·cy**, *n.*

Men·e·la·us (men′ə·lā′əs), *n. Gk. Legend.* king of Sparta, the husband of Helen.

men·folk (men′fōk′), *n.pl.* men.

men·ha·den (men·hā′dən), *n.*, *pl.* **-den**. *Am.* a sea fish common along the E coast of the United States. [< Algonquian]

me·ni·al (mē′ni·əl; mēn′yəl), *adj.* belonging to or suited to a servant; low; mean. —*n.* servant who does the humblest and most unpleasant tasks. [< AF, < *meiniée* household, ult. < L *mansio* habitation] —**me′ni·al·ly**, *adv.*

me·nin·ges (mə·nin′jēz), *n.pl.*, *sing.* **me·ninx** (mē′ningks). *Anat.* the three membranes that surround the brain and spinal cord. [< NL (pl.) < Gk.] —**me·nin·ge·al** (mə·nin′ji·əl), *adj.*

men·in·gi·tis (men′in·jī′tis), *n.* a very serious disease in which the membranes surrounding the brain or spinal cord are inflamed. —**men·in·git·ic** (men′ən·jit′ik), *adj.*

me·nis·cus (mə·nis′kəs), *n.*, *pl.* **-nis·cus·es**, **-nis·ci** (-nis′ī). 1. the curved upper surface of a column of liquid. 2. lens that is convex on one side and concave on the other. [< NL < Gk. *meniskos*, dim. of *mene* moon]

Men·non·ite (men′ən·īt), *n.* member of a Christian church opposed to infant baptism, taking oaths, holding public office, and military service.

Me·non (mē′non), *n.* **V. K. Krishna**, born 1897, Indian diplomat.

Meniscus lens

men·o·pause (men′ə·pôz), *n.* the final cessation of the menses, occurring normally between the ages of 45 and 50. [< NL < Gk. *men* month + *pausis* pause]

men·ses (men′sēz), *n.pl.* discharge of blood from the uterus that normally occurs every four weeks between puberty and the menopause. [< L, pl. of *mensis* month]

Men·she·vik (men′shə·vik), *n.*, *pl.* **Men·she·viks**, **Men·she·vi·ki** (men′shə·vē′ki). member of a Russian liberal political party (1903–1917) opposed to the more radical Bolsheviks.

men·stru·al (men′strü·əl), *adj.* 1. pertaining to the menses. 2. monthly.

men·stru·ate (men′strü·āt), *v.*, **-at·ed**, **-at·ing**. have a discharge of blood from the uterus, normally at intervals of four weeks. [< LL *menstruatus*, ult. < L *mens* month] —**men′stru·a′tion**, *n.*

men·sur·a·ble (men′shər·ə·bəl), *adj.* measurable. —**men′sur·a·bil′i·ty**, *n.*

men·su·ra·tion (men′shə·rā′shən), *n.* 1. act, art, or process of measuring. 2. branch of mathematics that deals with finding lengths, areas, and volumes. [< LL, ult. < L *mensura* MEASURE]

—ment, *suffix forming nouns from verbs or the stems of verbs.* 1. act or state or fact of ——ing, as in *enjoyment*, *management*. 2. state or condition or fact of being ——ed, as in *amazement*, *astonishment*. 3. product or result of ——ing, as in *pavement*. 4. means or instrument for ——ing, as in *inducement*. [< F < L *-mentum*]

men·tal (men′təl), *adj.* 1. of the mind: *a mental test.* 2. for the mind; done by the mind: *mental arithmetic.* 3. having a mental disease or weakness. 4. for insane people. [< LL, < L *mens* mind]

men·tal·i·ty (men·tal′ə·ti), *n.*, *pl.* **-ties**. mental capacity; mind.

men·tal·ly (men′təl·i), *adv.* 1. in the mind; with the mind. 2. with regard to the mind.

mental reservation, an unexpressed qualification of a statement.

mental telepathy, extrasensory perception.

men·thol (men′thol; -thōl; -thōl), *n.* a white, crystalline substance, $C_{10}H_{20}O$, obtained from oil of peppermint, used in medicine. [< G, < L *menta* mint + *oleum* oil]

men·tho·lat·ed (men′thə·lāt′id), *adj.* containing menthol.

men·tion (men′shən), *v.* 1. speak about; refer to. 2. not to mention, not even considering; besides. [< n.] —*n.* 1. a short statement (about); reference (to). 2. make mention of, mention. [< OF < L *mentio*] —**men′tion·a·ble**, *adj.* —**men′tion·er**, *n.*

men·tor (men′tər), *n.* a wise and trusted adviser. [< Gk.]

men·u (men′ū; mā′nū), *n.* 1. list of the food served at a meal; bill of fare. 2. the food served. [< F, small, detailed, < L *minutus* made small. Doublet of MINUTE².]

me·ow (mi·ou′), *n.* sound made by a cat. —*v.* make this sound. [imit.]

Meph·i·stoph·e·les (mef′ə·stof′ə·lēz), *n.* a powerful evil spirit; crafty devil. —**Meph·is·to·phe·li·an** (mef′is·tō·fē′li·ən; -fēl′yən), *adj.*

me·phit·ic (mi·fit′ik), *adj.* 1. having a nasty smell. 2. noxious; poisonous; pestilential. [< LL, < *mephitis* stench]

mer·can·tile (mér′kən·til; -tīl), *adj.* 1. of merchants or trade; commercial: *a mercantile firm*, *mercantile law*. 2. of or pertaining to mercantilism. [< F < Ital., < *mercante* MERCHANT]

mer·can·til·ism (mér′kən·til·iz′əm; -tīl-), *n.* 1. system which favored a balance of exports of commodities, over imports, and regulated a nation's agriculture, industry, and trade with that end in view. 2. mercantile principles, practices, or spirit. —**mer′can·til·ist**, *n.*

Mer·ca·tor's projection, method of drawing maps with straight instead of curved lines for latitude and longitude. [after G. *Mercator*, cartographer]

mer·ce·nar·y (mér′sə·ner′i), *adj.*, *n.*, *pl.* **-nar·ies**. —*adj.* 1. working for money only; acting with money as the motive. 2. done for money or gain. —*n.* soldier serving for pay in a foreign army. [< L, < *merces* wages] —**Syn.** *adj.* 1. hireling, grasping. —*n.* hireling.

mer·cer (mér′sər), *n. Brit.* dealer in cloth. [< OF *mercier*, ult. < L *merx* wares]

mer·cer·ize (mér′sər·īz), *v.*, **-ized**, **-iz·ing**. treat (cotton thread or cloth) with a chemical solution that strengthens it, gives it a silky luster, and makes it hold dyes better. [after J. *Mercer*, patentee of the process]

mer·chan·dise (mér′chən·dīz; -dīs), *n.*, *v.*, **-dised**, **-dis·ing**. —*n.* goods for sale; wares; articles bought and sold. —*v.* buy and sell; trade. [< F, < *marchand* MERCHANT] —**mer′chan·dis′er**, *n.*

mer·chant (mér′chənt), *n.* 1. person who buys and sells. 2. storekeeper. —*adj.* trading; pertaining to trade: *merchant ships*. [< OF *marchéant*, ult. < L *merx* wares]

mer·chant·a·ble (mér′chən·tə·bəl), *adj.* marketable.

mer·chant·man (mér′chənt·mən), *n.*, *pl.* **-men**. ship used in commerce.

merchant marine, ships used in commerce.

Mer·cia (mér′shə; -shi·ə), *n.* an ancient Anglian kingdom in C England. —**Mer′cian**, *adj.*, *n.*

mer·ci·ful (mér′si·fəl), *adj.* having mercy; showing or feeling mercy; full of mercy. —**mer′ci·ful·ly**, *adv.* —**mer′ci·ful·ness**, *n.* —**Syn.** compassionate, clement, kind, lenient. —**Ant.** relentless, implacable, unmerciful.

mer·ci·less (mér′si·lis), *adj.* without mercy; having no mercy; showing no mercy. —**mer′ci·less·ly**, *adv.* —**mer′ci·less·ness**, *n.* —**Syn.** relentless, implacable, pitiless, ruthless.

mer·cu·ri·al (mər·kyūr′i·əl), *adj.* 1. sprightly; quick; changeable; fickle. 2. caused by the use of mercury: *mercurial poisoning*. 3. containing mercury: *a mercurial ointment*. —**mer·cu′ri·al·ly**, *adv.* —**mer·cu′ri·al·ness**, *n.*

mer·cu·ric (mər·kyūr′ik), *adj. Chem.* of compounds, containing mercury in a bivalent state.

mer·cu·ro·chrome (mər·kyūr′ə·krōm′), *n.* 1. an iridescent green compound of mercury forming a red solution in water. 2. the solution, used as an antiseptic. 3. **Mercurochrome**, a trademark for this solution.

mer·cu·rous (mər·kyür′əs; mėr′kyə·rəs), *adj.* *Chem.* of compounds, containing mercury as a univalent radical.

mer·cu·ry (mėr′kyə·ri), *n.*, *pl.* **-ries.** 1. *Chem.* a heavy, silver-white metallic element, Hg, that is liquid at ordinary temperatures. 2. column of mercury in a thermometer or barometer. 3. **Mercury, Roman Myth.** messenger of the gods, the god of commerce, of skill of hand, quickness of wit, and eloquence, identified with Hermes by the Greeks. 4. **Mercury,** planet nearest the sun. [< L *Mercurius* (def. 3)]

mer·cy (mėr′si), *n.*, *pl.* **-cies.** 1. more kindness than justice requires; kindness beyond what can be claimed or expected. 2. kindly treatment; pity. 3. something to be thankful for; blessing. 4. **at the mercy of,** in the power of. [< OF < Med.L *merces* < L, reward] —**Syn.** 1. clemency, lenity, compassion, forbearance, grace.

mere[1] (mir), *adj., superl.* **mer·est.** nothing else than; only; simple: *the cut was the merest scratch.* [< L *merus* pure] —**Syn.** bare, sheer.

mere[2] (mir), *n.* *Poetic or Dial.* lake; pond. [OE]

Mer·e·dith (mer′ə·dith), *n.* George, 1828–1909, English novelist and poet.

mere·ly (mir′li), *adv.* simply; only; and nothing more; and that is all: *merely a matter of form.*

me·ren·gue (mā·reng′gā), *n.* a ballroom dance that originated in the Dominican Republic.

mer·e·tri·cious (mer′ə·trish′əs), *adj.* attractive in a showy way; alluring by false charms. [< L, < *meretrix* prostitute < *mereri* earn] —**mer′e·tri′cious·ly,** *adv.* —**mer′e·tri′cious·ness,** *n.*

mer·gan·ser (mər·gan′sər), *n.*, *pl.* **-sers** or (*esp. collectively*) **-ser.** any of several kinds of large ducks that have long, slender bills. The male has a crested head. [< NL, < *mergus* diver + *anser* goose]

merge (mėrj), *v.*, **merged, merg·ing.** 1. swallow up; absorb; combine and absorb; combine. 2. become swallowed up or absorbed in something else: *the twilight merges into darkness.* [< L *mergere* to dip] —**Syn.** 1. consolidate, fuse.

merg·er (mėr′jər), *n.* a merging; absorption; combination: *one big company was formed by the merger of four small ones.*

me·rid·i·an (mə·rid′i·ən), *n.* 1. circle passing through any place on the earth's surface and through the North and South Poles. 2. the half of such a circle from pole to pole. All the places on the same meridian have the same longitude. 3. the highest point: *the meridian of life is the prime of life.* [< OF < L *meridianus,* ult. < *medius* middle + *dies* day]

me·ringue (mə·rang′), *n.* 1. mixture made of egg whites beaten stiff and sweetened. 2. a small cake, etc., made of this mixture. [< F]

me·ri·no (mə·rē′nō), *n.*, *pl.* **-nos.** 1. kind of sheep with long, fine wool. 2. wool of this sheep. 3. a soft woolen yarn made from it. [< Sp.]

mer·it (mer′it), *n.* 1. goodness; worth; value: *the merits of Shakespeare's plays are obvious.* 2. thing that deserves praise or reward: *realistic thinking is one of his merits.* 3. real fact or quality, whether good or bad: *the judge will consider the case on its merits.* —*v.* deserve. [< F < L *meritum* earned] —**Syn.** 1. worthiness, excellence. —*v.* earn.

mer·i·to·ri·ous (mer′ə·tô′ri·əs; -tō′-), *adj.* deserving reward or praise; having merit; worthy. —**mer′i·to′ri·ous·ly,** *adv.* —**mer′i·to′ri·ous·ness,** *n.*

merle, merl (mėrl), *n.* *Poetic.* a European blackbird. [< F < L *merula*]

Mer·lin (mėr′lən), *n.* magician who helped King Arthur.

mer·maid (mėr′mād′), *n.* 1. maiden in fairy tales having the form of a fish from the waist down. 2. an expert woman swimmer. [< *mere*[2] + *maid*]

mer·man (mėr′man′), *n.*, *pl.* **-men.** 1. man in

Merle (ab. 10 in. long)

fairy tales having the shape of a fish from the waist down. 2. an expert swimmer.

mer·ri·ment (mer′i·mənt), *n.* laughter and gaiety; fun; mirth; merry enjoyment.

mer·ry (mer′i), *adj.*, **-ri·er, -ri·est.** 1. laughing; full of fun: *a merry reveler.* 2. gay; joyful: *a merry holiday, merry bells.* 3. *Archaic.* delightful. 4. **make merry,** laugh and be gay; have fun. [OE *myrge*] —**mer′ri·ly,** *adv.* —**mer′ri·ness,** *n.* —**Syn.** 1. jolly, jovial, gleeful. —**Ant.** 1. sad.

mer·ry-an·drew (mer′i·an′drü), *n.* clown.

mer·ry-go-round (mer′i·gō·round′), *n.* 1. set of animals and seats on a platform that goes round and round by machinery. 2. any whirl or rapid round: *a merry-go-round of parties.*

mer·ry·mak·ing (mer′i·māk′ing), *n.* 1. laughter and gaiety; fun. 2. gay festival; merry entertainment. —*adj.* gay and full of fun; engaged in merrymaking. —**mer′ry·mak′er,** *n.*

me·sa (mā′sə), *n.* *Am.* a small, high plateau with steep sides. [< Sp. < L *mensa* table]

Me·sa·bi Range (mə·sä′bi), a range of hills in NE Minnesota, containing great deposits of iron ore.

mé·sal·li·ance (mā·zal′i·əns; *Fr.* mā·zä·lyäns′), *n.* *French.* misalliance.

mes·cal (mes·kal′), *n.* *Am.* 1. an alcoholic drink made from the fermented juice of an agave plant. 2. the plant itself. 3. a small cactus whose buttonlike tops are dried and chewed as a stimulant by the Indians. [< Sp. < Aztec *mexcalli* liquor]

mes·dames (mā·däm′), *n.pl.* 1. pl. of **madam.** 2. pl. of **madame.** 3. ladies.

mes·de·moi·selles (mād·mwä·zel′), *n.* pl. of **mademoiselle.**

me·seems (mi·sēmz′), *v.*, *pt.* **me·seemed.** *Archaic.* it seems to me.

mesh (mesh), *n.* 1. open space of a net or sieve: *this net has half-inch meshes.* 2. **in mesh,** in gear; fitted together. 3. meshes, a. network. b. snares. —*v.* 1. catch or be caught in a net. 2. engage or become engaged: *the teeth of the small gear mesh with the teeth of a larger one.* [cf. OE *mæscre* net]

mes·mer·ism (mes′mər·iz·əm; mez′-), *n.* hypnotism. [for F. A. *Mesmer,* who popularized the doctrine] —**mes·mer·ic** (mes·mer′ik; mez-), *adj.* —**mes·mer′i·cal·ly,** *adv.* —**mes′mer·ist,** *n.*

mes·mer·ize (mes′mər·īz; mez′-), *v.*, **-ized, -iz·ing.** hypnotize. —**mes′mer·i·za′tion,** *n.* —**mes′mer·iz′er,** *n.*

mes·o·carp (mes′ə·kärp), *n.* the middle layer of the pericarp, such as the fleshy part of a peach. [< Gk. *mesos* middle + *karpos* fruit]

mes·o·derm (mes′ə·dėrm), *n.* the middle layer of cells in an embryo. [< Gk. *mesos* middle + *derma* skin] —**mes′o·der′mal,** *adj.*

mes·on (mes′on), **mes·o·tron** (mes′ə·tron), or **mes·o·ton** (-ton), *n.* *Physics.* a highly unstable heavy electron found in cosmic rays; particle having the same electric charge as an electron, but much greater mass. Theoretically, mesons exert nuclear forces of attraction.

Mes·o·po·ta·mi·a (mes′ə·pə·tā′mi·ə; -tām′yə), *n.* 1. ancient country in SW Asia, between the Tigris and Euphrates rivers. 2. former name of Iraq. —**Mes′o·po·ta′mi·an,** *adj.*, *n.*

mes·quite (mes·kēt′; mes′kēt), *n.* *Am.* tree or shrub growing in the SW United States and in Mexico. Cattle eat mesquite pods. [< Am.Sp. *mezquite* < Aztec]

mess (mes), *n.* 1. a dirty or untidy mass or group of things; dirty or untidy condition. 2. confusion; difficulty. 3. an unpleasant or unsuccessful affair or state of affairs. 4. group of people who take meals together regularly, esp. such a group in the army or navy. 5. meal of such a group: *the officers are at mess now.* 6. food that does not look or taste good. —*v.* 1. make dirty or untidy. 2. make a failure of; confuse; spoil. 3. take one's meals (with). 4. **mess about, mess around,** putter around. [< OF < L *missus* (thing) put (i.e., on the table)]

mes·sage (mes′ij), *n.* 1. words sent from one person to another. 2. official speech or writing:

the President's message to Congress. **3.** inspired words: *the message of a prophet.* [< OF, ult. < L *missus* sent] —**Syn. 1.** communication, letter, note, despatch.

mes·sa·line (mes′ə‑lēn′; mes′ə‑lēn), *n.* a thin, soft silk cloth with a surface like satin. [< F]

mes·sen·ger (mes′ən‑jər), *n.* **1.** person who carries a message or goes on an errand. **2.** sign that something is coming; forerunner. —**Syn. 1.** carrier, courier. **2.** precursor, herald.

Mes·si·ah (mə‑sī′ə), *n.* **1.** expected deliverer of the Jewish people. **2.** in Christian use, Jesus. **3.** any savior. [var. of LL *Messias,* < Gk. < Heb. *māshiaḥ* anointed] —**Mes·si′ah·ship,** *n.* —**Mes·si·an·ic** (mes′i·an′ik), *adj.*

mes·sieurs (mes′ərz; *Fr.* mā·syœ′), *n.pl.* **1.** pl. of monsieur. **2.** gentlemen.

Mes·si·na (mə‑sē′nə), *n.* seaport in NE Sicily.

mess·mate (mes′māt′), *n.* one of a group of people who eat together regularly.

Messrs., *n.* messieurs. ➤ Messrs. is the abbreviation of French *messieurs* but pronounced as English, mes′ərz. It is used as the plural of *Mr.* (*Messrs. Truman and Taft*) and sometimes, though rarely now in American usage, in addressing firms (*Messrs. Brown, Hubbell and Company*).

mess·y (mes′i), *adj.,* mess·i·er, mess·i·est. in a mess; like a mess; untidy; in disorder; dirty. —mess′i·ness, *n.*

mes·ti·za (mes‑tē′zə), *n.* a woman of mixed blood.

mes·ti·zo (mes‑tē′zō), *n., pl.* ‑zos, ‑zoes. **1.** person of mixed blood. **2.** person of Spanish and American Indian blood. **3.** native of the Philippine Islands having Chinese blood. [< Sp., ult. < L *mixtus* mixed]

met (met), *v.* pt. and pp. of meet[1].

met., metropolitan.

me·tab·o·lism (mə‑tab′ə‑liz‑əm), *n. Biol.* processes of building up food into living matter and using living matter until it is broken down into simpler substances or waste matter, giving off energy. [< Gk. *metabole* change < *meta‑* into a different position + *bole* a throwing] —**met·a·bol·ic** (met′ə‑bol′ik), *adj.*

met·a·car·pus (met′ə‑kär′pəs), *n., pl.* ‑pi (‑pī). **1.** part of a hand between the wrist and the fingers. **2.** part of a forefoot between the carpus and the phalanges. [< NL, ult. < Gk. *meta‑* after + *karpos* wrist] —**met′a·car′pal,** *adj., n.*

met·al (met′əl), *n., adj., v.,* ‑aled, ‑al·ing; *esp.* Brit. ‑alled, ‑al·ling. —*n.* **1.** substance such as iron, gold, silver, copper, lead, tin, aluminum, steel, bronze, and brass. **2.** *Chem.* any element whose atoms tend to lend electrons, or any mixture of such elements. **3.** broken stone, cinders, etc., used for roads and roadbeds. **4.** material; substance: *cowards are not made of the same metal as heroes.* —*adj.* made of metal. —*v.* furnish or cover with metal. [< OF < L < Gk. *metallon,* orig., mine]

metall., metallurgic; metallurgy.

me·tal·lic (mə‑tal′ik), *adj.* **1.** of, containing, or consisting of metal. **2.** like metal; characteristic of metal; that suggests metal: *a metallic luster, a metallic voice.* —**me·tal′li·cal·ly,** *adv.*

met·al·lif·er·ous (met′əl·if′ər·əs), *adj.* containing or yielding metal. [< L, < *metallum* metal + *ferre* to bear]

met·al·lur·gy (met′əl·ér′ji), *n.* science or art of separating metals from their ores and refining them for use. [< NL *metallurgia,* ult. < Gk. *metallon* metal + *ergon* work] —**met·al·lur′gic,** **met′al·lur′gi·cal,** *adj.* —**met′al·lur′gi·cal·ly,** *adv.* —**met′al·lur′gist,** *n.*

met·al·work·ing (met′əl·wèr′king), *n.* act of making things out of metal. —**met′al·work′,** *n.* —**met′al·work′er,** *n.*

met·a·mor·phism (met′ə‑môr′fiz·əm), *n.* **1.** change of form. **2.** change in the structure of a rock caused by pressure, heat, etc.

met·a·mor·phose (met′ə‑môr′fōz, ‑fōs), *v.,* ‑phosed, ‑phos·ing. change in form; transform: *the witch metamorphosed people into animals.*

met·a·mor·pho·sis (met′ə‑môr′fə·sis), *n., pl.* ‑ses (‑sēz). **1.** change of form. **2.** the changed form. **3.** a noticeable or complete change of character, appearance, or condition. [< L < Gk., ult. < *meta‑* over + *morphe* form] —**met′a·mor′phic,** *adj.*

met·a·phor (met′ə‑fər; ‑fôr), *n.* figure of speech in which a word or phrase that ordinarily means one thing is used of another thing in order to suggest a likeness between the two. [< F < L < Gk. *metaphora* transfer, ult. < *meta‑* over + *pherein* carry] —**met·a·phor·i·cal** (met′ə‑fôr′ə‑kəl; ‑for′‑), *adj.* —**met′a·phor′i·cal·ly,** *adv.* ➤ Metaphors and similes and analogies all make comparisons, but the three figures differ in form and in fullness. An *analogy* is usually a rather full comparison, showing or implying several points of similarity. A *simile* makes the comparison exact, labels it by an introductory word, *like* or *as.* A *metaphor* is the shortest, most compact of these comparisons; in it the likeness is implied rather than stated explicitly. Typically the writer asserts that one thing *is* another (in some respect), or suggests that it acts like or has some of the qualities of something else, as in the examples *a copper sky, a heart of stone.*

met·a·phys·i·cal (met′ə‑fiz′ə‑kəl), *adj.* **1.** of metaphysics. **2.** highly abstract; hard to understand. —**met′a·phys′i·cal·ly,** *adv.*

met·a·phys·ics (met′ə‑fiz′iks), *n.* branch of philosophy that tries to explain reality and knowledge; the philosophical study of the real nature of the universe. [< Med.L < Med.Gk. (*ta*) *metaphysika* for Gk. *ta meta ta physika* the (works) after the Physics; with ref. to philosophical works of Aristotle] —**met·a·phy·si·cian** (met′ə‑fə·zish′ən), *n.*

met·a·tar·sus (met′ə‑tär′səs), *n., pl.* ‑si (‑sī). **1.** part of a foot between the ankle and the toes. **2.** part (or bony part) of a hind foot between the tarsus and the phalanges. [< NL, < Gk. *meta‑* after + *tarsos* flat of the foot] —**met′a·tar′sal,** *adj.*

me·tath·e·sis (mə‑tath′ə·sis), *n., pl.* ‑ses (‑sēz). **1.** transposition of sounds, syllables, or letters in a word. **2.** *Chem.* interchange of atoms between two molecules. **3.** transposition; reversal. [< LL < Gk., transposition, ult. < *meta‑* over + *tithenai* set] —**met·a·thet·ic** (met′ə‑thet′ik), **met′a·thet′i·cal,** *adj.*

Met·a·zo·a (met′ə‑zō′ə), *n.pl.* a large zoölogical division comprising all animals which are composed of more than one cell. [< NL, ult. < Gk. *meta‑* after + *zoion* animal] —**met′a·zo′an,** *adj., n.*

mete[1] (mēt), *v.,* met·ed, met·ing. give to each a share of; distribute; allot. [OE *metan*]

mete[2] (mēt), *n.* boundary. [< OF < L *meta*]

met·em·psy·cho·sis (met′əm·si·kō′sis; mə‑temp′sə·kō′sis), *n., pl.* ‑ses (‑sēz). the passing of the soul at death into a new body. Some Oriental philosophies teach that by metempsychosis a person's soul lives again in an animal's body. [< L < Gk., < *meta‑* over + *empsychoein* to animate, ult. < *en* in + *psyche* soul]

me·te·or (mē′ti·ər), *n.* mass of stone or metal that comes toward the earth from outer space with enormous speed; shooting star. [< Gk. *meteoron* (thing) in the air < *meta‑* up + *‑aoros* lifted < *aeirein* lift]

me·te·or·ic (mē′ti·ôr′ik; ‑or′‑), *adj.* **1.** consisting of meteors. **2.** flashing like a meteor; brilliant and soon ended; swift. **3.** of the atmosphere. Wind and rain are meteoric phenomena. —**me′te·or′i·cal·ly,** *adv.*

me·te·or·ite (mē′ti·ər·īt), *n.* mass of stone or metal that has fallen to the earth from outer space. —**me·te·or·it·ic** (mē′ti·ər·it′ik), *adj.*

meteorol., **1.** meteorology. **2.** meteorologic.

me·te·or·ol·o·gy (mē′ti·ər·ol′ə·ji), *n.* science of the atmosphere and weather. —**me·te·or·o·log·ic** (mē′ti·ər·ə·loj′ik), **me′te·or·o·log′i·cal,** *adj.* —**me′te·or·o·log′i·cal·ly,** *adv.* —**me′te·or·ol′o·gist,** *n.*

me·ter[1] (mē′tər), *n.* **1.** unit of length in the metric system; 39.37 inches. **2.** the arrangement of beats or accents in a line of poetry. **3.** the arrangement of beats in music. Also, *esp. Brit.*

metre. [< F < L < Gk. *metron*] ❯ Meter is now more common, esp. in the U.S., than *metre*. The second *e* drops out in derivatives: *metric, metrical, metrics*.

me·ter² (mē′tər), *n.* 1. device for measuring. 2. device for measuring and recording the amount of gas, water, electricity, etc., used. —*v.* measure with a meter. Also, *esp.* Brit. **metre**. [< *mete¹*]

-meter, *word element.* 1. device for measuring, as in *speedometer*. 2. meter; 39.37 inches, as in *kilometer*. 3. having —— feet, as in *hexameter*. [< NL *-metrum* < Gk. *metron* measure]

meter maid, *Am.* woman assigned to enforce parking meter regulations.

Meth., Methodist.

meth·ane (meth′ān), *n. Chem.* a colorless, odorless, inflammable gas, CH₄, the simplest of the hydrocarbons. Methane comes from marshes, petroleum wells, volcanoes, and coal mines.

me·thinks (mi·thingks′), *v., pt.* **me·thought.** *Archaic.* it seems to me. [OE *mē thyncth* it seems to me]

meth·od (meth′əd), *n.* 1. way of doing something: *method of instruction.* 2. system in doing things; order in thinking: *work with method.* [< L < Gk. *methodos,* orig., pursuit < *meta-* after + *hodos* a way] —Syn. 1. mode, manner, way. 2. plan, design.

me·thod·i·cal (mə·thod′ə·kəl), **me·thod·ic** (-ik), *adj.* according to a method; systematic; orderly. —**me·thod′i·cal·ly,** *adv.* —**me·thod′i·cal·ness,** *n.*

Meth·od·ism (meth′əd·iz·əm), *n.* doctrine, organization, and manner of worship of the Methodist Church.

Meth·od·ist (meth′əd·ist), *n.* member of a church that had its origin in the teachings and work of John Wesley. —*adj.* of Methodists or Methodism. —**Meth′od·is′tic,** *adj.*

meth·od·ize (meth′əd·īz), *v.,* **-ized, -iz·ing.** reduce to a method; arrange with method. —**meth′od·iz′er,** *n.*

me·thought (mi·thôt′), *v. pt.* of methinks.

Me·thu·se·lah (mə·thü′zə·lə), *n.* 1. *Bible.* a man said to have lived 969 years. Gen. 5:27. 2. a very old man.

meth·yl (meth′əl), *n. Chem.* a univalent hydrocarbon radical, CH₃. [< F, ult. < Gk. *methy* wine + *hyle* wood]

methyl alcohol, *Chem.* wood alcohol, CH₃OH.

me·tic·u·lous (mə·tik′yə·ləs), *adj.* extremely or excessively careful about small details. [< L *meticulosus* < *metus* fear] —**me·tic′u·lous·ly,** *adv.*

mé·tier (mā·tyā′), *n.* trade; profession. [< F L *ministerium.* Doublet of MINISTRY.]

me·ton·y·my (mə·ton′ə·mi), *n.* use of the name of one thing for that of another which it naturally suggests. *Example:* The pen (power of literature) is mightier than the sword (force). [< LL < Gk. *metonymia,* lit., change of name < *meta-* over + dial. *onyma* name] —**met·o·nym·ic** (met′ə·nim′ik), **met′o·nym′i·cal,** *adj.* ❯ Metonymy is not only a common figure of speech (common in both formal literary and in colloquial usage) but it is one way in which the meanings of words change. Long use of the *crown* for *the king,* the *heart* for *courage* or for *sympathy,* and hundreds of other similar words has given them definite secondary meanings, separate senses in dictionary definitions.

me·tre (mē′tər), *n. Esp. Brit.* meter. ❯ See meter¹ for usage note.

met·ric (met′rik), *adj.* 1. of the meter or the system of measurement based on it. 2. metrical.

met·ri·cal (met′rə·kəl), *adj.* 1. of meter; having a regular arrangement of accents; written in verse, not in prose. 2. of, pertaining to, or used in measurement. —**met′ri·cal·ly,** *adv.*

metric system, a decimal system of measurement that uses the meter (39.37 in.) as its unit of length, the gram (.0022046 pound) as the unit of mass or weight, and the liter (61.024 cu. in. or 1 cubic decimeter) as the unit of volume.

metric ton, 1000 kilograms or 2204.62 avoirdupois pounds.

met·ro·nome (met′rə·nōm), *n.* a clocklike device with a pendulum that can be adjusted to tick at different speeds. [< Gk. *metron* measure + *-nomos* regulating] —**met·ro·nom·ic** (met′rə·nom′ik), *adj.*

Metronome

me·trop·o·lis (mə·trop′ə·lis), *n.* 1. the most important city of a country or region: *New York is the metropolis of the United States.* 2. a large, important center: *Chicago is a busy metropolis.* 3. the chief diocese of a church province. [< LL < Gk., *meter* mother + *polis* city]

met·ro·pol·i·tan (met′rə·pol′ə·tən), *adj.* of a large city; belonging to large cities: *metropolitan newspapers.* —*n.* 1. person who lives in a large city and knows its ways. 2. bishop who has authority over the bishops of a church province.

Met·ter·nich (met′ər·nik), *n.* Prince von, 1773–1859, Austrian diplomat and statesman.

met·tle (met′əl), *n.* 1. disposition; spirit; courage. 2. on one's mettle, ready to do one's best. [var. of *metal*] —**met′tled,** *adj.* —Syn. 1. ardor, enthusiasm.

met·tle·some (met′əl·səm), *adj.* full of mettle; spirited; courageous. —Syn. ardent, fiery.

Meuse (mūz), *n. Fr.* mœz), *n.* river flowing from NE France into the Rhine near its mouth.

Mev (mev), *n. Am.* million electron volts.

mew¹ (mū), *n.* sound made by a cat. —*v.* make this sound. [imit.]

mew² (mū), *n.* a sea gull; gull. [OE *mǣw*]

mewl (mūl), *v.* cry like a baby; whimper. [imit.]

mews (mūz), *n.* stables built around a court or alley.

Mex., 1. Mexican. 2. Mexico.

Mexican War, war between the United States and Mexico from 1846 to 1848.

Mex·i·co (mek′sə·kō), *n.* 1. country in North America, just S of W United States. 2. Gulf of, gulf of the Atlantic, S of the United States and E of Mexico. —**Mex′i·can,** *adj., n.*

Mexico City, capital of Mexico, in the S part.

mez·za·nine (mez′ə·nēn), *n.* a low story between two higher stories of a building, usually one just above and extending only part way over the ground floor. [< F < Ital., < *mezzano* middle < L *medianus*]

mez·zo (met′sō; mez′ō), *adj. Music.* middle; medium; half. [< Ital. < L *medius* middle]

mez·zo-so·pran·o (met′sō-sə·pran′ō; -prä′nō; mez′ō-), *n., pl.* -pran·os. 1. voice between soprano and contralto. 2. singer having such a voice.

mez·zo·tint (met′sō·tint′; mez′ō-), *n.* 1. picture engraved on copper or steel by polishing and scraping away parts of a roughened surface. 2. this method of engraving pictures. —*v.* engrave by this method. [< Ital. *mezzotinto* halftint]

MF, Middle French.

mf., *Music.* somewhat loud. [< Ital. *mezzo forte*]

mfg., manufacturing.

mfr., *pl.* mfrs. manufacturer.

Mg, *Chem.* magnesium.

mg., milligram; milligrams.

Mgr., 1. Manager. 2. Monsignor.

MHG, Middle High German.

mi (mē), *n. Music.* the third tone of the scale. [see GAMUT]

mi., 1. mile; miles. 2. mill; mills.

Mi·am·i (mī·am′i; -ə), *n.* city in SE Florida.

mi·as·ma (mī·az′mə; mi-), *n., pl.* -mas, -ma·ta (-mə·tə). harmful vapors arising from rotting organic matter. [< NL < Gk., pollution] —**mi·as′mal,** **mi·as·mat·ic** (mī′az·mat′ik), **mi·as′mic,** *adj.*

mi·ca (mī′kə), *n.* mineral that divides into

āge, cāre, fär; ēqual, tėrm; īce; ōpen, ôrder; pût, rüle, ūse; th, then; ə=a in about.

thin, partly transparent layers; isinglass. Mica is used in stove doors, where the heat might break glass. [< L, grain, crumb] —mi·ca·ceous (mī·kā′shəs), *adj.*

Mi·cah (mī′kə), *n.* **1.** a Hebrew prophet who lived in the eighth century B.C. **2.** book of the Old Testament.

mice (mīs), *n.* pl. of mouse.

Mich., **1.** Michaelmas. **2.** Michigan.

Mi·chael (mī′kəl), *n.* Saint, *Bible.* one of the archangels. He was the conqueror of Lucifer.

Mich·ael·mas (mik′əl·məs), *n.* *Esp. Brit.* September 29, church festival in honor of the archangel Michael.

Mi·chel·an·ge·lo (mī′kəl·an′jə·lō), *n.* 1475-1564, Italian sculptor, painter, and architect.

Mi·chel·son (mī′kəl·sən), *n.* Albert A., 1852-1931, American physicist.

Mich·i·gan (mish′ə·gən), *n.* **1.** a Middle Western State of the United States. *Capital:* Lansing. *Abbrev.:* Mich. **2.** Lake, one of the five Great Lakes, between the United States and Canada. —Mich·i·gan·der (mish′ə·gan′dər), Mich′i·gan·ite, *n. Am.*

Mick·ey Finn, mick·ey finn (mik′i fin′), *U.S. Slang.* a drugged drink.

mick·le (mik′əl), *adj., adv., n.* Archaic or Dial. much. [OE micel]

micro-, *word element.* **1.** small; very small, as in microörganism. **2.** one millionth of a ——, as in microfarad. **3.** that makes much use of the microscope, as in microbiology. [< Gk., < mikros small]

mi·crobe (mī′krōb), *n.* **1.** a microscopic organism, usually one of vegetable nature; germ. **2.** bacterium, esp. one causing disease. [< F, < Gk. mikros small + bios life] —mi·cro·bi·al (mī·krō′bi·əl), mi·cro′bic, *adj.*

mi·cro·cop·y (mī′krō·kop′i), *n., pl.* -cop·ies. a copy made on microfilm.

mi·cro·cosm (mī′krō·koz·əm), *n.* **1.** a little world; universe in miniature. **2.** man thought of as a miniature representation of the universe. [< F < LL < LGk. mikros kosmos little world] —mi′cro·cos′mic, mi′cro·cos′mi·cal, *adj.*

mi·cro·far·ad (mī′krō·far′əd; -ad), *n.* unit of electrical capacity; one millionth of a farad.

mi·cro·film (mī′krō·film′), *n.* film preserving the contents of newspapers, records, etc., in very small space. —*v.* record on microfilm.

mi·cro·groove (mī′krō·grüv′), *n.* a narrow groove used on long-playing phonograph records.

mi·crom·e·ter (mī·krom′ə·tər), *n.* **1.** instrument for measuring minute distances, angles, objects, etc., used with a microscope or telescope. **2.** micrometer caliper.

micrometer caliper, caliper having a screw with a very fine thread, used for very accurate measurement.

Micrometer

mi·cron (mī′kron), *n., pl.* mi·crons, mi·cra (mī′krə). one millionth of a meter. *Symbol:* μ [< NL < Gk., neut. adj., small]

Mi·cro·ne·sia (mī′krō·nē′zhə; -shə), *n.* group of small islands in the Pacific, E of the Philippines. —Mi′cro·ne′sian, *adj., n.*

mi·cro·ör·gan·ism (mī′krō·ôr′gən·iz·əm), *n.* animal or vegetable organism too small to be seen except with a microscope, as bacteria.

mi·cro·phone (mī′krə·fōn), *n.* instrument that changes sound waves into variations of an electric current. —mi·cro·phon·ic (mī′krə·fon′ik), *adj.*

mi·cro·scope (mī′krə·skōp), *n.* instrument with a lens or combination of lenses that make small things look larger. [< NL microscopium < Gk. mikros small + skopion means of viewing < skopeein look at]

mi·cro·scop·ic (mī′krə·skop′ik), **mi·cro·scop·i·cal** (-ə·kəl), *adj.* **1.** that cannot be seen without using a microscope; tiny. **2.** like a microscope; suggesting a microscope: *a microscopic eye for mistakes.* **3.** of a microscope; with a microscope. —mi′cro·scop′i·cal·ly, *adv.*

mi·cros·co·py (mī·kros′kə·pi; mī′krə·skō′pi), *n.* use of a microscope; microscopic investigation. —mi·cros′co·pist, *n.*

mi·cro·wave (mī′krō·wāv′), *n.* an electromagnetic wave, usually having a wave length of less than ten meters.

mid¹ (mid), *adj.* in the middle of; middle. [OE midd]

mid², 'mid (mid), *prep. Poetic.* amid. [var. of amid]

Mi·das (mī′dəs), *n.* Gk. Legend. a king whose touch turned everything to gold.

mid·brain (mid′brān′), *n.* the middle segment of the brain.

mid·chan·nel (mid′chan′əl), *n.* the middle part of a channel.

mid·con·ti·nent (mid′kon′tə·nənt), *n.* the middle part of a continent.

mid·day (mid′dā′), *n.* middle of the day; noon. —*adj.* of midday.

mid·dle (mid′əl), *adj.* **1.** halfway between; in the center; at the same distance from either end or side. **2.** in between; medium: *a man of middle size.* **3.** intermediate, esp. in time. **4.** between old and modern: *Middle English.* —*n.* **1.** point or part that is the same distance from each end or side or other limit; the central part. **2.** the middle part of a person's body; waist. **3.** something intermediate. [OE middel] —Syn. *n.* **1.** center, midst.

middle age, time of life between youth and old age; period from about 40 to about 55 years old. —mid′dle-aged′, *adj.*

Middle Ages, period of European history between ancient and modern times, from about 500 A.D. to about 1450 A.D.

middle C, *Music.* note on the first added line below the treble staff and the first above the bass staff.

middle class, people between the aristocracy or the very wealthy and the peasantry or working class.

middle ear, *Anat.* the tympanum.

Middle East, region from the E Mediterranean to India. The term has no exact geographical limits, but is usually taken to include the Near East.

Middle English, 1. period in the history of the English language between Old English and Modern English, lasting from about 1100 to about 1500. **2.** language of this period.

Middle French, the French language from 1400-1600.

Middle High German, the High German language from 1100-1450.

Middle Low German, the Low German language from 1100-1450.

mid·dle·man (mid′əl·man′), *n., pl.* -men. trader or merchant who buys goods from the producer and sells them to a retailer or directly to the consumer.

mid·dle·most (mid′əl·mōst), *adj.* in the exact middle; nearest the middle; midmost.

mid·dle-of-the-road (mid′əl·əv·thə·rōd′), *adj. Colloq.* avoiding extremes, as in politics, editorial policy, etc. —mid′dle-of-the-road′er, *n.*

middle term, term in the major and minor premises of a syllogism but not in the conclusion.

mid·dle·weight (mid′əl·wāt′), *n.* boxer or wrestler who weighs more than 147 pounds and less than 160 pounds.

Middle West, *Am.* part of the United States west of the Appalachian Mountains, east of the Rocky Mountains, and north of the Ohio River and the southern boundaries of Missouri and Kansas. Also, Midwest. —**Middle Western,** *Am.* —**Middle Westerner,** *Am.*

mid·dling (mid′ling), *adj.* medium in size, quality, grade, etc. —*adv. Colloq. or Dial.* moderately; fairly. —*n.* middlings, coarse particles of ground wheat mixed with bran. [< middle]

mid·dy (mid′i), *n., pl.* -dies. **1.** Colloq. midshipman. **2.** Am. middy blouse.

middy blouse, *Am.* a loose blouse like a sailor's.

midge (mij), *n.* **1.** a kind of very small insect; gnat. **2.** a very small person. [OE *mycg*]

midg·et (mij′it), *n.* **1.** a very small person; dwarf. **2.** something very small of its kind. [< *midge*]

Mid·i·an·ite (mid′i·ən·īt), *n.* member of a wandering tribe of Arabs that fought against the Israelites.

mid·i·ron (mid′ī′ərn), *n.* a golf club with a steel or iron head having a face of medium slope.

mid·land (mid′lənd), *n.* the middle part of a country; the interior. —*adj.* in or of the midland.

Mid·lands (mid′ləndz), *n.pl.* the central part of England; the midland counties.

mid·most (mid′mōst), *adj.* in the exact middle; nearest the middle.

mid·night (mid′nīt′), *n.* twelve o'clock at night; the middle of the night. —*adj.* of or like midnight; late at night.

midnight sun, sun seen at midnight in the arctic and antarctic regions during summer.

mid·rib (mid′rib′), *n. Bot.* the central vein of a leaf.

mid·riff (mid′rif), *n.* **1.** muscular wall separating the chest cavity from the abdomen; diaphragm. **2.** a woman's garment which leaves the middle portion of the body bare. [OE *midhrif* < *midd* mid + *hrif* belly]

mid·ship (mid′ship′), *adj.* in or of the middle of a ship.

mid·ship·man (mid′ship′mən), *n., pl.* -men. **1.** student at the U.S. Naval Academy at Annapolis or at any college that trains men for the navy. **2.** *Brit.* graduate of the British naval schools until he is made sublieutenant; officer of the same rank as such a graduate. **3.** formerly, a boy or young man who assisted the officers of a ship.

mid·ships (mid′ships′), *adv.* amidships.

midst[1] (midst), *n.* **1.** middle. **2.** in the midst of, in the middle of; among; surrounded by. ▶ midst. A rather formal word except in the prepositional phrase *in the midst of. In our midst* and so on are journalese for "with us," "in our town."

midst[2], **'midst** (midst), *prep.* amidst; amid.

mid·stream (mid′strēm′), *n.* middle of a stream.

mid·sum·mer (mid′sum′ər), *n.* **1.** middle of summer. **2.** time around June 21. —*adj.* in the middle of summer.

mid-Vic·to·ri·an (mid′vik·tô′ri·ən; –tō′–), *adj.* old-fashioned; strict in morals. —*n.* person with old-fashioned ideas and tastes, and strict in morals.

mid·way (mid′wā′), *adv., adj.* halfway; in the middle. —*n.* **1.** middle way or course. **2.** *Am.* place for side shows and other amusements at a fair.

Midway Islands, two small islands in the Pacific, belonging to the United States.

mid·week (mid′wēk′), *n.* the middle of the week. —*adj.* in the middle of the week.

Mid·west (mid′west′), *n. Am.* Middle West. —**Mid′west′ern,** *adj. Am.* —**Mid′west′ern·er,** *n. Am.*

mid·wife (mid′wīf′), *n., pl.* -wives. woman who helps women in childbirth. [OE *mid* with + *wīf* woman]

mid·wife·ry (mid′wīf′ə·ri; –wīf′ri), *n.* the helping of women in childbirth.

mid·win·ter (mid′win′tər), *n.* **1.** middle of winter. **2.** the time around December 21. —*adj.* in the middle of winter.

mid·year (mid′yir′), *adj.* happening in the middle of the year. —*n.* **midyears,** *Am., Colloq.* midyear examinations.

mien (mēn), *n.* manner of holding the head and body; way of acting and looking: *George Washington had the mien of a soldier.* [prob. < *demean;* infl. by F *mine* expression < Celtic] —Syn. bearing, demeanor, appearance.

miff (mif), *Colloq.* —*n.* a peevish fit; petty quarrel. —*v.* **1.** be offended; have a petty quarrel. **2.** offend slightly.

MIG, Mig (mig), *n.* a Russian-designed jet fighter plane.

might[1] (mīt), *v.* pt. of may. [OE *mihte*] ▶ See could for usage note.

might[2] (mīt), *n.* great power; strength. [OE *miht*] —Syn. force, puissance.

might·y (mīt′i), *adj.,* **might·i·er, might·i·est,** *adv.* —*adj.* **1.** possessing, characterized by, or showing strength or power; powerful; strong: *a mighty ruler, mighty force.* **2.** very great: *a mighty famine.* —*adv. Colloq.* very. —**might′i·ly,** *adv.* —**might′i·ness,** *n.* —Syn. *adj.* **1.** puissant, potent. **2.** huge, vast, enormous. —Ant. *adj.* **1.** weak, feeble, impotent.

mi·gnon·ette (min′yən·et′), *n.* plant with long, pointed clusters of small, fragrant, greenish-white flowers. [< F]

mi·graine (mī′grān), *n.* a severe headache, usually on one side only. Also, megrim. [< F < LL < Gk. *hemikrania* < *hemi–* half + *kranion* skull]

mi·grant (mī′grənt), *n.* person, animal, bird, or plant that migrates. —*adj.* migrating.

mi·grate (mī′grāt), *v.,* -grat·ed, -grat·ing. **1.** move from one place to settle in another: *pioneers from New England migrated to all parts of the United States.* **2.** go from one region to another with the change in the seasons: *most birds migrate to warmer countries in the winter.* [< L *migratus*]

mi·gra·tion (mī·grā′shən), *n.* **1.** a migrating. **2.** number of people or animals migrating together. **3.** change of position of an atom or atoms within a molecule. **4.** movement of ions toward an electrode during electrolysis. —**mi·gra′tion·al,** *adj.*

mi·gra·to·ry (mī′grə·tô′ri; –tō′–), *adj.* **1.** migrating; that migrates. **2.** of migration. **3.** wandering. —Syn. **3.** roving, nomad.

mi·ka·do, Mi·ka·do (mə·kä′dō), *n., pl.* -dos. title of the emperor of Japan. The Japanese seldom use this title except in poetry. [< Jap. lit., exalted gate]

mike (mīk), *n. Slang.* microphone.

mil (mil), *n.* unit of length, .001 of an inch, used in measuring the diameter of wires. [< L *mille* thousand]

mil., **1.** military. **2.** militia.

mi·la·dy (mi·lā′di), *n., pl.* -dies. **1.** my lady (used by continental Europeans in speaking to or of an English lady). **2.** an English lady.

Mi·lan (mi·lan′), *n.* city in N Italy. —**Mil·a·nese** (mil′ə·nēz′; –nēs′), *adj., n.*

milch (milch), *adj.* giving milk; kept for the milk it gives: *a milch cow.* [OE *–milce* milking < *mioluc* milk]

mild (mīld), *adj.* **1.** gentle; kind: *a mild, inoffensive man.* **2.** warm; temperate; moderate; not harsh or severe: *a mild climate.* **3.** soft or sweet to the senses; not sharp, sour, bitter, or strong in taste: *mild cheese.* [OE *milde*] —**mild′ly,** *adv.* —**mild′ness,** *n.* —Syn. **1.** tender, lenient, merciful. **2.** clement, pleasant, bland. —Ant. **1.** severe, austere. **2.** rigorous, harsh.

mil·dew (mil′dü; –dū), *n.* kind of fungus that appears on plants or on paper, clothes, leather, etc. —*v.* cover or become covered with mildew. [OE *mildēaw* honeydew] —**mil′dew·y,** *adj.*

mile (mīl), *n.* **1.** unit of measure equal to 5280 feet (a statute mile). **2.** geographical or nautical mile, the length of one minute of a great circle of the earth, officially fixed at 6080.27 feet in the U.S., and at 6080 feet in Great Britain. **3.** international nautical or air mile, an official measure equal to 6076.097 feet. [< L *milia* (*passum*), pl. of *mille* (*passus*) a thousand (paces)]

mile·age, mil·age (mīl′ij), *n.* **1.** miles covered or traveled. **2.** length, extent, or distance in miles. **3.** *Am.* allowance for traveling expenses at so much a mile.

mile·stone (mīl′stōn′), *n.* **1.** stone set up to

MIDRIB

show the distance in miles to a certain place. 2. an important event showing progress.

mi·lieu (mē·lyœ′), *n.* surroundings; environment. [< F]

mil·i·tant (mil′ə·tənt), *adj.* aggressive; fighting; warlike. —*n.* a militant person. [< L, serving as a soldier, ult. < *miles* soldier] —**mil′i·tan·cy,** *n.* —**mil′i·tant·ly,** *adv.*

mil·i·ta·rism (mil′ə·tə·riz′əm), *n.* 1. policy of making military organization and power very strong. 2. military spirit and ideals. —**mil′i·ta·rist,** *n.* —**mil′i·ta·ris′tic,** *adj.* —**mil′i·ta·ris′ti·cal·ly,** *adv.*

mil·i·ta·rize (mil′ə·tə·riz), *v.,* -rized, -riz·ing. 1. make the military organization of (a country) very powerful. 2. fill with military spirit and ideals. —**mil′i·ta·ri·za′tion,** *n.*

mil·i·tar·y (mil′ə·ter′i), *adj.* 1. of soldiers or war. 2. done by soldiers. 3. fit for soldiers. 4. suitable for war; warlike. 5. belonging to the army. —*n.* the army; soldiers. [< L, < *miles* soldier] —**mil′i·tar′i·ly,** *adv.* —**Syn.** *adj.* 4. martial.

military police, soldiers that act as police for the army.

mil·i·tate (mil′ə·tāt), *v.,* -tat·ed, -tat·ing. act; work; operate (*against* or *in favor of*): *bad weather militated against the success of the picnic.*

mi·li·tia (mi·lish′ə), *n.* army of citizens trained for war or any other emergency. [< L, < *miles* soldier] —**mi·li′tia·man,** *n.*

milk (milk), *n.* 1. the white liquid secreted by female mammals for the nourishment of their young. 2. any kind of liquid resembling this: *the milk of a coconut.* —*v.* 1. draw milk from (a cow, goat, etc.). 2. yield or produce milk. 3. drain contents, strength, information, wealth, etc., from: *the dishonest treasurer milked the club treasury.* 4. draw sap or poison from: *milk a rattlesnake.* [OE *mioluc*] —**milk′er,** *n.*

milk-and-wa·ter (milk′ən·wô′tər; -wot′ər), *adj.* weak; wishy-washy.

milk leg, painful swelling of the leg caused by clots in the veins.

milk·maid (milk′mād′), *n.* 1. woman who milks cows. 2. woman who works in a dairy.

milk·man (milk′man′), *n., pl.* -men. man who sells or delivers milk.

milk of magnesia, a milky, white medicine, Mg(OH)$_2$ in water, used as a laxative and antacid.

milk snake, *Am.* a small, harmless, gray snake.

milk·sop (milk′sop′), *n.* an unmanly fellow; coward. —**milk′sop′ism,** *n.*

milk sugar, lactose.

milk tooth, one of the first set of teeth; temporary tooth of a young child or animal.

milk·weed (milk′wēd′), *n. Am.* weed with white juice that looks like milk.

milk·y (mil′ki), *adj.,* milk·i·er, milk·i·est. 1. like milk; white as milk; whitish. 2. of milk; containing milk. 3. mild; weak; timid. —**milk′i·ness,** *n.*

Milkweed (2 to 3 ft. high)

Milky Way, a broad band of faint light that stretches across the sky at night. It is made up of countless stars, too far away to be seen separately without a telescope.

mill[1] (mil), *n.* 1. machine for grinding grain into flour or meal. 2. building containing such a machine. 3. any machine for crushing or grinding: *a coffee mill.* 4. machine for stamping, pressing, cutting, polishing, etc. 5. building where manufacturing is done. 6. the ridged edge of a coin. —*v.* 1. grind (grain) into flour or meal. 2. grind into powder or pulp. 3. manufacture. 4. cut a series of fine notches or ridges on the edge of (a coin): *a dime is milled.* 5. move around in confusion: *the frightened cattle began to mill.* [< LL *molinum* < L *mola* millstone]

mill[2] (mil), *n.* $.001, or ¹⁄₁₀ of a cent. Mills are used in figuring, but not as coins. [short for L *millesimum* one thousandth < *mille* thousand]

Mill (mil), *n.* John Stuart, 1806–1873, English economist and philosopher.

mill·dam (mil′dam′), *n.* dam built in a stream to supply water power for a mill.

mil·len·ni·um (mə·len′i·əm), *n., pl.* -ni·ums, -ni·a (-ni·ə). 1. period of a thousand years. 2. the period of a thousand years during which Christ is expected to reign on earth. Rev. 20:1–7. 3. period of righteousness and happiness. [< NL, < L *mille* thousand + *annus* year] —**mil·len′ni·al,** *adj.*

mil·le·pede (mil′ə·pēd), **mil·le·ped** (-ped), *n.* a small, wormlike arthropod that has two pairs of legs apiece for most of its segments. Also, **millipede, milliped.** [< L *millepeda* < *mille* thousand + *pes* foot]

mill·er (mil′ər), *n.* 1. one who owns or runs a mill, esp. a flour mill. 2. moth whose wings look as if they were powdered with flour.

mill·er's-thumb (mil′ərz·thum′), *n.* a small fresh-water fish with spiny fins.

mil·let (mil′it), *n.* 1. a very small grain used for food in Asia and Africa. 2. the plant that it grows on, often used for hay. [< F, ult. < L *milium*]

Mil·let (mi·lā′), *n.* Jean François, 1814–1875, French painter.

milli-, *word element.* one thousandth of a ——, as in *millimeter.* [< L, < *mille*]

mil·li·am·pere (mil′i·am′pir), *n.* one thousandth of an ampere.

mil·liard (mil′yərd; -yärd), *n.* thousand millions; 1,000,000,000. [< F, < L *mille* thousand]

mil·li·gram, *esp. Brit.* **mil·li·gramme** (mil′ə·gram), *n.* one thousandth of a gram.

mil·li·li·ter, *esp. Brit.* **mil·li·li·tre** (mil′ə·lē′tər), *n.* one thousandth of a liter.

mil·li·me·ter, *esp. Brit.* **mil·li·me·tre** (mil′ə·mē′tər), *n.* one thousandth of a meter, or .03937 inch.

mil·li·mi·cron (mil′ə·mī′kron), *n., pl.* -cra (-krə). the thousandth part of a micron.

mil·li·ner (mil′ə·nər), *n.* person who makes, trims, or sells women's hats. [var. of *Milaner,* dealer in goods from Milan, Italy, famous for straw]

mil·li·ner·y (mil′ə·ner′i; -nər·i), *n.* 1. women's hats. 2. business of making, trimming, or selling women's hats.

mil·lion (mil′yən), *n.* 1. one thousand thousand; 1,000,000. 2. a very large number. —*adj.* 1. one thousand thousand; 1,000,000. 2. very many. [< OF < Ital. *milione,* ult. < L *mille* thousand] —**mil′lionth,** *adj., n.*

mil·lion·aire, mil·lion·naire (mil′yən·ãr′), *n.* 1. person who has a million or more dollars, pounds, francs, etc. 2. very wealthy person.

mil·li·pede (mil′ə·pēd), **mil·li·ped** (-ped), *n.* millepede.

mill·pond (mil′pond′), *n.* pond supplying water to drive a mill wheel.

mill·race (mil′rās′), *n.* 1. current of water that drives a mill wheel. 2. channel in which it flows to the mill.

mill·stone (mil′stōn′), *n.* 1. either of a pair of round flat stones for grinding corn, wheat, etc. 2. a heavy burden.

mill·stream (mil′strēm′), *n.* the stream in a millrace.

mill wheel, wheel that supplies power for a mill.

mill·work (mil′wèrk′), *n.* 1. doors, windows, moldings, and other things made in a planing mill. 2. work done in a mill.

mill·wright (mil′rīt′), *n.* 1. person who designs, builds, or sets up mills or machinery for mills. 2. mechanic who sets up and takes care of the machinery in a factory, workshop, etc.

mi·lord (mi·lôrd′), *n.* 1. my lord (used by continental Europeans in speaking to or of an English lord or gentleman). 2. an English gentleman.

milque·toast (milk′tōst′), *n.* an extremely timorous person. [after comic-strip character, Mr. *Milquetoast*]

mil·reis (mil′rās′), *n., pl.* **-reis.** a former Brazilian silver coin and monetary unit.

milt (milt), *n.* 1. the sperm cells of male fishes with the milky fluid containing them. 2. the reproductive gland in male fishes. [OE *milte*]

Mil·ton (mil′tən), *n.* John, 1608–1674, English poet. —**Mil·ton·ic** (mil·ton′ik), **Mil·to·ni·an** (mil·tō′ni·ən), *adj.*

Mil·wau·kee (mil·wô′ki), *n.* city in SE Wisconsin, on Lake Michigan.

mime (mīm), *n., v.,* **mimed, mim·ing.** —*n.* 1. jester; clown. 2. a coarse farce among the ancient Greeks and Romans, using funny actions and gestures. 3. actor in such a farce. —*v.* imitate; mimic. [< L < Gk. *mimos*] —**mim′er,** *n.*

Mim·e·o·graph (mim′i·ə·graf′; -gräf′), *Am.* —*n.* 1. *Trademark.* machine for making copies of written or typewritten material. 2. mimeograph, any such machine. —*v.* mimeograph, make (copies) with a Mimeograph or similar machine. [< Gk. *mimeesthai* imitate + -GRAPH]

mi·met·ic (mi·met′ik; mī-), *adj.* 1. imitative. 2. make-believe. 3. exhibiting mimicry. [< Gk. *mimetikos* < *mimeesthai* imitate] —**mi·met′i·cal·ly,** *adv.*

mim·ic (mim′ik), *v.,* **-icked, -ick·ing,** *n., adj.* —*v.* 1. make fun of by imitating. 2. copy closely; imitate: *a parrot can mimic a person's voice.* 3. resemble closely: *some insects mimic leaves.* —*n.* person or thing that imitates. —*adj.* not real, but imitated or pretended for some purpose. [< L < Gk. *mimikos.* See MIME.]

Butterfly that mimics dead leaves

mim·ic·ry (mim′ik·ri), *n., pl.* **-ries.** 1. a mimicking. 2. protective mimicry, close resemblance of an animal to its surroundings or to some other animal.

mi·mo·sa (mi·mō′sə; -zə), *n.* tree, shrub, or plant growing in warm regions, and usually having fernlike leaves, and heads or spikes of small flowers. [< NL, < L *mimus* MIME; from mimicry of animal reactions]

min., 1. minimum. 2. minute; minutes.

mi·na (mī′nə), *n.* myna.

min·a·ret (min′ə·ret′; min′ə·ret), *n.* a slender, high tower of a Mohammedan mosque with one or more projecting balconies, from which a crier calls the people to prayer. [< F or Sp. < Ar. *manārat* lighthouse]

min·a·to·ry (min′ə·tô′ri; -tō′-), *adj.* menacing; threatening. [< LL, < L *minari* threaten, ult. < *minae* projecting points, threats] —**min′a·to′ri·ly,** *adv.*

mince (mins), *v.,* **minced, minc·ing,** *n.* —*v.* 1. chop up into very small pieces. 2. speak or do in an affectedly polite or elegant manner. 3. not to mince matters, to speak plainly and frankly. 4. walk with little short steps. —*n.* mincemeat. [< OF *mincier,* ult. < L *minutus* small] —**minc′er,** *n.*

mince·meat (mins′mēt′), *n.* mixture of chopped meat, apples, suet, raisins, spices, etc., used as a filling for pies.

minc·ing (min′sing), *adj.* 1. too polite; too nice. 2. walking with little short steps. —**minc′ing·ly,** *adv.*

mind (mīnd), *n.* 1. that which thinks, feels, and wills. 2. intellect. 3. person who has intelligence. 4. reason; sanity: *be out of one's mind.* 5. way of thinking and feeling: *change one's mind.* 6. desire, purpose, intention, or will: *have a good mind to do something.* 7. what one thinks or feels; opinions; sentiments: *speak your mind.* 8. attention; thought; mental effort: *keep your mind on your work.* 9. remembrance or recollection: *call to mind.* 10. have in mind, a. remember. b. think of; consider. c. intend; plan. 11. put in mind, remind. 12. set one's mind on, want very much. —*v.* 1. remember. 2. Archaic or Dial. remind. 3. attend to; give heed to: *mind my words!* 4. take notice; observe. 5. be careful concerning: *mind the step.* 6. be careful. 7. look after; take care of; tend: *mind the baby.* 8. obey: *mind your father and mother.* 9. feel concern about; object to: *mind parting from a friend.* 10. feel concern; object. [OE *gemynd*] —**mind′er,** *n.* —**Syn.** *n.* 1. understanding, reason, judgment, sense. 2. intelligence. 9. memory.

Min·da·na·o (min′də·nä′ō), *n.* the second largest island in the Philippines.

mind·ful (mīnd′fəl), *adj.* 1. having in mind: *mindful of the advice.* 2. taking thought; careful: *mindful of every step.* —**mind′ful·ly,** *adv.* —**mind′ful·ness,** *n.* —**Syn.** 1. aware, cognizant. 2. heedful, attentive.

mind·less (mīnd′lis), *adj.* 1. without intelligence; stupid. 2. not taking thought; careless. —**mind′less·ly,** *adv.*

Min·do·ro (min·dô′rō; -dō′-), *n.* island in the C Philippines.

mine[1] (mīn), *pron.* 1. belonging to me: *this book is mine.* 2. the one or ones belonging to me: *your shoes are black; mine are brown.* —*adj.* Archaic. my (used only before a vowel or *h,* or after a noun): *mine eyes, mine heart, sister mine.* [OE *mīn*]

mine[2] (mīn), *n., v.,* **mined, min·ing.** —*n.* 1. a large hole or space dug in the earth to get out something valuable. 2. rich or plentiful source: *a dictionary is a mine of information.* 3. *Mil.* container holding an explosive charge that is put under water and exploded by propeller vibrations (acoustic or sonic mine) or by magnetic attraction (magnetic mine), or laid on the ground or shallowly buried and exploded by contact with a vehicle, etc. (land mine). —*v.* 1. dig a mine; make a hole, space, passage, etc., below the earth. 2. dig into (the earth, a hill, etc.) for coal, ore, etc. 3. get (metal, etc.) from a mine. 4. dig in; make (passages, etc.) by digging. 5. put explosive mines in or under; lay explosive mines. [< F < Celtic]

mine field, 1. area throughout which explosive mines have been laid. 2. pattern of mines in such an area.

min·er (mīn′ər), *n.* worker in a mine.

min·er·al (min′ər·əl; min′rəl), *n.* 1. substance obtained by mining. Coal is a mineral. 2. any substance that is neither plant nor animal. —*adj.* 1. of minerals. 2. like a mineral. 3. containing minerals: *mineral water.* [< OF, ult. < mine MINE[2]]

min·er·al·, mineralogy.

min·er·al·ize (min′ər·əl·īz; min′rəl-), *v.,* **-ized, -iz·ing.** 1. convert into mineral substance; transform (metal) into an ore. 2. impregnate or supply with mineral substances. —**min′er·al·i·za′tion,** *n.* —**min′er·al·iz′er,** *n.*

min·er·al·o·gy (min′ər·al′ə·ji; -ol′ə-), *n.* science of minerals. —**min·er·a·log·i·cal** (min′ər·ə·loj′ə·kəl), *adj.* —**min′er·a·log′i·cal·ly,** *adv.* —**min′er·al′o·gist,** *n.*

mineral oil, 1. oil obtained from the earth. Kerosene is a mineral oil. 2. a colorless, odorless, tasteless oil obtained from petroleum, used as a laxative.

mineral water, water containing mineral salts or gases.

Mi·ner·va (mə·nér′və), *n. Roman Myth.* goddess of wisdom, the arts, and defensive war, identified with the Greek goddess Athena.

min·e·stro·ne (min′ə·strō′ni), *n.* a thick soup containing vegetables, vermicelli, etc. [< Ital.]

mine sweeper, ship used for dragging a harbor, the sea, etc., to remove mines laid by an enemy.

Ming (ming), *n.* the ruling Chinese dynasty from 1368 to 1644.

min·gle (ming′gəl), *v.,* **-gled, -gling.** 1. mix: *two rivers that join mingle their waters.* 2. associate: *mingle with important people.* 3. form by mixing; concoct. [ME *mengele(n)* < OE *mengan* mix] —**min′gler,** *n.* —**Syn.** 1. blend, fuse, combine.

min·i·a·ture (min′i·ə·chər; min′ə·chər), *n.* 1. anything represented on a small scale: *a miniature of the ship Mayflower.* 2. a very small painting, usually a portrait. **3. in miniature,** on a small scale; reduced in size. —*adj.* done or made on a very small scale; tiny. [< Ital. *miniatura* < Med.L *miniare* illuminate (a manuscript) < L, paint red, < *minium* red lead; confused with L *minutus* small] —**min′i·a·tur·ist,** *n.*

miniature camera, camera using narrow film (35 mm. or less).

min·im (min′əm), *n.* **1.** the smallest liquid measure, one sixtieth of a dram, or about a drop. **2.** *Music.* a half note. **3.** a very small amount. [< L *minimus* smallest]

min·i·mize (min′ə·mīz), *v.,* **-mized, -miz·ing. 1.** reduce to the least possible amount or degree: *minimize the effects of inflation.* **2.** state at the lowest possible estimate; make the least of: *minimize the help others have given.* —**min′i·mi·za′tion,** *n.* —**min′i·miz′er,** *n.*

min·i·mum (min′ə·məm), *n., pl.* **-mums, -ma** (-mə), *adj.* —*n.* the least possible amount; lowest amount: *eight hours' sleep is the minimum that children should have.* —*adj.* **1.** least possible: *minimum age for voting.* **2.** lowest: *minimum rate.* [< L, smallest (thing)] —**min′i·mal,** *adj.*

minimum wage, wage agreed upon or fixed by law as the lowest payable to certain employees.

min·ing (mīn′ing), *n.* **1.** working mines for ores, coal, etc. **2.** business of digging coal or ores from mines.

min·ion (min′yən), *n.* **1.** servant or follower willing to do whatever he is ordered. **2.** *Contemptuous.* darling; favorite. **3.** size of type; 7-point. [< F *mignon* petite, dainty]

min·is·ter (min′is·tər), *n.* **1.** clergyman serving a church; spiritual guide; pastor. **2.** person who is given charge of a department of the government: *the Minister of War.* **3.** person sent to a foreign country to represent his own government: *the United States Minister to France.* **4.** person or thing employed in carrying out (purpose, will, etc.). —*v.* **1.** act as a servant or nurse; be of service: *she ministers to the sick man's wants.* **2.** be helpful; give aid; contribute. [< L, servant < *minus* less, after *magister* MASTER] —Syn. *v.* **1.** serve, attend. **2.** help, assist.

min·is·te·ri·al (min′is·tir′i·əl), *adj.* **1.** of a minister. **2.** of the ministry. **3.** suitable for a clergyman. **4.** executive; administrative. **5.** subordinate; helping. —**min′is·te′ri·al·ly,** *adv.*

min·is·trant (min′is·trənt), *adj.* ministering. —*n.* one who ministers.

min·is·tra·tion (min′is·trā′shən), *n.* **1.** service as a minister of a church. **2.** help; aid.

min·is·try (min′is·tri), *n., pl.* **-tries. 1.** office, duties, or time of service of a minister. **2.** ministers of a church. **3.** ministers of a government. **4.** in England and in Europe, a government department under a minister. **5.** offices of such a department. **6.** a ministering or serving. [< L *ministerium* office, service; see MINISTER. Doublet of MÉTIER.]

Min·i·track (min′ə·trak′), *n.* a system for tracking rockets and missiles by radio signals, established by the Naval Research Laboratory. See also **moonwatch.**

min·i·ver (min′ə·vər), *n.* fur or combination of furs formerly much used for lining and trimming garments. [< OF *menu vair* small vair; see MENU; *vair* < L *varius* variegated]

mink (mingk), *n.* **1.** a weasellike animal that lives in water part of the time. **2.** its valuable brown fur. [appar. < Scand. (Sw.) *mänk*]

Minn., Minnesota.

Mink (total length ab. 2 ft.)

Min·ne·ap·o·lis (min′i·ap′ə·lis; -ap′lis), *n.* city in SE Minnesota, on the Mississippi.

min·ne·sing·er, Min·ne·sing·er (min′ə·sing′ər), *n.* a German lyrical poet and singer of the 12th, 13th, and 14th centuries. [< G, love singer]

Min·ne·so·ta (min′ə·sō′tə), *n.* a Middle West-

ern State of the United States. *Capital:* St. Paul. *Abbrev.:* Minn. —**Min′ne·so′tan,** *adj., n. Am.*

min·now (min′ō), *n.* **1.** a very small freshwater fish. **2.** any very tiny fish. [ME *minwe,* OE *myne*]

mi·nor (mī′nər), *adj.* **1.** smaller; lesser; less important: *a minor fault, a minor poet.* **2.** under legal age. **3.** *Music.* **a.** less by a half step than the corresponding major interval. **b.** noting a scale, mode, or key whose third tone is minor in relation to the fundamental tone. —*n.* **1.** person under the legal age of responsibility. **2.** *Am.* subject or course of study to which a student gives much time and attention, but less than to his major subject. —*v.* **minor in,** *Colloq.* have or take as a minor subject of study. [< L, lesser] —Syn. *adj.* **1.** subordinate, secondary, lower, inferior.

Mi·nor·ca (mə·nôr′kə), *n.* one of the Balearic Islands in the W Mediterranean, belonging to Spain.

mi·nor·i·ty (mə·nôr′ə·ti; mī-; -nor′-), *n., pl.* **-ties,** *adj.* —*n.* **1.** smaller number or part; less than half. **2.** condition or time of being under the legal age of responsibility. —*adj.* of or pertaining to a minority.

minor league, *Am.* any professional sports league or association, esp. in baseball, other than the major leagues.

Mi·nos (mī′nəs; -nos), *n. Gk. Myth.* **1.** king and lawgiver of Crete who became a judge in Hades. **2.** his grandson, who built the Labyrinth at Crete and kept the Minotaur in it.

Min·o·taur (min′ə·tôr), *n. Gk. Myth.* monster with a bull's head and a man's body, kept in the Labyrinth at Crete and fed with human flesh.

Minsk (minsk), *n.* city in the W Soviet Union.

min·ster (min′stər), *n. Esp. Brit.* **1.** church of a monastery. **2.** a large or important church; cathedral. [< LL *monasterium.* Doublet of MONASTERY.]

min·strel (min′strəl), *n.* **1.** singer or musician in the household of a lord in the Middle Ages. **2.** singer or musician who went about and sang or recited poems, often of his own making. **3.** *Am.* member of a company of actors, usually white men made up as Negroes, giving songs, music, and jokes supposed to have come from the Negroes. [< OF < LL *ministerialis* < L *ministerium* MINISTRY]

min·strel·sy (min′strəl·si), *n., pl.* **-sies. 1.** art or practice of a minstrel. **2.** collection of songs and ballads. **3.** company of minstrels.

mint¹ (mint), *n.* **1.** a sweet-smelling plant used for flavoring. Peppermint and spearmint are kinds of mint. **2.** piece of candy flavored with mint. [< L *menta,* akin to Gk. *minthe*]

mint² (mint), *n.* **1.** place where money is coined by public authority. **2.** a large amount: *a million dollars is a mint of money.* —*v.* **1.** coin (money). **2.** make or fabricate; originate. [< L *moneta* mint, money. Doublet of MONEY.] —**mint′er,** *n.*

mint·age (min′tij), *n.* **1.** a minting; coinage. **2.** product of minting; output of a mint. **3.** charge for coining; cost of coining.

min·u·end (min′yū·end), *n. Math.* number or quantity from which another is to be subtracted. In 100—23=77, the minuend is 100. [< L *minuendus* to be made smaller < *minus* less]

min·u·et (min′yū·et′), *n.* **1.** a slow, stately dance. **2.** music for it. [< F *menuet,* dim. of *menu* small]

mi·nus (mī′nəs), *prep.* **1.** less; decreased by: *5 minus 2 leaves 3.* **2.** *Colloq.* lacking: *a book minus its cover.* —*adj.* **1.** less than: *a mark of B minus is not so high as B.* **2.** showing subtraction: *the minus sign is —.* **3.** less than zero: *if you have no money, and owe someone 3 cents, you have —3¢.* —*n.* **1.** Also, **minus sign.** sign (—) meaning that the quantity following it is to be subtracted. **2.** minus quantity. **3.** deficiency or loss. [< L, less]

min·ute¹ (min′it), *n.* **1.** sixty seconds; one sixtieth of an hour. **2.** short time; instant: *that'll be over in a minute.* **3.** point of time: *come here this minute.* **4.** *Geom.* one sixtieth of a degree. 10°10′ means ten degrees and ten minutes. **5. minutes,** written summary; official record of proceedings of a society, board, committee, etc. **6. up to the minute,** up-to-date. [< OF < LL *minuta* small part. See MINUTE².]

mi·nute² (mī·nūt′; –nūt′; mə–), *adj.* **1.** very small: *microscopes are used to study minute organisms.* **2.** going into or concerned with very small details: *minute instructions.* [< L *minutus* made small < *minus* less. Doublet of MENU.] —**mi·nute′ly,** *adv.* —**mi·nute′ness,** *n.* —Syn. **1.** tiny, diminutive, little. **2.** detailed, particular.

min·ute hand (min′it), hand on a clock or watch that indicates minutes. It moves around the whole dial once in an hour.

min·ute·man (min′it·man′), *n., pl.* –men. *Am.* member of the American militia just before and during the Revolution, who were ready for military service at very short notice.

mi·nu·ti·ae (mi·nū′shi·ē; –nū′–), *n.pl.* very small matters; trifling details. [< L, smallness. See MINUTE².]

minx (mingks), *n.* a pert girl.

Mir·a·beau (mir′ə·bō), *n.* 1749–1791, French statesman and orator.

mir·a·cle (mir′ə·kəl), *n.* **1.** a wonderful happening that is contrary to or independent of the known laws of nature: *it would be a miracle if the sun should stand still in the heavens for an hour.* **2.** something marvelous; a wonder. **3.** remarkable example: *a miracle of patience.* **4.** a miracle play. [< OF < L *miraculum*, ult. < *mirus* wonderful]

miracle play, play based on Bible stories or on legends of the saints, produced during the Middle Ages.

mi·rac·u·lous (mə·rak′yə·ləs), *adj.* **1.** contrary to or independent of the known laws of nature. **2.** wonderful; marvelous. —**mi·rac′u·lous·ly,** *adv.* —**mi·rac′u·lous·ness,** *n.* —Syn. **1.** supernatural, incomprehensible. **2.** extraordinary, surprising.

mi·rage (mə·räzh′), *n.* **1.** a misleading appearance, usually in the desert or at sea, resulting from a reflection of some distant scene in such a way as to give the impression that it is near. **2.** illusion. [< F, < *mirer* look at. See MIRROR.]

mire (mīr), *n., v.,* **mired, mir·ing.** —*n.* **1.** soft deep mud; slush. **2.** bog; swamp. —*v.* **1.** get stuck in mire. **2.** stick in mire. **3.** soil with mud or mire. **4.** involve in difficulties. [< Scand. *mȳrr*] —Syn. *n.* **1.** ooze, slime.

mirk (mèrk), *n., adj.* murk.

mirk·y (mèr′ki), *adj.,* **mirk·i·er, mirk·i·est.** murky.

mir·ror (mir′ər), *n.* **1.** a looking glass; surface that reflects light. **2.** whatever reflects or gives a true description: *that book is a mirror of the times.* **3.** model; example; pattern: *that knight was a mirror of chivalry.* —*v.* reflect as a mirror does: *the still water mirrored the trees along the bank.* [< OF *mirour,* ult. < L *mirari* wonder, admire]

mirth (mèrth), *n.* merry fun; being joyous or gay; laughter. [OE *myrgth* < *myrge* merry] —**mirth′less,** *adj.* —**mirth′less·ly,** *adv.* —**mirth′less·ness,** *n.* —Syn. merriment, gaiety, jollity, glee, hilarity.

mirth·ful (mèrth′fəl), *adj.* merry; gay; laughing. —**mirth′ful·ly,** *adv.* —**mirth′ful·ness,** *n.*

mir·y (mīr′i), *adj.,* **mir·i·er, mir·i·est. 1.** muddy; swampy. **2.** dirty; filthy. —**mir′i·ness,** *n.*

mis-, *prefix.* **1.** bad, as in *misformation, misgovernment.* **2.** badly, as in *misform, mismade, mismake.* **3.** wrong, as in *mispronunciation, misvaluation.* **4.** wrongly, as in *misclassify, mislabel.* [OE *mis*(*s*)–, or in borrowed words < OF *mes*- < OHG *missi*–, *missa*–]

mis·ad·ven·ture (mis′əd·ven′chər), *n.* an unfortunate accident; bad luck; mishap.

mis·al·li·ance (mis′ə·lī′əns), *n.* an unsuitable alliance or association, esp. in marriage.

mis·an·thrope (mis′ən·thrōp; miz′–), **mis·an·thro·pist** (mis·an′thrə·pist), *n.* hater of mankind; person who dislikes or distrusts hu-

man beings. [< Gk., < *misein* hate + *anthropos* man] —**mis·an·throp·ic** (mis′ən·throp′ik; miz′–), —**mis·an·throp′i·cal,** *adj.* —**mis′an·throp′i·cal·ly,** *adv.*

mis·an·thro·py (mis·an′thrə·pi), *n.* hatred, dislike, or distrust of human beings.

mis·ap·ply (mis′ə·plī′), *v.,* **-plied, -ply·ing.** apply wrongly; make a wrong application or use of. —**mis·ap·pli·ca·tion** (mis′ap·lə·kā′shən), *n.*

mis·ap·pre·hend (mis′ap·ri·hend′), *v.* misunderstand. —**mis·ap·pre·hen·sion** (mis′ap·ri·hen′shən), *n.*

mis·ap·pro·pri·ate (mis′ə·prō′pri·āt), *v.,* **-at·ed, -at·ing. 1.** put to a wrong use. **2.** use dishonestly as one's own. —**mis′ap·pro′pri·a′tion,** *n.*

mis·be·come (mis′bi·kum′), *v.,* **-came, -come, -com·ing.** be unbecoming to; be unfit for: *swearing misbecomes a lady.* —**mis′be·com′ing,** *adj.*

mis·be·got·ten (mis′bi·got′ən), **mis·be·got** (–got′), *adj.* begotten unlawfully; illegitimate.

mis·be·have (mis′bi·hāv′), *v.,* **-haved, -hav·ing.** behave badly. —**mis′be·hav′ior,** *esp. Brit.* **mis′be·hav′iour,** *n.*

mis·be·lief (mis′bi·lēf′), *n.* **1.** a wrong or erroneous belief. **2.** belief in a religion that is not the regularly accepted one.

mis·be·lieve (mis′bi·lēv′), *v.,* **-lieved, -liev·ing. 1.** believe wrongly; hold an erroneous belief. **2.** disbelieve; doubt. —**mis′be·liev′er,** *n.*

misc., miscellaneous; miscellany.

mis·cal·cu·late (mis·kal′kyə·lāt), *v.,* **-lat·ed, -lat·ing.** calculate wrongly. —**mis′cal·cu·la′tion,** *n.*

mis·call (mis·kôl′), *v.* call by a wrong name.

mis·car·riage (mis·kar′ij), *n.* **1.** failure: *a miscarriage of justice.* **2.** failure to arrive: *the miscarriage of a letter.* **3.** birth of a baby before it is able to live.

mis·car·ry (mis·kar′i), *v.,* **-ried, -ry·ing. 1.** go wrong: *John's plans miscarried, and he could not come.* **2.** fail to arrive: *the letter must have miscarried.* **3.** have a miscarriage.

mis·ce·ge·na·tion (mis′ə·jə·nā′shən), *n. Am.* an interbreeding between different races. [< L *miscere* mix + *genus* race]

mis·cel·la·ne·ous (mis′ə·lā′ni·əs), *adj.* **1.** not all of one kind or nature: *a miscellaneous collection containing stones, stamps, birds' nests, and other things.* **2.** many-sided: *a miscellaneous writer.* [< L, < *miscellus* mixed, ult. < *miscere* mix] —**mis′cel·la′ne·ous·ly,** *adv.* —**mis′cel·la′ne·ous·ness,** *n.* —Syn. **1.** mixed, varied, assorted, heterogeneous.

mis·cel·la·ny (mis′ə·lā′ni), *n., pl.* **-nies. 1.** a miscellaneous collection; mixture. **2.** miscellanies, collection of miscellaneous articles in one book.

mis·chance (mis·chans′; –chäns′), *n.* misfortune; bad luck.

mis·chief (mis′chif), *n.* **1.** injury, usually done by some person; harm. **2.** conduct that causes harm or trouble, often without meaning it. **3.** one who does harm, often just in fun. **4.** merry teasing: *eyes full of mischief.* [< OF *meschief,* ult. < *mes*- bad (see MIS-) + *chever* come to an end < *chief* head < L *caput*] —Syn. **1.** damage, hurt, trouble.

mis·chie·vous (mis′chə·vəs), *adj.* **1.** harmful: *a mischievous belief.* **2.** full of mischief; naughty. **3.** full of pranks and teasing fun. —**mis′chie·vous·ly,** *adv.* —**mis′chie·vous·ness,** *n.* —Syn. **1.** hurtful, injurious. **3.** playful, teasing, roguish.

mis·ci·ble (mis′ə·bəl), *adj.* capable of being mixed. [< L *miscere* mix] —**mis′ci·bil′i·ty,** *n.*

mis·con·ceive (mis′kən·sēv′), *v.,* **-ceived, -ceiv·ing.** have wrong ideas about; misunderstand. —**mis·con·ceiv′er,** *n.* —**mis·con·cep·tion** (mis′kən·sep′shən), *n.*

mis·con·duct (*n.* mis·kon′dukt; *v.* mis′kən·dukt′), *n.* **1.** bad behavior. **2.** bad management: *misconduct of the business resulted in a loss.* —*v.* **1.** behave badly. **2.** manage badly.

mis·con·strue (mis′kən·strü′), *v.,* **-strued,**

-stru·ing. take in a wrong sense; misunderstand. —**mis·con·struc·tion** (mis'kən·struk'-shən), n.

mis·count (v. mis·kount'; n. mis'kount), v. count wrongly. —n. wrong count.

mis·cre·ant (mis'krē·ənt), adj. 1. having very bad morals; base. 2. Archaic. unbelieving. —n. 1. villain. 2. Archaic. unbeliever. [< OF, < mes- wrongly (see MIS-) + creant, ppr. of creire believe < L credere] —Syn. adj. 1. depraved, vile, detestable.

mis·cue (mis·kū'), n., v. -cued, -cu·ing. —n. a bad stroke in billiards that does not hit the ball squarely. —v. 1. make such a stroke. 2. Theater. miss one's cue.

mis·deal (v. mis·dēl'; n. mis'dēl'), v., -dealt (-delt'), -deal·ing. —v. deal wrongly, esp. at cards. —n. a wrong deal. —**mis·deal'er**, n.

mis·deed (mis·dēd'; mis'dēd'), n. a bad act; wicked deed. —Syn. misdemeanor, offense.

mis·de·mean (mis'di·mēn'), v. behave badly.

mis·de·mean·or, esp. Brit. **mis·de·mean·our** (mis'di·mēn'ər), n. 1. Law. a breaking of the law, not so serious as a felony. Disturbing the peace and breaking traffic laws are misdemeanors. 2. wrong deed. 3. bad behavior: all were punished for the misdemeanor of a few.

mis·di·rect (mis'də·rekt'; -dī-), v. direct wrongly. —**mis'di·rec'tion**, n.

mis·do (mis·dü'), v., -did, -done, -do·ing. do wrongly. —**mis·do'er**, n.

mis·doubt (mis·dout'), v. Archaic. 1. distrust. 2. fear. —n. suspicion.

mis·em·ploy (mis'em·ploi'), v. use wrongly or improperly. —**mis'em·ploy'ment**, n.

mi·ser (mī'zər), n. person who loves money for its own sake; one who lives poorly in order to save money and keep it. [< L, wretched] —Syn. skinflint, niggard.

mis·er·a·ble (miz'ər·ə·bəl; miz'rə·bəl), adj. 1. wretchedly unhappy: a sick child is often miserable. 2. causing trouble or unhappiness: a miserable cold. 3. poor; mean; wretched: they live in miserable surroundings. —n. a miserable person; one who is in misery. —**mis'er·a·ble·ness**, n. —**mis'er·a·bly**, adv. —Syn. adj. 1. disconsolate. 3. deplorable, pitiable, sordid.

mi·ser·ly (mī'zər·li), adj. of, like, or suited to a miser; stingy. —**mi'ser·li·ness**, n. —Syn. avaricious, niggardly, close.

mis·er·y (miz'ər·i; miz'ri), n., pl. -er·ies. 1. a miserable, unhappy state of mind: the misery of having no home or friends. 2. poor, mean, miserable circumstances: the misery of poverty. [< L miseria < miser wretched] —Syn. 1. wretchedness, distress, woe, grief, anguish.

mis·fea·sance (mis·fē'zəns), n. Law. the wrongful performance of a lawful act; wrongful and injurious exercise of lawful authority. [< OF mesfaisance < mes- wrong (see MIS-) + faire do < L facere]

mis·fire (mis·fīr'), v., -fired, -fir·ing, n. —v. fail to be fired or exploded properly. —n. instance of misfiring.

mis·fit (v. mis·fit'; n. mis'fit'), v., -fit·ted, -fit·ting, n. —v. fit badly. —n. 1. a bad fit. 2. a maladjusted individual.

mis·for·tune (mis·fôr'chən), n. 1. bad luck. 2. piece of bad luck; unlucky accident. —Syn. 1. adversity, trouble. 2. disaster, mischance, catastrophe. —Ant. 1. prosperity, success.

mis·give (mis·giv'), v., -gave, -giv·en, -giv·ing. cause to feel doubt, suspicion, or anxiety.

mis·giv·ing (mis·giv'ing), n. a feeling of doubt, suspicion, or anxiety: have misgivings about their safety. —Syn. foreboding, apprehension.

mis·gov·ern (mis·guv'ərn), v. govern or manage badly. —**mis·gov'ern·ment**, n.

mis·guide (mis·gīd'), v., -guid·ed, -guid·ing. lead into mistakes or wrongdoing; mislead. —**mis·guid'ance**, n. —**mis·guid'ed**, adj. —**mis·guid'ed·ly**, adv. —**mis·guid'er**, n.

mis·han·dle (mis·han'dəl), v., -dled, -dling. handle badly; maltreat.

mis·hap (mis'hap; mis·hap'), n. an unlucky accident. —Syn. misfortune, disaster.

mis·in·form (mis'in·fôrm'), v. give wrong or misleading information to. —**mis'in·for·ma'tion**, n.

mis·in·ter·pret (mis'in·tér'prit), v. interpret wrongly; explain wrongly; misunderstand. —**mis'in·ter'pre·ta'tion**, n. —Syn. misconstrue.

mis·judge (mis·juj'), v., -judged, -judg·ing. judge wrongly or unjustly. —**mis·judg'ment**, esp. Brit. **mis·judge'ment**, n.

mis·lay (mis·lā'), v., -laid, -lay·ing. 1. put in the wrong place. 2. put in a place and then forget where it is: mislay a sweater. —**mis·lay'er**, n.

mis·lead (mis·lēd'), v., -led, -lead·ing. 1. lead astray; cause to go in the wrong direction: the sign misled the traveler. 2. cause to do wrong; lead into wrongdoing: he was misled by his companions. 3. lead to think what is not so; deceive: his lies misled me. —**mis·lead'ing**, adj. —**mis·lead'ing·ly**, adv. —Syn. 1. misguide, misdirect. 3. delude, beguile, dupe.

mis·man·age (mis·man'ij), v., -aged, -ag·ing. manage badly. —**mis·man'age·ment**, n. —**mis·man'ag·er**, n.

mis·match (mis·mach'), v. match badly or unsuitably. —n. a bad or unsuitable match.

mis·mate (mis·māt'), v., -mat·ed, -mat·ing. mate unsuitably.

mis·name (mis·nām'), v., -named, -nam·ing. call by a wrong name.

mis·no·mer (mis·nō'mər), n. 1. name that describes wrongly. 2. error in naming. [< OF, < mes- wrongly (see MIS-) + nommer to name < L nominare. See NOMINATE.]

mi·sog·a·my (mi·sog'ə·mi), n. hatred of marriage. [< NL, ult. < Gk. misos hatred + gamos marriage] —**mi·sog'a·mist**, n.

mi·sog·y·ny (mi·soj'ə·ni), n. hatred of women. [< NL, ult. < Gk. misos hatred + gyne woman] —**mi·sog'y·nist**, n. —**mi·sog'y·nous**, adj.

mis·place (mis·plās'), v., -placed, -plac·ing. 1. put in the wrong place. 2. Colloq. put in a place and then forget where it is. 3. give (one's love or trust) to the wrong person. —**mis·place'ment**, n.

mis·play (mis·plā'), n. Am. a wrong play. —v. play wrongly.

mis·print (n. mis'print'; v. mis·print'), n. mistake in printing. —v. print wrongly.

mis·pri·sion (mis·prizh'ən), n. 1. a wrongful action or omission, esp. by a public official. 2. neglect to give notice of an act of treason or felony. [< OF, ult. < mes- wrongly (see MIS-) + prendre take < L prehendere]

mis·prize (mis·prīz'), v., -prized, -priz·ing. despise; undervalue; slight. [< OF, < mes- wrongly (see MIS-) + prisier PRIZE[2]]

mis·pro·nounce (mis'prə·nouns'), v., -nounced, -nounc·ing. pronounce incorrectly. —**mis·pro·nun·ci·a·tion** (mis'prə·nun'si·ā'-shən), n.

mis·quote (mis·kwōt'), v., -quot·ed, -quot·ing. quote incorrectly. —**mis'quo·ta'tion**, n.

mis·read (mis·rēd'), v., -read (-red'), -read·ing. 1. read wrongly: misread a sentence. 2. misunderstand; interpret wrongly: misread directions and get lost.

mis·rep·re·sent (mis'rep·ri·zent'), v. represent falsely; give a wrong idea of. —**mis'rep·re·sen·ta'tion**, n. —**mis'rep·re·sent'er**, n.

mis·rule (mis·rül'), n., v., -ruled, -rul·ing. —n. 1. bad or unwise rule. 2. disorder. —v. rule badly. —**mis·rul'er**, n.

miss[1] (mis), v. 1. fail to hit. 2. fail to find, get, meet, attend, use, catch, hear, read, do, solve, etc. 3. be unsuccessful; fail: miss in one's schemes. 4. let slip by; not seize: I missed my chance. 5. escape or avoid: barely miss being hit. 6. notice the absence of; feel keenly the absence of: I miss my mother when she goes away. 7. miss fire, a. of guns, fail to go off. b. fail. —n. failure to hit, attain, etc. [OE missan]

miss[2] (mis), n., pl. miss·es. 1. girl; young woman. 2. Miss, title put before a girl's or unmarried woman's name: Miss Brown, the Misses Brown, the Miss Browns. [short for mistress] ➤ miss. Plural misses, sometimes pronounced mis'-

ēz to distinguish from mis′iz (Mrs.): *the Misses Angel and Joyce.* When the misses are from the same family the plural could be, formally, *the Misses Smith;* colloquially, *the Miss Smiths. Miss* is used only with a person's name—except in humor or sales talk, or by a waiter, a servant, or the like.

Miss., Mississippi.

mis·sal (mis′əl), *n.* book containing the prayers, etc., for celebrating Mass throughout the year. [< Med.L, < LL *missa* mass]

mis·shape (mis-shāp′), *v.,* **-shaped, -shaped** or **-shap·en, -shap·ing.** shape badly; deform; make in the wrong shape. —**mis·shap′en,** *adj.*

mis·sile (mis′əl), *n.* **1.** object that is thrown, hurled, or shot, such as a stone, a bullet, an arrow, or a lance. **2.** a self-propelled bomb or rocket. —*adj.* capable of being thrown, hurled, or shot. [< L, ult. < *mittere* send]

mis·sile·man (mis′əl-mən), *n., pl.* **-men.** person who works with missiles and rockets.

miss·ing (mis′ing), *adj.* lacking; wanting; absent; not found; gone: *one book is missing.*

mis·sion (mish′ən), *n.* **1.** sending or being sent on some special work; errand: *he was sent on a mission to a foreign government.* **2.** group sent on some special business: *a mission was sent by the church.* **3.** business on which a mission is sent. **4.** station or headquarters of a religious mission. **5.** **missions,** an organized effort to spread the Christian religion. **6.** business or purpose in life; calling: *her mission seems to be to help others.* **7.** a definite military or naval operation involving a single airplane or a group of airplanes. —*v.* send on a mission; entrust with a mission. [< L *missio* < *mittere* send] —**mis′sion·al,** *adj.* —Syn. *n.* **2.** commission, delegation. **3.** message, charge, duty, trust.

mis·sion·ar·y (mish′ən-er′i), *n., pl.* **-ar·ies,** *adj.* —*n.* **1.** person sent on a religious mission. **2.** person who works to advance some cause or idea. —*adj.* of missions or missionaries.

Mis·sis·sip·pi (mis′ə-sip′i), *n.* **1.** the largest river in North America, flowing south through the United States from N Minnesota into the Gulf of Mexico. **2.** a Southern State of the United States. *Capital:* Jackson. *Abbrev.:* Miss. —Mis′sis·sip′pi·an, *adj.,* n. Am.

mis·sive (mis′iv), *n.* a written message; letter. [< Med.L *missivus,* ult. < L *mittere* send]

Mis·sou·ri (mi·zur′i; -ə), *n.* **1.** the longest river in the United States, flowing from SW Montana into the Mississippi. **2.** a Middle Western State of the United States. *Capital:* Jefferson City. *Abbrev.:* Mo. **3.** from Missouri, *Am., Slang.* not convinced until shown clear proof. —Missou′ri·an, *adj., n.* Am.

mis·speak (mis-spēk′), *v.,* **-spoke, -spo·ken, -speak·ing.** speak, utter, or pronounce wrongly or incorrectly.

mis·spell (mis-spel′), *v.,* **-spelled** or **-spelt, -spell·ing.** spell incorrectly.

mis·spell·ing (mis-spel′ing), *n.* an incorrect spelling.

mis·spend (mis-spend′), *v.,* **-spent, -spend·ing.** spend foolishly or wrongly; waste.

mis·spent (mis-spent′), *adj.* spent foolishly or wrongly. —*v.* pt. and pp. of misspend.

mis·state (mis-stāt′), *v.,* **-stat·ed, -stat·ing.** make wrong or misleading statements about. —**mis·state′ment,** *n.* Syn. misrepresent.

mis·step (mis-step′; mis′step), *n.* **1.** a wrong step. **2.** error or slip in conduct.

mist (mist), *n.* **1.** cloud of very fine drops of water in the air; fog. **2.** anything that dims, blurs, or obscures. **3.** haze before the eyes due to illness or tears. —*v.* **1.** come down in mist; rain in very fine drops. **2.** be covered with mist; become dim. **3.** cover with a mist; put a mist before; make dim: *tears misted her eyes.* [OE] —Syn. *n.* **1.** haze, drizzle.

mis·tak·a·ble (mis·tāk′ə-bəl), *adj.* that may be mistaken or misunderstood.

mis·take (mis-tāk′), *n., v.,* **-took, -tak·en, -tak·ing.** —*n.* error; blunder; misunderstanding: *I used your towel by mistake.* —*v.* **1.** mis-

understand (what is seen or heard). **2.** take wrongly; take (to be some other person or thing): *mistake a stick for a snake.* **3.** make a mistake. [< Scand. *mistaka*] —Syn. *n.* fault, oversight, slip.

mis·tak·en (mis-tāk′ən), *adj.* **1.** wrong in opinion; having made a mistake: *a mistaken person should admit his error.* **2.** wrong; wrongly judged; misplaced: *giving too much is a mistaken kindness.* —*v.* pp. of mistake. —**mis·tak′en·ly,** *adv.*

mis·ter (mis′tər), *n.* **1.** Mister, Mr., a title put before a man's name or the name of his office: *Mr. Smith, Mr. President.* **2.** *Colloq.* sir: *Good morning, mister.* —*v. Colloq.* address as "mister." [var. of *master*]

mis·tle·toe (mis′əl-tō), *n.* **1.** plant with small, waxy, white berries and yellow flowers, that grows as a parasite on certain trees. **2.** sprig of mistletoe, often used as a Christmas decoration. [OE *misteltān* < *mistel* mistletoe + *tān* twig]

Mistletoe growing on a tree

mis·took (mis-tuk′), *v.* pt. of mistake.

mis·tral (mis′trəl; mis·träl′), *n.* a cold, dry, northerly wind common in southern France and neighboring regions. [< F < Pr., orig., dominant, < L *magistralis* < *magister* master]

mis·treat (mis-trēt′), *v.* treat badly. —**mis·treat′ment,** *n.*

mis·tress (mis′tris), *n.* **1.** the woman who is at the head of a household. **2.** woman or country that is in control or can rule: *mistress of the seas.* **3.** woman who has a thorough knowledge or mastery: *a mistress of cookery.* **4.** *Brit.* a woman teacher. **5.** *Poetic.* woman loved and courted by a man. **6.** woman who improperly occupies the place of a wife. **7.** Mistress, title of courtesy for a married woman, usually abbreviated in writing to Mrs. and pronounced mis′iz, miz′iz, or miz. [< OF *maistresse* < *maistre* MASTER]

mis·tri·al (mis·trī′əl), *n.* **1.** trial having no effect in law because of some error in the proceedings. **2.** an inconclusive trial.

mis·trust (mis-trust′), *v.* feel no confidence in; doubt: *mistrust one's ability.* —*n.* lack of trust or confidence. —**mis·trust′er,** *n.* —**mis·trust′ful,** *adj.* —**mis·trust′ful·ly,** *adv.* —**mis·trust′ful·ness,** *n.* —**mis·trust′ing·ly,** *adv.* —**mis·trust′less,** *adj.* —Syn. *v.* suspect, distrust. —*n.* doubt, suspicion.

mist·y (mis′ti), *adj.,* **mist·i·er, mist·i·est.** **1.** of mist. **2.** characterized by mist; covered with mist. **3.** not clearly seen or outlined. **4.** as if seen through a mist; vague; indistinct. —**mist′i·ly,** *adv.* —**mist′i·ness,** *n.*

mis·un·der·stand (mis′un·dər·stand′), *v.,* **-stood, -stand·ing. 1.** understand wrongly. **2.** take in a wrong sense; give the wrong meaning to. —**mis′un·der·stand′ing,** *n.* —Syn. **1.** misapprehend, misconceive. **2.** misinterpret.

mis·un·der·stood (mis′un·dər·stud′), *v.* pt. and pp. of misunderstand. —*adj.* not understood; not properly appreciated.

mis·us·age (mis·ūs′ij; -ūz′-), *n.* **1.** a wrong or improper usage. **2.** ill usage; bad treatment.

mis·use (*v.* mis·ūz′; *n.* mis·ūs′), *v.,* **-used, -us·ing,** *n.* —*v.* **1.** use for the wrong purpose: *misuse a knife at the table by lifting food with it.* **2.** abuse; ill-treat: *misuse horses by loading them too heavily.* —*n.* a wrong or improper use. —Syn. *v.* **1.** misapply. **2.** maltreat.

mite¹ (mīt), *n.* any of various tiny animals that belong to the same class as spiders and live in foods, on plants, or on other animals. [OE *mīte*]

mite² (mīt), *n.* **1.** anything very small; little bit. **2.** coin of slight value. **3.** a very small child. [< MDu., ? ult. identical with *mite¹*]

mi·ter, *esp. Brit.* **mi·tre** (mī′tər), *n., v.,* **mi·tered, mi·ter·ing;** *esp. Brit.* **mi·tred, mi·tring.** —*n.* **1.** a tall, pointed, folded cap worn by bishops during sacred ceremonies. 2. the bevel on either of the pieces in a miter joint. —v. 1. bestow a miter on; make a bishop. 2. prepare (ends of wood) for joining in a miter joint. [< L < Gk. *mitra* headband] —mi'tered, *esp. Brit.* mi'tred, *adj.* —mi'ter·er, *n.*

miter joint, a right-angled joint made by cutting the ends of two pieces of wood on equal slants.

mit·i·gate (mit'ə·gāt), *v.*, -gat·ed, -gat·ing. make or become mild; make or become milder; make less severe or less intense: *mitigate a person's anger or pain, mitigate a punishment.* [< L *mitigatus* < *mitis* gentle] —mit'i·ga·ble, *adj.* —mit'i·ga'tive, *adj.* —mit'i·ga'tor, *n.* —mit·i·ga·to·ry (mit'ə·gə·tô'ri; -tō'-), *adj., n.*

Miter

mi·to·sis (mi·tō'sis; mī-), *n.* method of cell division in which the chromatin of the nucleus forms into a thread that separates into segments or chromosomes, each of which in turn separates longitudinally into two parts. [< NL, < Gk. *mitos* thread] —mi·tot·ic (mi·tot'ik; mī-), *adj.*

mitt (mit), *n.* 1. kind of long glove without fingers, or with very short fingers. 2. *Am.* glove used by baseball players. 3. mitten. [short for *mitten*]

mit·ten (mit'ən), *n.* 1. kind of winter glove covering the four fingers together and the thumb separately. 2. mittens, *Slang.* boxing gloves. [< F *mitaine* half glove]

mix (miks), *v.*, mixed or mixt, mix·ing, *n.* —v. 1. put together; stir well together: *mix ingredients to make a cake.* 2. prepare by putting different things together: *mix a cake.* 3. join: *mix business and pleasure.* 4. be or become mixed: *milk and water mix.* 5. associate together; get along together: *people mix well in a group like ours.* 6. mix up, a. confuse. b. involve; concern. —*n.* 1. mixture. 2. *Colloq.* mixed condition; mess. [< *mixt* mixed < F < L *mixtus* mixed] —mix'er, *n.* —Syn. *v.* 1. mingle, blend, combine, fuse, amalgamate. 5. fraternize. —Ant. *v.* 1. separate.

mixed (mikst), *adj.* 1. put together or formed by mixing; of different kinds combined: *mixed candies, mixed emotions.* 2. of different classes, kinds, etc.; not exclusive: *a mixed company.* 3. of or for persons of both sexes: *a mixed chorus.* 4. of different religions: *a mixed marriage.* 5. mixed up, *Colloq.* mentally confused.

mixed number, number consisting of a whole number and a fraction, such as 1½ or 16¾.

mix·ture (miks'chər), *n.* 1. a mixing or being mixed. 2. what has been mixed. 3. two or more substances mixed together, but not chemically combined. —Syn. 1. blending, fusing. 2. blend, compound, combination.

mix-up (miks'up'), *n. Colloq.* 1. confusion; mess. 2. a confused fight.

miz·zen (miz'ən), **miz·en,** *n. Naut.* 1. a fore-and-aft sail on the mizzenmast. 2. mizzenmast. [< F < Ital. < L *medianus* in the middle]

miz·zen·mast, miz·en·mast (miz'ən·mast'; -mäst'; -məst), *n. Naut.* mast nearest the stern in a two-masted or three-masted ship.

MLG, Middle Low German.

Mlle., *pl.* Mlles. Mademoiselle.

MM., Messieurs.

mm., millimeter; millimeters.

Mme., *pl.* Mmes. Madame.

Mn, *Chem.* manganese.

mne·mon·ic (ni·mon'ik), *adj.* 1. aiding the memory. 2. intended to aid memory. 3. of or pertaining to memory. [< Gk., < *mnamnasthai* remember]

Mo, *Chem.* molybdenum.

Mo., 1. Missouri. 2. Monday.

mo., 1. *pl.* mos. month. 2. months.

M.O., m.o., money order.

mo·a (mō'ə), *n.* a large extinct bird of New Zealand, something like an ostrich. [< Maori]

Mo·ab (mō'ab), *n.* an ancient kingdom in Syria. —Mo·ab·ite (mō'əb·īt), *n., adj.*

moan (mōn), *n.* 1. a long, low sound of suffer-ing. 2. any similar sound: *the moan of the wind.* —v. 1. make moans. 2. utter with a moan. 3. complain; grieve. 4. complain about; grieve for. [ME *man.* Cf. OE *mǣnan* complain.] —moan'ing·ly, *adv.* —Syn. *v.* 1. groan, wail. 3, 4. lament, bewail.

moat (mōt), *n.* a deep, wide ditch dug around a castle or town as a protection against enemies. Moats were usually kept filled with water. —v. surround with a moat. [< OF *mote* mound]

mob (mob), *n., v.,* mobbed, mob·bing. —n. 1. a large number of people, usually crowded closely together. 2. the common mass of people. 3. a lawless crowd, easily moved to act without thinking. —v. 1. crowd around in curiosity, anger, etc. 2. attack with violence, as a mob does. [short for L *mobile vulgus* fickle common people] —mob'ber, *n.* —Syn. *n.* 1. crowd, multitude.

mo·bile (mō'bəl; mō'bēl), *adj.* 1. movable; easy to move. 2. moving easily; changing easily: *a mobile mind adapts itself quickly.* —n. pieces of metal, wood, etc., suspended on wires or threads and so balanced as to move in a slight breeze, used decoratively. [< L, movable < *movere* move] —mo·bil·i·ty (mō·bil'ə·ti), *n.*

Mo·bile Bay (mō'bēl), part of the Gulf of Mexico that extends into SW Alabama.

mo·bi·lize (mō'bə·līz), *v.,* -lized, -liz·ing. 1. call (troops, warships, etc.) into active military service; organize for war. 2. assemble and prepare for war: *the troops mobilized quickly.* 3. put into motion or active use: *mobilize the wealth of a country.* [< F, < mobile MOBILE] —mo'bi·liz'a·ble, *adj.* —mo'bi·li·za'tion, *n.*

moc·ca·sin (mok'ə·sən), *n. Am.* 1. a soft leather shoe or sandal. 2. Also, water moccasin. a poisonous snake found in the southern part of the United States. [< Algonquian]

moccasin flower, *Am.* a pink or white orchid shaped somewhat like a slipper.

Mo·cha (mō'kə), *n.* Also, mocha. 1. a choice variety of coffee originally coming from Arabia. 2. kind of soft leather used for gloves. —*adj.* mocha, flavored with coffee.

mock (mok), *v.* 1. laugh at; make fun of. 2. make fun of by copying or imitating. 3. imitate; copy. 4. scoff. 5. make light of; pay no attention to. 6. deceive; disappoint. —*adj.* not real; copying; sham; imitation: *a mock battle.* —*n.* 1. an action or speech that mocks. 2. person or thing scorned or deserving scorn. 3. mockery; derision. 4. imitation. [< OF *mocquer*] —mock'er, *n.* —mock'ing, *adj.* —mock'ing·ly, *adv.* —Syn. *v.* 1. deride, ridicule, taunt, gibe. 3. mimic, ape. 6. delude, fool. —*adj.* feigned, pretended.

mock·er·y (mok'ər·i), *n., pl.* -er·ies. 1. a making fun; ridicule: *their mockery of John hurt his feelings.* 2. person or thing to be made fun of. 3. a bad copy or imitation. 4. a disregarding; setting at naught: *an unfair trial is a mockery of justice.* —Syn. 1. derision, sarcasm.

mock-he·ro·ic (mok'hi·rō'ik), *adj.* imitating or burlesquing what is heroic: *a mock-heroic poem.*

mock·ing·bird (mok'ing·bėrd'), *n. Am.* songbird of the S United States that imitates the notes of other birds.

mock orange, syringa.

mock turtle soup, soup made in imitation of green turtle soup.

mock-up (mok'up'), *n.* a full-sized model of an airplane, machine, etc., used for teaching purposes.

mo·dal (mō'dəl), *adj.* of or having to do with mode, manner, or form. —mo·dal·i·ty (mō·dal'ə·ti), *n.* —mod'al·ly, *adv.*

modal auxiliary, word like *may, can, must, would,* and *should,* that indicates the mood of the verb with which it is used.

mode (mōd), *n.* 1. manner or way in which a thing is done: *his mode of coming was unusual.* 2. style, fashion, or custom that prevails; the way most people are today: *bobbed hair became the mode about 1920.* 3. *Gram.* form of a verb that shows whether an act or state is thought of as a fact, command, etc.; mood. 4. *Music.* any of various arrangements of the tones of an octave.

5. *Statistics.* the most frequent of a set of measurements. [< L *modus* measure] —Syn. **1.** method. **2.** vogue.

mod·el (mod′əl), *n.*, *v.*, **–eled, –el·ing;** *esp. Brit.* **–elled, –el·ling,** *adj.* —*n.* **1.** a small copy: *a model of a ship.* **2.** figure in clay or wax that is to be copied in marble, bronze, etc.: *a model for a statue.* **3.** way in which a thing is made; style: *dresses of that model are becoming to me.* **4.** thing or person to be copied or imitated. **5.** person who poses for artists, photographers, etc. **6.** woman in a clothing store who puts on garments in order to show customers how they look. —*v.* **1.** make; shape; fashion; design; plan: *model a bird's nest in clay.* **2.** make models; design: *model in clay.* **3.** form (something) after a particular model: *model yourself on your father.* **4.** be a model. —*adj.* **1.** serving as a model. **2.** just right or perfect, esp. in conduct: *a model child.* [< F < Ital. *modello,* dim. of *modo* MODE] —mod′el·er, *esp. Brit.* mod′el·ler, *n.* —Syn. *n.* **4.** example, pattern, standard, prototype. –*v.* **1.** form, mold.

mod·er·ate (*adj., n.* mod′ər·it; *v.* mod′ər·āt), *adj., n., v.,* **–at·ed, –at·ing.** —*adj.* **1.** kept or keeping within proper bounds; not extreme: *moderate expenses.* **2.** not violent; calm: *moderate in speech or opinion.* **3.** fair; medium; not very large or good: *a moderate profit.* —*n.* person who holds moderate opinions. —*v.* **1.** make less violent. **2.** become less extreme or violent: *the wind is moderating.* **3.** act as moderator; preside (over). [< L *moderatus* regulated] —mod′er·ate·ly, *adv.* —mod′er·ate·ness, *n.* —Syn. *adj.* **2.** restrained, temperate. –*v.* **1, 2.** diminish, lessen. —Ant. *adj.* **1.** immoderate, extreme. **2.** intemperate.

mod·er·a·tion (mod′ər·ā′shən), *n.* **1.** a moderating. **2.** freedom from excess; proper restraint; temperance. **3.** calmness; lack of violence. **4. in moderation,** within limits; not going to extremes.

mod·e·ra·to (mod′ə·rä′tō), *adj. Music.* in moderate time. [< Ital.]

mod·er·a·tor (mod′ər·ā′tər), *n.* **1.** a presiding officer; chairman. **2.** arbitrator; mediator. **3.** *Nuclear Physics.* material used in a reactor to slow down fission. —mod′er·a′tor·ship, *n.*

mod·ern (mod′ərn), *adj.* **1.** of the present time; of times not long past: *television is a modern invention.* **2.** up-to-date; not old-fashioned. —*n.* **1.** person of modern times. **2.** person who has modern ideas and tastes. **3.** *Print.* a type characterized by bold vertical strokes and straight serifs. [< LL *modernus* < L *modo* just now] —mod′ern·ly, *adv.* —mod′ern·ness, *n.* —Syn. *adj.* **1.** new, recent, late. —Ant. *adj.* **1.** antique, ancient.

Modern English, the English language from about 1500 through the present.

mod·ern·ism (mod′ər·niz·əm), *n.* **1.** modern attitudes or methods; sympathy with what is modern. **2.** tendency in religion to interpret the teachings of the Bible or the church in accordance with modern scientific theories. **3.** a modern word or phrase. —mod′ern·ist, *n.* —mod′ern·is′tic, *adj.*

mo·der·ni·ty (mə·dér′nə·ti; mō–), *n., pl.* **–ties. 1.** a being modern. **2.** something modern.

mod·ern·ize (mod′ər·nīz), *v.,* **–ized, –iz·ing. 1.** make modern; bring up to present ways or standards. **2.** become modern. —mod′ern·i·za′tion, *n.* —mod′ern·iz′er, *n.*

mod·est (mod′ist), *adj.* **1.** not thinking too highly of oneself; not vain; humble. **2.** bashful; not bold; shy; held back by a sense of what is fit and proper. **3.** not calling attention to one's body; decent. **4.** not too great; not asking too much: *a modest request.* **5.** not gaudy; humble in appearance; quiet: *a modest little house.* [< L *modestus* in due measure < *modus* measure] —mod′est·ly, *adv.* —Syn. **1.** unpretentious, unassuming. **2.** diffident. —Ant. **1.** conceited, egotistical. **2.** bold, forward.

mod·es·ty (mod′is·ti), *n., pl.* **–ties. 1.** freedom from vanity; being modest or humble. **2.** shy-ness; bashfulness. **3.** being decent. —Syn. **1.** humility. **2.** diffidence.

mod·i·cum (mod′ə·kəm), *n.* a small or moderate quantity: *a modicum of common sense.* [< L, neut., moderate < *modus* measure]

mod·i·fi·ca·tion (mod′ə·fə·kā′shən), *n.* **1.** partial alteration or change. **2.** a modifying or being modified; a toning down: *a modification of one's claims.* **3.** limitation of meaning. **4.** modified form; variety.

mod·i·fi·er (mod′ə·fī′ər), *n.* **1.** word or group of words that limits another word or group of words. **2.** person or thing that modifies. ▶ **Modifiers** are words or groups of words that restrict, limit, or make more exact the meaning of other words. In these examples the words in italics modify the words in small caps: *a cold, windy* DAY; HE FAILED *miserably; a truly* GREAT . . . *a truly great* MAN. *Coming around the corner,* WE met him head on. *As we came around the corner,* we saw him boarding a trolley. In general the modifiers of nouns and pronouns are adjectives, participles, adjective phrases, adjective clauses; the modifiers of verbs, adjectives, and adverbs are adverbs, adverbial phrases, or clauses.

mod·i·fy (mod′ə·fī), *v.,* **–fied, –fy·ing. 1.** change (somewhat): *modify the terms of a lease.* **2.** make less; tone down; make less severe or strong: *modify his demands.* **3.** *Gram.* limit the meaning of; qualify. Adverbs modify verbs and adjectives. **4.** change (a vowel) by umlaut. [< L *modificare* limit < *modus* measure + *facere* make] —mod′i·fi′a·ble, *adj.* —Syn. **1.** alter. **2.** temper, moderate.

mod·ish (mōd′ish), *adj.* fashionable; stylish. —mod′ish·ly, *adv.* —mod′ish·ness, *n.*

mo·diste (mō·dēst′), *n.* maker of or dealer in women's gowns, hats, etc.; dressmaker. [< F]

mod·u·late (moj′ə·lāt), *v.,* **–lat·ed, –lat·ing. 1.** regulate; adjust; vary; soften; tone down. **2.** alter (the voice) for expression. **3.** *Music.* change from one key or note to another. **4.** *Music.* attune to a certain pitch or key. **5.** vary the frequency of (electrical waves). **6.** change (a radio current) by adding sound waves to it. [< L *modulatus,* ult. < *modus* measure] —mod′u·la′tor, *n.* —mod·u·la·to·ry (moj′ə·lə·tô′ri; –tō′–), *adj.*

mod·u·la·tion (moj′ə·lā′shən), *n.* **1.** a modulating or being modulated. **2.** *Music.* change from one key to another in the course of a piece. **3.** *Electronics.* a varying of high-frequency waves.

mod·ule (moj′ül), *n.* **1.** a standard or unit for measuring. **2.** the size of some part taken as a unit of measure. [< L *modulus,* dim. of *modus* measure. Doublet of MOLD[1].]

mo·dus op·e·ran·di (mō′dəs op′ə·ran′dī), *Latin.* method or manner of working.

Mo·gul (mō′gul; mō·gul′), *n.* **1.** Mongolian. **2.** one of the Mongol conquerors of India in the 16th century or one of their descendants. **3.** mogul, an important person.

mo·hair (mō′hār), *n.* **1.** cloth made from the long, silky hair of the Angora goat. **2.** a similar cloth made of wool and cotton or rayon. [ult. < Ar. *mukhayyar;* conformed to *hair*]

Mo·ham·med (mō·ham′id), *n.* 570?–632 A.D., founder and prophet of Islam, a religion widely accepted in Asia and Africa. Also, Mahomet, Muhammad.

Mo·ham·med·an (mō·ham′ə·dən), *adj.* of Mohammed or the religion founded by him. —*n.* follower of Mohammed; believer in the religion founded by him. Also, Mahometan, Muhammadan.

Mo·ham·med·an·ism (mō·ham′ə·dən·iz′əm), *n.* the Mohammedan religion. Also, Mahometanism, Muhammadanism.

Mo·ha·ve (mō·hä′vē), *n.* Mojave.

Mo·hawk (mō′hôk), *n., pl.* **–hawk, –hawks.** *Am.* member of a tribe of American Indians formerly living in central New York State.

Mo·he·gan (mō·hē′gən), *n. Am.* member of a tribe of American Indians formerly living in Connecticut. Also, Mahican.

āge, cãre, fär; ēqual, tėrm; īce; ōpen, ôrder; pŭt, rūle, ūse; tth, then; ə=a in about.

Mo·hi·can (mō-hē′kən), *n. Am.* member of a tribe of American Indians formerly living in the upper Hudson valley. Also, **Mahican.**

moi·e·ty (moi′ə·ti), *n., pl.* **-ties. 1.** half. **2.** part. [< OF < LL *medietas* half < L, the middle < *medius* middle]

moil (moil), *v.* work hard; drudge. —*n.* **1.** hard work; drudgery. **2.** trouble; confusion. [< OF *moillier* moisten < L *mollis* soft] —**moil′er,** *n.* —moil′ing·ly, *adv.*

moire (mwär; mwä·rā′; mô·rā′; mō–), *n.* fabric having a wavelike pattern; watered fabric. [< F, alter. of E *mohair*]

moi·ré (mwä·rā′; mô·rā′; mō–), *n.* moire. —*adj.* having a wavelike pattern; watered: *moiré silk.* [< F]

moist (moist), *adj.* **1.** slightly wet; damp: *moist ground.* **2.** rainy: *moist weather.* [< OF *moiste* < L *mucidus* moldy, musty < *mucus* mucus] —moist′ly, *adv.* —moist′ness, *n.* —Syn. **1.** humid, dank. —Ant. **1.** dry, arid, parched.

moist·en (mois′ən), *v.* **1.** make moist. **2.** become moist. —moist′en·er, *n.*

mois·ture (mois′chər), *n.* slight wetness; water or other liquid spread in very small drops in the air or on a surface.

Mo·ja·ve (mō·hä′vē), *n.* desert in S California. Also, **Mohave.**

mo·lar (mō′lər), *n.* tooth with a broad surface for grinding. A person's back teeth are molars. —*adj.* **1.** adapted for grinding. **2.** of the molar teeth. [< L, < *mola* mill]

mo·las·ses (mə·las′iz), *n. Am.* a sweet syrup obtained in making sugar from sugar cane. [< Pg. < LL *mellaceum* must < *mel* honey]

mold[1] (mōld), *n.* **1.** a hollow shape in which anything is formed or cast: *pour melted metal into a mold.* **2.** the shape or form which is given by a mold. **3.** model according to which anything is shaped. **4.** something shaped in a mold: *a mold of pudding.* **5.** nature; character. —*v.* **1.** form; shape: *mold candles from wax.* **2.** make or form into shape: *mold wax into candles.* Also, *esp. Brit.* **mould.** [< OF *modle* < L *modulus.* Doublet of MODULE.] —mold′a·ble, *adj.*

mold[2] (mōld), *n.* **1.** a woolly or furry, fungous growth, often greenish in color, that appears on food and other animal or vegetable substances when they are left too long in a warm, moist place. **2.** any of the fungi that produce such a growth. —*v.* **1.** become covered with mold. **2.** cover with mold. Also, *esp. Brit.* **mould.** [ME *moul,* earlier *muwle(n),* prob. infl. by *mold*[3]] —Syn. *n.* **1.** mildew.

mold[3] (mōld), *n.* loose earth; fine, soft, rich soil. Also, *esp. Brit.* **mould.** [OE *molde*]

mold·board (mōld′bôrd′; -bōrd′), *n.* a curved metal plate in a plow, that turns over the earth from the furrow. Also, *esp. Brit.* **mouldboard.**

mold·er[1] (mōl′dər), *v.* **1.** turn into dust by natural decay; crumble; waste away. **2.** cause to crumble or waste away. Also, *esp. Brit.* **moulder.** [prob. < *mold*[3]]

mold·er[2] (mōl′dər), *n.* one that molds. Also, *esp. Brit.* **moulder.**

mold·ing (mōl′ding), *n.* **1.** act of shaping. **2.** something molded. **3.** strip, usually of wood, used to support pictures, to cover electric wires, etc. **4.** decorative strip of wood, stone, plaster, etc. Also, *esp. Brit.* **moulding.**

mold·y (mōl′di), *adj.,* **mold·i·er, mold·i·est. 1.** covered with mold: *a moldy crust of bread.* **2.** musty; stale: *a moldy smell.* Also, *esp. Brit.* **mouldy.** —mold′i·ness, *n.*

mole[1] (mōl), *n.* a congenital spot on the skin, usually brown. [OE *māl*]

mole[2] (mōl), *n.* a small animal that lives underground most of the time. Moles have velvety fur and very small eyes. [ME *molle*]

Mole (total length ab. 7 in.)

mole[3] (mōl), *n.* breakwater. [< L *moles* mass]

mo·lec·u·lar (mə·lek′yə·lər), *adj.* pertaining to, caused by, or consisting of molecules. —mo·lec′u·lar·ly, *adv.*

molecular film, a layer one molecule thick.

mol·e·cule (mol′ə·kūl), *n.* **1.** *Physics, Chem.* the smallest particle into which a substance can be divided without chemical change. **2.** a very small particle. [< NL *molecula,* dim. of L *moles* mass]

mole·hill (mōl′hil′), *n.* **1.** a small mound or ridge of earth raised up by moles burrowing under the ground. **2.** something insignificant.

mole·skin (mōl′skin′), *n.* **1.** skin of the mole used as fur. **2.** a strong cotton fabric used for sportsmen's and laborers' clothing.

mo·lest (mə·lest′), *v.* meddle with and injure; interfere with and trouble; disturb. [< OF < L, < *molestus* troublesome < *moles* burden] —moles·ta·tion (mō′les·tā′shən; mol′es–), *n.* —mo·lest′er, *n.* —Syn. harass, harry.

Mo·lière (mō·lyär′), *n.* 1622–1673, greatest French writer of comedies.

moll (mol), *n. Slang.* **1.** a female companion of a criminal or vagrant. **2.** prostitute. [short for *Molly,* familiar var. of *Mary*]

mol·li·fy (mol′ə·fī), *v.,* **-fied, -fy·ing.** soften; appease; mitigate: *mollify a person or his wrath.* [< F < LL, < *mollis* soft + *facere* make] —mol′li·fi·ca′tion, *n.* —mol′li·fi′er, *n.* —mol′li·fy′ing·ly, *adv.* —Syn. calm, quiet, pacify, soothe.

mol·lusk, *esp. Brit.* **mol·lusc** (mol′əsk), *n.* animal having a soft body not composed of segments, and usually covered with a hard shell. Snails, mussels, oysters, and clams are mollusks. [< F < L *molluscus* soft (of a nutshell)] —mol·lus·can (mə·lus′kən), *adj., n.*

mol·ly·cod·dle (mol′i·kod′əl), *n., v.,* **-dled, -dling.** —*n.* boy or man accustomed to being fussed over and pampered; milksop. —*v.* coddle; pamper. [< *Molly* (familiar var. of *Mary*) + *coddle*] —mol′ly·cod′dler, *n.*

Mo·loch (mō′lok), *n.* **1.** a Semitic deity whose worship was marked by the sacrifice of children by their parents. **2.** anything conceived as requiring frightful sacrifice.

Mo·lo·kai (mō′lō·kī′), *n.* the fourth largest island of Hawaii; site of a leper colony.

Mo·lo·tov (mô′lə·tôf; -tof; mol′ə–), *n.* Viacheslav Mikhailovich, born 1890, Soviet statesman, foreign minister 1939–49 and 1953–56.

molt (mōlt), *v.* **1.** shed the feathers, skin, etc., before a new growth. Birds and snakes molt. **2.** shed (feathers, etc.). —*n.* act or time of doing this. Also, *esp. Brit.* **moult.** [ME *mout* < OE *mūtian* (as in *bemūtian* exchange for) < L *mutare* change] —molt′er, *n.*

molt·en (mōl′tən), *adj.* **1.** melted: *molten steel.* **2.** made by melting and casting: *a molten image.* —*v.* pp. of **melt.**

Mo·luc·cas (mə·luk′əz; mō–), *n.pl.* group of islands in E Indonesia, between Celebes and New Guinea. Also, **Spice Islands.**

mo·lyb·de·num (mə·lib′də·nəm; mol′ib·dē′nəm), *n. Chem.* a silver-white metallic element, Mo, of the chromium group. [< NL < L *molybdaena* < Gk., < *molybdos* lead]

mo·ment (mō′mənt), *n.* **1.** a very short space of time; instant: *in a moment, all was changed.* **2.** a present or other particular point of time: *we both arrived at the same moment.* **3.** importance: *a matter of moment.* **4.** tendency to cause rotation around a point or axis. [< L *momentum* < *movere* move. Doublet of MOMENTUM.] —Syn. **1.** second, minute. **3.** consequence, significance.

mo·men·tar·i·ly (mō′mən·ter′ə·li), *adv.* **1.** for a moment: *hesitate momentarily.* **2.** at every moment; from moment to moment: *danger momentarily increasing.* **3.** at any moment.

mo·men·tar·y (mō′mən·ter′i), *adj.* lasting only a moment. —mo′men·tar′i·ness, *n.* —Syn. fleeting, transitory, temporary.

mo·ment·ly (mō′mənt·li), *adv.* **1.** every moment; from moment to moment. **2.** at any moment. **3.** for a moment.

mo·men·tous (mō·men′təs), *adj.* very important. —mo·men′tous·ly, *adv.* —mo·men′tous·ness, *n.* —Syn. weighty, serious, critical. —Ant. trivial, trifling, paltry, insignificant.

mo·men·tum (mō·men′təm), *n., pl.* **-tums,**

-ta (-tə). **1.** force with which a body moves, the product of its mass and its velocity: *a falling object gains momentum as it falls*. **2.** impetus resulting from movement. [< L, moving power. Doublet of MOMENT.] —**Syn. 2.** impulse, force.

Mon., **1.** Monday. **2.** Monsignor.

Mon·a·co (mon′ə·kō; mə·nak′ō), *n.* a very small country within SE France, on the Mediterranean Sea.

mon·ad (mon′ad; mō′nad), *n.* **1.** unit. **2.** *Biol.* a very simple single-celled animal or plant. **3.** *Chem.* atom, element, or radical having a valence of one. [< LL < Gk. *monas* unit < *monos* alone]

mon·arch (mon′ərk), *n.* **1.** king, queen, emperor, etc.; hereditary sovereign; ruler. **2.** person or thing like a monarch. [< LL < Gk., < *monos* alone + *archein* rule]

mo·nar·chal (mə·när′kəl), *adj.* **1.** of a monarch. **2.** characteristic of a monarch. **3.** suitable for a monarch. —**mo·nar′chal·ly**, *adv.*

mo·nar·chic (mə·när′kik), *adj.* **1.** of or like a monarch or monarchy. **2.** favoring a monarchy. —**mo·nar′chi·cal·ly**, *adv.*

mon·ar·chism (mon′ər·kiz·əm), *n.* **1.** principles of monarchy. **2.** advocacy of monarchic principles. —**mon′ar·chist**, *n.*, *adj.* —**mon′ar·chis′tic**, *adj.*

mon·ar·chy (mon′ər·ki), *n.*, *pl.* **-chies. 1.** government by a monarch. **2.** nation governed by a monarch.

mon·as·ter·y (mon′əs·ter′i), *n.*, *pl.* **-ter·ies.** building where monks or nuns live a contemplative life according to fixed rules and under religious vows. [< LL < Gk. *monasterion*, ult. < *monos* alone. Doublet of MINSTER.] —**mon·as·te·ri·al** (mon′əs·tir′i·əl), *adj.*

mo·nas·tic (mə·nas′tik), **mo·nas·ti·cal** (-tə·kəl), *adj.* **1.** of monks or nuns: *monastic vows.* **2.** of monasteries. **3.** like that of monks or nuns. —*n.* monk. [< LL < LGk. *monastikos*, ult. < *monos* alone] —**mo·nas′ti·cal·ly**, *adv.*

mo·nas·ti·cism (mə·nas′tə·siz·əm), *n.* system or condition of living according to fixed rules, in groups shut off from the world, and devoted to religion.

mon·a·tom·ic (mon′ə·tom′ik), *adj. Chem.* **1.** having one atom in the molecule. **2.** containing one replaceable atom or group. **3.** monovalent.

Mon·day (mun′di; -dā), *n.* the second day of the week, following Sunday.

mon·e·tar·y (mon′ə·ter′i; mun′-), *adj.* **1.** of the coinage or currency of a country. The monetary unit in the United States is the dollar. **2.** of money: *a monetary reward.* [< LL *monetarius.* See MONEY.] —**mon′e·tar′i·ly**, *adv.*

mon·e·tize (mon′ə·tīz; mun′-), *v.*, **-tized, -tiz·ing. 1.** legalize as money. **2.** coin into money. —**mon′e·ti·za′tion**, *n.*

mon·ey (mun′i), *n.*, *pl.* **-eys. 1.** current coin; gold, silver, or other metal made into coins; bank notes, etc., representing gold or silver; any medium of exchange. **2.** a particular form or denomination of money. **3.** wealth. **4.** **make money, a.** get money. **b.** become rich. [< OF < L *moneta* mint, money < *Juno Moneta*, in whose temple money was coined. Doublet of MINT².] ►**money. 1.** Exact sums of money are usually written in figures: *72¢; $4.98; $5; $168.75; $42,810.* Round sums are more likely to be written in words: *two hundred dollars; a million and a half dollars.* In factual books or articles involving frequent references to sums of money, however, figures are often used throughout. **2.** In consecutive writing, amounts are usually written out when used adjectively: *A Million Dollar Baby in the Five and Ten Cent Store.* Informally, figures are often used: *an 85¢ seat.*

mon·ey·bag (mun′i·bag′), *n.* **1.** bag for money. **2.** **moneybags,** *Colloq.* **a.** wealth; riches. **b.** (*sing. in use*) a wealthy or avaricious person.

mon·eyed (mun′id), *adj.* **1.** having money; wealthy. **2.** consisting of or representing money.

money of account, a monetary denomination used in reckoning, especially one not issued

as a coin. In the United States, the mill is a money of account but not a coin. The nickel is a coin, but not a money of account.

money order, order for the payment of money, issued at one post office and payable at another.

mon·ger (mung′gər; mong′-), *n. Brit.* dealer in some sort of article: *a fishmonger.* [ult. < L *mango* trader < Gk.]

Mon·gol (mong′gəl; -gol; -gōl), *n.* **1.** member of the Asiatic race now inhabiting Mongolia and nearby parts of China and Siberia. **2.** Mongolian. —*adj.* **1.** of this race. **2.** Mongolian.

Mon·go·li·a (mong·gō′li·ə), *n.* vast region in Asia, N of China and S of W Siberia.

Mon·go·li·an (mong·gō′li·ən), *n.* **1.** member of the yellow race living in Asia, as the Chinese, Japanese, Siamese, etc. **2.** their language or languages. —*adj.* of Mongolia, the Mongolians, or their languages.

Mon·gol·oid (mong′gəl·oid), *adj.* resembling the Mongols; having characteristics of the Mongolian race. —*n.* person of Mongolian race.

Mongoose (total length ab. 2 ft.)

mon·goose, mon·goos (mong′gūs), *n.*, *pl.* **-goos·es.** a slender, ferretlike animal of India, used for destroying rats, and noted for its ability to kill certain poisonous snakes without being harmed. [< Marathi (lang. of W India) *mangūs*]

mon·grel (mung′grəl; mong′-), *n.* animal or plant of mixed breed, esp. a dog. —*adj.* of mixed breed, race, origin, nature, etc. [cf. OE *gemang* mixture]

mon·ies (mun′iz), *n.pl.* sums of money.

mon·ism (mon′iz·əm; mō′niz·əm), *n. Philos.* doctrine that the universe can be explained by one substance or principle. [< NL, < Gk. *monos* single] —**mon′ist**, *n.* —**mo·nis·tic** (mō·nis′tik), **mo·nis′ti·cal**, *adj.*

mo·ni·tion (mō·nish′ən), *n.* **1.** admonition; warning. **2.** an official or legal notice: *the bishop sent a monition to three clergymen.* [< L *monitio* < *monere* warn]

mon·i·tor (mon′ə·tər), *n.* **1.** pupil in school with special duties, such as helping to keep order and taking attendance. **2.** person who gives advice or warning. **3.** a low armored warship having one or more turrets for guns. **4.** a large lizard of Africa, Australia, and southern Asia. **5.** a receiver used for checking radio transmissions. —*v.* check (radio transmission) by listening in with a receiver. [< L, < *monere* admonish] —**mon·i·to·ri·al** (mon′ə·tô′ri·əl; -tō′-), *adj.* —**mon′i·tor·ship′**, *n.*

mon·i·to·ry (mon′ə·tô′ri; -tō′-), *adj.*, *n.*, *pl.* **-ries.** —*adj.* admonishing; warning. —*n.* letter containing admonition.

monk (mungk), *n.* man who gives up everything else for religion and enters a monastery to live. [< LL < LGk. *monachos* < Gk., individual, < *monos* alone]

mon·key (mung′ki), *n.*, *pl.* **-keys,** *v.*, **-keyed, -key·ing.** —*n.* **1.** one of the group of animals most closely resembling man. **2.** one of the smaller animals in this group, not a chimpanzee, gorilla, or other large ape. **3.** person, esp. a child, who is full of mischief. —*v. Am., Colloq.* play; fool; trifle. [prob. < MLG *Moneke*, son of Martin the Ape in story of Reynard]

mon·key·shine (mung′ki·shīn′), *n. Am., Slang.* a mischievous trick; clownish joke.

monkey wrench, wrench with a movable jaw that can be adjusted to fit different sizes of nuts.

monk·ish (mungk′ish), *adj.* (*derogatory substitute for* monastic). **1.** of a monk; having to do with monks. **2.** like a monk; characteristic of a monk. **3.** like monks or their way of life. —**monk′ish·ly**, *adv.* —**monk′ish·ness**, *n.*

monks·hood (mungks′hůd′), *n.* a kind of aconite, so called from its hooded flowers.

mono-, *word element.* one; single, as in *monogamy, monosyllable.* [< Gk., < *monos* single]

mon·o·bas·ic (mon'ō-bās'ik), *adj. Chem.* having but one hydrogen atom replaceable by an atom or radical of a base in forming salts.

mon·o·chrome (mon'ə-krōm), *n.* a painting, drawing, print, etc., in a single color or shades of a single color. [< Gk., < *monos* single + *chroma* color] —mon'o·chro·mat'ic, *adj.* —mon'o·chro'mic, mon'o·chro'mi·cal, *adj.* —mon'o·chrom'ist, *n.*

mon·o·cle (mon'ə-kəl), *n.* eyeglass for one eye. [< F < LL, one-eyed, < Gk. *mono-* single + L *oculus* eye] —mon'o·cled, *adj.*

Monocle

mon·o·cot·y·le·don (mon'ə-kot'ə-lē'dən), *n. Bot.* plant with only one cotyledon. —mon·o·cot·y·le·don·ous (mon'ə-kot'ə-lē'dən-əs; -led'ən-), *adj.*

mon·o·dy (mon'ə·di), *n., pl.* -dies. 1. a mournful song. 2. poem in which one person laments another's death. 3. *Music.* a. style of composition in which one part or melody predominates. b. composition in this style. [< LL < Gk. *monoidia*, ult. < *monos* single + *aeidein* sing] —mo·nod·ic (mə·nod'ik), *adj.* —mo·nod'i·cal·ly, *adv.*

mo·nog·a·my (mə·nog'ə·mi), *n.* 1. practice or condition of being married to only one person at a time. 2. habit of having only one mate. [< L < Gk., < *monos* single + *gamos* marriage] —mo·nog'a·mist, *n.* —mo·nog'a·mous, *adj.*

mon·o·gram (mon'ə·gram), *n.* a person's initials combined in one design. [< LL < Gk., < *monos* single + *gramma* letter] —mon·o·gram·mat·ic (mon'ə·grə·mat'ik), *adj.* —mon'o·grammed, *adj.*

mon·o·graph (mon'ə·graf; -gräf), *n.* book or article written on a particular subject: *Darwin's monograph on earthworms.* —mo·nog·ra·pher (mə·nog'rə·fər), *n.* —mon·o·graph'ic, *adj.*

mon·o·lith (mon'ə·lith), *n.* 1. a single large block of stone. 2. monument, column, statue, etc., formed of a single large block of stone. [< L < Gk., < *monos* single + *lithos* stone]

mon·o·lith·ic (mon'ə·lith'ik), *adj.* 1. of or pertaining to monoliths. 2. comprising an imposing, uniform, and harmonious whole: *a police state is a monolithic organization.*

mon·o·logue, mon·o·log (mon'ə·lôg; -log), *n.* 1. a long speech by one person in a group. 2. entertainment by a single speaker. 3. play for a single actor. 4. part of a play in which a single actor speaks alone. [< F < LGk., < *monos* single + *logos* speech, discourse] —mon'o·log·ist, mon'o·logu'ist, *n.*

mon·o·ma·ni·a (mon'ə·mā'ni·ə), *n.* 1. insanity on one subject only. 2. unreasonable interest or tendency. —mon·o·ma·ni·ac (mon'ə·mā'ni·ak), *n.* —mon·o·ma·ni·a·cal (mon'ə·mə·nī'ə·kəl), *adj.*

mon·o·met·al·lism (mon'ō·met'əl·iz·əm), *n.* use of one metal only as the standard of money values. —mon·o·me·tal·lic (mon'ō·mə·tal'ik), *adj.*

mo·no·mi·al (mō·nō'mi·əl), *Algebra.* —*adj.* consisting of a single word or term. —*n.* expression consisting of a single term. [< MONO- + -*nomial*, as in *binomial*]

mon·o·phon·ic (mon'ə·fon'ik), *adj.* reproducing sound by means of a single channel; not stereophonic.

mon·o·plane (mon'ə·plān), *n.* airplane with only one pair of wings.

mo·nop·o·list (mə·nop'ə·list), *n.* 1. person who has a monopoly. 2. person who favors monopoly. —mo·nop'o·lis'tic, *adj.*

mo·nop·o·lize (mə·nop'ə·līz), *v.,* -lized, -lizing. 1. have or get exclusive possession or control of: *this firm monopolizes thread production.* 2. occupy wholly; keep entirely to oneself: *the agent monopolized the conversation.* —mo·nop'o·li·za'tion, *n.* —mo·nop'o·liz'er, *n.*

mo·nop·o·ly (mə·nop'ə·li), *n., pl.* -lies. 1. exclusive control of a commodity or service: *the only milk company in town has a monopoly on milk delivery.* 2. such control granted by a government: *an inventor has a monopoly on his invention for a certain number of years.* 3. control that, though not exclusive, enables the person or company to fix prices. 4. a commercial product or service that is exclusively controlled or nearly so. 5. person or company that has a monopoly of some commodity or service. 6. the exclusive possession or control: *no one country has a monopoly of virtue.* [< L < Gk., < *monos* single + *poleein* sell]

mon·o·rail (mon'ə·rāl'), *n.* railway in which cars run on a single rail.

mon·o·syl·la·ble (mon'ə·sil'ə·bəl), *n.* word of one syllable. *Yes* and *no* are monosyllables. —mon·o·syl·lab·ic (mon'ə·sə·lab'ik), *adj.* —mon'o·syl·lab'i·cal·ly, *adv.*

mon·o·the·ism (mon'ə·thē·iz'əm), *n.* doctrine or belief that there is only one God. [< MONO- + Gk. *theos* god] —mon'o·the'ist, *n.* —mon·o·the·is'tic, *adj.* —mon'o·the·is'ti·cal·ly, *adv.*

mon·o·tone (mon'ə·tōn), *n.* sameness of tone, of style of writing, of color, etc. —*adj.* continuing on one tone; of one tone, style, or color.

mo·not·o·nous (mə·not'ə·nəs), *adj.* 1. continuing in the same tone. 2. not varying; without change. 3. wearying because of its sameness. —mo·not'o·nous·ly, *adv.* —mo·not'o·nousness, *n.* —Syn. 1. singsong. 2. unvarying, uniform. 3. tedious, humdrum, dull.

mo·not·o·ny (mə·not'ə·ni), *n.* 1. sameness of tone or pitch. 2. lack of variety. 3. wearisome sameness. [< Gk. *monotonia*, ult. < Gk. *monos* single + *tonos* tone]

mon·o·treme (mon'ə·trēm), *n.* one of the lowest order of mammals. Duckbills and echidnas are monotremes. [< MONO- + *trema* hole]

mon·o·type (mon'ə·tīp), *n., v.,* -typed, -typing. —*n. Am.* 1. a set of two machines (keyboard machine and casting machine) for making and setting type in separate letters. 2. Monotype. trademark for these machines. —*v.* set with a monotype machine.

mon·o·va·lent (mon'ə·vā'lənt), *adj. Chem.* having a valence of one.

mon·ox·ide (mon-ok'sīd), *n. Chem.* oxide containing one oxygen atom in each molecule.

Mon·roe (mən·rō'), *n.* James, 1758–1831, the fifth president of the United States, 1817–1825.

Monroe Doctrine, *Am.* doctrine that European nations should not interfere with American nations or try to acquire more territory in America.

Mon·ro·vi·a (mon·rō'vi·ə), *n.* capital of Liberia.

Mon·sei·gneur, mon·sei·gneur (môN·se·nyœr'), *n., pl.* **Mes·sei·gneurs; mes·sei·gneurs** (mā·se·nyœr'). 1. a French title of honor given to princes, bishops, and other persons of importance. 2. person bearing this title. [< F, my lord. See SEIGNEUR.]

mon·sieur (mə·syœ'), *n., pl.* **mes·sieurs** (mā·syœ'). Mr.; sir. [< F, earlier *mon sieur* my lord. See SIRE.]

Mon·si·gnor, mon·si·gnor (mon·sē'nyər), *n., pl.* **Mon·si·gnors, Mon·si·gno·ri** (mon'sē·nyō'ri; -nyō'-); **mon·si·gnors, mon·si·gno·ri.** 1. title given to certain dignitaries in the Roman Catholic Church. 2. person having this title. [< Ital., half-trans. of F *monseigneur* MONSEIGNEUR]

mon·soon (mon·sün'), *n.* 1. a seasonal wind of the Indian Ocean and S Asia, blowing from the SW from April to October and from the NE during the rest of the year. 2. a rainy season during which this wind blows from the SW. [< Du. < Pg. < Ar. *mausim* season]

mon·ster (mon'stər), *n.* 1. any animal or plant that is out of the usual course of nature. Centaurs, sphinxes, and griffins are imaginary monsters. 2. a huge creature or thing. 3. person too wicked to be human: *he is a monster of cruelty.* —*adj.* huge. [< OF < L *monstrum* divine warning < *monstrare* show] —Syn. *n.* 2. giant.

mon·stros·i·ty (mon·stros'ə·ti), *n., pl.* -ties. 1. monster. 2. a monstrous thing. 3. state or character of being monstrous.

mon·strous (mon'strəs), *adj.* 1. huge; enormous. 2. wrongly formed or shaped; like a monster. 3. so wrong or absurd as to be almost unheard of. 4. shocking; horrible; dreadful. —adv. Colloq. very; extremely. —**mon′strous·ly,** adv. —**mon′strous·ness,** n. —Syn. adj. 1. colossal, prodigious, stupendous. 4. atrocious.

Mont., Montana.

mon·tage (mon·täzh′), n. 1. the combination of several distinct pictures to make a composite picture. 2. a composite picture so made. 3. Motion Pictures. the use of a rapid succession of pictures, esp. to suggest a train of thought. [< F, < monter MOUNT¹]

Mon·taigne (mon·tān′), n. 1533–1592, French essayist.

Mon·tan·a (mon·tan′ə), n. a Western State of the United States. Capital: Helena. Abbrev.: Mont. —**Mon·tan′an,** adj., n.

Mont Blanc (Fr. môn blän′; Eng. mont blangk′), the highest mountain in the Alps, between France and Italy.

Mont·calm (mont·käm′), n. 1712–1759, French general defeated by the English at Quebec.

Mon·te Car·lo (mon′tē kär′lō), town in Monaco, noted as a gambling resort.

Mon·te·ne·gro (mon′tə·nē′grō), n. a former kingdom in S Europe, now a division of S Yugoslavia. —**Mon·te·ne·grin** (mon′tə·nē′grin), adj.,n.

Mon·ter·rey (mon′tə·rā′), n. city in NE Mexico.

Mon·tes·quieu (mon′tes·kū), n. 1689–1755, French writer about government.

Mon·te·vi·de·o (mon′tə·vi·dā′ō; –vid′i·ō), n. capital of Uruguay, on the Plata River.

Mon·te·zu·ma II (mon′tə·zū′mə), 1466?–1520, last Aztec emperor of Mexico, 1502–1520, defeated by Cortez.

Mont·gom·er·y (mont·gum′ər·i; –gum′ri), n. capital of Alabama, in the C part.

month (munth), n. 1. one of the 12 parts (Jan., Feb., etc.) into which the year is divided. 2. time from any day of one month to the corresponding day of the next month. [OE mōnath; akin to moon]

month·ly (munth′li), adj., adv., n., pl. -lies. —adj. 1. of or for a month; lasting a month. 2. done, happening, payable, etc., once a month. —adv. once a month; every month. —n. magazine published once a month.

Mon·ti·cel·lo (mon′tə·sel′ō), n. home of Thomas Jefferson, near Charlottesville, Va.

Mont·mar·tre (môn·mär′trə), n. section of Paris, noted for its night life.

Mont·pel·ier (mont·pēl′yər), n. capital of Vermont, in the C part.

Mont·re·al (mont′ri·ôl′), n. seaport in Quebec, on the St. Lawrence River.

Mont St. Mi·chel (môn san mē·shel′), a small island off the NW coast of France, famous for its abbey and fortress.

mon·u·ment (mon′yə·mənt), n. 1. something set up to keep a person or an event from being forgotten. A monument may be a building, pillar, arch, statue, tomb, or stone. 2. anything that keeps alive the memory of a person or an event. 3. enduring or prominent instance: the professor's researches were monuments of learning. 4. something set up to mark a boundary. 5. Obs. tomb; sepulcher; burial vault. [< L monumentum < monere remind]

mon·u·men·tal (mon′yə·men′təl), adj. 1. of a monument. 2. serving as a monument. 3. like a monument. 4. weighty and lasting; important. The Constitution of the United States is a monumental document. 5. very great: monumental ignorance. —**mon′u·men′tal·ly,** adv.

moo (mü), n., pl. moos, v., mooed, moo·ing. —n. sound made by a cow. —v. make this sound.

mooch (müch), v. Slang. 1. steal. 2. beg; get at another person's expense. —**mooch′er,** n.

mood¹ (müd), n. 1. state of mind or feeling. 2. moods, fits of depression or bad temper. [OE mōd spirit] —Syn. 1. humor, temper, inclination, disposition, vein.

mood² (müd), n. Gram. form of a verb that shows whether the act or state is thought of as

a fact, a command, etc.: the indicative mood. Also, mode. [alter. of mode; infl. by mood¹]

mood·y (müd′i), adj., mood·i·er, mood·i·est. 1. likely to have changes of mood. 2. often having gloomy moods. 3. sunk in sadness; gloomy; sullen. —**mood′i·ly,** adv. —**mood′i·ness,** n. —Syn. 3. melancholy, sad, ill-humored.

moon (mün), n. 1. a heavenly body that revolves around the earth once in approximately 28 days and reflects the sun's light so that it looks bright. 2. moon at a certain period of time: new moon (visible as slender crescent), half moon (visible as half circle), full moon (visible as circle), old moon (waning). 3. a lunar month. 4. moonlight. 5. satellite of any planet. 6. an artificial earth satellite. —v. wander about or gaze listlessly. [OE mōna] —**moon′like′,** adj.

moon·beam (mün′bēm′), n. ray of moonlight.

moon·calf (mün′kaf′; –käf′), n. a born fool.

moon·light (mün′līt′), n. light of the moon. —adj. 1. Also, **moon·lit** (mün′lit′). having the light of the moon. 2. while the moon is shining; by night.

moon·light·er (mün′līt·ər), n. person who holds more than one job at the same time.

moon·shine (mün′shīn′), n. 1. moonlight. 2. empty talk; empty show; nonsense. 3. Am., Colloq. intoxicating liquor unlawfully distilled or unlawfully smuggled into the country.

moon·shin·er (mün′shin·ər), n. Am., Colloq. person who makes intoxicating liquor contrary to law.

moon·stone (mün′stōn′), n. a whitish gem with a pearly luster, a variety of feldspar.

moon·struck (mün′struk′), **moon·strick·en** (–strik′ən), adj. dazed; crazed.

moon·watch (mün′woch′), n. optical tracking of man-made satellites, etc., chiefly by volunteer observers. See also Minitrack. —**moon′watch′-er,** n.

moor¹ (mür), v. 1. put or keep (a ship, etc.) in place by means of ropes or chains fastened to the shore or to anchors. 2. be made secure by ropes, anchors, etc. [ME more(n). Cf. OE mǣrels mooring rope.]

moor² (mür), n. Brit. open waste land, esp. if heather grows on it. [OE mōr]

Moor (mür), n. member of an Arab people living in NW Africa. In the eighth century A.D. the Moors conquered Spain. —**Moor′ish,** adj.

Moore (mür; mōr; môr), n. 1. George, 1852–1933, Irish author. 2. Thomas, 1779–1852, Irish poet.

moor hen, 1. a female red grouse. 2. Am. any of various wading birds, as the rail, coot, etc.

moor·ings (mür′ingz), n.pl. 1. ropes, cables, anchors, etc., by which a ship is fastened. 2. place where a ship is moored.

moor·land (mür′land′; –lənd), n. land covered with heather; moor.

moose (müs), n., pl. moose. 1. Am. animal like a large deer, living in Canada and the N United States. 2. the European elk. [< Algonquian]

moot (müt), adj. debatable; doubtful: a moot point. —v. 1. argue. 2. bring forward (a point, subject, case, etc.) for discussion. —n. assembly. [OE mōt meeting] —**moot′er,** n.

moot court, mock court, esp. one held in a law school to give students practice.

mop¹ (mop), n., v., mopped, mop·ping. —n. 1. bundle of coarse yarn, rags, cloth, etc., fastened at the end of a stick, for cleaning floors, etc. 2. a thick head of hair like a mop. —v. 1. wash or wipe up; clean with a mop. 2. wipe. 3. mop up, finish. [ME mappe]

mop² (mop), v., mopped, mop·ping, n. —v. 1. grimace. 2. mop and mow, make faces. —n. grimace.

mope (mōp), v., moped, mop·ing, n. —v. be indifferent and silent; be gloomy and sad. —n. 1.

person who mopes. **2. mopes,** low spirits.
—**mop′er,** n. —**mop′ish,** adj. —**mop′ish·ly,**
adv. —**mop′ish·ness,** n.

mop·pet (mop′it), n. child. [< obs. mop doll]

mo·raine (mə·rān′), n. mass of rocks, dirt,
etc., deposited at the side or end of a glacier.
[< F]

mor·al (môr′əl; mor′-), adj. **1.** good in character or conduct; virtuous according to civilized
standards of right and wrong; right; just: a
moral act, a moral man. **2.** capable of understanding right and wrong: a little baby is not a
moral being. **3.** having to do with character or
with the difference between right and wrong: a
moral question. **4.** based on the principles of
right conduct rather than on law or custom. **5.**
teaching a good lesson; having a good influence.
—n. **1.** lesson, inner meaning, or teaching of a
fable, a story, or an event. **2. morals,** a. behavior
in matters of right and wrong. b. character. c.
principles in regard to conduct. [< L moralis <
mos custom (pl., manners)] —**Syn.** adj. **1.**
righteous, upright, ethical.

mo·rale (mə·ral′; -räl′), n. moral or mental
condition as regards courage, confidence, enthusiasm, etc.: the morale of troops. [< F, fem.
of moral MORAL]

mor·al·ist (môr′əl·ist; mor′-), n. **1.** person
who thinks much about moral duties, sees the
moral side of things, and leads a moral life. **2.**
person who teaches, studies, or writes about
morals. —**mor′al·is′tic,** adj.

mo·ral·i·ty (mə·ral′ə·ti), n., pl. -ties. **1.** right
or wrong of an action. **2.** doing right; virtue. **3.**
system of morals; set of rules or principles of
conduct. **4.** moral instruction; moral lesson or
precept. **5.** drama popular during the 15th and
16th centuries, in which vices and virtues appear
as real people. —**Syn. 3.** ethics.

mor·al·ize (môr′əl·īz; mor′-), v., -ized, -iz-
ing. **1.** think, talk, or write about questions of
right and wrong. **2.** point out the lesson or inner
meaning of. **3.** improve the morals of. —**mor′-
al·i·za′tion,** n. —**mor′al·iz′er,** n.

mor·al·ly (môr′əl·i; mor′-), adv. **1.** in a moral
manner. **2.** in morals; as to morals. **3.** ethically:
things morally considered. **4.** practically: murder, to which he is morally, if not really, a party.

moral victory, defeat that has the effect on
the mind that a victory would have.

mo·rass (mə·ras′), n. piece of low, soft, wet
ground; swamp. [< Du. moeras < OF marais <
Gmc.]

mor·a·to·ri·um (môr′ə·tô′ri·əm; mor′-;
-tō′-), n., pl. -ri·ums, -ri·a (-ri·ə). **1.** a
legal authorization to delay payments of money
due. **2.** period during which such authorization
is in effect. [< NL, < L morari delay < mora a
delay]

Mo·ra·vi·a (mô·rā′vi·ə; mō-), n. province in
C Czechoslovakia. —**Mo·ra′vi·an,** adj., n.

mor·bid (môr′bid), adj. **1.** unhealthy; not
wholesome: a morbid liking for horror. **2.** caused
by disease; characteristic of disease; diseased:
cancer is a morbid growth. **3.** frightful; ghastly:
morbid events. [< L morbidus < morbus disease]
—**mor·bid′i·ty,** **mor′bid·ness,** n. —**mor′bid-
ly,** adv.

mor·dant (môr′dənt), adj. **1.** biting; cutting;
sarcastic. **2.** that fixes colors in dyeing. —n. **1.**
substance that fixes colors in dyeing. **2.** acid that
eats into metal. [< OF, ppr. of mordre bite < L
mordere] —**mor′dan·cy,** n. —**mor′dant·ly,** adv.

more (môr; mōr), adj. (used as comparative
of much and many, with the superlative most),
n., adv. (often used before adjectives and adverbs, and regularly before those of more than
two syllables, to form comparatives). —adj. **1.**
greater in number, quantity, amount, degree, or
importance: more men, more help. **2.** further;
additional: take more time. —n. **1.** a greater
number, quantity, amount, or degree: the more
they have, the more they want. **2.** an additional
amount: tell me more. —adv. **1.** in or to a greater
extent or degree: that hurts more. **2.** in addition;
further; longer; again: sing once more. **3.** be no
more, be dead. **4. more or less,** a. somewhat:

more or less accurate. b. nearly; approximately:
five miles more or less. [OE māra]

More (môr; mōr), n. Sir Thomas, 1478–1535,
English statesman and author, canonized in
1935.

more·o·ver (môr·ō′vər; mōr-), adv. also; besides; in addition to that: his power is absolute
and, moreover, hereditary. —**Syn.** furthermore,
also.

mo·res (mô′rēz; mō′-), n.pl. Sociol. traditional
rules; customs. [< L, manners]

Mor·gan (môr′gən), n. John Pierpont, 1837–
1913, American financier and art collector.

mor·ga·nat·ic (môr′gə·nat′ik), adj. designating or pertaining to a form of marriage in which
a man of high rank marries a woman of lower
rank with an agreement that neither she nor her
children shall have any claim to his rank or
property. [< NL morganaticus morning gift, ult.
< OHG morgan morning] —**mor′ga·nat′i·cal·ly,**
adv.

morgue (môrg), n. Am. **1.** place in which the
bodies of unknown persons found dead are kept
until they can be identified. **2.** in a newspaper
office, the reference library. [< F]

mor·i·bund (môr′ə·bund; mor′-), adj. dying.
[< L moribundus < mori die]
—**mor′i·bun′di·ty,** n. —**mor′i-
bund·ly,** adv.

mo·ri·on (mô′ri·on; mō′-), n.
helmet without a visor, shaped
somewhat like a hat. [< F < Sp.,
< morra crown of head]

Mor·mon (môr′mən), n. Am.
member of the Church of Jesus
Christ of Latter-day Saints,
founded in 1830 by Joseph Smith.
—adj. of or pertaining to the
Mormons or their religion. —**Mor′mon·ism,** n.

MORION

morn (môrn), n. Poetic. morning. [OE morgen]

morn·ing (môr′ning), n. **1.** the early part of
the day, ending at noon. **2.** dawn. **3.** the first or
early part of anything. —adj. of or in the morning. [ME morwening (see MORN); patterned on
evening] —**Syn.** n. **2.** daybreak, sunrise.

morn·ing-glo·ry (môr′ning·glô′ri; -glō′-),
n., pl. -ries. Am. a climbing vine with heart-
shaped leaves and funnel-shaped blue, lavender,
pink, or white flowers.

morning star, planet, esp. Venus, seen in the
eastern sky before sunrise.

Mo·ro (mô′rō; mō′-), n., pl. Mo·ros. **1.** member
of any of various tribes of Mohammedan Malays
in the S Philippine Islands. **2.** language of these
people.

Mo·roc·co (mə·rok′ō), n. **1.** country in NW
Africa, formerly partly under French, partly under
Spanish control; it became independent in 1956.
2. Marrakech. —**Mo·roc·can** (mə·rok′ən), adj.

mo·roc·co (mə·rok′ō), n., pl. -cos. **1.** a fine
leather made from goatskins, used in binding
books. **2.** leather imitating this.

mo·ron (mô′ron; mō′-), n. Am. **1.** person of
20 years or more who has the same intelligence
as an ordinary child from 8 to 12 years old. **2.**
Colloq. a feeble-minded person. [< Gk., neut.,
foolish, dull] —**mo·ron·ic** (mə·ron′ik), adj. Am.

mo·rose (mə·rōs′), adj. gloomy; sullen; ill-
humored. [< L morosus, orig., set in one's ways
< mos habit] —**mo·rose′ly,** adv. —**mo·rose′-
ness,** n. —**Syn.** moody, surly, gruff. —**Ant.** amiable, pleasant, genial.

Mor·pheus (môr′fi·əs; -fūs), n. Greek god of
dreams; popularly, the god of sleep. —**Mor·
phe·an,** adj.

mor·phine (môr′fēn), **mor·phi·a** (môr′-
fi·ə), n. drug made from opium, used to dull pain
and to cause sleep. [< F < G morphin < Mor-
pheus Morpheus]

mor·phol·o·gy (môr·fol′ə·ji), n. **1.** branch of
biology that deals with the forms and structure
of animals and plants. **2.** branch of the science
of language that deals with forms of words as
affected by inflection, derivation, etc. [< Gk.
morphe form + -LOGY] —**mor·pho·log·ic** (môr′-
fə·loj′ik), **mor′pho·log′i·cal,** adj. —**mor′pho·
log′i·cal·ly,** adv. —**mor·phol′o·gist,** n.

Mor·ris (môr′is; mor′-), *n.* William, 1834-1896, English poet, artist, and socialist writer.

Morris chair or **morris chair**, armchair with an adjustable back.

morris dance, or **morris**, *n.* an old English dance performed by people in fancy costumes.

mor·row (môr′ō; mor′o), *n.* **1.** the following day or time. **2.** *Archaic.* morning. **3.** tomorrow. [ME *morwe*, var. of *morwen* MORN]

Morse (môrs), *n.* Samuel F. B., 1791-1872, American inventor of the telegraph.

Morse alphabet or **code**, *Am.* a telegraphic alphabet made up of dots, dashes, and spaces.

mor·sel (môr′səl), *n.* **1.** a small bite; mouthful. **2.** piece; fragment. [< OF, dim. of *mors* a bite, ult. < L *mordere* bite]

mor·tal (môr′təl), *adj.* **1.** sure to die sometime: *all creatures are mortal.* **2.** of man; of mortals: *past all mortal aid.* **3.** of death: *the mortal hour.* **4.** causing death of the body: *mortal sin.* **5.** causing death: *a mortal wound.* **6.** to the death: *a mortal enemy.* **7.** very great; deadly: *mortal terror.* —*n.* **1.** a being that is sure to die sometime. **2.** man; human being. [< L *mortalis* < *mors* death] —**mor′tal·ly**, *adv.* —Syn. *adj.* **2.** human.

mor·tal·i·ty (môr·tal′ə·ti), *n.* **1.** mortal nature; being sure to die sometime. **2.** loss of life on a large scale: *the mortality from automobile accidents is very serious.* **3.** death rate; number of deaths per thousand cases of a disease, or per thousand persons in the population. **4.** mankind.

mor·tar[1] (môr′tər), *n.* mixture of lime, sand, and water, or of cement, sand, and water, for holding bricks or stones together. [< OF *mortier* < L *mortarium*]

mor·tar[2] (môr′tər), *n.* **1.** bowl of very hard material, in which substances may be pounded to a powder. **2.** a short cannon for shooting shells at high angles. [< L *mortarium* (through F for the meaning "cannon")]

mor·tar·board (môr′tər·bôrd′; -bōrd′), *n.* an academic cap with a flat, square top.

Mortar and pestle

mort·gage (môr′gij), *n., v.,* **-gaged, -gag·ing.** —*n.* **1.** claim on property, given to a person who has loaned money in case the money is not repaid when due. **2.** document that gives such a claim. —*v.* **1.** give a lender a claim to (one's property) in case a debt is not paid when due. **2.** put under some obligation; pledge. [< OF, < *mort* dead (< L *mortuus*) + *gage* pledge, GAGE[1]]

mort·ga·gee (môr′gi·jē′), *n.* person to whom property is mortgaged.

mort·ga·gor, mort·gag·er (môr′gi·jər), *n.* person who mortgages his property.

mor·ti·cian (môr·tish′ən), *n. Am.* undertaker.

mor·ti·fi·ca·tion (môr′tə·fə·kā′shən), *n.* **1.** shame; humiliation. **2.** cause of shame or humiliation. **3.** a mortifying or being mortified: *the mortification of the body by fasting.* —Syn. **1.** chagrin, embarrassment.

mor·ti·fy (môr′tə·fī), *v.,* **-fied, -fy·ing. 1.** make ashamed; humiliate: *a child's misconduct mortifies its parent.* **2.** overcome (bodily desires and feelings) by pain and self-denial: *saints often mortified their bodily cravings.* **3.** die; decay: *cut off an inflamed foot that has mortified.* [< OF < L *mortificare* kill < L *mors* death + *facere* make] —**mor′ti·fi′er**, *n.* —Syn. **1.** chagrin, embarrass, shame. **2.** restrain, repress, deny.

mor·tise, or **mor·tice** (môr′tis), *n., v.,* **-tised, -tis·ing; -ticed, -tic·ing.** —*n.* a rectangular hole in one piece of wood cut to receive a projection on another piece (called the tenon) so as to form a joint (**mortise and tenon joint**). —*v.* **1.** cut a mortise in. **2.** fasten by a mortise. [< F *mortaise* < Ar. *murtazz* fastened]

TENON
MORTISE
Mortise and tenon joint

mor·tu·ar·y (môr′chu·er′i), *n., pl.* **-ar·ies,** *adj.* —*n.* **1.** building where dead bodies are kept until burial. **2.** morgue. —*adj.* of death or burial. [< Med.L *mortuarium,* ult. < L *mors* death]

mos., months.

mo·sa·ic (mō·zā′ik), *n.* **1.** small pieces of stone, glass, wood, etc., of different colors inlaid to form a picture or design. **2.** such a picture or design. **3.** anything like a mosaic. —*adj.* formed by, pertaining to, or resembling such work. [< Med.L *mosaicus, musaicus* of the Muses. See MUSE.]

Mo·sa·ic (mō·zā′ik), **Mo·sa·i·cal** (-ə·kəl), *adj.* of Moses or of writings ascribed to him.

Mosaic design

Mosaic law, 1. the ancient laws of the Hebrews ascribed to Moses. **2.** part of the Bible where these laws are stated.

Mos·cow (mos′kou; -kō), *n.* capital of the Soviet Union, in the C part of European Russia.

Mo·selle (mō·zel′), *n.* river flowing from NE France into the Rhine in W Germany.

Mo·ses (mō′ziz; -zis), *n.* the great leader and lawgiver of the Israelites.

mo·sey (mō′zi), *v.,* **-seyed, -sey·ing.** *Am., Slang.* **1.** shuffle along. **2.** saunter; amble.

Mos·lem (moz′ləm; mos′-), *n., pl.* **-lems, -lem,** *adj.* Mohammedan. Also, **Muslem, Muslim.** [< Ar. *muslim* one who submits < *aslama* submit; akin to SALAAM]

mosque (mosk), *n.* a Mohammedan place of worship. [< F < Ital. < Ar. *masjid* < *sajada* prostrate oneself]

mos·qui·to (məs·kē′tō), *n., pl.* **-toes, -tos. 1.** a small, thin insect whose female gives a bite or sting that itches. Some kinds transmit malaria; some transmit yellow fever. **2.** a light, fast British bomber. [< Sp., dim. of *mosca* < L *musca* fly]

mosquito boat, a fast motorboat, carrying a gun or torpedo.

moss (môs; mos), *n.* **1.** very small, soft, green or brown plants that grow close together like a carpet on the ground, on rocks, on trees, etc. **2.** any of various similar plants. [OE *mos* bog]

Mos·sa·degh (môs′ə′deg′; mü′sä′dēk′), *n.* Mohammed, born 1880, Iranian statesman, prime minister of Iran from 1951 to 1953.

moss·back (môs′bak′; mos′-), *n. Am., Slang.* person whose ideas are out of date.

moss rose, a cultivated rose with mosslike growth on the calyx and stem.

moss·y (môs′i; mos′i), *adj.,* **moss·i·er, moss·i·est. 1.** covered with moss: *a mossy bank.* **2.** like moss: *mossy green.* —**moss′i·ness,** *n.*

most (mōst), *adj.* (used as superlative of **much** and **many, with the comparative more**), *n., adv.* (often used before adjectives and adverbs, and regularly before those of more than two syllables, to form superlatives). —*adj.* **1.** the greatest quantity, amount, measure, degree, or number of: *the winner gets the most money.* **2.** almost all: *most children like candy.* **3.** for the most part, mainly; usually. —*n.* **1.** the greatest quantity, amount, degree, or number: *he did most of the work.* **2.** at most or at the most, not more than. **3. make the most of,** make the best use of. —*adv.* **1.** in or to the greatest extent or degree: *which hurt most?* **2.** *Colloq.* almost; nearly. [OE *māst*]

-most, suffix forming superlatives, as in *foremost, inmost, topmost, uttermost.* [ME]

most·ly (mōst′li), *adv.* almost all; for the most part; mainly; chiefly.

Mo·sul (mō·sül′), *n.* city in N Iraq.

mot (mō), *n.* a clever or witty remark. [< F < L *muttum* grunt, word. Doublet of MOTTO.]

mote (mōt), *n.* speck, esp. of dust. [OE *mot*]

mo·tel (mō·tel′), *n. Am.* a hotel or group of cottages which provide sleeping, and often eating, accommodations for motorists. [blend of *motor* and *hotel*]

āge, cāre, fär; ēqual, tėrm; īce; ōpen, ôrder; pút, rüle, ūse; th, then; ə=a in about.

moth (môth; moth), *n., pl.* **moths** (môthz; môthz; môths; moths). 1. a small, winged insect that lays eggs in cloth, fur, etc. Its larvae eat holes in the material. 2. a broad-winged insect very much like a butterfly, but flying mostly at night. [OE *moththe*] —**moth′y,** *adj.*

moth ball, ball of naphthalene, used to keep moths away from wool, silk, fur, etc.

moth·ball (môth′bôl′; môth′–), *v.* 1. clean and cover (something) with a protective film to prepare it for temporary storage. 2. take (ships, aircraft, etc.) out of service for such storage.

moth-eat·en (môth′ēt′ən; môth′–), *adj.* 1. having holes made by moths. 2. out-of-date.

moth·er[1] (muth′ər), *n.* 1. a female parent. 2. person who is like a mother. 3. cause; source: *Necessity is the mother of invention.* 4. head of a female religious community; woman exercising control and responsibility like that of a mother. 5. a familiar name for an old woman. —*v.* 1. be mother of; act as mother to. 2. acknowledge oneself mother of or assume as one's own. —*adj.* 1. that is a mother. 2. like a mother. 3. of a mother. 4. native. [OE *mōdor*] —**moth′er·less,** *adj.*

moth·er[2] (muth′ər), *n.* a stringy, sticky substance formed in vinegar or on liquids turning to vinegar. Mother consists of bacteria. [special use of *mother*[1]]

mother country, 1. country where a person was born. 2. country in relation to its colonies or its natives.

moth·er·hood (muth′ər·hůd), *n.* 1. state of being a mother. 2. qualities of a mother. 3. mothers.

Mother Hub·bard (hub′ərd), a full, loose gown for women.

moth·er-in-law (muth′ər·in·lô′), *n., pl.* **moth·ers-in-law.** 1. mother of one's husband or wife. 2. *Colloq.* stepmother.

moth·er·land (muth′ər·land′), *n.* 1. one's native country. 2. land of one's ancestors.

moth·er·ly (muth′ər·li), *adj.* 1. of a mother. 2. like a mother; kindly. —**moth′er·li·ness,** *n.* —Syn. 2. maternal.

moth·er-of-pearl (muth′ər·əv·pérl′), *n.* the hard, rainbow-colored lining of certain shells, used to make buttons and ornaments; nacre.

Mother's Day, *Am.* the second Sunday of May, set apart in the United States in honor of mothers.

mother superior, woman who is the head of a convent of nuns.

mother tongue, 1. one's native language. 2. language to which other languages owe their origin.

mother wit, natural intelligence.

mo·tif (mō·tēf′), *n.* subject for development or treatment in art, literature, or music. [< F]

mo·tile (mō′təl), *adj. Biol.* able to move by itself. [< L *motus* moved] —**mo·til′i·ty,** *n.*

mo·tion (mō′shən), *n.* 1. change of position or place; movement; moving: *the motion of one's hand in writing.* 2. motions, actions; activities. 3. a formal suggestion made in a meeting or law court: *the motion to adjourn was carried.* —*v.* 1. make a movement, as of the hand or head, to show one's meaning. 2. show (a person) what to do by such a motion: *he motioned me out.* [< L *motio* < *movere* move] —Syn. *n.* 1. move, action, activity. –*v.* 1. gesticulate, gesture. —Ant. *n.* 1. stillness, immobility, repose.

mo·tion·less (mō′shən·lis), *adj.* not moving. —**mo′tion·less·ly,** *adv.* —**mo′tion·less·ness,** *n.* —Syn. inert, stationary, still, quiet.

motion picture, series of pictures shown on a screen in which people and things seem to move. Also, **moving picture.**

mo·ti·vate (mō′tə·vāt), *v.,* -vat·ed, -vat·ing. provide with a motive; act upon as a motive. —**mo′ti·va′tion,** *n.*

mo·tive (mō′tiv), *n.* 1. thought or feeling that makes one act: *his motive in going away was a wish to travel.* 2. motif. —*adj.* that makes something move: *steam is the motive power of this engine.* [< Med.L *motivum* moving (impulse) < L *movere* to move] —Syn. *n.* 1. incentive, impulse, inducement, reason.

mot·ley (mot′li), *n., pl.* **-leys,** *adj.* —*n.* suit of more than one color worn by clowns. —*adj.* 1. of different colors like a clown's suit. 2. made up of units not alike: *a motley collection.* [ME *motteley*]

mo·tor (mō′tər), *n.* 1. any thing or person that imparts motion, esp. an engine that makes a machine go. 2. a dynamo. 3. an internal-combustion engine. 4. automobile. —*adj.* 1. pertaining to a motor. 2. run by a motor. 3. having to do with motion. 4. having to do with bodily movements. Motor nerves arouse muscles to action. —*v.* travel by automobile. [< L, mover < *movere* to move]

Clown wearing a motley costume

mo·tor·boat (mō′tər·bōt′), *n.* boat that is run by a motor.

mo·tor·bus (mō′tər·bus′), **motor coach,** *n.* bus run by a motor.

mo·tor·cade (mō′tər·kād), *n. Am.* procession or long line of automobiles.

mo·tor·car (mō′tər·kär′), *n.* automobile.

motor court, *Am.* group of small buildings providing accommodations for travelers by automobile.

mo·tor·cy·cle (mō′tər·sī′kəl), *n.* a self-propelled, two-wheeled vehicle. —**mo·tor·cy·clist** (mō′tər·sī′klist), *n.*

mo·tor·ist (mō′tər·ist), *n.* person who drives an automobile.

mo·tor·ize (mō′tər·īz), *v.,* -ized, -iz·ing. 1. furnish with a motor. 2. supply (infantry units, cavalry, etc.) with motor-driven vehicles to facilitate maneuverability. —**mo′tor·i·za′tion,** *n.*

mo·tor·man (mō′tər·mən), *n., pl.* **-men.** 1. *Am.* man who runs an electric streetcar or train. 2. man who runs a motor.

motor truck, truck with an engine and chassis made for carrying heavy loads.

mot·tle (mot′əl), *v.,* -tled, -tling, *n.* —*v.* mark with spots or streaks of different colors. —*n.* a mottled coloring or pattern. [? < *motley*] —**mot′tler,** *n.*

mot·to (mot′ō), *n., pl.* -toes, -tos. a brief sentence adopted as a rule of conduct. [< Ital. < L *muttum* grunt, word. Doublet of мот.] —Syn. proverb, adage, saying, maxim.

mou·jik (mū·zhik′; mū′zhik), *n.* muzhik.

Mouk·den (mūk′den′; mūk′–), *n.* Mukden.

mould (mōld), *n., v. Esp. Brit.* mold. —**mould′a·ble,** *adj.*

mould·board (mōld′bôrd′; –bōrd′), *n. Esp. Brit.* moldboard.

mould·er (mōl′dər), *v., n. Esp. Brit.* molder.

mould·ing (mōl′ding), *n. Esp. Brit.* molding.

mould·y (mōl′di), *adj.,* mould·i·er, mould·i·est. *Esp. Brit.* moldy. —**mould′i·ness,** *n.*

moult (mōlt), *v., n. Esp. Brit.* molt.

mound (mound), *n.* 1. bank or heap of earth or stones. 2. a small hill. 3. *Am., Baseball.* the slightly elevated ground from which the pitcher pitches. —*v.* enclose with a mound; heap up. [OE *mund* protection; meaning infl. by *mount*[2]]

mount[1] (mount), *v.* 1. go up; ascend: *mount stairs.* 2. move or proceed upwards: *a flush mounts to the brow.* 3. rise; increase; rise in amount: *the costs are mounting.* 4. get up on: *mount a platform.* 5. get on a horse; get up on something: *mount and ride away.* 6. put on a horse; furnish with a horse: *the mounted police.* 7. put up high: *mounted on stilts.* 8. put in proper position or order for use: *mount specimens on slides.* 9. fix in a setting, on backing, a support, etc.: *mount a picture on cardboard.* 10. ornament: *pistols mounted with silver.* 11. have or carry (guns) as a fortress or ship does. 12. go or put on (guard) as a sentry or watch does. —*n.* 1. horse provided for riding. 2. a setting; backing; support. 3. act of mounting. 4. manner of mounting. [< OF *monter* < L *mons* mountain] —**mount′a·ble,** *adj.* —**mount′er,** *n.*

mount[2] (mount), *n.* mountain; high hill. [< L *mons*]

moun·tain (moun′tən), *n.* 1. very high hill. 2. mountains or mountain chain, a series of such hills. 3. something like a high hill:

mountain of rubbish. **4.** a huge amount. —*adj.* **1.** of or pertaining to mountains. **2.** living, growing, or found on mountains. **3.** resembling or suggesting a mountain. [< OF *montaigne* < *mont* MOUNT²] —Syn. *n.* **1.** elevation, peak.

mountain ash, any of several trees of the rose family with pinnate leaves, white flowers, and bright-red berries.

moun·tain·eer (moun′tə·nir′), *n.* **1.** person who lives in the mountains. **2.** person skilled in mountain climbing. —*v.* climb mountains.

mountain goat, *Am.* the white antelope of the Rocky Mountains.

mountain laurel, *Am.* an evergreen shrub with glossy leaves and pale-pink flowers.

mountain lion, *Am.* cougar.

Mountain goat (ab. 3 ft. high at the shoulder)

moun·tain·ous (moun′tə·nəs), *adj.* **1.** covered with mountain ranges. **2.** huge.

mountain sheep, *Am.* the wild sheep of the Rocky Mountains.

moun·te·bank (moun′tə·bangk), *n.* **1.** person who sells quack medicines in public, appealing to his audience by tricks, stories, jokes, etc. **2.** anybody who tries to deceive people. —*v.* act like a mountebank. [< Ital. *montambanco* for *monta in banco* mount-on-bench]

mount·ing (moun′ting), *n.* support, setting, or the like: *the mounting of a photograph.*

Mount Ver·non (vér′nən), home of George Washington in Virginia, on the Potomac River near Washington, D.C.

mourn (môrn; mōrn), *v.* **1.** grieve. **2.** feel or show sorrow over. [OE *murnan*] —mourn′er, *n.* —Syn. **1.** lament, sorrow, bewail.

mourn·ful (môrn′fəl; mōrn′-), *adj.* **1.** sad; sorrowful. **2.** gloomy; dreary. **3.** causing, or attended with, sorrow or mourning. —mourn′ful·ly, *adv.* —mourn′ful·ness, *n.* —Syn. **1.** doleful, dolorous, melancholy.

mourn·ing (môr′ning; mōr′-), *n.* **1.** sorrowing; lamentation. **2.** the wearing of black or some other color (white in the Orient), to show sorrow for a person's death. **3.** a draping of buildings, hanging flags at half-mast, etc., as signs of such sorrow. **4.** clothes, draperies, etc., to show such sorrow. —*adj.* of mourning; used in mourning. —mourn′ing·ly, *adv.*

mourning dove, *Am.* a wild dove of North America that makes a mournful sound.

mouse (*n.* mous; *v.* mouz), *n., pl.* **mice** (mīs), *v.,* **moused, mous·ing.** —*n.* **1.** a small, gray, gnawing animal. **2.** a shy, timid person. —*v.* **1.** hunt for mice; catch mice for food. **2.** search as a cat does; move about as if searching. [OE *mūs*]

MOUSE, Minimum Orbital Unmanned Satellite of Earth (the sphere about the size of a basketball which it is proposed to launch into an orbit around the earth).

mous·er (mouz′ər), *n.* animal that catches mice.

mousse (mūs), *n.* a fancy food made with whipped cream, either frozen or stiffened with gelatin: *chocolate mousse.* [< F, moss, < Gmc.]

mous·tache (mus′tash; məs·tash′), *n.* *Esp. Brit.* mustache.

mous·y (mous′i), *adj.,* **mous·i·er, mous·i·est. 1.** resembling or suggesting a mouse in color, odor, behavior, etc. **2.** quiet as a mouse. **3.** infested with mice.

mouth (*n.* mouth; *v.* mouth), *n., pl.* **mouths** (mouthz), *v.* —*n.* **1.** opening through which an animal takes in food. **2.** space containing tongue and teeth. **3.** a grimace. **4.** an opening suggesting a mouth: *the mouth of a river.* —*v.* **1.** seize or rub with the mouth. **2.** utter (words) in an affected or pompous way. **3.** speak oratorically. **4.** make grimaces. [OE *mūth*] —mouth·er (mouth′ər), *n.* —mouth′less, *adj.*

mouth·ful (mouth′fùl), *n., pl.* **-fuls. 1.** amount the mouth can hold. **2.** what is taken into the mouth at one time. **3.** a small amount.

mouth organ, harmonica.

mouth·piece (mouth′pēs′), *n.* **1.** the part of a pipe, horn, etc., that is placed in or against a person's mouth. **2.** piece placed at the mouth of something or forming its mouth. **3.** person, newspaper, etc., that speaks for others.

mouth·y (mouth′i; mouth′i), *adj.,* **mouth·i·er, mouth·i·est.** loud-mouthed. —mouth′i·ly, *adv.* —mouth′i·ness, *n.*

mov·a·ble, move·a·ble (mūv′ə·bəl), *adj.* **1.** that can be moved. **2.** that can be carried from place to place as personal possessions can. **3.** changing from one date to another in different years. Easter is a movable holy day. —*n.* **1.** piece of furniture that is not a fixture but can be moved to another house. **2.** Usually, **movables.** *Law.* personal property. —mov′a·bil′i·ty, move′a·bil′i·ty; mov′a·ble·ness, move′a·ble·ness, *n.* —mov′a·bly, move′a·bly, *adv.* —Syn. *adj.* **1.** mobile. **2.** portable, transportable.

move (mūv), *v.,* **moved, mov·ing,** *n.* —*v.* **1.** change the place or position of: *she moved her lips.* **2.** change place or position: *the trees move.* **3.** change one's abode: *we move next week.* **4.** make a move in a game; be moved in a game: *I move my bishop.* **5.** put or keep in motion: *the wind moves the trees.* **6.** cause to act: *castor oil moves the bowels.* **7.** act: *God moves in a mysterious way.* **8.** impel; rouse; excite: *power to move the masses.* **9.** affect with emotion; excite to tender feeling: *move men to tears.* **10.** make a formal request, application, or proposal: *propose: I move that we adjourn.* **11.** sell or be sold: *these dresses are moving slowly.* **12.** make progress: *the tale moves slowly.* **13.** exist; be active: *move in the best society.* **14.** turn; swing; operate: *most doors move on a hinge.* —*n.* **1.** right or time to move in a game. **2.** act of moving; movement. **3.** action toward a goal: *a move to disconcert his opponents.* **4.** on the move, moving about. [< AF < L *movere*] —mov′er, *n.* —Syn. *v.* **1, 2.** shift. **3.** remove, transfer. **8.** actuate, stimulate, prompt. **9.** influence.

move·ment (mūv′mənt), *n.* **1.** act or fact of moving: *movements of the legs.* **2.** change in the placing of troops or ships. **3.** the moving parts of a machine. The movement of a watch consists of many little wheels. **4.** *Music.* the kind of rhythm a piece has, its speed, etc. **b.** one division of a long musical selection. **5.** rhythmical structure or character. **6.** suggestion of action in a painting or sculpture. **7.** abundance of incidents; action. **8.** efforts and results of a group of people working together to bring about some one thing: *the movement for a safe and sane Fourth of July.* **9.** an emptying of the bowels. —Syn. **1.** motion, move, action, stir.

mov·ie (mūv′i), *n. Am., Colloq.* a motion picture.

mov·ing (mūv′ing), *adj.* **1.** that moves. **2.** causing motion; actuating. **3.** touching; pathetic: *a moving story.* —mov′ing·ly, *adv.*

moving picture, a motion picture.

mow¹ (mō), *v.,* **mowed, mowed or mown, mowing. 1.** cut down with a machine or a scythe. **2.** cut down the grass or grain from. **3.** cut down grass, etc. **4.** destroy in large numbers, as if by mowing. [OE *māwan*] —mow′er, *n.*

mow² (mou), *n.* **1.** place in a barn where hay, grain, or the like is piled or stored. **2.** pile or stack of hay, grain, etc., in a barn. [OE *mūga*]

mow³ (mō; mou), *v., n.* grimace. [< OF *moue*]

Mo·zam·bique (mō′zəm·bēk′), *n.* a Portuguese colony in SE Africa.

Mo·zart (mō′tsärt), *n.* Wolfgang Amadeus, 1756–1791, Austrian musical composer.

M.P., MP. 1. Member of Parliament. **2.** Metropolitan Police. **3.** Also, **MP.** Military Police.

mph, m.p.h., miles per hour.

Mr., Mr (mis′tər), *pl.* **Messrs.** mister, title put in front of a man's name or the name of his position.

Mrs. (mis′iz; miz′iz; miz), *pl.* **Mmes.** title put in front of a married woman's name.

Ms., MS., or **ms.,** *pl.* **Mss.; MSS.;** mss. manuscript.

M.S., M.Sc., Master of Science.

MSA, M.S.A., Mutual Security Agency.

Msgr., Monsignor.

M.S.T., MST, or **m.s.t.,** *Am.* Mountain Standard Time.

Mt., *pl.* **Mts.** Mount: *Mt. Everest.*

mt., mtn., *pl.* **mts.; mtns.** mountain.

mu (mū), *n.* the 12th letter of the Greek alphabet (M, μ).

much (much), *adj.,* more, most, *adv.,* more, most, *n.* —*adj.* in great quantity, amount, or degree: *much money, much time.* —*adv.* **1.** to a great extent or degree: *much pleased.* **2.** nearly; about: *this is much the same as the others.* —*n.* **1.** a great deal: *much of this is not true.* **2.** a great, important, or notable thing or matter: *the rain did not amount to much.* **3.** make much of, treat, represent, or consider as of great importance. [var. of OE *micel*] —**much′ness,** *n.*

mu·ci·lage (mū′sə·lij), *n.* **1.** *Am.* a gummy substance used to stick things together. **2.** substance like glue or gelatin in plants. [< F < LL *mucilago* musty juice < L *mucus* mucus]

mu·ci·lag·i·nous (mū′sə·laj′ə·nəs), *adj.* **1.** sticky; gummy. **2.** containing or secreting mucilage.

muck (muk), *n.* **1.** dirt; filth. **2.** moist farmyard manure. —*v.* **1.** soil or make dirty. **2.** put muck on. [< Scand. *myki*] —**muck′y,** *adj.*

muck·er (muk′ər), *n. Am., Slang.* a vulgar, ill-bred person.

muck·rake (muk′rāk′), *v.,* -raked, -rak·ing. *Am.* hunt for and expose corruption. —**muck′rak′er,** *n. Am.*

mu·cous (mū′kəs), *adj.* **1.** of or like mucus. **2.** containing or secreting mucus.

mucous membrane, *Anat., Zool.* lining of the nose, throat, and other cavities that are open to the air.

mu·cus (mū′kəs), *n.* a slimy substance that moistens the linings of the body. [< L]

mud (mud), *n.* soft, sticky, wet earth. [ME *mudde*] —Syn. mire, slime, ooze.

mud·dle (mud′əl), *v.,* -dled, -dling, *n.* —*v.* **1.** mix up; bring (things) into a mess. **2.** make confused or stupid or slightly drunk. **3.** think or act in a confused, blundering way. —*n.* mess; disorder; confusion. [< *mud*] —**mud′dler,** *n.*

mud·dy (mud′i), *adj.,* -di·er, -di·est, *v.,* -died, -dy·ing. —*adj.* **1.** of or like mud. **2.** having much mud; covered with mud. **3.** clouded with mud; dull; not pure: *muddy water, a muddy color.* **4.** confused; not clear. —*v.* make or become muddy. —**mud′di·ly,** *adv.* —**mud′di·ness,** *n.*

mud·guard (mud′gärd′), *n.* guard or shield so placed as to protect riders or passengers from mud thrown by the wheels of a vehicle.

mud hen, *Am.* water bird that looks like a large chicken. It lives in marshes.

mud puppy, *Am.* salamander that lives in water.

mu·ez·zin (mū·ez′in), *n.* crier who, at certain hours, calls Mohammedans to prayer. [< Ar. *mu'adhdhin*]

Mud hen (ab. 1 ft. long)

muff (muf), *n.* **1.** a covering of fur or other material for keeping both hands warm. One hand is put in at each end. **2.** a clumsy failure to catch a ball that comes into one's hands. —*v.* **1.** fail to catch (a ball) when it comes into one's hands. **2.** bungle. [< Du. < F *moufle*]

muf·fin (muf′ən), *n.* a small, round cake made of wheat flour, corn meal, or the like, eaten with butter and usually served hot.

muf·fle (muf′əl), *v.,* -fled, -fling, *n.* —*v.* **1.** wrap or cover up in order to keep warm and dry. **2.** wrap oneself in garments, etc. **3.** wrap in something in order to soften or stop the sound. **4.** dull or deaden (a sound). —*n.* **1.** a muffled

sound. **2.** thing that muffles. [< OF *enmoufler* wrap up < *moufle* muff]

muf·fler (muf′lər), *n.* **1.** wrap or scarf worn around the neck for warmth. **2.** thing used to deaden sound: *the muffler of a motor.*

muf·ti (muf′ti), *n., pl.* -tis for 2. **1.** ordinary clothes, not a uniform. **2.** a Mohammedan expounder of the laws of the Mohammedan religion. [< Ar. *mufti* (def. 2); def. 1 ? with ref. to informal costume traditional for a stage mufti]

mug (mug), *n., v.,* mugged, mug·ging. —*n.* **1.** a heavy earthenware or metal drinking cup with a handle. **2.** amount a mug holds. **3.** *Slang.* face. **4.** *Slang.* mouth. —*v. Slang.* attack (a person) from behind by locking the forearm around the neck and choking. [cf. Scand. (Norw.) *mugge;* defs. 3 and 4 from common shape of mugs in earlier times] —**mug′ger,** *n.*

Mug

mug·gy (mug′i), *adj.,* -gi·er, -gi·est. warm and humid; damp and close. [< *mug* fog < Scand. *mugga*] —**mug′gi·ness,** *n.*

mug·wump (mug′wump′), *n. Am.* an independent in politics. [< Algonquian *mukquomp* great man]

Mu·ham·mad (mù·ham′əd), *n.* Mohammed. —**Mu·ham′mad·an,** *adj., n.* —**Mu·ham′mad·an·ism,** *n.*

mu·jik (mū·zhik′; mü′zhik), *n.* muzhik.

Muk·den (mùk′den′; mük′-), *n.* city in Manchuria. Also, **Moukden, Shenyang.**

mu·lat·to (mə·lat′ō; myù-), *n., pl.* -toes. **1.** person having one white and one Negro parent. **2.** person having some white and some Negro blood. [< Sp. and Pg. *mulato* < *mulo* mule; from hybrid origin]

mul·ber·ry (mul′ber′i), *n., pl.* -ries. **1.** any of various trees such as the American mulberry that yields a berrylike fruit or the white mulberry whose leaves are used for feeding silkworms. **2.** the berrylike fruit of any of these trees. **3.** dark purplish red. [OE *mōrberie* < L *morum* mulberry + OE *berie* berry]

mulch (mulch), *n.* straw, leaves, loose earth, etc., spread on the ground around trees or plants, used to protect the roots from cold or heat, to prevent evaporation of moisture from the soil, etc. —*v.* cover with straw, leaves, etc. [OE *mylsc* mellow]

mulct (mulkt), *v.* **1.** deprive of something, as by deceit or a shrewd trick; deprive. **2.** punish by a fine. —*n.* fine; penalty. [< L *mulctare,* erroneous var. of *multare* < *multa* a fine]

mule¹ (mūl), *n.* **1.** offspring of the ass and horse, esp. of a male ass and a mare. **2.** *Colloq.* a stubborn person. **3.** kind of spinning machine. [< F < L *mula, mulus*]

mule² (mūl), *n.* kind of slipper that leaves the heel uncovered. [< F < Du. < L *mulleus* shoe of red leather]

mu·le·teer (mū′lə·tir′), *n.* driver of mules.

mul·ish (mūl′ish), *adj.* stubborn; obstinate. —**mul′ish·ly,** *adv.* —**mul′ish·ness,** *n.*

mull¹ (mul), *v. Am., Colloq.* think (about) without making much progress; ponder.

mull² (mul), *v.* make (wine, beer, etc.) into a warm drink, with sugar, spices, etc.

mul·lah (mul′ə; mùl′ə), *n.* in Mohammedan countries, a title of respect for one who is learned in the sacred law. [< Turk., Pers., Hind. *mullā* < Ar. *mawlā*]

mul·lein, mul·len (mul′ən), *n.* weed with coarse, woolly leaves and spikes of yellow flowers. [< AF *moleine*]

mul·let (mul′it), *n., pl.* -lets or (esp. collectively) -let. kind of edible fish. There are red mullets and gray mullets. [< OF *mulet* < L *mullus* red mullet < Gk. *myllos*]

mul·li·gan (mul′ə·gən), *n. Am., Slang.* stew of meat and vegetables.

mul·li·ga·taw·ny (mul′ə·gə·tô′ni), *n.* soup flavored with curry. [< Tamil *miḷagu-taṇṇir* pepper water]

mul·lion (mul′yən), *n.* a vertical bar between

the lights of a window, the panels in the wall of a room, or the like. —**mul′lioned,** *adj.*

multi-, *word element.* **1.** having many or several, as in *multiform.* **2.** many or several times, as in *multimillionaire.* [< L, < *multus* much, many]

mul·ti·cel·lu·lar (mul′ti·sel′yə·lər), *adj.* having more than one cell.

mul·ti·col·ored (mul′ti·kul′ərd), *adj.* having many colors.

mul·ti·far·i·ous (mul′tə·fãr′i·əs), *adj.* **1.** having many different parts, elements, forms, etc. **2.** many and various. [< L *multifarius*] —**mul′ti·far′i·ous·ly,** *adv.* —**mul′ti·far′i·ous·ness,** *n.*

mul·ti·form (mul′tə·fôrm), *adj.* having many different shapes, forms, or kinds. —**mul·ti·for·mi·ty** (mul′tə·fôr′mə·ti), *n.*

M, mullion.

mul·ti·lat·er·al (mul′ti·lat′ər·əl), *adj.* **1.** having many sides; many-sided. **2.** involving two or more nations. —**mul′ti·lat′er·al·ly,** *adv.*

mul·ti·mil·lion·aire (mul′ti·mil′yən·ãr′), *n. Am.* a millionaire many times over.

mul·ti·ple (mul′tə·pəl), *adj.* of, having, or involving many parts, elements, relations, etc.: *a man of multiple interests.* —*n.* number that contains another number a certain number of times without a remainder. 12 is a multiple of 3. [< F < LL *multiplus* manifold]

multiple sclerosis, disease which cripples and can destroy vital parts of the nervous system.

mul·ti·pli·cand (mul′tə·pli·kand′), *n.* number or quantity to be multiplied by another. [< L *multiplicandus* to be multiplied. See MULTI-PLY.]

mul·ti·pli·ca·tion (mul′tə·plə·kā′shən), *n.* **1.** a multiplying. **2.** a being multiplied.

mul·ti·plic·i·ty (mul′tə·plis′ə·ti), *n., pl.* -ties. a manifold variety; great many.

mul·ti·pli·er (mul′tə·plī′ər), *n.* **1.** number by which another number is to be multiplied. **2.** person or thing that multiplies.

mul·ti·ply (mul′tə·plī), *v.,* -plied, -ply·ing. **1.** increase in number or amount. **2.** take (a number or quantity) a given number of times. To multiply 16 by 3 means to take 16 three times, making 48. [< OF < L *multiplicare* < *multiplex* manifold] —**mul′ti·pli′a·ble,** *adj.* —Syn. **1.** augment, enlarge.

mul·ti·stage (mul′ti·stāj), *adj.* of a rocket or missile, having two or more propulsive sections, each operating after the preceding stage has burned out and separated.

mul·ti·tude (mul′tə·tüd; -tūd), *n.* **1.** a great many; crowd. **2.** the multitude, the common people. [< L, < *multus* much] —Syn. **1.** host, throng, horde, legion, army, swarm.

mul·ti·tu·di·nous (mul′tə·tü′də·nəs; -tū′-), *adj.* **1.** very numerous. **2.** including many parts, elements, items, or features. —**mul′ti·tu′di·nous·ly,** *adv.* —**mul′ti·tu′di·nous·ness,** *n.*

mul·ti·va·lent (mul′ti·vā′lənt; mul·tiv′ə-), *adj. Chem.* having a valence of three or more. —**mul′ti·va′lence,** *n.*

mul·ti·ver·si·ty (mul′tə·vėr′sə·ti), *n., pl.* -ties. a large educational institution comprising several universities.

mum (mum), *adj.* silent; saying nothing. —*interj.* be silent! say nothing! [ME; ? imit.]

mum·ble (mum′bəl), *v.,* -bled, -bling, *n.* —*v.* speak indistinctly. —*n.* a mumbling. [ME *momele(n),* ? < *mum*] —**mum′bler,** *n.*

mum·mer (mum′ər), *n.* **1.** person who wears a mask, fancy costume, etc., for fun. **2.** actor.

mum·mer·y (mum′ər·i), *n., pl.* -mer·ies. **1.** performance of mummers. **2.** useless or silly show or ceremony. [< OF *mommerie*]

mum·mi·fy (mum′ə·fī), *v.,* -fied, -fy·ing. **1.** make (a dead body) into a mummy; make like a mummy. **2.** dry or shrivel up. —**mum′mi·fi·ca′tion,** *n.*

mum·my (mum′i), *n., pl.* -mies, *v.,* -mied, -my·ing. —*n.* **1.** a dead body preserved from decay. Egyptian mummies have lasted more than 3000 years. **2.** a brown bituminous pigment. —*v.* mummify. [< Med.L < Ar. < Pers. *mūmiyā* < *mūm* wax]

mumps (mumps), *n.pl.* (*sing. in use*) a contagious disease marked by swelling of the face and difficulty in swallowing. [pl. of obs. *mump* grimace]

Egyptian mummy and coffin

munch (munch), *v.* chew vigorously and steadily; chew noisily. [appar. imit.]—**munch′-er,** *n.*

Mun·chau·sen (mun′chô·zən; -chou-), *n.* Baron, 1720–1797, supposed author of a book of incredible tales.

mun·dane (mun′dān), *adj.* **1.** of this world, not of heaven; earthly. **2.** of the universe; of the world. [< F < L, < *mundus* world] —**mun′dane·ly,** *adv.*

Mu·nich (mū′nik), *n.* **1.** city in SW Germany. **2.** an instance of appeasement which brings shame to the appeaser.

Munich Pact, pact signed September 29, 1938 by Germany, France, Great Britain, and Italy, by which the Sudetenland was given over to Germany.

mu·nic·i·pal (mū·nis′ə·pəl), *adj.* **1.** of or having to do with the affairs of a city, town, or other municipality. **2.** run by a city, town, etc. **3.** having local self-government. [< L *municipalis,* ult. < *munia* official duties + *capere* take on] —**mu·nic′i·pal·ly,** *adv.*

mu·nic·i·pal·i·ty (mū·nis′ə·pal′ə·ti), *n., pl.* -ties. city, town, or other district having local self-government.

mu·nif·i·cence (mū·nif′ə·səns), *n.* very great generosity. [< L, < *munificus* generous, ult. < *munus* gift + *facere* make]

mu·nif·i·cent (mū·nif′ə·sənt), *adj.* extremely generous. [< *munificence*] —**mu·nif′i·cent·ly,** *adv.* —Syn. bountiful, bounteous, lavish, liberal.

mu·ni·tion (mū·nish′ən), *n.* munitions, military supplies; materials used in war, such as guns, powder, or bombs. —*adj.* pertaining to military supplies. A munition plant is a factory for making munitions. —*v.* provide with military supplies. [< L, < *munire* fortify]

mu·ral (myūr′əl), *adj.* **1.** on a wall. **2.** of a wall; having to do with walls; like a wall. **3.** steep. —*n.* picture painted on a wall. [< F < L, < *murus* wall]

mur·der (mėr′dər), *n. Law.* the unlawful killing of a human being when it is planned beforehand. —*v.* **1.** kill thus. **2.** spoil; do very badly. [var. of obs. *murther,* OE *morthor*] —**mur′der·er,** *n.* —Syn. *v.* **1.** slay, assassinate, execute.

mur·der·ess (mėr′dər·is), *n.* woman who murders somebody.

mur·der·ous (mėr′dər·əs), *adj.* **1.** capable of killing: *a murderous blow.* **2.** ready to murder: *a murderous villain.* **3.** causing murder: *a murderous plot.* —**mur′der·ous·ly,** *adv.* —**mur′der·ous·ness,** *n.*

mu·ri·at·ic acid (myūr′i·at′ik), hydrochloric acid. [< L, < *muria* brine]

murk (mėrk), *n.* darkness; gloom. —*adj. Poetic.* dark; gloomy. Also, mirk. [< Scand. *myrkr*]

murk·y (mėr′ki), *adj.,* murk·i·er, murk·i·est. dark; gloomy. Also, mirky. —**murk′i·ly,** *adv.* —**murk′i·ness,** *n.*

Mur·mansk (mėr·mänsk′; mûr·mänsk′), *n.* seaport and railroad terminus in NW Soviet Union.

mur·mur (mėr′mər), *n.* **1.** a soft, low, indistinct sound that rises and falls a little and goes on without breaks: *murmur of a stream, murmur of voices in another room.* **2.** a sound in the heart or lungs, esp. an abnormal sound due to a leaky valve in the heart. **3.** a softly spoken word or speech. **4.** complaint made under the breath, not aloud. —*v.* **1.** make a soft, low, indistinct sound. **2.** utter in a murmur. **3.** complain under the breath; grumble. [< L *murmur*]

—**mur'mur·er**, *n.* —**mur'mur·ing**, *adj.* —**mur'-mur· ly**, *adv.* —**Syn.** *n.* 1. hum, babble. –*v.* 2. mumble, mutter.

mur·rain (mér'ən), *n.* an infectious disease of cattle. [< OF *morine*, ult. < L *mori die*]

Mur·ray (mér'i), *n.* river in SE Australia.

mus., 1. museum. 2. music; musical.

mus·ca·dine (mus'kə·din; –dīn), *n.* grape of the S United States.

mus·cat (mus'kat; –kət), *n.* a light-colored grape with the flavor or odor of musk. [< F < Pr. < LL *muscatus* with musk < *muscus* musk]

mus·ca·tel (mus'kə·tel'), *n.* 1. a strong, sweet wine made from muscat grapes. 2. the muscat grape. [< OF. See MUSCAT.]

mus·cle (mus'əl), *n., v.,* –**cled**, –**cling**. —*n.* 1. bundle of special tissue that can be tightened or loosened to move a part of the body. 2. this tissue. 3. strength. —*v.* **muscle in**, *Am., Slang.* force oneself into a situation where one is not wanted. [< F < L *musculus*, dim. of *mus* mouse; from appearance of certain muscles]

mus·cle-bound (mus'əl·bound'), *adj.* having some of the muscles stiff or tight, usually as a result of too much exercise.

Muscle Shoals, rapids of the Tennessee River in NW Alabama. Wilson Dam and other dams were built there to improve navigation, control floods, and produce electricity.

Mus·co·vite (mus'kə·vīt), *n., adj.* Russian.

Mus·co·vy (mus'kə·vi), *n. Archaic.* Russia.

mus·cu·lar (mus'kyə·lər), *adj.* 1. of the muscles; influencing the muscles. 2. having well-developed muscles; strong. 3. consisting of muscle. —**mus·cu·lar·i·ty** (mus'kyə·lar'ə·ti), *n.* —**mus'cu·lar·ly**, *adv.* —**Syn.** 2. sinewy, brawny, powerful. —**Ant.** 2. weak, feeble.

muscular dys·tro·phy (dis'trə·fi), a gradual wasting away and weakening of the muscles.

mus·cu·la·ture (mus'kyə·lə·chər), *n.* system or arrangement of muscles.

muse (mūz), *v.,* mused, mus·ing. 1. think in a dreamy way; think; meditate. 2. look thoughtfully. 3. say thoughtfully. [< OF *muser* loiter] —**mus'er**, *n.* —**Syn.** 1. ponder, reflect, ruminate.

Muse (mūz), *n.* 1. *Class. Myth.* one of the nine Greek goddesses of the fine arts and sciences. 2. Sometimes, **muse.** spirit that inspires a poet or composer. [< OF < L < Gk. *Mousa*]

mu·se·um (mū·zē'əm), *n.* building or rooms where a collection of objects illustrating science, art, ancient life, or other subjects is kept. [< L < Gk. *mouseion* seat of the Muses. See MUSE.]

mush[1] (mush), *n.* 1. *Am.* corn meal boiled in water. 2. a soft, thick mass. 3. *Colloq.* weak sentiment; silly talk. [var. of *mash.* Cf. Du. *moes.*]

mush[2] (mush), *n., v. Am.* journey on foot, usually with a dog sled across snow. [? for *mush on*, alter. of F *marchons* let us advance] —**mush'er**, *n.*

mush·room (mush'rüm; –rüm), *n.* 1. a small fungus, shaped like an umbrella, that grows very fast. Some mushrooms are good to eat; some are poisonous. 2. anything shaped or growing like a mushroom. —*adj.* 1. of or like a mushroom. 2. of very rapid growth. —*v.* 1. grow very fast. 2. flatten at one end. A bullet sometimes mushrooms when it hits a very hard object. [< F *mousseron*, ? < *mousse* moss < Gmc.]

Mushrooms (stalk 2 to 5 in. long)

mush·y (mush'i), *adj.,* mush·i·er, mush·i·est. 1. like mush; pulpy. 2. *Colloq.* weakly sentimental. —**mush'i·ness**, *n.*

mu·sic (mū'zik), *n.* 1. art of putting sounds together in beautiful or pleasing arrangements. 2. beautiful or pleasing arrangements of sounds. 3. a pleasant sound. 4. written or printed signs for tones. 5. appreciation of, or responsiveness to, musical sounds. 6. **face the music,** *Am., Colloq.* meet trouble boldly or bravely. 7. **set to music,** provide (the words of a song) with music. [< L < Gk. *mousike* (*techne*) art of the Muse. See MUSE.]

mu·si·cal (mū'zə·kəl), *adj.* 1. of music. 2.

sounding beautiful or pleasing; like music. 3. set to music; accompanied by music. 4. fond of music. 5. skilled in music. —**mu'si·cal·ly**, *adv.* —**mu'si·cal·ness**, *n.*

musical comedy, *Am.* a gay and amusing play in which plot and characterization are less important than singing, dancing, and costumes.

mu·si·cale (mū'zə·kal'), *n. Am.* a social gathering to enjoy music. [< F, short for *soirée musicale* musical evening]

music box, box or case containing apparatus for producing music mechanically.

music hall, 1. hall for musical entertainments. 2. *Esp. Brit.* theater for vaudeville.

mu·si·cian (mū·zish'ən), *n.* 1. person skilled in music. 2. person who sings or who plays on a musical instrument, especially one who does so for pay. 3. composer of music. —**mu·si'cian·ly**, *adj.*

mus·ing (mūz'ing), *adj.* dreamy; meditative. —**mus'ing·ly**, *adv.*

musk (musk), *n.* 1. substance with a strong and lasting odor, used in making perfumes. Musk is found in a special gland in the male musk deer. 2. the odor of musk. [< LL < LGk. < Pers. *mushk*]

musk deer, a small, hornless deer of central Asia, the male of which has a gland containing musk.

musk·el·lunge (mus'kə·lunj), *n., pl.* –**lunge.** *Am.* a large American pike. [< Ojibwa *mash-kinonge* great pike]

mus·ket (mus'kit), *n.* kind of old gun. Soldiers used muskets before rifles were invented. [< F < Ital. *moschetto*, orig., a kind of hawk < *mosca* fly < L *musca*]

mus·ket·eer (mus'kə·tir'), *n.* soldier armed with a musket.

mus·ket·ry (mus'kit·ri), *n.* 1. muskets. 2. shooting with muskets or rifles. 3. soldiers armed with muskets.

musk·mel·on (musk'mel'ən), *n.* kind of sweet, juicy melon; cantaloupe.

musk ox, an arctic animal, somewhat like an ox and even more like a sheep, that has a musky smell.

musk·rat (musk'rat'), *n., pl.* –**rats** or (*esp. collectively*) –**rat.** *Am.* 1. a water animal of North America, like a rat, but larger. 2. its valuable dark-brown fur.

musk·y (mus'ki), *adj.,* musk·i·er, musk·i·est. of musk; like musk; like that of musk.

Mus·lem, Mus·lim (muz'ləm; mus'–), *n., adj.* Moslem.

mus·lin (muz'lən), *Am.* —*n.* 1. a thin, fine cotton cloth, used for dresses, curtains, etc. 2. a heavier cotton cloth, used for sheets, undergarments, etc. —*adj.* made of muslin. [< F < Ital. *mussolina* < *Mussolo* Mosul, city in Iraq]

muss (mus), *U.S. Colloq.* —*v.* put into disorder; rumple. —*n.* disorder; mess. [var. of *mess*] —**muss'y**, *adj.*

mus·sel (mus'əl), *n.* 1. an edible salt-water mollusk that looks like a small clam, with black shells. 2. a fresh-water mollusk whose shells are used in making buttons. [< L *musculus* mussel, MUSCLE]

Mus·so·li·ni (mūs'ə·lē'ni), *n.* **Benito** (*Il Duce*), 1883–1945, leader of the Italian Fascists and prime minister of Italy 1922–1943.

Mus·sul·man (mus'əl·mən), *n., pl.* –**mans.** Mohammedan; Moslem.

must[1] (must; *unstressed* məst), *auxiliary verb, pt.* must, *n., adj.* –*aux. v.* 1. be obliged to; be forced to: *man must eat to live.* 2. ought to; should: *I must go home soon.* 3. be certain to (be, do, etc.): *I must seem very rude.* 4. be supposed or expected to: *you must have that book.* 5. *Must* is sometimes used with its verb omitted: *we must to horse, we must away.* —*n.* something necessary; obligation: *this rule is a must.* —*adj.* demanding attention or doing; necessary: *a must item, must legislation.* [OE *mōste*, pt.]

must[2] (must), *n.* the unfermented juice of the grape; new wine. [< L (*vinum*) *mustum* fresh (wine)]

mus·tache (mus'tash; məs·tash'), *n.* hair

growing on a man's upper lip. Also, *esp. Brit.* **moustache.** [< F < Ital. < Gk. *mystax* upper lip, mustache]

mus·ta·chio (məs·tä'shō), *n., pl.* **-chios.** mustache. —**mus·ta·chioed** (məs·tä'shōd), *adj.*

mus·tang (mus'tang), *n. Am.* the small, wild or half-wild horse of the American plains. [< Sp. *mestengo* untamed]

mus·tard (mus'tərd), *n.* **1.** a yellow powder or paste used as seasoning to give a pungent taste. **2.** plant from whose seeds it is made. [< OF *moustarde*, ult. < L *mustum* MUST²]

mustard gas, a poison gas, (ClCH₂CH₂)₂S, that causes burns, blindness, and death.

mustard plaster, poultice made of mustard and water, or of mustard, flour, and water.

mus·ter (mus'tər), *v.* **1.** assemble, as troops, the crew of a ship, etc.; gather together; collect: *muster soldiers.* **2.** summon: *muster up courage.* **3.** muster in, *Am.* enlist. **4.** muster out, *Am.* discharge. —*n.* **1.** assembly; collection. **2.** bringing together of men or troops for review or service. **3.** list of those mustered. **4.** the number mustered. **5.** pass muster, be inspected and approved; come up to the required standards. [< OF < L *monstrare* show < *monstrum* portent] —**Syn.** *v.* **1.** convene, marshal, array. —**Ant.** *v.* **1.** disband, dissolve, disorganize.

mus·ty (mus'ti), *adj.,* **-ti·er, -ti·est. 1.** having a smell or taste suggesting mold or damp; moldy. **2.** stale; out-of-date: *musty laws.* —**mus'ti·ly,** *adv.* —**mus'ti·ness,** *n.*

mut (mut), *n. Slang.* mutt.

mu·ta·ble (mū'tə·bəl), *adj.* **1.** liable to change: *mutable customs.* **2.** fickle: *a mutable person.* [< L, < *mutare* change] —**mu'ta·bil'i·ty, mu'ta·ble·ness,** *n.* —**mu'ta·bly,** *adv.* —**Syn. 1.** changeable, variable. **2.** inconstant.

mu·tant (mū'tənt), *n.* new variety of plant or animal resulting from mutation.

mu·tate (mū'tāt), *v.,* **-tat·ed, -tat·ing. 1.** change. **2.** produce mutations.

mu·ta·tion (mū·tā'shən), *n.* **1.** change; alteration. **2.** a new feature that appears suddenly in animals or plants and can be inherited. **3.** a new variety of animal or plant formed in this way. [< L, < *mutare* change] —**mu·ta'tion·al,** *adj.*

mute (mūt), *adj., n., v.,* **mut·ed, mut·ing.** —*adj.* **1.** not making any sound; silent. **2.** unable to speak; dumb. **3.** (of letters) not pronounced. **4.** *Law.* making no response when arraigned. —*n.* **1.** person who cannot speak. **2.** clip or pad put on a musical instrument to soften the sound. **3.** a silent letter. —*v.* put a clip or pad on a musical instrument to soften the sound. [< L *mutus*] —**mute'ly,** *adv.* —**mute'ness,** *n.*

mu·ti·late (mū'tə·lāt), *v.,* **-lat·ed, -lat·ing. 1.** cut, tear, or break off a part of; injure seriously by cutting, tearing, or breaking off some part. **2.** make (a story, song, etc.) imperfect by removing or damaging parts. [< L, < *mutilus* maimed] —**mu'ti·la'tion,** *n.* —**mu'ti·la'tive,** *adj.* —**mu'ti·la'tor,** *n.* —**Syn. 1.** maim, mangle, disfigure.

mu·ti·neer (mū'tə·nir'), *n.* person who takes part in a mutiny.

mu·ti·nous (mū'tə·nəs), *adj.* rebellious. —**mu'ti·nous·ly,** *adv.* —**mu'ti·nous·ness,** *n.* —**Syn.** riotous, insubordinate. —**Ant.** obedient, submissive, tractable, compliant.

mu·ti·ny (mū'tə·ni), *n., pl.* **-nies,** *v.,* **-nied, -ny·ing.** —*n.* open rebellion against lawful authority, esp. by sailors or soldiers against their officers. —*v.* take part in a mutiny; rebel. [< obs. *mutine* revolt < OF, < *mutin* rebellious, ult. < L *movere* move] —**Syn.** *n.* insurrection, revolt, uprising. —*v.* revolt.

mutt (mut), *n. Am., Slang.* **1.** dog, esp. a mongrel. **2.** a stupid person. Also, **mut.**

mut·ter (mut'ər), *v.* **1.** utter low and indistinctly with lips partly closed. **2.** complain; grumble. —*n.* **1.** act of muttering. **2.** muttered words. [< obs. *mutter murmur,* OE *mōtian* make a speech < *mōt* meeting] —**mut'ter·er,** *n.* —**mut'ter·ing·ly,** *adv.*

mut·ton (mut'ən), *n.* meat from a sheep. [< OF *moton* < Celtic]

mutton chop, 1. a small piece of mutton, usually from the ribs or loin, for broiling or frying. **2.** patch of whiskers on each side of the face, shaped somewhat like a chop.

mu·tu·al (mū'chŭ·əl), *adj.* **1.** done, said, felt, etc., by each toward the other; given and received: *mutual promises, mutual dislike.* **2.** each to the other: *mutual enemies.* **3.** *Colloq.* belonging to each of several: *our mutual friend.* [< L *mutuus* reciprocal] —**mu·tu·al·i·ty** (mū'chŭ·al'ə·ti), *n.* —**mu'tu·al·ly,** *adv.* —**Syn. 1.** reciprocal. **3.** common, joint.

Mutton chop whiskers

mu·zhik, mu·zjik (mü·zhik'; mü'zhik), *n.* a Russian peasant. Also, **moujik, mujik.**

muz·zle (muz'əl), *n., v.,* **-zled, -zling.** —*n.* **1.** nose, mouth, and jaws of a four-footed animal. **2.** cover of straps or wires to put over an animal's head to keep it from biting or eating. **3.** open front end of a gun, pistol, etc. —*v.* **1.** put a muzzle on. **2.** compel (a person) to keep silent about something. [< OF, < *muse* muzzle] —**muz'zler,** *n.*

muz·zle·load·er (muz'əl·lōd'ər), *n.* gun that is loaded through the muzzle.

MVD, M.V.D., the secret police of the Soviet Union.

my (mi), *pron.* belonging to me. —*interj. Colloq.* exclamation of surprise. [OE *min*]

my·ce·li·um (mī·sē'li·əm), *n., pl.* **-li·a** (-li·ə). the main part of a fungus, consisting of interwoven fibers. [< NL, < Gk. *mykes* mushroom]

My·ce·nae (mī·sē'nē), *n.* a very ancient city in Greece. —**My·ce·ne·an** (mī'si·nē'ən), *adj.*

my·col·o·gy (mī·kol'ə·ji), *n.* branch of botany that deals with fungi. [< Gk. *mykes* fungus + -LOGY] —**my·col'o·gist,** *n.*

my·na, my·nah (mī'nə), *n.* an Asiatic bird of the starling family. Also, **mina.** [< Hind. *mainā*]

Myn·heer (mīn·hâr'), *n.* **1.** Sir; Mr. **2.** mynheer, a Dutchman. [< Du. *mijnheer* my lord]

my·o·pi·a (mī·ō'pi·ə), *n.* near-sightedness. [< NL < Gk., ult. < *myein* shut + *ops* eye] —**my·op·ic** (mī·op'ik), *adj.*

myr·i·ad (mir'i·əd), *n.* **1.** ten thousand. **2.** a very great number: *there are myriads of stars.* —*adj.* **1.** ten thousand. **2.** countless. [< LL < Gk. *myrias* ten thousand, myriad]

myr·i·a·pod (mir'i·ə·pod'), *n.* arthropod having a wormlike body with many segments and many legs. Centipedes and millepedes are myriapods. [< Gk. *myrias* myriad + *pous* foot]

Myr·mi·don (mer'mə·don), *n.* **1.** one of a warlike people of ancient Thessaly who accompanied Achilles to the Trojan War. **2.** myrmidon, an obedient and unquestioning follower.

myrrh (mer), *n.* a fragrant, gummy substance with a bitter taste, used in medicines, perfumes, and incense. It is obtained from a shrub that grows in Arabia and eastern Africa. [< L < Gk., < Akkadian (group of extinct Semitic langs.) *murrū*]

myr·tle (mer'təl), *n.* **1.** an evergreen shrub of S Europe with shiny leaves, fragrant white flowers, and black berries. **2.** *Am.* a low, creeping, evergreen vine with blue flowers; periwinkle. [< OF *mirtile,* dim. of L *myrtus* < Gk. *myrtos*]

my·self (mī·self'), *pron., pl.* **ourselves. 1.** the emphatic form of me or I: *I myself will go.* **2.** reflexive form of me: *I hurt myself.* **3.** my real self; my normal self: *I am not myself today.*

My·sore (mī·sōr'; -sôr'), *n.* city in S India.

mys·te·ri·ous (mis·tir'i·əs), *adj.* **1.** full of mystery; hard to explain or understand; secret; hidden. **2.** suggesting mystery. —**mys·te'ri·ous·ly,** *adv.* —**mys·te'ri·ous·ness,** *n.* —**Syn. 1.** obscure, inexplicable, inscrutable. —**Ant. 1.** clear, plain, evident.

mys·ter·y¹ (mis'tər·i; mis'tri), *n., pl.* **-ter·ies. 1.** secret; something that is hidden or unknown.

2. thing, person, or situation about which there is something unexplained that arouses curiosity or speculation. 3. secrecy; obscurity. 4. something that is not explained or understood. 5. a religious conception or doctrine that human reason cannot understand. 6. a secret religious rite to which only initiated persons are admitted. 7. play based on the Bible. [< L < Gk. *mysterion*, ult. < *myein* close (i.e., the lips or eyes)] —Syn. 1. enigma, puzzle.

mys·ter·y² (mis′tər·i; mis′tri), n., pl. -ter·ies. *Archaic.* 1. craft; trade. 2. association of craftsmen or merchants; guild. [< Med.L *misterium* for L *ministerium* MINISTRY; form infl. by *mystery¹*]

mys·tic (mis′tik), n. person who believes that truth or God can be known through spiritual insight. —adj. mystical. [< L < Gk. *mystikos.* See MYSTERY¹.]

mys·ti·cal (mis′tə·kəl), adj. 1. having some secret meaning; beyond human understanding; mysterious. 2. spiritually symbolic. The lamb and the dove are mystical symbols of the Christian religion. 3. of or concerned with mystics or mysticism. 4. of or having to do with secret rites open only to the initiated. —mys′ti·cal·ly, adv. —mys′ti·cal·ness, n.

mys·ti·cism (mis′tə·siz·əm), n. 1. beliefs or mode of thought of mystics. 2. doctrine that truth or God may be known through spiritual insight, independent of the mind.

mys·ti·fy (mis′tə·fī), v., -fied, -fy·ing. 1. bewilder purposely; puzzle; perplex. 2. make mysterious; involve in mystery. —mys′ti·fi·ca′tion, n. —mys′ti·fy′ing·ly, adv. —Syn. 1. confuse, nonplus.

myth (mith), n. 1. legend or story, usually attempting to account for something in nature. 2. stories of this kind: *the realm of myth.* 3. any invented story. 4. an imaginary person or thing. [< NL < LL < Gk. *mythos* word, story] —Syn. 1. fable.

myth., mythological; mythology.

myth·i·cal (mith′ə·kəl), **myth·ic** (-ik), adj. 1. of myths; like a myth; in myths. 2. not real; made-up; imaginary. —myth′i·cal·ly, adv. —Syn. 2. fictitious.

my·thol·o·gy (mi·thol′ə·ji), n., pl. -gies. 1. myths collectively: *Greek mythology.* 2. study of myths. —myth·o·log·i·cal (mith′ə·loj′ə·kəl), myth′o·log′ic, —myth′o·log′i·cal·ly, adv. —my·thol′o·gist, n.

Myt·i·le·ne (mit′ə·lē′nē), n. a Greek island in the Aegean Sea.

N

N, n (en), n., pl. N's; n's. the 14th letter of the alphabet.

N, 1. *Chem.* nitrogen. 2. North; Northern.

n, *Algebra.* an indefinite number.

N., 1. Navy. 2. New. 3. Noon. 4. North; Northern. 5. November.

n., 1. neuter. 2. nominative. 3. north; northern. 4. noun. 5. number.

Na, *Chem.* sodium.

N.A., 1. National Army. 2. North America.

N.A.A.C.P., NAACP, National Association for the Advancement of Colored People.

nab (nab), v., nabbed, nab·bing. *Slang.* 1. catch or seize suddenly; grab. 2. arrest. [earlier *nap*, OE *hnæppan* strike]

na·bob (nā′bob), n. 1. nawab (def. 1). 2. a very rich man. [< Hind. *nawwāb* deputy governor. See NAWAB.] —na·bob·er·y (nā′bob′ər·i; nā·bob′-), n.

na·celle (nə·sel′), n. the enclosed part of an aircraft which contains the motors and in which passengers are carried. [< F < L *navicella*, double dim. of *navis* ship]

na·cre (nā′kər), n. mother-of-pearl. [< F, ? ult. < Pers. *nakāra* pearl oyster] —na·cre·ous (nā′kri·əs), adj.

na·dir (nā′dər; -dir), n. 1. the point in the heavens directly beneath the place where one stands; the point opposite the zenith. 2. the lowest point. [ult. < Ar. *nazir* opposite (i.e., to the zenith)]

nae (nā), adj., adv. *Scot.* no.

nag¹ (nag), v., nagged, nagging. irritate or annoy by peevish complaints; scold. [cf. Icel. *nagga* grumble] —nag′ger, n. —nag′ging·ly, adv.

nag² (nag), n. 1. a small riding horse. 2. *Colloq.* a horse. 3. an inferior horse. [cf. Du. *negge*]

Na·ga·sa·ki (nä′gə·sä′ki), n. seaport in W Japan: the second military use of the atomic bomb, Aug. 9, 1945.

Na·go·ya (nä·gō′yə), n. city in C Japan.

Na·guib (nə·gēb′), n. Mohammed, born 1901, Egyptian army officer, nominal chief executive of Egypt from 1952 to 1954.

Na·hua·tl (nä′wä·təl), n. language of the Aztecs, Toltecs, and other American Indian tribes of central Mexico and parts of Central America. —adj. of this language.

Na·hum (nā′əm; -həm), n. 1. a Hebrew prophet. 2. book of the Old Testament.

ZENITH

OBSERVER ON EARTH

NADIR

nai·ad (nā′ad; nī′-), n., pl. -ads, -a·des (-ə·dēz). 1. Also, Naiad. *Class. Myth.* nymph guarding a stream or spring. 2. a girl swimmer. [< L < Gk. *Naias;* akin to *naein* to flow]

na·ïf (nä·ēf′), adj. naïve.

nail (nāl), n. 1. a slender piece of metal to be hammered into or through wood to hold separate pieces together or to be used as a peg. 2. a thin, horny plate on the upper side of the end of a finger or toe. 3. on the nail, at once; immediately; without delay. 4. hit the nail on the head, guess or understand correctly; say or do something just right. —v. 1. fasten with a nail or nails. 2. hold or keep fixed. 3. *Colloq.* catch; seize. 4. *Colloq.* detect and expose (a lie, etc.). [OE *nægel*] —nail′er, n.

nain·sook (nān′sůk; nan′-), n. a very soft, fine cotton cloth. [< Hind., < *nain* eye + *sukh* pleasure]

Nai·ro·bi (nī·rō′bi), n. capital of Kenya, a country in E Africa.

na·ïve, na·ive (nä·ēv′), adj. simple in nature; like a child; artless; not sophisticated. Also, naïf. [< F, fem., < L *nativus* NATIVE] —na·ïve′ly, na·ive′ly, adv. —na·ïve′ness, na·ive′ness, n. —Syn. unaffected, artless, natural, open, sincere. ➤ naïve, naive. The form without the dieresis (*naive*) is gaining. It is unnecessary to keep the French masculine form *naïf* in English. *Naïve* can do all the work.

na·ïve·té, na·ive·te (nä·ēv′tā′), n. 1. unspoiled freshness. 2. a naïve action, remark, etc.

na·ked (nā′kid), adj. 1. with no clothes on; bare. 2. not covered; stripped: *a naked sword, naked fields.* 3. not protected; exposed. 4. without addition of anything else; plain: *the naked truth.* [OE *nacod*] —na′ked·ly, adv. —na′ked·ness, n. —Syn. 1. nude, unclothed, undressed. 2. uncovered. 3. unprotected, unguarded.

naked eye, eye not helped by a glass, telescope, or microscope.

NAM, N.A.M., National Association of Manufacturers.

nam·by–pam·by (nam′bi·pam′bi), adj., n., pl. -bies. —adj. weakly simple or sentimental; insipid: *valentines are often namby-pamby.* —n. 1. namby-pamby talk or writing. 2. a namby-pamby person. [alter. of *Ambrose Philips,* 18th cent. Brit. poet ridiculed by H. Carey, A. Pope]

name (nām), n., v., named, nam·ing. —n. 1. word or words by which a person, animal, place, or thing is spoken of or to. 2. word or words applied descriptively; appellation, title, or epithet: *call a person names.* 3. title or term as distinguished from fact: *liberty had become only a* *name.* 4. reputation; fame. 5. a famous person: *one of the great names of history.* 6. **in name only,** supposed to be, but not really so. 7. **in name of,** a. with appeal to the name of. b. acting for. —*v.* 1. give a name to: *name a newborn baby.* 2. call by name; mention by name: *three persons were named in the report.* 3. give the right name for: *can you name these flowers?* 4. mention; speak of; state: *name several reasons.* 5. specify or fix: *name a price.* 6. choose for some duty or office; nominate: *name Mr. Taft for president.* [OE *nama*] —**name′a·ble,** *adj.* —**nam′er,** *n.* —Syn. *n.* 2. designation, denomination. 4. renown, note. —*v.* 1. denominate, entitle, call. 2. designate. 6. appoint.

name·less (nām′lis), *adj.* 1. having no name: *a nameless grave.* 2. that cannot be named or described: *a strange, nameless longing.* 3. not fit to be mentioned. 4. not named. 5. unknown to fame; obscure. —**name′less·ness,** *n.*

name·ly (nām′li), *adv.* that is to say. ➤ namely. The beginning of wisdom in handling "introductory words" like *namely, that is, for example, such as* is to use them as seldom as possible. *Namely* belongs chiefly in routine expository prose. Very often it can be omitted altogether in compact, informal writing. When *namely* introduces a series of short items, it is more often followed by a comma than by a colon, but in formal style or in a long, rather complicated sentence, *namely* would usually be preceded by a semicolon.

name·sake (nām′sāk′), *n.* one having the same name as another, esp. one named after another.

nan·keen, nan·kin (nan·kēn′), *n.* a firm, yellow or buff cloth. [alter. of *Nanking*]

Nan·king (nan′king′), *n.* city in E China.

nan·ny goat (nan′i), *Colloq.* a female goat.

Nantes (nants; *Fr.* näṅt), *n.* 1. seaport in W France, on the Loire River. 2. **Edict of,** edict granting religious toleration to French Protestants (Huguenots), signed in 1598.

Nan·tuck·et (nan·tuk′it), *n.* island off Massachusetts, S of Cape Cod.

Na·o·mi (nā·ō′mi; nā′ō·mi), *n. Bible.* mother-in-law of Ruth, from whom she refused to part. Ruth I.

nap[1] (nap), *n., v.,* **napped, nap·ping.** —*n.* a short sleep. —*v.* 1. take a short sleep. 2. **napping,** off guard; unprepared. [OE *hnappian* sleep lightly]

nap[2] (nap), *n.* the soft, short, woolly threads or hairs on the surface of cloth. [< MDu. or MLG *noppe*] —**nap′less,** *adj.*

na·palm (nā′päm′; -pälm′), *n.* 1. a chemical substance used to thicken gasoline for use in certain military weapons. 2. the thickened gasoline.

nape (nāp; nap), *n.* the back of the neck.

na·per·y (nā′pər·i; nāp′ri), *n.* tablecloths, napkins, and doilies. [< obs. F *naperie* < *nape, nappe* < L *mappa* napkin]

naph·tha (nap′thə; naf′-), *n.* a liquid made from petroleum, coal tar, etc., used as fuel and to take spots from clothing. [< L < Gk., orig., an inflammable liquid issuing from the earth]

naph·tha·lene, naph·tha·line (naf′thə·lēn; nap′-), or **naph·tha·lin** (-lin), *n. Chem.* a white, crystalline hydrocarbon, $C_{10}H_8$, usually prepared from coal tar, used in making moth balls, dyes, disinfectants, etc.

nap·kin (nap′kin), *n.* 1. piece of cloth used at meals for protecting the clothing or for wiping the lips or fingers. 2. any similar piece, such as a baby's diaper or a small towel. [< F *nappe.* See NAPERY.]

Na·ples (nā′pəlz), *n.* seaport on the SW coast of Italy.

na·po·le·on (nə·pō′li·ən; -pōl′yən), *n.* 1. a former French gold coin worth 20 francs. 2. *Am.* kind of pastry with a cream or jam filling. [named for the *Napoleons*]

Na·po·le·on (nə·pō′li·ən; -pōl′yən), *n.* 1. (*Napoleon Bonaparte*), 1769–1821, French general and emperor of France, 1804–1815. 2. III (*Louis Na-*

poleon), 1808–1873, nephew of Napoleon I, president of France 1848–52 and emperor of France 1852–70. —**Na·po·le·on·ic** (nə·pō′li·on′ik), *adj.*

nar·cis·sism (när·sis′iz·əm), *n.* erotic feeling for oneself. —**nar·cis′sist,** *n.*

nar·cis·sus (när·sis′əs), *n., pl.* **-cis·sus·es, -cis·si** (-sis′ī). 1. a spring plant with yellow or white flowers and long, slender leaves. It grows from a bulb. 2. the flower. [< L < Gk.; assoc. (from the sedative effect of the plant) with *narke* numbness]

Nar·cis·sus (när·sis′əs), *n. Gk. Myth.* a beautiful youth who fell in love with his reflection in a spring. He pined away and was changed into the flower narcissus.

nar·co·sis (när·kō′sis), **nar·co·tism** (när′kə·tiz·əm), *n.* stupor; insensibility.

nar·cot·ic (när·kot′ik), *n.* 1. drug that produces drowsiness, sleep, dullness, or an insensible condition, and lessens pain by dulling the nerves: *opium is a powerful narcotic.* 2. anything that soothes or dulls. 3. person addicted to some narcotic drug or drugs. —*adj.* 1. having the properties and effects of a narcotic. 2. of or for persons addicted to narcotic drugs. [< L < Gk., < *narkoein* benumb < *narke* numbness] —Syn. *n.* 1. opiate, anodyne.

nard (närd), *n.* spikenard. [< L < Gk. *nardos* < Phoenician < Skt.]

nar·es (nār′ēz), *n.pl., sing.* **nar·is** (nār′is). *Anat.* the nasal passages; nostrils. [< L, pl.]

nar·ghi·le, nar·gi·le (när′gə·lē), *n.* an Oriental tobacco pipe in which the smoke is drawn through water. [ult. < Pers. *nārgīleh* < *nārgīl* coconut; from orig. material]

Nar·ra·gan·sett Bay (nar′ə·gan′sit), bay of the Atlantic, in E Rhode Island.

nar·rate (na·rāt′; nar′āt), *v.,* **-rat·ed, -rat·ing.** 1. tell (a story, etc.) of. 2. tell stories, etc. [< L, pp. of *narrare* relate] —**nar·ra′tor,** narrat′er, *n.* —Syn. 1. relate, recount, repeat.

nar·ra·tion (na·rā′shən), *n.* 1. act of telling. 2. the form of composition that relates an event or a story. Novels, short stories, histories, and biographies are forms of narration. 3. story; account. —Syn. 1. relation, recital. 3. narrative.

nar·ra·tive (nar′ə·tiv), *n.* 1. story. 2. narration; storytelling. —*adj.* that narrates: *a narrative poem.* —**nar′ra·tive·ly,** *adv.* —Syn. *n.* 1. tale, anecdote.

nar·row (nar′ō), *adj.* 1. not wide; having little width; of less than the specified, understood, or usual width: *narrow cloth.* 2. limited in extent, space, amount, range, scope, opportunity, etc.: *a narrow circle of friends.* 3. with little margin: *a narrow escape.* 4. lacking breadth of view or sympathy; not liberal; prejudiced: *narrow thought.* 5. close; careful; minute: *a narrow scrutiny.* 6. with barely enough to live on. 7. *Phonet.* pronounced with a narrow opening of the vocal organs; tense. —*n.* **narrows,** the narrow part of a river, strait, sound, valley, pass, etc. —*v.* make or become narrower; decrease in breadth, extent, etc.; limit. [OE *nearu*] —**nar′row·ly,** *adv.* —**nar′row·ness,** *n.* —Syn. *adj.* 2. limited, confined, strait, restricted. 4. illiberal, bigoted. 5. detailed, scrupulous. 6. scanty, meager, impoverished. —Ant. *adj.* 2. wide, broad.

nar·row-gauge (nar′ō·gāj′), *adj.* having railroad tracks less than 56½ inches apart.

nar·row-mind·ed (nar′ō·mīn′did), *adj.* lacking breadth of view or sympathy; prejudiced. —**nar′row-mind′ed·ly,** *adv.* —**nar′row-mind′ed·ness,** *n.* —Syn. illiberal, intolerant.

nar·whal, nar·wal (när′hwəl; -wəl), or **nar·whale** (-hwāl′), *n.* kind of arctic whale whose body is about 16 feet long. The male has a long tusk extending forward from the upper jaw. [< Dan. or Sw. *narhval* < *nār* corpse + *hval* whale]

na·sal (nā′zəl), *adj.* 1. of, in, or from the nose: *a nasal discharge.* 2. *Phonet.* requiring the nose passage to be open; spoken through the nose. *M, n,* and *ng* represent nasal sounds. —*n. Phonet.* a nasal sound. [< L *nasus* nose] —**na·sal·i·ty** (nā·zal′ə·ti), *n.* —**na′sal·ly,** *adv.*

na·sal·ize (nā'zəl·īz), v., -ized, -iz·ing. utter or speak with a nasal sound. —**na'sal·i·za'tion,** n.

nas·cent (nas'ənt; nā'sənt), adj. in the process of coming into existence; just beginning to exist, grow, or develop. [< L nascens, ppr. of nasci be born] —**nas'cen·cy,** n.

nascent state or **condition,** Chem. condition of a substance during its formation or its liberation from compounds.

Nash·ville (nash'vil), n. capital of Tennessee, in the C part.

Nas·sau (nas'ô), n. capital of the Bahamas.

Nas·ser (nas'ər), n. Gamal Abdel, born 1918, Egyptian army officer, premier of Egypt, 1954 and of the United Arab Republic, 1958.

na·stur·tium (nə·stėr'shəm), n. 1. plant with yellow, orange, and red flowers, and sharp-tasting seeds and leaves. 2. the flower. [< L, < nasus nose + torquere twist; from sharp odor]

Nasturtium

nas·ty (nas'ti; näs'-), adj., -ti·er, -ti·est. 1. disgustingly dirty; filthy. 2. morally filthy; vile: a nasty mind. 3. very unpleasant: nasty weather. [cf. Du. nestig] —**nas'ti·ly,** adv. —**nas'ti·ness,** n.

nat., 1. national. 2. native. 3. natural.

na·tal (nā'təl), adj. 1. of one's birth: one's natal day is his birthday. 2. Poetic. native. [< L natalis, ult. < nasci be born]

Na·tal (nə·tal'; -täl'), n. province of South Africa, on the E coast.

na·tant (nā'tənt), adj. swimming; floating; represented as swimming. [< L, ppr. of natare float, swim, ult. < nare swim]

na·ta·to·ri·al (nā'tə·tô'ri·əl; -tō'-), **na·ta·to·ry** (nā'tə·tô'ri; -tō'-), adj. pertaining to, adapted for, or characterized by swimming. [< LL, ult. < L natare swim. See NATANT.]

na·ta·to·ri·um (nā'tə·tô'ri·əm; -tō'-), n., pl. -ri·ums, -to·ri·a (-ri·ə). a swimming pool.

nathe·less (nāth'lis; nath'-), **nath·less** (nath'-), Archaic. —adv. nevertheless. —prep. notwithstanding. [OE nā thȳ lǣs never the less]

na·tion (nā'shən), n. 1. people occupying the same country, united under the same government, and mostly speaking the same language: the English nation. 2. a people, race, or tribe; those having the same descent, language, and history: the Scottish nation. [< L natio stock, race, ult. < nasci be born]

na·tion·al (nash'ən·əl; nash'nəl), adj. of a nation; belonging to a whole nation: national laws, a national disaster. —n. citizen of a nation. —**na'tion·al·ly,** adv.

national bank, bank chartered by a national government. In the United States, national banks belong to the Federal Reserve System.

National Guard, U.S. the reserve militia of the individual States of the U.S., called or ordered to serve the Federal government in time of war or national emergency.

na·tion·al·ism (nash'ən·əl·iz'əm; nash'nəl-), n. 1. patriotic feelings or efforts. 2. desire and plans for national independence. 3. form of socialism that advocates government ownership and control of all industries. —**na'tion·al·ist,** n. —**na'tion·al·is'tic,** adj. —**na'tion·al·is'ti·cal·ly,** adv.

na·tion·al·i·ty (nash'ən·al'ə·ti), n., pl. -ties. 1. nation. 2. condition of belonging to a nation. Citizens of the same country have the same nationality. 3. condition of being a nation: after the American Revolution the colonies attained nationality.

na·tion·al·ize (nash'ən·əl·īz; nash'nəl-), v., -ized, -iz·ing. 1. make national. 2. bring (land, industries, railroads, etc.) under the control or ownership of a nation. 3. make into a nation. —**na'tion·al·i·za'tion,** n.

na·tion·wide (nā'shən·wīd'), adj. extending throughout the nation: a nation-wide election.

na·tive (nā'tiv), n. 1. person born in a certain place or country. 2. person who has lived most or all of his life in a place. 3. one of the original inhabitants of a place, as contrasted with conquerors, settlers, visitors, etc., esp. one who belongs to a less civilized race. 4. member of a less civilized race, usually not white. 5. animal or plant that originated in a place. —adj. 1. born in a certain place or country: people born in New York are native sons and daughters of New York. 2. belonging to one because of his birth: one's native land. 3. belonging to one because of his country or the nation to which he belongs: a native costume. 4. born in a person; natural: native ability, native courtesy. 5. of or having to do with the original inhabitants, esp. those not white: native customs, native huts. 6. (of language) that one learns to speak first: one's native language. 7. referring to one who has learned (a particular language) as his first language: a native speaker of English. 8. originating, grown, or produced in a certain place: tobacco is native to America. 9. found pure in nature: native copper. 10. found in nature; not produced: native salt is refined for use. 11. in a natural state: the native beauty of the hills. 12. go native, live as the uncivilized natives do. [< L nativus innate, ult. < nasci be born] —**na'tive·ly,** adv. —**na'tive·ness,** n. —Syn. n. 3. aborigine. —adj. 4. inborn, innate, inherent. 5. aboriginal. 8. indigenous. —Ant. adj. 1. alien, foreign. 4. acquired, assumed.

na·tive-born (nā'tiv·bôrn'), adj. born in the place or country indicated.

na·tiv·i·ty (nə·tiv'ə·ti; nā-), n., pl. -ties. 1. birth. 2. horoscope. 3. the Nativity, a. birth of Christ. b. Christmas; December 25.

natl., national.

NATO, North Atlantic Treaty Organization.

nat·ty (nat'i), adj., -ti·er, -ti·est. trim and tidy; neatly smart in dress or appearance. —**nat'ti·ly,** adv. —**nat'ti·ness,** n.

nat·u·ral (nach'ə·rəl; nach'rəl), adj. 1. produced by nature; based on some state of things in nature: scenery has natural beauty. 2. not artificial: coal and oil are natural products. 3. born such: a natural fool. 4. instinctive; inborn: natural ability. 5. not cultivated or civilized. 6. coming in the ordinary course of events; normal: a natural death. 7. in accordance with the nature of things or the circumstances of the case: a natural response. 8. instinctively felt to be right and fair: natural rights. 9. like nature; true to nature: the picture looked natural. 10. free from affectation or restraint: a natural manner. 11. of or pertaining to nature: the natural sciences. 12. based on what is learned from nature: natural religion. 13. Music. neither sharp nor flat; without sharps and flats. 14. illegitimate: a natural son. —n. 1. that which is natural. 2. Music. a. a natural tone or note. b. sign (♮) used to cancel the effect of a preceding sharp or flat. c. a white key on the piano. 3. a half-witted person. 4. Colloq. an expert by nature. 5. Colloq. a sure success. [< L naturalis. See NATURE.] —**nat'u·ral·ness,** n. —Syn. adj. 4. innate, inherent. 6. regular, usual. 10. simple, ingenuous, artless, unaffected.

natural gas, a combustible gas formed naturally in the earth, consisting of methane with hydrogen and other gases.

natural history, the study of animals, plants, minerals, and other things in nature.

nat·u·ral·ism (nach'ə·rəl·iz'əm; nach'rəl-), n. 1. in art and literature, close adherence to nature and reality. 2. action based on natural instincts. 3. Philos. a view of the world which takes account only of natural elements and forces, excluding the supernatural or spiritual.

nat·u·ral·ist (nach'ə·rəl·ist; nach'rəl-), n. 1. person who makes a study of animals and plants. 2. writer or artist who represents life exactly as it is; extreme realist.

nat·u·ral·is·tic (nach'ə·rəl·is'tik; nach'rəl-), adj. 1. of natural history or naturalists. 2. of naturalism, esp. in art and literature. 3. of or in accordance with nature.

nat·u·ral·ize (nach'ə·rəl·īz; nach'rəl-), v., -ized, -iz·ing. 1. admit (a foreigner) to citizenship. 2. adopt (a foreign word or custom).

Chauffeur is a French word that has been naturalized in English. 3. introduce and make at home in another country: *the English oak has been naturalized in parts of Massachusetts.* 4. become like a native. [<nat′u·ral·i·za′tion, *n.*

nat·u·ral·ly (nach′ə·rəl·i; nach′rəl·i), *adv.* 1. in a natural way: *speak naturally.* 2. by nature: *a naturally obedient child.* 3. as might be expected; of course.

natural philosophy, physics.

natural resources, materials supplied by nature, as minerals and water power.

natural science, science of nature. Zoölogy, botany, and geology are natural sciences.

natural selection, the process by which animals and plants best adapted to their environment tend to survive.

na·ture (nā′chər), *n.* 1. the world; all things except those made by man. 2. sum total of the forces at work throughout the universe: *the laws of nature.* 3. the instincts or inherent tendencies directing conduct: *it is against nature for a mother to kill her child.* 4. reality: *true to nature.* 5. primitive, wild condition; condition of human beings before social organization. 6. natural character. 7. what a thing really is; quality; character. 8. sort; kind. 9. person of a particular character: *she is a gentle nature.* 10. physical being; vital powers: *food sufficient to sustain nature.* 11. by nature, because of the essential character of the person or thing. [<OF <L *natura* birth, character, ult. < *nasci* be born] —Syn. 2. universe, cosmos. 7. essence. 8. type, class. 9. disposition, temperament, personality.

naught (nôt), *n.* 1. nothing. 2. zero; 0. Also, **nought.** —*adj.* *adv.* Archaic. nought. [OE *nāwiht* < *nā* no + *wiht* wight]

naugh·ty (nô′ti), *adj.* *-ti·er,* *-ti·est.* 1. bad; not obedient. 2. somewhat improper. [< *naught* wicked] —naugh′ti·ly, *adv.* —naugh′ti·ness, *n.* —Syn. 1. evil, mischievous, disobedient.

nau·sea (nô′shə; -shi·ə; -si·ə), *n.* 1. the feeling that one has when about to vomit. 2. seasickness. 3. extreme disgust; loathing. [< L < Gk., < *naus* ship]

nau·se·ate (nô′shi·āt; -si-), *v.,* *-at·ed,* *-at·ing.* 1. cause nausea in; make sick. 2. feel nausea; become sick. —nau′se·a′tion, *n.*

nau·seous (nô′shəs; -shi·əs), *adj.* 1. causing nausea; sickening. 2. disgusting; loathsome. —nau′seous·ly, *adv.* —nau′seous·ness, *n.* —Syn. 2. revolting, repulsive, offensive.

naut., nautical.

nautch (nôch), *n.* an entertainment in India consisting of dancing by professional dancing girls. [< Hind. < Prakrit (an ancient lang. of India) *nachcha* dancing]

nau·ti·cal (nô′tə·kəl), *adj.* of or having to do with ships, sailors, or navigation. [< L < Gk. *nautikos,* ult. < *naus* ship] —nau′ti·cal·ly, *adv.* —Syn. maritime.

nautical mile, about 6080 feet.

nau·ti·lus (nô′tə·ləs), *n., pl.* *-lus·es,* *-li* (-lī). either of two kinds of cephalopod. The pearly nautilus has a spiral shell, pearly inside. The paper nautilus has saillike arms and a very thin shell. [< L < Gk. *nautilos,* orig., sailor, ult. < *naus* ship]

Pearly nautilus

nav., 1. naval. 2. navigation.

Nav·a·ho, Nav·a·jo (nav′ə·hō), *n., pl.* *-hos;* *-jos.* Am. member of a tribe of American Indians living in New Mexico, Arizona, and Utah.

na·val (nā′vəl), *adj.* 1. of or for warships or the navy: *a naval officer.* 2. having a navy: *the naval powers.* [< L, < *navis* ship]

Na·varre (nə·vär′), *n.* a former kingdom including parts of SW France and N Spain.

nave (nāv), *n.* the main part of a church or cathedral between the side aisles. The nave extends from the main entrance to the transepts. [< Med.L < L *navis* ship]

na·vel (nā′vəl), *n.* 1. the mark or scar in the middle of the surface of the abdomen. 2. center; middle. [OE *nafela*]

navel orange, *Am.* a seedless orange with a small growth at one end.

nav·i·cert (nav′ə·sért), *n.* certificate issued by British consulates identifying a ship's cargo.

navig., navigation.

nav·i·ga·ble (nav′ə·gə·bəl), *adj.* 1. that ships can travel on: *the Mississippi River is deep enough to be navigable.* 2. seaworthy: *the old ship is no longer navigable.* 3. that can be steered. —nav′i·ga·bil′i·ty, nav′i·ga·ble·ness, *n.* —nav′i·ga·bly, *adv.*

nav·i·gate (nav′ə·gāt), *v.,* *-gat·ed,* *-gat·ing.* 1. sail, manage, or steer (a ship, airplane, etc.). 2. sail on or over (a sea or river). 3. travel by water; sail. 4. convey (goods) by water. 5. sail through (the air) in an airship, etc. 6. manage a ship or airship. [< L, < *navis* ship + *agere* drive]

nav·i·ga·tion (nav′ə·gā′shən), *n.* 1. act or process of navigating. 2. art or science of finding a ship's or airplane's position and course. —nav′i·ga′tion·al, *adj.*

nav·i·ga·tor (nav′ə·gā′tər), *n.* 1. one who sails the seas. 2. one who has charge of the navigating of a ship or who is skilled in navigating. 3. explorer of the seas. 4. one who finds the position and course of an airship. 5. *Brit.* navvy.

nav·vy (nav′i), *n., pl.* *-vies.* *Brit.* an unskilled laborer who works on canals, railways, roads, etc. [short for *navigator* (def. 5)]

na·vy (nā′vi), *n., pl.* *-vies.* 1. all the ships of war of a country, with their men and the department that manages them. 2. officers and men of the navy. 3. *Archaic* or *Poetic.* fleet of ships. 4. Also, navy blue. a dark blue. [< OF *navie,* ult. < L *navis* ship]

navy bean, *Am.* the common white bean, dried for use.

na·wab (nə·wôb′), *n.* 1. a native ruler in India under the Mogul empire. 2. nabob (def. 2). [< Hind. < Ar. *nawwāb,* pl. of *nā′ib* deputy]

nay (nā), *adv.* 1. *Archaic.* no. 2. not only that, but also: *we are willing, nay eager to go.* —*n.* 1. no; a denial or refusal. 2. a negative vote or voter. [< Scand. *nei* < *ne* not + *ei* ever]

Naz·a·rene (naz′ə·rēn′; naz′ə·rēn), *n.* 1. person born or living in Nazareth. Jesus is often called "the Nazarene." 2. an early Christian.

Naz·a·reth (naz′ə·rəth), *n.* town in N Palestine where Jesus lived during his boyhood.

Na·zi (nä′tsi; nat′si), *n., pl.* Na·zis, *adj.* —*n.* 1. member or supporter of the National Socialist German Workers Party in Germany, organized under the leadership of Adolf Hitler. 2. adherent of Naziism in any country; fascist. —*adj.* of or having to do with the Nazis. [< G, short for *Na(tionalso)zi(alist)* National Socialist] ▶ *Nazi* was the name of a political party and is capitalized like *Republican* or *Democrat.* The type of party represented by the Nazis is usually referred to as *fascist.*

Na·zi·fy, na·zi·fy (nä′tsə·fī; nat′sə-), *v.,* *-fied,* *-fy·ing.* 1. place under control of the Nazis. 2. indoctrinate with Nazi views. —Na′zi·fi·ca′tion, na′zi·fi·ca′tion, *n.*

Na·zi·ism (nä′tsi·iz·əm; nat′si-), **Na·zism** (nä′tsiz·əm; nat′siz-), *n.* the doctrines of the Nazis, including totalitarian government and state control of industry, but opposition to communism.

Nb, *Chem.* niobium.

N.B., 1. New Brunswick. 2. (L *nota bene*) Also, **n.b.** note well; observe carefully.

N.C., North Carolina.

N.C.O., noncommissioned officer.

Nd, *Chem.* neodymium.

N. Dak., N.D., North Dakota.

Ne, *Chem.* neon.

NE, n.e., northeast; northeastern.

N.E., 1. New England. 2. northeast; northeastern.

Ne·an·der·thal man (ni·an′dər·täl), an extinct race, widespread in Europe in the old Stone Age.

Ne·a·pol·i·tan (nē′ə·pol′ə·tən), *adj.* of or pertaining to Naples. —*n.* native of Naples.

neap tide (nēp), the lowest level of high tide. Neap tide comes twice a month. [OE nēp]

near (nir), adv. 1. to or at a short distance; not far: *stand near.* 2. closely: *tribes near allied.* 3. *Colloq.* all but; almost. 4. **near at hand,** a. within easy reach. b. not far in the future. —adj. 1. close by; not distant; less distant: *the near side.* 2. intimate; familiar: *a near friend.* 3. closely related: *a near cousin.* 4. approximating or resembling closely: *near silk, near beer.* 5. left (opposed to *off* or *right*): *the near horse and the off horse make a team.* 6. short; direct: go by the *nearest route.* 7. by a close margin: *a near escape.* —prep. close to in space, time, condition, etc.: *regions near the equator.* —v. come or draw near; approach: *the ship neared the land.* [OE nēar, compar. of nēah nigh] —near′ness, n. —Syn. adj. 1. close, nigh.

near·by (nir′bī′), adj., adv. near; close at hand: *a nearby house; they went nearby to visit.*

Near East, 1. *U.S.* the Balkans and the countries of SW Asia. 2. *Brit.* the Balkans.

near·ly (nir′li), adv. 1. almost: *I nearly made the train.* 2. closely: *a fact that concerns you very nearly.* —Syn. 1. approximately, well-nigh.

near-sight·ed (nir′sīt′id), adj. seeing distinctly at a short distance only. —near′-sight′-ed·ly, adv. —near′-sight′ed·ness, n.

neat[1] (nēt), adj. 1. clean and in order: *a neat room.* 2. able and willing to keep things in order: *a neat child.* 3. well-formed; in proportion: *a neat design.* 4. skillful; clever: *a neat trick.* 5. *Esp. Brit.* without anything mixed in it: *he took a drink of brandy neat.* 6. free from deductions; net: *neat weight.* [< F < L nitidus gleaming < nitere shine] —neat′ly, adv. —neat′ness, n. —Syn. 1. tidy, trim, cleanly, nice. 4. deft, adroit. 5. undiluted, pure, clear. —Ant. 1. unkempt, slovenly, disorderly.

neat[2] (nēt), *Archaic.* —n.pl. or sing. cattle; cows; oxen. —adj. of the ox kind. [OE nēat]

neath, 'neath (nēth; nēth), prep. Poetic. beneath.

neat·herd (nēt′hėrd′), n. Archaic. cowherd.

neb (neb), n. 1. Scot. bill; beak. 2. nib. [OE nebb]

Nebr., Neb., Nebraska.

Ne·bras·ka (nə·bras′kə), n. a Middle Western State of the United States. *Capital:* Lincoln. *Abbrev.:* Nebr., Neb. —Ne·bras′kan, adj., n. Am.

Neb·u·chad·nez·zar (neb′yə·kəd·nez′ər; neb′ə-), **Neb·u·chad·rez·zar** (-rez′-), n. died 562 B.C., king of Babylon, 604?–562 B.C.

neb·u·la (neb′yə·lə), n., pl. -lae (-lē) -las. a bright spot like a small, bright cloud, visible in the sky at night. A nebula may be either a mass of luminous gas or a cluster of stars very far away from our sun and its planets. [< L, mist] —neb′u·lar, adj.

nebular hypothesis, theory that the sun and planets developed from a luminous mass of gas.

neb·u·los·i·ty (neb′yə·los′ə·ti), n., pl. -ties. 1. cloudlike quality. 2. nebula.

neb·u·lous (neb′yə·ləs), adj. 1. hazy; vague; indistinct; confused. 2. cloudlike. 3. of or like a nebula or nebulae. [< L, < nebula mist] —neb′-u·lous·ly, adv. —neb′u·lous·ness, n.

nec·es·sar·i·ly (nes′ə·ser′ə·li), adv. 1. because of necessity: *leaves are not necessarily green.* 2. as a necessary result: *war necessarily causes misery and waste.*

nec·es·sar·y (nes′ə·ser′i), adj., n., pl. -sar·ies. —adj. 1. that must be, be had, or be done: *death is a necessary end.* 2. involuntary: *hunger is a necessary response.* —n. thing impossible to do without: *food, clothing, and shelter are necessaries of life.* [< L, < necesse unavoidable, ult. < ne- not + cedere withdraw] —Syn. adj. 1. inevitable, required, indispensable, essential, requisite. ➤ necessary. Spelled with one c and two s's. Very often a verb is more direct and emphatic, less polite than a construction with nec-essary: *You must* [or *have to,* rather than *It is necessary that you*] *pay your tuition before receiving your class cards.*

ne·ces·si·tate (nə·ses′ə·tāt), v., -tat·ed, -tat-

ing. 1. make necessary: *his broken leg necessitated an operation.* 2. compel; force. —ne·ces′-si·ta′tion, n. —Syn. 1. require, demand.

ne·ces·si·tous (nə·ses′ə·təs), adj. very poor; needy. —ne·ces′si·tous·ly, adv. —ne·ces′si-tous·ness, n.

ne·ces·si·ty (nə·ses′ə·ti), n., pl. -ties. 1. fact of being necessary; extreme need: *the necessity of eating.* 2. that which cannot be done without: *water is a necessity.* 3. that which forces one to act in a certain way: *necessity often drives people to do disagreeable things.* 4. that which is inevitable: *night follows day as a necessity.* 5. need; poverty: *this poor family is in great necessity.* 6. of necessity, because it must be. —Syn. 1. exigency. 2. essential, requisite, requirement. 3. constraint, compulsion. ➤ necessity. The idiom is *necessity of doing* something (not *to do* or *for doing*): *I don't see the necessity of reading so many pages to get so few facts.* Often *need* will be more concise: *I don't see the need of reading so many pages. . . .*

neck (nek), n. 1. part of the body that connects the head with the shoulders. 2. part of a garment that fits the neck. 3. a narrow strip of land. 4. the slender part of a bottle, flask, retort, or other container. 5. the long, slender part of a violin, etc., between the body and the head. 6. any narrow part like a neck. 7. neck and neck, a. abreast. b. even in a race or contest. —v. Am., Slang. embrace amorously; hug; caress. [OE hnecca]

neck·band (nek′band′), n. a cloth band worn around the neck, either separately or as part of a garment.

neck·cloth (nek′klôth′; -kloth′), n. cloth worn round the neck; cravat.

neck·er·chief (nek′ər·chif), n. cloth worn round the neck.

neck·lace (nek′lis), n. string of jewels, gold, silver, beads, etc., worn around the neck as an ornament.

neck·piece (nek′pēs′), n. a fur scarf.

neck·tie (nek′tī′), n. a narrow band or a tie worn around the neck and tied in front.

neck·wear (nek′wâr′), n. collars, ties, and other articles that are worn around the neck.

ne·crol·o·gy (ne·krol′ə·ji), n., pl. -gies. 1. list of persons who have died. 2. notice of a person's death. [< Med.L < Gk. nekros dead body + -LOGY] —nec·ro·log·i·cal (nek′rə·loj′ə·kəl), adj. —nec′ro·log′i·cal·ly, adv.

nec·ro·man·cy (nek′rə·man·si), n. magic; a foretelling of the future by communicating with the dead. [< Med.L, L < Gk., < nekros dead body + manteia divination; confusion with L niger "black" led to interpretation as "black art"] —nec′ro·man′cer, n.

ne·crop·o·lis (ne·krop′ə·lis), n., pl. -lis·es. cemetery. [< NL < Gk., < nekros dead body + polis city]

ne·cro·sis (ne·krō′sis), n., pl. -ses (-sēz). death or decay (of a part of an animal or plant). [< NL < Gk., ult. < nekros dead body] —ne-crot·ic (ne·krot′ik), adj.

nec·tar (nek′tər), n. 1. Gk. Myth. the drink of the gods. 2. any delicious drink. 3. a sweet liquid found in many flowers. Bees gather nectar and make it into honey. [< L < Gk. nektar] —nec-tar·e·ous (nek·târ′i·əs), adj.

nec·tar·ine (nek′tər·ēn′; nek′tər·ēn), n. a kind of peach having no down on its skin.

née, nee (nā), adj. born. [< F, fem. pp. of naître be born < L nasci] ➤ Née is placed after the name of a married woman to show her maiden name: *Mrs. Smith, née Adams.*

need (nēd), n. 1. lack of a useful or desired thing: *his writing showed need of grammar.* 2. a useful or desired thing that is lacking: *in the jungle their need was fresh water.* 3. necessity: *there is no need to hurry.* 4. a situation or time of difficulty: *a friend in need.* 5. extreme poverty. 6. have need to, must; should; have to; ought to. 7. if need be, if it has to be. —v. 1. have need of; want; require: *need money.* 2. be necessary: *the rope cuts his hands more than needs.* 3. must; should; have to; ought to: *need*

she go? 4. be in want: *give to those that need.*
[OE *ned*] —need′er, *n.* —Syn. *n.* 2. exigency. 5.
want, destitution, indigence, privation. —*v.* 1.
lack. ➤ **need.** Note that *need* with the meaning
"must, should, have to" in rather formal usage is
used as an auxiliary—that is, like "must" and
"should" it has the third person singular form
need (rather than *needs*), it takes an infinitive
without *to,* and in negative and interrogative
constructions is used as the main verb, not as an
infinitive with *do, does.* Examples of typical use
are: (1) (*in interrogative constructions*): FOR-
MAL *Need she go?* INFORMAL *Does she need to go?*
(2) (*in negative constructions*): FORMAL *She
need not go.* INFORMAL *She doesn't need to go.*
(3) (*in affirmative constructions*): FORMAL *She
wonders if she need go.* INFORMAL *She wonders if
she needs to go.*

need·ful (nēd′fəl), *adj.* needed; necessary.
—need′ful·ly, *adv.* —need′ful·ness, *n.* —Syn.
requisite, required, indispensable, vital, essential.

nee·dle (nē′dəl), *n., v.,* –dled, –dling. —*n.* 1. a
very slender tool, sharp at one end and with a
hole or eye to pass a thread through, used in
sewing. 2. a slender rod used in knitting. 3. rod
with a hook at one end used in crocheting, etc.
4. a thin steel pointer on a compass or on electrical machinery. 5. end of a syringe used for
injecting something below the skin. 6. a phonograph needle. 7. the needle-shaped leaf of a fir
tree or pine tree. —*v.* 1. sew or pierce with, or as
with, a needle. 2. vex by repeated sharp prods,
gibes, etc.; goad or incite, as into hurrying. [OE
nēdl] —nee′dle·like′, *adj.*

needle point, embroidery made on a coarse,
stiff canvas cloth and used to cover chairs, foot-
stools, etc. —nee′dle·point′, *adj.*

need·less (nēd′lis), *adj.* not needed; unnecessary. —need′less·ly, *adv.* —need′less·ness, *n.*

needle valve, valve whose very small opening
is controlled by a slender, needle-shaped rod.

nee·dle·wom·an (nē′dəl·wùm′ən), *n., pl.*
–wom·en. 1. user of the needle. 2. woman who
earns her living by sewing.

nee·dle·work (nē′dəl·wėrk′), *n.* work done
with a needle; sewing; embroidery.

need·n't (nēd′ənt), need not.

needs (nēdz), *adv.* because of necessity; necessarily: *he needs must go where duty calls.*

need·y (nēd′i), *adj.,* need·i·er, need·i·est. very
poor; not having enough to live on. —need′i-
ness, *n.* —Syn. indigent, destitute, penniless.

ne'er (nâr), *adv. Esp. Poetic.* never.

ne'er-do-well (nâr′dü·wel′), *n.* a worthless
fellow; good-for-nothing person. —*adj.* worthless; good-for-nothing.

ne·far·i·ous (ni·fâr′i·əs), *adj.* very wicked;
villainous. [< L *nefarius,* ult. < *ne-* not + *fas*
right, orig., (divine) decree < *fari* speak] —ne-
far′i·ous·ly, *adv.* —ne·far′i·ous·ness, *n.* —Syn.
heinous, atrocious, infamous.

neg., negative; negatively.

ne·gate (ni·gāt′; nē′gāt), *v.,* –gat·ed, –gat·ing.
deny; nullify. [< L *negatus,* pp. of *negare* say
no]

ne·ga·tion (ni·gā′shən), *n.* 1. a denying; denial: *shaking the head is a sign of negation.* 2.
absence or opposite of some positive thing or
quality. Darkness is the negation of light.

neg·a·tive (neg′ə·tiv), *adj., n., v.,* –tived, –tiv-
ing. —*adj.* 1. saying no: *his answer was negative.* 2. not positive; consisting in the lack of the
opposite: *negative kindness means not being unkind.* 3. *Math.* counting down from zero; minus.
4. of the kind of electricity produced on resin
when it is rubbed with silk. 5. *Photog.* showing
the lights and shadows reversed: *the negative
image on a photographic plate.* 6. showing an
absence of the germs, symptoms, etc., of an illness. 7. *Biol.* moving or turning away from light,
the earth, etc. 8. resisting suggestions; very un-
coöperative. —*n.* 1. word or statement that says
no or denies. 2. the side that says no or denies in an argument. 3. a negative quality
or characteristic. 4. *Math.* a minus quantity.

5. kind of electricity produced on resin when it is
rubbed with silk. 6. the negative element in an
electric cell. 7. a photographic image in which
the lights and shadows are reversed. Prints are
made from it. 8. right of veto. 9. **in the negative,**
a. in favor of denying (a request, suggestion,
etc.). b. saying no; denying. —*v.* 1. say no to;
deny; vote against. 2. disprove. —neg′a·tive·ly,
adv. —neg′a·tive·ness, neg′a·tiv′i·ty, *n.*

neg·a·tiv·ism (neg′ə·tiv·iz′əm), *n.* tendency
to say or do the opposite of what is suggested.
—neg′a·tiv·is′tic, *adj.*

Neg·ev (neg′ev), **Neg·eb** (neg′eb), *n.* a desert
region in S Israel.

neg·lect (ni·glekt′), *v.* 1. give too little care or
attention to: *neglect one's health.* 2. leave undone; not attend to: *neglect an order.* 3. omit;
fail: *don't neglect to water the plants.* —*n.* 1. act
of neglecting; disregard. 2. want of attention to
what should be done. 3. a being neglected. [< L
neglectus < *neg-* not + *legere* pick up] —neg-
lect′er, neg·lec′tor, *n.* —Syn. *v.* 1. slight. 2. disregard, ignore, overlook. —*n.* 1. negligence, dere-
liction, slight. —Ant. *v.* 1. cherish, foster.

neg·lect·ful (ni·glekt′fəl), *adj.* careless; negligent. —neg·lect′ful·ly, *adv.* —neg·lect′ful·
ness, *n.*

neg·li·gee (neg′lə·zhā′; neg′lə·zhā), *French,*
né·gli·gé (nā·glē·zhā′), *n.* 1. a woman's loose
house gown. 2. easy, informal dress or attire.
[< F, fem. pp. of *négliger* NEGLECT]

neg·li·gence (neg′lə·jəns), *n.* 1. lack of proper
care or attention; neglect: *negligence was the
cause of the accident.* 2. carelessness; indifference. [< L, < *negligere* NEGLECT] —Syn. 1. re-
missness, inattention. 2. heedlessness.

neg·li·gent (neg′lə·jənt), *adj.* 1. neglectful;
given to neglect; showing neglect. 2. careless; indifferent. —neg′li·gent·ly, *adv.* —Syn. 1. remiss,
derelict. 2. regardless, heedless.

neg·li·gi·ble (neg′lə·jə·bəl), *adj.* that can be
disregarded: *a difference of a penny is negligi-
ble.* —neg′li·gi·bil′i·ty, neg′li·gi·ble·ness, *n.*
—neg′li·gi·bly, *adv.*

ne·go·tia·ble (ni·gō′shə·bəl; –shi·ə–), *adj.* 1.
capable of being negotiated or sold; whose ownership can be transferred. 2. that can be got
past or over. —ne·go′tia·bil′i·ty, *n.*

ne·go·ti·ate (ni·gō′shi·āt), *v.,* –at·ed, –at·ing.
1. talk over and arrange terms: *negotiate for
peace.* 2. arrange for: *they finally negotiated a
peace treaty.* 3. sell. 4. *Colloq.* get past or over:
*the car negotiated the sharp curve by slowing
down.* [< L, < *negotium* business < *neg-* not +
otium ease] —ne·go′ti·a′tor, *n.* —Syn. 1. parley, confer, consult.

ne·go·ti·a·tion (ni·gō′shi·ā′shən), *n.* a ne-
gotiating; arrangement: *negotiations for the
new school are nearly finished.*

Ne·gress (nē′gris), *n.* a Negro woman or girl.

Ne·gri·to (ni·grē′tō), *n., pl.* –tos, –toes. member of certain dwarfish Negroid peoples of SE
Asia and of Africa, esp. of the Philippine Islands
and East Indies.

Ne·gro (nē′grō), *n., pl.* –groes, *adj.* —*n.* 1.
person belonging to any of the black races of
Africa. 2. a colored person having some black
ancestors. —*adj.* of or pertaining to Negroes.
[< Sp. < L *niger* black]

Ne·groid (nē′groid), *adj.* resembling Negroes;
akin to the Negro race; of a Negro type. —*n.*
person of a Negroid race.

Ne·he·mi·ah (nē′ə·mī′ə), *n.* 1. a Hebrew
leader who rebuilt the walls of Jerusalem about
445 B.C. 2. book of the Old Testament.

Neh·ru (nā′rü), *n.* Jawaharlal, 1889–1964,
prime minister of India from 1947 to 1964.

neigh (nā), *n.* sound that a horse makes. —*v.*
make such a sound. [OE *hnǣgan*]

neigh·bor, *esp. Brit.* **neigh·bour** (nā′bər),
n. 1. one who lives near another. 2. person or
thing that is near another. —*v.* 1. live or be
near (to). 2. adjoin; border on. —*adj.* living or
situated near to another. [OE *nēahgebūr* < *nēah*
nigh + *gebūr* dweller, countryman] —neigh′-
bor·er, *esp. Brit.* neigh′bour·er, *n.* —neigh′bor-

ing, esp. Brit. **neigh′bour·ing**, adj. —**neigh′bor·ly**, esp. Brit. **neigh′bour·ly**, adj. —**neigh′bor·li·ness**, esp. Brit. **neigh′bour·li·ness**, n.

neigh·bor·hood, esp. Brit. **neigh·bour·hood** (nā′bər·hŭd), n. 1. region near some place or thing. 2. place; district: a good neighborhood. 3. people living near one another; people of a place. 4. nearness. 5. in the neighborhood of, Colloq. somewhere near; about. —adj. of or having to do with a neighborhood. —Syn. n. 1. vicinity. 2. locality.

nei·ther (nē′thər; nī′-), conj. 1. not either: neither you nor I will go. 2. nor yet: "they toil not, neither do they spin." —adj. not either: neither statement is true. —pron. not either. [ME, < ne not + EITHER]

Nel·son (nel′sən), n. Viscount Horatio, 1758-1805, English admiral.

nem·a·tode (nem′ə·tōd), adj. belonging to a class or group of worms characterized by an elongated, unsegmented, cylindrical body. —n. such a worm. Hookworms and trichinae are nematodes. [< NL, ult. < Gk. nema thread]

Nem·e·sis (nem′ə·sis), n., pl. -ses (-sēz). 1. the Greek goddess of vengeance. 2. nemesis, a. just punishment for evil deeds. b. person who punishes another for evil deeds. [< Gk., < nemein give what is due]

N. Eng., Northern England.

neo-, word element. 1. new. 2. recent. [< Gk., < neos]

ne·o·co·lo·ni·al·ism (nē′ō·kə·lō′ni·ə·liz′əm), n. the supposed policy or practice of a large nation to dominate politically or economically smaller nations, especially former colonies; imperialism. —**ne·o·co·lo′ni·al·ist**, n., adj.

ne·o·dym·i·um (nē′ō·dim′i·əm), n. Chem. a rare metallic element, Nd, found in certain rare minerals.

ne·o·lith·ic (nē′ə·lith′ik), adj. of the later Stone Age, when polished stone weapons and tools were made and used: neolithic man.

ne·ol·o·gism (nē·ol′ə·jiz·əm), **ne·ol·o·gy** (-ji), n., pl. -gisms, -gies. 1. use of new words or new meanings for old words. 2. a new word; new meaning for an old word. [< F, < Gk. neos new + logos word]

ne·o·my·cin (nē·ə·mī′sin), n. an antibiotic drug obtained from the soil.

ne·on (nē′on), n. Chem. an element, Ne, that is a colorless, odorless gas, forming a very small part of the air. Tubes containing neon are used in electric signs and television sets. [< NL < Gk., new]

ne·o-Na·zi·ism (nē′ō·nä′tsi·iz·əm; -nat′si-), **ne·o-Na·zism** (nē′ō·nä′tsiz·əm; -nat′siz-), n. movement to restore the former principles and beliefs of Nazism. —**ne′o-Na′zi**, n.

ne·o·phyte (nē′ə·fīt), n. 1. a new convert. 2. beginner; novice. [< L < Gk., < neos new + phyein to plant]

Ne·pal (nə·pôl′), n. country between India and Tibet.

ne·pen·the (ni·pen′thē), n. 1. drug supposed to bring forgetfulness of sorrow or trouble. 2. anything that does this. [< L < Gk., < ne- not + penthos grief] —**ne·pen′the·an**, adj.

neph·ew (nef′ū; esp. Brit. nev′ū), n. son of one's brother or sister; son of one's brother-in-law or sister-in-law. [< OF < L nepos]

ne·phri·tis (ni·frī′tis), n. inflammation of the kidneys, esp. Bright's disease. [< LL, Gk., < nephros kidney] —**ne·phrit·ic** (ni·frit′ik), adj.

nep·o·tism (nep′ə·tiz·əm), n. the showing of too much favor by one in power to his relatives, esp. by giving them desirable appointments. [< F < Ital., < nipote NEPHEW] —**nep′o·tist**, n.

Nep·tune (nep′tūn; -tŏon), n. 1. Roman Myth. the god of the sea, identified with the Greek god Poseidon. 2. a large planet too far from the earth to be seen with the naked eye.

nep·tu·ni·um (nep·tū′ni·əm; -tū′-), n. Chem. a radioactive element, Np, obtained by bombardment of uranium with neutrons, used in the atom bomb.

Ne·re·id, ne·re·id (nir′i·id), n. Gk. Myth. any of the sea nymphs who attended Poseidon.

Ne·ro (nir′ō), n. 37-68 A.D., Roman emperor, 54-68 A.D. —**Ne·ro·ni·an** (ni·rō′ni·ən), adj., n.

ner·va·tion (nėr·vā′shən), n. Bot., Zool. arrangement of nerves.

nerve (nėrv), n., v., nerved, nerv·ing. —n. 1. fiber or bundle of fibers connecting the brain or spinal cord with the eyes, ears, muscles, glands, etc. 2. mental strength; courage. 3. strength; vigor; energy. 4. Slang. rude boldness; impudence. 5. Bot. vein of a leaf. 6. Zool. one of the thicker lines in an insect's wing. 7. get on one's nerves, annoy or irritate one. 8. nerves, a. nervousness. b. attack of nervousness. —v. arouse strength or courage in: nerve oneself for a struggle. [< L nervus sinew, tendon]

nerve·less (nėrv′lis), adj. 1. without strength or vigor; feeble; weak. 2. without courage or firmness. 3. without nerves. —**nerve′less·ly**, adv. —**nerve′less·ness**, n.

nerv·ous (nėr′vəs), adj. 1. of the nerves: the nervous system of the body. 2. having delicate or easily excited nerves. 3. having or proceeding from nerves that are out of order: a nervous patient. 4. restless; uneasy; timid. 5. having nerves. 6. strong; vigorous: a nervous style of writing. —**nerv′ous·ly**, adv. —**nerv′ous·ness**, n. —**Syn.** 2. high-strung, excitable. 4. apprehensive. 6. energetic, forceful.

Leaf nerves

nervous system, Anat., Zool. system of nerves and nerve cells in a person or animal.

nerv·y (nėr′vi), adj., nerv·i·er, nerv·i·est. 1. Am., Slang. rude and bold. 2. Am. requiring courage or firmness. 3. strong; vigorous. 4. Brit. Colloq. highly excitable; nervous.

nes·cience (nesh′əns; nesh′i·əns), n. ignorance. [< LL, ult. < L ne- not + scire know] —**nes′cient**, adj.

-ness, suffix. 1. quality, state, or condition of being —— as blackness, preparedness. 2. —— action; —— behavior, as in some uses of carefulness, meanness. [OE -nes(s)] ❯ -ness, a living suffix, is freely used to form new words.

nest (nest), n. 1. a structure or place used by birds for laying eggs and rearing young. 2. place used by insects, fishes, turtles, rabbits, or the like, for depositing eggs or young. 3. a snug abode, retreat, or resting place. 4. place that swarms (usually with something bad): a nest of thieves. 5. the birds, animals, etc., living in a nest. 6. set or series (often from large to small) such that each fits within another: nest of drinking cups. —v. 1. build or have a nest. 2. settle or place in, or as if in, a nest. [OE]

nest egg, 1. a natural or artificial egg left in a nest to induce a hen to continue laying eggs there. 2. something laid up as a reserve.

nes·tle (nes′əl), v., -tled, -tling. 1. settle oneself comfortably or cozily: nestle into a chair. 2. be settled comfortably or cozily; be sheltered: the little house nestled among the trees. 3. press close in affection or for comfort: nestle up to one's mother. [OE nestlian < nest] —**nes′tler**, n.

nest·ling (nest′ling), n. 1. bird too young to leave the nest. 2. a young child.

Nes·tor (nes′tər), n. 1. Gk. Legend. the oldest and wisest of the Greeks at the siege of Troy. 2. a wise old man.

net¹ (net), n., v., net·ted, net·ting. —n. 1. an open fabric made of string, cord, thread, or hair, knotted together in such a way as to leave holes regularly arranged, as fish net, a mosquito net, a tennis net, etc. 2. anything like a net. 3. a lacelike cloth. 4. a trap or snare. —v. 1. catch in a net: net a fish. 2. cover, confine, or protect with a net. [OE nett] —**net′like**, adj. —**Syn.** n. 1. mesh, network, reticulation.

net² (net), adj., n., v., net·ted, net·ting. —adj. remaining after deductions; free from deductions. A net gain or profit is the actual gain after all working expenses have been paid. —n. the net weight, profit, price, etc. —v. gain: the sale netted me a good profit. [< F. See NEAT¹.]

neth·er (nethʹər), adj. lower. [OE neothera]

Neth·er·lands (neth′ər-ləndz), The. *n.* a small country in Europe, W of Germany and N of Belgium; Holland. —Neth′er·land′er, *n.*

Netherlands Indies, Dutch East Indies.

Netherlands West Indies, Dutch West Indies.

neth·er·most (neth′ər-mōst), *adj.* lowest.

nether world, world of the dead; hell.

net·ting (net′ing), *n.* a netted or meshed material: *mosquito netting, wire netting for window screens.*

net·tle (net′əl), *n., v.,* -tled, -tling. —*n.* kind of plant having sharp leaf hairs that sting the skin when touched. —*v.* sting the mind; irritate; provoke; vex. [OE *netele*] —Syn. *v.* exasperate, incense.

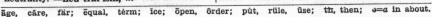

Nettle

net·work (net′wėrk), *n.* 1. a netting; net. 2. any netlike combination of things: *a network of railroads.* 3. group of radio or television stations connected together.

neu·ral (nur′əl), *adj.* of or pertaining to a nerve, neuron, or nervous system. [< Gk. *neuron* nerve]

neu·ral·gia (nù-ral′jə; nyù-), *n.* pain, usually sharp, along the course of a nerve. [< NL, < Gk. *neuron* nerve + *algos* pain] —neu·ral′gic, *adj.*

neu·ras·the·ni·a (nùr′əs-thē′ni·ə; nyùr′-; -thēn′yə), *n.* nervous exhaustion or weakness. [< NL, < Gk. *neuron* nerve + *asthenia* weakness] —neu·ras·then·ic (nùr′əs-then′ik; nyùr′-), *adj.*

neu·ri·tis (nù-rī′tis; nyù-), *n.* inflammation of a nerve or nerves. —neu·rit·ic (nù-rit′ik; nyù-), *adj.*

neu·rol·o·gy (nù-rol′ə·ji; nyù-rol′-), *n.* study of the nervous system and its diseases. —neu·ro·log·i·cal (nùr′ə·loj′ə·kəl; nyùr′-), *adj.* —neu·rol′o·gist, *n.*

neu·ron (nùr′on; nyùr′-), **neu·rone** (-ōn), *n.* one of the conducting cells of which the brain, spinal cord, and nerves are composed. [< Gk., nerve] —neu·ron·ic (nù·ron′ik; nyù-), *adj.*

neu·rop·a·thy (nù-rop′ə·thi; nyù-), *n.* disease of the nervous system. —neu·ro·path·ic (nùr′ə·path′ik; nyùr′-), neu′ro·path′i·cal, *adj.* —neu′ro·path′i·cal·ly, *adv.*

neu·rop·ter·ous (nù-rop′tər·əs; nyù-), *adj.* belonging to an order of insects having two pairs of wings with netlike veins. [< Gk. *neuron* nerve + *pteron* wing]

neu·ro·sis (nù-rō′sis; nyù-), *n., pl.* -ses (-sēz). a nervous disorder or disease, esp. one without apparent organic change. [< NL, < Gk., < *neuron* nerve]

neu·rot·ic (nù-rot′ik; nyù-), *adj.* 1. suffering from a nervous disease. 2. too nervous. —*n.* person suffering from neurosis.

neut., neuter.

neu·ter (nü′tər; nū′-), *adj.* 1. *Gram.* neither masculine nor feminine. *It* is a neuter pronoun. 2. *Zool.* having sex organs that are not fully developed. Worker bees are neuter. 3. being on neither side; neutral. —*n.* 1. *Gram.* a neuter word or form. 2. *Gram.* the neuter gender. 3. an animal, plant, or insect that is neuter. [< L, < *ne-* not + *uter* either]

neu·tral (nü′trəl; nū′-), *adj.* 1. on neither side in a quarrel or war. 2. of or belonging to a neutral country or neutral zone: *a neutral port.* 3. neither one thing nor the other; indefinite. 4. having little or no color; grayish. 5. *Chem.* neither acid nor alkaline. 6. *Elect.* neither positive nor negative. 7. *Biol.* neuter. —*n.* 1. a neutral person or country. 2. position of gears when they do not transmit motion from the engine to the wheels or other working parts. [< L *neutralis.* See NEUTER.] —neu′tral·ly, *adv.* —Syn. *adj.* 3. negative.

neu·tral·ist (nü′trəl·ist; nū′-), *n.* one who practices or advocates neutrality, esp. in international affairs. —*adj.* practicing or advocating neutrality. —neu′tral·ism, *n.*

neu·tral·i·ty (nü-tral′ə·ti; nū-), *n.* a being neutral; neutral character or status. —Syn. impartiality.

neu·tral·ize (nü′trəl·īz; nū′-), *v.,* -ized, -izing. 1. make neutral. 2. keep war out of. 3. make of no effect by some opposite force; counterbalance. 4. make chemically inert. 5. make electrically inert. —neu′tral·i·za′tion, *n.* —neu′tral·iz′er, *n.* —Syn. 3. counteract, offset.

neutral vowel. *Phonet.* schwa.

neu·tri·no (nü-trē′nō; nū-), *n. Physics.* a small, uncharged particle, usually considered to have a mass of zero.

neu·tron (nü′tron; nū′-), *n. Physics.* particle that is neutral electrically and has about the same mass as a proton. [< *neutr*(al) neither positively nor negatively charged + *-on* (after *electron, proton*)]

neutron bomb, a hydrogen bomb set off with little heat or shock effect. It releases highly lethal, short-lived neutrons.

Nev., Nevada.

Ne·vad·a (nə-vad′ə; -vä′də), *n.* a Western State of the United States. *Capital:* Carson City. *Abbrev.:* Nev. —Ne·vad′an, *adj., n. Am.*

nev·er (nev′ər), *adv.* 1. not ever; at no time: *he never has seen a more perfect copy.* 2. in no case; not at all; to no extent or degree: *never the wiser.* 3. never so, a. not even so. b. no matter how. [OE *nǣfre* < *ne* not + *ǣfre* ever]

nev·er·more (nev′ər·môr′; -mōr′), *adv.* never again.

nev·er·the·less (nev′ər·thə·les′), *adv.* however; none the less; for all that; in spite of it.

new (nü; nū), *adj.* 1. never having existed before; now first made, thought out, known or heard of, felt, or discovered: *a new invention.* 2. lately grown, come, or made; not old: *a new bud.* 3. now first used; not worn or used up: *a new path.* 4. different; changed: *he is a new man now.* 5. not familiar: *a new country to me.* 6. not yet accustomed: *new to the work.* 7. later; modern; recent: *new dances.* 8. just come; having just reached the position: *a new president.* 9. being the later or latest of two or more things of the same kind: *New England.* 10. further; additional; more: *he sought new information on the subject.* —*adv.* 1. newly; recently or lately; freshly. 2. again; anew. [OE *niwe*] —new′ish, *adj.* —new′ness, *n.* —Syn. *adj.* 1. novel, original. 3. fresh, unused. 5. unfamiliar, strange.

New·ark (nü′ərk; nū′-), *n.* city in NE New Jersey, near New York City.

New Bed·ford (bed′fərd), seaport in SE Massachusetts, formerly an important whaling port.

new·born (nü′bôrn′; nū′-), *adj.* 1. recently or only just born. 2. ready to start a new life.

New Bruns·wick (brunz′wik), province in SE Canada.

New·cas·tle (nü′kas′əl; -käs′-; nū′-), *n.* 1. Also, Newcastle-upon-Tyne (-tīn′). city in NE England. 2. carry coals to Newcastle, do something unnecessary.

new·com·er (nü′kum′ər; nū′-), *n.* person who has just come or who came not long ago.

New Deal, *Am.* the policies and measures advocated by President Franklin D. Roosevelt as a means of improving the economic and social welfare of the United States. —New Dealer, *Am.*

New Delhi, the capital of the republic of India, just S of old Delhi.

new·el (nü′əl; nū′-), *n.* the post at the top or bottom of a stairway that supports the railing. [< OF *noiel,* ult. < L *nux* nut; infl. by *noel* bud, ult. < L *nodus* knot]

New England, *Am.* the northeastern part of the United States. —New Englander, *Am.*

new·fan·gled (nü′fang′gəld; nū′-), *adj.* 1. lately come into fashion; of a new kind. 2. fond of novelty. [ME *newefangel* < *newe* new + *fange* (*n*) take]

Newel

New·found·land (nü′fənd·land′, nū′-; nü′-fənd·land′, nū′-; *for 3, also* nü·found′lənd, nū-), *n.* **1.** a large island in the Atlantic just off the E coast of Canada. **2.** a province in NE Canada that includes Newfoundland and Labrador. **3.** a shaggy, intelligent dog like a spaniel, but much larger. —New·found·land·er (nū-found'lən-dər; nū-), *n.*

New Frontier, *Am.* the policies and programs advocated by President John F. Kennedy.

New Guin·ea (gin'i), a large island north of Australia. Part of New Guinea belongs to Indonesia and part to Australia. Also, **Papua.**

New Hamp·shire (hamp'shər; -shir), a New England State of the United States. *Capital:* Concord. *Abbrev.:* N.H.

New Ha·ven (hā'vən), city in S Connecticut.

New Heb·ri·des (heb'rə-dēz), group of islands E of Australia, under joint rule of Great Britain and France.

New Jer·sey (jêr'zi), an Eastern State of the United States. *Capital:* Trenton. *Abbrev.:* N.J. —New Jer·sey·ite (jêr'zi-īt).

New Jerusalem, heaven.

New Latin, the Latin language after 1500.

new look, the, a general name for the innovations brought about in women's clothes in 1947.

new·ly (nū'li; nū'li), *adv.* **1.** lately; recently: *newly wedded.* **2.** again; freshly: *a newly revived scandal.* **3.** in a new way.

New·man (nū'mən; nū'-), *n.* John Henry, 1801–1890, English theologian and author who became a Roman Catholic and was made a cardinal.

New Mexico, a Southwestern State of the United States. *Capital:* Santa Fe. *Abbrev.:* N. Mex., N.M. —**New Mexican.**

new moon, moon when seen as a thin crescent with the hollow side on the left.

New Netherland, a former Dutch colony in America, from 1614 to 1664. England took possession of it in 1664 and divided it into the colonies of New York and New Jersey.

New Or·le·ans (ôr'li-ənz; *older* ôr-lēnz'), city in SE Louisiana, near the mouth of the Mississippi River.

news (nūz; nūz), *n.* **1.** something told as having just happened; information about something that has just happened or will soon happen. **2. break the news,** make something known; tell something. [ME *newes,* pl. of *newe* that which is new, adj. used as n.] —**Syn. 1.** tidings, advices, intelligence, information.

news·boy (nūz'boi'; nūz'-), *n.* boy who sells or delivers newspapers.

news·cast (nūz'kast'; -käst'; nūz'-), *n.* a radio broadcast of news. —**news'cast'er,** *n.* —**news'cast'ing,** *n.*

news·deal·er (nūz'dēl'ər; nūz'-), *n.* seller of newspapers and magazines.

news·let·ter (nūz'let'ər; nūz'-), *n.* a written or printed letter presenting an informal or confidential coverage of the news.

New South Wales, a state in SE Australia.

news·pa·per (nūz'pā'pər; nūz'-; nŭs'-; nŭs'-), *n.* sheets of paper printed every day or week, telling the news, carrying advertisements, and often having stories, poems, and useful information.

news·print (nūz'print'; nūz'-), *n.* kind of paper on which newspapers are usually printed.

news·reel (nūz'rēl'; nūz'-), *n. Am.* a motion picture showing current events.

news·stand (nūz'stand'; nūz'-), *n. Am.* place where newspapers and magazines are sold.

news·y (nūz'i; nūz'i), *adj.,* news·i·er, news·i·est, *n., pl.* news·ies. *Colloq.* —*adj.* full of news. —*n.* newsboy.

newt (nūt; nŭt), *n.* any of various small salamanders that live in water part of the time. [OE *efete;* ME *an ewt* taken as *a newt*]

New Testament, the part of the Bible which contains the life and teachings of Christ recorded by his followers, together with their own experiences and teachings.

New·ton (nū'tən; nū'-), *n.* Isaac, 1642–1727, English scientist and mathematician. —**New·to·ni·an** (nū-tō'ni-ən; nū-), *adj., n.*

New World, the Western Hemisphere; North America and South America. —**new'-world',** *adj.*

new year, 1. year approaching or newly begun. **2. New Year, New Year's, a. New Year's Day. b.** the first day or days of the year.

New Year's Day, New Year's, January 1, usually observed as a legal holiday.

New Year's Eve, the evening of Dec. 31.

New York, 1. an Eastern State of the United States. *Capital:* Albany. *Abbrev.:* N.Y. **2.** Also, **New York City.** seaport in SE New York State, at the mouth of the Hudson River. It is the largest city in the United States. —**New Yorker,** *Am.*

New York State Barge Canal, 1. system of canals in New York State. **2.** canal that connects Lake Erie and the Hudson River, including most of the Erie Canal.

New Zea·land (zē'lənd), a British dominion in the S Pacific, consisting of two main islands and various small ones. —**New Zealander.**

next (nekst), *adj.* following at once; nearest: *the next train, the next room.* —*adv.* **1.** the first time after this: *when you next come, bring it.* **2.** in the place or time or position that is nearest: *his name comes next.* **3.** next door to, a. in or at the house next to. b. almost; nearly. **4.** next to, a. nearest to. b. almost; nearly. —*prep.* nearest to: *the house next the church.* [OE *nēhst,* superl. of *nēah* nigh] —**Syn.** *adj.* closest.

next of kin, the nearest blood relative.

nex·us (nek'səs), *n., pl.* nex·us. **1.** connection; link. **2.** a connected series. [< L, ult. < *nectere* bind]

N.G., n.g., *Am., Colloq.* no good.

N.H., New Hampshire.

Ni, *Chem.* nickel.

N.I., Northern Ireland.

ni·a·cin (nī'ə-sin), *n.* nicotinic acid. [from trademark < ni(cotinic) ac(id)]

Ni·ag·a·ra (nī-ag'rə; -ag'ə-rə), *n.* **1.** a short river flowing from Lake Erie into Lake Ontario over Niagara Falls. **2.** Niagara Falls.

Niagara Falls, a great waterfall of the Niagara River, on the boundary between the United States and Canada.

nib (nib), *n., v.,* nibbed, nib·bing. —*n.* **1.** point of a pen; either of its parts. **2.** tip; point. **3.** a bird's bill; neb. —*v.* furnish with a nib. [var. of *neb*]

nib·ble (nib'əl), *v.,* -bled, -bling, *n.* —*v.* **1.** eat away with quick, small bites, as a rabbit or a mouse does. **2.** bite gently or lightly. —*n.* a nibbling; small bite. [cf. LG *nibbelen*] —**nib'bler,** *n.*

Ni·be·lung·en·lied (nē'bə-lúng'ən-lēt'), *n.* a German epic given its present form by an unknown author in S Germany during the first half of the 13th century.

nib·lick (nib'lik), *n.* a golf club with a short, flat, iron head having a slanting face, used when the ball is in a hole, close behind a bunker, etc.

Nic·a·ra·gua (nik'ə-rä'gwə), *n.* **1.** country in Central America. **2. Lake,** lake in S Nicaragua. —**Nic'a·ra'guan,** *adj., n.*

nice (nīs), *adj.,* nic·er, nic·est. **1.** pleasing; agreeable; satisfactory: *a nice face.* **2.** thoughtful; kind: *he was nice to us.* **3.** exact; precise; discriminating: *a nice ear for music.* **4.** minute; fine; subtle: *a nice distinction.* **5.** delicately skillful; requiring care, skill, or tact: *a nice problem.* **6.** exacting; particular; hard to please; fastidious; dainty: *nice in his eating.* **7.** proper; suitable. **8.** scrupulous: *too nice for a politician.* **9.** refined; cultured: *a nice accent.* [< OF, silly, < L *nescius* ignorant < *ne-* not + *scire* know] —**nice'ly,** *adv.* —**nice'ness,** *n.* —**Syn. 1.** gratifying, enjoyable. **3.** accurate. **6.** delicate. **7.** fitting, seemly. ▶ Nice is a counter word indicating mild approval, so general in meaning that it is of little use in writing.

Nice (nēs), *n.* a seaside resort in SE France.

Ni·cene Creed (nī-sēn'; nī'sēn), a formal statement of the chief tenets of Christian belief, based on that adopted in 325 A.D. and generally accepted throughout western Christendom.

ni·ce·ty (nī′sə·ti), *n.*, *pl.* **-ties.** 1. exactness; accuracy; delicacy: *television sets require nicety of adjustment.* 2. a fine point; small distinction; detail: *the niceties of scientific measurement.* 3. quality of being very particular; daintiness; refinement: *she has an air of nicety about her.* 4. something dainty or refined: *the niceties of living.* 5. to a nicety, just right.

niche (nich), *n.* 1. a recess or hollow in a wall for a statue, vase, etc. 2. a suitable place or position. [< F, ult. < L *nidus* nest] —**Syn.** 1. nook, cavity.

Nich·o·las (nik′ə·ləs; nik′ləs), *n.* 1. Saint, the patron saint of young people, sailors, travelers, and Russians. 2. **Saint, Santa Claus.** 3. **I,** 1796–1855, czar of Russia, 1825–1855. 4. **II,** 1868–1918, czar of Russia, 1894–1917; executed during the Russian Revolution.

Vase in a niche

nick (nik), *n.* place where a small bit has been cut or broken out; notch; groove. —*v.* 1. make a nick or nicks in. 2. cut into or through. 3. hit, guess, catch, etc., exactly. 4. *Slang.* trick, cheat, or defraud. [cf. OE *gehnycned* wrinkled]

nick·el (nik′əl), *n.*, *v.*, **-eled, -el·ing;** *esp. Brit.* **-elled, -el·ling.** —*n.* 1. *Chem.* a metallic element, Ni, that looks like silver and is somewhat like iron, much used as an alloy. 2. *Am.* a coin containing nickel; a United States five-cent piece. —*v.* cover or coat with nickel. [< Sw. < G *kupfernickel,* lit., copper devil; the ore resembles copper but yields none] ➤ **nickel.** Most words with this last syllable (-əl) are spelled *-le,* but *nickel* keeps the *-el* of its German origin.

nick·el·o·de·on (nik′ə·lō′di·ən), *n. Am.* a. place of amusement with motion-picture exhibitions, etc., to which the price of admission is only five cents. b. a juke box.

nickel plate, a thin coating of nickel deposited on a metal object to prevent rust, etc.

nick·el-plate (nik′əl·plāt′), *v.*, **-plat·ed, -plat·ing.** coat with nickel.

nick·nack (nik′nak′), *n.* knickknack.

nick·name (nik′nām′), *n.*, *v.*, **-named, -nam·ing.** —*n.* name added to a person's real name or used instead of it. —*v.* give a nickname to. [ME *ekename; an ekename* taken as *a nekename.* See EKE², NAME.]

Nic·o·si·a (nik′ō·sē′ə), *n.* capital of Cyprus.

nic·o·tine (nik′ə·tēn), **nic·o·tin** (-tin), *n.* poison contained in tobacco leaves. [< F; after J. *Nicot,* who introduced tobacco in France]

nic·o·tin·ic acid (nik′ə·tin′ik), a vitamin, C₆H₅NCOOH, which prevents pellagra.

nic·ti·tate (nik′tə·tāt), *v.*, **-tat·ed, -tat·ing.** wink. [< Med.L *nictitatus,* ult. < L *nictare* wink] —**nic′ti·ta′tion,** *n.*

nictitating membrane, a thin membrane, or inner or third eyelid, present in many animals, capable of being drawn across the eyeball.

niece (nēs), *n.* daughter of one's brother or sister; daughter of one's brother-in-law or sister-in-law. [< OF, ult. < L *neptis*]

nif·ty (nif′ti), *adj.*, **-ti·er, -ti·est.** *Am., Slang.* attractive; stylish.

Ni·ger (nī′jər), *n.* 1. republic in W Africa north of Dahomey, formerly part of French West Africa. 2. river flowing from W Africa into the S Atlantic.

Ni·ge·ri·a (nī·jir′i·ə), *n.* country in W Africa, a member of the British Commonwealth. —**Ni·ge′ri·an,** *adj., n.*

nig·gard (nig′ərd), *n.* a stingy person. —*adj.* stingy. [< Scand. *hnøggr* stingy]

nig·gard·ly (nig′ərd·li), *adj.* 1. stingy. 2. meanly small or scanty: *a niggardly gift.* —*adv.* stingily. —**nig′gard·li·ness,** *n.* —**Syn.** *adj.* 1. miserly, illiberal, stinting.

nig·ger (nig′ər), *n. Colloq., Offensive.* Negro. [< F < Sp. *negro* NEGRO]

nigh (nī), *adv., adj.*, **nigh·er, nigh·est** or **next,** *prep., v.* near. [OE *nēah*]

night (nīt), *n.* 1. the darkness between evening and morning; the time between sunset and sunrise. 2. the darkness of night; the dark. 3. the darkness of ignorance, sin, sorrow, old age, death, etc. 4. evening; nightfall. [OE *niht*]

night blindness, a condition of the eyes in which the sight is normal in the day or in a strong light, but is abnormally poor or wholly gone at night or in a dim light.

night·cap (nīt′kap′), *n.* 1. cap to be worn in bed. 2. *Colloq.* drink taken just before going to bed.

night club, place for dancing, eating, and entertainment, open only at night.

night·dress (nīt′dres′), *n.* nightgown.

night·fall (nīt′fôl′), *n.* the coming of night.

night·gown (nīt′goun′), *n.* a long, loose garment worn in bed.

night·hawk (nīt′hôk′), *n.* 1. kind of bird that flies and feeds mostly by night. 2. *Colloq.* person who stays up late.

night·in·gale (nīt′ən·gāl; nīt′ing-), *n.* a small, reddish-brown bird of Europe. The male sings sweetly at night as well as in the daytime. [for *nightgale,* OE *nihtegale* < *niht* night + *galan* sing]

Night·in·gale (nīt′ən·gāl; nīt′ing-), *n.* **Florence,** 1820–1910, Englishwoman who brought about great improvements in nursing.

Nightingale (6 to 7 in. long)

night letter, *Esp. U.S.* a long telegram sent at night at reduced rates.

night·long (nīt′lông′; -long′), *adj.* lasting all night. —*adv.* through the whole night.

night·ly (nīt′li), *adj.* 1. done, happening, or appearing every night. 2. done, happening, or appearing at night. —*adv.* 1. every night: *performances are given nightly.* 2. at night; by night. —**Syn.** *adj.* 2. nocturnal.

night·mare (nīt′mâr′), *n.* 1. a very distressing dream. 2. a very distressing experience. [< *night* + OE *mare* monster oppressing men during sleep] —**night′mar′ish,** *adj.*

night owl, *Colloq.* person who habitually stays up late.

night school, school held in the evening for persons who work during the day.

night·shade (nīt′shād′), *n.* any of various plants belonging to the same genus as the potato and the tomato. The black nightshade has black, poisonous berries. The **deadly nightshade,** or belladonna, has red berries.

night·shirt (nīt′shèrt′), *n.* a long, loose shirt worn by a man or boy in bed.

night spot, *Am., Colloq.* a night club.

night·time (nīt′tīm′), *n.* time between evening and morning.

night·walk·er (nīt′wôk′ər), *n.* 1. person who goes around at night for a bad purpose. 2. a large earthworm crawling around at night.

ni·hil·ism (nī′ə·liz·əm), *n.* 1. entire rejection of the usual beliefs in religion, morals, government, laws, etc. 2. *Philos.* the denial of all existence. 3. use of violent methods against a ruler. [< L *nihil* nothing] —**ni′hil·ist,** *n.* —**ni′hil·is′tic,** *adj.*

Ni·ke¹ (nī′kē; nē′kā), *n. Gk. Myth.* goddess of victory, usually represented with wings.

Ni·ke² (nī′kē; nē′kā), *n.* an antiaircraft rocket-propelled missile launched from the ground and guided by electronic signals from the ground. [after *Nike¹*]

nil (nil), *n.* nothing. [< L, earlier *nihil*]

Nile (nīl), *n.* a great river in Africa flowing north through Egypt into the Mediterranean.

nim·ble (nim′bəl), *adj.*, **-bler, -blest.** 1. active and sure-footed; light and quick; quick-moving: *goats are nimble in climbing among the rocks.* 2. quick to understand and to reply; clever: *a nimble mind.* [ME *nymel* < OE *niman* take] —**nim′ble·ness,** *n.* —**nim′bly,** *adv.* —**Syn.** 1. agile, lively, spry, brisk. —**Ant.** 1. slow, heavy.

āge, cāre, fär; ēqual, tèrm; īce; ōpen, ôrder; pùt, rūle, ūse; th, then; ə=a in about.

nim·bus (nim′bəs), n., -bus·es, -bi (-bī). 1. a light disk or other radiance about the head of a divine or sacred person in a picture. 2. a bright cloud surrounding a god, person, or thing. [< L, cloud]

Nim·rod (nim′rod), n. 1. Bible. a great hunter. Gen. 10:8 and 9. 2. hunter.

nin·com·poop (nin′kəm·pup), n. fool; simpleton; blockhead.

nine (nīn), n. 1. a cardinal number, one more than eight. 2. symbol of this number; 9. 3. set of nine persons or things. —adj. one more than eight; 9. [OE nigon]

nine·fold (nīn′fōld′), adj. 1. nine times as much or as many. 2. having nine parts. —adv. nine times as much or as many.

nine·pins (nīn′pinz′), n. (sing. in use) game in which nine large wooden pins are set up to be bowled down with a ball.

nine·teen (nīn′tēn′), n. 1. a cardinal number, nine more than ten. 2. symbol of this number; 19. —adj. nine more than ten; 19. —nine′teenth′, adj., n.

nine·ty (nīn′ti), n., pl. -ties, adj. —n. 1. a cardinal number, nine times ten. 2. symbol of this number; 90. —adj. nine times ten; 90. —nine·ti·eth (nīn′ti·ith), adj., n.

Nin·e·veh (nin′ə·və), n. an ancient city of Assyria.

nin·ny (nin′i), n., pl. -nies. fool.

ninth (nīnth), adj. 1. next after the eighth; last in a series of 9. 2. being one of 9 equal parts. —n. 1. next after the eighth; last in a series of 9. 2. one of nine equal parts. —ninth′ly, adv.

Ni·o·be (nī′ō·bē), n. Gk. Legend. mother whose fourteen beautiful children were slain because she boasted about them. Turned by Zeus into a stone fountain, she weeps forever for her children.

ni·o·bi·um (nī·ō′bi·əm), n. Chem. a steel-gray, rare metallic element, Nb, that resembles tantalum in chemical properties. Formerly, columbium. —ni·o·bic (nī·ō′bik; -ob′ik), ni·o·bous (nī·ō′bəs), adj.

nip¹ (nip), v., nipped, nip·ping, n. —v. 1. squeeze tight and suddenly; bite: the crab nipped my toe. 2. take off by biting, pinching, or snipping. 3. hurt at the tips; spoil; injure: plants nipped by frost. 4. have a sharp, biting effect on: cold winds nip your ears and nose. —n. 1. a tight squeeze; pinch; sudden bite. 2. injury caused by frost. 3. sharp cold; chill: there is a nip in the air on a frosty morning. 4. a small bit. 5. nip and tuck, Am., Colloq. even in a race or contest. [ME nyppen. Cf. Du. nijpen.] —Syn. v. 1. pinch. 2. clip, cut. 4. sting.

nip² (nip), n. a small drink.

nip·per (nip′ər), n. 1. one that nips. 2. a big claw of a lobster or crab. 3. Usually, nippers. pincers, forceps, pliers, or any tool that nips.

nip·ple (nip′əl), n. 1. a small projection through which the baby animal gets its mother's milk. 2. a rubber cap or mouthpiece of a baby's bottle. 3. anything shaped or used like a nipple.

Nip·pon (nip·pon′; nip′on), n. Japanese name of Japan. —Nip·pon·ese (nip′ən·ēz′; -ēs′), adj., n.

nip·py (nip′i), adj., -pi·er, -pi·est. biting; sharp.

nir·va·na, Nir·va·na (nir·vä′nə; -van′ə; nėr′-), n. the Buddhist idea of heavenly peace; perfect happiness reached by complete absorption of oneself into the supreme universal spirit. [< Skt., extinction, < nis- out + vā- blow]

Ni·sei (nē′sā′), n., pl. -sei. Am. a native-born U.S. or Canadian citizen whose parents were Japanese immigrants. [< Jap.]

Nis·sen hut (nis′ən), Mil. Quonset hut.

nit (nit), n. 1. egg of a louse or similar insect. 2. a very young louse or similar insect. [OE hnitu]

ni·ter, esp. Brit. **ni·tre** (nī′tər), n. 1. potassium nitrate, KNO₃, a salt obtained from potash, used in making gunpowder; saltpeter. 2. sodium nitrate, NaNO₃, used as a fertilizer. [< L < Gk. nitron]

ni·ton (nī′ton), n. Chem. early name of radon. [< NL, < L nitere to shine]

ni·trate (nī′trāt), n., v., -trat·ed, -trat·ing. —n. 1. Chem. salt or ester of nitric acid. 2. potassium nitrate, KNO₃, or sodium nitrate, NaNO₃, used as a fertilizer. —v. treat with nitric acid or a nitrate. —ni·tra′tion, n.

ni·tric acid (nī′trik), a clear, colorless liquid, HNO₃, that eats into flesh, clothing, metal, and other substances.

ni·tri·fy (nī′trə·fī), v., -fied, -fy·ing. 1. oxidize (ammonia compounds, etc.) to nitrites or nitrates, esp. by bacterial action. 2. impregnate (soil, etc.) with nitrates. [< F nitrifier. See NITER, -FY.] —ni′tri·fi·ca′tion, n.

ni·trite (nī′trīt), n. salt or ester of nitrous acid.

ni·tro·gen (nī′trə·jən), n. Chem. one of the elements, a colorless, odorless, tasteless gas, N, that forms about four-fifths of the air by volume. —ni·trog·e·nous (nī·troj′ə·nəs), adj.

ni·tro·glyc·er·in (nī′trə·glis′ər·in), **ni·tro·glyc·er·ine** (-in; -ēn), n. an oily, explosive liquid, C₃H₅(NO₃)₃, made by treating glycerin with nitric and sulfuric acids, used in dynamite.

ni·trous acid (nī′trəs), an acid, HNO₂, known only in solution.

nitrous oxide, a colorless gas, N₂O, that causes laughing and inability to feel pain; laughing gas. It is often used as an anesthetic by dentists.

nit·wit (nit′wit′), n. Am., Slang. stupid person.

nix¹ (niks), n., interj. Am., Slang. nothing; no. [< G nichts]

nix² (niks), n., pl. nix·es. a water fairy. [< colloq. Du. or G]

nix·ie (nik′si), n. a female water fairy.

Nix·on (nik′ən), n. Richard Milhous, born 1913, vice-president of the U.S., 1953–1961.

N.J., New Jersey.

N·kru·mah (en·krü′mə, nə·krü′mə), n. Kwame, born 1909, prime minister of the Gold Coast, 1952–1957, President of Ghana, 1957–1966.

NKVD, N.K.V.D., formerly, the secret police of the Soviet Union, now the MVD.

NL, New Latin.

NLRB, National Labor Relations Board.

N.M., N. Mex., New Mexico.

NNE, N.N.E., direction halfway between north and northeast.

NNW, N.N.W., direction halfway between north and northwest.

no¹ (nō), n., pl. noes, adj., adv. —n. 1. word used to deny, refuse, or disagree. 2. denial; refusal. 3. a negative vote or voter: the noes have it. [< adv.] —adj. not any; not a: he has no friends. [var. of none] —adv. 1. word used to deny, refuse, or disagree: Will you come? No. 2. not in any degree; not at all: he is no better. 3. not, chiefly in phrases like whether or no. [OE nā < ne not + ā ever] ▷ See yes for usage note.

no², No (nō), n., pl. no, nos, No, Nos. Japanese classical drama. [< Jap.]

No, Chem. nobelium.

No., 1. north; northern. 2. number. ▷ No. The abbreviation No. for number is written with a capital. It is appropriate chiefly in business and technical English. In the United States No. is not written with street numbers.

No·ah (nō′ə), n. Bible. man whom God told to make an ark (Noah's ark) to save himself, his family, and a pair of each kind of animal from the Flood. Gen. 5:28–10.

No·bel (nō·bel′), n. Alfred Bernhard, 1833–1896, Swedish inventor, founder of the Nobel prizes.

no·be·li·um (nō·bē′li·əm), n. Chem. a rare radioactive, artificial element, No [< Nobel Institute, where produced]

Nobel prizes, five money prizes established by Alfred B. Nobel to be given annually to those persons who have done most in physics, chemistry, medicine, literature, and the promotion of peace.

no·bil·i·ty (nō·bil′ə·ti), n., pl. -ties. 1. people of noble rank. Earls, counts, princes, and kings belong to the nobility. 2. noble birth; noble rank.

3. noble character. —**Syn. 1.** peerage. 3. greatness, magnanimity.

no·ble (nō′bəl), *adj.*, **-bler, -blest,** *n.* —*adj.* **1.** high and great by birth, rank, or title. **2.** high and great in character; showing greatness of mind; good: *a noble deed.* **3.** excellent; fine; splendid; magnificent: *a noble sight.* —*n.* person high and great by birth, rank, or title. [< F < L .*nobilis* renowned] —**no′ble·ness,** *n.* —**no′bly,** *adv.* —**Syn.** *adj.* **1.** aristocratic, high-born, patrician. **2.** honorable, worthy. **3.** imposing, stately. —*n.* nobleman, peer.

no·ble·man (nō′bəl·mən), *n., pl.* **-men.** man of noble rank, title, or birth.

no·blesse o·blige (nō·bles′ ō·blēzh′), *French.* persons of noble rank should behave nobly.

no·ble·wom·an (nō′bəl·wüm′ən), *n., pl.* **-wom·en.** woman of noble birth or rank.

no·bod·y (nō′bod·i), *pron., n., pl.* **-bod·ies.** —*pron.* no one; no person. —*n.* person of no importance. ➤ **Nobody, nothing, nowhere** are written as single words. *Nobody* and *nothing* are singular: *Nobody thinks that way any more. Nothing is further from the truth. The dog could be found nowhere.*

nock (nok), *n.* notch on a bow or arrow for the bowstring.

noc·tur·nal (nok·tėr′nəl), *adj.* **1.** of or in the night: *stars are a nocturnal sight.* **2.** active in the night: *the owl is a nocturnal bird.* **3.** closed by day, open by night: *a nocturnal flower.* [< LL *nocturnalis,* ult. < L *nox* night] —**noc·tur′nal·ly,** *adv.*

noc·turne (nok′tėrn), *n. Music.* a dreamy or pensive piece. [< F]

nod (nod), *v.,* **nod·ded, nod·ding,** *n.* —*v.* **1.** bow (the head) slightly and raise it again quickly. **2.** say yes by nodding. **3.** express by bowing the head: *nod consent.* **4.** let the head fall forward and bob about when sleepy or falling asleep. **5.** be sleepy; become careless and dull. **6.** droop, bend, or sway back and forth: *nodding plumes.* —*n.* a nodding of the head: *he gave us a nod as he passed.* [ME *nodden*] —**nod′der,** *n.*

nod·dle (nod′əl), *n. Colloq.* the head.

node (nōd), *n.* **1.** knot; knob; swelling. **2.** *Bot.* joint in a stem; part of a stem that normally bears a leaf or leaves. **3.** *Physics.* a point, line, or plane in a vibrating body at which there is comparatively no vibration. [< L *nodus* knot] —**nod′al,** *adj.*

nod·ule (noj′ül), *n.* **1.** a small knot, knob, or swelling. **2.** a small, rounded mass or lump: *nodules of pure gold.* [< L *nodulus,* dim. of *nodus* knot] —**nod·u·lar** (noj′ə·lər), *adj.*

no·ël (nō·el′), *n.* **1.** a Christmas song; carol. **2.** Noël, Christmas. [< F < L *natalis* natal (i.e. the natal day of Christ) < *nasci* be born]

nog·gin (nog′ən), *n.* **1.** a small cup or mug. **2.** a small drink; one fourth of a pint. **3.** *Am., Colloq.* a person's head.

no·how (nō′hou′), *adv. Colloq.* in no way; not at all.

noise (noiz), *n., v.,* **noised, nois·ing.** —*n.* **1.** a sound that is not musical or pleasant. **2.** a sound. **3.** din of voices and movements; loud shouting; outcry; clamor. —*v.* **1.** make a noise. **2.** talk much. **3.** spread the news of; tell: *it was noised abroad that the king was dying.* [< OF < L *nausea* NAUSEA] —**Syn.** *n.* **3.** babble, uproar, hubbub, tumult.

noise·less (noiz′lis), *adj.* making no noise: *a noiseless typewriter.* —**noise′less·ly,** *adv.* —**noise′less·ness,** *n.*

noi·some (noi′səm), *adj.* **1.** offensive; disgusting; smelling bad: *a noisome slum.* **2.** harmful; injurious: *a noisome pestilence.* [< *noy* (var. of *annoy*) + *some*¹] —**noi′some·ly,** *adv.* —**noi′some·ness,** *n.*

nois·y (noiz′i), *adj.,* **nois·i·er, nois·i·est. 1.** making much noise: *a noisy boy.* **2.** full of noise: *a noisy street.* **3.** having much noise with it: *a*

noisy game, a noisy quarrel. —**nois′i·ly,** *adv.* —**nois′i·ness,** *n.* —**Syn. 1.** shouting, clamorous, brawling, blatant.

nol-pros (nol′ pros′), *v.,* **-prossed, -pros·sing.** *Am.* discontinue (all or part of a lawsuit) and have a note of the fact put on the court record. [short for L *nolle prosequi* to be unwilling to prosecute]

nom., nominative.

no·mad (nō′mad; nom′ad), *n.* **1.** member of a tribe that moves from place to place to have pasture for its cattle. **2.** wanderer. —*adj.* **1.** wandering from place to place to find pasture. **2.** wandering. [< L < Gk., ult. < *nemein* to pasture]

no·mad·ic (nō·mad′ik), *adj.* of nomads or their life; wandering; roving. —**no·mad′i·cal·ly,** *adv.*

no·mad·ism (nō′mad·iz·əm; nom′ad–), *n.* the way that nomads live.

no man's land, 1. in war, the land between opposing lines of trenches. **2.** tract about which there is dispute.

nom de plume (nom′ də plüm′), a pen name; name used by a writer instead of his real name. [formed in E from F words]

Nome (nōm), *n.* seaport and mining town in W Alaska, on Bering Sea.

no·men·cla·ture (nō′mən·klā′chər; nō·men′klə–), *n.* set or system of names or terms: *the nomenclature of music.* [< L *nomenclatura* < *nomen* name + *calare* to call]

nom·i·nal (nom′ə·nəl), *adj.* **1.** being so in name only; not real: *the president is the nominal head of the club, but the secretary is the one who really runs its affairs.* **2.** so small that it is not worth considering; unimportant compared with the real value. [< L, < *nomen* name] —**nom′i·nal·ly,** *adv.*

nom·i·nate (nom′ə·nāt), *v.,* **-nat·ed, -nat·ing. 1.** name as candidate for an office: *three times Bryan was nominated for President, but he was never elected.* **2.** appoint for an office or duty: *the President nominated him as Secretary of State.* [< L, ult. < *nomen* name] —**nom′i·na′tor,** *n.* —**nom′i·na′tion,** *n.* —**Syn.** designate.

nom·i·na·tive (nom′ə·nə·tiv; -nā′tiv), *Gram.* —*adj.* **1.** showing the subject of a verb and words agreeing with the subject. **2.** being in or pertaining to that case. —*n.* **1.** the nominative case. **2.** a word in that case. *Who* and *I* are nominatives.

nom·i·nee (nom′ə·nē′), *n.* person who is nominated.

non–, *prefix.* not; not a; opposite of; lack of; failure of, as in *nonconformity, nonacceptance, nonpayment.* [< L *non* not]

If an adjective formed with *non–* is not defined in this dictionary, its meaning will be clear if *not* is put in place of the *non.* If a noun formed with *non–* is not defined, its meaning will be clear if *not, not a, the opposite of,* or *the absence of* is put in place of the *non. Non–* is a living prefix and may be used with any noun, adjective, or adverb; but if there is a commonly used word of the same meaning formed with *un–, in–,* or *dis–,* that word is usually preferable. Most of the words that have *non–* as the preferred usage, or as a respectable rival of *un–,* are listed below, or as regular entries.

non′ab·sorb′ent
non′ab·stain′er
non·ac′id
non′ac·tin′ic
non′ad·he′sive
non′ad·ja′cent
non′ad·jec·ti′val
non′ad·min′is·tra′tive
non′ad·mis′sion
non′ad·ver′bi·al
non·Af′ri·can
non′ag·gres′sive

non′ag·ri·cul′tur·al
non′al·co·hol′ic
non′al·le′giance
non′-A·mer′i·can
non-An′gli·can
non′ap·os·tol′ic
non′ap·peal′a·ble
non′ap·proach′a·ble
non′a·quat′ic
non-Ar′y·an
non′-A·si·at′ic
non′as·sess′a·ble

non·as·sign'a·ble
non'as·sim'i·la·ble
non'as·sim'i·la'tion
non'as·so'ci·a'tion
non'at·mos·pher'ic
non'a·tom'ic
non·bas'ic
non·be'ing
non'be·liev'er
non'bel·lig'er·ent
non·break'a·ble
non·burn'ing
non'ca·non'i·cal
non'cap·i·tal·is'tic
non'car·niv'o·rous
non'cat·a·stroph'ic
non'cat·e·gor'i·cal
non-Cath'o·lic
non·cel'lu·lar
non·cen'tral
non'-Chi·nese'
non-Chris'tian
non·civ'i·lized
non·clas'si·cal
non·cler'i·cal
non·clin'i·cal
non'co·a·lesc'ing
non'co·her'ent
non'co·he'sive
non'col·laps'i·ble
non·col·le'giate
non·com'bat
non'com·bus'ti·ble
non'com·mer'cial
non'com·mu'ni·ca·ble
non'com·mu'ni·cant
non·com'mu·nist
non'com·pet'ing
non'com·pet'i·tive
non'com·ple'tion
non'com·pul'sion
non'con·cur'rence
non'con·du'cive
non'con·duct'ing
non'con·duc'tion
non'con·form'ing
non'con·sec'u·tive
non'con·sent'
non'con·sent'ing
non·con'se·quence
non'con·serv'a·tive
non'con·sti·tu'tion·al
non'con·ta'gious
non'con·tem'po·rar'y
non'con·ti·nen'tal
non'con·tin'u·ance
non'con·tin'u·ous
non·con'tra·band
non'con·trac'tile
non'con·trac'tu·al
non'con·tra·dic'to·ry
non'con·trib'u·to'ry
non'con·tro·ver'sial
non'con·ver'gent
non'con·vert'i·ble
non'co·öp'er·a'tive
non'co·ör'di·na'tion
non'cor·rec'tive
non'cor·ro'sive
non'cre·a'tive
non·cred'i·tor
non·crim'i·nal
non·crit'i·cal
non·crys'tal·line
non·cu'mu·la'tive
non'de·cep'tive
non'de·cid'u·ous
non'de·duct'i·ble
non'de·fer'a·ble
non'de·his'cent
non'de·liv'er·a·ble
non'de·liv'er·y
non'dem·o·crat'ic
non'de·part·men'tal
non'de·par'ture
non'de·riv'a·ble
non'de·struc'tive

non'de·tach'a·ble
non'de·vel'op·ment
non'de·vo'tion·al
non'dic·ta·to'ri·al
non'di·dac'tic
non'dif·fu'sion
non·dir'i·gi·ble
non'dis·count'a·ble
non'dis·crim'i·na'tion
non'dis·pos'al
non'dis·tinc'tive
non'di·ver'gent
non'di·vis'i·ble
non·doc'tri·nal
non'dog·mat'ic
non·dra·mat'ic
non·driv'ing
non·du'ra·ble
non·du'ti·a·ble
non'dy·nas'tic
non·earn'ing
non·ed'i·ble
non·ed'u·ca·ble
non'ed·u·ca'tion·al
non'ef·fi'cient
non'e·las'tic
non'e·lec'tion
non'e·lec'tive
non'e·lec'tric
non'e·lec'tri·fied
non'e·mo'tion·al
non'en·force'a·ble
non'en·force'ment
non-Eng'lish
non'en·tailed'
non'en·vi'ron·men'tal
non'e·pis'co·pal
non'-E·pis'co·pa'lian
non'e·quiv'a·lent
non·eth'i·cal
non'-Eu·clid'e·an
non·eu·gen'ic
non'-Eu·ro·pe'an
non'e·van·gel'i·cal
non'ev·o·lu'tion·ar'y
non'ex·change'a·ble
non'ex·clu'sive
non'ex·ist'ence
non'ex·ist'ent
non'ex·ist'ing
non'ex·pan'si·ble
non'ex·plo'sive
non'ex·port'a·ble
non'ex·tend'ed
non'ex·ten'sile
non'ex·ten'sion
non'ex·tra·dit'a·ble
non'ex·tra'ne·ous
non·ex'tro·vert
non·fac'tu·al
non·fad'ing
non-Fas'cist
non·fed'er·al
non·fed'er·at'ed
non·fer'rous
non·fer'tile
non·fes'tive
non·feu'dal
non·fic'tion·al
non·fire'proof'
non·fis'cal
non·fis'sion·a·ble
non·flow'er·ing
non·fluc'tu·at'ing
non·fo'cal
non·for'feit·a·ble
non·for'fei·ture
non·freez'ing
non·func'tion·al
non·gas'e·ous
non-Ger'man
non'-Ger·man'ic
non-Goth'ic
non'gov·ern·men'tal
non·gran'u·lar
non-Greek'
non·green'
non'gre·gar'i·ous

non·hab'it·a·ble
non'-Hel·len'ic
non'he·red'i·tar'y
non·her'it·a·ble
non·her'i·tor
non·his·tor'ic
non·hon'or·ar'y
non·hu'man
non·hu'mor·ous
non'i·den'ti·cal
non'i·den'ti·ty
non'id·i·o·mat'ic
non·im·mu'ni·ty
non·im'mu·nized
non'im·pe'ri·al
non'im·por·ta'tion
non'im·preg'nat·ed
non'im·pres'sion·ist
non'in·clu'sive
non·in'crease
non'in·dict'a·ble
non'in·dict'ment
non'in·dig'e·nous
non'in·di·vid'u·al
non'in·dus'tri·al
non'in·fec'tion
non'in·fec'tious
non'in·fi·nite
non'in·flam'ma·ble
non'in·flam'ma·to'ry
non'in·flect'ed
non'in·flec'tion·al
non'in·form'a·tive
non'in·her'it·a·ble
non'in·struc'tion·al
non'in·stru·men'tal
non'in·ter·course
non'in·ter·fer'ence
non'in·ter·sect'ing
non'in·tox'i·cant
non'in·tox'i·cat'ing
non'in·tro·spec'tive
non·in'tro·vert
non'in·tu'i·tive
non·i'o·dized
non·i'on·ized
non-I'rish
non'ir·ra'di·at'ed
non·ir'ri·ga·ble
non'ir·ri·ga'tion
non·ir'ri·tant
non·ir'ri·tat'ing
non-Is'ra·el·ite
non'-I·tal'ian
non·it'er·a·tive
non'-Jap·a·nese'
non-Jew'
non-Jew'ish
non'ju·di'cial
non'ju·rid'i·cal
non'ju·ris'tic
non-Lat'in
non·le'gal
non·li'censed
non·liq'uid
non'liq·ui·dat'ing
non'liq·ui·da'tion
non·lit'er·ar'y
non'li·ti'gious
non'li·tur'gi·cal
non·liv'ing
non'lu·mi·nes'cent
non·lu'mi·nous
non'mag·net'ic
non·main'te·nance
non'ma·lig'nant
non·mal'le·a·ble
non·mar'i·tal
non·mar'riage·a·ble
non·mar'ry·ing
non·mar'tial
non·ma·te'ri·al
non'ma·te'ri·al·is'tic
non·ma·ter'nal
non'math·e·mat'i·cal
non'me·chan'i·cal
non·med'i·cal
non'me·dic'i·nal

non'me·lo'di·ous
non·melt'ing
non·mem'ber
non·mer'can·tile
non'met·al·lif'er·ous
non'met·a·phys'i·cal
non·me·te·or'ic
non-Meth'o·dist
non·met'ri·cal
non'met·ro·pol'i·tan
non·mi'gra·to'ry
non·mil'i·tant
non·mil'i·tar'y
non·min'er·al
non'min·is·te'ri·al
non·mi·rac'u·lous
non'-Mo·ham'med·an
non'-Mon·go'li·an
non-Mor'mon
non·mor'al
non-Mos'lem
non·mo'tile
non'mu·nic'i·pal
non·mus'cu·lar
non·mys'ti·cal
non·myth'i·cal
non·na'tion·al
non·na'tion·al·is'tic
non·nat'u·ral
non·nav'i·ga·ble
non'ne·ces'si·ty
non'ne·go'tia·ble
non·neu'tral
non-Nor'man
non-Norse'
non·nu'cle·ar
non·nu'cle·at'ed
non·nu'tri·tious
non·nu'tri·tive
non'-o·be'di·ence
non'ob·lig'a·to'ry
non'ob·serv'ance
non'ob·serv'er
non'ob·struc'tion·ist
non'oc·cu·pa'tion·al
non'oc·cur'rence
non·o'dor·ous
non'of·fi'cial
non·op'er·at'ing
non·op'er·a'tion
non·op'er·a'tive
non-o'ri·en'tal
non·orth'o·dox
non·ox'i·diz'a·ble
non·ox'i·diz'ing
non·ox'y·gen·at'ed
non'pa·cif'ic
non·pac'i·fist
non·pa'gan
non·pal'a·tal
non·par'
non·par'al·lel
non·par·a·lyt'ic
non·par·a·sit'ic
non·par'ent
non·pa·ren'tal
non'par·ish·ion·er
non'par·lia·men'ta·ry
non'pa·ro'chi·al
non'par·tic'i·pant
non'par·tic'i·pat'ing
non'par·tic'i·pa'tion
non·pas'ser·ine
non'pa·ter'nal
non'pa·ter'nal·is'tic
non'path·o·gen'ic
non·pay'ing
non·pay'ment
non'per·form'ance
non'per·form'er
non·pe·ri·od'i·cal
non·per'ish·a·ble
non·per'ma·nent
non·per'me·a·ble
non·per·mis'si·ble
non'per·pen·dic'u·lar
non'per·pet'u·al
non'per·se·cu'tion
non'per·sist'ence

non'phil·o·soph'i·cal
non'phys'i·cal
non'plan'e·tar'y
non'plas'tic
non·po·et'ic
non·poi'son·ous
non·po'lar·iz'a·ble
non-Pol'ish
non'po·lit'i·cal
non·po'rous
non'-Por·tu·guese'
non'pred'a·to'ry
non'pre·dic'ta·ble
non'pref·er·en'tial
non'pre·hen'sile
non'prej·u·di'cial
non'pre·par'a·to'ry
non'prep·o·si'tion·al
non'-Pres·by·te'ri·an
non'pre·scrip'tive
non'pres·er·va'tion
non'pres·i·den'tial
non'priest'ly
non'pro·duc'ing
non'pro·fes'sion·al
non'pro·fes·so'ri·al
non'prof·it·eer'ing
non'pro·gres'sive
non'pro·hib'i·tive
non'pro·lif'ic
non'pro·mis'cu·ous
non'pro·phet'ic
non'pro·pri'e·tar'y
non'pro·scrip'tive
non'pro·tec'tive
non-Prot'es·tant
non-Prus'sian
non·psy'chic
non·punc'tur·a·ble
non·pun'ish·a·ble
non·pu'ru·lent
non·ra'cial
non·ra'di·at'ing
non·rad'i·cal
non·ra'ta·ble
non·ra'tion·al
non're·ac'tive
non're·al'i·ty
non're·cip'ro·cal
non're·cip'ro·cat'ing
non'rec·og·ni'tion
non're·cov'er·a·ble
non're·cur'rent
non're·fill'a·ble
non're·fu'el·ing
non're·gen'er·at'ing
non're·gen'er·a'tive
non·re'gent
non·reg'i·ment'ed
non·reg'is·tered
non·reg'is·tra·ble
non·reign'ing
non·rel'a·tive
non're·li'gious
non're·mu'ner·a'tive
non're·new'a·ble
non're·pay'a·ble
non're·pent'ance
non're·pet'i·tive
non're·pro·duc'tive
non·res'i·dence
non·res'i·den·cy
non·res'i·den'tial
non're·solv'a·ble
non·res'o·nant
non're·strict'ed
non·res·ur·rec'tion
non're·ten'tive
non're·tir'ing
non're·turn'a·ble
non're·veal'ing
non're·ver'sal
non're·vers'i·ble
non're·vert'i·ble
non'rev·o·lu'tion·ar'y
non're·volv'ing
non'rhe·tor'i·cal
non·rhym'ing

non·rhyth'mic
non·rig'id
non'rit·u·al·is'tic
non·rit'ual
non-Ro'man
non'ro·man'tic
non·roy'al
non'roy·al·ist
non·ru'ral
non-Rus'sian
non'sac·er·do'tal
non'sac·ra·men'tal
non·sa'cred
non·sal'a·ble
non·sal'a·ried
non'-Scan·di·na'vi·an
non'schis·mat'ic
non'scho·las'tic
non'sci·en·tif'ic
non·sea'son·al
non·se'cret
non·se·cre'tive
non·se·cre·to'ry
non·sec'tion·al
non·sec'u·lar
non·sed'en·tar'y
non'se·lec'tive
non-Sem'ite
non'-Se·mit'ic
non·sen'si·tive
non·sen'si·tized
non·sen'so·ry
non·sen'tient
non·se'rous
non·ser'vile
non·sex'u·al
non'-Shake·spear'i·an
non·shar'ing
non·shrink'a·ble
non·sink'a·ble
non·Slav'ic
non·sleep'er
non·slip'per
non·smok'er
non·smok'ing
non·so'cial
non'so·cial·is'tic
non·sol'id
non·sol'vent
non-So'vi·et
non-Span'ish
non·spark'ling
non·spe'cial·ized
non'spe·cif'ic
non'spec·tac'u·lar
non·spec'tral
non·spec'u·la'tive
non·spher'i·cal
non·spir'it·u·al
non·spir'it·u·ous
non·spon·ta'ne·ous
non·stain'a·ble
non·stain'ing
non·stand'ard·ized
non·start'er
non·start'ing
non·stat'ic
non·sta'tion·ar'y
non·sta·tis'ti·cal
non·stat'u·to'ry
non·stim'u·lat'ing
non·stra·te'gic
non·stretch'a·ble
non·strik'er
non·strik'ing
non·struc'tur·al
non'sub·mis'sive
non'sub·scrib'er
non'sub·scrib'ing
non·sub·stan'tial
non'suc·cess'
non'suc·cess'ive
non'sup·port'er
non'sup·port'ing
non·sup'pu·ra'tive
non'sus·tain'ing
non-Swed'ish
non-Swiss'

non'syl·lab'ic
non'sym·met'ri·cal
non'sym'pa·thiz'er
non'symp·to·mat'ic
non'syn'chro·nous
non'syn·tac'tic
non'sys·tem·at'ic
non·tar'nish·a·ble
non·tax'a·ble
non·teach'a·ble
non·tech'ni·cal
non·ter'mi·na·ble
non·ter'mi·nal
non·ter·ri·to'ri·al
non'tes·ta·men'ta·ry
non'tex'tu·al
non'the·at'ri·cal
non·tox'ic
non'trans·fer'a·ble
non·trop'i·cal
non'tu·ber'cu·lous
non-Turk'ish
non·typ'i·cal
non·u'nit'ed
non·us'er

non·u'ter·ine
non·u·til'i·tar'i·an
non·vas'cu·lar
non've·ne're·al
non·ven'om·ous
non·ver'bal
non·ver·nac'u·lar
non·ver'ti·cal
non·vet'er·an
non·vi'a·ble
non·vi'bra·to'ry
non'vi·o·la'tion
non·vir'u·lent
non·vis'u·al
non·vis'u·al·ized
non·vit're·ous
non·vo'cal
non·vo·cal'ic
non'vo·ca'tion·al
non·vol'a·tile
non'vol·can'ic
non·vol'un·tar'y
non·vot'ing
non·work'er
non·work'ing
non·yield'ing

non·ac·cept·ance (non'ək·sep'təns), *n.* failure or refusal to accept.

non·age (non'ij; nō'nij), *n.* **1.** a being under the legal age of responsibility; minority. **2.** an early stage; period before maturity. [< AF, < *non–* not (< L) + *age* AGE]

non·a·ge·nar·i·an (non'ə·jə·nâr'i·ən; nō'-nə–), *n.* person who is 90 years old or between 90 and 100 years old. —*adj.* 90 years old or between 90 and 100 years old. [< L *nonagenarius* containing ninety]

non·ag·gres·sion (non'ə·gresh'-ən), *n.* lack of aggression.

non·a·gon (non'ə·gon), *n.* a plane figure having nine angles and nine sides. [< L *nonus* ninth + Gk. *gonia* angle]

Nonagon

non·ap·pear·ance (non'ə·pir'əns), *n.* fact of not appearing; failure to appear.

non·at·tend·ance (non'ə·ten'dəns), *n.* failure to be present.

nonce (nons), *n.* **1.** the one or particular occasion or purpose. **2. for the nonce,** for the present time or occasion. [ME (*for then*) *ones* (for the) once, taken as (*for the*) *nones*]

nonce word, word formed and used for a single occasion. ➤ **nonce word.** Strictly, a word used but once so far as existing writing shows; a word coined for the occasion and not attaining general use. *Unblack* in *unblack herself* would be called a nonce word. As a rule arbitrary coinages do not stick.

non·cha·lance (non'shə·ləns; non'shə·läns'), *n.* cool unconcern; indifference.

non·cha·lant (non'shə·lənt; non'shə·länt'), *adj.* without enthusiasm; coolly unconcerned; indifferent. [< F, < *non–* not (< L) + *chaloir* be warm < L *calere*] —**non'cha·lant·ly,** *adv.* —**Syn.** cool, careless.

non·com (non'kom'), *n. Colloq.* a noncommissioned officer.

non·com·bat·ant (non'kəm·bat'ənt; –kom'bə·tənt), *n.* person who is not a fighter in the army or navy in time of war; civilian. Surgeons, nurses, chaplains, etc., are noncombatants even though with the army. —*adj.* not fighting; civilian in wartime.

non·com·mis·sioned (non'kə·mish'ənd), *adj.* without a commission; not commissioned. Corporals and sergeants are noncommissioned officers.

non·com·mit·tal (non'kə·mit'əl), *adj. Am.* not committing oneself; not saying yes or no: *"I will think it over" is a noncommittal answer.* —**non'com·mit'tal·ly,** *adv.*

non·com·pli·ance (non'kəm·pli'əns), *n.* fact of not complying; failure to comply.

non com·pos men·tis (non' kom'pəs men'-tis), *Latin.* mentally unable to manage one's affairs; insane.

non·con·duc·tor (non′kən·duk′tər), *n.* substance that does not readily conduct heat, electricity, etc. Rubber is a nonconductor of electricity.

non·con·form·ance (non′kən·fôr′məns), *n.* fact of not conforming; failure to conform.

non·con·form·ist (non′kən·fôr′mist), *n.* **1.** person who refuses to conform to an established church. **2.** Usually, **Nonconformist.** Protestant who is not a member of the Church of England. —**non′con·form′i·ty,** *n.*

non·co·öp·er·a·tion (non′kō·op′ər·ā′shən), *n.* **1.** failure or refusal to coöperate. **2.** refusal to coöperate with a government for political reasons.

non·de·script (non′di·skript), *adj.* not easily classified; not of any one particular kind. —*n.* a nondescript person or thing. [< NON- + L *descriptus* (to be) described]

none[1] (nun), *pron.* **1.** not any: *we have none of that paper left.* **2.** no one; not one: *none of these is a typical case.* **3.** (*pl. in use*) no persons or things: *none have arrived.* **4.** no part; nothing: *she has none of her mother's beauty.* —*adv.* **1.** to no extent; in no way; not at all: *our supply is none too great.* **2.** none the less, nevertheless. [OE *nān* < *ne* not + *ān* one] ⟩ **none, no one.** *None* is a single word, but *no one* is often used instead of *none*, for emphasis. *None* may be either singular or plural, and probably now is more common with the plural: *None of the witnesses was required. She tried on ten hats, but none of them were attractive.*

none[2] (nōn), *n.* **1.** the fifth of the seven canonical hours. **2.** prayers or service for it. [< F, < L *nona.* See NOON.]

non·en·ti·ty (non·en′tə·ti), *n., pl.* **-ties.** **1.** person or thing of little or no importance. **2.** something that does not exist.

non·es·sen·tial (non′ə·sen′shəl), *adj.* not essential; not necessary. —*n.* person or thing not essential.

none·such (nun′such′), *n.* person or thing without equal or parallel. Also, **nonsuch.**

non·fic·tion (non·fik′shən), *n.* prose literature that is not a novel, short story, or other form of writing based on imaginary people and events. Biographies and histories are nonfiction.

non·ful·fill·ment,   non·ful·fil·ment (non′fûl·fil′mənt), *n.* failure to fulfill; failure to be fulfilled.

non·in·ter·ven·tion (non′in·tər·ven′shən), *n.* **1.** failure or refusal to intervene. **2.** systematic avoidance of any interference by a nation in the affairs of other nations or of its own states, etc.

non·ju·ror (non·jûr′ər), *n.* one who refuses to take a required oath.

non·met·al (non′met′əl), *n. Chem.* an element not having the character of a metal. Carbon and nitrogen are nonmetals.

non·me·tal·lic (non′mə·tal′ik), *adj. Chem.* not like a metal. Carbon, oxygen, sulfur, and nitrogen are nonmetallic chemical elements.

non·mor·al (non·môr′əl; -mor′-), *adj.* having no relation to morality; neither moral nor immoral.

non·ob·jec·tive (non′əb·jek′tiv), *adj.* pertaining to a school of art which seeks to represent forms nonexistent in the physical world.

non·pa·reil (non′pə·rel′), *adj.* having no equal. —*n.* **1.** person or thing having no equal. **2.** size of type; 6-point. This line is in nonpareil. [< F, < *non-* not (< L) + *pareil* equal, ult. < L *par*]

non·par·ti·san,   non·par·ti·zan (non-pär′tə·zən), *adj.* **1.** not partisan. **2.** *Am.* not supporting, or controlled by, any of the regular political parties.

non·plus (non·plus′; non′plus), *v.,* **-plused, -plus·ing;** *esp. Brit.* **-plussed, -plus·sing,** *n.* —*v.* puzzle completely; make unable to say or do anything. —*n.* a state of being nonplused. [< L *non plus* no further] —**Syn.** *v.* confound, confuse, mystify, embarrass. —*n.* confusion.

non·pro·duc·tive (non′prə·duk′tiv), *adj.* **1.** not productive. **2.** not directly connected with production. —**non′pro·duc′tive·ness,** *n.*

non·prof·it (non·prof′it), *adj.* not for profit; without profit.

non·pros (non′pros′), *v.,* **-prossed, -pros·sing.** enter a judgment against (a plaintiff) in a suit when he does not appear to prosecute it. [short for L *non prosequitur* he does not prosecute]

non·res·i·dent (non·rez′ə·dənt), *adj.* **1.** not residing in a particular place. **2.** not residing where official duties require one to reside. —*n.* a nonresident person.

non·re·sist·ant (non′ri·zis′tənt), *adj.* not resisting; passively obedient. —*n.* one who does not resist authority or force; one who maintains that violence should never be resisted by force. —**non′re·sist′ance,** *n.*

non·re·stric·tive (non′ri·strik′tiv), *adj.* (of a modifier) adding descriptive detail.

non·sched·uled (non′skej′ůld), *adj.* not operating or proceeding according to a regular schedule: *a nonscheduled airline.*

non·sec·tar·i·an (non′sek·tãr′i·ən), *adj.* not connected with any religious denomination.

non·sense (non′sens), *n.* words, ideas, or acts without meaning; foolish talk or doings; a plan or suggestion that is foolish. —**Syn.** foolishness.

non·sen·si·cal (non·sen′sə·kəl), *adj.* foolish; absurd. —**non·sen′si·cal·ly,** *adv.* —**non·sen′si·cal·ness,** *n.* —**Syn.** senseless, silly, preposterous.

non se·qui·tur (non sek′wə·tər), inference or conclusion that does not follow from the premises. [< L, it does not follow]

non·sked (non′sked′), *n.* a non-scheduled airline or non-scheduled airlines collectively.

non·skid (non′skid′), *adj.* made to resist skidding: *nonskid tires.*

non·stop (non′stop′), *adj., adv.* without stopping.

non·such (nun′such′), *n.* nonesuch.

non·suit (non′sūt′), *n. Law.* a judgment given against a person beginning a lawsuit who neglects to prosecute, or who fails to show a legal case, or who fails to bring sufficient evidence.

non·sup·port (non′sə·pôrt′; -pōrt′), *n.* **1.** lack of support. **2.** failure to provide for someone for whom one is legally responsible.

non·un·ion (non·ūn′yən), *adj.* **1.** not belonging to a trade union. **2.** not following trade-union rules. **3.** not recognizing or favoring trade unions. —**non·un′ion·ism,** *n.* —**non·un′ion·ist,** *n.*

non·vot·er (non·vōt′ər), *n.* person who does not vote.

noo·dle[1] (nü′dəl), *n.* a mixture of flour and water, or flour and eggs, like macaroni, but made in flat strips. [< G *nudel*]

noo·dle[2] (nü′dəl), *n. Slang.* head.

nook (nůk), *n.* **1.** a cozy little corner. **2.** a hidden spot; sheltered place. [ME *noke*]

noon (nün), *n.* **1.** twelve o'clock in the daytime; middle of the day. **2.** *Poetic.* midnight. **3.** the brightest, best, or highest point or period. —*adj.* of noon. [< L *nona* (*hora*) ninth (hour), 3 p.m.; the meaning shifted with a change in time of church service]

noon·day (nün′dā′), *n., adj.* noon.

no one, no-one (nō′wun′), no person; nobody.

noon·time (nün′tīm′),   **noon·tide** (-tīd′), *n.* noon.

noose (nüs), *n., v.,* **noosed, noos·ing.** —*n.* **1.** loop with a slip knot that tightens as the string or rope is pulled. **2.** snare. —*v.* **1.** make a noose with; tie a noose in. **2.** catch with a noose. **3.** snare. [prob. < OF < L *nodus* knot]

Noose

no-par (nō′pär′), *adj.* having no set face value: *a no-par share of stock.*

nor[1] (nôr; *unstressed* nər), *conj.* and not; or not; neither; and not either. *Nor* is used with a preceding *neither* or negative: *not a boy nor a girl stirred.* [OE (unstressed) *nā*(*hwæ*)*ther* < *ne* not + *ā*(*hwæ*)*ther* either. See OR.]

nor′, nor[2] (nôr), *n., adj., adv.* north.

Nor., **1.** North. **2.** Norway.

Nor·dic (nôr′dik), *adj.* designating, belonging

to, or pertaining to a race or type characterized by tall stature, blond hair, blue eyes, and long heads. —*n.* member of such a race. Scandinavians are Nordics. [< F, < *nord* north < Gmc.]

Nor·folk (nôr′fək), *n.* seaport in SE Virginia.

Norfolk jacket, a loose coat with a belt.

norm (nôrm), *n.* standard for a certain group; type; model; pattern: *in mathematics this class is above the norm for the senior year.* [< L *norma*]

nor·mal (nôr′məl), *adj.* **1.** of the usual standard; regular; usual: *the normal temperature of the human body is 98.6 degrees.* **2.** usual and desirable. **3.** not subjected to the treatment given to an experimental group. **4.** *Geom.* being at right angles. —*n.* **1.** the usual state or level: *two pounds above normal.* **2.** *Geom.* line or plane that is at right angles to another. [< L *normalis.* See NORM.] —**nor·mal·i·ty** (nôr·mal′ə·ti), **nor′mal·ness,** *n.* —**Syn.** *adj.* **1.** natural, typical, ordinary, common, everyday.

nor·mal·cy (nôr′məl·si), *n.* normal condition.

nor·mal·ize (nôr′məl·īz), *v.,* –ized, –iz·ing. make normal. —**nor′mal·i·za′tion,** *n.*

nor·mal·ly (nôr′məl·i), *adv.* in the normal way; regularly; if things are normal.

normal school, school where people are trained to be teachers.

Nor·man (nôr′mən), *n.* **1.** member of the mixed race, descended from the Scandinavians who settled in Normandy and from the French. **2.** one of the Scandinavian ancestors of these people; Northman. —*adj.* of the Normans or Normandy.

Norman Conquest, conquest of England by the Normans in 1066.

Nor·man·dy (nôr′mən·di), *n.* district in NW France. At one time Normandy was a duchy; later it was a province.

Nor·man-French (nôr′mən-french′), *n.* Anglo-French.

Norse (nôrs), *adj.* **1.** of or having to do with ancient Scandinavia, its people, or their language. **2.** of or having to do with Norway or its people. —*n.* **1.** (*pl. in use*) **a.** people of ancient Scandinavia; Norsemen; Northmen. **b.** Norwegians. **2.** language of the ancient Scandinavians; Old Norse. **3.** language of Norway.

Norse·man (nôrs′mən), *n., pl.* –men. member of a tall, blond race that lived in ancient Scandinavia; Northman. The Vikings were Norsemen.

north (nôrth), *n.* **1.** direction to which a compass needle points; direction to the right as one faces the setting sun. **2.** Also, **North,** part of any country toward the north. **3. North,** *Am.* the northern part of the United States; the States north of Maryland, the Ohio River, and Missouri. **4. North,** northern England (beyond the Humber). **5.** *Poetic.* the north wind. —*adj.* **1.** lying toward or situated in the north. **2.** originating in or coming from the north. **3. North,** in the northern part; northern: *North China.* —*adv.* **1.** toward the north. **2.** in the north. [OE]

North Africa, a region in the northern part of the continent of Africa, especially those countries bordering on or N of the Sahara.

North America, the northern continent of the Western Hemisphere. The United States, Mexico, and Canada are some of the countries in North America. —**North American.**

North Borneo, former British colony in NE Borneo. Now called Sabah.

North Cape, point of land in the Arctic Ocean at the N tip of Norway.

North Car·o·li·na (kar′ə·lī′nə), a Southern State of the United States. *Capital:* Raleigh. *Abbrev.:* N.C. —**North Car·o·lin·i·an** (kar′ə·lin′i·ən), *Am.*

North Da·ko·ta (də·kō′tə), a Middle Western State of the United States. *Capital:* Bismarck. *Abbrev.:* N. Dak., N.D. —**North Da·ko′tan,** *Am.*

north·east (nôrth′ēst′; *Naut.* nôr′-), *adj.* **1.** halfway between north and east. **2.** lying toward or situated in the northeast. **3.** originating in or coming from the northeast: *a northeast wind.* **4.** directed toward the northeast. —*n.* **1.** a north-

east direction. **2.** place that is in the northeast part or direction. —*adv.* **1.** toward the northeast. **2.** from the northeast. **3.** in the northeast.

north·east·er (nôrth′ēs′tər; *Naut.* nôr′-), *n.* wind or storm from the northeast.

north·east·er·ly (nôrth′ēs′tər·li; *Naut.* nôr′-), *adj., adv.* toward or from the northeast.

north·east·ern (nôrth′ēs′tərn; *Naut.* nôr′-), *adj.* **1.** toward the northeast. **2.** from the northeast. **3.** of or pertaining to the northeast.

north·east·ward (nôrth′ēst′wərd; *Naut.* nôr′-), *adv.* Also, **north′east′wards.** toward the northeast. —*adj.* **1.** toward the northeast. **2.** northeast. —*n.* northeast.

north·east·ward·ly (nôrth′ēst′wərd·li; *Naut.* nôr′-), *adj., adv.* **1.** toward the northeast. **2.** of winds, from the northeast.

north·er (nôr′thər), *n.* wind or storm from the north.

north·er·ly (nôr′thər·li), *adj., adv.* **1.** toward the north. **2.** from the north: *a northerly wind.* —**north·er·li·ness** (nôr′thər·li·nis), *n.*

north·ern (nôr′thərn), *adj.* **1.** toward the north. **2.** from the north. **3.** of or in the north. **4. Northern,** *Am.* of or in the N part of the United States. —**north·ern·most** (nôr′thərn·mōst), *adj.*

North·ern·er (nôr′thər·nər), *n.* **1.** *Am.* native or inhabitant of the North of the United States. **2.** northerner, native or inhabitant of the north.

Northern Hemisphere, the half of the earth that is north of the equator.

Northern Ireland, a self-governing district in NE Ireland that is a part of the United Kingdom of Great Britain and Northern Ireland.

northern lights, the aurora borealis.

Northern Rhodesia, former British protectorate in SE Africa. Now called Zambia.

North Island, the northernmost of the two main islands of New Zealand.

North Korea, country in Korea under Communist control.

north·land (nôrth′lənd), *n.* land in the north; the northern part of a country. —**north′land·er,** *n.*

North·man (nôrth′mən), *n., pl.* –men. **1.** Norseman. **2.** native or inhabitant of northern Europe.

North Pole, northern end of the earth's axis.

North Sea, a part of the Atlantic, E of Great Britain, W of Denmark, and S of Norway.

North Star, the bright star almost directly above the North Pole.

North·um·bri·an (nôr·thum′bri·ən), *n.* a dialect of Old English spoken in Northumbria, ancient kingdom in N England.

North Vietnam, country in Indochina under Communist control.

north·ward (nôrth′wərd; *Naut.* nôr′thərd), *adv.* Also, **north′wards.** toward the north. —*adj.* **1.** toward the north. **2.** north. —*n.* north.

north·ward·ly (nôrth′wərd·li), *adj., adv.* **1.** toward the north. **2.** of winds, from the north.

north·west (nôrth′west′; *Naut.* nôr′-), *adj.* **1.** halfway between north and west. **2.** lying toward or situated in the northwest. **3.** originating in or coming from the northwest: *a northwest wind.* **4.** directed toward the northwest. —*n.* **1.** a northwest direction. **2.** place that is in the northwest part or direction. **3. Northwest,** *Am.* Washington and Oregon. —*adv.* **1.** toward the northwest. **2.** from the northwest. **3.** in the northwest.

north·west·er (nôrth′wes′tər; *Naut.* nôr′-), *n.* wind or storm from the northwest.

north·west·er·ly (nôrth′wes′tər·li; *Naut.* nôr′-), *adj., adv.* **1.** toward the northwest. **2.** from the northwest.

north·west·ern (nôrth′wes′tərn; *Naut.* nôr′-), *adj.* **1.** toward or from the northwest. **2.** of the northwest. **3. Northwestern,** *Am.* of, having to do with, or in Washington or Oregon.

Northwest Territories, division of N Canada, between the Yukon Territory and Hudson Bay.

Northwest Territory, the former name for

lands now forming Ohio, Indiana, Illinois, Michigan, Wisconsin, and part of Minnesota.

north·west·ward (nôrth′west′wərd; *Naut.* nôr′-), *adv.* Also, **north′west′wards.** toward the northwest. —*adj.* **1.** toward the northwest. **2.** northwest. —*n.* northwest.

north·west·ward·ly (nôrth′west′wərd·li; *Naut.* nôr′-), *adj., adv.* **1.** toward the northwest. **2.** of winds, from the northwest.

Norw., Norway; Norwegian.

Nor·way (nôr′wā), *n.* a mountainous country in N Europe, west and north of Sweden.

Nor·we·gian (nôr·wē′jən), *adj.* of Norway, its people, or their language. —*n.* **1.** native or inhabitant of Norway. **2.** language of Norway.

nor′west·er (nôr·wes′tər), *n. Am.* a heavy, waterproof, oilskin coat worn by seamen.

Nor·wich (nôr′ij; -ich; nor′-), *n.* city in E England.

Nos., numbers.

nose (nōz), *n., v.,* **nosed, nos·ing.** —*n.* **1.** part of the face or head just above the mouth, serving as the opening for breathing and as the organ of smell. **2.** the organ of smell. **3.** sense of smell: *a dog with a good nose.* **4.** faculty for perceiving or detecting: *a reporter must have a nose for news.* **5.** part that stands out, as the bow of a ship or airplane. **6.** lead by the nose, have complete control over. **7.** pay through the nose, pay a great deal too much. **8.** turn up one's nose at, treat with contempt or scorn. **9.** under one's nose, in plain sight; very easy to notice. —*v.* **1.** discover by smell; smell out. **2.** smell; sniff. **3.** rub with the nose. **4.** push with the nose or forward end. **5.** push (one's way): *the boat nosed carefully between the rocks.* **6.** search (for); pry (into). **7.** nose out, find out by looking around quietly or secretly. [OE *nosu*]

nose bag, bag containing food, to be hung on a horse's head.

nose·band (nōz′band′), *n.* part of a bridle that goes over the animal's nose.

nose·bleed (nōz′blēd′), *n.* a bleeding from the nose.

nose cone, the front section of a ballistic missile, designed to carry a bomb to a target or instruments or a man into space. The nose cone usually separates from the rest of the missile after the fuel runs out.

nose dive, 1. a swift plunge straight downward by an airplane, etc. **2.** a sudden, sharp drop.

nose-dive (nōz′dīv′), *v.,* **-dived, -div·ing.** take a nose dive.

nose·gay (nōz′gā′), *n.* bouquet.

nose·piece (nōz′pēs′), *n.* **1.** part of a helmet that covers and protects the nose. **2.** noseband.

no show, *Am.* person who neglects to cancel his airline reservation after he decides not to make the trip.

nos·tal·gia (nos·tal′jə), *n.* homesickness. [< NL, < Gk. *nostos* homecoming + *algos* pain] —**nos·tal′gic,** *adj.*

nos·tril (nos′trəl), *n.* either of the two openings in the nose. Smells come into the sensitive parts of the nose through the nostrils. [OE *nosthyrl* < *nosu* nose + *thyrel* hole]

nos·trum (nos′trəm), *n.* **1.** medicine made by the person who is selling it; quack remedy; patent medicine. **2.** a pet scheme for producing wonderful results; a cure-all. [< L, ours, because it is usually prepared by the person recommending it]

nos·y, nos·ey (nōz′i), *adj.,* **nos·i·er, nos·i·est.** *Colloq.* prying; inquisitive.

not (not), *adv.* word that says no; a negative: *that is not true.* [unstressed var. of *nought*]

no·ta be·ne (nō′tə bē′nē), *Latin.* note well; observe what follows; take notice.

no·ta·ble (nō′tə·bəl), *adj.* worthy of notice; striking; remarkable: *a notable event.* —*n.* person who is notable: *many notables came to the President's reception.* [< L, < *notare* to note] —**no′ta·ble·ness, no′ta·bil′i·ty,** *n.* —**no′ta·bly,** *adv.* —**Syn.** *adj.* memorable, conspicuous, famous, signal.

no·ta·rize (nō′tə·rīz), *v.,* **-rized, -riz·ing.** certify (a contract, deed, will, etc.).

no·ta·ry pub·lic (nō′tə·ri), or **notary,** *n., pl.* **no·tar·ies public; notaries.** a public officer authorized to certify deeds and contracts, to record the fact that a certain person swears that something is true, and to attend to other legal matters. [< L *notarius* clerk, ult. < *nota* note] —**no·tar·i·al** (nō·târ′i·əl), *adj.*

no·ta·tion (nō·tā′shən), *n.* **1.** set of signs or symbols used to represent numbers, quantities, or other values: *the Arabic notation (1, 2, 3, 4, etc.).* **2.** the representing of numbers, quantities, or other values by symbols or signs. Music has a special system of notation, and so has chemistry. **3.** note to assist memory; record; jotting: *make a notation on the margin.* **4.** act of noting. —**no·ta′tion·al,** *adj.*

notch (noch), *n.* **1.** a V-shaped nick or cut made in an edge or on a curving surface: *the Indians cut notches on a stick to keep count of numbers.* **2.** *Am.* a deep, narrow pass or gap between mountains. **3.** *Colloq.* grade; step; degree. —*v.* **1.** make a notch or notches in. **2.** record by notches; score; tally. [< F *oche* < OF *oschier* to notch; *an och* taken as *a noch*] —**notched,** *adj.* —**notch′er,** *n.* —**Syn.** *n.* **1.** dent, indentation. —*v.* **1.** nick, dent.

note (nōt), *n., v.,* **not·ed, not·ing.** —*n.* **1.** words written down to remind one of something: *take notes of a lecture.* **2.** notice; heed: *take note of.* **3.** piece of information; comment; remark. **4.** a very short letter. **5.** letter from one government to another; diplomatic or official communication in writing. **6.** a single sound of definite pitch made by a musical instrument or a voice. **7.** *Music.* **a.** a written sign to show the pitch and length of a sound. **b.** a black or white key of a piano or other instrument. **8.** a bird's song or call. **9.** song; melody; tune. **10.** a significant sound or way of expression: *a note of anxiety in her voice.* **11.** sign, token, or proof of genuineness; characteristic or distinguishing feature. **12.** distinction, importance, or consequence: *a man of note.* **13.** a written promise to pay a certain sum of money at a certain time. **14.** certificate of a government or bank passing current as money. **15.** compare notes, exchange ideas or opinions. —*v.* **1.** write down as a thing to be remembered. **2.** observe carefully; give attention to; take notice of. **3.** mention specially. **4.** indicate; signify, or denote. [< OF < L *nota* mark] —**note′less,** *adj.* —**not′er,** *n.* —**Syn.** *n.* **2.** observation. **5.** message. **11.** mark, symbol, character. **12.** significance. —*v.* **1.** record. **2.** regard.

Notes in music:
A, whole note;
B, half note;
C, quarter note;
D, eighth note.

note·book (nōt′bùk′), *n.* book in which to write notes.

not·ed (nōt′id), *adj.* especially noticed; conspicuous; well-known; celebrated; famous: *Samson was noted for his strength, Shakespeare is the most noted English author.* —**not′ed·ly,** *adv.* —**not′ed·ness,** *n.* —**Syn.** renowned, distinguished. —**Ant.** obscure, unknown.

note paper, paper used for writing letters.

note·wor·thy (nōt′wėr′thi), *adj.* worthy of notice; remarkable: *a noteworthy achievement.* —**note′wor′thi·ly,** *adv.* —**note′wor′thi·ness,** *n.*

noth·ing (nuth′ing), *n.* **1.** not anything; no thing: *nothing arrived by mail.* **2.** thing that does not exist: *create a world out of nothing.* **3.** thing of no importance or significance; person of no importance: *people regard him as a nothing.* **4.** zero; naught. **5.** make nothing of, a. be unable to understand. b. fail to use or do. c. treat as unimportant or worthless. **6.** think nothing of, a. consider as easy to do. b. treat as unimportant or worthless. —*adv.* not at all: *be nothing wiser than before.* [< *no* + *thing*] ➤ See **nobody** for usage note.

noth·ing·ness (nuth′ing·nis), *n.* **1.** nonexistence. **2.** worthlessness. **3.** an unimportant or worthless thing. **4.** unconsciousness.

no·tice (nō′tis), *n., v.,* **-ticed, -tic·ing. 1.** observation; heed; attention: *escape one's notice.* **2.** information; warning: *the whistle blew to give notice of quitting time.* **3.** a written or printed sign; paper posted in a public place. 4. a warning that one will end an agreement with another at a certain time: *the servant gave notice.* 5. favorable attention. 6. paragraph or article about something: *the new book got a favorable notice.* 7. **take notice, give notice; observe; see.** —*v.* 1. take notice of; give attention to; perceive: *I noticed a big difference.* 2. give notice to; serve with a notice. 3. mention; refer to. [< F < L, < *notus* known] —Syn. *n.* 1. regard, note. 2. notification. 3. bulletin, placard. –*v.* 1. see, mark, note, heed.

no·tice·a·ble (nō′tis·ə·bəl), *adj.* 1. easily seen or noticed. 2. worth noticing. —**no′tice·a·bly,** *adv.* —Syn. 1. discernible, conspicuous.

no·ti·fi·ca·tion (nō′tə·fə·kā′shən), *n.* 1. a notifying. 2. notice: *have you received a notification of the meeting?*

no·ti·fy (nō′tə·fī), *v.,* –fied, –fy·ing. 1. give notice to; let know; inform; announce to: *notify us when there will be a test.* 2. make known; give notice of. [< F < L, < *notus* known + *facere* make] —**no′ti·fi′er,** *n.* —Syn. 1. apprise, acquaint. 2. proclaim, publish.

no·tion (nō′shən), *n.* 1. idea; understanding: *he has no notion of what I mean.* 2. opinion; belief: *one common notion is that red hair means a quick temper.* 3. intention: *he has no notion of risking his money.* 4. a foolish idea or opinion. 5. **notions,** *Am.* small useful articles; pins, needles, thread, tape, etc. [< L *notio,* ult. < *noscere* know] —Syn. 1. concept, impression.

no·tion·al (nō′shən·əl), *adj.* 1. having to do with ideas or opinions. 2. in one's imagination or thought only; not real. 3. *Am.* full of notions; having strange notions; fanciful. —**no′tion·al·ly,** *adv.*

no·to·ri·e·ty (nō′tə·rī′ə·ti), *n., pl.* –ties. 1. a being famous for something bad; ill fame: *a crime or scandal brings much notoriety to those involved in it.* 2. being widely known. 3. a well-known person.

no·to·ri·ous (nō·tô′ri·əs; –tō′–), *adj.* 1. well-known because of something bad; having a bad reputation. 2. well-known. [< Med.L *notorius* < L *notus* known] —**no·to′ri·ous·ly,** *adv.* —**no·to′ri·ous·ness,** *n.* ➤ **Notorious** means well-known for unsavory reasons: *a notorious cheat; famous* is well-known-for accomplishment or excellence: *a famous writer or aviator.*

Not·ting·ham (not′ing·əm), *n.* city in C England.

not·with·stand·ing (not′with·stan′ding; –with–), *prep.* in spite of: *he bought it notwithstanding the high price.* —*conj.* 1. in spite of the fact that: *notwithstanding there was need for haste, he still delayed.* 2. notwithstanding that, though. —*adv.* in spite of it; nevertheless: *it is raining; but I shall go, notwithstanding.*

nou·gat (nü′gət; –gä), *n.* a kind of soft candy containing nuts. [< F < Pr., ult. < L *nux* nut]

nought (nôt), *n.* naught. —*adj.* Archaic. of no value. Also, **naught.** —*adv.* Archaic. in no way; not at all. Also, **naught.** [see NAUGHT]

noun (noun), *n.* Gram. word used as the name of a person, place, thing, quality, event, etc. Words like *John, table, school, kindness, skill,* and *party* are nouns. —*adj.* used as a noun. [< OF *nom* < L *nomen* name] —**noun′al,** *adj.* ➤ **forms of nouns.** Nouns may be single words or compound words (*bathroom, bookcase, logrolling*) or they may be group words: *high school, hub cap, go-getter, motorcar.* Such nouns are given as main entries. English nouns change their forms to make the plural, most of them adding –s or –es: *boys, kindnesses, manufacturers.* Usually look under the singular form to get the meaning of a plural noun, and for questions about their use. English nouns change their form for case only in the genitive or possessive, typically by adding '*s: boy's, Harriet's.* Look under the uninflected form. A very few nouns in English have different forms for the masculine and feminine gender: *confidant— confidante, executor—executrix, actor—actress.* Such nouns are separately entered.

nour·ish (nėr′ish), *v.* 1. make grow, or keep alive and well, with food; feed: *milk nourishes a baby.* 2. maintain; foster: *nourish a hope.* [< OF *noriss–* < L *nutrire* feed] —**nour′ish·er,** *n.* —**nour′ish·ing,** *adj.* —**nour′ish·ing·ly,** *adv.* —Syn. 1. nurse, nurture. 2. support, encourage.

nour·ish·ment (nėr′ish·mənt), *n.* 1. food. 2. a nourishing or being nourished.

nou·veau riche (nü·vō rēsh′), *pl.* **nou·veaux riches** (nü·vō rēsh′). French. one who has recently become rich; often, one who makes a vulgar display of his wealth.

Nov., November.

no·va (nō′və), *n., pl.* –vae (–vē), –vas. Astronomy. a star that suddenly glows brightly, then gradually fades to its normal brightness. [< L, fem. of *novus* new]

No·va Sco·tia (nō′və skō′shə), province in SE Canada consisting chiefly of a peninsula that extends into the Atlantic. —**No′va Sco′tian.**

nov·el (nov′əl), *adj.* of a new kind or nature; strange; new: *flying gives people a novel sensation.* —*n.* story with characters and a plot, usually long enough to fill one or more volumes. [< Ital., < L *novella* new things, speech showing originality] —**nov′el·is′tic,** *adj.* —**nov′el·is′ti·cal·ly,** *adv.* —Syn. *adj.* unfamiliar. –*n.* tale, romance, narrative.

nov·el·ette (nov′əl·et′), *n.* a short novel, usually not long enough to fill a volume by itself.

nov·el·ist (nov′əl·ist), *n.* writer of novels.

no·vel·la (nō·vel′ə; *Ital.* nō·vel′lä), *n., pl.* –le (–lā). a short story with a simple plot: *Boccaccio's novelle are famous.* [< Ital. See NOVEL.]

nov·el·ty (nov′əl·ti), *n., pl.* –ties. 1. newness: *after the novelty of washing dishes wore off, Mary did not want to do it any more.* 2. a new or unusual thing: *staying up late was a novelty to the children.* 3. **novelties,** small, unusual articles; toys, cheap jewelry, etc. —Syn. 1. recentness, freshness. 2. innovation, rarity, curiosity.

No·vem·ber (nō·vem′bər), *n.* the 11th month of the year, having 30 days. [< L, < *novem* nine; from the order of the early Roman calendar]

no·ve·na (nō·vē′nə), *n., pl.* –nae (–nē). in the Roman Catholic Church, a religious exercise consisting of prayers or services on nine days, or sometimes nine corresponding days in consecutive months. [< Med.L, ult. < L *novem* nine]

nov·ice (nov′is), *n.* 1. one who is new to what he is doing; beginner. 2. person who is received into a religious group on trial before taking vows. Before becoming a monk or a nun, a person is a novice. [< OF < L, < *novus* new] —Syn. 1. tyro, apprentice.

no·vi·ti·ate, no·vi·ci·ate (nō·vish′i·it; –āt), *n.* 1. period of trial and preparation in a religious order. 2. novice. 3. house or rooms occupied by religious novices. 4. state or period of being a beginner in anything.

no·vo·caine, no·vo·cain (nō′və·kān), *n.* 1. an alkaloid compound, used as a local anesthetic. 2. **Novocain,** a trademark for this compound. [< L *novus* new + E (co)*caine*]

now (nou), *adv.* 1. at the present time: *he is here now.* 2. by this time: *the case is probably settled now.* 3. at once: *do it now!* 4. then; next: *if passed, the bill now goes to the president.* 5. at the time referred to: *the clock now struck three.* 6. a little while ago: *I just now saw him.* 7. under the present circumstances; as things are; as it is: *I would believe almost anything now.* 8. **Now** is also used to introduce or emphasize: *oh, come now!* —*n.* the present; this time. —*conj.* since; inasmuch as. —*interj.* be careful! please! [OE *nū*]

now·a·days (nou′ə·dāz′), *adv.* at the present day; in these times: *nowadays people travel in automobiles.* —*n.* the present day; these times.

no·way (nō′wā), **no·ways** (–wāz), *adv.* nowise.

no·where (nō′hwãr), *adv.* in no place; at no place; to no place: *go nowhere.* ➤ **nowhere near.** Colloquial and informal: *It was a good score but nowhere near as large as we'd hoped for.* For-

mal: *not so large as* or *not nearly so large as.*
See **nobody** for another usage note.

no·wise (nō′wiz), *adv.* in no way; not at all.

nox·ious (nok′shəs), *adj.* very harmful; poisonous: *noxious fumes, noxious teachings.* [< L, < *noxa* hurt] —**nox′ious·ly,** *adv.* —**nox′ious·ness,** *n.* —Syn. hurtful, unhealthful, deadly. —Ant. healthful, wholesome, beneficial.

noz·zle (noz′əl), *n.* tip put on a hose, etc., forming an outlet. [dim. of *nose*]

N.S., Nova Scotia.

N.T., New Testament.

nth (enth), *adj.* **1.** last in the series 1, 2, 3, 4 . . . n; being of the indefinitely large or small amount denoted by *n.* **2.** to the nth degree or power, a. to any degree or power. b. to the utmost.

nt. wt., net weight.

nu (nū; nū̇), *n.* the 13th letter (N, ν) of the Greek alphabet.

nu·ance (nü·äns′, nū̇-; nü̇′äns, nū̇′–), *n.* **1.** shade of expression, meaning, feeling, etc. **2.** shade of color or tone. [< F]

nub (nub), *n.* **1.** knob; protuberance. **2.** *Am., Colloq.* point or gist of anything. [appar. var. of *knob*]

nub·bin (nub′ən), *n.* **1.** a small lump or piece. **2.** *Am.* a small or imperfect ear of corn. [dim. of *nub*]

Nu·bi·a (nü′bi·ə; nū̇′–), *n.* region in NE Africa S of Egypt and bordering on the Red Sea. —**Nu′bi·an,** *n., adj.*

nu·bile (nü′bəl; nū̇′–), *adj.* old enough to be married; marriageable. [< L, < *nubere* take a husband] —**nu·bil′i·ty,** *n.*

nu·cle·ar (nü′kli·ər; nū̇′–), *adj.* forming a nucleus; having to do with nuclei.

nuclear fission, *Physics, Chem.* fission (def. 3).

nuclear fuel, *Physics.* a fissile substance which will sustain a chain reaction.

nuclear fusion, *Physics.* fusion (def. 4).

nuclear physics, branch of physics that is concerned with atoms and their nuclear structure.

nuclear reactor, *Physics.* reactor.

nu·cle·ate (*v.* nü′kli·āt, nū̇′–; *adj.* nü′kli·it, –āt, nū̇′–), *v.,* –**at·ed,** –**at·ing,** *adj.* —*v.* form into a nucleus or around a nucleus. —*adj.* having a nucleus. —**nu′cle·a′tion,** *n.* —**nu′cle·a′tor,** *n.*

nu·cle·on·ics (nü′kli·on′iks; nū̇′–), *n.* study and science of the behavior and characteristics of nucleons.

nu·cle·ons (nü′kli·onz; nū̇′–), *n.pl.* protons and neutrons of an atomic nucleus.

nu·cle·us (nü′kli·əs; nū̇′–), *n., pl.* –**cle·i** (–kli·ī), –**cle·us·es. 1.** a beginning to which additions are to be made. **2.** a central part or thing around which other parts or things are collected. **3.** *Physics.* a proton, or group of protons and electrons (sometimes including alpha particles), forming the central part of an atom and carrying a positive charge. **4.** *Chem.* the basic arrangement of atoms in a particular compound; kernel. **5.** *Biol.* an active body lying within the protoplasm of a cell of an animal or a plant, without which the cell cannot grow and divide. **6.** *Astron.* the dense central part of a comet's head. [< L, < *nux* nut] —Syn. **2.** center, core, heart.

nude (nüd; nū̇d), *adj.* naked; unclothed; bare. —*n.* **1.** a naked figure in painting, sculpture, or photography. **2.** the nude, a. the naked figure. b. a naked condition. [< L *nudus*] —**nude′ly,** *adv.* —**nude′ness,** *n.*

nudge (nuj), *v.,* **nudged, nudg·ing,** *n.* —*v.* push slightly; jog with the elbow to attract attention, etc. —*n.* a slight push or jog.

nud·ism (nüd′iz·əm; nū̇d′–), *n.* practice of going naked for health or as a fad. —**nud′ist,** *n., adj.*

nu·di·ty (nü′də·ti; nū̇′–), *n., pl.* –**ties. 1.** nakedness. **2.** something naked.

nu·ga·to·ry (nü′gə·tô′ri; –tō′–; nū̇′–), *adj.* **1.** trifling; worthless. **2.** ineffective; useless. [< L, < *nugari* to trifle < *nugae* trifles]

nug·get (nug′it), *n.* **1.** lump. **2.** lump of native gold. **3.** anything valuable: *nuggets of wisdom.* [? < *nug* lump]

nui·sance (nü′səns; nū̇′–), *n.* thing or person that annoys, troubles, offends, or is disagreeable: *flies are a nuisance.* [< OF, < *nuire* harm < L *nocere*] —Syn. annoyance, plague, trouble, inconvenience.

nuisance tax, tax that is annoying because it is collected in very small amounts from the consumer.

null (nul), *adj.* **1.** not binding; of no effect; as if not existing: *a promise obtained by force is legally null.* **2.** unimportant; useless; meaningless. **3.** not any; zero. **4. null and void,** without force or effect; worthless. [< L, < *ne*- not + *ullus* any]

nul·li·fy (nul′ə·fī), *v.,* –**fied,** –**fy·ing. 1.** make not binding; render void: *nullify a law.* **2.** make unimportant, useless, or meaningless; destroy; cancel. [< L, < *nullus* not any + *facere* make] —**nul′li·fi·ca′tion,** *n.* —**nul′li·fi′er,** *n.* —Syn. **1.** annul, repeal.

nul·li·ty (nul′ə·ti), *n., pl.* –**ties. 1.** futility; nothingness. **2.** a mere nothing. **3.** something of no legal force or validity.

Num., Numbers.

numb (num), *adj.* having lost the power of feeling or moving: *numb with cold.* —*v.* **1.** make numb. **2.** dull the feelings of: *numbed with grief.* [ult. < OE *numen* taken, seized] —**numb′ing·ly,** *adv.* —**numb′ly,** *adv.* —**numb′ness,** *n.* —Syn. *adj.* deadened, insensible, benumbed, paralyzed.

num·ber (num′bər), *n.* **1.** word or symbol used in counting; numeral. Two, fourteen, twenty-six, second, fourteenth, twenty-sixth, 2, 14, and 26 are numbers. **2.** a particular numeral that shows a thing's place in a series or identifies it: *a telephone number.* **3.** amount of units; sum; total: *the number of your fingers is ten.* **4.** quantity: *a number of reasons.* **5.** collection or company: *the number of saints.* **6.** one of a numbered series; single part of a program, etc. **7.** a single issue of a periodical. **8.** *Colloq.* a particular item or individual from a group or kind: *the dress she bought was a pretty little number.* **9.** *Gram.* property or feature of words that indicates whether they refer to one, or more than one, person or thing. *Boy, ox,* and *this* are in the singular number; *boys, oxen,* and *these* are in the plural number. **10.** form or group of forms indicating this. **11.** a number of, several; many. **12. numbers, a.** arithmetic. **b.** many: *numbers were turned away.* **c.** numerical preponderance. **d.** poetry. **e.** group of musical notes or measures. —*v.* **1.** mark with a number; assign a number to; distinguish with a number: *the pages of this book are numbered.* **2.** be able to show; have: *this city numbers a million inhabitants.* **3.** amount to: *a crew numbering 20 men.* **4.** reckon as one of a class or collection: *numbered among his followers.* **5.** fix the number of; limit: *his days are numbered.* **6.** count. [< OF < L *numerus*] —**num′ber·er,** *n.* ▶ **Number** is a collective noun, requiring a singular or plural verb according as the total or the individual units are meant: *A number of tickets have already been sold. The number of tickets sold is astonishing.* ▶ **numbers.** Usage varies in writing numbers that are parts of consecutive sentences. In general, newspapers and informal writing have figures for numbers over ten, words for smaller numbers; rather conservative magazine and book styles have figures for numbers over 100 except when they can be written in two words: INFORMAL (newspaper): *four, ten,* 15, 92, 114. FORMAL (book): *four, ten, fifteen, ninety-two,* 114. But practice is not consistent. See **amount** for another usage note.

num·ber·less (num′bər·lis), *adj.* **1.** very numerous; too many to count: *the fish in the sea are numberless.* **2.** without a number. —Syn. **1.** countless, myriad, infinite.

Num·bers (num′bərz), *n.* the fourth book of the Old Testament, dealing with the counting of the Israelites after they left Egypt.

numbers pool, an illegal lottery, esp. one basing its receipts on a large number of small bets, paying off on the occurrence of a specific number from an unpredictable source, as the daily baseball totals, etc.

nu·mer·a·ble (nū′mər·ə·bəl; nū′-), *adj.* that can be counted.

nu·mer·al (nū′mər·əl; nū′-), *n.* figure, letter, or word standing for a number; group of figures, letters, or words standing for a number: *Arabic numerals, Roman numerals.* —*adj.* of numbers; standing for a number. [< LL, < L *numerus* number]

nu·mer·ate (nū′mər·āt; nū′-), *v.*, -at·ed, -at·ing. 1. number; count; enumerate. 2. read (an expression in numbers). —*nu′mer·a′tion, n.*

nu·mer·a·tor (nū′mər·ā′tər; nū′-), *n.* 1. *Math.* number above the line in a fraction which shows how many parts are taken. In ⅜, 3 is the numerator. 2. person or thing that makes a count.

nu·mer·i·cal (nū·mer′ə·kəl; nū-), **nu·mer·ic** (-ik), *adj.* 1. of a number; having to do with numbers; in numbers; by numbers. 2. shown by numbers, not by letters: *10 is a numerical quantity.* —nu·mer′i·cal·ly, *adv.*

nu·mer·ous (nū′mər·əs; nū′-), *adj.* 1. very many. 2. in great numbers. —nu′mer·ous·ly, *adv.* —nu′mer·ous·ness, *n.* —Syn. 1. manifold, several, innumerable.

Nu·mid·i·a (nū·mid′i·ə; nū-), *n.* an ancient country in N Africa. —Nu·mid′i·an, *adj., n.*

nu·mis·mat·ics (nū′miz·mat′iks; -mis-; nū-), *n.* study of coins and medals. [< F < L *numisma* coin < Gk., < *nomizein* have in use] —nu′mis·mat′ic, nu′mis·mat′i·cal, *adj.* —nu·mis·ma·tist (nū·miz′mə·tist; -mis′-; nū-), *n.*

num·skull (num′skul′), *n. Colloq.* a stupid person; blockhead. [for *numb skull*]

nun (nun), *n.* woman who devotes her life to religion and lives under religious vows with a group of women like her. [ult. < LL *nonna*]

nun·ci·o (nun′shi·ō), *n., pl.* -ci·os. 1. ambassador from the pope to a government. 2. messenger. [< Ital. < L *nuntius* messenger]

nun·ner·y (nun′ər·i), *n., pl.* -ner·ies. building or buildings where nuns live; convent.

nup·tial (nup′shəl), *adj.* of marriage or weddings. —*n.* nuptials, a wedding; the wedding ceremony. [< L *nuptialis,* ult. < *nubere* take a husband]

Nu·rem·berg (nûr′əm·bėrg; nyûr′-), *n.* city in W Germany.

nurse (nėrs), *n., v.,* nursed, nurs·ing. —*n.* 1. person who takes care of the sick, the injured, or the old, or is trained to do this. 2. woman who cares for and brings up the young children or babies of another person. 3. one who feeds and protects. —*v.* 1. be a nurse; act as a nurse; work as a nurse. 2. act as a nurse for; wait on or try to cure (the sick); take care of (sick, injured, or old people). 3. cure or try to cure by care. 4. take care of and bring up (another's baby or young child). 5. nourish; protect; make grow: *nurse a plant, nurse a fire.* 6. use or treat with special care: *he nursed his sore arm by using it very little.* 7. hold closely; clasp fondly. 8. give milk to (a baby). 9. suck milk from a mother or nurse. [< OF < L *nutricia* < *nutrire* feed, nourish] —Syn. *v.* 5. nurture, cherish, foster.

nurse·maid (nėrs′mād′), *n.* maid employed to care for children.

nurs·er·y (nėr′sər·i; nėrs′ri), *n., pl.* -er·ies. 1. room set apart for the use of children and babies. 2. piece of ground or place where young trees and plants are raised for transplanting or sale. 3. place or condition that helps something to grow and develop: *poverty is a nursery of crime.*

nurs·er·y·man (nėr′sər·i·mən; nėrs′ri-), *n., pl.* -men. man who grows or sells young trees and plants.

nursery school, school for children not old enough to go to kindergarten.

nurs·ling, nurse·ling (nėrs′ling), *n.* baby that is being nursed.

nur·ture (nėr′chər), *v.,* -tured, -tur·ing, *n.* —*v.* 1. rear; bring up; care for; foster; train:

she nurtured the child as if he had been her own. 2. nourish. [< n.] —*n.* 1. rearing; bringing up; training; education: *the two sisters had received very different nurture, one at home and the other at a convent.* 2. nourishment. [< OF, ult. < L *nutrire* nourish] —nur′tur·er. *n.*

nut (nut), *n., v.,* nut·ted, nut·ting, *adj.* —*n.* 1. a dry fruit or seed with a hard, woody or leathery shell and a kernel inside which is good to eat. 2. kernel of a nut. 3. *Bot.* a hard, one-seeded fruit that does not open when ripe, such as an acorn. 4. a small block, usually of metal, that screws on to a bolt to tighten or hold something. 5. *Slang.* head. 6. *Slang.* a queer or crazy person. —*v.* gather nuts; seek for nuts. —*adj.* nuts, *U.S. Slang.* queer; crazy. [OE *hnutu*] —nut′like′, *adj.*

nut·crack·er (nut′krak′ər), *n.* 1. instrument for cracking the shells of nuts. 2. *Am.* any of several birds of the same family as the crow, that feed on nuts.

nut·gall (nut′gôl′), *n.* lump or ball that swells up on an oak tree where it has been injured by an insect.

nut·hatch (nut′hach′), *n.* a small, sharp-beaked bird that feeds on small nuts, seeds, and insects.

nut·meg (nut′meg), *n.* 1. a hard, spicy seed about as big as a marble, obtained from the fruit of an East Indian tree. The seed is grated and used for flavoring food. 2. the tree. [half-trans. of unrecorded OF *nois mugue,* var. of *nois muguete,* MUSK nut (nois < L *nux*)]

nu·tri·a (nū′tri·ə; nū′-), *n.* fur of the coypu. [< Sp. < L *lutra*]

nu·tri·ent (nū′tri·ənt; nū′-), *adj.* nourishing. —*n.* a nourishing substance. [< L, ppr. of *nutrire* nourish]

nu·tri·ment (nū′trə·mənt; nū′-), *n.* nourishment; food.

nu·tri·tion (nū·trish′ən; nū-), *n.* 1. food. 2. series of processes by which food is changed to living tissues. —nu·tri′tion·al, *adj.* —nu·tri′-tion·al·ly, *adv.* —nu·tri′tion·ist, *n.*

nu·tri·tious (nū·trish′əs; nū-), *adj.* valuable as food; nourishing. —nu·tri′tious·ly, *adv.* —nu·tri′tious·ness, *n.*

nu·tri·tive (nū′trə·tiv; nū′-), *adj.* 1. having to do with foods and the use of foods. 2. nutritious. —nu′tri·tive·ness, *n.*

nut·shell (nut′shel′), *n.* 1. shell of a nut. 2. in a nutshell, in very brief form; in a few words.

nut·ting (nut′ing), *n.* gathering nuts.

nut·ty (nut′i), *adj.,* -ti·er, -ti·est. 1. containing many nuts. 2. like nuts; tasting like nuts. 3. *Slang.* queer; crazy. —nut′ti·ness, *n.*

nux vom·i·ca (nuks vom′ə·kə), 1. medicine containing strychnine, made from the seed of a tree growing in the East Indies. 2. the seed. 3. the tree. [< Med.L, vomiting nut, < L *nux* nut + *vomere* vomit]

nuz·zle (nuz′əl), *v.,* -zled, -zling. 1. nestle; snuggle; cuddle. 2. poke or rub with the nose; press the nose against. [< *nose;* infl. by *nestle*]

NW, N.W., or **n.w.,** northwest; northwestern.

N.Y., New York State.

Ny·as·a·land (nī·as′ə·land′; nī-), *n.* former British protectorate in SE Africa. Now called Malawi.

N.Y.C., New York City.

ny·lon (nī′lon), *n.* 1. an extremely strong, elastic, and durable substance, used to make clothing, stockings, bristles, etc. 2. nylons, stockings made of nylon.

nymph (nimf), *n., pl.* nymphs for *1, 2,* nymphs or nym·phae (nim′fē) for *3.* 1. *Class. Myth.* one of the lesser goddesses of nature, who lived in seas, rivers, springs, hills, woods, or trees. 2. *Poetic.* a beautiful or graceful young woman. 3. insect in the stage of development between larva and adult insect. A nymph has no wings. [< OF < L < Gk. *nymphe*] —nym′phal, *adj.*

nym·pho·ma·ni·a (nim′fə·mā′ni·ə), *n.* an extreme and often uncontrollable sexual desire in a woman. —nym′pho·ma′ni·ac, *adj., n.*

N.Z., New Zealand.

O

O¹, o (ō), *n., pl.* **O's; o's. 1.** the 15th letter of the alphabet. **2.** something like the letter O in shape.

O² (ō), *interj.* oh!

O, 1. old. **2.** *Chem.* oxygen. **3.** zero.

O., 1. Ocean. **2.** October. **3.** Ohio. **4.** Old.

oaf (ōf), *n., pl.* **oafs. 1.** a very stupid child or man. **2.** a deformed child. **3.** a clumsy person. [OE *ælf* elf] —**oaf′ish,** *adj.* —**oaf′ish·ly,** *adv.* —**oaf′ish·ness,** *n.*

O·a·hu (ō-ä′hū), *n.* the third largest island of Hawaii.

oak (ōk), *n.* **1.** a large tree with hard, durable wood, jagged leaves, and nuts called acorns. **2.** its wood. **3.** tree or shrub resembling or suggesting an oak. —*adj.* made of oak: *an oak table.* [OE āc] —**oak′en,** *adj.*

oak apple or **gall,** lump or ball on an oak leaf or stem due to injury by an insect.

American oak: leaf and acorn.

Oak·land (ōk′lənd), *n.* city in W California.
Oak·ley (ōk′li), *n. Am., Slang.* See Annie Oakley.

Oak Ridge, city located on a U.S. government reservation in E Tennessee. Oak Ridge is an atomic-energy research center.

oa·kum (ō′kəm), *n.* a loose fiber obtained by untwisting and picking apart old ropes. Oakum is used for calking the seams or cracks on ships. [OE *ācumba* offcombings]

oar (ôr; ōr), *n.* **1.** pole with a flat end, used in rowing. **2.** put one's oar in, meddle; interfere. **3.** rest on one's oars, stop working or trying and take a rest. **4.** person who rows. —*v.* row. [OE ār] —**oared,** *adj.* —**oar′less,** *adj.*

oar·lock (ôr′lok′; ōr′-), *n.* a notch or U-shaped support in which the oar rests in rowing; rowlock.

oars·man (ôrz′mən; ōrz′-), *n., pl.* **-men. 1.** man who rows. **2.** man who rows well. —**oars′-man·like′,** *adj.* —**oars′man·ship,** *n.*

OAS, Organization of American States.

o·a·sis (ō-ā′sis), *n., pl.* **o·a·ses** (-sēz). a fertile spot in the desert where there is water. [< L, Gk.; appar. < Egyptian] —**o·a′sal, o·a·sit·ic** (ō′ə·sit′ik), *adj.*

oat (ōt), *n.* **1.** Usually, **oats.** a tall cereal grass whose grain is used in making oatmeal and as a food for horses. **2. oats,** grain of the oat plant. **3.** feel one's oats, *Am., Slang.* **a.** be lively or frisky. **b.** feel pleased or important and show it. **4.** sow one's wild oats, do the things that wild young people do before settling down. **5.** *Poetic.* a musical pipe made of an oat straw. [OE *āte*] —**oat′en,** *adj.*

oat·cake (ōt′kāk′), *n.* a thin cake made of oatmeal.

oath (ōth), *n., pl.* **oaths** (ōthz; ōths). **1.** a solemn promise or statement that something is true, which God or some holy person or thing is called on to witness. **2.** any statement or promise formally affirmed and taken as the equivalent of an oath. **3.** name of God or some holy person or thing used as an exclamation to add force to or express anger. **4.** a curse; swearword. [OE āth] —**Syn. 1.** vow. **2.** pledge. **4.** expletive, malediction.

oat·meal (ōt′mēl′), *n.* **1.** oats made into meal; ground oats; rolled oats. **2.** porridge made from oatmeal.

ob-, *prefix.* **1.** against; in the way; opposing; hindering. **2.** inversely; contrary to the usual position. **3.** toward; to. **4.** on; over. [< L *ob-* (also, by assimilation to the following consonant, *o-, oc-, of-, op-, os-*)]

O·ba·di·ah (ō′bə·dī′ə), *n.* **1.** a Hebrew prophet. **2.** book of the Old Testament containing his prophecies.

ob·bli·ga·to (ob′lə·gä′tō), *adj., n., pl.* **-tos.** *Music.* —*adj.* accompanying a solo, but having a distinct character and independent importance.

—*n.* such an accompaniment. [< Ital., lit. obliged]

ob·du·rate (ob′də·rit; -dyə-), *adj.* **1.** stubborn; unyielding: *an obdurate refusal.* **2.** hardened in feelings or heart; not repentant: *an obdurate criminal.* [< L, < *ob-* against + *durare* harden] —**ob′du·ra·cy, ob′du·rate·ness,** *n.* —**ob′du·rate·ly,** *adv.* —**Syn. 1.** obstinate, unbending, inexorable. **2.** callous, impenitent.

o·be·di·ence (ō-bē′di·əns), *n.* **1.** act or fact of doing what one is told; submission to authority or law. **2.** authority; rule, esp. ecclesiastical authority or rule. —**Syn. 1.** compliance, subservience. —**Ant. 1.** disobedience, defiance.

o·be·di·ent (ō-bē′di·ənt), *adj.* doing what one is told; willing to obey. [< L, ppr. of *oboedire* obey] —**o·be′di·ent·ly,** *adv.* —**o·be′di·ent·ness,** *n.* —**Syn.** docile, tractable, compliant, submissive. —**Ant.** disobedient, refractory.

o·bei·sance (ō-bā′səns; ō-bē′-), *n.* **1.** movement of the body expressing deep respect; deep bow: *the men made obeisance to the king.* **2.** deference; homage. [< OF *obeissance* obedience] —**o·bei′sant,** *adj.* —**o·bei′sant·ly,** *adv.*

ob·e·lisk (ob′ə·lisk), *n.* **1.** a tapering, four-sided shaft of stone with a top shaped like a pyramid. **2.** in printing, the dagger mark (†). [< L < Gk. *obeliskos,* dim. of *obelos* a spit] —**ob′e·lis′cal,** *adj.*

O·ber·am·mer·gau (ō′bər·äm′ər·gou′), *n.* village in SW Germany; site of the Passion Play.
O·ber·on (ō′bər·on), *n.* in Shakespeare's "*Midsummer Night's Dream,*" the king of the fairies, husband of Titania.

o·bese (ō-bēs′), *adj.* extremely fat. [< L *obesus* < *ob-* in addition + *edere* eat] —**o·bese′ness, o·bes·i·ty** (ō-bēs′ə·ti; ō·bes′-), *n.*

o·bey (ō-bā′), *v.* **1.** do what one is told: *the dog obeyed and went home.* **2.** follow the orders of: *obey your father.* **3.** yield to (authority or law or control). **4.** yield to the control of: *a car obeys the driver.* [< F < L, < *ob-* to + *audire* give ear] —**o·bey′er,** *n.* —**o·bey′ing·ly,** *adv.*

ob·fus·cate (ob·fus′kāt; ob′fus-), *v.,* **-cat·ed, -cat·ing.** darken; obscure; confuse; stupefy: *a man's mind may be obfuscated by liquor.* [< L, < *ob-* + *fuscus* dark] —**ob′fus·ca′tion,** *n.* —**ob·fus′ca·tor,** *n.*

o·bi (ō′bi), *n.* a long, broad sash worn by Japanese women and children. [< Jap.]

ob·i·ter dic·tum (ob′ə·tər dik′təm; ō′bə·tər), *pl.,* **ob·i·ter dic·ta** (dik′tə). **1.** an incidental statement. **2.** an incidental opinion, esp. one given by a judge. [< L, said by the way]

o·bit·u·ar·y (ō·bich′u·er′i), *n., pl.* **-ar·ies,** *adj.* —*n.* a notice of death, often with a brief account of the person's life. —*adj.* of a death; recording a death. [< Med.L *obituarius,* ult. < L *obire* (*mortem*) meet (death) < *ob-* up to + *ire* go]

obj., object; objective.

ob·ject (*n.* ob′jikt, -jekt; *v.* əb·jekt′), *n.* **1.** something that can be seen or touched; thing. **2.** person or thing toward which feeling, thought, or action is directed: *an object of charity.* **3.** person or thing that is pitiful, absurd, funny, or foolish. **4.** thing aimed at; end; purpose. **5.** *Philos.* thing that is or can be thought of. **6.** *Gram.* word or group of words toward which the action of the verb is directed or to which a preposition expresses some relation. In "He threw the ball to his brother," *ball* is the object of *threw,* and *brother* is the object of *to.* —*v.* **1.** make objections; be opposed; feel dislike: *many people object to loud noise.* **2.** give a reason against; bring forward in opposition; oppose: *mother objected that the weather was too wet to play outdoors.* [< L *objectus* < *ob-* toward, against + *jacere* to throw] —**ob·ject′ing·ly,** *adv.* —**ob′ject·less,** *adj.* —**ob·jec′tor,** *n.* —**Syn. n. 1.** article. **4.** goal, aim. —**Ant. v. 1.** acquiesce, approve, accede. **2.** agree.

ob·jec·ti·fy (əb·jek′tə·fī), v., **-fied, -fy·ing.** make objective: *experiments in chemistry objectify the teaching.* —**ob·jec′ti·fi·ca′tion,** n.

ob·jec·tion (əb·jek′shən), n. **1.** something said in objecting; reason or argument against something: *make objections to a plan.* **2.** feeling of disapproval or dislike: *an objection to working.* —Syn. **2.** opposition.

ob·jec·tion·a·ble (əb·jek′shən·ə·bəl), adj. **1.** likely to be objected to: *objectionable features of the plan.* **2.** unpleasant; disagreeable: *noise is objectionable in church.* —**ob·jec′tion·a·ble·ness,** n. —**ob·jec′tion·a·bly,** adv. —Syn. **2.** undesirable, offensive, obnoxious.

ob·jec·tive (əb·jek′tiv), n. **1.** something aimed at: *my objective this summer will be learning to play tennis better.* **2.** something real and observable. **3.** *Gram.* a. the objective case. b. word in that case. *Whom* and *me* are objectives. **4.** lens or lenses nearest to the thing seen through a telescope, microscope, etc. —adj. **1.** being the object of endeavor: *an objective point.* **2.** existing outside the mind as an actual object and not merely in the mind as an idea; real. Actions are objective; ideas are subjective. **3.** about outward things, not about the thoughts and feelings of the speaker, writer, painter, etc.; giving facts as they are without a bias toward either side; impersonal: *a scientist must be objective in his experiments.* **4.** *Gram.* showing the object of a verb or the object of a preposition. In "John hit me," *me* is in the objective case. —**ob·jec′tive·ly,** adv. —**ob·jec′tive·ness,** n. —Syn. n. **1.** object, aim, goal. –adj. **3.** impartial.

ob·jec·tiv·i·ty (ob′jek·tiv′ə·ti), n. intentness on objects external to the mind; external reality.

object lesson, a practical illustration of a principle.

ob·jet d'art (ôb·zhā där′), pl. **ob·jets d'art** (ôb·zhā där′). *French.* a small picture, vase, etc., of some artistic value.

ob·jur·gate (ob′jər·gāt; əb·jér′gāt), v., **-gated, -gat·ing.** reproach vehemently; upbraid violently; berate. [< L, < ob- + *jurgare* scold] —**ob′jur·ga′tion,** n. —**ob′jur·ga′tor,** n. —**ob·jur·ga·to·ry** (əb·jér′gə·tô′ri; -tō′-), adj. —**ob·jur′ga·to′ri·ly,** adv. —Syn. vituperate.

ob·late (ob′lāt; ob·lāt′), adj. flattened at the poles: *an oblate spheroid.* [< NL oblatus < ob- inversely + (pro)latus prolate] —**ob′late·ly,** adv. —**ob′late·ness,** n.

ob·la·tion (ob·lā′shən), n. **1.** an offering to God or a god. **2.** gift to a church or for other pious use. **3.** the offering of bread and wine in the Communion service. [< LL, < ob- up to + latus, pp. to *ferre* bring] —**ob·la′tion·al, ob·la·to·ry** (ob′lə·tô′ri; -tō′-), adj.

ob·li·gate (ob′lə·gāt), v., **-gated, -gat·ing,** adj. –v. bind morally or legally; pledge: *a witness in court is obligated to tell the truth.* –adj. bound morally or legally. [< L, < ob- to + *ligare* bind]

ob·li·ga·tion (ob′lə·gā′shən), n. **1.** duty under the law; duty due to a promise or contract; duty on account of social relationship or kindness received: *a wife's first obligation is to her husband and children.* **2.** a binding power (of a law, promise, sense of duty, etc.): *the one who did the damage is under obligation to pay for it.* **3.** a binding legal agreement; bond; contract: *the firm was not able to meet its obligations.* **4.** fact of being in debt for a favor, service, or the like. **5.** service; favor; benefit: *repay all obligations.* —**ob′li·ga′tion·al,** adj. —**ob′li·ga′tor,** n. —Syn. **1.** responsibility. **3.** covenant.

ob·lig·a·to·ry (ob·lig′ə·tô′ri; -tō′-; ob′lə·gə-), adj. binding morally or legally; required: *attendance at primary school is obligatory.* —**ob·lig′a·to′ri·ly,** adv. —**ob·lig′a·to′ri·ness,** n.

o·blige (ə·blīj′), v., **o·bliged, o·blig·ing. 1.** bind by a promise, contract, duty, etc.; compel; force: *the law obliges parents to send their children to school.* **2.** put under a debt of thanks for some favor; do a favor: *Grace obliged the crowd with a song.* [< OF < L, < ob- to + *ligare* bind]

—**o·blig′er,** n. —**o·blig′ing,** adj. —**o·blig′ing·ly,** adv. —**o·blig′ing·ness,** n. —Syn. **1.** constrain. **2.** accommodate.

ob·lique (əb·lēk′; military əb·līk′), adj., v., **-liqued, -liqu·ing.** —adj. **1.** not straight up and down; not straight across; slanting. In the diagram, AB, CD, EF, and GH are oblique lines. **2.** not straightforward; indirect: *she made an oblique reference to her illness, but did not mention it directly.* **3.** not narrated directly, but put into a reported form. –v. have or take an oblique direction; slant. [< L *obliquus*] —**ob·lique′ly,** adv. —**ob·liq·ui·ty** (əb·lik′wə·ti), ob·lique′ness, n.

oblique angle, any angle that is not a right angle.

oblique case, any case of a noun or pronoun except the nominative and vocative.

ob·lit·er·ate (əb·lit′ər·āt), v., **-at·ed, -at·ing.** remove all traces of; blot out; destroy: *rain obliterated the footprints.* [< L, < ob- + *litera* letter] —**ob·lit′er·a′tion,** n. —**ob·lit′er·a′tive,** adj. —**ob·lit′er·a′tive·ly,** adv. —**ob·lit′er·a′tor,** n. —Syn. efface, expunge, erase.

ob·liv·i·on (əb·liv′i·ən), n. **1.** condition of being entirely forgotten: *many ancient cities have long since passed into oblivion.* **2.** forgetfulness. [< L, < *oblivisci* forget]

ob·liv·i·ous (əb·liv′i·əs), adj. forgetful; not mindful: *oblivious of my surroundings.* —**ob·liv′i·ous·ly,** adv. —**ob·liv′i·ous·ness,** n. —Syn. unmindful, heedless, inattentive.

ob·long (ob′lông; -long), adj. longer than broad: *an oblong loaf of bread.* —n. rectangle that is not a square. [< L, < ob- + *longus* long]

Oblong

ob·lo·quy (ob′lə·kwi), n., pl. **-quies. 1.** public reproach; abuse; blame. **2.** disgrace; shame. [< LL, ult. < ob- against + *loqui* speak] —Syn. **1.** censure.

ob·nox·ious (əb·nok′shəs), adj. very disagreeable; offensive; hateful: *disgusting table manners are obnoxious.* [< L, < ob- + *noxa* injury] —**ob·nox′ious·ly,** adv. —**ob·nox′ious·ness,** n. —Syn. objectionable, odious.

o·boe (ō′bō), n. a wooden wind instrument in which a thin, poignant tone is produced by a double reed. [< Ital. < F *hautbois* HAUTBOY] —**o′bo·ist,** n.

obs., obsolete; used formerly but not now.

ob·scene (əb·sēn′), adj. offending modesty or decency; impure; filthy; vile. [< L *obscenus*] —**ob·scene′ly,** adv. —**ob·scen·i·ty** (əb·sen′ə·ti; -sē′nə-), obs·cene′ness, n. —Syn. indecent, gross, lewd, ribald.

ob·scur·ant·ism (əb·skyur′ən·tiz·əm), n. opposition to progress and the spread of knowledge. —**ob·scur′ant, ob·scur′ant·ist,** n., adj.

ob·scure (əb·skyur′), adj., **-scur·er, -scur·est,** v., **-scured, -scur·ing.** —adj. **1.** not clearly expressed: *an obscure passage in a book.* **2.** not expressing meaning clearly: *an obscure style of writing.* **3.** not well known; attracting no notice: *an obscure little village, an obscure poet.* **4.** not easily discovered; hidden: *an obscure path.* **5.** not distinct; not clear: *obscure sounds, an obscure view.* **6.** dark; dim: *an obscure corner.* **7.** indefinite: *an obscure brown, an obscure vowel.* –v. hide from view; make obscure; dim; darken: *clouds obscure the sun.* [< OF < L, < ob- up + *scur-* cover] —**ob·scu·ra′tion, ob·scure′ment,** n. —**ob·scure′ly,** adv. —**ob·scure′ness,** n. —**ob·scur′er,** n. —**ob·scur′ing·ly,** adv. —Syn. adj. **1.** ambiguous, vague, enigmatic, cryptic. **3.** unknown, undistinguished, humble. **4.** secluded. **6.** dusky, murky, gloomy. –v. eclipse, conceal.

ob·scu·ri·ty (əb·skyur′ə·ti), n., pl. **-ties. 1.** lack of clearness; difficulty in being understood: *the obscurity of the passage makes several interpretations possible.* **2.** something obscure: *poor writing is full of obscurities.* **3.** a being unknown: *Lincoln rose from obscurity to fame.* **4.** a little-known person or place. **5.** lack of light; dimness. —**Syn.** 1. ambiguity, vagueness. 5. darkness, shade.

ob·se·quies (ob'sə·kwiz), *n.pl.* funeral rites or ceremonies; stately funeral.

ob·se·qui·ous (əb·sē'kwi·əs), *adj.* polite or obedient from hope of gain or from fear; servile; fawning: *obsequious courtiers.* [< L, ult. < ob- after + *sequi* follow] —**ob·se'qui·ous·ly,** *adv.* —**ob·se'qui·ous·ness,** *n.* —**Syn.** slavish.

ob·serv·a·ble (əb·zér'və·bəl), *adj.* 1. that can be or is noticed; noticeable. 2. that can be or is observed: *Lent is observable by some churches.* —**observ'a·ble·ness,** *n.* —**ob·serv'a·bly,** *adv.*

ob·serv·ance (əb·zér'vəns), *n.* 1. act of observing or keeping laws or customs: *the observance of the Sabbath.* 2. act performed as a sign of worship or respect; religious ceremony: *church services are religious observances.* 3. rule or custom to be observed, esp. the rule of a religious order. —**Syn.** 1. celebration. 2. rite.

ob·serv·ant (əb·zér'vənt), *adj.* 1. quick to notice; watchful; observing: *an observant person.* 2. careful in observing (a law, rule, custom, etc.): *observant of the traffic rules.* —**ob·serv'ant·ly,** *adv.* —**Syn.** 1. heedful, regardful, attentive.

ob·ser·va·tion (ob'zər·vā'shən), *n.* 1. act, habit, or power of seeing and noting: *the trained observation of a doctor.* 2. fact of being seen; being seen; notice: *the tramp avoided observation.* 3. something seen and noted. 4. act of watching for some special purpose; study: *observation of nature.* 5. an observing of the altitude of the sun or other heavenly body in order to determine the latitude and longitude of one's position. 6. remark. —**ob'ser·va'tion·al,** *adj.* —**ob'ser·va'tion·al·ly,** *adv.* —**Syn.** 6. comment.

ob·serv·a·to·ry (əb·zér'və·tô'ri; -tō'-), *n.,* *pl.* -ries. 1. place or building with a telescope for observing the stars and other heavenly bodies. 2. place or building for observing facts or happenings of nature. 3. a high place or building giving a wide view. —**ob·serv'a·to'ri·al,** *adj.*

ob·serve (əb·zérv'), *v.,* -served, -serv·ing. 1. see and note; notice: *I observed nothing queer in his behavior.* 2. examine for some special purpose; study: *an astronomer observes the stars.* 3. remark: *"Bad weather," the captain observed.* 4. keep; follow in practice: *observe a rule.* 5. show regard for; celebrate: *observe the Sabbath.* [< L, < *ob-* over + *servare* watch, keep] —**observ'er,** *n.* —**ob·serv'ing,** *adj.* —**ob·serv'ing·ly,** *adv.* —**ob·serv'ing·ness,** *n.* —**Syn.** 1. perceive. 2. survey, watch. 3. comment, mention.

ob·sess (əb·ses'), *v.* fill the mind of; keep the attention of; haunt. [< L *obsessus* < *ob-* by + *sedere* sit] —**ob·ses'sive,** *adj.* —**ob·ses'sor,** *n.*

ob·ses·sion (əb·sesh'ən), *n.* 1. influence of a feeling, idea, or impulse that a person cannot escape. 2. the feeling, idea, or impulse itself.

ob·sid·i·an (ob·sid'i·ən), *n.* a hard, dark, glassy rock that is formed when lava cools. [< L *obsidianus*; named for *Obsius,* its discoverer]

ob·so·les·cent (ob'sə·les'ənt), *adj.* passing out of use; tending to become out of date. [< L *obsolescens,* ult. < *ob-* + *solere* to be accustomed] —**ob'so·les'cence,** *n.* —**ob'so·les'cent·ly,** *adv.*

ob·so·lete (ob'sə·lēt), *adj.* 1. no longer in use: *"eft" (meaning "again") is an obsolete word.* 2. out-of-date: *we still use this machine though it is obsolete.* [< L *obsoletus.* See OBSOLESCENT.] —**ob'so·lete·ly,** *adv.* —**ob'so·lete·ness,** *n.* ▶ Obsolete indicates a word no longer used (like *oft*—"often") or a meaning of a word no longer used (like *can* in the sense of "know," *dole* in the sense of "grief"). Expressions that have completely disappeared from use offer little trouble in writing. There is little temptation to refer to a *bottle* of hay, or to use *can* in the sense of "know." This dictionary contains only the more important obsolete words likely to be encountered in reading the older literature.

ob·sta·cle (ob'stə·kəl), *n.* something that stands in the way or stops progress: *blindness is an obstacle in most occupations.* [< OF < L *obstaculum* < *ob-* in the way of + *stare* stand] —**Syn.** obstruction, barrier, bar, impediment, hindrance.

ob·ste·tri·cian (ob'stə·trish'ən), *n.* physician whose specialty is obstetrics.

ob·stet·rics (ob·stet'riks), *n.* branch of medicine and surgery concerned with caring for and treating women in, before, and after childbirth. [< L, < *obstetrix* midwife < *ob-* by + *stare* to stand] —**ob·stet'ric, ob·stet'ri·cal,** *adj.*

ob·sti·na·cy (ob'stə·nə·si), *n.,* *pl.* -cies. 1. stubbornness. 2. an obstinate act. —**ob'sti·nance,** *n.* —**Syn.** 1. willfulness.

ob·sti·nate (ob'stə·nit), *adj.* 1. not giving in; stubborn: *an obstinate person.* 2. hard to control or treat: *an obstinate cough.* [< L *obstinatus,* ult. < *ob-* by + *stare* stand] —**ob'sti·nate·ly,** *adv.* —**ob'sti·nate·ness,** *n.* —**Syn.** 1. dogged, headstrong. 2. persistent, intractable. —**Ant.** 1. compliant, yielding, tractable.

ob·strep·er·ous (əb·strep'ər·əs), *adj.* 1. noisy; boisterous. 2. unruly; disorderly: *an obstreperous mob.* [< L, < *ob-* against + *strepere* make a noise] —**ob·strep'er·ous·ly,** *adv.* —**ob·strep'er·ous·ness,** *n.* —**Syn.** 1. clamorous, vociferous. 2. turbulent.

ob·struct (əb·strukt'), *v.* 1. make hard to pass through; block up: *fallen trees obstruct the road.* 2. be in the way of; hinder: *trees obstruct our view of the ocean.* [< L *obstructus* < *ob-* in the way of + *struere* pile] —**ob·struct'er, ob·struc'tor,** *n.* —**ob·struct'ing·ly,** *adv.* —**ob·struc'tive,** *adj.* —**ob·struc'tive·ly,** *adv.* —**ob·struc'tive·ness,** *n.* —**Syn.** 1. close, choke, clog. 2. impede. —**Ant.** 1. open, clear.

ob·struc·tion (əb·struk'shən), *n.* 1. thing that obstructs; something in the way. 2. a blocking; a hindering, esp. persistent or systematic attempts to stop or retard the progress of business in a legislative assembly, committee, or the like. —**ob·struc'tion·ism,** *n.* —**ob·struc'tion·ist,** *n.*

ob·tain (əb·tān'), *v.* 1. get or procure through diligence or effort; acquire: *obtain a prize, obtain possession of a house one has rented, obtain knowledge through study.* 2. be in use; be customary: *different rules obtain in different schools.* [< F < L, < *ob-* to + *tenere* hold] —**ob·tain'a·ble,** *adj.* —**ob·tain'er,** *n.* —**ob·tain'ment, ob·ten·tion** (əb·ten'shən), *n.* —**Syn.** 1. secure, gain, win.

ob·trude (əb·trüd'), *v.,* -trud·ed, -trud·ing. 1. put forward unasked and unwanted; force: *don't obtrude your opinions on others.* 2. come unasked and unwanted; force oneself; intrude. 3. push out; thrust forward. [< L, < *ob-* toward + *trudere* to thrust] —**ob·trud'er,** *n.* —**ob·tru'sion,** *n.*

ob·tru·sive (əb·trü'siv), *adj.* inclined to obtrude; intrusive. —**ob·tru'sive·ly,** *adv.* —**ob·tru'sive·ness,** *n.* —**Syn.** meddlesome, officious.

ob·tuse (ob·tūs'; -tüs'), *adj.* 1. not sharp or acute; blunt. 2. having more than 90° of angle but less than 180°: *an obtuse angle.* 3. slow in understanding; stupid: *too obtuse to take the hint.* 4. not sensitive; dull: *obtuse hearing.* [< L *obtusus* < *ob-* on + *tundere* to beat] —**ob·tuse'ly,** *adv.* —**ob·tuse'ness, ob·tu'si·ty,** *n.*

OBTUSE ANGLE   RIGHT ANGLE

ob·verse (*n.* ob'vérs; *adj.* ob·vérs', ob'vérs), *n.* 1. side of a coin, medal, etc., that has the principal design. 2. that face of anything that is meant to be turned toward the observer; front. 3. counterpart. —*adj.* 1. turned toward the observer. 2. being a counterpart to something else. [< L *obversus* < *ob-* toward + *vertere* to turn] —**ob·verse'ly,** *adv.*

ob·vi·ate (ob'vi·āt), *v.,* -at·ed, -at·ing. meet and dispose of; clear out of the way; remove: *a telephone call often obviates the necessity of writing.* [< L, < *obvius* in the way. See OBVIOUS.] —**ob'vi·a'tion,** *n.* —**ob'vi·a'tor,** *n.*

ob·vi·ous (ob'vi·əs), *adj.* easily seen or understood; clear to the eye or mind; not to be doubted: *too obvious to need proof.* [< L, < *obviam* in the way < *ob* across + *via* way] —**ob'vi·ous·ly,** *adv.* —**ob'vi·ous·ness,** *n.* —**Syn.** plain, manifest, evident, unmistakable.

oc·a·ri·na (ok'ə·rē'nə), *n.* a musical instrument shaped like a sweet potato, with finger holes and a whistlelike mouthpiece. [prob. dim. of Ital. *oca* goose; with ref. to the shape]

occas., occasional; occasionally.

oc·ca·sion (ə·kā′zhən), *n.* 1. a particular time: *we have met on several occasions.* 2. a special event: *jewels worn only on great occasions.* 3. event or circumstances causing a need. 4. a good chance; opportunity. 5. cause; reason: *the occasion of the quarrel.* 6. on occasion, now and then; once in a while. —*v.* cause; bring about: *his queer behavior occasioned a good deal of talk.* [< L *occasio*, ult. < *ob-* in the way of < *cadere* fall] —Syn. *n.* 1. instance. 5. ground.

oc·ca·sion·al (ə·kā′zhən·əl), *adj.* 1. happening or coming now and then, or once in a while: *occasional thunderstorms.* 2. caused by or used for some special time or event: *occasional poetry.* —**oc·ca′sion·al·ly,** *adv.*

Oc·ci·dent (ok′sə·dənt), *n.* 1. countries in Europe and America; the West. 2. occident, the west. [< L *occidens* < *ob-* + *cadere* to fall] —**Oc·ci·den·tal, oc·ci·den·tal** (ok′sə·den′təl), *adj., n.* —**oc′ci·den′tal·ly,** *adv.*

oc·cip·i·tal (ok·sip′ə·təl), *adj.* of or having to do with the back part of the head or skull. —**oc·cip′i·tal·ly,** *adv.*

oc·ci·put (ok′sə·pət), *n., pl.* **oc·cip·i·ta** (ok·sip′ə·tə). *Anat.* the back part of the head or skull. [< L, < *occipitium* < *ob-* + *caput* head]

oc·clude (ə·klüd′), *v.*, **–clud·ed, –clud·ing.** 1. stop up (a passage, pores, etc.); close. 2. shut in, out, or off. 3. *Chem.* absorb and retain (gases). 4. *Dentistry.* meet closely. [< L *occludere* < *ob-* up + *claudere* to close] —**oc·clud′ing·ly, oc·clu′sive·ly,** *adv.* —**oc·clu·sion** (ə·klü′zhən), *n.* —**oc·clu·sive** (ə·klü′siv), *adj.*

oc·cult (ə·kult′; ok′ult), *adj.* 1. beyond the bounds of ordinary knowledge; mysterious. 2. outside the laws of the natural world; magical. Astrology and alchemy are occult sciences. [< L *occultus* hidden] —**oc·cult′ism,** *n.* —**oc·cult′ist,** *n.* —**oc·cult′ly,** *adv.* —**oc·cult′ness,** *n.* —Syn. 1. secret, hidden, mystic.

oc·cul·ta·tion (ok′ul·tā′shən), *n.* concealment, esp. a hiding of one heavenly body by another passing between it and the observer.

oc·cu·pan·cy (ok′yə·pən·si), *n.* act or fact of occupying; holding (land, houses, a pew, etc.) by being in possession.

oc·cu·pant (ok′yə·pənt), *n.* 1. person who occupies. 2. person in actual possession of a house, estate, office, etc.

oc·cu·pa·tion (ok′yə·pā′shən), *n.* 1. business; employment; trade. 2. being occupied; possession; occupying: *the occupation of a town by the enemy.* —**oc′cu·pa′tion·al,** *adj.* —**oc′cu·pa′tion·al·ly,** *adv.* —Syn. 1. work, calling, pursuit.

occupational therapy, the treatment of persons having physical disabilities through specific types of exercises, work, etc., to promote rehabilitation.

oc·cu·py (ok′yə·pī), *v.*, **–pied, –py·ing.** 1. take up; fill: *the building occupies an entire block.* 2. keep busy; engage; employ: *sports often occupy a boy's attention.* 3. take possession of: *the enemy occupied our fort.* 4. keep possession of; hold: *a judge occupies an important position.* 5. live in: *the owner and his family occupy the house.* [< OF < L *occupare* seize < *ob-* onto + *cap-* grasp] —**oc′cu·pi′er,** *n.* —Syn. 2. absorb. 4. possess.

oc·cur (ə·kér′), *v.*, **–curred, –cur·ring.** 1. take place; happen: *storms often occur in winter.* 2. be found; exist: *e occurs in print more than any other letter.* 3. come to mind; suggest itself: *did it occur to you to close the window?* [< L, < *ob-* in the way of + *currere* run] —Syn. 1. befall, chance.

oc·cur·rence (ə·kér′əns), *n.* 1. an occurring: *the occurrence of storms.* 2. event: *an unexpected occurrence.* —**oc·cur′rent,** *adj.* —Syn. 2. incident, happening, episode.

o·cean (ō′shən), *n.* 1. the great body of salt water that covers almost three fourths of the

earth's surface. 2. any of its five main divisions; the Atlantic, Pacific, Indian, Arctic, and Antarctic oceans. 3. a vast expanse or quantity. [< L < Gk. *okeanos*] —**o·ce·an·ic** (ō′shi·an′ik), *adj.* —**o′ce·an′i·cal·ly,** *adv.* —Syn. 1. sea, main.

o·cean·aut (ō′shə·nôt), *n.* an explorer of an ocean or sea.

O·ce·an·i·a (ō′shi·an′i·ə), *n.* islands of the central and S Pacific. —**O′ce·an′i·an,** *adj., n.*

o·cean·og·ra·phy (ō′shən·og′rə·fi; ō′shi·ən-), *n.* branch of physical geography dealing with the ocean. —**o′cean·og′ra·pher,** *n.* —**o·cean·o·graph·ic** (ō′shən·ə·graf′ik; ō′shi·ən·ə-), **o′cean·o·graph′i·cal,** *adj.*

o·ce·lot (ō′sə·lot; os′ə-), *n. Am.* a spotted wildcat somewhat like a leopard, found from Texas through South America. [< F < Mex. *ocelotl*]

o·cher, o·chre (ō′kər), *n.* 1. any of various earths ranging in coloring from pale yellow to orange, brown, and red, used as pigments. 2. a brownish yellow. [< F < L < Gk., < *ochros* pale yellow] —**o′cher·ous** (ō′kər·əs), **o·chre·ous** (ō′kər·əs; ō′kri·əs), *adj.* —**o′cher·y, o·chry** (ō′kri), *adj.*

o'clock (ə·klok′), of or by the clock.

Oct., October.

oc·ta·gon (ok′tə·gon; -gən), *n.* a plane figure having eight angles and eight sides. —**oc·tag·o·nal** (ok·tag′ə·nəl), *adj.* —**oc·tag′on·al·ly,** *adv.*

Octagon

oc·ta·he·dron (ok′tə·hē′drən), *n., pl.* **-drons, -dra** (-drə). a solid figure having eight plane faces or sides. —**oc′ta·he′dral,** *adj.*

oc·tane (ok′tān), *n.* a colorless, liquid hydrocarbon, C_8H_{18}, that occurs in petroleum.

octane number or **rating,** a numerical rating of motor fuels, based on their antiknock properties.

oc·tave (ok′tiv; -tāv), *Music.* —*n.* 1. interval between a note and another note having twice or half as many vibrations per second. 2. the eighth note above or below a given tone. 3. series of notes or of keys of an instrument, filling the interval between a note and its octave. [< L *octavus* eighth] —**oc·ta·val** (ok·tā′vəl; ok′tə-), *adj.*

Oc·ta·vi·an (ok·tā′vi·ən), *n.* see Augustus.

oc·ta·vo (ok·tā′vō; -tä′-), *n., pl.* **-vos,** *adj.* —*n.* 1. the page size of a book in which each leaf is one eighth of a whole sheet of paper. 2. book having this size, usually about 6 by 9½ inches. —*adj.* having this size. [< Med.L *in octavo* in an eighth]

oc·tet, oc·tette (ok·tet′), *n.* 1. a musical composition for eight voices or instruments. 2. eight singers or players. 3. any group of eight. [< *octo-* eight + *-et,* patterned on *duet,* etc.]

octo-, oct-, or **octa-,** word element. eight, as in *octopus* and *octagon.* [< Gk., < *okto*]

Oc·to·ber (ok·tō′bər), *n.* the tenth month of the year, having 31 days. [< L, < *octo* eight; from the order of the Roman calendar]

oc·to·dec·i·mo (ok′tə·des′ə·mō), *n., pl.* **-mos.** 1. the page size of a book in which each leaf is one eighteenth of a whole sheet of paper. 2. a volume of this size. —*adj.* having this size. [< Med.L *in octodecimo* in an eighteenth]

oc·to·ge·nar·i·an (ok′tə·jə·nár′i·ən), *n.* person who is 80 years old or between 80 and 90 years old. —*adj.* 80 years old or between 80 and 90 years old. [< L *octogenarius* containing eighty] —**oc·tog·e·nar·y** (ok·toj′ə·ner′i), *adj., n.*

oc·to·pus (ok′tə·pəs), *n.* 1. a sea mollusk having a soft body and eight arms with suckers on them. 2. anything like an octopus; powerful, grasping organization with far-reaching influence. [< NL < Gk., < *okto* eight + *pous* foot]

oc·to·roon (ok′tə·rün′), *n. Am.* person having one eighth Negro blood or ancestry. [< *octo-* eight + (*quad*) *roon*]

oc·tu·ple (ok′tü·pəl; -tyü-), *adj., v.,* **-pled, -pling.** —*adj.* eightfold. —*v.* multiply by eight. [< L, < *octo* eight + *-plus* -fold] —**oc′tu·ply,** *adv.*

oc·u·lar (ok′yə·lər), *adj.* 1. of or having to do

with the eye: *an ocular muscle.* 2. like an eye. 3. received by actual sight; seen: *ocular proof.* —*n.* eyepiece of a telescope, microscope, etc. [< L, < *oculus* eye] —oc′u·lar·ly, *adv.*

oc·u·list (ok′yə·list), *n.* doctor skilled in the treatment of eye diseases.

O.D., Officer of the Day.

odd (od), *adj.* 1. left over: *the odd change.* 2. being one of a pair or set of which the rest is missing: *an odd stocking.* 3. extra; occasional; casual: *odd jobs, odd moments.* 4. with some extra: *six hundred odd children.* 5. leaving a remainder of 1 when divided by 2. 6. strange; peculiar; queer: *it is odd that I cannot remember his name.* [< Scand. *odda*–] —odd′ish, *adj.* —odd′ly, *adv.* —odd′ness, *n.* —Syn. 2. unmatched, unmated, single. 6. abnormal, freakish.

odd·ball (od′bôl′), *n. Am., Slang.* a very eccentric person.

odd·i·ty (od′ə·ti), *n., pl.* -ties. 1. strangeness; queerness; peculiarity. 2. a strange, queer, or peculiar person or thing. —Syn. 1. singularity. 2. freak, curiosity.

odds (odz), *n.pl. or sing.* 1. difference in favor of one and against another; advantage. 2. in games, extra allowance given to the weaker side. 3. at odds, quarreling; disagreeing. 4. odds and ends, things left over; extra bits; odd pieces; scraps; remnants. 5. the odds are, the chances are; the probability is.

ode (ōd), *n.* a lyric poem full of noble feeling expressed with dignity. [< F < LL < Gk. *ōidē,* ult. < *aeidein* sing] —od′ic, *adj.* —od′ist, *n.*

O·der (ō′dər), *n.* river flowing through W Poland into the Baltic Sea.

O·des·sa (ō·des′ə), *n.* seaport in the S Soviet Union, on the Black Sea.

O·din (ō′din), *n. Scand. Myth.* god of wisdom, culture, war, and the dead, identical with Anglo-Saxon Woden and German Wotan.

o·di·ous (ō′di·əs), *adj.* very displeasing; hateful; offensive. [< L, *odium* odium] —o′di·ous·ly, *adv.* —o′di·ous·ness, *n.* —Syn. detestable, abominable, abhorrent, repulsive.

o·di·um (ō′di·əm), *n.* 1. hatred; dislike. 2. reproach; blame. [< L, < *odisse* to hate] —Syn. 1. detestation. 2. disfavor, disgrace.

ODM, O.D.M., Office of Defense Mobilization.

o·dor, *esp. Brit.* **o·dour** (ō′dər), *n.* 1. smell: *the odor of roses, the odor of garbage.* 2. reputation. 3. fragrance; perfume. [< OF < L] —o′dored, *esp. Brit.* o′doured, *adj.* —o′dor·less, *esp. Brit.* o′dour·less, *adj.* —Syn. 1. scent. 2. esteem, estimation. 3. aroma, redolence.

o·dor·if·er·ous (ō′dər·if′ər·əs), *adj.* giving forth an odor; fragrant. —o′dor·if′er·ous·ly, *adv.* —o′dor·if′er·ous·ness, *n.*

o·dor·ous (ō′dər·əs), *adj.* giving forth an odor; having an odor; sweet-smelling; fragrant. —o′dor·ous·ly, *adv.* —o′dor·ous·ness, *n.* —Syn. aromatic, redolent.

O·dys·se·us (ō·dis′i·əs; ō·dis′ūs), *n. Gk. Legend.* Ulysses.

Od·ys·sey (od′ə·si), *n., pl.* -seys. 1. a long Greek epic poem by Homer, describing the ten years of wandering of Odysseus after the Trojan War and his return home. 2. Also, **odyssey.** any long series of wanderings and adventures.

OE, O.E., Old English (Anglo-Saxon).

oec·u·men·i·cal (ek′yü·men′ə·kəl), **oec·u·men·ic** (–ik), *adj. Brit.* ecumenical. —oec′u·men′i·cal·ly, *adv.*

Oed·i·pus (ed′ə·pəs; ē′də–), *n. Gk. Legend.* king who unknowingly killed his father and married his mother.

Oedipus complex, an early and morbidly strong attachment to the parent of the opposite sex, accompanied by dislike for the other parent.

o'er (ôr; ōr), *prep., adv. Poetic or Dial.* over.

oe·soph·a·gus (ē·sof′ə·gəs), *n., pl.* -gi (–jī). esophagus.

of (ov; uv; *unstressed* əv), *prep.* 1. belonging to: *the children of a family.* 2. made from: *a house of bricks.* 3. that has; containing; with: *a house of six rooms.* 4. that has a quality: *a look of pity.* 5. that is the same as; that is; named: *the city of Chicago.* 6. away from; from: *north of*

Boston. 7. having to do with; in regard to; concerning; about: *think well of someone.* 8. that has as a purpose: *the hour of prayer.* 9. by: *the writings of Shakespeare.* 10. as a result of having or using; through: *die of grief.* 11. out of: *she came of a noble family.* 12. among: *a mind of the finest.* 13. during: *of late years.* 14. in telling time, before: *ten minutes of six.* 15. *Of* connects nouns and adjectives having the meaning of a verb with what would be the object of the verb: *the eating of fruit, the drinking of milk.* [OE (unstressed) *of.* Cf. OFF.] ▶ **of, off.** *Of* is frequently used in colloquial and substandard doubling of prepositions—*inside of, off of, outside of. Inside of* and *outside of* are also used in informal writing, but not *off of,* which should be reduced to *off: He stepped off* [of] *the sidewalk.* ▶ The colloquial contraction *'ve* for *have* is often carelessly written *of: I could have* [or, *could've,* not *could of*] *gone if I'd wanted to. I ought to have* [not to *of*] *gone.*

OF, O.F., Old French.

off (ôf; of), *prep.* 1. not in the usual or correct position on or of; not on: *a button is off his coat.* 2. from; away from: *miles off the main road.* 3. leading from: *an alley off Main St.* 4. seaward from: *the ship anchored off Maine.* —*adv.* 1. from the usual or correct position, condition, etc.: *he took off his hat.* 2. away: *go off on a journey.* 3. distant in time: *Christmas is only five weeks off.* 4. so as to stop or lessen: *turn the water off.* 5. without work: *an afternoon off.* 6. in full; wholly: *clear of the table.* 7. on one's way: *we are off on a trip.* 8. be off, go away; leave quickly. 9. off and on, now and then; intermittently. —*adj.* 1. not connected; stopped: *the electricity is off.* 2. without work: *he pursues his hobby during off hours.* 3. in a specified condition in regard to money, property, etc.: *how well off are we?* 4. not very good; not up to average: *an off season for fruit.* 5. possible but not likely: *an off chance.* 6. more distant; farther: *the off side of a wall.* 7. on the right-hand side: *the nigh horse and the off horse make a team.* 8. seaward. —*interj.* 1. go away! stay away! 2. off with, a. take off. b. away with! —*n.* a being off; thing that *is* off. [OE (stressed) *of.* Cf. OF.] ▶ See of for usage note.

off., office; officer; official.

of·fal (ôf′əl; of′əl), *n.* 1. the waste parts of an animal killed for food. 2. garbage; refuse. [< *off + fall*]

off-beat (ôf′bēt′), *adj. Colloq.* unusual; beyond the ordinary, esp. in literature, art, music, etc.

off-col·or (ôf′kul′ər; of′–), *adj.* 1. defective in color. 2. *Am.* somewhat improper.

of·fend (ə·fend′), *v.* 1. hurt the feelings of; make angry; displease. 2. sin. [< OF < L, < *ob*-against + *fendere* strike] —of·fend′er, *n.* —of·fend′ing·ly, *adv.* —Syn. 1. affront, provoke, annoy, vex. 2. transgress.

of·fense, *esp. Brit.* **of·fence** (ə·fens′), *n.* 1. a breaking of the law; sin: *an offense against God and man.* 2. cause of wrongdoing. 3. condition of being offended; hurt feelings; anger. 4. act of offending; hurting someone's feelings: *no offense was meant.* 5. act of attacking: *a gun is a weapon of offense.* 6. those who are attacking. —of·fense′less, *esp. Brit.* of·fence′less, *adj.* —of·fense′less·ly, *esp. Brit.* of·fence′less·ly, *adv.* —Syn. 1. crime, misdemeanor, transgression. 3. resentment, displeasure.

of·fen·sive (ə·fen′siv), *adj.* 1. giving offense; irritating; annoying: *an offensive remark.* 2. unpleasant; disagreeable; disgusting: *an offensive odor.* 3. ready to attack; attacking. 4. used for attack; having to do with attack: *offensive weapons.* —*n.* 1. position or attitude of attack: *the army took the offensive.* 2. attack. —of·fen′sive·ly, *adv.* —of·fen′sive·ness, *n.* —Syn. *adj.* 2. displeasing, distasteful. 3. aggressive.

of·fer (ôf′ər; of′–), *v.* 1. hold out to be taken or refused; present: *he offered us his help.* 2. present to be seen or noticed. 3. present for sale. 4. bid as a price. 5. be willing if another approves: *he offered to help us.* 6. propose: *she offered a few ideas.* 7. present in worship: *offer prayers.* 8. give; show: *offer resistance.* 9. present itself; occur: *I will come if the opportunity offers.* 10. show intention; attempt; try: *offer to hit.* —*n.* act or fact of offering: *an offer of money, an offer to sing.* [ult. < L, < *ob-* to + *ferre* bring] —of′fer·er, of′fer·or, *n.* —Syn. *v.* 1. proffer, tender. 6. advance, suggest. 10. endeavor.

of·fer·ing (ôf′ər·ing; ŏf′ring; of′-), *n.* 1. the giving of something as an act of worship. 2. contribution. 3. act of one that offers.

of·fer·to·ry (ôf′ər·tō′ri; -tō′-; of′-), *n., pl.* -ries. 1. collection at a religious service. 2. verses said or the music sung or played while the offering is received. 3. in the Roman Catholic Church, part of the Mass at which bread and wine are offered to God. —of′fer·to′ri·al, *adj.* —of′fer·to′ri·al·ly, *adv.*

off·hand (ôf′hand′; of′-), *adv.* without previous thought or preparation. —*adj.* Also, off′-hand′ed. 1. done or made offhand. 2. casual; informal. —off′hand′ed·ly, *adv.* —off′hand′ed·ness, *n.* —Syn. *adj.* 1. unpremeditated, unstudied, impromptu, extemporaneous. 3. unceremonious.

of·fice (ôf′is; of′-), *n.* 1. place in which the work of a position is done; room or rooms for clerical work. 2. position, esp. in the public service. 3. duty of one's position; task; job; work: *a teacher's office is teaching.* 4. staff of persons carrying on work in an office. 5. an administrative department of a governmental organization. 6. act of kindness or unkindness; attention: *through the good offices of a friend, he was able to get a job.* 7. a religious ceremony or prayer. [< OF < L *officium* service] —Syn. 2. post, situation. 3. function, charge.

of·fice·hold·er (ôf′is·hōl′dər; of′-), *n.* a government official.

of·fi·cer (ôf′ə·sər; of′ə-), *n.* 1. person who commands others in the army or navy. 2. captain of a ship or any of his chief assistants. 3. person who holds a public, church, or government office. 4. person appointed or elected to an administrative position in a club, society, etc. —*v.* 1. provide with officers. 2. direct; conduct; manage. —of′fi·cer·less, *adj.* —of′fi·cer·ship′, *n.*

officer of the day, army or navy officer who has charge, for the time being, of the guards, prisoners, barracks, etc.

of·fi·cial (ə·fish′əl), *n.* 1. person who holds a public position or who is in charge of some public work or duty: *the President and Secretary of State are government officials.* 2. person holding office; officer: *bank officials.* —*adj.* 1. of or pertaining to an office: *an official uniform.* 2. having authority: *an official record.* [< L *officialis.* See OFFICE.] —of·fi′cial·dom, *n.* —of·fi′cial·ism, *n.* —of·fi′cial·ly, *adv.*

of·fi·ci·ate (ə·fish′i·āt), *v.,* -at·ed, -at·ing. 1. perform the duties of any office or position. 2. perform the duties of a priest or minister. —of·fi′ci·a′tion, *n.* —of·fi′ci·a′tor, *n.*

of·fic·i·nal (ə·fis′ə·nəl), *adj.* 1. kept in stock by druggists. 2. recognized by the pharmacopoeia. —*n.* an official drug. [< Med.L < L *officina* shop, ult. < *opus* work + *facere* do]

of·fi·cious (ə·fish′əs), *adj.* too ready to offer services or advice; minding other people's business; fond of meddling. [< L *officiosus* dutiful. See OFFICE.] —of·fi′cious·ly, *adv.* —of·fi′cious·ness, *n.* —Syn. meddlesome, intrusive.

off·ing (ôf′ing; of′-), *n.* 1. the more distant part of the sea as seen from the shore. 2. in the offing, a. just visible from the shore. b. within sight. c. not far off.

off·ish (ôf′ish; of′-), *adj. Colloq.* inclined to keep aloof; distant and reserved in manner. —off′ish·ly, *adv.* —off′ish·ness, *n.*

off·scour·ings (ôf′skour′ingz; of′-), *n.pl.* 1. filth; refuse. 2. low, worthless people.

off·set (*v.* ôf′set′, of′-; *n.* ôf′set′, of′-), *v.,* -set, -set·ting, *n.* —*v.* 1. make up for; balance: *the better roads offset the greater distance.* 2. set off or balance: *offset the better roads against the greater distance.* —*n.* 1. something which makes up for something else; compensation. 2.

process of printing in which the inked impression is first made on a rubber roller and then on the paper, instead of directly on paper. 3. ledge formed on a wall by lessening its thickness above. —Syn. *v.* 1. counterbalance, neutralize.

off·shoot (ôf′shŭt′; of′-), *n.* 1. shoot or branch growing out from the main stem of a plant, tree, etc. 2. anything coming, or thought of as coming, from a main part, stock, race, etc.

off·shore (ôf′shōr′; -shôr′; of′-), *adv., adj.* off or away from the shore.

off·side, off·side (ôf′sid′; of′-), *adj.* away from one's own or the proper side; being on the wrong side.

off·spring (ôf′spring′; of′-), *n.* 1. what is born from or grows out of something; child or children; descendant. 2. result; effect.

off·stage (ôf′stāj′; of′-), *adj.* away from the part of the stage that the audience can see.

off-the-cuff (ôf′thə·kuf′), *Colloq.* —*adj.* made without preparation; impromptu: *an off-the-cuff speech.* —*adv.* Also, **off the cuff.** without preparation.

oft (ôft; oft), *adv. Archaic.* often. [OE]

of·ten (ôf′ən; of′-; -tən), *adv.* in many cases; many times; frequently: *blame is often misdirected, he comes here often.* [ME, < *oft*] —Syn. generally, repeatedly. ► **often.** Pronouncing the *t* is usually a localism, but it is sometimes sounded in singing to make an emphatic syllable. *Oft* is archaic, used by amateur poets who have to count their syllables.

of·ten·times (ôf′ən·timz′; of′-), **oft·times** (ôft′timz′; of′-), *adv.* often.

o·gee (ō·jē′; ō′jē), *n.* an S-shaped curve or line. [< F *ogive*]

o·gle (ō′gəl), *v.,* o·gled, o·gling, *n.* —*v.* 1. look at with desire; make eyes at. 2. look with desire; make eyes. —*n.* an ogling look. [< Du. *oogelen* < *oog* eye] —o′gler, *n.*

Ogee arch

o·gre (ō′gər), *n.* giant or monster that supposedly eats people. [< F] —o·gre·ish (ō′gər·ish), o·grish (ō′grish), *adj.*

oh, Oh (ō), *interj., n., pl.* oh's, ohs; Oh's, Ohs. —*interj.* 1. word used before names in addressing persons: *Oh, Mary, look!* 2. expression of surprise, joy, grief, pain, and other feelings. —*n.* the exclamation, Oh.

O'Hare Airport (ō·hãr′), a major airport in Chicago, Illinois.

OHG, O.H.G., Old High German.

O·hi·o (ō·hi′ō), *n.* 1. a Middle Western State of the United States. *Capital:* Columbus. 2. river in the United States, flowing SW from Pittsburgh into the Mississippi. —O·hi′o·an, *adj., n. Am.*

ohm (ōm), *n.* unit of electrical resistance. One ohm is the resistance of a conductor through which one volt can send a current of one ampere. [named for G. S. *Ohm,* physicist] —ohm′ic, *adj.* —ohm′me′ter, *n.*

-oid, *suffix.* 1. like; like that of, as in *Mongoloid, amoeboid.* 2. thing like a, as in *spheroid, alkaloid.* [< Gk, < *eidos* form]

oil (oil), *n.* 1. any of several kinds of thick, fatty or greasy liquids that are lighter than water, that burn easily, and that dissolve in alcohol, but not in water. Mineral oils are used for fuel; animal and vegetable oils are used in cooking, medicine, and in many other ways. Essential or volatile oils, such as oil of peppermint, are distilled from plants, leaves, flowers, etc., and are thin and evaporate very quickly. 2. mineral oil; petroleum. 3. olive oil. 4. substance that resembles oil in some respect. 5. oil paint. 6. an oil painting. —*v.* 1. put oil on or in. 2. bribe. [< OF < L *oleum* < Gk. *elaion*] —oil′er, *n.*

oil cake, mass of linseed, cottonseed, etc., from which the oil has been pressed, used as a food for cattle and sheep or as a fertilizer.

oil·cloth (oil′klôth′; -kloth′), *n.* cloth made waterproof by coating it with paint or oil.

oil of vitriol, sulfuric acid.

oil paint or color, paint made by mixing pigment with oil.

oil painting, 1. picture painted with oil colors. **2.** art of painting with oil colors.

oil·skin (oil′skin′), *n.* **1.** cloth treated with oil to make it waterproof. **2.** Usually, **oilskins.** coat and trousers made of this cloth.

oil well, *Am.* well drilled in the earth to get oil.

oil·y (oil′i), *adj.*, **oil·i·er, oil·i·est. 1.** of oil. **2.** containing oil. **3.** covered or soaked with oil. **4.** like oil; smooth; slippery. —**oil′i·ly,** *adv.* —**oil′i·ness,** *n.*

oint·ment (oint′mənt), *n.* substance made from oil or fat, often containing medicine, used on the skin to heal or to make it soft and white. [< OF *oignement*, ult. < L *unguere* anoint; form infl. by *anoint*] —**Syn.** unguent, salve, balm.

O·jib·wa, O·jib·way (ō·jib′wä), *n., pl.* **-wa, -was; -way, -ways;** *adj.* **-wa.** *Am.* member of a large tribe of American Indians formerly living near the Great Lakes; Chippewa. —*adj.* of this tribe.

OK, O.K. (ō′kā′), *adj., adv., v.,* **OK'd, OK'ing; O.K.'d, O.K.'ing;** *n., pl.* **OK's; O.K.'s.** *Am. Colloq.* —*adj., adv.* all right; correct; approved. —*v.* endorse; approve. —*n.* approval. [prob. from the "O.K. Club," a Democratic club of New York City formed in 1840 by supporters of Martin Van Buren; so called in allusion to "Old Kinderhook," Van Buren having been born at Kinderhook, N.Y.] ≫ **OK, O.K.** Business and colloquial English for "correct, all right, approved." Occasionally spelled *okay,* rarely *okeh.*

o·ka·pi (ō·kä′pi), *n., pl.* **-pis, -pi.** an African animal like the giraffe, but smaller and with a much shorter neck. [< an African lang.]

o·kay (ō′kā′), *adj., adv., v., n. Am., Colloq.* OK.

o·keh (ō′kā′), *adj., adv., v., n. Colloq., Rare.* OK.

O·khotsk (ō·kotsk′), *n.* Sea of, sea E of the Soviet Union in Asia and N of Japan. It is part of the Pacific Ocean.

O·kie (ō′ki), *n., Am., Colloq.* a migratory farm worker, originally one from Oklahoma.

O·ki·na·wa (ō′kə·ni′wə), *n.* a large island in the Ryukyu group in the N Pacific; captured by the United States in 1945.

Okla., Oklahoma.

O·kla·ho·ma (ō′klə·hō′mə), *n.* a Southern State of the United States. *Capital:* Oklahoma City. *Abbrev.:* Okla. —**O′kla·ho′man,** *adj., n. Am.*

Oklahoma City, capital of Oklahoma, in the C part.

o·kra (ō′krə), *n.* **1.** plant cultivated for its sticky pods, which are used in soups and as a vegetable. **2.** the pods. [< West African lang.]

OL, Old Latin.

O·lav V (ō′läf), born 1903, king of Norway since 1957.

old (ōld), *adj.,* **old·er** or **eld·er, old·est** or **eld·est,** *n.* —*adj.* **1.** having existed long; aged: *an old wall.* **2.** of age; in age: *the baby is one year old.* **3.** of or pertaining to aged persons or things: *a good old age.* **4.** not new; made, used, or known long ago: *an old excuse.* **5.** made, used, or known very long ago; ancient: *an old tomb, the old language of Hellenic civilization.* **6.** much worn by age or use: *old clothes.* **7.** looking or seeming old. **8.** mature: *old for her years.* **9.** having much experience. **10.** former: *an old student.* **11.** earlier or earliest: *Old English.* **12.** no longer used: *an old spelling.* **13.** familiar; dear: *good old fellow.* **14.** *Colloq.* good; fine. **15.** of colors, dull and soft. —*n.* time long ago. [OE *eald*] —**old′ish,** *adj.* —**old′ness,** *n.* —**Syn.** *adj.* **3.** elderly. **5.** antique, antiquated. **6.** dilapidated, decayed, shabby, outworn. **9.** experienced, practiced. **12.** obsolete, superannuated.

old age, years of life from about 65 on.

old country, country an emigrant comes from, often Great Britain or Ireland.

old·en (ōl′dən), *adj. Poetic.* of old; old; ancient.

Old English, 1. period in the history of the English language before 1100. **2.** language of this

period; Anglo-Saxon. **3.** kind of black-letter type.

This is Old English.

old-fash·ioned (ōld′fash′ənd), *adj.* **1.** of an old fashion: *an old-fashioned dress.* **2.** keeping to old ways, ideas, etc.: *an old-fashioned house-keeper.*

old-fo·gy, old-fo·gey (ōld′fō′gi), or **old-fo·gy·ish, old-fo·gey·ish** (-ish), *adj.* out-of-date; behind the times.

Old French, the French language from about 800 A.D. to about 1400.

Old Glory, *Am.* flag of the United States.

Old High German, form of the German language that was spoken in S Germany from about 800 A.D. to 1100. Modern standard German is descended from Old High German.

Old Icelandic, Old Norse (def. 2).

Old Latin, the Latin language before the second century B.C.

old-line (ōld′līn′), *adj.* **1.** conservative. **2.** established.

old maid, 1. woman who has not married and seems unlikely to. **2.** a prim, fussy person. —**old′-maid′ish,** *adj.* —**Syn. 1.** spinster.

old master, 1. any great painter who lived before 1700. **2.** a painting by such a painter.

Old Norse, 1. Scandinavian speech from the Viking period to about 1300. **2.** the Icelandic language in the Middle Ages.

Old Saxon, the form of Low German spoken by the Saxons in NW Germany from about 800 A.D. to about 1100.

old school, group of people who have old-fashioned or conservative ideas.

old·ster (ōld′stər), *n. Colloq.* an old or older person.

old style, kind of type.

This line is printed in old style.

—**old′-style′,** *adj.*

Old Testament, the earlier part of the Bible, which contains the religious and social laws of the Hebrews, a record of their history, their important literature, and writings of their prophets.

old-time (ōld′tīm′), *adj.* of former times; like old times.

old-tim·er (ōld′tīm′ər), *n. Colloq.* person who has long been a resident, member, worker, etc.

old wives' tale, a foolish story or belief.

old-wom·an·ish (ōld′wŭm′ən·ish), *adj.* like, suggesting, or befitting an old woman; fussy.

old-world (ōld′wėrld′), *adj.* **1.** of or pertaining to the ancient world. **2.** belonging to or characteristic of a former period: *old-world courtesy.* **3.** Also, **Old-World.** of or pertaining to the Eastern Hemisphere; not American.

Old World, Europe, Asia, and Africa.

o·le·ag·i·nous (ō′li·aj′ə·nəs), *adj.* oily. [< L, < *olea* olive tree] —**o′le·ag′i·nous·ly,** *adv.* —**o′le·ag′i·nous·ness,** *n.*

o·le·an·der (ō′li·an′dər), *n.* a poisonous evergreen shrub with fragrant red, pink, or white flowers. [< Med.L]

o·le·ic acid (ō·lē′ik; ō′li·ik), an oily liquid, $C_{17}H_{33}COOH$, obtained by hydrolyzing various animal and vegetable oils and fats.

o·le·in (ō′li·in), *n.* ester of oleic acid and glycerin. Lard, olive oil, and cottonseed oil are mostly olein.

o·le·o·mar·ga·rine (ō′li·ō·mär′jə·rēn; -rin), **o·le·o·mar·ga·rin** (-rin), or **o·le·o** (ō′li·ō), *n. Am.* a substitute for butter made from animal fats and vegetable oils; margarine.

o·le·o·res·in (ō′li·ō·rez′ən), *n.* a natural or prepared solution of resin in oil.

ol·fac·tion (ol·fak′shən), *n.* **1.** act of smelling. **2.** sense of smell. [< L *olfactus,* pp. of *olfacere* smell at < *olere* emit a smell + *facere* make]

ol·fac·to·ry (ol·fak′tə·ri), *adj., n., pl.* **-ries.** —*adj.* Sometimes, **ol·fac′tive.** having to do with smelling; of smell. The nose is an olfactory organ. —*n.* an olfactory organ.

ol·i·garch (ol′ə·gärk), *n.* one of the members of an oligarchy.

Okra pods

ol·i·gar·chy (ol′ə·gär′ki), *n.*, *pl.* **-chies.** 1. form of government in which a few people have the power. 2. country or state having such a government. 3. the ruling few. [< Gk., ult. < *oligos* few + *archos* leader] —**ol′i·gar′chic, ol′i·gar′chi·cal,** *adj.* —**ol′i·gar′chi·cal·ly,** *adv.*

ol·ive (ol′iv), *n.* 1. kind of evergreen tree with gray-green leaves that grows in southern Europe and other warm regions. 2. fruit of this tree, with a hard stone and bitter pulp. 3. wood of the olive tree. 4. a yellowish green. 5. a yellowish brown. —*adj.* 1. yellowish-green. 2. yellowish-brown. [< F < L *oliva* < Gk. *elaia*]

olive branch, 1. anything offered as a sign of peace. 2. child.

olive oil, oil pressed from olives, used as food and in medicine.

ol·la (ol′ə), *n.* Am. 1. an earthen water jar or cooking pot. 2. a stew. [< Sp. < L]

ol·o·gy (ol′ə·ji), *n.*, *pl.* **-gies.** any science or branch of knowledge. [< connective -o- + -LOGY]

O·lym·pi·a (ō·lim′pi·ə), *n.* 1. plain in ancient Greece where games were held every four years in honor of Zeus. 2. capital of Washington, in the W part of the State. —**O·lym′pic,** *adj.*

O·lym·pi·ad, o·lym·pi·ad (ō·lim′pi·ad), *n.* celebration of the modern Olympic games.

O·lym·pi·an (ō·lim′pi·ən), *adj.* 1. pertaining to Olympia or to Mount Olympus. 2. like a god; heavenly. 3. rather too gracious; magnificent; superior.

O·lym·pic games (ō·lim′pik), 1. Also, Olympian games, contests in athletics, poetry, and music, held every four years by the ancient Greeks in honor of Zeus. 2. Also, the Olympics, modern athletic contests imitating the athletic contests of these games. They are held once every four years in a different country, and athletes from many nations compete in them.

O·lym·pus (ō·lim′pəs), *n.* 1. Mount, mountain in NE Greece, where the greater Greek gods were supposed to live. 2. heaven.

O·ma·ha (ō′mə·hô; -hä), *n.* city in E Nebraska.

O·mar Khay·yam (ō′mär kī·yäm′; kī′am), died 1123?, Persian poet.

o·ma·sum (ō·mā′səm), *n.*, *pl.* **-sa** (-sə). the third stomach of a cow or other ruminant. It receives the food when it is swallowed the second time. [< L]

o·me·ga (ō·meg′ə; ō·mē′gə; ō·mā′gə), *n.* 1. the last letter of the Greek alphabet (Ω or ω). 2. the last of any series; end. [< LGk. *o mega* big o]

om·e·let, om·e·lette (om′ə·lit; om′lit), *n.* eggs beaten up with milk or water, fried or baked, and then folded over. [< F *omelette*]

o·men (ō′mən), *n.* 1. sign of what is to happen; object or event that is believed to mean good or bad fortune. 2. prophetic meaning: *a bird of ill omen.* —*v.* be a sign of; presage. [< L] —**Syn.** *n.* 1. augury, portent, presage.

om·i·cron (om′ə·kron; ō′mə-), *n.* the 15th letter of the Greek alphabet (O or o). [< Gk. *o micron* small o]

om·i·nous (om′ə·nəs), *adj.* of bad omen; unfavorable; threatening: *those clouds look ominous for our picnic.* [< L, < *omen* omen] —**om′i·nous·ly,** *adv.* —**om′i·nous·ness,** *n.* —**Syn.** inauspicious, menacing, foreboding.

o·mis·sion (ō·mish′ən), *n.* 1. an omitting or being omitted. 2. thing omitted.

o·mit (ō·mit′), *v.*, **o·mit·ted, o·mit·ting.** 1. leave out: *omit a letter in a word.* 2. fail to do; neglect: *Mary omitted making her bed.* [< L *omittere* < *ob-* by + *mittere* let go] —**o·mit′tance,** *n.* —**o·mit′ter,** *n.* —**Syn.** 2. overlook, ignore, skip.

om·ni·bus (om′nə·bus), *n.*, *pl.* **-bus·es,** *adj.* —*n.* bus. —*adj.* covering many things at once: *an omnibus law.* [< L, for all]

om·ni·far·i·ous (om′nə·fār′i·əs), *adj.* of all forms, varieties, or kinds. [< L *omnifarius*] —**om′ni·far′i·ous·ness,** *n.*

om·nip·o·tence (om·nip′ə·təns), *n.* complete power; unlimited power.

om·nip·o·tent (om·nip′ə·tənt), *adj.* having all power; almighty. —*n.* the Omnipotent, God. [< L, < *omnis* all + *potens* being able] —**om·nip′o·tent·ly,** *adv.*

om·ni·pres·ence (om′nə·prez′əns), *n.* presence everywhere at the same time: *God's omnipresence.*

om·ni·pres·ent (om′nə·prez′ənt), *adj.* present everywhere at the same time.

om·nis·cience (om·nish′əns), *n.* knowledge of everything; complete or infinite knowledge. [< Med.L, < L *omnis* all + *scientia* knowledge]

om·nis·cient (om·nish′ənt), *adj.* having complete or infinite knowledge; knowing everything. —**om·nis′cient·ly,** *adv.*

om·niv·o·rous (om·niv′ə·rəs), *adj.* 1. eating every kind of food. 2. eating both animal and vegetable food. 3. taking in everything; fond of all kinds: *an omnivorous reader.* [< L, < *omnis* all + *vorare* eat greedily] —**om·niv′o·rous·ly,** *adv.* —**om·niv′o·rous·ness,** *n.*

Omsk (omsk), *n.* city in the C Soviet Union, in W Siberia.

on (on; ôn), *prep.* 1. above and supported by: *on the table.* 2. touching so as to cover, be around, etc.: *put the ring on her finger.* 3. close to: *a house on the shore.* 4. in the direction of; toward: *the workers marched on the capitol.* 5. against; upon: *the picture on the wall.* 6. by means of; by the use of: *this news is on good authority.* 7. in the condition of; in the process of; in the way of: *on half pay, on purpose, on duty.* 8. at the time of; during: *they greeted us on our arrival, on Sunday.* 9. in relation to; in connection with; concerning: *a book on animals.* 10. for the purpose of: *he went on an errand.* 11. in addition to: *defeat on defeat discouraged them.* 12. among: *who is on the committee?* —*adv.* 1. on something: *the walls are up, and the roof is on.* 2. to something: *hold on, or you may fall.* 3. toward something: *some played; the others looked on.* 4. farther: *march on.* 5. in or into a condition, process, manner, action, etc.: *turn the gas on.* 6. from a time; forward: *from that day on.* 7. with the indicated part forward: *head on.* 8. and so on, and more of the same. 9. on and on, without stopping. —*adj.* taking place: *the race is on.* [OE]

ON, O.N., Old Norse.

o·nan·ism (ō′nən·iz·əm), *n.* 1. in coitus, withdrawal before emission occurs. 2. masturbation. [< *Onan,* a proper name; see Gen. 38:9] —**o′nan·ist,** *n.*

once (wuns), *adv.* 1. one time: *he comes once a day.* 2. at some one time in the past; formerly: *a once powerful nation.* 3. even a single time; ever: *if the facts once become known.* 4. once and again, repeatedly. 5. once for all, finally or decisively. 6. once in a while, now and then. 7. once or twice, a few times. 8. once over, a single time over. —*n.* 1. a single occasion: *once is enough.* 2. at once, a. immediately. b. at one and the same time. —*conj.* if ever; whenever: *once you cross the river you are safe.* —*adj.* former: *a once friend.* [OE *ānes* < an ONE]

once-o·ver (wuns′ō′vər), *n.* Am., Slang. a single or brief inspection.

on·com·ing (on′kum′ing; ôn′-), *adj.* approaching. —*n.* approach.

one (wun), *n.* 1. a cardinal number, the first and lowest whole number. 2. symbol of this number; 1. 3. a single person or thing: *I gave him the one he wanted.* 4. at one, in agreement or harmony. 5. make one, a. form or be one of a number, assembly, or party. b. join together; unite in marriage. 6. one and all, everyone. 7. one by one, one after another. —*adj.* 1. a single: *one apple.* 2. some: *one day he will be sorry.* 3. the same: *they held one opinion.* 4. joined together; united: *they replied in one voice.* 5. a certain: *one John Smith was elected.* 6. all one, all the same. —*pron.* 1. some person or thing: *one of the poems was selected for the book.* 2. any person or thing: *one must work hard to achieve success.* 3. the same person or thing: *Dr. Jekyll and Mr. Hyde were one and*

āge, cāre, fär; ēqual, tėrm; īce; ōpen, ôrder; put, rūle, ūse; th, then; ə=a in about.

the same. [OE (stressed) *ān*. Cf. A, AN¹.] ▶ **one.**
The use of the impersonal pronoun *one* is characteristically formal, especially if it must be repeated: *One can't be too careful, can one?* (formal). *You can't be too careful, can you?* (informal). This repetition of *one*, often to avoid *I*,
often when *you* would be more natural, is deadly.
American usage stands firmly by older English
usage in referring back to *one* by *he, his, him*
(or *she, her*): *One is warned to be cautious if he
would avoid offending his friends and bringing
their displeasure down upon his head.*

one an·oth·er, one the other: *they struck at one
another, they were in one another's way.*

one-horse (wun'hôrs'), *adj.* **1.** drawn or
worked by a single horse. **2.** *U.S. Colloq.* of little
scope, capacity, or importance; minor; petty.

O·nei·da (ō-nī'də), *n. Am.* member of an
American Indian tribe formerly living in C New
York State.

O'Neill (ō-nēl'), *n.* Eugene (Gladstone), 1888–
1953, American dramatist.

one·ness (wun'nis), *n.* **1.** singleness. **2.** sameness. **3.** unity. **4.** agreement.

on·er·ous (on'ər-əs), *adj.* burdensome; oppressive. [< L *onerosus* < *onus* burden] —on'
er·ous·ly, *adv.* —on'er·ous·ness, *n.* —Syn.
heavy, weighty, arduous.

one·self (wun-self'), **one's self,** *pron.* **1.**
one's own self: *one should not praise oneself.* **2.**
be oneself. **a.** have full control of one's mind or
body. **b.** act naturally.

one-sid·ed (wun'sīd'id), *adj.* **1.** seeing only
one side of a question; partial; prejudiced. **2.**
uneven; unequal. **3.** having but one side.

one-step (wun'step'), *n., v., -stepped, -stepping.* —*n.* **1.** dance much like a quick walk. **2.**
music for it. —*v.* dance the one-step.

one-time (wun'tīm'), *adj.* of the past; former.

one-track (wun'trak'), *adj.* **1.** having only
one track. **2.** *Colloq.* understanding or doing
only one thing at a time; narrow.

one-up·man·ship (wun'up'mən-ship), *n.
Colloq.* skill of being able to gain the advantage
over one's opponent.

one-way (wun'wā'), *adj.* moving or allowing
movement in only one direction.

one-world·er (wun'wérl'dər), *n.* one who
advocates internationalism.

on·ion (un'yən), *n.* **1.** a bulblike root with a
sharp, strong smell and taste. **2.** the plant it
grows on. [< F < L *unio* onion, kind of pearl]

on·ion·skin (un'yən-skin'), *n.* a thin, glossy,
translucent paper.

on·look·er (on'lûk'ər; ôn'-), *n.* person who
watches without taking part; spectator. —on'
look'ing, *adj., n.*

on·ly (ōn'li), *adj.* **1.** by itself or themselves;
sole, single, or few of the kind or class: *an only
son.* **2.** best; finest: *he is the only writer for my
tastes.* —*adv.* **1.** merely; just: *he sold only two.*
2. and no one else; and nothing more; and that
is all: *only he remained.* **3.** if only, I wish: *if
only wars would cease!* **4.** only too, very: *she
was only too glad to help us.* —*conj.* except that;
but: *I would have gone only you objected.* [OE
ānlīc] —Syn. *adj.* **1.** solitary, unique. ▶ **only.**
The importance of the position of *only* has been
greatly exaggerated. Logically it should stand
immediately before the element modified: *I need
only six more to have a full hundred.* But usage
is not always logical, and in this construction
usage is conspicuously in favor of placing the
only before the verb of the statement. There is
no possible misunderstanding in the meaning of:
I only need six more to have a full hundred.

on·o·mat·o·poe·ia (on'ə·mat'ə·pē'ə), *n.* **1.**
formation of a name or word by imitating the
sound associated with the thing designated, as
in *buzz, hum, cuckoo, slap, splash.* **2.** adaptation
of the sound to the sense for rhetorical effect,
as in "the murmurous haunt of flies on summer
eves." [< L < Gk., < *onoma* word, name + *-poios*
making] —on'o·mat'o·poe'ic, on·o·mat·o·po·
et·ic (on'ə·mat'ə·pō·et'ik), *adj.* —on'o·mat'o·
po·et'i·cal·ly, *adv.*

On·on·da·ga (on'ən-dô'gə; -dä'-), *Am. n.*

member of a tribe of American Indians formerly
living in C New York State.

on·rush (on'rush'; ôn'-), *n.* a violent forward
rush.

on·set (on'set'; ôn'-), *n.* **1.** attack: *the onset of
the enemy took us by surprise.* **2.** beginning: *the
onset of this disease is gradual.* —Syn. **1.** assault,
onslaught. **2.** commencement, start.

on·shore (on'shôr'; -shōr'; ôn'-), *adv., adj.* **1.**
toward the land. **2.** on the land.

on·slaught (on'slôt'; ôn'-), *n.* a vigorous
attack.

Ont., Ontario.

On·tar·i·o (on-târ'i-ō), *n.* **1.** Lake, smallest
and easternmost of the five Great Lakes, between the U.S. and Canada. **2.** province in Canada, N of the Great Lakes. —On·tar'i·an, *adj., n.*

on-the-cuff (on'thə-kuf'), *Colloq.* —*adj.* **1.** to
buy on credit. **2.** to be paid for in installments.
—*adv.* Also, **on the cuff.** on credit.

on·to (on'tü; ôn'-), *prep.* on to; to a position
on. ▶ **onto, on to.** When *on* is an adverb and *to*
a preposition in a separate locution, they should
of course be written as two words: *The rest of
us drove on / to the city.* When the words make
a definite preposition, they are usually written
solid: *The team trotted onto the floor. They
looked out onto the park.* *Onto* is frequently used
as a colloquial double preposition when *on* or *to*
by itself would be used in writing: *They finally
got on* [colloquial, *onto*] *the bus. The crowd got
to* [colloquial, *onto*] *James Street.*

o·nus (ō'nəs), *n.* burden; responsibility. [< L]

on·ward (on'wərd; ôn'-), *adv.* Also, **on'wards.**
toward the front; further on; on; forward:
move onward. —*adj.* on; further on; toward the
front; forward: *an onward movement.*

on·yx (on'iks), *n.* a semiprecious variety of
quartz with layers of different colors and shades.
[< L < Gk., nail, claw]

oo·long (ü'lông; -long), *n.* a black tea consisting of leaves that were partially fermented
before they were dried. [< Chinese *wu-lung*
black dragon]

ooze¹ (üz), *v.*, **oozed, ooz·ing,** *n.* —*v.* **1.** pass out
slowly through small openings; leak out slowly
and quietly: *his courage oozed away as he
waited.* **2.** give out slowly: *the cut oozed blood.*
[< n.] —*n.* **1.** a slow flow. **2.** something that
oozes. [OE *wōs* juice] —oo'zy, *adj.* —oo'zi·ness,
n.

ooze² (üz), *n.* a soft mud or slime, esp. at the
bottom of a pond, river, or on the ocean bottom.
[OE *wāse* mud] —oo'zy, *adj.* —oo'zi·ness, *n.*

op., **1.** opus; opera. **2.** opposite.

o·pac·i·ty (ō-pas'ə·ti), *n., pl.* **-ties. 1.** a being
opaque; darkness; a being impervious to light.
2. something opaque.

o·pal (ō'pəl), *n.* a mineral, an amorphous form
of silica, found in many varieties and colors
(often a milky white), certain of which have a
peculiar rainbow play of colors and are valued
as gems. [< L *opalus* < Gk. *opallios* < Skt. *upala*
precious stone] —o·pal·ine (ō'pəl·in; -in), *adj.*

o·pal·esce (ō'pəl·es'), *v.*, **-esced, -esc·ing.** exhibit a play of colors like that of the opal.
—o'pal·es'cence, *n.* —o'pal·es'cent, *adj.*

o·paque (ō-pāk'), *adj.* **1.** not letting light
through; not transparent. **2.** not shining; dark;
dull. **3.** obscure; hard to understand. **4.** stupid.
—*n.* something opaque. [< L *opacus* dark, shady]
—o·paque'ly, *adv.* —o·paque'ness, *n.*

op art (op), optical art.

op. cit., in the work cited. [< L *opere citato*]

ope (ōp), *v.*, **oped, op·ing.** *Poetic.* open.

o·pen (ō'pən), *adj.* **1.** not shut; not closed: *an
open gate.* **2.** not having its door, gate, lid, etc.,
closed: *an open box.* **3.** not closed in: *an open
space.* **4.** unfilled; not taken: *a position still
open.* **5.** that may be entered, used, shared,
competed for, etc., by all: *an open market.* **6.**
accessible or available: *the only course still open.*
7. without prohibition or restriction: *open
season for hunting.* **8.** *Am., Colloq.* allowing
saloons, gambling, etc.: *an open town.* **9.** undecided; not settled: *an open question.* **10.** having no cover, roof, etc.; letting in air freely: *an*

open carriage. 11. not covered or protected; exposed: *open to temptation.* **12.** not obstructed: *an open view.* **13.** exposed to general view, knowledge, etc.; not secret: *open disregard of rules.* **14.** accessible to knowledge, sympathy, etc.: *an open mind.* **15.** having spaces or holes: *cloth of open texture.* **16.** *Music.* of a note, produced without aid of slide, key, etc. **17.** *Phonet.* uttered with relatively wide opening over the tongue. **18.** unreserved, candid, or frank: *an open face.* **19.** that is spread out; expanded: *an open newspaper.* **20.** generous; liberal: *give with an open hand.* **21.** *Mil.* of a city, town, etc., unfortified; protected from enemy attack under international law. **22. open to, a.** ready to take; willing to consider. **b.** liable to. **c.** to be had or used by. —*n.* **1.** an open or clear space; opening. **2.** the **open, a.** the open country, air, sea, etc. **b.** public view or knowledge. —*v.* **1.** afford access (into, to, etc.); have an opening. **2.** become open or more open; become accessible. **3.** cause to be open or more open; make accessible. **4.** clear of obstructions; make (a passage, etc.) clear; make (an opening): *open a channel through the ice.* **5.** make or become accessible; enlighten or become enlightened. **6.** lay bare; expose to view; uncover; disclose; reveal. **7.** come to view. **8.** expand, extend, or spread out; make or become less compact: *the ranks opened.* **9.** begin; start: *school opens today, open a meeting with prayer.* **10.** cut into. **11. open up, a.** make or become open. **b.** unfold; spread out. **c.** begin; start. [OE; akin to UP] —**o′pen·er,** *n.* —**o′pen·ly,** *adv.* —**o′pen·ness,** *n.* —**Syn.** *adj.* **1.** unclosed, ajar, unlocked. **4.** unoccupied, free. **9.** unsettled, abatable. **11.** uncovered, unprotected. **13.** public. **15.** perforated, porous. **18.** straightforward. **19.** unfolded, extended. —*v.* **6.** divulge. **9.** initiate, commence.

open air, out of doors. —**o′pen-air′,** *adj.*

open door, 1. free access to all. **2.** policy of admitting all nations to a country upon equal terms, esp. for trade. —**o′pen-door′,** *adj.*

open forum, forum or assembly for the discussion of questions of public interest, open to all who wish to take part.

o·pen-hand·ed (ō′pən-han′did), *adj.* generous; liberal. —**o′pen-hand′ed·ly,** *adv.* —**o′pen-hand′ed·ness,** *n.*

o·pen-heart·ed (ō′pən-här′tid), *adj.* **1.** frank; unreserved. **2.** kindly; generous. —**o′pen-heart′ed·ly,** *adv.* —**o′pen-heart′ed·ness,** *n.*

o·pen·ing (ō′pən·ing; ōp′ning), *n.* **1.** an open or clear space; gap; hole: *an opening in a wall.* **2.** the first part; beginning. **3.** a formal beginning: *a spring opening to show the new fashions.* **4.** place or position that is open or vacant. **5.** a favorable chance or opportunity. —**Syn. 1.** aperture, fissure, orifice. **2.** start, commencement, introduction. **4.** vacancy.

open letter, letter addressed to a person but published in a newspaper, magazine, etc.

o·pen-mind·ed (ō′pən-mīn′did), *adj.* having or showing a mind open to new arguments or ideas. —**o′pen-mind′ed·ly,** *adv.* —**o′pen-mind′ed·ness,** *n.*

open question, something undecided or uncertain.

open ses·a·me (ses′ə-mē), **1.** password at which doors or barriers fly open. **2.** a magical means of obtaining entrance.

open shop, *Am.* factory, shop, or other establishment that will employ both union and nonunion workers.

o·pen·work (ō′pən·wẽrk′), *n.* ornamental work that shows openings.

op·er·a¹ (op′ər·ə; op′rə), *n.* **1.** play that is mostly sung, with costumes, scenery, acting, and music to go with the singing. *Faust* and *Lohengrin* are well-known operas. **2.** branch of art represented by such plays: *the history of opera.* **3.** performance of an opera. **4.** theater where operas are performed. [< Ital., for *opera* in *musica* (a dramatic) work to music; *opera* < L, effort (akin to *opus* a work)]

op·er·a² (op′ə·rə), *n.* pl. of **opus.**

op·er·a·ble (op′ər·ə·bəl), *adj.* fit for, or admitting of, a surgical operation. —**op′er·a·ble·ness,** *n.* —**op′er·a·bly,** *adv.*

o·pé·ra bouffe (op′ər·ə büf′; *Fr.* ō·pā·rä büf′), *French.* comic opera.

opera glass or **glasses,** a small binocular telescope for use at the opera and in theaters. Opera glasses are like field glasses, but smaller.

Opera glasses

op·er·ate (op′ər·āt), *v.,* -**at·ed,** -**at·ing. 1.** be at work; run: *the machinery operates night and day.* **2.** manage; keep at work: *who operates this elevator?* **3.** produce an effect; work; act: *several causes operated to bring on the war.* **4.** produce a desired effect: *the medicine operated quickly.* **5.** do something to the body, usually with instruments, to improve health: *the doctor operated on the injured man.* **6.** carry on military movements. [< L *operatus* < *opus* a work, or *opera* effort] —**op′er·at′a·ble,** *adj.* —**op′er·at′a·ble·ness,** *n.* —**op′er·at′a·bly,** *adv.* —**Syn. 1.** perform, function.

op·er·at·ic (op′ər·at′ik), *adj.* of or like the opera. —**op′er·at′i·cal·ly,** *adv.*

op·er·a·tion (op′ər·ā′shən), *n.* **1.** act or fact of working. **2.** the way a thing works: *the operation of a machine.* **3.** action; activity: *the operation of brushing one's teeth.* **4.** in operation, a. running; working; in action. **b.** in use or effect. **5.** a process in some form of work or production. **6.** a business transaction, esp. a speculative one. **7.** something done to the body, usually with instruments, to improve health. **8.** movements of soldiers, ships, supplies, etc., for war purposes. **9.** *Math.* something done to a number or quantity. —**op′er·a′tion·al,** *adj.*

op·er·a·tive (op′ər·ā′tiv; -ə·tiv), *adj.* **1.** operating; effective: *the laws operative in a community.* **2.** of or concerned with surgical operations. —*n.* **1.** worker; laborer. **2.** *Am.* detective. —**op′er·a·tive·ly,** *adv.* —**op′er·a·tive·ness,** *n.*

op·er·a·tor (op′ər·ā′tər), *n.* **1.** person who operates. **2.** a skilled worker who operates a machine, telephone, telegraph, etc. **3.** person who runs a factory, mine, railroad, etc.

o·per·cu·lum (ō·pér′kyə·ləm), *n.,* pl. -**la** (-lə), -**lums.** *Bot., Zool.* a lidlike part or organ; any flap covering an opening. [< L, < *operire* cover]

op·er·et·ta (op′ər·et′ə), *n.,* pl. -**tas.** a short, amusing opera.

oph·thal·mi·a (of·thal′mi·ə), *n.* an acute infection of the membrane around the eye that may affect the eye, causing blindness. [< LL < Gk., < *ophthalmos* eye]

oph·thal·mic (of·thal′mik), *adj.* of or pertaining to the eye.

oph·thal·mol·o·gy (of′thal·mol′ə·ji), *n.* science that deals with the structure, functions, and diseases of the eye. —**oph·thal·mo·log·i·cal** (of·thal′mə·loj′ə·kəl), *adj.* —**oph′thal·mol′o·gist,** *n.*

o·pi·ate (ō′pi·it; -āt), *n.* **1.** drug that contains opium and so dulls pain or brings sleep. **2.** anything that quiets. —*adj.* **1.** containing opium. **2.** bringing sleep or ease. —**o·pi·at·ic** (ō′pi·at′ik), *adj.*

o·pine (ō·pīn′), *v.,* **o·pined, o·pin·ing.** *Humorous.* hold or express an opinion; think. [< L *opinari*] —**o·pin′er,** *n.*

o·pin·ion (ə·pin′yən), *n.* **1.** what one thinks; belief not so strong as knowledge; judgment. **2.** impression; estimate. **3.** a formal judgment by an expert; professional advice. [< L *opinio.* See OPINE.] —**o·pin′ion·al,** *adj.* —**o·pin′ion·al·ly,** *adv.* —**o·pin′ioned,** *adj.* —**Syn. 1.** view, notion, idea. **2.** sentiment. **3.** decision, verdict.

o·pin·ion·at·ed (ə·pin′yən·āt′id), *adj.* obstinate or conceited with regard to one's opinions; dogmatic. —**o·pin′ion·at′ed·ly,** *adv.* —**o·pin′ion·at′ed·ness,** *n.*

o·pin·ion·a·tive (ə·pin′yən·ā′tiv), *adj.* opinionated. —**o·pin′ion·a′tive·ly,** *adv.* —**o·pin′ion·a′tive·ness,** *n.*

o·pi·um (ō′pi·əm), *n.* a powerful drug that causes sleep and eases pain. It is also used to stimulate and intoxicate. Opium is made from a kind of poppy. [< L < Gk. *opion*, dim. of *opos* vegetable juice]

O·por·to (ō·pôr′tō; -pōr′-), *n.* seaport in NW Portugal, noted for port wine.

o·pos·sum (ə·pos′əm), *n. Am.* a small mammal that lives mostly in trees, common in the S United States. When caught, it pretends to be dead. [< Algonquian]

opp., 1. opposed. 2. opposite.

op·po·nent (ə·pō′nənt), *n.* person who is on the other side in a fight, game, or discussion; person fighting, struggling, or speaking against one. —*adj.* opposing. [< L, < *ob-* against + *ponere* place] —**Syn.** *n.* antagonist, adversary, enemy, rival, foe.

op·por·tune (op′ər·tūn′; -tūn′), *adj.* fortunate; well-chosen; favorable; suitable. [< L, favorable (of wind), < *ob portum* (*ferens*) (bringing) to port] —**op′por·tune′ly,** *adv.* —**op′por·tune′ness,** *n.*

op·por·tun·ism (op′ər·tūn′iz·əm; -tūn′-), *n.* policy or practice of adapting thought and action to particular circumstances rather than to general principles. —**op′por·tun′ist,** *n.* —**op′por·tun·is′tic,** *adj.* —**op′por·tun·is′ti·cal·ly,** *adv.*

op·por·tu·ni·ty (op′ər·tū′nə·ti; -tū′-), *n., pl.* -ties. a good chance; favorable time; convenient occasion. —**Syn.** opening.

op·pos·a·ble (ə·pōz′ə·bəl), *adj.* 1. capable of being opposed. 2. capable of being placed opposite something else. The human thumb is opposable to the fingers. —**op·pos′a·bil′i·ty,** *n.*

op·pose (ə·pōz′), *v.,* -posed, -pos·ing. 1. be against; be in the way of; act, fight, or struggle against; try to hinder; resist: *a swamp opposed the advance of the enemy.* 2. set up against; place in the way of: *let us oppose good nature to anger.* 3. put in contrast: *love is opposed to hate.* 4. put in front of; cause to face: *oppose one's finger to one's thumb.* [< OF, < *op-* (< L *ob-*) against + *poser* put, POSE] —**op·posed′,** *adj.* —**op·pos′er,** *n.* —**op·pos′ing,** *adj.* —**op·pos′ing·ly,** *adv.* —**Syn.** *v.* withstand, withstand.

op·po·site (op′ə·zit), *adj.* 1. placed against; as different in direction as can be: *the house straight across the street is opposite to ours.* 2. as different as can be; just contrary. *Sour is opposite to sweet.* 3. *Bot.* situated on diametrically opposed sides of an axis. —*n.* thing or person that is opposite. *Black is the opposite of white.* —*prep.* opposite to: *opposite the church.* [< L *oppositus* < *ob-* against + *ponere* place] —**op′po·site·ly,** *adv.* —**op′po·site·ness,** *n.* —**Syn.** *adj.* 2. antithetic, contradictory.

op·po·si·tion (op′ə·zish′ən), *n.* 1. action against; resistance. 2. a political party opposed to the party in power. —**op′po·si′tion·al,** *adj.*

op·press (ə·pres′), *v.* 1. govern harshly; keep down unjustly or by cruelty. 2. weigh down; lie heavily on; burden. [< Med.L *oppressare*, ult. < L *ob-* against + *premere* press] —**op·pres′sor,** *n.* —**Syn.** 2. overburden, crush.

op·pres·sion (ə·presh′ən), *n.* 1. an oppressing: *the oppression of the people by the nobles.* 2. a being oppressed: *they fought against oppression.* 3. cruel or unjust treatment. 4. a heavy, weary feeling. —**Syn.** 3. tyranny, persecution, despotism. 4. weariness, depression.

op·pres·sive (ə·pres′iv), *adj.* 1. harsh; severe; unjust. 2. hard to bear; burdensome. —**op·pres′sive·ly,** *adv.* —**op·pres′sive·ness,** *n.*

op·pro·bri·ous (ə·prō′bri·əs), *adj.* expressing scorn, reproach, or abuse. *Coward, liar,* and *thief* are opprobrious names. —**op·pro′bri·ous·ly,** *adv.* —**op·pro′bri·ous·ness,** *n.*

op·pro·bri·um (ə·prō′bri·əm), *n.* disgrace or reproach caused by shameful conduct; infamy. [< L, ult. < *ob-* + *probrum* infamy, reproach]

opt., 1. optative. 2. optics. 3. optional.

op·ta·tive (op′tə·tiv), *Gram.* —*adj.* expressing a wish. —*n.* 1. the optative mood. 2. verb in the optative mood. [< LL, < L *optare* wish] —**op′ta·tive·ly,** *adv.*

op·tic (op′tik), *adj.* of the eye; of the sense of sight. —*n. Colloq.* the eye. [< Med.L < Gk., < *op-* see]

op·ti·cal (op′tə·kəl), *adj.* 1. of the eye; visual: *an optical defect.* 2. made to assist sight: *an optical instrument.* 3. of vision and light in relation to each other. —**op′ti·cal·ly,** *adv.*

optical art, a form of abstract painting in which unusual optical illusions and effects are produced by means of highly complex geometrical designs; op art.

op·ti·cian (op·tish′ən), *n.* maker or seller of eyeglasses and other optical instruments.

op·tics (op′tiks), *n.* science that deals with light and vision.

op·ti·mal (op′tə·məl), *adj.* most favorable. —**op′ti·mal·ly,** *adv.*

op·ti·mism (op′tə·miz·əm), *n.* 1. tendency to look on the bright side of things. 2. belief that everything will turn out for the best. 3. doctrine that the existing world is the best of all possible worlds. [< NL, < L *optimus* best] —**op′ti·mist,** *n.* —**op′ti·mis′tic, op′ti·mis′ti·cal,** *adj.* —**op′ti·mis′ti·cal·ly,** *adv.*

op·ti·mum (op′tə·məm), *n., pl.* -mums, -ma (-mə), *adj.* —*n.* the best or most favorable point, degree, amount, etc., for the purpose. —*adj.* optimal. [< L]

op·tion (op′shən), *n.* 1. right or freedom of choice. 2. a choosing; choice. 3. right to buy something at a certain price within a certain time. [< L *optio*] —**Syn.** 2. preference, alternative.

op·tion·al (op′shən·əl), *adj.* left to one's choice; not required. —**op′tion·al·ly,** *adv.*

op·tom·e·try (op·tom′ə·tri), *n.* 1. measurement of visual powers. 2. practice or art of testing eyes in order to fit them with glasses. [< *opto-* sight (< Gk. *optos* seen) + *-metry* < Gk., < *metron* measure] —**op·tom′e·trist,** *n. Am.*

op·u·lent (op′yə·lənt), *adj.* 1. wealthy; rich. 2. abundant; plentiful. [< L *opulens* < *ops* power, resources] —**op′u·lence, op′u·len·cy,** *n.* —**op′u·lent·ly,** *adv.* —**Syn.** 1. affluent. 2. profuse.

o·pus (ō′pəs), *n., pl.* **op·e·ra** (op′ə·rə). a work; composition: *the violinist played his own opus, No. 16.* [< L]

or (ôr; *unstressed* ər), *conj.* 1. word used to express a choice, difference, etc.: *you can go or stay, is it sweet or sour?* 2. and if not; otherwise: *hurry, or you will be late.* 3. that is; being the same as: *this is the end or last part.* [OE (unstressed) ā(hwœ)ther < ā ever + hwœther either, whether]

-or, *suffix.* 1. person or thing that ——, as in *actor, accelerator, orator.* 2. act, state, condition, quality, characteristic, etc., esp. in words from Latin, as in *error, horror.* [< L] ≻ -or, -our. American spelling prefers -or in such words as *color, governor, honor.* When referring to Jesus Christ, *Saviour* is usually spelled with the *u* but in other senses without it. *Glamour* still survives, but the *u* is rapidly being dropped from this word. British usage is divided on this point, though of course to an American reader the words in *-our* are conspicuous. In quoting directly from British writings their spelling should be exactly followed, and in referring to British institutions, like the Labour Party, their usual spelling should be used.

or·a·cle (ôr′ə·kəl; or′-), *n.* 1. answer, often equivocal, given by a god through a priest or priestess, to some question. 2. place where the god gives answers. 3. priest, priestess, or other means by which the god's answer is given. 4. something regarded as an infallible guide or indicator. 5. a very wise person. [< OF < L *oraculum* < *orare,* orig., recite solemnly]

o·rac·u·lar (ô·rak′yə·lər), *adj.* 1. of or like an oracle. 2. with a hidden meaning that is difficult to make out. 3. very wise. —**o·rac′u·lar′i·ty** (ô·rak′yə·lar′ə·ti), *n.* —**o·rac′u·lar·ly,** *adv.*

o·ral (ō′rəl; ō′-), *adj.* 1. spoken; using speech: *an oral agreement.* 2. of the mouth: *the oral opening.* [< L *os* mouth] —**o′ral·ly,** *adv.* —**o′ral·ness,** *n.* —**Syn.** 1. verbal, vocal. ≻ oral, verbal. Strictly, *oral* means "spoken," and *verbal* means "in words"; but *verbal* has been so long used in the sense of *oral* that the sense is recognized in dictionaries: *an oral (or verbal) message.*

or·ange (ôr′inj; or′-), *n.* 1. a round, reddish-yellow, juicy fruit that grows in warm climates. 2. the tree it grows on. 3. fruit or tree that suggests an orange. 4. a reddish yellow. —*adj.* 1. of or like an orange. 2. reddish-yellow. [< OF < Sp. < Ar. < Pers. *nārang;* in OF blended with *or* gold]

or·ange·ade (ôr′inj·ād′; or′-), *n.* drink made of orange juice, sugar, and water.

orange pekoe, a black tea from Ceylon or India.

o·rang-u·tan (ō·rang′ú·tan′), **o·rang-ou·tang** (-tang′), or **o·rang** (ō·rang′), *n.* a large ape of the forests of Borneo and Sumatra, that has very long arms and long, reddish-brown hair. It lives mostly in trees and eats fruits and leaves. [< Malay, < *orang* man + *utan* wild]

o·rate (ô·rāt′; ō–; ôr′āt; ō′rāt), *v.,* -**rat·ed,** -**rat·ing.** *Colloq.* make an oration; talk in a grand manner. [< *oration*]

o·ra·tion (ô·rā′shən; ō–), *n.* a formal public speech delivered on a special occasion. [< L, < *orare* speak formally. Doublet of ORISON.] —Syn. address, harangue.

o·ra·tor (ôr′ə·tər; or′-), *n.* 1. person who makes an oration. 2. person who can speak very well in public.

or·a·to·ri·o (ôr′ə·tô′ri·ō; -tō′-; or′-), *n., pl.* -ri·os. a musical composition, usually based on a religious theme, for solo voices, chorus, and orchestra. [< Ital., orig., place of prayer < LL *oratorium* ORATORY²]

or·a·to·ry¹ (ôr′ə·tô′ri; -tō′-; or′-), *n.* 1. skill in public speaking; fine speaking. 2. art of public speaking. [< L (*ars*) *oratoria* oratorical (art)] —**or·a·tor·i·cal** (ôr′ə·tôr′ə·kəl; or′ə·tor′-), *adj.* —**or′a·tor′i·cal·ly,** *adv.* —Syn. 1. eloquence.

or·a·to·ry² (ôr′ə·tô′ri; -tō′-; or′-), *n., pl.* -ries. a small chapel; room set apart for prayer. [< LL *oratorium* < *orare* pray]

orb (ôrb), *n.* 1. sphere; globe. 2. sun, moon, planet, or star. 3. world. 4. *Esp. Poetic.* eyeball or eye. —*v.* form into a circle or sphere. [< L *orbis* circle] —**orbed,** *adj.* —Syn. *n.* 1. ball.

or·bic·u·lar (ôr·bik′yə·lər), *adj.* like a circle or sphere; rounded. —**or·bic·u·lar·i·ty** (ôr·bik′-yə·lar′ə·ti), *n.* —**or·bic′u·lar·ly,** *adv.*

or·bic·u·late (ôr·bik′yə·lit; -lāt), **or·bic·u·lat·ed** (-lāt′id), *adj.* orbicular. —**or·bic′u·late·ly,** *adv.*

or·bit (ôr′bit), *n., v.,* -**bit·ed,** -**bit·ing.** —*n.* 1. path of the earth or any one of the planets about the sun. 2. path of any heavenly body about another heavenly body. 3. regular course of life or experience. 4. sphere of influence. —*v.* 1. travel around (a body) in an orbit. 2. travel in an orbit. 3. place (a satellite) in an orbit. 4. of a satellite, etc., arrive in its orbit. [< L *orbita* wheel track < *orbis* wheel, circle] —**or′bit·al,** *adj.*

Orbit of the earth (E) around the sun. Arrows show direction.

or·chard (ôr′chərd), *n.* 1. piece of ground on which fruit trees are grown. 2. trees in an orchard. [OE *ortgeard* < *ort-* (appar. < L *hortus* garden) + *geard* yard¹]

or·ches·tra (ôr′kis·trə), *n.* 1. musicians playing at a concert, an opera, or a play. 2. instruments played together by the musicians in an orchestra. 3. part of a theater just in front of the stage, where the musicians sit. 4. *Am.* the main floor of a theater, esp. the part near the front. [< L < Gk., the space where the dancers performed, ult. < *orcheesthai* to dance] —**or·ches·tral** (ôr·kes′trəl), *adj.* —**or·ches′tral·ly,** *adv.*

or·ches·trate (ôr′kis·trāt), *v.,* -**trat·ed,** -**trat·ing.** compose or arrange (music) for performance by an orchestra. —**or′ches·tra′tion,** *n.*

or·chid (ôr′kid), *n.* 1. Also, **or·chis** (ôr′kis). plant with beautiful, queerly shaped flowers that

are formed of three petallike sepals and three petals, one petal being very different from the other two. b. its flower. 2. a light purple. —*adj.* light-purple. [< NL, ult. < L *orchis* < Gk., testicle; from shape of root.

ord., 1. order. 2. ordinance. 3. ordinary.

or·dain (ôr·dān′), *v.* 1. order; fix; decide; appoint: *the law ordains that the murderers shall be hanged.* 2. officially appoint or consecrate as a minister in a Christian church. [< OF < L *ordinare* < *ordo* order] —**or·dain′er,** *n.* —**or·dain′ment,** *n.* —Syn. 1. decree, prescribe.

or·deal (ôr·dēl′; -dē′əl; ôr′dēl), *n.* 1. a severe test or experience: *the ordeal of a visit to the dentist.* 2. in early times, an effort to decide the guilt or innocence of an accused person by making him do something dangerous like holding fire or taking poison. It was supposed that an innocent person would not be harmed by such danger. [OE *ordǣl* judgment] —Syn. 1. trial.

or·der (ôr′dər), *n.* 1. way one thing follows another: *in order of size, in alphabetical order.* 2. condition in which every part or piece is in its right place: *put a room in order.* 3. condition; state: *my affairs are in good order.* 4. way the world works; way things happen: *the order of nature.* 5. state or condition of things in which the law is obeyed and there is no trouble: *keep order.* 6. principles and rules by which a meeting is run. 7. a telling what to do; command: *the captain's orders.* 8. direction of a court or judge made in writing and not included in a judgment. 9. paper saying that money is to be given or paid, or something handed over: *a postal money order.* 10. statement or list of things telling a store or tradesman what you wish sent. 11. kind or sort: *ability of a high order.* 12. *Biol.* a group in the classifying of plants and animals that is below or smaller than a class, but larger than a family. 13. a social rank, grade, or class: *all orders of society.* 14. rank or position in the church: *the order of bishops.* 15. ordination. 16. brotherhood of monks, friars, or knights: *the Franciscan order.* 17. society to which one is admitted as an honor: *the Order of the Golden Fleece.* 18. a modern fraternal organization: *the Order of Masons.* 19. any one of the typical styles of columns and architecture: *the Doric, Ionic, and Corinthian orders.* 20. the regular form of worship for a given occasion. 21. *Am.* portion or serving of food served in a restaurant, etc. 22. **call to order,** ask to be quiet and start work. 23. **in order that,** so that; with the purpose that. 24. **in order to,** as a means to; to. 25. **in short order,** quickly. 26. **on the order of,** somewhat like; similar to. 27. **take orders,** become a clergyman. —*v.* 1. put in order; arrange: *order one's affairs.* 2. tell what to do; give an order; command; bid: *he ordered that the prisoners be handcuffed.* 3. give orders, directions, etc.: *please order for me.* 4. give (a store, etc.) an order for. 5. decide; will: *the gods ordered it otherwise.* 6. **order about** or **around,** send here and there; tell to do this and that. [< OF < L *ordo* row, rank] —**or′der·er,** *n.* —**or′der·less,** *adj.* —Syn. *n.* 1. sequence, succession. 7. injunction, mandate, direction. —*v.* 1. systematize, methodize, regulate. 2. direct, instruct.

or·der·ly (ôr′dər·li), *adj., n., pl.* -lies. —*adj.* 1. in order; with regular arrangement, method, or system. 2. keeping order; well-behaved or regulated. —*n.* 1. a noncommissioned officer or private soldier who attends a superior officer to carry orders, etc. 2. a hospital attendant who keeps things clean and in order. —**or′der·li·ness,** *n.* —Syn. *adj.* 1. methodical, systematic. 2. peaceable, peaceful, quiet.

or·di·nal (ôr′də·nəl), *adj.* 1. showing order or position in a series. First, second, third, etc., are ordinal numbers; one, two, three, etc., are cardinal numbers. 2. pertaining to an order of animals or plants. —*n.* 1. an ordinal number 2. book of special forms for certain church ceremonies. [< LL *ordinalis* < L *ordo* order] —**or′di·nal·ly,** *adv.* ➤ See **cardinal number** for usage note.

or·di·nance (ôr′də·nəns), *n.* rule or law made

by authority; decree. [< OF, ult. < L *ordinare* arrange, regulate] —Syn. canon, regulation.

or·di·nar·i·ly (ôr'də·ner'·ə·li; *emphatic* ôr'də-når'ə·li), *adv.* 1. usually; regularly. 2. to the usual extent.

or·di·nar·y (ôr'də·ner'i), *adj., n., pl.* -nar·ies. —*adj.* 1. usual; regular; customary: *for all ordinary purposes.* 2. somewhat below the average: *the speaker was ordinary and tiresome.* 3. *Law.* having jurisdiction by virtue of office, not by special delegation. —*n.* 1. meal served at a fixed price. 2. inn; dining room of an inn. 3. person who has authority in his own right, esp. a bishop or a judge. 4. form for saying Mass. 5. in ordinary, in regular service: *physician in ordinary to the king.* [< L *ordinarius*. See ORDER.] —**or'di·nar'i·ness,** *n.* —Syn. *adj.* 1. normal, habitual, wonted. 2. mediocre, inferior. —Ant. *adj.* 1. extraordinary, uncommon, exceptional.

or·di·nate (ôr'də·nit; -nāt), *n.* a vertical line drawn on a graph to define a point in a system of coördinates.

or·di·na·tion (ôr'də·nā'shən), *n.* 1. act or ceremony of ordaining. 2. fact or condition of being ordained.

ord·nance (ôrd'nəns), *n.* 1. cannon; artillery. 2. military weapons of all kinds. [var. of *ordinance*]

ore (ôr; ōr), *n.* rock, sand, or dirt containing some metal. [OE *ār* brass]

Oreg., Ore., Oregon.

Or·e·gon (ôr'ə·gon; -gən; or'-), *n.* a Northwestern State of the United States, on the Pacific coast. *Capital:* Salem. *Abbrev.:* Oreg., Ore. —**Or·e·go·ni·an** (ôr'ə·gō'ni·ən; or'-), *adj., n. Am.*

O·res·tes (ô·res'tēz; ō-), *n.* son of Agamemnon and Clytemnestra, who avenged the murder of his father by killing his mother. He was pursued by the Furies for this crime.

or·gan (ôr'gən), *n.* 1. any part of an animal or plant that is composed of various tissues organized to perform some particular function. An eye, lung, stomach, root, stamen, or pistil is an organ. 2. means of action; instrument. A court is an organ of government. 3. means of giving information or expressing opinions; newspaper or magazine that speaks for and gives the views of a political party or some other organization. 4. Also, **pipe organ.** a musical instrument made of pipes of different lengths, which are sounded by air blown by a bellows and played by keys. 5. any of various other musical instruments: a. a hand organ. b. a reed organ. c. a harmonica. [< L < Gk. *organon* instrument < *ergon* work]

or·gan·dy, or·gan·die (ôr'gən·di), *n., pl.* -dies. a fine, thin, stiff muslin, used for dresses. [< F *organdi*]

or·gan·ic (ôr·gan'ik), *adj.* 1. of the bodily organs; vital; affecting the structure of an organ: *an organic disease.* 2. produced by animal or plant activities. Starch is an organic compound. 3. having organs, as an organized physical structure, as plants and animals have; not of the mineral kingdom. 4. made up of related parts, but being a unit; coördinated: *the United States is an organic whole made up of 50 States.* 5. that is part of the structure or constitution of a person or thing; fundamental. 6. *Chem.* of or containing carbon: *organic compounds.* —Syn. 4. organized. 5. inherent, innate, constitutional.

or·gan·i·cal·ly (ôr·gan'ik·li), *adv.* 1. in an organic manner. 2. in organization. 3. as part of an organization.

organic chemistry, branch of chemistry that deals with compounds of carbon.

or·gan·ism (ôr'gən·iz·əm), *n.* 1. a living body having organs or an organized structure; individual animal or plant. 2. a very tiny animal or plant. 3. a whole made up of related parts that work together.

or·gan·ist (ôr'gən·ist), *n.* person who plays an organ.

or·gan·i·za·tion (ôr'gən·ə·zā'shən), *n.* 1. group of persons united for some purpose. Churches, clubs, and political parties are organizations. 2. thing made up of related parts, each having a special duty. 3. act or process of

organizing; grouping and arranging parts to form a whole. 4. way in which a thing's parts are arranged to work together. —**or'gan·i·za'tion·al,** *adj.* —Syn. 1. association.

organization man, man who belongs to and identifies himself fully with a company, party, or other organization and its purposes, methods, etc.

or·gan·ize (ôr'gən·iz), *v.,* -ized, -iz·ing. 1. put into working order; get together and arrange. 2. combine in a company, party, labor union, etc. 3. furnish with organs. [< LL, < *organum* ORGAN] —**or'gan·iz·a·ble,** *adj.* —**or'gan·iz·a·bil'i·ty,** *n.* —**or'gan·iz'er,** *n.* —Syn. 1. systematize, form.

organized labor, *Am.* workingmen who are organized into labor unions.

or·gasm (ôr'gaz·əm), *n.* the series of responses at the climax of copulation. [< NL *orgasmus* < Gk. *orgaein* swell, be excited] —**or·gas·tic** (ôr-gas'tik), *adj.*

or·gy (ôr'ji), *n., pl.* -gies. 1. a wild, drunken revel. 2. period of uncontrolled indulgence. 3. **orgies,** secret rites or ceremonies in the worship of certain Greek and Roman gods, esp. the god of wine, celebrated with drinking, wild dancing, and singing. [< L < Gk. *orgia* secret rites] —**or·gi·ac** (ôr'ji·ac), **or·gic** (ôr'jik), *adj.* —**or·gi·as·tic** (ôr'-ji·as'tik), *adj.* —**or'gi·as'ti·cal·ly,** *adv.*

o·ri·el (ô'ri·əl; ō'-), *n.* a bay window projecting from the outer face of a wall. [< OF *oriol* porch]

Oriel

o·ri·ent (*v.* ô'ri·ent, ō'-; *n., adj.* ô'ri·ənt, ō'-), *v.* 1. orient oneself, get in the right relations to the things or persons about one. 2. put facing east. 3. turn toward the east or in any indicated direction: *the building is oriented north and south.* —*n.* 1. the Orient, the East; countries in Asia. China and Japan are important nations of the Orient. 2. *Poetic.* the east. —*adj.* 1. *Poetic.* eastern. 2. rising. [< L *oriens* rising, with ref. to the rising sun]

O·ri·en·tal (ô'ri·en'təl; ō'-), *adj.* 1. Eastern; of the Orient. 2. **oriental,** eastern. —*n.* native of the East. Turks, Arabs, Persians, Hindus, and Chinese are Orientals. —**o'ri·en'tal·ly,** *adv.*

O·ri·en·tal·ism, o·ri·en·tal·ism (ô'ri·en'təl·iz·əm; ō'-), *n.* 1. Oriental character or characteristics. 2. knowledge of Oriental languages, literature, etc. —**O'ri·en'tal·ist, o'ri·en'tal·ist,** *n.*

o·ri·en·tate (ô'ri·en·tāt; ō'-), *v.,* -tat·ed, -tat·ing. orient.

o·ri·en·ta·tion (ô'ri·en·tā'shən; ō'-), *n.* 1. an orienting or being oriented. 2. a finding out of the actual facts or conditions and putting oneself in the right relation to them.

or·i·fice (ôr'ə·fis; or'-), *n.* mouth; opening; hole. [< F < L *orificium* < L *os* mouth + *facere* make] —**or·i·fi·cial** (ôr'ə·fish'əl; or'ə-), *adj.*

orig., 1. origin. 2. original; originally.

or·i·ga·mi (or'ə·gä'mi), *n.* Japanese art of folding paper to make decorative objects. [< Jap.]

or·i·gin (ôr'ə·jin; or'-), *n.* 1. thing from which anything comes; source; beginning. 2. parentage; ancestry; birth. [< L *origo* < *oriri* rise] —Syn. 1. root, cause.

o·rig·i·nal (ə·rij'ə·nəl), *adj.* 1. belonging to the beginning; first; earliest: *the original settlers.* 2. new; fresh; novel: *plan an original game for the party.* 3. able to do, make, or think something new; inventive. 4. not copied, imitated, or translated from something else. —*n.* 1. thing from which another is copied, imitated, or translated. 2. language in which a book was first written. 3. an unusual person; queer person. 4. origin; source. —**o·rig'i·nal·ly,** *adv.* —**o·rig'i·nal·ness,** *n.* —Syn. *adj.* 1. initial. 3. creative.

o·rig·i·nal·i·ty (ə·rij'ə·nal'ə·ti), *n.* 1. ability to do, make, or think up something new. 2. freshness; novelty. 3. a being original.

original sin, 1. *Theol.* a depravity, or tendency to evil, held to be innate in mankind and transmitted from Adam to the race in consequence of his sin. 2. *Rom. Cath. Theol.* privation of sanctifying grace in consequence of Adam's sin.

o·rig·i·nate (ə·rij′ə·nāt), v., **-nat·ed, -nat·ing. 1.** cause to be; invent. **2.** come into being; begin; arise. **—o·rig′i·na′tion,** n. **—o·rig′i·na′tive,** adj. **—o·rig′i·na′tor,** n.

O·ri·no·co (ō′ri·nō′kō; ō′-), n. a large river flowing from NW South America into the Atlantic.

o·ri·ole (ō′ri·ōl; ō′-), n. **1.** *Am.* any of several American birds having yellow- or orange-and-black feathers. **2.** any of several European birds having yellow-and-black feathers. [< NL *oriolus,* ult. < L *aurum* gold]

O·ri·on (ō·rī′ən; ō′-), n., *gen.* **Or·i·o·nis** (ōr′i·ō′nis; ōr′-). group of stars near the equator of the heavens.

Baltimore oriole
(ab. 7 in. long)

or·i·son (ōr′i·zən; ōr′-), n. *Archaic* or *Poetic.* prayer. [< OF < LL *oratio* prayer < L, speech, < *orare* pray. Doublet of ORATION.]

Ork·ney Islands (ōrk′ni), group of islands NE of and belonging to Scotland.

Or·lé·ans (ōr′li·ənz; *Fr.* ōr·lā·äN′), n. city in C France, on the Loire River.

Or·lon (ōr′lon), n. *Trademark.* a light-weight synthetic fiber that resists sun and rain, used for clothing, sails, awnings, etc.

Or·ly (ōr·lē′), n. a small town near Paris, site of a major international airport.

or·mo·lu (ōr′mə·lü), n. alloy of copper and zinc, used to imitate gold. [< F *or moulu* ground gold]

or·na·ment (n. ōr′nə·mənt; v. ōr′nə·ment), n. **1.** something pretty; something to add beauty: *jewelry and vases are ornaments.* **2.** use of ornaments. **3.** person or act that adds beauty, grace, or honor. —v. add beauty to; make more pleasing or attractive; decorate. [< OF < L, < *ornare* adorn] **—or′na·ment′er,** n. **—Syn.** n. **1.** adornment, decoration. —v. adorn, embellish.

or·na·men·tal (ōr′nə·men′təl), adj. **1.** of or having to do with ornament. **2.** for ornament; used as an ornament. **3.** decorative. —n. something ornamental. **—or′na·men′tal·ly,** adv.

or·na·men·ta·tion (ōr′nə·men·tā′shən), n. **1.** an ornamenting or being ornamented. **2.** decorations; ornaments.

or·nate (ōr·nāt′), adj. much adorned; much ornamented. [< L *ornatus* adorned] **—or·nate′ly,** adv. **—or·nate′ness,** n. **—Syn.** elaborate, showy.

or·ner·y (ōr′nər·i), adj. *Colloq.* or *Dial.* **1.** inferior. **2.** homely. **3.** mean in disposition. **4.** low; vile. [contraction of *ordinary*] **—or′ner·i·ness,** n. *Am.*

or·ni·thol·o·gy (ōr′nə·thol′ə·ji), n. study of birds. [< NL, < Gk. *ornis* bird + *-logos* treating of] **—or·ni·tho·log·i·cal** (ōr′nə·thə·loj′ə·kəl), adj. **—or′ni·thol′o·gist,** n.

or·ni·tho·rhyn·chus (ōr′nə·thə·ring′kəs), n. duckbill. [< Gk. *ornis* bird + *rhynchos* bill]

o·ro·tund (ō′rə·tund; ō′-), adj. **1.** strong, full, rich, and clear in voice or speech. **2.** pompous; bombastic. [alter. of L *ore rotundo,* lit., with round mouth] **—o′ro·tun′di·ty,** n.

or·phan (ōr′fən), n. child whose parents are dead; child whose father or mother is dead. —adj. **1.** of or for such children. **2.** without a father or mother or both. —v. make an orphan of. [< LL < Gk. *orphanos* bereaved] **—or′phan·hood,** n.

or·phan·age (ōr′fən·ij), n. **1.** home for orphans. **2.** being an orphan.

Or·phe·us (ōr′fi·əs; -fūs), n. *Gk. Myth.* musician who played his lyre so sweetly that animals and even trees and rocks followed him. **—Or′phe·an** (ōr·fē′ən), adj. **—Or·phic** (ōr′fik), adj.

or·ris, or·rice (ōr′is; ōr′-), n. **1.** orrisroot. **2.**

plant that it grows on; kind of iris. [appar. alter. of *iris*]

or·ris·root (ōr′is·rüt′; -rut′; ōr′-), n. a fragrant rootstock of a variety of iris, used in making perfume, toothpaste, etc.

or·tho·clase (ōr′thə·klās; -klāz), n. feldspar having two cleavages at right angles to each other. [< Gk. *orthos* straight + *klasis* cleavage] —or′tho·clas′tic, adj.

or·tho·don·tia (ōr′thə·don′shə; -shi·ə), n. branch of dentistry that deals with straightening and adjusting teeth. [< NL, < Gk. *orthos* straight + *odon* tooth] **—or′tho·don′tic,** adj. **—or′tho·don′tist,** n.

or·tho·dox (ōr′thə·doks), adj. **1.** generally accepted, esp. in religion. **2.** having generally accepted views or opinions, esp. in religion. **3.** approved by convention; usual; customary. [< LL < Gk., < *orthos* correct + *doxa* opinion] **—or′tho·dox′ly,** adv. **—Syn. 3.** accepted, conventional.

Orthodox Church, group of Christian churches in eastern Europe and western Asia that do not recognize the Pope as the supreme head of the Church.

or·tho·dox·y (ōr′thə·dok′si), n., pl. **-dox·ies.** orthodox practice, esp. in religion; being orthodox.

or·tho·ë·py (ōr·thō′ə·pi; ōr′thō-), n. **1.** correct pronunciation. **2.** part of grammar that deals with pronunciation; phonology. [< Gk., < *orthos* correct + *epos* utterance] **—or·tho·ëp·ic** (ōr′thō·ep′ik), adj. **—or·tho·ëp′i·cal,** adj. **—or·tho′ë·pist,** n.

or·thog·ra·phy (ōr·thog′rə·fi), n., pl. **-phies. 1.** correct spelling; spelling considered as right or wrong. **2.** art of spelling; study of spelling. [< L < Gk., *orthos* correct + *graphein* write] **—or·thog′ra·pher,** n. **—or·tho·graph·ic** (ōr′thə·graf′ik), or′tho·graph′i·cal, adj. **—or′tho·graph′i·cal·ly,** adv.

or·tho·pe·dics, or·tho·pae·dics (ōr′thə·pē′diks), n. branch of surgery that deals with the deformities and diseases of bones and joints, esp. in children. [< Gk. *orthos* correct + *paideia* rearing of children < *pais* child] **—or′tho·pe′dic, or′tho·pae′dic,** adj. **—or′tho·pe′dist, or′tho·pae′dist,** n.

or·thop·ter·ous (ōr·thop′tər·əs), adj. *Zool.* belonging to the order of insects including crickets, grasshoppers, cockroaches, etc. [< Gk. *orthos* straight + *pteron* wing]

or·to·lan (ōr′tə·lən), n. a European bunting, regarded as a specially delicate food. [< F < Pr. < L *hortulanus* of gardens < *hortus* garden]

-ory, suffix. **1.** ——ing, as in *contradictory.* **2.** of or pertaining to ——; of or pertaining to ——ion, as in *advisory, auditory.* **3.** characterized by ——ion, as in *adulatory.* **4.** serving to ——, as in *expiatory.* **5.** tending to ——; inclined to ——, as in *conciliatory.* **6.** place for ——; establishment for ——ing, as in *depository.* [< L *-orius, -orium*]

o·ryx (ō′riks; ō′-), n., pl. **o·ryx·es** or (esp. collectively) **o·ryx.** an African antelope with long, nearly straight horns. [< L < Gk., antelope, pickax; with ref. to pointed horns]

OS, O.S., Old Saxon.

Os, *Chem.* osmium.

O·sa·ka (ō·sä′kə), n. seaport in S Japan.

os·car (os′kər), n. *Am.* a small statuette awarded annually by the Academy of Motion Picture Arts and Sciences for the best performances, production, photography, etc., during the year. [supposedly from the remark, "He reminds me of my Uncle Oscar," made by the secretary of the Academy upon seeing one of the statuettes]

os·cil·late (os′ə·lāt), v., **-lat·ed, -lat·ing. 1.** swing to and fro like a pendulum; move to and fro between two points. **2.** cause to swing to and fro. **3.** vary between opinions, purposes, etc. **4.** cause an electric current to alternate at a high frequency. [< L *oscillatus*] **—os′cil·la′tor,** n. **—os·cil·la·to·ry** (os′ə·lə·tō′ri; -tō′-), adj.

os·cil·la·tion (os′ə·lā′shən), n. **1.** fact or process of oscillating. **2.** a single swing of a vibrating body. **3.** *Physics.* **a.** a single forward and backward surge of a charge of electricity. **b.** a rapid change in electromotive force. **c.** a single complete cycle of an electric wave.

os·cine (os′in; -in), *n.* any of a large group of perching birds that have well-developed vocal organs and usually sing. [< L *oscines*, pl., < *ob-* to + *canere* sing]

os·cu·late (os′kyə·lāt), *v.,* **-lat·ed, -lat·ing. 1.** kiss. **2.** come or bring into close contact. [< L, < *osculum* little mouth, kiss, dim. of *os* mouth] —**os′cu·la′tion,** *n.* —**os·cu·la·to·ry** (os′kyə·lə·tô′ri; -tō′-), *adj.*

-ose[1], *suffix.* **1.** full of; having much or many, as in *verbose.* **2.** inclined to; fond of, as in *jocose.* **3.** like, as in *schistose.* [< L *-osus*]

-ose[2], *suffix.* used to form chemical terms, esp. names of sugars and other carbohydrates, as in *fructose, lactose,* and of protein derivatives, as in *proteose.* [< F *-ose* in *glucose*]

o·sier (ō′zhər), *n.* **1.** *Esp. Brit.* kind of willow tree. **2.** *Esp. Brit.* a tough, flexible branch or twig of this tree. Osiers are woven into baskets. **3.** kind of American dogwood. —*adj.* made of osiers. [< F] —*o′siered, adj.*

O·si·ris (ō·sī′ris), *n.* the chief god of ancient Egypt, ruler of the lower world and judge of the dead.

Os·lo (oz′lō; os′-), *n.* capital of Norway, in the SE part. Until 1925 it was called Christiania.

os·mi·um (oz′mi·əm), *n. Chem.* a hard, heavy, grayish metallic element, Os, used for electric-light filaments, etc.

os·mo·sis (oz·mō′sis; os-), *n.* **1.** tendency of two fluids that are separated by something porous to go through it and become mixed. **2.** diffusion or spreading of fluids through a membrane or partition till they are mixed. [Latinized var. of *osmose* < Gk. *osmos* a thrust] —**os·mot·ic** (oz·mot′ik; os-), *adj.* —**os·mot′i·cal·ly,** *adv.*

os·prey (os′pri), *n., pl.* **-preys.** a large hawk that feeds on fish. [ult. < L *ossifraga* < *os* bone + *frangere* break]

Osprey (ab. 2 ft. long)

OSS, O.S.S., Office of Strategic Services.

Os·sa (os′ə), *n.* Mount, mountain in NE Greece. In Greek legend, when the giants made war on the gods, they piled Mount Ossa on Mount Olympus and Mount Pelion upon Mount Ossa in an attempt to reach heaven.

os·se·ous (os′i·əs), *adj.* **1.** bony. **2.** containing bones. [< L, < *os* bone] —**os′se·ous·ly,** *adv.*

os·si·fy (os′ə·fī), *v.,* **-fied, -fy·ing. 1.** change into bone; become bone. **2.** harden like bone; make or become fixed, hard-hearted, or very conservative. [< L *os* bone + *facere* make] —**os′si·fi·ca′tion,** *n.*

Os·si·ning (os′ə·ning), *n.* town in SE New York State, on the Hudson River. Sing Sing prison is located there.

Ost·end (ost·end′), *n.* seaport in NW Belgium noted as a summer resort.

os·ten·si·ble (os·ten′sə·bəl), *adj.* apparent; pretended; professed: *her ostensible purpose was borrowing sugar, but she really wanted to see the new furniture.* [< F < L *ostendere* show < *ob-* toward + *tendere* stretch] —**os·ten′si·bly,** *adv.*

os·ten·ta·tion (os′ten·tā′shən), *n.* a showing off; display intended to impress others. [< L *ostentatio,* ult. < *ob-* toward + *tendere* stretch] —**Syn.** parade, pomp. —**Ant.** modesty, reserve, simplicity.

os·ten·ta·tious (os′ten·tā′shəs), *adj.* **1.** done for display; intended to attract notice. **2.** showing off; liking to attract notice. —**os′ten·ta′-tious·ly,** *adv.* —**os′ten·ta′tious·ness,** *n.* —**Syn. 1.** showy, spectacular, pretentious, gaudy.

os·te·ol·o·gy (os′ti·ol′ə·ji), *n.* branch of anatomy that deals with bones. [< Gk. *osteon* bone + *-LOGY*] —**os·te·o·log·i·cal** (os′ti·ə·loj′ə·kəl), *adj.* —**os′te·ol′o·gist,** *n.*

os·te·op·a·thy (os′ti·op′ə·thi), *n.* treatment of diseases by manipulating the bones and muscles. [< Gk. *osteon* bone + *-PATHY*] —**os·te·o·path** (os′ti·ə·path), **os′te·op′a·thist,** *n. Am.* —**os′te·o·path′ic,** *adj. Am.* —**os′te·o·path′i·cal·ly,** *adv.*

ost·ler (os′lər), *n.* hostler.

os·tra·cism (os′trə·siz·əm), *n.* **1.** banishment from one's native country. **2.** a being shut out from society, from favor, from privileges, or from association with one's fellows.

os·tra·cize (os′trə·sīz), *v.,* **-cized, -ciz·ing. 1.** banish. **2.** shut out from society, from favor, from privileges, etc. [< Gk., < *ostrakon* tile, potsherd; orig. used in balloting] —**os′tra·ciz′a·ble,** *adj.* —**os′tra·ciz′er,** *n.*

os·trich (ôs′trich; os′-), *n.* a large African and Arabian bird that can run swiftly but cannot fly. [< OF < LL *avis struthio* < L *avis* bird, LL *struthio* < Gk. *strouthion* < *strouthos* ostrich]

O.T., OT, or **OT.,** Old Testament.

O·thel·lo (ə·thel′ō), *n.* a brave but jealous Moor, hero of Shakespeare's play *Othello.*

oth·er (uth′ər), *adj.* **1.** being the remaining one of two or more: *John is here, but the other boys are at school.* **2.** additional or further: *he and one other person.* **3.** not the same as one or more already mentioned: *come some other day.* **4.** different: *I would not have him other than he is.* **5.** every other, every second; alternate: *she buys cream every other day.* **6.** the other day (night, etc.), recently. —*pron.* **1.** the other one; not the same ones: *each praises the other.* **2.** another person or thing: *there are others to be considered.* **3.** of all others, more than all others. —*adv.* otherwise; differently: *I can't do other than to go.* [OE *ōther*] —**oth′er·ness,** *n.*

oth·er·wise (uth′ər·wīz′), *adv.* **1.** in a different way; differently: *I could not do otherwise.* **2.** in other ways: *he is noisy, but otherwise a very nice boy.* **3.** under other circumstances; in a different condition: *he reminded me of what I should otherwise have forgotten.* —*adj.* different: *it might have been otherwise.* —*conj.* or else; if not: *come at once; otherwise you will be too late.*

other world, world to come; life after death.

oth·er·world·ly (uth′ər·wérld′li), *adj.* of or devoted to another world, such as the world of mind or imagination, or the world to come. —**oth′er·world′li·ness,** *n.*

o·ti·ose (ō′shi·ōs; -ti-), *adj.* **1.** lazy; idle. **2.** ineffective; futile. **3.** superfluous; useless. [< L *otium* leisure] —**o′ti·ose·ly,** *adv.* —**o·ti·os·i·ty** (ō′shi·os′ə·ti; ō′ti-), *o′ti·ose·ness, n.*

o·tol·o·gy (ō·tol′ə·ji), *n.* science of the ear and its diseases. [< Gk. *ous* (*ot-*) ear + *-LOGY*] —**o·to·log·i·cal** (ō′tə·loj′ə·kəl), *adj.* —**o·tol′o·gist,** *n.*

Ot·ta·wa (ot′ə·wə; -wä), *n.* capital of Canada, in SE Ontario.

ot·ter (ot′ər), *n., pl.* **-ters** or (*esp. collectively*) **-ter. 1.** any of several mammals related to the minks and weasels, that are good swimmers and have webbed toes with claws. **2.** fur of any otter. [OE *oter*]

Ot·to·man (ot′ə·mən), *n., pl.* **-mans. 1.** Turk. **2. ottoman, a.** a low, cushioned seat without back or arms. **b.** a cushioned footstool.

Ottoman Empire, a former empire of the Turks in SE Europe, SW Asia, and N Africa; Turkish Empire.

ouch (ouch), *interj.* exclamation expressing sudden pain.

ought[1] (ôt), *auxiliary verb.* **1.** have a duty; be obliged: *you ought to obey your parents.* **2.** be right or suitable: *it ought to be allowed.* **3.** be wise: *I ought to go before it rains.* **4.** be expected: *at your age you ought to know better.* **5.** be very likely: *the fastest one ought to win the race.* [OE *āhte* (inf., *āgan* owe)] —**Syn. 1.** must, should.

ought[2] (ôt), *n., adv.* aught; anything.

ought[3] (ôt), *n. Colloq.* nought; zero; 0. [var. of *nought, a nought* taken as *an ought*]

Oui·ja (wē′jə), *n. Am. Trademark.* device used in fortunetelling that consists of a small board on legs that rests on a larger board marked with words, letters of the alphabet, or other characters. [< F *oui* yes + G *ja* yes]

ounce[1] (ouns), *n.* 1. unit of weight, 1/16 of a pound in avoirdupois, and 1/12 of a pound in troy weight. 2. measure for liquids; fluid ounce. 16 ounces = 1 pint. 3. a very small amount. [< OF < L *uncia* twelfth part. Doublet of INCH.]

ounce[2] (ouns), *n.* a grayish wild cat of C Asia with black spots, somewhat like a leopard. [< OF *once* for *lonce* < L *lynx* LYNX]

our (our; är), *pron.* of us; belonging to us. [OE *ūre*]

ours (ourz; ärz), *pron.* 1. of us; belonging to us: *this garden is ours.* 2. the one or ones belonging to us: *ours is a large house.*

our·self (our·self′; är-), *pron.* myself. ≻ Ourself is used by an author, king, judge, etc.: "*We will ourself reward the victor*," *said the queen.*

our·selves (our·selvz′; är-), *pron. pl.* 1. the emphatic form of we or us: *we did it ourselves.* 2. the reflexive form of us: *we hurt ourselves.*

-ous, *suffix.* 1. having; having much; full of, as in *joyous.* 2. characterized by, as in *zealous.* 3. having the nature of, as in *murderous.* 4. of or pertaining to, as in *monogamous.* 5. like, as in *thunderous.* 6. committing or practicing, as in *bigamous.* 7. inclined to, as in *amorous.* 8. *Chem.* implying a larger proportion of the element indicated by the word than *-ic* implies. *Stannous* means containing tin in larger proportions than a corresponding *stannic* compound. [< OF < L *-osus*]

ou·sel (ü′zəl), *n.* ouzel.

oust (oust), *v.* force out; drive out. [< AF *ouster,* (cf. F *ôter*) < L *obstare* block, hinder. See OBSTACLE.] —*Syn.* evict, expel, dispossess.

oust·er (ous′tər), *n.* 1. an ousting, esp. an illegal forcing of a person out of his property. 2. one that ousts.

out (out), *adv.* 1. away; forth: *rush out.* 2. not in or at a place, position, state, etc.: *out of fashion.* 3. into the open air: *he went out at noon.* 4. into society: *a young girl who came out last season.* 5. to or at an end: *fight it out.* 6. from the usual condition, place, position, etc.: *put the light out, turn your pockets out.* 7. so as to project or extend: *stand out.* 8. into or in existence, activity, or outward manifestation: *fever broke out.* 9. completely; effectively: *fit out an army.* 10. aloud; loudly: *speak out.* 11. to others: *give out the books.* 12. from a number, stock, store, source, cause, material, etc.: *she picked out a new coat.* 13. from a state of composure, satisfaction, or harmony: *feel put out.* 14. at a money loss: *be out ten dollars.* 15. out and away, by far. 16. out and out, thoroughly. —*adj.* 1. not in possession or control: *the Democrats are in, the Republicans out.* 2. not in use, action, etc.: *the fire is out.* 3. Baseball. not having its inning: *the out side.* 4. external; exterior; outer; outlying: *an out island.* 5. out for, looking for; trying to get. 6. out to, eagerly trying to. —*n.* 1. *Am., Baseball.* a being out or putting out. 2. person or thing that is out: *he was an out after the election.* 3. *Am., Colloq.* a way out; excuse: *an easy out.* 4. at outs or on the outs, *Colloq.* quarreling; disagreeing. —*v.* 1. go or come out. 2. put out. —*interj.* Archaic. begone! away! [OE *ūt*]

out-, *prefix.* 1. outward; forth; away, as in *outburst, outgoing.* 2. outside; at a distance, as in *outbuilding, outfield, outlying.* 3. more than; longer than, as in *outbid, outlive, outnumber.* 4. better than, as in *outdo, outrun, outsail.*

out-and-out (out′ən-out′), *adj.* thorough.

out·bal·ance (out-bal′əns), *v.,* –anced, –ancing. 1. weigh more than. 2. exceed in value, importance, influence, etc.

out·bid (out-bid′), *v.,* –bid, –bid or –bid·den, –bid·ding. bid higher than (someone else).

out·board (out′bōrd′; –bôrd′), *adj., adv.* 1. outside the hull of a ship or boat. 2. away from the middle of a ship or boat.

outboard motor, a portable gasoline motor attached to the back of a boat or canoe.

out·bound (out′bound′), *adj.* outward bound.

out·break (out′brāk′), *n.* 1. a breaking out. 2. riot; public disturbance. —*Syn.* 1. outburst, eruption. 2. uprising, insurrection.

out·build (out-bild′), *v.,* –built, –build·ing. build more or better than.

out·build·ing (out′bil′ding), *n.* shed or building built near a main building.

out·burst (out′bėrst′), *n.* a bursting forth.

out·cast (out′kast′; –käst′), *adj.* 1. cast out from home and friends; homeless; friendless. 2. rejected; discarded. —*n.* an outcast person or animal. —*Syn. adj.* 1. forsaken, forlorn. —*n.* castaway, exile.

out·class (out-klas′; –kläs′), *v.* be of higher class than; be much better than.

out·come (out′kum′), *n.* result; consequence.

out·crop (*n.* out′krop′; *v.* out-krop′), *n., v.,* –cropped, –crop·ping. —*n.* 1. a coming to the surface of the earth: *the outcrop of a vein of coal.* 2. part that comes to the surface. —*v.* come to the surface; appear.

out·cry (*n.* out′krī′; *v.* out-krī′), *n., pl.* –cries, *v.,* –cried, –cry·ing. —*n.* 1. a crying out; sudden cry or scream. 2. a great noise or clamor. 3. auction. —*v.* 1. cry out; cry aloud. 2. cry louder than. —*Syn. n.* 1. shout. 2. uproar.

out·date (out-dāt′), *v.,* –dat·ed, –dat·ing. make old-fashioned. —*out·dat′ed,* *adj.*

out·dis·tance (out-dis′təns), *v.,* –tanced, –tanc·ing. leave behind; outstrip.

out·do (out-dü′), *v.,* –did, –done, –do·ing. do more or better than; surpass. —*out·do′er,* *n.* —*Syn.* excel, exceed, overcome.

out·door (out′dōr′; –dôr′), *adj.* done, used, or living outdoors.

out·doors (out′dōrz′; –dôrz′), *Am.* —*adv.* out in the open air; not indoors or in the house. —*n.* the open air.

out·er (out′ər), *adj.* farther out; outside. —*out′er·most,* *adj., adv.* —*Syn.* outward, exterior, external.

outer space, 1. space beyond the pull of the earth's gravity. 2. space beyond the solar system; interstellar space.

out·face (out-fās′), *v.,* –faced, –fac·ing. 1. face boldly; defy. 2. stare down.

out·field (out′fēld′), *n. Am., Baseball.* a. the part of the field beyond the diamond or infield. b. the three players in the outfield.

out·field·er (out′fēl′dər), *n. Am., Baseball.* a player stationed in the outfield.

out·fit (out′fit), *n., v.,* –fit·ted, –fit·ting. —*n.* 1. all the articles necessary for any undertaking or purpose: *outfit for a camping trip, bride's outfit.* 2. *Am.* group working together. —*v.* furnish with everything necessary for any purpose; equip. —*out′fit′ter,* *n.* —*Syn. n.* 1. equipment.

out·flank (out-flangk′), *v.* 1. go or extend beyond the flank of (an opposing army, etc.); turn the flank of. 2. circumvent.

out·flow (out′flō′), *n.* 1. a flowing out: *an outflow of sympathy.* 2. that which flows out.

out·gen·er·al (out-jen′ər·əl; –jen′rəl), *v.,* –aled, –al·ing; *esp. Brit.* –alled, –al·ling. get the better of by superior strategy.

out·go (out′gō′), *n., pl.* –goes. what goes out or is paid out; amount that is spent.

out·go·ing (out′gō′ing), *adj.* departing; outward bound: *outgoing steamships.*

out·grow (out-grō′), *v.,* –grew, –grown, –grow·ing. 1. grow too large for. 2. grow beyond or away from; get rid of by growing older. 3. grow faster or taller than.

out·growth (out′grōth′), *n.* 1. a natural development, product, or result. 2. offshoot; something that has grown out. 3. a growing out or forth. —*Syn.* 1. outcome.

out·guess (out-ges′), *v.* get the better of.

out·house (out′hous′), *n.* 1. a separate building used in connection with a main building. 2. *Am.* an outdoor toilet.

out·ing (out′ing), *n.* a short pleasure trip;

walk or airing; holiday spent outdoors away from home.

out·land·er (out'lan'dər), *n.* 1. foreigner; alien. 2. *Colloq.* outsider; stranger.

out·land·ish (out·lan'dish), *adj.* 1. not familiar; queer. 2. looking or sounding as if it belonged to a foreign country. —**out·land'ish·ly,** *adv.* —**out·land'ish·ness,** *n.* —Syn. 1. odd, bizarre, strange.

out·last (out·last'; -läst'), *v.* last longer than.

out·law (out'lô'), *n.* 1. person outside the protection of the law; exile; outcast. 2. a lawless person; habitual criminal. —*v.* 1. make or declare (a person) an outlaw. 2. make or declare illegal: *outlaw war.* 3. deprive of legal force: *an outlawed debt cannot be collected.* [< Scand. *utlagi*] —**out'law'ry,** *n.* —Syn. *n.* 2. bandit, highwayman, desperado.

out·lay (*n.* out'lā'; *v.* out·lā'), *n., v.,* –laid, –lay·ing. —*n.* 1. a spending. 2. amount spent. —*v.* expend: *outlay money in improvements.*

out·let (out'let), *n.* 1. means or place of letting out or getting out: *outlet of a lake, outlet for one's energies.* 2. market for a product. —Syn. 1. vent, opening, exit, passage.

out·line (out'lin'), *n., v.,* –lined, –lin·ing. —*n.* 1. line that shows the shape of an object; line that bounds a figure. 2. a drawing or style of drawing that gives only outer lines. 3. a general plan; rough draft. 4. **in outline,** a. with only the outline shown. b. with only the main features. —*v.* 1. draw the outer line of. 2. give a plan of; sketch. —**out'lin'er,** *n.* —Syn. *n.* 1. contour, profile.

out·live (out·liv'), *v.,* –lived, –liv·ing. live or last longer than. —Syn. survive, outlast.

out·look (out'lùk'), *n.* 1. what one sees on looking out; view: *a pleasant outlook.* 2. what seems likely to happen; prospect: *the outlook for our picnic is not very good.* 3. way of thinking about things; attitude of mind; point of view: *a gloomy outlook on life.* 4. lookout; tower to watch from. —Syn. 1. prospect, scene.

out·ly·ing (out'li'ing), *adj.* lying outside the boundary; out-of-the-way; remote. —Syn. distant, isolated.

out·ma·neu·ver, out·ma·noeu·vre (out'mə·nü'vər), *v.,* –vered, –ver·ing; –vred, –vring. outdo in maneuvering; get the better of by maneuvering.

out·mod·ed (out·mōd'id), *adj.* out-of-date.

out·most (out'mōst), *adj.* farthest out.

out·num·ber (out·num'bər), *v.* be more than; exceed in number: *outnumbered three to one.*

out-of-date (out'əv·dāt'), *adj.* old-fashioned; not in present use. ▶ Out-of-date, out-of-doors are hyphenated in formal writing when they stand before a noun but not necessarily in informal writing: *His model is out of date* (not usually hyphenated). *He has an out-of-date model* (formal). *He has an out of date model* (informal).

out-of-doors (out'əv·dôrz'; -dōrz'), *adj.* Also, **out-of-door.** outdoor. —*n., adv.* outdoors. ▶ See out-of-date for usage note.

out-of-the-way (out'əv·thə·wā'), *adj.* 1. remote; unfrequented; secluded. 2. seldom met with; unusual: *out-of-the-way information.*

out·pa·tient (out'pā'shənt), *n.* patient receiving treatment at a hospital but not staying there.

out·play (out·plā'), *v.* surpass or defeat in playing.

out·point (out·point'), *v.* 1. score more points than. 2. sail closer to the wind than.

out·post (out'pōst'), *n.* 1. guard, or small number of soldiers, placed at some distance from an army or camp to prevent surprise. 2. place where they are stationed. 3. anything thought of as an outpost or advance guard. Missionaries and traders have been outposts of civilization.

out·pour (*n.* out'pôr'; –pōr'; *v.* out·pôr', –pōr'), *n.* 1. a pouring out. 2. that which is poured out. —*v.* pour out. —**out'pour'ing,** *n.*

out·put (out'pùt'), *n.* 1. amount produced; product or yield: *the daily output of automo-*

biles. 2. **a** putting forth: *a sudden output of effort.*

out·rage (out'rāj), *n., v.,* –raged, –rag·ing. —*n.* act showing no regard for the rights or feelings of others; act of violence; offense; insult. —*v.* 1. offend greatly; do violence to; insult. 2. break (the law, a rule of morality, etc.) openly; treat as nothing at all. [< OF, ult. < L *ultra* beyond] —Syn. *n.* affront, offense.

out·ra·geous (out·rā'jəs), *adj.* 1. that is or involves an outrage. 2. atrocious. 3. very offensive or insulting. —**out·ra'geous·ly,** *adv.* —**out·ra'geous·ness,** *n.* —Syn. 2. villainous, heinous.

out·rank (out·rangk'), *v. Am.* rank higher than.

ou·tré (ü·trā'), *adj.* eccentric; bizarre. [< F, pp. of *outrer* exaggerate, ult. < L *ultra* beyond]

out·reach (*v.* out·rēch'; *n.* out'rēch'), *v.* 1. reach beyond. 2. reach out; extend. —*n.* 1. a reaching out. 2. length of reach.

out·ride (out·rid'), *v.,* –rode, –rid·den, –rid·ing. 1. ride faster or better than. 2. of ships, last through (a storm).

out·rig·ger (out'rig'ər), *n.* framework ending in a float, extending outward from the side of a canoe to prevent upsetting. —**out'rigged',** **out'rig'gered,** *adj.*

out·right (out'rit'), *adv.* 1. altogether; entirely; not gradually: *sell a thing outright.* 2. openly; without restraint: *I laughed outright.* 3. at once. 4. straight out; straight ahead. —*adj.* 1. complete; thorough: *an outright loss.* 2. downright; straightforward; direct: *an outright refusal.* —**out'right'ness,** *n.*

out·run (out·run'), *v.,* –ran, –run, –run·ning. 1. run faster than. 2. leave behind; run beyond; pass the limits of.

out·sell (out·sel'), *v.,* –sold, –sell·ing. 1. sell more than. 2. sell for more than.

out·set (out'set'), *n.* a beginning.

out·shine (out·shin'), *v.,* –shone, –shin·ing. 1. shine more brightly than. 2. be more brilliant or excellent than; surpass.

out·side (*n., adj., adv.* out'sid'; *prep. also* out'-sid'), *n.* 1. side or surface that is out; outer part. 2. external appearance. 3. space or position without. 4. **at the outside,** *Colloq.* at the utmost limit. 5. **outside in,** so that what should be outside is inside; with the outside not showing. —*adj.* 1. on the outside; of or near the outside: *the outside leaves.* 2. not belonging to a certain group, set, district, etc. 3. being, acting, done, or originating without or beyond a wall, boundary, etc.: *outside noises.* 4. *Colloq.* highest; largest; reaching the utmost limit: *an outside estimate.* 5. situated on or toward the far side of any track or line that is not straight: *his outside skate held him up when he turned abruptly.* —*adv.* 1. on or to the outside. 2. outdoors. —*prep.* 1. *U.S. Colloq.* with the exception (of): *outside of John, none of us liked the play.* 2. out of; beyond the limits of. —Syn. *n.* 1. exterior.

out·sid·er (out'sid'ər), *n.* 1. person who is outside. 2. person not belonging to a particular group, set, company, party, district, etc.

out·size (out'siz'), *adj.* larger than the usual size. —*n.* article of clothing, etc., larger than the usual size.

out·skirts (out'skerts'), *n.pl.* the outer parts or edges of a town, district, etc.; outlying parts.

out·smart (out·smärt'), *v. U.S. Colloq.* outdo in cleverness.

out·spo·ken (out'spō'kən), *adj.* frank; not reserved: *outspoken criticism.* —**out'spo'ken·ly,** *adv.* —**out'spo'ken·ness,** *n.* —Syn. candid, blunt.

out·spread (*adj.* out'spred'; *v.* out·spred'), *adj., v.,* –spread, –spread·ing. spread out.

out·stand·ing (out·stan'ding), *adj.* 1. standing out from others; well-known; important. 2. unpaid. 3. projecting. —**out·stand'ing·ly,** *adv.* —**out·stand'ing·ness,** *n.*

out·stretched (out'strecht'), *adj.* extended.

out·strip (out·strip'), *v.,* –stripped, –strip·ping. 1. go faster than; leave behind in a race. 2. do better than; excel.

out·ward (out′wərd), *adj.* **1.** going toward the outside; turned toward the outside: *an outward motion.* **2.** outer: *to all outward appearances.* **3.** that can be seen; plain to see: *when that outward reformation took place.* **4.** seeming; on the surface: *the outward man.* —*adv.* Also, **out′wards. 1.** toward the outside; away. **2.** on the outside. —**out′ward·ness,** *n.* —**Syn.** *adj.* **2.** external, exterior, superficial.

out·ward·ly (out′wərd·li), *adv.* **1.** on the outside or outer surface. **2.** toward the outside. **3.** as regards appearance or outward manifestation.

out·wear (out·wãr′), *v.,* **-wore, -worn, -wearing. 1.** wear longer than. **2.** wear out.

out·weigh (out·wā′), *v.* **1.** weigh more than. **2.** exceed in value, importance, influence, etc.: *the advantages outweigh the disadvantages.*

out·wit (out·wit′), *v.,* **-wit·ted, -wit·ting.** get the better of by being more intelligent; be too clever for. —**out·wit′ter,** *n.* —**Syn.** circumvent, foil.

out·work (*n.* out′wẽrk′; *v.* out·wẽrk′), *n.* part of the fortifications of a place lying outside the main ones. —*v.* surpass in working; work harder or faster than.

ou·zel (ü′zəl), *n.* **1.** any of various European thrushes, esp. the blackbird. **2.** the water ouzel. Also, **ousel.** [OE ōsle]

o·va (ō′və), *n.* pl. of **ovum.**

o·val (ō′vəl), *adj.* **1.** egg-shaped. **2.** shaped like an ellipse. —*n.* something having an oval shape. [< NL, < L *ovum* egg] —**o′val·ly,** *adv.* —**o′val·ness,** *n.*

o·va·ry (ō′və·ri), *n.,* pl. **-ries. 1.** *Anat., Zool.* organ of a female in which eggs are produced. **2.** *Bot.* part of a plant enclosing the young seeds. [< NL, < L *ovum* egg] —**o·var·i·an** (ō·vãr′i·ən), *adj.*

o·vate (ō′vāt), *adj. Bot.* egg-shaped. —**o′vate·ly,** *adv.* —**o′vate·ness,** *n.*

o·va·tion (ō·vā′shən), *n.* an enthusiastic public welcome; burst of loud clapping or cheering. [< L, < *ovare* rejoice]

ov·en (uv′ən), *n.* **1.** space in a stove or near a fireplace, for baking food. **2.** a small furnace for heating or drying. [OE *ofen*]

o·ver (ō′vər), *prep.* **1.** above in place or position: *the roof over one's head.* **2.** above in authority, power, etc.: *we have a captain over us.* **3.** on; upon: *a blanket lying over a bed.* **4.** at all or various places on: *a blush came over her face.* **5.** above and to the other side of; across: *leap over a wall.* **6.** on the other side of: *lands over the sea.* **7.** out and down from: *he fell over the edge of the cliff.* **8.** more than; beyond: *it costs over ten dollars.* **9.** here and there on or in; roundabout; all through: *travel over Europe.* **10.** from end to end of: *over the wire.* **11.** during: *over many years.* **12.** in reference to; concerning; about: *quarrel over a matter.* **13.** while engaged on or concerned with: *fall asleep over one's work.* —*adv.* **1.** above: *hung over.* **2.** so as to cover the surface, or affect the whole surface: *rub something over.* **3.** from side to side; to the other side; across any intervening space: *sail over.* **4.** from one to another: *hand the money over.* **5.** on the other side; at some distance: *over in Europe, over by the hill.* **6.** down; out and down: *she went too near the edge and fell over.* **7.** so as to bring the upper side or end down or under: *turn over a page.* **8.** again; in repetition: *ten times over.* **9.** too (used chiefly in compounds), as in *overnice.* **10.** through a region, area, etc.: *travel all over.* **11.** from beginning to end: *read a thing over.* **12.** throughout or beyond a period of time: *please stay over till Monday.* **13.** in excess or addition: *receive the full sum and something over.* **14.** over again; once more. **15. over against, a.** opposite to; in front of. **b.** so as to bring out a difference. **16. over and above,** besides; in addition to. **17. over and over,** again and again. —*adj.* **1.** upper; higher up: *the over crust of a pie.* **2.** higher in authority, station, etc. (used chiefly in compounds), as in *overlord.* **3.** surplus; extra (used chiefly in compounds), as in *pay for overtime.*

4. too much; too great (used chiefly in compounds), as in *overuse of drugs.* **5.** at an end: *the play is over.* —*n.* amount in excess. [OE *ofer*] —**Ant.** *prep.* **1.** under, below, beneath.

over-, *prefix.* **1.** too; too much; too long, etc., as in *overcrowded, overfull, overburden, overpay, oversleep.* **2.** extra, as in *oversize, overtime.* **3.** over, as in *overflow, overlord, overseas, overthrow.*

If a word beginning with *over* is not specially defined in this dictionary, its meaning may be learned by putting *too* in place of *over* for adjectives and adverbs, *too much* or *excessive* in place of *over* for nouns, and —— *too much* in place of *over* —— for verbs. Adverbs in *-ly* and nouns in *-ness* formed from these adjectives will be understood from the meaning of the adjective in question. *Over-* is a living prefix and may be freely used to form new words.

overabound, *v.*
overabundance, *n.*
overabundant, *adj.*
overaccentuate, *v.*
overage, *adj.*
overambitious, *adj.*
overanxiety, *n.*
overanxious, *adj.*
overapprehensive, *adj.*
overarch, *v., n.*
overassertive, *adj.*
overassessment, *n.*
overattentive, *adj.*
overbashful, *adj.*
overblow, *v.*
overblown, *adj.*
overboastful, *adj.*
overbold, *adj.*
overbounteous, *adj.*
overbrilliant, *adj.*
overbrutal, *adj.*
overbuild, *v.*
overburden, *v.*
overburdensome, *adj.*
overburn, *v.*
overbusy, *adj.*
overbuy, *v.*
overcapable, *adj.*
overcapacity, *n.*
overcapitalization, *n.*
overcapitalize, *v.*
overcaptious, *adj.*
overcaptiousness, *n.*
overcareful, *adj.*
overcareless, *adj.*
overcaution, *n.*
overcautious, *adj.*
overcharitable, *adj.*
overcheap, *adj.*
overchildish, *adj.*
overcivil, *adj.*
overcivilized, *adj.*
overclean, *adj., v.*
overclever, *adj.*
overcomplex, *adj.*
overcompliant, *adj.*
overconfidence, *n.*
overconfident, *adj.*
overconscientious, *adj.*
overconscious, *adj.*
overconsciousness, *n.*
overconservative, *adj.*
overconsiderate, *adj.*
overcontribute, *v.*
overcook, *v.*
overcool, *adj., v.*
overcorrupt, *adj., v.*
overcourteous, *adj.*
overcovetous, *adj.*
overcredulous, *adj.*
overcritical, *adj.*
overcrowd, *v.*
overcultivate, *v.*
overcunning, *adj.*
overcurious, *adj.*
overdainty, *adj.*
overdear, *adj.*
overdecorate, *v.*

overdeliberate, *adj., v.*
overdelicate, *adj.*
overdemand, *v., n.*
overdesirous, *adj.*
overdevelop, *v.*
overdevelopment, *n.*
overdignified, *adj.*
overdiligence, *n.*
overdiligent, *adj.*
overdress, *v., n.*
overdry, *adj., v.*
overeager, *adj.*
overearly, *adj.*
overearnest, *adj.*
overeasy, *adj.*
overeat, *v.*
overeducate, *v.*
overelaborate, *adj., v.*
overelegant, *adj.*
overembellish, *v.*
overemotional, *adj.*
overemphasize, *v.*
overemphatic, *adj.*
overenthusiastic, *adj.*
overexcitable, *adj.*
overexcite, *v.*
overexercise, *v., n.*
overexert, *v.*
overexertion, *n.*
overexpand, *v.*
overexpansion, *n.*
overexposure, *n.*
overexuberant, *adj.*
overfacile, *adj.*
overfamiliar, *adj.*
overfanciful, *adj.*
overfar, *adj., adv.*
overfastidious, *adj.*
overfat, *adj.*
overfatigue, *n., v.*
overfearful, *adj.*
overfeed, *v.*
overfill, *v.*
overfluent, *adj.*
overfond, *adj.*
overfoolish, *adj.*
overfrail, *adj.*
overfrank, *adj.*
overfree, *adj.*
overfreely, *adv.*
overfrequency, *n.*
overfrequent, *adj., v.*
overfull, *adj.*
overfullness, *n.*
overgenerous, *adj.*
overgenial, *adj.*
overgentle, *adj.*
overgloomy, *adj.*
overgracious, *adj.*
overgrasping, *adj.*
overgrateful, *adj.*
overgratify, *v.*
overgraze, *v.*
overgreasy, *adj.*
overgreat, *adj.*
overgreedy, *adj.*
overhappy, *adj.*

āge, cãre, fär; ēqual, tẽrm; īce; ōpen, ôrder; put, rüle, ūse; th, then; ə=a in about.

overharden, *v.*
overhardy, *adj.*
overharsh, *adj.*
overhasty, *adj.*
overhaughty, *adj.*
overheat, *v., n.*
overheavy, *adj.*
overhigh, *adj.*
overhung, *adj.*
overidealistic, *adj.*
overillustrate, *v.*
overimaginative, *adj.*
overimpress, *v.*
overinclined, *adj.*
overindividualistic, *adj.*
overindulge, *v.*
overindulgence, *n.*
overindustrialize, *v.*
overinflate, *v.*
overinflation, *n.*
overinfluence, *n., v.*
overinsistent, *adj.*
overinsure, *v.*
overinventoried, *adj.*
overinvest, *v.*
overirrigate, *v.*
overirrigation, *n.*
overissue, *v., n.*
overjealous, *adj.*
overjoyful, *adj.*
overjudicious, *adj.*
overkeen, *adj.*
overkind, *adj.*
overlabor, *v.*
overlade, *v.*
overlarge, *adj.*
overlaudatory, *adj.*
overlavish, *adj.*
overlax, *adj.*
overleap, *v.*
overlearned, *adj.*
overleaven, *v., n.*
overliberal, *adj.*
overlively, *adj.*
overlogical, *adj.*
overlong, *adj., adv.*
overlusty, *adj.*
overluxuriant, *adj.*
overmany, *adj.*
overmasterful, *adj.*
overmature, *adj., v.*
overmeanness, *n.*
overmeasure, *n., v.*
overmeek, *adj.*
overmellow, *adj., v.*
overmerciful, *adj.*
overmerry, *adj.*
overmild, *adj.*
overmodest, *adj.*
overmodesty, *n.*
overmoist, *adj.*
overmortgage, *v., n.*
overmournful, *adj.*
overmultiply, *v.*
overnear, *adj.*
overneat, *adj.*
overnegligence, *n.*
overnegligent, *adj.*
overnervous, *adj.*
overnice, *adj.*
overnourish, *v.*
overnumerous, *adj.*
overobedient, *adj.*
overobese, *adj.*
overobsequious, *adj.*
overoffensive, *adj.*
overofficious, *adj.*
overpartial, *adj.*
overpassionate, *adj.*
overpatriotic, *adj.*
overpay, *v.*
overpayment, *n.*
overpeople, *v.*
overpessimistic, *adj.*
overplausible, *adj.*
overplentiful, *adj.*
overplump, *adj.*
overply, *v., n.*
overpolite, *adj.*
overpopular, *adj.*

overpopulate, *v.*
overpopulation, *n.*
overpopulous, *adj.*
overpositive, *adj.*
overpotent, *adj.*
overpowerful, *adj.*
overpraise, *n., v.*
overprecise, *adj.*
overpress, *v.*
overpresumptuous, *adj.*
overprize, *v.*
overproduce, *v.*
overproficient, *adj.*
overprolific, *adj.*
overprominent, *adj.*
overprompt, *adj., v.*
overprosperous, *adj.*
overproud, *adj.*
overprovide, *v.*
overprovoke, *v.*
overpunish, *v.*
overpunishment, *n.*
overquick, *adj.*
overquiet, *adj., v.*
overrash, *adj.*
overrate, *v.*
overrationalize, *v.*
overready, *adj., v.*
overrealistic, *adj.*
overrefined, *adj.*
overrefinement, *n.*
overreligious, *adj.*
overremiss, *adj.*
overresolute, *adj.*
overrestrain, *v.*
overrich, *adj.*
overrighteous, *adj.*
overripe, *adj.*
overripen, *v.*
overroast, *v.*
overrude, *adj.*
oversad, *adj.*
oversalt, *v.*
oversanguine, *adj.*
oversaturate, *v.*
oversaucy, *adj.*
overscented, *adj.*
overscrupulous, *adj.*
overseason, *v., adj.*
oversell, *v.*
oversensitive, *adj.*
oversentimental, *adj.*
overserious, *adj.*
overservile, *adj.*
oversevere, *adj.*
overseverity, *n.*
oversharp, *adj.*
overshort, *adj.*
overshorten, *v.*
oversilent, *adj.*
oversimple, *adj.*
oversimplicity, *n.*
oversimplify, *v.*
overskeptical, *adj.*
oversleep, *v.*
overslight, *adj., v.*
overslow, *adj.*
oversolemn, *adj.*
oversolicitous, *adj.*
oversoon, *adj., adv.*
oversophisticated, *adj.*
overspecialize, *v.*
overspeculate, *v.*
overspeculation, *n.*
overspend, *v.*
oversqueamish, *adj.*
overstiff, *adj.*
overstimulate, *v.*
overstimulation, *n.*
overstrain, *n., v.*
overstress, *v., n.*
overstrict, *adj.*
overstrident, *adj.*
overstrong, *adj.*
overstudious, *adj.*
overstudy, *n., v.*
oversubscribe, *v.*
oversubscription, *n.*
oversubtle, *adj.*

oversubtlety, *n.*
oversufficient, *adj.*
oversure, *adj.*
oversusceptible, *adj.*
oversuspicious, *adj.*
oversweet, *adj.*
oversystematic, *adj.*
oversystematize, *v.*
overtalkative, *adj.*
overtame, *adj., v.*
overtask, *v.*
overtechnical, *adj.*
overtedious, *adj.*
overteem, *v.*
overtenacious, *adj.*
overtender, *adj.*
overthrifty, *adj.*
overthrust, *v., n.*
overtimid, *adj.*
overtimorous, *adj.*
overtire, *v.*
overtrade, *v.*

overtrim, *v.*
overtrustful, *adj.*
overunionized, *adj.*
overuse, *n., v.*
overvaluation, *n.*
overvalue, *v.*
overvehement, *adj.*
overventilate, *v.*
overventuresome, *adj.*
overventurous, *adj.*
overviolent, *adj.*
overvote, *v., n.*
overwarm, *adj.*
overwary, *adj.*
overweaken, *v.*
overwealthy, *adj.*
overwear, *v.*
overwet, *adj., v.*
overwise, *adj.*
overwordy, *adj.*
overworry, *v., n.*
overzealous, *adj.*

o·ver·act (ō'vər-akt'), *v.* act to excess; overdo in acting; act (a part) in an exaggerated manner.

o·ver·ac·tive (ō'vər-ak'tiv), *adj.* too active; active to excess. —o'ver·ac'tive·ly, *adv.* —o'ver·ac·tiv'i·ty, *n.*

o·ver·all (ō'vər-ôl'), *adj.* 1. from one end to the other. 2. including everything. —*n.* overalls, *Am.* loose trousers worn over clothes to keep them clean. Overalls usually have a part that covers the chest.

o·ver·arm (ō'vər-ärm'), *adj., adv.* overhand (defs. 1 and 2).

o·ver·awe (ō'vər-ô'), *v.,* -awed, -aw·ing. overcome or restrain with awe. —Syn. intimidate, cow.

o·ver·bal·ance (ō'vər-bal'əns), *v.,* -anced, -anc·ing. 1. be greater than in weight, importance, value, etc. 2. cause to lose balance.

o·ver·bear (ō'vər-bâr'), *v.,* -bore, -borne, -bear·ing. 1. overcome by weight or force; oppress; master. 2. bear down by weight or force; overthrow; upset.

o·ver·bear·ing (ō'vər-bâr'ing), *adj.* inclined to dictate; forcing others to one's own will; domineering. —o'ver·bear'ing·ly, *adv.* —o'ver·bear'ing·ness, *n.* —Syn. dictatorial, imperious, arrogant, haughty. —Ant. meek, humble, lowly.

o·ver·bid (*v.* ō'vər-bid'; *n.* ō'vər-bid'), *v.,* -bid, -bid or -bid·den, -bid·ding, —*n.* 1. bid more than the value of (a thing). 2. bid higher than (a person). —*n.* a bid that is higher.

o·ver·board (ō'vər-bôrd'; -bōrd'), *adv.* 1. from a ship into the water. 2. throw overboard, a. throw into the water. b. *Colloq.* get rid of; give up; abandon; discard.

o·ver·cast (ō'vər-kast'; -käst'), *adj., v.,* -cast, -cast·ing. —*adj.* 1. cloudy; dark; gloomy: *the sky was overcast before the storm.* 2. sewed with overcast stitches. —*v.* 1. cover or be covered with clouds or darkness. 2. sew over and through (the edges of a seam) with long stitches to prevent raveling.

o·ver·charge (*v.* ō'vər-chärj'; *n.* ō'vər-chärj'), *v.,* -charged, -charg·ing, —*n.* 1. charge too high a price. 2. load too heavily. —*n.* 1. charge that is too great. 2. too heavy or too full a load.

o·ver·cloud (ō'vər-kloud'), *v.* 1. cloud over; become clouded over; darken. 2. make or become gloomy.

o·ver·coat (ō'vər-kōt'), *n. Am.* a heavy coat worn over the regular clothing.

o·ver·come (ō'vər-kum'), *v.,* -came, -come, -com·ing. 1. get the better of; win the victory over; conquer: *overcome an enemy, one's faults, etc.* 2. make weak or helpless: *overcome by weariness.* —o'ver·com'er, *n.* —Syn. 1. defeat, overpower, vanquish, master.

o·ver·do (ō'vər-dü'), *v.,* -did, -done, -do·ing. 1. do too much: *she overdid and became tired.* 2. exaggerate. 3. cook too much. 4. exhaust; tire. —Syn. 1. overwork. 2. overact. 4. fatigue.

o·ver·dose (*n.* ō'vər-dōs'; *v.* ō'vər-dōs'), *n., v.,* -dosed, -dos·ing. —*n.* too big a dose. —*v.* give too large a dose to.

o·ver·draft, o·ver·draught (ō'vər-draft';

–drăft′), *n.* **1.** an overdrawing of an account, as at a bank. **2.** amount of the excess.

o·ver·draw (ō′vər·drô′), *v.,* **–drew, –drawn, –draw·ing. 1.** draw from (a bank account, allowance, etc.) more than one has a right to. **2.** exaggerate.

o·ver·drive (*v.* ō′vər·drīv′; *n.* ō′vər·drīv′), *v.,* **–drove, –driv·en, –driv·ing,** *n.* —*v.* overwork. —*n.* an arrangement of gears whereby even more speed and less power are produced than in high. —o′ver·driv′en, *adj.*

o·ver·due (ō′vər·dū′; –dū′), *adj.* more than due; due some time ago but not yet arrived, paid, etc.: *the train is overdue.*

o·ver·es·ti·mate (*v.* ō′vər·es′tə·māt; *n.* ō′vər·es′tə·mit), *v.,* **–mat·ed, –mat·ing,** *n.* —*v.* estimate at too high a value, amount, rate, etc. —*n.* estimate that is too high. —o′ver·es·ti·ma′tion, *n.*

o·ver·flow (*v.* ō′vər·flō′; *n.* ō′vər·flō′), *v.,* **–flowed, –flown, –flow·ing,** *n.* —*v.* **1.** flow over the bounds: *rivers often overflow in the spring.* **2.** cover; flood: *the river overflowed my garden.* **3.** have the contents flowing over: *my cup is overflowing.* **4.** flow over the top of: *the milk is overflowing the cup.* **5.** extend out beyond; be too many for: *the crowd overflowed the little parlor and filled the hall.* **6.** be very abundant: *an overflowing harvest, overflowing kindness.* —*n.* an overflowing; excess. —o′ver·flow′ing, *adj.* —o′ver·flow′ing·ly, *adv.* —Syn. *v.* **2.** inundate, overrun, deluge. —*n.* superfluity.

o·ver·grow (ō′vər·grō′), *v.,* **–grew, –grown, –grow·ing. 1.** grow over. **2.** grow too fast; become too big. **3.** outgrow. —o′ver·grown′, *adj.*

o·ver·growth (ō′vər·grōth′), *n.* **1.** too great or too rapid growth. **2.** growth overspreading or covering something.

o·ver·hand (ō′vər·hand′), *adj., adv.* **1.** with the hand raised above the shoulder: *an overhand throw, pitch overhand.* **2.** with the knuckles upward. **3.** in sewing, over and over; with stitches passing successively over an edge. —*v. Am.* sew overhand. —o′ver·hand′ed, *adj.*

o·ver·hang (*v.* ō′vər·hang′; *n.* ō′vər·hang′), *v.,* **–hung, –hang·ing,** *n.* —*v.* **1.** hang over; project over. **2.** hang over so as to darken, sadden, or threaten. —*n.* **1.** something that projects: *the overhang of a roof.* **2.** amount of projecting.

o·ver·haul (ō′vər·hôl′), *v.* **1.** examine thoroughly so as to make any repairs or changes that are needed. **2.** gain upon; overtake. —o′ver·haul′ing, *n.*

o·ver·head (*adv.* ō′vər·hed′; *adj., n.* ō′vər·hed′), *adv.* in the sky; on the floor above; on high; above: *the stars overhead.* —*adj.* **1.** being, working, or passing overhead: *overhead wires.* **2.** applying to one and all; general. —*n.* general expenses or charges, such as rent, lighting, heating, taxes, repairs.

o·ver·hear (ō′vər·hir′), *v.,* **–heard, –hear·ing.** hear when one is not meant to hear: *overhear what they said.* —o′ver·hear′er, *n.*

o·ver·joy (ō′vər·joi′), *v.* make extremely joyful. —o′ver·joyed′, *adj.*

o·ver·lad·en (ō′vər·lād′ən), *adj.* overloaded.

o·ver·land (ō′vər·land′; –lənd), *adv., adj.* on or through land; by land.

o·ver·lap (*v.* ō′vər·lap′; *n.* ō′vər·lap′), *v.,* **–lapped, –lap·ping,** *n.* —*v.* lap over; cover and extend beyond: *shingles are laid to overlap each other.* —*n.* **1.** a lapping over. **2.** amount by which one thing laps over another. **3.** part that overlaps.

o·ver·lay (*v.* ō′vər·lā′; *n.* ō′vər·lā′), *v.,* **–laid, –lay·ing,** *n.* —*v.* **1.** lay or place (one thing) over or upon another. **2.** cover, overspread, or surmount with something, esp. to finish with a layer or applied decoration of something: *wood overlaid with gold.* —*n.* something laid over something else; layer or decoration; covering.

o·ver·lie (ō′vər·lī′), *v.,* **–lay, –lain, –ly·ing.** lie over or upon.

o·ver·load (*v.* ō′vər·lōd′; *n.* ō′vər·lōd′), *v.* load too heavily. —*n.* too great a load.

o·ver·look (ō′vər·lúk′), *v.* **1.** have a view of from above; be higher than: *this high window overlooks half the city.* **2.** fail to see: *here are the letters you overlooked.* **3.** pay no attention to; excuse: *overlook bad behavior this time.* **4.** manage; look after and direct. —o′ver·look′er, *n.* —Syn. **2.** disregard, ignore, slight, neglect. **3.** forgive, condone.

o·ver·lord (ō′vər·lôrd′), *n.* person who is lord over another lord or other lords. —o′ver·lord′-ship, *n.*

o·ver·ly (ō′vər·li), *adv.* overmuch; excessively; too.

o·ver·mas·ter (ō′vər·mas′tər; –mäs′–), *v.* overcome; overpower. —o′ver·mas′ter·ing, *adj.* —o′ver·mas′ter·ing·ly, *adv.*

o·ver·match (ō′vər·mach′), *v.* surpass.

o·ver·much (ō′vər·much′), *adj., adv., n.* too much.

o·ver·night (*adv.* ō′vər·nīt′; *adj., n.* ō′vər·nīt′), *adv.* **1.** during the night: *stay overnight.* **2.** on the night before. —*adj.* **1.** done, occurring, etc., during the night: *an overnight stop.* **2.** for the night: *an overnight bag.* **3.** of or pertaining to the night before. —*n.* the previous evening.

o·ver·pass (*v.* ō′vər·pas′, –päs′; *n.* ō′vər·pas′, –päs′), *v.,* **–passed or –past, –pass·ing,** *n.* —*v.* pass over (a region, bounds, etc.). —*n.* bridge over a road, railroad, canal, etc.

o·ver·play (ō′vər·plā′), *v.* **1.** play (a part, etc.) in an exaggerated manner. **2.** play better than; surpass; defeat.

o·ver·pow·er (ō′vər·pou′ər), *v.* **1.** overcome; master; overwhelm: *overpower one's enemies.* **2.** be so much greater that nothing else is felt: *sudden anger overpowered every other feeling.* —o′ver·pow′er·ing, *adj.* —o′ver·pow′er·ing·ly, *adv.* —Syn. **1.** conquer, vanquish, defeat, overthrow.

o·ver·pro·duc·tion (ō′vər·prə·duk′shən), *n.* **1.** production of more than is needed. **2.** production of more than can be sold at a profit.

o·ver·reach (ō′vər·rēch′), *v.* **1.** reach over or beyond. **2.** spread over. **3.** reach too far. **4.** cheat. **5.** overreach oneself, a. fail or miss by trying for too much. b. fail by being too crafty or tricky. —o′ver·reach′er, *n.* —Syn. **4.** defraud, swindle, dupe.

o·ver·ride (ō′vər·rīd′), *v.,* **–rode, –rid·den, –rid·ing. 1.** ride over; trample on. **2.** ride over (a region, place, etc.). **3.** act in spite of: *override objections.* **4.** prevail over: *a new rule overriding all previous ones.* **5.** tire out by riding; ride too much: *override a horse.*

o·ver·rule (ō′vər·rül′), *v.,* **–ruled, –rul·ing. 1.** rule or decide against (a plea, argument, objection, etc.); set aside. **2.** prevail over; be stronger than. —o′ver·rul′ing, *adj.* —o′ver·rul′ing·ly, *adv.* —Syn. **1.** override, reject.

o·ver·run (*v.* ō′vər·run′; *n.* ō′vər·run′), *v.,* **–ran, –run, –run·ning,** *n.* —*v.* **1.** spread over and spoil or harm in some way: *weeds had overrun the old garden.* **2.** spread over: *vines overran the wall.* **3.** run or go beyond; exceed: *the speaker overran the time set for him.* **4.** run over. **5.** overflow. —*n.* **1.** an overrunning. **2.** amount overrunning or carried over. —o′ver·run′ner, *n.* —Syn. *v.* **1.** invade, ravage, infest.

o·ver·sea (*adv.* ō′vər·sē′; *adj.* ō′vər·sē′), *adv., adj.* overseas.

o·ver·seas (*adv.* ō′vər·sēz′; *adj.* ō′vər·sēz′), *adv.* across the sea; beyond the sea. —*adj.* **1.** done, used, or serving overseas. **2.** of countries across the sea; foreign.

o·ver·see (ō′vər·sē′), *v.,* **–saw, –seen, –see·ing.** look after and direct (work or workers); superintend; manage. —Syn. supervise, inspect.

o·ver·se·er (ō′vər·sē′ər), *n.* one who oversees, superintends, or looks after the work of others. —o′ver·se′er·ship, *n.* —Syn. supervisor.

o·ver·set (*v.* ō′vər·set′; *n.* ō′vər·set′), *v.,* **–set, –set·ting,** *n.* —*v.* **1.** upset; overturn. **2.** overthrow. —*n.* overthrow.

o·ver·shad·ow (ō′vər·shad′ō), *v.* **1.** be more important than. **2.** cast a shadow over.

o·ver·shoe (ō′vər·shü′), *n. Am.* a rubber shoe

or a felt shoe with a rubber sole worn over another shoe to keep the foot dry and warm.

o·ver·shoot (ō′vər·shüt′), v., -shot, -shooting. 1. shoot over, higher than, or beyond. 2. go over, higher than, or beyond. 3. go too far.

o·ver·shot (adj. ō′vər·shot′; v. ō′vər·shot′), adj. 1. having the upper jaw projecting beyond the lower. 2. driven by water flowing over from above. —v. pt. and pp. of overshoot.

o·ver·sight (ō′vər·sīt′), n. 1. failure to notice or think of something. 2. watchful care. —Syn. 1. overlooking, inadvertence, omission, slip. 2. supervision, superintendence, charge.

o·ver·size (ō′vər·sīz′), adj. too big. —n. 1. size larger than the proper or usual size. 2. something larger than is necessary.

o·ver·skirt (ō′vər·skėrt′), n. Am. a. an outer skirt. b. a separate skirt over the upper part of the main skirt.

o·ver·spread (ō′vər·spred′), v., -spread, -spread·ing. spread over: a smile overspread his face.

o·ver·state (ō′vər·stāt′), v., -stat·ed, -stat·ing. state too strongly; exaggerate. —o′ver·state′ment, n.

o·ver·stay (ō′vər·stā′), v. stay beyond the time or continuance of.

o·ver·step (ō′vər·step′), v., -stepped, -stepping. go beyond; exceed: the government overstepped the bounds of its proper functions.

o·ver·stock (v. ō′vər·stok′; n. ō′vər·stok′), supply with more than is needed. —n. too great a stock or supply.

o·ver·strung (ō′vər·strung′), adj. too nervous or sensitive.

o·ver·stuffed (ō′vər·stuft′), adj. of furniture, with the whole surface covered by upholstery.

o·ver·sup·ply (v. ō′vər·sə·plī′; n. ō′vər·sə·plī′), v., -plied, -ply·ing, n., pl. -plies. —v. supply in excess. —n. an excessive supply.

o·vert (ō′vėrt; ō·vėrt′), adj. open; evident; not hidden; public: hitting someone is an overt act. [< OF, pp. of ovrir open < L aperire] —o′vert·ly, adv. —o′vert·ness, n. —Syn. plain, manifest, apparent.

o·ver·take (ō′vər·tāk′), v., -took, -tak·en, -tak·ing. 1. come up with: the blue car overtook ours. 2. come upon suddenly: a storm overtook the children.

o·ver·tax (ō′vər·taks′), v. 1. tax too heavily. 2. put too heavy a burden on. —o′ver·tax·a′tion, n.

o·ver·throw (v. ō′vər·thrō′; n. ō′vər·thrō′), v., -threw, -thrown, -throw·ing, n. —v. 1. take away the power of; defeat: overthrow a king. 2. put an end to; destroy: overthrow slavery. 3. overturn; upset; knock down. —n. a defeat; upset. —o′ver·throw′er, n. —Syn. v. 1. rout, conquer, vanquish, overcome. —n. destruction.

o·ver·time (n., adv., adj. ō′vər·tīm′; v. ō′vər·tīm′), n., adv., adj., v., -timed, -tim·ing. —n. extra time; time beyond the regular hours. —adv., adj. beyond the regular hours. —v. give too much time to: overtime a camera exposure.

o·ver·tone (ō′vər·tōn′), n. a fainter and higher tone heard along with the main or fundamental tone; harmonic.

o·ver·top (ō′vər·top′), v., -topped, -top·ping. 1. rise above; be higher than. 2. surpass; excel. —Syn. 2. outstrip.

o·ver·train (ō′vər·trān′), v. subject to or undergo so much athletic training that the condition is injured rather than improved; train to excess.

o·ver·ture (ō′vər·chər), n. 1. proposal; offer: the enemy is making overtures for peace. 2. Music. composition played by the orchestra as an introduction to an opera, oratorio, etc. [< OF < L apertura opening. Doublet of APERTURE.] —Syn. 1. proposition. 2. prelude.

o·ver·turn (v. ō′vər·tėrn′; n. ō′vər·tėrn′), v. 1. turn upside down. 2. upset; fall down; fall over. 3. make fall down; overthrow; destroy the power of. —n. an overturning. —o′ver·turn′er, n. —Syn. v. 1. invert. 2. capsize. 3. defeat, ruin.

o·ver·ween·ing (ō′vər·wēn′ing), adj. thinking too much of oneself; conceited; self-confi-

dent; presumptuous. [ppr. of overween < OVER- + ween expect (OE wēnan)] —o′ver·ween′ing·ly, adv. —o′ver·ween′ing·ness, n.

o·ver·weigh (ō′vər·wā′), v. 1. be greater than in weight, importance, etc.; outweigh. 2. oppress.

o·ver·weight (adj. ō′vər·wāt′; n. ō′vər·wāt′; v. ō′vər·wāt′), adj. having too much weight: a boy overweight for his age. —n. 1. too much weight. 2. extra weight. —v. overburden.

o·ver·whelm (ō′vər·hwelm′), v. 1. overcome completely; crush: overwhelm with grief. 2. cover completely as a flood would. [< OVER- + whelm roll, submerge (ME)] —o′ver·whelm′-ing, adj. —o′ver·whelm′ing·ly, adv.

o·ver·work (n. ō′vər·wėrk′; v. ō′vər·wėrk′), n., v., -worked or -wrought, -work·ing. —n. too much or too hard work. —v. 1. work too hard or too long. 2. cause to work too much. 3. spend too much work upon; elaborate to excess. See also overwrought. —Syn. v. 2. overtax, overburden, exhaust, fatigue.

o·ver·wrought (ō′vər·rôt′), adj. 1. wearied; excited: overwrought nerves. 2. too elaborate. 3. overworked.

Ov·id (ov′id), n. 43 B.C.–17? A.D., Roman poet.

o·vi·duct (ō′və·dukt), n. Anat., Zool. tube through which the ovum or egg passes from the ovary. [< NL < ovum egg + ductus DUCT]

o·vi·form (ō′və·fôrm), adj. egg-shaped. [< L ovum egg + -FORM]

o·vip·a·rous (ō·vip′ə·rəs), adj. Zool. producing eggs that are hatched after leaving the body. [< L, < ovum egg + parere bring forth] —o·vi·par·i·ty (ō′vi·par′ə·ti), n.

o·vi·pos·i·tor (ō′və·poz′ə·tər), n. in certain insects, an organ at the end of the abdomen, by which eggs are deposited. [< L ovum egg + positor placer < ponere to place] —o·vi·po·si·tion (ō′vi·pə·zish′ən), n.

o·void (ō′void), n. —o·voi·dal (ō·voi′dəl), adj. egg-shaped.

o·vule (ō′vūl), n. 1. Biol. a little ovum. 2. Bot. part of a plant that develops into a seed. [< NL ovulum, dim. of L ovum egg] —o′vu·lar, adj.

o·vum (ō′vəm), n., pl. o·va (ō′və). Biol. a female germ cell; egg. [< L, egg]

owe (ō), v., owed, ow·ing. 1. have to pay; be in debt for: owe interest on a mortgage. 2. be in debt: he is always owing for something. 3. be obliged or indebted for: we owe a great deal to our parents. 4. owe a grudge, feel ill will. [OE āgan]

ow·ing (ō′ing), adj. 1. that owes: a man owing money. 2. due; owed: pay what is owing. 3. owing to, on account of; because of; due to; as a result of: owing to the rain we did not go outdoors.

owl (oul), n. bird with a big head, big eyes, and a short, hooked beak. Owls hunt mice and small birds at night. [OE ūle] —owl′-ish, adj. —owl′ish·ly, adv. —owl′ish·ness, n. —owl′like′, adj.

American great horned owl (ab. 2 ft. long, from ears to tip of tail)

owl·et (oul′it), n. 1. a young owl. 2. a small owl.

own (ōn), adj. 1. of oneself or itself; belonging to oneself or itself: we have our own troubles, the house is her own. 2. in closest relationship: own brothers have the same parents. —n. 1. the one or ones belonging to oneself or itself: come into one's own. 2. of one's own, belonging to oneself. 3. on one's own, Colloq. on one's own account, responsibility, resources, etc. —v. 1. possess: he owns much land. 2. acknowledge; admit; confess: he owned his guilt. 3. acknowledge as one's own: his father will not own him. [OE āgen, orig. pp. of āgan owe] —own′er, n. —own′er·less, adj. —own′er·ship, n. —Syn. v. 1. have, hold. 2. concede, grant.

ox (oks), n., pl. ox·en. 1. the full-grown male of cattle, that has been castrated and is used as a draft animal or for beef. 2. any of a group of mammals with horns and cloven hoofs, including domestic cattle, buffaloes, bison, etc. [OE oxa] —ox′like′, adj.

ox·al·ic acid (oks·al′ik), a poisonous organic acid, $C_2H_2O_4 \cdot 2H_2O$, that occurs in many plants. It is used for bleaching, removing stains, making dyes, etc. [< F < L *oxalis* sorrel < Gk., < *oxys* sour]

ox·bow (oks′bō′), *n.* 1. *U.S.* a U-shaped piece of wood placed under and around the neck of an ox, with the upper ends inserted in the bar of the yoke. See the picture under yoke. 2. a U-shaped bend in a river.

ox·cart (oks′kärt′), *n.* cart drawn by oxen.

ox·en (ok′sən), *n.* pl. of ox.

ox·eye (oks′ī′), *n. Am.* 1. the common American daisy. 2. any of several plants like it.

ox·ford (oks′fərd), *n.* 1. kind of low shoe. 2. Also, **Oxford gray.** a very dark gray. [after *Oxford,* the city]

Ox·ford (oks′fərd), *n.* 1. city in S England. 2. the very old and famous English university located there.

ox·heart (oks′härt′), *n.* a large, heart-shaped cherry.

ox·i·da·tion (ok′sə·dā′shən), *n.* 1. an oxidizing. 2. a being oxidized.

ox·ide (ok′sīd; –sid), **ox·id** (–sid), *n. Chem.* compound of oxygen with another element or radical. [< F, < *ox(ygène)* oxygen + *(ac)ide* acid]

ox·i·dize (ok′sə·dīz), *v.,* –dized, –diz·ing. *Chem.* 1. combine with oxygen. When a substance burns or rusts, it is oxidized. 2. rust. 3. lose or cause to lose hydrogen. 4. change to a higher positive valence. —**ox′i·diz′a·ble,** *adj.* —**ox′i·di·za′tion,** *n.* —**ox′i·diz′er,** *n.*

ox·lip (oks′lip′), *n.* primrose that has clusters of pale-yellow flowers.

Ox·o·ni·an (oks·ō′ni·ən), *adj.* of or pertaining to Oxford University or Oxford. —*n.* member or graduate of Oxford University. [< Med.L *Oxonia* Oxford]

ox·y·a·cet·y·lene (ok′si·ə·set′ə·lēn), *adj.* of, pertaining to, or using a mixture of oxygen and acetylene.

oxyacetylene blowpipe or torch, tool with a very hot flame for welding or cutting

metals. It uses a mixture of oxygen and acetylene.

ox·y·gen (ok′sə·jən), *n. Chem.* gas without color or odor that forms about one fifth of the air. Animals and plants cannot live, and fire will not burn, without oxygen. Oxygen is a chemical element, O, present in a combined form in many substances. [< F, intended as "acidifying (principle)" < Gk. *oxys* sharp + –*genes* born, ult. < *gignesthai* be born] —**ox·y·gen·ic** (ok′sə·jen′ik), *adj.* —**ox·y·ge·nous** (ok·sij′ə·nəs), *adj.*

ox·y·gen·ate (ok′sə·jən·āt), **ox·y·gen·ize** (–īz), *v.,* –at·ed, –at·ing; –ized, –iz·ing. 1. treat or combine with oxygen. 2. oxidize. —**ox′y·gen·a′tion,** *n.* —**ox′y·gen·iz′a·ble,** *adj.*

oxygen mask, device worn over the nose and mouth by aviators at very high altitudes, through which supplementary oxygen is supplied from an attached container.

oxygen tent, a small tent that can be filled with oxygen, used in treating some diseases.

o·yez, o·yes (ō′yes; ō′yez), *interj., n.* hear! attend! a cry uttered, usually three times, by a public or court crier to command silence and attention before a proclamation, etc., is made. [< AF. hear ye! < *oyer* hear, var. of *oïr* < L *audire*]

oys·ter (ois′tər), *n.* kind of mollusk much used as food, having a rough, irregular shell in two halves. Oysters are found in shallow water along seacoasts. Some kinds yield pearls. [< OF < L < Gk. *ostreon*]

oyster crab, a small crab that lives harmlessly within the shell of a live oyster.

oyster plant, salsify.

oz., *pl.* ozs. ounce.

O·zark Mountains (ō′zärk), or **O·zarks,** *n.pl.* a low mountain range in S Missouri, N Arkansas, and E Oklahoma.

o·zone (ō′zōn), *n.* 1. form of oxygen, O_3, with a peculiar odor, produced by electricity and present in the air, esp. after a thunderstorm. 2. *Colloq.* pure air that is refreshing. [< F, < Gk. *ozein* smell + F –*one,* chem. suffix] —**o·zon·ic** (ō·zon′ik; ō·zō′nik), *adj.* —**o·zo·nif·er·ous** (ō′zə·nif′ər·əs), *adj.*

P

P, p (pē), *n., pl.* P's; p's. the 16th letter of the alphabet.

P, 1. *Chem.* phosphorus. 2. *Physics.* pressure.

p., 1. page. 2. participle. 3. past. 4. per. 5. pint. 6. *Baseball.* pitcher.

pa (pä), *n. Colloq.* papa; father.

Pa, *Chem.* protactinium.

Pa., Pennsylvania.

p.a., participial adjective.

pab·u·lum (pab′yə·ləm), *n.* food. [< L, fodder]

pace (pās), *n., v.,* paced, pac·ing. —*n.* 1. rate; speed: *a fast pace in walking.* 2. a step. 3. length of a step in walking; about 2½ feet. 4. way of stepping. The walk, trot, and canter are some of the paces of the horse. 5. a particular pace of some horses in which the feet on the same side are lifted and put down together. 6. put one through his paces, try one out; find out what one can do. —*v.* 1. set the pace for. 2. walk over with regular steps: *pace the floor.* 3. walk with regular steps. 4. measure by paces. 5. of horses, move at a pace. [< OF < L *passus* step] —**pac′er,** *n.* —Syn. *n.* 4. gait.

pace·mak·er (pās′māk′ər), *n.* person, animal, or thing that sets the pace. —**pace′mak′ing,** *n.*

pach·y·derm (pak′ə·dėrm), *n.* a thick-skinned mammal with hoofs, such as the elephant, hippopotamus, and rhinoceros. [< F < Gk., < *pachys* thick + *derma* skin] —**pach·y·der·ma·tous** (pak′ə·dėr′mə·təs), *adj.*

Pa·cif·ic (pə·sif′ik), *n.* the great ocean W of North and South America, extending to Asia and Australia. —*adj.* of, on, or near the Pacific Ocean.

pa·cif·ic (pə·sif′ik), **pa·cif·i·cal** (–ə·kəl), *adj.* 1. tending to make peace; making peace. 2. loving peace; not warlike. 3. peaceful; calm; quiet. [< L *pacificus,* ult. < *pax* peace + *facere* make] —**pa·cif′i·cal·ly,** *adv.* —Syn. 1. peaceable, conciliatory, appeasing. 3. placid, tranquil, serene. —Ant. 2. quarrelsome, belligerent.

pa·cif·i·cate (pə·sif′ə·kāt), *v.,* –cat·ed, –cat·ing. pacify. —**pac·if·i·ca·tion** (pas′ə·fə·kā′shən), *n.* —**pa·cif′i·ca′tor,** *n.* —**pa·cif·i·ca·to·ry** (pə·sif′ə·kə·tô′ri; –tō′–), *adj.*

pac·i·fi·er (pas′ə·fī′ər), *n.* 1. person or thing that pacifies. 2. a rubber nipple or ring given to a baby to suck.

pac·i·fism (pas′ə·fiz·əm), *n.* principle or policy of establishing and maintaining universal peace by settlement of all differences between nations by peaceful means. —**pac′i·fist,** *n.* —**pac·i·fis′tic,** *adj.* —**pac′i·fis′ti·cal·ly,** *adv.*

pac·i·fy (pas′ə·fī), *v.,* –fied, –fy·ing. 1. make calm; quiet down: *pacify a screaming baby.* 2. establish peace throughout: *soldiers were sent to pacify the country.* Also, pacificate. [< L *pacificare.* See PACIFIC.] —**pac′i·fi′a·ble,** *adj.* —**pac′i·fy′ing·ly,** *adv.*

pack¹ (pak), *n.* 1. bundle of things wrapped up or tied together for carrying. 2. amount packed: *this year's pack.* 3. set; lot; a number together: *a pack of thieves, a pack of lies.* 4. a number of animals hunting together; a number of dogs kept together for hunting. 5. a complete set of playing cards, usually 52. 6. a large area of floating pieces of ice pushed together. 7. a paste put on the face as a cosmetic treatment. 8. a wrapping of the body in cloths (hot or cold, wet

āge, cāre, fär; ēqual, tėrm; īce; ōpen, ôrder; pút, rüle, ūse; ŧℏ, then; ə=a in about.

or dry) as a medical treatment. **9.** the cloths, sheets, blankets, etc., so used. —*v.* **1.** put together in a bundle, box, bale, etc.: *pack your clothes in this bag.* **2.** put things together in a bundle, box, bale, etc.: *are you ready to pack?* **3.** fill with things; put one's things into: *pack your trunk.* **4.** fit together closely; admit of storing and shipping: *these goods pack well.* **5.** press or crowd closely together: *a hundred men were packed into one small room.* **6.** become packed; crowd together. **7.** put into a container to be sold or stored: *meat, fish, and vegetables are often packed in cans.* **8.** make tight with something that water, steam, air, etc., cannot leak through. **9.** load (an animal) with a pack; burden. **10.** *Am., Colloq.* carry, esp. as part of one's regular equipment: *pack a gun.* **11.** pack off, send away. **12.** send packing, send away in a hurry. [< MLG *packe*] —**pack′er,** *n.* —Syn. *n.* **1.** parcel, bale, package. —*v.* **5.** cram.

pack² (pak), *v.* arrange unfairly. To pack a jury or a convention is to fill it unfairly with those who will favor one side.

pack·age (pak′ij), *n., v.,* –aged, –ag·ing. —*n.* **1.** bundle of things packed or wrapped together; box with things packed in it; parcel. —*v.* put in a package. —Syn. *n.* packet, pack.

package deal, *Am., Colloq.* grouping of two or more items as a unit for sale, acceptance, etc.

package tour, a trip offered by a tourist agency as a unit including meals, tickets, etc.

pack animal, animal used for carrying loads.

pack·et (pak′it), *n.* a small package.

packet boat, boat that carries mail, passengers, and goods regularly on a fixed route.

pack horse, horse used to carry packs of goods.

pack·ing (pak′ing), *n.* **1.** material used to pack or to make watertight, steamtight, etc. **2.** act, process, or work of one that packs.

packing house, *Am.* place where meat, vegetables, etc., are prepared and packed to be sold.

pack·sad·dle (pak′sad′əl), *n.* saddle specially adapted for supporting the load on a pack animal.

pack train, *Am.* line or group of animals carrying loads.

pact (pakt), *n.* agreement; compact. [< L *pactum,* orig., agreed] —Syn. covenant, treaty.

pad¹ (pad), *n., v.,* pad·ded, pad·ding. —*n.* **1.** a cushionlike mass of soft material used for comfort, protection, or stuffing. **2.** a soft, stuffed saddle. **3.** one of the cushionlike parts on the bottom side of the feet of dogs, foxes, and some other animals. **4.** foot of a dog, fox, etc. **5.** the large floating leaf of the water lily. **6.** number of sheets of paper fastened along an edge or edges; tablet. **7.** cloth soaked with ink to use with a rubber stamp. **8.** launching pad. —*v.* **1.** fill with something soft; stuff: *a padded suit for football.* **2.** make (a written paper or speech) longer by using unnecessary words just to fill space. —pad′der, *n.* —Syn. *z.* **1.** cushion.

pad² (pad), *v.,* pad·ded, pad·ding, *n.* —*v.* **1.** walk; tramp; trudge. **2.** walk or trot softly. —*n.* a dull sound, as of footsteps on the ground. [< Du. or LG; akin to PATH]

pad·ding (pad′ing), *n.* **1.** material used to pad with, such as hair, cotton, or straw. **2.** unnecessary words used just to make a speech or a written paper longer.

pad·dle¹ (pad′əl), *n., v.,* –died, –dling. —*n.* **1.** a short oar with a broad blade at one end or both ends, used without resting it against the boat. **2.** act of paddling; a turn at the paddle. **3.** one of the broad boards fixed around a water wheel or a paddle wheel to push, or be pushed by, the water. **4.** a paddle-shaped piece of wood used for stirring, for mixing, for beating clothes, etc. —*v.* **1.** move (a boat or canoe) with a paddle or paddles. **2.** use a paddle to move a canoe, etc. **3.** row gently. **4.** *Am., Colloq.* beat or strike with a paddle; spank. —pad′dler, *n.*

pad·dle² (pad′əl), *v.,* –died, –dling. **1.** move the hands or feet about in water. **2.** toddle. —pad′dler, *n.*

pad·dle·fish (pad′əl·fish′), *n., pl.* –fish·es or (*esp. collectively*) –fish. a large fish whose long,

flat snout looks somewhat like a canoe paddle.

paddle wheel, wheel with paddles around it for propelling a ship on water.

pad·dock (pad′ək), *n.* **1.** a small field near a stable or house, used as a pasture. **2.** pen for horses at a race track. [var. of *parrock,* OE *pearroc* enclosed space, fence < Med.L *parricus* enclosure. Doublet of PARK.]

pad·dy, pad·i (pad′i), *n., pl.* pad·dies; pad·is. **1.** rice. **2.** rice in the husk, uncut or gathered. **3.** field of rice. [< Malay *padi*]

Pad·e·rew·ski (pad′ə·ref′ski), *n.* Ignace Jan, 1860–1941, Polish pianist, composer, and statesman.

pad·lock (pad′lok′), *n.* lock that can be put on and removed. It hangs by a curved bar, hinged at one end and snapped shut at the other. —*v.* fasten with a padlock.

pa·dre (pä′drā), *n.* **1.** father (used esp. with reference to a priest). **2.** chaplain in the army or navy. [< Ital., Sp., Pg. < L *pater* father]

Pad·u·a (paj′ủ·ə; pad′yủ·ə), *n.* city in NE Italy. —**Pa·do·va** (pä′dō·vä), *n.* Ital. name.

pae·an (pē′ən), *n.* song of praise, joy, or triumph. Also, pean. [< L < Gk. *paian* hymn to Apollo (called *Paian*)]

pae·di·at·rics (pē′di·at′riks), *n.* pediatrics.

pa·gan (pā′gən), *n.* **1.** person who is not a Christian, Jew, or Mohammedan; heathen. The ancient Greeks and Romans were pagans. **2.** person who has no religion. —*adj.* **1.** having to do with pagans; not Christian, Jewish, or Mohammedan. **2.** not religious. [< L *paganus,* lit., a rustic, later civilian, heathen < *pagus* village] —pa′gan·dom, *n.* —pa′gan·ish, *adj.* —pa′gan·ism, *n.*

Pag·a·ni·ni (pag′ə·nē′nē), *n.* Nicolò, 1784–1840, Italian violinist.

pa·gan·ize (pā′gən·īz), *v.,* –ized, –iz·ing. make or become pagan. —pa′gan·i·za′tion, *n.*

page¹ (pāj), *n., v.,* paged, pag·ing. —*n.* **1.** one side of a leaf or sheet of paper. **2.** print or writing on one side of a leaf. **3.** a record: *the pages of history.* **4.** happening or time considered as part of history: *the settling of the West is a glorious page in our history.* —*v.* number the pages of. [< F < L *pagina* < *pangere* fasten]

page² (pāj), *n., v.,* paged, pag·ing. —*n.* **1.** a boy servant; errand boy. **2.** youth who attends a person of rank. **3.** youth preparing to be a knight. —*v. Am.* try to find (a person) at a hotel, club, etc., by having his name called out by a page. [< OF < Ital., ult. < Gk. *paidion* lad, dim. of *pais* child]

pag·eant (paj′ənt), *n.* **1.** an elaborate spectacle; procession in costume; pomp; display: *the coronation of the new king was a splendid pageant.* **2.** a public entertainment that represents scenes from history, legend, or the like, esp. a drama or series of scenes played out-of-doors by local actors. **3.** empty show, not reality.

pag·eant·ry (paj′ənt·ri), *n., pl.* –ries. **1.** a splendid show; gorgeous display; pomp. **2.** mere show; empty display.

pag·i·na·tion (paj′ə·nā′shən), *n.* **1.** act of numbering the pages of books, etc. **2.** the figures with which pages are numbered.

pa·go·da (pə·gō′də), *n.* temple with many stories forming a tower. Pagodas are built in India, China, and Japan. [< Pg. *pagode* < Tamil *pagavadi*]

Pa·go Pa·go, Pa·go·pa·go (päng′ō·päng′ō; päng′ō·pä′gō; pä′gō·pä′gō), *n.* harbor in Samoa, in the SW Pacific. A United States naval station is located there.

paid (pād), *adj.* **1.** receiving money; hired. **2.** no longer owed; settled. **3.** cashed. —*v.* pt. and pp. of pay. ▶ paid, payed. *Paid* is the spelling of the past tense and past participle of *pay* (he paid his bills) in all senses except *he payed out a line, rope,* etc.

Pagoda

pail (pāl), *n.* **1.** a round container for carrying

liquids, etc.; bucket. 2. amount a pail holds. [OE *pægel;* ? < Med.L *pagella* a measure]

pail·ful (pāl′fúl), *n., pl.* **-fuls.** amount that fills a pail.

pain (pān), *n.* 1. a feeling of being hurt; suffering. 2. on pain of, under pain of, with the punishment or penalty of, unless a certain thing is done. 3. **pains,** trouble to do something; effort; care. —*v.* cause to suffer; give pain; hurt. [< OF < L *poena* penalty < Gk. *poine*] —**pain′less,** *adj.* —**pain′less·ly,** *adv.* —**pain′less·ness,** *n.* —**Syn.** *n.* 1. ache, pang, misery, anguish, agony, distress. -*v.* afflict, torture, torment. —**Ant.** *n.* 1. ease.

Paine (pān), *n.* **Thomas,** 1737–1809, English-American writer on politics and religion.

pain·ful (pān′fəl), *adj.* 1. causing pain; unpleasant; hurting. 2. difficult. —**pain′ful·ly,** *adv.* —**pain′ful·ness,** *n.* —**Syn.** 1. distressing, torturing, agonizing.

pains·tak·ing (pānz′tāk′ing), *adj.* very careful. —**pains′tak′ing·ly,** *adv.* —**Syn.** particular.

paint (pānt), *n.* 1. substance that can be (alone or mixed with some liquid) put on a surface to make a layer or film of white, black, or colored material. 2. coloring matter put on the face or body; rouge. [< v.] —*v.* 1. cover or decorate with paint: *paint a house.* 2. use paint. 3. represent (an object, etc.) in colors. 4. make pictures. 5. put on like paint: *paint iodine on a cut.* 6. picture vividly in words. [< OF < L *pingere*] —**paint′a·ble,** *adj.* —**paint′ed,** *adj.* —**paint′y,** *adj.* —**Syn.** *v.* 3. picture, sketch, portray.

paint·brush (pānt′brush′), *n.* brush for putting on paint.

paint·er[1] (pān′tər), *n.* 1. person who paints pictures; artist. 2. person who paints houses, woodwork, etc. [< OF, ult. < L *pictor* < *pingere* to paint]

paint·er[2] (pān′tər), *n.* a rope, usually fastened to the bow of a boat, for tying it to a ship, pier, etc. [? var. of *panter* net < OF < L < Gk. *panthera* net]

paint·er[3] (pān′tər), *n.* *Am.* the American panther or cougar. [var. of *panther*]

paint·ing (pān′ting), *n.* 1. something painted; picture. 2. act of one that paints. 3. art of representation, decoration, and creating beauty with paints.

pair (pār), *n., pl.* **pairs** or (*sometimes after a numeral*) **pair,** *v.* —*n.* 1. a set of two; two that go together: *a pair of gloves.* 2. two of a kind: *a pair of sizes, a pair of rascals.* 3. a single thing consisting of two parts that cannot be used separately: *a pair of scissors.* 4. two people who are married or are engaged to be married. 5. two animals that are mated. 6. two members on opposite sides in a deliberative body who arrange not to vote on a certain question. 7. the arrangement thus made. —*v.* 1. arrange in a pair or pairs. 2. form a pair or pairs. 3. join in love and marriage. 4. **pair off,** separate into a pair or pairs. [< F < L *paria* (neut. pl.) equals] ▷ **pair.** In business usage and in much informal usage the plural of *pair* is *pair* when it comes after a number: *six pair of socks.* In other positions *pairs* is the usual plural: *How many pairs of socks do you have? Pair of stairs* is an idiom now usually considered archaic or local, but is still occasionally found: *The building had only one pair* [flight] *of stairs.*

pais·ley (pāz′li), *n., pl.* **-leys,** *adj.* —*n.* a soft woolen cloth with a very elaborate and colorful pattern. —*adj.* made of paisley: *a paisley shawl.* [after *Paisley,* Scotland]

pa·ja·mas (pə·jä′məz), *n.pl.* 1. garments to sleep in, etc., consisting of a coat and loose trousers fastened at the waist. 2. loose trousers worn by Mohammedan men and women. Also, *esp. Brit.* pyjamas. [< Hind. < Pers., < *pāe* leg + *jāmah* garment]

Pak·i·stan (pak′ə·stan; pä′kə·stän), *n.* republic in S Asia, a member of the British Commonwealth of Nations.

pal (pal), *n., v.,* **palled, pal·ling.** —*n.* *Colloq.* comrade; chum; accomplice. —*v.* associate as pals. [< Gypsy, brother]

pal·ace (pal′is), *n.* 1. a grand house for a king, queen, bishop, or some other exalted personage to live in. 2. a very fine house or building. [< OF < L *palatium* Palatine Hill, location of emperor's palace] —**Syn.** 1. castle. 2. mansion, château.

pal·a·din (pal′ə·din), *n.* 1. one of the twelve knights in attendance on Charlemagne. 2. a knightly defender. [< F < Ital. *paladino.* See PALATINE.]

pa·lae·og·ra·phy (pā′li·og′rə·fi), *n.* paleography. —**pa′lae·og′ra·pher,** *n.* —**pa·lae·o·graph·ic** (pā′li·ə·graf′ik), **pa′lae·o·graph′i·cal,** *adj.*

pa·lae·o·lith·ic (pā′li·ə·lith′ik), *adj.* paleolithic.

pa·lae·on·tol·o·gy (pā′li·on·tol′ə·ji), *n.* paleontology. —**pa·lae·on·to·log·ic** (pā′li·on′tə·loj′ik), **pa′lae·on′to·log′i·cal,** *adj.* —**pa′lae·on′to·log′i·cal·ly,** *adv.* —**pa′lae·on·tol′o·gist,** *n.*

Pa·lae·o·zo·ic (pā′li·ə·zō′ik), *n., adj.* Paleozoic.

pal·an·quin, pal·an·keen (pal′ən·kēn′), *n.* a covered couch carried by poles resting on men's shoulders. [< Pg. *palanquim.* Cf. Skt. *palyanka* couch.]

pal·at·a·ble (pal′it·ə·bəl), *adj.* agreeable to the taste; pleasing. —**pal′at·a·bil′i·ty, pal′at·a·ble·ness,** *n.* —**pal′at·a·bly,** *adv.*

pal·a·tal (pal′ə·təl), *adj.* 1. *Anat.* of or pertaining to the palate. 2. *Phonet.* uttered with the aid of the palate. The *y* in *yet* is a palatal sound. —*n. Phonet.* a palatal sound.

pal·a·tal·ize (pal′ə·təl·īz), *v.,* **-ized, -iz·ing.** *Phonet.* change into a palatal sound. —**pal′a·tal·i·za′tion,** *n.*

pal·ate (pal′it), *n.* 1. roof of the mouth. The bony part in front is the hard palate, and the fleshy part in back is the soft palate. 2. sense of taste: *the new flavor pleased his palate.* [< L *palatum*]

pa·la·tial (pə·lā′shəl), *adj.* like a palace; fit for a palace; magnificent. —**pa·la′tial·ly,** *adv.*

pal·a·tine (pal′ə·tīn; -tin), *adj.* having royal rights in his own territory: *a count palatine.* [< L *palatinus* of the palatium or Palatine Hill, palace]

Pa·lau (pä·lou′), or **Palau Islands,** *n.* group of about 100 islands in the W Pacific, a part of the Caroline group. The chief islands were captured or neutralized by the United States in 1944.

pa·lav·er (pə·lav′ər; -lä′vər), *n.* 1. parley or conference, esp. between travelers and uncivilized natives. 2. talk. 3. smooth, persuading talk; fluent talk; flattery. —*v.* 1. talk. 2. talk fluently or flatteringly. [< Pg. < L *parabola* story, parable. Doublet of PARABLE, PAROLE.]

pale[1] (pāl), *adj.,* **pal·er, pal·est,** *v.,* **paled, pal·ing.** —*adj.* 1. without much color; whitish. 2. not bright; dim. —*v.* turn pale. [< OF < L *pallidus* < *pallere* be pale. Doublet of PALLID.] —**pale′ly,** *adv.* —**pale′ness,** *n.* —**pal′ish,** *adj.* —**Syn.** *adj.* 1. pallid, wan, ashen, colorless. 2. faint, indistinct. —**Ant.** *adj.* 1. rosy, ruddy, flushed.

pale[2] (pāl), *n., v.,* **paled, pal·ing.** —*n.* 1. a long, narrow board, pointed at the top, used for fences. 2. an enclosing or confining barrier. 3. an enclosed area; restricted region. 4. boundary: *outside the pale of civilized society.* —*v.* enclose with pales. [< OF < L *palus.* Doublet of POLE[1].]

pale·face (pāl′fās′), *n. Am.* a white person. The North American Indians are said to have called white people palefaces. —**pale′faced′,** *adj. Am.*

pa·le·og·ra·phy (pā′li·og′rə·fi), *n.* 1. ancient writing or ancient forms of writing. 2. study of ancient writings to determine the dates, origins, meaning, etc. Also, **palaeography.** [< Gk. *palaios* ancient + *graphe* writing] —**pa′le·og′ra·pher,** *n.* —**pa·le·o·graph·ic** (pā′li·ə·graf′ik), **pa′le·o·graph′i·cal,** *adj.*

pa·le·o·lith·ic (pā′li·ə·lith′ik), *adj.* of or having to do with the earlier part of the Stone Age, characterized by crudely chipped stone tools. Also, **palaeolithic.** [< Gk. *palaios* ancient + *lithos* stone]

pa·le·on·tol·o·gy (pā′li·on·tol′ə·ji), *n.* science of the forms of life existing long ago, as represented by fossil animals and plants. Also, **palaeontology**. [< Gk. *palaios* ancient + *on* being + -LOGY] —**pa·le·on·to·log·ic** (pā′li·on′tə·loj′ik), **pa·le·on·to·log·i·cal**, *adj.* —**pa·le·on·to·log′i·cal·ly**, *adv.* —**pa′le·on·tol′o·gist**, *n.*

Pa·le·o·zo·ic (pā′li·ə·zō′ik), *n.* an old geological era, or a group of rocks, whose fossils represent early forms of life. —*adj.* of this era or these rocks. Also, **Palaeozoic**. [< Gk. *palaios* ancient + *zoe* life]

Pa·ler·mo (pə·lär′mō), *n.* seaport and capital of Sicily, in the NW part.

Pal·es·tine (pal′əs·tīn), *n.* a former country in SW Asia, on the Mediterranean Sea, now divided into Israel and Arab-controlled territory. Also, **Canaan** or the **Holy Land**. —**Pal·es·tin·i·an** (pal′əs·tin′i·ən), *adj.*, *n.*

Pal·es·tri·na (pal′əs·trē′nə), *n.* Giovanni da, 1526?-1594, Italian composer.

pal·ette (pal′it), *n.* 1. a thin board, usually oval or oblong, with a thumb hole at one end, used by painters to lay and mix colors on. 2. set of colors on this board. [< F < VL. dim. of L *pala* spade]

Artist's palette

pal·frey (pôl′fri), *n.*, *pl.* —**freys**. a gentle riding horse, esp. one used by ladies. [< OF < LL. < Gk. *para*- beside + L *veredus* light horse]

pal·imp·sest (pal′imp·sest), *n.* parchment or other writing material from which one writing has been erased to make room for another. [< L < Gk. *palimpsestos* scraped again, ult. < *palin* again + *psein* rub smooth]

pal·ing (pāl′ing), *n.* 1. fence of pales. 2. a pale, as in a fence.

pal·i·sade (pal′ə·sād′), *n.*, *v.*, —**sad·ed**, —**sad·ing**. —*n.* 1. a long, strong wooden stake pointed at the top end. 2. fence of stakes set firmly in the ground to enclose or defend. 3. Usually, **palisades**. line of high, steep cliffs. —*v.* furnish or surround with a palisade. [< F, < *palisser* enclose with pales. See PALE².]

pall¹ (pôl), *n.* 1. a heavy cloth of black, purple, or white velvet spread over a coffin, a hearse, or a tomb. 2. something that spreads over or covers, esp. with darkness or gloom: *a pall of smoke.* —*v.* cover with or as with a pall. [< L *pallium* cloak]

pall² (pôl), *v.* 1. become distasteful or very tiresome because there has been too much of it. 2. cloy. [var. of *appall*] —**Syn.** 2. satiate, surfeit, glut.

pal·la·di·um¹ (pə·lā′di·əm), *n. Chem.* a rare silver-white metallic element, Pd, harder than platinum. [< NL; named after the asteroid *Pallas*]

pal·la·di·um² (pə·lā′di·əm), *n.* anything regarded as an important safeguard. [< L < Gk. *palladion*, dim. of Pallas; the statue of Pallas Athena overlooking Troy was thought to protect the city]

Pal·las (pal′əs), or **Pallas Athena**, *n.* Athena.

pall·bear·er (pôl′bâr′ər), *n. Am.* one of the men who walk with the coffin at a funeral.

pal·let¹ (pal′it), *n.* bed of straw; poor bed. [< OF *paillet* < *paille* straw < L *palea*]

pal·let² (pal′it), *n.* 1. a flat blade used by potters and others. 2. a painter's palette. 3. projection on a pawl. [var. of *palette*]

pal·li·ate (pal′i·āt), *v.*, —**at·ed**, —**at·ing**. 1. lessen without curing; mitigate: *palliate a disease.* 2. make appear less serious; excuse: *palliate a fault.* [< L, < *pallium* cloak] —**pal′li·a′tion**, *n.* —**pal′li·a′tive**, *adj.* —**pal′li·a′tive·ly**, *adv.* —**pal′li·a′tor**, *n.*

pal·lid (pal′id), *adj.* lacking color; pale: *a pallid complexion.* [< L *pallidus*. Doublet of PALE¹.] —**pal′lid·ly**, *adv.* —**pal′lid·ness**, *n.*

Pall Mall (pel′mel′; pal′mal′), street in London, noted for its clubs.

pal·lor (pal′ər), *n.* lack of color from fear, illness, death, etc.; paleness. [< L]

palm¹ (päm), *n.* 1. inside of the hand between the wrist and the fingers. 2. the corresponding part of a glove. 3. blade of an oar; any flat, widened part at the end of an armlike projection. 4. the flat, widened part of the horn of a deer. 5. width of a hand; 3 to 4 inches. —*v.* 1. conceal in the hand. 2. pass or get accepted (something not good). 3. palm off, pass off or get accepted by tricks, fraud, or false representation. [< OF < L *palma*]

palm² (päm), *n.* 1. any of many kinds of trees growing in warm climates, the majority of which are tall and have a bunch of large leaves at the top. 2. branch or leaf of a palm tree as a symbol of victory or triumph. 3. victory; triumph. [< L *palma* palm tree, palm¹] —**pal·ma·ceous** (pal·mā′shəs), *adj.*

Pal·ma (päl′mä), *n.* seaport in W Majorca, capital of the Balearic Islands.

pal·mate (pal′māt), **pal·mat·ed** (-id), *adj.* 1. *Bot.* shaped like a hand with the fingers spread out. 2. *Zool.* web-footed; webbed. —**pal′mate·ly**, *adv.*

Palm Beach, a winter resort in SE Florida.

palm·er¹ (päm′ər), *n.* 1. pilgrim returning from the Holy Land bringing a palm branch as a token. 2. pilgrim.

palm·er² (päm′ər), *n.* person who palms or conceals something.

pal·met·to (pal·met′ō), *n.*, *pl.* —**tos**, —**toes**. any of several kinds of palm trees with fan-shaped leaves, abundant on the SE coast of the United States.

palm·is·try (päm′is·tri), *n.* art of telling a person's fortune from the lines and marks in the palm of his hand. —**palm′ist**, *n.*

Palm Sunday, the Sunday before Easter Sunday.

palm·y (päm′i), *adj.*, **palm·i·er**, **palm·i·est**. 1. abounding in palms; shaded by palms. 2. flourishing; prosperous; glorious.

pal·o·mi·no (pal′ə·mē′nō), *n.*, *pl.* —**nos**. *Am.* a cream-colored horse of Arabian stock. Its mane and tail are usually lighter colored. [< Sp.]

pal·pa·ble (pal′pə·bəl), *adj.* 1. readily seen or heard and recognized; obvious. 2. that can be touched or felt. [< LL, < L *palpare* feel] —**pal′pa·bil′i·ty**, *n.* —**pal′pa·bly**, *adv.* —**Syn.** 1. perceptible, plain, evident, manifest. 2. tangible.

pal·pi·tate (pal′pə·tāt), *v.*, —**tat·ed**, —**tat·ing**. 1. beat very rapidly: *your heart palpitates when you are excited.* 2. quiver; tremble: *he palpitated with terror.* [< L, < *palpitare* to throb < *palpare* to pat] —**pal′pi·ta′tion**, *n.*

pal·pus (pal′pəs), **palp** (palp), *n.*, *pl.* **pal·pi** (pal′pī); **palps**. the jointed feeler attached to the mouth of insects, spiders, lobsters, etc. Palpi are organs of touch or taste. [< L]

PALPI

pal·sy (pôl′zi), *n.*, *pl.* —**sies**, *v.*, —**sied**, —**sy·ing**. —*n.* paralysis. —*v.* paralyze. [< OF < L *paralysis*. Doublet of PARALYSIS.] —**pal′sied**, *adj.*

pal·ter (pôl′tər), *v.* 1. talk or act insincerely; trifle deceitfully. 2. act carelessly; trifle. 3. haggle. —**pal′ter·er**, *n.*

pal·try (pôl′tri), *adj.*, —**tri·er**, —**tri·est**. almost worthless; trifling; petty; mean. [? < dial. *palt* trash] —**pal′tri·ly**, *adv.* —**pal′tri·ness**, *n.* —**Syn.** insignificant, trivial.

pam·pas (pam′pəz; -pəs), *n.pl.* the vast treeless plains of South America, esp. in Argentina. [< Sp. < Peruvian] —**pam·pe·an** (pam·pē′ən; pam′pi·ən), *adj.*

pam·per (pam′pər), *v.* indulge too much; allow too many privileges to: *pamper a child, pamper one's appetite.* [ME *pampere(n)*] —**pam′per·er**, *n.* —**Syn.** spoil, humor.

pam·phlet (pam′flit), *n.* 1. booklet in paper covers. 2. a brief essay treating some popular subject. [< Anglo-L *panfletus*, for *Pamphilet*, popular name for 12th-century poem, "Pamphilus, seu de Amore"] —**Syn.** 2. brochure, tract.

pam·phlet·eer (pam'flǝ·tir'), *n.* writer of pamphlets. —*v.* write and issue pamphlets.

pan (pan), *n., v.,* **panned, pan·ning.** —*n.* **1.** dish for cooking and other household uses, usually broad, shallow, and with no cover. **2.** anything like this. The dishes on a pair of scales are called pans. **3.** in old-fashioned guns, the hollow part of the lock that held a little gunpowder to set the gun off. —*v.* **1.** *Am., Colloq.* criticize severely; reprimand. **2.** pan out, *Am., Colloq.* turn out. **3.** *Am.* wash (gravel, sand, etc.) in a pan to get gold. [OE *panne*]

Pan (pan), *n. Gk. Myth.* god of forests, pastures, flocks, and shepherds, represented as a man with legs like a goat, who played on musical pipes.

pan-, *word element.* all, as in *Pan-American, Pan-Christian, pandemonium.* [< Gk. *pas,* masc., *pan,* neut.]

Pan., Panama.

pan·a·ce·a (pan'ǝ·sē'ǝ), *n.* remedy for all diseases or ills; cure-all. [< L < Gk. *panakeia,* ult. < *pan-* all + *akos* cure] —**pan'a·ce'an,** *adj.*

Pan·a·ma (pan'ǝ·mä, -mō; pan'ǝ·mä', -mō'), *n.* **1.** Isthmus of, a narrow neck of land connecting North America with South America. **2.** country on the Isthmus of Panama, on either side of the Canal Zone. **3.** Also, Panama City. seaport and capital of this country. —**Pan·a·ma·ni·an** (pan'ǝ·mä'ni·ǝn; -mä'-), *adj., n.*

Panama Canal, *Am.* canal cut across the Isthmus of Panama to connect the Atlantic and Pacific oceans, built and controlled by the United States.

Panama Canal Zone. See Canal Zone.

Panama hat, or **panama,** *n.* a fine hat woven from the young leaves of a palmlike plant of Central and South America.

Pan-A·mer·i·can (pan'ǝ·mer'ǝ·kǝn), *adj.* **1.** of all Americans. **2.** *Am.* including all the countries of North, Central, and South America. —**Pan'-A·mer'i·can·ism,** *n.*

Pan American Union, organization having representatives from each of the 21 American republics, formed to promote mutual coöperation and further the interests of peace.

Pa·nay (pä·nī'), *n.* one of the C islands in the Philippines.

pan·cake (pan'kāk'), *n., v.,* **-caked, -cak·ing.** —*n.* **1.** a thin, flat cake of batter, fried in a pan or on a griddle. **2.** a quick, almost flat landing made by an airplane. —*v.* make such a landing.

pan·cre·as (pan'kri·ǝs), *n. Anat., Zool.* gland near the stomach that discharges into the intestine a secretion that helps digestion. The pancreas of animals when used for food is called sweetbread. [< NL < Gk., < *pan* all + *kreas* flesh]

pan·cre·at·ic (pan'kri·at'ik), *adj.* of the pancreas. The pancreatic juice aids digestion.

pan·da (pan'dǝ), *n.* the giant panda, a bear-like mammal of Tibet, mostly white with black legs.

pan·de·mo·ni·um (pan'dǝ·mō'ni·ǝm), *n.* **1.** abode of all the demons. **2.** place of wild disorder or lawless confusion. **3.** a wild uproar or lawlessness. **4.** Pandemonium, hell's capital. [< NL, < Gk. *pan-* all + *daimon* demon]

pan·der (pan'dǝr), *n.* person who helps other people indulge low desires, passions, or vices. —*v.* **1.** supply material or opportunity for vices. **2.** act as pander for. [from name of character in story told by Boccaccio and Chaucer]

Pan·dit (pun'dit), *n.* Madame Vijaya Lakshmi, born 1900, Indian stateswoman; president of the United Nations General Assembly from 1953 to 1954.

Pan·do·ra (pan·dô'rǝ; -dō'-), *n. Gk. Legend.* the first woman, created by the gods to punish mankind for having learned the use of fire. Curiosity led her to open a box and thus let out all sorts of ills into the world. Only Hope remained at the bottom.

pan·dow·dy (pan·dou'di), *n., pl.* **-dies.** *Am.* a deep apple pie with top crust only.

pane (pān), *n.* a single sheet of glass in a win-

dow, a door, or a sash. [< OF < L *pannus* piece of cloth] —**paned,** *adj.*

pan·e·gyr·ic (pan'ǝ·jir'ik), *n.* **1.** speech or writing in praise of a person or thing. **2.** enthusiastic or extravagant praise. [< L < Gk., < *pan-* all + *agyris* assembly] —**pan'e·gyr'i·cal,** *adj.* —**pan'e·gyr'i·cal·ly,** *adv.* —**pan'e·gyr'ist,** *n.*

pan·el (pan'ǝl), *n., v.,* **-eled, -el·ing;** *esp. Brit.* **-elled, -el·ling.** —*n.* **1.** strip or surface that is different in some way from what is around it. A panel is often sunk below or raised above the rest, and used for a decoration. Panels may be in a door or other woodwork, on large pieces of furniture, or made as parts of a dress. **2.** picture, photograph, or design much longer than wide. **3.** list of persons called as jurors; the members of a jury. **4.** a group formed for discussion. —*v.* arrange in panels; furnish or decorate with panels. [< OF, piece, ult. < L *pannus* piece of cloth] —**pan'el·ist,** *n.*

Panels

panel discussion, the discussion of a particular issue by a selected group of people: *a panel discussion on racial discrimination.*

pan·el·ing, *esp. Brit.* **pan·el·ling** (pan'ǝl·ing), *n.* panels.

pang (pang), *n.* a sudden, short, sharp pain or feeling: *the pangs of a toothache, a pang of pity.* —*Syn.* ache, twinge.

pan·go·lin (pang·gō'lin), *n.* a scaly, toothless mammal of tropical Asia and Africa; scaly anteater. [< Malay *peng-goling* roller]

pan·han·dle¹ (pan'han'dǝl), *n.* **1.** handle of a pan. **2.** *Am.* a narrow strip of land projecting like a handle.

pan·han·dle² (pan'han'dǝl), *v.,* **-dled, -dling.** *Am., Colloq.* beg, esp. in the streets. —**pan'han'dler,** *n. Am.*

Pan·hel·len·ic, pan·hel·len·ic (pan'hǝ·len'ik), *adj.* **1.** pertaining to all members of the Greek race. **2.** pertaining to all college fraternities and sororities.

pan·ic (pan'ik), *n., adj., v.,* **-icked, -ick·ing.** —*n.* fear spreading through a multitude of people so that they lose control of themselves; unreasoning fear: *when the theater caught fire, there was a panic.* —*adj.* caused by panic; showing panic. —*v.* **1.** *Slang.* make laugh (an audience, etc.). **2.** go into a state of panic: *the audience panicked when the fire broke out.* [< F < L < Gk. *Panikos* of Pan (who caused fear)] —**pan'ick·y,** *adv.* —**pan'ic-strick'en, pan'ic-struck'.** *adj.* —*Syn. n.* alarm, terror, dread.

pan·i·cle (pan'ǝ·kǝl), *n. Bot.* a compound raceme; a loose, diversely branching flower cluster: *a panicle of oats.* [< L *panicula,* dim. of *panus* a swelling] —**pan'i·cled,** *adj.*

pan·ni·er (pan'i·ǝr), *n.* **1.** basket, esp. one of a pair of considerable size to be slung across the shoulders or across the back of a beast of burden. **2.** puffed drapery about the hips. [< OF < L *panarium* bread basket < *panis* bread]

Panicle

pan·o·ply (pan'ǝ·pli), *n., pl.* **-plies. 1.** a complete suit of armor. **2.** complete equipment or covering: *an Indian in panoply of paint and feathers.* [< Gk. *panoplia* < *pan-* all + *hopla* arms] —**pan'o·plied,** *adj.*

pan·o·ram·a (pan'ǝ·ram'ǝ; -rä'mǝ), *n.* **1.** a wide, unbroken view of a surrounding region. **2.** a complete survey of some subject: *a panorama of history.* **3.** a continuously passing or changing scene: *the panorama of city life.* [< PAN- + Gk. *horama* view] —**pan'o·ram'ic,** *adj.* —**pan'o·ram'i·cal·ly,** *adv.* —**pan'o·ram'ist** *n.*

Pan·pipe (pan'pīp'), **Pan's pipes,** *n.* an early musical instrument made of reeds or tubes of different lengths, fastened together in order of their length.

pan·sy (pan'zi), *n.*, *pl.* **–sies. 1.** variety of violet that has large flowers with flat, velvety petals usually of several colors. **2.** the flower. **3.** *Slang.* a male homosexual; effeminate man. [< F *pensée* thought. Cf. PENSIVE.]

pant (pant), *v.* **1.** breathe hard and quickly. **2.** speak with short, quick breaths. **3.** long eagerly. **4.** throb violently. —*n.* **1.** short quick breath. **2.** a throb. [? < OF *pantoisier* < VL *phantasiare* be oppressed with nightmare. See FANTASY.] —**Syn.** *v.* **1.** gasp, puff. **3.** yearn, hunger, crave.

pan·ta·lets, pan·ta·lettes (pan'tə·lets'), *n.pl.* **1.** long drawers extending to the ankles, formerly worn by women and girls. **2.** pair of trimmed pieces for attaching to the legs of drawers.

pan·ta·loon (pan'tə·lün'), *n.* **1.** in modern pantomime, a vicious, foolish old man, the butt and accomplice of the clown. **2.** pantaloons, trousers. [< F < Ital. *Pantalone*, a comic character in early Italian comedies]

pan·the·ism (pan'thē·iz·əm), *n.* **1.** belief that God and the universe are identical. **2.** worship of all the gods. —**pan'the·ist**, *n.* —**pan'the·is'·tic**, **pan'the·is'ti·cal**, *adj.* —**pan'the·is'ti·cal·ly**, *adv.*

Pan·the·on (pan'thi·on; pan·thē'ən), *n.* **1.** temple for all the gods, built at Rome about 27 B.C. and later used as a Christian church. **2.** pantheon, **a.** temple dedicated to all the gods. **b.** a public building containing tombs or memorials of the illustrious dead of a nation. **c.** all the deities of a people. [< L < Gk. *pantheion* < *pan–* all + *theos* god]

pan·ther (pan'thər), *n.*, *pl.* **–thers** or (*esp. collectively*) **–ther. 1.** cougar. **2.** leopard. **3.** jaguar. [< OF < L < Gk.]

pan·to·graph (pan'tə·graf; –gräf), *n.* instrument for copying plans, drawings, etc., on any scale desired. [< Gk. *pas* all + –GRAPH]

pan·to·mime (pan'tə·mīm), *n.*, *v.*, **–mimed, –mim·ing.** —*n.* **1.** a play without words, in which the actors express themselves by gestures. **2.** gestures without words. —*v.* express by gestures. [< L < Gk., < *pas* all + *mimos* mimic] —**pan·to·mim·ic** (pan'tə·mim'ik), *adj.* —**pan·to·mim·ist** (pan'tə·mim'ist), *n.*

pan·try (pan'tri), *n.*, *pl.* **–tries.** a small room in which food, dishes, silverware, table linen, etc., are kept. [< AF *panetrie*, ult. < L *panis* bread]

pants (pants), *n.pl. Colloq.* **1.** *Esp. U.S.* trousers. **2.** drawers, esp. women's. [short for *pantaloons*] ➤ pants, trousers. In formal usage the word for men's breeches is *trousers*; on the other levels the word is *pants.*

pan·zer (pan'zər), *adj.* armored. A panzer division consists largely of tanks. [< G, armor]

pap (pap), *n.* a soft food for infants or invalids. [cf. LG *pappe*]

pa·pa (pä'pə; pə·pä'), *n.* father; daddy.

pa·pa·cy (pā'pə·si), *n.*, *pl.* **–cies. 1.** position, rank, or authority of the Pope. **2.** time during which a pope rules. **3.** all the popes. **4.** government by the Pope. [< Med. L, < *papa* POPE]

pa·pal (pā'pəl), *adj.* **1.** of the Pope: *a papal letter.* **2.** of the papacy. **3.** of the Roman Catholic Church: *papal ritual.* —**pa'pal·ism**, *n.*

pa·paw (pô'pô), *n. Am.* **1.** a small North American tree bearing oblong, edible fruit with many beanlike seeds. **2.** this fruit. Also, pawpaw. [< Sp. *papaya.* See PAPAYA.]

pa·pa·ya (pə·pä'yə), *n.* **1.** a tropical American tree having a straight, palmlike trunk with a tuft of large leaves at the top and edible, melonlike fruit with yellowish pulp. **2.** the fruit. [< Sp. (def. 2), <.*papayo* (def. 1) < Carib]

pa·per (pā'pər), *n.* **1.** a material in thin sheets used for writing, printing, drawing, wrapping packages, covering walls, etc. Paper is made from wood pulp, rags, etc. **2.** piece or sheet of paper. **3.** piece or sheet of paper with writing or printing on it; document: *important papers were stolen.* **4.** wrapper, container, or sheet of paper containing something. **5.** newspaper. **6.**

article; essay. **7.** a written examination. **8.** a written promise to pay money; note. **9.** paper money. **10.** wallpaper. **11. on paper, a.** in writing or print. **b.** in theory. **12.** papers, documents telling who or what one is. —*adj.* **1.** of or pertaining to paper. **2.** made of paper: *paper dolls.* **3.** like paper; frail; thin; *almonds with paper shells.* **4.** existing only on paper: *when he tried to sell, his paper profits disappeared.* —*v.* **1.** cover with paper. **2.** supply with paper. **3.** write on paper. [< L *papyrus.* Doublet of PAPYRUS.] —**pa'per·er**, *n.* —**pa'per·like'**, *adj.*

pa·per·back (pā'pər·bak'), *n.* a small, inexpensive book bound in paper.

paper hanger, person whose business is to cover walls with wallpaper.

paper tiger, person or thing that appears to be strong or threatening, but is really weak.

pa·per·weight (pā'pər·wāt'), *n.* a small, heavy object put on papers to keep them from being scattered.

pa·per·work (pā'pər·wėrk'), *n.* clerical work, as the filling in of forms, planning, figuring, etc., incidental to some activity.

pa·per·y (pā'pər·i), *adj.* thin like paper.

pa·pier-mâ·ché (pā'pər·mə·shā'), *n.* a paper pulp mixed with some stiffener and molded when moist. It becomes hard and strong when dry. —*adj.* made of papier-mâché. [< F, chewed paper]

pa·pil·la (pə·pil'ə), *n.*, *pl.* **–pil·lae** (–pil'ē). **1.** a small, nipplelike projection. **2.** a small vascular process at the root of a hair or feather. **3.** one of certain small protuberances concerned with the senses of touch, taste, or smell. [< L, nipple]

pa·pist (pā'pist), *n.*, *adj. Contemptuous.* Roman Catholic. [< NL, < L *papa* POPE] —**pa·pis'·tic, pa·pis'ti·cal**, *adj.*

pa·poose, pap·poose (pa·püs'), *n. Am.* a North American Indian baby. [< Algonquian *papeisses* < *peisses* child]

pap·ri·ka, pap·ri·ca (pap·rē'kə; pap'rə–), *n.* a kind of red pepper not so strong as the ordinary kind. [< Hung.]

Pap·u·a (pap'yu̇·ə; pä'pu̇·ä), *n.* **1.** New Guinea. **2.** Territory of, the SE part of New Guinea, a territory belonging to Australia. —**Pap·u·an** (pap'yu̇·ən), *adj.*, *n.*

pa·py·rus (pə·pī'rəs), *n.*, *pl.* **–ri** (–rī). **1.** a tall water plant from which the ancient Egyptians, Greeks, and Romans made a kind of paper to write on. **2.** a writing material made from the pith of the papyrus plant. **3.** an ancient record written on papyrus. [< L < Gk. *papyros.* Doublet of PAPER.]

par (pär), *n.* **1.** equality; an equal level: *he is on a par with his brother in intelligence.* **2.** average or normal amount, degree, or condition: *feel below par.* **3.** the value of a bond, a note, a share of stock, etc., that is printed on it; face value: *stock selling above par.* **4.** the established normal value of the money of one country in terms of the money of another country. **5.** score in golf made by perfect playing. —*adj.* **1.** average; normal. **2.** of or at par. [< L, equal]

par., 1. paragraph. **2.** parallel.

Pa·rá (pä·rä'), *n.* Belém.

par·a·ble (par'ə·bəl), *n.* a short story used to teach some truth or moral lesson: *Jesus taught in parables.* [< L < Gk. *parabole* comparison < *para–* alongside + *bole* a throwing. Doublet of PALAVER, PAROLE.]

pa·rab·o·la (pə·rab'ə·lə), *n.*, *pl.* **–las.** a plane curve formed by the intersection of a cone with a plane parallel to a side of the cone. [< NL < Gk., juxtaposition. See PARABLE.]

Parabola

par·a·bol·ic (par'ə·bol'ik), *adj.* pertaining to, of the form of, or resembling a parabola. —**par'a·bol'i·cal·ly**, *adv.*

Par·a·cel·sus (par'ə·sel'səs), *n.* 1493?-1541, Swiss alchemist and physician.

par·a·chute (par'ə·shüt), *n.*, *v.*, **–chut·ed, –chut·ing.** —*n.* an umbrellalike apparatus used in descending safely through the air from a great height. —*v.* **1.** descend by, or as if by, a parachute. **2.** convey by a parachute. [< F, <

para- (< Ital., guard against!) + *chute* a fall]
—**par'a·chut'ist,** *n.*

pa·rade (pə·rād'), *n., v.,* -rad·ed, -rad·ing.
—*n.* 1. march for display; procession: *the circus
had a parade.* 2. group of people walking for
display or pleasure. 3. place where people walk
for pleasure. 4. a great show or display: *a
parade of one's wealth.* 5. a military display or
review of troops. 6. place used for the regular
parade of troops. —*v.* 1. march through with
display: *the performers and animals paraded
the streets.* 2. march in procession; walk proudly
as if in a parade. 3. make a great show of. 4.
come together in military order for review or
inspection. 5. assemble (troops) for review. [<
F < Sp. *parada,* ult. < Sp *parare* prepare] —**pa·
rad'er,** *n.* —**Syn.** *n.* 1. pageant, cavalcade. -*v.* 3.
display, flaunt.

par·a·digm (par'ə·dim; -dīm), *n.* 1. pattern;
example. 2. example of a noun, verb, pronoun,
etc., in all its inflections. [< L < Gk. *para-
deigma* pattern, ult. < *para-* side by side +
deiknunai to show] —**par·a·dig·mat·ic** (par'ə·
dig·mat'ik), *adj.*

par·a·dise (par'ə·dīs), *n.* 1. heaven. 2. place
or condition of great happiness. 3. place of great
beauty. 4. garden of Eden. [< L < Gk. < OPers.
pairidaēza park < *pairi-* around + *daēza* wall]
—**par'a·dis'al,** *adj.*

par·a·dox (par'ə·doks), *n.* 1. statement that
may be true but seems to say two opposite
things. "More haste, less speed" is a paradox. 2.
statement that is false because it says two opposite things. 3. person or thing that seems to
be full of contradictions. [< L < Gk., < *para-*
contrary to + *doxa* opinion] —**par'a·dox'i·cal,**
adj. —**par'a·dox'i·cal·ly,** *adv.* —**par'a·dox'i·
cal·ness,** *n.* ➤ See epigram for usage note.

par·af·fin, par·af·fine (par'ə·fin), *n.* 1. a
white, tasteless substance like wax, used for
making candles, for sealing jars, etc. 2. any
hydrocarbon of the methane series. —*v.* treat
with paraffin. [< G, < L *parum* too little +
affinis related; from its small affinity for other
substances] —**par'af·fin'ic,** *adj.*

par·a·gon (par'ə·gon), *n.* model of excellence
or perfection. [< OF < Ital. *paragone* touch-
stone]

par·a·graph (par'ə·graf; -gräf), *n.* 1. group
of sentences that belong together; distinct part
of a chapter, letter, or composition. It is customary to begin a paragraph on a new line and
to indent this line. 2. a separate note or item
of news in a newspaper. 3. sign (¶) used to
show where a paragraph begins or should begin.
—*v.* divide into paragraphs. [< LL < Gk. *para-
graphos* line (in the margin) marking a break
in sense < *para-* beside + *graphein* write]
—**par'a·graph'er,** *n.* —**par'a·graph'ic,** *adj.*
—**par'a·graph'i·cal·ly,** *adv.*

Par·a·guay (par'ə·gwā; -gwī), *n.* country in
C South America, between Bolivia, Brazil, and
Argentina. —**Par'a·guay'an,** *adj., n.*

par·a·keet (par'ə·kēt), *n.* any of various small
parrots, most of which have slender bodies and
long tails. Also, **parrakeet, parroket,**
or **parroquet.** [< OF < Ital. *parro-
chetto* < *parroco* parish priest]

par·al·lax (par'ə·laks), *n.* the
change or amount of change in the
direction in which an object is seen
or photographed, caused by a change
in the position of the observer or
camera. Seen from A, star S is in direction AS. Seen from B, it is in direction BS. The parallax is the difference between these two directions, or the
angle ASB. [< Gk. *parallaxis* alternation, ult.
< *para-* + *allassein* to change] —**par·al·lac·tic**
(par'ə·lak'tik), *adj.*

par·al·lel (par'ə·lel), *adj., n., v.,* -leled, -lel-
ing; *esp.* Brit. -lelled, -lel·ling. —*adj.* 1. at or
being the same distance apart everywhere, like
the two rails of a railroad track. 2. having the
same direction, course, or tendency. 3. similar;
corresponding: *parallel points in the characters
of different men.* —*n.* 1. a parallel line or sur-

face. 2. anything parallel in direction, course, or
tendency. 3. in geography: a. any of the imaginary circles around the earth parallel to the
equator, marking degrees of
latitude. b. the markings on a
map that represent these circles. 4. thing like or similar to
another. 5. comparison to
show likeness: *draw a parallel between this
winter and last winter.* 6. *Printing.* a pair
of vertical lines (‖) used as a mark of reference. —*v.* 1. be at the same distance from
throughout the length: *the street parallels the
railroad.* 2. cause to be or run parallel to. 3. be
like; be similar to: *your story closely parallels
what he told me.* 4. find a case which is similar
or parallel to. 5. compare in order to show likeness. [< L < Gk., < *para allelois* beside one
another] —**Syn.** *adj.* 3. analogous, like.

Parallel lines

par·al·lel·ism (par'ə·lel·iz'əm), *n.* 1. a being
parallel. 2. likeness; similarity; correspondence.

par·al·lel·o·gram (par'ə·
lel'ə·gram), *n.* a four-sided
figure whose opposite sides are
parallel and equal.

pa·ral·y·sis (pə·ral'ə·sis), *n.,
pl.* -ses (-sēz). 1. a lessening
or loss of the power of motion
or sensation in any part of the body. 2. disease
manifesting this symptom; palsy. 3. condition of
powerlessness or helpless inactivity; crippling:
a paralysis of trade. [< L < Gk., ult. < *para-*
from beside + *lyein* to loose. Doublet of PALSY.]
—**par·a·lyt·ic** (par'ə·lit'ik), *adj., n.*

Parallelograms

par·a·lyze, *esp.* Brit. **par·a·lyse** (par'ə·līz),
v., -lyzed, -lyz·ing; *esp.* Brit. -lysed, -lys·ing. 1.
affect with a lessening or loss of the power of
motion or feeling: *his left arm was paralyzed.* 2.
make powerless or helplessly inactive; cripple:
fear paralyzed my mind. —**par'a·ly·za'tion,** *esp.*
Brit. **par'a·ly·sa'tion,** *n.* —**Syn.** 2. stun, benumb.

par·a·me·ci·um (par'ə·mē'shi·əm; -si·əm), *n.,
pl.* -ci·a (-shi·ə; -si·ə). *Zool.* a one-celled animal
shaped like a slender slipper, that is covered
with cilia and has a groove along one side leading into an open mouth. Paramecia are free-
swimming and usually live in stagnant water.
[< NL, < Gk. *paramekes* oblong < *para-* on one
side + *mekos* length]

par·a·mount (par'ə·mount), *adj.* chief in importance; above others; supreme. [< AF *para-
mont* above < *par* by (< L *per*) + *amont* up
< L *ad montem* to the mountain] —**par'a·
mount·ly,** *adv.* —**Syn.** dominant.

par·a·mour (par'ə·mùr), *n.* 1. person who
takes the place of a husband or wife illegally.
2. *Archaic.* lover. [< OF, < *par amour* by love
< L *per amorem*]

Pa·ra·ná (pä'rə·nä'), *n.* river flowing S from
C Brazil into the Plata River.

par·a·noi·a (par'ə·noi'ə), *n.* a mental de-
rangement, esp. a chronic form of insanity
characterized by elaborate delusions. [< NL <
Gk., ult. < *para-* amiss + *nous* mind] —**par·a·
noi·ac** (par'ə·noi'ak), *adj., n.*

par·a·noid (par'ə·noid), *n.* person suffering
from paranoia. —**par'a·noid,** *adj.*

par·a·pet (par'ə·pet; -pit), *n.* 1. a low wall or
mound of stone, earth, etc., to protect soldiers.
2. a low wall at the edge of a balcony, roof,
bridge, etc. [< Ital., < *para* defend! (< L *parare*
prepare) + *petto* breast < L *pectus*]

par·a·pher·nal·ia (par'ə·fər·nāl'yə), *n.pl.* 1.
(*pl. in use*) personal belongings. 2. (*sometimes
sing. in use*) equipment; outfit. [< Med.L, ult.
< Gk., < *para-* besides + *pherne* dowry]

par·a·phrase (par'ə·frāz), *v.,* -phrased,
-phras·ing, *n.* —*v.* state the meaning of (a passage) in other words; translate freely. —*n.* expression of the meaning of a passage in other
words. [< F < L < Gk., < *para-* alongside of +
phrazein say] —**par'a·phras'er,** *n.* —**Syn.** *n.*
translation, version. ➤ A paraphrase is a restatement of a writer's ideas in different words.
It is now usually applied to digesting the contents of a passage in one's own words.

age, câre, fär; ēqual, tèrm; īce, ōpen, ôrder; pùt, rüle, ūse; tɦ, then; ə=a in about.

par·a·ple·gi·a (par′ə·plē′ji·ə), *n.* paralysis of the legs and the lower part of the trunk. [< NL < Gk., paralysis of one side of the body] —par·a·ple·gic (par′ə·plē′jik; -plej′ik), *adj., n.*

Pa·rá rubber (pä·rä′), rubber obtained from South American trees.

par·a·site (par′ə·sīt), *n.* **1.** animal or plant that lives on, with, or in another, from which it gets its food. **2.** person who lives on others without making any useful and fitting return; hanger-on: *beggars and tramps are parasites.* [< L < Gk., < *para-* alongside of + *sitos* food] —par·a·sit·ic (par′ə·sit′ik), par·a·sit′i·cal, *adj.* —par′a·sit′i·cal·ly, *adv.*

par·a·sol (par′ə·sôl; -sol), *n.* umbrella used to ward off the rays of the sun. [< F < Ital., < *para* ward off! + *sole* sun]

par·a·thy·roid glands (par′ə·thī′roid), small glands near the thyroid glands. Their secretion, which enables the body to use calcium, is necessary for life.

par·a·troop·er (par′ə·trüp′ər), *n.* soldier trained to use a parachute for descent from an aircraft into a battle area. [< *para*(*chute*) + *trooper*] —par′a·troops′, *n.pl.*

par·boil (pär′boil′), *v.* **1.** boil till partly cooked. **2.** overheat. [< F < LL, < *per-* thoroughly + *bullire* boil; *par-* confused with *part*]

par·cel (pär′səl), *n., v., -celed, -cel·ing; esp.* Brit. -celled, -cel·ling. —*n.* **1.** bundle of things wrapped or packed together; package. **2.** container with things packed in it. **3.** piece: *a parcel of land.* **4.** lot; pack: *a parcel of liars.* —*v.* **1.** make into a parcel or parcels. **2.** parcel out, divide into, or distribute in, portions. [< OF, ult. < L *particula*, dim. of *pars* part] —Syn. *n.* **1.** packet. **3.** lot, section.

parcel post, branch of the postal service which carries parcels.

parch (pärch), *v.* **1.** dry by heating; roast slightly: *parched corn.* **2.** make or become hot, dry, or thirsty. **3.** make excessively dry. —Syn. **1.** scorch, sear, singe, char.

par·chee·si, par·che·si, or **par·chi·si** (pär·chē′zi), *n.* game somewhat like backgammon, played by moving pieces according to throws of dice. [< Hind. *pachīsī* < *pachīs* twenty-five (highest throw)]

parch·ment (pärch′mənt), *n.* **1.** skin of sheep, goats, etc., prepared for use as a writing material. **2.** manuscript or document written on parchment. **3.** paper that looks like parchment. [< OF < LL < Gk. *pergamēnē* < *Pergamon* Pergamum, whence it came]

pard¹ (pärd), *n.* Archaic. leopard; panther. [< F < L Gk. *pardos*]

pard² (pärd), *n.* Am., Slang. partner; friend; companion. [for *partner*]

par·don (pär′dən), *n.* **1.** forgiveness. **2.** excuse. **3.** a setting free from punishment; ecclesiastical indulgence. **4.** a legal document setting a person free from punishment. [< v.] —*v.* **1.** forgive. **2.** excuse. **3.** set free from punishment: *the governor pardoned the criminal.* [< OF < LL, < L *per-* thoroughly + *donare* give] —par′don·a·ble, *adj.* —par′don·a·ble·ness, *n.* —par′don·a·bly, *adv.* —Syn. *n.* **1.** absolution, amnesty. —*v.* **1.** acquit, absolve. —Ant. *v.* **1.** punish. **3.** convict, condemn. ▶ See **excuse** for usage note.

par·don·er (pär′dən·ər), *n.* **1.** person who pardons. **2.** an ecclesiastical official charged with the granting of indulgences in the Middle Ages.

pare (pär), *v.,* pared, par·ing. **1.** cut, trim, or shave off the outer part of; peel: *pare an apple.* **2.** cut away from: *pare a layer from a corn.* **3.** cut away little by little: *pare down expenses.* [< F < L *parare* make ready. Doublet of PARRY.] —Syn. **1.** skin, strip.

par·e·gor·ic (par′ə·gôr′ik; -gor′-), *n.* a soothing medicine containing camphor and a very little opium. —*adj.* soothing. [< LL < Gk. *paregorikos* soothing, ult. < *para-* at the side of + *-agoros* speaking]

paren., *pl.* parens., parenthesis.

pa·ren·chy·ma (pə·reng′kə·mə), *n.* **1.** Anat., Zool. the essential tissue of an animal organ as distinguished from connective tissue, etc. **2.**

Bot. the fundamental cellular tissue of plants, which composes the softer parts of leaves, the pulp of fruits, the pith of stems, etc. [< Gk., < *para-* beside + *en-* in + *chyma* what is poured] —par·en·chym·a·tous (par′eng·kim′ə·təs), *adj.*

par·ent (pār′ənt), *n.* **1.** father or mother. **2.** any animal or plant that produces offspring. **3.** source; cause. [< OF < L *parens*, orig. active pp. of *parere* bring forth] —pa·ren·tal (pə·ren′təl), *adj.* —pa·ren′tal·ly, *adv.* —par′ent·hood, *n.*

par·ent·age (pār′ən·tij), *n.* **1.** descent from parents; family line; ancestry. **2.** being a parent.

parent element, Nuclear Physics. element that yields an isotope or daughter element through radioactive decay or nuclear bombardment.

pa·ren·the·sis (pə·ren′thə·sis), *n., pl.* -ses (-sēz). **1.** word, phrase, sentence, etc., inserted within a sentence to explain or qualify something. **2.** either or both of two curved lines ( ) used to set off such an expression. **3.** interval. [< L < Gk., ult. < *para-* beside + *en-* in + *thesis* a placing] —par·en·thet·ic (par′ən·thet′ik), par′en·thet′i·cal, *adj.* —par′en·thet′i·cal·ly, *adv.* ▶ Parentheses ( ). Parentheses (often called *curves* and by printers called *parens*) are sometimes used in writing, chiefly to enclose words, phrases, or whole sentences that add to the clearness of a statement without altering its meaning and that are allowed to stand outside the frame of the sentence. These additions are likely to be (1) illustrations, (2) definitions, or (3) added information thrown in for good measure, as in the first sentence of this paragraph, or in this sentence: *This bill, commonly called the Lockport plan, has been the basis of all later city-manager charters (there are now 438).* These uses are slightly stiff and belong most appropriately to rather formal exposition. Sometimes parentheses are used to mark an apologetic aside, as much as to say "You know this, but let me remind you"—though this use is less common today than formerly: *James Monroe (the fifth President) enunciated the doctrine in 1823.* Parentheses are often used to enclose the letters or figures that mark items in an enumeration, as in the second sentence (above) of this article, though this tends to make the numbers or letters more conspicuous than they deserve to be.

pa·ren·the·size (pə·ren′thə·sīz), *v.,* -sized, -siz·ing. insert as or in a parenthesis.

pa·re·sis (pə·rē′sis; par′ə-), *n.* an incomplete paralysis that affects the ability to move, but does not affect ability to feel. [< NL < Gk., a letting go, ult. < *para-* by + *hienai* let go] —pa·ret·ic (pə·ret′ik; -rē′tik), *adj., n.*

par ex·cel·lence (pär ek′sə·läns), French. above all others of the same sort.

par·fait (pär·fā′), *n.* a rich ice cream containing eggs and whipped cream and frozen without stirring. [< F, perfect]

par·he·li·on (pär·hē′li·ən; -hēl′yən), *n., pl.* -li·a (-li·ə; -yə). a bright circular spot on a solar halo. [< L < Gk., < *para-* beside + *helios* sun]

pa·ri·ah (pə·rī′ə; pä′ri·ə), *n.* **1.** outcast. **2.** Usually, **Pariah.** member of a low caste in S India and Burma. [< Tamil *paraiyar* drummer; because this caste provided the drummers at festivals]

pa·ri·e·tal (pə·rī′ə·təl), *adj.* **1.** of the wall of the body or of one of its cavities. **2.** Am. pertaining to, or having authority over, those within the buildings of a college: *a parietal committee.* —*n.* Also, **parietal bone.** either of two bones that form part of the side and top of the skull. [< LL, < L *paries* wall]

pa·ri·mu·tu·el (par′i·mū′chü·əl), *n.* **1.** system of betting on horse races in which those who have bet on the winning horses divide the money lost by the losers. **2.** machine for recording such bets. [< F, mutual wager]

par·ing (pār′ing), *n.* part pared off; skin; rind.

Par·is (par′is), *n.* capital of France, located in N France on the Seine. —Pa·ri·sian (pə·rizh′ən), *adj., n.*

Par·is (par′is), *n.* Gk. Legend. son of Priam, king of Troy, who caused the Trojan War by carrying off Helen, the wife of King Menelaus of Sparta.

Paris green, a poisonous, emerald-green powder containing arsenic, used as a pigment and in making sprays for killing insects.

par·ish (par'ish), *n.* **1.** district that has its own church and clergyman. **2.** people of a parish. **3.** *Am.* in Louisiana, a county. [< OF < LL < Gk., ult. < *para* near + *oikos* dwelling]

pa·rish·ion·er (pə·rish'ən·ər; -rish'nər), *n.* member of a parish.

par·i·ty (par'ə·ti), *n.* **1.** equality with regard to state, quality, degree, etc. **2.** similarity or close correspondence. **3.** balance between the market prices for a farmer's commodities and his own gross expenditures. [< L, < *par* equal]

park (pärk), *n.* **1.** land set apart for the pleasure of the public. **2.** land set apart for wild animals. **3.** grounds around a fine house. **4.** place to leave an automobile, etc., for a time. **5.** space where army vehicles and mules, supplies, and artillery are put when an army camps. —*v.* **1.** enclose in a park. **2.** *Am.* leave (an automobile, etc.) for a time in a certain place. **3.** arrange (army vehicles, artillery, etc.) in a park. **4.** *Colloq.* place, put, or leave. [< OF *parc* < L *parricus* enclosure. Doublet of PADDOCK.]

par·ka (pär'kə), *n.* **1.** a fur jacket with a hood, worn in Alaska and in NE Asia. **2.** *Am.* a long woolen shirt or jacket with a hood. [< Russ.]

parking meter, *Am.* device containing a clock mechanism which is operated by the insertion of coins. It allows an automobile a specified amount of time in a parking area for each coin.

park·way (pärk'wā'), *n.* a broad road with spaces planted with grass, trees, etc.

Parl., Parliament; Parliamentary.

par·lance (pär'ləns), *n.* way of speaking; talk; language. [< OF, < *parler* speak. See PARLEY.]

par·lay (pär'li; -lā), *Am.* —*v.* **1.** risk an original bet and its winnings on another bet. **2.** extend and exploit (something) with conspicuous success: *parlay a talent into a big business.* —*n.* such a bet. [alter. of *paroli* < F < Ital., grand cast at dice]

par·ley (pär'li), *n., pl.* -leys, *v.,* -leyed, -ley·ing. —*n.* **1.** conference; informal talk. **2.** an informal discussion with an enemy about terms of surrender, exchange of prisoners, etc. —*v.* discuss terms, esp. with an enemy. [< OF *parlée* < pp. of *parler* speak, ult. < L *parabola* PARABLE]

par·lia·ment (pär'lə·mənt), *n.* **1.** council or congress that is the highest lawmaking body of a country. **2.** Parliament, the national lawmaking body of Great Britain. It consists of the House of Lords and the House of Commons. [< OF *parlement.* See PARLEY.]

par·lia·men·tar·i·an (pär'lə·men·târ'i·ən), *n.* one skilled in parliamentary procedure or debate.

par·lia·men·ta·ry (pär'lə·men'tə·ri; -men'tri), *adj.* **1.** of a parliament. **2.** done by a parliament. **3.** according to the rules and customs of a parliament or other lawmaking body. **4.** having a parliament.

par·lor, *esp. Brit.* **par·lour** (pär'lər), *n.* **1.** room for receiving or entertaining guests; sitting room. **2.** room in a club or hotel used for reading and relaxation. **3.** *Am.* a decorated room used as a shop; shop: *a beauty parlor.* —*adj.* of or pertaining to a parlor. [< AF *parlur.* See PARLEY.]

parlor car, *Am.* railroad passenger car for day travel, more luxurious than ordinary cars.

par·lous (pär'ləs), *adj. Archaic* or *Dial.* **1.** perilous. **2.** very clever; shrewd. —*adv.* extremely. [var. of PERILOUS]

Par·me·san cheese (pär'mə·zan'; pär'mə·zan), a hard, dry Italian cheese made from skim milk.

Par·nas·sus (pär·nas'əs), *n.* **1.** Mount, mountain in S Greece, in ancient Greek times sacred to Apollo and the Muses. **2.** the fabled mountain of poets, whose summit is their goal. —**Par·nas·si·an** (pär·nas'i·ən), *adj.*

pa·ro·chi·al (pə·rō'ki·əl), *adj.* **1.** of, for, or in a parish: *a parochial school.* **2.** narrow; limited: *a parochial viewpoint.* [< OF < LL, < *parochia* PARISH] —**pa·ro'chi·al·ism,** *n.* —**pa·ro'chi·al·ly,** *adv.*

par·o·dy (par'ə·di), *n., pl.* -dies, *v.,* -died, -dy·ing. —*n.* **1.** a humorous imitation of a serious writing. A parody follows the form of the original, but changes its sense to nonsense. **2.** a poor imitation. —*v.* **1.** make fun of by imitating; make a parody on. **2.** imitate poorly. [< L < Gk. < *para*- beside + *oide* song] —**par'o·dist,** *n.*

pa·role (pə·rōl'), *n., v.,* -roled, -rol·ing. —*n.* **1.** word of honor: *the prisoner of war gave his parole not to try to escape.* **2.** conditional release from prison or jail before the full term is served. **3.** conditional freedom allowed in place of imprisonment. —*v. Am.* put on parole; release on parole. [< F, word, < L *parabola* PARABLE. Doublet of PARABLE, PALAVER.]

pa·rot·id (pə·rot'id), *Anat.* —*adj.* near the ear. The parotid glands, one in front of each ear, supply saliva to the mouth through the parotid ducts. —*n.* parotid gland. [< L < Gk. *parotis* < *para*- beside + *ous* ear]

par·ox·ysm (par'ək·siz·əm), *n.* **1.** a severe, sudden attack: *a paroxysm of coughing.* **2.** fit; convulsion: *a paroxysm of rage.* [< Med.L < Gk., ult. < *para*- + *oxynein* render acute] —**par'ox·ys'mal,** *adj.*

par·quet (pär·kā'; -ket'), *n., v.,* -queted, -quet·ing; *esp. Brit.* -quet·ted, -quet·ting. —*n.* **1.** an inlaid wooden flooring. **2.** *Am.* **a.** the main floor of a theater. **b.** part of the main floor of a theater from the orchestra to the parquet circle. —*v.* **1.** furnish with an inlaid wooden floor. **2.** make (flooring) of inlaid wood. [< F, dim of *parc* PARK]

Parquetry

parquet circle, *Am.* the part of the main floor of a theater that is under the balcony.

par·quet·ry (pär'kit·ri), *n., pl.* -ries. mosaic of wood used for floors, wainscoting, etc.

parr (pär), *n., pl.* parrs or (*esp. collectively*) parr. a young salmon before it is old enough to go to sea.

par·ra·keet (par'ə·kēt), **par·ro·ket,** or **par·ro·quet** (-ket), *n.* parakeet.

par·ri·cide[1] (par'ə·sīd), *n.* **1.** person who kills his parent. **2.** person who kills anybody whom he should revere. [< F < LL, < L *pater* father + -*cida* killer] —**par'ri·cid'al,** *adj.*

par·ri·cide[2] (par'ə·sīd), *n.* crime of killing one's parent or parents. [< F < LL, < L *pater* father + -*cidium* act of killing]

par·rot (par'ət), *n.* bird with a stout, hooked bill and often with bright-colored feathers. Some parrots can imitate sounds and repeat words and sentences. —*v.* repeat without understanding. [< F *Perrot,* dim. of *Pierre* Peter]

parrot fever, psittacosis.

par·ry (par'i), *v.,* -ried, -ry·ing, *n., pl.* -ries. —*v.* ward off; turn aside; evade (a thrust, stroke, weapon, question, etc.). —*n.* **1.** act of parrying; avoiding. **2.** Fencing. a special defensive movement. [< F < Ital. *parare* ward off < L *parare* prepare. Doublet of PARE.] —**Syn.** *v.* elude, avoid, avert.

parse (pärs), *v.,* parsed, pars·ing. **1.** analyze (a sentence) grammatically, telling its parts of speech and their uses in the sentence. **2.** describe (a word) grammatically, telling what part of speech it is, its form, and its use in a sentence. [< L *pars* (orationis) part (of speech)] —**pars'er,** *n.* ▶ parse. Parsing is describing the grammatical forms and functions of the words in a sentence. The sentence *A hermit lived in the ruined abbey* might be parsed: *Hermit* is a singular noun, subject of the verb *lived; in the ruined abbey* is an adverbial phrase of place; *abbey* is a singular noun object of the preposition *in,* modified by the adjective *ruined.*

Par·see, Par·si (pär'sē; pär·sē'), *n.* member

of a sun-worshiping sect in India descended from the Persians who first settled there in the early part of the eighth century A.D. —**Par′see·ism, Par′si·ism,** n.

par·si·mo·ni·ous (pär′sə·mō′ni·əs), adj. too economical; stingy. —**par′si·mo′ni·ous·ly,** adv. —Syn. frugal, stinting, miserly. —Ant. generous, liberal, lavish.

par·si·mo·ny (pär′sə·mō′ni), n. extreme economy; stinginess. [< L parsimonia < parcere to spare] —Syn. frugality, miserliness.

pars·ley (pärs′li), n., pl. -leys. a garden plant with finely divided, fragrant leaves, used to flavor food and to trim platters of meat. [OE petersilie, also < OF peresil; both < VL petrosilium < L < Gk., < petros rock + selinon parsley]

pars·nip (pärs′nip), n. 1. vegetable that is the long, tapering, whitish root of a plant belonging to the same family as the carrot. 2. the plant. [< OF < L pastinaca (cf. pastinare dig); form infl. by ME nep turnip]

par·son (pär′sən), n. 1. minister in charge of a parish. 2. any clergyman; minister. [< Med.L persona parson. Doublet of PERSON.] —Syn. 2. pastor, preacher, curate.

par·son·age (pär′sən·ij), n. house provided for a minister by a church.

part (pärt), n. 1. something less than the whole: part of an apple. 2. each of several equal quantities into which a whole may be divided: a dime is a tenth part of a dollar. 3. share: everyone must do his part. 4. side in a dispute or contest: he always takes his brother's part. 5. character in a play; the words spoken by a character. 6. a dividing line left in combing one's hair. 7. one of the voices or instruments in music. The four parts in singing are soprano, alto, tenor, and bass. 8. the musical score for a part. 9. ability; talent: a man of parts. 10. region; district; place: in foreign parts. 11. for one's part, as far as one is concerned. 12. in good part, in a friendly or gracious way. 13. in part, to some extent; partly. 14. part and parcel, a necessary part. 15. take part, take or have a share. [< L pars] —v. 1. divide into two or more pieces. 2. divide into shares; portion out. 3. force apart; divide: the policeman parted the crowd. 4. go apart; separate: the friends parted in anger. 5. break: the rope parted. 6. go away; depart. 7. die. 8. comb (the hair) away from a dividing line. 9. part company (with), end companionship. 10. part from, go away from; leave. 11. part with, give up; let go. —adj. less than the whole: part time. —adv. in some measure or degree; partly. [< OF < L partire < pars, n.] —part′ed, adj. —part′er, n. —Syn. n. 1. portion, piece, fragment, segment, section. —v. 1. sever, sunder, detach. ➤ part. On the part of is often a rather clumsy way of saying by, among, for, and the like: It resulted in less wild driving on the part of [by] young people.

part., 1. participle. 2. particular.

par·take (pär·tāk′), v., -took, -tak·en, -taking. 1. eat or drink some; take some. 2. take or have a share. 3. partake of, a. have a share in. b. have to some extent the nature or character of: her graciousness partakes of condescension. [< partaker, for part-taker] —par·tak′er, n.

par·terre (pär·tār′), n. Am. the part of the main floor of a theater under the balcony. [< F, on the ground]

par·the·no·gen·e·sis (pär′thə·nō·jen′ə·sis), n. Biol. reproduction without any male element. [< Gk. parthenos virgin + E genesis] —par·the·no·ge·net·ic (pär′thə·nō·jə·net′ik), adj.

Par·the·non (pär′thə·non), n. temple of Athena on the Acropolis in Athens, regarded as the finest example of Doric architecture.

Par·thi·a (pär′thi·ə), n. an ancient country in Asia SE of the Caspian Sea, now a part of NE Iran. —**Par′thi·an,** adj., n.

Parthian shot, a sharp parting remark or the like. The Parthians used to shoot their arrows at the enemy while pretending to retreat.

par·tial (pär′shəl), adj. 1. not complete; not total: a partial loss. 2. inclined to favor one side more than another; favoring unfairly. 3. favorably inclined: be partial to sports. [< LL,

< L pars part] —**par′tial·ly,** adv. —**par′tial·ness,** n. —Syn. 1. incomplete, imperfect. 2. biased, prejudiced, one-sided.

par·ti·al·i·ty (pär′shi·al′ə·ti; -shal′ə-), n., pl. -ties. 1. a favoring of one more than another or others; favorable prejudice; being partial: treat all the students without partiality. 2. a particular liking; fondness: a partiality for candy. —Syn. 1. bias, favoritism. 2. preference, bent.

par·tic·i·pant (pär·tis′ə·pənt), n. one who shares or participates. —adj. participating.

par·tic·i·pate (pär·tis′ə·pāt), v., -pat·ed, -pat·ing. have a share; take part. [< L participatus, ult. < pars part + capere take] —par·tic′i·pa′tion, n. —par·tic′i·pa′tor, n.

par·ti·cip·i·al (pär′tə·sip′i·əl), adj. of or having to do with a participle, as a participial adjective (a masked man, a becoming dress), a participial noun (in cutting ice, the fatigue of marching). —**par′ti·cip′i·al·ly,** adv.

par·ti·ci·ple (pär′tə·sip′əl), n. a form of a verb used as an adjective. [< OF, < participe a sharing < L participium. See PARTICIPATE.] ➤ A participle cannot be limited in person or number, but it retains the verbal attributes of tense, voice, power to take an object, and modification by adverbs. Examples: the girl writing sentences at the blackboard, the recently stolen silver, John having missed the boat. In these phrases, writing is a present participle; stolen is a past participle; having missed is a perfect participle.

par·ti·cle (pär′tə·kəl), n. 1. a very little bit. 2. prefix or suffix. 3. preposition, conjunction, article, or interjection. In, if, an, and ah are particles. 4. Physics. portion of matter so small that, though it possesses mass, it may be treated as a point without length, breadth, or thickness. [< L particula, dim. of pars part] —Syn. 1. mite, whit, iota, jot.

par·ti-col·ored (pär′ti·kul′ərd), adj. colored differently in different parts.

par·tic·u·lar (pər·tik′yə·lər), adj. 1. apart from others; considered separately; single: that particular chair is already sold. 2. belonging to some one person, thing, group, occasion, etc.; not general: a particular characteristic of a skunk is his smell. 3. different from others; unusual; special: a particular friend. 4. hard to please; wanting everything to be just right; very careful. 5. giving details; full of details: a particular account of the game. —n. 1. an individual part; item; point: the work is complete in every particular. 2. in particular, especially. [< OF < L particularis. See PARTICLE.] —Syn. adj. 2. individual, distinctive. 4. precise, exacting, fastidious. 5. detailed, minute.

par·tic·u·lar·i·ty (pər·tik′yə·lar′ə·ti), n., pl. -ties. 1. detailed quality; minuteness. 2. special carefulness. 3. attentiveness to details. 4. a particular feature or trait. 5. quality of being hard to please. 6. quality or fact of being particular.

par·tic·u·lar·ize (pər·tik′yə·lər·īz), v., -ized, -iz·ing. 1. mention particularly or individually; treat in detail. 2. mention individuals; give details. —par·tic′u·lar·i·za′tion, n.

par·tic·u·lar·ly (pər·tik′yə·lər·li), adv. 1. in a high degree; especially. 2. in a particular manner; in detail; minutely. —Syn. 1. principally, mainly.

part·ing (pär′ting), n. 1. departure; going away. 2. death. 3. a taking leave. 4. division; separation. 5. place of division or separation. —adj. 1. given, taken, done, etc., at parting: a parting request, a parting shot. 2. departing. 3. dividing; separating.

par·ti·san, par·ti·zan (pär′tə·zən), n. 1. a strong supporter of a person, party, or cause; one whose support is based on feeling rather than on reasoning. 2. guerrilla. —adj. of or like a partisan. [< F < Ital. partigiano < parte part] —**par′ti·san·ship′, par′ti·zan·ship′,** n. —Syn. n. 1. follower, adherent, disciple.

par·ti·tion (pär·tish′ən), n. 1. division into parts: the partition of a man's wealth when he dies. 2. portion; part. 3. wall between rooms, etc. —v. 1. divide into parts: partition a house into rooms. 2. dismember and distribute. 3. separate by a partition. [< L, < partire PART] —**par·ti′-**

tion·er, n. —par·ti'tion·ment, n. —Syn. n. 1. apportionment, distribution.

par·ti·tive (pär'tə·tiv), Gram. —n. word or phrase meaning a part of a collective whole. Some, few, and any are partitives. —adj. expressing a part of a collective whole: a partitive adjective. —par'ti·tive·ly, adv.

part·ly (pärt'li), adv. in part; in some measure or degree.

part·ner (pärt'nər), n. 1. one who shares. 2. member of a company or firm who shares the risk and profits of the business. 3. wife or husband. 4. companion in a dance. 5. player on the same team or side in a game. [var. of parcener < AF, < parçon PARTITION; infl. by part] —Syn. 1. sharer, partaker.

part·ner·ship (pärt'nər·ship), n. 1. a being a partner; joint interest; association: the partnership of marriage. 2. company or firm with two or more members who share in the risk and profits of the business. 3. the legal relation between persons who are legally partners in business. 4. the contract creating this relation.

part of speech, any one of the form classes which collectively include the total structure of a language. ➤ parts of speech. Although in our speaking and writing we are not conscious of using nouns or verbs or adjectives, we need to be able to identify the parts of speech if we are going to describe and discuss grammatically what we have written. It is useful to know whether we are using nouns or verbs, pronouns or prepositions. The traditional parts of speech in English are nouns, pronouns, adjectives, verbs, adverbs, prepositions, conjunctions, and interjections. One of the fundamental facts of English grammar is that a word may function as more than one part of speech: You may spell a word (noun), write a word picture (adjective), or word a message (verb). This shows that the part of speech to which a word belongs cannot be definitely decided by looking at the word by itself; we need to know how it is used.

par·tridge (pär'trij), n., pl. -tridg·es or (esp. collectively) -tridge. 1. any of several kinds of game birds belonging to the same group as the quail, pheasant, and grouse. 2. Am. in the United States, the ruffed grouse or the quail. [< OF < L < Gk. perdix]

Hungarian partridge (ab. 1 ft. long)

part song, song with parts in simple harmony for two or more voices, esp. one meant to be sung without an accompaniment.

par·tu·ri·ent (pär·tūr'i·ənt; -tyùr'-), adj. 1. bringing forth young; about to give birth to young. 2. pertaining to childbirth.

par·tu·ri·tion (pär'tù·rish'ən; -tyù-; -chù-), n. childbirth. [< L, < parturire to in labor, ult. < parere to bear]

par·ty (pär'ti), n., pl. -ties, adj. —n. 1. group of people doing something together: a scouting party of three soldiers. 2. a gathering for pleasure: on her birthday she had a party and invited her friends. 3. group of people wanting the same kind of government or action: the Democratic Party. 4. system of taking sides on public matters. 5. one who takes part in, aids, or knows about: he was a party to our plot. 6. each of the persons or sides in a contract, lawsuit, etc. 7. Colloq. person. —adj. of or pertaining to a party. [< OF partie < pp. of partir divide, PART] —Syn. n. 1. company, band. 3. faction, cabal, junto. ➤ See person for usage note.

party line, 1. Am. a telephone line by which two or more subscribers are connected with the exchange by one circuit. 2. Am. an abstract boundary line setting off the tenets of a political party. 3. policy advocated and followed by the Communist Party. —party liner, Am.

par value, face value.

par·ve·nu (pär'və·nü; -nū), n. one who has risen to a higher place than he is fit for; upstart. [< F, pp. of parvenir arrive < L, < per- through + venire come]

Pas·a·de·na (pas'ə·dē'nə), n. city in SW California, near Los Angeles.

Pas·cal (pas·kal'; pas'kəl), n. 1623–1662, French philosopher, mathematician, and physicist.

pas·chal (pas'kəl), adj. 1. of or having to do with the Jewish Passover. 2. of or having to do with Easter; used in Easter celebrations.

pa·sha (pə·shä'; pash'ə; pä'shə), n. 1. a former Turkish title of rank. 2. a civil or military official of high rank in Turkey. [< Turk., var. of bāshā < bash head]

pa·sha·lik, pa·sha·lic (pə·shä'lik), n. territory governed by a pasha.

pasque·flow·er (pask'flou'ər), n. any of several anemones with purple or white flowers that bloom early in the spring. [pasque < OF, Easter, < L < Gk. < Heb. pesaḥ Passover]

pass (pas; päs), v., passed, passed or past, pass·ing, n. —v. 1. go by; move past: pass another car on the road. 2. make one's way; move on; go: the salesman passed from house to house. 3. go from one to another; go about; circulate; be transferred or conveyed: his estate passed to his children. 4. cause to go from one to another; cause to circulate; hand around: the curious coin was passed around for examination. 5. get through or by: we passed the dangerous section of the road successfully. 6. go across or over: pass a threshold. 7. put or direct (a rope, string, etc.): he passed a rope around his waist for support. 8. go away; depart: the time for action had already passed. 9. cause to go, move onward, or proceed: pass troops in review. 10. discharge from the body. 11. be successful in (an examination, a course, etc.). 12. cause or allow to go through something; sanction or approve: pass accounts as correct. 13. ratify or enact: pass a bill or law. 14. be approved by a lawmaking body, etc.: the new ordinance passed the City Council. 15. come to an end; die. 16. go beyond; exceed; surpass: his performance passed all expectations. 17. use; spend: we passed the days pleasantly. 18. change: water passes from a liquid to a solid state when it freezes. 19. take place; happen: tell me all that passed. 20. be accepted (for or as): use silk or a material that will pass for silk. 21. cause to be accepted: the inspector passed the item after examining it. 22. express; pronounce: a judge passes sentence on guilty persons. 23. give a judgment or opinion: the judges passed on each contestant. 24. go without notice: he was rude, but let that pass. 25. let go without action. 26. leave out; omit: pass a dividend. 27. transfer (the ball, etc.) in football, hockey, and other games. 28. Cards. give up a chance to play a hand, refuse to play a hand, or refuse to bid. 29. thrust. 30. Fencing. make a thrust. 31. Am., Baseball. permit (a batter) to reach first base on balls, or as a result of being hit by a pitched ball. 32. promise: pass one's word. 33. bring to pass, accomplish; cause to be. 34. come to pass, take place; happen. 35. pass away, come to an end; die. 36. pass by, fail to notice; overlook; disregard. 37. pass off, a. go away. b. take place; be done. c. get accepted; pretend to be. 38. pass out, Colloq. faint; lose consciousness. 39. pass over, fail to notice; overlook; disregard. 40. pass up, Am. give up; renounce. —n. 1. act of passing; passage. 2. success in an examination, etc.; passing an examination but without honors. 3. permission or license to pass; free ticket. 4. state; condition: things have come to a strange pass. 5. motion of the hands: Dan made a pass at Dick. 6. a sleight-of-hand motion; manipulation; trick. 7. a narrow road, path, way, channel, etc.; narrow passage through the mountains. 8. transference of a ball, etc., as in football. 9. a causing to pass; a thrust, esp. in fencing. 10. Baseball. permitting a batter to reach first base on balls; walk. 11. Cards. act of allowing an opportunity to bid or raise to go by. [< OF passer, ult. < L passus step] —pass'er, n. —Syn. v. 2. proceed, advance. 8. recede, disappear, vanish. 13. sanction, confirm. 16. excel, transcend.

pass., 1. passenger. 2. passim. 3. passive.

pass·a·ble (pas′ə·bəl; päs′–), adj. 1. fairly good; moderate: a passable knowledge of geography. 2. that can be passed: a passable river. 3. current; valid: passable coin. 4. that may be enacted: a passable bill. —pass′a·ble·ness, n. —pass′a·bly, adv. —Syn. 1. tolerable, mediocre.

pas·sage (pas′ij), n. 1. hall or way through a building; passageway. 2. means of passing; way through: ask for passage through a crowd. 3. right, liberty, or leave to pass: the guard refused us passage. 4. a passing: the passage of time. 5. piece from a speech or writing: a passage from the Bible. 6. a going across; voyage: a stormy passage. 7. course; journey; progress. 8. a making into law by a favoring vote of a legislature: the passage of a bill. 9. interchange of communications, confidences, etc., between persons. 10. exchange of blows: passage at arms. 11. phrase or other division of a piece of music. [< OF, < passer PASS] —Syn. 1. corridor.

pas·sage·way (pas′ij·wā′), n. way along which one can pass; passage, as a hall or alley.

pass·book (pas′bůk′; päs′–), n. a little book in which a bank keeps an account of what a person puts in and takes out.

pas·sé (pa·sā′; pas′ā), adj. 1. past. 2. past its usefulness. 3. out of date. [< F, passed]

pas·sen·ger (pas′ən·jər), n. traveler in a train, bus, boat, etc. [< OF passagier < passage PASSAGE]

passenger pigeon, Am. kind of wild pigeon, now extinct, that flew far in very large flocks.

pass·er·by (pas′ər·bī′; päs′–), n., pl. pass·ers-by, one that passes by.

pas·ser·ine (pas′ər·in; –īn), adj. belonging or pertaining to the very large group of perching birds, including more than half of all birds. —n. a bird that perches. [< L, < passer sparrow]

pas·sim (pas′im), adv. Latin. here and there; in various places. ≽ Passim is used in referring to expressions found in several places in some book or books.

pass·ing (pas′ing; päs′–), adj. 1. that passes. 2. transient; fleeting. 3. cursory; incidental. 4. that is now happening. 5. allowing one to pass an examination or test: 75 will be a passing mark. —n. 1. act of one that passes; a going by; a departure. 2. means or place of passing. 3. in passing, as one proceeds or passes. —adv. Archaic. surpassingly; very. —Syn. adj. 2. transitory, momentary.

pas·sion (pash′ən), n. 1. very strong feeling. 2. violent anger; rage: he flew into a passion. 3. an ardent affection or sexual love between a man and a woman. 4. very strong liking: she has a passion for music. 5. object of a passion: music is her passion. 6. Archaic. suffering. 7. Often, Passion. the sufferings of Jesus on the cross or after the Last Supper. [< OF < L passio < pati suffer] —pas′sion·less, adj. —pas′sion·less·ly, adv. —pas′sion·less·ness, n. —Syn. 1. emotion. 2. fury.

pas·sion·ate (pash′ən·it), adj. 1. having or showing strong feelings. 2. easily moved to anger. 3. resulting from strong feeling: a passionate speech. —pas′sion·ate·ly, adv. —pas′sion·ate·ness, n. —Syn. 2. quick-tempered, irascible, fiery. 3. ardent, fervent, impassioned.

pas·sion·flow·er (pash′ən·flou′ər), n. 1. plant with showy flowers supposed to suggest the crown of thorns, the wounds, the nails, etc., of Christ's crucifixion. 2. the flower.

Passion Play, play representing the sufferings and death of Christ.

pas·sive (pas′iv), adj. 1. not acting in return; just being acted on without itself acting: a passive mind or disposition. 2. not resisting: the slaves gave passive obedience to their master. 3. inactive; quiescent; inert. 4. Gram. showing the subject as acted on. In "The window was broken by John," was broken is in the passive voice. —n. Gram. 1. a verb form that shows the subject as acted on. 2. the passive voice. [< L passivus < pati suffer] —pas′sive·ly, adv. —pas′sive·ness, pas·siv′i·ty, n. —Syn. adj. 1. impassive. 2. submissive, unresisting, patient.

pass·key (pas′kē′; päs′–), n., pl. –keys. 1. key for opening several locks. 2. a private key.

Pass·o·ver (pas′ō′vər; päs′–), n. an annual feast of the Jews in memory of the sparing of the Hebrews in Egypt. Exod. 12.

pass·port (pas′pôrt; –pōrt; päs′–), n. 1. a paper or book giving official permission to travel in a certain country, under the protection of one's own government. 2. anything that gives one admission or acceptance.

pass·word (pas′wėrd′; päs′–), n. a secret word that allows a person speaking it to pass a guard.

past (past; päst), adj. 1. gone by; ended: our troubles are past. 2. just gone by: the past year was full of trouble. 3. having served a term in office: a past president. 4. Gram. indicating time gone by, or former action or state: the past tense, a past participle. —n. 1. time gone by; time before; what has happened: life began far back in the past. 2. a past life or history: our country has a glorious past. 3. one's past life, esp. if hidden or unknown. 4. Gram. the past tense or a verb form in it. —prep. 1. beyond; farther on than: past the mark. 2. later than; after: it is past noon. 3. beyond in number, amount, or degree. 4. beyond the ability, range, scope, etc., of: absurd fancies that are past belief. —adv. so as to pass by or beyond: the cars go past once an hour. —v. pp. of pass.

pas·ta (päs′tə), n. any of certain foods made of grain, or such foods collectively; spaghetti, macaroni, etc. [< Ital.]

paste (pāst), n., v., past·ed, past·ing. —n. 1. mixture, such as flour and water boiled together, that will stick paper together. 2. dough for pastry. 3. a soft, doughlike mixture. Fish paste is pounded fish. 4. a hard, glassy material used in making imitations of precious stones. —v. 1. stick with paste. 2. Slang. strike, esp. with a fist; beat. [< OF < LL < Gk., pasta porridge]

paste·board (pāst′bôrd′; –bōrd′), n. a stiff material made of sheets of paper pasted together or of paper pulp pressed and dried.

pas·tel (pas·tel′; pas′tel), n. 1. kind of crayon used in drawing. 2. a drawing made with such crayons. 3. a soft, pale shade of some color. [< Ital., < LL pasta PASTE]

pas·ter (pās′tər), n. 1. slip to paste on or over something. 2. one that pastes.

pas·tern (pas′tərn), n. the part of a horse's foot between the fetlock and the hoof. [< OF pasturon, dim. of pasture tether for a horse, ult. < L pastor herdsman. See PASTOR.]

FETLOCK
PASTERN
HOOF

Pas·ter·nak (pas′tər·nak), n. Boris, 1890–1960, Russian poet and novelist.

Pas·teur (pas·tėr′), n. Louis, 1822–1895, French chemist.

pas·teur·ize (pas′chər·īz; –tər–), v., –ized, –iz·ing. heat (milk, etc.) to a high enough temperature to destroy harmful bacteria, etc. [after L. Pasteur] —pas′teur·i·za′tion, n.

pas·tille (pas·tēl′), **pas·til** (pas′til), n. 1. a flavored or medicated lozenge. 2. a small roll or cone of aromatic paste, burnt as a disinfectant, incense, etc. [< F < L pastillus roll, aromatic lozenge, dim. of panis bread]

pas·time (pas′tīm′; päs′–), n. a pleasant way of passing time; amusement; recreation.

past master, 1. one who has filled the office of master in a society, lodge, etc. 2. person who has much experience in any profession, art, etc.

pas·tor (pas′tər; päs′–), n. minister in charge of a church; spiritual guide. [< L, shepherd, < pascere feed] —pas′tor·ship, n.

pas·tor·al (pas′tər·əl; päs′–), adj. 1. of shepherds or country life. 2. simple or naturally beautiful like the country. 3. of a pastor or his duties. —n. 1. a pastoral play, poem, or picture. 2. letter from a bishop to his clergy or to the people of his church district. —pas′tor·al·ism, n. —pas′tor·al·ist, n. —pas′tor·al·ly, adv. —Syn. adj. 1. rural, rustic, country, bucolic.

pas·tor·ate (pas′tər·it; päs′–), **pas·tor·age** (–ij), n. 1. position or duties of a pastor. 2. term of service of a pastor. 3. pastors as a group.

past participle, participle that indicates time gone by, or a former action or state. *Played* and *thrown* are past participles in "She has played all day," "The ball should have been thrown to me." ➤ See participle for usage note.

past perfect, *n.* **1.** a verb form showing that an event was completed before a given past time; pluperfect. In "He had learned to read before he went to school," *had learned* is the past perfect of *learn.* **2.** the past perfect tense or a verb form in it. —*adj.* of or pertaining to this verb form.

pas·tra·mi (pəs·trä'mi), *n.* a smoked and well-seasoned cut of beef, esp. a shoulder cut. [< Yiddish]

pas·try (pās'tri), *n., pl.* **-tries. 1.** food made of baked flour paste, made rich with lard, butter, or a vegetable shortening. **2.** pies, tarts, and other foods wholly or partly made of rich flour paste. [< *paste*]

pas·tur·age (pas'chər·ij; päs'-), *n.* **1.** the growing grass and other plants for cattle, sheep, or horses to feed on. **2.** pasture land.

pas·ture (pas'chər; päs'-), *n., v.,* **-tured, -tur·ing.** —*n.* **1.** a grassy field or hillside; grasslands on which cattle, sheep, or horses can feed. **2.** the grass and other growing plants. —*v.* **1.** put (cattle, sheep, etc.) out to pasture. **2.** (of cattle, sheep, etc.) feed on (growing grass, etc.). [< LL *pastura* < L *pascere* feed] —pas'tur·a·ble, *adj.* —pas'tur·a·bil'i·ty, *n.* —pas'tur·er, *n.*

past·y (pās'ti), *adj.,* **past·i·er, past·i·est. 1.** like paste. **2.** pale. **3.** flabby. —past'i·ness, *n.*

pat[1] (pat), *v.,* **pat·ted, pat·ting,** *n.* —*v.* **1.** strike or tap lightly with something flat: *she patted the dough into a flat cake.* **2.** tap with the hand as a sign of sympathy, approval or affection: *pat a dog.* —*n.* **1.** a light stroke or tap with the hand or with something flat. **2.** sound made by patting. **3.** a small mass, esp. of butter, shaped by patting. [OE *potian* push]

pat[2] (pat), *adj.* apt; suitable: *a pat reply.* —*adv.* **1.** aptly; exactly; suitably. **2. stand pat,** *Colloq.* hold to things as they are and refuse to change. [prob. special use of *pat*[1]] —pat'ness, *n.*

Pat·a·go·ni·a (pat'ə·gō'ni·ə; -gōn'yə), *n.* region in the extreme south of South America. —Pat'a·go'ni·an, *adj., n.*

patch (pach), *n.* **1.** piece put on to mend a hole or a tear. **2.** piece of cloth, etc., put over a wound or a sore. **3.** pad over a hurt eye to protect it. **4.** piece of ground: *a garden patch.* **5.** scrap or bit of cloth left over. —*v.* **1.** protect or adorn with a patch or patches; put patches on; mend. **2.** piece together; make hastily. **3. patch up, a.** put an end to; settle. **b.** make right hastily or for a time. **c.** put together hastily or poorly. [ME *pacche*] —patch'er, *n.* —patch'y, *adj.* —patch'i·ly, *adv.* —patch'i·ness, *n.*

patch·work (pach'wérk'), *n.* **1.** pieces of cloth of various colors or shapes sewed together: *a patchwork quilt.* **2.** anything like this.

pate (pāt), *n.* **1.** top of the head; head. **2.** brains.

pâ·té de foie gras (pä·tā' də fwä grä'), *French.* paste made with livers of specially fattened geese.

pa·tel·la (pə·tel'ə), *n., pl.* **-tel·las, -tel·lae** (-tel'ē). kneecap. [< L, dim. of *patina* pan] —pa·tel'lar, *adj.*

pat·en (pat'ən), *n.* plate on which the bread is placed at the celebration of the Eucharist or Mass. [< OF < L *patina* pan, dish]

pat·ent (*n., adj. 1, v.* pat'ənt, esp. *Brit.* pā'tənt; *adj. 2, 3* pā'tənt, pat'ənt), *n.* **1.** a government grant to a person by which he is the only one allowed to make or sell a new invention for a certain number of years. **2.** invention that is patented. **3.** an official document from a government giving a right or privilege. —*adj.* **1.** given or protected by a patent. **2.** evident; plain: *it is patent that cats dislike dogs.* **3.** open. —*v.* get a patent for. [< L *patens* lying open] —pa·ten·cy (pā'tən·si), *n.* —pat'ent·a·ble, *adj.* —pat'ent·a·bil'i·ty, *n.* —pa·tent·ly (pā'tənt·li), *adv.* —pat'ent·or, *n.* —Syn. *adj.* **2.** manifest, obvious, apparent.

pat·ent leather (pat'ənt), *Am.* leather with a very glossy, smooth surface, usually black.

pa·ter (pā'tər), *n. Brit. Colloq.* father. [< L]

pa·ter·fa·mil·i·as (pā'tər·fə·mil'i·əs), *n.* father or head of a family. [< L, < *pater* father + *familias,* gen., of a family]

pa·ter·nal (pə·tér'nəl), *adj.* **1.** of or like a father; fatherly. **2.** related on the father's side of the family: *a paternal aunt, cousin, etc.* **3.** received or inherited from one's father: *Mary's blue eyes are a paternal inheritance.* [< LL, ult. < *pater* father] —pa·ter'nal·ly, *adv.*

pa·ter·nal·ism (pə·tér'nəl·iz·əm), *n.* management of the affairs of a country or group of people in the way that a father manages the affairs of his family and children. —pa·ter'nal·is'tic, *adj.* —pa·ter'nal·is'ti·cal·ly, *adv.*

pa·ter·ni·ty (pə·tér'nə·ti), *n.* **1.** being a father; fatherhood. **2.** paternal origin: *King Arthur's paternity was unknown.*

pa·ter·nos·ter (pat'ər·nos'tər; pā'tər-), *n.* **1.** the Lord's Prayer, esp. in Latin. **2.** one of the beads of a rosary on which the Lord's Prayer is said. [< L, our father]

Pat·er·son (pat'ər·sən), *n.* city in NE New Jersey.

path (path; päth), *n., pl.* **paths** (pathz; päthz). **1.** way made by people or animals walking, usually too narrow for automobiles or wagons. **2.** walk through a garden or park. **3.** line along which a person or thing moves; route; track: *the moon has a regular path through the sky.* **4.** way of acting or behaving. [OE *pæth*] —path'less, *adj.* —path'less·ness, *n.* —Syn. **1.** walk, trail, lane. **3.** course.

pa·thet·ic (pə·thet'ik), **pa·thet·i·cal** (-ə·kəl), *adj.* **1.** pitiful; arousing pity. **2.** of the emotions. [< LL < Gk. *pathetikos,* ult. < *pathein* suffer] —pa·thet'i·cal·ly, *adv.* —Syn. **1.** pitiable, moving, touching, affecting.

pathetic fallacy, attributing human emotions and characteristics to nature. ➤ pathetic fallacy. Crediting places and things with human emotions is known as the pathetic fallacy. A certain amount of such metaphor is natural and often successful. But the sea and clouds and winds and mountains have too often been given human emotions, or at least emotional adjectives, by amateur and professional melodramatists, so that now such figures are usually ineffective.

path·find·er (path'fīn'dər; päth'-), *n. Am.* one who finds a path or way.

path·o·gen·ic (path'ə·jen'ik), *adj.* producing disease. [< *patho-* (< Gk. *pathos* disease) + *-genic* (ult. < Gk. *gen-* produce)]

pathol., pathology.

pa·thol·o·gy (pə·thol'ə·ji), *n., pl.* **-gies. 1.** study of the causes and nature of diseases. **2.** unhealthy conditions and processes caused by a disease. [< *patho-* (< Gk. *pathos* disease) + -LOGY] —path·o·log·ic (path'ə·loj'ik), path·o·log'i·cal, *adj.* —path·o·log'i·cal·ly, *adv.* —pa·thol'o·gist, *n.*

pa·thos (pā'thos), *n.* quality in speech, writing, music, events, or a scene that arouses a feeling of pity or sadness. [< Gk. suffering, feeling]

path·way (path'wā'; päth'-), *n.* path.

-pathy, *suffix.* **1.** feeling, as in *antipathy.* **2.** disease, as in *neuropathy.* **3.** treatment of disease, as in *osteopathy.* [< Gk. *-patheia*]

pa·tience (pā'shəns), *n.* **1.** willingness to put up with waiting, pain, trouble, etc.; calm endurance without complaining or losing self-control. **2.** long, hard work; steady effort. **3.** solitaire (def. 1). —Syn. **1.** forbearance, resignation, calmness.

pa·tient (pā'shənt), *adj.* **1.** willing to put up with waiting, pain, trouble, etc.; enduring calmly without complaining or losing self-control. **2.** with steady effort or long, hard work; quietly persevering. —*n.* person who is being treated by a doctor. [< OF < L *patiens* suffering] —pa'tient·ly, *adv.* —Syn. *adj.* **1.** uncomplaining, resigned. —Ant. *adj.* **1.** impatient, restless, uneasy.

pat·i·na (pat′ə·nə), *n.* 1. film or incrustation, usually green, on the surface of old bronze. 2. film or coloring produced in the course of time on wood or other substance. [< Ital.]

pat·i·o (pat′i·ō; pä′ti·ō), *n., pl.* –i·os. *Am.* 1. an inner court or yard open to the sky. 2. terrace for outdoor eating, lounging, etc. [< Sp.]

pat·ois (pat′wä), *n., pl.* pat·ois (pat′wäz). dialect spoken by the common people of a district: *the patois of the French Canadians.* [< F]

pa·tri·arch (pä′tri·ärk), *n.* 1. father and ruler of a family or tribe. Abraham, Isaac, and Jacob were patriarchs. 2. person thought of as the father or founder of something. 3. a venerable old man. 4. bishop of the highest honor in the early Christian church or in the Greek Church. [< L < Gk., < *patria* family + *archos* leader] —pa′tri·ar′chal, pa′tri·ar′chic, *adj.* —pa′tri·ar′chal·ly, *adv.*

pa·tri·ar·chate (pä′tri·är′kit), *n.* position, dignity, or authority of a church patriarch.

pa·tri·ar·chy (pä′tri·är′ki), *n., pl.* –chies. form of social organization in which the father is head of the family and in which descent is reckoned in the male line, the children belonging to the father's clan.

pa·tri·cian (pə·trish′ən), *n.* 1. member of the nobility of ancient Rome. 2. noble; aristocrat. —*adj.* 1. of the patricians. 2. of high social rank; aristocratic. 3. suitable for an aristocrat. [< L *patricius* of the *patres* (senators, lit., fathers) at Rome] —pa·tri′cian·ism, *n.*

pat·ri·cide[1] (pat′rə·sīd), *n.* crime of killing one's father. [< LL, < L *pater* father + –*cidium* act of killing] —pat′ri·cid′al, *adj.*

pat·ri·cide[2] (pat′rə·sīd), *n.* one who kills his father. [< Med.L, < L *pater* father + –*cida* killer]

Pat·rick (pat′rik), *n.* Saint, 389?–461? A.D. British missionary and bishop who converted Ireland to Christianity. He is the patron saint of Ireland.

pat·ri·mo·ny (pat′rə·mō′ni), *n., pl.* –nies. 1. property inherited from one's father or ancestors. 2. property belonging to a church, monastery, or convent. 3. any heritage. [< L *patrimonium* < *pater* father] —pat′ri·mo′ni·al, *adj.*

pa·tri·ot (pä′tri·ət; –ot), *n.* person who loves and loyally supports his country. [< LL < Gk. *patriotes*, ult. < *patris* fatherland] —pa·tri·ot·ic (pä′tri·ot′ik), *adj.* —pa′tri·ot′i·cal·ly, *adv.*

pa·tri·ot·ism (pä′tri·ət·iz′əm), *n.* love and loyal support of one's country.

pa·tris·tic (pə·tris′tik), **pa·tris·ti·cal** (–tə·kəl), *adj.* pertaining to the early leaders, or fathers, of the Christian church or to their writings. —pa·tris′ti·cal·ly, *adv.*

pa·trol (pə·trōl′), *v.,* –trolled, –trol·ling, *n.* —*v.* 1. go the rounds as a watchman or a policeman does. 2. go around (a town, camp, etc.) to watch or guard. —*n.* 1. men who patrol: *the patrol was changed at midnight.* 2. a going of the rounds to watch or guard. 3. group of soldiers, ships, or airplanes, sent out to find out all they can about the enemy. 4. unit of eight boy scouts. [< F *patrouiller* paddle in mud] —pa·trol′ler, *n.*

pa·trol·man (pə·trōl′mən), *n., pl.* –men. *Am.* policeman, esp., who patrols a certain district.

patrol wagon, *Am.* a closed wagon or truck used by the police for carrying prisoners.

pa·tron (pä′trən), *n.* 1. one who buys regularly at a given store. 2. person who gives his approval and support to some person, art, cause, or undertaking. 3. a guardian saint or god. 4. in ancient Rome, an influential man who took certain persons under his protection. [< OF < L *patronus* < *pater* father. Doublet of PATROON.] —pa′tron·al, *adj.* —Syn. 2. sponsor.

pa·tron·age (pä′trən·ij; pat′rən–), *n.* 1. regular business given by customers. 2. favor, encouragement, or support given by a patron. 3. condescending favor: *an air of patronage.* 4. power to give jobs or favors: *the patronage of a Congressman.* 5. political jobs or favors.

pa·tron·ess (pä′trən·is; pat′rən–), *n.* 1. a woman patron. 2. lady who helps some entertainment with her name, money, or presence.

pa·tron·ize (pä′trən·īz; pat′rən–), *v.,* –ized, –iz·ing. 1. be a regular customer of; give regular business to. 2. act as a patron toward; support or protect. 3. treat in a condescending way: *we dislike to have anyone patronize us.* —pa′tron·iz′er, *n.* —pa′tron·iz′ing, *adj.* —pa′tron·iz′ing·ly, *adv.*

patron saint, saint regarded as the special guardian of a person, church, city, etc.

pat·ro·nym·ic (pat′rə·nim′ik), *n.* name derived from the name of a father or ancestor. Williamson is a patronymic. [< LL < Gk., < *pater* father + dial. *onyma* name]

pa·troon (pə·trün′), *n. Am.* owner of an estate in land who had certain privileges under the former Dutch governments of New York and New Jersey. [< Du. < L *patronus.* Doublet of PATRON.]

pat·ter[1] (pat′ər), *v.* make rapid taps: *bare feet pattered along the hard floor.* —*n.* series of quick taps or the sound they make. [< PAT[1]]

pat·ter[2] (pat′ər), *n.* 1. rapid and easy talk: *a magician's patter.* 2. talk of a class or group: *the patter of beggars and thieves.* —*v.* talk or say rapidly and easily, without much thought. [var. of *pater* in *paternoster*] —pat′ter·er, *n.*

pat·tern (pat′ərn), *n.* 1. arrangement of forms and colors; design: *the patterns of wallpaper, rugs, cloth, and jewelry.* 2. model or guide for something to be made. 3. a fine example; model to be followed. —*v.* make according to a pattern: *she patterned herself after her mother.* [< OF *patron* pattern, PATRON] —pat′tern·mak′er, *n.* —Syn. *n.* 1. motif. 3. ideal.

pat·ty (pat′i), *n., pl.* –ties. 1. Also, patty shell, *Am.* a hollow form of pastry filled with chicken, oysters, etc. 2. a small, round, flat piece of food or candy. [< F *pâté*]

pau·ci·ty (pô′sə·ti), *n.* 1. a small number; fewness. 2. a small amount; scarcity; lack. [< L, < *paucus* few]

Paul (pôl), *n.* Saint, died 67? A.D., Apostle who started Christian groups in many countries and wrote most of the epistles in the New Testament. —Paul·ine (pôl′īn; –ēn), *adj.*

Paul VI, born 1897, Pope since 1963.

paunch (pônch; pänch), *n.* 1. belly; stomach. 2. a large, protruding belly. [< OF *panche* < L *pantex*] —paunch′y, *adj.* —paunch′i·ness, *n.*

pau·per (pô′pər), *n.* a very poor person; person supported by charity. [< L, poor. Doublet of POOR.]

pau·per·ism (pô′pər·iz·əm), *n.* poverty.

pau·per·ize (pô′pər·īz), *v.,* –ized, –iz·ing. make a pauper of. —pau′per·i·za′tion, *n.*

pause (pôz), *v.,* paused, paus·ing, *n.* —*v.* 1. stop for a time; wait. 2. dwell; linger: *pause upon a word.* —*n.* 1. moment of silence; stop; rest. 2. a brief stop in speaking or reading. 3. *Music.* a sign (⌣ or ⌢) above or below a note, meaning that it is to be held for a longer time. [< F < L *pausis* < *pauein* to stop] —pause′less, *adj.* —pause′less·ly, *adv.* —paus′er, *n.* —paus′ing·ly, *adv.* —Syn. *v.* 1. hesitate, delay. —*n.* 2. intermission, break, hesitation.

pave (pāv), *v.,* paved, pav·ing. 1. cover (a street, sidewalk, etc.) with a pavement. 2. make smooth or easy; prepare. [< OF *paver*, ult. < L *pavire* beat, tread down] —pav′er, *n.*

pave·ment (pāv′mənt), *n.* 1. covering for streets, sidewalks, etc., made of stones, bricks, wood, asphalt, etc. 2. material used for paving.

pa·vil·ion (pə·vil′yən), *n.* 1. a light building, usually one somewhat open, used for shelter, pleasure, etc.: *a bathing pavilion.* 2. a large tent raised on posts; tent. 3. one of a group of buildings forming a hospital. —*v.* furnish with a pavilion; enclose or shelter in a pavilion. [< L *papilio* tent, butterfly]

pav·ing (pāv′ing), *n.* 1. material for pavement. 2. pavement.

paw (pô), *n.* 1. foot of an animal having claws. Cats and dogs have paws. 2. *Colloq.* hand. —*v.* 1. strike or scrape with the paws or feet: *the cat pawed the mouse.* 2. *Colloq.* handle awkwardly, roughly, or in too familiar a manner. [< OF *powe* < Gmc.] —paw′er, *n.*

pawl (pôl), *n.* a pivoted bar arranged to catch in the teeth of a ratchet wheel or the like so as to prevent movement backward or to impart motion.

pawn[1] (pôn), *v.* leave (something) with another person as security that borrowed money will be repaid: *he pawned his watch to buy food until he could get work.* [< n.] —*n.* 1. something left as security. 2. in pawn, in another's possession as security. 3. a pledge. [< OF < *pan*] —**pawn·er** (pôn'ər), **pawn·or** (pôn'ər; pôn·ôr'), *n.*

A, pawls; B, ratchet wheel.

pawn[2] (pôn), *n.* 1. *Chess.* one of the 16 pieces of lowest value. 2. person or thing used by someone for his own purposes. 3. an unimportant factor. [< AF, var. of OF *peon* < LL *pedo* foot soldier < L *pes* foot. Doublet of PEON.]

pawn·bro·ker (pôn'brō'kər), *n.* man who lends money at interest on articles that are left with him as security for the loan. —**pawn'bro'-king,** *n.*

Paw·nee (pô·nē'), *n. Am.* member of an American Indian tribe that lived near the forks of the Platte River.

pawn·shop (pôn'shop'), *n.* pawnbroker's shop.

paw·paw (pô'pô), *n. Am.* papaw.

pay (pā), *v.,* **paid** or (*Obs. except for def. 13*) **payed, pay·ing,** *n.* —*v.* 1. give (a person) what is due for things, work, etc. 2. give (money, etc.) due. 3. give money; pay what is owed. 4. give money for: *pay your way.* 5. hand over the amount of: *pay a debt.* 6. give; offer: *pay attention.* 7. be profitable to; be worth while to: *it pays me to keep that stock, it wouldn't pay me to take that job.* 8. yield as a return: *that stock pays me four per cent.* 9. be profitable: *it pays to be polite.* 10. recompense or requite; reward or punish: *he paid them for their insults by causing them trouble.* 11. suffer; undergo: *the one who does wrong must pay the penalty.* 12. pay off, a. give all the money that is owed; pay in full. b. get even with; get revenge on. 13. let out (a rope, etc.). 14. *Naut.* fall off to leeward. 15. **pay as you go,** *Am.* pay or discharge obligations as they are incurred. —*n.* 1. money or equivalent given for things or work; return for favors or hurts. 2. **in the pay of,** paid by and working for. 3. source of payment: *he is good pay.* [< OF < L *pacare* pacify < *pax* peace] —**pay·ee',** *n.* **pay'er,** *n.* —**Syn.** *v.* 1. compensate. —*n.* 1. compensation, remuneration. ➤ See **paid** for usage note.

pay·a·ble (pā'ə·bəl), *adj.* 1. required to be paid; due: *bills payable.* 2. that may be paid. —**Syn.** 1. owing, unpaid, outstanding.

pay dirt, *Am.* earth, ore, etc., containing enough metal to be worth mining.

pay·mas·ter (pā'mas'tər; -mäs'-), *n.* person whose job is to pay wages.

pay·ment (pā'mənt), *n.* 1. a paying. 2. amount paid. 3. reward or punishment. —**Syn.** 1. compensation, remuneration, settlement, discharge.

pay·off (pā'ôf'; -of'), *n.* 1. a paying of wages. 2. time of such payment. 3. returns from an enterprise, specific action, etc. 4. climax (of a story, situation, etc.).

pay roll, 1. list of persons to be paid and the amounts that each one is to receive. 2. the total amount to be paid to them.

payt., payment.

Pb, *Chem.* lead. [< L *plumbum*]

PC, *U.S. Navy.* a fast boat used esp. for anti-submarine patrolling.

pc., *pl.* **pcs.** piece.

pct., p.c., per cent.

Pd, *Chem.* palladium.

pd., paid.

P.D., 1. Police Department. 2. Also, **p.d.** per diem.

pea (pē), *n., pl.* **peas,** *Archaic* or *Brit. Dial.* **pease,** *adj.* —*n.* 1. the round seed in the pod of a plant, used as a vegetable. 2. the plant itself. 3.

seed or plant like a pea. —*adj.* of the size of a pea: *pea coal.* [< *pease,* orig. sing., later taken as a pl.]

peace (pēs), *n.* 1. freedom from war or strife of any kind. 2. public quiet, order, and security. 3. agreement between contending parties to end war: *the Peace of Paris.* 4. freedom from disturbance; quiet; calm: *peace of mind.* 5. hold or keep one's peace, be silent. —*interj.* keep still! stay quiet! [< OF < L *pax*] —**Syn.** *n.* 1. harmony, concord, amity. 3. reconciliation.

peace·a·ble (pēs'ə·bəl), *adj.* 1. liking peace; keeping peace: *peaceable people refrain from quarreling.* 2. peaceful: *a peaceable reign.* —**peace'a·ble·ness,** *n.* —**peace'a·bly,** *adv.* —**Syn.** 1. pacific, amicable, friendly. —**Ant.** 1. contentious, quarrelsome, belligerent.

Peace Corps, an agency of the U.S. government, set up in 1961 to provide people with technical skill to underdeveloped countries.

peace·ful (pēs'fəl), *adj.* 1. full of peace; quiet; calm. 2. liking peace; keeping peace. 3. of or having to do with peace. —**peace'ful·ly,** *adv.* —**peace'ful·ness,** *n.* —**Syn.** 1. tranquil, serene, placid. 2. peaceable, pacific.

peace·mak·er (pēs'māk'ər), *n.* person who makes peace. —**peace'mak'ing,** *n., adj.*

peace officer, policeman, sheriff, or constable.

peace pipe, *Am.* pipe smoked by American Indians as a token or pledge of peace.

peace·time (pēs'tīm'), *n.* a time of peace. —*adj.* of or pertaining to such a time.

peach[1] (pēch), *n.* 1. a juicy, nearly round fruit having a rough stone or pit. 2. tree that it grows on. 3. fruit or tree like a peach. 4. a yellowish pink. —*adj.* yellowish-pink. [< OF, ult. < L *Persicum (malum)* Persian apple < Gk.]

peach[2] (pēch), *v. Slang.* turn informer. [var. of *appeach* < AF var. of OF *empechier* hinder. See IMPEACH.]

peach·y (pēch'i), *adj.,* **peach·i·er, peach·i·est.** like a peach. —**peach'i·ness,** *n.*

pea·cock (pē'kok'), *n., pl.* -**cocks** or (*esp. collectively*) -**cock.** bird with beautiful green, blue, and gold feathers. The tail feathers have spots like eyes on them and can be spread out and held upright like a fan. [ult. < OE *pēa* (< L *pavo* peafowl) + *cock*[1]]

pea·fowl (pē'foul'), *n.* peacock or peahen.

pea·hen (pē'hen'), *n.* female of the peacock.

pea jacket, *Am.* a short coat of thick woolen cloth worn by sailors.

peak (pēk), *n.* 1. the pointed top of a mountain or hill. 2. mountain that stands alone. 3. the highest point. 4. any pointed end or top: *the peak of a beard, the peak of a roof.* 5. the front part or the brim of a cap, which stands out. —*v.* raise straight up; tilt up. [var. of *pick*[2]] —**Syn.** *n.* 3. summit, pinnacle, apex.

peaked[1] (pēkt; pēk'id), *adj.* having a peak; pointed.

peak·ed[2] (pēk'id), *adj.* thin. [< *peak,* v., look sick]

peal (pēl), *n.* 1. a loud, long sound: *a peal of thunder.* 2. the loud ringing of bells. 3. set of bells; chimes. —*v.* sound out in a peal; ring. [ME *pele*] —**Syn.** *v.* resound, reverberate, boom.

pe·an (pē'ən), *n.* paean.

pea·nut (pē'nut'), *n. Am.* 1. plant of the same family as the pea, whose pods ripen underground and contain large seeds which are used as nuts when roasted. 2. one of these pods containing seeds. 3. one of these seeds.

peanut butter, *Am.* food made of peanuts ground until soft and smooth.

pear (pãr), *n.* 1. a sweet, juicy fruit rounded at one end and smaller toward the stem end. 2. tree that it grows on. 3. fruit or plant like a pear. [< LL *pira* < L *pirum*] —**pear'-shaped',** *adj.*

pearl (pėrl), *n.* 1. a white or nearly white gem that has a soft shine like satin, formed inside the shell of a kind of oyster, or in other similar shellfish. 2. thing that looks like a pearl, such as

āge, cãre, fär; ēqual, tėrm; īce; ōpen, ôrder; pút, rüle, ūse; tʜ, then; ə=a in about.

a dewdrop or a tear. **3.** a very fine one of its kind. **4.** a very pale, clear, bluish gray. **5.** size of type; 5 point. This line is in pearl. —*adj.* **1.** very pale, clear bluish-gray. **2.** formed into small, round pieces: *pearl tapioca.* —*v.* hunt or dive for pearls. [< OF *perle;* ? akin to L *perna,* a bivalve] —**pearl′er,** *n.* —**pearl′y,** *adj.* —**pearl′i·ness,** *n.*

pearl gray, a soft, pale, bluish gray.

Pearl Harbor, harbor near Honolulu, on the S coast of Oahu island in the Hawaiian Islands; the U.S. naval base that was attacked treacherously by the Japanese on Dec. 7, 1941.

peart (pirt; pyert), *adj. Dial.* **1.** lively. **2.** clever. [var. of *pert*] —**peart′ly,** *adv.*

Pea·ry (pir′i), *n.* Robert Edwin, 1856–1920, American naval officer and arctic explorer, discoverer of the North Pole in 1909.

peas·ant (pez′ənt), *n.* farmer of the working class in Europe. [< AF var. of OF *paysant* < *pays* country, ult. < L *pagus* district]

peas·ant·ry (pez′ənt·ri), *n.* peasants.

pease (pēz), *n. Archaic or Brit. Dial.* pl. of pea. [< LL *pisa* < L *pisum* < Gk. *pison*]

pease·cod, peas·cod (pēz′kod′), *n.* pod of a pea.

peat (pēt), *n.* kind of turf, used as fuel after being dried. Peat is made of partly rotted moss and plants. —**peat′y,** *adj.*

pea·vey, pea·vy (pē′vi), *n., pl.* -veys; -vies. a strong stick that is tipped with an iron or steel point and has a hinged hook near the end. Lumbermen use peaveys in managing logs. [after J. *Peavey,* the inventor]

peb·ble (peb′əl), *n., v.,* -bled, -bling. —*n.* a small stone, usually worn and rounded by being rolled about by water. —*v.* prepare (leather) so that it has a grained surface. [OE *pæbbel* (in place names)] —**peb′bled, peb′bly,** *adj.*

pe·can (pi·kän′; -kan′; pē′kan), *n. Am.* **1.** an olive-shaped nut with a smooth, thin shell, that grows on a kind of hickory tree common in the S United States. **2.** tree that it grows on. [< Algonquian *pakan* hard-shelled nut]

pec·ca·dil·lo (pek′ə·dil′ō), *n., pl.* -loes, -los. a slight sin or fault. [< Sp. *pecadillo,* dim. of *pecado* sin < L *peccatum*]

pec·ca·ry (pek′ə·ri), *n., pl.* -ries or (*esp. collectively*) -ry. kind of wild pig found in South America and as far N as Texas. [< Carib *pakira*]

peck[1] (pek), *n.* **1.** unit of dry measure, eight quarts or one fourth of a bushel: *a peck of potatoes.* **2.** container holding just a peck, to measure with. **3.** a great deal: *a peck of trouble.* [ME *pec*]

peck[2] (pek), *v.* **1.** strike and pick with the beak, esp. with pounding movements. **2.** make by striking with the beak: *woodpeckers peck holes in trees.* **3.** aim with a beak; make a pecking motion. **4.** strike at and pick up with the beak: *a hen pecks corn.* **5.** *Colloq.* eat only a little, bit by bit. **6.** find fault. —*n.* **1.** stroke made with the beak. **2.** hole or mark made by pecking. **3.** *Colloq.* stiff, unwilling kiss. [akin to *pick*[1]] —**peck′er,** *n.*

pec·tin (pek′tin), *n.* substance that occurs in ripe fruits and makes fruit jelly stiff. [< Gk. *pēktos* congealing, curdling < *pegnynai* make stiff]

pec·to·ral (pek′tə·rəl), *adj.* of, in, or on the breast or chest. [< L, < *pectus* chest] —**pec′to·ral·ly,** *adv.*

pec·u·late (pek′yə·lāt), *v.,* -lat·ed, -lat·ing. steal (money or goods entrusted to one); embezzle. [< L *peculatus* having embezzled, ult. < *pecu* money, cattle] —**pec′u·la′tion,** *n.* —**pec′u·la′tor,** *n.*

pe·cu·liar (pi·kūl′yər), *adj.* **1.** strange; odd; unusual. **2.** belonging to one person or thing and not to another; special: *this book has a peculiar value.* [< L *peculiaris* of one's own < *peculium* property. See PECULATE.] —**pe·cul′iar·ly,** *adv.* —**Syn.** **1.** eccentric, queer, singular. **2.** particular, individual.

pe·cu·li·ar·i·ty (pi·kū′li·ar′ə·ti), *n., pl.* -ties. **1.** a being peculiar; strangeness; oddness; unusualness. **2.** thing or feature that is strange or odd. **3.** a peculiar or characteristic quality. **4.** a distinguishing quality or feature. —**Syn.** **1.** eccentricity. **3.** idiosyncrasy.

pe·cu·ni·ar·y (pi·kū′ni·er′i), *adj.* of or pertaining to money; in the form of money. [< L, < *pecunia* money. See PECULATE.] —**pe·cu′ni·ar′i·ly,** *adv.*

ped·a·gog·ic (ped′ə·goj′ik; -gō′jik), **ped·a·gog·i·cal** (-ə·kəl), *adj.* of teachers or teaching; of pedagogy. —**ped′a·gog′i·cal·ly,** *adv.*

ped·a·gogue, ped·a·gog (ped′ə·gog; -gōg), *n.* **1.** teacher. **2.** a narrow-minded teacher. [< OF < L < Gk. *paidagogos* < *pais* boy + *agogos* leader]

ped·a·go·gy (ped′ə·gō′ji; -goj′i), *n.* **1.** teaching. **2.** science or art of teaching.

ped·al (*n., v.* ped′əl; *adj.* ped′əl, pē′dəl), *n., v.,* -aled, -al·ing; *esp. Brit.* -alled, -al·ling, *adj.* —*n.* lever worked by the foot; the part on which the foot is placed to move any kind of machinery. Organs and pianos have pedals for changing the tone. —*v.* **1.** work or use the pedals of; move by pedals: *he pedaled his bicycle up the hill.* **2.** work pedals. —*adj.* of or having to do with the foot or feet. [< F < Ital. < L *pedale* (thing) of the foot < *pes* foot] —**ped′al·ist,** *n.*

ped·ant (ped′ənt), *n.* **1.** person who displays his knowledge in an unnecessary or tiresome way. **2.** a dull, narrow-minded teacher or scholar. [< Ital. *pedante,* ult. < Gk. *paideuein* educate] —**pe·dan·tic** (pi·dan′tik), *adj.* —**pe·dan′ti·cal·ly,** *adv.* —**pe·dan′ti·cism,** *n.*

ped·ant·ry (ped′ənt·ri), *n., pl.* -ries. **1.** an unnecessary or tiresome display of knowledge. **2.** overemphasis on book learning.

ped·dle (ped′əl), *v.,* -dled, -dling. **1.** carry from place to place and sell. **2.** sell or deal out in small quantities: *peddle candy.* **3.** travel about with things to sell. —**ped′dler, ped′ler** (ped′lər), *n.*

ped·er·as·ty (ped′ər·as′ti; pē′dər-), *n.* sexual intercourse of a male with a male. [< NL < Gk. *paiderastia* < *pais* boy + *eran* to love] —**ped′er·ast,** *n.*

ped·es·tal (ped′is·təl), *n., v.,* -taled, -tal·ing; *esp. Brit.* -talled, -tal·ling. —*n.* **1.** base on which a column or a statue stands. **2.** base of a tall vase, lamp, etc. **3.** base; support; foundation. —*v.* place on a pedestal. [< F < Ital. *piedestallo* < *pie* foot (< L *pes*) + *di* of + *stallo* STALL[1] (< Gmc.)]

pe·des·tri·an (pə·des′tri·ən), *n.* person who goes on foot; walker. —*adj.* **1.** going on foot; walking. **2.** without imagination; dull; slow. [< L *pedester* on foot < *pes* foot] —**pe·des′tri·an·ism,** *n.*

pe·di·a·tri·cian (pē′di·ə·trish′ən; ped′i-), **pe·di·a·trist** (pē′di·at′rist, ped′i-), *n.* doctor who specializes in pediatrics.

pe·di·at·rics (pē′di·at′riks; ped′i-), *n.* branch of medicine dealing with children's diseases and the care of babies and children. Also, *paediatrics.* [pl. of *pediatric* < Gk. *pais* child + *iatreia* medical treatment] —**pe′di·at′ric,** *adj.*

ped·i·cel (ped′ə·səl), *n.* a small stalk or stalklike part. [< NL *pedicellus,* ult. < L *pes* foot] —**ped·i·cel·lar** (ped′ə·sel′ər), *adj.*

ped·i·gree (ped′ə·grē), *n.* **1.** list of ancestors; family tree. **2.** ancestry; line of descent. [appar. < F *pied de grue* foot of a crane; from appearance of 3-branched mark used in genealogies] —**ped′i·greed,** *adj.*

ped·i·ment (ped′ə·mənt), *n.* the low triangular part on the front of buildings in the Greek style. —**ped·i·men·tal** (ped′ə·men′təl), *adj.*

pe·dom·e·ter (pi·dom′ə·tər), *n.* instrument for recording the number of steps taken and thus measuring the distance traveled. [< F, < *pedo-* (< L *pes* foot) + *-metre* -METER]

pe·dun·cle (pi·dung′kəl), *n. Bot., Zool.* stalk; stem; stalklike part. See the picture under pedicel. [< NL *pedunculus,* dim. of L *pes* foot] —**pe·dun′cled,** *adj.* —**pe·dun·cu·lar** (pi·dung′kyə·lər), *adj.*

peek (pēk), *v.* look quickly and slyly; peep. —*n.* a quick, sly look. [ME *piken*]

peel (pēl), *n.* Also, *peel′ing.* rind or outer covering of fruit, etc. —*v.* **1.** strip skin, rind, or bark from. 2. strip: *the Indians peeled the bark from trees to make canoes.* 3. come off: *when I was sunburnt, my skin peeled.* [var. of *pill,* appar. < L *pilare* to strip of hair] —peel′er, *n.* —Syn. *n.* skin, bark, husk, pod, shell. -*v.* 1. pare, flay.

Peel (pēl), *n.* Sir Robert, 1788–1850, British statesman, prime minister 1834–35 and 1841–46.

peep[1] (pēp), *v.* 1. look through a small or narrow hole or crack. 2. look when no one knows it. 3. look out, as if peeping; come partly out. 4. cause to stick out a little; show slightly. —*n.* 1. a look through a hole or crack; little look. 2. a secret look. 3. the first looking or coming out: *at the peep of day.* [? var. of *peek*] —peep′er, *n.* —Syn. *v.* 1. peer, peek.

peep[2] (pēp), *n.* a short, sharp sound made by a young bird. —*v.* 1. make such a sound. 2. speak in a thin, weak voice. [imit.] —peep′er, *n.*

peep·hole (pēp′hōl′), *n.* hole through which one may peep.

peer[1] (pir), *n.* 1. person of the same rank, ability, etc., as another; equal. 2. man who has a title; man who is high and great by birth or rank. A duke, marquis, earl, count, viscount, or baron is a peer. [< OF < L *par* equal] —Syn. 1. match.

peer[2] (pir), *v.* 1. look closely to see clearly, as a near-sighted person does: *she peered at the tag to read the price.* 2. come out slightly; peep out: *the sun was peering from behind a cloud.* [? var. of *appear*]

peer·age (pir′ij), *n.* 1. rank or dignity of a peer. 2. peers of a country. 3. book giving a list of the peers of a country.

peer·ess (pir′is), *n.* 1. wife or widow of a peer. 2. woman having the rank of peer in her own right.

peer·less (pir′lis), *adj.* without an equal; matchless: *a peerless leader.* —peer′less·ly, *adv.* —peer′less·ness, *n.* —Syn. unequaled, unsurpassed.

peeve (pēv), *v.,* peeved, peev·ing, *n. Colloq.* —*v.* make, become, or be peevish. —*n.* an annoyance.

pee·vish (pē′vish), *adj.* cross; fretful; complaining. [ME *pevysh*] —pee′vish·ly, *adv.* —pee′vish·ness, *n.* —Syn. petulant, pettish, irritable.

peg (peg), *n., v.,* pegged, peg·ging. —*n.* 1. pin or small bolt of wood, metal, etc., used to fasten parts together; to hang things on; to stop a hole, to make fast a rope or string, to mark the score in a game, etc. 2. a certain amount; degree. 3. take down a peg, lower the pride of; humble. 4. *Brit.* a small drink of alcoholic liquor. 5. *Colloq.* leg; wooden leg. —*v.* 1. fasten or hold with or as if with pegs. 2. work hard. 3. *Colloq.* aim; throw. [appar. < MDu. *pegge*] —peg′ger, *n.*

Peg·a·sus (peg′ə·səs), *n.* 1. *Gk. Myth.* horse with wings, the steed of the Muses. 2. group of stars in the northern sky.

peg top, 1. a wooden top spinning on a metal peg. 2. peg tops, trousers wide at the hips and gradually narrowing to the ankles. —peg′-top′, *adj.*

peign·oir (pān·wär′; pān′wär), *n.* a woman's dressing sack or gown. [< F, < *peigner* < L *pectinare* to comb < *pecten* a comb]

Pei·ping (pā′ping′; bā′-), *n.* Peking.

pe·jor·a·tive (pi·jôr′ə·tiv; -jor′-; pē′jə·rā′tiv; pej′-), *adj.* tending to make worse; disparaging. —*n.* a pejorative form or word. *Poetaster* is a pejorative of *poet.* [< LL, < *pejor* worse]

Pe·king (pē′king′), *n.* city in NE China, the capital of China for more than five centuries. From 1928 to 1949 called Peiping (pā′ping′; bā′-).

Pe·king·ese (pē′king-ēz′; -ēs′), **Pe·kin·ese** (-kən·ēz′; -ēs′), *n., pl.* -ese, *adj.* —*n.* 1. a small dog with long hair and

Pekingese

a pug nose. 2. native or inhabitant of Peking. —*adj.* of or having to do with Peking or its people.

pe·koe (pē′kō), *n.* kind of black tea. [< Chinese *pek-ho* white down; because the leaves are picked young with the "down" still on them]

pelf (pelf), *n.* money or riches, thought of as bad or degrading. [< OF *pelfre* spoils]

pel·i·can (pel′ə·kən), *n.* a large fish-eating water bird with a huge bill and a pouch for storing food. [< LL < Gk. *pelekan,* ? ult. < *pelekys* ax]

Pe·li·on (pē′li·ən), *n.* Mount, mountain in NE Greece. See Ossa, Mount.

pe·lisse (pə·lēs′), *n.* 1. coat lined or trimmed with fur. 2. woman's long cloak. [< F, ult. < LL *pelliceus* of fur < *pellis* skin]

pel·la·gra (pə·lag′rə; -lā′grə), *n.* disease marked by eruption on the skin, a nervous condition, and sometimes insanity, caused by improper food. [< Ital.] —pel·lag′rous, *adj.*

pel·let (pel′it), *n.* 1. a little ball of mud, paper, food, medicine, etc.; pill. 2. bullet. —*v.* hit with pellets. [< OF *pelote* < L *pila* ball]

pell-mell, pell·mell (pel′mel′), *adv.* 1. in a rushing, tumbling mass or crowd. 2. in headlong haste. —*adj.* headlong; tumultuous. —*n.* violent disorder or confusion. [< F *pêle-mêle,* latter element appar. < *mêler* mix]

pel·lu·cid (pə·lü′sid), *adj.* 1. transparent; clear: *a pellucid stream.* 2. clearly expressed; easy to understand: *pellucid language.* [< L *pellucidus,* ult. < *per-* through + *lucere* to shine] —pel·lu·cid·i·ty (pel′ü·sid′ə·ti), pel·lu′cid·ness, *n.* —pel·lu′cid·ly, *adv.*

Pel·o·pon·ne·sus, Pel·o·pon·ne·sos (pel′ə·pə·nē′səs), *n.* peninsula that constitutes the S part of Greece. —**Pel·o·pon·ne·sian** (pel′ə·pə·nē′shən; -zhən), *adj., n.*

pelt[1] (pelt), *v.* 1. throw things at; attack; assail: *pelt a dog with stones.* 2. beat heavily: *the rain came pelting down.* 3. throw: *the clouds pelted rain upon us.* 4. hurry. —*n.* 1. a pelting. 2. speed: *at full pelt.* —pelt′er, *n.*

pelt[2] (pelt), *n.* 1. skin of a sheep, goat, or small fur-bearing animal, before it is tanned. 2. skin. [prob. < *peltry*] —Syn. 1. hide, coat, fur.

pelt·ry (pel′tri), *n., pl.* -ries. 1. pelts; skins; furs. 2. a pelt. [< AF var. of OF *peleterie* < *pel* skin < L *pellis*]

pel·vis (pel′vis), *n., pl.* -ves (-vēz). 1. *Anat.* the basin-shaped cavity formed by the hipbones and the end of the backbone. 2. *Zool.* a corresponding cavity of any vertebrate. 3. *Anat., Zool.* bones forming this cavity. [< L, basin] —pel′vic, *adj.*

pem·mi·can (pem′ə·kən), *n. Am.* dried meat pounded into a paste with melted fat. [< Cree (N Am. Ind.) *pimikan* < *pimikew* he makes grease]

pen[1] (pen), *n., v.,* penned, pen·ning. —*n.* 1. a small metal instrument with a split point used for writing in ink. 2. tool to use in writing with ink; pen and holder together. 3. style of writing; writing. —*v.* write. [< OF < L *penna* feather]

pen[2] (pen), *n., v.,* penned or pent, pen·ning. —*n.* a small, closed yard for cows, sheep, pigs, chickens, etc. —*v.* 1. shut in a pen. 2. shut in; confine closely. [OE *penn*]

pen. peninsula.

pe·nal (pē′nəl), *adj.* 1. of, having to do with, or given as punishment: *penal laws, penal labor.* 2. liable to be punished: *robbery is a penal offense.* [< L, < *poena* punishment < Gk. *poine* fine] —pe′nal·ly, *adv.*

pe·nal·ize (pē′nəl·īz; pen′əl-), *v.,* -ized, -iz·ing. 1. declare punishable by law or by rule; set a penalty for: *fouls are penalized in most games.* 2. inflict a penalty on; punish: *our team was penalized five yards.* —pe′nal·i·za′tion, *n.*

pen·al·ty (pen′əl·ti), *n., pl.* -ties. 1. punishment: *the penalty for speeding is a fine of ten dollars.* 2. disadvantage imposed on a side or player for breaking rules. 3. disadvantage attached to some act or condition: *the penalties of old age.* 4. handicap.

pen·ance (pen′əns), *n.* 1. punishment borne to show sorrow for sin, to make up for a wrong done, and to obtain pardon. 2. sacrament of the Roman Catholic Church that includes contrition, confession, satisfaction, and absolution. [< OF < L *paenitentia* PENITENCE. Doublet of PENITENCE.]

Pe·nang (pi·nang′), *n.* settlement in the Federation of Malaya.

pe·na·tes, Pe·na·tes (pə·nā′tēz), *n.pl. Rom. Myth.* gods of the household, worshiped in ancient Rome. [< L, < *penus* interior of the house]

pence (pens), *n. Brit.* pl. of **penny.**

pen·chant (pen′chənt), *n.* a strong taste or liking; inclination: *a penchant for taking long walks.* [< F, ppr. of *pencher* to incline, ult. < L *pendere* hang]

pen·cil (pen′səl), *n., v.,* –ciled, –cil·ing; *esp. Brit.* –cilled, –cil·ling. —*n.* 1. a pointed tool to write or draw with. 2. object of like shape. 3. stick of coloring matter. 4. an artist's paintbrush. 5. set of lines, light rays, or the like, coming to a point or extending in different directions from a point. —*v.* 1. use a pencil on. 2. mark or write with a pencil. 3. draw or execute with a pencil. [< OF, ult. < L *penicillum,* double dim. of *penis* tail] —**pen′cil·er,** *esp. Brit.* **pen′cil·ler,** *n.* —**pen′cil·ing,** *esp. Brit.* **pen′cil·ling,** *n.*

pend (pend), *v.* remain undecided. [< L *pendere* hang]

pend·ant (pen′dənt), *n.* 1. a hanging ornament, such as a locket. 2. ornament hanging down from ceiling or roof. —*adj.* pendent.

pend·ent (pen′dənt), *adj.* 1. hanging: *the pendent branches of willow.* 2. overhanging. 3. pending. —*n.* pendant. —**pend′ent·ly,** *adv.* —**Syn.** *adj.* 1. suspended. 2. projecting.

pend·ing (pen′ding), *adj.* waiting to be decided or settled: *while the agreement was pending.* —*prep.* 1. while waiting for; until: *pending his return, let us get everything ready.* 2. during: *pending the investigation.* —**Syn.** *adj.* unsettled, undecided, impending.

pen·drag·on (pen·drag′ən), *n.* chief leader, title of ancient British chiefs. [< Welsh, < *pen* chief + *dragon* war leader, DRAGON] —**pen·drag′on·ship,** *n.*

pen·du·lous (pen′jə·ləs), *adj.* 1. hanging loosely: *the oriole builds a pendulous nest.* 2. swinging. [< L, < *pendere* hang] —**pen′du·lous·ly,** *adv.* —**pen′du·lous·ness,** *n.*

pen·du·lum (pen′jə·ləm; –dyə·ləm), *n.* weight so hung from a fixed point that it is free to swing to and fro. The movement of the works of a tall clock is often timed by a pendulum. [< NL, neut., < L *pendulus* PENDULOUS]

Pendulum. Dotted lines show motion.

Pe·nel·o·pe (pə·nel′ə·pē), *n. Gk. Legend.* the faithful wife of Odysseus who waited twenty years for his return.

pen·e·tra·ble (pen′ə·trə·bəl), *adj.* that can be penetrated. —**pen′e·tra·bil′i·ty, pen′e·tra·ble·ness,** *n.* —**pen′e·tra·bly,** *adv.*

pen·e·trate (pen′ə·trāt), *v.,* –trat·ed, –trating. 1. get into or through: *a bullet can penetrate a wall, or two inches into a wall.* 2. pierce through: *our eyes could not penetrate the darkness.* 3. make a way: *even where the trees were thickest, the sunshine penetrated.* 4. soak through; spread through: *the odor penetrated the whole house.* 5. see into; understand: *I could not penetrate the mystery.* 6. affect or impress very much. [< L *penetratus,* ult. < *penitus* inmost] —**pen′e·tra′tive,** *adj.* —**pen′e·tra′tive·ly,** *adv.* —**Syn.** 2. perforate, puncture. 4. permeate, pervade. 5. discern, comprehend.

pen·e·trat·ing (pen′ə·trāt′ing), *adj.* 1. sharp; piercing. 2. having an acute mind; understanding thoroughly. —**pen′e·trat′ing·ly,** *adv.*

pen·e·tra·tion (pen′ə·trā′shən), *n.* 1. act or power of penetrating. 2. act of entering a country and gaining influence there. 3. sharpness of intellect; insight. —**Syn.** 3. acumen, shrewdness, discernment.

pen·guin (pen′gwin; peng′–), *n.* a sea bird with flippers for diving and swimming in place of wings for flying.

pen·i·cil·lin (pen′ə·sil′in), *n.* a very powerful antibiotic made from a penicillium mold. [< *penicillium*]

pen·i·cil·li·um (pen′ə·sil′i·əm), *n., pl.* –cil·li·ums, –cil·li·a (–sil′i·ə). any of a certain genus of fungi. The mold on cheese is a penicillium. [< L *penicillus* small brush or tail. See PENCIL.]

pen·in·su·la (pən·in′sə·lə; –syə–), *n.* piece of land almost surrounded by water, or extending far out into the water. Florida is a peninsula. [< L, < *paene* almost + *insula* island] —**pen·in′su·lar,** *adj.* —**pen·in·su·lar·i·ty** (pən·in′sə·lar′ə·ti; –syə–), *n.*

pe·nis (pē′nis), *n., pl.* –nis·es (–nis·iz), –nes (–nēz). the male organ of copulation. [< L, tail]

pen·i·tence (pen′ə·təns), *n.* sorrow for sinning or doing wrong; repentance. [< OF < L *paenitentia* < *paenitere* repent. Doublet of PENANCE.]

pen·i·tent (pen′ə·tənt), *adj.* sorry for sinning or doing wrong; repenting. —*n.* 1. person who is sorry for sin or wrongdoing. 2. person who confesses and does penance for his sins under the direction of the church. —**pen′i·tent·ly,** *adv.* —**Syn.** *adj.* repentant, contrite, remorseful.

pen·i·ten·tial (pen′ə·ten′shəl), *adj.* 1. of, showing, or pertaining to penitence: *the penitential psalms express remorse for sin.* 2. of or pertaining to penance. —*n.* 1. a penitent. 2. book of rules about penances. —**pen′i·ten′tial·ly,** *adv.*

pen·i·ten·tia·ry (pen′ə·ten′shə·ri), *n., pl.* –ries, *adj.* —*n.* 1. prison for criminals. 2. *Am.* a state or Federal prison. —*adj.* 1. making one liable to punishment in a prison: *a penitentiary offense.* 2. used for punishment, discipline, and reformation: *penitentiary measures.* 3. of penance; penitential.

pen·knife (pen′nīf′), *n., pl.* –knives. a small pocketknife.

pen·man (pen′mən), *n., pl.* –men. 1. person whose handwriting is good. 2. writer.

pen·man·ship (pen′mən·ship), *n.* writing with pen, pencil, etc.; handwriting.

Penn (pen), *n.* William, 1644–1718, English Quaker who founded Philadelphia.

Penn., Penna., Pennsylvania.

pen name, name used by a writer instead of his real name.

pen·nant (pen′ənt), *n.* flag, usually long and narrow, used on ships in signaling, as a school banner, etc. [blend of *pendant* and *pennon*]

pen·ni·less (pen′i·lis), *adj.* without a cent of money; very poor. —**Syn.** destitute, indigent.

pen·non (pen′ən), *n.* 1. a long, triangular flag, originally carried on the lance of a knight. 2. flag or banner. [< OF *penon,* ult. < L *penna* feather] —**pen′noned,** *adj.*

Penn·syl·va·ni·a (pen′səl·vā′ni·ə; –vān′yə), *n.* an Eastern State of the United States. *Capital:* Harrisburg. *Abbrev.:* Penn., Penna., or Pa. —**Penn′syl·va′ni·an,** *adj., n.*

Pennsylvania Dutch, *Am.* 1. the descendants of 17th and 18th century immigrants to SE Pennsylvania from S Germany and Switzerland. 2. dialect of German with English intermixed, spoken by Pennsylvania Germans. ➤ As used in this expression, "Dutch" is a rendering of "Deutsch," meaning German. The expression "Pennsylvania Dutch" has become securely established but "Pennsylvania German" is the more accurate expression, "Dutch" being in this case erroneously associated with Holland.

Pennsylvania German, *Am.* 1. descendant of immigrants from S Germany and Switzerland who settled in SE Pennsylvania in the 17th and 18th centuries. 2. Pennsylvania Dutch (def. 2).

pen·ny (pen′i), *n., pl.* **pen·nies,** *esp. Brit.* (collectively for 2) **pence.** 1. cent; copper coin of the U.S. and Canada. 100 pennies = 1 dollar. 2. an English bronze coin equal to one twelfth of a shilling, or about one cent (1950). 3. sum of money. 4. a pretty penny, *Colloq.* a large sum of money. [OE *pending* < *Penda*, king of Mercia]

pen·ny·roy·al (pen'i·roi'əl), *n.* 1. *Am.* plant of the mint family. 2. a fragrant oil made from it.

pen·ny·weight (pen'i·wāt'), *n.* 24 grains or ½₀ of an ounce in troy weight.

pen·ny·wise (pen'i·wīz'), *adj.* saving in regard to small sums.

pen·ny·worth (pen'i·werth'), *n.* 1. as much as can be bought for a penny. 2. a small amount. 3. bargain.

pe·nol·o·gy (pē·nol'ə·ji), *n.* science of punishment of crime and management of prisons. [< Gk. *poine* fine + -LOGY] —**pe·no·log·i·cal** (pē'nə·loj'ə·kəl), *adj.* —**pe·nol'o·gist,** *n.*

pen·sile (pen'səl), *adj.* 1. hanging; pendent. 2. building a hanging nest. [< L *pensilis* < *pendere* hang]

pen·sion[1] (pen'shən), *n.* a regular payment to a person which is not wages. Pensions are often paid because of long service, special merit, injuries received, etc. —*v.* 1. give a pension to. 2. pension off, retire from service with a pension. [< OF < L *pensio* < *pendere* weigh, pay] —**pen'sion·a·ble,** *adj.* —**pen·sion·ar·y** (pen'shən·er'i), *adj., n.*

pen·sion[2] (päN·syôN'), *n.* French. boarding house.

pen·sion·er (pen'shən·ər), *n.* 1. person who receives a pension. 2. a hireling; dependent.

pen·sive (pen'siv), *adj.* 1. thoughtful in a serious or sad way. 2. melancholy. [< OF, < *penser* think < L *pensare* weigh, ponder < *pendere* weigh] —**pen'sive·ly,** *adv.* —**pen'sive·ness,** *n.* —Syn. 1. meditative, reflective. 2. sober, grave, sad.

pent (pent), *adj.* closely confined; penned; shut: *pent in the house all winter.* —*v.* pt. and pp. of pen[2].

pen·ta·gon (pen'tə·gon), *n.* 1. figure having five sides and five angles. 2. the Pentagon, United States Army headquarters building at Arlington, Virginia. [< LL < Gk., < *pente* five + *gonia* angle] —**pen·tag·o·nal** (pen·tag'ə·nəl), *adj.* —**pen·tag'o·nal·ly,** *adv.*

pen·tam·e·ter (pen·tam'ə·tər), *n.* poetry having five feet or measures in each line. —*adj.* consisting of five feet or measures. [< L < Gk., < *pente* five + *metron* meter]

Pen·ta·teuch (pen'tə·tūk; -tūk), *n.* the first five books of the Old Testament; Genesis, Exodus, Leviticus, Numbers, and Deuteronomy. [< L < Gk., < *pente* five + *teuchos* vessel, book] —**Pen'ta·teu'chal,** *adj.*

pen·tath·lon (pen·tath'lon), *n.* an athletic contest consisting of five different events. The person having the highest total score wins. [< Gk., < *pente* five + *athlon* contest]

pen·ta·va·lent (pen'tə·vā'lənt; pen·tav'ə·), *Chem.* —*adj.* having a valence of five. —*n.* atom or group of atoms have a valence of five.

Pen·te·cost (pen'tə·kôst; -kost), *n.* 1. the seventh Sunday after Easter, a Christian festival in memory of the descent of the Holy Ghost upon the Apostles. Acts 2. Also called Whitsunday. 2. a Jewish religious holiday, observed about seven weeks after the Passover, celebrating the harvest and also the giving of the law to Moses. [< L < Gk. *pentekoste* (*hemera*) fiftieth (day)] —**Pen'te·cos'tal,** pen'te·cos'tal, *adj.*

pent·house (pent'hous'), *n.* *Am.* apartment or house built on the top of a building. [ME *pentis* < OF *apentis*, ult. < L *appendere* APPEND]

pent-up (pent'up'), *adj.* closely confined.

pe·nult (pē'nult; pi·nult'), *n.* the next to the last syllable in a word. [< L *paenultima* (*syllaba*) next-to-last (syllable) < *paene* almost + *ultimus* last] —**pe·nul·ti·mate** (pi·nul'tə·mit), *adj., n.*

pe·num·bra (pi·num'brə), *n., pl.* **-brae** (-brē), **-bras.** 1. the partial shadow outside of the complete shadow formed by the sun, moon, etc., during an eclipse. 2. the grayish outer part of a sunspot. [< NL, < L *paene* almost + *umbra* shadow] —**pe·num'bral,** *adj.*

pe·nu·ri·ous (pi·nur'i·əs; -nyūr'-), *adj.* mean about spending or giving money; stingy. —**pe·nu'ri·ous·ly,** *adv.* —**pe·nu'ri·ous·ness,** *n.*

pen·u·ry (pen'yə·ri), *n.* very great poverty. [< L *penuria*]

pe·on (pē'on; -ən), *n.* 1. in Spanish America, a person doing work that requires little skill. 2. in SW United States and Mexico, a worker held for service to work off a debt. [< Sp. < LL *pedo* foot soldier. Doublet of PAWN[2].]

pe·on·age (pē'ən·ij), *n.* 1. condition or service of a peon. 2. *Am.* practice of holding persons to work off debts.

pe·o·ny (pē'ə·ni), *n., pl.* **-nies.** 1. a perennial garden plant with large, showy flowers. 2. its flower. [ult. < Gk. *paionia* < *Paion* physician of the gods; from plant's use in medicine]

peo·ple (pē'pəl), *n., pl.* **-ple** or (*for def.* 2) **-ples,** *v.,* **-pled, -pling.** —*n.* 1. men, women, and children; persons. 2. race; nation. 3. body of citizens of a state; the public. 4. persons of a place, class, or group. 5. the common people; lower classes. 6. persons in relation to a superior: *a king rules over his people.* 7. family; relatives. —*v.* fill with people; populate; stock with animals, etc.: *Europe very largely peopled America.* [< AF < L *populus*] —**peo'pler,** *n.* —Syn. *n.* 2. folk, tribe. 3. subjects, inhabitants, population.

people's front, popular front.

Pe·o·ri·a (pi·ô'ri·ə; -ō'-), *n.* city in C Illinois.

pep (pep), *n., v.,* **pepped, pepping.** *Am., Slang.* —*n.* spirit; energy; vim. —*v.* pep up, instill spirit or energy in. [short for *pepper*]

pep·lum (pep'ləm), *n., pl.* **-lums, -la** (-lə). 1. a short skirt attached about the waist; overskirt. 2. a full garment worn by ancient Greek women. [< L < Gk. *peplos*]

pep·per (pep'ər), *n.* 1. a seasoning with a hot taste, used for soups, meats, vegetables, etc. 2. plant bearing berries from which pepper is made. 3. any of several hollow, green or red vegetables with many seeds. They are eaten raw or cooked or pickled. 4. capsicum. —*v.* 1. season or sprinkle with pepper. 2. sprinkle thickly: *peppered with freckles.* 3. hit with small objects sent thick and fast: *we peppered the enemy's lines with our shot.* [< L < Gk. *piperi*]

pep·per·corn (pep'ər·kôrn'), *n.* a dried berry ground up to make black pepper.

pep·per·grass (pep'ər·gras'; -gräs'), *n.* a common weed with a peppery taste.

pep·per·mint (pep'ər·mint), *n.* 1. herb grown for its oil, used in medicine and in candy. 2. this oil. 3. candy flavored with peppermint oil.

pep·per·y (pep'ər·i), *adj.* 1. full of pepper; like pepper. 2. hot; sharp. 3. having a hot temper; easily made angry. —**pep'per·i·ness,** *n.*

pep·py (pep'i), *adj.,* **-pi·er, -pi·est.** *Am., Slang.* full of pep; energetic; lively; vigorous. —**pep'pi·ly,** *adv.* —**pep'pi·ness,** *n.*

pep·sin (pep'sin), *n.* 1. enzyme that helps to digest meat, eggs, cheese, and other proteins. 2. medicine to help digestion, containing it. [< Gk. *pepsis* digestion]

pep·tic (pep'tik), *adj.* 1. promoting digestion; digestive. 2. able to digest. 3. of or pertaining to pepsin. —*n.* substance promoting digestion. [< L < Gk., < *peptos* cooked]

pep·tone (pep'tōn), *n.* any of a class of diffusible and soluble substances into which meat, eggs, cheese, and other proteins are changed by pepsin or trypsin. —**pep·ton·ic** (pep·ton'ik), *adj.*

Pep·ys (pēps; peps; pep'is), *n.* Samuel, 1633-1703, English writer of a famous diary.

āge, cāre, fär; ēqual, tėrm; īce; ōpen, ôrder; pùt, rüle, ūse; th, then; ə=a in about.

Pe·quot (pē'kwot), *n. Am.* member of a tribe of American Indians in S New England.

per (pėr; pər), *prep.* **1.** for each: *a pound of candy per child, ten cents per pound.* **2.** through; by means of. [< L] ➤ Per (Latin, "through, by, by the, among," etc.) is most appropriate when used in phrases that are still close to their Latin originals—*per capita, per cent*—or in a definitely commercial setting—*$18 per week, $2.60 per yard, forty-four hours per week*—or in certain standardized technical phrases—*revolutions per minute.* Because of its commercial and technical connotation, *per* is less appropriate in general prose, where the English equivalent phrase usually fits more naturally: *$18 a week, 20¢ a quart, four times a year.*

per-, *prefix.* **1.** through; throughout. **2.** thoroughly; utterly; very. **3.** *Chem.* the maximum or a large amount of, as in *peroxide.* [< L]

per·ad·ven·ture (pėr'əd·ven'chər), *adv. Archaic.* perhaps. —*n.* chance; doubt.

per·am·bu·late (pər·am'byə·lāt), *v.,* -**lat·ed,** -**lat·ing.** walk through or about. [< L, < *per-* through + *ambulare* to walk] —**per·am'bu·la'tion,** *n.* —**per·am·bu·la·to·ry** (pər·am'byə·lə·tô'ri; -tō'-), *adj.*

per·am·bu·la·tor (pər·am'byə·lā'tər), *n.* **1.** a small carriage in which a baby is pushed about. **2.** person who perambulates.

per an·num (pər an'əm), per year; yearly; for each year: *a salary of $2500 per annum.*

per·cale (pər·kāl'; -kal'), *n.* a closely woven cotton cloth with a smooth finish. [< F < Pers. *pärgālā*]

per cap·i·ta (pər kap'ə·tə), for each person: *$40 for eight men is $5 per capita.*

per·ceive (pər·sēv'), *v.,* -**ceived,** -**ceiv·ing.** **1.** be aware of through the senses; see, hear, taste, smell, or feel. **2.** take in with the mind; observe. [< OF < L, < *per-* fully + *capere* grasp] —**per·ceiv'a·ble,** *adj.* —**per·ceiv'a·bly,** *adv.* —Syn. **2.** comprehend, apprehend, understand.

per cent, per·cent (pər sent'), *n.* hundredths; parts in each hundred. Five per cent (5%) of 40 is the same as ⁵⁄₁₀₀ × 40. [for LL *per centum*] ➤ Per cent is not followed by a period, and may be written as one word. It is informally used instead of *percentage* or even of *proportion: Only a small percent of the class was* [or *were*—collective agreement] *there.*

per cent., per centum, **1.** by the hundred. **2.** for or in every hundred.

per·cent·age (pər·sen'tij), *n.* **1.** rate or proportion of each hundred; part of each hundred: *what percentage of children were absent?* **2.** part; proportion: *a large percentage of school-books now have pictures.* **3.** allowance, commission, discount, rate of interest, etc., figured by per cent. **4.** *Am., Slang.* advantage or profit.

per·cen·tile (pər·sen'til; -təl; -til), *n.* any value in a series of points on a scale arrived at by dividing a group into a hundred equal parts in order of magnitude.

per·cept (pėr'sept), *n.* **1.** that which is perceived. **2.** understanding that is the result of perceiving.

per·cep·ti·ble (pər·sep'tə·bəl), *adj.* that can be perceived. —**per·cep'ti·bil'i·ty,** *n.* —**per·cep'ti·bly,** *adv.* —Syn. sensible, palpable, discernible, noticeable.

per·cep·tion (pər·sep'shən), *n.* **1.** act of perceiving: *his perception of the change came in a flash.* **2.** power of perceiving: *a keen perception.* **3.** percept. [< L *perceptio < percipere* PERCEIVE] —**per·cep'tion·al,** *adj.* —Syn. **1.** insight, apprehension, discernment, comprehension.

per·cep·tive (pər·sep'tiv), *adj.* **1.** having to do with perception. **2.** having the power of perceiving. —**per·cep'tive·ness,** *n.*

perch¹ (pėrch), *n.* **1.** bar, branch, or anything else on which a bird can come to rest. **2.** a rather high place or position. **3.** measure of length; rod; 5½ yards. **4.** measure of area; square rod; 30¼ square yards. —*v.* **1.** alight and rest; sit. **2.** sit rather high. **3.** place high up. [< OF < L *pertica* pole] —**perch'er,** *n.*

perch² (pėrch), *n., pl.* **perch·es** or (*esp. collec-*

tively) **perch. 1.** kind of small fresh-water fish, used for food. **2.** a similar salt-water fish. [< OF < L < Gk. *perke*]

per·chance (pər·chans'; -chäns'), *adv. Archaic* or *Poetic.* perhaps.

Per·che·ron (pėr'chə·ron; -shə-), *n.* one of a breed of large and strong horses.

per·cip·i·ent (pər·sip'i·ənt), *adj.* **1.** perceiving. **2.** having perception. —*n.* one that perceives. [< L *percipiens.* See PERCEIVE.] —**per·cip'i·ence,** *n.*

per·co·late (pėr'kə·lāt), *v.,* -**lat·ed,** -**lat·ing.** **1.** drip or drain through small holes or spaces. **2.** filter through; permeate. [< L, ult. < *per-* through + *colum* strainer] —**per'co·la'tion,** *n.*

per·co·la·tor (pėr'kə·lā'tər), *n.* kind of coffee pot in which boiling water drains through ground coffee.

per·cus·sion (pər·kush'ən), *n.* **1.** the striking of one body against another with force; stroke; blow. **2.** the striking of musical instruments to produce tones. [< L *percussio < per-* (intensive) + *quatere* strike, beat]

percussion instrument, a musical instrument (as a drum or cymbal) played by striking it.

per di·em (pər dī'əm), **1.** per day; for each day. **2.** allowance of so much every day. [< L, per day]

per·di·tion (pər·dish'ən), *n.* **1.** loss of one's soul and the joys of heaven. **2.** hell. **3.** utter loss. [< L, < *perdere* destroy < *per-* to destruction + *dare* give]

per·e·gri·nate (per'ə·grə·nāt), *v.,* -**nat·ed,** -**nat·ing.** travel; journey. —**per'e·gri·na'tion,** *n.* —**per'e·gri·na'tor,** *n.*

per·e·grine (per'ə·grin; -grīn; -grēn), *adj.* **per·e·grin** (-grin), *n.* a large falcon. [< L *peregrinus* from foreign parts, ult. < *per-* outside + *ager* (*Romanus*) the (Roman) territory. Doublet of PILGRIM.]

per·emp·to·ry (pər·emp'tə·ri; per'əmp·tô'ri; -tō'-), *adj.* **1.** imperious; positive: *a peremptory teacher.* **2.** allowing no denial or refusal: *a peremptory command.* **3.** leaving no choice; decisive; final; absolute: *a peremptory decree.* [< L *peremptorius* deadly, that puts an end to, ult. < *per-* to destruction + *emere,* orig., take] —**per·emp'to·ri·ly,** *adv.* —**per·emp'to·ri·ness,** *n.*

per·en·ni·al (pər·en'i·əl), *adj.* **1.** lasting for a very long time; enduring: *the perennial beauty of the hills.* **2.** *Bot.* having underground parts that live more than two years: *perennial garden plants.* —*n.* a perennial plant. [< L *perennis* lasting < *per-* through + *annus* year] —**per·en'ni·al·ly,** *adv.* —Syn. *adj.* **1.** abiding.

perf., **1.** perfect. **2.** perforated.

per·fect (*adj., n.* pėr'fikt; *v.* pər·fekt'), *adj.* **1.** without defect; faultless: *perfect work shows great care.* **2.** completely skilled; expert. **3.** having all its parts; complete. **4.** entire; utter: *a perfect stranger to us.* **5.** *Gram.* showing action or state completed at the time of speaking. There are three perfect tenses: perfect, past perfect, and future perfect. —*v.* **1.** remove all faults from; make perfect: *perfect a plan as it is being tried out.* **2.** improve. **3.** complete. —*n. Gram.* a. the perfect tense. b. a verb form in such tense. *Have eaten* is the perfect form of *eat.* [< OF < L *perfectus* completed < *per-* thoroughly + *facere* make, do] —**per'fect·ly,** *adv.* —**per'fect·ness,** *n.* —Syn. *adj.* **1.** flawless, impeccable. **3.** whole.

per·fect·i·ble (pər·fek'tə·bəl), *adj.* capable of becoming, or being made, perfect. —**per·fect'i·bil'i·ty,** *n.*

per·fec·tion (pər·fek'shən), *n.* **1.** perfect condition; faultlessness; highest excellence. **2.** a perfect person or thing. **3.** a making complete or perfect: *the perfection of plans.* **4.** to perfection, perfectly. —**per·fec'tion·ist,** *n.*

per·fec·tive (pər·fek'tiv), *adj.* tending to make perfect; conducive to perfection. —**per·fec'tive·ly,** *adv.* —**per·fec'tive·ness,** *n.*

per·fec·to (pər·fek'tō), *n., pl.* -**tos.** *Am.* a thick cigar that tapers nearly to a point at both ends. [< Sp., perfect]

per·fect par·ti·ciple, participle expressing action completed before the time of speaking or acting. In "Having written the letter, she mailed it," *having written* is a perfect participle. ❯ See participle for usage note.

per·fi·dy (pér'fə·di), *n., pl.* **–dies.** a breaking faith; base treachery; being false to a trust. [< L, ult. < *per-* + *fides* faith] —**per·fid·i·ous** (pər·fid'i·əs), *adj.* —**per·fid'i·ous·ly,** *adv.* —**per·fid'i·ous·ness,** *n.*

per·fo·rate (*v.* pér'fə·rāt; *adj.* pér'fə·rit, –rāt), *v.,* **–rat·ed, –rat·ing,** *adj.* —*v.* make a hole or holes through. —*adj.* pierced. [< L, < *per-* through + *forare* bore] —**per'fo·ra'tive,** *adj.* —**per'fo·ra'tor,** *n.*

per·fo·ra·tion (pér'fə·rā'shən), *n.* **1.** hole bored or punched through something: *the perforations in a sheet of stamps.* **2.** a perforating or being perforated.

per·force (pər·fôrs'; –fōrs'), *adv.* by necessity; necessarily.

per·form (pər·fôrm'), *v.* **1.** do: *perform work.* **2.** put into effect; carry out: *perform a task.* **3.** go through; render: *perform a piece of music.* **4.** do something, esp. act, play, sing, or do tricks in public. [< AF *performer,* var. of OF *parfournir* < *par-* completely + *-fournir* furnish, finish; infl. by *forme* form] —**per·form'er,** *n.* —**Syn.** 2. execute, accomplish, fulfill, achieve.

per·form·ance (pər·fôr'məns), *n.* **1.** a performing. **2.** thing performed; act; deed. **3.** the giving of a play, circus, or other show. —**Syn.** 1. execution, accomplishment, achievement, fulfillment. 2. exploit, feat. 3. production.

per·fume (*n.* pér'fūm, pər·fūm'; *v.* pər·fūm'), *n., v.,* **–fumed, –fum·ing.** —*n.* **1.** a sweet smell. **2.** liquid having the sweet smell of flowers. —*v.* **1.** fill with sweet odor: *flowers perfumed the air.* **2.** put a sweet-smelling liquid on. [< F < OItal. < L *per-* through + *fumare* to smoke] —**Syn.** *n.* 1. fragrance, scent, redolence, aroma.

per·fum·er (pər·fūm'ər), *n.* **1.** maker or seller of perfumes. **2.** one that perfumes.

per·fum·er·y (pər·fūm'ər·i), *n., pl.* **–er·ies. 1.** a perfume. **2.** perfumes. **3.** business of making or selling perfumes.

per·func·to·ry (pər·fungk'tə·ri), *adj.* **1.** done merely for the sake of getting rid of the duty; mechanical; indifferent: *the little boy gave his face a perfunctory washing.* **2.** acting in a perfunctory way. [< LL *perfunctorius,* ult. < L *perfungi* perform < *per-* to the end + *fungi* execute] —**per·func'to·ri·ly,** *adv.* —**per·func'to·ri·ness,** *n.* —**Syn.** 1. careless, superficial.

per·go·la (pér'gə·lə), *n.* arbor made of a trellis supported by posts. [< Ital.]

per·haps (pər·haps'; pər·aps'), *adv.* maybe; possibly. [ME *per happes* by chances. See PER, HAP.]

per·i·anth (per'i·anth), *n. Bot.* envelope of a flower, including the calyx and the corolla. [< NL, < Gk. *peri-* around + *anthos* flower]

per·i·car·di·tis (per'ə·kär·dī'tis), *n.* inflammation of the pericardium.

per·i·car·di·um (per'ə·kär'di·əm), *n., pl.* **–di·a** (–di·ə). a membranous sac enclosing the heart. [< Gk., < *peri-* around + *kardia* heart] —**per·i·car·di·ac** (per'ə·kär'di·ak), **per'i·car'di·al,** *adj.*

per·i·carp (per'ə·kärp), *n. Bot.* walls of a ripened ovary or fruit; seed vessel. [< NL < Gk., < *peri-* around + *karpos* fruit] —**per·i·car·pi·al** (per'ə·kär'pi·əl), *adj.*

Per·i·cles (per'ə·klēz), *n.* 490?–429 B.C., Athenian statesman, orator, and military commander. —**Per·i·cle·an** (per'ə·klē'ən), *adj.*

per·i·gee (per'ə·jē), *n. Astron.* point in the orbit of a heavenly body where it comes closest to the earth. See the picture under apogee. [< F < NL < Gk., < *peri-* near + *ge* earth] —**per'i·ge'al,** *adj.*

per·i·he·li·on (per'ə·hē'li·ən; –hēl'yən), *n., pl.* **–li·a** (–li·ə; –yə). *Astron.* point in its orbit where a heavenly body comes closest to the sun. See the picture under aphelion. [< NL, < Gk. *peri-* near + *helios* sun]

per·il (per'əl), *n., v.,* **–iled, –il·ing;** *esp. Brit.* **–illed, –il·ling.** —*n.* chance of harm; danger. —*v.* put in danger. [< F < L *periculum*] —**Syn.** *n.* jeopardy, hazard, risk.

per·il·ous (per'ə·ləs), *adj.* dangerous. —**per·il·ous·ly,** *adv.* —**Syn.** hazardous, risky, unsafe. —**Ant.** safe, secure.

pe·rim·e·ter (pə·rim'ə·tər), *n.* **1.** the outer boundary of a surface or figure. **2.** distance around such a boundary. [< L < Gk., < *peri-* around + *metron* measure] —**per·i·met·ric** (per'ə·met'rik), **per'i·met'ri·cal,** *adj.* —**per'i·met'ri·cal·ly,** *adv.*

per·i·ne·um (per'ə·nē'əm), *n., pl.* **–ne·a** (–nē'ə). region of the body between the thighs. —**per'i·ne'al,** *adj.*

pe·ri·od (pir'i·əd), *n.* **1.** portion of time, life, development, history, etc., having certain features or conditions. **2.** *Education.* a class hour devoted to the study of a single subject. **3.** the time of one complete cycle of a vibration, current, etc. **4.** portion of a game during which there is actual play. **5.** time during which a thing lasts, acts, etc. **6.** time needed for a disease to run its course. **7.** Also, **periods.** menses. **8.** dot (.) marking the end of most sentences or showing an abbreviation. **9.** pause at the end of a sentence. **10.** a complete sentence: *the orator spoke in stately periods.* —*adj.* characteristic of a certain period of time: *period furniture.* [< L < Gk. *periodos* a going around, cycle < *peri-* around + *hodos* a going] —**Syn.** *n.* 1. term, interval. ❯ **period** (.). 1. The principal function of the period is to mark the end of a statement, that is, the end of every completed sentence not definitely a question or exclamation. Sometimes sentences in the form of exclamations or questions are really to be regarded as statements. After such a sentence a writer may use the exclamation mark or question mark, but he will usually have a period if the tone is lacking in emotion or if he wishes to minimize the emotion of the sentence form he has chosen. 2. Period in combination with other marks. Most publishers prefer that a period coming at the end of a quotation be placed inside the quotation marks: *"The longer you put it off," he said, "the harder it's going to be."*

pe·ri·od·ic (pir'i·od'ik), *adj.* **1.** occurring, appearing, or done again and again at regular intervals: *periodic attacks of malaria.* **2.** happening every now and then: *a periodic fit of clearing up one's desk.* **3.** expressed in formal sentences whose meanings are not complete without the final words.

pe·ri·od·i·cal (pir'i·od'ə·kəl), *n.* magazine that appears regularly. —*adj.* **1.** of periodicals. **2.** published at regular intervals. **3.** periodic. —**pe'ri·od'i·cal·ly,** *adv.*

pe·ri·o·dic·i·ty (pir'i·ə·dis'ə·ti), *n., pl.* **–ties.** tendency to happen at regular intervals.

periodic law, *Chem.* law that the properties of elements change at regular intervals when the elements are arranged in the order of their atomic numbers.

periodic table, *Chem.* table in which the elements, arranged in the order of their atomic weights, are shown in related groups.

per·i·os·te·um (per'i·os'ti·əm), *n., pl.* **–te·a** (–ti·ə). the dense fibrous membrane covering the surface of bones except at the joints. [< NL < LL < Gk., < *peri-* around + *osteon* bone] —**per'i·os'te·al,** *adj.*

per·i·pa·tet·ic (per'ə·pə·tet'ik), *adj.* walking about; traveling from place to place. [< L < Gk., < *peri-* around + *patein* to walk; with ref. to Aristotle's manner of teaching]

pe·riph·er·al (pə·rif'ər·əl), *adj.* **1.** pertaining to, situated in, or forming an outside boundary. **2.** at the outside; external. —**pe·riph'er·al·ly,** *adv.*

pe·riph·er·y (pə·rif'ər·i), *n., pl.* **–er·ies. 1.** an outside boundary: *the periphery of a circle is called the circumference.* **2.** an external surface. [< LL < Gk., < *peri-* around + *pherein* carry]

per·i·phrase (per'ə·frāz), *n., v.,* **–phrased, –phras·ing.** —*n.* a roundabout way of speaking or writing; circumlocution. —v. express in a roundabout way.

per·iph·ra·sis (pə·rif'rə·sis), n., pl. **-ses** (-sēz). periphrase. [< L < Gk., ult. < peri- around + phrazein speak]

per·i·phras·tic (per'ə·fras'tik), adj. expressed in a roundabout way. —per'i·phras'ti·cal·ly, adv.

per·i·scope (per'ə·skōp), n. instrument that allows those in a submarine or trench to obtain a view of the surface. It is a tube with an arrangement of prisms or mirrors that reflect light rays down the tube. [< Gk. peri- around + skopeein to look] —per·i·scop·ic (per'ə·skop'ik), per'i·scop'i·cal, adj.

per·ish (per'ish), v. 1. lose life through violence, accident, privation, etc. 2. decay and disappear. 3. be destroyed: buildings perish in flames. [< OF periss- < L, < per- to destruction + ire go]

per·ish·a·ble (per'ish·ə·bəl), adj. liable to perish; liable to spoil or decay. —n. Usually, perishables. something perishable. —per'ish·a·ble·ness, n.

per·i·stal·sis (per'ə·stal'sis), n., pl. **-ses** (-sēz). movement in the wall of a hollow organ by which it propels its contents onward, esp. the wavelike, circular contractions of the alimentary canal. [< NL < Gk., ult. < peri- around + stellein wrap] —per·i·stal·tic (per'ə·stal'tik), adj.

per·i·style (per'ə·stīl), n. 1. row of columns surrounding a building, court, or the like. 2. space or court so enclosed. [< F < L < Gk., < peri- around + stylos pillar]

per·i·to·ne·um, per·i·to·nae·um (per'ə·tə·nē'əm), n., pl. **-ne·a; -nae·a** (-nē'ə). Anat. membrane that lines the walls of the abdomen and covers the organs in it. [< LL < Gk. peritonaion, neut. adj., stretched over, ult. < peri- around + teinein stretch] —per'i·to·ne'al, per'·i·to·nae'al, adj.

per·i·to·ni·tis (per'ə·tə·nī'tis), n. inflammation of the peritoneum.

per·i·wig (per'ə·wig), n. wig. [earlier perewyke. See PERUKE.]

per·i·win·kle¹ (per'i·wing'kəl), n. a low, trailing evergreen plant with blue flowers. The American periwinkle is called myrtle. [< L pervinca; infl. by periwinkle²]

per·i·win·kle² (per'i·wing'-kəl), n. a sea snail with a thick, cone-shaped, spiral shell, used for food. [OE pinewincle; pine-? < L pina mussel]

Periwinkle (ab. ¾ in. long)

per·jure (per'jər), v., -jured, -jur·ing. make (oneself) guilty of perjury. [< OF < L, < per- falsely + jurare swear] —per'jur·er, n.

per·ju·ry (per'jər·i), n., pl. -ries. act of swearing that something is true which one knows to be false.

perk (perk), v. 1. move, lift the head, or act briskly or saucily. 2. raise smartly or briskly: the sparrow perked up his tail. 3. make trim or smart. 4. put oneself forward briskly or assertively. —adj. perky. [ME perke(n)]

perk·y (per'ki), adj., perk·i·er, perk·i·est. smart; brisk; saucy; pert: a perky squirrel. —perk'i·ly, adv. —perk'i·ness, n.

per·ma·nent (per'mə·nənt), adj. lasting; intended to last: a permanent filling in a tooth. —n. Colloq. a permanent wave. [< L permanens staying to the end < per- through + manere stay] —per'ma·nence, per'ma·nen·cy, n. —per'ma·nent·ly, adv. —Syn. adj. abiding, enduring, durable. —Ant. adj. impermanent, temporary.

permanent wave, wave lasting several months, put in the hair by a special process.

per·man·ga·nate (pər·mang'gə·nāt), n. Chem. salt of an acid containing manganese.

per·me·a·ble (per'mi·ə·bəl), adj. that can be permeated. —per'me·a·bil'i·ty, n.

per·me·ate (per'mi·āt), v., -at·ed, -at·ing. 1. spread through the whole of; pass through; soak through: smoke permeated the house. 2. penetrate. [< L, < per- through + meare to pass] —per'me·a'tion, n. —per'me·a'tive, adj.

per·mis·si·ble (pər·mis'ə·bəl), adj. that may be permitted; allowable. —per·mis'si·bil'i·ty, n. —per·mis'si·bly, adv.

per·mis·sion (pər·mish'ən), n. formal or express allowance or consent. —Syn. leave, sufferance, authorization, sanction. —Ant. prohibition, refusal, denial.

per·mis·sive (pər·mis'iv), adj. 1. permitting; allowing. 2. permitted; allowed. —per·mis'sive·ly, adv. —per·mis'sive·ness, n.

per·mit (v. pər·mit'; n. per'mit, pər·mit'), v., -mit·ted, -mit·ting, n. —v. 1. allow (a person, etc.) to do something: permit me to explain. 2. let (something) be done or occur. 3. tolerate. 4. afford opportunity for: conditions permitting no delay. —n. 1. a formal, written order giving permission to do something: a permit to fish or hunt. 2. permission. [< L, < per- through + mittere let go] —per·mit'ter, n. —Syn. v. 1. sanction, authorize. 3. suffer. —n. 1. license.

per·mu·ta·tion (per'myù·tā'shən), n. 1. alteration. 2. Math. a. a changing of the order of a set of things; arranging in different orders. b. such an arrangement or group. The permutations of a, b, and c are abc, acb, bac, bca, cab, cba. [< L, < per- across + mutare to change]

Per·nam·bu·co (per'nəm·bū'kō), n. former name of Recife.

per·ni·cious (pər·nish'əs), adj. 1. that will destroy or ruin; causing great harm or damage: gambling is a pernicious habit. 2. fatal. [< L perniciosus, ult. < per- + nex death] —per·ni'cious·ly, adv. —per·ni'cious·ness, n. —Syn. 1. destructive, injurious, noxious, harmful.

pernicious anemia, a very severe disease in which the number of red corpuscles in the blood decreases.

per·nick·e·ty (pər·nik'ə·ti), adj. Colloq. 1. fastidious; fussy. 2. requiring carefulness and precision.

Pe·rón (pə·rōn'), n. Juan Domingo, born 1902, president of Argentina from 1946 to 1955.

per·o·ra·tion (per'ə·rā'shən), n. the last part of an oration or discussion. [< L, < per- to a finish + orare speak formally]

per·ox·ide (pər·ok'sīd), **per·ox·id** (-sid), n., v., -id·ed, -id·ing. —n. Chem. a. oxide of a given element or radical that contains the greatest, or an unusual, amount of oxygen. b. hydrogen peroxide. —v. bleach (hair) by applying peroxide (def. b).

per·pen·dic·u·lar (per'pən·dik'yə·lər), adj. 1. upright; standing straight up. 2. at right angles. —n. 1. a perpendicular line or plane. 2. a perpendicular position. [< OF < L, < perpendiculum plumb line, ult. < per- + pendere hang] —per'pen·dic'u·lar'i·ty, n. —per'pen·dic'u·lar·ly, adv. —Syn. adj. 1. vertical, plumb.

per·pe·trate (per'pə·trāt), v., -trat·ed, -trat·ing. do or commit (crime, fraud, trick, or anything bad or foolish). [< L, < per- (intensive) + patrare perform] —per'pe·tra'tion, n. —per'pe·tra'tor, n.

per·pet·u·al (pər·pech'ù·əl), adj. 1. lasting forever; eternal: the perpetual hills. 2. lasting throughout life: a perpetual income. 3. continuous; never ceasing: a perpetual stream of visitors. [< L, < perpetuus continuous] —per·pet'u·al·ly, adv. —per·pet'u·al·ness, n. —Syn. permanent, everlasting, enduring. 3. unceasing, incessant, constant.

per·pet·u·ate (pər·pech'ù·āt), v., -at·ed, -at·ing. make perpetual; keep from being forgotten. —per·pet'u·a'tion, n. —per·pet'u·a'tor, n.

per·pe·tu·i·ty (per'pə·tü'ə·ti; -tū'-), n., pl. -ties. state or fact of being perpetual; existence forever.

per·plex (pər·pleks'), v. 1. trouble with doubt; puzzle; bewilder. 2. make difficult to understand or settle; confuse. [orig. adj., < L perplexus confused < per- completely + plectere intertwine] —per·plex·ed·ly (pər·plek'sid·li), adv. —per·plex'ing, adj. —per·plex'ing·ly, adv. —Syn. 1. mystify, nonplus.

per·plex·i·ty (pər·plek′sə·ti), n., pl. –ties. 1. perplexed condition; confusion; being puzzled. 2. something that perplexes. —Syn. 1. bewilderment, uncertainty, doubt, dilemma.

per·qui·site (pér′kwə·zit), n. anything received for work besides the regular pay. [< Med.L perquisitum (thing) gained, ult. < L per- carefully + quaerere seek]

Per·ry (per′i), n. 1. Oliver Hazard, 1785–1819, American naval commander. 2. his brother, Matthew C., 1794–1858, American naval officer; induced Japan to open trade with the United States.

Pers., 1. Persia. 2. Persian.

pers., person; personal.

per se (pér sē′), Latin. by itself; in itself; intrinsically.

per·se·cute (pér′sə·kūt), v., –cut·ed, –cut·ing. 1. do harm to again and again; oppress. 2. punish for religious reasons. 3. annoy: persecuted by silly questions. [< persecution] —per′se·cu′tive, adj. —per′se·cu′tor, n. —Syn. 1. wrong, torment. 3. harass, worry, vex.

per·se·cu·tion (pér·sə·kū′shən), n. a persecuting or being persecuted. [< L persecutio, ult. < per- perseveringly + sequi follow]

Per·seph·o·ne (pər·sef′ə·nē), n. Gk. Myth. daughter of Zeus who was carried off by Hades, the king of the lower world, and made his queen. The Latin equivalent is Proserpina, often Anglicized as Proserpine.

Per·seus (pér′si·əs; pér′sūs), n. 1. Gk. Myth. hero who slew Medusa and rescued Andromeda from a sea monster. 2. group of stars in the northern sky.

per·se·ver·ance (pér′sə·vir′əns), n. a sticking to a purpose or an aim; never giving up what one has set out to do. —Syn. persistence, tenacity, diligence, pertinacity.

per·se·vere (pér′sə·vir′), v., –vered, –ver·ing. continue steadily in doing something hard; persist. [< F < L, < per- very + severus strict] —per′se·ver′ing·ly, adv.

Per·shing (pér′shing), n. John Joseph, 1860–1948, general in command of the American army during World War I.

Per·sia (pér′zhə; esp. Brit. –shə), n. country in SW Asia S of the Caspian Sea. Its name was officially changed to Iran in 1935.

Per·sian (pér′zhən; esp. Brit. –shən), adj. of or pertaining to Persia, its people, or their language. —n. 1. native or inhabitant of Persia. 2. language of Persia.

Persian Gulf, gulf of the Arabian Sea, between Persia and Arabia.

Persian lamb, a very curly fur from lambs of Persia and some parts of C Asia.

per·si·flage (pér′sə·fläzh), n. light, joking talk. [< F, < persifler banter, appar. < per- (< L) + siffler whistle, hiss < L sifilare]

per·sim·mon (pər·sim′ən), n. Am. 1. a North American tree with a plumlike fruit containing one to ten seeds. 2. fruit of this tree, very astringent when green but sweet and good to eat when very ripe. [< Algonquian]

per·sist (pər·sist′; –zist′), v. 1. continue firmly; refuse to stop or be changed. 2. last; stay; endure. 3. say again and again; maintain. [< L, < per- to the end + sistere stand] —Syn. 1. persevere.

per·sist·ent (pər·sis′tənt; –zis′–), adj. 1. persisting; having lasting qualities, esp. in the face of dislike, disapproval, or difficulties: a persistent worker. 2. lasting; going on; continuing: a persistent headache. —per·sist′ence, per·sist′en·cy, n. —per·sist′ent·ly, adv. —Syn. 1. persevering, untiring, insistent, tenacious.

per·son (pér′sən), n. 1. man, woman, or child; human being: four persons saw this. 2. character in a play or story. 3. a human body; bodily appearance: he has a fine person. 4. Law. a human being or corporation having rights and duties. 5. in person, a. in one's own individual character. b. with one's own bodily presence. 6. Gram. a. change in a pronoun or verb to show the per-

son speaking (first person), the person spoken to (second person), or the person or thing spoken of (third person). I and we are used for the first person; thou and you, for the second person; he, she, it, and they, for the third person. b. a form of a pronoun or verb giving such indication. Comes is third person singular of come. [< OF < L persona character, mask worn by actor. Doublet of PARSON.] —Syn. 1. individual. ➤ Person is the ordinary word for referring to a human being without making any particular distinction. Individual has the same meaning (though it is applied to single objects and animals as well) but emphasizes the person's singleness, aloneness, and is slightly heavy or pretentious unless that emphasis is needed. Party is legal or humorous.

per·son·a·ble (pér′sən·ə·bəl), adj. having a pleasing appearance; good-looking; attractive.

per·son·age (pér′sən·ij), n. 1. person of importance. 2. person. 3. character in a book, play, etc.

per·son·al (pér′sən·əl; pérs′nəl), adj. 1. individual; private: a personal letter. 2. done in person; directly by oneself, not through others or by letter: a personal visit. 3. of the body or bodily appearance: personal beauty. 4. having the nature of an individual rational being: a personal God. 5. about or against a person or persons: personal abuse. 6. inclined to make remarks to or ask questions of others: don't be too personal. 7. Gram. showing person. I, we, thou, you, he, she, it, and they are the personal pronouns. 8. of or having to do with possessions that can be moved, not land or buildings. —n. Am., Colloq. a short paragraph in a newspaper about a particular person or persons.

per·son·al·i·ty (pér′sən·nal′ə·ti), n., pl. –ties. 1. the personal or individual quality that makes one person be different or act differently from another: a baby two weeks old does not have much personality. 2. qualities of a person. 3. remark made about or against some person: personalities are not in good taste in general conversation. 4. person; personage. 5. being a person, not a thing. —Syn. 1. character, individuality.

per·son·al·ize (pér′sən·əl·īz; pérs′nəl–), v., –ized, –iz·ing. 1. make personal. 2. personify.

per·son·al·ly (pér′sən·əl·i; pérs′nəl·i), adv. 1. in person; not by the aid of others: see to the comforts of guests personally. 2. as far as oneself is concerned. 3. as a person: we like Mr. Hart personally.

per·so·na non gra·ta (pər·sō′nə non grā′tə), Latin. an unacceptable person.

per·son·ate (pér′sən·āt), v., –at·ed, –at·ing. 1. act the part of (a character in a play, etc.). 2. pretend to be. —per′son·a′tion, n. —per′son·a′tor, n.

per·son·i·fi·ca·tion (pər·son′ə·fə·kā′shən), n. 1. a striking example; type. 2. a representing as a person. 3. person or creature imagined as representing a thing or idea. 4. figure of speech in which a lifeless thing or quality is spoken of as if alive. ➤ Personification is a figure of speech in which an object or animal or quality or ideal is given some attributes of a human being: "Deal gently, Love, with him and her who live together now!"

per·son·i·fy (pər·son′ə·fi), v., –fied, –fy·ing. 1. be a type of; embody: Satan personifies evil. 2. regard or represent as a person. We often personify the sun and moon, referring to the sun as "he" and the moon as "she." —per·son′i·fi′er, n.

per·son·nel (pér′sə·nel′), n. persons employed in any work, business, or service. [< F, personal; adj. used as n.]

per·spec·tive (pər·spek′tiv), n. 1. art of picturing objects on a flat surface so as to give the appearance of distance. 2. effect of distance on the appearance of objects. 3. effect of the distance of events upon the mind. 4. view of things or facts in which they are in the right relations. —adj. drawn so as to show the proper perspec-

tive. [< Med.L *perspectiva* (*ars*) (science) of optics, ult. < L *per-* through + *specere* look] —**per·spec'tive·ly,** *adv.*

per·spi·ca·cious (pėr'spə·kā'shəs), *adj.* keen in observing and understanding; discerning. [< L *perspicax* sharp-sighted, ult. < *per-* through + *specere* to look] —**per'spi·ca'cious·ly,** *adv.* —**per·spi·cac·i·ty** (pėr'spə·kas'ə·ti), *n.* —Syn. shrewd, acute.

per·spi·cu·i·ty (pėr'spə·kū'ə·ti), *n.* clearness in expression; ease in being understood. —Syn. lucidity, plainness.

per·spic·u·ous (pər·spik'yū·əs), *adj.* clear; easily understood. [< L *perspicuus,* ult. < *per-* through + *specere* to look] —**per·spic'u·ous·ly,** *adv.* —**per·spic'u·ous·ness,** *n.*

per·spi·ra·tion (pėr'spə·rā'shən), *n.* 1. sweat. 2. sweating.

per·spire (pər·spīr'), *v.,* **-spired, -spir·ing.** sweat. [< L, < *per-* through + *spirare* breathe]

per·suade (pər·swād'), *v.,* **-suad·ed, -suad·ing.** 1. win over to do or believe; make willing or sure by urging, arguing, etc. 2. convince. 3. try to convince. 4. urge. [< L, < *per-* strongly + *suadere* to urge] —**per·suad'a·ble,** *adj.* —**per·suad'er,** *n.* —Syn. 1. induce, influence, impel, move. 4. coax.

per·sua·sion (pər·swā'zhən), *n.* 1. a persuading: *all our persuasion was of no use; she would not come.* 2. power of persuading. 3. firm belief. 4. religious belief; creed: *all Christians are not of the same persuasion.* 5. *Humorous.* kind; sort. —Syn. 3. conviction, opinion.

per·sua·sive (pər·swā'siv; -ziv), *adj.* able, intended, or fitted to persuade. —**per·sua'sive·ly,** *adv.* —**per·sua'sive·ness,** *n.* —Syn. winning, moving.

pert (pėrt), *adj.* 1. too forward or free in speech or action; saucy; bold. 2. *Colloq.* lively. [for *apert,* ME < OF, open < L *apertus;* infl. by OF *aspert* EXPERT] —**pert'ly,** *adv.* —**pert'ness,** *n.* —Syn. 1. impudent, impertinent. —Ant. 1. modest, retiring, humble, meek.

per·tain (pər·tān'), *v.* 1. belong or be connected as a part, possession, attribute, etc.: *we own the house and the land pertaining to it.* 2. refer; be related. "Pertaining to school" means "having to do with school." 3. be appropriate: *we had turkey and everything else that pertains to Thanksgiving Day.* [< OF < L, < *per-* across + *tenere* to reach]

Perth (pėrth), *n.* city in SW Australia.

per·ti·na·cious (pėr'tə·nā'shəs), *adj.* holding firmly to a purpose, action, or opinion; very persistent. [< L *pertinacia* firmness < *per-* very + *tenax* tenacious] —**per'ti·na'cious·ly,** *adv.* —**per'ti·na'cious·ness,** **per·ti·nac·i·ty** (pėr'tə·nas'ə·ti), *n.* —Syn. determined, dogged, stubborn, obstinate, tenacious.

per·ti·nent (pėr'tə·nənt), *adj.* having to do with what is being considered; relating to the matter in hand; to the point: *if your question is pertinent, I will answer it.* [< L, ppr. of *pertinere* PERTAIN] —**per'ti·nence, per'ti·nen·cy,** *n.* —**per'ti·nent·ly,** *adv.* —Syn. relevant, apt, appropriate.

per·turb (pər·tėrb'), *v.* disturb greatly; make uneasy or troubled: *Mother was much perturbed by my illness.* [< L, < *per-* thoroughly + *turbare* confuse] —**per·turb'a·ble,** *adj.* —**per·tur·ba·tion** (pėr'tər·bā'shən), *n.* —**per·turb'ed·ly,** *adv.* —Syn. excite, agitate, trouble, distress.

Pe·ru (pə·rü'), *n.* a mountainous country on the W coast of South America. —**Pe·ru·vi·an** (pə·rü'vi·ən), *adj., n.*

pe·ruke (pə·rük'), *n.* wig, esp. one worn by men in the 17th and 18th centuries. [< F *perruque*]

pe·rus·al (pə·rüz'əl), *n.* a perusing; reading: *the perusal of a letter.*

pe·ruse (pə·rüz'), *v.,* **-rused, -rus·ing.** 1. read through carefully. 2. read. [orig., use up, < L *per-* to the end + E *use*] —**pe·rus'a·ble,** *adj.* —**pe·rus'er,** *n.*

Peruvian bark, cinchona (def. 2).

per·vade (pər·vād'), *v.,* **-vad·ed, -vad·ing.** go or spread its influence, presence, etc., throughout; be throughout: *the odor of pines pervades*

the air. [< L, < *per-* through + *vadere* go] —**per·vad'er,** *n.* —**per·va·sion** (pər·vā'zhən), *n.* —**per·va·sive** (pər·vā'siv), *adj.* —**per·va'sive·ly,** *adv.* —**per·va'sive·ness,** *n.* —Syn. penetrate, permeate, impregnate.

per·verse (pər·vėrs'), *adj.* 1. contrary and willful; stubborn: *the perverse child did just what we told him not to do.* 2. persistent in wrong. 3. wicked. 4. not correct; wrong: *perverse reasoning.* [< L *perversus* turned away. See PERVERT.] —**per·verse'ly,** *adv.* —**per·verse'ness, per·ver'si·ty,** *n.* —Syn. 1. obstinate, wayward.

per·ver·sion (pər·vėr'zhən; -shən), *n.* 1. a turning or being turned to what is wrong; change to what is unnatural, abnormal, or wrong. 2. a perverted form. 3. an abnormal form of sexual behavior.

per·vert (*v.* pər·vėrt'; *n.* pėr'vėrt), *v.* 1. lead or turn from the right way or from the truth: *reading crime comics perverts our taste for good books.* 2. give a wrong meaning to: *his enemies perverted his friendly remark and made it into an insult.* 3. use for wrong purposes or in a wrong way: *a clever criminal perverts his talents.* 4. change from what is natural or normal. —*n.* a perverted person. [< L, < *per-* to destruction + *vertere* to turn] —**per·vert'er,** *n.* —**per·vert'i·ble,** *adj.* —Syn. *v.* 1. corrupt, debase, deprave. 2. misinterpret, distort, falsify. 3. misuse, misapply.

per·vi·ous (pėr'vi·əs), *adj.* 1. giving passage or entrance: *sand is easily pervious to water.* 2. open to influence, argument, etc. [< L, < *per-* through + *via* way] —**per'vi·ous·ness,** *n.*

pe·se·ta (pə·sā'tə), *n.* 1. unit of money of Spain, worth about 9 cents (1950). 2. a silver coin equal to one peseta. [< Sp., dim. of *pesa* weight. See PESO.]

pes·ky (pes'ki), *adj.,* **-ki·er, -ki·est.** *U.S. Colloq.* troublesome; annoying. [? alter. of *pesty* < *pest*]

pe·so (pā'sō), *n., pl.* **-sos.** any of various gold or silver coins of a dollar or less in value, used in Spanish-speaking countries. [< Sp., weight < L *pensum,* pp. of *pendere* weigh]

pes·si·mism (pes'ə·miz·əm), *n.* 1. tendency to look on the dark side of things or to see difficulties and disadvantages. 2. belief that things naturally tend to evil, or that life is not worth while. [< L *pessimus* worst] —**pes'si·mist,** *n.* —**pes'si·mis'tic,** *adj.* —**pes'si·mis'ti·cal·ly,** *adv.*

pest (pest), *n.* 1. thing or person that causes trouble, injuries, or destruction; nuisance. 2. pestilence. [< L *pestis* plague] —Syn. annoyance, curse. 2. plague, epidemic.

pes·ter (pes'tər), *v.* annoy; trouble; vex. [appar. < OF *empestrer* hobble (an animal); infl. by *pest*]

pest·house (pest'hous'), *n.* hospital for persons ill with highly infectious and dangerous diseases.

pes·tif·er·ous (pes·tif'ər·əs), *adj.* 1. bringing disease or infection. 2. *Colloq.* troublesome; annoying. [< L, < *pestis* plague + *ferre* bring] —**pes·tif'er·ous·ly,** *adv.* —Syn. 1. infectious, contagious.

pes·ti·lence (pes'tə·ləns), *n.* disease that spreads rapidly, causing many deaths. Smallpox, yellow fever, and the plague are pestilences. —**pes·ti·len·tial** (pes'tə·len'shəl), *adj.* —Syn. plague, epidemic, pest.

pes·ti·lent (pes'tə·lənt), *adj.* 1. often causing death. Smallpox is a pestilent disease. 2. harmful to morals; destroying peace: *the pestilent effects of war.* 3. troublesome; annoying. —**pes'ti·lent·ly,** *adv.*

pes·tle (pes'əl; pes'təl), *n., v.,* **-tled, -tling.** —*n.* 1. tool for pounding or crushing substances into a powder in a mortar. 2. any of various mechanical appliances for pounding or stamping. —*v.* pound or crush with a pestle. [< OF, < L *pistillum* < *pinsere* to pound. Doublet of PISTIL.]

pet¹ (pet), *n., adj., v.,* **pet·ted, pet·ting.** —*n.* 1. animal kept as a favorite and treated with affection. 2. a darling; a favorite. —*adj.* 1. treated as a pet. 2. showing affection: *a pet name.* 3. darling; favorite. —*v.* **1.** treat as a pet; stroke; pat. **2.** fondle and caress one of the opposite sex. —Syn. *v.* **1.** coddle, pamper, indulge, humor.

pet² (pet), *n.* fit of peevishness.

Pé·tain (pā·taN′), *n.* Henri Philippe, 1856–1951, French general.

pet·al (pet′əl), *n.* one of the parts of a flower that are usually colored. A rose has many petals. [< NL < Gk. *petalon* leaf, orig. neut. adj., outspread] —**pet′aled, pet′alled,** *adj.*

pe·tard (pi·tärd′), *n.* an explosive device formerly used in warfare to break doors or gates. [< F, < *péter* break wind, ult. < L *pedere*]

pet·cock (pet′kok′), *n.* a small faucet.

pe·ter (pē′tər), *v. Am., Colloq.* fail gradually (with *out*): *the gold lode petered out.*

Pe·ter (pē′tər), *n.* **1.** Saint (*"Simon Peter"*), died 67? A.D., one of the twelve disciples chosen by Jesus as his Apostles. **2.** either of two books in the New Testament that bear his name. **Peter I,** (*"the Great"*) 1672–1725, czar of Russia 1682–1725.

pet·i·ole (pet′i·ōl), *n. Bot.* the slender stalk by which a leaf is attached to the stem. [< L *petiolus*, dim. of *pes* foot] —**pet′i·o·late,** *adj.*

pet·it (pet′i), *adj. Law.* small; petty; minor: *petit larceny.* [< F, < VL stem *pit-* little. Doublet of PETTY.]

pe·tite (pə·tēt′), *adj.* little; of small size; tiny, esp. with reference to a woman or girl. —**pe·tite′ness,** *n.*

pet·it four (pet′i fôr′; fôr′), *pl.* **pet·its fours** (pet′i fôrz′; -fōrz′). small cakes or cookies. [< F, little oven]

pe·ti·tion (pə·tish′ən), *n.* **1.** a formal request to a superior or to one in authority for some privilege, right, benefit, etc.: *the people signed a petition asking the city council for a new sidewalk.* **2.** *Law.* a written application for an order of court or for some action by a judge. **3.** a respectful or humble request. **4.** prayer. **5.** that which is requested or prayed for. —*v.* **1.** ask earnestly; make a petition to. **2.** make a petition. **3.** pray. [< L, < *petere* seek] —**pe·ti·tion·a·ry** (pə·tish′ən·er′i), *adj.* —**pe·ti′tion·er,** *n.* —Syn. *n.* **1.** suit, entreaty, supplication. —*v.* **1.** entreat.

pet·it jury (pet′i), petty jury.

Pe·trarch (pē′trärk), *n.* 1304–1374, Italian poet, famous for his sonnets.

pet·rel (pet′rəl), *n.* any of a number of sea birds, esp. the stormy petrel. [appar. dim. of St. *Peter,* who walked on the sea]

pet·ri·fy (pet′rə·fī), *v.,* **-fied, -fy·ing. 1.** turn into stone; become stone. **2.** harden; stiffen; deaden. **3.** paralyze with fear, horror, or surprise. [< F *pétrifier,* ult. < L *petra* stone < Gk.] —**pet·ri·fac·tion** (pet′rə·fak′shən), **pet′ri·fi·ca′tion,** *n.* —Syn. **3.** benumb, stupefy.

pet·ro·chem·i·cal (pet′rō·kem′ə·kəl), *n.* a chemical compound or element obtained from petroleum or natural gas and wholly or partly from their hydrocarbons and intended for chemical markets. [< *petro-* (< Gk. *petra* rock, *petros* stone) + *chemical*] —**pet′ro·chem′is·try,** *n.*

Pet·ro·grad (pet′rə·grad), *n.* former name (1914–24) of Leningrad.

pe·trog·ra·phy (pi·trog′rə·fi), *n.* branch of geology that deals with the description and classification of rocks. [< *petro-* (< Gk. *petra* rock, *petros* stone) + *-graphy* < Gk. *graphein* write] —**pe·trog′ra·pher,** *n.*

pet·rol (pet′rəl), *n. Brit.* gasoline. [< F < Med.L *petroleum.* Doublet of PETROLEUM.]

pet·ro·la·tum (pet′rə·lā′təm), *n. Am.* **1.** salve or ointment made from petroleum. **2.** mineral oil. [< NL, < *petrol*]

pe·tro·le·um (pə·trō′li·əm), *n.* an oily liquid found in the earth. Gasoline, kerosene, and paraffin are made from petroleum. [< Med.L, < Gk. *petra* rock, *petros* stone + L *oleum* oil. Doublet of PETROL.]

pe·trol·o·gy (pi·trol′ə·ji), *n.* science of rocks,

---

including their origin, structure, changes, etc. [< *petro-* (< Gk. *petra* rock, *petros* stone) + -LOGY] —**pet·ro·log·ic** (pet′rə·loj′ik), **pet′ro·log′i·cal,** *adj.* —**pe·trol′o·gist,** *n.*

pet·ti·coat (pet′i·kōt), *n.* **1.** skirt that hangs from the waist or from the shoulders, worn beneath the dress by women, girls, and babies. **2.** skirt. **3.** *Slang.* woman; girl. —*adj.* female; feminine: *petticoat government.* [orig. *petty coat* little coat]

pet·ti·fog (pet′i·fog; -fôg), *v.,* **-fogged, -fogging.** carry on a petty or shifty law business. —**pet′ti·fog′ger,** *n.* —**pet′ti·fog′ging,** *n.*

pet·tish (pet′ish), *adj.* peevish; cross. —**pet′tish·ly,** *adv.* —**pet′tish·ness,** *n.*

pet·ty (pet′i), *adj.,* **-ti·er, -ti·est. 1.** having little importance or value; small. **2.** mean; narrow-minded. **3.** lower; subordinate. [< OF *petit.* Doublet of PETIT.] —**pet′ti·ly,** *adv.* —**pet′ti·ness,** *n.* —Syn. **1.** trifling, trivial, slight, paltry, insignificant. **3.** minor, inferior.

petty cash, sum of money kept on hand to pay small expenses.

petty jury, group of 12 persons chosen to decide a case in court. Also, petit jury.

petty larceny, theft in which the value of the property taken is less than a certain amount.

petty officer, a noncommissioned officer in the navy.

pet·u·lant (pech′ə·lənt), *adj.* peevish; subject to little fits of bad temper; irritable over trifles. [< L *petulans,* ult. < *petere* seek, aim at] —**pet′u·lance, pet′u·lan·cy,** *n.* —**pet′u·lant·ly,** *adv.*

pe·tu·ni·a (pə·tü′ni·ə; -nyə; -tū′-), *n.* **1.** plant with funnel-shaped flowers of white, pink, and various shades of purple. **2.** the flower. [< NL < F *petun* tobacco; < South Am.Ind.]

pew (pū), *n.* **1.** bench with a back, for people to sit on in a church. **2.** place in a church set apart for the use of a certain family or group of people. [< OF < L *podia,* pl., elevated place, balcony, PODIUM]

pe·wee (pē′wē), *n. Am.* **1.** a small American bird with an olive-colored or gray back. **2.** a phoebe or other small flycatcher. [imit.]

pe·wit (pē′wit; pū′it), *n.* **1.** the lapwing. **2.** the European black-headed gull. **3.** pewee. [imit.]

pew·ter (pū′tər), *n.* **1.** alloy of tin with lead, copper, or other metals. **2.** dishes or other utensils made of this alloy. —*adj.* made of pewter: *a pewter mug.* [< OF *peautre*]

pf., **1.** Also, **pfg.** pfennig. **2.** Also, **pfd.** preferred.

Pfc., *Mil.* private first class.

pfen·nig (pfen′ig), *n., pl.* **pfen·nigs, pfen·ni·ge** (pfen′i·gə). a German coin worth about a quarter of a cent (1953). [< G; akin to PENNY]

Pg., **1.** Portugal. **2.** Portuguese.

pha·e·ton (fā′ə·tən), *n.* **1.** a light, four-wheeled carriage. **2.** an open automobile of the touring car type. [< F, named for *Phaëthon,* son of Helios]

phag·o·cyte (fag′ə·sīt), *n.* leucocyte capable of absorbing and destroying waste or harmful material. [< Gk. *phagos* eating + E *-cyte* cell (< Gk. *kytos* hollow container)]

pha·lan·ger (fə·lan′jər), *n.* a small, tree-climbing marsupial of the Australian region. [< NL, < Gk. *phalangion* spiderweb < *phalanx* spider; with ref. to webbed toes]

pha·lanx (fā′langks; fal′angks), *n., pl.* **pha·lanx·es, pha·lan·ges** (fə·lan′jēz). **1.** in ancient Greece, a special battle formation of infantry fighting in close ranks with their shields joined and long spears overlapping each other. **2.** a compact or closely massed body of persons, animals, or things. **3.** any bone in the fingers or toes. [< L < Gk.]

phal·lus (fal′əs), *n., pl.* **phal·li** (fal′ī). **1.** *Anat.* penis. **2.** image of the penis, symbolizing the generative power of nature. [< L < Gk. *phallos*] —**phal′lic, phal′li·cal,** *adj.*

phan·tasm (fan′taz·əm), *n.* **1.** thing seen only in one's imagination; unreal fancy: *the phantasms of a dream or fever.* **2.** a supposed appear-

---

āge, cāre, fär; ēqual, tėrm; īce; ōpen, ôrder; put, rūle, ūse; th, then; ə=a in about.

ance of an absent person, living or dead. [< L < Gk. *phantasma* image, ult. < *phainein* show. Doublet of PHANTOM.] —phan·tas′mal, phan·tas′mic, *adj.* —phan·tas′mal·ly, *adv.*

phan·tas·ma·go·ri·a (fan·taz′mə·gôr′i·ə; –gō′–), *n.* a shifting scene of real things, illusions, imaginary fancies, deceptions, and the like. [< Gk. *phantasma* PHANTASM + ? *agora* assembly] —phan·tas′ma·go′ri·al, phan·tas·ma·gor·ic (fan·taz′mə·gôr′ik; –gor′–), *adj.*

phan·ta·sy (fan′tə·si; –zi), *n., pl.* –sies. fantasy.

phan·tom (fan′təm), *n.* 1. image of the mind: *phantoms of a dream.* 2. a vague, dim, or shadowy appearance; ghost. —*adj.* like a ghost; unreal: *a phantom ship.* [< OF < VL < Gk. *phantasma* image. Doublet of PHANTASM.] —Syn. *n.* 2. apparition, specter, wraith, spirit.

phantom order, a standing order for materials, esp. weapons, airplanes, etc., placed by the U.S. government with a firm, but not acted upon until an official signal for proceeding is given.

Phar·aoh (fâr′ō), *n.* title given to the kings of ancient Egypt.

phar·i·sa·ic (far′ə·sā′ik), **phar·i·sa·i·cal** (–ə·kəl), *adj.* 1. making an outward show of religion or morals without the real spirit. 2. thinking oneself more moral than others; hypocritical. 3. Pharisaic, of or pertaining to the Pharisees. —phar′i·sa′i·cal·ly, *adv.* —phar′i·sa′i·cal·ness, *n.*

phar·i·sa·ism (far′ə·sā·iz′əm), **phar·i·see·ism** (–sē·iz′əm), *n.* 1. rigid observance of the external forms of religion without genuine piety. 2. hypocrisy; self-righteousness. 3. Pharisaism, doctrine and practice of the Pharisees.

Phar·i·see (far′ə·sē), *n.* 1. member of an ancient Jewish sect that was very strict in keeping to tradition and the laws of its religion. 2. person who makes a show of religion rather than follows its spirit, and thinks he is much better than other men.

pharm., 1. pharmaceutic. 2. pharmacopoeia. 3. pharmacy.

phar·ma·ceu·tic (fär′mə·sü′tik), **phar·ma·ceu·ti·cal** (–tə·kəl), *adj.* pertaining to pharmacy. [< LL < Gk., ult. < *pharmakon* drug, poison] —phar′ma·ceu′ti·cal·ly, *adv.*

phar·ma·ceu·tics (fär′mə·sü′tiks), *n.* pharmacy (def. 1).

phar·ma·cist (fär′mə·sist), *n.* druggist.

phar·ma·col·o·gy (fär′mə·kol′ə·ji), *n.* science of drugs, their preparation, uses, and effects. [< Gk. *pharmakon* drug + –LOGY] —phar·ma·co·log·i·cal (fär′mə·kə·loj′ə·kəl), *adj.* —phar′ma·col′o·gist, *n.*

phar·ma·co·poe·ia (fär′mə·kə·pē′ə), *n.* book containing an official list and description of drugs and medicines. [< Gk., < *pharmakon* drug + *poieein* make] —phar′ma·co·poe′ial, *adj.*

phar·ma·cy (fär′mə·si), *n., pl.* –cies. 1. preparation and dispensing of drugs and medicines; occupation of a druggist; pharmaceutics. 2. place where drugs and medicines are prepared and sold; drugstore. [< LL < Gk., ult. < *pharmakon* drug]

pha·ryn·ge·al (fə·rin′ji·əl; far′in·jē′əl), **pha·ryn·gal** (fə·ring′gəl), *adj.* pertaining to or connected with the pharynx.

phar·yn·gi·tis (far′in·jī′tis), *n.* inflammation of the mucous membrane of the pharynx.

phar·ynx (far′ingks), *n., pl.* **phar·ynx·es,** **pha·ryn·ges** (fə·rin′jēz). *Anat., Zool.* tube or cavity that connects the mouth with the esophagus. [< NL < Gk.]

phase (fāz), *n.* 1. one of the changing states or stages of development of a person or thing: *at present John has no use for girls; that is a phase most boys go through.* 2. one side, part, or view (of a subject): *what phase of mathematics are you studying now?* 3. *Astron.* the apparent shape of the moon or of a planet at a given time. 4. *Physics.* a particular stage in a series of periodic changes or movements. 5. *Chem.* a homogeneous part of a heterogeneous system, separated from other parts by definite boundaries. [< NL < Gk.

phasis appearance < *phainein* show] —Syn. 2. aspect, facet. ➤ **Phase** means "aspect," "side" (as of a question). It is overused for *part, kind,* and so on: *a phase of college that I dislike.* See also the usage note under *faze.*

Ph.B., *Am.* Bachelor of Philosophy.

Ph.D., *Am.* Doctor of Philosophy.

pheas·ant (fez′ənt), *n., pl.* –ants or (*esp. collectively*) –ant. 1. a game bird with a long tail and brilliant feathers. 2. *Am.* the ruffed grouse. [< AF < Pr. < L < Gk. *phasianos,* lit., Phasian; with ref. to River Phasis in Colchis]

phe·nac·e·tin, phe·nac·e·tine (fə·nas′ə·tin), *n.* a white, crystalline powder, $C_{10}H_{13}NO_2$, used to relieve fever and pain.

phe·nix (fē′niks), *n.* phoenix.

phe·no·bar·bi·tal (fē′nō·bär′bə·tôl; –tal), *n.* a white powder, used as a hypnotic or sedative.

phe·nol (fē′nol; –nol), *n.* carbolic acid. —phe·no·lic (fi·nō′lik; –nol′ik), *adj.*

phe·nol·phthal·ein (fē′nōl·thal′ēn; –fthal′–; fē′nol–), *n.* a white powder, $C_{20}H_{14}O_4$, used in testing acidity, making dyes, medicines, etc.

phe·nom·e·nal (fə·nom′ə·nəl), *adj.* 1. of or pertaining to a phenomenon or phenomena. 2. having the nature of a phenomenon. 3. extraordinary: *a phenomenal memory.* —phe·nom′e·nal·ly, *adv.*

phe·nom·e·non (fə·nom′ə·non), *n., pl.* –na (–nə) or (*esp. for def. 2*) –nons. 1. fact, event, or circumstance that can be observed: *lightning is an electrical phenomenon.* 2. an extraordinary or remarkable thing or person. [< L < Gk. *phainomenon,* neut. ppr. of *phainesthai* appear] —Syn. 1. occurrence, manifestation. 2. wonder, marvel, prodigy.

phew (fū), *interj.* exclamation of disgust, impatience, surprise, etc.

phi (fī; fē), *n.* the 21st letter of the Greek alphabet (Φ, φ).

phi·al (fī′əl), *n.* a small bottle; vial. [< F < LL < L *phiala* < Gk. *phiale* a broad flat vessel]

Phi Be·ta Kap·pa (fī′ bā′tə kap′ə; bē′tə), *Am.* society composed of American college students and graduates who have ranked high in scholarship.

Phid·i·as (fid′i·əs), *n.* 500?–432? B.C., famous Greek sculptor. —Phid′i·an, *adj.*

Phil., 1. Philemon. 2. Philippians. 3. Philippine.

Phila., Philadelphia.

Phil·a·del·phi·a (fil′ə·del′fi·ə; –del′fyə), *n.* city in SE Pennsylvania, on the Delaware River.

phi·lan·der (fə·lan′dər), *v.* make love without serious intentions; flirt. [orig. n., < Gk., < *philos* loving + *aner* man; appar. taken as "loving man"] —phi·lan′der·er, *n.*

phi·lan·thro·py (fə·lan′thrə·pi), *n., pl.* –pies. 1. love of mankind shown by practical kindness and helpfulness to humanity. 2. thing that benefits humanity: *a hospital is a useful philanthropy.* [< LL < Gk., ult. < *philos* loving + *anthropos* man] —phil·an·throp·ic (fil′ən·throp′ik), phil′an·throp′i·cal, *adj.* —phil′an·throp′i·cal·ly, *adv.* —phi·lan′thro·pist, *n.* —Syn. 1. benevolence, charity.

phi·lat·e·ly (fə·lat′ə·li), *n.* the collecting, arranging, and study of postage stamps, stamped envelopes, post cards, etc. [< F, ult. < Gk. *philos* loving + *ateleia* exemption from tax; the stamp indicates the tax is paid] —phi·la·tel·ic (fil′ə·tel′ik), *adj.* —phil′a·tel′i·cal·ly, *adv.* —phi·lat′e·list, *n.*

Phi·le·mon (fə·lē′mən), *n.* book of the New Testament written by Paul.

phil·har·mon·ic (fil′här·mon′ik; fil′ər–), *adj.* devoted to music; loving music: *a musical club is often called a philharmonic society.* [< F, ult. < Gk. *philos* loving + *harmonia* music]

Phil·ip (fil′əp), *n.* one of the twelve disciples chosen by Jesus as his Apostles.

Philip II, 1. 382–336 B.C., king of Macedonia 359–336 B.C. and the father of Alexander the Great. 2. 1527–1598, king of Spain 1556–1598. He sent the Armada against England.

Phi·lip·pi (fə·lip′ī), *n.* city in ancient Macedonia.

Phi·lip·pi·ans (fə·lip′i·ənz), *n.* one of the books of the New Testament, a letter from Paul to the early Christians of Philippi.

Phi·lip·pic (fə·lip′ik), *n.* 1. any of several orations by Demosthenes denouncing King Philip of Macedonia. 2. any of several orations by Cicero denouncing Marcus Antonius. 3. philippic, a bitter attack in words.

Phil·ip·pine (fil′ə·pēn), *adj.* of or having to do with the Philippine Islands or their inhabitants. Also, Filipine, Filipino.

Philippine Islands, or **Philippines,** *n.pl.* group of 7083 islands in the W Pacific, SE of Asia and N of Australia.

Phi·lis·tine (fə·lis′tin; fil′əs·tēn; –tīn), *n.* 1. *Bible.* one of a warlike people in SW Palestine. 2. person who is commonplace in ideas and tastes. —*adj.* 1. of the Philistines. 2. lacking culture; commonplace. —**Phi·lis′tin·ism,** *n.*

phil·o·den·dron (fil′ə·den′drən), *n.* a tropical American climbing evergreen plant, often grown as a house plant for its smooth, shiny leaves.

phi·lol·o·gy (fi·lol′ə·ji), *n.* 1. an older name for linguistics. 2. the study of literary and other records. [< L < Gk., < *philos* loving + *logos* word, speech, story] —**phil·o·log·ic** (fil′ə·loj′ik), **phil′o·log′i·cal,** *adj.* —**phi·lol′o·gist, phi·lo·lo·gi·an** (fil′ə·lō′ji·ən; –jən), *n.*

phil·o·mel (fil′ə·mel), **phil·o·me·la** (fil′ə·mē′lə), *n. Poetic.* nightingale.

philos., philosophical; philosophy.

phi·los·o·pher (fə·los′ə·fər), *n.* 1. person who studies philosophy much. 2. person who has a system of philosophy. 3. person who shows the calmness of philosophy under hard conditions, accepting life and making the best of it.

philosophers′ stone, substance believed to have the power to change base metals into gold or silver.

phil·o·soph·i·cal (fil′ə·sof′ə·kəl), **phil·o·soph·ic** (–ik), *adj.* 1. of philosophy. 2. knowing much about philosophy. 3. devoted to philosophy. 4. wise; calm; reasonable. —**phil′o·soph′i·cal·ly,** *adv.*

phi·los·o·phize (fə·los′ə·fīz), *v.,* –**phized,** –**phiz·ing.** think or reason as a philosopher does; try to understand and explain things: *philosophize about life.* —**phi·los′o·phiz′er,** *n.*

phi·los·o·phy (fə·los′ə·fi), *n., pl.* –**phies.** 1. study of the truth or principles underlying all knowledge; study of the most general causes and principles of the universe. 2. explanation or theory of the universe. 3. system for guiding life. 4. the broad general principles of a particular subject: *the philosophy of history.* 5. a reasonable attitude; calmness. [< L < Gk., love of wisdom ult. < *philos* loving + *sophos* wise]

phil·ter, phil·tre (fil′tər), *n., v.,* –**tered,** –**ter·ing;** –**tred,** –**tring.** —*n.* 1. drug or potion used to make a person fall in love. 2. a magic drink. —*v.* charm by a potion. [< F < L < Gk. *philtron* love charm ult. < *philos* loving]

phle·bi·tis (fli·bī′tis), *n.* inflammation of a vein. —**phle·bit·ic** (fli·bit′ik), *adj.*

phle·bot·o·my (fli·bot′ə·mi), *n.* opening a vein to let blood; bleeding. [< LL < Gk., ult. < *phleps* vein + –*tomos* cutting] —**phle·bot′o·mist,** *n.*

phlegm (flem), *n.* 1. the thick discharge from the nose or throat that accompanies a cold. 2. sluggish disposition or temperament; indifference. 3. coolness; calmness. [< OF < LL < Gk. *phlegma* clammy humor (resulting from heat) < *phlegein* burn]

phleg·mat·ic (fleg·mat′ik), **phleg·mat·i·cal** (–ə·kəl), *adj.* 1. sluggish; indifferent. 2. cool; calm. —**phleg·mat′i·cal·ly,** *adv.*

phlox (floks), *n.* 1. plant with clusters of showy flowers in various colors. 2. the flower. [< L < Gk., a plant; lit., flame]

Phnom Penh (pə·nôm′ pen′), *n.* capital of Cambodia.

pho·bi·a (fō′bi·ə), *n.* a morbid or insane fear. [< NL < Gk. –*phobia* < *phobos* fear] —**pho′bic,** *adj.*

Phoe·be (fē′bē), *n.* 1. *Gk. Myth.* goddess of the moon, also called Artemis by the Greeks and Diana by the Romans. 2. *Poetic.* the moon.

phoe·be (fē′bē), *n. Am.* a small American bird with a grayish-olive back, a yellowish breast, and a low crest on the head. [imit., but accommodated to *Phoebe*]

Phoe·bus (fē′bəs), *n.* 1. *Gk. Myth.* Apollo, the god of the sun. 2. *Poetic.* the sun.

Phoe·ni·cia (fə·nish′ə), *n.* an ancient country in W Syria, on the Mediterranean Sea. —**Phoe·ni′cian,** *adj., n.*

phoe·nix (fē′niks), *n.* a mythical bird, the only one of its kind, said to live 500 or 600 years, to burn itself on a funeral pile, and to rise again from the ashes, fresh and beautiful, for another long life. Also, phenix. [< L < Gk. *phoinix,* prob. < Egyptian *bonu, bennu* heron]

Phoebe (ab. 7 in. long)

Phoe·nix (fē′niks), *n.* capital of Arizona, in the C part.

phone[1] (fōn), *n., v.,* **phoned, phon·ing.** *Am., Colloq.* telephone. ▷ Phone is the normal informal word for *telephone* as noun (*on the phone*) or verb (*phone me later*).

phone[2] (fōn), *n. Phonet.* a speech sound. [< Gk.]

pho·neme (fō′nēm), *n. Phonet.* one of a group of distinctive sounds that make up the words of a language. The words *cat* and *bat* are distinguished by their initial phonemes /k/ and /b/. A phoneme comprises several sounds (allophones) which are not meaningful in themselves. The *p* in *pit* and the *p* in *ship,* though differing slightly in pronunciation, belong to the one phoneme /p/. [< Gk. *phonema* a sound] —**pho·ne′mic,** *adj.*

pho·ne·mics (fə·nē′miks), *n.* branch of linguistics dealing with phonemes. —**pho·ne·mi·cist** (fə·nē′mə·sist), *n.*

phonet., phonetics.

pho·net·ic (fə·net′ik), *adj.* 1. of or having to do with speech sounds: *phonetic laws.* 2. representing speech sounds: *phonetic symbols.* [< NL < Gk., ult. < *phone* sound] —**pho·net′i·cal·ly,** *adv.*

pho·net·ics (fə·net′iks), *n.* science dealing with speech sounds and the art of pronunciation. —**pho·ne·ti·cian** (fō′nə·tish′ən), *n.*

phon·ic (fon′ik; fō′nik), *adj.* 1. of sound. 2. of speech sounds; phonetic. 3. voiced.

phon·ics (fon′iks; fō′niks), *n.* simplified phonetics for teaching reading.

pho·no·gen·ic (fō′nə·jen′ik), *adj. Am.* having voice qualities that are ideal for transmission by telephone.

pho·no·gram (fō′nə·gram), *n.* character or symbol representing a single speech sound, syllable, or word. [< *phono–* (< Gk. *phone* sound) + –GRAM] —**pho′no·gram′ic, pho′no·gram′mic,** *adj.*

pho·no·graph (fō′nə·graf; –gräf), *n. Am.* instrument that records and reproduces sounds. [< *phono–* (< Gk. *phone* sound) + –GRAPH] —**pho′no·graph′ic,** *adj. Am.* —**pho′no·graph′i·cal·ly,** *adv.*

pho·nol·o·gy (fō·nol′ə·ji), *n.* 1. system of sounds used in a language. 2. study of the sounds of a language, their history and changes. [< *phono–* (< Gk. *phone* sound) + –LOGY] —**pho·no·log·ic** (fō′nə·loj′ik), **pho′no·log′i·cal,** *adj.* —**pho′no·log′i·cal·ly,** *adv.* —**pho·nol′o·gist,** *n.*

pho·ny, pho·ney (fō′ni), *adj.,* –**ni·er,** –**ni·est;** –**ney·er,** –**ney·est;** *n., pl.* –**nies;** –**neys.** *Am., Slang.* —*adj.* not genuine; counterfeit; fraudulent. —*n.* fake; pretender. [< *fawney,* a gilt brass ring used by swindlers < Irish]

phos·gene (fos′jēn), *n.* a dangerous poisonous gas, COCl₂, used in war.

phos·phate (fos′fāt), *n.* 1. *Chem.* salt or ester of an acid containing phosphorus. 2. fertilizer containing such salts. 3. drink of carbonated water flavored with fruit syrup, and containing a little phosphoric acid.

phos·phide (fos′fīd; -fĭd), **phos·phid** (-fĭd), *n. Chem.* compound of phosphorus with a basic element or radical.

phos·pho·resce (fos′fə·res′), *v.,* -resced, -resc·ing. be luminous without noticeable heat. —**phos′pho·res′cence**, *n.* —**phos′pho·res′cent**, *adj.*

phos·phor·ic (fos·fôr′ik; -for′-), *adj. Chem.* pertaining to or containing phosphorus, esp. in its higher valence.

phosphoric acid, a colorless, odorless acid, H_3PO_4, containing phosphorus.

phos·pho·rous (fos′fə·rəs; fos·fô′-; -fō′-), *adj. Chem.* pertaining to or containing phosphorus, esp. in its lower valence.

phos·pho·rus (fos′fə·rəs), *n., pl.* -ri (-rī). *Chem.* a solid nonmetallic element, P, existing in two forms; one yellow, poisonous, inflammable, and luminous in the dark; the other red, nonpoisonous, and less inflammable. [< L < Gk. *phosphoros* the morning star < *phos* light + *pherein* bring]

phos·phu·ret·ed, phos·phu·ret·ted (fos′fy̆ə·ret′id), *adj. Chem.* combined with phosphorus.

pho·to (fō′tō), *n., pl.* -tos. *Colloq.* photograph. ➤ Photo as a clip from *photograph* is in colloquial use, but is not so widely current as, say, *phone* for *telephone,* because of the convenient substitute *picture.*

pho·to·e·lec·tric (fō′tō·i·lek′trik), *adj.* 1. pertaining to the electricity or electrical effects produced by light. 2. noting or pertaining to an apparatus for taking photographs by electric light.

photoelectric cell, cell or vacuum tube which produces variations in an electric current in accordance with variations in the light falling upon it.

pho·to·en·grav·ing (fō′tō·en·grāv′ing), *n.* 1. process by which plates to print from are produced with the aid of photography. 2. plate so produced. 3. picture printed from it. —**pho′to·en·grav′er,** *n.*

photo finish, *Am.* in racing, a finish so close that a photograph is required to decide the winner.

pho·to·flash lamp (fō′tə·flash′), an electrically fired lamp used to take instantaneous flashlight photographs.

pho·to·flood lamp (fō′tə·flud′), an electric lamp that gives very bright, sustained light, for taking pictures.

photog., photography.

pho·to·gen·ic (fō′tə·jen′ik), *adj.* 1. photographing very well, esp. in motion pictures: *a photogenic face.* 2. *Biol.* phosphorescent; luminescent. Certain bacteria are photogenic. [< *photo-* light (< Gk. *phos*) + *-genes* born, produced]

pho·to·graph (fō′tə·graf; -gräf), *n.* picture made with a camera. A photograph is made by the action of the light rays from the thing pictured coming through the lens of the camera onto a film spread over the surface of glass, paper, celluloid, or metal. —*v.* 1. take a photograph of. 2. take photographs. 3. look (clear, unnatural, etc.) in a photograph: *she does not photograph well.* [< *photo-* light (< Gk. *phos*) + -GRAPH]

pho·tog·ra·phy (fə·tog′rə·fi), *n.* the taking of photographs. —**pho·tog′ra·pher,** *n.* —**pho·to·graph·ic** (fō′tə·graf′ik), **pho′to·graph′i·cal,** *adj.* —**pho′to·graph′i·cal·ly,** *adv.*

pho·to·gra·vure (fō′tə·grə·vyur′; -grā′vyər), *n.* 1. photoengraving. 2. a metal plate on which a photograph has been engraved.

pho·tom·e·ter (fō·tom′ə·tər), *n.* instrument for measuring the intensity of light.

pho·tom·e·try (fō·tom′ə·tri), *n.* branch of physics dealing with measurements of the intensity of light. —**pho·to·met·ric** (fō′tə·met′rik), **pho′to·met′ri·cal,** *adj.* —**pho·tom′e·trist,** *n.*

pho·to·mon·tage (fō′tō·mon·täzh′; -môn-), *n.* montage that uses photographs.

pho·to·mu·ral (fō′tō·myur′əl), *n.* mural consisting of a greatly enlarged photograph or photographs.

pho·ton (fō′ton), *n. Physics.* unit of visible light, or in general, of radiant energy.

pho·to·play (fō′tə·plā′), *n. Am.* a motion-picture play.

pho·to·sen·si·tive (fō′tō·sen′sə·tiv), *adj.* readily stimulated to action by light.

pho·to·stat (fō′tə·stat), *n.* 1. Photostat, *Trademark.* a special camera for making copies of maps, drawings, pages of books, etc., directly on specially prepared paper. 2. photograph made with it. —*v.* make such a photograph of. —**pho′to·stat′ic,** *adj.*

pho·to·syn·the·sis (fō′tō·sin′thə·sis), *n.* process by which plant cells make sugar from carbon dioxide and water in the presence of chlorophyll and light.

pho·to·te·leg·ra·phy (fō′tō·tə·leg′rə·fi), *n.* 1. telegraphy by means of light, as with a heliograph. 2. the electric transmission of facsimiles of photographs. —**pho·to·tel·e·graph·ic** (fō′tō·tel′ə·graf′ik), *adj.*

pho·tot·ro·pism (fō·tot′rə·piz·əm), *n.* tendency to turn in response to light. [< *photo-* light (< Gk. *phos*) + Gk. *-tropos* turning]

phrase (frāz), *n., v.,* phrased, phras·ing. —*n.* 1. combination of words: *he spoke in simple phrases.* 2. expression often used: *"call up" is the common phrase for "get a telephone connection with."* 3. a short, striking expression. *Examples:* A Fair Deal; a war to end wars; liberty or death. 4. a group of words not containing a subject and predicate and used as a single word. *Examples:* in the house; coming by the church; to eat too fast. 5. a short part of a piece of music, usually containing four measures. —*v.* 1. express in a particular way: *she phrased her excuse politely.* 2. mark off or bring out the phrases of (a piece of music). [< L < Gk. *phrasis* < *phrazein* express] —**phras′al,** *adj.*

phra·se·ol·o·gy (frā′zi·ol′ə·ji), *n., pl.* -gies. selection and arrangement of words; particular way in which a person expresses himself in language: *the phraseology of the Bible.* —**phra·se·o·log·i·cal** (frā′zi·ə·loj′ə·kəl), *adj.*

phre·net·ic (fri·net′ik), **phre·net·i·cal** (-ə·kəl), *adj.* 1. frenzied; frenetic. 2. insane. [< OF < L < Gk. *phrenetikos.* Doublet of FRANTIC.] —**phre·net′i·cal·ly,** *adv.*

phre·nol·o·gy (fri·nol′ə·ji), *n. Am.* theory that the shape of the skull shows what sort of mind and character a person has. [< Gk. *phren* mind + -LOGY] —**phren·o·log·ic** (fren′ə·loj′ik), **phren′o·log′i·cal,** *adj.* —**phre·nol′o·gist,** *n.*

Phryg·i·a (frij′i·ə), *n.* an ancient country in the C and NW part of Asia Minor. —**Phryg′i·an,** *adj., n.*

phthi·sis (thī′sis), **phthis·ic** (tiz′ik), *n.* tuberculosis of the lungs; consumption. [< L < Gk., < *phthinein* waste away] —**phthis·i·cal** (tiz′ə·kəl), *adj.*

phy·lac·ter·y (fə·lak′tər·i), *n., pl.* -ter·ies. either of two small leather cases containing texts from the Jewish law, worn by orthodox Jews during prayer to remind them to keep the law. [< LL < Gk. *phylakterion* safeguard, ult. < *phylax* watchman]

phy·log·e·ny (fī·loj′ə·ni), *n., pl.* -nies. racial history; the origin and development (of a kind of animal or plant). [< G, < Gk. *phylon* race + *-geneia* origin] —**phy·lo·ge·net·ic** (fī′lō·jə·net′ik), **phy·lo·gen·ic** (fī′lō·jen′ik), *adj.* —**phy′lo·ge·net′i·cal·ly,** *adv.*

phy·lum (fī′ləm), *n., pl.* -la (-lə). a primary division of the animal or vegetable kingdom, usually equivalent to a subkingdom. [< NL < Gk. *phylon* race, stock]

phys·ic (fiz′ik), *n., v.,* -icked, -ick·ing. —*n.* 1. medicine, esp. one that moves the bowels. 2. art of healing; science and practice of medicine. —*v.* 1. move the bowels of. 2. give medicine to. 3. act like a medicine on; cure. [< L < Gk. *physike* (episteme) (knowledge) of nature, ult. < *phyein* produce]

phys·i·cal (fiz′ə·kəl), *adj.* 1. of the body:

physical exercise. **2.** of matter; material: *the tide is a physical force.* **3.** according to the laws of nature: *a physical impossibility.* **4.** of the science of physics. —**phys′i·cal·ly,** *adv.* —**Syn. 1.** bodily, corporal, corporeal.

physical chemistry, branch of chemistry that deals with the physical properties of substances and uses physical methods to solve chemical problems.

physical education, *Am.* instruction in how to exercise and take care of the body.

physical geography, study of land forms, climate, winds, ocean currents, and all other physical features of the earth.

physical science, 1. physics. **2.** physics, chemistry, geology, astronomy, and other sciences of physical facts.

phy·si·cian (fə·zish′ən), *n.* doctor of medicine.

phys·ics (fiz′iks), *n.* science that deals with matter and energy that do not involve change in composition, or with the action of different forms of energy on matter. Physics studies mechanics, heat, light, sound, and electricity. [pl. of *physic* (= Gk. *ta physika* the natural things)] —**phys′i·cist** (fiz′ə·sist), *n.*

phys·i·og·no·my (fiz′i·og′nə·mi; -i·on′ə-), *n., pl.* -mies. **1.** kind of features or type of face one has; one's face. **2.** art of estimating character from the features of the face or the form of the body. [< LL < Gk., < *physis* nature + *gnomon* judge] —**phys·i·og·nom·ic** (fiz′i·og·nom′ik; -i·ə-nom′ik), **phys·i·og·nom′i·cal,** *adj.* —**phys·i·og·nom′i·cal·ly,** *adv.* —**phys·i·og′no·mist,** *n.*

phys·i·og·ra·phy (fiz′i·og′rə·fi), *n.* **1.** physical geography. **2.** formerly, the science of nature in general. [< *physio-* (< Gk. *physis* nature) + *-graphy* (< Gk. *graphein* write)] —**phys·i·og′-ra·pher,** *n.* —**phys·i·o·graph·ic** (fiz′i·ə·graf′ik), **phys′i·o·graph′i·cal,** *adj.*

physiol., physiological; physiologist; physiology.

phys·i·ol·o·gy (fiz′i·ol′ə·ji), *n.* **1.** science dealing with the normal functions of living things or their organs: *animal physiology, human physiology, plant physiology.* **2.** all the functions and activities of a living thing or of one of its organs. [< L < Gk., < *physis* nature + *-logos* treating of] —**phys·i·o·log·i·cal** (fiz′i·ə-loj′ə·kəl), **phys′i·o·log′ic,** *adj.* —**phys′i·o·log′i·cal·ly,** *adv.* —**phys′i·ol′o·gist,** *n.*

phys·i·o·ther·a·py (fiz′i·ō·ther′ə·pi), *n.* treatment of diseases and defects by physical remedies, such as massage or electricity (rather than by drugs). [< *physio-* (< Gk. *physis* nature) + *therapy*]

phy·sique (fi·zēk′), *n.* bodily structure, organization, or development: *a man of strong physique.* [< F, physical. See PHYSIC.]

pi¹ (pī), *n., pl.* pis. **1.** *Math.* ratio of the circumference of any circle to its diameter, usually written as π. (π = 3.141592+.) **2.** the 16th letter of the Greek alphabet (Π, π). [def. 1 use of Gk. letter to mean Gk. *periphereia* PERIPHERY]

pi² (pī), *n., v.,* pied, pi·ing. —*n.* **1.** printing types all mixed up. **2.** any confused mixture. —*v.* mix up (type). Also, pie.

P.I., Philippine Islands.

pi·a·nis·si·mo (pē′ə·nis′ə·mō), *adj., adv., n., pl.* -mos, -mi (-mē). *Music.* —*adj.* very soft. —*adv.* very softly. —*n.* a passage played this way. [< Ital., superlative of *piano* soft. See PIANO².]

pi·an·ist (pi·an′ist; pē′ə·nist), *n.* person who plays the piano.

pi·an·o¹ (pi·an′ō), *n., pl.* -an·os. a large musical instrument whose tones come from many wires. The wires are sounded by hammers that are worked by striking keys on a keyboard. [for *pianoforte*]

pi·a·no² (pi·ä′nō), *Music.* —*adj.* soft. —*adv.* softly. [< Ital. < L *planus* plain. Doublet of PLAIN and PLAN.]

pi·an·o·for·te (pi·an′ə·fôr′tē, -fôr′-; pi·an′-

ə·fôrt, -fōrt), *n.* piano¹. [< Ital., < *piano* soft + *forte* loud]

pi·as·ter, pi·as·tre (pi·as′tər), *n.* **1.** coin worth from about ½ cent to about 3 cents (1950), used in Turkey, Egypt, Lebanon, Syria, etc. **2.** a former Spanish silver coin worth about a dollar.

pi·az·za (pi·az′ə), *n.* **1.** *Am.* a large porch along one or more sides of a house. **2.** an open public square in Italian towns. [< Ital. < L < Gk. *plateia* (*hodos*) broad (street). Doublet of PLACE and PLAZA.] —**Syn. 1.** veranda.

pi·broch (pē′brok), *n.* kind of musical piece performed on the bagpipe, usually warlike or sad. [< Scotch Gaelic *piobaireachd* pipe music, ult. < *piob* pipe]

pi·ca (pī′kə), *n.* **1.** size of type, 12 point.

This line is in pica.

2. this size used as a measure; about ⅙ inch. [< Anglo-L, name of a book of rules concerning holy days, supposed (? erroneously) to be printed in pica]

pic·a·dor (pik′ə·dôr), *n.* one of the horsemen who open a bullfight by irritating the bull with pricks of their lances. [< Sp., < *picar* pierce]

Pic·ar·dy (pik′ər·di), *n.* region in N France.

pic·a·resque (pik′ə·resk′), *adj.* dealing with rogues and their questionable adventures: *a picaresque novel.* [< Sp., < *picaro* rogue]

Pi·cas·so (pi·kä′sō), *n.* Pablo, born 1881, Spanish-French painter and sculptor.

pic·a·yune (pik′ə·ūn′), *Am.* —*n.* **1.** any coin of small value. **2.** an insignificant person or thing; trifle. —*adj.* Also, pic′a·yun′ish. small; petty; mean. [< Louisiana F *picaillon* coin worth 5 cents]

Pic·ca·dil·ly (pik′ə·dil′i), *n.* one of the main business streets of London.

pic·ca·lil·li (pik′ə·lil′i), *n.* relish made of chopped pickles, onions, tomatoes, etc., with hot spices.

pic·co·lo (pik′ə·lō), *n., pl.* -los. a small, shrill flute, sounding an octave higher than the ordinary flute. [< Ital., small]

pick¹ (pik), *v.* **1.** choose; select. **2.** pull away with the fingers; gather: *we pick fruit and flowers.* **3.** use a pick or pickax. **4.** pierce, dig into, or break up with something pointed. **5.** use something pointed to remove things from: *pick one's teeth, pick a bone.* **6.** prepare for use by removing feathers, waste parts, etc. **7.** pull apart. **8.** *Am.* use fingers with a plucking motion: *play a banjo by picking its strings.* **9.** seek and find occasion for; seek and find: *pick a quarrel.* **10.** pick a lock, open a lock with a pointed instrument, wire, etc. **11.** pick a pocket, steal from a person's pocket. **12.** pick at, a. pull on with the fingers, etc. b. eat only a little of at a time. c. *Colloq.* find fault with; nag. **13.** pick off, shoot one at a time. **14.** pick on, a. *Colloq.* find fault with. b. *Colloq.* annoy; tease. c. select. **15.** pick out, a. choose; select. b. distinguish (a thing) from surroundings. c. make out (the sense or meaning). **16.** pick over, a. look over carefully. b. prepare for use. **17.** pick up, a. take up. b. summon (courage, etc.). c. get by chance: *pick up a bargain.* d. learn without being taught. e. take up into a vehicle or ship. f. *Colloq.* improve. g. regain; find again. h. go faster; increase in speed. i. become acquainted with without being introduced. j. *Am.* tidy up; put in order. —*n.* **1.** choice; selection. **2.** the best or most desirable part. **3.** amount of a crop gathered at one time. **4.** thing held in the fingers and used to pull on the strings of a musical instrument. [ME *picke(n);* cf. OE *picung* pricking] —**pick′er,** *n.* —**pick′y,** *adj.*

pick² (pik), *n.* **1.** a heavy, sharp-pointed tool for breaking earth, rock, etc.; pickax. **2.** a sharp-pointed tool: *ice is broken into pieces with a pick.* [ME *picke,* var. of *pik* PIKE¹]

pick·a·back (pik′ə·bak′), *adv.* on the back or shoulders.

pick·a·nin·ny (pik′ə·nin′i), *n., pl.* -nies. *Am.* **1.** a small Negro child. **2.** any small child. [< Pg. *pequenino* very small]

pick·ax, pick·axe (pik′aks′), *n.* a heavy tool with a sharp point for breaking up dirt, rocks, etc.; pick.

picked (pikt), *adj.* 1. cleaned by picking. 2. specially selected for merit.

pick·er·el (pik′ər·əl; pik′rəl), *n.*, *pl.* -els or (*esp. collectively*) -el. *U.S. and Canada.* kind of large fresh-water fish with a long, narrow, pointed head. [dim. of *pike*²]

pick·et (pik′it), *n.* 1. *Am.* a pointed stake or peg driven into the ground to make a fence, to tie a horse to, etc. 2. a small body of troops, or a single man, posted at some place to watch for the enemy and guard against surprise. 3. person stationed by a labor union near a factory, store, etc., where there is a strike. Pickets try to prevent employees from working or customers from buying. 4. a person who takes part in a public demonstration or boycott to support a cause; demonstrator. —*v.* 1. enclose with pickets; fence. 2. tie to a picket. 3. station as pickets. 4. station pickets at or near: *picket a factory.* 5. act as a picket. [< F, dim. of *pic* a pick. See PICK²] —**pick′et·er**, *n.* —**pick′et·ing**, *n.* —Syn. *n.* 2. sentry, sentinel.

picket fence, fence made of pickets.

pick·ings (pik′ingz), *n.pl.* 1. amount picked. 2. things left over; scraps. 3. things stolen or received dishonestly.

pick·le (pik′əl), *n.*, *v.*, -led, -ling. —*n.* 1. salt water, vinegar, or other liquid in which meat and vegetables can be preserved. 2. cucumber preserved in pickle. 3. any other vegetable preserved in pickle. 4. *Colloq.* trouble; difficulty. 5. an acid bath for cleaning metal castings, etc. —*v.* 1. preserve in pickle: *pickled beets.* 2. clean with acid. [< MDu. *pekel*] —**pick′ler**, *n.*

pick·pock·et (pik′pok′it), *n.* person who steals from people's pockets.

pick·up (pik′up′), *n.* 1. a picking up. 2. *Slang.* a getting better; improvement. 3. acceleration; going faster; increase in speed. 4. *Colloq.* acquaintance made without an introduction. 5. *Slang.* a bracing drink. 6. *Radio.* a. reception of sounds for broadcasting. b. apparatus for such reception. c. place where it occurs. 7. *Television.* a. reception of images and their conversion into electric waves. b. apparatus that does this. 8. the part of a phonograph that transforms the varying of the groove in the record into electrical or sound waves. 9. *Am.* a small, light truck for light hauling.

pic·nic (pik′nik), *n.*, *v.*, -nicked, -nick·ing. —*n.* 1. a pleasure trip with a meal in the open air. 2. *Slang.* a very easy job. —*v.* 1. go on a picnic. 2. eat in picnic style. [< F *piquenique*] —**pic′nick·er**, *n.*

pi·cot (pē′kō), *n.* one of a number of fancy loops in embroidery, tatting, etc., or along the edge of lace, ribbon, etc. —*v.* trim with such loops. [< F, dim. of *pic* a pick. See PICK².]

pic·ric acid (pik′rik), an intensely bitter acid, C₆H₂(NO₂)₃OH, used as a dye and in explosives. [< Gk. *pikros* bitter]

Pict (pikt), *n.* member of a nationality formerly living in Scotland, esp. N Scotland. —**Pict′ish,** *adj.*

pic·to·graph (pik′tə·graf; -gräf), *n.* picture used as a sign or symbol. [< L *pictus* painted + -GRAPH] —**pic′to·graph′ic,** *adj.* —**pic′to·graph′i·cal·ly,** *adv.* —**pic·tog·ra·phy** (pik·tog′rə·fi), *n.*

Pictographs for "weeping" and "forest"

pic·to·ri·al (pik·tô′ri·əl; -tō′-), *adj.* 1. pertaining to pictures; expressed in pictures. 2. making a picture for the mind; vivid. 3. illustrated by pictures: *a pictorial magazine.* 4. having to do with painters or painting. —*n.* magazine in which pictures are an important feature. —**pic·to′ri·al·ly,** *adv.*

pic·ture (pik′chər), *n.*, *v.*, -tured, -tur·ing. —*n.* 1. a drawing, painting, portrait, or photograph; a print of any of these. 2. scene. 3. something beautiful. 4. a visible image: *the picture in a mirror.* 5. a mental image: *memory's pictures.* 6. likeness: *he is the picture of his*

father. 7. example; embodiment: *she was the picture of despair.* 8. a motion picture. 9. a vivid description. —*v.* 1. draw, paint, etc.; make into a picture. 2. imagine: *it is hard to picture life a hundred years ago.* 3. describe vividly. [< L *pictura* < *pingere* to paint] —**pic′tur·a·ble,** *adj.* —**pic′tur·a·ble·ness,** *n.* —**pic′tured,** *adj.*

picture show, *Am.* a motion picture.

pic·tur·esque (pik′chər·esk′), *adj.* 1. quaint or interesting enough to be used as the subject of a picture: *a picturesque old mill.* 2. vivid. —**pic′tur·esque′ly,** *adv.* —**pic′tur·esque′ness,** *n.*

picture tube, the cathode-ray tube of a television receiver, the front of which constitutes the screen on which the picture being transmitted is reproduced.

picture window, a large window designed to give a wide view.

pid·dle (pid′əl), *v.*, -dled, -dling. do anything in a trifling or ineffective way. —**pid′dler,** *n.* —**pid′dling,** *adj.*

pidg·in English (pij′ən), one of several forms of English, with reduced grammatical structure and vocabulary, used in W Africa, Australia, Melanesia, and formerly in China, as a trade or communication jargon. Also, **pigeon English.** [*pidgin*, Chinese alter. of *business*]

pie¹ (pī), *n.* fruit, meat, etc., enclosed in pastry and baked. [ME *pye*]

pie² (pī), *n.* magpie. [< OF < L *pica*]

pie³ (pī), *n.*, *v.*, pied, pie·ing. pi². [? extended use of *pie*¹]

pie·bald (pī′bôld′), *adj.* spotted in two colors: *a piebald horse.* —*n.* a spotted horse. [appar. < *pie*² + *bald*; with ref. to dark color of magpie]

piece (pēs), *n.*, *v.*, pieced, piec·ing. —*n.* 1. one of the parts into which a thing is divided or broken; bit. 2. portion; part; small quantity: *piece of land, piece of bread.* 3. a single thing of a set or class: *this set of china has 144 pieces.* 4. coin. 5. example; instance: *piece of nonsense.* 6. a single composition in an art: *a new piece at a theater.* 7. gun; cannon. 8. quantity in which goods are made: *she bought the whole piece of muslin.* 9. figure, disk, block, or the like, used in playing checkers, chess, and other games. 10. **of a piece,** of the same kind; in keeping. —*v.* 1. make or repair by adding or joining pieces. 2. join the pieces of. [< OF < VL *pettia* fragment < Celtic] —**piec′er,** *n.* —**piec′ing,** *n.* —Syn. *n.* 1. fragment, scrap, section.

pièce de ré·sis·tance (pyes də rā·zēs·täNs′), *French.* 1. the chief dish of a meal. 2. the main article in any collection.

piece goods, fabrics sold by the piece.

piece·meal (pēs′mēl′), *adv.* 1. piece by piece; a little at a time. 2. piece from piece; to pieces; into fragments. —*adj.* done piece by piece.

piece of eight, an old Spanish dollar.

piece·work (pēs′werk′), *n.* work paid for by the amount done, not by the time it takes. —**piece′work′er,** *n.*

pied (pīd), *adj.* having patches of two or more colors; many-colored. [< *pie*²; with ref. to magpie's plumage]

pie·plant (pī′plant′; -plänt′), *n.* *Am.* rhubarb.

pier (pir), *n.* 1. structure extending into the water, used as a walk or a landing place. 2. breakwater. 3. one of the solid supports on which the arches of a bridge rest; any solid support of masonry. 4. the solid part of a wall between windows, doors, etc. [< Med.L *pera*]

pierce (pirs), *v.*, pierced, pierc·ing. 1. go into; go through: *a tunnel pierces the mountain.* 2. make a hole in; bore into or through: *a nail pierced the tire of our car.* 3. force a way; force a way through or into: *the cold pierces to my bones, the wind pierces our shelter.* 4. sound sharply through, as a cry through the air. 5. make a way through with the eye or mind: *pierce a disguise, pierce a mystery.* 6. affect sharply. [< OF *percier*, ult. < L *pertusus* pierced] —**pierc′er,** *n.* —**pierc′ing,** *adj.* —**pierc′ing·ly,** *adv.* —**pierc′ing·ness,** *n.* —Syn. 2. prick, perforate, puncture.

Pierce (pirs), *n.* Franklin, 1804-1869, the 14th president of the United States, 1853-1857.

Pi·e·ri·an (pī·ir′i·ən), *adj.* of the Muses.

Pierre (pir), *n.* capital of South Dakota.

pi·e·tism (pī′ə·tiz·əm), *n.* 1. deep piety. 2. pretended piety. —**pi′e·tist**, *n.* —**pi′e·tis′tic**, **pi′-e·tis′ti·cal**, *adj.*

pi·e·ty (pī′ə·ti), *n., pl.* **-ties.** 1. a being pious; reverence for God; devotion to religion. 2. dutiful regard for one's parents or other elders. 3. a pious act, remark, belief, etc. [< OF < L *pietas* < *pius* pious. Doublet of PITY.]

pif·fle (pif′əl), *n.* Colloq. silly talk; nonsense.

pig (pig), *n.* 1. a swine or hog, a domestic animal raised for its meat. 2. a young hog. 3. pork. 4. Colloq. person who seems or acts like a pig. 5. an oblong mass of metal that has been run into a mold while hot. [OE *picg* (in *picg-bred* acorn, lit., pig-bread)] —**pig′like′**, *adj.*

pi·geon (pij′ən), *n.* 1. kind of bird with a plump body and short legs; dove. 2. Slang. person who is easily tricked. [< OF < VL < LL *pipio* squab]

pigeon English, pidgin English.

pigeon hawk, a small hawk.

pi·geon·hole (pij′ən·hōl′), *n., v.,* **-holed, -hol·ing.** —*n.* one of a set of boxlike compartments for holding papers and other articles in a desk, a cabinet, etc. —*v.* 1. put in a pigeonhole; put away. 2. classify and lay aside in memory where one can refer to it. 3. put aside with the idea of dismissing, forgetting, etc.

pi·geon·toed (pij′ən·tōd′), *adj.* having the toes or feet turned inward.

pig·ger·y (pig′ər·i), *n., pl.* **-ger·ies.** place where pigs are kept.

pig·gish (pig′ish), *adj.* like a pig; greedy; filthy. —**pig′gish·ly**, *adv.* —**pig′gish·ness**, *n.*

pig·gy, pig·gie (pig′i), *n., pl.* **-gies,** *adj.* —*n.* a little pig. —*adj.* greedy.

pig·gy-back, pig·gy·back (pig′i·bak′), Colloq. —*adj.* designating the carrying of anything that usually moves alone by a larger vehicle, etc., as a trailer truck by a railroad flatcar. —*v.* pickaback.

pig·head·ed (pig′hed′id), *adj.* stupidly obstinate or stubborn.

pig iron, crude iron as it first comes from the blast furnace or smelter, usually cast into oblong masses called pigs.

pig·ment (pig′mənt), *n.* coloring matter. The color of a person's hair, skin, and eyes is due to pigment in the cells of the body. [< L *pigmentum*, ult. < *pingere* to paint. Doublet of PIMENTO.] —**pig·men·ta·ry** (pig′mən·ter′i), *adj.*

pig·men·ta·tion (pig′mən·tā′shən), *n.* deposit of pigment in the tissue of a living animal or plant, causing coloration or discoloration.

pig·my, Pig·my (pig′mi), *n., pl.* **-mies,** *adj.* pygmy.

pig·skin (pig′skin′), *n.* 1. skin of a pig. 2. leather made from it. 3. Am., Colloq. football.

pig·sty (pig′stī′), **pig·pen** (-pen′), *n., pl.* **-sties; -pens.** 1. pen where pigs are kept. 2. a filthy place.

pig·tail (pig′tāl′), *n.* 1. braid of hair hanging from the back of the head. 2. twist of tobacco.

pike¹ (pīk), *n.* a long wooden shaft with a sharp-pointed metal head; spear. [OE *pīc* pick] —**pike′man**, *n.*

pike² (pīk), *n.* a large fresh-water fish with a long, narrow, pointed head. [for *pikefish*. See PICK².]

pike³ (pīk), *n.* turnpike. [for *turnpike*]

pik·er (pīk′ər), *n. Am., Slang.* person who does things in a small or cheap way.

Pike's Peak (pīks), mountain of the Rocky Mountains, in C Colorado.

pike·staff (pīk′staf′; -stäf′), *n., pl.* **-staves** (-stāvz′). staff or shaft of a pike or spear.

pi·las·ter (pə·las′tər), *n.* a rectangular pillar, esp. when it forms part of a wall from which it projects somewhat. [< F < Ital. *pilastro* < L *pila* pillar] —**pi·las′tered**, *adj.*

Soldier holding a pike

Pi·late (pī′lət), *n.* Pontius, Roman governor of Judea, 26-36? A.D. During his rule Christ was crucified.

pi·lau, pi·law (pi·lô′), **pi·laf** (pi·läf′), *n.* an Oriental dish consisting of rice boiled with mutton, fowl, or the like, and flavored with spices, raisins, etc. [< Pers. *pilāw*]

pil·chard (pil′chərd), *n.* 1. sardine. 2. a small sea fish like it.

pile¹ (pīl), *n., v.,* **piled, pil·ing.** —*n.* 1. many things lying one upon another in a more or less orderly way: *pile of wood.* 2. mass like a hill or mound: *pile of dirt.* 3. heap of wood on which a dead body or sacrifice is burned. 4. a large structure or mass of buildings. 5. Colloq. a large amount. 6. Am., Colloq. a large amount of money; fortune. 7. Nuclear Physics. former name of a reactor. 8. Elect. a. series of plates of different metals, arranged alternately with cloth or paper wet with acid between them, for producing an electric current. b. any similar arrangement for producing an electric current; battery. —*v.* 1. make into a pile; heap evenly; heap up. 2. gather or rise in piles. 3. cover with large amounts. 4. go in a confused, rushing crowd. [< OF < L *pila* pillar] —**piled**, *adj.* —Syn. *n.* 1. heap, stack.

pile² (pīl), *n., v.,* **piled, pil·ing.** —*n.* a heavy beam driven into the earth, often under water, to help support a bridge, wharf, etc. —*v.* furnish with piles; drive piles into. [< L *pilum* javelin]

pile³ (pīl), *n.* 1. a soft, thick nap on velvet, plush, and many carpets. 2. a soft, fine hair or down; wool. [< L *pilus* hair] —**piled**, *adj.*

piles (pīlz), *n.pl.* swelling of blood vessels at the anus, often painful; hemorrhoids.

pil·fer (pil′fər), *v.* steal in small quantities; steal. [< OF *pelfrer* rob. Cf. PELF.] —**pil′fer·er**, *n.* —Syn. filch, embezzle.

pil·grim (pil′grəm), *n.* 1. person who goes on a journey to a sacred or holy place as an act of religious devotion. 2. traveler; wanderer. 3. Pilgrim, Am. one of the Puritan settlers of Plymouth Colony in 1620. [< AF < Med.L *peregrinus* pilgrim < L, foreigner. Doublet of PEREGRINE.] —Syn. 1. crusader. 2. wayfarer.

pil·grim·age (pil′grə·mij), *n.* 1. a pilgrim's journey; journey to some sacred place as an act of religious devotion. 2. a long journey. 3. life thought of as a journey.

pil·ing (pīl′ing), *n.* 1. piles or heavy beams driven into the ground, etc. 2. structure made of piles.

pill (pil), *n.* 1. medicine made up into a tiny ball to be swallowed whole. 2. a very small ball of anything. 3. Slang. ball, esp. a baseball or golf ball. 4. Slang. an unpleasant person. [< MDu. or MLG < L *pilula*, dim. of *pila* ball]

pil·lage (pil′ij), *v.,* **-laged, -lag·ing.** *n.* —*v.* rob with violence; plunder: *pirates pillaged the towns along the coast.* —*n.* plunder; robbery. [< OF, < *piller* plunder < VL *pillare*] —**pil′lag·er**, *n.* —Syn. *v.* sack, strip.

pil·lar (pil′ər), *n.* 1. a slender, upright structure; column. Pillars are usually made of stone, wood, or metal and used as supports or ornaments for a building. Sometimes a pillar stands alone as a monument. 2. anything slender and upright like a pillar. 3. an important support. A person of strong character or important position is a pillar of society. 4. from pillar to post, from one thing or place to another without any definite purpose. [< OF *piler*, ult. < L *pila* pillar] —**pil′lared**, *adj.* —Syn. 3. upholder.

pill·box (pil′boks′), *n.* 1. box, usually shallow and often round, for holding pills. 2. a small, low fortress with very thick walls and roof.

pil·lion (pil′yən), *n.* pad attached behind a saddle for a person to sit on. [< Scotch Gaelic *pillin*, dim. of *pell* cushion < L *pellis* skin]

pil·lo·ry (pil′ə·ri), *n., pl.* **-ries,** *v.,* **-ried, -ry·ing.** —*n.* frame of wood with holes through which a person's head and hands were put, formerly used as a punishment, being set up in a public place where the crowd could make fun of the offender. —*v.* 1. put in the pillory. 2.

expose to public ridicule, contempt, or abuse. [< OF *pellori* < Pr. *espilori*]

pil·low (pil'ō), *n.* 1. bag or case filled with feathers, down, or other soft material. 2. cushion; pad. —*v.* rest on a pillow. [ult. < L *pulvinus*] —**pil'low·like**', *adj.* —**pil'low·y**, *adj.*

pil·low·case (pil'ō·kās'), **pil·low·slip** (-slip'), *n.* a cotton or linen cover pulled over a pillow.

pi·lose (pī'lōs), *adj.* covered with soft hair; hairy. [< L, < *pilus* hair]

pi·lot (pī'lət), *n.* 1. man who steers a ship. 2. man whose business is steering ships in or out of a harbor or through dangerous waters. A ship takes on a pilot before coming into a strange harbor. 3. person who steers an airplane, airship, or balloon. 4. guide; leader. 5. device that controls the action of one part of a machine, motor, etc. —*v.* 1. act as the pilot of; steer. 2. guide; lead. [< F < Ital. *pilota*] —**pi'lot·less**, *adj.* —Syn. *n.* 1. steersman, helmsman.

pi·lot·age (pī'lət·ij), *n.* 1. piloting. 2. the fee paid for a pilot's service.

pilot biscuit or **bread**, *Am.* a ship biscuit; large, flat cracker.

pilot fish, a small, bluish fish found in warm seas, often accompanying sharks.

pilot light, a small light kept burning all the time and used to light a main light whenever desired.

pilot plant, the equipment necessary to carry out on a small scale for test purposes, for eliminating production problems, etc., a process for which full-scale operations are planned.

pi·men·to (pi·men'tō), *n., pl.* -tos. 1. kind of sweet pepper, used as a vegetable, relish, and stuffing for green olives. 2. allspice. 3. tree that allspice grows on. [< Sp. < Med.L *pigmentum* spice < LL, vegetable juice, < L, pigment. Doublet of PIGMENT.]

pi·mien·to (pi·myen'tō), *n., pl.* -tos. a sweet pepper. [< Sp. See PIMENTO.]

pimp (pimp), *n., v.* pander.

pim·per·nel (pim'pər·nel), *n.* 1. a small scarlet, purple, or white flower that closes in bad weather. 2. plant it grows on. [< OF *pimprenele*, ult. < VL *piperinus* of peppercorns < L *piper* PEPPER]

pim·ple (pim'pəl), *n.* a small, inflamed swelling of the skin. [cf. OE *piplian* grow pimply] —**pim'pled**, *adj.* —**pim'ply**, *adj.*

pin (pin), *n., v.*, **pinned**, **pin·ning**. —*n.* 1. a short, slender piece of wire with a point at one end and a head at the other, for fastening things together. 2. badge with a pin or clasp to fasten it to the clothing. 3. ornament that has a pin or clasp; brooch. 4. peg made of wood or metal, used to fasten things together, hold something, hang things on, etc. 5. a belaying pin. 6. peg that holds an oar in place. 7. peg in a violin, etc., to which a string is fastened. 8. a bottle-shaped piece of wood used in the game of ninepins, tenpins, etc. 9. *Colloq.* leg. 10. stick for the flag marking a hole on a golf course. 11. something small or worthless. 12. **on pins and needles**, very anxious or uneasy. —*v.* 1. fasten with a pin or pins; put a pin through. 2. fasten or attach firmly to or on. 3. hold fast in one position. 4. bind to an undertaking or pledge. [OE *pinn* peg]

pin·a·fore (pin'ə·fôr'; -fōr'), *n.* 1. a child's apron that covers most of the dress. 2. a light dress without sleeves. [< pin + *afore*]

pin·ball (pin'bôl'), *n.* game in which a ball rolls down a board studded with pins or pegs into numbered compartments.

pinball machine, a gambling device used for playing pinball.

pince-nez (pans'nā'; pins'-), *n.* eyeglasses kept in place by a spring that pinches the nose. [< F, pinch-nose]

pin·cers (pin'sərz), *n.pl.* or *sing.* 1. tool for gripping and holding tight, made like scissors but with jaws instead of blades. 2. a large claw of crabs, lobsters, etc., which can be used to pinch or nip; pair of claws. 3. *Mil.* operation in which the enemy is surrounded and crushed by

the meeting of columns driven on each side of him. [< OF, < *pincier* to pinch]

pinch (pinch), *v.* 1. squeeze between two hard edges; squeeze with thumb and forefinger. 2. press so as to hurt; squeeze. 3. cause sharp discomfort or distress to. 4. cause to shrink or become thin: *a face pinched by hunger.* 5. limit closely; stint: *be pinched for space.* 6. be stingy. 7. *Slang.* arrest. 8. *Slang.* steal. —*n.* 1. a squeeze between two hard edges; squeeze with thumb and forefinger. 2. sharp pressure that hurts; squeeze. 3. as much as can be taken up with the tips of finger and thumb: *a pinch of salt.* 4. sharp discomfort or distress: *the pinch of hunger.* 5. time of special need; emergency. 6. *Slang.* arrest. 7. *Slang.* stealing. [< OF *pincier*] —**pinch·er**, *n.* —**Syn.** *v.* 1. nip, tweak. 3. afflict. —*n.* 3. bit, dash. 5. hardship, strait, difficulty.

pinch·beck (pinch'bek), *n.* alloy of zinc and copper, used in imitation of gold.

pinch·ers (pin'chərz), *n. pl.* or *sing.* pincers.

pinch-hit (pinch'hit'), *v.*, **-hit**, **-hit·ting**. *Am.* 1. bat for another baseball player when a hit is badly needed. 2. take another's place in an emergency. —**pinch hitter**.

pin·cush·ion (pin'kush'ən), *n.* a small cushion to stick pins in until needed.

Pin·dar (pin'dər), *n.* 522?–443? B.C. Greek lyric poet. —**Pin·dar·ic** (pin·dar'ik), *adj.*

pin·dling (pin'dling), *adj. Am., Colloq.* puny.

pine[1] (pīn), *n.* 1. any of a group of evergreen trees that have cones, and clusters of needleshaped leaves that grow out from temporary scalelike leaves. Pines are valuable for timber, turpentine, resin, tar, etc. 2. its wood. [< L *pinus*]

pine[2] (pīn), *v.*, **pined**, **pin·ing**. 1. long eagerly; yearn. 2. waste away with pain, hunger, grief, or desire. [OE, < *pīn*, *n.*, torture < L *poena* penalty < Gk. *poinē*] —**Syn.** 2. languish, droop.

pin·e·al body or **gland** (pin'i·əl), a small body of unknown function, present in the brain of all vertebrates having a cranium. [< F < L *pinea* pine cone < *pinus* pine]

pine·ap·ple (pīn'ap'əl), *n.* 1. a large, juicy fruit growing in hot climates, that looks somewhat like a large pine cone. 2. plant with slender, stiff leaves that it grows on. 3. *Am., Slang.* a hand grenade or bomb.

pin·e·y (pīn'i), *adj.*, **pin·i·er**, **pin·i·est**. piny.

pin·feath·er (pin'feth'ər), *n.* an undeveloped feather that looks like a small stub.

Ping Pong (ping' pong'), *n. Trademark.* game like tennis, played on a table with small wooden rackets and a light, hollow celluloid ball. [imit.]

pin·head (pin'hed'), *n.* 1. the head of a pin. 2. something very small or worthless. —**pin'head'ed**, *adj.*

pin·ion[1] (pin'yən), *n.* 1. the last joint of a bird's wing. 2. wing. 3. any one of the stiff flying feathers of the wing. —*v.* 1. cut off or tie the pinions (of a bird) to prevent flying. 2. bind; bind the arms of; bind (to something). [< OF *pignon*, ult. < L *pinna* feather. Cf. PINION[2].] —**pin'ioned**, *adj.*

pin·ion[2] (pin'yən), *n.* a small gear with teeth that fit into those of a larger gear or rack. [< F *pignon* < OF, battlement, ult. < L *pinna* pinnacle]

pink[1] (pingk), *n.* 1. color obtained by mixing red with white; light or pale red. 2. Often, **Pink**. person who tends toward communism. 3. the highest degree or condition: *in the pink of health.* 4. plant with spicy-smelling flowers of various colors, mostly white, pink, and red. A carnation is a variety of pink. 5. this plant's flower. —*adj.* 1. pale-red. 2. moderately radical. —**pink'ish**, *adj.* —**pink'ish·ness**, *n.*

pink[2] (pingk), *v.* 1. prick or pierce with a sword, spear, or dagger. 2. cut the edge of (cloth) in small scallops or notches. 3. ornament with small, round holes. [ME *pynke(n)* < OE *pynca* point] —**pinked**, *adj.* —**pink'er**, *n.*

pink·eye (pingk'ī'), *n. Am.* a contagious disease characterized by inflammation and soreness of the membrane that lines the eyelids and covers the eyeball.

pink·ie (pingk′ĭ), *n. Esp. U.S.* the smallest finger.

pin money, 1. allowance of money made by a man to his wife or daughter for her own use. 2. a small amount of money used to buy extra things for one's own use.

pin·na (pin′ə), *n., pl.* **pin·nae** (pin′ē), **pin·nas.** feather, wing, or winglike part. [< L] —**pin′nal,** *adj.*

pin·nace (pin′is), *n.* 1. a ship's boat. 2. a very small schooner. [< F < Ital. *pinaccia* or Sp. *pinaza*, ult. < L *pinus* pine]

pin·na·cle (pin′ə·kəl), *n., v.,* **-cled, -cling.** —*n.* 1. a high peak or point of rock. 2. the highest point. 3. a slender turret or spire. —*v.* 1. put on a pinnacle. 2. furnish with pinnacles. [< OF < L *pinnaculum,* dim. of *pinna* wing, point] —**pin′na·cled,** *adj.* —**Syn.** *n.* 2. apex, top, zenith, acme.

pin·nate (pin′āt; -ĭt), *adj.* 1. like a feather. 2. *Bot.* having leaflets on each side of a stalk. [< L, < *pinna* feather] —**pin′nate·ly,** *adv.*

pi·noch·le, pi·noc·le (pē′-nuk′əl; -nok′-), *n. Am.* game played with 48 cards, in which points are scored according to the value of certain combinations of cards.

Pinnate leaf

pi·ñon (pin′yən; pēn′yōn), *n. Am.* 1. pine, esp. of the Rocky Mountain region, producing large edible seeds. 2. its seed. [< Sp., < *piña* pine cone]

pin·point (pin′point′), *v.* aim at accurately; determine precisely. —*adj.* extremely accurate or precise: *pinpoint bombing.*

pin·point·ing (pin′poin′ting), *n. Am.* accurate, precise aim.

pint (pīnt), *n.* 1. unit of measure equal to half a quart. 2. container holding a pint. [< F < MDu. *pinte* plug]

pin·tle (pin′təl), *n.* pin or bolt, esp. one upon which something turns, as in a hinge. [OE *pintel* penis]

pin·to (pin′tō), *adj., n., pl.* **-tos.** *Am.* —*adj.* spotted in two colors; piebald. —*n.* 1. *W.* a pinto horse. 2. Also, **pinto bean.** a mottled variety of kidney bean. [< Sp., painted]

pin-up (pin′up′), *n.* 1. picture of a very attractive girl, pinned up on a wall, usually by admirers personally unacquainted. 2. a very attractive girl. —*adj.* very attractive: *a pin-up girl.*

pin·wheel (pin′hwēl′), *n.* 1. kind of firework that revolves when lighted. 2. toy made of a paper wheel fastened to a stick by a pin so that it revolves in the wind.

pin·worm (pin′wėrm′), *n.* a small, threadlike worm infesting the rectum, esp. of children.

pin·y (pīn′ĭ), *adj.,* **pin·i·er, pin·i·est.** 1. abounding in or covered with pine trees: *piny mountains.* 2. pertaining to or suggesting pine trees: *a piny odor.* Also, **piney.**

pi·o·neer (pī′ə·nir′), *n.* 1. *Am.* person who settles in a part of the country that has not been occupied before except by primitive tribes. 2. person who goes first, or does something first, and so prepares a way for others. 3. one of a group of soldiers who make roads, build bridges, dig trenches, etc.; engineer. —*v.* prepare or open up for others; take the lead in doing. [< F *pionnier* < OF *peon* foot soldier. See PEON.]

pi·ous (pī′əs), *adj.* 1. having or showing reverence for God; religious. 2. done or used from real or pretended religious motives. [< L *pius*] —**pi′ous·ly,** *adv.* —**pi′ous·ness,** *n.* —**Syn.** 1. godly, devout, reverent, holy. —**Ant.** 1. impious, irreligious, irreverent.

pip¹ (pip), *n.* seed of an apple, orange, etc. [short for *pippin*]

pip² (pip), *n.* 1. a contagious disease of birds, characterized by the secretion of thick mucus in

the mouth and throat. 2. *Colloq.* a slight illness. [< MDu. < VL *pippita* < L *pituita* phlegm]

pip³ (pip), *n.* one of the spots on playing cards, dominoes, or dice. [earlier *peep;* orig. uncert.]

pip⁴ (pip), *v.,* **pipped, pip·ping.** 1. peep; chirp. 2. break through (the shell). [? var. of *peep*]

pipe (pīp), *n., v.,* **piped, pip·ing.** —*n.* 1. tube through which a liquid or gas flows. 2. any tube-like thing or part, esp. a tube with a bowl of clay, wood, etc., at one end, for smoking. 3. quantity of tobacco a pipe will hold. 4. a musical instrument with a single tube into which the player blows. 5. pipes, set of musical tubes: *the pipes of Pan.* 6. pipes, bagpipe. 7. any one of the tubes in an organ. 8. a shrill sound, voice, or song. 9. a boatswain's whistle. 10. cask for wine. [< VL *pipa* < L *pipare* chirp; (def. 10) < OF] —*v.* 1. carry by means of a pipe or pipes. 2. supply with pipes. 3. play on a pipe. 4. make a shrill noise; sing in a shrill voice. 5. sing; utter. 6. give orders, signals, etc., with a boatswain's whistle. 7. summon by a pipe. 8. **pipe down,** *Am., Slang.* be quiet; shut up. 9. **pipe up,** a. begin to play (music). b. *Slang.* speak. 10. trim (a dress, etc.) with a cordlike fold. [< L *pipare* chirp] —**pip′er,** *n.*

pipe dream, *Colloq.* an impractical idea.

pipe·ful (pīp′fūl), *n., pl.* **-fuls.** quantity sufficient to fill the bowl of a pipe.

pipe line, *Am.* 1. line of pipes for carrying oil or other liquids. 2. source of information, usually secret.

pipe-line (pīp′līn′), *v.,* **-lined, -lin·ing.** *Am.* 1. carry by a pipe line. 2. provide with a pipe line.

pipe organ, *Am.* organ (def. 4).

pi·pette, pi·pet (pī·pet′; pī-), *n.* a slender pipe or tube for transferring or measuring liquids. [< F, dim. of *pipe* pipe]

pip·ing (pīp′ing), *n.* 1. pipes. 2. material for pipes. 3. a shrill sound. 4. music of pipes. 5. a narrow band of material, sometimes containing a cord, used for trimming along edges and seams. —*adj.* 1. shrill. 2. piping hot, very hot.

pip·it (pip′it), *n.* a small bird somewhat like a lark, that sings while flying. [imit.]

pip·kin (pip′kin), *n.* 1. a small earthen pot. 2. a small wooden pail.

pip·pin (pip′ən), *n.* any of several kinds of apple. [< OF *pepin*]

pi·quant (pē′kənt), *adj.* 1. stimulating to the mind, interest, etc.: *a piquant bit of news.* 2. pleasantly sharp; stimulating to the taste: *a piquant sauce.* 3. fresh; dashing. [< F, pricking, stinging] —**pi′quan·cy, pi′quant·ness,** *n.* —**pi′quant·ly,** *adv.* —**Syn.** 1. clever, smart, lively.

pique (pēk), *n., v.,* **piqued, pi·quing.** —*n.* a feeling of anger at being slighted; wounded pride. —*v.* 1. cause such a feeling in; wound the pride of. 2. arouse; stir up: *the curiosity of the boys was piqued by the locked trunk.* 3. **pique** oneself on or upon, feel proud about. [< F *piquer* prick, sting] —**Syn.** *n.* displeasure, resentment, irritation. —*v.* 1. offend, sting, nettle.

pi·qué (pi·kā′), *n.* a cotton fabric with narrow ribs or raised stripes. [< F, quilted, pp. of *piquer* stitch, prick]

pi·ra·cy (pī′rə·si), *n., pl.* **-cies.** 1. robbery on the sea. 2. act of publishing or using a book, play, piece of music, etc., without the author's permission. [< Med.L < Gk. *peirateia*]

Pi·rae·us (pī·rē′əs), *n.* the port of Athens.

Pi·ran·del·lo (pir′ən·del′ō), *n.* Luigi, 1867-1936, Italian dramatist, poet, and novelist.

pi·rate (pī′rit), *n., v.,* **-rat·ed, -rat·ing.** —*n.* 1. one who attacks and robs ships unlawfully; robber on the sea. 2. ship used by pirates. 3. any pillager. 4. user of another's creation, esp. writing, without permission and for his own gain. —*v.* 1. be a pirate; plunder; rob. 2. publish or use without the author's permission. 3. use illegally. [< L < Gk., < *peiraein* to attack] —**pi·rat·i·cal** (pī·rat′ə·kəl), *adj.* —**pi·rat′i·cal·ly,** *adv.*

pir·ou·ette (pir′u·et′), *n., v.,* **-et·ted, -et·ting.** —*n.* a whirling about on one foot or on the

āge, cāre, fär; ēqual, tėrm; īce; ōpen, ôrder; pùt, rüle, ūse; th, then; ə=a in about.

toes, as in dancing. —*v.* whirl in this way. [< F, spinning top] —**pir′ou·et′ter, pir′ou·et′tist,** *n.*

Pi·sa (pē′zə), *n.* city in NW Italy, famous for its leaning tower.

pis·ca·to·ri·al (pis′kə·tô′ri·əl; -tō′-), **pis·ca·to·ry** (pis′kə·tô′ri; -tō′-), *adj.* of or pertaining to fishermen or fishing. [< L, ult. < *piscis* fish] —**pis′ca·to′ri·al·ly,** *adv.*

Pis·ces (pis′ēz), *n.pl., gen.* **Pis·ci·um** (pish′i·əm). 1. the Fishes, a northern constellation that was considered to have the shape of fishes. 2. the 12th sign of the zodiac.

pis·mire (pis′mīr′), *n.* ant. [cf. Norw. *myre*]

pis·ta·chi·o (pis·tä′shi·ō; -tash′i·ō), *n., pl.* **-chi·os.** 1. a greenish nut having a flavor that suggests almond. 2. a small tree that it grows on. 3. its flavor. 4. a light green. [< Ital. < L < Gk. *pistakion* < *pistake* the tree < OPers.]

pis·til (pis′təl), *n.* part of a flower that produces seeds, consisting, when complete, of an ovary, a style, and a stigma.
[< NL *pistillum* < L, PESTLE. Doublet of PESTLE.] —**pis·til·late** (pis′tə·lit, -lāt), *adj.*

pis·tol (pis′təl), *n., v.,* **-toled, -tol·ing;** *esp. Brit.* **-tolled, -tol·ling.** —*n.* a small, short gun held and fired with one hand. —*v.* fire at with a pistol. [< F < G < Czech *pist′al*]

pis·tole (pis·tōl′), *n.* a former gold coin of Spain. [< F, coin, PISTOL]

pis·ton (pis′tən), *n.* a short cylinder, or a flat, round piece of wood or metal, fitting closely inside a tube or hollow cylinder in which it is moved back and forth by some force (often the pressure of steam). A piston receives or transmits motion by means of a rod (**piston rod**) that is attached to it. [< F < Ital. *pistone* < *pistare* pound, ult. < L *pistus,* pp. of *pinsere* pound]

pit¹ (pit), *n., v.,* **pit·ted, pit·ting.** —*n.* 1. a natural hole in the ground. 2. hole dug into the earth. 3. hollow on the surface of anything; hole. 4. a little hole or scar, such as is left by smallpox. 5. a covered hole used as a trap for wild animals. 6. an unsuspected danger. 7. *Brit.* a. the rear part of the main floor of a theater, where the seats are cheaper. b. people who sit there. 8. *Am.* part of the floor of an exchange devoted to a special business: *the wheat pit.* 9. place where dogs or cocks are made to fight. 10. hell, or part of it. —*v.* 1. mark with small pits or scars. 2. set to fight or compete; match: *the little man pitted his brains against the big man's strength.* [ult. < L *puteus* well] —**pit′ted,** *adj.* —Syn. *n.* 2. excavation. 6. snare, pitfall.

pit² (pit), *n., v.,* **pit·ted, pit·ting.** —*n. Am.* the hard seed of a cherry, peach, plum, date, etc.; stone. —*v.* remove pits from (fruit). [< Du., kernel]

pitch¹ (pich), *v.* 1. throw; fling; hurl; toss. 2. *Am.* throw (a baseball, etc.) for the batter to hit. 3. fix firmly in the ground; set up: *pitch a tent.* 4. take up a position; settle. 5. fall or plunge forward. 6. plunge with the bow rising and then falling: *the ship pitched about in the storm.* 7. set at a certain point, degree, or level. 8. determine the key of (a tune, etc.). 9. slope. 10. pitch in, *Colloq.* work vigorously. 11. pitch into, *Colloq.* attack. 12. pitch on or upon, choose; select. —*n.* 1. throw; fling; hurl; toss. 2. point; position; degree. 3. degree of highness or lowness of a sound. Notes in music with a low pitch have a slower rate of vibration than those with a high pitch. 4. height. 5. act or manner of pitching. 6. that which is pitched. 7. amount of slope. 8. distance between the successive teeth of a cogwheel. 9. distance between two things in a machine. [ME *picche(n)*] —**pitch′ing,** *adj., n.* —Syn. *v.* 1. cast, heave.

pitch² (pich), *n.* 1. a black, sticky substance made from tar or turpentine, used to cover the seams of ships, to cover roofs, to make pavements, etc. 2. resin from certain evergreen trees. —*v.* cover with pitch. [< L *pix*]

pitch·blende (pich′blend′), *n.* mineral consisting largely of uranium oxide, occurring in black, pitchlike masses. Pitchblende is a source of radium, uranium, and actinium.

pitched battle, battle with troops properly arranged.

pitch·er¹ (pich′ər), *n.* container for holding and pouring liquids, with a lip on one side and a handle on the other. [< OF *pichier*]

pitch·er² (pich′ər), *n.* 1. person who pitches. 2. *Am.* player on a baseball team who throws the ball for the batter to hit.

pitch·er·ful (pich′ər·fůl), *n., pl.* **-fuls.** quantity sufficient to fill a pitcher.

pitcher plant, plant with leaves shaped somewhat like a pitcher.

Pitcher plant (1 to 2 ft. high)

pitch·fork (pich′fôrk′), *n.* a large fork with a long handle, for lifting and throwing hay, etc. —*v.* lift and throw with a pitchfork.

pitch pine, *Am.* a pine tree from which pitch or turpentine is obtained.

pitch·y (pich′i), *adj.* 1. full of pitch. 2. like pitch; sticky. 3. black. —**pitch′i·ness,** *n.*

pit·e·ous (pit′i·əs), *adj.* to be pitied; moving the heart; deserving pity. —**pit′e·ous·ly,** *adv.* —**pit′e·ous·ness,** *n.* —Syn. affecting.

pit·fall (pit′fôl′), *n.* 1. a hidden pit to catch animals in. 2. any trap or hidden danger.

pith (pith), *n.* 1. the central, spongy tissue of plant stems. 2. a similar soft tissue: *pith of an orange.* 3. an important or essential part: *pith of a speech.* 4. strength; energy. [OE *pitha*] —Syn. 3. substance, essence, gist. 4. vigor, force.

Pith·e·can·thro·pus (pith′ə·kan·thrō′pəs; -kan′thrə·pəs), *n., pl.* **-pi** (-pī). an extinct ape man, whose existence is assumed from remains found in Java, 1891–92. [< NL, < Gk. *pithekos* ape + *anthropos* man]

pith·y (pith′i), *adj.* 1. full of substance, meaning, force, or vigor: *pithy phrases.* 2. of or like pith. 3. having much pith: *a pithy orange.* —**pith′i·ly,** *adv.* —**pith′i·ness,** *n.* —Syn. 1. pregnant, concise.

pit·i·a·ble (pit′i·ə·bəl), *adj.* 1. to be pitied; moving the heart; deserving pity. 2. deserving contempt; mean; to be scorned. —**pit′i·a·ble·ness,** *n.* —**pit′i·a·bly,** *adv.* —Syn. 1. lamentable, deplorable. 2. contemptible, insignificant.

pit·i·ful (pit′i·fəl), *adj.* 1. to be pitied; moving the heart; deserving pity. 2. feeling pity; feeling sorrow for the trouble of others. 3. deserving contempt; mean; to be scorned. —**pit′i·ful·ly,** *adv.* —**pit′i·ful·ness,** *n.* —Syn. 1. touching, affecting, distressing, pathetic. 2. compassionate, merciful. 3. despicable, contemptible.

pit·i·less (pit′i·lis), *adj.* without pity or mercy. —**pit′i·less·ly,** *adv.* —**pit′i·less·ness,** *n.* —Syn. merciless, ruthless.

Pitt (pit), *n.* 1. **William,** 1708–1778, English statesman. 2. his son, **William,** 1759–1806, prime minister of England 1783–1801 and 1804–1806.

pit·tance (pit′əns), *n.* 1. a small allowance of money. 2. a small amount or share. [< OF *pitance,* ult. < L *pietas* PIETY]

Pitts·burgh (pits′bėrg), *n.* city in SW Pennsylvania.

pi·tu·i·tar·y (pi·tū′ə·ter′i; -tū′-), *n.* 1. the pituitary gland. 2. medicine made from it. [< L, < *pituita* phlegm]

pituitary gland or **body,** a small, oval endocrine gland situated beneath the brain, that secretes hormones that promote growth, stimulate other glands, etc.

pit·y (pit′i), *n., pl.* **pit·ies,** *v.,* **pit·ied, pit·y·ing.** —*n.* 1. sympathy; sorrow for another's suffering or distress; feeling for the sorrows of others. 2. cause for pity or regret; thing to be sorry for. 3. have or take pity on, show pity for. —*v.* 1. feel pity for. 2. feel pity. [< OF < L *pietas.* Doublet of PIETY.] —**pit′i·er,** *n.* —**pit′y·ing·ly,** *adv.* —Syn. *n.* 1. compassion, commiseration, condolence. —Ant. *n.* 1. ruthlessness.

Pi·us XII (pī′əs), 1876-1958, Pope from 1939 to 1958.

piv·ot (piv′ət), *n.* **1.** shaft, pin, or point on which something turns. **2.** that on which something turns, hinges, or depends; central point. —*v.* **1.** mount on, attach by, or provide with a pivot. **2.** turn on a pivot. [< F] —piv′ot·al, *adj.*

pix·i·lat·ed (pik′sə·lāt′id), *adj. Am.* slightly crazy; confused; bewildered.

pix·y, pix·ie (pik′si), *n., pl.* pix·ies. fairy or elf.

piz·za (pēt′sə), *n.* a large, flat cake of bread dough covered with cheese, tomato sauce, spices, etc., and baked. [< Ital.]

piz·zi·ca·to (pit′sə·kä′tō), *adj., n., pl.* -ti (-tē). *Music.* —*adj.* played by plucking the strings with the finger instead of using the bow, as on a violin. —*n.* a note or passage so played. [< Ital., picked]

pk., *pl.* pks. **1.** park. **2.** peak. **3.** peck.

pkg., *pl.* pkgs. package.

pl., 1. place. **2.** plural.

pla·ca·ble (plā′kə·bəl; plak′ə-), *adj.* forgiving; easily quieted; mild. —pla′ca·bil′i·ty, pla′ca·ble·ness, *n.* —pla′ca·bly, *adv.*

plac·ard (*n.* plak′ärd; *v.* plə·kärd′, plak′ärd), *n.* notice to be posted in a public place; poster. —*v.* put placards on or in. [< F, < *plaque* plaque]

pla·cate (plā′kāt; plak′āt), *v.*, -cat·ed, -cat·ing. soothe or satisfy the anger of; make peaceful: *placate a person one has offended.* [< L *placatus*] —pla′cat·er, *n.* —pla·ca·tion (plā·kā′-shən), *n.* —pla·ca·tive (plā′kə·tiv; plak′ə-), pla·ca·to·ry (plā′kə·tô′ri; -tō′-; plak′ə-), *adj.*

place (plās), *n., v.,* placed, plac·ing. —*n.* **1.** part of space occupied by a person or thing. **2.** city, town, village, district, etc. **3.** building or spot used for a certain purpose. A store or office is a place of business. **4.** house; house and grounds; dwelling. **5.** part or spot in something: *the dentist filled the decayed place in the tooth.* **6.** reasonable ground or occasion. **7.** the proper or natural position: *books in place on shelves.* **8.** rank; position; way of life. **9.** position in time: *the performance went too slowly in several places.* **10.** space; room; space or seat for a person. **11.** situation; post or office; official employment or position. **12.** duty; business: *it is not my place to find fault.* **13.** step or point in order of proceeding: *in the first place, the room is too small; in the second place, it is too dirty.* **14.** *Arith.* position of a figure in a number. **15.** position among the leaders at the finish of a race. **16.** a short street or court. **17.** in place of, instead of. **18.** out of place, a. not in the proper or usual place. b. inappropriate or ill-timed. **19.** take place, happen; occur. —*v.* **1.** put (in a spot, position, condition, or relation). **2.** put in the proper position, with the proper person, etc.: *place an order, place sentries.* **3.** *Am.* give the place, position, or condition of; identify: *I remember his name, but I cannot place him.* **4.** appoint (a person) to a post or office; find a situation, etc., for. **5.** be among the three leaders at the finish of a race, usually the second. [< L < Gk. *plateia* (*hodos*) broad way < *platys* broad. Doublet of PLAZA, PIAZZA.] —plac′er, *n.* —Syn. *v.* **1.** locate, set, lay.

place kick, kick given a football after it has been put on the ground.

place-kick (plās′kik′), *v.* make a place kick.

place·ment (plās′mənt), *n.* **1.** a placing or being placed; location; arrangement. **2.** the finding of work or a job for a person. **3.** *Football.* a placing of the ball on the ground for an attempt to kick a goal by a place kick.

pla·cen·ta (plə·sen′tə), *n., pl.* -tae (-tē), -tas. organ by which the fetus is attached to the wall of the womb and nourished. [< NL < L, flat cake, < Gk. *plakounta*, accus., < *plax* flat surface] —pla·cen′tal, *adj.*

plac·er (plas′ər), *n. Am.* place where gold or other minerals can be washed out of loose sand or gravel. [< Am.Sp., sandbank; akin to PLAZA]

placer mining, *Am.* the washing of loose sand or gravel for gold or other minerals.

plac·id (plas′id), *adj.* calm; peaceful; quiet: *a placid lake.* [< L, < *placere* please] —pla·cid·i·ty (plə·sid′ə·ti), plac′id·ness, *n.* —plac′id·ly, *adv.*

plack·et (plak′it), *n.* an opening or slit at the top of a skirt to make it easy to put on.

pla·gia·rism (plā′jə·riz·əm), *n.* **1.** act of plagiarizing. **2.** idea, expression, plot, etc., taken from another and used as one's own. [< L *plagiarius* kidnaper] —pla′gia·rist, *n.* —pla′gia·ris′tic, *adj.* —pla′gia·ris′ti·cal·ly, *adv.*

pla·gia·rize (plā′jə·rīz), *v.*, -rized, -riz·ing. take and use as one's own (the thoughts, writings, inventions, etc., of another), esp. to take and use (a passage, plot, etc., from the work of another writer). —pla′gia·riz′er, *n.*

pla·gia·ry (plā′jə·ri), *n., pl.* -ries. **1.** plagiarism. **2.** one who plagiarizes.

plague (plāg), *n., v.,* plagued, pla·guing. —*n.* **1.** a very dangerous disease that spreads rapidly and often causes death. The plague is common in Asia and has several times swept through Europe. **2.** thing or person that torments, vexes, annoys, troubles, offends, or is disagreeable. —*v.* **1.** cause to suffer from a plague. **2.** vex; annoy; bother. [< L *plaga* blow, pestilence < dial. Gk. *plaga* blow] —pla′guer, *n.* —Syn. *n.* **2.** nuisance, trouble, bother. —*v.* **2.** trouble, worry, pester, tease.

pla·guy, pla·guey (plā′gi), *adj. Colloq.* troublesome; annoying. —pla′gui·ly, *adv.*

plaice (plās), *n., pl.* plaice or (*occasionally*) plaic·es. a kind of flatfish. [< OF < LL *platessa* flatfish < Gk. *platys* flat]

plaid (plad), *n.* **1.** any cloth with a pattern of checks or crisscross stripes. **2.** a pattern of this kind. **3.** a long piece of woolen cloth, usually having a pattern of checks or stripes in many colors, worn about the shoulders by the Scottish Highlanders. —*adj.* having a pattern of checks or crisscross stripes: *a plaid dress.* [< Scotch Gaelic *plaide*] —plaid′ed, *adj.*

plain (plān), *adj.* **1.** easy to understand; easily seen or heard; clear. **2.** without ornament or decoration; simple. **3.** without figured pattern, varied weave, or variegated color. **4.** not rich or highly seasoned. **5.** common; ordinary; simple in manner: *a plain man of the people.* **6.** not pretty: *a plain girl.* **7.** not very hard; easy. **8.** frank; honest; sincere. **9.** flat; level; smooth. —*adv.* in a plain manner; clearly. —*n.* **1.** a flat stretch of land. **2.** plains, *Am.* prairies. [< OF < L *planus* flat. Doublet of PIANO², PLAN.] —plain′ish, *adj.* —plain′ly, *adv.* —plain′ness, *n.* —Syn. *adj.* **1.** apparent, manifest, evident, obvious. **2.** unadorned, untrimmed. **6.** homely.

plain-clothes man (plān′klōz′; -klōthz′), detective wearing ordinary clothes when on duty.

plains·man (plānz′mən), *n., pl.* -men. *Am.* man who lives on the plains.

plain song, vocal music used in the Christian church from the earliest times. Plain song is sung in unison. It is rhythmical, although the beats are not regular.

plain-spo·ken (plān′spō′kən), *adj.* plain or frank in speech.

plaint (plānt), *n.* **1.** complaint. **2.** *Archaic.* lament.

plain·tiff (plān′tif), *n.* person who begins a lawsuit. [< OF *plaintif* complaining. See PLAINTIVE.]

plain·tive (plān′tiv), *adj.* mournful; sad. [< OF, ult. < L *planctus* complaint] —plain′tive·ly, *adv.* —plain′tive·ness, *n.* —Syn. doleful, sorrowful.

plait (plāt, plat *for 1*; plāt, plēt *for 2*), *n., v.* **1.** braid. **2.** pleat. [< OF *pleit*, ult. < L *plicare* to fold] —plait′ed, *adj.* —plait′ing, plait′work′, *n.*

plan (plan), *n., v.,* planned, plan·ning. —*n.* **1.** way of making or doing something that has been worked out beforehand; scheme of arrangement. **2.** a drawing or diagram to show how a garden, a floor of a house, a park, etc., is arranged. **3.** a definite intention or undertaking. —*v.* **1.** think out beforehand how something is to be made or done; design, scheme, or devise; make plans. 2. make a drawing or diagram of. [< F, lit., a plane, < L *planus*; with ref. to a PIANO².] —**plan′less**, *adj.* —**plan′less·ly**, *adv.* —**plan′less·ness**, *n.* —planned, *adj.* —plan′ner. *n.* —Syn. *n.* 1. method, design, plot. –*v.* 1. contrive, intend, purpose.

plane¹ (plān), *n.*, *adj.*, *v.*, **planed**, **plan·ing.** —*n.* 1. any flat or level surface. 2. level; grade: *try to keep your work on a high plane.* 3. a thin, flat or curved supporting surface of an airplane. 4. airplane. 5. surface such that if any two points on it are joined by a straight line, the line will be contained wholly in the surface. —*adj.* 1. flat; level. 2. contained in a flat or level surface: *a plane figure.* 3. of or having to do with such surfaces. –*v.* 1. glide as an airplane does. 2. rise slightly out of the water while moving. [< L *planum* level place]

plane² (plān), *n.*, *v.*, **planed**, **plan·ing.** —*n.* 1. a carpenter's tool with a blade for smoothing or removing wood. 2. machine for smoothing or removing metal. –*v.* 1. smooth with a plane. 2. remove with a plane. [< F, ult. < LL *plana*]

plan·er (plān′ər), *n.* machine for planing wood or for finishing flat surfaces on metal.

plan·et (plan′it), *n.* 1. one of the heavenly bodies (except comets and meteors) that move around the sun. Mercury, Venus, the earth, Mars, Jupiter, Saturn, Uranus, Neptune, and Pluto are planets. 2. formerly the sun, the moon, Mercury, Venus, Mars, Jupiter, or Saturn. [< Gk. *planetes* < *planaesthai* wander]

plan·e·tar·i·um (plan′ə·tār′i·əm), *n.*, *pl.* **-i·a** (-i·ə). 1. apparatus that shows the movements of the sun, moon, planets, and stars by projecting lights on the inside of a dome. 2. room or building with such an apparatus.

plan·e·tar·y (plan′ə·ter′i), *adj.* 1. of a planet; having to do with planets. 2. wandering; erratic. 3. terrestrial; mundane. 4. pertaining to a form of transmission for varying the speed in automobiles. 5. moving in an orbit.

plane tree, or **plane,** *n.* a tall, spreading tree with broad leaves and bare patches on the trunk. The American plane tree is also called the buttonwood or sycamore. [< F < L < Gk. *platanos* < *platys* broad]

plank (plangk), *n.* 1. a long, flat piece of sawed timber thicker than a board. 2. *Am.* article or feature of the platform of a political party, etc. 3. **walk the plank,** walk off a plank extending from a ship's side over the water. Pirates used to make their prisoners do this. –*v.* 1. cover or furnish with planks. 2. *Am.* cook on a board: *planked steak.* 3. *Colloq.* put or set with force: *he planked down the package.* 4. *Am., Colloq.* pay at once: *she planked out her money.* [< OF < L *planca*] —**plank′er**, *n.* —**plank′ing**, *n.*

plant (plant; plänt), *n.* 1. a living thing that is not an animal. Trees, shrubs, herbs, fungi, algae, etc., are plants. 2. a living thing that has leaves, roots, and a soft stem, and is small in contrast with a tree or shrub. 3. a young growth ready to be set out in another place. 4. the buildings, machinery, etc., used in manufacturing some article. 5. buildings, equipment, etc., for any purpose: *a college plant.* 6. *Slang.* scheme to trap, trick, mislead, or deceive. –*v.* 1. put or set in the ground to grow. 2. furnish; stock; put seed in. 3. *Am.* deposit (young fish, spawn, oysters) in a river, lake, etc. 4. set firmly; put; place. 5. *Slang.* deliver (a blow, etc.). 6. establish or set up (a colony, city, etc.). 7. implant (principles, doctrines, etc.). 8. *Slang.* hide, as something stolen. [< L *planta* sprout] —**plant′-ing**, *n.* —Syn. *v.* 4. fix, implant.

Plan·tag·e·net (plan·taj′ə·nit), *n.* member of the royal family that ruled England from 1154 to 1485.

plan·tain¹ (plan′tən), *n.* 1. kind of large banana. 2. plant that it grows on. [< Sp. *plántano*]

plan·tain² (plan′tən), *n.* a common weed with large, spreading leaves close to the ground and long, slender spikes carrying flowers and seeds. [< OF < L *plantago*]

plan·ta·tion (plan·tā′shən), *n.* 1. a large farm or estate on which cotton, tobacco, sugar, etc., are grown. The work on a plantation is done by laborers who live there. 2. a large group of trees or other plants that have been planted. 3. colony. [< L *plantatio* a planting. See PLANT.]

plant·er (plan′tər; plän′-), *n.* 1. man who owns or runs a plantation. 2. machine for planting. 3. person who plants.

plan·ti·grade (plan′tə·grād), *adj.* walking on the whole sole of the foot. —*n.* a plantigrade animal, as the bear. [< L *planta* sole + *gradi* to walk]

plant louse, aphid.

plaque (plak), *n.* 1. an ornamental tablet of metal, porcelain, etc. 2. a platelike ornament or badge. [< F < Du. *plak* flat board]

plash (plash), *v.*, *n.* splash. —**plash′y**, *adj.*

plas·ma (plaz′mə), **plasm** (plaz′əm), *n.* 1. the liquid part of blood or lymph, as distinguished from the corpuscles. 2. the watery part of milk, as distinguished from the globules of fat. 3. protoplasm. [< LL < Gk., something formed or molded, < *plassein* to mold] —**plas′mic**, **plas·mat·ic** (plaz·mat′ik), *adj.*

plas·ter (plas′tər; pläs′-), *n.* 1. a soft mixture of lime, sand, and water that hardens in drying, used for covering walls or ceilings. 2. plaster of Paris. 3. a medical preparation consisting of some substance spread on cloth, that will stick to the body and protect cuts, relieve pain, etc. –*v.* 1. cover with plaster. 2. spread with anything thickly. 3. make smooth and flat. 4. apply a plaster to. 5. apply like a plaster. [< Med.L *plastrum* < L *emplastrum* < Gk., < *en-* on + *plassein* to mold] —**plas′ter·er**, *n.* —**plas′ter·ing**, **plas′ter·work′**, *n.* —**plas′ter·y**, *adj.*

plaster of Paris, a mixture of powdered gypsum (a white material) and water, which hardens quickly, used for making molds, cheap statuary, etc.

plas·tic (plas′tik), *adj.* 1. molding or giving shape to material. 2. concerned with molding or modeling. Sculpture is a plastic art. 3. easily molded or shaped. Clay, wax, and plaster are plastic substances. 4. easily influenced; impressionable. —*n.* any of various substances that harden and retain their shape after being molded or shaped when softened by heat, pressure, etc. Glass, celluloid, Bakelite, vulcanite, and nylon are plastics. [< L < Gk. *plastikos*, ult. < *plassein* to form, shape] —**plas′ti·cal·ly**, *adv.* —**plas·tic·i·ty** (plas·tis′ə·ti), *n.*

plastic surgery, surgery that restores, remedies, or improves the outer appearance of the body.

Pla·ta (plä′tä), *n.* a large inlet of the Atlantic in SE South America between Argentina and Uruguay. The Uruguay and Paraná rivers empty into the Plata River.

plate (plāt), *n.*, *v.*, **plat·ed**, **plat·ing.** —*n.* 1. dish, usually round, that is almost flat. 2. contents of such a dish. 3. something having a similar shape. 4. dishes and food served to one person at a meal. 5. dishes or utensils of silver or gold. 6. dishes and utensils covered with a thin layer of silver or gold. 7. a thin, flat sheet or piece of metal. 8. armor made of such pieces of metal. 9. a platelike part, organ, or structure. Some reptiles and fishes have a covering of horny or bony plates. 10. a thin, flat piece of metal on which something is engraved. Plates are used for printing pictures. 11. something printed from such a piece of metal. 12. a metal copy of a page of type. 13. *Photog.* a thin sheet of glass coated with chemicals that are sensitive to light. 14. *Am., Baseball.* the home base. 15. piece of metal or other firm material with false teeth set into it. 16. a thin cut of beef from the lower end of the ribs. 17. part of a vacuum tube to which the electrons flow. 18. timber laid horizontally to receive the ends of other timbers. –*v.* 1. cover with a thin layer of silver, gold, or other metal. 2. cover with metal plates for protection. 3. make a plate from (type) for printing. [< OF, ult. < VL *plattus* flat < Gk. *platys*] —**plate′like′**, *adj.* —**plate′mak′er**, *n.* —**plate′mak′ing**, *n.* —**plat′er**, *n.*

pla·teau (pla·tō′), *n.*, *pl.* -teaus, -teaux (-tōz′). 1. plain in the mountains or at a height above the sea; large, high plain. 2. *Psychol.* period when a learner is assimilating previous knowledge without apparent progress in new learning. [< F < OF *platel*, dim. of *plat* flat]

plate·ful (plāt′fùl), *n.*, *pl.* -fuls. as much as a plate will hold.

plate glass, thick and very clear glass used for large windowpanes, mirrors, etc.

plat·en (plat′ən), *n.* 1. a flat metal plate in a printing press, that presses the paper against the inked type. 2. roller against which the paper rests in a typewriter. [< OF *platine* < *plat* flat. See PLATE.]

plat·form (plat′fôrm), *n.* 1. a raised level surface. There usually is a platform beside the track at a railroad station. A hall usually has a platform for speakers. 2. *Am.* in a railroad car, the separate floor space at the end. 3. *Am.* plan of action or statement of principles of a political party. 4. *Obs.* plan; chart; map; design. [< F *plateforme* flat form] —**plat′formed,** *adj.*

plat·ing (plāt′ing), *n.* 1. a thin layer of silver, gold, or other metal. 2. a covering of metal plates. 3. action of one that plates.

plat·i·num (plat′ə·nəm), *n.* 1. *Chem.* a heavy precious metal, Pt, that looks like silver and does not tarnish or melt easily. It is a chemical element. 2. shade of gray suggestive of platinum. [< NL, ult. < Sp. *plata* silver]

plat·i·tude (plat′ə·tüd; -tūd), *n.* 1. a dull or commonplace remark, esp. one given out solemnly as if it were fresh and important. 2. flatness; triteness; dullness. [< F, < *plat* flat] —**plat′i·tu′di·nist, plat·i·tu·di·nar·i·an** (plat′ə·tü′də·nãr′i·ən; -tū′-), *n.* —**plat′i·tu′di·nous,** *adj.*

Pla·to (plā′tō), *n.* 427?–347? B.C., Greek philosopher who was the pupil of Socrates and the teacher of Aristotle.

Pla·ton·ic (plə·ton′ik), *adj.* 1. of or pertaining to Plato or his philosophy. 2. Also, **platonic.** friendly but not loverlike. 3. idealistic; not practical. —**Pla·ton′i·cal·ly, pla·ton′i·cal·ly,** *adv.*

Pla·to·nism (plā′tə·niz′əm), *n.* philosophy or doctrines of Plato or his followers. —**Pla′to·nist,** *n.* —**Pla′to·nis′tic,** *adj.*

pla·toon (plə·tün′), *n.* 1. group of soldiers acting as a unit. A platoon is smaller than a company and larger than a squad. 2. a small group. [< F *peloton* group, little ball, dim. of *pelote* ball. See PELLET.]

Platte (plat), *n.* river flowing from C Nebraska into the Missouri River.

plat·ter (plat′ər), *n.* 1. a large, shallow dish for holding or serving food, esp. meat and fish. 2. *Am., Slang.* a phonograph record. [< AF *plater* < OF *plat* flat]

plat·y·pus (plat′ə·pəs), *n.*, *pl.* -pus·es, -pi (-pī). duckbill. [< NL < Gk., < *platys* flat + *pous* foot]

plau·dit (plô′dit), *n.* Usually, **plaudits.** round of applause; enthusiastic expression of approval or praise. [alter. of L *plaudite* applaud!]

plau·si·ble (plô′zə·bəl), *adj.* 1. appearing true, reasonable, or fair. 2. apparently worthy of confidence but often not really so: *a plausible liar.* [< L *plausibilis* deserving applause, pleasing < *plaudere* applaud] —**plau′si·bil′i·ty, plau′si·ble·ness,** *n.* —**plau′si·bly,** *adv.*

Plau·tus (plô′təs), *n.* 254?–184 B.C., Roman writer of comedies.

play (plā), *n.* 1. fun; sport; recreation. 2. a turn, move, or act in a game. 3. act of carrying on a game. 4. **in play,** a. acting; operating. b. as a joke. 5. way of carrying on a game. 6. a story written for or presented as a dramatic performance; drama. 7. action: *foul play.* 8. light, quick movement or change: *the play of sunlight on leaves, the play of color in an opal.* 9. freedom for action, movement, etc. 10. operation; working. 11. gambling. —*v.* 1. have fun; do something in sport; take part in a game. 2. do in sport; imitate in sport. 3. do; perform: *he played a mean trick.* 4. take part in (a game): *play tag.*

5. take part in a game against. 6. cause to play. 7. act on a stage, or as if on a stage; act a part. 8. act the part of (a character in a play, etc.); act (a drama). 9. give theatrical performances in: *play the larger cities.* 10. act in a specified way: *play sick.* 11. *Am.* make believe; imitate in fun as a basis for play: *play cowboys.* 12. make music. 13. produce (music) on an instrument. 14. perform on (a musical instrument). 15. move lightly, quickly, or freely: *a breeze played on the water.* 16. cause to act, move, or work; direct (on, over, along): *play a hose on a burning building.* 17. put into action in a game: *play your ten of hearts.* 18. operate with continued or repeated action: *a fountain played in the garden.* 19. allow (a hooked fish) to exhaust itself by pulling on the line. 20. act carelessly; do foolish things: *don't play with matches.* 21. gamble; bet. 22. *Am.* bet on: *he plays the races.* 23. play into the hands of, act so as to give the advantage to. 24. play on or upon, take advantage of; make use of. 25. play up to, *Slang.* try to get the favor of; flatter. [OE *plegan* to exercise] —**play′a·ble,** *adj.* —**Syn.** *n.* 1. amusement, pastime, game, frolic. 9. liberty, scope, room. —*v.* 1. frolic, revel. 15. flutter, flicker. 21. stake, wager.

play·bill (plā′bil′), *n.* program of a play.

play·boy (plā′boi′), *n.* *Am., Slang.* man, usually wealthy, whose chief interest is in having a good time.

play·er (plā′ər), *n.* 1. person who plays. 2. actor in a theater. 3. musician. 4. thing or device that plays.

player piano, *Am.* piano played by machinery.

play·fel·low (plā′fel′ō), *n.* playmate.

play·ful (plā′fəl), *adj.* 1. full of fun; fond of playing. 2. joking; not serious. —**play′ful·ly,** *adv.* —**play′ful·ness,** *n.* —**Syn.** 1. sportive, frolicsome. 2. humorous, jocular, bantering, jesting.

play·go·er (plā′gō′ər), *n.* person who goes often to the theater.

play·ground (plā′ground′), *n.* place for outdoor play.

play·house (plā′hous′), *n.* 1. *Am.* a small house for a child to play in. 2. a toy house for a child; doll house. 3. theater.

playing card, card used in playing games like bridge, poker, hearts, euchre, and pinochle; one of a set of 52 cards including 4 suits (spades, hearts, diamonds, and clubs) of 13 cards each.

play·let (plā′lit), *n.* a short drama.

play·mate (plā′māt′), *n.* one who plays with another.

play·off (plā′ôf′; -of′), *n.* an extra game or round played to settle a tie.

play on words, pun.

play·thing (plā′thing′), *n.* thing to play with; toy.

play·time (plā′tīm′), *n.* time for playing.

play·wright (plā′rīt′), *n.* writer of plays; dramatist.

pla·za (plä′zə; plaz′ə), *n.* a public square in a city or town. [< Sp. < L < Gk. *plateia* broad way. Doublet of PLACE and PIAZZA.]

plea (plē), *n.* 1. request; appeal: *a plea for pity.* 2. excuse; defense: *the man's plea was that he did not see the signal.* 3. answer made by a defendant to a charge against him in a law court. [< OF < L *placitum* (that) which pleases] —**Syn.** 1. entreaty, prayer. 2. justification, vindication.

plead (plēd), *v.*, **plead·ed** or **plead** (pled), **plead·ing.** 1. offer reasons for or against; argue. 2. ask earnestly; make an earnest appeal. 3. offer as an excuse: *the woman who stole pleaded poverty.* 4. speak for or against in a law court: *he had a good lawyer to plead his case.* 5. conduct a case in a law court. 6. answer to a charge in a law court: *the prisoner pleaded guilty.* [< OF < VL *placitare,* ult. < L *placere* please] —**plead′er,** *n.* —**plead′ing,** *adj.* —**plead′ing·ly,** *adv.* —**Syn.** 2. entreat, supplicate, implore, beseech.

pleas·ant (plez′ənt), *adj.* 1. pleasing; agreeable; giving pleasure. 2. easy to get along with;

friendly. 3. fair; not stormy. [< OF *plaisant*, ppr. of *plaisir* please < L *placere*] —**pleas′ant‧ly**, *adv.* —**pleas′ant‧ness**, *n.* —Syn. 1. delightful, enjoyable. 2. congenial, amiable.

pleas‧ant‧ry (plez′ənt‧ri), *n., pl.* –ries. 1. a good-natured joke; witty remark. 2. joking. —Syn. 1. witticism, jest. 2. drollery, banter, raillery.

please (plēz), *v.,* pleased, pleas‧ing. 1. be agreeable to. 2. be agreeable. 3. wish; think fit. 4. be the will of. 5. may it please you (now used merely as a polite addition to requests or commands). [< OF < L *placere*] —**pleased**, *adj.* —**pleas′ing**, *adj.* —**pleas′ing‧ly**, *adv.* —**pleas′ing‧ness,** *n.* —Syn. 1. gratify, content, suit.

pleas‧ur‧a‧ble (plezh′ər‧ə‧bəl; plā′zhər-), *adj.* pleasant; agreeable. —**pleas′ur‧a‧ble‧ness,** *n.* —**pleas′ur‧a‧bly,** *adv.*

pleas‧ure (plezh′ər; plā′zhər), *n.* 1. a feeling of being pleased; enjoyment; delight. 2. something that pleases; cause of joy or delight. 3. worldly or frivolous enjoyment. 4. one's will, desire, or choice: *what is your pleasure in this matter?*

Dress with a pleated skirt

pleat (plēt), *n.* a flat, usually narrow, fold made in cloth by doubling it on itself. —*v.* fold or arrange in pleats. [var. of *plait*] —**pleat′er,** *n.*

plebe (plēb), *n. Am.* member of the lowest class at the U.S. Military Academy at West Point, the Naval Academy at Annapolis, or the Air Force Academy at Colorado Springs. [< *plebe*(ian)]

ple‧be‧ian (pli‧bē′ən), *n.* 1. one of the common people of ancient Rome. 2. one of the common people. 3. a common, vulgar person. —*adj.* 1. of the plebeians. 2. of the common people. 3. common; vulgar. [< L, < *plebs* the common people] —**ple‧be′ian‧ism,** *n.*

pleb‧i‧scite (pleb′ə‧sīt; -sit), *n.* a direct vote by the qualified voters of a state on some important question. [< L, < *plebs* the common people + *scitum* decree] —**ple‧bis‧ci‧tar‧y** (pli‧bis′ə‧ter′i), **pleb‧i‧scit‧ic** (pleb′ə‧sit′ik), *adj.*

plec‧trum (plek′trəm), *n., pl.* –trums, –tra (-trə). a small piece of ivory, horn, metal, etc., used for plucking the strings of a mandolin, lyre, zither, etc. [< L < Gk. *plektron* < *plessein* to strike]

pled (pled), *v. Colloq.* pt. and pp. of **plead**.

pledge (plej), *n., v.,* pledged, pledg‧ing. —*n.* 1. a solemn promise. 2. something that secures or makes safe; security. 3. condition of being held as security. 4. person who has promised to join an organization but is serving a probationary period before membership. 5. sign; token. 6. the drinking of a health or toast. 7. **take the pledge**, promise not to drink alcoholic liquor. —*v.* 1. promise solemnly. 2. cause to promise solemnly; bind by a promise. 3. give as security. 4. drink a health to. [< OF < Med.L *plebium* < Gmc.; akin to PLIGHT²] —**pledg‧ee** (plej′ē′), *n. Law.* —**pledg′er;** *Law* **pledg‧or, pledg‧or** (plej′ôr′), *n.* —Syn. *n.* 1. covenant, vow. 2. surety, guarantee.

Ple‧ia‧des (plē′ə‧dēz; plī′-), *n.pl.* group of hundreds of stars. Six can normally be seen with the naked eye.

ple‧na‧ry (plē′nə‧ri; plen′ə-), *adj.* 1. full; complete; entire; absolute. 2. attended by all of its qualified members. [< LL, < L *plenus* full]

plen‧i‧po‧ten‧ti‧ar‧y (plen′ə‧pə‧ten′shi‧er′i; -shə‧ri), *n., pl.* –ar‧ies, *adj.* —*n.* person, esp. a diplomatic agent, having full power or authority. —*adj.* having or giving full power and authority. [< Med.L, ult. < L *plenus* full + *potens* powerful]

plen‧i‧tude (plen′ə‧tüd; -tūd), *n.* fullness; completeness; abundance. [< L, < *plenus* full] —**plen‧i‧tu‧di‧nous** (plen′ə‧tü′də‧nəs; -tū′-), *adj.*

plen‧te‧ous (plen′ti‧əs), *adj.* plentiful. —**plen′te‧ous‧ly,** *adv.* —**plen′te‧ous‧ness,** *n.*

plen‧ti‧ful (plen′ti‧fəl), *adj.* more than enough; ample; abundant: *ten gallons of gasoline is a plentiful supply for a seventy-mile trip.* —**plen′ti‧ful‧ly,** *adv.* —**plen′ti‧ful‧ness,** *n.* —Syn. bountiful, copious, profuse. —Ant. scarce, scant, insufficient.

plen‧ty (plen′ti), *n., pl.* –ties, *adj., adv.* —*n.* 1. a full supply; all that one needs; large enough number or quantity: *there is plenty of time.* 2. quality or condition of being plentiful; abundance: *years of peace and plenty.* —*adj.* enough; abundant: *six potatoes will be plenty.* —*adv. Colloq.* quite; fully: *plenty good enough.* [< OF < L *plenitas* fullness < *plenus* full] —Syn. *n.* 1. profusion, copiousness. ➤ **Plenty** as an adverb is colloquial. It is in good informal use but would rarely be found in formal writing.

ple‧num (plē′nəm), *n., pl.* –nums, –na (-nə). full assembly, as of the upper and lower houses of a legislature. [< L, full]

ple‧o‧nasm (plē′ə‧naz‧əm), *n.* 1. use of more words than are necessary to express an idea. *Both of the two twins* is a pleonasm. 2. an unnecessary word, phrase, or expression. [< LL < Gk., ult. < *pleon* more] —**ple′o‧nast,** *n.* —**ple′o‧nas′tic,** *adj.* —**ple′o‧nas′ti‧cal‧ly,** *adv.*

pleth‧o‧ra (pleth′ə‧rə), *n.* excessive fullness; too much; superabundance. [< NL < Gk., < *plethein* be full] —**ple‧thor‧ic** (ple‧thôr′ik; -thor′-; pleth′ə‧rik), *adj.*

pleu‧ra (plur′ə), *n., pl.* pleu‧rae (plur′ē). a thin membrane covering the lungs and folded back to make a lining for the thorax or chest cavity. [< NL < Gk., rib] —**pleu′ral,** *adj.*

pleu‧ri‧sy (plur′ə‧si), *n.* inflammation of the thin membrane covering the lungs and lining the thorax. —**pleu‧rit‧ic** (plu‧rit′ik), *adj.*

Plex‧i‧glas (plek′sə‧glas′, -gläs′), *n. Trademark.* a light, transparent thermoplastic, often used in place of glass. [< *pl*(*astic*) + (*fl*) *exi*(*ble*) + *glas*(*s*)]

plex‧us (plek′səs), *n., pl.* –us‧es, –us. network of nerves, blood vessels, etc. [< L, < *plectere* to twine, braid]

pli‧a‧ble (plī′ə‧bəl), *adj.* 1. easily bent; flexible; supple: *willow twigs are pliable.* 2. easily influenced; adaptable; yielding: *he is too pliable to be a good leader.* [< F, < *plier* bend] —**pli′a‧bil′i‧ty, pli′a‧ble‧ness,** *n.* —**pli′a‧bly,** *adv.*

pli‧ant (plī′ənt), *adj.* 1. bending easily; flexible; supple. 2. easily influenced; yielding. [< OF, bending. See PLY².] —**pli′an‧cy, pli′ant‧ness,** *n.* —**pli′ant‧ly,** *adv.* —Syn. 1. pliable, limber. 2. compliant, adaptable, tractable. —Ant. 1. rigid, stiff. 2. resolute, firm.

pli‧er (plī′ər), *n.* 1. pliers (*sometimes sing. in use*) or pair of pliers, a small pincers with long jaws, for bending wire, holding small objects, etc. 2. one who or that which plies.

Pliers

plight¹ (plīt), *n.* condition or state, usually bad. [< AF *plit*, orig., manner of folding, ult. < L *plicare* to fold; confused with *plight²*] —Syn. predicament, dilemma, scrape, fix.

plight² (plīt), *v.* 1. pledge; promise. 2. plight one's troth, a. promise to be faithful. b. promise to marry. —*n.* a solemn promise; pledge. [OE *pliht* danger]

plinth (plinth), *n.* the lower, square part of the base of a column. [< L < Gk. *plinthos*]

Plin‧y (plin′i), *n.* 1. ("the Elder"), 23–79 A.D., Roman naturalist and writer. 2. ("the Younger"), his nephew, 61?–113? A.D., Roman orator, statesman, and writer.

plod (plod), *v.,* plod‧ded, plod‧ding, *n.* —*v.* 1. walk heavily; trudge. 2. walk slowly or heavily along: *we plod the path of toil.* 3. work patiently with effort: *plod away at one's lessons.* —*n.* 1. act of plodding; course of plodding. 2. sound as of a heavy tread. —**plod′der,** *n.* —**plod′ding,** *adj.* —**plod′ding‧ly,** *adv.* —**plod′ding‧ness,** *n.*

plot (plot), *n., v.,* plot‧ted, plot‧ting. —*n.* 1. a secret plan, esp. an evil one: *two men formed a plot to rob the bank.* 2. plan or main story of a play, novel, poem, etc. 3. a small piece of ground: *a garden plot.* 4. map; diagram. —*v.* 1. plan secretly with others; plan. 2. divide (land) into plots. 3. make a map or diagram of. 4. mark the position of (something) on a map or diagram. [OE, patch of ground; meaning infl. by complot a joint plot (< F)] —plot'less, adj. —plot'less·ly, adv. —plot'less·ness, n. —plot'ted, adj. —plot'ter, n. —Syn. n. 1. intrigue, conspiracy. -v. 1. scheme, contrive, conspire, intrigue.

plov·er (pluv'ər; plō'vər), n. bird with a short tail and a bill like that of a pigeon. [< AF, ult. < L pluvia rain]

plow, plough (plou), n. 1. a big, heavy implement for cutting the soil and turning it over. 2. machine for removing snow; snowplow. —v. 1. turn up (soil) with a plow. 2. use a plow. 3. move as a plow does; advance slowly and with effort. 4. remove with a plow or as if with a plow: plow up old roots. 5. furrow: plow a field, wrinkles plowed in one's face by time. 6. cut the surface of (water). 7. Brit. Slang. flunk (a student). [OE plōg] —plow'er, plough'er, n. —plow'ing, plough'ing, n.

plow·man, plough·man (plou'mən), n., pl. -men. 1. man who guides a plow. 2. a farm worker.

plow·share, plough·share (plou'shãr'), n. blade of a plow, the part that cuts the soil.

pluck (pluk), v. 1. pull off; pick. 2. pull at; pull; tug; jerk. 3. pull on (the strings of a musical instrument). 4. pull feathers or hair off: pluck a chicken. 5. Slang. rob; swindle. 6. Brit., Colloq. reject (a candidate) in an examination. 7. pluck up, a. pull up. b. gather up (courage, spirit, etc.). —n. 1. act of picking or pulling. 2. courage. [OE pluccian] —plucked, adj. —pluck'er, n. —pluck'less, adj. —pluck'less·ness, n. —Syn. v. 1. gather. 2. tweak, twitch. -n. 2. resolution, stamina, spirit.

pluck·y (pluk'i), adj., pluck·i·er, pluck·i·est. having or showing courage. —pluck'i·ly, adv. —pluck'i·ness, n.

plug (plug), n., v., plugged, plug·ging. —n. 1. piece of wood, etc., used to stop up a hole. 2. device to make an electrical connection. 3. hydrant. 4. cake of pressed tobacco; piece of this cut off for chewing. 5. a spark plug. 6. Colloq. an advertisement, esp. one put in a radio program. 7. Am., Colloq. a worn-out or inferior horse. 8. Am., Colloq. a man's high silk hat. —v. 1. stop up or fill with a plug. 2. Slang. hit; shoot. 3. Colloq. work steadily; plod. 4. Colloq. work steadily for by advertisements or publicity. 5. plug in, make an electrical connection by inserting a plug. [< MDu. plugge] —plug'ger, n. —plug'ging, n., adj. —plug'less, adj. —plug'like', adj.

plug-ug·ly (plug'ug'li), n., pl. -lies. Am. Slang. ruffian.

plum (plum), n. 1. a roundish, juicy fruit with a smooth skin and a stone or pit. 2. tree that it grows on. 3. raisin in a pudding, cake, etc. 4. sugarplum. 5. something very good or desirable. 6. Finance. dividend declared over and above the number normally declared. 7. a dark, bluish purple. [< VL pruna < L prunum < Gk. proumnon. Doublet of PRUNE.] —plum'like', adj.

plum·age (plüm'ij), n. feathers of a bird: a parrot has bright plumage. [< OF. < plume PLUME]

plumb (plum), n. 1. a small weight used on the end of a line to find the depth of water or to see if a wall is vertical. 2. out of plumb or off plumb, not vertical. —adj. 1. vertical. 2. Colloq. complete; thorough. —adv. 1. vertically. 2. Colloq. completely; thoroughly. 3. exactly; precisely. —v. 1. make vertical. 2. test or adjust by a plumb line; test; sound: plumb the depths of the lake. 3. get to the bottom of: no one could plumb the mystery. [< OF < L plumbum lead]

plumb bob, plumb (n. def. 1).

plumb·er (plum'ər), n. man whose work is putting in and repairing water pipes and fixtures in buildings. [< OF plombier, ult. < L plumbum lead]

plumb·ing (plum'ing), n. 1. work or trade of a plumber. 2. the water pipes and fixtures in a building: bathroom plumbing.

plumb line, line with a plumb at the end.

plume (plüm), n., v., plumed, plum·ing. —n. 1. a large, long feather; feather. 2. a feather, bunch of feathers, or tuft of hair worn as an ornament on a hat, helmet, etc. 3. the hollow cylinder of spray thrown up by an underwater atomic explosion. —v. 1. furnish with plumes. 2. smooth or arrange the feathers of: the eagle plumed its wing. 3. plume oneself on, be proud of; show pride concerning. [< OF < L pluma] —plumed, adj. —plume'like', adj.

plum·met (plum'it), n. plumb (def. 1). —v. plunge; drop. [< OF plommet < plomb lead; see PLUMB]

plu·mose (plü'mōs), adj. 1. feathered. 2. feathery. —plu'mose·ly, adv. —plu·mos·i·ty (plü·mos'ə·ti), n.

plump¹ (plump), adj. rounded out; attractively fat. —v. make plump; become plump. [cf. MDu. plomp, MLG plump blunt, thick] —plump'ly, adv. —plump'ness, n. —Syn. adj. chubby, pudgy.

plump² (plump), v. 1. fall or drop heavily or suddenly: all out of breath, she plumped down on a chair. 2. cast all of one's vote for a single candidate. —n. Colloq. a sudden plunge; heavy fall. —adv. 1. heavily or suddenly: he ran plump into me. 2. directly; bluntly. —adj. direct; downright; blunt. [cf. Du. plompen, LG plumpen, and plump¹] —plump'er, n.

plum·y (plüm'i), adj. 1. having plumes. 2. adorned with plumes. 3. feathery.

plun·der (plun'dər), v. 1. rob by force; rob: pirates plundered the town. 2. despoil; fleece; embezzle: the dishonest cashier plundered $10,000 from the bank. —n. 1. things taken in plundering; booty; loot: they carried off the plunder in their ships. 2. act of robbing by force. [< G plündern] —plun'der·er, n. —plun'der·ous, adj. —Syn. v. 1. loot, sack. -n. 1. spoils.

plunge (plunj), v., plunged, plung·ing, n. —v. 1. throw or thrust with force into a liquid, place, or condition. 2. throw oneself into water, danger, a fight, etc.). 3. rush; dash. 4. pitch suddenly and violently. 5. Slang. gamble heavily. —n. 1. act of plunging. 2. a dive into the water. 3. a rapid dash. [< OF plungier, ult. < L plumbum lead] —plung'ing, adj. —plung'ing·ly, adv. —Syn. v. 1. immerse, submerge, dip. 2. leap, dive.

plung·er (plun'jər), n. 1. one that plunges. 2. part of a machine that acts with a plunging motion. 3. a reckless speculator.

plunk (plungk), v. 1. pluck (a banjo, guitar, etc.). 2. throw, push, put, drop, etc., heavily or suddenly. —n. Colloq. act or sound of plunking. —adv. with a plunk. [imit.]

plu·per·fect (plü'pér'fikt), n., adj. past perfect. [short for L plus quam perfectum more than perfect]

plu·ral (plùr'əl), adj. 1. containing or pertaining to more than one. 2. Gram. designating that class of words or forms which indicate or imply more than one. —n. Gram. form of a word to show that it means more than one; plural number. Books is the plural of book; men, of man; are, of is; we, of I; these, of this. [< L pluralis < plus more]

plu·ral·i·ty (plü·ral'ə·ti), n., pl. -ties. 1. Am. difference between the largest number of votes and the next largest in an election. 2. the greater number; the majority. 3. a large number; multitude. 4. state or fact of being plural.

plu·ral·ize (plùr'əl·īz), v., -ized, -iz·ing. make plural; express in the plural form.

plu·ral·ly (plùr'əl·i), adv. in the plural number.

plus (plus), prep. 1. added to: 3 plus 2 equals 5. 2. and also: the work of an engineer requires intelligence plus experience. —adj. 1. and more: his mark was B plus. 2. showing addition: the plus sign. 3. positive; positively electrified. —n. 1. the plus sign (+). 2. an added quantity. 3. a positive quantity. 4. surplus; gain. [< L, more]

plus fours, loose, baggy knickers that come down below the knee.

plush (plush), *n.* fabric like velvet but thicker and softer. —*adj. Slang.* luxurious; expensive. [< F *pluche*, ult. < L *pilus* hair] —**plushed,** *adj.* —**plush′y,** *adj.* —**plush′i·ness,** *n.*

Plu·tarch (plü′tärk), *n.* 46?–120? A.D., Greek who wrote biographies of famous Greeks and Romans.

Plu·to (plü′tō), *n.* 1. *Class. Myth.* god of the lower world. He was also called Hades by the Greeks and Dis by the Romans. 2. the planet that is farthest from the sun. —**Plu·to·ni·an** (plü·tō′ni·ən), **Plu·ton·ic** (plü·ton′ik), *adj.*

plu·toc·ra·cy (plü·tok′rə·si), *n., pl.* —**cies.** 1. government in which the rich rule. 2. a ruling class of wealthy people. [< Gk., < *ploutos* wealth + *kratos* power]

plu·to·crat (plü′tə·krat), *n.* 1. person who has power or influence because of his wealth. 2. a wealthy person. —**plu′to·crat′ic,** *adj.* —**plu′to·crat′i·cal·ly,** *adv.*

plu·to·ni·um (plü·tō′ni·əm), *n.* a radioactive element, Pu, derived from neptunium, important in atomic fission. [< L, neut., < *Pluto*]

plu·vi·al (plü′vi·əl), *adj.* 1. of or pertaining to rain; rainy. 2. caused by rain. [< L, < *pluvia* rain]

plu·vi·ous (plü′vi·əs), *adj.* rainy.

ply[1] (plī), *v.,* **plied, ply·ing.** 1. work with; use: *the dressmaker plies her needle.* 2. keep up work on; work away at or on: *we plied the water with our oars.* 3. work busily or steadily. 4. urge again and again: *the enemy plied our messenger with questions.* 5. supply with in a pressing manner: *ply a person with food or drink.* 6. go back and forth regularly between certain places: *a bus plies between the station and the hotel.* 7. go back and forth regularly on: *boats ply the river.* [ult. var. of *apply*] —**ply′er,** *n.*

ply[2] (plī), *n., pl.* **plies.** thickness; fold; twist. Three-ply rope is made up of three twists. [< F *pli* < OF < L *plicare* to fold]

Plym·outh (plim′əth), *n.* 1. seaport in SW England, on the English Channel. 2. town in SE Massachusetts, founded by the Pilgrims in 1620.

Plymouth Rock, *Am.* rock at Plymouth, Massachusetts, on which the Pilgrims are said to have landed in 1620.

ply·wood (plī′wüd′), *n.* board or boards made of several thin layers of wood glued together.

Pm, *Chem.* promethium.

P.M., 1. Postmaster. 2. Prime Minister.

p.m., P.M., 1. after noon. [< L *post meridiem*] 2. the time from noon to midnight. ➤ See a.m. for usage note.

p.n., participial noun.

pneu·mat·ic (nü·mat′ik; nū–), *adj.* 1. filled with or containing air. 2. worked by air. 3. having to do with air and other gases. 4. pertaining to pneumatics. —*n.* tire containing air. [< L < Gk., < *pneuma* wind] —**pneu·mat′i·cal·ly,** *adv.*

pneu·mat·ics (nü·mat′iks; nū–), *n.* branch of physics that deals with the pressure, elasticity, weight, etc., of air and other gases.

pneu·mo·nia (nü·mō′nyə; –ni·ə; nū–), *n.* disease in which the lungs are inflamed. [< NL < Gk., < *pneumon* lung] —**pneu·mon·ic** (nü·mon′ik; nū–), *adj.*

Po (pō), *n.* river in NW Italy.

Po, *Chem.* polonium.

P.O., 1. postal order. 2. post office.

poach[1] (pōch), *v.* 1. trespass (on another's land), esp. to hunt or fish. 2. take (game or fish) without any right. [< early F *pocher* poke out < Gmc.; akin to POKE[1]] —**poach′er,** *n.*

poach[2] (pōch), *v.* cook (an egg) by breaking it into boiling water. [< OF *pochier* < *poche* cooking spoon < Celtic] —**poach′a·ble,** *adj.*

Po·ca·hon·tas (pō′kə·hon′təs), *n.* 1595?–1617, American Indian girl, said to have saved the life of Captain John Smith.

pock (pok), *n.* pimple, mark, or pit on the skin, caused by smallpox and certain other diseases. [OE *pocc*] —**pocked,** *adj.*

pock·et (pok′it), *n.* 1. a small bag sewed into clothing. 2. a hollow place; enclosed place. 3. a small bag or pouch. 4. bag at the corner or side

of a pool or billiard table. 5. hole in the earth containing gold or other ore; single lump of ore. 6. any current or condition in the air that causes an airplane to drop suddenly. —*v.* 1. shut in; hem in. 2. place in one's pocket. 3. hold back; suppress; hide: *he pocketed his pride and said nothing.* 4. take and endure, without doing anything about it: *he pocketed the insult.* 5. take secretly or dishonestly: *Tom pocketed all the profits.* —*adj.* 1. meant to be carried in a pocket: *a pocket handkerchief.* 2. small enough to go in a pocket; diminutive. [< AF *pokete,* dim. of *poke* POKE[2]] —**pock′et·y,** *adj.*

pocket battleship, warship smaller than a cruiser but carrying much larger guns.

pock·et·book (pok′it·bůk′), *n.* 1. *Am.* a woman's purse. 2. case for carrying money, papers, etc., in a pocket.

pock·et·ful (pok′it·fůl), *n., pl.* –**fuls.** as much as a pocket will hold.

pock·et·knife (pok′it·nīf′), *n., pl.* –**knives.** a small knife with one or more blades that fold into the handle.

pocket veto, *Am.* method by which the President can veto a bill by failing to sign it at the end of a session within ten days after Congress adjourns.

pock·mark (pok′märk′), *n.* pock. —**pock′-marked′,** *adj.*

pod (pod), *n., v.,* **pod·ded, pod·ding.** —*n.* 1. a bivalve shell or case in which plants like beans and peas grow their seeds. 2. a dehiscent fruit or pericarp with more than one seed. —*v.* 1. produce pods. 2. fill out into a pod.

Pod of peas

podg·y (poj′i), *adj.,* **podg·i·er, podg·i·est.** short and fat; pudgy. —**podg′i·ness,** *n.*

po·di·a·try (pō·dī′ə·tri), *n.* chiropody. [< Gk. *pous* foot + E –*iatry* treatment < Gk. *iatreia*] —**po·di′a·trist,** *n.*

po·di·um (pō′di·əm), *n., pl.* –**di·a** (–di·ə). 1. a raised platform. 2. an animal structure that serves as a foot. [< L < Gk. *podion,* dim. of *pous* foot]

Po·dunk (pō′dungk), *n. Am.* 1. name of a mythical town noted for its small size, dullness, and lack of progress. 2. any small or insignificant town or village. [< Algonquian, appar., a neck or corner of land; orig., an Indian place name, later used derisively to refer to any insignificant town]

Poe (pō), *n.* Edgar Allan, 1809–1849, American poet, critic, and writer of tales.

po·em (pō′əm; pōm), *n.* 1. an arrangement of words in lines with a regularly repeated accent; composition in verse. 2. composition showing great beauty or nobility of language or thought. 3. a beautiful thing. [< L < Gk. *poema,* var. of *poiema* < *poeein,* var. of *poieein* make, compose]

po·e·sy (pō′ə·si; –zi), *n., pl.* –**sies.** 1. *Poetic.* poetry. 2. *Archaic.* art of poetry. [< OF, ult. < Gk. *poesis* < var. of *poiesis* composition]

po·et (pō′it), *n.* 1. person who writes poetry. 2. person who has great ability to feel and express beauty. [< L < Gk. *poetes*]

po·et·as·ter (pō′it·as′tər), *n.* writer of rather poor poetry. [< NL, < *poet* + –*aster* denoting inferiority (< L)]

po·et·ess (pō′it·is), *n.* a woman poet.

po·et·ic (pō·et′ik), **po·et·i·cal** (–ə·kəl), *adj.* 1. having to do with poems or poets. 2. suitable for poems or poets. *Alas, o'er,* and *blithe* are poetic words. 3. consisting of poems. 4. showing beautiful or noble language, imagery, or thought. —**po·et′i·cal·ly,** *adv.*

po·et·ics (pō·et′iks), *n.* 1. part of literary criticism that deals with the nature and laws of poetry. 2. treatise on poetry.

poet laureate, *pl.* **poets laureate.** 1. in Great Britain, poet appointed by the king or queen to write poems in celebration of court and national events. 2. the official poet of any country, state, etc.

po·et·ry (pō′it·ri), *n.* 1. poems: *a collection of poetry.* 2. art of writing poems. 3. poetic quality; poetic spirit or feeling. [< LL, < L *poeta* POET]

po·grom (pō'grom'; pō'grəm), *n.* an organized massacre, esp. of Jews. [< Russ., devastation]

poi (poi), *n.* a Hawaiian food made of the root of the taro. [< Hawaiian]

poign·ant (poin'ənt; -yənt), *adj.* 1. very painful; piercing: *poignant suffering.* 2. keen; intense: *a subject of poignant interest.* 3. sharp to the taste or smell: *poignant sauces.* [< OF, ppr. of *poindre* prick < L *pungere*] —**poign'an·cy,** *n.* —**poign'ant·ly,** *adv.* —Syn. 1. severe, penetrating. 3. pungent.

poi·lu (pwä'lü), *n.* nickname for a French soldier. [< F, orig., hairy, ult. < L *pilus* hair]

poin·set·ti·a (poin·set'i·ə), *n.* Am. plant with large, scarlet leaves that look like flower petals. [< NL; named after J. R. *Poinsett,* its discoverer]

point (point), *n.* 1. a sharp end; something having a sharp end. 2. a tiny round mark; dot. 3. *Math.* something that has position but not extension. 4. place; spot: *stop at this point.* 5. any particular or definite position, condition, or time; degree; stage: *boiling point.* 6. item; detail: *he answered my questions point by point.* 7. a distinguishing mark or quality: *one's good points.* 8. a physical characteristic or feature of an animal. 9. the main idea or purpose; important or essential thing. 10. a particular aim, end, or purpose. 11. each of the 32 positions indicating direction marked at the circumference of the card of a compass. 12. the interval between any two adjacent points of a compass; 11 degrees 15 minutes. 13. piece of land with a sharp end sticking out into the water; cape. 14. unit of credit, scoring, or measuring; unit of price quotations: *the university accredited him with five points for the semester's work, stock that has gone up a point.* 15. unit for measuring type; about ½₂ inch. 16. a decimal point. 17. *Am., Colloq.* hint; suggestion. 18. lace made with a needle. 19. *Brit.* a railroad switch. 20. *Phonet.* a diacritical mark used in Semitic languages, indicating the vowel sound. 21. any punctuation mark, esp. a period. 22. at the point of, in the act of; very near to. 23. **in point,** pertinent. 24. **in point of,** as regards. 25. **make a point of,** insist upon. 26. **on the point of,** just about; on the verge of. —*v.* 1. sharpen. 2. mark with dots; punctuate. 3. indicate position or direction, or direct attention with, or as if with, the finger. 4. show with the finger; call attention to. 5. direct a finger, weapon, etc. 6. have a specified direction: *the signboard points north.* 7. of a dog, show the presence of game by standing rigid and looking toward it. 8. **point off,** mark off with points or dots. 9. **point out,** show or call attention to. [< OF *point* mark, moment and *pointe* sharp point, both ult. < L *pungere* to prick] —**point'a·ble,** *adj.* —Syn. *n.* 1. prick, goad. 4. location, position. 6. particular. 7. trait, characteristic. 10. object. –*v.* 5. aim, level.

point-blank (point'blangk'), *adj.* 1. aimed straight at the mark. 2. plain and blunt; direct: *a point-blank question.* —*adv.* 1. straight at the mark. 2. plainly and bluntly; directly: *one boy gave excuses, but the other refused point-blank.* —Syn. *adj.* 2. straightforward.

point·ed (poin'tid), *adj.* 1. having a point or points: *a pointed roof.* 2. sharp; piercing: *a pointed wit.* 3. directed; aimed. 4. emphatic: *he showed her pointed attention.* —**point'ed·ly,** *adv.* —**point'ed·ness,** *n.* —Syn. 1. peaked. 4. emphasized, direct, marked.

point·er (poin'tər), *n.* 1. one that points. 2. a long, tapering stick used in pointing things out on a map, blackboard, etc. 3. hand of a clock, meter, etc. 4. a short-haired hunting dog trained to show where game is by standing still and directing its nose toward the location. 5. *Colloq.* hint; suggestion.

Point Four, the fourth point in a U.S. governmental program instituted by President Truman, which grants aid to economically undeveloped countries.

point lace, lace made with a needle.

point·less (point'lis), *adj.* 1. without a point.

2. without force or meaning. —**point'less·ly,** *adv.* —**point'less·ness,** *n.* —Syn. 2. insipid, inane, witless.

point of view, 1. position from which objects are considered. 2. attitude of mind.

poise (poiz), *v.,* **poised, pois·ing,** *n.* —*v.* 1. balance. 2. be balanced. 3. hold supported or raised: *poise a spear.* 4. hang supported or suspended. —*n.* 1. balance. 2. general composure; stability. 3. suspense. [< OF *peser* weigh < L *pensare* intensive of *pendere* weigh] —Syn. *n.* 1. equilibrium. 2. equanimity, steadiness.

poi·son (poi'zən), *n.* 1. drug or other substance very dangerous to life and health. Strychnine and opium are poisons. 2. anything dangerous or deadly. —*v.* 1. kill or harm by poison. 2. put poison in or on. 3. have a dangerous or harmful effect on. —*adj.* poisonous. [< OF < L *potio* potion. Doublet of POTION.] —**poi'son·er,** *n.* —**poi'son·ing,** *n.*

poison ivy, Am. plant with glossy, green, compound leaves of three leaflets each, that causes a painful rash on most people if they touch it.

poi·son·ous (poi'zən·əs), *adj.* 1. containing poison; very harmful to life and health. 2. having a dangerous or harmful effect. —**poi'son·ous·ly,** *adv.* —**poi'son·ous·ness,** *n.* —Syn. 2. noxious, destructive.

poke[1] (pōk), *v.,* **poked, pok·ing,** *n.* —*v.* 1. push against with something pointed; thrust into; thrust; push. 2. pry. 3. make by poking. 4. go lazily; loiter. —*n.* 1. a poking; thrust; push. 2. a slow, lazy person. [ME. Cf. MDu., MLG *poken.*] —Syn. *v.* 1. prod, nudge. 2. search, grope. 4. idle, dawdle.

poke[2] (pōk), *n.* 1. *Now Dial.* bag; sack. 2. *Archaic.* pocket. [ME; akin to OE *pocca*]

Poke bonnet

poke[3] (pōk), *n.* poke bonnet. [? *n.* use of *poke*[1]]

poke[4] (pōk), *n.* pokeweed. [< Algonquian]

poke·ber·ry (pōk'ber'i), *n., pl.* **-ries.** 1. berry of the pokeweed. 2. pokeweed.

poke bonnet, bonnet with a projecting brim.

pok·er[1] (pōk'ər), *n.* 1. one that pokes. 2. a metal rod for stirring a fire.

pok·er[2] (pōk'ər), *n. Am.* a card game in which the players bet on the value of the cards that they hold in their hands. [? < F *poque*]

poker face, Am., Colloq. face that does not show one's thoughts or feelings.

poke·weed (pōk'wēd'), *n.* Am. a tall weed of North America with juicy, purple berries and poisonous roots.

pok·y, pok·ey (pōk'i), *adj.,* **pok·i·er, pok·i·est.** 1. puttering; slow; dull. 2. small and dull; petty; mean. 3. shabby. [< *poke*[1]]

Pol., Polish.

Po·land (pō'lənd), *n.* country in C Europe.

po·lar (pō'lər), *adj.* 1. of or near the North or South Pole: *the polar regions.* 2. having to do with a pole or poles. 3. of the poles of a magnet, electric battery, etc. 4. opposite in character, like the poles of a magnet: *love and hatred are polar feelings or attitudes.* 5. *Chem.* ionizing when dissolved or fused. [< Med.L, < L *polus* POLE[2]]

polar bear, a large, white bear of the arctic regions.

Po·lar·is (pō·lãr'is), *n.* the North Star; polestar.

po·lar·i·ty (pō·lar'ə·ti), *n.* 1. the possession of an axis with reference to which certain physical properties are determined. A magnet or battery has polarity. 2. a positive or negative polar condition, as in electricity.

po·lar·i·za·tion (pō'lər·ə·zā'shən), *n.* 1. production or acquisition of polarity. 2. process by which gases produced during electrolysis are deposited on electrodes of a cell, giving rise to a reverse electromotive force. 3. *Optics.* a state, or the production of a state, in which rays of light exhibit different properties in different directions.

po·lar·ize (pō′lər·īz), v., -ized, -iz·ing. give polarity to; cause polarization in. —po′lar·iz′a·ble, adj. —po′lar·iz′a·bil′i·ty, n. —po′lar·iz′er, n.

pole¹ (pōl), n., v., poled, pol·ing. —n. 1. a long, slender piece of wood, etc.: a telephone pole, a flag pole. 2. measure of length; rod; 5½ yards. 3. measure of area; square rod; 30¼ square yards. —v. Am. make (a boat) go with a pole. [< L palus stake. Doublet of PALE².]

pole² (pōl), n. 1. either end of the earth's axis. The North Pole and the South Pole are opposite each other. 2. each of the two points in which the earth's axis, when extended, cuts the celestial sphere, about which the stars seem to revolve. 3. either of two parts where opposite forces are strongest. A magnet or battery has both a positive pole and a negative pole. 4. either end of the axis of any sphere. [< L < Gk. polos]

Pole (pōl), n. native or inhabitant of Poland.

pole·cat (pōl′kat′), n. 1. a small, dark-brown European animal with a very disagreeable odor. 2. Am. the North American skunk.

po·lem·ic (pə·lem′ik), n. 1. argument; dispute; controversy. 2. a vigorous controversialist. —adj. Also, po·lem′i·cal. of controversy or disagreement; of dispute. [< Gk. polemikos belligerent < polemos war] —po·lem′i·cal·ly, adv.

po·lem·ics (pə·lem′iks), n. art or practice of disputation or controversy, esp. in theology.

pole·star (pōl′stär′), n. 1. the North Star. 2. a guiding principle; guide.

pole vault, vault over a high, horizontal bar by using a long pole. —pole vaulter. —pole vaulting.

po·lice (pə·lēs′), n., v., -liced, -lic·ing. —n. 1. persons whose duty is keeping order and arresting people who break the law. 2. department of government that keeps order and arrests persons who break the law. 3. regulation and control of a community, esp. with reference to matters of public order, safety, health, morals, etc.; public order. —v. keep order in: police the streets. [< F < L < Gk. politeia polity. Doublet of POLICY¹, POLITY.]

police dog, a kind of large, strong dog that looks like a wolf; German shepherd dog.

po·lice·man (pə·lēs′mən), n., pl. -men. member of the police.

police state, state strictly policed by governmental authority, thus demonstrating only a minimum of social, economic, and political liberty. —police statism.

po·lice·wom·an (pə·lēs′wům′ən), n., pl. -wom·en. woman who is a member of the police.

pol·i·cy¹ (pol′ə·si), n., pl. -cies. 1. plan of action; way of management: it is a poor policy to promise more than you can do. 2. action or procedure conforming to prudence or expediency: his policy was highly responsible for his good business. 3. practical wisdom; prudence. 4. political skill or shrewdness. [< OF < L < Gk. politeia polity. Doublet of POLICE, POLITY.] —Syn. 3. shrewdness.

pol·i·cy² (pol′ə·si), n., pl. -cies. 1. a written agreement about insurance. 2. Am. method of gambling by betting on numbers drawn in a lottery. [< F < Ital. pólissa < L < Gk. apodeixis declaration]

pol·i·cy·hold·er (pol′ə·si·hōl′dər), n. Am. one who holds an insurance policy.

po·li·o (pō′li·ō), n. Am., Colloq. poliomyelitis.

po·li·o·my·e·li·tis (pō′li·ō·mī′ə·lī′tis; pol′i·ō-), n. 1. infantile paralysis. 2. any inflammation of the gray matter of the spinal cord. [< NL, < Gk. polios gray + myelos marrow]

pol·ish (pol′ish), v. 1. make smooth and shiny, esp. by friction: polish shoes. 2. become smooth and shiny. 3. remove by smoothing. 4. put into a better condition; improve. 5. make elegant; refine. 6. polish off, Colloq. get done with; finish. —n. 1. substance used to give smoothness or shine: silver polish. 2. polished condition; smoothness. 3. a polishing or being polished. 4.

culture; elegance; refinement. [< OF poliss- < L polire] —pol′ished, adj. —pol′ish·er, n. —Syn. v. 1. burnish, brighten.

Pol·ish (pōl′ish), adj. of or pertaining to Poland, its people, or their language. —n. language of Poland.

Polish Corridor, strip of land assigned after World War I to Poland in order to give that country access to the sea. It separated East Prussia from the rest of Germany, and was a source of friction between Poland and Germany until the outbreak of World War II.

Po·lit·bu·ro (pə·lit′byůr′ō), n. the Communist Party executive committee which examines and controls policy and matters of state in the Soviet Union.

po·lite (pə·līt′), adj. 1. having or showing good manners; behaving properly. 2. refined; elegant. [< L politus polished] —po·lite′ly, adv. —po·lite′ness, n. —Syn. 1. gracious, civil, courteous. 2. polished, cultured. —Ant. 1. impolite.

pol·i·tic (pol′ə·tik), adj. 1. wise in looking out for one's own interests; prudent: a politic person. 2. scheming; crafty. 3. expedient; judicious. 4. political: the state is a body politic. [< L < Gk., ult. < polis city-state] —pol′i·tic·ly, adv. —Syn. 1. shrewd, astute, sagacious.

po·lit·i·cal (pə·lit′ə·kəl), adj. 1. of or concerned with politics. 2. having to do with citizens or government: treason is a political offense. 3. of politicians or their methods. 4. having a definite system of government. —po·lit′i·cal·ly, adv.

political economy, economics. —political economist.

political science, science of the principles and conduct of government.

pol·i·ti·cian (pol′ə·tish′ən), n. 1. person who gives much time to political affairs; person who is experienced in politics. 2. person active in politics chiefly for his own profit or that of his party. 3. person holding a political office. 4. statesman.

pol·i·tics (pol′ə·tiks), n. sing. or pl. 1. management of political affairs: Franklin D. Roosevelt was engaged in politics for many years. 2. political affairs. 3. political principles or opinions. 4. political methods or maneuvers. 5. science and art of government. ▶ Politics is construed as either a singular or plural word but should not be both in the same passage: In almost any group, politics is a subject which will arouse controversy. Republican politics were offensive to Federalists.

pol·i·ty (pol′ə·ti), n., pl. -ties. 1. government. 2. a particular form or system of government. 3. community with a government; state. [< obs. F < L < Gk. politeia polity, ult. < polis city-state. Doublet of POLICE, POLICY¹.]

Polk (pōk), n. James Knox, 1795–1849, the 11th president of the United States, 1845–1849.

pol·ka (pōl′kə; pō′-), n., v., -kaed, -ka·ing. —n. 1. a kind of lively dance. 2. music for it. —v. dance a polka. [< F < G, prob. < Slavic]

pol·ka dot (pō′kə), 1. Am. dot or round spot repeated to form a pattern on cloth. 2. pattern or fabric with such dots. —pol′ka-dot′ted, adj. Am.

poll (pōl), n. 1. a voting; collection of votes. 2. number of votes cast. 3. the results of these votes. 4. list of persons, esp. a list of voters. 5. polls, Am. place where votes are cast and counted. 6. a survey of public opinion concerning a particular subject. 7. the head. —v. 1. receive (as votes). 2. vote; cast (a vote). 3. take or register the votes of. 4. cut off or cut short the hair, wool, horns, branches, etc., of. [cf. MDu. pol(le) top, MLG pol head]

pol·len (pol′ən), n. a fine, yellowish powder formed on the anthers of flowers. Grains of pollen carried to the pistils of flowers fertilize them. [< L, mill dust]

pol·li·nate (pol′ə·nāt), v., -nat·ed, -nat·ing. carry pollen from stamens to pistils of; shed pollen on. —pol′li·na′tion, n.

pol·li·wog, pol·ly·wog (pol′i·wog), n. tadpole. [cf. ME polwigle. See POLL, WIGGLE.]

poll·ster (pōl′stər), *n.* one who takes a public-opinion poll.

poll tax, a tax on every person, or on every person of a specified class, esp. as a prerequisite to the right to vote in public elections.

pol·lute (pə·lüt′), *v.,* **-lut·ed. -lut·ing. 1.** make dirty; defile: *to pollute water.* **2.** desecrate. [< L *pollutus*] —**pol·lut′er,** *n.* —**pol·lu′tion,** *n.* —Syn. **1.** befoul, taint.

Pol·lux (pol′əks), *n.* **1.** *Gk. and Roman Myth.* one of the twin sons of Zeus and Leda. Pollux was immortal; his brother, Castor, was mortal. **2.** one of the two brightest stars in the constellation Gemini.

Pol·ly·an·na (pol′i·an′ə), *n. Am.* an irrepressible optimist. [from the heroine of stories by Eleanor Porter, American writer]

po·lo (pō′lō), *n.* game played by men on horseback with long-handled mallets and a wooden ball. [? ult. < Tibetan *pulu*] —**po′lo·ist,** *n.*

Po·lo (pō′lō), *n.* Marco, 1254?–1324?, Italian who wrote of his travels in Asia.

po·lo·naise (pol′ə·nāz′; pō′lə-), *n.* **1.** a slow, stately dance in three-quarter time. **2.** music for it. [< F, fem. adj., lit., Polish]

po·lo·ni·um (pə·lō′ni·əm), *n.* a radioactive element, Po, occurring in pitchblende. [< NL, < Med.L *Polonia* Poland]

pol·troon (pol·trün′), *n.* a wretched coward. [< F < Ital., < *poltro* lazy, orig., bed] —**poltroon′er·y,** *n.* —**pol·troon′ish,** *adj.*

poly-, *word element.* more than one; many; extensive, as in *polyangular, polylinguist, polynuclear.* [< Gk., < *polys* much, many]

pol·y·an·dry (pol′i·an′dri), *n.* practice of having more than one husband at the same time. [< Gk., < *polys* many + *aner* man, husband] —**pol′y·an′drous,** *adj.*

pol·y·an·thus (pol′i·an′thəs), *n.* **1.** oxlip. **2.** kind of narcissus bearing clusters of small, yellow or white flowers. [< NL < Gk., < *polys* many + *anthos* flower]

pol·y·eth·yl·ene (pol′i·eth′ə·lēn), *n.* an odorless, flexible, chemically inert plastic made by polymerizing ethylene, used in industry, for garden hose, freezer containers, etc.

po·lyg·a·my (pə·lig′ə·mi), *n.* practice or condition of having more than one wife at the same time. [< Gk., < *polys* many + *gamos* marriage] —**po·lyg′a·mist,** *n.* —**po·lyg′a·mous,** *adj.*

pol·y·glot (pol′i·glot), *adj.* **1.** knowing several languages. **2.** written in several languages. —*n.* person who knows several languages. [< Gk., < *polys* many + *glotta* tongue] —**pol′y·glot′tal, pol′y·glot′tic,** *adj.*

pol·y·gon (pol′i·gon), *n.* a plane figure having more than four angles and four sides. [< L < Gk., < *polys* many + *gonia* angle] —**po·lyg·o·nal** (pə·lig′ə·nəl, *adj.* —**po·lyg′o·nal·ly,** *adv.*

pol·y·he·dron (pol′i·hē′dron), *n., pl.* **-drons, -dra** (-drə). a solid figure having many faces. [< NL < Gk., < *polys* many + *hedra* seat, side] —**pol′y·he′dral,** *adj.*

pol·y·mer (pol′i·mər), *n. Chem.* any of two or more polymeric compounds.

pol·y·mer·ic (pol′i·mer′ik), *adj. Chem.* having the same elements combined in the same proportions by weight, but differing in molecular weight. Acetylene, C_2H_2, and benzene, C_6H_6, are polymeric compounds. [< Gk., < *polys* many + *meros* part]

pol·y·mer·ize (pol′i·mər·īz; pə·lim′ər-), *v.,* **-ized, -iz·ing.** combine so as to form a polymer. —**po·lym·er·ism** (pə·lim′rə·iz·əm; pol′i·mər-), *n.* —**po·lym·er·i·za·tion** (pə·lim′ər·ə·zā′shən; pol′i·mər-), *n.*

pol·y·mor·phous (pol′i·môr′fəs), **pol·y·mor·phic** (-fik), *adj.* having, assuming, or passing through many or various forms, stages, etc. [< Gk., < *polys* many + *morphe* form] —**pol′y·mor′phism,** *n.*

Pol·y·ne·sia (pol′ə·nē′zhə; -shə), *n.* group of many small islands in the Pacific, E of Australia and the Philippines.

Pol·y·ne·sian (pol′ə·nē′zhən; -shən), *n.* **1.** member of the brown race inhabiting Polynesia. **2.** the languages of Polynesia, including Maori, Hawaiian, etc. —*adj.* of or pertaining to Polynesia, its inhabitants, or their languages.

pol·y·no·mi·al (pol′i·nō′mi·əl), *n.* an algebraic expression consisting of two or more terms. ab, x^3y, and $3npq$ are monomials; $ab+x^3y$ and $pq-p^3+q$ are polynomials. —*adj.* consisting of two or more terms. *Homo sapiens* is a polynomial expression. [< POLY- + *-nomial,* as in *binomial*]

pol·yp (pol′ip), *n.* **1.** *Zool.* a rather simple form of water animal, not much more than a saclike stomach with fingerlike tentacles around the edge to gather in food. Polyps often grow in colonies, with their bases connected. Corals and sea anemones are polyps. **2.** *Pathol.* tumor arising from a mucous or serous surface. [< F < L < Gk., < *polys* many + *pous* foot]

pol·y·phon·ic (pol′i·fon′ik), *adj. Music.* having two or more voices or parts, each with an independent melody, but all harmonizing; contrapuntal.

po·lyph·o·ny (pə·lif′ə·ni), *n.* polyphonic composition; counterpoint. [< Gk., < *polys* many + *phone* voice]

pol·y·syl·la·ble (pol′i·sil′ə·bəl), *n.* word of more than three syllables. —**pol·y·syl·lab·ic** (pol′i·sə·lab′ik), **pol′y·syl·lab′i·cal,** *adj.* —**pol′y·syl·lab′i·cal·ly,** *adv.*

pol·y·tech·nic (pol′i·tek′nik), *adj.* pertaining to or dealing with many arts or sciences: *a polytechnic school.* —*n.* a technical school.

pol·y·the·ism (pol′i·thē·iz′əm), *n.* belief in more gods than one. The religion of the Greeks was polytheism. [< F, ult. < Gk. *polys* many + *theos* god] —**pol′y·the′ist,** *n.* —**pol′y·the·is′tic, pol′y·the·is′ti·cal,** *adj.*

pom·ace (pum′is), *n.* apple pulp or similar fruit pulp before or after the juice has been pressed out. [ult. < Med.L *pomacium* cider < L *pomum* apple]

po·ma·ceous (pə·mā′shəs), *adj.* belonging to the same family of plants as the apple.

po·made (pə·mād′; -mäd′), *n., v.,* **-mad·ed, -mad·ing.** —*n.* Also, **po·ma·tum** (pə·mā′təm; -mä′-). a perfumed ointment for the scalp and hair. —*v.* put pomade on. [< F < Ital. *pommata* < L *pomum* fruit]

pome (pōm), *n.* apple or any fruit like it; fruit consisting of firm, juicy flesh surrounding a core that contains several seeds. Apples, pears, and quinces are pomes. [< OF, ult. < L *pomum* apple]

pome·gran·ate (pom′gran′it; pum′-; pum·gran′it), *n.* **1.** a reddish-yellow fruit with a thick skin, red pulp, and many seeds. **2.** tree it grows on. [< OF, < *pome* fruit (ult. < L *pomum*) + *grenate* having grains < L, < *granum* grain]

Pom·er·a·ni·a (pom′ər·ā′ni·ə), *n.* region on the Baltic Sea, now chiefly in Poland.

Pom·er·a·ni·an (pom′ər·ā′ni·ən), *n.* a small dog with a sharp nose, pointed ears, and long, thick, silky hair.

pom·mel (pum′əl; pom′-), *n., v.,* **-meled, -mel·ing;** *esp. Brit.* **-melled, -mel·ling.** —*n.* **1.** part of a saddle that sticks up at the front. **2.** a rounded knob on the hilt of a sword, dagger, etc. —*v.* beat with the fists; strike; beat. Also, **pummel.** [< OF *pomel,* ult. < L *pomum* apple] —**pom′mel·er,** *esp. Brit.* **pom′mel·ler,** *n.*

po·mol·o·gy (pə·mol′ə·ji), *n.* branch of science that deals with fruits and fruit growing. [< NL *pomologia.* See POME, -LOGY.] —**po·mo·log·i·cal** (pō′mə·loj′ə·kəl), *adj.* —**po·mol′o·gist,** *n.*

pomp (pomp), *n.* **1.** a stately display; splendor; magnificence: *the king was crowned with great pomp.* **2.** a showy display. [< OF < L < Gk. *pompe* parade] —Syn. **1.** flourish, grandeur.

pom·pa·dour (pom′pə·dôr; -dōr), *n.* **1.** arrangement of a woman's hair in which it is

Pompadour

puffed high over the forehead. 2. *Am.* arrangement of a man's hair in which it is brushed straight up and back from the forehead. [from the Marquise de *Pompadour*]

Pom·pa·dour (pom′pə·dôr; –dōr; –dur), *n.* Marquise de, 1721–1764, mistress of Louis XV of France.

pom·pa·no (pom′pə·nō), *n., pl.* –nos. *Am.* 1. a food fish of the West Indies and neighboring coasts of North America. 2. a somewhat similar fish of the California coast. [< Sp.]

Pom·pe·ii (pom·pā′; –pā′ē), *n.* city in ancient Italy, buried by an eruption of Mount Vesuvius in 79 A.D. —**Pom·pe·ian** (pom·pā′ən; –pē′-), *adj., n.*

Pom·pey (pom′pi), *n.* 106–48 B.C., Roman general and statesman.

pom-pom (pom′pom), *n.* a one-pounder automatic anti-aircraft cannon. [imit.]

pom·pon (pom′pon), *n.* 1. an ornamental tuft or ball of feathers, silk, or the like, worn on a hat or dress, on the shoes, etc. 2. kind of chrysanthemum or dahlia with very small, rounded flowers. [< F, < *pompe* POMP]

pom·pous (pom′pəs), *adj.* 1. trying to seem magnificent; fond of display; acting proudly; self-important: *a pompous manner.* 2. (of language, style, etc.) ostentatiously lofty. 3. magnificent; stately. —**pom·pos·i·ty** (pom·pos′ə·ti), pom′pous·ness, *n.* —**pom′pous·ly,** *adv.*

Ponce de Le·ón (pons′ də lē′ən; *Sp.* pôn′thä thä lā·ôn′, pôn′sä), Juan, 1460?–1521, Spanish soldier who discovered Florida.

pon·cho (pon′chō), *n., pl.* –chos. *Am.* a large piece of cloth, often waterproof, with a slit in the middle for the head to go through. [< Am. Sp. < Araucanian (S Am.Ind.) *pontho*]

pond (pond), *n.* body of still water, smaller than a lake. Ponds are often artificially formed. [orig. var. of *pound*³] —**pond′y,** *adj. Am.*

pon·der (pon′dər), *v.* consider carefully; meditate. [< OF < L *ponderare* weigh < *pondus* weight] —**pon′der·a·ble,** *adj.* —**pon′der·a·bil′i·ty,** *n.* —**pon′der·er,** *n.* —**pon′der·ing·ly,** *adv.*

pon·der·ous (pon′dər·əs), *adj.* 1. very heavy. 2. heavy and clumsy. 3. dull; tiresome. [< L, < *pondus* weight] —**pon′der·ous·ly,** *adv.* —**pon′der·ous·ness,** pon·der·os·i·ty (pon′dər·os′ə·ti), *n.* —**Syn.** 1. weighty, massive. 2. unwieldy.

pone (pōn), *n. Am., S.* 1. bread made of corn meal. 2. loaf or cake of this bread. [< Algonquian]

pon·gee (pon·jē′), *n.* kind of soft silk, usually left in natural brownish-yellow color. [? < dial. Chinese *pun-chi* home-woven]

pon·iard (pon′yərd), *n.* dagger. [< F *poignard*, ult. < L *pugnus* fist]

pon·tiff (pon′tif), *n.* 1. the Pope. 2. bishop. 3. a high priest; chief priest. [< F < L *pontifex*, a high priest of Rome, prob. < *pons* bridge + *facere* make]

pon·tif·i·cal (pon·tif′ə·kəl), *adj.* 1. of or pertaining to the Pope; papal. 2. of or pertaining to a bishop. —*n.* pontificals, vestments and marks of dignity used by cardinals and bishops at certain ecclesiastical functions or ceremonies. —**pon·tif′i·cal·ly,** *adv.*

pon·tif·i·cate (pon·tif′ə·kit; –kāt), *n., v.,* –cat·ed, –cat·ing. —*n.* office or term of office of a pontiff. —*v.* speak pompously.

pon·toon (pon·tün′), *n.* 1. a low, flat-bottomed boat. 2. such a boat, or some other floating structure, used as one of the supports of a temporary bridge. 3. a sealed box containing air, used in raising sunken boats, etc. 4. either of the two boat-shaped parts of an airplane, for landing on or taking off from water. [< F < L *ponto* < *pons* bridge]

pontoon bridge, a temporary bridge supported by low, flat-bottomed boats or other floating structures.

po·ny (pō′ni), *n., pl.* –nies. 1. kind of small horse. 2. *Am., Colloq.* translation of a book, which a pupil uses instead of translating the book himself. 3. *Am., Colloq.* a small glass of alcoholic liquor. [< F *poulenet*, ult. < L *pullus* foal]

pony express, *Am.* system of carrying mail, etc., by men on fast ponies or horses.

pooch (püch), *n. Am., Slang.* dog.

pood (püd), *n.* a Russian weight equal to about 36 pounds. [< Russ., ult. < L *pondus* weight]

poo·dle (pü′dəl), *n.* one of an intelligent breed of pet dogs with thick hair. Some poodles have wiry, curly hair; others have long, silky hair. [< G *pudel* < dial. G *pudeln* splash water]

pooh (pü), *interj., n.* exclamation of contempt.

pooh-pooh (pü′pü′), *v.* express contempt for; make light of. —*interj.* exclamation of contempt.

pool¹ (pül), *n.* 1. a small body of still water; small pond. 2. a still, deep place in a stream. 3. puddle. 4. tank of water to swim or bathe in. [OE *pōl*]

pool² (pül), *n.* 1. game played on a special table with six pockets. The players try to drive balls into the pockets with long sticks called cues. 2. things or money put together by different persons for common advantage. 3. *Am.* arrangement between several companies, groups, etc., to prevent competition by controlling prices. 4. persons who form a pool. 5. *Am.* stake played for in some games. —*v. Am.* put (things or money) together for common advantage. [< F *poule* booty, orig., hen < LL *pulla* chick]

pool·room (pül′rüm′; –rüm′), *n. Am.* 1. room or place in which the game of pool is played. 2. place where people bet on races.

Poo·na (pü′nə), *n.* city in W India, SE of Bombay.

poop (püp), *n.* 1. Also, **poop deck.** deck at the stern above the ordinary deck, often forming the roof of a cabin. 2. stern of a ship. —*v.* break over the stern of (a ship). [< OF < Ital. < L *puppis* stern]

POOP

poor (pur), *adj.* 1. having few things or nothing; needy. 2. characterized by or showing poverty. 3. not good in quality; lacking something needed. 4. scanty. 5. needing pity; unfortunate. 6. not favorable: *a poor chance for recovery.* —*n.* the poor, persons who are needy; poor people. [< OF < L *pauper.* Doublet of PAUPER.] —**poor′ly,** *adv., adj.* —**poor′ness,** *n.* —**Syn.** *adj.* 1. indigent, destitute, impoverished, straitened. 4. inadequate, insufficient. 6. inauspicious.

poor·house (pur′hous′), *n.* house in which paupers live at public expense.

pop¹ (pop), *v.,* popped, pop·ping, *n., adv.* —*v.* 1. make a short, quick, explosive sound. 2. move, go, or come suddenly or unexpectedly. 3. thrust or put suddenly. 4. put (a question) suddenly. 5. *Colloq.* shoot. 6. burst open with a pop. 7. *Am.* heat or roast (popcorn) until it bursts with a pop. 8. bulge. 9. *Am., Baseball.* hit a short, high ball over the infield. —*n.* 1. a short, quick, explosive sound. 2. shot from a gun, etc. 3. a nonalcoholic carbonated drink. —*adv.* with a pop; suddenly; unexpectedly. [imit.]

pop² (pop), *adj. Colloq.* 1. popular. 2. having to do with pop art. —*n.* 1. a popular song. 2. pop art.

pop³ (pop), *n. Am.* 1. father. 2. any elderly man. [short for *papa*]

pop., 1. popular. 2. population.

pop art, a form of painting and sculpture that uses themes of a popular nature, such as comic strips and advertisements. —**pop art′ist.**

pop·corn (pop′kôrn′), *n. Am.* 1. kind of Indian corn, the kernels of which burst open and puff out when heated. 2. the white, puffed-out kernels.

Pope, pope (pōp), *n.* the supreme head of the Roman Catholic Church: *the Pope, the last three popes.* [< LL *papa* pope < L, tutor, bishop, < Gk. *pap(p)as* father]

Pope (pōp), *n.* Alexander, 1688–1744, English poet.

pop·gun (pop′gun′), *n.* a toy gun that shoots with a popping sound.

pop·in·jay (pop′in·jā), *n.* a vain, overtalkative person; conceited, silly person. [< OF < Sp. < Ar. *babbaghā′* < Pers.]

pop·ish (pōp'ish), *adj. Contemptuous.* pertaining to the Roman Catholic Church. —**pop'ish·ly,** *adv.* —**pop'ish·ness,** *n.*

pop·lar (pop'lər), *n.* **1.** any of several trees that grow very rapidly and produce light, soft wood, such as the cottonwood and the aspen. **2.** wood of such a tree. [< OF *poplier* < L *populus*]

pop·lin (pop'lən), *n.* a ribbed dress fabric, made of silk and wool, cotton and wool, or cotton. [< F < Ital. *papalina,* fem., papal, from the papal capital of Avignon]

Po·po·cat·e·pet·l (pō'pō·kat'ə·pet'əl), *n.* volcano in S Mexico, near Mexico City.

pop·o·ver (pop'ō'vər), *n. Am.* a very light and hollow muffin.

pop·per (pop'ər), *n.* **1.** one that pops. **2.** *Am.* a wire basket or metal pan used for popping popcorn, esp. over an open fire.

pop·py (pop'i), *n., pl.* **-pies. 1.** kind of plant with showy red, yellow, or white flowers. **2.** the extract from any of these plants. Opium is made from one kind of poppy. **3.** the flower. **4.** a bright red. [ult. < L *papaver*]

pop·py·cock (pop'i·kok'), *n., interj. Am., Colloq.* nonsense; bosh.

pop·u·lace (pop'yə·lis), *n.* the common people. [< F < Ital. *popolaccio,* ult. < L *populus* people]

pop·u·lar (pop'yə·lər), *adj.* **1.** liked by acquaintances or associates. **2.** liked by most people: *a popular song.* **3.** of the people; by the people; representing the people: *the United States has a popular government.* **4.** widespread among many people; common. **5.** suited to or intended for ordinary people: *popular prices.* [< L, < *populus* people] —**pop'u·lar·ly,** *adv.* —Syn. **4.** general, prevailing, current.

popular front, Popular Front, coalition of communist, socialist, and moderate political parties against fascism, esp. in France. Also, **people's front.**

pop·u·lar·i·ty (pop'yə·lar'ə·ti), *n.* a being liked generally.

pop·u·lar·ize (pop'yə·lər·īz), *v.,* **-ized, -izing.** make popular. —**pop'u·lar·i·za'tion,** *n.* —**pop'u·lar·iz'er,** *n.*

popular vote, *Am.* the vote of the entire electorate thought of as including all the people.

pop·u·late (pop'yə·lāt), *v.,* **-lat·ed, -lat·ing. 1.** inhabit: *a densely populated city.* **2.** furnish with inhabitants: *Europeans populated America.* [< Med.L *populatus,* ult. < L *populus* people] —**pop'u·la'tor,** *n.*

pop·u·la·tion (pop'yə·lā'shən), *n.* **1.** people of a city or a country. **2.** the number of people. **3.** part of the inhabitants distinguished in any way from the rest: *the Negro population.* **4.** act or process of furnishing with inhabitants. **5.** *Statistics.* aggregate of individuals or items used for various measurements.

Pop·u·list (pop'yə·list), *n. Am.* member of a political party formed in the United States in 1891 that advocated government control of the railroads, etc. —**Pop'u·lism,** *n. Am.* —**Pop'u·lis'tic,** *adj. Am.*

pop·u·lous (pop'yə·ləs), *adj.* full of people; having many people per square mile. —**pop'u·lous·ly,** *adv.* —**pop'u·lous·ness,** *n.*

por·ce·lain (pôr'sə·lin, pôr'-; pôrs'lin, pôrs'-), *n.* very fine earthenware; china. [< F < Ital. *porcellana* a kind of shell]

porch (pôrch; pōrch), *n.* **1.** a covered entrance to a building. **2.** *Am.* veranda. [< OF < L *porticus.* Doublet of PORTICO.]

por·cine (pôr'sīn, -sin), *adj.* **1.** of pigs or hogs. **2.** like or characteristic of pigs or hogs. [< L, < *porcus* pig]

por·cu·pine (pôr'kyə·pīn), *n.* rodent covered with spines or quills. [< OF *porc-espin,* ult. < L *porcus* pig + *spina* thorn]

Porcupine
(total length ab. 3 ft.)

pore¹ (pôr; pōr), *v.,* **pored, por·ing. 1.** study long and steadily: *he would rather pore over a book than play.* **2.** meditate or ponder intently. —**por'er,** *n.*

pore² (pôr; pōr), *n.* a very small opening. Sweat comes through the pores in the skin. [< F < L < Gk. *poros,* lit., passage]

por·gy (pôr'gi), *n., pl.* **-gies** or (*esp. collectively*) **-gy.** *Am.* any of various salt-water food fishes, such as the scup and the sea bream.

pork (pôrk; pōrk), *n.* **1.** meat of a pig or hog used for food. **2.** *Am., Slang.* money supplied by Federal or State appropriations, taxes, etc., spent to confer local benefits for political reasons. [< OF < L *porcus* pig] —**pork'like',** *adj.*

pork·er (pôr'kər; pōr'-), *n.* pig, esp. one fattened to eat.

pork·y (pôr'ki; pōr'-), *adj., n., pl.* **pork·ies.** —*adj.* of or like pork; fat. —*n. Am., Colloq.* porcupine.

por·nog·ra·phy (pôr·nog'rə·fi), *n.* obscene writings or pictures. [ult. < Gk. *porne* harlot + -*graphos* writing about] —**por·no·graph·ic** (pôr'nə·graf'ik), *adj.*

po·rous (pô'rəs; pō'-), *adj.* full of pores or tiny holes; permeable by water, air, etc. Cloth, blotting paper, and ordinary flowerpots are porous. —**po·ros·i·ty** (pô·ros'ə·ti; pō-), **po'rous·ness,** *n.* —**po'rous·ly,** *adv.*

por·phy·ry (pôr'fə·ri), *n., pl.* **-ries.** a hard, red or purplish rock of Egypt containing white crystals. [< F, ult. < Gk. *porphyra* purple dye of shellfish] —**por·phy·rit·ic** (pôr'fə·rit'ik), *adj.*

por·poise (pôr'pəs), *n., pl.* **-pois·es** or (*esp. collectively*) **-poise. 1.** a sea animal from five to eight feet long, somewhat like a small whale. Porpoises eat fish. **2.** any of several other small sea animals, as the common dolphin. [< OF *porpeis,* ult. < L *porcus* hog + *piscis* fish]

por·ridge (pôr'ij; por'-), *n.* food made of oatmeal or other cereal boiled in water or milk. [var. of *pottage*]

por·rin·ger (pôr'in·jər; por'-), *n.* a small dish from which soup, porridge, bread and milk, etc., can be eaten.

port¹ (pôrt; pōrt), *n.* **1.** place where ships and boats can be sheltered from storms; harbor. **2.** place where ships and boats can load and unload; city or town with a harbor. **3.** port of entry. [< L *portus*] —Syn. **1.** bay, inlet, cove.

port² (pôrt; pōrt), *n. Naut.* porthole. [< L *porta* gate]

port³ (pôrt; pōrt), *n.* the left side of a ship, when facing the bow. —*adj.* on the left side of a ship. —*v.* turn or shift to the left side.

port⁴ (pôrt; pōrt), *n.* **1.** way of holding one's head and body; bearing. **2.** position of a weapon when ported. —*v.* bring, hold, or carry (a rifle or sword) across and close to the body with the barrel or blade near the left shoulder. [< F < L *portare* carry] —Syn. *n.* **1.** carriage, demeanor, air.

port⁵ (pôrt; pōrt), *n.* a strong, sweet wine that is dark red or tawny. [from *Oporto,* Portuguese city]

Port., Portugal; Portuguese.

port·a·ble (pôr'tə·bəl; pōr'-), *adj.* capable of being carried; easily carried. —**port'a·bil'i·ty,** *n.*

por·tage (pôr'tij; pōr'-), *n.* **1.** *Am.* a carrying of boats, provisions, etc., overland from one river, lake, etc., to another. **2.** place over which this is done. **3.** act of carrying. **4.** cost of carrying. —*v. Am.* carry (boats, goods, etc.) overland from one river or lake to another.

por·tal (pôr'təl; pōr'-), *n.* door, gate, or entrance, usually an imposing one. [< Med.L, < L *porta* gate]

portal-to-portal pay, wages paid to an employee for the time he spends reaching his specific job location after having arrived on the grounds of the employer.

Port Arthur, 1. seaport in NE China, on the Yellow Sea. **2.** city in SE Texas.

Port-au-Prince (pôrt′ō-prins′; pōrt′-), *n.* seaport and capital of Haiti.

por·cul·lis (pôrt-kul′is; pōrt-), *n.* a strong gate or grating of iron sliding up and down in grooves, used to close the gateway of an ancient castle or fortress. [< OF *porte coleice* sliding gate, ult. < L *porta* gate + *colare* filter through] —*porte·cul′lised, adj.*

Porte (pôrt; pōrt), *n.* the Turkish government before 1923.

por·tend (pôr-tend′; pōr-), *v.* indicate beforehand; be a portent of: *black clouds portend a storm.* [< L, < *por-* before + *tendere* extend] —**Syn.** foreshadow, betoken, forebode.

por·tent (pôr′tent; pōr′-), *n.* 1. a warning or coming evil; sign; omen. 2. ominous or fateful significance. —**Syn.** 1. token, presage.

por·ten·tous (pôr-ten′təs; pōr-), *adj.* 1. indicating evil to come; ominous; threatening. 2. amazing; extraordinary. —**por·ten′tous·ly,** *adv.* —**por·ten′tous·ness,** *n.* —**Syn.** 1. foreboding. 2. wonderful, marvelous.

por·ter¹ (pôr′tər; pōr′-), *n.* 1. man employed to carry burdens or baggage. 2. *Am.* attendant in a parlor car or sleeping car. [< OF, ult. < L *portare* carry]

por·ter² (pôr′tər; pōr′-), *n.* 1. doorkeeper; gatekeeper. 2. janitor. [< OF < LL, < L *porta* gate]

por·ter³ (pôr′tər; pōr′-), *n.* a heavy, dark-brown beer. [short for *porter's ale* (i.e., ale for a *porter¹*)]

Por·ter (pôr′tər; pōr′-), *n.* **William Sydney,** real name of O. Henry.

por·ter·house (pôr′tər·hous′; pōr′-), or **porterhouse steak,** *n. Am.* a choice beefsteak containing the tenderloin. [supposedly so called because made popular about 1814 by the keeper of a N.Y. porterhouse (place where porter and other liquors were sold)]

por·fo·lio (pôrt·fō′li·ō; pōrt-), *n., pl.* **-li·os.** 1. brief case. 2. position and duties of a cabinet member or a minister of state. [< Ital. *portafoglio,* ult. < L *portare* carry + *folium* sheet, leaf]

port·hole (pôrt′hōl′; pōrt′-), *n.* an opening in a ship's side to let in light and air. Also, **port.**

por·ti·co (pôr′tə·kō; pōr′-), *n., pl.* **-coes, -cos.** roof supported by columns, forming a porch or a covered walk. [< Ital. < L *porticus.* Doublet of PORCH.] —**por′ti·coed,** *adj.*

por·tiere, por·tière (pôr·tyâr′; pōr-), *n.* curtain hung at a doorway. [< F, < *porte* door]

por·tion (pôr′shən; pōr′-), *n.* 1. part; share. 2. quantity of food served for one person. 3. the part of an estate that goes to an heir; property inherited. 4. dowry. 5. one's lot; fate. —*v.* 1. divide into parts or shares. 2. give (a thing to a person) as share; give a portion, inheritance, dowry, etc., to. [< OF < L *portio*] —**por′tion·er,** *n.* —**por′tion·less,** *adj.* —**Syn.** *n.* 1. division, piece, quota, allotment. 5. destiny.

Port·land (pôrt′lənd; pōrt′-), *n.* 1. seaport in SW Maine. 2. seaport in NW Oregon.

Portland cement, kind of cement made by burning limestone and clay in a kiln, used in making mortar and concrete.

port·ly (pôrt′li; pōrt′-), *adj.,* **-li·er, -li·est.** 1. stout; corpulent. 2. stately; dignified. [< *port⁴*] —**port′li·ness,** *n.*

por·man·teau (pôrt·man′tō; pōrt-), *n., pl.* **-teaus, -teaux** (-tōz). *Esp. Brit.* a traveling bag with two compartments. [< F, < *porter* carry + *manteau* mantle]

Por·to Ri·co (pôr′tō rē′kō; pōr′-), former name of Puerto Rico. —**Porto Rican.**

por·trait (pôr′trit; -trāt; pōr′-), *n.* 1. picture of a person, esp. of the face. 2. picture in words; description. [< F, orig. pp. of *portraire* portray]

por·trai·ture (pôr′tri·chər; pōr′-), *n.* 1. act of portraying. 2. portrait.

por·tray (pôr·trā′; pōr-), *v.* 1. picture in words; describe. 2. make a picture of. 3. represent on the stage. [< OF < L, < *pro-* forth + *trahere* draw] —**por·tray′a·ble,** *adj.* —**por·tray′al,** *n.* —**por·tray′er,** *n.* —**Syn.** 1. depict. 3. impersonate, act.

Port Sa·id (sä·ēd′), seaport in NE Egypt, at the Mediterranean end of the Suez Canal.

Ports·mouth (pôrts′məth; pōrts′-), *n.* seaport in S England, on the English Channel.

Por·tu·gal (pôr′chə·gəl; pōr′-), *n.* country in SW Europe, just W of Spain.

Por·tu·guese (pôr′chə·gēz′; -gēs′) *n., pl.* **-guese,** *adj.* —*n.* 1. native or inhabitant of Portugal. 2. language of Portugal. Portuguese is also the chief language of Brazil. —*adj.* of or pertaining to Portugal, its people, or their language.

Portuguese Guinea, a Portuguese colony in NW Africa.

Portuguese India, former colony belonging to Portugal, on the W coast of India.

por·tu·lac·a (pôr′chə·lak′ə; pōr′-), *n.* a low-growing plant with thick, fleshy leaves and variously colored flowers. [< L, purslane]

pose (pōz), *n., v.,* **posed, pos·ing.** —*n.* 1. position of the body; way of holding the body. 2. attitude assumed for effect; pretense; affectation: *she takes the pose of being an invalid when really she is well and strong.* —*v.* 1. hold a position: *he posed an hour for his portrait.* 2. put in a certain position; put: *the artist posed him before painting his picture.* 3. put on an attitude for effect; make a false pretense: *he posed as a rich man though he owed more than he owned.* 4. put forward for discussion; state: *pose a question.* [< F *poser* < LL *pausare* pause < L *pausa* a pause; in Romance lang. infl. by stem *pos-* of L *ponere* place (from meaning "cause to pause, set down") and influence spread to many compounds, e.g., *compose, dispose, oppose*]

Po·sei·don (pə·sī′dən), *n. Gk. Myth.* god of the sea and of horses, identified by the Romans with Neptune.

Po·sen (pō′zən), *n.* city in W Poland. *Polish,* Poznań.

pos·er¹ (pōz′ər), *n.* person who poses.

pos·er² (pōz′ər), *n.* a very puzzling problem.

po·seur (pō·zér′), *n.* an affected person; one who poses to impress others. [< F, < *poser* pose]

pos·it (poz′it), *v.* lay down or assume as a fact or principle; affirm; postulate. [< L *positus,* pp. of *ponere* set, place]

po·si·tion (pə·zish′ən), *n.* 1. place where a thing or person is. 2. way of being placed: *sit in a more comfortable position.* 3. proper place. 4. condition with reference to place or circumstances: *the army maneuvered for position before attacking.* 5. job. 6. rank; standing, esp. high standing. 7. way of thinking; set of opinions: *what is your position on this question?* [< L *positio* < *ponere* to set] —**po·si′tion·al,** *adj.* —**Syn.** 1. situation, site, location, spot. 5. post, office. 6. status.

pos·i·tive (poz′ə·tiv), *adj.* 1. admitting no question; without doubt; sure. 2. too sure; too confident: *her positive manner annoys people.* 3. definite; emphatic. 4. that can be thought of as real and present. Light is a positive thing; darkness is only the absence of light. 5. showing that a particular disease, condition, germ, etc., is present. 6. that definitely does something or adds something; practical: *don't just make criticisms; give us some positive help.* 7. tending in the direction thought of as that of increase or progress: *motion in the direction that the hands of a clock move is positive.* 8. counting up from zero; plus: *five above zero is a positive quantity.* 9. of the kind of electricity produced by rubbing glass with silk; lacking electrons. 10. *Photog.* having the lines and shadows in the same position as in the original. 11. *Gram.* of the simple form of an adjective or adverb. —*n.* 1. a positive degree or quantity. 2. a positive quality or characteristic. 3. plate in a battery from which the current flows into the wire. 4. print made from a photographic film or plate. 5. *Gram.* the simple form of an adjective or adverb, as distinct from the comparative and superlative. Fast is the positive; *faster* is the comparative; *fastest* is the superlative. [< L *positivus,* ult. < *ponere* to set] —**pos′i·tive·ly,** *adv.* —**pos′i·tive·ness,** *n.* —**Syn.** *adj.* 1. unquestionable, unmistakable, indisputable. **2.** arbitrary, dogmatic, peremptory. **>** Positive degree of adjectives and adverbs is the simple adjective form (*poor, high, slow-witted*) or adverb form (*slow, bitterly*).

pos·i·tiv·ism (pos'ə·tiv·iz'əm), *n.* **1.** a philosophical system which deals only with positive facts and phenomena, rejecting abstract speculation. **2.** assurance; dogmatism. —**pos'i·tiv·ist**, *n.* —**pos'i·tiv·is'tic**, *adj.*

pos·i·tron (poz'ə·tron), *n. Physics.* particle having the same magnitude of mass and charge as an electron, but exhibiting a positive charge; positive electron.

poss., **1.** possession. **2.** possessive.

pos·se (pos'ē), *n.* group of men summoned by a sheriff to help him: *the posse pursued the thief.* [< Med.L, power, < L, v., be able]

pos·sess (pə·zes'), *v.* **1.** own; have. **2.** hold as property; hold; occupy. **3.** control; influence strongly. **4.** control by an evil spirit: *he fought like one possessed.* **5.** maintain; keep. **6.** *Archaic.* take; win. [< OF, < *possession* < L, < *possidere* possess] —**pos·sessed'**, *adj.* —**pos·ses'sor**, *n.* —**pos·ses'sor·ship**, *n.*

pos·ses·sion (pə·zesh'ən), *n.* **1.** a possessing; holding. **2.** ownership. **3.** thing possessed; property. **4.** territory under the rule of a country: *Alaska is a possession of the United States.* **5.** domination by a particular feeling, idea, etc. **6.** self-control. —Syn. **1.** tenure. **3.** belonging.

pos·ses·sive (pə·zes'iv), *adj.* **1.** of possession. **2.** *Gram.* showing possession. *My, your, his,* and *our* are possessive forms of the pronouns. **3.** desirous of ownership: *a possessive nature.* **4.** asserting or claiming ownership: *a possessive manner.* —*n. Gram.* **1.** the possessive case. **2.** possessive form of a word. In "the boy's books," *boy's* is a possessive. —**pos·ses'sive·ly**, *adv.* —**pos·ses'sive·ness**, *n.*

pos·set (pos'it), *n.* a hot drink made of milk, alcoholic liquor, and spices.

pos·si·bil·i·ty (pos'ə·bil'ə·ti), *n., pl.* -ties. **1.** a being possible: *there is a possibility that the train may be late.* **2.** a possible thing or person.

pos·si·ble (pos'ə·bəl), *adj.* **1.** that can be; that can be done; that can happen: *come if possible.* **2.** that can be true or a fact: *it is possible that he went.* **3.** that can be done, chosen, etc., properly: *the only possible candidate.* [< L, < *posse* be able]

pos·si·bly (pos'ə·bli), *adv.* **1.** by any possibility; no matter what happens: *I cannot possibly go.* **2.** perhaps: *possibly you are right.*

pos·sum (pos'əm), *n. Am.* opossum. **2.** play possum, put on a false appearance; pretend.

post¹ (pōst), *n.* **1.** piece of timber, metal, or the like, set upright, usually as a support: *posts of a door or bed.* **2.** post, line, etc., where a race starts or ends. —*v.* **1.** fasten (a notice) up in a place where it can easily be seen. **2.** make known by, or as if by, a posted notice; make public: *post a reward.* **3.** *Am.* protect (land) from trespassers by putting up notices. **4.** put (a name) in a list that is published or posted up. **5.** cover (a wall, etc.) with notices or bills. [< L *postis*]

post² (pōst), *n.* **1.** place where a soldier, policeman, etc., is stationed. **2.** a military station; fort. **3.** soldiers occupying a military station. **4.** *Am.* a local branch of a veterans' organization. **5.** job or position. **6.** *Am.* a trading station, esp. in an uncivilized or unsettled country. —*v.* station at a post; place troops at a particular point: *post guards at the door.* [< F < Ital. < L *positus* stationed] —**post'ed**, *adj.* —Syn. *n.* **5.** employment, office.

post³ (pōst), *n.* **1.** an established system for carrying letters, papers, packages, etc.; the mail. **2.** *Esp. Brit.* a single mail; the letters, etc., thus delivered: *this morning's post.* **3.** one of a series of fixed stations along a route for furnishing relays of men and horses for carrying letters, etc., and supplying service to travelers by post horse, post chaise, etc. —*v.* **1.** send by post; mail. **2.** travel with post horses or by post chaise. **3.** travel with speed; hasten. **4.** rise and fall in the saddle in rhythm with the horse's trot. **5.** *Colloq.*

inform. **6.** *Bookkeeping.* transfer (an entry) from journal to ledger. —*adv.* by post; speedily. [< F < Ital. < L *posita*, fem., placed] —**post'ed**, *adj.*

post-, *prefix.* after, as in *postgraduate, postmortem, postscript.* [< L, < *post*, prep., adv., after, behind]

post·age (pōs'tij), *n.* amount paid on anything sent by mail.

postage stamp, an official stamp placed on mail to show that postage has been paid.

post·al (pōs'təl), *adj.* having to do with mail and post offices. —*n. Am.* Also, **postal card. post card.**

post bel·lum (pōst bel'əm), *Latin.* after the war.

post·boy (pōst'boi'), *n.* **1.** a mail carrier. **2.** man who rides one of the horses drawing a carriage.

post card, 1. a card with a government postage stamp printed on it. **2.** any card, esp. one with a picture on one side, for sending a message by mail.

post chaise, a hired carriage used for traveling before there were railroads.

post·date (pōst'dāt'), *v.*, **-dat·ed, -dat·ing.** give a later date than the true date to (a letter, check, etc.).

post·er (pōs'tər), *n.* a large printed sheet or notice put up in some public place.

pos·te·ri·or (pos·tir'i·ər), *adj.* **1.** situated behind; back; rear; hind. **2.** later; coming after. [< L, compar. of *posterus* subsequent < *post* after] —**pos·te·ri·or·i·ty** (pos·tir'i·ôr'ə·ti; -or'-), *n.* —**pos·te'ri·or·ly**, *adv.*

pos·ter·i·ty (pos·ter'ə·ti), *n.* **1.** generations of the future. **2.** all of a person's descendants. [< L, < *posterus*. See POSTERIOR.]

pos·tern (pōs'tərn; pos'-), *n.* **1.** a back door or gate. **2.** any small door or gate. —*adj.* **1.** of or like a postern. **2.** rear; lesser: *the castle had a postern door.* [< OF *posterne*, ult. < L *posterus* behind. See POSTERIOR.]

Post Exchange, shop at a military post that sells cigarettes, candy, etc., to soldiers.

post·grad·u·ate (pōst·graj'ù·it), *Am.* —*n.* student who continues studying in college or at school after graduation. —*adj.* **1.** taking a course of study after graduation. **2.** of or for postgraduates.

post·haste (pōst'hāst'), *n.* great haste. —*adv.* very speedily; in great haste.

post horse, horse hired by travelers.

post·hu·mous (pos'chù·məs), *adj.* **1.** born after the death of the father. **2.** published after the death of the author. **3.** happening after death. [< LL *posthumus*, var. of L *postumus* last; *h* by confusion with *humus* earth, in sense of "burial"] —**post'hu·mous·ly**, *adv.*

pos·til·ion, pos·til·lion (pōs·til'yən; pos-), *n.* man who rides one of the horses drawing a carriage. [< F *postillon*]

post·lude (pōst'lüd), *n.* a concluding musical piece or movement. [< *post-* + (*pre*)*lude*]

post·man (pōst'mən), *n., pl.* -men. man who carries and delivers mail for the government.

post·mark (pōst'märk'), *n.* an official mark stamped on mail to cancel the postage stamp and record the place and date of mailing. —*v.* stamp with a postmark.

post·mas·ter (pōst'mas'tər; -mäs'-), *n.* person in charge of a post office. —**post'mas'ter·ship**, *n.*

postmaster general, *pl.* **postmasters general.** person at the head of the postal system of a country.

post·me·rid·i·an (pōst'mə·rid'i·ən), *adj.* occurring after noon; of or pertaining to the afternoon.

post me·rid·i·em (pōst mə·rid'i·əm), after noon. *Abbrev.* p.m., P.M. [< L, after midday]

post·mis·tress (pōst'mis'tris), *n.* woman in charge of a post office.

post·mor·tem (pōst·môr'təm), *adj.* after death. —*n.* autopsy. [< L, after death]

post·na·tal (pōst·nā′təl), *adj.* after birth.

post office, 1. place where mail is handled and postage stamps are sold. **2.** Often, **Post Office.** the government department that takes charge of mail. **3.** *Am.* kind of kissing game.

post·paid (pōst′pād′), *adj.* with the postage paid for.

post·pone (pōst·pōn′), *v.,* **-poned, -pon·ing.** put off till later; put off to a later time; delay. [< L < *post-* after + *ponere* put] —**post·pon′a·ble,** *adj.* —**post·pone′ment,** *n.* —**post·pon′er,** *n.* —Syn. defer.

post·pran·di·al (pōst·pran′di·əl), *adj.* after-dinner; *postprandial speeches.* [< POST- + L *prandium* lunch]

post·rid·er (pōst′rīd′ər), *n. Am.* man who carries mail on horseback.

post road, 1. road or route over which mail is or was carried. **2.** road with stations which furnish horses.

post·script (pōst′skript), *n.* addition to a letter, written after the writer's name has been signed. [< L *postscriptum,* orig. neut. pp., < *post-* after + *scribere* write] —**post′script·al,** *adj.*

pos·tu·late (*n.* pos′chə·lit; *v.* pos′chə·lāt), *n., v.,* **-lat·ed, -lat·ing.** —*n.* a fundamental principle; necessary condition: *one postulate of geometry is that a straight line may be drawn between any two points.* —*v.* **1.** assume without proof as a basis of reasoning; take for granted. **2.** require as a fundamental principle or necessary condition. **3.** require; demand; claim. [< L *postulatum,* orig. neut. pp., demanded] —**pos′tu·la′tion,** *n.* —**pos′tu·la′tion·al,** *adj.* —**pos′tu·la′tor,** *n.*

pos·tur·al (pos′chər·əl), *adj.* of or pertaining to posture.

pos·ture (pos′chər), *n., v.,* **-tured, -tur·ing.** —*n.* **1.** position of the body; way of holding the body: *good posture is important for health.* **2.** condition; situation; state. —*v.* **1.** take a certain posture. **2.** put in a certain posture. **3.** pose for effect. [< F < L *positura* < *ponere* to place] —**pos′tur·er, pos′tur·ist,** *n.*

post·war (pōst′wôr′), *adj.* after the war.

po·sy (pō′zi), *n., pl.* **-sies. 1.** flower. **2.** bunch of flowers; bouquet. [var. of *poesy*]

pot (pot), *n., v.,* **pot·ted, pot·ting.** —*n.* **1.** a round, deep container made of metal or earthenware. There are many different kinds of pots. **2.** pot and what is in it; amount a pot can hold. **3.** alcoholic liquor. **4.** basket used to catch fish, lobsters, etc. **5.** *Colloq.* all the money bet at one time. —*v.* **1.** put into a pot. **2.** take a pot shot at; shoot. [OE *pott*]

po·ta·ble (pō′tə·bəl), *adj.* fit for drinking. —*n.* Usually, **potables.** anything drinkable. [< LL, < L *potare* to drink] —**po′ta·bil′i·ty,** *n.*

pot·ash (pot′ash′), *n.* **1.** any of several substances made from wood ashes and used in soap, fertilizers, etc., mainly impure potassium carbonate. **2.** potassium. [< Du. *potasch,* lit., pot ash]

po·tas·si·um (pə·tas′i·əm), *n. Chem.* a soft, silver-white metallic element, K, occurring in nature only in compounds. [< NL < E *potash*]

potassium bromide, a white, crystalline substance, KBr, used in medicine, photography, etc.

potassium cyanide, a very poisonous white, crystalline substance, KCN, used for removing gold from ore, electroplating, killing insects, etc.

potassium nitrate, a colorless, crystalline substance, KNO₃, used as an oxidizing agent, in gunpowder, explosives, etc.; niter; saltpeter.

po·ta·tion (pō·tā′shən), *n.* **1.** act of drinking. **2.** a drink, esp. of alcoholic liquor. [< L, < *potare* to drink]

po·ta·to (pə·tā′tō), *n., pl.* **-toes. 1.** a starchy tuber that is a main item in the food of many countries; Irish potato. **2.** plant producing these tubers, and having trumpet-shaped flowers that are white or white with blue stripes. **3.** sweet potato. [< Sp. *patata* < Haitian]

potato beetle or **bug,** *Am.* beetle with black and yellow stripes that damages potato plants.

potato chip, *Am.* a thin slice of raw potato fried in deep fat.

pot·bel·ly (pot′bel′i), *n., pl.* **-lies.** a distended or protuberant belly. —**pot′bel′lied,** *adj.*

pot·boil·er (pot′boil′ər), *n. Colloq.* work of literature or art produced merely to make a living.

po·tent (pō′tənt), *adj.* **1.** powerful; having great power: *a potent remedy for a disease.* **2.** having sexual power. **3.** producing powerful physical or chemical effects. **4.** exercising great moral influence: *his good deeds had potent effects on his comrades.* [< L *potens*] —**po′ten·cy, po′tence, po′tent·ness,** *n.* —**po′tent·ly,** *adv.* —Syn. **1.** mighty, strong.

po·ten·tate (pō′tən·tāt), *n.* **1.** person having great power. **2.** king, queen, emperor or other ruler.

po·ten·tial (pə·ten′shəl), *adj.* **1.** possible as opposed to actual; capable of coming into being or action. **2.** *Gram.* expressing possibility by the use of *may, might, can, could,* etc.: *the potential mood of a verb.* **3.** *Physics.* noting energy which is due to position and not to motion. A suspended weight has potential energy. —*n.* **1.** something potential; possibility. **2.** amount of electrification of a point with reference to some standard. [< LL, ult. < L *potens* potent] —**po·ten·ti·al·i·ty** (pə·ten′shi·al′ə·ti), *n.* —**po·ten′tial·ly,** *adv.*

poth·er (poth′ər), *n.* confusion; disturbance; fuss. —*v.* bother; fuss.

pot·herb (pot′érb′; -hérb′), *n.* **1.** any plant whose leaves and stems are boiled as a vegetable, such as spinach. **2.** plant used as seasoning in cooking. Sage and parsley are potherbs.

pot·hook (pot′hůk′), *n.* **1.** hook for hanging a pot or kettle over an open fire. **2.** rod with a hook for lifting hot pots, etc. **3.** an S-shaped stroke in writing, esp. one made by children in learning to write.

pot·house (pot′hous′), *n.* place where beer or ale is sold.

po·tion (pō′shən), *n.* a drink, esp. one that is used as a medicine or poison, or in magic. [< L *potio.* Doublet of POISON.]

pot·luck (pot′luk′), *n.* whatever food happens to be ready or on hand for a meal.

Po·to·mac (pə·tō′mək), *n.* river flowing from E West Virginia between Maryland and Virginia, into Chesapeake Bay.

pot·pie (pot′pī′), *n. Am.* **1.** a baked meat pie. **2.** stew with dumplings.

pot·pour·ri (pō′pů·rē′; pot·půr′i), *n.* **1.** a musical or literary medley. **2.** a fragrant mixture of dried flower petals and spices. [< F, trans. of Sp. *olla podrida* rotten pot < L *olla* pot, VL *putrita,* fem. pp. of *putrire* to rot < L *puter* soft, rotten]

Pots·dam (pots′dam), *n.* city in N Germany, near Berlin; locale of the conferences between Truman, Churchill (succeeded by Attlee), and Stalin, in 1945.

pot·sherd (pot′shérd′), *n.* a broken piece of earthenware. [< *pot* + *sherd,* var. of *shard*]

pot shot, 1. shot taken at game merely to provide a meal, with little regard to the rules of sport. **2.** quick shot at an animal or person from close range without careful aim.

pot·tage (pot′ij), *n.* a thick soup. [< OF *potage* < *pot* pot < Gmc.]

pot·ted (pot′id), *adj.* **1.** put into a pot. **2.** cooked and preserved in pots or cans.

pot·ter¹ (pot′ər), *n.* person who makes pots, dishes, vases, etc., out of clay. [OE *pottere* < *pott* pot]

pot·ter² (pot′ər), *v. Esp. Brit.* putter. [< earlier *pote* poke, OE *potian* push; akin to *put*] —**pot′ter·er,** *n.* —**pot′ter·ing·ly,** *adv.*

potter's field, piece of ground used for burying people who have no friends or money.

potter's wheel, a rotating horizontal disk upon which clay is molded into dishes, etc.

pot·ter·y (pot′ər·i), *n., pl.* **-ter·ies. 1.** pots, dishes, vases, etc., made from clay and hardened by heat. **2.** art or business of making them. **3.** place where they are made.

pouch (pouch), *n.* 1. bag; sack: *a postman's pouch.* 2. a baglike fold of skin: *a kangaroo carries its young in a pouch.* —*v.* 1. put into a pouch. 2. form a pouch. [< OF *pouche, poche* < Gmc.; akin to POKE²] —**pouched,** *adj.*

poul·ter·er (pōl′tər·ər), *n.* dealer in poultry.

poul·tice (pōl′tis), *n., v.,* -ticed, -tic·ing. —*n.* a soft, moist mass of mustard, herbs, etc., applied to the body as a medicine. —*v.* put a poultice on. [ult. < L *pultes,* pl. of *puls* mush]

poul·try (pōl′tri), *n.* chickens, turkeys, geese, ducks, etc. [< OF, < *poulet* PULLET]

pounce (pouns), *v.,* pounced, pounc·ing, *n.* —*v.* 1. come down with a rush and seize. 2. dash, come, or jump suddenly. —*n.* a sudden swoop or pouncing.

pound¹ (pound), *n., pl.* pounds or (*esp. collectively*) pound. 1. unit of weight. 1 pound avoirdupois = 16 ounces. 1 pound troy = 12 ounces. 2. Also, **pound sterling.** unit of money of Great Britain, worth about $2.80 (1950). 1 pound = 20 shillings. [< L *pondo,* orig., *libra pondo* a pound by weight]

pound² (pound), *v.* 1. hit hard again and again; hit heavily: *he pounded the door with his fist.* 2. beat hard; throb: *after running fast you can feel your heart pound.* 3. make into a powder or pulp by pounding. —*n.* 1. act of pounding. 2. a heavy or forcible blow. [OE *pūnian*] —**pound′er,** *n.* —**Syn.** *v.* 1. thump, strike, beat. 3. pulverize.

pound³ (pound), *n.* 1. an enclosed place in which to keep stray animals. 2. enclosure for keeping, confining, or trapping animals. 3. place of confinement. —*v.* shut up in a pound; confine. [OE *pund-*]

Pound (pound), *n.* **Ezra (Loomis),** born 1885, American poet.

pound·age (poun′dij), *n.* tax, commission, rate, etc., of so much per pound of English money or per pound of weight.

pound·al (poun′dəl), *n. Physics.* amount of force that, acting for one second on a mass of one pound, gives it a velocity of one foot per second. 1 poundal = 13,825 dynes.

pound cake, cake made with a pound of sugar and a pound of butter for each pound of flour, and plenty of eggs.

pound-fool·ish (pound′fül′ish), *adj.* foolish or careless in regard to large sums.

pour (pôr; pōr), *v.* 1. cause to flow in a steady stream. 2. flow in a steady stream. —*n.* 1. a pouring. 2. a heavy rain. [ME *poure(n)*] —**pour′er,** *n.* —**pour′ing·ly,** *adv.*

pout (pout), *v.* 1. thrust or push out the lips, as a displeased or sulky child does. 2. swell out; protrude. 3. look sullen or displeased. —*n.* 1. a pushing out of the lips when displeased or sulky. 2. display of sullenness. [ME *poute(n)*] —**pout′er,** *n.* —**pout′ing·ly,** *adv.*

pout·y (pou′ti), *adj. Am., Colloq.* inclined to pout; peevish.

pov·er·ty (pov′ər·ti), *n.* 1. condition of being poor: *their tattered clothing and broken furniture indicated their great poverty.* 2. lack of what is needed: *poverty of the soil.* 3. a small amount: *poverty of ideas.* [< OF < L *paupertas* < *pauper* poor] —**Syn.** 1. indigence, destitution, privation. 2. deficience. 3. dearth, paucity.

pov·er·ty-strick·en (pov′ər·ti·strik′ən), *adj.* extremely poor.

POW, prisoner of war.

pow·der (pou′dər), *n.* 1. a solid reduced to dust by pounding, crushing, or grinding. 2. some special kind of powder: *face powder.* 3. gunpowder. —*v.* 1. make into powder. 2. become powder. 3. sprinkle or cover with powder. 4. apply powder (to the face, etc.). 5. sprinkle. [< OF *poudre* < L *pulvis* dust] —**pow′der·er,** *n.* —**pow′der·y,** *adj.*

powder blue, a light blue.

powder horn, flask for carrying gunpowder, made of an animal's horn.

Powder horn

powder puff, a soft puff or pad for applying powder to the skin.

pow·er (pou′ər), *n.* 1. strength; might; force. 2. ability to do or act. 3. particular ability. 4. control; authority; influence; right. 5. political ascendancy in a government. 6. **in power,** having control or authority. 7. person, thing, body, or nation having legal authority or influence. 8. energy or force that can do work: *running water produces power to run mills.* 9. capacity for exerting mechanical force, as measured by the rate at which it is exerted or at which the work is done. Power is expressed in foot-pounds per minute, ergs per second, horsepower, watts, etc. 10. product of a number multiplied by itself. 16 is the 4th power of 2. 11. capacity of an instrument to magnify. The higher the power of a telescope or microscope the more details you can see. 12. Often, **powers.** deity; divinity. [ME, n. < AF, v. < OF *poër* < VL *potere* for L *posse* be able] —**pow′ered,** *adj.* —**Syn.** 1. vigor, potency. 3. faculty. 4. command, sway, domination.

pow·er·boat (pou′ər·bōt′), *n.* boat propelled by an engine on board; motorboat.

pow·er·ful (pou′ər·fəl), *adj.* 1. having great power or force; mighty; strong. 2. *Colloq.* great in number or amount. —**pow′er·ful·ly,** *adv.* —**pow′er·ful·ness,** *n.* —**Syn.** 1. potent.

pow·er·house (pou′ər·hous′), *n.* a building containing boilers, engines, dynamos, etc., for generating power.

pow·er·less (pou′ər·lis), *adj.* without power; helpless. —**pow′er·less·ly,** *adv.* —**pow′er·less·ness,** *n.* —**Syn.** weak, impotent.

power of attorney, a written statement giving one person legal power to act for another.

power politics, in international affairs, diplomacy which uses the threat of superior military power.

power station, powerhouse.

pow·wow (pou′wou′), *Am.* —*n.* 1. an American Indian ceremony, usually accompanied by magic, feasting, and dancing, performed for the cure of disease, success in hunting, etc. 2. council or conference of or with American Indians. 3. *Colloq.* any conference or meeting. —*v.* hold a powwow; confer. [< Algonquian]

pox (poks), *n.* 1. any disease that covers the body or parts of the body with sores, such as chicken pox or smallpox. 2. syphilis. [var. of *pocks,* pl. of POCK]

Poz·nań (pôz′nän′y), *n.* Polish name of **Posen.**

pp., 1. pages. 2. past participle. 3. pianissimo.

P.P., Parcel Post.

p.p., 1. parcel post. 2. past participle. 3. postpaid.

ppr., **p.pr.,** present participle.

Pr, *Chem.* praseodymium.

Pr., Provençal.

pr., 1. *pl.* prs. pair. 2. present. 3. price.

P.R., Puerto Rico.

prac·ti·ca·ble (prak′tə·kə·bəl), *adj.* 1. that can be done; capable of being put into practice: *a practicable idea.* 2. that can be used: *a practicable road.* [< F, < *pratiquer* PRACTICE; infl. by Med.L *practicare* to practice] —**prac′ti·ca·bil′i·ty,** **prac′ti·ca·ble·ness,** *n.* —**prac′ti·ca·bly,** *adv.* —**Syn.** 1. possible, feasible.

prac·ti·cal (prak′tə·kəl), *adj.* 1. having to do with action or practice rather than thought or theory. 2. fit for actual practice. 3. useful. 4. having good sense. 5. engaged in actual practice or work. 6. being such in effect; virtual. 7. earlier *practic* < LL < Gk. *praktikos* < *prassein* do] —**prac·ti·cal·i·ty** (prak′tə·kal′ə·ti), **prac′ti·cal·ness,** *n.* ▶ **Practical** and its derivatives give some trouble, partly because we slur syllables in pronunciation—*practically* becoming prak′tik·li or even prak′t′li, *practicability* becoming prak′tə·bil′ə·ti—and it is a temptation to spell the word as it is spoken rather than the recognized written form. **Practical,** adjective: *a practical scheme, he has a practical mind; practically,* adverb: *they were practically* *minded,* colloquial in phrases like "practically all there"; **practicable,** adjective: *a practicable method;* **practicability,** noun: *they questioned the practicability of the idea.*

practical joke, trick played on a person to have a laugh at him.

prac·ti·cal·ly (prak′tik·li), adv. 1. really; in effect. 2. *Colloq.* almost; nearly. 3. in a practical way; in a useful way. 4. by actual practice.

prac·tice (prak′tis), n., v., -ticed, -tic·ing. —n. 1. action done many times over for skill. 2. skill gained by experience or exercise: *he was out of practice at batting.* 3. action or process of doing or being something. 4. the usual way; custom. 5. the working at or following of a profession or occupation: *engaged in the practice of law.* 6. business of a doctor or lawyer: *Dr. Adams sold his practice.* 7. *Law.* an established method of conducting legal proceedings. [< v.] —v. Also, **practise.** 1. do (some act) again and again to learn to do it well. 2. do usually; make a custom of. 3. follow, observe, or use day after day. 4. work at or follow as a profession, act, or occupation. 5. practice a profession. 6. give training to; drill. [< OF *practiser,* ult. < LL *practicus* PRACTICAL] —**prac′tic·er,** n. —Syn. n. 1. drill, exercise. 4. habit. –v. 6. exercise, train.

prac·ticed, prac·tised (prak′tist), adj. experienced; skilled; expert; proficient. —Syn. versed, accomplished.

prac·tise (prak′tis), v., -tised, -tis·ing. prac·tice. —**prac′tis·er,** n.

prac·ti·tion·er (prak·tish′ən·ər; -tish′nər), n. person engaged in the practice of a profession: *a medical practitioner.*

prae·no·men (prē·nō′mən), n., pl. -nom·i·na (-nom′ə·nə). the first or personal name of a Roman citizen. [< L, < *prae-* before + *nomen* name] —**prae·nom·i·nal** (prē·nom′ə·nəl), adj.

prae·tor (prē′tər), n. magistrate or judge in ancient Rome. A praetor ranked next below a consul. [< L, ult. < *prae-* before + *ire* go] —**prae·to·ri·al** (prē·tô′ri·əl; -tō′-), adj. —**prae·to′ri·an,** n.

prag·mat·ic (prag·mat′ik), **prag·mat·i·cal** (-ə·kəl), adj. 1. concerned with practical results or values; of or pertaining to pragmatism: *a pragmatic philosophy.* 2. busy; active. 3. matter-of-fact; practical. 4. meddlesome; interfering. 5. conceited; opinionated. [< L < Gk. *pragmatikos* efficient, ult. < *prassein* do] —**prag·mat′i·cal·ly,** adv. —**prag·mat′i·cal·ness,** n.

prag·ma·tism (prag′mə·tiz·əm), n. 1. *Am.* philosophy that tests the value and truth of ideas by their practical consequences. 2. a pragmatic quality or condition. 3. officiousness. 4. dogmatism. 5. a matter-of-fact way of viewing things. —**prag′ma·tist,** n.

Prague (präg), *Czech,* Pra·ha (prä′hä). n. capital of Czechoslovakia.

prai·rie (prār′i), n. *Am.* a large area of level or rolling land with grass but no trees. [< F, ult. < L *pratum* meadow]

prairie chicken, *Am.* any of several grouse of the prairies of North America.

prairie dog, *Am.* animal like a woodchuck but smaller. Prairie dogs bark.

Prairie chicken (ab. 1½ ft. from bill to end of tail)

prairie schooner, *Am.* a large covered wagon used by emigrants in crossing the plains of North America before the railroads were built.

prairie wolf, *Am.* coyote.

praise (prāz), n., v., praised, prais·ing. —n. 1. saying that a thing or person is good; words that tell the worth or value of a thing or person. 2. words or song setting forth the glory and goodness of God. —v. 1. express approval or admiration of. 2. worship in words or song: *praise God.* [< OF *preisier,* ult. < L *pretium* price] —**prais′er,** n. —Syn. n. 1. commendation, acclaim. –v. 1. commend, extol, laud, applaud. —Ant. n. 1. condemnation, censure. –v. 1. condemn, criticize.

praise·wor·thy (prāz′wér′ᵺi), adj. worthy

of praise; deserving approval. —**praise′wor′thi·ly,** adv. —**praise′wor′thi·ness,** n.

pra·line (prä′lēn), n. *Am.* a small cake of brown candy made of sugar and nuts, usually pecans or almonds. [< F; invented by the cook of Marshal Duplessis-*Praslin*]

pram (pram), n. *Brit. Colloq.* perambulator; baby carriage.

prance (prans; präns), v., pranced, pranc·ing, n. —v. 1. spring about on the hind legs: *horses prance when they feel lively.* 2. ride on a horse doing this. 3. move gaily or proudly; swagger. 4. caper; dance. —n. a prancing. —**pranc′er,** n. —**pranc′ing·ly,** adv.

prank¹ (prangk), n. piece of mischief; playful trick. On April Fool's Day people play pranks on each other. —**prank′ish,** adj. —**prank′ish·ly,** adv. —**prank′ish·ness,** n. —**prank′ster,** n.

prank² (prangk), v. 1. dress in a showy way; adorn. 2. make a show or display. [cf. MLG *prank* showiness]

pra·se·o·dym·i·um (prā′zi·ō·dim′i·əm), n. *Chem.* a rare metallic element, Pr, of the same group as cerium. [< NL, ult. < Gk. *prasios* leek-green + E (*di*)*dymium,* a rare element, < Gk. *didymos* twin]

prate (prāt), v., prat·ed, prat·ing, n. —v. talk a great deal in a foolish way. —n. empty or foolish talk. [cf. MDu., MLG *praten*] —**prat′er,** n. —**prat′ing·ly,** adv. —Syn. v., n. prattle, chatter, babble.

prat·tle (prat′əl), v., -tled, -tling, n. —v. 1. talk as a child does; tell freely and carelessly. 2. talk or tell in a foolish way. 3. sound like baby talk; babble. —n. 1. simple, artless talk. 2. baby talk; foolish talk. 3. a sound like baby talk; babble. [< *prate*] —**prat′tler,** n. —**prat′tling·ly,** adv.

prawn (prôn), n. any of several edible shellfish much like shrimp but larger. [ME *prane*]

pray (prā), v. 1. speak to God in worship; enter into spiritual communion with God; offer worship. 2. make earnest request to God or to any other object of worship: *pray for help, pray for one's family.* 3. ask earnestly: *pray God for help* or *to help.* 4. ask earnestly for. 5. bring or get by praying. 6. please: *pray come with me.* [< OF < L *precari* < *prex* prayer] —**pray′er,** n. —Syn. 3. entreat, implore, beseech, beg.

prayer (prâr), n. 1. act of praying. 2. thing prayed for. 3. form of words to be used in praying. 4. form of worship; religious service consisting mainly of prayers. 5. an earnest or humble request. [< OF *preiere,* ult. < L *prex* prayer] —**prayer′ful,** adj. —**prayer′ful·ly,** adv. —**prayer′ful·ness,** n. —Syn. 5. entreaty, appeal.

praying mantis, mantis.

pre-, *prefix.* before in place, time, order, or rank, as in *prepay, prevision, prewar.* [< L *prae-*] ➤ **pre-.** The prefix *pre-,* meaning before in time (*preëxist, pre-Victorian*), or in place (*precerebral*), or rank (*preëminent*), (1) requires a dieresis on *e,* or is separated by a hyphen from, the root to which it is joined when the root begins with *e: preëminent, pre-eminent; preëmpt, pre-empt; preëxistence, pre-existence;* and (2) takes a hyphen when the root is a proper name: *pre-American, pre-Elizabethan.* To other words it is joined directly: *prearrange, predominant, preheat, preview, prewar.*

preach (prēch), v. 1. speak publicly on a religious subject. 2. deliver (a sermon). 3. make known by preaching; proclaim: *preach the Gospel.* 4. give earnest advice. [< OF < L *praedicare* declare, preach. Doublet of PREDICATE.] —**preach′ing,** n. —**preach′ing·ly,** adv.

preach·er (prēch′ər), n. person who preaches; clergyman; minister.

preach·i·fy (prēch′ə·fī), v., -fied, -fy·ing. preach or moralize too much.

preach·ment (prēch′mənt), n. 1. a preaching. 2. a long, tiresome sermon or speech.

preach·y (prēch′i), adj., preach·i·er, preach·i·est. *Colloq.* 1. inclined to preach. 2. suggestive of preaching.

pre·am·ble (prē′am′bəl), n. a preliminary statement; introduction to a speech or a writing.

[< F < Med.L *praeambulum*, orig. neut. adj., walking before, ult. < L *prae-* before + *ambulare* to walk]

pre·ar·range (prē'ə·rānj'), *v.*, -ranged, -rang·ing. arrange beforehand. —pre'ar·range'ment, *n.*

pre·a·tom·ic (prē'ə·tom'ik), *adj. Am.* before Aug. 6, 1945, the first military use of the atom bomb, at Hiroshima.

preb·end (preb'ənd), *n.* 1. salary given to a clergyman connected with a cathedral or a collegiate church. 2. Also, **preb·en·dar·y** (preb'ən·der'i). clergyman who has a prebend. [< LL *praebenda* allowance < L (things) to be furnished < *praebere* furnish] —**pre·ben·dal** (pri·ben'dəl), *adj.*

pre·can·cel (prē·kan'səl), *v.*, -celed, -cel·ing; *esp. Brit.* -celled, -cel·ling. cancel (postage stamps) before use.

pre·car·i·ous (pri·kãr'i·əs), *adj.* 1. dependent on the will or pleasure of another. 2. not safe or secure; uncertain; dangerous; risky: *a soldier leads a precarious life.* [< L *precarius*, orig., obtainable by entreaty, ult. < *prex* prayer] —pre·car'i·ous·ly, *adv.* —pre·car'i·ous·ness, *n.* —Syn. 2. insecure, perilous, hazardous. —Ant. 2. certain, secure, safe, sure.

pre·cau·tion (pri·kô'shən), *n.* 1. a taking care beforehand: *proper precaution is prudent.* 2. care taken beforehand; thing done beforehand to ward off evil or secure good results. —pre·cau·tion·ar·y (pri·kô'shən·er'i), pre·cau'tion·al, *adj.*

pre·cede (prē·sēd'), *v.*, -ced·ed, -ced·ing. 1. go before; come before: *Mr. Hoover preceded Mr. Roosevelt as President.* 2. be higher than in rank or importance: *a major precedes a captain.* [< L, < *prae-* before + *cedere* go]

prec·e·dence (pres'ə·dəns; pri·sēd'əns), **prec·e·den·cy** (-dən·si), *n.*, *pl.* -denc·es; -den·cies. 1. act or fact of preceding. 2. higher position or rank; greater importance: *take precedence over all others.* 3. right to precede others in ceremonies or social affairs; social superiority.

prec·e·dent (*n.* pres'ə·dənt; *adj.* pri·sēd'ənt, pres'ə·dənt), *n.* case that may serve as an example or reason for a later case. —*adj.* preceding. [< L *praecedens.* See PRECEDE.] —prec·e·den·tial (pres'ə·den'shəl), *adj.* —pre·ced·ent·ly (pri·sēd'ənt·li; pres'ə·dənt·li), *adv.*

pre·ced·ing (prē·sēd'ing), *adj.* going before; coming before; previous.

pre·cen·tor (pri·sen'tər), *n.* person who leads and directs the singing of a church choir or congregation. [< LL *praecentor*, ult. < L *prae-* before + *canere* sing] —pre·cen·to·ri·al (prē'sen·tô'ri·əl; -tō'-), *adj.* —pre·cen'tor·ship, *n.*

pre·cept (prē'sept), *n.* rule of action or behavior; maxim. [< L *praeceptum*, orig. neut. pp., enjoined, anticipated < *prae-* before + *capere* take] —Syn. teaching, adage, axiom.

pre·cep·tor (pri·sep'tər), *n.* instructor. —pre·cep·to·ri·al (prē'sep·tô'ri·əl; -tō'-), pre·cep'to·ral, *adj.* —pre·cep'tor·ship, *n.*

pre·ces·sion (prē·sesh'ən), *n.* act, fact, or condition of going first; precedence. —pre·ces'sion·al, *adj.*

pre·cinct (prē'singkt), *n.* 1. district within certain boundaries, for governmental, administrative, or other purposes: *an election precinct, a police precinct.* 2. space within a boundary: *the school precincts.* 3. Often, **precincts.** boundary; limit. [< Med.L *praecinctum*, orig. neut. pp., enclosed < *prae-* before + *cingere* gird]

pre·ci·os·i·ty (presh'i·os'ə·ti), *n.*, *pl.* -ties. too much refinement; affectation. [< OF *preciosité* < *précieux* precious] ▶ See precious for usage note.

pre·cious (presh'əs), *adj.* 1. worth much; valuable. Gold, platinum, and silver are often called the precious metals. 2. much loved; dear. 3. too nice; overrefined. 4. *Colloq.* very great. —*adv. Colloq.* very. —*n.* darling. [< OF < L *pretiosus* < *pretium* value] —pre'cious·ly, *adv.* —pre'cious·ness, *n.* —Syn. *adj.* 1. costly, expensive. 2.

beloved. ▶ **precious, preciosity.** Applied to style, *precious* and *preciosity* (rarely *preciousness*) mean "excessive attention to, fastidiousness in the use of words," or, less often, "too great care in pronunciation."

precious stone, jewel; gem.

prec·i·pice (pres'ə·pis), *n.* a very steep cliff; almost vertical slope. [< F < L, < *praeceps* steep, lit. headlong, < *prae-* first + *caput* head]

pre·cip·i·tant (pri·sip'ə·tənt), *adj.* 1. very sudden or abrupt. 2. acting in a hasty or rash manner. 3. falling or rushing headlong. —*n. Chem.* substance that causes another substance in solution in a liquid to be deposited in solid form. —pre·cip'i·tance, pre·cip'i·tan·cy, *n.* —pre·cip'i·tant·ly, *adv.*

pre·cip·i·tate (*v.* pri·sip'ə·tāt; *adj., n.* pri·sip'ə·tāt, -tit), *v.*, -tat·ed, -tat·ing, *adj., n.* —*v.* 1. hasten the beginning of; bring about suddenly: *precipitate a war.* 2. throw headlong; hurl. 3. *Chem.* separate (a substance) out from a solution as a solid. 4. *Physics, Meteorol.* a. condense from vapor in the form of rain, dew, etc. b. be condensed in this way. —*adj.* 1. very hurried; sudden: *a precipitate drop in the temperature.* 2. with great haste and force; plunging or rushing; hasty; rash. 3. headlong. —*n.* 1. *Chem.* substance, usually crystalline, separated out from a solution as a solid. 2. *Physics, Meteorol.* condensed moisture, usually in the form of rain or snow. [< L, < *praeceps* headlong. See PRECIPICE.] —pre·cip'i·tate·ly, *adv.* —pre·cip'i·tate·ness, *n.* —pre·cip'i·ta'tive, *adj.* —pre·cip'i·ta'tor, *n.*

pre·cip·i·ta·tion (pri·sip'ə·tā'shən), *n.* 1. act or state of precipitating; throwing down or falling headlong. 2. a hastening or hurrying. 3. a sudden bringing on: *precipitation of a war without warning.* 4. unwise or rash rapidity; sudden haste. 5. the separating out of a substance from a solution as a solid. 6. substance separated out from a solution as a solid. 7. the depositing of moisture in the form of rain, dew, or snow. 8. amount that is precipitated.

pre·cip·i·tous (pri·sip'ə·təs), *adj.* 1. like a precipice; very steep: *precipitous cliffs.* 2. hasty; rash. —pre·cip'i·tous·ly, *adv.* —pre·cip'i·tous·ness, *n.*

pré·cis (prā'sē; prā·sē'), *n.*, *pl.* -cis. abstract; summary. [< F, orig. adj., PRECISE]

pre·cise (pri·sīs'), *adj.* 1. exact; accurate; definite: *the precise sum was 34½ cents.* 2. careful. 3. strict; scrupulous. [< L *praecisus* abridged < *prae-* in front + *caedere* to cut] —pre·cise'ly, *adv.* —pre·cise'ness, *n.* —Syn. 1. correct. 3. punctilious.

pre·ci·sion (pri·sizh'ən), *n.* accuracy; exactness: *precision of a machine.* —pre·ci'sion·ist, *n.* —Syn. correctness, definiteness.

pre·clude (pri·klüd'), *v.*, -clud·ed, -clud·ing. shut out; make impossible; prevent. [< L, < *prae-* before + *claudere* to shut] —pre·clu·sion (pri·klü'zhən), *n.* —pre·clu·sive (pri·klü'siv), *adj.* —pre·clu'sive·ly, *adv.* —Syn. exclude, prohibit.

pre·co·cious (pri·kō'shəs), *adj.* 1. developed earlier than usual. 2. developed too early. [< L *praecox*, ult. < *prae-* before (its time) + *coquere* ripen] —pre·co'cious·ly, *adv.* —pre·co'cious·ness, pre·coc·i·ty (pri·kos'ə·ti), *n.*

pre·con·ceive (prē'kən·sēv'), *v.*, -ceived, -ceiv·ing. form an idea or opinion of beforehand. —pre·con·cep·tion (prē'kən·sep'shən), *n.*

pre·con·cert (prē'kən·sērt'), *v.* arrange beforehand: *a preconcerted signal.* —pre'con·cert'ed·ly, *adv.*

pre·cur·sor (pri·kėr'sər), *n.* forerunner. [< L *praecursor*, ult. < *prae-* before + *currere* run] —Syn. predecessor, herald.

pre·cur·so·ry (pri·kėr'sə·ri), *adj.* indicative of something to follow; introductory.

pred., predicate.

pre·da·cious, pre·da·ceous (pri·dā'shəs), *adj.* living by prey; predatory. [< L *praedari* rob < *praeda* prey] —pre·dac·i·ty (pri·das'ə·ti), *n.* —pre·da'cious·ness, pre·da'ceous·ness, *n.*

age, cãre, fär; ēqual, tėrm; īce; ōpen, ôrder; pũt, rũle, ũse; th, then; ə=a in about.

pred. adj., predicate adjective.

pred·a·to·ry (pred′ə·tô′ri; -tō′-), *adj.* **1.** of or inclined to plundering or robbery. **2.** preying upon other animals. Hawks and owls are predatory birds. [< L, ult. < *praeda* prey] —pred′a·to′ri·ly, *adv.* —pred′a·to′ri·ness, *n.* —Syn. **1.** marauding, thieving, rapacious.

pred·e·ces·sor (pred′ə·ses′ər), *n.* **1.** person holding a position or office before another: *John Adams was Jefferson's predecessor.* **2.** thing that came before another. **3.** ancestor; forefather. [< LL *praedecessor,* ult. < *prae-* before + *decedere* retire]

pre·des·ti·nate (*v.* prē·des′tə·nāt; *adj.* prē·des′tə·nit, -nāt), *v.,* -nat·ed, -nat·ing, *adj.* —*v.* **1.** decree or ordain beforehand. **2.** foreordain by divine purpose. —*adj.* foreordained. —pre·des′ti·na′tor, *n.* —Syn. *v.* **1.** predetermine, predestine.

pre·des·ti·na·tion (prē′des·tə·nā′shən), *n.* **1.** an ordaining beforehand; destiny; fate. **2.** action of God in deciding beforehand what shall happen. **3.** doctrine that by God's decree certain souls will be saved and others lost.

pre·des·tine (prē·des′tən), *v.,* -tined, -tin·ing. determine or settle beforehand; foreordain.

pre·de·ter·mine (prē′di·tér′mən), *v.,* -mined, -min·ing. **1.** determine or decide beforehand. **2.** direct or impel beforehand (to something). —pre′de·ter′mi·na·ble, *adj.* —pre′de·ter′mi·na′tion, *n.*

pred·i·ca·ble (pred′ə·kə·bəl), *adj.* that can be predicated or affirmed. —pred′i·ca·bil′i·ty, pred′i·ca·ble·ness, *n.* —pred′i·ca·bly, *adv.*

pre·dic·a·ment (pri·dik′ə·mənt), *n.* **1.** an unpleasant, difficult, or dangerous situation. **2.** any condition, state, or situation. [< LL *praedicamentum* quality, category < L *praedicare* PREDICATE] —pre·dic·a·men·tal (pri·dik′ə·men′təl), *adj.* —Syn. **1.** plight, strait, fix, dilemma.

pred·i·cate (*n.,* *adj.* pred′ə·kit; *v.* pred′ə·kāt), *n., adj., v.,* -cat·ed, -cat·ing. —*n.* Gram. word or words expressing what is said about the subject. Examples: Men *work*. The men *dug wells*. The men *are soldiers*. —*adj.* Gram. belonging to the predicate. In "Horses are strong," *strong* is a **predicate adjective.** —*v.* **1.** found or base (a statement, action, etc.) on something. **2.** declare, assert, or affirm to be real or true: *most religions predicate life after death.* [< L, < *prae-* before + *dicare* make known. Doublet of PREACH.] —pred′i·ca′tion, *n.* —pred′i·ca′tive, *adj.* —pred′i·ca′tive·ly, *adv.* ➤ predicate. A predicate is the verb and its dependent words that complete the meaning of the subject of a subordinate or independent clause. It may be a verb of complete meaning (The big bell *tolled*), a verb and adverbial modifier (The sun *went behind the cloud*), a transitive verb and its object (He *finally landed the big fish*), a linking verb and complement (The oldest member of a family *is usually the first to go*). Two verbs depending upon one subject are known as a compound predicate: The three of them *washed* and *wiped* the whole lot in fifteen minutes.

pre·dict (pri·dikt′), *v.* tell beforehand; prophesy. [< L, < *prae-* before + *dicere* say] —pre·dict′a·ble, *adj.* —pre·dic′tive, *adj.* —pre·dic′tive·ly, *adv.* —pre·dic′tor, *n.* —Syn. foretell, presage.

pre·dic·tion (pri·dik′shən), *n.* **1.** act of predicting. **2.** thing predicted; prophecy.

pre·di·gest (prē′di·jest′; -dī-), *v.* **1.** digest beforehand. **2.** treat (food) by an artificial process, similar to digestion, in order to make it more digestible. —pre′di·ges′tion, *n.*

pre·di·lec·tion (prē′də·lek′shən; pred′ə-), *n.* a liking; preference. [< F, ult. < L *prae-* before + *diligere* choose] —Syn. partiality, predisposition.

pre·dis·pose (prē′dis·pōz′), *v.,* -posed, -pos·ing. give an inclination or tendency to; make liable or susceptible: *a cold predisposes a person to other diseases.* —pre·dis·po·si·tion (prē′dis·pə·zish′ən), *n.*

pre·dom·i·nant (pri·dom′ə·nənt), *adj.* **1.** having more power, authority, or influence than others; superior. **2.** prevailing; most noticeable. —pre·dom′i·nance, pre·dom′i·nan·cy, *n.* —pre·dom′i·nant·ly, *adv.* —Syn. **1.** controlling, ruling. —Ant. **1.** subordinate, secondary. ➤ **Predominant** is the adjective: *a predominant sentiment, a sentiment predominant in the village.* **Predominate** is the verb: *This sentiment predominated in the village.* These words are heavy for prevailing, prevail, or some such word.

pre·dom·i·nate (pri·dom′ə·nāt), *v.,* -nat·ed, -nat·ing. be greater in power, strength, influence, or numbers. —pre·dom′i·nat′ing·ly, *adv.* —pre·dom′i·na′tion, *n.* —pre·dom′i·na′tor, *n.* ➤ See predominant for usage note.

pre·ëm·i·nent, pre-em·i·nent (pri·em′ə·nənt), *adj.* standing out above all others; superior to others. —pre·ëm′i·nence, pre·em′i·nence, *n.* —pre·ëm′i·nent·ly, pre·em′i·nent·ly, *adv.*

pre·ëmpt, pre-empt (pri·empt′), *v.* **1.** secure before someone else can; acquire or take possession of beforehand. **2.** settle on (land) with the right to buy it before others. [< *preëmption*] —pre·ëmp′tive, pre·emp′tive, *adj.* —pre·ëmp′tor, pre·emp′tor, *n.*

pre·ëmp·tion, pre-emp·tion (pri·emp′shən), *n.* a preëmpting or being preëmpted. [< L *prae-* before + *emptio* buying < *emere* to buy]

preen (prēn), *v.* **1.** smooth or arrange (the feathers) with the beak, as a bird does. **2.** dress (oneself) carefully. —preen′er, *n.*

pre·ëx·ist, pre-ex·ist (prē′ig·zist′), *v.* exist beforehand, or before something else. —pre′ëx·ist′ence, pre′ex·ist′ence, *n.* —pre′ëx·ist′ent, pre′ex·ist′ent, *adj.*

pref., **1.** preface. **2.** preferred. **3.** prefix.

pre·fab (prē·fab′), *n., v.,* -fabbed, -fab·bing. *Am.* —*n.* a prefabricated house. —*v.* prefabricate.

pre·fab·ri·cate (prē·fab′rə·kāt), *v.,* -cat·ed, -cat·ing. make all standardized parts of (a house, etc.). The erection of a prefabricated house requires merely the assembling of the various sections. —pre·fab′ri·cat′ed, *adj.* —pre′fab·ri·ca′tion, *n.*

pref·ace (pref′is), *n., v.,* -aced, -ac·ing. —*n.* introduction to a book, writing, or speech: *this book has a preface written by the author.* —*v.* **1.** introduce by written or spoken remarks; give a preface to. **2.** be a preface to; begin. [< OF, ult. < L, < *prae-* before < *fari* speak] —pref′ac·er, *n.*

pref·a·to·ry (pref′ə·tô′ri; -tō′-), **pref·a·to·ri·al** (pref′ə·tô′ri·əl; -tō′-), *adj.* of or like a preface; given as a preface; introductory; preliminary. —pref′a·to′ri·ly, pref′a·to′ri·al·ly, *adv.*

pre·fect (prē′fekt), *n.* **1.** title of various military and civil officers in ancient Rome and elsewhere. **2.** the chief administrative official of a department of France. [< L *praefectus,* orig. pp., put in charge < *prae-* in front + *facere* make] —pre·fec·to·ral (pri·fek′tə·rəl), pre·fec·to·ri·al (prē′fek·tô′ri·əl; -tō′-), *adj.*

pre·fec·ture (prē′fek·chər), *n.* office, jurisdiction, territory, or official residence of a prefect. —pre·fec·tur·al (pri·fek′chər·əl), *adj.*

pre·fer (pri·fér′), *v.,* -ferred, -fer·ring. **1.** like better; choose rather. **2.** put forward; present: *in a few words he preferred his claim to the property.* **3.** promote; advance. [< L, < *prae-* before + *ferre* carry] —pre·fer′rer, *n.* ➤ **prefer.** The better idiom is with *to*: *I prefer "Babbitt" to "Main Street." He preferred going by train to going in their car.* **Had rather . . . than** is less formal and more used: *He had [he'd] rather go by train than in their car.*

pref·er·a·ble (pref′ər·ə·bəl; pref′rə·bəl), *adj.* to be preferred; more desirable. —pref′er·a·bil′i·ty, pref′er·a·ble·ness, *n.* —pref′er·a·bly, *adv.*

pref·er·ence (pref′ər·əns; pref′rəns), *n.* **1.** act or attitude of liking better: *my preference is for beef rather than lamb.* **2.** thing preferred; first choice: *Helen's preference in reading is a detective story.* **3.** a prior favor, choice, right, or claim. **4.** favoritism. —Syn. **2.** selection, election.

pref·er·en·tial (pref'ər·en'shəl), *adj.* of, giving, or receiving preference. —**pref'er·en'tial·ly,** *adv.*

preferential shop, shop giving preference to union members in hiring, promotion, etc.

pre·fer·ment (pri·fér'mənt), *n.* 1. advancement; promotion. 2. position or office giving social or financial advancement, esp. one in the church.

preferred stock, *Am.* stock on which dividends must be paid before any can be paid on the common stock.

pre·fig·ure (prē·fig'yər), *v.,* -ured, -ur·ing. 1. represent beforehand by a figure or type. 2. imagine to oneself beforehand. —**pre·fig·u·ra·tion** (prē'fig·yə·rā'shən), **pre·fig'ure·ment,** *n.* —**pre·fig·ur·a·tive** (prē·fig'yər·ə·tiv), *adj.*

pre·fix (*n.* prē'fiks; *v.* prē·fiks'), *n.* a syllable, syllables, or word put at the beginning of a word to change its meaning or to form a new word, as in prepaid, *unlike.* —*v.* put before. We prefix *Mr.* to a man's name. [< L *praefixus* < *prae-* in front + *figere* fix] —**pre·fix·al** (prē'fik·səl; prē·fik'səl), *adj.*

preg·na·ble (preg'nə·bəl), *adj.* open to attack; assailable. —**preg'na·bil·i·ty,** *n.*

preg·nan·cy (preg'nən·si), *n., pl.* -cies. pregnant quality or condition.

preg·nant (preg'nənt), *adj.* 1. having an embryo or embryos developing in the uterus; being with child or young. 2. filled; loaded. 3. fertile; rich; abounding. 4. very significant. [< L *praegnans* < *prae-* before + *gen-* to bear] —**preg'nant·ly,** *adv.*

pre·hen·sile (pri·hen'səl), *adj.* adapted for seizing, grasping, or holding on. Many monkeys have prehensile tails. [< F, ult. < L *prehendere* to grasp] —**pre·hen·sil·i·ty** (prē'hen·sil'ə·ti), *n.*

pre·his·tor·ic (prē'his·tôr'ik; -tor'-), **pre·his·tor·i·cal** (-ə·kəl), *adj.* of or belonging to periods before recorded history. —**pre'his·tor'i·cal·ly,** *adv.*

pre·judge (prē·juj'), *v.,* -judged, -judg·ing. judge beforehand; judge without knowing all the facts. —**pre·judg'er,** *n.* —**pre·judg'ment,** *esp. Brit.* **pre·judge'ment,** *n.*

prej·u·dice (prej'ə·dis), *n., v.,* -diced, -dic·ing. —*n.* 1. opinion formed without taking time and care to judge fairly: *a prejudice against doctors.* 2. harm; injury. —*v.* 1. cause a prejudice in; fill with prejudice: *one unfortunate experience prejudiced him against all lawyers.* 2. damage; harm; injure. [< F < L, < *prae-* before + *judicium* judgment] —**Syn.** *n.* 1. bias, prepossession. ▷ **prejudice.** Remember the spelling of *prejudice* by associating it with *pre-judge* and the adjective *prej·u·di·cial.*

prej·u·di·cial (prej'ə·dish'əl), *adj.* causing prejudice or disadvantage; hurtful. —**prej'u·di'cial·ly,** *adv.* —**Syn.** detrimental, damaging.

prel·a·cy (prel'ə·si), *n., pl.* -cies. 1. position or rank of a prelate. 2. prelates. 3. church government by prelates.

prel·ate (prel'it), *n.* clergyman of high rank, such as a bishop. [< Med.L, < L *praelatus* one preferred, orig. pp. to L *praeferre* PREFER] —**prel'ate·ship,** *n.*

prelim, preliminary.

pre·lim·i·nar·y (pri·lim'ə·ner'i), *adj., n., pl.* -nar·ies. —*adj.* coming before the main business; leading to something more important. —*n.* a preliminary step; something preparatory. [< NL, ult. < L *prae-* before + *limen* threshold] —**pre·lim'i·nar'i·ly,** *adv.* —**Syn.** *adj.* preparatory, prefatory, introductory.

prel·ude (prel'ūd; prē'lūd), *n., v.,* -ud·ed, -ud·ing. —*n.* 1. anything serving as an introduction; preliminary performance: *the organ prelude to a church service.* 2. Music. a. a prefatory or introductory piece to a main composition, such as a fugue or suite. b. a brief composition, usually based on a short figure or motive. —*v.* be a prelude or introduction to. [< F < Med.L, ult. < L *prae-* before + *ludere* play] —**pre·lud·er** (pri·lūd'ər; prel'yə·dər), *n.*

pre·ma·ture (prē'mə·chúr'; -túr'; -tyúr'),

adj. 1. before the proper time; too soon. 2. overhasty; precipitate. —**pre'ma·ture'ly,** *adv.* —**pre'ma·ture'ness, pre'ma·tu'ri·ty,** *n.*

pre·med·i·cal (prē·med'ə·kəl), *adj.* preparing for the study of medicine.

pre·med·i·tate (prē·med'ə·tāt), *v.,* -tat·ed, -tat·ing. consider or plan beforehand: *a deliberate, premeditated murder.* —**pre·med'i·tat'ed,** *adj.* —**pre·med'i·tat'ed·ly,** *adv.* —**pre·med·i·ta'tion,** *n.* —**pre·med'i·ta'tor,** *n.*

pre·mier (*n.* pri·mir', prē'mi·ər; *adj.* prē'mi·ər, prem'yər), *n.* prime minister. —*adj.* first in rank; chief. [< F, first < L *primarius* PRIMARY] —**pre·mier'ship,** *n.*

pre·mière (pri·mir'; prə·myãr'), *n.* a first public performance. [< F, orig. fem. of *premier.* See PREMIER.]

prem·ise (*n.* prem'is; *v.* pri·mīz'), *n., v.,* -ised, -is·ing. —*n.* 1. Logic. a statement assumed to be true and used to draw a conclusion. *Example:* Major premise: Children should go to school. Minor premise: He is a child. Conclusion: He should go to school. 2. premises, a. house or building with its grounds. b. Law. property forming the subject of a document. —*v.* set forth as an introduction or explanation; mention beforehand. [< Med.L *praemissa,* orig. fem. pp., < L *prae-* before + *mittere* send]

pre·mi·um (prē'mi·əm), *n.* 1. reward; prize: *some magazines give premiums for obtaining new subscriptions.* 2. something more than the ordinary price or wages. 3. amount of money paid for insurance: *he pays premiums on his life insurance four times a year.* 4. excess value of one form of money over another of the same nominal value. 5. unusual or unfair value: *giving money to beggars may put a premium on idleness.* 6. **at a premium,** a. at more than the usual value or price. b. very valuable; much wanted. [< L *praemium* reward]

pre·mo·ni·tion (prē'mə·nish'ən; prem'ə-), *n.* 1. a forewarning. 2. presentiment. [< earlier F < L, ult. < *prae-* before + *monere* warn] —**pre·mon·i·to·ry** (pri·mon'ə·tô'ri; -tō'-), *adj.* —**pre·mon'i·to'ri·ly,** *adv.*

pre·na·tal (prē·nā'təl), *adj.* previous to birth. —**pre·na'tal·ly,** *adv.*

pre·oc·cu·py (prē·ok'yə·pī), *v.,* -pied, -py·ing. 1. take up all the attention of: *the question of getting to New York preoccupied her mind.* 2. occupy beforehand; take possession of before others: *our favorite seats had been preoccupied.* —**pre·oc'cu·pan·cy,** *n.* —**pre·oc·cu·pa·tion** (prē·ok'yə·pā'shən; prē'ok-), *n.* —**pre·oc'cu·pied,** *adj.*

pre·or·dain (prē'ôr·dān'), *v.* decide or settle beforehand; foreordain. —**pre'or·dain'ment,** **pre·or·di·na·tion** (prē'ôr·də·nā'shən), *n.*

prep (prep), *adj. Colloq.* preparatory.

prep., 1. preparatory. 2. preposition.

pre·paid (prē·pād'), *v.* pt. and pp. of **prepay.**

prep·a·ra·tion (prep'ə·rā'shən), *n.* 1. a preparing. 2. a being prepared. 3. thing done to prepare for something. 4. medicine, food, or other substance made by a special process.

pre·par·a·to·ry (pri·par'ə·tô'ri; -tō'-), *adj.* 1. of or for preparation; preparing: *a preparatory school.* 2. as an introduction; preliminary. —**pre·par'a·to'ri·ly,** *adv.*

pre·pare (pri·pãr'), *v.,* -pared, -par·ing. 1. make ready; get ready. 2. make by a special process. [< L, < *prae-* before + *parere* make ready] —**pre·par·ed·ly** (pri·pãr'id·li), *adv.* —**pre·par'er,** *n.* —**Syn.** 2. devise, contrive, concoct.

pre·par·ed·ness (pri·pãr'id·nis; -pãrd'nis), *n.* 1. a being prepared; readiness. 2. possession of adequate military forces and defenses.

pre·pay (prē·pā'), *v.,* -paid, -pay·ing. 1. pay in advance. 2. pay for in advance. —**pre·pay'a·ble,** *adj.* —**pre·pay'ment,** *n.*

pre·pon·der·ant (pri·pon'dər·ənt), *adj.* 1. weighing more; being stronger or more numerous; having more power or influence. 2. chief; most important. —**pre·pon'der·ance, pre·pon'der·an·cy,** *n.* —**pre·pon'der·ant·ly,** *adv.*

pre·pon·der·ate (pri·pon'dər·āt), v., -at·ed, -at·ing. 1. be greater than; outweigh. 2. be greater than something else in weight, power, force, influence, number, amount, etc.: *oaks and maples preponderate in our woods.* 3. be chief; be most important. [< L *praeponderatus* outweighed, ult. < *prae*- before + *pondus* weight] —pre·pon'der·at'ing·ly, *adv.* —pre·pon'der·a'tion, *n.*

prep·o·si·tion (prep'ə·zish'ən), *n. Gram.* word that shows certain relations between other words. *With, for, by,* and *in* are prepositions in the sentence "A man *with* rugs *for* sale walked *by* our house, *in* the morning." [< L *praepositio*, ult. < *prae*- before + *ponere* place] —prep'o·si'tion·al, *adj.* —prep'o·si'tion·al·ly, *adv.* ➤ **preposition at end of sentence.** It was once fashionable for textbooks to put a stigma upon prepositions standing at the end of their constructions (*What did you do it for?*)—a rule which probably came from Latin grammar, in which prepositions do not come at the end. But postponing the preposition is a characteristic English idiom, even though it runs contrary to our usual tendency to keep words of a construction close together. In fact it is so generally the normal word order that the real danger is in clumsiness from trying to avoid a preposition at the end of a clause or sentence: *Tell me what it is to which you object* [what you object to]. *To whatever authority we may appeal, he will quibble over the method to be adopted* [whatever authority we may appeal to . . .]. It is possible to object to this word order on the ground of emphasis, on the principle that "Sentences should end with words that deserve distinction." In speech of course there is no trouble, since we depress the voice enough to remove any undue emphasis from a final *to* or *on;* on the printed page it is slightly harder to keep this relative stress, though when such a sentence occurs in a natural, colloquial style the rhythm will usually take care of the stress. Extreme cases are possible (like the boy's "What did you bring that book for me to be read to out of for?"); but there is no reason for hesitating to let a preposition fall at the end if natural idiom and rhythm place it there.

pre·pos·sess (prē'pə·zes'), v. 1. fill with a favorable feeling or opinion. 2. fill with a feeling or opinion. —pre'pos·sess'ing, *adj.* —pre'pos·sess'ing·ly, *adv.* —pre'pos·sess'ing·ness, *n.* —pre'pos·ses'sion, *n.*

pre·pos·ter·ous (pri·pos'tər·əs; -trəs), *adj.* contrary to nature, reason, or common sense; absurd; senseless. [< L *praeposterus* in reverse order, ult. < *prae*- before + *post* after] —pre·pos'ter·ous·ly, *adv.* —pre·pos'ter·ous·ness, *n.* —Syn. foolish, silly, irrational, ridiculous.

pre·puce (prē'pūs), *n.* foreskin. [< F < L *praeputium*.] —pre·pu·tial (pri·pū'shəl), *adj.*

pre·req·ui·site (prē·rek'wə·zit), *n.* something required beforehand: *a high-school course is the usual prerequisite to college work.* —*adj.* required beforehand.

pre·rog·a·tive (pri·rog'ə·tiv), *n.* right or privilege that nobody else has: *the government has the prerogative of coining money.* [< L *praerogativa*, orig. fem. adj., asked to vote first, ult. < *prae*- before + *rogare* ask]

Pres., President.

pres., 1. present. 2. pressure.

pres·age (*n.* pres'ij; *v.* pri·sāj'), *n., v.,* -aged, -ag·ing. —*n.* 1. sign felt as a warning; omen. 2. prophetic significance: *an occurrence of dire presage.* 3. a feeling that something is about to happen. —*v.* give warning (of); predict: *some people think that a circle around the moon presages a storm.* [< L, ult. < *prae*- before + *sagus* prophetic] —pre·sag'er, *n.* —pre·sag'ing·ly, *adv.*

pres·by·ter (prez'bə·tər; pres'-), *n.* 1. an elder in the early Christian church. 2. in the Presbyterian church, a minister or a lay elder. 3. in the Episcopal church, a minister or a priest. [< L, elder, < Gk. *presbyteros,* compar. of *presbys* old. Doublet of PRIEST.] —pres·byt·er·al (prez·bit'ər·əl; pres-), *adj.*

Pres·by·te·ri·an (prez'bə·tir'i·ən; pres'-), *adj.* 1. being or naming a Protestant denomination or church governed by elected presbyters or elders all of equal rank. 2. of the Presbyterian church. —*n.* member of the Presbyterian church. —Pres'by·te'ri·an·ism, *n.*

pres·by·ter·y (prez'bə·ter'i; pres'-), *n., pl.* -ter·ies. 1. in the Presbyterian church, a meeting or court of all the ministers and certain of the elders within a district. 2. district under the jurisdiction of such a meeting or court. 3. part of a church set aside for the clergy.

pre·school (prē'skül'), *adj.* before the age of going to regular school.

pre·sci·ence (prē'shi·əns; presh'i-), *n.* knowledge of things before they exist or happen; foreknowledge; foresight. [< LL < L *praesciens* < *prae*- before + *scire* know] —pre'sci·ent, *adj.* —pre'sci·ent·ly, *adv.*

pre·scribe (pri·skrīb'), v., -scribed, -scrib·ing. 1. order; direct: *good citizens do what the laws prescribe.* 2. order as a remedy or treatment: *the doctor prescribed quinine.* 3. give medical advice. [< L, < *prae*- before + *scribere* write] —pre·scrib'er, *n.* —Syn. 1. command, designate, ordain.

pre·script (*n.* prē'skript; *adj.* pri·skript', prē'skript), *n.* 1. that which is prescribed. 2. order; direction. —*adj.* prescribed.

pre·scrip·tion (pri·skrip'shən), *n.* 1. order; direction. 2. a written direction for preparing and using a medicine. 3. the medicine. —pre·scrip'tive, *adj.* —pre·scrip'tive·ly, *adv.* —pre·scrip'tive·ness, *n.*

pres·ence (prez'əns), *n.* 1. fact or condition of being present in a place. 2. place where a person is: *the messenger was admitted to my presence.* 3. physical nearness, as of an audience, or a person of very high rank: *the knight retired from the royal presence.* 4. appearance; bearing: *man of noble presence.* 5. something present, esp. a ghost, spirit, or the like. 6. **in the presence of,** in the sight or company of. [< OF < L, < *praesens* PRESENT¹]

presence of mind, ability to think calmly and quickly when taken by surprise.

pres·ent¹ (prez'ənt), *adj.* 1. being in the place or thing in question; at hand, not absent. 2. at this time; being or occurring now. 3. *Gram.* denoting action now going on or a state now existing. *Go* is the present tense: *went* is the past tense. —*n.* 1. the present time: *at present people need courage.* 2. *Gram.* the present tense or a verb form in that tense. 3. **by these presents,** *Law.* by this document. [< L *praesens* < *prae*- before + *esse* be]

pre·sent² (*v.* pri·zent'; *n.* prez'ənt), *v.* 1. give: *he presented a gift to his hostess.* 2. offer; offer formally: *the servant presented the sandwiches to each guest.* 3. bring before the mind; offer for consideration: *he presented reasons for his action.* 4. offer to view or notice: *the new City Hall presents a fine appearance.* 5. bring before the public: *our school presented a play.* 6. set forth in words. 7. hand in; send in: *the grocer presented his bill.* 8. introduce (one person to another); introduce formally: *presented at court.* 9. direct; point; turn. 10. **present arms,** bring a rifle, etc., to a vertical position in front of the body. —*n.* thing given; gift. [< OF < L *praesentare* < *praesens* PRESENT¹] —pre·sent'er, *n.* —Syn. *n.* donation, benefaction.

pre·sent·a·ble (pri·zen'tə·bəl), *adj.* 1. fit to be seen. 2. suitable in appearance, dress, manners, etc., for being introduced into society or company. 3. suitable to be offered or given. —pre·sent'a·bil'i·ty, present'a·ble·ness, *n.* —pre·sent'a·bly, *adv.*

pres·en·ta·tion (prez'ən·tā'shən; prē'zen-), *n.* 1. a giving. 2. gift. 3. a bringing forward; offering to be considered: *the presentation of a plan.* 4. an offering to be seen; showing: *the presentation of a play.* 5. a formal introduction. —pres'en·ta'tion·al, *adj.*

pres·ent-day (prez'ənt·dā'), *adj.* of the present time.

pre·sen·ti·ment (pri·zen'tə·mənt), *n.* a feeling or impression that something is about to happen; vague sense of approaching misfortune; foreboding. [< MF, ult. < L *prae*– before + *sentire* to sense] **—pre·sen·ti·men·tal** (pri·zen′tə·men′təl), *adj.*

pres·ent·ly (prez′ənt·li), *adv.* before long; soon: *the clock will strike presently.*

pre·sent·ment (pri·zent′mənt), *n.* 1. presentation. 2. representation on the stage or by a portrait.

present participle, *Gram.* participle that expresses present time. *Examples: rising prices, growing fear of war.* ➤ See participle for usage note.

present perfect, *Gram.* tense indicating action now completed, constructed in English by *have* with a past participle. In "I have completed my work," *have completed* is a present perfect.

present tense, *Gram.* tense that expresses time that is now.

pre·serv·a·tive (pri·zér′və·tiv), *n.* any substance that will prevent decay or injury: *salt is a preservative for meat.* —*adj.* that preserves.

pre·serve (pri·zérv′), *v.,* –served, –serv·ing, *n.* —*v.* 1. keep from harm or change; keep safe; protect. 2. keep up; maintain. 3. keep from spoiling: *ice helps to preserve food.* 4. prepare (food) to keep it from spoiling. Boiling with sugar, salting, smoking, and pickling are different ways of preserving food. —*n.* 1. Usually, **preserves.** fruit cooked with sugar and sealed from the air. 2. place where wild animals or fish are protected. [< OF < LL, < L *prae*– before + *servare* keep] **—pre·serv′a·ble,** *adj.* **—pres·er·va·tion** (prez′ər·vā′shən), *n.* **—pre·serv′er,** *n.* —Syn. *v.* 1. save, defend, shield, guard.

pre·side (pri·zid′), *v.,* –sid·ed, –sid·ing. 1. hold the place of authority; have charge of a meeting. 2. have authority; have control. [< L, < *prae*– before + *sedere* sit] **—pre·sid′er,** *n.*

pres·i·den·cy (prez′ə·dən·si; prez′dən·si), *n., pl.* –cies. 1. Often, **Presidency.** office of president. 2. time during which a president is in office.

pres·i·dent (prez′ə·dənt; prez′dənt), *n.* 1. the chief officer of a company, college, society, club, etc. 2. Often, **President.** the highest executive officer of a republic. [< L *praesidens* presiding. See PRESIDE.] **—pres·i·den·tial** (prez′ə·den′shəl), *adj.* **—pres′i·den′tial·ly,** *adv.*

pres·i·dent-e·lect (prez′ə·dənt·i·lekt′; prez′dənt–), *n. Am.* president elected but not yet inaugurated.

pre·sid·i·um (pri·sid′i·əm), *n.* a governmental administrative committee in the Soviet Union. [< L *praesidium* a presiding over. See PRESIDE.]

press¹ (pres), *v.* 1. use force or weight steadily against; push with steady force. 2. squeeze; squeeze out. 3. extract juice from by squeezing. 4. use force steadily. 5. clasp; hug. 6. make smooth; flatten. 7. push forward; keep pushing. 8. move by pushing steadily (up, down, against, etc.). 9. urge onward; cause to hurry. 10. crowd; throng. 11. urge (a person); keep asking; entreat. 12. lay stress upon; insist on. 13. constrain; compel; force. 14. urge for acceptance. 15. harass; oppress; trouble. 16. weigh heavily upon (the mind, a person, etc.). 17. demand prompt action; be urgent. —*n.* 1. a pressing; pressure; push. 2. pressed condition. 3. any of various instruments or machines for exerting pressure. 4. machine for printing; printing press. 5. establishment for printing books, etc. 6. process or art of printing. 7. go to press, begin to be printed. 8. newspapers and periodicals and those who write for them. 9. notice given in newspapers or magazines. 10. crowd; throng. 11. a pressing forward or together; crowding. 12. urgency; hurry. 13. cupboard for clothes, books, etc. [< OF < L *pressare* < *mere* to press] **—press′er,** *n.*

press² (pres), *v.* 1. force into service, usually naval or military. 2. seize and use. [earlier *prest* < OF *prester* furnish, ult. < L *praesto* ready]

press agent, *Am.* agent in charge of publicity for a person, organization, etc.

press·ing (pres′ing), *adj.* requiring immediate action or attention; urgent. **—press′ing·ly,** *adv.* **—press′ing·ness,** *n.*

press·man (pres′mən), *n., pl.* –men. man who operates or has charge of a printing press.

pres·sure (presh′ər), *n.* 1. the continued action of a weight or force: *the pressure of the wind filled the sails of the boat.* 2. force per unit of area: *there is a pressure of 20 pounds to the inch on this tire.* 3. state of trouble or strain: *pressure of poverty.* 4. a compelling force or influence: *he changed his mind under pressure from others.* 5. need for prompt or decisive action; urgency: *pressure of business.* 6. electromotive force. [< OF < L *pressura* < *mere* to press] **—pres′sur·al,** *adj.*

pressure cooker, *Am.* an airtight apparatus for cooking with steam under pressure.

pressure group, any business, professional, or labor group which attempts to further its interests in the state or national legislatures.

pres·sur·ize (presh′ər·iz), *v.,* –ized, –iz·ing. keep the atmospheric pressure inside of the cabin of an airplane at a normal level in spite of the altitude.

press·work (pres′wèrk′), *n.* 1. the working or management of a printing press. 2. work done by a printing press.

pres·ti·dig·i·ta·tion (pres′tə·dij′ə·tā′shən), *n.* sleight of hand. [< F < L *praestigiator* juggler; form infl. by F *preste* quick and L *digitus* finger] **—pres′ti·dig′i·ta′tor,** *n.*

pres·tige (pres·tēzh′; pres′tij), *n.* reputation, influence, or distinction based on what is known of one's abilities, achievements, opportunities, associations, etc. [< F, magic spell, ult. < L *praestigiae* tricks]

pres·to (pres′tō), *adv., adj., n., pl.* –tos. —*adv.* quickly. —*adj.* quick. —*n.* a quick part in a piece of music. [< Ital., ult. < L *praesto*, *adv.*, ready]

Prest·wick (prest′wik), *n.* a small community near Glasgow, Scotland; site of a major international airport.

pre·sume (pri·züm′), *v.,* –sumed, –sum·ing. 1. take for granted without proving; suppose: *the law presumes innocence until guilt is proved.* 2. take upon oneself; venture; dare: *may I presume to tell you you are wrong?* 3. take an unfair advantage (used with *on* or *upon*): *don't presume on a person's good nature by borrowing from him every week.* [< L *praesumere* take for granted < *prae*– before + *sumere* take] **—pre·sum′a·ble,** *adj.* **—pre·sum′a·bly, pre·sum·ed·ly** (pri·züm′id·li), *adv.* **—pre·sum′er,** *n.* **—pre·sum′ing·ly,** *adv.*

pre·sump·tion (pri·zump′shən), *n.* 1. act of presuming. 2. thing taken for granted: *since he had the stolen jewels, the presumption was that he was the thief.* 3. cause or reason for presuming; probability. 4. unpleasant boldness: *it is presumption to go to a party when one has not been invited.* —Syn. 4. forwardness, effrontery.

pre·sump·tive (pri·zump′tiv), *adj.* 1. based on likelihood; presumed. 2. presumptive heir, heir presumptive. 3. giving ground for presumption or belief: *presumptive evidence of his guilt.* **—pre·sump′tive·ly,** *adv.*

pre·sump·tu·ous (pri·zump′chü·əs), *adj.* acting without permission or right; too bold; forward. **—pre·sump′tu·ous·ly,** *adv.* **—pre·sump′tu·ous·ness,** *n.* —Syn. overbold, impudent, arrogant. —Ant. unassuming, modest, meek, humble.

pre·sup·pose (prē′sə·pōz′), *v.,* –posed, –pos·ing. 1. take for granted in advance; assume beforehand: *let us presuppose that he wants more money.* 2. require as a necessary condition; imply: *a fight presupposes fighters.* **—pre·sup·po·si·tion** (prē′sup·ə·zish′ən), *n.*

pret., preterit.

pre·tend (pri·tend′), *v.* 1. make believe. 2. claim falsely: *she pretends to like you, but talks about you behind your back.* 3. claim falsely to have: *she pretended illness.* 4. claim: *I don't pretend to be a musician.* 5. lay claim: *James Stuart pretended to the English throne.* 6. venture; attempt: *I cannot pretend to judge between them.* [< L, < *prae-* before + *tendere* to stretch] —**pre·tend′ed,** *adj.* —**pre·tend′ed·ly,** *adv.* —**pre·tend′ing·ly,** *adv.* —Syn. 3. simulate, feign. 4. profess, allege.

pre·tend·er (pri·ten′dər), *n.* 1. person who pretends. 2. person who makes claims to a throne without just right.

pre·tense, *esp. Brit.* **pre·tence** (pri·tens′; prē′tens), *n.* 1. make-believe; pretending. 2. a false appearance: *under pretense of picking up the handkerchief, she took the money.* 3. a false claim: *the girls made a pretense of knowing the boys' secret.* 4. claim. 5. a showing off; display: *her manner is free from pretense.* 6. anything done to show off. [< AF *pretensse,* ult. < L *praetendere* PRETEND] —Syn. 5. ostentation.

pre·ten·sion (pri·ten′shən), *n.* 1. claim: *the young prince has pretensions to the throne.* 2. a putting forward of a claim. 3. a pretentious display.

pre·ten·tious (pri·ten′shəs), *adj.* 1. making claims to excellence or importance: *a pretentious person, book, or speech.* 2. doing things for show or to make a fine appearance: *a pretentious style of entertaining guests.* [< F *prétentieux,* ult. < L *praetendere* PRETEND] —**pre·ten′tious·ly,** *adv.* —**pre·ten′tious·ness,** *n.*

pret·er·it, pret·er·ite (pret′ər·it), *Gram.* —*n.* a verb form that expresses occurrence in the past; past tense. *Obeyed* is the preterit of *obey; spoke, of speak;* and *saw,* of *see.* —*adj.* expressing past time. [< L *praeteritus,* ult. < *praeter-* past + *ire* go]

pre·ter·nat·u·ral (prē′tər·nach′ə·rəl; -nach′rəl), *adj.* 1. out of the ordinary course of nature; abnormal. 2. due to something above or beyond nature; supernatural. [< Med.L, ult. < L *praeter-* beyond + *natura* NATURE] —**pre′ter·nat′u·ral·ly,** *adv.* —**pre′ter·nat′u·ral·ness,** *n.*

pre·text (prē′tekst), *n.* a false reason concealing the real reason; pretense; excuse. [< L, ult. < *prae-* in front + *texere* to weave]

Pre·to·ri·a (pri·tô′ri·ə; -tō′-), *n.* the administrative capital of the Republic of South Africa, in the NE part.

pret·ti·fy (prit′ə·fī), *v.,* -**fied,** -**fy·ing.** *Contemptuous.* make pretty, esp. overly pretty.

pret·ty (prit′i), *adj.,* -**ti·er,** -**ti·est,** *n., pl.* -**ties,** *adv.* —*adj.* 1. pleasing (used to describe people and things that are good-looking in a feminine or childish way, dainty, sweet, charming, etc., but not stately, grand, elegant, or very important). 2. too dainty or delicate. 3. *Colloq.* considerable in amount or extent. 4. *Usually ironically.* excellent. —*n. pl.* pretties. pretty persons or things. —*adv.* fairly; rather. [OE *prættig* cunning < *prætt* trick] —**pret′ti·ly,** *adv.* —**pret′ti·ness,** *n.* —**pret′ty·ish,** *adj.*

pret·zel (pret′səl), *n. Am.* a hard biscuit, usually in the form of a knot, salted on the outside. [< G *brezel* < L *bracchium* < Gk. *brachion* arm]

pre·vail (pri·vāl′), *v.* 1. exist in many places; be in general use. 2. be the most usual or strongest. 3. be the stronger; win the victory; succeed. 4. be effective. 5. prevail on, upon, or with, persuade. [< L, < *prae-* before + *valere* have power]

pre·vail·ing (pri·vāl′ing), *adj.* 1. that prevails; having superior force or influence; victorious. 2. in general use; common. —**pre·vail′ing·ly,** *adv.* —**pre·vail′ing·ness,** *n.*

prev·a·lent (prev′ə·lənt), *adj.* widespread; in general use; common: *colds are prevalent in the winter.* [< L *praevalens,* ppr. of *praevalere* PREVAIL] —**prev′a·lence,** *n.* —**prev′a·lent·ly,** *adv.* —Syn. usual, ordinary.

pre·var·i·cate (pri·var′ə·kāt), *v.,* -**cat·ed,** -**cat·ing.** turn aside from the truth in speech or act; lie. [< L *praevaricatus* having made a sham accusation, ult. < *prae-* before + *varicus* straddling < *varus* crooked] —**pre·var′i·ca′tion,** *n.* —**pre·var′i·ca′tor,** *n.*

pre·vent (pri·vent′), *v.* 1. keep (from). 2. keep from happening: *rain prevented the game.* 3. hinder. [< L, < *prae-* before + *venire* come] —**pre·vent′a·ble, pre·vent′i·ble,** *adj.* —**pre·vent′er,** *n.* —Syn. 1. restrain, check, stop.

pre·ven·tion (pri·ven′shən), *n.* 1. a preventing. 2. something that prevents.

pre·ven·tive (pri·ven′tiv), **pre·vent·a·tive** (-tə·tiv), *adj.* that prevents: *preventive measures against disease.* —*n.* something that prevents: *vaccination is a preventive against smallpox.* —**pre·ven′tive·ly,** *adv.* —**pre·ven′tive·ness,** *n.*

preventive war, an aggressive war waged against another nation, supposedly started in anticipation of attack by that nation.

pre·view (prē′vū′), *n.* 1. a previous view, inspection, survey, etc. 2. *Am.* the advance showing of scenes from a motion picture. —*v.* view beforehand.

pre·vi·ous (prē′vi·əs), *adj.* 1. coming or going before; that came before; earlier. 2. *Colloq.* quick. 3. **previous to,** before. [< L *praevius* leading the way < *prae-* before + *via* road] —**pre′vi·ous·ly,** *adv.* —**pre′vi·ous·ness,** *n.* —Syn. 1. prior, preceding, former.

pre·vi·sion (prē·vizh′ən), *n.* foresight; foreknowledge. —**pre·vi′sion·al,** *adj.*

pre·war (prē′wôr′), *adj.* before the war.

prey (prā), *n.* 1. animal hunted or seized for food, esp. by another animal: *mice and birds are the prey of cats.* 2. habit of hunting and killing other animals for food: *bird of prey.* 3. person or thing injured; victim: *be a prey to fear or disease.* —*v.* prey on or upon, a. hunt or kill for food. b. be a strain upon; injure; irritate. c. rob; plunder. [< OF < L *praeda*] —**prey′er,** *n.*

Pri·am (prī′əm), *n.* king of Troy at the time of the Trojan War.

price (prīs), *n., v.,* **priced, pric·ing.** —*n.* 1. amount for which a thing is sold or can be bought. 2. reward offered for the capture of a person alive or dead. 3. what must be given, done, undergone, etc., to obtain a thing. 4. value; worth. —*v.* 1. put a price on; set the price of. 2. ask the price of; find out the price of. 3. **price a person out of the market,** prohibit a person from buying by setting prices too high. 4. **price goods out of the market,** eliminate products, as competitors of similar products, by pricing too high. [< OF < L *pretium*] —**priced,** *adj.* —**pric′er,** *n.* —Syn. *n.* 1. charge, cost.

price·less (prīs′lis), *adj.* 1. extremely valuable. 2. *Slang.* amusingly absurd. —**price′less·ness,** *n.*

price support, a program of the United States government under which farmers may secure loans against their crops of certain agricultural commodities at a specified amount per bushel, bale, etc.

prick (prik), *n.* 1. a sharp point. 2. a little hole or mark made by a sharp point. 3. a pricking. 4. a sharp pain. —*v.* 1. make a hole in with a sharp point. 2. mark with a sharp point. 3. **prick up,** point upward. 4. cause sharp pain to. 5. spur; urge on. [OE *prica* point] —**pricked,** *adj.* —**prick′er,** *n.* —**prick′ing,** *adj.* —**prick′ing·ly,** *adv.* —Syn. *v.* 1. puncture, pierce. 4. sting, hurt. 5. goad, incite.

prick·le (prik′əl), *n., v.,* -**led,** -**ling.** —*n.* 1. a small, sharp point; thorn; spine. 2. a stinging or smarting sensation. —*v.* 1. feel a prickly or smarting sensation. 2. cause such a sensation in. [OE *pricel* < *prica* point]

prick·ly (prik′li), *adj.,* -**li·er,** -**li·est.** 1. having many sharp points like thorns. 2. sharp and stinging; itching. —**prick′li·ness,** *n.*

prickly heat, *Am.* a red, itching rash on the skin caused by inflammation of the sweat glands.

prickly pear, *Am.* 1. a pear-shaped, edible fruit of a species of cactus. 2. plant that it grows on.

pride (prīd), *n., v.,* **prid·ed, prid·ing.** —*n.* 1. a high opinion of one's own worth or possessions. 2. pleasure or satisfaction in something concerned with oneself: *take pride in keeping our house clean.* 3. something that one is proud of. 4. too high an opinion of oneself. 5. scorn of others. 6. the best part: *in the pride of manhood.* —*v.* pride oneself on, be proud of. [OE *prȳde* < *prūd* PROUD] —**pride′ful,** *adj.* —**pride′-**

ful·ly, *adv.* —**pride′ful·ness**, *n.* —**pride′less**, *adj.* —Syn. *n.* 4. vanity, arrogance.

priest (prēst), *n.* 1. a special servant of a god, who performs certain public religious acts. 2. clergyman or minister of a Christian church. 3. clergyman authorized to administer the sacraments and pronounce absolution. [ult. < L *presbyter.* Doublet of PRESBYTER.] —**priest′hood**, *n.* —**priest′less**, *adj.* —**priest′like′**, *adj.*

priest·craft (prēst′kraft′; -kräft′), *n.* skill, methods, etc., of priests, esp. when applied to worldly ends.

priest·ess (prēs′tis), *n.* woman who serves at an altar or in sacred rites.

priest·ly (prēst′li) *adj.* -li·er, -li·est. 1. of or pertaining to a priest. 2. suitable for a priest. —**priest′li·ness**, *n.*

prig (prig), *n.* person who is too particular about speech and manners, and prides himself on being better than others. —**prig′gish**, *adj.* —**prig′gish·ly**, *adv.* —**prig′gish·ness**, *n.*

prig·ger·y (prig′ər·i), *n.*, *pl.* -ger·ies. conduct or character of a prig.

prim (prim), *adj.*, **prim·mer**, **prim·mest.** stiffly precise, neat, proper, or formal. —**prim′ly**, *adv.* —**prim′ness**, *n.* —Syn. prudish, demure.

pri·ma·cy (prī′mə·si), *n.*, *pl.* -cies. 1. a being first in order, rank, importance, etc. 2. position or rank of a church primate. 3. in the Roman Catholic Church, the supreme power of the Pope. [< Med.L, < L *primas* of first rank. See PRIMATE.]

pri·ma don·na (prē′mə don′ə), *pl.* **pri·ma don·nas.** the principal woman singer in an opera. [< Ital., first lady]

pri·ma fa·ci·e (prī′mə fā′shi·ē; fā′shi), at first view; before investigation. [< L, abl. of *prima facies* first appearance]

pri·mal (prī′məl), *adj.* 1. of early times; first; primeval. 2. chief; fundamental. [< Med.L, < L *primus* first] —**pri′mal·ly**, *adv.*

prim·a·quine (prim′ə·kwin), *n.* a synthetic compound used in treating malaria.

pri·ma·ri·ly (prī′mer′ə·li; -mə·rə-; *emphatic* prī·mâr′ə·li), *adv.* 1. chiefly; principally. 2. at first; originally.

pri·ma·ry (prī′mer′i; -mə·ri), *adj.*, *n.*, *pl.* -ries. —*adj.* 1. first in time; first in order. 2. from which others have come; original; fundamental. 3. first in importance; chief. —*n.* 1. anything that is first in order, rank, or importance. 2. a primary color. 3. *Am.* a meeting or gathering of the voters of a political party in an election district to choose candidates for office. [< L *primarius* first in rank < *primus* first] —**pri′ma·ri·ness**, *n.* —Syn. 3. principal.

primary accent, 1. the strongest accent in the pronunciation of a word. 2. mark (′) used to show this.

primary colors, pigments or colors that are, or are thought to be, fundamental. Red, yellow, and blue are the primary colors in pigments.

pri·mate (prī′mit; -māt), *n.* 1. archbishop or bishop ranking above all other bishops in a country or church province. 2. any of the highest order of animals, including people, apes, and monkeys. [< L *primas* of first rank < *primus* first] —**pri′mate·ship**, *n.* —**pri·ma·tial** (prī·mā′shəl), *adj.*

prime¹ (prīm), *adj.* 1. first in rank; chief. 2. first in time or order; fundamental; original. 3. first in quality; first-rate; excellent. 4. that cannot be divided without a remainder by any whole number except itself and 1. 7, 11, and 13 are prime numbers. 5. having no common divisor but 1. 2 is prime to 9. —*n.* 1. the best time; best condition. 2. the best part. 3. the first part; beginning. 4. springtime. 5. early manhood or womanhood; youth. 6. a prime number. 7. one of the sixty minutes in a degree. 8. the mark (′): a. indicating a minute. b. used in various ways, as to distinguish one symbol from another. [ult. < L *primus* first] —**prime′ness**, *n.*

prime² (prīm), *v.*, **primed**, **prim·ing.** 1. supply (a gun) with powder. 2. cover (a surface) with a first coat of paint or oil so that paint will not soak in. 3. equip (a person) with information, words, etc. 4. pour water into (a pump) to start action.

prime meridian, meridian from which the longitude east and west is measured. It passes through Greenwich, England, and its longitude is 0°.

prime minister, the chief minister of a government; the head of the cabinet.

prim·er¹ (prim′ər), *n.* 1. a first book in reading. 2. a first book; beginner's book. 3. great primer, 18-point type. 4. long primer, 10-point type. [< Med.L *primarius* PRIMARY]

prim·er² (prīm′ər), *n.* 1. person or thing that primes. 2. cap or cylinder containing a little gunpowder, used for firing a charge.

pri·me·val (prī·mē′vəl), *adj.* 1. of the first ages, esp. of the world. 2. dating from the first ages or earliest times. 3. characteristic of the first ages or earliest times; primitive. [< L *primaevus* early in life < *primus* first + *aevum* age] —**pri·me′val·ism**, *n.* —**pri·me′val·ly**, *adv.* —**pri·me′val·ness**, *n.*

prim·ing (prīm′ing), *n.* 1. powder or other material used to set fire to an explosive. 2. a first coat of paint, sizing, etc.

prim·i·tive (prim′ə·tiv), *adj.* 1. of early times; of long ago: *primitive people often lived in caves.* 2. first of the kind: *primitive Christians.* 3. very simple; such as people had early in human history. 4. original; primary. —*n.* 1. artist belonging to an early period, esp. before the Renaissance. 2. picture by such an artist. [< L, ult. < *primus* first] —**prim′i·tive·ly**, *adv.* —**prim′i·tive·ness**, *n.* —**prim′i·tiv·ism**, *n.* —Syn. *adj.* 1. ancient, aboriginal, primeval.

pri·mo·gen·i·tor (prī′mə·jen′ə·tər), *n.* 1. ancestor; forefather. 2. the earliest ancestor. [< LL, < L *primus* first + *genitor* begetter]

pri·mo·gen·i·ture (prī′mə·jen′ə·chər), *n.* 1. state, condition, or fact of being the first-born of the children of the same parents. 2. right or principle of inheritance or succession by the first-born, esp. the inheritance of a family estate by the eldest son. [< Med.L *primogenitura*, ult. < L *primus* first + *gignere* beget] —**pri·mo·gen·i·tal** (prī′mə·jen′ə·təl), *adj.*

pri·mor·di·al (prī·môr′di·əl), *adj.* 1. existing at the very beginning; primitive. 2. original; elementary. [< L, < *primordium* beginning] —**pri·mor′di·al·ism**, *n.* —**pri·mor′di·al·i·ty**, *n.* —**pri·mor′di·al·ly**, *adv.*

primp (primp), *v.* 1. dress (oneself) for show; prink. 2. dress carefully.

prim·rose (prim′rōz′), *n.* Also, **prim·u·la** (prim′yə·lə). 1. any of a large group of plants with flowers of various colors. The common primrose of Europe is pale yellow. 2. the flower. —*adj.* 1. pale-yellow. 2. gay; pleasant. [< Med.L *prima rosa* first rose]

Primrose

prin., principal.

prince (prins), *n.* 1. a male member of a royal family; esp., in Great Britain, a son or grandson of a king or queen. 2. sovereign. 3. ruler of a small state subordinate to a king or emperor. 4. the greatest or best of a group; chief. [< OF < L *princeps* chief] —**prince′dom**, *n.* —**prince′like′**, *adj.* —**prince′ship**, *n.*

Prince Albert, *Am.* a long, double-breasted coat.

prince consort, prince who is the husband of a queen or empress ruling in her own right.

Prince Edward Island, province of Canada on an island in the Gulf of St. Lawrence, just N of Nova Scotia.

prince·ly (prins′li), *adj.*, -li·er, -li·est. 1. of a prince or his rank; royal. 2. like a prince; noble. 3. fit for a prince; magnificent. —**prince′li·ness**, *n.* —Syn. 3. sumptuous, splendid.

Prince of Wales, title conferred on the eldest son, or heir apparent, of the British sovereign.

prin·cess (prin′ses; -sis), *n.* 1. daughter of a

king or queen; daughter of a king's or queen's son. 2. wife or widow of a prince. 3. woman having the rank of a prince. —**prin′cess·ly,** *adv.*

prin·cesse, prin·cess (prin·ses′; prin′sis), *adj.* of women's clothing, one-piece and close-fitting.

prin·ci·pal (prin′sə·pəl), *adj.* most important; main; chief. —*n.* 1. a chief person; one who gives orders. 2. *Am.* the head, or one of the heads, of a primary or secondary school. 3. sum of money on which interest is paid. 4. money or property from which income is received. 5. person who hires another person to act for him. 6. person directly responsible for a crime. 7. person responsible for the payment of a debt that another person has endorsed. [< L *principalis* < *princeps* chief] —**prin′ci·pal·ship′,** *n.* —**Syn.** *adj.* cardinal, foremost, prime, leading. —**Ant.** *adj.* minor, secondary. **➤ principal, principle.** Associate *principal* as an adjective (the *principal* reason) with other adjectives ending in –*al:* historical, political, musical. *Principal* as a noun is probably an abbreviation of a phrase in which it was originally an adjective: the *principal* that draws interest was once the *principal sum;* the *principal* of a school, the *principal teacher;* the *principal* in a legal action, the *principal party;* the *principals* in the cast of a play or movie, the *principal actors.* These are the most common uses of *principal* as a noun. The noun meaning a general truth (the *principles* of science) or a rule of conduct (a man of high *principles*) is *principle.*

prin·ci·pal·i·ty (prin′sə·pal′ə·ti), *n., pl.* –ties. 1. a small state or country ruled by a prince. 2. country from which a prince gets his title. 3. supreme power.

prin·ci·pal·ly (prin′sə·pəl·i; –sip·li), *adv.* for the most part; chiefly; mainly.

principal parts, the main parts of a verb, from which the rest can be derived. **➤** The **principal parts** of English verbs are the infinitive (*ask*), the past tense form (*asked*), the past participle (*asked*), and the present participle (*asking*). This dictionary lists all infinitives as main entries. Immediately after the pronunciation, in small boldface, the principal parts of all verbs, except those formed by adding –*ed* or –*ing* directly to the infinitive without any change in the infinitive, are given in this order: past tense (*fell*), past participle (*fallen*), present participle (*falling*). If the forms of the past tense and the past participle are identical, only one form is given. Thus, under *probe,* two forms only are given: *probed* is both the past tense and the past participle, *probing* the present participle.

prin·ci·pate (prin′sə·pāt), *n.* 1. a chief place or authority. 2. principality. [< L, < *princeps* chief]

prin·ci·ple (prin′sə·pəl), *n.* 1. truth that is a foundation for other truths: the *principles of democratic government.* 2. a fundamental belief: *religious principles.* 3. rule of action or conduct: *make it a principle to save some money each week.* 4. uprightness; honor: *a man of principle.* 5. rule of science explaining how things act: *the principle by which a machine works.* 6. method of operation. 7. source; origin. 8. one of the elements that compose a substance, esp. one that gives some special quality or effect: *the bitter principle in a drug.* [< OF < L *principium* < *princeps* chief] **➤** See **principal** for usage note.

prink (pringk), *v.* 1. dress (oneself) for show. 2. fuss over one's appearance. —**prink′er,** *n.*

print (print), *v.* 1. use type, blocks, plates, etc., and ink or dye to stamp words, pictures, designs, etc., on paper or the like. 2. stamp letters, words, etc., on with type, etc., and ink. 3. cause to be printed; publish. 4. produce books, newspapers, etc., by printing press. 5. make (words or letters) the way they look in print instead of in writing. 6. make with such letters: *print your name clearly.* 7. stamp with designs, patterns, pictures, etc.: *machines print wallpaper, cloth,* etc. 8. fix: *the scene is printed on my memory.* 9. take an impression from type,

etc. 10. produce a photograph by transmission of light through (a negative). —*n.* 1. printed words, letters, etc.: *this book has clear print.* 2. printed condition. 3. **in print,** a. in printed form. b. of books, etc., still available for purchase from the publisher. 4. **out of print,** no longer sold by the publisher. 5. picture or design printed from a block or plate. 6. cloth with a pattern printed on it. 7. mark made by pressing or stamping: *the print of a foot.* 8. photograph produced from a negative. [< OF *priente,* ult. < L *premere* to press] —**print′a·ble,** *adj.* —**print′er,** *n.* —**print′less,** *adj.*

print., printing.

printer's devil, a young helper or errand boy in a printing shop.

print·ing (prin′ting), *n.* 1. the producing of books, newspapers, etc., by impression from movable types, plates, etc. 2. printed words, letters, etc. 3. all the copies printed at one time. 4. letters made like those in print.

printing press, machine for printing from types, plates, etc.

pri·or¹ (prī′ər), *adj.* 1. coming before; earlier: *a prior engagement.* 2. **prior to,** coming before in time, order, or importance; earlier than; before. [< L] **➤** *Prior to* is heavy (often journalese) for *before: Prior to* [before] *coming here he had been at Stanford.*

pri·or² (prī′ər), *n.* officer usually ranking next below an abbot, in a monastery or religious house. [< Med.L, n. use of L *prior* PRIOR¹] —**pri·or·ate** (prī′ər·it), **pri′or·ship,** *n.*

pri·or·ess (prī′ər·is), *n.* woman holding a position corresponding to that of a prior.

pri·or·i·ty (prī·ôr′ə·ti; –or′–), *n., pl.* –ties. 1. a being earlier in time. 2. a coming before in order or importance: *fire engines have priority over other traffic.* 3. *U.S.* a governmental rating giving right of way, esp. in passage, to persons or things important in national defense, essential affairs of state, etc., in order of importance. —**Syn.** 1. antecedence. 2. superiority, supremacy.

pri·o·ry (prī′ə·ri), *n., pl.* –ries. a religious house governed by a prior or prioress. A priory is often, but not necessarily, dependent on an abbey.

prism (priz′əm), *n.* 1. solid whose bases or ends have the same size and shape and are parallel to one another, and each of whose sides has two pairs of parallel edges. 2. a transparent prism, usually with three-sided ends, that separates white light passing through it into the colors of the rainbow. [< LL < Gk. *prisma* < *priein* to saw] —**pris′mal,** *adj.*

Prisms

pris·mat·ic (priz·mat′ik), **pris·mat·i·cal** (–ə·kəl), *adj.* 1. of or like a prism. 2. formed by a transparent prism. 3. varied in color; brilliant. —**pris·mat′i·cal·ly,** *adv.*

pris·on (priz′ən), *n.* place where a person is shut up against his will, esp. a public building where criminals are confined. [< OF < L *prehensio* arrest < *prehendere* seize]

pris·on·er (priz′ən·ər; priz′nər), *n.* 1. person who is confined in prison. 2. person taken by the enemy in war. 3. person arrested and held for trial.

pris·sy (pris′i), *adj.,* –si·er, –si·est. *Am., Colloq.* too easily shocked; overnice.

pris·tine (pris′tēn; –tin; –tīn), *adj.* as it was in its earliest time or state; original; primitive. [< L *pristinus*]

prith·ee (pri̱th′i), *interj. Archaic.* I pray thee: *prithee, come hither.*

pri·va·cy (prī′və·si), *n., pl.* –cies. 1. condition of being private; being away from others. 2. absence of publicity; secrecy.

pri·vate (prī′vit), *adj.* 1. not for the public; for just a few special people or for one: *a private car.* 2. not public; individual; personal: *my private opinion.* 3. secret; confidential: *a private pocket.* 4. secluded: *some private corner.* 5. having no public office: *a private citizen.* —*n.* 1. a common soldier, not an officer. 2. **in private,** a.

not publicly. **b.** secret. [< L *privatus* apart from the state, orig. pp., set apart, deprived < *privus* one's own. Doublet of PRIVY.] —**pri′vate·ly,** *adv.* —**pri′vate·ness,** *n.* —Syn. *adj.* 2. particular. 4. isolated, sequestered, solitary.

private enterprise, business as conducted without public (governmental) control or ownership.

pri·va·teer (prī′və·tir′), *n.* **1.** an armed ship owned by private persons and holding a government commission to attack and capture enemy ships. **2.** commander or one of the crew of a privateer. —*v.* cruise as a privateer.

pri·va·tion (prī·vā′shən), *n.* **1.** lack of the comforts or of the necessities of life. **2.** loss; absence. [< L *privatio.* See PRIVATE.] —Syn. **1.** need, destitution.

priv·a·tive (priv′ə·tiv), *Gram.* —*adj.* expressing privation or denial of something. *Un-* is a privative prefix. —*n.* a privative prefix or suffix. —**priv′a·tive·ly,** *adv.*

priv·et (priv′it), *n.* any of several evergreen shrubs with small leaves, much used for hedges.

Privet

priv·i·lege (priv′ə·lij), *n.,* *v.,* -leged, -leg·ing. —*n.* a special right, advantage, or favor. —*v.* give a privilege to. [< L *privilegium* law applying to one individual < *privus* individual + *lex* law] —**priv′i·leged,** *adj.* —Syn. *n.* liberty, license, prerogative.

priv·i·ly (priv′ə·li), *adv.* secretly.

priv·y (priv′i), *adj., n., pl.* **priv·ies.** —*adj.* **1.** private. **2.** privy to, having secret or private knowledge of. —*n.* a small outhouse used as a toilet. [< OF < L *privatus.* Doublet of PRIVATE.]

privy council, group of personal advisers to a ruler. —privy councilor.

privy seal, in Great Britain, the seal affixed to minor documents or to grants, etc., close up afterwards to receive the great seal.

prize¹ (prīz), *n.* **1.** reward won after trying against other people. **2.** reward worth working for. —*adj.* **1.** given as a prize. **2.** that has won a prize. **3.** worthy of a prize. [var. of ME *prise* PRICE] —Syn. *n.* **1.** award, premium.

prize² (prīz), *n.* thing or person that is taken or captured, esp. an enemy's ship taken at sea. [< F *prise,* n., seizure < L *prehensa,* fem. pp., seized]

prize³ (prīz), *v.,* prized, priz·ing. **1.** value highly. **2.** estimate the value of. [< OF *prisier,* var. of *preisier* PRAISE] —prized, *adj.*

prize⁴ (prīz), *v.,* prized, priz·ing. *Esp. Brit.* raise or move by force; pry.

prize court, a court that makes decisions concerning ships and other property captured at sea during a war.

prize fight, fight with fists which people pay money to see. —prize fighter. —prize fighting.

prize ring, 1. a square space enclosed by ropes, used for prize fights. **2.** prize fighting.

pro¹ (prō), *adv., n., pl.* pros. —*adv.* in favor of; for. —*n.* reason in favor of. The pros and cons of a question are the arguments for and against it.

pro² (prō), *n., adj., pl.* pros, *adj. Colloq.* professional. [short for *professional*]

pro-, *prefix.* **1.** before, as in *proscenium.* **2.** forward, as in *proceed, project.* **3.** forth; out, as in *prolong, proclaim.* **4.** on the side of; in favor of; in behalf of, as in *pro-British.* [def. 1 < Gk. *pro;* defs. 2, 3, 4 < L *pro*]

prob., probably.

prob·a·bil·i·ty (prob′ə·bil′ə·ti), *n., pl.* -ties. **1.** quality or fact of being likely or probable; chance. **2.** in all probability, probably. **3.** something likely to happen: *a storm is one of the probabilities for tomorrow.* **4.** in statistics, likelihood of an event happening, as measured by the relative frequency of events of the kind in the course of experience.

prob·a·ble (prob′ə·bəl), *adj.* **1.** likely to happen: *cooler weather is probable.* **2.** likely to be true: *the probable cause of the accident.* **3.** affording ground for belief: *probable evidence.* [< L, < *probare* PROVE] —prob′a·bly, *adv.*

pro·bate (prō′bāt), *n., adj., v.,* -bat·ed, -bat·ing. *Law.* —*n.* the official proving of a will as genuine. —*adj.* of or concerned with the probating of wills: *a probate court.* —*v.* prove by legal process the genuineness of (a will). [< L *probatum,* orig., neut. pp., made good < *probus* good]

pro·ba·tion (prō·bā′shən), *n.* **1.** trial or testing of conduct, character, qualifications, etc. **2.** any act or process of testing: *admitted to college on probation.* **3.** *Am.* system of letting young offenders against the law, or first offenders, go free without receiving the punishment which they are sentenced to unless there is a further offense. —pro·ba′tion·al, pro·ba·tion·ar·y (prō·bā′shən·er′i), *adj.*

pro·ba·tion·er (prō·bā′shən·ər), *n.* person who is on probation. —pro·ba′tion·er·ship′, *n.*

probe (prōb), *v.,* probed, prob·ing, *n.* —*v.* **1.** search into; examine thoroughly; investigate. **2.** search; penetrate: *probe into a secret.* **3.** examine or explore with a probe. —*n.* **1.** a thorough examination; investigation. **2.** *Am.* investigation, usually by a legislative body, in an effort to discover evidences of law violation. **3.** a slender instrument with a rounded end for exploring the depth or direction of a wound, a cavity in the body, etc. [< LL *proba,* n., < L *probare* PROVE. Doublet of PROOF.] —prob′er, *n.* —prob′ing, *n.* —prob′ing·ly, *adv.*

pro·bi·ty (prō′bə·ti; prob′ə-), *n.* uprightness; honesty; high principle. [< L, < *probus* righteous] —Syn. integrity, sincerity.

prob·lem (prob′ləm), *n.* **1.** question; difficult question. **2.** matter of doubt or difficulty. **3.** something to be worked out: *a problem in arithmetic.* —*adj.* that causes difficulty: *a problem child.* [< L < Gk. *problema* < *proballein* propose < *pro-* forward + *ballein* to throw]

prob·lem·at·ic (prob′ləm·at′ik), **prob·lem·at·i·cal** (-ə·kəl), *adj.* having the nature of a problem; doubtful; uncertain; questionable. —prob′lem·at′i·cal·ly, *adv.*

pro bo·no pub·li·co (prō bō′nō pub′lə·kō), *Latin.* for the public welfare.

pro·bos·cis (prō·bos′is), *n., pl.* -bos·cis·es (-bos′is·iz), -bos·ci·des (-bos′ə·dēz). **1.** an elephant's trunk. **2.** a long, flexible snout. **3.** the mouth parts of some insects, developed to great length for sucking. **4.** *Humorous.* a person's nose. [< L < Gk. *proboskis*]

pro·ce·dure (prə·sē′jər), *n.* **1.** way of proceeding; method of doing things. **2.** the customary manners or ways of conducting business: *legal procedure.* **3.** a particular course or mode of action. [< F, < *procéder* PROCEED] —pro·ce′dur·al, *adj.*

pro·ceed (*v.* prə·sēd′; *n.* prō′sēd), *v.* **1.** go on after having stopped; move forward: *please proceed with your story.* **2.** be carried on; take place: *the trial may proceed.* **3.** carry on any activity: *he proceeded to light his pipe.* **4.** come forth; issue; go out: *heat proceeds from fire.* **5.** begin and carry on an action at law. —*n.* Usually, **proceeds,** money obtained from a sale, etc. [< L, < *pro-* forward + *cedere* to move] —pro·ceed′er, *n.* —Syn. *v.* **1.** advance, progress. **4.** emanate. —Ant. *v.* **1.** stop, halt, pause.

pro·ceed·ing (prə·sēd′ing), *n.* **1.** action; conduct; what is done. **2.** proceedings, **a.** action in a case in a law court. **b.** record of what was done at the meetings of a society, club, etc. —Syn. **1.** performance, doing.

proc·ess (pros′es; *esp. Brit.* prō′ses), *n.* **1.** forward movement; progress; course. **2.** set of actions or changes in a special order: *by what process or processes is cloth made from wool?* **3.** part that grows out or sticks out. **4.** a written command or summons to appear in a law court. —*v.* treat or prepare by some special method. —*adj.* treated or prepared by some special method. [< F < L *processus* progress < *procedere* PROCEED] —Syn. *n.* **2.** method, procedure, operation.

processing tax, a federal tax placed on processes involved in handling certain commodities, esp. agricultural commodities.

pro·ces·sion (prə·sesh′ən), *n.* **1.** something that moves forward; persons marching or riding: *a funeral procession.* **2.** an orderly moving forward: *march in procession.* —*Syn.* **1.** cavalcade, train, parade.

pro·ces·sion·al (prə·sesh′ən·əl), *adj.* **1.** of a procession. **2.** used or sung in a procession. —*n.* **1.** processional music. **2.** book containing hymns, etc., for use in religious processions. —**pro·ces′sion·al·ly,** *adv.*

pro·claim (prə·klām′), *v.* make known publicly and officially; declare publicly: *war was proclaimed, proclaim him king.* [< L, < pro- forth + clamare to shout] —**pro·claimed′,** *adj.* —**pro·claim′er,** *n.* —*Syn.* publish, announce.

proc·la·ma·tion (prok′lə·mā′shən), *n.* an official announcement; public declaration: *the President's annual Thanksgiving proclamation.* —**pro·clam·a·to·ry** (prō·klam′ə·tô′rĭ, -tō′-), *adj.* —*Syn.* edict, decree.

pro·cliv·i·ty (prō·kliv′ə·tĭ), *n., pl.* **-ties.** tendency; inclination. [< L, ult. < pro- forward + clivus slope] —*Syn.* bias, bent, proneness.

pro·con·sul (prō·kon′səl), *n.* governor or military commander of an ancient Roman province with duties and powers like a consul's. [< L, from the phrase *pro consule* in place of a consul] —**pro·con′su·lar,** *adj.* —**pro·con′su·late, pro·con′sul·ship,** *n.*

pro·cras·ti·nate (prō·kras′tə·nāt), *v.,* **-nated, -nat·ing.** put things off until later; delay; delay repeatedly. [< L *procrastinatus,* ult. < pro- forward + cras tomorrow] —**pro·cras′ti·na′tion,** *n.* —**pro·cras′ti·na′tive, pro·cras·ti·na·to·ry** (prō·kras′tə·nə·tô′rĭ, -tō′-), *adj.* —**pro·cras′ti·na′tor,** *n.* —*Syn.* defer, postpone.

pro·cre·ate (prō′krĭ·āt), *v.,* **-at·ed, -at·ing. 1.** become father to; beget. **2.** produce offspring. **3.** bring into being; produce. [< L, < pro- forth + creare create] —**pro′cre·a′tion,** *n.* —**pro′cre·a′tive,** *adj.* —**pro′cre·a′tor,** *n.*

Pro·crus·tes (prō·krus′tēz), *n. Gk. Legend.* robber who stretched his victims or cut off their legs to make them fit the length of his bed. —**Pro·crus·te·an** (prō·krus′tĭ·ən), *adj.*

proc·tor (prok′tər), *n.* **1.** official in a university or school who keeps order. **2.** person employed to manage another's case in a law court. [short for *procurator*] —**proc·to·ri·al** (prok·tô′rĭ·əl, -tō′-), *adj.* —**proc′tor·ship,** *n.*

pro·cum·bent (prō·kum′bənt), *adj.* lying face down; prone; prostrate. [< L *procumbens* leaning forward]

proc·u·ra·tor (prok′yə·rā′tər), *n.* **1.** agent. **2.** a financial agent or administrator of an imperial Roman province. [< L, < *procurare.* See PROCURE.] —**proc·u·ra·to·ri·al** (prok′yə·rə·tô′ri·əl, -tō′-), *adj.* —**proc′u·ra′tor·ship,** *n.*

pro·cure (prō·kyūr′), *v.,* **-cured, -cur·ing. 1.** obtain by care or effort; get: *procure evidence.* **2.** bring about; cause: *procure a person's death.* **3.** obtain (women) for the gratification of lust. [< L *procurare* manage, ult. < pro- before + cura care] —**pro·cur′a·ble,** *adj.* —**pro·cure′ment,** *n.* —**pro·cur′er,** *n.* —*Syn.* **1.** acquire, gain, win, secure.

Pro·cy·on (prō′sĭ·on), *n.* star of the first magnitude in Canis Minor.

prod (prod), *v.,* **prod·ded, prod·ding,** *n.* —*v.* **1.** poke or jab with something pointed: *prod an animal with a stick.* **2.** stir up; urge on: *prod a lazy boy.* —*n.* **1.** poke; thrust. **2.** a sharp-pointed stick; goad. [OE *prod-,* as in *prodbor* borer] —**prod′der,** *n.*

prod·i·gal (prod′ə·gəl), *adj.* **1.** spending too much; wasting money or other resources; wasteful. **2.** abundant; lavish. —*n.* person who is wasteful or extravagant; spendthrift. [< earlier F, ult. < L *prodigus* wasteful] —**prod′i·gal·ly,** *adv.* —*Syn. adj.* **1.** extravagant. —*Ant. adj.* **1.** frugal, saving, stingy.

prod·i·gal·i·ty (prod′ə·gal′ə·tĭ), *n., pl.* **-ties. 1.** wasteful or reckless extravagance. **2.** rich abundance; profuseness.

pro·di·gious (prə·dij′əs), *adj.* **1.** very great in size, quantity, or extent; enormous; huge. **2.** very great in degree; excessive. **3.** wonderful;

marvelous. —**pro·di′gious·ly,** *adv.* —**pro·di′gious·ness,** *n.*

prod·i·gy (prod′ə·jĭ), *n., pl.* **-gies. 1.** marvel; wonder: *an infant prodigy.* **2.** a marvelous example. [< L *prodigium* omen]

pro·duce (*v.* prə·dūs′, -dūs′; *n.* prod′ūs, -ūs, prō′dūs, -dūs), *v.,* **-duced, -duc·ing,** *n.* —*v.* **1.** make: *this factory produces stoves.* **2.** bring about; cause: *hard work produces success.* **3.** bring forth; supply; create: *hens produce eggs.* **4.** yield offspring, crops, products, dividends, interest, etc. **5.** bring forward; show: *produce your proof.* **6.** bring (a play, etc.) before the public. —*n.* what is produced; yield: *vegetables are a garden's produce.* [< L, < pro- forth + ducere bring] —**pro·duc′i·ble,** *adj.* —*Syn. v.* **1.** manufacture. **2.** effect, occasion. **3.** furnish, yield. **5.** exhibit.

pro·duc·er (prə·dūs′ər; -dūs′-), *n.* **1.** one that produces. **2.** person who grows or makes things that are to be used or consumed by others. **3.** *Am.* one who has general charge of the production of motion pictures.

prod·uct (prod′əkt), *n.* **1.** that which is produced; result of work or of growth: *factory products, farm products.* **2.** *Math.* number or quantity resulting from multiplying.

pro·duc·tion (prə·duk′shən), *n.* **1.** act of producing; creation; manufacture. **2.** something that is produced.

pro·duc·tive (prə·duk′tiv), *adj.* **1.** producing; bringing forth: *hasty words are productive of quarrels.* **2.** producing food or other articles of commerce: *productive labor.* **3.** producing abundantly; fertile: *a productive farm.* —**pro·duc′tive·ly,** *adv.* —**pro·duc·tiv·i·ty** (prō′duk·tiv′ə·tĭ), **pro·duc′tive·ness,** *n.*

pro·em (prō′em), *n.* introduction; preface. [< L < Gk., < pro- before + oime song] —**pro·e·mi·al** (prō·ē′mĭ·əl), *adj.*

prof (prof), *n. Am., Colloq.* professor.

Prof., prof., professor.

prof·a·na·tion (prof′ə·nā′shən), *n.* act of showing contempt or disregard toward something holy; desecration. —**pro·fan·a·to·ry** (prə·fan′ə·tô′rĭ, -tō′-), *adj.* —*Syn.* defilement, debasement, sacrilege.

pro·fane (prə·fān′), *adj., v.,* **-faned, -fan·ing.** —*adj.* **1.** not sacred; worldly: *profane literature.* **2.** with contempt or disregard for God or holy things: *profane language.* —*v.* **1.** treat (holy things) with contempt or disregard. **2.** put to wrong or unworthy use. [< F < L *profanus* not sacred < pro- in front (outside) of + fanum shrine] —**pro·fane′ly,** *adv.* —**pro·fane′ness,** *n.* —**pro·fan′er,** *n.* —*Syn. adj.* **2.** irreligious, irreverent, blasphemous.

pro·fan·i·ty (prə·fan′ə·tĭ), *n., pl.* **-ties. 1.** use of profane language; swearing. **2.** a being profane; lack of reverence.

pro·fess (prə·fes′), *v.* **1.** lay claim to; claim: *I don't profess to be an expert.* **2.** declare openly: *he professed his loyalty to the United States.* **3.** declare one's belief in: *Christians profess Christ and the Christian religion.* **4.** have as one's profession or business: *profess law.* [< professed] —**pro·fess′ing,** *adj.* —*Syn.* **1.** assume, pretend. **2.** own, aver, acknowledge.

pro·fessed (prə·fest′), *adj.* **1.** alleged; pretended. **2.** avowed or acknowledged; openly declared. **3.** having taken the vows of, or been received into, a religious order. [< L *professus* < pro- forth + fateri confess] —**pro·fess·ed·ly** (prə·fes′id·lĭ), *adv.*

pro·fes·sion (prə·fesh′ən), *n.* **1.** occupation requiring an education, esp. law, medicine, teaching, or the ministry. **2.** people engaged in such an occupation. **3.** act of professing; open declaration: *a profession of friendship.* —*Syn.* **3.** avowal.

pro·fes·sion·al (prə·fesh′ən·əl; -fesh′nəl), *adj.* **1.** of or pertaining to a profession; appropriate to a profession: *the professional gravity of a doctor.* **2.** engaged in a profession: *a professional man.* **3.** making a business or trade of something that others do for pleasure: *a professional ballplayer.* **4.** undertaken or engaged in by professionals rather than amateurs: *a professional ball game.* 5. making a business of something not properly to be regarded as a business: *a professional politician.* —*n.* person who does this. —**pro·fes′sion·al·ism,** *n.* —**pro·fes′sion·al·ly,** *adv.*

pro·fes·sion·al·ize (prə·fesh′ən·əl·īz; -fesh′nəl-), *v.,* -ized, -iz·ing. make or become professional. —**pro·fes′sion·al·i·za′tion,** *n.*

pro·fes·sor (prə·fes′ər), *n.* 1. teacher of the highest rank in a college or university. 2. *Colloq.* teacher. 3. person who professes. [< L See PROFESSED.] —**pro·fes′sor·dom,** *n.* —**pro·fes·so·ri·al** (prō′fə·sō′ri·əl; -sō′-; prof′ə-), *adj.* —**pro′fes·so′ri·al·ly,** *adv.* —**pro·fes′sor·ship,** **pro·fes·sor·ate** (prə·fes′ər·it), *n.*

prof·fer (prof′ər), *v.* offer for acceptance: *proffer services.* —*n.* an offer made: *proffers of peace.* [< AF *proffrir* < *pro-* forth (< L *pro-*) + *offrir* OFFER] —**prof′fer·er,** *n.* —Syn. *v.* tender.

pro·fi·cien·cy (prə·fish′ən·si), *n., pl.* -cies. a being proficient; knowledge; skill.

pro·fi·cient (prə·fish′ənt), *adj.* advanced in any art, science, or subject; skilled; expert: *proficient in music.* —*n.* an expert. [< L *proficiens* making progress < *pro-* forward + *facere* make] —**pro·fi′cient·ly,** *adv.* —Syn. *adj.* versed, qualified, adept, competent.

pro·file (prō′fīl), *n., v.,* -filed, -fil·ing. —*n.* 1. a side view. 2. outline. 3. a drawing of a transverse vertical section of a building, bridge, etc. 4. a short and vivid biographical sketch. —*v.* 1. draw a profile of. 2. portray vividly in a biographical sketch. [< Ital., < *profilare* draw in outline < L *pro-* forth + *filum* thread] —**pro′fil·ist,** *n.*

Profile of Lincoln

prof·it (prof′it), *n.* 1. Often, profits. gain from a business; what is left when the cost of carrying on the business is subtracted from the money taken in. 2. gain from any transaction. 3. advantage; benefit. —*v.* 1. make profit; gain in a material sense. 2. get advantage; gain; benefit: *profit by one's mistakes.* 3. be an advantage or benefit. [< OF < L *profectus* advance < *proficere.* See PROFICIENT.] —**prof′it·er,** *n.* —**prof′it·less,** *adj.* —**prof′it·less·ly,** *adv.* —Syn. *n.* 2. returns, proceeds. 3. welfare.

prof·it·a·ble (prof′it·ə·bəl), *adj.* 1. yielding a financial profit. 2. giving a gain or benefit; useful. —**prof′it·a·ble·ness,** *n.* —**prof′it·a·bly,** *adv.* —Syn. 1. lucrative. 2. beneficial.

prof·it·eer (prof′ə·tir′), *n.* person who makes an unfair profit by taking advantage of public necessity. —*v.* seek or make such excessive profits. —**prof′it·eer′ing,** *n.*

prof·li·ga·cy (prof′lə·gə·si), *n.* 1. great wickedness; vice. 2. reckless extravagance.

prof·li·gate (prof′lə·git), *adj.* 1. very wicked; shamelessly bad. 2. recklessly extravagant. —*n.* person who is very wicked or extravagant. [< L *profligatus* ruined] —**prof′li·gate·ly,** *adv.* —**prof′li·gate·ness,** *n.*

pro·found (prə·found′), *adj.* 1. very deep: *a profound sleep.* 2. deeply felt; very great: *profound respect.* 3. going far deeper than what is easily understood: *a profound thinker.* 4. low: *a profound bow.* [< OF < L *profundus* < *pro-* away + *fundus* bottom] —**pro·found′ly,** *adv.* —**pro·fun·di·ty** (prə·fun′də·ti), **pro·found′ness,** *n.* —Syn. 3. abstruse, recondite.

pro·fuse (prə·fūs′), *adj.* 1. very abundant: *profuse thanks.* 2. spending or giving freely; lavish; extravagant: *profuse with one's money.* [< L *profusus* poured forth < *pro-* forth + *fundere* pour] —**pro·fuse′ly,** *adv.* —**pro·fuse′ness,** *n.* —Syn. 1. bountiful, copious.

pro·fu·sion (prə·fū′zhən), *n.* 1. great abundance. 2. extravagance; lavishness. —**pro·fu·sive** (prə·fū′siv), *adj.*

pro·gen·i·tor (prō·jen′ə·tər), *n.* ancestor in the direct line; forefather. [< L, < *pro-* forth + *gignere* beget] —**pro·gen·i·to·ri·al** (prō·jen′ə·tō′ri·əl; -tō′-), *adj.* —**pro·gen′i·tor·ship′,** *n.*

pro·gen·i·ture (prō·jen′ə·chər), *n.* 1. a begetting; birth. 2. offspring.

prog·e·ny (proj′ə·ni), *n., pl.* -nies. children; offspring; descendants. [< OF < L *progenies.* See PROGENITOR.]

pro·ges·ter·one (prō·jes′tər·ōn), **pro·ges·tin** (-jes′tin), *n.* a hormone, $C_{21}H_{30}O_2$, derived from a body which develops in the ovary, used in disorders of pregnancy and menstruation.

prog·na·thous (prog′nə·thəs; prog·nā′-), *adj.* having the jaws protruding beyond the upper part of the face. [< Gk. *pro-* forward + *gnathos* jaw]

prog·no·sis (prog·nō′sis), *n., pl.* -ses (-sēz). 1. forecast of the probable course of a disease. 2. estimate of what will probably happen. [< LL < Gk., ult. < *pro-* before + *gignoskein* recognize] —**prog·nos·tic** (prog·nos′tik), *adj.*

prog·nos·ti·cate (prog·nos′tə·kāt), *v.,* -cated, -cat·ing. predict from facts; forecast. —**prog·nos·ti·ca·ble** (prog·nos′tə·kə·bəl), *adj.* —**prog·nos′ti·ca′tion,** *n.* —**prog·nos′ti·ca′tive,** *adj.* —**prog·nos′ti·ca′tor,** *n.*

pro·gram, *esp. Brit.* **pro·gramme** (prō′gram; -grəm), *n., v.,* -grammed, -gram·ming. —*n.* 1. list of items or events; list of performers, etc.: *the program filled four pages.* 2. items composing an entertainment: *the entire program was delightful.* 3. plan of what is to be done: *a school program.* 4. a set of instructions fed into a computer. —*v.* 1. arrange plans of operation for (a computing mechanism, automation system, group of workers, etc.). 2. put (an item) on a program, as in a theatrical entertainment, plan of operation, etc. [< LL < Gk. *programma* proclamation, ult. < *pro-* forth + *graphein* write] —**pro·gram·mat·ic** (prō′grə·mat′ik), *adj.*

prog·ress (*n.* prog′res, *esp. Brit.* prō′gres; *v.* prə·gres′), *n.* 1. advance; growth; development; improvement: *the progress of the arts and sciences.* 2. a moving forward; going ahead: *make rapid progress on a journey.* —*v.* 1. get better; advance; develop: *we progress in learning step by step.* 2. move forward; go ahead: *the war had progressed some time.* [< L *progressus,* ult. < *pro-* forward + *gradi* walk] —Syn. *v.* 1. improve, grow.

pro·gres·sion (prə·gresh′ən), *n.* 1. a moving forward; going ahead: *a slow method of progression.* 2. *Math.* succession of quantities in which there is always the same relation between each quantity and the one succeeding it. 2, 4, 6, 8, 10 are in arithmetical progression. 2, 4, 8, 16 are in geometrical progression. —**pro·gres′sion·al,** *adj.*

pro·gres·sive (prə·gres′iv), *adj.* 1. making progress; advancing to something better; improving: *a progressive nation.* 2. favoring progress; wanting improvement in government, etc. 3. moving forward; going ahead. 4. going from one to the next. 5. *Gram.* showing the action as going on. Is reading, was reading, and has been reading are progressive forms of read. —*n.* 1. person who favors progress. 2. Progressive, *Am.* member of a Progressive Party. —**pro·gres′sive·ly,** *adv.* —**pro·gres′sive·ness,** *n.*

Progressive Party, *Am.* 1. a political party formed in 1912 under the leadership of Theodore Roosevelt. 2. a similar political party organized in 1924 and led by Senator Robert M. La Follette. 3. a political party founded in 1948 and led, until outbreak in 1950 of the war in Korea, by Henry A. Wallace.

pro·hib·it (prō·hib′it), *v.* 1. forbid by law or authority: *picking flowers in the park is prohibited.* 2. prevent. [< L *prohibitus* < *pro-* away + *habere* keep] —**pro·hib′it·ed,** *adj.*

pro·hi·bi·tion (prō′ə·bish′ən), *n.* 1. act of prohibiting or forbidding. 2. law or order that prohibits. 3. *Am.* law or laws against making or selling alcoholic liquors. —**pro·hi·bi′tion·ist,** *n.*

pro·hib·i·tive (prō·hib′ə·tiv), **pro·hib·i·to·ry** (-ə·tō′ri; -tō′-), *adj.* prohibiting; preventing. —**pro·hib′i·tive·ly,** *adv.* —**pro·hib′i·to′ri·ly,** *adv.* —**pro·hib′i·tive·ness,** *n.*

proj·ect (*n.* proj′ekt; *v.* prə·jekt′), *n.* 1. a plan;

scheme. 2. an undertaking; enterprise. —v. 1. plan; scheme. 2. stick out: *the rocky point projects far into the water.* 3. cause to stick out or protrude. 4. throw or cast forward: *a cannon projects shot.* 5. cause to fall on a surface: *motion pictures are projected on the screen, trees project shadows on the grass.* 6. draw lines through (a point, line, figure, etc.) and reproduce it on a surface. [< L *projectus* < *pro-* forward + *jacere* to throw] —pro·ject′ed, *adj.* —pro·ject′ing, *adj.* —Syn. *v.* 1. devise, contrive. 2. protrude, bulge, jut.

pro·jec·tile (prə·jek′təl), *n.* object that can be thrown, hurled, or shot, such as a stone or bullet. —*adj.* 1. capable of being thrown, hurled, or shot. 2. forcing forward; impelling.

pro·jec·tion (prə·jek′shən), *n.* 1. part that projects or sticks out. 2. a sticking out. 3. a throwing or casting forward: *the projection of a cannon ball from a cannon.* 4. *Geom.* the projecting of a figure, etc., upon a surface. 5. the casting forward, usually upon a screen, of an image, esp. from a motion-picture machine. 6. representation, upon a flat surface, of all or part of the surface of the earth or the celestial sphere. 7. a forming of projects or plans. 8. *Psychol.* the treating of what is essentially subjective as objective and external.

pro·jec·tor (prə·jek′tər), *n.* 1. apparatus for projecting a picture on a screen. 2. person who forms projects.

pro·late (prō′lāt), *adj.* lengthened along one direction.

pro·le·tar·i·an (prō′lə·tãr′i-ən), *adj.* of or belonging to the proletariat. —*n.* person belonging to the proletariat. [< L *proletarius* furnishing the state only with children < *proles* offspring] —pro′le·tar′i·an·ism, *n.*

pro·le·tar·i·at (prō′lə·tãr′i·ət), *n.* class of people that depend on daily work for a living; laboring class.

pro·lif·ic (prə·lif′ik), *adj.* 1. producing offspring abundantly. 2. producing much: *a prolific tree.* [< Med.L, < L *proles* offspring + *facere* make] —pro·lif′i·ca·cy (prə·lif′ə·kə·si), pro·lif′ic·ness, *n.* —pro·lif′i·cal·ly, pro·lif′ic·ly, *adv.*

pro·lix (prō·liks′; prō′liks), *adj.* using too many words; too long; tedious. [< L *prolixus* stretched out] —pro·lix·i·ty (prō·lik′sə·ti), pro·lix′ness, *n.* —pro·lix′ly, *adv.* —Syn. wordy, verbose, long-winded, tiresome, wearisome.

pro·logue, pro·log (prō′lôg; -log), *n.* 1. speech or poem addressed to the audience by one of the actors at the beginning of a play. 2. introduction to a novel, poem, or other literary work. 3. any introductory act or event. [< L < Gk. < *pro-* before + *logos* speech]

pro·long (prə·lông′; -long′), *v.* make longer; extend. [< LL, < *pro-* forth + *longus* long] —pro·long′a·ble, *adj.* —pro·long·a·tion (prō′lông·gā′shən; -long-), pro·long′ment, *n.* —pro·longed′, *adj.* —pro·long′er, *n.* —Syn. lengthen, stretch, protract.

prom (prom), *n. Am., Colloq.* dance or ball given by a college or high-school class. [short for *promenade*]

prom·e·nade (prom′ə·nād′; -näd′), *n., v.,* -nad·ed, -nad·ing. —*n.* 1. walk for pleasure or display: *the Easter promenade.* 2. a public place for such a walk. 3. march of all the guests at the opening of a formal dance. —*v.* 1. walk about or up and down for pleasure or for display. 2. walk through. [< F, < *promener* take for a walk] —prom′e·nad′er, *n.*

Pro·me·the·us (prə·mē′thi·əs; -thūs), *n. Gk. Myth.* a Titan who stole fire from heaven and taught men its use. Zeus punished him by chaining him to a rock. —Pro·me·the·an (prə·mē′thi·ən), *adj.*

pro·me·thi·um (prə·mē′thi·əm), *n. Chem.* a rare metallic element, Pm. Formerly, illinium.

prom·i·nence (prom′ə·nəns), *n.* 1. quality or fact of being prominent. 2. something that juts out, esp. upward.

prom·i·nent (prom′ə·nənt), *adj.* 1. well-known; important: *a prominent citizen.* 2. easy to see: *a single tree in a field is prominent.* 3. standing out; projecting: *some insects have prominent eyes.* [< L *prominens* < *pro-* forward + *men-* jut] —prom′i·nent·ly, *adv.* —Syn. 1. eminent, leading. 2. conspicuous. 3. jutting, protuberant.

pro·mis·cu·ous (prə·mis′kyū·əs), *adj.* 1. mixed and in disorder: *a promiscuous heap of clothing.* 2. making no distinctions; not discriminating: *promiscuous friendships.* 3. *Colloq.* casual. [< L *promiscuus* < *phrase pro miscus as common < miscere* mix] —pro·mis′cu·ous·ly, *adv.* —pro·mis′cu·ous·ness, prom·is·cu·i·ty (prom′is·kū′ə·ti; prō′mis-), *n.* —Syn. 1. miscellaneous.

prom·ise (prom′is), *n., v.,* -ised, -is·ing. —*n.* 1. words, said or written, binding a person to do or not to do something. 2. indication of what may be expected: *the clouds give promise of rain.* 3. indication of future excellence; something that gives hope of success: *a young scholar who shows promise.* —*v.* 1. make a promise of (something) to (a person, etc.). 2. give one's word; make a promise. 3. give indication or hope of; give ground for expectation. [< L *promissum,* orig. neut. pp., promised < *pro-* before + *mittere* put] —prom′is·er, *n.* —Syn. *n.* 1. vow, pledge, covenant.

Promised Land, 1. *Bible.* country promised by God to Abraham and his descendants; Canaan. Gen. 15:18; 17:1-8. 2. heaven.

prom·is·ing (prom′is·ing), *adj.* likely to turn out well; hopeful. —prom′is·ing·ly, *adv.*

prom·is·so·ry (prom′ə·sô′ri; -sō′-), *adj.* containing a promise.

promissory note, a written promise to pay a stated sum of money to a certain person at a certain time.

prom·on·to·ry (prom′ən·tô′ri; -tō′-), *n., pl.* -ries. a high point of land extending from the coast into the water; headland. [< Med.L *promontorium,* var. of L *promunturium*] —prom′on·to′ri·al, *adj.*

pro·mote (prə·mōt′), *v.,* -mot·ed, -mot·ing. 1. raise in rank, condition, or importance: *be promoted from clerk to manager.* 2. help to grow or develop; help to success: *promote peace.* 3. help to organize; start: *promote a new company.* 4. *Am.* advance (a pupil) from one class or grade to another. 5. *Am.* further the sale of (an article) by advertising. [< L *promotus* < *pro-* forward + *movere* to move] —pro·mot′a·ble, *adj.* —pro·mot′er, *n.* —pro·mo′tion, *n.* —pro·mo′tive, *adj.* —Syn. 1. advance, elevate, exalt.

prompt (prompt), *adj.* 1. ready and willing; on time; quick: *be prompt to obey.* 2. done at once; made without delay: *prompt punishment.* —*v.* 1. cause (someone) to do something: *his curiosity prompted him to ask questions.* 2. give rise to; suggest; inspire: *a kind thought prompted the gift.* 3. remind (a learner, speaker, actor) of the words or actions needed. [< L *promptus,* orig. pp., brought forth < *pro-* forward + *emere* orig., take. Doublet of PRONTO.] —prompt′er, *n.* —prompt′ly, *adv.* —prompt′ness, promp·ti·tude (promp′tə·tüd; -tūd), *n.* —Syn. *adj.* 1. punctual, speedy, swift. 2. immediate. —*v.* 1. incite, impel, induce.

pro·mul·gate (prō·mul′gāt; esp. *Brit.* prom′əl-gāt), *v.,* -gat·ed, -gat·ing. 1. proclaim formally; announce officially: *promulgate the king's decree.* 2. spread far and wide: *promulgate knowledge.* [< L, < *pro-* forth + unrecorded *mulgare,* intensive of *mulgere,* orig., to press] —pro·mul·ga·tion (prō′mul·gā′shən; prom′əl-), *n.* —pro·mul·ga·tor (prō·mul′gā·tər; prom′əl-gā′-), *n.*

pron., 1. pronoun. 2. pronunciation.

prone (prōn), *adj.* 1. inclined; liable: *we are prone to think evil of people we dislike.* 2. lying face down. 3. lying flat. [< L *pronus*] —prone′ly, *adv.* —prone′ness, *n.*

prong (prông; prong), *n.* one of the pointed ends of a fork, antler, etc. —*v.* pierce or stab with a prong. [ME *prange*] —pronged, *adj.*

prong·horn (prông′hôrn′; prong′-), *n., pl.*

-horns or (*esp. collectively*) -horn. animal like an antelope, found on the plains of W North America.

pro·nom·i·nal (prō·nom'ə·nəl), *adj.* of pronouns; having the nature of a pronoun. —pro·nom'i·nal·ly, *adv.*

pro·noun (prō'noun), *n.* 1. one of the parts of speech, comprising words used to indicate without naming. 2. a word that does this; word used instead of a noun. *Examples:* I, we, you, he, it, they, who, whose, which, this, mine, whatever. [< F < L, < *pro-* in place of + *nomen* noun]

Pronghorn
(ab. 3 ft. high at the shoulder)

pro·nounce (prə·nouns'), *v.*, -nounced, -nounc·ing. 1. make the sounds of; speak: *pronounce your words clearly.* 2. pronounce words. 3. give an opinion or decision: *only an expert should pronounce on this case.* 4. declare (a person or thing) to be: *the doctor pronounced her cured.* 5. declare formally or solemnly: *the judge pronounced sentence on the criminal.* [< OF < L, ult. < *pro-* forth + *nuntius* announcement] —pro·nounce'a·ble, *adj.* —pro·nounc'er, *n.*

pro·nounced (prə·nounst'), *adj.* 1. strongly marked; decided. —pro·nounc·ed·ly (prə·noun'sid·li), *adv.*

pro·nounce·ment (prə·nouns'mənt), *n.* 1. a formal statement. 2. opinion; decision.

pron·to (pron'tō), *adv. Am., Colloq.* promptly; quickly. [< Sp. < L *promptus* prompt. Doublet of PROMPT.]

pro·nun·ci·a·men·to (prə·nun'si·ə·men'tō, -shi·ə-), *n., pl.* -tos. a formal announcement; proclamation; manifesto. [< Sp., < *pronunciar* pronounce]

pro·nun·ci·a·tion (prə·nun'si·ā'shən), *n.* 1. way of pronouncing: *this book gives the pronunciation of each main word.* 2. a pronouncing.

proof (prüf), *n.* 1. way or means of showing beyond doubt the truth of something. 2. establishment of the truth of anything. 3. act of testing; trial. 4. condition of having been tested and approved. 5. a trial impression from type, an engraved or etched plate, or a photographic negative. A book is first printed in proof so that errors can be corrected. 6. the degree of strength of alcoholic liquors. —*adj.* 1. of tested value against something: *proof against being taken by surprise.* 2. of standard strength. [< OF *prueve* < LL *proba* < L *probare* prove. Doublet of PROBE.] —proof'less, *adj.* —Syn. *n.* 2. confirmation, certification, corroboration. 3. examination, assay.

-proof, *suffix.* protected against; safe from, as in *fireproof, bombproof.*

proof·read (prüf'rēd'), *v.*, -read (-red'), -read·ing. *Am.* read (printers' proofs, etc.) and mark errors to be corrected. —proof'read'er, *n. Am.*

prop (prop), *v.*, propped, prop·ping, *n.* —*v.* 1. hold up by placing a support under or against. 2. support; sustain. —*n.* thing or person used to support another. [cf. MDu. *proppe*] —prop'less, *adj.* —Syn. *n.* support, brace, stay.

prop·a·gan·da (prop'ə·gan'də), *n.* 1. systematic efforts to spread opinions or beliefs. 2. opinions or beliefs thus spread. [< NL *congregatio de propaganda fide* congregation concerning propagating the faith] —prop'a·gan'dism, *n.* —prop'a·gan'dist, *n.* —prop'a·gan·dis'tic, *adj.*

prop·a·gan·dize (prop'ə·gan'dīz), *v.*, -dized, -diz·ing. 1. propagate or spread (doctrines, etc.) by propaganda. 2. carry on propaganda.

prop·a·gate (prop'ə·gāt), *v.*, -gat·ed, -gat·ing. 1. produce offspring. 2. reproduce. 3. increase in number: *trees propagate themselves by seeds.* 4. cause to increase in number by the production of young. 5. spread (news, knowledge, etc.): *propagate the principles of science.* 6. pass on; send further: *sound is propagated by vibrations.* [< L *propagatus*] —prop·a·ga·ble (prop'ə·gə·bəl), *adj.* —prop'a·ga·bil'i·ty, *n.* —prop'a·ga'tion, *n.* —prop'a·ga'tive, *adj.* —prop'a·ga'-

tor, *n.* —Syn. 3. multiply. 5. extend, diffuse, circulate, transmit.

pro·pa·tri·a (prō pā'tri·ə; pat'ri·ə), *Latin.* for one's country or native land.

pro·pel (prə·pel'), *v.*, -pelled, -pel·ling. drive forward; force ahead: *propel a boat by oars.* [< L, < *pro-* forward + *pellere* to push] —pro·pel'la·ble, *adj.*

pro·pel·lant (prə·pel'ənt), *n.* something that propels, esp. the fuel of a missile or rocket.

pro·pel·lent (prə·pel'ənt), *adj.* propelling. —*n.* one that propels.

pro·pel·ler (prə·pel'ər), *n.* 1. device consisting of a revolving hub with blades, for propelling boats, airplanes, etc. 2. one that propels.

pro·pen·si·ty (prə·pen'sə·ti), *n., pl.* -ties. a natural inclination or bent. [< L *propensus* inclined < *pro-* forward + *pendere* hang]

prop·er (prop'ər), *adj.* 1. correct; right; fitting: *night is the proper time to sleep, and bed the proper place.* 2. according to recognized usage: *use a word in its proper sense.* 3. strictly so called; in the strict sense of the word: *no shellfish are fishes proper.* 4. decent; respectable: *proper conduct.* 5. belonging exclusively or distinctively: *qualities proper to a substance.* 6. *Gram.* belonging to one or a few; not common to all. *John Adams* is a proper name. 7. *Colloq.* complete; thorough. [< OF < L *proprius*] —prop'er·ly, *adv.* —prop'er·ness, *n.* —Syn. 1. suitable, becoming, appropriate. 4. seemly. ➤ **proper adjectives.** Proper nouns used as adjectives, and adjectives directly derived from proper names and still referring to the place or person, are capitalized. After proper adjectives lose the sense of referring to their origins, they become simple adjectives and are not capitalized: *the French language, American interests, Roman ruins* (but *roman type*).

proper fraction, a fraction less than 1, as ³⁄₄, ¹⁄₈, ⁵⁄₈, and ¹⁹⁹⁄₁₀₀₀.

proper noun, noun naming a particular person or thing, as *John* or *Chicago.* ➤ **proper nouns.** Considerable care needs to be taken to spell and pronounce the names of people, places, companies, institutions as the people most concerned with them wish to have them spelled and pronounced. Many are rare or in some way extraordinary: *Thames* (temz), *Worcester* (wús'tər), *San Joaquin* (san' wä·kēn'). Many fairly common names occur in various forms: *How—Howe, Harvey—Hervey, Cohen—Cohn—Kohen, Mac—Mc–M'*, and so on. Special care is needed with names having silent letters or some peculiarity of spelling or phrasing: *Pittsburgh, Lindbergh,* the Johns Hopkins University, the State University of Iowa, the Ohio State University. Getting proper names in the right form is courtesy as well as accuracy.

prop·er·ty (prop'ər·ti), *n., pl.* -ties. 1. thing or things owned; possession or possessions. 2. ownership. 3. piece of land or real estate. 4. quality or power belonging specially to something: *soap has the property of removing dirt.* 5. **properties,** furniture, weapons, etc. (everything except scenery and clothes), used in staging a play. [< OF *propriete* < L, < *proprius* one's own] —prop'er·tied, *adj.*

proph·e·cy (prof'ə·si), *n., pl.* -cies. 1. a foretelling of future events. 2. thing told about the future. 3. a divinely inspired utterance, revelation, writing, etc. [< OF < L < Gk., < *prophetes* PROPHET]

proph·e·sy (prof'ə·sī), *v.*, -sied, -sy·ing. 1. tell what will happen; foretell; predict. 2. speak when or as if divinely inspired. 3. utter in prophecy. —proph'e·si'er, *n.* —Syn. 1. prognosticate.

proph·et (prof'it), *n.* 1. person who tells what will happen. 2. person who preaches what he thinks has been revealed to him. 3. **the Prophets,** books of the Old Testament written by prophets. [< L < Gk. *prophetes*, ult. < *pro-* before + *phanai* speak] —proph'et·hood, proph'et·ship, *n.*

proph·et·ess (prof'it·is), *n.* a woman prophet.

pro·phet·ic (prə-fet′ik), **pro·phet·i·cal** (-ə-kəl), *adj.* 1. belonging to a prophet; such as a prophet has: *prophetic power.* 2. containing prophecy: *a prophetic saying.* 3. giving warning of what is to happen; foretelling. —**pro·phet′i·cal·ly**, *adv.*

pro·phy·lac·tic (prō′fə-lak′tik; prof′ə-), *adj.* protecting from disease. —*n.* medicine or treatment that protects against disease. [< Gk. *pro-phylaktikos*, ult. < *pro-* before + *phylassein* to guard] —**pro′phy·lac′ti·cal·ly**, *adv.*

pro·phy·lax·is (prō′fə-lak′sis; prof′ə-), *n.* 1. protection from disease. 2. treatment to prevent disease. [< NL, < Gk. *pro-* before + *phylaxis* protection]

pro·pin·qui·ty (prō-ping′kwə-ti), *n.* 1. nearness in place, esp. personal nearness. 2. nearness of blood; kinship. [< L *propinquitas*, ult. < *prope* near]

pro·pi·ti·ate (prə-pish′i-āt), *v.*, **-at·ed, -at·ing.** prevent or reduce the anger of; win the favor of; appease or conciliate. [< L, ult. < *propitius* PROPITIOUS] —**pro·pi′ti·a′tion**, *n.* —**pro·pi′ti·a′tor**, *n.* —**pro·pi·ti·a·to·ry** (prə-pish′i-ə-tô′ri; -tō′-), **pro·pi′ti·a′tive**, *adj.*

pro·pi·tious (prə-pish′əs), *adj.* 1. favorable: *propitious weather for our trip.* 2. favorably inclined; gracious. [< L *propitius*, orig., falling forward < *pro-* forward + *petere* go toward] —**pro·pi′tious·ly**, *adv.* —**pro·pi′tious·ness**, *n.* —Syn. 1. auspicious, promising.

pro·po·nent (prə-pō′nənt), *n.* 1. person who makes a proposal or proposition. 2. favorer; supporter.

pro·por·tion (prə-pôr′shən; -pōr′-), *n.* 1. relation in size, number, amount, or degree of one thing compared to another: *each man's pay will be in proportion to his work.* 2. a proper relation between parts: *his short legs were not in proportion to his long body.* 3. proportions, a. size; extent. b. dimensions. 4. part; share: *a large proportion of Nevada is desert.* 5. an equality of ratios. *4 is to 2 as 10 is to 5 is a proportion.* —*v.* fit (one thing to another) so that they go together: *the designs in that rug are well proportioned.* [< L, < phrase *pro portione* in relation to the part] —**pro·por′tion·a·ble**, *adj.* —**pro·por′tion·a·bly**, *adv.* —**pro·por′tioned**, *adj.* —**pro·por′tion·er**, *n.* —**pro·por′tion·less**, *adj.* —**pro·por′tion·ment**, *n.*

pro·por·tion·al (prə-pôr′shən-əl; -pōrsh′nəl; -pōr′-), *adj.* in the proper proportion; corresponding: *the increase in price is proportional to the improvement in the car.* —*n.* one of the terms of a proportion in mathematics. —**pro·por′tion·al′i·ty**, *n.* —**pro·por′tion·al·ly**, *adv.*

pro·por·tion·ate (prə-pôr′shən-it; -pōrsh′nit; -pōr′-), *adj.* in the proper proportion; proportioned; proportional. —**pro·por′tion·ate·ly**, *adv.*

pro·pos·al (prə-pōz′əl), *n.* 1. what is proposed; plan; suggestion. 2. offer of marriage. —Syn. 1. proposition, overture.

pro·pose (prə-pōz′), *v.*, **-posed, -pos·ing.** 1. put forward for consideration, discussion, acceptance, etc.; suggest. 2. present (the name of someone) for office, membership, etc. 3. intend; plan. 4. make an offer of marriage. [< F, < *pro-* forth (< L) + *poser* POSE] —**pro·pos′a·ble**, *adj.* —**pro·posed′**, *adj.* —**pro·pos′er**, *n.* —Syn. 1. offer, recommend, move.

prop·o·si·tion (prop′ə-zish′ən), *n.* 1. what is offered to be considered; proposal. 2. statement. 3. statement that is to be proved true. 4. problem to be solved. 5. *Am., Colloq.* a business enterprise; an affair to be dealt with; an undertaking. 6. *Am., Colloq.* person or thing to be dealt with. —**prop′o·si′tion·al**, *adj.* —**prop′o·si′tion·al·ly**, *adv.* ➤ **Proposition** is originally a business word for *offer, plan, proposal,* which is inappropriate in general usage. "I have a proposition for you" = "I have a plan. . . ."

pro·pound (prə-pound′), *v.* put forward; propose: *propound a theory.* [earlier *propone* < L, < *pro-* before + *ponere* set] —**pro·pound′er**, *n.*

pro·pri·e·tar·y (prə-prī′ə-ter′i), *adj., n., pl.* **-tar·ies.** —*adj.* 1. belonging to a proprietor: *proprietary rights.* 2. holding property: *the proprietary class.* 3. owned by a private person or company: *a proprietary medicine.* —*n.* 1. owner. 2. group of owners. 3. ownership.

pro·pri·e·tor (prə-prī′ə-tər), *n.* owner. [alter. of *proprietary* < LL, < L *proprietas* property, ownership < *proprius* one's own] —**pro·pri·e·to·ri·al** (prə-prī′ə-tô′ri·əl; -tō′-), *adj.* —**pro·pri·e·to′ri·al·ly**, *adv.* —**pro·pri′e·tor·ship′**, *n.* —**pro·pri′e·to′ry**, *adj.*

pro·pri·e·tress (prə-prī′ə-tris), *n.* a woman owner or manager.

pro·pri·e·ty (prə-prī′ə-ti), *n., pl.* **-ties.** 1. quality of being proper; fitness. 2. proper behavior. 3. **the proprieties,** conventional standards or requirements of proper behavior. [< L, < *proprius* proper] —Syn. 1. aptness, suitability. 2. respectability, decency.

pro·pul·sion (prə-pul′shən), *n.* 1. a driving forward or onward. 2. a propelling force or impulse. —**pro·pul′sive, pro·pul·so·ry** (prə-pul′sə-ri), *adj.*

pro ra·ta (prō rā′tə; rä′tə), in proportion. [< L *pro rata* (*parte*) according to the portion figured (for each)]

pro·rate (prō-rāt′; prō′rāt′), *v.*, **-rat·ed, -rat·ing.** *Am.* distribute or assess proportionally. [< *pro rata*] —**pro·rat′a·ble**, *adj.*

pro·rogue (prō-rōg′), *v.*, **-rogued, -rogu·ing.** discontinue the regular meetings of (a lawmaking body) for a time. [< F < L *prorogare* defer < *pro-* forward + *rogare* ask for] —**pro·ro·ga·tion** (prō′rə·gā′shən), *n.* —**pro·ro′guer**, *n.*

pro·sa·ic (prō-zā′ik), *adj.* like prose; matter-of-fact; ordinary; not exciting. —**pro·sa′i·cal·ly**, *adv.* —**pro·sa′ic·ness**, *n.* —Syn. commonplace, humdrum, dull, tedious.

pro·sce·ni·um (prō-sē′ni-əm), *n., pl.* **-ni·a** (-ni-ə). part of the stage in front of the curtain. [< L < Gk., < *pro-* in front of + *skene* stage, orig., tent]

pro·scribe (prō-skrīb′), *v.*, **-scribed, -scrib·ing.** 1. prohibit as wrong or dangerous; condemn. 2. put outside of the protection of the law; outlaw. 3. forbid to come into a certain place; banish. [< L, < *pro-* openly, publicly + *scribere* write] —**pro·scrib′er**, *n.* —**pro·scrip·tion** (prō-skrip′shən), *n.* —**pro·scrip′tive**, *adj.* —**pro·scrip′tive·ly**, *adv.* —**pro·scrip′tive·ness**, *n.* —Syn. 1. forbid, interdict. 3. exile.

prose (prōz), *n., adj., v.*, **prosed, pros·ing.** —*n.* 1. the ordinary form of spoken or written language; plain language not arranged in verses. 2. dull, ordinary talk. —*adj.* 1. of or in prose. 2. lacking imagination; matter-of-fact; commonplace. —*v.* talk or write in a dull, commonplace way. [< F < L *prosa* (*oratio*) straight (speech), ult. < *pro-* forward + *vertere* to turn] —**pro·sa·ist** (prō′zā·ist), **pros′er**, *n.*

pros·e·cute (pros′ə-kūt), *v.*, **-cut·ed, -cut·ing.** 1. bring before a court of law: *reckless drivers will be prosecuted.* 2. bring a case before a law court. 3. carry out; follow up: *he prosecuted an inquiry into reasons for the company's failure.* 4. carry on (a business or occupation). [< L *prosecutus* pursued < *pro-* forth + *sequi* follow] —**pros′e·cut′a·ble**, *adj.* —**pros′e·cu′tor**, *n.* —**pros′e·cu′tor·ship**, *n.*

pros·e·cu·tion (pros′ə-kū′shən), *n.* 1. the carrying on of a lawsuit. 2. side that starts action against another in a law court. 3. a carrying out; following up.

pros·e·lyte (pros′ə-līt), *n., v.*, **-lyt·ed, -lyt·ing.** —*n.* person who has been converted from one opinion, religious belief, etc., to another. —*v.* convert from one opinion, religious belief, etc., to another. [< L < Gk. *proselytos*, orig., one from another land] —**pros′e·lyt′er**, *n.* —**pros′e·lyt′ism**, *n.*

pros·e·lyt·ize (pros′ə-lit·īz′; -lə·tīz′), *v.*, **-ized, -iz·ing.** make converts. —**pros′e·lyt·i·za′tion**, *n.* —**pros′e·lyt·iz′er**, *n.*

Pro·ser·pi·na (prō-sér′pə-nə), **Pro·ser·pi·ne** (prō-sér′pə-nē; pros′ər·pīn), *n. Roman Myth.* Persephone.

pro·sit (prō′sit), *interj.* to your health! [< L, may it benefit]

pro·slav·er·y (prō-slāv′ər·i; -slāv′ri), *adj.* favoring slavery.

pros·o·dy (pros'ə·di), *n.* science of poetic meters and versification. [< L < Gk., all the features (accent, modulation, etc.) that characterize speech < *pros* in addition to + *oide* song, poem] —**pro·sod·ic** (prə·sod'ik), **pro·sod'i·cal,** *adj.* —**pro·sod'i·cal·ly,** *adv.* —**pros'o·dist,** *n.*

pros·pect (pros'pekt), *n.* **1.** thing expected or looked forward to. **2.** act of looking forward; expectation: *the prospect of a vacation is pleasant.* **3.** outlook for the future. **4. in prospect,** expected; looked forward to. **5.** person who may become a customer, candidate, etc. **6.** view; scene: *the prospect from the mountain.* —*v.* search: *prospect for gold.* [< L, ult. < *pro-* forward + *specere* to look] —**pros'pect·less,** *n.* —Syn. **1.** **2.** anticipation. **6.** sight.

pro·spec·tive (prə·spek'tiv), *adj.* probable; expected. —**pro·spec'tive·ly,** *adv.* —**pro·spec'tive·ness,** *n.*

pros·pec·tor (pros'pek·tər; prə·spek'-), *n. Am.* one who explores or examines a region for gold, silver, oil, etc.

pro·spec·tus (prə·spek'təs), *n.* a printed statement describing and advertising something. [< L, PROSPECT]

pros·per (pros'pər), *v.* **1.** be successful; have good fortune; flourish. **2.** make successful. [< OF < L, < *prosperus* prosperous] —**pros'per·er,** *n.* —**pros'per·ing·ly,** *adv.*

pros·per·i·ty (pros·per'ə·ti), *n., pl.* **-ties.** prosperous condition; good fortune; success.

pros·per·ous (pros'pər·əs), *adj.* **1.** successful; thriving; doing well; fortunate. **2.** favorable; helpful. [< L *prosperus*] —**pros'per·ous·ly,** *adv.* —**pros'per·ous·ness,** *n.* —Syn. **1.** flourishing, rich, wealthy. —Ant. **1.** unsuccessful, needy, poor.

pros·tate (pros'tāt), or **prostate gland,** *n.* a large gland surrounding the male urethra in front of the bladder. [< Med.L < Gk. *prostates* one standing in front, ult. < *pro-* before + *stenai* to stand] —**pro·stat·ic** (prō·stat'ik), *adj.*

pros·ti·tute (pros'tə·tüt; -tūt), *n., v.,* **-tut·ed, -tut·ing.** —*n.* **1.** woman who practices unlawful, esp. indiscriminate, sexual intercourse for gain or hire. **2.** person who does base things for money. —*v.* **1.** put to an unworthy or base use. **2.** submit to sexual intercourse for gain or hire. [< L *prostitutus* < *pro-* publicly + *statuere* cause to stand] —**pros'ti·tu'tion,** *n.* —**pros'ti·tu'tor,** *n.*

pros·trate (pros'trāt), *v.,* **-trat·ed, -trat·ing,** *adj.* —*v.* **1.** lay down flat; cast down: *the captives prostrated themselves before the conqueror.* **2.** make very weak or helpless; exhaust: *sickness often prostrates people.* —*adj.* **1.** lying flat with face downward. **2.** lying flat. **3.** overcome; helpless: *a prostrate enemy.* [< L *prostratus* < *pro-* forth + *sternere* strew] —**pros·tra'tion,** *n.* —Syn. *adj.* **1,** **2.** prone.

pros·y (prōz'i), *adj.,* **pros·i·er, pros·i·est.** like prose; commonplace; dull; tiresome. —**pros'i·ly,** *adv.* —**pros'i·ness,** *n.*

prot·ac·tin·i·um (prōt'ak·tin'i·əm), *n. Chem.* a very rare radioactive metallic element, Pa. Formerly, **protoactinium.**

pro·tag·o·nist (prō·tag'ə·nist), *n.* **1.** the main character in a play, story, or novel. **2.** any main or leading character. [< Gk., ult. < *protos* first + *agon* contest]

pro·te·an (prō'ti·ən; prō·tē'ən), *adj.* readily assuming different forms or characters; exceedingly variable. [< *Proteus*]

pro·tect (prə·tekt'), *v.* **1.** shield from harm or danger; shelter; defend; guard. **2.** guard (home industry) against foreign goods by taxing any which are brought into the country. [< L *tectus* < *pro-* in front + *tegere* to cover] —**pro·tect'ing,** *adj.* —**pro·tect'ing·ly,** *adv.* —**pro·tect'ing·ness,** *n.* —**pro·tec'tor,** *n.* —**pro·tec'tor·ship,** *n.* —Syn. **1.** secure, fortify.

pro·tec·tion (prə·tek'shən), *n.* **1.** act of protecting; condition of being kept from harm; defense: *we have policemen for our protection.* **2.** thing or person that prevents damage: *an apron is a protection when doing dirty work.* **3.** system of taxing foreign goods so that people are more likely to buy goods made in their own country; the opposite of free trade. **4.** passport. —**pro·tec'tion·ism,** *n.* —**pro·tec'tion·ist,** *n.* —Syn. **1.** guard, security. **2.** shield, safeguard, bulwark.

pro·tec·tive (prə·tek'tiv), *adj.* **1.** being a defense; protecting: *the hard protective covering of a turtle.* **2.** preventing injury to those around: *a protective device on a machine.* **3.** guarding against foreign-made goods by putting a high tax or duty on them. —**pro·tec'tive·ly,** *adv.* —**pro·tec'tive·ness,** *n.*

pro·tec·tor·ate (prə·tek'tər·it), *n.* a weak country under the protection and partial control of a strong country. Parts of Africa are European protectorates.

pro·té·gé (prō'tə·zhā), *n.* person under the protection or kindly care of another. [< F, pp. of *protéger* < L *protegere* PROTECT]

pro·té·gée (prō'tə·zhā), *n.* a woman protégé.

pro·tein (prō'tēn; -tē·in), **pro·te·id** (prō'tē·id), *n.* a complex compound containing nitrogen that is a necessary part of the cells of animals and plants. —*adj.* of or containing protein. [< G, < Gk. *proteios* of the first quality]

pro tem., pro tempore.

pro tem·po·re (prō tem'pə·rē), *Latin.* for the time being; temporarily.

pro·test (*n.* prō'test; *v.* prə·test'), *n.* **1.** statement that denies or objects strongly: *yield after protest.* **2.** a solemn declaration: *a protest of innocence.* **3. under protest,** unwillingly; though objecting. **4.** a written statement by a notary public that a bill, note, check, etc., has been presented to someone who has refused to pay it or accept it. —*v.* **1.** make objections; object. **2.** object to: *protest a decision.* **3.** declare solemnly; assert: *the accused man protested his innocence.* **4.** state that (a check, note, bill, etc.) has not been paid. [< OF < L, ult. < *pro-* forth + *testis* witness] —**pro·test'er,** *n.* —**pro·test'ing·ly,** *adv.*

Prot·es·tant (prot'is·tənt), *n.* **1.** a member of any of certain Christian churches which ultimately have split off from the Roman Catholic Church since the sixteenth century. Baptists, Presbyterians, Methodists, Quakers, and many others are Protestants. **2. protestant,** person who protests.

Protestant Episcopal Church, a Protestant church in the U.S. that has about the same principles and beliefs as the Church of England.

Prot·es·tant·ism (prot'is·tənt·iz'əm), *n.* **1.** the religion of Protestants. **2.** their principles and beliefs. **3.** Protestants or Protestant churches as a group.

prot·es·ta·tion (prot'is·tā'shən), *n.* **1.** a solemn declaration; protesting. **2.** a formal dissent or disapproval; protest.

Pro·te·us (prō'ti·əs; -tūs), *n. Gk. Myth.* a sea god who had the power of assuming many different forms.

pro·to·ac·tin·i·um (prō'tō·ak·tin'i·əm), *n. Chem.* former name of protactinium.

pro·to·col (prō'tə·kol; -kōl), *n.* **1.** a first draft or record from which a document, esp. a treaty, is prepared. **2.** rules of etiquette of the diplomatic corps. [< OF < Med.L < Gk. *protokollon* a first leaf (with date and contents) glued onto a papyrus roll < *protos* first + *kolla* glue] —**pro·to·col·ic** (prō'tə·kol'ik; -kōl'-), *adj.*

pro·ton (prō'ton), *n.* a tiny particle carrying one unit of positive electricity. All atoms are built up of electrons and protons. [< Gk., neut. adj., first]

pro·to·plasm (prō'tə·plaz·əm), *n.* living matter; the substance that is the physical basis of life; the living substance of all plant and animal cells. [< G, < Gk. *protos* first + *plasma* something molded < *plassein* mold] —**pro'to·plas'mic,** *adj.*

pro·to·type (prō'tə·tīp), *n.* the first or primary type of anything; the original or model: *a modern ship has its prototype in the hollowed log used by savages.* —**pro'to·typ'al, pro·to·typ·ic** (prō'tə·tip'ik), **pro'to·typ'i·cal,** *adj.*

Pro·to·zo·a (prō'tə·zō'ə), *n.pl.* protozoans. [< NL, pl., < Gk. *protos* first + *zoion* animal]

pro·to·zo·an (prō'tə·zō'ən), *n.* animal that consists of a single cell. —*adj.* belonging to or pertaining to the single-celled animals. —**pro'to·zo'al,** *adj.*

pro·tract (prō·trakt'), *v.* 1. draw out; lengthen in time: *protract a visit.* 2. slide out; thrust out; extend. 3. draw by means of a scale and protractor. [< L *protractus* < *pro-* forward + *trahere* drag] —**pro·tract'ed,** *adj.* —**pro·tract'-ed·ly,** *adv.* —**pro·tract'ed·ness,** *n.* —**pro·tract'-i·ble,** *adj.* —**pro·trac'tion,** *n.* —**pro·trac'tive,** *adj.*

pro·trac·tile (prō·trak'təl), *adj.* capable of being lengthened out, or of being thrust forth.

pro·trac·tor (prō·trak'tər), *n.* instrument for drawing or measuring angles.

pro·trude (prō·trüd'), *v.,* –trud·ed, –trud·ing. 1. thrust forth; stick out: *the saucy child protruded her tongue.* 2. be thrust forth; project: *her teeth protrude too far.* [< L, < *pro-* forward + *trudere* to thrust] —**pro·tru·sion** (prō·trü'-zhən), *n.* —**pro·tru·sive** (prō·trü'siv), *adj.;* **trud'ent,** *adj.* —**pro·tru'sive·ly,** *adv.* —**pro·tru'sive·ness,** *n.*

pro·tu·ber·ance (prō·tü'bər·əns; –tū'–), **pro·tu·ber·an·cy** (–ən·si), *n., pl.* –anc·es; –cies. 1. protuberant quality or condition. 2. part that sticks out; bulge; swelling.

pro·tu·ber·ant (prō·tü'bər·ənt; –tū'–), *adj.* bulging out; sticking out; prominent. [< LL *protuberans* bulging, ult. < *pro-* forward + *tuber* lump] —**pro·tu·ber·an·tial** (prō·tü'bər·an'shəl; –tū'–), *adj.* —**pro·tu'ber·ant·ly,** *adv.*

proud (proud), *adj.* 1. thinking well of oneself. 2. feeling or showing pleasure or satisfaction. 3. having a becoming sense of what is due oneself, one's position, or character: *too proud to fight.* 4. thinking too well of oneself; haughty; arrogant. 5. highly honorable, creditable, or gratifying: *a proud moment.* 6. proceeding from or due to pride. 7. majestic; magnificent: *proud cities.* 8. proud of, thinking well of; being well satisfied with. [< OF *prod, prud* valiant < LL *prode* of use < L *prōdesse* be useful] —**proud'ly,** *adv.* —**proud'ness,** *n.* —**Syn.** 4. overbearing, disdainful, vain. —**Ant.** 4. meek, humble.

proud flesh, formation of too many grainlike particles of flesh during the healing of a wound or sore.

Proust (prüst), *n.* Marcel, 1871–1922, French novelist.

Prov., 1. Provençal. 2. Proverbs.

prov., provincialism.

prove (prüv), *v.,* **proved, proved** or **prov·en, prov·ing.** 1. establish as true; make certain. 2. establish the genuineness or validity of, esp. of a will. 3. be found to be: *this book proved interesting.* 4. try out; test; subject to some testing process: *prove a new gun.* 5. *Math.* verify the correctness of (some statement). [< OF < L *probare < probus* worthy] —**prov'a·ble,** *adj.* —**prov'a·ble·ness,** *n.* —**prov'a·bly,** *adv.* —**prov'er,** *n.* —**Syn.** 1. corroborate, verify, confirm. 2. probate.

Pro·ven·çal (prō'vən·säl'; prov'ən–), *n.* 1. native or inhabitant of Provence. 2. language of Provence.

Pro·vence (prô·väNs'), *n.* part of SE France, ancient Rome's first province.

prov·en·der (prov'ən·dər), *n.* 1. dry food for animals, such as hay or corn. 2. *Colloq.* food. [< OF < L *praebenda.* See PREBEND.]

prov·erb (prov'ėrb), *n.* 1. a short wise saying used for a long time by many people. 2. a well-known case: *he is a proverb for carelessness.* 3. Proverbs, book of the Old Testament made up of sayings of the wise men of Israel, including Solomon.

pro·ver·bi·al (prə·vėr'bi·əl), *adj.* 1. of proverbs; expressed in a proverb; like a proverb: *proverbial brevity, proverbial wisdom, a proverbial saying.* 2. that has become a proverb: *the proverbial stitch in time.* 3. well-known: *the proverbial loyalty of dogs.* —**pro·ver'bi·al·ly,** *adv.*

pro·vide (prə·vīd'), *v.,* –vid·ed, –vid·ing. 1. supply; furnish: *sheep provide us with wool.* 2.

supply means of support; arrange to supply means of support: *a father provides for his family.* 3. take care for the future: *provide for old age.* 4. state as a condition beforehand: *the rules provide that dues must be paid monthly.* 5. get ready; prepare beforehand. [< L, < *pro-* ahead + *videre* see. Doublet of PURVEY.] —**pro·vid'a·ble,** *adj.* —**pro·vid'er,** *n.*

pro·vid·ed (prə·vīd'id), *conj.* on the condition that; if: *she will go provided her friends can go also.*

prov·i·dence (prov'ə·dəns), *n.* 1. God's care and help. 2. care for the future; good management. 3. Providence, God.

Prov·i·dence (prov'ə·dəns), *n.* capital of Rhode Island, in the NE part.

prov·i·dent (prov'ə·dənt), *adj.* 1. having or showing foresight: *provident men lay aside money for their families.* 2. economical; frugal. [< L *providens.* See PROVIDE.] —**prov'i·dent·ly,** *adv.* —**Syn.** 1. foreseeing, prudent. 2. thrifty.

prov·i·den·tial (prov'ə·den'shəl), *adj.* 1. of or proceeding from divine power or influence. 2. fortunate. —**prov'i·den'tial·ly,** *adv.*

pro·vid·ing (prə·vīd'ing), *conj.* on the condition that: *I shall go providing it doesn't rain.*

prov·ince (prov'ins), *n.* 1. one of the main divisions of a country. Canada is made up of provinces instead of states. 2. **the provinces,** part of a country outside the capital or the largest cities. 3. proper work or activity. 4. division; department: *the province of literature.* 5. an ancient Roman territory outside Italy, ruled by a Roman governor. [< F < L *provincia*]

pro·vin·cial (prə·vin'shəl), *adj.* 1. of a province. 2. belonging or peculiar to some particular province or provinces rather than to the whole country; local: *provincial English.* 3. lacking refinement or polish; narrow: *a provincial point of view.* —*n.* 1. person born or living in a province. 2. a provincial person. —**pro·vin·ci·al·i·ty** (prə·vin'shi·al'ə·ti), *n.* —**pro·vin'cial·ly,** *adv.*

pro·vin·cial·ism (prə·vin'shəl·iz·əm), *n.* 1. provincial manners, habit of thought, etc. 2. narrow-mindedness. 3. word, expression, or way of pronunciation peculiar to a district of a country.

pro·vi·sion (prə·vizh'ən), *n.* 1. statement making a condition: *a provision of the lease is that the rent must be paid promptly.* 2. a taking care for the future. 3. care taken for the future; arrangement made beforehand: *there is a provision for making the building larger if necessary.* 4. that which is made ready; supply; stock. 5. **make provision,** take care for the future; make arrangements beforehand. 6. **provisions,** supply of food and drinks. —*v.* supply with provisions. —**pro·vi'sion·er,** *n.*

pro·vi·sion·al (prə·vizh'ən·əl), *adj.* for the time being; temporary: *a provisional agreement, a provisional governor.* —**pro·vi'sion·al·ly,** *adv.*

pro·vi·so (prə·vī'zō), *n., pl.* –sos, –soes. sentence or part of a sentence in a contract, or other agreement, that states a condition; condition: *Tom was promoted with the proviso that he was to be put back if he failed any subject.* [< L, it being provided, < *providere* PROVIDE]

pro·vi·so·ry (prə·vī'zə·ri), *adj.* 1. containing a proviso; conditional. 2. provisional. —**pro·vi'so·ri·ly,** *adv.*

prov·o·ca·tion (prov'ə·kā'shən), *n.* 1. act of provoking. 2. something that stirs one up; cause of anger: *angry without provocation.*

pro·voc·a·tive (prə·vok'ə·tiv), *adj.* 1. irritating; vexing. 2. tending or serving to call forth action, thought, laughter, anger, etc.: *a remark provocative of mirth.* —*n.* something that rouses or irritates. —**pro·voc'a·tive·ly,** *adv.* —**pro·voc'a·tive·ness,** *n.*

pro·voke (prə·vōk'), *v.,* –voked, –vok·ing. 1. make angry; vex. 2. stir up; excite: *an insult provokes a person to anger.* 3. bring about; start into action; cause. [< L, < *pro-* forth + *vocare* to call] —**pro·vok'er,** *n.* —**pro·vok'ing,** *adj.* —**pro·vok'ing·ly,** *adv.* —**Syn.** 1. irritate, exasperate, nettle. 2. rouse, kindle, incite

prov·ost (prov′əst), *n.* **1.** person appointed to superintend or preside, such as the head of certain colleges or churches. **2.** the chief magistrate in a Scottish town. [< Med.L *propositus* for *praepositus*, orig. pp. < *prae-* at the head of + *ponere* to place] —prov′ost·ship, *n.*

prov·ost marshal (prō′vō), **1.** in the army, an officer acting as head of police in a camp or district. **2.** in the navy, an officer charged with the safekeeping of prisoners until their trial by court-martial.

prow (prou), *n.* **1.** the pointed front part of a ship or boat; bow. **2.** something like it. [< F < Ital. < L < Gk. *proira*]

prow·ess (prou′is), *n.* **1.** bravery; daring. **2.** brave or daring acts. **3.** unusual skill or ability. [< OF *proece* < *prod* valiant. See PROUD.] —prow′ess·ful, *adj.* —Syn. **1.** courage, valor. —Ant. **1.** cowardice, timidity.

prowl (proul), *v.* **1.** go about slowly and secretly hunting for something to eat or steal: *many wild animals prowl at night.* **2.** wander. —*n.* act of prowling. [ME *prolle(n)*] —prowl′er, *n.* —prowl′ing·ly, *adv.* —Syn. *v.* **1.** slink, sneak, skulk.

prowl car, *Am.* a police car connected with headquarters by radio telephone.

prox·i·mal (prok′sə·məl), *adj.* situated toward the point of origin or attachment. [< L *proximus* nearest] —prox′i·mal·ly, *adv.*

prox·i·mate (prok′sə·mit), *adj.* **1.** next; nearest. **2.** approximate. [< LL *proximatus* approached < *proximus* nearest] —prox′i·mate·ly, *adv.* —prox′i·mate·ness, *n.*

prox·im·i·ty (proks·im′ə·ti), *n.* nearness: *she and her cat enjoy the proximity of the fire.* [< L, < *proximus* nearest]

proximity fuse, *Am.* a tiny radio device set in the nose of a projectile that causes the shell to explode at a position where maximum damage will ensue.

prox·i·mo (prok′sə·mō), *adv.* in or of the coming month. [short for L *proximo mense* during next month]

prox·y (prok′si), *n., pl.* **prox·ies. 1.** action of a deputy or substitute. **2.** agent; deputy; substitute. **3.** a writing authorizing a proxy to act or vote for a person. **4.** vote so given. [ME *prokecye,* alter. of *procuracy* the office of proctor. See PROCURE.]

prude (prüd), *n.* person who is too proper or too modest about sex; person who puts on extremely proper or modest airs. [< F, ult. < OF *prod* worthy. See PROWESS.] —prud′ish, *adj.* —prud′ish·ly, *adv.* —prud′ish·ness, *n.*

pru·dence (prü′dəns), *n.* **1.** wise thought before acting; good judgment. **2.** good management; economy. —Syn. **1.** foresight, care, caution.

pru·dent (prü′dənt), *adj.* planning carefully ahead of time; sensible; discreet: *a prudent man saves part of his wages.* [< L *prudens,* var. of *providens* PROVIDENT] —pru′dent·ly, *adv.* —Syn. judicious, wise, careful, cautious. —Ant. foolish, rash, thoughtless, indiscreet.

pru·den·tial (prü·den′shəl), *adj.* of, marked by, or showing prudence. —pru·den′tial·ly, *adv.*

prud·er·y (prüd′ər·i), *n., pl.* **-er·ies. 1.** extreme modesty or propriety, esp. when not genuine. **2.** a prudish act or remark.

prune¹ (prün), *n.* kind of dried sweet plum. [< F < L *prunum.* Doublet of PLUM.]

prune² (prün), *v.,* pruned, prun·ing. **1.** cut out useless or undesirable parts from. **2.** cut superfluous or undesirable twigs or branches from (a bush, tree, etc.). [< OF *proognier*] —prun′er, *n.*

pruning hook, implement with a hooked blade, used for pruning vines, etc.

pru·ri·ent (prur′i·ənt), *adj.* having lustful thoughts or wishes. [< L *pruriens* itching, being wanton] —pru′ri·ence, pru′ri·en·cy, *n.* —pru′ri·ent·ly, *adv.*

Prus·sia (prush′ə), *n.* a former state in N Germany. —Prus′sian, *adj., n.*

Prussian blue, a deep-blue pigment, essentially a cyanogen compound of iron.

prus·sic acid (prus′ik), a deadly poison that smells like bitter almonds; hydrocyanic acid.

pry¹ (prī), *v.,* pried, pry·ing, *n., pl.* **pries.** —*v.* look with curiosity; peep: *she is always prying into other people's affairs.* —*n.* an inquisitive person. [ME *prie(n)*] —pry′ing·ly, *adv.*

pry² (prī), *v.,* pried, pry·ing, *n., pl.* **pries.** —*v.* **1.** raise or move by force. **2.** get with much effort: *I pried the secret out of him.* [< n.] —*n.* lever for prying. [< *prize* a lever, taken as a pl.]

Ps., Psalm; Psalms.

P.S., 1. postscript. **2.** Public School.

psalm (säm), *n.* **1.** a sacred song or poem. **2.** Psalm, any of the 150 sacred songs or hymns that together form a book of the Old Testament. —*v.* celebrate or praise in psalms. [< LL < Gk. *psalmos*]

psalm·book (säm′bùk′), *n.* collection of metrical translations of the Psalms prepared for public worship.

psal·mo·dy (sä′mə·di; sal′mə-), *n., pl.* **-dies. 1.** act, practice, or art of singing psalms or hymns. **2.** psalms or hymns. [< LL < Gk., < *psalmos* psalm + *oide* song] —psal·mod·ic (sal·mod′ik), *adj.* —psal′mo·dist, *n.*

Psalms (sämz), *n.pl.* book of the Old Testament consisting of 150 psalms.

Psal·ter (sôl′tər), *n.* **1.** the Book of Psalms. **2.** Sometimes, psalter, a prayer book containing the Psalms for liturgical or devotional use. [< L < Gk. *psalterion* PSALTERY]

psal·ter·y (sôl′tər·i; -tri), *n., pl.* **-ter·ies.** an ancient musical instrument played by plucking the strings. [< L < Gk. *psalterion,* orig., stringed instrument < *psallein* pluck]

Man playing a psaltery

pseu·do (sü′dō), *adj.* **1.** false; sham; pretended. **2.** having only the appearance of. [< Gk. *pseudes* false]

pseu·do·nym (sü′də·nim), *n.* name used by an author instead of his real name. [< Gk. *pseudonymon* < *pseudes* false + dial. *onyma* name]

pshaw (shô), *interj., n.* exclamation expressing impatience, contempt, etc.

psi (sī; psē), *n.* the 23rd letter of the Greek alphabet (Ψ, ψ).

psit·ta·co·sis (sit′ə·kō′sis), *n.* a contagious disease of parrots and other birds, communicable to people; parrot fever. [< NL, < Gk. *psittakos* parrot]

pso·ri·a·sis (sə·rī′ə·sis), *n.* a chronic skin disease characterized by dry, scaling patches. [< NL < Gk., ult. < *psora* itch]

P.S.T., PST, or **p.s.t.,** *Am.* Pacific Standard Time.

Psy·che (sī′kē), *n.* **1.** Gk. *Myth.* the human soul or spirit pictured as a beautiful young girl, usually with butterfly wings. In the ancient myth, Psyche was loved by Cupid and was made immortal. **2.** psyche, a. the human soul or spirit. **b.** the mind.

psy·chi·a·try (sī·kī′ə·tri; si-), *n.* study and treatment of mental diseases. [< PSYCHO- + Gk. *iatreia* cure] —psy·chi·at·ric (sī′ki·at′rik), psy′chi·at′ri·cal, *adj.* —psy′chi·at′ri·cal·ly, *adv.* —psy·chi′a·trist, *n.*

psy·chic (sī′kik), *adj.* Also, psy′chi·cal. **1.** of the soul or mind; mental. **2.** outside the known laws of physics; supernatural. **3.** especially susceptible to psychic influences. —*n.* medium (def. 5). [< Gk., < *psyche* soul, mind] —psy′chi·cal·ly, *adv.*

psycho-, psych-, *word element.* mind, as in *psychoanalysis.* [< Gk. *psyche* soul, mind]

psy·cho·a·nal·y·sis (sī′kō·ə·nal′ə·sis), *n.* **1.** the minute examination of a mind or minds to discover the underlying mental causes producing certain mental and nervous disorders. **2.** analysis of mind or personality. —psy·cho·an·a·lyst (sī′kō·an′ə·list), *n.* —psy·cho·an·a·lyt·ic (sī′kō·an′ə·lit′ik), psy′cho·an′a·lyt′i·cal, *adj.* —psy′cho·an′a·lyt′i·cal·ly, *adv.*

āge, cãre, fär; ēqual, térm; īce; ōpen, ôrder; pùt, rüle, üse; th, then; ə=a in about.

psy·cho·an·a·lyze (sī'kō·an'ə·līz), v., **-lyzed**, **-lyz·ing.** examine by psychoanalysis. **—psy'-cho·an'a·lyz'er,** n.

psychological moment, 1. the very moment to get the desired effect in the mind. **2.** the critical moment.

psychological warfare, systematic efforts to affect morale, loyalty, etc., esp. of large national groups.

psy·chol·o·gy (sī·kol'ə·ji), n., pl. **-gies. 1.** the science of mind. Psychology tries to explain why people act, think, and feel as they do. **2.** the mental states and processes of a person or persons; mental nature and behavior: Mrs. Jones knew her husband's psychology. [< NL, < Gk. psyche soul, mind + -logos treating of] **—psy·cho·log·i·cal** (sī'kə·loj'ə·kəl), **psy'cho·log'ic,** adj. **—psy'cho·log'i·cal·ly,** adv. **—psy·chol'o·gist,** n.

psy·cho·neu·ro·sis (sī'kō·nū·rō'sis; -nyū-), n., pl. **-ses** (-sēz). neurosis of psychic origin; mental illness without organic lesion. **—psy·cho·neu·rot·ic** (sī'kō·nū·rot'ik; -nyū-), adj.

psy·cho·path·ic (sī'kə·path'ik), adj. **1.** of or pertaining to mental diseases. **2.** having a mental disease. **3.** likely to become insane.

psy·chop·a·thy (sī·kop'ə·thi), n. **1.** mental disease. **2.** mental eccentricity or instability so extreme as to border on insanity.

psy·cho·sis (sī·kō'sis), n., pl. **-ses** (-sēz). any severe form of mental disturbance or disease. [< NL < Gk., < psyche soul, mind] **—psy·chot·ic** (sī·kot'ik), adj.

psy·cho·so·mat·ic (sī'kō·sə·mat'ik), adj. of or pertaining to both mind and body.

psychosomatic medicine, the use of the methods and principles of psychology in the treatment of physical ailments.

psy·cho·ther·a·py (sī'kō·ther'ə·pi), n. treatment of disease by mental influences.

Pt, Chem. platinum.

pt., pl. (for 1, 3, 4) **pts. 1.** part. **2.** past tense. **3.** pint. **4.** point. **5.** preterit.

P.T.A., Am. Parent-Teacher Association.

ptar·mi·gan (tär'mə·gən), n., pl. **-gans** or (esp. collectively) **-gan.** any of several kinds of grouse found in mountainous and cold regions. [< Scotch Gaelic tārmachan]

PT boat, U.S. Navy. a small, fast motorboat which carries torpedoes, depth bombs, etc.

pter·i·do·phyte (ter'ə·dō·fīt'), n. any of the highest group of seedless plants having roots, stems, and leaves. Ferns and horsetails are pteridophytes. [< Gk. pteris fern + E -phyte < Gk. phyton plant]

pter·o·dac·tyl (ter'ə·dak'təl), n. an extinct flying reptile that had wings somewhat like a bat's. [< Gk. pteron wing + daktylos finger, toe]

Ptol·e·ma·ic (tol'ə·mā'ik), adj. of or having to do with the astronomer Ptolemy. The Ptolemaic system of astronomy taught that the earth was the fixed center of the universe, around which the heavenly bodies moved.

Ptol·e·my (tol'ə·mi), n. **1.** Claudius, Greek mathematician, astronomer, and geographer at Alexandria. He lived about 130 A.D. **2.** any of a certain family of Egyptian rulers who ruled Egypt from 323 B.C. to 30 B.C.

pto·maine, pto·main (tō'mān; tō·mān'), n. a substance, often poisonous, produced in decaying matter. Improperly canned foods may contain ptomaines. [< Ital., < Gk. ptoma corpse]

Pu, Chem. plutonium.

pub (pub), n. Brit. Slang. public house (def. 1).

pu·ber·ty (pū'bər·ti), n. the physical beginning of manhood and womanhood. Puberty comes at about 14 in boys and about 12 in girls. [< L pubertas < pubes adult]

pu·bes·cent (pū·bes'ənt), adj. **1.** arriving or arrived at puberty. **2.** Bot., Zool. covered with down or fine short hair. [< L pubescens reaching puberty < pubes adult] **—pu·bes'cence,** n.

pu·bis (pū'bis), n., pl. **-bes** (-bēz). part of either hipbone that, with the corresponding part of the other, forms the front of the pelvis. [< NL os pubis bone of the groin] **—pu'bic,** adj.

pub·lic (pub'lik), adj. **1.** of, belonging to, or concerning the people as a whole: public affairs. **2.** done, made, acting, etc., for the people as a whole: public relief. **3.** open to all the people; serving all the people: a public park. **4.** of or engaged in the affairs or service of the people: a public official. **5.** known to many or all; not private: the fact became public. **6.** international: public law. —n. **1.** the people in general; all the people. **2.** a particular section of the people; clientele: a popular actor has a large public. **3.** in public, not in private or secretly; openly. [< L publicus, ult. < populus the people] **—pub'lic·ly,** adv.

pub·li·can (pub'lə·kən), n. **1.** Brit. keeper of a pub. **2.** a tax collector of ancient Rome.

pub·li·ca·tion (pub'lə·kā'shən), n. **1.** book, newspaper, or magazine; anything that is published. **2.** the printing and selling of books, newspapers, magazines, etc. **3.** act of making known; fact or state of being made known; public announcement. [< L, ult. < publicus PUBLIC]

public domain, 1. Am. lands belonging to the state or federal government. **2. in the public domain,** of works, material, etc., available for unrestricted use because unprotected by copyright or patent.

public enemy, Am. person who is a menace to the public.

public house, 1. Brit. place where alcoholic liquor is sold to be drunk; saloon. **2.** inn; hotel.

pub·li·cist (pub'lə·sist), n. **1.** person skilled or trained in law or in public affairs. **2.** writer on law, politics, or public affairs.

pub·lic·i·ty (pub·lis'ə·ti), n. **1.** public notice: the publicity that actors desire. **2.** measures used for getting, or the process of getting, public notice: a campaign of publicity for a new automobile. **3.** being public; being seen by or known to everybody: in the publicity of the street.

pub·li·cize (pub'lə·sīz), v., **-cized, -ciz·ing.** give publicity to.

public opinion, opinion of the people in a country, community, etc.

public relations, activities of an organization, army, etc., that are concerned with giving the general public a better understanding of its policies and purposes, by giving out news through the newspapers, magazines, radio, motion pictures, etc.

public school, 1. Am. a free school maintained by taxes. **2.** in England, an endowed private boarding school.

pub·lic-spir·it·ed (pub'lik·spir'it·id), adj. having or showing an unselfish desire for the public good.

public utility, company formed or chartered to render services to the public, such as a company furnishing electricity or gas, a railroad, a streetcar or bus line, etc.

public works, Am. things built by the government at public expense and for public use, such as roads, docks, canals, and waterworks.

pub·lish (pub'lish), v. **1.** prepare and offer (a book, paper, map, piece of music, etc.) for sale or distribution. **2.** make publicly or generally known: don't publish the faults of your friends. **3.** announce formally or officially. [< OF publier, ult. < L publicus PUBLIC; modeled after punish, etc.] **—pub'lish·a·ble,** adj. **—Syn. 2.** divulge, reveal, disclose. **—Ant. 2.** suppress, withhold.

pub·lish·er (pub'lish·ər), n. person or company whose business is to publish books, newspapers, magazines, etc.

Puc·ci·ni (pū·chē'ni), n. Giacomo, 1858–1924, Italian musical composer.

Puck (puk), n. **1.** a mischievous fairy in English folklore, who appears in Shakespeare's play A Midsummer Night's Dream. **2. puck,** a mischievous spirit; goblin. **b.** a rubber disk used in the game of ice hockey. [OE pūca goblin] **—puck'ish,** adj. **—puck'ish·ness,** n.

puck·a (puk'ə), adj. in India: **1.** reliable; good. **2.** solid; substantial. **3.** permanent. Also, **pukka.** [< Hind. pakkā cooked, ripe]

puck·er (puk'ər), v. draw into wrinkles or irregular folds: *pucker one's brow.* —*n.* an irregular fold; wrinkle. [appar. < *poke²*] —**Syn.** *v.* crease, corrugate, purse.

pud·ding (pud'ing), *n.* **1.** a soft cooked food, usually sweet, as rice pudding. **2.** kind of sausage. **3.** anything soft like a pudding.

pud·dle (pud'əl), *n., v.* –dled, –dling. —*n.* **1.** a small pool of water, esp. dirty water. **2.** a small pool of any liquid. **3.** wet clay and sand stirred into a paste. —*v.* **1.** make wet or muddy. **2.** mix up wet clay and sand into a thick paste. **3.** use a mixture of wet clay and sand to stop water from running through. **4.** stir (melted iron) along with an oxidizing agent to make wrought iron. [cf. OE *pudd* ditch] —**pud'dler,** *n.* —**pud'dly,** *adj.*

pud·dling (pud'ling), *n.* act or process of converting pig iron into wrought iron by stirring the molten metal along with an oxidizing agent.

pudg·y (puj'i), *adj.,* pudg·i·er, pudg·i·est. short and fat or thick. —**pudg'i·ly,** *adv.* —**pudg'i·ness,** *n.*

pueb·lo (pweb'lō), *n., pl.* –los. *Am.* **1.** an Indian village built of adobe and stone. There were many pueblos in the SW United States. **2.** Pueblo, an Indian living in a pueblo. [< Sp., people, < L *populus*]

pu·er·ile (pū'ər·il), *adj.* foolish for a grown person to say or do; childish. [< L, < *puer* boy] —**pu'er·ile·ly,** *adv.* —**pu'er·il'i·ty,** pu'er·ileness, *n.* —**Syn.** juvenile, silly, immature.

pu·er·per·al (pū·ėr'pər·əl), *adj.* of or pertaining to childbirth. [< NL, ult. < L *puer* child + *parere* to bear]

Puer·to Ri·co (pwer'tō rē'kō), island in the E part of the West Indies. It is a commonwealth affiliated with the United States, with autonomy in local affairs. Formerly, Porto Rico. —**Puerto Rican.**

puff (puf), *v.* **1.** blow with short, quick blasts. **2.** breathe quick and hard. **3.** give out puffs; move with puffs: *the engine puffed out of the station.* **4.** move or come in puffs: *smoke puffed out of the chimney.* **5.** smoke: *puff a cigar.* **6.** swell with air or pride: *he puffed out his cheeks.* **7.** arrange in soft, round masses. **8.** praise in exaggerated language. —*n.* **1.** a short, quick blast: *a puff of wind.* **2.** a small quantity of air, smoke, etc., blown out in short, quick blasts. **3.** a quick, hard breath. **4.** act or process of swelling. **5.** a soft round mass, as of hair. **6.** a small pad for putting powder on the skin, etc. **7.** a light pastry filled with whipped cream, jam, etc. **8.** extravagant praise. **9.** portion of material gathered and held down at the edges but left full in the middle, as in dresses, etc. [OE *pyffan*] —**puff'y,** *adj.* —**puff'i·ly,** *adv.* —**puff'i·ness,** *n.*

puff adder, a large and very poisonous African snake that puffs up the upper part of its body when excited.

puff·ball (puf'bôl'), *n.* any of various ballshaped fungi characterized by spore cases that give off a cloud of tiny spores when suddenly broken.

puff·er (puf'ər), *n.* **1.** person or thing that puffs. **2.** *Am.* any of various fishes capable of inflating the body.

puf·fin (puf'ən), *n.* a sea bird of the N Atlantic that has a high, narrow, furrowed, parti-colored bill. [ME *poffin*]

pug¹ (pug), *n.* **1.** a small, tan dog with a curly tail and a short, turned-up nose. **2.** pug nose.

pug² (pug), *n. Slang.* pugilist.

Pu·get Sound (pū'jit), long narrow bay of the Pacific between NW Washington and Vancouver Island.

pu·gi·lism (pū'jə·liz·əm), *n.* art of fighting with the fists; boxing. [< L *pugil* boxer] —**pu'gi·list,** *n.* —**pu'gi·lis'tic,** *adj.* —**pu'gi·lis'ti·cal·ly,** *adv.*

pug·na·cious (pug·nā'shəs), *adj.* having the habit of fighting; fond of fighting; quarrelsome. [< L *pugnax,* ult. < *pugnus* fist] —**pug·na'cious·ly,** *adv.* —**pug·nac·i·ty** (pug·nas'ə·ti), pug·na'cious·ness, *n.* —**Syn.** combative.

pug nose, a short, turned-up nose. —**pug-nosed** (pug'nōzd'), *adj.*

pu·is·sant (pū'i·sənt; pū·is'ənt; pwis'ənt), *adj. Archaic.* powerful; mighty; strong. [< OF, being powerful, ult. < var. of L *posse* be able] —**pu'is·sance,** *n.* —**pu'is·sant·ly,** *adv.*

puke (pūk), *n., v.,* puked, puk·ing. vomit.

puk·ka (puk'ə), *adj.* pucka.

Pu·las·ki (pū·las'ki), *n.* Count Casimir, 1748–1779, Polish nobleman who was a general in the American Revolutionary army.

pul·chri·tude (pul'krə·tūd; –tüd), *n.* beauty. [< L, < *pulcher* beautiful] —**pul·chri·tu·di·nous** (pul'krə·tü'də·nəs; –tū'–), *adj. Am.*

pule (pūl), *v.,* puled, pul·ing. cry in a thin voice, as a sick child does; whimper; whine. —**pul'er,** *n.* —**pul'ing,** *adj.* —**pul'ing·ly,** *adv.*

Pu·litz·er Prize (pū'lit·sər; pûl'it–), *Am.* any one of various annual prizes for the best American drama, novel, biography, history, book of verse, editorial, and cartoon, established by Joseph Pulitzer, an American journalist, 1847–1911, and first awarded in 1917.

pull (pul), *v.* **1.** draw or haul toward oneself or itself, or in a particular direction, or into a particular position: *pull a trigger, pull a sled up a hill.* **2.** tug with the fingers, etc.: *pull at one's tie.* **3.** move, usually with effort or force: *the train pulled out of the station.* **4.** draw out; extract: *pull a tooth.* **5.** be drawn: *this yarn pulls apart easily.* **6.** tear; rip. **7.** stretch too far; strain: *the runner pulled a ligament in his leg.* **8.** row: *pull for the shore.* **9.** be provided or rowed with: *the boat pulls eight oars.* **10.** hold back, esp. to keep from winning: *pull one's punches in a fight.* **11.** *Slang.* perform; carry through: *don't pull any tricks.* **12.** *Printing.* take (an impression or proof). **13.** pull oneself together, gather one's faculties, energy, etc. **14.** pull through, get through a difficult or dangerous situation. **15.** pull together, work in harmony; get on together. —*n.* **1.** act or effort of pulling. **2.** force expended in pulling. **3.** act of rowing. **4.** a difficult climb, journey, or other effort. **5.** handle, rope, ring, or other thing to pull by. **6.** *Am., Slang.* influence; advantage. [OE *pullian*] —**pull'er,** *n.* —**Syn.** *v.* **1.** drag, tow.

pul·let (pul'it), *n.* a young hen, usually less than a year old. [< OF *poulette,* dim. of *poule* hen < L *pulla*]

pul·ley (pul'i), *n., pl.* –leys. **1.** wheel with a grooved rim in which a rope can run, and so change the direction of the pull. **2.** set of such wheels used to increase the power applied. [< OF *poulie,* ult. < Gk. *polos* axle]

PULLEY

Pull·man (pul'mən), or **Pullman car,** *n.* **1.** a railroad car with berths and small rooms for passengers to sleep in. **2.** a railroad car with specially comfortable seats; parlor car. [after G. M. Pullman, the inventor]

pull·o·ver (pul'ō'vər), *n.* sweater put on by pulling it over the head.

pul·mo·nar·y (pul'mə·ner'i), *adj.* **1.** of or pertaining to the lungs. Tuberculosis and pneumonia are pulmonary diseases. **2.** having lungs. [< L, < *pulmo* lung]

Pul·mo·tor (pul'mō'tər; pûl'–), *n. Trademark.* device for producing artificial breathing, for use on persons who have almost drowned or smothered. [< L *pulmo* lung + E *motor*]

pulp (pulp), *n.* **1.** the soft part of any fruit or vegetable. **2.** the soft inner part of a tooth, containing blood vessels and nerves. **3.** any soft wet mass. Paper is made from wood pulp. **4.** *Am., Slang.* magazine printed on cheap paper, and usually containing matter of a cheap, sensational nature. —*v.* reduce to pulp. [< L *pulpa*] —**pulp'er,** *n.* —**pulp'y,** *adj.* —**pulp'i·ness,** *n.*

pul·pit (pul'pit), *n.* **1.** platform or raised structure in a church from which the minister preaches. **2.** the pulpit, preachers or preachings. [< LL *pulpitum* < L, scaffold, platform]

pulp·wood (pulp'wŭd'), n. 1. wood reduced to pulp for making paper. 2. wood suitable for making paper.

pul·que (pŭl'kā; pŭl'ki), n. Am. an alcoholic drink made from the fermented juice of the agave, much used in Mexico and Central America. [< Sp. < Mex. dial.]

pul·sate (pul'sāt), v., -sat·ed, -sat·ing. 1. expand and contract rhythmically; beat; throb. 2. vibrate; quiver. [< L pulsatus, pp. of pulsare, frequentative of pellere to beat. Doublet of PUSH.] —**pul·sa'tion**, n. —**pul·sa·tive** (pul'sə-tiv), **pul·sa·to·ry** (pul'sə·tô'ri; -tō'-), adj.

pulse[1] (puls), n., v., pulsed, puls·ing. —n. 1. the beating of the heart; changing flow of blood in the arteries caused by the beating of the heart. 2. any regular, measured beat. 3. feeling; sentiment: the pulse of the nation. —v. beat; throb; vibrate. [< L pulsus < pellere to beat]

pulse[2] (puls), n. peas, beans, and lentils, used as food. [< OF < L puls porridge]

pulse·jet (puls'jet'), n. a type of jet engine into which the air necessary for the burning of the fuel is admitted by valves in spurts.

pul·ver·ize (pul'vər·īz), v., -ized, -iz·ing. 1. grind to powder or dust. 2. become dust. 3. break to pieces; demolish. [< LL pulverizare < L pulvis dust] —**pul'ver·iz'a·ble**, adj. —**pul'ver·i·za'tion**, n. —**pul'ver·iz'er**, n.

pu·ma (pū'mə), n. cougar [< Sp. < Kechua (S Am.Ind.)]

pum·ice (pum'is), n., v., -iced, -ic·ing. —n. Also, **pumice stone**, a light, spongy stone thrown up from volcanoes, used for cleaning, smoothing, and polishing. —v. clean, smooth, or polish with pumice. [< OF < L pumex] —**pu·mi·ceous** (pū-mish'əs), adj.

pum·mel (pum'əl), v., -meled, -mel·ing; esp. Brit. -melled, -mel·ling. pommel.

pump[1] (pump), n. apparatus or machine for forcing liquids, air, or gas into or out of things. —v. 1. move (liquids, air, etc.) by a pump. 2. blow air into. 3. remove water, etc., from by a pump. 4. work a pump. 5. work as a pump does. 6. move up and down like a pump handle. 7. move by, or as if by, a pump handle: he pumped my hand. 8. draw, force, etc., as if from a pump. 9. get information out of; try to get information out of. [appar. < F pompe, ? < Gmc.] —**pump'er**, n.

Hand pump: A and B, valves; C, water

pump[2] (pump), n. a low shoe with no fasteners.

pum·per·nick·el (pum'pər·nik'əl), n. Am. a heavy, dark bread made of unbolted rye. [< G]

pump·kin (pump'kin; pung'kin), n. 1. a large, roundish, orange-yellow fruit of a trailing vine, used for making pies, as food for stock, etc. 2. vine that it grows on. [alter. (with substitution of -KIN) of earlier pumpion < L < Gk. pepon]

pun (pun), n., v., punned, pun·ning. —n. a humorous use of a word where it can have different meanings; play on words. —v. make puns. —**pun'ner**, n. —**pun'ning·ly**, adv.

punch[1] (punch), v. 1. hit with the fist. 2. Am. herd or drive cattle. —n. 1. a quick thrust or blow. 2. Colloq. vigorous force or effectiveness. [? var. of pounce] —**punch'er**, n. —Syn. v. 1. strike, poke, thump.

punch[3] (punch), v. 1. pierce, cut, stamp, force, or drive with a punch: the train conductor punches tickets. 2. make (a hole) with a punch or any pointed instrument. —n. 1. a tool or apparatus for piercing, perforating, or stamping materials, impressing a design, forcing nails beneath a surface, driving bolts out of holes, and the like. 2. tool for making holes. [short for puncheon a stamping tool used by goldsmiths] —**punch'er**, n. —Syn. v. 2. puncture.

punch[3] (punch), n. drink made of different liquids mixed together. [prob. < Hind. panc five, through number of ingredients in drink]

Punch (punch), n. 1. a hook-nosed, humpbacked doll who quarrels violently with his wife

Judy in the puppet show **Punch and Judy**. 2. pleased as Punch, very much pleased. [var. of punchinello]

pun·cheon (pun'chən), n. 1. a large cask for liquor. 2. amount that it holds. 3. Am. slab of timber, or a piece of a split log, with the face roughly smoothed. [< OF poinchon, ult. < L pungere pierce]

pun·chi·nel·lo (pun'chə·nel'ō), n., pl. -los, -loes. clown. [< dial. Ital. Pulcinella, prob. ult. < L pullus chick]

punching bag, a leather bag filled with air or stuffed, to be hung up and punched with the fists for exercise.

punc·til·i·o (pungk·til'i·ō), n., pl. -i·os. 1. detail of honor, conduct, ceremony, etc. 2. care in attending to such details. [< Ital. < Sp. puntillo, ult. < L punctum point]

punc·til·i·ous (pungk·til'i·əs), adj. 1. very careful and exact: be punctilious in obeying the doctor's orders. 2. paying strict attention to details of conduct and ceremony. —**punc·til'i·ous·ly**, adv. —**punc·til'i·ous·ness**, n. —Syn. 1. precise, scrupulous. 2. particular. —Ant. 1. negligent.

punc·tu·al (pungk'chù·əl), adj. prompt; on time: punctual to the minute. [< Med.L, < L punctus POINT] —**punc'tu·al'i·ty**, **punc'tu·al·ness**, n. —**punc'tu·al·ly**, adv.

punc·tu·ate (pungk'chù·āt), v., -at·ed, -at·ing. 1. use periods, commas, and other marks to help make the meaning clear. 2. put punctuation marks in. 3. interrupt now and then. 4. give point or emphasis to: he punctuated his remarks with gestures. [< Med.L, < L punctus POINT] —**punc'tu·a'tor**, n.

punc·tu·a·tion (pungk'chù·ā'shən), n. use of periods, commas, and other marks to help make the meaning clear. ≻ See pp. 21–24 for a discussion of punctuation.

punctuation marks, marks used in writing or printing to help make the meaning clear, such as periods, commas, question marks, colons, etc.

punc·ture (pungk'chər), n., v., -tured, -turing. —n. 1. hole made by something pointed. 2. act or process of puncturing. —v. 1. make a hole in with something pointed. 2. have or get a puncture. 3. reduce, spoil, or destroy as if by a puncture. [< L punctura < pungere prick] —**punc'tur·a·ble**, adj. —Syn. v. 1. pierce, prick, perforate.

pun·dit (pun'dit), n. 1. a very learned Hindu. 2. any very learned person; expert; authority. [< Hind. < Skt. pandita learned]

pun·gent (pun'jənt), adj. 1. sharply affecting the organs of taste and smell: the pungent smell of burning leaves. 2. sharp; biting: pungent criticism. 3. acutely distressing. 4. stimulating to the mind; keen; lively: a pungent wit [< L pungens pricking] —**pun'gen·cy**, n. —**pun'gent·ly**, adv. —Syn. 1. piquant, spicy. 2. caustic, sarcastic, 3. poignant.

pun·ish (pun'ish), v. 1. cause pain, loss, or discomfort to for some fault or offense: punish a disobedient child. 2. cause pain, loss, or discomfort for: punish theft. 3. Colloq. deal with severely, roughly, or greedily. [< OF puniss- < L < poena penalty] —**pun'ish·a·ble**, adj. —**pun'ish·a·bil'i·ty**, **pun'ish·a·ble·ness**, n. —**pun'isher**, n. —Syn. 1. chastise, chasten, discipline.

pun·ish·ment (pun'ish·mənt), n. 1. a punishing or being punished. 2. something inflicted as a penalty in punishing. 3. pain, suffering, or loss. 4. Colloq. severe or rough treatment.

pu·ni·tive (pū'nə·tiv), **pu·ni·to·ry** (-tô'ri; -tō'-), adj. 1. concerned with punishment. 2. inflicting punishment. —**pu'ni·tive·ly**, adv. —**pu'ni·tive·ness**, n.

Pun·jab (pun·jäb'; pun'jäb), n. a former province in N India, now divided between the republic of India and Pakistan.

punk (pungk), Am. —n. 1. a preparation that burns very slowly, often used to light fireworks. 2. decayed wood used as tinder. —adj. Slang. poor or bad in quality. [? < Am.Ind.]

pun·ster (pun'stər), n. person fond of making puns.

punt[1] (punt), *n.* **1.** a shallow, flat-bottomed boat having square ends, usually moved by pushing with a pole against the bottom of a river, etc. **2.** kick given to a football dropped from the hands before it touches the ground. —*v.* **1.** propel (a boat) by pushing with a pole against the bottom of a river, pond, etc. **2.** kick (a football) before it touches the ground after dropping it from the hands. [< L *ponto*] —**punt′er,** *n.*

punt[2] (punt), *v.* **1.** bet against the banker in a card game. **2.** gamble. [< F *ponter* < Sp., ult. < L *punctum* point] —**punt′er,** *n.*

pu·ny (pū′ni), *adj.,* **-ni·er, -ni·est. 1.** of less than usual size and strength; weak. **2.** petty; not important. [< OF *puisne* later-born < *puis* (ult. < L *postea*) afterwards + *ne* born < L *natus*] —**pu′ni·ly,** *adv.* —**pu′ni·ness,** *n.* —**Syn. 1.** undeveloped, stunted, small, feeble. **2.** trivial, insignificant. —**Ant. 1.** robust.

pup (pup), *n., v.,* **pupped, pup·ping.** —*n.* **1.** a young dog; puppy. **2.** a young fox, wolf, seal, etc. **3.** a silly, conceited young man. —*v.* bring forth pups. [var. of *puppy*]

pu·pa (pū′pə), *n., pl.* **-pae** (-pē), **-pas. 1.** stage between the larva and the adult in the development of many insects. **2.** form of an insect in this stage. Most pupae are inactive and some, such as those of many moths, are enclosed in a tough case or cocoon. [special NL use of L, girl, doll] —**pu′pal,** *adj.*

pu·pil[1] (pū′pəl), *n.* person who is learning in school or being taught by someone. [< OF < L *pupillus, pupilla* ward < *pupus* boy, *pupa* girl] —**pu′pil·like′,** *adj.* —**Syn.** scholar, student, learner.

pu·pil[2] (pū′pəl), *n.* the expanding and contracting opening in the iris of the eye, through which light passes to the retina. [< L *pupilla,* orig., little doll, dim. of *pupa* girl, doll]

pup·pet (pup′it), *n.* **1.** a small doll. **2.** figure made to look like a person and moved by wires, strings, or the hands. **3.** anybody who is not independent, waits to be told how to act, and does what somebody else says. [earlier *poppet* < F, < L *pupa* girl, doll]

pup·py (pup′i), *n., pl.* **-pies. 1.** a young dog. **2.** a silly, conceited young man. [prob. < F *poupée* doll, ult. < L *pupa*] —**pup′py·hood,** *n.*

pur (pėr), *n., v.,* **purred, pur·ring. purr.**

pur·blind (pėr′blīnd′), *adj.* **1.** nearly blind. **2.** slow to discern or understand. [earlier *pur blind* pure blind] —**pur′blind·ly,** *adv.* —**pur′blind·ness,** *n.*

pur·chase (pėr′chəs), *v.,* **-chased, -chas·ing,** *n.* —*v.* **1.** get by paying a price; buy. **2.** get in return for something: *purchase safety at the cost of happiness.* **3.** hoist, haul, or draw by the aid of some mechanical device. —*n.* **1.** act of buying. **2.** thing bought. **3.** a firm hold to help move something or to keep from slipping. **4.** device for obtaining such a hold. [< AF *purchacer* pursue < *pur-* forth (< L *pro-*) + *chacer* CHASE[1]] —**pur′chas·a·ble,** *adj.* —**pur′chas·er,** *n.*

pur·dah (pėr′də), *n.* in India, a curtain serving to screen women from the sight of men or strangers. [< Hind. < Pers. *pardah* veil, curtain]

pure (pyúr), *adj.* **1.** not mixed with anything else; unadulterated; genuine: *pure gold.* **2.** perfectly clean; spotless: *pure hands.* **3.** perfect; correct; without defects: *speak pure French.* **4.** nothing else than; mere; sheer: *pure accident.* **5.** with no evil; without sin; chaste: *the pure in heart.* **6.** abstract or theoretical (opposed to *applied*): *pure mathematics.* **7.** of unmixed descent: *a pure Indian family.* —*n.* that which is pure. [< OF < L *purus*] —**pure′ly,** *adv.* —**pure′ness,** *n.* —**Syn.** *adj.* **1.** unalloyed. **2.** immaculate. **3.** faultless. **4.** utter, absolute. **5.** virtuous, innocent.

pu·rée, pu·ree (pyú·rā′; pyúr′ā), *n., v.,* **-réed, -ré·ing; -reed, -re·ing.** —*n.* **1.** food boiled to a pulp and pushed through a sieve. **2.** a thick soup. —*v.* make into a purée. [< F, < *purer* to strain]

pur·ga·tion (pėr·gā′shən), *n.* a purging.

pur·ga·tive (pėr′gə·tiv), *n.* medicine that empties the bowels. —*adj.* purging. —**pur′ga·tive·ly,** *adv.* —**pur′ga·tive·ness,** *n.*

pur·ga·to·ry (pėr′gə·tô′ri; -tō′-), *n., pl.* **-ries. 1.** in the belief of the Roman Catholics, a temporary condition or place in which the souls of those who have died penitent are purified from venial sin or the effects of sin by punishment. **2.** any condition or place of temporary suffering or punishment. [< Med.L *purgatorium,* orig. neut. adj., purging < L *purgare* PURGE] —**pur′ga·to′ri·al,** *adj.*

purge (pėrj), *v.,* **purged, purg·ing,** *n.* —*v.* **1.** wash away all that is not clean from; make clean. **2.** become clean. **3.** clear of any undesired thing or person, such as air in a water pipe or opponents in a nation. **4.** empty (the bowels). —*n.* **1.** act of purging. **2.** medicine that purges. **3.** elimination of undesired persons from a nation or party. [< OF < L *purgare* cleanse, ult. < *purus* pure + *agere* drive] —**purge′a·ble,** *adj.* —**purg′er,** *n.*

pu·ri·fy (pyúr′ə·fī), *v.,* **-fied, -fy·ing. 1.** make pure. **2.** become pure. [< OF < L, < *purus* pure + *facere* make] —**pu′ri·fi·ca′tion,** *n.* —**pu′ri·fi′er,** *n.* —**Syn. 1.** cleanse, purge.

pur·ism (pyúr′iz·əm), *n.* **1.** avoidance of all words and expressions that are not acceptable. **2.** insistence that others do this. —**pur′ist,** *n.* —**pu·ris′tic, pu·ris′ti·cal,** *adj.*

Pu·ri·tan (pyúr′ə·tən), *n.* **1.** member of a group in the Church of England during the 16th and 17th centuries who wanted simpler forms of worship and stricter morals. Many Puritans settled in New England. **2. puritan,** person who is very strict in morals and religion. —*adj.* **1.** of the Puritans. **2. puritan,** very strict in morals and religion. —**Pu′ri·tan·ism, pu′ri·tan·ism,** *n.* —**Syn.** *adj.* **2.** austere, straitlaced, puritanical.

pu·ri·tan·i·cal (pyúr′ə·tan′ə·kəl), **pu·ri·tan·ic** (-ik), *adj.* very strict or too strict in morals or religion. —**pu′ri·tan′i·cal·ly,** *adv.* —**pu′ri·tan′i·cal·ness,** *n.*

pu·ri·ty (pyúr′ə·ti), *n.* **1.** freedom from dirt or mixture; clearness; cleanness. **2.** freedom from evil; innocence. **3.** freedom from foreign or inappropriate elements or characteristics; correctness: *purity of style.* [< L, < *purus* pure]

purl[1] (pėrl), *v.* flow with rippling motions and a murmuring sound. —*n.* a purling motion or sound. [? < Scand. (Norw.) *purla*]

purl[2] (pėrl), *v.* knit with inverted stitches. —*n.* inversion of stitches in knitting, producing a ribbed appearance. [< *pirl* twist, of uncert. orig.]

pur·lieu (pėr′lū), *n.* **1.** piece of land on the border of a forest, esp. one formerly included in the forest and still in part subject to the forest laws. **2.** one's haunt or resort; one's bounds. **3.** any frequenting, neighboring, or outlying region or district. [alter. of earlier *puraley* (infl. by F *lieu* place) < AF, < *poraler* go through]

pur·loin (pėr·loin′), *v.* steal. [< AF *purloigner* remove < *pur-* forth (< L *pro-*) + *loin* afar < L *longe*] —**pur·loin′er,** *n.*

pur·ple (pėr′pəl), *n., adj., v.,* **-pled, -pling.** —*n.* **1.** a dark color made by mixing red and blue. **2.** purple cloth or clothing, esp. as worn by emperors, kings, etc., to indicate high rank. **3.** imperial, royal, or high rank: *a prince is born to the purple.* —*adj.* **1.** of the color of purple. **2.** imperial; royal. **3.** brilliant; gorgeous; gaudy. —*v.* make or become purple. [< L < Gk. *porphyra,* a shellfish, or the purple dye from it] —**pur′plish, pur′ply,** *adj.*

purple martin, *Am.* a large, blue-black swallow of the U.S.

pur·port (*v.* pėr·pôrt′, -pōrt′, pėr′pôrt, -pōrt; *n.* pėr′pôrt, -pōrt), *v.* **1.** claim; profess: *the document purported to be official.* **2.** have as its main idea; mean. —*n.* meaning; main idea. [< AF < *pur-* forth (< L *pro-*) + *porter* carry < L *portare*] —**pur′port·less,** *adj.* —**Syn.** *n.* sense, gist, signification.

pur·pose (pėr′pəs), *n., v.,* **-posed, -pos·ing.** —*n.* **1.** something one has in mind to get or do;

plan; aim; intention. 2. object or end for which a thing is made, done, used, etc. 3. **on purpose,** with a purpose; not by accident. 4. **to good purpose,** with good results. 5. **to little** or **no purpose,** with few or no results. —*v.* plan; aim; intend. [< OF *purposer* PROPOSE] —**pur′pose·ful,** *adj.* —**pur′pose·ful·ly,** *adv.* —**pur′pose·ful·ness,** *n.* —**pur′pose·less,** *adj.* —**pur′pose·less·ly,** *adv.* —**pur′pose·less·ness,** *n.* —Syn. *n.* 1. intent, design. —*v.* propose, contemplate, design.

pur·pose·ly (pér′pəs·li), *adv.* on purpose; intentionally.

purr (pér), *n.* a low murmuring sound such as a cat makes when pleased. —*v.* make this sound. Also, **pur.** [imit.]

purse (pérs), *n.*, *v.*, **pursed, purs·ing.** —*n.* 1. a little bag or case for carrying money around with one. 2. money; resources; treasury. 3. sum of money: *a purse was made up for the victims of the fire.* —*v.* draw together; press into folds or wrinkles. [< LL < Gk. *byrsa* hide, skin]

purs·er (pér′sər), *n.* officer who keeps the accounts of a ship, pays wages, and attends to other matters of business.

purs·lane (pérs′lān; –lin), *n.* a common plant that has small, yellow flowers and small, thick leaves. [< OF *porcelaine,* alter. of L *porcilaca,* var. of *portulaca*]

pur·su·ance (pər·sü′əns), *n.* a following; carrying out; pursuit: *in pursuance of his duty, the policeman risked his life.*

pur·su·ant (pər·sü′ənt), *adj.* pursuant to, following; acting according to; in accordance with. —**pur·su′ant·ly,** *adv.*

Purslane

pur·sue (pər·sü′), *v.*, **–sued, –su·ing.** 1. follow to catch or kill; chase. 2. proceed along; follow in action; follow: *pursue a wise course.* 3. strive for; try to get; seek: *pursue pleasure.* 4. carry on; keep on with: *pursue the study of French.* 5. continue to annoy or trouble: *pursue a teacher with questions.* [< AF *pursuer* < L *prosequi.* See PROSECUTE.] —**pur·su′a·ble,** *adj.* —**pur·su′er,** *n.* —Syn. 1. hunt, track.

pur·suit (pər·süt′), *n.* 1. act of pursuing: *in pursuit of a fleeing enemy.* 2. the pursuing of something to be gained or attained: *pursuit of wealth.* 3. occupation: *literary pursuits.*

pursuit plane, a fighter aircraft that has high speed, a high rate of climb, and can be maneuvered with ease.

pur·sui·vant (pér′swi·vənt), *n.* 1. officer below a herald in rank. 2. follower; attendant. [< OF *poursuivant* pursuing. See PURSUE.]

pur·sy (pér′si), *adj.*, **–si·er, –si·est.** 1. short-winded or puffy. 2. fat. [< AF *pursif,* var. of OF *polsif* < *polser* pant, PULSATE] —**pur′si·ness,** *n.*

pu·ru·lent (pyúr′ə·lənt; pyúr′yə-), *adj.* full of pus; discharging pus; like pus. [< L *purulentus* < *pus* pus] —**pu′ru·lence, pu′ru·len·cy,** *n.* —**pu′ru·lent·ly,** *adv.*

pur·vey (pər·vā′), *v.* supply (food or provisions); provide; furnish: *purvey meat for an army.* [< AF *porveier* < L *providere.* Doublet of PROVIDE.] —**pur·vey′a·ble,** *adj.* —**pur·vey′or,** *n.*

pur·vey·ance (pər·vā′əns), *n.* 1. a purveying. 2. provisions; supplies.

pur·view (pér′vū), *n.* range of operation, activity, concern, etc.; scope; extent. [< AF *purveu,* orig. pp. of *porveier* purvey]

pus (pus), *n.* a yellowish-white liquid formed by inflammation of infected tissue in the body, that consists of white blood cells, bacteria, serum, etc. [< L] —**pus′sy,** *adj.*

push (púsh), *v.* 1. move (something) away by pressing against it. 2. move up, down, back, forward, etc., by pressing: *push him outdoors.* 3. move from shore. 4. thrust. 5. press hard: *push with all one's might.* 6. go forward by force: *push on at rapid pace.* 7. force (one's way). 8. make go forward; urge: *he pushed his plans cleverly.* 9. continue with; follow up: *push a claim.* 10. extend: *Alexander pushed his conquests still farther east.* 11. urge the use, sale,

etc., of. —*n.* 1. act of pushing. 2. hard effort; determined advance. 3. *Colloq.* force; energy. [< OF < L *pulsare* beat, PULSATE. Doublet of PULSATE.] —**push′er,** *n.* —**push′ing,** *adj.* —**push′ing·ly,** *adv.* —Syn. *v.* 2. shove, drive. 8. hasten, promote.

push button, *Am.* a small button or knob pushed to turn an electric current on or off.

push·cart (púsh′kärt′), *n.* a light cart pushed by hand.

Push·kin (púsh′kin), *n.* Alexander, 1799–1837, Russian poet and writer.

push·o·ver (púsh′ō′vər), *n. Am., Slang.* 1. something very easy to do. 2. person very easy to beat in a contest.

pu·sil·lan·i·mous (pū′sə·lan′ə·məs), *adj.* cowardly; mean-spirited; faint-hearted. [< L, < *pusillus* little + *animus* courage] —**pu·sil·la·nim·i·ty** (pū′sə·lə·nim′ə·ti), *n.* —**pu′sil·lan′i·mous·ly,** *adv.* —Syn. timorous, spiritless, feeble. —Ant. brave, valiant, courageous.

puss (pús), *n.* 1. cat. 2. hare. 3. girl.

puss·y (pús′i), *n., pl.* **puss·ies.** cat.

puss·y·foot (pús′i·fút′), *v., n., pl.* **–foots.** *Slang.* —*v. Am.* 1. move softly and cautiously to avoid being seen. 2. be cautious and timid about revealing one's opinions or committing oneself. —*n.* person who pussyfoots. —**puss′y·foot′er,** *n. Am.* —**puss′y·foot′ing,** *n., adj.*

pussy willow, *Am.* a small American willow with silky catkins.

pus·tule (pus′chúl), *n.* 1. pimple containing pus. 2. any swelling like a pimple or blister, such as the pustules of chicken pox. [< L, < *pus* pus] —**pus·tu·lar** (pus′-chə·lər), *adj.*

Pussy willow

put (pút), *v.*, **put, put·ting,** *n.* —*v.* 1. cause to be in some place or position; place; lay: *put your hand in mine.* 2. cause to be in some state, condition, position, relation, etc.: *the murderer was put to death.* 3. express: *a teacher should put things clearly.* 4. propose or submit for answer, consideration, deliberation, etc.: *put a question.* 5. take one's course; go; turn; proceed: *the ship put out to sea.* 6. throw or cast (a 16-lb. ball, etc.) from the hand placed close to the shoulder. 7. set at a particular place, point, amount, etc., in a scale of estimation; appraise: *he puts the distance at five miles.* 8. apply: *a doctor puts his skill to good use.* 9. impose: *put a tax on gasoline.* 10. assign; attribute: *he put a wrong construction on my action.* 11. **put about, a.** put (a ship) on the opposite tack. **b.** change direction. 12. **put aside, away,** or **by,** save for future use. 13. **put down, a.** put an end to; suppress. **b.** write down. **c.** pay as a down payment. 14. **put in, a.** *Colloq.* spend (time) as specified. **b.** enter port. **c.** enter a place for safety, supplies, etc. 15. **put off, a.** lay aside; postpone. **b.** bid or cause to wait. **c.** get rid of. 16. **put on, a.** take on oneself. **b.** pretend. 17. **put out, a.** extinguish (fire). **b.** confuse; embarrass. **c.** distract, disturb, or interrupt. **d.** destroy (an eye, etc.). **e.** cause to be out in a game. **f.** publish. 18. **put through,** carry out successfully. 19. **put to it,** force to a course; put in difficulty. 20. **put up, a.** offer; give; show. **b.** make. **c.** build. **d.** lay aside. **e.** put in usual place. **f.** preserve (fruit, etc.). **g.** give lodging or food to. **h.** *Colloq.* incite. **i.** *Slang.* plan beforehand craftily. 21. **put upon,** impose upon; take advantage of; victimize. 22. **put up with,** bear with patience; tolerate. —*n.* a throw or cast. [cf. OE *putung* impulse] —Syn. *v.* 1. set, deposit.

pu·ta·tive (pū′tə·tiv), *adj.* supposed; reputed. [< L, < *putare* think] —**pu′ta·tive·ly,** *adv.*

pu·tre·fac·tion (pū′trə·fak′shən), *n.* decay; rotting. —**pu′tre·fac′tive,** *adj.*

pu·tre·fy (pū′trə·fī), *v.*, **–fied, –fy·ing.** rot; decay. [< OF < L, ult. < *puter* rotten + *fieri* become] —**pu′tre·fi′er,** *n.* —Syn. decompose.

pu·tres·cent (pū·tres′ənt), *adj.* 1. becoming putrid; rotting. 2. pertaining to putrefaction. [< L *putrescens* growing rotten, ult. < *puter* rotten] —**pu·tres′cence,** *n.*

pu·trid (pū′trid), *adj.* 1. rotten; foul. 2. thoroughly corrupt or depraved; extremely bad. [< L *putridus*, ult. < *puter* rotten] **—pu'trid·ly,** *adv.* **—pu'trid·ness, pu·trid'i·ty,** *n.*

Putsch (pŭch), *n. German.* uprising; insurrection.

putt (put), *v.* strike (a golf ball) gently and carefully in an effort to make it roll into the hole. —*n.* the stroke itself. [var. of *put*]

put·tee, put·ty (put'ĭ; pu·tē'), *n., pl.* **-tees; -ties.** 1. a long, narrow strip of cloth wound round the leg from ankle to knee, worn by sportsmen, soldiers, etc. 2. gaiter of cloth or leather reaching from ankle to knee, worn by soldiers, riders, etc. [< Hind. *paṭṭī* bandage, strip]

put·ter¹ (put'ər), *v.* keep busy in a rather useless way. Also, *esp. Brit.* **potter.** [var. of *potter²*] **—put'ter·er,** *n.*

putt·er² (put'ər), *n.* 1. person who putts. 2. a golf club used in putting.

put·ter³ (put'ər), *n.* one that puts.

putt·ing green (put'ĭng), the smooth turf or sand around a golf hole.

put·ty (put'ĭ), *n., pl.* **-ties,** *v.,* **-tied, -ty·ing.** —*n.* a soft mixture of whiting and linseed oil, used for fastening panes of glass, etc. —*v.* stop up or cover with putty. [< F *potée*, orig., potful < *pot* pot] **—put'ti·er,** *n.*

put-up (pŭt'up'), *adj. Colloq.* planned beforehand, or deliberately, in a secret or crafty manner.

puz·zle (puz'əl), *n., v.,* **-zled, -zling.** —*n.* 1. a hard problem. 2. problem or task to be done for fun. 3. puzzled condition. —*v.* 1. make unable to answer, solve, or understand something; perplex. 2. be perplexed. 3. exercise one's mind on something hard. 4. puzzle out, find out by thinking or trying hard. 5. puzzle over, think hard about; try hard to do or work out. **—puz'zle·ment,** *n.* **—puz'zler,** *n.* **—Syn.** *n.* 3. bewilderment, quandary. —*v.* 1. bewilder, mystify.

Pvt., Private.

PWA, Public Works Administration.

pwt., pennyweight.

PX, P.X., Post Exchange.

py·e·mi·a, py·ae·mi·a (pī·ē'mi·ə), *n.* form of blood poisoning caused by bacteria that produce pus. [< NL, < Gk. *pyon* pus + *haima* blood]

Pyg·ma·li·on (pig·māl'i·ən; -māl'yən), *n.* a Greek sculptor who fell in love with a statue he had made.

pyg·my (pig'mĭ), *n., pl.* **-mies,** *adj.* —*n.* 1. a very small person; dwarf. 2. **Pygmy,** member of any of various Negroid races of Africa, SE Asia, Philippine Islands, etc. —*adj.* very small. Also, **pigmy, Pigmy.** [< L < Gk. *pygmaioi*, orig. pl. adj., dwarfish < *pygme* cubit, fist]

py·ja·mas (pə·jä'məz; -jam'əz), *n.pl. Esp. Brit.* pajamas.

py·lon (pī'lon), *n.* 1. post or tower for guiding aviators. 2. a tall steel framework used to carry high-tension wires across country. 3. gateway, particularly of an Egyptian temple. [< Gk., gateway, < *pyle* gate]

py·lo·rus (pī·lô'rəs; -lō'-; pə-), *n., pl.* **-ri** (-rī). the opening that leads from the stomach into the intestine. [< LL < Gk. *pyloros*, orig., gatekeeper < *pyle* gate + *horos* watching] **—py·lor·ic** (pī·lôr'ĭk; -lor'-; pə-), *adj.*

Pyong·yang (pyung'yäng'), *n.* capital of North Korea.

py·or·rhe·a, py·or·rhoe·a (pī'ə·rē'ə), *n.* disease of the gums in which pockets of pus

form about the teeth, the gums shrink, and the teeth become loose. [< NL, < Gk. *pyon* pus + *rhoia* a flow < *rhein* to flow] **—py'or·rhe'al, py'or·rhoe'al,** *adj.*

Pyramids

pyr·a·mid (pir'ə·mid), *n.* 1. a solid having triangular sides meeting in a point. 2. thing or things having the form of a pyramid. 3. the **Pyramids,** the huge, massive stone pyramids, serving as royal tombs, built by the ancient Egyptians. —*v.* 1. be or put in the form of a pyramid. 2. raise or increase (costs, wages, etc.) gradually. 3. increase (one's operations) in buying or selling stock on margin by using the profits to buy or sell more. [< L < Gk. *pyramis* < Egyptian] **—py·ram·i·dal** (pə·ram'ə·dəl), *adj.* **—pyr·am'i·dal·ly,** *adv.* **—pyr'a·mid'ic, pyr'a·mid'i·cal,** *adj.* **—pyr'a·mid'i·cal·ly,** *adv.*

pyre (pir), *n.* 1. pile of wood for burning a dead body. 2. any pile to be burned. [< L *pyra* < Gk., < *pyr* fire]

Pyr·e·nees (pir'ə·nēz), *n.pl.* mountain range between France and Spain. **—Pyr·e·ne·an** (pir'ə·nē'ən), *adj.*

py·ret·ic (pī·ret'ĭk), *adj.* 1. of or having to do with fever. 2. producing fever. 3. feverish. [< NL, < Gk. *pyretos* fever < *pyr* fire]

Py·rex (pī'reks), *Am.* —*n. Trademark.* kind of glassware that will not break when heated. —*adj.* Also, **pyrex.** made of Pyrex.

pyr·i·dox·ine (pir'ə·dok'sēn; -sin), *n.* vitamin B_6, $C_8H_{11}O_3N$, essential to human nutrition, found in wheat germ, fish liver, etc.

py·ri·tes (pī·rī'tēz; pə-; pī'rīts), *n.* 1. iron pyrites, a mineral which has a yellow color and glitters so that it suggests gold; fool's gold. 2. any of various compounds of sulfur and a metal. [< L < Gk., flint, < *pyr* fire]

py·rog·ra·phy (pī·rog'rə·fĭ; pī-), *n.* art of burning designs on wood, leather, etc. [< *pyro-* (< Gk. *pyr* fire) + *-graphy* < Gk. *graphein* write] **—py·ro·graph·ic** (pī'rə·graf'ĭk; pir'ə-), *adj.*

py·ro·ma·ni·a (pī'rə·mā'ni·ə), *n.* an insane desire to set things on fire. [< *pyro-* (< Gk. *pyr* fire) + *mania*] **—py·ro·ma·ni·ac** (pī'rə·mā'ni·ak), *n.* **—py·ro·ma·ni·a·cal** (pī'rə·mə·nī'ə·kəl), *adj.*

py·ro·tech·nics (pī'rə·tek'niks), *n.* 1. Also, **py'ro·tech'ny. a.** the making of fireworks. **b.** use of fireworks. **c.** display of fireworks. 2. a brilliant or sensational display. [< *pyro-* (< Gk. *pyr* fire) + *technics*] **—py'ro·tech'nic, py'ro·tech'ni·cal,** *adj.*

py·rox·y·lin, py·rox·y·line (pī·rok'sə·lin), *n.* any of various substances made by nitrating certain forms of cellulose, as guncotton.

Pyr·rhic victory (pir'ĭk), victory won at too great cost, so named after Pyr·rhus (pir'əs), a Greek king, 318?–272 B.C., who invaded Italy and won a battle but with an enormous loss of life.

Py·thag·o·ras (pi·thag'ə·rəs), *n.* 582?–500? B.C., Greek philosopher, religious teacher, and mathematician. **—Py·thag·o·re·an** (pi·thag'ə·rē'ən), *adj., n.*

Pyth·i·as (pith'i·əs), *n. Roman Legend.* man famous for his devoted friendship with Damon.

py·thon (pī'thon; -thən), *n.* 1. any of several large snakes of the Old World that are related to the boas and kill their prey by crushing. 2. any large boa. [< L < Gk.]

Q

Q, q (kū), *n., pl.* **Q's; q's.** the 17th letter of the alphabet.

Q., question.

q., 1. quart. 2. question.

Q.E.D., which was to be proved. [< L *quod erat demonstrandum*]

qt., 1. quantity. 2. *pl.* **qt., qts.** quart.

quack¹ (kwak), *n.* sound a duck makes. —*v.* make such a sound. [imit.] **—quack'y,** *adj.*

quack² (kwak), *n.* 1. a dishonest person who pretends to be a doctor. 2. an ignorant pretender to knowledge or skill of any sort. —*adj.* 1. used

āge, cāre, fär; ēqual, tėrm; īce; ōpen, ôrder; pụt, rüle, ūse; th, then; ə=a in about.

by quacks. 2. not genuine. [short for *quack-salver*] —quack′er·y, *n.* —quack′ish, *adj.* —quack′ish·ly, *adv.* —Syn. *n.* 2. charlatan, mountebank, impostor.

quack·sal·ver (kwak′sal·vər), *n.* a quack doctor. [< earlier Du., < *quacken* boast of + *salf* salve]

quad[1] (kwod), *n. Colloq.* quadrangle of a college.

quad[2] (kwod), *n. Colloq.* quadruplet.

quad·ran·gle (kwod′rang′gəl), *n.* 1. a four-sided space or court wholly or nearly surrounded by buildings. 2. the buildings around a quadrangle. 3. quadrilateral. [< LL *quadrangulum* < L *quadri-* four + *angulus* angle] —quad·ran·gu·lar (kwod·rang′gyə-lər), *adj.* —quad·ran′gu·lar·ly, *adv.*

quad·rant (kwod′rənt), *n.* 1. quarter of a circle or of its circumference. 2. instrument used in astronomy, navigation, etc., for measuring altitudes. [< L *quadrans* a fourth]

Quadrants

quad·rate (*adj.*, *n.* kwod′rit; –rāt; *v.* kwod′rāt), *adj.*, *n.*, *v.*, -rat·ed, -rat·ing. —*adj.* square; rectangular. —*n.* something square or rectangular. —*v.* conform. [< L, < *quadrus* square < *quattuor* four]

quad·rat·ic (kwod·rat′ik), *Algebra.* —*adj.* involving a square or squares, but no higher powers. $x^2 + 3x + 2 = 12$ is a quadratic equation. —*n.* a quadratic equation. —quad·rat′i·cal·ly, *adv.*

quad·rat·ics (kwod·rat′iks), *n.* branch of algebra that deals with quadratic equations.

quad·ra·ture (kwod′rə·chər), *n.* 1. act of squaring. 2. the finding of a square equal in area to a given surface bounded by a circle or other curve. [< L *quadratura*. See QUADRATE.]

quad·ren·ni·al (kwod·ren′i·əl), *adj.* 1. occurring every four years: *a quadrennial presidential election.* 2. of or for four years. [< L *quadriennium* < *quadri-* four + *annus* year] —quad·ren′ni·al·ly, *adv.*

quad·ri·lat·er·al (kwod′rə·lat′-ər·əl), *adj.* having four sides and four angles. —*n.* a plane figure having four sides and four angles. [< L, < *quadri-* four + *latus* side]

Quadrilaterals

qua·drille (kwə·dril′), *n.* 1. a square dance for four couples. 2. music for it. [< F < Sp. *cuadrilla* troop < *cuadro* battle square < L *quadrus* square]

quad·ril·lion (kwod·ril′yən), *n.* 1. in the United States and France, 1 followed by 15 zeros. 2. in Great Britain, 1 followed by 24 zeros. [< F, < *quadri-* four (< L) + MILLION] —quad·ril′lionth, *adj.*, *n.*

quad·riv·i·um (kwod·riv′i·əm), *n.* in the Middle Ages, arithmetic, geometry, astronomy, and music, the more advanced four of the seven liberal arts. [< LL < L, crossroads, < *quadri-* four + *via* way] —quad·riv′i·al, *adj.*

quad·roon (kwod·rün′), *n.* person having one fourth Negro blood; child of a mulatto and a white person. [< Sp. *cuarterón* < *cuarto* fourth]

quad·ru·ped (kwod′rû·ped), *n.* animal that has four feet. —*adj.* having four feet. [< L, < *quadru-* four + *pes* foot]

quad·ru·ple (kwod′rû·pəl; kwod·rü′-), *adj.*, *n.*, *v.*, -pled, -pling. —*adj.* 1. fourfold; consisting of four parts; including four parts or parties. 2. four times; four times as great. —*n.* number, amount, etc., four times as great as another. —*v.* make or become four times as great. [< L *quadruplus* < *quadru-* four + -*plus* fold] —quad′ru·ply, *adv.*

quad·ru·plet (kwod′rû·plit; kwod·rü′-), *n.* 1. one of four children born at a birth. 2. group of four.

quad·ru·pli·cate (*adj.*, *n.* kwod·rü′plə·kit; kwod·rü′plə·kāt), *adj.*, *v.*, -cat·ed, -cat·ing, *n.* —*adj.* fourfold; quadruple. —*v.* make fourfold; quadruple. —*n.* one of four things, esp. four copies of a document, exactly alike. [< L *quad-*

ruplicatus, ult. < *quadru-* four + *plicare* to fold] —quad·ru′pli·ca′tion, *n.*

quaff (kwäf; kwaf; kwôf), *v.* drink in large draughts; drink freely. —*n.* a quaffing. —quaff′er, *n.*

quag·gy (kwag′i; kwog′i), *adj.*, -gi·er, -gi·est. miry; swampy. [prob. < *quag* bog] —quag′gi·ness, *n.*

quag·mire (kwag′mīr′; kwog′-), *n.* 1. a boggy or miry place. 2. a difficult situation. [< *quag* bog + *mire*] —quag′mir′y, *adj.*

qua·hog, qua·haug (kwô′hog, –hôg; kwə-hog′, –hôg′), *n. Am.* a roundish, edible American clam; hard clam. [< Algonquian]

quail[1] (kwāl), *n.*, *pl.* quails or (*esp. collectively*) quail. *Am.* any of various game birds belonging to the same group as fowls and partridges, esp. the bobwhite. [< OF *quaille* < Gmc.]

Quail or bobwhite
(ab. 10 in. long)

quail[2] (kwāl), *v.* be afraid; lose courage; shrink back in fear: *the slave quailed at his master's look.* —quail′er, *n.* —Syn. tremble, quake, cower, flinch.

quaint (kwānt), *adj.* strange or odd in an interesting, pleasing, or amusing way. [< OF *cointe* pretty < L *cognitus* known] —quaint′ly, *adv.* —quaint′ness, *n.*

quake (kwāk), *v.*, quaked, quak·ing, *n.* —*v.* shake; tremble: *quake with fear.* —*n.* 1. a shaking; trembling. 2. earthquake. [OE *cwacian*] —quak′er, *n.* —quak′ing, *adj.* —quak′ing·ly, *adv.* —quak′y, *adj.* —Syn. *v.* quiver, shudder, shiver.

Quak·er (kwāk′ər), *n.* member of a Christian group called the Society of Friends. Quakers refuse to go to war or to take oaths; their clothes, manners, and religious services are very plain and simple. —Quak′er·ish, *adj.* —Quak′er·ism, *n.* —Quak′er·ly, *adj.*

Quak·er·ess (kwāk′ər·is), *n.* a Quaker woman or girl.

qual·i·fi·ca·tion (kwol′ə·fə·kā′shən), *n.* 1. that which makes a person fit for a job, task, office, etc.: *to know the way is one qualification for a guide.* 2. that which limits, changes, or makes less free and full: *his pleasure had one qualification; his friends could not enjoy it, too.* 3. modification; limitation; restriction: *the statement was made without any qualification.*

qual·i·fied (kwol′ə·fīd), *adj.* 1. having the desirable or required qualifications; fitted; adapted. 2. modified; limited; restricted. —qual′i·fied·ly, *adv.* —qual′i·fied·ness, *n.*

qual·i·fy (kwol′ə·fī), *v.*, -fied, -fy·ing. 1. make fit or competent: *qualify oneself for a job.* 2. become fit; show oneself fit: *when did he qualify?* 3. furnish with legal power; make legally capable. 4. make less strong; change somewhat; limit; modify: *qualify your statement that dogs are loyal by adding "usually."* 5. modify the strength or flavor of: *qualify a glass of water with rum.* 6. *Gram.* limit or modify the meaning of. Adverbs qualify verbs. [< Med.L, < L *qualis* of what sort + *facere* make] —qual′i·fi′a·ble, *adj.* —qual′i·fi′er, *n.* —qual′i·fy′ing·ly, *adv.* —Syn. 1. prepare, equip. 5. moderate, diminish, reduce.

qual·i·ta·tive (kwol′ə·tā′tiv), *adj.* concerned with quality or qualities. —qual′i·ta′tive·ly, *adv.*

qualitative analysis, *Chem.* testing of something to find out what chemical substances are in it.

qual·i·ty (kwol′ə·ti), *n.*, *pl.* -ties. 1. something special about an object that makes it what it is: *one quality of iron is hardness; one quality of sugar is sweetness.* 2. characteristic; attribute: *she has many fine qualities.* 3. the kind that anything is: *that is a poor quality of cloth.* 4. nature; disposition; temper: *trials often test a man's quality.* 5. character; position; relation:

Dr. Smith was present, but in quality of friend, not as physician. **6.** fineness; merit; excellence: *look for quality rather than quantity.* **7.** high rank; good or high social position. **8.** people of high rank. **9.** the character of sounds aside from pitch and volume or intensity. [< L, < *qualis* < what sort] —Syn. **1.** property. **2.** trait, feature.

qualm (kwäm), *n.* **1.** a sudden disturbing feeling in the mind; misgiving: *I tried the test with some qualms.* **2.** disturbance or scruple of conscience: *feel qualms at staying away from church.* **3.** a feeling of faintness or sickness, esp. of nausea, that lasts for just a moment. [OE *cwealm* pain] —**qualm′ish,** *adj.* —**qualm′ish·ly,** *adv.* —**qualm′ish·ness,** *n.* —Syn. **1.** uneasiness, doubt.

quan·da·ry (kwon′də·rĭ; -drĭ), *n., pl.* **-ries.** state of perplexity or uncertainty; dilemma. —Syn. predicament, difficulty, puzzle.

quan·ti·ta·tive (kwon′tə·tā′tiv), *adj.* **1.** concerned with quantity. **2.** that can be measured. —**quan′ti·ta′tive·ly,** *adv.* —**quan′ti·ta′tive·ness,** *n.*

quantitative analysis, *Chem.* a testing of something to find out how much there is of each chemical substance in it.

quan·ti·ty (kwon′tə·tĭ), *n., pl.* **-ties.** **1.** amount: *use equal quantities of nuts and raisins in the cake.* **2.** a large amount; large number: *a baker buys flour in quantity.* **3.** *Math.* something that is measurable. **4.** *Music.* length of a note. **5.** length of a sound or syllable in speech. [< L, < *quantus* how much]

quan·tum (kwon′təm), *n., pl.* **-ta** (-tə). *Physics.* **a.** the smallest amount of energy capable of existing independently. **b.** this amount of energy regarded as a unit. [< L, neut. adj., how much]

quantum theory, *Physics.* theory that whenever energy is transferred, the transfer occurs in pulsations or stages rather than continuously, and that the amount transferred during each stage is a definite quantity.

quar·an·tine (kwôr′ən·tēn; kwor′-), *v.,* **-tined, -tin·ing,** *n.* —*v.* **1.** keep away from others for a time to prevent the spread of an infectious disease: *people with smallpox are quarantined.* **2.** isolate for a time for any reason. —*n.* **1.** state of being quarantined: *the house was in quarantine for three weeks.* **2.** detention, isolation, and other measures taken to prevent the spread of an infectious disease. **3.** place where people, animals, plants, ships, etc., are held until it is sure that they have no infectious diseases, insect pests, etc. **4.** time during which they are held. [< Ital., < *quaranta* forty < L *quadraginta*; with ref. to 40 days as the orig. period of isolation]

quar·rel¹ (kwôr′əl; kwor′-), *n., v.,* **-reled, -rel·ing;** *esp. Brit.* **-relled, -rel·ling.** —*n.* **1.** an angry dispute or disagreement; breaking off of friendly relations. **2.** cause for a dispute or disagreement; reason for breaking off friendly relations: *a bully likes to pick quarrels.* **3.** cause for complaint. —*v.* **1.** dispute or disagree angrily; break off friendly relations. **2.** find fault: *it is useless for a girl to quarrel with fate because she is not a boy.* [< OF < L *querella,* var. of *querela* complaint] —**quar′rel·er,** *esp. Brit.* **quar′rel·ler,** *n.* —Syn. *n.* **1.** dissension, contention, controversy, wrangle. —*v.* **1.** differ, wrangle, squabble.

quar·rel² (kwôr′əl; kwor′-), *n.* **1.** bolt or arrow used with a crossbow. [< OF < Med.L *quadrellus,* dim. of L *quadrus* square]

quar·rel·some (kwôr′əl·səm; kwor′-), *adj.* too ready to quarrel; fond of fighting and disputing. —**quar′rel·some·ly,** *adv.* —**quar′rel·some·ness,** *n.* —Syn. choleric, irascible, disputatious.

quar·ry¹ (kwôr′ĭ; kwor′ĭ), *n., pl.* **-ries,** *v.,* **-ried, -ry·ing.** —*n.* place where stone is dug, cut, or blasted out for use in building. —*v.* obtain from a quarry. [< Med.L *quareia,* ult. < L *quadrus* square] —**quar′ri·er,** *n.*

quar·ry² (kwôr′ĭ; kwor′ĭ), *n., pl.* **-ries.** **1.** animal chased in a hunt; game; prey. **2.** anything hunted or eagerly pursued. [< OF, < *cuir* hide < L *corium*]

quart (kwôrt), *n.* **1.** measure for liquids, equal to one fourth of a gallon. **2.** measure for dry things, equal to one eighth of a peck. **3.** container holding a quart. [< F < L *quarta,* fem. adj., fourth]

quar·ter (kwôr′tər), *n.* **1.** one fourth; half of a half; one of four equal or corresponding parts. **2.** *Am.* one fourth of a dollar; 25 cents. **3.** a silver coin of the United States and Canada worth 25 cents. **4.** one fourth of an hour; moment marking this period. **5.** one fourth of a year; 3 months. **6.** one of the four periods of the moon, lasting about 7 days each. **7.** one fourth of a school year. **8.** region; place. **9.** section; district: *the Mexican quarter.* **10.** certain part of a community, group, etc.: *the bankers′ theory was not accepted in other quarters.* **11. at close quarters,** very close together; almost touching. **12. quarters, a.** place to live or stay. **b.** proper position or station. **13.** point of the compass; direction: *in what quarter is the wind?* **14.** mercy shown a defeated enemy in sparing his life. **15.** leg and its adjoining parts. **16.** *Naut.* part of a ship's side near the stern. **17.** *Heraldry.* one of four (or more) parts into which a shield is divided by lines at right angles. **18.** emblem occupying the upper right fourth of a shield. **19.** *Am.* quarterback. —*v.* **1.** divide into quarters. **2.** give a place to live in: *soldiers were quartered in all the houses of the town.* **3.** live or stay in a place. **4.** cut the body of (a person) into quarters; dismember. **5.** *Naut.* blow on a ship's quarter. **6.** place or bear (coats of arms) in quarters of a shield. —*adj.* being one of four equal parts; being equal to only about one fourth of full measure. [< OF < L *quartarius* a fourth < *quartus* fourth]

quar·ter·back (kwôr′tər·bak′), *n. Am., Football.* one of four players behind the line.

quar·ter·deck (kwôr′tər·dek′), *n.* part of the upper deck between the mainmast and the stern, used esp. by the officers of a ship.

quar·tered (kwôr′tərd), *adj.* **1.** divided into quarters. **2.** furnished with rooms or lodging. **3.** *Heraldry.* divided or arranged in quarters.

Quartered arms

quar·ter·ly (kwôr′tər·lĭ), *adj., adv., n., pl.* **-lies.** —*adj.* happening, done, etc., four times a year. —*adv.* once each quarter of a year. —*n.* magazine published every three months.

quar·ter·mas·ter (kwôr′tər·mas′tər; -mäs′-), *n.* **1.** in the army, an officer who has charge of providing quarters, clothing, fuel, transportation, etc., for troops. **2.** in the navy, an officer on a ship who has charge of the steering, the compasses, signals, etc. —**quar′ter·mas′ter·ship,** *n.*

quarter note, *Music.* note equal to one fourth of a whole note.

quar·ter·saw (kwôr′tər·sô′), *v.,* **-sawed, -sawed** or **-sawn, -saw·ing.** saw (a log) lengthwise into quarters and then into boards.

quarter section, *Am.* piece of land, usually square, containing 160 acres.

quarter sessions. 1. an English court, held quarterly, that has limited criminal jurisdiction and certain other powers. **2.** any of various other courts held quarterly.

quar·ter·staff (kwôr′tər·staf′; -stäf′), *n., pl.* **-staves** (-stāvz′). an old English weapon consisting of a stout pole 6 to 8 feet long, tipped with iron.

quar·tet, quar·tette (kwôr·tet′), *n.* **1.** group of four musicians (singers or players). **2.** piece of music for four voices or instruments. **3.** any group of four. [< F < Ital., < *quarto* fourth < *quartus*]

quar·to (kwôr′tō), *n., pl.* **-tos,** *adj.* —*n.* **1.** the page size, usually about 9 by 12 inches, of a book in which each leaf is one fourth of a whole sheet of paper. **2.** book having this size. —*adj.* having this size. [< Med.L *in quarto* in the fourth (of a sheet)]

quartz (kwôrts), *n.* a very hard mineral composed of silica, SiO₂. Common quartz crystals are colorless and transparent, but amethyst, jasper, and many other colored stones are quartz. [< G *quarz*]

quash¹ (kwosh), *v.* put down completely; crush: *quash a revolt.* [< OF *quasser* < L *quassare* shatter, intensive of *quatere* to shake]

quash² (kwosh), *v.* make void; annul. [< OF < LL *cassare* < *cassus* null; infl. in OF by *quasser* QUASH¹]

qua·si (kwā′sī; -zī; kwä′sī; -zī), *adj.* seeming; not real; halfway. —*adv.* seemingly; not really; partly; almost. [< L]

quasi-, *prefix.* form of **quasi** used in combination, as in *quasi-official.*

quas·sia (kwosh′ə), *n.* 1. a bitter drug obtained from the wood of a tropical American tree, used as a tonic and as a substitute for hops. 2. the wood. 3. the tree. [< NL; named after *Quassi,* Surinam Negro who first used the bark as a fever remedy]

quat·rain (kwot′rān), *n.* stanza or poem of four lines. [< F, < *quatre* four < L *quattuor*]

quat·re·foil (kat′ər.foil′; kat′rə-), *n.* 1. leaf or flower composed of four leaflets or petals. 2. an architectural ornament having four lobes. [< OF *quatre* four (< L *quattuor*) + *feuille* FOIL²]

qua·ver (kwā′vər), *v.* 1. shake tremulously; tremble: *the old man's voice quavered.* 2. trill in singing or in playing on an instrument. 3. sound, speak, or sing in trembling tones. —*n.* 1. a quavering or tremulous shake, esp. in the voice. 2. trill in singing or in playing on an instrument. 3. *Music.* an eighth note. [frequentative of *quave* shake, ME *cwavien*] —qua′ver·er, *n.* —qua′ver·ing·ly, *adv.* —qua′ver·y, *adj.*

quay (kē), *n.* a solid landing place where ships load and unload, often built of stone. [< OF *kay* < Celtic]

Quay

Que., Quebec.

quean (kwēn), *n.* 1. a bold, impudent girl or woman; hussy. 2. prostitute. [OE *cwene*]

quea·sy (kwē′zī), *adj.,* -si·er, -si·est. 1. inclined to nausea; easily upset. 2. tending to unsettle the stomach. 3. uneasy; uncomfortable. 4. squeamish; fastidious. —quea′si·ly, *adv.* —quea′si·ness, *n.*

Que·bec (kwi·bek′), *n.* 1. province in E Canada. 2. its capital, on the St. Lawrence River.

queen (kwēn), *n.* 1. wife of a king. 2. a woman ruler. 3. woman who is very important, stately, or beautiful. 4. a fully developed female in a colony of bees, ants, etc., that lays eggs. There is usually only one queen in a hive of bees. 5. a playing card bearing a picture of a queen. 6. piece in chess that can move in any straight or diagonal row. 7. the chief, best, finest, etc.: *the rose, queen of flowers.* —*v.* act like a queen. [OE *cwēn*] —queen′dom, *n.* —queen′hood, queen′ship, *n.* —queen′less, *adj.* —queen′like′, *adj.*

Queen Anne's lace, *Am.* the wild carrot, that bears a dainty white bloom.

queen dowager, widow of a king.

queen·ly (kwēn′lī), *adj.,* -li·er, -li·est, *adv.* —*adj.* 1. of a queen; fit for a queen. 2. like a queen; like a queen's. —*adv.* in a queenly manner; as a queen does. —queen′li·ness, *n.*

queen mother, widow of a former king and mother of a reigning king or queen.

Queens (kwēnz), *n.* borough of New York City, on Long Island E of Brooklyn.

Queens·land (kwēnz′lənd), *n.* a state in E Australia.

queer (kwir), *adj.* 1. strange; odd: *a queer remark for her to make.* 2. amusingly odd: *a queer little house.* 3. strange or odd from a conventional point of view; peculiar; eccentric: *queer opinions.* 4. mentally unbalanced; deranged. 5. *Colloq.* of questionable character; suspicious. 6. *Slang.* counterfeit. —*v. Slang.* spoil; ruin. [< G

quer oblique] —queer′er, *n.* —queer′ish, *adj.* —queer′ly, *adv.* —queer′ness, *n.* —Syn. *adj.* 1. singular, curious, unusual. 2. quaint. 3. freakish, bizarre. —Ant. *adj.* 1. ordinary, usual.

quell (kwel), *v.* 1. put down (disorder, rebellion, etc.); subdue: *quell a mutiny.* 2. put an end to; extinguish: *quell one's hopes.* 3. quiet or allay (feelings, etc.). [OE *cwellan* to kill] —quell′er, *n.* —Syn. 1. crush, overpower, suppress.

Que·moy (ki·moi′), *n.* a small island about 15 mi. off the coast of SE China.

quench (kwench), *v.* 1. put an end to; stop: *quench a thirst.* 2. drown out; put out: *water will quench a fire.* 3. cool suddenly by plunging into water or other liquid. [OE, as in *ācwencan*] —quench′a·ble, *adj.* —quench′er, *n.* —quench′less, *adj.* —Syn. 1. allay, slake. 2. extinguish, check, stifle, suppress.

quer·u·lous (kwer′ə·ləs; kwer′yə-), *adj.* 1. complaining; faultfinding. 2. fretful; peevish. [< L *querulus* < *queri* complain] —quer′u·lous·ly, *adv.* —quer′u·lous·ness, *n.* —Syn. 2. petulant.

que·ry (kwir′ī), *n., pl.* -ries, *v.,* -ried, -ry·ing. —*n.* 1. question; inquiry. 2. the sign (?) put after a question or used to express doubt about something written or printed. —*v.* 1. ask; ask about; inquire into. 2. ask questions. 3. express doubt about. [< Med.L *quere* < L *quaere* ask!]

quest (kwest), *n.* 1. search; hunt. 2. expedition of knights. 3. object sought for. —*v.* search or seek for; hunt. [< OF < VL *quaesita* < L *quaerere* seek] —quest′er, *n.* —quest′ful, *adj.*

ques·tion (kwes′chən), *n.* 1. thing asked; sentence in interrogative form, addressed to someone to get information: *what was your question?* 2. a judicial examination or trial; interrogation. 3. matter of doubt or dispute; controversy: *a question arose about the ownership of the property.* 4. matter to be talked over, investigated, considered, etc.; problem: *the question of prohibition.* 5. proposal to be voted on. 6. the taking of a vote on a proposal. 7. **beside the question,** off the subject. 8. **beyond** or **without question,** without doubt; not to be disputed. 9. **call in question,** dispute; challenge. 10. **in question,** a. under consideration or discussion. b. in dispute. 11. **out of the question,** impossible. —*v.* 1. ask in order to find out; seek information from. 2. ask; inquire. 3. doubt; dispute: *I question the truth of his story.* [< AF < L *quaestio,* ult. < *quaerere* ask] —ques′tion·a·ry (kwes′chən·er′ī), *adj., n.* —ques′tion·er, *n.* —ques′tion·ing, *adj.* —ques′tion·ing·ly, *adv.* —Syn. *n.* 1. query, inquiry. —*v.* 1. interrogate, query.

ques·tion·a·ble (kwes′chən·ə·bəl), *adj.* 1. open to question or dispute; doubtful; uncertain. 2. of doubtful propriety, honesty, morality, respectability, or the like. —ques′tion·a·ble·ness, *n.* —ques′tion·a·bly, *adv.* —Syn. 1. debatable, disputable, controvertible. 2. dubious, suspicious.

question mark, mark (?) put after a question in writing or printing. ➤ **question mark** (?). a. The principal use of the question mark is as the end stop to a question: *what was the real reason?* b. A question mark may or may not be used after a request that is phrased as a question, depending on the formality of the style: *Will you please return this at your earliest convenience?* (formal). *Will you please return this at your earliest convenience* (informal). c. A question mark is no longer used after an indirect question: *He wanted to know what the real reason was.*

ques·tion·naire (kwes′chən·âr′), *n.* list of questions, usually a written or printed list.

quet·zal (ket·säl′), **que·zal** (kā·säl′), *n.* a Central American bird having brilliant golden-green and scarlet plumage. The male has long, flowing tail feathers. [< Sp. < Mex. *quetzalli,* the bird's tail feather]

queue (kū), *n., v.,* queued, queu·ing. —*n.* 1. braid of hair hanging down from the back of the head. 2. *Esp. Brit.* a long line of people, automobiles, etc. —*v. Esp. Brit.* form or stand in a long line. [< F < L *coda,* var. of *cauda* tail]

Chinese queue

Que·zon City (kā·sôn′), newly-built city on the northeast edge of Manila. It replaced Manila in 1948 as the capital of the Philippines.

Que·zon y Mo·li·na (kā′sôn ē mō·lē′nä), Manuel Luis, 1878–1944, Philippine statesman and patriot.

quib·ble (kwib′əl), *n.*, *v.*, -bled, -bling. —*n.* an unfair and petty evasion of the point or truth by using words with a double meaning: *a legal quibble.* —*v.* evade the point or the truth by twisting the meaning of words. —**quib′bler**, *n.*

quick (kwik), *adj.* 1. fast and sudden; swift: *a quick turn.* 2. coming soon; prompt: *a quick reply.* 3. not patient; hasty: *a quick temper.* 4. brisk: *a quick fire.* 5. acting quickly; ready; lively. 6. understanding or learning quickly. 7. *Archaic.* living. —*n.* 1. the tender, sensitive flesh under a fingernail or toenail. 2. the tender, sensitive part of one's feelings: *their insults cut him to the quick.* 3. a vital or important part. 4. living persons: *the quick and the dead.* —*adv.* quickly. [OE *cwic* alive] —**quick′ish**, *adj.* —**quick′ness**, *n.* —Syn. *adj.* 1. rapid, speedy, fleet. 3. precipitate, impatient, irascible. 5. nimble, agile. —Ant. *adj.* 1. slow, sluggish.

quick·en (kwik′ən), *v.* 1. move more quickly; hasten: *quicken your pace.* 2. stir up; make alive: *quicken hot ashes into flames, quicken one's imagination.* 3. become more active or alive: *his pulse quickened.* —**quick′en·er**, *n.* —Syn. 1. hurry, expedite, accelerate. 2. rouse, stimulate, animate. —Ant. 1. check, retard.

quick-freeze (kwik′frēz′), *v.*, -froze, -frozen, -freez·ing. subject (food) to rapid freezing to prepare it for storing at freezing temperatures. —**quick freezing.**

quick·ie (kwik′i), *n. Slang.* 1. a motion picture, novel, or the like, produced cheaply and in haste. 2. a short drink of alcoholic liquor.

quick·lime (kwik′lim′), *n.* a white, alkaline substance obtained by burning limestone and used for making mortar; unslaked lime.

quick·ly (kwik′li), *adv.* in a quick manner.

quick·sand (kwik′sand′), *n.* soft, wet sand, very deep, that will not support one's weight.

quick·set (kwik′set′), *n. Esp. Brit.* plant or cutting, esp. of hawthorn, set to grow in a hedge.

quick·sil·ver (kwik′sil′vər), *n.* the metal mercury. —*v.* coat with mercury.

quick·step (kwik′step′), *n.* 1. step used in marching in quick time. 2. a lively dance step. 3. music in a brisk march rhythm.

quick-tem·pered (kwik′tem′pərd), *adj.* easily angered.

quick time, a fast speed of marching. In quick time, soldiers march four miles an hour.

quick-wit·ted (kwik′wit′id), *adj.* having a quick mind; mentally alert. —**quick′-wit′ted·ly**, *adv.* —**quick′-wit′ted·ness**, *n.*

quid[1] (kwid), *n.* 1. piece to be chewed. 2. bite of chewing tobacco. [OE *cwidu* cud]

quid[2] (kwid), *n.*, *pl.* **quid.** *Brit. Slang.* one pound, or 20 shillings.

quid·di·ty (kwid′ə·ti), *n.*, *pl.* -ties. 1. essence. 2. quibble. [< Med.L *quidditas* whatness < L *quid* what]

quid·nunc (kwid′nungk′), *n.* newsmonger; gossip; inquisitive person. [< L, what now]

quid pro quo (kwid′ prō kwō′), *Latin.* compensation; one thing in return for another.

qui·es·cence (kwi·es′əns), **qui·es·cen·cy** (–ən·si), *n.* absence of activity; quietness.

qui·es·cent (kwi·es′ənt), *adj.* quiet; still; motionless; inactive. [< L *quiescens* resting < *quies*, n., rest] —**qui·es′cent·ly**, *adv.*

qui·et[1] (kwi′ət), *adj.* 1. not moving; still: *remain quiet.* 2. moving very little: *a quiet current.* 3. free from disturbance; tranquil: *a quiet conscience.* 4. not giving offense or causing disorder; peaceable: *quiet neighbors.* 5. not disturbed by emotion; calm; contented: *a quiet mind or spirit.* 6. free from noise or sound: *a quiet neighborhood.* 7. free from fuss or bustle: *quiet manners.* 8. not active: *a quiet market, quiet games.* 9. not glaring or showy; in good

taste: *quiet colors.* —*v.* make or become quiet. —*adv.* quietly. [< L *quietus* resting, ult. < *quies* quiet[2]. Doublet of COY and QUIT, adj.] —**qui′et·er**, *n.* —**qui′et·ly**, *adv.* —**qui′et·ness**, *n.*

qui·et[2] (kwi′ət), *n.* 1. state of rest; stillness; absence of motion or noise. 2. freedom from disturbance; peace. [< L *quies*]

qui·e·tude (kwi′ə·tūd; -tōōd), *n.* quietness; stillness; calmness.

qui·e·tus (kwi·ē′təs), *n.* a final getting rid of anything; finishing stroke. [< Med.L *quietus est* he is discharged. See QUIET[1].]

quill (kwil), *n.* 1. a large, stiff feather. 2. the hollow stem of a feather. 3. anything made from the hollow stem of a feather, such as a pen, toothpick, etc. 4. a stiff, sharp hair or spine. A porcupine has quills on its back. [ME *quil*]

quilt (kwilt), *n.* 1. bedcover made of two pieces of cloth with a soft pad between, held in place by lines of stitching. 2. bedcover. 3. anything resembling a quilt. —*v.* 1. *Am.* make quilts. 2. stitch together with a soft lining: *quilt a bathrobe.* 3. sew in lines or patterns. [< OF < L *culcita* cushion] —**quilt′ed**, *adj.* —**quilt′er**, *n.*

quilting bee, *Am.* a friendly gathering of women to make a quilt.

quince (kwins), *n.* 1. a hard, yellowish fruit, used for preserves. 2. tree it grows on. 3. a similar shrub or tree grown for its blossoms. [orig. pl. of ME *quyne* < OF *cooin* < L *cotoneum*]

qui·nine (kwi′nin), **quin·in** (kwin′in), *n.* 1. a bitter, colorless, crystalline drug made from the bark of a cinchona tree, used for colds, malaria, and fevers. 2. any of various compounds of quinine that are used as medicine. [< Sp. *quina* < Kechua (S Am.Ind.) *kina* bark]

quinine water, a carbonated drink containing a small amount of quinine and a little lemon, lime, or orange juice.

quin·quen·ni·al (kwin·kwen′i·əl), *adj.* 1. occurring every five years. 2. of, or for five years. [< L *quinquennium* < *quinque* five + *annus* year]

quin·sy (kwin′zi), *n.* tonsillitis with pus; very sore throat with an abscess in the tonsils. [< Med.L *quinancia* < LL < Gk. *kynanche*, orig., dog's collar < *kyon* dog + *anchein* choke]

quint (kwint), *n. Colloq.* quintuplet.

quin·tal (kwin′təl), *n.* a hundredweight.

quin·tes·sence (kwin·tes′əns), *n.* 1. pure essence; purest form. 2. the most perfect example of something. [< Med.L *quinta essentia* fifth essence, trans. of Gk. *pempte ousia*]

quin·tes·sen·tial (kwin′tə·sen′shəl), *adj.* having the nature of a quintessence; of the purest or most perfect kind.

quin·tet, quin·tette (kwin·tet′), *n.* 1. group of five musicians (singers or players). 2. piece of music for five voices or instruments. 3. any group of five. [< F < Ital., < *quinto* fifth < L *quintus*]

Quin·til·ian (kwin·til′yən), *n.* 35?–95? A.D., Roman writer on rhetoric and oratory.

quin·til·lion (kwin·til′yən), *n.* 1. in the United States and France, 1 followed by 18 zeros. 2. in Great Britain, 1 followed by 30 zeros. [< L *quintus* fifth + E MILLION] —**quin·til′lionth**, *adj.*, *n.*

quin·tu·ple (kwin′tū·pəl; -tyū-; kwin·tū′pəl; -tū′-), *adj.*, *v.*, -pled, -pling, *n.* —*adj.* 1. fivefold; consisting of five parts. 2. five times as great. —*v.* make or become five times as great. —*n.* number, amount, etc., five times as great as another. [< F, < L *quintus* fifth; patterned on *quadruple*]

quin·tu·plet (kwin′tū·plit; -tyū-; kwin·tū′plit; -tū′-; -tup′lit), *n.* 1. one of five children born at a birth. 2. any group or combination of five.

quip (kwip), *n.*, *v.*, quipped, quip·ping. —*n.* 1. a clever or witty saying. 2. a sharp, cutting remark. 3. quibble. 4. something odd or strange. —*v.* make quips. [for earlier *quippy* < L *quippe* indeed!, I dare say] —**quip′ster**, *n.*

quire (kwir), *n.* 24 or 25 sheets of paper of the same size and quality. [< OF *quaier*, ult. < L *quaterni* four each]

quire² (kwīr), n. Archaic. choir.

quirk (kwėrk), n. 1. a peculiar way of acting. 2. a clever or witty saying. 3. quibble. 4. a sudden twist or turn. 5. flourish in writing. —**quirk′y**, adj.

quirt (kwėrt), n. Am. riding whip with a short, stout handle and a lash of braided leather. [? < Sp. cuerda cord]

quis·ling (kwiz′ling), n. any person who treacherously helps to prepare the way for enemy occupation of his own country. [after Vidkun Quisling, Norwegian puppet ruler for the Nazis]

quit (kwit), v., quit or quit·ted, quit·ting, adj. —v. 1. stop: the men quit work when the whistle blew. 2. stop working. 3. leave: he quit his room in anger. 4. give up; let go. 5. pay back; pay off (a debt). 6. free; clear; rid. —adj. free; clear; rid: I gave him money to be quit of him. [(v.) < OF < Med.L quietare discharge < L quietus QUIET¹; (adj.) < OF quite < L quietus. Doublet of QUIET¹ and COY.]

quit·claim (kwit′klām′), Law. —n. 1. the giving up of a claim. 2. document stating that somebody gives up a claim. —v. give up claim to (a possession, etc.).

quite (kwīt), adv. 1. completely; wholly; entirely: a hat quite out of fashion. 2. actually; really; positively: quite the thing. 3. Colloq. to a considerable extent or degree: quite pretty. [orig. adj., var. of quit in sense of "clear"] ► quite. In formal English quite means "entirely, wholly," as in "quite gone." In informal and colloquial English, it is reduced in meaning to "somewhat, very, rather": I am quite tired. We went quite a long way. This meaning passes over into a number of convenient colloquial phrases: quite a few, quite a little, quite a lot.

Qui·to (kē′tō), n. capital of Ecuador, in the N part.

quit·rent (kwit′rent′), n. rent paid in money, instead of services rendered under a feudal system.

quits (kwits), adj. 1. on even terms by repayment or retaliation. 2. be quits with, get even with; have revenge on.

quit·tance (kwit′əns), n. 1. release from debt or obligation. 2. the paper certifying this; a receipt. 3. repayment.

quit·ter (kwit′ər), n. Am., Colloq. person who gives up easily.

quiv·er¹ (kwiv′ər), v., n. shake; shiver; tremble. [cf. OE cwiferlīce actively] —**quiv′er·ing**, adj. —**quiv′er·ing·ly**, adv.

quiv·er² (kwiv′ər), n. case to hold arrows. [< AF quivere, prob. < Gmc.] —**quiv′ered**, adj.

qui vive? (kē vēv′), 1. who goes there? 2. on the qui vive, watchful; alert. [< F, lit., (long) live who?; expecting such a reply as Vive le roi! Long live the king!]

Qui·xo·te (kē·hō′te; kwik′sət), n. Don. See Don Quixote.

quix·ot·ic (kwiks·ot′ik), **quix·ot·i·cal** (-ə-kəl), adj. 1. resembling Don Quixote; extravagantly chivalrous or romantic. 2. visionary; not practical. —**quix·ot′i·cal·ly**, adv. —**quix·ot′ism** (kwik′sə·tiz·əm), **quix·ot·i·cism** (kwiks·ot′ə·siz·əm), **quix·ot·ry** (kwik′sə·tri), n.

quiz (kwiz), v., quizzed, quiz·zing, n., pl. quiz·zes. —v. 1. examine informally by questions; test the knowledge of. 2. make fun of. —n. 1. Am. an informal written or oral examination; test. 2. person who makes fun of others. —**quiz′zer**, n. —**quiz′zing**, adj. —**quiz′zing·ly**, adv.

quiz·zi·cal (kwiz′ə·kəl), adj. 1. odd; queer; comical. 2. that suggests making fun of others; teasing. —**quiz′zi·cal·i·ty**, **quiz′zi·cal·ness**, n. —**quiz′zi·cal·ly**, adv.

quoin (koin; kwoin), n. 1. an external angle of a wall or building. 2. stone forming an outside angle of a wall; cornerstone. 3. a wedge-shaped piece of wood, metal, etc. [var. of coin]

quoit (kwoit), n. 1. a heavy, flattish iron or rope ring thrown to encircle a peg stuck in the ground or to come as close to it as possible. 2. **quoits** (sing. in use), game so played. The game of quoits is often played with horseshoes.

quon·dam (kwon′dəm), adj. that once was; former. [< L, at one time]

Quon·set hut (kwon′sit), a prefabricated metal building with a semicircular roof. [first used at Quonset (R.I.) naval air base]

quo·rum (kwô′rəm; kwō′-), n. number of members of any society or assembly that must be present if the business done is to be legal or binding. [< L, of whom]

quot., quotation.

quo·ta (kwō′tə), n. share of a total due from or to a particular district, state, person, etc. [< Med.L, < L quota pars how large a part]

quot·a·ble (kwōt′ə·bəl), adj. 1. that can be quoted. 2. that can be quoted with propriety. 3. suitable for quoting. —**quot′a·bil′i·ty**, **quot′a·ble·ness**, n. —**quot′a·bly**, adv.

quo·ta·tion (kwō·tā′shən), n. 1. somebody's words repeated exactly by another person; passage quoted from a book, speech, etc.: from what author does this quotation come? 2. quoting: quotation is a habit of some preachers. 3. the stating of the current price of a stock, commodity, etc. 4. the price so stated: what was today's market quotation on wheat? —**quo·ta′tion·al**, adj. —**quo·ta′tion·al·ly**, adv.

quotation mark, one of a pair of marks used to indicate the beginning and end of a quotation. ► quotation marks (" "). 1. methods of indicating quotations. a. Double quotes (" ") are the usual marks. The mark before the quoted matter is the open quote, and the one after is the close quote. b. The use of single quotes (') is common in England and is increasing in the United States. They are used by The Atlantic Monthly and by many publishers in some of their books. The single quotes are as accurate as the double and are much less spotty on the page. c. For quotations within quotations, double and single quotes are alternated. If you begin with the double marks: " ' . . . ' "; if you begin with the single: ' " . . . " ' If there are quotations within two such quotations, continue to alternate the double and single quotes as needed. 2. principal uses of quotation marks. a. One of the forms of quotation marks is used to indicate all passages taken from another writer, whether a phrase or a page or more, unless the quoted material is set off by wider indention than the rest (see Punctuation, p. 23). b. There are no half quotes. A sentence is either an exact quotation, in quotation marks, or else it isn't and so is not quoted. A speech summarized or quoted "indirectly" is not marked: The manager told me, "I work harder in one day keeping the girls busy than they work all week" (direct quotation). The manager told me that he worked harder in one day keeping the girls busy than they worked all week (indirect quotation). [Not: The manager told me "that he worked harder in one day keeping the girls busy than they worked all week."] c. Some adventurous writers of fiction do not use quotation marks in the dialogue of their stories, but the practice is not common. 3. quotation marks and other marks. a. When a question mark or an exclamation mark ends a quotation, it is placed inside the quotes: "Don't go near that wire!" he shouted. Then in a calm voice she asked, "Why couldn't you have said so in the first place?" When a question mark or exclamation mark belongs to a sentence that includes a quotation, it is placed after the quotes: Was this "a war to end all wars"? b. Most publishers put commas and periods inside the close quotes, whether they belong with the quotation or not. The reason for this is that the quotes help fill the small spot of white that would be left if the comma or period came outside. Some writers follow the conventions that apply to the exclamation and question marks, putting comma or period inside the quotes if it belongs with the quotation, outside if it belongs with the quoting sentence, but this usage is much less common.

quote (kwōt), v., quot·ed, quot·ing, n. —v. 1. repeat the exact words of; give words or passages from. 2. repeat exactly the words of another or a passage from a book. 3. bring forward as an example or authority. 4. give the price of. —*n.* 1. quotation. 2. a quotation mark. [< Med.L *quotare* number chapters < L *quotus* which (in sequence)] —quot'er, *n.*

quoth (kwōth), *v. Archaic.* said. [pt. of *queathe* (OE *cwethan.* See BEQUEATH.]

quo·tid·i·an (kwō·tid'i·ən), *adj.* reappearing daily; daily. —*n.* something, esp. a fever or ague, that occurs daily. [< L *quotidianus,* var.

of *cottidianus* < *cottidie* daily < *quotus* which (in sequence) + *dies* day]

quo·tient (kwō'shənt), *n. Math.* number obtained by dividing one number by another. [< L *quotiens* how many times]

q.v., which see. [< L *quod vide*] ⟩ q.v. is used as a reference to another book, article, etc., already mentioned, or as a cross reference within the same work.

R

R, r (är), *n., pl.* R's; r's. 1. the 18th letter of the alphabet. 2. the three R's, reading, writing, and arithmetic.

R., 1. King. [< L *rex*] 2. Queen. [< L *regina*] 3. railroad; railway. 4. Republican. 5. River.

r., 1. radius. 2. railroad; railway. 3. road. 4. rod. 5. ruble. 6. rupee.

Ra (rä), *n. Egyptian Myth.* the sun god and supreme deity.

Ra, *Chem.* radium.

rab·bet (rab'it), *n., v.,* –bet- ed, –bet·ing. —*n.* 1. cut, groove, or slot made on the edge or sur-

RABBETS

face of a board or the like, to receive the end or edge of another piece of wood shaped to fit it. 2. joint so made. —*v.* 1. cut or form a rabbet in. 2. join with a rabbet. [< OF *rabat* a beating down < *rabattre.* See REBATE.]

rab·bi (rab'ī), *n., pl.* –bis. teacher of the Jewish religion; pastor of a Jewish congregation. [< L < Heb., my master]

rab·bin·i·cal (rə·bin'ə·kəl), **rab·bin·ic** (–ik), *adj.* of or pertaining to rabbis, their learning, writings, etc. —rab·bin'i·cal·ly, *adv.*

rab·bit (rab'it), *n.* 1. a burrowing mammal about as big as a cat, with soft fur and long ears. 2. its fur. [ME *rabet*]

rabbit fever, *Am.* tularemia.

rab·ble (rab'əl), *n.* 1. a disorderly crowd; mob. 2. the rabble, *Contemptuous.* the lower classes. [cf. Du. *rabbelen* prattle]

Rab·e·lais (rab'ə·lā), *n.* François, 1495?-1553, French writer, famous for his lively satire and coarse humor. —Rab·e·lai·si·an (rab'ə·lā'zi·ən; –zhən), *adj.*

rab·id (rab'id), *adj.* 1. unreasonably extreme; fanatical; violent. 2. furious; raging. 3. having rabies; mad. [< L *rabidus* < *rabere* be mad] —rab'id·ly, *adv.* —rab'id·ness, ra·bid'i·ty, *n.*

ra·bies (rā'bēz), *n.* hydrophobia (def. 1). [< L, madness] —ra·bi·et·ic (rā'bi·et'ik), *adj.*

rac·coon (ra·kün'), *n. Am.* 1. a small, grayish flesh-eating mammal with a bushy, ringed tail, that lives mostly in trees and is active at night. 2. its fur. Also, **racoon.** [< Algonquian]

race¹ (rās), *n., v.,* raced, rac·ing. —*n.* 1. contest of speed, as in running, driving, riding, sailing, etc. 2. Often, races. a series of horse races run at a set time over a regular course. 3. any contest that suggests a race: *a political race.* 4. onward movement; regular course: *the race of life.* 5. a strong or fast current of water. 6. channel of a stream. 7. channel leading water to or from a place where its energy is utilized. —*v.* 1. engage in a contest of speed. 2. try to beat in a contest of speed; run a race with. 3. cause to run in a race. 4. run, move, or go swiftly. 5. cause to run, move, or go swiftly. 6. of a motor, wheel, etc., run too fast when load or resistance is lessened without corresponding lessening of power. [< Scand. *rās*] —rac'er, *n.*

race² (rās), *n.* 1. group of persons connected by common descent or origin. 2. a great division of mankind having certain physical peculiarities in common: *the white race, the yellow race.* 3. a particular variety of animals or plants. 4. a natural kind of living creatures: *the human race, the race of fishes.* 5. any group, class, or kind, esp. a class of persons: *the brave race of seamen.* 6. condition of belonging to a particular stock, or the qualities, etc., due to this: *race was of*

importance to Hitler. [< F < Ital. *razza*] —ra·cial (rā'shəl), *adj.* —ra'cial·ly, *adv.*

ra·ceme (rā·sēm'; rə–), *n.* a simple flower cluster having its flowers on nearly equal stalks along a stem, the lower flowers blooming first. The lily of the valley has racemes. [< L *racemus* cluster. Doublet of RAISIN.] —ra·cemed', *adj.* —rac·e·mose (ras'ə·mōs), *adj.*

race suicide, *Am.* extinction of a people that tends to result when, by deliberate limitation of the number of children, the birth rate falls below the death rate.

race track or **course,** ground laid out for racing.

ra·chi·tis (rə·kī'tis), *n.* rickets. [< NL < Gk. *rhachis* backbone] —ra·chit·ic (rə·kit'ik), *adj.*

Rach·ma·ni·noff (räk·mä'ni·nôf), *n.* Sergei, 1873-1943, Russian pianist and composer.

Ra·cine (ra·sēn'), *n.* Jean Baptiste, 1639-1699, French poet and dramatist.

rac·ism (rās'iz·əm), **ra·cial·ism** (rā'shəl·iz- əm), *n.* 1. exaggeration of inherent racial differences. 2. prejudice in favor of certain races. —rac'ist, *n.*

rack¹ (rak), *n.* 1. frame with bars, shelves, or pegs to hold, arrange, or keep things on, such as a hat rack, tool rack, or baggage rack. 2. framework set on a wagon for carrying hay, straw, etc. 3. instrument formerly used for torturing people by stretching them. 4. cause or condition of great suffering in body or mind. 5. bar with pegs or teeth on one edge, into which teeth on the rim of a wheel can fit. 6. on the rack, in great pain; suffering very much. —*v.* 1. hurt very much: *racked with grief.* 2. stretch; strain. [prob. < MDu. or MLG *recke*]

WHEEL

RACK

Rack (def. 5)

rack² (rak), *n.* wreck. [var. of *wrack*]

rack³ (rak), *n.* a horse's gait, similar to a pace; single-foot. —*v.* go thus.

rack·et¹ (rak'it), *n.* 1. a loud noise; loud talk; din. 2. *U.S. Colloq.* a dishonest scheme for getting money from people by threatening violence or damage. 3. *U.S. Colloq.* any dishonest scheme. 4. *U.S. Slang.* occupation. [? imit.]

rack·et², **rac·quet** (rak'it), *n.* a light, wide bat made of network stretched on a frame, used for games like tennis. [< F *raquette* < Ar. *rāha* palm of the hand] ⟩ **racket.** The spelling *racquet* is an affectation. Write *tennis racket.*

rack·et·eer (rak'ə·tir'), *Am., Slang.* —*n.* person who extorts money by threatening violence or damage. —*v.* extort money by threatening violence or damage. —rack'et·eer'ing, *n. Am.*

rac·on·teur (rak'on·tér'), *n.* person clever in telling stories, anecdotes, etc. [< F]

ra·coon (ra·kün'), *n.* raccoon.

rac·y (rās'i), *adj.,* rac·i·er, rac·i·est. 1. vigorous; lively. 2. having an agreeably peculiar taste or flavor. 3. risqué. —rac'i·ly, *adv.* —rac'i·ness, *n.* —Syn. 1. forcible, spirited. 2. piquant, spicy.

ra·dar (rā'där), *n. Am.* 1. instrument for determining the distance and direction of unseen objects by the reflection of radio waves. 2. other instruments and techniques which have developed from this. 3. process by which the reflection of the radio waves is measured. [short for ra(dio) d(etecting) a(nd) r(anging)]

āge, câre, fär; ēqual, tèrm; īce; ōpen, ôrder; pùt, rüle, ūse; th, then; ə=a in about.

radar fence or **screen,** *Am.* a protective chain of radar stations placed around an area.

radar island, *Am.* a large platform at sea, supported by steel stilts, on which is situated radar equipment to detect the approach of enemy aircraft.

ra·di·al (rā′di·əl), *adj.* arranged like or in radii or rays. —**ra′di·al·ly,** *adv.*

ra·di·ance (rā′di·əns), **ra·di·an·cy** (—ən·si), *n.* 1. vivid brightness. 2. radiation.

ra·di·ant (rā′di·ənt), *adj.* 1. shining; bright; beaming: *a radiant smile.* 2. sending out rays of light or heat: *the sun is a radiant body.* 3. sent off in rays from some source; radiated. [< L *radians* beaming < *radius* ray]

Radial arrangement

ra·di·ate (rā′di·āt), *v.,* -at·ed, -at·ing, *adj.* —*v.* 1. give out rays of: *the sun radiates light and heat.* 2. give out rays; shine: *the sun radiates.* 3. issue in rays. 4. give out; send forth: *her face radiates joy.* 5. spread out from a center: *roads radiate from the city.* —*adj.* radiating from a center. [< L *radiatus.* See RADIANT.] —**ra′di·ate·ly,** *adv.* —**ra′di·a′tive,** *adj.*

ra·di·a·tion (rā′di·ā′shən), *n.* 1. act or process of giving out rays of light, heat, sounds, or electricity. 2. energy radiated; ray or rays.

radiation sickness, a systemic disease resulting from overexposure to radioactivity.

ra·di·a·tor (rā′di·ā′tər), *n. Am.* 1. a heating device consisting of a set of pipes through which steam or hot water passes. 2. device for cooling circulating water, as on an automobile.

rad·i·cal (rad′ə·kəl), *adj.* 1. going to the root; fundamental. 2. favoring extreme changes or reforms; extreme. —*n.* 1. person who favors extreme changes or reforms. 2. *Chem.* an atom or group of atoms acting as a unit in chemical reactions. Ammonium (NH₄) is a radical in NH₄OH. 3. *Math.* the sign (√) put before an expression to show that some root of it is to be extracted. 4. *Gram.* root. [< LL, < L *radix* root] —**rad′i·cal·ism, rad′i·cal·ness,** *n.* —**rad′i·cal·ly,** *adv.* —Syn. *adj.* 1. basic.

ra·di·i (rā′di·ī), *n.* pl. of radius.

ra·di·o (rā′di·ō), *n.,* pl. -di·os, *adj., v.,* -di·oed, -di·o·ing. —*n. Am.* 1. way of sending and receiving words, music, etc., by electric waves, without connecting wires. 2. apparatus for receiving and making audible the sounds so sent. —*adj.* 1. *Am.* of, pertaining to, used in, or sent by radio. 2. of or having to do with radio frequencies higher than 15,000 per second. —*v.* transmit or send out by radio. [independent use of *radio*-, abstracted from *radiotelegraphy,* etc.]

radio-, *word element.* 1. radio, as in *radiotelegraphy.* 2. radial, as in *radiosymmetrical.* 3. radiant energy, as in *radiograph.* 4. radioactive, as in *radioelement, radioisotope.* [< *radius*]

ra·di·o·ac·tive (rā′di·ō·ak′tiv), *adj. Physics, Chem.* giving off radiant energy in the form of alpha, beta, or gamma rays by the breaking up of atoms. —**ra′di·o·ac·tiv′i·ty,** *n.*

ra·di·o·bi·ol·o·gy (rā′di·ō·bī·ol′ə·ji), *n.* branch of biology dealing with the effects of radioactivity on living organisms. —**ra′di·o·bi′o·log′i·cal,** *adj.* —**ra′di·o·bi·ol′o·gist,** *n.*

ra·di·o·car·bon (rā′di·ō·kär′bən), *n.* carbon 14.

ra·di·o·gram (rā′di·ō·gram′), *n.* 1. message transmitted by radio. 2. radiograph.

ra·di·o·graph (rā′di·ō·graf′; -gräf′), *n.* an X-ray picture. —*v.* make an X-ray picture of. —**ra′di·og′ra·pher** (ra′di·og′rə·fər), *n.* —**ra′di·o·graph′ic, ra′di·o·graph′i·cal,** *adj.* —**ra′di·og′ra·phy,** *n.*

ra·di·o·i·so·tope (rā′di·ō·ī′sə·tōp), *n.* a radioactive isotope derived artificially from an element not normally radioactive, often as a by-product of atomic research, the operation of an atomic furnace, etc.

ra·di·o·sonde (rā′di·ō·sond′), *n.* a radio transmitter dropped by parachute to broadcast temperature, humidity, etc.

radio strontium, strontium 90.

ra·di·o·tel·e·graph (rā′di·ō·tel′ə·graf; -gräf′), *n.* telegraph worked by radio. —*v.* telegraph by radio. —**ra′di·o·tel′e·graph′ic,** *adj.*

ra·di·o·te·leg·ra·phy (rā′di·ō·tə·leg′rə·fi), *n.* telegraphing by radio.

ra·di·o·tel·e·phone (rā′di·ō·tel′ə·fōn), *n., v.,* -phoned, -phon·ing. —*n.* Also, **ra′di·o·phone′.** a radio transmitter using voice communication. —*v.* telephone by radio. —**ra′di·o·tel·e·phon′ic** (rā′di·ō·tel′ə·fon′ik), *adj.*

ra·di·o·tel·e·phon·y (rā′di·ō·tə·lef′ə·ni), *n.* radio communication by means of voice signals.

ra·di·o·tel·e·scope (rā′di·ō·tel′ə·skōp), *n.* large network of wires on a frame forming an antenna that can receive radio signals from outer space, used to find new stars, track satellites, etc.

ra·di·o·ther·a·py (rā′di·ō·ther′ə·pi), *n.* treatment of disease by means of X rays or radioactive agencies.

rad·ish (rad′ish), *n.* 1. a small, crisp root with a red or white skin, used as a relish and in salads. 2. the plant. [< L *radix* root]

ra·di·um (rā′di·əm), *n. Chem.* a radioactive metallic element, Ra, found in very small amounts in uranium ores such as pitchblende, used in treating cancer and in making luminous paint. Radium atoms are constantly breaking up and in this process give off alpha, beta, and gamma rays. [< NL, < L *radius* ray]

ra·di·us (rā′di·əs), *n.,* pl. -di·i (-di·ī), -di·us·es. 1. any line going straight from the center to the outside of a circle or a sphere. 2. a circular area measured by the length of its radius. 3. *Anat.* that one of the two bones of the forearm which is on the thumb side. [< L, ray, rod] Doublet of RAY¹.]

Each line from C (center) is a radius.

ra·don (rā′don), *n.* a rare element, Rn, given off by radium, that is a radioactive gas. [< *radium*]

R.A.F., Royal Air Force (of Great Britain).

raf·fi·a (raf′i·ə), *n.* 1. fiber from the leafstalks of a species of palm growing in Madagascar, used in making baskets, etc. 2. the raffia palm. [< Malagasy (the language of Madagascar)]

raf·fle (raf′əl), *n., v.,* -fled, -fling. —*n.* sale in which many people each pay a small sum for a chance of getting an article. —*v.* 1. sell (an article) by a raffle. 2. hold a raffle. [ME *rafle* a dice game < OF, plundering, stripping, ult. < Du. *rafelen* ravel, pluck]

raft¹ (raft; räft), *n.* logs or boards fastened together to make a floating platform. [< Scand. *raptr* log]

raft² (raft; räft), *n. Colloq.* a large number; abundance. [var. of *raff* heap < *riffraff*]

raft·er (raf′tər; räf′-), *n.* a slanting beam of a roof. [OE *ræfter*]

rag¹ (rag), *n.* 1. a torn or waste piece of cloth. 2. a small piece of cloth. 3. rags, clothing that is much torn or worn. 4. a contemptuous or humorous term for some article of clothing, a flag, a theater curtain, a piece of paper money, etc. —*adj.* made from rags. [< Scand. *rögg* shaggy tuft] —Syn. *n.* 3. tatters.

rag² (rag), *v.,* **ragged, rag·ging,** *n. Slang.* —*v.* 1. scold. 2. tease. —*n.* a ragging.

rag·a·muf·fin (rag′ə·muf′ən), *n.* 1. a ragged, disreputable fellow. 2. a ragged child.

rage (rāj), *n., v.,* **raged, rag·ing.** —*n.* 1. violent anger: *a voice quivering with rage.* 2. a fit of violent anger: *be in a rage.* 3. a violent desire: *the rage to kill.* 4. fierce violence; fury: *the rage of a savage tiger.* 5. what everybody wants for a short time; the fashion. —*v.* be furious with anger. 2. speak or act with furious anger. 3. act violently; move, proceed, or continue with great violence: *a storm is raging.* [< OF < VL *rabia* < L *rabies*] —**rage′ful,** *adj.* —**rage′ful·ly,** *adv.* —Syn. *n.* 1. fury, frenzy, wrath. 5. vogue, fad.

rag·ged (rag′id), *adj.* 1. worn or torn into rags. 2. wearing torn or badly worn-out clothing. 3. not straight and tidy; rough. 4. having loose shreds or bits. 5. having rough or sharp points; uneven; jagged: *ragged rocks.* —**rag′ged·ly,** *adv.* —**rag′ged·ness,** *n.* —Syn. 1. rent, tattered, frayed. 5. craggy, rocky, broken.

rag·lan (rag′lən), *n.* a loose topcoat or overcoat with sleeves cut so as to continue up to the collar. [after Lord *Raglan,* British general]

ra·gout (ra·gü′), *n.* a highly seasoned stew of meat and vegetables. [< F, < *ragoûter* restore the appetite]

rag·time (rag′tīm′), *n. Am., Colloq.* 1. musical rhythm with accents falling at unusual places. 2. syncopated music; jazz.

rag·weed (rag′wēd′), *n.* any of several coarse weeds of the aster family whose pollen is one of the most common causes of hay fever.

rah (rä), *interj., n. Am.* hurrah.

raid (rād), *n.* 1. attack; sudden attack. 2. a sudden attack, usually by a small force having no intention of holding the territory invaded. 3. an entering and seizing what is inside. —*v.* 1. attack suddenly. 2. force a way into; enter and seize what is in. 3. engage in a raid. [northern form of OE *rād* a riding. Cf. ROAD.] —raid′er, *n.*

rail¹ (rāl), *n.* 1. bar of wood or of metal. There are stair rails, fence rails, rails protecting monuments, etc. 2. one of the two parallel bars of a railroad track. 3. railroad: *ship by rail.* 4. the upper part of the bulwarks of a ship. —*v.* 1. furnish with rails. 2. enclose with bars. [< OF < L *regula* straight rod. Double of RULE.]

rail² (rāl), *v.* complain bitterly; use violent and reproachful language. [< F *railler,* ult. < LL *ragere* to scream. Doublet of RALLY².] —rail′er, *n.* —**Syn.** scold, reproach.

rail³ (rāl), *n., pl.* rails or (*esp. collectively*) rail. any of numerous small birds with short wings, narrow bodies, strong legs, long toes, and a harsh cry, that live in marshes and swamps. [< F *râle* < VL *rascla;* prob. imit.]

Rail (10 in. long)

rail·ing (rāl′ing), *n.* 1. fence made of rails. 2. material for rails. 3. rails.

rail·ler·y (rāl′ər·i), *n., pl.* -ler·ies. 1. good-humored ridicule; joking; teasing. 2. a bantering remark. [< F *raillerie.* See RAIL².]

rail·road (rāl′rōd′), *n. Esp. U.S.* 1. road or track with parallel steel rails on which the wheels of the cars go. 2. tracks, stations, trains, and other property of a system of transportation that uses rails, together with the people who manage them. —*v. Am.* 1. send by railroad; carry on a railroad. 2. work on a railroad. 3. *Colloq.* send along quickly or too quickly to be fair. 4. *Slang.* commit to prison on unfounded charges in order to be rid of. —rail′road′er, *n.* —rail′road′ing, *n. Am.*

rail·way (rāl′wā′), *n.* 1. *Esp. Brit.* railroad. 2. track made of rails.

rai·ment (rā′mənt), *n. Archaic.* clothing; garments. [short for *arraiment.* See ARRAY.]

rain (rān), *n.* 1. water falling in drops from the clouds. 2. the fall of such drops. 3. a thick, fast fall of anything. —*v.* 1. fall in drops of water. 2. fall like rain. 3. pour like rain; send like rain. [OE *regn*] —rain′less, *adj.*

rain·bow (rān′bō′), *n.* bow or arch of seven colors (violet, indigo, blue, green, yellow, orange, and red) seen sometimes in the sky, or in mist or spray, when the sun shines on it from behind one.

rain check, *Am.* ticket for future use, given to the spectators at a baseball game or other outdoor performance stopped by rain.

rain·coat (rān′kōt′), *n. Am.* a waterproof coat worn for protection from rain.

rain·drop (rān′drop′), *n.* drop of rain.

rain·fall (rān′fôl′), *n.* 1. shower of rain. 2. amount of water in the form of rain, snow, etc., falling within a given time and area.

Rai·nier (rə·nir′; rā–), *n.* **Mount,** mountain in W Washington. Also, **Mount Tacoma.**

rain·mak·er (rān′māk′ər), *n.* one who seeks to produce rain, as by supernatural or artificial means. —rain′mak′ing, *n., adj.*

rain·storm (rān′stôrm′), *n.* storm with much rain.

rain·y (rān′i), *adj.,* rain·i·er, rain·i·est. 1. having rain; having much rain. 2. bringing rain. 3. wet with rain. —rain′i·ness, *n.*

raise (rāz), *v.,* raised, rais·ing, *n.* —*v.* 1. lift up: *raise one's hand.* 2. set upright: *raise the overturned lamp.* 3. cause to rise: *raise a cloud of dust.* 4. put or take into a higher position; make higher or nobler; elevate: *raise a man to manager.* 5. increase in amount, price, pay, etc.: *raise the rent.* 6. increase in degree, intensity, or force: *raise the temperature.* 7. make louder or of higher pitch: *raise your voice.* 8. in games, bid or bet more than (another player's bid or bet, or another player). 9. gather together; collect; manage to get: *the leader raised an army.* 10. breed; grow: *raise wheat, dogs, etc.* 11. bring into existence: *raise a storm.* 12. cause to appear: *raise a ghost.* 13. cause; bring about: *a funny remark raises a laugh.* 14. utter: *raise a shout.* 15. build; create; produce; start; set up: *raise a monument.* 16. rouse; stir up: *the dog raised a rabbit from the underbrush.* 17. bring up; rear: *parents raise their children.* 18. cause to become light: *raised bread.* 19. bring back to life: *raise the dead.* 20. put an end to: *raise the siege of a fort.* 21. come in sight of: *the ship raised land.* —*n.* 1. a raised place. 2. increase in amount, price, pay, etc. 3. amount of such an increase. [< Scand. *reisa*] —rais′a·ble, *adj.* —rais′er, *n.* —**Syn.** *v.* 1. hoist, heave. 4. promote, advance, exalt. 9. muster. 10. produce, cultivate. ➤ **raise,** rear. *Rear* is now formal in the sense of *rearing* a child or of being *reared. Bring up* in this sense is current in all levels of usage. *Raised* is good informal usage: *I was born and raised in Maine.*

rai·sin (rā′zən), *n.* a sweet dried grape. [< OF < L *racemus* grape cluster. Doublet of RACEME.]

raj (räj), *n.* in India, rule; dominion.

ra·jah, ra·ja (rä′jə), *n.* ruler or chief in India, Java, Borneo, etc. [< Hind. *rājā* < Skt.] —ra′jah·ship, ra′ja·ship, *n.*

rake¹ (rāk), *n., v.,* raked, rak·ing. —*n.* a long-handled tool having a bar at one end with teeth in it, used for smoothing the soil or gathering together loose leaves, hay, straw, etc. —*v.* 1. move with a rake: *rake the leaves off the grass.* 2. use a rake. 3. gather; gather together. 4. search carefully. 5. fire guns along the length of (a ship, line of soldiers, etc.). [OE *raca*]

rake² (rāk), *n.* a profligate or dissolute person. [short for *rakehell* a roué]

rake³ (rāk), *n., v.,* raked, rak·ing. slant; slope.

rake-off (rāk′ôf′, -of′), *n. Slang.* share or portion, often an amount taken or received unlawfully.

rak·ish (rāk′ish), *adj.* 1. smart; jaunty; dashing. 2. immoral; dissolute. —rak′ish·ly, *adv.* —rak′ish·ness, *n.* —**Syn.** 2. licentious.

Ra·leigh (rô′li), *n.* 1. Sir **Walter,** 1552?–1618, English soldier, explorer, statesman, and author. 2. capital of North Carolina, in the C part.

ral·ly¹ (ral′i), *v.,* -lied, -ly·ing, *n., pl.* -lies. —*v.* 1. bring together; bring together again; get in order again: *rally the fleeing troops.* 2. pull together; revive: *rally your energy for one last effort.* 3. come together in a body for a common purpose or action. 4. call (persons) together, as for common action. 5. come to the assistance of a person, party, or cause: *he rallied to the side of his friend.* 6. recover health and strength: *the sick man may rally now.* 7. recover more or less from a drop in price: *the market rallied.* —*n.* 1. act or fact of rallying; recovery. 2. a coming together; mass meeting: *a political rally.* 3. act or fact of hitting the ball back and forth several times in tennis and similar games. [< F *rallier* < *re-* again + *allier* ALLY]

ral·ly² (ral′i), *v.,* -lied, -ly·ing. make fun of; tease. [< F *railler* rail². Doublet of RAIL².] —ral′ly·ing·ly, *adv.* —**Syn.** banter, joke.

ram (ram), *n., v.,* rammed, ram·ming. —*n.* 1. a male sheep. 2. machine or part of a machine that strikes heavy blows. 3. **Ram,** Aries. —*v.* 1. butt against; strike head on; strike violently. 2. push hard; drive down or in by heavy blows. [OE *ramm*] —ram′mer, *n.* —**Syn.** *v.* 2. stuff, cram.

ram·ble (ram′bəl), v., **-bled, -bling,** n. —v. **1.** wander about. **2.** talk or write about first one thing and then another with no useful connections. **3.** spread irregularly in various directions: *vines rambled over the wall.* —n. a walk for pleasure, not to go to any special place. —ram′-bler, n. —Syn. v. **1.** roam, rove, saunter.

ram·bunc·tious (ram-bungk′shəs), adj. Am., Slang. **1.** wild and uncontrollable; unruly. **2.** noisy and violent; boisterous.

ram·e·kin, ram·e·quin (ram′ə-kin), n. **1.** a small, separately cooked portion of some food, esp. one topped with cheese and bread crumbs. **2.** a small baking dish holding enough for one portion. [< F *ramequin* < Du.]

ram·i·fy (ram′ə-fī), v., **-fied, -fy·ing.** divide or spread out into branchlike parts. [< F < Med.L. < L *ramus* branch + *facere* make] —ram′i·fi·ca′tion, n.

ram·jet (ram′jet′), n. a type of jet engine in which the fuel is fed into air compressed by the speed of the airplane, guided missile, etc., in which it is contained.

ramp¹ (ramp), n. a sloping way connecting two different levels of a building, road, etc.; slope. [< F *rampe* < *ramper.* See RAMP².]

ramp² (ramp), v. **1.** rush wildly about; behave violently. **2.** jump or rush with fury. [< F *ramper* creep]

ram·page (n. ram′pāj; v. ram-pāj′, ram′pāj), n., v., **-paged, -pag·ing.** —n. fit of rushing wildly about; wild outbreak. —v. rush wildly about; behave violently; rage. [? < ramp²]

ramp·ant (ram′pənt), adj. **1.** growing without any check. **2.** unchecked. **3.** angry; excited; violent. **4.** *Heraldry.* standing up on the hind legs. [< OF, ramping] —ramp′an·cy, n. —ramp′ant·ly, adv. —Syn. **2.** unrestrained, unbridled. **3.** furious, raging.

Lion rampant (def. 4)

ram·part (ram′pärt), n. **1.** a wide bank of earth, often with a wall on top, built around a fort to help defend it. **2.** anything that defends; protection. [< F, < *remparer* fortify, ult. < L *re-* back + *ante* before + *parare* prepare]

ram·rod (ram′rod′), n. **1.** rod for ramming down the charge in a gun that is loaded from the muzzle. **2.** rod for cleaning the gun barrel.

ram·shack·le (ram′shak′əl), adj. loose and shaky; likely to come apart. [? ult. < *ransack*]

ran (ran), v. pt. of run.

ranch (ranch), n. **1.** *Western U.S.* a very large farm and its buildings for raising cattle, horses, etc. **2.** any farm or farming establishment: *a chicken ranch.* **3.** persons employed or living on a ranch. —v. Am. work on or manage a ranch. [< Sp., group of persons who eat together] —ranch′er, ranch′man, n.

ranch house, 1. a one-story dwelling, like most houses on a ranch, having a low roof. **2.** main house on a ranch, where the owner or manager and his family live.

ran·cid (ran′sid), adj. **1.** stale; spoiled: *rancid fat.* **2.** tasting or smelling like stale fat or butter. [< L *rancidus* < *rancere* be rank] —ran′cid·ly, adv. —ran′cid·ness, ran·cid′i·ty, n.

ran·cor, esp. Brit. **ran·cour** (rang′kər), n. bitter resentment or ill will; extreme hatred or spite. [< OF < LL, rankness, < L *rancere* be rank] —ran′cor·ous, adj. —ran′cor·ous·ly, adv. —ran′cor·ous·ness, n. —Syn. malice, animosity.

ran·dom (ran′dəm), adj. by chance; with no plan. —n. at random, by chance; with no plan or purpose. [< OF *randon* rapid rush] —Syn. adj. accidental, casual, haphazard.

ra·nee (rä′nē), n. wife of a rajah. Also, rani. [< Hind. *rānī* < Skt. *rājñī*]

rang (rang), v. pt. of ring².

range (rānj), n., v., **ranged, rang·ing,** adj. —n. **1.** distance between certain limits; extent: *a range of prices from 5 cents to 25 dollars.* **2.** distance a gun can shoot. **3.** distance from a gun, etc., of an object aimed at. **4.** place to practice shooting. **5.** land for grazing. **6.** row or line of mountains. **7.** row; line. **8.** rank, class, or order.

9. stove for cooking. [< v.] —v. **1.** vary within certain limits: *prices ranging from $5 to $10.* **2.** wander; rove; roam. **3.** wander over: *buffalo once ranged these plains.* **4.** search (an area). **5.** put in a row or rows. **6.** put in groups or classes. **7.** put in a line on someone's side: *loyal citizens ranged themselves with the king.* **8.** run in a line; extend: *a boundary ranging east and west.* **9.** be found; occur: *a plant ranging from Canada to Mexico.* —adj. of or on land for grazing. [< OF *ranger* array, ult. < *reng* line, RANK¹] —Syn. n. **1.** scope, reach, latitude. **7.** series, sequence. –v. **2.** ramble. **6.** arrange, classify, class.

rang·er (rān′jər), n. **1.** person employed to guard a tract of forest. **2.** Am. one of a body of armed men employed in ranging over a region to police it. **3.** Also, **Ranger.** *U.S. Army.* a soldier in World War II trained for raids and surprise attacks; commando. —rang′er·ship, n.

Ran·goon (rang-gün′), n. capital and chief port of Burma, in the S part.

rang·y (rān′ji), adj., **rang·i·er, rang·i·est.** slender and long-limbed: *a rangy horse.* —rang′i·ness, n. Am.

ra·ni (rä′nē), n. ranee.

rank¹ (rangk), n. **1.** row or line, usually of soldiers, placed side by side. **2.** ranks, a. army; soldiers. b. rank and file. **3.** position; grade; class: *the rank of colonel, in the first rank.* **4.** high position: *a duke is a man of rank.* —v. **1.** arrange in a row or line. **2.** have a certain rank: *New York State ranks first in wealth.* **3.** put in some special order in a list: *rank the States for area.* **4.** outrank: *a major ranks a captain.* [ult. < OF *reng* < Gmc.] —Syn. n. **3.** standing, status.

rank² (rangk), adj. **1.** large and coarse: *rank grass.* **2.** growing richly. **3.** producing a dense but coarse growth: *rank swamp land.* **4.** having a strong, bad smell or taste: *rank tobacco.* **5.** strongly marked; extreme: *rank ingratitude.* **6.** coarse; not decent. [OE *ranc* proud] —rank′ly, adv. —rank′ness, n. —Syn. **4.** tainted, rancid.

rank and file, a. common soldiers, not officers. b. the common people.

ran·kle (rang′kəl), v., **-kled, -kling.** be sore; cause soreness; continue to give pain: *the insult rankled.* [ult. < OF *draoncler* < Med.L *dracunculus* sore, dim. of L *draco* serpent]

ran·sack (ran′sak), v. **1.** search thoroughly through: *ransack the desk for the lost letter.* **2.** rob; plunder. [< Scand. *rannsaka,* lit., search a house < *rann* house + *-saka* search] —ran′sack·er, n. —Syn. **1.** rummage, explore.

ran·som (ran′səm), n. price paid or demanded before a captive is set free. —v. **1.** obtain the release of (a captive) by paying a price. **2.** redeem. [< OF *rançon* < L *redemptio.* Doublet of REDEMPTION.] —ran′som·er, n.

rant (rant), v. speak wildly, extravagantly, violently, or noisily. —n. an extravagant, violent, or noisy speech. [< MDu. *ranten*] —rant′er, n. —rant′ing·ly, adv. —Syn. v. declaim, rave.

rap¹ (rap), n., v., **rapped, rap·ping.** —n. **1.** a quick, light blow; a light, sharp knock. **2.** Am., Slang. blame; rebuke: *take the rap.* —v. **1.** knock sharply; tap. **2.** say sharply: *rap out an answer.* [? imit.] —Syn. v. **1.** thump, whack, bang.

rap² (rap), n. Colloq. the least bit.

ra·pa·cious (rə-pā′shəs), adj. **1.** seizing by force; plundering. **2.** grasping; greedy. **3.** of animals, living by the capture of prey. [< L *rapax* grasping < *rapere* seize] —ra·pa′cious·ly, adv. —ra·pa′cious·ness, n. —ra·pac·i·ty (rə-pas′ə-ti), n. —Syn. **2.** avaricious. **3.** predatory.

rape¹ (rāp), n., v., **raped, rap·ing.** —n. **1.** a seizing and carrying off by force. **2.** the crime of having sexual intercourse with a woman or girl forcibly and against her will. —v. **1.** seize and carry off by force. **2.** force (a woman or girl) to have sexual intercourse against her will. [< L *rapere* seize] —rap′ist, n.

rape² (rāp), n. a small plant whose leaves are used as food for sheep and hogs and whose seeds yield an oil (rape oil) that is used as a lubricant, etc. [< L *rapa, rapum*]

Raph·a·el (raf′l·əl; rä′fi·əl), n. **1.** 1483–1520, Italian painter. **2.** one of the chief angels.

rap·id (rap′id), *adj.* **1.** moving, acting, or doing with speed: *a rapid worker.* **2.** going on or forward at a fast rate: *rapid growth.* —*n.* Usually, **rapids,** *Am.* part of a river's course where the water rushes quickly. [< L *rapidus* < *rapere* hurry away] —**ra·pid·i·ty** (rə·pid′ə·ti), **rap′id·ness,** *n.* —**rap′id·ly,** *adv.* —**Syn.** *adj.* **1.** fleet, speedy.

ra·pi·er (rā′pi·ər), *n.* a light sword used for thrusting. [< MF *rapière* < *râpe* grater, RASP; with ref. to the perforated guard]

rap·ine (rap′ən), *n.* robbing by force and carrying off; plundering. [< L *rapina*]

rap·port (ra·pôrt′; –pōrt′; *Fr.* rä·pôr′), *n.* agreement; harmony. [< F, < *rapporter* bring back]

rap·proche·ment (rä·prôsh·män′), *n. French.* establishment or renewal of friendly relations. [< F, < *rapprocher* bring near]

rap·scal·lion (rap·skal′yən), *n.* rascal; rogue; scamp. [earlier *rascallion* < *rascal*]

rapt (rapt), *adj.* **1.** lost in delight. **2.** so busy thinking of or enjoying one thing that one does not know what else is happening. **3.** carried away in body or spirit from earth, life, or ordinary affairs. **4.** showing or caused by a rapt condition. [< L *raptus* seized] —**rapt′ly,** *adv.* —**rapt′ness,** *n.* —**Syn.** **1.** enraptured, ecstatic. **2.** engrossed, spellbound, absorbed. **3.** transported.

rap·to·ri·al (rap·tô′ri·əl, –tō′–), *adj.* **1.** adapted for seizing prey. **2.** belonging or pertaining to an order of birds of prey, such as the eagles, hawks, etc. [ult. < L *raptor* robber < *rapere* seize]

rap·ture (rap′chər), *n.* **1.** a strong feeling that absorbs the mind; very great joy. **2.** Often, **raptures.** expression of great joy. [< *rapt*] —**Syn.** **1.** transport, ecstasy, bliss.

rap·tur·ous (rap′chər·əs), *adj.* full of rapture; expressing or feeling rapture. —**rap′tur·ous·ly,** *adv.* —**rap′tur·ous·ness,** *n.*

rare¹ (rãr), *adj.,* **rar·er, rar·est.** **1.** seldom seen or found: *a rare bird.* **2.** not happening often; unusual: *a rare event.* **3.** thin; not dense. [< L *rarus*] —**rare′ness,** *n.* —**Syn.** **1.** scarce. **2.** infrequent, uncommon. **3.** rarefied, tenuous.

rare² (rãr), *adj.,* **rar·er, rar·est.** not cooked much: *a rare steak.* [OE *hrēr*]

rare·bit (rãr′bit), *n.* Welsh rabbit.

rare earth, oxide of a rare-earth metal.

rare-earth metals (rãr′ẽrth′), rare metallic elements having atomic numbers 57 to 71.

rar·e·fy (rãr′ə·fī), *v.,* **–fied, –fy·ing. 1.** make or become less dense. **2.** refine; purify. [< L, *rarus* rare + *facere* make] —**rar·e·fac·tion** (rãr′ə·fak′shən), *n.* —**rar′e·fac′tive,** *adj.*

rare·ly (rãr′li), *adv.* **1.** seldom; not often: *things rarely seen.* **2.** unusually; unusually well: *a rarely carved panel.* ➤ **Rarely ever** (*I rarely ever go*) is an established colloquial idiom, a simplification of the more formal *rarely if ever.*

rar·i·ty (rãr′ə·ti), *n., pl.* **–ties. 1.** something rare. **2.** fewness; scarcity. **3.** lack of density; thinness.

ras·cal (ras′kəl), *n.* a bad, dishonest person. Sometimes *rascal* is used jokingly, as when one calls a child a little rascal. —*adj.* low; mean; dishonest. [< OF *rascaille* < *rasque* filth, ult. < L *radere* scratch] —**ras·cal·i·ty** (ras·kal′ə·ti), *n.* —**ras′cal·ly,** *adv.*

rase (rāz), *v.,* **rased, ras·ing.** raze.

rash¹ (rash), *adj.* too hasty; careless; reckless; taking too much risk. [ME *rasch* quick] —**rash′ly,** *adv.* —**rash′ness,** *n.* —**Syn.** headlong, heedless, impetuous, foolhardy. —**Ant.** deliberate.

rash² (rash), *n.* a breaking out with many small red spots on the skin. Scarlet fever causes a rash. [< OF *rasche,* ult. < L *radere* scratch]

rash·er (rash′ər), *n.* a thin slice of bacon or ham for frying or broiling.

rasp (rasp), *v.* **1.** make a harsh, grating sound: *the file rasped.* **2.** utter with a grating sound: *rasp out a command.* **3.** have a harsh or irritating effect (on); grate: *rasp on one's* nerves. **4.** scrape with a rough instrument. —*n.* **1.** a harsh, grating sound. **2.** a coarse file with pointlike teeth. [< OF *rasper* < Gmc.] —**rasp′ing,** *adj.*

rasp·ber·ry (raz′ber′i; –bri; räz′–), *n., pl.* **–ries. 1.** a small fruit, usually red or black, that grows on bushes. **2.** bush that it grows on. **3.** *Slang.* sound of disapproval or derision made with the tongue and lips. [< earlier *raspis* raspberry + *berry*]

Ras·pu·tin (ras·pū′tən), *n.* 1871–1916, Russian monk who had great influence over the family of Czar Nicholas II.

rat (rat), *n., v.,* **rat·ted, rat·ting.** —*n.* **1.** a long-tailed rodent like a mouse but larger. Rats are gray, black, brown, or white. **2.** a low, mean, disloyal person. **3. smell a rat,** suspect a trick or scheme. **4.** *Am.* pad worn to puff out a woman's hair. —*v.* **1.** hunt for rats; catch rats. **2.** behave in a low, mean, disloyal way. [OE *ræt*]

rat·a·ble (rāt′ə·bəl), *adj.* **1.** capable of being rated. **2.** *Brit.* taxable. —**rat′a·bil′i·ty, rat′-a·ble·ness,** *n.* —**rat′a·bly,** *adv.*

ra·tan (ra·tan′), *n.* rattan.

ratch·et (rach′it), *n.* **ratch** (rach), *n.* wheel or bar with teeth that come against a catch so that motion is permitted in one direction but not in the other. [< F < Ital. *rocchetto,* ult. < Gmc.]

RATCHET
CATCH

rate (rāt), *n., v.,* **rat·ed, rat·ing.** —*n.* **1.** quantity, amount, or degree measured in proportion to something else: *the rate of interest is 6 cents on the dollar.* **2.** degree of speed or progress: *a rapid rate.* **3.** price: *we pay the regular rate.* **4.** class; grade; rating. **5.** *Brit.* tax on property for some local purpose. **6. at any rate, a.** in any case; under any circumstances. **b.** at least. **7. at that** or **this rate,** in that or this case; under such circumstances. —*v.* **1.** put a value on. **2.** consider; regard. **3.** put in a certain class or grade, as a ship or sailor. **4.** be regarded; be classed; rank. [< OF < Med.L *rata* (*pars*) fixed (amount), pp. of L *reri* reckon] —**rat′er,** *n.* —**Syn.** *n.* **4.** rank, order. —*v.* **1.** appraise, assess.

rate·pay·er (rāt′pā′ər), *n.* Brit. taxpayer.

rath·er (rath′ər; räth′–), *adv.* **1.** more readily; more willingly. **2.** more properly or justly; with better reason. **3.** more truly: *late Monday night or, rather, early Tuesday morning.* **4.** (with verbs) in some degree: *he rather felt that this was unwise.* **5.** to some extent; somewhat; more than a little: *rather good.* **6.** on the contrary. **7. had rather,** would more willingly; prefer to. —*interj. Colloq.* yes, indeed! certainly! very much so! [OE *hrathor,* compar. of *hrathe* quickly] ➤ See **had** for usage note.

raths·kel·ler (räts′kel′ər), *n. Am.* restaurant selling alcoholic drinks, usually below street level. [< G, < *rat*(*haus*) town hall + *keller* cellar]

rat·i·fy (rat′ə·fī), *v.,* **–fied, –fy·ing.** confirm; approve: *the Senate must ratify a treaty to make it binding.* [< OF < Med.L, ult. < L *ratus* fixed + *facere* make] —**rat′i·fi·ca′tion,** *n.* —**rat′i·fi′er,** *n.* —**Syn.** sanction, authorize.

rat·ing (rāt′ing), *n.* **1.** class; grade. **2.** position in a class or grade: *the rating of a seaman.* **3.** an amount fixed as a rate: *a rating of 80% in English.* **4.** estimate of credit standing.

ra·ti·o (rā′shi·ō; –shō), *n., pl.* **–ti·os. 1.** relative magnitude. "He has sheep and cows in the ratio of 10 to 3" means that he has ten sheep for every three cows, or 3⅓ times as many sheep as cows. **2.** quotient. The ratio of 6 to 10 is %₀. The ratio of 10 to 6 is ¹%. **3.** proportional relation; rate. [< L, reckoning, < *reri* reckon. Doublet of RATION, REASON.]

ra·ti·oc·i·nate (rash′i·os′ə·nāt), *v.,* **–nat·ed, –nat·ing.** carry on a process of reasoning; reason. [< L *ratiocinatus* < *ratio.* See RATIO.] —**ra′ti·oc′i·na′tion,** *n.* —**ra′ti·oc′i·na′tive,** *adj.* —**ra′ti·oc′i·na′tor,** *n.*

ra·tion (rash′ən; rā′shən), *n.* **1.** a fixed allowance of food; daily allowance of food for a person or animal: *a balanced ration.* **2.** portion of anything dealt out: *rations of sugar, of coal, etc.* —*v.* **1.** supply with rations: *ration an army.* **2.** allow only certain amounts to: *ration citizens when supplies are scarce.* **3.** distribute in limited amounts: *ration food to the public in wartime.* [< F < Med.L *ratio* < L, reckoning. Doublet of RATIO, REASON.] —**ra′tion·ing,** *n.* —Syn. *n.* **2.** share, allotment. ➤ ration (rations). *Ration* is pronounced rash′ən or rā′shən, the former esp. in the Army and wherever rations are handled in large quantities (or numbers).

ra·tion·al (rash′ən·əl; rash′nəl), *adj.* **1.** sensible; reasonable; reasoned out: *act in a rational way.* **2.** able to think and reason clearly: *as children grow older, they become more rational.* **3.** of reason; based on reasoning. **4.** *Math.* expressible in finite terms; involving no root that cannot be extracted. [< L *rationalis.* See RATIO.] —**ra·tion·al·i·ty** (rash′ən·al′ə·ti), *n.* —**ra′tion·al·ly,** *adv.* —Syn. **1.** sound, wise, judicious, sane. —Ant. **1.** unreasonable.

ra·tion·al·ism (rash′ən·əl·iz′əm; rash′nəl-), *n.* principle or habit of accepting reason as the supreme authority in matters of opinion, belief, or conduct. —**ra′tion·al·ist,** *n.* —**ra′tion·al·is′tic,** *adj.* —**ra′tion·al·is′ti·cal·ly,** *adv.*

ra·tion·al·ize (rash′ən·əl·īz; rash′nəl-), *v.,* **-ized, -iz·ing.** **1.** make rational or conformable to reason. **2.** treat or explain in a rational manner. **3.** find (often unconsciously) an explanation or excuse for. **4.** find excuses for one's desires. —**ra′tion·al·i·za′tion,** *n.* —**ra′tion·al·iz′er,** *n.*

rat·line, rat·lin (rat′lən), *n. Naut.* one of the small ropes that cross the shrouds of a ship, used as steps for going aloft.

RATO, *Aeronautics.* rocket assist for take-off.

rats·bane (rats′bān′), *n.* any poison for rats.

rat·tan (ra·tan′), *n.* **1.** kind of palm with a very long stem. **2.** stems of such palm trees, used for wickerwork, canes, etc. **3.** cane or switch made from a piece of such a stem. Also, **ratan.** [ult. < Malay *rotan*]

rat·ter (rat′ər), *n.* **1.** animal that catches rats. **2.** one who deserts his associates.

rat·tle (rat′əl), *v.,* **-tled, -tling,** *n.* —*v.* **1.** make a number of short, sharp sounds. **2.** cause to rattle. **3.** move with short, sharp sounds: *the cart rattled down the street.* **4.** talk quickly, on and on. **5.** say quickly. **6.** *Am., Colloq.* confuse; embarrass. —*n.* **1.** a number of short, sharp sounds: *the rattle of empty bottles.* **2.** sound in the throat, occurring in some diseases of the lungs and also often just before death. **3.** toy, instrument, etc., that makes a noise when it is shaken. **4.** *Am.* series of horny pieces at the end of a rattlesnake's tail. [ME *ratelen;* prob. imit.]

rat·tle·brain (rat′əl·brān′), *n.* a giddy, thoughtless person.

rat·tler (rat′lər), *n.* **1.** *Am., Colloq.* rattlesnake. **2.** one that rattles.

rat·tle·snake (rat′əl·snāk′), *n. Am.* a poisonous snake with a thick body and a broad triangular head, that makes a rattling noise with its tail.

rat·tle·trap (rat′əl·trap′), *n.* **1.** a rattling, rickety wagon or other vehicle. **2.** any shaky, rattling object.

rat·ty (rat′i), *adj.,* **-ti·er, -ti·est. 1.** of or like rats. **2.** full of rats. **3.** *Slang.* shabby.

rau·cous (rô′kəs), *adj.* hoarse; harsh-sounding. [< L *raucus*] —**rau′cous·ly,** *adv.* —**rau′cous·ness, rau·ci·ty** (rô′sə·ti), *n.*

rav·age (rav′ij), *v.,* **-aged, -ag·ing,** *n.* —*v.* lay waste; damage greatly; destroy. —*n.* violence; destruction; great damage. [< F, < *ravir* RAVISH] —**rav′ag·er,** *n.* —Syn. *v.* devastate, despoil, desolate, ruin. —*n.* havoc, waste.

rave (rāv), *v.,* **raved, rav·ing.** **1.** talk wildly: *an excited, angry person raves.* **2.** talk with too much enthusiasm: *she raved about her food.* **3.** howl; roar; rage. [? < OF *raver,* var. of *rêver* to dream] —Syn. **1.** storm, rant.

rav·el (rav′əl), *v.,* **-eled, -el·ing;** *esp. Brit.* **-elled, -el·ling,** *n.* —*v.* **1.** separate the threads of; fray. **2.** fray out; separate into threads. **3.** make plain or clear; unravel. **4.** become tangled, involved, or confused. **5.** tangle; involve. —*n.* an unraveled thread or fiber. [prob. < MDu. *ravelen*] —**rav′el·er,** *esp. Brit.* **rav′el·ler,** *n.*

rav·el·ing, *esp. Brit.* **rav·el·ling** (rav′əl·ing; rav′ling), *n.* something raveled out; a thread drawn from a woven or knitted fabric.

ra·ven (rā′vən), *n.* a large black bird like a crow but larger. —*adj.* deep, glossy black. [OE *hræfn*]

Raven (ab. 2 ft. long)

rav·en·ing (rav′ən·ing), *adj.* greedy and hungry.

rav·en·ous (rav′ən·əs), *adj.* **1.** very hungry. **2.** greedy. **3.** rapacious. —**rav′en·ous·ly,** *adv.* —**rav′en·ous·ness,** *n.*

ra·vine (rə·vēn′), *n.* a long, deep, narrow gorge worn by running water.

rav·ing (rāv′ing), *adj.* **1.** that raves; delirious; frenzied; raging. **2.** *Colloq.* remarkable; extraordinary. —*n.* delirious, incoherent talk.

rav·i·o·li (rav′i·ō′li), *n.pl.* small, thin pieces of dough filled with chopped meat, cheese, etc., cooked in boiling water and served with a seasoned tomato sauce. [< Ital., ult. < L *rapum* beet]

rav·ish (rav′ish), *v.* **1.** fill with delight. **2.** carry off by force. **3.** rape. [< OF *raviss-* < L *rapere* seize] —**rav′ish·er,** *n.* —**rav′ish·ment,** *n.*

rav·ish·ing (rav′ish·ing), *adj.* very delightful; enchanting. —**rav′ish·ing·ly,** *adv.*

raw (rô), *adj.* **1.** not cooked: *raw oysters.* **2.** in the natural state; not manufactured, treated, or prepared: *raw materials, raw hides.* **3.** not experienced; not trained: *a raw soldier.* **4.** damp and cold: *raw weather.* **5.** with the skin off; sore: *a raw spot.* **6.** brutally or coarsely frank. **7.** *Slang.* harsh; unfair: *a raw deal.* —*n.* **1.** the raw flesh. **2.** a raw or sore spot on the body. [OE *hrēaw*] —**raw′ly,** *adv.* —**raw′ness,** *n.* —Syn. *adj.* **2.** unworked, unrefined. **3.** unskilled, inexperienced. **4.** chilly, bleak.

Ra·wal·pin·di (rä′wəl·pin·di), *n.* capital of Pakistan, in the NW part.

raw-boned (rô′bōnd′), *adj.* gaunt.

raw·hide (rô′hīd′), *n., v.,* **-hid·ed, -hid·ing.** —*n.* **1.** the untanned skin of cattle. **2.** *Am.* rope or whip made of this. —*v. Am.* whip with a rawhide.

ray[1] (rā), *n.* **1.** line or beam of light. **2.** line or stream of heat, electricity, or energy. **3.** any stream of particles moving in the same line. **4.** a thin line like a ray, coming out from a center. **5.** part like a ray. The petals of a daisy and the arms of a starfish are rays. **6.** a slight trace; faint gleam. —*v.* send forth in rays; radiate. [< OF < L *radius.* Doublet of RADIUS.]

ray[2] (rā), *n.* any of several varieties of fishes, related to the sharks, that have broad, flat bodies with very broad pectoral fins. [< F < L *raia*]

ray·on (rā′on), *n. Am.* fiber or fabric made from cellulose treated with chemicals. Rayon is used instead of silk, wool, and cotton. [< ray[1]]

raze (rāz), *v.,* **razed, raz·ing.** tear down; destroy completely. Also, **rase.** [< F *raser* scrape, ult. < L *radere*]

ra·zor (rā′zər), *n.* tool with a sharp blade to shave with. [< OF *rasor* < *raser.* See RAZE.]

ra·zor·back (rā′zər·bak′), *n.* kind of thin, half-wild hog with a ridged back.

razz (raz), *Am., Slang.* —*v.* laugh at; make fun of. —*n.* derision. [< raspberry]

raz·zle-daz·zle (raz′əl·daz′əl), *Slang.* —*n.* performance that is fast, flashy, or showy and may also trick the eye. —*adj.* spectacular; flashy.

Rb, *Chem.* rubidium.

R.C. **1.** Red Cross. **2.** Roman Catholic.

rd. **1.** road. **2.** Rd., Road. **3.** rod; rods.

R.D., Rural Delivery.

re[1] (rā; rē), *n. Music.* the second tone of a scale. [see GAMUT]

re[2] (rē), *prep.* with reference to; about; concerning. [for L *in re* in the matter of]

Re, *Chem.* rhenium.

re–, *prefix.* **1.** again; anew; once more, as in *reappear, rebuild, reheat, reopen.* **2.** back, as in *recall, repay, replace.* [< L; also (before vowels), *red–*] ► The prefix re–, meaning "again," is separated from the word to which it is joined: (1) by a dieresis or hyphen when that word begins with e: *reënact, re-enact; reënlist; reënlist, re-enter, re-enter; reëxamine, re-examine;* and (2) by a hyphen when the form with hyphen can have a slightly different meaning from the form without: *reform,* to change, improve—*re-form,* to shape again; *recover,* to regain—*re-cover,* to cover again; and (3) by a hyphen (rarely) for emphasis, as in "he was now *re-seated* in fair comfort," or in informal or humorous compounds, *re-re-married.* Ordinarily there is no hyphen: *rearrange, refine, remit.*

The meaning of each of the following words is found by adding *again* or *anew* to the main part. The pronunciation of the main part is not changed.

re′ab·sorb′
re′ab·sorp′tion
re′ac·cept′
re′ac·com′mo·date
re′ac·com′pa·ny
re′ac·cuse′
re′a·dapt′
re′ad·dress′
re′ad·journ′
re′ad·just′
re′ad·just′ment
re′ad·mis′sion
re′ad·mit′
re′ad·mit′tance
re′a·dopt′
re′ad·vance′
re′af·firm′
re′af·firm′ance
re′af·fir·ma′tion
re′a·line′ment
re·an′i·mate
re·an·i·ma′tion
re′a·noint′
re′ap·pear′
re′ap·pear′ance
re′ap·pli·ca′tion
re′ap·ply′
re′ap·point′
re′ap·point′ment
re′ap·por′tion
re′ap·por′tion·ment
re′as·cend′
re′as·sem′ble
re′as·sem′bly
re′as·sert′
re′as·ser′tion
re′as·sess′
re′as·sign′
re′as·sign′ment
re′as·so′ci·ate
re′as·sume′
re′as·sump′tion
re′at·tach′
re′at·tain′
re′at·tempt′
re′a·wak′en
re·bap′tism
re′bap·tize′
re·bill′
re·bind′
re·birth′
re·born′
re·build′
re·built′
re·cap′i·tal·ize
re·charge′
re·char′ter
re·check′
re·choose′
re·chris′ten
re·cir′cle
re·cir′cu·late
re·clothe′
re·coin′
re·col′or
re′com·bi·na′tion

re′com·bine′
re·com′fort
re′com·mence′
re·com·mit′tal
re′com·pose′
re′con·ceal′
re·con′cen·trate
re′con·den·sa′tion
re′con·dense′
re′con·firm′
re·con′quer
re′con·quest
re·con′se·crate
re′con·sign′
re·con′sol·i·date
re′con·sol′i·da′tion
re·con′sti·tute
re′con·sti·tu′tion
re′con·vene′
re′con·ver′sion
re′con·vert′
re′con·vert′er
re′con·vey′
re′con·vey′ance
re·cop′y
re·cross′
re·crown′
re′crys·tal·li·za′tion
re·crys′tal·lize
re′de·cay′
re′de·ceive′
re′de·cide′
re′de·cline′
re·dec′o·rate
re′dec·o·ra′tion
re·ded′i·cate
re′ded·i·ca′tion
re′de·feat′
re′de·fend′
re′de·fy′
re·de·liv′er·y
re·dem′on·strate
re′dem·on·stra′tion
re′de·ny′
re′de·pos′it
re′de·scend′
re′de·scribe′
re′de·ter′mine
re′de·vel′op
re′di·gest′
re·dis′count
re′dis·cov′er
re′dis·cov′er·y
re·dis′trib·ute
re′dis·tri·bu′tion
re′di·vide′
re·do′
re′draft′
re·draw′
re·dress′
re·dry′
re·ëd′it
re·ëd′i·tor
re·ëd′u·cate

re′ëd·u·ca′tion
re′e·ject′
re′e·lec′tion
re′em·bark′
re′e·merge′
re′e·mer′gence
re·ëm′i·grate
re·ëm′pha·sis
re·ëm′pha·size
re′en·act′
re′en·act′ment
re′en·gage′
re′en·gage′ment
re′en·grave′
re·ën′list
re·ën·list′ment
re·ën′ter
re·ën′try
re′es·tab′lish
re′es·tab′lish·ment
re′ex·am′i·na′tion
re′ex·am′ine
re′ex·hib′it
re′ex·port′
re′ex·por·ta′tion
re·fash′ion
re·fas′ten
re·fit′
re·flow′
re·fold′
re·forge′
re·forg′er
re·for′ti·fy
re·frac′ture
re·frame′
re·fu′el
re·fur′nish
re·gath′er
re·gild′
re·gird′
re·glaze′
re·glo′ri·fy
re·glue′
re·grade′
re·group′
re·han′dle
re·heat′
re·heel′
re′ig·nite′
re′im·pose′
re′im·po·si′tion
re′im·press′
re′im·print′
re′im·pris′on
re′im·pris′on·ment
re′in·duce′
re′in·fect′
re′in·fec′tion
re′in·flame′
re′in·flate′
re′in·form′
re′in·fuse′
re′in·scribe′
re′in·sert′
re′in·ser′tion
re′in·spect′
re′in·spec′tion
re′in·spire′
re′in·stall′
re′in·stal·la′tion
re′in·stall′ment
re′in·struct′
re′in·sur′ance
re′in·sure′
re′in·sur′er
re·in′te·grate
re′in·te·gra′tion
re′in·ter′
re′in·ter′ment
re′in·ter′ro·gate
re′in·tro·duce′
re′in·tro·duc′tion
re′in·vent′
re′in·vest′
re′in·ves′ti·gate
re′in·vest′ment
re′in·vig′or·ate
re′in·vig′or·a′tion

re′in·vite′
re·is′sue
re·kin′dle
re·la′bel
re·lace′
re·lance′
re·latch′
re·laun′der
re·learn′
re·light′
re·line′
re·liq′ui·date
re·live′
re·load′
re·loan′
re·lo′cate
re′lo·ca′tion
re·made′
re·make′
re·mar′riage
re·mar′ry
re·match′
re·meas′ure
re·mi′grate
re·mil′i·ta·rize
re·mix′
re·mod′i·fy
re·mold′
re·name′
re·nom′i·nate
re′nom·i·na′tion
re·no′ti·fy
re·num′ber
re′ob·tain′
re′oc·cu·pa′tion
re·oc′cu·py
re·o′pen
re′op·pose′
re·or′der
re·pack′
re·pack′er
re·paint′
re·pa′per
re·pass′
re·pave′
re·ped′dle
re·pe′nal·ize
re·peo′ple
re·phrase′
re·plant′
re·plas′ter
re·play′
re·pledge′
re·pol′ish
re·pop′u·late
re·pour′
re·prime′
re·proc′ess
re′pro·claim′
re′pro·mul′gate
re·prove′
re′pub·li·ca′tion
re·pub′lish
re·pur′chase
re·pur′chas·er
re·pu′ri·fy
re·pur′pose
re′pur·sue′
re·quick′en
re·rate′
re·read′
re·reel′
re·roll′
re·route′
re·run′
re·sad′dle
re·sal′a·ble
re′sale′
re·seal′
re·seed′
re·seek′
re·seize′
re·sell′
re·serve′
re·set′tle
re·set′tle·ment
re·shape′
re·sharp′en

re·ship'
re·ship'ment
re·shuf'fle
re·sift'
re·sight'
re·soak'
re·sold'
re·sol'der
re·sole'
re'so·lid'i·fy
re·sound'
re·spell'
re·spread'
re·sprin'kle
re·stack'
re·stamp'
re·start'
re·state'
re·state'ment
re·stip'u·late
re·stock'
re·strength'en
re·stress'
re·strike'
re·string'
re·strive'
re·stud'y
re·sum'mon
re'sup·ply'
re·sur'face
re·surge'
re'sur·vey'
re·teach'

re·tell'
re·test'
re·tes'ti·fy
re·think'
re·tie'
re·told'
re·trans'fer
re'trans·late'
re·tri'al
re·try'
re·turf'
re·type'
re'up·hol'ster
re·use'
re·u'ti·lize
re·val'u·ate
re'val·u·a'tion
re·val'ue
re·vi'brate
re·vict'ual
re·vis'it
re·vi'tal·ize
re·vote'
re·voy'age
re·warm'
re·wash'
re·wa'ter
re·weigh'
re·wind'
re·wire'
re·word'
re·work'
re·write'

reach (rēch), v. 1. get to; come to; arrive at: *reach the top of a hill, the end of a book, an agreement,* etc. 2. stretch; stretch out: *reach toward or after something.* 3. extend in space, time, operation, effect, influence, etc. (to): *the power of Rome reached to the ends of the known world.* 4. extend to: *the radio reaches millions.* 5. get or come; function: *farther than the eye can reach.* 6. get in touch with by anything extended, cast, etc.; touch: *the anchor reached bottom.* 7. make a stretch of certain length with the hand, etc.: *I cannot reach to the top of the wall.* 8. move to touch or seize something; try to get: *the man reached for his gun.* 9. get at; influence: *men are reached by flattery.* 10. amount to; be equal to: *sums reaching a considerable amount.* 11. take or pass with the hand: *please reach me the newspaper.* —n. 1. a stretching out; reaching: *make a reach for the rope.* 2. extent or distance of reaching: *out of one's reach.* 3. range; power; capacity: *the reach of the mind.* 4. a continuous stretch or extent. [OE *rǣcan*] —reach'a·ble, adj. —reach'er, n. —Syn. v. 1. attain, gain.

re·act (ri·akt'), v. 1. act back; have an effect on the one that is acting: *unkindness often reacts on the unkind person.* 2. act in response: *dogs react to kindness by showing affection.* 3. act chemically: *acids react on metals.* 4. return to a previous state, level, etc.

re·act (rē·akt'), v. act over again.

re·act·ance (ri·ak'təns), n. Elect. that part of the impedance of an alternating current which is due to self-induction and capacity.

re·ac·tion (ri·ak'shən), n. 1. action in the opposite direction: *fever is a common reaction from a chill.* 2. a political tendency toward a previous state of affairs. 3. action in response to some influence or force: *our reaction to a joke is to laugh.* 4. Chem. action of two substances on each other. ≻ Reaction has escaped from chemistry and the biological sciences to become a counter word for any response of feeling or idea: *Let me have your reaction to* [often *on*] *this.* The objection to *reaction* in such use is the objection to all counter words. It tends to crowd out more appropriate or more exact words—*opinion, attitude, feeling, response, impression,* and any number of words for exact feelings and opinions.

re·ac·tion·ar·y (ri·ak'shən·er'i), adj., n., pl. -ar·ies. —adj. marked by or favoring reaction. —n. person who favors reaction, esp. in politics.

re·ac·tor (ri·ak'tər), n. Nuclear Physics. a special assembly for the production of a limited

release of nuclear (or atomic) energy, consisting of layers of fissionable material, such as uranium, spaced with moderators, such as graphite and heavy water, which slow down the speed and number of the neutrons intended for splitting the uranium nuclei; pile; nuclear reactor; atomic furnace.

read¹ (rēd), v., read (red), read·ing. 1. get the meaning of (writing or printing): *the blind read with their fingers.* 2. speak (printed or written words): *read this story to me.* 3. show by letters, figures, signs, etc.: *the thermometer reads 70 degrees.* 4. give as the word or words in a particular passage: *for "fail," a misprint, read "fall."* 5. study: *read law.* 6. get the meaning of; understand: *God reads men's hearts.* 7. give the meaning of; interpret: *a prophet reads the future.* 8. introduce (something not expressed or directly indicated) by one's manner of understanding or interpreting: *read a hostile intent in a friendly letter.* 9. produce a certain impression when read; mean: *this does not read like a child's composition.* 10. admit of being read or interpreted: *a rule that reads two different ways.* 11. bring or put by reading: *he reads himself to sleep.* 12. read out of, expel from (a political party, etc.). [OE *rǣdan* counsel]

read² (red), adj. having knowledge gained by reading; informed. [orig. pp. of *read¹*]

read·a·ble (rēd'ə·bəl), adj. 1. easy to read; interesting. 2. capable of being read. —read'a·bil'i·ty, read'a·ble·ness, n. —read'a·bly, adv.

read·er (rēd'ər), n. 1. person who reads. 2. person employed to read manuscripts and estimate their fitness for publication. 3. proofreader. 4. one who reads or recites to entertain an audience. 5. book for learning and practicing reading.

read·ing (rēd'ing), n. 1. act or process of getting the meaning of writing or printing. 2. a speaking out loud of written or printed words; public recital. 3. the study of books, etc. 4. written or printed matter read or to be read. 5. thing shown by letters, figures, or signs: *the reading of the thermometer was 96 degrees.* 6. the form of a given word or passage in a particular edition of a book: *no two editions have the same reading for that passage.* 7. interpretation. 8. extent to which one has read; literary knowledge. —adj. 1. that reads. 2. used in or for reading. 3. having a taste for reading.

Read·ing (red'ing), n. city in SE Pennsylvania.

read·y (red'i), adj., read·i·er, read·i·est, v., read·ied, read·y·ing, n. —adj. 1. prepared for action or use at once; prepared: *dinner is ready.* 2. properly equipped, finished, or arranged: *ships ready for battle.* 3. willing: *ready to face trial.* 4. quick; prompt: *a ready welcome.* 5. quick in thought or action; dexterous: *ready wit.* 6. apt; likely; liable: *too ready to find fault.* 7. immediately available: *ready money.* —v. make ready; prepare. —n. condition or state of being fit for action. [< OE *rǣde* ready] —read'i·ly, adv. —read'i·ness, n. —Syn. adj. 3. disposed. 4. unhesitating. 5. nimble. 6. prone.

read·y-made (red'i·mād'), adj. made for anybody who will buy; not made to order.

re·a·gent (rē·ā'jənt), n. substance used to detect the presence of other substances by the chemical reactions it causes.

re·al¹ (rē'əl; rēl), adj. 1. existing as a fact; not imagined or made up; actual; true: *a real experience, the real reason.* 2. genuine: *a real diamond.* 3. pertaining to things. 4. Law. noting or pertaining to immovable property. Lands and houses are called real property. 5. Math. either rational or irrational, not imaginary. [< LL *realis* < L *res* matter] —re'al·ness, n. —Syn. 1. positive, certain, substantial. 2. authentic. ≻ real, really. *Real* is not used in formal writing except as an adjective: *a real experience, a real chore.* In substandard use, *real* is an adverb, a more emphatic *very: Write real soon. It's real pretty. Really* is both an informal and a formal adverb: *a really successful party.*

re·al² (rē'əl; Sp. rä·äl'), n., pl. re·als, Sp. re·a·les (rä·ā'lās). a former small Spanish silver coin, worth about 12½ cents. [< Sp. < L *regalis* regal. Doublet of REGAL, ROYAL.]

real estate, land together with the buildings, trees, water, etc. on it.

re·al·ism (rē′əl·iz·əm), *n*. **1.** practical tendency. **2.** in art and literature, the picturing of life as it actually is. **3.** doctrine that material objects have a real existence independent of our consciousness of them. **4.** doctrine that general ideas have a real existence independent of the mind. —**re′al·ist**, *n*. —**re·al·is′tic**, *adj*. —**re·al·is′ti·cal·ly**, *adv*.

re·al·i·ty (ri·al′ə·ti), *n*., *pl*. **-ties. 1.** actual existence; true state of affairs: *ghosts have no place in reality*. **2.** a real thing; actual fact. **3.** in reality, really; actually; in fact; truly.

re·al·i·za·tion (rē′əl·ə·zā′shən), *n*. **1.** clear understanding; full awareness; perception. **2.** a realizing or being realized. **3.** exchange of property for its money value.

re·al·ize (rē′əl·iz), *v*., **-ized, -iz·ing. 1.** understand clearly; be fully aware of: *she realizes how hard you worked*. **2.** make real; bring into actual existence. **3.** cause to seem real. **4.** change (property) into money. **5.** obtain as a return or profit: *he realized $10,000*. **6.** bring as a return or profit. —**re′al·iz′a·ble**, *adj*. —**re′al·iz′er**, *n*. —Syn. **1.** comprehend. **2.** achieve, accomplish.

re·al·ly (rē′əl·i; rēl′i), *adv*. **1.** actually: *things as they really are*. **2.** genuinely; truly: *really extraordinary*. **3.** indeed: *Oh, really?* ➤ See real[1] for usage note.

realm (relm), *n*. **1.** kingdom. **2.** region or sphere in which something rules or prevails. **3.** a particular field of something: *the realm of biology*. [< OF *relaime* < *reial* REGAL]

Re·al·tor (rēl′tər; rē′əl-; -tôr), *n*. *Am*., *Trademark*. person engaged in the real estate business who is a member or affiliated member of the National Association of Real Estate Boards.

re·al·ty (rē′əl·ti), *n*. real estate.

real wages, wages measured in actual purchasing power.

ream[1] (rēm), *n*. 480 or 500 sheets of paper of the same size and quality. [< OF < Sp. < Ar. *rizmah* bundle]

ream[2] (rēm), *v*. enlarge or shape (a hole). [OE *rȳman* enlarge < *rūm* room]

ream·er (rēm′ər), *n*. tool for reaming.

reap (rēp), *v*. **1.** cut (grain). **2.** gather (a crop). **3.** cut grain or gather a crop from. **4.** get as a return or reward: *reap profits*. **5.** get a return. [OE *repan*] —**reap′a·ble**, *adj*. —**reap′er**, *n*.

re·ap·praise (rē′ə·prāz′), *v*., **-praised, -prais·ing.** give new consideration to the worth, desirability, etc. of. —**re′ap·prais′al**, *n*.

rear[1] (rir), *n*. **1.** the back part; back. **2.** space or position behind, or at the back of, anything. **3.** the last part of an army, fleet, etc. **4.** at or in the rear of, behind. —*adj*. at or in the back. [var. of *arrear*] —**rear′most**, *adj*.

rear[2] (rir), *v*. **1.** make grow; help to grow; bring up: *rear children*. **2.** set up; build: *rear a temple*. **3.** raise; lift up: *rear one's head*. **4.** of an animal, rise on the hind legs; rise. [OE *rēran* raise < *risan* rise] —**rear′er**, *n*. —Syn. **1.** foster. **2.** erect, construct. **3.** elevate, hoist. ➤ See raise for usage note.

rear admiral, a naval officer ranking next above a commodore and next below a vice-admiral.

re·arm (rē·ärm′), *v*. **1.** arm again; arm oneself again. **2.** supply with new or better weapons. —**re·ar·ma·ment** (rē·är′mə·mənt), *n*.

re·ar·range (rē′ə·rānj′), *v*., **-ranged, -rang·ing. 1.** arrange in a new or different way. **2.** arrange again. —**re′ar·range′ment**, *n*.

rear·ward (rir′wərd), *adv*., *adj*. toward or in the rear.

rea·son (rē′zən), *n*. **1.** cause; motive: *I have my own reasons for doing this*. **2.** justification; explanation. **3.** ability to think and draw conclusions. **4.** right thinking; good sense. **5.** sanity. **6.** by reason of, on account of; because of. —*v*. **1.** think; think logically: *man can reason*. **2.** draw conclusions or inferences from facts or premises. **3.** consider; discuss; argue. [< OF

< L *ratio*. Doublet of RATIO, RATION.] —**rea′son·er**, *n*. —Syn. *n*. **1.** ground. **3.** intellect. –*v*. **2.** infer, deduce. ➤ **reason . . . is because.** In formal English the construction beginning "The reason is . . ." is completed by a noun or a noun clause, to balance the noun *reason*: *The reason for my poor work in French was my intense dislike of the subject* (noun). *The reason for my poor work in French was that I disliked the subject intensely* (noun clause). But in speech not many noun clauses introduced by *that* are used and the connective that most obviously stresses the notion of reason is *because*, so that in colloquial English we should probably find: *The reason for my poor work in French was because I didn't like the subject*.

rea·son·a·ble (rē′zən·ə·bəl; rēz′nə-), *adj*. **1.** according to reason; sensible; not foolish. **2.** not asking too much; fair; just. **3.** not high in price; inexpensive. **4.** able to reason. —**rea′son·a·ble·ness**, **rea′son·a·bil′i·ty**, *n*. —**rea′son·a·bly**, *adv*.

rea·son·ing (rē′zən·ing; rēz′ning), *n*. **1.** process of drawing conclusions from facts. **2.** reasons; arguments.

re·as·sure (rē′ə·shur′), *v*., **-sured, -sur·ing. 1.** restore to confidence. **2.** assure again or anew. —**re·as·sur′ance**, *n*. —**re′as·sur′ing·ly**, *adv*.

re·bate (rē′bāt; ri·bāt′), *n*., *v*., **-bat·ed, -bat·ing.** —*n*. return of part of money paid; partial refund; discount. —*v*. give as a rebate. [< OF *rabattre* beat down < *re-* back + *abattre* ABATE] —**re′bat·er**, *n*. —Syn. *n*. deduction, allowance.

re·bec, re·beck (rē′bek), *n*. a musical instrument, somewhat like a violin, used in the Middle Ages. [< MF, var. of OF *rebebe*, ult. < Ar. *rabāb*]

Re·bec·ca (ri·bek′ə), *n*. *Bible*. the wife of Isaac and the mother of Esau and Jacob. Gen. 24 and 25.

reb·el (*n*., *adj*. reb′əl; *v*. ri·bel′), *n*., *adj*., *v*., **re·belled, re·bel·ling.** —*n*. person who resists or fights against authority instead of obeying. [< *v*.] —*adj*. defying law or authority: *the rebel army*. —*v*. **1.** resist or fight against law or authority. **2.** feel a great dislike or opposition. [< OF < L *rebellare*, ult. < *re-* again + *bellum* war. Doublet of REVEL.] —Syn. *n*. revolter, insurgent. –*v*. **1.** revolt, mutiny.

re·bel·lion (ri·bel′yən), *n*. **1.** active, armed resistance to one's government. **2.** resistance to any power or restriction. —Syn. **1.** revolt, insurrection, revolution, sedition.

re·bel·lious (ri·bel′yəs), *adj*. **1.** defying authority; acting like a rebel. **2.** hard to treat or deal with. **3.** of or characteristic of rebels or rebellion. —**re·bel′lious·ly**, *adv*. —**re·bel′lious·ness**, *n*. —Syn. **1.** mutinous, seditious. **2.** disobedient, intractable. —Ant. **2.** submissive.

re·bound (*v*. ri·bound′; *n*. rē′bound′, ri·bound′), *v*. **1.** spring back. **2.** cause to spring back. —*n*. a springing back. —Syn. *v*. **1.** recoil.

re·broad·cast (rē·brôd′kast′; -kåst′), *v*., **-cast** or **-cast·ed, -cast·ing**, *n*. —*v*. **1.** broadcast again or anew. **2.** relay by broadcast (messages, speeches, etc.), received from a broadcasting station). —*n*. program, etc., rebroadcast.

re·buff (ri·buf′), *n*. a blunt or sudden check to a person who makes advances, offers help, makes a request, etc. —*v*. give a rebuff to. [< F < Ital. *ribuffo*] —Syn. *v*. check, repulse, snub.

re·buke (ri·būk′), *v*., **-buked, -buk·ing**, *n*. —*v*. express disapproval of; reprove. —*n*. expression of disapproval; scolding. [< AF *rebuker*. Cf. OF *rebuchier* < *re-* back + *buchier* to strike] —**re·buk′er**, *n*. —**re·buk′ing·ly**, *adv*. —Syn. *v*. chide.

re·bus (rē′bəs), *n*. representation of a word or phrase by pictures suggesting the syllables or words. A picture of a cat on a log is a rebus for *catalog*. [< L, by means of objects]

re·but (ri·but′), *v*., **-but·ted, -but·ting.** oppose by evidence on the other side or by argument; try to disprove. [< AF, OF *reboter* < *re-* back + *boter* BUTT²] —**re·but′ter**, *n*.

re·but·tal (ri·but′əl), *n*. a rebutting.

rec., **1.** receipt. **2.** recipe. **3.** record.

re·cal·ci·trant (ri·kal′sə·trənt), *adj*. resisting authority or control; disobedient. —*n*. person

---

āge, cāre, fär; ēqual, tėrm; īce; ōpen, ôrder; put, rüle, ūse; tħ, then; ə=a in about.

who is recalcitrant. [< L *recalcitrans* kicking back, ult. < *re-* back + *calx* heel] —**re·cal'ci·trance, re·cal'ci·tran·cy,** *n.*

re·call (*v.* ri·kôl'; *n.* ri·kôl', rē'kôl'), *v.* **1.** call back to mind; remember. **2.** call back; order back: *the ambassador was recalled.* **3.** bring back: *recalled to life.* **4.** take back; withdraw: *recall an edition of a book.* **5.** remove (a public official) from office by vote of the people. —*n.* **1.** a recalling to mind. **2.** a calling back; ordering back. **3.** a taking back; revocation; annulment. **4.** removal of a public official from office by vote of the people. —**re·call'a·ble,** *adj.* —**re·call'ment,** *n.* —**Syn.** *v.* **1.** recollect. **2.** summon. **4.** revoke, cancel, retract, repeal.

re·cant (ri·kant'), *v.* **1.** take back formally or publicly; withdraw or renounce (a statement, opinion, purpose, etc.): *after careful study the scholar recanted his first opinion.* **2.** renounce an opinion or allegiance: *the prisoner would not recant.* [< L *recantare,* ult. < *re-* back + *canere* sing] —**re·can·ta·tion** (rē'kan·tā'shən), *n.* —**re·cant'er,** *n.* —**Syn.** **1.** abjure, forswear.

re·cap (rē'kap'; rē·kap'), *v.,* **-capped, -capping,** *n.* —*v.* put a strip of rubber or similar material on (a worn surface of an automobile tire), by cementing and vulcanizing. —*n.* tire that has been recapped.

re·ca·pit·u·late (rē'kə·pich'ə·lāt), *v.,* **-lat·ed, -lat·ing.** repeat or recite the main points of; tell briefly; sum up. —**re'ca·pit'u·la·tion,** *n.* —**re'ca·pit'u·la'tive, re·ca·pit·u·la·to·ry** (rē'kə·pich'- ə·lə·tō'rĭ; -tō'-), *adj.* —**re'ca·pit'u·la'tor,** *n.*

re·cap·ture (rē·kap'chər), *v.,* **-tured, -turing,** *n.* —*v.* capture again; have again. —*n.* a taking or being taken a second time.

re·cast (*v.* rē·kast', -käst'; *n.* rē'kast', -käst'), *v.,* **-cast, -cast·ing,** *n.* —*v.* **1.** cast again or anew. **2.** make over; remodel. —*n.* a recasting.

recd., rec'd., received.

re·cede (ri·sēd'), *v.,* **-ced·ed, -ced·ing 1.** go or move backward: *he receded from view.* **2.** slope backward: *a receding chin.* **3.** withdraw: *recede from a plan.* [< L, < *re-* back + *cedere* go] —**re·ced'ence,** *n.* —**Syn.** **1.** retreat, retire.

re·ceipt (ri·sēt'), *n.* **1.** a written statement that money, a package, a letter, etc., has been received. **2.** receipts, money received; amount or quantity received. **3.** a receiving or being received: *on receipt of the news he went home.* **4.** recipe. —*v.* *Am.* write on (a bill, etc.) that something has been received or paid for. [< OF < L *recepta,* fem. pp. of *recipere* RECEIVE] ➤ receipt, recipe (ri·sēt'; res'ə·pē). Both words mean "directions for making something." Locally one or the other may be preferred by cooks, but they are interchangeable in actual meaning. *Receipt* also means "a written acknowledgment for something received."

re·ceiv·a·ble (ri·sēv'ə·bəl), *adj.* **1.** fit for acceptance. **2.** on which payment is to be received.

re·ceive (ri·sēv'), *v.,* **-ceived, -ceiv·ing. 1.** take (something offered or sent); take into one's hands or possession: *receive gifts.* **2.** have (something) bestowed, conferred, etc.: *receive a name.* **3.** be given; get: *receive a letter from home.* **4.** take, accept, admit, or get something: *"Freely ye have received."* **5.** take; support; bear; hold: *the boat received a heavy load.* **6.** take or let into the mind. **7.** accept as true or valid: *a theory widely received.* **8.** agree to listen to: *receive confession.* **9.** experience; suffer; endure: *receive a blow.* **10.** let into one's house, society, etc. **11.** admit to a place; give shelter to: *receive strangers.* **12.** admit to a state or condition: *receive a person into the church.* **13.** be at home to friends and visitors: *she receives on Tuesdays.* **14.** *Radio.* change electrical waves into sound signals. [< OF < L, < *re-* back + *capere* take] —**Syn.** **11.** greet, welcome.

re·ceiv·er (ri·sēv'ər), *n.* **1.** person who receives. **2.** thing that receives. **3.** *Am.* part of a telephone held to the ear. **4.** a receiving set for radio, telephone, telegraph, etc. **5.** *Law.* person appointed to take charge of the property of others.

re·ceiv·er·ship (ri·sēv'ər·ship), *n. Law.* **1.** position of a receiver in charge of the property

of others. **2.** condition of being in the control of a receiver.

re·cent (rē'sənt), *adj.* **1.** done or made not long ago: *recent events.* **2.** not long past; modern: *a recent period in history.* [< L *recens*] —**re'cent·ly,** *adv.* —**re'cent·ness, re'cen·cy,** *n.* —**Syn.** **1.** new, fresh.

re·cep·ta·cle (ri·sep'tə·kəl), *n.* any container or place used to put things in to keep them conveniently. Bags, baskets, and vaults are all receptacles. [< L *receptaculum,* ult. < *recipere* RECEIVE]

re·cep·tion (ri·sep'shən), *n.* **1.** act of receiving: *calm reception of bad news.* **2.** fact of being received. **3.** manner of receiving: *a warm reception.* **4.** a gathering to receive and welcome people.

re·cep·tion·ist (ri·sep'shən·ist), *n.* person employed to receive callers, as in a doctor's office.

re·cep·tive (ri·sep'tiv), *adj.* able, quick, or willing to receive ideas, suggestions, impressions, etc. —**re·cep'tive·ly,** *adv.* —**re·cep·tiv·i·ty** (rē'- sep·tiv'ə·ti), **re·cep'tive·ness,** *n.*

re·cep·tor (ri·sep'tər), *n.* cell or group of cells sensitive to stimuli; sense organ.

re·cess (*n.* rē'ses *for 1,* ri·ses', rē'ses *for 2 and 3; v.* ri·ses'), *n.* **1.** time during which work stops: *there will be a short recess before the next meeting.* **2.** part in a wall set back from the rest; alcove; niche. **3.** an inner place or part; quiet, secluded place. —*v.* **1.** take a recess: *the convention recessed until this afternoon.* **2.** place in a recess; set back. **3.** make a recess in: *recess a wall.* [< L *recessus* a retreat < *recedere* RECEDE] —**Syn.** **1.** intermission, respite.

re·ces·sion[1] (ri·sesh'ən), *n.* **1.** a sloping backward. **2.** an indented place in a wall, etc. **3.** withdrawal. **4.** period of temporary business reduction, shorter and less extreme than a depression. [< L *recessio* < *recedere* RECEDE]

re·ces·sion[2] (rē·sesh'ən), *n.* a ceding back to a former owner. [< *re-* + *cession*]

re·ces·sion·al (ri·sesh'ən·əl), *adj.* sung or played while the clergy and the choir retire from the church at the end of a service. —*n.* a recessional hymn or piece of music.

re·ces·sive (ri·ses'iv), *adj.* likely to go back; receding. —**re·ces'sive·ly,** *adv.*

recessive character, the one of any pair of opposite characters that is latent and subordinate in an animal or plant, when both are present in the germ plasm.

Re·ci·fe (rə·sē'fə), *n.* seaport in E Brazil. Former name, Pernambuco.

rec·i·pe (res'ə·pē), *n.* **1.** set of directions for preparing something to eat. **2.** set of directions for preparing any thing or result. [< L, take! imperative of *recipere* take, RECEIVE] ➤ See receipt for usage note.

re·cip·i·ent (ri·sip'i·ənt), *n.* person or thing that receives something. —*adj.* receiving; willing to receive. [< L *recipiens.* See RECEIVE.] —**re·cip'i·ence, re·cip'i·en·cy,** *n.*

re·cip·ro·cal (ri·sip'rə·kəl), *adj.* **1.** in return: *although I gave him many presents, I had no reciprocal gifts from him.* **2.** mutual: *reciprocal liking.* **3.** *Gram.* expressing mutual action or relation. In "The two children like each other," *each other* is a reciprocal pronoun. —*n.* **1.** thing which is reciprocal to something else; counterpart. **2.** number so related to another that when multiplied together they give 1. 3 is the reciprocal of ⅓, and ⅓ is the reciprocal of 3. [< L *reciprocus* returning] —**re·cip'ro·cal·i·ty,** *n.* —**re·cip'ro·cal·ly,** *adv.*

re·cip·ro·cate (ri·sip'rə·kāt), *v.,* **-cat·ed, -cat·ing. 1.** give, do, feel, or show in return: *reciprocate favors.* **2.** move or cause to move with an alternating backward and forward motion. [< L, < *reciprocus* returning] —**re·cip'ro·ca'tion,** *n.* —**re·cip'ro·ca'tive, re·cip·ro·ca·to·ry** (ri·sip'rə·kə·tō'rĭ; -tō'-), *adj.*

rec·i·proc·i·ty (res'ə·pros'ə·ti), *n.* **1.** reciprocal state; mutual action. **2.** a mutual exchange, esp. an exchange of special privileges in regard to trade between two countries.

re·cit·al (ri·sīt′əl), n. 1. act of reciting; telling facts in detail. 2. story; account. 3. a musical entertainment, given usually by a single performer. —Syn. 2. narration, narrative.

rec·i·ta·tion (res′ə·tā′shən), n. 1. a reciting. 2. Am. a reciting of a prepared lesson by pupils before a teacher. 3. a repeating of something from memory. 4. piece repeated from memory.

rec·i·ta·tive (res′ə·tə·tēv′), n. Music. 1. a style of music halfway between speaking and singing. Operas often contain long passages of recitative. 2. passage, part, or piece in this style.

re·cite (ri·sīt′), v., -cit·ed, -cit·ing. 1. say over; repeat: recite a lesson. 2. Am. repeat something from memory; say part of a lesson. 3. give an account of in detail: recite one's adventures. 4. repeat (a poem, speech, etc.) to entertain an audience. [< L recitare < re- again + citare appeal to] —re·cit′er, n. —Syn. 1. rehearse. 3. relate, narrate.

reck (rek), v. Archaic. 1. care; heed. 2. be important or interesting; matter. [OE reccan]

reck·less (rek′lis), adj. rash; heedless; careless. —reck′less·ly, adv. —reck′less·ness, n.

reck·on (rek′ən), v. 1. find the number or value of; count: reckon the cost before you decide. 2. consider; judge; account: he is reckoned the best speller in the class. 3. Colloq. think; suppose. 4. depend; rely: you can reckon on our help. 5. settle; settle accounts. 6. reckon with, take into consideration. [OE (ge)recenian] —reck′on·er, n. —Syn. 1. compute, calculate. 2. regard, deem, esteem. 4. bank. ➤ See calculate for usage note.

reck·on·ing (rek′ən·ing; rek′ning), n. 1. method of computing; count; calculation. 2. settlement of an account. 3. bill, esp. at an inn or tavern. 4. calculation of the position of a ship. 5. position calculated.

re·claim (ri·klām′), v. 1. bring back to a useful, good condition. 2. demand the return of. —re·claim′a·ble, adj. —re·claim′er, n.

rec·la·ma·tion (rek′lə·mā′shən), n. a reclaiming or being reclaimed; restoration to a useful, good condition.

re·cline (ri·klīn′), v., -clined, -clin·ing. lean back; lie or lay down. [< L, < re- back + -clinare lean] —re·clin′er, n.

re·cluse (n. rek′lüs, ri·klüs′; adj. ri·klüs′), n. person who lives shut up or withdrawn from the world, as for religious or personal reasons. —adj. shut up or apart from the world. [< OF < L reclusus shut up < re- back + claudere shut] —re·clu·sion (ri·klü′zhən), n.

rec·og·ni·tion (rek′əg·nish′ən), n. 1. a knowing again; recognizing or being recognized: by a good disguise he escaped recognition. 2. acknowledgment: insist on complete recognition of rights. 3. favorable notice; acceptance. 4. a formal acknowledgment conveying approval or sanction. [< L recognitio]

re·cog·ni·zance (ri·kog′nə·zəns; -kon′ə-), n. Law. 1. bond binding a person to do some particular act. 2. sum of money to be forfeited if the act is not performed. [< OF reconoissance < reconoistre RECOGNIZE. Doublet of RECONNAISSANCE.]

rec·og·nize (rek′əg·nīz), v., -nized, -niz·ing. 1. know again: I could scarcely recognize my old friend. 2. identify: recognize a person from a description. 3. acknowledge acquaintance with; greet. 4. acknowledge; accept; admit: recognize an official's authority. 5. take notice of: wait till the chairman recognizes you. 6. show appreciation of. 7. acknowledge and agree to deal with: recognize a new government that has come to power. [< OF reconoistre < L, < re- again + com- (intensive) + (g)noscere learn. Doublet of RECONNOITER.] —rec′og·niz′a·ble, adj. —rec′og·niz′a·bly, adv. —rec′og·nized, adj. —rec′og·niz′er, Law re·cog·ni·zor (ri·kog′nə·zôr′; -kon′ə-), n.

re·coil (v. ri·koil′; n. ri·koil′, rē′koil), v. 1. draw back; shrink back: recoil at seeing a snake. 2. spring back: the gun recoiled when I fired. 3. react: revenge often recoils on the avenger. —n. a recoiling. [< OF reculer] —re·coil′er, n.

re·col·lect (rē′kə·lekt′), v. 1. collect again. 2. recover control of (oneself).

rec·ol·lect (rek′ə·lekt′), v. 1. call back to mind; remember. 2. bethink (oneself). —rec′ol·lec′tion, n. —rec′ol·lec′tive, adj.

rec·om·mend (rek′ə·mend′), v. 1. speak in favor of; suggest favorably. 2. advise. 3. make pleasing or attractive: the position of the camp recommends it as a summer home. 4. hand over for safekeeping. —rec′om·mend′a·ble, adj. —rec·om·mend·a·to·ry (rek′ə·men′də·tô′ri; -tō′-), adj. —rec′om·mend′er, n.

rec·om·men·da·tion (rek′ə·men·dā′shən), n. 1. a recommending. 2. anything that recommends a person or thing. 3. words of advice or praise. 4. thing recommended.

re·com·mit (rē′kə·mit′), v., -mit·ted, -mit·ting. 1. commit again. 2. refer again to a committee. —re·com·mit′ment, re·com·mit·tal (rē′kə·mit′əl), n.

rec·om·pense (rek′əm·pens), v., -pensed, -pens·ing. —v. 1. pay (a person); pay back; reward. 2. make a fair return for (an action, anything lost, damage done, hurt received, etc.). —n. payment; reward; return; amends. [< LL recompensare, ult. < L re- back + com- with, against + pendere weigh out in payment] —Syn. v. 1. repay, compensate, remunerate, requite.

rec·on·cile (rek′ən·sīl), v., -ciled, -cil·ing. 1. make friends again. 2. settle (a quarrel, disagreement, etc.). 3. make agree; bring into harmony. 4. make satisfied; make no longer opposed. [< L, ult. < re- back + concilium bond of union] —rec′on·cil′a·ble, adj. —rec′on·cil′a·bil′i·ty, rec′on·cil′a·ble·ness, n. —rec′on·cil′a·bly, adv. —rec′on·cil′er, n.

rec·on·cil·i·a·tion (rek′ən·sil′i·ā′shən), rec·on·cile·ment (rek′ən·sīl′mənt), n. 1. a reconciling; bringing together again in friendship. 2. a being reconciled; settlement or adjustment of disagreements, differences, etc. —rec·on·cil·i·a·to·ry (rek′ən·sil′i·ə·tô′ri; -tō′-), adj.

rec·on·dite (rek′ən·dīt; ri·kon′dīt), adj. 1. hard to understand; profound. 2. little known; obscure. 3. concealed. [< L reconditus stored away, ult. < re- back + com- up + dare put] —rec′on·dite·ly, adv. —rec′on·dite·ness, n.

re·con·di·tion (rē′kən·dish′ən), v. put in good condition by repairing, making over, etc.

re·con·nais·sance (ri·kon′ə·səns), n. examination or survey, esp. for military purposes. [< F. Doublet of RECOGNIZANCE.]

rec·on·noi·ter, rec·on·noi·tre (rek′ə·noi′tər; rē′kə-), v., -tered, -ter·ing; -tred, -tring. approach and examine or observe in order to learn something; make a survey of (the enemy, the enemy's strength or position, a region, etc.) in order to gain information for military purposes. [< F. Doublet of RECOGNIZE.] —rec′on·noi′ter·er, rec′on·noi′trer, n.

re·con·sid·er (rē′kən·sid′ər), v. consider again. —re′con·sid′er·a′tion, n.

re·con·struct (rē′kən·strukt′), v. rebuild; make over. —re′con·struc′tive, adj.

re·con·struc·tion (rē′kən·struk′shən), n. 1. a reconstructing. 2. thing reconstructed. 3. Reconstruction, Am. a. process by which the Southern States after the Civil War were reorganized and their relations with the national government were reëstablished. b. period when this was done, 1865–1877.

re·cord (v. ri·kôrd′; n., adj. rek′ərd), v. 1. set down in writing so as to keep for future use: record what the speaker says. 2. put in some permanent form; keep for remembrance: we record history in books. 3. put on a phonograph disk. —n. 1. thing written or kept. 2. an official written account: a secretary keeps a record of what is done at a meeting. 3. an official copy of a document. 4. Am. disk or cylinder used on a phonograph. 5. the known facts about what a person, animal, ship, etc., has done: a fine record at school. 6. Am. a criminal record. 7. the best yet done; best amount, rate, speed, etc., yet attained: hold the record for the high jump. 8. a recording or being recorded: what happened is a *matter of record*. **9. off the record**, not to be recorded or quoted. **10. on record**, recorded. —*adj.* making or affording a record: *a record wheat crop*. [< OF < L *recordari* remember, ult. < *re-* back + *cor* heart, mind]

re·cord·er (ri·kôr′dər), *n.* **1.** person whose business is to make and keep records. **2.** part of a machine that records. —**re·cord′er·ship**, *n.*

re·cord·ing (ri·kôr′ding), *n.* **1.** a phonograph record. **2.** the original transcription of any sound or combination of sounds.

re·count (ri·kount′), *v.* tell in detail; give an account of: *recount the happenings of the day*. [< OF, < *re-* again + *conter* relate, COUNT¹]

re·count (*n.* rē′kount′; *v.* rē·kount′), *n.* a second count. —*v.* count again.

re·coup (ri·küp′), *v.* **1.** make up for: *he recouped his losses*. **2.** repay. [< F, < *re-* back + *couper* cut] —**re·coup′ment**, *n.*

re·course (rē′kôrs; -kōrs; ri·kôrs′; -kōrs′), *n.* **1.** an appealing; turning for help or protection. **2.** person or thing appealed to or turned to for help or protection. **3. have recourse to**, appeal to; turn to for help. [< OF < L *recursus* retreat, ult. < *re-* back + *currere* run]

re·cov·er (ri·kuv′ər), *v.* **1.** get back (something lost, taken away, or stolen). **2.** make up for (something lost or damaged) : *recover lost time*. **3.** bring back to life, health, one's senses, or normal condition. **4.** get well; get back to a normal condition. **5.** get back to the proper position or condition: *he started to fall but recovered himself*. **6.** obtain by judgment in a law court. **7.** obtain judgment in one's favor in a law court. **8.** rescue; deliver. **9.** regain in usable form; reclaim. Many useful substances are now recovered from materials that used to be thrown away. [< OF < L *recuperare*. Doublet of RECUPERATE.] —**re·cov′er·a·ble**, *adj.* —**re·cov′er·er**, *n.*

re·cov·er (rē·kuv′ər), *v.* put a new cover on.

re·cov·er·y (ri·kuv′ər·i; -kuv′ri), *n.*, *pl.* **-er·ies. 1.** a recovering. **2.** a coming back to health or normal condition. **3.** a getting back something that was lost, taken away, or stolen. **4.** a getting back to a proper position or condition.

rec·re·ant (rek′ri·ənt), *adj.* **1.** cowardly. **2.** disloyal; traitorous. —*n.* **1.** coward. **2.** traitor. [< OF, confessing oneself beaten, ult. < L *re-* back + *credere* believe] —**rec′re·ance, rec′re·an·cy**, *n.* —**rec′re·ant·ly**, *adv.* —**Syn.** *adj.* **1.** craven.

rec·re·ate (rek′ri·āt), *v.*, **-at·ed, -at·ing. 1.** refresh with games, pastimes, exercises, etc. **2.** take recreation. [< L *recreatus* restored < *re-* again + *creare* create] —**rec′re·a′tive**, *adj.*

re·create (rē′kri·āt′), *v.*, **-at·ed, -at·ing.** create anew. —**re′-cre·a′tion**, *n.*

rec·re·a·tion (rek′ri·ā′shən), *n.* play; amusement. Walking, gardening, and reading are quiet forms of recreation. —**rec′re·a′tion·al**, *adj.*

re·crim·i·nate (ri·krim′ə·nāt), *v.*, **-nat·ed, -nat·ing.** accuse (someone) in return. [< Med.L, ult. < L *re-* back + *crimen* charge] —**re·crim′i·na′tion**, *n.* —**re·crim′i·na′tive, re·crim′i·na·to·ry** (ri·krim′ə·nə·tô′ri; -tō′-), *adj.*

re·cru·des·cence (rē′krü·des′əns), **re·cru·des·cen·cy** (-ən·si), *n.* a breaking out afresh; renewed activity. [< L *recrudescere*, ult. < *re-* again + *crudus* raw] —**re′cru·des′cent**, *adj.*

re·cruit (ri·krüt′), *n.* **1.** a newly enlisted soldier or sailor. **2.** a new member of any group or class. —*v.* **1.** get (men) to join an army or navy. **2.** strengthen or supply (an army, navy, etc.) with new men. **3.** get (new members). **4.** replenish. [< F *recruter* < OF *recrue* new growth, ult. < L *re-* back + *crescere* grow] —**re·cruit′er**, *n.* —**re·cruit′ment**, *n.*

rec·tal (rek′təl), *adj.* of the rectum.

rec·tan·gle (rek′tang′gəl), *n.* a four-sided figure with four right angles. [< LL, < L *rectus* right + *angulus* angle]

rec·tan·gu·lar (rek·tang′gyə·lər), *adj.* shaped like a rectangle. —**rec·tan′gu·lar′i·ty**, *n.* —**rec·tan′gu·lar·ly**, *adv.*

rec·ti·fy (rek′tə·fī), *v.*, **-fied, -fy·ing. 1.** make right; put right; adjust; remedy: *admit a mis-*

take and be willing to rectify it. **2.** change (an alternating current) into a direct current. **3.** purify; refine. [< LL, < L *rectus* right + *facere* make] —**rec′ti·fi′a·ble**, *adj.* —**rec′ti·fi·ca′tion**, *n.* —**rec′ti·fi′er**, *n.* —**Syn. 1.** correct, amend.

rec·ti·lin·e·ar (rek′tə·lin′i·ər), *adj.* **1.** forming a straight line. **2.** bounded or formed by straight lines. **3.** characterized by straight lines. **4.** in a straight line. [< L *rectus* straight + E *linear*] —**rec′ti·lin′e·ar·ly**, *adv.*

rec·ti·tude (rek′tə·tüd; -tūd), *n.* upright conduct or character; honesty; righteousness. [< LL, < L *rectus* straight] —**Syn.** integrity, virtue.

rec·tor (rek′tər), *n.* **1.** clergyman in the Protestant Episcopal Church or the Church of England who has charge of a parish. **2.** priest in the Roman Catholic Church who has charge of a congregation or religious house. **3.** head of a school, college, or university. [< L, ruler, < *regere* rule] —**rec·to·ri·al** (rek·tô′ri·əl; -tō′-), *adj.* —**rec′tor·ship**, *n.*

rec·to·ry (rek′tə·ri; rek′tri), *n., pl.* **-ries. 1.** a rector's house. **2.** *Brit.* a rector's benefice with all its rights, tithes, and lands.

rec·tum (rek′təm), *n.* the lowest part of the large intestine. [< NL, for L *intestinum rectum* straight intestine]

re·cum·bent (ri·kum′bənt), *adj.* lying down; reclining; leaning. [< L *recumbens* reclining] —**re·cum′ben·cy**, *n.* —**re·cum′bent·ly**, *adv.*

re·cu·per·ate (ri·kü′pər·āt; -kū′-), *v.*, **-at·ed, -at·ing. 1.** recover from sickness, exhaustion, loss, etc. **2.** restore to health, strength, etc. **3.** regain. [< L *recuperatus* recovered. Doublet of RECOVER.] —**re·cu′per·a′tion**, *n.* —**re·cu′per·a′tive**, *adj.* —**re·cu′per·a′tive·ness**, *n.* —**re·cu′per·a′tor**, *n.*

re·cur (ri·kėr′), *v.*, **-curred, -cur·ring. 1.** come up again; occur again; be repeated: *leap year recurs every four years*. **2.** return in thought or speech. [< L, < *re-* back + *currere* run]

re·cur·rent (ri·kėr′ənt), *adj.* **1.** recurring; occurring again; repeated. **2.** turned back so as to run in the opposite direction. —**re·cur′rence**, *n.* —**re·cur′rent·ly**, *adv.*

re·curve (ri·kėrv′), *v.*, **-curved, -curv·ing.** curve back; bend back.

red (red), *n., adj.*, **red·der, red·dest.** —*n.* **1.** the color of blood. **2.** any shade of that color. **3.** a red pigment or dye. **4.** red cloth or clothing. **5.** a red or reddish person, animal, or thing. **6. Red**, *a.* radical; revolutionary. Communists, extreme socialists, and anarchists are called Reds. **b.** an inhabitant of the Soviet Union. **7.** *Am.*, *Colloq.* **in the red**, in debt; losing money. **8. see red**, *Colloq.* become very angry. —*adj.* **1.** having the color of blood, being like it, or suggesting it. **2.** sore; inflamed. **3.** blushing. **4. Red**, *a.* extremely radical; revolutionary. **b.** pertaining to the Soviet Union. [OE *rēad*] —**red′dish**, *adj.* —**red′ness**, *n.*

re·dact (ri·dakt′), *v.* put into literary form; prepare for publication; edit. [< L *redactus* reduced < *re-* back + *agere* bring] —**re·dac′tion**, *n.* —**re·dac′tor**, *n.*

red·breast (red′brest′), *n. Am.* robin.

red·bud (red′bud′), *n. Am.* tree that has many small, pink, budlike flowers early in the spring.

red·cap (red′kap′), *n. Am.* porter at a railroad station, bus station, etc., usually wearing a red cap as part of his uniform.

Red Cross, an international organization to care for the sick and wounded in war and to relieve suffering caused by floods, fire, diseases, and other calamities.

red deer, 1. deer native to the forests of Europe and Asia, and formerly very abundant in England. **2.** *Am.* the common American deer in its summer coat.

red·den (red′ən), *v.* **1.** make or become red. **2.** blush.

re·deem (ri·dēm′), *v.* **1.** buy back: *property on which money has been lent is redeemed when the loan is paid back*. **2.** pay off: *we redeemed the mortgage*. **3.** carry out; make good; fulfill: *we redeem a promise by doing what we said we would*. **4.** set free; rescue; save: *redeemed from*

Rectangles

sin. **5.** make up for; balance: *a redeeming fea-ture.* [< L *redimere* < *re-* back + *emere* buy] —re·deem'a·ble, *adj.* —re·deem'er, *n.* —Syn. 1. repurchase, regain. 4. liberate, deliver, release.

re·demp·tion (rĭ·demp'shən), *n.* **1.** a redeeming. **2.** a being redeemed. **3.** deliverance; rescue. **4.** deliverance from sin; salvation. [< L *redemptio* < *redimere* REDEEM. Doublet of RANSOM.] —re·demp'tive, re·demp'to·ry, *adj.*

re·de·ploy (rē'di·ploi'), *v.* *Mil.* change the po-sition of troops from one theater of war to another. —re'de·ploy'ment, *n.*

red flag, 1. symbol of rebellion, revolution, etc. **2.** sign of danger. **3.** thing that stirs up anger.

red-hand·ed (red'han'did), *adj.* **1.** having hands red with blood. **2.** in the very act of crime. —red'-hand'ed·ly, *adv.* —red'-hand'ed·ness, *n.*

red·head (red'hed'), *n.* **1.** person having red hair. **2.** kind of duck resembling the canvasback, that has a red head. —red'-head'ed, *adj.*

red herring, 1. the common smoked herring. **2.** something used to draw attention away from the real issue.

red-hot (red'hot'), *adj.* **1.** red with heat; very hot. **2.** very enthusiastic; excited; violent. **3.** fresh from the source.

red·in·gote (red'ing·gōt), *n.* **1.** a man's outer coat with long skirts that overlap in front, now no longer worn. **2.** a somewhat similar coat now worn by women. [< F < E *riding coat*]

Redingote (def. 1)

red·in·te·grate (red·in'tə·grāt), *v.,* -grat·ed, -grat·ing. make or be-come whole again; renew; reëstab-lish. [< L, ult. < *re-* again + *integer* whole] —red·in'te·gra'tion, *n.* —red·in'te·gra'tive, *adj.*

re·di·rect (rē'də·rekt'; -dī-), *v.* direct again or anew. —*adj. Am., Law.* noting or pertaining to a second examination of a witness by the party calling him, after cross-examination. —re'di·rec'tion, *n.*

re·dis·trict (rē·dis'trikt), *v. Am.* divide into districts again.

red lead, red oxide of lead, Pb₃O₄, used in paint, in making glass, etc.

red-let·ter (red'let'ər), *adj.* **1.** marked by red letters. **2.** memorable; especially happy.

red-light district (red'līt'), *Am.* district containing many brothels. Formerly they were often indicated by red lights.

red man, an American Indian.

red·o·lent (red'ə·lənt), *adj.* **1.** having a pleas-ant smell; fragrant. **2.** smelling strongly; giving off an odor: *a house redolent of fresh paint.* **3.** suggesting thoughts or feelings: *"Ivanhoe" is a name redolent of romance.* [< L *redolens* emit-ting scent < *re-* back + *olere* to smell] —red'o-lence, red'o·len·cy, *n.* —red'o·lent·ly, *adv.*

re·dou·ble (rē·dub'əl), *v.,* -bled, -bling, *n.* —*v.* **1.** double again. **2.** increase greatly; double. **3.** repeat; echo. **4.** double back. **5.** *Games.* dou-ble an opponent's double. —*n.* act of redoubling; a double of a double. [< F *redoubler*] —re·dou'-ble·ment, *n.*

re·doubt (rĭ·dout'), *n.* a small fort standing alone. [< F *redoute* < Ital. < Med.L *reductus* re-treat < *reducere.* See REDUCE.]

re·doubt·a·ble (rĭ·dout'ə·bəl), *adj.* that should be feared or dreaded. [< OF, < *redouter* dread < *re-* again + *douter* DOUBT] —re·doubt'-a·ble·ness, *n.* —re·doubt'a·bly, *adv.*

re·dound (rĭ·dound'), *v.* come back as a result; contribute. [< OF < L *redundare* overflow, ult. < *re-* back + *unda* wave]

red pepper, 1. plant that has a podlike fruit that turns red when ripe. The sweet pepper and cayenne are kinds of red pepper. **2.** cayenne pepper.

re·dress (*v.* rĭ·dres'; *n.* rē'dres; rĭ·dres'), *v.* set right; repair; remedy: *redress the wrongs of the poor.* —*n.* a setting right; reparation; relief. [< F, < *re-* again + *dresser* (see DRESS)] —re·dress'-a·ble, *adj.* —re·dress'er, re·dres'sor, *n.*

Red River, river flowing from NW Texas into the Mississippi.

Red Sea, the narrow sea between Arabia and Africa, a part of the Indian Ocean.

red·skin (red'skin'), *n. Am.* American Indian.

red·start (red'stärt'), *n. Am.* a fly-catching warbler of America. [< *red* + *start* tail]

red tape, too much attention to details and forms. —red'-tape', *adj.*

red·top (red'top'), *n. Am.* kind of grass grown for forage and pasture.

re·duce (rĭ·dūs'; -dūs'), *v.,* -duced, -duc·ing. **1.** make less; make smaller; decrease: *reduce expenses, reduce weight.* **2.** become less or be made less: *everything reduces at last to this.* **3.** make lower in degree, intensity, etc.; weaken; dilute. **4.** bring down; lower: *misfortune reduced that poor woman to begging.* **5.** bring to a certain state, form, or condition; change: *reduce a noisy class to order.* **6.** change to another form: *reduce a statement to writing.* **7.** conquer; subdue. **8.** restore to its proper place or normal condition. **9.** *Chem.* **a.** combine with hydrogen. **b.** remove oxygen from. **c.** change (a compound) so that the valence of the positive element is lower. **10.** treat (a photographic negative) so as to make (it) less dense. [< L, < *re-* back + *ducere* bring] —re·duc'er, *n.* —re·duc'i·ble, *adj.* —re·duc'i-bil'i·ty, *n.* —re·duc'i·bly, *adv.* —Syn. 1. lessen, diminish. 4. humble, debase, degrade.

reducing agent, any chemical substance that reduces or removes the oxygen in a com-pound.

re·duc·ti·o ad ab·sur·dum (rĭ·duk'shi·ō ad ab·sér'dəm), *Latin.* reduction to absurdity.

re·duc·tion (rĭ·duk'shən), *n.* **1.** a reducing or being reduced. **2.** amount by which a thing is re-duced. **3.** form of something produced by reduc-ing; copy of something on a smaller scale. —re·duc'tion·al, *adj.* —re·duc'tive, *adj.*

re·dun·dan·cy (rĭ·dun'dən·si), **re·dun·dance** (-dəns), *n., pl.* -cies; danc·es. **1.** more than is needed. **2.** a redundant thing, part, or amount. **3.** the use of too many words for the same idea.

re·dun·dant (rĭ·dun'dənt), *adj.* **1.** extra; not needed. **2.** using too many words for the same idea; wordy. [< L, ppr. of *redundare* REDOUND] —re·dun'dant·ly, *adv.*

re·du·pli·cate (*v.* rĭ·dū'plə·kāt, -dū'-; *adj.* rĭ·dū'plə·kit, -kāt, -dū'-), *v.,* -cat·ed, -cat·ing, *adj.* —*v.* double; repeat. —*adj.* doubled or re-peated. —re·du'pli·ca'tion, *n.* —re·du'pli·ca'-tive, *adj.*

red·wood (red'wud'), *n. Am.* **1.** a California evergreen tree that sometimes grows to a height of 300 feet. **2.** its brownish-red wood.

re·ech·o, re·ech·o (rē·ek'ō), *v.,* -ech·oed, -ech·o·ing; -ech·oed, -ech·o·ing, *n., pl.* -ech-oes; -ech·oes. —*v.* echo back. —*n.* echo of an echo.

reed (rēd), *n.* **1.** a kind of tall grass with a hol-low jointed stalk that grows in wet places. **2.** such stalks. **3.** thing made from the stalk of a reed or anything like it. A musical instrument played by blowing through it and an arrow are both reeds. **4.** a thin piece of wood or metal in a musical instrument that produces sound when a current of air moves it. —*adj.* producing tones by means of reeds: *a reed organ.* [OE *hrēod*]

reed organ, a musical instrument producing tones by means of small metal reeds.

reed·y (rēd'i), *adj.,* reed·i·er, reed·i·est. **1.** full of reeds. **2.** made of a reed or reeds. **3.** like a reed or reeds. **4.** sounding like a reed instrument: *a thin, reedy voice.* —reed'i·ness, *n.*

reef¹ (rēf), *n.* a narrow ridge of rocks or sand at or near the surface of the water. [ult. < Scand. *rif*]

reef² (rēf), *n.* part of a sail that can be rolled or folded up to reduce its size. —*v.* re-duce the size of (a sail) by rolling or folding up a part of it. [< Scand. *rif* rib, reef. Cf. REEF¹.]

Beefed sail

reef·er¹ (rēf′ər), *n.* **1.** *Naut.* one who reefs. **2.** a short coat of thick cloth, worn esp. by sailors and fishermen. [< *reef*²]

reef·er² (rēf′ər), *n. Am., Slang.* cigarette containing marijuana. [< *reef*², in sense of "roll up"]

reef knot, square knot.

reek (rēk), *n.* a strong, unpleasant smell; vapor. —*v.* **1.** send out vapor or a strong, unpleasant smell. **2.** be wet with sweat or blood. [OE *rēc*] —**reek′er,** *n.* —**reek′y,** *adj.*

reel¹ (rēl), *n.* **1.** frame turning on an axis, for winding thread, yarn, a fish line, rope, wire, etc. **2.** spool; roller. **3. a.** spool for film. **b.** *Am.* length of motion-picture film rolled on a large spool. **4. off the reel,** *Colloq.* quickly and easily. —*v.* **1.** wind on a reel. **2.** draw with a reel or by winding: *reel in a fish.* **3.** reel off, say, write, or make in a quick, easy way. [OE *hrēol*]

reel² (rēl), *v.* **1.** sway, swing, or rock under a blow, shock, etc. **2.** sway in standing or walking. **3.** be in a whirl; be dizzy. **4.** go with swaying or staggering movements. **5.** sway; stagger; waver. —*n.* a reeling or staggering movement. [special use of *reel*¹]

reel³ (rēl), *n.* **1.** a lively dance. **2.** music for it. [special use of *reel*²]

re·en·force, re-en·force (rē′en·fôrs′; -fôrs′), *v., -forced, -forc·ing.* reinforce. —**re′·en·force′ment, re′-en·force′ment,** *n.*

re·en·try (rē′en′tri), *n.* an entering again or return, esp. of a ballistic missile into the earth's atmosphere.

reeve (rēv), *v.,* reeved or rove, reev·ing. pass (a rope) through a hole, ring, etc.

ref., **1.** referee. **2.** reference. **3.** referred.

re·fec·tion (ri·fek′shən), *n.* **1.** refreshment by food or drink. **2.** meal; repast.

re·fec·to·ry (ri·fek′tə·ri), *n., pl.* -ries. a room for meals, esp. in a monastery, convent, or school. [< LL *refectorium*, ult. < L *reficere* refresh < *re-* again + *facere* make]

re·fer (ri·fèr′), *v., -ferred, -fer·ring.* **1.** direct attention: *the minister often refers to the Bible.* **2.** relate; apply: *the rule refers only to special cases.* **3.** send or direct for information, help, or action: *we referred him to the boss.* **4.** turn for information or help: *writers often refer to a dictionary.* **5.** hand over; submit: *let's refer the dispute to the umpire.* **6.** consider as belonging or due; assign: *many people refer their failures to bad luck.* [< L, < *re-* back + *ferre* take] —**refer·a·ble** (ref′ər·ə·bəl), **re·fer′ra·ble,** *adj.* —**re·fer′rer,** *n.* —Syn. **1.** allude, advert. **6.** attribute.

ref·er·ee (ref′ər·ē′), *n., v.,* -eed, -ee·ing. —*n.* **1.** a judge of play in games and sports. **2.** person to whom something is referred for decision or settlement. —*v.* act as referee; act as referee in.

ref·er·ence (ref′ər·əns), *n.* **1.** a referring or being referred. **2.** direction of the attention: *this history contains many references to larger histories.* **3.** statement, book, etc., to which the attention is directed: *you will find that reference on page 16.* **4.** use for information or help: *a dictionary is a book of reference.* **5.** person who can give information about another person's character or ability. **6.** statement about someone's character or ability. **7.** relation; respect; regard: *a test without reference to age.* **8. in** or **with reference to,** about; concerning. **9. make reference to,** mention. —*adj.* used for information or help: *a reference library.* —**ref·er·en·tial** (ref′-ər·en′shəl), *adj.* —**ref′er·en′tial·ly,** *adv.*

ref·er·en·dum (ref′ər·en′dəm), *n., pl.* -dums, -da (-də). **1.** *Am.* process of submitting a law already passed by the lawmaking body to a direct vote of the citizens for approval or rejection. **2.** the submitting of any matter to a direct vote. [< L, that which must be referred. See REFER.]

ref·er·ent (ref′ər·ənt), *n.* object or class of objects, act, situation, quality, idea, or fancy to which a word refers.

re·fill (*v.* rē·fil′; *n.* rē′fil′), *v.* fill again. —*n.* material to refill a thing. —**re·fill′a·ble,** *adj.*

re·fine (ri·fīn′), *v., -fined, -fin·ing.* **1.** free from impurities: *sugar, oil, and metals are refined be-*

fore being used. **2.** make or become fine, polished, or cultivated: *reading good books helps to refine one's speech.* **3.** make very fine, subtle, or exact. —**re·fin′er,** *n.* —Syn. **1.** purify.

re·fined (ri·fīnd′), *adj.* **1.** freed from impurities: *refined sugar.* **2.** freed or free from grossness, coarseness, crudeness, vulgarity, or the like. **3.** well-bred. **4.** subtle: *refined distinctions.* **5.** minutely precise: *refined measurements.* —**re·fin·ed·ly** (ri·fīn′id·li), *adv.* —Syn. **2.** polished, cultured.

re·fine·ment (ri·fīn′mənt), *n.* **1.** fineness of feeling, taste, manners, or language. **2.** act or result of refining. **3.** improvement. **4.** a fine point; subtle distinction. **5.** an improved, higher, or extreme form of something.

re·fin·er·y (ri·fīn′ər·i), *n., pl.* -er·ies. a building and machinery for purifying metal, sugar, petroleum, or other things.

re·fit (rē·fit′), *v., -fit·ted, -fit·ting.* —*v.* **1.** fit, prepare, or equip for use again. **2.** get fresh supplies. —*n.* a refitting.

re·flect (ri·flekt′), *v.* **1.** turn back or throw back (light, heat, sound, etc.): *the sidewalks reflect heat on a hot day.* **2.** give back an image; give back a likeness or image of: *a mirror reflects your face and body.* **3.** reproduce or show like a mirror: *the newspaper reflected the owner's opinions.* **4.** think; think carefully: *take time to reflect before doing important things.* **5.** cast blame, reproach, or discredit: *bad behavior reflects on home training.* **6.** serve to cast or bring: *a brave act reflects credit on the person who does it.* **7.** cast back light, heat, etc.: *a mirror reflects.* [< L, < *re-* back + *flectere* to bend] —**re·flect′er,** *n.* —**re·flect′i·ble,** *adj.* —Syn. **4.** meditate, ponder, deliberate.

re·flec·tion, *esp. Brit.* **re·flex·ion** (ri·flek′-shən), *n.* **1.** a reflecting or being reflected. **2.** something reflected. **3.** likeness; image. **4.** thinking; careful thinking: *on reflection, the plan seemed too dangerous.* **5.** idea or remark resulting from careful thinking; idea; remark. **6.** remark, action, etc., that casts blame or discredit. **7.** blame; discredit. **8. angle of reflection,** angle which a ray of light, or the like, reflected from a surface, makes with a perpendicular to that surface at the point of reflection. See diagram under incidence. —**re·flec′tion·al,** *esp. Brit.* **re·flex′-ion·al,** *adj.*

re·flec·tive (ri·flek′tiv), *adj.* **1.** reflecting: *a reflective surface.* **2.** thoughtful: *a reflective look.* —**re·flec′tive·ly,** *adv.* —**re·flec′tive·ness, re·flec·tiv·i·ty** (rē′flek·tiv′ə·ti), *n.*

re·flec·tor (ri·flek′tər), *n.* any thing, surface, or device that reflects light, heat, sound, etc.

re·flex (*adj., n.* rē′fleks; *v.* ri·fleks′), *adj.* **1.** not voluntary; coming as a direct response to a stimulation of some sensory nerve cells. Sneezing is a reflex act. **2.** bent back; turned back. —*n.* **1.** action in direct response to a stimulation of some nerve cells. Sneezing, vomiting, and shivering are reflexes. **2.** something reflected; image; reflection: *a law should be a reflex of the will of the people.* —*v.* bend back; turn back. [< L *reflexus,* pp. of *reflectere.* See REFLECT.] —**re·flex′i·ble,** *adj.* —**re·flex′i·bil′i·ty,** *n.* —**re′flex·ly,** *adv.* —**re·flex·ive** (ri·flek′siv), *Gram.* —*adj.* **1.** of a verb, expressing an action in which the object of the action is the same as the subject. **2.** of a pronoun, indicating that it is the same as a preceding person or thing. —*n.* a reflexive verb or pronoun. In "The boy hurt himself," *hurt* and *himself* are reflexives. —**re·flex′ive·ly,** *adv.* —**re·flex′ive·ness, re·flex·iv·i·ty** (rē′fleks·iv′ə·ti), *n.* ⟩ Reflexive pronouns in English are made of the personal pronouns plus the suffix *-self* or *-selves.* They are called reflexive because the action of the verb is directed toward the subject of the construction: *He shaves himself.* *She bought herself two hats.*

ref·lu·ent (ref′lü·ənt), *adj.* flowing back; ebbing.

re·flux (rē′fluks), *n.* a flowing back; the ebb of a tide.

re·for·est (rē·fôr′ist; -for′-), *v.* replant (woodland) with trees. —**re′for·est·a′tion,** *n.*

re·form (ri·fôrm′), *v.* **1.** improve by some alteration of form, arrangement, etc.: *reform the calendar.* 2. change from worse to better: *reform a bad boy by understanding treatment.* 3. cause (a person) to abandon wrong or evil ways of life or conduct, and to adopt right ones. 4. put an end to (abuses, disorders, etc.); correct (errors, etc.). —*n.* 1. improvement by alteration of arrangement, etc. 2. an instance of this: *political reform, social reforms.* 3. changing one's manner of life, conduct, etc., for the better. [< L, ult. < *re-* again + *forma* form] —re·form′a·ble, *adj.* —re·form′a·tive, *adj.* —re·formed′, *adj.* —reform′ist, *n.* —**Syn.** *v.* 4. rectify.

re-form (rē·fôrm′), *v.* 1. form again. 2. take a new shape.

ref·or·ma·tion (ref′ər·mā′shən), *n.* 1. a reforming or being reformed; change for the better; improvement. 2. **Reformation,** the religious, social, and political movement in Europe in the 16th century that led to the establishment of Protestant churches. —ref′or·ma′tion·al, *adj.*

re·form·a·to·ry (ri·fôr′mə·tô′ri; -tō′-), *adj. n., pl. -ries.* —*adj.* serving to reform; intended to reform. —*n.* Also, *Am.* reform school. an institution for reforming young offenders against the laws; a prison for young criminals.

re·form·er (ri·fôr′mər), *n.* person who reforms, or tries to reform, some state of affairs, custom, etc.; supporter of reforms.

re·fract (ri·frakt′), *v.* bend (a ray) from a straight course: *water refracts light.* In the diagram, the ray of light SP in passing into the water is refracted from its original direction SPL to SPR. [< L *refractus* broken up < *re-* back + *frangere* to break] —re·frac′tive, *adj.* —re·frac′tive·ly, *adv.* —re·frac′tive·ness, *n.* —re·frac·tiv·i·ty (rē′frak·tiv′ə·ti), *n.* —re·frac′tor, *n.*

re·frac·tion (ri·frak′shən), *n.* the turning or bending of a ray of light when it passes obliquely from one medium into another of different density.

re·frac·to·ry (ri·frak′tə·ri), *adj.* 1. hard to manage; stubborn; obstinate: *mules are refractory.* 2. not yielding readily to treatment: *a refractory cough.* 3. *Mining.* hard to melt, reduce, or work. —re·frac′to·ri·ly, *adv.* —re·frac′to·ri·ness, *n.*

re·frain¹ (ri·frān′), *v.* hold oneself back: *refrain from wrongdoing.* [< OF < L, < *re-* back + *frenum* bridle] —**Syn.** forbear, abstain, desist.

re·frain² (ri·frān′), *n.* 1. phrase or verse repeated regularly in a song or poem. 2. music for it. [< OF, ult. < VL *refrangere* break off. See REFRACT.]

re·fran·gi·ble (ri·fran′jə·bəl), *adj.* capable of being refracted. [< *re-* + *frangere* to break] —re·fran′gi·bil′i·ty, re·fran′gi·ble·ness, *n.*

re·fresh (ri·fresh′), *v.* make or become fresh again; renew. [< OF, < *re-* again + *fresche* fresh] —re·fresh′ing, *adj.* —re·fresh′ing·ly, *adv.* —re·fresh′ing·ness, *n.* —**Syn.** freshen, renovate, revive, enliven.

re·fresh·er (ri·fresh′ər), *adj.* serving to reinstate knowledge or abilities, or to bring a person new needed knowledge. —*n.* person or thing that refreshes.

re·fresh·ment (ri·fresh′mənt), *n.* 1. a refreshing or being refreshed. 2. thing that refreshes. 3. refreshments, food or drink.

re·frig·er·ant (ri·frij′ər·ənt), *adj.* 1. refrigerating; cooling. 2. reducing bodily heat or fever. —*n.* 1. something that cools. 2. a liquid convertible into a gas at low temperature, used in mechanical refrigeration.

re·frig·er·ate (ri·frij′ər·āt), *v.,* -at·ed, -at·ing. make or keep cold or cool. [< L *refrigeratus,* ult. < *re-* again + *frigus* cold] —re·frig′er·a′tion, *n.*

re·frig·er·a·tor (ri·frij′ər·ā′tər), *n. Am.* box, room, etc., for keeping foods, etc., cool, as by means of ice or some other cooling agent.

ref·uge (ref′ūj), *n.* shelter or protection from danger, trouble, etc. [< OF < L, < *re-* back + *fugere* flee] —**Syn.** safety, security.

ref·u·gee (ref′yə·jē′; ref′yə·jē), *n.* person who flees for refuge or safety, esp. to a foreign country, as in time of persecution or war.

re·ful·gent (ri·ful′jənt), *adj.* shining brightly; radiant; splendid. [< L, < *re-* back + *fulgere* shine] —re·ful′gence, *n.* —re·ful′gent·ly, *adv.*

re·fund¹ (*v.* ri·fund′; *n.* rē′fund), *v.* pay back. —*n.* return of money paid. [< L, < *re-* back + *fundere* pour] —re·fund′er, *n.* —re·fund′ment, *n.*

re·fund² (rē·fund′), *v.* change (a debt, loan, etc.) into a new form. [< *re-* + *fund*]

re·fur·bish (rē·fėr′bish), *v.* polish up again; do up anew; brighten; renovate.

re·fus·al (ri·fūz′əl), *n.* 1. act of refusing. 2. right to refuse or take a thing before it is offered to others. —**Syn.** 1. denial, dissent.

re·fuse¹ (ri·fūz′), *v.,* -fused, -fus·ing. 1. decline to accept; reject: *refuse an offer.* 2. deny (a request, demand, invitation); decline to give or grant: *refuse admittance.* 3. decline (to do something): *refuse to discuss the question.* 4. decline to accept or consent: *she is free to refuse.* [< OF *refuser* < L *refusus,* pp. of *refundere.* See REFUND¹.] —re·fus′a·ble, *adj.* —re·fus′er, *n.*

ref·use² (ref′ūs), *n.* useless stuff; waste; rubbish. —*adj.* discarded. [< OF *refus,* pp. of *refuser* REFUSE¹.] —**Syn.** *n.* trash, dregs.

re·fute (ri·fūt′), *v.,* -fut·ed, -fut·ing. prove a claim, opinion, or argument) to be false or incorrect. [< L *refutare*] —ref·u·ta·ble (ref′yə·tə·bəl; ri·fū′tə-), *adj.* —ref′u·ta·bil′i·ty, *n.* —ref′u·ta·bly, *adv.* —ref·u·ta·tion (ref′yə·tā′shən), *n.* —re·fut′er, *n.* —**Syn.** disprove, rebut.

reg., 1. regiment. 2. register; registered. 3. regular; regularly. 4. regulation.

re·gain (ri·gān′), *v.* 1. get again or anew; recover: *regain health.* 2. get back to; reach again: *regain the shore.* —re·gain′a·ble, *adj.* —re·gain′er, *n.* —re·gain′ment, *n.*

re·gal (rē′gəl), *adj.* 1. belonging to a king; royal. 2. kinglike; fit for a king. [< L *regalis* < *rex* king. Doublet of ROYAL, REAL².] —re′gal·ly, *adv.* —**Syn.** 2. stately, splendid, magnificent.

re·gale (ri·gāl′), *v.,* -galed, -gal·ing. 1. entertain agreeably; delight with something pleasing. 2. entertain with a choice repast; feast. [< F, ult. < MDu. *vale* wealth] —re·gale′ment, *n.*

re·ga·li·a (ri·gā′li·ə; -gāl′yə), *n.pl.* 1. the emblems of royalty. Crowns, scepters, etc., are regalia. 2. the emblems or decorations of any society, order, etc. [< L, royal things, neut. pl. of *regalis* REGAL.]

re·gard (ri·gärd′), *v.* 1. consider; think of: *he is regarded as the best doctor in town.* 2. think highly of; care for; respect: *she always regards her parents' wishes.* 3. heed: *none regarded her screams.* 4. look at; look closely at; watch: *he regarded me sternly.* 5. concern; relate to: *I do not believe you as regards that.* —*n.* 1. consideration; thought; care: *have regard for the feelings of others.* 2. a look; steady look. 3. esteem; favor; good opinion. 4. regards, good wishes; an expression of esteem. 5. point; particular matter. 6. in or with regard to, about; concerning; relating to. 7. without regard to, not considering. [< F, < *re-* back + *garder* GUARD] —re·gard′a·ble, *adj.* —re·gard′er, *n.* —**Syn.** *v.* 1. deem, hold, account. 2. esteem. —*n.* 1. concern.

re·gard·ful (ri·gärd′fəl), *adj.* 1. heedful; observant; mindful. 2. considerate; respectful. —re·gard′ful·ly, *adv.* —re·gard′ful·ness, *n.*

re·gard·ing (ri·gär′ding), *prep.* with regard to; concerning; about: *a prophecy regarding the future.*

re·gard·less (ri·gärd′lis), *adj.* having or showing no regard; careless. —*adv.* 1. without regard. 2. *Am., Colloq.* with complete disregard of expense or consequence. —re·gard′less·ly, *adv.* —re·gard′less·ness, *n.*

re·gat·ta (ri·gat′ə), *n.* 1. a boat race. 2. a series of boat races. [< dial. Ital.]

re·gen·cy (rē′jən·si), *n., pl. -cies.* 1. position,

office, or function of a regent or group of regents. 2. government consisting of regents. 3. time during which there is a regency.

re·gen·er·ate (v. ri·jen′ər·āt; adj. ri·jen′ər-it), v., -at·ed, -at·ing, adj. —v. 1. improve the moral condition of; put new life and spirit in. 2. reform. 3. grow again; form (new tissue, a new part, etc.) to replace what is lost. —adj. made over in better form; formed anew morally or spiritually. [< L regeneratus made over, ult. < re- again + genus birth] —re·gen·er·a·cy (ri·jen′ər·ə·si), n. —re·gen′er·a′tion, n. —re·gen′er·a′tive, adj. —re·gen′er·a·tive·ly, adv. —re·gen′er·a′tor, n.

re·gent (rē′jənt), n. 1. person who rules when the regular ruler is absent or unfit. 2. member of a governing board. —adj. acting as a regent. [< L regens ruling] —re′gent·ship, n.

reg·i·cide¹ (rej′ə·sīd), n. person who kills a king. [< L rex king + E -cide < L -cida killer]

reg·i·cide² (rej′ə·sīd), n. crime of killing a king. [< L rex king + E -cide < L -cidium killing]

re·gime, ré·gime (ri·zhēm′; rā–), n. 1. system of government or rule; prevailing system. 2. system of living; regimen. [< F < L regimen. Doublet of REGIMEN.]

reg·i·men (rej′ə·men; –mən), n. set of rules or habits of diet, exercise, or manner of living intended to improve health, reduce weight, etc. [< L, < regere to rule. Doublet of REGIME.]

reg·i·ment (n. rej′ə·mənt; v. rej′ə·ment), n. 1. unit of an army consisting of several companies of soldiers organized into one large group, usually commanded by a colonel. A regiment is larger than a battalion and smaller than a brigade. 2. a large number. —v. 1. form into a regiment or organized group. 2. treat in a strict or uniform manner: a totalitarian state regiments its citizens. [< LL regimentum rule < regere to rule]

reg·i·men·tal (rej′ə·men′təl), adj. of or pertaining to a regiment. —n. regimentals, military uniform. —reg′i·men′tal·ly, adv.

reg·i·men·ta·tion (rej′ə·men·tā′shən), n. 1. formation into organized or uniform groups. 2. a making uniform. 3. subjection to control.

Re·gi·na (ri·jī′nə), n. city in S Canada, capital of the province of Saskatchewan.

re·gion (rē′jən), n. 1. any large part of the earth's surface: the region of the equator. 2. place; space; area: an unhealthful region. 3. Anat. part of the body: the region of the heart. 4. sphere; domain: the region of art. [< L regio < regere to direct]

re·gion·al (rē′jən·əl), adj. of or in a particular region: a regional storm. —re′gion·al·ly, adv.

reg·is·ter (rej′is·tər), n. 1. list; record: a register of attendance is kept in our school. 2. book in which a list or record is kept. 3. thing that records. A cash register shows the amount of money taken in. 4. registration or registry. 5. registrar. 6. an opening with an arrangement to regulate the amount of air or heat that passes through. 7. range of a voice or an instrument. 8. the exact fit of lines, columns, colors, etc., in printing. —v. 1. write in a list or record: register the names of the new members. 2. have one's name written in a list or record: a person must register before he can vote. 3. indicate; record: the thermometer registers 90 degrees. 4. show (surprise, joy, anger, etc.) by the expression on one's face or by actions. 5. have (a letter, parcel, etc.) recorded in a post office, paying extra postage for special care in delivery. 6. of lines, columns, colors, etc., fit or correspond exactly in printing. [< Med.L registrum < L registum, neut. pp., recorded < re- back + gerere carry] —reg′is·tered, adj. —reg′is·ter·er, n. —reg·is·tra·ble (rej′is·trə·bəl), adj.

reg·is·trar (rej′is·trär′), n. official who keeps a register; official recorder. [var. of register < register]

reg·is·tra·tion (rej′is·trā′shən), n. 1. a registering. 2. an entry in a register. 3. number of people registered. —reg′is·tra′tion·al, adj.

reg·is·try (rej′is·tri), n., pl. –tries. 1. a registering; registration. 2. place where a register is kept; office of registration. 3. book in which a list or record is kept; register.

reg·nant (reg′nənt), adj. 1. ruling. 2. exercising sway or influence; predominant. 3. prevalent; widespread. [< L regnans ruling < regnum kingdom]

re·gress (v. ri·gres′; n. rē′gres), v. go back; move in a backward direction. —n. a going back; movement backward. [< L regressus a return < re- back + gradi go] —re·gres′sion, n.

re·gret (ri·gret′), n., v., -gret·ted, -gret·ting. —n. 1. sorrowful longing for what is gone; sense of loss: it is a matter of regret that I could not see my mother before leaving. 2. the feeling of being sorry for some fault, act, etc., of one's own: regret for discourtesy shown or injustice done. 3. regrets, feelings of sorrow for what is lost, gone, done, or past: recall: waste time in useless regrets. 4. Usually, regrets, a polite reply declining an invitation. —v. feel regret about. [< OF regreter < OE grētan, cry, greet] —re·gret′ful, adj. —re·gret′ful·ly, adv. —re·gret′ful·ness, n. —re·gret′ta·ble, adj. —re·gret′ta·bly, adv. —re·gret′ter, n.

reg·u·lar (reg′yə·lər), adj. 1. fixed by custom or rule; usual; normal: six o'clock was his regular hour of rising. 2. following some rule or principle; according to rule: a period is the regular ending for a sentence. 3. coming, acting, or done again and again at the same time: Saturday is a regular holiday. 4. steady; habitual: a regular customer. 5. even in size, spacing, or speed; well-balanced: regular features, regular teeth. 6. symmetrical. 7. having all its angles equal and all its sides equal. 8. orderly; methodical: lead a regular life. 9. properly fitted or trained. 10. Gram. having the usual changes of form to show tense, number, person, etc. 11. Colloq. thorough; complete. 12. permanently organized: the regular army. 13. of or belonging to the permanent army of a country. 14. of, pertaining to, or conforming to the requirements of a political party or other established organization: the regular candidate. 15. belonging to a religious order bound by certain rules. —n. 1. member of a regularly paid group of any kind: the army was made up of regulars and volunteers. 2. Am. a party member who faithfully stands by his party. [< L, < regula RULE] —reg′u·lar′i·ty, n. —reg′u·lar·ly, adv. —Syn. adj. 1. typical, standard. 4. constant.

reg·u·lar·ize (reg′yə·lər·īz′), v., -ized, -iz·ing. make regular. —reg′u·lar·i·za′tion, n.

reg·u·late (reg′yə·lāt), v., -lat·ed, -lat·ing. 1. control by rule, principle, or system: private schools regulate the behavior of students. 2. keep at some standard: regulate the temperature of the room. 3. adjust so as to ensure correct working: regulate a watch. 4. put in good condition: regulate digestion. [< LL, < regula RULE] —reg′u·lat′a·ble, reg·u·la·ble (reg′yə·lə·bəl), adj. —reg′u·la′tive, adj.

reg·u·la·tion (reg′yə·lā′shən), n. 1. control by rule, principle, or system: without regulation there can be no coöperation between men. 2. rule; law: traffic regulations. —adj. 1. according to or required by a regulation; standard: a regulation uniform. 2. usual; ordinary.

reg·u·la·tor (reg′yə·lā′tər), n. 1. person or thing that regulates. 2. device in a clock or watch to make it go faster or slower. 3. a very accurate clock used as a standard of time. —reg·u·la·to·ry (reg′yə·lə·tô′ri, –tō′–), adj.

re·gur·gi·tate (rē·gėr′jə·tāt), v., -tat·ed, -tat·ing. 1. rush, surge, or flow back, as liquids, gases, undigested food, etc. 2. throw up, as food from the stomach. [< Med.L regurgitatus, ult. < L re- back + gurges whirlpool] —re·gur′gi·ta′tion, n.

re·ha·bil·i·tate (rē′hə·bil′ə·tāt), v., -tat·ed, -tat·ing. 1. restore to a good condition; make over in a new form: rehabilitate an old house. 2. restore to former standing, rank, rights, privileges, reputation, etc. [< Med.L, ult. < L re- again + habilis fit (see ABLE)] —re′ha·bil′i·ta′tion, n.

re·hash (v. rē·hash'; n. rē'hash), v. deal with again; work up (old material) in a new form. —n. 1. a rehashing. 2. something old put in a different form.

re·hearse (ri·hèrs'), v., -hearsed, -hears·ing. 1. practice (a play, part, etc.) for a public performance. 2. drill or train (a person, etc.) by repetition. 3. tell in detail; repeat. [< OF, < re- again + hercier to harrow, ult. < L hirpex rake] —re·hears'al, n. —re·hears'er, n. —Syn. 3. narrate, relate, recount.

Reich (rīh), n. German. Germany; the German state.

reichs·mark (rīhs'märk'), n., pl. -marks, -mark. the unit of money of Germany established in 1924.

Reichs·tag (rīhs'täk'), n. the former elective legislative assembly of Germany.

reign (rān), n. 1. period of power of a ruler: Queen Victoria's reign lasted sixty-four years. 2. royal power. 3. existence everywhere; prevalence. —v. 1. be a ruler: a king reigns over his kingdom. 2. exist everywhere; prevail: on a still night silence reigns. [< OF < L regnum < regere to rule]

Reign of Terror, a period of the French Revolution from about March, 1793, to July, 1794, during which many persons considered undesirable by the ruling group were ruthlessly executed.

re·im·burse (rē'im·bèrs'), v., -bursed, -bursing. pay back: you reimburse a person for expenses made for you. [< re- + obs. imburse < Med.L, < L in- into + LL bursa purse; patterned on F rembourser] —re'im·burse'ment, n. —re'im·burs'er, n.

re·im·port (v. rē'im·pôrt', -pōrt'; n. rē·im'-pôrt, -pōrt), v. import (something previously exported). —n. reimportation.

re·im·por·ta·tion (rē'im·pôr·tā'shən; -pōr-), n. 1. an importing of something previously exported. 2. goods reimported.

Reims (rēmz; Fr. raNs), n. city in N France. Also, **Rheims.**

rein (rān), n. 1. a long, narrow strap or line fastened to a bridle or bit, by which to guide and control an animal. 2. a means of control and direction. 3. **give rein to,** let move or act freely, without guidance or control. —v. 1. check or pull with reins. 2. guide and control. [< OF rene, ult. < L retinere hold back, RETAIN]

re·in·car·nate (rē'in·kär'nāt), v., -nat·ed, -nat·ing. give a new body to (a soul). —re'in·car·na'tion, n.

rein·deer (rān'dir'), n., pl. -deer. kind of large deer with branching horns, living in northern regions, used to pull sleighs and also for meat. [< Scand. hreindȳri < hreinn reindeer + dȳr animal]

re·in·force (rē'in·fôrs', -fōrs'), v., -forced, -forc·ing. 1. strengthen with new force or materials: reinforce an army, a bridge, etc. 2. strengthen: reinforce an argument, etc. Also, **reënforce, re-enforce.** —re'in·forc'er, n.

reinforced concrete, concrete with metal embedded in it to make the structure stronger.

re·in·force·ment (rē'in·fôrs'mənt; -fōrs'-), n. 1. act of reinforcing. 2. a being reinforced. 3. something that reinforces. 4. reinforcements, extra soldiers or warships. Also, **reënforcement, re-enforcement.**

re·in·state (rē'in·stāt'), v., -stat·ed, -stat·ing. restore to a former position or condition; establish again. —re'in·state'ment, n.

re·it·er·ate (rē·it'ər·āt), v., -at·ed, -at·ing. say or do several times; repeat (an action, demand, etc.) again and again. [< L, ult. < re- again + iterum again] —re·it'er·a'tion, n. —re·it'er·a'tive, adj. —re·it'er·a'tive·ly, adv.

re·ject (v. ri·jekt'; n. rē'jekt), v. 1. refuse to take, use, believe, accept, acknowledge, hear, consider, grant, etc.: he tried to join the army but was rejected. 2. throw away as useless or unsatisfactory: reject all apples with soft spots. 3. vomit. —n. a rejected person or thing. [< L rejectus < re- back + jacere to throw] —re·ject'a·ble, adj. —re·ject'er, n. —re·ject'ing·ly,

adv. —re·jec'tion, n. —Syn. v. 1. decline, rebuff, repulse.

re·joice (ri·jois'), v., -joiced, -joic·ing. 1. be glad; be filled with joy. 2. make glad; fill with joy. [< OF rejoiss-, ult. < L re- again + gaudere be glad] —re·joic'er, n. —re·joic'ing, n. —re·joic'ing·ly, adv. —Syn. 2. cheer, delight.

re·join[1] (rē·join'), v. 1. join or unite again. 2. join the company of again. [< re- + join]

re·join[2] (ri·join'), v. answer; reply. [< F, < re- back + joindre join]

re·join·der (ri·join'dər), n. an answer to a reply; response. —Syn. retort.

re·ju·ve·nate (ri·jü'və·nāt), v., -nat·ed, -nat·ing. make young or vigorous again; give youthful qualities to. [< re- + L juvenis young] —re·ju've·na'tion, n. —re·ju've·na'tor, n.

re·lapse (ri·laps'), v., -lapsed, -laps·ing, n. —v. fall or slip back into a former state, way of acting, etc.: relapse into silence. —n. a relapsing. [< L relapsus < re- back + labi to slip] —re·laps'er, n.

re·late (ri·lāt'), v., -lat·ed, -lat·ing. 1. give an account of; tell: the traveler related his adventures. 2. connect in thought or meaning: "better" and "best" are related to "good." 3. be connected in any way: we are interested in what relates to ourselves. [< L relatus, pp. to referre < re- back + ferre bring] —re·lat'er, re·la'tor, n. —Syn. 1. recount, recite, narrate. 3. refer, pertain.

re·lat·ed (ri·lāt'id), adj. 1. connected. 2. belonging to the same family; connected by a common origin. —re·lat'ed·ness, n. —Syn. 2. allied, cognate, akin.

re·la·tion (ri·lā'shən), n. 1. connection in thought or meaning: your answer has no relation to the question. 2. connection between persons, groups, countries, etc.: the relation of mother and child. 3. person who belongs to the same family as another, such as a father, brother, aunt, etc.; relative. 4. reference; regard: we must plan with relation to the future. 5. act of telling; account: we were interested in his relation of his adventures. —re·la'tion·al, adj. —Syn. 2. alliance, relationship, affiliation.

re·la·tion·ship (ri·lā'shən·ship), n. 1. connection. 2. condition of belonging to the same family.

rel·a·tive (rel'ə·tiv), n. 1. person who belongs to the same family as another, such as father, brother, aunt, etc. 2. a relative pronoun, adjective, or adverb. —adj. 1. related or compared to each other: consider the relative merits of your proposal and mine. 2. relative to, a. about; concerning. b. in proportion to. 3. depending for meaning on a relation to something else. East is a relative term. 4. Gram. introducing a subordinate clause; referring to another person or thing. In "The man who wanted it is gone," who is a relative pronoun, and who wanted it is a relative clause. —rel'a·tive·ness, n. ▶ **relative clauses.** A relative clause is an adjective clause introduced by a relative pronoun, that, which, or who: The rain that began in the morning kept on all night. A relative clause stands immediately after the noun it modifies. In the sentence above, the clause modifies rain. In colloquial and informal English relative clauses often have no pronoun: The ideas we held in common were few indeed. [Formal: The ideas that we held. . . .] ▶ **relative pronouns.** The relative pronouns are as, that, what, whatever, which (of which, whose), who (whose, whom), whoever: Somebody, who [or whom] I don't know, shouted, "Put 'em out." That refers to persons or things; who to persons. Which refers to animals or objects or situations, and also to collective nouns even if they refer to persons.

rel·a·tive·ly (rel'ə·tiv·li), adv. 1. in a relative manner; in relation to something else; comparatively: a relatively small difference. 2. in relation or with reference (to): the value of one thing relatively to other things. 3. in proportion (to): a subject little understood relatively to its importance.

rel·a·tiv·i·ty (rel′ə·tiv′ə·ti), *n.* 1. a being relative. 2. *Physics.* character of being relative rather than absolute, as ascribed to motion or velocity. 3. theory expressed in certain equations by Einstein. According to it, the only velocity we can measure is velocity relative to some body; observers on any celestial body may regard that body as motionless except for its rotation and acceleration and obtain the same observations as they would on any other celestial body, and will then obtain always the same value for the velocity of light; the mass of a moving body increases in dependence on its velocity; in a certain sense space is curved.

re·lax (ri·laks′), *v.* 1. loosen up; make or become less stiff or firm: *relax when you dance.* 2. make or become less strict or severe; lessen in force: *discipline is relaxed on the last day of school.* 3. reduce strain and worry; be lazy and carefree: *take a vacation and relax.* 4. weaken. [< L *relaxare*, ult. < *re-* back + *laxus* loose. Doublet of RELEASE.] —**re·lax·ed·ly** (ri·lak′sid·li), *adv.* —**re·lax′er,** *n.*

re·lax·a·tion (rē′lak·sā′shən), *n.* 1. a loosening: *relaxation of the muscles.* 2. a lessening of strictness, severity, force, etc. 3. relief from work or effort; recreation; amusement.

re·lay (rē′lā; ri·lā′), *n.* 1. a fresh supply, esp. of horses or men. 2. a relay race. 3. one part of a relay race. 4. *Elect.* an electromagnetic device in which a weak current controls a stronger current, used in transmitting telegraph or telephone messages over long distances. —*v.* 1. take and carry farther. 2. *Elect.* transmit by relay. [< OF *relais* reserve pack of hounds, etc., ult. < *re-* back + *laier* leave < Gmc.]

re·lay (rē·lā′), *v.,* -laid, -lay·ing. lay again.

re·lay race (rē′lā), race in which each member of a team runs only his share of the way.

re·lease (ri·lēs′), *v.,* -leased, -leas·ing, *n.* —*v.* 1. let go; let loose: *the prisoner was released.* 2. set free; relieve: *release from a promise.* 3. give up (legal right, claim, etc.); make over to another (property, etc.). 4. *Am.* permit to be published, shown, sold, etc. —*n.* 1. a letting go; setting free: *the release of the slaves.* 2. freedom; relief: *release from pain.* 3. part that releases other parts of a machine. 4. *Law.* a. surrender of right, estate, etc., to another. b. document that does this. 5. *Am.* permission for publication, exhibition, sale, etc. 6. article, statement, etc., distributed for publication. [< OF *relaissier* < L *relaxare.* Doublet of RELAX.] —**re·leas′a·ble,** *adj.* —**re·lease′ment,** *n.* —**re·leas′er,** *n.*

re·lease (rē·lēs′), *v.,* -leased, -leas·ing. lease again.

rel·e·gate (rel′ə·gāt), *v.,* -gat·ed, -gat·ing. 1. send away, usually to a lower position or condition. 2. send into exile; banish. 3. hand over (a matter, task, etc.). [< L, < *re-* back + *legare* to despatch] —**rel·e·ga·ble** (rel′ə·gə·bəl), *adj.* —**rel′e·ga′tion,** *n.*

re·lent (ri·lent′), *v.* become less harsh or cruel; be more tender and merciful. [ult. < L *re-* again + *lentus* slow] —**re·lent′ing·ly,** *adv.*

re·lent·less (ri·lent′lis), *adj.* without pity; unyielding; harsh. —**re·lent′less·ly,** *adv.* —**re·lent′less·ness,** *n.* —**Syn.** ruthless, implacable.

rel·e·vant (rel′ə·vənt), *adj.* bearing upon or connected with the matter in hand; to the point: *be sure your questions are relevant.* [< L *relevans* refreshing, ult. < *re-* back + *levis* light] —**rel′e·vance,** **rel′e·van·cy,** *n.* —**rel′e·vant·ly,** *adv.* —**Syn.** pertinent, applicable, appropriate.

re·li·a·ble (ri·lī′ə·bəl), *adj.* worthy of trust; that can be depended on: *reliable sources of news.* —**re·li′a·bil′i·ty, re·li′a·ble·ness,** *n.* —**re·li′a·bly,** *adv.* —**Syn.** dependable, trustworthy.

re·li·ance (ri·lī′əns), *n.* 1. trust; dependence. 2. confidence. 3. thing on which one depends.

re·li·ant (ri·lī′ənt), *adj.* 1. relying; depending. 2. confident. 3. relying on oneself.

rel·ic (rel′ik), *n.* 1. thing, custom, etc., that remains from the past. 2. something belonging to a holy person, kept as a sacred memorial. 3. keepsake; souvenir. 4. relics, remains; ruins. [< OF < L *reliquiae,* pl., remains]

rel·ict (rel′ikt), *n.* widow. [< Med.L *relicta,* orig. fem. pp. of L *relinquere.* See RELINQUISH.]

re·lief (ri·lēf′), *n.* 1. the lessening of, or freeing from, a pain, burden, difficulty, etc. 2. something that lessens or frees from pain, burden, difficulty, etc.; help given to poor people; aid; help. 3. something that makes a pleasing change or lessens strain. 4. release from a post of duty, as by the coming of a substitute. 5. change of persons on duty. 6. persons who relieve others from duty; person who does this. 7. reinforcements. 8. projection or apparent projection of figures and designs from a surface in sculpture, drawing, painting, etc. 9. figure or design standing out from the surface from which it is cut, shaped, or stamped. 10. form of any part of the earth's surface with special regard to differences in elevation. 11. in relief, standing out from a surface. 12. distinctness, as with reference to a background. [< OF, < *relever* RELIEVE] —**Syn.** 2. succor, remedy.

relief map, map that shows the different heights of a surface by using shading, colors, solid materials, etc.

re·lieve (ri·lēv′), *v.,* -lieved, -liev·ing. 1. make less; make easier; reduce the pain or trouble of: *aspirin will relieve a headache.* 2. set free: *your coming relieves me of the bother of writing a long letter.* 3. bring aid to; help: *soldiers were sent to relieve the fort.* 4. give variety or a pleasing change to: *a black dress relieved by red trimming.* 5. free (a person on duty) by taking his place. 6. make stand out more clearly. [< OF < L *relevare* lighten. See RELEVANT.] —**re·liev′a·ble,** *adj.* —**re·liev′er,** *n.* —**Syn.** 1. mitigate, alleviate.

re·li·gion (ri·lij′ən), *n.* 1. recognition of and belief in a superhuman power or powers to whom obedience, reverence, and worship are due. 2. the feeling or the spiritual attitude of those recognizing such a superhuman power. 3. manifestation of such feeling in conduct or life. 4. any system of faith in and worship of a Supreme Being or a god or gods: *the Christian religion, the religion of the Mohammedans.* 5. sense of obligation. [< L *religio* respect for what is sacred]

re·li·gi·os·i·ty (ri·lij′i·os′ə·ti), *n.* affectation of religious feeling.

re·li·gious (ri·lij′əs), *adj.* 1. of or connected with religion: *religious meetings.* 2. much interested in religion; devoted to the worship of God or gods: *an intensely religious person.* 3. belonging to an order of monks, nuns, friars, etc. 4. of or connected with such an order. 5. strict: *religious care.* —*n.* 1. monk, nun, friar, etc.; member of a religious order. 2. such persons collectively. —**re·li′gious·ly,** *adv.* —**re·li′gious·ness,** *n.*

re·lin·quish (ri·ling′kwish), *v.* 1. give up; desist from: *relinquish all hope, bad habits, etc.* 2. give over (to); renounce or surrender (a possession, right, etc.). 3. let go (something held, the hold, etc.). [< OF *relinquiss-,* ult. < L *re-* behind + *linquere* leave] —**re·lin′quish·er,** *n.* —**re·lin′quish·ment,** *n.* —**Syn.** 1. abandon, resign.

rel·i·quar·y (rel′ə·kwer′i), *n.,* pl. -quar·ies. a small box or other receptacle for a relic or relics. [< OF *reliquaire* < *relique* RELIC]

rel·ique (rel′ik; *Fr.* rə·lēk′), *n.* relic. [< F]

rel·ish (rel′ish), *n.* 1. a pleasant taste; good flavor: *hunger gives relish to simple food.* 2. something to add flavor to food. Olives and pickles are relishes. 3. slight dash (of something). 4. liking; appetite; enjoyment. —*v.* 1. make pleasing to the taste. 2. like the taste or flavor of. 3. take pleasure in; enjoy. [earlier *reles* < OF, remainder, < *relesser* RELEASE] —**rel′ish·a·ble,** *adj.* —**rel′ish·er,** *n.* —**rel′ish·ing·ly,** *adv.* —**Syn.** *n.* 1. savor. 3. trace, touch, smack.

re·luc·tance (ri·luk′təns), **re·luc·tan·cy** (-tən·si), *n.* 1. a reluctant feeling or action; unwillingness. 2. slowness in action because of unwillingness.

re·luc·tant (ri·luk′tənt), *adj.* 1. unwilling; showing unwillingness. 2. slow to act because unwilling. [< L *reluctans* struggling against, ult.

< *re*- back + *lucta* wrestling] —re·luc′tant·ly, *adv.* —Syn. 1. loath, averse.

re·ly (ri·lī′), *v.*, -lied, -ly·ing. depend; trust: *rely on your own efforts.* [< OF < L *religare* bind fast < *re*- back + *ligare* bind]

re·main (ri·mān′), *v.* 1. continue in a place; stay: *remain in the city.* 2. continue without change as to some form, state, or quality specified: *remain active in business.* 3. be left after a part, quantity, or number has been taken away or destroyed: *the years of life that remain.* 4. be left as not included; be still to be dealt with: *some objections remain.* —n. remains, a. what is left. b. a dead body. [< OF < L, < *re*- back + *manere* stay] —Syn. *v.* 1. abide, rest, sojourn.

re·main·der (ri·mān′dər), *n.* 1. the part left over; the rest: *if you take 2 from 9, the remainder is 7.* 2. copies of a book left over after the sale has practically ceased. —Syn. 1. residue, remnant, balance, surplus.

re·mand (ri·mand′, -mänd′), *v.* 1. send back. 2. send back (a prisoner or an accused person) to prison. —n. a remanding. [< LL, < L *re*- back + *mandare* consign] —re·mand′ment, *n.*

re·mark (ri·märk′), *v.* 1. say, write, or comment casually. 2. notice; observe: *did you remark his expression?* —n. 1. something said in few words; short statement. 2. act of noticing; observation. [< F, < *re*- again + *marquer* to mark] —Syn. *v.* 2. note, regard. —n. 1. comment.

re·mark·a·ble (ri·mär′kə·bəl), *adj.* worthy of notice; unusual. —re·mark′a·ble·ness, *n.* —re·mark′a·bly, *adv.* —Syn. notable, noteworthy, extraordinary, singular. —Ant. commonplace.

Rem·brandt (rem′brant), *n.* 1606–1669, Dutch painter and etcher.

re·me·di·a·ble (ri·mē′di·ə·bəl), *adj.* that can be remedied or cured. —re·me′di·a·bly, *adv.*

re·me·di·al (ri·mē′di·əl), *adj.* remedying; curing; helping; relieving: *remedial reading.* —re·me′di·al·ly, *adv.*

rem·e·dy (rem′ə·di), *n., pl.* -dies, *v.*, -died, -dy·ing. —n. 1. a means of removing or relieving diseases or any bad condition; cure. 2. *Law.* legal means of enforcing a right or redressing a wrong. —v. put or make right; cure. [< L *remedium*] —rem′e·di·less, *adj.* —Syn. *n.* 1. restorative, corrective.

re·mem·ber (ri·mem′bər), *v.* 1. have (something) come into the mind again; call to mind; recall. 2. recall something. 3. keep in mind; take care not to forget. 4. have memory: *dogs remember.* 5. make a gift to; reward; tip. 6. mention (a person) as sending friendly greetings; recall to the mind of another. [< OF < L, ult. < *re*- again + *memor* mindful of] —re·mem′ber·a·ble, *adj.* —re·mem′ber·er, *n.*

re·mem·brance (ri·mem′brəns), *n.* 1. power to remember; act of remembering; memory. 2. state of being remembered. 3. keepsake; souvenir. 4. remembrances, greetings.

re·mem·branc·er (ri·mem′brən·sər), *n.* person or thing that reminds one; reminder.

re·mind (ri·mīnd′), *v.* make (one) think (of something); cause to remember. —re·mind′er, *n.*

rem·i·nisce (rem′ə·nis′), *v.*, -nisced, -nisc·ing. talk or think about past experiences or events.

rem·i·nis·cence (rem′ə·nis′əns), *n.* 1. a remembering; recalling past happenings, etc. 2. Often, reminiscences. account of something remembered; recollection. [< L, ult. < *reminisci* remember] —rem′i·nis′cent, *adj.* —rem′i·nis′cent·ly, *adv.*

re·miss (ri·mis′), *adj.* careless; slack; neglectful; negligent: *be remiss in one's duty.* [< L *remissus* < *re*- back + *mittere* send] —re·miss′ness, *n.* —Syn. derelict, thoughtless.

re·mis·si·ble (ri·mis′ə·bəl), *adj.* that can be remitted. —re·mis′si·bil′i·ty, *n.*

re·mis·sion (ri·mish′ən), *n.* 1. a letting off (from debt, punishment, etc.). 2. pardon; forgiveness. 3. a lessening (of pain, force, labor, etc.).

re·mit (ri·mit′), *v.*, -mit·ted, -mit·ting. 1. send money to a person or place: *enclosed is our bill; please remit.* 2. send (money due). 3. refrain from carrying out; refrain from exacting; cancel: *remit a punishment or fine.* 4. pardon; forgive: *power to remit sins.* 5. make less; decrease: *remit one's efforts.* 6. become less. 7. send back, esp. to prison. [< L *remittere* send back. See REMISS.] —re·mit′ta·ble, *adj.* —re·mit′tal, *n.* —re·mit′ter, *n.*

re·mit·tance (ri·mit′əns), *n.* 1. a sending money to someone at a distance. 2. the money that is sent.

re·mit·tent (ri·mit′ənt), *adj.* lessening for a time; lessening at intervals. —re·mit′tent·ly, *adv.*

rem·nant (rem′nənt), *n.* a small part left. [< OF *remenant*, ppr. of *remenoir* REMAIN] —Syn. rest, fragment.

re·mod·el (rē·mod′əl), *v.*, -eled, -el·ing; *esp. Brit.* -elled, -el·ling. 1. model again. 2. make over: *remodel an old barn into a house.*

re·mon·e·tize (rē·mun′ə·tīz; -mon′-), *v.*, -tized, -tiz·ing. *Am.* restore to use as legal tender, esp. silver. —re·mon′e·ti·za′tion, *n. Am.*

re·mon·strance (ri·mon′strəns), *n.* protest; complaint.

re·mon·strant (ri·mon′strənt), *adj.* remonstrating; protesting. —n. person who remonstrates. —re·mon′strant·ly, *adv.*

re·mon·strate (ri·mon′strāt), *v.*, -strat·ed, -strat·ing. 1. say in protest; object. 2. reason or plead in protest. [< Med.L *remonstratus* pointed out, ult. < L *re*- back + *monstrum* sign] —re·mon·stra′tion (rē′mon·strā′shən; rem′ən-), *n.* —re·mon·stra·tive (ri·mon′strə·tiv), *adj.* —re·mon·stra·tor (ri·mon′strā·tər), *n.*

re·morse (ri·môrs′), *n.* deep, painful regret for having done wrong. [< L *remorsus* torment, ult. < *re*- back + *mordere* to bite] —re·morse′ful, *adj.* —re·morse′ful·ly, *adv.* —re·morse′ful·ness, *n.* —re·morse′less, *adj.* —re·morse′less·ly, *adv.* —re·morse′less·ness, *n.* —Syn. compunction, contrition.

re·mote (ri·mōt′), *adj.*, -mot·er, -mot·est. 1. far away; far off: *a remote country.* 2. out of the way; secluded: *a remote village.* 3. distant: *a remote relative.* 4. slight; faint: *I haven't the remotest idea what you mean.* [< L *remotus*, pp. of *removere* REMOVE] —re·mote′ly, *adv.* —re·mote′ness, *n.*

remote control, control from a distance usually by electrical connection or radio signal.

re·mount (*v.* rē·mount′; *n.* rē′mount′, rē·mount′), *v.* 1. mount again. 2. furnish with fresh horses. —n. a fresh horse, or a supply of fresh horses, for use.

re·mov·a·ble (ri·müv′ə·bəl), *adj.* that can be removed. —re·mov′a·bil′i·ty, re·mov′a·ble·ness, *n.* —re·mov′a·bly, *adv.*

re·mov·al (ri·müv′əl), *n.* 1. a removing; taking away: *after the removal of the soup, fish was served.* 2. change of place: *removal to larger quarters.* 3. dismissal from an office or position.

re·move (ri·müv′), *v.*, -moved, -mov·ing, *n.* —v. 1. move from a place or position; take off; take away: *remove your hat.* 2. get rid of; put an end to: *remove all doubt.* 3. kill. 4. dismiss from an office or position: *the governor removed the mayor for failing to do his duty.* 5. go or move away. —n. 1. a moving away. 2. change of residence. 3. step or degree of distance: *at every remove the mountain seemed smaller.* [< OF < L, < *re*- back + *movere* to move] —re·mov′er, *n.* —Syn. *v.* 1. dislodge, shift, displace.

re·moved (ri·müvd′), *adj.* 1. distant; remote. 2. separated by one or more steps or degrees of relationship.

re·mu·ner·ate (ri·mū′nər·āt), *v.*, -at·ed, -at·ing. pay for work, services, trouble, etc.; reward. [< L *remuneratus*, ult. < *re*- back + *munus* gift] —re·mu′ner·a′tion, *n.* —re·mu′ner·a·tive (ri·mū′nər·ā′tiv; -ə·tiv), *adj.* —re·mu′ner·a′tive·ly, *adv.* —re·mu′ner·a′tor, *n.* —Syn. recompense, repay.

Re·mus (rē′məs), *n. Roman Myth.* the twin

brother of Romulus. As children they were nursed by a wolf; later Romulus founded Rome and slew Remus for leaping contemptuously over the wall of his new city.

ren·ais·sance (ren′ə·säns′; ren′ə·säns; ri·nā′-səns), n. 1. revival; new birth. 2. the **Renaissance, a.** the great revival of art and learning in Europe during the 14th, 15th, and 16th centuries. **b.** period of time when this revival occurred. **c.** style of art, architecture, etc., of this period. [< F, < *renaître* be born again, ult. < L *renasci*. See RENASCENT.] ➤ **renaissance, renascence.** The first spelling is the more common. The word is capitalized when it refers to the period of history, not when referring to a revival, as "the prewar renaissance in American poetry."

re·nal (rē′nəl), adj. of or pertaining to the kidneys. [< L, < *ren* kidney]

re·nas·cence (ri·nas′əns; -nā′səns), n. 1. revival; new birth; renewal. 2. a being renascent. 3. the Renascence, the Renaissance.

re·nas·cent (ri·nas′ənt; -nā′sənt), adj. being born again; reviving; springing again into being or vigor. [< L, < *re*- again + *nasci* be born]

rend (rend), v., **rent, rend·ing. 1.** pull apart violently; tear: *wolves will rend a lamb.* **2.** split: *lightning rent the tree.* **3.** disturb violently: *a mind rent by doubt.* **4.** remove with force or violence. [OE *rendan*] —**rend′er,** n. —Syn. 1. rip, sunder, sever.

ren·der (ren′dər), v. 1. cause to become; make: *an accident has rendered him helpless.* **2.** give; do: *what service has he rendered?* **3.** offer for consideration, approval, payment, etc.; hand in; report: *the treasurer rendered an account of all the money spent.* **4.** give in return: *render thanks.* **5.** pay as due: *render tribute to a conqueror.* **6.** bring out the meaning of; represent: *the actor rendered the part of Hamlet well.* **7.** play or sing (music). **8.** change from one language to another; translate. **9.** melt (fat, etc.); clarify or extract by melting. [< OF *rendre* < L *reddere* give as due, pay < *re*- as due + *dare* give; infl. by L *prendere* take] —**ren′der·a·ble,** adj. —**ren′der·er,** n. —Syn. 6. interpret.

ren·dez·vous (rän′də·vü), n., pl. **-vous** (-vüz), v., **-voused** (-vüd), **-vous·ing** (-vü′ing). —n. 1. an appointment or engagement to meet at a fixed place or time; meeting by agreement. 2. a meeting place; gathering place. 3. place agreed on for a meeting at a certain time, esp. of troops or ships. —v. Am. meet at a rendezvous. [< F, < *rendez-vous* betake yourself!]

ren·di·tion (ren·dish′ən), n. 1. a rendering. 2. Am. the rendering of a dramatic part, music, etc., so as to bring out the meaning. 3. translation.

ren·e·gade (ren′ə·gād), n. deserter from a religious faith, a political party, etc.; traitor. —adj. deserting; disloyal; like a traitor. [< Sp. < Med.L *renegatus* denied. See RENEGE.] —Syn. n. recreant, backslider.

re·nege (ri·nig′), v., **-neged, -neg·ing,** n. —v. 1. fail to play a card of the suit that is led, although you have one. 2. *Colloq.* back out; fail to keep a promise. —n. in cardplaying, failure to follow suit when able to do so. [< Med.L, < L *re*- back + *negare* deny] —**re·neg′er,** n.

re·new (ri·nü′; -nū′), v. 1. make new again; make like new; restore. 2. begin again; get again; say, do, or give again: *renew an attack, renew one's efforts.* **3.** replace by new material or a new thing of the same sort; fill again. 4. give or get for a new period: *renew a lease.* **5.** renew a lease, note, etc. —**re·new′a·ble,** adj. —**re·new·ed·ly** (ri·nü′id·li; -nū′-), adv. —Syn. 1. repair, renovate, remodel. 2. recommence, resume.

re·new·al (ri·nü′əl; -nū′-), n. a renewing or being renewed.

ren·net (ren′it), n. substance containing rennin, used for making cheese and junket. [ME, < *rennen* RUN]

ren·nin (ren′in), n. enzyme in the gastric juice that coagulates or curdles milk.

Re·no (rē′nō), n. city in W Nevada.

Re·noir (rə·nwär′), n. Pierre Auguste, 1841–1919, French painter.

re·nounce (ri·nouns′), v., **-nounced, -nounc·ing. 1.** declare formally that one gives up; give up entirely; give up: *renounce a right, claim, or title.* **2.** disown; cast off: *renounce a wicked son.* [< F < L, ult. < *re*- back + *nuntius* message] —**re·nounce′ment,** n. —**re·nounc′er,** n. —Syn. 1. abandon, forsake, relinquish.

ren·o·vate (ren′ə·vāt), v., **-vat·ed, -vat·ing.** make new again; make like new; restore to good condition. [< L, ult. < *re*- again + *novus* new] —**ren′o·va′tion,** n. —**ren′o·va′tor,** n.

re·nown (ri·noun′), n. fame. [< AF *renoun,* ult. < L *re*- repeatedly + *nomen* name] —**re·nowned′,** adj. —Syn. celebrity, distinction.

rent (rent), n. 1. a regular payment for the use of property. 2. *Economics.* what is paid for the use of natural resources. —v. 1. pay for the use of (property): *we rent a house from Mr. Smith.* 2. receive pay for the use of (property): *he rents several other houses.* **3.** be leased or let for rent: *this farm rents for $1500 a year.* [< OF *rente,* ult. < L *reddere* RENDER] —**rent′a·ble,** adj. —**rent′er,** n.

rent² (rent), n. a torn place; tear; split. —adj. torn; split. —v. pt. and pp. of **rend.** [orig. v., var. of *rend*]

rent·al (ren′təl), n. amount received or paid as rent. —adj. of or in rent.

re·nun·ci·a·tion (ri·nun′si·ā′shən), n. a giving up of a right, title, possession, etc.; renouncing.

re·or·gan·i·za·tion (rē′ôr·gən·ə·zā′shən), n. 1. reorganizing. 2. being reorganized.

re·or·gan·ize (rē·ôr′gən·īz), v., **-ized, -iz·ing. 1.** organize anew; form again; arrange in a new way. 2. form a new company to operate (a business in the hands of a receiver). —**re·or′gan·iz′er,** n.

Rep., 1. Representative. 2. Republican.

re·pair¹ (ri·pãr′), v. 1. put in good condition again; mend: *he repairs shoes.* 2. make up for: *how can I repair the harm done?* —n. 1. act or work of repairing: *make repairs on the school building.* 2. instance or piece of repairing. 3. condition fit to be used: *keep the roads in repair.* 4. condition with respect to repairing: *a house in bad repair.* [< L, < *re*- again + *parare* prepare] —**re·pair′a·ble,** adj. —**re·pair′er,** n. —**re·pair′man,** n. —Syn. v. 1. restore, renovate.

re·pair² (ri·pãr′), v. go (to a place). [< OF < LL *repatriare* return to one's own country. Doublet of REPATRIATE.]

rep·a·ra·ble (rep′ə·rə·bəl), adj. that can be repaired or remedied. —**rep′a·ra·bly,** adv.

rep·a·ra·tion (rep′ə·rā′shən), n. 1. a giving of satisfaction or compensation for wrong or injury done. 2. compensation for wrong or injury. 3. Usually, **reparations.** compensation for the devastation of territory during war. 4. a repairing or being repaired. —**re·par·a·tive** (ri·par′ə·tiv), **re·par·a·to·ry** (ri·par′ə·tô′ri; -tō′-), adj.

rep·ar·tee (rep′ər·tē′), n. 1. a witty reply or replies. 2. talk characterized by clever and witty replies. 3. cleverness and wit in making replies. [< F, < *repartir* reply, ult. < L *re*- back + *pars* part]

re·past (ri·past′; -päst′), n. 1. meal; attractive meal; food. 2. a taking of food. [< OF, ult. < L *re*- again + *pascere* feed]

re·pa·tri·ate (rē·pā′tri·āt), v., **-at·ed, -at·ing.** send back or restore to one's own country: *the prisoners of war were repatriated.* [< LL *repatriatus,* ult. < L *re*- back + *patria* native land. Doublet of REPAIR².] —**re·pa′tri·a′tion,** n.

re·pay (ri·pā′), v., **-paid, -pay·ing. 1.** pay back; give back: *repay money borrowed.* 2. make return for: *repay a kindness.* 3. make return to: *the boy's success repaid the teacher for her efforts.* —**re·pay′a·ble,** adj. —**re·pay′er,** n. —**re·pay′ment,** n. —Syn. 1. refund, reimburse.

re·peal (ri·pēl′), v. do away with; revoke; abrogate: *the Stamp Act was finally repealed.* —n. act of repealing; abrogation: *vote for the repeal of a law.* [< AF *repeler,* alter. of OF *rapeler* < *re*- back + *apeler* to call. See APPEAL.] —**re·peal′a·ble,** adj. —**re·peal′er,** n. —Syn. v. 1. rescind, annul.

re·peat (ri·pēt′), v. 1. do or make again: *repeat an error*. 2. say again: *repeat a word for emphasis*. 3. say over; recite: *repeat a poem from memory*. 4. say after another says: *repeat the oath after me*. 5. tell to another or others: *do not repeat the secret*. 6. vote more than once in an election. —n. 1. a repeating. 2. thing repeated. 3. *Music*. a. passage to be repeated. b. sign indicating this, usually a row of dots. [< L *repetere* attack again < *re-* again + *petere* aim at] —re·peat′a·ble, adj. —re·peat′ed, adj. —re·peat′ed·ly, adv.

re·peat·er (ri·pēt′ər), n. 1. *Am*. gun that fires several shots without reloading. 2. *Am*. person who votes more than once in an election. 3. one that repeats.

re·pel (ri·pel′), v., **-pelled, -pel·ling**. 1. force back; drive back or away: *repel the enemy*. 2. cause to move apart or away: *oil and water repel each other*. 3. be displeasing to; cause disgust in: *her manner repels me*. 4. refuse to admit or accept; reject: *repel a suggestion*. [< L, < *re-* back + *pellere* to drive] —re·pel′lence, re·pel′len·cy, n. —re·pel′ler, n.

re·pel·lent (ri·pel′ənt), adj. 1. unattractive; disagreeable. 2. repelling; driving back.

re·pent (ri·pent′), v. 1. feel sorry for sin and seek forgiveness. 2. feel sorry for; regret: *repent one's choice*. [< OF *repentir*, ult. < L *re-* repeatedly + *paenitere* cause to regret] —re·pent′er, n. —Syn. 1. deplore, rue.

re·pent·ance (ri·pen′təns), n. 1. sorrow for doing wrong. 2. sorrow; regret. —re·pent′ant, adj. —re·pent′ant·ly, adv. —Syn. 1. contrition.

re·per·cus·sion (rē′pər·kush′ən), n. 1. an indirect influence or reaction from an event. 2. sound flung back; echo. 3. a springing back; rebound; recoil. [< L *repercussio*, ult. < *re-* back + *per-* thoroughly + *quatere* to beat] —re′per·cus′sive, adj.

rep·er·toire (rep′ər·twär; -twôr), n. the list of plays, operas, parts, pieces, etc., that a company or performer is prepared to perform. [< F < LL *repertorium*. Doublet of REPERTORY.]

rep·er·to·ry (rep′ər·tô′ri, -tō′-), n., pl. **-ries**. 1. repertoire. 2. store or stock of things ready for use. 3. storehouse. [< LL *repertorium* inventory, ult. < *reperire* find, get. Doublet of REPERTOIRE.]

rep·e·ti·tion (rep′ə·tish′ən), n. 1. a repeating: *repetition helps learning*. 2. thing repeated. —re·pet·i·tive (ri·pet′ə·tiv), adj.

rep·e·ti·tious (rep′ə·tish′əs), adj. full of repetitions; repeating in a tiresome way. —rep′e·ti′tious·ly, adv. —rep′e·ti′tious·ness, n.

re·pine (ri·pīn′), v., **-pined, -pin·ing**. be discontented; fret; complain. [< *re-* + *pine²*]

re·place (ri·plās′), v., **-placed, -plac·ing**. 1. fill or take the place of; supersede. 2. get another in place of. 3. put back; put in place again; restore. —re·place′a·ble, adj. —re·place′ment, n. —re·plac′er, n.

re·plen·ish (ri·plen′ish), v. fill again; provide a new supply for: *replenish a wardrobe*. [< OF *repleniss-*, ult. < L *re-* again + *plenus* full] —re·plen′ish·er, n. —re·plen′ish·ment, n.

re·plete (ri·plēt′), adj. abundantly supplied; filled. [< L, < *re-* again + *plere* fill] —re·ple′tion, re·plete′ness, n. —Syn. full, abounding.

rep·li·ca (rep′lə·kə), n. copy; reproduction. [< Ital., < *replicare* reproduce. See REPLY.]

re·ply (ri·plī′), v., **-plied, -ply·ing**, n., pl. **-plies**. —v. 1. answer in words or writing: *reply to a question*. 2. answer by suitable action: *reply to the enemy's fire*. 3. return as an answer: *not know what to reply*. 4. *Law*. answer a defendant's plea. —n. 1. act of replying. 2. an answer in words or writing; response. 3. answer by some action: *his reply was a blow*. [< OF < L *replicare* unroll < *re-* back + *plicare* to fold]

re·port (ri·pôrt′; -pōrt′), n. 1. account of something seen, heard, read, done, or considered. 2. an account officially expressed, generally in writing. 3. the sound of a shot or an explosion. 4. common talk; rumor. 5. reputation. —v. 1. make a report of; announce. 2. give a formal account of; state officially. 3. take down in writing; write an account of. 4. make a report. 5. act as reporter. 6. describe. 7. present; present oneself: *report for duty at 9 a.m.* 8. announce as a wrongdoer; denounce. [< OF < L, < *re-* back + *portare* carry] —re·port′a·ble, adj. —Syn. n. 1. narrative, description. 4. gossip, hearsay. –v. 1. tell, relate, narrate.

re·port·er (ri·pôr′tər; -pōr′-), n. 1. person who reports. 2. person who gathers news for a newspaper. —rep·or·to·ri·al (rep′ər·tô′ri·əl; -tō′-), adj.

re·pose¹ (ri·pōz′), n., v., **-posed, -pos·ing**. —n. 1. rest; sleep: *do not disturb her repose*. 2. quietness; ease: *repose of manner*. 3. peace; calmness. —v. 1. lie at rest: *repose upon a bed*. 2. lay to rest: *repose yourself in the hammock*. 3. rest from work or toil; take a rest. 4. trust (in); rely (on). [< F < LL, cause to rest, < *re-* again + *pausare* to pause] —re·pose′ful, adj. —re·pose′ful·ly, adv. —re·pose′ful·ness, n.

re·pose² (ri·pōz′), v., **-posed, -pos·ing**. put; place. [< L *repos-* < *reponere* replace. See POSE.]

re·pos·i·to·ry (ri·poz′ə·tô′ri; -tō′-), n., pl. **-ries**. 1. place or container where things are stored or kept. 2. confidant.

re·pos·sess (rē′pə·zes′), v. 1. possess again; get possession of again. —re′pos·ses′sion, n.

rep·re·hend (rep′ri·hend′), v. reprove (a person), as for a fault; rebuke; blame. [< L, orig., pull back < *re-* back + *prehendere* grasp]

rep·re·hen·si·ble (rep′ri·hen′sə·bəl), adj. deserving reproof, rebuke, or blame. —rep′re·hen′si·bil′i·ty, rep′re·hen′si·ble·ness, n. —rep′re·hen′si·bly, adv.

rep·re·hen·sion (rep′ri·hen′shən), n. reproof; rebuke; blame.

rep·re·sent (rep′ri·zent′), v. 1. stand for; be a sign or symbol of: *the stars in our flag represent the States*. 2. express by some sign, symbol, etc.: *represent speech by writing*. 3. act in place of; speak and act for: *we chose a committee to represent us*. 4. act for (a constituency, etc.) by deputed right in exercising a voice in legislation or government. 5. act the part of: *each child will represent an animal at the party*. 6. show in a picture, statue, carving, etc.; give a likeness of; portray. 7. be a type of; be an example of. 8. describe; set forth. 9. bring before the mind; make one think of. [< L, < *re-* back + *praesentare* to PRESENT²] —rep′re·sent′a·ble, adj.

rep·re·sen·ta·tion (rep′ri·zen·tā′shən), n. 1. act of representing. 2. condition or fact of being represented: "*Taxation without representation is tyranny*." 3. representatives considered as a group. 4. likeness; picture; model. 5. protest; complaint. 6. account; statement. —rep′re·sen·ta′tion·al, adj. —rep′re·sen·ta′tion·al·ly, adv.

rep·re·sent·a·tive (rep′ri·zen′tə·tiv), n. 1. person appointed to act or speak for others. 2. **Representative**, *Am*. member of the House of Representatives. 3. example; type. —adj. 1. having its citizens represented by chosen persons. 2. representing. 3. enough like all those of its kind to stand for all the rest. —rep′re·sent′a·tive·ly, adv. —rep′re·sent′a·tive·ness, n. —Syn. n. 1. agent, deputy.

re·press (ri·pres′), v. 1. prevent from acting; check; repress an impulse to cough. 2. keep down; put down: *the dictator repressed the revolt*. [< L *repressus* < *re-* back + *premere* press] —re·press′er, n. —re·press′i·ble, adj. —re·pres′sive, adj. —re·pres′sive·ly, adv. —re·pres′sive·ness, n. —Syn. 1. curb, restrain. 2. suppress.

re·pres·sion (ri·presh′ən), n. 1. act of repressing. 2. state of being repressed.

re·prieve (ri·prēv′), v., **-prieved, -priev·ing**, n. —v. 1. delay the execution of (a person condemned to death). 2. give relief from any evil or trouble. —n. 1. delay in carrying out a punishment, esp. of the death penalty. 2. temporary relief from any evil or trouble. [prob. var. of *reprove* in sense of "retest"]

rep·ri·mand (rep′rə·mand; -mänd), n. a severe or formal reproof. —v. reprove severely or formally. [< F *réprimande* < *réprimer* REPRESS]

āge, cāre, fär; ēqual, tėrm; īce; ōpen, ôrder; pút, rūle, ūse; t̄h, then; ə=a in about.

re·print (v. rē·print', n. rē'print'), v. print again; print a new impression of. —n. a reprinting; a new impression of printed work.

re·pris·al (ri·prīz'əl), n. injury done in return for injury, esp. by one nation to another. [< OF reprisaille, ult. < L reprehendere REPREHEND]

re·proach (ri·prōch'), n. 1. blame. 2. disgrace. 3. cause or occasion of blame or discredit. 4. object of blame, censure, or disapproval. —v. blame. [< F reprocher] —re·proach'a·ble, adj. —re·proach'er, n. —re·proach'ing·ly, adv. —re·proach'less, adj. —Syn. n. 1. censure. 2. discredit. -v. upbraid, censure, reprove, rebuke.

re·proach·ful (ri·prōch'fəl), adj. full of or expressing reproach. —re·proach'ful·ly, adv. —re·proach'ful·ness, n.

rep·ro·bate (rep'rə·bāt), n., adj., v., -bat·ed, -bat·ing. —n. an unprincipled scoundrel. —adj. morally abandoned; unprincipled. —v. disapprove; condemn; censure. [< LL reprobatus reproved < L re- dis- + probare approve. Doublet of REPROVE.] —rep'ro·ba'tion, n. —rep'ro·ba'tive, adj. —rep'ro·ba'tive·ly, adv. —Syn. adj. depraved, corrupt, base.

re·pro·duce (rē'prə·dūs'; -dūs'), v., -duced, -duc·ing. 1. produce again: a radio reproduces sounds. 2. make a copy of: a camera will reproduce a picture. 3. produce offspring: most plants reproduce by seeds. —re'pro·duc'er, n. —re'pro·duc'i·ble, adj. —Syn. 1. propagate, generate.

re·pro·duc·tion (rē'prə·duk'shən), n. 1. a reproducing or being reproduced. 2. a copy. 3. process by which animals and plants produce individuals like themselves.

re·pro·duc·tive (rē'prə·duk'tiv), adj. 1. that reproduces. 2. for or concerned with reproduction. —re'pro·duc'tive·ly, adv. —re'pro·duc'tive·ness, n.

re·proof (ri·prüf'), n. words of blame or disapproval.

re·prove (ri·prüv'), v., -proved, -prov·ing. express disapproval of; find fault with; rebuke; blame. [< OF < LL reprobare. Doublet of REPROBATE.] —re·prov'a·ble, adj. —re·prov'al, n. —re·prov'er, n. —re·prov'ing·ly, adv.

rep·tile (rep'təl), n. 1. a cold-blooded animal that creeps or crawls, such as a snake, lizard, turtle, alligator, or crocodile. 2. a low, mean person. —adj. 1. of or like a reptile; crawling; creeping. 2. low; mean. [< LL, orig. neut. adj., < L repere crawl]

rep·til·i·an (rep·til'i·ən), adj. 1. of or pertaining to reptiles. 2. like a reptile; base; mean. —n. a reptile.

re·pub·lic (ri·pub'lik), n. nation or state in which the citizens elect representatives to manage the government. [< L res publica public interest, state]

re·pub·li·can (ri·pub'lə·kən), adj. 1. of a republic; like that of a republic. 2. Republican, Am. of or having to do with the Republican Party. 3. favoring a republic. —n. 1. person who favors a republic. 2. Republican, Am. member of the Republican Party.

re·pub·li·can·ism (ri·pub'lə·kən·iz'əm), n. 1. republican government. 2. republican principles; adherence to republican principles. 3. Republicanism, Am. principles or policies of the Republican Party.

Republican Party, Am. one of the two main political parties in the United States.

re·pu·di·ate (ri·pū'di·āt), v., -at·ed, -at·ing. 1. refuse to accept; reject: repudiate a doctrine. 2. refuse to acknowledge or pay: repudiate a debt. 3. cast off; disown: repudiate a son. [< L, < repudium divorce] —re·pu'di·a'tion, n. —re·pu'di·a'tive, adj. —re·pu'di·a'tor, n. —Syn. 1. disclaim. 3. renounce.

re·pug·nance (ri·pug'nəns), **re·pug·nan·cy** (-nən·si), n. strong dislike, distaste, or aversion.

re·pug·nant (ri·pug'nənt), adj. 1. distasteful; disagreeable; offensive. 2. objecting; averse; opposed. [< L repugnans resisting < re- back + pugnare to fight] —re·pug'nant·ly, adv. —Syn. 1. objectionable.

re·pulse (ri·puls'), v., -pulsed, -puls·ing, n. —v. 1. drive back; repel. 2. refuse to accept; reject: she coldly repulsed him. —n. 1. a driving back; being driven back: after the second repulse, the enemy surrendered. 2. refusal; rejection. [< L repulsus, pp. of repellere REPEL] —re·puls'er, n. —Syn. v. 2. rebuff, snub.

re·pul·sion (ri·pul'shən), n. 1. strong dislike or aversion. 2. repulse; repelling or being repelled. 3. Physics. action of bodies that repel each other, or an inherent force by which bodies are forced apart.

re·pul·sive (ri·pul'siv), adj. 1. causing strong dislike or aversion: snakes are repulsive to some people. 2. tending to drive back or repel. —re·pul'sive·ly, adv. —re·pul'sive·ness, n.

rep·u·ta·ble (rep'yə·tə·bəl), adj. having a good reputation; well thought of; in good repute. —rep'u·ta·bil'i·ty, rep'u·ta·ble·ness, n. —rep'u·ta·bly, adv. —Syn. respectable, estimable.

rep·u·ta·tion (rep'yə·tā'shən), n. 1. what people think and say the character of a person or thing is; character in the opinion of others. 2. good name; good reputation. 3. fame. —Syn. 1. estimation, name. 2. repute.

re·pute (ri·pūt'), n., v., -put·ed, -put·ing. —n. 1. reputation. 2. good reputation. —v. suppose to be; consider; suppose: he is reputed the richest man in the State. [< L, < re- over + putare think]

re·put·ed (ri·pūt'id), adj. accounted or supposed to be such: the reputed author. —re·put'ed·ly, adv.

re·quest (ri·kwest'), v. 1. ask for; ask as a favor: request a loan from the bank. 2. ask: he requested her to go with him. —n. 1. act of asking: at our request. 2. what is asked for: grant my request. 3. state of being asked for or sought after: a good dancer is in great request. 4. by request, in response to a request. [< OF requeste, ult. < L re- again + quaerere ask] —Syn. v. 1. beg, beseech, entreat. n. 3. demand.

Req·ui·em, req·ui·em (rek'wi·əm; rē'kwi-), n. 1. Mass for the dead; musical church service for the dead. 2. music for it. [< L, accus. of requies rest; the first word of the Mass]

re·quire (ri·kwīr'), v., -quired, -quir·ing. 1. have need for; need; want: we shall require more help. 2. make necessary. 3. put under an obligation or necessity: circumstances require us to submit. 4. order to do something. [< L requirere. See REQUEST.] —re·quir'er, n.

re·quire·ment (ri·kwīr'mənt), n. 1. need; thing needed: patience is a requirement in teaching. 2. demand; thing demanded: fulfill all requirements for graduation.

req·ui·site (rek'wə·zit), adj. required by circumstances; needed; necessary: the qualities requisite for a leader. —n. thing needed: food and air are requisites for life. —req'ui·site·ly, adv. —req'ui·site·ness, n. —Syn. adj. essential, indispensable.

req·ui·si·tion (rek'wə·zish'ən), n. 1. act of requiring. 2. a demand made, esp. a formal written demand. 3. state of being required for use or called into service. 4. essential condition; requirement. —v. 1. demand or take by authority. 2. make demands upon.

re·quit·al (ri·kwīt'əl), n. repayment; payment; return.

re·quite (ri·kwīt'), v., -quit·ed, -quit·ing. 1. pay back; make return for: requite evil with good. 2. make retaliation for; avenge. 3. make return to. [< re- + quite, var. of quit] —re·quite'ment, n. —re·quit'er, n. —Syn. 1. repay, reward. 2. punish.

re·re·dos (rir'dos), n. a screen or a decorated part of the wall behind an altar. [< AF, ult. < rere REAR[1] + dos back (< L dossum, var. of dorsum)]

re·scind (ri·sind'), v. deprive of force; repeal; cancel; rescind a law or treaty. [< L, < re- back + scindere to cut] —re·scind'a·ble, adj. —re·scind'er, n. —re·scind'ment, n.

re·scis·sion (ri·sizh'ən), n. a rescinding.

res·cue (res'kū), v., -cued, -cu·ing, n. —v. save from danger, capture, harm, etc.; free;

deliver. —*n.* a saving or freeing from danger, capture, harm, etc. [< OF *rescoure*, ult. < L *re-* back + *ex* out + *quatere* to shake] —**res'cu·er,** *n.* —**Syn.** *v.* liberate, release.

re·search (ri·sérch'; rē'sérch), *n.* a careful hunting for facts or truth; inquiry; investigation. —*v.* make researches. [< MF *recerche.* See RE-, SEARCH.]

re·search·er (ri·sér'chər; rē'sér-), *n.* person who makes researches; investigator. ➤ *Researcher* has been added to the English vocabulary as a needed shortening for *research worker.*

re·seat (rē·sēt'), *v.* 1. seat again. 2. put a new seat on.

re·sem·blance (ri·zem'bləns), *n.* likeness; similar appearance: *twins often show great resemblance.*

re·sem·ble (ri·zem'bəl), *v.*, **-bled, -bling.** be like or similar to; have likeness to in form, figure, or qualities. [< OF *resembler*, ult. < L *re-* again + *similis* similar] —**re·sem'bler,** *n.*

re·sent (ri·zent'), *v.* feel injured and angry at; feel indignation at: *resent an insult.* [< F *ressentir*, ult. < L *re-* back + *sentire* feel] —**re·sent'er,** *n.* —**re·sent'ful,** *adj.* —**re·sent'ful·ly,** *adv.* —**re·sent'ful·ness,** *n.*

re·sent·ment (ri·zent'mənt), *n.* the feeling that one has at being injured or insulted; indignation.

res·er·va·tion (rez'ər·vā'shən), *n.* 1. a keeping back; hiding in part; something not expressed: *a mental reservation.* 2. a limiting condition: *agree without reservation.* 3. *Am.* land set aside for a special purpose. The government has set apart Indian reservations. 4. *Am.* arrangement to keep a thing for a person; securing of accommodations, etc. 5. something reserved.

re·serve (ri·zėrv'), *v.*, **-served, -serv·ing,** *n.*, *adj.* —*v.* 1. keep back; hold back: *reserve criticism.* 2. set apart for a special purpose: *time reserved for recreation.* 3. save for use later: *reserve enough money for your fare home.* 4. set aside for the use of a particular person or persons: *reserve a table.* —*n.* 1. the actual cash in a bank or assets that can be turned into cash quickly: *banks must keep a reserve of money.* 2. *Mil.* a. body of soldiers kept ready to help the main army in battle. b. reserves, soldiers or sailors not in active service but ready to serve if needed. 3. public land set apart for a special purpose: *a forest reserve.* 4. anything kept back for future use. 5. fact, state, or condition of being kept, set apart, or saved for use later. 6. habit of keeping back or restraining one's thoughts, feelings, and affairs to oneself; self-restraint. —*adj.* kept in reserve; forming a reserve. [< L, < *re-* back + *servare* keep] —**Syn.** *v.* 1. retain, withhold. 2. allot. –*n.* 6. constraint, reticence.

re·served (ri·zėrvd'), *adj.* 1. kept in reserve; kept by special arrangement. 2. set apart. 3. self-restrained in action or speech. —**re·serv·ed·ly** (ri·zėr'vid·li), *adv.* —**re·serv'ed·ness,** *n.* —**Syn.** 1. withheld, retained. 3. restrained, reticent.

re·serv·ist (ri·zėr'vist), *n.* soldier or sailor not in active service but available if needed.

res·er·voir (rez'ər·vwär; -vôr), *n.* 1. place where water is collected and stored for use. 2. anything to hold a liquid. 3. place where anything is collected and stored. 4. a great supply. [< F, < *réserver* RESERVE]

re·set (*v.* rē·set'; *n.* rē'set'), *v.*, **-set, -set·ting,** *n.* —*v.* set again: *a broken arm must be reset.* —*n.* 1. act of resetting. 2. thing reset.

re·side (ri·zīd'), *v.*, **-sid·ed, -sid·ing.** 1. live (in or at) for a long time; dwell. 2. be (in); exist (in): *her charm resides in her happy smile.* 3. of rights, powers, etc., be vested in; rest in. [< L *residere* < *re-* back + *sedere* settle] —**re·sid'er,** *n.*

res·i·dence (rez'ə·dəns), *n.* 1. house; home. 2. act or fact of residing. 3. period of residing in a place. 4. **in residence,** living in a place while on duty or doing active work. —**Syn.** 1. abode, dwelling, habitation.

res·i·den·cy (rez'ə·dən·si), *n.*, *pl.* **-cies.** 1. residence. 2. formerly, the official residence of a representative of the governor general of India at a native court.

res·i·dent (rez'ə·dənt), *n.* 1. person living in a place, not a visitor. 2. an official sent to live in a foreign land to represent his country. —*adj.* 1. dwelling in a place; residing. 2. living in a place while on duty or doing active work. 3. of birds, not migratory.

res·i·den·tial (rez'ə·den'shəl), *adj.* 1. of, pertaining to, or fitted for residences. 2. pertaining to residence: *residential qualifications.*

re·sid·u·al (ri·zij'ü·əl), *adj.* 1. of or forming a residue; remaining; left over. 2. *Math.* left after subtraction. —*n.* 1. remainder. 2. *Math.* a residual quantity.

re·sid·u·ar·y (ri·zij'ü·er'i), *adj.* entitled to the remainder of an estate.

res·i·due (rez'ə·dü; -dū), *n.* what remains after a part is taken; remainder. [< F < L *residuum*, neut. adj., left over. Doublet of RESIDUUM.]

re·sid·u·um (ri·zij'ü·əm), *n.*, *pl.* **-sid·u·a** (-zij'ü·ə). residue; remainder. [< L. Doublet of RESIDUE.]

re·sign (ri·zīn'), *v.* 1. give up a job, position, etc. 2. give up (a job); give back (a commission); renounce (a claim). 3. resign oneself, submit quietly; adapt oneself without complaint. [< OF < L *resignare* unseal, ult. < *re-* back + *signum* seal]

res·ig·na·tion (rez'ig·nā'shən), *n.* 1. act of resigning. 2. a written statement giving notice that one resigns. 3. patient acceptance; quiet submission. —**Syn.** 3. acquiescence, meekness.

re·signed (ri·zīnd'), *adj.* accepting what comes without complaint. —**re·sign·ed·ly** (ri·zīn'id·li), *adv.* —**re·sign'ed·ness,** *n.*

re·sil·i·ence (ri·zil'i·əns; -zil'yəns), **re·sil·i·en·cy** (-i·ən·si; -yən·si), *n.* 1. elasticity. 2. cheerfulness.

re·sil·i·ent (ri·zil'i·ənt; -zil'yənt), *adj.* 1. springing back; returning to the original form or position after being bent, compressed, or stretched. 2. readily recovering; buoyant; cheerful. [< L *resiliens* < *re-* back + *salire* to jump]

res·in (rez'ən), *n.* a sticky yellow or brown substance that flows from certain plants and trees, esp. the pine and fir. It is also derived chemically and is used in medicine and varnish. The harder portion remaining after heating is called rosin. [< L *resina*] —**res'in·ous,** *adj.* —**res'in·ous·ly,** *adv.* —**res'in·y,** *adj.*

re·sist (ri·zist'), *v.* 1. act against; strive against; oppose: *resist the adoption of a plan.* 2. act against something; oppose something: *do not resist.* 3. strive successfully against; keep from: *unable to resist laughing.* 4. withstand the action or effect of (an acid, storm, etc.): *resist rust.* [< L, < *re-* back + *sistere* make a stand] —**re·sist'er,** *n.* —**re·sist'i·ble,** *adj.* —**re·sist'i·bil'i·ty,** *n.* —**Syn.** 1. withstand, defy.

re·sist·ance (ri·zis'təns), *n.* 1. act of resisting. 2. power to resist: *resistance to disease.* 3. thing or act that resists; opposing force; opposition. 4. people in a country occupied or controlled by another country who organize and fight for their freedom: *the French resistance in World War II.* 5. *Elect.* property of a conductor that opposes the passage of a current and changes electric energy into heat. —**re·sist'ant,** *adj.*

re·sist·less (ri·zist'lis), *adj.* 1. that cannot be resisted. 2. *Rare.* lacking power to resist.—**re·sist'less·ly,** *adv.* —**re·sist'less·ness,** *n.*

re·sis·tor (ri·zis'tər), *n. Elect.* a conducting body or device used in an electric circuit, etc., because of its resistance.

res·o·lute (rez'ə·lüt), *adj.* 1. firmly determined; set or fixed in purpose. 2. firm and bold in pursuing purposes. [< L *resolutus*, pp. of *resolvere* RESOLVE] —**res'o·lute·ly,** *adv.* —**res'o·lute·ness,** *n.* —**Syn.** 1. steadfast, unshaken.

res·o·lu·tion (rez'ə·lü'shən), *n.* 1. act of resolving or determining. 2. thing decided on; thing determined. 3. determination. 4. a formal expression of opinion. **5.** a breaking into parts. **6.** act or result of solving; solution.

re·solve (ri·zolv′), *v.*, **-solved, -solv·ing,** *n.* —*v.* **1.** make up one's mind; determine; decide: *resolve to do better work.* **2.** break into parts; break up; distinguish parts within: *resolve a spectrum into its various lines.* **3.** answer and explain; solve: *his letter resolved all our doubts.* **4.** decide by vote: *it was resolved that our school have a lunchroom.* **5.** change: *the assembly resolved itself into a committee.* —*n.* **1.** thing determined on: *he kept his resolve to do better.* **2.** firmness in carrying out a purpose; determination. [< L, < *re-* un- + *solvere* loosen] —re·solv′a·ble, *adj.* —re·solv′a·bil′i·ty, *n.* —re·solv′er, *n.* —Syn. *v.* **1.** purpose, intend.

re·solved (ri·zolvd′), *adj.* determined; resolute. —re·solv·ed·ly (ri·zol′vid·li), *adv.* —re·solv′ed·ness, *n.*

res·o·nance (rez′ə·nəns), *n.* **1.** resounding quality; being resonant: *the resonance of an organ.* **2.** *Physics.* a reinforcing and prolonging of sound by reflection or by vibration of other objects. **3.** *Elect.* condition of an electrical circuit adjusted to allow the greatest flow of current at a certain frequency.

res·o·nant (rez′ə·nənt), *adj.* **1.** resounding; continuing to sound; echoing. **2.** tending to increase or prolong sounds. **3.** of or in resonance. [< L *resonans,* ult. < *re-* back + *sonus* sound] —res′o·nant·ly, *adv.*

res·o·na·tor (rez′ə·nā′tər), *n.* something that produces resonance; appliance for increasing sound by resonance.

res·or·cin·ol (rez·ôr′sə·nol; -nōl), **res·or·cin** (-sin), *n.* a colorless, crystalline substance, $C_6H_4(OH)_2$, that is used in medicine as an antiseptic, and in making dyes, drugs, etc.

re·sort (ri·zôrt′), *v.* **1.** go; go often: *many people resort to the beaches in hot weather.* **2.** turn for help: *resort to violence.* —*n.* **1.** an assembling; going to often: *a park is a place of popular resort in good weather.* **2.** place people go to: *a summer resort.* **3.** act of turning for help. **4.** person or thing turned to for help. [< OF, < *re-* back + *sortir* go out] —re·sort′er, *n.*

re·sound (ri·zound′), *v.* **1.** give back sound; echo. **2.** give back (sound); echo (sound). **3.** sound loudly. **4.** be filled with sound. **5.** repeat loudly; proclaim loudly; celebrate. [< L, ult. < *re-* back + *sonus* sound] —re·sound′er, *n.* —re·sound′ing, *adj.* —re·sound′ing·ly, *adv.*

re·source (ri·sôrs′; -sōrs′; rē′sôrs; -sōrs), *n.* **1.** any source of supply, support, or aid. **2.** resources, **a.** the actual and potential wealth of a country. **b.** means of raising money and supplies; funds. **c.** available means or capabilities of any kind. **3.** any means of getting success or getting out of trouble. **4.** skill in meeting difficulties, getting out of trouble, etc. [< F *ressource,* ult. < L *re-* again + *surgere* rise]

re·source·ful (ri·sôrs′fəl; -sōrs′-), *adj.* good at thinking of ways to do things; quick-witted. —re·source′ful·ly, *adv.* —re·source′ful·ness, *n.*

re·spect (ri·spekt′), *n.* **1.** honor; esteem: *show respect to those who are older.* **2.** consideration; regard: *show respect for other people's property.* **3.** respects, expressions of respect; regards. **4.** point; matter; detail: *a plan unwise in many respects.* **5.** relation; reference: *plan with respect to the future.* —*v.* **1.** feel or show honor or esteem for: *respect the President.* **2.** show consideration for: *respect the feelings of others.* **3.** relate to; refer to. [< L *respectus,* pp. of *respicere* look back, have regard for < *re-* back + *specere* to look] —re·spect′er, *n.* —Syn. *n.* **1.** reverence, veneration. **4.** particular, feature.

re·spect·a·bil·i·ty (ri·spek′tə·bil′ə·ti), *n., pl.* -ties. **1.** respectable quality or condition. **2.** respectable social standing.

re·spect·a·ble (ri·spek′tə·bəl), *adj.* **1.** worthy of respect; having a good reputation: *respectable citizens obey the laws.* **2.** having fair social standing; honest and decent: *his parents were poor but respectable people.* **3.** fairly good; moderate in size or quality: *a respectable but not brilliant record.* **4.** good enough to use; fit to be

seen. —re·spect′a·ble·ness, *n.* —re·spect′a·bly, *adv.*

re·spect·ful (ri·spekt′fəl), *adj.* showing respect; polite. —re·spect′ful·ly, *adv.* —re·spect′ful·ness, *n.*

re·spect·ing (ri·spek′ting), *prep.* with regard to; about; concerning.

re·spec·tive (ri·spek′tiv), *adj.* belonging to each; particular; individual: *go to your respective rooms.*

re·spec·tive·ly (ri·spek′tiv·li), *adv.* as regards each one in his turn or in the order mentioned.

res·pi·ra·tion (res′pə·rā′shən), *n.* **1.** act of inhaling and exhaling; breathing. **2.** a single breath. **3.** the processes by which an animal, plant, or living cell secures oxygen from the air or water, distributes it, combines it with substances in the tissues, and gives off carbon dioxide.

res·pi·ra·tor (res′pə·rā′tər), *n.* **1.** a device, usually of gauze, worn over the nose and mouth to prevent inhaling harmful substances. **2.** device used in giving artificial respiration.

res·pi·ra·to·ry (res′pə·rə·tô′ri; -tō′-; ri·spīr′ə-), *adj.* pertaining to or used for breathing.

re·spire (ri·spīr′), *v.,* -spired, -spir·ing. inhale and exhale; breathe. [< L, < *re-* regularly + *spirare* breathe]

res·pite (res′pit), *n., v.,* -pit·ed, -pit·ing. —*n.* **1.** time of relief and rest; lull. **2.** a putting off; delay, esp. in carrying out a sentence of death; reprieve. —*v.* give a respite to. [< OF < VL *respectus* delay < LL, expectation, < L *respectare* wait for. See RESPECT.]

re·splend·ent (ri·splen′dənt), *adj.* very bright; shining; splendid: *the queen was resplendent with jewels.* [< L *resplendens* glittering < *re-* back + *splendere* to shine] —re·splend′ence, re·splend′en·cy, *n.* —re·splend′ent·ly, *adv.*

re·spond (ri·spond′), *v.* **1.** answer; reply. **2.** act in answer; react: *nerves respond to a stimulus.* [< OF < L, < *re-* in return + *spondere* promise]

re·spond·ent (ri·spon′dənt), *adj.* answering; responding. —*n.* **1.** person who responds. **2.** *Law.* defendant, esp. in a divorce case.

re·sponse (ri·spons′), *n.* **1.** an answer by word or act. **2.** words said or sung by the congregation or choir in answer to the minister. **3.** reaction of body or mind to a stimulus. [< L *responsum,* orig. neut. pp. of *respondere* RESPOND] —Syn. **1.** rejoinder, reply.

re·spon·si·bil·i·ty (ri·spon′sə·bil′ə·ti), *n., pl.* -ties. **1.** a being responsible; obligation: *a little child does not feel much responsibility.* **2.** thing for which one is responsible. A task, a debt, and little children to care for are responsibilities. —Syn. **1.** accountability.

re·spon·si·ble (ri·spon′sə·bəl), *adj.* **1.** obliged or expected to account (for): *each pupil is responsible for the care of the books given him.* **2.** deserving credit or blame: *the bad weather is responsible for the small attendance.* **3.** trustworthy; reliable: *a responsible person should take care of the money.* **4.** involving obligation or duties: *the presidency is a very responsible position.* **5.** able to tell right from wrong; able to think and act reasonably: *insane people are not responsible.* —re·spon′si·ble·ness, *n.* —re·spon′si·bly, *adv.* —Syn. **1.** accountable, answerable. —Ant. **3.** negligent, careless.

re·spon·sive (ri·spon′siv), *adj.* **1.** making answer; responding: *a responsive glance.* **2.** easily moved; responding readily: *be responsive to kindness.* —re·spon′sive·ly, *adv.* —re·spon′sive·ness, *n.*

rest¹ (rest), *n.* **1.** sleep: *have a good night's rest.* **2.** ease after work or effort: *allow an hour for rest.* **3.** freedom from anything that tires, troubles, disturbs, or pains; quiet: *rest after work.* **4.** absence of motion: *bring a machine to rest.* **5.** support: *a rest for a billiard cue.* **6.** place of rest: *a rest for sailors.* **7.** *Music.* a pause. **b.** mark to show a pause. **8.** death; the grave. **9.** at

rest, a. asleep. **b.** not moving. **c.** free from pain, trouble, etc. **d.** dead. **10.** lay to rest, bury. —*v.* **1.** be asleep or still: *lie down and rest.* **2.** be free from work, effort, care, trouble, etc.: *teachers rest in the summer.* **3.** stop moving; cause to stop moving: *the ball rested at the bottom of the hill.* **4.** give rest to; refresh by rest: *rest one's horses.* **5.** lie, recline, sit, lean, etc., for rest or ease: *he spent the whole day resting in a chair.* **6.** be supported: *the ladder rests against the wall.* **7.** be fixed: *our eyes rested on the open book.* **8.** be at ease: *don't let Mrs. White rest until she promises to visit us.* **9.** be or become inactive; let remain inactive: *let the matter rest, rest the matter there.* **10.** place for support; lay; lean: *rest one's head in one's hands.* **11.** rely (on); trust (in); depend; be based: *our hope rests on you.* **12.** cause to rely or depend; base: *we rest our hope on you.* **13.** be found; be present: *in a democracy, government rests with the people.* **14.** be dead; lie in the grave. **15.** *Am.* end voluntarily the introduction of evidence in (a case at law): *the lawyer rested his case.* [OE]

rest² (rest), *n.* what is left; those that are left. —*v.* continue to be: *you may rest assured that I will keep my promise.* [< F *reste,* ult. < L *restare* be left < *re—* back + *stare* stand]

res·tau·rant (res′tə-rənt, –ränt; –trənt, –tränt), *n. Am.* place to buy and eat a meal. [< F, orig. ppr. of *restaurer* RESTORE]

res·tau·ra·teur (res′tə-rə-tér′), *n.* keeper of a restaurant.

rest·ful (rest′fəl), *adj.* **1.** full of rest; giving rest. **2.** quiet; peaceful. —rest′ful·ly, *adv.* —rest′ful·ness, *n.*

res·ti·tu·tion (res′tə-tü′shən; –tū′–), *n.* **1.** a giving back of what has been lost or taken away. **2.** act of making good any loss, damage, or injury. [< L *restitutio,* ult. < *re—* again + *statuere* set up] —**Syn.** 1. return, restoration. 2. reparation, amends.

res·tive (res′tiv), *adj.* **1.** restless; uneasy. **2.** hard to manage. **3.** refusing to go ahead; balky. [< OF *restif* motionless < *rester* REST², v.] —res′tive·ly, *adv.* —res′tive·ness, *n.*

rest·less (rest′lis), *adj.* **1.** unable to rest; uneasy: *the dog seemed restless.* **2.** without rest or sleep; not restful: *a restless night.* **3.** rarely or never still or quiet; always moving. —rest′less·ly, *adv.* —rest′less·ness, *n.*

res·to·ra·tion (res′tə-rā′shən), *n.* **1.** restoring or being restored; bringing back to a former condition. **2.** something restored. **3.** the Restoration, **a.** the reëstablishment of the monarchy in 1660 under Charles II of England. **b.** period from 1660 to 1688 in England during which Charles II and James II reigned.

re·stor·a·tive (ri-stôr′ə-tiv; –stōr′–), *adj.* capable of restoring; tending to restore health or strength. —*n.* something that does so.

re·store (ri-stôr′; –stōr′), *v.,* –stored, –storing. **1.** bring back; establish again: *restore order.* **2.** bring back to a former condition or to a normal condition: *the old house has been restored.* **3.** give back; put back: *restore stolen goods to the owner.* [< OF < L *restaurare*] —restor′er, *n.*

re·strain (ri-strān′), *v.* **1.** hold back; keep down; keep in check; keep within limits: *restrain your curiosity.* **2.** keep in prison; confine. [< OF < L *restringere* RESTRICT] —re·strain′a·ble, *adj.* —re·strain·ed·ly (ri-strān′id·li), *adv.* —re·strain′er, *n.* —**Syn.** 1. detain, repress, curb, check.

re·straint (ri-strānt′), *n.* **1.** a restraining or being restrained. **2.** means of restraining. **3.** tendency to restrain natural feeling; reserve. —**Syn.** 1. restriction, limitation, check, curb.

restraint of trade, limitation or prevention of free competition in business.

re·strict (ri-strikt′), *v.* keep within limits; confine: *restrict the membership to twelve.* [< L *restrictus* < *re—* back + *stringere* draw tight] —re·strict′ed, *adj.* —re·strict′ed·ly, *adv.*

re·stric·tion (ri-strik′shən), *n.* **1.** a restrict-

ing or being restricted. **2.** something that restricts; limiting condition or rule: *restrictions on the use of the playground.*

re·stric·tive (ri-strik′tiv), *adj.* restricting; limiting. Some laws are prohibitive; some are only restrictive. —re·stric′tive·ly, *adv.* ⟩ A restrictive modifier defines, limits, identifies the word it refers to, that is, it gives a fact that sets it off from other things of the same class. If the restrictive modifier is omitted, the statement either becomes meaningless, as in the first sentence below, or else it has quite a different meaning, as in the second: "It was quite a different looking person *who walked out into the cold frosty air a few minutes later.*" "The right of the dictatorships *to decide how long this wholesale killing goes on* is unquestioned." The italicized elements in these sentences are restrictive and should stand as they are here, not set off by commas.

re·sult (ri-zult′), *n.* **1.** that which happens because of something; what is caused: *the result of the fall was a broken leg.* **2.** good or useful result: *we want results, not talk.* **3.** quantity, value, etc., obtained by calculation. —*v.* **1.** be a result; follow as a consequence: *sickness often results from eating too much.* **2.** have as a result; end: *eating too much often results in sickness.* [< L *resultare* rebound, ult. < *re—* back + *salire* spring] —**Syn.** *n.* 1. consequence, outcome, conclusion.

re·sult·ant (ri-zul′tənt), *adj.* resulting. —*n.* **1.** result. **2.** *Physics.* any force that has the same effect as two or more forces acting together.

re·sume (ri-züm′), *v.,* –sumed, –sum·ing. **1.** begin again; go on: *resume reading where we left off.* **2.** get or take again: *those standing may resume their seats.* [< L, < *re—* again + *sumere* take up] —re·sum′a·ble, *adj.* —re·sum′er, *n.*

ré·su·mé (rez′u·mā′), *n.* summary. [< F, orig. pp. of *résumer* resume]

re·sump·tion (ri-zump′shən), *n.* a resuming: *the resumption of duties after absence.* —re·sump′tive, *adj.*

re·sur·gent (ri-sér′jənt), *adj.* rising or tending to rise again. —re·sur′gence, *n.*

re·sur·rect (rez′ə·rekt′), *v.* **1.** raise from the dead; bring back to life. **2.** bring back to sight, use, etc.

res·ur·rec·tion (rez′ə·rek′shən), *n.* **1.** a coming to life again; rising from the dead. **2.** the Resurrection, the rising again of Christ after His death and burial. **3.** a being alive again after death. **4.** restoration from decay, disuse, etc.; revival. [< L *resurrectio,* ult. < *re—* again + *surgere* rise] —res′ur·rec′tion·al, *adj.*

re·sus·ci·tate (ri·sus′ə·tāt), *v.,* –tat·ed, –tat·ing. bring or come back to life or consciousness; revive. [< L *resuscitatus,* ult. < *re—* again + *sub—* up + *citare* rouse] —re·sus′ci·ta′tion, *n.* —re·sus′ci·ta′tive, *adj.* —re·sus′ci·ta′tor, *n.*

re·tail (*n., adj.. v.* 1 rē′tāl; *v.* 2 ri·tāl′), *n.* **1.** sale of goods in small quantities at a time: *our grocer buys at wholesale and sells at retail.* **2.** at retail, in small lots or quantities. —*adj.* of or engaged in selling in small quantities: *the retail trade, a retail merchant.* —*v.* **1.** sell or be sold in small quantities. **2.** tell over again: *retail gossip.* [< OF, scrap, ult. < *re—* back + *taillier* cut (see TALLY)] —re′tail·er, *n.*

re·tain (ri·tān′), *v.* **1.** continue to have or hold; keep: *china dishes retain heat longer than metal pans do.* **2.** hold or keep in possession: *retain television rights.* **3.** keep in mind; remember. **4.** employ by payment of a fee: *he retained a lawyer.* [< OF < L, < *re—* back + *tenere* hold] —re·tain′a·ble, *adj.* —re·tain′ment, *n.*

re·tain·er¹ (ri·tān′ər), *n.* person who serves a person of rank; vassal; attendant; follower.

re·tain·er² (ri·tān′ər), *n.* fee paid to secure services. [< F *retenir,* n. use of inf., RETAIN]

re·take (*v.* rē·tāk′; *n.* rē′tāk′), *v.,* –took, –taken, –tak·ing, *n.* —*v.* **1.** take again. **2.** take back. —*n.* **1.** a retaking. **2.** *Am., Colloq.* in motion pictures, another photographing or photograph of a scene. —re·tak′er, *n.*

re·tal·i·ate (ri·tal′i·āt), *v.*, –at·ed, –at·ing. pay back wrong, injury, etc.; return like for like, usually to return evil for evil. [< L *retaliatus* < *re–* in return + *tal–* pay] —re·tal′i·a′tion, *n.* —re·tal·i·a·to·ry (ri·tal′i·ə·tô′ri; –tō′–), re·tal′i·a′tive, *adj.*

re·tard (ri·tärd′), *v.* make slow; delay the progress of; keep back; hinder: *bad roads retarded the car.* [< L, ult. < *re–* back + *tardus* slow] —re·tar·da·tion (rē′tär·dā′shən), *n.* —re·tard′er, *n.* —Syn. detain, impede.

re·tard·ed (ri·tär′did), *adj.* slow in development; backward: *retarded children.*

retch (rech), *v.* make efforts to vomit; make movements like those of vomiting. [OE *hræcan* clear the throat]

ret′d., **1.** retained. **2.** returned.

re·ten·tion (ri·ten′shən), *n.* **1.** a retaining or being retained. **2.** power to retain. **3.** ability to remember.

re·ten·tive (ri·ten′tiv), *adj.* **1.** able to hold or keep. **2.** able to remember. —re·ten′tive·ly, *adv.* —re·ten′tive·ness, re·ten·tiv·i·ty (rē′ten·tiv′ə·ti), *n.*

ret·i·cence (ret′ə·səns), **ret·i·cen·cy** (–sən·si), *n.* tendency to be silent or say little; reserve in speech.

ret·i·cent (ret′ə·sənt), *adj.* disposed to keep silent or say little; not speaking freely; reserved in speech. [< L *reticens* keeping silent < *re–* back + *tacere* be silent] —ret′i·cent·ly, *adv.* —Syn. reserved, taciturn.

re·tic·u·la·tion (ri·tik′yə·lā′shən), *n.* **1.** a netlike formation, arrangement, or appearance; network. **2.** one of the meshes of a network. [< L, ult. < *reticulum,* dim. of *rete* net]

ret·i·cule (ret′ə·kūl), *n.* a woman's small handbag. [< F < L *reticulum.* See RETICULATION.]

ret·i·na (ret′ə·nə), *n., pl.* –nas, –nae (–nē). layer of cells at the back of the eyeball that is sensitive to light and receives the images of things looked at. [< Med.L, < L *retinacula,* pl., band, reins] —ret′i·nal, *adj.*

ret·i·nue (ret′ə·nü; –nū), *n.* group of attendants or retainers; following: *a king's retinue.* [< OF, orig. fem. pp. of *retenir* RETAIN]

re·tire (ri·tīr′), *v.*, –tired, –tir·ing. **1.** go away to be quiet: *she retired to a convent.* **2.** go to bed: *we retire early.* **3.** give up an office, occupation, etc.: *our teachers retire at 65.* **4.** remove from an office, occupation, etc.: *retire most of the officers after a war.* **5.** withdraw or lead back (troops); retreat. **6.** withdraw (money) from circulation. **7.** take up and pay off (bonds, loans, etc.). **8.** put out (a batter, side, etc.) in baseball and cricket. [< F, < *re–* back + *tirer* draw]

re·tired (ri·tīrd′), *adj.* **1.** withdrawn from one's occupation: *a retired sea captain.* **2.** secluded; shut off; hidden. —Syn. **2.** remote.

re·tire·ment (ri·tīr′mənt), *n.* **1.** a retiring or being retired; withdrawal. **2.** a quiet way or place of living: *she lives in retirement.*

re·tir·ing (ri·tīr′ing), *adj.* shrinking from society or publicity; reserved; shy. —re·tir′ing·ly, *adv.* —re·tir′ing·ness, *n.* —Syn. bashful, modest.

re·tort¹ (ri·tôrt′), *v.* **1.** reply quickly or sharply. **2.** return in kind; turn back on: *retort blow for blow.* —*n.* a sharp or witty reply. [< L *tortus* thrown back < *re–* back + *torquere* twist]

re·tort² (ri·tôrt′; rē′tôrt), *n.* container used for distilling or decomposing substances by heat. [< Med.L *retorta,* orig. fem. pp. See RETORT¹.]

A, retort; B, receiver; C, flame to heat retort; D, water to keep receiver cool.

re·touch (rē·tuch′), *v.* improve (a photographic negative, etc.) by new touches or slight changes.

re·trace (ri·trās′), *v.*, –traced, –trac·ing. go back over: *we retraced our steps to where we started.* [< F, < *re–* back + *tracer* TRACE¹] —re·trace′a·ble, *adj.*

re·trace (rē·trās′), *v.*, –traced, –trac·ing. trace over again: *re-trace these drawings.* —re·trace′a·ble, *adj.*

re·tract (ri·trakt′), *v.* **1.** draw back or in: *the dog snarled and retracted his lips.* **2.** withdraw; take back: *retract an offer or an opinion.* [< L *retractare,* ult. < *re–* back + *trahere* draw] —re·tract′a·ble, *adj.* —re·tract′a·bil·i·ty, *n.* —re·trac′tive, *adj.* —re·trac′tor, *n.* —Syn. **2.** revoke, rescind, recall.

re·trac·ta·tion (rē′trak·tā′shən), *n.* a retracting of a promise, statement, etc.

re·trac·tile (ri·trak′təl), *adj.* capable of being drawn back or in. —re·trac·til·i·ty (rē′trak·til′ə·ti), *n.*

re·trac·tion (ri·trak′shən), *n.* **1.** a drawing or being drawn back or in. **2.** withdrawal of a promise, statement, etc. **3.** retractile power.

re·tread (*v.* rē·tred′; *n.* rē′tred′), *v.*, –tread-ed, –tread·ing, *n.* —*v.* put a new tread on. —*n.* a retreaded tire.

re·treat (ri·trēt′), *v.* **1.** go or move back; withdraw. **2.** make a forced withdrawal: *the enemy retreated before the advance of our soldiers.* —*n.* **1.** act of going back or withdrawing. **2.** forced withdrawal, often in a hurried and disorderly manner. **3.** signal for retreat: *the drums beat a retreat.* **4.** signal on a bugle or drum, given in the army at sunset. **5.** a safe, quiet place; place of rest or refuge. [< OF *retraite,* orig. pp. of *retraire* < L *retrahere* RETRACT] —Syn. *n.* **1.** withdrawal, retirement. **5.** shelter.

re·trench (ri·trench′), *v.* **1.** cut down or reduce (expenses, etc.). **2.** reduce expenses: *we must retrench.* [< earlier F *retrencher.* See RE–, TRENCH.] —re·trench′er, *n.* —re·trench′ment, *n.* —Syn. **1.** curtail, diminish.

ret·ri·bu·tion (ret′rə·bū′shən), *n.* a deserved punishment; return for evil done, or sometimes for good done. [< L, ult. < *re–* back + *tribuere* assign] —re·trib·u·tive (ri·trib′yə·tiv), re·trib·u·to·ry (ri·trib′yə·tô′ri; –tō′–), *adj.* —re·trib′u·tive·ly, *adv.*

re·trieve (ri·trēv′), *v.*, –trieved, –triev·ing, *n.* —*v.* **1.** get again; recover: *retrieve a lost pocket-book.* **2.** bring back to a former or better condition; restore: *retrieve one's fortunes.* **3.** make good; make amends for; repair: *retrieve a mistake.* **4.** find and bring to a person: *a dog can be trained to retrieve game.* **5.** find and bring back killed or wounded game. —*n.* act of retrieving; recovery; possibility of recovery. [< OF, < *re–* again + *trouver* find] —re·triev′a·ble, *adj.* —re·triev′al, *n.*

re·triev·er (ri·trēv′ər), *n.* **1.** one that retrieves. **2.** dog trained to find killed or wounded game and bring it to a hunter.

retro–, *prefix.* backward; back; behind, as in *retrogress.* [< L, < *retro,* adv.]

ret·ro·ac·tive (ret′rō·ak′tiv), *adj.* acting back; having an effect on what is

Labrador retriever (ab. 2 ft. high at the shoulder)

past. A retroactive law applies to events that occurred before the law was passed. —ret′ro·ac′tive·ly, *adv.* —ret′ro·ac·tiv′i·ty, *n.*

ret·ro·cede (ret′rə·sēd′), *v.*, –ced·ed, –ced·ing. go back; recede. [< L, < *retro–* backward + *cedere* go]

ret·ro·grade (ret′rə·grād), *adj., v.*, –grad·ed, –grad·ing. —*adj.* **1.** moving backward; retreating. **2.** becoming worse. —*v.* **1.** move or go backward. **2.** fall back toward a worse condition; grow worse; decline. [< L, ult. < *retro–* backward + *gradi* go]

ret·ro·gress (ret′rə·gres; ret′rə·gres′), *v.* **1.** move backward; go back. **2.** become worse. [< L *retrogressus,* pp. of *retrogradi.* See RETROGRADE.] —ret′ro·gres·sion, *n.* —ret′ro·gres′sive, *adj.* —ret′ro·gres′sive·ly, *adv.*

ret·ro·spect (ret′rə·spekt), *n.* **1.** survey of past time, events, etc.; thinking about the past. **2.** in retrospect, when looking back. —*v.* think

of (something past). [ult. <L *retrospectus* <
retro- back + *specere* to look] —ret′ro·spec′-
tion, *n.* —ret′ro·spec′tive, *adj.* —ret′ro·spec′-
tive·ly, *adv.*

ret·rous·sé (ret′rü·sā′), *adj.* turned up: *a
retroussé nose.* [<F]

re·turn (ri·tėrn′), *v.* 1. go back; come back:
my brother will return this summer. 2. bring,
give, send, hit, put, or pay back: *return that
book to the library.* 3. yield: *the concert returned about $50 over expenses.* 4. report or
announce officially: *the jury returned a verdict
of guilty.* 5. reply: *"No!" he returned crossly.*
6. elect to a lawmaking body. —*n.* 1. a going or
coming back; happening again. 2. thing returned.
3. a bringing, giving, sending, hitting, or putting
back: *a poor return for kindness.* 4. Often, returns. profit; amount received. 5. in return,
as a return; to return something. 6. report;
account: *election returns.* 7. reply. —*adj.* 1. of or
pertaining to a return: *a return ticket.* 2. sent,
given, done, etc., in return: *a return game.* [<
OF *retourner.* See RE-, TURN.] —re·turn′a·ble,
adj. —Syn. *v.* 5. respond, rejoin. —*n.* 1. recur-
rence, reappearance.

re·turn·ee (ri·tėrn′ē′; ri·tėrn′ē′), *n.* person
who has returned.

re·un·ion (rē·ūn′yən), *n.* 1. a coming together
again. 2. a social gathering of persons who have
been separated or who have interests in common.

re·u·nite (rē′ū·nīt′), *v.* —nit·ed, —nit·ing.
bring or come together again. —re′u·nit′a·ble,
adj. —re′u·nit′er, *n.*

Reu·ther (rü′thər), *n.* Walter, born 1907,
American labor leader, president of the CIO
since 1952.

rev (rev), *n., v.,* revved, rev·ving. *Colloq.* —*n.* a
revolution (of an engine or motor). —*v.* increase
the speed of (an engine or motor).

Rev., 1. Revelation. 2. Reverend.

rev., revised; revision.

re·vamp (rē·vamp′), *v. Am.* patch up; repair.

re·veal (ri·vēl′), *v.* 1. make known: *never reveal my secret.* 2. display; show. [<L, ult. <*re-*
back + *velum* veil] —re·veal′a·ble, *adj.* —re-
veal′er, *n.* —re·veal′ment, *n.*

rev·eil·le (rev′ə·lē), *n.* a signal on a bugle or
drum to waken soldiers or sailors in the morning. [<F *réveillez (-vous)* awaken!, ult. <L
re- again + *ex-* up + *vigil* awake]

rev·el (rev′əl), *v.,* -eled, -el·ing; *esp. Brit.*
-elled, -el·ling, *n.* —*v.* 1. take great pleasure
(in): *the children revel in country life.* 2. make
merry; take part in boisterous merrymaking.
—*n.* a noisy good time; merrymaking: *the New
Year's revels.* [<OF <L *rebellare.* Doublet of
REBEL.] —rev′el·er, *esp. Brit.* rev′el·ler, *n.*

rev·e·la·tion (rev′ə·lā′shən), *n.* 1. act of
making known. 2. the thing made known. 3.
God's disclosure of Himself and of His will to His
creatures. 4. Revelation, often, Revelations. the
last book of the New Testament.

rev·el·ry (rev′əl·ri), *n., pl.* -ries. boisterous
reveling or festivity; wild merrymaking.

re·venge (ri·venj′), *n., v.,* -venged, -veng·ing.
—*n.* 1. harm done in return for a wrong; vengeance. 2. desire for vengeance. —*v.* 1. do harm in
return for. 2. be revenged or revenge oneself,
get revenge. [<OF *revengier,* ult. <L *re-* back +
vindicare avenge. See VINDICATE.] —re·veng′er, *n.*

re·venge·ful (ri·venj′fəl), *adj.* feeling or
showing a strong desire for revenge. —re·venge′-
ful·ly, *adv.* —re·venge′ful·ness, *n.*

rev·e·nue (rev′ə·nū; -nū), *n.* 1. money coming in;
income. 2. the income of a government from taxation, excise duties, customs, etc., appropriated
to the payment of public expenses. [<F, orig.
fem. pp. of *revenir* <L *re-* back + *venire* come]

re·ver·ber·ant (ri·vėr′bər·ənt), *adj.* rever-
berating.

re·ver·ber·ate (ri·vėr′bər·āt), *v.,* -at·ed, -at-
ing. 1. echo back. 2. cast or be cast back; reflect
(light or heat). [<L *reverberatus* beaten back,
ult. <*re-* back + *verbera* a blow] —re·ver′ber-
a′tion, *n.* —re·ver·ber·a·to·ry (ri·vėr′bər·ə·tô′ri;
-tō′-), *adj.*

re·vere¹ (ri·vir′), *v.,* -vered, -ver·ing. love and

respect deeply; honor greatly; show reverence
for. [<L, <*re-* back + *vereri* be awed]

re·vere² (ri·vir′), *n.* revers.

Re·vere (ri·vir′), *n.* Paul, 1735–1818, American
patriot.

rev·er·ence (rev′ər·əns; rev′rəns), *n., v.,*
-enced, -enc·ing. —*n.* 1. a feeling of deep respect, mixed with wonder, awe, and love. 2. a
deep bow. 3. his or your Reverence, title used
in speaking of or to a clergyman. —*v.* regard
with reverence; revere. —Syn. *n.* 1. veneration,
adoration.

rev·er·end (rev′ər·ənd; rev′rənd), *adj.* worthy
of great respect. —*n.* 1. Reverend, title for
clergymen. 2. *Colloq.* clergyman. [<L *reverendus*
to be respected. See REVERE¹.]

rev·er·ent (rev′ər·ənt; rev′rənt), *adj.* feeling
reverence; showing reverence. [<L *reverens*
revering. See REVERE¹.] —rev′er·ent·ly, *adv.*

rev·er·en·tial (rev′ər·en′shəl), *adj.* reverent.
—rev′er·en′tial·ly, *adv.* —rev′er·en′tial·ness, *n.*

rev·er·ie (rev′ər·i), *n.* dreamy
thoughts; dreamy thinking of pleasant things: *indulge in reveries about
the future.* Also, revery. [<F, <
rêver to dream] —rev′er·ist, *n.*

re·vers (rə·vir′; -vār′), *n., pl.
-vers (-virz′; -vārz′).* part of a
garment turned back to show the
lining or facing. Also, revere. [<F,
REVERSE]

Revers
on a dress

re·ver·sal (ri·vėr′səl), *n.* change to the opposite; reversing or being reversed.

re·verse (ri·vėrs′), *n., adj., v.,* -versed, -vers-
ing. —*n.* 1. the opposite or contrary: *she did
the reverse of what I ordered.* 2. gear that reverses the movement of machinery. 3. a change
to bad fortune; check; defeat: *unexpected reverses.* 4. the back: *the reverse of a medal.* —*adj.*
1. turned backward; opposite or contrary in
position or direction: *the reverse side of a
record.* 2. acting in a manner opposite or contrary to that which is usual. 3. causing an
opposite or backward movement. —*v.* 1. turn the
other way; turn inside out; turn upside down:
reverse that gun. 2. change to the opposite. 3.
repeal; annul: *the court reversed its decree.* 4.
Mach. cause to act in a backward or opposite
direction. [<L *reversus,* pp. of *revertere* turn
around. See REVERT.] —re·verse′ly, *adv.* —re-
vers′er, *n.* —Syn. *n.* 3. setback, failure.

re·vers·i·ble (ri·vėr′sə·bəl), *adj.* 1. that can
be reversed; that can reverse. 2. finished on both
sides so that either can be used as the right side.
—re·vers′i·bil′i·ty, re·vers′i·ble·ness, *n.* —re·
vers′i·bly, *adv.*

re·ver·sion (ri·vėr′zhən; -shən), *n.* 1. return
to a former condition, practice, belief, etc.; return. 2. return of property to the grantor or his
heirs. 3. right to possess a certain property
under certain conditions. —re·ver′sion·al, *adj.*
—re·ver·sion·ar·y (ri·vėr′zhən·er′i; -shən-), *adj.*

re·vert (ri·vėrt′), *v.* 1. go back; return: *if a
man dies without heirs, his property reverts to
the State.* 2. *Biol.* go back to an antecedent state
of development. [<OF <L, <*re-* back + *vertere*
turn] —re·vert′i·ble, *adj.*

rev·er·y (rev′ər·i), *n., pl.* -er·ies. reverie.

re·view (ri·vū′), *v.* 1. study again; look at
again: *he reviewed the scene of the crime.* 2.
look back on: *before falling asleep, Helen reviewed the day's happenings.* 3. examine again;
look at with care: *let's review the situation.* 4.
Law. reëxamine. A superior court may review
decisions of a lower court. 5. inspect formally:
the President reviewed the fleet. 6. examine to
give an account of: *Mr. Brown reviews books for
a living.* 7. review books, etc. —*n.* 1. a studying
again. 2. a looking back on; survey. 3. *Law.*
reëxamination of the decision or proceedings
in a case. 4. an examination or inspection, esp.
a formal inspection of military or naval forces.
5. account of a book, play, etc., giving its merits
and faults. 6. magazine containing articles on
subjects of current interest, including accounts

āge, cãre, fär; ēqual, tėrm; īce; ōpen, ôrder; put, rüle, ūse; th, then; ə=a in about.

of books, etc.: *a law review, a movie review*. 7. revue. [< F *revue*, orig. pp., seen again, ult. < L *re-* again + *videre* see] —re·view′a·ble, *adj*.

re·view·er (ri·vū′ər), *n*. 1. person who reviews. 2. person who writes articles discussing books, plays, etc.

re·vile (ri·vīl′), *v*., –viled, –vil·ing. heap reproaches on; abuse with words. [< OF *reviler* despise < *re-* again + *vil* VILE] —re·vile′ment, *n*. —re·vil′er, *n*. —re·vil′ing·ly, *adv*. —Syn. berate.

re·vise (ri·vīz′), *v*., –vised, –vis·ing, *n*. —*v*. 1. read carefully in order to correct; look over and change; examine and improve. 2. change; alter. —*n*. 1. process of revising. 2. a revised form or version. 3. a proof sheet printed after corrections have been made. [< F *reviser*, ult. < L *re-* again + *videre* see] —re·vis′er, re·vi′sor, *n*.

Revised Version, the revised form of the Authorized Version of the Bible (1881, 1885).

re·vi·sion (ri·vizh′ən), *n*. 1. act or work of revising: *a revision of taxes*. 2. a revised form: *a revision of his book*. —re·vi′sion·al, *adj*.

re·vi·sion·ist (ri·vizh′ə·nist), *n*. 1. one who favors or supports revision. 2. a Communist who tends to a flexible interpretation of Marxism, in accordance with changing national needs.

re·viv·al (ri·vīv′əl), *n*. 1. a bringing or coming back to life or consciousness. 2. restoration to vigor or health. 3. a bringing or coming back to style, use, activity, etc. 4. an awakening or increase of interest in religion. 5. *Am*. Also, re·vival meeting. special services or efforts made to awaken or increase interest in religion.

re·viv·al·ist (ri·vīv′əl·ist), *n*. person who holds special services to awaken interest in religion.

re·vive (ri·vīv′), *v*., –vived, –viv·ing. 1. bring back or come back to life or consciousness: *revive a half-drowned person*. 2. bring or come back to a fresh, lively condition: *flowers revive in water*. 3. make or become fresh; restore: *hot coffee revived the cold, tired man*. 4. bring back or come back to notice, use, fashion, memory, activity, etc.: *an old play is sometimes revived on the stage*. [< L, < *re-* again + *vivere* live] —re·viv′er, *n*. —Syn. 3. refresh, hearten.

re·viv·i·fy (rē·viv′ə·fī), *v*., –fied, –fy·ing. restore to life; give new life to. —re·viv′i·fi·ca′-tion, *n*. —re·viv′i·fi′er, *n*.

rev·o·ca·ble (rev′ə·kə·bəl), *adj*. that can be repealed, canceled, or withdrawn. —rev′o·ca·bil′i·ty, *n*. —rev′o·ca·bly, *adv*.

rev·o·ca·tion (rev′ə·kā′shən), *n*. repeal; canceling; withdrawal.

rev·o·ca·to·ry (rev′ə·kə·tô′ri, –tō′–), *adj*. revoking; recalling; repealing.

re·voke (ri·vōk′), *v*., –voked, –vok·ing, *n*. —*v*. 1. take back; repeal; cancel; withdraw: *the king revoked his decree*. 2. fail to follow suit in playing cards when one can and should. —*n. Cards*. a failure to follow suit when one can and should. [< L, < *re-* back + *vocare* call] —re·vok′er, *n*.

re·volt (ri·vōlt′), *n*. act or state of rebelling: *the fleet was already in revolt*. —*v*. 1. turn away from and fight against a leader; rise against the government's authority: *the people revolted against the dictator*. 2. turn away with disgust: *revolt at a bad smell*. 3. cause to feel disgust. [< F < Ital. *rivolta*, ult. < L *revolvere* REVOLVE] —re·volt′er, *n*. —Syn. *n*. rebellion, revolution, sedition. —*v*. 3. repel, sicken.

re·volt·ing (ri·vōl′ting), *adj*. disgusting; repulsive. —re·volt′ing·ly, *adv*.

rev·o·lu·tion (rev′ə·lü′shən), *n*. 1. a complete overthrow of an established government or political system. 2. a complete change: *the automobile caused a revolution in ways of traveling*. 3. movement, real or apparent, in a circle or curve around some point: *one revolution of the earth around the sun takes a year*. 4. act or fact of turning round a center or axis; rotation: *the revolution of the earth causes day and night*. 5. time or distance of one revolution. 6. a complete cycle or series of events: *the revolution of the four seasons fills a year*. [< L *revolutio* < *revolvere* REVOLVE]

rev·o·lu·tion·ar·y (rev′ə·lü′shən·er′i), *adj*., *n.*, *pl.* –ar·ies. —*adj*. 1. of or connected with a revolution. 2. bringing or causing great changes. 3. Revolutionary, *Am*. of or pertaining to the American Revolution, or those who fought in it. —*n*. revolutionist.

Revolutionary War, *Am*. the war from 1775 to 1783 by which the thirteen American colonies won independence from England.

rev·o·lu·tion·ist (rev′ə·lü′shən·ist), *n*. person who advocates, or takes part in, a revolution.

rev·o·lu·tion·ize (rev′ə·lü′shən·īz), *v*., –ized, –iz·ing. 1. cause a revolution in the government of. 2. change completely; produce a very great change in.

re·volve (ri·volv′), *v*., –volved, –volv·ing. 1. move in a circle; move in a curve round a point: *the moon revolves around the earth*. 2. turn round a center or axis; rotate: *the wheels of a moving car revolve*. 3. turn over in the mind; consider from many points of view. [< L, < *re-* back + *volvere* roll] —re·volv′a·ble, *adj*. —re·volv′ing, *adj*. —Syn. 3. ponder, study.

re·volv·er (ri·vol′vər), *n. Am*. pistol that can be fired several times without loading it again.

re·vue (ri·vū′), *n*. a theatrical entertainment with singing, dancing, parodies of recent plays, humorous treatments of happenings and fads of the year, etc. [< F. See REVIEW.]

re·vul·sion (ri·vul′shən), *n*. a sudden, violent change or reaction. [< L *revulsio*, ult. < *re-* back + *vellere* tear away]

re·ward (ri·wôrd′), *n*. 1. return made for something done. 2. a money payment given or offered for the detection or capture of offenders against the law, the return of lost property, etc. —*v*. 1. give a reward to: *reward a person for his services*. 2. give a reward for: *reward his past services liberally*. 3. be a reward for: *the good results rewarded him for his efforts*. [< var. of OF *regarder* REGARD] —re·ward′a·ble, *adj*. —re·ward′er, *n*. —Syn. *v*. 1. recompense, repay.

Rey·kja·vik (rā′kyə·vēk′), *n*. capital and seaport of Iceland, in the SW part.

Rey·nolds (ren′əldz), *n*. Sir Joshua, 1723–1792, English portrait painter.

R.F., r.f., radio frequency.

R.F.D., *Am*. Rural Free Delivery.

Rh, *Chem*. rhodium.

rhap·sod·ic (rap·sod′ik), rhap·sod·i·cal (–ə·kəl), *adj*. of or characteristic of rhapsody; extravagantly enthusiastic; ecstatic.

rhap·so·dize (rap′sə·dīz), *v*., –dized, –diz·ing. talk or write with extravagant enthusiasm.

rhap·so·dy (rap′sə·di), *n.*, *pl.* –dies. 1. utterance or writing marked by extravagant enthusiasm. 2. *Music*. an instrumental composition irregular in form. [< L < Gk. *rhapsoidia* verse-composition, ult. < *rhaptein* to stitch] —rhap′so·dist, *n*.

rhe·a (rē′ə), *n*. any of several large birds of South America that are much like the ostrich, but are smaller and have three toes instead of two.

Rhea (ab. 4½ ft. from bill to tail)

Rhee (rē), *n*. Syngman, 1875–1965, Korean statesman; president of South Korea, 1948–1960.

Rheims (rēmz; *Fr*. raɴs), *n*. Reims.

Rhen·ish (ren′ish), *adj*. of the river Rhine or the regions near it. —*n*. Rhine wine.

rhe·ni·um (rē′ni·əm), *n. Chem*. a rare, hard, grayish metallic element, Re, that has chemical properties similar to those of manganese. [< L *Rhenus* Rhine]

rhe·o·stat (rē′ə·stat), *n. Elect*. instrument for regulating the strength of an electric current by introducing different amounts of resistance into the circuit. [< Gk. *rheos* current + *statos* standing still] —rhe′o·stat′ic, *adj*.

rhe·sus (rē′səs), *n*. a small, yellowish-brown monkey with a short tail, found in India. [from a character in the *Iliad*]

Rhe·sus factor (rē′səs), Rh factor.

rhet·o·ric (ret′ə·rik), *n.* 1. art of using words in speaking or writing. 2. book about this art. 3. mere display in language. [< L < Gk. *rhetorike* (*techne*) art of an orator]

rhe·tor·i·cal (ri·tôr′ə·kəl; –tor′–), *adj.* 1. of or pertaining to rhetoric. 2. using rhetoric. 3. intended especially for display; artificial. 4. oratorical. —**rhe·tor′i·cal·ly,** *adv.*

rhetorical question, question asked only for effect, not for information.

rhet·o·ri·cian (ret′ə·rish′ən), *n.* person skilled in rhetoric.

rheum (rüm), *n.* 1. a watery discharge, such as mucus, tears, or saliva. 2. catarrh; cold. [< OF < L < Gk. *rheuma* a flowing < *rheein* to flow] —**rheum′y,** *adj.*

rheu·ma·tism (rü·mat′ik), *adj.* 1. of rheumatism. 2. having rheumatism; liable to have rheumatism. —*n.* person who has rheumatism.

rheumatic fever, an acute disease that often has very harmful aftereffects.

rheu·ma·tism (rü′mə·tiz·əm), *n.* disease with inflammation, swelling, and stiffness of the joints. [< L < Gk., ult. < *rheuma* RHEUM]

Rh factor, substance often found in the blood of human beings and the higher mammals. Blood containing this substance (**Rh positive**) does not combine favorably with blood lacking it (**Rh negative**). Also, **Rhesus factor.** [first discovered in the blood of the rhesus monkey]

rhi·nal (rī′nəl), *adj.* of or pertaining to the nose; nasal.

Rhine (rīn), *n.* river flowing from C Switzerland through Germany and the Netherlands into the North Sea.

rhine·stone (rīn′stōn′), *n.* an imitation diamond, made of glass. [trans. of F *caillou du Rhin*]

Rhine wine, wine, usually a white wine, produced in the valley of the Rhine.

rhi·ni·tis (rī·nī′tis), *n.* inflammation of the nose or its mucous membrane. [< NL, < Gk. *rhis* nose]

rhi·noc·er·os (rī·nos′-ər·əs), *n., pl.* **-os·es** or (*esp. collectively*) **-os.** a large, thick-skinned animal of Africa and Asia with one or two upright horns on the snout. [< L < Gk. *rhinokeros*, ult. < *rhis* nose + *keras* horn]

rhi·zome (rī′zōm), *n.* a rootlike stem lying along or under the ground, which usually produces roots below and shoots from the upper surface; rootstock. [< Gk., ult. < *rhiza* root]

Forms of rhizome: S, Solomon's-seal; T, trillium; J, jack-in-the-pulpit.

rho (rō), *n.* the 17th letter of the Greek alphabet (P, ρ).

Rhode Island (rōd), a New England State of the United States. *Capital:* Providence. *Abbrev.:* R.I. —**Rhode Islander,** *Am.*

Rhodes (rōdz), *n.* a Greek island, formerly Italian, in the Aegean Sea, just SW of Asia Minor. —**Rho·di·an** (rō′di·ən), *adj., n.*

Rho·de·sia (rō·dē′zhə), *n.* region in S Africa including **Southern Rhodesia** and the former British protectorate of **Northern Rhodesia.** —**Rho·de′sian,** *adj., n.*

rho·di·um (rō′di·əm), *n.* *Chem.* a grayish-white metallic element, Rh, forming salts that give rose-colored solutions. [< Gk. *rhodon* rose]

rho·do·den·dron (rō′də·den′-drən), *n.* an evergreen shrub somewhat like an azalea with beautiful pink, purple, or white flowers. [< NL < Gk., < *rhodon* rose + *dendron* tree]

rhom·boid (rom′boid), *n.* parallelogram with equal opposite sides that is not a rectangle. —*adj.* Also, **rhom·boi′dal.** shaped like a rhombus or rhomboid.

Rhomboids

rhom·bus (rom′bəs), **rhomb** (rom; romb), *n., pl.* **rhom·bus·es, rhom·bi** (–bī); **rhombs.** parallelogram with equal sides, having two obtuse angles and two acute angles; diamond. [< L < Gk. *rhombos*] —**rhom′-bic,** *adj.*

Rhone, French **Rhône** (rōn), *n.* river flowing from S Switzerland through SE France into the Mediterranean Sea.

Rhombuses

rhu·barb (rü′bärb), *n.* 1. a garden plant with very large leaves, whose sour stalks are used for making sauce, pies, etc. 2. the stalks. 3. the sauce made of them. 4. *Am., Colloq.* a heated dispute, usually marked by derisive comment. [< OF]

rhum·ba (rum′bə), *n.* rumba.

rhyme (rīm), *v.,* **rhymed, rhym·ing,** *n.* —*v.* 1. sound alike in the last part. *Long* and *song* rhyme. *Go to bed* rhymes with *sleepy head.* 2. put or make into rhyme: *rhyme a translation.* 3. make rhymes. 4. use (a word) with another that rhymes with it: *rhyme "love" and "dove."* —*n.* 1. agreement in the final sounds of words or lines. 2. word or line having the same last sound as another. *Cat* is a rhyme for *mat.* 3. verses or poetry with a regular return of similar sounds. 4. without rhyme or reason, having no system or sense. Also, **rime.** [< OF < L < Gk. *rhythmos* rhythm. Doublet of RHYTHM.] —**rhym′er,** *n.* ▶ **rhyme, rime.** The simpler spelling seems to be gaining slowly on *rhyme.* It was the original spelling in English.

rhyme·ster (rīm′stər), *n.* maker of rather poor rhymes or verse. Also, **rimester.**

rhythm (riᵺ′əm), *n.* 1. movement with a regular repetition of a beat, accent, rise and fall, or the like: *the rhythm of dancing, the rhythm of the tides, the rhythm of one's heartbeats.* 2. repetition of an accent; arrangement of beats in a line of poetry. 3. grouping by accents or beats: *triple rhythm.* [< L < Gk. *rhythmos* < *rheein* to flow. Doublet of RHYME.]

rhyth·mi·cal (riᵺ′mə·kəl), **rhyth·mic** (–mik), *adj.* having rhythm; of or pertaining to rhythm. —**rhyth′mi·cal·ly,** *adv.*

R.I., Rhode Island.

ri·al (rī′əl), *n.* an Iranian silver coin and unit of money.

Ri·al·to (ri·al′tō), *n.* 1. a former business district of Venice. 2. a famous bridge in Venice that crosses the Grand Canal. 3. *Am.* the theater district along Broadway in New York City.

rib (rib), *n., v.,* **ribbed, rib·bing.** —*n.* 1. one of the curved bones extending from the backbone and enclosing the upper part of the body. 2. cut of meat containing a rib. 3. piece that forms a frame. An umbrella has ribs. 4. a thick vein of a leaf. 5. ridge in cloth, knitting, etc. —*v.* 1. furnish or strengthen with ribs. 2. mark with riblike ridges. 3. *Slang.* tease; mock. [OE *ribb*] —**ribbed,** *adj.*

rib·ald (rib′əld), *adj.* offensive in speech; coarsely mocking. —*n.* a ribald person. [< OF *ribauld,* ult. < MDu. *ribe* prostitute] —**Syn.** *adj.* irreverent, indecent, obscene, indelicate, gross.

rib·ald·ry (rib′əld·ri), *n.* ribald language.

rib·and, rib·band (rib′ənd), *n.* *Archaic.* ribbon.

rib·bon (rib′ən), *n.* 1. strip or band of silk, satin, velvet, etc. 2. a narrow strip of cloth: *torn to ribbons.* 3. *Am.* band charged with ink for use in a typewriter. 4. a long, narrow strip of anything. —*v.* 1. adorn with ribbons. 2. separate into ribbons. [< OF *ruban* < Gmc.] —**rib′-boned,** *adj.*

ri·bo·fla·vin (rī′bō·flā′vin), *n.* constituent of the vitamin B complex, $C_{17}H_{20}N_4O_6$, present in liver, eggs, milk, spinach, etc.; lactoflavin; vitamin B₂; vitamin G. [< *ribose* (ult. < *gum arabic*) + L *flavus* yellow]

rice (rīs), *n., v.,* **riced, ric·ing.** —*n.* 1. the starchy seeds or grain of a plant grown in warm climates. Rice is an important food in India,

China, and Japan. 2. the plant itself. —*v.* reduce to a form like rice: *rice potatoes.* [< OF < Ital., ult. < Gk. *oryza* < Iranian]

rice paper, a thin paper made from the straw of rice.

ric·er (rīs′ər), *n. Am.* utensil for ricing cooked potatoes, etc., by pressing them through small holes.

rich (rich), *adj.* 1. having much money or property: *a rich man.* 2. abundantly supplied with resources: *the United States is rich in oil and coal.* 3. abundant: *a rich supply.* 4. producing or yielding abundantly; fertile: *rich soil, a rich mine.* 5. valuable: *rich spoils.* 6. costly; elegant: *rich dress.* 7. having many desirable elements or qualities, esp. containing plenty of butter, eggs, flavoring, etc. 8. (of colors, sounds, smells, etc.) deep; full; vivid. 9. *Colloq.* amusing. 10. *Colloq.* ridiculous; absurd. —*n.pl.* rich people. [OE *rīce* < Celtic] —**rich′ly,** *adv.* —**rich′ness,** *n.* —Syn. *adj.* 1. wealthy, affluent, opulent, well-to-do, moneyed. 3. plentiful, bountiful, copious. 4. productive, fruitful, fecund. 6. expensive, sumptuous, gorgeous, luxurious.

Rich·ard I (rich′ərd), ("Richard the Lion-Hearted," "Richard Coeur de Lion") 1157–1199, king of England, 1189–1199.

Rich·e·lieu (rish′ə·lū), *n.* Duke of, 1585–1642, French cardinal and statesman.

rich·es (rich′iz), *n.pl.* wealth; abundance of property; much money, land, goods, etc. [< OF *richesse* < *riche* rich < Gmc. See RICH.]

Rich·mond (rich′mənd), *n.* 1. capital of Virginia, a river port in the E part of the State on the James River. 2. borough of New York City consisting of Staten Island.

rick (rik), *n.* stack of hay, straw, etc., esp. one made so that the rain will run off it. —*v.* form into a rick or ricks. [OE *hrēac*]

rick·ets (rik′its), *n.* disease of childhood, caused by lack of vitamin D or calcium, that results in softening, and sometimes bending, of the bones; rachitis. [appar. alter. of *rachitis;* infl. by *wrick* wrench, strain]

rick·et·y (rik′it·i), *adj.* 1. liable to fall or break down; shaky: *a rickety old chair.* 2. having rickets; suffering from rickets. 3. feeble in the joints. —**rick′et·i·ness,** *n.* —Syn. 1. ramshackle.

rick·shaw, rick·sha (rik′shô), *n.* jinrikisha.

rick·ey (rik′i), *n. Am.* drink consisting of the juice of a lime, alcoholic liquor, esp. gin, and carbonated water. [supposedly from a personal name]

ric·o·chet (rik′ə·shā′), *n., v.,* -cheted (-shād′), -chet·ing (-shā′ing); esp. *Brit.* -chet·ted (-shet′id; -shād′), -chet·ting (-shet′ing; -shā′ing). —*n.* the skipping or jumping motion of an object as it goes along a flat surface. —*v.* move in this way. [< F]

rid (rid), *v.,* rid or rid·ded, rid·ding. 1. make free (from): *what will rid a house of rats?* 2. be rid of, be freed from. 3. get rid of, a. get free from. b. do away with. [OE (*ge*)*ryddan* to clear land] —**rid′der,** *n.*

rid·dance (rid′əns), *n.* a clearing away or out; removal.

rid·dle¹ (rid′əl), *n., v.,* -dled, -dling. —*n.* 1. a puzzling question, statement, problem, etc. *Example:* When is a door not a door? *Answer:* When it is ajar. 2. person or thing that is hard to understand, explain, etc. —*v.* speak in riddles. [OE *rǣdels* < *rǣdan* guess, explain; ME *redels* taken as pl.] —**rid′dler,** *n.* —**rid′dling·ly,** *adv.* —Syn. *n.* 1. enigma, puzzle, conundrum.

rid·dle² (rid′əl), *v.,* -dled, -dling. —*v.* 1. make many holes in: *the door of the fort was riddled with bullets.* 2. sift: *riddle gravel.* —*n.* a coarse sieve. [OE *hriddel* sieve]

ride (rīd), *v.,* rode or (*Archaic*) rid (rid), rid·den (rid′ən) or (*Archaic*) rid, rid·ing, *n.* —*v.* 1. sit on and manage a horse, camel, bicycle, etc.: *he rides every morning.* 2. sit on and manage: *ride a bicycle or a horse.* 3. admit of being ridden: *a horse that rides easily.* 4. be carried along in or by anything: *ride on a train.* 5. ride over, along, or through (a road, boundary, region, etc.). 6. be mounted on; be carried

on: *the eagle rides the winds.* 7. do or perform: *ride a race.* 8. move on; float; float along: *the ship rode the waves and now rides at anchor in the harbor.* 9. *Colloq.* make fun of; tease. 10. cause to ride or be carried: *ride a man on a rail as punishment.* 11. control, dominate, or tyrannize over: *be ridden by foolish fears.* 12. ride down, a. knock down. b. overcome. c. overtake by riding. d. exhaust by riding. 13. ride out, a. withstand (a gale, etc.) without damage. b. endure successfully. 14. ride up, move up from the proper position: *that coat rides up at the back.* —*n.* 1. a trip on the back of a horse, in a carriage, car, train, boat, etc. 2. path, road, etc. made for riding. [OE *rīdan*] —**ride′a·ble,** *adj.*

rid·er (rīd′ər), *n.* 1. person who rides. 2. anything added to a record, document, legislative bill, or statement after it was supposed to be completed. —**rid′er·less,** *adj.* —Syn. 2. amendment, addition.

ridge (rij), *n., v.,* ridged, ridg·ing. —*n.* 1. the long and narrow upper part of something: *the ridge of an animal's back.* 2. line where two sloping surfaces meet: *the ridge of a roof.* 3. a long, narrow chain of hills or mountains: *the Blue Ridge of the Appalachian Mountains.* 4. any raised narrow strip: *the ridges on corduroy cloth.* —*v.* 1. form or make into ridges. 2. cover or mark with ridges. [OE *hrycg*] —**ridg′y,** *adj.*

ridge·pole (rij′pōl′), *n.* the horizontal timber along the top of a roof or tent.

rid·i·cule (rid′ə·kūl), *v.,* -culed, -cul·ing, *n.* —*v.* laugh at; make fun of. —*n.* laughter in mockery; words or actions that make fun of somebody or something. [< F < L *ridiculum,* neut. adj., RIDICULOUS] —**rid′i·cul′er,** *n.* —Syn. *v.* deride, mock, taunt, twit, scoff. —*n.* derision, raillery, sarcasm.

ri·dic·u·lous (ri·dik′yə·ləs), *adj.* deserving ridicule; absurd; laughable. [< L *ridiculus* < *ridere* to laugh] —**ri·dic′u·lous·ly,** *adv.* —**ri·dic′u·lous·ness,** *n.* —Syn. nonsensical, preposterous, ludicrous.

Rif (rif), *n.* Er, a mountainous region in N Morocco, along the Mediterranean coast.

rife (rīf), *adj.* 1. happening often; numerous; widespread. 2. full; abounding: *the land was rife with rumors of war.* [OE *rīfe*] —**rife′ness,** *n.*

Riff (rif), *n.* native or inhabitant of Er Rif. —**Riff·i·an** (rif′i·ən), *adj., n.*

rif·fle (rif′əl), *n., v.,* -fled, -fling. —*n.* 1. *Am.* a rapid. 2. *Am.* a ripple. 3. act of shuffling cards. —*v.* shuffle (cards) by bending the edges slightly so that the two divisions of the deck slide into each other.

riff·raff (rif′raf′), *n.* 1. worthless people. 2. trash. —*adj.* worthless. [< OF *rif et raf* every scrap < *rifler* RIFLE² + *raffler* carry off (see RAFFLE)]

ri·fle¹ (rī′fəl), *n., v.,* -fled, -fling. —*n.* 1. *Am.* gun with spiral grooves in its barrel to spin the bullet as it is fired. 2. such a gun that is fired from the shoulder. 3. soldier armed with a rifle. —*v.* cut spiral grooves in (a gun). [ult. < F *rifler* to scratch, groove, RIFLE²]

ri·fle² (rī′fəl), *v.,* -fled, -fling. 1. search and rob; ransack and rob. 2. steal; take away. 3. strip bare. [< OF *rifler* < Gmc.] —**ri′fler,** *n.*

ri·fle·man (rī′fəl·mən), *n., pl.* -men. 1. *Am.* soldier armed with a rifle. 2. man who uses a rifle.

ri·fling (rī′fling), *n.* 1. act or process of cutting spiral grooves in a gun barrel. 2. system of spiral grooves in a rifle.

rift (rift), *n., v.* split; break; crack. [< Scand. *ript*] —**rift′y,** *adj.*

rig (rig), *v.,* rigged, rig·ging, *n.* —*v.* 1. equip (a ship) with masts, sails, ropes, etc. 2. move (a shroud, boom, stay, etc.) to its proper place. 3. equip; fit out. 4. *Colloq.* dress. 5. get ready for use. 6. put together in a hurry or by using odds and ends. 7. arrange dishonestly for one's own advantage. —*n.* 1. arrangement of masts, sails, ropes, etc., on a ship. A schooner has a fore-and-aft rig. 2. *Colloq.* dress. 3. outfit; equipment. 4. *Am., Colloq.* carriage, with its horse or horses. [< Scand. (Dan.) *rigge*] —**rigged,** *adj.* —**rig′ger,** *n.*

Ri·ga (rē'gə), *n.* seaport in and capital of Latvia.

rig·ging (rig'ing), *n.* 1. ropes, chains, etc., used to support and work the masts, yards, sails, etc., on a ship. 2. tackle; equipment.

right (rīt), *adj.* 1. good; just; lawful: *right conduct.* 2. correct; true: *the right answer.* 3. proper; fitting: *say the right thing.* 4. favorable: *if the weather is right, we'll go.* 5. healthy; normal: *be in one's right senses.* 6. meant to be seen; most important: *the right side of cloth.* 7. opposite of left; belonging or pertaining to the side of anything which is turned east when the main side is turned north: *one's right hand or right glove.* 8. straight: *a right line.* 9. formed by a line drawn to another line or surface by the shortest course: *a right angle, a right cone.* 10. *Archaic.* rightful; real: *the right owner.* —*adv.* 1. in a way that is good, just, or lawful: *he acted right when he told the truth.* 2. correctly; truly: *she guessed right.* 3. properly; well: *it serves you right to lose if you cheat.* 4. favorably: *turn out right.* 5. in a good or suitable condition: *put things right.* 6. to the right hand: *turn right.* 7. exactly; just; precisely: *put it right here.* 8. *Am.* at once; immediately: *stop playing right now.* 9. (used in some titles) very: *right honorable.* 10. *Colloq.* or *Dial.* extremely. 11. in a straight line; directly: *look me right in the eye.* 12. completely: *his hat was knocked right off.* 13. right away; at once; immediately. 14. **right off**, at once; immediately. —*n.* 1. that which is right: *know the difference between right and wrong.* 2. a just claim, title, or privilege: *the right to vote.* 3. fair treatment; justice. 4. blow struck with the right hand. 5. the right side or what is on the right side. 6. the **Right**, often **the right**. part of a lawmaking body, made up of conservative or reactionary political groups, that sits on the right of the presiding officer. 7. **by right** or **by rights**, justly; properly. 8. **in the right**, right. 9. **to rights**, *Colloq.* in or into proper condition; order, etc. —*v.* 1. make correct: *right errors.* 2. put in order: *right a room.* 3. do justice to: *right the oppressed.* 4. get or put into proper position: *the ship righted as the wave passed.* [OE *riht*] —**right′a·ble**, *adj.* —**right′less**, *adj.* —**right′ly**, *adv.* —**right′ness**, *n.* —**Syn.** *adj.* 1. equitable, ethical. 2. accurate. 3. fit, seemly, due, appropriate. 4. suitable, propitious. 6. principal, front, upper. —*n.* 1. equity, morality, virtue. 2. prerogative. —*v.* 1. rectify, emend. 2. adjust. 3. vindicate. ▶ **right.** In the sense of "extremely," *right* is a localism (*we'll be right glad to see you*).

right a·bout-face (rīt'ə-bout'fās'), turn in the opposite direction.

right angle, angle of 90 degrees.

right-an·gled (rīt'ang'gəld), *adj.* containing a right angle or right angles; rectangular.

Right angle

right·eous (rī'chəs), *adj.* 1. doing right; virtuous; behaving justly. 2. morally right or justifiable: *righteous indignation.* —**right′eous·ly**, *adv.* —**right′eous·ness**, *n.* —**Syn.** 1. upright, just.

right·ful (rīt'fəl), *adj.* 1. according to law; by rights: *the rightful owner of this dog.* 2. just and right; proper: *one's rightful position.* —**right′ful·ly**, *adv.* —**right′ful·ness**, *n.* —**Syn.** 1. lawful. 2. due.

right-hand (rīt'hand'), *adj.* 1. on or to the right. 2. of, for, or with the right hand. 3. most helpful or useful.

right-hand·ed (rīt'han'did), *adj.* 1. using the right hand more easily and readily than the left. 2. done with the right hand. 3. made to be used with the right hand. 4. turning from left to right: *a right-handed screw.* —**right′-hand′ed·ness**, *n.*

right·ist (rīt'ist), *n.* person who has conservative or reactionary ideas in politics. —*adj.* having conservative or reactionary ideas in politics.

right-mind·ed (rīt'mīn'did), *adj.* having right opinions or principles.

right·o (rīt'ō), *interj. Brit.* all right!

right of way, 1. right to go first; precedence over all others. 2. right to pass over property belonging to someone else. 3. *Am.* strip of land on which a railroad, power line, etc., is built.

right triangle, triangle one of whose angles is a right angle.

right wing, the conservative or reactionary members, as of a political party. —**right-wing** (rīt'wing'), *adj.* —**right-wing·er** (rīt'wing'ər), *n.*

rig·id (rij'id), *adj.* 1. stiff; firm; not bending: *a rigid support.* 2. inflexible; strict; not changing: *rigid rules.* 3. severely exact; rigorous: *a rigid examination.* 4. of an airship, having its shape and dimensions maintained by a firm framework. [< L *rigidus* < *rigere* be stiff] —**ri·gid′i·ty, rig′id·ness**, *n.* —**rig′id·ly**, *adv.* —**Syn.** 1. unyielding, unbending, hard. 2. stringent.

rig·ma·role (rig'mə-rōl), *n.* foolish talk; words without meaning; nonsense. [earlier *ragman roll* < *ragman* list + *roll*]

rig·or, *esp. Brit.* **rig·our** (rig'ər), *n.* 1. strictness; severity; harshness: *the rigors of a long, cold winter.* 2. stiffness; rigidity. [< OF < L, < *rigere* be stiff] —**Syn.** 1. sternness, austerity.

rig·or mor·tis (rig'ər môr'tis), the stiffening of the muscles after death. [< L, stiffness of death]

rig·or·ous (rig'ər·əs), *adj.* 1. very severe; harsh; strict: *the rigorous discipline in a prison.* 2. thoroughly logical and scientific; exact: *the rigorous methods of science.* —**rig′or·ous·ly**, *adv.* —**rig′or·ous·ness**, *n.* —**Syn.** 1. stern.

rile (rīl), *v.,* **riled, ril·ing.** *Esp. U.S. Colloq.* 1. irritate; vex. 2. make (water) muddy. [var. of *roil*]

Ri·ley (rī'li), *n.* James Whitcomb, 1853–1916, American poet.

rill (ril), *n.* a tiny stream; little brook. [cf. Du *ril* groove, furrow]

rim (rim), *n., v.,* **rimmed, rim·ming.** —*n.* an edge, border, or margin on or around anything: *the rim of a wheel.* —*v.* form or put a rim around. [OE *rima*] —**rim′less**, *adj.* —**rimmed**, *adj.*

rime¹ (rīm), *v.,* **rimed, rim·ing,** *n.* rhyme. —**rim′er**, *n.* ▶ See **rhyme** for usage note.

rime² (rīm), *n., v.,* **rimed, rim·ing.** —*n.* white frost; hoarfrost. —*v.* cover with rime. [OE *hrīm*] —**rim′y**, *adj.*

rime·ster (rīm'stər), *n.* rhymester.

rind (rīnd), *n.* the firm outer covering (of fruits, plants, cheeses, etc.). [OE]

ring¹ (ring), *n., v.,* **ringed, ring·ing.** —*n.* 1. circle: *dance in a ring.* 2. a thin circle of metal or other material: *a napkin ring.* 3. the outer edge or border of a coin, plate, wheel, or anything round. 4. a circular layer of wood produced yearly in a tree trunk. 5. an enclosed space for races, games, circus performances, etc. The ring for a prize fight is square. 6. **the ring**, prize fighting. 7. competition; rivalry; contest: *in the ring for election to the Senate.* 8. group of people combined for a selfish or bad purpose. —*v.* 1. put a ring around; enclose. 2. provide with a ring. 3. form a ring or rings. 4. cut away the bark in a ring around a tree or branch. [OE *hring*] —**ringed**, *adj.* —**ring′er**, *n.*

ring² (ring), *v.,* **rang, rung, ring·ing.** —*v.* 1. give forth a clear sound, as a bell does. 2. cause to give forth a clear ringing sound: *ring the bell.* 3. cause a bell to sound: *did you ring?* 4. make (a sound) by ringing: *the bells rang a joyous peal.* 5. call to church, prayers, etc., by ringing bells. 6. announce or proclaim by ringing; usher; conduct: *ring out the old year.* 7. proclaim or repeat loudly everywhere: *ring a person's praises.* 8. resound; sound loudly: *the room rang with shouts of laughter.* 9. be filled with report or talk. 10. sound: *his words rang true.* 11. have a sensation as of sounds of bells: *my ears ring.* 12. call on the telephone. 13. **ring in**, *Colloq.* bring in dishonestly or trickily. 14. **ring off**, end a telephone call. —*n.* 1. act of ringing. 2. sound of a bell or like a bell. 3. a characteristic sound or quality, indicating genuineness of the reverse. 4. call on the telephone. [OE *hringan*] —**ring′er**, *n.*

ring·lead·er (ring'lēd'ər), *n.* person who leads others in opposition to authority or law.

ring·let (ring′lit), *n.* **1.** a little ring. **2.** curl: *wear hair in ringlets.* —**ring′let·ed,** *adj.*

ring·mas·ter (ring′mas′tər; –mäs′–), *n.* man in charge of the performances in the ring of a circus.

ring·side (ring′sīd′), *n.* **1.** place just outside the ring at a circus, prize fight, etc. **2.** place affording a close view.

ring·worm (ring′werm′), *n.* a contagious skin disease, caused by parasites and characterized by ring-shaped patches.

rink (ringk), *n.* **1.** sheet of ice for skating. **2.** a smooth floor for roller skating. [< Scotch < OF *renc* course, RANK¹]

rinse (rins), *v.,* **rinsed, rins·ing,** *n.* —*v.* **1.** wash with clean water: *rinse the soap out of your hair.* **2.** wash lightly: *rinse your mouth with water and soda.* —*n.* a rinsing. [< OF *reincer,* ult. < L *recens* fresh] —**rins′er,** *n.*

Ri·o de Ja·nei·ro (rē′ō dā zhə·nãr′ō; dī jə·nir′ō, or **Ri·o** (rē′ō), *n.* former capital of Brazil, a seaport on the SE coast.

Ri·o Grande (rē′ō grand′; gran′dē), river flowing from SW Colorado into the Gulf of Mexico.

ri·ot (rī′ət), *n.* **1.** disturbance of the peace by an unlawful assembly of persons: *a race riot.* **2.** wild disorder; violent confusion. **3.** loose living; wild reveling. **4.** bright display: *the garden was a riot of color.* **5.** read the riot act, give orders for disturbance to cease. **6.** run riot, a. act without restraint. b. grow wildly or luxuriantly. —*v.* **1.** behave in a wild, disorderly way. **2.** revel. [< OF *riote* dispute, ult. < L *rugire* to roar] —**ri′ot·er,** *n.* —**Syn.** *n.* **1.** outbreak, tumult, insurrection. **2.** brawl, uproar.

ri·ot·ous (rī′ət·əs), *adj.* **1.** taking part in a riot. **2.** boisterous; disorderly: *riotous conduct, riotous glee.* —**ri′ot·ous·ly,** *adv.* —**ri′ot·ous·ness,** *n.* —**Syn.** **2.** turbulent, tumultuous.

rip¹ (rip), *v.,* **ripped, rip·ping,** *n.* —*v.* **1.** cut roughly; tear apart; tear off: *rip the cover off this box.* **2.** become torn apart. **3.** cut or pull out (the threads in the seams of a garment). **4.** saw (wood) along the grain, not across the grain. **5.** *Colloq.* move fast or violently. **6.** *Colloq.* speak or say with violence: *rip out an oath.* —*n.* a torn place; seam burst in a garment. [ME *rippe(n)*] —**rip′per,** *n.* —**Syn.** *v.* **1.** rend, tear.

rip² (rip), *n.* **1.** *Am.* stretch of rough water made by cross currents meeting. **2.** a swift current made by the tide. [? special use of *rip¹*]

R.I.P., may he or she (they) rest in peace. [< L < *Requiescat* (*requiescant*) *in pace*]

ri·par·i·an (ri·pãr′i·ən; rī–), *adj.* of or on the bank of a river, a lake, etc.: *riparian rights.* [< L, < *ripa* riverbank]

rip cord, cord which, when pulled, opens a parachute.

ripe (rīp), *adj.,* **rip·er, rip·est. 1.** full-grown and ready to be gathered and eaten: *ripe fruit.* **2.** resembling ripe fruit in ruddiness and fullness. **3.** fully developed and fit to use: *ripe knowledge.* **4.** ready to break or be lanced: *a ripe boil.* **5.** ready: *ripe for mischief.* **6.** far enough along. **7.** advanced in years. [OE *rīpe*] —**ripe′ly,** *adv.* —**ripe′ness,** *n.* —**Syn.** **1.** mellow, mature, matured.

rip·en (rīp′ən), *v.* become or make ripe. —**rip′-en·er,** *n.*

rip·ping (rip′ing), *adj. Esp. Brit. Slang.* fine; splendid. —**rip′ping·ly,** *adv.*

rip·ple (rip′əl), *n., v.,* **–pled, –pling.** —*n.* **1.** a very little wave. **2.** anything that seems like a tiny wave: *ripples in sand.* **3.** sound that reminds one of little waves: *a ripple of laughter.* —*v.* **1.** make a sound like rippling water. **2.** form or have ripples. **3.** flow with ripples on the surface. **4.** make little ripples on. —**rip′pler,** *n.* —**rip′pling,** *adj.* —**rip′pling·ly,** *adv.* —**rip′ply,** *adj.*

rip·roar·ing (rip′rōr′ing; –rôr′–), *adj. Am., Slang.* hilarious; uproarious.

rip·saw (rip′sô′), *n.* saw for cutting wood along the grain, not across the grain.

rise (rīz), *v.,* **rose, ris·en** (riz′ən), **ris·ing,** *n.* —*v.* **1.** get up from a lying, sitting, or kneeling position: *rise from a chair.* **2.** get up from sleep or rest: *rise at dawn.* **3.** go up; come up; move up; ascend: *fog rises from a river.* **4.** extend upward: *the tower rises to a height of 60 feet.* **5.** slope upward: *hills rise in the distance.* **6.** cause to rise. **7.** go higher; increase: *prices are rising.* **8.** advance to a higher level of action, thought, feeling, expression, rank, position, etc.: *he rose from errand boy to president.* **9.** become louder or of higher pitch. **10.** come above the horizon: *the sun rises in the morning.* **11.** start; begin: *quarrels often rise from trifles.* **12.** come into being or action: *the wind rose.* **13.** be built up, erected, or constructed: *houses are rising on the edge of town.* **14.** become more animated or more cheerful: *his spirits rose.* **15.** revolt; rebel. **16.** grow larger and lighter: *yeast makes dough rise.* **17.** come to life again. **18.** bring a meeting or session to an end. **19.** rise to, be equal to; be able to deal with: *they rose to the occasion.* —*n.* **1.** an upward movement; ascent: *the rise of a balloon.* **2.** the coming of a fish to the surface of the water to seize bait, etc. **3.** an upward slope. **4.** piece of rising or high ground; hill. **5.** the vertical height of a step, slope, arch, etc. **6.** increase. **7.** advance in rank, power, etc. **8.** origin; beginning: *rise of a stream in a mountain.* **9.** give rise to, start; begin; cause; bring about. [OE *rīsan*] —**Syn.** *v.* **1.** arise, stand. **10.** appear, emerge. **16.** swell, increase. —*n.* **6.** augmentation. ➤ In referring to people, **arise** is formal and poetic; **rise** is rather formal; **get up** is informal and colloquial.

ris·er (rīz′ər), *n.* **1.** person or thing that rises: *an early riser.* **2.** the vertical part of a step.

ris·i·bil·i·ty (riz′ə·bil′ə·ti), *n., pl.* **–ties. 1.** ability or inclination to laugh. **2.** Often, **risibilities,** *Am.* desire to laugh; sense of humor.

ris·i·ble (riz′ə·bəl), *adj.* **1.** able or inclined to laugh. **2.** of laughter; used in laughter. **3.** causing laughter; amusing; funny. [< LL *risibilis,* ult. < L *ridere* to laugh]

ris·ing (rīz′ing), *n.* **1.** act of one that rises. **2.** revolt. **3.** something that rises; prominence. **4.** quantity of dough set to rise. —*adj.* **1.** that rises. **2.** advancing to adult years: *the rising generation.* —*prep.* **1.** approaching; about: *rising nine years.* **2.** *Am., Colloq.* rather more than; above: *rising a thousand men.*

risk (risk), *n.* **1.** chance of harm or loss; danger. **2.** person or thing with reference to the chance of loss from insuring him or it. —*v.* **1.** expose to the chance of harm or loss: *a soldier risks his life.* **2.** take the risk of: *they risked getting wet.* [< F *risque* < Ital., *risicare* to dare] —**risk′er,** *n.* —**Syn.** *n.* **1.** hazard, peril, jeopardy, venture. –*v.* **1.** hazard, endanger, imperil, jeopardize.

risk·y (ris′ki), *adj.,* **risk·i·er, risk·i·est. 1.** full of risk; dangerous. **2.** somewhat improper; risqué. —**risk′i·ly,** *adv.* —**risk′i·ness,** *n.* —**Syn.** **1.** hazardous, perilous, precarious, unsafe.

ris·qué (ris·kā′), *adj.* suggestive of indecency; somewhat improper. [< F, pp. of *risquer* to RISK]

rite (rīt), *n.* **1.** a solemn ceremony. The church has rites for baptism, marriage, and burial. **2.** any customary ceremony or observance. **3.** a particular form or system of ceremonies. [< L *ritus*] —**rite′less,** *adj.*

rit·u·al (rich′u·əl), *n.* **1.** form or system of rites. The rites of baptism, marriage, and burial are parts of the ritual of the church. **2.** book containing rites or ceremonies. **3.** the carrying out of rites. —*adj.* of rites; done as a rite: *ritual laws, a ritual dance.* [< L, < *ritus* rite] —**rit′u·al·ly,** *adv.*

rit·u·al·ism (rich′u·əl·iz′əm), *n.* **1.** fondness for ritual; insistence upon ritual. **2.** study of ritual practices or religious rites. —**rit′u·al·ist,** *n.* —**rit′u·al·is′tic,** *adj.* —**rit′u·al·is′ti·cal·ly,** *adv.*

ri·val (rī′vəl), *n., adj., v.,* **–valed, –val·ing;** *esp. Brit.* **–valled, –val·ling.** —*n.* **1.** person who wants and tries to get the same thing as another; one who tries to equal or do better than another. **2.** thing that will bear comparison with something else; equal; match. —*adj.* wanting the same thing as another; being a rival. —*v.* **1.** try to equal or outdo. **2.** engage in rivalry; compete. **3.** equal; match. [< L *rivalis* using the same stream

◄ *rivus* stream] —ri′val·less, *adj.* —Syn. *n.* 1. competitor, contestant, antagonist. —*v.* 2. vie.

ri·val·ry (rī′vəl·ri), *n., pl.* -ries. action, position, or relation of a rival or rivals; competition. —Syn. contest.

rive (rīv), *v.,* rived, rived or riv·en (riv′ən), riv·ing. tear apart; split; cleave. [< Scand. *rifa*]

riv·er (riv′ər), *n.* 1. a large natural stream of water. 2. any abundant stream or flow. [< OF *rivere* < L *riparius* of a riverbank < *ripa* bank] —riv′ered, *adj.* —riv′er·less, *adj.*

Ri·ve·ra (rē·vä′rä), *n.* Diego, 1886–1957, Mexican painter, esp. of murals.

riv·er·head (riv′ər·hed′), *n.* source of a river.

riv·er·side (riv′ər·sīd′), *n.* bank of a river. —*adj.* on the bank of a river: *a riverside path.*

riv·et (riv′it), *n.* a metal bolt with each end hammered into a head. Rivets fasten heavy steel beams together. —*v.* 1. fasten with a rivet or rivets. 2. fasten firmly; fix firmly. [< OF, < *river* fix < VL *ripare* come to shore < L *ripa* bank] —riv′et·er, *n.*

Riv·i·er·a (riv′i·âr′ə), *n.* section of France and Italy along the Mediterranean Sea, famous as a resort.

riv·u·let (riv′yə·lit), *n.* a very small stream. [< Ital. *rivoletto,* ult. < L *rivus* stream]

rm., *pl.* rms. 1. ream. 2. room.

Rn, *Chem.* radon.

R.N., 1. registered nurse. 2. Royal Navy.

roach¹ (rōch), *n. Am.* cockroach. [short for *cockroach*]

roach² (rōch), *n., pl.* roach·es or (*esp. collectively*) roach. 1. a European fresh-water fish related to the carp. 2. any of various similar fishes, such as the American sunfish. [< OF *roche*]

road (rōd), *n.* 1. highway between places; way made for teams or automobiles to travel on. 2. way or course. 3. *Am.* railroad. 4. Also, roadstead. place near the shore where ships can ride at anchor. 5. on the road, *Am.* traveling, esp. as a salesman. 6. take to the road, *Archaic.* become a highwayman. [OE *rād* a riding] —road′less, *adj.* —Syn. 1. roadway, turnpike, thoroughfare.

road agent, *Am., W.* highwayman.

road·bed (rōd′bed′), *n. Am.* foundation of a road or of a railroad.

road·block (rōd′blok′), *n.* an obstacle.

road·house (rōd′hous′), *n.* restaurant in the country where people can stop for refreshments and sometimes entertainment.

road metal, broken stone, cinders, etc., used for roads and roadbeds.

road runner, *Am.* a long-tailed bird of the deserts of the SW United States, related to the cuckoo.

road·side (rōd′sīd′), *n.* side of a road. —*adj.* beside a road.

road·ster (rōd′stər), *n. Am.* an open automobile with one seat.

road·way (rōd′wā′), *n.* 1. road. 2. the part of a road used by wheeled vehicles.

roam (rōm), *v.* 1. go about with no special plan or aim; wander: *roam through the fields.* 2. wander over. —*n.* a walk or trip with no special aim; wandering. [ME *rome(n)*] —roam′er, *n.* —Syn. *v.* 1. ramble, rove, stray, stroll.

roan (rōn), *adj.* yellowish- or reddish-brown sprinkled with gray or white. —*n.* a roan horse. [< F < Sp. *roano*]

Ro·a·noke Island (rō′ə·nōk), island just off the NE coast of North Carolina.

roar (rôr; rōr), *v.* 1. make a loud, deep sound; make a loud noise: *a lion roars.* 2. utter loudly: *roar out a command.* 3. make or put by roaring: *the crowd roared itself hoarse.* 4. laugh loudly. 5. move with a roar: *the train roared past us.* —*n.* a loud, deep sound; loud noise. [OE *rārian*] —roar′er, *n.* —Syn. *v.* 1. bellow, bawl, howl, yell.

roast (rōst), *v.* 1. cook by dry heat; cook before a fire; bake. 2. prepare by heating: *roast coffee, roast a metal ore.* 3. make or become very hot. 4.

be baked. 5. *Colloq.* make fun of; ridicule. —*n.* 1. piece of roasted meat; piece of meat to be roasted. 2. rule the roast, be master. —*adj.* roasted: *roast beef.* [< OF *rostir* < Gmc.]

roast·er (rōs′tər), *n.* 1. pan used in roasting. 2. chicken, young pig, etc., fit to be roasted. 3. person or thing that roasts.

rob (rob), *v.,* robbed, rob·bing. 1. take away from by force or threats; steal from. 2. steal. [< OF *robber* < Gmc.] —rob′ber, *n.* —Syn. 1. plunder, pillage, loot.

rob·ber·y (rob′ər·i; rob′ri), *n., pl.* -ber·ies. 1. act of robbing. 2. *Law.* the felonious taking of the property of another from his person or from his immediate presence, against his will, by violence or intimidation. —Syn. 1. theft.

robe (rōb), *n., v.,* robed, rob·ing. —*n.* 1. a long, loose outer garment. 2. garment that shows rank, office, etc.: *a judge's robe.* 3. a covering or wrap. —*v.* put a robe on; dress. [< OF, orig., plunder, booty. Cf. ROB.] —robed, *adj.*

Rob·ert I (rob′ərt), ("*Robert the Bruce*"), 1274–1329, king of Scotland, 1306–1329.

Robes·pierre (rōbz′pir), *n.* Maximilien de, 1758–1794, one of the chief leaders of the French Revolution and of the Reign of Terror.

rob·in (rob′ən), *n.* 1. *Am.* a large American thrush with a reddish breast. 2. a small European bird with a yellowish-red breast. [< OF, dim. of *Robert*]

Robin Hood, *English Legend.* leader of an outlaw band of Sherwood Forest who robbed the rich and helped the poor.

rob·in's-egg blue (rob′ənz·eg′), *Am.* greenish blue.

Rob·in·son (rob′ən·sən), *n.* Edwin Arlington, 1869–1935, American poet.

ro·bot (rō′bət; rob′ət), *n.* 1. a machine-made man; mechanical device that does some of the work of human beings. 2. person who acts or works in a dull, mechanical way. [invented by Karel Capek for his play, *R.U.R.*; suggested by Czech *robota* work, *robotnik* serf]

robot bomb, a jet-propelled airplane, steered by a mechanical device, without a pilot, which carries a heavy charge of explosives; buzz bomb.

ro·bust (rō·bust′; rō′bust), *adj.* 1. strong and healthy; sturdy: *a robust person, a robust mind.* 2. suited to or requiring bodily strength: *robust exercises.* 3. rough; rude. [< L *robustus,* orig., oaken < *robur* oak] —ro·bust′ly, *adv.* —ro·bust′ness, *n.* —Syn. 1. hardy, stalwart, stout.

roc (rok), *n.* in Arabian tales, a bird having enormous size and strength. [< Ar. *rukhkh*]

Roch·es·ter (roch′es·tər), *n.* city in W New York State.

rock¹ (rok), *n.* 1. a large mass of stone. 2. any piece of stone; a stone. 3. *Geol.* a. the mass of mineral matter of which the earth's crust is made up. b. a particular layer or kind of such matter. 4. something firm like a rock; support; defense. 5. source of peril or disaster. 6. anything that suggests a rock. 7. on the rocks, a. wrecked; ruined. b. *Colloq.* bankrupt. —*adj.* made of rock. [< OF *roque* < VL *rocca*]

rock² (rok), *v.* 1. move backward or forward, or from side to side; sway. 2. put (to sleep, rest, etc.) with swaying movements. 3. move or sway violently with emotion. —*n.* a rocking movement. [OE *roccian*] —Syn. *v.* 1. swing, roll.

rock bottom, *Am.* the very bottom; lowest level.

rock-bot·tom (rok′bot′əm), *adj. Am.* down to the very bottom; very lowest.

rock-bound (rok′bound′), *adj.* surrounded by rocks; rocky.

rock candy, sugar in the form of large, hard crystals.

rock crystal, a colorless, transparent variety of quartz that is often used for jewelry, ornaments, etc.

Rock·e·fel·ler (rok′ə·fel′ər), *n.* 1. John D., 1839–1937, American capitalist and philanthropist. 2. his son, John D., 1874–1960, American capitalist and philanthropist. 3. his grandson,

Nelson A., born 1908, American political leader, governor of New York since 1959.

rock·er (rok′ər), *n.* 1. one of the curved pieces on which a cradle, rocking chair, etc., rocks. 2. a rocking chair. 3. any of various devices that operate with a rocking motion.

rock·et (rok′it), *n.* a self-propelling device operating by means of gases escaping from a nozzle or jet at the rear of a combustion chamber. The rocket principle is used in some types of projectiles, and as at least part of the driving power in some aircraft.

rock·et·ry (rok′ət·ri), *n.* 1. the science of designing and firing rockets or missiles. 2. rockets collectively: *long-range rocketry.*

rock garden, *Am.* garden with flowers planted among rocks.

rocking chair, *Am.* chair mounted on rockers, or on springs, so that it can rock back and forth.

rocking horse, toy horse on rockers.

rock-ribbed (rok′ribd′), *adj.* 1. having ridges of rock. 2. unyielding.

rock salt, salt in large crystals.

rock wool, woollike fibers made from rock or slag and used for insulation and soundproofing.

rock·y[1] (rok′i), *adj.,* rock·i·er, rock·i·est. 1. full of rocks. 2. made of rock. 3. like rock; hard; firm.

rock·y[2] (rok′i), *adj.,* rock·i·er, rock·i·est. 1. likely to rock; shaky. 2. unpleasantly uncertain. 3. *Am., Slang.* sickish; weak; dizzy. —**rock′i·ness,** *n.*

Rocky Mountain goat, *Am.* the white antelope of the Rocky Mountains.

Rock·y Mountains (rok′i), or **Rockies,** *n.pl. Am.* the chief group of mountain ranges in W North America, extending from Alaska to N Mexico.

ro·co·co (rō·kō′kō; rō′kə·kō′), *n.* style of architecture and decoration with elaborate ornamentation, combining shellwork, scrolls, foliage, etc., much used in the first half of the 18th century. —*adj.* of or pertaining to this style. [< F, < *rocaille* shellwork]

rod (rod), *n.* 1. a thin, straight bar of metal or wood. 2. anything like a rod in shape. 3. a stick used to beat or punish. 4. punishment. 5. a long, light pole; fishing rod. 6. a measure of length; 5½ yards or 16½ feet. A square rod is 30¼ square yards or 272¼ square feet. 7. stick used to measure with. 8. *Am., Slang.* pistol. 9. power; authority; tyranny. 10. a divining rod. 11. a cylindrical bacterium. 12. **spare the rod,** fail to punish. [OE *rodd*]

rode (rōd), *v.* pt. of ride.

ro·dent (rō′dənt), *n.* any of a group of mammals having teeth especially adapted for gnawing wood and similar material. Rats, mice, and squirrels, are rodents. —*adj.* 1. gnawing. 2. of or like a rodent. [< L *rodens* gnawing]

ro·de·o (rō′di·ō; rō·dā′ō), *n., pl.* **-de·os.** *Am.* 1. contest or exhibition of skill in roping cattle, riding horses, etc. 2. *W.* the driving together of cattle. [< Sp., < *rodear* go around]

Ro·din (rō·daN′), *n.* Auguste, 1840–1917, French sculptor.

roe[1] (rō), *n.* 1. fish eggs. 2. the spawn of various crustaceans. [ME *rowe*]

roe[2] (rō), *n., pl.* **roes** or (*esp. collectively*) **roe.** a small deer of Europe and Asia, with forked antlers. [OE *rā*]

roe·buck (rō′buk′), *n.* a male roe deer.

Roent·gen rays (rent′gən), X rays. Also, **Röntgen rays.** [after W. K. *Roentgen,* physicist]

rog·er (roj′ər), *interj. U.S. Slang.* O.K.; message received and understood. [from the signaler's word for the letter *r,* for "received"]

rogue (rōg), *n.* 1. a tricky, dishonest, or worthless person; cheat; rascal. 2. a mischievous person. 3. animal with a savage nature that lives apart from the herd. [? short for earlier *roger* beggar] —**Syn.** 1. knave, scoundrel, scamp.

ro·guer·y (rō′gər·i), *n., pl.* **-guer·ies.** 1. conduct of rogues; dishonest trickery. 2. playful

mischief. —**Syn.** 1. knavery, rascality, fraud. 2. mischievousness, waggery.

rogues' gallery, *Am.* collection of photographs of known criminals.

ro·guish (rō′gish), *adj.* 1. dishonest; rascally. 2. playfully mischievous. —**ro′guish·ly,** *adv.* —**ro′guish·ness,** *n.* —**Syn.** 1. knavish, tricky, fraudulent. 2. waggish, sportive.

roil (roil), *v.* 1. make (water, etc.) muddy by stirring up sediment. 2. disturb; irritate; vex. [< earlier F *ruiler* mix mortar, ult. < L *regula* rule] —**roil′y,** *adj.*

rois·ter (rois′tər), *v.* be boisterous; revel noisily; swagger. [< OF *ruistre* rude, ult. < L *rus* the country] —**rois′ter·er,** *n.* —**rois′ter·ous,** *adj.*

ROK (rok), *n.* 1. Republic of Korea. 2. a soldier in the South Korean army.

role, rôle (rōl), *n.* 1. an actor's part in a play: *the leading role.* 2. part played in real life. [< F, the roll (of paper, etc.) on which a part is written] ▶ **Role** (*a role in a play*) is still conservatively spelled with the circumflex (*rôle*) but in common usage the accent has been dropped.

roll (rōl), *v.* 1. move along by turning over and over: *a ball rolls.* 2. wrap around on itself or on some other thing: *roll the string into a ball.* 3. form by rolling into a cylinder: *roll a cigarette.* 4. move or be moved on wheels: *the car rolled along.* 5. move smoothly; sweep along: *the years roll on.* 6. turn around; revolve. 7. perform a periodical revolution in an orbit. 8. move from side to side: *the ship rolled in the waves.* 9. turn over, or over and over: *the horse rolled in the dust.* 10. walk with a swaying gait. 11. rise and fall in gentle slopes: *rolling country.* 12. make flat or smooth with a roller; spread out with a rolling pin, etc. 13. put ink on with a roller. 14. make deep, loud sounds: *thunder rolls.* 15. beat (a drum) with rapid continuous strokes. 16. *Am., Slang.* rob (a person who is drunk or otherwise helpless) by, or as if by, turning him over in searching through his pockets. 17. utter with full, flowing sound: *the organ rolled out the stirring hymn.* 18. utter with a trill: *roll one's r's.* 19. *Colloq.* have more than enough: *be rolling in money.* 20. **roll up,** increase; pile up or become piled up. —*n.* 1. something rolled up; cylinder formed by rolling (often forming a definite measure): *a roll of carpet.* 2. a more or less rounded, cylindrical, or rolled-up mass. 3. continued motion up and down, or from side to side. 4. rapid continuous beating on a drum. 5. a deep, loud sound: *the roll of thunder.* 6. act of rolling. 7. motion like that of waves; undulation: *the roll of a prairie.* 8. maneuver in which an airplane makes a complete turn about its longitudinal axis while maintaining a horizontal direction of flight. 9. record; list; list of names: *call the roll.* 10. kind of bread or cake. 11. *Am., Slang.* paper money rolled up. 12. **strike off the rolls,** expel from membership. [< OF *roller,* ult. < L *rota* wheel] —**roll′a·ble,** *adj.* —**Syn.** *v.* 2. curl, coil. 4. wheel. 6. gyrate. 8. rock, sway, lurch. —*n.* 1. coil. 9. scroll, roster, register, catalogue.

roll call, the calling of a list of names, as of soldiers, pupils, etc., to find out who are present.

roll·er (rōl′ər), *n.* 1. thing that rolls; cylinder on which something is rolled along or rolled up. 2. cylinder of metal, stone, wood, etc., used for smoothing, pressing, crushing, etc. 3. a long, swelling wave. 4. person who rolls something.

roller bearing, *Am.* a bearing in which the shaft turns on rollers to lessen friction.

roller coaster, *Am.* railway for amusement, consisting of inclined tracks along which small cars roll, bump, etc.

roller skate, *Am.* a skate with small wheels instead of a runner, for use on a floor or sidewalk.

roll·er-skate (rōl′ər·skāt′), *v.,* **-skat·ed, -skat·ing.** *Am.* move on roller skates.

rol·lick·ing (rol′ik·ing), *adj.* jolly; merry; lively. Also, **rol·lick·some** (-səm), *adj.*

roll·ing (rōl′ing), *n.* action, motion, or sound of anything that rolls or is being rolled: *the rolling of a ball, the rolling of thunder.* —*adj.* 1. that rolls. 2. *Am.* of land, rising and falling in gentle slopes. **3.** swaying from side to side: *a rolling gait.* **4.** turning or folding over, as a collar. —Syn. *adj.* **2.** undulating, wavy, hilly.

rolling mill, 1. factory where metal is rolled into sheets and bars. **2.** machine for doing this.

rolling pin, cylinder of wood or glass for rolling out dough.

rolling stock, locomotives and cars of a railroad.

ro·ly-po·ly (rō′li·pō′li), *adj., n., pl.* -lies. —*adj.* short and plump. —*n.* **1.** a short, plump person or animal. **2.** a pudding made of jam or fruit spread on a rich dough, rolled up and cooked. [appar. < *roll*]

Rom., 1. Roman. **2.** Romanic. **3.** *Bible.* Romans.

Ro·ma·ic (rō·mā′ik), *n.* the everyday speech of modern Greece. —*adj.* of or pertaining to this speech.

ro·maine (rō·mān′), *n.* variety of lettuce having long green leaves with crinkly edges, which are joined loosely at the base. [< F, fem. adj., Roman]

Ro·man (rō′mən), *adj.* **1.** of or pertaining to Rome or its people. **2.** of or pertaining to the Roman Catholic Church. **3.** roman, of or in roman type. —*n.* **1.** native, inhabitant, or citizen of Rome. **2.** a Roman Catholic. **3.** roman, style of type most used in printing and typewriting. Most of this dictionary is in roman.

Roman candle, kind of firework consisting of a tube that shoots out balls of fire, etc.

Roman Catholic, 1. of, pertaining to, or belonging to the Christian church that recognizes the Pope as the supreme head. **2.** member of this church. —**Roman Catholicism.**

ro·mance (*n.* rō·mans′, rō′mans; *v.* rō·mans′), *n., v.,* -manced, -manc·ing. —*n.* **1.** a love story. **2.** story or poem telling of heroes, love, colorful adventures, or noble deeds: *the romances about King Arthur and his knights.* **3.** romantic character, quality, or spirit. **4.** interest in adventure and love. **5.** a love affair. **6.** a made-up story. —*v.* **1.** make up romances. **2.** think or talk in a romantic way. **3.** exaggerate; lie. [ult. < OF *romanz,* ult. < VL *romanice* in a Romance language < L *Romanus* Roman < *Roma* Rome] —**ro·manc′er,** *n.*

Romance languages, French, Italian, Spanish, Portuguese, Rumanian, Provençal, and other languages that came from Latin, the language of the Romans.

Roman Empire, empire of ancient Rome that lasted from 27 B.C. to 395 A.D.

Ro·man·esque (rō′mən·esk′), *n.* style of architecture using round arches and vaults, popular in Europe during the early Middle Ages, between the periods of Roman and Gothic architecture. —*adj.* of, in, or having to do with this style of architecture.

Romanesque architecture

Ro·ma·ni·a (rō·mā′ni·ə; -mān′yə), *n.* Rumania. —**Ro·ma′ni·an,** *adj., n.*

Ro·man·ic (rō·man′ik), *adj.* derived from Latin. French, Italian, and Spanish are Romanic languages. —*n.* a Romanic language.

Ro·man·ize (rō′mən·īz), *v.,* -ized, -iz·ing. **1.** make or become Roman in character. **2.** make or become Roman Catholic. —**Ro′man·i·za′tion,** *n.*

Roman nose, nose having a prominent bridge.

Roman numerals, numerals like XXIII, LVI, and MDCCLX, in which I = 1, V = 5, X = 10, L = 50, C = 100, D = 500, and M = 1000.
➤ **Roman numerals** (i, ii, cxlvi . . .) are occasionally used to number units in rather short series, as in outlines, chapters of a book, acts of a play, though now less often than formerly. The preliminary pages of books are almost always numbered with Roman numerals. Sometimes they are used on title pages for the date, and on very formal inscriptions. In Roman

numerals a small number preceding a larger is to be subtracted from the larger (ix = 9).

Ro·ma·nov, Ro·ma·noff (rō′mə·nôf; rō·mä′nôf; -nof), *n.* the royal family of Russia from 1613 to 1917.

Roman rite, in the Roman Catholic Church, form of ceremony used in celebrating Mass and in administering sacraments in the diocese of Rome.

Ro·mans (rō′mənz), *n.* book of the New Testament, an epistle written by Saint Paul to the Christians of Rome.

ro·man·tic (rō·man′tik), *adj.* **1.** characteristic of romances or romance; appealing to fancy and the imagination: *romantic tales of love and war.* **2.** having ideas or feelings suited to romance: *a romantic schoolgirl.* **3.** suited to a romance. **4.** fond of making up fanciful stories. **5.** representing life in literature or art as one pleases; not realistic and not classical. Romantic writing usually tells about the unusual and adventurous aspects of life and uses complete freedom of form and expression. —*n.* a romantic person. [< F *romantique* < earlier *romant* a ROMANCE] —**ro·man′ti·cal·ly,** *adv.* —Syn. *adj.* **1.** imaginative, fanciful. **2.** sentimental.

ro·man·ti·cism (rō·man′tə·siz·əm), *n.* **1.** romantic spirit or tendency. **2.** the romantic tendency in literature and art (contrasted with classicism or with realism). —**ro·man′ti·cist,** *n.*

Rom·a·ny (rom′ə·ni), *n., pl.* -nies, *adj.* —*n.* **1.** Gypsy. **2.** language of the Gypsies. —*adj.* belonging or pertaining to the Gypsies, their customs, or their language.

Rom. Cath., Roman Catholic.

Rome (rōm), *n.* **1.** capital of Italy, on the Tiber River. Rome was the center of the ancient Roman civilization and the capital of the ancient Roman Empire. The headquarters of the Pope and the Roman Catholic Church are in Rome. **2.** the ancient Roman republic or the ancient Roman Empire. **3.** the Roman Catholic Church.

Ro·me·o (rō′mi·ō), *n.* hero of Shakespeare's play *Romeo and Juliet.*

romp (romp), *v.* play in a rough, boisterous way; rush, tumble, and punch in play. —*n.* **1.** a rough, lively play or frolic. **2.** girl or boy who likes to romp. [ult. var. of *ramp,* v.] —**romp′er,** *n.* —**romp′ish,** *adj.* —**romp′ish·ness,** *n.*

romp·ers (romp′ərz), *n.pl.* a loose outer garment, worn by young children at play.

Rom·u·lus (rom′yə·ləs), *n. Roman Myth.* the founder and first king of Rome, who, together with his brother, Remus, was nourished by a wolf.

ron·deau (ron′dō; ron·dō′), *n., pl.* -deaux (-dōz; -dōz′). a short poem with thirteen (or ten) lines. The opening words are used in two places as a refrain. [< OF, var. of *rondel* RONDEL]

ron·del (ron′del), *n.* a short poem, usually with fourteen lines and two rhymes. The initial couplet is repeated in the middle and at the end. [< OF, orig. dim. of *rond* ROUND]

ron·do (ron′dō; ron·dō′), *n., pl.* -dos. *Music.* a work or movement having one principal theme to which return is made after the introduction of each subordinate theme.

Rönt·gen rays (rent′gən), Roentgen rays.

rood (rüd), *n.* **1.** *Archaic.* the cross on which Christ died. **2.** a representation of it; crucifix. **3.** 40 square rods; one fourth of an acre. [OE *rōd*]

roof (rüf; ruf), *n.* **1.** the top covering of a building. **2.** something like it: *the roof of a cave, of a car, of the mouth, etc.* —*v.* cover with a roof; form a roof over. [OE *hrōf*] —**roof′er,** *n.* —**roof′less,** *adj.*

roof garden, *Am.* **1.** garden on the flat roof of a building. **2.** roof or top story of a building, ornamented with plants, etc., and used for a restaurant, theater, etc.

roof·ing (rüf′ing; ruf′-), *n.* **1.** act of covering with a roof. **2.** material used for roofs, as shingles.

āge, cãre, fär; ēqual, tėrm; īce; ōpen, ôrder; pũt, rũle, ũse; th, then; ə=a in about.

rook¹ (rŭk), *n.* **1.** a European crow that often nests in trees near buildings. **2.** person who cheats at cards, dice, etc. —*v.* cheat. [OE *hrōc*]

rook² (rŭk), *n.* one of the pieces with which the game of chess is played; castle. [< OF, ult. < Pers. *rukh*]

rook·er·y (rŭk′ər·i), *n.*, *pl.* **-er·ies. 1.** a breeding place of rooks; colony of rooks. **2.** a breeding place or colony where other birds or animals are crowded together. **3.** a crowded, dirty, and poor tenement house or group of such houses.

Rook (ab. 19 in. long)

rook·ie (rŭk′i), *n. Slang.* **1.** an inexperienced recruit. **2.** beginner; novice. **3.** *Am.* beginner at baseball.

room (rüm; rům), *n.* **1.** a part of a house, or other building, with walls separating it from the rest of the building of which it is a part. **2.** rooms, lodgings. **3.** people in a room. **4.** space occupied by, or available for, something: *there is little room to move in a crowd.* **5.** opportunity: *room for improvement.* —*v.* **1.** occupy a room; lodge. **2.** provide with a room. [OE *rūm*] —**Syn.** *n.* **1.** chamber, apartment. **5.** scope, range.

room·er (rüm′ər; rům′-), *n. Am.* person who lives in a rented room or rooms in another's house; lodger.

room·ette (rüm·et′; rům-), *n.* a small private bedroom on some Pullman cars.

room·ful (rüm′fůl; rům′-), *n.*, *pl.* **-fuls. 1.** enough to fill a room. **2.** people or things in a room.

rooming house, *Am.* house with rooms to rent.

room·mate (rüm′māt′; rům′-), *n. Am.* person who shares a room with another or others.

room·y (rüm′i; rům′-), *adj.*, **room·i·er, room·i·est.** having plenty of room; large; spacious. —**room′i·ly,** *adv.* —**room′i·ness,** *n.*

roor·back (rür′bak), *n. Am.* a false story or slander about a candidate for office, circulated for political effect. [from *Roorback's Tour,* an alleged travel book published in 1844 which was said to contain a damaging statement about the character of James K. Polk]

Roo·se·velt (rō′zə·velt), *n.* **1.** (Anna) Eleanor, 1884–1962, American author and stateswoman, wife of Franklin D. Roosevelt. **2.** Franklin Delano, 1882–1945, the 32nd president of the United States, 1933–1945. **3.** Theodore, 1858–1919, the 26th president of the United States, 1901–1909.

roost (rüst), *n.* **1.** bar, pole, or perch on which birds rest or sleep. **2.** place for birds to roost in. **3.** *Am.* place to rest or stay. **4. rule the roost,** *Am., Colloq.* be master. —*v.* sit as birds do on a roost; settle for the night. [OE *hrōst*]

roost·er (rüs′tər), *n.* a male domestic fowl.

root¹ (rüt; růt), *n.* **1.** part of a plant that grows downward, usually into the ground, to hold the plant in place, absorb water and mineral foods from the soil, and often to store food material. **2.** any underground part of a plant. **3.** something like a root in shape, position, use, etc.: *the root of a tooth, the roots of the hair.* **4.** thing from which other things grow and develop; cause; source: *"The love of money is the root of all evil."* **5.** take root, a. send out roots and begin to grow. b. become firmly fixed. **6.** the essential part; base. **7.** *Math.* a. quantity that produces another quantity when multiplied by itself a certain number of times. 2 is the square root of 4 and the cube root of 8 (2x2= 4, 2x2x2= 8). b. quantity that satisfies an equation when substituted for an unknown quantity. In the equation $x^2+2x-3=0$, 1 and −3 are the roots. **8.** *Gram.* a. word from which others are derived. *Room* is the root of *roominess, roomer, roommate,* and *roomy.* b. an alleged ultimate element of language. **9.** the fundamental tone of a chord. —*v.* **1.** send out roots and begin to grow; become fixed in the ground: *some plants root* quickly. **2.** cause to send out roots. **3.** fix firmly: *rooted to the spot by surprise.* **4.** become firmly fixed. **5.** pull, tear, or dig (up, out, etc.) by the roots; get completely rid of. [< Scand. *rōt*] —**root′less,** *adj.* —**root′y,** *adj.*

root² (rüt; růt), *v.* **1.** dig with the snout, as swine do. **2.** poke; pry; search. [OE *wrōtan*] —**root′er,** *n.*

root³ (rüt; růt), *v. Am., Slang.* cheer or support a contestant, etc., enthusiastically. [prob. < earlier *rout* to shout, roar < Scand. *rauta*] —**root′er,** *n. Am.*

root beer, *Am.* a soft drink made from the juice of the roots of certain plants, such as sarsaparilla, sassafras, etc.

root·ed (rüt′id; růt′-), *adj.* **1.** having roots. **2.** having taken root; firmly implanted: *a rooted belief.* —**root′ed·ly,** *adv.* —**root′ed·ness,** *n.*

root hair, a hairlike outgrowth from a root that absorbs water and dissolved minerals from the soil.

root·let (rüt′lit; růt′-), *n.* a little root.

root·stock (rüt′stok′; růt′-), *n.* rhizome.

rope (rōp), *n., v.,* **roped, rop·ing.** —*n.* **1.** a strong, thick line or cord made by twisting smaller cords together. **2.** *Am., W.* lasso. **3.** number of things twisted or strung together: *a rope of pearls.* **4.** cord or noose for hanging a person. **5.** death by being hanged. **6.** a sticky, stringy mass. **7. know the ropes, a.** know the various ropes of a ship. **b.** *Slang.* know about a business or activity. —*v.* **1.** tie, bind, or fasten with a rope. **2.** enclose or mark off with a rope. **3.** *Am.* catch (a horse, calf, etc.) with a lasso. **4.** form a sticky, stringy mass. **5.** rope in, *Am., Slang.* get or lead in by tricking. [OE *rāp*]

rop·y (rōp′i), *adj.,* **rop·i·er, rop·i·est. 1.** forming sticky threads; stringy: *a ropy syrup.* **2.** like a rope or ropes. —**rop′i·ly,** *adv.* —**rop′i·ness,** *n.*

Roque·fort (rōk′fərt), *n.* **1.** a strongly flavored French cheese made of goats' milk, veined with mold. **2.** cheese of similar flavor made from cows' milk.

ror·qual (rôr′kwəl), *n.* any of the whalebone whales having a dorsal fin; any finback. [< F < Norw. *röyrkval*]

Ror·schach test (rôr′shäk), a psychological test which measures personality traits, general intelligence, etc., based on the subject's interpretation of ten different ink blot designs.

ro·sa·ry (rō′zə·ri), *n., pl.* **-ries. 1.** string of beads for keeping count in saying a series of prayers. **2.** a series of prayers. [< Med.L *rosarium* < L, rose garden, ult. < *rosa* rose¹]

rose¹ (rōz), *n.* **1.** flower that grows on a bush with thorny stems. Roses are red, pink, white, or yellow and usually smell very sweet. **2.** the bush itself. **3.** any of various related or similar plants or flowers. **4.** a pinkish-red color. **5.** something shaped like a rose or suggesting a rose. —*adj.* pinkish-red. [< L *rosa*]

rose² (rōz), *v.* pt. of **rise.**

ro·se·ate (rō′zi·it; -āt), *adj.* **1.** rose-colored; rosy. **2.** cheerful; optimistic. —**ro′se·ate·ly,** *adv.*

rose beetle or **bug,** beetle destructive to roses.

rose·bud (rōz′bud′), *n.* bud of a rose.

rose·bush (rōz′bůsh′), *n.* shrub or vine bearing roses.

rose-col·ored (rōz′kul′ərd), *adj.* **1.** pinkish-red. **2.** bright; cheerful; optimistic.

rose·mar·y (rōz′mār′i), *n., pl.* **-mar·ies.** an evergreen shrub whose leaves yield a fragrant oil used in making perfume. [< L *ros maris,* lit., dew of the sea; assoc. with *rose* and *Mary*]

rose of Sharon, shrub with bright flowers; althea.

ro·sette (rō·zet′), *n.* ornament, object, or arrangement shaped like a rose. Rosettes are often made of ribbon. Carved or molded rosettes are used in architecture. [< F, dim. of *rose* ROSE¹]

rose water, water made fragrant with oil of roses.

rose window, an ornamental circular window, esp. one with a pattern of small sections that radiate from a center.

rose·wood (rōz'wůd'), *n.* **1.** a beautiful reddish wood used in fine furniture. **2.** the tropical tree that it comes from.

Rosh Ha·sha·na (rosh' hə·shä'nə; rōsh'), the Jewish New Year.

ros·in (roz'ən), *n.* a hard, yellow substance that remains when turpentine is evaporated from pine resin. Rosin is rubbed on violin bows and on the shoes of acrobats to keep them from slipping. —*v.* cover or rub with rosin. [var. of *resin*]

Ross (rôs; ros), *n.* Betsy, 1752–1836, American woman who is said to have made the first American flag.

Ros·set·ti (rō·set'i; -zet'i), *n.* **1.** Dante Gabriel, 1828–1882, English poet and painter. **2.** his sister, Christina Georgina, 1830–1894, English poet.

Ros·si·ni (rô·sē'ni), *n.* Gioacchino Antonio, 1792–1868, Italian composer of operas.

ros·ter (ros'tər), *n.* **1.** list giving each person's name and duties. **2.** any list. [< Du. *rooster*]

Ros·tov (ros·tôf'; -tof'), *n.* city and port in S Soviet Union, on the Don River.

ros·trum (ros'trəm), *n.*, *pl.* -trums, -tra (-trə). platform for public speaking. [< L, beak, < *rodere* gnaw; with ref. to the speakers' platform in the Roman forum, which was decorated with the beaks of captured war galleys] —*ros'tral, adj.* —*Syn.* stage, dais.

ros·y (rōz'i), *adj.* ros·i·er, ros·i·est. **1.** like a rose; rose-red; pinkish-red. **2.** made of roses. **3.** bright; cheerful. —*ros'i·ly, adv.* —*ros'i·ness, n.*

rot (rot), *v.*, rot·ted, rot·ting, *n.* —*v.* **1.** decay; spoil. **2.** cause to decay. —*n.* **1.** process of rotting; decay. **2.** rotten matter. **3.** a disease of plants and animals, esp. of sheep. **4.** *Esp. Brit. Slang.* nonsense; rubbish. [OE *rotian*] —*Syn. v.* 1, 2. decompose, putrefy, corrupt.

ro·ta·ry (rō'tə·ri), *adj.* **1.** turning like a top or a wheel; rotating. **2.** having parts that rotate. **3.** of an airplane engine, having radially arranged cylinders that revolve around a common fixed crankshaft.

ro·tate (rō'tāt), *v.*, -tat·ed, -tat·ing. **1.** move around a center or axis; turn in a circle; revolve. Wheels, tops, and the earth rotate. **2.** change in a regular order; take turns or cause to take turns: *farmers rotate crops.* [< L *rotatus* < *rota* wheel] —*ro'tat·a·ble, adj.* —*ro'tat·a·bly, adv.* —*ro·ta·tive* (rō'tə·tiv), *adj.* —*ro'ta·tor, n.*

ro·ta·tion (rō·tā'shən), *n.* **1.** act or process of moving around a center or axis; turning in a circle; revolving. **2.** the turning of the earth. **3.** change in a regular order. **4.** in rotation, in turn; in regular succession. —*ro·ta'tion·al, ro·ta·to·ry* (rō'tə·tô'ri; -tō'-), *adj.*

rotation of crops, varying the crops grown in the same field to keep the soil from losing its fertility.

R.O.T.C., Reserve Officers' Training Corps.

rote (rōt), *n.* **1.** a set, mechanical way of doing things. **2.** by rote, by memory without thought of the meaning.

ro·to·gra·vure (rō'tə·grə·vyůr'; -grā'vyər), *n.* **1.** process of printing from an engraved copper cylinder on which the pictures, letters, etc., have been depressed instead of raised. **2.** *Am.* a print or section of a newspaper made by this process. [< L *rota* wheel + E *gravure*]

ro·tor (rō'tər), *n.* the rotating part of a machine or apparatus. [short for *rotator*]

rot·ten (rot'ən), *adj.* **1.** decayed; spoiled: *a rotten egg.* **2.** foul; bad-smelling: *rotten air.* **3.** not in good condition; unsound; weak: *rotten ice.* **4.** corrupt; dishonest. **5.** *Slang.* bad; nasty. [< Scand. *rotinn*] —*rot'ten·ly, adv.* —*rot'ten·ness, n.* —*Syn.* 1. decomposed. 2. putrid, fetid.

rot·ter (rot'ər), *n. Esp. Brit. Slang.* a thoroughly worthless or objectionable person.

Rot·ter·dam (rot'ər·dam'), *n.* seaport in SW Netherlands.

ro·tund (rō·tund'), *adj.* **1.** round; plump: *a rotund face.* **2.** sounding rich and full; full-

toned: *a rotund voice.* [< L *rotundus*, ult. < *rota* wheel. Doublet of ROUND.] —*ro·tun'di·ty, ro·tund'ness, n.* —*ro·tund'ly, adv.*

ro·tun·da (rō·tun'də), *n.* **1.** a circular building or part of a building, esp. one with a dome. **2.** a large, high, circular room. [< L, fem. adj. See ROTUND.]

rou·ble (rü'bəl), *n.* ruble.

rou·é (rü·ā'; rü'ā), *n.* a dissipated man; rake. [< F, orig. pp. of *rouer* break on the wheel; first applied to 18th-century group of profligates]

Rou·en (rü·än'), *n.* city in N France.

rouge (rüzh), *n.*, *v.*, rouged, roug·ing. —*n.* **1.** a red powder, paste, or liquid for coloring the cheeks or lips. **2.** a red powder, chiefly ferric oxide, used for polishing metal, jewels, etc. —*v.* color with rouge. [< F, red]

rough (ruf), *adj.* **1.** not smooth; not level; not even: *rough boards, rough bark.* **2.** without polish or fine finish: *rough diamonds.* **3.** without luxury and ease: *rough life in camp.* **4.** not completed or perfected; done as a first try; without details: *a rough drawing, a rough idea.* **5.** coarse and tangled: *a dog with a rough coat of hair.* **6.** likely to hurt others; harsh; not gentle: *rough manners.* **7.** disorderly; riotous: *a rough crowd.* **8.** unpleasant; hard; severe: *in for a rough time.* **9.** requiring merely strength rather than intelligence or skill: *rough work.* **10.** stormy: *rough weather.* **11.** violently disturbed or agitated: *a rough sea.* **12.** harsh to the ear **or** taste: *rough sounds, rough wines.* **13.** *Phonet.* pronounced with an aspirate; having the sound of *h.* —*n.* **1.** a coarse, violent person. **2.** rough ground. **3.** a rough thing or condition. **4.** any portion of a golf course on which grass, weeds, etc., are untrimmed. **5. in the rough,** not polished or refined; coarse; crude. —*v.* **1.** make or become rough; roughen. **2.** treat roughly. **3.** shape or sketch roughly. **4. rough it,** live without comforts and conveniences. —*adv.* in a rough manner. [OE *rūh*] —*rough'er, n.* —*rough'ish, adj.* —*rough'ly, adv.* —*rough'ness, n.* —*Syn. adj.* 1. uneven, irregular, broken, jagged. 2. unfinished, untrimmed, uncut, crude. 3. uncultivated, unpolished. 4. approximate, imperfect, incomplete, preliminary. 5. shaggy, bristly. 6. discourteous, impolite, uncivil. 7. boisterous, tumultuous. 8. drastic, rigorous. 10. inclement.

rough·age (ruf'ij), *n.* **1.** rough or coarse material. **2.** the coarser parts or kinds of food, as bran, fruit skins, and straw.

rough-and-read·y (ruf'ənd·red'i), *adj.* **1.** rough and crude, but good enough for the purpose; roughly effective. **2.** showing rough vigor rather than refinement.

rough-and-tum·ble (ruf'ənd·tum'bəl), *Am.* —*adj.* with little regard for rules; roughly vigorous; boisterous. —*n.* a rough-and-tumble fight or struggle.

rough-dry (ruf'drī'), *v.*, -dried, -dry·ing. dry (clothes) after washing without ironing them.

rough·en (ruf'ən), *v.* make or become rough.

rough-hew (ruf'hū'), *v.*, -hewed, -hewed or -hewn, -hew·ing. **1.** hew (timber, stone, etc.) roughly or without smoothing or finishing. **2.** give crude form to.

rough·house (ruf'hous'), *n.*, *v.*, -housed, -hous·ing. *Slang.* —*n.* rough play; rowdy conduct; disorderly behavior. —*v. Am.* act in a rough or disorderly way.

rough·neck (ruf'nek'), *n. Slang.* a rough, coarse fellow.

rough·rid·er (ruf'rīd'ər), *n. Am.* **1.** man used to rough, hard riding. **2.** person who breaks in and rides rough, wild horses. **3. Roughriders,** members of a volunteer cavalry regiment organized by Theodore Roosevelt during the Spanish-American War.

rough·shod (ruf'shod'), *adj.* **1.** having horseshoes with sharp calks to prevent slipping. **2. ride roughshod over,** show no consideration for; treat roughly.

rou·lette (rü·let'), *n.*, *v.*, -let·ted, -let·ting. —*n.* **1.** a gambling game in which the players bet on the turn of a wheel. 2. a small wheel with sharp teeth for making lines of marks, dots, or perforations. —*v.* mark or perforate with a roulette. [< F, ult. < *roue* < L *rota* wheel]

Rou·ma·ni·a (rü·mā′nĭ·ə; -mān′yə), *n.* Rumania. —**Rou·ma′ni·an**, *adj., n.*

round (round), *adj.* 1. shaped like a ball, a ring, a cylinder, or the like; having a circular or curved outline or surface: *a round hoop.* 2. plump: *her figure was short and round.* 3. by, with, or involving a circular movement. The waltz is a round dance. 4. full; complete; large: *a good round sum of money.* 5. plainly expressed; plain-spoken; frank: *scold in good round terms.* 6. with a full tone: *a mellow, round voice.* 7. *Phonet.* spoken with the lips rounded. *O* is a round vowel. —*n.* 1. anything shaped like a ball, circle, cylinder, or the like. The rungs of a ladder are sometimes called rounds. 2. a fixed course ending where it begins: *the watchman makes his rounds.* 3. movement in a circle or about an axis: *the earth's yearly round.* 4. a series (of duties, events, etc.); routine: *a round of pleasures.* 5. section of a game or sport: *a round in a fight.* 6. discharge of firearms by a group of soldiers at the same time. 7. bullets, powder, etc., for such a shot. 8. a single outburst of applause, cheers, etc. 9. dance in which the dancers move in a circle. 10. a short song, sung by several persons or groups beginning one after the other. The "Three Blind Mice" is a round. 11. form of sculpture in which the figures are apart from any background. 12. cut of beef just above the hind leg. 13. **go the round**, be passed, told, shown, etc., by many people from one to another. —*v.* 1. make or become round: *round the corners of a table.* 2. go wholly or partly around: *the ship rounded Cape Horn.* 3. turn around; wheel about: *the bear rounded and faced the hunters.* 4. *Phonet.* utter (a vowel) with a small circular opening of the lips. 5. **round off** or **out,** a. make or become round. b. finish; complete. 6. **round up,** draw or drive together. —*adv.* 1. in a circle; with a whirling motion: *wheels go round.* 2. on all sides; in every direction: *the travelers were compassed round by dangers.* 3. in circumference: *the pumpkin measures 50 inches round.* 4. by a longer road or way: *we went round by the candy store on our way home.* 5. from one to another: *a report is going round.* 6. through a round of time: *summer will soon come round again.* 7. about; around: *he doesn't look fit to be round.* 8. here and there: *just looking round.* 9. for all: *there is just enough cake to go round.* —*prep.* 1. on all sides of: *bullets fell round him.* 2. so as to encircle or surround: *build a fence round the yard.* 3. so as to make a turn to the other side of: *walk round the corner.* 4. in a circuit or course through; to all or various parts of: *we took our cousins round the town.* 5. about; around: *stand still and look round one.* 6. here and there in: *all round the city.* 7. **get** or **come round** a person, a. outwit him. b. wheedle him. [< OF < L *rotundus.* Doublet of ROTUND.] —**round′ish,** *adj.* —**round′ish·ness,** *n.* —**round′ness,** *n.* —Syn. *adj.* 1. cylindrical, spherical, globular. 2. rotund, stout. —*n.* 1. ring. 3. revolution, cycle. 4. succession. ▶ **round, around.** In colloquial and informal usage *round* and *around* are used interchangeably, with a definite tendency to use *round* (or to clip the *a* of *around* so short that it would be taken for *round*). In formal English there is some tendency to keep *around* to mean "here and there" or "in every direction" and *round* for "in a circular motion" or "in a reverse motion": *I have looked all around; there aren't any around here. He is going round the world; everyone turned round. Around* is colloquial and informal in the sense of "about, near": *He had around $200 in bills. Is anybody around* [that is, *around here*]? *Round* has no apostrophe.

round·a·bout (round′ə·bout′), *adj.* indirect: *a roundabout route, hear in a roundabout way.* —*n.* 1. an indirect way, course, or speech. 2. a short, tight jacket for men or boys. 3. *Esp. Brit.* merry-go-round. —Syn. *adj.* circuitous.

round dance, 1. dance performed by couples and characterized by circular or revolving movements. 2. formerly, dance with dancers in a circle.

roun·de·lay (roun′də·lā), *n.* song in which a phrase or a line is repeated again and again. [< OF *rondelet,* dim. of *rondel* RONDEL; infl. by *lay*[4]]

round·er (roun′dər), *n. Slang.* 1. *Am.* person who makes the rounds of places of amusement, esp. of disreputable places. 2. formerly, a spendthrift or drunkard.

Round·head (round′hed′), *n.* a Puritan in England during the English civil wars, 1642–1652.

round·house (round′hous′), *n. Am.* a circular building for storing or repairing locomotives, that is built about a turntable.

round·ly (round′lĭ), *adv.* 1. in a round manner. 2. bluntly; severely. 3. fully; completely.

round number, 1. a whole number without a fraction. 2. number in even tens, hundreds, thousands, etc. 3874 in round numbers would be 3900 or 4000.

round robin, petition, protest, etc., with the signatures written in a circle, so that it is impossible to tell who signed first.

round-shoul·dered (round′shōl′dərd), *adj.* having the shoulders bent forward.

round table, 1. group of persons assembled for an informal discussion, etc. 2. **Round Table,** a. table around which King Arthur and his knights sat. b. King Arthur and his knights. —**round′-ta′ble,** *adj.*

round trip, *Am.* trip to a place and back again.

round·up (round′up′), *n.* 1. *Am., W.* a. act of driving or bringing cattle together from long distances. b. the men and horses that do this. 2. any similar gathering.

round·worm (round′wẽrm′), *n.* any of a group of unsegmented worms that have long, round bodies, as the hookworm and trichina.

rouse (rouz), *v.,* **roused, rous·ing,** *n.* —*v.* arouse; wake up; stir up: *I was roused by the telephone, the dogs roused a deer from the bushes, he was roused to anger by the insult.* —*n.* a rousing. —**rous′er,** *n.* —**rous′ing,** *adj.* —**rous′ing·ly,** *adv.* —Syn. *v.* awaken, excite.

Rous·seau (rü·sō′), *n.* Jean Jacques, 1712–1778, French philosopher.

roust·a·bout (roust′ə·bout′), *n. Am.* an unskilled laborer on wharves, ships, ranches, etc.

rout[1] (rout), *n.* 1. flight of a defeated army in disorder. 2. a complete defeat. 3. a noisy, disorderly crowd; mob; rabble. —*v.* 1. put to flight. 2. defeat completely. [< OF *route* detachment, ult. < L *rumpere* to break]

rout[2] (rout), *v.* 1. put (out); force (out): *rout the lazy boys out of bed.* 2. dig with the snout. [var. of *root*[2]]

route (rüt; rout), *n., v.,* **rout·ed, rout·ing.** —*n.* way to go; road: *go the northern route.* —*v.* 1. arrange the route for. 2. send by a certain route. [< OF < L *rupta* (*via*) (a way) opened up, (a passage) forced < *rumpere* break] —Syn. *n.* path, course, passage. ▶ **route.** The pronunciation (rüt) is general, but (rout) is used in the army and colloquially as of newspaper and delivery routes.

rou·tine (rü·tēn′), *n.* a fixed, regular method of doing things; habitual doing of the same things in the same way. —*adj.* using routine: *routine methods.* [< F, < *route* ROUTE] —**rou·tin′ism,** *n.* —**rou·tin′ist,** *n.*

rove[1] (rōv), *v.,* **roved, rov·ing.** wander; wander about; roam: *rove over the fields and woods.* —**rov′er,** *n.* —Syn. ramble, range, stroll.

rove[2] (rōv), *v.* pt. and pp. of *reeve*[2].

row[1] (rō), *n.* 1. line of people or things 2. line of seats, as in a theater. 3. street with a line of buildings on either side. 4. **hard row to hoe,** *Am.* a difficult thing to do. [OE *rāw*] —Syn. 1. file, series, rank.

row[2] (rō), *v.* 1. use oars to propel a boat. 2. propel (a boat, etc.) by the use of oars. 3. convey in a rowboat: *we were rowed to the shore.* 4. perform (a race, etc.) by rowing. —*n.* **1.** act of using oars. **2.** trip in a rowboat. [OE *rōwan*] —**row′er**, *n.*

row³ (rou), *n.* **1.** a noisy quarrel; disturbance; clamor. **2.** *Colloq.* squabble. —*v.* **1.** *Colloq.* quarrel noisily; make noise. **2.** *Colloq.* scold; upbraid.

row·an (rō′ən; rou′-), *n.* **1.** the mountain ash. **2.** its red, berrylike fruit. [< Scand. (Norw.) *raun*]

row·boat (rō′bōt′), *n.* boat moved by oars.

row·dy (rou′di), *n., pl.* **-dies,** *adj.,* **-di·er, -di·est.** *Am.* —*n.* a rough, disorderly, quarrelsome person. —*adj.* rough; disorderly; quarrelsome. —**row′di·ly,** *adv.* —**row′di·ness,** *n. Am.* —**row′dy·ish,** *adj. Am.* —**row′dy·ish·ly,** *adv.* —**row′dy·ish·ness,** *n.* —**row′dy·ism,** *n. Am.*

row·el (rou′əl), *n., v.,* **-eled, -el·ing;** *esp. Brit.* **-elled, -el·ling.** —*n.* a small wheel with sharp points, attached to the end of a spur. —*v.* use a rowel on. [< OF *roel,* ult. < L *rota* wheel]

row·lock (rō′lok), *n.* oarlock.

roy·al (roi′əl), *adj.* **1.** of kings and queens: *the royal family.* **2.** belonging to a king or queen: *royal power.* **3.** favored or encouraged by a king or queen; serving a king or queen: *the Royal Academy.* **4.** from or by a king or queen: *a royal command.* **5.** appropriate for a king; splendid: *a royal welcome.* **6.** like a king; noble. **7.** fine; excellent. **8.** beyond the common or ordinary in size, quality, etc. —*n.* a small mast or sail set above the topgallant. [< OF < L *regalis.* Doublet of REGAL, REAL².] —**roy′al·ly,** *adv.* —**Syn.** *adj.* **2.** regal, kingly, imperial. **5.** magnificent. **6.** majestic, august, stately.

roy·al·ist (roi′əl·ist), *n.* supporter of a king or of a royal government.

royal palm, *Am.* a tall palm tree that has a whitish trunk and is often planted for ornament.

roy·al·ty (roi′əl·ti), *n., pl.* **-ties. 1.** a royal person; royal persons. Kings, queens, princes, and princesses are royalty. **2.** rank or dignity of a king or queen; royal power. **3.** kingliness; royal quality; nobility. **4.** share of the receipts or profits paid to an owner of a patent or copyright; payment for the use of any of various rights.

r.p.m., revolutions per minute.

R.R., 1. railroad. **2.** Right Reverend.

R.S.F.S.R., Russian Soviet Federated Socialist Republic.

R.S.V.P., please answer. [< F *répondez s'il vous plaît*]

Ru, *Chem.* ruthenium.

rub (rub), *v.,* **rubbed, rub·bing,** *n.* —*v.* **1.** move (one thing) back and forth (against another); move (two things) together: *rub your hands to warm them.* **2.** move one's hand or an object over the surface of; push and press along the surface of: *the nurse rubbed my lame back.* **3.** press as it moves: *that door rubs on the floor.* **4.** make or bring (to some condition) by sliding the hand or some object: *rub silver bright.* **5.** irritate or make sore by rubbing. **6. rub down,** rub (the body); massage. —*n.* **1.** act of rubbing. **2.** something that rubs or hurts the feelings. **3.** difficulty. [ME *rubbe(n)*] —**Syn.** *v.* **4.** polish, burnish, furbish. **5.** chafe.

rub·ber¹ (rub′ər), *n.* **1.** an elastic substance obtained from the milky juice of various tropical plants, or by various chemical processes. Rubber will not let air or water through. **2.** something made from this substance. We wear rubbers on our feet when it rains. **3.** person or thing that rubs. —*adj.* made of rubber. —*v. Am., Slang.* stretch the neck or turn the head to look at something. —**rub′ber·y,** *adj.*

rub·ber² (rub′ər), *n.* **1.** a series of games of an odd number, usually three, the last of which is played to decide the contest when each side has won the same number of games. **2.** the deciding game in a series of this kind.

rub·ber·ize (rub′ər·īz), *v.,* **-ized, -iz·ing.** cover or treat with rubber.

rub·ber·neck (rub′ər·nek′), *Am., Slang.* —*v.* stretch the neck or turn the head to look at something; stare. —*n.* person who does this.

rubber plant, 1. any plant yielding rubber. **2.** an ornamental house plant with oblong, shining, leathery leaves.

rubber stamp, *Am., Colloq.* person or group that approves or endorses something without thought.

rub·ber-stamp (rub′ər-stamp′), *v. Colloq.* approve or endorse (a policy, bill, etc.) without thought.

rub·bish (rub′ish), *n.* **1.** waste stuff of no use; trash. **2.** silly words and thoughts; nonsense. —**rub′bish·y,** *adj.* —**Syn. 1.** litter, debris, refuse, garbage.

rub·ble (rub′əl), *n.* **1.** rough broken stones, bricks, etc. **2.** masonry made of this. [ME *robel*] —**rub′bly,** *adj.*

rub·down (rub′doun′), *n.* a rubbing of the body; massage.

rube (rüb), *n. Am., Slang.* an unsophisticated countryman. [< the name *Reuben*]

Ru·bens (rü′bənz), *n.* Peter Paul, 1577-1640, Flemish painter.

Ru·bi·con (rü′bə·kon), *n.* **1.** a small river in Italy which Julius Caesar crossed to start a civil war that made him master of Rome. **2.** **cross the Rubicon,** make an important decision from which one cannot turn back.

ru·bi·cund (rü′bə·kund), *adj.* reddish; ruddy. [< L *rubicundus* < *rubere* be red] —**ru′bi·cun′di·ty,** *n.*

ru·bid·i·um (rü·bid′i·əm), *n. Chem.* a silver-white metallic element, Rb, resembling potassium. [< NL, < L *rubidus* red; its spectrum has red lines]

ru·ble (rü′bəl), *n.* a Russian monetary unit and silver coin or piece of paper money, worth about 25 cents (1950). Also, **rouble.**

ru·bric (rü′brik), *n.* **1.** title or heading of a chapter, a law, etc., written or printed in red or in special lettering. **2.** any heading. **3.** direction for the conducting of religious services inserted in a prayer book, ritual, etc. [< L *rubrica* red coloring matter < *ruber* red] —**ru′bri·cal,** *adj.* —**ru′bri·cal·ly,** *adv.*

ru·by (rü′bi), *n., pl.* **-bies,** *adj.* —*n.* **1.** a clear, hard, red precious stone. **2.** its color. —*adj.* deep, glowing red. [< OF *rubi,* ult. < L *rubeus* red]

ruche (rüsh), *n.* full pleating or frill of lace, ribbon, net, etc., used as trimming for women's dresses. [< F, orig., beehive]

ruch·ing (rüsh′ing), *n.* trimming made of ruches.

ruck·us (ruk′əs), *n. Am., Slang.* a noisy disturbance or uproar.

rud·der (rud′ər), *n.* **1.** a hinged, flat piece of wood or metal at the rear end of a boat or ship, by which it is steered. **2.** a similar piece in an airplane, dirigible, etc. [OE *rōthor*] —**rud′dered,** *adj.* —**rud′der·less,** *adj.*

rud·dy (rud′i), *adj.,* **-di·er, -di·est. 1.** red. **2.** healthy red: *ruddy cheeks.* [OE *rudig*] —**rud′di·ly,** *adv.* —**rud′di·ness,** *n.* —**Syn. 1.** reddish, rubicund, florid. **2.** rosy.

rude (rüd), *adj.,* **rud·er, rud·est. 1.** impolite; not courteous: *it is rude to stare, a rude reply.* **2.** roughly made or done; without finish or polish; coarse: *rude tools, a rude cabin.* **3.** rough in manner or behavior; violent; harsh: *rude hands, a rude shock.* **4.** harsh to the ear; unmusical. **5.** not having learned much; rather wild; barbarous: *rude tribes.* [< L *rudis*] —**rude′ly,** *adv.* —**rude′ness,** *n.* —**Syn. 1.** uncivil, discourteous, impertinent, impudent. **2.** unwrought, raw, crude. **5.** primitive, uncivilized.

ru·di·ment (rü′də·mənt), *n.* **1.** part to be learned first; beginning: *the rudiments of grammar.* **2.** something in an early stage; an organ or part incompletely developed in size or structure. [< L *rudimentum* < *rudis* rude] —**ru·di·men·tal** (rü′də·men′təl), *adj.*

ru·di·men·ta·ry (rü′də·men′tə·ri; -tri), *adj.* **1.** to be learned or studied first; elementary. **2.** in an early stage of development; incompletely developed. —**ru′di·men′ta·ri·ly,** *adv.* —**ru′di·men′ta·ri·ness,** *n.* —**Syn. 2.** embryonic.

rue[1] (rü), v., rued, ru·ing, n. —v. 1. be sorry for; regret. 2. Archaic. feel sorrow. —n. Archaic. sorrow; regret. [OE hrēowan] —ru'er, n.

rue[2] (rü), n. a strong-smelling plant with yellow flowers and bitter leaves. [< OF < L ruta, ? < Gk. rhytē]

rue·ful (rü'fəl), adj. 1. sorrowful; unhappy; mournful: a rueful expression. 2. causing sorrow or pity: a rueful sight. —rue'ful·ly, adv. —rue'ful·ness, n. —Syn. 1. doleful, woeful, lugubrious, melancholy.

ruff[1] (ruf), n. 1. a deep frill stiff enough to stand out, worn around the neck by men and women in the 16th century. 2. collar of specially marked feathers or hairs on the neck of a bird or animal. [akin to ruffle[1]] —ruffed, adj.

Ruff

ruff[2] (ruf), v. trump in a card game. —n. act of trumping. [< early F roffle]

ruffed grouse, Am. a North American game bird with a tuft of feathers on each side of the neck. It is in some places called a partridge and in others a pheasant.

ruf·fi·an (ruf'i·ən), n. a rough, brutal, or cruel person. —adj. Also, ruf'fi·an·ly. rough, lawless, and brutal. [< early F] —ruf'fi·an·ism, n. —Syn. n. bully, rowdy, rough, hoodlum.

ruf·fle[1] (ruf'əl), v., -fled, -fling. —v. 1. make rough or uneven; wrinkle: a breeze ruffled the lake. 2. gather into a ruffle. 3. trim with ruffles. 4. disturb; annoy. 5. become ruffled. —n. 1. roughness or unevenness in some surface; wrinkling. 2. strip of cloth, ribbon, or lace gathered along one edge and used for trimming. 3. disturbance; annoyance. 4. disorder; confusion. [cf. Scand. hrufla scratch] —ruf'fler, n. —Syn. v. 1. rumple, roughen, disorder, disarrange. 4. disquiet, discompose, agitate, vex.

ruf·fle[2] (ruf'əl), n., v., -fled, -fling. —n. a low, steady beating of a drum. —v. beat (a drum) in this way. [? imit.]

rug (rug), n. 1. a heavy floor covering. 2. a thick, warm cloth used as covering. [< Scand. (Norw. dial.) rugga coarse covering]

Rug·by (rug'bi), n. 1. town in C England. 2. a famous school for boys there. 3. Also, Rugby football. one form of the game of football.

rug·ged (rug'id), adj. 1. covered with rough projections; rough and uneven: rugged rocks, a rugged ascent. 2. Am. sturdy or strong rather than elegant; robust; vigorous. 3. wrinkled; furrowed: a rugged brow. 4. roughly irregular; hard in outline and form: rugged features. 5. tempestuous; severe: rugged weather, rugged times. 6. harsh; stern. 7. rough and rude; unpolished; unrefined. [< Scand. (Sw.) rugga roughen. Cf. RUG.] —rug'ged·ly, adv. —rug'ged·ness, n. —Syn. 1. broken, craggy, scraggy. 2. hardy. 6. austere, unfeeling, hard.

Ruhr (rür; Ger. rür), n. 1. river in W Germany flowing into the Rhine. 2. a rich mining and industrial region along this river.

ru·in (rü'ən), n. 1. very great damage; destruction; overthrow; decay: his enemies planned the duke's ruin. 2. condition of destruction, decay, or downfall: the house had gone to ruin and neglect. 3. cause of destruction, decay, or downfall: drink was his ruin. 4. ruins, that which remains after destruction or decay, esp. a building, wall, etc., that has fallen to pieces. 5. bankruptcy. —v. 1. bring to ruin; destroy; spoil: the rain has ruined my new hat. 2. come to ruin. 3. dishonor (a woman). 4. make bankrupt. [< L ruina a collapse] —ru'in·a·ble, adj. —ru'in·er, n. —Syn. n. 1. wreck, havoc. 2. dilapidation, ruination. —v. 1. overthrow, overwhelm, demolish, wreck.

ru·in·a·tion (rü'ə·nā'shən), n. ruin; destruction; downfall.

ru·in·ous (rü'ə·nəs), adj. 1. bringing ruin; causing destruction. 2. fallen into ruins; in ruins. —ru'in·ous·ly, adv. —ru'in·ous·ness, n.

rule (rül), n., v., ruled, rul·ing. —n. 1. statement of what to do and not to do; a law; principle governing conduct, action, arrangement,

etc.: obey the rules of the game. 2. order by a law court referring to only one particular case. 3. set of rules; code, esp. a code observed by a religious order. 4. control; government: in a democracy the people have the rule. 5. a regular method; thing that usually happens or is done; what is usually true: fair weather is the rule in Arizona. 6. a straight strip used to measure or as a guide to drawing. 7. a thin, type-high strip of metal, for printing a line or lines. 8. as a rule, usually. —v. 1. make a rule; decide. 2. make a formal decision. 3. decide formally or authoritatively; decree: the judge ruled the question out of order. 4. exercise highest authority; control; govern; direct. 5. prevail; be current: prices of wheat and corn ruled high all the year. 6. mark with lines. 7. mark off. 8. rule a thing out, decide that it does not belong in. [< OF < L regula straight stick < regere to guide. Doublet of RAIL[1].] —rul'a·ble, adj. —Syn. n. 1. regulation, order, precept. 4. direction, authority, dominion, sway. —v. 4. manage, dominate, domineer, sway.

rule of three, method of finding the fourth term in a mathematical proportion when three are given.

rule of thumb, 1. rule based on experience or practice rather than on scientific knowledge. 2. a rough practical method of procedure.

rul·er (rül'ər), n. 1. person who governs. 2. a straight strip of wood, metal, etc., used in drawing lines or in measuring.

rul·ing (rül'ing), n. 1. a decision of a judge or court. 2. ruled lines. —adj. 1. that rules; governing. 2. controlling; predominating; prevalent. —rul'ing·ly, adv.

rum[1] (rum), n. 1. an alcoholic liquor made from sugar cane, molasses, etc. 2. alcoholic liquor.

rum[2] (rum), adj. Esp. Brit. Slang. odd; queer.

Rum., Rumanian.

Ru·ma·ni·a (rü·mā'ni·ə; -mān'yə), n. country in S Europe. Also, Romania, Roumania.

Ru·ma·ni·an (rü·mā'ni·ən; -mān'yən), adj. of or pertaining to Rumania, its inhabitants, or language. —n. 1. native or inhabitant of Rumania. 2. language of Rumania. Also, Romanian, Roumanian.

rum·ba (rum'bə), n., v., -baed, -ba·ing. —n. 1. a Negro Cuban dance. 2. Am. dance imitative of this, characterized by sensuous movements. 3. music for such a dance. —v. dance the rumba. Also, rhumba. [< Sp., prob. < African lang.]

rum·ble (rum'bəl), v., -bled, -bling, n. —v. 1. make a deep, heavy, continuous sound. 2. move with such a sound. 3. utter with such a sound. —n. 1. a deep, heavy, continuous sound: the far-off rumble of thunder. 2. Am., Slang. a teenage gang fight. 3. the rear part of an automobile or carriage containing an extra seat or a place for baggage. [? ult. imit.] —rum'bler, n. —rum'bling, adj.

ru·mi·nant (rü'mə·nənt), n. animal that chews the cud, as cows, sheep, camels, etc. —adj. 1. belonging to the group of ruminants. 2. meditative; reflective. [< L ruminans chewing a cud < rumen gullet] —ru'mi·nant·ly, adv.

ru·mi·nate (rü'mə·nāt), v., -nat·ed, -nat·ing. 1. chew the cud. 2. chew again: a cow ruminates its food. 3. ponder; meditate. [< L ruminatus < rumen gullet] —ru'mi·nat'ing, adj. —ru'mi·nat'ing·ly, adv. —ru'mi·na'tion, n. —ru'mi·na'tive, adj. —ru'mi·na'tive·ly, adv. —ru'mi·na'tor, n. —Syn. 3. muse, reflect.

rum·mage (rum'ij), v., -maged, -mag·ing, n. —v. 1. search thoroughly by moving things about. 2. search in a disorderly way. 3. pull from among other things; bring to light. —n. 1. a rummaging search. 2. odds and ends. [< early F arrumage < arrumer stow cargo]

rum·my[1] (rum'i), adj., -mi·er, -mi·est. Slang. odd; strange; queer.

rum·my[2] (rum'i), n. Am. a kind of card game.

ru·mor, esp. Brit. **ru·mour** (rü'mər), n. 1. a story or statement talked of as news without any proof that it is true. 2. vague, general talk: rumor has it that Italy will quarrel with France. —v. tell or spread by rumor. [< OF < L] —Syn. n. 1. report, gossip, hearsay.

rump (rump), *n.* **1.** the hind part of the body of an animal, where the legs join the back. **2.** cut of beef from this part. **3.** an unimportant or inferior part; remnant. [< Scand. (Dan.) *rumpe*]

rum·ple (rum′pəl), *v.,* **-pled, -pling,** *n.* —*v.* crumple; crush; wrinkle. —*n.* wrinkle; crease. [cf. MDu. *rompel*] —**rum′ply,** *adj.* —**Syn.** *v.* pucker, crease, disorder.

rum·pus (rum′pəs), *n. Colloq.* **1.** a noisy quarrel; disturbance. **2.** noise; uproar.

rum·run·ner (rum′run′ər), *n. Am.* person or ship that smuggles alcoholic liquor.

run (run), *v.,* **ran, run, run·ning,** *n.* —*v.* **1.** go faster than walking: *run to the house.* **2.** go hurriedly; hasten: *run to a person's aid.* **3.** flee: *run for your life.* **4.** cause to run; cause to move: *run a horse up and down.* **5.** perform by, or as by, running: *run errands.* **6.** go; move; keep going: *this train runs to Buffalo.* **7.** go on; proceed: *prices of hats run as high as $50.00.* **8.** creep; trail; climb: *vines run along the sides of the road.* **9.** run along (a way, path, etc.): *run the course until the end.* **10.** pursue; chase (game, etc.): *run a fox.* **11.** pass or cause to pass quickly: *time runs on.* **12.** trace; draw: *run that report back to its source.* **13.** stretch; extend: *shelves run along the walls.* **14.** drive; force; thrust: *run a knife into a person.* **15.** flow; flow with: *the streets ran blood.* **16.** discharge fluid, mucus, or pus: *my nose runs.* **17.** bring or come into a certain named condition: *the well ran dry.* **18.** have a specified character, quality, form, size, etc.: *these potatoes run large.* **19.** spread: *the color ran when the dress was washed.* **20.** continue; last: *a lease to run two years.* **21.** have currency or be current; occur. **22.** *Law.* have legal force. **23.** take part in a race or contest. **24.** *Am.* be a candidate for election. **25.** *Am.* agree upon or support in an election for office. **26.** expose oneself to: *run a risk.* **27.** move easily, freely, or smoothly; keep operating: *a rope runs in a pulley.* **28.** cause to move easily, freely, or smoothly; cause to keep operating: *run a machine.* **29.** be worded or expressed: *how does the first verse run?* **30.** *Am.* conduct; manage: *run a business.* **31.** go about without restraint; run wild; grow without restraint. **32.** of fish, move together in large numbers. **33.** drop stitches; ravel. **34.** sew by pushing a needle in and out with even stitches in a line. **35.** get past or through: *enemy ships tried to run the blockade.* **36.** smuggle: *run rum.* **37.** *Am.* publish (an advertisement, story, etc.) in a newspaper: *he ran an ad in the evening paper.* **38.** soften; become liquid; melt. **39.** shape by melting. **40. run across,** *Am.* meet by chance. **41. run down, a.** cease to go; stop working. **b.** pursue till caught or killed; hunt down. **c.** knock down by running against. **d.** speak evil against. **e.** decline or reduce in vigor or health. **f.** fall off, diminish, or decrease; deteriorate. **42. run for it,** run for safety. **43. run in, a.** *Slang.* arrest and put in jail. **b.** pay a short visit. **44. run into, a.** meet by chance. **b.** crash into; collide with. **45. run off, a.** cause to be run or played. **b.** print. **46. run out,** come to an end; become exhausted. **47. run out of,** use up; have no more. **48. run over, a.** a ride or drive over. **b.** overflow. **c.** go through quickly. **49. run through, a.** consume or spend rapidly or recklessly. **b.** pierce. **50. run up,** *Colloq.* make quickly. —*n.* **1.** act of running: *set out at a run.* **2.** spell or period of causing (a machine, etc.) to operate; amount of anything produced in such a period: *during a run of eight hours the factory produced a run of 100 cars.* **3.** spell of causing something liquid to run or flow, or the amount that runs: *the run of sap from maple trees.* **4.** trip: *the ship reached port after a six weeks' run.* **5.** unit of score in baseball or cricket. **6.** a continuous spell or course; continuous extent: *a run of bad luck.* **7.** succession of performances: *this play has had a two-year run.* **8.** onward movement; progress; course; trend: *the run of events.* **9.** a continuous series or succession of something; succession of demands: *a run on the bank.* **10.** *Music.* a rapid succession of tones. **11.** kind or class: *the com-*

mon *run of mankind.* **12.** freedom to go over or through, or to use: *the guests were given the run of the house.* **13.** number of fish moving together: *a run of salmon.* **14.** stretch or enclosed space for animals: *a chicken run.* **15.** place where stitches have slipped out or become undone: *a run in a stocking.* **16.** flow or rush of water, etc.; small stream. **17.** a run for one's money, **a.** strong competition. **b.** satisfaction for one's efforts. **18. in the long run,** on the whole; in the end. **19. on the run, a.** hurrying. **b.** in retreat or rout. [< pp. of OE *rinnan* run] —**Syn.** *v.* **1.** scamper, scurry, scuttle, sprint, gallop. **2.** hurry, rush, race, speed. **8.** twine.

run·a·bout (run′ə·bout′), *n.* **1.** *Am.* a light automobile or carriage with a single seat. **2.** a small motorboat. **3.** person who runs about from place to place.

run·a·round (run′ə·round′), *n. Am., Slang.* avoidance; evasion.

run·a·way (run′ə·wā′), *n.* person, horse, etc., that runs away. —*adj.* **1.** out of control. **2.** done by runaways. **3.** easily won.

run-down (run′doun′), *adj.* **1.** tired; sick. **2.** falling to pieces; partly ruined. **3.** that has stopped going or working. —*n.* a summary listing: *give me a quick run-down of the important facts in the case.*

rune (rün), *n.* **1.** any letter of an ancient Teutonic alphabet. **2.** mark that looks like a rune and has some mysterious, magic meaning. **3.** verse or sentence that has a magic meaning. [< Scand. *rūn*]

rung¹ (rung), *v.* pp. of **ring²**.

rung² (rung), *n.* **1.** a round rod or bar used as a step of a ladder. **2.** crosspiece set between the legs of a chair or as part of the back or arm of a chair. **3.** spoke of a wheel. **4.** bar of wood having a similar shape and use. [OE *hrung*]

ru·nic (rü′nik), *adj.* **1.** consisting of runes; written in runes; marked with runes. **2.** like a rune.

run·nel (run′əl), **run·let** (-lit), *n.* a small stream or brook. [OE *rynel* < *rinnan* run]

run·ner (run′ər), *n.* **1.** person, animal, or thing that runs; racer. **2.** messenger. **3.** person who runs or works a machine, etc. **4.** something in or on which something else runs or moves. **5.** *Am.* either of the narrow pieces on which a sleigh or sled slides. **6.** *Am.* blade of a skate. **7.** a long, narrow strip: *runners of linen and lace on bureaus.* **8.** smuggler. **9.** a slender stem that takes root along the ground, thus producing new plants. **10.** a raveled place.

Runner of a strawberry plant

run·ner-up (run′ər-up′), *n.* player or team that takes second place in a contest.

run·ning (run′ing), *n.* **1.** act of a person or thing that runs: *running a store, running a race.* **2.** that which runs. **3. be in the running,** have a chance to win. **4. be out of the running,** have no chance to win. —*adj.* **1.** cursive: *a running hand.* **2.** discharging matter: *a running sore.* **3.** flowing. **4.** liquid. **5.** going or carried on continuously: *a running comment.* **6.** current: *the running month.* **7.** repeated continuously: *a running pattern.* **8.** following in succession: *for three nights running.* **9.** prevalent. **10.** moving or proceeding easily or smoothly. **11.** (of a rope, etc.) moving when pulled or hauled. **12.** (of a knot or noose) slipping or sliding easily. **13.** (of plants) creeping or climbing. **14.** that is measured in a straight line. **15.** of the run of a train, bus, etc. **16.** performed with or during a run: *a running leap.* **17.** operating as a machine.

running board, *Am.* a metal piece along the side of some automobiles, near the ground.

running head, a heading printed at the top of each page of a book, etc.

running knot, knot so made as to slide along the rope.

running mate, *Am.* candidate running on the

same ticket with another, but for a subordinate office, as a candidate for Vice-President.

running noose, noose with a running knot.

Run·ny·mede (run′i·mēd), *n.* meadow near London where King John granted the Magna Charta in 1215.

run-off (run′ôf′; -of′), *n.* **1.** something that runs off. **2.** a final, deciding race or contest.

run-of-the-mill (run′əv·t͟hə·mil′), *adj.* without particular merit; ordinary.

runt (runt), *n.* **1.** a stunted animal, person, or plant. **2.** ox or cow of a small breed. [OE *hrunta* (in sword name) < *hrung* RUNG²] —**runt′y,** *adj.*

run·way (run′wā′), *n.* **1.** way, track, groove, trough, or the like, along which something moves, slides, etc. **2.** *Am.* the beaten track of deer or other animals. **3.** an enclosed place for animals to run in. **4.** strip having a hard surface on which planes land and take off.

ru·pee (rü·pē′), *n.* a unit of money of India or Pakistan, worth about 21 cents (1966). [< Hind. *rūpiyah* < Skt. *rūpya* silver]

ru·pi·ah (rü·pē′ə), *n.* the unit of money of Indonesia, worth about 2¼ cents (1966).

rup·ture (rup′chər), *n., v.,* -**tured,** -**tur·ing.** —*n.* **1.** a break; breaking: *the rupture of a blood vessel.* **2.** the sticking out of some tissue or organ of the body through the wall of the cavity that should hold it in; hernia. —*v.* **1.** break; burst; break off. **2.** affect with or suffer hernia. [< L *ruptura* < *rumpere* burst]

ru·ral (rur′əl), *adj.* in, belonging to, or like that of the country. [< L *ruralis* < *rus* country] —**ru′ral·ly,** *adv.* —**Syn.** agrarian, rustic.

ruse (rüz; rüs), *n.* trick; stratagem. [< F, < *ruser* dodge, RUSH¹] —**Syn.** artifice, dodge, wile.

rush¹ (rush), *v.* **1.** move with speed or force: *we rushed along.* **2.** attack with much speed and force: *they rushed the enemy.* **3.** come, go, pass, act, etc., with speed or haste: *tears rush to the eyes.* **4.** send, push, force, etc., with speed or haste: *rush a message.* **5.** *Am. Slang.* keep company with (a girl) constantly. —*n.* **1.** act of rushing: *the rush of the flood.* **2.** busy haste; hurry: *the rush of city life.* **3.** effort of many people to go somewhere or get something: *the Christmas rush.* **4.** eager demand; pressure: *a sudden rush of business.* **5.** attempt to carry the ball through the opposing line in football. **6.** *Am.* scrimmage held as a form of sport between bodies of students. **7.** **rushes,** in motion pictures, the first prints of recent shots projected for cutting, criticism, etc. **8. with a rush,** suddenly; quickly. —*adj.* requiring haste: *a rush order.* [orig., force out of place by violent impact; cf. OE *hrȳsc* a blow] —**rush′er,** *n.* —**rush′ing,** *adj.* —**rush′ing·ly,** *adv.* —**Syn. v. 1.** dash, hurry.

rush² (rush), *n.* **1.** plant with pithy or hollow stems, that grows in wet ground. **2.** stem of such a plant, used for making chair seats, baskets, etc. **3.** something of little or no value. [OE *rysc*]

rush hour, *Am.* time when traffic is heaviest.

rusk (rusk), *n.* **1.** piece of bread or cake toasted in the oven. **2.** a kind of light, soft, sweet biscuit. [< Sp., Pg. *rosca* roll]

Rus·kin (rus′kin), *n.* **John,** 1819–1900, English author, art critic, and social reformer.

Russ (rus), *n., pl.* **Russ,** *adj.* Russian.

Russ., Russian.

rus·set (rus′it), *adj.* yellowish-brown; reddish-brown. —*n.* **1.** yellowish brown; reddish brown. **2.** coarse, russet-colored cloth. The peasants used to wear russet. **3.** kind of apple with a rough brownish skin. [< OF *rousset,* ult. < L *russus* red] —**rus′set·y,** *adj.*

Rus·sia (rush′ə), *n.* **1.** the Soviet Union. **2.** the European part of the Soviet Union, including White Russia, the Ukraine, Georgia, etc., and part of the Russian Soviet Federated Socialist Republic. **3.** a former empire in E Europe and NW Asia ruled by a czar, with its capital at St. Petersburg.

Russia leather, or russia, *n.* a fine, smooth leather, often dark-red, produced by careful tanning and dyeing.

Rus·sian (rush′ən), *adj.* of or pertaining to Russia, its people, or their language. —*n.* **1.** native or inhabitant of Russia, esp. a member of

the dominant Slavic race of Russia. **2.** language of Russia.

Russian Soviet Federated Socialist Republic, the largest republic in the Union of Soviet Socialist Republics, approximately the same size as the former empire of Russia.

Russian thistle, *Am.* a large weed with spiny branches that develops into a tumbleweed.

rust (rust), *n.* **1.** the reddish-brown or orange coating that forms on iron or steel when exposed to air or moisture. **2.** any film or coating on any other metal due to oxidization, etc. **3.** a plant disease that spots leaves and stems. **4.** a reddish brown or orange. —*v.* **1.** become covered with rust. **2.** coat with rust. **3.** have or cause to have the disease rust. —*adj.* reddish-brown or orange. [OE *rūst*] —**rust′less,** *adj.*

rus·tic (rus′tik), *adj.* **1.** belonging to or suitable for the country; rural. **2.** simple; plain: *his rustic speech and ways made him uncomfortable in the city school.* **3.** rough; awkward. **4.** made of branches with the bark still on them. —*n.* a country person. [< L, < *rus* country] —**rus′ti·cal·ly,** *adv.*

rus·ti·cate (rus′tə·kāt), *v.,* -**cat·ed,** -**cat·ing.** **1.** go to or stay in the country. **2.** send to the country. **3.** send (a student) away from a university or college as a punishment. [< L, < *rusticus* RUSTIC] —**rus′ti·ca′tion,** *n.* —**rus′ti·ca′tor,** *n.*

rus·tic·i·ty (rus·tis′ə·ti), *n., pl.* -**ties. 1.** rustic quality, characteristic, or peculiarity. **2.** rural life. **3.** awkwardness; ignorance.

rus·tle (rus′əl), *n., v.,* -**tled,** -**tling.** —*n.* sound that leaves make when moved by the wind; sound like this. —*v.* **1.** make such a sound. **2.** move or stir (something) so that it makes such a sound: *rustle the papers.* **3.** *Am., Slang.* act, do, or get with energy. **4.** *Am., Colloq.* steal (cattle, etc.). [OE *hrūxlian* make noise] —**rus′tling,** *adj.* —**rus′tling·ly,** *adv.*

rus·tler (rus′lər), *n. Am.* **1.** *Slang.* an active, energetic person. **2.** *Colloq.* a cattle thief.

rust·proof (rust′prüf′), *adj.* resisting rust.

rust·y (rus′ti), *adj.,* **rust·i·er, rust·i·est. 1.** covered with rust; rusted: *a rusty knife.* **2.** made by rust. **3.** colored like rust. **4.** faded: *a rusty black.* **5.** damaged by lack of use. **6.** out of practice. —**rust′i·ly,** *adv.* —**rust′i·ness,** *n.*

rut¹ (rut), *n., v.,* **rut·ted, rut·ting.** —*n.* **1.** track made in the ground by wheels. **2.** a fixed or established way of acting. —*v.* make ruts in. [? var. of *route*] —**Syn. n. 1.** furrow, groove.

rut² (rut), *n., v.,* **rut·ted, rut·ting.** —*n.* **1.** sexual excitement of deer, goats, sheep, etc., occurring at regular intervals. **2.** period during which it lasts. —*v.* be in rut. [< OF < L *rugitus* bellowing < *rugire* bellow]

ru·ta·ba·ga (rü′tə·bā′gə; -beg′ə), *n.* kind of large yellow turnip. [< Swed. (dial.) *rotabagge*]

Ruth (rüth), *n.* **1.** *Bible.* the wife of Boaz, famous for her devotion to her mother-in-law, Naomi. **2.** book of the Old Testament that tells about her.

ru·the·ni·um (rü·thē′ni·əm), *n. Chem.* a brittle gray metal, Ru. It is an element similar to platinum. [< NL, < Med.L *Ruthenia* Russia; because discovered in the Urals] —**ru·then·ic** (rü·then′ik; -thē′nik), *adj.* —**ru·the′ni·ous,** *adj.*

ruth·less (rüth′lis), *adj.* having no pity; showing no mercy; cruel. —**ruth′less·ly,** *adv.* —**ruth′less·ness,** *n.* —**Syn.** merciless, pitiless.

rut·ty (rut′i), *adj.,* -**ti·er,** -**ti·est.** full of ruts.

R.V., Revised Version (of the Bible).

Ry., railway.

-ry, *suffix.* **1.** occupation or work of a ——, as in *dentistry, chemistry.* **2.** act of a ——, as in *mimicry.* **3.** quality, state, or condition of a ——, as in *rivalry.* **4.** group of ——s, considered collectively, as in *jewelry, peasantry.* [short form of *-ery*]

rye (rī), *n.* **1.** a hardy annual plant widely grown in cold regions. **2.** its seeds or grain. **3.** flour made from them. **4.** Also, **rye whiskey,** *Am.* whiskey made from rye. [OE *ryge*]

Ryu·kyu Islands (rü′kü′), chain of 55 islands extending from Japan to Taiwan.

S

S, s (es), *n., pl.* **S's; s's,** *adj.* —*n.* **1.** the 19th letter of the alphabet. **2.** anything shaped like an S. —*adj.* shaped like an S.

S, 1. south; southern. **2.** *Chem.* sulfur.

S., 1. *pl.* **SS.** Saint. **2.** Saturday. **3.** September. **4.** South; south. **5.** Southern; southern. **6.** Sunday.

s., 1. second. **2.** shilling; shillings. **3.** singular. **4.** south; southern.

Sa, *Chem.* samarium.

S.A., 1. Salvation Army. **2.** South Africa. **3.** South America. **4.** South Australia.

Saar (sär; *Ger.* zär), *n.* **1.** river flowing from NE France through W Germany. **2.** Also, **Saar Basin,** region in W Germany in its valley.

Sa·bah (sä′bä), *n.* state in Malaysia; formerly called North Borneo.

Sab·bath (sab′əth), *n.* **1.** day of the week used for rest and worship. Sunday is the Christian Sabbath; Saturday is the Jewish Sabbath. **2.** sabbath, period of rest, quiet, etc. —*adj.* of or belonging to the Sabbath. [< L < Gk. < Heb., < *shabath* rest]

Sab·bat·i·cal (sə·bat′ə·kəl), **Sab·bat·ic** (-ik), *adj.* **1.** of or suitable for the Sabbath. **2.** sabbatical, **a.** of or for a rest from work. **b.** *Am.* denoting a time of absence from duty for purposes of study and travel given to teachers: *sabbatical leave.* [< Gk. *sabbatikos.* See SABBATH.] —Sab·bat′i·cal·ly, —sab·bat′i·cal·ly, *adv.*

sa·ber, *esp. Brit.* **sa·bre** (sā′bər), *n., v.,* **-bered, -ber·ing;** *esp. Brit.* **-bred, -bring.** —*n.* a heavy, curved sword with a sharp edge, used by cavalry. —*v.* strike, wound, or kill with a saber. [< F *sabre,* alter. of *sable,* ult. < Hung., < *szabni* cut] —sa′bered, *esp. Brit.* sa′bred, *adj.* —sa′ber·like′, *esp. Brit.* sa′bre·like′, *adj.*

Sa·bine (sā′bīn), *n.* member of a tribe in C Italy which was conquered by the Romans in the third century B.C.

Sable (ab. 1½ ft. long, without the tail)

sa·ble (sā′bəl), *n.* **1.** a small flesh-eating mammal valued for its dark brown, glossy fur. **2.** its fur. —*adj. Poetic.* black; dark. [< OF, ult. < Slavic] —sa′ble·ness, *n.*

sab·ot (sab′ō; *Fr.* sà·bō′), *n.* **1.** shoe hollowed out of a single piece of wood, worn by peasants in France, Belgium, etc. **2.** a coarse leather shoe with a thick wooden sole. [< F]

sab·o·tage (sab′ə·täzh), *n., v.,* **-taged, -tag·ing.** —*n.* **1.** damage done to work, tools, machinery, etc., by workmen as an attack or threat against an employer. **2.** such damage done by civilians of a conquered nation to injure the conquering forces. **3.** damage done by enemy agents or sympathizers in an attempt to slow down a nation's war effort. —*v.* damage or destroy deliberately. [< F, < *saboter* bungle, walk noisily < *sabot* sabot]

sab·o·teur (sab′ə·tér′), *n.* person who practices sabotage. [< F]

sa·bra (sä′brə), *n., pl.* **sa·brot** (sä·brōt′). *Hebrew.* person born in Israel.

sac (sak), *n.* a baglike part in an animal or plant, often one containing liquids, as the sac of a honeybee. [< L *saccus* SACK¹] —sac′like′, *adj.*

SAC, S.A.C., Strategic Air Command.

sac·cha·rin (sak′ə·rin), *n.* a very sweet substance obtained from coal tar, used as a substitute for sugar in some diets, as for diabetes.

sac·cha·rine (sak′ə·rin), *adj.* sugary; very sweet: *a saccharine smile.* —*n.* saccharin. [< Med.L *saccharum* sugar < Gk. *sakcharon*] —sac′cha·rine·ly, —sac′cha·rin′i·ty, *adv.*

sac·er·do·tal (sas′ər·dō′təl), *adj.* of priests or of the priesthood; priestly. [< L, < *sacerdos* priest < *sacer* holy] —sac′er·do′tal·ly, *adv.*

sa·chem (sā′chəm), *n. Am.* chief of an American Indian tribe. [< Algonquian]

sa·chet (sa·shā′; *esp. Brit.* sash′ā), *n.* **1.** a small bag or pad containing perfumed powder. **2.** perfumed powder. [< F, dim. of *sac* sack¹]

sack¹ (sak), *n.* **1.** a large bag made of coarse cloth. **2.** such a bag with what is in it: *two sacks of corn.* **3.** *U.S.* any sack or what is in it: *a sack of candy.* **4.** Also, **sacque,** a loose coat, esp. for women and children. **5.** *Esp. Brit. Slang.* a discharge from employment. —*v.* **1.** put into a sack or sacks. **2.** *Esp. Brit. Slang.* discharge from employment. [< L < Gk. < Heb. *saq*]

sack² (sak), *v.* plunder (a captured city). —*n.* a plundering of a captured city. [< F *sac* < Ital. *sacco*] —sack′er, *n.* —Syn. *v.* pillage, devastate.

sack³ (sak), *n.* sherry or other strong, light-colored wine. [< F (*vin*) *sec* dry (wine) < L *siccus*]

sack·but (sak′but), *n.* a musical wind instrument of the Middle Ages, somewhat like the trombone. [< F *saquebute* < *saquer* pull + *bouter* push]

sack·cloth (sak′klôth′; -kloth′), *n.* **1.** coarse cloth for making sacks. **2.** coarse cloth worn as a sign of mourning or penitence.

sack·ful (sak′fůl), *n., pl.* **-fuls.** enough to fill a sack.

sack·ing (sak′ing), *n.* coarse cloth for making sacks, etc.

sacque (sak), *n.* sack¹, def. 4.

sac·ra·ment (sak′rə·mənt), *n.* **1.** a solemn religious ceremony of the Christian church. Baptism is a sacrament. **2.** Often, **Sacrament.** the Eucharist, or Lord's Supper; the bread alone. **3.** something especially sacred. **4.** sign; token; symbol. **5.** a solemn promise; oath. [< L *sacramentum,* ult. < *sacer* holy] —sac′ra·men·tal (sak′rə·men′təl), *adj.* —sac′ra·men′tal·ly, *adv.*

Sac·ra·men·to (sak′rə·men′tō), *n.* capital of California, in the C part.

sa·cred (sā′krid), *adj.* **1.** belonging to or dedicated to God or a god; holy: *the sacred altar, a sacred building.* **2.** connected with religion; religious: *sacred music, sacred writings.* **3.** worthy of reverence: *the sacred memory of a dead hero.* **4.** dedicated to some person, object, or purpose: *a monument sacred to the memory of a dead hero.* **5.** that must not be violated or disregarded: *sacred oaths, the king's person is sacred.* [orig. pp. of ME *sacren* < *sacre*(*n*) sanctify < L, < *sacer* holy] —sa′cred·ly, *adv.* —sa′cred·ness, *n.*

Sacred College, the cardinals of the Roman Catholic Church collectively. The Sacred College elects and advises the Pope.

sac·ri·fice (sak′rə·fīs), *n., v.,* **-ficed, -fic·ing.** —*n.* **1.** act of offering to a god; the thing offered: *the ancient Hebrews killed animals on the altars as sacrifices to God.* **2.** a giving up one thing for another. **3.** the thing given up or devoted. **4.** loss: *sell a house at a sacrifice.* **5.** Also, **sacrifice hit,** *Am.* bunt or fly in baseball that helps the runner to advance although the batter is put out. —*v.* **1.** give or offer to a god. **2.** permit injury or disadvantage to, for the sake of something else; give up: *a mother will sacrifice her life for her children.* **3.** offer or make a sacrifice. **4.** sell at a loss: *sacrifice a house.* **5.** *Am., Baseball.* help (a runner) to advance by a sacrifice. [< OF < L *sacrificium,* ult. < *sacra* rites + *facere* perform] —sac′ri·fic′er, *n.* —Syn. *n.* **1.** immolation.

sac·ri·fi·cial (sak′rə·fish′əl), *adj.* **1.** having to do with sacrifice. **2.** used in a sacrifice. —sac′ri·fi′cial·ly, *adv.*

sac·ri·lege (sak′rə·lij), *n.* an intentional injury to anything sacred; disrespectful treatment of anyone or anything sacred. [< OF < L *sacrilegium* temple robbery < *sacrum* sacred object + *legere* pick up] —Syn. profanation.

sac·ri·le·gious (sak′rə·lij′əs; –lē′jəs), *adj.* injurious or insulting to sacred persons or things. [< **sac′ri·le′gious·ly**, *adv.* —**sac′ri·le′gious·ness**, *n.* —**Syn.** impious, irreverent.

sac·ris·tan (sak′ris·tən), *n.* person in charge of a sacristy. [< Med.L, ult. < L *sacer* holy. Doublet of SEXTON.]

sac·ris·ty (sak′ris·ti), *n.*, *pl.* –**ties.** place where the sacred vessels, robes, etc., of a church are kept. [< Med.L *sacristia*, ult. < L *sacer* holy]

sac·ro·sanct (sak′rō·sangkt), *adj.* set apart as sacred; consecrated; very holy or sacred. [< L, ult. < *sacer* sacred + *sancire* consecrate] —**sac′ro·sanc′ti·ty, sac′ro·sanct·ness,** *n.*

sa·crum (sā′krəm), *n.*, *pl.* –**cra** (–krə) –**crums.** bone at the lower end of the spine, which is formed by the joining of several vertebrae and which makes the back of the pelvis. [< LL (*os*) *sacrum* sacred (bone); from its being offered as a dainty in sacrifices] —**sa′cral,** *adj.*

sad (sad), *adj.*, **sad·der, sad·dest. 1.** not happy; full of sorrow; grieving: *sad looks.* **2.** causing sorrow; distressing: *a sad disappointment.* **3.** dull in color; dark. **4.** extremely bad: *a sad mess.* **5.** *Dial.* of food, damp and heavy; soggy. [OE *sæd* sated] —**sad′ly,** *adv.* —**sad′ness,** *n.* —**Syn. 1.** melancholy, miserable, dejected, despondent, downcast, disconsolate. **2.** lamentable, deplorable, grievous. —**Ant. 1.** glad, cheerful, happy.

sad·den (sad′ən), *v.* make or become sad. —**Syn.** depress, dishearten, distress.

sad·dle (sad′əl), *n.*, *v.*, –**dled, –dling.** —*n.* **1.** seat for a rider on a horse's back, on a bicycle, etc. **2.** part of a harness that holds the shafts, or to which a checkrein is attached. **3.** thing shaped or placed like a saddle. **4.** ridge between two mountain peaks. **5.** piece of meat consisting of the upper back portion of an animal. **6.** in the **saddle,** in a position of control. —*v.* **1.** put a saddle on. **2.** put as a burden or responsibility on; burden. [OE *sadol*]

sad·dle·bag (sad′əl·bag′), *n.* one of a pair of bags laid over an animal's back behind the saddle.

sad·dle·bow (sad′əl·bō′), *n.* the front part of a saddle, which sticks up.

sad·dler (sad′lər), *n.* person who makes or sells saddles and harness.

sad·dler·y (sad′lər·i), *n.*, *pl.* –**dler·ies. 1.** work or shop of a saddler. **2.** *Am.* saddles, harness, and other equipment for horses.

Sad·du·cee (saj′ə·sē), *n.* one of a Jewish sect, of the time of Christ, that denied the resurrection of the dead. —**Sad′du·ce′an,** *n.*, *adj.* —**Sad′du·cee′ism,** *n.*

sa·dism (sā′diz·əm; sad′iz–), *n.* **1.** perverse cruelty. **2.** cruelty indulged in as a sexual perversion. [< F; from the Count de *Sade,* who wrote of it] —**sa′dist,** *n.*, *adj.* —**sa·dis·tic** (sə·dis′tik; sā–), *adj.* —**sa·dis′ti·cal·ly,** *adv.*

sad sack, *U.S. Slang.* a poor bewildered soldier who blunders his way through the mazes of army life. **2.** any bewildered, blundering person. [from the comic strip by Sgt. George Baker]

sa·fa·ri (sə·fä′ri), *n.*, *pl.* –**ris. 1.** journey or hunting expedition in eastern Africa. **2.** a long trip. [< Ar.]

safe (sāf), *adj.*, **saf·er, saf·est,** *n.* —*adj.* **1.** free from harm or danger: *keep money in a safe place.* **2.** not harmed: *return from war safe and sound.* **3.** out of danger; secure: *we feel safe with the dog in the house.* **4.** put beyond power of doing harm: *a criminal safe in prison.* **5.** careful: *a safe move.* **6.** that can be depended on: *a safe guide.* —*n.* **1.** a steel or iron box for money, jewels, papers, etc. **2.** place made to keep things safe: *a meat safe.* [< OF *sauf* < L *salvus*] —**safe′ly,** *adv.* —**safe′ness,** *n.* —**Syn.** *adj.* **2.** unharmed, unscathed. **5.** trustworthy, reliable.

safe·con·duct (sāf′kon′dukt), *n.* **1.** privilege of passing safely through a region, esp. in time of war. **2.** paper granting this privilege.

safe·guard (sāf′gärd′), *v.* keep safe; guard against hurt or danger; protect: *pure food laws safeguard our health.* —*n.* protection; defense.

safe·keep·ing (sāf′kēp′ing), *n.* protection.

safe·ty (sāf′ti), *n.*, *pl.* –**ties,** *adj.* —*n.* **1.** quality or state of being safe; freedom from harm or danger. **2.** device to prevent injury. —*adj.* giving safety; making harm unlikely.

safety belt, 1. belt attached to the seat of an airplane, automobile, etc. that keeps a person from being thrown forward or upward. **2.** life belt.

safety match, match that will ignite only when rubbed on a specially prepared surface.

safety pin, pin bent back on itself to form a spring and having a guard that covers the point.

safety razor, *Am.* razor having the blade protected to prevent cutting the skin.

safety valve, 1. valve in a steam boiler or the like that opens and lets steam or fluid escape when the pressure becomes too great. **2.** a harmless outlet for anger, nervousness, etc.

saf·fron (saf′rən), *n.* **1.** an orange-yellow coloring matter obtained from a kind of crocus, used to color and flavor food, etc. **2.** an autumn crocus with purple flowers having orange-yellow stigmas. **3.** an orange yellow. —*adj.* orange-yellow. [< F *safran,* ult. < Ar. *za′farān*]

sag (sag), *v.*, **sagged, sag·ging,** *n.* —*v.* **1.** sink under weight or pressure; bend down in the middle: *a sagging board.* **2.** hang down unevenly: *a sagging door.* **3.** become less firm or elastic; droop; sink: *sagging spirits.* **4.** *Am., Colloq.* decline in value. —*n.* **1.** a sagging. **2.** place where anything sags. [cf. Du. *zakken* sink]

sa·ga (sä′gə), *n.* **1.** an old Norse story of heroic deeds. **2.** any story of heroic deeds. [< Scand.]

sa·ga·cious (sə·gā′shəs), *adj.* **1.** wise in a keen, practical way; shrewd. **2.** intelligent. [< L *sagax*] —**sa·ga′cious·ly,** *adv.* —**sa·ga′cious·ness,** *n.* —**Syn. 1.** keen, sharp-witted, astute.

sa·gac·i·ty (sə·gas′ə·ti), *n.*, *pl.* –**ties.** keen, sound judgment; mental acuteness; shrewdness. —**Syn.** insight, acumen, perspicacity.

sag·a·more (sag′ə·môr; –mōr), *n. Am.* in some American Indian tribes, a chief or great man.

sage¹ (sāj), *adj.*, **sag·er, sag·est,** *n.* —*adj.* **1.** wise. **2.** showing wisdom or good judgment: *a sage reply.* —*n.* a profoundly wise man. [< OF, ult. < L *sapere* be wise] —**sage′ly,** *adv.* —**sage′ness,** *n.* —**Syn.** *adj.* **1.** learned. **2.** prudent.

sage² (sāj), *n.* **1.** a plant whose leaves are used as seasoning and in medicine. **2.** its dried leaves. **3.** salvia. **4.** *Am.* sagebrush. [< OF *sauge* < L *salvia.* Doublet of SALVIA.]

SAGE (sāj), *n.* Semi-Automatic Ground Environment, a proposed network of radar installations across the United States, each unit of which will feed data by wire to centralized electronic computers.

sage·brush (sāj′brush′), *n. Am.* a grayish-green shrub, common on the dry plains of the W United States.

sage grouse, *Am.* a very large grouse common on the plains of W North America.

sage hen, *Am.* **1.** sage grouse. **2.** a female sage grouse.

Sag·it·tar·i·us (saj′ə·tār′i·əs), *n.* **1.** a southern constellation that was thought of as arranged in the shape of a centaur drawing a bow. **2.** the ninth sign of the zodiac; the Archer.

sa·go (sā′gō), *n.*, *pl.* –**gos. 1.** a starchy food used in making puddings, etc. **2.** a palm tree (sago palm) from whose pith this starchy food is made. [< Malay *sagu*]

Sa·ha·ra (sə·hãr′ə; –hā′rə), *n.* the great desert in N Africa.

sa·hib (sä′ib), *n.* sir; master. Natives in India used to call a European "sahib" when speaking to or of him. [< Hind. < Ar. *çāhib* lord]

said (sed), *v.* pt. and pp. of **say.** —*adj.* named or mentioned before: *the said witness.*

Sai·gon (sī·gon′), *n.* capital of South Vietnam.

sail (sāl), *n.* **1.** piece of cloth spread to the wind to make a ship move through the water. **2.** sails: *our ship had all sail spread.* **3.** something like a sail, as the arm of a windmill. **4.** ship. **5.** trip on a boat with sails or on any other vessel. **6.** set sail, begin a trip by water. **7.** take in sail, **a.** lower or lessen the sails of a ship. **b.** lessen one's hopes, ambitions, etc. **8.** under sail, with the sails spread out. —*v.* **1.** travel on water by the action of wind on sails. 2. travel on a steamboat, airship, etc. 3. move smoothly like a ship with sails: *the eagle sailed by.* 4. sail upon, over, or through: *sail the seas.* 5. manage a ship or boat: *learn to sail.* 6. manage or navigate (a ship or boat). 7. begin a trip by water: *we sail at 2 p.m.* 8. sail into, *Slang.* a. attack; beat. b. criticize; scold. [OE *segl*] —**sail′ing**, *n.* —**sail′less**, *adj.* —Syn. v. 1. navigate, cruise.

sail·boat (sāl′bōt′), *n.* boat that is moved by a sail or sails.

sail·cloth (sāl′klôth′; -kloth′), *n.* canvas or other material used for making sails.

sail·er (sāl′ər), *n.* a ship with reference to its sailing power: *a fast sailer.*

sail·fish (sāl′fish′), *n., pl.* -fish·es or (*esp. collectively*) -fish. *Am.* a large salt-water fish that has a long, high fin on its back.

sail·or (sāl′ər), *n.* 1. person whose work is sailing. 2. person who works on a ship. 3. member of a ship's crew, not an officer. 4. a flat-brimmed hat modeled after the kind of hat sailors used to wear years ago. —*adj.* like that of a sailor: *a sailor suit.* —**sail′or·ly**, *adj.*

saint (sānt), *n.* 1. a very holy person; true Christian. 2. person who has gone to heaven. 3. person declared a saint by the Roman Catholic Church. 4. in some religious bodies, a designation applied by the members to themselves. 5. person like a saint. —*v.* 1. make a saint of; canonize. 2. call or consider a saint. —*adj.* holy; sacred. [< OF < L *sanctus* consecrated] —**saint′hood, saint′ship,** *n.* —**saint′like′,** *adj.*

Saint. For places beginning with "Saint" look under the St. words.

Saint Ber·nard (bər-närd′), a big, tan-and-white, intelligent dog with a large head.

saint·ed (sān′tid), *adj.* 1. declared to be a saint. 2. thought of as a saint; gone to heaven. 3. sacred; very holy. 4. saintly.

Saint-Gau·dens (sānt-gō′dənz), *n.* Augustus, 1848–1907, American sculptor.

saint·ly (sānt′li), *adj.,* -li·er, -li·est. 1. like a saint; very holy. 2. very good. —**saint′li·ness,** *n.*

Saint Patrick's Day, March 17.

Saint-Saëns (saṅ-säṅs′), *n.* (Charles) Camille, 1835–1921, French composer and pianist.

Saint Val·en·tine's Day (val′ən·tīnz), February 14.

saith (seth), *v. Archaic.* says.

Sai·pan (sī-pän′; -pan′), *n.* one of the Marianas Islands, in the W Pacific; captured by American forces, 1944.

sake[1] (sāk), *n.* 1. cause; account; interest: *for appearances' sake.* 2. purpose; end. 3. for the sake of, a. because of; on account of: *for the sake of appearances.* b. to help; to please. 4. for your own sake, on your own account; to help yourself. [OE *sacu* cause at law]

sa·ke[2] (sä′kē), *n.* a Japanese fermented alcoholic beverage made from rice. [< Jap.]

Sak·ha·lin (sak′ə-lēn; -lin), *n.* a Russian island E of Siberia, between the Sea of Okhotsk and the Sea of Japan.

sal (sal), *n.* salt, used esp. in druggists' terms, such as *sal ammoniac.* [< L]

sa·laam (sə-läm′), *n.* 1. a greeting in the Orient that means "Peace." 2. a very low bow, with the palm of the right hand placed on the forehead. —*v.* 1. greet with a salaam. 2. make a salaam. [< Ar. *salām* peace]

sal·a·ble (sāl′ə-bəl), *adj.* that can be sold; fit to be sold; easily sold. Also, saleable. —**sal′a·bil′i·ty, sal′a·ble·ness,** *n.* —**sal′a·bly,** *adv.* —Syn. marketable, merchantable, purchasable.

sa·la·cious (sə-lā′shəs), *adj.* lustful; lewd; obscene; indecent. [< L *salax*] —**sa·la′cious·ly,** *adv.* —**sa·la′cious·ness, sa·lac·i·ty** (sə-las′ə-ti), *n.* —Syn. lecherous, lascivious.

sal·ad (sal′əd), *n.* 1. raw, green vegetables, such as lettuce, cabbage, and celery, served with a dressing. Often cold meat, fish, eggs, cooked vegetables, or fruits are used along with, or instead of, the raw green vegetables. 2. any green vege-

table that can be eaten raw. [< OF < Pr. *salada,* ult. < L *sal* salt]

salad days, days of youthful inexperience.

sal·a·man·der (sal′ə-man′dər), *n.* 1. any of various lizardlike amphibians with long tails and short limbs. 2. a mythical lizard or reptile supposed to live in fire. [< OF < L < Gk. *salamandra*] —**sal·a·man·drine** (sal′ə-man′drin), *adj.*

Salamander

sa·la·mi (sə-lä′mi), *n.* a kind of sausage. [< Ital., pl. of *salame,* ult. < L *sal* salt]

sal ammoniac, ammonium chloride.

sal·a·ry (sal′ə-ri; sal′ri), *n., pl.* -ries. fixed pay for regular work. [< AF < L *salarium* soldier's allowance for salt < *sal* salt] —**sal′a·ried,** *adj.* —**sal′a·ry·less,** *adj.* —Syn. stipend, wages.

sale (sāl), *n.* 1. act of selling; exchange of goods for money: *no sale yet this morning.* 2. amount sold: *today's sales were larger than yesterday's.* 3. chance to sell; demand; market: *there is almost no sale now for carriages.* 4. a selling at lower prices than usual: *a sale on suits.* 5. auction. 6. for or on sale, to be sold. [OE *sala*]

sale·a·ble (sāl′ə-bəl), *adj.* salable. —**sale′a·bil′i·ty, sale′a·ble·ness,** *n.* —**sale′a·bly,** *adv.*

Sa·lem (sā′ləm), *n.* 1. seaport in NE Massachusetts, settled in 1626. 2. capital of Oregon, in the NW part.

sal·e·ra·tus (sal′ə-rā′təs), *n.* sodium bicarbonate. [< NL *sal aeratus* aerated salt]

sales·girl (sālz′gėrl′), *n. Am.* girl whose work is selling in a store.

sales·la·dy (sālz′lā′di), *n., pl.* -dies. *Am.* saleswoman.

sales·man (sālz′mən), *n., pl.* -men. man whose work is selling.

sales·man·ship (sālz′mən-ship), *n.* 1. work of a salesman. 2. ability at selling.

sales·peo·ple (sālz′pē′pəl), *n.pl. Am.* salespersons.

sales·per·son (sālz′pér′sən), **sales·clerk** (-klėrk′), *n.* person whose work is selling in a store.

sales·room (sālz′rüm′; -rum′), *n. Am.* room where things are sold or shown for sale.

sales tax, tax based on the amount received for articles sold.

sales·wom·an (sālz′wum′ən), *n., pl.* -wom·en. woman whose work is selling in a store.

sal·i·cyl·ic acid (sal′ə-sil′ik), *Chem.* a solid white substance, $C_7H_6O_3$, used as a mild antiseptic and preservative, and as a medicine for rheumatism, gout, etc. Aspirin is a common preparation of salicylic acid.

sa·li·ent (sā′li·ənt; sāl′yənt), *adj.* 1. standing out; easily seen or noticed; prominent; striking: *the salient features in a landscape, the salient points in a speech.* 2. pointing outward; projecting: *a salient angle.* —*n.* 1. a salient angle or part. 2. part of a fort or line of trenches that projects toward the enemy. [< L *saliens* leaping] —**sa′li·ence, sa′li·en·cy,** *n.* —**sa′li·ent·ly,** *adv.* —Syn. adj. 1. noticeable, conspicuous.

sa·line (sā′līn; sā′lin), *adj.* like salt; salty. —*n.* medicine containing a salt. [< L *sal* salt] —**sa·lin·i·ty** (sā·lin′ə·ti), *n.*

sa·li·va (sə-lī′və), *n.* liquid that the salivary glands secrete into the mouth to keep it moist, aid in chewing, and start digestion. [< L]

sal·i·var·y gland (sal′ə-ver′i), any of various glands that empty their secretions into the mouth. The salivary glands of human beings and most other vertebrates are digestive glands that secrete saliva containing enzymes, salts, etc.

sal·i·vate (sal′ə-vāt), *v.,* -vat·ed, -vat·ing. 1. produce a large secretion of saliva in. 2. secrete saliva. —**sal′i·va′tion,** *n.*

Salk (sôlk), *n.* Jonas E., born 1914, American doctor who developed a vaccine (Salk vaccine) effective against some types of infantile paralysis.

sal·low (sal′ō), *adj.* having a sickly, yellowish color or complexion. —*v.* make yellowish. [OE *salu*] —**sal′low·ish,** *adj.* —**sal′low·ness,** *n.*

sal·ly (sal′i), *n., pl.* **–lies,** *v.,* **–lied, –ly·ing.** —*n.* 1. a sudden attack made from a defensive position; sortie. 2. a sudden rushing forth. 3. trip; excursion. 4. a sudden start into activity. 5. outburst. 6. a witty remark. —*v.* 1. go suddenly from a defensive position to attack an enemy. 2. set out briskly. 3. set out on an excursion or trip. [< F *saillie,* ult. < L *salire* to leap]

sal·ma·gun·di (sal′mə·gun′di), *n.* 1. dish of chopped meat, anchovies, eggs, onions, oil, etc. 2. any mixture, medley, or miscellany. [< F *salmigondis,* ult. < Ital. *salami conditi* pickled sausages]

salm·on (sam′ən), *n., pl.* **-ons** or (*esp. collectively*) **-on,** *adj.* —*n.* 1. a large marine and fresh-water fish with silvery scales and yellowish-pink flesh, common in the N Atlantic near the mouths of large rivers which it ascends in order to spawn. 2. a variety of this species confined to lakes (landlocked salmon). 3. any of various fishes of the same family but different genera, which are common in the N Pacific and the rivers flowing into it. 4. a yellowish-pink color. —*adj.* yellowish-pink. [< OF < L *salmo*]

Salmon

salmon trout, *Am.* kind of trout resembling a salmon.

Sa·lo·me (sə·lō′mē), *n.* daughter of Herodias, whose dancing so pleased Herod that he gave her the head of John the Baptist. Matt. 14:3–11.

sa·lon (sə·lon′), *n., pl.* **-lons.** 1. a large room for receiving or entertaining guests. 2. assembly of guests in such a room. 3. place used to exhibit works of art. [< F < Ital. *salone* < *sala* hall]

Sal·o·ni·ka (sal′ə·nē′kə; sə·lon′ə·kə; sal′ə·nī′kə), *n.* seaport in NE Greece.

sa·loon (sə·lün′), *n.* 1. *Am.* place where alcoholic drinks are sold and drunk. 2. a large room for general or public use: *the dining saloon of a ship.* [< F *salon* SALON] —**Syn.** 1. tavern, bar.

sa·loon·keep·er (sə·lün′kēp′ər), *n. Am.* man who keeps a saloon (def. 1).

sal·si·fy (sal′sə·fi), *n.* 1. a root with an oysterlike flavor, eaten as a vegetable. 2. the purpleflowered plant having this root. [< F < Ital. < L *saxifraga.* Doublet of SAXIFRAGE.]

sal soda, sodium carbonate.

salt (sôlt), *n.* 1. a white substance found in the earth and in sea water; sodium chloride. Salt is used to season and preserve food. 2. *Chem.* a compound derived from an acid by replacing the hydrogen wholly or partly by a metal or an electropositive radical. Baking soda is a salt. 3. that which gives liveliness, piquancy, or pungency to anything. 4. saltcellar. 5. *Colloq.* sailor. 6. wit. 7. **salts,** a. medicine that causes movements of the bowels. b. smelling salts. 8. **salt of the earth,** the best people. 9. **with a grain of salt,** with some reservation or allowance. 10. **worth one's salt,** worth one's support, wages, etc. —*adj.* 1. containing salt. 2. tasting like salt. 3. overflowed with or growing in salt water: *saltmarshes.* 4. cured or preserved with salt. 5. sharp or pungent; to the point; lively: *salt speech.* —*v.* 1. mix or sprinkle with salt: *salt an egg.* 2. cure or preserve with salt: *salt meat.* 3. provide with salt: *salt cattle.* 4. make pungent; season: *talk salted with wit.* 5. salt a mine, *Am.* put ore, gold dust, or the like into a mine to create a false impression of value. 6. **salt away** or **down,** a. pack with salt to preserve. b. *Am., Slang.* store away. [OE *sealt*] —**salt′ed,** *adj.* —**salt′er,** *n.* —**salt′ish,** *adj.* —**salt′less,** *adj.*

salt·cel·lar (sôlt′sel′ər), *n.* shaker or dish for holding salt, used on the table.

Salt Lake City, capital of Utah, in the N part.

salt lick, *Am.* place where natural salt is found on the surface of the ground and where animals go to lick it up.

salt·pe·ter, salt·pe·tre (sôlt′pē′tər), *n.* 1. potassium nitrate; niter. 2. kind of fertilizer; sodium nitrate. [< Med.L *sal petrae* salt of rock]

salt·wa·ter (sôlt′wô′tər; -wot′ər), *adj.* 1. consisting of or containing salt water. 2. living in the sea or in water like sea water.

salt·y (sôl′ti), *adj.,* **salt·i·er, salt·i·est.** 1. containing salt; tasting of salt. 2. to the point; witty and a bit improper: *a salty remark.* —**salt′i·ly,** *adv.* —**salt′i·ness,** *n.*

sa·lu·bri·ous (sə·lü′bri·əs), *adj.* healthful. [< L *salubris* < *salus* good health] —**sa·lu′bri·ous·ly,** *adv.* —**sa·lu′bri·ous·ness, sa·lu·bri·ty** (sə·lü′brə·ti), *n.*

sal·u·tar·y (sal′yə·ter′i), *adj.* 1. beneficial: *salutary advice.* 2. good for the health; wholesome: *salutary exercise.* [< L *salutaris* < *salus* good health] —**sal′u·tar′i·ly,** *adv.* —**sal′u·tar′i·ness,** *n.* —**Syn.** 1. profitable, useful.

sal·u·ta·tion (sal′yə·tā′shən), *n.* 1. a greeting; saluting: *a man raises his hat in salutation.* 2. something uttered, written, or done to salute. You begin a letter with a salutation, such as "Dear Sir."

sa·lu·ta·to·ri·an (sə·lü′tə·tô′ri·ən; -tō′-), *n. Am.* in American colleges and schools, student who delivers the salutatory address.

sa·lu·ta·to·ry (sə·lü′tə·tô′ri; -tō′-), *adj., n., pl.* **-ries.** *Am.* —*adj.* expressing greeting; welcoming. —*n.* an opening address welcoming guests at the graduation of a class.

sa·lute (sə·lüt′), *v.,* **-lut·ed, -lut·ing,** *n.* —*v.* 1. honor in a formal manner by raising the hand to the head, by firing guns, or by dipping flags: *salute the flag.* 2. meet with kind words, a bow, a kiss, etc.; greet: *salute one's friends.* 3. make a bow, gesture, or the like to: *he took off his hat to salute her.* 4. come to; meet: *shouts of welcome saluted their ears.* 5. make a salute: *salute properly.* —*n.* 1. act of saluting; sign of welcome, farewell, or honor. 2. position of the hand, gun, etc., in saluting. [< L *salutare* greet < *salus* good health] —**sa·lut′er,** *n.* —**Syn.** *v.* 2. welcome, hail.

Sal·va·dor (sal′və·dôr), *n.* El Salvador. —**Sal·va·do·ran** (sal′və·dô′rən; -dō′-), **Sal·va·do·ri·an** (sal′və·dô′ri·ən; -dō′-), *adj., n.*

sal·vage (sal′vij), *n., v.,* **-vaged, -vag·ing.** —*n.* 1. act of saving a ship or its cargo from wreck, capture, etc. 2. payment for saving it. 3. rescue of property from fire, etc. 4. property salvaged: *the salvage from a shipwreck or a fire.* —*v.* save from fire, shipwreck, etc. [< F, or < Med.L *salvagium,* ult. < L *salvus* safe] —**sal′vag·er,** *n.*

sal·va·tion (sal·vā′shən), *n.* 1. a saving or being saved. 2. person or thing that saves. Christians believe that Christ is the salvation of the world. 3. a saving of the soul; deliverance from sin and from punishment for sin. [< LL, ult. < L *salvus* safe]

Salvation Army, organization to spread religion and help the poor, founded in England in 1865 by William Booth. —**Sal·va′tion·ist,** *n.*

salve¹ (sav; säv), *n., v.,* **salved, salv·ing.** —*n.* 1. a soft, greasy substance put on wounds and sores; healing ointment. 2. something soothing: *kind words are a salve to hurt feelings.* —*v.* 1. put salve on. 2. soothe; smooth over: *he salved his conscience by the thought that his lie harmed no one.* [OE *sealf*] —**Syn.** *n.* 1. unguent.

salve² (salv), *n., v.,* **salved, salv·ing.** save from loss or destruction; salvage. [< SALVAGE]

sal·ver (sal′vər), *n.* tray. [< F < Sp. *salva,* orig., foretasting, ult. < L *salvus* safe]

sal·vi·a (sal′vi·ə), *n.* 1. a garden plant with racemes of bright-red flowers; scarlet sage. 2. any plant of the same family. [< L, prob. < *salvus* healthy; with ref. to its supposed healing properties. Doublet of SAGE².]

sal·vo (sal′vō), *n., pl.* **-vos, -voes.** 1. the discharge of several guns at the same time as a broadside or as a salute. 2. a round of cheers or applause. [< Ital., ult. < L *salve* haill, be in good health!]

sal vo·la·ti·le (sal′ vō·lat′ə·lē), *Latin.* 1. a salt of ammonium, NH₄CO₃. 2. an aromatic solution of this salt used to relieve faintness, headache, etc.

Salz·burg (sôlz′bėrg), *n.* city in W Austria. Annual music festivals are held there.

Sam., Samuel, the name of two books of the Bible.

S. Am., South America; South American.

Sa·mar (sä′mär), *n.* island in the Philippine Islands.

sam·a·ra (sam′ə·rə; sə·mär′ə), *n.* any dry fruit that has a winglike extension and does not split open when ripe. [< L, elm seed]

Sa·mar·i·a (sə·mãr′i·ə), *n.* **1.** district in the N part of ancient Palestine. **2.** the chief city of this district.

Sa·mar·i·tan (sə·mar′ə·tən), *n.* **1.** native or inhabitant of Samaria. **2.** the good Samaritan. —*adj.* of or pertaining to Samaria or its people.

Samara of a maple tree

sa·mar·i·um (sə·mãr′i·əm), *n. Chem.* a rare metal, Sm or Sa, an element of the cerium group.

Sam·ar·kand, Sam·ar·cand (sam′ər·kand′), *n.* city in Uzbek, Soviet Union in Asia, N of Afghanistan.

sam·ba (sam′bə), *n.* an African dance adapted and modified in Brazil.

Sam Browne belt, a military belt having a supporting piece passing over the right shoulder, worn by officers.

same (sām), *adj.* **1.** not another; identical: *we came back the same way we went.* **2.** just alike; not different: *her name and mine are the same.* **3.** unchanged in character, condition, etc.: *he is the same kind old man.* **4.** just spoken of; aforesaid. —*pron.* **1.** the same person or thing. **2.** the same, in the same manner. *Sea* and *see* are pronounced the same. **3.** all the same, notwithstanding; nevertheless. **4.** just the same, a. in the same manner. b. nevertheless. [OE] —*same′ness, n.* —Syn. *adj.* **2.** similar, like, corresponding. —Ant. *adj.* **2.** different, dissimilar, unlike. ➤ Same is used as a pronoun in such expressions as *"The same happened to me once"* and popularly in *"I'll take the same," "more of the same."* In these the reference is to something in the context or situation. *Same* as a pronoun is also characteristic of legal and business use: *"and enclose check for same"* where better style would have *it* or *them* instead of *same.*

sam·ite (sam′īt; sā′mīt), *n.* a heavy, rich silk fabric, sometimes interwoven with gold, worn in the Middle Ages. [< OF < Med.Gk. *hexamiton* < Gk. *hex* six + *mitos* thread]

Sa·mo·a (sə·mō′ə), *n.* group of islands in the S Pacific. Several of these islands (American Samoa) belong to the United States and the rest (Western Samoa) are independent. —Sa·mo′an, *adj., n.*

Sa·mos (sā′mos), *n.* a Greek island off W Turkey in the Aegean Sea. —Sa·mi·an (sā′mi·ən), *adj., n.*

Sam·o·thrace (sam′ə·thrās), *n.* a Greek island off NE Greece in the Aegean Sea.

sam·o·var (sam′ə·vär; sam′ə·vär′), *n.* a metal urn used for heating water for tea. [< Russ., lit., self-boiler]

samp (samp), *n. Am.* **1.** a coarsely ground corn. **2.** porridge made of this. [< Algonquian]

sam·pan (sam′pan), *n.* any of various small boats of China, etc. A sampan is sculled by one or more oars at the stern. [< Chinese < Pg.; orig. uncert.]

Sampan

sam·ple (sam′pəl; säm′-), *n., adj., v.,* -pled, -pling. —*n.* part to show what the rest is like; one thing to show what the others are like: *pushing people aside to get in a car is a sample of his bad manners.* —*adj.* serving as a sample: *a sample copy.* —*v.* take a part of; test a part of: *sample a cake.* [var. of *essample,* var. of *example*] —Syn. *n.* specimen, example.

sam·pler (sam′plər; säm′-), *n.* **1.** person who samples. **2.** piece of cloth embroidered to show skill in needlework.

Sam·son (sam′sən), *n.* **1.** *Bible.* man who had very great strength. **2.** any very strong man.

Sam·u·el (sam′yü·əl), *n.* **1.** a Hebrew leader, judge, and prophet of ancient times. **2.** either of two books in the Old Testament.

sam·u·rai (sam′ü·rī), *n., pl.* -rai. **1.** the military class in feudal Japan. **2.** member of this class. [< Jap.]

San An·to·ni·o (san an·tō′ni·ō), city in S Texas.

san·a·tive (san′ə·tiv), **san·a·to·ry** (san′ə·tō′ri; -tō′-), *adj.* healing; having power to cure. [< LL, ult. < L *sanus* healthy]

san·a·to·ri·um (san′ə·tō′ri·əm; -tō′-), *n., pl.* -to·ri·ums, -to·ri·a (-tō′ri·ə; -tō′-). sanitarium; health resort. [< NL, neut. of LL *sanatorius* health-giving, ult. < L *sanus* healthy]

sanc·ti·fied (sangk′tə·fīd), *adj.* **1.** consecrated. **2.** sanctimonious.

sanc·ti·fy (sangk′tə·fī), *v.,* -fied, -fy·ing. **1.** make holy: *a life of sacrifice had sanctified her.* **2.** set apart as sacred; observe as holy: *"Lord, sanctify this our offering to Thy use."* **3.** make free from sin. **4.** justify; make right. [< L, < *sanctus* holy + *facere* make] —*sanc′ti·fi·ca′tion, n.* —*sanc′ti·fi′er, n.*

sanc·ti·mo·ni·ous (sangk′tə·mō′ni·əs), *adj.* making a show of holiness; putting on airs of sanctity. —*sanc′ti·mo′ni·ous·ly, adv.* —*sanc′ti·mo′ni·ous·ness, n.*

sanc·ti·mo·ny (sangk′tə·mō′ni), *n.* show of holiness; airs of sanctity.

sanc·tion (sangk′shən), *n.* **1.** permission with authority; support; approval: *the sanction of the law.* **2.** ratification; confirmation. **3.** *Law.* provision of a law enacting a penalty for disobedience to it or a reward for obedience. **4.** *International Law.* action by several nations toward another, intended to force it to obey international law, as a blockade, military force, etc. —*v.* **1.** authorize; approve; allow: *her conscience does not sanction stealing.* **2.** ratify; confirm. [< L, < *sancire* ordain] —*sanc′tion·er, n.* —Syn. *n.* **1.** approbation, countenance.

sanc·ti·ty (sangk′tə·ti), *n., pl.* -ties. **1.** holiness; saintliness; godliness. **2.** sacredness; holy character: *the sanctity of a church.* **3.** a sacred thing. [< L, < *sanctus* holy]

sanc·tu·ar·y (sangk′chù·er′i), *n., pl.* -ar·ies. **1.** a sacred place. A church is a sanctuary. **2.** part of a church around the altar. **3.** a sacred place of worship or protection. **4.** any asylum or place of refuge: *a bird sanctuary.* **5.** immunity from the law; refuge; protection. [< L, ult. < *sanctus* holy] —Syn. **1.** church, temple, shrine.

sanc·tum (sangk′təm), *n.* **1.** a sacred place. **2.** a private room or office where a person can be undisturbed. [< L, orig. neut. adj., holy]

sand (sand), *n.* **1.** tiny grains of worn-down or disintegrated rocks. **2.** sands, tract or region composed mainly of sand. **3.** sand in an hourglass. **4.** *Am., Slang.* courage; pluck. —*v.* **1.** sprinkle with sand. **2.** clean, smooth, or polish with sand, sandpaper, etc. [OE]

san·dal (san′dəl), *n., v.,* -daled, -dal·ing; *esp. Brit.* -dalled, -dal·ling. —*n.* **1.** kind of shoe made of a sole fastened to the foot by straps. **2.** kind of cutout slipper. —*v.* furnish with sandals. [< F < L, ult. < Gk. *sandalon*] —*san′daled, esp. Brit.* **san′dalled,** *adj.*

Sandals: A (def. 1); B (def. 2).

san·dal·wood (san′dəl·wùd′), *n.* **1.** a fragrant wood used for making boxes, fans, etc., and burned as incense. **2.** the tree that it comes from.

sand·bag (sand′bag′), *n., v.,* -bagged, -bag·ging. —*n.* **1.** bag filled with sand, used to protect trenches, as a ballast on balloons, etc. **2.** *Am.* a small bag of sand used as a club. —*v.* **1.** furnish with sandbags. **2.** hit or stun with a sandbag. —*sand′bag′ger, n.*

sand·bank (sand′bangk′), *n.* ridge of sand.

sand bar, *Am.* ridge of sand formed by the action of tides or currents.

sand·blast (sand′blast′; -bläst′), *n.* **1.** blast of air or steam containing sand, used to clean, grind, cut, or decorate hard surfaces, such as glass, stone, or metal. 2. apparatus used to apply such a blast. —v. use a sandblast on.

San Di·e·go (san di·ā′gō), seaport in SW California.

sand·man (sand′man′), n. the fabled man said to make children sleepy, by sprinkling sand on their eyes.

sand·pa·per (sand′pā′pər), n. a strong paper with a layer of sand glued on it, used for smoothing, cleaning, or polishing. —v. smooth, clean, or polish with this.

sand·pip·er (sand′pīp′ər), n. a small bird with a long bill, living on sandy shores.

sand·stone (sand′stōn′), n. kind of rock formed mostly of sand.

sand·storm (sand′stôrm′), n. storm of wind that bears along clouds of sand.

Sandpiper
(ab. 7 in. long)

sand·wich (sand′wich), n. two or more slices of bread with meat, jelly, cheese, or some other filling between them. —v. put in (between): *he was sandwiched between two fat women.* [from the Earl of *Sandwich*]

Sandwich Islands, former name of the Hawaiian Islands.

sandwich man, Colloq. man carrying two advertising boards hung from his shoulders, one before him and one behind.

sand·y (san′di), adj., sand·i·er, sand·i·est. 1. containing or consisting of sand; covered with sand. 2. yellowish-red: *sandy hair.* 3. shifting like sand; not stable. —sand′i·ness, n.

sane (sān), adj., san·er, san·est. 1. having a healthy mind; not crazy. 2. having or showing good sense; sensible. [< L *sanus* healthy] —sane′ly, adv. —sane′ness, n. —Syn. 1. sound, rational.

San·for·ize (san′fər·īz), v., -ized, -iz·ing. Am. shrink (cotton or linen cloth) by a patented process before it is tailored. [after *Sanford L. Cluett*, the inventor]

San Fran·cis·co (san frən·sis′kō), a large seaport in W California.

San Francisco Bay, inlet of the Pacific on which San Francisco and Oakland, California, are located.

sang (sang), v. pt. of sing.

sang-froid (sän·frwä′), n. coolness of mind; calmness; composure. [F, lit., cold blood]

san·gui·nar·y (sang′gwə·ner′i), adj. 1. with much blood or bloodshed; bloody: *a sanguinary battle.* 2. delighting in bloodshed; bloodthirsty. [< L *sanguinarius < sanguis* blood] —san′gui·nar·i·ly, adv. —san′gui·nar·i·ness, n.

san·guine (sang′gwin), adj. 1. naturally cheerful and hopeful: *a sanguine disposition.* 2. confident; hopeful: *sanguine of success.* 3. having a healthy red color; ruddy: *a sanguine complexion.* 4. sanguinary. [< L *sanguineus.* See SANGUINARY.] —san′guine·ly, adv. —san′guine·ness, n. —Syn. 1. optimistic.

san·i·tar·i·an (san′ə·tãr′i·ən), n. person familiar with, or engaged in, sanitary work. —adj. sanitary.

san·i·tar·i·um (san′ə·tãr′i·əm), n., pl. -tar·i·ums, -tar·i·a (-tãr′i·ə). 1. establishment, esp. in a good climate, for treatment of the sick or convalescent; sanatorium. 2. health resort. [< L *sanitas* health < *sanus* healthy]

san·i·tar·y (san′ə·ter′i), adj. 1. of or pertaining to health; favorable to health; preventing disease: *sanitary regulations.* 2. free from dirt and filth. [< F *sanitaire*, ult. < L *sanus* healthy] —san′i·tar·i·ly, adv. —san′i·tar·i·ness, n. —Syn. 1. healthful, hygienic.

san·i·ta·tion (san′ə·tā′shən), n. the working out and practical application of sanitary measures.

san·i·ty (san′ə·ti), n. 1. soundness of mind; mental health. 2. soundness of judgment; sensibleness; reasonableness. [< L, < *sanus* healthy]

San Jo·se (san′ hō·zā′), city in W California.

San Jo·sé (san′ hō·zā′; Sp. säng′ hō·sā′), capital of Costa Rica.

San Jose scale, a scale insect very injurious to fruit trees, shrubs, etc. It was brought into the United States from China.

San Juan (san hwän′), seaport in and capital of Puerto Rico, in the NE part.

sank (sangk), v. pt. of sink.

San Ma·ri·no (sän′ mä·rē′nō), an independent republic in the E part of the Italian peninsula.

sans (sanz; Fr. sän), prep. Archaic or French. without. [< F < L *absentia* (abl.) in the absence (of), infl. by L *sine* without]

San Sal·va·dor (san sal′və·dôr), 1. island of the C Bahamas. 2. capital of El Salvador.

sans-cu·lotte (sanz′kyù·lot′), n. 1. in the French Revolution, a contemptuous term for a republican of the poorer class, adopted by the revolutionists as a designation of honor. 2. any extreme republican or revolutionary. [< F, without knee breeches] —sans′-cu·lot′tic, adj. —sans′-cu·lot′tism, n.

San·skrit, San·scrit (san′skrit), n. the ancient literary language of India.

San·ta (san′tə, san′ti for 1; san′tə, sän′tä for 2), n. 1. Am. Santa Claus. 2. a Spanish or an Italian word meaning *saint*, used in combinations.

San·ta Cat·a·li·na (san′tə kat′ə·lē′nə), an island resort off the coast of S California.

San·ta Claus (san′tə klôz′), Am. Saint Nicholas, the saint of Christmas-giving, according to modern conception, a jolly old man with a white beard, clad in a fur-trimmed red costume.

San·ta Fe (san′tə fā′), capital of New Mexico, in the N part.

Santa Fe Trail, Am. an early trade route between Independence, Missouri, and Santa Fe, New Mexico.

San·ti·a·go (san′ti·ä′gō; Sp. sän·tyä′gō), n capital of Chile, in the C part.

San·to Do·min·go (san′tō də·ming′gō), 1. capital of Dominican Republic. Formerly called Ciudad Trujillo. 2. Dominican Republic.

São Pau·lo (soun pou′lù), city in S Brazil.

São Sal·va·dor (soun säl′və·dôr′), Bahia.

sap[1] (sap), n. 1. liquid that circulates through a plant, carrying water, food, etc., as blood does in animals. Rising sap carries water and salt from the roots; sap traveling downward carries sugar, gums, resins, etc. 2. any life-giving liquid. 3. sapwood. 4. Slang. a silly, stupid person; fool. [OE *sæp*] —sap′less, adj.

sap[2] (sap), v., sapped, sap·ping, n. —v. 1. dig under or wear away the foundation of. 2. weaken; use up: *the extreme heat sapped our strength.* 3. dig protected trenches. 4. approach (the enemy's position) by means of such trenches. —n. trench dug to approach the enemy's position. [< F or Ital. < LL *sappa* spade]

sap·head (sap′hed′), n. Colloq. a silly, stupid person; fool. —sap′head·ed, adj.

sa·pi·ent (sā′pi·ənt), adj. wise; sage. [< L *sapiens* being wise] —sa′pi·ence, sa′pi·en·cy, n. —sa′pi·ent·ly, adv.

sap·ling (sap′ling), n. 1. a young tree. 2. a young person.

sap·o·dil·la (sap′ə·dil′ə), n. 1. a large evergreen tree of tropical America that yields chicle and bears large, edible berries that look and taste somewhat like pears. 2. the fruit.

sap·o·na·ceous (sap′ə·nā′shəs), adj. soapy. [< Med.L, < L *sapo* soap] —sap′o·na′ceous·ness, sap·o·nac·i·ty (sap′ə·nas′ə·ti), n.

sa·pon·i·fy (sə·pon′ə·fī), v., -fied, -fy·ing. 1. make (a fat or oil) into soap by treating with an alkali. 2. become soap. [< NL, < L *sapo* soap + *facere* make] —sa·pon′i·fi′a·ble, adj. —sa·pon′i·fi·ca′tion, n. —sa·pon′i·fi′er, n.

sap·per (sap′ər), n. Brit. soldier employed in the construction of trenches, fortifications, field-works, etc. [< SAP[2]]

sap·phire (saf′īr), n. 1. a bright-blue precious stone, that is hard and clear like a diamond. 2. a bright blue. 3. variety of corundum. —adj. bright-blue. [< L < Gk. *sappheiros*]

Sap·pho (saf′ō), *n.* Greek lyric poetess of Lesbos who lived about 600 B.C. —**Sap′phic,** *adj.*

sap·py (sap′l), *adj., -pi·er, -pi·est.* 1. full of sap. 2. vigorous; energetic. 3. *Slang.* silly; foolish. —**sap′pi·ly,** *adv.* —**sap′pi·ness,** *n.*

sap·ro·phyte (sap′rō·fīt), *n.* a vegetable organism that lives on decaying organic matter. Certain fungi are saprophytes. [< Gk. *sapros* rotten + E *-phyte* < Gk. *phyton* plant] —**sap·ro·phyt·ic** (sap′rō·fit′ik), *adj.*

sap·suck·er (sap′suk′ər), *n. Am.* a small American woodpecker that feeds on the sap and sapwood of trees.

sap·wood (sap′wùd′), *n.* the soft, new, living wood between the bark and the hard, inner wood of most trees.

Sapsucker
(ab. 8 in.
long)

Sar·a·cen (sar′ə·sən), *n.* 1. an Arab. 2. a Mohammedan at the time of the Crusades. —*adj.* of or pertaining to the Saracens. —**Sar·a·cen·ic** (sar′ə·sen′ik), **Sar′a·cen′·i·cal,** *adj.*

Sar·ah (sār′ə), *n. Bible.* the wife of Abraham and the mother of Isaac.

Sa·ra·je·vo, Sa·ra·ye·vo (sä′rä·yā′vō), *n.* city in C Yugoslavia; assassination of Austrian archduke, 1914, precipitated World War I.

Sar·a·to·ga Springs (sar′ə·tō′gə), *n.* city and health resort in E New York State.

Sa·ra·wak (sə·rä′wäk; *native* -wä), *n.* former British colony in NW Borneo; now part of Malaysia.

sar·casm (sär′kaz·əm), *n.* 1. a sneering or cutting remark; ironical taunt. 2. act of making fun of a person to hurt his feelings; bitter irony. [< LL < Gk. *sarkasmos* < *sarkezein* sneer, strip off flesh < *sarx* flesh] ▶ Sarcasm is a quality of some statements, a note of bitterness or reproach. The statement may be ironical (that is, to be interpreted differently depending on point of view), or it may be direct. The sarcasm lies in its harshness, an intention to hurt feelings.

sar·cas·tic (sär·kas′tik), *adj.* using sarcasm; sneering; cutting. —**sar·cas′ti·cal·ly,** *adv.* —Syn. ironical, satirical, taunting, caustic.

sar·co·ma (sär·kō′mə), *n., pl.* -mas, -ma·ta (-mə·tə). any of various harmful tumors of connective tissue. [< NL < Gk., ult. < *sarx* flesh] —**sar·co·ma·toid** (sär·kō′mə·toid), **sar·co·ma·tous** (sär·kō′mə·təs; -kom′ə-), *adj.*

sar·coph·a·gus (sär·kof′ə·gəs), *n., pl.* -gi (-jī), -gus·es. a stone coffin, esp. an ornamental one. [< L < Gk., orig., flesh-eating (stone) < *sarx* flesh + *phagein* eat]

sard (särd), *n.* a brownish-red variety of chalcedony, used in jewelry.

sar·dine (sär·dēn′), *n., pl.* -dines or (*esp. collectively*) -dine. kind of small fish preserved in oil for food. [< F < Ital. < L *sardina* < *sarda*]

Sar·din·i·a (sär·din′i·ə), *n.* a large Italian island in the Mediterranean Sea, W of Italy. —**Sar·din′·i·an,** *adj.*

sar·don·ic (sär·don′ik), *adj.* bitter; sarcastic; scornful; mocking: *a fiend's sardonic laugh.* [< F < L < Gk. *Sardonios,* a supposed Sardinian plant that produced hysterical convulsions] —**sar·don′i·cal·ly,** *adv.*

sar·do·nyx (sär′də·niks), *n.* variety of onyx containing layers of chalcedony. [< L < Gk. *sardonyx*]

Sar·gent (sär′jənt), *n.* John Singer, 1856–1925, American portrait painter.

sa·ri (sä′ri), *n., pl.* -ris. a long piece of cotton or silk, the outer garment of Hindu women, worn wound around the body with one end thrown over the head. [< Hind.]

Sark (särk), *n.* one of the Channel Islands.

sa·rong (sə·rông′; -rong′), *n.* a rectangular piece of cloth, usually a brightly colored printed material, worn as a skirt by men and women in the Malay Archipelago, East Indies, etc. [< Malay *sārong*]

sar·sa·pa·ril·la (sas′pə·ril′ə; sär′sə·pə-), *n.* 1. a tropical American plant of the smilax genus, or its root. 2. *Am.* a cooling drink made from

the root. [< Sp. *zarzaparilla* < *zarza* bramble + *parra* vine]

Sar·to (sär′tō), *n.* Andrea del, 1486–1531, Florentine painter.

sar·to·ri·al (sär·tô′ri·əl; -tō′-), *adj.* of tailors or their work. [< L *sartorius* of a tailor, ult. < *sarcire* to patch] —**sar·to′ri·al·ly,** *adv.*

sash[1] (sash), *n.* a long, broad strip of cloth or ribbon, worn as an ornament round the waist or over one shoulder. [ult. < Ar. *shāsh* turban]

sash[2] (sash), *n.* 1. frame for the glass of a window or door. 2. such frames. —*v.* furnish with sashes. [alter. of *chassis,* taken as pl.]

sa·shay (sa·shā′), *v. Am., Colloq.* glide, move, or go about.

Sas·katch·e·wan (sas·kach′ə·won), *n.* province in W Canada.

sas·sa·fras (sas′ə·fras), *n. Am.* 1. a slender American tree that has fragrant, yellow flowers and bluish-black fruit. 2. the aromatic dried bark of its root, used in medicine and to flavor candy, soft drinks, etc. 3. the flavor. [< Sp. *sasafras*]

sas·sy (sas′l), *adj.,* -si·er, -si·est. *U.S. Dial.* saucy.

sat (sat), *v.* pt. and pp. of sit.

Sat., Saturday.

Sa·tan (sā′tən), *n.* the evil spirit; the enemy of goodness; the Devil. [< L < Gk. < Heb. *sātān* adversary] —**sa·tan·ic** (sā·tan′ik; sə-), **sa·tan′·i·cal,** *adj.* —**sa·tan′i·cal·ly,** *adv.*

satch·el (sach′əl), *n.* a small bag for carrying clothes, books, etc.; handbag. [< OF < L *saccellus,* double dim. of *saccus* SACK[1]]

sate[1] (sāt), *v.,* sat·ed, sat·ing. 1. satisfy fully (any appetite or desire). 2. supply with more than enough, so as to disgust or weary. [alter. of *sade* (OE *sadian* glut; cf. SAD) under infl. of L *satiare* SATIATE]

sate[2] (sat; sāt), *v., Archaic,* pt. and pp. of sit.

sa·teen (sa·tēn′), *n.* a cotton cloth made to imitate satin, often used for lining sleeves. [var. of *satin*]

sat·el·lite (sat′ə·līt), *n.* 1. a small planet that revolves around a larger planet. 2. a sphere or other object launched into an orbit around the earth. 3. follower or attendant upon a person of importance. 4. a subservient or obsequious follower. 5. country nominally independent but actually controlled by a more powerful country. [< L *satelles* attendant]

sa·ti·a·ble (sā′shi·ə·bəl; sā′shə·bəl), *adj.* that can be satiated. —**sa′ti·a·bil′i·ty, sa′ti·a·ble·ness,** *n.* —**sa′ti·a·bly,** *adv.*

sa·ti·ate (sā′shi·āt), *v.,* -at·ed, -at·ing. 1. feed fully; satisfy fully. 2. supply with too much; weary or disgust with too much. [< L, < *satis* enough] —**sa′ti·a′tion,** *n.* —Syn. 2. surfeit, glut, cloy, overfeed, stuff.

sa·ti·e·ty (sə·tī′ə·ti), *n.* the feeling of having had too much; satiated condition. [< L *satietas.* See SATIATE.]

sat·in (sat′ən), *n.* a silk or rayon cloth with one very smooth, glossy side. —*adj.* of or like satin; smooth and glossy. [< OF, ult. < VL *seta* silk] —**sat·in′like′,** *adj.* —**sat′in·y,** *adj.*

sat·in·wood (sat′ən·wùd′), *n.* 1. the beautiful smooth wood of an East Indian tree, used to ornament furniture, etc. 2. the tree itself.

sat·ire (sat′īr), *n.* 1. use of sarcasm or irony to attack or ridicule a habit, idea, custom, etc. 2. poem, essay, story, etc., that attacks or ridicules in this way. [< L *satira,* var. of (*lanx*) *satura* full (dish)]

sa·tir·i·cal (sə·tir′ə·kəl), **sa·tir·ic** (-ik), *adj.* of satire; containing satire; fond of using satire. —**sa·tir′i·cal·ly,** *adv.* —**sa·tir′i·cal·ness,** *n.* —Syn. sarcastic, ironical, cutting, caustic, sneering.

sat·i·rist (sat′ə·rist), *n.* writer of satires; person who uses satire.

sat·i·rize (sat′ə·rīz), *v.,* -rized, -riz·ing. attack with satire; criticize with mockery; seek to improve by ridicule. —**sat′i·riz′er,** *n.*

sat·is·fac·tion (sat′is·fak′shən), *n.* 1. fulfillment; satisfying. 2. condition of being satisfied or pleased or contented. 3. anything that makes us feel pleased or contented. 4. payment of debt; discharge of obligation; making up for wrong or injury done. 5. give satisfaction, a. satisfy. b. fight a duel because of an insult. —**Syn.** 1. gratification. 2. contentment, complacency. 4. reparation, atonement, expiation. —**Ant.** 2. discontent, dissatisfaction.

sat·is·fac·to·ry (sat'is·fak'tə·ri; -tri), *adj.* satisfying; good enough to satisfy. —**sat'is·fac'to·ri·ly,** *adv.* —**sat'is·fac'to·ri·ness,** *n.* —**Syn.** gratifying, pleasing, adequate, sufficient.

sat·is·fy (sat'is·fī), *v.,* **-fied, -fy·ing.** 1. give enough to: fulfill (desires, hopes, demands, etc.); put an end to (needs, wants, etc.): *satisfy one's appetite.* 2. fully meet (an objection, doubt, demand, etc.). 3. make contented; please: *are you satisfied now?* 4. give satisfaction. 5. pay (a debt or creditor): *satisfy a bill.* 6. make right (a wrong); make reparation to (a person): *satisfy claims for damage.* 7. set free from doubt; convince: *he was satisfied that it was an accident.* 8. make up for a wrong or injury. [< OF < L, < *satis* enough + *facere* do] —**sat'is·fi'a·ble,** *adj.* —**sat'is·fi'er,** *n.* —**sat'is·fy'ing·ly,** *adv.* —**Syn.** 1. gratify, appease, content. 5. liquidate, discharge. 6. settle, recompense, remunerate.

sa·trap (sā'trap; sat'rap), *n.* 1. ruler, often a tyrant, who is subordinate to a higher ruler. 2. governor of a province under the ancient Persian monarchy. [< L < Gk. *satrapes* < OPers.]

sa·trap·y (sā'trə·pi; sat'rə-), *n., pl.* **-trap·ies.** province or authority of a satrap.

sat·u·ra·ble (sach'ə·rə·bəl), *adj.* that can be saturated. —**sat'u·ra·bil'i·ty,** *n.*

sat·u·rate (sach'ə·rāt), *v.,* **-rat·ed, -rat·ing.** 1. soak thoroughly; fill full: *saturate the moss with water before planting the bulbs in it.* 2. cause (a substance) to unite with the greatest possible amount of another substance. A saturated solution (of sugar, salt, etc.) is one that cannot dissolve any more (sugar, salt, etc.). [< L *saturatus* glutted < *satur* full] —**sat'u·rat'er,** *n.* —**Syn.** 1. steep, drench, imbue.

sat·u·ra·tion (sach'ə·rā'shən), *n.* 1. act or process of saturating. 2. fact of being saturated; saturated condition.

saturation point, 1. point at which a substance will take up no more of another substance. 2. condition in which a person can endure no more.

Sat·ur·day (sat'ər·di; -dā), *n.* the seventh day of the week, following Friday.

Sat·urn (sat'ərn), *n.* 1. *Roman Myth.* the god of agriculture, identified with the Greek Cronus. 2. *Astron.* large planet that has rings around it.

Sat·ur·na·li·a (sat'ər·nā'li·ə; -nāl'yə), *n.pl.* 1. the ancient Roman festival of Saturn, celebrated in December with riotous feasting and unrestrained merrymaking. 2. saturnalia, period of unrestrained revelry and license. —**Sat'ur·na'li·an,** *adj.* **sat'ur·na'li·an,** *adj.*

sat·ur·nine (sat'ər·nīn), *adj.* gloomy; grave; taciturn. [< *Saturn;* those born under the planet's sign are supposed to be morose] —**sat'ur·nine·ly,** *adv.* —**sat'ur·nine·ness, sat·ur·nin·i·ty** (sat'ər·nin'ə·ti), *n.*

sat·yr (sat'ər; sā'tər), *n.* 1. *Gk. Myth.* deity of the woods, part man and part beast. The satyrs were followers of Bacchus, the god of wine. 2. man who is beastly in thought and action. [< L < Gk. *satyros*] —**sa·tyr·ic** (sə·tir'ik), *adj.*

sauce (sôs), *n., v.,* **sauced, sauc·ing.** —*n.* 1. something, usually a liquid, served with food to make it taste better: *tomato sauce.* 2. *Am.* stewed fruit: *applesauce.* 3. something that adds interest or relish. 4. *Colloq.* sauciness. —*v.* 1. season. 2. *Colloq.* be saucy to. [< OF < L *salsa,* fem. adj., salted, ult. < *sal* salt]

sauce·pan (sôs'pan'), *n.* a metal dish with a handle, used for stewing, boiling, etc.

sau·cer (sô'sər), *n.* 1. a shallow dish to set a cup on. 2. something round and shallow like a saucer. [< OF *saucier* sauce dish < *sauce* SAUCE] —**sau'cer·less,** *adj.*

sau·cy (sô'si), *adj.,* **-ci·er, -ci·est.** 1. showing lack of respect; rude. 2. pert; smart: *a saucy hat.* [< SAUCE] —**sau'ci·ly,** *adv.* —**sau'ci·ness,** *n.*

Sa·u·di Arabia (sä·ti'di), country in C Arabia.

sauer·kraut (sour'krout'), *n. Am.* cabbage cut fine, salted, and allowed to ferment. [< G, < *sauer* sour + *kraut* cabbage]

Saul (sôl), *n. Bible.* 1. the first king of Israel. 1 Sam. 9–31. 2. the original name of the apostle Paul. Acts 9:1–31.

saun·ter (sôn'tər; sän'-), *v.* walk along slowly and happily; stroll: *saunter through the park.* —*n.* 1. a leisurely or careless gait. 2. a stroll. —**saun'ter·er,** *n.* —**saun'ter·ing·ly,** *adv.*

sau·ri·an (sô'ri·ən), *adj.* of or belonging to the lizards, or to the lizards and certain other reptiles. —*n.* 1. lizard. 2. any similar reptile, such as a crocodile or dinosaur. [< NL, < Gk. *sauros* lizard]

sau·sage (sô'sij), *n.* chopped pork, beef, or other meats, seasoned and usually stuffed into a thin tube. [< OF < LL *salsicia,* ult. < L *sal* salt]

sau·té (sō·tā'), *adj., n., v.,* **-téed, -té·ing.** —*adj.* cooked or browned in a little fat. —*n.* dish of food cooked in this way. —*v.* fry quickly in a little fat. [< F, pp., jumped]

sau·terne (sō·tėrn'), *n.* a French white wine. [from *Sauterne,* in France, where the grapes are grown]

sav·age (sav'ij), *adj.* 1. wild or rugged, as country or scenery. 2. not civilized; barbarous: *savage customs.* 3. fierce, ferocious, or cruel: *a savage dog.* —*n.* 1. member of a people in the lowest stage of development or cultivation. 2. a fierce, brutal, or cruel person. [< OF *sauvage* < LL *salvaticus,* ult. < L *silva* forest] —**sav'age·ly,** *adv.* —**sav'age·ness,** *n.* —**Syn.** *adj.* 1. uncultivated. 2. uncivilized. 3. brutal, pitiless.

sav·age·ry (sav'ij·ri), *n., pl.* **-ries.** 1. an uncivilized condition: *live in savagery.* 2. fierceness; cruelty; brutality.

sa·van·na, sa·van·nah (sə·van'ə), *n.* a treeless plain. [< earlier Sp. *zavana* < Carib]

Sa·van·nah (sə·van'ə), *n.* seaport in E Georgia.

sa·vant (sə·vänt'; sav'ənt), *n., pl.* **sa·vants.** man of learning or science. [< earlier F ppr. of *savoir* know < L *sapere* be wise]

save[1] (sāv), *v.,* **saved, sav·ing.** 1. make safe from harm, danger, loss, etc.; rescue: *save a drowning man.* 2. keep safe from harm, danger, hurt, loss, etc.; protect: *save one's honor.* 3. lay aside; store up: *save pieces of string.* 4. keep from spending or wasting: *save your strength.* 5. avoid expense or waste: *save in every way you can.* 6. lay up money; add to one's property: *save for a bicycle.* 7. prevent; make less: *save work, save trouble.* 8. treat carefully to lessen wear, weariness, etc.: *large print saves one's eyes.* 9. *Theol.* set free from sin and its results: *Christ came to save the world.* [< OF < LL *salvare* < L *salvus* safe] —**sav'a·ble, sav·e·a·ble,** *adj.* —**sav'er,** *n.* —**Syn.** 1. deliver, redeem. 2. safeguard, shield, preserve.

save[2] (sāv), *prep.* except; but: *work every day save Sundays.* —*conj. Archaic.* unless. [var. of *safe,* in sense of "not being involved"]

sav·ing (sāv'ing), *adj.* 1. that saves. 2. accustomed to save; economical. 3. making a reservation: *a saving clause.* —*n.* 1. act or way of saving money, time, etc.: *it will be a saving to take this short cut.* 2. that which is saved. 3. savings, money saved. —*prep.* 1. save; except. 2. with all due respect to or for: *saving your presence.* —*conj.* with the exception of. —**sav'ing·ly,** *adv.* —**sav'ing·ness,** *n.* —**Syn.** *adj.* 1. redeeming, redemptory, preserving. 2. thrifty, provident, sparing, frugal.

savings bank, bank which pays interest even on small deposits.

sav·ior, *esp. Brit.* **sav·iour** (sāv'yər), *n.* 1. one who saves or rescues. 2. the Saviour, Jesus Christ.

sa·voir-faire (sav'wär·fâr'), *n.* knowledge of just what to do; tact. [< F, lit., knowing how to act]

sa·vor, *esp. Brit.* **sa·vour** (sā′vər), *n.* **1.** taste or smell; flavor: *the soup has a savor of onion.* **2.** a pleasing flavor; interesting quality. **3.** a distinctive quality; noticeable trace. —*v.* **1.** taste or smell (*of*): *a sauce that savors of lemon.* **2.** enjoy the savor of; taste with pleasure. **3.** have the quality or nature (*of*): *a request that savors of a command.* [< OF < L *sapor*] —sa′vor·er, *esp. Brit.* sa′vour·er, *n.* —sa′vor·less, *esp. Brit.* sa′vour·less, *adj.* —sa′vor·ous, *esp. Brit.* sa′vour·ous, *adj.*

sa·vor·y[1], *esp. Brit.* **sa·vour·y** (sā′vər·i), *adj.*, -vor·i·er, -vor·i·est; -vour·i·er, -vour·i·est, *n., pl.* -vor·ies; -vour·ies. —*adj.* **1.** pleasing in taste or smell. **2.** morally pleasing; agreeable. —*n. Brit.* a savory or appetizing dish served at the end of a dinner. [< OF *savoure,* ult. < L *sapor* taste] —sa′vor·i·ly, *esp. Brit.* sa′vour·i·ly, *adv.* —sa′vor·i·ness, *esp. Brit.* sa′vour·i·ness, *n.* —Syn. *adj.* **1.** appetizing, palatable, tasty, toothsome.

sa·vor·y[2] (sā′vər·i), *n., pl.* -vor·ies. any of several fragrant herbs used for seasoning food. [< L *satureia*]

Sa·voy (sə·voi′), *n.* the royal house of Italy from 1861 to 1946.

sa·voy (sə·voi′), *n.* kind of cabbage with wrinkled leaves. [after *Savoy,* a region in France]

Sa·voy·ard (sə·voi′ərd), *n.* actor, producer, or warm admirer of Gilbert and Sullivan's operas, many of which were first produced at the Savoy Theater, London.

sav·vy (sav′i), *v.,* -vied, -vy·ing, *n. Am., Slang.* —*v.* know; understand. —*n.* understanding; intelligence; sense. [partly < F *savez(-vous)?* do you know?, partly < Sp. *sabe* or *sabes* you know; both ult. < L *sapere* be wise]

saw[1] (sô), *n., v.,* sawed, sawed or sawn, sawing. —*n.* tool for cutting, made of a thin blade with sharp teeth on the edge. —*v.* **1.** cut with a saw. **2.** make or form with a saw. **3.** use a saw. **4.** be sawed: *wood that saws easily.* [OE *sagu*] —saw′er, *n.*

saw[2] (sô), *v.* pt. of see[1].

saw[3] (sô), *n.* a wise saying; proverb. "A stitch in time saves nine" is a familiar saw. [OE *sagu;* akin to SAY]

saw·buck (sô′buk′), *n. Am.* **1.** sawhorse. **2.** *Slang.* a ten-dollar bill. [(def. 1) < Du. *zaagbok;* (def. 2) with ref. to the x-shaped ends of a sawyer's sawbuck, X being the Roman numeral for 10]

saw·dust (sô′dust′), *n.* particles of wood made by sawing.

saw·fish (sô′fish′), *n., pl.* -fish·es or (*esp. collectively*) -fish. fish like a shark, with a long, flat snout like a saw.

saw·horse (sô′hôrs′), *n.* frame for holding wood that is being sawed.

saw·mill (sô′mil′), *n.* a building where machines saw timber into planks, boards, etc.

sawn (sôn), *v.* pp. of saw[1].

saw·yer (sô′yər), *n. Am.* man whose work is sawing timber.

sax·horn (saks′hôrn′), *n.* a brass musical instrument like a trumpet, having valves, a loud full tone, and a wide range. [after A. *Sax,* the inventor]

sax·i·frage (sak′sə·frij), *n.* a low, spreading plant with rosettes of thick leaves with silvery, toothed edges, often grown in rock gardens. [< L *saxifraga,* ult. < *saxum* rock + *frangere* break. Doublet of SALSIFY.]

Sax·on (sak′sən), *n.* **1.** member of a German tribe dwelling in NW Germany in ancient times. With the Angles and Jutes, the Saxons conquered Britain in the fifth and sixth centuries A.D. **2.** language of the Saxons. **3.** native of Saxony in modern Germany. —*adj.* pertaining to the early Saxons or their language.

Sax·o·ny (sak′sə·ni), *n.* a former state in E Germany.

sax·o·phone (sak′sə·fōn), *n.* a brass musical instrument with keys for the fingers and a reed mouthpiece. [after A. *Sax,* the inventor] —sax′o·phon′ist, *n.*

say (sā), *v.,* said, say·ing, *n.* —*v.* **1.** speak: *what did you say?* **2.** put into words; express; declare: *say what you think.* **3.** recite; repeat: *say your prayers.* **4.** suppose; take for granted: *you can learn in, say, ten lessons.* **5.** express an opinion: *it is hard to say.* **6.** that is to say, that is; in other words. **7.** to say nothing of, without mentioning. —*n.* **1.** what a person says or has to say: *I have had my say.* **2.** chance to say something. **3.** the say, power; authority: *who has the say in this matter?* [OE *secgan*] —say′a·ble, *adj.* —say′er, *n.* —Syn. *v.* **1.** utter, articulate, enunciate. **2.** announce, tell, assert. ▸ Say is the general word for speaking. Talk implies a continued "saying." State implies a formal "saying" (compare *statement*) and is better kept for this meaning (not *Mr. Owen stated that he was ready if we were*). In labeling the speeches of characters in a story, *said* is the best word to use, since it attracts least attention, unless there is reason for using a more specific word.

say·est (sā′ist), **sayst** (sāst), *v. Archaic.* say. "Thou sayest" means "you say."

say·ing (sā′ing), *n.* **1.** something said; statement. **2.** proverb. **3.** go without saying, be too obvious to need mention. —Syn. **1.** utterance, declaration, assertion. **2.** adage, saw, maxim.

say·so (sā′sō′), *n. Colloq.* **1.** an unsupported statement. **2.** authority; power.

Sb, *Chem.* antimony.

SBA, S.B.A., Small Business Administration.

Sc, *Chem.* scandium.

Sc., Scotch; Scottish.

sc., **1.** scene. **2.** science. **3.** scilicet. **4.** scruple.

S.C., **1.** Signal Corps. **2.** South Carolina.

s.c., small capitals.

scab (skab), *n., v.,* scabbed, scab·bing. —*n.* **1.** crust that forms over a sore during healing. **2.** *Am., Slang.* workman who will not join a labor union or who takes a striker's place. —*v.* **1.** become covered with a scab. **2.** *Am.* act or work as a scab. [< Scand. (Dan.) *skab*]

scab·bard (skab′ərd), *n.* sheath or case for the blade of a sword, etc. [< AF *escaubers,* pl.]

scab·by (skab′i), *adj.,* -bi·er, -bi·est. **1.** covered with scabs. **2.** consisting of scabs. **3.** *Colloq.* low; mean. —scab′bi·ly, *adv.* —scab′bi·ness, *n.*

sca·bies (skā′bēz′, -bi·ēz), *n.* disease of the skin caused by mites that live as parasites under the skin and cause itching. [< L, itch, < *scabere* to scratch] —sca·bi·et·ic (skā′bi·et′ik), *adj.*

sca·brous (skā′brəs), *adj.* **1.** somewhat indelicate, salacious, or risqué. **2.** full of difficulties; harsh. **3.** rough with minute projections. [< LL, < L *scaber* scaly] —sca′brous·ly, *adv.* —sca′brous·ness, *n.*

scad (skad), *n. Am., Slang.* Usually, scads. a large quantity. [< Scand. (Norw.) *skadd;* akin to SHAD]

scaf·fold (skaf′əld), *n.* **1.** a temporary structure for holding workmen and materials during the erection, repair, or decoration of a building. **2.** a raised platform on which criminals are put to death. —*v.* furnish or support with a scaffold. [< var. of OF *eschaffaut,* from same source as *catafalque*]

scaf·fold·ing (skaf′əl·ding), *n.* **1.** scaffold. **2.** materials for scaffolds.

scal·a·wag (skal′ə·wag), *n. Am., Colloq.* a good-for-nothing person; scamp; rascal.

scald[1] (skôld), *v.* **1.** burn with hot liquid or steam. **2.** pour boiling liquid over; use boiling liquid on. **3.** heat or be heated almost to boiling, but not quite. —*n.* **1.** burn caused by hot liquid or steam. **2.** *Am.* a browning of foliage by very hot weather. **3.** any of several parasitic plant diseases. [< dial. OF *escalder* < LL, < L *ex-* very + *calidus* hot]

scald[2] (skôld, skäld), *n.* skald.

scale[1] (skāl), *n., v.,* scaled, scal·ing. —*n.* **1.** one of the thin, flat, hard plates forming the outer covering of some fishes, snakes, and lizards. **2.** a thin layer like a scale: *scales of skin peel* *off after scarlet fever.* **3.** one of the parts that unite to cover a bud in winter. **4.** Also, **scale insect.** insect that has a shieldlike covering under which it hides and feeds. —*v.* **1.** remove scales from. **2.** come off in scales. **3.** remove in thin layers. [< OF *escale* < Gmc.] —**scal′a·ble,** *adj.* —**scale′less,** *adj.* —**scale′like′,** *adj.*

scale² (skāl), *n., v.,* **scaled, scal·ing.** —*n.* **1.** dish or pan of a balance. **2.** Usually, **scales.** a balance; instrument for weighing. **3.** Scales, Libra. **4. turn the scales,** decide. —*v.* **1.** weigh: *he scales 180 pounds.* **2.** weigh in scales; measure; compare. [< Scand. *skāl;* akin to SHALE, SHELL]

scale³ (skāl), *n., v.,* **scaled, scal·ing.** —*n.* **1.** series of steps or degrees; scheme of graded amounts: *a scale of wages ranging from $5 to $15 a day.* **2.** series of marks made along a line at regular distances to use in measuring. A thermometer has a scale. **3.** instrument marked in this way, used for measuring, etc. **4.** size of a plan, map, drawing, or model compared with what it represents: *a map drawn to the scale of one inch for each 100 miles.* **5.** relative size or extent: *entertain on a large scale.* **6.** *Music.* series of tones ascending or descending in pitch. —*v.* **1.** *U.S.* reduce by a certain proportion: *all prices were scaled down 10 per cent.* **2.** make according to a scale. **3.** climb; climb over. [< L *scala* ladder] —**scal′er,** *n.*

sca·lene (skā·lēn′; skā′lēn), *adj.* of a triangle, having three unequal sides. [< LL < Gk. *skalenos,* orig., staggering]

scal·lion (skal′yən), *n.* **1.** kind of onion. **2.** shallot. **3.** leek. [< OF < L *(caepa) Ascalonia* (onion) from Ascalon, in Palestine]

scal·lop (skol′əp; skal′–), *n.* **1.** shellfish somewhat like a clam. In some species the large muscle that opens and closes the shell is edible. **2.** one of the two parts of the shell. **3.** one of a series of curves on an edge of a dress, etc. —*v.* **1.** bake with sauce and bread crumbs in a dish; escallop: *scalloped oysters, scalloped tomatoes.* **2.** make with a series of curves on: *she scallops the edge of the paper.* Also, **scollop.** [< OF *escalope* shell < Gmc.] —**scal′lop·er,** *n.*

Shell of scallop (def. 1)

scalp (skalp), *n.* **1.** skin and hair on the top and back of the head. **2.** part of this skin and hair cut off as a token of victory. —*v. Am.* **1.** cut or tear the scalp from. **2.** buy and sell to make small quick profits. **3.** trade in (tickets to theaters, games, etc.). [< Scand. *skālpr* sheath] —**scalp′er,** *n.*

scal·pel (skal′pəl), *n.* a small, straight knife used by surgeons. [< L *scalpellum,* dim. of *scalprum* knife]

scal·y (skāl′i), *adj.,* **scal·i·er, scal·i·est.** **1.** covered with scales; having scales like a fish. **2.** suggesting scales. —**scal′i·ness,** *n.*

scamp (skamp), *n.* rascal; rogue; worthless person. —*v.* do (work, etc.) in a hasty, careless manner. [< dial. *scamp* roam, prob. < *scamper*] —**scamp′er,** *n.* —**scamp′ish,** *adj.*

scam·per (skam′pər), *v.* run quickly. —*n.* a quick run. [ult. < OF *escamper* run away, ult. < L *ex*– out of + *campus* field]

scan (skan), *v.,* **scanned, scan·ning.** —*v.* **1.** look at closely; examine with care. **2.** *Colloq.* glance at; look over hastily. **3.** mark off (lines of poetry) into feet. *Example:* Sing′ a song′ of six′pence. **4.** be according to the rules for marking off lines of poetry into feet. **5.** *Electronics, Television.* expose bits of a surface in rapid succession to beams of electrons in order to transmit a picture. —*n.* act or fact of scanning. [< LL *scandere* < L, climb] —**scan′ner,** *n.*

Scand., **1.** Scandinavia. **2.** Scandinavian.

scan·dal (skan′dəl), *n.* **1.** a shameful action that brings disgrace or offends public opinion. **2.** damage to reputation; disgrace. **3.** public talk about a person that will hurt his reputation; evil gossip. [< L < Gk. *skandalon* trap. Doublet of SLANDER.] —**Syn. 2.** discredit, disrepute, dishonor. **3.** slander, calumny, defamation.

scan·dal·ize (skan′dəl·īz), *v.,* **-ized, -iz·ing.**

offend by something wrong or improper; shock. —**scan′dal·i·za′tion,** *n.* —**scan′dal·iz′er,** *n.*

scan·dal·mon·ger (skan′dəl·mung′gər; –mong′–), *n.* person who spreads scandal and evil gossip.

scan·dal·ous (skan′dəl·əs), *adj.* **1.** disgraceful to reputation; shameful; shocking. **2.** spreading scandal or slander; slandering. —**scan′dal·ous·ly,** *adv.* —**scan′dal·ous·ness,** *n.* —**Syn. 1.** disreputable, infamous. **2.** slanderous.

Scan·di·na·vi·a (skan′də·nā′vi·ə; –nāv′yə), *n.* **1.** Norway, Sweden, and Denmark. **2.** peninsula on which Norway and Sweden are located.

Scan·di·na·vi·an (skan′də·nā′vi·ən; –nāv′yən), *adj.* of Scandinavia, its people, or their languages. —*n.* **1.** native or inhabitant of Scandinavia. **2.** languages of Scandinavia and Iceland, both modern and historical.

scan·di·um (skan′di·əm), *n. Chem.* a rare metallic element, Sc. [< NL, < L *Scandia* dinavia]

scan·sion (skan′shən), *n.* the marking off of lines of poetry into feet; scanning. [< L *scansio* < *scandere* scan]

scant (skant), *adj.* **1.** not enough in size or quantity: *her coat was short and scant.* **2.** barely enough; barely full; bare. **3.** scant of, having not enough: *scant of breath.* —*v.* make scant; cut down; limit; stint. [< Scand. *skamt,* neut. adj., short] —**scant′ly,** *adv.* —**scant′ness,** *n.*

scant·ling (skant′ling), *n.* **1.** a small beam or piece of timber, often used as an upright piece in the frame of a building. **2.** *Am.* small beams or timbers. [var. of *scantillon* < OF *escantillon.* ult. < LL *cantus* corner < Gk. *kanthos* corner of the eye]

scant·y (skan′ti), *adj.,* **scant·i·er, scant·i·est.** **1.** not enough: *his scanty clothing did not keep out the cold.* **2.** barely enough; meager: *a scanty harvest.* —**scant′i·ly,** *adv.* —**scant′i·ness,** *n.* —**Syn. 1.** scant, inadequate, insufficient.

Sca·pa Flow (skap′ə flō′), a sea area among the Orkney Islands, N of Scotland.

scape·goat (skāp′gōt′), *n.* person or thing made to bear the blame for the mistakes or sins of others. [< *scape,* var. of *escape* + *goat.* The ancient Jewish high priests used to lay the sins of the people upon a goat which was then driven out into the wilderness.]

scape·grace (skāp′grās′), *n.* a reckless, good-for-nothing person; scamp.

scap·u·la (skap′yə·lə), *n., pl.* **-lae** (-lē), **-las.** shoulder blade. [< L]

scap·u·lar (skap′yə·lər), *adj.* of the shoulder or shoulder blade. —*n.* **1.** in the Roman Catholic Church, a loose, sleeveless garment hanging from the shoulders, worn by certain religious orders. **2.** two small pieces of woolen cloth joined by string passed over the shoulders, worn under the ordinary clothing by Roman Catholics as a mark of religious devotion. [< NL < LL, < L *scapula* shoulder]

scar (skär), *n., v.,* **scarred, scar·ring.** —*n.* **1.** mark left by a healed cut, wound, burn, or sore. **2.** any mark like this. —*v.* **1.** mark with a scar. **2.** form a scar; heal. [< OF < L < Gk. *eschara* scab, hearth]

scar·ab (skar′əb), *n.* **1.** beetle, esp. the sacred beetle of the ancient Egyptians. **2.** image of this beetle, much used in ancient Egypt as a charm or ornament. [< F < L *scarabaeus*]

Scarab (def. 2) : A, side; B, top.

scar·a·mouch (skar′ə·mouch′; –müsh′), *n.* **1.** a cowardly braggart. **2.** rascal. [< F < Ital. *scaramuccia.* See SKIRMISH]

scarce (skārs), *adj.,* **scarc·er, scarc·est,** *adv.* —*adj.* **1.** hard to get; rare: *a scarce book.* **2.** not abundant or plentiful: *some commodities are scarce in wartime.* **3. make oneself scarce,** *Colloq.* a. go away. b. stay away. —*adv.* scarcely. [< OF *escars,* ult. < L *ex*– out + *carpere* pluck] —**scarce′ness,** *n.* —**Syn. adj. 2.** scant.

scarce·ly (skārs′li), *adv.* **1.** not quite; barely: *we could scarcely see through the thick fog.* **2.**

decidedly not: *he can scarcely have said that.* **3.** very probably not: *I will scarcely pay that much.* —**Syn. 1.** hardly. ⟩ **scarcely.** In writing there is danger of falling into a concealed double negative when using *scarcely. Scarcely* means "not probably." Consequently in formal and informal English a sentence like *For a while we couldn't scarcely see a thing* should read *For a while we could scarcely see a thing.*

scar·ci·ty (skãr′sə·ti), *n., pl.* **-ties.** too small a supply; lack; rarity. —**Syn.** insufficiency, deficiency, dearth, want, rareness.

scare (skãr), *v.,* **scared, scar·ing,** *n.* —*v.* **1.** frighten. **2.** scare up, *Colloq.* get; raise. —*n.* **1.** fright. **2.** frightened condition. [< Scand. *skirra* < *skjarr* timid] —**scar′er,** *n.* —**scar′ing·ly,** *adv.* —**Syn.** *v.* **1.** terrify, alarm, startle.

scare·crow (skãr′krō′), *n.* **1.** figure of a man dressed in old clothes, set in a field to frighten birds away from crops. **2.** person dressed in ragged clothes. **3.** anything that fools people into being frightened.

scare·head (skãr′hed′), *n. U.S. Colloq.* headline in large print.

scarf[1] (skãrf), *n., pl.* **scarfs,** *esp. Brit.* **scarves. 1.** a long, broad strip of silk, lace, etc., worn about the neck, shoulders, head, or waist. **2.** necktie with hanging ends. **3.** a long strip of cloth, etc., used as a cover for a bureau, table, piano, etc. [prob. < dial. OF *escarpe* < Gmc.]

scarf[2] (skãrf), *n., pl.* **scarfs,** *v.* —*n.* joint in which the ends of beams are cut so that they lap over and join firmly. —*v.* join by a scarf. [< Scand. (Sw.) *skarva*]

Scarfs

scar·i·fy (skãr′ə·fī), *v.,* **-fied, -fy·ing. 1.** make scratches or cuts in the surface of (the skin, etc.). **2.** criticize severely; hurt the feelings of. **3.** loosen (soil) without turning it over. [< LL, < L *scarifare* < Gk., < *skariphos* stylus] —**scar′i·fi·ca′tion,** *n.* —**scar′i·fi′er,** *n.*

scar·la·ti·na (skãr′lə·tē′nə), *n.* **1.** scarlet fever. **2.** a mild form of scarlet fever.

scar·let (skãr′lit), *n.* **1.** a very bright red, much lighter than crimson. **2.** cloth or clothing having this color. —*adj.* very bright red. [< OF *escarlate,* ? ult. < Pers. *saqalāt* rich cloth]

scarlet fever, a very contagious disease characterized by scarlet rash, sore throat, and fever.

scarlet runner, a tall bean vine of tropical America that has showy scarlet flowers, and long pods with large black seeds; kidney bean.

scarlet sage, salvia.

scarlet tanager, *Am.* the common tanager of North America. The male has black wings and tail and a scarlet body.

scarp (skãrp), *n.* **1.** a steep slope. **2.** the inner slope or side of a ditch surrounding a fortification. —*v.* make into a steep slope; slope steeply. [< Ital. *scarpa* < Gmc.]

scarves (skãrvz), *n. Esp. Brit.* pl. of **scarf**[1].

scar·y (skãr′i), *adj.,* **scar·i·er, scar·i·est.** *Colloq.* **1.** causing fright or alarm. **2.** easily frightened.

scat (skat), *v.,* **scat·ted, scat·ting.** *Colloq.* go off in a great hurry.

scathe (skã#), *n., v.,* **scathed, scath·ing.** —*n.* hurt; harm. —*v.* **1.** criticize severely. **2.** *Archaic.* hurt; harm. [< Scand. *skathi* injury]

scathe·less (skã#′lis), *adj.* without harm.

scath·ing (skã#′ing), *adj.* bitterly severe. —**scath′ing·ly,** *adv.*

scat·ter (skat′ər), *v.* **1.** throw here and there; sprinkle: *scatter ashes on the icy sidewalk.* **2.** separate and drive off in different directions: *scatter the mob.* **3.** separate and go in different directions: *the hens scattered.* —*n.* act or fact of scattering. [akin to *shatter*] —**scat′ter·er,** *n.* —**Syn.** *v.* **1.** strew, sow, spread. **2.** disperse.

scat·ter·brain (skat′ər·brān′), *n.* a thoughtless, heedless person. —**scat′ter·brained′,** *adj.*

scaup duck (skôp), widgeon. [var. of *scalp*]

scav·enge (skav′inj), *v.,* **-enged, -eng·ing. 1.** cleanse. **2.** act as scavenger. [< *scavenger*]

scav·en·ger (skav′in·jər), *n.* **1.** person who cleans streets, etc., taking away the dirt and filth. **2.** animal that feeds on decaying matter. [alter. of *scavager,* lit., inspector < *scavage* toll < OF, < *escauwer* inspect < Flemish *scauwen*]

sce·nar·i·o (si·nãr′i·ō; -nä′ri-), *n., pl.* **-nar·i·os.** outline of a motion picture, giving the main facts about the scenes, persons, and acting; outline of any play, opera, etc. [< Ital., ult. < L *scena* SCENE]

sce·nar·ist (si·nãr′ist; -nä′rist), *n.* person who writes scenarios.

scene (sēn), *n.* **1.** time, place, circumstances, etc., of a play or story: *the scene of the novel is laid in Virginia during the Civil War.* **2.** the painted screens, hangings, etc., used in a theater to represent places: *the scene represents a city street.* **3.** part of an act of a play: *the king comes to the castle in Act I, Scene 2.* **4.** a particular incident of a play: *the trial scene in the "Merchant of Venice."* **5.** action, incident, situation, etc., occurring in reality or represented in literature or art: *the scene of one's childhood.* **6.** view; picture: *the boats make a pretty scene.* **7.** show of strong feeling in front of others; exhibition; display: *make a scene.* **8. behind the scenes, a.** out of sight of the audience. **b.** privately; secretly, not publicly. [< L < Gk. *skene,* orig., tent, where actors changed costumes]

scen·er·y (sēn′ər·i; sēn′ri), *n., pl.* **-er·ies. 1.** the painted hangings, fittings, etc., used in a theater to represent places. **2.** the general appearance of a landscape: *mountain scenery.*

sce·nic (sē′nik; sen′ik), *adj.* **1.** of or pertaining to natural scenery; having much fine scenery: *a scenic route.* **2.** of or belonging to the stage of a theater; dramatic; theatrical: *scenic effects.* **3.** representing an action, incident, situation, etc., in art. —**sce′ni·cal·ly,** *adv.*

scent (sent), *n.* **1.** smell: *the scent of roses.* **2.** sense of smell: *bloodhounds have a keen scent.* **3.** smell left in passing: *dogs follow a fox by the scent.* **4.** perfume. **5.** means by which a thing or a person can be traced: *the police are on the scent of the thieves.* —*v.* **1.** smell: *the dog scented a rabbit.* **2.** hunt by using the sense of smell: *the dog scented about for the trail.* **3.** perfume. **4.** fill with odor: *roses scent the air.* **5.** have a suspicion of; be aware of: *I scent trouble.* [< OF *sentir* smell < L *sentire* feel]

scep·ter, *esp. Brit.* **scep·tre** (sep′tər), *n., v.,* **-tered, -ter·ing;** *esp. Brit.* **-tred, -tring.** —*n.* **1.** the rod or staff carried by a ruler as a symbol of royal power or authority. **2.** royal or imperial power or authority. —*v.* furnish with a scepter. [< OF < L < Gk. *skeptron* staff] —**scep′tered,** *esp. Brit.* **scep′tred,** *adj.*

scep·tic (skep′tik), *n., adj.* skeptic.

scep·ti·cal (skep′tə·kəl), *adj.* skeptical.

scep·ti·cism (skep′tə·siz·əm), *n.* skepticism.

sched·ule (skej′ùl), *n., v.,* **-uled, -ul·ing.** —*n.* **1.** a written or printed statement of details; list. A timetable is a schedule of the coming and going of trains. **2.** a classified or tabular statement. —*v.* **1.** make a schedule of; enter in a schedule. **2.** *Am., Colloq.* plan or arrange to be, have, or do something at a definite future date: *schedule the convention for the fall.* [< OF < LL *schedula,* dim. of L *scheda* < Gk. *schede* sheet of papyrus] —**sched′u·lar,** *adj.*

Scheldt (skelt), *n.* river flowing from N France through Belgium into the North Sea.

sche·mat·ic (skē·mat′ik), *adj.* pertaining to or having the nature of a diagram, plan, or scheme; diagrammatic. —**sche·mat′i·cal·ly,** *adv.*

scheme (skēm), *n., v.,* **schemed, schem·ing.** —*n.* **1.** program of action; plan: *a scheme for extracting gold from sea water.* **2.** plan of action to attain some end, often one characterized by self-seeking or intriguing: *a scheme to cheat the government.* **3.** system of connected things, parts, thoughts, etc.: *the color scheme of a room.* —*v.* plan; plot. [< L < Gk. *schema* figure, appearance] —**schem′er,** *n.* —**Syn.** *n.* **1.** design, project. **2.** intrigue, machination, plot.

schem·ing (skēm′ing), *adj.* making tricky

schemes; crafty. —**schem'ing·ly**, adv. —Syn. plotting, intriguing, designing, wily.

Sche·nec·ta·dy (skə·nek'tə·di), n. city in E New York State.

scher·zo (sker'tsō), n., pl. –zos, –zi (–tsi). a light or playful part of a sonata or symphony. [< Ital. < G scherz joke]

Schick test (shik), test to determine susceptibility to or immunity from diphtheria, made by injecting a dilute diphtheria toxin under the skin. [after Dr. B. Schick]

Schil·ler (shil'ər), n. Johann Friedrich von, 1759–1805, German poet and dramatist.

schil·ling (shil'ing), n. unit of money used in Austria, worth about 7 cents (1953). [< G]

schism (siz'əm), n. 1. division because of some difference of opinion about religion. 2. division into hostile groups. [< L < Gk. schisma < schizein to split]

schis·mat·ic (siz·mat'ik), adj. Also, schis·mat'i·cal. 1. causing or likely to cause schism. 2. inclined toward, or guilty of, schism. —n. person who tries to cause a schism or takes part in a schism. —schis·mat'i·cal·ly, adv.

schist (shist), n. kind of crystalline rock that splits easily into layers. [< F < L < Gk. schistos cleft < schizein to split]

schiz·oid (skiz'oid), adj. 1. having schizophrenia. 2. resembling schizophrenia.

schiz·o·phre·ni·a (skiz'ə·frē'ni·ə; –frēn'yə), n. psychosis characterized by dissociation from environment and deterioration of personality. [< NL, < Gk. schizein to split + phren mind] —schiz·o·phren·ic (skiz'ə·fren'ik), adj., n.

Schles·wig-Hol·stein (shles'wig·hōl'stīn), n. a former province in NW Germany.

schnapps, schnaps (shnäps), n. 1. Hollands. 2. any spirituous liquor. [< G]

schnau·zer (shnou'zər), n. a wire-haired German terrier with a long head and heavy eyebrows, mustache, and beard. [< G, lit., snarler < schnauze snout]

schnor·kle, schnor·kel (shnôr'kəl), n. snorkel.

schol·ar (skol'ər), n. 1. a learned person; person having much knowledge. 2. student who is given money by some institution to help him continue his studies. 3. pupil at school; learner. [< LL, < L schola SCHOOL[1]] —Syn. 3. student.

schol·ar·ly (skol'ər·li), adj. 1. of, befitting, or like that of a scholar: scholarly habits. 2. having much knowledge; learned. 3. fond of learning; studious. —schol'ar·li·ness, n.

schol·ar·ship (skol'ər·ship), n. 1. possession of knowledge gained by study; quality of learning and knowledge. 2. grant of money to help a student continue his studies.

scho·las·tic (skə·las'tik), adj. Also, scho·las'ti·cal. 1. of schools, scholars, or education; academic: scholastic achievements. 2. of or like scholasticism. —n. 1. Often, Scholastic. person who favors scholasticism. 2. theologian and philosopher in the Middle Ages. [< L < Gk., ult. < schole school] —scho·las'ti·cal·ly, adv.

scho·las·ti·cism (skə·las'tə·siz·əm), n. 1. system of theological and philosophical teaching dominant in the Middle Ages, based chiefly on the authority of the church fathers and of Aristotle, and characterized by a formal method of discussion. 2. adherence to the teachings of the schools or to traditional doctrines and methods.

scho·li·ast (skō'li·ast), n. an ancient commentator upon the classics. [< LL < LGk. scholiastes] —scho'li·as'tic, adj.

school[1] (skül), n. 1. place for teaching and learning. 2. a regular course of meetings of teachers and pupils for instruction. 3. session of such a course. 4. those who are taught and their teachers. 5. any place, situation, experience, etc., as a source of instruction or training: the school of adversity. 6. those who exhibit in practice the same general methods, principles, tastes, or intellectual bent: the Dutch school of painting, a gentleman of the old school. 7. a particular department or group in a university. 8. room, rooms, building, or group of buildings where a group of teachers and pupils meet. 9. place of

training or discipline. —v. 1. educate in a school; teach. 2. train; discipline: school yourself to control your temper. [< L < Gk. schole, orig., leisure] —school'a·ble, adj. —Syn. n. 1. academy.

school[2] (skül), n. a large group of the same kind of fish or water animals swimming together. [< Du. Cf. SHOAL[2].]

school·book (skül'bŭk'), n. book for study in schools.

school·boy (skül'boi'), n. boy attending school.

school·fel·low (skül'fel'ō), n. companion at school.

school·girl (skül'gėrl'), n. girl attending school.

school·house (skül'hous'), n. a building used as a school.

school·ing (skül'ing), n. 1. instruction in school; education received at school. 2. cost of instruction. 3. the training of a horse and rider.

school·man (skül'mən), n., pl. –men. 1. man engaged in teaching or in managing a school. 2. Often, Schoolman. teacher in a university of the Middle Ages; medieval theologian.

school·mas·ter (skül'mas'tər; –mäs'–), n. man who teaches in or manages a school.

school·mate (skül'māt'), n. companion at school.

school·room (skül'rüm'; –rum'), n. room in which pupils are taught.

school·teach·er (skül'tēch'ər), n. person who teaches in a school.

schoon·er (skün'ər), n. Am. 1. ship with two or more masts and fore-and-aft sails. 2. prairie schooner. 3. Colloq. a large glass for beer. [< scoon, skim, prob. < Scand.]

Scho·pen·hau·er (shō'pən·hou'ər), n. Arthur, 1788–1860, German philosopher.

schot·tische (shot'ish), n. 1. a dance somewhat like the polka. 2. music for it. [< G, lit., Scottish]

Schu·bert (shü'bərt), n. Franz, 1797–1828, Austrian composer.

Schu·mann (shü'män), n. Robert (Alexander), 1810–1856, German composer.

Schu·man plan (shü'mən), plan providing for the pooling of the coal and steel resources of France, Italy, West Germany, Belgium, the Netherlands, and Luxemburg. The coal and steel production is supervised by a joint high authority.

Schuyl·kill (skül'kil), n. river flowing from E Pennsylvania into the Delaware River at Philadelphia.

schwa (shwä), n. an unstressed vowel sound such as a in about or u in circus, represented by the symbol ə; neutral vowel. [< G < Heb. sh'wa]

sci., science; scientific.

sci·at·ic (sī·at'ik), adj. 1. of the hip. 2. affecting the sciatic nerves. [< LL < Gk. ischiadikos < ischion hip joint]

sci·at·i·ca (sī·at'ə·kə), n. pain in a sciatic nerve and its branches; neuralgia of the hips, thighs, and legs. —sci·at'i·cal, adj.

sciatic nerve, a large nerve along the back part of the thigh and leg.

sci·ence (sī'əns), n. 1. knowledge of facts and laws based upon observation and arranged in an orderly system. 2. branch of such knowledge. Biology, chemistry, physics, and astronomy are natural sciences. Economics and sociology are social sciences. Agriculture and engineering are applied sciences. 3. a natural science. 4. skill; technique. 5. Science, Am. Christian Science. [< OF < L scientia knowledge < scire know]

science fiction, a novel or short story based on some actual or fanciful elements of science.

sci·en·tif·ic (sī'ən·tif'ik), adj. 1. trained in or using the facts and laws of science, or some branch of science: a scientific farmer. 2. of or pertaining to science or the sciences; used in science: scientific instruments. 3. based on or conforming to the principles of science: the scientific method. 4. systematic; exact. 5. expert: a scientific boxer. [< LL, < scientia knowledge + facere make] —sci'en·tif'i·cal·ly, adv.

sci·en·tist (sī'ən·tist), *n.* **1.** person who is trained in, or is familiar with, science. **2.** Scientist, *Am.* Christian Scientist.

scil·i·cet (sĭl'ə·set), *adv.* to wit; namely. [< L, < *scire* to know + *licet* it is allowed]

scim·i·tar, scim·i·ter (sĭm'ə·tər), *n.* a short, curved sword used by Turks, Persians, etc. Also, simitar. [< Ital. *scimitarra*]

scin·til·la (sĭn·tĭl'ə), *n.* spark; particle; trace. [< L, spark. Doublet of TINSEL.]

scin·til·late (sĭn'tə·lāt), *v.,* -lat·ed, -lat·ing. sparkle; flash; twinkle: *the snow scintillates in the sun like diamonds.* [< L, < *scintilla* spark] —scin'til·lat'ing, *adj.* —scin'til·la'tion, *n.*

sci·o·lism (sī'ə·lĭz·əm), *n.* superficial knowledge. [< LL *sciolus* knowing little, ult. < *scire* know] —sci'o·list, *n.* —sci'o·lis'tic, *adj.*

sci·on (sī'ən), *n.* **1.** bud or branch cut for grafting. **2.** Also, cion. descendant. [< OF *cion*]

scis·sor (sĭz'ər), *v.* cut with scissors.

scis·sors (sĭz'ərz), *n.pl.* **1.** tool or instrument for cutting that has two sharp blades so fastened that they will work toward each other. **2.** a wrestling hold with the legs. [< OF *cisoires,* pl., < LL *cisorium,* sing., tool for cutting, ult. < L *caedere* cut; confused with L *scissor* cutter]

scle·ro·sis (sklĭ·rō'sĭs), *n., pl.* -ses (-sēz). a hardening of a tissue or part of the body by an increase of connective tissue or the like. [< Med.L < Gk., < *skleros* hard] —scle·ro'sal, *adj.*

scle·rot·ic (sklĭ·rŏt'ĭk), *n.* the hard, white outer membrane of the eye. —*adj.* **1.** of or pertaining to the sclerotic. **2.** of, with, or having sclerosis.

scoff (skŏf; skof), *v.* make fun to show one does not believe something; mock. —*n.* **1.** mocking words or acts. **2.** something ridiculed or mocked. [< Scand. (Dan.) *skuffe* deceive] —scoff'er, *n.*

scoff·law (skŏf'lô'; skof'-), *n. Am.* person who habitually disregards the law, esp. law dealing with operation of motor vehicles.

scold (skōld), *v.* **1.** find fault with; blame with angry words: *scold a naughty boy.* **2.** find fault; talk angrily: *don't scold.* —*n.* person who scolds, esp. a noisy, scolding woman. [prob. < Scand. *skäld* poet, in sense of "lampooner"] —scold'er, *n.* —scold'ing, *adj., n.* —scold'ing·ly, *adv.* —Syn. *v.* **1.** chide, berate, abuse, revile, upbraid, censure.

scol·lop (skŏl'əp), *n., v.* scallop.

sconce (skons), *n.* bracket projecting from a wall, used to hold a candle or other light. [< Med.L *sconsa,* ult. < L *abscondere* hide]

scone (skōn; skon), *n.* a thick, flat, round cake cooked on a griddle; a similar cake baked in an oven. Some scones taste much like bread; some are like buns. [prob. < MDu. *schoon(brot)* fine (bread)]

Sconce

scoop (skŭp), *n.* **1.** tool like a shovel. **2.** part of a dredge, steam shovel, etc., that holds coal, sand, etc. **3.** a large ladle. **4.** a kitchen utensil to take out flour, sugar, etc. **5.** amount taken up at one time by a scoop. **6.** act of taking up. **7.** place hollowed out. **8.** *Am., Slang.* a. the publishing of a piece of news before a rival newspaper does. b. the piece of news. —*v.* **1.** take up or out with a scoop, or as a scoop does. **2.** hollow out; dig out; make by scooping. **3.** *Am., Slang.* publish a piece of news before (a rival newspaper). [partly < MDu. *schoepe* bucket, partly < MDu. *schoppe* shovel]

scoop·ful (skŭp'fûl), *n., pl.* -fuls. enough to fill a scoop.

scoot (sküt), *Colloq.* —*v.* go quickly; dart. —*n.* act of scooting. [prob. < Scand.; akin to SHOOT]

scoot·er (sküt'ər), *n.* **1.** a vehicle consisting of two wheels, one in front of the other, and a footboard between, steered by a handle bar and propelled by pushing against the ground with one foot. **2.** a similar vehicle run by a motor.

scope (skōp), *n.* **1.** distance the mind can reach; extent of view: *very hard words are not within the scope of a child's understanding.* **2.** space; opportunity: *football gives scope for courage*

and quick thinking. [< Ital., ult. < Gk. *skopos* aim, object] —Syn. **1.** range, compass. **2.** room.

sco·pol·a·mine (skō·pŏl'ə·mēn), *n.* drug, C17H21NO4, used as a depressant and to produce twilight sleep. [< NL *Scopola,* a genus of plants (named after G. A. *Scopoli,* naturalist) + E *amine*]

scor·bu·tic (skôr·bū'tĭk), **scor·bu·ti·cal** (-tə·kəl), *adj.* **1.** pertaining to or of the nature of scurvy. **2.** affected with scurvy. [< NL, < *scorbutus* scurvy < F *scorbut* < Gmc.]

scorch (skôrch), *v.* **1.** burn slightly; burn on the outside: *scorch a shirt in ironing it.* **2.** dry up; wither: *grass scorched by the sun.* **3.** damage as if by heat. **4.** criticize with burning words. —*n.* a slight burn. —scorch'ing, *adj.*

scorched earth, **1.** destruction by government orders of all things useful to an invading army. **2.** of or pertaining to such destruction.

scorch·er (skôr'chər), *n.* **1.** person or thing that scorches. **2.** *Colloq.* a very hot day. **3.** *Colloq.* person who rides very fast.

score (skōr; skôr), *n., v.,* scored, scor·ing. —*n.* **1.** record of points made in a game, contest, test, etc.: *the score was 9 to 2 in our favor.* **2.** amount owed; debt; account. **3.** reason; ground: *don't worry on that score.* **4.** a written or printed piece of music arranged for different instruments or voices: *the score of a musical comedy.* **5.** a group or set of twenty; twenty: *a score or more were present.* **6.** scores, a great number: *scores died in the epidemic.* **7.** pay off or settle a score, get even for an injury or wrong. —*v.* **1.** make, as points in a game, contest, test, etc. **2.** make points; succeed. **3.** keep a record of (the number of points in a game, contest, etc.). **4.** gain or win as an addition to the score: *he scored five runs for our team.* **5.** gain or win: *score a success.* **6.** keep a record of, as an amount owed; mark; set down. **7.** arrange (a piece of music) for different instruments or voices. **8.** cut; scratch; mark; line. **9.** *Am., Colloq.* blame or scold severely. [< Scand. *skor* notch] —scor'er, *n.*

scorn (skôrn), *v.* **1.** look down upon; think of as mean or low; despise: *scorn a traitor.* **2.** reject or refuse as low or wrong: *the judge scorned to take a bribe.* —*n.* **1.** a feeling that a person, animal, or act is mean or low; contempt. **2.** person, animal, or thing that is scorned or despised. [< OF *escarn* < Gmc.] —scorn'er, *n.* —Syn. *v.* **1.** disdain, spurn. —*n.* **1.** disdain.

scorn·ful (skôrn'fəl), *adj.* showing contempt; mocking; full of scorn. —scorn'ful·ly, *adv.* —scorn'ful·ness, *n.* —Syn. contemptuous, disdainful, derisive.

Scor·pi·o (skôr'pĭ·ō), *n.* **1.** a southern constellation that was thought of as arranged in the shape of a scorpion. **2.** the eighth sign of the zodiac; the Scorpion.

scor·pi·on (skôr'pĭ·ən), *n.* **1.** a small animal belonging to the same group as the spider and having a poisonous sting in its tail. **2.** a whip or scourge. **3.** Scorpion, Scorpio. [< L, ult. < Gk. *skorpios*]

Scorpion (1 to 8 in. long)

Scot (skot), *n.* native or inhabitant of Scotland.

scot (skot), *n.* one's share of a payment; payment; tax. [< Scand. *skot*]

Scot., **1.** Scotch; Scottish. **2.** Scotland.

Scotch (skoch), *adj.* Scottish. —*n.* **1.** the people of Scotland. **2.** Scottish (def. 2). **3.** whiskey made in Scotland.

scotch (skoch), *v.* **1.** stamp on; make harmless: *scotch a snake without killing it.* **2.** cut or gash.

Scotch-Gael·ic (skoch'gāl'ĭk), *n.* the Celtic language of the Scottish Highlanders; Erse.

Scotch·man (skoch'mən), **Scots·man** (skots'-), *n., pl.* -men. native or inhabitant of Scotland.

Scotch terrier, kind of short-legged terrier with rough, wiry hair and pointed ears.

scot-free (skot'frē'), *adj.* free from injury, punishment, etc.; unharmed.

Sco·tia (skō'shə), n. Poetic. Scotland.

Scot·land (skot'lənd), n. division of Great Britain N of England.

Scotland Yard, 1. headquarters of the London police. 2. the London police, esp. the department that does detective work.

Scots (skots), adj. 1. Scottish. 2. in the older Scottish currency. —n. people of Scotland.

Scott (skot), n. Sir Walter, 1771–1832, Scottish novelist and poet.

Scot·ti·cism (skot'ə·siz·əm), n. way of speaking peculiar to the Scottish dialect.

Scot·tish (skot'ish), adj. of or pertaining to Scotland, its people, or their language. —n. 1. Scotch (def. 1). 2. dialect of English spoken by the people of Scotland.

scoun·drel (skoun'drəl), n. person without honor or good principles; villain; rascal. —scoun'drel·ly, adj.

scour¹ (skour), v. 1. clean or polish by vigorous rubbing. 2. remove dirt and grease from (anything) by rubbing. 3. make clear by flowing through or over: the stream had scoured a channel. 4. clean; cleanse. —n. act of scouring. [prob. < MDu. < OF escurer, ult. < L ex- completely + cura care] —scour'er, n.

scour² (skour), v. 1. move quickly over. 2. go swiftly in search or pursuit. [prob. < OF escourre run forth, ult. < L ex- out + currere run]

scourge (skėrj), n., v., scourged, scourg·ing. —n. 1. a whip. 2. any means of punishment. 3. some thing or person that causes great trouble or misfortune. —v. 1. whip; punish. 2. trouble very much; afflict. [< OF escorge, ult. < L ex- out + corium a hide] —scourg'er, n.

scout¹ (skout), n. 1. a trained observer who reconnoiters a region to get information about the enemy. 2. airplane, ship, etc., used to reconnoiter enemy positions and territory. 3. one who acts as a scout. 4. person belonging to the Boy Scouts or Girl Scouts. 5. Slang. fellow; person: he's a good scout. —v. 1. act as a scout; hunt around to find something: go out and scout for wood. 2. observe or examine to get information. [< OF < escouter listen < L auscultare] —scout'er, n. —scout'ing·ly, adv.

scout² (skout), v. 1. refuse to believe in; reject with scorn. 2. scoff. [< Scand. skúta taunt] —scout'er, n.

scout·mas·ter (skout'mas'tər; -mäs'-), n. man in charge of a troop or band of Boy Scouts.

scow (skou), n. Am. a large, flat-bottomed boat used to carry freight, sand, etc. [< Du. schouw]

scowl (skoul), v. 1. look angry or sullen by lowering the eyebrows; frown. 2. express with a scowl. —n. an angry, sullen look; frown. [< Scand. (Dan.) skule] —scowl'er, n. —scowl'ing, adj. —scowl'ing·ly, adv.

Scowl

scrab·ble (skrab'əl), v., -bled, -bling, n. —v. 1. scratch or scrape about with hands, claws, etc. 2. scramble. 3. scrawl; scribble. —n. a scraping; scramble; scrawl. [< Du. schrabbelen, frequentative of schrabben scratch]

scrag (skrag), n., v., scragged, scrag·ging. —n. 1. a lean, skinny person or animal. 2. a lean, bony part. 3. Slang. neck. —v. Slang. wring the neck of; hang.

scrag·gly (skrag'li), adj., -gli·er, -gli·est. rough; irregular; ragged.

scrag·gy (skrag'i), adj., -gi·er, -gi·est. 1. lean; thin. 2. scraggly. —scrag'gi·ness, n.

scram (skram), v., scrammed, scram·ming. Am., Slang. go at once. [short for scramble]

scram·ble (skram'bəl), v., -bled, -bling, n. —v. 1. make one's way by climbing, crawling, etc.: scramble up a rocky hill. 2. struggle with others for something: scramble for the ball. 3. mix together in a confused way. 4. Am. cook (eggs) with the whites and yolks mixed together. —n. 1. a climb or walk over rough ground. 2. struggle to possess: the scramble for wealth. [var. of scrabble] —scram'bler, n. —scram'bling·ly, adv.

Scran·ton (skran'tən), n. city in NE Pennsylvania.

scrap¹ (skrap), n., v., scrapped, scrap·ping. —n. 1. a small piece; little bit; small part left over. 2. bit of something written or printed. 3. scraps, old metal fit only to be melted and made again. —v. 1. make into scraps; break up. 2. throw aside as useless or worn out. [< Scand. skrap]

scrap² (skrap), n., v., scrapped, scrap·ping. Slang. fight; quarrel; struggle. [var. of scrape] —scrap'per, n.

scrap·book (skrap'bůk'), n. book in which pictures or clippings are pasted and kept.

scrape (skrāp), v., scraped, scrap·ing, n. —v. 1. rub with something sharp or rough; make smooth or clean thus: scrape your muddy shoes with this old knife. 2. remove by rubbing with something sharp or rough: the man scraped some paint off the table. 3. rub with a harsh sound; rub harshly: the branch of the tree scraped against the window. 4. collect by scraping or with difficulty: scrape together enough money for one year at college. 5. manage with difficulty: that family can just scrape along. 6. bow with a drawing back of the foot. —n. 1. act of scraping. 2. a scraped place. 3. a harsh, grating sound. 4. position hard to get out of; difficulty. [< Scand. skrapa] —scrap'er, n.

scrap iron, broken or waste pieces of old iron.

scrap·ple (skrap'əl), n. Am. scraps of pork boiled with corn meal, made into cakes, sliced, and fried. [< scrap¹]

scrap·py¹ (skrap'i), adj., -pi·er, -pi·est. made up of odds and ends; fragmentary; disconnected. —scrap'pi·ly, adv. —scrap'pi·ness, n.

scrap·py² (skrap'i), adj., -pi·er, -pi·est. Slang. fond of fighting. —scrap'pi·ly, adv. —scrap'pi·ness, n.

scratch (skrach), v. 1. break, mark, or cut slightly with something sharp or rough: don't scratch the paint. 2. tear or dig with the nails or claws: the cat scratched him. 3. rub or scrape to relieve itching, to give sensory pleasure, or from force of habit; rub some part of one's body in this way: he scratched his head. 4. rub with a harsh noise; rub: this pen scratches. 5. write in a hurry or carelessly. 6. scrape out; strike out; draw a line through. 7. withdraw (a horse, etc.) from a race or contest. 8. make a living by hard work and economy. —n. 1. mark made by scratching: there are scratches on this new desk. 2. a very slight cut. 3. sound of scratching: the scratch of a pen. 4. any act of scratching. 5. the starting place of a race; starting place, time, or status of a competitor who has neither allowance nor penalty. 6. from scratch, from nothing. 7. up to scratch, up to standard. —adj. collected or prepared hastily, and often of poor quality. [alter. of earlier scrat, infl. by obs. cratch; ult. orig. uncert.] —scratch'er, n.

scratch hit, hit in baseball that the batter is credited with because of some circumstance, although it would ordinarily have been useless.

scratch pad, pad of paper for hurried writing.

scratch·y (skrach'i), adj., scratch·i·er, scratch·i·est. 1. that scratches, scrapes, or grates. 2. consisting of mere scratches. —scratch'i·ly, adv. —scratch'i·ness, n.

scrawl (skrôl), v. write or draw poorly or carelessly. —n. poor, careless handwriting. —scrawl'er, n. —scrawl'y, adj.

scraw·ny (skrô'ni), adj., -ni·er, -ni·est. Am., Colloq. lean; thin; skinny. [< Scand. (dial. Norw.) skran] —scraw'ni·ness, n. Am.

scream (skrēm), v. 1. make a loud, sharp, piercing cry. People scream in fright, in anger, and in sudden pain. 2. utter loudly. 3. laugh loudly. —n. 1. a loud, sharp, piercing cry. 2. something extremely funny. [< Scand. skrœma scare] —scream'er, n. —scream'ing, adj.

screech (skrēch), v. make a loud, piercing cry. —n. a loud, piercing cry. [earlier scritch, imit.] —screech'er, n. —screech'y, adj.

screech owl, 1. any of various small owls having hornlike tufts of feathers. 2. owl that screeches, as distinguished from one that hoots.

screed (skrēd), *n.* a long speech or writing. [< var. of OE *screade* shred]

screen (skrēn), *n.* **1.** a covered frame that hides, protects, or separates. **2.** wire woven together with small openings in between: *put the screens on the windows.* **3.** an ornamental partition. **4.** anything like a screen. **5.** surface on which motion pictures, etc., are shown. **6.** the screen, motion pictures; films. **7.** sieve for sifting sand, gravel, coal, seed, etc. **8.** *Physics.* barrier against some special form of energy. —*v.* **1.** shelter, protect, or hide with, or as with, a screen: *screen one's face from the fire with a fan, the mother tried to screen her guilty son.* **2.** show (a motion picture) on a screen. **3.** photograph with a motion-picture camera. **4.** adapt (a story, etc.) for reproduction as a motion picture. **5.** be suitable for reproducing on a motion-picture screen. **6.** sift (sand, gravel, coal, etc.) with a sieve. [< OF *escren* < Gmc.] —**screen′-a·ble,** *adj.* —**screen′er,** *n.* —Syn. *n.* **1.** shield, protection, fender. —*v.* **1.** shield, defend, cover, conceal.

screw (skrü), *n.* **1.** kind of nail, with a ridge twisted evenly round its length: *turn the screw to the right to tighten it.* **2.** cylinder with a ridge winding round it. **3.** part into which this cylinder fits and advances. **4.** propeller of a boat or any other thing that turns like a screw or looks like one. **5.** a turn of a screw. **6.** a screwing motion. **7.** a former instrument of torture for compressing the thumbs. **8.** a very stingy person; miser. **9. put the screws on,** use pressure or force to get something. —*v.* **1.** turn as one turns a screw; twist: *screw the lid on the jar.* **2.** turn like a screw; be fitted for being put together or taken apart by a screw or screws. **3.** wind; twist. **4.** fasten or tighten with a screw or screws. **5.** force, press, or stretch tight by using a screw or screws. **6.** force to do something; force (prices) down; force (people) to tell or to give up; force people to tell or give up something. **7.** distort. **8.** gather for an effort: *screw up one's courage.* [< OF *escroue* nut]

Wood screws (def. 1)

screw·ball (skrü′bôl′), *n. Slang.* an eccentric person.

screw·driv·er (skrü′drīv′ər), **screw driver,** *n.* tool for putting in or taking out screws by turning them.

screw propeller, a revolving hub with radiating blades for propelling a ship, aircraft, etc.

scrib·ble (skrib′əl), *v.,* –bled, –bling, *n.* —*v.* **1.** write or draw carelessly or hastily: *scribble a note.* **2.** make marks that do not mean anything. —*n.* something scribbled. [< Med.L *scribillare,* ult. < L *scribere* write] —**scrib′bler,** *n.*

scribe (skrīb), *n.* **1.** person whose occupation is writing. Before printing was invented, there were many scribes. **2.** teacher of the Jewish law. **3.** writer; author. [< L *scriba* < *scribere* write] —**scrib′al,** *adj.*

scrim (skrim), *n.* a loosely woven cotton or linen material, much used for window curtains.

scrim·mage (skrim′ij), *n., v.,* –maged, –maging. —*n.* **1.** a rough fight or struggle. **2.** play in football that takes place when the two teams are lined up and the ball is snapped back. —*v.* **1.** take part in a rough fight or struggle. **2.** in football, take part in a scrimmage. Also, *esp. Brit.* **scrummage.** [ult. var. of *skirmish*]

scrimp (skrimp), *v.* **1.** be sparing of; use too little of. **2.** be very economical; stint; skimp: *many parents have to scrimp to keep their children in school.* **3.** treat stingily or very economically.

scrimp·y (skrimp′i), *adj.,* scrimp·i·er, scrimp-i·est. scanty; meager. —**scrimp′i·ly,** *adv.*

scrip (skrip), *n.* **1.** a writing. **2.** receipt, certificate, or other document showing a right to something, esp. a certificate entitling the holder to a fraction of a share of stock. **3.** paper money in amounts of less than a dollar, formerly issued in the United States. [var. of *script*]

script (skript), *n.* **1.** written letters, figures, signs, etc.; handwriting: *German script.* **2.** style

of type that looks like handwriting. **3.** manuscript of a play or actor's part. **4.** manuscript used in broadcasting. [< L *scriptum,* orig. neut. pp., written] —**script′writ′er,** *n.*

scrip·ture (skrip′chər), *n.* **1.** any sacred writing. **2.** Scripture. Also, the Scriptures, the Holy Scripture. the Bible. [< L *scriptura* a writing < *scribere* write] —**scrip′tur·al, Scrip′tur·al,** *adj.* —**scrip′tur·al·ly, Scrip′tur·al·ly,** *adv.*

scriv·en·er (skriv′nər), *n. Archaic.* clerk; notary. [< obs. *scrivein* < OF *escrivein,* ult. < L *scribere* write]

scrod (skrod), *n. Am.* a young cod, esp. one cut up for cooking. [< MDu. *schrode* piece cut off]

scrof·u·la (skrof′yə·lə), *n.* form of tuberculosis characterized by the enlargement of the lymph glands, esp. those in the neck. [< Med.L, sing. < L *scrofulae,* pl. < *scrofa* a sow] —**scrof′u·lous,** *adj.* —**scrof′u·lous·ly,** *adv.* —**scrof′u·lous·ness,** *n.*

scroll (skrōl), *n.* **1.** roll of parchment or paper, esp. one with writing on it. **2.** ornament resembling a partly unrolled sheet of paper, or having a spiral or coiled form. [alter. of *scrow* (infl. by *roll*), ult. < OF *escroe* scrap < Gmc.]

Scroll (def. 2)

scroll saw, a very narrow saw for cutting thin wood in curved or ornamental patterns.

Scrooge (skrüj), *n.* the old miser in Dickens's story *A Christmas Carol.*

scro·tum (skrō′təm), *n., pl.* -ta (-tə). pouch that contains the testicles. [< L] —**scro′tal,** *adj.*

scrounge (skrounj), *v.,* scrounged, scrounging. *Slang.* pilfer. —**scroung′er,** *n.*

scrub¹ (skrub), *v.,* scrubbed, scrub·bing, *n.* —*v.* **1.** rub hard; wash or clean by rubbing. **2.** wash. —*n.* a scrubbing. [? < MDu. *schrubben*] —**scrub′ber,** *n.*

scrub² (skrub), *n.* **1.** low, stunted trees or shrubs. **2.** anything small, or below the usual size. **3.** *Am.* player not on the regular team, etc. —*adj.* **1.** small; poor; inferior: *a scrub ball team.* **2.** *Am.* of or for players not on the regular team. [var. of SHRUB] —**scrub′by,** *adj.*

scruff (skruf), *n.* nape of the neck.

scrum·mage (skrum′ij), *n., v.,* –maged, –maging. *Esp. Brit.* scrimmage. —**scrum′mag·er,** *n.*

scrump·tious (skrump′shəs), *adj. Am., Slang.* elegant; splendid; first-rate.

scru·ple (skrü′pəl), *n., v.,* –pled, –pling. —*n.* **1.** a feeling of doubt about what one ought to do. **2.** a feeling of uneasiness that keeps a person from doing something. **3.** a weight of 20 grains. Three scruples make 1 dram. **4.** a very small amount. —*v.* **1.** hesitate or be unwilling (to do something): *he does not scruple to deceive.* **2.** have scruples. [< L *scrupulus,* orig. dim. of *scrupus* sharp stone]

scru·pu·lous (skrü′pyə·ləs), *adj.* **1.** having or showing a strict regard for what is right. **2.** attending thoroughly to details; very careful: *pay scrupulous attention.* —**scru·pu·los·i·ty** (skrü′pyə·los′ə·ti), scru′pu·lous·ness, *n.* —**scru′pu·lous·ly,** *adv.* —Syn. **1.** conscientious.

scru·ti·nize (skrü′tə·nīz), *v.,* –nized, –niz·ing. examine closely; inspect carefully. —**scru′ti·niz′er,** *n.* —**scru′ti·niz′ing·ly,** *adv.*

scru·ti·ny (skrü′tə·ni), *n., pl.* –nies. close examination; careful inspection. [< LL *scrutinium* < L *scrutari* ransack]

scu·ba (skü′bə), *n.* underwater breathing equipment used by skin divers. [< *s*(elf) -*c*(ontained) *u*(nderwater) *b*(reathing) *a*(pparatus)]

scud (skud), *v.,* scud·ded, scud·ding, *n.* —*v.* run or move swiftly: *clouds scudding across the sky.* —*n.* **1.** a scudding. **2.** clouds or spray driven by the wind. [? var. of *scut* a short tail, esp. of a rabbit or deer [< Scand. *skutr* stern]; first applied to a running of a hare]

scuff (skuf), *v.* **1.** walk without lifting the feet; shuffle. **2.** wear or injure the surface of by hard use. —*n.* a scuffing. [var. of SCUFFLE]

scuf·fle (skuf′əl), *v.,* –fled, –fling, *n.* —*v.* **1.** struggle or fight in a rough, confused manner.

2. shuffle. —*n.* 1. a confused, rough struggle or fight. 2. a shuffling. [< Scand. (Sw.) *skuffa* push] —scuf'fler, *n.* —Syn. *n.* 1. tussle, scrimmage.

scull (skul), *n.* 1. oar worked with a side twist over the end of a boat to make it go. 2. one of a pair of oars used, one on each side, by a single rower. 3. act of propelling by sculls. 4. a light racing boat for one or more rowers. —*v.* propel (a boat), by a scull or by sculls. —scull'er, *n.*

Man sculling

scul·ler·y (skul'ər·i; skul'ri), *n.*, *pl.* -ler·ies. *Esp. Brit.* a small room where the dirty, rough work of a kitchen is done. [< OF *escuelerie*, ult. < L *scutella* platter]

scul·lion (skul'yən), *n. Archaic.* servant who does the dirty, rough work in a kitchen. [< OF *escouillon* swab, cloth]

sculp·tor (skulp'tər), *n.* person who carves or models figures; artist in sculpture.

sculp·tress (skulp'tris), *n.* a woman sculptor.

sculp·ture (skulp'chər), *n.*, *v.*, -tured, -tur·ing. —*n.* 1. art of carving or modeling figures. Sculpture includes the cutting of statues from blocks of marble or wood, casting in bronze, and modeling in clay or wax. 2. sculptured work; piece of such work. —*v.* 1. carve or model. 2. cover or ornament with sculpture. [< L, < *sculpere* carve] —sculp'tur·al, *adj.* —sculp'tur·al·ly, *adv.* —sculp'tured, *adj.*

scum (skum), *n.*, *v.*, scummed, scum·ming. —*n.* 1. a thin layer that rises to the top of a liquid; *green scum floats on the pond.* 2. low, worthless people. —*v.* 1. form scum; become covered with scum. 2. skim. [? < MDu. *schuum*]

scum·my (skum'i), *adj.*, -mi·er, -mi·est. 1. of or containing scum. 2. low; worthless.

scup (skup), *n.* a narrow, high-backed sea fish used for food, found on E coast of the U.S.

scup·per (skup'ər), *n.* an opening in the side of a ship to let water run off the deck.

scup·per·nong (skup'ər·nông; -nong), *n. Am.* a large, yellowish-green grape grown in the S United States. [from *Scuppernong* River, North Carolina]

scurf (skėrf), *n.* small scales of dead skin; dandruff. [< Scand. *skurf*] —scurf'y, *adj.*

scur·ri·lous (skėr'ə·ləs), *adj.* 1. coarsely joking. 2. abusive and indecent. [< L, < *scurra* buffoon] —scur'ri·lous·ly, *adv.* —scur'ri·lous·ness, *scur·ril·i·ty* (skə·ril'ə·ti), *n.*

scur·ry (skėr'i), *v.*, -ried, -ry·ing, *n.*, *pl.* -ries. —*v.* run or cause to run quickly; hurry. —*n.* a hasty running; hurrying; flurry.

scur·vy (skėr'vi), *n.*, *adj.*, -vi·er, -vi·est. —*n.* disease characterized by swollen and bleeding gums, livid spots on the skin, and prostration, due to lack of vitamin C in the diet. Scurvy used to be common among sailors when they had little to eat except bread and salt meat. —*adj.* low; mean; contemptible: *a scurvy trick.* [< scurf] —scur'vi·ly, *adv.* —scur'vi·ness, *n.*

scut·tle¹ (skut'əl), *n.* kind of bucket for holding or carrying coal. [< L *scutella* platter]

scut·tle² (skut'əl), *v.*, -tled, -tling, *n.* scamper; scurry. [var. of *scuddle* < *scud*] —scut'tler, *n.*

scut·tle³ (skut'əl), *n.*, *v.*, -tled, -tling. —*n.* an opening in the deck or side of a ship, with a lid or cover. —*v.* 1. cut a hole or holes through the bottom or sides of (a ship) to sink it. 2. cut a hole or holes in the deck of (a ship) to salvage the cargo. [? < F < Sp. *escotilla* hatchway] —scut'tler, *n.*

scut·tle·butt (skut'əl·but'), *n. U.S. Navy Slang.* rumor and stories not based on fact.

Scyl·la (sil'ə), *n.* 1. a dangerous rock opposite the whirlpool Charybdis, at the extreme SW tip of Italy. 2. between Scylla and Charybdis, between two dangers, one of which must be met.

scythe (sīth), *n.*, *v.*, scythed, scyth·ing. —*n.* a long, slightly curved blade on a long handle, for cutting grass, etc. —*v.* cut with a scythe. [OE *sithe;* spelling infl. by L *scindere* to cut]

Scyth·i·a (sith'i·ə), *n.* an ancient region of Europe and Asia N of the Black and Caspian seas and eastward. —Scyth'i·an, *adj., n.*

S. Dak., S.D., South Dakota.

Se, *Chem.* selenium.

SE, S.E., southeast; southeastern.

sea (sē), *n.* 1. any large body of salt water, smaller than an ocean, partly or wholly enclosed by land: *the North Sea.* 2. the ocean. 3. a large, heavy wave. 4. the swell of the ocean. 5. an overwhelming amount or number. 6. at sea, a. out on the sea. b. puzzled; confused. [OE *sæ*]

sea anemone, a flowerlike polyp with a fleshy, cylindrical body and a mouth surrounded by many tentacles.

sea bass, 1. a common food fish of the Atlantic coast with a peculiar tail fin. 2. any of various similar fishes.

sea·bee (sē'bē'), *n.* member of the construction battalion of the U.S. Navy, composed of mechanics, carpenters, welders, etc., who normally take no part in combat. [from the initials *C.B.,* for Construction Battalion]

sea·board (sē'bôrd'; -bōrd'), *n.* land near the sea; seacoast; seashore: *the Atlantic seaboard.*

sea bream, any of certain fishes belonging to the family which includes scups, porgies, etc.

sea calf, the common seal, often called the harbor seal.

sea·coast (sē'kōst'), *n.* land along the sea.

sea cow, 1. manatee, dugong, or any similar mammal living in the sea. 2. walrus.

sea cucumber, any of a group of small echinoderms, most of which have flexible bodies that look somewhat like cucumbers.

sea dog, 1. a sailor, esp. one with long experience. 2. the common seal.

sea elephant, kind of very large seal, the male of which has a trunklike snout.

sea·far·er (sē'fâr'ər), *n. Poetic.* 1. sailor. 2. traveler on the sea.

sea·far·ing (sē'fâr'ing), *adj.* traveling or working on the sea. —*n.* 1. a sailor's life. 2. act or fact of traveling by sea.

sea·food (sē'füd'), *n. Am.* edible salt-water fish and shellfish.

sea·girt (sē'gėrt'), *adj. Poetic.* surrounded by the sea.

sea·go·ing (sē'gō'ing), *adj.* 1. going by sea. 2. fit for going to sea.

sea green, light bluish green.

sea gull, gull¹.

sea horse, 1. a kind of small fish (2 to 10 inches long) with a prehensile tail and a head suggesting that of a horse. 2. walrus. 3. a fabulous sea animal with the foreparts of a horse and the hind parts of a fish.

Sea horse

seal¹ (sēl), *n.* 1. design stamped on a piece of wax, etc., to show ownership or authenticity; a paper, circle, mark, etc., representing it. The seal of the United States is attached to important government papers. 2. stamp for marking things with such a design: *a seal with one's initials on it.* 3. thing that fastens or closes something tightly. 4. pledge: *under seal of secrecy.* 5. mark; sign. 6. set one's seal to, a. put one's seal on. b. approve. —*v.* 1. mark (a document) with a seal as evidence of authenticity or confirmation. 2. ratify, certify, or make binding (an agreement, etc.). 3. mark with a seal as evidence of legal or standard exactness, measure, quality, etc. 4. fasten (a letter, etc.) with a seal, wax, etc. 5. place a seal upon (a closed door, etc.) so that it cannot be opened without breaking the seal. 6. close tightly; shut; fasten. 7. settle; determine. 8. decide beyond recall. 9. give a sign that (a thing) is true: *seal a promise with a kiss.* [< OF, ult. < L *sigillum,* dim. of *signum* sign] —seal'a·ble, *adj.* —seal'er, *n.*

seal² (sēl), *n.*, *pl.* seals or (*esp. collectively*) seal for 1, *v.* —*n.* 1. a marine carnivorous mammal with large flippers, living usually in cold regions. Some

Fur seal
(6 ft. long)

kinds are hunted for their valuable fur. 2. the fur. 3. leather made from the skin of a seal. —v. hunt seals. [OE *seolh*] —seal'er, *n.*

sea legs, *Colloq.* legs accustomed to walking steadily on a rolling or pitching ship.

sea level, surface of the sea, esp. when half-way between mean high and low water. Heights of mountains are measured as so many feet above sea level.

sea lily, crinoid.

sealing wax, a hard kind of wax made of resin and shellac, soft when heated, used for sealing letters, packages, etc.

sea lion, a large seal of the Pacific coast.

seal·skin (sēl'skin'), *n.* 1. skin of the fur seal, prepared for use. 2. garment made of this fur.

Sea·ly·ham (sē'li·ham; –əm), *n.* one of a breed of white wire-haired terriers with short legs and square jaws.

seam (sēm), *n.* 1. line formed by sewing two pieces of cloth, canvas, leather, etc., together. 2. any line where edges join. 3. any mark or line like a seam. 4. *Geol.* layer; stratum. —v. 1. sew the seam of; join with a seam. 2. mark (the face, etc.) with wrinkles, scars, etc. 3. crack open. [OE *sēam*] —seam'less, *adj.*

sea·man (sē'mən), *n.,* *pl.* –men. 1. sailor. 2. sailor who is not an officer. —sea'man·like', sea'man·ly, *adj.*

sea·man·ship (sē'mən·ship), *n.* skill in managing a ship.

sea mew, gull[1].

seam·stress (sēm'stris), *n.* woman whose work is sewing. Also, **sempstress.**

seam·y (sēm'i), *adj.,* seam·i·er, seam·i·est. 1. having or showing seams. 2. worst; least pleasant: *the seamy side of life.* —seam'i·ness, *n.*

sé·ance (sā'äns), *n.* 1. a sitting; session. 2. a meeting of people trying to communicate with spirits of the dead by the help of a medium. [< F, < *seoir* sit < L *sedere*]

sea·plane (sē'plān'), *n.* hydroplane (def. 2).

sea·port (sē'pōrt'; –pôrt'), *n.* port or harbor on the seacoast; city or town with a harbor that ships can reach from the sea.

sear (sir), *v.* 1. burn or char the surface of. 2. make hard or unfeeling. 3. dry up; wither. —*n.* mark made by searing. —*adj.* Also, **sere.** dried up; withered. [OE *sēar; v.* < adj.]

search (sérch), *v.* 1. try to find by looking; seek: *search for a lost cat.* 2. go through and examine carefully and in detail, esp. for something concealed: *search a ship.* 3. probe: *the doctor searched the wound.* 4. search out, a. look for. b. find by searching. —*n.* 1. act of searching; examination. 2. in search of, trying to find; looking for. [< OF *cerchier*, ult. < L *circus* circle] —search'a·ble, *adj.* —search'er, *n.*

search·ing (sér'ching), *adj.* 1. examining carefully. 2. piercing; sharp. —search'ing·ly, *adv.*

search·light (sérch'līt'), *n.* 1. device that can throw a very bright beam of light in any direction desired. 2. the beam of light.

search warrant, a legal document authorizing the search of a house or building for stolen goods, criminals, etc.

sea·shore (sē'shōr'; –shôr'), *n.* land along the sea.

sea·sick (sē'sik'), *adj.* sick because of a ship's motion. —sea'sick'ness, *n.*

sea·side (sē'sīd'), *n.* seacoast; seashore.

sea·son (sē'zən), *n.* 1. one of the four periods of the year; spring, summer, autumn, or winter. 2. any period of time marked by something special: *the Christmas season.* 3. time when something is occurring, active, at its best, or in fashion: *the baseball season.* 4. a period of time: *a bad season.* 5. a suitable or fit time. 6. in season, a. at the right or proper time. b. in the time or condition for eating, hunting, etc. c. early enough. —v. 1. improve the flavor of: *season soup with salt.* 2. give interest or character to: *season conversation with wit.* 3. make fit for use by a period of keeping or treatment: *wood is seasoned for building by drying and*

hardening it. 4. become fit for use. 5. accustom; make used: *soldiers are seasoned to battle by experience in war.* 6. make less severe; soften: *season justice with mercy.* [< OF < L *satio* a sowing < *serere* to sow] —sea'son·er, *n.* ⟩ seasons. Spring, summer, fall, autumn, and so on are not capitalized except for stylistic emphasis, as sometimes in poetry or nature essays.

sea·son·a·ble (sē'zən·ə·bəl; sēz'nə·bəl), *adj.* 1. suitable to the season: *seasonable weather.* 2. coming at the right or proper time: *seasonable aid.* —sea'son·a·ble·ness, *n.* —sea'son·a·bly, *adv.* —Syn. 2. opportune, timely, convenient.

sea·son·al (sē'zən·əl), *adj.* having to do with the seasons; depending on a season; happening at regular intervals. —sea'son·al·ly, *adv.*

sea·son·ing (sē'zən·ing; sēz'ning), *n.* 1. something that gives a better flavor, as salt, pepper, or spices. 2. something that gives interest or character: *a speech with a seasoning of humor.*

seat[1] (sēt), *n.* 1. thing to sit on. 2. place to sit. 3. place in which one has the right to sit: *a seat in Congress.* 4. that part of a chair, bench, stool, etc., on which one sits. 5. that part of the body on which one sits, or the clothing covering it. 6. manner of sitting, as on horse-back. 7. that on which anything rests; base. —v. 1. set or place on a seat: *seat a person on a chair.* 2. have seats for (a specified number). 3. provide with a seat or seats. 4. put a seat on. 5. be seated, a. sit down. b. be sitting. c. be situated. [< Scand. *sǣti*] —seat'er, *n.*

seat[2] (sēt), *n.* 1. an established place or center. 2. residence; home. —v. fix in a particular or proper place; settle; locate: *seated in the west* [OE *sǣte*]

SEATO, Southeast Asian Treaty Organization.

Se·at·tle (sē·at'əl), *n.* seaport in W Washington, on Puget Sound.

sea urchin, a small sea animal with a spiny shell.

sea·ward (sē'wərd), *adv.* Also, **sea'wards.** toward the sea. —*adj.* lying, facing, or tending toward the sea. —*n.* direction toward the sea.

Sea urchin (2 to 6 in. in diameter)

sea·way (sē'wā'), *n.* 1. a way over the sea. 2. the open sea. 3. progress of a ship through the waves. 4. a rough sea. 5. an inland waterway that is deep enough to permit ocean shipping.

sea·weed (sē'wēd'), *n.* any plant or plants growing in the sea.

sea·wor·thy (sē'wėr'tнi), *adj.* fit for sailing on the sea; able to stand storms at sea. —sea'wor'thi·ness, *n.*

se·ba·ceous (si·bā'shəs), *adj.* 1. pertaining to fat; fatty; greasy. 2. secreting a fatty matter, as certain glands. [< L, < *sebum* grease]

Se·bas·to·pol (si·bas'tə·pōl), *n.* Sevastopol.

SEC, Securities and Exchange Commission.

sec., 1. secant. 2. *pl.* secs. second. 3. secondary. 4. secretary. 5. *pl.* secs. section. 6. security.

se·cant (sē'kant; –kant), *n.* 1. *Geom.* line that intersects. 2. *Trigonometry.* a. a straight line drawn from the center of a circle through one extremity of an arc to the tangent from the other extremity of the same arc. b. ratio of the length of this line to the length of the radius of the circle. [< L *secans* cutting]

se·cede (si·sēd'), *v.,* –ced·ed, –ced·ing. withdraw formally from an organization. [< L, < *se-* apart + *cedere* go] —se·ced'er, *n.*

se·ces·sion (si·sesh'ən), *n.* 1. a formal withdrawing from an organization. 2. Often, **Secession,** *Am.* the withdrawal from the Union of eleven Southern States in 1860–61, which brought on the Civil War. —se·ces'sion·ist, *n.*

se·clude (si·klüd'), *v.,* –clud·ed, –clud·ing. keep apart from company; shut off from others. [< L *secludere* < *se-* apart + *claudere* shut]

se·clud·ed (si·klüd'id), *adj.* shut off from others; undisturbed. —se·clud'ed·ly, *adv.* —se·clud'ed·ness, *n.* —Syn. withdrawn, isolated.

se·clu·sion (si·klü′zhən), n. 1. a secluding or being secluded; retirement. 2. a secluded place. —**se·clu′sive,** adj. —**se·clu′sive·ly,** adv. —**se·clu′sive·ness,** n.

sec·ond[1] (sek′ənd), adj. 1. next after the first: the second house on the block. 2. below the first; inferior: the second officer. 3. another; other: her second self. —adv. in the second group, division, rank, etc.; secondly. —n. 1. person or thing that is second. 2. seconds, articles below first quality. Seconds have some defect. 3. person who supports or aids another; backer: the prize fighter had a second. —v. 1. support; back up; assist: second another person's idea. 2. express approval or support of. 3. act as second to (a prize fighter, etc.). [< F < L secundus < sequi follow] —**sec′ond·er,** n.

sec·ond[2] (sek′ənd), n. 1. ⅟₆₀ of a minute; ⅟₃₆₀₀ of an hour. 2. a very short time. 3. ⅟₃₆₀₀ of a degree of an angle. 12° 10′ 30″ means 12 degrees, 10 minutes, 30 seconds. [< F < Med.L secunda (minuta) second (minute), i.e., the result of the second division of the hour into sixty parts]

sec·ond·ar·y (sek′ən·der′i), adj., n., pl. -ar·ies. —adj. 1. next after the first in order, place, time, etc. 2. not main or chief; having less importance. 3. not original; derived. —n. person or thing that is secondary, second in importance, or subordinate. —**sec′ond·ar′i·ly,** adv. —**sec′ond·ar′i·ness,** n. —Syn. adj. 2. subordinate, subsidiary, auxiliary, inferior, minor.

secondary accent, Phonet. 1. a stress accent that is weaker than the strongest stress in a word (primary accent), but stronger than no stress. The second syllable of ab·bre′vi·a′tion has a secondary accent. 2. mark (′) used to show this.

secondary school, Am. high school.

second childhood, a foolish or childish condition caused by old age.

sec·ond-class (sek′ənd·klas′; -kläs′), adj. of inferior grade or quality; second-rate. —adv. on a second-class ship, train, etc.

sec·ond-hand (sek′ənd·hand′), adj. 1. not original; obtained from another: second-hand information. 2. not new; used already by someone else. 3. dealing in used goods: a second-hand bookshop.

second hand, hand on a clock or watch, pointing to the seconds, that moves around the dial once in a minute.

second lieutenant, Mil. an army officer who ranks next below a first lieutenant.

sec·ond·ly (sek′ənd·li), adv. in the second place; second.

second nature, habit, quality, knowledge, etc., that a person has acquired and had for so long that it seems to be almost a part of his nature.

second person, Gram. form of a pronoun or verb used to indicate the person spoken to.

sec·ond-rate (sek′ənd·rāt′), adj. 1. rated as second-class. 2. inferior. —adv. in an inferior manner. —**sec′ond-rat′er,** n.

second sight, the supposed power of seeing distant objects or future events as if they were present. —**sec′ond-sight′ed,** adj.

se·cre·cy (sē′krə·si), n., pl. -cies. 1. condition of being secret: an affair conducted in strict secrecy. 2. ability to keep things secret. 3. tendency to conceal; lack of frankness.

se·cret (sē′krit), adj. 1. done, made, or conducted without the knowledge of others: a secret marriage. 2. keeping to oneself what one knows: be as secret as the grave. 3. known only to a few: a secret society. 4. kept from sight; hidden: a secret drawer. 5. retired; secluded: a secret place. 6. very hard to understand or discover. —n. 1. something secret or hidden; mystery. 2. thing known only to a few. 3. a hidden cause or reason. 4. in secret, secretly; in private; not openly. [< F < L secretus set apart < se apart + cernere separate. Doublet of SECRETE.] —**se′cret·ly,** adv. —**se′cret·ness,** n. —Syn. adj. 1. surreptitious, clandestine, underhand. 2. uncommunicative, secretive, reticent. 4. concealed, covered. 6. obscure, recondite, esoteric.

secret agent, agent of the government secret service.

sec·re·tar·i·al (sek′rə·tār′i·əl), adj. of a secretary; having to do with a secretary.

sec·re·tar·i·at (sek′rə·tār′i·ət; -at), n. 1. office or position of secretary. 2. group of secretaries. 3. place where a secretary transacts business.

sec·re·tar·y (sek′rə·ter′i), n., pl. -tar·ies. 1. person who writes letters, keeps records, etc., for a person, company, club, etc. 2. person who has charge of a department of the government. The Secretary of the Treasury is the head of the Treasury Department. 3. a writing desk with a set of drawers and often with shelves for books. [< LL secretarius confidential officer < L secretum, n., SECRET] —**sec′re·tar′y·ship,** n.

secretary bird, a large, long-legged African bird of prey that feeds on reptiles, so called because its crest suggests pens stuck over the ear.

se·crete (si·krēt′), v., -cret·ed, -cret·ing. 1. keep secret; hide. 2. Biol. separate and elaborate from the blood. [< L secretus. Doublet of SECRET.] —**se·cre′tor** so·cret′er, n.

se·cre·tion (si·krē′shən), n. 1. substance that is secreted by some part of an animal or plant. 2. process or function of an animal body, executed in the glands, by which various substances, as bile, are separated and elaborated from the blood. —**se·cre·tion·ar·y** (si·krē′shən·er′i), se·cre′tion·al, adj.

se·cre·tive (si·krē′tiv), adj. 1. having the habit of secrecy; not frank and open. 2. causing or aiding secretion. —**se·cre′tive·ly,** adv. —**se·cre′tive·ness,** n. —Syn. 1. reticent, reserved.

se·cre·to·ry (si·krē′tə·ri), adj., n., pl. -ries. —adj. secreting; of or causing secretion. —n. organ of the body that secretes.

secret service, 1. branch of a government that makes secret investigations. 2. an official service that is secret. 3. Secret Service, Am. branch of the U.S. Treasury Department concerned with discovering and preventing counterfeiting, with protecting the President, and, in wartime, with espionage.

sect (sekt), n. 1. group of people having the same principles, beliefs, or opinions. 2. a religious group separated from an established church. [< L secta party, school < sequi follow]

sec·tar·i·an (sek·tār′i·ən), adj. 1. of or pertaining to a sect. 2. characteristic of one sect only. —n. 1. a devoted member of a sect, esp. a narrow-minded or strongly prejudiced member. 2. member of a sect. —**sec·tar′i·an·ism,** n.

sec·tion (sek′shən), n. 1. part cut off; part; division; slice: divide the cake into sections. 2. one of several parts that can be put together to form a whole: the sections of a pipe. 3. division of a book: Chapter X has seven sections. 4. region; part of a country, city, etc.: a town has a business section, residential sections, etc. 5. act of cutting. 6. a representation of a thing as it would appear if cut straight through. 7. district one mile square. —v. cut into sections. [< L, < secare cut]

sec·tion·al (sek′shən·əl), adj. 1. pertaining to a particular section; local. 2. made of sections: a sectional bookcase. —**sec′tion·al·ism,** n. —**sec′tion·al·ist,** n. —**sec′tion·al·ly,** adv.

sec·tor (sek′tər), n. 1. Geom. a plane figure bounded by two radii and the included arc of a circle, ellipse, or the like. 2. Mil. a clearly defined area which a given unit protects or covers with fire; part of a front held by a unit. 3. instrument consisting of two rulers connected by a joint. A sector is used in measuring or drawing angles. [< LL, < L, cutter, < secare cut] —**sec·to·ri·al** (sek·tô′ri·əl; -tō′-), adj.

sec·u·lar (sek′yə·lər), adj. 1. worldly, not religious or sacred: secular music. 2. living in the world; not belonging to a religious order. —n. a secular priest. [< L, < saeculum age, world] —**sec′u·lar·ism,** n. —**sec′u·lar·ist,** n. —**sec′u·lar·is′tic,** adj. —**sec′u·lar·ly,** adv.

sec·u·lar·ize (sek′yə·lər·īz), v., -ized, -iz·ing. 1. make secular or worldly; separate from religious connection or influence: secularize the *schools.* 2. transfer (property) from the possession of the church to that of the government. —sec′u·lar·i·za′tion, *n.* —sec′u·lar·iz′er, *n.*

se·cure (si·kyúr′), *adj., v.,* –cured, –cur·ing. —*adj.* 1. safe against loss, attack, escape, etc.: *a secure hiding place.* 2. sure; certain; that can be counted on: *our victory is secure.* 3. free from care or fear: *a secure old age.* 4. firmly fastened; not liable to give way: *the boards of this bridge do not look secure.* —*v.* 1. make safe; protect. 2. make a creditor sure of payment, as by a mortgage or bond. 3. make oneself safe; be safe. 4. make (something) sure or certain. 5. make firm or fast: *secure the locks on the windows.* 6. get; obtain: *secure your tickets early.* [< L, < *se-* free from + *cura* care. Doublet of SURE.] —se·cure′ly, *adv.* —se·cure′ness, *n.* —se·cur′er, *n.* —Syn. *adj.* 1. guarded, protected, impregnable, unassailable. 2. assured. 3. confident. 4. fast, firm, stable, immovable. –*v.* 1. guard, defend, shield. 4. assure, insure. 5. fasten, tie, moor. 6. acquire, procure.

se·cu·ri·ty (si·kyúr′ə·ti), *n., pl.* –ties. 1. freedom from danger, care, or fear; feeling or condition of being safe. 2. certainty. 3. something that secures or makes safe: *a watchdog is a security against burglars.* 4. Usually, **securities.** bond or stock certificate: *these railroad securities can be sold for $5000.* 5. something given as a pledge that a person will fulfill some duty, promise, etc.: *a life-insurance policy may serve as security for a loan.* 6. person who agrees to be responsible for another. —Syn. 1. confidence. 3. safety, protection, defense.

secy., sec′y., secretary.

se·dan (si·dan′), *n.* 1. *Am.* a closed automobile seating four or more persons. 2. sedan chair.

sedan chair, a covered chair carried on poles by two men.

Sedan chair

se·date (si·dāt′), *adj.* quiet; calm; serious. [< L *sedatus* calmed] —se·date′ly, *adv.* —se·date′ness, *n.* —Syn. composed, staid, unruffled.

sed·a·tive (sed′ə·tiv), *n.* 1. medicine that lessens pain or excitement. 2. anything soothing or calming. —*adj.* 1. lessening pain or excitement. 2. soothing; calming.

sed·en·tar·y (sed′ən·ter′i), *adj.* 1. used to sitting still much of the time: *sedentary people.* 2. that keeps one sitting still much of the time: *a sedentary occupation.* 3. moving little and rarely. 4. *Zool.* fixed to one spot; not migratory. [< L *sedentarius*, ult. < *sedere* sit] —sed′en·tar′i·ly, *adv.* —sed′en·tar′i·ness, *n.*

sedge (sej), *n.* a grasslike plant that grows in wet places. [OE *secg*] —sedged, sedg′y, *adj.*

sed·i·ment (sed′ə·mənt), *n.* 1. matter that settles to the bottom of a liquid. 2. *Geol.* matter deposited, as by water. [< F < L, < *sedere* settle] —sed·i·men·ta·tion (sed′ə·men·tā′shən), *n.*

sed·i·men·ta·ry (sed′ə·men′tə·ri), **sed·i·men·tal** (–təl), *adj.* 1. of or having to do with sediment. 2. formed from sediment. —sed′i·men′ta·ri·ly, *adv.*

se·di·tion (si·dish′ən), *n.* speech or action causing discontent or rebellion against the government; incitement to discontent or rebellion. [< L *seditio* < *se-* apart + *ire* go] —se·di·tion·ar·y (si·dish′ən·er′i), *adj.* —Syn. revolt, insurrection, mutiny, riot, insubordination.

se·di·tious (si·dish′əs), *adj.* 1. stirring up discontent or rebellion. 2. taking part in sedition; guilty of sedition. 3. pertaining to sedition. —se·di′tious·ly, *adv.* —se·di′tious·ness, *n.*

se·duce (si·dūs′; –dūs′), *v.,* –duced, –duc·ing. 1. tempt to wrongdoing; persuade to do wrong. 2. lead away from virtue; lead astray; beguile. 3. entice (a woman) to a surrender of chastity. [< L, < *se-* aside + *ducere* lead] —se·duc′er, *n.* —se·duc′i·ble, *adj.* —se·duc′ing·ly, *adv.* —se·duc·tion (si·duk′shən), se·duce′ment, *n.* —Syn. 1. corrupt. 2. mislead. 3. betray.

se·duc·tive (si·duk′tiv), *adj.* alluring; capti-

vating; charming. —se·duc′tive·ly, *adv.* —se·duc′tive·ness, *n.*

sed·u·lous (sej′ə·ləs), *adj.* hard-working; diligent; painstaking. [< L *sedulus* < *se dolo* without deception] —se·du·li·ty (si·dū′lə·ti; –dū′–), sed′u·lous·ness, *n.* —sed′u·lous·ly, *adv.* —Syn. industrious, assiduous, persevering, untiring.

see¹ (sē), *v.,* saw, seen, see·ing. 1. perceive with the eyes; look at: *see that black cloud.* 2. examine with the eyes; view; observe: *see a tennis match.* 3. have the power of sight: *the blind do not see.* 4. perceive with the mind; understand: *I see what you mean.* 5. find out; learn: *please see who it is.* 6. take care; make sure: *see that the work is properly done.* 7. think; consider: *you may go if you see fit to do so.* 8. have knowledge or experience of: *that coat has seen hard wear.* 9. attend; escort; go with: *see a girl home.* 10. meet; have a talk with: *he wishes to see you alone.* 11. call on: *will you see him at his home?* 12. receive a call from: *if he comes, will you see him?* 13. visit; attend: *we saw the World's Fair.* 14. in poker, etc., to meet (a bet) by staking an equal sum. 15. **see through, a.** understand the real character or hidden purpose of. **b.** go through with; finish. **c.** watch over or help through a difficulty. [OE *sēon*] —see′a·ble, *adj.* —Syn. 1. behold, descry, espy, discern, notice, note. 2. watch, witness, regard. 4. apprehend.

see² (sē), *n.* 1. position or authority of a bishop. 2. diocese; bishopric. [< OF *sie* < L *sedes* abode]

seed (sēd), *n., pl.* **seeds, seed,** *v.* —*n.* 1. thing from which a flower, vegetable, or other plant grows; small grainlike fruit. 2. bulb, sprout, or any part of a plant from which a new plant will grow. 3. germ. 4. Often, **seeds.** children; descendants. 5. semen; sperm. 6. **go to seed, a.** come to the time of yielding seeds. **b.** come to the end of vigor, usefulness, prosperity, etc. —*v.* 1. sow with seeds; scatter seeds over: *the farmer seeded his field with corn.* 2. sow (seeds): *dandelions seed themselves.* 3. remove the seeds from: *seed raisins.* 4. *Am.* scatter or distribute (the names of players) so that the best players do not meet in the early part of a tournament. 5. scatter dry ice or other chemicals into (clouds) from an airplane in an effort to produce rain artificially. [OE *sǣd*] —seed′er, *n.* —seed′less, *adj.* —seed′like′, *adj.*

seed·case (sēd′kās′), *n.* any pod, capsule, or other dry, hollow fruit that contains seeds.

seed·ing (sēd′ing), *n.* 1. act or fact of distributing seeds. 2. *Sports.* distribution of players in a tournament. 3. in rain making, the dropping of dry ice or other chemicals into clouds.

seed leaf, cotyledon.

seed·ling (sēd′ling), *n.* 1. a young plant grown from a seed. 2. a small young tree less than three feet high.

seed vessel, pericarp.

seed·y (sēd′i), *adj.,* seed·i·er, seed·i·est. 1. full of seed. 2. gone to seed. 3. *Colloq.* shabby; no longer fresh or new: *seedy clothes.* —seed′i·ly, *adv.* —seed′i·ness, *n.*

see·ing (sē′ing), *n.* sight. —*adj.* that sees. —*conj.* in view of the fact; considering: *seeing that it is 10 o'clock, we will wait no longer.*

Seeing Eye, organization that breeds and trains dogs as guides for blind people. It is located at Morristown, a town in New Jersey.

seek (sēk), *v.,* sought, seek·ing. 1. try to find; look for: *seek a new home.* 2. hunt; search: *seek for something lost.* 3. try to get: *friends sought his advice.* 4. try; attempt: *he seeks to make peace.* 5. go to: *being sleepy, he sought his bed.* 6. *Archaic.* go. [OE *sēcan*] —seek′er, *n.*

seem (sēm), *v.* 1. appear; appear to be: *he seemed a very old man.* 2. appear to oneself: *I still seem to hear the music.* 3. appear to exist: *there seems no need to wait longer.* 4. appear to be true or to be the case: *it seems likely to rain.* [< Scand. *sœma* conform to] —seem′er, *n.*

seem·ing (sēm′ing), *adj.* apparent; that appears to be: *a seeming advantage.* —*n.* appearance; likeness. —seem′ing·ly, *adv.* —seem′ing·ness, *n.*

seem·ly (sēm′li), *adj.*, **-li·er, -li·est**, *adv.* —*adj.*
1. suitable; proper. 2. having a pleasing appearance. —*adv.* properly; becomingly. —**seem′li·ness,** *n.* —Syn. *adj.* **1.** becoming, decorous.

seen (sēn), *v.*, pp. of **see**[1].

seep (sēp), *v.* ooze; trickle; leak: *water seeps through sand.* [? OE *sīpian*] —**seep′y,** *adj.*

seep·age (sēp′ij), *n.* 1. a seeping; leakage. 2. moisture or liquid that seeps.

seer (sir *for 1, 3;* sē′ər *for 2*), *n.* 1. person who foresees or foretells future events; prophet. 2. one that sees. 3. one who tells fortunes.

seer·ess (sir′is), *n.* woman who is a seer.

seer·suck·er (sir′suk′ər), *n.* cloth with alternate strips of plain and crinkled material. [< Hind. < Pers. *shir o shakkar*, lit., milk and sugar]

see·saw (sē′sô′), *n.* 1. plank resting on a support near its middle so the ends can move up and down. 2. moving up and down on such a plank. 3. motion up and down or back and forth. —*v.* 1. move up and down on a balanced plank. 2. move up and down or back and forth. —*adj.* moving up and down or back and forth. [varied reduplication of *saw*[1]]

seethe (sēth), *v.*, **seethed, seeth·ing.** 1. boil. 2. bubble and foam: *seething waters.* 3. be excited; be disturbed: *seething with discontent.* 4. soak; steep. [OE *sēothan*] —**seeth′ing·ly,** *adv.*

seg·ment (seg′mənt), *n.* 1. part cut, marked, or broken off; division; section: *an orange is easily pulled apart into its segments.* 2. *Geom.* part of a circle, sphere, etc., cut off by a line or plane. —*v.* divide into segments. [< L *segmentum* < *secare* to cut] —**seg·men·tal** (seg·men′təl), **seg·men·tar·y** (seg′mən·ter′i), *adj.* —**seg′men·tal·ly,** *adv.* —Syn. *n.* 1. portion, piece.

The shaded part is a segment of the circle.

seg·men·ta·tion (seg′mən·tā′shən), *n.* division into segments.

se·go lily (sē′gō) or **sego,** *n.*, *pl.* **-gos.** *Am.* plant that has trumpet-shaped flowers, common in the SW part of the United States. [< Am.Ind.]

seg·re·gate (*v.* seg′rə·gāt; *adj.* seg′rə·git, -gāt), *v.*, **-gat·ed, -gat·ing,** *adj.* —*v.* 1. separate from others; set apart; isolate. 2. separate from the rest and collect in one place, as in crystallization. —*adj.* segregated. [< L *segregatus* < *se-* apart from + *grex* herd] —**seg′re·ga′tive,** *adj.* —**seg′re·ga′tor,** *n.*

seg·re·ga·tion (seg′rə·gā′shən), *n.* 1. a segregating or being segregated. 2. separation of Negroes from other racial groups, esp. in schools, theaters, etc.

seg·re·ga·tion·ist (seg′rə·gā′shən·ist), *n.* one who believes in the separation of Negroes from other racial groups.

sei·gneur (sēn·yér′), *n.* a feudal lord or landowner. [< F. Doublet of SEIGNIOR and SIEUR.] —**sei·gneu·ri·al** (sēn·yûr′i·əl), *adj.*

seign·ior (sēn′yər), *n.* 1. lord; lord of a manor; gentleman. 2. title of respect. [< OF < acc. of L *senior* SENIOR. Doublet of SEIGNEUR and SIEUR.]

Seine (sān), *n.* river flowing from E France into the English Channel.

seine (sān), *n.*, *v.*, **seined, sein·ing.** —*n.* a fishing net that hangs straight down in the water. It has floats at the upper edge and sinkers at the lower. —*v.* 1. fish with a seine. 2. catch with a seine. [< L < Gk. *sagene*]

seis·mic (sīz′mik; sīs′-), *adj.* 1. of earthquakes or an earthquake. 2. caused by an earthquake. [< Gk. *seismos* earthquake < *seiein* to shake]

seis·mo·graph (sīz′mə·graf; -gräf; sīs′-), *n.* instrument for recording the direction, intensity, and duration of earthquakes. [< *seismo-* (< Gk. *seismos* earthquake) + –GRAPH] —**seis·mog·ra·pher** (sīz·mog′rə·fər; sīs-), *n.* —**seis′mo·graph′ic,** *adj.* —**seis·mog′ra·phy,** *n.*

seis·mol·o·gy (sīz·mol′ə·ji; sīs-), *n.* study of earthquakes and other movements of the earth's crust. [< *seismo-* (< Gk. *seismos* earthquake) + –LOGY] —**seis·mo·log·i·cal** (sīz′mə·loj′ə·kəl; sīs′-), **seis′mo·log′ic,** *adj.* —**seis′mo·log′i·cal·ly,** *adv.* —**seis·mol′o·gist,** *n.*

seize (sēz), *v.*, **seized, seiz·ing.** 1. take hold of suddenly; clutch; grasp. 2. grasp with the mind. 3. grasp and use: *seize an opportunity.* 4. take possession of by force. 5. take possession of or come upon suddenly: *a fever seized him.* 6. take possession of by legal authority: *seize smuggled goods.* 7. take into custody; capture: *men were seized for rioting.* 8. *Law.* put in possession of; possess. 9. *Naut.* bind; lash; make fast: *seize one rope to another.* 10. seize on or upon, a. take hold of suddenly. b. take possession of. [< OF *seisir*, ult. < Gmc.] —**seiz′a·ble,** *adj.* —**seiz′er,** *Law* **sei·zor** (sē′zər; -zôr), *n.* —Syn. 1. grip, snatch, grab, nab. 4. appropriate, confiscate.

sei·zure (sē′zhər), *n.* 1. act of seizing: *seizure of smuggled goods.* 2. condition of being seized: *after his seizure he was imprisoned.* 3. a sudden attack of disease.

se·lah (sē′lə), *n.* a Hebrew word occurring frequently in the Psalms, probably meaning "Pause here."

sel·dom (sel′dəm), *adv.* rarely; not often: *he is seldom ill.* [OE *seldum*] —**sel′dom·ness,** *n.*

se·lect (si·lekt′), *v.* choose; **pick** out: *select the book you want.* —*adj.* 1. picked as best; chosen specially: *a select crew.* 2. choice; superior. 3. careful in choosing; particular as to friends, company, etc.: *a very select club.* [< L *selectus* < *se-* apart + *legere* choose] —**se·lect′ly,** *adv.* —**se·lect′ness,** *n.* —**se·lec′tor,** *n.* —Syn. *v.* cull, elect. —*adj.* 2. picked.

se·lect·ee (si·lek′tē′), *n.* person drafted for military service by the United States in 1940 and later.

se·lec·tion (si·lek′shən), *n.* 1. choice. 2. person, thing, or group chosen. 3. the selecting of animals or plants to survive. —**se·lec′tion·ist,** *n.*

se·lec·tive (si·lek′tiv), *adj.* 1. selecting; having the power to select. 2. having to do with selection. 3. *Elect.* responding to oscillations of a certain frequency only. —**se·lec′tive·ly,** *adv.* —**se·lec′tive·ness,** *n.*

Selective Service, selection of persons from the total manpower of a country for compulsory military service; draft.

se·lec·tiv·i·ty (si·lek′tiv′ə·ti), *n.* 1. quality of being selective. 2. property of a circuit, instrument, or the like, by virtue of which it responds to electric oscillations of a particular frequency; esp., the ability of a radio receiving set to receive certain frequencies or waves to the exclusion of others.

se·lect·man (si·lekt′mən), *n.*, *pl.* **-men.** *Am.* one of a board of town officers in New England, chosen each year to manage certain public affairs.

Se·le·ne (si·lē′nē), *n.* *Gk. Myth.* goddess of the moon.

sel·e·nite (sel′ə·nīt; si·lē′-), *n.* variety of gypsum, found in transparent crystals and foliated masses. [< L < Gk. *selenites* (*lithos*) (stone) of the moon < *selene* moon; its brightness was supposed to vary with the moon]

se·le·ni·um (si·lē′ni·əm), *n.* *Chem.* a nonmetallic element, Se, resembling sulfur in chemical properties. Because its electrical resistance varies with the amount of light, it is used in photoelectric cells. [< NL, < Gk. *selene* moon]

self (self), *n.*, *pl.* **selves,** *adj.*, *pron.*, *pl.* **selves.** —*n.* 1. one's own person: *his very self.* 2. one's own welfare, interests, etc.: *a selfish person puts self first.* 3. nature, character, etc., of a person or thing: *one's former self.* —*adj.* being the same throughout; all of one kind, quality, color, material, etc. —*pron.* myself; himself; herself; yourself: *a check made payable to self.* [OE]
➤ Self as a suffix forms the reflexive pronouns: *myself, yourself, himself, herself, itself, oneself, ourselves, yourselves, themselves.* These are used chiefly for emphasis (*I can do that myself*) or as a reflexive object (*I couldn't help myself*).

self–, *prefix.* 1. of or over oneself, etc., as in *self-conscious, self-control.* 2. by or in oneself, etc., as in *self-inflicted, self-evident.* 3. to or for oneself, etc., as in *self-addressed, self-respect.* 4. automatic; automatically, as in *self-starter, self-closing.* [< *self*]

self-a·base·ment (self′ə·bās′mənt), n. abasement of self.

self-ab·hor·rence (self′ab·hôr′əns; –hor′–), n. abhorrence of self.

self-ab·ne·ga·tion (self′ab′nə·gā′shən), n. self-denial.

self-ab·sorbed (self′ab·sôrbd′; –zôrbd′), adj. absorbed in one's own thoughts, affairs, etc. —self-ab·sorp·tion (self′ab·sôrp′shən; –zôrp′–), n.

self-a·buse (self′ə·būs′), n. 1. abuse of oneself. 2. masturbation.

self-act·ing (self′ak′ting), adj. working of itself: a self-acting machine. —self′-ac′tor, n.

self-ad·dressed (self′ə·drest′), adj. addressed to oneself.

self-as·ser·tion (self′ə·sér′shən), n. insistence on one's own wishes, opinions, claims, etc. —self′-as·ser′tive, adj. —self′-as·ser′tive·ly, adv.

self-as·sur·ance (self′ə·shúr′əns), n. self-confidence. —self′-as·sured′, adj.

self-cen·tered, esp. Brit. **self-cen·tred** (self′sen′tərd), adj. 1. occupied with one's own interests and affairs. 2. selfish. 3. being a fixed point around which other things move. —self′-cen′tered·ness, esp. Brit. self′-cen′tred·ness, n.

self-col·ored (self′kul′ərd), adj. 1. of one uniform color. 2. of the natural color.

self-com·mand (self′kə·mand′; –mänd′), n. control of oneself.

self-com·mun·ion (self′kə·mūn′yən), n. communion with oneself.

self-com·pla·cent (self′kəm·plā′sənt), adj. pleased with oneself; self-satisfied. —self′-com·pla′cence, self′-com·pla′cen·cy, n. —self′-com·pla′cent·ly, adv.

self-con·ceit (self′kən·sēt′), n. conceit; too much pride in oneself or one's ability. —self′-con·ceit′ed, adj. —self′-con·ceit′ed·ness, n.

self-con·fi·dence (self′kon′fə·dəns), n. belief in one's own ability, power, judgment, etc.; confidence in oneself. —self′-con′fi·dent, adj. —self′-con′fi·dent·ly, adv.

self-con·scious (self′kon′shəs), adj. made conscious of how one is appearing to others; embarrassed, esp. by the presence or the thought of other people and their attitude toward one; shy. —self′-con′scious·ly, adv. —self′-con′scious·ness, n.

self-con·se·quence (self′kon′sə·kwens), n. sense of one's own importance.

self-con·sist·ent (self′kən·sis′tənt), adj. consistent with oneself or itself; having its parts or elements in agreement. —self′-con·sist′en·cy, n.

self-con·tained (self′kən·tānd′), adj. 1. saying little; reserved. 2. containing in oneself or itself all that is necessary; independent of what is external. 3. having all its working parts contained in one case, cover, or framework: a watch is self-contained. —self′-con·tain′ment, n.

self-con·tra·dic·tion (self′kon′trə·dik′shən), n. 1. contradiction of oneself or itself. 2. statement containing elements that are contradictory. —self′-con′tra·dic′to·ry, adj.

self-con·trol (self′kən·trōl′), n. control of one's actions, feelings, etc. —self′-con·trolled′, adj.

self-de·cep·tive (self′di·sep′tiv), adj. deceiving oneself. —self′-de·cep′tion, n.

self-de·fense, esp. Brit. **self-de·fence** (self′di·fens′), n. defense of one's own person, property, reputation, etc. —self′-de·fen′sive, adj.

self-de·ni·al (self′di·nī′əl), n. sacrifice of one's own desires and interests; going without things one wants. —self′-de·ny′ing, adj. —self′-de·ny′ing·ly, adv. —Syn. self-sacrifice, abstemiousness, austerity. —Ant. self-indulgence.

self-de·ter·mi·na·tion (self′di·tér′mə·nā′shən), n. 1. direction from within only, without influence or force from without. 2. the deciding by the people of a nation what form of government they shall have, without reference to the wishes of any other nation. —self′-de·ter′mined, adj. —self′-de·ter′min·ing, adj.

self-de·vo·tion (self′di·vō′shən), n. self-sacrifice. —self′-de·vo′tion·al, adj.

self-dis·ci·pline (self′dis′ə·plin), n. careful control and training of oneself.

self-ed·u·cat·ed (self′ej′ù·kāt′id), adj. self-taught; educated by one's own efforts. —self′-ed′u·ca′tion, n.

self-ef·face·ment (self′i·fās′mənt), n. act or habit of modestly keeping oneself in the background. —self′-ef·fac′ing, adj.

self-es·teem (self′es·tēm′), n. 1. self-respect. 2. conceit.

self-ev·i·dent (self′ev′ə·dənt), adj. evident by itself; needing no proof. —self′-ev′i·dence, n. —self′-ev′i·dent·ly, adv.

self-ex·am·i·na·tion (self′ig·zam′ə·nā′shən), n. examination into one's own state, conduct, motives, etc.

self-ex·ist·ent (self′ig·zis′tənt), adj. 1. existing independently of any other cause. 2. having an independent existence. —self′-ex·ist′ence, n.

self-ex·plan·a·to·ry (self′iks·plan′ə·tō′ri; –tō′–), **self-ex·plain·ing** (–iks·plān′ing), adj. explaining itself; obvious.

self-ex·pres·sion (self′iks·presh′ən), n. expression of one's personality.

self-fill·ing (self′fil′ing), adj. that can fill itself.

self-gov·ern·ment (self′guv′ərn·mənt), n. 1. government of a group by its own members. 2. self-control. —self′-gov′erned, adj. —self′-gov′ern·ing, adj.

self-heal (self′hēl′), n. weed with blue or purple flowers, formerly supposed to heal wounds.

self-help (self′help′), n. a helping oneself; getting along without assistance from others. —self′-help′ful, adj.

self-im·por·tant (self′im·pôr′tənt), adj. having or showing too high an opinion of one's own importance. —self′-im·por′tance, n. —self′-im·por′tant·ly, adv.

self-im·posed (self′im·pōzd′), adj. imposed on oneself by oneself.

self-im·prove·ment (self′im·prüv′mənt), n. improvement of one's character, mind, etc., by one's own efforts. —self′-im·prov′ing, adj.

self-in·duced (self′in·düst′; –dūst′), adj. 1. induced by itself; induced by oneself. 2. produced by self-induction.

self-in·duc·tion (self′in·duk′shən), n. the inducing of an electric current in a circuit by a varying current in that circuit.

self-in·dul·gence (self′in·dul′jəns), n. gratification of one's own desires, passions, etc., with too little regard for the welfare of others. —self′-in·dul′gent, adj. —self′-in·dul′gent·ly, adv.

self-in·flict·ed (self′in·flik′tid), adj. inflicted on oneself by oneself.

self-in·ter·est (self′in′tər·ist; –trist), n. 1. interest in one's own welfare with too little care for the welfare of others; selfishness. 2. personal advantage. —self′-in′ter·est·ed, adj.

self·ish (sel′fish), adj. 1. caring too much for oneself; caring too little for others. 2. characterized by or showing care solely or chiefly for oneself: selfish motives. —self′ish·ly, adv. —self′ish·ness, n.

self-knowl·edge (self′nol′ij), n. knowledge of one's own character, ability, etc.

self·less (self′lis), adj. having no regard or thought for self; unselfish. —self′less·ly, adv. —self′less·ness, n.

self-love (self′luv′), n. 1. love of oneself; selfishness. 2. conceit. —self′-lov′ing, adj.

self-made (self′mād′), adj. 1. made by oneself. 2. successful through one's own efforts.

self-mov·ing (self′müv′ing), adj. that can move by itself.

self-pit·y (self′pit′i), n. pity for oneself. —self′-pit′y·ing, adj. —self′-pit′y·ing·ly, adv.

self-pol·li·na·tion (self′pol′ə·nā′shən), n. transfer of pollen from a stamen to a pistil of the same flower.

self-pos·sessed (self'pə·zest'), *adj.* having or showing control of one's feelings and acts; not excited, embarrassed, or confused; calm. —**self'·pos·ses'sion**, *n.* —Syn. composed, collected, poised, assured, unruffled.

self-praise (self'prāz'), *n.* praise of oneself.

self-pres·er·va·tion (self'prez'ər·vā'shən), *n.* preservation of oneself from harm or destruction.

self-pro·tec·tion (self'prə·tek'shən), *n.* protection of oneself.

self-re·cord·ing (self'ri·kôr'ding), *adj.* recording automatically.

self-reg·is·ter·ing (self'rej'is·tər·ing), *adj.* registering automatically.

self-reg·u·lat·ing (self'reg'yə·lāt'ing), *adj.* regulating oneself or itself. —**self'-reg'u·la'tion**, *n.* —**self'-reg'u·la'tive**, *adj.*

self-re·li·ance (self'ri·lī'əns), *n.* reliance on one's own acts, abilities, etc. —**self'-re·li'ant**, *adj.* —**self'-re·li'ant·ly**, *adv.*

self-re·proach (self'ri·prōch'), *n.* blame by one's own conscience. —**self'-re·proach'ful**, *adj.*

self-re·spect (self'ri·spekt'), *n.* respect for oneself; proper pride. —**self'-re·spect'ing**, *adj.*

self-re·straint (self'ri·strānt'), *n.* restraint imposed on oneself by oneself; self-control. —**self'-re·strained'**, *adj.*

self-right·eous (self'rī'chəs), *adj.* thinking that one is more moral than others; thinking that one is very good and pleasing to God. —**self'-right'eous·ly**, *adv.* —**self'-right'eous·ness**, *n.*

self-sac·ri·fice (self'sak'rə·fīs), *n.* sacrifice of one's own interests and desires, as for one's duty or another's welfare. —**self'-sac'ri·fic'ing**, *adj.*

self-same (self'sām'), *adj.* very same. —**self'-same'ness**, *n.*

self-sat·is·fied (self'sat'is·fīd), *adj.* pleased with oneself. —**self'-sat'is·fac'tion**, *n.*

self-seek·ing (self'sēk'ing), *adj.* selfish. —*n.* selfishness. —**self'-seek'er**, *n.*

self-serv·ice (self'sėr'vis), *n.* act or process of serving oneself in a restaurant, store, etc.

self-start·er (self'stär'tər), *n.* an electric motor or other device used to start an engine automatically. —**self'-start'ing**, *adj.*

self-styled (self'stīld'), *adj.* called by oneself.

self-suf·fi·cient (self'sə·fish'ənt), *adj.* **1.** asking no help; independent. **2.** conceited. —**self'-suf·fi'cien·cy**, *n.*

self-suf·fic·ing (self'sə·fīs'ing), *adj.* self-sufficient. —**self'-suf·fic'ing·ness**, *n.*

self-sup·port (self'sə·pôrt', -pōrt'), *n.* unaided support of oneself. —**self'-sup·port'ed**, *adj.*

self-sup·port·ing (self'sə·pôr'ting; -pōr'-), *adj.* earning one's expenses; getting along without help.

self-sus·tain·ing (self'səs·tān'ing), *adj.* self-supporting. —**self'-sus·tain'ing·ly**, *adv.*

self-taught (self'tôt'), *adj.* taught by oneself without aid from others.

self-willed (self'wild'), *adj.* insisting on having one's own way; objecting to doing what others ask or command.

self-wind·ing (self'wīn'ding), *adj.* that is wound automatically.

sell (sel), *v.*, **sold, sell·ing**, *n.* —*v.* **1.** exchange for money or other payment: *sell a house.* **2.** deal in; keep for sale: *grocers sell canned goods.* **3.** be given in exchange; be on sale; be sold: *strawberries sell at a high price in January.* **4.** give up; betray, esp. for a price or to gain some advantage: *sell one's country.* **5.** *Am.* cause to be accepted, approved, or adopted by representations and methods characteristic of salesmanship: *sell an idea to the public.* **6.** *Colloq.* win acceptance, approval, or adoption: *an idea that will sell.* **7.** *Slang.* cheat; trick; hoax. **8. sell one's life dearly,** do much damage to adversaries before being killed. **9. sell out, a.** sell all that one has of; get rid of by selling. **b.** *Am., Slang.* betray for a secret bargain. —*n. Slang.* cheat; trick; hoax. [OE *sellan*] —Syn. *v.* **1.** vend, barter, trade.

sell·er (sel'ər), *n.* **1.** person who sells. **2.** thing considered with reference to its sale: *this book is a best seller.*

sell-out (sel'out'), *n.* **1.** *Am., Slang.* a selling out; betrayal. **2.** *Colloq.* performance of a play, etc., for which no unsold seats are left.

Selt·zer (selt'sər), *n.* a bubbling mineral water containing salt, sodium, calcium, and magnesium carbonates. [< G *Selterser* < *Selters*, place where it is found]

sel·vage, sel·vedge (sel'vij), *n.* edge of a fabric finished off to prevent raveling; border; edge. [< *self* + *edge*; because it serves itself as an edge]

selves (selvz), *n.* pl. of **self**: *he had two selves.*

se·man·tic (sə·man'tik), **se·man·ti·cal** (-tə·kəl), *adj.* pertaining to signification or meaning.

se·man·tics (sə·man'tiks), *n.* **1.** *Linguistics.* the scientific study of the meanings and the development of meanings of words; semasiology. **2.** the scientific study of the relations between symbols or signs and what they denote, including the emotional and unconscious reactions of individuals to particular symbols. [< LL < Gk. *semantikos* having meaning, ult. < *sema* sign] —**se·man'ti·cist**, *n.*

sem·a·phore (sem'ə·fôr; -fōr), *n.*, *v.*, **-phored, -phor·ing.** —*n.* apparatus for signaling; upright post or structure with movable arms, an arrangement of lanterns, flags, etc., used in railroad signaling. —*v.* signal by semaphore. [< Gk. *sema* signal + *-phoros* carrying] —**sem·a·phor·ic** (sem'ə·fôr'ik; -fōr'-), *adj.*

RED LIGHT — STOP; YELLOW LIGHT — CAUTION; GREEN LIGHT — PROCEED
Railroad semaphores

Se·ma·rang (sə·mä'räng), *n.* seaport in N Java.

se·ma·si·ol·o·gy (sə·mā'si·ol'ə·ji; -zi·ol'-), *n.* semantics.

sem·blance (sem'bləns), *n.* **1.** likeness; copy. **2.** the outward aspect; appearance. **3.** an assumed or unreal appearance. [< OF, < *sembler* seem, ult. < L *similis* similar]

se·men (sē'mən), *n.* fluid containing the male reproductive cells. [< L, seed]

se·mes·ter (sə·mes'tər), *n. Am.* half of a school year. [< G < L *semestris* semiannual, ult. < *sex* six + *mensis* month] —**se·mes'tral**, *adj.*

semi-, *prefix.* **1.** half, as in *semicircle.* **2.** partly; incompletely, as in *semicivilized.* **3.** twice. Semi——ly means in each half of a ——, or twice in a ——, as in *semimonthly.* [< L] ➤ Semi- is not usually hyphened except before proper names (*semi-Christian*) or words beginning with *i* (*semi-invalid*).

sem·i·an·nu·al (sem'i·an'yü·əl), *adj.* **1.** occurring every half year. **2.** lasting a half year. —**sem'i·an'nu·al·ly**, *adv.*

sem·i·ar·id (sem'i·ar'id), *adj.* having very little rainfall.

sem·i·breve (sem'i·brēv'), *n. Music.* whole note.

sem·i·cir·cle (sem'i·sėr'kəl), *n.* half of a circle. —**sem·i·cir·cu·lar** (sem'i·sėr'kyə·lər), *adj.* —**sem'i·cir'cu·lar·ly**, *adv.*

semicircular canal, *Anat.* any of three curved, tubelike canals in the inner part of the ear that help us keep our balance.

sem·i·civ·i·lized (sem'i·siv'ə·līzd), *adj.* partly civilized. —**sem'i·civ'i·li·za'tion**, *n.*

sem·i·co·lon (sem'i·kō'lən), *n.* mark of punctuation (;) that shows a separation not so complete as that shown by a period. ➤ A semicolon (;) marks a degree of separation between sentence elements considerably greater than that marked by a comma, and often nearly as great as that marked by a period. There are a few situations in which a semicolon is likely to be employed by all writers, but in most situations its use depends upon appropriateness to a writer's style. The situations in which a semicolon is most likely to be used are those involving separation of units that contain smaller elements separated by commas, as (1) items in a series,

(2) enumerations, **(3)** lists of figures, **(4)** scores, or **(5)** clauses with commas in them. A semicolon may also be used to separate coördinate clauses which are not closely related, (1) when no connective is expressed, (2) when the clauses are connected by a conjunctive adverb such as *however, moreover, nevertheless,* or *consequently* (each of which is relatively heavy and tends to be used as a connective between clauses which are long and formally joined), and (3) when the clauses are connected by a coördinating conjunction but the connection is not close or if the clauses are long. Except for these instances, the use of semicolons is largely a stylistic matter. They tend to slow up the reading and are consequently fewer in narrative than in exposition. In informal styles commas would be used in preference or if the distinction between clauses is considerable two sentences would be written.

sem·i·con·scious (sem'i·kon'shəs), *adj.* half-conscious; not fully conscious. **—sem'i·con'scious·ly,** *adv.* **—sem'i·con'scious·ness,** *n.*

sem·i·de·tached (sem'i·di·tacht'), *adj.* partly detached, used esp. of either of two houses joined by a common wall but separated from other buildings.

sem·i·fi·nal (sem'i·fī'nəl), *n.* one of the two rounds, matches, etc., that immediately precede the final one. **—adj.** designating or pertaining to such a round, match, etc.

sem·i·flu·id (sem'i·flü'id), *adj.* imperfectly fluid; extremely viscous. **—n.** a substance neither solid nor liquid; one that flows but is very thick. **—sem'i·flu·id'i·ty,** *n.*

sem·i·liq·uid (sem'i·lik'wid), *adj., n.* semifluid. **—sem'i·li·quid'i·ty,** *n.*

sem·i·month·ly (sem'i·munth'li), *adj., adv., n., pl.* **-lies.** **—adj.** occurring or appearing twice a month. **—adv.** twice a month. **—n.** something that occurs or appears twice a month; magazine or paper published twice a month.

sem·i·nal (sem'ə·nəl), *adj.* 1. of or pertaining to semen or seed. 2. like seed; having the possibility of future development. **—sem'i·nal·ly,** *adv.*

sem·i·nar (sem'ə·när), *n.* 1. group of college or university students doing research under direction. 2. course of study or work for such a group. [< G < L *seminarium* plant nursery, hotbed < *semen* seed. Doublet of SEMINARY.]

sem·i·nar·y (sem'ə·ner'i), *n., pl.* **-nar·ies.** 1. school, esp. one beyond high school. 2. academy or boarding school, esp. for young women. 3. school or college for training students to be priests, ministers, etc. [< L *seminarium.* Doublet of SEMINAR.]

sem·i·na·tion (sem'ə·nā'shən), *n.* a sowing; propagation; dissemination.

sem·i·nif·er·ous (sem'ə·nif'ər·əs), *adj.* 1. bearing or producing seed. 2. conveying or containing semen.

Sem·i·nole (sem'ə·nōl), *n., pl.* **-nole, -noles,** *adj. Am.* **—n.** member of a tribe of American Indians living in Florida and Oklahoma. **—adj.** of or having to do with this tribe.

sem·i·of·fi·cial (sem'i·ə·fish'əl), *adj.* partly official; having some degree of authority. **—sem'i·of·fi'cial·ly,** *adv.*

se·mi·ot·ics (sē'mi·ot'iks), *n.* science of signs or symbols. [< Gk. *semeion* sign]

sem·i·per·me·a·ble (sem'i·pér'mi·ə·bəl), *adj.* permeable to some substances but not to others.

sem·i·pre·cious (sem'i·presh'əs), *adj.* having value but not great value.

sem·i·qua·ver (sem'i·kwā'vər), *n. Music.* sixteenth note.

sem·i·skilled (sem'i·skild'), *adj.* partly skilled.

sem·i·sol·id (sem'i·sol'id), *adj.* partly solid. **—n.** a partly solid substance.

Sem·ite (sem'īt; sē'mīt), *n.* member of the linguistic family that includes the Hebrews, Arabs, Syrians, Phoenicians, Assyrians, etc.

Se·mit·ic (sə·mit'ik), *adj.* of or pertaining to the Semites or their languages. **—n.** group of languages including Hebrew, Arabic, etc.

sem·i·trop·i·cal (sem'i·trop'ə·kəl), *adj.* halfway between tropical and temperate.

sem·i·vow·el (sem'i·vou'əl), *n.* a vowel sound which does not form the center of a syllable, as *w, y,* in *win, yet.*

sem·i·week·ly (sem'i·wēk'li), *adj., adv., n., pl.* **-lies.** **—adj. Am.** occurring or appearing twice a week. **—adv.** twice a week. **—n.** something that occurs or appears twice a week; magazine or paper published twice a week.

sem·i·year·ly (sem'i·yir'li), *adj., adv., n., pl.* **-lies.** **—adj.** occurring or appearing twice a year. **—adv.** twice a year. **—n.** something that occurs or appears twice a year.

sem·o·li·na (sem'ə·lē'nə), *n.* the parts of hard wheat remaining after the flour has been sifted through, used in making puddings, macaroni, etc. [< Ital. *semolino,* ult. < L *simila* fine flour]

sem·pi·ter·nal (sem'pi·tér'nəl), *adj.* everlasting; eternal. [< LL *sempiternalis,* ult. < L *semper* forever] **—sem·pi·ter·ni·ty** (sem'pi·tér'nə·ti), *n.*

semp·stress (sem'stris; semp'-), *n.* seamstress.

Sen., sen., 1. Senate; Senator. 2. Senior.

sen (sen), *n., pl.* **sen.** a Japanese copper or bronze coin, equal to $\frac{1}{100}$ of a yen.

sen·ate (sen'it), *n.* 1. a governing or lawmaking assembly. The highest council of state in ancient Rome was called the senate. 2. **Senate,** *Am.* the upper house of Congress or of a State legislature. 3. the upper house of the legislature of certain other countries, as Canada, Australia, etc. 4. a governing, advisory, or disciplinary body, as in certain universities. [< L *senatus* < *senex* old man]

sen·a·tor (sen'ə·tər), *n.* member of a senate. **—sen·a·to·ri·al** (sen'ə·tô'ri·əl; -tō'-), *adj.* **—sen'a·to'ri·al·ly,** *adv.* **—sen'a·tor·ship',** *n.*

send (send), *v.,* **sent, send·ing.** 1. cause to go: *send ten men, send forth smoke.* 2. compel or force to go: *the enemy's fire sent them running.* 3. cause to be carried: *send a letter.* 4. cause to come, occur, be, etc.: *God sends rain.* 5. drive; impel; throw: *send a ball.* 6. *Elect.* transmit. 7. send a message or messenger: *send for a doctor.* 8. give (*forth, out,* etc.): *send forth light.* 9. of a ship, to pitch. [OE *sendan*] **—send'er,** *n.* **—Syn.** 1. dispatch. 5. hurl, cast. 8. emit.

send-off (send'ôf'; -of'), *n. Am.* 1. a friendly demonstration in honor of a person setting out on a journey, course, career, etc. 2. *Colloq.* a start (favorable or unfavorable) given to a person or thing.

Sen·e·ca (sen'ə·kə), *n. Am.* member of the largest tribe of the Iroquois Confederacy of American Indians.

Sen·e·gal (sen'ə·gôl'), *n.* 1. republic in W Africa on the Atlantic, formerly part of French West Africa. 2. river in W Africa flowing into the Atlantic. **—Sen·e·gal·ese** (sen'ə·gôl·ēz'; -ēs'; -gəl-), *adj., n.*

se·nes·cent (sə·nes'ənt), *adj.* growing old; beginning to show old age. [< L *senescens* growing old, ult. < *senex* old] **—se·nes'cence,** *n.*

sen·es·chal (sen'ə·shəl), *n.* steward in charge of a royal palace, nobleman's estate, etc., in the Middle Ages. Seneschals often had the powers of judges or generals. [< OF; from a Gmc. compound "old servant"]

se·nile (sē'nīl; -nil), *adj.* 1. of old age. 2. showing the weakness of old age. 3. caused by old age. [< L, < *senex* old] **—se·nil·i·ty** (sə·nil'ə·ti), *n.*

sen·ior (sēn'yər), *adj.* 1. older. 2. the older; designating a father whose son has the same given name: *John Parker, Senior.* 3. higher in rank or longer in service: *Mr. Jones is the senior member of the firm of Jones and Brown.* 4. *Am.* of or pertaining to the graduating class. **—n.** 1. an older person: *Paul is his brother's senior by two years.* 2. person of higher rank or longer service. 3. *Am.* member of the graduating class. [< L, compar. of *senex* old. Doublet of SIRE.]

āge, cāre, fär; ēqual, tėrm; īce; ōpen, ôrder; pút, rüle, ūse; ŧħ, then; ə=a in about.

senior high school, *Am.* school attended after junior high school. It usually has grades 10, 11, and 12.

sen·ior·i·ty (sēn·yôr'ə·ti; -yor'-), *n., pl.* **-ties.** superiority in age or standing; state or fact of being older.

sen·na (sen'ə), *n.* **1.** laxative extracted from the dried leaves of any of several cassia plants. **2.** the dried leaves of any of these plants. **3.** the cassia plant, or a plant similar to it. [< NL < Ar. *sanā*]

Sen·nach·er·ib (sə·nak'ər·ib), *n.* died 681 B.C., king of Assyria, 705–681 B.C.

se·ñor (sā·nyôr'), *n., pl.* **-ño·res** (-nyō'rās). *Spanish.* **1.** as a term of address, sir. **2.** as a title, Mr. **3.** gentleman.

se·ño·ra (sā·nyō'rä), *n. Spanish.* **1.** Mrs.; Madame. **2.** lady.

se·ño·ri·ta (sā'nyō·rē'tä), *n. Spanish.* **1.** Miss. **2.** a young lady.

sen·sa·tion (sen·sā'shən), *n.* **1.** action of the senses; power to see, hear, feel, taste, smell, etc.: *a dead body is without sensation.* **2.** capacity to respond to stimulation. **3.** a mental condition produced through an organ of sense. **4.** feeling: *he had a sad sensation.* **5.** strong or excited feeling: *the announcement of war caused a sensation.* **6.** cause of such feeling. [< LL *sensatio,* ult. < L *sensus* SENSE]

sen·sa·tion·al (sen·sā'shən·əl), *adj.* **1.** arousing strong or excited feeling. **2.** trying to arouse strong or excited feeling. **3.** of the senses; having to do with sensation. —**sen·sa'tion·al·ist,** *n.* —**sen·sa'tion·al·is'tic,** *adj.* —**sen·sa'tion·al·ly,** *adv.* —Syn. **1.** exciting, thrilling, dramatic.

sen·sa·tion·al·ism (sen·sā'shən·əl·iz'əm), *n.* **1.** sensational methods; sensational writing, language, etc. **2.** the philosophical theory or doctrine that all ideas are derived solely through sensation.

sense (sens), *n., v.,* **sensed, sens·ing.** —*n.* **1.** power of the mind to know what happens outside itself. Sight, hearing, touch, taste, and smell are senses. **2.** the feeling produced through these senses. **3.** understanding; appreciation: *everyone thinks he has a sense of humor.* **4.** Usually, **senses.** normal, sound condition of mind. **5.** judgment; intelligence: *common sense would have prevented the accident.* **6.** meaning: *a gentleman in every sense of the word.* **7.** what is sensible, reasonable, or intelligent: *talk sense.* **8.** the general opinion: *the sense of the assembly was clear before the vote.* **9.** direction; course. **10.** in a sense, in some respects; to some degree. **11.** make sense, be understandable; be reasonable. —*v.* **1.** be aware; feel. **2.** *Colloq.* understand. [< L *sensus* < *sentire* perceive] —Syn. *n.* **2.** perception, sensation. **3.** apprehension. **4.** rationality. **5.** wisdom, sagacity. **6.** signification.

sense·less (sens'lis), *adj.* **1.** unconscious. **2.** foolish; stupid. **3.** meaningless, as words. —**sense'less·ly,** *adv.* —**sense'less·ness,** *n.*

sense organ, eye, ear, or other part of the body by which a person or an animal receives sensations of heat, colors, sounds, smells, etc.

sen·si·bil·i·ty (sen'sə·bil'ə·ti), *n., pl.* **-ties. 1.** ability to feel or perceive: *some drugs lessen a person's sensibilities.* **2.** sensitiveness. **3.** fineness of feeling: *she has an unusual sensibility for colors.* **4.** Usually, **sensibilities.** sensitive feelings. **5.** sensibilities, emotional capacities. **6.** capacity for higher or more refined feelings. **7.** tendency to feel hurt or offended too easily. **8.** awareness; consciousness. —Syn. **2.** susceptibility, impressibility.

sen·si·ble (sen'sə·bəl), *adj.* **1.** having or showing good judgment; wise. **2.** aware; conscious. **3.** that can be noticed. **4.** that can be perceived by the senses. **5.** sensitive. [< LL *sensibilis,* ult. < L *sentire* feel] —**sen'si·ble·ness,** *n.* —**sen'si·bly,** *adv.* —Syn. **1.** judicious, discreet, sagacious, practical, hard-headed. **2.** sentient, cognizant. **3.** perceptible, appreciable.

sen·si·tive (sen'sə·tiv), *adj.* **1.** receiving impressions readily: *the eye is sensitive to light.* **2.** easily affected or influenced: *a thermometer is sensitive to temperature.* **3.** easily hurt or of-fended. [< Med.L *sensitivus* < L *sensus* SENSE] —**sen'si·tive·ly,** *adv.* —**sen'si·tiv'i·ty, sen'si·tive·ness,** *n.* —Syn. **2.** impressionable, impressible, susceptible.

sensitive plant, a tropical American plant whose leaflets fold together when touched.

sen·si·tize (sen'sə·tīz), *v.,* **-tized, -tiz·ing.** make sensitive. —**sen'si·ti·za'tion,** *n.* —**sen'si·tiz'er,** *n.*

sen·so·ry (sen'sə·ri), **sen·so·ri·al** (sen·sō'-ri·əl; -sō'-), *adj.* of or pertaining to sensation.

sen·su·al (sen'shù·əl), *adj.* **1.** pertaining to the bodily senses rather than to the mind or soul: *sensual pleasures.* **2.** caring too much for the pleasures of the senses. **3.** lustful; lewd. **4.** of or pertaining to the senses or sensation. [< LL, < L *sensus* SENSE] —**sen'su·al·ism,** *n.* —**sen'su·al·ist,** *n.* —**sen'su·al·is'tic,** *adj.* —**sen'su·al·ly,** *adv.* —Syn. **2.** voluptuous, self-indulgent. **3.** wanton, lecherous. —Ant. **3.** continent, chaste.

sen·su·al·i·ty (sen'shù·al'ə·ti), *n., pl.* **-ties. 1.** sensual nature. **2.** excessive indulgence in the pleasures of the senses. **3.** lewdness.

sen·su·al·ize (sen'shù·əl·īz), *v.,* **-ized, -iz·ing.** make sensual. —**sen'su·al·i·za'tion,** *n.*

sen·su·ous (sen'shù·əs), *adj.* **1.** of or derived from the senses; having an effect on the senses; perceived by the senses: *the sensuous thrill of a warm bath,* a *sensuous love of color.* **2.** enjoying the pleasures of the senses. —**sen'su·ous·ly,** *adv.* —**sen'su·ous·ness,** *n.*

sent (sent), *v.* pt. and pp. of send.

sen·tence (sen'təns), *n., v.,* **-tenced, -tenc·ing.** —*n.* **1.** group of words that expresses a complete thought. **2.** decision. **3.** opinion pronounced on some particular subject. **4.** *Law.* a. a decision by a judge on the punishment of a criminal. b. the punishment itself. **5.** *Obs.* proverb. **6.** in music, a period. —*v.* pronounce punishment on. [< F < L *sententia,* orig., opinion < *sentire* feel] —**sen'tenc·er,** *n.* —**sen·ten'tial** (sen·ten'shəl), *adj.*

sen·ten·tious (sen·ten'shəs), *adj.* **1.** full of meaning; saying much in few words. **2.** speaking as if one were a judge settling a question. **3.** inclined to make wise sayings; abounding in proverbs. **4.** characterized by or given to pompous moralizing. [< L, < *sententia* SENTENCE] —**sen·ten'tious·ly,** *adv.* —**sen·ten'tious·ness,** *n.* —Syn. **1.** pithy. **3.** epigrammatic.

sen·tient (sen'shənt), *adj.* **1.** that can feel; of or having feeling. **2.** characterized by sensation or feeling. —*n.* one that feels. [< L *sentiens* feeling] —**sen'tience, sen'tien·cy,** *n.* —**sen'tient·ly,** *adv.*

sen·ti·ment (sen'tə·mənt), *n.* **1.** mixture of thought and feeling. Admiration, patriotism, and loyalty are sentiments. **2.** feeling, esp. refined or tender feeling. **3.** thought or saying that expresses feeling. **4.** a mental attitude. **5.** a personal opinion. [< LL, < L *sentire* feel] —Syn. **2.** emotion, sentimentality. **3.** maxim, epigram. **5.** view, thought.

sen·ti·men·tal (sen'tə·men'təl), *adj.* **1.** having or showing much tender feeling: *sentimental poetry.* **2.** likely to act from feelings rather than from logical thinking. **3.** of or dependent on sentiment. **4.** having too much sentiment. —**sen'ti·men'tal·ly,** *adv.* —Syn. **4.** emotional, gushing.

sen·ti·men·tal·ism (sen'tə·men'təl·iz·əm), *n.* **1.** tendency to be influenced by sentiment rather than reason. **2.** excessive indulgence in sentiment. **3.** feeling expressed too openly or commonly or sentimentally. —**sen'ti·men'tal·ist,** *n.*

sen·ti·men·tal·i·ty (sen'tə·men·tal'ə·ti), *n., pl.* **-ties.** sentimental quality, behavior, etc.

sen·ti·men·tal·ize (sen'tə·men'təl·īz), *v.,* **-ized, -iz·ing. 1.** indulge in sentiment; affect sentiment. **2.** make sentimental. **3.** be sentimental about.

sen·ti·nel (sen'tə·nəl), *n., v.,* **-neled, -nel·ing;** *esp. Brit.* **-nelled, -nel·ling.** —*n.* **1.** one stationed to keep watch and guard against surprises. **2.** stand sentinel, act as a sentinel; keep watch. —*v.* **1.** watch over as a sentinel does. **2.**

furnish with sentinels. 3. post as sentinels. [< F < Ital. *sentinella*]

sen·try (sen'tri), *n.*, *pl.* **–tries.** 1. sentinel. 2. watch; guard: *we stood sentry over the sleepers.* [? abbrev. of *centrinel*, var. of *sentinel*]

Seoul (sōl; sā·ül'; *Brit.* sā·ōl'), *n.* city in W Korea, capital of the Korean republic. *Japanese, Keijo.*

se·pal (sē'pəl), *n.* one of the leaf-like divisions of the calyx, or outer covering, of a flower. [< NL *sepalum*, short for L *separatum petalum* separate petal] —**se'paled,** *esp. Brit.* **se'palled,** *adj.*

PETAL

SEPAL

sep·a·ra·ble (sep'ə·rə·bəl; sep'rə-bəl), *adj.* that can be separated. —**sep'a·ra·bil'i·ty, sep'a·ra·ble·ness,** *n.* —**sep'a·ra·bly,** *adv.*

sep·a·rate (*v.* sep'ə·rāt; *adj., n.* sep'ə·rit, sep'rit), *v.*, **–rat·ed, –rat·ing,** *adj., n.* —*v.* 1. put apart: *separate persons fighting.* 2. disconnect, disjoin, or disunite (what is connected): *separate church and state.* 3. become parted or disengaged: *the rope separated under the strain.* 4. put out of or remove from personal association: *separated from one's wife.* 5. withdraw from association or relations: *the partners have separated.* 6. keep apart as by an intervening barrier, space, etc.: *the Atlantic separates Europe from America.* 7. part or divide (a mass, whole, etc.) into individuals, elements, etc.: *separate a mixture.* 8. take by such parting or dividing: *separate metal from ore.* —*adj.* 1. disconnected: *separate fragments.* 2. being or standing apart: *a row of separate houses.* 3. shut off, one from another: *separate confinement.* 4. existing or maintained independently: *separate organizations.* 5. unconnected; distinct: *two separate questions.* 6. individual; particular: *each separate item.* —*n.* something separate. [< L, < *se-* apart + *parare* get] —**sep'a·rate·ly,** *adv.* —**sep'a·rate·ness,** *n.* —**sep'a·ra'tive,** *adj.* —**sep'a·ra'tor,** *n.* —**Syn.** *v.* 2. disengage, detach.

sep·a·ra·tion (sep'ə·rā'shən), *n.* 1. a separating or being separated. 2. line or point of separating. 3. *Law.* a. a divorce. b. the living apart of husband and wife by agreement.

sep·a·ra·tist (sep'ə·rā'tist; sep'ə·rə-; sep'rə-), *n.* member of a group that separates or withdraws from a larger group. —**sep·a·ra·tism** (sep'ə·rə·tiz'əm; sep'rə-), *n.*

se·pi·a (sē'pi·ə), *n.* 1. a brown paint or ink prepared from the inky fluid of cuttlefish. 2. a dark-brown color. —*adj.* 1. dark-brown. 2. done in sepia: *a sepia print.* [< L < Gk.]

se·poy (sē'poi), *n.* formerly, a native of India who was a soldier in the British army. [< Pg. < Hind. < Pers. *sipāhī* soldier < *sipāh* army]

sep·sis (sep'sis), *n.* blood poisoning. [< NL < Gk., putrefaction, < *sepein* to rot]

Sept., September.

Sep·tem·ber (sep·tem'bər), *n.* the ninth month, containing 30 days. [< L, < *septem* seven; from the order of the Roman calendar]

sep·ten·ni·al (sep·ten'i·əl), *adj.* 1. lasting seven years. 2. occurring every seven years. [< L *septennium* seven-year period < *septem* seven + *annus* year] —**sep·ten'ni·al·ly,** *adv.*

sep·tet, sep·tette (sep·tet'), *n.* 1. a musical composition for seven voices or instruments. 2. seven singers or players. 3. any group of seven. [< G, < L *septem* seven; modeled after *duet*]

sep·tic (sep'tik), *adj.* 1. causing infection or putrefaction. 2. infected. [< L < Gk., < *sepein* to rot] —**sep·tic·i·ty** (sep·tis'ə·ti), *n.*

sep·ti·ce·mi·a (sep'tə·sē'mi·ə), *n.* blood poisoning, esp. a form in which microörganisms as well as their toxins are absorbed by the blood. [< NL < Gk. *septikos* septic (see under *sepein* to rot) + *haima* blood] —**sep'ti·ce'mic,** *adj.*

septic tank, tank in which sewage is acted on by bacteria.

sep·til·lion (sep·til'yən), *n.* 1. in the United States and France, 1 followed by 24 zeros. 2. in Great Britain, 1 followed by 42 zeros. [< F (< L *septem* seven), modeled after *million* MILLION] —**sep·til'lionth,** *adj., n.*

sep·tu·a·ge·nar·i·an (sep'chů·ə·jə·nār'i·ən; -tū-), **sep·tu·ag·e·nar·y** (-aj'ə·ner'i), *adj., n., pl.* **–nar·i·ans; –nar·ies.** —*adj.* of the age of 70 years, or between 70 and 80 years old. —*n.* person who is 70, or between 70 and 80, years old. [< L, ult. < *septuaginta* seventy]

sep·tum (sep'təm), *n., pl.* **–ta** (-tə). a dividing wall; partition. [< L, a fence, < *saepire* hedge in] —**sep'tal,** *adj.*

sep·tu·ple (sep'tů·pəl; -tyů-; sep·tū'pəl; -tū'-), *adj., v.,* **–pled, –pling.** —*adj.* seven times as great; sevenfold. —*v.* make seven times as great. [< LL *septuplus* < L *septem* seven + *-plus* -fold]

sep·ul·cher, *esp. Brit.* **sep·ul·chre** (sep'əl·kər), *n., v.,* **–chered, –chering;** *esp. Brit.* **–chred, –chring.** —*n.* place of burial; tomb; grave. —*v.* bury (a dead body) in a sepulcher. [< OF < L *sepulcrum* < *sepelire* bury]

se·pul·chral (sə·pul'krəl), *adj.* 1. of sepulchers or tombs. 2. of burial. 3. deep and gloomy; dismal. —**se·pul'chral·ly,** *adv.*

seq., the following. [< L *sequens*]

se·quel (sē'kwəl), *n.* 1. that which follows; continuation. 2. something that follows as a result of some earlier happening; result. 3. a complete story continuing an earlier one about the same people. [< L, < *sequi* follow] —**Syn.** 2. consequence, outcome.

se·quence (sē'kwəns), *n.* 1. the coming of one thing after another; succession; order of succession. 2. a connected series. 3. something that follows; result. [< LL, ult. < L *sequi* follow]

se·quent (sē'kwənt), *adj.* 1. following; subsequent. 2. following in order; consecutive. 3. following as a result; consequent. —*n.* that which follows; result; consequence. [< L *sequens* following]

se·quen·tial (si·kwen'shəl), *adj.* 1. sequent. 2. forming a sequence or connected series. —**se·quen'tial·ly,** *adv.*

se·ques·ter (si·kwes'tər), *v.* 1. remove or withdraw from public use or from public view. 2. take away (property) for a time from an owner until a debt is paid or some claim is satisfied. 3. seize by authority; take and keep. [< L, < *sequester* trustee, mediator < *sequi* follow] —**se·ques'tered,** *adj.*

se·ques·trate (si·kwes'trāt), *v.,* **–trat·ed, –trat·ing.** 1. confiscate. 2. *Archaic.* sequester.

se·ques·tra·tion (sē'kwes·trā'shən; si·kwes'-), *n.* 1. the seizing and holding of property until legal claims are satisfied. 2. forcible or authorized seizure; confiscation. 3. separation or withdrawal from others; seclusion.

se·quin (sē'kwin), *n.* 1. a small spangle used to ornament dresses, scarfs, etc. 2. a former Italian gold coin. [< F < Ital. *zecchino* < *zecca* mint < Ar. *sikka* a stamp] —**se'quined,** *adj.*

se·quoi·a (si·kwoi'ə), *n. Am.* either of two species of very tall evergreen trees of California. [< NL, < *Sequoya* (Cherokee *Sikwayi*), an Indian who invented a system of Cherokee writing]

se·rag·li·o (si·ral'yō; -räl'-), *n., pl.* **–rag·li·os.** the women's quarters of a Mohammedan house or palace; harem. [< Ital. *serraglio*, ult. < L *serare* lock up; infl. by Turk. *serāi* palace]

se·ra·pe (sə·rä'pē), *n. Am.* shawl or blanket, often having bright colors, worn by Spanish American Indians. [< dial. Sp.]

ser·aph (ser'əf), *n., pl.* **–aphs, –a·phim** (-ə·fim). one of the highest order of angels. [< *seraphim*, pl., < LL < Heb.] —**se·raph·ic** (sə·raf'ik), **se·raph'i·cal,** *adj.* —**se·raph'i·cal·ly,** *adv.*

Serb (sėrb), *n.* 1. native or inhabitant of Serbia. 2. language of Serbia. —*adj.* of Serbia, its people, or their language.

Ser·bi·a (sėr'bi·ə), *n.* district in SE Yugoslavia, formerly a country. —**Ser'bi·an,** *adj., n.*

sere (sir), *adj.* sear. [var. of *sear*]

ser·e·nade (ser'ə·nād'), *n., v.,* **–nad·ed, –nad·ing.** —*n.* 1. music played or sung outdoors at night, esp. by a lover under his lady's window. 2. piece of music suitable for such a perform-

---

āge, cāre, fär; ēqual, tėrm; īce; ōpen, ôrder; pút, rüle, ūse; th, then; ə=a in about.

ance. —*v.* **1.** sing or play to in this way. **2.** sing or play a serenade. [< F < Ital. *serenata,* ult. < L *serenus* serene] —ser′e·nad′er, *n.*

ser·en·dip·i·ty (ser′ən·dip′ə·ti), *n.* the facility to find, by accident, interesting or unexpected facts, proofs, etc. [a coined word]

se·rene (sə·rēn′), *adj.* **1.** peaceful; calm: *a serene smile.* **2.** clear; bright; not cloudy. [< L *serenus*] —se·rene′ly, *adv.* —se·rene′ness, *n.* —Syn. **1.** tranquil, placid, undisturbed.

se·ren·i·ty (sə·ren′ə·ti), *n., pl.* **-ties. 1.** quiet peace; calmness. **2.** clearness; brightness.

serf (sėrf), *n.* **1.** slave who cannot be sold off the land, but passes from one owner to another with the land. **2.** person who is mistreated, underpaid, etc. [< F < L *servus* slave] —serf′dom, *n.*

serge (sėrj), *n.* a kind of cloth having slanting lines or ridges on its surface. [< F, ult. < L *serica* (*vestis*) silken (garment) < Gk., < *Seres* the Chinese]

ser·geant (sär′jənt), *n.* **1.** *U.S. Army.* **a.** an officer ranking next above a corporal. Sergeants and corporals are noncommissioned officers. **b.** a noncommissioned officer next above a corporal and next below sergeant first class, formerly next below staff sergeant. **2.** a police officer ranking next above an ordinary policeman and next below a captain or lieutenant. **3.** sergeant at arms. Also, *esp. Brit.* serjeant. [< OF < L *serviens,* ppr. of *servire* serve] —ser·gean·cy (sär′jən·si), ser′geant·ship, *n.*

sergeant at arms, **ser·geant-at-arms** (sär′jənt·ət·ärmz′), *n., pl.* sergeants at arms; ser·geants-at-arms. officer who keeps order in a legislature, law court, etc.

sergeant first class, *U.S. Army.* since 1948, a noncommissioned officer next below master sergeant and next above sergeant.

se·ri·al (sir′i·əl), *n.* story published or broadcast one part at a time, once a week, every day, etc. —*adj.* **1.** of or having to do with a serial. **2.** published or broadcast one part at a time. **3.** of, arranged in, or making a series. [< NL, < L *series* SERIES] —se′ri·al′i·ty, *n.* —se′ri·al·ly, *adv.*

serial number, an individual number given to a person, article, etc.

se·ri·a·tim (sir′i·ā′tim; ser′i-), *adv.* in a series; one after the other. [< Med.L]

se·ries (sir′iz), *n., pl.* **-ries. 1.** number of similar things in a row: *a series of rooms opened off the long hall.* **2.** number of things placed one after another. **3.** number of things, events, etc., coming one after the other: *a series of rainy days.* **4.** an electrical arrangement with the positive pole or terminal of one battery, etc., connected to the negative pole or terminal of the next. **5.** *Math.* **a.** succession of terms related by some law, and consequently predictable. **b.** their sum. [< L, < *serere* join] ▶ series. Commas are used between the items of a series of three or more short items, although usage is divided over the insertion of a comma before the last item of the series. Many writers, esp. in an informal style, do not use one: *He finished the packing by including his toothbrush, comb [,] and shaving equipment.*

ser·if (ser′if), *n.* a thin or smaller line used to finish off a main stroke of a letter, as at the top and bottom of M.

se·ri·o·com·ic (sir′i·ō·kom′ik), **se·ri·o·com·i·cal** (-ə·kəl), *adj.* partly serious and partly comic. —se′ri·o·com′i·cal·ly, *adv.*

se·ri·ous (sir′i·əs), *adj.* **1.** thoughtful; grave: *a serious mood.* **2.** in earnest; not joking; sincere: *he was serious about the subject.* **3.** needing thought; important: *racial prejudice is a serious problem.* **4.** important because it may do much harm; dangerous: *serious trouble.* [< LL *seriosus* < L *serius* earnest] —se′ri·ous·ly, *adv.* —se′ri·ous·ness, *n.* —Syn. **1.** solemn, sober. **3.** weighty, momentous. **4.** critical, alarming.

ser·jeant (sär′jənt), *n.* *Esp. Brit.* sergeant. —ser′jeant·cy, ser′jeant·ship, *n.*

ser·mon (sėr′mən), *n.* **1.** a public talk on religion or something connected with religion. **2.** a serious talk about morals, conduct, duty, etc. **3.** a long, tiresome speech. [< L *sermo* a talk]

ser·mon·ize (sėr′mən·īz), *v.,* **-ized, -iz·ing. 1.** give a sermon; preach. **2.** preach or talk seriously to; lecture. —ser′mon·iz′er, *n.*

Sermon on the Mount, Christ's sermon to his disciples, as reported in Matt. 5–7 and Luke 6:20–49.

se·rol·o·gy (si·rol′ə·ji), *n.* science of serums. —se·ro·log·i·cal (sir′ə·loj′ə·kəl), *adj.* —se·rol′o·gist, *n.*

se·rous (sir′əs), *adj.* **1.** of or having to do with serum. **2.** like serum; watery. Tears are drops of a serous fluid. —se·ros·i·ty (si·ros′ə·ti), *n.*

ser·pent (sėr′pənt), *n.* **1.** snake; big snake. **2.** a sly, treacherous person. [< L *serpens,* orig., creeping]

ser·pen·tine (sėr′pən·tēn; -tīn), *adj.* **1.** of or like a serpent. **2.** winding; twisting. **3.** cunning; sly; treacherous. [< LL, < L *serpens* serpent] —ser·pen·ti·nous (sėr′pən·tē′nəs; -tī′-), *adj.*

ser·rate (ser′āt; -it), **ser·rat·ed** (-āt·id), *adj.* notched like the edge of a saw; toothed. [< L, < *serra* a saw] —ser·ra′tion, *n.*

Serrate leaf

ser·ried (ser′id), *adj.* crowded closely together. [< F *serré,* pp. of *serrer* press close]

se·rum (sir′əm), *n., pl.* **se·rums,** se·ra (sir′ə). **1.** a clear, pale-yellow, watery part of the blood that separates from the clot when blood coagulates. **2.** liquid used to prevent or cure a disease, usually obtained from the blood of an animal that has been made immune to the disease. Diphtheria antitoxin is a serum. **3.** any watery animal liquid. Lymph is a serum. [< L, whey]

serv·ant (sėr′vənt), *n.* **1.** person employed in a household. **2.** person employed by another. Policemen and firemen are public servants. **3.** person devoted to any service. Ministers are called the servants of God. [< OF, ppr. of *servir* SERVE] —ser′vant·less, *adj.*

serve (sėrv), *v.,* served, serv·ing, *n.* —*v.* **1.** be a servant of; give service to; work for or in: *serve an employer.* **2.** be a servant; give service; work: *he served as butler.* **3.** wait on at table; bring food or drink to. **4.** put (food or drink) on the table: *the maid served the first course.* **5.** go through a term of service as a soldier, etc.: *he served in the army.* **6.** supply; furnish; supply with something needed: *what can we serve you with?* **7.** help; aid: *let me know if I can serve you in any way.* **8.** be useful; be what is needed; be of use: *a grasshopper will serve as bait.* **9.** be useful to; fulfill: *this will serve my purpose.* **10.** be favorable or suitable; satisfy: *the ship will sail when the wind and tide serve.* **11.** treat: *the punishment served him right.* **12.** pass; spend: *the thief served a term in prison.* **13.** deliver (an order from a court, etc.); present (with an order from a court, etc.): *he was served with a notice to appear in court.* **14.** put (the ball) in play by hitting it in tennis and similar games. **15.** operate (a gun, etc.). **16.** *Naut.* bind or wind (a rope, etc.) with small cord to strengthen or protect it. —*n.* act or way of serving a tennis ball. [< OF < L, < *servus* slave]

serv·er (sėr′vər), *n.* **1.** person who serves. **2.** tray for dishes.

serv·ice (sėr′vis), *n., v.,* **-iced, -ic·ing.** —*n.* **1.** helpful act or acts; conduct that is useful to others: *he performed many services for his country.* **2.** supply; arrangements for supplying: *the train service was good.* **3.** occupation or employment as a servant: *go into service.* **4.** work for others; performance of duties; work: *the services of a doctor.* **5.** aid; assistance: *may I be of service to you?* **6.** advantage; benefit: *that will be of service to you.* **7.** department of government or public employment; the persons engaged in it: *the civil service, the air service.* **8.** the army or navy: *we entered the service together.* **9.** duty in the army or navy: *be on active service.* **10.** a religious meeting, ritual, or ceremony. **11.** regard; respect; devotion. **12.** manner of serving food; the food served. **13.** set of dishes, etc.: *a solid silver tea service.* **14.** *Law.* the serv-

ing of a process or writ upon a person. **15.** in
tennis, etc., act or manner of putting the ball in
play; the ball as put into play. **16.** *Naut.* a small
cord wound about a rope, etc., to strengthen or
protect it. **17.** at one's service, ready to do what
one wants. **18.** of service, helpful; useful. —*v.*
make fit for service; keep fit for service. [< OF
< L *servitium* < *servus* slave]

serv·ice·a·ble (sér′vis·ə·bəl), *adj.* **1.** capable
of giving good service; useful. **2.** useful for a long
time; able to stand much use. **3.** *Archaic.* willing
to be useful. —**serv′ice·a·bil′i·ty, serv′ice·a·ble·
ness,** *n.* —**serv′ice·a·bly,** *adv.*

serv·ice·man (sér′vis·man′), *n.,* *pl.* —**men.**
member of the armed forces.

service station, 1. *Am.* place for supplying
automobiles with gasoline, oil, water, etc. **2.**
place where repairs, parts, adjustments, etc.,
can be obtained for mechanical or electrical
devices.

ser·vi·ette (sér′vi·et′), *n.* napkin. [< F]

ser·vile (sér′vəl), *adj.* **1.** like that of slaves;
mean; base: *servile flattery.* **2.** of slaves; pertaining to slaves. **3.** fit for a slave. **4.** yielding
through fear, lack of spirit, etc. [< L, < *servus*
slave] —**serv′vile·ly,** *adv.* —**ser′vil′i·ty, ser′vile·
ness,** *n.* —**Syn. 1.** slavish, cringing, fawning,
groveling. —**Ant. 1.** imperious, haughty.

ser·vi·tor (sér′və·tər), *n.* servant; attendant.
[< OF < LL, < L *servire* SERVE] —**ser·vi·to·ri·al**
(sér′və·tô′ri·əl; -tō′-), *adj.*

ser·vi·tude (sér′və·tüd; -tūd), *n.* **1.** slavery;
bondage. **2.** forced labor as a punishment. [< L,
< *servus* slave]

ser·vo·mech·a·nism (sér′vō·mek′ə·niz·əm),
n. any of the various control devices by means of
which data affecting the operation of a machine
or machines, as in automation, is acted upon
automatically. Typically, a servomechanism includes a small motor (**servomotor**) which corrects or modifies an operation or process in
response to a changed condition.

ses·a·me (ses′ə·mē), *n.* **1.** an Oriental plant.
2. its seeds, used for food and in medicine. **3.**
See **open sesame.** [< Gk. < Semitic]

ses·qui·cen·ten·ni·al (ses′kwi-
sen·ten′i·əl), *n.* a 150th anniversary or its celebration. —*adj.*
pertaining to, or marking the completion of, a period of a century
and a half. [< L *sesqui–* one and a
half + E *centennial*]

ses·sile (ses′əl), *adj. Bot., Zool.*
attached by the base instead of by
a stem. [< L *sessilis* sitting < *sedere*
sit]

Sessile
leaves

ses·sion (sesh′ən), *n.* **1.** a sitting
or meeting of a court, council, legislature, etc.: *Congress is now in session.* **2.** a
series of such sittings. **3.** a single continuous
term or period of such sittings. **4.** period of lessons and study. **5.** in session, meeting. [< L
sessio < *sedere* sit] —**ses′sion·al,** *adj.*

ses·tet (ses·tet′), *n.* **1.** a musical sextet. **2.** the
last six lines of a sonnet. [< Ital. *sestetto,* ult.
< L *sex* six]

set (set), *v.,* **set, set·ting,** *adj.,* *n.* —*v.* **1.** put in
some place; put; place. **2.** put in the right place,
position, or condition: *set a broken bone.* **3.** adjust according to a standard: *set a clock.* **4.** put
in some condition or relation: *a spark set the
woods on fire, set a person at ease.* **5.** put (a
price, etc.); fix the value of at a certain amount
or rate. **6.** put as the measure of esteem of a
person or thing: *set great store by a thing.* **7.**
post, appoint, or station for the purpose of performing some duty: *set a detective on a person.*
8. fix; arrange; appoint: *set a limit.* **9.** provide
for others to follow: *set a good example.* **10.** put
in a fixed, rigid, or settled state: *set one's teeth.*
11. become fixed; make or become firm or hard:
jelly sets as it cools. **12.** put in a frame or other
thing that holds: *set a diamond in gold.* **13.**
adorn; ornament. **14.** go down; sink below the
horizon: *the sun sets.* **15.** put (a hen) to sit on
eggs to hatch them; place (eggs) under a hen to

be hatched. **16.** of a hen, sit on eggs. **17.** of a dog,
indicate the position of game by standing stiffly
and pointing with the nose. **18.** hang or fit in
a particular manner: *that coat sets well.* **19.**
have a direction; tend: *the current sets to the
south.* **20.** begin to move: *he set out across the
river.* **21.** begin to apply; begin to apply oneself:
have you set to work? **22.** form fruit in the
blossom. **23.** adapt; fit: *set words to music.* **24.**
arrange (music) for certain voices or instruments. **25.** in printing, put (type) in the order
required. **26.** set about, start work upon; begin:
set about your washing. **27. set against, a.** make
unfriendly or hostile toward. **b.** balance; compare. **28. set apart,** reserve. **29. set aside, a.** put
to one side. **b.** put by for later use. **c.** discard,
dismiss, or leave out; reject; annul. **30. set back,**
stop; hinder; check. **31. set bread,** mix batter or
dough and leave it to rise. **32. set down, a.** deposit or let alight; put down. **b.** put down in
writing or printing. **c.** consider; ascribe. **33. set
forth, a.** make known; express; declare. **b.** start
to go. **34. set in, a.** begin. **b.** blow or flow towards
the shore. **35. set off, a.** explode. **b.** start to go.
c. increase by contrast. **36. set on** or **upon, a.**
attack. **b.** urge to attack. **37. set out, a.** start to
go. **b.** spread out to show, sell, or use. **c.** plant.
38. set sail, a. hoist and spread the sails. **b.**
start on a journey by ship. **c.** *Colloq.* fly away.
39. set to, a. begin. **b.** begin fighting. **40. set up,
a.** build. **b.** begin; start. **c.** put up; raise in place,
position, power, pride, etc. **d.** claim; pretend.
41. set up for, claim or pretend to be. —*adj.* **1.**
fixed or appointed beforehand; established: *a
set time, set rules.* **2.** fixed; rigid: *a set smile.* **3.**
settled; obstinate: *a man set in his ways.* **4.** firm;
hard. —*n.* **1.** number of things or persons belonging together; outfit: *a set of dishes.* **2.**
scenery of a play. **3.** device for receiving or sending by radio, telephone, telegraph, etc. **4.** way a
thing is put or placed; form; shape: *his jaw had
a stubborn set.* **5.** direction; tendency; course;
drift. **6.** warp; bend; displacement: *a set to the
right.* **7.** slip or shoot for planting. **8.** a young
fruit just formed from a blossom. **9.** act or manner of setting. **10.** group of six or more games
in tennis. One side must win at least two more
than the other side. **11.** a dog's pointing in the
presence of game. [OE *settan*] —**Syn. v. 1.** post,
locate, plant. **8.** ordain, prescribe. **14.** decline,
wane. —*adj.* **1.** determined, prescribed. **3.** unyielding. —*n.* **1.** collection, group. ▶ **set, sit.**
People and things *sit* (past tense, *sat*) or they
are *set* (past tense, *set*), meaning "placed": *I
like to sit in a hotel lobby. She set the soup down.*
A hen, however, *sets* [on her eggs].

set·back (set′bak′), *n.* **1.** a check to progress;
reverse. **2.** a setting back at different heights of
the outside wall in a tall building to give better
light and air in the street. **3.** a lessening in the
thickness of a wall. **4.** a flat, plain projection of
a wall.

set·screw (set′skrü′), *n.* a machine screw
used to fasten gears, pulleys, etc., to a shaft.

set·tee (se·tē′), *n.* sofa or long bench with a
back and, usually, arms. [< *set*]

set·ter (set′ər), *n.* **1.** person or thing that sets.
2. a long-haired hunting dog, trained to stand
motionless and point his nose toward the game
that he scents.

set·ting (set′ing), *n.* **1.** frame or other thing
in which something is set. The mounting of a
jewel is its setting. **2.** scenery of a play. **3.** place,
time, etc., of a play or story. **4.** surroundings;
background. **5.** music composed to go with certain words. **6.** the eggs that a hen sets on for
hatching. **7.** act of one that sets.

set·tle[1] (set′əl), *v.,* **-tled, -tling. 1.** determine;
decide; agree (upon): *have you settled on a
time?* **2.** put or be put in order; arrange: *settle
one's affairs.* **3.** pay; arrange payment: *settle a
bill.* **4.** take up residence in (a new country or
place): *settle in New York.* **5.** establish colonies
(in). **6.** set or be set in a fairly permanent
position, place, or way of life: *we are settled in
our new home.* **7.** put or come to rest in a particular place; put in or come to a definite con-

dition: *his cold settled in his lungs*. 8. arrange in or come to a desired or comfortable position: *the cat settled herself in the chair*. 9. make or become quiet: *this drug will settle your nerves*. 10. go down; sink. 11. of liquid, make or become clear. 12. of dregs, sink or cause to sink to the bottom. 13. make or become firm and compact. 14. **settle down**, a. live a more regular life. b. direct steady effort or attention. 15. **settle upon** or **on**, give (property, etc.) to by law. [OE *setlan* < *setl* settle²] —Syn. 1. fix, set. 9. compose, calm. 10. descend, fall.

set·tle² (set′əl), *n*. a long bench. [OE *setl*]

set·tle·ment (set′əl·mənt), *n*. 1. act of settling or state of being settled. 2. establishment in life. 3. deciding; determining: *settlement of a date*. 4. arrangement: *settlement of a dispute*. 5. payment: *settlement of a debt*. 6. the settling of persons in a new country. 7. colony. 8. group of buildings and the people living in them. 9. place in a poor, neglected neighborhood where work for its improvement is carried on. 10. the settling of property upon someone. 11. amount so given.

set·tler (set′lər), *n*. 1. person who settles. 2. person who settles in a new country.

set·tlings (set′lingz), *n.pl.* things in a liquid which settle to the bottom; sediment.

set-to (set′tü′), *n., pl.* -tos. *Colloq.* a fight; dispute.

set-up (set′up′), *n*. 1. *Am., Slang.* manner of holding the head and body; carriage; bearing. 2. arrangement of apparatus, machinery, etc. 3. arrangement of an organization. 4. *Am., Slang.* a prize fight, game, etc., that has been fixed. 5. carbonated water or any other beverage used to mix with whiskey, gin, etc.

Se·vas·to·pol (si·vas′tə·pōl), *n*. seaport in SW Russia, on the Black Sea. Also, **Sebastopol**.

sev·en (sev′ən), *n*. 1. a cardinal number, one more than six. 2. symbol of this number; 7. 3. card with seven spots. —*adj*. one more than six. [OE *seofon*]

sev·en·fold (sev′ən·fōld′), *adj*. 1. seven times as much or as many. 2. having seven parts. —*adv*. seven times as much or as many.

seven seas, all the oceans; the Arctic, Antarctic, North Atlantic, South Atlantic, North Pacific, South Pacific, and Indian oceans.

sev·en·teen (sev′ən·tēn′), *n*. 1. a cardinal number, seven more than ten. 2. symbol of this number; 17. —*adj*. seven more than ten. —**seven·teenth** (sev′ən·tēnth′), *adj., n*.

sev·enth (sev′ənth), *adj*. 1. next after the sixth; last in a series of 7. 2. being one of 7 equal parts. —*n*. 1. next after the sixth; last in a series of 7. 2. one of 7 equal parts. 3. *Music.* a. interval between two tones that are seven degrees apart. b. combination of two such tones. —**sev′enth·ly,** *adv*.

seventh heaven, 1. the highest part of heaven. 2. the highest place or condition of joy and happiness.

sev·en·ty (sev′ən·ti), *n., pl.* -ties, *adj*. —*n*. 1. a cardinal number, seven times ten. 2. symbol of this number; 70. —*adj*. seven times ten. —**sev′en·ti·eth,** *adj., n*.

sev·er (sev′ər), *v*. 1. part; separate; divide: *a church severed into two factions*. 2. cut off; break off: *sever the rope*. [< OF, ult. < L *separare* SEPARATE] —**sev′er·a·ble**, *adj*. —**sev′er·er,** *n*.

sev·er·al (sev′ər·əl; sev′rəl), *adj*. 1. being more than two or three but not many: *gain several pounds*. 2. individually separate; different: *on three several occasions*. 3. pertaining to separate individuals or to a separate individual; respective: *the boys went their several ways*. 4. considered separately; single: *each several one of a group*. 5. various: *several steps in a process*. —*n*. more than two or three but not many; some; a few: *several have given their consent*. [< AF, ult. < L *separ* distinct < *separare* SEPARATE]

sev·er·al·ly (sev′ər·əl·i; sev′rəl·i), *adv*. 1. separately; singly; individually. 2. respectively.

sev·er·ance (sev′ər·əns; sev′rəns), *n*. 1. a severing or being severed; separation; division. 2. a breaking off: *the severance of diplomatic relations*.

severance pay, additional pay granted to departing employees, based on seniority.

se·vere (sə·vir′), *adj.*, -ver·er, -ver·est. 1. very strict; stern; harsh: *the judge imposed a severe penalty on the criminal*. 2. serious; grave: *a severe illness*. 3. very plain or simple; without ornament: *a severe style of architecture*. 4. sharp; violent: *a severe criticism*. 5. difficult: *a severe test*. 6. rigidly exact, accurate, or methodical: *severe reasoning*. [< L *severus*] —**se·vere′ly,** *adv*. —**se·vere′ness,** *n*. —Syn. 1. rigorous, rough, hard. 3. chaste, unadorned. 4. cutting, keen. 5. trying, critical. 6. precise, rigid. —Ant. 1. kind, gentle.

se·ver·i·ty (sə·ver′ə·ti), *n., pl.* -ties. 1. strictness; sternness; harshness. 2. simplicity of style or taste; plainness. 3. violence; sharpness. 4. seriousness. 5. accuracy; exactness. 6. something severe.

Sev·ern (sev′ərn), *n*. river flowing from C Wales through W England into the Bristol Channel.

Se·ville (sə·vil′), *n*. city in SW Spain.

sew (sō), *v.*, sewed, sewed or sewn, sew·ing. 1. work with needle and thread. 2. fasten with stitches. 3. close with stitches. [OE *seowian*] —**sew′a·ble,** *adj*. —**sew′er,** *n*.

sew·age (sü′ij), *n*. the waste matter that passes through sewers.

sew·er (sü′ər), *n*. an underground pipe or channel for carrying off waste water and refuse. [< OF *seviere* sluice from a pond, ult. < L *ex* out + *aqua* water]

sew·er·age (sü′ər·ij), *n*. 1. removal of waste matter by sewers. 2. system of sewers. 3. sewage.

sew·ing (sō′ing), *n*. work done with a needle and thread; something to be sewed. —*adj*. for sewing; used in sewing.

sewn (sōn), *v*. pp. of sew.

sex (seks), *n*. 1. one of the two divisions of human beings, animals, etc. Men, bulls, and roosters are of the male sex; women, cows, and hens are of the female sex. 2. the character of being male or female: *people were admitted without regard to age or sex*. 3. attraction of one sex for the other. 4. the fair, gentle, or weaker sex, women. —*adj*. of or having to do with sex. [< L *sexus*] —**sex′less,** *adj*. —**sex′less·ly,** *adv*. —**sex′less·ness,** *n*.

sex·a·ge·nar·i·an (sek′sə·jə·nãr′i·ən), **sex·ag·e·nar·y** (seks·aj′ə·ner′i), *adj., n., pl.* -nar·i·ans; -nar·ies. —*adj*. of the age of 60 years, or between 60 and 70 years old. —*n*. person who is 60, or between 60 and 70 years old. [< L, ult. < *sexaginta* sixty]

sex appeal, *Am.* personal charm tending to draw together persons of the opposite sex.

sex·tant (seks′tənt), *n*. 1. instrument used by navigators, surveyors, etc., for measuring the angular distance between two objects. Sextants are used at sea to measure the altitude of the sun, a star, etc., in order to determine latitude and longitude. 2. one sixth of a circle. [< L *sextans* a sixth < *sex* six]

sex·tet, sex·tette (seks·tet′), *n*. 1. piece of music for six voices or instruments. 2. six singers or players. 3. any group of six. [alter. of *sestet* after L *sex* six]

sex·til·lion (seks·til′yən), *n*. 1. in the United States and France, 1 followed by 21 zeros. 2. in Great Britain, 1 followed by 36 zeros. [< F (< L *sextus* sixth), modeled after *million* MILLION] —**sex·til′lionth,** *adj., n*.

sex·ton (seks′tən), *n*. man who takes care of a church. [< OF < Med.L *sacristanus* sacristan. Doublet of SACRISTAN.]

sex·tu·ple (seks′tü·pəl; -tyü-; seks·tü′pəl; -tü′-), *adj., n., v.*, -pled, -pling. —*adj*. 1. consisting of six parts; sixfold. 2. six times as great. 3. *Music.* characterized by six beats to the measure. —*n*. number or amount six times as great as another. —*v*. make or become six times as great. [< L *sextus* sixth; modeled after *quadruple*]

sex·tu·plet (seks′tü·plit; -tyü-; seks·tü′plit; -tü′-), *n*. one of six children, animals, etc., born of the same mother at the same time.

sex·u·al (sek'shū·əl), *adj.* **1.** of or pertaining to sex. **2.** of or between the sexes. **3.** having sex; separated into two sexes. —**sex'u·al'i·ty,** *n.* —**sex'u·al·ly,** *adv.*

sex·y (sek'si), *adj. Slang.* **1.** charming or attractive sexually. **2.** sexually exciting. **3.** preoccupied or concerned with sex.

Sgt., Sergeant.

shab·by (shab'i), *adj.,* -bi·er, -bi·est. **1.** much worn. **2.** wearing old or much worn clothes. **3.** not generous; mean; unfair. [< *shab* scab, OE *sceabb*] —**shab'bi·ly,** *adv.* —**shab'bi·ness,** *n.*

shack (shak), *n. Am.* a roughly built hut or cabin; house in bad condition. [? ult. < *ramshackle*]

shack·le (shak'əl), *n., v.,* -led, -ling. —*n.* **1.** a metal band fastened around the ankle or wrist of a prisoner, slave, etc. Shackles are usually fastened to each other, the wall, floor, etc., by chains. **2.** link fastening together the two rings for the ankles and wrists of a prisoner. **3.** anything that prevents freedom of action, thought, etc. **4.** thing for fastening or coupling. **5.** shackles, fetters; chains. —*v.* **1.** put shackles on. **2.** restrain; hamper. **3.** fasten or couple with a shackle. [OE *sceacel*] —**shack'ler,** *n.*

shad (shad), *n., pl.* shad or (*for different kinds*) shads. any of several salt-water fishes related to the herrings that ascend rivers in the spring to spawn. [OE *sceadd*]

shad·ber·ry (shad'ber'i), *n., pl.* -ries. *Am.* **1.** fruit of the shadbush. **2.** shadbush.

shad·bush (shad'bush'), *n. Am.* a North American shrub or small tree with white flowers and berrylike fruit, which blossoms about the time when shad appear in the rivers.

shade (shād), *n., v.,* shad·ed, shad·ing. —*n.* **1.** a partly dark place, not in the sunshine. **2.** a slight darkness or coolness afforded by something that cuts off light: *the shade of a tree.* **3.** place or condition of comparative obscurity. **4.** the shades, darkness of evening or night. **5.** the shades, Class. Myth. Hades. **6.** something that shuts out light: *pull down the shades of the windows.* **7.** lightness or darkness of color. **8.** the dark part of a picture. **9.** a very small difference, amount, or degree: *a shade too long.* **10.** a darkening look, feeling, etc.; shadow; cloud: *a shade of doubt troubled her.* **11.** ghost; spirit. **12.** in or into the shade, **a.** out of the light. **b.** in or into a condition of being unknown or unnoticed. —*v.* **1.** screen from light; keep light from; reduce light on. **2.** make darker than the rest. **3.** make dark or gloomy. **4.** show small differences; change little by little. **5.** lessen slightly. [OE *sceadu*] —**shade'less,** *adj.* —**shad'er,** *n.*

shad·ing (shād'ing), *n.* **1.** a covering from the light. **2.** use of black or color to give the effect of shade in a picture. **3.** a slight variation or difference of color, character, etc.

shad·ow (shad'ō), *n.* **1.** shade made by some person, animal, or thing. **2.** shade; darkness; partial shade. **3.** the shadows, darkness after sunset. **4.** the dark part of a place or picture. **5.** a little bit; small degree; slight suggestion. **6.** ghost; a faint image. **7.** a reflected image. **8.** person who follows another closely and secretly, as a spy, detective, etc. **9.** a constant companion; follower. **10.** sadness; gloom. **11.** obscurity. **12.** a gloomy or troubled look or expression. **13.** protection; shelter. **14.** in or under the shadow of, very near to. —*v.* **1.** protect from light; shade. **2.** cast a shadow on. **3.** represent faintly. **4.** follow closely and secretly. **5.** make sad or gloomy. **6.** represent in a prophetic way. **7.** shadow forth, represent faintly. [from oblique case forms of OE *sceadu* shade] —**shad'ow·er,** *n.* —**shad'ow·less,** *adj.*

shad·ow·box·ing (shad'ō·bok'sing), *n.* boxing with an imaginary opponent for exercise or training.

shad·ow·y (shad'ō·i), *adj.* **1.** having much shadow or shade; shady. **2.** like a shadow; dim, faint, or slight. **3.** not real; ghostly. —**shad'ow·i·ly,** *adv.* —**shad'ow·i·ness,** *n.* —**Syn.** **1.** dark, obscure. **2.** fleeting, vague.

shad·y (shād'i), *adj.,* shad·i·er, shad·i·est. **1.** in the shade; shaded. **2.** giving shade. **3.** Colloq. of doubtful honesty, character, etc. **4.** on the shady side of, older than; beyond the age of. —**shad'i·ly,** *adv.* —**shad'i·ness,** *n.*

shaft (shaft; shäft), *n.* **1.** the long, slender stem of an arrow, spear, etc. **2.** arrow; spear. **3.** something like an arrow or spear aimed at a person. **4.** ray or beam of light. **5.** one of the two wooden poles between which a horse is harnessed to a carriage, etc. **6.** column. **7.** the main part of a column. **8.** flagpole. **9.** bar to support parts of a machine that turn, or to help move parts. **10.** handle of a hammer, ax, golf club, etc. **11.** stem; stalk. **12.** rib of a feather. **13.** a deep passage sunk in the earth. The entrance to a mine is called a shaft. **14.** a well-like passage: *an elevator shaft.* [OE *sceaft*] —**shaft'ed,** *adj.*

shag (shag), *n., v.,* shagged, shag·ging. —*n.* **1.** rough, matted hair, wool, etc. **2.** a mass of this: *the shag of a dog.* **3.** the long, rough nap of some kinds of cloth. **4.** cloth having such a nap. **5.** a coarse tobacco cut into shreds. —*v.* make rough or shaggy, esp. with vegetation. [OE *sceacga*]

shag·bark (shag'bärk'), *n. Am.* **1.** a hickory tree with very rough bark. **2.** nut of this tree.

shag·gy (shag'i), *adj.,* -gi·er, -gi·est. **1.** covered with a thick, rough mass of hair, wool, etc. **2.** long, thick, and rough: *shaggy eyebrows.* [< *shag*] —**shag'gi·ly,** *adv.* —**shag'gi·ness,** *n.*

shah (shä), *n.* Usually, Shah. a title of the ruler of Iran. [< Pers.]

shake (shāk), *v.,* shook, shak·en, shak·ing, *n.* —*v.* **1.** move quickly backwards and forwards, up and down, or from side to side: *shake a rug.* **2.** bring, throw, force, rouse, scatter, etc., by or as if by movement: *shake snow off one's clothes.* **3.** be shaken: *sand shakes off easily.* **4.** clasp (hands) in greeting, congratulating, etc., another: *shake hands.* **5.** tremble: *he is shaking with cold.* **6.** make tremble: *the explosion shook the town.* **7.** totter; waver. **8.** cause to totter or waver: *shake the very foundations of society.* **9.** disturb; make less firm: *his lie shook my faith in his honesty.* **10.** trill. **11.** *Am., Slang.* get rid of: *can't you shake him?* **12.** shake down, **a.** bring or throw down by shaking. **b.** cause to settle down. **c.** bring into working order. **d.** *Am., Slang.* get money from dishonestly. **13.** shake off, get rid of. **14.** shake up, **a.** shake hard. **b.** stir up. **c.** jar in body or nerves. —*n.* **1.** act or fact of shaking: *a shake of the head.* **2.** *Am., Colloq.* earthquake. **3.** drink made by shaking ingredients together: *a milk shake.* **4.** *Slang.* moment: *I'll be there in two shakes.* **5.** rapid alternation of a note with a tone above or below it; trill. **6.** crack in a growing tree; fissure. **7.** no great shakes, *Am., Colloq.* not unusual, extraordinary, or important. [OE *sceacan*] —**shak'ing,** *n.* —**shak'ing·ly,** *adv.* —**Syn.** *v.* **5.** quiver, shiver.

shake·down (shāk'doun'), *n.* **1.** *Am., Slang.* an exaction of money, etc., by compulsion. **2.** a bringing into working order by practice.

shake-out, shake·out (shāk'out'), *n. Colloq.* reorganization or change that involves the removal or omission of some persons, items, etc.

shak·er (shāk'ər), *n.* **1.** person who shakes something. **2.** machine or utensil used in shaking. **3.** *Am.* container in which drinks are mixed by shaking. **4.** *Am.* container for pepper, salt, etc., having a perforated top. **5.** **Shaker,** *Am.* member of an American religious sect, so called from movements of the body that form part of their worship.

Shake·speare, Shak·spere, Shak·speare (shāk'spir), *n.* William, 1564–1616, England's greatest poet and dramatist. —**Shakespear'i·an, Shake·spear'e·an, Shak·sper'i·an, Shak·sper'e·an,** *adj., n.*

shake-up (shāk'up'), *n.* a sudden and complete change.

shak·o (shak'ō), *n., pl.* shak·os. a high, stiff military hat with a plume or other ornament. See picture above. [< Hung. *csákó* peaked (cap)]

Shako

shak·y (shāk′ĭ), *adj.*, **shak·i·er, shak·i·est. 1.** shaking: *a shaky voice.* **2.** liable to break down; weak: *a shaky porch.* **3.** not to be depended on; not reliable. —**shak′i·ly,** *adv.* —**shak′i·ness,** *n.*

shale (shāl), *n.* a fine-grained rock, formed from clay or mud, that splits easily into thin layers. [OE *scealu* shell] —**shal′y,** *adj.*

shall (shal; *unstressed* shəl), *v., pres.* **shall,** *2nd sing. also* (*Poetic*) **shalt;** *past* **should,** *2nd sing. also* (*Archaic*) **should·est** or **shouldst. 1.** (used to denote future time): *we shall miss you.* **2.** (used to express promise or determination): *you shall hear from us, he shall not do it.* [OE *sceal* (inf., *sculan*) **] > shall, will.** The usage of *shall* and *will* has never been uniform in English, although some grammarians have attempted to insist on uniformity. The general practices in the more common situations needing these words are as follows: **1.** *Informal and Colloquial usage.* **a.** *Simple future.* In speech and informal writing the prevailing use in the United States, and in many other parts of the English-speaking world, is to use *will* in all persons: *I, you, he, she, we, you, they will ask.* This informal usage would appear in more printed matter if editors did not revise the copy to bring it in line with formal usage. **b.** *Emphatic future.* In expressing determination in the future or for some special emphasis, informal and colloquial usage is divided. In speech the determination is expressed by stress, which may be used on either word: *I shall′ go, I will′ go.* There seems to be a general tendency to use *shall* in all persons as the emphatic form: *I, you, he, she, we, you, they shall ask.* **c.** *Contractions.* In speaking and in informal writing where contractions are used, the future becomes *I'll, you'll, he'll,* and so on. *Won't* is used for *will not* (formed from an obsolete *woll* and *not*) and *shan't* for *shall not.* **d.** *In questions. Shall* is likely to be used in the first and third persons, and *will* in the second in asking questions, but practice is not consistent: *Shall I go? Will you go?* In the negative, *won't* is the more common: *Won't I look funny in that? What won't he think of next?* **2.** *Formal Usage.* In formal English many writers and editors use *shall* in the first person, *will* in the second and third persons in making the future tense: *I shall ask, he will ask.* In the emphatic future, expressing determination on the part of the speaker, formal English reverses this use of *shall* and *will: I will ask, he shall ask.* In asking questions a few people use the form of *shall* or *will* in a question that the answerer would use in his reply. This usage is distinctly formal: *Shall you go?* Answer: *I shall* (*shall not*) *go.*

shal·lop (shal′əp), *n.* a small, light open boat with sail or oars. [< F *chaloupe* < Du. *sloepe.* Doublet of SLOOP.]

shal·lot (shə·lot′), *n.* **1.** a small plant much like an onion, but with a bulb composed of sections or cloves. **2.** bulb or clove of this plant. **3.** a small brown onion. [ult. < F *eschalotte,* alter. of OF *eschaloigne* SCALLION]

shal·low (shal′ō), *adj.* not deep: *shallow water, a shallow mind.* —*n.* a shallow place. —*v.* **1.** become less deep. **2.** make less deep. [prob. ult. < OE *sceald*] —**shal′low·ness,** *n.*

sham (sham), *n., adj., v.,* **shammed, shamming.** —*n.* **1.** pretense; fraud. **2.** counterfeit; imitation. —*adj.* **1.** counterfeit; imitation. **2.** pretended; feigned. —*v.* pretend; feign. [orig. dial. var. of *shame*] —**sham′mer,** *n.*

sham·ble¹ (sham′bəl), *v.,* **-bled, -bling,** *n.* —*v.* walk awkwardly or unsteadily. —*n.* a shambling walk. [prob. ult. special use of *shamble²*; with ref. to the straddling legs of a bench]

sham·ble² (sham′bəl), *n.* **1.** shambles (*often sing. in use*), slaughter house. **2.** shambles (*often sing. in use*), place of butchery or of great destruction and confusion. [< L *scamellum,* dim. of *scamnum* bench; orig., a table on which meat was sold]

shame (shām), *n., v.,* **shamed, sham·ing.** —*n.* **1.** a painful feeling of having done something wrong, improper, or silly: *blush with shame.* **2.** a disgrace; dishonor. **3.** fact to be sorry about: *it is a shame to be so wasteful.* **4.** person or thing

to be ashamed of; cause of disgrace. **5.** sense of what is decent or proper. **6. for shame!** shame on you! **7. put to shame, a.** disgrace; make ashamed. **b.** surpass; make dim by comparison. —*v.* **1.** cause to feel shame. **2.** drive or force by shame. **3.** bring disgrace upon. [OE *sceamu*] —**sham′er,** *n.* —Syn. *n.* **1.** humiliation, mortification. —*v.* **1.** humiliate, mortify.

shame·faced (shām′fāst′), *adj.* **1.** bashful; shy. **2.** showing shame and embarrassment. —**shame·fac·ed·ly** (shām′fās′ĭd·lĭ; shām′fāst′-lĭ), *adv.* —**shame′fac′ed·ness,** *n.*

shame·ful (shām′fəl), *adj.* **1.** causing shame; bringing disgrace. **2.** scandalous. —**shame′fully,** *adv.* —**shame′ful·ness,** *n.* —Syn. **1.** dishonorable. **2.** immodest, indecent.

shame·less (shām′lĭs), *adj.* **1.** without shame. **2.** not modest. **3.** insensible to disgrace. —**shame′less·ly,** *adv.* —**shame′less·ness,** *n.* —Syn. **2.** impudent, brazen.

sham·my (sham′ĭ), *n., pl.* **-mies.** chamois.

sham·poo (sham·pū′), *v.,* **-pooed, -poo·ing,** *n.* —*v.* **1.** wash (the hair or scalp). **2.** massage. —*n.* **1.** a washing of the hair or scalp. **2.** preparation used for shampooing. **3.** massage. [< Hind. *champo,* lit., press!] —**sham·poo′er,** *n.*

sham·rock (sham′rok), *n.* **1.** a bright-green leaf composed of three parts. The shamrock is the national emblem of Ireland. **2.** any of various plants that have leaves like this, such as white clover, wood sorrel, etc. [< Irish *seamróg,* dim. of *seamar* clover]

Shamrock

Shang·hai (shang′hī′), *n.* seaport in E China.

shang·hai (shang′hī; shang·hī′), *v.,* **-haied, -hai·ing.** *Am.* **1.** make unconscious by drugs, liquor, etc., and put on a ship to serve as a sailor. **2.** bring by trickery or force. [with ref. to the practice of securing sailors by foul means for long voyages, often to *Shanghai*]

Shan·gri·la, Shan·gri-La (shang′grĭ·lä′), *n.* an idyllic earthly paradise. [an inaccessible land in *Lost Horizon,* a novel by James Hilton]

shank (shangk), *n.* **1.** the part of the leg between the knee and the ankle. **2.** the corresponding part in animals. **3.** the whole leg. **4.** any part like a leg, stem, or shaft. **5.** the body of a printing type. **6.** the narrow part of a shoe, connecting the broad part of the sole with the heel. **7.** part that connects the handle and acting portion of a tool, instrument, etc. **8.** the latter end or part of anything. **9. go** or **ride on shank's mare,** walk. [OE *sceanca*] —**shanked,** *adj.*

Shan·non (shan′ən), *n.* river flowing from N Eire into the Atlantic.

shan't (shant; shänt), shall not.

Shan·tung (shan′tung′ *for 1, 2; *shan′tung *for 3*), *n.* **1.** province in NE China. **2.** peninsula in the E part of this province. **3. shantung,** a heavy pongee, a kind of soft silk.

shan·ty¹ (shan′tĭ), *n., pl.* **-ties.** *Am.* a roughly built hut or cabin. [< Irish *seantig* hut]

shan·ty² (shan′tĭ), *n., pl.* **-ties.** chantey.

shape (shāp), *n., v.,* **shaped, shap·ing.** —*n.* **1.** the outward contour or outline; form; figure: *the shape of a triangle.* **2.** something that has form or figure: *a hooded and cloaked shape.* **3.** an assumed appearance: *take the shape of a cat.* **4.** the particular form or character which a thing has: *a gift in the shape of money.* **5.** definite form or character: *things are taking shape.* **6.** proper form or orderly arrangement: *put a thing into shape.* **7.** *Am.* condition: *his affairs are in bad shape.* **8.** a mold; pattern. [OE (*ge*)*sceap*] —*v.* **1.** form: *the child shapes clay into balls.* **2.** take shape; assume form: *his plan is shaping well.* **3.** adapt in form: *shape a sleeve to a person's arm.* **4.** give definite form or character to: *shape a dress.* **5.** direct; plan: *shape one's course in life.* **6.** express in words: *shape a question.* **7.** mold; pattern. **8. shape up, a.** take on a certain form or appearance; develop. **b.** show a certain tendency. [OE *sceapen,* pp. of *scieppan* create] —**shap′er,** *n.* —Syn. *v.* **1.** cast, build.

SHAPE, Supreme Headquarters, Allied Powers in Europe.

shape·less (shāp'lis), *adj.* 1. without definite shape. 2. having an unattractive shape. —**shape'less·ly,** *adv.* —**shape'less·ness,** *n.*

shape·ly (shāp'li), *adj.*, **-li·er, -li·est.** having a pleasing shape; well-formed. —**shape'li·ness,** *n.*

shape-up (shāp'up'), *n.* a system of hiring longshoremen whereby the men line up each work day to be selected for work by the foreman.

shard (shärd), *n.* 1. a broken piece; fragment. 2. piece of broken earthenware or pottery. 3. the hard case that covers a beetle's wing. [OE *sceard*]

share[1] (shār), *n.*, *v.*, **shared, shar·ing.** —*n.* 1. part belonging to one individual; portion; part: *do your share of the work.* 2. a definite fraction of some property owned in common; each of the parts into which the ownership of a company or corporation is divided: *the ownership of this railroad is divided into several million shares.* —*v.* 1. use together; enjoy together; have in common. 2. divide into parts, each taking a part. 3. have a share; take part. [OE *scearu* division] —**shar'er,** *n.* —**Syn.** *n.* 1. allotment, quota.

share[2] (shār), *n.* plowshare. [OE *scear*]

share·crop (shār'krop'), *v.*, **-cropped, -crop·ping.** *Am.* farm or raise (a crop) on share. —**share'crop'ping,** *n. Am.*

share·crop·per (shār'krop'ər), *n. Am.* person who farms land for the owner in return for part of the crops.

share·hold·er (shār'hōl'dər), *n.* person owning shares of stock.

shark[1] (shärk), *n.* any of a group of fishes, mostly marine, certain species of which are large and ferocious, and destructive to other fishes and sometimes dangerous to man.

shark[2] (shärk), *n.* 1. a dishonest person who preys on others. 2. *Am., Slang.* person unusually good at something; expert. [< G *schork,* var. of *schurke* scoundrel]

shark·skin (shärk'skin'), *n.* cloth made from fine threads of wool, rayon, or cotton, used in suits.

sharp (shärp), *adj.* 1. having a thin cutting edge or a fine point: *a sharp knife, a sharp pencil.* 2. having a point; not rounded: *a sharp nose.* 3. with a sudden change of direction: *a sharp turn.* 4. very cold: *a sharp wind.* 5. severe; biting: *sharp words.* 6. feeling somewhat like a cut or prick; affecting the senses keenly: *a sharp pain.* 7. clear; distinct: *the sharp contrast between black and white.* 8. quick; brisk: *a sharp walk.* 9. fierce; violent: *a sharp struggle.* 10. keen; eager: *a sharp appetite.* 11. being aware of things quickly: *a sharp eye, sharp ears.* 12. watchful; wide-awake: *a sharp watch.* 13. quick in mind; shrewd; clever: *sharp at a bargain.* 14. high in pitch; shrill. 15. *Music.* a. above the true pitch; raised a half step in pitch: *F sharp.* b. having sharps in the signature. 16. pronounced with breath and not with voice; voiceless. —*adv.* 1. promptly; exactly: *come at one o'clock sharp.* 2. in a sharp manner; in an alert manner; keenly: *look sharp!* 3. suddenly: *pull a horse up sharp.* —*n.* 1. *Music.* a. tone one half step above a given tone. b. the sign (♯) that shows this. 2. swindler; sharper. [OE *scearp*] —**sharp'ly,** *adv.* —**sharp'ness,** *n.* —**Syn.** *adj.* 2. angular, pointed. 4. nipping, cutting. 5. sarcastic, tart. 6. piercing, intense. 11. quick, discerning. 13. cunning, astute.

sharp·en (shär'pən), *v.* make or become sharp. —**sharp'en·er,** *n.*

sharp·er (shär'pər), *n.* 1. swindler. 2. cardsharp.

sharp·shoot·er (shärp'shüt'ər), *n.* 1. person who shoots very well. 2. soldier chosen to do accurate shooting. —**sharp'shoot'ing,** *n.*

sharp-wit·ted (shärp'wit'id), *adj.* having or showing a quick, keen mind.

Shas·ta (shas'tə), *n.* **Mount,** a volcanic peak in N California.

shat·ter (shat'ər), *v.* 1. break into pieces: *a stone shattered the window.* 2. disturb greatly; destroy: *a shattered mind.* 3. damage.

shave (shāv), *v.*, **shaved, shaved** or **shav·en, shav·ing,** *n.* —*v.* 1. remove hair with a razor; cut hair from (the face, chin, etc.) with a razor. 2. cut off (hair) with a razor. 3. cut off in thin slices; cut in thin slices. 4. cut very close. 5. come very close to; graze. —*n.* 1. the cutting off of hair with a razor. 2. tool for shaving, scraping, removing thin slices, etc. 3. a thin slice. 4. a narrow miss or escape. [OE *sceafan*]

shav·en (shāv'ən), *adj.* 1. shaved. 2. closely cut. 3. tonsured. —*v.* pp. of shave.

shav·er (shāv'ər), *n.* 1. person who shaves. 2. instrument for shaving. 3. *Colloq.* youngster.

shave·tail (shāv'tāl'), *n. Am., Slang.* a new second lieutenant.

Sha·vi·an (shā'vi·ən), *adj.* of, pertaining to, or characteristic of George Bernard Shaw.

shav·ing (shāv'ing), *n.* 1. Often, **shavings.** a very thin piece or slice. 2. act or process of cutting hair from the face, chin, etc., with a razor.

Shaw (shô), *n.* **George Bernard,** 1856–1950, Irish dramatist, critic, novelist, and social reformer.

shawl (shôl), *n.* a square or oblong piece of cloth to be worn about the shoulders or head. [< Pers. *shāl*]

Shaw·nee (shô·nē'), *n., pl.* **-nee, -nees.** *Am.* member of a tribe of American Indians formerly living in Tennessee and South Carolina, now in Oklahoma.

shay (shā), *n. Colloq.* chaise.

she (shē), *pron., sing. nom.* **she,** *poss.* **her** or **hers,** *obj.* **her;** *pl. nom.* **they,** *poss.* **their** or **theirs,** *obj.* **them;** *n., pl.* **shes.** —*pron.* 1. girl, woman, or female animal spoken about or mentioned before. 2. anything thought of as female and spoken about or mentioned before. —*n.* girl; woman; female animal. [OE *hēo*]

sheaf (shēf), *n., pl.* **sheaves** (shēvz). bundle of things of the same sort bound together or so arranged that they can be bound together: *a sheaf of wheat, a sheaf of arrows.* [OE *scēaf*]

shear (shir), *v.*, **sheared** or (*Archaic*) **shore, sheared** or **shorn, shear·ing,** *n.* —*v.* 1. cut with shears or scissors. 2. cut the wool or fleece from. 3. cut close; cut off; cut. —*n.* 1. act or process of shearing. 2. that which is taken off by shearing. 3. one blade of a pair of shears. 4. pair of shears. [OE *sceran*] —**shear'er,** *n.*

shears (shirz), *n.pl.* 1. large scissors. 2. any cutting instrument resembling scissors. [OE *scēar*]

sheath (shēth), *n., pl.* **sheaths** (shēthz). 1. case or covering for the blade of a sword, knife, etc. 2. any similar covering, esp. on an animal or plant. [OE *scēath*] —**sheath'less,** *adj.*

sheathe (shēth), *v.*, **sheathed, sheath·ing.** 1. put (a sword, etc.) into a sheath. 2. enclose in a case or covering. —**sheath'er,** *n.*

She·ba (shē'bə), *n.* 1. an ancient country in S Arabia. 2. **Queen of,** queen who visited Solomon to learn of his great wisdom. I Kings 10:1–13.

she·bang (shə·bang'), *n. U.S. Slang.* 1. outfit; concern. 2. affair; event.

shed[1] (shed), *n.* a building used for shelter, storage, etc., usually having only one story: *a wagon shed, a train shed.* [OE *sced* shelter]

shed[2] (shed), *v.*, **shed, shed·ding.** 1. pour out; let fall: *the girl shed tears.* 2. throw off: *a snake sheds its skin.* 3. throw off a covering, hair, etc.: *that snake has just shed.* 4. scatter abroad; give forth: *flowers shed perfume.* 5. cause to flow: *he shed his enemy's blood.* 6. shed blood, destroy life; kill. [OE *scēadan*] —**shed'der,** *n.* —**Syn.** 2. molt, discard. 4. emit, diffuse, disperse.

she'd (shēd), 1. she had. 2. she would.

sheen (shēn), *n.* brightness; luster. Satin and polished silver have a sheen. [OE *scēne* bright]

sheep (shēp), *n., pl.* **sheep.** 1. animal raised for wool and mutton. 2. a weak, timid, or stupid person. 3. leather made from the skin of sheep. [OE *scēap*]

Sheep

sheep·cote (shēp′kōt′), *n.* shelter for sheep.

sheep dog, collie or other dog trained to help a shepherd watch and tend sheep.

sheep·fold (shēp′fōld′), *n.* pen for sheep.

sheep·herd·er (shēp′hèr′dər), *n. Am.* person who watches and tends large numbers of sheep while they are grazing on unfenced land.

sheep·ish (shēp′ish), *adj.* 1. awkwardly bashful or embarrassed. 2. like a sheep; timid; weak; stupid. —**sheep′ish·ly,** *adv.* —**sheep′ish·ness,** *n.*

sheep·man (shēp′man′), *n., pl.* -men. 1. *Am.* person who owns and raises sheep. 2. sheepherder.

sheep·skin (shēp′skin′), *n.* 1. skin of a sheep, esp. with the wool on it. 2. leather or parchment made from it. 3. *Am., Colloq.* diploma.

sheep sorrel, a kind of sorrel with reddish flowers.

sheer¹ (shir), *adj.* 1. very thin; almost transparent. 2. unmixed with anything else; complete: *sheer weariness.* 3. straight up and down; steep: *a sheer drop of 100 feet.* —*adv.* 1. completely; quite. 2. very steeply. —*n.* dress of transparent material worn over a slip. [OE *scīr* bright; vowel from Scand. *skærr* bright] —**sheer′ly,** *adv.* —**sheer′ness,** *n.* —**Syn.** *adj.* 2. unadulterated, pure, absolute, utter. 3. abrupt, precipitous.

sheer² (shir), *v.* turn from a course; turn aside; swerve. —*n.* 1. a turning of a ship from its course. 2. the upward curve of a ship's deck or lines from the middle toward each end. [var. of *shear,* v.]

sheet¹ (shēt), *n.* 1. a large piece of linen or cotton cloth used to sleep on or under. 2. a broad, thin piece of anything. 3. a single piece of paper. 4. newspaper. 5. a broad, flat surface: *a sheet of water.* 6. *Poetic.* a sail. —*v.* furnish or cover with a sheet. [OE *scēte*]

sheet² (shēt), *n.* 1. rope that controls the angle at which a sail is set. 2. **sheets,** space at the bow or stern of an open boat. [OE *scēata*]

sheet anchor, 1. a large anchor used only in emergencies. 2. a final reliance or resource.

sheet·ing (shēt′ing), *n.* 1. cotton or linen cloth for bed sheets. 2. a lining or covering of timber or metal, used to protect a surface.

sheet metal, metal in thin pieces or plates.

sheet music, music printed on unbound sheets of paper.

Shef·field (shef′ēld), *n.* city in C England.

sheik, sheikh (shēk), *n.* 1. an Arab chief or head of a family, village, or tribe. 2. a Mohammedan religious leader. 3. title of respect used by Mohammedans. 4. *Slang.* lady-killer. [< Ar. *shaikh,* orig., old man]

shek·el (shek′əl), *n.* 1. an ancient silver coin of the Hebrews that weighed about half an ounce. 2. **shekels,** *Slang.* coins; money. [< Heb. *sheqel*]

shel·drake (shel′drāk′), *n., pl.* -drakes or (*esp. collectively*) -drake. 1. any of various large ducks of Europe and Asia, many of which have variegated plumage. 2. any merganser. [< obs. *sheld* variegated + *drake*]

shelf (shelf), *n., pl.* **shelves. 1.** a thin, flat piece of wood, metal, stone, etc., fastened to a wall or frame to hold things, such as books, dishes, etc. 2. anything like a shelf. 3. **on the shelf,** put aside as no longer useful or desirable. [prob. < LG *schelf*]

shell (shel), *n.* 1. a hard outside covering of an animal, such as of a mollusk, turtle, etc. 2. the hard outside covering of a nut, seed, fruit, etc. 3. outer part or appearance. 4. *Am.* a very light racing boat. 5. a casing of pastry, used for pies, tarts, etc. 6. a hollow projectile for a cannon, etc., filled with an explosive charge; cartridge. 7. something like a shell, as the framework of a house. 8. a shy, reserved attitude. 9. **retire into one's shell,** become shy and reserved; refuse to join in conversation, etc., with others. —*v.* 1. take out of a shell. 2. fall or come out of the shell. 3. come away or fall off as an outer covering does. 4. separate (grains of corn) from the cob. 5. bombard by cannon fire. 6. **shell out,** *Colloq.* hand over (money); pay up. [OE *sciell*] —**shell′er,** *n.* —**shell′·less,** *adj.* —**shell′·like′,** *adj.* —**shell′y,** *adj.*

she'll (shēl), 1. she shall. 2. she will.

shel·lac (shə·lak′), *n., v.,* -lacked, -lack·ing. —*n.* 1. liquid that gives a smooth, shiny appearance to wood, metal, etc. Shellac is made from a resinous substance dissolved in alcohol. 2. the resinous substance used. —*v.* 1. put shellac on; cover or fasten with shellac. 2. *Colloq.* completely defeat. [< *shell* + *lac¹*; trans. of F *laque en écailles* lac in thin plates] —**shel·lack′er,** *n.*

Shel·ley (shel′i), *n.* Percy Bysshe, 1792–1822, English poet.

shell·fire (shel′fīr′), *n.* the firing of explosive shells or projectiles.

shell·fish (shel′fish′), *n., pl.* -fish·es or (*esp. collectively*) -fish. a water animal (not a fish in the ordinary sense) having a shell. Oysters, clams, crabs, and lobsters are shellfish.

shell·proof (shel′prüf′), *adj.* secure against shells, bombs, etc.

shell shock, any of the many types of nervous or mental disorder resulting from the strain of war. —**shell′-shocked′,** *adj.*

shel·ter (shel′tər), *n.* 1. something that covers or protects from weather, danger, or attack. 2. protection; refuge. —*v.* 1. protect; shield; hide. 2. find shelter. —**shel′ter·er,** *n.* —**shel′ter·ing·ly,** *adv.* —**shel′ter·less,** *adj.* —**Syn.** *n.* 1. safeguard, defense, shield. —*v.* 1. screen, harbor.

shelve¹ (shelv), *v.,* **shelved, shelv·ing.** 1. put on a shelf. 2. lay aside. 3. furnish with shelves. [ult. < *shelf*]

shelve² (shelv), *v.,* **shelved, shelv·ing.** slope gradually.

shelves (shelvz), *n. pl.* of **shelf.**

shelv·ing (shel′ving), *n.* 1. wood, metal, etc., for shelves. 2. shelves.

she·nan·i·gan (shə·nan′ə·gən), *n. Am., Colloq.* Usually, **shenanigans.** mischief or trickery.

Shen·yang (shen′yang′), *n.* Mukden.

She·ol (shē′ōl), *n.* 1. a Hebrew name for the abode of the dead. 2. **sheol,** *Colloq.* hell.

shep·herd (shep′ərd), *n.* 1. man who takes care of sheep. 2. person who cares for and protects. 3. a spiritual guide; pastor. 4. **the Good Shepherd,** Jesus Christ. —*v.* 1. take care of. 2. guide; direct. [OE *scēaphierde* < *scēap* sheep + *hierde* herder < *heord* herd]

shepherd dog, sheep dog.

shep·herd·ess (shep′ər·dis), *n.* woman who takes care of sheep.

sher·bet (shèr′bət), *n.* 1. a frozen dessert made of fruit juice, sugar, and water, milk, or whites of eggs. 2. a cooling drink made of fruit juice, sugar, and water, popular in the Orient. [< Turk., Pers. < Ar. *sharbah* drink]

sher·iff (sher′if), *n.* the most important law-enforcing officer of a county. A sheriff appoints deputies to help him keep order in the county. [OE *scirgerēfa* < *scir* shire + *gerēfa* reeve] —**sher′iff·dom,** *n.*

Sher·man (shèr′mən), *n.* William Tecumseh, 1820–1891, Union general in the Civil War.

sher·ry (sher′i), *n., pl.* -ries. a strong wine made in S Spain, or a wine like it made elsewhere. It varies in color from pale yellow to brown. [earlier *sherris* (taken as pl.) wine from *Xeres,* Spanish town]

Sher·wood Forest (shèr′wu̇d), a royal forest near Nottingham, where Robin Hood is said to have lived.

she's (shēz), 1. she is. 2. she has.

Shet·land Islands (shet′lənd), group of British islands NE of Scotland.

Shetland pony, a small, sturdy, rough-coated pony, originally from the Shetland Islands.

shew (shō), *v.,* **shewed, shewn, shew·ing,** *n. Esp. Brit. or Archaic.* show.

shib·bo·leth (shib′ə·lith), *n.* any test word, watchword, or pet phrase of a political party, a class, sect, etc. [< Heb., stream; used as a password by the Gileadites to distinguish the fleeing Ephraimites, because they could not pronounce *sh.* Judges 12:4–6]

shied (shīd), *v.* pt. and pp. of **shy.**

shield (shēld), n. 1. piece of armor carried on the arm to protect the body in battle. 2. piece of fabric worn inside a dress at the armpit. 3. a covering for moving parts of machinery. 4. anything used to protect. 5. something shaped like a shield. —v. 1. be a shield to; protect; defend. 2. serve as a shield. [OE sceld] —shield′er, n.

Knight holding a shield

shift (shift), v. 1. change from one place, position, person, sound, etc., to another; change: shift blame or responsibility, the scene shifts. 2. be rather dishonest; scheme. 3. manage to get along; contrive: when his parents died, Tom had to shift for himself. 4. get rid of. 5. get along by indirect methods; employ shifts. 6. change the position of (the gears of an automobile). —n. 1. a substituting in the place of another person or thing; change: there are two shifts of work at the factory. 2. group of workmen; group: this man is on the night shift. 3. time during which such a group works. 4. way of getting on; scheme; trick: he tried every shift. 5. change in the arrangement of the players before a football is put into play. 6. make shift, a. manage to get along. b. manage with effort or difficulty. c. do as well as one can. 7. Archaic. a woman's chemise. [OE sciftan arrange] —shift′er, n. —Syn. v. 1. transfer. —n. 2. crew, gang. 4. expedient.

shift·less (shift′lis), adj. lazy; inefficient. —shift′less·ly, adv. —shift′less·ness, n.

shift·y (shif′ti), adj., shift·i·er, shift·i·est. 1. full of shifts; well able to look out for oneself. 2. not straightforward; tricky. —shift′i·ly, adv. —shift′i·ness, n.

Shi·ko·ku (shi-kō′kü), n. island that is part of Japan, in the SW part.

shil·le·lagh, shil·la·lah, shil·le·lah (shə-lā′li; –lə), n. Irish. a stick to hit with; cudgel. [from Shillelagh, Irish village]

shil·ling (shil′ing), n. 1. a British money of account and silver coin, worth about 14 cents (1950). 2. formerly, a corresponding piece of money of one of the thirteen American colonies. [OE scilling]

shil·ly-shal·ly (shil′i-shal′i), adj., adv., v., -lied, -ly·ing, n. —adj. vacillating; wavering; hesitating; undecided. —adv. in a vacillating or hesitating manner. —v. be undecided; vacillate; hesitate. —n. inability to decide; hesitation. [reduplication of shall I?]

Shi·loh (shī′lō), n. town in the C part of ancient Palestine.

shi·ly (shī′li), adv. shyly.

shim·mer (shim′ər), v. gleam faintly. —n. a faint gleam or shine. [OE scimerian] —shim′mer·y, adj.

shim·my (shim′i), n., pl. -mies, v., -mied, -my·ing. —n. 1. Am., Slang. a jazz dance with much shaking of the body. 2. an unusual shaking or vibration. —v. 1. Am. dance the shimmy. 2. shake; vibrate. [var. of chemise (taken as pl.)]

shin (shin), n., v., shinned, shin·ning. —n. 1. the front part of the leg from the knee to the ankle. 2. the lower part of the foreleg in beef cattle. —v. climb. [OE scinu]

shin·bone (shin′bōn′), n. tibia.

shin·dig (shin′dig), n. Am., Slang. a merry or noisy dance, party, etc. [? < shin + dig, a blow on the shin]

shine (shīn), v., shone or shined, shin·ing, n. —v. 1. send out light; be bright with light; reflect light; glow: the sun shines. 2. do very well; be brilliant; excel: a shining athlete. 3. make bright; polish: shine shoes. 4. cause to shine: shine a light. 5. shine up to, try to please and get the friendship of. —n. 1. light; brightness. 2. luster; polish; gloss, as of silk. 3. fair weather; sunshine. 4. polish put on shoes. 5. Slang. fancy; liking. 6. Slang. trick; prank. 7. take a shine to, Slang. become fond of; like. [OE scīnan] —Syn. v. 1. beam, gleam. —n. 1. radiance, gleam.

shin·er (shīn′ər), n. 1. person or thing that shines. 2. a small American fresh-water fish with glistening scales. 3. Slang. a black eye. 4. Brit. Slang. guinea; sovereign.

shin·gle[1] (shing′gəl), n., v., -gled, -gling. —n. 1. a thin piece of wood, etc., used to cover roofs, etc. Shingles are laid in overlapping rows with the thicker ends exposed. 2. Am., Colloq. a small signboard, esp. for a doctor's or lawyer's office. 3. a short haircut. —v. 1. cover with shingles: shingle a roof. 2. cut (the hair) short. [var. of earlier shindle < L scindula] —shin′gler, n.

shin·gle[2] (shing′gəl), n. Esp. Brit. 1. coarse gravel. 2. beach or other place covered with this. —shin′gly, adj.

shin·gles (shing′gəlz), n. sing. or pl. a virus disease that causes painful irritation of a group of nerves and an outbreak of itching spots or blisters. [< Med.L cingulus, var. of L cingulum girdle; trans. of Gk. zoster girdle, shingles]

shin·ing (shīn′ing), adj. 1. that shines; bright. 2. brilliant; outstanding. —shin′ing·ly, adv. —Syn. 1. glowing, radiant, glistening.

shin·ny (shin′i), n., pl. -nies, v., -nied, -ny·ing. —n. 1. a simple kind of hockey. 2. a hockey stick. —v. play shinny. [< shin]

Shin·to (shin′tō), n. 1. Also, Shin′to·ism. the native religion of Japan, primarily a system of nature worship and ancestor worship. 2. adherent of this religion. —adj. of or pertaining to Shinto. —Shin′to·ist, n., adj.

shin·y (shīn′i), adj., shin·i·er, shin·i·est. 1. shining; bright. 2. worn to a glossy smoothness: a coat shiny from hard wear. —shin′i·ness, n.

ship (ship), n., v., shipped, ship·ping. —n. 1. a large seagoing vessel with masts and sails. 2. any large vessel for use on water or in air, as a steamship, a battleship, an airship, etc. 3. officers and crew of a vessel. —v. 1. put, take, or receive on board a ship. 2. go on board a ship. 3. send or carry from one place to another by a ship, train, truck, etc. 4. engage for service on a ship. 5. take a job on a ship. 6. take in (water) over the side, as a vessel does when the waves break over it. [OE scip]

-ship, suffix. 1. office, status, or rank of ——, as in clerkship, governorship. 2. quality, state, or condition of ——, as in kinship. 3. act, acts, power, or skill of ——, as in horsemanship, dictatorship. 4. relation between ——s, as in cousinship, comradeship. [OE -scipe]

ship biscuit, a kind of hard biscuit used on shipboard; hardtack.

ship·board (ship′bôrd′; -bōrd′), n. 1. ship. 2. on shipboard, on or inside a ship.

ship·build·er (ship′bil′dər), n. person who designs or constructs ships. —ship′build′ing, n., adj.

ship·load (ship′lōd′), n. a full load for a ship.

ship·mas·ter (ship′mas′tər; -mäs′-), n. master, commander, or captain of a ship.

ship·mate (ship′māt′), n. a fellow sailor on a ship.

ship·ment (ship′mənt), n. 1. act of shipping goods. 2. goods sent at one time to a person, firm, etc.

ship of the line, a sailing warship carrying 74 or more guns.

ship·own·er (ship′ōn′ər), n. person who owns a ship or ships.

ship·per (ship′ər), n. person who ships goods.

ship·ping (ship′ing), n. 1. act or business of sending goods by water, rail, etc. 2. a body of ships. 3. their total tonnage. 4. the ships of a nation, city, or business.

ship·shape (ship′shāp′), adj. in good order; trim. —adv. in a trim, neat manner.

ship·wreck (ship′rek′), n. 1. destruction or loss of a ship. 2. a wrecked ship. 3. destruction; ruin. —v. 1. wreck; ruin; destroy. 2. suffer shipwreck.

ship·wright (ship′rīt′), n. man who builds or repairs ships.

ship·yard (ship′yärd′), n. place near the water where ships are built or repaired.

shire (shīr), *n.* one of the counties into which Great Britain is divided. [OE *scīr*]

shirk (shérk), *v. Am.* avoid or get out of doing (work, a duty, etc.). —*n.* person who shirks or does not do his share. [? < G *schurke* rascal] —shirk′er, *n.* —Syn. *v.* evade, shun, neglect.

shirr (shér), *Am.* —*v.* 1. draw up or gather (cloth) on parallel threads. 2. bake (eggs) in a shallow dish with butter, etc. —*n.* a shirred arrangement of cloth, etc.

shirt (shért), *n.* 1. garment for the upper part of a man's body. 2. undergarment for the upper part of the body. [OE *scyrte*. Cf. SKIRT.]

shirt·ing (shér′ting), *n.* cloth for shirts.

shirt-sleeve (shért′slēv′), *adj. Am.* informal.

shirt·waist (shért′wāst′), *n. Am.* a woman's loose waist or blouse, worn with a separate skirt.

Shi·va (shē′və), *n.* Siva.

shiv·er[1] (shiv′ər), *v.* shake with cold, fear, etc. —*n.* a shaking from cold, fear, etc. [ME *schivere*(*n*)] —shiv′er·y, *adj.* —Syn. *v.* quake.

shiv·er[2] (shiv′ər), *v.* break into small pieces. —*n.* a small piece; splinter.

shoal[1] (shōl), *adj.* shallow. —*n.* 1. place where the water is shallow. 2. sandbank or sand bar that makes the water shallow: *wrecked on the shoals.* —*v.* become shallow. [OE *sceald* shallow]

shoal[2] (shōl), *n.* a large number; crowd: *a shoal of fish.* —*v.* form into a shoal. [OE *scolu*]

shoat (shōt), *n.* a young pig able to feed itself. Also, **shote.**

shock[1] (shok), *n.* 1. a sudden, violent shake, blow, or crash. 2. a sudden, violent, or upsetting disturbance. 3. a collapsing or weakening of the body or mind caused by some violent impression on the nerves: *suffer from shock.* 4. *Colloq.* paralysis. 5. disturbance produced by an electric current passing through the body. —*v.* 1. strike together violently. 2. cause to feel surprise, horror, or disgust. 3. give an electric shock to. [prob. < F *choc, n., choquer, v.*] —shock′er, *n.* —Syn. 1. concussion, collision, jolt. *v.* 1. jar, jolt, collide. 2. horrify, startle, scandalize.

shock[2] (shok), *Am.* —*n.* group of cornstalks or bundles of grain set up on end together. —*v.* make into shocks. [? < LG or MDu. *schok*] —shock′er, *n.*

shock[3] (shok), *n.* a thick, bushy mass.

shock absorber, anything that absorbs or lessens shocks.

shock·ing (shok′ing), *adj.* 1. causing intense and painful surprise. 2. offensive; disgusting; revolting. 3. *Colloq.* very bad. —shock′ing·ly, *adv.* —shock′ing·ness, *n.* —Syn. 1. appalling. 2. outrageous, scandalous.

shock therapy, treatment of psychotic disorder through shock induced by chemical or electrical means.

shock troops, troops chosen and specially trained for making attacks.

shock wave, disturbance of the atmosphere created by the movement of an aircraft, rocket, etc. at velocities greater than that of sound.

shod (shod), *v.* pt. and pp. of shoe.

shod·dy (shod′i), *n., pl.* -dies, *adj.* -di·er, -di·est. —*n.* 1. an inferior kind of wool made of woolen waste, old rags, yarn, etc. 2. anything inferior made to look like what is better. —*adj.* 1. made of woolen waste. 2. falsely claiming superiority. 3. *Am.* making vulgar pretensions. —shod′di·ly, *adv.* —shod′di·ness, *n.*

shoe (shü), *n., pl.* shoes, (*Archaic*) shoon; *v.,* shod, shoe·ing. —*n.* 1. an outer covering, usually of leather, for a person's foot. 2. thing like a shoe in shape or use. 3. a horseshoe. 4. the part of a brake that presses on a wheel; wheel drag. 5. the outer case of an automobile tire. 6. a sliding plate or contact by which an electric car takes current from the third rail. 7. **in another's shoes,** in another's place, situation, etc. —*v.* furnish with a shoe or shoes. [OE *scōh*]

shoe·horn (shü′hôrn′), *n.* piece of metal, horn, etc., inserted at the heel of a shoe to make it slip on easily.

shoe·lace (shü′lās′), *n.* cord, braid, or leather strip for fastening a shoe.

shoe·mak·er (shü′māk′ər), *n.* man who makes or mends shoes. —shoe′mak′ing, *n.*

shoe·string (shü′string′), *n.* 1. shoelace. 2. *Am., Colloq.* a very small amount of money used to start or carry on a business, investment, etc.

shoe tree, form for keeping a shoe in shape or for stretching it.

sho·gun (shō′gun; -gün), *n.* a hereditary commander in chief of the Japanese army. The shoguns were the real rulers of Japan for hundreds of years until 1867. [< Jap. < Chinese *chiang chun* army leader]

shone (shōn), *v.* pt. and pp. of shine.

shook (shuk), *v.* pt. of shake.

shoon (shün), *n.pl. Archaic.* shoes.

shoot (shüt), *v.,* shot, shoot·ing, *n.* —*v.* 1. hit, wound, or kill with a bullet, arrow, etc.: *shoot a rabbit.* 2. send swiftly: *he shot question after question at us.* 3. fire or use (a gun, etc.). 4. of a gun, etc., send a bullet: *this gun shoots straight.* 5. move suddenly and swiftly: *a car shot by us, he shot back the bolt.* 6. pass quickly along, through, over, or under: *shoot Niagara Falls in a barrel.* 7. come forth from the ground; grow; grow rapidly. 8. take (a picture) with a camera; photograph. 9. project sharply: *a cape that shoots out into the sea.* 10. vary with some different color, etc.: *her dress was shot with threads of gold.* 11. measure the altitude of: *shoot the sun.* 12. send (a ball, etc.) toward the goal, pocket, etc. —*n.* 1. shooting practice. 2. trip, party, or contest for shooting. 3. a new part growing out; young bud or stem. [OE *scēotan*] —shoot′er, *n.* —Syn. *v.* 9. jut, extend.

shooting star, star seen falling or darting through the sky; meteor.

shop (shop), *n., v.,* shopped, shop·ping. —*n.* 1. place where things are sold; store. 2. place where things are made or repaired. 3. place where a certain kind of work is done: *a barber shop.* 4. talk shop, talk about one's work. —*v.* visit stores to look at or to buy things. [OE *sceoppa*] —shop′per, *n.*

shop·keep·er (shop′kēp′ər), *n.* person who carries on business in a shop or store.

shop·lift·er (shop′lif′tər), *n.* person who steals goods from a shop or store while pretending to be a customer. —shop′lift′ing, *n.*

shop·talk (shop′tôk′), *n.* the colloquial vocabulary of an occupation. ❯ **shoptalk.** Any occupation from law to ditchdigging has its shoptalk. For the most part shoptalk consists of the necessary names for materials, processes, tools, etc. The workman needs names for hundreds of things the layman doesn't know exist. These words are appropriate and necessary in informal speaking or writing about the particular occupation in which they are used. They are usually out of place in formal writing.

shop·worn (shop′wôrn′; -wōrn′), *adj.* soiled by being displayed or handled in a store.

shore[1] (shôr; shōr), *n.* 1. land at the edge of a sea, lake, etc. 2. land near a sea. 3. land. 4. **in shore,** in or on the water, near to the shore or nearer to the shore. 5. **off shore,** in or on the water, not far from the shore. [? < LG or MDu. *schore*] —shore′less, *adj.* —Syn. 1. coast, beach, strand.

shore[2] (shôr; shōr), *n., v.,* shored, shor·ing. —*n.* prop placed against or beneath something to support it. —*v.* prop up or support with shores. [? < MDu. *schore* prop]

shore[3] (shôr; shōr), *v. Archaic.* pt. of shear.

shore·line (shôr′līn′; shōr′-), *n.* line where shore and water meet.

shore patrol, the policing branch of the U.S. Navy.

shore·ward (shôr′wərd; shōr′-), *adv., adj.* toward the shore.

shor·ing (shôr′ing; shōr′-), *n.* shores or props for supporting a building, ship, etc.

shorn (shôrn; shōrn), *v.* pp. of shear.

Frame of a ship supported by shores

short (shôrt), *adj.* **1.** not long; of small extent from end to end: *a short distance.* **2.** not long for its kind: *a short tail.* **3.** not tall: *a short man, short grass.* **4.** extending or reaching but a little way: *a short memory.* **5.** less than the right amount, measure, standard, etc.: *the cashier is short in his accounts.* **6.** not having enough; scanty: *short allowance.* **7.** not reaching a mark or the like: *a short throw.* **8.** concise; brief: *a short essay.* **9.** so brief as to be rude: *a short answer.* **10.** short of, a. not up to; less than: *nothing short of your best work will satisfy me.* b. not having enough of: *short of ready cash.* **11.** *Phonet.* of vowels or syllables, occupying a relatively short time in utterance. The vowels are short in *fat, net, pin, not, up.* **12.** breaking or crumbling easily, as pastry. **13.** *Am.* not possessing at the time of sale the stocks or commodities that one sells. **14.** noting or pertaining to sales of stocks or commodities that the seller does not possess. —*adv.* **1.** so as to be or make short: *cut a thing short.* **2.** abruptly; suddenly: *the horse stopped short.* **3.** briefly. **4.** on the near side of an intended or particular point: *the throw fell short.* **5.** without going the full length (of): *stop short of actual crime.* **6.** without possessing at the time the stocks, etc., sold: *it is risky to sell short.* **7.** fall short, a. fail to reach. b. be insufficient. **8.** run short, a. not have enough. b. not be enough. —*n.* **1.** something short, esp. a short sound or syllable. **2.** *Elect.* a short circuit. **3.** *Am.* person who has sold short. **4.** a short sale. **5.** shorts, a. knee breeches. b. short, loose trousers worn in sports; trunks. c. mixture of bran and coarse meal. **6.** in short, briefly. [OE *sceort*] —**short′ish,** *adj.* —**short′ness,** *n.* —**Syn.** *adj.* **6.** deficient, inadequate. **8.** terse, succinct. **9.** abrupt, curt, sharp.

short·age (shôr′tij), *n.* **1.** *Am.* too small an amount; lack. **2.** amount by which something is deficient. —**Syn.** **1.** deficiency, inadequacy.

short·bread (shôrt′bred′), *n.* a rich cake or cooky that crumbles easily.

short·cake (shôrt′kāk′), *n.* **1.** cake made of rich biscuit dough and shortening, covered or filled with berries or other fruit. **2.** a sweet cake filled with fruit.

short·change (shôrt′chānj′), *v.,* **-changed, -chang·ing.** *Am., Colloq.* **1.** give less than the right change to. **2.** cheat. —**short′-chang′er,** *n.*

short circuit, a side circuit of electricity or relatively low resistance, connecting two points of a larger electric current so as to carry most of the current.

short-cir·cuit (shôrt′sér′kit), *v.* **1.** make a short circuit in. **2.** make a short circuit.

short cut, *Am.* a less distant or quicker way.

short·en (shôr′tən), *v.* **1.** make shorter; cut off. **2.** become shorter. **3.** make rich with butter, lard, etc. **4.** take in (sail). —**short′en·er,** *n.* —**Syn.** **1.** abridge, curtail, condense.

short·en·ing (shôr′tən·ing; shôrt′ning), *n.* butter, lard, or other fat, used to make pastry, cake, etc., crisp or crumbly.

short·hand (shôrt′hand′), *n.* method of rapid writing that uses symbols in place of letters, syllables, words, and phrases; stenography. For example, the symbols in the picture mean "Your letter was received today." —*adj.* **1.** using shorthand. **2.** written in shorthand.

A sample of shorthand

short·hand·ed (shôrt′han′did), *adj.* not having enough workmen or helpers. —**short′-hand′ed·ness,** *n.*

short·horn (shôrt′hôrn′), *n.* any of a breed of cattle with short horns, raised for beef.

short-lived (shôrt′livd′; -livd′), *adj.* living only a short time; lasting only a short time.

short·ly (shôrt′li), *adv.* **1.** in a short time; before long; soon. **2.** in a few words; briefly. **3.** briefly and rudely.

short shrift, little mercy, respite, or delay.

short-sight·ed (shôrt′sīt′id), *adj.* **1.** near-sighted; not able to see far. **2.** lacking in foresight; not prudent. —**short′-sight′ed·ly,** *adv.* —**short′-sight′ed·ness,** *n.*

short·stop (shôrt′stop′), *n.* *Am.* a baseball player stationed between second base and third base.

short story, a prose story with a full plot, but much shorter than a novel.

short-tem·pered (shôrt′tem′pərd), *adj.* easily made angry; quick-tempered.

short-term (shôrt′térm′), *adj.* falling due in a short time.

short ton, 2000 pounds avoirdupois.

short wave, a radio wave having a wave length of 60 meters or less. —**short′-wave′,** *adj.*

short-wave (shôrt′wāv′), *v.,* **-waved, -waving.** transmit by short waves.

short-wind·ed (shôrt′win′did), *adj.* getting out of breath too quickly; having difficulty in breathing. —**short′-wind′ed·ness,** *n.*

shot[1] (shot), *n., pl.* **shots** or (for defs. 2, 3) **shot** or **shots,** *v.,* **shot·ted, shot·ting.** —*n.* **1.** act of shooting. **2.** tiny ball or balls of lead; bullets. **3.** a single ball for a gun or cannon. **4.** discharge of a gun or cannon. **5.** any missile sent with force. **6.** distance a weapon can shoot; range. **7.** person who shoots: *he is a good shot.* **8.** an aimed stroke or throw in a game. **9.** a metal ball, usually weighing 16 pounds. **10.** remark aimed at some person or thing: *she made a parting shot.* **11.** an attempt; try: *make a shot at the job.* **12.** picture taken with a camera; photograph: *he took a shot of the beautiful scene.* **13.** *Slang.* drink: *a shot of whiskey.* **14.** *Slang.* dose: *a shot of some drug.* **15.** a long shot, an attempt at something difficult. **16.** put the shot, send a heavy metal ball as far as one can with one push. —*v.* load or weight with shot. [OE *sceot*]

shot[2] (shot), *v.* pt. and pp. of **shoot.** —*adj.* woven so as to show a play of colors: *blue silk shot with gold.*

shote (shōt), *n.* shoat.

shot·gun (shot′gun′), *n.* *Am.* a smoothbore gun for firing cartridges filled with small shot.

should (shud; *unstressed* shəd), *v.* **1.** pt. of **shall.** See **shall** for ordinary uses. **2.** *Should* has special uses: a. to express duty: *you should try to make fewer mistakes.* b. to make statements less direct or blunt: *I should not call her beautiful.* c. to express uncertainty: *if John should win the prize, how happy he would be.* d. to make statements about something that might have happened but did not: *I should have gone if you had asked me.* e. to express a condition or reason for something: *he was pardoned on the condition that he should leave the country.* [OE *sceolde*]

➤ **should, would. 1.** FUTURE EXPRESSING DOUBT. *Should* and *would* are used in statements that carry some doubt or uncertainty about the statement made. They are also used in polite or unemphatic requests: *They should be there by Monday.* [Contrast: *They will be there by Monday.*] *Would you please shut the door on your way out?* [Contrast: *Will you please . . .*] In the first person both *should* and *would* are used: *I would be much obliged if you could do this, I should be much obliged if you could do this.* Usage is so much divided on the choice between these forms that one's feeling is probably the safest guide. **2.** OTHER USES OF SHOULD AND WOULD. *Should* as an auxiliary used with all persons expresses a mild sense of obligation, weaker than *ought: I should pay this bill.* [Contrast: *I ought to pay this bill.*] In indirect discourse *should* and *would* represent the future tense of the direct speech: Direct: *"I will be ready at three," Mildred said.* Indirect: *Mildred said that she would be ready at three.*

shoul·der (shōl′dər), *n.* **1.** the part of the body to which an arm or foreleg or wing is attached. **2.** shoulders, the two shoulders and the upper part of the back. **3.** part of a garment covering this. **4.** foreleg and adjoining parts of a slaughtered animal. **5.** a shoulderlike part or projec-

āge, cāre, fär; ēqual, térm; īce; ōpen, ôrder; pút, rüle, ūse; th, then; ə=a in about.

tion. **6. shoulder to shoulder, a.** side by side; together. **b.** with united effort. —*v.* **1.** take upon or support with the shoulder or shoulders: *shoulder a tray.* **2.** bear (a burden, blame, etc.); assume (responsibility, expense, etc.). **3.** push with the shoulders: *he shouldered his way through the crowd.* **4. shoulder arms,** hold a rifle almost upright with the barrel resting in the hollow of the shoulder and the butt in the hand. [OE *sculdor*]

shoulder blade, the flat bone of the shoulder; scapula.

should·n't (shūd'ənt), should not.

shouldst (shūdst), **should·est** (shūd'ist), *v. Archaic.* 2nd pers. sing. of should.

shout (shout), *v.* **1.** call or cry loudly and vigorously. **2.** talk or laugh very loudly. **3.** express by a shout or shouts. —*n.* **1.** a loud, vigorous call or cry. **2.** a loud outburst of laughter. [? ult. var. of *scout²*] —**shout'er,** *n.*

shove (shuv), *v.,* **shoved, shov·ing,** *n.* —*v.* **1.** push. **2. shove off, a.** push away from the shore; row away. **b.** *Am., Slang.* leave; start. —*n.* push. [OE *scūfan*] —**shov'er,** *n.* —**Syn.** *v.* **1.** thrust, jostle, elbow.

shov·el (shuv'əl), *n., v.,* **-eled, -el·ing;** *esp. Brit.* **-elled, -el·ling.** —*n.* **1.** tool with a broad scoop, used to lift and throw loose matter: *a coal shovel, a steam shovel.* **2.** a shovelful. —*v.* **1.** lift and throw with a shovel. **2.** make with a shovel: *shovel a path.* **3.** work with a shovel. **4.** throw in large quantities: *shovel the food into one's mouth.* [OE *scofl*] —**shov'el·er,** *esp. Brit.* **shov'el·ler,** *n.*

shov·el·board (shuv'əl·bôrd'; -bôrd'), *n.* shuffleboard.

shov·el·ful (shuv'əl·fûl), *n., pl.* **-fuls.** as much as a shovel can hold.

show (shō), *v.,* **showed, shown** or **showed, show·ing,** *n.* —*v.* **1.** let be seen; put in sight: *she showed her new hat.* **2.** reveal; manifest; disclose: *he showed himself a noble man.* **3.** be in sight; appear; be seen: *anger showed in his face.* **4.** point out: *show him the way.* **5.** direct; guide: *show him out.* **6.** make clear; explain. **7.** make clear to; explain to: *show us how to do the problem.* **8.** prove: *he showed that it was true.* **9.** grant; give: *show mercy, show favor.* **10.** *Colloq.* be first, second, or third in a race. **11. show off,** make a show (of); display (one's good points, etc.). **12. show up, a.** expose. **b.** stand out. **c.** *Colloq.* put in an appearance. —*n.* **1.** display: *the jewels made a fine show.* **2.** display for effect: *a house furnished for show, not comfort.* **3.** any kind of public exhibition or display: *a horse show.* **4.** a showing: *the club voted by a show of hands.* **5.** appearance: *a sorry show.* **6.** false appearance: *a show of sincerity.* **7.** trace; indication: *a show of oil in a region.* **8.** *Colloq.* entertainment. **9.** *Colloq.* chance. **10.** object of scorn; something odd; queer sight: *don't make a show of yourself.* **11. for show,** for effect; to attract attention. Also, *esp. Brit.* or *Dial.* shew. [OE *scēawian* look at] —**show'er,** *n.* —**Syn.** *v.* **5.** conduct, usher. —*n.* **6.** pretext, pretense. ≥ **show.** Colloquial, or theatrical shoptalk, in the sense of "a play" and usually humorous or substandard for a dignified public performance, as of a concert; informal when applied to the movies (short for *picture show*). Informal and colloquial for "chance": *They didn't have a show of winning.*

show·boat (shō'bōt'), *n. Am.* steamboat with a theater for plays.

show·case (shō'kās'), *n.* a glass case to display and protect articles in stores, museums, etc.

show·down (shō'doun'), *n. Am., Colloq.* a forced disclosure of facts, purposes, etc.

show·er (shou'ər), *n.* **1.** a short fall of rain. **2.** anything like a fall of rain: *a shower of hail, tears, sparks from an engine.* **3.** *Am.* party for giving presents to a woman about to be married. **4.** *Am.* a shower bath. —*v.* **1.** rain for a short time. **2.** come in a shower. **3.** send in a shower; pour down. [OE *scūr*] —**show'er·y,** *adj.*

shower bath, bath in which water pours down on the body from above in small jets.

show·man (shō'mən), *n., pl.* **-men. 1.** man who manages a show. **2.** person skilled in showmanship or publicity. —**show'man·ship,** *n.*

shown (shōn), *v.* pp. of show.

show-off (shō'ôf'; -of'), *n.* **1.** a showing off. **2.** *Colloq.* person who shows off.

show·room (shō'rüm'; -rûm'), *n.* room used for the display of goods or merchandise.

show·y (shō'i), *adj.,* **show·i·er, show·i·est. 1.** making a display; striking; conspicuous. A peony is a showy flower. **2.** ostentatious. —**show'i·ly,** *adv.* —**show'i·ness,** *n.* —**Syn. 2.** gaudy, garish. —**Ant. 2.** unostentatious, quiet, modest.

shrank (shrangk), *v.* pt. of shrink.

shrap·nel (shrap'nəl), *n.* **1.** shell filled with bullets and powder, arranged to explode in the air and scatter the bullets over a large area. **2.** fragments scattered by such a shell on explosion. [after the inventor, H. *Shrapnel,* British officer]

shred (shred), *n., v.,* **shred·ded** or **shred, shred·ding.** —*n.* **1.** a very small piece torn off or cut off; very narrow strip; scrap. **2.** fragment; particle; bit. —*v.* tear or cut into small pieces. [OE *scrēade*] —**shred'der,** *n.*

shrew (shrü), *n.* **1.** a bad-tempered, quarrelsome woman. **2.** a mouselike animal with a long snout and brownish fur, that eats insects and worms. [OE *scrēawa*] —**shrew'ish,** *adj.* —**shrew'ish·ly,** *adv.* —**shrew'ish·ness,** *n.*

Shrew
(total length ab. 5 in.)

shrewd (shrüd), *adj.* **1.** having a sharp mind; showing a keen wit; clever. **2.** keen; sharp. [earlier *shrewed,* < *shrew, v.,* in sense of "scold"] —**shrewd'ly,** *adv.* —**shrewd'ness,** *n.* —**Syn. 1.** astute, discerning.

shriek (shrēk), *n.* **1.** a loud, sharp, shrill sound. **2.** a loud, shrill laugh. —*v.* **1.** make such a sound. **2.** utter loudly and shrilly. [akin to Scand. *skrækja*] —**shriek'er,** *n.*

shrift (shrift), *n. Archaic.* confession to a priest, followed by the imposing of penance and the granting of absolution. [< L *scriptus* written]

shrike (shrīk), *n.* bird with a strong, hooked beak that feeds on large insects, frogs, and sometimes on other birds. [OE *scric*]

shrill (shril), *adj.* **1.** having a high pitch; high and sharp in sound; piercing. Crickets, locusts, and katydids make shrill noises. **2.** full of shrill sounds. —*v.* **1.** make a shrill sound. **2.** sound sharply. —*n.* a shrill sound. —*adv.* with a shrill sound. [ME *shrille*] —**shrill'ness,** *n.* —**shrill'ly,** *adv.*

shrimp (shrimp), *n., pl.* **shrimps** or for 1 (*esp. collectively*) **shrimp. 1.** a small, long-tailed shellfish, used for food. **2.** a small or insignificant person.

Shrimp (2 in. long)

shrine (shrīn), *n., v.,* **shrined, shrin·ing.** —*n.* **1.** case, box, etc., holding a holy object. **2.** tomb of a saint, etc. **3.** place of worship. **4.** place or object considered as sacred because of its memories, history, etc. —*v.* enclose in a shrine or something like a shrine. [< L *scrinium* case]

shrink (shringk), *v.,* **shrank** or **shrunk, shrunk** or **shrunk·en, shrink·ing.** —*v.* **1.** draw back. **2.** become smaller. **3.** make smaller; cause to contract. —*n.* a shrinking. [OE *scrincan*] —**shrink'a·ble,** *adj.* —**shrink'er,** *n.* —**shrink'ing·ly,** *adv.* —**Syn.** *v.* **1.** retreat, recoil, quail, flinch. **2, 3.** shrivel, decrease.

shrink·age (shringk'ij), *n.* **1.** fact or process of shrinking. **2.** amount or degree of shrinking.

shrive (shrīv), *v.,* **shrove** or **shrived, shriv·en** (shriv'ən) or **shrived, shriv·ing.** *Archaic.* **1.** hear the confession of, impose penance on, and grant absolution to. **2.** make confession. **3.** hear confessions. **4. shrive oneself,** confess to a priest and do penance. [< L *scribere* write]

shriv·el (shriv′əl), v., –eled, –el·ing; esp. Brit. –elled, –el·ling. dry up; wither; shrink and wrinkle.

Shrop·shire (shrop′shir; –shər), n. county in W England.

shroud (shroud), n. 1. cloth or garment in which a dead person is wrapped for burial. 2. something that covers, conceals, or veils. 3. Usually, **shrouds**, Naut. rope from a mast to the side of a ship. Shrouds help support the mast. —v. 1. wrap for burial. 2. cover; conceal; veil. [OE scrūd] —shroud′less, adj.

shrove (shrōv), v. pt. of shrive.

Shrove·tide (shrōv′tīd′), n. the three days, Shrove Sunday, Monday, and Tuesday, before Ash Wednesday, the first day of Lent.

shrub (shrub), n. a woody plant smaller than a tree, usually with many separate stems starting from or near the ground; bush. [OE scrybb brush] —shrub′by, adj. —shrub′bi·ness, n. —shrub′like′, adj.

shrub·ber·y (shrub′ər·i; shrub′ri), n., pl. –ber·ies. shrubs.

shrug (shrug), v., shrugged, shrug·ging, n. —v. raise (the shoulders) as an expression of dislike, doubt, indifference, impatience, etc. —n. a raising of the shoulders in this way.

shrunk (shrungk), v. pp. and pt. of shrink.

shrunk·en (shrungk′ən), adj. grown smaller; shriveled. —v. pp. of shrink.

shuck (shuk), n. husk; pod. —v. remove the shucks from. —shuck′er, n.

shucks (shuks), interj. Am., Colloq. exclamation of disgust, regret, impatience, etc.

shud·der (shud′ər), v. tremble with horror, fear, cold, etc. —n. a trembling; quivering. [ME shodder(en), frequentative of OE scūdan shake]

shuf·fle (shuf′əl), v., –fled, –fling, n. —v. 1. walk without lifting the feet: the old man shuffles feebly along. 2. scrape or drag (the feet). 3. dance with a shuffle. 4. mix (cards, etc.) so as to change the order. 5. put, bring, come about, or answer in a tricky way. 6. shuffle off, be rid of. —n. 1. a scraping or dragging movement of the feet. 2. dance with a shuffle. 3. a shuffling of cards. 4. right or turn to shuffle (cards). 5. trick; unfair act; evasion. [? < LG schuffeln; akin to SHOVE] —Syn. v. 5. dodge, equivocate, quibble.

shuf·fle·board (shuf′əl·bôrd′; –bōrd′), n. a game played by pushing large disks along a surface to certain spots. Also, shovelboard.

shun (shun), v., shunned, shun·ning. keep away from; avoid. [OE scunian] —shun′ner, n.

shunt (shunt), v. 1. move out of the way; turn aside. 2. sidetrack; put aside; get rid of. 3. switch (a train) from one track to another. 4. Elect. carry by means of a shunt. —n. 1. a turning aside; shift. 2. a railroad switch. 3. Elect. wire or other conductor joining two points in a circuit and forming a path through which a part of the current will pass. [? < shunt]

shut (shut), v., shut, shut·ting, adj. —v. 1. close (a receptacle or opening) by pushing or pulling a lid, door, some part, etc., into place: shut a box. 2. close (eyes, a knife, a book, etc.) by bringing parts together. 3. close tight; close securely; close doors or other openings of: shut a house for the summer. 4. become shut; be closed. 5. enclose; confine: shut in prison. 6. shut down, a. close by lowering. b. close (a factory or the like) for a time; stop work. c. Colloq. put a stop or check on. 7. shut in, keep from going out. 8. shut off, close; obstruct; check; bar. 9. shut out, a. keep from coming in. b. defeat (a team) without allowing it to score. 10. shut up, a. shut the doors and windows of. b. Colloq. stop talking. c. keep from going out. —adj. closed; fastened up; enclosed. [OE scyttan bolt up]

shut·down (shut′doun′), n. Am. a closing of a factory, or the like, for a time; shutting down.

shut·in (shut′in′), Am. —adj. confined. —n. person who is kept from going out by sickness, weakness, etc.

shut·out (shut′out′), n. 1. Am. defeat of a team without allowing it to score. 2. lockout.

shut·ter (shut′ər), n. 1. a movable cover for a window. 2. a movable cover, slide, etc., for closing an opening. The device that opens and closes in front of the lens of a camera is the shutter. 3. person or thing that shuts. —v. put a shutter or shutters on or over. [< shut]

shut·tle (shut′əl), n., v., –tled, –tling. —n. 1. instrument that carries the thread from one side of the web to the other in weaving. 2. instrument on which thread is wound. Shuttles are used in tatting (a kind of lacemaking). 3. the sliding container that carries the lower thread in a sewing machine. 4. Am. a shuttle train. —v. move quickly to and fro. [OE scutel a dart < scēotan to shoot]

shut·tle·cock (shut′əl·kok′), n. a cork with feathers stuck in one end, which is hit by a battledore.

shuttle train, Am. train that runs back and forth over a short distance.

shy[1] (shī), adj., shy·er, shy·est or shi·er, shi·est, v., shied, shy·ing, n., pl. shies. —adj. 1. uncomfortable in company; bashful. 2. easily frightened away; timid. 3. cautious; wary. 4. Colloq. short in amount, degree, etc., to a certain extent. 5. fight shy of, keep away from; avoid. 6. shy of, Colloq. having little; lacking. —v. 1. start back or aside suddenly. 2. shrink. —n. a sudden start to one side. [OE scēoh] —shy′er, n. —shy′ly, adv. —shy′ness, n. —Syn. adj. 1. retiring, modest. 3. suspicious, distrustful, chary. —Ant. adj. 1. forward, bold.

shy[2] (shī), v., shied, shy·ing, n., pl. shies. —v. throw quickly and suddenly: the boy shied a stone at the tree. —n. a sudden, quick throw.

Shy·lock (shī′lok), n. 1. the relentless and revengeful moneylender in Shakespeare's play The Merchant of Venice. 2. a greedy moneylender.

shy·ster (shī′stər), n. Am., Colloq. lawyer or other person who uses improper or questionable methods in his business or profession.

si (sē), n. the seventh tone of the musical scale. [see GAMUT]

Si, Chem. silicon.

S.I., 1. Sandwich Islands. 2. Staten Island.

Si·am (sī·am′; sī′am), n. 1. Official name, Thailand. country in SE Asia between Burma and Laos and Cambodia. 2. Gulf of, gulf of the South China Sea, E and S of Siam.

Si·a·mese (sī′ə·mēz′; –mēs′), adj., n., pl. –mese. —adj. of or pertaining to Siam, its people, or their language. —n. 1. native of Siam. 2. language of Siam.

sib (sib), adj. related by blood; closely related; akin. —n. 1. kinsman or relative. 2. one's kin. 3. brother or sister. [OE sibb]

Si·be·li·us (si·bā′li·əs), n. Jean, 1865–1957, Finnish composer.

Si·be·ri·a (sī·bir′i·ə), n. region in N Asia, extending from the Ural Mountains to the Pacific. It is part of the Soviet Union. —Si·be′ri·an, adj., n.

sib·i·lant (sib′ə·lənt), adj. 1. hissing. 2. making, having, or representing a hissing sound. —n. a hissing sound, letter, or symbol. S and sh are sibilants. [< L sibilans hissing] —sib′i·lance, sib′i·lan·cy, n. —sib′i·lant·ly, adv.

sib·ling (sib′ling), n. one of two or more children of a family. —adj. of or pertaining to a brother or sister.

sib·yl (sib′əl), n. 1. any of several prophetesses that the ancient Greeks and Romans consulted about the future. 2. prophetess; fortuneteller; witch. [< L < Gk. sibylla] —si·byl·ic (si·bil′ik), sib·yl·line (sib′ə·lēn; –lin; –līn), adj.

sic[1] (sik), adv. Latin. so; thus. ▶ Sic in brackets is sometimes used to mark an error in quoted matter: The letter was headed "Danbury, Connecticut [sic], Jan. 2." It is sometimes also used, however, simply to indicate that exact quotation is being made, without reference to its correctness.

sic[2] (sik), v., sicked, sick·ing. 1. set upon or

attack. 2. incite to set upon or attack. [var. of *seek*]

Sic·i·ly (sis′ə·li), *n.* the largest island in the Mediterranean, a department of Italy. —**Si·cil·ian** (si·sil′yən), *adj., n.*

sick (sik), *adj.* 1. in poor health; having some disease; ill. 2. *Esp. Brit. Colloq.* vomiting; inclined to vomit; feeling nausea. 3. for a sick person; connected with sickness. 4. showing sickness. 5. weary; tired. 6. disgusted. 7. affected with sorrow or longing: *sick at heart.* 8. not in the proper condition. —*n.* sick people. [OE *sēoc*] —**sick′ish,** *adj.* —**sick′ish·ly,** *adv. Am.* —**sick′ish·ness,** *n.* —**Syn.** *adj.* 1. unwell, ailing, indisposed. ▷ **sick,** **ill.** Ill is the more formal word. The two words mean the same, except that colloquially and in British usage *sick* is often specialized to mean "nauseated."

sick bay, place on a ship used as a hospital.

sick·bed (sik′bed′), *n.* bed of a sick person.

sick·en (sik′ən), *v.* 1. become sick. 2. make sick. —**sick′en·er,** *n.* —**sick′en·ing,** *adj.* —**sick′en·ing·ly,** *adv.*

sick headache, migraine.

sick·le (sik′əl), *n.* tool consisting of a short, curved blade on a short handle, used for cutting grass, etc. [< L *secula*] —**sick′le-shaped′,** *adj.*

Sickle

sick·ly (sik′li), *adj.,* **-li·er, -li·est,** *adv., v.,* **-lied, -ly·ing.** —*adj.* 1. often sick; not strong; not healthy. 2. of or pertaining to sickness. 3. causing sickness. 4. faint; weak; pale. —*adv.* in a sick manner. —*v.* make sickly, esp. in appearance. —**sick′li·ness,** *n.* —**Syn.** *adj.* 1. ailing, indisposed. —**Ant.** *adj.* 1. healthy, strong.

sick·ness (sik′nis), *n.* 1. condition of being sick; illness; disease. 2. nausea; vomiting.

side (sīd), *n., adj., v.,* **sid·ed, sid·ing.** —*n.* 1. surface or line bounding a thing: *the sides of a square.* 2. one of the two surfaces of an object that is not the front, back, top, or bottom: *there is a door at the side of the house.* 3. either of the two surfaces of paper, cloth, etc.: *write only on one side of the paper.* 4. a particular surface: *the outer and inner sides of a hollow ball.* 5. aspect; phase: *all sides of a question.* 6. either the right or the left part of a thing; either part or region beyond a central line: *the east side of a city.* 7. either the right or the left part of the body of a person or an animal: *a pain in one's side.* 8. slope of a hill or bank. 9. group of persons opposed to another group: *both sides are ready for the contest.* 10. position, course, attitude, or part of one person or party against another: *be on the winning side of a dispute.* 11. part of a family; line of descent: *the man is English on his mother's side.* 12. on the side, *Am., Colloq.* in addition to one's ordinary duties. 13. side by side, beside one another. 14. take sides, place oneself with one person or group against another. —*adj.* 1. at one side; on one side: *the side aisles of a theater.* 2. from one side: *a side view.* 3. toward one side: *a side glance.* 4. less important: *a side issue.* —*v.* side with, take the part of; favor (one among opposing or differing groups or persons). [OE *side*]

side arms, sword, revolver, bayonet, etc., carried at the side or in the belt.

side·board (sīd′bôrd′; -bōrd′), *n.* piece of dining-room furniture. A sideboard has drawers and shelves for holding silver and linen, and space on top for dishes.

side·burns (sīd′bėrnz′), *n.pl. Am.* short whiskers just below the hairline on both cheeks. [alter. of *burnsides,* from A.E. *Burnside,* American general]

Sideburns

side·kick (sīd′kik′), *n. Am., Slang.* partner or very close friend.

side light, 1. light coming from the side. 2. incidental information about a subject.

side line, 1. line at the side of something. 2. line that marks the limit of play on the side of the field in football, etc. 3. side lines, space just outside these lines. 4. *Am.* an additional line of goods or business.

side·line (sīd′līn′), *v.,* **-lined, -lin·ing.** force or be forced out of participation by injury or illness.

side·long (sīd′lông′; -long′), *adj., adv.* to one side; toward the side.

side·piece (sīd′pēs′), *n.* piece forming a side or part of a side, or fixed by the side, of something.

si·de·re·al (sī·dir′i·əl), *adj.* 1. of or pertaining to the stars. 2. measured by the apparent daily motion of the stars. A sidereal day is about four minutes shorter than a mean solar day. [< L *sidereus* astral < *sidus* star]

side·sad·dle (sīd′sad′əl), *n.* a woman's saddle so made that both of the rider's legs are on the same side of the horse.

side show, 1. a small show in connection with a principal one. 2. any minor proceeding or affair connected with a more important one.

side·slip (sīd′slip′), *n., v.,* **-slipped, -slip·ping.** —*n.* 1. a slip to one side. 2. the slipping to one side of an airship. —*v.* slip to one side.

side step, 1. a step or stepping to one side. 2. step at the side of a ship, vehicle, etc.

side-step (sīd′step′), *v.,* **-stepped, -step·ping.** *Am.* 1. step aside. 2. avoid by stepping aside; evade: *side-step a responsibility.* —**side′-step′per,** *n. Am.*

side·swipe (sīd′swīp′), *v.,* **-swiped, -swip·ing,** *n. Am.* —*v.* hit with a sweeping blow along the side. —*n.* a sweeping blow along the side.

side·track (sīd′trak′), *Am.* —*n.* a short railroad track to which a train may be switched from a main track. —*v.* 1. switch (a train, etc.) to a sidetrack. 2. put aside; turn aside.

side·walk (sīd′wôk′), *n. Am.* place to walk at the side of a street, usually paved.

side·ward (sīd′wərd), *adj.* directed toward one side. —*adv.* Also, **side′wards.** toward one side.

side·way (sīd′wā′), *adv., adj.* sideways. —*n.* 1. a side street, not a main road; byway. 2. sidewalk.

side·ways (sīd′wāz′), **side·wise** (-wīz′), *adv., adj.* 1. toward one side. 2. from one side. 3. with one side toward the front.

side·wheel (sīd′hwēl′), *adj. Am.* having a paddle wheel on each side. —**side′-wheel′er,** *n. Am.*

side whisker, hair growing long on the side of the face. —**side′-whis′kered,** *adj.*

sid·ing (sīd′ing), *n.* 1. a short railroad track to which cars can be switched from a main track. 2. *Am.* boards forming the sides of a wooden building.

si·dle (sī′dəl), *v.,* **-dled, -dling,** *n.* —*v.* 1. move sideways. 2. move sideways slowly so as not to attract attention. —*n.* movement sideways.

siege (sēj), *n., v.,* **sieged, sieg·ing.** —*n.* 1. the surrounding of a fortified place by an army trying to capture it, mainly by shutting off its supplies; besieging or being besieged. 2. *Am.* any long or persistent effort to overcome resistance; any long-continued attack: *siege of illness.* 3. lay siege to, a. besiege. b. attempt to win or get by long and persistent effort. —*v.* besiege. [< OF, ult. < L *sedere* sit]

Sieg·fried (sēg′frēd), *n.* in German legends, a hero who killed a dragon, won a treasure, and rescued the Valkyrie, Brunhild, from an enchanted sleep.

si·en·na (si·en′ə), *n.* 1. a yellowish-brown coloring matter (raw sienna) made from earth containing iron. 2. a reddish-brown coloring matter (burnt sienna) made by roasting earth containing iron. 3. a yellowish brown or reddish brown. [short for Ital. *terra di Sien(n)a* earth of Siena, a city in Italy]

si·er·ra (si·er′ə), *n. Am.* chain of hills or mountains with jagged peaks. [< Sp., lit., a saw < L *serra*]

Si·er·ra Ne·vad·a (si·er′ə nə·vad′ə; nə·vä′də), a mountain range in E California.

si·es·ta (si·es′tə), *n.* a nap or rest taken at noon or in the afternoon. [< Sp.]

sieur (syœr), *n.* an old French title of rank or respect. [F < VL *seiorem* < accus. of L *senior* SENIOR. Doublet of SEIGNEUR and SEIGNIOR.]

sieve (siv), *n.*, *v.*, **sieved**, **siev·ing**. —*n.* utensil having holes that let liquids and smaller pieces pass through, but not the larger pieces. Shaking flour through a sieve removes lumps. —*v.* put through a sieve. [OE *sife*]

Sieve

sift (sift), *v.* 1. separate large pieces of from small by shaking in a sieve. 2. put through a sieve. 3. use a sieve. 4. fall through, or as if through, a sieve: *the snow sifted softly down.* 5. examine very carefully: *sift the evidence.* [OE *siftan < sife* sieve] —**sift'er**, *n.*

sigh (sī), *v.* 1. let out a very long, deep breath because one is sad, tired, relieved, etc. 2. say or express with a sigh. 3. make a sound like a sigh. 4. wish very much; long. 5. lament with sighing: *sigh over one's unhappy fate.* —*n.* act or sound of sighing. [ME *sighe(n)*, ult. < OE *sican*] —**sigh'er**, *n.* —**sigh'ing·ly**, *adv.*

sight (sīt), *n.* 1. power of seeing; vision: *birds have better sight than dogs.* 2. act of seeing; look; glance; gaze: *love at first sight.* 3. limit or range of seeing: *land was in sight.* 4. view; glimpse: *I caught a sight of him.* 5. something worth seeing: *see the sights of the city.* 6. something that looks queer: *her clothes were a sight.* 7. device on a gun, surveying instrument, etc., to assist in taking aim or observing. 8. observation taken with a telescope or other instrument; aim with a gun, etc. 9. at or on sight, as soon as seen. 10. catch sight of, see. 11. out of sight of, a. where one cannot see: *out of sight of land.* b. where one cannot be seen by. —*v.* 1. see: *at last Columbus sighted land.* 2. take a sight or observation of. 3. aim by means of sights. 4. adjust the sight (of a gun, etc.). 5. provide with sights. [OE *(ge)siht*]

sight draft, *Am.* draft payable on presentation.

sight·less (sīt'lis), *adj.* 1. blind. 2. not in sight; invisible.

sight·ly (sīt'li), *adj.*, **-li·er**, **-li·est**. 1. pleasing to the sight. 2. affording a fine view. —**sight'li·ness**, *n.*

sight·see·ing (sīt'sē'ing), *n.*, *adj.* going around to see objects or places of interest. —**sight'se'er**, *n.*

sig·ma (sig'mə), *n.* the 18th letter of the Greek alphabet (Σ,σ,ς).

sign (sīn), *n.* 1. any mark used to mean, represent, or point out something. +, −, and ÷ are mathematical signs. 2. motion or gesture intended to express or convey an idea: *we talked to them by signs.* 3. an inscribed board, space, etc., serving for advertisement, information, etc. 4. indication: *no signs of life.* 5. indication of a coming event: *signs of a storm.* 6. trace; vestige: *the hunter found signs of deer.* 7. in astronomy, any of the twelve divisions of the zodiac. —*v.* 1. attach one's name to: *he signed the letter.* 2. attach one's name to show authority, agreement, obligation, etc.; write one's name. 3. write: *sign your initials here.* 4. hire by a written agreement: *sign a new player.* 5. accept employment: *they signed for three years.* 6. give a sign to; signal: *sign someone to enter.* 7. communicate by gesture: *sign assent.* 8. mark with a sign. 9. sign away, assign. 10. sign off, stop broadcasting. 11. sign over, hand over by signing one's name. [< OF < L *signum*]

sig·nal (sig'nəl), *n.*, *v.*, **-naled**, **-nal·ing**; *esp. Brit.* **-nalled**, **-nal·ling**, *adj.* —*n.* 1. sign giving notice of something. 2. in card games, a bid or play that gives certain information to one's partner. 3. *Radio.* a. any impulse, sound, etc., transmitted or received. b. the modulation of a carrier wave. —*v.* 1. make a signal or signals (to). 2. make known by a signal or signals. —*adj.* 1. used as a signal or in signaling. 2. remarkable; striking; notable. [< F, ult. < L *signum* sign] —**sig'nal·er**, *esp. Brit.* **sig'nal·ler**, *n.* —**Syn.** *adj.* 2. conspicuous, outstanding.

Signal Corps, *Am.* part of the United States army in charge of signaling and communication by telegraph, telephone, radio, etc.

sig·nal·ize (sig'nəl·īz), *v.*, **-ized**, **-iz·ing**. make stand out; make notable.

sig·nal·ly (sig'nəl·i), *adv.* remarkably; strikingly; notably.

sig·nal·man (sig'nəl·mən; -man'), *n.*, *pl.* **-men**. man in charge of the signals on a railroad, in the army or navy, etc.

sig·na·to·ry (sig'nə·tô'ri; -tō'-), *n.*, *pl.* **-ries**, *adj.* —*n.* a signer of a document. —*adj.* signing.

sig·na·ture (sig'nə·chər), *n.* 1. a person's name written by himself. 2. a writing of one's name. 3. *Music.* signs printed at the beginning of a staff to show the pitch, key, and time of a piece. 4. *Printing.* a. letter or number printed at the bottom of the first page of every sheet, telling how it is to be folded and arranged in pages. b. sheet with such a mark, esp. when folded. 5. tune, etc., used to identify a radio program. [< LL *signatura*, ult. < L *signum* sign]

sign·board (sīn'bôrd'; -bōrd'), *n.* board having a sign, notice, advertisement, etc., on it.

sig·net (sig'nit), *n.* a small seal: *the order was sealed with the king's signet.* [< OF, ult. < L *signum* seal]

sig·nif·i·cance (sig·nif'ə·kəns), **sig·nif·i·can·cy** (-kən·si), *n.* 1. importance; consequence. 2. meaning. 3. expressiveness; significant quality. —**Syn.** 1. moment, gravity. 2. import, sense.

sig·nif·i·cant (sig·nif'ə·kənt), *adj.* 1. full of meaning; important; of consequence. 2. having a meaning; expressive. 3. having or expressing a hidden meaning. [< L, ppr. of *significare* SIGNIFY] —**sig·nif'i·cant·ly**, *adv.* —**Syn.** 1. weighty, momentous. 2. meaningful, telling.

sig·ni·fi·ca·tion (sig'nə·fə·kā'shən), *n.* 1. meaning; sense. 2. act or process of signifying. Signification relies largely upon words and gestures. —**sig·nif·i·ca·tive** (sig·nif'ə·kā'tiv), *adj.*

sig·ni·fy (sig'nə·fī), *v.*, **-fied**, **-fy·ing**. 1. be a sign of; mean. 2. make known by signs, words, or actions. 3. have importance; be of consequence; matter: *what a fool says does not signify.* [< L, < *signum* sign + *facere* make] —**sig'ni·fi'er**, *n.* —**Syn.** 1. represent, denote, imply, suggest. 2. indicate.

sign of the zodiac, any of the twelve divisions of the zodiac. Each of them is named after a group of stars.

si·gnor (sē·nyôr'), *n. Italian.* 1. Mr.; sir. 2. gentleman.

si·gno·ra (sē·nyô'rä), *n.*, *pl.* **-re** (-rä). *Italian.* 1. Mrs. 2. lady.

si·gno·re (sē·nyô'rā), *n.*, *pl.* **-ri** (-rē). *Italian.* 1. gentleman. 2. sir.

si·gno·ri·na (sē'nyô·rē'nä), *n.*, *pl.* **-ne** (-nä). *Italian.* 1. Miss. 2. a young lady.

sign·post (sīn'pōst'), *n.* guidepost.

Sikh (sēk), *n.* member of a religious sect of N India, famous as fighters.

si·lage (sī'lij), *n.* green food for farm animals, preserved in a silo.

si·lence (sī'ləns), *n.*, *v.*, **-lenced**, **-lenc·ing**, *interj.* —*n.* 1. absence of sound or noise; stillness. 2. a keeping still; not talking. 3. omission of mention. 4. secrecy. —*v.* stop the speech or noise of; make silent; quiet. —*interj.* be silent! [< OF < L, ult. < *silere* be silent] —**Syn.** *n.* 1. hush, quiet. 2. reticence, reserve.

si·lenc·er (sī'lən·sər), *n.* 1. person or thing that silences. 2. muffler on an internal-combustion engine. 3. device for deadening the sound of a gun.

si·lent (sī'lənt), *adj.* 1. quiet; still; noiseless: *the silent hills.* 2. not speaking; saying little or nothing: *a silent person.* 3. not spoken; not said out loud: *a silent prayer.* The *e* in *time* is a silent letter. 4. not active; taking no open or active part: *a silent partner.* 5. omitting mention. [< L *silens* being silent] —**si'lent·ly**, *adv.* —**si'lent·ness**, *n.* —**Syn.** 1. hushed. 2. speechless, dumb, reticent, taciturn.

Si·le·sia (si·lē'shə; -zhə; sī-), *n.* region in C Europe, now included for the most part in Poland and Czechoslovakia. —**Si·le'sian**, *adj.*, *n.*

si·lex (sī'leks), *n.* 1. silica. 2. Silex. *Trademark.* a coffee maker made of glass that resists heat. [< L, flint]

sil·hou·ette (sil'ů·et'), *n., v.,* -et·ted, -et·ting. —*n.* 1. an outline portrait cut out of a black paper or filled in with some single color. 2. a dark image outlined against a lighter background. —*v.* show in outline. [after E. de *Silhouette*, French politician]

sil·i·ca (sil'ə·kə), *n. Chem.* a hard, white or colorless substance, silicon dioxide, SiO_2. Flint, quartz, and sand are forms of silica. [< NL, < L *silex* flint]

sil·i·cate (sil'ə·kit; -kāt), *n. Chem.* compound containing silicon with oxygen and an alkali. Mica, soapstone, asbestos, and feldspar are silicates.

Silhouette

sil·i·con (sil'ə·kən), *n. Chem.* a nonmetallic element, Si, found only combined with other substances. [< *silica*]

sil·i·co·sis (sil'ə·kō'sis), *n.* disease of the lungs caused by continually breathing air filled with dust from quartz or silicates.

silk (silk), *n.* 1. a fine, soft thread spun by silkworms. 2. cloth made from it. 3. garment of such material. 4. anything like silk: *corn silk.* —*adj.* of, like, or pertaining to silk. [OE *sioloc* < Slavic < Gk. *serikos* < *Seres* the Chinese]

silk·en (sil'kən), *adj.* 1. made of silk: *a silken dress.* 2. like silk; smooth, soft, and glossy: *silken hair.* 3. wearing silk clothes.

silk-stock·ing (silk'stok'ing), *Am.* —*adj.* elegant; aristocratic: *a silk-stocking affair.* —*n.* an elegant, aristocratic person.

silk·worm (silk'wėrm'), *n.* caterpillar that spins silk to form a cocoon.

silk·y (sil'ki), *adj.,* silk·i·er, silk·i·est. 1. like silk; smooth, soft, and glossy. 2. of silk. —**silk'i·ly,** *adv.* —**silk'i·ness,** *n.*

sill (sil), *n.* 1. piece of wood or stone across the bottom of a door, window, or house frame. 2. a large, wooden beam on which the wall of a house, etc., rests. [OE *syll*]

sil·ly (sil'i), *adj.,* -li·er, -li·est, *n., pl.* -lies. —*adj.* 1. without sense or reason; foolish. 2. *Archaic.* simple; innocent; harmless. 3. *Archaic.* simple-minded; unsophisticated; ignorant. 4. *Colloq.* stunned; dazed. —*n.* a silly person. [OE *sǣlig* happy < *sǣl* happiness] —**sil'li·ly,** *adv.* —**sil'li·ness,** *n.* —**Syn.** *adj.* 1. senseless, nonsensical, ridiculous.

si·lo (sī'lō), *n., pl.* -los, *v.,* -loed, -lo·ing. —*n.* an airtight building or pit in which green food for farm animals is preserved. —*v.* preserve in a silo. [< Sp. < L < Gk. *siros* graincellar]

silt (silt), *n.* very fine earth, sand, etc., carried by moving water and deposited as sediment. —*v.* fill or choke up with silt. [prob. akin to SALT] —**silt'y,** *adj.*

sil·van (sil'vən), *adj.* sylvan.

sil·ver (sil'vər), *n.* 1. *Chem.* a shining white, precious metallic element, Ag, used for coins, jewelry, spoons, dishes, etc. 2. coins made from this metal. 3. utensils or dishes made from it: *table silver.* 4. something like silver. 5. the color of silver. —*adj.* 1. made of or plated with silver. 2. of or pertaining to silver. 3. having the color of silver. 4. having a clear ringing sound like that of silver dropped on a hard surface. 5. eloquent: *a silver tongue.* 6. of or advocating the use of silver as a standard of money. 7. indicating the 25th anniversary. —*v.* cover or coat with silver or something like silver: *silver a mirror.* [OE *siolfor*] —**sil'ver·er,** *n.* —**sil'ver·like',** *adj.*

sil·ver·fish (sil'vər·fish'), *n., pl.* -fish·es or (esp. collectively) -fish. any of various silvercolored insects which damage books and things made of paper.

silver fox, *Am.* 1. fox whose fur is composed of black hairs with white bands near the tips. 2. this fur.

silver lining, the brighter side of a sad or unfortunate situation.

silver nitrate, *Chem.* a white, crystalline salt, $AgNO_3$, obtained by treating silver with

nitric acid. It is used in medicine as an antiseptic, in photography, dyeing, etc.

sil·ver-plat·ed (sil'vər·plāt'id), *adj.* covered with a thin layer of silver or similar material.

sil·ver·smith (sil'vər·smith'), *n.* person who makes articles of silver.

sil·ver-tongued (sil'vər·tungd'), *adj.* eloquent.

sil·ver·ware (sil'vər·wãr'), *n.* articles made of silver; utensils or dishes made from silver.

sil·ver·y (sil'vər·i), *adj.* 1. like silver; like that of silver. 2. containing silver; covered with silver. —**sil'ver·i·ness,** *n.*

sim·i·an (sim'i·ən), *adj.* like or characteristic of an ape or monkey. —*n.* ape; monkey. [< L *simia* ape]

sim·i·lar (sim'ə·lər), *adj.* 1. much the same; alike; like. 2. *Geom.* of figures, having the same shape. [< F *similaire* < L *similis* like] —**sim'i·lar·ly,** *adv.*

sim·i·lar·i·ty (sim'ə·lar'ə·ti), *n., pl.* -ties. 1. a being similar; likeness; resemblance. 2. point of resemblance. —**Syn.** 1. semblance, analogy.

sim·i·le (sim'ə·lē), *n.* an expressed comparison of two different things or ideas. *Examples:* a face like marble, as brave as a lion. [< L, neut. adj., like] ▶ See metaphor for usage note.

si·mil·i·tude (sə·mil'ə·tüd; -tūd), *n.* 1. similarity; likeness; resemblance. 2. comparison. 3. copy; image. [< L, < *similis* like]

sim·i·tar (sim'ə·tər), *n.* scimitar.

Sim·la (sim'lə), *n.* the former summer capital of India, in the N part.

sim·mer (sim'ər), *v.* 1. make a murmuring sound while boiling gently. 2. keep at or just below the boiling point; boil gently. 3. be on the point of breaking out: *simmering anger, simmering rebellion.* 4. **simmer down,** cool off; calm down. —*n.* 1. process of cooking at or just below the boiling point. 2. state of simmering.

si·mo·le·on (sə·mō'li·ən), *n. Am., Slang.* dollar.

Si·mon Peter (sī'mən). See Peter, Saint.

si·mon-pure (sī'mən·pyůr'), *adj. Am., Colloq.* real; genuine; authentic. [from *Simon Pure,* the name of a Quaker in Mrs. Centlivre's comedy *A Bold Stroke for a Wife*]

si·mo·ny (sī'mə·ni; sim'ə-), *n.* 1. the making of money out of sacred things. 2. sin of buying or selling positions, promotions, etc., in the church. [< LL *simonia*, from *Simon Magus*, who tried to buy the power of conferring the Holy Spirit. Acts 8:9–24.] —**si'mon·ist,** *n.*

si·moom (si·müm'), **si·moon** (-mün'), *n.* a hot, suffocating, sand-laden wind of the deserts of Arabia, Syria, and N Africa. [< Ar. *semūm*]

simp (simp), *n. Am., Slang.* simpleton; fool.

sim·per (sim'pər), *v.* 1. smile in a silly, affected way. 2. express by a simper; say with a simper. —*n.* a silly, affected smile. —**sim'per·er,** *n.* —**sim'per·ing·ly,** *adv.* —**Syn.** *v.* 1. smirk.

sim·ple (sim'pəl), *adj.,* -pler, -plest, *n.* —*adj.* 1. easy to do or understand: *simple language.* 2. having few parts; not complex; not involved; elementary: *simple arithmetic.* 3. with nothing added; bare; mere: *the simple truth.* 4. without ornament; not rich or showy; plain: *simple clothes.* 5. natural; not affected; not showing off: *a pleasant simple manner.* 6. honest; sincere: *a simple heart.* 7. not subtle; not sophisticated; innocent; artless: *a simple child.* 8. common; ordinary: *a simple soldier.* 9. humble: *his parents were simple people.* 10. dull; stupid; weak in mind. 11. *Bot.* not divided into parts: *a simple leaf.* 12. *Zool.* not compound. 13. *Chem.* composed of only one element. —*n.* 1. a foolish, stupid person. 2. something simple. 3. plant used in medicine; medicine made from it. [< OF < L *simplex*] —**sim'ple·ness,** *n.* —**Syn.** *adj.* 3. pure, absolute. 5. unassuming, unpretentious. 6. open, straightforward. 7. naïve, ingenuous.

sim·ple-heart·ed (sim'pəl·här'tid), *adj.* 1. having or showing a simple, unaffected nature. 2. guileless; sincere. —**sim'ple-heart'ed·ness,** *n.*

simple machine, any of the elementary devices or mechanical powers on which other machines are based. The lever, wedge, pulley, wheel and axle, inclined plane, and screw are often called the six simple machines.

sim·ple-mind·ed (sim'pəl·mīn'did), *adj.* **1.** artless; inexperienced. **2.** ignorant; foolish; stupid. **3.** feeble-minded. —**sim'ple-mind'ed·ly,** *adv.* —**sim'ple-mind'ed·ness,** *n.*

sim·ple·ton (sim'pəl·tən), *n.* a silly person; fool. [< *simple*]

sim·plic·i·ty (sim·plis'ə·ti), *n., pl.* **-ties. 1.** a being simple. **2.** freedom from difficulty; clearness. **3.** plainness. **4.** absence of show or pretense; sincerity. **5.** lack of shrewdness; dullness. [< L, < *simplex* simple]

sim·pli·fy (sim'plə·fī), *v.,* **-fied, -fy·ing.** make simpler; make plainer or easier. —**sim'pli·fi·ca'tion,** *n.* —**sim'pli·fi'er,** *n.*

sim·ply (sim'pli), *adv.* **1.** in a simple manner. **2.** without much ornament; without pretense or affectation; plainly: *simply dressed.* **3.** merely; only: *he did not simply cry, he yelled.* **4.** foolishly: *act as simply as an idiot.* **5.** absolutely.

sim·u·la·crum (sim'yə·lā'krəm), *n., pl.* **-cra** (-krə), **-crums. 1.** a faint, shadowy, or unreal likeness; mere semblance. **2.** image. [< L, ult. < *similis* like]

sim·u·late (sim'yə·lāt), *v.,* **-lat·ed, -lat·ing.** *adj.* —*v.* **1.** pretend; feign. **2.** act like; look like; imitate: *certain insects simulate leaves.* —*adj.* simulated. [< L *simulatus* < *similis* like] —**sim'·u·la'tion,** *n.* —**sim'u·la'tive,** *adj.* —**sim'u·la'tive·ly,** *adv.* —**sim'u·la'tor,** *n.* —**Syn.** *v.* **1.** sham.

si·mul·cast (sī'məl·kast'; -käst'), *v.,* **-cast** or **-cast·ed, -cast·ing.** transmit a program over radio and television simultaneously. [< *simul(taneous)* + *(broad)cast*]

si·mul·ta·ne·ous (sī'məl·tā'ni·əs; sim'əl-), *adj.* existing, done, or happening at the same time. [< Med.L *simultaneus* simulated; confused in sense with L *simul* at the same time] —**si'mul·ta'ne·ous·ly,** *adv.* —**si'mul·ta'ne·ous·ness,** *n.* —**Syn.** coincident, contemporaneous.

sin (sin), *n., v.,* **sinned, sin·ning.** —*n.* **1.** a breaking of the law of God deliberately. **2.** an immoral act; wrongdoing. **3.** offense: *sins against good taste.* —*v.* **1.** break the law of God. **2.** do wrong. **3.** offend. [OE *synn*]

Si·nai (sī'nī), *n.* Mount, *Bible.* the mountain from which the law was given to Moses.

since (sins), *prep.* **1.** from a past time continuously till now: *the package has been ready since noon.* **2.** at any time between (some past time or event and the present): *we have not seen him since Saturday.* —*conj.* **1.** in the course of the period following the time when: *he has not written since he left us.* **2.** continuously from or counting from the time when: *he has been busy ever since he came.* **3.** because: *since you ask, I will tell you.* —*adv.* **1.** from then till now: *he got sick last Saturday and has been in bed ever since.* **2.** at some time between a particular past time and the present: *at first he refused but since has accepted.* **3.** before now; ago: *I heard that old joke long since.* [ME *sinnes, synnes, sithnes* < OE *siththan* then, later < *sith* late] ➤ See **because** for usage note.

sin·cere (sin·sir'), *adj.,* **-cer·er, -cer·est.** free from pretense or deceit; genuine; real. [< L *sincerus*] —**sin·cere'ly,** *adv.* —**sin·cere'ness,** *n.* —**Syn.** true, heartfelt, honest.

sin·cer·i·ty (sin·ser'ə·ti), *n., pl.* **-ties.** freedom from pretense or deceit; honesty.

sine (sīn), *n. Math.* in a right triangle, the ratio of the length of the side opposite an acute angle to the length of the hypotenuse. In the diagram, the sine of angle a = BC/AB, the sine of angle b = AC/AB. [< L *sinus* bend, bosom, trans. of Ar. *jaib* sine, bosom]

si·ne·cure (sī'nə·kyūr; sin'ə-), *n.* an extremely easy job; position requiring little or no work and usually paying well. [< Med.L (*beneficium*) *sine cura* (benefice) without cure (of souls)]

si·ne di·e (sī'nē dī'ē), without a day fixed for future action: *the committee adjourned sine die.* [< L, without a day]

si·ne qua non (sī'nē kwā non'), something essential; indispensable condition. [< L, lit., without which not]

sin·ew (sin'ū), *n.* **1.** a tough, strong band or cord that joins muscle to bone; tendon. **2.** strength; energy. **3.** means of strength; source of power. —*v.* furnish with sinews; strengthen as by sinews. [OE *sionu*] —**sin'ew·less,** *adj.*

sin·ew·y (sin'ū·i), *adj.* **1.** having strong sinews; strong; powerful. **2.** vigorous; forcible. **3.** like sinews; tough; stringy. —**sin'ew·i·ness,** *n.*

sin·ful (sin'fəl), *adj.* full of sin; wicked; wrong. —**sin'ful·ly,** *adv.* —**sin'ful·ness,** *n.* —**Syn.** depraved, immoral, evil.

sing (sing), *v.,* **sang** or **sung, sung, sing·ing,** *n.* —*v.* **1.** make music with the voice: *he sings on the concert stage.* **2.** utter musically: *he almost seemed to sing his lines from the play.* **3.** chant; intone: *the priest sings Mass.* **4.** make pleasant musical sounds: *birds sing.* **5.** bring, send, put, etc., with or by singing: *sing the baby to sleep.* **6.** tell in song or poetry: *he sang the deeds of heroes.* **7.** proclaim: *sing a person's praises.* **8.** make a ringing, whistling, humming, or buzzing sound. **9.** have a sensation of a ringing, buzzing, or humming sound. **10.** sing out, call loudly; shout. —*n.* **1.** a singing, ringing, or whistling sound. **2.** a singing, esp. in a group. [OE *singan*] —**Syn.** *v.* **1.** carol, warble, croon. **4.** chirp.

sing., singular.

Sin·ga·pore (sing'gə·pôr; -pōr; sing'ə-), *n.* **1.** seaport on an island off the S tip of the Malay Peninsula. **2.** state including this city and island, forming a part of Malaysia.

singe (sinj), *v.,* **singed, singe·ing,** *n.* —*v.* **1.** burn a little. **2.** burn the ends or edges of. **3.** remove by a slight burning. —*n.* a minor burn. [OE *sengan*]

sing·er (sing'ər), *n.* **1.** person who sings. **2.** bird that sings. —**Syn.** **1.** chorister, vocalist, songster. **2.** songbird.

sing·ing (sing'ing), *n.* **1.** sound made by one that sings. **2.** a ringing in the ears. —*adj.* that sings.

sin·gle (sing'gəl), *adj., n., v.,* **-gled, -gling.** —*adj.* **1.** one and no more; only one: *a single piece of paper.* **2.** for only one; individual: *a single bed.* **3.** without others; alone: *he came to the party single.* **4.** not married: *a single man.* **5.** having only one on each side: *the knights engaged in single combat.* **6.** *Bot.* having only one set of petals, as a wild rose. **7.** consisting of one part, element, or member; not double; not multiple: *single houses.* **8.** sincere; honest; genuine: *single devotion to a cause.* —*n.* **1.** a single thing or person. **2.** *Am., Baseball.* hit that allows the batter to reach first base only. **3.** *Cricket.* hit for which one run is scored. **4.** game for two people only. **5.** singles, game played with only one person on each side. —*v.* **1.** pick from among others: *the teacher singled Harry out for praise.* **2.** *Am., Baseball.* make a hit that allows the reaching of first base. [< OF < L *singulus*] —**sin'gle·ness,** *n.* —**Syn.** *adj.* **1.** sole. **3.** solitary. **4.** unmarried, celibate.

sin·gle-breast·ed (sing'gəl·bres'tid), *adj.* overlapping across the breast just enough to fasten with only one row of buttons.

single file, line of persons or things arranged one behind another.

sin·gle-foot (sing'gəl·fût'), *n. Am.* gait of a horse in which one foot is put down at a time. —*v.* go at a single-foot. —**sin'gle-foot'er,** *n. Am.*

sin·gle-hand·ed (sing'gəl·han'did), *adj.* **1.** without help from others; working alone. **2.** using, requiring, or managed by only one hand or only one person. —**sin'gle-hand'ed·ly,** *adv.*

sin·gle-heart·ed (sing'gəl·här'tid), *adj.* **1.** free from deceit; sincere. **2.** having only one purpose. —**sin'gle-heart'ed·ness,** *n.*

sin·gle-mind·ed (sing'gəl·mīn'did), *adj.* **1.** sincere; straightforward. **2.** having only one purpose in mind. —**sin'gle-mind'ed·ly,** *adv.* —**sin'gle-mind'ed·ness,** *n.*

sin·gle·stick (sing'gəl·stik'), *n.* **1.** stick held

in one hand, used in fencing. 2. fencing with such a stick.

single tax, 1. tax on one kind of property only. 2. *Am.* tax on land only.

sin·gle·ton (sing′gəl·tən), *n.* 1. something occurring singly or apart from others. 2. a playing card that is the only one of a suit in a person's hand.

sin·gle-track (sing′gəl·trak′), *adj.* 1. having only a single track. 2. able to go or act in only one way.

sin·gle·tree (sing′gəl·trē′), *n. Am.* whiffletree.

sin·gly (sing′gli), *adv.* 1. by itself; individually; separately: *consider each point singly.* 2. one by one; one at a time: *misfortunes never come singly.* 3. by one's own efforts; without help.

Sing Sing (sing′ sing′), *Am.* a State prison at Ossining, New York.

sing·song (sing′sông′; -song′), *n.* 1. a monotonous, up-and-down rhythm. 2. a monotonous tone or sound in speaking. 3. a monotonous or jingling verse. —*adj.* monotonous in rhythm.

sin·gu·lar (sing′gyə·lər), *adj.* 1. extraordinary; unusual: *a scene of singular beauty.* 2. strange; queer; peculiar: *a series of singular nocturnal happenings.* 3. being the only one of its kind: *an event singular in history.* 4. *Gram.* one in number. *Boy* is singular; *boys* is plural. 5. separate; individual; private: *a singular matter.* —*n. Gram.* 1. the singular number. 2. a word in the singular number. [< L, < *singulus* single] —**sin·gu·lar·i·ty** (sing′gyə·lar′ə·ti), **sin′gu·lar·ness,** *n.* —**sin′gu·lar·ly,** *adv.* —**Syn.** *adj.* 1. exceptional, uncommon, remarkable. 2. odd, curious, eccentric. 3. unique.

sin·is·ter (sin′is·tər), *adj.* 1. showing ill will; threatening: *a sinister rumor, a sinister look.* 2. bad; evil; dishonest. 3. disastrous; unfortunate. 4. on the left; left. 5. in heraldry, situated to the right of the one looking at the escutcheon. [< L, left; the left side being considered unlucky] —**sin′is·ter·ly,** *adv.* —**sin′is·ter·ness,** *n.* —**Syn.** 1. ominous.

sink (singk), *v.,* **sank** or **sunk, sunk** or **sunken, sink·ing,** *n.* —*v.* 1. go down; fall slowly; go lower and lower: *the sun is sinking.* 2. make go down; make fall: *lack of rain sank the reservoirs.* 3. go under: *the ship sank with all her crew.* 4. make go under: *the submarine sank two ships.* 5. become lower or weaker: *the wind has sunk down.* 6. make lower; reduce: *sink your voice to a whisper.* 7. pass gradually (into a state of sleep, silence, oblivion, etc.). 8. enter; penetrate: *let the lesson sink into your mind.* 9. make go deep; dig: *the men are sinking a well.* 10. invest (money) unprofitably. 11. become worse, as in health, morale, reputation, or social status: *sink into poverty, his spirits sank.* —*n.* 1. a shallow basin or tub with a drainpipe. 2. drain; sewer. 3. place of vice or corruption. 4. a low-lying area in land where waters collect, or where they disappear by sinking downward or by evaporation. [OE *sincan*] —**sink′a·ble,** *adj.* —**Syn.** *v.* 1. subside, descend, fall, settle, decline. 3. submerge. 6. diminish.

sink·er (singk′ər), *n.* 1. person or thing that sinks. 2. a lead weight for sinking a fishing line or net. 3. *Am., Slang.* doughnut.

sinking fund, fund formed by a government, corporation, or the like, usually by periodically setting aside certain amounts of money to accumulate at interest, for the paying off of a debt.

sin·less (sin′lis), *adj.* without sin. —**sin′less·ly,** *adv.* —**sin′less·ness,** *n.*

sin·ner (sin′ər), *n.* person who sins or does wrong.

sin·u·ous (sin′yu·əs), *adj.* 1. having many curves or turns; winding. 2. indirect; morally crooked. [< L, < *sinus* curve] —**sin′u·ous·ly,** *adv.* —**sin′u·ous·ness, sin·u·os·i·ty** (sin′yu·os′ə·ti), *n.*

si·nus (sī′nəs), *n.* 1. cavity in a bone of the skull. 2. a long, narrow abscess with a small opening. 3. a curved hollow; cavity. [< L]

si·nus·i·tis (sī′nəs·ī′tis), *n.* inflammation of a sinus, esp. a nasal sinus.

Si·on (sī′ən), *n.* Zion.

Sioux (sü), *n., pl.* **Sioux** (sü; süz), *adj. Am.* —*n.* member of a tribe of American Indians of the Midwestern U.S. —*adj.* of this tribe. —**Siou·an** (sü′ən), *adj. Am.*

sip (sip), *v.,* **sipped, sip·ping,** *n.* —*v.* 1. drink little by little. 2. drink from little by little. —*n.* 1. act of sipping. 2. a very small drink. [OE *sypian* take in moisture] —**sip′per,** *n.*

si·phon (sī′fən), *n.* 1. a bent tube through which liquid can be drawn over the edge of one container into another at a lower level by air pressure. 2. bottle for soda water with a tube through which the liquid is forced out by the pressure of the gas in the bottle. —*v.* draw off by means of a siphon or pass through a siphon. Also, **syphon.** [< L < Gk., pipe]

sir (sėr; *unstressed* sər), *n.* 1. a respectful or formal term of address used to a man. 2. **Sir,** a. title of a knight or baronet: *Sir Walter Scott.* b. title of respect or honor, used to a man. 3. title of respect formerly used before a man's name or a noun designating his profession. 4. Mr. or Master. [var. of *sire*]

sire (sīr), *n., v.,* **sired, sir·ing.** —*n.* 1. a male ancestor. 2. the male parent. 3. title of respect used formerly to a great noble and now to a king. —*v.* be the father of. [< OF < VL *seior* < L *senior,* nom., older. Doublet of SENIOR.]

si·ren (sī′rən), *n.* 1. *Gk. Myth.* nymph who, by her sweet singing, lured sailors to destruction upon the rocks. 2. woman who lures, tempts, or entices. 3. a kind of whistle consisting of a disk pierced with holes and rotating over a stream of compressed air, steam, or the like. —*adj.* Also, **si·ren·ic** (sī·ren′ik). of a siren; tempting; charming. [< L < Gk. *seiren*]

Sir·i·us (sir′i·əs), *n.* the brightest (fixed) star in the sky; the Dog Star. —**Sir′i·an,** *adj.*

sir·loin (sėr′loin), *n.* cut of beef from the part of the loin in front of the rump. [< var. of OF *surlonge* < *sur* over (< L *super*) + *longe* LOIN]

si·roc·co (sə·rok′ō), *n., pl.* **-cos.** 1. a hot, dry, dust-laden wind blowing from N Africa across the Mediterranean and S Europe. 2. a moist, warm, south or southeast wind in these same regions. 3. any hot, unpleasant wind. [< F < Ital. < Ar. *shoruq* < *sharq* east]

sir·up (sir′əp; sėr′-), *n.* syrup. —**sir′up·y,** *adj.*

sis (sis), *n. Am., Colloq.* sister.

sis·al (sis′əl; sī′səl), or **sisal hemp,** *n.* 1. a strong, white fiber, used for making rope, twine, etc. 2. plant that it comes from. [from *Sisal,* town in Yucatán]

sis·sy (sis′i), *n., pl.* **-sies.** 1. sister. 2. *Am., Colloq.* boy or man who behaves too much like a girl. [dim. of *sis,* < *sister*] —**sis′sy·ish,** *adj.*

sis·ter (sis′tər), *n.* 1. daughter of the same parents or parent. 2. person or thing resembling or closely associated with another. 3. a female fellow member of a society, church, etc. 4. member of a religious order of women; nun: *Sisters of Charity.* —*adj.* being a sister; related as if by sisterhood. [< Scand. *systir*] —**sis′ter·ly,** *adj.* —**sis′ter·li·ness,** *n.*

sis·ter·hood (sis′tər·hud), *n.* 1. bond between sisters; feeling of sister for sister. 2. persons joined as sisters; association of women with some common aim, characteristic, belief, profession, etc. Nuns form a sisterhood.

sis·ter-in-law (sis′tər·in·lô′), *n., pl.* **sis·ters-in-law.** 1. sister of one's husband or wife. 2. wife of one's brother. 3. wife of the brother of one's husband or wife.

Sis·y·phus (sis′ə·fəs), *n. Gk. Myth.* king condemned forever to roll a heavy stone up a steep hill in Hades, only to have it roll down again.

sit (sit), *v.,* **sat** or (*Archaic*) **sate, sit·ting.** 1. rest on the lower part of the body, with the weight off the feet: *she sat in a chair.* 2. seat; cause to sit: *she sat her guests at the table.* 3. sit on: *he sat his horse well.* 4. have place or position: *the clock has sat on that shelf for years.* 5. have a seat in an assembly, etc.; be a member of a council: *sit in Congress.* 6. hold a session: *the court sits next month.* 7. place oneself in a position for having one's picture made; pose. 8. be in a state of rest; remain inactive. 9. perch: *a bird sat on the fence.* 10. cover eggs

so that they will hatch; brood. **11.** fit: *the coat sits well.* **12. sit down,** take a seat; put oneself in a sitting position. **13. sit in,** take part (in a game, conference, etc.). **14. sit on** or **upon, a.** sit in judgment or council on. **b.** have a seat on a jury, commission, etc. **c.** *Slang.* check, rebuke, or snub. **15. sit up, a.** raise the body to a sitting position. **b.** keep such a position. **c.** stay up instead of going to bed. **d.** *Colloq.* start up in surprise. [OE *sittan*] —**Syn. 8.** rest, repose.
➤ See set for usage note.

sit-down strike (sit′doun′), or **sit-down,** *n. Am.* strike in which the workers stay in the factory, store, etc., without working until their demands are met or an agreement is reached.

site (sīt), *n.* position or place (of anything). [< L *situs*]

sit-ter (sit′ər), *n.* **1.** person who sits. **2.** a baby sitter.

sit-ting (sit′ing), *n.* **1.** act of one that sits. **2.** a meeting or session of a legislature, court, etc. **3.** time of remaining seated.

sitting duck, an easy target or mark.

sit-u-ate (sich′u̇·āt), *v.,* -at-ed, -at-ing. place; locate. [< LL, < L *situs* location]

sit-u-at-ed (sich′u̇·āt′id), *adj.* **1.** placed; located. **2.** of persons, being in certain circumstances. ➤ *Situated,* when followed by a preposition, is usually an unnecessary sentence element: *He traveled to a small town in Canada called Picton,* [situated] *in Ontario.*

sit-u-a-tion (sich′u̇·ā′shən), *n.* **1.** position; location; place. **2.** circumstances; case; condition: *act reasonably in all situations.* **3.** place to work; job. **4.** a critical state of affairs in a play, novel, etc. —**Syn. 1.** site, station. **3.** post.

Si-va (sē′və; shē′-), *n. Hindu Myth.* one of the three chief divinities, known as "the Destroyer." Also, Shiva. —**Si′va·ism,** *n.* —**Si′va·ist,** *n.* —**Si′va·is′tic,** *adj.*

six (siks), *n.* **1.** a cardinal number, one more than five. **2.** symbol of this number; 6. **3.** card or die with six spots. **4. at sixes and sevens, a.** in confusion. **b.** in disagreement. —*adj.* one more than five. [OE *siex*]

six-fold (siks′fōld′), *adj.* **1.** six times as much or as many. **2.** having six parts. —*adv.* six times as much or as many.

six-pence (siks′pəns), *n.* **1.** six British pennies; six pence. **2.** a British coin having this value, worth about 6 cents (1950).

six-pen-ny (siks′pen′i; -pən·i), *adj.* **1.** worth or costing sixpence. **2.** of little worth; cheap. **3.** two-inch: *sixpenny nails.*

six-shoot-er (siks′shüt′ər), *n. Am.* revolver that can fire six shots without being reloaded.

six-teen (siks′tēn′), *n.* **1.** a cardinal number, six more than ten. **2.** symbol of this number; 16. —*adj.* six more than ten. —**six-teenth** (siks′tēnth′), *adj., n.*

sixteenth note, a musical note having one sixteenth of the time value of a whole note; semiquaver.

Sixteenth notes

sixth (siksth), *adj.* **1.** next after the fifth; last in a series of 6. **2.** being one of 6 equal parts. —*n.* **1.** next after the fifth; last in a series of 6. **2.** one of six equal parts. —**sixth′ly,** *adv.*

sixth sense, an unusual power of perception; intuition.

six-ty (siks′ti), *n., pl.* -ties, *adj.* —*n.* **1.** a cardinal number, six times ten. **2.** symbol of this number; 60. —*adj.* six times ten. —**six′ti·eth,** *adj., n.*

six-ty-fourth note (siks′ti·fôrth′; -fōrth′), a musical note having the time value of one sixty-fourth of a whole note.

siz-a-ble, size-a-ble (sīz′ə·bəl), *adj.* fairly large. —**siz′a·ble·ness, size′a·ble·ness,** *n.* —**siz′a·bly, size′a·bly,** *adv.*

size¹ (sīz), *n., v.,* sized, siz-ing, *adj.* —*n.* **1.** amount of surface or space a thing takes up: *the size of a city.* **2.** extent; amount; magnitude: *size of an industry, undertaking, etc.* **3.** a great extent or magnitude: *seek size rather than quality.* **4.** one of a series of measures: *his shoes* are size 10. **5.** *Colloq.* the actual condition; true description. **6.** of a size, of the same size. —*v.* **1.** arrange according to size or in sizes. **2.** make of certain size. **3. size up,** *Am., Colloq.* **a.** form an opinion of; estimate. **b.** come up to some size or grade. —*adj.* having size. [ult. var. of *assize,* in sense of "to set standard of weights and measures"] —**Syn.** *n.* **1.** area. **2.** volume. **3.** bulk.
➤ *Size* as an adjective, as in *a small size hat,* has come into general usage from the commercial fields. *Sized,* as in *a small-sized hat,* would be expected but now occurs more frequently only in formal English.

size² (sīz), *n., v.,* sized, siz-ing. —*n.* Also, siz-ing (sīz′ing). a sticky substance made from glue, starch, etc., used to glaze paper, cover plastered walls, stiffen cloth, etc. —*v.* coat or treat with size. [? special use of *size¹*]

siz-zle (siz′əl), *v.,* -zled, -zling, *n.* —*v.* **1.** make a hissing sound, as fat does when frying. **2.** *Colloq.* be extremely hot. —*n.* a hissing sound.

skald (skôld; skäld), *n.* a Scandinavian poet and singer of ancient times. Also, scald. [< Scand. *skáld*]

skate¹ (skāt), *n., v.,* skat-ed, skat-ing. —*n.* **1.** frame with a blade that can be fastened to a shoe so that a person can glide over ice. **2.** a shoe with such a blade fastened to it. **3.** a roller skate. —*v.* glide or move along on skates. [< Du. *schaats* < OF *escache* stilt < Gmc.] —**skat′er,** *n.*

skate² (skāt), *n., pl.* skates or (*esp. collectively*) skate. a kind of broad, flat fish. [< Scand. *skata*]

skate-board (skāt′bôrd′; -bōrd′), *n.* narrow board resembling a surfboard, with roller-skate wheels attached to each end, used for skating.

Barn-door skate (ab. 4 ft. long)

skein (skān), *n.* **1.** a small, coiled bundle of yarn or thread. There are 120 yards in a skein of cotton yarn. **2.** a confused tangle. [< OF *escaigne*]

skel-e-ton (skel′ə·tən), *n.* **1.** the bones of a body, fitted together in their natural places. The skeleton is a frame that supports the muscles, organs, etc. **2.** a very thin person or animal. **3.** frame: *the steel skeleton of a building.* **4.** outline. —*adj.* **1.** of, like, or consisting of a skeleton. **2.** greatly reduced in numbers; fractional: *a skeleton crew.* [< NL < Gk., neut. adj., dried up] —**skel′e·tal,** *adj.* —**skel′e·ton·less,** *adj.*

skep-tic (skep′tik), *n.* **1.** person who questions the truth of theories or apparent facts; doubter. **2.** person who doubts or questions the possibility or certainty of our knowledge of anything. **3.** person who doubts the truth of religious doctrines. —*adj.* doubting; skeptical. Also, **sceptic.** [< L < Gk. *skeptikos* reflective]

skep-ti-cal (skep′tə·kəl), *adj.* **1.** of or like a skeptic; inclined to doubt; not believing easily. **2.** questioning the truth of theories or apparent facts. Also, **sceptical.** —**skep′ti·cal·ly,** *adv.* —**skep′ti·cal·ness,** *n.* —**Syn. 1.** doubting, incredulous, disbelieving, distrustful.

skep-ti-cism (skep′tə·siz·əm), *n.* **1.** a skeptical attitude; doubt; unbelief. **2.** doubt or unbelief with regard to religion. **3.** doctrine that nothing can be proved absolutely. Also, **scepticism.**

sketch (skech), *n.* **1.** a rough, quickly done drawing, painting, or design. **2.** outline; plan. **3.** a short description, story, play, etc. —*v.* **1.** make a sketch of; draw roughly. **2.** make sketches. [< Du. *schets* < Ital. *schizzo,* ult. < L < Gk. *schedios* impromptu] —**sketch′a·ble,** *adj.* —**sketch′er,** *n.* —**Syn.** *n.* **2.** draft, brief.

sketch-book (skech′bu̇k′), *n.* **1.** book to draw or paint sketches in. **2.** book of short descriptions, stories, plays, etc.

sketch-y (skech′i), *adj.,* sketch-i-er, sketch-i-est. **1.** like a sketch; having or giving only outlines or main features. **2.** incomplete; done very roughly. —**sketch′i·ly,** *adv.* —**sketch′i·ness,** *n.*

skew (skū), *adj.* **1.** twisted to one side; slanting. **2.** having a part that deviates from a straight line, right angle, etc. 3. unsymmetrical. —n. a twisting or slanting position. —v. 1. slant; twist. 2. give a slanting form, position, direction, etc., to. 3. turn aside; swerve. 4. represent unfairly; distort. 5. squint. [< dial. OF *eskiuer* shy away from, eschew < Gmc.]

skew·er (skū′ər), n. a long pin of wood or metal stuck through meat to hold it together while it is cooking. —v. fasten with or as if with a skewer or skewers.

ski (skē; *Norw.* shē), n., pl. skis, ski, v., skied, ski·ing. —n. one of a pair of long, slender pieces of hard wood, that can be fastened to the shoes to enable a person to glide over snow. —v. glide over the snow on skis. [< Norw.] —ski′er, n.

skid (skid), n., v., skid·ded, skid·ding. —n. 1. a slip or slide sideways. 2. piece of wood or metal to prevent a wheel from going round. 3. a timber, frame, etc., on which something rests, or on which something heavy may slide. 4. runner on the bottom of an airplane to enable the airplane to skid along the ground when landing. 5. **on the skids,** *Slang.* headed for dismissal, failure, or other disaster. —v. 1. slip or slide sideways while moving: *the car skidded.* 2. slide along without going round, as a wheel does when held by a skid. 3. slide along on a skid or skids. [cf. OFris. *skid* stick of wood] —skid′der, n.

skiff (skif), n. 1. a light rowboat. 2. a small, light boat. [< F < Ital. *schifo* < Gmc.]

skill (skil), n. 1. ability gained by practice, knowledge, etc.; expertness. 2. ability to do things well with one's body or with tools. [< Scand. *skil* distinction] —skilled, adj. —skill′less, adj. —Syn. 1. facility, proficiency. 2. dexterity, deftness, adroitness.

skil·let (skil′it), n. a shallow pan with a long handle, used for frying.

skill·ful, skil·ful (skil′fəl), adj. 1. having skill; expert: *a skillful surgeon.* 2. showing skill: *a skillful production.* —skill′ful·ly, skil′ful·ly, adv. —skill′ful·ness, skil′ful·ness, n. —Syn. 1, 2. dexterous, deft, adroit, proficient.

skim (skim), v., skimmed, skim·ming, n. —v. 1. remove from the top: *the cook skims the cream from the milk.* 2. take something from the top of. 3. move lightly over: *his skates skimmed the ice.* 4. glide along: *the swallows were skimming by.* 5. send skimming: *skim a flat stone over the water.* 6. read hastily or carelessly. 7. become covered with a thin layer of ice, scum, etc. 8. cover with a thin layer of ice, scum, etc. —n. 1. that which is skimmed off. 2. act of skimming. [prob. < OF *escumer* < *escume* scum < Gmc.] —skim′mer, n.

skim milk, milk from which the cream has been removed.

skimp (skimp), v. 1. supply in too small an amount. 2. be very saving or economical. 3. do imperfectly. —skimp′ing·ly, adv.

skimp·y (skimp′i), adj., skimp·i·er, skimp·i·est. 1. scanty; not enough. 2. too saving or economical. —skimp′i·ly, adv. —skimp′i·ness, n.

skin (skin), n., v., skinned, skin·ning. —n. 1. the covering of the body in persons, animals, fruits, etc., esp. when soft and flexible. 2. hide; pelt. 3. container made of skin for holding liquids. 4. any outer covering. —v. 1. take the skin off. 2. shed skin. 3. *Slang.* swindle of money, etc.; cheat. [< Scand. *skinn*] —skin′less, adj. —skin′ner, n.

skin-deep (skin′dēp′), adj. shallow; slight.

skin diver, swimmer equipped to go skin diving.

skin diving, swimming about easily under water for long periods of time equipped with oxygen tanks and other gear.

skin·flint (skin′flint′), n. a stingy person.

skin·ny (skin′i), adj., -ni·er, -ni·est. 1. very thin; very lean. 2. like skin. —skin′ni·ness, n.

skip (skip), v., skipped, skip·ping, n. —v. 1. leap lightly; spring; jump. 2. leap lightly over: *skip rope.* 3. send bounding along a surface: *skip stones on a lake.* 4. go bounding along a surface. 5. pass over; fail to notice; omit: *skip a page.* 6. *U.S.* advance in school, bypassing one or more grades. 7. *Am., Colloq.* leave in a hurry. —n. 1. a light spring or leap. 2. a passing over. [cf. Scand. (MSw.) *skuppa*] —skip′per, n.

skip·per (skip′ər), n. 1. captain of a ship, esp. of a small trading or fishing boat. 2. any captain or leader. —v. act as leader of. [< MDu. *schipper* < *schip* ship]

skirl (skérl), v. *Scot.* of bagpipes, sound loudly and shrilly. —n. sound of a bagpipe. [< Scand. (dial. Norw.) *skrylla*]

skir·mish (skér′mish), n. 1. a slight fight between small groups of soldiers. 2. a slight conflict, argument, contest, etc. —v. take part in a skirmish. [< OF *eskirmiss-*, orig., ward off < Gmc.] —skir′mish·er, n.

skirt (skért), n. 1. the part of a dress that hangs from the waist. 2. a woman's or girl's garment that hangs from the waist. 3. something like a skirt. 4. border; edge. 5. Usually, **skirts.** outskirts. 6. *Slang.* woman or girl. 7. one of the flaps hanging from the sides of a saddle. —v. 1. border or edge. 2. pass along the border or edge; pass along the border or edge of: *skirt a town to avoid traffic.* 3. be, lie, live, etc., along the border of: *many suburban areas skirt New York City.* [< Scand. *skyrta* shirt] —skirt′er, n.

skit (skit), n. a short sketch that contains humor or satire. [cf. Scand. *skyti* shooter]

skit·tish (skit′ish), adj. 1. apt to start, jump, or run; easily frightened. 2. fickle; changeable. 3. coy. [prob. < Scand. root akin to *skjōta* shoot] —skit′tish·ly, adv. —skit′tish·ness, n.

skit·tles (skit′əlz), n. 1. game in which the players try to knock down nine wooden pins by rolling or throwing wooden disks or balls at them. 2. *Chess.* a quick practice game. 3. **beer and skittles,** enjoyment; pleasure. [< Scand. (Dan.) *skyttel* shuttle]

skoal (skōl), n., interj. a Scandinavian word used in drinking a health. —v. drink the health of. [< Dan., Norw. *skaal* < ONorse *skāl* bowl]

Skt., Sanskrit.

sku·a (skū′ə), or **skua gull,** n. any of several large brown sea birds that are related to the gulls; jaeger. [cf. Scand. *skūfr*]

skul·dug·ger·y (skul·dug′ər·i; -dug′ri), n. *Am., Colloq.* trickery; dishonesty.

skulk (skulk), v. 1. keep out of sight to avoid danger, work, duty, etc.; hide or lurk in a cowardly way. 2. move in a stealthy, sneaking way. —n. person who skulks. [< Scand. (Dan.) *skulke*] —skulk′er, n. —skulk′ing·ly, adv.

skull (skul), n. 1. the bones of the head; the group of bones around the brain. 2. head; brain. [< Scand. (dial. Norw.) *skul* shell] —skulled, adj. —skull′less, adj.

skull·cap (skul′kap′), n. a close-fitting cap without a brim.

Skunk
(total length ab. 2 ft.)

skunk (skungk), n. 1. a black, bushy-tailed animal, usually with white stripes along its back. It is about the size of a cat and gives off a very strong, unpleasant smell when frightened or attacked. 2. fur of this animal, used on coats, etc. 3. *Colloq.* a mean, contemptible person. —v. *Slang.* defeat utterly. [< Algonquian]

skunk cabbage, *Am.* a low, ill-smelling, broad-leaved plant, growing commonly in moist ground.

sky (skī), n., pl. skies, v., skied or skyed, sky·ing. —n. 1. Often, **skies.** the covering over the world; the region of the clouds or the upper air. 2. Often, **skies.** the heavens or firmament. 3. the celestial heaven. 4. **out of a clear sky,** suddenly; unexpectedly. 5. **to the skies,** very highly. —v. hit, throw, or raise high into the air. [< Scand. *skȳ* cloud]

sky·lark (skī′lärk′), n. the common European lark, a small bird that sings very sweetly as it flies toward the sky. —v. play pranks; frolic. —sky′lark·er, n.

sky·light (skī′līt′), n. window in a roof or ceiling.

sky·line (skī′līn′), n. 1. horizon. 2. outline of buildings, mountains, trees, etc., as seen against the sky.

sky pilot, *Slang.* clergyman; chaplain.

sky·rock·et (skī′rok′it), *n.* rocket. —*v. Am., Colloq.* rise much and quickly, as prices, etc.

sky·sail (skī′sāl′; -səl), *n.* in a square-rigged ship, a light sail set at the top of the mast above the royal.

sky·scrap·er (skī′skrāp′ər), *n. Am.* a very tall building.

sky·ward (skī′wərd), *adj.* directed toward the sky. —*adv.* Also, **sky′wards.** toward the sky.

sky·writ·ing (skī′rīt′ing), *n.* the tracing of words, etc., against the sky from an airplane, using smoke or some similar substance.

slab (slab), *n.* **1.** a broad, flat, thick piece (of stone, wood, meat, etc.). **2.** a rough outside piece cut from a log. [ME *slabbe*]

slack¹ (slak), *adj.* **1.** not tight or firm; loose: *the rope was slack.* **2.** careless: *she is a slack housekeeper.* **3.** slow: *a slack pace.* **4.** not active; not brisk; dull: *business is slack at this season.* —*n.* **1.** part that hangs loose: *the slack of a rope.* **2.** a dull season; quiet period: *a slack in business.* **3.** a stopping of a strong flow of the tide or a current of water. —*v.* **1.** make slack; let up on: *they did not slack their pace.* **2.** be or become slack; let up: *their pace slacked.* **3.** slake (lime). **4.** slack off, **a.** loosen. **b.** lessen one's efforts. **5.** slack up, slow down; go more slowly. —*adv.* in a slack manner. [OE *slæc*] —**slack′ly,** *adv.* —**slack′ness,** *n.* —**Syn.** *adj.* **2.** negligent, lax, remiss, indolent.

slack² (slak), *n.* dirt, dust, and small pieces left after coal is screened; small coal. [< Du. *slak* < G *schlacke*]

slack·en (slak′ən), *v.* **1.** make slower. **2.** become slower. **3.** become less active, vigorous, brisk, etc. **4.** make looser: *slacken the rope.* **5.** become loose. —**slack′en·er,** *n.* —**Syn.** **1.** retard.

slack·er (slak′ər), *n. Colloq.* person who shirks work or evades his duty.

slacks (slaks), *n.pl.* loose trousers.

slag (slag), *n., v.,* **slagged, slag·ging.** —*n.* **1.** the rough, hard waste left after metal is separated from ore by melting. **2.** a light, spongy lava. —*v.* form slag; change into slag. [< MLG *slagge*] —**slag′gy,** *adj.*

slain (slān), *v.* pp. of **slay.**

slake (slāk), *v.,* **slaked, slak·ing. 1.** satisfy (thirst, revenge, wrath, etc.); cause to be less active, intense, etc. **2.** put out (a fire). **3.** change (lime) from CaO to Ca(OH)₂ (**slaked lime**) by leaving it in the moist air or putting water on it. **4.** become less active, vigorous, intense, etc. [OE *slacian* < *slæc* slack] —**Syn. 1, 2.** quench.

sla·lom (slä′lōm; slä′ləm), *n.* in skiing, a race over a downhill, twisting course. [< Norw.]

slam¹ (slam), *v.,* **slammed, slam·ming,** *n.* —*v.* **1.** shut with force and noise; close with a bang. **2.** throw, push, hit, or move hard with force. **3.** *Am., Colloq.* criticize harshly. —*n.* **1.** a violent and noisy closing, striking, etc.; bang. **2.** *Am., Colloq.* harsh criticism.

slam² (slam), *n.* the winning of 12 (**little** or **small slam**) or all 13 (**grand slam**) tricks in the game of bridge.

slam-bang (slam′bang′), *adj. Slang.* forceful.

slan·der (slan′dər; slän′-), *n.* **1.** a false statement meant to do harm. **2.** the spreading of false reports. —*v.* **1.** talk falsely about. **2.** speak or spread slander. [< OF *esclandre* scandal < L *scandalum*. Doublet of SCANDAL.] —**slan′der·er,** *n.* —**Syn.** *n.* **1.** defamation, calumny, libel. —*v.* **1.** defame, calumniate.

slan·der·ous (slan′dər·əs; -drəs; slän′-), *adj.* **1.** containing a slander. **2.** speaking or spreading slanders. —**slan′der·ous·ly,** *adv.* —**slan′der·ous·ness,** *n.*

slang (slang), *n.* **1.** words, phrases, etc., usually characterized by a special vividness or coloring, and not generally used in formal English. *Cop* and *highbrow* are slang. **2.** the specialized language of a particular class of people. —**slang′y,** *adj.* —**slang′i·ly,** *adv.* —**slang′i·ness,** *n.*

slank (slangk), *v. Archaic.* pt. of **slink.**

slant (slant; slänt), *v.* slope. —*n.* **1.** slope. **2.** *Am.* mental attitude; way of regarding some-

thing. —*adj.* sloping. [? < Scand. (Norw.) *slent* stratum] —**slant′ing,** *adj.* —**slant′ing·ly,** *adv.* —**slant′ly,** *adv.* —**Syn.** *n.* **1.** incline, pitch.

slant·wise (slant′wīz′; slänt′-), *adv.* Also, **slant·ways** (slant′wāz′; slänt′-). in a slanting manner; obliquely. —*adj.* slanting; oblique.

slap (slap), *n., v.,* **slapped, slap·ping,** —*n.* **1.** a blow with the open hand or with something flat. **2.** a direct insult or rebuff. —*v.* **1.** strike with the open hand or with something flat. **2.** put, dash, or cast with force. —*adv.* **1.** straight; directly. **2.** suddenly. [< LG *slappe*] —**slap′per,** *n.*

slap·dash (slap′dash′), *adv.* hastily and carelessly. —*adj.* hasty and careless. —*n.* hasty, careless action, methods, or work.

slap-hap·py (slap′hap′i), *adj. U.S.* groggy; witless.

slap·jack (slap′jak′), *n. Am.* griddlecake.

slap·stick (slap′stik′), *Am.* —*n.* **1.** device made of two long, narrow sticks fastened so as to slap together loudly when a clown, actor, etc., hits somebody with it. **2.** comedy full of rough play. —*adj.* full of rough play. In slapstick comedy, the actors knock each other around to make people laugh.

slash (slash), *v.* **1.** cut with a sweeping stroke of a sword, knife, etc.; gash: *he slashed the bark off the tree with his knife.* **2.** make a slashing stroke. **3.** cut or slit to let a different cloth or color show through. **4.** whip severely; lash. **5.** criticize sharply, severely, or unkindly. **6.** *Am.* cut down severely; reduce a great deal. **7.** cut out parts of (a book, etc.); change greatly (a book, etc.). —*n.* **1.** a sweeping, slashing stroke. **2.** a cut or wound made by such a stroke. **3.** *Am.* an open space in a forest, usually littered with chips, broken branches, etc. **4.** *Am.* litter of chips, broken branches, etc. [ME *slaschen*] —**slash′er,** *n.* —**slash′ing,** *adj., n.*

slat (slat), *n., v.,* **slat·ted, slat·ting.** —*n.* a long, thin, narrow piece of wood or metal. —*v.* furnish with slats. [ult. < OF *esclat* split piece]

slate (slāt), *n., v.,* **slat·ed, slat·ing,** *adj.* —*n.* **1.** a bluish-gray rock that splits easily into thin, smooth layers. Slate is used to cover roofs and for blackboards. **2.** a thin piece of this rock. **3.** a dark, bluish gray. **4.** *Am.* list of candidates, officers, etc., to be considered for appointment, nomination, etc. —*v.* **1.** cover with slate. **2.** list on a slate. —*adj.* dark bluish-gray. [< OF *esclate*, var. of *esclat* slat] —**slat′er,** *n.* —**slat′y,** *adj.*

slat·tern (slat′ərn), *n.* woman who is dirty, careless, or untidy in her dress, her ways, her housekeeping, etc. [< *slatter* slop; orig. uncert.] —**slat′tern·ly,** *adj.* —**slat′tern·li·ness,** *n.*

slaugh·ter (slô′tər), *n.* a killing; butchering. —*v.* kill; butcher. [< Scand. *slātr* butcher-meat] —**slaugh′ter·er,** *n.* —**Syn.** *n.* slaying, murder.

slaughter house, place where animals are killed for food.

Slav (släv; slav), *n.* member of a group of peoples in E Europe whose languages are related. Russians, Poles, Czechs, Slovaks, Bulgarians, and Yugoslavs are Slavs. —*adj.* of or having to do with the Slavs.

slave (slāv), *n., v.,* **slaved, slav·ing.** —*n.* **1.** person who is the property of another. Slaves were bought and sold like horses. **2.** person who is controlled or ruled by some desire, habit, or influence: *a slave of drugs.* **3.** person who works like a slave. **4.** ant that is captured and forced to work for other ants. —*v.* work extremely hard and for long hours. [< OF < Med.L *Sclavus* Slav < LGk. *Sklabos*] —**slave′less,** *adj.*

slave driver, *Am.* **1.** overseer of slaves. **2.** an exacting taskmaster.

slave·hold·ing (slāv′hōl′ding), *adj.* owning slaves. —*n.* the owning of slaves. —**slave′hold′-er,** *n.*

slav·er¹ (slāv′ər), *n.* **1.** dealer in slaves. **2.** ship used in the slave trade.

slav·er² (slav′ər), *v.* **1.** let saliva run from the mouth. **2.** wet with saliva. —*n.* **1.** saliva running from the mouth. **2.** gross flattery. [< Scand. *slafra*] —**slav′er·er,** *n.*

slav·er·y (slāv′ər·ḭ; slāv′rḭ), *n.* **1.** condition of being a slave. Many African Negroes were captured and sold into slavery. **2.** custom of owning slaves. **3.** condition like that of a slave. **4.** hard work like that of a slave. —**Syn. 1.** bondage, serfdom, thraldom, servitude.

Slav·ic (slāv′ĭk; slav′-), *adj.* of or pertaining to the Slavs or their languages. —*n.* language or group of languages spoken by the Slavs.

slav·ish (slāv′ish), *adj.* **1.** of or pertaining to a slave or slaves. **2.** like a slave; mean; base. **3.** weakly submitting. **4.** like that of slaves; fit for slaves. **5.** lacking originality and independence. —**slav′ish·ly,** *adv.* —**slav′ish·ness,** *n.* —**Syn. 3.** servile, cringing, groveling, abject.

Sla·vo·ni·a (slə·vō′nḭ·ə), *n.* region in S Europe, now in N Yugoslavia.

Sla·vo·ni·an (slə·vō′nḭ·ən), *adj.* **1.** of or pertaining to Slavonia or its people. **2.** Slavic. —*n.* **1.** native of Slavonia. **2.** Slav. **3.** the Slavic language or languages.

slaw (slô), *n. Am.* coleslaw. [< Du. *sla,* contraction of *salade* SALAD]

slay (slā), *v.,* **slew, slain, slay·ing.** kill with violence. [OE *slēan*] —**slay′er,** *n.*

slea·zy (slē′zḭ), *adj.,* **-zi·er, -zi·est.** flimsy and poor: *sleazy cloth.* —**slea′zi·ly,** *adv.* —**slea′zi·ness,** *n.*

sled (sled), *n., v.,* **sled·ded, sled·ding.** —*n.* a wooden framework mounted on runners for use on snow or ice. —*v.* **1.** ride on a sled. **2.** carry on a sled. [< MDu. *sledde*] —**sled′der,** *n.*

sled·ding (sled′ĭng), *n. Am.* **1.** a riding on a sled. **2.** hard sledding, unfavorable conditions.

sledge¹ (slej), *n., v.,* **sledged, sledg·ing.** —*n.* sled; sleigh. —*v.* **1.** carry on a sledge. **2.** ride in a sledge. [< MDu. *sleedse*]

sledge² (slej), *n., v.,* **sledged, sledg·ing.** —*n.* a sledge hammer (def. 1). —*v.* pound or strike with a sledge. [OE *slecg*]

sledge hammer, 1. a large, heavy hammer. **2.** anything powerful and crushing.

sleek (slēk), *adj.* **1.** soft and glossy; smooth: *sleek hair.* **2.** having smooth, soft skin, hair, fur, etc.: *a sleek cat.* **3.** smooth of speech, manners, etc.: *a sleek salesman.* —*v.* **1.** smooth. **2.** make smooth and glossy; make tidy. [var. of *slick*] —**sleek′er,** *n.* —**sleek′ly,** *adv.* —**sleek′ness,** *n.* —**sleek′y,** *adj.*

sleep (slēp), *v.,* **slept, sleep·ing.** —*n.* —*v.* **1.** rest body and mind; be without ordinary consciousness. **2.** be in a condition like sleep. **3.** pass in sleeping: *sleep away the morning.* **4.** be asleep in: *he slept the sleep of exhaustion.* **5.** sleep off, get rid of by sleeping. —*n.* **1.** a condition in which body and mind are very inactive, occurring naturally and regularly in animals. **2.** state or condition like sleep. **3.** last sleep, death. [OE *slæpan*] —**sleep′ing,** *adj., n.* —**sleep′less,** *adj.* —**sleep′less·ly,** *adv.* —**sleep′less·ness,** *n.* —**Syn.** *v.* **1.** slumber, doze, drowse, nap, snooze. —*n.* **1.** slumber, doze, drowse, snooze, nap.

sleep·er (slēp′ər), *n.* **1.** person or thing that sleeps. **2.** *Am.* a sleeping car. **3.** a horizontal beam. **4.** a tie to support a railroad track. **5.** *Colloq.* person, animal, or thing that does very much better in a contest of any sort than was anticipated.

sleeping bag, *Am.* a waterproof bag, usually warmly lined, to sleep in out of doors.

sleeping car, *Am.* a railroad car with berths for passengers to sleep in.

sleeping sickness, disease causing fever, inflammation of the brain, sleepiness, and usually death. One kind is carried by the tsetse fly.

sleep·walk·ing (slēp′wôk′ĭng), *n.* act of walking while asleep. —*adj.* that walks about while asleep. —**sleep′walk′er,** *n.*

sleep·y (slēp′ḭ), *adj.,* **sleep·i·er, sleep·i·est. 1.** ready to go to sleep; inclined to sleep. **2.** not active; quiet. —**sleep′i·ly,** *adv.* —**sleep′i·ness,** *n.* —**Syn. 1.** drowsy, slumberous.

sleet (slēt), *n.* **1.** half-frozen rain. **2.** the coating of thin ice that coats trees, houses, etc., during winter rains. —*v.* come down in sleet. [ME] —**sleet′y,** *adj.* —**sleet′i·ness,** *n.*

sleeve (slēv), *n., v.,* **sleeved, sleev·ing.** —*n.* **1.** the part of a garment that covers the arm. **2.** tube into which a rod or another tube fits. **3.** laugh in or up one's sleeve, be amused but not show it. **4.** up one's sleeve, in reserve; ready for use when needed. —*v.* furnish with sleeves. [OE *sliefe*] —**sleeved,** *adj.* —**sleeve′less,** *adj.*

sleigh (slā), *n.* —*n.* carriage or cart mounted on runners for use on ice or snow. —*v.* travel or ride in a sleigh. [< Du. *slee,* var. of *slede* sled] —**sleigh′er,** *n. Am.* —**sleigh′ing,** *n. Am.*

sleight (slīt), *n.* **1.** skill; dexterity. **2.** a clever trick. [< Scand. *slœgth* < *slœgr* sly]

sleight of hand, 1. skill and quickness in moving the hands. **2.** tricks or skill of a modern magician; juggling.

slen·der (slen′dər), *adj.* **1.** long and thin; not big around: *a slender girl.* **2.** slight; small; scanty: *a slender meal, a slender hope.* [ME *slendre, sclendre*] —**slen′der·ly,** *adv.* —**slen′der·ness,** *n.* —**Syn. 1.** slim, spare, lank, lean.

slen·der·ize (slen′dər·īz), *v.,* **-ized, -iz·ing. 1.** make slender. **2.** cause to look slender.

slept (slept), *v.* pt. and pp. of **sleep.**

sleuth (slūth), *n.* **1.** bloodhound. **2.** *Am.* detective. —*v. Am.* be or act like a detective. [< Scand. *slōth* trail]

sleuth·hound (slūth′hound′), *n. Colloq.* **1.** bloodhound. **2.** detective.

slew¹ (slū), *v.* pt. of **slay.**

slew² (slū), *v., n.* turn; swing; twist. Also, **slue.**

slew³ (slū), *n.* a swampy place; marshy inlet. Also, **slough** *Am.,* **slue.** [var. of *slough¹*]

slew⁴ (slū), *n. Am., Colloq.* lot; large number or amount. Also, **slue.** [? < Irish *sluagh* host, crowd]

slice (slīs), *n., v.,* **sliced, slic·ing.** —*n.* **1.** a thin, flat, broad piece cut from something. **2.** knife or spatula with a thin, broad blade. **3.** part; share. **4.** *Golf.* a slicing hit. —*v.* **1.** cut into slices. **2.** cut (off) as a slice. **3.** remove, spread, make smooth, etc., by using a slice. **4.** divide into parts or shares. **5.** *Golf.* hit (a ball) so that it curves to one's right, if right-handed. [< OF *esclice* thin chip < Gmc.] —**slic′er,** *n.*

slick (slik), *adj.* **1.** sleek; smooth: *slick hair.* **2.** slippery; greasy. **3.** *Colloq.* clever; ingenious. **4.** sly; tricky. **5.** smooth of speech, manners, etc. [ME *slike;* akin to OE *slician* make smooth] —*v.* **1.** make sleek or smooth. **2.** make smart or pretentious. —*n.* **1.** a smooth place or spot. **2.** *Am., Slang.* magazine printed on heavy, glossy paper. —*adv.* **1.** smoothly; slyly; cleverly. **2.** directly. [OE *slician*] —**slick′ly,** *adv.* —**slick′ness,** *n.*

slick·er (slik′ər), *n. Am.* **1.** a long, loose waterproof coat. **2.** *Colloq.* a sly, tricky person.

slide (slīd), *v.,* **slid** (slid), **slid** or **slid·den** (slid′ən), **slid·ing.** —*n.* —*v.* **1.** move smoothly along a surface: *slide on ice.* **2.** move easily or quietly or secretly: *the thief slid in the window.* **3.** pass without heeding or being heeded: *let things slide.* **4.** pass by degrees; slip: *slide into bad habits.* **5.** pass quietly or secretly: *time slid by.* —*n.* **1.** act of sliding. **2.** a smooth surface for sliding on. **3.** *Am.* mass of earth, snow, etc., sliding down. **4.** the sliding down of such a mass. **5.** a small, thin sheet of glass on which objects are put for microscopic examination. [OE *slīdan*] —**slid′er,** *n.* —**slid′ing,** *adj.* —**Syn.** *v.* **1.** glide.

slide rule, device marked with logarithmic scales, used by engineers, physicists, etc., for making rapid calculations.

sliding scale, 1. scale of wages, prices, taxes, etc., that can be adjusted according to certain conditions. **2.** a slide rule.

slight (slīt), *adj.* **1.** not much; not important; small: *the event had slight consequence.* **2.** not big around; slender: *a slight person.* **3.** frail; flimsy: *a slight excuse.* —*v.* treat as of little value; pay too little attention to; neglect: *slight work, feel slighted.* —*n.* a slighting treatment; act of neglect. [OE *–sliht* level, as in *eorthslihtes* level with the ground] —**slight′er,** *n.* —**slight′ing,** *adj.* —**slight′ing·ly,** *adv.* —**slight′ness,** *n.* —**Syn.** *adj.* **1.** inconsiderable, trivial, trifling. **2.** slim, thin. —*v.* disregard.

sli·ly (slī′lḭ), *adv.* slyly.

slim (slĭm), *adj.*, slim·mer, slim·mest, *v.*, slimmed, slim·ming. —*adj.* 1. slender; thin. 2. small; slight; weak: *a slim answer.* —*v.* 1. make slim. 2. become slim. [< Du., bad] —slim′ly, *adv.* —slim′mish, *adj.* —slim′ness, *n.*

slime (slīm), *n.*, *v.*, slimed, slim·ing. —*n.* 1. soft, sticky mud or something like it. 2. a sticky substance given off by snails, slugs, fish, etc. 3. disgusting filth. —*v.* 1. cover or smear with or as with slime. 2. remove slime from. [OE *slīm*]

slim·y (slīm′ĭ), *adj.*, slim·i·er, slim·i·est. 1. covered with slime. 2. of or like slime. 3. disgusting; filthy. —slim′i·ly, *adv.* —slim′i·ness, *n.*

sling (slĭng), *n.*, *v.*, slung, sling·ing. —*n.* 1. strip of leather with a string fastened to each end, for throwing stones. 2. a throw; hurling. 3. a hanging loop of cloth fastened around the neck to support a hurt arm. 4. loop of rope, band, chain, etc., by which heavy objects are lifted, carried, or held. 5. *Am.* drink consisting of liquor, sugar, and water. [< v.] —*v.* 1. throw with a sling. 2. throw; cast; hurl; fling. 3. raise, lower, etc., with a sling. 4. hang in a sling; hang so as to swing loosely. 5. *Am.* *Slang.* mix; serve. [< Scand. *slyngva*] —sling′er, *n.*

A, sling for lifting; B, sling lifting a barrel.

sling·shot (slĭng′shot′), *n.* a Y-shaped stick with a rubber band fastened to its prongs, used to shoot pebbles, etc.

slink (slĭngk), *v.*, slunk or (*Archaic*) slank, slunk, slink·ing. move in a sneaking, guilty manner; sneak. [OE *slincan*] —slink′ing·ly, *adv.*

slip[1] (slĭp), *v.*, slipped or (*Archaic*) slipt, slipped, slip·ping, *n.* —*v.* 1. go or move smoothly, quietly, easily, or quickly: *she slipped out of the room, time slips by, the ship slips through the waves.* 2. slide; move out of place: *the knife slipped and cut him.* 3. slide suddenly without wanting to: *he slipped on the icy sidewalk.* 4. cause to slip; put, pass, or draw smoothly, quietly, or secretly: *she slipped the ring from her finger, slip the note into Mary's hand.* 5. put or take (something) easily or quickly: *slip on your coat, slip off your shoes.* 6. pass without notice; pass through neglect; escape: *don't let this opportunity slip.* 7. get loose from; get away from; escape from: *the dog has slipped his collar, your name has slipped my mind.* 8. let go; release: *he slipped the hound, the ship has slipped anchor and is off.* 9. make a mistake or error. 10. let slip, tell without meaning to. 11. slip one over on, *Colloq.* get the advantage of, esp. by trickery. 12. slip up, *Am.*, *Colloq.* make a mistake or error. —*n.* 1. act or fact of slipping. 2. thing that can be slipped on or off; covering: *pillows are covered by slips.* 3. a sleeveless garment worn under a dress. 4. mistake; error: *he makes slips in grammar.* 5. *Am.* space for ships between wharves or in a dock. 6. an inclined platform alongside of the water, on which ships are built or repaired. [prob. < MLG *slippen*]

slip[2] (slĭp), *v.*, slipped or (*Archaic*) slipt, slipped, slip·ping, *n.* —*v.* cut branches from (a plant) to grow new plants; take (a part) from a plant. —*n.* 1. a narrow strip of paper, wood, etc. 2. a young, slender person. 3. a small branch or twig cut from a plant, used to grow a new plant. [prob. < MDu., MLG *slippe* a cut]

slip cover, a removable cloth cover for over-stuffed furniture.

slip knot, 1. knot made to slip along the rope or cord around which it is made. 2. knot that can be undone by a pull.

slip-on (slĭp′on; -ôn′), *adj.* 1. that can be put on or taken off easily or quickly. 2. that must be put on or taken off over the head. —*n.* a slip-on glove, blouse, sweater, etc.

slip·per (slĭp′ər), *n.* 1. a kind of light, low shoe. 2. person or thing that slips. —*v.* hit or beat with a slipper. —slip′pered, *adj.*

slip·per·y (slĭp′ər·ĭ; slĭp′rĭ), *adj.*, -per·i·er, -per·i·est. 1. causing or likely to cause slipping. 2. slipping away easily. 3. shifty; tricky. [ME alter. of OE *slipor* slippery] —slip′per·i·ness, *n.*

slippery elm, *Am.* 1. an elm tree of E North America having an inner bark which becomes slippery when moistened. 2. the inner bark.

slip·shod (slĭp′shod′), *adj.* 1. careless in dress, habits, speech, etc.; untidy; slovenly. 2. shuffling: *a slipshod gait.* 3. wearing shoes worn down at the heel. —slip′shod′ness, *n.*

slipt (slĭpt), *v.* *Archaic.* pt. of slip.

slip-up (slĭp′up′), *n.* *Colloq.* mistake; error.

slit (slĭt), *v.*, slit, slit·ting, *n.* —*v.* cut or tear in a straight line; make a long, straight cut or tear in. —*n.* a straight, narrow cut, tear, or opening. [OE *slīte*] —slit′ter, *n.*

slith·er (slĭth′ər), *v.* slide down or along a surface, esp. unsteadily; go with a sliding motion. —*n.* such a movement; a slide. [OE *slidrian*]

sliv·er (slĭv′ər), *n.* 1. a long, thin piece that has been split off, broken off, or cut off; splinter. 2. a loose fiber of wool, cotton, etc. —*v.* split or break into slivers. [ult. < OE *slīfan* split] —sliv′er·er, *n.*

slob (slob), *n.* 1. *Irish.* mud. 2. *Slang.* a stupid, untidy, or clumsy person. [prob. < Irish *slab* mud < Gmc.]

slob·ber (slob′ər), *v.* 1. let liquid run out from the mouth. 2. wet or smear with saliva, etc. 3. speak in a silly, sentimental way. —*n.* 1. saliva or other liquid running out from the mouth. 2. silly, sentimental talk or emotion. [prob. ult. < Du. *slabberen*] —slob′ber·er, *n.* —slob′ber·ing, *adj.* —slob′ber·ing·ly, *adv.* —slob′ber·y, *adj.* —slob′ber·i·ness, *n.*

sloe (slō), *n.* 1. a dark-purple, plumlike fruit. 2. a thorny shrub that it grows on; blackthorn. [OE *slāh*]

sloe gin, alcoholic beverage flavored with sloe.

slog (slog), *v.*, slogged, slog·ging, *n.* —*v.* 1. hit hard. 2. plod heavily. —*n.* a hard blow. [var. of *slug*[2]] —slog′ger, *n.*

slo·gan (slō′gən), *n.* 1. word or phrase used by a business, club, political party, etc., to advertise its purpose; motto. 2. a war cry; battle cry. [< Scotch Gaelic, < *sluagh* army + *gairm* cry]

sloop (slüp), *n.* sailboat having one mast, a mainsail, a jib, and sometimes other sails. [< Du. *sloep*, earlier *sloepe*. Doublet of SHALLOP.]

slop[1] (slop), *v.*, slopped, slop·ping, *n.* —*v.* 1. spill liquid upon; spill; splash. 2. splash through mud, slush, or water. 3. slop over, *Am.*, *Slang.* show too much feeling, enthusiasm, etc. —*n.* 1. liquid carelessly spilled or splashed about. 2. Often, **slops.** dirty water; liquid garbage. 3. a thin liquid mud or slush. 4. Often, **slops.** liquid or semiliquid food that is weak or not appetizing. [cf. OE *cūsloppe* cow slobber]

slop[2] (slop), *n.* 1. a loose outer garment, such as a jacket or smock. 2. **slops,** a. cheap ready-made clothing. b. clothes, bedding, etc., supplied to sailors on a ship. [OE, as in *oferslop* overgarment]

slope (slōp), *v.*, sloped, slop·ing, *n.* —*v.* 1. go up or down at an angle: *the land slopes toward the sea.* 2. cause to go up or down at an angle. —*n.* 1. any line, surface, land, etc., that goes up or down at an angle. 2. amount of slope. [< OE *slopen*, pp. of *-slūpan* slip] —slop′er, *n.* —slop′ing, *adj.* —slop′ing·ly, *adv.* —slop′ing·ness, *n.* —Syn. v. 1. incline.

slop·py (slop′ĭ), *adj.*, -pi·er, -pi·est. 1. very wet; slushy. 2. splashed or soiled with liquid. 3. *Colloq.* careless; slovenly. 4. *Colloq.* weak; silly. —slop′pi·ly, *adv.* —slop′pi·ness, *n.*

slosh (slosh), *n.* 1. slush. 2. *Colloq.* a watery or weak drink. —*v.* 1. splash in slush, mud, or water. 2. *Am.* go about idly. —slosh′y, *adj.*

slot (slot), *n.*, *v.*, slot·ted, slot·ting. —*n.* a small, narrow opening or depression. —*v.* make a slot or slots in.

Sloth (ab. 2 ft. long)

sloth (slōth; slôth), *n.* 1. unwillingness to work or exert oneself; laziness; idleness. 2. *Archaic.* slowness. 3. a very slow-moving animal of South and Central America that lives in trees. Sloths hang upside down from tree branches. [< *slow*] —Syn. 1. sluggishness, indolence.

sloth·ful (slôth′fəl; slôth′-), *adj.* unwilling to work or exert oneself; lazy; idle. —**sloth′ful·ly,** *adv.* —**sloth′ful·ness,** *n.* —Syn. sluggish.

slot machine, machine, esp. for gambling, that is worked by dropping a coin into a slot.

slouch (slouch), *v.* 1. stand, sit, walk, or move in an awkward, drooping manner: *the weary man slouched along.* 2. droop or bend downward. —*n.* 1. a bending forward of head and shoulders; awkward, drooping way of standing, sitting, or walking. 2. *Esp. U.S.* an awkward, slovenly, or inefficient person. —**slouch′ing,** *adj.* —**slouch′y, adj.** —**slouch′i·ly,** *adv.* —**slouch′i·ness,** *n.*

slough¹ (slou *for 1 and 3*; slü *for 2*), *n.* 1. *Am.* a soft, deep muddy place; mud hole. 2. *Am.* slew³. 3. hopeless discouragement; degradation. [OE *slōh*] —**slough′y, adj.**

slough² (sluf), *n.* 1. the old skin shed or cast off by a snake. 2. layer of dead skin or tissue that drops or falls off as a wound, sore, etc., heals. —*v.* 1. drop off; throw off; shed. 2. be shed or cast; drop or fall. 3. discard (a losing card). [ME *slugh(e), slouh*] —**slough′y, adj.**

Slo·vak (slō′vak), *n.* 1. member of a Slavic people living in Slovakia. The Slovaks are closely related to the Bohemians and the Moravians. 2. their language. —*adj.* of or having to do with Slovakia, its people, or their language.

Slo·va·ki·a (slō·vä′ki·ə; –vak′i·ə), *n.* region in E Czechoslovakia, under the control of Germany 1939–45. —**Slo·va′ki·an,** *adj., n.*

slov·en (sluv′ən), *n.* person who is untidy, dirty, or careless in dress, appearance, habits, work, etc. —*adj.* untidy; dirty; careless. [? ult. < Flem. *sloef* dirty, Du. *slof* careless]

Slo·vene (slō′vēn), *n.* 1. member of a Slavic group of people living in Slovenia. The Slovenes are closely related to the Croats, Serbians, and other southern Slavs. 2. their language. —*adj.* of or having to do with Slovenia, its people, or their language; Slovenian.

Slo·ve·ni·a (slō·vē′ni·ə; –vēn′yə), *n.* region in NW Yugoslavia. —**Slo·ve′ni·an,** *adj., n.*

slov·en·ly (sluv′ən·li), *adj.,* –li·er, –li·est, *adv.* —*adj.* untidy, dirty, or careless in dress, appearance, habits, work, etc. —*adv.* in a slovenly manner. —**slov′en·li·ness,** *n.* —Syn. *adj.* unkempt, slatternly, slipshod.

slow (slō), *adj.* 1. taking a long time; taking longer than usual; not fast or quick: *a slow journey.* 2. behind time; running at less than proper speed: *a slow runner.* 3. indicating time earlier than the correct time: *a slow clock.* 4. causing a low or lower rate of speed: *a slow track.* 5. burning or heating slowly or gently: *a slow flame.* 6. sluggish; naturally inactive: *a slow pupil.* 7. dull; not interesting: *this book is very slow.* —*v.* 1. make slow or slower; reduce the speed of: *slow down a car.* 2. become slow; go slower: *slow up when you go through a town.* —*adv.* in a slow manner. [OE *slāw*] —**slow′ly,** *adv.* —**slow′ness,** *n.* —Syn. *adj.* 1. lingering, dilatory, delaying, leisurely. 7. wearisome, tiresome. —Ant. *adj.* 1. fast, swift, fleet, rapid.

slow-mo·tion (slō′mō′shən), *adj.* 1. moving at less than normal speed. 2. showing action at much less than its actual speed.

sludge (sluj), *n.* 1. soft mud; mire; slush. 2. a soft, thick, muddy mixture, deposit, sediment, etc. 3. small broken pieces of floating ice.

slue¹ (slü), *v.,* slued, slu·ing, *n.* slew².

slue² (slü), *n.* slew³.

slue³ (slü), *n.* slew⁴.

slug¹ (slug), *n.* 1. a slow-moving animal like a snail, without a shell or with only a very small shell. 2. caterpillar or larva that looks like a slug. 3. any slow-moving person, animal, wagon, etc. 4. piece of lead or other metal for firing from a gun. 5. *Am.* lump of metal. 6. *Am., Printing.* a strip of metal used to space lines of type. A slug is more than ⅟₁₆ of an inch in thickness. b. line of type cast in one piece by a linotype machine. [? < Scand. (dial. Sw.) *slogga* be sluggish]

slug² (slug), *v.,* slugged, slug·ging, *n. Colloq.* —*v.* 1. hit hard with the fist. 2. strike violently. —*n.* a hard blow with the fist. —**slug′ger,** *n.* —**slug′ging,** *n.*

slug·gard (slug′ərd), *n.* a lazy, idle person. —*adj.* lazy; idle. [ult. < *slug¹*] —**slug′gard·ly,** *adj.*

slug·gish (slug′ish), *adj.* 1. slow-moving; not active; lacking energy or vigor. 2. lazy; idle. [< *slug¹*] —**slug′gish·ly,** *adv.* —**slug′gish·ness,** *n.* —Syn. 1. dull, inert. 2. slothful, indolent.

sluice (slüs), *n., v.,* sluiced, sluic·ing. —*n.* 1. structure with a gate for holding back or controlling the water of a canal, river, or lake. 2. Also, sluice gate. gate that holds back or controls the flow of water. When the water behind a dam gets too high, the sluices are opened. 3. water held back or controlled by such a gate. 4. thing that controls the flow or passage of anything. 5. *Am.* a long, sloping trough through which water flows, used to wash gold from sand, dirt, or gravel. 6. channel for carrying off water. —*v.* 1. let out or draw off (water) by opening a sluice. 2. flow or pour in a stream; rush. 3. flush or cleanse with a rush of water; pour or throw water over. 4. *Am.* wash (gold) from sand, dirt, or gravel in a sluice. 5. send (logs, etc.) along a channel of water. [< OF *escluse,* ult. < L *ex–* out + *claudere* shut]

Sluice (def. 2)

slum (slum), *n., v.,* slummed, slum·ming. —*n.* 1. street, alley, etc., in a crowded, dirty part of a city or town. 2. the slums, a crowded, dirty part of a city or town, where the poorest people live. —*v.* go into or visit the slums. —**slum′mer,** *n.* —**slum′ming,** *n.*

slum·ber (slum′bər), *v.* 1. sleep. 2. pass in sleep. 3. be inactive: *the volcano had slumbered for years.* —*n.* 1. a light sleep. 2. an inactive state or condition. [ult. < OE *slūma,* n.] —**slum′ber·er,** *n.* —**slum′ber·less,** *adj.*

slum·ber·ous (slum′bər·əs), **slum·brous** (–brəs), *adj.* 1. sleepy. 2. causing or inducing sleep. 3. of or suggestive of sleep. 4. inactive; sluggish. 5. calm; quiet.

slump (slump), *v.* drop heavily; fall suddenly. —*n.* a heavy or sudden fall.

slung (slung), *v.* pt. and pp. of sling.

slunk (slungk), *v.* pt. and pp. of slink.

slur (slėr), *v.,* slurred, slur·ring, *n.* —*v.* 1. pass lightly over; go through hurriedly or in a careless way: *slur over a person's faults.* 2. pronounce indistinctly: *many persons slur "how do you do."* 3. speak or write sounds, letters, etc., so indistinctly that they run into each other. 4. *Music.* a. sing or play (two or more tones of different pitch) without a break; run together in a smooth, connected manner. b. mark with a slur. 5. harm the reputation of; insult; slight. —*n.* 1. a slurred pronunciation, sound, etc. 2. *Music.* a. a slurring of tones. b. a curved mark (⌢) indicating this. 3. blot or stain (upon reputation); insulting or slighting remark: *slur on a person's good name.* [ME *slor* mud] —**slur′ring·ly,** *adv.*

A slur in music

slush (slush), *n.* 1. partly melted snow; snow and water mixed. 2. soft mud. 3. silly, sentimental talk, writing, etc. 4. grease. —**slush′y, adj.** —**slush′i·ness,** *n.*

slut (slut), *n.* 1. a dirty, untidy woman. 2. woman of loose morals. 3. a female dog. —**slut′tish,** *adj.* —**slut′tish·ly,** *adv.* —**slut′tish·ness,** *n.*

sly (slī), *adj.,* sly·er, sly·est, or sli·er, sli·est, *n.* —*adj.* 1. able to do things without letting others know; acting secretly: *a sly thief.* 2. cunning; crafty; tricky; wily: *a sly plot.* 3. such as a sly person or animal would use: *she asked sly questions.* 4. playfully mischievous or knowing: *a sly wink.* —*n.* on the sly, in a sly way; secretly. [< Scand. *slœgr*] —**sly′ish,** *adj.* —**sly′ly,** *adv.* —**sly′ness,** *n.* —Syn. *adj.* 1. surreptitious, stealthy, furtive. 2. artful, subtle.

Sm, *Chem.* samarium.

smack[1] (smak), *n.* **1.** a slight taste or flavor. **2.** trace; suggestion. —*v.* have a smack. [OE *smæcc*] —Syn. *n.* **2.** touch, dash, tinge.

smack[2] (smak), *v.* **1.** open (the lips) quickly so as to make a sharp sound. **2.** kiss loudly. **3.** slap. **4.** crack (a whip, etc.). —*n.* **1.** a smacking movement of the lips. **2.** the sharp sound made in this way. **3.** a loud kiss, slap, or crack. —*adv. Colloq.* **1.** directly; squarely. **2.** suddenly and sharply; with or as if with a smack. [ult. imit.]

smack[3] (smak), *n.* a small sailboat with one mast. [prob. < Du. *smak*]

smack·ing (smak'ing), *adj.* lively, brisk, or strong.

small (smôl), *adj.* **1.** not large; little; not large as compared with other things of the same kind: *a small house.* **2.** not great in amount, degree, extent, duration, value, strength, etc.: *a small dose, small hope of success.* **3.** not important: *a small matter.* **4.** not prominent; of low social position; humble; poor: *both the great and the small mourned Lincoln's death.* **5.** having little land, capital, etc.: *a small farmer, a small dealer.* **6.** gentle; soft; low: *a small, murmuring purr.* **7.** mean; not generous: *a small nature.* **8.** of letters, not capital. **9.** feel small, be ashamed or humiliated. —*adv.* **1.** into small pieces. **2.** in low tones. **3.** in a small manner. —*n.* **1.** that which is small. **2.** the small, narrow, or scanty part. [OE *smæl*] —**small'ish,** *adj.* —**small'ness,** *n.* —Syn. *adj.* **1.** diminutive, undersized, tiny, minute. **2.** slight, inconsiderable. **3.** trifling, insignificant, trivial. **7.** selfish, illiberal, stingy.

small arms, weapons easily carried by a person, such as rifles or revolvers.

small capital, a capital letter that is slightly smaller than the regular capital letter. This line shows 5½-point REGULAR CAPITALS and SMALL CAPITALS.

small fry, 1. babies or children; small or young creatures. **2.** small fish. **3.** unimportant people or things.

small hours, the early hours of the morning.

small potatoes, *Am.* an unimportant person or thing; unimportant persons or things.

small·pox (smôl'poks'), *n.* a very contagious disease characterized by fever and blisterlike eruptions on the skin that often leave permanent scars shaped like little pits.

small talk, conversation about unimportant matters; chat.

smart (smärt), *v.* **1.** feel sharp pain: *his eyes smarted.* **2.** cause sharp pain. **3.** feel distress or irritation: *he smarted from the scolding.* **4.** suffer: *he shall smart for this.* —*n.* a sharp pain: *the smart of a cut.* —*adj.* **1.** sharp; severe: *a smart blow.* **2.** keen; active; lively: *a smart pace.* **3.** clever; bright; shrewd: *a smart child.* **4.** fresh and neat; in good order: *smart in his uniform.* **5.** stylish; fashionable; *smart hotels.* **6.** *Colloq.* or *Dial.* fairly large; considerable. —*adv.* in a smart manner. [OE *smeart*] —**smart'ly,** *adv.* —**smart'ness,** *n.* —Syn. *adj.* **1.** stinging, vigorous, forceful. **3.** precocious, gifted, talented. **4.** trim, spruce, natty.

smart al·eck (al'ik), *Am.* a conceited, obnoxious person.

smart·en (smär'tən), *v.* **1.** improve in appearance; brighten. **2.** make or become brisker.

smart·weed (smärt'wēd'), *n.* weed growing in wet places, which causes a smarting sensation when brought into contact with the skin.

smash (smash), *v.* **1.** break into pieces with violence and noise: *smash a window.* **2.** destroy; shatter; ruin: *smash an argument.* **3.** be broken to pieces: *the dishes smashed on the floor.* **4.** become ruined. **5.** rush violently; crash: *the car smashed into a tree.* **6.** crush; defeat: *smash an attack.* **7.** hit (a tennis ball) with a hard, fast overhand stroke. **8.** *Colloq.* hit a hard blow. —*n.* **1.** a violent breaking; shattering; crash: *smash of two automobiles.* **2.** sound of a smash or crash: *the smash of broken glass.* **3.** a crushing defeat; disaster. **4.** a business failure; bankruptcy. **5.** a hard, fast overhand stroke in tennis.

6. *Colloq.* a hard blow. **7. to smash, a.** into broken pieces; into bits. **b.** to ruin. [blend of SMACK[2] and MASH] —**smash'er,** *n.*

smash-up (smash'up'), *n.* **1.** *Am.* a bad collision; wreck. **2.** a business failure; bankruptcy. **3.** a great misfortune; disaster.

smat·ter (smat'ər), *n.* slight knowledge. [cf. Sw. *smattra* rattle] —**smat'ter·er,** *n.*

smat·ter·ing (smat'ər·ing), *n.* slight or superficial knowledge. —**smat'ter·ing·ly,** *adv.*

smaze (smāz), *n.* combination of smoke and haze in the air. [blend of *smoke* and *haze*]

smear (smir), *v.* **1.** cover or stain with anything sticky, greasy, or dirty. **2.** rub or spread (oil, grease, paint, etc.). **3.** rub or wipe (a brush, hand, cloth, etc.) so as to make a mark or stain. **4.** receive a mark or stain; be smeared. **5.** harm; soil; spoil. **6.** injure a person's reputation by malicious charges. **7.** *U.S. Slang.* defeat decisively; rout. —*n.* **1.** mark or stain left by smearing. **2.** a malicious attack. [OE *smeoru* grease]

smell (smel), *v.,* **smelled** or **smelt** (smelt), **smell·ing,** *n.* —*v.* **1.** perceive with the nose: *smell smoke.* **2.** use the sense of smelling. **3.** give out a smell. **4.** give out a bad smell; have a bad smell. **5.** find a trace or suggestion of, as through shrewdness: *smell trouble brewing.* **6.** have the smell (of); have the trace (of): *the plan smells of trickery.* **7.** hunt or find by smelling or as if by smelling: *smell out a thief.* —*n.* **1.** act of smelling. **2.** sense of smelling. **3.** quality in a thing that affects the sense of smell: *the smell of smoke.* **4.** trace; suggestion. [ME *smelle(n)*] —**smell'a·ble,** *adj.* —**smell'er,** *n.* —**smell'y,** *adj.* —Syn. *n.* **3.** odor, scent, aroma.

smelling salts, a form of ammonia inhaled to relieve faintness, headaches, etc.

smelt[1] (smelt), *v.* **1.** melt (ore) in order to get the metal out of it. **2.** refine (impure metal) by melting. [< MDu., MLG *smelten*]

smelt[2] (smelt), *n., pl.* **smelts** or (*esp. collectively*) **smelt.** a small, edible sea fish with silvery scales. [OE]

smelt·er (smel'tər), *n.* **1.** *Am.* place where ores or metals are smelted. **2.** furnace for smelting ores.

smi·lax (smī'laks), *n.* **1.** a twining, trailing plant or vine, much used by florists in decoration. **2.** any of a large group of woody vines with prickly stems, umbrella-shaped clusters of flowers, and blackish or red berries. [< L < Gk.]

Smilax

smile (smīl), *v.,* **smiled, smil·ing,** *n.* —*v.* **1.** look pleased or amused; show pleasure, favor, kindness, amusement, etc., by an upward curve of the mouth. **2.** look pleasant or agreeable; look with favor: *fortune smiled upon the enterprise.* **3.** bring, put, drive, etc., by smiling: *smile one's tears away.* **4.** give (a smile). **5.** express by a smile: *she smiled consent.* **6.** show scorn, disdain, etc., by a curve of the mouth: *she smiled bitterly.* —*n.* **1.** act of smiling. **2.** a favoring look or regard; pleasant look or aspect. [ME *smile(n)*] —**smile'less,** *adj.* —**smil'er,** *n.* —**smil'ing·ly,** *adv.* —**smil'ing·ness,** *n.*

smirch (smérch), *v.* soil with soot, dirt, dust, dishonor, disgrace, etc. —*n.* a dirty mark; blot. [? < OF *esmorcher* torture] —**smirch'er,** *n.*

smirk (smérk), *v.* smile in an affected, silly, self-satisfied way. —*n.* an affected, silly, self-satisfied smile. [OE *smearcian* to smile] —**smirk'er,** *n.* —**smirk'ing·ly,** *adv.*

smite (smīt), *v.,* **smote, smit·ten** or **smit** (smit), **smit·ing. 1.** strike; strike or hit hard. **2.** come with force (upon). **3.** charm; enamor. **4.** affect with a sudden pain, disease, etc. **5.** strike down; punish severely; destroy. [OE *smītan*]

smith (smith), *n.* **1.** man who makes or shapes things out of metal. **2.** blacksmith. [OE]

Smith (smith), *n.* **1.** Adam, 1723–1790, Scottish political economist. **2.** Alfred Emanuel, 1873–1944, American political leader. **3.** Captain John,

1580–1631, English explorer and early settler of Virginia. **4.** Joseph, 1805–1844, founder of the Mormon Church.

smith·er·eens (smith′ər·ēnz′), *n.pl. Colloq.* small pieces; bits.

smith·y (smith′ĭ; smith′ĭ), *n., pl.* **smith·ies.** workshop of a smith, esp. a blacksmith. [< *smith*]

smit·ten (smit′ən), *adj.* **1.** hard hit; struck. **2.** suddenly and strongly affected. **3.** very much in love. —*v.* pp. of smite.

smock (smok), *n.* a loose outer garment worn to protect clothing. —*v.* ornament (a smock, dress, etc.) with a honeycomb pattern made of lines of stitches crossing each other diagonally. [OE *smocc*] —**smock′ing,** *n.*

smog (smog), *n.* a combination of smoke and fog in the air. [blend of *smoke* and *fog*]

smoke (smōk), *n., v.,* **smoked, smok·ing.** —*n.* **1.** a visible mixture of gases and particles of carbon which rises when anything burns; cloud caused by anything burning. **2.** something resembling this. **3.** that which is smoked; cigar, cigarette, pipe, etc. **4.** act of smoking tobacco. **5.** *Am.* a spell at smoking a pipe, cigar, etc.: *a short smoke.* —*v.* **1.** give off smoke or steam, or something like it. **2.** expose to the action of smoke. **3.** cure (meat, fish, etc.) by smoking. **4.** drive (out) by smoke, or as if by smoke. **5.** draw into the mouth and puff out the smoke of burning tobacco or the like. **6.** make, bring, pass, etc., by smoking. **7.** color, darken, or stain with smoke. **8.** smoke out. **a.** drive out with smoke. **b.** find out and make known. [OE *smoca*] —Syn. **2.** find, fume, reek, vapor.

smoke·house (smōk′hous′), *n. Am.* a building or place in which meat, fish, etc., are treated with smoke to keep them from spoiling.

smoke·less (smōk′lĭs), *adj.* **1.** making or giving off little or no smoke: *smokeless powder.* **2.** having little or no smoke.

smok·er (smōk′ər), *n.* **1.** person who smokes tobacco. **2.** Also, **smoking car,** *Am.* a railroad car or a part of it where smoking is allowed. **3.** *Am.* an informal gathering of men for smoking and entertainment.

smoke screen, mass of thick smoke used to hide a ship, airplane, etc., from the enemy.

smoke·stack (smōk′stak′), *n.* **1.** a tall chimney. **2.** pipe that discharges smoke, etc.

smok·y (smōk′ĭ), *adj.,* **smok·i·er, smok·i·est. 1.** giving off much smoke. **2.** full of smoke. **3.** darkened or stained with smoke. **4.** like smoke or suggesting smoke: *a smoky taste.* —**smok′i·ly,** *adv.* —**smok′i·ness,** *n.*

Smoky Mountains. See Great Smoky Mountains.

smol·der (smōl′dər), *v.* **1.** burn and smoke without flame. **2.** exist inwardly with little or no outward sign. **3.** show suppressed feeling: *the angry man's eyes smoldered.* —*n.* a slow, smoky burning without flame; smoldering fire. Also, **smoulder.** [var. of ME *smorther* SMOTHER] —**smol′der·ing·ly,** *adv.*

Smol·lett (smol′ĭt), *n.* **Tobias,** 1721–1771, English novelist.

smooth (smūth), *adj.* **1.** having an even surface, like glass, silk, or still water; flat; level: *smooth stones.* **2.** free from unevenness or roughness: *smooth sailing.* **3.** without lumps: *smooth sauce.* **4.** without hair: *a smooth face.* **5.** without trouble or difficulty; easy: *a smooth course of affairs.* **6.** calm; serene: *a smooth temper.* **7.** polished; pleasant; polite: *a smooth talker.* **8.** insincerely pleasant and polite. **9.** not harsh in sound or taste: *smooth verses, smooth wine.* —*v.* **1.** make smooth or smoother. **2.** make calmer. **3.** make easy. **4.** remove (projections, etc.). **5.** smooth over, make (something) seem less wrong or unpleasant. —*adv.* in a smooth manner. —*n.* **1.** act of smoothing. **2.** smooth part or place. [OE *smōth*] —**smooth′er,** *n.* —**smooth′ly,** *adv.* —**smooth′ness,** *n.* —Syn. *adj.* **1.** plain, sleek, glossy. **6.** placid, unruffled.

smooth·bore (smūth′bôr′; -bōr′), *Am.* —*adj.* not rifled. —*n.* a smoothbore gun.

smooth-tongued (smūth′tungd′), *adj.* speaking smoothly; agreeable; suave; plausible.

smor·gas·bord, smör·gås·bord (smôr′gəs·bôrd), *n. Am.* an elaborate Scandinavian meal, featuring a large variety of hors d'oeuvres. [< Sw., lit., bread-and-butter table]

smote (smōt), *v.* pt. of smite.

smoth·er (smuth′ər), *v.* **1.** make unable to get air; kill by depriving of air. **2.** be unable to breathe freely; suffocate. **3.** cover thickly. **4.** deaden or put out by covering thickly: *smother a fire.* **5.** keep back; check; suppress: *he smothered a sharp reply.* **6.** cook in a covered pot or baking dish: *smothered chicken.* —*n.* cloud of dust, smoke, spray, etc. [ME *smorther,* n. < OE *smorian* suffocate] —**smoth′er·er,** *n.*

smoul·der (smōl′dər), *v., n.* smolder.

smudge (smuj), *n., v.,* **smudged, smudg·ing.** —*n.* **1.** a dirty mark; smear. **2.** a smoky fire made to drive away insects or to protect fruit from frost. —*v.* mark with dirty streaks; smear. —**smudg′y,** *adj.* —**smudg′i·ly,** *adv.* —**smudg′i·ness,** *n.*

smug (smug), *adj.,* **smug·ger, smug·gest. 1.** too pleased with one's own goodness, cleverness, respectability, etc.; self-satisfied; complacent. **2.** sleek; neat; trim. [prob. < Du., LG *smuk* spruce, adj.] —**smug′ly,** *adv.* —**smug′ness,** *n.*

smug·gle (smug′əl), *v.,* **-gled, -gling. 1.** bring into or take out of a country secretly and against the law. **2.** bring, take, put, etc., secretly. [< LG *smuggeln*] —**smug′gler,** *n.*

smut (smut), *n., v.,* **smut·ted, smut·ting.** —*n.* **1.** soot, dirt, etc. **2.** place soiled with smut. **3.** indecent, obscene talk or writing; obscenity. **4.** a plant disease in which the ears of grain are changed to a black dust. —*v.* **1.** soil or be soiled with smut. **2.** become affected with smut. [OE *smitte*; infl. by *smudge, smutch*]

smutch (smuch), *v., n.* smudge.

Smuts (smuts), *n.* **Jan Christiaan,** 1870–1950, South African political leader and general.

smut·ty (smut′ĭ), *adj.,* **-ti·er, -ti·est. 1.** soiled with smut, soot, etc.; dirty. **2.** indecent; obscene. **3.** having the plant disease called smut. —**smut′ti·ly,** *adv.* —**smut′ti·ness,** *n.*

Smyr·na (smér′nə), *n.* former name of Izmir.

Sn, *Chem.* tin. [< L *stannum*]

snack (snak), *n.* **1.** a light meal. **2.** share; portion. [< MLG *snakken*]

snaf·fle (snaf′əl), *n., v.,* **-fled, -fling.** —*n.* a slender, jointed bit used on a bridle. —*v.* **1.** put a snaffle on (a horse, etc.). **2.** control or manage by a snaffle. [cf. Du. *snavel* beak]

sna·fu (sna·fū′), *adj., v.,* **-fued, -fu·ing.** *Slang.* —*adj.* being in great disorder; snarled; confused. —*v.* **1.** put in disorder or in a chaotic state. **2.** mishandle. [from initial letters of "situation normal—all fouled up"]

snag (snag), *n., v.,* **snagged, snag·ging.** —*n.* **1.** *Am.* tree or branch held fast in a river or lake. **2.** any sharp or rough projecting point, such as the broken end of a branch. **3.** a hidden or unexpected obstacle. —*v.* **1.** *Am.* run or catch on a snag. **2.** hinder. [? < Scand. (dial. Norw.) *snage* point of land] —**snagged,** *adj.* —**snag′gy,** *adj.*

snag·gle·tooth (snag′əl·tüth′), *n., pl.* **-teeth.** tooth that grows apart from or beyond the others. —**snag′gle-toothed′,** *adj.*

snail (snāl), *n.* **1.** a small, soft-bodied mollusk that crawls very slowly. Most snails have spirally coiled shells on their backs into which they can withdraw for protection. **2.** a lazy, slow-moving person. [OE *snegel*]

Snail

snake (snāk), *n., v.,* **snaked, snak·ing.** —*n.* **1.** a long, slender, crawling reptile without limbs. Some snakes are venomous. **2.** a sly, treacherous person. —*v.* **1.** move, wind, or curve like a snake. **2.** *Am., Colloq.* drag; haul. **3.** *Colloq.* jerk. [OE *snaca*] —**snake′like′,** *adj.*

snak·y (snāk′ĭ), *adj.,* **snak·i·er, snak·i·est. 1.** of a snake or snakes. **2.** like a snake; like the curving and turning of a snake; twisting; winding. **3.** having many snakes. **4.** sly; venomous; treacherous. —**snak′i·ly,** *adv.* —**snak′i·ness,** *n.*

snap (snap), *v.,* **snapped, snap·ping,** *n., adj.*

adv. —*v.* **1.** make or cause to make a sudden, sharp sound: *this wood snaps as it burns.* **2.** move, shut, catch, etc., with a snap: *the latch snapped.* **3.** break suddenly or sharply: *the violin string snapped.* **4.** become suddenly unable to endure a strain: *his nerves snapped.* **5.** make a sudden, quick bite or snatch: *the dog snapped up the meat.* **6.** seize suddenly: *she snapped at the chance to go to Europe.* **7.** speak quickly and sharply: *"Silence!" snapped the teacher.* **8.** move quickly and sharply: *the soldiers snapped to attention.* **9.** *Am.* take a snapshot of. **10.** snap into it, *Am., Colloq.* move quickly; hurry. —*n.* **1.** a quick, sharp sound. **2.** a sudden, sharp breaking or the sound of breaking. **3.** a quick, sudden bite or snatch. **4.** quick, sharp speech. **5.** *Am., Colloq.* liveliness; dash; vim. **6.** a short spell of weather: *a cold snap.* **7.** fastener; clasp, esp. one making a snapping sound. **8.** a thin, crisp cooky. **9.** *Am., Colloq.* snapshot. **10.** *Am., Slang.* an easy job, piece of work, etc. —*adj.* **1.** *Am.* made or done suddenly; offhand: *snap judgment.* **2.** that moves, shuts, catches, etc., with a snap. **3.** *Slang.* easy. —*adv.* in a brisk or sharp manner. [< MDu., MLG *snappen*]

snap·drag·on (snap′drag′ən), *n.* a garden plant with showy flowers of crimson, purple, white, yellow, etc.

snap·per (snap′ər), *n.* **1.** person or thing that snaps. **2.** a snapping turtle. **3.** a red fish of tropical seas used for food.

snapping turtle, *Am.* a large, savage turtle of American rivers that has powerful jaws with which it snaps at its prey.

snap·pish (snap′ish), *adj.* **1.** apt to snap. **2.** quick and sharp in speech or manner; impatient. —**snap′pish·ly,** *adv.* —**snap′pish·ness,** *n.* —Syn. **2.** testy, crabbed, cross, irascible, petulant.

snap·py (snap′i), *adj.,* **-pi·er, -pi·est. 1.** snappish; sharp. **2.** quick or sudden. **3.** snapping or crackling in sound: *a snappy fire.* **4.** *Colloq.* having snap, crispness, smartness, liveliness, etc. —**snap′pi·ly,** *adv.* —**snap′pi·ness,** *n.*

snap·shot (snap′shot′), *n., v.,* -shot·ted, -shot·ting. —*n.* **1.** photograph taken in an instant. **2.** a quick shot taken without time for careful aim. —*v.* take a snapshot of.

snare (snār), *n., v.,* snared, snar·ing. —*n.* **1.** noose for catching small animals and birds. **2.** trap. **3.** one of the strings of gut or rawhide stretched across the bottom of a snare drum. —*v.* **1.** catch with a snare. **2.** trap: *snared by a lie.* [< Scand. *snara*] —**snar′er,** *n.*

snare drum, a small drum with strings of gut or rawhide stretched across the bottom to make a rattling sound.

snarl[1] (snärl), *v.* **1.** growl sharply and show one's teeth. **2.** speak harshly in a sharp, angry tone. **3.** say or express with a snarl. —*n.* **1.** act of snarling. **2.** a sharp, angry growl. **3.** sharp, angry words. [earlier *snar*; cf. MDu., MLG *snarren* rattle; akin to SNORE] —**snarl′er,** *n.* —**snarl′ing,** *adj.* —**snarl′ing·ly,** *adv.*

snarl[2] (snärl), *n.* **1.** tangle: *she combed the snarls out of her hair.* **2.** confusion: *his legal affairs were in a snarl.* —*v.* **1.** tangle or become tangled. **2.** confuse. [ult. < *snare* or its source] —**snarl′y,** *adj.*

snatch (snach), *v.* **1.** seize suddenly; grasp hastily. **2.** take suddenly. **3.** save or attain by quick action: *snatch victory from defeat.* **4.** snatch at, **a.** try to seize or grasp; seize; grasp. **b.** eagerly take advantage of. —*n.* **1.** act of snatching. **2.** a short time. **3.** a small amount; bit; scrap. [cf. MDu. *snakken*] —**snatch′er,** *n.* —Syn. *v.* **1.** grab, catch, snap. **2.** pluck, wrest.

snatch·y (snach′i), *adj.* done or occurring in snatches; disconnected. —**snatch′i·ly,** *adv.*

sneak (snēk), *v.* **1.** move in a stealthy, sly way. **2.** get, put, pass, take, in a stealthy, sly way. **3.** *Colloq.* steal. **4.** act in a mean, contemptible, cowardly way. **5.** sneak out of, avoid by slyness. —*n.* **1.** act of sneaking. **2.** person who sneaks; cowardly, contemptible person. [cf. OE *snican*] —**sneak′ing,** *adj.* —**sneak′ing·ly,** *adv.* —**sneak′y,** *adj.* —**sneak′i·ly,** *adv.* —**sneak′i·ness,** *n.* —Syn. *v.* **1.** slink, skulk, lurk.

sneak·er (snēk′ər), *n.* **1.** *Am., Colloq.* a light canvas shoe with a soft rubber sole. **2.** a sneak.

sneak thief, person who takes advantage of open doors, windows, or other easy opportunities to steal.

sneer (snir), *v.* **1.** show scorn or contempt by looks or words. **2.** utter with scorn or contempt. **3.** bring, put, force, etc., by sneering. —*n.* look or words expressing scorn or contempt. [ME *snere(n)*; akin to SNORE, SNARL] —**sneer′er,** *n.* —**sneer′ing,** *adj.* —**sneer′ing·ly,** *adv.* —Syn. *v.* **1.** scoff, jeer, gibe, flout, mock.

sneeze (snēz), *v.,* sneezed, sneez·ing, *n.* —*v.* **1.** expel air suddenly and violently through the nose and mouth by an involuntary spasm. **2.** sneeze at, *Colloq.* treat with contempt; despise. —*n.* a sudden, violent expelling of air through the nose and mouth. [var. of earlier *fnese(n)*, OE *fnēosan*] —**sneez′er,** *n.* —**sneez′ing,** *n.*

snick·er (snik′ər), **snig·ger** (snig′ər), *n.* a half-suppressed and usually disrespectful laugh; sly or silly laugh; giggle. —*v.* laugh in this way. [imit.] —**snick′er·er, snig′ger·er,** *n.* —**snick′er·ing·ly, snig′ger·ing·ly,** *adv.*

snide (snīd), *adj. Colloq.* **1.** slyly insinuating. **2.** derogatory.

sniff (snif), *v.* **1.** draw air through the nose in short, quick breaths that can be heard. **2.** clear one's nasal passages thus. **3.** smell with sniffs. **4.** try the smell of. **5.** draw in through the nose with the breath: *he sniffed the medicine.* **6.** suspect; detect. —*n.* **1.** act or sound of sniffing. **2.** a single breathing in of something; breath. [akin to *snivel*] —**sniff′er,** *n.* —**sniff′ing·ly,** *adv.* —**sniff′y,** *adj.*

snif·fle (snif′əl), *v.,* -fled, -fling, *n.* —*v.* **1.** breathe audibly through a partly clogged nose. **2.** sniff again and again. —*n.* **1.** a sniffling. **2.** the sniffles, **a.** fit of sniffling; tendency to sniffle. **b.** a slight cold in the head. —**snif′fler,** *n.*

snip (snip), *v.,* snipped, snip·ping, *n.* —*v.* cut with a small, quick stroke or series of strokes with scissors. —*n.* **1.** act of snipping. **2.** a small piece cut off. **3.** *Colloq.* a small or unimportant person. [< Du., LG *snippen*]

snipe (snīp), *n., pl.* snipes or (*esp. collectively*) snipe, *v.,* sniped, snip·ing. —*n.* any of various marsh birds with long bills. —*v.* **1.** hunt snipe. **2.** shoot, as at soldiers one at a time as a sportsman shoots at game; shoot from a concealed place. [< Scand. *snīpa*] —**snip′er,** *n.*

Snipe (ab. 11 in. long from tip of beak to tip of tail)

snip·pet (snip′it), *n.* **1.** a small piece snipped off. **2.** *Colloq.* a small or unimportant person.

snip·py (snip′i), *adj.,* -pi·er, -pi·est. **1.** *Colloq.* sharp; curt. **2.** *Colloq.* haughty; disdainful. **3.** made up of scraps or fragments. —**snip′pi·ness,** *n.*

snitch[1] (snich), *v. Slang.* snatch; steal. —**snitch′er,** *n.*

snitch[2] (snich), *Slang.* —*v.* be an informer; tell tales. —*n.* informer. —**snitch′er,** *n.*

sniv·el (sniv′əl), *v.,* -eled, -el·ing; *esp. Brit.* -elled, -el·ling, *n.* —*v.* **1.** cry with sniffling. **2.** put on a show of grief; whine. **3.** run at the nose; sniffle. —*n.* **1.** whining. **2.** sniffling. [akin to OE *snofl* mucus] —**sniv′el·er,** *esp. Brit.* **sniv′el·ler,** *n.*

snob (snob), *n.* person who cares too much for rank, wealth, position, etc., and too little for real merit; person who tries too hard to please those above him and too little to please those below him. —**snob′ber·y,** *n.* —**snob′bish,** *adj.* —**snob′bish·ly,** *adv.* —**snob′bish·ness,** *n.*

snood (snüd), *n.* **1.** band or ribbon formerly worn around the hair by young unmarried women in Scotland and northern England. **2.** net or bag worn over a woman's hair. **3.** a baglike hat. —*v.* bind (hair) with a snood. [OE *snōd*]

snoop (snüp), *Am., Colloq.* —*v.* go about in a sneaking, prying way; prowl; pry. —*n.* **1.** person who snoops. **2.** act of snooping. [< Du. *snoepen* eat in secret] —**snoop′er,** *n. Am.* —**snoop′y,** *adj.*

snoot·y (snōōt′ĭ), *adj.*, snoot·i·er, snoot·i·est. *U.S. Colloq.* snobbish; conceited.

snooze (snōōz), *v.*, snoozed, snooz·ing, *n. Colloq.* —*v.* take a nap; sleep; doze. —*n.* nap; doze.

snore (snōr; snôr), *v.*, snored, snor·ing, *n.* —*v.* breathe during sleep with a harsh, rough sound. —*n.* the sound so made. [ME *snore(n)*]

snor·kel (snôr′kəl), *n.* a periscopelike intake and exhaust shaft for Diesel engines which allows submarines to remain submerged for a very long period of time. Also, schnorkle, schnorkel. [< LG, slang for nose < unrecorded MLG *snorkeln*, frequentative of *snorken* snore because it is the nose of the submarine)]

snort (snôrt), *v.* 1. force the breath violently through the nose with a loud, harsh sound: *the horse snorted.* 2. make a sound like this. 3. show contempt, defiance, anger, etc., by snorting. 4. say or express with a snort. —*n.* act of snorting; the sound made. [< *snore*] —snort′er, *n.*

snout (snout), *n.* 1. the projecting part of an animal's head that contains the nose, mouth, and jaws. Pigs, dogs, and crocodiles have snouts. 2. anything like an animal's snout. 3. *Colloq.* a large or ugly nose. [ME *snoute*]

snout beetle, *Am.* a small, snouted beetle that eats grain, nuts, and fruit.

snow (snō), *n.* 1. water vapor frozen into crystals that fall to earth in soft, white flakes and spread upon it as a white layer. 2. a fall of snow. 3. *Poetic.* pure whiteness. 4. *Slang.* cocaine or heroin. —*v.* 1. fall as snow: *snow all day.* 2. let fall or scatter as snow. 3. cover, block up, etc., with snow or as if with snow. 4. snow in, *Am.* shut in by snow. 5. snow under, a. cover with snow. b. *Am., Colloq.* overwhelm. [OE *snāw*]

snow·ball (snō′bôl′), *n.* 1. ball made of snow pressed together. 2. *Am.* shrub with white flowers in large clusters like balls. —*v.* 1. throw balls of snow at. 2. increase rapidly by additions like a snowball. —snow′ball′ing, *n.*

snow·bank (snō′bangk′), *n.* a large mass or drift of snow.

snow·ber·ry (snō′ber′ĭ), *n.*, *pl.* -ries. *Am.* 1. a North American shrub that bears clusters of white berries in the fall. 2. the berry.

snow·bird (snō′bėrd′), *n.* 1. a small American bird that has a slate-gray back and a white breast, and is often seen in flocks during the winter. 2. the snow bunting.

snow·blind (snō′blīnd′), *adj.* temporarily or partly blind from exposure of the eyes to the glare of snow. —snow blindness.

snow bunting, a small, white finch with black and brownish markings that inhabits cold regions.

snow-capped (snō′kapt′), *adj.* having its top covered with snow.

snow·drift (snō′drift′), *n.* 1. mass or bank of snow piled up by the wind. 2. snow driven before the wind.

snow·drop (snō′drop′), *n.* a small plant with white flowers that blooms early in the spring.

snow·fall (snō′fôl′), *n.* 1. a fall of snow. 2. amount of snow falling in a certain time and area.

snow·flake (snō′flāk′), *n.* a small, feathery piece of snow.

snow job, *Am., Slang.* something used to overwhelm, as a flow of fast, persuasive talk.

snow·plow (snō′plou′), *n. Am.* machine for clearing away snow from streets, railroad tracks, etc.

snow·shed (snō′shed′), *n. Am.* a long shed built over a railroad track to protect it from snowslides.

snow·shoe (snō′shōō′), *n. Am.* a light, wooden frame with strips of leather stretched across it. Trappers in the far North wear snowshoes on their feet to keep from sinking in deep, soft snow.

snow·slide (snō′slīd′), *n. Am.* 1. the sliding down of a mass of snow on a steep slope. 2. the mass of snow that slides.

snow·storm (snō′stôrm′), *n. Am.* storm with much snow.

snow-white (snō′hwīt′), *adj.* white as snow.

snow·y (snō′ĭ), *adj.*, snow·i·er, snow·i·est. 1. having snow. 2. covered with snow. 3. like snow; white as snow. —snow′i·ly, *adv.* —snow′i·ness, *n.*

snub (snub), *v.*, snubbed, snub·bing, *n.*, *adj.* —*v.* 1. treat coldly, scornfully, or with contempt. 2. check or stop (a boat, horse, etc.) suddenly. —*n.* 1. cold, scornful, or disdainful treatment. 2. a sudden check or stop. 3. a sharp rebuke. —*adj.* short and turned up at the tip: *a snub nose.* [< Scand. *snubba* reprove] —snub′ber, *n.*

snub-nosed (snub′nōzd′), *adj.* having a snub nose.

snuff¹ (snuf), *v.* 1. draw in through the nose; draw up into the nose. 2. examine by smelling; sniff; smell. 3. take powdered tobacco into the nose by snuffing; use snuff. —*n.* 1. powdered tobacco taken into the nose. 2. act of snuffing. 3. amount snuffed. 4. *Slang.* up to snuff, up to the usual standards. [< MDu. *snuffen* sniff] —snuff′y, *adj.* —snuff′i·ness, *n.*

snuff² (snuf), *v.* 1. cut or pinch off the burned wick of. 2. put out (a candle); extinguish. 3. snuff out, a. put out; extinguish. b. put an end to suddenly and completely. —*n.* the burned part of a candlewick. —snuff′er, *n.*

snuff·ers (snuf′ərz), *n.pl.* small tongs for taking off burned wick or putting out the light of a candle.

Snuffers

snuf·fle (snuf′əl) *v.*, -fled, -fling, *n.* —*v.* 1. breathe noisily through a partly clogged nose. 2. smell; sniff. 3. speak, sing, etc., through the nose or with a nasal tone. —*n.* 1. act or sound of snuffling. 2. the snuffles, fit of snuffling; stuffed-up condition of the nose, caused by a cold, hay fever, etc. [ult. < *snuff¹* or its source] —snuf′fler, *n.* —snuf′fling·ly, *adv.*

snug (snug), *adj.*, snug·ger, snug·gest, *v.*, snugged, snug·ging, *adv.* —*adj.* 1. comfortable; warm; sheltered: *a snug corner.* 2. neat; trim; compact: *a snug cabin.* 3. well-built; seaworthy: *a snug ship.* 4. fitting closely. 5. small but sufficient: *a snug income.* —*v.* make snug. —*adv.* in a snug manner. [cf. Sw. *snygg* neat, trim] —snug′ly, *adv.* —snug′ness, *n.*

snug·gle (snug′əl), *v.*, -gled, -gling. 1. lie or press closely for warmth or comfort or from affection; nestle. 2. draw closely. [< *snug*]

so¹ (sō; *unstressed before consonants* sə), *adv.* 1. in this way; in that way; in the same way; as shown: *hold your pen so.* 2. as stated: *is that really so?* 3. in the aforesaid state or condition: *it has long been so.* 4. to this degree; to that degree: *do not walk so fast.* 5. to such a degree; to the same degree: *he was not so cold as she was.* 6. very: *you are so kind.* 7. very much: *my head aches so.* 8. for this reason; for that reason; accordingly; therefore: *the dog was hungry; so we fed it.* 9. likewise; also: *she likes dogs and so does he.* 10. and so, a. likewise; also. b. accordingly. 11. so as, with the result or purpose. 12. so far, up to this point. 13. so that, a. with the result that. b. with the purpose that. c. provided that; if. —*conj.* 1. with the result that; in order that: *go away so I can rest.* 2. with the purpose or intention that: *I did the work so he would not need to.* 3. on the condition that; if: *so it be done, I care not who does it.* —*interj.* 1. well! 2. let it be that way! all right! 3. is that true? —*pron.* 1. more or less; approximately: *a pound or so.* 2. the same: *a drunkard usually remains so.* [OE *swā*]

so² (sō), *n. Music.* sol.

So., South; south; southern.

soak (sōk), *v.* 1. make very wet; wet through; saturate. 2. let remain in water or other liquid until wet clear through. 3. become very wet; remain until wet clear through. 4. make its way; enter; go: *water will soak through the earth.* 5. suck: *a sponge soaks up water.* 6. drink heavily. 7. *Am., Slang.* punish severely; strike hard; defeat thoroughly. 8. *Am., Slang.* make pay too much; charge or tax heavily. 9. soak up, a. absorb. b. take into the mind. —*n.* 1. act or process of soaking. 2. state of being soaked. 3.

Slang. a heavy drinker. [OE *socian*] —**soak′er,** *n.* —**soak′ing·ly,** *adv.*

so-and-so (sō′ənd·sō′), *n., pl.* **-sos.** some person or thing not named.

soap (sōp), *n.* **1.** substance used for washing, usually made of a fat and caustic soda or potash. **2.** *Chem.* any metallic salt of an acid derived from a fat. **3.** *Am., Slang.* money, esp. as used for bribery. —*v.* rub or treat with soap. [OE *sāpe*]

soap·ber·ry (sōp′ber′i; –bər·i), *n., pl.* **-ries.** **1.** the fruit of any of certain tropical trees, used as a substitute for soap. **2.** any of the trees bearing such fruit.

soap·box (sōp′boks′), *Am. n.* an empty box used as a temporary platform by agitators or other speakers addressing gatherings on the streets. —*v.* address an audience on the public street. —**soap′box′er,** *n. Am.*

soap opera, *Am.* a daytime radio or television drama presented in serial form, usually featuring emotional domestic situations.

soap·stone (sōp′stōn′), *n.* stone that feels somewhat like soap, used for griddles, hearths, etc.

soap·suds (sōp′sudz′), *n.pl.* bubbles and foam made with soap and water.

soap·y (sōp′i), *adj.,* **soap·i·er, soap·i·est.** **1.** covered with soap or soapsuds. **2.** containing soap. **3.** like soap; smooth; greasy. —**soap′i·ly,** *adv.* —**soap′i·ness,** *n.*

soar (sôr; sōr), *v.* **1.** fly at a great height; fly upward: *an eagle soars.* **2.** rise beyond what is common and ordinary; aspire: *his ambition soared to the throne.* **3.** fly or move through the air by means of rising air currents. —*n.* **1.** act of soaring. **2.** height attained in soaring. [< OF *essorer,* ult. < L *ex-* out + *aura* breeze] —**soar′er,** *n.* —**soar′ing·ly,** *adv.*

sob (sob), *v.,* **sobbed, sob·bing,** *n., adj.* —*v.* **1.** cry or sigh with short, quick breaths. **2.** put, send, etc., by sobbing: *she sobbed herself to sleep.* **3.** make a sound like a sob. **4.** utter with sobs. —*n.* a catching of short, quick breaths because of grief, etc. —*adj. Am., Slang.* intended to arouse feelings of pity, sadness, etc.: *sob stories.* [prob. ult. imit.] —**sob′bing,** *n.* —**sob′bing·ly,** *adv.*

so·ber (sō′bər), *adj.* **1.** not drunk. **2.** temperate; moderate: *a sober, hard-working life.* **3.** quiet; serious; solemn: *a sober expression.* **4.** calm; sensible: *a judge's sober opinion.* **5.** free from exaggeration: *sober facts.* **6.** quiet in color: *dressed in sober gray.* **7.** showing self-control. —*v.* **1.** make or become sober. **2. sober up** or **off,** recover from too much alcoholic drink. [< OF < L *sobrius*] —**so′ber·ly,** *adv.* —**so′ber·ness,** *n.* —**Syn.** *adj.* **1.** unintoxicated. **2.** abstinent, abstemious. **4.** dispassionate, rational, deliberate, sane. **6.** subdued, somber, dull. —**Ant.** *adj.* **1.** intoxicated, drunk. **3.** light-hearted, gay.

so·ber-mind·ed (sō′bər·mīn′did), *adj.* having or showing a sober mind; self-controlled; sensible. —**so′ber-mind′ed·ness,** *n.*

so·bri·e·ty (sə·brī′ə·ti), *n., pl.* **-ties.** **1.** soberness. **2.** temperance in the use of strong drink. **3.** moderation. **4.** quietness; seriousness.

so·bri·quet (sō′brə·kā′), *n.* nickname. Also, **soubriquet.** [< F]

so-called (sō′kôld′), *adj.* **1.** called thus. **2.** called thus improperly or incorrectly. ➤ **so-called.** If you have to use *so-called,* don't duplicate the idea by putting the name of the so-called object in quotes: Not *the so-called "champion,"* but *the so-called champion.* The word is rather stiff, and in informal writing quotations marks would often be used instead *(the "champion"). So-called* is usually hyphened when it precedes its principal word but not when it follows: *Their so-called liberal views were merely an echo of the conservative attitude* [their "liberal" views were . . .]. *Their justice, so called, smacked of partiality.*

soc·cer (sok′ər), *n.* game played between two teams of eleven men each, using a round ball; association football. The ball may be struck with any part of the body except the hands and arms. [< *assoc.,* abbrev. of *association*]

so·cia·ble (sō′shə·bəl), *adj.* **1.** liking company; friendly. **2.** marked by conversation and companionship: *we had a sociable afternoon together.* —*n. Am.* an informal social gathering. —**so′cia·bil′i·ty, so′cia·ble·ness,** *n.* —**so′cia·bly,** *adv.* —**Syn.** *adj.* **1.** affable, agreeable, genial.

so·cial (sō′shəl), *adj.* **1.** pertaining to or concerned with human beings in their relations to each other. **2.** of or dealing with the living conditions, health, etc., of human beings: *social problems.* **3.** living, or liking to live, with others: *man is a social being.* **4.** for companionship or friendliness; pertaining to companionship or friendliness: *a social club.* **5.** liking company: *she has a social nature.* **6.** connected with fashionable society: *a social leader.* **7.** living together in organized communities: *ants and bees are social insects.* **8.** venereal. —*n.* a social gathering or party. [< L, < *socius* companion, orig. adj., sharing in] —**so′cial·ly,** *adv.* —**so′cial·ness,** *n.*

so·cial·ism (sō′shəl·iz·əm), *n.* **1.** theory or system of social organization by which the means of production and distribution are owned collectively and controlled through the government. **2.** a political movement advocating or associated with this system. —**so′cial·ist,** *n., adj.* —**so′cial·is′tic,** *adj.*

Socialist Party, political party that favors and supports socialism.

so·cial·ite (sō′shəl·īt), *n.* a prominent person in society.

so·cial·ize (sō′shəl·īz), *v.,* **-ized, -iz·ing.** **1.** make social. **2.** make fit for living with others. **3.** adapt to community needs. **4.** establish or regulate in accordance with socialism. —**so′cial·i·za′tion,** *n.*

socialized medicine, the providing of medical care and hospital services for all classes of society, esp. through governmental subsidization and administration.

social register, *Am.* list of people who are prominent in fashionable society.

social science, study of people, their activities, and their customs in relationship to others. History, sociology, economics, and civics are social sciences.

social security, system of federal old-age pensions for employed persons. The government pays part of the pension, part is deducted from the employee's salary, and part is paid by his employer.

social work, social service, work directed toward the betterment of social conditions in a community. Child welfare bureaus, milk stations, district nursing organizations, etc., are forms of social work. —**social worker.**

so·ci·e·ty (sə·sī′ə·ti), *n., pl.* **-ties.** **1.** group of persons joined together for a common purpose or by a common interest. A club, a fraternity, a lodge, or an association may be called a society. **2.** all the people; the people of any particular time or place; their activities and customs: *the good of society demands that wrongdoing be punished.* **3.** company; companionship. **4.** social intercourse. **5.** fashionable people; their doings. [< L *societas* < *socius* sharing in]

Society Islands, group of French islands in the S Pacific that includes Tahiti.

Society of Friends. See friend (def. 4).

Society of Jesus. See Jesuit.

so·ci·ol·o·gy (sō′si·ol′ə·ji; –shi-), *n.* study of the nature, origin, and development of human society and community life; science of social facts. Sociology deals with the facts of crime, poverty, marriage, divorce, the church, the school, etc. [< L *socius* companion + -LOGY] —**so′ci·o·log′i·cal** (sō′si·ə·loj′ə·kəl; –shi-), *adj.* —**so′ci·o·log′i·cal·ly,** *adv.* —**so′ci·ol′o·gist,** *n.*

sock[1] (sok), *n.* a short stocking, esp. one that reaches about halfway to the knee. [< L *soccus* a light shoe worn by actors in comedy]

sock[2] (sok), *Slang.* —*v.* strike or hit hard. —*n.* a hard blow. —*adv.* squarely; right.

āge, cāre, fär; ēqual, tėrm; īce; ōpen, ôrder; pùt, rüle, ūse; th, then; ə=a in about.

sock·et (sok′it), *n.* **1.** a hollow part or piece for receiving and holding something. Eyes are set in sockets. **2.** a connecting place for electric wires and plugs. [< AF *soket* < *soc* plowshare < Celtic]

Soc·ra·tes (sok′rə·tēz), *n.* 469–399 B.C., Athenian philosopher. —**So·crat·ic** (sō·krat′ik), *adj.*

Socratic method, use of a series of questions to lead a pupil to think, to make an opponent contradict himself, etc.

SOCKET
Ball-
and-
socket
joint

sod (sod), *n., v.,* **sod·ded, sod·ding.** —*n.* **1.** ground covered with grass. **2.** piece or layer of this containing the grass and its roots. —*v.* cover with sods. [< MDu., MLG *sode*]

so·da (sō′də), *n.* **1.** sodium carbonate; washing soda. **2.** sodium bicarbonate; baking soda. **3.** sodium hydroxide; caustic soda. **4.** soda water. **5.** soda water flavored with fruit juice or syrup, and often containing ice cream. [< Med.L]

soda ash, partly purified sodium carbonate.

so·dal·i·ty (sō·dal′ə·ti), *n., pl.* **-ties. 1.** fellowship; friendship. **2.** an association, society, or fraternity. **3.** in the Roman Catholic Church, a society with religious or charitable purposes. [< L, < *sodalis* sociable]

soda water, water charged with carbon dioxide to make it bubble and fizz, often served with the addition of syrup, ice cream, etc.

sod·den (sod′ən), *adj.* **1.** soaked through. **2.** heavy and moist. **3.** dull-looking; stupid. [old pp. of *seethe*] —**sod′den·ness,** *n.*

so·di·um (sō′di·əm), *n. Chem.* a soft, silver-white metallic element, Na, occurring in nature only in compounds. Salt and soda contain sodium. [< *soda*]

sodium bicarbonate, a powdery white substance, NaHCO₃, used in cooking, medicine, etc.; baking soda.

sodium carbonate, a salt, Na₂CO₃, that occurs in a powdery white form and in a hydrated crystalline form; washing soda. It is used for softening water, making soap and glass, etc.

sodium chloride, common salt, NaCl.

sodium hydroxide, a white solid, NaOH, that is a strong, corrosive alkali; caustic soda.

sodium nitrate, colorless crystals, NaNO₃, used in making fertilizers, explosives, etc.; Chile saltpeter.

Sod·om (sod′əm), *n. Bible.* an ancient city near the Dead Sea which was destroyed by fire from heaven because of the wickedness of its inhabitants. Gen. 18 and 19.

sod·om·y (sod′əm·i), *n.* unnatural sexual intercourse, esp. of one man with another or of a human being with an animal. [< OF *sodomie* < *Sodome* Sodom]

so·ev·er (sō·ev′ər), *adv.* **1.** in any case; in any way; in any degree: *no matter how long soever the work may take.* **2.** of any kind; at all.

so·fa (sō′fə), *n.* a long, upholstered seat or couch having a back and arms. [< F < Ar. *ṣoffah*]

So·fi·a (sō′fi·ə; sō·fē′ə), *n.* capital of Bulgaria.

soft (sôft; soft), *adj.* **1.** not hard; yielding readily to touch or pressure: *a soft pillow.* **2.** not hard compared with other things of the same kind: *lead is a soft metal.* **3.** not hard or sharp; gentle and graceful: *soft shadows, soft outlines.* **4.** fine in texture; not rough or coarse; smooth: *soft skin.* **5.** not loud: *a soft voice.* **6.** pleasant; mild; not sharp: *soft air.* **7.** not glaring or harsh: *soft light.* **8.** gentle; kind; tender: *a soft heart.* **9.** containing no mineral salts which interfere with the action of soap: *soft water.* **10.** *Colloq.* easy; easygoing: *a soft way to earn money.* **11.** weak; unmanly: *soft from lack of exercise.* **12.** silly; weak-minded: *he is soft in the head.* **13.** *Phonet.* pronounced as a fricative or an affricate, rather than as an explosive sound. The *c* and *g* in *city* and *gem* are "soft"; in *corn* and *get* they are "hard." —*adv.* softly; quietly; gently. —*n.* that which is soft; soft part. —*interj. Archaic.* hush! stop! [OE *sōfte*] —**soft′ish,** *adj.* —**soft′ly,** *adv.* —**soft′ness,** *n.* —**Syn.** *adj.* **1.** pliable, flexible. **5.** low. **8.** sympathetic.

soft·ball (sôft′bôl′; soft′-), *n. Am.* a modified kind of baseball employing a larger, softer ball.

soft-boiled (sôft′boild′; soft′-), *adj.* boiled only a little so as to keep (egg yolks, etc.) soft.

soft coal, bituminous coal.

soft drink, drink that contains no alcohol.

soft·en (sôf′ən; sof′-), *v.* **1.** make or become softer. **2.** lessen ability to resist invasion or attack through preliminary bombing, etc. —**soft′en·er,** *n.* —**soft′en·ing,** *n.* —**Syn. 1.** melt.

soft goods, textiles, groceries, etc. —**soft-goods** (sôft′gŭdz′; soft′-), *adj.*

soft-heart·ed (sôft′här′tid; soft′-), *adj.* gentle; kind; tender. —**soft′-heart′ed·ness,** *n.*

soft palate. See palate (def. 1).

soft soap, 1. a liquid or semiliquid soap. **2.** *Colloq.* flattery.

soft-soap (sôft′sōp′; soft′-), *v. Colloq.* flatter. —**soft′-soap′er,** *n.*

soft·wood (sôft′wŭd′; soft′-), *n.* **1.** in forestry, tree that has needles or does not have broad leaves. **2.** wood of such a tree.

soft·y (sôf′ti; sof′-), *n., pl.* **soft·ies.** *Colloq.* a person who is easily imposed upon.

sog·gy (sog′i), *adj.,* **-gi·er, -gi·est. 1.** thoroughly wet; soaked: *a soggy washcloth.* **2.** damp and heavy: *soggy bread.* —**sog′gi·ness,** *n.*

soil¹ (soil), *n.* **1.** ground; earth; dirt. **2.** a particular kind of earth: *sandy soil.* **3.** something thought of as a place for growth. **4.** land; country. [< AF < L *solium* seat, infl. by L *solum* soil] —**soiled,** *adj.*

soil² (soil), *v.* **1.** make dirty: *he soiled his clean clothes.* **2.** become dirty: *white shirts soil easily.* **3.** spot; stain: *the splashing paint soiled the wall.* **4.** disgrace; dishonor: *soil the family name.* **5.** corrupt morally. —*n.* a spot; stain. [< OF *soillier,* ult. < L *suile* pigsty < *sus* pig] —**Syn.** *v.* **1.** daub, begrime, besmirch. **4.** sully, defile.

soil bank, a program of the United States government for reducing farm surpluses by paying farmers in certain crops to leave a certain amount of acreage unplanted.

soi·ree, soi·rée (swä·rā′), *n.* an evening party or social gathering. [< F, < *soir* evening]

so·journ (*v.* sō·jėrn′, sō′jėrn; *n.* sō′jėrn), *v.* stay for a time. —*n.* a brief stay. [< OF *sojorner,* ult. < L *sub* under + *diurnus* of the day] —**so·journ′er,** *n.* —**so·journ′ment,** *n.*

Sol (sol), *n.* **1.** the Roman god of the sun, identified with the Greek god Helios. **2.** sun. [< L]

sol (sōl), *n. Music.* the fifth tone of the scale. Also, **so.** [see GAMUT]

sol·ace (sol′is), *n., v.,* **-aced, -ac·ing.** —*n.* comfort; relief. —*v.* comfort; relieve. [< OF < L *solacium* < *solari* console] —**sol′ace·ment,** *n.* —**Syn.** *n.* consolation, cheer.

so·lar (sō′lər), *adj.* **1.** of the sun: *a solar eclipse.* **2.** having to do with the sun: *solar phenomena.* **3.** coming from the sun: *solar energy.* **4.** measured or determined by the earth's motion in relation to the sun: *a solar year.* **5.** working by means of the sun's light or heat: *a solar machine.* [< L, < *sol* sun]

solar battery, a device to trap sunlight and convert it into electrical energy.

so·lar·i·um (sə·lãr′i·əm), *n., pl.* **-lar·i·a** (-lãr′i·ə). room, porch, etc., where people can lie or sit in the sun. [< L, < *sol* sun]

solar plexus, network of nerves situated at the upper part of the abdomen, behind the stomach and in front of the aorta.

solar system, sun and all the planets, satellites, comets, etc., that revolve around it.

sold (sōld), *v.* pt. and pp. of sell.

sol·der (sod′ər), *n.* **1.** metal or alloy that can be melted and used for joining or mending metal surfaces, parts, etc. **2.** anything that unites firmly or joins closely. —*v.* **1.** fasten, mend, or join with solder. **2.** unite firmly; join closely. **3.** mend; repair; patch. [< OF *soldure,* ult. < L *solidus* solid] —**sol′der·er,** *n.*

sol·dier (sōl′jər), *n.* **1.** man who serves in an army. **2.** an enlisted man in the army, not a commissioned officer. **3.** man having skill or experience in war. **4.** person who serves in any cause. —*v.* **1.** act or serve as a soldier. **2.** *Colloq.* pretend to work but do very little. [< OF, < *soulde* pay < L *solidus*, a Roman coin] —**sol′-dier·ly**, *adj.* —**sol′dier·li·ness**, *n.*

soldier of fortune, man serving or ready to serve as a soldier under any government for money, adventure, or pleasure.

sol·dier·y (sōl′jər·i), *n.* **1.** soldiers. **2.** military training or knowledge.

sole[1] (sōl), *adj.* **1.** one and only; single: *the sole survivor, sole heir.* **2.** only: *the sole grounds for action were based on hearsay.* **3.** of or for only one person or group and not others; exclusive: *the sole right of use.* **4.** without help; alone: *a sole undertaking.* **5.** *Law.* unmarried. [< L *solus*] —**sole′ness**, *n.*

sole[2] (sōl), *n.*, *v.*, **soled, sol·ing.** —*n.* **1.** the bottom or under surface of the foot. **2.** bottom of a shoe, slipper, boot, etc. **3.** piece cut in the same shape. **4.** the under surface; under part; bottom. —*v.* put a sole on. [< L *solea* < *solum* bottom, ground] —**soled,** *adj.*

sole[3] (sōl), *n.*, *pl.* **soles** or (*esp. collectively*) **sole.** a kind of flatfish. European sole is valued highly as food. [< F < L *solea,* orig., *sole*[2]]

sol·e·cism (sol′ə·siz·əm), *n.* **1.** violation of the grammatical or other accepted usages of a language; mistake in using words. "I done it" is a solecism. **2.** mistake in social behavior; breach of good manners or etiquette. **3.** any error. [< L < Gk. *soloikismos,* supposedly < *Soloi,* Greek colony in Cilicia] —**sol′e·cist,** *n.* —**sol′e·cis′tic,** *adj.* —**sol′e·cis′ti·cal·ly,** *adv.*

sole·ly (sōl′li), *adv.* **1.** as the only one or ones; alone: *solely responsible for the accident.* **2.** only: *the plant can be found solely in the United States.* **3.** wholly: *a solely fictitious story.*

sol·emn (sol′əm), *adj.* **1.** serious; grave; earnest: *a solemn face.* **2.** causing serious or grave thoughts. **3.** done with form and ceremony. **4.** connected with religion; sacred. **5.** legally correct. [< L *sollemnis*] —**sol′emn·ly,** *adv.* —**sol′-emn·ness,** *n.* —**Syn. 2.** impressive, sobering.

so·lem·ni·ty (sə·lem′nə·ti), *n.*, *pl.* **-ties. 1.** solemn feeling; seriousness; impressiveness. **2.** Often, **solemnities.** a solemn, formal ceremony.

sol·em·nize (sol′əm·nīz), *v.*, **-nized, -niz·ing. 1.** observe with ceremonies. **2.** hold or perform (a ceremony or service). **3.** make serious or grave. —**sol′em·ni·za′tion,** *n.*

sol-fa (sōl′fä′), *n.* system of singing the syllables *do, re, mi, fa, sol, la, ti, do* to tones of the scale. [< Ital., < *sol* + *fa.* See GAMUT.]

so·lic·it (sə·lis′it), *v.* **1.** try to obtain orders or business: *solicit for a business firm.* **2.** ask earnestly for: *solicit advice.* **3.** make appeals or requests: *solicit for contributions.* **4.** of a prostitute, accost men with immoral offers. **5.** influence to do wrong; tempt; entice. [< L *sol(l)icitare* < *sol(l)icitus* wholly moved] —**so·lic′i·ta′-tion,** *n.* —**Syn. 2.** request, beg.

so·lic·i·tor (sə·lis′ə·tər), *n.* **1.** person who entreats or requests. **2.** *Am.* person who seeks trade, business, donations, etc. **3.** *Law.* **a.** in England, a lawyer. A solicitor prepares a case, and a barrister pleads it. **b.** lawyer for a town, city, etc. —**so·lic′i·tor·ship′,** *n.*

solicitor general, *pl.* **solicitors general. 1.** a law officer who assists the attorney general and ranks next below him. **2.** *Am.* the chief law officer in a State having no attorney general.

so·lic·i·tous (sə·lis′ə·təs), *adj.* **1.** showing care or concern; anxious; concerned: *parents are solicitous for their children's progress.* **2.** desirous; eager. [< L *sol(l)icitus.* See SOLICIT.] —**so·lic′i·tous·ly,** *adv.* —**so·lic′i·tous·ness,** *n.*

so·lic·i·tude (sə·lis′ə·tūd), *n.* anxious care; anxiety; concern. —**so·lic·i·tu·di·nous** (sə·lis′ə·tū′də·nəs; -tū′-), *adj.*

sol·id (sol′id), *adj.* **1.** not a liquid or a gas: *solid particles floating in water.* **2.** not hollow: *a solid ball of matter.* **3.** having three dimensions; cubic: *a solid foot.* **4.** dense; thick; heavy: *solid masses of smoke.* **5.** strongly put together; hard; firm: *solid construction.* **6.** alike throughout: *the cloth is a solid blue.* **7.** firmly united:

the country was solid for peace. **8.** real; serious: *chemistry and physics are solid subjects.* **9.** genuine: *solid comfort.* **10.** that can be depended on: *he is a solid citizen.* **11.** having good judgment; sound; sensible; intelligent: *a solid book by a solid thinker.* **12.** financially sound or strong: *a solid business.* **13.** whole; entire: *I waited three solid hours.* **14.** undivided; continuous: *a solid row of houses.* **15.** having the lines of type not separated by leads; having few open spaces. **16.** having length, breadth, and thickness. **17.** written without a hyphen. *Earthworm* is a solid word. **18.** *Am., Colloq.* in favor; on a firm basis: *I was pretty solid with him.* **19.** *Slang.* excellent. —*n.* **1.** substance or body that is not a liquid or a gas. **2.** body that has length, breadth, and thickness. [< L *solidus*] —**sol′id·ly,** *adv.* —**sol′id·ness,** *n.* —**Syn. *adj.* 5.** compact, stable. **7.** unanimous. **9.** sound, real. **10.** reliable.

sol·i·dar·i·ty (sol′ə·dar′ə·ti), *n.*, *pl.* **-ties.** unity or fellowship arising from common responsibilities and interests.

so·lid·i·fy (sə·lid′ə·fī), *v.*, **-fied, -fy·ing. 1.** make or become solid; harden. **2.** unite firmly. —**so·lid′i·fi′a·ble,** *adj.* —**so·lid′i·fi·ca′tion,** *n.*

so·lid·i·ty (sə·lid′ə·ti), *n.*, *pl.* **-ties.** a being solid; firmness; hardness; density.

sol·i·dus (sol′ə·dəs), *n.*, *pl.* **-di** (-dī). **1.** a Roman gold coin introduced by Constantine. **2.** a sloping line (/) used to separate shillings from pence (as 2/6 for 2 shillings, 6 pence), and generally as a dividing line, as in dates, fractions, etc.

so·lil·o·quize (sə·lil′ə·kwīz), *v.*, **-quized, -quiz·ing. 1.** talk to oneself. **2.** speak a soliloquy. —**so·lil′o·quist** (sə·lil′ə·kwist), **so·lil′o·quiz′er,** *n.* —**so·lil′o·quiz′ing·ly,** *adv.*

so·lil·o·quy (sə·lil′ə·kwi), *n.*, *pl.* **-quies. 1.** a talking to oneself. **2.** speech made by an actor to himself when alone on the stage. It reveals his thoughts and feelings to the audience, but not to the other characters in the play. [< LL, < L *solus* alone + *loqui* speak]

sol·i·taire (sol′ə·tār), *n.* **1.** a card game played by one person. **2.** diamond or other gem set by itself. [< F < L *solitarius.* Doublet of SOLITARY.]

sol·i·tar·y (sol′ə·ter′i), *adj.*, *n.*, *pl.* **-tar·ies.** —*adj.* **1.** alone; single; only: *a solitary passenger.* **2.** without companions; away from people; lonely: *a solitary kind of life.* —*n.* person living alone, away from people. [< L *solitarius,* ult. < *solus* alone. Doublet of SOLITAIRE.] —**sol′i·tar′-i·ly,** *adv.* —**sol′i·tar′i·ness,** *n.* —**Syn. *adj.* 1.** lone, sole. **2.** unattended, remote, secluded.

sol·i·tude (sol′ə·tūd), *n.* **1.** a being alone. **2.** a lonely place. **3.** loneliness. [< L, < *solus* alone] —**Syn. 1.** seclusion, isolation.

sol·mi·za·tion (sol′mə·zā′shən), *n.* system of singing the syllables, esp. the sol-fa syllables, to the tones of the scale. [< F *solmisation,* ult. < *sol* + *mi.* See GAMUT.]

so·lo (sō′lō), *n.*, *pl.* **-los, -li** (-lē), *adj.*, *v.* —*n.* **1.** piece of music for one voice or instrument. **2.** anything done without a partner, companion, instructor, etc. **3.** *Cards.* **a.** any of certain games in which one person plays alone against others. **b.** bid to play without discarding. —*adj.* **1.** arranged for and performed by one voice or instrument. **2.** playing the solo part. **3.** without a partner, companion, instructor, etc.; alone. —*v.* fly alone. [< Ital., alone, < L *solus*]

so·lo·ist (sō′lō·ist), *n.* person who performs a solo or solos.

Sol·o·mon (sol′ə·mən), *n.* **1.** king of Israel, in the tenth century B.C., a son of David. Solomon was famous for his wisdom. I Kings 3:5–28. **2.** man of great wisdom.

Solomon Islands, group of islands in the S Pacific, NE of Australia.

Sol·o·mon's-seal (sol′ə·mənz·sēl′), *n.* a kind of plant that has small flowers hanging from the bases of the leaves and a rootstock with seallike scars.

So·lon (sō′lən; -lon), *n.* **1.** 638?–558? B.C., Athenian lawgiver. **2.** a wise man; sage. **3.** *Am.* member of a legislative assembly. —**So·lo·ni·an** (sō·lō′ni·ən), **So·lon·ic** (sō·lon′ik), *adj.*

so long, *Colloq.* good-by; farewell.

sol·stice (sol′stis), *n.* either of the two times in the year when the sun is at its greatest distance from the celestial equator. In the Northern Hemisphere, June 21 or 22, the summer solstice, is the longest day of the year and December 21 or 22, the winter solstice, is the shortest. [< OF < L *solstitium,* ult. < *sol* sun + *sistere* stand still] —**sol·sti·tial** (sol·stish′əl), *adj.*

sol·u·ble (sol′yə·bəl), *adj.* 1. that can be dissolved or made into liquid. 2. that can be solved. [< L *solubilis* < *solvere* dissolve] —**sol′u·bil′i·ty,** sol′u·ble·ness, *n.* —**sol′u·bly,** *adv.*

so·lu·tion (sə·lü′shən), *n.* 1. the solving of a problem. 2. explanation. 3. process of dissolving; changing of a solid or gas to a liquid by treatment with a liquid. 4. liquid or mixture formed by dissolving. 5. a separating into parts. 6. condition of being dissolved. Sugar and salt can be held in solution in water. [< L *solutio* a loosing < *solvere* loosen] —**so·lu′tion·al,** *adj.*

solve (solv), *v.,* **solved, solv·ing.** find the answer to; clear up; explain. [< L *solvere* loosen] —**solv′a·ble,** *adj.* —**solv′a·bil′i·ty,** solv′a·ble·ness, *n.* —**solv′er,** *n.*

sol·vent (sol′vənt), *adj.* 1. able to pay all that one owes. 2. able to dissolve. —*n.* 1. substance, usually a liquid, that can dissolve other substances. 2. thing that solves. [< L *solvens* loosening, paying] —**sol′ven·cy,** *n.*

Sol·y·man (sol′i·mən), *n.* 1494?–1566, sultan of the Turkish Empire at the height of its power, 1520–1566. Also, **Suleiman.**

So·ma·lia (sə·mä′lyə), *n.* republic in E Africa, including the former British and Italian Somaliland.

So·ma·li·land (sə·mä′li·land′), *n.* region in E Africa divided into French and (formerly) British and Italian colonies, and including part of Ethiopia.

so·mat·ic (sō·mat′ik), *adj.* 1. of or pertaining to the body. 2. pertaining to the cavity of the body, or its walls. [< Gk., < *soma* body] —**so·mat′i·cal·ly,** *adv.*

som·ber, *esp. Brit.* **som·bre** (som′bər), *adj.* 1. dark; gloomy. 2. melancholy; dismal. [< F *sombre*] —**som′ber·ly,** *esp. Brit.* **som′bre·ly,** *adv.* —**som′ber·ness,** *esp. Brit.* **som′bre·ness,** *n.* —Syn. 1. cloudy, murky. 2. depressing, sad.

som·bre·ro (som·brãr′ō), *n., pl.* **-bre·ros.** *Am.* a broad-brimmed hat worn in the SW United States, Mexico, etc. [< Sp., ult. < L *umbra* shade]

Sombrero

some (sum; *unstressed* səm), *adj.* 1. certain, but not known or named: *some people sleep more than others.* 2. a number of: *he was here some weeks ago.* 3. a quantity of: *have some water.* 4. a; any: *ask some girl to come here.* 5. about: *some twenty people saw it.* 6. *Am., Colloq.* notable; big; good: *that was some storm!* —*pron.* 1. certain unnamed persons or things: *some think so.* 2. a certain number or quantity: *may I have some of that?* —*adv.* 1. *Colloq.* to some degree or extent; somewhat: *he is some better today.* 2. *Am., Colloq.* to a great extent or extent: *that's going some!* [OE *sum*]

-some[1], *suffix.* 1. tending to, as in *frolicsome.* 2. causing, as in *awesome, troublesome.* 3. to a considerable degree, as in *lonesome.* [OE -*sum*]

-some[2], *suffix.* group of, as in *twosome, foursome.* [< *some*]

some·bod·y (sum′bod′i; -bə·di), *pron., n., pl.* **-bod·ies.** —*pron.* person not known or named; some person; someone. —*n.* person of importance.

some·how (sum′hou), *adv.* 1. in a way not known or not stated; in one way or another. 2. somehow or other, in one way or another.

some·one (sum′wun; -wən), *pron., n.* some person; somebody.

som·er·sault (sum′ər·sôlt), **som·er·set** (-set), *n.* 1. a roll or jump, turning the heels over the head. 2. **turn a somersault,** somer-

sault. —*v.* perform a somersault. Also, **summersault.** [< earlier F *sombresault* < Pr., ult. < L *supra* over + *saltus* jump]

Som·er·ville (sum′ər·vil), *n.* city in E Massachusetts, near Boston.

some·thing (sum′thing), *n.* 1. some thing; particular thing not named or known: *he has something on his mind.* 2. a certain amount or quantity; part; little: *something yet of doubt remains.* 3. thing or person of some value or importance: *he thinks he's something.* 4. thing or person that is to a certain extent an example of what is named: *Einstein is something of a violinist.* —*adv.* somewhat; to some extent or degree: *he is something like his father.*

some·time (sum′tīm), *adv.* 1. at an indefinite time in the future: *come over sometime.* 2. at an indefinite point of time: *sometime last March.* —*adj.* former: *a sometime pupil.*

some·times (sum′tīmz), *adv.* now and then; at times: *he comes to visit sometimes.*

some·what (sum′hwot), *adv.* to some extent or degree; slightly: *somewhat round.* —*n.* some part; some amount: *somewhat of a musician.*

some·where (sum′hwãr), *adv.* 1. in or to some place; in or to one place or another: *he lives somewhere in the neighborhood.* 2. at some time: *it happened somewhere in the last century.* —*n.* an undetermined or unspecified place.

Somme (sôm), *n.* river in N France.

som·nam·bu·late (som·nam′byə·lāt), *v.,* **-lat·ed, -lat·ing.** walk in one's sleep.

som·nam·bu·lism (som·nam′byə·liz·əm), *n.* sleepwalking. [< L *somnus* sleep + *ambulare* walk] —**som·nam′bu·list,** *n.* —**som·nam′bu·lis′tic,** *adj.* —**som·nam′bu·lis′ti·cal·ly,** *adv.*

som·nif·er·ous (som·nif′ər·əs), *adj.* 1. causing sleep. 2. sleepy. [< L, < *somnus* sleep + *ferre* bring] —**som·nif′er·ous·ly,** *adv.*

som·no·lent (som′nə·lənt), *adj.* sleepy; drowsy. [< L, < *somnus* sleep] —**som′no·lence, som′no·len·cy,** *n.* —**som′no·lent·ly,** *adv.*

son (sun), *n.* 1. a male child. 2. a male descendant. 3. boy or man attached to country, etc., as a child is to its parents. 4. anything thought of as a son in relation to its origin. 5. term of address to a boy or man from an older person, priest, etc. 6. the Son, Jesus Christ. [OE *sunu*]

so·nant (sō′nənt), *adj.* 1. of sound; having sound; sounding. 2. *Linguistics.* syllabic. 3. *Phonet.* voiced. —*n.* 1. *Linguistics.* a syllabic sound (opposed to *consonant*). 2. *Phonet.* voiced sound. [< L *sonans* sounding < *sonus,* n., sound] —**so′nance,** *n.* —**so·nan·tal** (sō·nan′təl), *adj.*

so·na·ta (sə·nä′tə), *n.* piece of music, usually for the piano, having three or four movements in contrasted rhythms but related keys. [< Ital., lit., sounded (on an instrument, as distinguished from sung), ult. < L *sonus* sound]

song (sông; song), *n.* 1. something to sing; short poem set to music. 2. poetry that has a musical sound. 3. piece of music for, or as if for, a poem that is to be sung. 4. act or practice of singing. 5. any sound like singing: *the song of the brook.* 6. a mere trifle; low price: *buy things for a song.* 7. **song and dance,** *Am., Slang.* explanation or account, not necessarily true, and often intended to impress or deceive. [OE *sang*]

song·bird (sông′bėrd′; song′-), *n.* 1. bird that sings. 2. a woman singer.

Song of Solomon, The, a book of the Old Testament. Also, **Song of Songs.**

song sparrow, a small North American songbird with black, brown, and white feathers.

song·ster (sông′stər; song′-), *n.* 1. singer. 2. writer of songs or poems. 3. songbird.

song·stress (sông′stris; song′-), *n.* 1. a woman singer. 2. a woman writer of songs or poems; poetess. 3. a female songbird.

song thrush, 1. the wood thrush. 2. a European bird noted for its song; the mavis.

son·ic (son′ik), *adj.* 1. of, having to do with, or using sound waves. 2. having to do with the rate at which sound travels in air (1087 feet per second).

sonic barrier or **wall,** point at which an airplane or projectile attains the same rate of speed as sound. Air disturbances are encountered at this point.

sonic mine, *Mil.* container holding an explosive charge that is put under water and exploded by propeller vibrations; acoustic mine.

son-in-law (sun'in-lô'), *n., pl.* **sons-in-law.** the husband of one's daughter.

son·net (son'it), *n.* poem having 14 lines, usually in iambic pentameter, and a certain arrangement of rhymes. Elizabethan and Italian sonnets differ in the arrangement of the rhymes. [< F *sonet,* < Ital. < L *sonus* sound]

son·net·eer (son'ə-tir'), *n.* writer of sonnets. —*v.* write sonnets.

son·ny (sun'i), *n., pl.* **-nies.** little son. > Sonny is used as a pet name, or as a way of speaking to a little boy.

so·no·rous (sə-nô'rəs; -nō'-), *adj.* 1. giving out or having a deep, loud sound. 2. full and rich in sound. 3. having an impressive sound; high-sounding. [< L *sonorus,* ult. < *sonus* sound] —**so·nor·i·ty** (sə-nôr'ə-ti; -nor'-), **so·no'rous·ness,** *n.* —**so·no'rous·ly,** *adv.*

Soo·chow (su'chou'), *n.* former name of Wuhsien.

soon (sün), *adv.* 1. in a short time; before long: *I will see you again soon.* 2. before the usual or expected time; early: *why have you come so soon?* 3. promptly; quickly: *do it soon!* 4. readily; willingly: *I would as soon ride as walk.* [OE *sōna* at once] —**soon'ness,** *n.* —**Syn.** 1. shortly, presently. > **sooner (than).** After *no sooner* the connective used is *than,* not *when: The fly had no sooner hit the water than* [not *when*] *a huge trout snapped at it.*

soot (sut; süt), *n.* a black substance in the smoke from burning coal, wood, oil, etc. —*v.* cover or blacken with soot. [OE *sōt*]

sooth (süth), *Archaic.* —*n.* truth. —*adj.* true. —*adv.* in truth. [OE *sōth*] —**sooth'ly,** *adv.*

soothe (süth), *v.,* **soothed, sooth·ing.** 1. quiet; calm; comfort. 2. make less painful; relieve; ease. [OE *sōthian*] —**sooth'er,** *n.* —**sooth'ing,** *adj.* —**sooth'ing·ly,** *adv.* —**sooth'ing·ness,** *n.*

sooth·say·er (süth'sā'ər), *n.* person who claims to tell what will happen; person who makes predictions. —**sooth'say'ing,** *n.*

soot·y (sut'i; süt'i), *adj.,* **soot·i·er, soot·i·est.** 1. covered or blackened with soot. 2. dark-brown or black; dark-colored. —**soot'i·ly,** *adv.* —**soot'i·ness,** *n.*

sop (sop), *n., v.,* **sopped, sop·ping.** —*n.* 1. piece of food dipped or soaked in milk, broth, etc. 2. something given to soothe or quiet; bribe. —*v.* 1. dip or soak. 2. take up (water, etc.); wipe; mop. 3. be drenched. 4. drench. [OE *sopp*]

soph·ism (sof'iz·əm), *n.* 1. a clever but misleading argument; argument based on false or unsound reasoning. 2. fallacy. [< L < Gk., ult. < *sophos* clever]

soph·ist (sof'ist), *n.* 1. a clever but misleading reasoner. 2. Often, **Sophist. a.** one of a class of teachers of rhetoric, philosophy, ethics, etc., in ancient Greece. **b.** any member of this class at a later date who was concerned with clever, rather than sound, argument. 3. man of learning. —**so·phis'ti·cal** (sə-fis'tə-kəl), **so·phis'tic,** *adj.* —**so·phis'ti·cal·ly,** *adv.* —**so·phis'ti·cal·ness,** *n.*

so·phis·ti·cate (*v.* sə-fis'tə-kāt; *adj., n.* sə-fis'tə-kāt, -kit), *v.,* **-cat·ed, -cat·ing,** *adj., n.* —*v.* 1. make experienced in worldly ways; cause to lose one's natural simplicity and frankness. 2. mislead. 3. use sophistry; quibble. 4. involve in sophistry. —*adj.* sophisticated. —*n.* a sophisticated person. [< Med.L *sophisticatus.* See SOPHISM.]

so·phis·ti·cat·ed (sə-fis'tə-kāt'id), *adj.* 1. experienced in worldly ways; lacking in natural simplicity or frankness. 2. appealing to the tastes of sophisticated people. 3. misleading.

so·phis·ti·ca·tion (sə-fis'tə-kā'shən), *n.* 1. a lessening or loss of naturalness, simplicity, or frankness; worldly experience or ideas; artificial ways. 2. sophistry.

soph·ist·ry (sof'is·tri), *n., pl.* **-ries.** 1. unsound

reasoning. 2. a clever but misleading argument. 3. art, practice, or learning of the ancient Greek sophists, esp. of their type of argument.

Soph·o·cles (sof'ə-klēz), *n.* 495?–406? B.C., Greek tragic poet. —**Soph·o·cle·an** (sof'ə-klē'-ən), *adj.*

soph·o·more (sof'ə-môr; sof'môr; -mōr), *n.* student in the second year of high school or college. —*adj.* of or pertaining to second-year students. [< *sophom,* var. of *sophism*]

soph·o·mor·ic (sof'ə-môr'ik; sof·mor'ik; -mor'-), **soph·o·mor·i·cal** (-ə-kəl), *adj.* 1. of, pertaining to, or like a sophomore or sophomores. 2. *Am.* conceited and pretentious but crude and ignorant. 3. intellectually immature. —**soph'o·mor'i·cal·ly,** *adv.*

so·po·rif·ic (sō'pə·rif'ik; sop'ə-), *adj.* 1. causing or tending to cause sleep. 2. sleepy; drowsy. —*n.* drug that causes sleep. [< L *sopor* deep sleep + *facere* make]

sop·ping (sop'ing), *adj.* soaked; drenched.

sop·py (sop'i), *adj.,* **-pi·er, -pi·est.** soaked; very wet.

so·pra·no (sə-pran'ō; -prä'nō), *n., pl.* **-pra·nos, -pra·ni** (-prä'nē), *adj.* —*n.* 1. the highest singing voice in women and boys. 2. singer with such a voice. 3. a soprano part. —*adj.* of, sung by, or composed for a soprano. [< Ital., < *sopra* above < L *supra*]

Sor·bonne (sôr·bon'), *n.* seat of the faculties of letters and science of the University of Paris.

sor·cer·er (sôr'sər·ər), *n.* person who practices magic with the aid of evil spirits; magician.

sor·cer·ess (sôr'sər·is), *n.* woman who practices magic with the aid of evil spirits; witch.

sor·cer·y (sôr'sər·i), *n., pl.* **-cer·ies.** magic performed with the aid of evil spirits; witchcraft. [< OF *sorcerie,* ult. < L *sors* lot] —**sor'cer·ous,** *adj.* —**sor'cer·ous·ly,** *adv.* —**Syn.** necromancy.

sor·did (sôr'did), *adj.* 1. dirty; filthy. 2. caring too much for money; meanly selfish; mean; low; base. [< L *sordidus* dirty < *sordere* be dirty] —**sor'did·ly,** *adv.* —**sor'did·ness,** *n.* —**Syn.** 1. foul, squalid. 2. ignoble, degraded.

sore (sôr; sōr), *adj.,* **sor·er, sor·est,** *n.* —*adj.* 1. painful; aching; tender; smarting: *a sore throat, a sore finger.* 2. suffering bodily pain from wounds, etc.: *his body was very sore.* 3. sad; distressed: *the suffering of the poor makes her heart sore.* 4. easily angered or offended; irritable; touchy. 5. *Colloq.* offended; angered; vexed. 6. causing pain, misery, anger, or offense; vexing: *a sore subject.* 7. severe; distressing. —*n.* 1. a painful place on the body where the skin or flesh is broken or bruised. 2. cause of pain, sorrow, sadness, anger, offense, etc. [OE *sār*] —**sore'ly,** *adv.* —**sore'ness,** *n.*

sore·head (sôr'hed'; sōr'-), *n. Am., Colloq.* person who is angry or offended. —**sore'head'ed,** *adj.*

sor·ghum (sôr'gəm), *n.* 1. a tall cereal plant resembling corn. One variety has a sweet juice used for making molasses or syrup, others provide food for livestock either by their grain or as hay, and still others furnish material for brushes or brooms. 2. *Am.* molasses or syrup made from a sorghum plant. [< NL < Ital. < Med.L *surgum*]

Sorghum

so·ror·i·ty (sə-rôr'ə-ti; -ror'-), *n., pl.* **-ties.** 1. a sisterhood. 2. *Am.* club or society of women or girls. There are student sororities in many American colleges. [prob. < Med.L *sororitas* < L *soror* sister]

sor·rel¹ (sôr'əl; sor'-), *adj.* reddish-brown. —*n.* 1. a reddish-brown color. 2. a reddish-brown horse. [< OF *sorel* < *sor* yellowish-brown]

sor·rel² (sôr'əl; sor'-), *n.* any of several plants with sour leaves. [< OF *surele* < *sur* sour < Gmc.]

sor·row (sor'ō; sôr'ō), *n.* 1. grief; sadness; regret: *his sorrow was caused by the death of his brother.* 2. cause of grief, sadness, or regret; trouble; suffering; misfortune: *her sorrows have* aged her. —v. **1.** feel or show grief, sadness, or regret. **2.** be sad; feel sorry; grieve. [OE *sorg*] —**sor′row·er,** n. —**sor′row·ing·ly,** adv. —**Syn.** n. **1.** unhappiness. **2.** affliction, woe.

sor·row·ful (sor′ə·fəl; sôr′–), adj. **1.** full of sorrow; feeling sorrow; sad. **2.** showing sorrow. **3.** causing sorrow. —**sor′row·ful·ly,** adv. —**sor′row·ful·ness,** n. —**Syn. 1, 2,** unhappy, mournful.

sor·ry (sor′i; sôr′–), adj., **–ri·er, –ri·est. 1.** feeling pity, regret, sympathy, etc.; sad: *be sorry for a loss.* **2.** wretched; poor; pitiful: *a sorry sight.* **3.** melancholy; dismal; gloomy. [OE *sārig* < *sār* sore] —**sor′ri·ly,** adv. —**sor′ri·ness,** n.

sort (sôrt), n. **1.** kind; class: *what sort of work does he do?* **2.** character; quality; nature: *art of a certain sort.* **3.** person or thing of a certain kind or quality: *he is a good sort.* **4.** way; fashion; manner. **5.** of sorts, a. of one kind or another. b. of a poor or mediocre quality. **6.** out of sorts, ill, cross, or uncomfortable. **7.** sort of (*used adverbially*), *Colloq.* somewhat; rather. —v. **1.** arrange by kinds or classes; arrange in order. **2.** separate from others; put. [< OF, ult. < L *sors,* orig., lot] —**sort′a·ble,** adj. —**sort′er,** n. —**Syn.** v. **1.** assort, classify, class, select. ➤ See **kind²** for usage note.

sor·tie (sôr′tē), n. **1.** a sudden attack by troops from a defensive position. **2.** a single round trip of an aircraft on a tactical mission. [< F, < *sortir* go out]

S O S (es′ō′es′), **1.** signal of distress consisting of the letters *s o s* of the international Morse alphabet (. . . — — — . . .), used in wireless telegraphy. **2.** *Colloq.* any urgent call for help.

so-so, so·so (sō′sō′), or **so so,** adj. neither very good nor very bad, but inclining toward bad. —adv. passably; indifferently; tolerably.

sot (sot), n. person made stupid and foolish by drinking too much alcohol; drunkard. [< Med.L *sottus*] —**sot′tish,** adj. —**sot′tish·ly,** adv. —**sot′tish·ness,** n.

sot·to vo·ce (sot′ō vō′chē), **1.** in an undertone. **2.** aside; privately. [< Ital., lit., below (normal) voice]

sou (sü), n. **1.** a former French coin, worth 5 centimes or 1/20 of a franc. **2.** anything of little value. [F, ult. < L *solidus,* a Roman coin]

sou·brette (sü·bret′), n. **1.** maidservant or lady's maid in a play or opera, esp. one displaying coquetry, pertness, and a spirit of intrigue; lively or pert young woman character. **2.** actress or singer taking such a part. [< F < Pr. *soubreto* coy < *soubra* set aside]

sou·bri·quet (sü′brə·kā), n. sobriquet.

souf·flé (sü·flā′; sü′flā), n. a frothy baked dish, usually made light by beaten eggs. —adj. puffed up. [< F, orig. pp. of *souffler* puff up]

sough (suf; sou), v. make a rustling or murmuring sound. —n. such a sound. [OE *swōgan*]

sought (sôt), v. pt. and pp. of **seek.**

soul (sōl), n. **1.** the part of the human being that thinks, feels, and makes the body act; the spiritual part of a person. **2.** energy of mind or feelings; spirit: *his writing has no soul.* **3.** cause of inspiration and energy: *he was the soul of the reform movement.* **4.** the essential part: *brevity is the soul of wit.* **5.** person: *don't tell a soul.* **6.** embodiment: *the soul of honor.* **7.** spirit of a dead person. **8.** upon my soul! as I hope to be saved! indeed! [OE *sāwol*]

soul·ful (sōl′fəl), adj. **1.** full of feeling; deeply emotional. **2.** expressing or suggesting a deep feeling. —**soul′ful·ly,** adv. —**soul′ful·ness,** n.

soul·less (sōl′lis), adj. having no soul; without spirit or noble feelings. —**soul′less·ly,** adv.

sound¹ (sound), n. **1.** what can be heard; auditory sensation. **2.** vibrations causing this sensation. Sound travels in waves. **3.** noise, note, tone, etc., whose quality indicates its source or nature: *the sound of fighting.* **4.** distance within which a noise may be heard. **5.** *Phonet.* one of the set of conventional vocal elements used in the oral communication of a language: *a vowel sound.* **6.** effect produced on the mind by what is heard: *a warning sound.* **7.** mere noise without meaning. —v. **1.** make a sound or noise: *the horn sounded.* **2.** cause to sound: *sound a horn.* **3.** be heard:

the bells sounded in his ears. **4.** test by noting sounds: *sound a person's lungs.* **5.** order or direct by a sound: *sound a retreat.* **6.** make known; announce; utter: *sound his praises.* **7.** seem: *that excuse sounds queer.* **8.** be filled with sound. [< OF *son* < L *sonus*]

sound² (sound), adj. **1.** free from injury, decay, or defect: *sound fruit.* **2.** free from disease; healthy: *a sound body and mind.* **3.** strong; safe; secure: *a sound business firm.* **4.** solid: *sound rock.* **5.** correct; right; reasonable; reliable: *sound advice.* **6.** without any legal defect: *a sound title.* **7.** having orthodox or conventional ideas: *politically sound.* **8.** honorable; loyal: *sound behavior.* **9.** thorough; hearty: *a sound whipping, a sound sleep.* —adv. deeply; thoroughly. [OE (*ge*) *sund*] —**sound′ly,** adv. —**sound′ness,** n. —**Syn.** adj. **1.** uninjured, unhurt.

sound³ (sound), v. **1.** measure the depth of (water) by letting down a weight fastened to the end of a line. **2.** examine or test by a line arranged to bring up a sample. **3.** inquire into the feelings, inclination, etc., of (a person): examine; investigate: *sound him out on the idea.* **4.** go toward the bottom; dive: *the whale sounded.* [< OF *sonder,* prob. < Gmc. source of *sound⁴*] —**sound′a·ble,** adj. —**sound′er,** n. —**Syn. 1.** fathom. **3.** probe, question, interrogate.

sound⁴ (sound), n. **1.** a narrow passage of water joining two seas, or between the mainland and an island: *Long Island Sound.* **2.** arm of the sea: *Puget Sound.* **3.** a sac in fishes containing air or gas that helps them in floating. [OE *sund* swimming; partly < Scand. *sund* strait]

sound barrier, point approximating the speed of sound (761 miles per hour at sea level) at which an aircraft creates a shock wave and is subjected to various unusual stresses.

sound·ing (soun′ding), adj. **1.** that sounds. **2.** resounding. **3.** sounding fine, but useless.

sound·ings (soun′dingz), n.pl. **1.** Often, **soundings.** measuring the depth of water by letting down a weight fastened to the end of a line. **2.** depths of water found by measuring in this way. **3.** water not more than 600 feet deep.

sound·less (sound′lis), adj. without sound; making no sound. —**sound′less·ly,** adv.

sound·proof (sound′prüf′), adj. not letting sound pass through. —v. make soundproof.

sound track, record of words, music, etc., made along one edge of a motion-picture film.

soup¹ (süp), n. a liquid food made by boiling meat, vegetables, fish, etc. [< F *soupe* < Gmc.]

soup² (süp), v. **soup up,** *Slang.* increase the horsepower of (a motor, etc.); add additional power to. [< *supe(rcharge)*]

soup·çon (süp·sôn′; süp′sôn), n. a slight trace or flavor. [< F]

soup·y (süp′i), adj., **soup·i·er, soup·i·est.** like soup.

sour (sour), adj. **1.** having a taste like vinegar or lemon juice: *most green fruit is sour.* **2.** fermented; spoiled: *sour milk.* **3.** having a sour or rank smell. **4.** disagreeable; bad-tempered; peevish: *a sour remark.* **5.** cold and wet; damp: *sour weather.* —v. **1.** make or become sour; turn sour. **2.** make or become peevish, bad-tempered, or disagreeable. —n. **1.** something sour. **2.** *Am.* an acid beverage containing alcohol. —adv. in a sour manner. [OE *sūr*] —**sour′ish,** adj. —**sour′ly,** adv. —**sour′ness,** n. —**Syn.** adj. **1.** acid, acidulous, tart. **2.** rancid, curdled. **4.** bitter.

source (sôrs; sōrs), n. **1.** beginning of a brook or river; fountain; spring. **2.** place from which anything comes or is obtained. **3.** person, book, statement, etc., that supplies information. [< OF, ult. < L *surgere* rise, surge]

sour·dough (sour′dō′), n. *Am., Colloq.* prospector or pioneer in Alaska or Canada. [so called from their practice of saving a lump of sour dough from each breadmaking to start fermentation in subsequent baking]

sour grapes, thing that a person pretends not to want because he cannot have it.

sour gum, *Am.* the tupelo.

souse (sous), v., **soused, sous·ing,** n. —v. **1.** plunge into liquid; drench; soak in a liquid. **2.**

soak in vinegar, brine, etc.; pickle. 3. *Am. Slang.* make or become intoxicated. —*n.* 1. a plunging into a liquid. 2. liquid used for pickling. 3. something soaked or kept in pickle, esp. the head, ears, and feet of a pig. 4. *Am., Slang.* drunkard. [ult. < OF *sous* pickled pork < Gmc.]

south (south), *n.* 1. direction to the right as one faces the rising sun; direction just opposite north. 2. Also, **South.** part of any country toward the south. 3. **South,** *Am.* the part of the United States lying south of the Mason-Dixon Line, the Ohio River, Missouri, and Kansas. —*adj.* 1. lying toward or situated in the south. 2. originating in or coming from the south: *a south wind.* 3. **South,** in the southern part; southern: *South China.* —*adv.* 1. toward the south. 2. in the south. [OE *sūth*]

South Africa, Republic of, country in S Africa. —**South African.**

South African Dutch, Afrikaans.

South America, continent in the Western Hemisphere, SE of North America. —**South American.**

South·amp·ton (south-amp′tən; -hamp′-), *n.* seaport in S England.

South Bend, city in N Indiana.

South Carolina, a Southern State of the United States. *Capital:* Columbia. *Abbrev.:* S.C. —**South Carolinian,** *Am.*

South China Sea. See China Sea.

South Da·ko·ta (də·kō′tə), a Middle Western State of the United States. *Capital:* Pierre. *Abbrev.:* S. Dak. —**South Da·ko′tan,** *Am.*

South·down (south′doun′), *n.* any of an English breed of small, hornless sheep.

south·east (south′ēst′; *Naut.* sou′-), *adj.* 1. halfway between south and east. 2. lying toward or situated in the southeast. 3. originating in or coming from the southeast. 4. directed toward the southeast. —*n.* 1. a southeast direction. 2. place that is in the southeast part or direction. —*adv.* 1. toward the southeast. 2. in the southeast.

south·east·er (south′ēs′tər; *Naut.* sou′-), *n.* wind or storm from the southeast.

south·east·er·ly (south′ēs′tər·li; *Naut.* sou′-), *adj., adv.* 1. toward the southeast. 2. from the southeast.

south·east·ern (south′ēs′tərn; *Naut.* sou′-), *adj.* 1. toward the southeast. 2. from the southeast. 3. of or pertaining to the southeast.

south·east·ward (south′ēst′wərd; *Naut.* sou′-), *adv.* Also, **south′east′wards.** toward the southeast. —*adj.* 1. toward the southeast. 2. southeast. —*n.* southeast.

south·east·ward·ly (south′ēst′wərd·li; *Naut.* sou′-), *adj., adv.* 1. toward the southeast. 2. of winds, from the southeast.

south·er (south′ər), *n.* wind or storm from the south.

south·er·ly (suth′ər·li), *adj., adv.* 1. toward the south. 2. from the south. —**south′er·li·ness,** *n.*

south·ern (suth′ərn), *adj.* 1. toward the south. 2. from the south. 3. of or in the south. 4. **Southern,** *Am.* of or in the S part of the United States. —**south·ern·most** (suth′ərn·mōst), *adj.*

Southern Cross, four bright stars in the form of a cross, used in finding the direction south.

south·ern·er (suth′ər·nər), *n.* 1. native or inhabitant of the south. 2. **Southerner,** *Am.* native or inhabitant of the South of the U.S.

Southern Hemisphere, the half of the earth that is south of the equator.

Southern Rhodesia, a self-governing British territory in SE Africa.

South·ey (suth′i; south′i), *n.* Robert, 1774-1843, English poet.

South Island, largest island of New Zealand.

South Korea, country in Korea.

south·land (south′lənd; -land′), *n.* land in the south; southern part of a country.

south·paw (south′pô′), *Slang.* —*n. Am.* a left-handed baseball pitcher. —*adj.* left-handed.

South Pole, the southern end of the earth's axis.

South Sea Islands, islands in the S Pacific; Oceania. —**South Sea Islander.**

South Vietnam, country in Indochina, S of the 17th parallel.

south·ward (south′wərd; *Naut.* suth′ərd), *adv.* Also, **south′wards.** toward the south. —*adj.* 1. toward the south. 2. south. —*n.* south.

south·ward·ly (south′wərd·li), *adj., adv.* 1. toward the south. 2. of winds, coming from the south.

south·west (south′west′; *Naut.* sou′-), *adj.* 1. halfway between south and west. 2. lying toward or situated in the southwest. 3. originating in or coming from the southwest: *a southwest wind.* 4. directed toward the southwest. —*n.* 1. a southwest direction. 2. place that is in the southwest part or direction. 3. **Southwest,** *Am.* New Mexico, Arizona, and S California. —*adv.* 1. toward the southwest. 2. from the southwest. 3. in the southwest.

south·west·er (south′wes′tər *for 1;* sou′- *for 2*), *n.* 1. wind or storm from the southwest. 2. sou′wester.

south·west·er·ly (south′wes′tər·li; *Naut.* sou′-), *adj., adv.* 1. toward the southwest. 2. from the southwest.

south·west·ern (south′wes′tərn; *Naut.* sou′-), *adj.* 1. toward the southwest. 2. from the southwest. 3. of the southwest; pertaining to the southwest. 4. **Southwestern,** *Am.* of, having to do with, or in New Mexico, Arizona, or S California.

south·west·ward (south′west′wərd; *Naut.* sou′-), *adv.* Also, **south′west′wards.** toward the southwest. —*adj.* 1. toward the southwest. 2. southwest. —*n.* southwest.

south·west·ward·ly (south′west′wərd·li; *Naut.* sou′-), *adj., adv.* 1. toward the southwest. 2. of winds, from the southwest.

sou·ve·nir (sü′və·nir′; sü′və·nir), *n.* 1. something to remind one of a place, person, or occasion; keepsake. 2. a memory. [< F, orig. inf., < L *subvenire* come to mind < *sub-* up + *venire* come] —**Syn.** 1. memento, remembrance, reminder, token.

sou′west·er (sou′wes′tər), *n.* a waterproof hat having a broad brim behind to protect the neck, worn esp. by seamen.

Sou'wester

sov·er·eign (sov′rən), *n.* 1. king or queen; supreme ruler; monarch. 2. a British gold coin, worth 20 shillings. —*adj.* 1. having the rank or power of a sovereign. 2. greatest in rank or power. 3. independent of the control of other governments. 4. above all others; supreme; greatest. 5. very excellent or powerful. [< OF *soverain,* ult. < L *super* over] —**sov′ereign·ly,** *adv.* —**Syn.** *adj.* 4. paramount, chief.

sov·er·eign·ty (sov′rən·ti), *n., pl.* -ties. 1. supreme power or authority. State sovereignty was the doctrine that each State was superior to and independent of the United States in power over its own territory. 2. rank, power, or jurisdiction of a sovereign. —**Syn.** 1. supremacy.

so·vi·et (sō′vi·et; -it; sov′i-), *n.* 1. council; assembly. 2. Often, **Soviet,** in the Soviet Union: a. either of two elected local assemblies **(village soviets, town soviets).** b. any of the pyramid of larger assemblies elected by local assemblies, culminating in the **Union Congress of Soviets** or **Supreme Soviet.** —*adj.* 1. of or pertaining to soviets. 2. **Soviet,** of or pertaining to the Soviet Union. [< Russ., council] —**sol′vi·et·dom,** *n.* —**so·vi·et·ism** (sō′vi·it·iz′əm; sov′i-), *n.* —**so′vi·et·ist,** *adj.*

so·vi·et·ize (sō′vi·it·iz; sov′i-), *v.,* -ized, -izing. change to a soviet government. —**so·vi·et·i·za·tion** (sō′vi·it′ə·zā′shən; sov′i-), *n.*

Soviet Russia, 1. the Russian Soviet Federated Socialist Republic. 2. Soviet Union.

Soviet Union, union of fifteen Soviet republics in E Europe and W and N Asia, the largest of which is the Russian Soviet Federated Socialist Republic. Full name, **Union of Soviet Socialist Republics.**

sow[1] (sō), *v.*, **sowed, sown** (sōn) **or sowed, sow-ing.** **1.** scatter (seed) on the ground; plant (seed); plant seed in. **2.** scatter seed. **3.** scatter (anything). [OE *sāwan*] —**sow'er,** *n.*

sow[2] (sou), *n.* fully grown female pig. [OE *sū*]

soy (soi), **soy·a** (soi'ə), *n.* **1.** a Chinese and Japanese sauce for fish, meat, etc., made from fermented soybeans. **2.** soybean. [< Jap. < Chinese, < *shi* condiment + *yu* oil]

soy·bean (soi'bēn'), *n.* **1.** a bean widely grown in China, Japan, and the United States. **2.** plant that it grows on.

SP, S.P., shore patrol.

Sp., **1.** Spain. **2.** Spaniard. **3.** Spanish.

sp., **1.** special. **2.** species. **3.** specific. **4.** specimen. **5.** spelling.

spa (spä), *n.* **1.** a mineral spring. **2.** place where there is a mineral spring. [after *Spa,* Belgian resort city]

space (spās), *n., v.,* **spaced, spac·ing.** —*n.* **1.** unlimited room or place extending in all directions: *the earth moves through space.* **2.** limited place or room: *a space 2½ by 4 by 8 inches.* **3.** extent or area of ground, surface, etc.: *the trees covered acres of space.* **4.** distance of place: *a space of ten miles.* **5.** length of time: *a space of two hours.* **6.** *Archaic.* an interval of time; a while. **7.** time in which to do something; opportunity. **8.** part of a surface; blank between words, etc. **9.** *Printing.* one of the blank types used to separate words, etc. **10.** *Music.* one of the intervals between the lines of a staff. **11.** accommodations on a train, etc. —*v.* **1.** fix the space or spaces of; separate by spaces. **2.** divide into spaces. [< OF < L *spatium*] —**spac'er,** *n.*

space age, period characterized by development of means of flight and travel in outer space.

space platform or **station,** a structure consisting of a satellite in orbit around the earth, used as an observatory or a launching site for travel in outer space.

space ship, a projected type of aircraft capable of interplanetary travel.

space suit, an airtight suit designed to protect travelers in outer space from radiation, heat, and lack of oxygen by imitating the conditions of the earth's atmosphere.

spa·cious (spā'shəs), *adj.* containing much space; with plenty of room; vast. —**spa'cious·ly,** *adv.* —**spa'cious·ness,** *n.* —**Syn.** extensive, broad, capacious, large, roomy. —**Ant.** cramped.

spade[1] (spād), *n., v.,* **spad·ed, spad·ing.** —*n.* **1.** tool for digging; a kind of shovel. **2.** call a spade a spade, call a thing by its real name; speak plainly and frankly. —*v.* dig with a spade. [OE *spadu*] —**spad'er,** *n.*

spade[2] (spād), *n.* **1.** a black figure (♠) used on playing cards. **2.** a playing card bearing such figures. **3. spades,** suit of playing cards bearing such figures, usually the highest ranking suit. [< Ital. < L < Gk. *spathe* sword, broad blade]

spa·dix (spā'diks), *n., pl.* **spa-dix·es, spa·di·ces** (spā·dī'sēz). spike composed of minute flowers on a fleshy stem. A spadix is usually enclosed in a petallike leaf called a spathe, as in the jack-in-the-pulpit and the calla lily. [< L < Gk., palm branch]

spa·ghet·ti (spə·get'ı), *n.* long, slender sticks made of a mixture of flour and water, soft when cooked. [< Ital., pl. dim. of *spago* cord]

Spain (spān), *n.* country in SW Europe.

spake (spāk), *v. Archaic.* pt. of **speak.**

span[1] (span), *n., v.,* **spanned, span·ning.** —*n.* **1.** the distance between the tip of a man's thumb and the tip of his little finger when the hand is spread out; about 9 inches. **2.** distance between two supports: *the arch had a fifty-foot span.* **3.** part between two supports: *the bridge crossed the river in three spans.* **4.** a short length of time: *"A life's but a span."* **5.** the full extent: *the span of life, the span of memory.* —*v.* **1.** measure by the hand spread out. **2.** extend over: *a bridge spanned the river.* [OE *spann*]

span[2] (span), *n. Am.* pair of horses or other animals harnessed and driven together. [< Du., LG, < *spannen* stretch, yoke]

span[3] (span), *v. Archaic.* pt. of **spin.**

span·gle (spang'gəl), *n., v.,* **-gled, -gling.** —*n.* **1.** a small piece of glittering metal used for decoration. **2.** any small bright bit: *this rock shows spangles of gold.* —*v.* **1.** decorate with spangles. **2.** sprinkle with small bright bits: *the sky is spangled with stars.* **3.** glitter. [dim. of earlier *spang,* prob. < MDu. *spange* brooch] —**span'gler,** *n.* —**span'gly,** *adj.*

Span·iard (span'yərd), *n.* native or inhabitant of Spain.

span·iel (span'yəl), *n.* **1.** any of various breeds of dogs, usually of small or medium size with long, silky hair and drooping ears. **2.** person who yields too easily to others. [< OF *espagneul,* orig., Spanish < L *Hispania* Spain]

Span·ish (span'ish), *adj.* of Spain; pertaining to Spain, its people, or their language. —*n.* **1.** the people of Spain. **2.** the language of Spain.

Spanish America, *Am.* countries and islands S of the United States, in which the principal language is Spanish. —**Spanish American,** *Am.*

Spanish Main, 1. originally, the mainland of America adjacent to the Caribbean Sea, esp. between the mouth of the Orinoco River and the Isthmus of Panama. **2.** in later use, the Caribbean Sea.

Spanish moss, *Am.* plant growing on the branches of certain trees, from which it hangs in gray streamers, found in the S United States.

spank (spangk), *v.* strike with the open hand, a slipper, etc., esp. on the buttocks. —*n.* a blow with the open hand, a slipper, etc.; slap. [imit.]

spank·er (spangk'ər), *n.* **1.** a fore-and-aft sail on the mast nearest the stern. **2.** *Colloq.* anything fine, large, unusual for its kind, etc.

spank·ing (spangk'ing), *adj.* **1.** blowing briskly. **2.** quick and vigorous. **3.** *Colloq.* unusually fine, great, large, etc. [cf. Dan. *spanke* strut]

span·ner (span'ər), *n.* **1.** one that spans. **2.** tool for holding and turning a nut, bolt, etc.

spar[1] (spär), *n., v.,* **sparred, spar·ring.** —*n.* **1.** a stout pole used to support or extend the sails of a ship; mast, yard, gaff, boom, etc., of a ship. **2.** the main beam of an airplane wing. —*v.* provide (a ship) with spars. [ME *sparre.* Cf. Scand. *sparri,* MDu. *sparre.*]

spar[2] (spär), *v.,* **sparred, spar·ring,** *n.* —*v.* **1.** make motions of attack and defense with the arms and fists; box. **2.** dispute. —*n.* **1.** a boxing match. **2.** dispute.

spar[3] (spär), *n.* a shiny mineral that splits into flakes easily. [OE *spær*] —**spar'ry,** *adj.*

SPAR, Spar (spär), *n.* member of the SPARS, the Women's Reserve of the U.S. Coast Guard Reserve. [< S(*emper*) *Par*(*atus*) always ready, the motto of the Coast Guard]

spare (spãr), *v.,* **spared, spar·ing,** *adj.,* **spar·er, spar·est,** *n.* —*v.* **1.** show mercy to; refrain from harming or destroying: *he spared his enemy.* **2.** make (a person, etc.) free from (something); relieve or exempt (a person, etc.) from (something): *he did the work to spare you the trouble.* **3.** show consideration for; save from labor, pain, etc.: *spare a person's feelings.* **4.** use in small quantities or not at all; be saving of: *spare gas or coal.* **5.** refrain from: *don't spare the expense.* **6.** be saving. **7.** get along without; do without: *can you spare a dime?* —*adj.* **1.** free for other use: *spare time.* **2.** extra; in reserve: *a spare tire.* **3.** thin; lean: *a spare person.* **4.** small in quantity; meager; scanty. —*n.* a spare thing, part, tire, etc. [OE *sparian*] —**spare'ly,** *adv.* —**spare'ness,** *n.* —**spar'er,** *n.* —**Syn.** *adj.* **3.** lank, gaunt.

spare·rib (spãr'rib'), *n.* rib of pork having less meat than the ribs near the loins.

spar·ing (spãr'ing), *adj.* **1.** that spares. **2.** economical; frugal. —**spar'ing·ly,** *adv.* —**spar'-ing·ness,** *n.* —**Syn.** **2.** parsimonious, stingy.

spark (spärk), *n.* **1.** a small bit of fire: *a spark from his match caused the fire.* **2.** *Elect.* flash given off when electricity jumps across an open space. **3.** flash; gleam: *a spark of light.* **4.** a small amount: *a spark of interest.* **5.** trace of life. —*v.* **1.** flash; gleam. **2.** send out small bits of fire; produce sparks. **3.** fire (one's associates, etc.) with enthusiasm; enliven. [OE *spearca*]

spark² (spärk), *n.* beau; lover. —*v. Colloq.* be a beau or lover; court; woo. [? < Scand. *sparkr* lively] —spark'ish, *adj.*

spar·kle (spär'kəl), *v.,* -kled, -kling, *n.* —*v.* 1. send out little sparks, esp. as fire. 2. shine; glitter; flash; gleam. 3. be brilliant; be lively. 4. bubble: *a sparkling drink.* 5. cause to sparkle. —*n.* 1. a little spark. 2. shine; glitter; flash; gleam. 3. brilliance; liveliness. [< *spark¹*] —spar'kling, *adj.* —spar'kling·ly, *adv.*

spar·kler (spär'klər), *n.* 1. person or thing that sparkles. 2. firework that sends out little sparks. 3. a sparkling gem; diamond. 4. *Colloq.* a bright eye.

spark plug, *Am.* 1. device in the cylinder of a gasoline engine by which the mixture of gasoline and air is exploded by an electric spark. 2. *Colloq.* one who fires his companions or associates with enthusiasm and determination.

spar·row (spar'ō), *n.* any of many small finches, such as the song sparrow, the English sparrow, and the chipping sparrow. [OE *spearwa*]

English sparrow (ab. 6 in. long)

sparse (spärs), *adj.,* spars·er, spars·est. 1. thinly scattered; occurring here and there: *a sparse population.* 2. scanty; meager. [< L *sparsus,* pp. of *spargere* scatter] —sparse'ly, *adv.* —sparse'ness, spar·si·ty (spär'sə·ti), *n.*

Spar·ta (spär'tə), *n.* one of the most important cities in ancient Greece, famous for its soldiers.

Spar·tan (spär'tən), *adj.* 1. of Sparta or its people. 2. like the Spartans; simple, frugal, severe, and sternly disciplined. —*n.* 1. native or inhabitant of Sparta. 2. person who is like the Spartans. —Spar'tan·ism, *n.*

spasm (spaz'əm), *n.* 1. a sudden, abnormal, involuntary contraction of a muscle or muscles. 2. any sudden, brief fit or spell of unusual energy or activity: *a spasm of temper.* [< L < Gk. *spasmos* < *spaein* draw up, tear away]

spas·mod·ic (spaz·mod'ik), **spas·mod·i·cal** (-ə·kəl), *adj.* 1. pertaining to spasms; resembling a spasm. 2. sudden and violent, but brief; occurring very irregularly. 3. having or showing bursts of excitement. —spas·mod'i·cal·ly, *adv.* —Syn. 2. jerky, fitful, intermittent.

spas·tic (spas'tik), *adj.* 1. caused by a spasm or spasms. 2. of, having to do with, or characterized by spasms. —*n.* person suffering from a tonic contraction of a muscle or muscles. —spas'ti·cal·ly, *adv.*

spat¹ (spat), *n., v.,* spat·ted, spat·ting. —*n.* 1. a slight quarrel. 2. a light blow; slap. —*v.* 1. *Am.* quarrel slightly. 2. slap lightly. [? imit.]

spat² (spat), *v.* pt. and pp. of spit¹.

spat³ (spat), *n.* Usually, spats. a short gaiter covering the ankle. [short for *spatterdash*]

spate (spāt), *n.* 1. flood; freshet. 2. a heavy downpour of rain. 3. a sudden outburst. [ME; akin to OE *spātan* to spit]

spathe (spāth), *n. Bot.* a large bract or pair of bracts that enclose a flower cluster. The calla lily has a white spathe around a yellow flower cluster. See the picture under spadix. [< Gk., palm branch, oar blade] —spathed, *adj.*

spa·tial (spā'shəl), *adj.* 1. of or pertaining to space. 2. existing in space. —spa·ti·al·i·ty (spā'shi·al'ə·ti), *n.* —spa'tial·ly, *adv.*

spat·ter (spat'ər), *v.* 1. scatter or dash in drops or particles. 2. fall in drops or particles: *rain spatters on the sidewalk.* 3. strike in a shower; strike in a number of places. 4. splash or spot with mud, slander, disgrace, etc. —*n.* 1. a spattering: *a spatter of bullets.* 2. sound of spattering. 3. a splash or spot. [cf. Du., LG *spatten* spout] —spat'ter·ing·ly, *adv.*

spat·ter·dash (spat'ər·dash'), *n.* Usually, spatterdashes. a long gaiter worn to keep the trousers or stockings from being splashed with mud, etc. [< *spatter* + *dash*]

spat·u·la (spach'ə·lə), *n.* tool with a broad, flat, flexible blade, used for mixing drugs, spreading paints, frostings, etc. [< L, dim. of *spatha* flat blade < Gk. *spathe*] —spat'u·lar, *adj.*

spav·in (spav'ən), *n.* disease of horses in which a bony swelling forms at the hock, causing lameness. [< OF *espavain*] —spav'ined, *adj.*

Spatulas: A, cake knife; B, palette knife.

spawn (spôn), *n.* 1. eggs of fish, frogs, shellfish, and the like. 2. young newly hatched from such eggs. 3. a swarming brood; offspring. 4. product; result. —*v.* 1. bring forth; give birth to. [< OF < L *expandere* spread out. Doublet of EXPAND.]

spay (spā), *v.* remove the ovaries of. [< AF *espeier,* ult. < OF *espee* sword < L *spatha.* See SPADE².]

speak (spēk), *v.,* spoke or (*Archaic*) spake, spo·ken or (*Archaic*) spoke, speak·ing. 1. say words; talk: *do not speak to me.* 2. utter orally; say: *speak a person's name.* 3. make a speech: *who is going to speak at the forum?* 4. tell; express; make known: *speak the truth.* 5. use (a language): *do you speak French?* 6. express an idea, feeling, etc.; communicate: *his actions spoke of honor.* 7. make a plea, request, application, etc.; appeal: *speak for seats ahead of time.* 8. speak to or with. 9. of dogs, bark when told. 10. so to speak, to speak in such a manner. 11. speak for, a. speak in the interest of; represent. b. ask or apply for. 12. speak of, mention; refer to. 13. speak out or up, speak loudly, clearly, or freely. [OE *specan*] —speak'a·ble, *adj.*

speak·eas·y (spēk'ēz'i), *n., pl.* -eas·ies. *Am., Slang.* place where alcoholic liquors are sold contrary to law.

speak·er (spēk'ər), *n.* 1. person who speaks. 2. a presiding officer. —speak'er·ship, *n.*

Speaker of the House, *Am.* the presiding officer of the House of Representatives.

speak·ing (spēk'ing), *n.* act, utterance, or discourse of a person who speaks. —*adj.* 1. that speaks. 2. used in, suited to, or involving speech: *within speaking distance.* 3. permitting conversation: *a speaking acquaintance with a person.* 4. highly expressive: *speaking eyes.* 5. lifelike: *a speaking likeness.* —speak'ing·ly, *adv.*

spear¹ (spir), *n.* weapon with a long shaft and a sharp-pointed head. —*v.* pierce with a spear. [OE *spere*] —spear'er, spear'man, *n.*

spear² (spir), *n.* sprout or shoot of a plant: *a spear of grass.* —*v.* sprout or shoot into a long stem. [var. of *spire*; infl. by *spear¹*]

spear·head (spir'hed'), *n.* 1. the sharp-pointed striking end of a spear. 2. part that comes first in an attack, undertaking, etc.

spear·mint (spir'mint'), *n.* common mint, a fragrant herb much used for flavoring.

spec., special.

spe·cial (spesh'əl), *adj.* 1. of a particular kind; distinct from others; not general: *a special key.* 2. being a particular one: *a special day.* 3. pertaining to a particular thing, etc.: *the special features of a plan.* 4. having a particular function, purpose, etc.: *special legislation.* 5. specific, as a statement. 6. different from what is ordinary or usual: *a special occasion, special honors.* 7. exceptional in amount or degree: *special importance.* 8. great: *a special friend.* —*n.* 1. a special train, car, bus, etc. 2. any special person or thing. 3. a special edition of a newspaper. 4. *Am.* in a store, restaurant, etc., a product which is specially featured. [< L, < *species* appearance] —spe'cial·ly, *adv.* —spe'cial·ness, *n.*

spe·cial·ist (spesh'əl·ist), *n.* person who devotes or restricts himself to one particular branch of study, business, etc. —spe'cial·ism, *n.* —spe·cial·is'tic, *adj.*

spe·ci·al·i·ty (spesh'i·al'ə·ti), *n., pl.* -ties. 1. a special or distinctive quality or characteristic. 2. a special point; particular; detail. 3. specialty.

spe·cial·ize (spesh'əl·īz), *v.,* -ized, -iz·ing. 1. pursue some special branch of study, work, etc.: *many students specialize in engineering.* 2. adapt to special conditions; give special form, use, duty, etc., to; limit. 3. develop in a special way; take on a special form, use, etc. 4. mention specially; specify. 5. go into particulars. —**spe′cial·i·za′tion,** *n.* —**spe′cial·iz′er,** *n.*

spe·cial·ty (spesh′əl·ti), *n., pl.* –ties. 1. a special study; special line of work, profession, trade, etc. 2. product, article, etc., to which special attention is given. 3. a special character; special quality. 4. a special or particular characteristic; peculiarity. 5. a special point or item; particular; detail.

spe·cie (spē′shi), *n.* money in the form of coins; metal money. [< L (in) *specie* (in) kind, abl. of *species* kind]

spe·cies (spē′shiz), *n., pl.* –cies. 1. group of animals or plants that have certain permanent characteristics in common. 2. kind; sort; distinct kind or sort. 3. appearance; form; shape. 4. the species, the human race. [< L, orig., appearance. Doublet of SPICE.] ≫ Species has the same form in both singular and plural, though some distinguish in pronunciation: singular, spē′shiz; plural, spē′shēz.

specif., specific; specifically.

spe·cif·ic (spi·sif′ik), *adj.* 1. definite; precise; particular: *a specific rule.* 2. characteristic of or peculiar to something: *a scaly skin is a specific feature of snakes.* 3. curing some particular disease. —*n.* 1. any specific statement, quality, etc. 2. a cure for some particular disease. Quinine is a specific for malaria. [< LL, < L *species* sort + *facere* make] —**spe·cif′i·cal·ly,** *adv.* —**spec·i·fic·i·ty** (spes′ə·fis′ə·ti), **spe·cif′ic·ness,** *n.*

spec·i·fi·ca·tion (spes′ə·fə·kā′shən), *n.* 1. act of specifying; definite mention; detailed statement of particulars. 2. a detailed description of the dimensions, materials, etc., for a building, road, dam, boat, etc. 3. something specified; particular item, article, etc.

specific gravity, ratio of the weight of a given volume of any substance to that of the same volume of some other substance taken as a standard, water being used for solids and liquids, and hydrogen or air for gases.

spec·i·fy (spes′ə·fī), *v.,* –fied, –fy·ing. 1. mention or name definitely; state or describe in detail: *specify what you want.* 2. include in the specifications. [< LL, < *specificus* SPECIFIC] —**spec′i·fi′a·ble,** *adj.* —**spec′i·fi′er,** *n.*

spec·i·men (spes′ə·mən), *n.* 1. one of a group or class taken to show what the others are like; single part, thing, etc., regarded as an example of its kind. 2. *Colloq.* a human being; person. [< L, < *specere* to view]

spe·cious (spē′shəs), *adj.* making a good appearance; seeming desirable, reasonable, or probable, but not really so. [< L, < *species* appearance] —**spe′cious·ly,** *adv.* —**spe′cious·ness,** *n.*

speck (spek), *n.* 1. a small spot; stain. 2. a tiny bit; particle. —*v.* mark with specks. [OE *specca*]

speck·le (spek′əl), *n.,* –led, –ling. —*n.* a small spot or mark. —*v.* mark with speckles.

specs (speks), *n.pl. Colloq.* spectacles.

spec·ta·cle (spek′tə·kəl), *n.* 1. thing to look at; sight. 2. a public show or display. 3. spectacles, pair of glasses to help a person's sight or to protect his eyes. [< L *spectaculum,* ult. < *specere* to view] —**spec′ta·cled,** *adj.* —Syn. 2. exhibition, parade, pageant.

spec·tac·u·lar (spek·tak′yə·lər), *adj.* 1. making a great display. 2. pertaining to a spectacle or show. —*n.* a television program running for an hour or more and involving outstanding performers and costly production. —**spec·tac′u·lar′i·ty,** *n.* —**spec·tac′u·lar·ly,** *adv.*

spec·ta·tor (spek′tā·tər; spek·tā′-), *n.* person who watches without taking part. [< L, < *spec·tare* to watch < *specere* to view] —**spec·ta·to·ri·al** (spek′tə·tô′ri·əl; –tō′-), *adj.* —Syn. observer, witness, onlooker, bystander, beholder.

spec·ter, *esp. Brit.* **spec·tre** (spek′tər), *n.* ghost. [< L *spectrum* appearance. See SPEC·TRUM.]

spec·tral (spek′trəl), *adj.* 1. of or like a specter; ghostly. 2. of or produced by the spectrum:

spectral colors. —**spec·tral·i·ty** (spek·tral′ə·ti), **spec′tral·ness,** *n.* —**spec′tral·ly,** *adv.*

spec·tro·scope (spek′trə·skōp), *n.* instrument for obtaining and examining the spectrum of a ray from any source. —**spec·tro·scop·ic** (spek′trə·skop′ik), **spec′tro·scop′i·cal,** *adj.* —**spec′tro·scop′i·cal·ly,** *adv.*

spec·tros·co·py (spek·tros′kə·pi; spek′trə·skō′pi), *n.* 1. science having to do with the examination and analysis of spectra. 2. use of the spectroscope. —**spec·tros′co·pist,** *n.*

spec·trum (spek′trəm), *n., pl.* –tra (–trə), –trums. 1. *Physics.* the band of colors formed when a beam of light is broken up by being passed through a prism or by some other means. A rainbow has all the colors of the spectrum: red, orange, yellow, green, blue, indigo, and violet. 2. band of colors formed when any radiant energy is broken up. The ends of such a band are not visible to the eye, but are studied by photography, heat effects, etc. 3. *Radio.* the wave-length range between 30,000 meters and 3 centimeters. [< L, appearance, < *specere* to view]

spec·u·late (spek′yə·lāt), *v.,* –lat·ed, –lat·ing. 1. reflect; meditate; consider; conjecture. 2. buy or sell when there is a large risk, with the hope of making a profit from future price changes. [< L, < *specula* watchtower]

spec·u·la·tion (spek′yə·lā′shən), *n.* 1. thought; reflection; conjecture. 2. a buying or selling when there is a large risk, with the hope of making a profit from future price changes.

spec·u·la·tive (spek′yə·lā′tiv; –lə·tiv), *adj.* 1. thoughtful; reflective. 2. theoretical rather than practical. 3. risky. 4. of or involving speculation in land, stocks, etc. —**spec′u·la′tive·ly,** *adv.* —**spec′u·la′tive·ness,** *n.*

spec·u·la·tor (spek′yə·lā′tər), *n.* 1. person who speculates. 2. person who buys tickets for shows, games, etc., in advance, hoping to sell them later at a higher price.

spec·u·lum (spek′yə·ləm), *n., pl.* –la (–lə), –lums. 1. a mirror of polished metal. A reflecting telescope contains a speculum. 2. a surgical instrument for enlarging an opening in order to examine a cavity. [< L, mirror < *specere* to view]

speech (spēch), *n.* 1. act of speaking; talk. 2. power of speaking. 3. manner of speaking. 4. what is said; the words spoken. 5. a public talk. 6. language. [OE *spǣc*] —**speech′ful,** *adj.* —**speech′ful·ness,** *n.* —Syn. 1. discourse.

speech·i·fy (spēch′ə·fī), *v.,* –fied, –fy·ing. *Humorous or Depreciatory.* make a speech or speeches. —**speech′i·fi′er,** *n.*

speech·less (spēch′lis), *adj.* 1. not able to speak. 2. silent. —**speech′less·ly,** *adv.* —**speech′less·ness,** *n.*

speed (spēd), *n., v.,* sped (sped) or speed·ed, speed·ing. —*n.* 1. a swift or rapid movement: *the speed of a rocket.* 2. rate of movement: *at full speed.* 3. arrangement of gears to give a certain rate of movement. An automobile usually has three speeds forward and one backward. 4. *Archaic.* good luck; success. —*v.* 1. go fast: *the boat sped over the water.* 2. make go fast: *speed a horse.* 3. make go faster: *speed production.* 4. help forward; promote: *speed an undertaking.* 5. send fast. 6. *Archaic.* give success to: *God speed you.* 7. speed up, go or cause to go faster; increase in speed. [OE *spēd*] —**speed′ster,** *n.* —Syn. *n.* 1. rapidity, celerity, quickness, haste.

speed·boat (spēd′bōt′), *n.* motorboat built to go fast.

speed·er (spēd′ər), *n.* person or thing that speeds, esp. a person who drives an automobile at a higher speed than is legal or safe.

speed·om·e·ter (spēd·om′ə·tər), *n.* instrument to indicate speed.

speed·up (spēd′up′), *n.* a speeding up; increase in speed.

speed·way (spēd′wā′), *n. Am.* road or track for fast driving.

speed·well (spēd′wel), *n.* any of various low plants with blue, purple, pink, or white flowers; veronica.

speed·y (spēd′i), *adj.*, speed·i·er, speed·i·est. 1. moving, going, or acting with speed: *speedy workers.* 2. done with or characterized by speed: *speedy progress.* 3. rapidly coming or brought to pass: *a speedy change.* 4. coming, given, or arrived at, quickly or soon; prompt: *a speedy decision.* —speed′i·ly, *adv.* —speed′i·ness, *n.*

spe·le·ol·o·gy (spē′li·ol′ə·ji), *n.* branch of science dealing with caves. —spe′le·ol′o·gist, *n.*

spell¹ (spel), *v.*, spelled or spelt, spell·ing. 1. write or say the letters of (a word) in order: *spell a word.* 2. write or say the letters of a word in order: *she cannot spell well.* 3. make up or form (a word). 4. mean: *delay spells danger.* 5. spell out, a. explain simply and lucidly. b. read with difficulty. [< OF *espeller* < Gmc.]

spell² (spel). *n.* 1. word or set of words having magic power. 2. fascination; charm. 3. cast a spell on, fascinate. 4. under a spell, fascinated. [OE, story]

spell³ (spel). *n.*, *v.*, spelled, spell·ing. —*n.* 1. period of work or duty: *the sailor's spell at the wheel was four hours.* 2. Colloq. period or time of anything. 3. *Am.*, Colloq. attack of illness, indisposition, etc. 4. period during which a particular kind of weather prevails. 5. relief of one person by another in doing something. [ME; akin to v.] —*v.* 1. Colloq. work in place of (another) for a while. 2. give an interval of rest to. 3. take an interval of rest. [OE *spelian*, v.]

spell·bind (spel′bīnd′), *v.*, –bound, –binding. make spellbound, fascinate; enchant. —spell′bind′er, *n.*

spell·bound (spel′bound′), *adj.* too interested to move; fascinated; enchanted.

spell·er (spel′ər), *n.* 1. person who spells words. 2. book for teaching spelling.

spell·ing (spel′ing), *n.* 1. the writing or saying of the letters of a word in order. 2. way that a word is spelled.

spelling bee, *Am.* a spelling contest.

Spen·cer (spen′sər), *n.* Herbert, 1820–1903, English philosopher. —Spen·ce·ri·an (spen·sir′i·ən), *adj.*, *n.*

spend (spend), *v.*, spent, spend·ing. 1. pay out: *how much money did you spend?* 2. pay out money: *earn before you spend.* 3. use (labor, words, time, etc.) on some object, etc.: *don't spend any more time on that job.* 4. pass (time) in a particular manner: *spend a day at the beach.* 5. wear out; exhaust: *the storm has spent its force.* [OE *spendan* < L *expendere.* Doublet of EXPEND.] —spend′a·ble, *adj.* —spend′er, *n.*

spend·thrift (spend′thrift′), *n.* person who wastes money. —*adj.* extravagant with money.

Spen·ser (spen′sər), *n.* Edmund, 1552?–1599, English poet, author of *The Faerie Queene.* —Spen·se·ri·an (spen·sir′i·ən), *adj.*, *n.*

spent (spent), *v.* pt. and pp. of spend. —*adj.* 1. used up. 2. worn out; tired: *a spent swimmer.*

sperm¹ (spėrm), *n.* 1. the fluid of a male animal that fertilizes the eggs of the female. 2. one of the male germ cells in it. [< L < Gk. *sperma* seed < *speirein* sow]

sperm² (spėrm), *n.* 1. spermaceti. 2. a sperm whale. 3. sperm oil.

sper·ma·cet·i (spėr′mə·set′i; –sē′ti), *n.* a whitish, waxy substance obtained from the oil in the head of the sperm whale and used in making fine candles, ointments, cosmetics, etc. [< Med.L *sperma ceti* sperm of a whale]

sper·mat·ic (spėr·mat′ik), **sper·mic** (spėr′mik), *adj.* 1. of or pertaining to sperm; seminal; generative. 2. pertaining to a sperm gland.

sper·ma·to·phyte (spėr′mə·tə·fīt′), *n.* plant that produces seeds. The spermatophytes form the largest division of the plant kingdom. [< spermato– (< Gk. *sperma* seed) + –phyte (< Gk. *phyton* plant)] —sper·ma·to·phyt·ic (spėr′mə·tə·fit′ik), *adj.*

sper·ma·to·zo·ön (spėr′mə·tə·zō′ən), *n.*, *pl.* –zo·a (–zō′ə). the male reproductive cell. A spermatozoön unites with an ovum to fertilize it. [< spermato– (< Gk. *sperma* seed) + Gk. *zoion* animal)] —sper′ma·to·zo′al, sper′ma·to·zo′ic, *adj.*

sperm oil, a light-yellow oil from the sperm whale, used for lubricating.

sperm whale, a large, square-headed, toothed whale that has a large cavity in its head filled with sperm oil and spermaceti.

spew (spū), *v.* throw out; cast forth; vomit. Also, spue. [OE *spiwan*] —spew′er, *n.*

sp. gr., specific gravity.

sphag·num (sfag′nəm), *n.* 1. any of various soft mosses, found chiefly on the surface of bogs. 2. a mass or quantity of this moss used by gardeners in potting and packing plants, in surgery for dressing wounds, etc. [< NL < Gk. *sphagnos*, kind of moss]

sphere (sfir), *n.*, *v.*, sphered, spher·ing. —*n.* 1. a round body whose surface is at all points equally distant from the center; globe; ball. 2. place or surroundings in which a person or thing exists, acts, works, etc.: *woman's sphere.* 3. range; extent; region: *sphere of influence.* 4. any of the stars or planets. 5. a supposed hollow globe, with the earth at its center, enclosing the stars, sun, and planets. 6. the heavens; the sky. —*v.* 1. enclose in or as if in a sphere. 2. form into a sphere. 3. set aloft. [< L < Gk. *sphaira*]

spher·i·cal (sfer′ə·kəl), *adj.* 1. shaped like a sphere. 2. of or pertaining to a sphere or spheres. —spher′i·cal′i·ty, spher′i·cal·ness, sphe·ric·i·ty (sfi·ris′ə·ti), *n.*

sphe·roid (sfir′oid), *n.* 1. a body shaped somewhat like a sphere. 2. a solid generated by the revolution of an ellipse about one of its axes. —*adj.* almost spherical. —sphe·roi′dal, *adj.* —sphe·roi′dal·ly, —sphe·roi·dic·i·ty (sfir′oi·dis′ə·ti), sphe·roi′di·ty, *n.*

sphinc·ter (sfingk′tər), *n.* Anat. a ringlike muscle that surrounds an opening or passage to close it. [< LL < Gk. *sphinkter* < *sphingein* squeeze] —sphinc′ter·al, sphinc·te·ri·al (sfingk·tir′i·əl), sphinc·ter·ic (sfingk·ter′ik), *adj.*

sphinx (sfingks), *n.*, *pl.* sphinx·es, sphin·ges (sfin′jēz). 1. statue of a lion's body with the head of a man, ram, or hawk. 2. Sphinx, a huge statue with a man's head and a lion's body, near Cairo, Egypt. 3. Sphinx, *Gk. Legend.* monster with the head of a woman, the body of a lion, and wings. The Sphinx proposed a riddle to every passer-by and killed those unable to guess it. 4. a puzzling or mysterious person. [< L < Gk.]

Sphinx

spice (spīs), *n.*, *v.*, spiced, spic·ing. —*n.* 1. seasoning. Pepper, cinnamon, cloves, ginger, and nutmeg are common spices. 2. a spicy, fragrant odor. 3. something that adds flavor or interest. 4. a slight touch or trace. —*v.* 1. put spice in; season: *spiced pickles.* 2. add flavor or interest to. [< OF, ult. < L *species* sort. Doublet of SPECIES.] —spiced, *adj.* —spic′er, *n.*

Spice Islands, Moluccas.

spick-and-span (spik′ənd·span′), *adj.* neat and clean; spruce or smart; fresh; new: *a spick-and-span uniform.* [short for *spick-and-span-new; spick,* var. of *spike; span-new* < Scand. *spān-nȳr* < *spānn* chip + *nȳr* new]

spic·ule (spik′ūl), *n.* 1. a small, slender, sharp-pointed piece, usually bony or crystalline. 2. such a piece, as the skeletal element of sponges, etc. 3. a small spike of flowers. [< L *spiculum*, dim. of *spicum*, var. of *spica* ear of grain]

spic·y (spīs′i), *adj.*, spic·i·er, spic·i·est. 1. flavored with spice. 2. like spice. 3. lively; keen. 4. somewhat improper. —spic′i·ly, *adv.* —spic′i·ness, *n.* —Syn. 2. aromatic, fragrant.

spi·der (spī′dər), *n.* 1. any of the eight-legged, wingless arachnids, many of which spin webs to catch insects for food. 2. something like or suggesting a spider. 3. *Am.* a frying pan with a handle. 4. *Am.* frame with three legs to

Garden spider

support a pot or pan over a fire. [OE *spīthra* < *spinnan* spin] —**spi′der·y**, *adj.*

spi·der·wort (spī′dər·wėrt′), *n.* a trailing plant that takes root at the knots of its stems and has clusters of flowers.

spiel (spēl), *Am., Slang.* —*n.* talk; speech; harangue, esp. one of a cheap, noisy nature. —*v.* talk; speak. [< dial. G, play] —**spiel′er**, *n. Am.*

spiff·y (spif′i), *adj.*, **spiff·i·er, spiff·i·est.** *Slang.* smart; neat; trim.

spig·ot (spig′ət), *n.* **1.** *U.S.* faucet. **2.** peg or plug used to stop the small hole of a cask, barrel, etc.

spike¹ (spīk), *n., v.,* **spiked, spik·ing.** —*n.* **1.** a large, strong nail. **2.** a sharp-pointed spike or part. —*v.* **1.** fasten with spikes. **2.** provide with spikes. **3.** pierce or injure with a spike. **4.** put an end or stop to; make useless; block. **5.** *Am., Slang.* add liquor to (a drink, etc.). [< Scand. *spīk*] —**spike′like′**, *adj.* —**spik′er**, *n.*

spike² (spīk), *n.* **1.** ear of grain. **2.** a long, pointed flower cluster. [< L *spica*]

spike·let (spīk′lit), *n.* a small spike or flower cluster.

spike·nard (spīk′nərd; -närd), *n.* **1.** a sweet-smelling ointment used by the ancients. **2.** the fragrant East Indian plant from which it was probably obtained. [< Med.L *spica nardi* ear of nard]

spile (spīl), *n., v.,* **spiled, spil·ing.** —*n.* **1.** peg or plug of wood used to stop the small hole of a cask or barrel. **2.** *Am.* spout for drawing off sap from the sugar maple. —*v.* **1.** stop up (a hole) with a plug. **2.** furnish with a spout. [cf. MDu., MLG *spile*]

spill¹ (spil), *v.,* **spilled or spilt, spill·ing,** *n.* —*v.* **1.** let (liquid or any matter in loose pieces) run or fall: *spill milk or salt.* **2.** fall or flow out: *water spilled from the pail.* **3.** shed (blood). **4.** *Colloq.* cause to fall from a horse, car, boat, etc. **5.** let wind out of (a sail). **6.** *Slang.* make known; tell. —*n.* **1.** a spilling. **2.** quantity spilled. **3.** *Colloq.* a fall. [OE *spillan*] —**spill′er**, *n.*

spill² (spil), *n.* **1.** splinter. **2.** piece of wood or paper used to light candles, etc. [? ult. var. of *spile*]

spill·way (spil′wā′), *n.* channel or passage for the escape of surplus water from a dam, river, etc.

spin (spin), *v.,* **spun or** (*Archaic*) **span, spun, spin·ning,** *n.* —*v.* **1.** draw out and twist (cotton, flax, wool, etc.) into thread. **2.** make (thread, yarn, etc.) by drawing out and twisting cotton, wool, flax, etc. **3.** make (a thread, web, cocoon, etc.) by giving out from the body sticky material that hardens into thread: *spiders spin webs.* **4.** make (glass, gold, etc.) into thread. **5.** turn or make turn rapidly: *the boy spins his top.* **6.** feel dizzy: *my head spun after the rough boat ride.* **7.** run, ride, drive, etc., rapidly: *spin across the water in a boat.* **8.** fabricate; produce; tell: *spin yarns about adventures at sea.* **9.** shape (sheet metal) into hollow, rounded form during rotation on a lathe or wheel by pressure with a suitable tool. **10. spin out,** make long and slow; draw out; prolong. —*n.* **1.** a spinning. **2.** a rapid run, ride, drive, etc. **3.** a flight maneuver in which an airplane loses altitude rapidly and descends in a vertical spiral path. [OE *spinnan*] —**Syn.** *v.* **5.** twirl, whirl, rotate, revolve.

spin·ach (spin′ich; -ij), *n.* **1.** a plant whose green leaves are boiled and eaten. **2.** the leaves. [< OF *(e)spinache* < Med.L < Sp. *espinaca* < Ar. *isbānakh*]

spi·nal (spī′nəl), *adj.* of the spine or backbone; pertaining to the backbone. —**spi′nal·ly,** *adv.*

spinal column, the spine; the backbone.

spinal cord, a thick, whitish cord of nerve tissue in the backbone or spine.

spin·dle (spin′dəl), *n., v.,* **-dled, -dling.** —*n.* **1.** the rod or pin used in spinning to twist, wind, and hold thread. **2.** any rod or pin that turns around, or on which something turns, such as an axle, axis, shaft, mandrel, or either of the two shaftlike parts of a lathe that hold the piece that is to be turned. **3.** *Am.* rod or post fixed to a rock, reef, or shoal to warn navigators. —*v.*

grow tall and slender; grow too tall and slender. [OE *spinel* < *spinnan* spin]

spin·dle·legs (spin′dəl·legz′), **spin·dle·shanks** (-shangks′), *n.pl.* **1.** long, thin legs. **2.** *Colloq.* (*sing. in use*) person with long, thin legs. —**spin·dle-leg·ged** (spin′dəl·leg′id; -legd′), **spin·dle-shanked** (spin′dəl·shangkt′), *adj.*

spin·dling (spin′dling), *adj.* very long and slender; too tall and thin.

spin·dly (spin′dli), *adj.*, **-dli·er, -dli·est.** spindling.

spin·drift (spin′drift′), *n.* spray blown or dashed up from the waves. Also, **spoondrift.**

spine (spīn), *n.* **1.** series of small bones down the middle of the back; backbone. **2.** anything like a backbone; long, narrow ridge or support. **3.** a stiff, sharp-pointed outgrowth on a plant or animal; thorn or something like it. A cactus has spines; so has a porcupine. **4.** the supporting back portion of a book cover. [< L *spina*, orig. thorn] —**spined,** *adj.* —**spine′like′,** *adj.*

spine·less (spīn′lis), *adj.* **1.** without spines. **2.** having no backbone. **3.** without moral force, resolution, or courage; weak-willed; feeble. —**spine′less·ly,** *adv.* —**spine′less·ness,** *n.*

spin·et (spin′it; spi·net′), *n.* **1.** an old-fashioned musical instrument like a small harpsichord. **2.** a compact upright piano. [< F < Ital. *spinetta,* prob. after G. *Spinetti,* Italian inventor]

spin·na·ker (spin′ə·kər), *n. Naut.* a large, triangular sail carried by yachts on the side opposite the mainsail when running before the wind. [supposedly from *Sphinx,* a yacht on which first used]

spin·ner (spin′ər), *n.* person, animal, or thing that spins.

spin·ner·et (spin′ər·et), *n.* organ by which spiders, silkworms, etc., spin their threads.

spin·ning (spin′ing), *adj.* that spins. —*n.* act or procedure of one that spins.

spinning jenny, an early type of spinning machine having more than one spindle, whereby one person could spin a number of threads at the same time.

spinning wheel, a large wheel and a spindle arranged for spinning cotton, flax, wool, etc., into thread or yarn.

Spi·no·za (spi·nō′zə), *n.* 1632–1677, Dutch philosopher.

spin·ster (spin′stər), *n.* **1.** an unmarried woman. **2.** an elderly woman who has not married; old maid. **3.** woman who spins flax, wool, etc., into thread. —**spin′ster·hood, spin′ster·ship,** *n.* —**spin′ster·ish,** *adj.*

spin·y (spī′ni), *adj.*, **spin·i·er, spin·i·est.** **1.** covered with spines; having spines; thorny: *a spiny cactus, a spiny porcupine.* **2.** spinelike. **3.** difficult; troublesome. —**spin′i·ness,** *n.*

spi·ra·cle (spī′rə·kəl; spir′ə-), *n.* an opening for breathing. Insects take in air through tiny spiracles. A whale breathes through a spiracle in the top of its head. [< L *spiraculum* < *spirare* breathe] —**spi·rac·u·lar** (spī·rak′yə·lər), *adj.*

spi·rae·a, spi·re·a (spī·rē′ə), *n.* any of various shrubs that have clusters of small white, pink, or red flowers with five petals. [< L < Gk. *speiraia*]

spi·ral (spī′rəl), *n., adj., v.,* **-raled, -ral·ing;** *esp. Brit.* **-ralled, -ral·ling.** —*n.* **1.** a winding and gradually widening coil; the shape of a watch spring; the shape of the thread of a screw. **2.** a single turn of a spiral. **3.** *Economics.* a constantly augmented increasing or decreasing: *an inflationary spiral.* —*adj.* coiled, as a snail's shell. —*v.* **1.** move in a spiral. **2.** form into a spiral. [< Med.L, < L *spira* a coil < Gk. *speira*] —**spi′ral·ly,** *adv.*

Spirals

spi·rant (spī′rənt), *n. Phonet.* fricative. [< L *spirans* breathing]

spire (spīr), *n., v.,* **spired, spir·ing.** —*n.* **1.** the top part of a tower or steeple that narrows to a point. See the picture under **steeple.** **2.** anything tapering and pointed. —*v.* **1.** shoot up. **2.** furnish with a spire. [OE *spīr*] —**spired,** *adj.* —**spire′like′,** *adj.* —**spir′y,** *adj.*

spir·it (spir′it), *n.* **1.** the immaterial part of man; soul: *he is present in spirit, though absent in body.* **2.** man's moral, religious, or emotional nature. **3.** a supernatural being. **4.** a vital principle (in man, etc.). **5. the Spirit,** a. God. b. the Holy Ghost. **6.** Often, **spirits.** state of mind; disposition; temper: *he is in good spirits.* **7.** influence that stirs up and rouses: *a spirit of reform.* **8.** person; personality: *a noble spirit.* **9. spirits,** vigor; liveliness; cheerfulness. **10.** courage; vigor; liveliness: *a race horse must have spirit.* **11.** enthusiasm and loyalty. **12.** the real meaning or intent: *the spirit of a law.* **13.** Often, **spirits.** solution in alcohol: *spirits of camphor.* **14.** Often, **spirits.** strong alcoholic liquor: *he drinks beer but no spirits.* **15. out of spirits,** sad; gloomy. —*v.* **1.** stir up; encourage; cheer. **2.** carry (away or off) secretly: *the child has been spirited away.* **3.** conjure (up). [< L *spiritus*, orig., breath < *spirare breathe.* Doublet of SPRITE.] —**spir′it·less,** *adj.* —**spir′it·less·ly,** *adv.* —**spir′it·less·ness,** *n.* —**Syn.** *n.* **3.** phantom, specter, apparition. **6.** humor, mood. **10.** animation, mettle, vivacity. **11.** ardor, zeal.

spir·it·ed (spir′it·id), *adj.* lively; dashing. —**spir′it·ed·ly,** *adv.* —**spir′it·ed·ness,** *n.*

spirit level, instrument used to find out whether a surface is level. When the bubble of air in the glass tube of a spirit level is exactly at the middle of the tube, the surface is level.

spir·it·u·al (spir′i·chů·əl), *adj.* **1.** of the spirit or soul. **2.** caring much for things of the spirit or soul. **3.** having to do with the church: *spiritual lords.* **4.** sacred; religious. —*n.* **1.** a matter of religion or the church. **2.** a sacred song or hymn as sung by the Negroes of the southern United States. —**spir′it·u·al·ly,** *adv.* —**spir′it·u·al·ness, spir′it·u·al′i·ty,** *n.*

spir·it·u·al·ism (spir′i·chů·əl·iz′əm), *n.* **1.** *Am.* belief that spirits of the dead communicate with the living, esp. through persons called mediums. **2.** insistence on the spiritual; doctrine that spirit alone is real. —**spir′it·u·al·ist,** *n.* —**spir′it·u·al·is′tic,** *adj.*

spir·it·u·al·ize (spir′i·chů·əl·īz′), *v.,* –**ized,** –**iz·ing.** make spiritual. —**spir′it·u·al·i·za′tion,** *n.*

spir·it·u·ous (spir′i·chů·əs), *adj.* **1.** containing alcohol. **2.** distilled, not fermented. —**spir·i·tu·os′i·ty** (spir′i·chů·os′ə·ti), **spir′it·u·ous·ness,** *n.*

spi·ro·chete, spi·ro·chaete (spī′rə·kēt), *n.* any of the bacteria that have a spiral shape. [< NL, < Gk. *speira* coil + *chaite* hair] —**spi′ro·che′tal, spi′ro·chae′tal,** *adj.*

spirt (spėrt), *v., n.* spurt.

spit¹ (spit), *v.,* **spat** or **spit, spit·ting,** *n.* —*v.* **1.** throw out saliva from the mouth: *a cat spits when angry.* **2.** throw out: *the gun spits fire.* —*n.* **1.** the liquid produced in the mouth; saliva. **2.** noise or act of spitting. **3.** a frothy or spitlike secretion given off by some insects. **4. the spit of,** *Colloq.* just like. [OE *spittan*] —**spit′ter,** *n.*

spit² (spit), *n., v.,* **spit·ted, spit·ting.** —*n.* **1.** a sharp-pointed, slender rod or bar on which meat is roasted. **2.** a narrow point of land running into the water. —*v.* pierce; stab. [OE *spitu*]

spit·ball (spit′bôl′), *n. Am.* **1.** a small ball of chewed-up paper, used as a missile. **2.** *Baseball.* variety of curve pitched by moistening one side of the ball with saliva.

spite (spīt), *n., v.,* **spit·ed, spit·ing.** —*n.* **1.** ill will; grudge. **2. in spite of,** not prevented by; notwithstanding. —*v.* show ill will toward; annoy. [ult. < *despite*] —**spite′ful,** *adj.* —**spite′ful·ly,** *adv.* —**spite′ful·ness,** *n.*

spit·fire (spit′fīr′), *n.* **1.** person, esp. a woman or girl, who has a quick and fiery temper. **2.** something that sends forth fire, such as a cannon or some kinds of fireworks. —*adj.* of or like a spitfire.

Spits·ber·gen (spits′bėr′gən), *n.* group of Norwegian islands in the Arctic Ocean, N of Norway.

spit·tle (spit′əl), *n.* saliva; spit. [< *spit*]

spit·toon (spi·tün′), *n. Am.* cuspidor.

spitz (spits), or **spitz dog,** *n.* Pomeranian. [< G, pointed]

spiv (spiv), *n. Brit. Colloq.* dealer in the black market.

splash (splash), *v.* **1.** cause (water, mud, etc.) to fly about. **2.** dash liquid about: *the baby splashes in his tub.* **3.** cause to scatter a liquid about: *he splashed the oars as he rowed.* **4.** dash in scattered masses or drops: *the waves splashed on the beach.* **5.** wet, spatter, or soil. **6.** fall, move, or go with a splash or splashes. **7.** mark with spots or patches. —*n.* **1.** sound of splashing; splashing. **2.** spot of liquid splashed upon a thing. **3.** spot; patch. **4. make a splash,** *Colloq.* attract attention; cause excitement. [alter. of *plash,* *n.,* < OE *plæsc* puddle] —**splash′er,** *n.* —**splash′y,** *adj.*

splat (splat), *n.* a broad, flat piece of wood, esp. the central upright part of the back of a chair.

splat·ter (splat′ər), *v., n.* splash; spatter. [blend of *spatter* and *splash*]

splay (splā), *v.* **1.** spread out. **2.** spread; flare. —*adj.* **1.** spread out. **2.** wide and flat. —*n.* **1.** spread; flare. **2.** a slanting surface. [< *display*]

splay·foot (splā′fůt′), *n., pl.* –**feet.** a broad, flat foot, esp. one turned outward. —**splay′foot′ed,** *adj.*

spleen (splēn), *n.* **1.** a ductless gland at the left of the stomach in man, and near the stomach or intestine in other vertebrates. People used to think that the spleen caused low spirits, bad temper, and spite. **2.** bad temper; spite; anger. **3.** low spirits. [< L < Gk. *splen*] —**spleen′ful,** *adj.* —**spleen′ish, spleen′y,** *adj.*

splen·did (splen′did), *adj.* **1.** brilliant in appearance, color, etc.: *a splendid sight to see.* **2.** richly handsome; gorgeous; magnificent: *splendid jewels.* **3.** glorious: *a splendid name in history.* **4.** strikingly admirable: *splendid talents.* **5.** *Colloq.* very good; fine; excellent: *a splendid chance.* [< L *splendidus* < *splendere* be bright] —**splen′did·ly,** *adv.* —**splen′did·ness,** *n.*

splen·dif·er·ous (splen·dif′ər·əs), *adj. Am.* splendid; magnificent; fine.

splen·dor, esp. *Brit.* **splen·dour** (splen′dər), *n.* **1.** great brightness; brilliant light. **2.** magnificent show; pomp; glory. [< L, < *splendere* be bright] —**splen′dor·ous,** *adj.*

sple·net·ic (spli·net′ik), *adj.* **1.** pertaining to the spleen. **2.** bad-tempered; irritable; peevish. [< LL, < *splen* SPLEEN] —**sple·net′i·cal·ly,** *adv.*

splice (splīs), *v.,* **spliced, splic·ing,** *n.* —*v.* **1.** join together (ropes, etc.) by weaving together ends that have been untwisted. **2.** join together (two pieces of timber) by overlapping. **3.** *Slang.* marry. —*n.* a joining of ropes or timbers by splicing. [< MDu. *splissen*] —**splic′er,** *n.*

Splicing

splint (splint), *n.* **1.** arrangement of wood, metal, plaster, etc., to hold a broken or dislocated bone in place. **2.** a thin strip of wood, such as is used in making baskets. [< MDu., MLG *splinte*]

splin·ter (splin′tər), *n.* a thin, sharp piece of wood, bone, glass, etc. —*adj.* pertaining to dissenting groups that break away from regular political groups, religious organizations, etc.: *a splinter party.* —*v.* split or break into splinters. [< MDu.] —**splin′ter·y,** *adj.*

split (split), *v.,* **split, split·ting,** *n., adj.* —*v.* **1.** break or cut from end to end, or in layers. **2.** separate into parts; divide. **3.** divide into different groups, factions, parties, etc., as by discord. **4.** *Physics, Chem.* a. divide (a molecule) into two or more individual atoms. b. divide (an atomic nucleus) into two portions of approximately equal mass by forcing the absorption of a neutron. **5.** burst. **6. split hairs,** make too fine distinctions. **7. split one's vote or ticket,** *Am.* vote for candidates of different parties. —*n.* **1.** division in a group, party, etc.: *there was a split in the Republican Party.* **2.** a splitting; break; crack. **3.** *Slang.* share; portion. **4.** Often, **splits.** an acrobatic trick of sinking to the floor with

the legs spread far apart in opposite directions.
5. bottle of a drink half the usual size. 6. *Colloq.*
a sweet dish made of sliced fruit, ice cream, etc.
—*adj.* broken or cut from end to end; divided.
[< MDu. *splitten*] —**split′ter,** *n.*

split infinitive, infinitive having an adverb
between *to* and the verb. *Example:* He wants to
never work, but to always play. ❯ **split infinitive.** The word order in which an adverb comes
between the *to* and the verb in an infinitive (She
asked them *to please sit down*) is called a split
infinitive. Awkward split infinitives are avoided:
*After a while I was able to, although not very
accurately, distinguish the good customers from
the sulky ones.*

split-lev-el (split′lev′əl), *adj.* (of a house)
having certain rooms on a level less than a full
story higher than others.

split-ting (split′ing), *adj.* **1.** that splits. **2.**
very severe; extreme; violent.

splotch (sploch), *n.* a large, irregular spot;
splash. —*v.* make splotches on. [? blend of *spot*
and *blotch*] —**splotch′y,** *adj.*

splurge (splėrj), *n., v.,* **splurged, splurg·ing.**
Am., Colloq. —*n.* a showing off. —*v.* **1.** show off.
2. spend extravagantly.

splut-ter (splut′ər), *v.* **1.** talk in a hasty, confused, or incoherent way. **2.** make spitting or
popping noises; sputter. —*n.* a spluttering.
—**splut′ter·er,** *n.*

spoil (spoil), *v.,* **spoiled** or **spoilt** (spoilt),
spoil·ing, *n.* —*v.* **1.** damage; injure; destroy:
rain spoiled the picnic. **2.** be damaged; become
bad or unfit for use: *fruit spoils if kept too long.*
3. injure the character or disposition of, esp. by
excessive indulgence: *spoil a child.* **4.** take by
force; steal; rob. —*n.* **1.** Often, **spoils.** things
taken by force; things won: *the soldiers carried
the spoils back to their own land.* **2.** an object of
plundering; prey. **3.** Usually, **spoils.** government
offices and positions filled by the successful political party. [< OF *espoillier,* ult. < L *spolium,*
n.] —**spoil′a·ble,** *adj.* —**spoil′er,** *n.* —**Syn.** *v.* **1.**
ruin, wreck. **2.** deteriorate, decay, rot. **4.** plunder, pillage, sack, ravage. —*n.* **1.** loot.

spoil·age (spoil′ij), *n.* **1.** act of spoiling. **2.** that
which is spoiled.

spoils·man (spoilz′mən), *n., pl.* **-men.** *Am.*
person who gets or tries to get a government
office or job as a reward for his service to the
successful political party.

spoils system, *Am.* the system or practice in
which public offices with their salaries and advantages are at the disposal of the victorious
political party for its own purposes and in its
own (rather than the public) interest.

Spo·kane (spō·kan′), *n.* city in E Washington.

spoke[1] (spōk), *v.* **1.** pt. of speak. **2.** *Archaic.*
pp. of speak.

spoke[2] (spōk), *n., v.,* **spoked, spok·ing.** —*n.* **1.**
one of the bars from the center of a wheel to the
rim. **2.** rung of a ladder. **3.** put a spoke in one's
wheel, stop or hinder a person. —*v.* furnish with
spokes. [OE *spāca*]

spo·ken (spō′kən), *v.* pp. of speak. —*adj.* **1.**
expressed with the mouth; uttered; told: *the
spoken word.* **2.** speaking in a certain way: *a
soft-spoken man.*

spokes·man (spōks′mən), *n., pl.* **-men.** person
who speaks for another or others.

spo·li·a·tion (spō′li·ā′shən), *n.* **1.** a plundering or despoiling; robbery. **2.** the plundering of
neutrals at sea in time of war. [< L, ult. <
spolium booty] —**spo′li·a′tive,** *adj.* —**spo′li·a′-
tor,** *n.*

spon·dee (spon′dē), *n.* a foot or measure in
poetry consisting of two long or accented syllables. The spondee is used to vary other meters.
[< L < Gk., < *sponde* libation; orig. used in
songs accompanying libations] —**spon·da·ic**
(spon·dā′ik), *adj.*

sponge (spunj), *n., v.,* **sponged, spong·ing.**
—*n.* **1.** a kind of sea animal having a tough,
fiberlike skeleton or framework. **2.** its light
framework used for soaking up water in bathing, cleaning, etc. **3.** a sponging. **4.** something
like a sponge, such as bread dough, a kind of
cake, a kind of pudding, etc **5.** *Colloq.* person

who continually lives at the expense of others;
parasite. **6. throw up the sponge,** give up; admit
defeat. —*v.* **1.** wipe or rub with a wet sponge;
make clean or damp in this way. **2.** absorb. **3.**
Colloq. live or profit at the expense of another in
a mean way. [< L < Gk. *spongia*] —**sponge′-
like′,** *adj.* —**spong′er,** *n.* —**spon′gy,** *adj.*
—**spon′gi·ness,** *n.*

sponge cake, a light, spongy cake made with
eggs, sugar, flour, etc., but no butter.

spon·son (spon′sən), *n.* **1.** part projecting from
the side of a ship or boat, used for support or
protection. **2.** an air-filled section on either side
of an airplane, canoe, etc., to steady it.

spon·sor (spon′sər), *n.* **1.** person who is responsible for a person or thing: *the sponsor of a
law.* **2.** person who takes vows for an infant at
baptism; godfather or godmother. **3.** a surety. **4.**
company, store, or other business firm that pays
the costs of a radio or television program advertising its products. —*v.* act as sponsor for. [< L,
< *spondere* give assurance] —**spon·so·ri·al**
(spon·sô′ri·əl; -sō′-), *adj.* —**spon′sor·ship,** *n.*

spon·ta·ne·i·ty (spon′tə·nē′ə·ti), *n., pl.* **-ties.**
1. a state, quality, or fact of being spontaneous.
2. a spontaneous action, movement, etc.

spon·ta·ne·ous (spon·tā′ni·əs), *adj.* **1.** caused
by natural impulse or desire; not forced or compelled; not planned beforehand: *a spontaneous
cheer.* **2.** taking place without external cause or
help; caused entirely by inner forces. **3.** growing
or produced naturally; not planted, cultivated,
etc. [< LL, < L *sponte* of one's own accord]
—**spon·ta′ne·ous·ly,** *adv.* —**spon·ta′ne·ous·
ness,** *n.* —**Syn. 1.** voluntary, unbidden.

spontaneous combustion, the bursting
into flame of a substance without anyone's
having set it on fire. In spontaneous combustion,
the heat produced by chemical action within the
substance itself causes it to catch on fire.

spoof (spüf), *v., n.* *Slang.* trick; hoax; joke.
[coined by A. Roberts, British comedian]

spook (spük), *n.* *Am., Colloq.* ghost; specter.
[< Du.] —**spook′ish,** *adj.* —**spook′y,** *adj., Am.*

spool (spül), *n.* **1.** a cylinder of wood or metal
on which thread, wire, etc., is wound. **2.** something like a spool in shape or use. —*v.* wind on
a spool. [< MDu. *spoele*] —**spool′er,** *n.*

spoon (spün), *n.* **1.** utensil consisting of a
small, shallow bowl at the end of a handle and
used to take up or stir food or drink. **2.** something shaped like a spoon, as a lure used in
casting or trolling for fish. **3.** a kind of golf club
with a wooden head that has more loft than a
brassie. —*v.* **1.** take up in a spoon. **2.** *Slang.*
make love in a silly way. [OE *spōn* chip, shav-
ing]

spoon·bill (spün′bil′), *n.* **1.** a long-legged
wading bird that has a long, flat bill with a
spoon-shaped tip. **2.** any of various birds that
have a similar bill. —**spoon′-billed′,** *adj.*

spoon·drift (spün′drift′), *n.* spindrift.

spoon·ful (spün′fůl), *n., pl.* **-fuls.** as much as
a spoon can hold.

spoor (spůr), *n.* trail of a wild animal; track.
—*v.* track by or follow a spoor. [< Du.]

spo·rad·ic (spə·rad′ik), **spo·rad·i·cal** (-ə-
kəl), *adj.* **1.** appearing or happening at intervals
in time: *sporadic outbreaks.* **2.** being or occurring apart from others; isolated. **3.** appearing
in scattered instances: *sporadic cases of scarlet
fever.* **4.** occurring singly, or widely apart in
locality. [< Med.L < Gk. *sporadikos* scattered,
ult. < *spora* a sowing] —**spo·rad′i·cal·ly,** *adv.*

spo·ran·gi·um (spə·ran′ji·əm), *n., pl.* **-gi·a**
(-ji·ə). *Bot.* receptacle containing spores; spore
case. The little brown spots sometimes seen on
the under side of ferns are sporangia. [< NL,
< Gk. *spora* seed + *angeion* vessel]

spore (spôr; spōr), *n., v.,* **spored, spor·ing.** —*n.*
1. a single cell capable of growing into a new
plant or animal. Ferns produce spores. **2.** germ;
seed. —*v.* produce spores. [< NL < Gk. *spora*
seed]

spo·ro·phyte (spô′rə·fīt; spō′-), *n.* any plant
or generation of a plant that produces asexual
spores.

spor·ran (spôr′ən; spor′-), *n.* in a Scottish Highland costume, a large purse, commonly of fur, hanging from the belt in front. [< Scotch Gaelic *sporan*]

sport (spôrt; spōrt), *n.* 1. form of amusement or play; game; contest. Baseball, football, golf, tennis, fishing, hunting, and racing are outdoor sports. 2. amusement; play; fun. 3. playful joking: *say a thing in sport*. 4. object of ridicule: *don't make sport of the lame boy*. 5. object of a joke; plaything: *his hat blew off and became the sport of the wind*. 6. person of sportsmanlike or admirable qualities. 7. *Colloq.* one who is willing to take a chance; good fellow: *be a sport*. 8. *Am., Colloq.* gambler. 9. *Am., Slang.* a cheap, showy person. 10. *Biol.* animal or plant that varies suddenly or in a marked manner from the normal type. 11. **make sport of**, make fun of; laugh at; ridicule. —*v.* 1. amuse oneself with some pleasant pastime. 2. jest, as in fun; ridicule. 3. *Colloq.* display: *sport a new hat*. 4. trifle. —*adj.* of sports; suitable for sports. [ult. short for *disport*] —**sport′er**, *n.* —**sport′ful**, *adj.* —**sport′ful·ly**, *adv.* —**sport′ful·ness**, *n.* —**Syn.** *n.* 2. diversion, pastime, recreation.

sport·ing (spôr′ting; spōr′-), *adj.* 1. of, interested in, or engaging in sports. 2. playing fair. 3. willing to take a chance. 4. *Colloq.* involving risk; uncertain. —**sport′ing·ly**, *adv.*

spor·tive (spôr′tiv; spōr′-), *adj.* playful; jocose; merry. —**spor′tive·ly**, *adv.* —**spor′tive·ness**, *n.*

sports (spôrts; spōrts), *adj.* of sports; suitable for sports: *a sports dress*.

sports·man (spôrts′mən; spōrts′-), *n., pl.* -men. 1. person who takes part in sports, esp. hunting, fishing, or racing. 2. person who likes sports. 3. person who plays fair. 4. person who is willing to take a chance. —**sports′man·like′**, **sports′man·ly**, *adj.* —**sports′man·ship**, *n.*

sports·wom·an (spôrts′wùm′ən; spōrts′-), *n.* a woman sportsman.

sport·y (spôr′ti; spōr′-), *adj.*, **sport·i·er**, **sport·i·est**. *Colloq.* 1. gay or fast; flashy; vulgar. 2. smart in dress, appearance, manners, etc. —**sport′i·ness**, *n.*

spot (spot), *n., v.,* **spot·ted**, **spot·ting**, *adj.* —*n.* 1. mark, stain, or speck, as on a surface: *a spot of ink on the paper*. 2. a moral stain or flaw: *his character is without spot*. 3. a small part unlike the rest: *his tie is blue with white spots*. 4. place: *a spot in the country*. 5. *Colloq.* a small amount; little bit: *a spot of lunch*. 6. **hit the spot**, *Colloq.* be just right; be satisfactory. 7. **on the spot**, a. at the very place. b. at once. c. *Am., Slang.* in trouble or difficulty. d. *Slang.* marked for death. 8. *Am., Colloq.* with the value in dollars designated by a number; a bank note: *a ten spot*. —*v.* 1. make spots on: *spot a dress*. 2. become spotted; have spots: *this fabric will spot*. 3. place in a certain spot; scatter in various spots: *lookouts were spotted all along the coast*. 4. *Colloq.* pick out; find out; recognize: *spot a friend in the crowd*. 5. blemish; stain: *he spotted his reputation by lying repeatedly*. —*adj.* 1. on hand; ready: *a spot answer*. 2. pertaining to or involving immediate cash payment: *a spot transaction*. 3. *Radio.* originating from a local station. [ME] —**spot′less**, *adj.* —**spot′less·ly**, *adv.* —**spot′less·ness**, *n.* —**spot′ta·ble**, *adj.* —**Syn.** *n.* 1. blotch, blot, fleck.

spot cash, *Am.* money paid just as soon as the goods are delivered or the work is done.

spot check, *Am.* 1. a brief, rough sampling. 2. a checkup made without warning.

spot·light (spot′līt′), *n.* 1. a strong light thrown upon a particular place or person. 2. the lamp that gives the light: *a spotlight in a theater*. 3. a powerful light, as on an automobile, that can be pointed in any direction. 4. conspicuous attention; public notice.

spot·ted (spot′id), *adj.* 1. stained with spots: *a spotted reputation*. 2. marked with spots: *a spotted dog*. —**spot′ted·ness**, *n.*

spotted fever, any of various fevers characterized by spots on the skin.

spot·ter (spot′ər), *n.* 1. person or thing that spots, esp. one that locates enemy positions. 2. civilian who watches for enemy aircraft over a city, town, etc. 3. *Am.* person employed to keep watch on employees for evidence of dishonesty or other misconduct.

spot·ty (spot′i), *adj.*, **-ti·er**, **-ti·est**. 1. having spots; spotted. 2. not of uniform quality. —**spot′ti·ly**, *adv.* —**spot′ti·ness**, *n.*

spous·al (spouz′əl), *n.* Often, **spousals**. the ceremony of marriage. —*adj.* of or pertaining to marriage.

spouse (spous; spouz), *n.* husband or wife. [< OF < L *sponsus*, *sponsa*, pp. of *spondere* bind oneself] —**spouse′less**, *adj.*

spout (spout), *v.* 1. throw out (a liquid) in a stream or spray: *the fountain spouted water*. 2. flow out with force: *water spouted from a break in the pipe*. 3. speak in loud tones with affected emotion: *the actor spouted his lines*. —*n.* 1. stream; jet. 2. pipe for carrying off water. 3. tube or lip by which liquid is poured. A teakettle, a coffee pot, and a syrup jug have spouts. [cf. MDu. *spouten*] —**spout′er**, *n.* —**spout′less**, *adj.* —**Syn.** *v.* 2. spurt, gush, jet, squirt. 3. declaim.

sprain (sprān), *v.* injure (a joint or muscle) by a sudden twist or wrench: *sprain your ankle*. —*n.* injury caused in this way.

sprang (sprang), *v.* pt. of **spring**.

sprat (sprat), *n.* a small food fish related to the herring, found along the Atlantic coast of Europe. [OE *sprott*]

sprawl (sprôl), *v.* 1. toss or spread the limbs about, as an infant or animal lying on its back. 2. lie or sit with the limbs spread out, esp. ungracefully. 3. stretch out (the limbs) as in sprawling. 4. spread out in an irregular or awkward manner: *a sprawling vine*. 5. move awkwardly. —*n.* act or position of sprawling. [OE *sprēawlian*] —**sprawl′er**, *n.* —**sprawl′y**, *adj.*

spray[1] (sprā), *n.* 1. liquid going through the air in small drops. 2. something like this: *a spray of bullets*. 3. instrument that sends a liquid out as spray. —*v.* 1. scatter spray on; sprinkle. 2. scatter spray. 3. direct numerous small missiles, etc., upon. [? < MDu. *sprayen*] —**spray′er**, *n.*

spray[2] (sprā), *n.* 1. a small branch or piece of some plant with its leaves, flowers, or fruit. 2. an ornament like this.

spread (spred), *v.*, **spread**, **spread·ing**, *n., adj.* —*v.* 1. cover or cause to cover a large or larger area; stretch out; unfold; open: *spread rugs on the floor*. 2. move further apart: *spread out your fingers*. 3. lie; extend: *fields of corn spread out before us*. 4. scatter; distribute: *he spread the news*. 5. cover with a thin layer: *spread bread with butter*. 6. put as a thin layer: *spread the paint evenly*. 7. be put as a thin layer: *this paint spreads evenly*. 8. set (a table) for a meal. 9. put food on (a table). 10. **spread oneself**, *Colloq.* a. try hard to make a good impression. b. display one's abilities fully. c. brag. —*n.* 1. expansion; diffusion: *the spread of news*. 2. the extent of spreading: *the spread of a deer's antlers*. 3. capacity for spreading: *the spread of an elastic material*. 4. *Colloq.* food put on the table; feast. 5. *Am.* a cloth covering for a bed, table, etc. 6. *Am.* something spread. Butter and jam are spreads. 7. *Am.* in a newspaper, an article given conspicuous treatment, as by display across two or more columns. —*adj.* stretched out; expanded; extended. [OE *sprēdan*] —**spread′er**, *n.* —**Syn.** *v.* 1. unroll, unfurl, expand, stretch. 4. circulate, disseminate.

spread eagle, a boastful person.

spread-ea·gle (spred′ē′gəl), *adj., v.,* **-gled**, **-gling**. —*adj.* 1. having the form of an eagle with wings spread out. 2. *Am.* boastful: *spread-eagle oratory*. —*v.* stretch out flat and sprawling; tie with arms and legs outstretched.

spree (sprē), *n.* **1.** a lively frolic. **2.** spell of drinking intoxicating liquor.

sprig (sprig), *n.* **1.** shoot, twig, or small branch. **2.** ornament or design shaped like a sprig. **3.** *Contemptuous.* a young man. —**sprig′gy,** *adj.*

spright·ly (sprīt′li), *adj.,* -li·er, -li·est, *adv.* —*adj.* lively; gay. —*adv.* in a lively manner. [< *spright,* var. of *sprite*] —**spright′li·ness,** *n.* —Syn. *adj.* spirited, animated, vivacious.

spring (spring), *v.,* sprang or sprung, sprung, spring·ing, *n., adj.* —*v.* **1.** move rapidly or suddenly; leap; jump: *spring into the air.* **2.** fly back or away as if by elastic force: *a trap springs.* **3.** cause to spring; cause to act by a spring: *spring a trap.* **4.** come from some source; arise; grow: *great industries sprang up.* **5.** begin to move, act, grow, etc., suddenly; burst forth: *sparks sprang from the fire.* **6.** bring out, produce, or make suddenly: *spring a surprise on someone.* **7.** crack or split, as a bat. **8.** become bent or warped, as boards. **9.** of game, rouse from cover. **10.** *Slang.* release (a person) from jail, as by bail. **11.** spring a leak, crack and begin to let water through. **12.** spring a mine, cause the gunpowder or other explosive in a mine to explode. —*n.* **1.** leap or jump: *a spring over the fence.* **2.** an elastic device that returns to its original shape after being pulled or held out of shape: *beds have wire springs.* **3.** elastic quality: *the old man's knees have lost their spring.* **4.** a flying back from a forced position. **5.** season (in North America, March, April, May) when plants begin to grow. **6.** a small stream of water coming from the earth. **7.** source; origin; cause: *springs of action.* **8.** the first and freshest period: *the spring of life.* **9.** a split or crack, as in a mast. **10.** a bend or warp, as in a board. —*adj.* **1.** having a spring or springs. **2.** resting on springs. **3.** of, pertaining to, characteristic of, or suitable for the season of spring: *spring hats.* **4.** from a spring: *spring water.* [OE *springan*] —**spring′er,** *n.* —Syn. *v.* **1.** bound, vault, skip, hop. **2.** rebound, recoil. **4.** originate, issue, emanate, emerge. **5.** shoot, rush, dart, fly. —*n.* **1.** bound, vault. **3.** resiliency, buoyancy.

spring·board (spring′bôrd′; -bōrd′), *n.* **1.** a projecting board from which persons dive. **2.** an elastic board used in vaulting, etc.

spring·bok (spring′bok′), *n., pl.* -boks or (*esp. collectively*) -bok. a gazelle or small antelope of South Africa. [< Du., springing buck]

spring fever, *Am.* a listless, lazy feeling felt by some people, caused by the first sudden warm weather of spring.

Spring·field (spring′fēld), *n.* **1.** capital of Illinois, in the C part. **2.** city in S Massachusetts.

spring·halt (spring′hôlt′), *n.* stringhalt.

spring lock, a lock that fastens automatically by a spring.

spring tide, 1. the high tide at its highest level, coming at the time of the new moon or the full moon. **2.** any great flood, swell, or rush.

spring·time (spring′tīm′), **spring·tide** (-tīd′), *n.* the season of spring.

spring·y (spring′i), *adj.,* spring·i·er, spring·i·est. **1.** that springs; elastic. **2.** having many springs of water. —**spring′i·ly,** *adv.* —**spring′i·ness,** *n.*

sprin·kle (spring′kəl), *v.,* -kled, -kling, *n.* —*v.* **1.** scatter in drops or tiny bits: *sprinkle ashes on an icy sidewalk.* **2.** spray or cover with small drops: *sprinkle flowers with water.* **3.** dot or vary with something scattered here and there. **4.** be sprinkled. **5.** rain a little. —*n.* **1.** a sprinkling; small quantity. **2.** a light rain. [cf. Du. *sprenkelen*] —**sprin′kler,** *n.* —**sprin′kling,** *n.* —Syn. *v.* **1.** strew, spatter, besprinkle.

sprint (sprint), *v.* run at full speed, esp. for a short distance. —*n.* **1.** a short race at full speed. **2.** a short period of intense activity. [ME *sprente(n)*] —**sprint′er,** *n.*

sprit (sprit), *n. Naut.* a small pole that supports and stretches a sail. [OE *sprēot*]

sprite (sprīt), *n.* elf; fairy; goblin. [< OF *esprit* spirit < L *spiritus.* Doublet of SPIRIT.]

sprit·sail (sprit′sāl′; -səl), *n. Naut.* sail supported and stretched by a sprit.

sprock·et (sprok′it), *n.* **1.** one of a set of projections on the rim of a wheel, arranged so as to fit into the links of a chain. The sprockets keep the chain from slipping. **2.** wheel made with sprockets.

Sprocket wheel

sprout (sprout), *v.* **1.** begin to grow: *buds sprout.* **2.** put forth shoots, sprouts, buds, etc.: *seeds sprout, potatoes sprout.* **3.** cause to grow: *the rain has sprouted the corn.* **4.** develop rapidly. **5.** *Colloq.* remove sprouts from. —*n.* **1.** a shoot of a plant. **2.** sprouts, Brussels sprouts. [OE, as in *āsprūtan*] —Syn. *v.* **2.** germinate, bud.

spruce[1] (sprüs), *n.* **1.** a coniferous evergreen tree with needle-shaped leaves. **2.** its wood. [ult. var. of *Pruce* Prussia]

spruce[2] (sprüs), *adj.,* spruc·er, spruc·est, *v.,* spruced, spruc·ing. —*adj.* neat; trim. —*v.* make or become spruce: *John spruced himself up for dinner.* [? special use of earlier *Spruce* Prussia (i.e., made in Prussia, therefore smart-looking)] —**spruce′ly,** *adv.* —**spruce′ness,** *n.* —Syn. *adj.* smart, dapper, jaunty.

sprung (sprung), *v.* pp. of spring.

spry (sprī), *adj.,* spry·er, spry·est, or spri·er, spri·est. active; lively; nimble: *a mouse is a spry animal.* —**spry′ly,** *adv.* —**spry′ness,** *n.*

spt., seaport.

spud (spud), *n., v.,* spud·ded, spud·ding. —*n.* **1.** tool with a narrow blade for digging up or cutting the roots of weeds. **2.** tool like a chisel for removing bark. **3.** *Colloq.* potato. —*v.* remove with a spud. [cf. Dan. *spyd* spear]

spue (spū), *v.,* spued, spu·ing. spew.

spume (spūm), *n., v.,* spumed, spum·ing. foam; froth. [< L *spuma*] —**spu′mous, spum′y,** *adj.*

spu·mo·ne (spə·mō′nē), *n.* a type of Italian ice cream, usually containing fruit, nuts, etc. [< Ital.]

spun (spun), *v.* pt. and pp. of spin.

spunk (spungk), *n.* **1.** *Colloq.* courage; pluck; spirit; mettle. **2.** tinder or punk. **3.** get (one's) spunk up, *Colloq.* show courage, pluck, or spirit. [< Irish or Scotch Gaelic < L *spongia* SPONGE]

spunk·y (spungk′i), *adj.,* spunk·i·er, spunk·i·est. **1.** *Colloq.* courageous; plucky; spirited. **2.** quick-tempered; angry. —**spunk′i·ly,** *adv.* —**spunk′i·ness,** *n.*

spun rayon, yarn made from rayon threads. When woven, spun rayon often resembles linen cloth.

spur (spér), *n., v.,* spurred, spur·ring. —*n.* **1.** a pricking instrument worn on a horseman's heel for urging a horse on. **2.** anything that urges on: *ambition is a spur.* **3.** something like a spur; point sticking out: *a spur of rock.* **4.** ridge projecting from or subordinate to the main body of a mountain or mountain range. **5.** any short branch: *a spur of a railroad.* **6.** on the spur of the moment, on a sudden impulse. **7.** win one's spurs, attain distinction. —*v.* **1.** prick with spurs. **2.** ride quickly. **3.** strike or wound with a spur or spurs. **4.** urge on: *pride spurred the boy to fight.* **5.** provide with a spur or spurs. [OE *spura*] —**spur′less,** *adj.* —**spur′like′,** *adj.*

Horseman's spur

spurge (spérj), *n.* euphorbia. [< OF *espurge,* ult. < L *ex* out + *purgare* purge]

spu·ri·ous (spyür′i·əs), *adj.* **1.** not coming from the right source; not genuine; false; sham: *a spurious document.* **2.** illegitimate. [< L *spurius*] —**spu′ri·ous·ly,** *adv.* —**spu′ri·ous·ness,** *n.*

spurn (spérn), *v.* **1.** refuse with scorn; scorn: *the judge spurned the bribe.* **2.** show scorn. **3.** strike with the foot; kick away. —*n.* **1.** disdainful rejection; contemptuous treatment. **2.** a kick. [OE *spurnan*] —**spurn′er,** *n.* —Syn. *v.* **1.** reject, despise, contemn.

spurt (spért), *v.* **1.** flow suddenly in a stream or jet; gush out; squirt. **2.** cause to gush out. **3.** put forth great energy for a short time; show great activity for a short time: *the runners* *spurted near the end of the race.* —*n.* **1.** a sudden rushing forth; jet: *spurts of flame.* **2.** a great increase of effort or activity for a short time. Also, **spirt.** [var. of *sprit,* OE *spryttan*]

sput·nik (sput′nik; spūt′–), *n.* any of a group of earth satellites containing scientific instruments or animals, put into orbit by the Soviet Union. [< Russ., companion, satellite]

sput·ter (sput′ər), *v.* **1.** make spitting or popping noises: *sputtering firecrackers.* **2.** throw out (drops of saliva, bits of food, etc.) in excitement or in talking too fast. **3.** say (words or sounds) in haste and confusion. —*n.* **1.** confused talk. **2.** a sputtering; sputtering noise. [< SPOUT] —**sput′ter·er,** *n.* —**sput′ter·ing·ly,** *adv.*

spu·tum (spū′təm), *n., pl.* –ta (–tə). **1.** saliva; spit. **2.** what is coughed up from the lungs and spat out. [< L, < *spuere* spit]

spy (spī), *n., pl.* **spies,** *v.,* **spied, spy·ing.** —*n.* **1.** person who keeps secret watch on the action of others. **2.** person who, in time of war, tries to get information about the enemy, usually by visiting the enemy's territory in disguise or under false pretenses. —*v.* **1.** find out or try to find out by careful observation; search. **2.** keep secret watch. **3.** catch sight of; see: *he spied a plane overhead.* [< OF *espier* < Gmc.]

spy·glass (spī′glas′; –gläs′), *n.* a small telescope.

spy·mas·ter (spī′mas′tər; –mäs′–), *n.* person who directs the activities of, and acts as a clearing agent for, an organized group of spies (**spy ring**).

sq., **1.** square. **2.** the following.

squab (skwob), *n.* a very young bird, esp. a young pigeon.

squab·ble (skwob′əl), *n., v.,* **–bled, –bling.** —*n.* a petty, noisy quarrel. —*v.* take part in a petty, noisy quarrel. —**squab′bler,** *n.*

squad (skwod), *n., v.,* **squad·ded, squad·ding.** —*n.* **1.** a number (varying in different army branches) of soldiers grouped for drill, inspection, or work. A squad is the smallest tactical unit in an army. **2.** any small group of persons working together. —*v.* **1.** form into squads. **2.** assign to a squad. [< F < Ital. *squadra* SQUARE]

squad car, *Am.* a police patrol car.

squad·ron (skwod′rən), *n.* **1.** a part of a naval fleet used for special service. **2.** a body of cavalry usually having from 120 to 200 men. **3.** a formation of airplanes, usually two or three flights, that fly or fight together. **4.** any group. [< Ital. *squadrone* < *squadra* SQUARE]

squal·id (skwol′id), *adj.* filthy; degraded; wretched. [< L *squalidus* < *squalere* be filthy] —**squal′id·ly,** *adv.* —**squal′id·ness,** **squa·lid′i·ty,** *n.*

squall[1] (skwôl), *n.* **1.** a sudden, violent gust of wind, often with rain, snow, or sleet. **2.** *Colloq.* commotion; trouble. —*v.* blow in a squall. [cf. Sw. *skval-regn*] —**squall′y,** *adj.*

squall[2] (skwôl), *v.* cry out loudly; scream violently: *the baby squalled.* —*n.* a loud, harsh cry. [< Scand. *skvala* cry out] —**squall′er,** *n.*

squal·or (skwol′ər), *n.* misery and dirt; filth. [< L, < *squalere* be filthy]

squan·der (skwon′dər), *v.* spend foolishly; waste. —**squan′der·er,** *n.* —**squan′der·ing·ly,** *adv.*

square (skwãr), *n., adj.,* **squar·er, squar·est,** *v.,* **squared, squar·ing,** *adv.* —*n.* **1.** a plane figure with four equal sides and four equal angles (□). **2.** anything of or near this shape. **3.** *Am.* space in a city or town bounded by streets on four sides. **4.** *Am.* distance along one side of such a space; block. **5.** an open space in a city or town bounded by streets on four sides, often planted with grass, trees, etc. **6.** *Am.* any similar open space, as at the meeting of streets. **7.** body of troops drawn up in a square form. **8.** an L-shaped or T-shaped instrument used for making or testing right angles. **9.** Also, **square number,** *Math.* product obtained when a number is multiplied by itself. 16 is the square of 4. **10. on the square, a.** at right angles. **b.** *Colloq.* justly; fairly; honestly. —*adj.* **1.** having four

equal sides and four right angles. **2.** of a specified length on each side of a square: *a room ten feet square.* **3.** designating a unit representing an area in the form of a square: *a square inch.* **4.** having breadth more nearly equal to length or height than is usual: *a square jaw.* **5.** forming a right angle: *a square corner.* **6.** straight; level; even, as a surface. **7.** leaving no balance; even: *make accounts square.* **8.** just; fair; honest: *a square deal.* **9.** straightforward; direct: *a square refusal.* **10.** multiplied by itself. **11.** solid and strong. —*v.* **1.** make square; make rectangular; make cubical. **2.** mark out in squares. **3.** bring to the form of a right angle. **4.** make straight, level, or even. **5.** adjust; settle: *square accounts.* **6.** agree; conform: *his acts do not square with his promises.* **7.** *Math.* **a.** find the equivalent of in square measure. **b.** multiply by itself. **c.** find a square equivalent to. **8. square away, set the sails so that the ship will stay before the wind. 9. square off,** *Colloq.* put oneself in a position of defense or attack. **10. square oneself,** *Colloq.* **a.** make up for something one has said or done. **b.** get even. **11. square the circle, a.** find a square equal in area to a circle. **b.** try to do something impossible. —*adv.* **1.** *Colloq.* fairly or honestly. **2.** so as to be square; in square or rectangular form; at right angles. [< OF *esquar(r)e,* ult. < L *ex* out + *quadrus* square] —**square′ly,** *adv.* —**square′ness,** *n.* —**squar′er,** *n.* —**squar′ish,** *adj.* — Syn. *adj.* **8.** equitable. **9.** absolute, downright.

square dance, dance performed by a set of couples arranged in some set form. The quadrille and Virginia reel are square dances. —**square dancer,** —**square dancing.**

square deal, *Am., Colloq.* fair and honest treatment.

square knot, knot whose free ends come out alongside the other parts. It will not slip and is easily untied.

square meal, *Am.* a substantial or satisfying meal.

square measure, system of measurement of volume in square units. 144 square inches = 1 square foot.

square-rigged (skwãr′rigd′), *adj. Naut.* having the principal sails set at right angles across the masts. —**square′-rig′ger,** *n.*

square root, number that produces a given number when multiplied by itself. The square root of 16 is 4.

square sail, a four-sided sail.

square shooter, *Am., Colloq.* a fair and honest person.

squash[1] (skwosh), *v.* **1.** press until soft or flat; crush. **2.** make a squashing sound; move with a squashing sound. **3.** put an end to; stop by force. **4.** *Colloq.* silence with a crushing argument, reply, etc. **5.** crowd; squeeze. —*n.* **1.** something squashed; a crushed mass. **2.** a squashing. **3.** a squashing sound. **4.** game somewhat like handball and tennis. [< OF *esquasser,* ult. < L *ex* out + *quassare* shake] —**squash′er,** *n.*

squash[2] (skwosh), *n. Am.* **1.** fruit of any of various vinelike plants, often eaten as a vegetable or made into a pie. **2.** plant it grows on. [< Algonquian]

Summer squash

Winter squash

squash·y (skwosh′i), *adj.,* **squash·i·er, squash·i·est.** **1.** easily squashed. **2.** soft and wet. —**squash′i·ly,** *adv.* —**squash′i·ness,** *n.*

squat (skwot), *v.,* **squat·ted,** or **squat, squat·ting,** *adj., n.* —*v.* **1.** crouch on the heels. **2.** sit on the ground or floor with the legs drawn up closely beneath or in front of the body. **3.** seat (oneself) with the legs drawn up. **4.** *Am.* settle on another's land without title or right. **5.** settle on public land to acquire ownership of it under government sanction. —*adj.* **1.** crouching: *a squat figure sat in front of the fire.* **2.** short and thick; low and broad. —*n.* act of squatting; squatting posture. [< OF *esquatir* crush, ult. <

L *ex-* out + *coactus* forced < *co-* together + *agere* drive] **—squat′ter,** *n.*

squat·ty (skwot′i), *adj.,* **-ti·er, -ti·est.** short and thick; low and broad.

squaw (skwô), *n. Am.* 1. an American Indian woman or wife. 2. *Slang.* woman or wife. [< Algonquian]

squawk (skwôk), *v.* 1. make a loud, harsh sound; *hens and ducks squawk when frightened.* 2. utter harshly and loudly. 3. *Slang.* complain loudly. —*n.* 1. a loud, harsh sound. 2. *Slang.* a loud complaint. **—squawk′er,** *n.*

squeak (skwēk), *v.* 1. make a short, sharp, shrill sound: *a mouse squeaks.* 2. cause to squeak. 3. utter with a squeak. 4. *Slang.* turn informer; confess. —*n.* 1. a short, sharp, shrill sound. 2. narrow squeak, *Colloq.* a narrow escape. [cf. Sw. *sqväka* croak] **—squeak′er,** *n.* **—squeak′y,** *adj.* **—squeak′i·ly, squeak′ing·ly,** *adv.* **—squeak′i·ness,** *n.*

squeal (skwēl), *v.* 1. make a long, sharp, shrill cry: *a pig squeals when it is hurt.* 2. utter sharply and shrilly. 3. *Slang.* turn informer. —*n.* a long, sharp, shrill cry. [imit.] **—squeal′er,** *n.*

squeam·ish (skwēm′ish), *adj.* 1. too proper, modest, etc.; easily shocked. 2. too particular; too scrupulous. 3. slightly sick at one's stomach. 4. easily turned sick. 5. dainty; delicate; fastidious. [var. of earlier *squeamous* < AF *escoymous*] **—squeam′ish·ly,** *adv.* **—squeam′ish·ness,** *n.*

squee·gee (skwē′jē), *n., v.,* **-geed, -gee·ing.** —*n.* 1. implement edged with rubber or the like, for sweeping water from surfaces. 2. any of various similar devices. —*v.* sweep, scrape, or press with a squeegee.

squeeze (skwēz), *v.,* **squeezed, squeez·ing,** *n.* —*v.* 1. press hard: *don't squeeze the kitten.* 2. hug: *she squeezed her child.* 3. force by pressing: *I can't squeeze another thing into my trunk.* 4. burden; oppress: *a blackmailer squeezes his victims.* 5. get by pressure, force, or effort: *the dictator squeezed money from the people.* 6. apply pressure to in order to extract something: *squeeze oranges.* 7. yield to pressure: *sponges squeeze easily.* 8. force a way: *squeeze through a crowd.* —*n.* 1. a tight pressure: *a squeeze of the hand.* 2. act of squeezing. 3. fact of being squeezed. 4. hug. 5. crush; crowding. 6. a small amount of juice, etc., obtained by squeezing. 7. *Colloq.* situation from which escape is difficult. [ult. < OE *cwȳsan*] **—squeez′a·ble,** *adj.* **—squeez′er,** *n.* **—Syn.** *v.* 1. compress, pinch. 2. clasp, embrace.

squelch (skwelch), *Colloq.* —*v.* 1. cause to be silent; crush: *she squelched him with a look of contempt.* 2. strike or press on with crushing force. —*n.* a crushing retort. [earlier *quelch,* blend of QUELL and SQUASH] **—squelch′er,** *n.*

squib (skwib), *n., v.,* **squibbed, squib·bing.** —*n.* 1. a short, witty attack in speech or writing; sharp sarcasm. 2. a broken firecracker. 3. a small firework that burns with a hissing noise and finally explodes. —*v.* write squibs.

squid (skwid), *n., pl.* **squids** or (*esp. collectively*) **squid.** a sea mollusk that is like a cuttlefish, but has a longer body, a pair of tail fins, and one pair of tentacles much longer than the others. Small squids are much used as bait.

squint (skwint), *v.* 1. look with the eyes partly closed: *squint in the sun.* 2. hold (the eyes) partly closed: *the sun makes her squint her eyes.* 3. look sideways. 4. be cross-eyed. 5. run or go obliquely. —*n.* 1. act of squinting. 2. a sidelong look; hasty look; look. 3. tendency to look sideways. 4. inclination; tendency. 5. cross-eyed condition. [< *asquint*] **—squint′er,** *n.* **—squint′ing·ly,** *adv.*

squire (skwīr), *n., v.,* **squired, squir·ing.** —*n.* 1. in England, a country gentleman, esp. the chief landowner in a district. 2. *Am.* in the United States, a justice of the peace or a local judge. 3. a young man of noble family who attended a knight till he himself was made a knight. 4. attendant. 5. a woman's escort. —*v.* 1. attend as a squire. 2. escort (a lady). [ult. var. of *esquire*]

squirm (skwėrm), *v.* 1. wriggle; writhe; twist. 2. show great embarrassment, annoyance, con-

fusion, etc. —*n.* a wriggle; writhe; twist. [? imit.] **—squirm′y,** *adj.*

squir·rel (skwėr′əl; skwėrl), *n.* 1. a small, bushy-tailed animal that lives in trees. 2. its gray, reddish, or dark-brown fur. [< AF *esquirel* < L *sciurus* < Gk., < *skia* shadow + *oura* tail]

squirt (skwėrt), *v.* 1. force out (liquid) through a narrow opening. 2. come out in a jet or stream. —*n.* 1. act of squirting. 2. jet of liquid, etc. 3. *Colloq.* an insignificant person who is impudent or self-assertive. **—squirt′er,** *n.* **—squirt′ing,** *adj.*

Sr, *Chem.* strontium.

Sr., 1. senior. 2. Sir.

S.R.O., standing room only.

S.S., 1. Secretary of State. 2. Secret Service. 3. steamship. 4. Sunday school.

SSE, S.S.E., direction halfway between south and southeast.

SS Troops, a select military unit of fanatical Nazis who served as a bodyguard to Hitler.

SSW, S.S.W., direction halfway between south and southwest.

St., 1. Saint. 2. Strait. 3. Street.

st., 1. stanza. 2. stet. 3. stone (weight). 4. street.

stab (stab), *v.,* **stabbed, stab·bing,** *n.* —*v.* 1. pierce or wound with a pointed weapon. 2. thrust with or as with a pointed weapon: *stab at an adversary.* 3. penetrate suddenly and sharply; pierce. 4. wound sharply or deeply in the feelings. 5. **stab in the back,** attempt to injure in a sly, treacherous manner; slander. —*n.* 1. thrust or blow made with a pointed weapon; any thrust. 2. wound made by stabbing. 3. an injury to the feelings. 4. *Colloq.* an attempt. [ult. akin to *stub*] **—stab′ber,** *n.* **—Syn.** *v.* 2. jab.

sta·bil·i·ty (stə·bil′ə·ti), *n., pl.* **-ties.** 1. a being fixed in position; firmness. 2. permanence. 3. steadfastness of character, purpose, etc. **—Syn.** 1. fixedness, steadiness, equilibrium.

sta·bi·lize (stā′bə·līz), *v.,* **-lized, -liz·ing.** 1. make stable or firm. 2. prevent changes in; hold steady: *stabilize prices.* 3. keep (an airplane, etc.) steady by special construction or automatic devices. **—sta′bi·li·za′tion,** *n.*

sta·bi·liz·er (stā′bə·līz′ər), *n.* 1. person or thing that makes something stable. 2. device for keeping an airplane, ship, etc., steady.

sta·ble¹ (stā′bəl), *n., v.,* **-bled, -bling.** —*n.* 1. a building where horses or cattle are kept and fed. 2. group of animals housed in such a building. 3. Often, **stables.** buildings and grounds where race horses are quartered and trained. 4. group of race horses belonging to one owner. 5. persons caring for such a group. —*v.* put, keep, or live in a stable. [< OF < *stabulum*] **—sta′-bler,** *n.* **—sta′bling,** *n.*

sta·ble² (stā′bəl), *adj.* 1. not likely to move or change; steadfast; firm; steady. 2. lasting without change; permanent. 3. able to return to its original position. 4. *Chem., Nuclear Physics.* a. in a balanced condition; not readily destroyed or decomposed. b. resisting molecular change. [< F < L *stabilis*] **—sta′ble·ness,** *n.* **—sta′bly,** *adv.* **—Syn.** 1. constant, unwavering. 2. fixed.

sta·ble·boy (stā′bəl·boi′), *n.* boy who works in a stable.

stac·ca·to (stə·kä′tō), *Music.* —*adj.* with breaks between the successive tones; disconnected; abrupt. —*adv.* in a staccato manner. [< Ital., lit., detached]

stack (stak), *n.* 1. a large pile of hay, straw, etc. Haystacks are often round and arranged to shed water. 2. pile of anything, usually in orderly arrangement: *a stack of wood.* 3. number of rifles arranged to form a cone or pyramid. 4. *Colloq.* a large quantity. 5. chimney. 6. Usually, **stacks.** rack with shelves for books. 7. Usually, **stacks,** *Am.* part of a library in which the main collection of books is shelved. —*v.* 1. pile or arrange in a stack: *stack hay, firewood, guns, etc.* 2. *Am.* arrange (playing cards) unfairly. 3. have **the cards stacked against one,** be at a great disadvantage. [< Scand. *stakkr*] **—stack′er,** *n.*

sta·di·um (stā′di·əm), *n., pl.* **-di·ums, -di·a** (-di·ə). an oval or U-shaped structure with rows of seats around a large open space for athletic games. [< L < Gk. *stadion*]

staff (staf; stäf), *n., pl.* **staves** or **staffs** for 1 and 2, **staffs** for 3-5, *v.* —*n.* 1. stick; pole; rod: *the flag hangs on a staff.* 2. something that supports or sustains: *bread is called the staff of life.* 3. group assisting a chief; group of employees. 4. group of officers that makes plans for an army or navy but does no fighting. 5. *Music.* the five lines and the four spaces between them on which music is written. —*v.* provide with a staff. [OE *stæf*]

Musical staff

staff officer, officer who helps make plans for an army or navy but does no actual fighting.

staff sergeant, *U.S. Army.* formerly, a noncommissioned officer of the third grade.

stag (stag), *n.* 1. a full-grown male deer. 2. the male of various other animals, esp. one castrated when full grown. 3. man who goes to a dance, party, etc., alone or with other men. 4. *Am., Colloq.* dinner, party, etc., attended by men only. —*adj.* attended by, or for men only. [OE *stagga*]

stage (stāj), *n., v.,* **staged, stag·ing.** —*n.* 1. the raised platform in a theater on which the actors perform. 2. the theater; the drama; actor's profession: *Shakespeare wrote for the stage.* 3. scene of action: *the stage of politics.* 4. a section of a rocket or missile having its own motor and fuel. A three-stage rocket has three motors, one in each stage, which separate one after another from the rocket after use. 5. platform; flooring. 6. place of rest on a journey; regular stopping place. 7. distance between two places of rest on a journey; distance between stops. 8. stagecoach; bus. 9. one step or degree in a process; period of development: *the first stage of a disease.* 10. **by easy stages,** a little at a time; slowly; often stopping. 11. **on the stage,** being an actor or actress. —*v.* 1. put on a stage; arrange: *the play was excellently staged.* 2. be suited to the theater: *that scene will not stage well.* 3. *Am.* arrange to have an effect: *the angry people staged a riot.* [< OF *estage,* ult. < L *stare* stand]

stage·coach (stāj′kōch′), *n.* coach carrying passengers and parcels over a regular route.

stage·craft (stāj′kraft′; -kräft′), *n.* the art of writing, adapting, or presenting plays.

stage·hand (stāj′hand′), *n.* person whose work is moving scenery, arranging lights, etc., in a theater.

stage-struck (stāj′struk′), *adj.* wanting very much to become an actor or actress.

stage whisper, 1. a loud whisper on a stage meant for the audience to hear. 2. whisper meant to be heard by others than the person addressed.

stag·ger (stag′ər), *v.* 1. sway or reel (from weakness, a heavy load, or drunkenness). 2. make sway or reel: *the blow staggered him.* 3. become unsteady; waver. 4. hesitate. 5. cause to hesitate or become confused. 6. confuse or astonish greatly. 7. make helpless. 8. arrange in a zigzag order or way. 9. arrange (times of beginning work, lunch periods, etc.) in overlapping intervals, so as to relieve traffic, utilize a plant better, increase the efficiency of workers, etc. —*n.* 1. a swaying; reeling. 2. **staggers** (*sing. in use*), a nervous disease of horses, cattle, etc., that makes them stagger or fall suddenly. 3. a staggered arrangement or order. [ult. < Scand. *stakra*] —**stag′ger·er,** *n.* —**stag′ger·ing·ly,** *adv.*

stag·ing (stāj′ing), *n.* 1. a temporary platform or structure of posts and boards for support, as in building; scaffolding. 2. act or process of putting a play on the stage. 3. a traveling by stages or by stagecoach.

stag·nant (stag′nənt), *adj.* 1. not running or flowing. 2. foul from standing still. 3. not active; sluggish; dull. [< L *stagnans* stagnating. See STAGNATE.] —**stag′nan·cy,** *n.* —**stag′nant·ly,** *adv.* —**Syn.** 1. motionless, quiet, inactive.

stag·nate (stag′nāt), *v.,* **-nat·ed, -nat·ing.** 1. be stagnant; become stagnant. 2. make stagnant. [< L, < *stagnum* standing water] —**stag·na′tion,** *n.*

stag·y (stāj′i), *adj.,* **stag·i·er, stag·i·est.** 1. of or pertaining to the stage. 2. suggestive of the stage; theatrical. 3. artificial; pompous; affected. —**stag′i·ly,** *adv.* —**stag′i·ness,** *n.*

staid (stād), *adj.* having a settled, quiet character; sober; sedate. —*v. Archaic.* pt. and pp. of *stay*[1]. [orig. pp. of *stay*[1] in sense of "restrain"] —**staid′ly,** *adv.* —**staid′ness,** *n.* —**Syn.** *adj.* grave, serious, steady, composed.

stain (stān), *n.* 1. discoloration; spot. 2. patch of different color. 3. cause of reproach; blemish. —*v.* 1. discolor with spots; soil. 2. bring reproach upon; blemish. 3. color in a particular way. 4. produce a stain. 5. become stained. [earlier *distain* < OF *desteindre* take out the color, ult. < L *dis-* off + *tingere* dye] —**stain′a·ble,** *adj.* —**stain′er,** *n.* —**stain′less,** *adj.* —**stain′less·ly,** *adv.* —**stain′less·ness,** *n.* —**Syn.** *n.* 3. stigma. —*v.* 2. defile.

stainless steel, steel containing chromium, nickel, or some other metal that prevents rusting or staining.

stair (stãr), *n.* 1. one of a series of steps for going from one level or floor to another. 2. set of such steps. 3. **stairs,** series of steps for going from one level or floor to another. [OE *stæger*] ➤ See **pair** for usage note.

stair·case (stãr′kās′), *n.* flight of stairs with its framework; stairs.

stair·way (stãr′wā′), *n. Am.* a way up and down by stairs; stairs.

stake[1] (stāk), *n., v.,* **staked, stak·ing.** —*n.* 1. stick or post pointed at one end for driving into the ground. 2. stick or post to which a person is bound and burned alive. 3. **the stake,** execution by burning. 4. **pull up stakes,** *Am., Colloq.* move away. —*v.* 1. fasten to a stake or with a stake. 2. *Am.* mark, protect, etc. (a claim) with stakes; mark the boundaries of. [OE *staca*] —**stak′er,** *n.*

stake[2] (stāk), *v.,* **staked, stak·ing,** *n.* —*v.* 1. risk (money or something valuable) on the result of a game or on any chance. 2. *Am., Slang.* grubstake. 3. *Am., Slang.* furnish with money or materials. —*n.* 1. money risked; what is staked. 2. Often, **stakes,** the prize in a race or contest. 3. something to gain or lose; interest; share in a property. 4. **at stake,** to be won or lost; risked. —**stak′er,** *n.* —**Syn.** *v.* 1. bet, wager.

stake·hold·er (stāk′hōl′dər), *n.* person who takes care of what is bet and pays it to the winner.

Sta·kha·no·vism (stə·kä′nə·viz·əm), *n.* in the Soviet Union, a system of rewarding individual enterprise (in factories, etc.) and thereby increasing output; a form of piecework.

Sta·kha·no·vite (stə·kä′nə·vīt), *n.* worker who increases his output under Stakhanovism.

sta·lac·tite (stə·lak′tīt; stal′ək-), *n.* a formation of lime, shaped like an icicle, hanging from the roof of a cave. Stalactites and stalagmites are formed by dripping water that contains lime. [< NL, < Gk. *stalaktos* dripping < *stalassein* trickle] —**stal·ac·tit·ic** (stal′ək·tit′ik), **stal·ac·tit′i·cal,** *adj.* —**stal′ac·tit′i·cal·ly,** *adv.*

sta·lag·mite (stə·lag′mīt; stal′əg-), *n.* a formation of lime, shaped like a cone, built up on the floor of a cave. [< NL, < Gk. *stalagmos* a drop < *stalassein* trickle] —**stal·ag·mit·ic** (stal′əg·mit′ik), **stal′ag·mit′i·cal,** *adj.* —**stal′ag·mit′i·cal·ly,** *adv.*

Stalactites and stalagmites

stale (stāl), *adj.,* **stal·er, stal·est,** *v.,* **staled, stal·ing.** —*adj.* 1. not fresh; hard and dry: *stale bread.* 2. no longer new or interesting: *a stale joke.* 3. out of condition: *go stale from too much running.* —*v.* make or become stale. [ME] —**stale′ly,** *adv.* —**stale′ness,** *n.* —**Syn.** *adj.* 2. trite, hackneyed, banal.

stale·mate (stāl′māt′), *n., v.,* **-mat·ed, -mat·ing.** —*n.* **1.** *Chess.* position of the pieces when no move can be made by a player in his turn without putting the king in check, thus forcing a drawn game. **2.** any position in which no action can be taken; complete standstill. —*v.* put in such a position; bring to a complete standstill. [< ME *stale* stalemate (prob. < AF *estale* standstill) + MATE²]

Sta·lin (stä′lin), *n.* Joseph, 1879-1953, Soviet political leader.

Sta·lin·grad (stä′lin·grad; -gräd), *n.* former name of Volgograd.

stalk¹ (stôk), *n.* **1.** stem or main axis of a plant. **2.** any slender, supporting or connecting part of a plant. A flower or leaf blade may have a stalk. **3.** any similar part of an animal. The eyes of a crawfish are on stalks. [ME *stalke*] —**stalk′less,** *adj.* —**stalk′like′,** *adj.* —**stalk′y,** *adj.*

stalk² (stôk), *v.* **1.** approach (wild animals) without being seen or heard by them. **2.** pursue (an animal or a person) without being seen or heard. **3.** spread silently and steadily: *disease stalked through the land.* **4.** walk with slow, stiff, or haughty strides. —*n.* **1.** a haughty gait. **2.** a stalking. [OE, as in *bestealcian* steal along] —**stalk′er,** *n.*

stalk·ing-horse (stôk′ing·hôrs′), *n.* **1.** horse or figure of a horse, behind which a hunter conceals himself in stalking game. **2.** anything used to hide plans or acts; pretext.

stall¹ (stôl), *n.* **1.** place in a stable for one animal. **2.** *Esp. Brit.* a small place for selling things. **3.** seat in the choir of a church. **4.** *Brit.* seat in the front part of a theater. **5.** of an airplane, condition of stalling. —*v.* **1.** live in a stall, stable, kennel, etc. **2.** put or keep in a stall. **3.** stop or bring to a standstill, usually contrary to one's wish. **4.** stick fast in mud, snow, etc.; come to a standstill. **5.** of an airplane, lose so much speed that it cannot be controlled. **6.** put an airplane in a stall. [OE *steall*] —**stalled,** *adj.*

stall² (stôl), *Slang.* —*n.* pretext, esp. as a means of delay. —*v.* **1.** pretend; evade; deceive. **2.** delay. [< AF *estal* decoy < Gmc.]

stal·lion (stal′yən), *n.* an uncastrated male horse, esp. one kept for breeding purposes. [< OF *estalon* < Gmc.]

stal·wart (stôl′wərt), *adj.* **1.** strongly built: *a stalwart body.* **2.** strong and brave: *a stalwart knight.* **3.** firm; steadfast: *a stalwart supporter.* —*n.* **1.** a stalwart person. **2.** a loyal supporter of a political party. [OE *stœlwierthe* serviceable < *stathol* position + *wierthe* worthy] —**stal′wart·ly,** *adv.* —**stal′wart·ness,** *n.* —Syn. *adj.* **1.** sturdy, stout, muscular, powerful. **2.** bold.

sta·men (stā′mən), *n., pl.* **sta·mens, stam·i·na** (stam′ə·nə). part of a flower that contains the pollen, consisting of a slender, threadlike stem or filament and an anther. [< L, warp, thread] —**sta′mened,** *adj.*

stam·i·na (stam′ə·nə), *n.* strength; endurance. [< L, threads (of life, spun by the Fates)]

stam·mer (stam′ər), *v.* **1.** repeat the same sound, esp. involuntarily, in an effort to speak; hesitate in speaking. **2.** utter thus: *stammer an excuse.* —*n.* a stammering; stuttering. [OE *stamerian*] —**stam′mer·er,** *n.* —**stam′mer·ing·ly,** *adv.*

stamp (stamp), *v.* **1.** bring down (one's foot) with force. **2.** walk in this way: *she stamped out of the room.* **3.** fix firmly or deeply: *the scene was stamped in her memory.* **4.** pound; crush; trample; tread: *she stamped out the fire.* **5.** impress, cut, etc. (a design). **6.** show to be of a certain quality or character; indicate: *his speech stamps him as an educated man.* **7.** put postage on. **8.** stamp out, **a.** put out by stamping. **b.** put an end to by force. —*n.* **1.** act of stamping. **2.** a heavy metal piece used to crush or pound rock, etc. **3.** mill or machine that crushes rock, etc. **4.** instrument that cuts, shapes, or impresses a design on (paper, wax, metal, etc.); thing that puts a mark on. **5.** the mark made with it. **6.** an official mark or seal. **7.** impression; marks: *her face bore the stamp of suffering.* **8.** kind; type: *men of his stamp are rare.* **9.** a small piece of paper with a sticky back, put on letters, papers,

parcels, etc., to show that a charge has been paid. [ME *stampe(n)*] —**stamped,** *adj.* —**stamp′er,** *n.*

stam·pede (stam·pēd′), *n., v.,* **-ped·ed, -ped·ing.** *Am.* —*n.* **1.** a sudden scattering or headlong flight of a frightened herd of cattle or horses. **2.** any headlong flight of a large group. **3.** a general rush. —*v.* **1.** scatter or flee in a stampede. **2.** make a general rush. **3.** cause to stampede. [< Mex.Sp. *estampida* (in Sp., uproar) < *estampar* stamp, ult. < Gmc.] —**stam·ped′er,** *n. Am.*

stance (stans), *n.* position of the feet of a player when making a stroke in golf or other games. [< F, ult. < L *stare* stand]

stanch¹ (stänch; stanch), *v.* **1.** stop or check the flow of (blood, etc.). **2.** stop the flow of blood from (a wound). **3.** cease flowing. Also, **staunch.** [< OF *estanchier*] —**stanch′er,** *n.* —**stanch′less,** *adj.*

stanch² (stänch; stanch), *adj.* **1.** firm; strong; substantial: *stanch walls, a stanch defense.* **2.** loyal; steadfast. **3.** watertight: *a stanch boat.* Also, **staunch.** [< OF *estanche,* fem.] —**stanch′ly,** *adv.* —**stanch′ness,** *n.* —Syn. **2.** constant, true, faithful, steady, unswerving.

STANCHIONS

stan·chion (stan′shən), *n.* an upright bar, post, or support (in a window, in a stall for cattle, on a ship, etc.). [< OF *estanchon,* ult. < L *stare* stand]

stand (stand), *v.,* **stood, stand·ing,** *n.* —*v.* **1.** be upright on one's feet (opposed to *sit, lie,* etc.). **2.** have specified height when upright: *he stands six feet in his socks.* **3.** rise to one's feet: *he stood when she entered the room.* **4.** be set upright; be placed; be located: *the box stands over there.* **5.** set upright or in an indicated position, condition, etc.: *stand the box here.* **6.** be in a certain place, rank, scale, etc.: *he stood first in his class.* **7.** take or keep a certain position: *"Stand back!"* **8.** take and keep a way of thinking or acting: *stand for fair play.* **9.** be in a special condition: *he stands innocent of any wrong.* **10.** be unchanged; hold good; remain the same: *the rule against lateness will stand.* **11.** stay in place; last: *the old house has stood for many years.* **12.** gather and stay: *tears stood in her eyes.* **13.** put up with; tolerate: *she won't stand any nonsense.* **14.** undergo; bear; endure: *stand trial.* **15.** withstand without being hurt or giving way: *cloth that will stand wear.* **16.** *Colloq.* bear the expense of: *stand treat.* **17.** hold a specified course: *the ship stood out to sea.* **18.** stop moving; halt; stop: *"Stand!" cried the sentry.* **19.** stand a chance, have a chance. **20.** stand by, **a.** be near. **b.** side with; help; support. **c.** keep; maintain. **d.** be or get ready for use, action, etc. **21.** stand for, **a.** represent; mean. **b.** be on the side of; take the part of; uphold. **c.** be a candidate for. **d.** *Am., Colloq.* put up with. **e.** sail or steer toward. **22.** stand in, *Colloq.* be associated or friendly; be on good terms. **23.** stand off, keep off; keep away. **24.** stand on, **a.** be based on; depend on. **b.** demand; assert; claim. **25.** stand out, **a.** project. **b.** be noticeable or prominent. **c.** refuse to yield. **26.** stand pat, *Am.* hold to things as they are and refuse to change. **27.** stand up, **a.** get to one's feet. **b.** endure; last. **28.** stand up for, take the part of; defend; support. **29.** stand up to, meet or face boldly. —*n.* **1.** a halt; stop. **2.** stop for defense, resistance, etc.: *make a last stand.* **3.** *Am.* a halt on a theatrical tour to give a performance. **4.** place where a person stands; position. **5.** a raised place where people can sit or stand. **6.** something to put things on or in. **7.** place or fixtures for a small business: *stand that sells newspapers.* **8.** group of growing trees or plants. [OE *standan*] —**stand′er,** *n.* —Syn. *v.* **10.** continue. **11.** endure. —*n.* **1.** pause, stay, rest. **4.** post, station, site.

stand·ard (stan′dərd), *n.* **1.** anything taken as a basis of comparison; model; rule: *good standards of living, your work is not up to standard.* **2.** an authorized weight or measure. **3.** flag, emblem, or symbol. **4.** an upright support: *the floor lamp has a long standard.* **5.** tree or shrub with one tall, straight stem. —*adj.* **1.** used as a standard; according to rule. **2.** having recognized excellence or authority. **3.** indicating a specified manner of speaking and writing which is approved by a particular society: *standard English.* [< OF *estandart* < Gmc.] —**Syn.** *n.* **1.** criterion, gauge, pattern, prototype.

stand·ard·bear·er (stan'dərd-bâr'ər), *n.* **1.** officer or soldier who carries a flag or standard. **2.** person who carries a banner in a procession. **3.** a conspicuous leader of a movement, political party, etc.

stand·ard·ize (stan'dər-dīz), *v.*, —**ized**, —**iz·ing**. **1.** make standard in size, shape, weight, quality, strength, etc.: *the parts of an automobile are standardized.* **2.** regulate by a standard. **3.** test by a standard. —**stand'ard·i·za'tion**, *n.* —**stand'ard·iz'er**, *n.*

standard of living, way of living that a person or community considers necessary to provide enough material things for comfort, happiness, etc.

standard time, time officially adopted for a region or country.

stand-by (stand'bī'), *n., pl.* —**bys**. **1.** person or thing that can be relied upon; chief support; ready resource. **2.** ship kept in readiness for emergencies. **3.** order or signal to stand by.

stand·ee (stan-dē'), *n. Am.* person who has to stand in a theater, etc.

stand-in (stand'in'), *n.* **1.** *Colloq.* favorable position; good standing. **2.** *Am.* person whose work is standing in the place of a motion-picture actor or actress while the lights, camera, etc., are being arranged.

stand·ing (stan'ding), *n.* **1.** position; reputation: *men of good standing.* **2.** duration: *a habit of long standing.* **3.** act of standing; place of standing. —*adj.* **1.** straight up; erect. **2.** done from an erect position: *a standing jump.* **3.** established; permanent: *a standing army.* **4.** that stands: *a standing lamp.* **5.** not flowing; stagnant. —**Syn.** *adj.* **1.** upright, perpendicular. **3.** lasting, enduring.

standing room, 1. space to stand in. **2.** space to stand in after all the seats are taken.

Stan·dish (stan'dish), *n.* Miles, 1584?–1656, the military leader of the colony at Plymouth, Massachusetts.

stand-off (stand'ôf'; -of'), *Am.* —*n.* **1.** a standing off or apart; reserve; aloofness. **2.** situation involving a balance between opposing elements; a tie or draw, as in a game. —*adj.* standing off or apart; reserved; holding aloof. —**stand'-off'ish**, *adj.* —**stand'-off'ish·ness**, *n.*

stand-pat (stand'pat'), *Am., Colloq.* —*adj.* standing firm for things as they are; opposing any change. —*n.* standpatter.

stand·pat·ter (stand'pat'ər), *n. Am., Colloq.* person who stands firm for things as they are and opposes any change, esp. in politics.

stand·pipe (stand'pīp'), *n.* a large vertical pipe or tower to hold water.

stand·point (stand'point'), *n.* point at which one stands to view something; point of view; mental attitude.

stand·still (stand'stil'), *n.* a complete stop; halt; pause: *during the strike, production came to a standstill.*

stang (stang), *v. Archaic or Obs.* pt. of sting.

stan·hope (stan'hōp; stan'əp), *n.* a kind of light, open, one-seated carriage with two or four wheels. [after F. *Stanhope,* British clergyman]

stank (stangk), *v.* pt. of stink.

stan·nic (stan'ik), *adj. Chem.* containing tin with a valence of four.

stan·nous (stan'əs), *adj. Chem.* containing tin with a valence of two.

stan·num (stan'əm), *n. Chem.* tin. [< LL]

stan·za (stan'zə), *n.* group of lines of poetry, commonly four or more, arranged according to a fixed plan; verse of a poem. [< Ital., orig., stopping place, ult. < L *stare* stand] —**stan·za·ic** (stan-zā'ik), *adj.* —**stan·za'i·cal·ly**, *adv.*

sta·pes (stā'pēz), *n. Anat.* the innermost of the three small bones in the middle ear; the stirrup bone.

sta·ple[1] (stā'pəl), *n., v.*, —**pled**, —**pling**. —*n.* **1.** a U-shaped piece of metal with pointed ends. Staples are driven into doors, etc., to hold hooks, pins, or bolts. **2.** a bent piece of wire used to hold together papers, parts of a book, etc. —*v.* fasten with a staple or staples. [OE *stapol* post] —**sta'pler**, *n.*

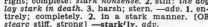

Staple (def. 1)

sta·ple[2] (stā'pəl), *n., adj., v.*, —**pled**, —**pling**. —*n.* **1.** the most important or principal article grown or manufactured in a place. Cotton is the staple in many Southern States. **2.** a chief element or material. **3.** a raw material. **4.** fiber of cotton, wool, etc. **5.** *Archaic.* the principal market of a place; chief center of trade. —*adj.* **1.** most important; principal. **2.** established in commerce: *a staple trade.* **3.** regularly produced in large quantities for the market. —*v.* sort according to fiber: *staple wool.* [< OF *estaple* mart < Gmc.] —**sta'pler**, *n.*

star (stär), *n., v.*, **starred**, **star·ring**, *adj.* —*n.* **1.** any of the heavenly bodies appearing as bright points in the sky at night. **2.** any heavenly body except the moon, the planets, comets, and meteors. **3.** a plane figure having five points, or sometimes six, like these: ✿☼. **4.** thing having or suggesting this shape. **5.** asterisk (*). **6.** *Am.* in the United States, a representation of a star symbolizing one of the States in the Union. **7.** person who is distinguished in some art, profession, or other field: *an athletic star.* **8.** a celebrated actor, singer, etc., esp. one who plays the lead in a performance: *a movie star.* **9.** a heavenly body considered as influencing people and events: *born under a lucky star.* **10.** fate; fortune. **11.** see stars, *Colloq.* see flashes of light as a result of a hard blow on the head. —*v.* **1.** set with stars; ornament with stars. **2.** mark with a star or an asterisk. **3.** be prominent; be a leading performer: *star in many movies.* **4.** present as a star. —*adj.* chief; best; leading; excellent. [OE *steorra*] —**star'less**, *adj.* —**star'like'**, *adj.*

star·board (stär'bərd; -bôrd; -bōrd), *n.* the right side of a ship, when facing forward. —*adj.* on the right side of a ship. —*v.* turn (the helm) to the right side. —*adv.* toward the right side. [OE *stēorbord.* See STEER[1], BOARD.]

starch (stärch), *n.* **1.** a white, tasteless food substance. Potatoes, wheat, rice, and corn contain much starch. **2.** preparation of it used to stiffen clothes, curtains, etc. **3.** starches, foods containing much starch. **4.** a stiff, formal manner; stiffness. **5.** *Slang.* vigor. —*v.* stiffen (clothes, curtains, etc.) with starch. [OE *stercan* (in *stercedferhth* stout-hearted) < *stearc* stiff, strong] —**starch'y**, *adj.* —**starch'i·ness**, *n.*

Star Chamber, 1. in English history, a court that used arbitrary, secret, and unfair methods of trial. It was abolished in 1641. **2.** any court, committee, or group like this.

star·dom (stär'dəm), *n.* **1.** condition of being a star actor or performer. **2.** star actors or performers as a group.

stare (stâr), *v.*, **stared**, **star·ing**, *n.* —*v.* **1.** look long and directly with the eyes wide open. A person stares in wonder, surprise, stupidity, curiosity, or from mere rudeness. **2.** bring to a named condition by staring: *stare one down.* **3.** gaze at. **4.** be very striking or glaring. **5.** stare one in the face, be very evident; seem likely to happen soon. —*n.* a long and direct look with the eyes wide open. [OE *starian*] —**star'er**, *n.* —**star'ing**, *adj.* —**star'ing·ly**, *adv.* —**Syn.** *v.* **1.** gaze, gape.

star·fish (stär'fish'), *n., pl.* —**fish·es** or (*esp. collectively*) —**fish**. a star-shaped sea animal.

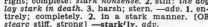

Starfish
(ab. 5 in. across)

stark (stärk), *adj.* **1.** downright; complete: *stark nonsense.* **2.** stiff: *the dog lay stark in death.* **3.** harsh; stern. —*adv.* **1.** entirely; completely. **2.** in a stark manner. [OE *stearc* stiff, strong] —**stark'ly**, *adv.*

star·let (stär'lĭt), *n.* 1. a young actress or singer who is being coached for leading roles in motion pictures. 2. a little star.

star·ling (stär'lĭng), *n.* 1. a common European bird which nests about buildings and is easily tamed. 2. *Am.* a kind of American blackbird. [OE *stærling*]

star·lit (stär'lĭt'), *adj.* lighted by the stars.

star-of-Beth·le·hem (stär'əv-bĕth'lĭ-əm; -lə-hĕm), *n.* plant of the lily family that grows from a small bulb and has a tall cluster of white, star-shaped flowers.

star·ry (stär'ĭ), *adj.*, -ri·er, -ri·est. 1. lighted by stars; containing many stars: *a starry sky.* 2. shining like stars: *starry eyes.* 3. like a star in shape. 4. of or having to do with stars. —**star'ri·ly**, *adv.* —**star'ri·ness**, *n.*

Stars and Stripes, *Am.* the flag of the United States.

Star-Span·gled Banner (stär'spang'gəld), *Am.* 1. the American national anthem. The words were composed by Francis Scott Key during the War of 1812. 2. Stars and Stripes.

start (stärt), *v.* 1. get in motion; set out; begin a journey: *the train started on time.* 2. begin: *start a book.* 3. set moving, going, acting, etc.: *cause to set out; cause to begin: start an automobile.* 4. enable to set out on a journey, course of action, etc.: *start a person in business.* 5. give a sudden, involuntary jerk or twitch; move suddenly: *he started in surprise.* 6. come, rise, or spring out suddenly: *tears started from her eyes.* 7. burst or stick out: *eyes seeming to start from their sockets.* 8. rouse: *start a rabbit.* 9. become loose. 10. cause to become loose: *start a run in a stocking.* 11. start in, out, or up, start. —*n.* 1. the beginning of a movement, act, journey, race, etc. 2. a setting in motion. 3. chance of starting a career, etc.: *his father gave him his start.* 4. a sudden movement; jerk. 5. a beginning ahead of others; advantage: *he got the start of his rivals.* 6. spurt of activity: *work by fits and starts.* 7. place, line, etc., where a race begins. [< var. of OE *styrtan* leap up] —**start'er**, *n.* —**Syn.** *v.* 1. embark, leave, go. 2. commence, initiate.

star·tle (stär'təl), *v.*, -tled, -tling, *n.* —*v.* 1. frighten suddenly; surprise. 2. move suddenly in fear or surprise. —*n.* a sudden shock of surprise or fright. [OE *steartlian* struggle] —**star'tler**, *n.* —**star'tling**, *adj.* —**star'tling·ly**, *adv.* —**Syn.** *v.* 1. scare, alarm, shock, stun.

star·va·tion (stär·vā'shən), *n.* 1. a starving. 2. suffering from extreme hunger; being starved.

starve (stärv), *v.*, starved, starv·ing. 1. die because of hunger. 2. suffer severely because of hunger or a need. 3. weaken or kill with hunger. 4. force or subdue by lack of food: *they starved the enemy into surrendering.* 5. *Colloq.* feel hungry. 6. have a strong desire or craving. 7. weaken or destroy by lack of something needed. 8. starve for, suffer from lack of: *starve for news.* [OE *steorfan* die] —**starv'er**, *n.*

starve·ling (stärv'lĭng), *adj.* starving; hungry. —*n.* person, animal, etc., that is suffering from lack of food.

stash (stăsh), *Am., Slang.* —*v.* hide or put away for safekeeping or future use. —*n.* what is hidden or put away.

state (stāt), *n., v.,* stat·ed, stat·ing, *adj.* —*n.* 1. condition of a person or thing, as with respect to constitution, structure, or the like: *in an excited state, ice is water in a solid state.* 2. a person's position in life; rank; station: *humble state.* 3. high style of living; dignity; pomp: *a coach of state.* 4. Also, State. a. nation. b. one of several organized political groups of people that together form a nation. The State of Texas is one of the United States. 5. the civil government; highest civil authority: *affairs of state.* 6. the States, (*chiefly in British use*) the United States. 7. lie in state, lie in an open coffin to be seen by people before being buried. —*v.* 1. tell in speech or writing; express; say: *state one's views.* 2. set forth in proper or definite form: *state a problem.* —*adj.* 1. used on or reserved for very formal and special occasions; ceremonious; formal: *state robes.* 2. State or state, *Am.* maintained, controlled, or established by a State: *a State road.* 3. of or pertaining to civil government or authority: *state control.* [< L *status* condition, position < *stare* stand; common in L phrase *status rei publicae* condition of the republic] —**stat'a·ble, state'·a·ble**, *adj.* —**state'·hood**, *n.* —**Syn.** *n.* 1. situation, circumstances. 2. standing, status. 3. grandeur, magnificence. —*v.* 1. declare. ➤ See say for usage note.

state·craft (stāt'kraft'; -kräft'), *n.* 1. statesmanship. 2. crafty statesmanship.

stat·ed (stāt'ĭd), *adj.* 1. said; told. 2. fixed; settled. —**stat'ed·ly**, *adv.*

State·house (stāt'hous'), *n. U.S.* building in which the legislature of a State meets.

state·ly (stāt'lĭ), *adj.*, -li·er, -li·est. dignified; imposing; grand; majestic. —**state'li·ness**, *n.*

state·ment (stāt'mənt), *n.* 1. act or manner of stating something. 2. something stated; report: *a written statement.* 3. summary of an account, showing the amount owed or due.

Stat·en Island (stăt'ən), island in New York Bay, S of Manhattan Island, that is a part of New York City.

state·room (stāt'rüm'; -rûm'), *n. Am.* a private room on a ship or railroad train.

state's evidence, 1. *Am.* testimony given in court by a criminal against his associates in a crime. 2. turn state's evidence, *Am.* testify in court against one's associates in a crime.

state·side (stāt'sīd'), **states·side** (stāts'-sīd'), *Am.* —*adj.* of or in the United States. —*adv.* in or in the direction of the United States.

states·man (stāts'mən), *n., pl.* -men. person skilled in the management of public or national affairs. —**states'man·like', states'man·ly**, *adj.*

states·man·ship (stāts'mən·shĭp), *n.* the qualities of a statesman; skill in the management of public affairs.

state socialism, form of socialism in which government control, management, or ownership is used to improve social conditions.

States' rights, *Am.* powers belonging to the separate States of the United States, under the Constitution. The doctrine of States' rights holds that all powers not specially delegated by the Constitution to the national government, nor denied by it to the States, belong to the States.

States' Rights Democrat, States' Righter, or **State Righter,** *Am.* a Dixiecrat.

states·wom·an (stāts'wûm'ən), *n., pl.* -wom·en. a woman statesman.

stat·ic (stăt'ĭk), **stat·i·cal** (-ə·kəl), *adj.* 1. at rest; standing still: *civilization does not remain static, but changes constantly.* 2. characterized by stability and lack of change: *a static society.* 3. *Elect.* having to do with stationary electrical charges that balance each other. Static electricity can be produced by rubbing a glass rod with a silk cloth. 4. of or pertaining to atmospheric electricity that interferes with radio reception. —*n. Am., Elect.* 1. atmospheric electricity. 2. interference due to such electricity. [< Gk. *statikos* causing to stand] —**stat'i·cal·ly**, *adv.*

stat·ics (stăt'ĭks), *n.pl.* (*sing. in use*). branch of mechanics that deals with objects at rest or forces that balance each other.

sta·tion (stā'shən), *n.* 1. place in which anything stands; place which a person is appointed to occupy in the performance of some duty; assigned post: *the policeman took his station at the corner.* 2. a regular stopping place, as on a railroad or bus line. 3. building or structure at such a stopping place; depot. 4. a building or place equipped for some particular kind of work, research, etc.: *a postal station.* 5. place or equipment for sending out or receiving programs, messages, etc., by radio. 6. social position; rank. —*v.* assign a station to; place. [< L, < *stare* stand] —**Syn.** *n.* 1. position, location, situation. 6. standing, status. —*v.* post.

sta·tion·ar·y (stā'shən·ĕr'ĭ), *adj.* 1. having a fixed station or place; not movable. 2. standing still; not moving. 3. not changing in size, number, activity, etc. [< L, < *statio* STATION]

sta·tion·er (stā'shən·ər), *n.* person who sells

paper, pens, pencils, ink, etc. [< Med.L *stationarius* shopkeeper, orig., stationary, as distinct from a roving peddler]

sta·tion·er·y (stā′shən·er′i), *n.* writing materials; paper, cards, and envelopes.

station wagon, *Am.* closed automobile, usually having a tailboard, a flat top, and rows of seats behind the driver.

stat·ism (stāt′iz·əm), *n.* a highly centralized governmental control of the economy of a state or nation.

sta·tis·tic (stə·tis′tik), *adj.* statistical. —*n.* a numerical fact.

sta·tis·ti·cal (stə·tis′tə·kəl), *adj.* of or pertaining to statistics; consisting of or based on statistics. —**sta·tis′ti·cal·ly,** *adv.*

stat·is·ti·cian (stat′is·tish′ən), *n.* expert in statistics.

sta·tis·tics (stə·tis′tiks), *n.* 1. (*pl. in use*) numerical facts about people, the weather, business conditions, etc. Statistics are collected and classified systematically. 2. (*sing. in use*) science of collecting and classifying such facts in order to show their significance. [ult. < G < NL *statisticus* political, ult. < L *status* STATE]

stat·u·ar·y (stach′u·er′i), *n., pl.* **-ar·ies,** *adj.* —*n.* statues. —*adj.* of or for statues.

stat·ue (stach′ü), *n.* image of a person or animal carved in stone or wood, cast in bronze, or modeled in clay or wax. [< F < L *statua,* ult. < *stare* stand]

stat·u·esque (stach′ü·esk′), *adj.* like a statue in dignity, formal grace, or classic beauty. —**stat′u·esque′ly,** *adv.* —**stat′u·esque′ness,** *n.*

stat·u·ette (stach′ü·et′), *n.* a small statue.

stat·ure (stach′ər), *n.* 1. height. 2. development; physical, mental, or moral growth. [< OF < L *statura* < *stare* stand]

sta·tus (stā′təs; stat′əs), *n.* 1. condition; state. 2. social or professional standing; position; rank: *his status as a doctor.* 3. legal position. [< L, < *stare* stand]

status quo (kwō), **status in quo,** the way things are; the existing state of affairs. [< L, the state in which]

stat·ute (stach′üt), *n.* 1. law enacted by a legislative body. 2. a law; decree. [< F *statut,* ult. < L *statuere* establish, ult. < *stare* stand]

statute law, written law; law established by statutes or legislative enactments.

stat·u·to·ry (stach′u·tô′ri; -tō′-), *adj.* 1. pertaining to a statute. 2. fixed by statute. 3. punishable by statute. —**stat′u·to′ri·ly,** *adv.*

St. Au·gus·tine (ô′gəs·tēn), city in NE Florida, the oldest city in the United States.

staunch (stônch; stänch), *v., adj.* stanch. —**staunch′ly,** *adv.* —**staunch′ness,** *n.*

stave (stāv), *n., v.,* staved or stove, stav·ing. —*n.* 1. one of the curved pieces of wood that form the sides of a barrel, tub, etc. 2. stick or staff. 3. rung of a ladder. 4. verse or stanza of a poem or song. 5. the musical staff. —*v.* 1. break a hole in (a barrel, boat, etc.). 2. become smashed or broken in. 3. furnish with staves. 4. **stave off,** put off; keep back; delay or prevent. [< *staves,* pl. of *staff*]

staves (stāvz), *n.* 1. pl. of staff. 2. pl. of stave.

stay¹ (stā), *v.,* stayed, or staid, stay·ing, *n.* —*v.* 1. continue to be as indicated; remain: *stay clean.* 2. live for a while; dwell: *stay at a hotel.* 3. stop; halt: *we have no time to stay.* 4. pause; wait: *stay awhile.* 5. remain for: *stay to dinner.* 6. put an end to for a while: *stay proceedings.* 7. *Am., Colloq.* satisfy (hunger, appetite, etc.). 8. put off; delay: *stay judgment.* 9. restrain; check: *stay the spread of disease.* 10. endure: *unable to stay to the end of a race.* 11. *Archaic.* remain. —*n.* 1. a staying; a stop; time spent: *a pleasant stay in the country.* 2. check; restraint: *a stay on his activity.* 3. delay in carrying out the order of a court: *the judge granted the condemned man a stay for an appeal.* 4. *Colloq.* staying power; endurance. [< OF *ester* stand < L *stare*] —**stay′er,** *n.* —Syn. *v.* 2. reside, lodge, sojourn, abide. 4. linger, tarry, delay.

stay² (stā), *n., v.,* stayed, stay·ing. —*n.* 1. a support; prop; brace. 2. stays, corset. —*v.* support; prop; hold up. [prob. ult. < OF *estayer* < Gmc.] —**stay′er,** *n.* —Syn. *v.* brace, sustain.

stay³ (stā), *n., v.,* stayed, stay·ing. —*n.* 1. a strong rope, often of wire, which supports a mast of a ship. 2. any rope or chain similarly used. —*v.* 1. support or secure with stays. 2. of a ship, change to the other tack. [OE *stæg*]

stay·sail (stā′sāl′; -səl), *n.* a sail fastened on a stay or rope.

St. Croix (sānt kroi′), largest of the Virgin Islands, belonging to the United States.

stead (sted), *n.* 1. the place of a person or thing as occupied by a successor or substitute. 2. **stand in good stead,** be of advantage or service to. [OE *stede*]

stead·fast (sted′fast; -fäst; -fəst), *adj.* firmly fixed; constant; not moving or changing. Also, **stedfast.** —**stead′fast·ly,** *adv.* —**stead′fast·ness,** *n.* —Syn. unwavering, unswerving.

stead·y (sted′i), *adj.,* stead·i·er, stead·i·est, *v.,* stead·ied, stead·y·ing, *n., pl.* stead·ies. —*adj.* 1. firmly fixed; firm; not swaying or shaking: *hold a ladder steady.* 2. changing little; uniform; regular: *steady progress.* 3. not easily excited; calm: *steady nerves.* 4. reliable; having good habits: *a steady young man.* 5. resolute; steadfast: *steady friendship.* 6. keeping nearly upright in a heavy sea. —*v.* 1. make or keep steady. 2. become steady. —*n. Am., Slang.* a person's regular companion or sweetheart. [< stead] —**stead′i·er,** *n.* —**stead′i·ly,** *adv.* —**stead′i·ness,** *n.* —Syn. *adj.* 2. undeviating, invariable, constant. 4. trustworthy, dependable, sober. 5. unwavering, unfaltering.

steak (stāk), *n.* slice of meat or fish for broiling or frying. *Steak* often means *beefsteak.* [< Scand. *steik*]

steal (stēl), *v.,* stole, sto·len, steal·ing, *n.* —*v.* 1. take (something) that does not belong to one; take dishonestly: *steal money.* 2. take, get, or do secretly: *steal a look at someone.* 3. take, get, or win by art, charm, or gradual means: *she steals all hearts.* 4. move secretly or quietly: *she stole out of the house.* 5. move slowly or gently: *the years steal by.* 6. *Am., Baseball.* run to (a base) without being helped by a hit or error. —*n.* 1. *Colloq.* act of stealing. 2. *Colloq.* the thing stolen. 3. *Am.* a corrupt deal, highly remunerative to its perpetrators. [OE *stelan*] —**steal′er,** *n.* —**steal′ing·ly,** *adv.* —Syn. *v.* 1. pilfer, filch, purloin. 4. sneak, skulk, slink.

stealth (stelth), *n.* secret or sly action. [< steal]

stealth·y (stel′thi), *adj.,* stealth·i·er, stealth·i·est. done in a secret manner; secret; sly. —**stealth′i·ly,** *adv.* —**stealth′i·ness,** *n.* —Syn. furtive, sneaking, underhand, surreptitious.

steam (stēm), *n.* 1. water in the form of vapor or gas. Steam is used to heat houses, run engines, etc. 2. any vapor. 3. *Colloq.* power; energy; force. —*v.* 1. give off steam: *a cup of steaming coffee.* 2. rise in steam. 3. move by steam: *the ship steamed off.* 4. cook, soften, or freshen by steam. 5. become covered with condensed steam, as a mirror. —*adj.* 1. moved by steam. 2. operated by steam. 3. providing heat with steam. 4. carrying steam. [OE *stēam*] —**steam′y,** *adj.* —**steam′i·ly,** *adv.* —**steam′i·ness,** *n.*

steam·boat (stēm′bōt′), *n.* boat moved by steam.

steam engine, engine operated by steam, typically one in which a sliding piston in a cylinder is moved by the expansive action of steam generated in a boiler.

steam·er (stēm′ər), *n.* 1. steamboat; steamship. 2. engine run by steam. 3. container in which something is steamed.

steam fitter, man who installs and repairs steam pipes, radiators, boilers, etc. —**steam fitting.**

steam roller, 1. a heavy roller moved by steam, used to crush and level materials in making roads. 2. *Colloq.* means of crushing opposition.

āge, câre, fär; ēqual, tėrm; īce; ōpen, ôrder; pùt, rüle, ūse; tħ, then; ə=a in about.

steam·roll·er (stēm'rōl'ər), v. Colloq. crush.

steam·ship (stēm'ship'), n. ship moved by steam.

steam shovel, Am. machine for digging, operated by steam.

ste·ap·sin (sti·ap'sin), n. a digestive enzyme secreted in the pancreatic juice, which changes fats into glycerol and fatty acids. [blend of stea(rin) and (pe)psin]

ste·a·rin (stē'ə·rin; stir'in), n. 1. Chem. a colorless, odorless substance, $C_8H_5O_3(C_{17}H_{35}CO)_8$, that is the chief constituent of many animal and vegetable fats. 2. a mixture of fatty acids used for making candles, solid alcohol, etc. [< F stéarine < Gk. stear fat] —ste·ar·ic (sti·ar'ik; stir'ik), adj.

sted·fast (sted'fast; -fäst; -fəst), adj. steadfast.

steed (stēd), n. 1. horse, esp. a riding horse. 2. a high-spirited horse. [OE stēda] —steed'less, adj.

steel (stēl), n. 1. iron mixed with carbon so that it is very hard, strong, and tough. Most tools are made from steel. 2. something made from steel. 3. sword. 4. steellike hardness, strength, or color: nerves of steel. —adj. 1. made of steel. 2. like steel in hardness, strength, or color: steel nerves. —v. 1. point, edge, or cover with steel. 2. make hard or strong like steel. [OE stēle] —steel'y, adj. —steel'i·ness, n.

steel·work·er (stēl'wér'kər), n. person who works in a place where steel is made.

steel·works (stēl'wérks'), n. pl or sing. place where steel is made.

steel·yard (stēl'yärd; stil'yərd), n. a scale for weighing. A steelyard has unequal arms, the longer one having a movable weight and the shorter a hook for holding the object to be weighed.

Steelyard

steen·bok (stēn'bok'; stān'-), n. any of various small African antelopes frequenting rocky places. Also, steinbok. [< Du., < steen stone + bok buck]

steep[1] (stēp), adj. 1. having a sharp slope; almost straight up and down. 2. Am., Colloq. unduly high; extravagant; unreasonable: a steep price. —n. a steep slope. [OE stēap] —steep'ly, adv. —steep'ness, n. —Syn. adj. 1. precipitous, abrupt.

steep[2] (stēp), v. 1. soak: let the tea steep in boiling water for five minutes. 2. immerse; imbue: ruins steeped in gloom. —n. 1. a soaking. 2. liquid in which something is soaked. [prob. < OE stēap bowl] —steep'er, n.

stee·ple (stē'pəl), n. a high tower on a church, usually with a spire. [OE stēpel < stēap steep] —stee'pled, adj.

SPIRE
STEEPLE

stee·ple·chase (stē'pəl·chās'), n. 1. a horse race over a course having ditches, hedges, and other obstacles. 2. a horse race across country. —stee'ple·chas'er, n.

stee·ple·jack (stē'pəl·jak'), n. man who climbs steeples, tall chimneys, or the like, to make repairs, etc.

steer[1] (stir), v. 1. guide the course of (anything in motion): steer a ship, an automobile, an airplane, etc. 2. be guided: this car steers easily. 3. guide a ship, automobile, airship, etc.: the pilot steered for the harbor. 4. direct one's way or course: steer between extremes. 5. steer clear of, keep away from; avoid. —n. Am., Slang. an idea or a suggested course of action. [OE stēoran] —steer'a·ble, adj. —steer'er, n.

steer[2] (stir), n. 1. a young ox, usually two to four years old. 2. any male of beef cattle. [OE stēor]

steer·age (stir'ij), n. part of a passenger ship occupied by passengers traveling at the cheapest rate.

steers·man (stirz'mən), n., pl. -men. person who steers a ship. —steers'man·ship, n.

stein (stīn), n. a beer mug. [< G, stone]

stein·bock (stīn'bok'), n. steenbok.

stel·lar (stel'ər), adj. 1. of or pertaining to the stars; of or like a star. 2. chief: a stellar role. [< L, < stella star]

stel·late (stel'āt; -it), adj., **stel·lat·ed** (-āt·id), adj. spreading out like the points of a star; star-shaped. [< L, < stella star] —stel'late·ly, adv.

stem[1] (stem), n., v., stemmed, stem·ming. —n. 1. the main part of a plant above the ground. The stem supports the branches, etc. 2. the part of a flower, a fruit, or a leaf that joins it to the plant or tree. 3. anything like or suggesting the stem of a plant: the stem of a goblet, the stem of a pipe, etc. 4. Gram. the unchanged part in a series of inflectional forms. 5. Naut. the bow or front end of a boat. 6. from stem to stern, from one end of the ship to the other. —v. 1. remove the stem from (a leaf, fruit, etc.). 2. stem from, Am. originate or spring from. [OE stemn] —stem'less, adj. —stemmed, adj. —stem'mer, n.

stem[2] (stem), v., stemmed, stem·ming. 1. stop; check; dam up. 2. make progress against: stem the swift current. [< Scand. stemma]

stem-wind·ing (stem'wīn'ding), adj. Am. of a watch, wound by turning a knob on the stem. —stem'wind'er, n. Am.

stench (stench), n. a very bad smell; stink. [OE stenc < stincan smell] —stench'y, adj.

sten·cil (sten'səl), n., v. -ciled, -cil·ing; esp. Brit. -cilled, -cil·ling. —n. 1. a thin sheet of metal, paper, etc., having letters or designs cut through it. When it is laid on a surface and ink or color is spread on, these letters or designs are made on the surface. 2. the letters or designs so made. —v. mark or paint with a stencil. [ult. < OF estanceler ornament with colors, ult. < L scintilla spark] —sten'cil·er, esp. Brit. sten'cil·ler, n.

ste·nog·ra·pher (stə·nog'rə·fər), n. Am. person whose work is stenography and typewriting.

ste·nog·ra·phy (stə·nog'rə·fi), n. 1. method of rapid writing that uses symbols in place of letters, sounds, and words. 2. act of writing in such symbols. [< Gk. stenos narrow + E -graphy (< Gk. graphein write)] —sten·o·graph·ic (sten'ə·graf'ik), sten'o·graph'i·cal, adj. —sten'o·graph'i·cal·ly, adv.

Sten·o·type (sten'ə·tīp), n. 1. Trademark. kind of typewriter used in stenotypy. 2. stenotype, letter or group of letters used for a sound, word, or phrase in stenotypy. [< Gk. stenos narrow + E type] —sten'o·typ'ist, n.

sten·o·typ·y (sten'ə·tīp'i; stə·not'ə·pi), n. 1. form of shorthand that uses ordinary letters. 2. use of a stenotype machine to record speeches, etc.

sten·to·ri·an (sten·tô'ri·ən; -tō'-), adj. very loud or powerful in sound. [from Stentor, a Greek herald in the Trojan War, whose voice was as loud as the voices of fifty men] —stento'ri·an·ly, adv.

step (step), n., v., stepped, step·ping. —n. 1. a movement made by lifting the foot and putting it down again in a new position, as in walking, running, etc. 2. distance covered by one such movement: she was three steps away when he called her back. 3. a short distance; little way: the school is only a step away. 4. way of walking, dancing, etc.: a brisk step. 5. pace uniform with that of another or others or in time with music: keep step, be in step. 6. pace in marching. 7. steps, movements or course in walking: retrace one's steps. 8. place for the foot in going up or coming down: a rung of a ladder is a step. 9. sound made by putting the foot down: hear steps. 10. footprint: see steps in the mud. 11. an action, as toward a result: the college took steps to prevent epidemics. 12. a degree in a scale; a grade in rank. 13. Music. a. a degree of the staff or the scale. b. interval between two successive degrees of the scale. 14. steps, stepladder. 15. in dancing, a combination of movements. 16. step by step, little by little; slowly. 17. watch one's step, be careful. [< v.] —v. 1. move by stepping: step forward. 2. walk a short distance: *step this way.* **3.** press with the foot, as on the starter of an automobile. **4.** measure (a distance, ground, etc.) by steps: *step off the distance.* **5.** put the foot down: *step on a worm.* **6.** make or arrange like a flight of steps. **7.** *Colloq.* go fast. **8.** come as if by a step: *step into a good job.* **9.** **step down,** a. come down. b. decrease. **10. step in,** come in; intervene; take part. **11. step on it,** *Colloq.* go faster; hurry up. **12. step out,** *Am., Colloq.* go out for entertainment. **13. step up,** a. go up. b. *Am., Colloq.* increase. [OE *steppan*] —**Syn.** *n.* **11.** measure.

step—, *prefix.* related by the remarriage of a parent, not by blood, as in *stepmother, stepsister.* [OE *stēop—*]

step·broth·er (step'bru th'ər), *n.* a stepfather's or stepmother's son by a former marriage.

step·child (step'chīld'), *n., pl.* **—chil·dren.** child of one's husband or wife by a former marriage.

step·daugh·ter (step'dô'tər), *n.* daughter of one's husband or wife by a former marriage.

step·fa·ther (step'fä'thər), *n.* man who has married one's mother after the death or divorce of one's real father. —**step'fa'ther·ly,** *adj.*

step-in (step'in'), *adj.* of garments, shoes, etc., put on by being stepped into.

step·lad·der (step'lad'ər), *n.* ladder with flat steps instead of rungs.

step·moth·er (step'muth'ər), *n.* woman who has married one's father after the death or divorce of one's real mother.

steppe (step), *n.* **1.** the Steppes, the vast Russian plains in SE Europe and in Asia. **2.** a vast treeless plain. [< Russ. *step*]

stepped-up (step'up'), *adj. Am., Colloq.* speeded up or intensified; increased.

step·per (step'ər), *n.* person, etc., that steps.

stepping stone, anything serving as a means of advancing or rising.

step·sis·ter (step'sis'tər), *n.* a stepfather's or stepmother's daughter by a former marriage.

step·son (step'sun'), *n.* son of one's husband or wife by a former marriage.

stept (stept), *v. Poetic* pt. and pp. of **step.**

-ster, *suffix.* **1.** one that —s, as in *fibster.* **2.** one that makes —, as in *maltster, rhymester.* **3.** one that is —, as in *youngster.* **4.** special meanings, as in *gangster, roadster, teamster.* [OE *-estre, -istre*]

stere (stir), *n.* a cubic meter. [< F < Gk. *stereos* solid]

ster·e·o (ster'i·ō; stir'—), *adj., n., pl. -e·os.* —*adj.* **1.** in photography, optics, etc., reproducing or simulating binocular vision. **2.** in acoustics, stereophonic. —*n.* **1.** a stereophonic system of sound reproduction. **2.** stereotype (defs. 1 and 2).

ster·e·o·phon·ic (ster'i·ə·fon'ik; stir'—), *adj.* reproducing or simulating the acoustic effect of a sound as it would be heard with both ears. —**ster'e·o·phon'i·cal·ly,** *adv.*

ster·e·op·ti·con (ster'i·op'tə·kən; stir'—), *n. Am.* an improved form of magic lantern, having a powerful light. [< NL, < Gk. *stereos* solid + *optikos* relating to vision]

ster·e·o·scope (ster'i·ə·skōp'; stir'—), *n.* instrument through which two pictures of the same object or scene are viewed, one by each eye. The object or scene thus viewed appears to have three dimensions. —**ster·e·o·scop·ic** (ster'i·ə·skop'ik; stir'—), **ster'e·o·scop'i·cal,** *adj.* —**ster·e·os·co·pist** (ster'i·os'kə·pist; stir'—), *n.*

Stereoscope

ster·e·o·type (ster'i·ə·tīp'; stir'—), *n., v.,* **-typed, -typ·ing.** —*n.* **1.** process of making metal plates by taking a mold of composed type and making from this mold a cast in type metal. **2.** a printing plate cast from a mold. **3.** the making or use of such plates. **4.** a fixed

form; something that never changes; convention. —*v.* **1.** make a stereotype of. **2.** print from stereotypes. **3.** give a fixed or settled form to.

ster·e·o·typed (ster'i·ə·tīpt'; stir'—), *adj.* **1.** printed from a stereotype. **2.** conventional.

ster·ile (ster'əl), *adj.* **1.** free from living germs: *a doctor's instruments must be kept sterile.* **2.** barren: *sterile land.* **3.** not producing offspring: *a sterile cow.* **4.** not producing results: *sterile hopes.* [< L *sterilis*] —**ster'ile·ly,** *adv.* —**ste·ril·i·ty** (stə·ril'ə·ti), *n.*

ster·i·lize, ster·i·lise (ster'ə·līz), *v.,* **-lized, -liz·ing;** *esp. Brit.* **-lised, -lis·ing.** **1.** free from living germs: *the water had to be sterilized by boiling to make it fit to drink.* **2.** deprive of fertility. —**ster'i·li·za'tion,** *esp. Brit.* **ster'i·li·sa'tion,** *n.* —**ster'i·liz'er,** *esp. Brit.* **ster'i·lis'er,** *n.*

ster·ling (ster'ling), *n.* **1.** British money. **2.** sterling silver or things made of it. —*adj.* **1.** of British money; payable in British money. **2.** of standard quality; containing 92.5 per cent pure silver. **3.** made of sterling silver. **4.** genuine; excellent; dependable. [prob. ult. < OE *steorra* star (as on certain early coins)]

sterling silver, silver 92.5 per cent pure.

stern[1] (stern), *adj.* **1.** severe; strict; harsh: *a stern master, a stern frown.* **2.** hard; not yielding; firm: *stern necessity.* **3.** grim: *stern mountains.* [OE *stirne*] —**stern'ly,** *adv.* —**stern'ness,** *n.* —**Syn.** **1.** austere, rigorous, exacting. **2.** rigid.

stern[2] (stern), *n.* the hind part of a ship or boat. [prob. < Scand. *stjōrn* steering] —**stern·most** (stern'mōst), *adj.*

Sterne (stern), *n.* Laurence, 1713–1768, English novelist.

ster·num (ster'nəm), *n., pl.* **-na** (-nə), **-nums.** *Anat., Zool.* the breastbone. [< NL < Gk.]

ster·nu·ta·tion (ster'nyə·tā'shən), *n.* act of sneezing. —**ster·nu·ta·tive** (stər·nū'tə·tiv), *adj.*

ster·to·rous (ster'tə·rəs), *adj.* making a heavy snoring sound. [< NL, < L *stertere* snore] —**ster'to·rous·ly,** *adv.* —**ster'to·rous·ness,** *n.*

stet (stet), *n., v.,* **stet·ted, stet·ting.** —*n.* "let it stand," a direction on printer's proof, a manuscript, or the like, to retain canceled matter (usually accompanied by a row of dots under or beside the matter). —*v.* mark for retention. [< L, let it stand]

steth·o·scope (steth'ə·skōp), *n.* instrument used by doctors when listening to sounds in the lungs, heart, etc. [< Gk. *stethos* chest + E *-scope* < Gk. *skopeein* watch] —**steth·o·scop·ic** (steth'ə·skop'ik), *adj.* —**ste·thos'co·py,** *n.*

Stet·tin (shte·tēn'), *n.* seaport in NW Poland.

ste·ve·dore (stē'və·dôr; -dōr), *n. Am.* man who loads and unloads ships. [< Sp. *estivador,* ult. < L *stipare* pack down]

Ste·ven·son (stē'vən·sən), *n.* **1.** Ad·lai (ad'lā) Ew·ing (ū'ing), 1900–1965, American political leader, governor of Illinois 1948–1953. **2.** Robert Louis, 1850–1894, Scottish author of novels, essays, etc.

stew (stü; stū), *v.* **1.** cook by slow boiling. **2.** *Colloq.* worry; fret. —*n.* **1.** food cooked by slow boiling: *beef stew.* **2.** *Colloq.* state of worry; fret. [< OF *estuver* < VL *extufare* < L *ex-* out + Gk. *typhos* vapor] —**stewed,** *adj.*

stew·ard (stü'ərd; stū'—), *n.* **1.** man who manages another's property or financial affairs. **2.** man who takes charge of the food and table service for a club, ship, railroad train, etc. **3.** employee on a ship who waits on table, attends to staterooms, etc. **4.** person appointed to manage a dinner, ball, show, etc. [OE *stigweard* < *stig* hall, sty + *weard* keeper, ward]

stew·ard·ess (stü'ər·dis; stū'—), *n.* **1.** a woman steward. **2.** woman employed on shipboard, an airplane, etc., to wait upon passengers.

St. He·le·na (hə·lē'nə), a British island in the S Atlantic; place of Napoleon's exile.

stib·i·um (stib'i·əm), *n. Chem.* antimony, Sb. [< L < Gk. *stibi*] —**stib'i·al,** *adj.*

stick[1] (stik), *n., v.,* **sticked, stick·ing.** —*n.* **1.** branch or shoot of a tree or shrub cut or broken off. **2.** a long, thin piece of wood. **3.** such a piece of wood shaped for a special use: *a walking stick.* 4. something like a stick in shape: *a stick of candy.* 5. the bat or thin, curved wand used in hockey, lacrosse, etc. 6. *Colloq.* a stiff, awkward, or stupid person. 7. lever used to work certain main controls of an airplane. 8. the sticks, *Am., Colloq.* the outlying districts; backwoods. —*v.* furnish with a stick or sticks to support or prop. [OE *sticca*] —Syn. *n.* 2. rod, staff.

stick² (stik), *v.,* **stuck, stick·ing.** —*v.* 1. pierce with a pointed instrument; thrust into; stab. 2. kill by stabbing or piercing. 3. fasten by thrusting the point or end into or through something: *he stuck a flower in his buttonhole.* 4. thrust or fix on something pointed: *stick a potato on a fork.* 5. put into a position: *don't stick your head out of the window.* 6. be thrust; extend (from, out, through, up, etc.): *his arms stick out of his coat sleeves.* 7. fasten by causing to adhere; attach: *stick a stamp on a letter.* 8. keep close: *the boy stuck to his mother's heels.* 9. be or become fastened; become fixed; be at a standstill: *our car stuck in the mud.* 10. bring to a stop: *our work was stuck by the breakdown of the machinery.* 11. keep on; hold fast: *stick to a task, stick to the same old idea.* 12. *Colloq.* puzzle. 13. be puzzled; hesitate. 14. *Slang.* put into a position involving labor, expense, loss, or the like. 15. *Slang.* charge exorbitantly; impose upon; cheat. 16. **stick around,** *Slang.* stay or wait nearby. 17. **stick at,** hesitate or stop for. 18. **stick out,** a. stand out; be plain. b. *Colloq.* put up with until the end. 19. **stick up,** *Slang.* hold up; rob. 20. **stick up for,** *Colloq.* support; defend. —*n.* a thrust. [OE *stician*]

stick·er (stik′ər), *n.* 1. person or thing that sticks. 2. *Am.* a gummed label. 3. *Am.* bur; thorn. 4. *Colloq.* puzzle.

stick·le (stik′əl), *v.,* **-led, -ling.** 1. make objections about trifles; insist stubbornly. 2. feel difficulties about trifles; have objections. [prob. ult. < OE *stihtan* arrange] —**stick′ler,** *n.*

stick·le·back (stik′əl·bak′), *n., pl.* **-backs** or (*esp. collectively*) **-back,** a small scaleless fish with a row of sharp spines on the back. The male builds an elaborate nest for the eggs.

stick·pin (stik′pin′), *n. Am.* pin worn in a necktie for ornament.

stick-to-it·ive·ness (stik′tü′it·iv·nis), *n. Am., Colloq.* perseverance.

stick-up (stik′up′), *n. Am., Slang.* holdup; robbery.

stick·y (stik′i), *adj.,* **stick·i·er, stick·i·est.** 1. that sticks; adhesive: *sticky glue.* 2. covered or smeared with adhesive material: *flypaper is sticky.* 3. of weather, humid. —**stick′i·ly,** *adv.* —**stick′i·ness,** *n.* —Syn. 1. viscous, glutinous, mucilaginous.

stiff (stif), *adj.* 1. not easily bent: *a stiff collar.* 2. hard to move: *stiff hinges.* 3. not able to move easily: *he was stiff and sore.* 4. drawn tight; tense: *a stiff cord.* 5. not fluid; firm: *stiff jelly.* 6. dense; compact: *stiff soil.* 7. not easy or natural in manner; formal: *a stiff bow, a stiff style of writing.* 8. strong and steady in motion: *a stiff breeze.* 9. hard to deal with; hard: *a stiff examination.* 10. firm in purpose; stubborn: *a stiff argument.* 11. strong: *a stiff drink.* 12. *Colloq.* more than seems suitable: *a stiff price.* —*n.* 1. *Slang.* corpse. 2. *Slang.* a stiff, formal, or priggish person. 3. *Am., Slang.* a rough, clumsy person. [OE *stif*] —**stiff′ish,** *adj.* —**stiff′ly,** *adv.* —**stiff′ness,** *n.* —Syn. *adj.* 1. inflexible, inelastic. 7. stilted, affected, constrained, ceremonious. 9. harsh, severe, rigorous. 12. immoderate, excessive.

stiff·en (stif′ən), *v.* make or become stiff. —**stiff′en·er,** *n.* —**stiff′en·ing,** *n., adj.*

stiff-necked (stif′nekt′), *adj.* 1. having a stiff neck. 2. stubborn; obstinate.

sti·fle (stī′fəl), *v.,* **-fled, -fling.** 1. stop the breath of; smother: *the smoke stifled the firemen.* 2. be unable to breathe freely: *I am stifling in this close room.* 3. keep back; suppress; stop: *stifle a yawn, stifle a rebellion.* [< Scand. *stifla* dam up] —**sti′fler,** *n.* —**sti′fling,** *adj.* —**sti′fling·ly,** *adv.* —Syn. 1, 2. choke, strangle. 3. extinguish, repress, muzzle, muffle.

stig·ma (stig′mə), *n., pl.* **stig·mas, stig·ma·ta** (stig′mə·tə). 1. mark of disgrace; stain or reproach on one's reputation. 2. a distinguishing mark or sign. 3. *Zool.* a small mark, spot, pore, or the like on an animal. 4. *Pathol.* a spot on the skin, esp. one that bleeds or turns red. 5. *Bot.* the part of the pistil of a plant that receives the pollen. 6. *Archaic.* a special mark burned on a slave or criminal. [< L < Gk.] —**stig·mat·ic** (stig·mat′ik), *adj., n.*

stig·ma·tize (stig′mə·tīz), *v.,* **-tized, -tiz·ing.** 1. set some mark of disgrace upon; reproach. 2. brand. —**stig′ma·ti·za′tion,** *n.* —**stig′ma·tiz′er,** *n.*

stile (stīl), *n.* 1. step or steps for getting over a fence or wall. 2. turnstile. [OE *stigel < stīgan* climb]

sti·let·to (stə·let′ō), *n., pl.* **-tos, -toes,** *v.,* **-toed, -to·ing.** —*n.* a dagger with a narrow blade. —*v.* stab or kill with a stiletto. [< Ital., ult. < L *stilus* pointed instrument]

still¹ (stil), *adj.* 1. without motion; without noise; quiet; tranquil: *a still scene.* 2. soft; low; subdued: *a still small voice.* 3. without waves: *still water.* 4. not bubbling: *still wine.* 5. not showing motion: *still feet.* —*v.* 1. make quiet: *still a crying child.* 2. become quiet. 3. calm; relieve. —*n.* 1. *Poetic.* a silence. 2. photograph of a person or other subject at rest. 3. *Am.* an individual picture or frame of a motion picture used in advertising. —*adv.* 1. at this or that time: *he came yesterday and he is still here.* 2. up to this or that time: *the matter is still unsettled.* 3. in the future as in the past: *it will still be here.* 4. even; yet: *still more, still worse.* 5. yet; nevertheless: *though rebuffed, he still tries.* 6. without moving; quietly. 7. *Archaic* or *Poetic.* steadily; constantly; always. —*conj.* yet; nevertheless: *I can see your point of view; still I don't agree with you.* [OE *still*] —**still′ness,** *n.* —Syn. *adj.* 1. stationary, silent. 3. calm, undisturbed. —*v.* 1. silence, hush, tranquilize, pacify.

still² (stil), *n.* 1. apparatus for distilling liquids, esp. one used in making alcohol. 2. distillery. [n. use of *still,* short form of *distill*]

still·born (stil′bôrn′), *adj.* dead when born.

still life, 1. inanimate objects, as flowers, pottery, etc., shown in a picture. 2. picture containing such things. —**still′-life′,** *adj.*

still·ly (adv. stil′li; adj. stil′i), *adv., adj.,* **-li·er, -li·est.** —*adv.* calmly; quietly. —*adj. Poetic.* quiet; calm.

stilt (stilt), *n.* one of a pair of poles, each with a support for the foot at some distance above the ground, used in walking through shallow water, or by children for amusement. [ME *stilte*]

stilt·ed (stil′tid), *adj.* stiffly dignified or formal: *stilted conversation.* —**stilt′ed·ly,** *adv.* —**stilt′ed·ness,** *n.* —Syn. pompous.

stim·u·lant (stim′yə·lənt), *n.* 1. food, drug, medicine, etc., that temporarily increases the activity of some part of the body. Tea, coffee, and alcoholic drinks are stimulants. 2. motive, influence, etc., that rouses one to action. —*adj.* stimulating.

stim·u·late (stim′yə·lāt), *v.,* **-lat·ed, -lat·ing.** 1. spur on; stir up; rouse to action. 2. increase temporarily the functional activity of (a part of the body, etc.). 3. excite with alcoholic liquor; intoxicate. 4. act as a stimulant or a stimulus. [< L, < *stimulus* goad] —**stim′u·lat′er, stim′u·la′tor,** *n.* —**stim′u·la′tion,** *n.* —Syn. 1. prick, goad, incite, encourage, impel, urge.

stim·u·la·tive (stim′yə·lā′tiv; -lə·tiv), *adj.* tending to stimulate; stimulating. —*n.* stimulus.

stim·u·lus (stim′yə·ləs), *n., pl.* **-li** (-lī). 1. something that stirs to action or effort. 2. something that excites some part of the body to activity. [< L, orig., goad]

sting (sting), *v.,* **stung** or (*Archaic* or *Obs.*) **stang, stung, sting·ing,** *n.* —*v.* 1. prick with a small point; wound: *be stung by a bee.* 2. pain sharply: *stung by ridicule.* 3. have a prickly or smarting feeling. 4. cause a feeling like that of a

sting: *mustard stings.* **5.** drive or stir up as if by a sting: *their ridicule stung him into making a sharp reply.* **6.** *Slang.* impose upon; charge exorbitantly. —*n.* **1.** act of stinging. **2.** prick; wound: *put mud on the sting to take away the pain.* **3.** the sharp-pointed part of an insect, animal, or plant that pricks or wounds and often poisons. **4.** sharp pain: *the sting of defeat.* **5.** thing that causes a sharp pain. **6.** thing that drives or urges sharply. [OE *stingan*] —**sting′-er,** *n.* —**sting′ing·ly,** *adv.* —**sting′ing·ness,** *n.* —**sting′less,** *adj.*

sting ray, *Am.* a broad, flat fish that can inflict severe wounds with its sharp spines.

stin·gy (stin′ji), *adj.,* –gi·er, –gi·est. **1.** reluctant to spend or give money; close-fisted; not generous: *he saved money without being stingy.* **2.** scanty; meager. [akin to STING] —**stin′gi·ly,** *adv.* —**stin′gi·ness,** *n.* —Syn. **1.** miserly, parsimonious, niggardly, penurious.

stink (stingk), *n., v.,* **stank** or **stunk, stunk, stink·ing.** —*n.* a very bad smell. —*v.* **1.** have a bad smell. **2.** cause to have a very bad smell. **3.** have a very bad reputation; be in great disfavor. [OE *stincan* to smell] —**stink′er,** *n.* —**stink′-ing,** *adj.* —**stink′ing·ly,** *adv.*

stink·bug (stingk′bug′), *n. Am.* any bad-smelling bug.

stink·weed (stingk′wēd′), *n. Am.* any of various ill-smelling plants, as the jimson weed.

stint (stint), *v.* **1.** keep on short allowance; be saving or careful in using or spending; limit: *the parents stinted themselves of food to give it to their children.* **2.** be saving; get along on very little. —*n.* **1.** limit; limitation: *give without stint.* **2.** amount or share set aside. **3.** task assigned: *a daily stint.* [OE *styntan* blunt] —**stint′er,** *n.* —**stint′ing·ly,** *adv.* —**stint′less,** *adj.*

stipe (stīp), *n. Bot.* stalk; stem. [< F < L *stipes* trunk]

sti·pend (stī′pend), *n.* **1.** fixed or regular pay; salary. **2.** any periodic payment. [< L *stipendium* < *stips* wages, orig., coin + *pendere* weigh out]

sti·pen·di·ar·y (stī·pen′di·er′i), *adj., n., pl.* –ar·ies. —*adj.* performing services for regular pay; receiving a stipend. —*n.* person who receives a stipend.

stip·ple (stip′əl), *v.,* –pled, –pling, *n.* —*v.* **1.** paint, draw, or engrave by dots. **2.** produce this effect on. **3.** apply (paint) by this method. —*n.* **1.** Also, **stip′pling,** this method of painting, drawing, or engraving. **2.** effect produced by this method. **3.** stippled work. [< Du. *stippelen*] —**stip′pler,** *n.*

stip·u·late (stip′yə·lāt), *v.,* –lat·ed, –lat·ing. arrange definitely; demand as a condition of agreement. [< L *stipulatus,* pp. of *stipulari* stipulate] —**stip′u·la′tor,** *n.* —**stip·u·la·to·ry** (stip′yə·lə·tô′ri; –tō′–), *adj.*

stip·u·la·tion (stip′yə·lā′shən), *n.* **1.** act of stipulating. **2.** a definite arrangement; agreement. **3.** a condition in an agreement or bargain.

stip·ule (stip′ūl), *n. Bot.* one of the pair of little leaf-like parts at the base of a leaf stem. [< L *stipula,* akin to *stipes* trunk. Doublet of STUBBLE.] —**stip·u·lar** (stip′yə·lər), *adj.* —**stip′uled,** *adj.*

stir¹ (stėr), *v.,* **stirred,** **stir·ring,** *n.* —*v.* **1.** move: *the wind stirs the leaves.* **2.** move about: *no one was stirring in the house.* **3.** circulate; be current: *is any news stirring?* **4.** mix by moving around with a spoon, fork, stick, etc.: *stir sugar into one's coffee.* **5.** be mixed with a spoon or the like: *this dough stirs hard.* **6.** set going; affect strongly; excite: *John stirs the other children to mischief.* **7.** become active, much affected, or excited: *the countryside was stirring with new life.* —*n.* **1.** movement. **2.** excitement. **3.** act of stirring. **4.** a jog; thrust; poke.

[OE *styrian*] —**stir′rer,** *n.* —Syn. *v.* **6.** rouse, animate, agitate. —*n.* **1.** motion, activity, bustle.

stir² (stėr), *n. Slang.* prison.

stir·ring (stėr′ing), *adj.* **1.** moving; active; lively: *stirring times.* **2.** rousing; exciting: *a stirring speech.* —**stir′ring·ly,** *adv.* —Syn. **1.** bustling, brisk. **2.** stimulating, inspiring.

stir·rup (stėr′əp; stir′–), *n.* **1.** a support for the rider's foot, hung from a saddle. **2.** piece somewhat like a stirrup used as a support. [OE *stigrāp* < *stige* climbing + *rāp* rope]

Stirrups

stirrup bone, the stapes.

stitch (stich), *n.* **1.** one complete movement of a threaded needle through cloth in sewing. **2.** one complete movement in knitting, crocheting, embroidering, etc. **3.** a particular method of taking stitches: *buttonhole stitch.* **4.** loop of thread, etc., made by a stitch. **5.** piece of cloth or clothing. **6.** *Colloq.* a small bit. **7.** a sudden, sharp pain. —*v.* **1.** make stitches in; fasten with stitches. **2.** sew. [OE *stice* puncture] —**stitch′er,** *n.* —**stitch′ing,** *n.*

sti·ver (stī′vər), *n.* **1.** a Dutch coin, ¹⁄₂₀ of a guilder, worth about 1½ cents (1950). **2.** anything having small value. [< Du. *stuiver*]

St. John, one of the Virgin Islands belonging to the United States.

St. John's, capital of Newfoundland.

St.-John's-wort (sānt·jonz′wėrt′), *n.* shrub or plant that has many clusters of showy yellow flowers.

St. Lawrence, 1. river in North America flowing from Lake Ontario into the Gulf of St. Lawrence. **2.** Gulf of, gulf in E Canada.

St. Lawrence Seaway, waterway that links the Great Lakes to the Atlantic Ocean by means of canals and the St. Lawrence River.

St. Lou·is (lü′is; lü′i), city in E Missouri, on the Mississippi River.

St.-Mi·hiel (saN′mē·yel′), *n.* town in NE France: battle, World War I, 1918.

St.-Mo·ritz (sānt·mə·rits′), *n.* a fashionable winter resort in SE Switzerland.

stoat (stōt), *n.* **1.** the ermine, esp. in its summer coat of brown. **2.** weasel.

stock (stok), *n.* **1.** things for use or for sale; supply used as it is needed: *this store keeps a large stock of toys.* **2. in stock,** ready for use or sale; on hand. **3. out of stock,** lacking, either temporarily or permanently; no longer on hand. **4.** amount of something saved or collected. **5.** cattle or other farm animals; livestock. **6.** the subscribed capital of a company or corporation, divided into transferable shares of uniform amount; shares in a company. **7.** fund that is a debt owed by a nation, city, etc., to individuals who receive a fixed rate of interest. **8.** a related group of people, animals, or plants; race; family: *she is of old New England stock.* **9.** part used as a support or handle; part to which other parts are attached: *the wooden stock of a rifle.* **10.** raw material: *rags are used as a stock for making paper.* **11.** broth in which meat or fish has been cooked, used as a base for soups, sauces, etc. **12.** various plays produced by a company at a single theater. **13.** something lifeless and stupid. **14.** butt for ridicule. **15.** trunk or stump of a tree; main stem of a plant. **16. the stocks, a.** a wooden frame with holes to put a person's feet and sometimes his hands through, used as a punishment. **b.** a wooden frame on which a ship or boat is built. **17.** tree or plant that furnishes cuttings for grafting. **18. take stock, a.** find out how much stock one has on hand. **b.** make an estimate or examination. **19. take stock in,** *Colloq.* take an interest in; consider important; trust. —*v.* **1.** lay in a supply of; supply: *stock fodder for the winter months.* **2.** lay in a supply. **3.** keep regularly for use or for sale: *a toy store stocks toys.* **4.** fasten to or provide with a stock. **5.** provide with wild life; stock a lake with fish.* **6.** furnish with horses, cattle, etc.: *stock a farm.* —*adj.* **1.** kept on hand regularly: *stock sizes.* 2. in common use; commonplace; everyday: *a stock topic of conversation.* 3. designating or pertaining to the raising of livestock. 4. of or pertaining to stock or stocks. [OE *stocc*] —**Syn.** 1. fund, store, goods, merchandise, wares. *-v.* 1. furnish, store, replenish.

stock·ade (stok·ād′), *n., v.,* –ad·ed, –ad·ing. —*n.* 1. defense made of large, strong posts set upright in the ground. 2. pen or other enclosed space made with upright posts, stakes, etc. —*v.* protect, fortify, or surround with a stockade. [< F *estacade,* ult. < Pr. *estaca* stake < Gmc.]

stock·bro·ker (stok′brō′kər), *n.* person who buys and sells stocks and bonds for others for a commission. —**stock′bro′ker·age, stock′bro′king,** *n.*

stock car, *Am.* a railroad freight car for livestock.

stock company, 1. company whose capital is divided into shares. 2. *Am.* a theatrical company employed more or less permanently under the same management, usually at one theater, to perform many different plays.

stock exchange, 1. place where stocks and bonds are bought and sold. 2. association of brokers and dealers in stocks and bonds.

stock·hold·er (stok′hōl′dər), *n.* owner of stocks or shares in a company. —**stock′hold′ing,** *n., adj.*

Stock·holm (stok′hōm; –hōlm), *n.* seaport and capital of Sweden, in the SE part.

stock·i·net (stok′ə·net′), *n. Esp. Brit.* an elastic, machine-knitted fabric used for making underwear, etc.

stock·ing (stok′ing), *n.* 1. a close-fitting, knitted covering of wool, cotton, Nylon, etc., for the foot and leg. 2. something like a stocking. [< *stock* stocking] —**stock′inged,** *adj.* —**stock′ing·less,** *adj.*

stock·man (stok′mən), *n., pl.* –men. 1. man who raises livestock. 2. man in charge of a stock of materials or goods.

stock market, 1. a stock exchange. 2. the buying and selling in such a place. 3. prices of stocks and bonds.

stock·pile (stok′pīl′), *n., v.,* –piled, –pil·ing. —*n.* 1. a supply of raw materials, essential items, etc., built up and held in reserve for use during time of emergency or shortage. 2. such a reserve of atomic weapons for warfare. —*v.* collect or bring together a stockpile.

stock raising, *Am.* the raising of livestock. —**stock raiser.**

stock-still (stok′stil′), *adj.* motionless.

stock·y (stok′i), *adj.,* stock·i·er, stock·i·est. having a solid or sturdy form or build; thick for its height. —**stock′i·ly,** *adv.* —**stock′i·ness,** *n.*

stock·yard (stok′yärd′), *n. Am.* place with pens and sheds for cattle, sheep, hogs, and horses. Livestock is kept in a stockyard before being sent to market or slaughtered.

stodg·y (stoj′i), *adj.,* stodg·i·er, stodg·i·est. 1. dull or uninteresting; tediously commonplace: *a stodgy book.* 2. heavy: *stodgy food.* —**stodg′i·ly,** *adv.* —**stodg′i·ness,** *n.*

sto·gy, sto·gie (stō′gi), *n., pl.* –gies. *Am.* a long, slender, cheap cigar. [from *Conestoga,* town in Pa.]

Sto·ic (stō′ik), *n.* 1. member of a school of ancient Greek philosophy which taught that men should be free from passion, unmoved by life's happenings, and should submit without complaint to unavoidable necessity. 2. stoic, person who remains calm, represses his feelings, and is indifferent to pleasure and pain. —*adj.* 1. pertaining to this philosophy, or to its followers. 2. stoic, stoical. [< L < Gk. *stoikos,* lit., pertaining to a *stoa* portico (esp. the portico in Athens where Zeno taught)]

sto·i·cal (stō′ə·kəl), *adj.* calm or austere; impassive. —**sto′i·cal·ly,** *adv.* —**sto′i·cal·ness,** *n.*

Sto·i·cism (stō′ə·siz·əm), *n.* 1. philosophy of the Stoics. 2. stoicism, patient endurance; indifference to pleasure and pain.

stoke (stōk), *v.,* stoked, stok·ing. 1. poke, stir

up, and feed (a fire); tend the fire of (a furnace). 2. tend a fire. [< *stoker*]

stoke·hole (stōk′hōl′), *n.* 1. hole through which fuel is put into a furnace. 2. space in front of furnaces where men shovel in coal and take out ashes.

stok·er (stōk′ər), *n.* 1. man who tends the fires of a furnace or boiler. 2. a mechanical device for tending and feeding a furnace. [< Du., < *stoken* stoke]

stole[1] (stōl), *v.* pt. of steal.

stole[2] (stōl), *n.* 1. a narrow strip of silk or other material worn around the neck by a clergyman during certain church functions. 2. a woman's collar or scarf of fur or cloth with ends hanging down in front. [< L < Gk. *stole* robe]

sto·len (stō′lən), *v.* pp. of steal.

stol·id (stol′id), *adj.* hard to arouse; not easily excited; showing no emotion; seeming dull. [< L *stolidus*] —**sto·lid′i·ty, stol′id·ness,** *n.* —**stol′id·ly,** *adv.* —**Syn.** impassive, stodgy.

sto·ma (stō′mə), *n., pl.* sto·ma·ta (stō′mə·tə; stom′ə-). a small opening; mouth; pore. [< NL < Gk., mouth]

stom·ach (stum′ək), *n.* 1. the most important part of the body for receiving and digesting food. 2. the part of the body containing the stomach; abdomen; belly. 3. appetite. 4. desire; liking: *I have no stomach for that kind of writing.* —*v.* 1. take into the stomach. 2. be able to eat or keep in one's stomach. 3. put up with; bear; endure: *he could not stomach such insults.* [< OF < L < Gk., < *stoma* mouth] —**stom′ach·al,** *adj.* —**sto·mach·ic** (stō·mak′ik), **sto·mach′i·cal,** *adj., n.*

stom·ach·er (stum′ək·ər), *n.* a part of a woman's dress covering the stomach and chest.

Lady wearing a stomacher

stone (stōn), *n., pl.* stones (but for def. 7 stone), *adj., v.,* stoned, ston·ing. —*n.* 1. hard mineral matter that is not metal; rock: *a wall of stone.* 2. piece of rock: *some boys throw stones.* 3. piece of rock of definite size, shape, etc., used for a particular purpose, as a gravestone, tombstone, grindstone, or millstone. 4. something hard and rounded like a stone, which sometimes forms in the kidneys or gall bladder causing sickness and pain. 5. gem; jewel. 6. a hard seed: *peach stones, plum stones.* 7. *Brit.* unit of weight equal to 14 pounds. 8. cast the first stone, be the first to criticize. —*adj.* 1. made of stone. 2. pertaining to stone. 3. made of stoneware or coarse clay. —*v.* 1. put stone on; line with stone. 2. throw stones at; drive by throwing stones; kill by throwing stones: *Saint Stephen was stoned.* 3. take stones or seeds out of: *stone cherries or plums.* [OE *stān*] —**stone′less,** *adj.* —**ston′er,** *n.* —**Syn.** 1. boulder. 2. pebble.

Stone Age, a prehistoric period when people used tools and weapons made from stone.

stone-blind (stōn′blīnd′), *adj.* totally blind.

stone bruise, bruise caused by a stone, esp. one on the sole of the foot.

stone·cut·ter (stōn′kut′ər), *n.* one that cuts or carves stones. —**stone′cut′ting,** *n.*

stone-deaf (stōn′def′), *adj.* totally deaf.

Stone·henge (stōn′henj), *n.* a prehistoric ruin in S England, consisting of huge slabs of stone, mostly upright.

stone·ma·son (stōn′mā′sən), *n.* person who cuts stone or builds walls, etc., of stone. —**stone′ma′son·ry,** *n.*

stone·ware (stōn′wār′), *n.* a coarse, hard, glazed pottery.

stone·work (stōn′wėrk′), *n.* 1. work in stone. 2. the part of a building made of stone. —**stone′work′er,** *n.*

ston·y (stōn′i), *adj.,* ston·i·er, ston·i·est. 1. having many stones: *the beach is stony.* 2. pertaining to or characteristic of stone. 3. resembling stone: *a stony mass.* 4. without expression

or feeling: *a stony stare.* **—ston′i·ly,** *adv.*
—ston′i·ness, *n.* **—Syn. 3.** rocky, flinty, ada-
mantine. **4.** glassy.

stood (stůd), *v.* pt. and pp. of **stand**.

stooge (stüj), *n., v.,* **stooged, stoog·ing.** *Am.,
Slang.* **—n. 1.** person on the stage who asks questions of a comedian and is the butt of the comedian's jokes. **2.** person who plays a compliant,
subordinate role. **—v. 1.** act as a stooge. **2.** play
a compliant, subordinate role.

stool (stül), *n.* **1.** seat without back or arms.
2. a similar article used to rest the feet on, or
to kneel on. **3.** stump or root of a plant from
which shoots grow. **4.** movement of the bowels;
waste matter from the bowels. **5.** article or place
to be used as a toilet. [< OE *stōl*]

stool pigeon, *Am.* **1.** pigeon used to lead other
pigeons into a trap. **2.** *Slang.* a spy for the
police; informer.

stoop[1] (stüp), *v.* **1.** bend forward: *stoop over a
desk.* **2.** carry head and shoulders bent forward:
stoop from old age. **3.** of trees, precipices, etc.,
bend forward and downward. **4.** lower oneself;
descend: *stoop to retaliate.* **—n. 1.** a forward
bend. **2.** a forward bend of the head and shoulders. **3.** condescension. [OE *stūpian*] **—stoop′er,**
n. **—stoop′ing·ly,** *adv.* **—Syn. v. 1.** bow, incline.
4. condescend, deign.

stoop[2] (stüp), *n. Am.* porch or platform at the
entrance of a house. [< Du. *stoep*]

stop (stop), *v.,* **stopped** or (*Poetic*) **stopt, stopping,** *n.* **—v. 1.** keep from moving, acting, doing,
being, etc.: *stop a clock, stop a speaker.* **2.** cut
off; withhold: *stop supplies.* **3.** put an end to;
interrupt; check: *his clever reply stopped the
derogatory remarks.* **4.** *Colloq.* stay; halt: *stop
at a hotel.* **5.** leave off moving, acting, doing,
being, etc.; cease: *all work stopped.* **6.** close by
filling; fill holes in; close: *stop a hole, a leak, a
wound, etc.* **7.** close (a vessel) with a cork, plug,
or the like; shut up (something) in a closed
vessel or place: *stop a bottle.* **8.** block; obstruct:
a fallen tree stopped traffic. **9.** check (a blow,
stroke, etc.); parry; ward off. **10. stop off,** *Am.,
Colloq.* stop for a short stay. **11. stop over,** a.
make a short stay. b. *Am., Colloq.* stop in the
course of a trip. **—n. 1.** a stopping or being
stopped; ending of movement or action; check.
2. thing that stops; obstacle. **3.** place where a
stop is made. **4.** any piece or device that serves
to check or control movement or action in a
mechanism. **5.** a punctuation mark. **6.** *Music.* a.
thing that controls pitch of an instrument. b. in
organs, a graduated set of pipes of the same
kind, or the knob or handle that controls them.
7. *Phonet.* a. a sudden, complete stopping of the
breath stream, followed by its sudden release.
b. consonant that involves such a stopping. *P,
t, k, b, d, g* are stops. **8.** put a stop to, stop;
end. [ult. < L *stuppa* tow < Gk. *styppē*]
—stopped, *adj.* **—Syn. v. 2.** discontinue, intermit. **3.** hinder, deter, impede, prevent, arrest,
suspend. **5.** desist, pause. **—n. 1.** obstruction,
interruption, suspension. ➤ **Stop** is colloquial
in the United States in the sense of "stay": *We
stopped two days in Los Angeles.* It is the normal
British usage.

stop·cock (stop′kok′), *n.* faucet; valve.

stop·gap (stop′gap′), *n.* a temporary substitute. **—adj.** serving as a stopgap.

stop·o·ver (stop′ō′vər), *n. Am.* a stopping over
in the course of a journey, esp. with the privilege of proceeding later on the ticket originally
issued for the journey.

stop·page (stop′ij), *n.* **1.** a stopping or being
stopped. **2.** block; obstruction.

stop·per (stop′ər), *n.* **1.** plug or cork for closing
a bottle, tube, etc. **2.** person or thing that stops.
—v. close or fit with a stopper.

stop·ple (stop′əl), *n., v.,* **-pled, -pling. —n.**
stopper for a bottle, etc. **—v.** close or fit with a
stopper.

stop watch, a watch having a hand that can
be stopped or started at any instant. A stop
watch indicates fractions of a second and is
used for timing races and contests.

stor·age (stôr′ij; stōr′-), *n.* **1.** act or fact of
storing goods. **2.** condition of being stored. **Cold
storage** is used to keep eggs and meat from
spoiling. **3.** place for storing: *she has put her
furniture in storage.* **4.** price for storing.

storage battery, a battery of cells which
transform electrical energy into chemical
changes when a current flows through them in
one direction, and yield electrical energy by the
reversal of these changes.

store (stôr; stōr), *n., v.,* **stored, stor·ing. —n.
1.** *Am.* place where goods are kept for sale. **2.**
thing or things laid up for use; supply; stock.
3. *Esp. Brit.* place where supplies are kept for
future use. **4. in store,** on hand; in reserve;
saved for the future. **5. set store by,** value;
esteem. **—v. 1.** supply or stock. **2.** put away for
future use; lay up. **3.** put in a warehouse or
place used for preserving. [< OF *estorer,* orig.,
restore < L *instaurare*] **—stor′a·ble,** *adj.*
—stor′er, *n.*

store·house (stôr′hous′; stōr′-), *n.* place
where things are stored: *this factory has many
storehouses for its products, a library is a storehouse of information.*

store·keep·er (stôr′kēp′ər; stōr′-), *n. Am.*
person who has charge of a store or stores.

store·room (stôr′rüm′; -rům′; stōr′-), *n.*
room where things are stored.

sto·rey (stôr′i; stōr′-), *n., pl.* **-reys.** *Esp. Brit.*
story[2].

sto·ried[1] (stô′rid; stō′-), *adj.* **1.** celebrated in
story or history. **2.** ornamented
with designs representing happenings in history or legend.

sto·ried[2], *esp. Brit.* **sto·reyed**
(stô′rid; stō′-), *adj.* having stories or floors: *a two-storied house.*

stork (stôrk), *n.* a large, long-
legged wading bird with a long
neck and a long bill. [OE *storc*]

storm (stôrm), *n.* **1.** a strong
wind with rain, snow, hail, or
thunder and lightning. In deserts there are storms of sand.
2. a heavy fall of rain, snow, or
hail; violent outbreak of thun-
der and lightning. **3.** anything like a storm: *a
storm of arrows.* **4.** a violent outburst or disturbance: *a storm of angry words.* **5.** a violent
attack: *the castle was taken by storm.* **—v. 1.**
blow hard; rain; snow; hail. **2.** be violent; rage:
she storms when something goes wrong. **3.** speak
loudly and angrily: *storm in reply.* **4.** rush violently: *storm out of the room.* **5.** attack violently: *the troops stormed the city.* [OE]
—storm′er, *n.* **—storm′less,** *adj.* **—Syn. v. 2.**
fume, rant. **5.** assault, assail.

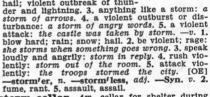

Stork
(ab. 3 ft. tall)

storm cellar, *Am.* cellar for shelter during
cyclones, tornadoes, etc.

storm troops, members of the private army
formed by Adolf Hitler around 1923 and dis-
banded in 1934. **—storm trooper.**

storm·y (stôr′mi), *adj.,* **storm·i·er, storm·i-
est. 1.** having storms; likely to have storms;
troubled by storms. **2.** rough and disturbed; violent. **—storm′i·ly,** *adv.* **—storm′i·ness,** *n.*
—Syn. 1. tempestuous, blustery, windy. **2.** wild.

stormy petrel, **1.** any of several small black-
and-white sea birds called petrels, whose presence is supposed to give warning of a storm. **2.**
anyone believed likely to cause trouble or to
indicate trouble.

Stor·thing, Stor·ting (stôr′ting′; stōr′-),
n. the national parliament of Norway.

sto·ry[1] (stô′ri; stō′-), *n., pl.* **-ries,** *v.,* **-ried,
-ry·ing. —n. 1.** account of some happening or
group of happenings. **2.** such an account, either
true or made-up, intended to interest the reader
or hearer; tale. **3.** *Colloq.* falsehood. **4.** stories as
a branch of literature: *a character famous in
story.* **5.** plot of a play, novel, etc. **6.** *Am.* a newspaper article, or material for such an article.
—v. ornament with stories or pictures: *storied
tapestries.* [< AF *estorie* < L *historia* history.
Doublet of HISTORY.] **—Syn. *n.* 1.** relation, nar-

rative, recital, record, chronicle. **2.** anecdote, fable, legend, novel. **3.** fib, lie.

sto·ry² (stô/ri; stō/-), *n., pl.* **-ries.** **1.** set of rooms on the same floor forming a complete horizontal section of a building; one of the structural divisions in the height of a building: *a house of two stories.* **2.** each of a series of divisions or stages of anything placed horizontally one above the other. Also, *esp. Brit.* **storey.** [? ult. special use of *story¹* in sense of "row of historical statues across a building front"]

sto·ry·tell·er (stô/ri·tel/ər; stō/-), *n.* **1.** person who tells stories. **2.** *Colloq.* person who tells falsehoods; liar. **—sto/ry·tell/ing,** *n., adj.*

stoup (stüp), *n.* **1.** vessel of varying size for liquids, as a cup, flagon, or tankard. **2.** basin for holy water at the entrance of a church. [< Scand. *staup*]

stout (stout), *adj.* **1.** fat and large: *a stout body.* **2.** strongly built; firm; strong: *a stout wall.* **3.** brave; bold: *a stout heart.* **4.** not yielding; stubborn: *stout resistance.* **—n.** **1.** a strong, dark-brown beer. **2.** person who is stout. **3.** Usually, **stouts.** clothing made specially for fat and large people. [< OF *estout* strong < Gmc. root *stolt-* proud < L *stultus* foolish] **—stout/ly,** *adv.* **—stout/ness,** *n.* **—Syn.** *adj.* **1.** stocky, plump, portly, corpulent, obese. **2.** durable, tough, sturdy, hardy, vigorous. **3.** valiant. **4.** determined, resolute.

stout-heart·ed (stout/här/tid), *adj.* brave; bold; courageous. **—stout/-heart/ed·ly,** *adv.* **—stout/-heart/ed·ness,** *n.*

stove¹ (stōv), *n.* apparatus for cooking and heating. There are wood, coal, gas, oil, and electric stoves. [OE *stofa* warm bathing room]

stove² (stōv), *v.* pt. and pp. of **stave.**

stove·pipe (stōv/pīp/), *n.* **1.** pipe of sheet metal serving as the chimney of a stove, or to connect a stove with the chimney flue. **2.** *Am., Colloq.* a tall silk hat.

stow (stō), *v.* **1.** pack: *the cargo was stowed in the ship's hold.* **2.** pack things closely in, as for storage or reserve; fill by packing. **3. stow away,** hide on a ship, airplane, etc., to get a free ride. [ult. < OE *stōw* place] **—stow/er,** *n.*

stow·age (stō/ij), *n.* **1.** act of stowing. **2.** room or place for stowing. **3.** what is stowed. **4.** a charge for stowing something.

stow·a·way (stō/ə·wā/), *n.* person who hides on a ship, train, etc., to get a free passage or to escape secretly.

Stowe (stō), *n.* Mrs. **Harriet (Elizabeth) Beecher,** 1811–1896, American writer.

St. Paul, capital of Minnesota, in the SE part.

St. Pe·ters·burg (pē/tərz·berg), the former capital of Russia under the czars, now called Leningrad.

stra·bis·mus (strə·biz/məs), *n.* a disorder of vision due to the turning of one eye·or both eyes from the normal position so that both cannot be directed at the same point or object at the same time. [< NL < Gk., ult. < *strabos* squint-eyed] **—stra·bis/mal, stra·bis/mic,** *adj.*

strad·dle (strad/əl), *v.,* **-dled, -dling,** *n.* **—v.** **1.** walk, stand, or sit with the legs wide apart. **2.** have a leg on each side of (a horse, bicycle, chair, ditch, etc.). **3.** *Am., Colloq.* a. avoid taking sides. b. attempt to favor both sides of (a question, etc.). **—n.** **1.** a straddling. **2.** distance straddled. [< var. of *stride*] **—strad/dler,** *n.* **—strad/dling·ly,** *adv.*

Strad·i·var·i·us (strad/ə·vãr/i·əs), *n.* **1.** Antonius, 1644–1737, Italian violin maker. **2.** violin, viola, or cello made by him.

strafe (strāf; sträf), *v.,* **strafed, straf·ing.** *Slang.* **1.** of aircraft, machine-gun and bomb enemy ground positions at close range. **2.** shell or bombard heavily. [from the German slogan *Gott strafe England* God punish England] **—straf/er,** *n.*

strag·gle (strag/əl), *v.,* **-gled, -gling.** **1.** wander about in a scattered fashion: *cows straggled along the lane.* **2.** stray from the rest; wander away. **3.** spread in an irregular, rambling manner. **—strag/gler,** *n.* **—strag/gling·ly,** *adv.* **—strag/gly,** *adj.*

straight (strāt), *adj.* **1.** without a bend or curve: *a straight path.* **2.** leading or going directly to some point; direct: *straight aim.* **3.** evenly formed or set: *hold the shoulders straight.* **4.** frank; honest; upright: *straight conduct.* **5.** in proper order or condition; right; correct: *keep your accounts straight.* **6.** continuous: *in straight succession.* **7.** *Am.* thoroughgoing or unreserved: *a straight Republican.* **8.** *Am.* unmodified; undiluted: *straight whiskey.* **9.** *Colloq.* reliable: *a straight tip.* **10.** in poker, made up of a sequence of five cards: *a straight flush.* **11.** *Am., Slang.* with no deduction, regardless of how many are bought: *cigars ten cents straight.* **—adv.** **1.** in a line: *walk straight.* **2.** in a straight form or position: *sit straight.* **3.** directly: *he went straight home.* **4.** frankly; honestly; uprightly: *live straight.* **5.** continuously: *drive straight on.* **6.** without qualification of any kind. **7. straight away** or **off,** at once. **—n.** **1.** straight form, position, or line. **2.** a straight part, as of a race course. **3.** *Am.* in poker, a sequence of five cards. [OE *streht,* pp. of *streccan* stretch] **—straight/ly,** *adv.* **—straight/ness,** *n.* **—Syn.** *adj.* **1.** undeviating, unswerving, unbroken. **4.** honorable. **—Ant.** *adj.* **1.** crooked, curving.

straight·a·way (strāt/ə·wā/), *n.* a straight course. **—adj.** in a straight course.

straight·en (strāt/ən), *v.* **1.** make or become straight. **2.** put in the proper order or condition. **—straight/en·er,** *n.*

straight-for·ward (strāt/fôr/wərd), *adj.* **1.** honest; frank. **2.** going straight ahead; direct. **—adv.** Also, **straight/for/wards.** directly or continuously ahead. **—straight/for/ward·ly,** *adv.* **—straight/for/ward·ness,** *n.*

straight-out (strāt/out/), *adj.* *Am., Colloq.* out-and-out; complete; thorough.

straight·way (strāt/wā/), *adv.* at once; immediately.

strain¹ (strān), *v.* **1.** draw tight; stretch: *the weight strained the rope.* **2.** pull hard: *the dog strained at his leash.* **3.** stretch as much as possible: *strain every nerve.* **4.** use to the utmost: *she strained her eyes to see.* **5.** injure by too much effort or by stretching: *strain a muscle.* **6.** be injured by too much effort. **7.** stretch or force beyond the proper limit: *strain the truth.* **8.** make a very great effort. **9.** press or pour through a strainer. **10.** drip through. **11.** press closely; squeeze; hug. **—n.** **1.** force or weight that stretches. **2.** a great or excessive effort: *the strain of lifting a heavy weight.* **3.** injury caused by too much effort or by stretching: *the strain of worry.* **4.** any severe, trying, or wearing pressure: *the strain of worry.* **5.** its effect on the body or mind. **6.** Often, **strains.** part of a piece of music; melody; song. **7.** manner or style of doing or speaking. [< OF < L *stringere* draw tight] **—strained,** *adj.* **—Syn.** *v.* **1.** pull, tighten. **2.** tug. **5.** wrench. **10.** percolate.

strain² (strān), *n.* **1.** line of descent; race; stock; breed. **2.** group of animals or plants that form a part of a breed, race, or variety. **3.** an inherited quality; hereditary character or disposition. **4.** trace or streak. [var. of OE *strēon* gain, begetting]

strain·er (strān/ər), *n.* thing that strains, as a filter, a sieve, or a colander.

strait (strāt), *n.* **1.** Often, **straits** (*sing. in use*). a narrow channel connecting two larger bodies of water. **2.** Often, **straits.** difficulty; need; distress. **3.** *Archaic.* isthmus. **—adj.** *Archaic.* **1.** narrow. **2.** strict. [< OF < L *strictus* drawn tight. Doublet of STRICT.] **—strait/ly,** *adv.* **—strait/ness,** *n.* **—Syn.** *n.* **2.** perplexity, dilemma.

strait·en (strāt/ən), *v.* **1.** limit by the lack of something, esp. money; restrict: *in straitened circumstances.* **2.** restrict in range, extent, amount, etc. **3.** *Archaic.* confine.

strait jacket, a strong coat that holds the arms close to the sides, used to keep a violent person from harming himself or others.

strait-laced (strāt/lāst/), *adj.* very strict in matters of conduct; prudish.

Straits Settlements, a former British colony in SE Asia.

strand¹ (strand), *v.* **1.** run aground; drive on

the shore. 2. bring or come into a helpless position. —*n. Poetic.* shore. [OE]

strand[2] (strand), *n.* 1. one of the threads, strings, or wires that are twisted together to make a rope. 2. thread or string: *a strand of pearls, a strand of hair.* —*v.* break a strand or strands of.

strange (strānj), *adj.*, **strang·er, strang·est,** *adv.* —*adj.* 1. unusual; queer; peculiar: *a strange accident.* 2. not known, seen, or heard of before; unfamiliar: *strange faces, strange language.* 3. unaccustomed (to); inexperienced (at): *strange to a job.* 4. out of place; not at home: *the farmer felt strange in the city.* —*adv. Colloq.* in a strange manner: *act strange.* [< OF < L *extraneus* foreign. Doublet of EXTRANEOUS.] —**strange′ly,** *adv.* —**strange′ness,** *n.* —Syn. *adj.* 1. odd, uncommon, singular, remarkable. 2. foreign, alien, new, novel. —Ant. *adj.* 1. usual.

stran·ger (strān′jər), *n.* 1. person not known, seen, or heard of before: *he was a stranger to us.* 2. person or thing new to a place: *a stranger in town.* 3. person who is out of place or not at home in something: *he is a stranger to your method of working.* 4. visitor; guest. 5. person from another country.

stran·gle (strang′gəl), *v.*, **–gled, –gling.** 1. kill by squeezing the throat to stop the breath. 2. suffocate; choke. 3. choke down; suppress; keep back. [< OF < L < Gk. *strangalaein,* ult. < *strangos* twisted] —**stran′gler,** *n.* —Syn. 2. throttle, stifle, smother.

strangle hold, 1. a wrestling hold for stopping an opponent's breath. 2. anything that suppresses or hinders free movement, development, etc.

stran·gu·late (strang′gyə·lāt), *v.*, **–lat·ed, –lat·ing.** 1. compress or constrict so as to stop the circulation in, or hinder the action of. 2. strangle; choke. [< L *strangulatus.* See STRANGLE.] —**stran′gu·la′tion,** *n.*

strap (strap), *n.*, *v.*, **strapped, strap·ping.** —*n.* 1. a narrow strip of leather or other material that bends easily. 2. a narrow band or strip of cloth. 3. a narrow strip for fastening things, holding things together, etc. 4. a narrow strip of leather to sharpen razors on; strop. —*v.* 1. fasten with a strap. 2. beat with a strap. 3. sharpen on a strap or strop. [var. of *strop*] —**strap′like′,** *adj.* —**strap′per,** *n.*

strap·hang·er (strap′hang′ər), *n. Colloq.* passenger in a streetcar, train, etc., who cannot get a seat and stands holding on to a strap.

strap·ping (strap′ing), *adj. Colloq.* tall, strong, and healthy.

stra·ta (strā′tə; strat′ə), *n.* pl. of stratum.

strat·a·gem (strat′ə·jəm), *n.* scheme or trick for deceiving the enemy; trick; trickery. [< F < L < Gk. *strategema,* ult. < *strategos* general. See STRATEGY.] —Syn. artifice, ruse, maneuver.

stra·te·gic (strə·tē′jik), **stra·te·gi·cal** (–jə·kəl), *adj.* 1. of strategy; based on strategy; useful in strategy. 2. important in strategy. 3. pertaining to raw material necessary for warfare which must be obtained, at least partially, from an outside country. 4. of an air force or bombing, specially made or trained for destroying enemy bases, industry, or communications behind the lines of battle. —**stra·te′gi·cal·ly,** *adv.*

strategic hamlet, a village fortified militarily against attacks by guerrillas.

strat·e·gist (strat′ə·jist), *n.* person trained or skilled in strategy.

strat·e·gy (strat′ə·ji), *n.*, *pl.* **–gies.** 1. Also, **strategics.** science or art of war; planning and directing of military movements and operations. 2. plan based on this. 3. the skillful planning and management of anything. [< Gk. *strategia* < *strategos* general < *stratos* army + *agein* lead]

Strat·ford-on-A·von (strat′fərd·on·ā′vən; –av′ən), **Stratford-upon-Avon,** *n.* town in C England on the Avon River; Shakespeare's birthplace and burial place.

strat·i·fy (strat′ə·fī), *v.*, **–fied, –fy·ing.** arrange in layers or strata; form into

layers or strata. —strat′i·fi·ca′tion, *n.*

strat·o·sphere (strat′ə·sfir; strā′tə–), *n.* the upper region of the atmosphere, which begins about seven miles above the earth. In the stratosphere, temperature varies little with changes in altitude, and the winds are chiefly horizontal. [< L *stratus* a spreading out + E *sphere*] —strat·o·spher·ic (strat′ə·sfer′ik; strā′tə–), *adj.*

strat·o·vi·sion (strat′ə·vizh′ən), *n.* method of using airplanes in the stratosphere to broadcast television.

Strata

stra·tum (strā′təm; strat′əm), *n.*, *pl.* **stra·ta, stra·tums.** 1. layer of material. esp. one of several parallel layers placed one upon another. 2. social level; group having about the same education, culture, development, etc. 3. *Geol.* layer of one kind of sedimentary rock. [< NL < L, neut. pp. of *sternere* spread]

Strauss (strous), *n.* 1. Johann, 1804–1849, Austrian composer. 2. his son, Johann, 1825–1899, Austrian composer, esp. of waltzes. 3. Richard, 1864–1949, German composer and conductor.

straw (strô), *n.* 1. the stalks or stems of grain after drying and threshing. Straw is used for bedding for horses and cows, for making hats, and for many other purposes. 2. stem or stalk, as of wheat, rye, etc. 3. a hollow tube for sucking up beverages, etc. 4. bit; trifle. 5. catch at a straw, try anything in desperation. —*adj.* 1. made of straw. 2. worthless. 3. sham; fictitious. [OE *strēaw*] —straw′y, *adj.*

straw·ber·ry (strô′ber′i; –bər·i), *n.*, *pl.* **–ries.** 1. a small, juicy, red fruit. 2. plant that it grows on.

straw-hat (strô′hat′), *Am.* —*n.* a summer theater. —*adj.* pertaining to summer theaters.

straw vote, *Am.* an unofficial vote taken to find out general opinion.

stray (strā), *v.* 1. lose one's way; wander; roam. 2. turn from the right course; go wrong. —*adj.* 1. wandering; lost. 2. scattered. 3. isolated: *a stray copy of a book.* —*n.* wanderer; lost animal. [< OF *estraier,* ult. < L *extra vagari* roam outside] —stray′er, *n.* —Syn. *v.* 1. rove, straggle. 2. err, deviate.

streak (strēk), *n.* 1. a long, thin mark or line: *a streak of lightning.* 2. layer: *bacon has streaks of fat and streaks of lean.* 3. strain; element: *a streak of humor.* 4. *Am., Colloq.* a brief period; spell: *a streak of luck.* 5. like a streak, *Colloq.* very fast; at full speed. —*v.* 1. put long, thin marks or lines on; cause to have streaks. 2. become streaked. 3. *Colloq.* move very fast; go at full speed. [OE *strica*] —streak′y, *adj.* —streak′i·ly, *adv.* —streak′i·ness, *n.*

stream (strēm), *n.* 1. flow of liquid; running water, as a river or a brook. 2. any steady flow: *a stream of words, a stream of light.* —*v.* 1. flow. 2. move steadily; move swiftly: *soldiers streamed out of the fort.* 3. pour out: *the wound streamed blood.* 4. be so wet as to drip in a stream: *streaming eyes.* 5. float or wave: *flags streamed in the wind.* [OE *strēam*]

stream·er (strēm′ər), *n.* 1. any long, narrow, flowing thing: *streamers of ribbon hung from her hat.* 2. a long, narrow flag. 3. stream of light, esp. one appearing in some forms of the aurora borealis. 4. a newspaper headline that runs all the way across the page.

stream·let (strēm′lit), *n.* a small stream.

stream·line (strēm′līn′), *adj.*, *n.*, *v.*, **–lined, –lin·ing.** —*adj.* having a shape that offers the least possible resistance in passing through air or water. —*n.* 1. a streamline shape. 2. path of a particle in a steadily flowing mass of fluid. —*v.* 1. give a streamline shape to, as an airplane or automobile. 2. bring up to date.

stream·lined (strēm′līnd′), *adj.* 1. streamline. 2. brought up to date; made more efficient.

street (strēt), *n.* 1. road in a city or town, usually with buildings on both sides. 2. place or way for automobiles, wagons, etc., to go. 3. people

āge, cāre, fär; ēqual, tėrm; īce; ōpen, ôrder; pùt, rüle, ūse; th, then; ə = a in about.

who live in the buildings on a street. [< LL (via) strata paved (road), pp. of L sternere lay out]

street·car (strēt'kär'), n. car that runs in the streets, usually on rails, and carries passengers.

street·walk·er (strēt'wôk'ər), n. prostitute who walks the streets soliciting business.

strength (strengkth; strength), n. 1. quality of being strong; power; force; vigor: Samson was a man of great strength. 2. power to resist or endure: strength of a wire, strength of a fort. 3. number of soldiers, warships, etc.; quota. 4. effective force: the strength of an argument. 5. vigor of feeling, language, action, etc.: a novel of great strength. 6. degree of strength, as of a beverage, chemical, or drug. 7. intensity, as of light, color, sound, flavor, or odor. 8. something that makes strong; support: God is our strength. 9. on the strength of, relying or depending on; with the support or help of. [OE, < strang strong] —strength'less, adj.

strength·en (strengk'thən; streng'-), v. make or grow stronger. —strength'en·er, n.

stren·u·ous (stren'yü·əs), adj. very active; full of energy. [< L strenuus] —stren'u·ous·ly, adv. —stren'u·ous·ness, n. —Syn. vigorous.

strep·to·coc·cus (strep'tə·kok'əs), n., pl. -coc·ci (-kok'sī). any of a group of spherical bacteria that multiply by dividing in only one direction, usually forming chains, and cause scarlet fever and other serious infections. [< NL, < Gk. streptos curved + kokkos grain] —strep·to·coc·cic (strep'tə·kok'sik), strep·to·coc·cal (strep'tə·kok'əl), adj.

strep·to·my·cin (strep'tō·mī'sin), n. a powerful substance similar to penicillin, effective against tuberculosis, typhoid fever, and certain other bacterial infections. [< Gk. streptos curved + mykes fungus]

stress (stres), n. 1. distressing, painful, or adverse force or influence: the stress of hunger. 2. severe strain upon endurance, feelings, etc.: do something under stress. 3. great effort: won by stress of arms. 4. physical pressure, pull, or other force exerted on one thing by another: the stress of a load or weight. 5. emphasis; importance: lay stress upon promptness. 6. the relative loudness in the pronunciation of syllables, words in a sentence, etc.; accent. —v. 1. put pressure upon. 2. treat as important; emphasize. 3. pronounce with stress. [partly < distress, partly < OF estrecier, ult. < L strictus drawn tight] —Syn. n. 5. significance.

stretch (strech), v. 1. draw out; extend (oneself, body, limbs, wings, etc.) to full length: the blow stretched him out on the ground. 2. continue over a distance; extend from one place to another; fill space; spread: the highway stretches from coast to coast. 3. extend one's body or limbs: stretch out on the couch. 4. reach out; hold out: he stretched out his hand for the money. 5. draw out to greater length or size: stretch the shoe a little. 6. become longer or wider without breaking: rubber stretches. 7. make great effort. 8. extend beyond proper limits: he stretched the law to suit his purpose. —n. 1. an unbroken length; extent: a stretch of water. 2. period; term: for hours at a stretch. 3. Slang. term of imprisonment. 4. course, direction. 5. one of the two straight sides of a race course, esp. the part of the course between the last turn and the finish line. 6. a stretching or being stretched. [OE streccan] —stretch'a·ble, adj. —Syn. v. 5. lengthen, elongate.

stretch·er (strech'ər), n. 1. one that stretches: a glove stretcher. 2. canvas stretched on a frame for carrying the sick, wounded, or dead.

stretch-out (strech'out'), n. Colloq. a postponement, esp. of the date when defense orders must be filled.

strew (strü), v., strewed, strewed or strewn, strew·ing. 1. scatter; sprinkle. 2. cover with something scattered or sprinkled. 3. be scattered over; be sprinkled over. [OE strēowian]

stri·at·ed (strī'āt·id), **stri·ate** (strī'it; -āt), adj. striped; streaked; furrowed. [< L striatus] —stri·a'tion, n.

strick·en (strik'ən), adj. 1. affected, as by

wounds, diseases, trouble, sorrows, etc.: a stricken deer. 2. deeply affected: stricken with grief. 3. stricken in years, old. —v. pp. of strike.

strict (strikt), adj. 1. very careful in following a rule: strict observance of a law. 2. harsh; severe: a strict parent. 3. rigorously enforced or maintained: strict discipline. 4. exact; precise; accurate: he told the strict truth. 5. perfect; complete; absolute: in strict confidence. [< L strictus bound tight. Doublet of STRAIT.] —strict'ly, adv. —strict'ness, n. —Syn. 2. austere, stern, exacting, rigorous.

stric·ture (strik'chər), n. 1. an unfavorable criticism; critical remark. 2. an unhealthy narrowing of some duct or tube of the body. [< L strictura < stringere bind tight]

stride (strīd), v., strode, strid·den (strid'ən), strid·ing, n. —v. 1. walk with long steps. 2. pass with one long step: he strode over the brook. 3. straddle: stride a fence. —n. 1. a long step. 2. distance covered by a stride. 3. hit one's stride, reach one's regular speed or normal activity. 4. make great or rapid strides, make great progress; advance rapidly. 5. take in one's stride, do or take without difficulty, hesitation, or special effort. [OE strīdan] —strid'er, n.

stri·dent (strī'dənt), adj. harsh-sounding; creaking; shrill. [< L stridens sounding harshly] —stri'dence, stri'den·cy, n. —stri'dent·ly, adv.

strid·u·late (strij'ə·lāt), v., -lat·ed, -lat·ing. produce a shrill, grating sound, esp. to do so as a cricket or katydid does, by rubbing together certain parts of the body. —strid'u·la'tion, n. —strid'u·la'tor, n. —strid·u·la·to·ry (strij'ə·lə·tô'ri; -tō'-), adj.

strife (strīf), n. 1. quarreling; fighting; discord. 2. a quarrel; fight. [< OF estrif < Gmc. Cf. STRIVE.] —Syn. 1. conflict. 2. struggle.

strike (strīk), v., struck, struck or strick·en, strik·ing, n. —v. 1. deal a blow to: strike a person. 2. deal; give: strike a blow in self-defense. 3. make by stamping, printing, etc.: strike a coin. 4. set or be set on fire by hitting or rubbing: strike a match. 5. fall upon, as light or sound does. 6. come into collision with: the ship struck a rock. 7. impress: the plan strikes me as silly. 8. sound: the clock struck, the clock struck midnight. 9. make (dumb, blind, etc.) suddenly, as if by a blow: the news struck them dumb. 10. affect deeply; afflict suddenly; overcome (by death, disease, suffering, fear, etc.): they were struck with terror. 11. attack: the enemy will strike at dawn. 12. occur to: an amusing thought struck her. 13. Am. find or come upon (ore, oil, water, etc.). 14. Am. come across suddenly or unexpectedly: strike a friend's name in a newspaper, strike a new way of doing things. 15. stop work to get better pay, shorter hours, etc.: the coal miners struck. 16. cross; rub: strike out the last word, strike his name off the list. 17. take away by a blow; take away: strike off his head. 18. go quickly or suddenly; go: we struck out across the fields. 19. assume: he struck an attitude. 20. take root; send down (a root or roots): the roots of oaks strike deep. 21. get by figuring: strike an average. 22. make; decide; enter upon: the employer and the workmen have struck an agreement. 23. lower or take down (a sail, flag, tent, etc.). 24. make level; make level with the top edge of a measure. 25. take hold of the bait: the fish are striking well today. 26. strike a balance, find the difference between the two sides of an account. 27. strike camp, take down tents. 28. strike home, reach a person or object as intended. 29. strike it rich, Am., Colloq. a. find rich ore, oil, etc. b. have a sudden or unexpected great success. 30. strike off, take off. 31. strike oil, Am., Colloq. a. find oil while boring. b. Slang. meet with great luck. 32. strike out, a. cross out; rub out. b. Am., Baseball. fail to hit three times: the batter struck out. c. Am., Baseball. cause to fail to hit three times: the pitcher struck out six men. 33. strike up, begin: strike up a friendship. —n. 1. act of striking. 2. a general quitting of work in order to force an employer or employers to agree to the workers' demands, as for higher wages. 3. Am., Baseball.

failure of the batter to hit a pitched ball, or any act ruled equivalent to this. 4. *Bowling.* a. an upsetting of all the pins with the first ball bowled. b. the score so made. 5. *Am.* act or fact of finding rich ore in mining, oil in boring, etc. 6. *Am.* any sudden success. 7. **on strike,** stopping work to get more pay, shorter hours, etc. [OE *strican* rub, stroke] —Syn. *v.* 1. smite, beat, buffet, slap. 13. discover.

strike·break·er (strīk′brāk′ər), *n.* person who helps to break up a strike of workers by taking a striker's job or by furnishing persons who will do so.

strike·break·ing (strīk′brāk′ing), *n.* forceful measures taken to halt a strike.

strik·er (strīk′ər), *n.* 1. person or thing that strikes. 2. worker who is on strike.

strik·ing (strīk′ing), *adj.* 1. that strikes. 2. engaged in a strike. 3. attracting attention; very noticeable. —**strik′ing·ly,** *adv.* —**strik′ing·ness,** *n.* —Syn. 3. remarkable, impressive.

Strind·berg (strind′bèrg), *n.* **Johan August,** 1849–1912, Swedish author.

string (string), *n., v.,* **strung, strung** or (*Rare*) **stringed, string·ing.** —*n.* 1. a thick thread, small cord or wire, or very thin rope, used for tying packages, etc. 2. such a thread with things on it: *she wore a string of beads around her neck.* 3. a special cord for musical instruments, bows, etc.: *the strings of a violin.* 4. **strings,** violins, cellos, and other stringed instruments. 5. anything used for tying: *apron strings.* 6. a cordlike part of plants. 7. a number of things that can form in a line or row: *a string of cars, a string of horses.* 8. *Am., Colloq.* condition: *an offer with a string attached to it.* 9. **on a string,** under control. 10. **pull strings, a.** direct the actions of others secretly. b. use secret influence. —*v.* 1. put on a string: *string beads.* 2. furnish with strings: *he had his tennis racket strung.* 3. tie with string; hang with a string or rope. 4. tighten the strings of. 5. make tense or excited: *her nerves were strung up to a high pitch.* 6. remove strings from: *string the beans.* 7. form into a string or strings. 8. move in a line or series: *the cars kept stringing along.* 9. arrange in a line or a row. 10. **string out,** *Am., Colloq.* prolong; stretch; extend: *the program was strung out too long.* 11. *Slang.* fool; hoax. 12. **string up,** *Colloq.* hang. [OE *streng*] —**string′er,** *n.* —**string′less,** *adj.* —**string′like′,** *adj.* —Syn. *n.* 1. twine. 7. series, succession, chain.

string bean, *Am.* 1. any of various bean plants, the unripe pod of which is used as a vegetable. 2. pod of any of these plants.

stringed instrument, a musical instrument having strings.

strin·gent (strin′jənt), *adj.* 1. strict; severe: *stringent laws.* 2. *Am.* lacking ready money; tight: *a stringent market for loans.* 3. convincing; forcible: *stringent arguments.* [< L *stringens* binding tight] —**strin′gen·cy, strin′gent·ness,** *n.* —**strin′gent·ly,** *adv.* —Syn. 1. rigid, rigorous, exacting, binding.

string·halt (string′hôlt′), *n.* a diseased condition of horses that causes jerking of the hind legs in walking. Also, **springhalt.**

string·y (string′i), *adj.,* **string·i·er, string·i·est.** 1. of or like a string or strings. 2. forming strings: *a stringy syrup.* 3. having tough fibers: *stringy roots.* 4. sinewy or wiry: *a stringy man.* —**string′i·ness,** *n.*

strip[1] (strip), *v.,* **stripped** or (*Rare*) **stript, strip·ping.** 1. make bare or naked; undress (a person, thing, etc.). 2. undress (oneself). 3. take off the covering of. 4. dismantle (guns, ships, etc.). 5. take away: *the boys stripped the fruit from the trees.* 6. rob. 7. separate the leaves from the stalks of (tobacco). 8. tear off the teeth of (a gear, etc.). 9. break the thread of (a bolt, nut, etc.). 10. strip of, a. take away from; deprive of. b. rob of (money, possessions, etc.). [OE, as in *bestrīepan* to plunder] —**strip′per,** *n.* —Syn. 3. skin, peel. 8. plunder, despoil.

strip[2] (strip), *n., v.,* **stripped, strip·ping.** —*n.* 1. a long, narrow, flat piece (of cloth, paper,

bark, etc.). 2. *Am.* a comic strip. —*v.* cut into strips. [prob. < MLG *strippe* strap]

strip[3] (strip), *n.* 1. a long, narrow runway for airplanes to take off from and land on. 2. a portable runway made of steel sheets.

stripe[1] (strip), *n., v.,* **striped, strip·ing.** —*n.* 1. a long, narrow band different from the rest of a surface or thing: *a tiger has stripes.* 2. a particular style or pattern of such bands. 3. a striped fabric. 4. **stripes,** number or combination of strips of braid on the sleeve of a uniform to show rank, length of service, etc. 5. sort; type: *a man of quite a different stripe.* —*v.* mark with stripes. [< MDu.] —**striped,** *adj.* —Syn. *n.* 1. streak, line, bar.

stripe[2] (strip), *n.* a stroke or lash with a whip. [? special use of *stripe*[1]]

strip·ling (strip′ling), *n.* boy just coming into manhood; youth; lad.

strip tease, *Am.* an act in burlesque in which a woman removes her clothing to a musical accompaniment. —**strip′-tease′,** *adj.* —**strip′-teas′er,** *n.*

strive (strīv), *v.,* **strove, striv·en** (striv′ən), **striv·ing.** 1. try hard; work hard: *strive for self-control.* 2. struggle vigorously, as in opposition or resistance: *strive against the stream.* 3. fight. [< OF *estriver* < Gmc.] —**striv′er,** *n.* —**striv′ing·ly,** *adv.* —Syn. 1. endeavor. 2, 3. contend, battle.

strode (strōd), *v.* pt. of **stride.**

stroke[1] (strōk), *n., v.,* **stroked, strok·ing.** —*n.* 1. act of striking; blow: *a stroke of lightning.* 2. sound made by striking: *we arrived at the stroke of three.* 3. piece of luck, fortune, etc., befalling one: *a stroke of bad luck.* 4. a single complete movement to be made again and again: *he swims a fast stroke.* 5. a throb or pulsing, as of the heart. 6. movement or mark made by a pen, pencil, brush, etc. 7. a single vigorous effort; very successful effort: *a bold stroke for liberty.* 8. an act, piece, or amount of work, etc. 9. a sudden attack (of disease). 10. attack of paralysis; apoplexy. 11. rower who sets the time for the other oarsmen on a crew. 12. a single pull of an oar. 13. keep stroke, make strokes at the same time. —*v.* be the stroke of (a crew). [prob. ult. < *strike* or its source] —**strok′er,** *n.*

stroke[2] (strōk), *v.,* **stroked, strok·ing,** *n.* —*v.* move the hand gently over: *stroke a kitten.* —*n.* such a movement. [OE *strācian*]

stroll (strōl), *v.* 1. take a quiet walk for pleasure; walk. 2. go from place to place: *strolling gypsies.* 3. stroll along or through. —*n.* a leisurely walk. —Syn. *v.* 1. saunter, ramble, roam.

stroll·er (strōl′ər), *n.* 1. wanderer. 2. a strolling player or actor. 3. a kind of light baby carriage.

Strom·bo·li (strom′bō·li), *n.* an Italian island in the Mediterranean, just N of Sicily.

strong (strông; strong), *adj.* 1. having much force or power: *a strong wind, a strong pull, strong muscles.* 2. able to last, endure, resist, etc.: *a strong fort.* 3. especially able, powerful, or competent in some specified respect: *strong in mathematics.* 4. not easily influenced, changed, etc.; firm: *a strong will.* 5. of great force or effectiveness: *strong arguments.* 6. having a certain number: *a group that is 100 strong.* 7. having much of the quality expected: *a strong rope, a strong acid, strong tea.* 8. clear and firm; loud: *a strong voice.* 9. containing much alcohol: *a strong drink.* 10. having much flavor or odor: *strong seasoning.* 11. having an unpleasant taste or smell: *strong butter.* 12. intense: *a strong light.* 13. vigorous; forceful: *a strong speech.* 14. hearty; zealous: *a strong prejudice.* 15. distinct; marked: *a strong likeness.* 16. *Gram.* inflecting by a vowel change within the stem of the word rather than by adding endings. *Examples:* find, found; give, gave. 17. *Phonet.* stressed. 18. characterized by steady or advancing prices: *a strong market for rubber.* —*adv.* with force; powerfully; vigorously; in a strong manner. [OE *strang*]

āge, cāre, fär; ēqual, tėrm; īce, ōpen, ôrder; pút, rüle, ūse; tн, then; ə=a in about.

—**strong′ly**, *adv.* —**strong′ness**, *n.* —Syn. *adj.*
1. mighty, potent. 2. invincible. 5. cogent.

strong-arm (strông′ärm′; strong′-), *Am.*
—*adj. Colloq.* using or involving the use of force
or violence. —*v.* use force or violence on.

strong·box (strông′boks′; strong′-), *n.* a
strongly made box to hold valuable things.

strong drink, drink containing much alcohol.

strong·hold (strông′hōld′; strong′-), *n.* a
strong place; safe place; fort; fortress.

strong-mind·ed (strông′mīn′did; strong′-),
adj. 1. having a strong mind; mentally vigorous.
2. independent; mannish. —**strong′-mind′ed·ly**,
adv. —**strong′-mind′ed·ness**, *n.*

stron·ti·um (stron′shi·əm; -ti·əm), *n. Chem.*
a hard, yellowish metallic element, Sr, resembling calcium. [< NL, < *Strontian*, a parish in
Scotland] —**stron·tic** (stron′tik), *adj.*

strontium 90, a radioactive isotope of strontium, produced esp. by the explosion of a hydrogen bomb, that produces cancer of the bone if
absorbed in sufficient quantity by humans;
radio strontium.

strop (strop), *n., v.*, **stropped, strop·ping**. —*n.*
a leather strap used for sharpening razors. —*v.*
sharpen on a strop. [ult. < L *stroppus* band <
Gk. *strophos*] —**strop′per**, *n.*

stro·phe (strō′fē) *n.* 1. the part of an ancient
Greek ode sung by the chorus when moving from
right to left. 2. group of lines of poetry; stanza.
[< Gk., orig., a turning (i.e., section sung by
the chorus while turning)] —**stroph·ic** (strof′-
ik; strō′fik), **stroph′i·cal**, *adj.*

strove (strōv), *v.* pt. of strive.

strow (strō), *v.*, **strowed, strown or strowed,
strow·ing**. *Archaic.* strew.

struck (struk), *v.* pt. and pp. of strike. —*adj.*
closed or affected in some way by a strike of
workers.

struc·tur·al (struk′chər·əl), *adj.* 1. used in
building. **Structural steel** is steel made into
beams, girders, etc. 2. of or pertaining to structure or structures. —**struc′tur·al·ly**, *adv.*

struc·ture (struk′chər), *n.* 1. a building;
something built. 2. anything composed of parts
arranged together. 3. manner of building; way
parts are put together; construction. 4. arrangement of parts, elements, etc.: *the structure of
a molecule.* [< L *structura* < *struere* arrange]

stru·del (strü′dəl; *Ger.* shtrü′dəl), *n.* a pastry,
usually filled with fruit or cheese. [< G]

strug·gle (strug′əl), *v.*, **-gled, -gling**, *n.* —*v.*
1. make great efforts with the body; try hard;
work hard against difficulties: *struggle for existence.* 2. bring, put, etc., by struggling: *struggle
oneself out of a tight place.* 3. get, move, or
make one's way with great effort: *the old man
struggled to his feet.* —*n.* 1. great effort; hard
work. 2. fighting; conflict. —**strug′gler**, *n.*
—**strug′gling**, *adj.* —**strug′gling·ly**, *adv.* —Syn.
v. 1. strive, labor, toil, cope, contend. —*n.* 1.
exertion, labor, endeavor. 2. strife, contest.

strum (strum), *v.*, **strummed, strum·ming**, *n.*
—*v.* play on (a stringed musical instrument)
unskillfully or carelessly. —*n.* 1. act of strumming. 2. sound of strumming. —**strum′mer**, *n.*

strum·pet (strum′pit), *n.* prostitute.

strung (strung), *v.* pt. and pp. of string.

strut[1] (strut), *v.*, **strut·ted, strut·ting**, *n.* —*v.*
walk in a vain, important manner. —*n.* a strut-
ting walk. [OE *strūtian*]
—**strut′ter**, *n.* —**strut′ting·ly**,
adv.

strut[2] (strut), *n.* a supporting
piece; brace. [ult. akin to
strut[1]]

strych·nine (strik′nin; -nēn;
-nīn), **strych·nin** (-nin), *n.* a poisonous
drug consisting of colorless crystals obtained
from nux vomica and related plants. It is used
in medicine in small doses as a tonic. [< F, < L
< Gk. *strychnos* nightshade]

St. Thomas, one of the Virgin Islands.

Stu·art (stü′ərt; stū′-), *n.* 1. the royal family
that ruled Scotland from 1371 to 1603 and England and Scotland from 1603 to 1714. 2. Mary.
See **Mary, Queen of Scots**.

stub (stub), *n., adj., v.*, **stubbed, stub·bing**.
—*n.* 1. a short piece that is left: *the stub of a
pencil.* 2. the short piece of each leaf in a check-
book, etc., kept as a record. 3. something unusually short and blunt. 4. *Am.* butt of a cigar or
cigarette. 5. pen having a short, blunt point. 6.
stump of a tree. —*adj.* short and thick. —*v.*
Esp. U.S. strike (one's toe) against something.
[OE] —**stub′ber**, *n.*

stub·ble (stub′əl), *n.* 1. Usually, **stubbles.** the
lower ends of stalks of grain left in the ground
after the grain is cut. 2. any short, rough
growth. [< OF < LL *stupula*, var. of L *stipula*
stem. Doublet of STIPULE.] —**stub′bled**, *adj.*
—**stub′bly**, *adj.*

stub·born (stub′ərn), *adj.* 1. fixed in purpose
or opinion; not giving in to argument or requests. 2. unreasonably obstinate: *a stubborn
child.* 3. obstinately maintained or performed:
stubborn resistance. 4. hard to deal with or
manage; refractory: *facts are stubborn things.*
[prob. ult. < *stub*] —**stub′born·ly**, *adv.* —**stub′-
born·ness**, *n.* —Syn. 1. unyielding, resolute. 2.
obdurate, perverse, headstrong.

stub·by (stub′i), *adj.*, **-bi·er, -bi·est**. 1. short
and thick. 2. short, thick, and stiff. 3. having
many stubs or stumps. —**stub′bi·ness**, *n.*

stuc·co (stuk′ō), *n., pl.* **-coes, -cos**, *v.*, **-coed,
-co·ing**. —*n.* plaster for covering exterior walls
of buildings. —*v.* cover with stucco. [< Ital. <
Gmc.] —**stuc′co·er**, *n.* —**stuc′co·work′**, *n.*

stuck (stuk), *v.* pt. and pp. of stick[2].

stuck-up (stuk′up′), *adj. Colloq.* too proud;
conceited; vain; haughty.

stud[1] (stud), *n., v.*, **stud·ded, stud·ding**. —*n.*
1. nailhead, knob, etc., sticking out from a surface: *the belt was ornamented with silver studs.*
2. a kind of small detachable button used in
men's shirts. 3. post to which boards are nailed
in making walls in houses. 4. a projecting pin,
slug, or the like on a machine. —*v.* 1. set with
studs or something like studs. 2. be set or scattered over. 3. set like studs; scatter at intervals.
4. provide with studs. [OE *studu*]

stud[2] (stud), *n.* 1. collection of horses kept for
breeding, hunting, etc. 2. place where such a
collection is kept. 3. *Am.* stallion. [OE *stōd*]

stu·dent (stü′dənt; stū′-), *n.* 1. person who
studies. 2. person who is studying in a school,
college, or university. [< L *studens*, orig., being
eager] —**stu′dent·ship**, *n.*

stud·horse (stud′hôrs′), *n.* stallion.

stud·ied (stud′id), *adj.* 1. resulting from
study; carefully considered. 2. done on purpose;
resulting from deliberate effort. —**stud′ied·ly**,
adv. —**stud′ied·ness**, *n.*

stu·di·o (stü′di·ō; stū′-), *n., pl.* **-di·os**, *adj.*
—*n.* 1. workroom of a painter, sculptor, photographer, etc. 2. place where motion pictures are
made. 3. place where a radio program is given.
—*adj.* of, pertaining to, or suitable for a studio.
[< Ital. < L *studium* study, enthusiasm. Doublet
of STUDY.]

stu·di·ous (stü′di·əs; stū′-), *adj.* 1. fond of
study. 2. showing careful consideration; careful; thoughtful; zealous: *studious of the comfort
of others.* —**stu′di·ous·ly**, *adv.* —**stu′di·ous·
ness**, *n.* —Syn. 2. earnest, attentive.

stud·y (stud′i), *n., pl.* **stud·ies**, *v.*, **stud·ied,
stud·y·ing**. —*n.* 1. effort to learn by reading or
thinking. 2. a careful examination; investigation: *make a study of plants.* 3. cultivation of a
particular branch of learning: *the study of
chemistry.* 4. something that is studied: *socio-
logical studies.* 5. something deserving attentive
consideration: *his face was a study.* 6. a room
for study, reading, writing, etc. 7. work of literature or art that deals in careful detail with
one particular subject: *a study of modern
poetry.* 8. sketch for a picture, story, etc. 9.
earnest effort, or the object of endeavor or effort. 10. deep thought; reverie. —*v.* 1. try to
learn. 2. examine carefully: *we studied the map.*
3. consider with care; think (out); plan: *the
prisoner studied ways to escape.* [< L *studium*,
orig., eagerness. Doublet of STUDIO.] —**stud′i·er**,
n. —Syn. *v.* 2. investigate, scrutinize. 3. ponder.

stuff (stuf), *n.* 1. what a thing is made of; material. 2. a woolen fabric. 3. thing or things; substance. 4. goods; belongings. 5. worthless material; useless things. 6. silly words and thoughts; nonsense. 7. inward qualities; character. —*v.* 1. pack full; fill. 2. *Am., Slang.* fill (a ballot box) with fraudulent votes. 3. stop (up); block; choke (up). 4. fill the skin of (a dead animal) to make it look as it did when alive. 5. fill (a chicken, turkey, etc.) with seasoned bread crumbs, etc. 6. force; push; thrust. 7. eat too much. [< OF *estoffe*, ult. < Gk. *styphein* pull together] —**stuff′er**, *n.* —**Syn.** *n.* 5. refuse, rubbish, trash. —*v.* 1. cram, crowd.

stuffed shirt, *Am., Slang.* man of insignificant abilities but of pompous or imposing manners.

stuff·ing (stuf′ing), *n.* 1. act of one that stuffs. 2. material used to fill or pack something. 3. seasoned bread crumbs, etc., used to stuff a chicken, turkey, etc., before cooking.

stuff·y (stuf′i), *adj.,* **stuff·i·er, stuff·i·est.** 1. lacking fresh air: *a stuffy room.* 2. lacking freshness or interest; dull: *a stuffy conversation.* 3. stopped up: *a cold makes one's head feel stuffy.* 4. *Colloq.* easily shocked or offended; prim. 5. *Am., Colloq.* angry; sulky. —**stuff′i·ly**, *adv.* —**stuff′i·ness**, *n.*

stul·ti·fy (stul′tə·fī), *v.,* **-fied, -fy·ing.** 1. cause to appear foolish or absurd; reduce to foolishness or absurdity. 2. make futile. [< LL, < L *stultus* foolish + *facere* make] —**stul·ti·fi·ca·tion** (stul′tə·fə·kā′shən), *n.* —**stul′ti·fi′er**, *n.*

stum·ble (stum′bəl), *v.,* **-bled, -bling,** *n.* —*v.* 1. trip by striking the foot against something. 2. cause to stumble. 3. walk unsteadily. 4. speak, act, etc., in a clumsy or hesitating way: *stumble through a speech.* 5. make a mistake; do wrong. 6. come by accident or chance: *stumble across an old friend.* —*n.* 1. a wrong act; mistake. 2. a stumbling. [cf. Norw. *stumla*] —**stum′bler**, *n.* —**stum′bling·ly**, *adv.*

stumbling block, obstacle; hindrance.

stump (stump), *n.* 1. the lower end of a tree or plant, left after the main part is cut off. 2. part of an arm, leg, tooth, etc., left after part is removed. 3. stub: *the stump of a pencil, cigar, etc.* 4. person with a short, thick build. 5. a wooden leg. 6. *Slang.* leg. 7. *Am.* place where a political speech is made. 8. a heavy step. 9. sound made by stiff walking or heavy steps. 10. *Am., Colloq.* a dare; challenge. 11. **up a stump,** *Am., Colloq.* unable to act, answer, etc.; impotent; baffled. —*v.* 1. *Am.* make political speeches in: *the candidates for governor will stump the State.* 2. walk in a stiff, clumsy way. 3. *Am., Colloq.* make unable to answer, do, etc.; embarrass. 4. *Am., Colloq.* dare; challenge. [cf. MLG *stump*] —**stump′y**, *adj.* —**stump′i·ly**, *adv.* —**stump′i·ness**, *n.*

stun (stun), *v.,* **stunned, stun·ning,** *n.* —*v.* 1. make senseless; knock unconscious. 2. daze; bewilder; shock; overwhelm. —*n.* a stunning; being stunned. [OE *stunian* crash, resound; infl. by OF *estoner* resound, stun] —**Syn.** *v.* 2. stupefy, dumfound, astound, amaze.

stung (stung), *v.* pt. and pp. of **sting.**

stunk (stungk), *v.* pt. and pp. of **stink.**

stun·ner (stun′ər), *n.* 1. person, thing, or blow that stuns. 2. *Colloq.* a very striking or attractive person or thing.

stun·ning (stun′ing), *adj.* 1. *Colloq.* having striking excellence, beauty, etc. 2. that stuns or dazes; bewildering. —**stun′ning·ly**, *adv.*

stunt[1] (stunt), *v.* check in growth or development: *lack of proper food stunts a child.* —*n.* 1. a stunting. 2. a stunted creature. [OE, foolish]

stunt[2] (stunt), *Colloq.* —*n. Am.* feat to attract attention; act showing boldness or skill. —*v.* 1. perform stunts. 2. perform stunts with.

stu·pe·fac·tion (stü′pə·fak′shən; stū′-), *n.* 1. dazed or senseless condition; stupor. 2. overwhelming amazement.

stu·pe·fy (stü′pə·fī; stū′-), *v.,* **-fied, -fy·ing.** 1. make stupid, dull, or senseless. 2. overwhelm

with amazement; astound. [< L, < *stupere* be amazed + *facere* make] —**stu′pe·fi′er**, *n.* —**stu′pe·fy′ing·ly**, *adv.* —**Syn.** 1. deaden, blunt.

stu·pen·dous (stü·pen′dəs; stū-), *adj.* amazing; marvelous; immense: *Niagara Falls is a stupendous sight.* [< L *stupendus* < *stupere* be amazed] —**stu·pen′dous·ly**, *adv.* —**stu·pen′dous·ness**, *n.*

stu·pid (stü′pid; stū′-), *adj.* 1. not intelligent; dull: *a stupid person.* 2. not interesting: *a stupid book.* 3. dazed; senseless. —*n. Colloq.* a stupid person. [< L *stupidus*] —**stu·pid·i·ty** (stü·pid′ə·ti; stū-), **stu′pid·ness**, *n.* —**stu′pid·ly**, *adv.* —**Syn.** *adj.* 1. heavy, stolid, dense, slow-witted. 2. uninspiring, vapid, flat. —**Ant.** *adj.* 1. clever. 2. lively.

stu·por (stü′pər; stū′-), *n.* a dazed condition; loss or lessening of the power to feel. [< L] —**stu′por·ous**, *adj.* —**Syn.** lethargy, torpor.

stur·dy (ster′di), *adj.,* **-di·er, -di·est.** 1. strong; stout: *sturdy legs.* 2. not yielding; firm: *sturdy resistance, sturdy defenders.* [< OF *esturdi* violent, orig., dazed] —**stur′di·ly**, *adv.* —**stur′di·ness**, *n.* —**Syn.** 1. hardy, robust, muscular, vigorous. 2. resolute, unyielding.

stur·geon (ster′jən), *n., pl.* **-geons** or (*esp. collectively*) **-geon.** a large food fish whose long body has a tough skin with rows of bony plates. Caviar and isinglass are obtained from sturgeons. [< AF, ult. < Gmc.]

Sturgeon (ab. 6 ft. long)

stut·ter (stut′ər), *v.* repeat (the same sound) involuntarily or spasmodically in an effort to speak. —*n.* act or habit of stuttering. [< dial. *stut.* Cf. Du. *stotteren.*] —**stut′ter·er**, *n.* —**stut′ter·ing·ly**, *adv.*

Stutt·gart (stut′gärt), *n.* city in SW Germany.

Stuy·ve·sant (stī′və·sənt), *n.* **Peter**, 1592–1672, Dutch governor of the colony of New Netherland 1646–1664.

St. Vi·tus's dance (vī′təs·iz), **St. Vitus dance**, chorea.

sty[1] (stī), *n., pl.* **sties.** 1. pen for pigs. 2. any filthy place. [OE *stig*]

sty[2], **stye** (stī), *n., pl.* **sties; styes.** *Med.* a small, inflamed swelling on the edge of the eyelid. A sty is like a small boil. [prob. < ME *styanye* (taken to mean "sty on eye"), ult. < OE *stigend* rising + *ēage* eye]

Styg·i·an (stij′i·ən), *adj.* 1. pertaining to the river Styx or the lower world; infernal. 2. dark; gloomy.

style (stīl), *n., v.,* **styled, styl·ing.** —*n.* 1. fashion: *dress in the latest styles.* 2. manner; method; way: *the Gothic style of architecture.* 3. way of writing or speaking: *a pedantic style.* 4. good style: *she dresses in style.* 5. literary or artistic excellence: *his painting lacks style.* 6. an official name; title: *salute him with the style of King.* 7. a pointed instrument for writing, drawing, etching, etc. 8. pointer on a dial, chart, etc. 9. *Bot.* the stemlike part of the pistil of a flower containing the stigma at its top. 10. rules of spelling, punctuation, etc., used by printers. 11. way of reckoning time and dates. Our present calender, since 1752, is New Style. Old Style dates are a few days earlier. Washington was born Feb. 11, 1732, Old Style. —*v.* name; call: *Joan of Arc was styled "the Maid of Orleans."* [< OF < L *stilus*, orig., pointed writing instrument; infl. in modern spelling by Gk. *stylos* column] —**style′less**, *adj.*

style·book (stīl′bùk′), *n.* 1. *Am.* book containing rules of punctuation, capitalization, etc., used by printers, writers, etc. 2. book showing fashions.

styl·ish (stīl′ish), *adj.* having style; fashionable. —**styl′ish·ly**, *adv.* —**styl′ish·ness**, *n.*

styl·ist (stīl′ist), *n.* 1. writer or speaker who has a good literary style. 2. person who designs or advises concerning interior decorations, clothes, etc. —**sty·lis·tic** (stī·lis′tik), *adj.* —**sty·lis′ti·cal·ly**, *adv.*

styl·ize (stīl'īz), v., –ized, –iz·ing. conform to a particular or to a conventional style. —styl'i·za'tion, n.

sty·lus (stī'ləs), n. 1. a pointed instrument for writing on wax. 2. a needlelike point used in making or playing phonograph records. [< L *stilus*. See STYLE.]

sty·mie (stī'mi), n., v., –mied, –mie·ing. —n. Golf. a. an opponent's ball on a putting green when it is directly between the player's ball and the hole for which he is playing and when the distance between the balls is more than six inches. b. occurrence of a ball in such a position, or the position of the ball. —v. 1. hinder with a stymie or as a stymie does. 2. block completely.

styp·tic (stip'tik), adj. Also, **styp'ti·cal.** able to stop or check bleeding; astringent. —n. something that stops or checks bleeding by contracting the tissue. Alum is a common styptic. [< L < Gk. *styptikos* < *styphein* constrict] —styp·tic'i·ty (stip·tis'ə·ti), n.

Styx (stiks), n. Gk. Myth. river in the lower world, across which the souls of the dead were ferried into Hades.

sua·sion (swā'zhən), n. an advising or urging; persuasion. [< L *suasio* < *suadere* persuade] —sua·sive (swā'siv), sua·so·ry (swā'sə·ri), adj. —sua'sive·ly, adv. —sua'sive·ness, n.

suave (swäv), adj. smoothly agreeable or polite. [< F < L *suavis* agreeable] —suave'ly, adv. —sua·vi·ty (swä'və·ti; swav'ə–), suave'ness, n.

sub (sub), n., adj., v., subbed, sub·bing. Colloq. —n., adj. 1. substitute. 2. submarine. 3. subordinate. —v. act as a substitute.

sub–, prefix. 1. under; below, as in *submarine.* 2. down; further; again, as in *subclassify, sublease.* 3. near; nearly, as in *subarctic.* 4. a. lower; subordinate; assistant, as in *subaltern.* b. of less importance, as in *subhead.* 5. resulting from further division, as in *subatom.* 6. in a comparatively small degree or proportion; slightly; somewhat, as in *subacid.* [< L *sub,* prep.; also (by assimilation to the following consonant), *su–, suc–, suf–, sug–, sum–, sup–*]

sub., 1. subscription. 2. substitute. 3. suburban.

sub·ac·id (sub·as'id), adj. slightly acid. —sub·a·cid·i·ty (sub'ə·sid'ə·ti), n.

sub·al·tern (sə·bôl'tərn; sub'əl·tėrn), n. 1. Esp. Brit. a commissioned officer in the army, ranking below a captain. 2. one who has a subordinate position. —adj. 1. Esp. Brit. ranking below a captain. 2. having lower rank; subordinate. [< LL, < L *sub–* under + *alternus* alternate]

sub·arc·tic (sub·ärk'tik; –är'tik), adj. near, or just below, the arctic region; pertaining to or occurring in regions just S of the arctic circle.

sub·at·om (sub·at'əm), n. any constituent of an atom. Protons and electrons are subatoms. —sub·a·tom·ic (sub'ə·tom'ik), adj.

sub·com·mit·tee (sub'kə·mit'i), n. a small committee chosen from a larger general committee for some special duty.

sub·con·scious (sub·kon'shəs), adj. 1. existing or operating in one's mind but not felt: *subconscious worries, subconscious thoughts.* 2. not wholly conscious. —n. subconscious thoughts, feelings, impulses, etc. —sub·con'scious·ly, adv. —sub·con'scious·ness, n.

sub·con·tract (n. sub·kon'trakt; v. sub·kon'trakt, sub'kən·trakt'), n. contract for carrying out a previous contract or a part of it. —v. make a subcontract; make a subcontract for. —sub·con'trac·tor, n.

sub·cu·ta·ne·ous (sub'kū·tā'ni·əs), adj. 1. under the skin. 2. placed or performed under the skin. —sub'cu·ta'ne·ous·ly, adv.

sub·deb (sub'deb'), n. Am., Colloq. a young girl soon to make her debut in society.

sub·di·vide (sub'də·vīd'; sub'də·vīd'), v., –vid·ed, –vid·ing. divide again; divide into smaller parts. —sub·di·vis·i·ble (sub'də·viz'ə·bəl), adj.

sub·di·vi·sion (sub'də·vizh'ən; sub'də·vizh'-ən), n. 1. division into smaller parts. 2. part of a part. 3. tract of land divided into building lots. —sub'di·vi'sion·al, adj.

sub·due (səb·dü'; –dū'), v., –dued, –du·ing. 1. conquer and bring into subjection: *the Spaniards subdued the Indian tribes in Mexico.* 2. overpower by a superior force; overcome. 3. overcome by persuasion or kindness, or by inspiring awe or fear. 4. repress (feelings, impulses, etc.): *we subdued a desire to laugh.* 5. tone down; soften: *a subdued light.* [ult. < L *subducere* draw away < *sub–* from under + *ducere* lead; infl. in meaning by L *subdere* subdue] —sub·du'a·ble, adj. —sub·dued', adj. —sub·dued'ly, adv. —sub·dued'ness, n. —sub·du'er, n. —Syn. 1. vanquish. 2. quell. 4. restrain. 5. lower, reduce.

sub·head (sub'hed'), **sub·head·ing** (–ing), n. 1. a subordinate head or title. 2. a subordinate division of a head or title.

subj., 1. subject. 2. subjunctive.

sub·ja·cent (sub·jā'sənt), adj. situated below; underlying. [< L, < *sub–* below + *jacere* lie] —sub·ja'cen·cy, n. —sub·ja'cent·ly, adv.

sub·ject (n., adj. sub'jikt; v. səb·jekt'), n. 1. something thought about, discussed, studied, etc.: *a subject of conversation.* 2. person who owes allegiance to a government and lives under its protection. 3. person under the power, control, or influence of another. 4. person or thing that undergoes or experiences something: *the dog was the subject of their experiment.* 5. Gram. word or words referring to the person or thing that performs or, when the verb is passive, receives the action of the verb. 6. theme or melody on which a musical work or movement is based. 7. object, scene, incident, etc., represented in art. —adj. 1. under some power or influence: *we are subject to our country's laws.* 2. exposed: *subject to ridicule.* 3. likely to have: *subject to headaches.* 4. being dependent or conditional: *subject to your approval.* —v. 1. bring under some power or influence: *Rome subjected all Italy to her rule.* 2. cause to undergo or experience something: *subject a person to ridicule.* [< L *subjectus* placed under < *sub* under + *jacere* throw] —Syn. n. 1. theme, topic, thesis, text. –v. 1. subdue, subordinate.

sub·jec·tion (səb·jek'shən), n. 1. a bringing under some power or influence; conquering: *the subjection of the rebels took years.* 2. condition of being under some power or influence: *women used to live in subjection to men.* —sub·jec'tion·al, adj.

sub·jec·tive (səb·jek'tiv), adj. 1. existing in the mind; belonging to the person thinking rather than to the object thought of: *base your subjective opinions on objective facts.* 2. about the thoughts and feelings of the speaker, writer, painter, etc.; personal: *a subjective poem.* 3. Gram. pertaining to or constituting the subject of a sentence. —sub·jec'tive·ly, adv. —sub·jec'tive·ness, n.

sub·jec·tiv·i·ty (sub'jek·tiv'ə·ti), n. subjective quality; existence in the mind only.

sub·join (sub·join'), v. add at the end; append.

sub·ju·gate (sub'jə·gāt), v., –gat·ed, –gat·ing. subdue; conquer. [< L, < *sub–* under + *jugum* yoke] —sub'ju·ga'tion, n. —sub'ju·ga'tor, n.

sub·junc·tive (səb·jungk'tiv), Gram. —n. 1. the mood of a verb which expresses a state, act, or event as possible, conditional, or dependent, rather than as actual. 2. verb in this mood. —adj. noting or pertaining to this mood. [< LL *subjunctivus,* ult. < L *sub–* under + *jungere* join] —sub·junc'tive·ly, adv.

sub·king·dom (sub·king'dəm; sub'king'–), n. any primary division of the animal kingdom, usually called a phylum.

sub·lease (n. sub'lēs'; v. sub·lēs', sub'lēs'), n., v., –leased, –leas·ing. —n. lease granted by a person who rents the property himself. —v. grant or take a sublease of. —sub·les·see (sub'-les·ē'), n. —sub·les·sor (sub·les'ôr; sub'les·ôr'), n.

sub·let (sub·let'; sub'let'), v., –let, –let·ting. 1. rent to another (something which has been rented to oneself). 2. give part of (a contract) to another.

sub·lieu·ten·ant (sub'lü·ten'ənt), n. 1. a subordinate lieutenant. 2. in the British army, an officer ranking next below a lieutenant.

sub·li·mate (v. sub'lə·māt; adj., n. sub'lə·mit,

–māt), v., –mat·ed, –mat·ing, adj., n. —v. 1. purify; refine. 2. Chem. sublime (a solid substance). 3. Psychol. divert the energy of primitive drives into behavior that is socially and ethically on a higher plane. —adj. sublimated. —n. Chem. material obtained when a substance is sublimed. [< L sublimatus, orig., raised < sublimis lofty] —sub'li·ma'tion, n.

sub·lime (səb·līm'), adj., n., v., –limed, –liming. —adj. 1. elevated in thought, sentiment, language, deed, etc.; lofty; noble: sublime courage. 2. inspiring awe or veneration; majestic. —n. that which is lofty, noble, exalted, etc. —v. 1. Chem. a. convert (a solid substance) by heat into a vapor, which on cooling condenses again to solid form, without apparent liquefaction. b. cause to be given off by this or some analogous process. 2. make lofty or sublime. [< L sublimis] —sub·lime'ly, adv. —sub·lime'ness, n. —Syn. adj. 2. grand, magnificent.

sub·lim·i·nal (sub·lim'ə·nəl; –lī'mə–), adj. 1. subconscious; below the threshold of consciousness: subliminal perception. 2. too weak or small to be felt or noticed.

sub·lim·i·ty (səb·lim'ə·ti), n., pl. –ties. 1. lofty excellence; grandeur; majesty; exalted state. 2. a sublime person or thing.

sub·ma·chine gun (sub'mə·shēn'), a lightweight automatic or semiautomatic gun, designed to be fired from the shoulder or hip.

sub·mar·gin·al (sub·mär'jə·nəl), adj. not productive enough to be worth cultivating, developing, etc., as land. —sub·mar'gin·al·ly, adv.

sub·ma·rine (n. sub'mə·rēn'; adj. sub'mə·rēn'), n. boat that can operate under water, used in warfare for discharging torpedoes, etc. —adj. 1. placed, growing, or used below the surface of the sea. 2. of, pertaining to, or carried on by submarine boats. —sub'ma·rine'ly, adv.

sub·max·il·lar·y (sub·mak'sə·ler'i), adj. of or pertaining to the lower jaw or lower jawbone.

sub·merge (səb·mérj'), v., –merged, –merging. 1. put under water; cover with water. 2. cover; bury: his talent was submerged by his shyness. 3. sink under water; go below the surfaces. [< L, < sub– under + mergere plunge] —sub·mer'gence, n. —sub·mer'gi·ble, adj. —Syn. 1. plunge, immerse, submerse.

sub·merse (səb·mérs'), v., –mersed, –mersing. submerge. [< L submersus, pp. of submergere SUBMERGE] —sub·mers'i·ble, adj., n. —sub·mer·sion (səb·mér'zhən; –shən), n.

sub·mis·sion (səb·mish'ən), n. 1. a submitting; yielding to the power, control, or authority of another. 2. obedience; humbleness. 3. a referring or being referred to the consideration or judgment of another or others. —Syn. 1. compliance, acquiescence, surrender.

sub·mis·sive (səb·mis'iv), adj. yielding to the power, control, or authority of another. —sub·mis'sive·ly, adv. —sub·mis'sive·ness, n.

sub·mit (səb·mit'), v., –mit·ted, –mit·ting. 1. yield to the power, control, or authority of another or others; surrender; yield: submit to arrest. 2. refer to the consideration or judgment of another or others: submit a report. 3. represent or urge in a respectful manner. [< L, < sub– under + mittere let go] —sub·mit'tal, n. —sub·mit'ter, n. —Syn. 1. comply. —Ant. 1. resist.

sub·nor·mal (sub·nôr'məl), adj. below normal; inferior to the normal. —sub·nor·mal·i·ty (sub'nôr·mal'ə·ti), n.

sub·or·di·nate (adj., n. sə·bôr'də·nit; v. sə·bôr'də·nāt), adj., n., v., –nat·ed, –nat·ing. —adj. 1. inferior in rank. 2. inferior in importance; secondary. 3. under the control or influence of something else; dependent. A complex sentence has one main clause and one or more subordinate clauses. 4. subordinating. Because, since, if, as, and whether are subordinate conjunctions. —n. a subordinate person or thing. —v. make subordinate. [< Med.L, ult. < L sub– under + ordo order] —sub·or'di·nate·ly, adv. —sub·or'di·nate·ness, n. —sub·or'di·na'tive, adj. —Syn. adj. 3. subject.

sub·or·di·na·tion (sə·bôr'də·nā'shən), n. 1.

a subordinating or being subordinated. 2. subordinate position or importance. 3. submission to authority; willingness to obey; obedience.

sub·orn (sə·bôrn'), v. 1. persuade or cause (a witness) to give false testimony in court. 2. persuade or cause (a person) to do an evil deed. [< L, < sub– secretly + ornare equip] —sub·or·na·tion (sub'ôr·nā'shən), n. —sub·orn'er, n.

sub·poe·na, sub·pe·na (sə·pē'nə), n., v., –naed, –na·ing. Law. —n. an official written order commanding a person to appear in law court. —v. summon with such an order. [< NL sub poena under penalty]

sub·ro·ga·tion (sub'rō·gā'shən), n. act of substituting for another, esp. the substitution of one person for another as a creditor.

sub ro·sa (sub rō'zə), in strict confidence; privately. [< L, under the rose]

sub·scribe (səb·skrīb'), v., –scribed, –scribing. 1. promise to give or pay (a sum of money): he subscribed $5 to the hospital fund. 2. write one's name at the end of a document, etc.; sign one's name: John Hancock was the first man to subscribe to the Declaration of Independence. 3. show one's consent or approval by signing: thousands of citizens subscribed the petition. 4. give one's consent or approval; agree: he will not subscribe to anything unfair. 5. subscribe to or for, promise to take and pay for, as a magazine, newspaper, etc. [< L, < sub– under + scribere write] —sub·scrib'er, n.

sub·script (sub'skript), adj. written underneath or low on the line. —n. number, letter, etc., written underneath and to one side of a symbol. In H_2SO_4 the 2 and 4 are subscripts. [< L subscriptus. See SUBSCRIBE.]

sub·scrip·tion (səb·skrip'shən), n. 1. a subscribing. 2. money subscribed; contribution. 3. the right obtained for the money: his subscription to the newspaper expires next week. 4. sum of money raised by a number of persons: we are raising a subscription for a new hospital. 5. signature. 6. assent or agreement expressed by signing one's name. —sub·scrip'tive, adj.

sub·sec·tion (sub'sek'shən; sub·sek'shən), n. part of a section.

sub·se·quent (sub'sə·kwənt), adj. 1. coming after; following; later: subsequent events. 2. subsequent to, after; following; later than: on the day subsequent to your call. [< L, < sub– up + sequi follow] —sub'se·quence, n. —sub'se·quen·tial (sub'sə·kwen'shəl), adj. —sub'se·quent·ly, adv. —sub'se·quent·ness, n.

sub·serve (səb·sérv'), v., –served, –serving. be of use or service in helping along (a purpose, action, etc.).

sub·ser·vi·ent (səb·sér'vi·ənt), adj. 1. tamely submissive; slavishly polite and obedient; servile. 2. useful as a means to help a purpose or end; serviceable. [< L, < sub– under + servire serve] —sub·ser'vi·ence, sub·ser'vi·en·cy, n. —sub·ser'vi·ent·ly, adv.

sub·side (səb·sīd'), v., –sid·ed, –sid·ing. 1. sink to a lower level: after the rain stopped the flood waters subsided. 2. grow less; die down; become less active: the storm finally subsided. 3. fall to the bottom; settle. [< L, < sub– down + sidere settle] —sub·sid·ence (səb·sīd'əns; sub'sə·dəns), n. —Syn. 2. abate, decrease, ebb.

sub·sid·i·ar·y (səb·sid'i·er'i), adj., n., pl. –ar·ies. —adj. 1. useful to assist or supplement; auxiliary; supplementary. 2. subordinate; secondary. —n. 1. thing or person that assists or supplements. 2. company having over half of its stock owned or controlled by another company. [< L subsidium reserve troops] —sub·sid'i·ar'i·ly, adv.

sub·si·dize (sub'sə·dīz), v., –dized, –diz·ing. 1. aid or assist with a grant of money. 2. buy the aid or assistance of with a grant of money. —sub'si·di·za'tion, n. —sub'si·diz'er, n.

sub·si·dy (sub'sə·di), n., pl. –dies. grant or contribution of money, esp. one made by a government to a private industry, a church, school, etc. [< L subsidium aid, reserve troops]

sub·sist (səb·sist'), v. 1. continue to be; exist:

many superstitions still subsist. **2.** keep alive; live: *people in the far north subsist on fish and meat.* [< L, < *sub–* up to + *sistere* stand]

sub·sist·ence (səb·sis′təns), *n.* **1.** existence; continuance. **2.** state or fact of keeping alive; living. **3.** means of keeping alive; livelihood. —**sub·sist′ent,** *adj.*

sub·soil (sub′soil′), *n.* layer of earth that lies just under the surface soil.

sub·son·ic (sub·son′ik), *adj.* having to do with or designed for use at a speed less than that of sound.

sub·stance (sub′stəns), *n.* **1.** what a thing consists of; matter; material: *ice and water are the same substance.* **2.** the real, main, or important part of anything. **3.** the real meaning: *give the substance of the speech in your own words.* **4.** solid quality: *claims lacking substance.* **5.** body: *a soup with substance.* **6.** wealth; property. **7.** a particular kind of matter: *the little pond is covered with a green substance.* **8.** in substance, **a.** essentially; mainly. **b.** really; actually. [< OF < L, < *substare* stand firm < *sub–* up to + *stare* stand] —**sub′stance·less,** *adj.* —**Syn. 2.** essence, nature. **3.** purport, gist.

sub·stand·ard (sub·stan′dərd; sub′stan′-dərd), *adj.* below standard.

sub·stan·tial (səb·stan′shəl), *adj.* **1.** real; actual: *not a ghost or a dream, but a substantial person.* **2.** large; important; ample: *a substantial improvement.* **3.** strong; firm; solid: *a substantial building.* **4.** in the main; in essentials: *the two stories were in substantial agreement.* **5.** well-to-do; wealthy. [< L, < *substantia* SUBSTANCE] —**sub·stan·ti·al·i·ty** (səb·stan′shi·al′ə·ti), *n.* —**sub·stan′tial·ly,** *adv.* —**sub·stan′tial·ness,** *n.*

sub·stan·ti·ate (səb·stan′shi·āt), *v.,* **-at·ed, -at·ing. 1.** establish by evidence; prove: *substantiate a claim.* **2.** give concrete or substantial form to. —**sub·stan′ti·a′tion,** *n.* —**sub·stan′ti·a′tive,** *adj.* —**sub·stan′ti·a′tor,** *n.*

sub·stan·tive (sub′stən·tiv), *n. Gram.* noun or pronoun; any adjective, phrase, or clause used as a noun. —*adj.* **1.** *Gram.* **a.** used as a noun; of the nature of a noun. **b.** showing or expressing existence. The verb *to be* is the substantive verb. **2.** independent. **3.** real; actual. **4.** essential. [< LL *substantivus,* ult. < *substare.* See SUB-STANCE.] —**sub·stan·ti·val** (sub′stən·tī′vəl), *adj.* —**sub′stan·ti′val·ly,** *adv.* —**sub′stan·tive·ly,** *adv.* —**sub′stan·tive·ness,** *n.*

sub·sta·tion (sub′stā′shən), *n.* a branch station.

sub·sti·tute (sub′stə·tüt; -tūt), *n., v.,* **-tut·ed, -tut·ing,** *adj.* —*n.* thing used instead of another; person taking the place of another. —*v.* **1.** put in the place of another. **2.** take the place of another. —*adj.* put in or taking the place of another. [< L *substitutus* < *sub–* instead + *statuere* establish] —**sub′sti·tut′er,** *n.* —**sub·sti·tu·tion·ar·y** (sub′stə·tü′shən·er′i; -tū′-), *adj.* —**Syn.** *n.* makeshift, expedient, alternate, deputy, proxy, representative. —*v.* **2.** replace.

sub·sti·tu·tion (sub′stə·tü′shən; -tū′-), *n.* use of one thing for another; putting (one person or thing) in the place of another; taking the place of another. —**sub′sti·tu′tion·al,** *adj.* —**sub′sti·tu′tion·al·ly,** *adv.*

sub·stra·tum (sub·strā′təm; -strat′əm), *n.,* pl. **-stra·ta** (-strā′tə; -strat′ə), **-stra·tums. 1.** layer lying under another. **2.** subsoil. **3.** basis. —**sub·stra′tal,** *adj.* —**sub·stra′tive,** *adj.*

sub·struc·ture (sub′struk′chər; sub·struk′-), *n.* structure forming a foundation. —**sub·struc′tur·al,** *adj.*

sub·ten·ant (sub·ten′ənt; sub′-ten′-), *n.* a tenant of a tenant; one who rents land, a house, or the like, from a tenant. —**sub·ten′an-cy,** *n.*

sub·tend (səb·tend′), *v. Geom.* extend under or be opposite to; stretch across. [< L, < *sub–* under + *tendere* stretch]

sub·ter·fuge (sub′tər·fūj), *n.* trick, excuse, or expedient used to escape something unpleasant. [< LL, ult. < L *subter–* from under + *fugere* flee] —**Syn.** artifice, ruse.

sub·ter·ra·ne·an (sub′tə·rā′ni·ən), **sub·ter·ra·ne·ous** (-əs), *adj.* **1.** underground. **2.** carried on secretly; hidden. [< L, < *sub–* under + *terra* earth] —**sub′ter·ra′ne·an·ly, sub′ter·ra′ne·ous·ly,** *adv.*

sub·tile (sut′əl; sub′til), *adj.* subtle. —**sub′-tile·ly,** *adv.* —**sub′tile·ness, sub·til·i·ty** (sub-til′ə·ti), *n.*

sub·ti·tle (sub′tī′təl), *n.* an additional or subordinate title of a book or article.

sub·tle (sut′əl), *adj.* **1.** delicate and elusive; thin; fine: *a subtle odor of perfume.* **2.** faint; mysterious: *a subtle smile.* **3.** having a keen, quick mind; discerning; acute: *a subtle understanding.* **4.** sly; crafty; tricky: *subtle schemers.* **5.** insidious in operation: *a subtle drug.* [< OF < L *subtilis,* orig., woven underneath] —**sub′-tle·ness,** *n.* —**sub′tly,** *adv.* —**Syn. 1.** tenuous, rare. **3.** discriminating, refined. **4.** artful, cunning, designing.

sub·tle·ty (sut′əl·ti), *n., pl.* **-ties. 1.** a subtle quality. **2.** something subtle.

sub·tract (səb·trakt′), *v.* **1.** *Math.* take away (one number from another). **2.** take away (something) from a whole. [< L *subtractus* < *sub–* from under + *trahere* draw] —**sub·tract′er,** *n.* —**sub·trac′tion,** *n.* —**sub·trac′tive,** *adj.*

sub·tra·hend (sub′trə·hend), *n. Math.* number or quantity to be subtracted from another. In 10—2=8, the subtrahend is 2. [< L, < *subtrahere* SUBTRACT]

sub·treas·ur·y (sub′trezh′ər·i; -trezh′ri; sub-trezh′-), *n., pl.* **-ur·ies. 1.** a branch treasury. **2.** *Am.* any branch of the United States treasury. —**sub′treas′ur·er,** *n.*

sub·trop·i·cal (sub·trop′ə·kəl), *adj.* **1.** bordering on the tropics; nearly tropical. **2.** pertaining to or occurring in a region between tropical and temperate. —**sub·trop·ics** (sub′trop′iks; sub-trop′-), *n.pl.*

sub·urb (sub′ėrb), *n.* **1.** district, town, or village just outside the boundaries of a city. **2.** Usually, **suburbs,** outlying parts. **3. the suburbs,** residential sections near the boundary of a city. [< L *suburbium* < *sub–* below + *urbs* city]

sub·ur·ban (sə·bér′bən), *adj.* **1.** pertaining to a suburb; in a suburb. **2.** characteristic of a suburb or its inhabitants. —**sub·ur·ban·ite** (sə·bér′bən·īt), *n.*

sub·ur·bi·a (sə·bér′bi·ə), *n.* the suburbs.

sub·ven·tion (səb·ven′shən), *n.* money granted, esp. by a government or some other authority, to aid or support some cause, institution, or undertaking; subsidy. —**sub·ven·tion·ar·y** (səb·ven′shən·er′i), *adj.*

sub·ver·sion (səb·vér′zhən; -shən), *n.* **1.** overthrow; destruction; ruin. **2.** anything that tends to overthrow or destroy; cause of ruin. —**sub·ver′sion·ar·y,** *adj.*

sub·ver·sive (səb·vér′siv), *adj.* tending to overthrow; destructive; causing ruin. —*n.* person who seeks to overthrow or undermine (a government, etc.).

sub·vert (səb·vért′), *v.* **1.** ruin (something established or existing); overthrow; destroy; cause the downfall, ruin, or destruction of. **2.** undermine the principles of; corrupt. [< L, < *sub–* up from under + *vertere* turn] —**sub·vert′er,** *n.* —**sub·vert′i·ble,** *adj.*

sub·way (sub′wā′), *n.* **1.** an underground passage. **2.** *Am.* an electric railroad beneath the surface of the streets in a city.

suc·ceed (sək·sēd′), *v.* **1.** turn out well; do well; have success: *he finally succeeded.* **2.** accomplish what is attempted or intended: *the attack succeeded beyond all expectations.* **3.** come next after; follow; take the place of: *week succeeds week.* **4.** come next after another; follow another: *when Edward VIII abdicated, George VI succeeded to the throne.* [< L, < *sub–* up (to) + *cedere* go] —**suc·ceed′er,** *n.* —**Syn. 1.** prosper, thrive, flourish.

suc·cess (sək·ses′), *n.* **1.** a favorable result; wished-for ending; good fortune: *efforts crowned with success.* **2.** the gaining of wealth, position, etc.: *he has had little success in life.* **3.** person or thing that succeeds: *he was a success in busi-*

B

A C

The chord AC subtends the arc ABC.

ness. **4.** result; outcome; fortune: *what success did you have?* [< L *successus* < *succedere* SUCCEED]

suc·cess·ful (sək·ses′fəl), *adj.* having success; ending in success; prosperous; fortunate. —**suc·cess′ful·ly**, *adv.* —**suc·cess′ful·ness**, *n.*

suc·ces·sion (sək·sesh′ən), *n.* **1.** group of things happening one after another; series: *a succession of events.* **2.** the coming of one person or thing after another: *a succession of kings.* **3.** the right or process by which one person takes the office, rank, estate, or other rights or liabilities of another person in accordance with law or custom. **4.** set or arrangement of persons having such a right of succeeding. **5. in succession,** one after another. —**suc·ces′sion·al,** *adj.* —**suc·ces′sion·al·ly,** *adv.*

suc·ces·sive (sək·ses′iv), *adj.* coming one after another; following in order: *it rained for three successive days.* —**suc·ces′sive·ness,** *n.* —**Syn.** consecutive, sequent.

suc·ces·sive·ly (sək·ses′iv·li), *adv.* one after another; in order.

suc·ces·sor (sək·ses′ər), *n.* **1.** one that follows. **2.** person who succeeds another in office, position, or ownership of property. —**suc·ces′sor·ship,** *n.*

suc·cinct (sək·singkt′), *adj.* expressed briefly and clearly; expressing much in few words; concise. [< L *succinctus,* pp. of *succingere* tuck up clothes for action < *sub-* up + *cingere* gird] —**suc·cinct′ly,** *adv.* —**suc·cinct′ness,** *n.* —**Syn.** compressed, condensed, terse.

suc·cor, *esp. Brit.* **suc·cour** (suk′ər), *n.* help; relief; aid. —*v.* help or aid, esp. in difficulty, want or distress. [< OF *sucurs,* ult. < L *succurrere* run to help < *sub-* up (to) + *currere* run] —**suc′cor·a·ble,** *esp. Brit.* **suc′cour·a·ble,** *adj.* —**suc′cor·er,** *esp. Brit.* **suc′cour·er,** *n.*

suc·co·tash (suk′ə·tash), *n.* *Am.* corn and beans cooked together. [< Algonquian]

suc·cu·lent (suk′yə·lənt), *adj.* **1.** juicy: *a succulent fruit.* **2.** interesting; not dull. **3.** having thick, fleshy leaves and stems. [< L, < *succus* juice] —**suc′cu·lence,** **suc′cu·len·cy,** *n.* —**suc′cu·lent·ly,** *adv.*

suc·cumb (sə·kum′), *v.* **1.** give way; yield: *he succumbed to temptation.* **2.** die. **3.** succumb to, die of. [< L, < *sub-* down + *-cumbere* lie]

such (such), *adj.* **1.** of that kind; of the same kind or degree: *I never have seen such a sight.* **2.** of the kind that; of a particular kind: *the food, such as it was, was plentiful.* **3.** of the kind already spoken of or suggested: *tea, coffee, and such commodities.* **4.** so great, so bad, so good, etc.: *he is such a liar.* **5.** some; certain: *in such and such a town.* —*pron.* **1.** such a person or thing: *take from the blankets such as you need.* **2. as such,** as being what is indicated or implied: *a leader, as such, deserves obedience.* [OE *swylc, swelc* < *swa* so + *lic* like] ➤ **Such.** As an intensive, *such* is colloquial and informal: *it was such a hot day, such nice people.* In formal writing the construction would be avoided or completed: *such nice people as they are.* Generally accepted constructions with *such* are: *There was such a crowd that* [not: so that] *we couldn't even get to the door. The invitation is extended to such nonmembers as are interested.* (As is a relative pronoun. A more informal construction would be: *The invitation is extended to all nonmembers who are interested.) A good lecturer? There's no such thing.* (*No such a thing* is colloquial and substandard.) As a coördinating conjunction, introducing examples, *such as* has a comma before but not after: *He was interested in all sorts of outlandish subjects, such as palmistry, numerology, and phrenology.*

such·like (such′līk′), *adj.* of such kind; of a like kind. —*pron.* things of such kind: *"deceptions, disguises, and suchlike."*

suck (suk), *v.* **1.** draw into the mouth: *lemonade can be sucked through a straw.* **2.** draw something from with the mouth: *suck oranges.* **3.** draw milk from the breast or a bottle. **4.** draw or be drawn by sucking: *he sucked at his pipe.* **5.**

drink; take; absorb: *a sponge sucks in water.* **6.** draw in; swallow: *the whirlpool sucked down the boat.* **7.** hold in the mouth and lick: *the child sucked a lollipop.* —*n.* **1.** act of sucking. **2.** a sucking force or sound. **3.** that which is sucked. [OE *sūcan*]

suck·er (suk′ər), *n.* **1.** animal or thing that sucks. **2.** *Am.* any of various freshwater fishes that suck in food or have mouths that suggest sucking. **3.** organ for sucking or holding fast by a sucking force. **4.** *Bot.* a shoot growing from an underground stem or root. **5.** pipe or tube through which something is drawn by suction. **6.** *Am., Colloq.* person easily deceived. **7.** *Colloq.* lollipop. —*v.* **1.** take suckers from (corn, tobacco, etc.). **2.** form suckers.

Sucker (ab. 2 ft. long)

suck·le (suk′əl), *v.,* **-led, -ling. 1.** feed with milk from the breast, udder, etc. **2.** nourish; bring up. [< *suck*] —**suck′ler,** *n.*

suck·ling (suk′ling), *n.* a very young animal or child, esp. one not yet weaned. —*adj.* **1.** very young. **2.** not yet weaned; sucking.

Su·cre (sü′krä), *n.* one of the two capitals (La Paz is the other) of Bolivia, in the S part.

su·crose (sü′krōs), *n.* *Chem.* ordinary sugar, $C_{12}H_{22}O_{11}$, obtained from sugar cane, sugar beets, etc. [< F *sucre* SUGAR]

suc·tion (suk′shən), *n.* **1.** the drawing of a liquid, gas, etc., into a space by sucking out or removing part of the air. **2.** the force caused by sucking out or removing part of the air in a space. —*adj.* causing a suction; working by suction. [< L *suctio* < *sugere* suck] —**suc·to·ri·al** (suk·tô′ri·əl; -tō′-), *adj.*

Su·dan (sü·dan′), *n.* **1.** a vast region in Africa, S of the Sahara Desert and Egypt. **2.** Formerly, **Anglo-Egyptian Sudan,** country in NE Africa, under the control of Great Britain and Egypt. —**Su·da·nese** (sü′də·nēz′; -nēs′), *adj., n.*

Sudanese Republic, Republic of Mali.

sud·den (sud′ən), *adj.* **1.** happening unexpectedly: *a sudden storm.* **2.** made or done unexpectedly: *a sudden decision, act, etc.* **3.** appearing unexpectedly: *a sudden turn in the road.* —*n.* **all of a sudden,** in a sudden manner. [< OF < L *subitaneus* < *subitus* sudden] —**sud′den·ly,** *adv.* —**sud′den·ness,** *n.* —**Syn.** *adj.* **2.** abrupt, hasty.

Su·de·ten·land (sü·dā′tən·land′), *n.* a mountainous region in N Czechoslovakia.

suds (sudz), *n.pl.* **1.** soapy water. **2.** bubbles and foam on soapy water. **3.** any froth or foam. **4.** *Slang.* beer. [? < MDu. *sudse* bog] —**suds′y,** *adj.*

sue (sü), *v.,* **sued, su·ing. 1.** start a lawsuit against. **2.** take action in law: *sue for damages.* **3.** beg or ask; make petition; plead: *messengers came suing for peace.* **4.** *Archaic.* make love to; woo. [< AF *suer,* ult. < L *sequi* follow] —**su′er,** *n.*

suède (swād), *n.* **1.** a soft leather that has a velvety nap on one or both sides. **2.** a kind of cloth that has a similar appearance. —*adj.* made of suede. [< F, lit., Sweden]

su·et (sü′it), *n.* the hard fat about the kidneys and loins of cattle or sheep. Beef suet is used in cooking and for making tallow. [dim. of AF *sue* tallow < L *sebum*] —**su′et·y,** *adj.*

Su·ez (sü′ez; sü·ez′), *n.* Isthmus of, the isthmus between Asia and Africa, a part of Egypt.

Suez Canal, canal across the Isthmus of Suez, connecting the Mediterranean and Red seas, controlled by Egypt.

suf·fer (suf′ər), *v.* **1.** undergo, experience, or be subjected to (pain, grief, injury, etc.): *his health suffered from overwork.* **2.** undergo any action, process, etc.: *suffer change.* **3.** allow; permit: *"Suffer the little children to come unto me."* **4.** bear with patiently; tolerate; endure: *I will not suffer such insults.* [< L, < *sub-* up + *ferre* bear] —**suf′fer·a·ble,** *adj.* —**suf′fer·a·ble·ness,** *n.* —**suf′fer·a·bly,** *adv.* —**suf′fer·er,** *n.*

suf·fer·ance (suf′ər·əns; suf′rəns), *n.* **1.** permission given only by a failure to object or prevent. **2.** power to bear or endure; patient endurance. **3. on sufferance,** allowed or tolerated, but not really wanted.

suf·fer·ing (suf'ər·ing; suf'ring), *n.* pain; the enduring of pain. —**suf'fer·ing·ly**, *adv.* —Syn. distress, agony, misery.

suf·fice (sə·fīs'), *v.*, **–ficed, –fic·ing. 1.** be enough or adequate: *the money will suffice for one year.* **2.** satisfy; content: *a small amount sufficed him.* [< L *sufficere* < *sub*- up (to) + *facere* make] —**suf·fic'er**, *n.* —**suf·fic'ing·ly**, *adv.* —**suf·fic'ing·ness**, *n.*

suf·fi·cien·cy (sə·fish'ən·si), *n.*, *pl.* **–cies. 1.** a sufficient amount; large enough supply. **2.** state or fact of being sufficient; adequacy. **3.** self-confidence.

suf·fi·cient (sə·fish'ənt), *adj.* as much as is needed; enough: *sufficient proof.* —**suf·fi'cient·ly**, *adv.* —Syn. adequate, ample.

suf·fix (*n.* suf'iks; *v.* sə·fiks', suf'iks), *n.* an addition made at the end of a word to change the meaning or form a new word. *-er, -ment, -less, -ic, -able,* and *-ible* are suffixes. —*v.* add at the end; put after. [< NL < L *suffixum*, neut. pp. < *sub*- upon + *figere* fasten] —**suf·fix'al** (suf'ik·səl), *adj.* —**suf·fix·ion** (sə·fik'shən), *n.*

suf·fo·cate (suf'ə·kāt), *v.*, **–cat·ed, –cat·ing. 1.** kill by stopping the breath. **2.** keep from breathing; hinder in breathing. **3.** die for lack of air. **4.** smother; suppress. [< L *suffocatus* < *sub*- up + *fauces* throat] —**suf·fo·cat'ing·ly**, *adv.* —**suf'fo·ca'tion**, *n.* —**suf'fo·ca'tive**, *adj.*

suf·fra·gan (suf'rə·gən), *n.* **1.** bishop consecrated to assist another bishop. **2.** any bishop considered in relation to his archbishop. —*adj.* assisting. [< OF, ult. < L *suffragium* suffrage]

suf·frage (suf'rij), *n.* **1.** a vote; a vote for some person or thing. **2.** *Am.* the right to vote. The United States granted suffrage to women in 1920. [< L *suffragium*]

suf·fra·gette (suf'rə·jet'), *n.* woman who advocated suffrage for women.

suf·fra·gist (suf'rə·jist), *n.* person who favors giving suffrage to more people, esp. to women. —**suf'fra·gism,** *n.*

suf·fuse (sə·fūz'), *v.*, **–fused, –fus·ing.** overspread (with a liquid, dye, etc.): *eyes suffused with tears.* [< L *suffusus* < *sub*- (up from) under + *fundere* pour] —**suf·fu·sion** (sə·fū'zhən), *n.* —**suf·fu·sive** (sə·fū'siv), *adj.*

sug·ar (shug'ər), *n.* **1.** a sweet substance, $C_{12}H_{22}O_{11}$, obtained chiefly from sugar cane or beets and used extensively in food products. **2.** any of the class of carbohydrates to which this substance belongs: *grape sugar, milk sugar.* —*v.* **1.** put sugar in; sweeten with sugar. **2.** cover with sugar; sprinkle with sugar. **3.** form sugar: *honey sugars if kept too long.* **4.** *Am.* make maple sugar. **5.** sugar off, *Am.* complete the boiling down of syrup. **6.** cause to seem pleasant or agreeable. [< OF, ult. < Ar. *sukkar* < Pers. *shakar* < Skt. *çarkarā*, orig., grit] —**sug'ar·less,** *adj.* —**sug'ar·y,** *adj.* —**sug'ar·i·ness,** *n.*

sugar beet, a large beet with a white root that yields sugar.

sugar cane, a very tall grass with a strong, jointed stem and flat leaves, growing in warm regions. Sugar cane is the main source of sugar.

sug·ar·coat (shug'ər·kōt'), *v.* **1.** cover with sugar. **2.** cause to seem more pleasant or agreeable. —**sug'ar·coat'ing,** *n.*

Sugar cane

sug·ar·plum (shug'ər·plum'), *n.* piece of candy; bonbon.

sug·gest (səg·jest'; sə·jest'), *v.* **1.** bring to mind; call up the thought of: *the thought of summer suggests swimming.* **2.** propose: *John suggested having a party.* **3.** show in an indirect way; hint: *his yawns suggested that he would like to go to bed.* [< L *suggestus* < *sub*- up + *gerere* bring] —**sug·gest'er,** *n.* —Syn. **2.** advise, recommend. **3.** insinuate, intimate.

sug·gest·i·ble (səg·jes'tə·bəl; sə·jes'-), *adj.* **1.** capable of being influenced by suggestion. **2.** that can be suggested. —**sug·gest'i·bil'i·ty,** *n.*

sug·ges·tion (səg·jes'chən; sə·jes'-), *n.* **1.** a suggesting: *the trip was made at his suggestion.*

2. state of being suggested. **3.** thing suggested: *the picnic was an excellent suggestion.* **4.** indirect indication or hint, esp. one that suggests improper or indecent ideas. **5.** the calling up of one idea by another because they are connected or associated in some way. **6.** a very small amount; slight trace: *speak with a suggestion of a foreign accent.* —Syn. **3.** proposal, recommendation.

sug·ges·tive (səg·jes'tiv; sə·jes'-), *adj.* **1.** tending to suggest ideas, acts, or feelings. **2.** *Am.* tending to suggest something improper or indecent. —**sug·ges'tive·ly,** *adv.* —**sug·ges'tive·ness,** *n.*

su·i·cide¹ (sü'ə·sīd), *n.* **1.** the killing of oneself on purpose. **2.** destruction of one's own interests or prospects. **3.** commit suicide, kill oneself on purpose. [< NL, < L *sui* of oneself + *-cidium* act of killing] —**su'i·cid'al,** *adj.* —**su'i·cid'al·ly,** *adv.*

su·i·cide² (sü'ə·sīd), *n.* person who kills himself on purpose. [< NL, < L *sui* of oneself + *-cida* killer]

su·i ge·ne·ris (sü'ī jen'ə·ris; sü'ī), *Latin.* of his, her, its, or their peculiar kind; unique.

suit (süt), *n.* **1.** set of clothes to be worn together, esp. a man's outer garments. **2.** case in a law court; application to a court for justice: *he started a suit to collect damages for his injuries.* **3.** one of the four sets of cards (spades, hearts, diamonds, and clubs). **4.** request; asking; wooing: *his suit was successful and she married him.* **5.** set or series of like things; suite. **6.** follow suit, **a.** play a card of the same suit as that first played. **b.** follow the example of another. —*v.* **1.** provide with clothes: *he was suited by a fashionable tailor.* **2.** make suitable; make fit: *suit the punishment to the offense.* **3.** be suitable for; agree with: *a cold climate suits apples and wheat, but not oranges.* **4.** be suitable; be convenient; fit: *which date suits best?* **5.** be becoming to: *her blue hat suits her complexion.* **6.** please; satisfy: *it is hard to suit everyone.* **7.** suit oneself, do as one pleases. [< AF *suite*, ult. < L *sequi* follow. Doublet of SUITE.] —Syn. *v.* **2.** adapt, adjust, accommodate. **6.** gratify, content.

suit·a·ble (süt'ə·bəl), *adj.* right for the occasion; fitting; proper. —**suit'a·bil'i·ty,** **suit'a·ble·ness,** *n.* —**suit'a·bly,** *adv.* —Syn. appropriate, meet, seemly.

suit·case (süt'kās'), *n.* a flat, rectangular traveling bag.

suite (swēt; *also* süt *for* 3), *n.* **1.** a connected series of rooms to be used by one person or family. **2.** set or series of like things. **3.** set of furniture that matches. **4.** *Music.* **a.** series of connected instrumental movements. **b.** set of dance tunes. **5.** group of attendants. [< F. Doublet of SUIT.]

suit·ing (süt'ing), *n.* cloth for making suits.

suit·or (süt'ər), *n.* **1.** man who is courting a woman. **2.** person bringing suit in a law court. **3.** anyone who sues or petitions. —**suit'or·ship,** *n.*

su·ki·ya·ki (sü'ki·yä'ki), *n.* a Japanese dish of thin strips of beef and diced vegetables, cooked briefly in sauce. [< Jap.]

Su·la·we·si (sü'lä·wä'si), *n.* a large island in E Indonesia. Formerly, Celebes.

Su·lei·man (sü'lā·män'), *n.* Solyman.

sul·fa (sul'fə), *adj.* of or pertaining to a family of drugs containing sulfurous anhydride (SO_2) and derived from sulfanilamide, used in treating various bacterial infections. —*n.* a sulfa drug. Also, **sulpha.**

sul·fa·di·a·zine (sul'fə·dī'ə·zēn; -zin), *n.* a substance derived from sulfanilamide and used in treating various infections.

sul·fa·nil·a·mide (sul'fə·nil'ə·mīd; -mid), *n.* a white, crystalline substance, derived from coal tar and used in treating various infections. Sulfanilamide was the first sulfa drug to be widely used. Also, **sulphanilamide.**

sul·fa·pyr·i·dine (sul'fə·pir'ə·dēn; -din), *n.* a substance derived from sulfanilamide, used mainly to combat pneumonia.

sul·fate (sul'fāt), *n.*, *v.*, **–fat·ed, –fat·ing.** —*n.* any salt of sulfuric acid. —*v.* **1.** combine, treat, or impregnate with sulfuric acid or with a sulfate or sulfates. 2. convert into a sulfate. 3. form a deposit of a lead sulfate compound on (the lead plates of a storage battery). Also, **sulphate.**

sul·fa·thi·a·zole (sul′fə·thī′ə·zōl; -zol), *n.* a widely used sulfa drug, $C_6H_9N_3O_2S_2$, used especially in treating pneumonia. Also, **sulphathiazole.**

sul·fide (sul′fīd), **sul·fid** (-fid), *n. Chem.* any compound of sulfur with another element or radical. Also, **sulphide, sulphid.**

sul·fite (sul′fīt), *n. Chem.* any salt of sulfurous acid. Also, **sulphite.**

sul·fur (sul′fər), *n.* 1. *Chem.* a light-yellow substance, S, that burns with a blue flame and a stifling odor. It is a nonmetallic chemical element. 2. a greenish yellow. —*adj.* greenish-yellow. Also, **sulphur.** [< L *sulfur, sulpur*] —**sul·fu·re·ous** (sul·fyūr′i·əs), *adj.* —**sul·fu′re·ous·ly,** *adv.* —**sul·fu′re·ous·ness,** *n.*

sul·fu·rate (sul′fə·rāt; -fyə-), *v.,* -rat·ed, -rat·ing. combine, treat, or impregnate with sulfur, the fumes of burning sulfur, or the like. Also, **sulphurate.** —**sul′fu·ra′tion,** *n.*

sulfur dioxide, *Chem.* a heavy, colorless gas, SO_2, that has a sharp odor, used as a bleach, disinfectant, preservative, and refrigerant.

sul·fu·ric (sul·fyūr′ik), *adj. Chem.* pertaining to or containing sulfur with a valence of six. Also, **sulphuric.**

sulfuric acid, oil of vitriol, a heavy, colorless, oily, very strong acid, H_2SO_4, a dibasic acid of sulfur. Sulfuric acid is used in making explosives and fertilizers, in refining petroleum, etc.

sul·fur·ous (sul′fər·əs; -fyər-; in *Chem.,* also sul·fyūr′əs), *adj.* 1. *Chem.* containing sulfur with a valence of four. 2. of or pertaining to sulfur. 3. containing sulfur. 4. like sulfur; like burning sulfur. 5. of or like the fires of hell; hellish. Also, **sulphurous.**

sulfurous acid, *Chem.* H_2SO_3, a colorless solution of sulfur dioxide in water, used as a bleach, reducing agent, etc.

sulk (sulk), *v.* hold aloof in a sullen manner; be sulky. —*n.* 1. a sulking. 2. a fit of sulking. 3. **sulks,** the ill humor shown by sulking. [< *sulky*] —**sulk′er,** *n.*

sulk·y (sul′ki), *adj.,* sulk·i·er, sulk·i·est, *n., pl.* sulk·ies. —*adj.* silent and bad-humored because of resentment; sullen. —*n.* a light carriage with two wheels, for one person. [cf. OE *āsolcen* lazy] —**sulk′i·ly,** *adv.* —**sulk′i·ness,** *n.*

Sulky racing

sul·len (sul′ən), *adj.* 1. silent because of bad humor or anger: *the sullen child refused to answer my question.* 2. showing bad humor or anger: *a sullen act.* 3. gloomy; morose; dismal: *the sullen skies threatened rain.* [< OF *solain,* ult. < L *solus* alone] —**sul′len·ly,** *adv.* —**sul′len·ness,** *n.* —**Syn.** 1. sulky. 2. churlish, surly, grouchy. 3. glum. —**Ant.** 1. sociable, amiable.

Sul·li·van (sul′ə·vən), *n.* Sir Arthur Seymour, 1842–1900, English composer who collaborated with W. S. Gilbert.

sul·ly (sul′i), *v.,* -lied, -ly·ing, *n., pl.* -lies. soil; stain; tarnish. [OE *sōlian* < *sōl* dirty]

sul·pha (sul′fə), *adj., n.* sulfa.

sul·pha·nil·a·mide (sul′fə·nil′ə·mīd; -mid), *n.* sulfanilamide.

sul·phate (sul′fāt), *n., v.,* -phat·ed, -phat·ing. sulfate.

sul·pha·thi·a·zole (sul′fə·thī′ə·zōl; -zol), *n.* sulfathiazole.

sul·phide (sul′fīd), **sul·phid** (-fid), *n.* sulfide.

sul·phite (sul′fīt), *n.* sulfite.

sul·phur (sul′fər), *n., adj.* sulfur. —**sul·phu·re·ous** (sul·fyūr′i·əs), *adj.* —**sul·phu′re·ous·ly,** *adv.* —**sul·phu′re·ous·ness,** *n.*

sul·phu·rate (sul′fə·rāt; -fyə-), *v.,* -rat·ed, -rat·ing. sulfurate. —**sul′phu·ra′tion,** *n.*

sul·phu·ric (sul·fyūr′ik), *adj.* sulfuric.

sul·phur·ous (sul′fər·əs; -fyər-; in *Chem.,* also sul·fyūr′əs), *adj.* sulfurous.

sul·tan (sul′tən), *n.* ruler of a Mohammedan country. Turkey was ruled by a sultan until 1922. [ult. < Ar. *sultān*] —**sul·tan·ic** (sul·tan′ik), *adj.* —**sul′tan·ship,** *n.*

sul·tan·a (sul·tan′ə; -tä′nə), *n.* 1. wife of a sultan. 2. mother, sister, or daughter of a sultan. 3. a small seedless raisin.

sul·tan·ate (sul′tən·āt), *n.* 1. position, authority, or period of rule of a sultan. 2. territory ruled over by a sultan.

sul·try (sul′tri), *adj.,* -tri·er, -tri·est. 1. oppressively hot, close, and moist: *we expect sultry weather during July.* 2. hot. [ult. < *swelter*] —**sul′tri·ly,** *adv.* —**sul′tri·ness,** *n.*

Su·lu Archipelago (sü′lü), group of islands in the SW part of the Philippine Islands.

sum (sum), *n., v.,* summed, sum·ming. —*n.* 1. total of two or more numbers or things taken together. 2. *Colloq.* problem in arithmetic. 3. the whole amount; total amount: *it represents the sum of my work.* 4. substance or gist of a matter: *the sum of his speech was this.* 5. amount of money: *he paid a large sum for the house.* 6. *Archaic.* the highest point. —*v.* 1. find the total of. 2. make a total of. 3. **sum up,** a. collect into a whole. b. express briefly. c. review the chief points (of). [< L *summa,* orig. fem. adj., highest] —**sum′less,** *adj.*

su·mac, su·mach (sü′mak; shü′-), *n.* 1. a shrub or small tree which has divided leaves that turn scarlet in the autumn and cone-shaped clusters of red fruit. 2. its dried leaves, used in tanning and dyeing. [< OF < Ar. *summāq*]

Sumac

Su·ma·tra (sù·mä′trə), *n.* a large island in W Indonesia, off the SE coast of Asia. —**Su·ma′tran,** *adj., n.*

sum·ma cum lau·de (súm′ə kùm lou′də; sü′mä kum lô′dē), with the highest honor.

sum·ma·rize (sum′ə·rīz), *v.,* -rized, -riz·ing. make or represent a summary of; give only the main points of; express briefly. —**sum′ma·ri·za′tion,** *n.* —**sum′ma·riz′er,** *n.*

sum·ma·ry (sum′ə·ri), *n., pl.* -ries, *adj.* —*n.* a brief statement giving the main points: *a summary of a book.* —*adj.* 1. concise and comprehensive; brief. 2. direct and prompt; without delay or formality: *summary jurisdiction.* [< L, < *summa* sum] —**sum·ma·ri·ly** (sum′ə·rə·li; emphatic sə·mer′ə·li), *adv.* —**sum′ma·ri·ness,** *n.* —**Syn.** *n.* abstract, digest, synopsis, résumé. —*adj.* 1. short, terse, succinct.

sum·ma·tion (sum·ā′shən), *n.* 1. process of finding the sum or total; addition. 2. the total. 3. *Law.* the final presentation of facts and arguments by the opposing counsel.

sum·mer (sum′ər), *n.* 1. season of the year between spring and autumn. 2. the warmest season. —*adj.* of summer; coming in summer. —*v.* 1. pass the summer: *summer at the seashore.* 2. keep or feed during the summer; arrange or manage during the summer. [OE *sumor*] —**sum′mer·y,** *adj.*

sum·mer·house (sum′ər·hous′), *n.* a building in a park or garden in which to sit in warm weather.

sum·mer·sault (sum′ər·sôlt), *n., v.* somersault.

summer solstice. See solstice.

summer squash, any of various squashes used as a summer vegetable.

sum·mit (sum′it), *n.* 1. the highest point; top. 2. the highest level of authority, especially the leaders of individual governments, as dealing in international affairs. [< F *sommet,* ult. < L *summus* highest] —**sum′mit·al,** *adj.* —**Syn.** apex, pinnacle, zenith.

sum·mon (sum′ən), *v.* 1. call with authority, esp. to some particular duty; order to come; send for: *summon men to defend their country.* 2. call together: *summon an assembly.* 3. call upon: *summon a fort to surrender.* 4. stir to

āge, cāre, fär; ēqual, tėrm; īce; ōpen, ôrder; pùt, rüle, ūse; ŧħ, then; ə=a in about.

action; rouse: *the fire alarm summoned the people.* [< L *summonere* hint to < *sub-* secretly + *monere* warn]

sum·mon·er (sum′ən·ər), *n.* **1.** person who summons. **2.** formerly, a petty officer whose duty was to warn persons to appear in court.

sum·mons (sum′ənz), *n.*, *pl.* **-mons·es**, *v.* —*n.* **1.** an order to appear at a certain place, esp. in a law court. **2.** a command; message; signal. —*v. Colloq.* summon to court. [< OF *somonse* < *somondre* SUMMON]

sump (sump), *n.* pit or reservoir for collecting water, oil, etc. [< MDu. *somp* or MLG *sump* swamp]

sump·ter (sump′tər), *n.* horse or mule for carrying baggage. —*adj.* load-carrying. [< OF *sommetier*, ult. < L *sagma* packsaddle < Gk.]

sump·tu·ar·y (sump′chù·er′i), *adj.* having to do with the spending of money; regulating expenses: *sumptuary laws.* [< L, < *sumptus* expense < *sumere* spend]

sump·tu·ous (sump′chù·əs), *adj.* **1.** costly. **2.** luxuriously fine or elegant. [< L, < *sumptus* expense < *sumere* spend] —**sump·tu·os·i·ty** (sump′chù·os′ə·ti), **sump′tu·ous·ness,** *n.* —**sump′tu·ous·ly,** *adv.* —**Syn. 1.** expensive.

sun (sun), *n.*, *v.*, **sunned, sun·ning.** —*n.* **1.** the brightest object in the sky; the heavenly body around which the earth and planets revolve. **2.** the light and warmth of the sun: *sit in the sun.* **3.** any heavenly body made up of burning gas and having satellites. **4.** something like the sun in brightness or splendor. **5.** day. **6.** year. **7. from sun to sun,** from sunrise to sunset. **8. in the sun,** in an advantageous or comfortable position. **9. under the sun,** on earth; in the world. —*v.* **1.** expose to the sun's rays: *she suns herself each day.* **2.** warm or dry in the sunshine: *she suns the clothes after washing them.* [OE *sunne*] —**sun′less,** *adj.* —**sun′less·ness,** *n.*

Sun., Sunday.

sun·beam (sun′bēm′), *n.* ray of sunlight.

sun·bon·net (sun′bon′it), *n.* a large bonnet that shades the face and neck.

sun·burn (sun′bėrn′), *n.*, *v.*, **-burned** or **-burnt, -burn·ing.** —*n.* **1.** a burning of the skin by the sun's rays. A sunburn is often red and painful. **2.** the color of red or tan resulting from sunburn. —*v.* **1.** burn the skin by the sun's rays; burn the skin of. **2.** become burned by the sun.

sun·dae (sun′di), *n. Am.* an individual portion of ice cream with syrup, crushed fruits, nuts, etc., over it.

Sun·day (sun′di; -dā), *n.* **1.** the first day of the week. **2.** the day of rest and worship among Christians.

Sunday school. 1. school held on Sunday for teaching religion. **2.** its members. ➤ **Sunday school.** Capitalize only the *Sunday* except in names of particular Sunday schools: *Sunday school, the Methodist Sunday School.*

sun·der (sun′dər), *v.* separate; part; sever; split. —*n.* **in sunder,** apart. [OE *sundrian* < *sundor* apart] —**sun′der·ance,** *n.* —**Syn.** *v.* divide, disjoin, disconnect.

sun·di·al (sun′di′əl), *n.* instrument for telling the time of day by the position of a shadow cast by the sun.

sun·dog (sun′dôg′; -dog′), *n.* **1.** parhelion. **2.** a small or incomplete rainbow.

sun·down (sun′doun′), *n.* sunset; the time of sunset.

sun·dried (sun′drīd′), *adj.* dried by the sun.

sun·dries (sun′driz), *n.pl.* sundry things; items not named; odds and ends.

sun·dry (sun′dri), *adj.* several; various. —*n.* **all and sundry,** all, both collectively and individually. [OE *syndrig* separate < *sundor* apart]

sun·fish (sun′fish′), *n.*, *pl.* **-fish·es** or (*esp. collectively*) **-fish. 1.** a large fish with tough flesh that lives in tropical or temperate seas. **2.** *Am.* a small fresh-water fish of North America, used for food.

sun·flow·er (sun′flou′ər), *n.* **1.** a tall plant having large yellow flowers with brown centers. **2.** any of various similar plants.

sung (sung), *v.* pt. and pp. of **sing.**

sun·glass·es (sun′glas′iz; -gläs′-), *n.pl.* spectacles to protect the eyes from the glare of the sun, usually made with colored glass.

sunk (sungk), *v.* pt. and pp. of **sink.**

sunk·en (sungk′ən), *adj.* **1.** sunk: *a sunken ship.* **2.** submerged: *a sunken rock.* **3.** situated below the general level: *a sunken garden.* **4.** fallen in; hollow: *sunken eyes.* —*v.* pp. of **sink.**

sun·light (sun′līt′), *n.* the light of the sun.

sun·lit (sun′lit′), *adj.* lighted by the sun.

sun·ny (sun′i), *adj.,* **-ni·er, -ni·est. 1.** having much sunshine: *a sunny day.* **2.** exposed to, lighted by, or warmed by the direct rays of the sun: *a sunny room.* **3.** like the sun; like sunshine. **4.** bright; cheerful; happy. —**sun′ni·ly,** *adv.* —**sun′ni·ness,** *n.* —**Syn. 3.** shining, radiant.

sun·rise (sun′rīz′), **sun·up** (sun′up′), *n.* **1.** the rising of the sun. **2.** the first appearance of the sun in the morning. **3.** the time when the top of the sun rises above the horizon.

sun·set (sun′set′), *n.* **1.** the setting of the sun. **2.** the last appearance of the sun in the evening. **3.** the time when the top of the sun goes below the horizon.

sun·shade (sun′shād′), *n.* **1.** parasol. **2.** protection against the sun.

sun·shine (sun′shīn′), *n.* **1.** the shining of the sun; light or rays of the sun. **2.** brightness; cheerfulness; happiness. —**sun′shin′y,** *adj.*

sun·spot (sun′spot′), *n.* one of the dark spots that appear at regular intervals of time on the sun.

sun·stroke (sun′strōk′), *n.* a sudden illness caused by the sun's rays or by too much heat.

sun·ward (sun′wərd), *adj.* toward or facing the sun. —*adv.* Also, **sun′wards.** toward the sun.

Sun Yat-sen (sùn′ yät′sen′), 1867–1925, Chinese revolutionary leader and statesman.

sup¹ (sup), *v.*, **supped, sup·ping. 1.** eat the evening meal; take supper. **2.** give a supper to or for. [< OF *soper* < Gmc.]

sup² (sup), *v.*, **supped, sup·ping,** *n.* sip. [OE *sūpan*]

sup. 1. superior. **2.** superlative. **3.** supplement; supplementary. **4.** supra.

su·per (sü′pər), *n. Colloq.* **1.** supernumerary. **2.** superintendent. —*adj. Slang.* superfine; excellent.

super-, *prefix.* **1.** over; above, as in *superimpose, superstructure.* **2.** besides, as in *superadd, supertax.* **3.** in high proportion; to excess; exceedingly, as in *superabundant, supersensitive.* **4.** surpassing, as in *superman, supernatural.* [< L *super* over, above]

su·per·a·ble (sü′pər·ə·bəl), *adj.* capable of being overcome; surmountable. —**su′per·a·bil′i·ty,** *n.*

su·per·a·bound (sü′pər·ə·bound′), *v.* **1.** be very abundant. **2.** be too abundant.

su·per·a·bun·dant (sü′pər·ə·bun′dənt), *adj.* **1.** very abundant. **2.** more than enough. —**su′per·a·bun′dance,** *n.* —**su′per·a·bun′dant·ly,** *adv.*

su·per·add (sü′pər·ad′), *v.* add besides; add further. —**su·per·ad·di·tion** (sü′pər·ə·dish′ən), *n.*

su·per·an·nu·ate (sü′pər·an′yü·āt), *v.*, **-at·ed, -at·ing. 1.** retire on a pension because of age or infirmity. **2.** make old-fashioned or out-of-date. [< Med.L *superannatus* more than a year old < L *super annum* beyond a year; infl. in spelling by *annuus* annual] —**su′per·an′nu·a′tion,** *n.*

su·per·an·nu·at·ed (sü′pər·an′yü·āt′id), *adj.* **1.** retired on a pension. **2.** too old for work, service, etc. **3.** old-fashioned; out-of-date.

su·per·a·tom·ic bomb (sü′pər·ə·tom′ik), the hydrogen bomb.

su·perb (sù·pérb′), *adj.* **1.** stately; majestic; magnificent; splendid: *superb jewels, superb beauty.* **2.** rich; elegant; sumptuous. **3.** first-rate; excellent: *a superb book.* [< L *superbus*] —**su·perb′ly,** *adv.* —**su·perb′ness,** *n.* —**Syn. 1.** grand, imposing, beautiful.

su·per·car·go (sü′pər·kär′gō), *n., pl.* –goes, –gos. officer on a merchant ship who has charge of the cargo and the business affairs of the voyage. —su′per·car′go·ship, *n.*

su·per·charge (sü′pər·chärj′), *v.,* –charged, –charg·ing. 1. charge to excess. 2. use a supercharger on. 3. pressurize.

su·per·charg·er (sü′pər·chär′jər), *n.* blower, pump, etc., in an internal-combustion engine for forcing more of the mixture of air and gasoline vapor into the cylinders than the action of the pistons would draw.

su·per·cil·i·ous (sü′pər·sil′i·əs), *adj.* haughty, proud, and contemptuous; disdainful. [< L, < *supercilium* eyebrow < *super-* above + *cel-* cover] —su′per·cil′i·ous·ly, *adv.* —su′per·cil′i·ous·ness, *n.* —Ant. humble, modest, meek.

su·per·dread·nought (sü′pər·dred′nôt), *n.* a very large and heavily armed battleship.

su·per·er·o·ga·tion (sü′pər·er′ə·gā′shən), *n.* the doing of more than duty requires. [< LL, < L *super-* over + *erogare* pay out]

su·per·er·og·a·to·ry (sü′pər·ə·rog′ə·tô′ri, –tō′–), *adj.* 1. doing more than duty requires. 2. unnecessary; superfluous.

su·per·fi·cial (sü′pər·fish′əl), *adj.* 1. of or pertaining to the surface: *superficial measurement.* 2. on or at the surface: *a superficial wound.* 3. concerned with or understanding only what is on the surface; not thorough; shallow: *a superficial education.* 4. without profound effects or significance: *superficial changes.* 5. apparent rather than real: *superficial piety.* [< L, < *superficies* surface < *super-* above + *facies* form] —su·per·fi·ci·al·i·ty (sü′pər·fish′i·al′ə·ti), su′per·fi′cial·ness, *n.* —su′per·fi′cial·ly, *adv.*

su·per·fine (sü′pər·fīn′), *adj.* 1. very fine; extra fine. 2. too refined; too nice. —su′per·fine′ly, *adv.* —su′per·fine′ness, *n.*

su·per·flu·i·ty (sü′pər·flü′ə·ti), *n., pl.* –ties. 1. a greater amount than is needed; excess. 2. something not needed. —Syn. 1. superabundance, surfeit.

su·per·flu·ous (sù·pér′flü·əs), *adj.* 1. more than is needed. 2. needless. [< L, ult. < *super-* over + *fluere* flow] —su′per·flu·ous·ly, *adv.* —su′per·flu·ous·ness, *n.* —Syn. 1. excessive. 2. unnecessary, useless.

Su·per·fort (sü′pər·fôrt′; –fōrt′), **Su·per·for·tress** (–fôr′tris), *n.* a heavy, four-engine bomber of the U.S. Air Force.

su·per·heat (sü′pər·hēt′), *v.* 1. heat very hot; heat too hot; heat hotter than usual. 2. heat (a liquid) above its boiling point without producing vaporization. 3. heat (steam) apart from water until it resembles a dry or perfect gas. —su′per·heat′er, *n.*

su·per·het·er·o·dyne (sü′pər·het′ər·ə·dīn), *Radio.* —*adj.* of or pertaining to a kind of reception which reduces modulated waves (above audibility) to a lower frequency and in later stages rectifies the signals to audio-frequency amplification. —*n.* a superheterodyne radio receiving set.

su·per·high·way (sü′pər·hī′wā), *n.* an express highway.

su·per·hu·man (sü′pər·hü′mən), *adj.* 1. above or beyond what is human. 2. above or beyond ordinary human power, experience, etc. —su·per·hu·man·i·ty (sü′pər·hü·man′ə·ti), su′per·hu′man·ness, *n.* —su′per·hu′man·ly, *adv.*

su·per·im·pose (sü′pər·im·pōz′), *v.,* –posed, –pos·ing. 1. put on top of something else. 2. put or join as an addition. —su·per·im·po·si·tion (sü′pər·im′pə·zish′ən), *n.*

su·per·in·duce (sü′pər·in·düs′; –dūs′), *v.,* –duced, –duc·ing. bring in or develop as an addition. —su·per·in·duc·tion (sü′pər·in·duk′shən), *n.*

su·per·in·tend (sü′prin·tend′; sü′pər·in–), *v.* oversee and direct (work or workers); manage (a place, institution, etc.). —su′per·in·tend′ence, su′per·in·tend′en·cy, *n.* —Syn. supervise, administer, conduct.

su·per·in·tend·ent (sü′prin·ten′dənt; sü′pər·in–), *n.* person who oversees, directs, or

manages. —*adj.* superintending. —su′per·in·tend′ent·ship, *n.* —Syn. *n.* supervisor, controller.

su·pe·ri·or (sə·pir′i·ər; sù–), *adj.* 1. above the average; very good; excellent: *superior work in school.* 2. higher in quality or quantity; better; greater: *superior numbers of soldiers.* 3. higher in position, rank, importance, etc.: *superior officer.* 4. showing a feeling of being above others; proud: *superior airs, superior manners.* 5. *Printing.* higher than the main line of type. In x²y³, the ² and ³ are superior symbols. 6. superior to, a. higher than; above. b. better than; greater than. c. not giving in to; above yielding to. —*n.* 1. person who is superior: *a captain is a lieutenant's superior.* 2. head of a monastery or convent. [< L, compar. of *superus,* adj., above < *super,* prep., above] —su·pe·ri·or·i·ty (sə·pir′i·ôr′ə·ti; –or′–; sù–), *n.* —su·pe′ri·or·ly, *adv.*

Su·pe·ri·or (sə·pir′i·ər; sù–), *n.* Lake, the largest and northernmost of the five Great Lakes, between the United States and Canada.

superl., superlative.

su·per·la·tive (sə·pér′lə·tiv; sù–), *adj.* 1. of the highest kind; above all others; supreme: *King Solomon had superlative wisdom.* 2. *Gram.* expressing the highest degree of comparison of an adjective or adverb. *Fairest, best,* and *most slowly* are the superlative forms of *fair, good,* and *slowly.* —*n.* 1. person or thing above all others; supreme example. 2. *Gram.* a. the superlative degree. b. form or combination of words that shows this degree. 3. **talk in superlatives,** exaggerate. [< L *superlativus,* ult. < *super-* beyond + *latus,* pp. to *ferre* carry] —su·per′la·tive·ly, *adv.* —su·per′la·tive·ness, *n.*

su·per·man (sü′pər·man′), *n., pl.* –men. 1. man having more than human powers. 2. man so able as to seem superhuman.

super market, *Am.* a large grocery store in which customers select their purchases from open shelves and pay for them on a cash-and-carry basis.

su·per·nal (sù·pér′nəl), *adj.* 1. heavenly; divine. 2. lofty; exalted. [< L *supernus* < *super* above] —su·per′nal·ly, *adv.*

su·per·nat·u·ral (sü′pər·nach′ər·əl; –nach′rəl), *adj.* above or beyond what is natural. —*n.* **the supernatural,** supernatural agencies, influences, or phenomena. —su′per·nat′u·ral·ism, *n.* —su′per·nat′u·ral·ist, *n., adj.* —su′per·nat′u·ral·is′tic, *adj.* —su′per·nat′u·ral·ly, *adv.* —su′per·nat′u·ral·ness, *n.*

su·per·nu·mer·ar·y (sü′pər·nü′mər·er′i; –nū′–), *adj., n., pl.* –ar·ies. —*adj.* more than the usual or necessary number; extra. —*n.* 1. an extra person or thing. 2. *Theater.* person who appears on the stage but has no lines to speak.

su·per·pose (sü′pər·pōz′), *v.,* –posed, –pos·ing. place above or on something else. [< F, < *super-* above + *poser* POSE] —su·per·pos′a·ble, *adj.*

su·per·scribe (sü′pər·skrīb′), *v.,* –scribed, –scrib·ing. 1. write (words, letters, one's name, etc.) above, on, or outside of something. 2. address (a letter or parcel). [< LL, < L, < *super-* above + *scribere* write]

su·per·script (sü′pər·skript), *adj.* written above. —*n.* number, letter, etc., written above and to one side of a symbol. In aˣbⁿ the ˣ and the ⁿ are superscripts. —su′per·scrip′tion, *n.*

su·per·sede (sü′pər·sēd′), *v.,* –sed·ed, –sed·ing. 1. take the place of; cause to be set aside; displace. 2. fill the place of; replace. [< L *supersedere* be superior to, refrain from < *super-* above + *sedere* sit] —su′per·sed′ence, su·per·se·dure (sü′pər·sē′jər), *n.* —su′per·sed′er, *n.*

su·per·sen·si·tive (sü′pər·sen′sə·tiv), *adj.* extremely or morbidly sensitive. —su′per·sen′si·tive·ly, *adv.* —su′per·sen′si·tive·ness, *n.*

su·per·son·ic (sü′pər·son′ik), *adj.* 1. of or pertaining to sound waves beyond the limit of human audibility (above frequencies of 20,000 cycles per second). 2. greater than the speed of sound in air (1087 feet per second). 3. capable of moving at a speed greater than the speed of sound.

su·per·sti·tion (sü′pər·stish′ən), *n.* 1. an unreasoning fear of what is unknown or mysterious; unreasoning expectation. **2.** belief or practice founded on ignorant fear or mistaken reverence. **3.** any blindly accepted and unreasonable belief. [< L *superstitio* < *super* above + *stare* stand]

su·per·sti·tious (sü′pər·stish′əs), *adj.* full of superstition; likely to believe superstitions; caused by or pertaining to superstition. —**su′per·sti′tious·ly,** *adv.* —**su′per·sti′tious·ness,** *n.*

su·per·struc·ture (sü′pər·struk′chər), *n.* **1.** structure built on something else. **2.** all of a building above the foundation. **3.** *Naut.* parts of a ship above the main deck. —**su′per·struc′tur·al,** *adj.*

su·per·tax (sü′pər·taks′), *n.* tax in addition to a normal tax.

su·per·vene (sü′pər·vēn′), *v.,* -**vened,** -**ven·ing.** come as something additional or interrupting. [< L, < *super*- upon + *venire* come] —**su·per·ven·ience** (sü′pər·vēn′yəns), **su·per·ven·ion** (sü′pər·ven′shən), *n.* —**su′per·ven′ient,** *adj.*

su·per·vise (sü′pər·vīz′), *v.,* -**vised,** -**vis·ing.** look after and direct (work or workers, a process, etc.); oversee; superintend. [< Med.L *supervisus* < L *super*- over + *videre* see] —**su′per·vi′sor,** *n.* —**su′per·vi′sor·ship,** *n.* —**su·per·vi·so·ry** (sü′pər·vī′zə·ri), *adj.*

su·per·vi·sion (sü′pər·vizh′ən), *n.* management; direction; oversight.

su·pine (sü·pīn′), *adj.* **1.** lying flat on the back. **2.** lazily inactive; listless. [< L *supinus*] —**su·pine′ly,** *adv.* —**su·pine′ness,** *n.* —**Syn. 2.** languid, indolent, inert.

supp., suppl., supplement.

sup·per (sup′ər), *n.* the evening meal; meal eaten early in the evening if dinner is near noon, or late in the evening if dinner is at six or later. [< OF *soper,* orig. inf., SUP¹] —**sup′per·less,** *adj.*

sup·plant (sə·plant′; -plänt′), *v.* **1.** take the place of; displace or set aside. **2.** take the place of by unfair methods or by treacherous means. [< L *supplantare* trip up < *sub*- under + *planta* sole of the foot] —**sup·plan·ta·tion** (sup′lan-tā′shən), **sup·plant′ment,** *n.* —**sup·plant′er,** *n.*

sup·ple (sup′əl), *adj.,* -**pler,** -**plest,** *v.,* -**pled,** -**pling.** —*adj.* **1.** bending easily: *supple leather.* **2.** readily adaptable to different ideas, circumstances, people, etc.; yielding: *a supple mind.* **3.** limber; lithe: *supple movements.* —*v.* make or grow supple. [< OF < L *supplex* submissive] —**sup′ple·ly,** *adv.* —**sup′ple·ness,** *n.* **Syn.** *adj.* **1.** pliant, pliable, flexible. —**Ant.** *adj.* **1.** stiff.

sup·ple·ment (*n.* sup′lə·mənt; *v.* sup′lə·ment), *n.* **1.** something added to complete a thing, or to make it larger or better. **2.** *Math.* amount needed to make an angle or arc equal 180 degrees. —*v.* supply what is lacking in; add to; complete. [< L *supplementum,* ult. < *sub*- up + -*plere* fill] —**sup′ple·men·ta′tion,** *n.* —**sup′ple·ment′er,** *n.* —**Syn.** *n.* **1.** addition.

sup·ple·men·ta·ry (sup′lə·men′tə·ri; -tri), **sup·ple·men·tal** (-men′təl), *adj.* **1.** additional. **2.** added to supply what is lacking. **3.** *Math.* of or pertaining to the relationship of two angles whose sum is 180 degrees. —**sup′ple·men′ta·ri·ly,** *adv.*

Angle ABC is supplementary to angle ABD.

sup·pli·ant (sup′li·ənt), *adj.* asking humbly and earnestly: *a suppliant prayer for help.* —*n.* person who asks humbly and earnestly. [< F, ppr. of *supplier* SUPPLICATE] —**sup′pli·ant·ly,** *adv.* —**sup′pli·ant·ness,** *n.*

sup·pli·cant (sup′lə·kənt), *n., adj.* suppliant. [< L *supplicans,* ppr. of *supplicare* SUPPLICATE] —**sup′pli·cant·ly,** *adv.*

sup·pli·cate (sup′lə·kāt), *v.,* -**cat·ed,** -**cat·ing.** **1.** beg humbly and earnestly. **2.** pray humbly. [< L *supplicatus* < *sub*- down + *plicare* bend] —**sup′pli·cat′ing·ly,** *adv.* —**sup′pli·ca′tion,** *n.* —**sup′pli·ca′tor,** *n.* —**sup·pli·ca·to·ry** (sup′lə·kə·tô′ri; -tō′-), *adj.* —**Syn. 1.** implore, entreat, beseech, petition.

sup·ply¹ (sə·plī′), *v.,* -**plied,** -**ply·ing,** *n., pl.* -**plies.** —*v.* **1.** furnish; provide: *supply a person with money, clothing, etc.* **2.** make up for (a loss,

lack, absence, etc.): *supply a deficiency.* **3.** satisfy (a want, need, etc.): *supply the demand.* **4.** fill (a place, vacancy, pulpit, etc.) as a substitute: *a stump supplied the place of a chair.* —*n.* **1.** quantity ready for use; stock; store: *a supply of pencils and erasers.* **2.** quantity of an article in the market ready for purchase: *a supply of coffee.* **3.** one that supplies a vacancy. **4.** act of supplying. **5.** sum of money provided by Congress, or a like body, to meet the expenses of government. **6.** **supplies,** any necessary material things. Supplies for an army include food, clothing, medicines, etc. [< OF < L, < *sub*- up + -*plere* fill] —**sup·pli′er,** *n.* —**Syn.** *v.* **1.** afford.

sup·ply² (sup′li), *adv.* supplely.

sup·port (sə·pôrt′; -pōrt′), *v.* **1.** keep from falling; hold up: *walls support the roof.* **2.** give strength or courage to; keep up; help: *support one's endeavors.* **3.** provide shelter, clothing, etc. for: *a man should support his family.* **4.** be in favor of; back; second: *he supports the President.* **5.** advocate or uphold (a theory, etc.): *support socialism.* **6.** help prove; bear out: *the facts support his claim.* **7.** *Milit.* assist or protect (another unit) in combat: *artillery fire supported the infantry attack.* **8.** put up with; bear; endure. **9.** act with (a leading actor); assist; attend. **10.** act (a part or character) with success. —*n.* **1.** act of supporting; condition of being supported; help; aid: *he needs our support.* **2.** maintenance: *support of a family.* **3.** person or thing that supports; prop. **4.** *Milit.* **a.** assistance or protection given by one element or unit to another. **b.** unit which helps another unit in battle: *aviation may be used as a support for infantry.* **c.** part of any unit held back at the beginning of an attack as reserve. [< OF < L *supportare* bring up < *sub*- up + *portare* carry] —**sup·port′er,** *n.* —**sup·port′ing·ly,** *adv.* —**sup·port′less,** *adj.* —**Syn.** *v.* **1.** sustain, prop, brace. **2.** further, encourage. **3.** maintain, keep. **6.** verify, substantiate, confirm. **8.** undergo, suffer, tolerate. —*n.* **1.** assistance.

sup·port·a·ble (sə·pôr′tə·bəl; -pōr′-), *adj.* capable of being supported; bearable or endurable; sustainable; maintainable. —**sup·port′a·bil′i·ty, sup·port′a·ble·ness,** *n.* —**sup·port′a·bly,** *adv.*

sup·pose (sə·pōz′), *v.,* -**posed,** -**pos·ing.** **1.** assume (something) for the sake of argument: *suppose the distance is one mile.* **2.** consider as a possibility: *suppose we wait until tomorrow.* **3.** assume as true; believe: *suppose a document to be authentic.* **4.** take for granted; assume: *I supposed that you had gone.* **5.** think: *what do you suppose I'll do?* **6.** involve as necessary; imply: *an invention supposes an inventor.* [< OF, < *sub*- under + *poser* POSE] —**sup·pos′a·ble,** *adj.* —**sup·pos′a·bly,** *adv.* —**sup·pos′er,** *n.* —**Syn. 4.** presume, expect.

sup·posed (sə·pōzd′), *adj.* accepted as true; considered as possible or probable; assumed. —**sup·pos·ed·ly** (sə·pōz′id·li), *adv.*

sup·pos·ing (sə·pōz′ing), *conj.* in the event that; if: *supposing it rains, shall we go?*

sup·po·si·tion (sup′ə·zish′ən), *n.* **1.** act of supposing. **2.** thing supposed; belief; opinion. —**sup′po·si′tion·al,** *adj.* —**sup′po·si′tion·al·ly,** *adv.* —**Syn. 2.** assumption, conjecture.

sup·press (sə·pres′), *v.* **1.** put an end to; stop by force; put down: *suppress a revolution.* **2.** keep in; hold back; keep from appearing: *suppress a yawn.* **3.** withhold from disclosure or publication: *each nation suppressed news that was not favorable to it.* **4.** check the flow of; stop: *suppress bleeding.* [< L *suppressus* < *sub*- down + *premere* press] —**sup·press′er, sup·pres′sor,** *n.* —**sup·press′i·ble,** *adj.* —**sup·pres′sive,** *adj.* —**Syn. 1.** subdue, quell, crush. **2.** restrain, repress.

sup·pres·sion (sə·presh′ən), *n.* **1.** a putting down by force or authority; putting an end to: *the suppression of the revolt.* **2.** a keeping in; holding back: *suppression of a fear.*

sup·pu·rate (sup′yə·rāt), *v.,* -**rat·ed,** -**rat·ing.** form pus; discharge pus; fester. [< L *suppuratus* < *sub*- under + *pus* pus] —**sup′pu·ra′tion,** *n.* —**sup′pu·ra′tive,** *adj.*

su·pra (sü′prə), *adv.* **1.** above. **2.** before in a book or writing. [< L]

su·pra·na·tion·al (sü´prə-nash´ən-əl; -nash´-nəl), *adj.* above a nation or state, as in power or authority.

su·pra·re·nal (sü´prə-rē´nəl), *adj.* **1.** adrenal. **2.** pertaining to or connected with a suprarenal. —*n.* a ductless gland, situated on or near the kidney, that furnishes a secretion called adrenalin. [< *supra-* above (< L) + L *renes* kidneys]

su·prem·a·cy (sə-prem´ə-si; sü-), *n.* **1.** state of being supreme. **2.** supreme authority or power. —Syn. **2.** domination, predominance, mastery.

su·preme (sə-prēm´; sü-), *adj.* **1.** highest in rank or authority: *the supreme commander.* **2.** highest in degree; greatest; utmost: *supreme disgust.* **3.** highest in quality: *supreme courage.* **4.** last: *the supreme moment.* **5. make the supreme sacrifice,** give one's life; die. [< L *supremus,* ult. < *super* above] —**su·preme′ly,** *adv.* —**su·preme′ness,** *n.* —Syn. **1.** chief, paramount.

Supreme Being, God.

Supreme Court, 1. *Am.* **a.** the highest court in the United States, which meets at Washington, D.C. It consists of a chief justice and eight associate justices. **b.** the highest court in some States. **2.** a similar court in other countries.

Supt., supt., superintendent.

Su·ra·ba·ya (sü´rä-bä´yä), *n.* seaport in NE Java.

su·rah (sùr´ə), *n.* a soft twilled silk. [after *Surat,* India]

sur·cease (sėr-sēs´), *n. Archaic.* end; cessation. [< OF *sursis,* pp. of *surseoir* refrain < L *supersedere.* See SUPERSEDE.]

sur·charge (*n.* sėr´chärj´; *v.* sėr-chärj´), *n., v.,* **-charged, -charg·ing.** —*n.* **1.** an extra charge. **2.** an additional mark printed on a postage stamp to change its value, date, etc. —*v.* **1.** charge extra. **2.** overcharge. **3.** overload: *a heart surcharged with grief.* **4.** print a surcharge on (a postage stamp). [< OF, < *sur-* over (< L *super-*) + *charg(i)er* CHARGE] —**sur·charg′er,** *n.*

sur·cin·gle (sėr´sing-gəl), *n.* a strap or belt around a horse's body to keep a saddle, blanket, or pack in place. [< OF, < *sur-* over (< L *super-*) + *cengle* girdle < L *cingula*]

sur·coat (sėr´kōt´), *n.* an outer coat, esp. a garment worn by knights over their armor. [< OF, < *sur-* over (< L *super-*) + *cote* COAT]

surd (sėrd), *n.* **1.** *Phonet.* a sound uttered without vibration of the vocal cords. The sounds of *f, k, p, s* (as in *sit*), and *t* are surds. **2.** *Math.* quantity that cannot be expressed in whole numbers. *Example:* $\sqrt{2}$. —*adj.* **1.** *Phonet.* uttered without vibrations of the vocal chords. **2.** *Math.* that cannot be expressed in whole numbers. [< L *surdus* unheard]

Surcoat

sure (shùr), *adj., v.,* sur·er, sur·est, *adv.* —*adj.* **1.** free from doubt: *be sure of one's friends.* **2.** confident: *sure of success in the end.* **3.** fully persuaded; convinced: *sure of a person's guilt.* **4.** certain (to do, be, happen, etc.): *he is sure to come.* **5.** to be trusted; safe; reliable: *a sure messenger.* **6.** never missing, slipping, etc.; unfailing; unerring: *sure aim, a sure touch.* **7.** admitting of no doubt or question: *sure proof.* **8.** firm or stable: *stand on sure ground.* **9.** *Archaic.* secure or safe. **10. be sure,** be careful; do not fail. **11. for sure,** surely; certainly. **12. make sure, a.** act so as to make something certain. **b.** get sure knowledge. **13. to be sure,** surely; certainly. —*adv. Colloq.* surely; certainly. [< OF < L *securus.* Doublet of SECURE.] —**sure′ness,** *n.* —Syn. *adj.* **5.** trustworthy. **6.** infallible. ▶ **Sure** is primarily an adjective: *sure footing, are you sure?* As an adverb, *sure* instead of *surely* or equivalent to *certainly* or *yes,* is colloquial: *Sure, I'm coming. That sure is fine of you.*

sure-foot·ed (shùr´fùt´id), *adj.* not liable to stumble, slip, or fall. —**sure′-foot′ed·ness,** *n.*

sure·ly (shùr´li), *adv.* **1.** undoubtedly; certainly: *half a loaf is surely better than none.* **2.** without mistake; without missing, slipping, etc.;

firmly: *the goat leaped surely from rock to rock.* **3.** as must be believed: *surely you are mistaken.* **4.** without fail: *slowly but surely.*

sure·ty (shùr´ə-ti), *n., pl.* **-ties. 1.** security against loss, damage, or failure to do something: *an insurance company gives surety.* **2.** person who agrees to be responsible for another. **3.** *Archaic.* a sure thing; certainty. —**sur′e·ty·ship,** *n.* —Syn. **1.** guaranty, pledge.

surf (sėrf), *n.* waves or swell of the sea breaking on the shore or upon shoals, reefs, etc.

sur·face (sėr´fis), *n., adj., v.,* **-faced, -fac·ing.** —*n.* **1.** the outside of anything: *the surface of a golf ball, the surface of a mountain.* **2.** any face or side of a thing: *a cube has six surfaces.* **3.** that which has length and breadth but no thickness: *a plane surface in geometry.* **4.** extent or area of outer face. **5.** the outward appearance, esp. as distinguished from the inner nature: *he is very kind below the surface.* —*adj.* **1.** of or on the surface; pertaining to the surface. **2.** apparent rather than real; superficial: *surface manners.* —*v.* put a surface on; make smooth: *surface a road.* [< MF, < *sur-* above (< L *super-*) + *face* FACE] —**sur′fac·er,** *n.*

sur·face-to-sur·face (sėr´fis-tü-sėr´fis), *adj.* launched from the ground to intercept and destroy a flying aircraft, missile, etc.

surf·board (sėrf´bôrd´; -bōrd´), *n.* a long, narrow board for riding the surf.

surf·boat (sėrf´bōt´), *n.* a strong boat specially made for use in heavy surf. —**surf′boat′man,** *n.*

sur·feit (sėr´fit), *n.* **1.** too much; excess, esp. in eating or drinking. **2.** disgust caused by excess or satiety. —*v.* overfeed; satiate. [< OF *surfait,* orig. pp., overdone < *sur-* above (< L *super-*) + *faire* do < L *facere*] —Syn. *v.* glut.

surg., surgery; surgical.

surge (sėrj), *v.,* surged, surg·ing, *n.* —*v.* **1.** rise and fall; move like waves: *the crowd surged through the streets.* **2.** increase suddenly; rush: *blood surged to his face.* —*n.* **1.** a swelling wave; sweep or rush of waves; something like a wave: *a surge of anger.* **2.** the swelling and rolling of the sea. **3.** a surging, wavelike volume or body of something. **4.** *Elect.* a sudden rush of current; violent oscillation. **5.** a slipping back. [ult. <prob. through OF) < L *surgere* rise] —**surg′y,** *adj.*

sur·geon (sėr´jən), *n.* doctor who performs operations. [< AF *surgien,* OF *cirurgien* < *cirurgie* SURGERY] —**sur′geon·cy,** *n.*

sur·ger·y (sėr´jər-i), *n., pl.* **-ger·ies. 1.** the art and science of treating diseases, injuries, etc., by operations and instruments. Malaria can be cured by medicine, but a ruptured appendix requires surgery. **2.** office, laboratory, or operating room of a surgeon. [< OF *surgerie, cirurgerie,* < *cirurgie* < L < Gk. *cheirourgia,* ult. < *cheir* hand + *ergon* work]

sur·gi·cal (sėr´jə-kəl), *adj.* **1.** of or having to do with surgery. **2.** used in surgery. **3.** performed by a surgeon. —**sur′gi·cal·ly,** *adv.*

Su·ri·nam (sùr´ə-nam), *n.* an autonomous Dutch territory in the N part of South America.

sur·ly (sėr´li), *adj.,* **-li·er, -li·est.** bad-tempered and unfriendly; rude; gruff. [ult. < *sir,* in sense of "lord"] —**sur′li·ly,** *adv.* —**sur′li·ness,** *n.* —Syn. sullen, churlish, cross. —Ant. genial.

sur·mise (*v.* sər-mīz´; *n.* sər-mīz´, sėr´mīz), *v.,* **-mised, -mis·ing.** —*v.* form a conjecture (regarding); guess. —*n.* **1.** a mental conception; conjecture. **2.** a matter of conjecture. [< OF, accusation, ult. < *sur-* upon (< L *super-*) + *mettre* put < L *mittere* send] —**sur·mis′er,** *n.*

sur·mount (sər-mount´), *v.* **1.** rise above. **2.** be above or on top of: *the peak surmounts the valley.* **3.** go up and across: *surmount a hill.* **4.** overcome: *he surmounted many difficulties.* [< OF, < *sur-* over (< L *super-*) + *monter* MOUNT] —**sur·mount′a·ble,** *adj.*

sur·name (sėr´nām´), *n., v.,* **-named, -nam·ing.** —*n.* **1.** a last name; family name. **2.** name added to a person's real name. William I of England had the surname "the Conqueror." —*v.* give an added name to; call by a surname. [< F, < *sur-* over (< L *super-*) + *nom* name < L *nomen;* infl. by E *name*]

sur·pass (sər·pas′; -päs′), v. 1. do better than; be greater than; excel: *his work surpassed expectations.* 2. be too much or too great for; go beyond; exceed: *the horrors of the battlefield surpassed description.* [< F, < *sur-* beyond + *passer* pass] —**sur·pass′a·ble,** adj. —**sur·pass′er,** n. —**sur·pass′ing·ly,** adv. —**sur·pass′ing·ness,** n. —Syn. 1. outdo, outstrip, outrun, eclipse.

sur·plice (sér′plis), n. a broad-sleeved, white gown worn by clergymen and choir singers over their other clothes. [< OF, < *sur-* over (< L *super-*) + *pelice* fur garment, ult. < L *pellis* hide] —**sur′pliced,** adj.

sur·plus (sér′pləs; -plus), n. 1. amount over and above what is needed; extra quantity left over; excess. 2. excess of assets over liabilities. —adj. more than is needed; excess: *surplus wheat and cotton are shipped abroad.* [< OF, < *sur-* over (< L *super-*) + *plus* PLUS] —**sur·plus·age** (sér′plus·ij), n. —Syn. n. 1. residue, remainder.

sur·prise (sər·prīz′; sə-), n., v., -prised, -pris·ing, adj. —n. 1. a feeling caused by something unexpected. 2. something unexpected. 3. a catching unprepared; coming upon suddenly. 4. take by surprise, a. catch unprepared; come on suddenly and unexpectedly. b. astonish. —v. 1. cause to feel surprised; astonish: *the magician's trick surprised me.* 2. catch unprepared; come upon suddenly: *the enemy surprised the fort.* 3. lead or bring (a person, etc.) unawares: *the news surprised her into tears.* —adj. that is not expected; surprising: *a surprise party, a surprise visit.* [< OF, < *sur-* over (< L *super-*) + *prendre* take < L *prehendere*] —**sur·pris′al,** n. —**sur·pris′ed·ly** (sər·prīz′id·li; sə-), adv. —**sur·pris′er,** n. —Syn. n. 1. astonishment, amazement, wonder. -v. 1. amaze, astound, dumfound.

sur·pris·ing (sər·prīz′ing; sə-), adj. causing surprise. n. —**sur·pris′ing·ly,** adv. —**sur·pris′ing·ness,** n. —Syn. astonishing, amazing, striking.

sur·re·al·ism (sə·rē′əl·iz·əm), n. a modern movement in painting, sculpture, literature, etc., that tries to show what takes place in the subconscious mind. —**sur·re′al·ist,** n., adj. —**sur·re′al·is′tic,** adj. —**sur·re′al·is′ti·cal·ly,** adv.

sur·ren·der (sə·ren′dər), v. 1. give up; give (oneself or itself) up; yield: *the captain had to surrender to the enemy, surrender oneself to grief.* —n. act of surrendering. [< OF *sur-* over (< L *super-*) + *rendre* RENDER] —**sur·ren′der·er,** n. —Syn. v. relinquish, resign, abandon.

sur·rep·ti·tious (sér′əp·tish′əs), adj. 1. stealthy; secret. 2. secret and unauthorized. [< L *surrepticius,* ult. < *sub-* secretly + *rapere* snatch] —**sur′rep·ti′tious·ly,** adv. —**sur′rep·ti′tious·ness,** n.

sur·rey (sér′i), n., pl. -reys. Am. a light, four-wheeled carriage having two seats. [after *Surrey,* England]

sur·ro·gate (n. sér′ə·gāt, -git; v. sér′ə·gāt), n., v., -gat·ed, -gat·ing. —n. 1. a substitute; deputy, esp. the deputy of a bishop. 2. Am. in certain States, a judge having charge of the probate of wills, the administration of estates, etc. —v. put into the place of another; substitute for another. [< L *surrogatus* substituted < *sub-* instead + *rogare* ask for] —**sur′ro·gate·ship′,** n.

sur·round (sə·round′), v. 1. shut in on all sides; extend around: *a high fence surrounds the field.* 2. encircle: *they surrounded the invalid with every comfort.* [< AF *surrounder* surpass < LL *superundare* overflow < L *super-* over + *unda* wave; infl. in meaning by *round*] —**sur·round′er,** n. —Syn. 1. enclose, encompass.

sur·round·ing (sə·roun′ding), n. 1. that which surrounds. 2. surroundings, surrounding things, conditions, etc. —adj. enclosing; surrounding; enveloping.

sur·tax (sér′taks′), n. an additional or extra tax. [< F *surtaxe* < *sur-* over + *taxe* tax]

sur·tout (sér·tüt′, -tü′), n. a man's overcoat. [< F, < *sur-* over + *tout* all]

sur·veil·lance (sər·vāl′əns; -yəns), n. 1. watch kept over a person: *the police kept the criminal under strict surveillance.* 2. supervision. [< F, < *sur-* over (< L *super-*) + *veiller* watch < L *vigilare*] —**sur·veil′lant,** adj.

sur·vey (v. sər·vā′; n. sér′vā, sər·vā′), v., n., pl. -veys. —v. 1. look over; view; examine: *survey a field of study.* 2. measure for size, shape, position, boundaries, etc.: *men are surveying the land before it is divided into house lots.* 3. survey land. —n. 1. a general look; view. 2. a formal examination or inspection. 3. a written statement or description of this. 4. a careful measurement. 5. map, plan, or description of such a measurement. [< AF *surveier,* ult. < L *super-* over + *videre* see] —**sur·vey′a·ble,** adj.

sur·vey·ing (sər·vā′ing), n. 1. business or act of making surveys of land. 2. mathematical instruction in the principles and art of making surveys.

sur·vey·or (sər·vā′ər), n. 1. person who surveys, esp. land. 2. a customs official who finds out the quantity and value of things brought in from another country. —**sur·vey′or·ship,** n.

surveyor's measure, system of measuring used by surveyors. The unit is usually a chain 66 ft. long with links 7.92 in. long. 100,000 square links = 1 square acre.

sur·viv·al (sər·vīv′əl), n. 1. act or fact of surviving; continuance of life; living or lasting longer than others. 2. person, thing, custom, belief, etc., that has lasted from an earlier time.

sur·vive (sər·vīv′), v., -vived, -viv·ing. 1. live longer than; remain alive after: *he survived his wife by three years; survive an accident.* 2. exist longer than: *the crops survived the drought.* 3. continue to exist; remain: *books have survived from the time of the Egyptians.* [< AF, < *sur-* over (< L *super-*) + *vivre* live < L *vivere*] —**sur·viv′ing,** adj. —**sur·vi′vor, sur·viv′er,** n.

sus·cep·ti·bil·i·ty (sə·sep′tə·bil′ə·ti), n., pl. -ties. 1. quality or state of being susceptible; readiness to receive impressions; sensitiveness. 2. susceptibilities, sensitive feelings.

sus·cep·ti·ble (sə·sep′tə·bəl), adj. 1. easily influenced by feelings or emotions; very sensitive: *a susceptible heart.* 2. susceptible of, a. capable of receiving or undergoing: *oak is susceptible of a high polish.* b. sensitive to. 3. susceptible to, easily affected by; liable to; open to: *vain people are susceptible to flattery.* [< LL *susceptibilis,* ult. < L *sub-* up + *capere* take] —**sus·cep′ti·ble·ness,** n. —**sus·cep′ti·bly,** adv. —Syn. 1. impressionable, tender.

sus·pect (v. səs·pekt′; n. sus′pekt; adj. sus′pekt, səs·pekt′), v. 1. imagine to be so; think likely: *the old fox suspected danger.* 2. believe guilty, false, bad, etc., without proof: *the policeman suspected the thief of lying.* 3. feel no confidence in; doubt: *the judge suspected the truth of the thief's excuse.* 4. be suspicious. —n. person suspected. —adj. open to suspicion; suspected. [< L, < *sub-* under + *specere* look] —**sus·pect′a·ble,** adj. —**sus·pect′er,** n. —Syn. v. 1. surmise, conjecture.

sus·pend (səs·pend′), v. 1. hang down by attaching to something above: *the lamp was suspended from the ceiling.* 2. hold in place as if by hanging: *smoke suspended in still air.* 3. stop for a while: *suspend work.* 4. stop payment; be unable to pay one's debts. 5. remove or exclude for a while from some privilege or job: *he was suspended for bad conduct.* 6. refrain from concluding definitely; keep undecided; put off: *the court suspended judgment till next Monday.* [< L, < *sub-* up + *pendere* hang] —Syn. 1. dangle, swing. 3. interrupt, intermit, delay. 6. defer, withhold. —Ant. 3. continue, proceed.

sus·pend·er (səs·pen′dər), n. 1. suspenders, straps worn over the shoulders to hold up the trousers. 2. Brit. garter.

sus·pense (səs·pens′), n. 1. condition of being uncertain: *the detective story kept me in suspense until the last chapter.* 2. anxious uncertainty; anxiety: *mothers feel suspense when their children are very sick.* 3. condition of being undecided: *the matter hung in suspense for a few days.* [< OF (en) *suspens* (in) abeyance, ult. < L *suspensus.* See SUSPEND]

sus·pen·sion (səs·pen′shən), n. 1. a suspending or being suspended. 2. support on which something is suspended. 3. a temporary abolishment or setting aside of a law, rule, etc. 4. arrangement of springs for supporting the body of an automobile, railroad car, etc. 5. *Physics.* a. mixture in which very small particles of a solid remain suspended without dissolving. b. the condition of the solid in such a mixture. c. a solid in such condition. 6. *Physical Chem.* a system of finely divided particles kept in motion by the molecules of a liquid, gas, etc., or by agitation. 7. *Music.* a. a holding back of the progression of a part in harmony by prolonging a tone in one chord into the following chord, usually producing a temporary discord. b. the tone so prolonged. 8. stoppage of payment of debts or claims because of financial inability or insolvency; business failure. —**Syn. 1.** interruption, intermission, stop, postponement, respite.

sus·pen·sion bridge, bridge hung on cables or chains between towers.

Suspension bridge

sus·pen·so·ry (səs-pen'sə-ri), *adj.*, *n.*, *pl.* -ries. —*adj.* 1. holding up; supporting. 2. stopping for a while; leaving undecided. —*n.* a muscle, ligament, bandage, etc., that holds up or supports a part of the body.

sus·pi·cion (səs-pish'ən), *n.* 1. state of mind of a person who suspects; suspecting: *the real thief tried to turn suspicion toward others.* 2. condition of being suspected: *they are above suspicion.* 3. an instance of suspecting something. 4. a vague notion: *he never had a suspicion that it was true.* 5. a very small amount; slight trace; suggestion: *she spoke with a suspicion of spite.* 6. **on suspicion,** because of being suspected. 7. **under suspicion,** suspected. [< L. See SUSPECT.] —**Syn. 1.** doubt, distrust, misgiving. ► **suspicion.** As a verb *suspicion* (nobody *suspicioned who it was*) is substandard. *Suspect* is the formal and informal verb.

sus·pi·cious (səs-pish'əs), *adj.* 1. causing one to suspect: *a man was hanging about the house in a suspicious manner.* 2. feeling suspicion; suspecting: *our dog is suspicious of strangers.* 3. showing suspicion: *the dog gave a suspicious sniff at my leg.* —**sus·pi'cious·ly,** *adv.* —**sus·pi'cious·ness,** *n.* —**Syn. 1.** questionable, doubtful. 2. distrustful, mistrustful.

sus·pire (səs-pīr'), *v.*, -pired, -pir·ing. *Poetic.* 1. sigh. 2. breathe; breathe forth. [< L, < *sub*-up + *spirare* breathe] —**sus·pi·ra·tion** (sus'pə-rā'shən), *n.*

Sus·que·han·na (sus'kwə-han'ə), *n.* river flowing from C New York State through Pennsylvania and Maryland into Chesapeake Bay.

sus·tain (səs-tān'), *v.* 1. keep up; keep going: *hope sustains him in his misery.* 2. supply with food, provisions, etc.: *sustain an army.* 3. hold up; support: *arches sustain the weight of the roof.* 4. bear; endure: *the sea wall sustains the shock of the waves.* 5. suffer; experience: *sustain a great loss.* 6. allow; admit; favor: *the court sustained his suit.* 7. agree with; confirm. [< OF < L, < *sub*- up + *tenere* hold] —**sus·tain'a·ble,** *adj.* —**sus·tain·ed·ly** (səs-tān'id-li), *adv.* —**sus·tain'er,** *n.* —**sus·tain'ment,** *n.* —**Syn. 1.** aid, assist, comfort, relieve. 4. stand. 5. undergo. 7. corroborate, sanction.

sustaining program, *Radio.* program having no sponsor but maintained at the expense of a station or network.

sus·te·nance (sus'tə-nəns), *n.* 1. food. 2. means of living; support.

sut·ler (sut'lər), *n.* person who follows an army and sells provisions, etc., to the soldiers. [< earlier Du. *soeteler* < *soetelen* ply a low trade] —**sut'ler·ship,** *n.*

sut·tee (su-tē', sut'ē), *n.* 1. a Hindu widow who throws herself on the burning funeral pile of her husband. 2. former Hindu custom of burning a widow with the body of her husband. [< Hind. < Skt. *satī* faithful wife] —**sut·tee'ism,** *n.*

su·ture (sü'chər), *n.*, *v.*, -tured, -tur·ing. —*n.* 1. seam formed in sewing up a wound. 2. method of doing this. 3. one of the stitches or fastenings used. 4. a sewing together or a joining as if by

sewing. 5. *Anat.* line where two bones, esp. of the skull, join. —*v.* unite by suture or as if by a suture. [< L, < *suere* sew] —**su'tur·al,** *adj.*

su·ze·rain (sü'zə·rin; -rān), *n.* 1. a feudal lord. 2. state or government exercising political control over a dependent state. [< F, < *sus* above (< L *sursum* upward), modeled on *souverain* sovereign]

su·ze·rain·ty (sü'zə·rin·ti; -rān'-), *n.*, *pl.* -ties. position or authority of a suzerain.

s.v., under the word or heading. [< L *sub verbo* or *sub voce*]

svelte (svelt), *adj.* slender; lithe. [< F]

SW, S.W., s.w., southwest; southwestern.

Sw., 1. Sweden. 2. Swedish.

swab (swob), *n.*, *v.*, swabbed, swab·bing. —*n.* 1. a mop for cleaning decks, floors, etc. 2. a bit of sponge, cloth, or cotton for cleansing some part of the body or for applying medicine to it. 3. a cleaner for a tube. 4. *Slang.* an awkward, clumsy person. —*v.* clean with a swab; apply a swab to: *swab a person's throat.* Also, **swob.** [< *swabber*, < Du. *zwabber* < *zwabben* swab] —**swab'ber,** *n.*

swad·dle (swod'əl), *v.*, -dled, -dling, *n.* —*v.* bind (a baby) with long, narrow strips of cloth; wrap tightly with clothes, bandages, etc. —*n.* cloth used for swaddling. [OE *swæthel* band-(age); akin to SWATHE]

swaddling clothes, long, narrow strips of cloth for wrapping a newborn infant.

swag (swag), *n.* 1. *Slang.* things stolen; booty; plunder; dishonest political gains. 2. *Australian.* bundle of personal belongings. 3. an ornamental festoon of flowers, leaves, ribbons, etc. [prob. < Scand. (dial. Norw.) *svagga* sway]

swag·ger (swag'ər), *v.* 1. walk with a bold, rude, or superior air; strut about or show off in a vain or insolent way. 2. boast or brag noisily. 3. bluster; affect by bluster; bluff. —*n.* a swaggering way of walking or acting. —*adj. Colloq.* very fashionable. [< *swag*] —**swag'ger·er,** *n.* —**swag'ger·ing·ly,** *adv.*

swagger stick, a short, light stick or cane, sometimes carried by soldiers.

swain (swān), *n. Archaic or Poetic.* 1. lover. 2. a young man who lives in the country. [< Scand. *sveinn* boy] —**swain'ish,** *adj.* —**swain'ish·ness,** *n.*

swale (swāl), *n. Am.* a low, wet piece of land; low place. [cf. Scand. *svalr* cool]

swal·low[1] (swol'ō), *v.* 1. take into the stomach through the throat: *swallow food.* 2. perform the act of swallowing: *I cannot swallow.* 3. take in; absorb: *the waves swallowed up the swimmer.* 4. *Colloq.* believe too easily; accept without question or suspicion: *he will swallow any story.* 5. put up with; take meekly; accept without opposing or desisting: *he had to swallow the insult.* 6. take back: *swallow words said in anger.* 7. keep back; keep from expressing: *she swallowed her displeasure and smiled.* —*n.* 1. a swallowing: *he took the medicine at one swallow.* 2. amount swallowed at one time. [< OE *swelgan*] —**swal'low·a·ble,** *adj.* —**swal'low·er,** *n.*

swal·low[2] (swol'ō), *n.* 1. a small, swift-flying bird with a deeply forked tail, noted for the extent and quickness of its migratory movements. 2. a martin or other bird of the same family as the swallow. 3. any of certain swifts that resemble swallows. [OE *swealwe*] —**swal'low·like',** *adj.*

swal·low·tail (swol'ō-tāl'), *n.* 1. thing shaped like or suggesting the deeply forked tail of a swallow. 2. a swallow-tailed coat. —**swal'low-tailed',** *adj.*

swallow-tailed coat, a man's coat with tails, worn at formal evening parties.

Swallow-tailed coat

swam (swam), *v.* pt. of swim.

swa·mi (swä'mi), *n.*, *pl.* -mis. title of a Hindu religious teacher. [< Hind., master, < Skt. *svāmin*]

swamp (swomp; swômp), *n.* wet, soft land. —*v.* 1. plunge or sink in a swamp or in water. 2. fill with water and sink: *their boat swamped, the wave swamped the boat.* 3. overwhelm or be overwhelmed as by a flood; make or become helpless. [akin to SUMP] —swamp′ish, *adj.* —swamp′less, *adj.* —swamp′y, *adj.* —Syn. *n.* marsh, morass, bog, fen, slough, quagmire.

swamp·land (swomp′land'; swômp′-), *n.* tract of land covered by swamps.

swan (swon; swôn), *n.* 1. a large, graceful water bird with a long, slender, curving neck, and in most species a pure white plumage in the adult. 2. a sweet singer; poet. [OE] —swan′like', *adj.*

swan dive, *Am.* a graceful dive in which the legs are held straight from the toes to the hips, the back is curved, and the arms are spread like the wings of a gliding bird.

swang (swang), *v. Archaic and Dial.* pt. of swing.

swank (swangk), *Slang.* —*v.* show off; bluff; swagger. —*n.* 1. a showing off. 2. style; smartness; dash. —*adj.* Also, swank′y, stylish; smart; dashing. [cf. OE *swancor* lithe] —swank′i·ly, *adv.* —swank′i·ness, *n.*

swan's-down, **swans·down** (swonz′doun'; swônz′-), *n.* 1. the soft down of a swan, used for trimming, powder puffs, etc. 2. a fine, thick, soft cloth made from wool or cotton, used for babies' coats, bathrobes, etc.

swan song, 1. song which a dying swan is supposed to sing. 2. a person's last piece of work.

swap (swop), *v.*, swapped, swap·ping, *n. Colloq.* exchange; barter; trade. Also, swop. —swap′per, *n.*

sward (swôrd), *n.* a grassy surface; turf. —*v.* cover with sward or turf. [OE *sweard* skin] —sward′y, *adj.*

sware (swâr), *v. Archaic.* pt. of swear.

swarm[1] (swôrm), *n.* 1. group of bees that leave a hive and fly off together to start a new colony. 2. group of bees settled together in a hive. 3. a large group of insects flying or moving about together. 4. aggregation of free-floating or free-swimming cells or unicellular organisms. 5. group of persons or things moving about in a confused mass; crowd. —*v.* 1. of bees, fly off together to start a new colony. 2. fly or move about in great numbers; be in very great numbers. 3. be crowded: *the swamp swarms with mosquitoes.* 4. crowd. [OE *swearm*] —swarm′er, *n.* —Syn. *n.* 5. multitude, throng.

swarm[2] (swôrm), *v.* climb; shin.

swart (swôrt), *adj.* dark; swarthy. [OE *sweart*] —swart′ness, *n.*

swarth (swôrth), *adj. Archaic.* swarthy.

swarth·y (swôr′thi; -thi), *adj.*, swarth·i·er, swarth·i·est. dark-colored or having a dark skin. [earlier *swarfy* < *swarf* grit, OE *geswearf*] —swarth′i·ly, *adv.* —swarth′i·ness, *n.*

swash (swosh), *v.* dash (water, etc.) about; splash. —*n.* such action or sound. [prob. imit.] —swash′er, *n.* —swash′ing·ly, *adv.*

swash·buck·ler (swosh′buk'lər), *n.* a swaggering swordsman, bully, or boaster. [< *swash* + *buckler*] —swash′buck'ling, swash′buck'ler-ing, *n.*, *adj.*

swas·ti·ka (swos′tə·kə), *n.* an ancient symbol or ornament consisting of a cross with arms of equal length, each arm having a continuation at right angles, and all four continuations turning the same way. The swastika with arms turning clockwise was adopted as the symbol of the Nazis in Germany. [< Skt., < *svasti* luck < *su* well + *as* be]

swat (swot), *v.*, swat·ted, swat·ting, *n. Colloq.* —*v.* hit with a smart or violent blow. —*n.* a smart or violent blow. —swat′ter, *n.*

swatch (swoch), *n.* sample of cloth or other material.

swath (swoth; swôth), *n.* 1. the space covered by a single cut of a scythe or by one cut of a mowing machine. 2. row of grass, grain, etc., cut by a scythe or mowing machine. 3. a strip. 4. cut a wide swath, make a showy display; splurge. [OE *swæth* track, trace]

swathe[1] (swāth), *v.*, swathed, swath·ing, *n.* —*v.* 1. wrap up closely or fully. 2. bind; wrap;

bandage. 3. envelop or surround like a wrapping. —*n.* a wrapping; bandage. [OE *swathian*]

swathe[2] (swāth), *n.* swath.

sway (swā), *v.* 1. swing back and forth; swing from side to side, or to one side: *the tree sways in the wind.* 2. make move; cause to sway: *the wind sways the grass.* 3. move to one side; turn aside; change in opinion, feeling, etc.: *nothing could sway his political beliefs.* 4. incline to one side; lean. 5. influence; control; rule. —*n.* 1. a swaying. 2. influence; control; rule. [< Scand. *sveigja*] —sway′er, *n.* —sway′ing·ly, *adv.* —Syn. *v.* 1. wave, fluctuate, oscillate.

sway·back (swā′bak'), *n.* hollow or sag of the back. —*adj.* sway-backed.

sway-backed (swā′bakt'), *adj.* 1. of horses, etc., strained in the back by overwork or the like. 2. having the back sagged or hollowed to an unusual degree.

swear (swâr), *v.*, swore or (*Archaic*) sware, sworn, swear·ing. 1. make a solemn statement, appealing to God or some other sacred being or object for confirmation; take oath. 2. declare, calling God to witness; make solemn oath; declare on oath. 3. bind by an oath; require to promise: *members of the club were sworn to secrecy.* 4. admit to office or service by administering an oath to: *swear a witness.* 5. promise solemnly; vow. 6. bring, set, take, etc., by swearing: *swear a person's life away.* 7. utter (an oath). 8. use profane language; curse. 9. swear by, a. name as one's witness in taking an oath. b. have great confidence in. 10. swear in, admit to office or service by giving an oath. 11. swear off, promise to give up. [OE *swerian*] —swear′er, *n.*

sweat (swet), *n.*, *v.*, sweat or sweat·ed, sweat·ing. —*n.* 1. moisture coming through the pores of the skin. 2. fit or condition of sweating: *he was in a cold sweat from fear.* 3. process of sweating or of being sweated. 4. *Colloq.* fit of suffering, anxiety, impatience, or anything that might make a person sweat. 5. moisture given out by something or gathered on its surface. —*v.* 1. give out moisture through the pores of the skin. 2. cause to sweat. 3. cause to give off moisture; ferment: *sweat tobacco in preparing it for use.* 4. come out in drops; ooze. 5. send out in drops. 6. wet or stain with sweat. 7. give out moisture; collect moisture from the air: *a pitcher of ice water sweats on a hot day.* 8. *Colloq.* suffer from anxiety, impatience, etc. 9. cause to work hard and under bad conditions: *that employer sweats his workers.* 10. *Colloq.* work very hard. 11. *Slang.* subject (a person) to a brutal or unfair questioning, etc., in order to extract information. 12. heat (solder) till it melts; join (metal parts) by heating. 13. heat (metal) in order to remove an easily fusible constituent. [OE *swætan*] —sweat′less, *adj.* —sweat′y, *adj.* —sweat′i·ly, *adv.* —sweat′i·ness, *n.*

sweat·er (swet′ər), *n.* a knitted jacket, usually of wool.

sweat gland, a small gland, just under the skin, that secretes sweat.

sweat·shop (swet′shop'), *n. Am.* place where workers are employed at low pay for long hours under bad conditions.

Swede (swēd), *n.* native or inhabitant of Sweden.

Swe·den (swē′dən), *n.* country in N Europe, E and S of Norway.

Swe·den·borg (swē′dən·bôrg), *n.* Emanuel, 1688–1772, Swedish philosopher, scientist, and mystic. —Swe·den·bor·gi·an (swē′dən·bôr′ji·ən), *n.*, *adj.* —Swe′den·bor′gi·an·ism, *n.*

Swed·ish (swēd′ish), *adj.* of or pertaining to Sweden, its people, or their language. —*n.* 1. people of Sweden. 2. language of Sweden.

sweep (swēp), *v.*, swept, sweep·ing, *n.* —*v.* 1. clean or clear (a floor, etc.) with a broom, brush, etc.; use a broom or something like one to remove dirt; brush: *sweep the steps.* 2. move, drive, or take away with or as with a broom, brush, etc.: *the wind sweeps the snow into drifts.* 3. move with a sweeping motion; carry along: *a flood swept away the bridge.* 4. trail upon: *her dress sweeps the ground.* 5. pass over with a steady movement: *her fingers swept the strings of the harp.* 6. move swiftly; pass swiftly: *guerrillas swept down on the town.* 7. move with dignity: *she swept out of the room.* 8. move or extend in a long course or curve: *the shore sweeps to the south for miles.* —*n.* 1. act of sweeping; clearing away; removing: *he made a clean sweep of all his debts.* 2. a steady, driving motion or swift onward course of something: *the sweep of the wind.* 3. a smooth, flowing motion or line; dignified motion: *the sweep of verse.* 4. a curve; bend: *the sweep of a road.* 5. a swinging or curving motion: *strong sweeps of a scythe.* 6. a continuous extent; stretch: *a wide sweep of farming country.* 7. reach; range; extent: *the mountain is beyond the sweep of your eye.* 8. sweeps, sweepings. 9. person who sweeps chimneys, streets, etc. 10. a long oar. 11. a long pole used to raise or lower a bucket from a well. 12. a sweepstakes contest. [OE (*ge*) *swēpa* sweepings] —sweep′er, *n.*

sweep·ing (swēp′ing), *adj.* 1. passing over a wide space: *a sweeping glance.* 2. having wide range: *a sweeping victory, a sweeping statement.* —*n.* sweepings, dust, rubbish, scraps, etc., swept out or up. —sweep′ing·ly, *adv.* —sweep′ing·ness, *n.*

sweep·stakes (swēp′stāks′), **sweep·stake** (-stāk′), *n.* 1. scheme for gambling on horse races, etc. People buy tickets, and the money they pay goes to the drawer or drawers of winning tickets. 2. the race or contest. 3. prize in such a race or contest.

sweet (swēt), *adj.* 1. having a taste like sugar or honey: *this pie is too sweet.* 2. having a pleasant taste or smell: *sweet flowers.* 3. pleasant; attractive; charming: *a sweet child, a sweet smile.* 4. fresh; not sour, salty, bitter, or spoiled: *sweet butter.* 5. *Music. Slang.* played in a slow, sentimental style. 6. working easily or smoothly: *a sweet ship, a sweet engine.* 7. of soil, good for farming. 8. dear; darling. 9. be sweet on, *Colloq.* be in love with. —*n.* 1. something sweet. 2. *Brit.* a sweet dessert. b. sweets, a. candy or other sweet things. b. pleasant or agreeable things. 4. sweetheart. —*adv.* in a sweet manner. [OE *swēte*] —sweet′ish, *adj.* —sweet′ish·ly, *adv.* —sweet′ish·ness, *n.* —sweet′ly, *adv.* —sweet′ness, *n.* —Syn. *adj.* 1. saccharine. 2. fragrant, perfumed. 3. agreeable, pleasing, winning. —Ant. *adj.* 1. sour, tart.

sweet alyssum, a common low-growing plant with clusters of small white flowers.

sweet·bread (swēt′bred′), *n.* the pancreas or thymus of a calf, lamb, etc., used as meat.

sweet·bri·er, sweet·bri·ar (swēt′brī′ər), *n.* eglantine.

sweet corn, *Am.* a kind of corn that is eaten when it is soft and that is canned for food. Sweet corn is sometimes called green corn.

sweet·en (swēt′ən), *v.* 1. make or become sweet. 2. make pleasant or agreeable. —sweet′en·er, *n.*

sweet·en·ing (swēt′ən·ing; swēt′ning), *n.* something that sweetens.

sweet flag, a water plant with long sword-shaped leaves and a pungent, aromatic rootstock.

sweet gum, *Am.* 1. a North American tree with star-shaped leaves that turn scarlet in the fall. 2. balsam from this tree.

sweet·heart (swēt′härt′), *n.* 1. a loved one; lover. 2. girl or woman loved. —Syn. 1. suitor, beau, swain.

sweet·meats (swēt′mēts′), *n.pl.* 1. candy; candied fruits; sugar-covered nuts; bonbons. 2. preserves.

sweet pea, 1. an annual climbing plant with delicate, fragrant flowers of various colors. 2. the flower.

sweet pepper, 1. a mild-flavored species of pepper plant. 2. its fruit.

sweet potato, *Am.* 1. a sweet, thick yellow or reddish root of a vine, used as a vegetable. 2. the vine that it grows on.

sweet-tem·pered (swēt′tem′pərd), *adj.* having a gentle or pleasant nature.

sweet william or **William,** plant with dense, rounded clusters of small flowers, that belongs to the same family as the pink.

swell (swel), *v.,* **swelled, swelled** or **swol·len, swell·ing,** *n., adj.* —*v.* 1. grow or make bigger: *bread dough swells as it rises, his head swelled where he bumped it.* 2. be larger or thicker in a particular place; stick out; cause to stick out: *a barrel swells in the middle.* 3. increase in amount, degree, force, etc.: *savings may swell into a fortune.* 4. rise or cause to rise above the level: *hills swell gradually from the plain.* 5. rise in waves: *the waters swelled in the ocean.* 6. grow or make louder: *swell the chorus.* 7. *Colloq.* become or make proud or conceited. —*n.* 1. act of swelling; increase in amount, degree, force, etc. 2. condition of being swollen. 3. part that swells out. 4. piece of higher ground; rounded hill. 5. a long, unbroken wave or waves. 6. a swelling tone or sound. 7. *Music.* a. crescendo followed by diminuendo. b. sign for this (< >). 8. device in an organ to control the volume of sound. 9. *Colloq.* a fashionable person, esp. one with high social rank. —*adj.* 1. *Colloq.* stylish; grand. 2. *Slang.* excellent; first-rate. [OE *swellan*] —Syn. *v.* 1. expand, inflate, distend, dilate. 2. bulge.

Sweet william

swell·ing (swel′ing), *n.* an increase in size; swollen part. —*adj.* 1. that swells; increasing. 2. of language, elevated; high-flown; turgid; bombastic. —swell′ing·ly, *adv.*

swel·ter (swel′tər), *v.* 1. suffer from heat. 2. perspire freely; sweat. —*n.* a sweltering condition. [ult. < OE *sweltan* die] —swel′ter·ing, *adj.* —swel′ter·ing·ly, *adv.*

swept (swept), *v.* pt. and pp. of sweep.

swept-back (swept′bak′), *adj.* (of the wings of an airplane) extending outward and sharply backward from the fuselage.

swerve (swėrv), *v.,* **swerved, swerv·ing,** *n.* —*v.* turn aside. —*n.* a turning aside: *the swerve of the ball made it hard to hit.* [OE *sweorfan* rub, file] —swerv′er, *n.* —Syn. *v.* deviate, diverge.

swift (swift), *adj.* 1. moving very fast: *a swift automobile.* 2. coming or happening quickly: *a swift response.* 3. quick, rapid, or prompt to act, etc.: *swift to suspect.* —*adv.* in a swift manner. —*n.* a small bird with long wings, somewhat like a swallow. [OE] —swift′ly, *adv.* —swift′ness, *n.* —Syn. *adj.* 1. fleet. 2. speedy. 3. expeditious.

Swift (swift), *n.* Jonathan, 1667–1745, British satirist.

swig (swig), *n., v.,* **swigged, swig·ging.** *Colloq.* —*n.* a deep drink. —*v.* drink heartily or greedily. —swig′ger, *n.*

swill (swil), *n.* 1. kitchen refuse, esp. when partly liquid; garbage; slops. Swill is usually fed to swine. 2. a deep drink. 3. any liquid matter. [< >] —*v.* 1. drink greedily; drink too much. 2. fill with drink. 3. wash by flooding too much with water. [OE *swilian*] —swill′er, *n.*

swim (swim), *v.,* **swam** or (*Archaic*) **swum, swim, swim·ming,** *n.* —*v.* 1. move along on or in the water by using arms, legs, fins, etc.: *fish swim.* 2. swim across: *swim a lake.* 3. make swim: *he swam his horse across the stream.* 4. float. 5. be overflowed or flooded with: *her eyes were swimming with tears.* 6. go smoothly; glide. 7. be dizzy; whirl: *my head swims!* —*n.* 1. act, time, motion, or distance of swimming. 2. the swimming bladder of a fish. 3. the swim, the current of affairs, activities, etc. [OE *swimman*] —swim′mer, *n.*

swim·ming·ly (swim′ing·li), *adv.* with great ease or success.

swin·dle (swin′dəl), *v.,* **-dled, -dling,** *n.* —*v.* 1. cheat; defraud: *honest merchants do not swindle their customers.* 2. get by fraud. —*n.* an act of swindling; cheat or fraud. [< *swindler*]

swin·dler (swin′dlər), *n.* person who cheats or defrauds. [< G *schwindler* < *schwindeln* be dizzy, act thoughtlessly, cheat]

swine (swin), *n., pl.* **swine.** 1. hogs; pigs. 2. a

hog. 3. a coarse or beastly person. [OE *swīn*] —swin'ish, *adj.* —swin'ish·ly, *adv.* —swin'ish·ness, *n.*

swine·herd (swīn'hėrd'), *n.* person who tends pigs or hogs.

swing (swing), *v.*, **swung** or (*Archaic and Dial.*) **swang**, **swung**, **swing·ing**, *n.*, *adj.* —*v.* 1. move back and forth, esp. with a regular motion: *the hammock swings.* 2. turn on a hinge or as if on a hinge: *the door swings smoothly.* 3. move in a curve: *he swung the automobile around the corner, swing a bat.* 4. move with a free, swaying motion: *the soldiers came swinging down the street.* 5. hang: *swing a hammock between two trees.* 6. *Am., Colloq.* manage or influence successfully: *swing a business deal.* 7. play (music) as swing. —*n.* 1. act or manner of swinging. 2. amount of swinging. 3. seat hung from ropes in which one may sit and swing. 4. a swinging gait or movement. 5. *Colloq.* shift or period of work. 6. a swinging blow. 7. freedom of action. 8. movement; activity. 9. Often, **swing music.** jazz music in which the players improvise freely on the original melody. 10. **in full swing,** going on actively and completely; without restraint. —*adj.* of or pertaining to swing (def. 9) or its style. [OE *swingan* beat] —swing'er, *n.* —swing'ing·ly, *adv.* —**Syn.** v. 1. sway, rock, oscillate. 5. suspend.

swinge (swinj), *v.*, **swinged**, **swinge·ing.** *Archaic.* beat; whip. [OE *swengan* < *swingan* beat] —swing'er, *n.*

swinge·ing (swin'jing), *adj. Colloq.* very forcible; very large; first-rate.

swin·gle·tree (swing'gəl·trē'), *n.* whiffletree.

swing shift, in factories, etc., the working hours between the day and night shifts, usually from 4 p.m. to midnight. [from playing of swing music for workers] —**swing shifter.**

swipe (swīp), *n.*, *v.*, **swiped**, **swip·ing.** —*n.* 1. *Colloq.* a sweeping stroke; hard blow. 2. a well sweep. —*v.* 1. *Colloq.* strike with a sweeping blow. 2. *Am., Slang.* steal. [cf. OE *swipu* scourge] —swip'er, *n.*

swirl (swėrl), *v.* 1. move or drive along with a twisting motion; whirl: *dust swirling in the air.* 2. twist; curl. —*n.* 1. a swirling movement; whirl; eddy. 2. a twist; curl. [cf. Du. *zwirrelen* whirl]

swish (swish), *v.* 1. move with a thin, light, hissing or brushing sound; make such a sound: *the whip swished through the air.* 2. cause to swish: *she swished the stick.* —*n.* a swishing movement or sound. [? imit.]

Swiss (swis), *adj.* 1. of or having to do with Switzerland or its people. 2. characteristic of Switzerland or its people. —*n.* 1. native or inhabitant of Switzerland. 2. people of Switzerland.

Swiss chard (chärd), any of several varieties of beets whose leaves are often eaten as a vegetable. [< F *carde*]

Swiss cheese, a firm, pale-yellow or whitish cheese with many large holes.

switch (swich), *n.* 1. a slender stick used in whipping. 2. a stroke; lash: *a switch of a whip.* 3. bunch of long hair worn by a woman in addition to her own hair. 4. a slender, flexible shoot or piece of a plant stem. 5. device for shifting a train from one track to another. 6. device for turning an electric current off or on. 7. a turn; change; shift: *a switch of votes to another candidate.* —*v.* 1. whip; lash. 2. move or swing like a switch. 3. *Am.* change, turn, or shift (a car, train, etc.) onto another track. 4. turn (an electric current, etc.) off or on. [prob. < var. of LG *swutsche*] —switch'er, *n.* —switch'like', *adj.*

switch·back (swich'bak'), *n. Am.* 1. a road climbing a steep grade in a zigzag course. 2. a roller coaster.

switch·board (swich'bôrd'; -bōrd'), *n. Am.* panel containing the necessary switches, meters, etc., for opening, closing, combining, or controlling electric circuits. A telephone switchboard has plugs or switches for connecting one line to another.

switch·man (swich'mən), *n., pl.* **-men.** man in charge of one or more railroad switches.

switch·yard (swich'yärd'), *n. Am.* a railroad yard where cars are switched from one track to another, put together to make trains, etc.

Switz·er·land (swit'sər-lənd), *n.* a small country in C Europe, N of Italy.

A, swivel; B, hook turning freely in swivel; C, chain.

swiv·el (swiv'əl), *n., v.,* **-eled, -el·ing;** *esp. Brit.* **-elled, -el·ling.** —*n.* 1. a fastening that allows the thing fastened to turn round freely upon it. 2. support allowing free motion of an attached part on a horizontal plane. 3. support on which a chair can revolve. 4. in a chain, a link having two parts, one of which turns freely in the other. 5. support on which a gun can turn round; gun that turns on such a support. —*v.* 1. turn on a swivel. 2. fasten or support by a swivel. 3. swing round; rotate; turn. [ult. < OE *swīfan* move] —swiv'el·like', *adj.*

swivel chair, *Am.* chair having a seat that turns on a swivel.

swob (swob), *n., v.,* **swobbed, swob·bing.** swab. —swob'ber, *n.*

swol·len (swōl'ən), *adj.* 1. swelled; tumid. 2. bombastic. —*v.* pp. of swell.

swoon (swün), *v.* 1. faint: *she swoons at the sight of blood.* 2. fade or die away gradually. —*n.* a faint. [ult. < OE *geswōgen* in a swoon] —swoon'ing·ly, *adv.*

swoop (swüp), *v.* 1. come down with a rush; descend in a sudden, swift attack: *the soldiers swooped upon the enemy.* 2. take at once stroke; snatch. —*n.* a rapid downward rush; sudden, swift descent or attack. [ult. < OE *swāpan* sweep] —swoop'er, *n.*

swop (swop), *v.,* **swopped, swop·ping,** *n.* swap. —swop'per, *n.*

sword (sôrd; sōrd), *n.* 1. weapon, usually metal, with a long, sharp blade fixed in a handle or hilt. 2. **at swords' points,** very unfriendly. 3. **cross swords,** a. fight. b. quarrel; dispute. 4. **put to the sword,** kill with a sword; slaughter in war. 5. the sword, a. war. b. military power. [OE *sweord*] —sword'less, *adj.* —sword'like', *adj.* —**Syn.** 1. rapier, saber, blade.

sword·fish (sôrd'fish'; sōrd'-), *n., pl.* **-fish·es** or (*esp. collectively*) **-fish.** a very large salt-water food fish with a long swordlike projection from its upper jaw.

Atlantic swordfish (ab. 7 ft. long)

sword grass, any of various grasses or plants with swordlike leaves.

sword knot, a looped strap, ribbon, or the like attached to the hilt of a sword, serving as a means of supporting it from the wrist or as an ornament.

sword·man (sôrd'mən; sōrd'-), *n., pl.* **-men.** *Archaic.* swordsman.

sword·play (sôrd'plā'; sōrd'-), *n.* action, practice, or art of wielding a sword; fencing. —sword'play'er, *n.*

swords·man (sôrdz'mən; sōrdz'-), *n., pl.* **-men.** 1. person skilled in using a sword. 2. person using a sword; fencer. 3. soldier. —swords'man·ship, *n.*

swore (swôr; swōr), *v.* pt. of swear.

sworn (swôrn; swōrn), *v.* pp. of swear. —*adj.* 1. having taken an oath; bound by an oath. 2. declared, promised, etc., with an oath.

'swounds (zwoundz; zoundz), *interj. Archaic.* a shortened form of *God's wounds,* used as an oath.

swum (swum), *v.* 1. pp. of swim. 2. *Archaic.* pt. of swim.

swung (swung), *v.* pt. and pp. of swing.

syb·a·rite (sib'ə·rīt), *n.* person who cares very much for luxury and pleasure. [< *Sybarite,* an inhabitant of *Sybaris,* ancient town in Italy known for its luxury] —syb'a·rit'ic (sib'ə·rit'-ik), *adj.* —syb'a·rit'i·cal·ly, *adv.*

syc·a·more (sik'ə·mōr; -mōr), *n.* 1. *Am.* a

shade tree, the buttonwood. 2. in England, a kind of maple. 3. in Egypt and Syria, a kind of fig tree. [< L < Gk. *sykomoros*]

syc·o·phant (sik′ə-fənt), *n.* a servile or self-seeking flatterer. [< L < Gk. *sykophantes* informer, slanderer] —**syc′o·phan·cy,** *n.* —**syc·o·phan·tic** (sik′ə-fan′tik), **syc′o·phan′ti·cal,** *adj.* —**syc′o·phan′ti·cal·ly,** *adv.* —**Syn.** fawner, parasite.

Syd·ney (sid′ni), *n.* the largest city and most important seaport in Australia.

syl·lab·ic (sə-lab′ik), *adj.* 1. of or pertaining to syllables; consisting of syllables. 2. *Phonet.* forming a separate syllable. The second *l* in *little* is syllabic. 3. representing a syllable. 4. pronounced syllable by syllable. —*n. Phonet.* a syllabic sound. —**syl·lab′i·cal·ly,** *adv.*

syl·lab·i·cate (sə-lab′ə-kāt), *v.,* -cat·ed, -cat·ing. form or divide into syllables. —**syl·lab′i·ca′tion,** *n.*

syl·lab·i·fy (sə-lab′ə-fī), *v.,* -fied, -fy·ing. divide into syllables. —**syl·lab′i·fi·ca′tion,** *n.*

syl·la·ble (sil′ə-bəl), *n., v.,* -bled, -bling. —*n.* 1. part of a word pronounced as a unit, consisting of a vowel alone or with one or more consonants. *American* is a word of four syllables. *Spasm* is a word of two syllables. *This* is a word of one syllable. 2. letter or group of letters representing a syllable in writing and printing. 3. the slightest bit; word: *do not breathe a syllable of this.* —*v.* pronounce in syllables; utter distinctly; utter. [< OF < L < Gk. *syllabe*, a taking together < *syn-* together + *labein* take]

syl·la·bus (sil′ə-bəs), *n., pl.* -bus·es, -bi (-bī). a brief statement of the main points of a speech, a book, a course of study, etc. [< NL, erroneous reading of L, Gk. *sittyba* parchment label] —**Syn.** abstract, synopsis.

syl·lo·gism (sil′ə-jiz·əm), *n.* 1. a form of argument or reasoning, consisting of two statements and a conclusion drawn from them. *Example:* All trees have roots; an oak is a tree; therefore, an oak has roots. 2. reasoning in this form; deduction. [< L < Gk., ult. < *syn-* together + *logos* a reckoning] —**syl′lo·gis′tic,** *adj.* —**syl′lo·gis′ti·cal·ly,** *adv.*

sylph (silf), *n.* 1. a slender, graceful girl or woman. 2. a slender, graceful spirit of the air. [< NL *sylphes,* pl.; a coinage of Paracelsus] —**sylph′like′, sylph′ish, sylph′y,** *adj.*

syl·van (sil′vən), *adj.* of or pertaining to the woods; in the woods; consisting of woods; having woods. —*n.* person or animal inhabiting or frequenting a woodland region. Also, **silvan.** [< L, < *silva* forest]

sym., 1. symbol. 2. symphony. 3. symptom.

sym·bol (sim′bəl), *n., v.,* -boled, -bol·ing; *esp. Brit.* -bolled, -bol·ling. —*n.* something that stands for or represents something else; emblem; sign: *the lion is the symbol of courage, the marks +, −, ×, and + are symbols for add, subtract, multiply, and divide.* —*v.* symbolize. [< L < Gk. *symbolon* token, ult. < *syn-* together + *ballein* throw] —**Syn.** *n.* token, figure.

sym·bol·ic (sim·bol′ik), **sym·bol·i·cal** (-ə-kəl), *adj.* 1. used as a symbol: *a lily is symbolic of purity.* 2. of, pertaining to, or expressed by a symbol; using symbols. —**sym·bol′i·cal·ly,** *adv.* —**sym·bol′i·cal·ness,** *n.*

sym·bol·ism (sim′bəl·iz·əm), *n.* 1. use of symbols; representation by symbols. 2. system of symbols. 3. symbolic meaning or character.

sym·bol·ist (sim′bəl·ist), *n.* 1. person who uses symbols or symbolism. 2. artist or writer who makes much use of colors, sounds, etc., as symbols.

sym·bol·is·tic (sim′bəl·is′tik), *adj.* of symbolism or symbolists. —**sym′bol·is′ti·cal·ly,** *adv.*

sym·bol·ize (sim′bəl·īz), *v.,* -ized, -iz·ing. 1. be a symbol of; stand for; represent. 2. represent by a symbol or symbols. 3. use symbols. —**sym′bol·i·za′tion,** *n.* —**sym′bol·iz′er,** *n.*

sym·me·try (sim′ə·tri), *n., pl.* -tries. 1. a regular, balanced arrangement on opposite sides of a line or plane, or around a center or axis. 2.

pleasing proportions between the parts of a whole; well-balanced arrangement of parts; harmony. [< L < Gk., < *syn-* together + *metron* measure] —**sym·met·ri·cal** (si·met′rə·kəl), **sym·met′ric,** *adj.* —**sym·met′ri·cal·ly,** *adv.* —**sym·met′ri·cal·ness,** *n.* —**sym′me·trist,** *n.*

sym·pa·thet·ic (sim′pə·thet′ik), *adj.* 1. having or showing kind feelings toward others; sympathizing. 2. *Colloq.* approving; agreeing. 3. enjoying the same things and getting along well together. —**sym′pa·thet′i·cal·ly,** *adv.* —**Syn.** 1. compassionate, commiserating, tender. 3. harmonious, congenial.

sym·pa·thize (sim′pə·thīz), *v.,* -thized, -thiz·ing. 1. feel or show sympathy. 2. share in or agree with a feeling or opinion; have sympathy. 3. be in approving accord. 4. agree or accord with. —**sym′pa·thiz′er,** *n.* —**sym′pa·thiz′ing·ly,** *adv.*

sym·pa·thy (sim′pə·thi), *n., pl.* -thies. 1. having the same feeling: *they were in complete sympathy.* 2. a sharing of another's sorrow or trouble. 3. agreement; approval; favor: *enlist the sympathy of the public.* [< L < Gk., < *syn-* together + *pathos* feeling] —**Syn.** 1. harmony, affinity, concord. 2. compassion, commiseration, tenderness, condolence.

sym·pho·ny (sim′fə·ni), *n., pl.* -nies. 1. an elaborate musical composition for an orchestra. It usually has three or more movements in different rhythms but related keys. 2. harmony of sounds. 3. harmony of colors: *in autumn the woods are a symphony in red, brown, and yellow.* [< L < Gk. *symphonia* harmony, concert, band < *syn-* together + *phone* voice, sound] —**sym·phon·ic** (sim·fon′ik), *adj.*

sym·po·si·um (sim·pō′zi·əm), *n., pl.* -si·ums, -si·a (-zi-ə). 1. a collection of the opinions of several persons on some subject. 2. a meeting for the discussion of some subject. [< L < Gk., < *syn-* together + *posis* drinking] —**sym·po·si·ac** (sim·pō′zi·ak), *adj.*

symp·tom (simp′təm), *n.* 1. sign; indication: *quaking knees and paleness are symptoms of fear.* 2. a noticeable change in the normal working of the body that indicates or accompanies disease, sickness, etc. [< LL < Gk. *symptoma* a happening, ult. < *syn-* together + *piptein* fall] —**symp′tom·less,** *adj.* —**Syn.** 1. token, mark.

symp·to·mat·ic (simp′tə·mat′ik), **symp·to·mat·i·cal** (-ə·kəl), *adj.* 1. being a sign; signifying; indicative: *riots are symptomatic of political or social unrest.* 2. indicating or accompanying a disease, etc.: *the infection caused a symptomatic fever.* 3. having to do with symptoms of disease, etc. —**symp′to·mat′i·cal·ly,** *adv.*

syn-, *prefix.* with; together; jointly; at the same time, as in *synchronous, synopsis,* and *synthesis.* [< Gk. *syn* with, together; also (by assimilation to the following consonant, *sy-*, *syl-*, *sym-*, *sys-*]

syn., synonym.

syn·a·gogue (sin′ə·gôg; -gog), *n.* 1. assembly of Jews for religious instruction and worship. 2. a building used by Jews for religious instruction and worship. [< L < Gk. *synagoge,* lit. assembly, ult. < *syn-* together + *agein* bring] —**syn·a·gog·i·cal** (sin′ə·goj′ə·kəl), **syn·a·gog·al** (sin′ə·gôg′əl; -gog′-), *adj.*

syn·apse (si·naps′; sin′aps), *n.* place where a nerve impulse passes from one nerve cell to another. [< Gk. *synapsis* conjunction < *syn-* together + *haptein* fasten]

syn·chro·mesh (sing′krə·mesh′), *n.* gear or system of gears in an automobile so constructed as to mesh with a minimum of friction and noise when the driver shifts from one speed to another.

syn·chro·nism (sing′krə·niz·əm), *n.* 1. state of being synchronous. 2. occurrence at the same time; agreement in time. 3. arrangement of historical events or persons according to their dates. —**syn′chro·nis′tic, syn′chro·nis′ti·cal,** *adj.* —**syn′chro·nis′ti·cal·ly,** *adv.*

syn·chro·nize (sing′krə·nīz), *v.,* -nized, -niz-

ing. 1. occur at the same time; agree in time. **2.** move or take place at the same rate and exactly together. **3.** make agree in time: *synchronize all the clocks in a building.* **4.** assign to the time or period. [< Gk., < *synchronos* SYNCHRONOUS] —**syn′chro·ni·za′tion,** *n.* —**syn′chro·niz′er,** *n.*

syn·chro·nous (sing′krə·nəs), *adj.* **1.** occurring at the same time; simultaneous. **2.** moving or taking place at the same rate and exactly together. **3.** *Physics, Elect., etc.* having the same frequency, or the same frequency and phase. [< LL < Gk., < *syn-* together + *chronos* time] —**syn′chro·nous·ly,** *adv.* —**syn′chro·nous·ness,** *n.*

syn·co·pate (sing′kə·pāt; sin′-), *v.,* **-pat·ed, -pat·ing. 1.** shorten by omitting sounds from the middle, as in syncopating *Gloucester* to *Gloster.* **2.** *Music.* **a.** begin (a tone) on an unaccented beat and hold it into an accented one. **b.** employ tones so affected in (a passage, piece, etc.). [< LL, < *syncope* SYNCOPE] —**syn′co·pa′tor, syn′co·pat′er,** *n.*

syn·co·pa·tion (sing′kə·pā′shən; sin′-), *n.* a syncopating or being syncopated. Jazz and ragtime are forms of syncopation in music.

syn·co·pe (sing′kə·pē; sin′-), *n.* contraction of a word by omitting sounds from the middle, as in *ne′er* for never. [< LL < Gk. *synkope,* orig., a cutting off, ult. < *syn-* together + *koptein* cut] —**syn·cop·ic** (sin·kop′ik), **syn·cop·tic** (sin·kop′tik), *adj.*

syn·dic (sin′dik), *n.* **1.** person who manages the business affairs of a university or other corporation. **2.** magistrate. [< LL < Gk. *syndikos* advocate < *syn-* together + *dike* justice]

syn·di·cal·ism (sin′də·kəl·iz′əm), *n.* a plan to put industry and government under the control of labor unions. —**syn′di·cal·ist,** *n.* —**syn′di·cal·is′tic,** *adj.*

syn·di·cate (*n.* sin′də·kit; *v.* sin′də·kāt), *n., v.,* **-cat·ed, -cat·ing. 1.** combination of persons or companies to carry out some undertaking, esp. one requiring a large capital investment. **2.** association for purchasing articles, stories, etc., and publishing them simultaneously in a number of newspapers or periodicals in various places. **3.** body of syndics. **4.** *Am. Slang.* group of criminals at the head of a city's or country's criminal activity. —*v.* **1.** combine into a syndicate. **2.** manage by a syndicate. **3.** publish through a syndicate. [< F *syndicat* < *syndic* SYNDIC] —**syn′di·ca′tion,** *n.* —**syn′di·ca′tor,** *n.*

syn·ec·do·che (si·nek′də·kē), *n.* a figure of speech by which a part is put for the whole, or the whole for a part, the special for the general, or the general for the special, or the like. *Example:* a factory employing 500 *hands* (persons). [< LL < Gk. *synekdoche,* ult. < *syn-* with + *ex-* out + *dechesthai* receive] —**syn·ec·doch·ic** (sin′ek·dok′ik), **syn′ec·doch′i·cal,** *adj.*

Synge (sing), *n.* **John Millington,** 1871–1909, Irish author of plays and poems.

syn·od (sin′əd), *n.* **1.** assembly called together under authority to discuss and decide church affairs; church council. **2.** court of the Presbyterian Church ranking next above the presbytery. **3.** assembly; convention; council. [< LL < Gk., < *syn-* together + *hodos* a going] —**syn′od·al,** *adj.*

syn·od·ic (si·nod′ik), **syn·od·i·cal** (-ə·kəl), *adj.* **1.** having to do with the conjunctions of the heavenly bodies. The synodic period of the moon is the time between one new moon and the next. **2.** of or pertaining to a synod. —**syn·od′i·cal·ly,** *adv.*

syn·o·nym (sin′ə·nim), *n.* **1.** word having a meaning that is the same or nearly the same as that of another word in a language (contrasted with *antonym*). *Fleet* is a synonym of *swift.* **2.** word or expression accepted as another name for something. *Reds* has become a synonym for *communists.* [< LL < Gk. *synonymon,* orig. neut. adj., SYNONYMOUS] —**syn′o·nym′ic, syn′o·nym′i·cal, syn′o·nym′i·cal·ly,** *adv.* —**syn·o·nym·i·ty** (sin′ə·nim′ə·ti), *n.*

syn·on·y·mous (si·non′ə·məs), *adj.* having

the same or nearly the same meaning. [< Med.L < Gk., < *syn-* together + (dial.) *onyma* name] —**syn·on′y·mous·ly,** *adv.*

syn·on·y·my (si·non′ə·mi), *n., pl.* **-mies. 1.** character of being synonymous; equivalence in meaning. **2.** study of synonyms. **3.** use or coupling of synonyms in discourse for emphasis or amplification. **4.** set, list, or system of synonyms.

syn·op·sis (si·nop′sis), *n., pl.* **-ses** (-sēz). a brief statement giving a general view of some subject, book, play, etc.; summary. [< LL < Gk., < *syn-* together + *opsis* a view] —**Syn.** digest.

syn·op·tic (si·nop′tik), **syn·op·ti·cal** (-tə·kəl), *adj.* **1.** giving a general view. **2.** Often, **Synoptic.** taking a common view. *Matthew, Mark,* and *Luke* are called the Synoptic Gospels because they are most alike in contents, order, and statement. —**syn·op′ti·cal·ly,** *adv.* —**syn·op′tist,** *n.* —**syn′op·tis′ti·cal·ly,** *adv.*

syn·tac·ti·cal (sin·tak′tə·kəl), **syn·tac·tic** (-tik), *adj.* of or pertaining to syntax; in accordance with the rules of syntax. —**syn·tac′ti·cal·ly,** *adv.*

syn·tax (sin′taks), *n. Gram.* **1.** construction or use of a word, phrase, or clause in a sentence. **2.** sentence structure; arrangement of the words of a language into phrases, clauses, and sentences. **3.** part of grammar dealing with this. [< LL < Gk. *syntaxis,* ult. < *syn-* together + *tassein* arrange]

syn·the·sis (sin′thə·sis), *n., pl.* **-ses** (-sēz). **1.** combination of parts or elements into a whole (opposite of *analysis*). **2.** a complex whole made up of parts or elements combined. **3.** *Chem.* formation of a compound or a complex substance by the chemical union of its elements, combination of simpler compounds, etc. Alcohol, ammonia, and rubber can be artificially produced by synthesis. [< L < Gk. < *syn-* together + *theinai* put] —**syn′the·sist,** *n.*

syn·the·size (sin′thə·sīz), *v.,* **-sized, -siz·ing. 1.** combine into a complex whole. **2.** make up by combining parts or elements. **3.** treat synthetically.

syn·thet·ic (sin·thet′ik), **syn·thet·i·cal** (-ə·kəl), *adj.* **1.** of or pertaining to synthesis. **2.** proceeding by or involving synthesis (opposite of *analytic*): *synthetic chemistry.* **3.** made artificially: *synthetic rubies.* **4.** using many compound words; tending to combine words: *German is a more synthetic language than French.* —**syn·thet′i·cal·ly,** *adv.*

syph·i·lis (sif′ə·lis), *n.* a contagious venereal disease communicated by contact or congenitally. [< NL < *Syphilus,* hero of Fracastoro's poem describing the disease, 1530] —**syph·i·lit·ic** (sif′ə·lit′ik), *adj., n.*

sy·phon (sī′fən), *n., v.* siphon.

Syr·a·cuse (sir′ə·kūs), *n.* city in C New York State.

Syr·i·a (sir′i·ə), *n.* **1.** country in W Asia. From 1958 to 1961, it united with Egypt to form the United Arab Republic. **2.** an ancient country N of Palestine and Arabia, along the E end of the Mediterranean. —**Syr′i·an,** *adj., n.*

Syr·i·ac (sir′i·ak), *adj.* of or having to do with Syria or its language. —*n.* the ancient language of Syria.

sy·rin·ga (sə·ring′gə), *n.* a shrub with fragrant white flowers blooming in early summer; mock orange. [< NL, < Gk. *syrinx* shepherd's pipe]

Syringa

sy·ringe (sə·rinj′; sir′inj), *n., v.,* **-ringed, -ring·ing.** —*n.* device fitted with a piston or rubber bulb for drawing in a quantity of fluid and then forcing it out in a stream. Syringes are used for cleaning wounds, injecting fluids into the body, etc. —*v.* clean, wash, inject, etc., by means of a syringe. [< Gk. *syrinx* pipe]

syr·inx (sir′ingks), *n., pl.* **sy·rin·ges** (sə·rin′jēz), **syr·inx·es. 1.** the vocal organ of birds, situated where the trachea divides into the right and left bronchi. **2.** *Anat.* the Eustachian tube. **3.** Panpipe. [< L < Gk., shepherd's pipe]

syr·up (sir′əp; sér′-), *n.* a sweet, thick liquid. Sugar boiled with water or fruit juices makes a syrup. Also, **sirup.** [< OF *sirop* < Ar. *sharāb* drink] —**syr′up·like′,** *adj.* —**syr′up·y,** *adj.*

sys·tem (sis′təm), *n.* 1. set of things or parts forming a whole: *a mountain system, the digestive system.* 2. an ordered group of facts, principles, beliefs, etc.: *a system of philosophy.* 3. a coördinated body of methods: *system of government, education, etc.* 4. plan; scheme; method: *a system for betting.* 5. an orderly way of getting things done: *work that shows system.* 6. the body as a whole. 7. group of heavenly bodies forming a whole that follows certain natural laws. 8. the world; universe. [< LL < Gk. *systema* < *syn-* together + *stesai* cause to stand] —**sys′tem·less,** *adj.* —**Syn.** 4. arrangement. 5. organization.

sys·tem·at·ic (sis′təm·at′ik), **sys·tem·at·i·cal** (-ə·kəl), *adj.* 1. according to a system; having a system, method, or plan. 2. arranged in or comprising an ordered system. 3. orderly in arranging things or in getting things done. 4. concerned with classification. —**sys′tem·at′i·cal·ly,** *adv.* —**Ant.** 3. unsystematic, unmethodical.

sys·tem·a·tize (sis′təm·ə·tīz), *v.,* **-tized, -tiz-ing.** arrange according to a system; make into a system; make more systematic. —**sys′tem·a·ti·za′tion,** *n.* —**sys′tem·a·tiz′er,** *n.*

sys·tem·ic (sis·tem′ik), *adj.* 1. of or pertaining to a system. 2. pertaining to a particular system of parts or organs of the body. 3. pertaining to or affecting the body as a whole. —**sys·tem′i·cal·ly,** *adv.*

sys·tem·ize (sis′təm·īz), *v.,* **-ized, -iz·ing.** systematize. —**sys′tem·i·za′tion,** *n.* —**sys′tem·iz′er,** *n.*

sys·to·le (sis′tə·lē), *n.* the normal rhythmical contraction of the heart, esp. that of the ventricles, which drives the blood into the aorta and the pulmonary artery. [< NL < Gk., contraction, < *syn-* together + *stellein* wrap] —**sys·tol·ic** (sis·tol′ik), *adj.*

T

T, t (tē), *n., pl.* **T's; t's.** 1. the 20th letter of the alphabet. 2. to a T, exactly; perfectly.

T., 1. Territory. 2. Testament. 3. Tuesday.

t., 1. teaspoon. 2. temperature. 3. in the time of. [< L *tempore*] 4. tenor. 5. tense. 6. territory. 7. time. 8. ton; tons.

Ta, *Chem.* tantalum.

tab (tab), *n., v.,* **tabbed, tab·bing.** —*n.* 1. a small flap, strap, loop, or piece. 2. tag; label. 3. keep tab on, *Am.* keep track of; keep a check on. —*v.* furnish or ornament with a tab or tabs.

tab·ard (tab′ərd), *n.* 1. a short, loose coat worn by heralds. 2. mantle worn over armor by knights. [< OF *tabart*]

Ta·bas·co (tə·bas′kō), *n. Am., Trademark.* a kind of pungent sauce, used on fish, meat, etc., prepared from the fruit of a variety of capsicum.

tab·by (tab′i), *n., pl.* **-bies,** *adj.* —*n.* 1. a brown or gray cat with dark stripes. 2. a female cat. 3. a spiteful female gossip. 4. taffeta. —*adj.* brown or gray with dark stripes. [< F < Ar. *'attābi* (def. 4), from a section of Bagdad where it was first made]

tab·er·na·cle (tab′ər·nak′əl), *n.* 1. a temporary dwelling; tent. 2. the human body thought of as the temporary dwelling of the soul. 3. place of worship for a large audience. 4. a Jewish temple. 5. tomb, shrine, etc., with a canopy. 6. container for something holy or precious, as the consecrated bread used in the Mass. [< L *tabernaculum* tent < *taberna* cabin] —**tab·er·nac·u·lar** (tab′ər·nak′yə·lər), *adj.*

ta·ble (tā′bəl), *n., v.,* **-bled, -bling.** —*n.* 1. piece of furniture having a smooth, flat top on legs. 2. food put on a table to be eaten. 3. the persons seated at a table: *the whole table laughed at his joke.* 4. a flat surface; plateau. 5. very condensed tabulated information; list. 6. a thin, flat piece of wood, stone, metal, etc.; tablet. 7. matter inscribed or written on tables. 8. lay the table, make the table ready for a meal. 9. on the table, in parliamentary procedure, on the table of the presiding officer so that the discussion is put off. 10. turn the tables, reverse conditions or circumstances completely. —*v.* 1. put on a table. 2. make a list or condensed statement of. 3 *Am.* put off discussing (a bill, motion, etc.). [< L *tabula* plank, tablet] —**Syn.** *n.* 5. schedule, synopsis.

tab·leau (tab′lō), *n., pl.* **-leaux** (-lōz), **-leaus.** 1. a striking scene; picture. 2. representation of a picture, statue, scene, etc., by a person or group posing in appropriate costume. [< F, dim. of *table* TABLE]

ta·ble·cloth (tā′bəl·klôth′; -kloth′), *n.* cloth for covering a table.

ta·ble d'hôte (tā′bəl dōt′; tab′əl), a meal served at a fixed time and price. [< F, lit., host's table]

ta·ble·land (tā′bəl·land′), *n.* a high plain; plateau.

ta·ble·spoon (tā′bəl·spün′), *n.* 1. a spoon larger than a teaspoon or dessert spoon, used to serve vegetables, etc.; a standard unit of measure in cookery. 2. tablespoonful.

ta·ble·spoon·ful (tā′bəl·spün′fùl), *n., pl.* **-fuls.** as much as a tablespoon holds. 3 teaspoonfuls = 1 tablespoonful. 1 tablespoonful = ½ fluid ounce.

tab·let (tab′lit), *n.* 1. number of sheets of writing paper fastened together at the edge. 2. a small, flat surface with an inscription. 3. a small, flat piece of medicine, candy, etc.: *aspirin tablets.* 4. a small, flat sheet of stone, wood, ivory, etc., used to write or draw on. [< F, < *table* TABLE]

ta·ble·ware (tā′bəl·wār′), *n.* dishes, knives, forks, spoons, etc., used at meals.

tab·loid (tab′loid), *n.* 1. a newspaper, usually having half the ordinary size newspaper page, that has many pictures and gives the news in short articles. 2. *Tabloid. Trademark.* tablet of medicine. —*adj.* compressed in or as in a tabloid; condensed. [< *tablet*]

ta·boo, ta·bu (tə·bü′), *adj., v.,* **-booed, -boo·ing; -bued, -bu·ing,** *n., pl.* **-boos; -bus.** —*adj.* 1. forbidden; prohibited; banned: *a taboo word.* 2. set apart as sacred or cursed. Among the Polynesians certain things, places, and persons are taboo. —*v.* forbid; prohibit; ban. —*n.* 1. a prohibition; a ban: *place a taboo on gambling.* 2. system or act of setting things apart as sacred or cursed. [< Tongan (lang. of the Tonga Islands in the S Pacific) *tabu*] ➤ **taboo, tabu.** Both spellings are used. *Tabu* looks un-English and is probably an affectation except for some scientists writing of primitive life.

ta·bor, ta·bour (tā′bər), *n.* a small drum, used to accompany a pipe or fife. [< OF *tabur;* of Oriental orig.]

tab·o·ret, tab·ou·ret (tab′ə·ret; tab′ə·ret′), *n.* 1. a small, low stand or table. 2. stool. 3. frame for embroidery. 4. a small tabor.

Ta·briz (tä·brēz′), *n.* city in NW Iran.

tab·u·lar (tab′yə·lər), *adj.* 1. of or arranged in tables or lists; written or printed in columns. 2. computed by the use of tables. 3. flat like a table: *a tabular rock.* —**tab′u·lar·ly,** *adv.*

tab·u·late (*v.* tab′yə·lāt; *adj.* tab′yə·lit, -lāt), *v.,* **-lat·ed, -lat·ing,** *adj.* —*v.* arrange (facts, figures, etc.) in tables or lists. —*adj.* shaped like

Tabard (def. 1)

Tabor

S
T

āge, cāre, fär; ēqual, tėrm; īce; ōpen, ôrder; pùt, rüle, ūse; ŦH, then; ə=a in about.

a table; tabular. —**tab′u·la′tion**, *n*. —**tab′u·la′tor**, *n*.

ta·chom·e·ter (tə·kom′ə·tər), *n*. any of various instruments for measuring or indicating the speed of a machine, a river, the blood, etc. [< Gk. *tachos* speed + –METER] —**ta·chom′e·try**, *n*.

tac·it (tas′it), *adj*. 1. unspoken; silent: *a tacit prayer*. 2. implied or understood without being openly expressed: *tacit reproach*. [< L *tacitus*, pp. of *tacere* be silent] —**tac′it·ly**, *adv*.

tac·i·turn (tas′ə·tėrn), *adj*. speaking very little; not fond of talking. [< *tacitus* TACIT] —**tac·i·tur·ni·ty** (tas′ə·tėr′nə·ti), *n*. —**tac′i·turn·ly**, *adv*. —**Syn**. silent, reserved, reticent.

Tac·i·tus (tas′ə·təs), *n*. 55?–120? A.D., Roman historian.

tack (tak), *n*. 1. a short, sharp-pointed nail or pin having a broad, flat head: *carpet tacks*. 2. stitch used as a temporary fastening. 3. *Naut*. direction in which a ship moves in regard to the position of her sails. When on port tack, a ship has the wind on her left. 4. a zigzag movement; one of the movements in a zigzag course. 5. course of action or conduct: *he took the wrong tack to get what he wanted*. 6. *Naut*. a. rope to hold in place a corner of some sails. b. corner to which this is fastened. —*v*. 1. fasten with tacks. 2. attach; add: *he tacked a postscript to the end of the letter*. 3. *Naut*. a. sail in a zigzag course against the wind. b. change from one tack to another. [< dial. OF *taque* nail < Gmc.] —**tack′er**, *n*.

tack·le (tak′əl), *n*., *v*., **–led**, **–ling**. —*n*. 1. equipment; apparatus; gear: *fishing tackle*. 2. ropes and pulleys for lifting, lowering, or moving. 3. act of tackling. 4. *Am*., *Football*. player between the guard and the end on either side of the line. —*v*. 1. try to deal with: *everyone has his own problems to tackle*. 2. lay hold of; seize: *tackle a thief*. 3. *Football*. seize and stop (an opponent having the ball) by bringing to the ground. 4. harness. [< MDu., MLG *takel*] —**tack′ler**, *n*.

Tackles for lifting

tack·y (tak′i), *adj*., **tack·i·er**, **tack·i·est**. *Am*., *Colloq*. shabby; dowdy.

Ta·co·ma (tə·kō′mə), *n*. 1. seaport in W Washington. 2. **Mount**, Mount Rainier.

tac·o·nite (tak′ə·nīt), *n*. kind of rock consisting of about 30 per cent iron ore. [< *Taconic* system of strata < *Taconic* Mts. (Mass. and Vt.)]

tact (takt), *n*. ability to say and do the right things; skill in dealing with people or handling difficult situations. [< L *tactus* sense of feeling < *tangere* touch] —**Syn**. discernment, address.

tact·ful (takt′fəl), *adj*. 1. having tact. 2. showing tact. —**tact′ful·ly**, *adv*. —**tact′ful·ness**, *n*.

tac·ti·cal (tak′tə·kəl), *adj*. 1. of or concerning tactics. 2. pertaining to the disposal of military or naval forces in supporting action against an enemy. 3. characterized by adroit procedure and skillful expedients. —**tac′ti·cal·ly**, *adv*.

tac·ti·cian (tak·tish′ən), *n*. person skilled or trained in tactics.

tac·tics (tak′tiks), *n*. 1. (*sing. in use*) art or science of disposing military or naval forces in action. 2. (*pl. in use*) the operations themselves. 3. (*pl. in use*) procedures to gain advantage or success; methods. [< NL < Gk. *taktike* (*techne*) the art of arranging < *tassein* arrange]

tac·tile (tak′təl), *adj*. 1. of or pertaining to touch. 2. that can be felt by touch. [< L *tactilis* < *tangere* touch] —**tac·til′i·ty**, *n*.

tact·less (takt′lis), *adj*. 1. without tact: *a tactless person*. 2. showing no tact: *a tactless reply*. —**tact′less·ly**, *adv*. —**tact′less·ness**, *n*.

tad·pole (tad′pōl′), *n*. a very young frog or toad at the stage when it has a tail and lives in water. [< ME *tadde* toad + *pol* poll (head); appar. "a toad that is all head"]

Ta·dzhik (tä·jek′), *n*. a soviet republic in C Asia.

tael (tāl), *n*. 1. a weight of E Asia equal to 1⅓ ounces avoirdupois. 2. a Chinese unit of money. [< Pg. < Malay *tahil*]

ta·en (tān), *Poetic*. taken.

taf·fe·ta (taf′ə·tə), *n*. 1. a rather stiff silk cloth with a smooth, glossy surface. 2. a similar cloth of linen, rayon, etc. [< OF < Pers. *tāftah* silk or linen]

taff·rail (taf′rāl′), *n*. a rail around a ship's stern. [< Du. *tafereel* panel, dim. of *tafel* TABLE]

taf·fy (taf′i), *n*. 1. a kind of chewy candy made of brown sugar or molasses boiled down, often with butter. 2. *Colloq*. flattery. Also, **toffee**, **toffy**.

Taft (taft), *n*. **William Howard**, 1857–1930, the 27th president of the United States, 1909–1913; chief justice of the Supreme Court, 1921–1930.

tag¹ (tag), *n*., *v*., **tagged**, **tag·ging**. —*n*. 1. piece of card, paper, leather, etc., to be tied or fastened to something: *a price tag*, *a name tag*. 2. a small, hanging piece; loose end; tatter. 3. a metal point at the end of a string. A shoelace has a tag on each end. 4. the last line or lines of a song, play, actor's speech, etc. —*v*. 1. furnish with a tag or tags. 2. *Colloq*. follow closely.

tag² (tag), *n*., *v*., **tagged**, **tag·ging**. —*n*. a children's game in which the player who is "it" chases the others until he touches one. The one touched is then "it" and must chase the others. —*v*. *Am*. touch or tap with the hand, as in tag.

Ta·hi·ti (tə·hē′ti), *n*. one of the Society Islands in the S Pacific. —**Ta·hi·ti·an** (tə·hē′ti·ən; –hē′shən), *adj*., *n*.

tail (tāl), *n*. 1. the hinder part of an animal's body. esp. when prolonged beyond the rest. 2. something like an animal's tail: *the tail of a kite*. 3. the after portion of an airplane. 4. *Astron*. the luminous train extending from the head of a comet. 5. the hind part of anything; back; rear; conclusion. 6. a long braid or tress of hair. 7. **tails**, **a**. the reverse side of a coin. **b**. *Am*., *Colloq*. coat with long tails, worn on formal occasions. **c**. full dress. 8. **turn tail**, run away from danger, trouble, etc. —*v*. 1. furnish with a tail. 2. form a tail. 3. follow close behind; form the tail of. 4. *Slang*. follow closely and secretly. 5. join (one thing) to the end of another. 6. be fastened by an end. —*adj*. 1. at the tail, back, or rear. 2. coming from behind: *a tail wind*. [OE *tægel*] —**tail′less**, *adj*. —**tail′like**, *adj*.

tail·board (tāl′bôrd′; –bōrd′), *n*. board at the back end of a truck, wagon, etc. that can be let down or removed when loading or unloading.

tail gate, **tail·gate** (tāl′gāt′), *n*. tailboard.

tail light or **lamp**, light, usually red, at the back end of an automobile, wagon, train, etc.

tai·lor (tā′lər), *n*. man whose business is making or repairing clothes. —*v*. 1. make by tailor's work. 2. fit or furnish with clothes made by a tailor. [< AF *taillour*, ult. < LL *taliare* cut < L *talea* rod, cutting] —**tai′lor·ing**, *n*.

tai·lor·bird (tā′lər·bėrd′), *n*. a small bird of Asia and Africa that stitches leaves together to form and hide its nest.

tai·lor-made (tā′lər·mād′), *adj*. made by, or as if by, a tailor; simple and fitting well.

tail·piece (tāl′pēs′), *n*. 1. piece forming the end or added at the end. 2. in printing, a small decorative engraving placed at the end of a chapter, etc.

tail spin, a downward, spinning movement of an airplane, with the nose first.

tail wind, wind coming from behind.

taint (tānt), *n*. stain or spot; trace of decay, corruption, or disgrace. —*v*. 1. give a taint to; spoil. 2. become tainted; decay. [partly var. of *attaint*; partly < OF *teint*, pp. of *teindre* dye < L *tingere*] —**Syn**. *n*. blemish. —*v*. 1. infect.

Tai·pei, **Tai·peh** (tī′pe′), *n*. capital of Taiwan.

Tai·wan (tī′wän′), *n*. island off the SE China coast, since 1949 the seat of the Chinese nationalist government.

take (tāk), *v*., **took**, **tak·en**, **tak·ing**, *n*. —*v*. 1. lay hold of; grasp: *he took her by the hand*. 2. seize; catch; capture: *take an animal in a trap*. 3. get into one's hold, control, possession, etc.: *take one's pen in hand*. 4. receive by way of payment: *he won't take a penny less*. 5. accept: *take my advice, I won't take a refusal*. 6. receive into some relationship: *he took a wife, she takes boarders*. 7. receive in an indicated manner: *she* took the news calmly. **8.** receive into the body or system. **9.** win: *he took first prize.* **10.** contract (disease): *take cold.* **11.** proceed to occupy: *he took a seat.* **12.** use (a vehicle) as a means of travel: *take a train.* **13.** use; make use of: *take the opportunity.* **14.** indulge in: *take a vacation.* **15.** submit to; put up with: *take hard punishment.* **16.** need; require: *it will take courage.* **17.** occupy; use up: *it will take all day.* **18.** choose; select: *take the shortest way home.* **19.** remove by death: *pneumonia took him.* **20.** take away; detract: *her paleness takes from her beauty.* **21.** subtract: *take 3 from 7 and you have 4.* **22.** lead: *where will this road take me?* **23.** go with; escort: *take her home.* **24.** carry: *take your lunch along.* **25.** do; make; obtain by some special method: *take a photograph.* **26.** form and hold in mind; feel: *take pride in one's work.* **27.** find out: *take my temperature.* **28.** act; have effect: *the vaccination took.* **29.** understand: *do you take my meaning?* **30.** assume as a fact; suppose: *I take it the train was late.* **31.** regard; consider: *let us take an example.* **32.** assume (responsibility, blame, etc.): *she took charge of the household.* **33.** assume or adopt (a symbol, badge, etc.): *she took the veil.* **34.** engage; hire; lease: *take a house.* **35.** write down; record: *take dictation.* **36.** receive and pay for regularly: *take a newspaper.* **37.** photograph. **38.** *Gram.* be used with. **39.** affected by: *marble takes a polish.* **40.** please; attract; charm: *it took her fancy.* **41.** attract and hold: *the scene took his eye.* **42.** go: *take to the woods.* **43.** attempt to get over, through, etc., or succeed in so doing: *my horse took the fence easily.* **44.** become: *he took sick.* **45.** begin to grow; strike root. **46.** can be taken: *it takes apart easily.* **47.** take after, be like; resemble. **48.** take amiss, a. misinterpret. **b.** be offended at. **49.** take back, withdraw; retract. **50.** take down, a. write down. **b.** lower the pride of. **51.** take for, suppose to be. **52.** take in, a. receive; admit. **b.** make smaller. **c.** understand. **d.** deceive; trick; cheat. **53.** take in vain, use (a name) carelessly or irreverently. **54.** take it out on, *Colloq.* relieve one's anger or annoyance by scolding or hurting. **55.** take off, a. leave the ground or water: *three airplanes took off at the same time.* **b.** *Colloq.* give an amusing imitation of; mimic. **56.** take on, a. engage; hire. **b.** undertake to deal with. **c.** *Colloq.* show great excitement, grief, etc. **57.** take one's time, not hurry. **58.** take over, take the ownership or control of. **59.** take the floor, rise to speak, as in a legislative body, club, etc. **60.** take to, form a liking for; become fond of. **61.** take up, a. soak up; absorb. **b.** make smaller. **c.** begin; undertake. **d.** pay off. **e.** lift. **62.** take up with, *Colloq.* begin to associate or be friendly with. —*n.* **1.** amount taken: *a great take of fish.* **2.** act of taking. **3.** that which is taken. **4.** act or process of making a photograph or scene in a motion picture. [< Scand. *taka*] —**tak′er,** *n.* —Syn. *v.* **15.** endure, undergo, bear, experience. **21.** deduct, abstract. **40.** captivate, delight.

take-home pay (tāk′hōm′), wages or salary remaining after taxes, insurance fees, etc., have been deducted.

take-off (tāk′ôf′, -of′), *n.* **1.** *Colloq.* an amusing imitation; mimicking. **2.** the leaving of the ground in leaping or in beginning a flight in an airplane; taking off. **3.** the place or point at which one takes off.

tak·est (tāk′ist), *v. Archaic.* take.

tak·eth (tāk′ith), *v. Archaic.* takes.

tak·ing (tāk′ing), *adj.* **1.** attractive; pleasing; winning: *a taking smile.* **2.** *Colloq.* infectious. —*n.* **1.** act of taking or state of being taken. **2.** that which is taken. **3. takings,** money taken in; receipts. —**tak′ing·ly,** *adv.* —**tak′ing·ness,** *n.*

talc (talk), *n.,* *v.,* **talcked, talck·ing; talced** (talkt), **talc·ing** (tal′king). —*n.* a soft, smooth mineral, used in making talcum powder, tailors' chalk, etc. —*v.* treat or rub with talc. [< Med.L *talcum* < Ar. *ṭalq* < Pers. *talk*]

tal·cum (tal′kəm), *n.* **1.** talcum powder. **2.** talc.

talcum powder, powder made of purified white talc, for use on the face and body.

tale (tāl), *n.* **1.** narrative; story: *he told us tales of his boyhood.* **2.** falsehood; lie. **3.** piece of gossip or scandal. **4.** the full number; total; count. **5.** tell tales, spread gossip or scandal. [OE *talu*]

tale·bear·er (tāl′bâr′ər), *n.* person who spreads gossip or scandal; telltale. —**tale′bear′ing,** *n., adj.*

tal·ent (tal′ənt), *n.* **1.** a special natural ability; ability: *a talent for music.* **2.** people who have talent. **3.** an ancient unit of weight or money, varying with time and place. [< L < Gk. *talanton*] —**tal′ent·ed,** *adj.* —**tal′ent·less,** *adj.* —Syn. **1.** aptitude, faculty, capacity, gift.

ta·ler (tä′lər), *n., pl.* **-ler.** thaler.

tales·man (tālz′mən; tā′lēz-), *n., pl.* **-men.** person chosen from among the bystanders or those present in court to serve on a jury when too few of those originally summoned are qualified to be on a jury. [< Med.L *tales* (de circumstantibus) such (of the bystanders) + *man*]

tale·tell·er (tāl′tel′ər), *n.* talebearer. —**tale′tell′ing,** *n., adj.*

tal·is·man (tal′is·mən; -iz-), *n., pl.* **-mans.** **1.** a stone, ring, etc., engraved with figures or characters supposed to have magic power; charm. **2.** anything that acts as a charm. [< Ar. < LGk. *telesma* < Gk., initiation into the mysteries, < *teleein* perform] —**tal·is·man·ic** (tal′is·man′ik; -iz-) —**tal′is·man′i·cal·ly,** *adv.*

talk (tôk), *v.* **1.** use words; speak: *a child learns to talk.* **2.** use in speaking: *talk sense, talk French.* **3.** bring, put, drive, influence, etc., by talk: *talk a person to sleep.* **4.** discuss: *talk politics, talk business.* **5.** consult; confer: *talk with one's doctor.* **6.** spread ideas by other means than speech: *talk by signs.* **7.** make sounds that suggest speech: *the birds were talking loudly.* **8.** gossip; report; rumor: *she talked behind their backs.* **9. talk back,** *Am., Colloq.* answer rudely or disrespectfully. **10. talk down,** make silent by talking louder or longer. **11. talk over,** a. discuss; consider together. **b.** persuade or convince by arguing. —*n.* **1.** the use of words; spoken words; speech; conversation. **2.** informal speech. **3.** a way of talking: *baby talk.* **4.** conference; council. **5.** gossip; report; rumor. **6.** mere empty speech. **7.** a subject for talk or gossip: *she is the talk of the town.* [ME *talke(n)*, ult. akin to *tell*] —Syn. *v.* **1.** converse. ➤ See say for usage note.

talk·a·tive (tôk′ə·tiv), *adj.* having the habit of talking a great deal; fond of talking. —**talk′a·tive·ly,** *adv.* —**talk′a·tive·ness,** *n.* —Syn. loquacious, garrulous, communicative, voluble. —Ant. taciturn, reticent, silent.

talk·er (tôk′ər), *n.* **1.** person who talks. **2.** a talkative person. —Syn. **1.** speaker, lecturer.

talk·ie (tôk′i), *n. Colloq.* **1.** *Am.* a motion picture with sound. **2. the talkies,** the sound-picture industry.

talk·ing-to (tôk′ing·tü′), *n., pl.* **-tos.** *Colloq.* a scolding.

tall (tôl), *adj.* **1.** higher than the average: *a tall building.* **2.** of the specified height: *six feet tall.* **3.** *Colloq.* high or large in amount: *a tall price.* **4.** *Am., Colloq.* hard to believe; exaggerated: *a tall tale.* [OE (ge)*tæl* prompt, active] —**tall′ness,** *n.* —Syn. **1.** lofty, towering.

Tal·la·has·see (tal′ə·has′i), *n.* capital of Florida, in the N part.

Tal·ley·rand (tal′i·rand), *n.* 1754–1838, French statesman and diplomat, noted for his craftiness.

Tal·linn (täl′in), *n.* capital and seaport of Estonia, on the Gulf of Finland.

tal·low (tal′ō), *n.* the hard fat from sheep, cows, etc., used for making candles and soap. —*v.* smear with tallow. [ME *talgh*] —**tal′low·y,** *adj.*

tal·ly (tal′i), *n., pl.* **-lies,** *v.,* **-lied, -ly·ing.** —*n.* **1.** stick of wood in which notches are cut to represent numbers, formerly used to show the amount of a debt or payment. **2.** anything on which a score or account is kept. **3.** a notch or mark made on a tally. **4.** account; reckoning; score: *a tally of a game.* **5.** label; tag: *the tally* *on a box.* **6.** anything corresponding to a certain other thing; duplicate; counterpart. **7.** correspondence; agreement. —*v.* **1.** mark on a tally; count up: *tally a score.* **2.** label; tag: *tally suitcases.* **3.** agree; correspond: *your account tallies with mine.* **4.** cause to fit, suit, or correspond. [< OF, ult. < L *talea* rod] —tal′li·er, *n.* —**Syn.** *v.* **1.** record, score, register. **3.** accord, conform.

tal·ly·ho (*n.* tal′i·hō′; *interj.* tal′i·hō′), *n., pl.* -hos, *interj. Esp. Brit.* —*n.* **1.** a coach drawn by four horses. **2.** a sounding of "tallyho" by a hunter. —*interj.* a hunter's cry on catching sight of the fox.

tally sheet, *Am.* a sheet on which a record or score is kept, esp. a record of votes.

Tal·mud (tal′mud), *n.* the sixty-three volumes containing the Jewish civil and canonical law. —Tal·mud′ic, Tal·mud′i·cal, *adj.* —Tal′mud·ist, *n.* —Tal′mud·is′tic, *adj.*

tal·on (tal′ən), *n.* **1.** claw of a bird of prey; claw. **2.** talons, clawlike fingers; grasping hands. [< OF, heel, ult. < L *talus* ankle] —tal′oned, *adj.*

ta·lus[1] (tā′ləs), *n., pl.* -li (-lī). *Anat.* the uppermost bone of the tarsus; anklebone; astragalus. [< L]

ta·lus[2] (tā′ləs), *n.* **1.** a slope. **2.** a sloping side or face of a wall, rampart, parapet, or other fortification. **3.** a sloping mass of rocky fragments lying at the base of a cliff or the like. [< F < L]

tam (tam), *n.* tam-o′-shanter.

ta·ma·le (tə·mä′lē), *n. Am.* a Mexican food made of corn meal and minced meat, seasoned with red peppers, wrapped in cornhusks, and roasted or steamed. [< Am.Sp. < Mex. *tamalli*]

tam·a·rack (tam′ə·rak), *n. Am.* an American larch tree. [< Algonquian]

tam·a·rind (tam′ə·rind), *n.* **1.** a tropical tree grown for its wood and fruit. **2.** its fruit, used in foods, drinks, and medicine. [ult. < Ar. *tamrhindi*, lit., date of India]

tam·bou·rine (tam′bə·rēn′), *n.* a small drum with metal disks, played by striking it with the knuckles or by shaking it. [< F *tambourin*, dim. of *tambour* drum]

Tambourine

tame (tām), *adj.*, tam·er, tam·est, *v.*, tamed, tam·ing. —*adj.* **1.** taken from the wild state and made obedient: *a tame bear.* **2.** without fear; gentle: *the squirrels are very tame.* **3.** without spirit; dull: *a tame story.* —*v.* **1.** make tame; break in. **2.** become tame. **3.** deprive of courage; tone down; subdue. [OE *tam*] —tame′a·ble, tam′a·ble, *adj.* —tame′ly, *adv.* —tame′ness, *n.* —tam′er, *n.* —**Syn.** *adj.* **1.** domesticated, domestic, docile. -*v.* **3.** curb, repress.

tame·less (tām′lis), *adj.* that has never been tamed; that cannot be tamed. —tame′less·ness, *n.*

Tam·er·lane (tam′ər·lān), *n.* 1333?–1405, Mongol conqueror of most of S and W Asia.

Tam·il (tam′əl), *n.* **1.** one of the Dravidian people of S India. **2.** their language. —*adj.* of or pertaining to the Tamils or their language.

Tam·ma·ny (tam′ə·ni), *Am.* —*n.* organization of politicians in the Democratic Party of New York City. —*adj.* of or having to do with this organization, its politics, methods, or members. [from the name of a Delaware Indian chief of the 17th cent.]

tam-o′-shan·ter (tam′ə·shan′-tər), *n.* a Scotch cap. Also, tam. [from the name of the hero in a poem by Burns]

Tam-o′-Shanter

tamp (tamp), *v.* **1.** pack down: *tamp the earth about a newly planted tree.* **2.** in blasting, to fill (the hole containing explosive) with dirt, etc. —tamp′er, *n.*

Tam·pa (tam′pə), *n.* seaport in W Florida.

tam·per (tam′pər), *v.* **1.** meddle; meddle improperly. **2.** tamper with, a. bribe; corrupt. b. change so as to damage or falsify. [ult. var. of *temper*] —tam′per·er, *n.*

Tam·pi·co (tam·pē′kō), *n.* seaport in E Mexico.

tam·pi·on (tam′pi·ən), *n.* **1.** a wooden plug

placed in the muzzle of a gun to keep out dampness and dust. **2.** plug for the top of an organ pipe.

tam·pon (tam′pon), *n.* plug of cotton or the like inserted in a wound, etc., to stop bleeding or absorb secretions. —*v.* fill or plug with a tampon. [< F]

tan (tan), *v.*, tanned, tan·ning, *n.*, *adj.* —*v.* **1.** make (a hide) into leather by soaking in a special liquid containing tannin. **2.** make brown from exposure to sun and air. **3.** become brown. **4.** *Colloq. thrash.* —*n.* **1.** the brown color of a person's skin resulting from being in the sun and air. **2.** a yellowish brown. **3.** bark used in tanning hides. **4.** tannin. —*adj.* yellowish-brown. [< Med.L *tannare*] —tan′ning, *n.*

tan·a·ger (tan′ə·jər), *n.* any of various small American oscine birds. The males are usually brilliantly colored. [< NL < Tupi *tangara*]

tan·bark (tan′bärk′), *n.* crushed bark used in tanning hides.

tan·dem (tan′dəm), *adv.* one behind the other: *drive horses tandem.* —*adj.* having animals, seats, parts, etc., arranged tandem. —*n.* **1.** two horses so harnessed. **2.** a carriage drawn by two horses so harnessed. **3.** a bicycle with two seats, one behind the other. [< L, at length, < *tam* so]

tang (tang), *n.* **1.** a strong taste or flavor: *the tang of mustard, the salt tang of sea air.* **2.** a distinctive flavor or quality. **3.** a smack, touch, or suggestion of something. **4.** a long, slender projecting point, strip, or prong forming the part of a chisel, file, etc., that fits into the handle. [< Scand. *tangi* point] —tang′y, *adj.*

Tan·gan·yi·ka (tang′gən·yē′kə; tan′-), *n.* **1.** a republic in E Africa, formerly a United Nations trust territory administered by Great Britain. It is joined in a federation, Tanzania, with Zanzibar. **2.** Lake, lake in C Africa.

tan·gent (tan′jənt), *adj.* **1.** touching. **2.** *Geom.* touching at one point only and not intersecting. These circles are tangent ⌒⌒. —*n.* **1.** *Geom.* a tangent line, curve, or surface. **2.** *Trigon.* in a right triangle, the ratio of the length of the side opposite to an (acute) angle to the length of the side (not the hypotenuse) adjacent to the angle. **3. fly off or go off at a tangent,** change suddenly from one course of action or thought to another. [< L *tangens* touching] —tan′gen·cy, *n.* —tan·gen′tial (tan·jen′shəl), *adj.* —tan·gen·ti·al·i·ty (tan·jen′shi·al′ə·ti), *n.* —tan·gen′tial·ly, *adv.*

tan·ge·rine (tan′jə·rēn′), *n.* a small, deep-colored orange with a very loose peel. [< *Tangier*]

tan·gi·ble (tan′jə·bəl), *adj.* **1.** capable of being touched or felt by touch: *ghosts are visible but not tangible.* **2.** real; definite: *a tangible reason.* —*n.* tangibles, things whose value is easily appraised; material assets. [< LL *tangibilis* < *tangere* touch] —tan′gi·bil′i·ty, tan′gi·ble·ness, *n.* —tan′gi·bly, *adv.* —**Syn.** *adj.* **2.** substantial, perceptible, evident.

Tan·gier (tan·jir′), *n.* seaport in NW Africa, on the Strait of Gibraltar, in an international zone.

tan·gle (tang′gəl), *v.*, -gled, -gling, *n.* —*v.* **1.** twist and twine together in a confused mass. **2.** catch and hold in or as in a net. **3.** involve in something that hampers or obstructs. **4.** bewilder; confuse: *the news tangled his thoughts.* —*n.* **1.** a confused mass; snarl. **2.** a tangled condition. **3.** perplexity. [prob. var. of *tagle* entangle < Scand. (dial. Sw.) *taggla* disorder] —tan′gle·ment, *n.* —tan′gler, *n.* —tan′gly, *adj.* —**Syn.** *v.* **1.** entangle, snarl, interweave, interlace. **2.** entrap, ensnare, enmesh. —**Ant.** *v.* **1.** disentangle.

tan·go (tang′gō), *n., pl.* -gos, *v.*, -goed, -going. —*n.* **1.** a Spanish-American dance with special music and many steps, figures, and poses. **2.** music for it. —*v.* dance the tango. [< Sp.]

tank (tangk), *n.* **1.** a large container for liquid or gas. **2.** a swimming pool. **3.** *Mil.* an armored combat vehicle carrying machine guns and cannons and moving on an endless track on each side. —*v.* put or store in a tank. [ult. < OF *estanc* pool]

tank·age (tangk′ij), *n.* **1.** the capacity of a tank or tanks. **2.** storage in tanks. **3.** the price charged for storage in tanks. **4.** waste matter from slaughterhouse tanks.

tank·ard (tangk′ərd), *n.* a large drinking mug with a handle and a hinged cover.

tank car, a railroad car with a tank for carrying liquids or gases.

tank·er (tangk′ər), *n.* ship with tanks for carrying oil or other liquid freight.

tan·ner (tan′ər), *n.* person whose work is tanning hides.

Tankard

tan·ner·y (tan′ər·i), *n., pl.* -ner·ies. place where hides are tanned.

tan·nic (tan′ik), *adj. Chem.* of or obtained from tanbark or tannin.

tan·nin (tan′ən), **tannic acid**, *n. Chem.* acid obtained from the bark or galls of oaks, etc., and from certain other plants. It is used in tanning, dyeing, making ink, and in medicine.

tan·sy (tan′zi), *n., pl.* -sies. a coarse, strong-smelling plant with large, toothed leaves and clusters of small yellow flowers. Tansy was formerly much used in cooking and medicine. [< OF < LL < Gk. *athanasia*, orig., immortality]

tan·ta·lize (tan′tə·līz), *v.,* -lized, -liz·ing. torment or tease by keeping something desired in sight but out of reach, or by holding out hopes that are repeatedly disappointed. [< *Tantalus*] —tan′ta·liz′ing·ly, *adv.* —Syn. plague, vex.

tan·ta·lum (tan′tə·ləm), *n. Chem.* a rare, grayish metallic element, Ta, that is very resistant to acids. [< *Tantalus;* because it will not absorb acid]

Tan·ta·lus (tan′tə·ləs), *n. Gk. Legend.* a Greek king punished in the lower world by having to stand up to his chin in water, under branches laden with fruit. Whenever he tried to drink or eat, the water or fruit withdrew from his reach.

tan·ta·mount (tan′tə·mount), *adj.* equivalent. [prob. < AF *tant amunter* amount to as much. See AMOUNT.]

tan·trum (tan′trəm), *n. Colloq.* fit of bad temper or ill humor.

Tan·za·ni·a (tan·zə·nē′ə), *n.* republic in E Africa consisting of the former British trust territory of Tanganyika and the adjacent island of Zanzibar.

Tao·ism (tou′iz·əm), *n.* one of the three main religions of China, founded on the doctrines of the ancient philosopher, Lao-tse. —Tao′ist, *n., adj.* —Tao·is′tic, *adj.*

tap¹ (tap), *v.,* tapped, tap·ping, *n.* —*v.* **1.** strike lightly: *tap on a window.* **2.** cause to strike lightly: *she tapped her foot on the floor.* **3.** make, put, etc., by light blows: *tap a rhythm, tap time, tap the ashes out of a pipe.* **4.** repair with a tap (def. **3**). —*n.* **1.** a light blow: *there was a tap at the door.* **2.** sound of a light blow. **3.** piece of leather added to the sole or heel of a shoe to repair it. **4.** taps, *Am.* a signal on a bugle or drum at which all lights in the soldiers' or sailors' quarters must be put out. [< OF *taper*]

tap² (tap), *n., v.,* tapped, tap·ping. —*n.* **1.** a stopper or plug to close a hole in a cask containing liquid. **2.** a means of turning on or off a flow of liquid; faucet. **3.** a certain kind or quality of liquor. **4.** *Colloq.* room in which liquor is sold and drunk. **5. on tap**, **a.** ready to be let out of a keg or barrel and served. **b.** ready for use; on hand. **6.** place where an electric connection is or can be made. **7.** tool for cutting threads of internal screws. —*v.* **1.** make a hole in to let out liquid. **2.** draw the plug from: *tap a cask.* **3.** furnish with a tap. **4.** let out (liquid) by piercing or by drawing a plug. **5.** let out liquid from by surgery. **6.** penetrate to; open up: *this highway taps a large district.* **7.** make a connection on: *tap a telegraph wire.* **8.** make internal screw threads in. [OE *tæppa*]

ta·pa (tä′pə), *n.* **1.** an unwoven cloth of the Pacific islands, made by steeping and beating the inner bark of a mulberry tree. **2.** the bark. [< Polynesian]

tap dance, dance in which the steps are accented by loud taps of the foot, toe, or heel.

tap-dance (tap′dans′; -däns′), *v.,* -danced, -danc·ing. do a tap dance.

tape (tāp), *n., v.,* taped, tap·ing. —*n.* **1.** a long, narrow woven strip of cotton, linen, etc. **2.** a long, narrow strip of other material: *steel tape.* Sound is recorded on a kind of plastic tape. **3.** strip, string, etc., stretched across a race track at the finish line. **4.** adhesive. —*v.* **1.** furnish with tape or tapes. **2.** fasten or wrap with tape. [OE *tæppe*]

tape·line (tāp′līn′), **tape measure**, *n.* a long strip of cloth or steel marked in inches, feet, etc., for measuring.

ta·per (tā′pər), *v.* **1.** make or become gradually smaller toward one end: *a church spire tapers off to a point.* **2.** grow less gradually; diminish. [< n.] —*n.* **1.** a very slender candle; long wick coated with wax. **2.** a gradual decrease of force, capacity, etc. [OE *tapor*] —ta′per·ing·ly, *adv.*

tape recorder, device for recording sound magnetically on a plastic tape. Sound waves activate the microphone transmitting electric impulses to an electromagnet through which the voice is reproduced on tape as it moves across it.

tape recording, **1.** the recording of sound on a tape. **2.** the sound thus recorded.

tap·es·try (tap′is·tri), *n., pl.* -tries, *v.,* -tried, -try·ing. —*n.* **1.** fabric with pictures or designs woven in it, used to hang on walls, cover furniture, etc. **2.** a picture in tapestry. —*v.* **1.** picture in tapestry. **2.** cover with tapestry; cover with a pattern like that of tapestry. [< F *tapisserie,* ult. < *tapis* < Gk. *tapetion,* dim. of *tapes* carpet]

tape·worm (tāp′wėrm′), *n.* a long, flat worm that lives during its adult stage as a parasite in the intestine of man and other vertebrates.

tap·i·o·ca (tap′i·ō′kə), *n.* a starchy food obtained from the root of the cassava plant. [ult. < Tupi-Guarani *tipioca*]

ta·pir (tā′pər), *n.* a large piglike animal of tropical America that has a flexible snout. [< Tupi *tapira*]

tap·room (tap′rüm′; -rûm′), *n. Esp. Brit.* barroom.

tap·root (tap′rüt′; -rût′), *n. Bot.* a main root growing downward.

tar¹ (tär), *n., v.,* tarred, tar·ring, *adj.* —*n.* a black, sticky substance obtained by the distillation of wood or coal. —*v.* **1.** cover or smear with tar. **2. tar and feather,** *Am.* pour heated tar on and cover with feathers as a punishment. —*adj.* of, like, or covered with tar. [OE *teoru*]

tar² (tär), *n.* sailor. [special use of *tar¹*]

tar·an·tel·la (tar′ən·tel′ə), *n.* **1.** a whirling southern Italian dance in very quick rhythm. **2.** music for this dance. [< Ital.]

ta·ran·tu·la (tə·ran′chə·lə), *n., pl.* -las, -lae (-lē), a large, hairy spider whose bite is painful, if not dangerous. People used to think that its bite caused an insane desire to dance. [< Med.L. ult. < L *Tarentum* Taranto, city in Italy]

Tarantula (body ab. 1 in. long)

tar·dy (tär′di), *adj.,* -di·er, -di·est. **1.** behind time; late. **2.** slow. [< F, ult. < L *tardus*] —tar′-di·ly, *adv.* —tar′di·ness, *n.*

tare¹ (tär), *n.* **1.** vetch. **2.** *Bible.* any of various injurious weeds. [cf. MDu. *tarwe* wheat]

tare² (tär), *n., v.,* tared, tar·ing. —*n.* **1.** the difference between the gross weight and the net weight of an article being shipped. It is usually the weight of the materials in which the article is wrapped or packed. **2.** a deduction made from the gross weight to allow for this. —*v.* ascertain, note, or allow for the tare of. [< F, ult. < Ar. *ṭarḥah* < *ṭaraḥa* reject]

tar·get (tär′git), *n.* **1.** device, usually circular, to be aimed at in shooting practice or contests. **2.** anything aimed at. **3.** object of abuse, scorn, criticism, etc.: *he was the target for their caustic remarks.* [< F *targuete,* ult. < Gmc.]

āge, cāre, fär; ēqual, tėrm; īce; ōpen, ôrder; pùt, rüle, ūse; tɦ, then; ə=a in about.

tar·iff (tar′if), *n.* **1.** list of duties or taxes on imports or exports. **2.** system of duties or taxes on imports or exports. **3.** any duty or tax in such a list or system: *a tariff on jewelry.* **4.** any table or scale of prices. [< Ital. < Ar. *tarif* information]

tarn (tärn), *n. Brit.* a small lake or pool in the mountains. [< Scand. *tjörn*]

tar·nish (tär′nish), *v.* **1.** dull the luster or brightness of. **2.** lose luster or brightness. **3.** cast a stain upon; sully: *his actions tarnished his reputation.* **4.** become dim or sullied. —*n.* **1.** loss of luster or brightness. **2.** a tarnished coating. [< F *terniss-* < *terne* dark, ? < Gmc.] —tar′nish·a·ble, *adj.* —Syn. v. **1.** dim, discolor, blacken.

ta·ro (tä′rō), *n., pl.* **-ros. 1.** a starchy root grown for food in the Pacific islands and other tropical regions. **2.** the plant, grown for ornament also. [< Polynesian]

tar·pau·lin (tär-pô′lən), *n.* **1.** canvas, or other coarse strong cloth, made waterproof. **2.** sheet of this used as a covering. [< *tar*¹ + *pall* in sense of "covering"]

tar·pon (tär′pon), *n., pl.* **-pons** or (*esp. collectively*) **-pon.** a large, silver-colored fish found in the warmer parts of the Atlantic Ocean.

Tar·quin (tär′kwin), *n.* one of a family of kings of early Rome, whose rule ended 510 B.C.

tar·ry¹ (tar′i), *v.* **-ried, -ry·ing. 1.** remain; stay. **2.** wait; delay. **3.** *Archaic.* wait for. —tar′ri·er, *n.*

tar·ry² (tär′i), *adj.* **-ri·er, -ri·est. 1.** of tar; like tar. **2.** covered with tar.

tar·sal (tär′səl), *adj.* of or pertaining to the tarsus. —*n.* bone or cartilage in the ankle.

tar·sus (tär′səs), *n., pl.* **-si** (-sī). *Anat.* **a.** the ankle. **b.** the group of small bones composing it. **2.** *Zool.* **a.** shank of a bird's leg. **b.** the last segment of an insect's leg. [< NL < Gk. *tarsos* sole of the foot, orig., crate]

tart¹ (tärt), *adj.* **1.** having a sharp taste; sour. **2.** sharp: *a tart reply.* [OE *teart*] —tart′ly, *adv.* —tart′ness, *n.*

tart² (tärt), *n.* **1.** pastry filled with cooked fruit, jam, etc. In the United States, a tart is small and the fruit shows; in England, any fruit pie is a tart. **2.** *Slang.* prostitute. [< OF *tarte;* def. 2 orig. a term of endearment]

tar·tan (tär′tən), *n.* **1.** a plaid woolen cloth. Each Scottish Highland clan has its own pattern of tartan. **2.** the pattern or design itself. —*adj.* **1.** made of tartan. **2.** of, like, or pertaining to tartan.

Tar·tar (tär′tər), *n.* **1.** member of a mixed horde of Mongols and Turks who overran Asia and E Europe during the Middle Ages. Tartars now live in parts of the Soviet Union and C and W Asia. **2.** tartar, person who has a bad temper. —*adj.* of or pertaining to a Tartar or Tartars. Also, Tatar.

tar·tar (tär′tər), *n.* **1.** an acid substance deposited on the inside of wine casks. After it is purified, this substance is called cream of tartar and is used with baking soda to make baking powder. **2.** a hard substance deposited on the teeth. [< F *tartre,* ? < Ar.] —tar·tar·e·ous (tär-tār′i·əs), *tar′tar·ous, adj.*

tar·tar·ic (tär-tär′ik; -tär′-), *adj.* of or pertaining to tartar; containing tartar; derived from tartar.

tartaric acid, *Chem.* a colorless crystalline compound, $C_4H_6O_6$, obtained from grapes, etc.

Tar·ta·rus (tär′tə·rəs), *n. Gk. Myth.* **1.** place of punishment below Hades. **2.** underworld; Hades. —Tar·tar·e·an (tär-tär′i·ən), *adj.*

Tash·kent (tash·kent′), *n.* city in the S Soviet Union in Asia.

task (task; täsk), *n.* **1.** work to be done; piece of work; duty. **2.** call or take to task, blame; scold; reprove. —*v.* **1.** put a task on; force to work. **2.** burden; strain. [< dial. OF *tasque,* var. of *taxa* < L *taxare* tax] —task′er, *n.* —Syn. *n.* **1.** assignment, undertaking, job, stint.

task force, *Mil.* a temporary group of units, esp. naval units, assigned to one commander for carrying out a specific operation.

task·mas·ter (task′mas′tər; täsk′mäs′-), *n.* person who sets tasks for others to do.

Tas·ma·ni·a (taz-mā′ni·ə; -mān′yə), *n.* island S of Australia, a state of the Commonwealth of Australia. —Tas·ma′ni·an, *adj., n.*

Tass (tas), *n.* an agency of the Soviet Union which collects and distributes news.

tas·sel (tas′əl), *n., v.,* **-seled, -sel·ing;** *esp. Brit.* **-selled, -sel·ling.** —*n.* **1.** a hanging bunch of threads, small cords, beads, etc., fastened together at one end. **2.** something like this: *corn has tassels.* —*v.* **1.** put tassels on. **2.** grow tassels. [< OF, mantle fastener]

taste (tāst), *n., v.,* **tast·ed, tast·ing.** —*n.* **1.** flavor: *a sweet, sour, salty, or bitter taste.* **2.** the sense by which the flavor of things is perceived. **3.** act of tasting. **4.** a little bit; sample: *take a taste of a cake.* **5.** a liking: *suit your own taste.* **6.** ability to perceive and enjoy what is appropriate, harmonious, or excellent: *a man of taste.* **7.** a manner or style that shows such ability: *her house is furnished in excellent taste.* **8.** to the king's or queen's taste, perfectly; very satisfactorily. —*v.* **1.** try the flavor of (something) by taking a little into the mouth. **2.** get the flavor of by the sense of taste: *she tasted almond in the cake.* **3.** have a particular flavor: *the soup tastes of onion.* **4.** eat or drink a little bit (of). **5.** experience; have: *taste freedom.* **6.** have experience: *taste of pleasure.* **7.** *Archaic.* relish; enjoy. [< OF *taster,* orig., feel] —tast′a·ble, *adj.* —Syn. n. **1.** savor, tang, smack. **5.** inclination, predilection, fondness.

taste bud, any of certain small groups of cells in the lining of the tongue or mouth that are sense organs of taste.

taste·ful (tāst′fəl), *adj.* **1.** having good taste. **2.** showing or done in good taste. —taste′ful·ly, *adv.* —taste′ful·ness, *n.*

taste·less (tāst′lis), *adj.* **1.** without taste. **2.** without good taste; in poor taste. —taste′less·ly, *adv.* —taste′less·ness, *n.* —Syn. **1.** insipid, flat, vapid.

tast·er (tās′tər), *n.* person who tastes, esp. one whose work is judging the quality of wine, tea, coffee, etc., by the taste.

tast·y (tās′ti), *adj.,* **tast·i·er, tast·i·est.** *Colloq.* **1.** tasting good; pleasing to the taste. **2.** having or showing good taste. —tast′i·ly, *adv.* —tast′i·ness, *n.*

tat (tat), *v.,* **tat·ted, tat·ting.** make a kind of lace by looping and knotting (threads) with a shuttle.

Ta·tar (tä′tər), *n., adj.* Tartar. —Ta·tar·i·an (tä·tär′i·ən), Ta·tar·ic (tä·tär′ik), *adj.*

tat·ter (tat′ər), *n.* **1.** a torn piece; rag. **2.** tatters, torn or ragged clothing. —*v.* **1.** tear or wear to pieces; make ragged. **2.** become worn or ragged. [ult. < Scand., var. of *tötturr* rag] —tat′tered, *adj.*

tat·ting (tat′ing), *n.* **1.** process or work of making a kind of lace by looping and knotting cotton or linen thread with a shuttle. **2.** lace made in this way.

tat·tle (tat′əl), *v.,* **-tled, -tling,** *n.* —*v.* **1.** tell tales or secrets. **2.** say or reveal by tattling. **3.** talk foolishly; gossip. **4.** utter idly or foolishly. —*n.* idle or foolish talk; gossip; telling tales or secrets. [cf. MDu. *tatelen* stutter] —tat′tler, *n.* —tat′tling, *adj.* —tat′tling·ly, *adv.*

tat·tle·tale (tat′əl·tāl′), *n., adj. Am., Colloq.* telltale.

tat·too¹ (ta·tü′), *n., pl.* **-toos. 1.** a signal on a bugle, drum, etc., calling soldiers or sailors to their quarters at night. **2.** series of raps, taps, etc.: *the hail beat a loud tattoo on the windowpane.* [< Du. *taptoe* < *tap* taproom + *toe* to, shut] —tat·too′er, *n.*

tat·too² (ta·tü′), *v.,* **-tooed, -too·ing,** *n., pl.* **-toos.** —*v.* **1.** mark (the skin) with designs or patterns by pricking it and putting in colors. **2.** mark (a design) on the skin in this way: *the sailor had a ship tattooed on his arm.* —*n.* **1.** act of tattooing. **2.** mark or design made by tattooing. [< Polynesian *tatau*] —tat·too′er, *n.*

tau (tô; tou), *n.* the 19th letter (T, τ) of the Greek alphabet.

taught (tôt), v. pt. and pp. of teach.

taunt (tônt; tänt), v. 1. subject to mockery; jeer at; reproach. 2. get or drive by taunts: *they taunted him into taking the dare.* —*n.* a bitter or insulting remark. —taunt′er, *n.* —taunt′-ing·ly, *adv.* —Syn. v. 1. deride, ridicule, gibe.

taupe (tōp), *n., adj.* dark, brownish gray. [< F, orig., mole, < L *talpa*]

Tau·rus (tô′rəs), *n., gen.* –ri (–rī). 1. the Bull, a zodiacal constellation. 2. the second sign of the zodiac. [< L, bull]

taut (tôt), *adj.* 1. tightly drawn: *a taut rope.* 2. tense: *taut nerves.* 3. in neat condition; tidy. [earlier *taught*, appar. var. of TIGHT] —taut′ly, *adv.* —taut′ness, *n.*

tau·tog (tô·tog′; –tôg′), *n. Am.* a food fish common on the Atlantic coast of the United States. [< Algonquian]

tau·tol·o·gy (tô·tol′ə·ji), *n., pl.* –gies. saying a thing over again in other words without adding clearness or force; useless repetition. *Example:* the modern college student of today. [< LL < Gk. *tautologia*, ult. < to *auto* the same (thing) + *legein* say] —tau·to·log·i·cal (tô′tə·loj′ə·kəl), *adj.* —tau′to·log′i·cal·ly, *adv.*

tav·ern (tav′ərn), *n.* 1. place where alcoholic drinks are sold and drunk; saloon. 2. inn. [< OF < L *taberna*, orig., rude dwelling]

taw (tô), *n.* 1. game of marbles. 2. a fancy marble used for shooting. 3. the line from which the players shoot.

taw·dry (tô′dri), *adj.,* –dri·er, –dri·est. showy and cheap; gaudy. [ult. alter. of *St. Audrey,* from cheap laces sold at St. Audrey's fair in Ely, England] —taw′dri·ly, *adj.* —taw′dri·ness, *n.*

taw·ny (tô′ni), *adj.,* –ni·er, –ni·est, *n.* —*adj.* brownish-yellow: *a lion has a tawny skin.* —*n.* a brownish yellow. [< OF *tane*, pp. of *taner* TAN] —taw′ni·ness, *n.*

tax (taks), *n.* 1. money paid by people for the support of the government. 2. a burden, duty, or demand that oppresses; strain. —*v.* 1. put a tax on: *tax imports, tax cigarettes.* 2. lay a heavy burden on; be hard for: *the job taxed his strength.* 3. reprove; accuse: *they taxed him with rudeness.* 4. examine and fix (the costs of a lawsuit, etc.). [< L *taxare*, orig., censure] —tax′er, *n.* —Syn. v. 2. assessment, levy, impost, duty, excise. –v. 2. strain, task.

tax·a·ble (tak′sə·bəl), *adj.* liable to be taxed; subject to taxation. —tax′a·bil′i·ty, tax′a·ble·ness, *n.* —tax′a·bly, *adv.*

tax·a·tion (taks·ā′shən), *n.* 1. a taxing: *taxation is necessary to provide roads, schools, and police.* 2. a tax imposed. 3. amount people pay for the support of the government; taxes.

tax·ex·empt (taks′ig·zempt′), *adj.* free from taxes; not taxed.

tax·i (tak′si), *n., pl.* tax·is, *v.,* tax·ied, tax·i·ing or tax·y·ing. —*n. Am.* taxicab. —*v.* 1. ride in a taxi. 2. of an airplane, move slowly on the surface of the ground or water under its own power.

tax·i·cab (tak′si·kab′), *n.* automobile for hire, with a meter (taximeter) to record the amount to be paid. [contraction of *taximeter cab; taximeter* < F, < *taxe* fare, TAX + *mètre* METER]

tax·i·der·my (tak′sə·dėr′mi), *n.* art of preparing the skins of animals and stuffing and mounting them in lifelike form. [< Gk. *taxis* arrangement (< *tassein* arrange) + *derma* skin] —tax′i·der′mal, tax′i·der′mic, *adj.* —tax′i·der′mist, *n.*

tax·on·o·my (taks·on′ə·mi), *n.* 1. classification, esp. in relation to its principles or laws. 2. branch of science dealing with classification. [< F, < Gk. *taxis* arrangement (< *tassein* arrange) + *-nomos* assigning] —tax·o·nom·ic (tak′sə·nom′ik), tax′o·nom′i·cal, *adj.* —tax′o·nom′i·cal·ly, *adv.* —tax·on′o·mist, *n.*

tax·pay·er (taks′pā′ər), *n.* 1. person who pays a tax or is required by law to do so. 2. a building erected to provide enough income to pay the taxes on the land on which it is built.

Tay·lor (tā′lər), *n.* 1. Jeremy, 1613–1667, English bishop and author. 2. Zachary, 1784–1850,

the 12th president of the United States, 1849–1850.

Tb, *Chem.* terbium.

t.b., 1. trial balance. 2. tuberculosis.

tbs., tbsp., tablespoon; tablespoons.

Tc, *Chem.* technetium.

Tchai·kov·sky, Tchai·kow·sky (chī·kôf′ski), *n.* Tschaikowsky.

Te, *Chem.* tellurium.

Tea leaves and flowers

tea (tē), *n.* 1. the dried and prepared leaves of a certain shrub, from which a drink is made by infusion with hot water. 2. the shrub itself. 3. the drink so made. 4. *Esp. Brit.* a meal in the late afternoon or early evening, at which tea is commonly served. 5. an afternoon reception at which tea is served. 6. something to drink prepared from some other thing: *beef tea.* [< dial. Chinese *t'e*]

tea·cart (tē′kärt′), *n.* a small table on wheels, used in serving tea.

teach (tēch), *v.,* taught, teach·ing. 1. show how to do; make understand: *teach a dog tricks.* 2. give instruction to: *he teaches well.* 3. give lessons in: *he teaches mathematics.* 4. give instruction; act as teacher: *she teaches for a living.* [OE *tǣcan* show] —teach′a·ble, *adj.* —teach′a·bil′i·ty, teach′a·ble·ness, *n.* —teach′a·bly, *adv.* ➤ See learn for usage note.

teach·er (tēch′ər), *n.* person who teaches, esp. one who teaches in a school. —teach′er·ship, *n.*

teach·ing (tēch′ing), *n.* 1. work or profession of a teacher. 2. act of one who teaches. 3. instruction; precept; doctrine.

teaching machine, device that gives information in a series of units and checks how well the information has been learned by a set of questions.

tea·cup (tē′kup′), *n.* 1. cup for drinking tea. 2. the quantity that such a cup may hold.

tea·cup·ful (tē′kup·ful), *n., pl.* –fuls. as much as a teacup holds, usually four fluid ounces.

teak (tēk), *n.* 1. a large tree of the East Indies with a hard, durable, yellowish-brown wood. 2. this wood, used for shipbuilding, making fine furniture, etc. [< Pg. < Malayalam *tēkka*]

tea·ket·tle (tē′ket′əl), *n.* kettle for heating water to make tea, etc.

teal (tēl), *n., pl.* teals or (*esp. collectively*) teal. any of several varieties of small freshwater duck.

team (tēm), *n.* 1. number of people working or acting together, esp. one of the sides in a match: *a football team, a debating team.* 2. two or more horses or other animals harnessed together to work. —*v.* 1. join together in a team. 2. drive a team. 3. work, carry, etc., with a team. [OE *tēam*]

team·mate (tēm′māt′), *n.* a fellow member of a team.

team·ster (tēm′stər), *n.* man whose work is driving a team of horses or hauling things with a truck.

team·work (tēm′wėrk′), *n. Am.* the acting together of a number of people to make the work of the group successful and effective.

tea·pot (tē′pot′), *n.* a container with a handle and a spout for making and serving tea.

tear¹ (tir), *n.* 1. Also, tear′drop′. a drop of salty fluid secreted by the lachrymal gland, coming or flowing from the eye. b. something like or suggesting a tear. 2. in tears, shedding tears; crying. [OE *tēar*] —tear′less, *adj.* —tear′y, *adj.*

tear² (tār), *v.,* tore, torn, tear·ing, *n.* —*v.* 1. pull apart by force: *tear a box open.* 2. make by pulling apart: *she tore a hole in her dress.* 3. make a hole or a rent in by a pull: *the nail tore her coat.* 4. pull hard or violently: *he tore at the hindering ropes.* 5. cut badly; wound: *the jagged stone tore his skin.* 6. rend; divide: *the party was torn by two factions.* 7. remove by effort: *he could not tear himself from that spot.* 8. make miserable; distress: *she was torn by anguish.* 9. become torn: *lace tears easily.* 10. *Colloq.* move with great haste: *an automobile* came tearing along. —n. 1. a torn place. 2. act or process of tearing. 3. a rushing movement; dash. 4. a violent rage; tantrum. 5. Am., Slang. spree. [OE teran] —tear'er, n. —Syn. v. 1. rip.

tear·ful (tir'fəl), adj. 1. full of tears; weeping. 2. causing tears; sad. —tear'ful·ly, adv. —tear'ful·ness, n. —Syn. 2. mournful.

tear gas (tir), gas that irritates the eyes, causing tears and temporary blindness, used esp. in breaking up riots.

tea·room (tē'rüm'; -rúm'), n. a room or shop where tea, coffee, and light meals are served.

tease (tēz), v., teased, teas·ing, n. —v. 1. vex or worry by jokes, questions, requests, etc.; annoy. 2. beg: the child teases for everything he sees. 3. comb out; shred (wool, etc.). 4. raise nap on (cloth). —n. 1. person who teases. 2. act of teasing or state of being teased. [OE tǣsan] —teas'er, n. —teas'ing·ly, adv. —Syn. v. 1. irritate, torment, plague, badger, pester.

tea·sel (tē'zəl), n., v., -seled, -sel·ing; esp. Brit. -selled, -sel·ling. —n. 1. a plant with stiff, prickly flower heads. 2. one of these used for raising nap on cloth. 3. a mechanical device used for the same purpose. —v. raise a nap on (cloth) with teasels. Also, teazel, teazle. [OE tǣsel] —tea'sel·er, esp. Brit. tea'sel·ler, n.

tea·spoon (tē'spün'), n. 1. a spoon smaller than a tablespoon, commonly used to stir tea or coffee; a standard unit of measure in cookery. 2. teaspoonful.

tea·spoon·ful (tē'spün·fúl'), n., pl. -fuls. as much as a teaspoon holds. 1 teaspoonful = ⅓ tablespoon. 1 teaspoonful = 1½ fluid drams.

teat (tēt; tit), n. protuberance on the breast or udder in female mammals, where the milk ducts discharge; nipple. [< OF tete < Gmc.]

tea·zel (tē'zəl), n., v., -zeled, -zel·ing; esp. Brit. -zelled, -zel·ling. teasel.

tea·zle (tē'zəl), n., v., -zled, -zling. teasel.

tech., 1. technical. 2. technology.

tech·ne·ti·um (tek·nē'shi·əm), n. Chem. an artificially produced metallic element, Tc.

tech·nic (tek'nik), n. technique. —adj. technical. [< Gk., < techne art, skill, craft]

tech·ni·cal (tek'nə·kəl), adj. 1. of or pertaining to a mechanical or industrial art or applied science: a technical school. 2. of or pertaining to the special facts of a science or art: electrolysis, tarsus, and proteid are technical words. 3. treating a subject technically; using technical terms: a technical lecture. 4. skilled in a particular art, trade, etc.: a technical man. 5. of or pertaining to any art or science: technical skill in singing. 6. by the rules of a certain science, art, game, etc. [< technic] —tech'ni·cal·ly, adv. —tech'ni·cal·ness, n.

tech·ni·cal·i·ty (tek'nə·kal'ə·ti), n., pl. -ties. 1. a technical matter, point, detail, term, expression, etc. 2. technical quality or character.

technical sergeant, U.S. Army. formerly, a noncommissioned officer of the second grade, above a staff sergeant and below a master sergeant.

tech·ni·cian (tek·nish'ən), n. 1. person experienced in the technicalities of a subject. 2. person skilled in the technique of an art.

Tech·ni·col·or (tek'nə·kul'ər), n. Am., Trademark. a special process by which three-color photographs are combined in one film.

tech·nics (tek'niks), n. 1. study or science of an art or of arts in general, esp. of the mechanical or industrial arts. 2. technic or technique.

tech·nique (tek·nēk'), n. 1. method or way of performing the mechanical details of an art; technical skill. 2. a special method or system used to accomplish something. [< F]

tech·noc·ra·cy (tek·nok'rə·si), n. government by technical experts. [< Gk. techne craft + E -cracy < Gk. kratos rule, strength] —tech'no·crat (tek'nə·krat), n. —tech'no·crat'ic, adj.

tech·nol·o·gy (tek·nol'ə·ji), n. 1. the science of the industrial arts: engineering is studied at a school of technology. 2. technical words, terms, or expressions used in an art, science, etc. [< Gk. technologia systematic treatment < techne art + -logos treating of] —tech·no-

log·i·cal (tek'nə·loj'ə·kəl), tech'no·log'ic, adj. —tech'no·log'i·cal·ly, adv. —tech·nol'o·gist, n.

ted·der (ted'ər), n. Am. machine that spreads out hay for drying. [cf. Scand. tethja spread manure]

Te De·um (tē dē'əm), 1. a hymn of praise and thanksgiving sung in Roman Catholic and Anglican churches at morning service, and also on special occasions. 2. music for this hymn. [< L, the first words of the hymn]

te·di·ous (tē'di·əs; tē'jəs), adj. long and tiring. [< LL, < L taedium TEDIUM] —te'di·ous·ly, adv. —te'di·ous·ness, n. —Syn. tiresome, wearisome, monotonous, dull, dreary.

te·di·um (tē'di·əm), n. state of being wearisome; tediousness. [< L, < taedet it is wearisome]

tee (tē), n., v., teed, tee·ing. —n. 1. the mark aimed at in quoits or other games. 2. a mark or place from which a player starts in playing each hole in golf. 3. a little mound of sand or dirt on which a golf ball is placed when a player drives; piece of wood, rubber, or other material used instead of the sand or dirt. —v. 1. put a (golf ball) on a tee. 2. tee off, drive (a golf ball) from a tee.

teem (tēm), v. be full (of); abound; swarm: the swamp teemed with mosquitoes. [OE tēman < tēam progeny] —teem'ing·ly, adv.

teen·ag·er (tēn'āj'ər), n. a young person in his or her teens.

teens (tēnz), n.pl. the years of life from 13 to 19 inclusive. [OE -tiene]

tee·pee (tē'pē), n. tepee.

tee·ter (tē'tər), n. a seesaw. —v. move unsteadily; waver; seesaw. [var. of titter < Scand. titra shake]

teeth (tēth), n. pl. of tooth.

teethe (tēth), v., teethed, teeth·ing. grow teeth; have teeth grow through the gums.

tee·to·tal (tē·tō'təl), adj. 1. of, pertaining to, advocating, or pledged to total abstinence from alcoholic liquor. 2. Colloq. absolute, complete, or entire. [< total, with initial letter repeated] —tee·to'tal·er, esp. Brit. tee·to'tal·ler, n. —tee·to'tal·ism, n. —tee·to'tal·ist, n.

Te·gu·ci·gal·pa (tā·gü'sē·gäl'pä), n. capital of Honduras, in the S part.

teg·u·ment (teg'yə·mənt), n. a natural covering of an animal body, or of any part of it, as a turtle's shell. [< L tegumentum < tegere cover]

Te·he·ran, Te·hran (te'ə·rän'; -ran'; -hə-), n. capital of Iran, in the N part.

tel., 1. telegram. 2. telegraph. 3. telephone.

Tel A·viv (tel' ə·vēv'), the former provisional capital of Israel, in the W part.

tele-, tel-, word element. 1. over a distance; far. 2. television, as in televerbiage. [< Gk. tele far]

tel·e·cast (tel'ə·kast'; -käst'), v., -cast or -cast·ed, -cast·ing, n. —v. broadcast by television. —n. a television program. [< tele(vision) + (broad)cast] —tel'e·cast'er, n.

tel·e·con (tel'ə·kon), n. 1. device that flashes messages sent by teletype from long distances on a screen, thus enabling groups in widely scattered places to hold conferences. 2. conference held by means of a telecon. [(radio-) tele(type) + con(ference)]

tel·e·gen·ic (tel'ə·jen'ik), adj. suitable for telecasting.

tel·e·gram (tel'ə·gram), n. Am. message sent by telegraph. —tel'e·gram'mic, adj.

tel·e·graph (tel'ə·graf; -gräf), n. apparatus, system, or process for sending messages by electricity. —v. 1. send (a message) by telegraph. 2. send a message to by telegraph. —te·leg·ra·pher (tə·leg'rə·fər), esp. Brit. te·leg'ra·phist, n. —tel'e·graph'ic, tel'e·graph'i·cal, adj. —tel'e·graph'i·cal·ly, adv. —Syn. v. 1, 2. wire.

te·leg·ra·phy (tə·leg'rə·fi), n. the making or operating of telegraphs.

Te·lem·a·chus (tə·lem'ə·kəs), n. Gk. Myth. son of Odysseus and Penelope. When Odysseus returned from the Trojan War, Telemachus helped him slay Penelope's insolent suitors.

tel·e·ol·o·gy (tel'i·ol'ə·ji; tē'li–), *n.* 1. fact or quality of being purposeful. 2. purpose or design as shown in nature. 3. doctrine that mechanisms alone cannot explain the facts of nature, and that purposes have causal power. 4. doctrine that all things in nature were made to fulfill a plan or design. [< NL, < Gk. *telos* end + *–logos* treating of] —**tel·e·o·log·i·cal** (tel'i·ə·loj'ə·kəl; tē'li–), *adj.* —**tel'e·ol'o·gist,** *n.*

te·lep·a·thy (tə·lep'ə·thi), *n.* communication of one mind with another by means beyond what is ordinary or normal. —**tel·e·path·ic** (tel'ə·path'ik), *adj.* —**tel'e·path'i·cal·ly,** *adv.* —**te·lep'a·thist,** *n.*

tel·e·phone (tel'ə·fōn), *n., v.,* –phoned, –phon·ing. *Am.* —*n.* apparatus, system, or process for transmitting sound or speech by electricity. —*v.* 1. talk through a telephone; send (a message) by telephone. 2. talk to by telephone. [< *tele–* far + *–phone* < Gk. *phone* sound, voice] —**tel'e·phon'er,** *n.* —**tel·e·phon·ic** (tel'ə·fon'ik), *adj.* —**tel'e·phon'i·cal·ly,** *adv.*

te·leph·o·ny (tə·lef'ə·ni), *n.* the making or operating of telephones.

tel·e·pho·to (tel'ə·fō'tō), *adj.* of or having to do with telephotography.

tel·e·pho·to·graph (tel'ə·fō'tə·graf; –gräf), *n.* 1. picture taken with a camera having a telephoto lens. 2. picture sent by telegraphy. Telephotographs in newspapers are often called wire photos. —*v.* 1. take a picture with a camera having a telephoto lens. 2. send a picture by telegraphy.

tel·e·pho·tog·ra·phy (tel'ə·fə·tog'rə·fi), *n.* 1. method or process of photographing distant objects by using a camera with a telephoto lens. 2. method or process of sending and reproducing pictures by telegraph. —**tel·e·pho·to·graph·ic** (tel'ə·fō'tə·graf'ik), *adj.*

telephoto lens, lens used in a camera for producing an enlarged image of a distant object.

Tel·e·promp·ter (tel'ə·promp'tər), *n. Trademark.* a device consisting of a moving band that gives a prepared speech line for line, used by speakers who are being televised. [< *tele*(vision) *prompter*]

tel·e·ran (tel'ə·ran), *n.* system of navigation for aircraft which utilizes television for transmitting radar mappings and other data. [short for *Tele-*(vision) *R*(adar) *A*(ir) *N*(avigation)]

tel·e·scope (tel'ə·skōp), *n., v.,* –scoped, –scop·ing, *adj.* —*n.* an instrument for making distant objects appear nearer and larger. The stars are studied by means of telescopes. —*v.* 1. force or be forced together one inside another like the sliding tubes of some telescopes: *when two railroad trains crash into each other, the cars are sometimes telescoped.* 2. shorten; condense. —*adj.* telescopic. [< NL, < Gk. *tele* far + *–skopion* instrument for observing < *skopeein* watch]

Man using a telescope

tel·e·scop·ic (tel'ə·skop'ik), **tel·e·scop·i·cal** (–ə·kəl), *adj.* 1. of or having to do with a telescope. 2. obtained or seen by means of a telescope: *a telescopic view of the moon.* 3. visible only through a telescope. 4. far-seeing. 5. consisting of parts that slide one inside another like the tubes of some telescopes. —**tel'e·scop'i·cal·ly,** *adv.*

te·les·co·py (tə·les'kə·pi), *n.* science or art of constructing or using telescopes.

tel·e·type (tel'ə·tīp), *n., v.,* –typed, –typ·ing. —*n.* 1. Teletype, *Trademark.* a telegraphic apparatus for sending and receiving signals by means of two instruments resembling typewriters. 2. system of sending signals by Teletype. —*v.* send (a message) by Teletype.

tel·e·type·writ·er (tel'ə·tīp'rīt'ər), *n.* a machine like a typewriter, used in teletyping.

tel·e·view (tel'ə·vū'), *v.* watch by means of television. —**tel'e·view'er,** *n.*

tel·e·vise (tel'ə·viz), *v.,* –vised, –vis·ing. 1. send by television. 2. see by television.

tel·e·vi·sion (tel'ə·vizh'ən), *n.* 1. process of transmitting the image of an object, scene, or event by radio or wire so that a person in some other place can see it at once. In television, waves of light from an object are changed into electric waves which are transmitted by radio or wire, and then changed back into waves of light that produce an image of the object on a screen. 2. apparatus on which these images may be seen.

tell (tel), *v.,* told, tell·ing. 1. put in words; say: *tell the truth.* 2. tell to; inform: *tell us about it.* 3. make known: *don't tell where the money is.* 4. tell something: *he was always telling, never doing.* 5. give evidence (of): *the smashed automobile told a sad story.* 6. act as talebearer; reveal or divulge (something secret or private): *promise not to tell.* 7. recognize; know; distinguish: *he couldn't tell which house it was.* 8. say plainly or positively: *I cannot tell exactly what happened.* 9. say to; order; command: *tell him to stop!* 10. say to with force: *I don't like it, I tell you.* 11. count; count one by one: *the nun tells her beads.* 12. have effect or force: *every blow told.* 13. tell off, a. count off; count off and detach for some special duty. b. strike back sharply in words; castigate. 14. tell time, know what time it is by the clock. [OE *tellan* < *talu* tale] —Syn. 1. utter. 3. mention.

tell·er (tel'ər), *n.* 1. person who tells. 2. person who counts, esp. votes. 3. person in a bank who takes in, gives out, and counts money.

tell·ing (tel'ing), *adj.* having effect or force; striking: *a telling blow.* —**tell'ing·ly,** *adv.*

tell·tale (tel'tāl'), *n.* 1. person who tells tales on others; person who reveals private or secret matters from malice. 2. thing that informs or warns. —*adj.* telling what is not supposed to be told; revealing.

tel·lu·ri·um (te·lùr'i·əm), *n. Chem.* a rare silver-white element, Te, resembling sulfur in its chemical properties and usually occurring in nature combined with gold, silver, or other metals. [< NL, < L *tellus* earth]

Tel·star (tel'stär'), *n. Trademark.* small earth satellite to amplify and relay microwave signals of television, telephone, etc.

tem·blor (tem·blôr'), *n. Am.* earthquake. [< Sp., < *tamblar* tremble]

te·mer·i·ty (tə·mer'ə·ti), *n.* reckless boldness; rashness. [< L, < *temere* heedlessly] —Syn. foolhardiness, audacity. —Ant. caution, wariness.

temp., 1. temperature. 2. temporary.

Tem·pel·hof (tem'pəl·hōf), *n.* suburb of Berlin, site of a major international airport.

tem·per (tem'pər), *n.* 1. state of mind; disposition; condition: *she was in a good temper.* 2. angry state of mind: *in her temper she broke a vase.* 3. calm state of mind: *he became angry and lost his temper.* 4. mental constitution; temperament: *he is calm in temper.* 5. the hardness, toughness, etc., of a mixture: *the temper of the clay was right for shaping.* 6. substance added to something to modify its properties or qualities. —*v.* 1. tone down; moderate; soften: *temper justice with mercy.* 2. bring or be brought to a proper or desired condition by mixing or preparing. Steel is tempered by heating it and working it till it has the proper degree of hardness. 3. tune or adjust the pitch of (an instrument, a voice, etc.). [< L *temperare,* orig., observe due measure < *tempus* time, interval] —Syn. *n.* 1. mood, humor. —*v.* 1. qualify.

tem·per·a (tem'pər·ə), *n.* a method of painting in which colors are mixed with whites of egg or other substances instead of oil. [< Ital.]

tem·per·a·ment (tem'pər·ə·mənt; –prə·mənt), *n.* 1. a person's nature or disposition: *she has a nervous temperament.* 2. an unusual nature or disposition that is not inclined to submit to ordinary rules or restraints: *an actress often has temperament.* 3. Music. the tuning of pianos, organs, etc., so that the tones are available in different keys or tonalities. [< L, < *temperare* TEMPER]

tem·per·a·men·tal (tem′pər·ə·men′təl; -prə-men′-), *adj.* **1.** due to temperament; constitutional: *cats have a temperamental dislike for water.* **2.** showing a strongly marked individual temperament. **3.** subject to moods and whims; easily irritated; sensitive. —**tem′per·a·men′tal·ly,** *adv.*

tem·per·ance (tem′pər·əns; -prəns), *n.* **1.** moderation in action, speech, habits, etc. **2.** moderation in the use of alcoholic drinks. **3.** the principle and practice of not using alcoholic drinks at all. **4.** *Archaic.* self-control. —**Syn.** 3. abstinence.

tem·per·ate (tem′pər·it; -prit), *adj.* **1.** not very hot and not very cold: *a temperate climate.* **2.** self-restrained; moderate: *he spoke in a temperate manner.* **3.** moderate in using alcoholic drinks; abstemious. [< L, pp. of *temperare* TEM-PER] —**tem′per·ate·ly,** *adv.* —**tem′per·ate·ness,** *n.* —**Syn.** 2. calm, dispassionate.

Temperate Zone, temperate zone, either of the two parts of the earth between the tropics and the polar circles.

tem·per·a·ture (tem′pər·ə·chər; -prə·chər), *n.* **1.** degree of heat or cold. The temperature of freezing water is 32 degrees Fahrenheit. **2.** degree of heat of a living body. **3.** the excess of this above the normal (98.6 degrees Fahrenheit in adult humans); fever: *the sick man had 3 degrees of temperature.* [< L *temperatura,* ult. < *tempus* time, season]

tem·pered (tem′pərd), *adj.* **1.** softened; moderated. **2.** having a (specified) state of mind: *a good-tempered person.* **3.** treated so as to become hard but not too brittle: *tempered steel.*

tem·pest (tem′pist), *n.* **1.** a violent storm with much wind. **2.** a violent disturbance. —*v.* disturb violently. [< OF *tempest(e)* < var. of L *tempestas* < *tempus* time, season]

tem·pes·tu·ous (tem·pes′chŭ·əs), *adj.* **1.** stormy: *a tempestuous night.* **2.** violent: *a tempestuous argument.* —**tem·pes′tu·ous·ly,** *adv.* —**tem·pes′tu·ous·ness,** *n.*

Tem·plar (tem′plər), *n.* **1.** member of a religious and military order founded among the Crusaders about 1118 to protect the Holy Sepulchre and pilgrims to the Holy Land. **2.** Knight Templar (def. 2).

tem·ple¹ (tem′pəl), *n., v.,* -pled, -pling. —*n.* **1.** a building used for the service or worship of a god or gods. **2.** Also, **Temple.** any of three temples in ancient Jerusalem built at different times by the Jews. **3.** any large building devoted to art, music, or the like. —*v.* provide with a church or temple. [< L *templum*] —**tem′pled,** *adj.* —**tem′ple·less,** *adj.* —**Syn.** n. 1. sanctuary, tabernacle.

tem·ple² (tem′pəl), *n.* the flattened part on either side of the forehead. [< OF, ult. < L *tempus*]

tem·po (tem′pō), *n., pl.* -pos, -pi (-pē). **1.** *Music.* time or rate of movement; proper or characteristic speed of movement. **2.** rhythm; characteristic rhythm, as of work, activity, etc. [< Ital., time, < L *tempus.* Doublet of TENSE².]

tem·po·ral¹ (tem′pə·rəl; -prəl), *adj.* **1.** of time. **2.** lasting for a time only. **3.** of this life only. **4.** not religious or sacred; worldly. [< L, < *tempus* time] —**tem·po·ral·i·ty** (tem′pə·ral′ə·ti), *n.* —**tem′po·ral·ly,** *adv.* —**Syn.** 2. temporary, transient. 3. earthly, terrestrial, mundane.

tem·po·ral² (tem′pə·rəl; -prəl), *adj.* of the temples or sides of the forehead. [< L, < *tempus* temple²]

tem·po·rar·y (tem′pə·rer′i), *adj.* lasting for a short time only; used for the time being; not permanent. [< L, < *tempus* time] —**tem·po·rar·i·ly** (tem′pə·rer′ə·li; emphatic tem′pə·râr′ə·li), *adv.* —**tem′po·rar′i·ness,** *n.* —**Syn.** transient, transitory, fleeting. —**Ant.** permanent, abiding, lasting.

tem·po·rize (tem′pə·rīz), *v.,* -rized, -riz·ing. **1.** evade immediate action or decision in order to gain time, avoid trouble, etc. **2.** fit one's acts to the time or occasion. **3.** come to terms; effect a compromise. [< MF *temporiser,* ult. < L *tempus* time] —**tem′po·ri·za′tion,** *n.* —**tem′po·riz′er,** *n.* —**tem′po·riz′ing·ly,** *adv.*

tempt (tempt), *v.* **1.** make, or try to make (a person) do something: *the sight of food tempted the hungry man to steal.* **2.** appeal strongly to; attract: *his offer tempted me.* **3.** act presumptuous toward; provoke: *it is tempting Providence to go in that old boat.* **4.** *Archaic.* test. [< L *temptare* try] —**tempt′a·ble,** *adj.* —**tempt′er,** *n.* —**Syn.** 1. lure, inveigle, decoy. 2. allure, entice.

temp·ta·tion (temp·tā′shən), *n.* **1.** a tempting. **2.** fact or state of being tempted. **3.** instance of this. **4.** thing that tempts. —**Syn.** 4. attraction, lure, enticement, inducement.

tempt·ing (temp′ting), *adj.* that tempts; alluring; inviting. [< F, < *tenir* hold < L *tenere*] —**tempt′ing·ly,** *adv.* —**tempt′ing·ness,** *n.*

tempt·ress (temp′tris), *n.* woman who tempts.

tem·pus fu·git (tem′pəs fū′jit), *Latin.* time flies.

ten (ten), *n.* **1.** a cardinal number, one more than nine. **2.** symbol of this number; 10. —*adj.* one more than nine; 10. [OE *tēn*]

ten·a·ble (ten′ə·bəl), *adj.* capable of being held or defended: *a tenable position, a tenable theory.* [< F, < *tenir* hold < L tenere] —**ten′a·bil′i·ty, ten′a·ble·ness,** *n.* —**ten′a·bly,** *adv.*

te·na·cious (ti·nā′shəs), *adj.* **1.** holding fast: *the tenacious jaws of a bulldog.* **2.** persistent: *a tenacious salesman.* **3.** able to remember: *a tenacious memory.* **4.** holding fast together; not easily pulled apart. **5.** sticky. [< L *tenax* < *tenere* hold] —**te·na′cious·ly,** *adv.* —**te·na′cious·ness,** *n.* —**Syn.** 2. stubborn, obstinate. 3. retentive.

te·nac·i·ty (ti·nas′ə·ti), *n.* **1.** firmness in holding fast. **2.** stubbornness; persistence. **3.** ability to remember. **4.** firmness in holding together; toughness. **5.** stickiness.

ten·an·cy (ten′ən·si), *n., pl.* -cies. **1.** state of being a tenant; occupying and paying rent for land or buildings. **2.** property so held. **3.** length of time a tenant occupies a property.

ten·ant (ten′ənt), *n.* **1.** person paying rent for the temporary use of the land or buildings of another person. **2.** person or thing that occupies: *birds are tenants of the trees.* —*v.* hold or occupy as a tenant; inhabit. [< F, orig. ppr. of *tenir* hold < L *tenere*] —**ten′ant·a·ble,** *adj.* —**ten′ant·less,** *adj.* —**ten′ant·ship,** *n.*

ten·ant·ry (ten′ənt·ri), *n., pl.* -ries. **1.** all the tenants on an estate. **2.** tenancy.

Ten Commandments, the ten rules for living and for worship that God revealed to Moses on Mount Sinai, according to the Bible. Exod. 20:2–17; Deut. 5:6–22.

tend¹ (tend), *v.* **1.** be apt; incline (to): *fruit tends to decay.* **2.** move (toward); be directed: *the coastline tends to the south here.* [< OF < L *tendere* stretch, aim. Doublet of TENDER².]

tend² (tend), *v.* **1.** attend to by work, services, care, etc.: *he tends shop for his father.* **2.** watch over and care for: *a nurse tends her patient.* [< *attend*] —**Syn.** 2. guard, protect.

tend·en·cy (ten′dən·si), *n., pl.* -cies. **1.** inclination; leaning: *he has a tendency to get angry easily.* **2.** a natural disposition to move, proceed, or act in some direction or toward some point, end, or result: *the tendency of falling bodies toward the earth.* **3.** trend or drift, as of a book, discourse, etc. [< Med.L *tendentia* < L *tendere* tend¹] —**ten·den′tial** (ten·den′shəl), *adj.* —**Syn.** 1. bent, propensity, proneness.

ten·der¹ (ten′dər), *adj.* **1.** not hard or tough; soft: *tender meat.* **2.** not strong and hardy; delicate: *tender young grass.* **3.** kind; affectionate; loving: *she spoke in tender words to the child.* **4.** not rough or crude; gentle: *he patted the dog with tender hands.* **5.** young; immature: *a tender age.* **6.** sensitive; painful; sore: *a tender wound.* **7.** feeling pain or grief easily: *she has a tender nature.* **8.** considerate; careful: *he handles people in a tender manner.* **9.** requiring careful or tactful handling: *a tender situation.* [< OF < L *tener*] —**ten′der·ly,** *adv.* —**ten′der·ness,** *n.* —**Syn.** 2. fragile, weak. 3. compassionate, merciful. 4. mild, sympathetic. —**Ant.** 1. tough. 3. cruel. 4. harsh, rough.

ten·der² (ten′dər), *v.* **1.** offer formally: *he tendered his thanks.* **2.** *Law.* offer (money, goods, etc.) in payment of a debt or other obligation, esp. in exact accordance with provided terms. —*n* 1. a formal offer: *she refused his tender of marriage.* 2. thing offered. Money that must be accepted as payment for a debt is called legal tender. [< F *tendre* < L *tendere* extend. Doublet of TEND¹.] —ten'der·a·ble, *adj.* —ten'der·er, *n.* —Syn. *v.* 1. proffer, present. —*n.* 1. proposal, proffer, overture.

tend·er³ (ten'dər), *n.* 1. person or thing that tends another. 2. a small boat carried or towed by a big one and used for landing passengers. 3. a small ship used for carrying supplies and passengers to and from larger ships. 4. the car attached behind a locomotive and used for carrying coal, oil, water, etc. [< tend²]

ten·der·foot (ten'dər·fůt'), *n., pl.* -foots, -feet. *Am., Colloq.* 1. newcomer to pioneer life. 2. person not used to rough living and hardships. 3. an inexperienced person; beginner.

ten·der-heart·ed (ten'dər·här'tid), *adj.* kindly; sympathetic. —ten'der-heart'ed·ness, *n.*

ten·der·loin (ten'dər·loin'), *n. Am.* 1. a tender part of the loin of beef or pork. 2. Tenderloin, a. a police precinct in New York City affording police officers good opportunities for graft. b. a similar district in other cities where gambling, prostitution, etc., flourish.

ten·don (ten'dən), *n. Anat.* a tough, strong band or cord of tissue that joins a muscle to a bone or some other part; sinew. [< Med.L *tendo* < Gk. *tenon*; infl. by L *tendere* stretch]

ten·dril (ten'drəl), *n.* 1. *Bot.* a threadlike part of a climbing plant that attaches itself to something and helps support the plant. 2. something similar: *tendrils of hair.* [< F *tendrillon*, ult. < L *tener* tender]

Tendrils on a grape vine

ten·e·ment (ten'ə·mənt), *n.* 1. any house or building to live in; dwelling house. 2. part of a house or building occupied by a tenant as a separate dwelling. 3. a tenement house. [< OF, ult. < L *tenere* hold] —ten·e·men·tal (ten'ə·men'təl), ten·e·men·ta·ry (ten'ə·men'tə·ri), *adj.*

tenement house, *Am.* a building divided into sets of rooms occupied by separate families, esp. such a building in the poorer sections of large cities.

ten·et (ten'it; *esp. Brit.* tē'nit), *n.* doctrine, principle, belief, or opinion held as true. [< L, he holds]

ten·fold (ten'fōld'), *adj.* 1. ten times as much or as many. 2. having ten parts. —*adv.* ten times as much or as many.

Tenn., Tennessee.

Ten·nes·see (ten'ə·sē'), *n.* 1. a Southern State of the United States. *Capital:* Nashville. *Abbrev.:* Tenn. 2. river flowing from E Tennessee into the Ohio River. —Ten'nes·se'an, *n., adj. Am.*

ten·nis (ten'is), *n.* a game played by two or four players on a specially marked, oblong court (tennis court), in which a ball is knocked back and forth over a net with a racket (tennis racket). [< AF *tenetz* hold!, ult. < L *tenere*]

Ten·ny·son (ten'ə·sən), *n.* Alfred (*1st Baron Tennyson*) 1809–1892, English poet.

ten·on (ten'ən), *n.* the end of a piece of wood cut so as to fit into a hole (the mortise) in another piece and so form a joint. See the picture under mortise. —*v.* 1. cut so as to form a tenon. 2. fit together with tenon and mortise. [< OF, ult. < L *tenere* hold]

ten·or (ten'ər), *n.* 1. the general tendency; course: *the tenor of his life has been calm.* 2. the general meaning or drift: *the tenor of a speech.* 3. *Music.* a. the adult male voice ranging between the baritone and alto voices. b. part sung by, or written for, such a voice. c. singer or instrument with such a voice or compass. —*adj. Music.* of or for the tenor. [< L, orig., a holding on, < *tenere* hold]

ten·pins (ten'pinz'), *n.* 1. (*sing. in use*) game played with ten wooden pins at which a ball is bowled to knock them down. 2. (*pl. in use*) the pins used.

tense¹ (tens), *adj.*, tens·er, tens·est, *v.*, tensed, tens·ing. —*adj.* 1. stretched tight; strained to stiffness: *a tense rope.* 2. in a state of mental or nervous strain: *a tense person.* 3. characterized by a strain upon the nerves or feelings: *a tense moment.* —*v.* stretch tight; stiffen: *he tensed his muscles for the leap.* [< L *tensus* stretched] —tense'ly, *adv.* —ten'si·ty, tense'ness, *n.* —Syn. *adj.* 1. taut, rigid. —Ant. *adj.* 1. loose, lax, relaxed.

tense² (tens), *n. Gram.* 1. a form of a verb showing the time of the action or state shown. 2. set of such forms for the various persons. [< OF *tens* time < L *tempus.* Doublet of TEMPO.]
▶ **tenses** of verbs. 1. *Sequence of Tenses.* When the verb of a main clause is in the past tense, the verb in a subordinate clause is also in the past tense: *The old man wondered whether the train had arrived.* A present infinitive is, however, usual after a past verb: *They intended to stop* [not: to have stopped] *only an hour in the village.* 2. *Consistent Use of Tenses.* It is confusing to a reader to find tenses shifted without definite reason, as in these sentences: I *sit* down at my desk early with intentions of spending the next four hours studying. Before many minutes *passed,* I *hear* a great deal of noise down on the floor below me; a water fight is in progress. . . . Shifts of this sort should be carefully avoided.

ten·sile (ten'səl), *adj.* 1. of or having to do with tension: *steel has great tensile strength.* 2. capable of being stretched; ductile. —ten·sil'i·ty, *n.*

ten·sion (ten'shən), *n.* 1. a stretching. 2. a stretched condition: *the tension of the spring is caused by the weight.* 3. mental strain: *a mother feels tension when her baby is sick.* 4. strained condition of relations: *political tension.* 5. stress caused by the action of a pulling force. 6. device to control the pull or strain on something. 7. *Elect.* voltage. 8. pressure of a gas. [< LL *tensio* < L *tendere* stretch] —ten'sion·al, *adj.*

ten·sor (ten'sər; -sôr), *n. Anat.* muscle that stretches or tightens some part of the body. [< NL]

tent (tent), *n.* a portable shelter, usually made of canvas, supported by a pole or poles. —*v.* 1. live in a tent. 2. cover with a tent. [< OF *tente,* ult. < L *tendere* stretch] —tent'like', *adj.*

ten·ta·cle (ten'tə·kəl), *n.* 1. *Zool.* a long, slender, flexible growth on the head or around the mouth of an animal, used to touch, hold, or move; feeler. 2. *Bot.* a sensitive, hairlike growth on a plant. [< NL *tentaculum* < L *tentare* feel out] —ten·tac·u·lar (ten·tak'yə·lər), *adj.*

ten·ta·tive (ten'tə·tiv), *adj.* done as a trial or experiment; experimental: *a tentative plan.* [< Med.L, < L *tentare* try out] —ten'ta·tive·ly, *adv.* —ten'ta·tive·ness, *n.*

tent caterpillar, *Am.* a caterpillar that spins tentlike silken webs in which it lives.

ten·ter (ten'tər), *n.* framework on which cloth is stretched so that it may set or dry evenly without shrinking. —*v.* stretch (cloth) on a tenter. [ult. < L *tentus,* pp. of *tendere* stretch]

ten·ter·hook (ten'tər·hůk'), *n.* 1. one of the hooks or bent nails that hold the cloth stretched on a tenter. 2. **on tenterhooks,** in painful suspense; anxious.

tenth (tenth), *adj.* 1. next after the 9th; last in a series of 10. 2. being one of 10 equal parts. —*n.* 1. next after the 9th; last in a series of 10. 2. one of 10 equal parts. —tenth'ly, *adv.*

ten·u·i·ty (ten·ū'ə·ti; ti·nū'-), *n.* rarefied condition; thinness; slightness.

ten·u·ous (ten'yů·əs), *adj.* 1. thin; slender: *tenuous filaments.* 2. not dense: *air ten miles above the earth is very tenuous.* 3. having slight importance; not substantial. [< L *tenuis* thin] —ten'u·ous·ly, *adv.* —ten'u·ous·ness, *n.*

ten·ure (ten'yər), *n.* 1. a holding of property, esp. real property; possessing. 2. length of time of holding or possessing: *the President's tenure*

āge, cāre, fär; ēqual, tėrm; īce; ōpen, ôrder; půt, rüle, ūse; tн, then; ə=a in about.

of office is four years. 3. manner of holding land, buildings, etc., from a feudal lord or superior. [< OF, ult. < L tenere hold] —ten·u·ri·al (ten·yür′i·əl), adj. —ten·u′ri·al·ly, adv.

te·pee (tē′pē), n. Am. tent of the American Indians; wigwam. Also, teepee. [< Am.Ind. (Dakota) tipi]

tep·id (tep′id), adj. slightly warm; lukewarm. [< L tepidus] —te·pid′i·ty, tep′id·ness, n. —tep′id·ly, adv.

Tepees

ter·bi·um (tér′bi·əm), n. Chem. a rare metallic element, Tb, of the yttrium group. [< terb-, abstracted from Ytterby, Swedish town]

ter·cen·te·nar·y (tér·sen′tə·ner′i; tér′sen·ten′ə·ri), adj., n., pl. -nar·ies. —adj. having to do with a period of 300 years. —n. 1. a period of 300 years. 2. a 300th anniversary. [< L ter three times + E centenary]

ter·cet (tér′sit; tér·set′), n. 1. a group of three lines rhyming together, or connected by rhyme with the adjacent group or groups of three lines. 2. Music. triplet. [< F < Ital. terzetto, ult. < L tertius third]

ter·gi·ver·sate (tér′jə·vər·sāt′), v., -sat·ed, -sat·ing. 1. change one's attitude or opinions with respect to a cause or subject. 2. shift or shuffle; evade. [< L tergiversatus, ult. < tergum back + vertere turn] —ter′gi·ver·sa′tion, n. —ter′gi·ver·sa′tor, n.

term (térm), n. 1. word or phrase used in a recognized and definite sense in some particular subject, science, art, business, etc.: medical terms. 2. a set period of time; length of time that a thing lasts: term of office. 3. one of the long periods into which the school year is divided: the fall term. 4. one of the periods of time when certain law courts are in session. 5. an appointed time for the payment of rent, interest, wages, etc. 6. Math. a. one of the members in a proportion or ratio. b. one of the parts of a compound algebraic expression. In $13ax^2-2bxy+y$, $13ax^2$, $2bxy$, and y are the terms. 7. terms, a. conditions: the terms of a treaty. b. way of speaking: in flattering terms. c. personal relations: on good terms, on speaking terms. 8. bring to terms, compel to agree, assent, or submit. —v. name; call: he might be termed handsome. [< OF terme < L terminus end, boundary line. Doublet of TERMINUS.] —term′less, adj. —Syn. n. 3. semester. 7a. stipulations.

ter·ma·gant (tér′mə·gənt), n. a violent, quarreling, scolding woman. —adj. violent; quarreling; scolding. [ult. < OF Tervagan, fictitious Moslem deity] —ter′ma·gan·cy, n.

ter·mi·na·ble (tér′mə·nə·bəl), adj. 1. that can be ended, as an agreement, contract, etc. 2. coming to an end after a certain time: a loan terminable in 10 years. —ter′mi·na·bil′i·ty, tér′mi·na·ble·ness, n. —ter′mi·na·bly, adv.

ter·mi·nal (tér′mə·nəl), adj. 1. at the end; forming the end part: a terminal bud. 2. coming at the end: terminal leave. 3. having to do with a term. 4. at the end of a railroad line. 5. marking a boundary, limit, or end. —n. 1. the end; end part. 2. Am. station, sheds, tracks, etc., at either end of a railroad line. 3. Elect. device attached to an apparatus, by means of which an electrical connection is established. —ter′mi·nal·ly, adv.

ter·mi·nate (tér′mə·nāt), v., -nat·ed, -nat·ing. 1. bring to an end; put an end to: terminate a partnership. 2. come to an end: his contract terminates soon. 3. occur at or form the end of; bound; limit. [< L, < terminus end] —ter′mi·na′tive, adj. —ter′mi·na·tive·ly, adv. —ter′mi·na′tor, n. —Syn. 1. conclude, finish, close.

ter·mi·na·tion (tér′mə·nā′shən), n. 1. an ending or being ended. 2. an end part. 3. Gram. ending of a word; inflection. —ter′mi·na′tion·al, adj. —Syn. 1. conclusion. 2. bound.

ter·mi·nol·o·gy (tér′mə·nol′ə·ji), n., pl. -gies. the special words or terms used in a science, art, business, etc.: medical terminology. —ter·mi·no·log·i·cal (tér′mə·nə·loj′ə·kəl), adj.

ter·mi·nus (tér′mə·nəs), n., pl. -ni (-nī), -nus·es. 1. either end of a railroad line, bus line, etc. 2. city or station at the end of a railroad line, bus line, etc. 3. an ending place; final point; goal; end. 4. a stone post, etc., marking a boundary or limit. [< L. Doublet of TERM.]

ter·mite (tér′mīt), n. any of the various soft-bodied insects that look like pale-colored ants and are often called white ants. Termites are very destructive to buildings, furniture, provisions, etc. [< NL termes, special use of L, woodworm] —ter·mit·ic (tér·mit′ik), adj.

tern (térn), n. a sea bird like a gull but with a more slender body and bill and a long, forked tail. [< Scand. (Dan.) terne]

Terp·sich·o·re (térp·sik′ə·rē), n. Gk. Myth. the Muse of dancing.

terp·si·cho·re·an (térp′sə·kə·rē′ən), adj. 1. having to do with dancing: the terpsichorean art. 2. Terpsichorean, of or pertaining to Terpsichore. —n. Colloq. dancer.

ter·race (ter′is), n., v., -raced, -rac·ing. —n. 1. a flat, raised piece of land; raised level. 2. street along the side or top of a slope. 3. row of houses on such a street. 4. a paved outdoor space adjoining a house, used for lounging, dining, etc. 5. the flat roof of a house, esp. of an Oriental or Spanish house. —v. form into a terrace or terraces; furnish with terraces. [< OF, ult. < L terra earth]

Terraces (def. 1)

ter·ra cot·ta (ter′ə kot′ə), 1. a kind of hard, brownish-red earthenware, used for vases, statuettes, etc. 2. a dull brownish red. [< Ital., < terra earth + cotta baked] —ter′ra-cot′ta, adj.

ter·ra fir·ma (ter′ə fér′mə), solid earth. [< L]

ter·rain (te·rān′; ter′ān), n. land; tract of land, esp. considered as to its extent and natural features in relation to its use in warfare. [< F, ult. < L terra land]

ter·ra·my·cin (ter′ə·mī′sin), n. an antibiotic derived from a soil microörganism, used in the treatment of syphilis, some rheumatic diseases, certain bacterial infections, etc. [< L terra earth + Gk. mykes fungus]

ter·ra·pin (ter′ə·pin), n. Am. a fresh-water or tidewater North American turtle used for food. [< Algonquian]

ter·rar·i·um (tə·rār′i·əm), n., pl. -i·ums, -i·a (-i·ə). vivarium for land animals. [< NL, < L terra land]

ter·res·tri·al (tə·res′tri·əl), adj. 1. of or having to do with the earth: terrestrial magnetism. 2. of land, not water: islands and continents make up the terrestrial parts of the earth. 3. living on the ground; not in the air or water or in trees: a terrestrial creature. 4. growing on land; growing in the ground: terrestrial plants. 5. worldly; earthly: terrestrial matters. [< L terrestris < terra earth] —ter·res′tri·al·ly, adv.

ter·ri·ble (ter′ə·bəl), adj. 1. causing great fear; dreadful; awful: a terrible leopard. 2. distressing; severe: the terrible suffering caused by war. 3. Colloq. extremely bad, unpleasant, etc.: a terrible temper. [< L, < terrere terrify] —ter′ri·ble·ness, n. —ter′ri·bly, adv. —Syn. 1. frightful, appalling, horrible, shocking.

ter·ri·er (ter′i·ər), n. a kind of small, active dog, formerly used to pursue prey into its burrow, occurring in numerous breeds, as the fox terrier, Airedale, Scotch terrier, etc. [< F, ult. < L terra earth]

ter·rif·ic (tə·rif′ik), adj. 1. causing great fear; terrifying. 2. Colloq. very great, severe, etc. [< L, < terrere terrify + -ficus making] —ter·rif′i·cal·ly, adv.

ter·ri·fy (ter′ə·fī), v., -fied, -fy·ing. fill with great fear; frighten very much. [< L, < terrere terrify + facere make] —ter′ri·fied·ly, adv. —ter′ri·fi′er, n. —ter′ri·fy′ing·ly, adv. —Syn. scare, alarm, horrify, appal, dismay.

ter·ri·to·ri·al (ter′ə·tô′ri·əl; -tō′-), adj. 1. of or having to do with territory. 2. Territorial, Am. of or having to do with a U.S. Territory. 3.

ōī or restricted to a particular territory or district. 4. Also, **Territorial**, *Brit.* organized for home defense. —*n.* **Territorial**, *Brit.* soldier of a Territorial force. —**ter′ri·to′ri·al·ism**, *n.* —**ter′ri·to′ri·al·ist**, *n.* —**ter′ri·to′ri·al·ly**, *adv.*

ter·ri·to·ry (ter′ə·tô′ri; -tō′-), *n., pl.* **-ries.** 1. land; region: *much territory in Africa is desert.* 2. land belonging to a government; land under the rule of a distant government. Gibraltar is British territory. 3. **Territory**, *Am.* district not admitted as a State but having its own lawmaking body. The Virgin Islands is a territory. 4. region assigned to a salesman or agent. 5. the facts investigated by some branch of science or learning: *the territory of biochemistry.* [< L *territorium* < *terra* land]

ter·ror (ter′ər), *n.* 1. great fear. 2. a feeling or cause of great fear. 3. *Colloq.* person or thing that causes much trouble and unpleasantness. [< L] —**ter′ror·less**, *adj.* —**Syn.** 1. fright, alarm, dread, consternation.

ter·ror·ism (ter′ər·iz·əm), *n.* 1. a terrorizing; use of terror. 2. condition of fear and submission produced by frightening people. 3. method of opposing a government internally through the use of terror. —**ter′ror·ist**, *n.* —**ter′ror·is′tic**, *adj.*

ter·ror·ize (ter′ər·īz), *v.,* **-ized, -iz·ing.** 1. fill with terror. 2. rule or subdue by causing terror. —**ter′ror·i·za′tion**, *n.* —**ter′ror·iz′er**, *n.*

ter·ry (ter′i), or **terry cloth**, *n., pl.* **-ries.** a rough cloth made of uncut looped yarn.

terse (tėrs), *adj.,* **ters·er, ters·est.** brief and to the point (said of writing, speaking, writers, or speakers). [< L *tersus*, pp. of *tergere* rub, polish] —**terse′ly**, *adv.* —**terse′ness**, *n.*

ter·ti·ar·y (tėr′shi·er′i; tėr′shə·ri), *adj., n., pl.* **-ar·ies.** —*adj.* of the third degree, order, rank, formation, etc.; third. —*n.* one of a bird's flight feathers. [< L, < *tertius* third]

tes·sel·late (*v.* tes′ə·lāt; *adj.* tes′ə·lit, -lāt), *v.,* **-lat·ed, -lat·ing,** *adj.* —*v.* make of small squares or blocks, or in a checkered pattern. —*adj.* made in this way. [< L *tessellatus*] —**tes′sel·la′tion**, *n.*

Tessellated

test (test), *n.* 1. a determining of presence, quality, or genuineness; examination; trial. 2. means of trial: *trouble is a test of character.* 3. *Chem.* a. examination of a substance to see what it is or what it contains, esp. by reagents, spectroscope, etc. b. process or substance used in such an examination. 4. *Educ.* a form of questioning and measuring used to evaluate retention of knowledge, capability, etc. —*v.* examine by a test; try out. [< OF, vessel used in assaying, < L *testum* earthen vessel] —**test′a·ble**, *adj.* —**test′er**, *n.*

Test., Testament.

tes·ta·ment (tes′tə·mənt), *n.* 1. *Law.* written instructions telling what to do with a person's property after his death; will. 2. **Testament**, a. a main division of the Bible; the Old Testament or the New Testament. b. *Colloq.* the New Testament. [< L, ult. < *testis* witness]

tes·ta·men·ta·ry (tes′tə·men′tə·ri; -tri), *adj.* 1. of or having to do with a testament or will. 2. given, done, or appointed by a testament or will. 3. in a testament or will. —**tes′ta·men′ta·ri·ly**, *adv.*

tes·tate (tes′tāt), *adj.* having made and left a valid will. —*n.* person who has left a valid will.

tes·ta·tor (tes′tā·tər; tes·tā′tər), *n.* person who makes a will, esp. one who has died leaving a valid will.

tes·ta·trix (tes·tā′triks), *n., pl.* **-tri·ces** (-trə·sēz). woman who makes a will; woman who has died leaving a will.

tes·ti·cle (tes′tə·kəl), *n.* one of the two sex glands in the male which secrete the spermatozoa. [< L *testiculus*, dim. of *testis* TESTIS] —**tes·tic·u·lar** (tes·tik′yə·lər), *adj.*

tes·ti·fy (tes′tə·fī), *v.,* **-fied, -fy·ing.** 1. give evidence; bear witness: *the excellence of Shake-*

speare's plays testifies to his genius. 2. give evidence of; bear witness to: *he testified that the paper was in my possession.* 3. declare solemnly; affirm. 4. *Law.* declare or give evidence under oath in a law court. [< L, < *testis* witness + *facere* make] —**tes′ti·fi·ca′tion**, *n.* —**tes′ti·fi′er**, *n.*

tes·ti·mo·ni·al (tes′tə·mō′ni·əl), *n.* 1. certificate of character, conduct, qualifications, value, etc.; recommendation. 2. something given or done to show esteem, admiration, gratitude, etc. —*adj.* given or done as a testimonial. —**Syn.** *n.* 1. credential, voucher.

tes·ti·mo·ny (tes′tə·mō′ni), *n., pl.* **-nies.** 1. statement of a witness under oath, used for evidence or proof: *a witness gave testimony that Mr. Doe was at home at 9 p.m.* 2. evidence: *the pupils presented their teacher with a watch in testimony of their respect and affection.* 3. an open declaration or profession of one's faith. [< L, < *testis* witness] —**Syn.** 1. attestation, affirmation, deposition. 2. witness, proof.

tes·tis (tes′tis), *n., pl.* **-tes** (-tēz). testicle. [< L, witness (of virility)]

tes·tos·ter·one (tes·tos′tər·ōn), *n.* a hormone, $C_{19}H_{28}O_2$, usually obtained from bulls' testicles.

test pilot, a pilot employed to test new or experimental airplanes by subjecting them to greater than normal stress.

test tube, a thin glass tube closed at one end, used in making chemical tests.

tes·tu·do (tes·tū′dō; -tū′-), *n., pl.* **-di·nes** (-də·nēz). 1. among the ancient Romans, a movable shelter with a strong and usually fireproof arched roof, used for protection in siege operations. 2. a shelter formed by a body of troops overlapping their shields above their heads. 3. some other sheltering contrivance. [< L, lit., tortoise < *testa* shell]

tes·ty (tes′ti), *adj.,* **-ti·er, -ti·est.** easily irritated; impatient. [< AF *testif* headstrong < *teste* head < L *testa* pot] —**tes′ti·ly**, *adv.* —**tes′ti·ness**, *n.* —**Syn.** irascible, peevish, petulant, cross.

tet·a·nus (tet′ə·nəs), *n.* a disease caused by bacilli entering the body through wounds, characterized by violent spasms, stiffness of many muscles, and even death. Tetanus of the lower jaw is called lockjaw. [< L < Gk. *tetanos* < *teinein* stretch] —**te·tan·ic** (ti·tan′ik), *adj.*

tête-à-tête (tāt′ə·tāt′), *adv.* two together in private: *they dined tête-à-tête.* —*adj.* of or for two people in private. —*n.* 1. a private conversation between two people. 2. *Am.* an S-shaped seat built so that two people can sit facing one another. [< F, head to head]

teth·er (teth′ər), *n.* 1. rope or chain for fastening an animal so that it can graze only within certain limits. 2. **at the end of one's tether**, at the end of one's resources or endurance. —*v.* fasten with a tether. [prob. < *Scand.* *tjōthr*]

tet·ra·he·dron (tet′rə·hē′drən), *n., pl.* **-drons, -dra** (-drə). *Geom.* a solid bounded by four plane sides. The most common tetrahedron is a pyramid whose base and three sides are equilateral triangles. [< LGk., < *tettares* four + *hedra* seat, base] —**tet′ra·he′dral**, *adj.* —**tet′ra·he′dral·ly**, *adv.*

Tetrahedron

te·tral·o·gy (te·tral′ə·ji), *n., pl.* **-gies.** series of four connected dramas, operas, etc. [< Gk., < *tettares* four + *logos* discourse]

te·tram·e·ter (te·tram′ə·tər), *adj.* consisting of four measures or feet. —*n.* line of verse having four measures or feet. [< L < Gk., < *tettares* four + *metron* measure]

tet·rarch (tet′rärk; tē′trärk), *n.* 1. the ruler of a part (originally a fourth part) of a province in the ancient Roman Empire. 2. any subordinate ruler. [< L < Gk., < *tettares* four + *archos* ruler] —**te·trar·chic** (te·trär′kik; tē-), *adj.*

tet·ra·va·lent (tet′rə·vā′lənt; te·trav′ə-), *adj.* *Chem.* having a valence of four.

te·trox·ide (te·trok′sid; -sid), **te·trox·id**

(–sid), *n.* any oxide having four atoms of oxygen in each molecule.

tet·ter (tet′ər), *n.* an itching skin disease. Eczema is a tetter. [OE *teter*]

Teu·ton (tü′tən; tū′-), *n.* **1.** German. **2.** member of a group of N Europeans that includes Germans, Dutch, and Scandinavians. —*adj.* German.

Teu·ton·ic (tü·ton′ik; tū-), *adj.* **1.** of or pertaining to the ancient Germanic tribes. **2.** German. **3.** of or having to do with the Teutons or their languages. —*n.* Germanic.

Tex., Texas.

Tex·as (tek′səs), *n.* a Southern State of the United States. *Capital:* Austin. *Abbrev.:* Tex. —Tex′an, *adj.*, *n. Am.*

Texas tower, *Am.*, *Slang.* a radar island (from its resemblance to the steel structures built in the Gulf of Mexico for drilling oil).

text (tekst), *n.* **1.** the main body of reading matter in a book: *this history contains 300 pages of text.* **2.** the original words of a writer. A text is often changed here and there when it is copied. **3.** any one of the various wordings of a poem, play, etc. **4.** the printed words on a page, as distinguished from margins, illustrations, etc. **5.** a short passage in the Bible, used as the subject of a sermon or as proof of some belief. **6.** topic; subject. **7.** textbook. [ult. < L *textus*, orig., texture < *texere* weave]

text·book (tekst′bŭk′), *n.* book for regular study by pupils. Most arithmetics and geographies are textbooks.

tex·tile (teks′til; –til), *adj.* **1.** woven. Cloth is a textile fabric. **2.** suitable for weaving. Cotton and wool are common textile materials. **3.** of or having to do with weaving: *the textile art.* —*n.* **1.** a woven fabric; cloth. **2.** material suitable for weaving. [< L, < *texere* weave]

tex·tu·al (teks′chü·əl), *adj.* of a text; pertaining to a text. A misprint is a textual error. —tex′tu·al·ly, *adv.*

tex·ture (teks′chər), *n.* **1.** arrangement of threads in a woven fabric. Burlap has a much coarser texture than a linen handkerchief. **2.** arrangement of the parts of anything; structure; constitution; make-up. Sandstone and granite have different textures. [< L, < *texere* weave] —tex′tur·al, *adj.* —tex′tur·al·ly, *adv.* —tex′tured, *adj.* —tex′ture·less, *adj.*

Th, *Chem.* thorium.

Thack·er·ay (thak′ər·i), *n.* William Makepeace, 1811–1863, English novelist.

Thai·land (tī′land), *n.* country in SE Asia bordered by Burma and Laos and Cambodia. It is the official name of Siam. See map at Malaysia.

thal·a·mus (thal′ə·məs), *n.*, *pl.* -mi (-mī). **1.** a part of the brain where a nerve emerges or appears to emerge. The optic thalami are two large, oblong masses of gray matter forming a part of the midbrain. **2.** *Bot.* a receptacle of a flower. [< L, inside room, < Gk. *thalamos*] —tha·lam·ic (thə·lam′ik), *adj.*

tha·ler (tä′lər), *n.*, *pl.* -ler. a former German silver coin, worth about 71½ cents. Also, taler.

thal·li·um (thal′i·əm), *n.* a soft, malleable, rare metallic element, Tl. [< NL, < Gk. *thallos* green shoot (from green band of spectrum)]

thal·lo·phyte (thal′ə·fīt), *n.* any of a large group of plants that have no leaves, stems, or roots. Bacteria, algae, fungi, and lichens are thallophytes. [< Gk. *thallos* green shoot + *phyton* plant] —thal·lo·phyt·ic (thal′ə·fit′ik), *adj.*

thal·lus (thal′əs), *n.*, *pl.* -li (-ī), -lus·es. a plant not divided into leaves, stem, and root. Mushrooms, toadstools, and lichens are thalli. [< NL < Gk. *thallos* green shoot]

Thames (temz), *n.* river flowing from SW England through London into the North Sea.

than (ŧẖan; *unstressed* ŧẖən), *conj.* **1.** in comparison with; compared to that which: *this train is faster than that one.* **2.** except; besides: *how else can we come than on foot?* **3.** than whom, compared to whom. [OE] ▶ Than is a conjunction introducing the second member of an unequal comparison: *You will get there earlier than*

I will. Since the clause with *than* is usually verbless (*than he, than I*), it appears rather as a preposition and in colloquial and substandard usage is often followed by an accusative as in: *You'll get there earlier than me* (colloquial and substandard). *Than whom* is an idiom used in all levels: *We admire the good manners and kindness of Mary, than whom there is no nicer person. Than* is the idiom after *no sooner: He had no sooner opened the door than the flames flared up. Then* is often carelessly written for *than.*

thane (thān), *n.* **1.** man who ranked between an earl and an ordinary freeman in early England. Thanes held lands of the king or lord and gave military service in return. **2.** a Scottish baron or lord. Also, thegn. [OE *thegn*] —thane′ship, *n.*

thank (thangk), *v.* **1.** say that one is pleased and grateful for something given or done; express gratitude to. **2.** have oneself to thank, be to blame. —*n.* **1.** thanks, a. I thank you. b. expression of gratitude and pleasure for something given or done. c. a feeling of kindness received; gratitude. **2.** thanks to, a. thanks be given to. b. owing to; because of. [OE *thanc*, orig., thought] —thank′er, *n.*

thank·ful (thangk′fəl), *adj.* feeling or expressing thanks; grateful. —thank′ful·ly, *adv.* —thank′ful·ness, *n.*

thank·less (thangk′lis), *adj.* **1.** not feeling or expressing thanks; not grateful. **2.** not likely to be rewarded with thanks; not appreciated. —thank′less·ly, *adv.* —thank′less·ness, *n.*

thanks·giv·ing (thangks·giv′ing), *n.* **1.** a giving of thanks. **2.** expression of thanks. **3.** day set apart to acknowledge God's favor. **4.** Thanksgiving, *Am.* Thanksgiving Day.

Thanksgiving Day, *Am.* a day set apart every year to acknowledge God's favor, usually the last Thursday in November.

that (ŧẖat; *unstressed* ŧẖət), *adj.* **1.** indicating some person, thing, idea, etc., already mentioned, understood, or to be emphasized: *do you know that boy?* **2.** indicating the farther of two or more things: *shall I buy this dress or that one we saw yesterday?* **3.** showing contrast: *this hat is prettier but that one costs less.* —*pron.* **1.** some person, thing, idea, etc., already mentioned, understood, or to be emphasized: *that is the right way, that's a good boy!* **2.** the farther of two or more things: *I like that better.* **3.** something contrasted: *which hat do you want, this or that?* **4.** who; whom; which: *the boy that I know, the hat that I want.* **5.** when; at or in which: *the year that we went abroad.* **6.** at that, *Colloq.* a. with no more talk, work, etc. b. *Am.* considering everything. **7.** in that, because. **8.** that's that, *Colloq.* that is settled or decided. —*conj.* that is used: **1.** to introduce a noun clause that is the subject or object of a verb: *that he will be here on time is not certain, I know that 6 and 4 are 10.* **2.** to show purpose: *he ran fast that he might not be late.* **3.** to show result: *he ran so fast that he was five minutes early.* **4.** to show cause: *I wonder what happened, not that I care.* **5.** to express a wish: *oh, that she were here!* **6.** to show anger, surprise, etc.: *that one so fair should be so false.* —*adv.* to such an extent or degree; so: a. (with adjectives and adverbs of quantity or degree): *he cannot stay up that late.* b. *Colloq.* or *Dial.* (with other adjectives and adverbs): *I am that sad I could cry.* [OE *thæt*]

thatch (thach), *n.* **1.** straw, rushes, palm leaves, etc., used as a roof or covering. **2.** roof or covering of thatch. —*v.* roof or cover with thatch. [OE *thæc*] —thatch′er, *n.* —thatch′y, *adj.*

Thatched roof

thau·ma·tur·gy (thô′mə·tėr′ji), *n.* the working of wonders or miracles; magic. [< Gk., ult. < *thauma* marvel + *orgos* working < *ergon* work] —thau′ma·tur′gic, thau′ma·tur′gi·cal, *adj.*

thaw (thô), *v.* **1.** melt: *the pond thaws in April.* **2.** become warm enough to melt ice, snow, etc.: *if the sun stays out, it will probably thaw today.* **3.**

make or become free of frost, ice, etc.: *our sidewalk thawed yesterday.* 4. make or become less stiff and formal in manner; soften: *his shyness thawed under her kindness.* —*n.* 1. a thawing. 2. weather above the freezing point (32 degrees); time of melting. 3. a becoming less stiff and formal in manner; softening. [OE *thawian*] —thaw'er, *n.* —thaw'less, *adj.*

the¹ (*unstressed before a consonant* thə; *unstressed before a vowel* thi; *stressed* thē), *definite article.* The word the shows that a certain one (or ones) is meant. Various special uses are: (1) to mark a noun as indicating something well-known or unique: *the Alps.* (2) with or as part of a title: *the Duke of Wellington.* (3) to mark a noun as indicating the best-known or most important of its kind: *the place to dine.* (4) to mark a noun as being used generically: *the dog is a quadruped.* (5) to indicate a part of the body or a personal belonging: *hang the head in shame.* (6) before adjectives used as nouns: *visit the sick, a love of the beautiful.* (7) distributively; to denote any one separately: *candy at one dollar the pound.* [OE thē, thel] ➤ the. The repetition of the article before the various nouns of a series emphasizes their distinctness: *The color, the fragrance, and their beautiful patterns of these flowers make them universal favorites; the color, fragrance, and pattern of these flowers are distinctive.*

the² (thə; thi), *adv.* The word the is used to modify an adjective or adverb in the comparative degree: (1) signifying "in or by that," "on that account," "in some or any degree": *if you start now, you will be back the sooner.* (2) used correlatively, in one instance with relative force and in the other with demonstrative force, and signifying "by how much . . . by so much," "in what degree . . . in that degree": *the more the merrier, the sooner the better.* [OE thȳ, thē, thon]

the·a·ter, *esp. Brit.* **the·a·tre** (thē'ə·tər), *n.* 1. place where plays are acted; place where motion pictures are shown. 2. place that looks like a theater in its arrangement of seats. 3. place of action: *theater of a war.* 4. plays; writing and producing plays; the drama. [< L < Gk. *theatron*]

the·at·ri·cal (thi·at'rə·kəl), *adj.* Also, **theat'ric.** 1. of or pertaining to the theater or actors. 2. suggesting a theater or acting; for display or effect; artificial. —*n.* theatricals, a. dramatic performances, esp. as given by amateurs. b. matters pertaining to the stage and acting. c. actions of a theatrical or artificial character. —the·at'ri·cal·ism, *n.* —the·at·ri·cal·i·ty (thi·at'rə·kal'ə·ti), the·at'ri·cal·ness, *n.* —the·at'ri·cal·ly, *adv.* —Syn. *adj.* 1. dramatic, histrionic. 2. affected, assumed.

Thebes (thēbz), *n.* 1. an ancient city on the Nile, now in ruins, formerly a center of Egyptian civilization. 2. city in ancient Greece. —The·ban (thē'bən), The·ba·ic (thē·bā'ik), *adj.*

thee (thē), *pron.* the objective case of thou. [OE thē]

theft (theft), *n.* 1. act of stealing. 2. an instance of stealing. [OE *thēoft* < *thēof* thief] —Syn. 1. thievery, pilfering, larceny, robbery.

thegn (thān), *n.* thane.

the·ine (thē'ēn; -in), **the·in** (-in), *n. Chem.* caffeine.

their (thār), *pron.* the possessive case of they, used before a noun. [< Scand *their(r)a*]

theirs (thārz), *pron.* 1. of them; belonging to them: *those books are theirs, not mine.* 2. the one or ones belonging to them: *our house is white; theirs is brown.*

the·ism (thē'iz·əm), *n.* belief in one God, the creator and ruler of the universe. [< Gk. *theos* god] —the'ist, *n.* —the·is'tic, *adj.* —the·is'ti·cal·ly, *adv.*

them (them; *unstressed* thəm), *pron.* the objective case of they. [< Scand. *theim*]

theme (thēm), *n.* 1. topic, as of a speech, discussion, book, etc.; subject. 2. a short written composition. 3. *Music.* a. the principal melody in a piece of music. b. a short melody repeated in

different forms in an elaborate musical composition. 4. a melody used to identify a particular radio or television program. [< L < Gk. *thema*, lit., something set down] —the·mat·ic (thē·mat'ik), *adj.* —the·mat'i·cal·ly, *adv.*

The·mis·to·cles (thə·mis'tə·klēz), *n.* 527?–460? B.C., Athenian leader and statesman.

them·selves (them·selvz'; thəm-), *pron.* 1. the emphatic form of they or them: *they did it themselves.* 2. the reflexive form of them: *they injured themselves.*

then (then), *adv.* 1. at that time: *prices were then lower.* 2. soon afterwards: *the noise stopped, and then began again.* 3. next in time or place: *first comes spring, then summer.* 4. at another time: *now one boy does best and then another.* 5. also; besides: *the dress seems too good to discard, and then it is so becoming.* 6. in that case; therefore: *if you didn't know, then you should have said so.* 7. but then, but at the same time; but on the other hand. 8. then and there, at that time and place; at once and on the spot. —*n.* that time: *by then we shall know the result.* —*adj.* being at that time; existing then: *the then President.* [OE *thænne*] ➤ Then is a conjunctive adverb. Often the connection between clauses is made closer by using and then: *The next three hours we spent in sightseeing; then we settled down to business. He ate a good meal, and then he took a nap before starting home again. Then too is overused as a connective in amateur writing: A reader enjoys a fast-moving story; then too he may enjoy finding something that will set him thinking.* Better: *A reader enjoys a fast-moving story, and he may also enjoy finding something that will set him thinking.* ➤ then, than. These words are often carelessly confused in writing. *Then* is an adverb of time, *than* a conjunction in clauses of comparison: *Then the whole crowd went to the drugstore. I think that book was better than any other novel I read last year.*

thence (thens), *adv.* 1. from that place; from there: *a few miles thence is a river.* 2. for that reason; therefore: *you didn't work, thence no pay.* 3. from that time; from then: *a few years thence.* [ME *thennes* < OE *thanan(e)*]

thence·forth (thens'fôrth'; -fôrth'), **thence·for·ward** (-fôr'wərd), **thence·for·wards** (-wərdz), *adv.* from then on; from that time forward.

the·oc·ra·cy (thi·ok'rə·si), *n., pl.* -cies. 1. government in which God is recognized as the supreme civil ruler and His laws are taken as the laws of the state. 2. government by priests. 3. country or nation governed by a theocracy. [< Gk., < *theos* god + *kratos* rule] —the·o·crat·ic (thē'ə·krat'ik), the'o·crat'i·cal, *adj.* —the'o·crat'i·cal·ly, *adv.*

the·od·o·lite (thi·od'ə·līt), *n.* a surveying instrument for measuring horizontal and vertical angles. —the·od·o·lit·ic (thi·od'ə·lit'ik), *adj.*

theol., theology.

the·o·lo·gian (thē'ə·lō'jən; -ji·ən), *n.* person skilled or trained in theology.

the·o·log·i·cal (thē'ə·loj'ə·kəl), **the·o·log·ic** (-ik), *adj.* 1. of or pertaining to theology. 2. referring to the nature and will of God. —the'o·log'i·cal·ly, *adv.*

the·ol·o·gy (thi·ol'ə·ji), *n., pl.* -gies. 1. study of the nature of God and His relations to man and the universe. 2. study of religion and religious beliefs. 3. system of religious beliefs. [< Gk., < *theos* god + *logos* treating of] —the·ol'o·gist, *n.*

the·o·rem (thē'ə·rəm), *n.* 1. statement in mathematics to be proved. 2. statement of mathematical relations that can be expressed by an equation or formula. 3. statement or rule that can be proved to be true. [< L < Gk. *theorema* < *theorein* consider] —the·o·re·mat·ic (thē'ə·rə·mat'ik), *adj.*

the·o·ret·i·cal (thē'ə·ret'ə·kəl), **the·o·ret·ic** (-ik), *adj.* 1. planned or worked out in the mind, not from experience; based on theory, not on fact; limited to theory. 2. dealing with theory only; not practical. —the'o·ret'i·cal·ly, *adv.*

the·o·re·ti·cian (thē'ə·rə·tish'ən), *n.* person who knows much about the theory of an art, science, etc.

the·o·rist (thē'ə·rist), *n.* person who forms theories.

the·o·rize (thē'ə·rīz), *v.,* **-rized, -riz·ing.** form a theory or theories; speculate. —**the'o·ri·za'tion,** *n.* —**the'o·riz'er,** *n.*

the·o·ry (thē'ə·ri), *n., pl.* **-ries. 1.** explanation; explanation based on thought; explanation based on observation and reasoning. **2.** the principles or methods of a science or art rather than its practice: *the theory of music.* **3.** abstract knowledge. **4.** thought or fancy as opposed to fact or practice. [< LL < Gk., < *theorein* consider] —**Syn. 1.** hypothesis, principle, doctrine.

the·os·o·phy (thi·os'ə·fi), *n.* a philosophy or religion that claims to have a special insight into the divine nature through spiritual self-development. Modern theosophy includes many of the teachings of Buddhism and Brahmanism. [< Med.L < LGk., ult. < Gk. *theos* god + *sophos* wise] —**the·o·soph·ic** (thē'ə·sof'ik), **the'o·soph'i·cal,** *adj.* —**the'o·soph'i·cal·ly,** *adv.* —**the·os'o·phist,** *n.*

ther·a·peu·tic (ther'ə·pū'tik), **ther·a·peu·ti·cal** (-tə·kəl), *adj.* having to do with the treatment or curing of disease; curative. [< NL, ult. < Gk. *therapeuein* cure, treat < *theraps* attendant] —**ther'a·peu'ti·cal·ly,** *adv.*

ther·a·peu·tics (ther'ə·pū'tiks), *n.* branch of medicine that deals with the remedial treatment of disease; therapy.

ther·a·peu·tist (ther'ə·pū'tist), *n.* person who specializes in therapeutics.

ther·a·py (ther'ə·pi), *n., pl.* **-pies.** treatment of diseases. —**ther'a·pist,** *n.*

there (thãr; *unstressed* thər), *adv.* **1.** in or at that place: *sit there.* **2.** to or into that place: *go there at once.* **3.** at that point in an action, speech, etc.: *you have done enough, you may stop there.* **4.** in that matter, particular, or respect: *you are mistaken there.* **5.** *There* is also used in sentences in which the verb comes before its subject: *is there a drugstore near here?* **6.** *There* is used to call attention to some person or thing: *there goes the bell.* —*n.* that place: *from there go on to New York.* —*interj. There* is also used to express satisfaction, triumph, dismay, encouragement, comfort, etc.: *there, there! don't cry.* —*adj.* **all there,** *Colloq.* **a.** wide-awake; alert. **b.** sane; not crazy. [OE *thãr*]

there·a·bouts (thãr'ə·bouts'), **there·a·bout** (-bout'), *adv.* **1.** near that place. **2.** near that time. **3.** near that number or amount.

there·af·ter (thãr·af'tər; -äf'-), *adv.* **1.** after that; afterward. **2.** accordingly.

there·at (thãr·at'), *adv.* **1.** when that happened; at that time. **2.** because of that; because of it. **3.** at that place; there.

there·by (thãr·bī'; thãr'bī), *adv.* **1.** by means of that; in that way. **2.** in connection with that: *thereby hangs a tale.* **3.** near there.

there·for (thãr·fôr'), *adv.* for that; for this; for it.

there·fore (thãr'fôr; -fōr), *adv.* for that reason; as a result of that; consequently. —**Syn.** hence, wherefore, then, accordingly.

there·from (thãr·from'; -frum'), *adv.* from that; from this; from it.

there·in (thãr·in'), *adv.* **1.** in that place; in it. **2.** in that matter; in that way.

there·in·to (thãr·in'tü; thãr'in·tü'), *adv.* **1.** into that place; into it. **2.** into that matter.

there·of (thãr·ov'; -uv'), *adv.* **1.** of that; of it. **2.** from it; from that source.

there·on (thãr·on'; -ôn'), *adv.* **1.** on that; on it. **2.** immediately after that.

there·to (thãr·tü'), *adv.* **1.** to that; to it. **2.** in addition to that; also.

there·to·fore (thãr'tə·fôr'; -fōr'), *adv.* before that time; until then.

there·un·der (thãr·un'dər), *adv.* **1.** under that; under it. **2.** under the authority of that; according to that.

there·un·to (thãr·un'tü; thãr'un·tü'), *adv.* to that; to it.

there·up·on (thãr'ə·pon'; -pôn'), *adv.* **1.** immediately after that. **2.** because of that; therefore. **3.** on that; on it. **4.** with reference to that.

there·with (thãr·with'; -with'), *adv.* **1.** with that; with it. **2.** in addition to that; also. **3.** immediately after that; then.

there·with·al (thãr'with·ôl'), *adv.* **1.** with that; with this; with it. **2.** in addition to that; also.

ther·mal (ther'məl), *adj.* Also, **ther·mic** (ther'mik). **1.** of or pertaining to heat. **2.** warm; hot. —*n.* in aeronautics and aerodynamics, a current of rising warm air. [< Gk. *therme* heat] —**ther'mal·ly, ther'mi·cal·ly,** *adv.*

thermal barrier, heat barrier.

thermo-, therm-, *word element.* heat. [< Gk. *therme*]

ther·mo·dy·nam·ic (ther'mō·dī·nam'ik; -dī-), **ther·mo·dy·nam·i·cal** (-ə·kəl), *adj.* **1.** of or having to do with thermodynamics. **2.** using force due to heat or to the conversion of heat into mechanical energy.

ther·mo·dy·nam·ics (ther'mō·dī·nam'iks; -dī-), *n.* branch of physics that deals with the relations between heat and mechanical energy.

ther·mo·e·lec·tric·i·ty (ther'mō·i·lek'tris'ə·ti; -ē'lek-), *n.* electricity produced directly by heat. —**ther'mo·e·lec'tric, ther'mo·e·lec'tri·cal,** *adj.* —**ther'mo·e·lec'tri·cal·ly,** *adv.*

ther·mom·e·ter (thər·mom'ə·tər), *n.* instrument for measuring temperature, as by means of the expansion and contraction of mercury or alcohol in a capillary tube and bulb. —**ther·mo·met·ric** (ther'mə·met'rik), *adj.*

ther·mo·nu·cle·ar (ther'mō·nü'kli·ər; -nū'-), *adj.* of or designating the fusion of atoms (as in the hydrogen bomb) through very high temperature: *a thermonuclear reaction.*

ther·mo·plas·tic (ther'mō·plas'tik), *adj.* becoming soft and capable of being molded when heated. —*n.* such a material, esp. a plastic.

Ther·mop·y·lae (thər·mop'ə·lē), *n.* a mountain pass in Greece. In 480 B.C., a few Spartan soldiers defended it against a great army of Persians until every Spartan was killed.

Ther·mos (ther'məs), *n. Trademark.* bottle, flask, or jug having a case or jacket that heat cannot pass through easily. It will keep its contents at about their original temperature for hours. [< Gk. *thermos* hot]

ther·mo·stat (ther'mə·stat), *n.* an automatic device that responds to conditions of temperature by turning heat on or off, opening a valve, sounding an alarm, etc. [< THERMO- + Gk. *-states* that stands] —**ther'mo·stat'ic,** *adj.* —**ther'mo·stat'i·cal·ly,** *adv.*

the·sau·rus (thi·sô'rəs), *n., pl.* **-ri** (-rī). **1.** treasury; storehouse. **2.** a dictionary, encyclopedia, or other book that is a storehouse of information. [< L < Gk. *thesauros.* Doublet of TREASURE.]

these (thēz), *adj., pron.* pl. of **this.**

The·se·us (thē'si·əs; -sūs), *n. Gk. Legend.* the principal hero of Athens. He rid the Athens area of evildoers, killed the Minotaur, and escaped from the Labyrinth with the help of Ariadne.

the·sis (thē'sis), *n., pl.* **-ses** (-sēz). **1.** proposition or statement to be debated or to be maintained against objections. **2.** subject for a composition. **3.** essay; essay presented by a candidate for a diploma or degree. [< L < Gk., orig., a setting down]

Thes·pi·an (thes'pi·ən), *adj.* of or having to do with the drama or tragedy; dramatic; tragic. —*n.* actor or actress. [< *Thespis,* Greek poet]

Thes·sa·lo·ni·ans (thes'ə·lō'ni·ənz), *n.* either of two books of the New Testament written by Saint Paul.

Thes·sa·lon·i·ca (thes'ə·lon'ə·kə; -lə·nī'kə), *n.* the ancient name of Salonika. —**Thes·sa·lo·ni·an** (thes'ə·lō'ni·ən), *adj., n.*

Thes·sa·ly (thes'ə·li), *n.* district in E Greece.

the·ta (thā'tə; thē'tə), *n.* the eighth letter (Θ, θ) of the Greek alphabet.

The·tis (thē'tis), *n. Gk. Myth.* one of the Nereids, the mother of Achilles.

thews (thūz), *n.pl.* 1. muscles. 2. sinews. [OE *thēaw* habit]

they (thā), *pron., nom.*, they; *poss.*, their, theirs, of them, of theirs; *obj.*, them. 1. nom. pl. of he, she, or it. 2. *Colloq.* some people; any people; persons. [< Scand. *their*] ➤ They is colloquially used as an indefinite pronoun but generally it is not so used in writing: Colloquial: *They have had no serious accidents at that crossing for over two years.* Written: *There have been no serious accidents* . . . .

thi·a·mine (thī'ə·min; -mēn), **thi·a·min** (-min), *n.* a complex organic compound, $C_{12}H_{17}$ ClN_4OS, found in cereals, yeast, etc., or prepared synthetically. Its chloride, vitamin B_1, aids in preventing beriberi, etc.

Thi·bet (ti·bet'), *n.* Tibet. —**Thi·bet'an**, *adj., n.*

thick (thik), *adj.* 1. with much space from one side to the opposite side; not thin: *a thick wall.* 2. measuring between two opposite sides: *two inches thick.* 3. set close together; dense: *thick hair.* 4. many and close together; abundant: *bullets thick as hail.* 5. filled; covered: *thick with flies.* 6. like glue or syrup; rather dense of its kind: *thick soup.* 7. not clear; foggy: *thick air.* 8. not clear in sound; hoarse: *a thick voice.* 9. stupid; dull. 10. *Colloq.* very friendly; intimate. 11. *Colloq.* too much to be endured. —*adv.* in a thick manner. —*n.* 1. that which is thick. 2. the thickest part: *in the thick of the fight.* 3. **thick and thin**, good times and bad; easy situations and hard. [OE *thicce*] —**thick'ly**, *adv.* —**thick'ness**, *n.* —Syn. *adj.* 3, close, compact, crowded. 4. plentiful, numerous. 7. misty, hazy. 8. indistinct, inarticulate, muffled. 9. slow, obtuse.

thick·en (thik'ən), *v.* 1. make or become thick or thicker. 2. make or become more dense, foggy, hoarse, obscure, or complicated. —**thick'en·er**, *n.* —Syn. 1. coagulate, congeal, condense.

thick·en·ing (thik'ən·ing; thik'ning), *n.* 1. material or ingredient used to thicken something. 2. a thickened part.

thick·et (thik'it), *n.* shrubs, bushes, or small trees growing close together. [OE *thiccet* < *thicce* thick] —**thick'et·ed**, *adj.* —Syn. shrubbery, copse, brake.

thick-head·ed (thik'hed'id), *adj.* stupid; dull. —**thick'-head'ed·ness**, *n.*

thick·set (thik'set'), *adj.* 1. thickly set: *a thick-set hedge.* 2. thick in form or build: *a thick-set man.* —*n.* 1. thicket. 2. a thick hedge.

thick-skinned (thik'skind'), *adj.* 1. having a thick skin. 2. not sensitive to criticism, reproach, rebuff, or the like.

thief (thēf), *n., pl.* **thieves** (thēvz). person who steals, esp. one who steals secretly and without using force. [OE *thēof*] —Syn. robber, pilferer, filcher.

thieve (thēv), *v.*, **thieved, thiev·ing.** steal. [OE *thēofian* < *thēof* thief] —**thiev'ish**, *adj.* —**thiev'ish·ly**, *adv.* —**thiev'ish·ness**, *n.*

thiev·er·y (thēv'ər·i; thēv'ri), *n., pl.* **-er·ies.** act of stealing; theft.

thigh (thī), *n.* 1. in man, the part of the leg between the hip and the knee. 2. a corresponding part of the hind limbs of other animals. [OE *thēoh*]

thigh·bone (thī'bōn'), *n.* bone of the leg between the hip and the knee; femur.

thill (thil), *n.* either of the shafts between which a single animal drawing a vehicle is placed. [ME *thille*]

thim·ble (thim'bəl), *n.* 1. a small metal cap worn on the finger to protect it when pushing the needle in sewing. 2. a short metal tube. 3. a metal ring fitted in a rope, to save wear on the rope. [OE *thȳmel* < *thūma* thumb]

thim·ble·rig (thim'bəl·rig'), *n., v.*, **-rigged, -rig·ging.** —*n.* a swindling game using a small ball or pea and three thimblelike cups. —*v.* cheat thus or in like manner. —**thim'ble·rig'ger**, *n.*

thin (thin), *adj.*, **thin·ner, thin·nest**, *adv.*, *v.*,

thinned, thin·ning. —*adj.* 1. with little space from one side to the opposite side; not thick: *thin paper, thin wire.* 2. having little flesh; slender; lean: *a thin person.* 3. not set close together; scanty: *thin hair.* 4. not dense: *thin mountain air.* 5. few and far apart; not abundant: *the actors played to a thin audience.* 6. not like glue or syrup; of less substance than usual: *thin milk.* 7. not deep or strong: *a shrill thin voice.* 8. having little depth, fullness, or intensity: *a thin color, thin liquor.* 9. easily seen through; flimsy: *a thin excuse.* 10. poor; feeble: *a thin joke.* —*adv.* in a thin manner. —*v.* make or become thin. [OE *thynne*] —**thin'ly**, *adv.* —**thin'ner**, *n.* —**thin'ness**, *n.* —**thin'nish**, *adj.* —Syn. *adj.* 1. narrow, slim, attenuated. 2. spare, gaunt, emaciated, wasted, skinny, lank. 5. sparse.

thine (thīn), *Mainly Archaic or Poetic.* —*pron.* 1. belonging to thee; yours. 2. the one or ones belonging to thee; yours. —*adj.* thy; your. [OE *thin*]

thing[1] (thing), *n.* 1. any inanimate object: *what are those things in the field?* 2. that which cannot be specifically designated or precisely described: *the box had a brass thing on it, what sort of thing is it?* 3. whatever is spoken or thought of; fact, event, idea, etc.: *a strange thing happened.* 4. a matter; affair; business: *how are things going?* 5. performance; deed: *the President's decision was a great thing.* 6. person or creature: *I felt sorry for the poor thing.* 7. particular; respect: *good in all things.* 8. **things**, a. belongings; possessions. b. clothes. 9. **know a thing or two**, *Colloq.* be experienced or wise. 10. **make a good thing of**, *Colloq.* profit from. 11. **see things**, have hallucinations. 12. **the thing**, a. the fashion or style. b. the important fact or idea. [OE] ➤ **Thing** is often deadwood: *Religion is a personal thing.* [Religion is personal.] *The first thing you do is to* [First you] *get a few small twigs burning.*

thing[2] (thing; ting), *n.* in Scandinavian countries, a legislative assembly, court of law, or other public meeting. Also, **ting**. [< Icelandic]

think (thingk), *v.*, **thought, think·ing.** 1. form or conceive in the mind: *think unkind thoughts.* 2. use the mind: *think clearly.* 3. have in the mind: *he thought that he would go.* 4. have an idea: *he had thought of her as still a child.* 5. have an opinion; believe: *do what you think fit.* 6. reflect; consider: *I must think before answering.* 7. imagine: *you can't think how surprised I was.* 8. remember: *I can't think of his name.* 9. intend: *he thinks to escape punishment.* 10. expect: *I did not think to find you here.* 11. make, bring, affect, etc., by thinking: *he thought himself into a dilemma.* 12. have consideration or regard: *think of others first.* 13. have a (high, low, or other) opinion: *think well of a person.* 14. **think aloud**, say what one is thinking. 15. **think better of**, a. think more favorably of. b. change one's mind concerning. 16. **think out**, a. plan or discover by thinking. b. solve or understand by thinking. c. think through to the end. 17. **think over**, consider carefully. 18. **think through**, think about until one reaches an understanding or conclusion. 19. **think twice**, think again before acting; hesitate. 20. **think up**, plan or discover by thinking. [OE *thencan*] —**think'a·ble**, *adj.* —**think'er**, *n.* —Syn. 5. deem, judge, opine, hold. 6. ponder, meditate, speculate. 7. conceive. 8. recollect, recall. 9. purpose, plan, mean.

think·ing (thingk'ing), *adj.* 1. that thinks; reasoning. 2. thoughtful or reflective. —*n.* thought. —**think'ing·ly**, *adv.* —Syn. *adj.* 2. contemplative, pensive, cogitative.

thin-skinned (thin'skind'), *adj.* 1. having a thin skin. 2. sensitive to criticism, reproach, rebuff, or the like; touchy. —**thin'-skinned'ness**, *n.*

third (thėrd), *adj.* 1. next after the second; last in a series of three. 2. being one of three equal parts. —*n.* 1. next after the second; last in a series of three. 2. one of three equal parts. 3. *Music.* a. tone three degrees from another tone. **b.** interval between such tones. **c.** combination of such tones. [OE *thirda*, var. of *thridda* < *thrēo* three] —**third′ly**, *adv.*

third-class (thềrd′klas′; -kläs′), *adj.* **Am.** of or belonging to a third class; inferior. —*adv.* on a third-class ship, train, etc.

third degree, Am., Colloq. use of torture by the police to force a person to give information or make a confession.

third estate, persons not in the nobility or clergy; common people.

third person, Gram. form of a pronoun or verb used to refer to the person spoken of. *He, she, it,* and *they* are pronouns of the third person.

third rail, Am. rail paralleling the ordinary rails of a railroad and carrying a powerful electric current.

third-rate (thềrd′rāt′), *adj.* **1.** of a third class. **2.** distinctly inferior.

Third Reich, the totalitarian state in Germany (1933–1945) under Adolf Hitler.

third world, the world of neutral, or non-aligned nations in the cold war between Communist and Western nations.

thirst (thềrst), *n.* **1.** a dry, painful feeling caused by having nothing to drink; desire or need for something to drink. **2.** a strong desire: *a thirst for excitement.* —*v.* **1.** feel thirst; be thirsty. **2.** have a strong desire. [OE *thurst*]

thirst·y (thềrs′ti), *adj.*, **thirst·i·er, thirst·i·est. 1.** feeling thirst; having thirst. **2.** without water or moisture; dry. **3.** having a strong desire; eager. —**thirst′i·ly,** *adv.* —**thirst′i·ness,** *n.*

thir·teen (thềr′tēn′), *n.* **1.** a cardinal number, three more than ten. **2.** symbol of this number; 13. —*adj.* three more than ten; 13. —**thir·teenth** (thềr′tēnth′), *adj.*, *n.*

thir·ty (thềr′ti), *n.*, *pl.* **-ties,** *adj.* —*n.* **1.** a cardinal number, three times ten. **2.** symbol of this number; 30. —*adj.* three times ten; 30. —**thir′ti·eth,** *adj.*, *n.*

thir·ty-sec·ond note (thềr′ti·sek′ənd) *Music.* a note ½d of a whole note (♪). Also, **demisemiquaver.**

this (this), *pron.*, *pl.* **these,** *adj.*, *adv.* —*pron.* **1.** the person, thing, event, quality, condition, idea, etc., that is present, mentioned, or referred to now: *this is the best, after this you must go home.* **2.** the one emphasized or contrasted with another called "that": *this is newer than that.* —*adj.* present; near; spoken of; referred to: *this minute, this child, this idea.* —*adv.* to this extent or degree; so: *you can have this much.* [OE] **▶ This,** like *that,* is often used to refer to the idea of a preceding clause or sentence: *He had always had his own way at home, and this made him a poor roommate.*

this·tle (this′əl), *n.* plant with a prickly stalk and leaves. The purple thistle is the national flower of Scotland. [OE *thistel*] —**this·tly** (this′li), *adj.*

this·tle·down (this′əl·doun′), *n.* the down or fluff of a thistle.

thith·er (thith′ər; thith′ər), *adv.* to that place; toward that place; there. —*adj.* on that side; farther. [OE *thider*]

thith·er·ward (thith′ər·wərd; thith′-), **thith·er·wards** (-wərdz), *adv.* toward that place; in that direction.

tho, tho′ (thō), *conj.*, *adv.* though.

thole (thōl), *n.* or **thole·pin** (thōl′pin′), *n.* a peg on the side of a boat to hold an oar in rowing. [OE *tholl*]

Tholes: A, single; B, double.

Thom·as (tom′əs), *n.* one of the twelve disciples chosen by Jesus as apostles. He at first doubted the resurrection. John 20:24–29.

Thomp·son submachine gun (tomp′sən) *Trademark.* a .45-caliber, air-cooled, automatic weapon, carried and operated by one man.

thong (thông; thong), *n.* **1.** a narrow strip of leather, etc., esp. used as a fastening. **2.** lash of a whip. [OE *thwang*]

Thor (thôr), *n.* the ancient Scandinavian god of thunder.

tho·rax (thō′raks; thô′-), *n.*, *pl.* **-rax·es, -ra·ces** (-rə·sēz). **1.** the part of the body between the neck and the abdomen. A man's chest is his thorax. **2.** the second division of an insect's body, between the head and the abdomen. [< L < Gk.] —**tho·rac·ic** (thō·ras′ik; thō-), *adj.*

Tho·reau (thə·rō′; thô′rō), *n.* Henry David, 1817–1862, American author and naturalist.

tho·ri·um (thō′ri·əm; thô′-), *n. Chem.* a radioactive metallic element, Th, present in certain rare minerals. [< NL, < *Thor*] —**thor·ic** (thôr′ik; thor′ik), *adj.*

thorn (thôrn), *n.* **1.** a sharp-pointed growth on a stem or branch of a tree or plant. **2.** tree or plant that has thorns on it. **3.** something that annoys or causes discomfort. [OE] —**thorn′less,** *adj.* —**thorn′like′,** *adj.* —*Syn. n.* **1.** spine, prickle.

thorn apple, 1. fruit of the hawthorn; haw. **2.** hawthorn. **3.** jimson weed.

thorn·y (thôr′ni), *adj.*, **thorn·i·er, thorn·i·est. 1.** full of thorns. **2.** troublesome; annoying: *a thorny problem.* —**thorn′i·ly,** *adv.* —**thorn′i·ness,** *n.* —*Syn.* **1.** spiny, prickly. **2.** vexatious, difficult.

thor·o (thềr′ō), *adj.* thorough. —**thor′o·ly,** *adv.*

tho·ron (thō′ron; thô′-), *n. Chem.* a rare element, Tn or Th Em, a radioactive gas.

thor·ough (thềr′ō), *adj.* **1.** being all that is needed; complete. **2.** doing all that should be done and slighting nothing. Also, **thoro.** [OE *thuruh,* var. of *thurh* through] —**thor′ough·ly,** *adv.* —**thor′ough·ness,** *n.* —*Ant.* **1.** partial. **2.** superficial, cursory.

thor·ough·bred (thềr′ō·bred′), *adj.* **1.** of pure breed or stock. **2.** well-bred; thoroughly trained. —*n.* **1.** a thoroughbred horse or other animal. **2.** a well-bred or thoroughly trained person.

thor·ough·fare (thềr′ō·fâr′), *n.* **1.** a passage, road, or street open at both ends. **2.** a main road; highway.

thor·ough·go·ing (thềr′ō·gō′ing), *adj.* thorough; complete.

those (thōz), *adj.*, *pron.* pl. of that.

thou (thou), *pron.* you; the one spoken to. —*v.* address familiarly as thou. [OE *thū*] **▶ Thou** is now archaic or poetical and replaced in general use by *you,* except in Biblical English in addressing God and as used by Quakers.

though (thō), *conj.* **1.** in spite of the fact that; notwithstanding the fact that: *though it was pouring, they went out.* **2.** yet; still; nevertheless: *he is better, though not entirely cured.* **3.** even if; granting or supposing that: *though I fail, I shall try again.* **4.** as though, as if; as it would be if. —*adv.* however: *I am sorry about our quarrel; you began it, though.* Also, **tho, tho′.** [ME *thoh*]

thought (thôt), *n.* **1.** what one thinks; idea; notion: *do you understand my thought?* **2.** the ideas of people of a certain place, class, or time: *18th-century thought.* **3.** power or process of thinking; mental activity: *thought helps solve problems.* **4.** reasoning: *he applied thought to the question.* **5.** consideration; attention; regard: *give some thought to others.* **6.** intention: *his thought was to avoid controversy, we had thoughts of going.* **7.** expectation: *I had no thought of seeing you here.* **8.** a little bit; trifle: *be a thought more polite.* —*v.* pt. and pp. of think. [OE *thōht*] —*Syn. n.* **1.** concept, opinion, belief. **3.** cogitation, deliberation, meditation, reflection, contemplation. **6.** purpose, design.

thought control, the strict limiting or regimentation of ideas, reasoning, etc., in all individuals so as to conform to that of a particular group, government, etc.

thought·ful (thôt′fəl), *adj.* **1.** full of thought; thinking. **2.** careful; heedful. **3.** careful of others; considerate. —**thought′ful·ly,** *adv.* —**thought′ful·ness,** *n.* —*Syn.* **1.** reflective, meditative, contemplative, pensive. **3.** attentive, regardful.

thought·less (thôt′lis), *adj.* **1.** without thought. **2.** doing things without thinking; careless. **3.** showing little or no care or regard for

others; not considerate. —**thought′less·ly,** adv.
—**thought′less·ness,** n. —Syn. 1. unthinking,
unreflecting. 2. rash, indiscreet. 3. remiss.

thou·sand (thou′zənd), n. 1. a cardinal number, ten times one hundred. 2. symbol of this
number; 1000. —adj. ten times one hundred;
1000. [OE *thūsend*] —**thou·sandth** (thou′zənth),
adj., n.

thou·sand·fold (thou′zənd·fōld′), adj. 1.
1000 times as much or as many. 2. having 1000
parts. —adv. 1000 times as much or as many.

Thousand Islands, group of about 1500
islands in the St. Lawrence River, near Lake
Ontario. Some belong to Canada, and some to
the United States.

Thrace (thrās), n. region in SE Europe.

thrall (thrôl), n. 1. person in bondage; slave.
2. thralldom. [< Scand. *thrǣll*]

thrall·dom, thral·dom (thrôl′dəm), n.
bondage; slavery.

thrash (thrash), v. 1. beat: *the man thrashed
the boy for stealing the apples.* 2. move violently;
toss: *the patient thrashed about in his bed.* 3.
thresh (wheat, etc.). 4. **thrash out,** settle by
thorough discussion. 5. **thrash over,** go over
again and again. —n. act of thrashing; beating.
[var. of *thresh*]

thrash·er (thrash′ər), n. 1. person or thing
that threshes. 2. Also, **thrasher shark.** thresher
(def. 3). 3. *Am.* any of several American birds
related to the mockingbird.

thread (thred), n. 1. cotton, silk, flax, etc.,
spun out into a fine cord. 2. a filament of glass,
metal, etc. 3. something long and slender like
a thread: *threads of gold could be
seen in the ore.* 4. the main thought
that connects the parts of a story,
speech, etc. 5. the course of life
thought of as a thread spun by the
Fates and cut at their pleasure. 6.
the winding, sloping ridge of a
screw, etc. —v. 1. pass a thread
through: *thread a needle.* 2. fix
(beads, etc.) upon a thread or string that is
passed through them. 3. form into a thread:
cook the syrup until it threads. 4. pass like a
thread through; pervade. 5. make one's way
through; make (one's way) carefully; go on a
winding course: *he threaded his way through
the crowd.* 6. form a thread on (a screw, etc.).
[OE *thrǣd*] —**thread′er,** n. —**thread′like′,** adj.

Thread
(def. 6)

thread·bare (thred′bãr′), adj. 1. having the
nap worn off; worn so much that the threads
show. 2. wearing clothes worn to the threads;
shabby. 3. old and worn; stale: *a threadbare
excuse.* —**thread′bare′ness,** n. —Syn. 3. hackneyed, trite.

threat (thret), n. 1. statement of what will be
done to hurt or punish someone. 2. sign or
cause of possible evil or harm. [OE *thrēat*]
—Syn. 1. menace, intimidation.

threat·en (thret′ən), v. 1. make a threat
against: *threaten a person.* 2. utter threats: *do
you mean to threaten?* 3. say what will be done
to hurt or punish: *threaten with imprisonment.*
4. be a sign of (possible evil or harm, etc.):
black clouds threaten rain. 5. be a cause of
possible evil or harm to: *a flood threatened the
city.* [OE *thrēatnian*] —**threat′en·er,** n.
—**threat′en·ing·ly,** adv. —Syn. 1. menace,
intimidate. 4. portend, presage, forebode.

three (thrē), n. 1. a cardinal number, one
more than two. 2. symbol of this number; 3.
3. set of three persons or things. —adj. one more
than two; 3. [OE *thrēo*] —Syn. n. 3. trio, triplet.

three-D, 3-D (thrē′dē′), n. three dimensional
(motion picture).

three·fold (thrē′fōld′), adj. 1. three times as
much or as many. 2. having three parts. —adv.
three times as much or as many.

three-mile limit (thrē′mīl′), distance from
the shore that, according to international law, is
included within the jurisdiction of the state
possessing the coast.

three·pence (thrip′əns; threp′əns), n. 1. three
British pennies; three pence. 2. coin of this

value, worth about 3 cents (1950). Also, **thrip-
pence.**

three-ply (thrē′plī′), adj. having three thicknesses, layers, folds, or strands.

three R's, reading, writing, and arithmetic.

three·score (thrē′skôr′; -skōr′), adj. three
times twenty; 60.

three·some (thrē′səm), n. 1. group of three
people. 2. game played by three people. 3. the
players.

thren·o·dy (thren′ə·di), n., pl. –dies. song of
lamentation, esp. at a person's death. [< Gk.,
< *threnos* lament + *oide* song] —**thre·no·di·al**
(thri·nō′di·əl), **thre·nod·ic** (thri·nod′ik), adj.
—**thren′o·dist,** n.

thresh (thresh), v. 1. separate the grain or
seeds from (wheat, etc.), as by beating with a
flail. 2. toss about; move violently; thrash. 3.
thresh out, settle by thorough discussion. 4.
thresh over, go over again and again. [OE
threscan]

thresh·er (thresh′ər), n. 1. person or thing
that threshes. 2. machine used for separating the
grain or seeds from wheat, etc. 3. Also, **thresher
shark.** a large shark with a very long tail.

thresh·old (thresh′ōld; thresh′hōld), n. 1.
piece of wood or stone under a door. 2. doorway.
3. point of entering; beginning point: *the scientist was on the threshold of an important discovery.* 4. in physiology and psychology, the
minimum stimulus adequate to produce the
specified response: *the threshold of consciousness.* [OE *thresc(w)old*]

threw (thrü), v. pt. of throw.

thrice (thrīs), adv. 1. three times. 2. very; extremely. [ME *thries* < OE *thriga* thrice]

thrift (thrift), n. absence of waste; saving;
economical management; habit of saving. [<
thrive] —**thrift′less,** adj. —**thrift′less·ly,** adv.
—**thrift′less·ness,** n. —Syn. economy, frugality.

thrift·y (thrif′ti), adj., thrift·i·er, thrift·i·est.
1. careful in spending; economical; saving. 2.
thriving; flourishing; prosperous: *a thrifty
plant.* —**thrift′i·ly,** adv. —**thrift′i·ness,** n.
—Syn. 1. provident, frugal, sparing.

thrill (thril), n. 1. a shivering, exciting feeling.
2. a thrilling quality, as of a play or story. 3. a
quivering; vibration. —v. 1. give a shivering,
exciting feeling to. 2. have such a feeling. 3.
quiver; tremble. [var. of *thirl,* OE *thyrlian* pierce
< *thurh* through] —**thrill′ing,** adj. —**thrill′-
ing·ly,** adv. —**thrill′ing·ness,** n. —Syn. v. 3.
vibrate, throb.

thrill·er (thril′ər), n. 1. person or thing that
thrills. 2. *Colloq.* a sensational play or story,
esp. one involving a murder.

thrip·pence (thrip′əns), n. threepence.

thrive (thrīv), v., throve or thrived, thrived or
thriv·en (thriv′ən), thriv·ing. be successful;
grow rich; grow strong; prosper. [< Scand.
thrifa(sk)] —**thriv′er,** n. —**thriv′ing,** adj.
—**thriv′ing·ly,** adv. —Syn. flourish.

thro′, thro (thrü), prep., adv., adj. through.

throat (thrōt), n. 1. the front of the neck. 2.
the passage from the mouth to the stomach or
the lungs. 3. any narrow passage: *the throat of
a mine.* 4. **jump down one's throat,** attack or
criticize a person with sudden violence. 5. **lump
in the throat,** a feeling of inability to swallow.
6. **stick in one's throat,** be hard or unpleasant
to say. [OE *throte*]

throat·y (thrōt′i), adj., throat·i·er, throat·i·
est. 1. produced or modified in the throat, as
sounds: *a throaty sound.* 2. of a woman's voice,
low-pitched and resonant. —**throat′i·ly,** adv.
—**throat′i·ness,** n.

throb (throb), v., throbbed, throb·bing, n. —v.
1. beat rapidly or strongly: *the long climb made
her heart throb.* 2. beat steadily. 3. quiver;
tremble. —n. 1. a rapid or strong beat: *a throb
of pain shot through his head.* 2. a steady beat:
the throb of a pulse. 3. a quiver; tremble.
—**throb′ber,** n. —**throb′bing·ly,** adv. —**throb′-
less,** adj. —Syn. v. 1. pulsate, palpitate.

throe (thrō), n. 1. a violent pang; great pain.
2. throes, a. pains of childbirth. b. anguish;

āge, cãre, fär; ēqual, tẽrm; īce; ōpen, ôrder; pùt, rüle, ūse; ŧħ, then; ə=a in about.

agony. **c.** a desperate struggle; violent disturbance. [earlier throwe; see THROW]

throm·bo·sis (throm·bō′sis), *n.* a coagulation of blood in a blood vessel or in the heart during life. [< NL < Gk., ult. < *thrombos* clot] —**throm·bot·ic** (throm·bot′ik), *adj.*

throne (thrōn), *n., v.,* throned, thron·ing. —*n.* 1. chair on which a king, queen, bishop, or other person of high rank sits during ceremonies. 2. power or authority of a king, queen, etc. —*v.* enthrone. [< L < Gk. *thronos*] —**throne′less,** *adj.*

throng (thrông; throng), *n.* a crowd; multitude. —*v.* 1. crowd; fill with a crowd. 2. come together in a crowd; go or press in large numbers. [OE (ge)*thrang*] —**Syn.** *n.* host, mass, pack.

thros·tle (thros′əl), *n. Dial.* a thrush, esp. the song thrush. [OE]

throt·tle (throt′əl), *n., v.,* –tled, –tling. —*n.* 1. valve regulating the flow of steam, gasoline vapor, etc., to an engine. 2. lever, pedal, etc., working such a valve. 3. throat. —*v.* 1. stop the breath of by pressure on the throat; strangle. 2. choke; suffocate. 3. check or stop the flow of; suppress: *high tariffs throttle trade between countries.* 4. lessen the speed of (an engine) by closing a throttle. [< *throat*] —**throt′tler,** *n.*

through (thrü), *prep.* 1. from end to end of; from side to side of; between the parts of; from beginning to end of: *pass through a door, cut a tunnel through a mountain.* 2. here and there in; over; around: *travel through a country.* 3. because of; by reason of: *they ran through fear.* 4. by means of: *we found out through him.* 5. having reached the end of; finished with: *be through one's work.* —*adv.* 1. from end to end; from side to side; between the parts: *the bullet hit the wall and went through.* 2. completely: *chilled through.* 3. from beginning to end: *read a letter through.* 4. along the whole distance; all the way: *the train goes through to Boston.* 5. to a favorable conclusion: *he pulled through.* 6. **through and through,** completely; thoroughly. —*adj.* 1. going all the way without change: *a through train, a through street.* 2. having reached the end; finished: *I am almost through.* Also, **thro, thro′, thru.** [earlier *thourgh,* OE *thurh*]

through·out (thrü·out′), *prep.* all the way through; through all; in every part of. —*adv.* in every part.

throve (thrōv), *v.* pt. of thrive.

throw (thrō), *v.,* threw, thrown, throw·ing, *n.* —*v.* 1. cast; toss; hurl: *throw a ball.* 2. bring to the ground: *his horse threw him.* 3. put, send, build, etc., hastily: *throw a bridge across a river, throw a man into prison.* 4. turn, direct, or move, esp. quickly: *she threw us a glance.* 5. move (a lever, etc.) that connects or disconnects parts of a switch, clutch, or other mechanism. 6. connect or disconnect thus. 7. shed. 8. *Am., Colloq.* let an opponent win (a race, game, etc.), as for money or other ulterior motives. 9. throw away, **a.** get rid of; discard. **b.** waste. **c.** fail to use. 10. throw back, revert to an ancestral type. 11. throw cold water on, discourage by being indifferent or unwilling. 12. throw in, add as a gift. 13. throw off, **a.** get rid of. **b.** *Colloq.* produce (a poem, etc.) in an offhand manner. 14. throw oneself at, try very hard to get the love, friendship, or favor of. 15. throw open, **a.** open suddenly or widely. **b.** remove all obstacles or restrictions from. 16. throw out, **a.** get rid of; discard. **b.** reject. 17. throw over, give up; discard; abandon. 18. throw up, **a.** *Colloq.* vomit. **b.** give up; abandon. **c.** build rapidly. —*n.* 1. a cast, toss, etc. 2. distance a thing is or may be thrown. 3. scarf; light covering. 4. movement of a reciprocating part of a machine from its central position to its extreme position. 5. length of the arm or radius of a crank. [OE *thrāwan* twist] —**throw′er,** *n.* —**Syn.** *v.* 1. fling, pitch, heave, sling.

throw·back (thrō′bak′), *n.* 1. a throwing back. 2. setback or check. 3. reversion to an ancestral type or character; an example of this.

thru (thrü), *prep., adv., adj.* through.

thrum (thrum), *v.,* thrummed, thrum·ming, *n.* —*v.* 1. play on a stringed instrument by pluck-

ing the strings: *thrum a guitar.* 2. drum or tap idly with the fingers. —*n.* the sound made by such playing or tapping. [imit.] —**thrum′mer,** *n.*

thrush (thrush), *n.* 1. any of a large group of migratory songbirds that includes the robin, the bluebird, the wood thrush, etc. 2. a brown bird with a spotted white breast, that has a very sweet song. [OE *thrÿsce*]

thrust (thrust), *v.,* thrust, thrust·ing, *n.* —*v.* 1. push with force. 2. stab: *thrust a knife into an apple.* 3. put forcibly into some position, condition, etc.: *thrust oneself into danger.* —*n.* 1. a forcible push; drive. 2. a stab. 3. attack. 4. in mechanics, architecture, etc., the force of one thing pushing on another. 5. the endwise push exerted by the rotation of a propeller. [< Scand. *thrÿsta*] —**thrust′er,** *n.* —**Syn.** *n.* 1. shove, punch, lunge.

thru·way (thrü′wā′), *n.* an express highway.

Thu·cyd·i·des (thü·sid′ə·dēz), *n.* 460?–400? B.C., Greek historian.

thud (thud), *n., v.,* thud·ded, thud·ding. —*n.* 1. a dull sound. 2. a blow or thump. —*v.* hit, move, or strike with a thud. [OE *thyddan* strike]

thug (thug), *n.* 1. ruffian; cutthroat. 2. member of a former religious organization of robbers and murderers in India. [< Hind. *ṭhag* < Skt. *sthaga* rogue]

thu·li·um (thü′li·əm), *n. Chem.* a rare element, Tm, of the yttrium group.

thumb (thum), *n.* 1. the short, thick finger of the human hand, next to the forefinger. 2. part that covers the thumb. 3. **thumbs down,** sign of disapproval or rejection. 4. **thumbs up,** sign of approval or acceptance. 5. **under the thumb of,** under the power or influence of. —*v.* 1. soil or wear by handling with the thumbs: *the books were badly thumbed.* 2. turn pages of (a book, etc.) rapidly, reading only portions. 3. handle awkwardly. 4. **thumb a ride,** get a ride by signaling. [OE *thūma*] —**thumb′like′,** *adj.*

thumb·nail (thum′nāl′), *n.* 1. nail of the thumb. 2. something very small or short. —*adj.* very small or short.

thumb·screw (thum′skrü′), *n.* 1. a screw made so that its head can be easily turned with the thumb and a finger. 2. an old instrument of torture that squeezed the thumbs.

Thumbscrews (def. 1)

thumb·tack (thum′tak′), *n. Am.* tack with a broad, flat head, that can be pressed into a wall, board, etc., with the thumb.

thump (thump), *v.* 1. strike with something thick and heavy: *he thumped the table with his fist.* 2. strike against (something) heavily and noisily: *the shutters thumped the wall in the wind.* 3. make a dull sound; pound: *the hammer thumped against the wood.* 4. beat violently: *his heart thumped.* 5. beat or thrash severely. —*n.* 1. a blow with something thick and heavy; heavy knock. 2. the dull sound made by a blow, knock, or fall. [imit.] —**thump′er,** *n.* —**Syn.** *n.* 1. whack, bang.

thun·der (thun′dər), *n.* 1. the loud noise that often follows a flash of lightning, caused by a disturbance of the air resulting from the discharge of electricity. 2. any noise like thunder. 3. threat; denunciation. 4. **steal one's thunder,** use another's idea or method without asking him or giving him credit. —*v.* 1. give forth thunder. 2. make a noise like thunder. 3. utter very loudly; roar: *thunder a reply.* 4. threaten; denounce. [OE *thunor*] —**thun′der·er,** *n.*

thun·der·bolt (thun′dər·bōlt′), *n.* 1. a flash of lightning and the thunder that follows it. 2. something sudden, startling, and terrible: *the news of his death came as a thunderbolt.*

thun·der·clap (thun′dər·klap′), *n.* 1. a loud crash of thunder. 2. something sudden or startling.

thun·der·cloud (thun′dər·kloud′), *n.* a dark, electrically charged cloud that brings thunder and lightning.

thun·der·head (thun′dər·hed′), *n.* one of the round, swelling masses of cumulus clouds often appearing before thunderstorms and frequently developing into thunderclouds.

thun·der·ous (thun′dər·əs; -drəs), *adj.* 1. producing thunder. 2. making a noise like thunder. —thun′der·ous·ly, *adv.*

thun·der·show·er (thun′dər·shou′ər), *n.* a shower with thunder and lightning.

thun·der·squall (thun′dər·skwôl′), *n.* squall with thunder and lightning.

thun·der·storm (thun′dər·stôrm′), *n.* storm with thunder and lightning.

thun·der·struck (thun′dər·struk′), *adj.* overcome, as if hit by a thunderbolt; astonished; amazed.

Thurs., Thur., Thursday.

Thurs·day (thérz′di; -dā), *n.* the fifth day of the week, following Wednesday.

thus (thus), *adv.* 1. in this way; in the way just stated, indicated, etc.; in the following manner: *he spoke thus.* 2. accordingly; consequently; therefore: *thus we decided that he was wrong.* 3. to this extent or degree; so: *thus far.* [OE]

thwack (thwak), *v.* strike vigorously with a stick or something flat. —*n.* a sharp blow with a stick or something flat. —thwack′er, *n.*

thwart (thwôrt), *v.* oppose and defeat; keep from doing something. —*n.* 1. a seat across a boat, on which a rower sits. 2. a brace in a canoe. —*adj.* lying across. —*adv.* across; crosswise. [< Scand. *thvert*, neut., transverse] —thwart′er, *n.* —Syn. *v.* obstruct, block, balk, foil, frustrate.

thy (thī), *pron., adj. Mainly Archaic or Poetic.* your. [OE *thin*]

thyme (tīm), *n.* a small plant that has a mintlike fragrance. The leaves of the common **garden thyme** are used for seasoning. The common **wild thyme** is a creeping evergreen. [< L < Gk. *thymon*] —thy′mic (tī′mik), *adj.*

thy·mol (thī′mōl; -mol), *n.* a drug, $C_{10}H_{13}OH$, obtained from thyme, used as an antiseptic.

thy·mus (thī′məs), *adj.* of or pertaining to the thymus gland. —*n.* the thymus gland. [< NL < Gk. *thymos*] —thy′mic (thī′mik), *adj.*

thymus gland, a small ductless gland near the base of the neck. The thymus of calves is used for food and called sweetbread.

thy·roid (thī′roid), *n.* 1. the thyroid gland. 2. medicine made from the thyroid glands of animals, used in the treatment of goiter, obesity, etc. 3. the thyroid cartilage. —*adj.* of or pertaining to the thyroid gland or thyroid cartilage. [ult. < Gk. *thyreoeides* shieldlike < *thyreos* oblong shield] —thy·roi′dal, *adj.*

thyroid cartilage, the principal cartilage of the larynx; Adam's apple.

thyroid gland or body, an important ductless gland in the neck of vertebrates that affects growth and metabolism. Goiter is an enlargement or a disorder of the thyroid gland.

thy·rox·in (thī·rok′sin), **thy·rox·ine** (-sēn), *n.* the principal secretion of the thyroid gland.

thyr·sus (thér′səs), *n., pl.* **-si** (-sī). staff or spear tipped with an ornament like a pine cone and sometimes wrapped round with ivy and vine branches, borne by Dionysus and his followers.

thy·self (thī·self′), *pron.* yourself.

ti (tē), *n. Music.* the seventh tone of the scale. [see GAMUT]

Ti, *Chem.* titanium.

ti·ar·a (tī·ār′ə; tī·ä′rə), *n.* 1. a band of gold, jewels, or flowers worn around the head as an ornament. 2. the triple crown of the Pope. 3. an ancient Persian headdress for men. [< L < Gk.]

Ti·ber (tī′bər), *n.* river flowing from C Italy past Rome into the Mediterranean.

Ti·be·ri·us (tī·bir′i·əs), *n.* 42 B.C.–37 A.D., Roman emperor 14 A.D.–37 A.D.

Ti·bet (ti·bet′), *n.* former country on a lofty plateau in S Asia. Now a province of China. Also, Thibet. —Ti·bet′an, *adj., n.*

tib·i·a (tib′i·ə), *n., pl.* **-i·ae** (-i·ē), **-i·as.** 1. *Anat.* the inner and thicker of the two bones of the leg from the knee to the ankle; shinbone. 2. an ancient flute. [< L] —tib′i·al, *adj.*

tic (tik), *n.* a habitual, involuntary twitching of the muscles, esp. those of the face. [< F]

tick¹ (tik), *n.* 1. a sound made by a clock or watch. 2. a sound like it. 3. *Colloq.* moment; instant. 4. a small mark. We use √ or / as a tick. —*v.* 1. make a tick, as a clock. 2. mark off: *the clock ticked away the minutes.* 3. mark with a tick; check: *he ticked off the items one by one.* [prob. ult. imit.]

tick² (tik), *n.* a tiny insect or spider that lives on animals and sucks their blood. [OE *ticia*]

Tick

tick³ (tik), *n.* 1. the cloth covering of a mattress or pillow. 2. *Colloq.* ticking. [prob. ult. < L *theca* case < Gk. *theke*]

tick·er (tik′ər), *n.* 1. person or thing that ticks. 2. a telegraphic instrument that prints market reports or news on **ticker tape,** a tape made of paper. 3. *Slang.* watch; clock. 4. *Slang.* the heart.

tick·et (tik′it), *n.* 1. a card or piece of paper that gives its holder a right or privilege: *a theater ticket.* 2. *Am., Colloq.* summons given to an offender to appear in court, usually with reference to traffic violations: *a ticket for speeding.* 3. a card or piece of paper attached to something to show its price, etc. 4. *Am.* the list of candidates to be voted on that belong to one political party. —*v.* put a ticket on; mark with a ticket. [< F *étiquette* ticket, ETIQUETTE]

ticket of leave, *Brit.* a permit giving a convict his liberty before his sentence has expired, provided he obeys certain conditions.

tick·ing (tik′ing), *n.* a strong cotton or linen cloth, used to cover mattresses and pillows and to make tents and awnings.

tick·le (tik′əl), *v.,* **-led, -ling,** *n.* —*v.* 1. touch lightly causing little thrills, shivers, or wriggles. 2. have a feeling like this; cause to have such a feeling: *my nose tickles.* 3. excite pleasantly; amuse: *the story tickled him.* 4. play, stir, get, etc., with light touches or strokes. —*n.* 1. a tingling or itching feeling. 2. a tickling. —tick′ler, *n.*

tick·lish (tik′lish), *adj.* 1. sensitive to tickling: *a ticklish person.* 2. requiring careful handling; delicate; risky: *a ticklish situation.* 3. easily upset; unstable: *a canoe is a ticklish craft.* 4. easily offended. —tick′lish·ness, *n.*

Ti·con·der·o·ga (tī′kon·dər·ō′gə), *n.* village and old fort on Lake Champlain, in New York State.

tid·al (tīd′əl), *adj.* 1. of tides; having tides; caused by tides. 2. depending on the tide.

tidal wave, 1. a large, destructive ocean wave produced by an earthquake, hurricane, etc. 2. either of two great swellings of the ocean surface (due to the attraction of the moon and sun) that move around the globe on opposite sides and cause the tides. 3. any great movement or manifestation of feeling, opinion, or the like.

tid·bit (tid′bit′), *n.* a very pleasing bit of food, news, etc. Also, titbit. [< *tid* nice + *bit* morsel]

tid·dly·winks (tid′li·wingks′), **tid·dle·dy·winks** (tid′əl·di·wingks′), *n.* a game played with small, colored disks that are snapped into a little cup.

tide (tīd), *n., v.,* **tid·ed, tid·ing.** —*n.* 1. the rise and fall of the ocean about every twelve hours, caused by the attraction of the moon and the sun. 2. anything that rises and falls like the tide: *the tide of popular opinion.* 3. stream; current; flood. 4. season; time. 5. turn the tide, change from one condition to the opposite. —*v.* 1. carry as the tide does. 2. tide over, help along for a time. [OE *tid,* orig., time]

tide·land (tīd′land′), *n.* submerged coastal land within the historical boundaries of a State and belonging to that State (according to a bill passed by the Congress of the U.S. in May 1953).

tide·wa·ter (tīd′wô′tər; -wot′ər), *n.* 1. water having tides. 2. seacoast. —*adj.* of or along tidewater.

ti·dings (tī′dingz), *n.pl.* news; information. [OE *tidung* < *tidan* happen]

ti·dy (tī′di), *adj.,* **-di·er, -di·est,** *v.,* **-died, -aying,** *n., pl.* **-dies.** —*adj.* 1. neat and in order;

a tidy room. **2.** inclined to keep things neat and in order: *a tidy person.* **3.** considerable; fairly large: *a tidy sum of money.* **4.** *Colloq.* fairly good. —*v.* put in order; make tidy. —*n.* a small cover to keep the back of a chair, etc., from becoming dirty or worn. [ult. < OE *tīd* time] —**ti′di·er,** *n.* —**ti′di·ly,** *adv.* —**ti′di·ness,** *n.* —**Syn.** *adj.* **1.** trim, orderly.

tie (tī), *v.,* **tied, ty·ing,** *n.* —*v.* **1.** fasten with string or the like; bind: *tie a package.* **2.** arrange to form a bow or knot: *tie one's apron strings.* **3.** tighten and fasten the string or strings of: *tie one's shoes.* **4.** fasten, join, or connect in any way. **5.** restrain; restrict; limit: *he did not want to be tied to a steady job.* **6.** make the same score; be equal in points: *the two teams tied.* **7.** make the same score as: *Harvard tied Yale in football.* **8.** tie down, limit; confine; restrict. **9.** tie up. **a.** tie firmly or tightly. **b.** wrap up. **c.** hinder; stop. **d.** keep (money or property) from being used, sold, or given away. —*n.* **1.** anything connecting or holding together two or more things or parts. **2.** cord, chain, etc., used for tying. **3.** a knot; ornamental knot. **4.** necktie. **5.** thing that unites; bond; obligation: *family ties.* **6.** beam, rod, or the like that connects or holds together two or more parts. **7.** *Am.* one of the transverse beams to which the rails of a railroad are fastened. **8.** equality in points, votes, etc. **9.** match or contest in which this occurs. **10.** *Music.* a curved line set above or below notes that are to be played or sung continuously. **11.** ties, low, laced shoes. [OE *tīgan* < *tēag* rope] —**ti′er,** *n.* —**Syn.** *v.* **1.** secure. **4.** tether.

Musical tie

Tien·tsin (tin′tsin′), *n.* city in NE China.

tier (tir), *n.* **1.** row; range; rank: *a tier of oars.* **2.** one of a series of rows arranged one above another: *tiers of seats at a baseball game.* —*v.* **1.** arrange in tiers. **2.** rise in tiers. [< F, orig., order] —**tiered,** *adj.*

Tier·ra del Fue·go (tyer′ə del fwā′gō), group of islands at the S end of South America. Part belongs to Argentina, part to Chile.

tie-up (tī′up′), *n.* **1.** a stopping of work or operations on account of a strike, storm, accident, etc. **2.** *Colloq.* connection; relation.

tiff (tif), *n.* **1.** a little quarrel. **2.** a slight ill humor. —*v.* **1.** have a little quarrel. **2.** be slightly peevish; be in a huff.

tif·fin (tif′ən), *n.* in India, lunch. [prob. < *tiff* drink, of uncert. orig.]

Tif·lis (tif′lis), *n.* city in SE Georgia in the Soviet Union.

ti·ger (tī′gər), *n.* **1.** a large, fierce Asiatic animal of the cat family that has dull-yellow fur striped with black. **2.** *Am., Colloq.* an extra yell at the end of a cheer. [< L < Gk. *tigris*] —**ti′ger·ish, ti′grish, ti′ger·like′,** *adj.*

tiger lily, a lily that has dull-orange flowers spotted with black.

ti·ger's-eye (tī′gərz·ī′), **ti·ger-eye** (tī′gər·ī′), *n.* a golden-brown semiprecious stone with a changeable luster, composed chiefly of quartz, colored with iron oxide.

tight (tīt), *adj.* **1.** firm; held firmly; packed or put together firmly: *a tight knot.* **2.** drawn; stretched: *a tight canvas.* **3.** close; fitting closely; fitting too closely: *tight clothing.* **4.** *Dial.* well-built; trim; neat. **5.** not letting water, air, or gas in or out. **6.** hard to deal with or manage; difficult: *his lies got him in a tight place.* **7.** *Colloq.* almost even; close: *it was a tight race.* **8.** hard to get; scarce: *money is tight just now.* **9.** *Colloq.* stingy. **10.** *Slang.* drunk. —*adv.* **1.** firmly. **2.** sit tight, *Colloq.* keep the same position, opinion, etc. [OE *getyht,* pp. of *tyhtan* stretch] —**tight′ly,** *adv.* —**tight′ness,** *n.* —**Syn.** *adj.* **1.** close, compact. **2.** taut, tense. **3.** snug, close-fitting.

tight·en (tīt′ən), *v.* **1.** make tight. **2.** become tight. —**tight′en·er,** *n.*

tight-fist·ed (tīt′fis′tid), *adj.* stingy.

tight-lipped (tīt′lipt′), *adj.* **1.** keeping the lips firmly together. **2.** saying little or nothing.

tight·rope (tīt′rōp′), *n.* rope stretched tight on which acrobats perform. —*adj.* of or pertaining to a tightrope.

tights (tīts), *n.pl.* a close-fitting garment worn by acrobats, dancers, etc.

tight-wad (tīt′wod′), *n.* *Am., Slang.* a stingy person.

ti·gress (tī′gris), *n.* a female tiger.

Ti·gris (tī′gris), *n.* river flowing from SE Turkey through Iraq, where it joins the Euphrates River and empties into the Persian Gulf.

tike (tīk), *n.* tyke.

til·de (til′də), *n.* **1.** a diacritical mark (~) used over *n* in Spanish when it is pronounced *ny,* as in *cañon* (kä·nyōn′). **2.** in the pronunciations in this book, a mark used over *a* to show that it is pronounced as in *fare* (fãr). [< Sp. < L *titulus* title]

tile (tīl), *n., v.,* **tiled, til·ing.** —*n.* **1.** a thin piece of baked clay, stone, etc. Tiles are used for covering roofs, paving floors, and ornamenting. **2.** pipe for draining land. **3.** tiles collectively. **4.** *Colloq.* a stiff hat; high silk hat. —*v.* put tiles on or in. [< L *tegula*] —**til′er,** *n.*

til·ing (tīl′ing), *n.* **1.** tiles collectively. **2.** the work of covering with tiles. **3.** work consisting of tiles.

till[1] (til), *prep., conj.* until; up to the time of; up to the time when. [OE *til*] ❯ **till, until.** These two words are not distinguishable in meaning. Use *till* or *until* according to the stress or the feel of the phrase you want. *Until* is most often used at the beginning of sentences or clauses: *Until he went to college, he never had thought of his speech. He had never thought of his speech till* [until] *he went to college.*

till[2] (til), *v.* cultivate (land); plow. [OE *tilian*] —**till′a·ble,** *adj.* —**till′er,** *n.*

till[3] (til), *n.* **1.** a small drawer for money under or behind a counter. **2.** formerly, a drawer or tray for keeping valuables. [ult. < OE *–tyllan* draw, as in *betyllan* lure]

till·age (til′ij), *n.* **1.** cultivation of land. **2.** fact or condition of being tilled. **3.** tilled land. **4.** crops growing on tilled land.

till·er (til′ər), *n.* bar or handle used to turn the rudder in steering a boat. [< OF *telier* weaver's beam, ult. < L *tela* web, loom] —**till′er·less,** *adj.*

tilt (tilt), *v.* **1.** slope; slant; lean; tip: *this table tilts.* **2.** rush, charge, or fight with lances. **3.** engage in a joust, contest, etc. **4.** point or thrust (a lance). **5.** tilt at, attack; fight; protest against. **6.** tilt at windmills, attack imaginary enemies. —*n.* **1.** a slope; sloping position. **2.** act or fact of tilting; state of being tilted. **3.** a fight on horseback with lances. **4.** any dispute or quarrel. **5.** full tilt, at full speed; with full force: *his car ran full tilt against the tree.* [ult. < OE *tealt* shaky] —**tilt′er,** *n.*

tim·bal (tim′bəl), *n.* kettledrum. [< F *timbale,* ult. < Ar. *aṭ-ṭabl* the drum]

tim·bale (tim′bəl), *n.* **1.** minced meat, fish, vegetables, etc., prepared with a sauce and cooked in a mold. **2.** a mold made of pastry. [< F, orig., TIMBAL]

tim·ber (tim′bər), *n.* **1.** *U.S.* wood used for building and making things. **2.** a large piece of wood used in building. Beams and rafters are timbers. **3.** growing trees; forests. —*v.* cover, support, or furnish with timber. [OE] —**tim′bered,** *adj.* —**tim′ber·ing,** *n.* —**tim′ber·land′,** *n.*

timber hitch, knot used to fasten a rope around a spar, post, etc.

timber line, *Am.* line beyond which trees will not grow on mountains and in the polar regions because of the cold.

timber wolf, *Am.* a large gray or brindled wolf of North America.

tim·bre (tim′bər; tam′–), *n.* the quality in sounds that distinguishes a certain voice, instrument, etc., from other voices, instruments, etc. Notes of the same pitch and loudness may differ in timbre. [< OF, ult. < Gk. *tympanon* kettledrum. Doublet of TYMPANUM.]

tim·brel (tim′brəl), *n.* tambourine. —**tim′-breled,** *Brit.* **tim′brelled,** *adj.*

Tim·buk·tu (tim·buk′tü; tim′buk·tü′), *n.* city in NW Africa.

time (tīm), *n., v.,* **timed, tim·ing,** *adj.* —*n.* **1.**

all the days there have been or ever will be; the past, present, and future: *space and time are two fundamental conceptions.* **2.** a limited extent of time, as between two successive events: *a long time.* **3.** a particular period of time: *for the time being.* **4.** epoch: *the time of the Stuarts.* **5.** a particular point in time: *what time is it?* **6.** a particular part of a year, day, etc.: *dinner time.* **7.** a prescribed or allotted term or period, as of one's life: *"one man in his time plays many parts."* **8.** the right part or point of time: *it is time to eat.* **9.** occasion: *this time we will succeed.* **10.** each occasion of a recurring action or event: *do a thing five times.* **11.** *Colloq.* term in prison. **12.** way of reckoning time: *daylight-saving time.* **13.** condition of life: *war brings hard times.* **14.** experience during a certain time: *a good time.* **15.** *Music.* **a.** rate of movement in music; rhythm: *march time, waltz time.* **b.** length of a note or rest in music. **16.** amount of time that one has worked or should work. **17.** pay for this: *give me my time.* **18.** free time; leisure: *have time to read.* **19.** times, multiplied by; ×. **20. against time,** trying to finish before a certain time. **21. at the same time,** however; nevertheless. **22. at times,** now and then; once in a while. **23. behind the times,** old-fashioned; out of date. **24. for the time being,** for the present; for now. **25. from time to time,** now and then; once in a while. **26. in good time, a.** at the right time. **b.** soon; quickly. **27. in time, a.** after a while. **b.** soon enough. **c.** in the right rate of movement in music, dancing, marching, etc. **28. on time, a.** at the right time; not late. **b.** with time in which to pay. **29. time after time, time and again,** again and again. **30. time out of mind,** beyond memory or record. —*v.* **1.** measure the time of: *time a race.* **2.** do at regular times; do in rhythm with; set the time of: *the dancers time their steps to the music.* **3.** choose the moment or occasion for. —*adj.* **1.** of or pertaining to time. **2.** provided with a clocklike mechanism so that it will explode or ignite at a given moment: *a time bomb.* **3.** payable at a date in the future. **4.** pertaining to purchases to be paid for at a future date. [OE *tíma*] —**Syn.** *n.* **2.** while, interval. **4.** era, age. **15a.** measure, tempo. ➤ **time.** The various time relationships are expressed in subordinate clauses introduced by the conjunctions *after, as, as long as, as often as, as soon as, before, since, till, when, whenever, while.*

time·card (tīm′kärd′), *n. Am.* **1.** card for recording the amount of time that a person works. **2.** card showing the times of trains, etc.

time clock, *Am.* clock with a device to record the time when workers arrive and leave.

time exposure, 1. exposure of a photographic film for a certain time, longer than a half second. **2.** photograph taken in this way. —**time′-expo′sure,** *adj.*

time-hon·ored, *esp. Brit.* **time-hon·oured** (tīm′on′ərd), *adj.* honored because old and established.

time·keep·er (tīm′kēp′ər), *n.* **1.** person or thing that keeps time. **2.** timepiece.

time·less (tīm′lis), *adj.* **1.** never ending; eternal. **2.** referring to no special time.

time·ly (tīm′li), *adj.*, -**li·er,** -**li·est.** at the right time. —**time′li·ness,** *n.* —**Syn.** seasonable, opportune, convenient, appropriate, fitting, suitable.

time·piece (tīm′pēs′), *n.* clock or watch.

tim·er (tīm′ər), *n.* **1.** person or thing that times. **2.** timekeeper. **3.** in an internal-combustion engine, an automatic device that causes the spark for igniting the charge to occur just at the time required.

time·serv·ing (tīm′sėr′ving), *adj., n.* shaping one's conduct to conform with the opinions of the time or of persons in power, esp. for selfish reasons. —**time′serv′er,** *n.*

time·ta·ble (tīm′tā′bəl), *n.* schedule showing the times when trains, boats, busses, airplanes, etc., arrive and depart.

time·worn (tīm′wôrn′; -wōrn′), *adj.* worn by long existence or use.

tim·id (tim′id), *adj.* easily frightened; shy.

[< L *timidus*] —**tim′id·ly,** *adv.* —**tim′id·ness,** *n.* —**Syn.** fearful, timorous, shrinking, retiring, bashful.

ti·mid·i·ty (ti·mid′ə·ti), *n.* state or character of being timid; shyness.

tim·ing (tīm′ing), *n.* regulation of the speed of motions, musical tempo, play of cards, etc., to secure the greatest possible effect.

tim·or·ous (tim′ər·əs), *adj.* easily frightened; timid. [< Med.L. < L *timor* fear] —**tim′or·ous·ly,** *adv.* —**tim′or·ous·ness,** *n.*

tim·o·thy (tim′ə·thi), *n. Am.* a kind of coarse grass with long, cylindrical spikes, often grown for hay. [after *Timothy* Hanson, early American cultivator]

Tim·o·thy (tim′ə·thi), *n.* **1.** a disciple of the Apostle Paul. **2.** either of the two books of the New Testament written as letters by Paul to Timothy.

tim·pa·ni (tim′pə·ni), *n.pl., sing.* -**no** (-nō). kettledrums. [< Ital., pl. of *timpano* TYMPANUM] —**tim′pa·nist,** *n.*

tin (tin), *n., adj., v.,* **tinned, tin·ning.** —*n.* **1.** *Chem.* a metallic element, Sn, resembling silver in color and luster but softer and cheaper. **2.** tin plate. **3.** any can, box, pan, or other container made of tin: *a pie tin.* —*adj.* made of tin. —*v.* **1.** cover with tin. **2.** *Brit.* put up in tin cans or tin boxes; can. [OE] —**tin′like′,** *adj.*

tinc·ture (tingk′chər), *n., v.,* -**tured,** -**tur·ing.** —*n.* **1.** solution of medicine in alcohol: *tincture of iodine.* **2.** trace; tinge. **3.** color; tint. —*v.* **1.** give a trace or tinge to. **2.** imbue: *words tinctured with piety.* **3.** color; tint. [< L *tinctura* < *tingere* tinge]

tin·der (tin′dər), *n.* anything that catches fire easily. **2.** material used to catch fire from a spark. [OE *tynder*] —**tin′der·like′,** *adj.*

tin·der·box (tin′dər·boks′), *n.* **1.** box for holding tinder, flint, and steel for making a fire. **2.** a very inflammable thing or person.

tine (tīn), *n.* a sharp projecting point or prong: *the tines of a fork.* [OE *tind*] —**tined,** *adj.*

tin foil, a very thin sheet of tin, or tin and lead, used as a wrapping for candy, tobacco, etc.

ting[1] (ting), *v.* make or cause to make a clear ringing sound. —*n.* such a sound. [imit.]

ting[2] (ting), *n.* thing[2].

tinge (tinj), *v.,* **tinged, tinge·ing** or **ting·ing,** *n.* —*v.* **1.** color slightly: *a drop of ink will tinge a glass of water.* **2.** add a trace of some quality to; change slightly: *sad memories tinged their present joy.* —*n.* **1.** a slight coloring or tint. **2.** a very small amount; trace. [< L *tingere*] —**ting′er,** *n.* —**tin·gi·ble** (tin′jə·bəl), *adj.*

tin·gle (ting′gəl), *v.,* -**gled,** -**gling,** *n.* —*v.* **1.** have a feeling of thrills or a pricking, stinging feeling. **2.** cause this feeling in: *shame tingled his cheeks.* **3.** be thrilling: *the newspaper story tingled with excitement.* **4.** tinkle; jingle. —*n.* **1.** a pricking, stinging feeling. **2.** a tinkling; jingling. [prob. var. of *tinkle*] —**tin′gler,** *n.* —**tin′gling·ly,** *adv.*

tink·er (tingk′ər), *n.* **1.** man who mends pots, pans, etc. **2.** unskilled or clumsy work; activity that is rather useless. **3.** person who does such work. —*v.* **1.** mend; patch. **2.** work or repair in an unskilled or clumsy way. **3.** work or keep busy in a rather useless way. [ult. < *tin*] —**tink′er·er,** *n.*

tin·kle (ting′kəl), *v.,* -**kled,** -**kling,** *n.* —*v.* **1.** make short, light, ringing sounds: *little bells tinkle.* **2.** cause to tinkle. **3.** move with a tinkle. **4.** call, make known, etc., by tinkling: *the little clock tinkled out the hours.* —*n.* series of short, light, ringing sounds: *the tinkle of sleigh bells.* [ult. imit.] —**tin′kler,** *n.* —**tin′kling,** *n., adj.*

tin·ner (tin′ər), *n.* **1.** person who works in a tin mine. **2.** person who works with tin. **3.** *Brit.* a canner.

tin·ny (tin′i), *adj.,* -**ni·er,** -**ni·est.** **1.** of tin; containing tin. **2.** like tin in looks or sound. —**tin′ni·ly,** *adv.* —**tin′ni·ness,** *n.*

tin-pan alley (tin′pan′), *Am.* district frequented by musicians, song writers, and song publishers.

āge, cāre, fär; ēqual, tėrm; īce; ōpen, ôrder; pùt, rüle, ūse; tħ, then; ə=a in about.

tin plate, thin sheets of iron or steel coated with tin. Ordinary tin cans are made of tin plate.

tin·sel (tin'səl), n., v., -seled, -sel·ing; esp. Brit. -selled, -sel·ling; adj. —n. 1. glittering copper, brass, etc., in thin sheets, strips, threads, etc., used to trim Christmas trees, etc. 2. anything showy but having little value. 3. a thin cloth woven with threads of gold, silver, or copper. —v. trim with tinsel. —adj. of or like tinsel; showy but not worth much. [< F étincelle spark < L scintilla spark. Doublet of SCINTILLA.] —tin'sel·ly, adj.

tin·smith (tin'smith'), n. person who works with tin; maker of tinware.

tint (tint), n. 1. variety of a color: several tints of blue. 2. a delicate or pale color. 3. variety of a color produced by mixing it with white. 4. in engraving, a uniform shading of fine lines. —v. put a tint on; color slightly. [earlier tinct < L tinctus a dyeing < tingere to dye] —tint'er, n.

tin·tin·nab·u·la·tion (tin'ti·nab'yə·lā'shən), n. Am. the ringing of bells. [ult. < L tintinnabulum bell]

Tin·to·ret·to (tin'tə·ret'ō), n. 1518–1594, Venetian painter.

tin·type (tin'tīp'), n. Am. photograph taken on a sheet of enameled tin or iron.

tin·ware (tin'wãr'), n. articles made of tin.

ti·ny (tī'ni), adj., -ni·er, -ni·est. very small; wee. —Syn. little, minute, microscopic, infinitesimal.

-tion, suffix. 1. act or state of _____ing, as in addition, opposition. 2. condition or state of being _____ed, as in exhaustion. 3. result of _____ing, as in apparition. [< L -tio]

tip¹ (tip), n., v., tipped, tip·ping. —n. 1. the terminal portion; end; point: the tips of the fingers. 2. the uppermost portion; summit; top: the tip of a steeple. 3. a small piece put on the end of something. —v. put a tip on; furnish with a tip. [ME tippe] —Syn. 1. extremity.

tip² (tip), v., tipped, tip·ping. n. —v. 1. slope; slant: she tipped the table toward her. 2. upset; overturn. 3. take off (a hat) in salutation. —n. a slope; slant. —tip'per, n. —Syn. v. 1. tilt, incline, lean. 2. capsize, overthrow.

tip³ (tip), n., v., tipped, tip·ping. —n. 1. a small present of money. 2. piece of secret information: a tip on a race horse. 3. a useful hint, suggestion, etc. 4. a light, sharp blow; tap. —v. 1. give a small present of money to. 2. give secret information to. 3. give a tip. 4. hit lightly and sharply; tap. 5. tip off, Am., Colloq. a. give secret information to. b. warn. —tip'per, n.

tip-off (tip'ôf'; -of'), n. Colloq. 1. piece of secret information. 2. Am. a warning.

Tip·per·a·ry (tip'ər·ãr'i), n. 1. county in S Eire. 2. town located there. 3. a song popular during World War I.

tip·pet (tip'it), n. 1. scarf for the neck and shoulders with ends hanging down in front, esp. a long black scarf worn by clergy in choir. 2. a long, narrow, hanging part of a hood, sleeve, or scarf. [prob. < tip¹]

Tippet (def. 2)

tip·ple (tip'əl), v., -pled, -pling, n. —v. drink (alcoholic liquor) often. —n. an alcoholic liquor. —tip'pler, n.

tip·ster (tip'stər), n. Colloq. person who makes a business of furnishing private or secret information for use in betting, speculation, etc.

tip·sy (tip'si), adj., -si·er, -si·est. 1. tipping easily; unsteady; tilted. 2. somewhat intoxicated but not thoroughly drunk. [prob. < tip²] —tip'si·ly, adv. —tip'si·ness, n.

tip·toe (tip'tō'), n., v., -toed, -toe·ing, adj., adv. —n. 1. the tips of the toes. 2. on tiptoe, a. walking on one's toes. b. eager. c. in a secret manner. —v. walk on the tips of the toes. —adj. 1. standing or walking on tiptoe. 2. eagerly expectant. 3. cautious; stealthy. —adv. on tiptoe.

tip·top (tip'top'), n. the very top; highest point. —adj. 1. at the very top or highest point. 2. Colloq. first-rate; excellent. —tip'top'per, n.

ti·rade (tī'rād; tə·rād'), n. 1. a long, vehement speech. 2. a long, scolding speech. [< F < Ital. tirata < tirare shoot]

Ti·ra·na (ti·rä'nə), n. capital of Albania, in the C part.

tire¹ (tīr), v., tired, tir·ing. 1. make weary: the work tired him. 2. become weary: he tired easily. 3. tire out, make very weary. [OE tȳrian] —Syn. 1. exhaust, fatigue, fag, jade. —Ant. 1. refresh, revive.

tire² (tīr), n., v., tired, tir·ing. —n. a band of rubber or metal around a wheel. —v. furnish with a tire. Also, Brit. tyre. [< attire, in sense of "covering"]

tired (tīrd), adj. weary; wearied; exhausted. —tired'ly, adv. —tired'ness, n.

tire·less (tīr'lis), adj. 1. never becoming tired; requiring little rest: a tireless worker. 2. never stopping: tireless efforts. —tire'less·ly, adv. —tire'less·ness, n. —Syn. 1. indefatigable.

tire·some (tīr'səm), adj. tiring; boring: a tiresome speech. —tire'some·ly, adv. —tire'some·ness, n. —Syn. exhausting, fatiguing, wearisome, tedious, irksome.

ti·ro (tī'rō), n., pl. -ros. tyro.

Ti·rol (ti·rōl'; tī'rōl; tir'ol; tir'əl), n. region in the Alps, partly in Austria and partly in Italy. Also, Tyrol. —Tir·o·lese (tir'ə·lēz'; -lēs'), Ti·ro·le·an (ti·rō'li·ən), adj., n.

tis·sue (tish'ü), n., v., -sued, -su·ing. —n. 1. Biol. substance forming the parts of animals and plants; a mass of cells: brain tissue, skin tissue. 2. a thin, light cloth. 3. web; network: her whole story was a tissue of lies. 4. tissue paper. —v. make into a tissue; weave. [< OF tissu, orig. pp. of tistre weave < L texere]

tissue paper, a very thin, soft paper.

tit¹ (tit), n. 1. titmouse. 2. any of various other small birds. [cf. Scand. tittr titmouse]

tit² (tit), n. nipple; teat. [OE titt]

Ti·tan (tī'tən), n. 1. Gk. Myth. one of a family of giants who ruled the world before the gods of Olympus. Prometheus and Atlas were Titans. 2. Also, titan. person or thing having enormous size, strength, power, etc.; giant. 3. the sun thought of as a god. —adj. Titanic.

Ti·ta·ni·a (ti·tā'ni·ə), n. in Shakespeare's "Midsummer Night's Dream," the queen of the fairies.

Ti·tan·ic (tī·tan'ik), adj. 1. of or like the Titans. 2. Also, titanic. having great size, strength, or power; gigantic; huge.

ti·ta·ni·um (ti·tā'ni·əm; ti-), n. Chem. a metallic element, Ti, occurring in various minerals. When isolated it is a dark-gray powder with a metallic luster. [< Titan] —ti·tan·ic (tī·tan'ik; ti-), adj.

tit·bit (tit'bit'), n. tidbit. [var. of tidbit]

tit for tat, blow for blow; like for like.

tithe (tīth), n., v., tithed, tith·ing. —n. 1. one tenth. 2. Often, tithes. Brit. tax of one tenth of the yearly produce of land, animals, and personal work, paid for the support of the church and the clergy. 3. a very small part. 4. any small tax, levy, etc. —v. 1. put a tax of a tenth on. 2. pay a tithe on. 3. give one tenth of one's income to the church or to charity. [OE teogotha tenth] —tith'er, n.

ti·tian (tish'ən), n. an auburn or golden red used extensively by Titian. —adj. auburn; golden-red.

Ti·tian (tish'ən), n. 1477?–1576, Italian painter.

tit·il·late (tit'ə·lāt), v., -lat·ed, -lat·ing. 1. excite pleasantly; stimulate agreeably. 2. tickle. [< L] —tit'il·la'tion, n. —tit'il·la'tor, n.

tit·i·vate, tit·ti·vate (tit'ə·vāt), v., -vat·ed, -vat·ing. Colloq. dress up; make smart; prink. [? ult. < tidy] —tit'i·va'tion, tit'ti·va'tion, n. —tit'i·va'tor, tit'ti·va'tor, n.

tit·lark (tit'lärk'), n. a small bird like a lark; pipit.

ti·tle (tī'təl), n., v., -tled, -tling. —n. 1. the name of a book, poem, picture, song, etc. 2. the title page or all the material on it. 3. name showing rank, occupation, or condition in life. King, duke, lord, countess, captain, doctor, professor, Madame, and Miss are titles. 4. any descriptive name. **5.** a first-place position; championship: *the tennis title.* **6.** *Law.* **a.** a legal right to the possession of property. **b.** evidence showing such a right. **c.** document giving such evidence. **7.** a recognized right; claim. —*v.* call by a title; name. [< OF < L *titulus.* Doublet of TITTLE.] —**ti′tled,** *adj.*

title page, the page at the beginning of a book that contains the title, the author's name, etc.

title role, the part or character for which a play is named. Hamlet is a title role.

tit·mouse (tit′mous′), *n., pl.* **-mice.** any of certain small birds with short bills and dull-colored feathers, as the chickadee. [ME *titmose* < *tit* titmouse + OE *māse* titmouse]

Ti·to (tē′tō), *n.* **Marshal** (*Josip Broz* or *Brozovich*), born 1892, Yugoslav premier since 1945.

Ti·to·ism (tē′tō-iz·əm), *n.* principles and practices of Marshal Tito, esp. the stressing of a form of Communism that places national interests above international interests. —**Ti′to·ist,** *n., adj.*

ti·trate (tī′trāt; tit′rāt), *v.,* **-trat·ed, -trat-ing,** *n.* —*v.* analyze (a solution) by titration. —*n.* solution to be analyzed in this way. [< F, < *titre* quality, TITLE]

ti·tra·tion (tī-trā′shən; ti–), *n.* process of determining the amount of some substance present in a solution by measuring the amount of a different substance that must be added to cause a chemical change.

tit·ter (tit′ər), *v.* laugh in a half-restrained manner; giggle. —*n.* such a laugh. —**tit′ter·er,** *n.* —**tit′ter·ing·ly,** *adv.*

tit·tle (tit′əl), *n.* **1.** a very little bit; particle; whit. **2.** a small stroke or mark over a letter in writing or printing. The dot over an *i* is a tittle. [< Med.L *titulus* diacritical mark < L, title. Doublet of TITLE.]

tit·tle-tat·tle (tit′əl·tat′əl), *n., v.,* **-tled, -tling.** gossip. —**tit′tle-tat′tler,** *n.*

tit·u·lar (tich′ə-lər; tit′yə–), *adj.* **1.** in title or name only: *he is a titular prince without any power.* **2.** having a title. **3.** pertaining to a title. [< L *titulus* title] —**tit′u·lar·ly,** *adv.*

Ti·tus (tī′təs), *n.* **1.** convert and companion of Saint Paul. **2.** epistle of the New Testament written to Titus by Saint Paul.

tiz·zy (tiz′i), *n., pl.* **-zies.** *Slang.* a very excited state; dither.

Tl, *Chem.* thallium.

Tm, *Chem.* thulium.

Tn, *Chem.* thoron.

tn., ton.

TNT, T.N.T., trinitrotoluene, a colorless solid used as an explosive in grenades, torpedoes, etc.

to (tü; *unstressed* tu̇, tə), *prep.* **1.** in the direction of: *go to the right.* **2.** as far as; until: *rotten to the core, faithful to the end.* **3.** for; for the purpose of: *he came to the rescue.* **4.** toward or into the position, condition, or state of: *he went to sleep.* **5.** so as to produce, cause, or result in: *to her horror, the beast approached.* **6.** into: *she tore the letter to pieces.* **7.** along with; with: *we danced to the music.* **8.** compared with: *the score was 9 to 5.* **9.** in agreement or accordance with: *it is not to my liking.* **10.** belonging with; of: *the key to my room.* **11.** in honor of: *drink to the king.* **12.** on; against: *fasten it to the wall.* **13.** about; concerning: *what did he say to that?* **14.** in: *four apples to the pound.* **15.** To is used to show action toward: *give the book to me, speak to her.* **16.** To is used with the infinitive form of verbs: *he likes to read, the birds began to sing.* —*adv.* **1.** toward a person, thing, or point implied or understood; forward: *he wore his cap wrong side to.* **2.** together; touching; closed: *the door slammed to.* **3.** to action or work: *we turned to gladly.* **4.** to consciousness: *she came to.* **5.** to and fro, first one way and then back again; back and forth. [OE *tō*] ➤ See infinitive for usage note.

toad (tōd), *n.* **1.** a small animal somewhat like a frog, living most of the time on land rather than in water. See the picture in the next column. **2.** any tailless amphibian; any frog. [OE *tāde*] —**toad′like′,** *adj.*

toad·fish (tōd′fish′), *n.* fish with a thick head, a wide mouth, and slimy skin without scales.

toad·stool (tōd′stül′), *n.* **1.** mushroom. **2.** a poisonous mushroom.

toad·y (tōd′i), *n., pl.* **toad·ies,** *v.,* **toad·ied, toad·y·ing.** —*n.* a fawning flatterer. —*v.* **1.** act like a toady. **2.** fawn upon; flatter. —**toad′y·ish,** *adj.* —**toad′y·ism,** *n.*

Toad
(ab. 3 in. long)

to-and-fro (tü′ənd-frō′), *adj.* back-and-forth.

toast¹ (tōst), *n.* bread browned by heat. [< v.] —*v.* **1.** brown by heat. **2.** heat thoroughly. [< OF *toster,* ult. < L *torrere* parch] —**toast′er,** *n.*

toast² (tōst), *n.* **1.** person or thing whose health is proposed and drunk: *"the King" was the first toast drunk by the officers.* **2.** a call on another or others to drink to some person or thing. **3.** act of drinking to the health of a person or thing. —*v.* **1.** propose as a toast; drink to the health of. **2.** drink toasts. [from the custom of putting toast into drinks]

toast·mas·ter (tōst′mas′tər; –mäs′–), *n.* **1.** person who presides at a dinner and introduces the speakers. **2.** person who proposes toasts.

to·bac·co (tə-bak′ō), *n., pl.* **-cos, -coes. 1.** the prepared leaves of certain plants of the nightshade family, used for smoking or chewing or as snuff. **2.** one of these plants. [< Sp. *tabaco* < Carib]

to·bac·co·nist (tə-bak′ə-nist), *n.* dealer in tobacco.

To·ba·go (tō-bā′gō), *n.* former British island in the West Indies, near Venezuela; it joined with Trinidad and became independent in 1962.

to·bog·gan (tə-bog′ən), *Am.* —*n.* a long, narrow, flat sled without runners. —*v.* **1.** slide downhill on such a sled. **2.** decline sharply and rapidly in value. [< F (Canadian) *tabagane* < Algonquian] —**to·bog′gan·er, to·bog′gan·ist,** *n.*

toc·ca·ta (tə-kä′tə), *n. Music.* composition for the piano or organ intended to exhibit the player's technique. [< Ital., orig. pp. of *toccare* touch]

toc·sin (tok′sən), *n.* **1.** alarm sounded on a bell; warning signal. **2.** bell used to sound an alarm. [< F < Pr. *tocasenh* < *tocar* strike + *senh* bell]

to·day, to-day (tə-dā′), *n.* this day; the present time. —*adv.* **1.** on this day. **2.** at the present time; now. [OE *tō dæge*] ➤ **today. 1.** *Today* (like *tonight* and *tomorrow*) is hyphened now only by formal writers and by conservative publishers, or by people who learned to spell when the hyphen was generally used. **2.** *Today, of today* are often deadwood, adding nothing to the meaning of a statement already placed in the present: *Economic conditions* [of today] *are more unsettled than they have been for years.*

tod·dle (tod′əl), *v.,* **-dled, -dling,** *n.* —*v.* walk with short, unsteady steps, as a baby does. —*n.* **1.** act of toddling. **2.** such a way of walking.

tod·dler (tod′lər), *n.* child just learning to walk.

tod·dy (tod′i), *n., pl.* **-dies. 1.** fermented palm sap. **2.** drink made of whiskey, brandy, etc., with hot water and sugar. [< Hind. *tāṛī* palm sap < *tāṛ* palm]

to-do (tə-dü′), *n., pl.* **-dos.** *Colloq.* fuss; bustle; commotion.

toe (tō), *n., v.,* **toed, toe·ing.** —*n.* **1.** one of the five end parts of the foot. **2.** the part of a stocking, shoe, etc., that covers the toes. **3.** the fore part of a foot or hoof. **4.** anything like a toe: *the toe and heel of a golf club.* **5. on one's toes,** ready for action; alert. —*v.* **1.** touch or reach with the toes: *toe a line.* **2.** turn the toes in walking, standing, etc.: *toe in, toe out.* **3.** furnish with a toe or toes. **4.** drive (a nail) slantwise. **5.** fasten by nails driven slantwise. [OE *tā*] —**toe′less,** *adj.* —**toe′like′,** *adj.*

toe·nail (tō′nāl′), *n.* **1.** the nail growing on a toe of the human foot. **2.** in carpentry, a nail driven obliquely.

āge, cãre, fär; ēqual, tẽrm; īce; ōpen, ôrder; pu̇t, rüle, ūse; ŧħ, then; ə=a in about.

tof·fee, tof·fy (tôf′i; tof′i), *n.*, *pl.* **-fees;**
-fies. taffy.

tog (tog), *n.*, *v.*, **togged, tog·ging.** —*n.* 1. garment. 2. togs, *Colloq.* clothes. —*v.* clothe; dress.
[prob. ult. < F *toge* cloak or L *toga*]

to·ga (tō′gə), *n.*, *pl.* **-gas, -gae** (-jē). 1. a loose
outer garment worn by men of ancient Rome.
2. robe of office. [< L] —**to·gaed** (tō′gəd), *adj.*

to·geth·er (tə·geth′ər), *adv.* 1. with each
other; in company: *they were standing together.*
2. in or into one gathering, company, mass, or
body: *call people together, consider several cases
together.* 3. taken or considered collectively:
this one cost more than all the others together.
4. into or in union, contact, collision, etc.: *sew
things together, the cars came together with a
crash.* 5. so as to form a connected whole or
compact body: *squeeze a thing together, that
argument does not hang together well.* 6. in
friendly relations; in agreement: *we were together in the enterprise.* 7. with mutual action;
reciprocally: *confer together.* 8. without a stop
or break; continuously: *he worked for days
together.* 9. at the same time: *you cannot have
both together.* 10. together with, along with.
[OE *tōgædere* < *tō* to + *gædere* together]

tog·ger·y (tog′ər·i), *n. Colloq.* garments;
clothes.

tog·gle (tog′əl), *n.*, *v.*, **-gled, -gling.** —*n.* 1.
pin, bolt, or rod put through the eye of a rope
or the link of a chain to keep it in place, to
hold two ropes together, to serve as a hold for
the fingers, etc. 2. a toggle joint, or a device
furnished with one. —*v.* furnish
with a toggle; fasten with a toggle.

toggle joint, a kneelike joint
that transmits pressure at right
angles.   Toggle joint

To·go (tō′gō), *n.* republic in W Africa, formerly
a French trust territory and part of Togoland.

To·go·land (tō′gō·land′), *n.* a former German
protectorate in W Africa, on the Gulf of Guinea,
later under British and French control.

toil¹ (toil), *n.* hard work; labor. —*v.* 1. work
hard. 2. move with difficulty, pain, or weariness.
[< AF, ? ult. < L *tudicula* olive press] —**toil′er,**
n. —**Syn.** *n.* drudgery, travail, effort, exertion.
—*v.* labor, drudge, slave.

toil² (toil), *n.* Often, **toils.** net; snare: *the thief
was caught in the toils of the law.* [< F *toile,*
lit., cloth < L *tela* web]

toi·let (toi′lit), *n.* 1. bathroom. 2. a water
closet. 3. process of dressing, including bathing,
combing the hair, etc. 4. Also, **toi·lette** (toi·let′).
a person's dress; costume. —*adj.* of or for the
toilet. [< F *toilette,* dim. of *toile.* See TOIL².]

toi·let·ry (toi′lit·ri), *n.*, *pl.* **-ries.** soap, face
powder, perfumery, etc., used for the toilet.

toilet water, a fragrant liquid not so strong
as perfume.

toil·some (toil′səm), *adj.* requiring hard work;
laborious; wearisome. —**toil′some·ly,** *adv.*
—**toil′some·ness,** *n.* —**Syn.** tiring, fatiguing.

toil·worn (toil′wôrn′; -wōrn′), *adj.* worn by
toil; showing the effects of toil.

To·kay (tō·kā′), *n.* 1. a rich, sweet wine made
near Tokay, a town in Hungary. 2. the large,
firm, reddish, sweet grape from which it is made.

to·ken (tō′kən), *n.* 1. something serving to indicate some fact, feeling, event, etc.; mark or sign:
wear black as a token of mourning. 2. sign of
friendship; keepsake. 3. piece of metal stamped
for a higher value than the metal is worth.
Tokens are used for some purposes instead of
money. 4. piece of metal indicating a right or
privilege. 5. something that is a sign of genuineness or authority. 6. *Archaic.* a signal. 7. by the
same token, moreover. 8. in token of, as a token
of; to show. —*adj.* having only the semblance of;
serving as a symbol; nominal; partial: *a token
payment, token resistance.* [OE *tācen*] —**Syn.** *n.*
1. symbol, indication. 2. memento, memorial.

to·ken·ism (tō′kə·niz·əm), *n. Am.* the making
of token signs of eliminating racial segregation.

To·kyo, To·ki·o (tō′ki·ō), *n.* capital of
Japan, in the SE part.

told (tōld), *v.* 1. pt. and pp. of **tell.** 2. all told,
including all.

To·le·do (tə·lē′dō), *n.* 1. city in NW Ohio. 2.
city in C Spain. 3. a fine sword or sword blade
made in Toledo, Spain.

tol·er·a·ble (tol′ər·ə·bəl), *adj.* 1. able to be
borne or endured. 2. fairly good: *in tolerable
health.* [< L, < *tolerare* tolerate] —**tol′er·a·ble-
ness,** *n.* —**tol′er·a·bly,** *adv.* —**Syn.** 1. bearable,
endurable, sufferable, supportable. 2. passable,
mediocre, ordinary, indifferent.

tol·er·ance (tol′ər·əns), *n.* 1. a willingness
to be tolerant and patient toward people whose
opinions or ways differ from one's own. 2. the
power of enduring or resisting the action of a
drug, poison, etc. 3. action of tolerating. 4. an
allowed amount of variation from a standard,
as in the weight of coins or the size of a wire,
bolt, shaft, or other product. —**Syn.** 1. indulgence, sufferance, liberality.

tol·er·ant (tol′ər·ənt), *adj.* 1. willing to let
other people do as they think best; willing to
endure beliefs and actions of which one does not
approve. 2. able to endure or resist the action
of a drug, poison, etc. —**tol′er·ant·ly,** *adv.*

tol·er·ate (tol′ər·āt), *v.*, **-at·ed, -at·ing.** 1.
allow; permit. 2. bear; endure. 3. endure or
resist the action of (a drug, poison, etc.). [< L
toleratus] —**tol′er·a′tive,** *adj.* —**tol′er·a′tor,** *n.*

tol·er·a·tion (tol′ər·ā′shən), *n.* 1. willingness
to put up with beliefs and actions of which one
does not approve; tolerance. 2. recognition of a
person's right to worship as he thinks best
without loss of civil rights or social privileges;
freedom of worship. —**Syn.** 1. indulgence.

toll¹ (tōl), *v.* 1. sound with single strokes slowly
and regularly repeated: *bells were tolled all over
the country at the President's death.* 2. call, announce, etc., by tolling. —*n.* 1. a stroke or sound
of a bell. 2. act or fact of tolling. [akin to OE
-tyllan draw. See TILL³.] —**toll′er,** *n.*

toll² (tōl), *n.* 1. tax or fee paid for some right
or privilege: *we pay a toll when we use the
bridge.* 2. right to collect tolls. 3. charge for a
certain service: *there is a toll on long-distance
telephone calls.* 4. something paid, lost, suffered,
etc.: *automobile accidents take a heavy toll of
human lives.* —*v.* collect tolls from; take as toll.
[< L < Gk. *telonion* toll house, ult. < *telos* tax]
—**toll′a·ble,** *adj.* —**toll′er,** *n.*

toll bridge, bridge at which a toll is charged.

toll call, a long-distance telephone call.

toll·gate (tōl′gāt′), *n.* gate where toll is collected.

toll·keep·er (tōl′kēp′ər), *n.* person who collects the toll at a tollgate.

Tol·stoy, Tol·stoi (tol′stoi), *n.* Count Lev
(*Eng.* Leo) Nikolaevich, 1828–1910, Russian
novelist and social reformer.

Tol·tec (tol′tek), *n.* one of an Indian people
supposed to have ruled in Mexico before the
Aztecs and to have given them their culture.
—*adj.* Also, **Tol′tec·an.** of or pertaining to this
people.

tol·u·ene (tol′yu·ēn), *n.* a colorless liquid,
$C_6H_5CH_3$, somewhat like benzene, obtained from
coal tar and coal gas and used as a solvent and
for making explosives, dyes, etc.

tom, Tom (tom), *n.* the male of various animals; male. [< *Tom,* proper name, short for
Thomas]

tom·a·hawk (tom′ə·hôk), *Am.* —*n.* a light ax
used by North American Indians as a weapon
and a tool. —*v.* strike or kill with a tomahawk.
[< Algonquian]

to·ma·to (tə·mā′tō; -mä′-), *n.*, *pl.* **-toes.** 1. a
juicy fruit used as a vegetable. Most tomatoes
are red, but some kinds are yellow. 2. the plant
it grows on. [< Sp. < Mex. *tomatl*]

tomb (tüm), *n.* grave, vault, mausoleum, etc.,
for a dead body. —*v.* put in a tomb; shut up as if
in a tomb. [< OF < LL < Gk. *tymbos*] —**tomb′-
less,** *adj.* —**tomb′like′,** *adj.*

tom·boy (tom′boi′), *n.* girl who likes to play
boys' games; boisterous, romping girl. —**tom′-
boy′ish,** *adj.*

tomb·stone (tüm′stōn′), *n.* stone that marks
a tomb or grave.

tom·cat (tom′kat′), *n.* a male cat.

tome (tōm), *n.* book, esp. a large, heavy book. [< F < L < Gk. *tomos*, orig., piece cut off]

tom·fool (tom′fūl′), *n.* a silly fool; stupid person.

tom·fool·er·y (tom′fūl′ər·i), *n., pl.* **-er·ies.** silly behavior; nonsense.

Tom·my, tom·my (tom′i), or **Tommy At·kins** (at′kinz), *n., pl.* **-mies.** nickname for a British soldier.

Tommy gun, tommy gun, *Am., Colloq.* a Thompson submachine gun. —**Tommy gunner, tommy gunner.**

tom·my·rot (tom′i·rot′), *n. Slang.* nonsense; rubbish; foolishness.

to·mor·row, to·mor·row (tə·môr′ō; -mor′ō), *n.* the day after today. —*adv.* on the day after today. ⊳ See **today** for usage note.

Tomsk (tômsk), *n.* city in C Soviet Union.

Tom Thumb, 1. a diminutive hero of folk tales. **2.** anything that is very small; any dwarf.

tom·tit (tom′tit′), *n.* a small bird, esp. a titmouse.

tom-tom (tom′tom′), *n.* **1.** a native drum, usually beaten with the hands. **2.** a monotonous, rhythmic drumbeat. [< Hind. *tam-tam*] —**tom′tom′mer,** *n.*

ton (tun), *n.* **1.** measure of weight; 2000 pounds in the United States and Canada, 2240 pounds in England. **2.** measure of volume that varies with the thing measured; it is about equal to the space occupied by a ton's weight of the particular stuff. Thus a ton of stone is 16 cubic feet. **3.** unit of measure of internal capacity of a ship; 100 cubic feet. **4.** unit of measure of carrying capacity of a ship; 40 cubic feet. **5.** unit to measure weight of water a ship will displace; 35 cubic feet, the weight of a long ton of sea water. **6. long ton,** 2240 pounds. **7. metric ton,** 1000 kilograms. **8. short ton,** 2000 pounds. [var. of *tun*]

ton·al (tōn′əl), *adj.* of or pertaining to tones or tone. —**ton′al·ly,** *adv.*

to·nal·i·ty (tō·nal′ə·ti), *n., pl.* **-ties. 1.** *Music.* **a.** sum of relations, melodic and harmonic, existing between the tones of a scale or musical system. **b.** a key or system of musical tones. **2.** the color scheme of a painting, etc.

tone (tōn), *n., v.,* **toned, ton·ing.** —*n.* **1.** any sound considered with reference to its quality, pitch, strength, source, etc.: *sweet, shrill, or loud tones.* **2.** quality of sound. **3.** *Music.* **a.** a musical sound; musical sound of definite pitch and character. **b.** the difference in pitch between two notes. C and D are one tone apart. **4.** a particular way of sounding, modulation, or intonation of the voice: *speak in surly tones.* **5.** manner of speaking or writing: *a moral tone, a vulgar tone.* **6.** spirit; character; style: *a tone of quiet elegance prevails in her home, the moral tone of the city was bad.* **7.** distinction; elegance: *her home had tone.* **8.** state of mind; temper. **9.** normal healthy condition; vigor. **10.** effect of color and of light and shade in a picture. **11.** shade of color. —*v.* **1.** harmonize: *this rug tones in well with the wallpaper and furniture.* **2.** give a tone to. **3.** change the tone of. **4.** intone. **5. tone down,** soften. **6. tone up,** give more sound, color, or vigor to; strengthen. [< L < Gk. *tonos,* orig., a stretching, taut string] —**tone′less,** *adj.* —**tone′less·ly,** *adv.* —**tone′less·ness,** *n.* —**ton′er,** *n.* —Syn. *n.* **1.** note.

tong (tông; tong), *n.* **1.** in China, an association or club. **2.** *Am.* a secret Chinese organization or club in the United States. [< Chinese *t'ang, t'ong,* orig., meeting hall]

tongs (tôngz; tongz), *n.pl.* (*sometimes sing. in use*) tool with two hinged or pivoted arms for seizing, holding, or lifting. [OE *tang*]

tongue (tung), *n., v.,* **tongued, tongu·ing.** —*n.* **1.** the movable piece of flesh in the mouth, used in tasting and, by people, for talking. **2.** an animal's tongue used as food. **3.** power of speech. **4.** way of speaking; speech; talk: *a flattering tongue.* **5.** the language of a people: *the English tongue.* **6.** something shaped or used like a tongue. **7.** the strip of leather under the laces of a shoe. **8.** a narrow strip of land running out into water. **9.** a movable piece inside a bell that swings and rings. **10.** a vibrating reed or the like in a musical instrument. **11. hold one's tongue,** keep still. **12. on the tip of one's tongue, a.** almost spoken. **b.** ready to be spoken. **13. with tongue in cheek,** with intent to mislead, esp. in jest. —*v.* **1.** modify tones of (a flute, cornet, etc.) with the tongue. **2.** use the tongue. **3.** touch with the tongue. **4.** project like a tongue. [OE *tunge*] —**tongue′less,** *adj.*

tongue-tie (tung′tī′), *n., v.,* **-tied, -ty·ing.** —*n.* impeded motion of the tongue, esp. caused by shortness of the membrane binding its under side. —*v.* render tongue-tied.

tongue-tied (tung′tīd′), *adj.* **1.** having the motion of the tongue hindered. **2.** unable to speak because of shyness, embarrassment, etc.

ton·ic (ton′ik), *n.* **1.** anything that gives strength; medicine to give strength. **2.** *Music.* the first note of a scale; keynote. —*adj.* **1.** restoring to health and vigor; giving strength; bracing. **2.** characterized by continuous contraction of the muscles: *a tonic convulsion.* **3.** *Music.* **a.** pertaining to a tone or tones. **b.** of or based on a keynote. **4.** having to do with tone or accent in speaking. **5.** *Phonet.* accented or stressed. [< Gk. *tonikos < tonos* TONE] —**ton′i·cal·ly,** *adv.*

to·nic·i·ty (tō·nis′ə·ti), *n.* **1.** a tonic quality or condition. **2.** the property of possessing bodily tone.

to·night, to·night (tə·nīt′), *n.* the night of this day; this night. —*adv.* on or during this night. ⊳ See **today** for usage note.

ton·nage (tun′ij), *n.* **1.** the carrying capacity of a ship expressed in tons of 100 cubic feet. **2.** the freight-carrying capacity of a ship. **3.** the total amount of shipping in tons. **4.** duty or tax on ships at so much a ton. **5.** weight in tons. Also, **tunnage.**

ton·neau (tun·ō′), *n., pl.* **-neaus** or **-neaux** (-ōz′). the rear part of an automobile body, with seats for passengers. [< F, lit., cask, ult. < Gmc.] —**ton·neaued** (tun·ōd′), *adj.*

ton·sil (ton′səl), *n. Anat.* either of the two oval masses of glandular tissue on the sides of the throat, just back of the mouth. [< L *tonsillae,* pl.] —**ton′sil·lar, ton′sil·ar,** *adj.*

ton·sil·lec·to·my (ton′sə·lek′tə·mi), *n., pl.* **-mies.** *Surgery.* removal of the tonsils.

ton·sil·li·tis (ton′sə·lī′tis), *n.* inflammation of the tonsils. —**ton·sil·lit·ic** (ton′sə·lit′ik), *adj.*

ton·so·ri·al (ton·sō′ri·əl; -sô′-), *adj. Esp. Humorous.* of or pertaining to a barber or his work. [< L *tonsorius,* ult. < *tondere* to shear]

ton·sure (ton′shər), *n., v.,* **-sured, -sur·ing.** —*n.* **1.** a clipping of the hair or shaving of a part or the whole of the head of a person entering the priesthood or an order of monks. **2.** the shaved part of the head of a priest or monk. —*v.* shave the head of. [< L *tonsura < tondere* shear, shave] —**ton′sured,** *adj.*

ton·tine (ton′tēn; ton·tēn′), *n.* system of annuity or insurance in which subscribers share a fund. The shares of survivors increase as members die, until the last gets all that is left. —*adj.* of or pertaining to such a system.

too (tü), *adv.* **1.** also; besides: *young, clever, and rich too.* **2.** beyond what is desirable, proper, or right; more than enough: *too long, too much.* **3.** very; exceedingly: *I am only too glad to help.* [var. of *to*] ⊳ **too.** In formal English *too* is not used to modify a past participle unless it has become an adjective: Formal: *I was too much surprised to say anything.* Informal: *I was too surprised to say anything.* General Usage: *I am too tired* [an adjective] *to think.* When *too* comes within a construction it is usually set off by commas, but in informal writing it usually is not when it comes at the end: *I'm going too.* Formal: *I'm going, too.*

took (tůk), *v.* pt. of **take.**

tool (tül), *n.* **1.** a knife, hammer, saw, shovel, or any instrument used in doing work. **2.** person used by another like a tool: *he is a tool of the party boss.* **3.** a part of a machine that cuts, bores, smooths, etc. **4.** the whole of such a machine. —*v.* **1.** use a tool on. **2.** work with a tool. **3.** ornament with a tool. **4.** *Brit. Colloq.* drive or ride in a horse-drawn vehicle at a rather speedy rate. [OE *tōl*] —**tool′er,** *n.* —Syn. *n.* **1.** implement, utensil.

tool·ing (tül′ing), *n.* **1.** work done with a tool. **2.** ornamentation made with a tool.

toot (tüt), *n.* sound of a horn, whistle, etc. —*v.* **1.** give forth a short blast. **2.** sound (a horn, whistle, etc.) in short blasts. [prob. ult. imit.] —**toot′er,** *n.*

tooth (tüth), *n.,* *pl.* **teeth,** *v.* —*n.* **1.** one of the hard bonelike parts in the mouth, used for biting and chewing. **2.** something like a tooth, as one of the projecting parts of a comb, rake, or saw. **3.** taste, relish, or liking (for): *a sweet tooth.* **4. fight tooth and nail,** fight fiercely, with all one's force. —*v.* **1.** furnish with teeth; put teeth on. **2.** indent; cut teeth on the edge of. **3.** interlock as cogwheels do. **4.** bite; gnaw. [OE *tōth*] —**toothed,** *adj.* —**tooth′less,** *adj.*

Teeth
M, molars;
B, bicuspids;
C, canine;
I, incisors.

tooth·ache (tüth′āk′), *n.* pain in a tooth or the teeth.

tooth·brush (tüth′brush′), *n.* a small brush for cleaning the teeth.

tooth·paste (tüth′pāst′), *n. Am.* paste used in cleaning the teeth.

tooth·pick (tüth′pik′), *n.* a small, pointed piece of wood or a sharpened quill for removing bits of food from between the teeth.

tooth·some (tüth′səm), *adj.* pleasing to the taste; tasting good. —**tooth′some·ly,** *adv.* —**tooth′some·ness,** *n.* —Syn. savory, delicious.

top[1] (top), *n.,* *adj.,* *v.,* **topped, top·ping.** —*n.* **1.** the highest point or part: *the top of a mountain.* **2.** the upper end or surface: *the top of a table.* **3.** the highest or leading place, rank, etc.: *he is at the top of his class.* **4.** one that occupies the highest or leading position: *he is top in his profession.* **5.** the highest point, pitch, or degree: *the top of one's voice.* **6.** the best or most important part: *top of the morning.* **7.** cover of an automobile, can, etc. **8.** head. **9.** the upper part of a shoe or boot. **10.** bunch of hair, fibers, etc. **11. from top to toe,** a. from head to foot. b. completely. **12. on top,** with success; with victory. **13. over the top,** over the front of a trench to attack. —*adj.* **1.** pertaining to, situated at, or forming the top: *the top shelf.* **2.** highest in degree; greatest: *at top speed.* **3.** chief; foremost: *top honors.* —*v.* **1.** put a top on: *top a box.* **2.** be on top of; be the top of: *a church tops the hill.* **3.** reach the top of: *they topped the mountain.* **4.** rise high; rise above: *the sun topped the horizon.* **5.** exceed in height, amount, number, etc.: *the expense topped $100,000.* **6.** do better than; outdo; excel: *his story topped all the rest.* **7.** hit (a ball) above center. **8. top off,** complete; finish; end. [OE *topp*] —Syn. *n.* **1.** crest, crown, apex, summit, pinnacle. —*v.* **1.** cap, crown.

top[2] (top), *n.* **1.** toy that spins on a point. **2. sleep like a top,** sleep soundly. [OE *topp*]

to·paz (tō′paz), *n.* **1.** a crystalline mineral that occurs in various forms and colors. Transparent yellow topaz is used as a gem. **2.** any of various other minerals, as a yellow variety of sapphire **(oriental topaz)** or a yellow variety of quartz **(false topaz).** [< L < Gk. *topazos*]

top boot, 1. a high boot having the upper part of different material and made to look as if turned down. **2.** any boot with a high top. —**top′-boot′ed,** *adj.*

top·coat (top′kōt′), *n.* overcoat; loose overcoat; lightweight overcoat.

To·pe·ka (tə·pē′kə), *n.* capital of Kansas, in the NE part.

top·er (tōp′ər), *n.* person who drinks a great deal of alcoholic liquor.

top·flight (top′flīt′), *adj.* of highest rank or quality.

top·gal·lant (top′gal′ənt; *Naut.* tə·gal′ənt), *n.* the mast or sail above the topmast; the third section of a mast above the deck. —*adj.* next above the topmast.

top hat, a tall, black silk hat worn by men in formal clothes.

top·heav·y (top′hev′i), *adj.* too heavy at the top. —**top′-heav′i·ness,** *n.*

top·ic (top′ik), *n.* **1.** subject that people think, write, or talk about: *the topics of the day.* **2.** a short phrase or sentence used in an outline to give the main point of a part of a speech, writing, etc. [sing. of *topics* < L *topica* < Gk. *(ta) topika,* a study of logical and rhetorical commonplaces (by Aristotle) < *topos* place]

top·i·cal (top′ə·kəl), *adj.* **1.** having to do with topics of the day; of current interest. **2.** of or using topics; having to do with the topics of a speech, writing, etc. **3.** limited to a certain spot or part of the body; local. —**top′i·cal·ly,** *adv.*

top·knot (top′not′), *n.* a knot of hair or a tuft of feathers on the top of the head. —**top′-knot′ted,** *adj.*

top·lev·el (top′lev′əl), *adj.* of or having the highest authority or rank.

top·loft·y (top′lôf′ti; -lof′ti), *adj. Colloq.* lofty in character or manner; haughty; pompous; pretentious. —**top′loft′i·ness,** *n.*

top·mast (top′mast′; -mäst′; *Naut.* -məst), *n.* the second section of a mast above the deck.

top·most (top′mōst), *adj.* highest.

top·notch (top′noch′), *adj. Am., Colloq.* first-rate; best possible.

to·pog·ra·pher (tə·pog′rə·fər), *n.* **1.** person who knows much about topography. **2.** person who accurately describes the surface features of a place or region.

to·pog·ra·phy (tə·pog′rə·fi), *n.,* *pl.* **-phies. 1.** the accurate and detailed description or drawing of places or their surface features. **2.** the surface features of a place or region. The topography of a region includes hills, valleys, streams, lakes, bridges, tunnels, roads, etc. [< LL < Gk., < *topos* place + *graphein* write] —**top·o·graph·ic** (top′ə·graf′ik), **top′o·graph′i·cal,** *adj.* —**top′o·graph′i·cal·ly,** *adv.*

top·per (top′ər), *n.* **1.** one who tops. **2.** *Slang.* an excellent, first-rate person or thing. **3.** *Colloq.* a top hat. **4.** *Colloq.* topcoat. **5.** a woman's short coat.

top·ple (top′əl), *v.,* **-pled, -pling. 1.** fall forward; tumble down: *the chimney toppled onto the roof.* **2.** throw over or down; overturn: *the wrestler toppled his opponent.* **3.** hang over in an unsteady way: *beneath toppling crags.*

tops (tops), *adj. Slang.* of the highest degree in quality, excellence, etc.

top·sail (top′sāl′; *Naut.* -səl), *n.* the second sail above the deck on a mast.

top secret, a most important and highly guarded secret.

top·se·cret (top′sē′krit), *adj.* of utmost secrecy; extremely confidential.

top sergeant, *Am., Colloq.* the first sergeant of a military company.

top·side (top′sīd′), *n.* the upper part of a ship's side, esp. the part above the water line.

top·soil (top′soil′), *n.* the upper part of the soil; soil above the subsoil.

top·sy-tur·vy (top′si·tėr′vi), *adv., adj., n., pl.* **-vies.** —*adv.* **1.** upside down. **2.** in confusion or disorder. —*adj.* **1.** turned upside down; inverted. **2.** confused; disordered. —*n.* **1.** inversion of the natural order or state. **2.** confusion; disorder. [prob. ult. < *top*[1] + *tirve* overturn, akin to OE *tearflian* roll over] —**top′sy-tur′vi·ly,** *adv.* —**top′sy-tur′vi·ness,** *n.*

toque (tōk), *n.* hat without a brim; small hat with very little brim. [< F]

to·rah, to·ra (tô′rə; tō′-), *n.* **1.** in Jewish usage, instruction, doctrine, or law. **2.** the Torah, Mosaic law; the Pentateuch. [< Heb.]

Toque

torch (tôrch), *n.* **1.** light to be carried around or stuck in a holder on a wall. A piece of pine wood or anything that burns easily makes a good torch. **2.** device for producing a very hot flame, used esp. to burn off paint, to solder metal, and to melt metal. **3.** *Brit.* a stick-shaped electric lamp; flashlight. **4.** something thought of as a source of enlightenment: *the torch of civilization.* [< OF *torche*, prob. ult. < L *torquere* twist]

torch·bear·er (tôrch′bãr′ər), *n.* one who carries a torch.

torch·light (tôrch′līt′), *n.* light of a torch or torches.

tore (tôr; tōr), *v.* pt. of tear².

tor·e·a·dor (tôr′i·ə·dôr), *n.* a Spanish bullfighter, usually mounted. [< Sp., ult. < *toro* bull < L *taurus*]

to·ri·i (tō′ri·ē; tō′-), *n., pl.* **-ri·i.** gateway at the entrance to a Japanese temple, built of two uprights and two crosspieces. [< Jap.]

tor·ment (*v.* tôr·ment′; *n.* tôr′ment), *v.* **1.** cause very great pain to. **2.** worry or annoy very much. —*n.* **1.** cause of very great pain. **2.** very great pain. **3.** cause of very much worry or annoyance. [< OF *tormenter*, ult. < L *tormentum*, orig., twisted sling < *torquere* twist] —**torment′ing**, *adj.* —**tor·ment′ing·ly**, *adv.* —**torment′ing·ness**, *n.* —**tor·men′tor**, **tor·ment′er**, *n.* —**Syn.** *v.* **1.** torture, persecute, distress, afflict. **2.** tease, plague, harass. –*n.* **2.** agony, anguish, misery, distress.

torn (tôrn; tōrn), *v.* pp. of tear².

tor·na·do (tôr·nā′dō), *n., pl.* **-does, -dos. 1.** *Am.* an extremely violent and destructive whirlwind, moving forward as a whirling funnel extending down from a mass of dark clouds. **2.** any extremely violent windstorm. **3.** violent outburst. [alter. of Sp. *tronada* < *tronar* thunder] —**tornad·ic** (tôr·nad′ik), *adj. Am.*

To·ron·to (tə·ron′tō), *n.* city in SE Canada, on Lake Ontario.

tor·pe·do (tôr·pē′dō), *n., pl.* **-does,** *v.,* **-doed, -do·ing.** —*n.* **1.** *Am.* a large, cigar-shaped shell that contains explosives and travels by its own power. Torpedoes are sent under water to blow up enemy ships. **2.** a submarine mine, shell, etc., that explodes when hit. **3.** *Am.* an explosive put on a railroad track which makes a loud noise for a signal when a wheel of the engine runs over it. —*v.* attack or destroy with a torpedo. [< L, the electric ray (a fish), orig., numbness]

torpedo boat, a small, fast warship used for attacking with torpedoes.

tor·pid (tôr′pid), *adj.* **1.** dull in nature; inactive; sluggish. **2.** not moving or feeling. Snakes are torpid all winter in cold climates. [< L *torpidus*] —**tor·pid′i·ty, tor′pid·ness,** *n.* —**tor′pid·ly,** *adv.* —**Syn.** **1.** lethargic, apathetic.

tor·por (tôr′pər), *n.* a torpid condition. [< L] —**tor·por·if·ic** (tôr′pər·if′ik), *adj.*

torque (tôrk), *n.* **1.** force causing rotation. **2.** the amount of turning power exerted by a shaft. **3.** necklace of twisted metal. The ancient Gauls and Britons wore torques. [< L *torques*]

tor·rent (tôr′ənt; tor′-), *n.* **1.** a violent, rushing stream of water. **2.** a heavy downpour. **3.** any violent, rushing stream; flood: *a torrent of abuse.* [< L *torrens* boiling, parching]

tor·ren·tial (tô·ren′shəl; to-), *adj.* of, caused by, or like a torrent. —**tor·ren′tial·ly,** *adv.*

Tor·ri·cel·li (tôr′ə·chel′i), *n.* **Evangelista,** 1608–1647, Italian physicist who invented the barometer. —**Tor′ri·cel′li·an,** *adj.*

tor·rid (tôr′id; tor′-), *adj.* **1.** very hot. Brazil is in the Torrid Zone. July is a torrid month. **2.** hotly ardent; passionate. [< L *torridus*] —**tor·rid′i·ty, tor′rid·ness,** *n.* —**tor′rid·ly,** *adv.*

Torrid Zone, the very warm region between the tropic of Cancer and the tropic of Capricorn. The equator divides the Torrid Zone.

tor·sion (tôr′shən), *n.* **1.** act or process of twisting. **2.** state of being twisted. **3.** *Mechanics.* **a.** the twisting of a body by two equal and opposite forces. **b.** the internal tendency of a twisted object to return to its previous condition. [< LL *torsio* < *torquere* twist] —**tor′sion·al,** *adj.* —**tor′sion·al·ly,** *adv.* —**tor′sion·less,** *adj.*

tor·so (tôr′sō), *n., pl.* **-sos, -si** (-sē). **1.** the trunk or body of a statue without any head,

arms, or legs. **2.** the trunk of the human body. [< Ital., orig., stalk < L < Gk. *thyrsos* wand]

tort (tôrt), *n. Law.* a civil (not criminal) wrong for which the law requires damages (except a breach of contract). [< OF < Med.L *tortum* injustice < L *torquere* turn awry, twist]

tor·til·la (tôr·tē′yə), *n. Am., S.W.* a thin, flat, round corn cake. [< Sp.]

tor·toise (tôr′təs), *n., pl.* **-tois·es, -toise. 1.** turtle, esp. one living on land. **2.** a slow-moving person or thing. [< Med.L *tortuca*, ult. < L *torquere* twist]

tortoise shell, the mottled yellow-and-brown shell of a turtle or tortoise. Tortoise shell is much used for combs and ornaments. —**tor′toise-shell′,** *adj.*

tor·tu·ous (tôr′chù·əs), *adj.* **1.** full of twists, turns, or bends; twisting; winding; crooked. **2.** mentally or morally crooked; not straightforward. [< L *tortuosus*, ult. < *torquere* twist] —**tor′tu·ous·ly,** *adv.* —**tor′tu·ous·ness,** *n.* —**Syn. 1.** sinuous, serpentine, zigzag, circuitous. —**Ant. 1.** direct.

tor·ture (tôr′chər), *n., v.,* **-tured, -tur·ing.** —*n.* **1.** act or fact of inflicting very severe pain. Torture was formerly used to make people give evidence about crimes, or to make them confess. **2.** very severe pain. —*v.* **1.** cause very severe pain to. **2.** twist the meaning of. **3.** twist or force out of its natural form: *winds tortured the trees.* [< L *tortura* < *torquere* twist] —**tor′turer,** *n.* —**tor′tur·ing·ly,** *adv.* —**Syn.** *n.* **2.** agony, anguish, misery, distress. –*v.* **1.** torment, rack, persecute, distress.

To·ry (tô′ri; tō′-), *n., pl.* **-ries,** *adj.* —*n.* **1.** in British politics, originally a member of the party that favored the greatest possible amount of royal power, etc. Strictly speaking, there is no Tory party in modern England, although members of the Conservative Party are often called Tories. **2.** *Am.* an American who favored England at the time of the American Revolution. **3.** Also, **tory.** one advocating conservative principles. —*adj.* **1.** of or pertaining to Tories. **2.** Also, **tory.** opposed to change; conservative. —**To′ry·ism,** *n.*

Tos·ca·ni·ni (tos′kə·nē′ni), *n.* **Arturo,** 1867–1957, Italian conductor in the United States.

toss (tôs; tos), *v.,* **tossed** or (*Poetic*) **tost, toss·ing,** *n.* —*v.* **1.** throw lightly with the palm upward; cast; fling: *toss a ball.* **2.** throw about; pitch about: *the ship is tossed by the waves.* **3.** lift quickly; throw upward: *she tossed her head, he was tossed by the bull.* **4.** throw a coin to decide something by the side that falls upward. **5.** throw oneself about in bed; roll restlessly. **6.** toss off, **a.** do or make quickly and easily. **b.** drink all at once. —*n.* **1.** distance to which something is or can be tossed. **2.** a throw; tossing. [? < Scand. (dial. Norw.) *tossa* strew] —**toss′er,** *n.*

toss-up (tôs′up′; tos′-), *n.* **1.** a tossing of a coin to decide something. **2.** an even chance.

tot¹ (tot), *n.* a little child.

tot² (tot), *v.,* **tot·ted, tot·ting,** *n. Esp. Brit. Colloq.* —*v.* add; total. —*n.* a total.

to·tal (tō′təl), *adj., n., v.,* **-taled, -tal·ing:** *esp. Brit.* **-talled, -tal·ling.** —*adj.* **1.** whole; entire: *the total amount expended.* **2.** complete: *a total failure, total indifference.* —*n.* the whole amount; sum. —*v.* **1.** find the sum of; add. **2.** reach an amount of; amount to. [< Med.L, < L *totus* all] —**to′tal·ly,** *adv.* —**Syn.** *n.* whole, aggregate.

to·tal·i·tar·i·an (tō′tal·ə·tãr′i·ən), *adj.* of or having to do with a government controlled by one political group that permits no other political groups. —*n.* person in favor of totalitarianism. —**to·tal′i·tar′i·an·ism,** *n.*

to·tal·i·ty (tō·tal′ə·ti), *n., pl.* **-ties. 1.** entirety. **2.** the total amount.

total war, war in which all the resources of a nation are used, and in which attack is made not only on the armed forces of the opponent, but also (subject to certain limitations) on all its people and property.

tote (tōt), *v.,* **tot·ed, tot·ing,** *n. Am., Colloq.* —*v.* carry; haul. —*n.* **1.** act or course of toting. **2.** thing toted. —**tot′er,** *n. Am.*

to·tem (tō′təm), n. Am. **1.** among American Indians, a natural object, often an animal, taken as the emblem of a tribe, clan, family, etc. **2.** image of a totem. [< Algonquian] —**to·tem·ic** (tō·tem′ik), n. Am. —**to·tem′i·cal·ly,** adv. —**to′tem·ism,** n. Am. —**to′tem·ist,** n. —**to′tem·is′tic,** adj.

totem pole, Am. pole carved and painted with representations of totems, erected by the Indians of the NW coast of America, esp. in front of their houses.

tot·ter (tot′ər), v. **1.** stand or walk with shaky, unsteady steps. **2.** be unsteady; shake as if about to fall. **3.** shake; tremble. —n. a tottering. —**tot′ter·er,** n. —**tot′ter·ing·ly,** adv. —**tot′ter·y,** adj. —Syn. v. **1.** wobble, stagger.

tou·can (tū′kan; tü·kän′), n. a bright-colored bird of tropical America, with an enormous beak. [< Carib]

touch (tuch), v. **1.** put the hand or some other part of the body on or against: *he touched my hand.* **2.** put (one thing) against another; make contact: *he touched the post with his foot.* **3.** be against; come against: *your sleeve is touching the butter.* **4.** be in contact: *our hands touched.* **5.** be adjacent to: *a part of the road touched the river.* **6.** strike lightly or gently: *touch the strings of a harp.* **7.** Geom. be tangent to. **8.** injure slightly: *the flowers were touched by the frost.* **9.** affect with some feeling: *the story touched us.* **10.** mark; color: *a gray dress touched with blue.* **11.** have to do with; concern: *the matter touches your interests.* **12.** speak of; deal with; refer to; treat lightly: *our conversation did not touch on that.* **13.** handle; use: *he won't touch liquor or tobacco.* **14.** reach; come up to: *his head almost touches the ceiling.* **15.** Colloq. come near in quality: *there's nothing that can touch this.* **16.** stop at; visit in passing: *the ship touched port.* **17.** make a brief stop: *most ships touch at that port.* **18.** Slang. borrow from: *touch a man for a quarter.* **19.** touch off, **a.** represent exactly or cleverly. **b.** cause to go off; fire. **20.** touch on or upon, **a.** mention; treat lightly. **b.** come close to. **21.** touch up, **a.** change a little; improve: *touch up a photograph.* **b.** rouse. —n. **1.** a touching or being touched: *a bubble bursts at a touch.* **2.** the sense by which a person perceives things by feeling, handling, or coming against them: *the blind have a keen touch.* **3.** sensation so caused: *an object with a slimy touch.* **4.** a coming or being in contact: *the touch of their hands.* **5.** a detail in any artistic work: *a story with charming poetic touches.* **6.** a close relation of communication, sympathy, etc.: *a newspaper keeps one in touch with the world.* **7.** act or manner of playing a musical instrument: *a pianist with an excellent touch.* **8.** the way the keys of an instrument work. **9.** a distinctive manner or quality: *the work showed an expert's touch.* **10.** a slight amount; little bit: *a touch of salt.* **11.** a slight attack: *a touch of fever.* **12.** Slang. an asking for or getting money, as a gift or a loan. [< OF *touchier*] —**touch′a·ble,** adj. —**touch′er,** n. —Syn. v. **6.** tap. **9.** move. —n. **10.** trace, tinge, shade, dash.

touch and go, an uncertain or risky situation. —**touch′-and-go′,** adj.

touch·back (tuch′bak′), n. Am. act of touching the football to the ground by a player behind his own goal line when driven there by the other side.

touch·down (tuch′doun′), n. Am. **1.** act of a player in putting the football on the ground behind the opponents' goal line. **2.** the score made in this way.

touched (tucht), adj. **1.** Colloq. slightly crazed. **2.** stirred emotionally.

touch·hole (tuch′hōl′), n. a small opening in an old-time gun through which the gunpowder inside was set on fire.

touch·ing (tuch′ing), adj. arousing tender feeling. —prep. concerning; about. —**touch′ing·ly,** adv. —**touch′ing·ness,** n. —Syn. adj. affecting, moving, pathetic.

touch-me-not (tuch′mi·not′), n. plant whose ripe seed pods burst open when touched.

touch·stone (tuch′stōn′), n. **1.** a black stone used to test the purity of gold or silver by the color of the streak made on the stone by rubbing it with the metal. **2.** any means of testing; a test.

touch·y (tuch′i), adj., touch·i·er, touch·i·est. **1.** apt to take offense at trifles; too sensitive. **2.** requiring skill in handling; ticklish; precarious: *loading bombs is a touchy job.* —**touch′i·ly,** adv. —**touch′i·ness,** n.

tough (tuf), adj. **1.** bending without breaking: *leather is tough.* **2.** hard to cut, tear, or chew: *tough cloth, tough meat.* **3.** stiff; sticky: *tough clay.* **4.** strong; hardy: *a tough plant, a tough beard.* **5.** hard; difficult: *tough work.* **6.** hard to bear; bad; unpleasant: *a tough experience.* **7.** hard to influence; stubborn. **8.** vigorous; severe; violent: *a tough struggle.* **9.** Am. rough; disorderly: *a tough neighborhood.* —n. U.S. a rough person; rowdy. [OE *tōh*] —**tough′ly,** adv. —**tough′ness,** n. —Syn. adj. **1.** firm, strong. **4.** sturdy, stout. **5.** laborious, arduous. **6.** trying.

tough·en (tuf′ən), v. make or become tough or tougher. —**tough′en·er,** n.

Tou·lon (tū·lon′), n. seaport in SE France.

Tou·louse (tü·lüz′), n. city in S France.

tou·pee (tü·pā′), n. a wig or patch of false hair worn to cover a bald spot. [< F *toupet* < OF *toupe* tuft]

tour (tŭr), v. **1.** travel from place to place. **2.** travel through: *last year they toured Europe.* **3.** walk around in: *tour the museum.* [< n.] —n. **1.** a long journey. **2.** a short journey; a walk around: *a tour of the boat.* **3.** a turn to do something; a shift of work or duty, esp. at one place. **4.** on tour, touring, said esp. of theatrical companies and traveling entertainers. [< F < L *tornus* turner's wheel, lathe < Gk. *tornos.* Cf. TURN.] —**tour′er,** n.

tour de force (tŭr də fôrs′), French. a notable feat of strength or ingenuity.

touring car, an open automobile for five or more passengers.

tour·ist (tŭr′ist), n. person traveling for pleasure.

tourist camp, Am. camp providing such accommodations as tourists need.

tourist class, on ships, the passenger accommodations next below the most expensive class.

tour·na·ment (tėr′nə·mənt; tŭr′-), n. **1.** a meeting for exercises and sports; the activities at such a meeting. **2.** contest of many persons in some sport: *a golf tournament.* **3.** contest between two groups of knights on horseback who fought for a prize. [< OF *torneiement* < *torneier* TOURNEY]

tour·ney (tėr′ni; tŭr′-), n., pl. -neys, v., -neyed, -ney·ing. —n. tournament. —v. take part in a tournament. [< OF *torneier,* ult. < L *tornus.* See TURN.]

tour·ni·quet (tŭr′nə·ket; -kā; tėr′-), n. device for stopping bleeding by compressing a blood vessel, such as a bandage tightened by twisting with a stick, or a pad pressed down by a screw. [< F, < *tourner* to turn]

Tourniquet: B, blood vessel.

tou·sle (tou′zəl), v., -sled, -sling, n. —v. put into disorder; make untidy; muss: *tousled hair.* —n. a disordered mass, esp. of hair. [< ME *touse(n)*]

Tous·saint L'Ou·ver·ture (tü·saN′ lü·ver·tyr′), 1743–1803, Negro general and political leader in Haiti.

tout (tout), Colloq. —v. **1.** try to get (customers, jobs, votes, etc.). **2.** Esp. Brit. spy out (information about race horses). **3.** Am. give special information about race horses. **4.** praise highly and insistently. —n. person who touts. [< var. of OE *tȳtan* peep out] —**tout′er,** n.

tout à fait (tü·tä·fe′), French. entirely; completely.

tout en·sem·ble (tü·tän·säN′blə), French. the general effect; the assemblage of parts or details, considered as forming a whole.

tow[1] (tō), v. pull by a rope, chain, etc. —n. **1.**

act of towing. 2. condition of being pulled along by a rope, chain, etc.: *the launch had the sailboat in tow.* 3. that which is towed. 4. the rope, chain, etc., used. 5. **in tow, a.** being towed. **b.** under one's care or influence. [OE *togian* drag] —**tow′er,** *n.*

tow² (tō), *n.* the coarse, broken fibers of flax, hemp, etc. —*adj.* made from tow. [OE *tōw-* a spinning]

tow·age (tō′ij), *n.* 1. a towing. 2. act or state of being towed. 3. charge for towing.

to·ward (*prep.* tôrd, tōrd, tə·wôrd′; *adj.* tôrd, tōrd), *prep.* Also, *esp. Brit.* **towards.** 1. in the direction of: *walk toward the north.* 2. with respect to; regarding; about; concerning: *he was friendly toward the idea.* 3. near: *toward two o'clock.* 4. for: *give money toward a person's expenses.* —*adj.* 1. about to happen; impending. 2. *Archaic.* apt; docile. [OE *tōweard* < *tō* to + *-weard* -ward]

tow·boat (tō′bōt′), *n.* tugboat.

tow·el (tou′əl), *n., v.,* **-eled, -el·ing;** *esp. Brit.* **-elled, -el·ling.** —*n.* piece of cloth or paper for wiping and drying something wet. —*v.* dry with a towel. [< OF *toaille* < Gmc.]

tow·el·ing, *esp. Brit.* **tow·el·ling** (tou′əl·ing), *n.* material used for towels, esp. cotton.

tow·er (tou′ər), *n.* 1. a high structure. It stands alone or forms part of a church, castle, or other building. 2. defense; protection. —*v.* rise high up. [< OF < L *turris*] —**tow′er·y,** *adj.* —Syn. *n.* 1. spire, steeple, turret. 2. citadel, fortress.

tow·er·ing (tou′ər·ing), *adj.* 1. very high. 2. very great. 3. very violent. —**tow′er·ing·ly,** *adv.*

tow·head (tō′hed′), *n.* 1. a head of very light, pale-yellow hair. 2. *Am.* person having such hair. —**tow′head′ed,** *adj.*

tow·line (tō′līn′), *n.* rope, chain, etc., for towing.

town (toun), *n.* 1. a large group of houses and buildings, smaller than a city. 2. any large place with many people living in it. 3. the people of a town. 4. the part of a town or city where the stores and office buildings are. 5. *Am.* in some States of the United States, as in New England, a municipal corporation with less elaborate organization and powers than a city. 6. *Am.* in other States of the United States a township. 7. **go to town, a.** achieve success. **b.** participate actively. —*adj.* 1. of a town or towns. 2. characteristic of towns. [OE *tūn*]

town clerk, official who keeps the records of a town.

town crier, a public crier in a city or town.

town hall, a building used for a town's business.

town house, house in town, belonging to a person who also has a house in the country.

town meeting, 1. a general meeting of the inhabitants of the town. 2. *Am.* in New England, a meeting of the qualified voters of a town for the transaction of public business.

town·ship (toun′ship), *n.* 1. in the U.S. and Canada, an administrative division of a county, with varying corporate powers. 2. *Am.* in U.S. surveys of public land, a region or district of 6 miles square. 3. formerly in England, a parish or one of the local divisions or districts of a large parish.

towns·man (tounz′mən), *n., pl.* **-men.** 1. person who lives in a town. 2. person who lives in one's own town. 3. *Am.* selectman.

towns·peo·ple (tounz′pē′pəl), **towns·folk** (-fōk′), *n.pl.* the people of a town.

tow·path (tō′path′; -päth′), *n.* a path along the bank of a canal or river for use in towing boats.

tow·rope (tō′rōp′), *n.* rope used for towing.

tox·e·mi·a, tox·ae·mi·a (toks·ē′mi·ə), *n.* a form of blood poisoning, esp. one in which the toxins produced by certain microörganisms enter the blood. [< NL, < L *toxicum* poison (see TOXIC) + Gk. *haima* blood] —**tox·e′mic, tox·ae′mic,** *adj.*

tox·ic (tok′sik), *adj.* poisonous; of poison:

caused by poison. [< Med.L. *toxicus,* ult. < Gk. *toxikon (pharmakon)* (poison) for shooting arrows < *toxon* bow] —**tox·ic·i·ty** (toks·is′ə·ti), *n.*

tox·i·col·o·gy (tok′sə·kol′ə·ji), *n.* science that deals with poisons, their effects, antidotes, detection, etc. [< Gk. *toxikon* poison (see TOXIC) + -LOGY] —**tox·i·co·log·i·cal** (tok′sə·kə·loj′ə·kəl), *adj.* —**tox′i·co·log′i·cal·ly,** *adv.* —**tox′i·col′o·gist,** *n.*

tox·in (tok′sən), *n.* any poisonous product of animal or vegetable metabolism, esp. one of those produced by bacteria and constituting the causative agents in such diseases as tetanus, diphtheria, etc. [< *toxic*]

toy (toi), *n.* 1. something for a child to play with; plaything. 2. thing that has little value or importance. 3. something small or diminutive like a plaything. —*adj.* of, made as, or like a plaything. —*v.* amuse oneself; play; trifle. —**toy′er,** *n.* —Syn. *n.* 2. trifle, knickknack, trinket.

tp., township.

Tr., *Chem.* terbium.

tr., 1. transitive. 2. translation; translator. 3. transpose. 4. treasurer.

trace¹ (trās), *n., v.,* **traced, trac·ing.** —*n.* 1. footprint or other mark left; track; trail: *traces of rabbits on the snow.* 2. mark, token, or evidence of the former existence, presence, or action of something; vestige: *the explorer found traces of an ancient city.* 3. a very small amount; little bit: *there wasn't a trace of gray in her hair.* 4. thing marked out or drawn. [< v.] —*v.* 1. follow by means of marks, tracks, or signs: *trace deer.* 2. follow the course of: *trace one's family back.* 3. find signs of; observe. 4. find out by search, examination, etc. 5. mark out; draw: *the spy traced a plan of the fort.* 6. copy by following the lines of. 7. decorate with tracery. [< OF *tracer,* ult. < L *trahere* drag] —**trace′a·ble,** *adj.* —**trace′a·bil′i·ty, trace′a·ble·ness,** *n.* —**trace′a·bly,** *adv.* —**trace′less,** *adj.* —**trace′less·ly,** *adv.*

trace² (trās), *n.* 1. either of the two straps, ropes, or chains by which an animal pulls a wagon, carriage, etc. 2. **kick over the traces,** throw off control; become unruly. [< OF *traiz,* pl., ult. < L *trahere* drag]

trac·er (trās′ər), *n.* 1. person or thing that traces. 2. machine for making tracings of drawings, plans, etc. 3. *Am.* inquiry sent from place to place to trace a missing person, letter, parcel, etc. 4. firework attached to a bullet to show its course. 5. *Physics, Chem.* an element (**tracer element**) or atom (**tracer atom**), usually radioactive, which can be traced and observed in a biological process or used to detect small quantities of its isotope in analysis.

trac·er·y (trās′ər·i; trās′ri), *n., pl.* **-er·ies.** 1. ornamental work consisting of intersecting or ramified ribs, bars, or the like, as in the upper part of a Gothic window. 2. any delicate interlacing work of lines, threads, etc., as in carving and embroidery.

Tracery

tra·che·a (trā′ki·ə; trə·kē′ə), *n., pl.* **-che·ae** (-ki·ē; -kē′ē). 1. the windpipe. 2. in insects and other arthropods, the air-conveying tube of the respiratory system. [< LL, ult. < Gk. *tracheia (arteria),* lit., rough (windpipe)] —**tra′che·al,** *adj.*

tra·cho·ma (trə·kō′mə), *n.* 1. a contagious inflammation of the eyelids. Trachoma is very common in the Orient. 2. granular eyelids, a much less serious condition. [< NL < Gk., roughness, < *trachys* rough] —**tra·chom·a·tous** (trə·kom′ə·təs; -kō′mə-), *adj.*

trac·ing (trās′ing), *n.* 1. copy of something made by marking or drawing over it. 2. line made by marking or drawing.

track (trak), *n.* 1. footprint: *the tracks of a rabbit.* 2. mark left by a wheel or any moving object: *the tracks of a truck.* 3. line of travel or motion; path; trail; road: *a track in the woods.* 4. course of action or conduct: *go on in*

āge, cāre, fär; ēqual, tèrm; īce; ōpen, ôrder; pùt, rüle, ūse; tʜ, then; ə=a in about.

the same track year after year. **5.** line of metal rails for cars to go on. **6.** a course for running or racing: *a race track.* **7.** the sport made up of contests in running, jumping, throwing, etc. **8.** in one's tracks, *Am., Colloq.* right where one is. **9. keep track of,** keep within one's sight, knowledge, or attention. **10. lose track of,** *Am.* fail to keep track of. **11. make tracks,** *Am., Colloq.* go very fast; run away. **12. off the track,** off the subject; wrong. **13. on the track,** on the subject; right. *—v.* **1.** *Am.* make footprints or other marks on (a floor, etc.): *don't track the floor.* **2.** *Am.* bring (snow or mud) into a place on one's feet: *track mud into the house.* **3.** follow by means of footprints, marks, smell, etc.: *track a bear.* **4.** trace in any way: *track down a criminal.* [< OF *trac*] **—track'er,** *n.* **—track'less,** *adj.* **—track'less·ly,** *adv.*

track·age (trak'ij), *n. Am.* **1.** all the tracks of a railroad. **2.** the right of one railroad to use the tracks of another.

track meet, *Am.* series of contests in running, jumping, throwing, etc.

tract[1] (trakt), *n.* **1.** stretch of land, water, etc.; extent; region; area. **2.** *Anat.* system of related parts or organs in the body: *the digestive tract.* **3.** period of time. [< L *tractus,* orig., hauling < *trahere* drag. Doublet of TRAIT.]

tract[2] (trakt), *n.* **1.** a little book or pamphlet on a religious subject. **2.** any little book or pamphlet. [appar. < L *tractatus,* a handling, ult. < *trahere* drag]

trac·ta·ble (trak'tə·bəl), *adj.* **1.** easily managed or controlled; easy to deal with; docile. **2.** easily worked, as copper or gold. [< L, < *tractare.* See TREAT.] **—trac·ta·bil'i·ty, tract'a·ble·ness,** *n.* **—tract'a·bly,** *adv.*

trac·tile (trak'təl), *adj.* capable of being drawn out to a greater length. **—trac·til'i·ty,** *n.*

trac·tion (trak'shən), *n.* **1.** a drawing or pulling; a being drawn. **2.** the drawing or pulling of loads along a road, track, etc. **3.** kind of power used for this. Electric traction is used on some railroads. **4.** friction: *wheels slip on ice because there is too little traction.* [< Med.L *tractio* < L *trahere* drag] **—trac'tion·al,** *adj.* **—trac·tive** (trak'tiv), *adj.*

trac·tor (trak'tər), *n.* **1.** something used for drawing or pulling. **2.** *Am.* engine on wheels, used for pulling wagons, plows, etc., along roads or over fields. **3.** airplane with the propeller in front of the wings. [< Med.L, < L *trahere* drag]

trade (trād), *n., v.,* **trad·ed, trad·ing.** *—n.* **1.** a buying and selling; exchange of goods; commerce: *foreign trade.* **2.** *Am., Colloq.* a bargain; business deal: *he made a good trade.* **3.** *Am., Colloq.* a political arrangement or deal. **4.** kind of work; business, esp. one requiring skilled mechanical work: *a carpenter or plumber learns his trade.* **5.** people in the same kind of work or business: *the building trade.* **6.** *Am., Colloq.* customers: *that store has a lot of trade.* **7. the trades,** the trade winds. *—v.* **1.** buy and sell; exchange goods; be in commerce: *trade with England.* **2.** exchange: *trade seats.* **3.** make an exchange: *if you don't like your book, I'll trade with you.* **4.** bargain; deal. **5. trade in,** *Am.* give an automobile, radio, etc., as payment or part payment for something. **6. trade off,** get rid of by trading. **7. trade on,** take advantage of. [< MDu., MLG, *track*] **—Syn.** *n.* **1.** traffic, dealing. **4.** occupation, craft, profession. *—v.* **1.** barter. **3.** swap.

trade-in (trād'in'), *n. Am.* thing given or accepted as payment or part payment for something.

trade-last (trād'last'; -läst'), *n. Am.* a second-hand complimentary statement passed to the benefiting person in exchange for a similar type of statement.

trade·mark (trād'märk'), *n.* mark, picture, name, or letters owned and used by a manufacturer or merchant to distinguish his goods from the goods of others. *—v.* **1.** distinguish by means of a trademark. **2.** register the trademark of.

trade name, 1. name used by a manufacturer or merchant for some article that he sells. **2.** a

special name used for any thing by those who buy and sell it. **3.** name under which a company does business.

trad·er (trād'ər), *n.* **1.** person who trades. **2.** ship used in trading.

trade school, school where trades are taught.

trades·man (trādz'mən), *n., pl.* **-men.** storekeeper; shopkeeper. **—Syn.** merchant, dealer, trader.

trades·peo·ple (trādz'pē'pəl), *n.pl.* storekeepers; shopkeepers.

trade union, *esp. Brit.* **trades union, 1.** association of workers in any trade or craft to protect and promote their interests. **2.** a labor union. **—trade unionism,** *esp. Brit.* **trades unionism. —trade unionist,** *esp. Brit.* **trades unionist.**

trade wind, a wind blowing steadily toward the equator from about 30° north latitude to about 30° south latitude. North of the equator, it blows from the northeast; south of the equator, from the southeast.

trading post, a store or station of a trader, esp. in wild or uncivilized places.

tra·di·tion (trə·dish'ən), *n.* **1.** the handing down of beliefs, opinions, customs, stories, etc., from parents to children. **2.** what is handed down in this way. **3.** a transmitted or inherited way of thinking or acting. **4.** the unwritten laws and doctrines received from Moses. **5.** the unwritten precepts and doctrines received from Christ and his apostles. [< L *traditio* < *tradere* hand down < *trans-* over + *dare* give. Doublet of TREASON.] **—tra·di'tion·ist,** *n.*

tra·di·tion·al (trə·dish'ən·əl; -dish'nəl), *adj.* **1.** of tradition. **2.** handed down by tradition. **3.** according to tradition. **4.** customary. **—tra·di'tion·al·ly,** *adv.* **—Syn. 2.** legendary.

tra·duce (trə·dūs'; -dūs'), *v.,* **-duced, -duc·ing.** speak evil of (a person) falsely; slander. [< L *traducere* parade in disgrace < *trans-* across + *ducere* lead] **—tra·duce'ment,** *n.* **—tra·duc'er,** *n.* **—tra·duc'ing·ly,** *adv.* **—Syn.** defame, calumniate, asperse.

Tra·fal·gar (trə·fal'gər), *n.* **1.** Cape, cape in SW Spain, on the Atlantic. **2.** a naval battle near this cape in 1805. Napoleon's fleet was defeated by a British fleet under Nelson.

traf·fic (traf'ik), *n., v.,* **-ficked, -fick·ing.** *—n.* **1.** people, automobiles, wagons, ships, etc., coming and going along a way of travel. **2.** their movement along such a way. **3.** a buying and selling; commerce; trade. **4.** business done by a railroad line, steamship line, etc.; number of passengers or amount of freight carried. **5.** intercourse; dealings. *—v.* carry on trade; buy; sell; exchange: *the men trafficked with the natives for ivory.* [< OF < Ital., < *trafficare* < *tras-* across (< L *trans-*) + *ficcare* shove, poke, ult. < L *figere* fix] **—traf'fick·er,** *n.*

tra·ge·di·an (trə·jē'di·ən), *n.* **1.** actor in tragedies. **2.** writer of tragedies.

tra·ge·di·enne (trə·jē'di·en'), *n.* actress in tragedies.

trag·e·dy (traj'ə·di), *n., pl.* **-dies. 1.** a serious play having an unhappy ending. *Hamlet* is a tragedy. **2.** the writing of such plays. **3.** a very sad or terrible happening. [< L < Gk. *tragoidia* < *tragos* goat (connection obscure) + *oide* song]

trag·ic (traj'ik), **trag·i·cal** (-ə·kəl), *adj.* **1.** of or having to do with tragedy: *a tragic actor.* **2.** very sad; dreadful: *a tragic death.* [< L < Gk. *tragikos*] **—trag'i·cal·ly,** *adv.* **—trag'i·cal·ness,** *n.*

trag·i·com·e·dy (traj'i·kom'ə·di), *n., pl.* **-dies. 1.** play having both tragic and comic elements. *The Merchant of Venice* is a tragicomedy. **2.** incident or situation in which serious and comic elements are blended. **—trag·i·com·ic** (traj'i·kom'ik), **trag'i·com'i·cal,** *adj.* **—trag'i·com'i·cal·ly,** *adv.*

trail (trāl), *v.* **1.** pull or drag along behind: *they trailed the heavy rope as they walked.* **2.** be drawn along behind: *her dress trails on the ground.* **3.** grow along: *poison ivy trailed by the road.* **4.** follow in a long, uneven line: *the ten campers trailed their leader down the mountainside.* **5.** follow along behind; follow: *the dog* *trailed him constantly.* 6. form a track or trail: *smoke trailed from the engine.* 7. go along slowly: *the snake trailed through the long grass.* 8. hunt by track or smell: *trail a deer.* 9. tread down (grass) to make a path. 10. pass little by little: *her voice trailed off into silence.* —*n.* 1. anything that follows along behind: *the car left a trail of dust behind it.* 2. track or smell: *the trail of the rabbit.* 3. path across a wild or unsettled region. 4. *Mil.* the lower end of a gun carriage. [< OF *trailler* tow, ult. < L *tragula* dragnet] —**trail′ing·ly,** *adv.*

trail·er (trāl′ər), *n.* 1. person or animal that follows a trail. 2. a trailing plant; vine that grows along the ground. 3. a vehicle, often large, designed to be pulled along the highway by an automobile, truck, etc., esp., by a truck lacking a body of its own. 4. *Am.* a mobile furnished house pulled by an automobile; trailer coach. 5. *Am.* a few scenes shown to advertise a forthcoming motion picture.

trailer coach, a small furnished house on either two or four wheels, pulled by an automobile.

trailer park, the grounds, equipped with utilities and other facilities, for accommodating trailer coaches.

trailing arbutus, *Am.* arbutus (def. 1).

train (trān), *n.* 1. a connected line of railroad cars moving along together. 2. line of people, animals, wagons, trucks, etc., moving along together: *a train of covered wagons.* 3. series or succession of proceedings, events, circumstances, etc.: *a long train of misfortunes.* 4. series of connected ideas, etc.: *one's train of thought.* 5. in machinery, a series of connected parts, such as wheels and pinions, through which motion is transmitted. 6. something that is drawn along behind; trailing part: *the train of a dress.* 7. group of followers. [< v.] —*v.* 1. bring up; rear; teach: *train a child.* 2. make skillful by teaching and practice: *train women as nurses.* 3. make or become fit by exercise and diet: *runners train for races.* 4. point; aim: *train cannon upon a fort.* 5. bring into a particular position: *train the vine around this post.* [< OF *trainer* < L *trahere* drag] —**train′a·ble,** *adj.* —**train′er,** *n.* —**Syn.** *n.* 2. row, chain, line, file, procession. —*v.* 1. educate, instruct, discipline.

train·ee (trān·ē′), *n.* 1. person who is receiving training. 2. *U.S. Army.* a newly inducted person who is receiving basic military training.

train·ing (trān′ing), *n.* 1. practical education in some art, profession, etc.: *training for teachers.* 2. development of strength and endurance. 3. good condition maintained by exercise, diet, etc.

train·load (trān′lōd′), *n.* as much as a train can hold or carry.

train·man (trān′mən), *n., pl.* **-men.** 1. *Am.* man who works on a railroad train. 2. brakeman.

trait (trāt; *Brit.* trā), *n.* a distinguishing feature or quality; characteristic. [< F, ult. < L *trahere* drag. Doublet of TRACT¹.]

trai·tor (trā′tər), *n.* 1. person who betrays his country or ruler. 2. person who betrays a trust, duty, friend, etc. [< OF, ult. < L *traditor,* ult. < *trans-* over + *dare* give] —**Syn.** 1. turncoat.

trai·tor·ous (trā′tər·əs), *adj.* like a traitor; treacherous; faithless. —**trai′tor·ous·ly,** *adv.* —**trai′tor·ous·ness,** *n.* —**Syn.** perfidious, disloyal, false. —**Ant.** faithful, loyal, constant.

tra·jec·to·ry (trə·jek′tə·ri; -trī), *n., pl.* **-ries.** the curved path of a projectile, comet, or planet. [< Med.L *trajectorius* throwing across, ult. < L *trans-* across + *jacere* throw]

tram (tram), *n.* 1. Also, **tram′car′,** *Brit.* streetcar. 2. a truck or car on which loads are carried in coal mines. [< MDu., MLG *trame* beam]

tram·mel (tram′əl), *n., v.,* **-meled, -mel·ing;** *esp. Brit.* **-melled, -mel·ling.** —*n.* 1. Usually, **trammels.** anything that hinders or restrains: *the trammels of custom or etiquette.* 2. a fine net to catch fish, birds, etc. 3. hook to hold pots, etc., over the fire. 4. a shackle for controlling the motions of a horse. 5. instrument for drawing an ellipse. —*v.* 1. hinder; restrain. 2. entangle. [< OF < L *tremaculum* < *tres* three + *macula* mesh]

tramp (tramp), *v.* 1. walk heavily: *he tramped across the room in his heavy boots.* 2. step heavily; tread: *he tramped on the flowers.* 3. go on foot; walk: *we tramped through the streets.* 4. walk steadily; march: *the soldiers tramped mile after mile.* 5. travel through on foot. 6. go or wander as a tramp. —*n.* 1. sound of a heavy step. 2. a long, steady walk; hike. 3. man who wanders about and begs. 4. a freight ship that takes a cargo when and where it can. [? < LG *trampen*] —**tramp′er,** *n.* —**Syn.** *v.* 4. plod, trudge. —*n.* 3. vagabond, hobo, vagrant, beggar.

tram·ple (tram′pəl), *v.,* **-pled, -pling,** *n.* —*v.* 1. tread heavily on; crush. 2. tread heavily. 3. treat cruelly, harshly, or scornfully. 4. **trample under foot, trample on** or **upon,** treat cruelly, harshly, or scornfully. —*n.* act or sound of trampling. [< *tramp*] —**tram′pler,** *n.*

trance (trans; trans), *n., v.,* **tranced, tranc·ing.** —*n.* 1. state or condition of unconsciousness somewhat like sleep. 2. a dazed or stunned condition. 3. a dreamy, absorbed, or hypnotic condition that is like a trance. 4. a high emotion; rapture. —*v.* hold in a trance; enchant. [< OF *transe,* ult. < L *trans-* across + *ire* go]

tran·quil (trang′kwil; tran′-), *adj.,* **-quil·er, -quil·est;** *esp. Brit.* **-quil·ler, -quil·lest.** calm; peaceful; quiet. [< L *tranquillus*] —**tran′quil·ly,** *adv.* —**tran′quil·ness,** *n.* —**Syn.** placid, serene.

tran·quil·ize, tran·quil·lize (trang′kwil·īz; tran′-), *v.,* **-ized, -iz·ing; -lized, -liz·ing.** 1. make calm, peaceful, or quiet. 2. become tranquil. —**Syn.** 1. pacify, compose, allay, soothe, still.

tran·quil·iz·er, tran·quil·liz·er (trang′kwil·īz′ər), *n.* any of various nonbarbiturate drugs that reduce tension, abate nervous strain, etc.

tran·quil·li·ty, tran·quil·i·ty (trang·kwil′ə·ti; tran-), *n.* calmness; peacefulness; quiet.

trans-, *prefix.* 1. across; over; through, as in *transcortical, transfluent, transflux, transisthmian.* 2. beyond; on the other side of, as in *Transjordan, transcend.* 3. across, etc.; and also beyond, on the other side of, as in *transarctic, transequatorial, transmarine, transoceanic, transpolar,* and many other geographical terms, such as *trans-Adriatic, trans-African, trans-Algerian.* [< L *trans,* prep.]

trans., 1. transactions. 2. transitive. 3. translation. 4. transportation.

trans·act (tran·zakt′; tran·akt′), *v.* 1. attend to; manage; do. 2. carry on business; deal. [< L *transactus* accomplished < *trans-* through + *agere* drive] —**trans·ac′tor,** *n.* —**Syn.** 1. perform, conduct.

trans·ac·tion (tran·zak′shən; tran·ak′-), *n.* 1. the carrying on (of business). 2. fact of being transacted. 3. piece of business. 4. **transactions,** records, reports, etc., of a learned society or the like. —**Syn.** 2. proceeding, deal, matter, affair.

trans·at·lan·tic (trans′ət·lan′tik; tranz′-), *adj.* 1. crossing the Atlantic. 2. on the other side of the Atlantic.

tran·scend (tran·send′), *v.* 1. go beyond the limits or powers of; exceed; be above. 2. be higher or greater than; excel. 3. be superior or extraordinary. [< L *transcendere* < *trans-* beyond + *scandere* climb] —**Syn.** 2. outdo, outstrip.

tran·scend·ent (tran·sen′dənt), *adj.* 1. surpassing ordinary limits; excelling; superior; extraordinary. 2. existing apart from the universe. —**tran·scend′ence, tran·scend′en·cy,** *n.* —**tran·scend′ent·ly,** *adv.* —**tran·scend′ent·ness,** *n.* —**Syn.** 1. unequaled, unrivaled, peerless, supreme.

tran·scen·den·tal (tran′sen·den′təl), *adj.* 1. transcendent. 2. supernatural. 3. obscure; incomprehensible; fantastic. —**tran′scen·den′tal·ly,** *adv.*

tran·scen·den·tal·ism (tran′sen·den′təl·iz·əm), *n.* 1. transcendental quality, thought, language, or philosophy. 2. any philosophy based upon the doctrine that the principles of reality are to be discovered by a study of the processes of thought, not from experience. 3. *Am.* the religious and philosophical doctrines of Emerson and others in New England about 1840, which had an important influence on American thought and literature. **4.** obscurity; incomprehensibility; fantasy. **—tran′scen·den′tal·ist,** *n.*

trans·con·ti·nen·tal (trans′kon·tə·nen′təl), *adj.* **1.** crossing a continent. **2.** on the other side of a continent.

tran·scribe (tran·skrīb′), *v.,* **–scribed, –scribing. 1.** copy in writing or in typewriting. **2.** set down in writing or print. **3.** arrange (a piece of music) for a different instrument or voice. **4.** make a recording or phonographic record of for broadcasting. **5.** broadcast a phonographic record. [< L, < *trans-* over + *scribere* write] **—tran·scrib′er,** *n.*

tran·script (tran′skript), *n.* **1.** a written or typewritten copy. **2.** a copy or reproduction of anything. **—tran·scrip′tive,** *adj.*

tran·scrip·tion (tran·skrip′shən), *n.* **1. a** transcribing; copying. **2.** transcript; copy. **3.** arrangement of a piece of music for a different instrument or voice. **4.** arrangement of music, etc., on a record for use in broadcasting. **5.** act or fact of broadcasting such a record.

tran·sept (tran′sept), *n.* **1.** the shorter part of a cross-shaped church. **2.** either end of this part. [< Med.L, ult. < L *trans-* across + *saeptum* fence] **—tran·sep′tal,** *adj.*

Transepts: I, def. 1; II, def. 2.

trans·fer (*v.* trans·fér′; trans′fér; *n.* trans′fér), *v.,* **–ferred, –fer·ring,** *n.* **—v. 1.** convey or remove from one person or place to another; hand over: *transfer a title to land.* **2.** convey (a drawing, design, pattern) from one surface to another. **3.** change from one streetcar, bus, train, etc., to another. **—n. 1.** a transferring or being transferred. **2.** thing transferred, as a drawing, pattern, etc., printed from one surface onto another. **3.** ticket allowing a passenger to continue his journey on another streetcar, bus, train, etc. [< L, < *trans-* across + *ferre* bear] **—trans·fer′a·ble,** *adj.* **—trans′fer·a·bil′i·ty,** *n.* **—trans·fer′ence,** *n.* **—trans·fer′rer,** *n.*

trans·fig·u·ra·tion (trans·fig′yə·rā′shən), *n.* **1.** a change in form or appearance; transformation. **2. the Transfiguration, a.** the change in appearance of Christ on the mountain. Matt. 17; Mark 9. **b.** the church festival on August 6 in honor of this.

trans·fig·ure (trans·fig′yər), *v.,* **–ured, –uring. 1.** change in form or appearance; transform: *new paint had transfigured the old house.* **2.** change so as to glorify; exalt. [< L, < *trans-* across + *figura* figure] **—trans·fig′ure·ment,** *n.*

trans·fix (trans·fiks′), *v.* **1.** pierce through. **2.** fasten by piercing through with something pointed. **3.** make motionless (with amazement, terror, etc.). [< L *transfixus* < *trans-* through + *figere* fix] **—trans·fix·ion** (trans·fik′shən), *n.*

trans·form (trans·fôrm′), *v.* **1.** change in form or appearance. **2.** change in condition, nature, or character. **3.** change (one form of energy) into another. A dynamo transforms mechanical energy into electricity. **4.** change (an electric current) into one of higher or lower voltage. [< L, < *trans-* across + *forma* form] **—trans·form′a·ble,** *adj.* **—trans·form′a·tive** (trans·fôr′mə·tiv), *adj.* **—Syn. 2.** transmute, metamorphose. **3.** convert.

trans·for·ma·tion (trans′fər·mā′shən), *n.* **1.** a transforming. **2.** wig worn by women.

trans·form·er (trans·fôr′mər), *n.* **1.** person or thing that transforms. **2.** *Elect.* device for changing an alternating current into one of higher or lower voltage.

trans·fuse (trans·fūz′), *v.,* **–fused, –fus·ing. 1.** pour from one container into another. **2.** transfer (blood) from one person or animal to another. **3.** infuse; instill: *the speaker transfused his enthusiasm into the audience.* [< L *transfusus* < *trans-* across + *fundere* pour] **—trans·fus′er,** *n.* **—trans·fus′i·ble,** *adj.*

trans·fu·sion (trans·fū′zhən), *n.* act or fact of transfusing.

trans·gress (trans·gres′; tranz-), *v.* **1.** break a law, command, etc.; sin. **2.** go contrary to; sin

against. **3.** go beyond (a limit or bound): *her manners transgressed the bounds of good taste.* [< L *transgressus* having gone beyond < *trans-* across + *gradi* to step] **—trans·gres′sor,** *n.* **—Syn. 3.** overstep, overpass, transcend.

trans·gres·sion (trans·gresh′ən; tranz-), *n.* a transgressing; breaking a law, command, etc.; sin. **—Syn.** violation, offense, fault, misdeed.

tran·ship (tran·ship′), *v.,* **–shipped, –shipping.** transship. **—tran·ship′ment,** *n.*

tran·sient (tran′shənt), *adj.* **1.** passing soon; fleeting; not lasting. **2.** *Am.* passing through and not staying long: *a transient guest.* **3.** *Music.* introduced casually and not necessary to the harmony. **—n.** *Am.* a visitor or boarder who stays for a short time. [< L *transiens* passing through < *trans-* through + *ire* go] **—tran′sience, tran′sien·cy,** *n.* **—tran′sient·ly,** *adv.* **—tran′sient·ness,** *n.* **—Syn.** *adj.* **1.** transitory, evanescent, momentary, temporary, ephemeral. **—Ant.** *adj.* **1.** abiding, enduring, permanent.

tran·sis·tor (tran·zis′tər), *n. Electronics.* a small crystal device consisting mainly of germanium, which amplifies electricity by controlling the flow of electrons. [< *trans-* + L *sistere* send, convey]

trans·it (tran′sit; -zit), *n., v.,* **–it·ed, –it·ing. —n. 1.** a passing across or through. **2.** a carrying or being carried across or through: *the goods were damaged in transit.* **3.** transition or change. **4.** instrument used in surveying to measure angles. **5.** *Astron.* **a.** an apparent passage of a heavenly body across the meridian of a place. **b.** passage of a small heavenly body across the disk of a larger one. **—v.** pass; pass across; pass through. [< L *transitus* < *transire.* See TRANSIENT.] **—trans·it·a·ble,** *adj.*

tran·si·tion (tran·zish′ən), *n.* **1.** a change or passing from one condition, place, thing, activity, topic, etc., to another. **2.** *Music.* a change of key. [< L *transitio* < *transire.* See TRANSIENT.] **—tran·si′tion·al,** *adj.* **—tran·si′tion·al·ly,** *adv.*

tran·si·tive (tran′sə·tiv), *adj.* **1.** *Gram.* of verbs, taking a direct object. *Bring* and *raise* are transitive verbs. **2.** involving transition. **—n.** a transitive verb. **—tran′si·tive·ly,** *adv.* **—tran′si·tive·ness,** *n.* ▷ See verb for usage note.

tran·si·to·ry (tran′sə·tô′ri; -tō′-; -zə-), *adj.* passing soon or quickly; lasting only a short time. **—tran′si·to′ri·ly,** *adv.* **—tran′si·to′ri·ness,** *n.*

Trans·jor·dan (trans·jôr′dən; tranz-), *n.* former name of Jordan (def. 2).

trans·late (trans·lāt′; tranz-; trans′lāt; tranz′-), *v.,* **–lat·ed, –lat·ing. 1.** change from one language into another. **2.** change into other words. **3.** explain the meaning of. **4.** change from one place, position, or condition to another. [< L *translatus,* pp. to *transferre.* See TRANSFER.] **—trans·lat′a·ble,** *adj.* **—trans·lat′a·ble·ness,** *n.* **—trans·la′tor,** *n.* **—Syn. 2.** paraphrase, render.

trans·la·tion (trans·lā′shən; tranz-), *n.* **1.** act of translating. **2.** result of translating; version. **—Syn. 2.** interpretation, rendering.

trans·lit·er·ate (trans·lit′ər·āt; tranz-), *v.,* **–at·ed, –at·ing.** change (letters, words, etc.) into corresponding characters of another alphabet or language, as to transliterate the Greek χ as *ch* and φ as *ph,* or transliterate Arabic words into English letters. [< TRANS- + L *litera* letter] **—trans·lit′er·a′tion,** *n.* **—trans·lit′er·a′tor,** *n.*

trans·lu·cent (trans·lü′sənt; tranz-), *adj.* letting light through without being transparent. Frosted glass is translucent. [< L, < *trans-* through + *lucere* shine] **—trans·lu′cence, trans·lu′cen·cy,** *n.* **—trans·lu′cent·ly,** *adv.*

trans·mi·grate (trans·mī′grāt; tranz-), *v.,* **–grat·ed, –grat·ing. 1.** move from one place or country to another; migrate. **2.** pass at death into another body. **—trans′mi·gra′tion,** *n.* **—trans·mi′gra·tor,** *n.* **—trans·mi′gra·to·ry** (trans·mī′grə·tô′ri; -tō′-; tranz-), *adj.*

trans·mis·si·ble (trans·mis′ə·bəl; tranz-), *adj.* capable of being transmitted: *a transmissible disease.* **—trans·mis′si·bil′i·ty,** *n.*

trans·mis·sion (trans·mish′ən; tranz-), *n.* **1.** a sending over; passing on; passing along; letting through: *mosquitoes are the only means of* *transmission of malaria.* 2. fact of being transmitted. 3. something transmitted. 4. the part of an automobile that transmits power from the engine to the rear axle. 5. passage through space of radio waves from the transmitting station to the receiving station. —**trans·mis'sive**, *adj.*

trans·mit (trans·mit'; tranz–), *v.,* –**mit·ted,** –**mit·ting.** 1. send over; pass on; pass along; let through. 2. communicate, as information, news, etc. 3. pass on to successors or posterity. 4. send out (signals, voice, music, etc.) by radio. [< L, < *trans–* across + *mittere* send] —**trans·mit'tal,** **trans·mit'tance,** *n.* —**trans·mit'ti·ble,** *adj.*

trans·mit·ter (trans·mit'ər; tranz–), *n.* 1. person or thing that transmits something. 2. that part of a telegraph or telephone by which messages are sent. 3. apparatus for sending out signals, voice, music, etc., by radio.

trans·mute (trans·mūt'; tranz–), *v.,* –**mut·ed,** –**mut·ing.** change from one nature, substance, or form into another. We can transmute water power into electrical power. [< L, < *trans–* thoroughly + *mutare* change] —**trans·mut'a·ble,** *adj.* —**trans·mut'a·bil'i·ty,** **trans·mut'a·ble·ness,** *n.* —**trans·mut'a·bly,** *adv.* —**trans'mu·ta'tion,** *n.* —**trans·mut'er,** *n.*

trans·o·ce·an·ic (trans'ō·shi·an'ik; tranz'–), *adj.* 1. crossing the ocean. 2. on the other side of the ocean.

tran·som (tran'səm), *n.* 1. *Am.* window over a door or other window, usually hinged for opening. 2. a horizontal bar across a window; crossbar separating a door from the window over it. [< L *transtrum,* orig., crossbeam] —**tran'somed,** *adj.*

tran·son·ic (tran·son'ik), *adj.* transsonic.

trans·pa·cif·ic (trans'pə·sif'ik), *adj.* 1. crossing the Pacific. 2. on the other side of the Pacific.

trans·par·en·cy (trans·pâr'ən·si; –par'–), *n.,* *pl.* –**cies.** 1. Also, **trans·par'ence.** transparent quality or condition. 2. something transparent. 3. picture, design, or the like, made visible by light shining through from behind.

trans·par·ent (trans·pâr'ent; –par'–), *adj.* 1. transmitting light so that bodies beyond or behind can be distinctly seen. Window glass is transparent. 2. frank: *a boy of transparent honesty.* 3. easily seen through or detected: *transparent excuses.* [< Med.L *transparens* showing light through < L *trans–* through + *parere* appear] —**trans·par'ent·ly,** *adv.* —**trans·par'ent·ness,** *n.* —Syn. 1. limpid, pellucid, sheer. 2. open, candid. 3. obvious, manifest.

tran·spire (tran·spīr'), *v.,* –**spired,** –**spir·ing.** 1. *Am.* take place; happen. 2. leak out; become known. 3. pass off or send off in the form of vapor through a wall or surface, as from the human body or from leaves. [< Med.L, < L *trans–* through + *spirare* breathe] —**tran·spi·ra'tion** (tran'spə·rā'shən), *n.*

trans·plant (trans·plant'; –plänt'), *v.* 1. plant again in a different place. 2. remove from one place to another. 3. bring (a colony, etc.) from one country to another for settlement. 4. transfer (skin, an organ, etc.) from one person, animal, or part of the body to another. —**transplant'a·ble,** *adj.* —**trans'plan·ta'tion,** *n.* —**trans·plant'er,** *n.*

trans·port (*v.* trans·pôrt', –pōrt'; *n.* trans'-pôrt; –pōrt'), *v.* 1. carry from one place to another: *wheat is transported from farms to mills.* 2. carry away by strong feeling: *transported with joy.* 3. send away to another country as a punishment. 4. kill. —*n.* 1. a carrying from one place to another: *trucks are much used for transport.* 2. ship used to carry men and supplies. 3. airplane that transports passengers, mail, freight, etc. 4. a strong feeling. 5. a transported convict. [< L, < *trans–* across + *portare* carry] —**trans·port'-a·ble,** *adj.* —**trans·port·a·bil'i·ty,** *n.* —**trans·port·a·tive** (trans·pôr'tə·tiv; –pōr'–), **trans·por'tive,** *adj.* —**trans·port'er,** *n.*

trans·por·ta·tion (trans'pər·tā'shən), *n.* 1. a transporting. 2. state of being transported. 3. *Am.* means of transport. 4. *Am.* cost of transport; ticket for transport. 5. a sending away to another country as a punishment.

trans·pose (trans·pōz'), *v.,* –**posed,** –**pos·ing.** 1. change the position or order of; interchange. 2. change the usual order of (letters or words). 3. *Music.* change the key of. 4. in algebra, transfer (a term) to the other side of an equation, changing plus to minus or minus to plus. [< F *transposer.* See TRANS–, POSE.] —**trans·pos'a·ble,** *adj.* —**trans·pos'a·bil'i·ty,** *n.* —**trans·pos·er,** *n.* —**trans·po·si·tion** (trans'pə·zish'ən), **trans·pos'al,** *n.* —**trans'po·si'tion·al,** *adj.*

trans·ship (trans·ship'), *v.,* –**shipped,** –**shipping.** transfer from one ship, train, car, etc., to another. Also, **tranship.** —**trans·ship'ment,** *n.*

trans·son·ic (trans·son'ik), *adj.* moving at a speed close to the speed of sound, 700–780 miles per hour. Also, **transonic.**

tran·sub·stan·ti·a·tion (tran'səb·stan'shi·ā'shən), *n.* 1. a changing of one substance into another. 2. *Rom. Cath. Church.* the changing of the substance of the bread and wine of the Eucharist into the substance of the body and blood of Christ, only the appearance of the bread and wine remaining.

Trans·vaal (trans·väl'; tranz–), *n.* province of the Union of South Africa, in the NE part.

trans·ver·sal (trans·vér'səl; tranz–), *adj.* transverse. —*n.* a line intersecting two or more other lines. —**trans·ver'sal·ly,** *adv.*

Lines AB and CD are transversals.

trans·verse (trans·vérs'; tranz–; trans'vérs; tranz'–), *adj.* lying across; placed crosswise; crossing from side to side: *transverse beams.* —*n.* 1. something transverse. 2. *Geom.* the longer axis of an ellipse. [< L *transversus* < *trans–* across + *vertere* turn] —**trans·verse'ly,** *adv.*

trap (trap), *n., v.,* **trapped, trap·ping.** —*n.* 1. thing or means for catching animals; snare. 2. trick or other means for catching someone off guard. 3. a trap door. 4. a device in a pipe to prevent the escape of air, water, gas, etc. 5. a light, two-wheeled carriage. 6. a device to throw clay pigeons, etc., into the air to be shot at. 7. **traps,** drums, cymbals, bells, gongs, etc. —*v.* 1. catch in a trap. 2. set traps for animals. 3. provide with a trap. 4. stop with a trap. 5. *Am.* make a business of catching animals in traps for their furs. [OE *træppe*] —Syn. *n.* 2. stratagem, artifice.

trap door, door in a floor or roof.

tra·peze (trə·pēz'; tra–), *n.* 1. a short horizontal bar hung by ropes like a swing, used in gymnasiums and circuses. 2. trapezium. [< F < LL < Gk. *trapezion,* dim. of *trapeza* table] —**tra·pez'ist,** *n.*

tra·pe·zi·um (trə·pē'zi·əm), *n., pl.* –**zi·ums,** –**zi·a** (–zi·ə). 1. *Geom.* a. a four-sided plane figure having no sides parallel. b. *Brit.* trapezoid (def. 1a). 2. *Anat.* bone in the wrist, at the base of the thumb. [< LL < Gk. *trapezion,* orig., little table. See TRAPEZE.]

Trapezium (def. 1a)

trap·e·zoid (trap'ə·zoid), *n.* 1. *Geom.* a. a four-sided plane figure having two sides parallel and two sides not parallel. b. *Brit.* trapezium (def. 1a). 2. *Anat.* bone in the wrist at the base of the forefinger. [< NL < Gk., < *trapeza* table + *eidos* form] —**trap'e·zoi'dal,** *adj.*

Trapezoids (def. 1a)

trap·per (trap'ər), *n.* person who traps, esp. a man who traps wild animals for their furs.

trap·pings (trap'ingz), *n.pl.* 1. ornamental coverings for a horse. 2. things worn; ornaments: *trappings of a king and his court.*

Trap·pist (trap'ist), *n.* monk belonging to an extremely austere branch of the Cistercian order established in 1664. —*adj.* of or pertaining to the Trappists. [< F *trappiste,* from the monastery of *La Trappe*]

trap·shoot·ing (trap'shüt'ing), *n.* shooting at clay pigeons, etc., thrown into the air. —**trap'shoot'er,** *n.*

āge, cāre, fär; ēqual, tėrm; īce; ōpen, ôrder; pùt, rüle, ūse; th, then; ə=a in about.

trash (trash), n. 1. worthless stuff; rubbish. 2. broken or torn bits; leaves, twigs, husks, etc., broken or cut off to aid growth or prepare something for use. 3. foolish notions, talk, or writing; nonsense. 4. a disreputable or worthless person. 5. worthless people collectively. [cf. Scand. (dial. Norw.) *trask*] —Syn. 1. debris, litter, refuse, garbage.

trash·y (trash′i), adj., **trash·i·er**, **trash·i·est**. like or containing trash; worthless. —**trash′i·ly**, adv. —**trash′i·ness**, n.

trau·ma (trô′mə; trou′-), n., pl. **-ma·ta** (-mə-tə), **-mas**. 1. a physical or psychic wound; injury. 2. the condition (neurosis, etc.) produced by it. [< Gk., wound]

trau·mat·ic (trô·mat′ik; trou-), adj. 1. of, pertaining to, or produced by a wound or injury. 2. for or dealing with the treatment of wounds or injuries.

trav·ail (trav′āl; trə·vāl′), n. 1. toil; labor. 2. trouble; hardship. 3. the pains of childbirth. —v. 1. toil; labor. 2. suffer the pains of childbirth. [< OF, ult. < LL *trepalium* torture device, prob. < L *tres* three + *palus* stake]

trav·el (trav′əl), v., **-eled**, **-el·ing**; esp. Brit. **-elled**, **-el·ling**, n. —v. 1. go from one place to another; journey: *travel across the country*. 2. go from place to place selling things: *he travels for a large firm*. 3. move in a fixed course, as a moving part in a machine does. 4. move; proceed; pass: *light and sound travel in waves*. 5. walk or run: *a deer travels many miles in a day*. 6. pass through or over: *travel a road*. —n. 1. movement in general. 2. going in trains, ships, cars, etc., from one place to another; journeying. 3. travels, journeys. [var. of *travail*] —**trav′el·er**, esp. Brit. **trav′el·ler**, n.

trav·eled, esp. Brit. **trav·elled** (trav′əld), adj. 1. having journeyed widely. 2. much used by travelers.

traveling salesman, Am. person whose work is going from place to place selling things for a company.

trav·e·logue, **trav·e·log** (trav′ə·lôg; -log), n. Am. lecture describing travel or a motion picture depicting travel.

trav·erse (v., adv. trav′ərs, trə·vėrs′; n., adj. trav′ərs), v., **-ersed**, **-ers·ing**, n., adj., adv. —v. 1. pass across, over, or through: *traverse a plain*. 2. walk or move in a crosswise direction; move back and forth. 3. oppose; hinder; thwart: *traverse his designs*. 4. deny: *he traversed their accusations*. —n. 1. act of crossing. 2. something put or lying across. 3. opposition; obstacle; hindrance. —adj. lying across; being across. —adv. across; crosswise. [< OF *traverser* < travers TRANSVERSE] —**trav′ers·a·ble**, adj. —**trav′ers·er**, n.

trav·es·ty (trav′is·ti), n., pl. **-ties**, v., **-tied**, **-ty·ing**. —n. 1. imitation of a serious literary work in such a way as to make it seem ridiculous. 2. any treatment or imitation that makes a serious thing seem ridiculous. —v. make (a serious subject or matter) ridiculous; imitate in an absurd or grotesque way. [< F *travesti* disguised, ult. < L *trans-* over + *vestire* dress]

trawl (trôl), n. 1. a strong net dragged along the bottom of the sea. 2. Am. line supported by buoys and having many short lines with baited hooks attached to it. —v. 1. fish with a net by dragging it along the bottom of the sea. 2. fish with lines supported by buoys. 3. catch (fish) with such a net or lines. [< MDu. *traghel* < L *tragula* dragnet. Cf. TRAIL.]

trawl·er (trôl′ər), n. Am. 1. person who trawls. 2. boat used in trawling.

tray (trā), n. 1. a flat, shallow holder or container with a low rim around it. 2. tray with dishes of food on it. 3. a shallow box that fits into a trunk, cabinet, etc. [OE *trēg*]

treach·er·ous (trech′ər·əs), adj. 1. not to be trusted; not faithful; disloyal: *the treacherous soldier carried reports to the enemy*. 2. having a false appearance of strength, security, etc.; not reliable; deceiving: *thin ice is treacherous*. —**treach′er·ous·ly**, adv. —**treach′er·ous·ness**, n.

treach·er·y (trech′ər·i), n., pl. **-er·ies**. 1. a breaking of faith; treacherous behavior; deceit.

2. treason. [< OF *trecherie* < *trechier* cheat] —Syn. 1. faithlessness, perfidy.

trea·cle (trē′kəl), n. Brit. molasses, esp. that produced during the refining of sugar. [< OF *triacle* antidote < L < Gk. *theriake*, ult. < *ther* wild beast]

tread (tred), v., trod or (Archaic) trode, trodden or trod, tread·ing, n. —v. 1. set the feet on; walk on or through; step across: *tread the streets*. 2. press under the feet; trample; crush: *tread grapes*. 3. dominate harshly; repress. 4. make, form, or do by walking: *tread a path*. 5. tread on air, feel happy and gay. 6. tread on one's toes, offend or annoy one. 7. tread the boards, be an actor or actress; play a part in a play. 8. tread water, keep oneself from sinking by moving the feet up and down. —n. 1. act or sound of treading; step: *the tread of marching feet*. 2. way of walking: *he walks with a heavy tread*. 3. the part of stairs or a ladder that a person steps on. 4. the part of a wheel or tire that touches the ground. 5. distance between opposite wheels of an automobile. 6. sole of the foot or of a shoe. [OE *tredan*] —**tread′er**, n.

trea·dle (tred′əl), n., v., **-dled**, **-dling**. —n. 1. lever worked by the foot to operate a machine: *the treadle of a sewing machine*. 2. Brit. pedal of a bicycle. —v. work a treadle. [OE *tredel* < *tredan* tread] —**trea′dler**, n.

tread·mill (tred′mil′), n. 1. apparatus to turn something by having a person or animal walk on the moving steps of a wheel or of a sloping, endless belt. 2. any wearisome or monotonous round of work or life.

treas., treasurer; treasury.

trea·son (trē′zən), n. betrayal of one's country or ruler. [< AF *treson* < L *traditio*. Doublet of TRADITION.]

trea·son·a·ble (trē′zən·ə·bəl; trēz′nə·bəl), **trea·son·ous** (-əs), adj. of treason; involving treason; traitorous. —**trea′son·a·ble·ness**, n. —**trea′son·a·bly**, adv.

treas·ure (trezh′ər; trā′zhər), n., v., **-ured**, **-ur·ing**. —n. 1. wealth or riches stored up; valuable things. 2. any thing or person that is much loved or valued. —v. 1. value highly. 2. put away for future use; store up. [< OF *tresor* < L < Gk. *thesauros*. Doublet of THESAURUS.]

treas·ur·er (trezh′ər·ər; trezh′rər; trā′zhər-ər; trāzh′rər), n. person in charge of money. —**treas′ur·er·ship′**, n.

treas·ure-trove (trezh′ər·trōv′; trā′zhər-), n. 1. money, jewels, or other treasure that a person finds, esp. if the owner of it is not known. 2. any valuable discovery. [< AF *tresor trové* treasure found]

treas·ur·y (trezh′ər·i; trezh′ri; trā′zhər·i; trāzh′ri), n., pl. **-ur·ies**. 1. place where money is kept. 2. money owned; funds. 3. department that has charge of the income and expenses of a country. 4. place where treasure is kept. 5. book or person thought of as a valued source.

treat (trēt), v. 1. act toward in some specified manner: *the driver treats his horses well*. 2. think of; consider; regard: *treat a matter as unimportant*. 3. deal with to relieve or cure: *the dentist is treating my tooth*. 4. deal with to bring about some special result: *treat a metal plate with acid in engraving*. 5. deal with; discuss: *this magazine treats the progress of medicine*. 6. express in literature or art: *treat a theme realistically*. 7. discuss terms; arrange terms: *messengers came to treat for peace*. 8. entertain with food, drink, or amusement: *treat guests to tea*. 9. pay the cost of entertainment. 10. treat of, deal with; discuss. —n. 1. act of treating. 2. gift of food, drink, or amusement. 3. anything that gives pleasure. [< OF *tretier* < L *tractare*, orig., drag violently, handle, frequentative of *trahere* drag] —**treat′a·ble**, adj. —**treat′er**, n.

trea·tise (trē′tis), n. book or writing dealing with some subject. A treatise is more formal and systematic than most books or writings. [< AF *tretiz*, ult. < L *tractare* TREAT]

treat·ment (trēt′mənt), n. 1. act or process of treating. 2. way of treating. 3. thing done or used to treat something else, as a disease.

trea·ty (trē′tĭ), *n.*, *pl.* **–ties.** agreement, esp. one between nations, signed and approved by each nation. [< OF *traite*, orig. pp. of *traiter* TREAT]

tre·ble (treb′əl), *adj.*, *v.*, **–bled, –bling,** *n.* —*adj.* 1. three times; threefold; triple. 2. *Music.* a. of or for the treble. b. shrill; high-pitched. —*v.* make or become three times as much: *treble one's money.* —*n.* 1. *Music.* a. the highest part in music; soprano. b. voice, singer, or instrument that takes this part. 2. a shrill, high-pitched voice or sound. [< OF < L *triplus* triple. Doublet of TRIPLE.] —**tre·bly** (treb′lĭ), *adv.*

treble clef, *Music.* symbol indicating that the pitch of the notes on a staff is above middle C.

tree (trē), *n.*, *v.*, **treed, tree·ing.** —*n.* 1. a large perennial plant with a woody trunk, branches, and leaves. 2. less accurately, any of certain other plants that resemble trees in form or size. 3. piece or structure of wood for some special purpose: *clothes tree, shoe tree.* 4. diagram with branches showing how the members of a family are related. 5. up a tree, a. chased up a tree. b. *Am., Colloq.* in a difficult position. —*v.* 1. furnish with a tree (beam, bar, wooden handle, etc.). 2. stretch (a shoe) on a tree. 3. *Am.* chase up a tree: *the cat was treed by a dog.* [OE trēo] —**tree′less,** *adj.* —**tree′less·ness,** *n.* —**tree′like′,** *adj.*

tree frog, 1. a small frog that lives in trees. 2. a tree toad.

tree·nail (trē′nāl′; tren′əl; trun′əl), *n.* a round pin of hard wood for fastening timbers together. Also, **trenail.**

tree of heaven, ailanthus.

tree toad, *Am.* a small toad living in trees, that has adhesive disks or suckers on its toes.

tre·foil (trē′foil), *n.* 1. plant having threefold leaves, as the common clovers. 2. ornament like a threefold leaf. [< OF < L, < *tri-* three + *folium* leaf] —**tre′foiled,** *adj.*

Trefoils (def. 2)

trek (trek), *v.*, **trekked, trek·king,** *n.* —*v.* 1. travel by ox wagon; migrate. 2. travel slowly by any means; travel. —*n.* 1. act of trekking. 2. journey. 3. stage of a journey between one stopping place and the next. [< Du. *trekken*, orig., draw, pull] —**trek′ker,** *n.*

trel·lis (trel′ĭs), *n.* frame of light strips of wood or metal crossing one another with open spaces in between; lattice, esp. one supporting growing vines. —*v.* 1. furnish with a trellis. 2. support on a trellis. 3. cross as in a trellis. [< OF *trelis,* ult. < L *trilix* triple-twilled]

trem·a·tode (trem′ə·tōd; trē′mə-), *n.* flatworm that lives as a parasite in or on other animals. —*adj.* belonging to the group of trematodes. [< NL, < Gk. *trematodes* holed < *trema* hole]

trem·ble (trem′bəl), *v.*, **–bled, –bling,** *n.* —*v.* 1. shake because of fear, excitement, weakness, cold, etc. 2. feel fear, anxiety, etc. —*n.* a trembling. [< OF *trembler,* ult. < L *tremulus* TREMULOUS] —**trem′bler,** *n.* —**trem′bling,** *adj.* —**trem′bling·ly,** *adv.* —Syn. *v.* 1. shiver, quake, shudder, quiver, vibrate.

trem·bly (trem′blĭ), *adj.* trembling; tremulous.

tre·men·dous (trĭ·men′dəs), *adj.* 1. dreadful; awful. 2. *Colloq.* very great; enormous: *a tremendous house.* 3. *Colloq.* extraordinary: *have a tremendous time.* [< L *tremendus,* lit., to be trembled at < *tremere* tremble] —**tre·men′dous·ly,** *adv.* —**tre·men′dous·ness,** *n.* —Syn. 1. frightful, horrible. 2. immense, monstrous.

trem·o·lo (trem′ə·lō), *n.*, *pl.* **–los.** *Music.* 1. a trembling or vibrating quality in tones. The tremolo is used to express emotion. 2. device in an organ used to produce this quality. [< Ital. Doublet of TREMULOUS.]

trem·or (trem′ər), *n.* 1. an involuntary shaking or trembling: *a nervous tremor in the voice.* 2. vibration. 3. thrill of emotion or excitement. [< L] —**trem′or·less,** *adj.* —Syn. 1. quaking, quivering.

trem·u·lous (trem′yə·ləs), *adj.* 1. trembling; quivering. 2. timid; fearful. 3. vibratory. [< L *tremulus* < *tremere* tremble. Doublet of TREMOLO.] —**trem′u·lous·ly,** *adv.* —**trem′u·lous·ness,** *n.* —Syn. 1. shaking, vibrating.

tre·nail (trē′nāl′; tren′əl; trun′əl), *n.* treenail.

trench (trench), *n.* 1. a long, narrow ditch with earth thrown up in front to protect soldiers. 2. a deep furrow; ditch; cut. —*v.* 1. surround with a trench; fortify with trenches. 2. dig a trench in. 3. dig ditches. 4. trench on or upon, a. trespass upon. b. come close to; border on. [< OF *trenchier,* cut, appar. ult. < L *truncare* < *truncus* mutilated]

trench·ant (tren′chənt), *adj.* 1. sharp; keen; cutting: *trenchant wit.* 2. vigorous; effective: *a trenchant policy.* 3. clear-cut; distinct: *in trenchant outline against the sky.* [< OF, cutting. See TRENCH.] —**trench′an·cy, trench′ant·ness,** *n.* —**trench′ant·ly,** *adv.*

trench·er (tren′chər), *n.* a wooden platter on which meat was formerly served and carved. [< AF *trenchour* knife, ult. < *trenchier* to cut. See TRENCH.]

trench fever, an infectious fever that is transmitted by lice and often affects soldiers in the trenches.

trench mouth, 1. a contagious inflammation of the mouth and gums. 2. any inflammation of the mouth and gums.

trend (trend), *n.* a general direction; course; tendency. —*v.* have a general direction; tend; run. [OE *trendan*]

Tren·ton (tren′tən), *n.* capital of New Jersey, in the W part.

tre·pan (trĭ·pan′), *n.*, *v.*, **–panned, –pan·ning.** —*n.* 1. a cylindrical saw for cutting out part of the skull. 2. a boring tool. —*v.* bore through with a trepan. [< Med.L < Gk. *trypanon* < *trypaein* bore]

tre·phine (trĭ·fīn′; -fēn′), *n.*, *v.*, **–phined, –phin·ing.** —*n.* an improved form of the trepan. —*v.* operate on with a trephine. [earlier *trafine,* alter. by inventor Woodall of *trapan* (var. of *trepan*) after L *tres fines* three ends]

trep·i·da·tion (trep′ə·dā′shən), *n.* 1. nervous dread; fear; fright. 2. a trembling. [< L, ult. < *trepidus* alarmed]

tres·pass (tres′pəs), *v.* 1. go on somebody's property without any right. 2. go beyond the limits of what is right, proper, or polite: *I won't trespass on your time any longer.* 3. do wrong; sin. —*n.* 1. act or fact of trespassing. 2. a wrong; a sin. 3. an unlawful act done by force against the person, property, or rights of another. [< OF *trespasser* < *tres-* across (< L *trans-*) + *passer* PASS] —**tres′pass·er,** *n.* —Syn. *v.* 1. intrude, encroach, infringe, invade. —*n.* 1. encroachment, infringement. 2. transgression, offense.

tress (tres), *n.* a lock, curl, or braid of hair. [< F *tresse*] —**tressed** (trest), *adj.*

tres·tle (tres′əl), *n.* 1. frame used as a support, consisting usually of a horizontal beam fixed at each end to a pair of spreading legs. 2. a supporting framework, as for carrying railroad tracks across a gap. [< OF *trestel* crossbeam, ult. < L *transtrum*]

Trestle (def. 1)

trey (trā), *n.* card, die, or domino with three spots. [< OF *trei* < L *tres* three]

tri-, *word element.* 1. three; having three; having three parts, as in *triangle.* 2. three times; into three parts, as in *trisect.* 3. *Chem.* containing three atoms, etc., of the substance specified, as in *trioxide.* 4. once in three; every third, as in *trimonthly.* [< L or Gk.]

tri·ad (trī′ad; -əd), *n.* 1. group of three, esp. of three closely related persons or things. 2. *Music.* chord of three tones. 3. *Chem.* element, atom, or radical having a valence of three. [< L < Gk. *trias* < *tri-* three]

tri·al (trī′əl), *n.* 1. the examining and deciding of a case in court. 2. process of trying or testing. 3. condition of being tried or tested:

he is employed on trial. **4.** trouble; hardship: *lack of money causes many trials.* **5.** cause of trouble or hardship. **6.** attempt; effort. —*adj.* **1.** of or pertaining to trial. **2.** done or used by way of trial, test, proof, or experiment. [< AF, < *trier* TRY] —Syn. *n.* **2.** experiment, examination. **4.** misfortune, sorrow. **6.** essay, endeavor.

trial balance, comparison of debit and credit totals in a ledger. If they are not equal, there is an error.

trial jury, group of 12 persons chosen to decide a case in court.

tri·an·gle (trī′ang′gəl), *n.* **1.** a plane figure having three sides and three angles. **2.** something shaped like a triangle. **3.** a musical instrument consisting of a triangle of steel that is struck with a steel rod. **4.** two men in love with the same woman; two women in love with the same man. [< L, < *tri*– three + *angulus* corner]

tri·an·gu·lar (trī·ang′gyə·lər), *adj.* **1.** shaped like a triangle; three-cornered. **2.** concerned with three persons, groups, etc. —tri·an·gu·lar·i·ty (trī·ang′gyə·lar′ə·ti), *n.* —tri·an′gu·lar·ly, *adv.*

tri·an·gu·late (*v.* trī·ang′gyə·lāt; *adj.* trī·ang′gyə·lit; –lāt), *v.*, –lat·ed, –lat·ing, *adj.* —*v.* **1.** divide into triangles. **2.** survey (a region) by dividing (it) into triangles and measuring their angles. **3.** find by trigonometry: *triangulate the height of a mountain.* **4.** make triangular. —*adj.* triangular. —tri·an′gu·la′tion, *n.* —tri·an′gu·la′tor, *n.*

tribe (trīb), *n.* **1.** group of people united by race and customs under the same leaders. **2.** class or set of people. **3.** class, kind, or sort of animals, plants, or other things. **4.** one of the twelve divisions of the ancient Hebrews. **5.** in ancient Rome, one of the three divisions of the Roman people. [< L *tribus*] —trib′al, *adj.* —trib′al·ism, *n.* —trib′al·ly, *adv.* —tribe′ship, *n.* —Syn. **1.** clan, family.

tribes·man (trībz′mən), *n., pl.* –men. member of a tribe.

trib·u·la·tion (trib′yə·lā′shən), *n.* great trouble; severe trial; affliction. [< LL *tribulatio,* ult. < L *tribulum* threshing sledge] —Syn. oppression, distress.

tri·bu·nal (tri·bū′nəl; trī–), *n.* **1.** court of justice; place of judgment. **2.** place where judges sit in a law court. [< L, < *tribunus* TRIBUNE¹]

trib·une¹ (trib′ūn), *n.* **1.** official in ancient Rome chosen by the plebeians to protect their rights and interests. **2.** defender of the people. [< L *tribunus* < *tribus* tribe] —trib′une·ship, *n.* —trib·u·ni·cial, trib·u·ni·tial (trib′yə·nish′əl), *adj.*

trib·une² (trib′ūn), *n.* a raised platform; rostrum. [< Ital. *tribuna* tribunal]

trib·u·tar·y (trib′yə·ter′i), *n., pl.* –tar·ies, *adj.* —*n.* **1.** stream that flows into a larger stream or body of water. The Ohio River is a tributary of the Mississippi River. **2.** one that pays tribute. —*adj.* **1.** flowing into a larger stream or body of water. **2.** paying tribute; required to pay tribute. **3.** contributing; helping. —trib′u·tar′i·ly, *adv.*

trib·ute (trib′ūt), *n.* **1.** money paid by one nation to another for peace or protection or because of some agreement. **2.** any forced payment, as a tax, etc. **3.** an acknowledgment of thanks or respect; compliment. Memorial Day is a tribute to our dead soldiers. [< L, < *tribuere* allot < *tribus* tribe]

trice¹ (trīs), *v.*, **triced, tric·ing.** *Naut.* haul up and fasten with a rope: *trice up a sail.* [< MDu. *trisen* hoist < *trise* pulley]

trice² (trīs), *n.* a very short time; moment; instant. [abstracted from phrase *at a trice* at a pull. See TRICE¹.]

tri·ceps (trī′seps), *n. Anat.* the large muscle at the back of the upper arm. It extends or straightens the arm. [< NL < L, three-headed; < *tri*– three + *caput* head]

tri·chi·na (tri·kī′nə), *n., pl.* –nae (–nē). a small, slender worm that lives in the intestines and muscles of man and some animals. [< NL < Gk., fem. adj., of hair < *thrix* hair]

trich·i·no·sis (trik′ə·nō′sis), *n.* disease due to the presence of trichinae in the intestines and muscular tissues. —trich·i·nous (trik′ə-nəs), trich·i·nosed (trik′ə·nōzd; –nōst), *adj.*

trick (trik), *n.* **1.** something done to deceive or cheat. **2.** something pretended or unreal; illusion: *the false message was a trick to get him to leave town.* **3.** a clever act; feat of skill: *we enjoyed the tricks of the trained animals.* **4.** the best way of doing or dealing with something: *the trick of making pies.* **5.** piece of mischief; prank: *play a trick on a person.* **6.** a peculiar habit or way of acting: *he has a trick of pulling at his collar.* **7.** the cards played in one round. **8.** a turn at steering a ship. **9.** *Am., Colloq.* a young girl; child. **10. do** or **turn the trick,** do what one wants done. —*v.* **1.** deceive; cheat. **2.** play tricks. **3.** dress. **4. trick out,** dress up; ornament. —*adj.* **1.** of or having the nature of a trick or tricks. **2.** made for or used in tricks. [< OF *trique*] —trick′er, *n.* —Syn. *n.* **1.** artifice, stratagem, subterfuge, ruse. **3.** exploit, stunt. **6.** peculiarity, mannerism. —*v.* **1.** defraud, cozen, delude. **3.** array, attire.

trick·er·y (trik′ər·i; trik′ri), *n., pl.* –er·ies. use of tricks; deception; cheating. —Syn. artifice, stratagem, imposture, duplicity.

trick·le (trik′əl), *v.*, –led, –ling, *n.* —*v.* **1.** flow or fall in drops or in a small stream: *tears trickled down her cheeks.* **2.** cause to flow in drops or in a small stream: *he trickled the water into the container.* **3.** come, go, pass, etc., slowly and unevenly: *people began to trickle into the theater.* —*n.* **1.** a small flow or stream. **2.** a trickling. [? earlier *strickle,* ult. < *strike*] —Syn. *v.* **1.** drip, dribble, ooze, leak.

trick·ster (trik′stər), *n.* cheat.

trick·y (trik′i), *adj.,* **trick·i·er, trick·i·est. 1.** full of tricks; deceiving; cheating. **2.** crafty; wily. **3.** not doing what is expected; dangerous or difficult to handle. —trick′i·ly, *adv.* —trick′i·ness, *n.* —Syn. **1.** deceptive, deceitful. **2.** artful.

tri·col·or, *esp. Brit.* **tri·col·our** (trī′kul′-ər), *adj.* having three colors. —*n.* **1.** flag having three colors. **2.** the flag of France. —tri′col′-ored, *esp. Brit.* tri′col′oured, *adj.*

tri·cot (trē′kō), *n.* **1.** a knitted fabric made by hand or machine. **2.** a kind of woolen cloth.

tric·o·tine (trik′ə·tēn′), *n.* a kind of twilled woolen cloth.

tri·cus·pid (trī·kus′pid), *adj.* Also, **tri·cus′pi·dal.** having three points or flaps. —*n.* a tricuspid tooth. [< L *tricuspis* three-pointed < *tri*– three + *cuspis* tip]

tri·cy·cle (trī′sə·kəl; –sik′əl), *n.* a three-wheeled vehicle worked by pedals or handles. [< F. See TRI–, CYCLE.] —tri′cy·cler, tri′cy·clist, *n.*

tri·dent (trī′dənt), *n.* a three-pronged spear. —*adj.* three-pronged. [< L, < *tri*– three + *dens* tooth]

tri·den·tate (trī·den′tāt), *adj.* having three teeth or teethlike points; three-pronged.

tried (trīd), *adj.* tested; proved. —*v.* pt. and pp. of *try.*

tri·en·ni·al (trī·en′i·əl), *adj.* **1.** lasting three years. **2.** occurring every three years. —*n.* **1.** period of three years. **2.** event that occurs every three years. **3.** the third anniversary of an event. [< L *triennium* three-year period < *tri*– three + *annus* year] —tri·en′ni·al·ly, *adv.*

Tri·este (trī·est′), *n.* seaport on the N Adriatic Sea, under administration of the United Nations from 1947 to 1954, when it was returned to Italy.

tri·fle (trī′fəl), *n., v.,* **–fled, –fling.** —*n.* **1.** thing having little value or importance. **2.** a small amount; little bit: *a trifle of sugar.* **3.** a small amount of money: *he sold the picture for a mere trifle.* **4.** a rich dessert made of sponge cake, whipped cream, custard, fruit, wine, etc. —*v.* **1.** talk, act, or treat lightly, not seriously. **2.** play or toy (*with*). **3.** spend (time, effort, money, etc.) on things having little value: *she had trifled away the whole morning.* [< OF *trufle*] —tri′fler, *n.* —Syn. *n.* **1.** triviality, trinket, knickknack. –*v.* **2.** fiddle. **3.** dally, dawdle, waste, idle.

tri·fling (trī′fling), *adj.* **1.** having little value;

not important; small. 2. frivolous; shallow. —*n.* trifling behavior; worthless activity. —**tri′fling·ly,** *adv.* —**tri′fling·ness,** *n.* —Syn. *adj.* 1. trivial, paltry, petty, insignificant. 2. foolish, vain.

tri·fo·li·ate (trī·fō′li·it; —āt), **tri·fo·li·at·ed** (-āt′id), *adj.* having three leaves, or three parts like leaves. Clover is trifoliate.

Trifoliate leaf

tri·fo·ri·um (trī·fō′ri·əm; -fō′-), *n., pl.* **-ri·a** (-ri·ə). gallery in a church above a side aisle or transept. [< Med.L, appar. < L *tri-* three + *foris* door]

trig (trig), *adj., v.,* **trigged, trig·ging.** —*adj.* 1. neat; trim; smart-looking. 2. in good physical condition. —*v.* **trig up,** *Chiefly Dial.* make trim.

trig., trigonometric; trigonometry.

trig·ger (trig′ər), *n., v.,* **-gered, -ger·ing.** —*n.* 1. the small lever pulled back by the finger in firing a gun. 2. lever pulled or pressed to release a spring, catch, etc. 3. **quick on the trigger,** *Am.* a. quick to shoot. b. *Colloq.* quick to act; mentally alert. —*v.* 1. set off (an explosion). 2. *Colloq.* initiate; start: *trigger an outburst of violence.* [ult. < Du. *trekker* < *trekken* pull]

trigon., trigonometry.

trig·o·nom·e·try (trig′ə·nom′ə·tri), *n.* branch of mathematics that deals with the relations between the sides and angles of triangles (plane or spherical) and the calculations based on these. [< NL, ult. < Gk. *tri-* three + *gonia* angle + *metron* measure] —**trig·o·no·met·ric** (trig′ə·nə·met′rik), **trig′o·no·met′ri·cal,** *adj.* —**trig′o·no·met′ri·cal·ly,** *adv.*

tri·he·dron (trī·hē′drən), *n., pl.* **-drons, -dra** (-drə). figure formed by three planes meeting at a point. —**tri·he′dral,** *adj.*

tri·lat·er·al (trī·lat′ər·əl), *adj.* having three sides. —**tri·lat′er·al·ly,** *adv.*

trill (tril), *v.* 1. sing, play, sound, or speak with a tremulous, vibrating sound. 2. of birds, sing or warble. 3. *Phonet.* pronounce with rapid vibration of the tongue, etc. The Spanish trill the letters *rr.* —*n.* 1. act or sound of trilling. 2. *Music.* a quick alternation of two notes either a tone or a half tone apart. 3. *Phonet.* a. a rapid vibration of the tongue, etc. b. consonant pronounced by such a vibration, as Spanish *rr.* [< Ital. *trillare* < Gmc.]

tril·lion (tril′yən), *n.* 1. in the United States and France, 1 followed by 12 zeros. 2. in Great Britain, 1 followed by 18 zeros. —*adj.* one trillion in amount. [< F, < *tri-* three, modeled on *million* million] —**tril′lionth,** *adj., n.*

tril·li·um (tril′i·əm), *n.* plant of the same family as the lily, with three leaves around a single flower. [< NL, < L *tri-* three]

tri·lo·bite (trī′lə·bīt), *n.* an extinct arthropod, with three divisions of the body and jointed limbs. [< NL, < Gk. *tri-* three + *lobos* lobe] —**tri·lo·bit·ic** (trī′lə·bit′ik), *adj.*

tril·o·gy (tril′ə·ji), *n., pl.* **-gies.** three plays, operas, novels, etc., that, while each is complete in itself, fit together to make a related series. [< Gk., < *tri-* three + *logos* story]

trim (trim), *v.,* **trimmed, trim·ming,** *adj.,* **trim·mer, trim·mest,** *n., adv.* —*v.* 1. put in good order; make neat by cutting away parts: *trim a hedge.* 2. remove (parts that are not needed or not neat): *trim dead leaves off plants.* 3. decorate: *trim a Christmas tree.* 4. balance (a boat, airplane, etc.) by arranging the load carried. 5. change (opinions, etc.) to suit circumstances. 6. try to please both sides. 7. *Naut.* arrange (the sails) to fit wind and direction. 8. *Colloq.* defeat; beat. 9. *Colloq.* scold. —*adj.* in good condition or order; neat: *a trim maid appeared.* —*n.* 1. good condition or order: *get in trim for a race.* 2. condition; order: *that ship is in poor trim for a voyage.* 3. trimming: *the trim on a dress.* 4. equipment; outfit. 5. *Naut.* a. set of a ship in the water. b. adjustment of sails with reference to the wind and direction. 6. *Am.* the visible woodwork inside a building. —*adv.* in a trim manner. [OE *trymman* strengthen, make ready] —**trim′ly,** *adv.* —**trim′mer,** *n.* —**trim′ness,** *n.* —Syn. *v.* 2. cut, clip, prune. 3. deck, adorn, garnish.

trim·e·ter (trim′ə·tər), *n.* poetry having three feet or measures in each line. —*adj.* consisting of three feet or measures. [< L < Gk., < *tri-* three + *metron* measure]

trim·ming (trim′ing), *n.* 1. decoration; ornament. 2. *Colloq.* a defeat; beating. 3. *Colloq.* a scolding. 4. **trimmings,** a. parts cut away in trimming. b. *Colloq.* additions to simple food: *turkey with all the trimmings.*

Trin·i·dad (trin′ə·dad), *n.* former British island in the West Indies, near Venezuela; it joined with Tobago and became independent in 1962.

Trin·i·tar·i·an (trin′ə·tãr′i·ən), *adj.* 1. believing in the Trinity. 2. pertaining to the Trinity. —*n.* person who believes in the Trinity. —**Trin′i·tar′i·an·ism,** *n.*

tri·ni·tro·tol·u·ene (trī·nī′trō·tol′yu·ēn), **tri·ni·tro·tol·u·ol** (-yu·ōl; -ol), *n. Chem.* a powerful explosive, $CH_2C_6H_2(NO_2)_3$, known as TNT.

Trin·i·ty (trin′ə·ti), *n.* the union of Father, Son, and Holy Ghost in one divine nature.

trin·i·ty (trin′ə·ti), *n., pl.* **-ties.** group of three; triad. [< OF < L, < *trinus* triple]

trin·ket (tring′kit), *n.* 1. any small fancy article, bit of jewelry, or the like. 2. trifle.

tri·no·mi·al (trī·nō′mi·əl), *n.* expression or name consisting of three terms. a+bx²—2 is a trinomial. —*adj.* consisting of three terms. [< *tri-* + *-nomial* from *binomial*] —**tri·no′mi·al·ly,** *adv.*

tri·o (trē′ō), *n., pl.* **tri·os.** 1. piece of music for three voices or instruments. 2. three singers or players. 3. any group of three. [< Ital., ult. < L *tres* three]

tri·ox·ide (trī·ok′sīd; -sid), **tri·ox·id** (-sid), *n. Chem.* any oxide having three atoms of oxygen in each molecule.

trip (trip), *n., v.,* **tripped, trip·ping.** —*n.* 1. a traveling about; journey; voyage. 2. a loss of footing; stumble; slip. 3. act of catching a person's foot to throw him down. 4. mistake; blunder. 5. a light, quick tread; stepping lightly. 6. a projecting part, catch, or the like for starting or checking some movement. [< v.] —*v.* 1. lose footing; stagger and fall; stumble: *trip on the stairs.* 2. cause to stumble and fall: *the loose board tripped him.* 3. make a mistake; do something wrong: *he tripped on that difficult question.* 4. cause to make a mistake or blunder: *the difficult question tripped him.* 5. take light, quick steps: *she tripped across the floor.* 6. *Mach.* release or operate suddenly (a catch, clutch, etc.); operate, start, or set free (a mechanism, weight, etc.). 7. **trip it,** skip; dance. [< OF *tripper* < Gmc.] —Syn. *n.* 1. excursion, tour, jaunt. —*v.* 5. skip, caper.

tri·par·tite (trī·pär′tīt), *adj.* 1. divided into three parts. 2. having three corresponding parts or copies. 3. made or shared by three parties. —**tri·par′tite·ly,** *adv.* —**tri·par·ti·tion** (trī′pär·tish′ən), *n.*

tripe (trīp), *n.* 1. the walls of the first and second stomachs of an ox, etc., used as food. 2. *Slang.* something foolish, worthless, offensive, etc. [< OF, entrails, < Ar. *tharb*]

trip·ham·mer (trip′ham′ər), *n.* a heavy hammer raised and then let fall by machinery.

tri·ple (trip′əl), *adj., n., v.,* **-pled, -pling.** —*adj.* 1. having three parts. 2. three times as much or as many. —*n.* 1. number, amount, etc., that is three times as much or as many. 2. *Am., Baseball.* hit by which a batter gets to third base. —*v.* 1. make or become three times as much or as many. 2. *Baseball.* hit a triple. [< L, < *tres* three + *-plus* fold. Doublet of TREBLE.] —**tri·ply** (trip′li), *adv.*

triple play, *Am., Baseball.* play that puts three men out.

trip·let (trip′lit), *n.* 1. one of three children born at the same time from the same mother. 2. group of three. 3. *Music.* group of three notes to be performed in the time of two. [< *triple*]

triple time, time or rhythm in music having three beats to the measure.

trip·li·cate (*v.* trip′lə·kāt; *adj., n.* trip′lə·kit), *v.,* –cat·ed, –cat·ing, *adj., n.* —*v.* make threefold; triple. —*adj.* triple; threefold. —*n.* 1. one of three things exactly alike. 2. in triplicate, with three copies exactly alike. [< L *triplicatus* < *triplex* threefold] —trip'li·ca'tion, *n.*

tri·pod (trī'pod), *n.* a stool, frame, or stand with three legs, as one for supporting a camera. [< L < Gk., < *tri*– three + *pous* foot] —trip·o·dal (trip'ə·dəl), tri·pod'ic, *adj.*

Trip·o·li (trip'ə·li), *n.* 1. region in N Africa. It was a Turkish province and later an Italian colony; it is now included in Libya. 2. seaport in NW Libya. —Tri·pol·i·tan (tri·pol'ə·tən), *adj., n.*

trip·per (trip'ər), *n.* 1. person or thing that trips. 2. device in a machine that releases a catch, etc.

trip·ping (trip'ing), *adj.* 1. that trips. 2. light and quick. —trip'ping·ly, *adv.*

trip·tych (trip'tik), *n.* 1. a set of three panels side by side, having pictures, carvings, or the like, on them. 2. a hinged, three-leaved writing tablet. [< Gk. *triptychos* threelayered < *tri*– three + *ptyx* fold]

tri·reme (trī'rēm), *n.* an ancient ship with three rows of oars, one above the other, on each side. [< L, < *tri*– three + *remus* oar]

Trireme.
Diagram shows position of rowers.

tri·sect (trī·sekt'), *v.* 1. divide into three parts. 2. *Geom.* divide into three equal parts. [< TRI– + L *sectus,* pp. of *secare* cut] —tri·sec'tion, *n.* —tri·sec'tor, *n.*

Tris·tram (tris'trəm), **Tris·tan** (–tən), *n.* a legendary knight of Britain at the time of King Arthur. His love for Iseult is the subject of many stories and poems and of an opera by Wagner.

tri·syl·la·ble (trī·sil'ə·bəl; trī–), *n.* word of three syllables, as *educate.* —tri·syl·lab·ic (tris'ə·lab'ik; trī'sə–), tris'yl·lab'i·cal, *adj.* —tris'yl·lab'i·cal·ly, *adv.*

trite (trīt), *adj.,* trit·er, trit·est. worn out by use; no longer new or interesting; commonplace. [< L *tritus* rubbed away] —trite'ly, *adv.* —trite'ness, *n.* —Syn. hackneyed, stereotyped, banal, stale. —Ant. original, new, fresh, vivid.

trit·i·um (trit'i·əm; trish'i·əm), *n. Chem.* an isotope of hydrogen, T or H³, the explosive used in a hydrogen bomb.

Tri·ton (trī'tən), *n.* 1. *Class. Myth.* a sea god having the head and body of a man and the tail of a fish. 2. triton, *Physics, Chem.* nucleus of a tritium atom.

trit·u·rate (trich'ə·rāt), *v.,* –rat·ed, –rat·ing, *n.* —*v.* rub, crush, or grind into a very fine powder. —*n.* any substance that is ground into a very fine powder. [< LL *trituratus* threshed, ult. < L *terere* rub] —trit'u·ra'tion, *n.* —trit'u·ra'tor, *n.*

tri·umph (trī'umf), *n.* 1. victory; success: *the triumphs of science.* 2. joy because of victory or success: *bring home the prize in triumph.* 3. something that is successful: *the new dress was a triumph.* 4. a Roman procession in honor of a victorious general. —*v.* 1. gain victory; win success: *our team triumphed over theirs.* 2. gain the mastery; prevail: *his sense of duty triumphed.* 3. rejoice because of victory or success. [< L *triumphus*] —tri·um·phal (trī·um'fəl), *adj.* —tri·um'phal·ly, *adv.* —tri'umph·er, *n.* —Syn. *n.* 1. conquest, achievement. 2. exultation, elation. —*v.* 1. succeed, conquer. 3. exult, glory.

tri·um·phant (trī·um'fənt), *adj.* 1. victorious; successful. 2. prevailing. 3. rejoicing because of victory or success. —tri·um'phant·ly, *adv.* —Syn. 3. exultant, jubilant.

tri·um·vir (trī·um'vər), *n., pl.* –virs, –vi·ri (–və·rī). one of three men who shared the same public office in ancient Rome. [< L, abstracted from phrase *trium virorum* of three men] —trium'vi·ral, *adj.*

tri·um·vi·rate (trī·um'və·rit; –rāt), *n.* 1. position or term of office of a triumvir. 2. government by three men together. 3. any association of three in office or authority. 4. any group of three.

tri·une (trī'ūn), *adj.* three in one: *the triune*

God. [< TRI– + L *unus* one] —tri·u·ni·ty (trīū'nə·ti), *n.*

tri·va·lent (trī·vā'lənt; triv'ə–), *adj. Chem.* having a valence of three. —tri·va'lence, triva'len·cy, *n.*

triv·et (triv'it), *n.* a stand or support with three legs or feet. Trivets are used over fires and under platters. [< L *tri*– three + OE –*fēte* footed]

triv·i·a (triv'i·ə), *n.pl.* trifles; trivialities.

triv·i·al (triv'i·əl), *adj.* 1. not important; trifling; insignificant. 2. *Archaic.* not new or interesting; ordinary. [< L *trivialis* vulgar, orig., of the crossroads, ult. < *tri*– three + *via* road] —triv'i·al·ly, *adv.* —triv'i·al·ness, *n.* —Syn. 1. paltry, slight, unimportant, small. —Ant. 1. important, momentous, serious.

triv·i·al·i·ty (triv'i·al'ə·ti), *n., pl.* –ties. 1. trivial quality. 2. a trivial thing, remark, affair, etc.; trifle.

tro·che (trō'kē), *n.* a small medicinal tablet or lozenge, usually round. [< obs. *trochisk* < F < LL < Gk. *trochiskos,* dim. of *trochos* wheel]

tro·chee (trō'kē), *n.* a foot or measure in poetry consisting of two syllables, the first accented and the second unaccented or the first long and the second short. [< L < Gk. *trochaios,* orig., running] —tro·cha·ic (trō·kā'ik), *adj., n.*

trod (trod), *v.* pt. and pp. of tread.

trod·den (trod'ən), *v.* pp. of tread.

trode (trōd), *v. Archaic.* pt. of tread.

trog·lo·dyte (trog'lə·dīt), *n.* 1. a cave man. 2. person living in seclusion; hermit. 3. person unacquainted with affairs of the world. [< L < Gk., < *trogle* cave + *dyein* go in] —trog·lo·dyt·ic (trog'lə·dit'ik), trog'lo·dyt'i·cal, *adj.*

Tro·jan (trō'jən), *adj.* of or pertaining to Troy or its people. —*n.* 1. native or inhabitant of Troy. 2. person who shows courage or energy: *they all worked like Trojans.*

Trojan horse, 1. *Gk. Legend.* a huge wooden horse in which the Greeks concealed soldiers and brought them into Troy during the Trojan War. 2. an enemy group stationed inside of a country to sabotage its industry and defense preparations.

Trojan War, *Gk. Legend.* a ten years' war carried on by the Greeks against Troy to get back Helen of Troy, who was carried off by Paris, son of King Priam.

troll¹ (trōl), *v.* 1. sing in a full, rolling voice. 2. sing in the manner of a round. 3. fish with a moving line. 4. roll. —*n.* 1. song whose parts are sung in succession. 2. reel of a fishing rod. 3. lure or bait for fishing. [< OF *troller* wander < Gmc.] —troll'er, *n.*

troll² (trōl), *n.* in Scandinavian folklore, an ugly dwarf or giant living underground in caves, etc. [< Scand.]

trol·ley (trol'i), *n., pl.* –leys. 1. *Am.* pulley moving against a wire to carry electricity to a streetcar, electric engine, etc. 2. *Am.* a trolley car. 3. pulley running on an overhead track, used to support and move a load. 4. *Brit.* truck; handcart. [prob. < *troll*¹ in sense of "roll"]

trolley car, *Am.* streetcar propelled electrically. The current is often taken from an overhead wire by means of a trolley.

trol·lop (trol'əp), *n.* 1. an untidy or slovenly woman. 2. prostitute.

Trol·lope (trol'əp), *n.* Anthony, 1815–1882, English novelist.

trom·bone (trom'bōn; trom·bōn'), *n.* a large brass musical instrument, usually with a sliding piece for varying the length of the tube. [< Ital., < *tromba* trumpet < Gmc.] —trom'bon·ist, *n.*

troop (trüp), *n.* 1. group or band of persons. 2. herd, flock, or swarm. 3. a cavalry unit, esp. armored, having 60 to 100 men commanded by a captain. A troop corresponds to a company in other branches of the army. 4. unit of 16 or 32 boy scouts. 5. troops, soldiers. —*v.* 1. gather in troops or bands; move together. 2. come or go in great numbers: *children trooped across the* _street._ 3. walk; go; go away. 4. form into troops. [< F, ult. < LL _troppus_ herd < Gmc.] —Syn. _n._ 1. squad, crowd, multitude, throng.

troop·er (trüp′ər), _n._ 1. soldier in a troop of cavalry. 2. a mounted policeman. 3. a cavalry horse.

troop·ship (trüp′ship′), _n._ ship used to carry soldiers; transport.

trope (trōp), _n._ 1. the use of a word or phrase in a sense different from its ordinary meaning. 2. word or phrase so used. [< L < Gk. _tropos_ turn] —trop′ist, _n._

tro·phy (trō′fi), _n._, _pl._ **-phies.** 1. captured arms, flags, etc., of a defeated enemy set up on the field of battle or elsewhere in memorial of victory. 2. anything serving as a memorial of victory: _a golf trophy._ [< F < L < Gk. _tropaion_ < _trope_ rout, orig., turn] —tro′phied, _adj._

trop·ic (trop′ik), _n._ 1. either of the two circles around the earth, one 23.45 degrees north and one 23.45 degrees south of the equator. The tropic of Cancer is the northern circle, and the tropic of Capricorn is the southern circle. 2. _Astron._ either of two circles in the celestial sphere, the limits reached by the sun in its apparent journey north and south. 3. **tropics, Tropics,** zone between latitudes 23½ degrees north and south or between 30 degrees north and south, the hottest part of the earth. —_adj._ of the tropics; belonging to the Torrid Zone. [< L < Gk. _tropikos_ pertaining to a turn < _trope_ turn]

trop·i·cal (trop′ə·kəl), _adj._ 1. of or having to do with the tropics; inhabiting the tropics: _tropical fruit._ 2. very hot; burning or fervent. 3. of a trope or tropes; used in a sense different from its ordinary meaning; figurative. —trop′i·cal·ly, _adv._

tro·pism (trō′piz·əm), _n._ _Biol._ tendency of an animal or plant to turn or move in response to a stimulus. [< Gk. _trope_ a turning] —tro·pis′tic, _adj._

trop·o·sphere (trop′ə·sfir), _n._ layer of the atmosphere between the earth and the stratosphere, within which there is a steady fall of temperature with increasing altitude. Most cloud formations occur in the troposphere.

trot (trot). _v._ **trot·ted, trot·ting,** _n._ —_v._ 1. of horses, etc., go at a gait between a walk and a run by lifting the right forefoot and the left hind foot at about the same time. 2. ride a horse at a trot. 3. make (a horse, etc.) trot. 4. run, but not fast. 5. trot out, _Colloq._ bring out for others to see. —_n._ 1. the motion or gait of a trotting horse. 2. a brisk, steady movement. 3. _Am., Slang._ translation of a book, used by a pupil instead of doing the translating himself. [< OF _trotter_ < Gmc.]

trot·line (trot′lin′), _n._ in fishing, a long line with short lines and baited hooks attached at regular intervals.

Trot·sky (trot′ski), _n._ Leon, 1879–1940, Russian revolutionary leader and political theorist.

trot·ter (trot′ər), _n._ 1. horse that trots. 2. a horse bred and trained to trot. 3. the foot of a sheep or a pig used for food.

trou·ba·dour (trü′bə·dôr; -dōr; -dùr), _n._ one of the lyric poets of S France, E Spain, and N Italy from the 11th to the 13th centuries. The troubadours wrote mainly about love and chivalry. [< F < Pr. _trobador,_ ult. < LL _tropus_ song < L, TROPE]

trou·ble (trub′əl), _v._ **-bled, -bling,** _n._ —_v._ 1. cause distress or worry to: _the lack of business troubled him._ 2. cause bodily pain or inconvenience to: _his shoulder troubled him._ 3. require extra work or effort of: _he troubled his relatives for help._ 4. stir up; make turbid; disturb: _troubled waters._ 5. cause oneself inconvenience: _don't trouble to come to the door._ 6. worry: _John troubled over the matter._ —_n._ 1. distress; worry; difficulty: _financial trouble._ 2. disturbance; agitation: _political troubles._ 3. a physical

disorder; ailment; disease. 4. an unfortunate position or circumstance: _he got into trouble with the authorities._ 5. extra work; bother; effort: _take the trouble._ 6. person, thing, or event that causes trouble: _he was always a trouble to her._ [< OF _troubler,_ ult. < L _turba_ turmoil] —trou′bler, _n._ —trou′bling·ly, _adv._ —Syn. _v._ 1. grieve, harass, afflict, annoy. 4. agitate. 5. bother. —_n._ 1. grief, anxiety, tribulation, affliction. 5. inconvenience, labor, toil.

trou·ble·mak·er (trub′əl·māk′ər), _n._ person who is always causing trouble for others.

trou·ble·shoot·er (trub′əl·shüt′ər), _n._ _Am._ person who discovers and eliminates causes of trouble.

trou·ble·some (trub′əl·səm), _adj._ 1. causing trouble; annoying. 2. laborious; difficult. —trou′ble·some·ly, _adv._ —trou′ble·some·ness, _n._ —Syn. 1. disturbing, distressing, harassing, vexatious, bothersome.

trou·blous (trub′ləs), _adj._ 1. disturbed; restless. 2. troublesome.

trough (trôf, trof; _dial._ trôth, troth), _n._ 1. a long, narrow container for holding food or water. 2. something shaped like this: _a trough for kneading dough._ 3. channel for carrying water; gutter. 4. a long hollow between two ridges, etc.: _trough between waves._ [OE _trōh_]

trounce (trouns), _v._, **trounced, trounc·ing.** 1. beat; thrash. 2. _Colloq._ defeat, as in a contest.

troupe (trüp), _n._ _Am._ troop; band; company, esp. a group of actors, singers, or acrobats. [< F]

troup·er (trüp′ər), _n._ 1. _Am._ member of a theatrical troupe. 2. an old, experienced actor.

trou·sers (trou′zərz), _n.pl._ a two-legged outer garment reaching from the waist to the ankles or knees. [< _trouse_ < Irish _triubhas_] —Syn. breeches, pants, knickerbockers. ➤ See pants for usage note.

trous·seau (trü·sō′; trü′sō), _n._, _pl._ **-seaux** (-sōz′; -sōz), **-seaus,** a bride's outfit of clothes, linen, etc. [< F, orig., bundle]

trout (trout), _n._, _pl._ **trouts** or (_esp. collectively_) **trout.** any of certain fresh-water food and game fishes of the salmon family. [< L < Gk. _troktes,_ lit., gnawer < _trogein_ gnaw]

trow·el (trou′əl), _n._, _v._, **-eled, -el·ing;** _esp. Brit._ **-elled, -el·ling.** —_n._ 1. tool for spreading or smoothing plaster or mortar. 2. tool for taking up plants, loosening dirt, etc. —_v._ 1. apply or smooth with a trowel. 2. dig up or loosen with a trowel. [< OF, ult. < L _trulla_ ladle < _trua_ skimmer] —trow′el·er, _esp. Brit._ trow′el·ler, _n._

Troy (troi), _n._ an ancient city in NW Asia Minor.

troy weight, a standard system of weights used for gems and precious metals. One pound troy equals a little over four-fifths of an ordinary pound. 24 grains = 1 pennyweight; 20 pennyweights = 1 ounce; 12 ounces = 1 pound. [after _Troyes,_ France]

tru·ant (trü′ənt), _n._ 1. child who stays away from school without permission. 2. person who neglects duty. 3. **play truant,** a. stay away from school without permission. b. stay away from work or duties. —_adj._ 1. staying away from school without permission. 2. neglecting duty. 3. lazy. 4. wandering. [< OF, prob. < Celtic] —tru′an·cy, _n._ —tru′ant·ly, _adv._

truce (trüs), _n._ 1. a stop in fighting; peace for a short time. 2. a rest from trouble or pain; respite.

Tru·cial States (trü′shəl), a group of seven small states in E Arabia, on the Persian Gulf, under British influence.

truck¹ (truk), _n._ 1. a strongly built automobile, cart, wagon, etc., for carrying heavy loads. 2. frame on small wheels for moving trunks, etc. 3. frame with two or more pairs of wheels for supporting the end of a railroad car, locomotive, etc. 4. a small wheel. 5. a wooden disk at the top of a flagstaff or mast with holes for the ropes. —_v._ 1. carry on a truck. 2. drive a truck. —_adj._ of or for a truck; used on trucks. [? < L _trochus_ iron hoop < Gk. _trochos_ wheel] —truck′-age, _n._

truck² (truk), *n.* **1.** *Am.* vegetables raised for market. **2.** small articles of little value; odds and ends. **3.** *Colloq.* rubbish; trash. **4.** *Colloq.* dealings. **5.** exchange; barter. **6.** payment of wages in goods, etc., rather than in money. [< v.] —*v.* exchange; barter. —*adj.* of or having to do with truck. [< OF *troquer*]

truck·er (truk'ər), *n.* **1.** person who drives a truck. **2.** person whose business is carrying goods, etc., by trucks.

truck·le¹ (truk'əl), *v.,* -led, -ling, *n.* —*v.* give up or submit tamely; be servile: *that man got his position by truckling to his superiors and flattering them.* —*n.* a truckle bed. [ult. < *truckle bed,* formerly used by servants and inferiors] —**truck'ler,** *n.* —**truck'ling·ly,** *adv.* —**Syn.** *v.* yield, submit, cringe, knuckle.

truck·le² (truk'əl), *v.,* -led, -ling, *n.* —*v.* move on rollers. —*n.* a small wheel. [< L *trochlea* < Gk. *trochilea* sheaf of a pulley]

truckle bed, a low bed moving on small wheels or casters. It can be pushed under a regular bed when not in use. [< *truckle²* + *bed*]

truck·man (truk'mən), *n., pl.* -men. man who drives a truck.

truc·u·lent (truk'yə·lənt), *adj.* fierce, savage, and cruel. [< L *truculentus* < *trux* fierce] —**truc'u·lence, truc'u·len·cy,** *n.* —**truc'u·lent·ly,** *adv.*

trudge (truj), *v.,* trudged, trudg·ing, *n.* —*v.* walk, esp. wearily or with effort. —*n.* a hard or weary walk. —**trudg'er,** *n.*

true (trü), *adj.,* tru·er, tru·est, *n., v.,* trued, tru·ing, *adv.* —*adj.* **1.** agreeing with fact; not false: *a true account of the events of the war.* **2.** real; genuine: *true gold.* **3.** free from deceit; sincere: *have a true interest in a person's welfare.* **4.** faithful; loyal: *a true patriot.* **5.** agreeing with a standard; right; proper; correct; exact; accurate: *a true copy, a true voice, true to type.* **6.** representative of the class named: *a sweet potato is not a true potato.* **7.** rightful; lawful: *the true heir.* **8.** reliable; sure: *a true sign.* **9.** accurately formed, fitted, or placed: *a true angle.* **10.** steady in direction, force, etc.; unchanging: *the arrow made a true course through the air.* **11. come true,** happen as expected; become real. —*n.* **1.** that which is true. **2.** exact or accurate formation, position, or adjustment: *a slanting door is out of true.* —*v.* make true; shape, place, or make in the exact position, form, etc., required. —*adv.* in a true manner; truly; exactly. [OE *triewe*] —**true'ness,** *n.* —**Syn.** *adj.* 4. constant, stanch.

true bill, *Law.* bill of indictment found by a grand jury to be supported by enough evidence to justify hearing the case.

true-blue (trü'blü'), *adj.* **1.** unchanging. **2.** stanch; loyal.

true·love (trü'luv'), *n.* a faithful lover; sweetheart.

truf·fle (truf'əl; trü'fəl), *n.* a fungus that grows underground, valued as a food. [prob. ult. < F *truffe*]

tru·ism (trü'iz·əm), *n.* statement that almost everybody knows is true. —**tru·is'tic,** *adj.*

trull (trul), *n.* prostitute; strumpet.

tru·ly (trü'li), *adv.* **1.** in a true manner; exactly; rightly; faithfully. **2.** in fact; really.

Tru·man (trü'mən), *n.* Harry S, born 1884, the 33rd president of the United States, 1945-1953.

trump (trump), *n.* **1.** any playing card of a suit that for the time ranks higher than the other suits. **2.** the suit itself. **3.** *Colloq.* a fine, dependable person. —*v.* **1.** take (a trick, card, etc.) with a trump. **2.** play a card of this suit. **3.** be better than; surpass; beat. **4.** make (up) to deceive. [alter. of *triumph*]

trump·er·y (trump'ər·i; trump'ri), *n., pl.* -er·ies, *adj.* —*n.* something showy but without value; worthless ornaments; useless stuff; nonsense. —*adj.* showy but without value; trifling; worthless. [< F, < *tromper* deceive]

trum·pet (trum'pit), *n.* **1.** a musical wind instrument that has a powerful tone, commonly a curved tube with a flaring bell at one end. **2.** thing shaped like a trumpet, as an ear trumpet

to aid hearing. **3.** a sound like that of a trumpet. —*v.* **1.** blow a trumpet. **2.** make a sound like a trumpet, as an elephant. **3.** proclaim loudly or widely. [< OF *trompette,* ult. < Gmc.]

trum·pet·er (trum'pit·ər), *n.* **1.** person who blows a trumpet. **2.** one who proclaims or announces something. **3.** *Am.* a large North American wild swan. **4.** a large South American bird with long legs and neck, related to the cranes. **5.** a kind of domestic pigeon.

trun·cate (trung'kāt), *v.,* -cat·ed, -cat·ing, *adj.* —*v.* cut off a part of. —*adj.* **1.** cut off; blunt, as if cut off: *the truncate leaf of the tulip tree.* **2.** *Geom.* cut off at the apex or vertex by a plane. **3.** *Zool.* cut off spiral shell, lacking the apex. [< L, < *truncus* maimed] —**trun'cate·ly,** *adv.* —**trunca'tion,** *n.*

Truncate leaf

trun·cheon (trun'chən), *n.* **1.** *Esp. Brit.* stick; club: *a policeman's truncheon.* **2.** staff of office or authority: *a herald's truncheon.* [< OF *tronchon,* ult. < L *truncus* TRUNK]

trun·dle (trun'dəl), *v.,* -dled, -dling, *n.* —*v.* **1.** roll along; bowl along. **2.** whirl; revolve. —*n.* **1.** a rolling; rolling along. **2.** a small wheel; caster. **3.** bed, truck, etc., on small wheels or casters. [OE -*tryndel,* as in *sintryndel* round] —**trun'dler,** *n.*

trundle bed, truckle bed.

trunk (trungk), *n.* **1.** the main stem of a tree. **2.** a big box for holding clothes, etc., when traveling. **3.** a body without the head, arms, and legs. **4.** enclosed compartment in an automobile for storing luggage, spare tire, tools, etc. **5.** the main part of anything: *the trunk of a column.* **6.** line between telephone exchanges. **7.** *Am.* the main line of a railroad, canal, etc. **8.** an elephant's snout. **9. trunks,** *Am.* very short trousers or breeches worn by athletes, swimmers, acrobats, etc. —*adj.* main; chief: *the trunk line of a railroad.* [< L *truncus,* maimed]

trunk hose, full, baglike breeches reaching halfway down the thigh, or lower. Trunk hose were worn in the 16th and 17th centuries.

trun·nion (trun'yən), *n.* either of the two round projections of a cannon, one on each side, which support it on its carriage. [< F *trognon* trunk, ult. < L *truncus*; infl. by F *moignon* stump of an amputated limb]

truss (trus), *v.* **1.** tie; fasten. **2.** support (a roof, bridge, etc.) with trusses. **3.** bundle; pack. —*n.* **1.** beams or other supports connected to support a roof, bridge, etc. **2.** appliance, bandage, pad, etc., used for support, esp. a pad with a belt or spring used in cases of hernia. **3.** bundle; pack. **4.** bundle of hay (56 to 60 pounds) or straw (36 pounds). **5.** *Naut.* an iron fitting by which a lower yard is fastened to the mast. [< OF *trusser,* ult. < L *torquere* twist] —**truss'er,** *n.*

Trusses (def. 1)

trust (trust), *n.* **1.** firm belief in the honesty, truthfulness, justice, or power of a person or thing; faith. **2.** person or thing trusted: *God is our trust.* **3.** confident expectation or hope: *our trust is that she will soon be well.* **4.** confidence in the ability or intention of a person to pay at some future time for goods, etc.; credit. **5.** something managed for the benefit of another; something committed to one's care. **6.** obligation or responsibility imposed on one in whom confidence or authority is placed: *breach of trust.* **7.** condition of one in whom trust has been placed: *a position of trust.* **8.** keeping; care: *the will was left in my trust.* **9.** *Law.* a confidence reposed in a person by making him nominal owner of property, which he is to hold, use, or dispose of for the benefit of another. **10.** a group of men or companies that controls much of a certain kind of business: *the steel trust.* **11.** group of businessmen or firms having a central committee that controls stock of the constituent companies, thus simplifying management and defeating competition. **12. in trust,** as a thing taken charge of for another. **13. on trust, a.** on business credit;

with payment later. **b.** without investigation.
—*v.* **1.** have faith; rely; be confident: *trust in God.* **2.** believe firmly in the honesty, truth, justice, or power of; have faith in: *he is a man to be trusted.* **3.** rely on; depend on: *a forgetful man should not trust his memory.* **4.** commit to the care of; leave without fear: *can I trust the keys to him?* **5.** hope; believe: *I trust you can come.* **6.** give business credit to: *the store will trust us.* **7.** trust to, rely on; depend on. —*adj.* **1.** managing for an owner. A trust company undertakes to manage property for anyone. **2.** of or pertaining to trust or trusts; held in trust. [< Scand. *traust*] —**trust′a·ble,** *adj.* —**trust′-er,** *n.* —**Syn.** *n.* **1.** confidence, credence, reliance. **6.** charge, commission, duty. –*v.* **4.** entrust.

trust·bust·er (trust′bust′ər), *n. Colloq.* a government official or other person who breaks up, or seeks to break up, business trusts.

trus·tee (trus·tē′), *n.* person responsible for the property or affairs of another person, or of a company, institution, etc. —**trus·tee′ship,** *n.*

trust·ful (trust′fəl), *adj.* ready to confide; ready to have faith; trusting; believing. —**trust′-ful·ly,** *adv.* —**trust′ful·ness,** *n.* —**Syn.** confiding, credulous, unsuspicious, naïve.

trust·ing (trus′ting), *adj.* that trusts; trustful. —**trust′ing·ly,** *adv.* —**trust′ing·ness,** *n.*

trust·wor·thy (trust′wėr′tⁱĭ), *adj.* that can be depended on; reliable. —**trust′wor′thi·ly,** *adv.* —**trust′wor′thi·ness,** *n.* —**Syn.** dependable, faithful.

trust·y (trus′tĭ), *adj.,* trust·i·er, trust·i·est, *n.,* *pl.* trust·ies. —*adj.* that can be depended on; reliable. —*n.* **1.** one that is trusted. **2.** *Am.* convict who is given special privileges because of his good behavior. —**trust′i·ly,** *adv.* —**trust′i·ness,** *n.*

truth (trᵫth), *n.,* *pl.* **truths** (trᵫthz; trᵫths). **1.** that which is true. **2.** state or character of being true. **3.** conformity with fact or reality. **4.** a true, exact, honest, sincere, or loyal quality or nature. **5.** in truth, truly; really; in fact. [OE *triewth* < *triewe* true] —**Syn.** **1.** fact, verity, reality. **3.** exactness, correctness, precision. **4.** veracity.

truth·ful (trᵫth′fəl), *adj.* **1.** telling the truth. **2.** conforming to truth. —**truth′ful·ly,** *adv.* —**truth′ful·ness,** *n.* —**Syn.** **1.** veracious, sincere, honest, candid. **2.** exact, accurate, correct.

truth serum, a popular name for a drug under the influence of which a person will reveal thoughts, etc., that he has been suppressing.

try (trī), *v.,* **tried, try·ing,** *n.,* *pl.* **tries.** —*v.* **1.** attempt; endeavor; strive: *he tried to do the work.* **2.** attempt to do or accomplish: *it seems easy until you try it.* **3.** experiment on or with; make trial of: *try a new invention.* **4.** find out about; test: *try one's luck.* **5.** *Law.* investigate in a law court: *the man was tried and found guilty.* **6.** subject to trials; afflict: *Job was greatly tried.* **7.** put to severe test; strain: *her mistakes try my patience.* **8.** make pure by melting or boiling. **9.** try on, put on to test the fit, looks, etc. **10.** try out, *Am.* **a.** test the effect or result of. **b.** test to find out about. **c.** enter as a competitor. **d.** make pure by melting or boiling. —*n.* an attempt; test; experiment [< OF *trier* cull] —**Syn.** *v.* **8.** purify.

try·ing (trī′ing), *adj.* hard to endure; annoying; distressing. —**try′ing·ly,** *adv.* —**try′ing·ness,** *n.* —**Syn.** severe, difficult, vexing.

try·out (trī′out′), *n. Am., Colloq.* test made to ascertain fitness for a specific purpose.

tryp·sin (trip′sin), *n.* an enzyme in the digestive juice secreted by the pancreas. Trypsin changes proteins into peptones. [irreg. < Gk. *tripsis* rubbing < *tribein* rub] —**tryp·tic** (trip′tik), *adj.*

try·sail (trī′sāl′; -səl), *n. Naut.* a small fore-and-aft sail used in stormy weather.

try square, instrument for drawing right angles and testing the squareness of anything.

tryst (trist), *n.* **1.** appointment to meet at a certain time and place. **2.** a meeting thus prearranged. **3.** place of meeting. [< OF *triste*]

tsar (zär; tsär), *n.* czar.

tsar·e·vitch (zär′ə·vich; tsär′-), *n.* czarevitch.

tsa·ri·na (zä·rē′nə; tsä-), *n.* czarina.

Tschai·kow·sky, Tschai·kov·sky (chī-kôf′ski), *n.* Pëtr (*Eng.* Peter) Ilich, 1840–1893, Russian composer. Also, Tchaikovsky, Tchaikowsky.

tset·se fly (tset′sē), or **tsetse,** *n.* any of the bloodsucking flies of Africa, some of which spread sleeping sickness. Also, tzetze fly, tzetze. [*tsetse* < Bantu]

Tsetse fly. Lines show actual size.

Tsing·tao (tsing′tou′), *n.* seaport in E China.

tsp., teaspoon.

T square, a T-shaped ruler used for making parallel lines, etc. The shorter arm slides along the edge of the drawing board, which serves as a guide.

Tu, *Chem.* thulium.

Tu., Tuesday. Also, Tues.

tub (tub), *n.,* *v.,* **tubbed, tub·bing.** —*n.* **1.** a large, open container for washing or bathing. **2.** bathtub. **3.** *Colloq.* bath: *he takes a cold tub every morning.* **4.** a round wooden container for holding butter, lard, etc. **5.** as much as a tub can hold. **6.** *Colloq.* a clumsy, slow boat or ship. —*v.* **1.** place or put in a tub. **2.** wash or bathe in a tub. [cf. MDu., MLG *tubbe*] —**tub′ba·ble,** *adj.* —**tub′ber,** *n.* —**tub′like′,** *adj.*

tu·ba (tü′bə; tū′-), *n.* a very large instrument of the trumpet class, of low pitch. [< L, war trumpet]

tub·by (tub′i), *adj.,* –bi·er, –bi·est. tub-shaped; short and fat. —**tub′bi·ness,** *n.*

tube (tüb; tūb), *n.* **1.** a long pipe of metal, glass, rubber, etc., used to hold or carry liquids or gases. **2.** a small cylinder of thin, easily bent metal with a cap that screws on the open end, used for holding toothpaste, paint, etc. **3.** tunnel in which an underground railroad runs. **4.** *Colloq.* the railway itself. **5.** anything like a tube. **6.** *Am., Electronics.* an electron tube. **7.** *Biol.* any hollow, cylindrical vessel or organ. [< L *tubus*] —**tubed,** *adj.* —**tube′like′,** *adj.*

tu·ber (tü′bər; tū′-), *n.* **1.** *Bot.* the thick part of an underground stem. A potato is a tuber. **2.** tubercle. [< L, lump]

tu·ber·cle (tü′bər·kəl; tū′-), *n.* **1.** a small, rounded projection or excrescence. **2.** a small, rounded swelling or knob on an animal or plant. **3.** a swelling caused by tuberculosis. [< L *tuberculum,* dim. of *tuber* lump]

tu·ber·cu·lar (tə·bėr′kyə·lər; tü-; tū-), *adj.* **1.** having tubercles. **2.** pertaining to tubercles. **3.** having tuberculosis. **4.** pertaining to tuberculosis. —**tu·ber′cu·lar·ly,** *adv.*

tu·ber·cu·lo·sis (tə·bėr′kyə·lō′sis; tü-; tū-), *n.* an infectious disease affecting various tissues of the body, but most often the lungs. Tuberculosis of the lungs is often called consumption. [< NL, < L *tuberculum* TUBERCLE] —**tu·ber·cu·lous** (tə·bėr′kyə·ləs; tü-; tū-), *adj.*

tube·rose (tüb′rōz′; tūb′-; tü′bə·rōs; tū′-), *n.* a bulbous plant with a spike of fragrant white flowers.

tu·ber·ous (tü′bər·əs; tū′-), *adj.* **1.** bearing tubers. **2.** of or like tubers. **3.** covered with rounded knobs or swellings. —**tu·ber·os·i·ty** (tü′bər·os′ə·ti; tū′-), *n.*

tub·ing (tüb′ing; tūb′-), *n.* **1.** material in the form of a tube: *rubber tubing.* **2.** tubes collectively. **3.** a piece of tube.

tu·bu·lar (tü′byə·lər; tū′-), *adj.* **1.** shaped like a tube; round and hollow. **2.** of or pertaining to a tube or tubes. —**tu′bu·lar·ly,** *adv.*

tuck (tuk), *v.* **1.** thrust into some narrow space or into some retired place: *he tucked the letter into his pocket.* **2.** thrust the edge or end of (a garment, covering, etc.) closely into place: *tuck your shirt in.* **3.** cover snugly: *tuck the children in bed.* **4.** draw close together; fold; contract; pucker. **5.** sew a fold in (a garment) for trimming or to make it shorter or tighter. **6.** sew tucks. —*n.* **1.** a fold sewed in a garment. **2.** any tucked piece or part. [ME *tuken* stretch, OE *tūcian* torment]

tuck·er[1] (tuk′ər), n. 1. piece of muslin, lace, etc., worn around the neck or over the chest. 2. person or thing that tucks. 3. Am. device on a sewing machine for making tucks.

tuck·er[2] (tuk′ər), v. Am., Colloq. tire; weary.

Tu·dor (tü′dər; tū′-), n. 1. the royal family that ruled England from 1485 to 1603. Henry VII, Henry VIII, Edward VI, Mary, and Elizabeth I were English rulers who belonged to the House of Tudor. 2. member of the Tudor family.

Tues., Tuesday. Also, **Tu.**

Tues·day (tüz′di; -dā; tūz′-), n. the third day of the week, following Monday.

tuft (tuft), n. 1. bunch of feathers, hair, grass, etc., held together at one end. 2. clump of bushes, trees, etc. 3. cluster of flowers, leaves, etc. —v. 1. put tufts on; furnish with tufts; divide into tufts. 2. grow in tufts. 3. put tufts on (a mattress, comforter, etc.) to keep the padding in place. [? < OF touffe < LL tufa helmet crest] —tuft′ed, adj. —tuft′er, n.

tug (tug), v., **tugged, tug·ging**, n. —v. 1. pull with force or effort; pull hard. 2. strive hard; toil. 3. tow by a tugboat. —n. 1. a hard pull. 2. a hard strain, struggle, effort, or contest. 3. tugboat. 4. one of a pair of long leather straps by which a horse pulls a wagon, cart, etc. [akin to tow] —tug′ger, n. —tug′ging·ly, adv.

tug·boat (tug′bōt′), n. a small, powerful boat used to tow other boats.

tug of war, 1. contest between two teams pulling at the ends of a rope, each trying to drag the other over a line marked between them. 2. any hard struggle.

Tugboat

tu·i·tion (tü·ish′ən; tū-), n. 1. teaching; instruction. 2. money paid for instruction. [< L tuitio protection < tueri watch over] —tu·i′tion·al, tu·i′tion·a·ry (tü·ish′ən·er′i; tū-), adj.

tu·la·re·mi·a, tu·la·rae·mi·a (tü′lə·rē′mi·ə), n. Am. an infectious disease of rabbits and other rodents that is sometimes transmitted to people; rabbit fever. [< (bacterium) tular(ense), the organism that causes the disease + -emia < Gk. haima blood]

tu·lip (tü′lip; tū′-), n. 1. any of certain plants of the same family as the lily, that grow from bulbs and have large cup-shaped flowers. Most tulips bloom in the spring. 2. the flower. 3. the bulb. [ult. < Turk. tülbend < Pers. dulband turban. Doublet of TURBAN.]

tulip tree, Am. a large North American tree with greenish-yellow flowers like tulips.

tulle (tül), n. a thin, fine silk net. [after Tulle, French town]

Tul·sa (tul′sə), n. city in NE Oklahoma, on the Arkansas River.

tum·ble (tum′bəl), v., **-bled, -bling**, n. —v. 1. fall: tumble down the stairs. 2. fall rapidly in value or price. 3. throw over or down; cause to fall. 4. roll or toss about. 5. move in a hurried or awkward way. 6. turn over; rumple; muss. 7. perform leaps, springs, somersaults, etc. —n. 1. a fall. 2. confusion; disorder. [ult. < OE tumbian dance about] —Syn. v. 4. pitch, wallow.

tum·ble·bug (tum′bəl·bug′), n. a beetle that rolls up a ball of dung in which it deposits eggs from which larvae develop.

tum·ble-down (tum′bəl·doun′), adj. ready to fall down; dilapidated.

tum·bler (tum′blər), n. 1. person who performs leaps, springs, etc.; acrobat. 2. a drinking glass; the contents of a glass. 3. part in the lock that must be moved from a certain position in order to release the bolt. 4. a kind of pigeon that turns over and over while flying. 5. a toy figure that rocks when touched but rights itself.

tum·ble·weed (tum′bəl·wēd′), n. Am. plant growing in the W United States, that breaks off from its roots and is blown about by the wind.

tum·brel, tum·bril (tum′brəl), n. 1. a farmer's cart. 2. cart that carried prisoners to be executed. 3. a two-wheeled covered cart for carrying ammunition and military tools. [prob. < OF tomberel cart < tomber fall]

tu·me·fy (tü′mə·fī; tū′-), v., **-fied, -fy·ing**. swell. [< L, < tumere swell + facere make] —tu·me·fac·tion (tü′mə·fak′shən; tū′-), n.

tu·mid (tü′mid; tū′-), adj. 1. swollen. 2. swollen with big words; pompous. [< L tumidus < tumere swell] —tu·mid′i·ty, tu′mid·ness, n. —tu′mid·ly, adv.

tu·mor, esp. Brit. **tu·mour** (tü′mər; tū′-), n. 1. a swelling. 2. a bodily growth caused by disease. [< L] —tu′mor·ous, adj.

tu·mult (tü′mult; tū′-), n. 1. noise; uproar. 2. a violent disturbance or disorder. 3. a mental or emotional disturbance. 4. confusion; excitement. [< L tumultus] —Syn. 2. brawl, outbreak.

tu·mul·tu·ous (tə·mul′chü·əs; tü-; tū-), adj. 1. characterized by tumult; very noisy or disorderly; violent. 2. greatly disturbed. 3. rough; stormy. —tu·mul′tu·ous·ly, adv. —tu·mul′tu·ous·ness, n. —Syn. 1. boisterous, turbulent.

tun (tun), n., v., **tunned, tun·ning**. —n. 1. a large cask for holding liquids. 2. formerly, a measure of capacity of liquor, equal to 252 gallons. —v. put into or store in a tun or tuns. [OE tunne, prob. < Celtic]

tu·na (tü′nə), or **tuna fish**, n. Am. 1. a large sea fish closely related to the tunny, used for food. It sometimes grows to a length of ten feet or more. 2. the tunny. [< Amer. Sp., ult. < L tunnus TUNNY]

tun·dra (tun′drə; tún′-), n. a vast, level, treeless plain in the arctic regions. [< Russ.]

tune (tün; tūn), n., v., **tuned, tun·ing**. —n. 1. a pleasing, rhythmical succession of musical sounds forming a melody; air. 2. the proper pitch: he can't sing in tune. 3. mood; manner; tone: he'll soon change his tune. 4. agreement; harmony: a person out of tune with his surroundings is unhappy. 5. due agreement, as of television or radio instruments, circuits, etc., with respect to frequency. 6. sing a different tune, talk or behave differently. 7. to the tune of, Colloq. to the amount or sum of. —v. 1. express musically. 2. be in tune; be in harmony. 3. put in tune: a man is tuning the piano. 4. adjust (a radio) into resonance with a transmitted signal. 5. fit; adapt. 6. tune in, adjust a radio to hear (what is wanted). 7. tune out, adjust a radio to get rid of (a signal or interference that is unwanted). 8. tune up, a. bring (musical instruments) to the same pitch. b. Colloq. begin to play, or sing, cry, etc. c. get into the best working order. [var. of tone] —tun′a·ble, tune′a·ble, adj. —tun′a·ble·ness, n. —tun′a·bly, adv. —tun′er, n. —Syn. n. 4. accord, concord.

tune·ful (tün′fəl; tūn′-), adj. musical; melodious. —tune′ful·ly, adv. —tune′ful·ness, n.

tune·less (tün′lis; tūn′-), adj. without tune; not musical. —tune′less·ly, adv. —tune′less·ness, n.

tung·sten (tung′stən), n. Chem. former name of wolfram, a metallic element, W, used in making steel and for electric lamp filaments. [< Swed., < tung heavy + sten stone]

tu·nic (tü′nik; tū′-), n. 1. garment like a shirt or gown, worn by the ancient Greeks and Romans. 2. any garment like this. 3. a woman's garment extending below the waist or over the skirt. 4. a short, close-fitting coat worn by soldiers, policemen, etc. 5. a natural covering of a plant, animal, part of an animal, etc. [< L tunica]

tuning fork, a small, two-pronged steel instrument that, when struck, vibrates at a fixed, constant, known rate and so makes a musical tone of a certain pitch.

Tuning fork

Tu·nis (tü′nis; tū′-), n. 1. seaport and capital of Tunisia, in the NE part. 2. Tunisia. 3. a former Barbary State in N Africa.

Tu·ni·sia (tü·nish′ə; tū-), n. country in N Africa, formerly under French control. It became independent in 1959. —Tu·ni′sian, adj., n.

tun·nage (tun′ij), n. tonnage.

tun·nel (tun′əl), n., v., **-neled, -nel·ing**; esp.

Brit. **-nelled, -nel·ling.** —n. an underground passage, esp. an underground roadway for a railroad, a passage in a mine, or an animal's burrow. —v. 1. make as or like a tunnel: tunnel a passage. 2. make a tunnel through or under. 3. make a tunnel. [< OF tonel cask < tonne tun] —tun′nel·er, esp. Brit. tun′nel·ler, n.

tun·ny (tun′i), n., pl. **-nies** or (esp. collectively) **-ny.** a large sea fish of the mackerel family, used for food. [< F, ult. < Gk. thynnos]

tu·pe·lo (tū′pə·lō; tū′-), n., pl. **-los.** Am. 1. a large North American tree of the dogwood family; sour gum. 2. its strong, tough wood. [< Am.Ind.]

Tu·pi-Gua·ra·ni (tū·pē′gwä′rä·nē′), n. a native linguistic stock of C South America, occurring particularly along the lower Amazon.

tup·pence (tup′əns), n. twopence.

tur·ban (tér′bən), n. 1. a scarf wound around the head or around a cap, worn by men in Oriental countries. 2. hat or headdress like this. [< Turk. < Ar. < Pers. dul-band. Doublet of TULIP.] —tur′baned, adj.

Turban

tur·bid (tér′bid), adj. 1. muddy; thick; not clear: a turbid river. 2. dense: turbid clouds. 3. confused; disordered: a turbid imagination. [< L, < turba turmoil] —tur′bid·ness, n.

tur·bine (tér′bən; -bīn), n. an engine or motor in which a wheel with vanes is made to revolve by the force of water, steam, or air. [< F < L turbo whirling object or motion]

tur·bo·fan (tér′bō·fan′), n. a turbojet engine in which a turbine-driven fan forces air through ducts directly into the hot turbine.

tur·bo·jet (tér′bō·jet′), n. a jet-propulsion engine having a turbine-driven air compressor. A turbojet employs a jet of hot gases in producing thrust.

tur·bo·prop (tér′bō·prop′), n. an adaptation of the turbojet, in which a propeller, driven by a shaft from the turbine, provides most of the thrust. [turbo– (< turbine) + prop(eller)]

tur·bot (tér′bət), n., pl. **-bots** or (esp. collectively) **-bot.** 1. a large European flatfish, much valued as food. 2. any of various similar fishes, such as certain flounders. [< OF tourbout]

tur·bu·lent (tér′byə·lənt), adj. 1. disorderly; unruly; violent. 2. greatly disturbed: turbulent water. 3. disturbing. [< L turbulentus < turba turmoil] —tur′bu·lence, tur′bu·len·cy, n. —tur′bu·lent·ly, adv. —Syn. 1. boisterous, uproarious, obstreperous. 2. tumultuous, stormy.

tu·reen (tə·rēn′; tū-), n. a deep, covered dish for serving soup, etc. [< F terrine earthen vessel, ult. < L terra earth]

turf (térf), n., pl. **turfs,** v. —n. 1. grass with its matted roots; sod. 2. piece of this. 3. peat. 4. Usually, the turf. a. a race track for horses. b. horse racing. —v. cover with turf. [OE]

turf·man (térf′mən), n., pl. **-men.** person interested in horse racing.

Tur·ge·nev (tür·gā′nyef), n. Ivan Sergeevich, 1818–1883, Russian novelist.

tur·ges·cent (tér·jes′ənt), adj. swelling; becoming swollen. [< L turgescens] —tur·ges′-cence, tur·ges′cen·cy, n.

tur·gid (tér′jid), adj. 1. swollen; bloated. 2. using big words and elaborate comparisons; bombastic. [< L turgidus] —tur·gid′i·ty, tur′-gid·ness, n. —tur′gid·ly, adv. —Syn. 1. inflated.

Tu·rin (tūr′ən; tyūr′-), n. city in NW Italy.

Turk (térk), n. native or inhabitant of Turkey; Mohammedan who lives in Turkey.

Turk., 1. Turkey. 2. Turkish.

Tur·ke·stan, Tur·ki·stan (tér′kə·stan′; -stän′), n. region in W and C Asia. Part of Turkestan belongs to China, part to the Soviet Union, and part to Afghanistan.

tur·key (tér′ki), n., pl. **-keys.** 1. Am. a large domesticated American bird. 2. its flesh, used for food. 3. Am., Slang. play or motion picture that is a failure. 4. talk turkey, Am., Colloq. talk frankly and bluntly. [ult. < Turkey]

Tur·key (tér′ki), n. country in W Asia and SE Europe.

turkey buzzard, Am. vulture of South and Central America and S United States, having a bare, reddish head and dark plumage.

Turk·ish (tér′kish), adj. of Turkey or the Turks. —n. the language of the Turks.

Turkish bath, a kind of bath in which the bather is kept in a heated room until he sweats freely and then is bathed and massaged.

Turkish Empire, Ottoman Empire.

turkish towel, a thick cotton towel with a long nap made of uncut loops.

tur·mer·ic (tér′mər·ik), n. 1. a yellow powder prepared from the root of an East Indian plant, used as a seasoning, as a yellow dye, in medicine, etc. 2. the plant itself. 3. its root. [< Med.L terra merita, lit., worthy earth < L terra earth + merere deserve]

tur·moil (tér′moil), n. commotion; tumult.

turn (térn), v. 1. move round as a wheel does; rotate: the merry-go-round turned. 2. cause to move round as a wheel does: turn a crank. 3. move part way around: turn over on your back. 4. do by turning; open, close, make lower, higher, tighter, looser, etc., by moving around: turn a key in the lock. 5. take a new direction: the road turns to the north here. 6. give a new direction to: he turned his steps to the north. 7. change the posture or position of; invert; reverse: turn a page. 8. change: turn water into ice. 9. change so as to be: she turned pale. 10. change for or to a worse condition; sour; spoil: warm weather turns milk. 11. give form to; make: he can turn pretty compliments. 12. put out of order; unsettle: praise turns his head. 13. depend: it all turns on the result of the election. 14. cause to go, send, etc.: turn a person from one's door. 15. turn (the eyes, face, etc.) in another direction; avert: she turned her face away. 16. put or apply to some purpose, use, etc.: turn money to good use. 17. direct (thought, desire, etc.): turn one's thoughts toward God. 18. direct eyes, thoughts, etc.: he turned his thoughts toward home. 19. be directed; be changed. 20. drive back; stop: turn a punch. 21. move to the other side of; go round; get beyond: turn the corner. 22. pass (a certain age, time, etc.): he has turned forty. 23. make in a lathe. 24. take form in a lathe. 25. make sick; become sick. 26. become dizzy. 27. bend back or blunt (the edge of). 28. of leaves, change color. 29. turn down, a. bend downward. b. place with face downward. c. Am. refuse: turn down a plan. d. lower by turning something. 30. turn in, a. turn and go in. b. Colloq. go to bed. c. give back. d. exchange. 31. turn off, a. shut off. b. put out (a light). 32. turn on, a. start the flow of; put on. b. attack; resist; oppose. c. depend on. 33. turn out, a. put out; shut off. b. let go out. c. drive out. d. come or go out: everyone turned out for the circus. e. make; produce. f. result. g. become. h. equip; fit out. 34. turn over, a. give; hand over; transfer: turn over a job to someone. b. think about carefully; consider in different ways. c. buy and then sell; use in business. d. invest and get back (capital). e. change in position, esp. change from lying on one side to lying on the other. f. convert to different use. g. do business to the amount of (sum specified). 35. turn to, a. refer to. b. go to for help. c. get busy; set to work. 36. turn up, a. fold up or over. b. make (a lamp, etc.) burn stronger. c. make (a radio) louder. d. be directed upwards. e. appear. —n. 1. motion like that of a wheel. 2. change of direction: a turn to the left. 3. place where there is a change in direction: a turn in the road. 4. a change: a turn for the better. 5. a twist: a turn of rope. 6. time for action which comes in due rotation or order to each of a number of persons, etc.: it's your turn now. 7. time or spell of action: have a turn at a thing. 8. deed; act: a good turn. 9. inclination; bent: he has a turn for mathematics. 10. need: will this serve your turn? 11. a walk, drive, or ride: a turn in the park. 12. spell of dizziness or faintness. 13. Colloq. a nervous shock. 14. Music. a grace consisting of a principal tone with those above and below it. 15. form; style: *a happy turn of expression.* 16. at every turn, every time; without exception. 17. by turns, one after another. 18. in turn, in proper order. 19. out of turn, not in proper order. 20. take turns, play, act, etc., one after another in proper order. 21. to a turn, to just the right degree. 22. turn about, turn and turn about, one after another in proper order. [< L *tornare* turn on a lathe < *tornus* lathe < Gk. *tornos.* Cf. TOUR.] —turn′er, *n.* —Syn. *v.* 1. revolve, spin, twirl. 5. shift, veer. 8. convert, transform, transmute. −*n.* 1. revolution, rotation. 9. tendency, bias, aptitude. 10. requirement, convenience.

turn·buck·le (tėrn′buk′əl), *n.* a short, hollow piece turning on a screw, used to unite and tighten two parts.

turn·coat (tėrn′kōt′), *n.* person who changes his party or principles; renegade.

turn·down (tėrn′doun′), *adj.* that is or can be turned down: *a turndown collar.*

turning point, point at which a notable change takes place.

tur·nip (tėr′nəp), *n.* 1. any of certain plants of the same family as the cabbage, with large, roundish roots that are used as vegetables. The white turnip and the Swedish turnip or rutabaga are common turnips. 2. the root of any of these plants. [prob. ult. < *turn* (from its rounded shape) + ME *nepe* turnip < L *napus*]

turn·key (tėrn′kē′), *n.*, *pl.* -keys. person in charge of the keys of a prison; keeper of a prison.

turn·out (tėrn′out′), *n.* 1. a gathering of people. 2. output. 3. act of turning out. 4. a railroad siding. 5. way in which somebody or something is equipped; equipment. 6. a horse or horses and carriage.

turn·o·ver (tėrn′ō′vər), *n.* 1. a turning over; upset. 2. the amount of changing from one job to another: *employers wish to reduce labor turnover.* 3. the paying out and getting back of the money involved in a business transaction: *the store reduced prices to make a quick turnover.* 4. the number of times money is invested and reinvested. 5. the total amount of business done in a given time: *he made a profit of $6000 on a turnover of $90,000.* 6. a small pie made by folding half the crust over the filling and upon the other half. —*adj.* having a part that turns over: *a turnover collar.*

turn·pike (tėrn′pīk′), *n.* 1. gate where toll is paid. 2. Also, **turnpike road.** road that has, or used to have, a gate where toll is paid.

turn·stile (tėrn′stīl′), *n.* post with two crossed bars that turn, set in an entrance.

turn·stone (tėrn′stōn′), *n.* a small migratory shore bird that turns over stones in search of food.

turn·ta·ble (tėrn′tā′bəl), *n.* 1. a revolving circular platform used for turning things around. 2. the rotating disk on a phonograph upon which records are placed.

tur·pen·tine (tėr′pən·tīn), *n.*, *v.*, -tined, -tin·ing. —*n.* 1. an oil obtained from various cone-bearing trees. Turpentine is used in mixing paints and varnishes, in medicine, etc. 2. the mixture of oil and resin from which the prepared oil is made. —*v.* treat with turpentine. [< L < Gk., < *terebinthos* turpentine tree]

tur·pi·tude (tėr′pə·tüd; -tūd), *n.* shameful wickedness; baseness. [< L, < *turpis* vile]

tur·quoise (tėr′koiz; -kwoiz), *n.* 1. a sky-blue or greenish-blue precious stone. 2. a sky blue; greenish blue. —*adj.* sky-blue; greenish-blue. [< F, orig. fem. adj., Turkish]

tur·ret (tėr′it), *n.* 1. a small tower, often on the corner of a building. 2. a low armored structure which revolves and within which guns are mounted. 3. a similar structure for gunners on armored tanks. 4. cockpit in a military aircraft usually enclosed by a strong, transparent plastic material and sometimes containing movable machine guns. [< OF *touret*, ult. < L *turris* tower] —tur′ret·ed, *adj.*

tur·tle (tėr′təl), *n.* 1. any of certain marine reptiles having the body enclosed in a hard shell from which the head, tail, and four legs protrude. 2. turn turtle, turn bottom side up. [< Sp. *tortuga* tortoise; infl. by E *turtle* turtledove]

tur·tle·dove (tėr′təl·duv′), *n.* a kind of small, slender dove, noted for the affection that the mates have for each other. [*turtle* < L *turtur*]

Tus·ca·ny (tus′kə·ni), *n.* district in C Italy. —Tus′can, *adj.*, *n.*

tusk (tusk), *n.* 1. a very long, pointed, projecting tooth. Elephants have tusks. 2. any tusklike tooth or part. —*v.* gore with a tusk; dig or tear with tusks. [ME *tuske*, var. of OE *tux*, var. of *tusc*] —tusked (tuskt), *adj.* —tusk′less, *adj.*

Tusks of a walrus

tus·sah (tus′ə), *n.* 1. a coarse Asiatic silk. 2. the silkworm that makes it. [< Hind. *tasar* shuttle]

tus·sle (tus′əl), *v.*, -sled, -sling, *n.* struggle; wrestle; scuffle. [var. of *tousle*]

tus·sock (tus′ək), *n.* a tuft of growing grass or the like.

tu·te·lage (tü′tə·lij; tū′-), *n.* 1. guardianship; protection. 2. instruction. 3. state of being in the charge of a guardian or tutor.

tu·te·lar·y (tü′tə·ler′i; tū′-), *adj.*, *n.*, *pl.* -lar·ies —*adj.* Also, **tu·te·lar** (-lər). 1. protecting; guardian: *a tutelary saint.* 2. of a guardian; used as a guardian. —*n.* a tutelary saint, spirit, divinity, etc. [< L, < *tutela* protection]

tu·tor (tü′tər; tū′-), *n.* 1. a private teacher. 2. *Am.* teacher below the rank of instructor at a college or university. 3. in English universities, a college official appointed to advise students, direct their work, etc. —*v.* 1. teach; instruct, esp. individually or privately. 2. train; discipline. 3. *Am.*, *Colloq.* be taught by a tutor. 4. *Am.* act as tutor. [< L, *guardian*, < *tueri* watch over] —tu·to·ri·al (tü·tô′ri·əl; tū–), *adj.* —tu·to′ri·al·ly, *adv.* —tu′tor·ship, *n.*

tut·ti-frut·ti (tü′ti·frü′ti), *n.* 1. preserve of mixed fruits. 2. ice cream containing a variety of fruits or fruit flavorings. —*adj.* flavored by mixed fruits. [< Ital., all fruits]

Tu·tu·i·la (tü′tü·ē′lä), *n.* a large island in Samoa that belongs to the United States.

tux (tuks), *n. Am.*, *Colloq.* tuxedo.

tux·e·do, Tux·e·do (tuk·sē′dō), *n.*, *pl.* -dos, -does. *Am.* a man's coat for evening wear, made without tails. [after *Tuxedo* Park, N. Y.]

TV, television.

TVA, Tennessee Valley Authority.

TV dinner, a frozen meal on a tray ready to be heated and served.

twad·dle (twod′əl), *n.*, *v.*, -dled, -dling. —*n.* silly, feeble, tiresome talk or writing. —*v.* talk or write in such a way. —twad′dler, *n.*

twain (twān), *n.*, *adj. Archaic or Poetic.* two. [OE *twēgen*]

Twain (twān), *n.* Mark, 1835–1910, American writer, author of *Huckleberry Finn.* His real name was Samuel Langhorne Clemens.

twang (twang), *n.* 1. a sharp ringing or vibrating sound. 2. a sharp nasal tone. —*v.* 1. make or cause to make a sharp, ringing sound: *the banjos twanged.* 2. play, pluck, shoot, etc., with a twang. 3. speak with a sharp nasal tone.

tweak (twēk), *v.* seize and pull with a sharp jerk and twist. —*n.* a sharp pull and twist. [< var. of OE *twiccian* pluck]

tweed (twēd), *n.* 1. a woolen cloth with a rough surface, usually woven of yarns of two or more colors. 2. suit, etc., made of this cloth. 3. **tweeds,** clothes made of tweed. [said to be misreading of *tweel*, var. of *twill*]

tweet (twēt), *n.*, *interj.* the note of a young bird. —*v.* utter such a sound.

tweet·er (twēt′ər), *n.* a small loud-speaker designed esp. to reproduce high treble sounds.

tweez·ers (twēz′ərz), *n.pl.* small pincers for pulling out hairs, picking up small objects, etc. [< *tweeze* instrument case, ult. < F *étui* < OF *estuier* keep < LL *studiare* be zealous]

twelfth (twelfth), *adj.* 1. next after the 11th; last in a series of 12. 2. being one of 12 equal parts. —*n.* **1.** next after the 11th; last in a series of 12. **2.** one of 12 equal parts.

twelve (twelv), *n.* **1.** a cardinal number, one more than 11. **2.** symbol of this number; 12. **3.** set of twelve persons or things. **4. the Twelve,** Twelve Apostles, the twelve disciples and associates of Jesus who were chosen as His Apostles. —*adj.* one more than 11; 12. [OE *twelf*]

twelve·fold (twelv′fōld′), *adj.* **1.** twelve times as much or as many. **2.** having 12 parts. —*adv.* twelve times as much or as many.

twelve·month (twelv′munth′), *n.* twelve months; a year.

twen·ty (twen′ti), *n., pl.* **-ties,** *adj.* —*n.* **1.** a cardinal number, two times ten. **2.** symbol of this number; 20. —*adj.* two times ten. —**twen′ti·eth,** *adj., n.*

twice (twīs), *adv.* **1.** two times. **2.** doubly. [ME *twies* < OE *twiga* twice]

twid·dle (twid′əl), *v.,* **-dled, -dling,** *n.* —*v.* **1.** twirl: *twiddle one's pencil.* **2.** play with idly. **3.** twiddle one's thumbs, a. keep turning one's thumbs idly about each other. **b.** do nothing; be idle. —*n.* a twirl. —**twid′dler,** *n.*

twig (twig), *n.* a slender shoot of a tree or other plant; very small branch. [OE *twigge*] —**twigged,** *adj.* —**twig′less,** *adj.*

twi·light (twī′līt′), *n.* **1.** the faint light reflected from the sky before the sun rises and after it sets. **2.** time when this light prevails. **3.** any faint light. **4.** condition or period after or before full development, glory, etc. —*adj.* of twilight; like that of twilight: *the twilight hour.* [ME, < *twi-* two + *light*¹]

twilight sleep, a semiconscious condition produced by the hypodermic injection of scopolamine and morphine, in order to lessen the pains of childbirth.

twill (twil), *n.* **1.** cloth woven in raised diagonal lines. **2.** a diagonal line or pattern formed by such weaving. —*v.* weave (cloth) in this way. [OE *twilic* < L *bilix* with a double thread < *bi-* two + *licium* thread] —**twilled,** *adj.*

twin (twin), *n., adj., v.,* **twinned, twin·ning.** —*n.* **1.** one of two children or animals born at the same time from the same mother. Twins sometimes look just alike. **2.** one of two persons or things exactly alike. **3. Twins, Gemini.** —*adj.* **1.** being a twin: *twin sisters.* **2.** being one of two things very much alike: *twin beds.* **3.** having two like parts. —*v.* **1.** give birth to twins. **2.** join closely; pair. [OE *twinn*]

twine (twīn), *n., v.,* **twined, twin·ing.** —*n.* **1.** a strong thread or string made of two or more strands twisted together. **2.** a twisting; twisting together. **3.** a twist; twisted thing. —*v.* **1.** twist together. **2.** encircle; enfold; wreathe. **3.** wind. [OE *twin*] —**twin′er,** *n.*

twinge (twinj), *n., v.,* **twinged, twing·ing.** —*n.* a sudden sharp pain: *a twinge of rheumatism, a twinge of remorse.* —*v.* **1.** feel such pain. **2.** cause such pain in. [OE *twengan* pinch] —**Syn.** *n.* ache, pang, cramp.

twin·kle (twing′kəl), *v.,* **-kled, -kling,** *n.* —*v.* **1.** shine with quick little gleams. **2.** move quickly: *the dancer's feet twinkled.* **3.** wink; blink. **4.** cause to twinkle. —*n.* **1.** a twinkling; sparkle; gleam. **2.** a quick motion. **3.** a quick motion of the eye; wink; blink. **4.** time required for a wink. [OE *twinclian*] —**twin′kler,** *n.* —**Syn.** *v.* **1.** sparkle, scintillate, glitter.

twin·kling (twing′kling), *n.* **1.** a little, quick gleam. **2.** an instant. —**twin′kling·ly,** *adv.*

twirl (twėrl), *v.* **1.** revolve rapidly; spin; whirl. **2.** turn round and round idly; twiddle. **3.** twist; curl; flourish. **4.** *Am.* throw (a baseball); pitch. —*n.* **1.** a twirling; spin; whirl; turn. **2.** a twist; curl; flourish. [blend of *twist* and *whirl*] —**twirl′er,** *n.*

twist (twist), *v.* **1.** turn; wind: *she twisted her ring on her finger.* **2.** wind together: *twist flowers into a wreath.* **3.** turn around. **4.** give a spiral form to. **5.** make (a ball) go round while moving in a curved direction. **6.** have a winding shape; curve or bend in any way: *the path twists in and out among the rocks.* **7.** curve; crook; bend. **8.** force out of shape or place: *his*

face was twisted with pain. **9.** give a wrong meaning to: *twist a person's words.* [< n.] —*n.* **1.** a curve; crook; bend. **2.** a spin; twirl. **3.** a twisting; being twisted. **4.** anything made by twisting: *a twist of bread.* **5.** a thread, cord, or rope made of two or more strands twisted together. **6.** a peculiar bias or inclination: *his answer showed a mental twist.* **7.** torsional strain or stress. [OE *–twist,* as in *mæsttwist* mast rope, stay] —**twist′a·ble,** *adj.* —**twist′ed·ly,** *adv.* —**twist′ing·ly,** *adv.* —**Syn.** *v.* **2.** twine, coil, interweave, intertwine. **8.** contort, distort.

twist·er (twis′tər), *n.* **1.** person or thing that twists. **2.** *Am., Baseball.* a curved pitched ball. **3.** *Am.* whirlwind; tornado; cyclone.

twit (twit), *v.,* **twit·ted, twit·ting,** *n.* —*v.* jeer at; reproach; taunt; tease. —*n.* a reproach; taunt. [OE *ætwītan* < *æt* at + *wītan* blame]

twitch (twich), *v.* **1.** move with a quick jerk. **2.** pull with a sudden tug or jerk; pull (at). —*n.* **1.** a quick jerky movement of some part of the body. **2.** a short, sudden pull or jerk. [akin to OE *twiccian* pluck] —**twitch′er,** *n.* —**twitch′ing,** *adj.* —**twitch′ing·ly,** *adv.*

twit·ter (twit′ər), *n.* **1.** sound made by birds; chirping. **2.** a titter; giggle. **3.** an excited condition. —*v.* **1.** make a twittering sound. **2.** chirp. **3.** titter; giggle. **4.** tremble with excitement. [imit.] —**twit′ter·er,** *n.*

'twixt (twikst), *prep. Poetic or Dial.* betwixt.

two (tü), *n., pl.* **twos,** *adj.* —*n.* **1.** a cardinal number, one more than one. **2.** symbol of this number; 2. **3.** set of two persons or things. **4.** a playing card, die face, etc., with two spots. **5. in two,** in two parts or pieces. **6. put two and two together,** form an obvious conclusion from the facts. —*adj.* one more than one; 2. [OE *twā*]

two-by-four (tü′bī·fôr′; -fōr′), *adj.* **1.** measuring two inches, feet, etc., by four inches, feet, etc. **2.** *Am., Colloq.* small; narrow; limited. —*n. Am.* piece of lumber 4 inches wide and 2 inches thick. Two-by-fours are much used in building.

two-edged (tü′ejd′), *adj.* **1.** having two edges; cutting both ways. **2.** effective either way.

two-faced (tü′fāst′), *adj.* **1.** having two faces. **2.** deceitful; hypocritical. —**two-fac·ed·ly** (tü′fās′id·li; -fāst′li), *adv.* —**two′-fac′ed·ness,** *n.*

two·fold (tü′fōld′), *adj.* **1.** two times as much or as many; double. **2.** having two parts. —*adv.* two times as much or as many; doubly.

two-hand·ed (tü′han′did), *adj.* **1.** having two hands. **2.** using both hands equally well. **3.** involving the use of both hands; requiring both hands to wield or manage: *a two-handed sword.* **4.** requiring two persons to operate: *a two-handed saw.* **5.** engaged in by two persons: *a two-handed game.*

two·pence (tup′əns), *n.* **1.** two British pennies; two pence. **2.** coin of this value (since 1662 coined only on special occasions). It is worth about two cents (1950). Also, **tuppence.**

two-pen·ny (tup′ən·i), *adj.* **1.** worth twopence. **2.** trifling; worthless.

two-ply (tü′plī′), *adj.* having two thicknesses, folds, layers, or strands.

two·some (tü′səm), *n.* **1.** group of two people. **2.** game played by two people. **3.** the players.

two-step (tü′step′), *n., v.,* **-stepped, -stepping.** —*n.* **1.** a dance in march time. **2.** music for it. —*v.* dance the two-step.

-ty¹, *suffix.* tens, as in *sixty, seventy, eighty.* [OE *-tig*]

-ty², *suffix.* fact, quality, state, condition, etc., of being——, as in *safety, sovereignty, surety. -ity* is often used instead of *-ty,* as in *artificiality, complexity, humidity.* [< OF, < L *-tas*]

ty·coon (tī·kün′), *n.* **1.** *Colloq.* an important businessman. **2.** title given by foreigners to the Japanese shogun. [< Jap. *taikun* < Chinese *tai* great + *kiun* lord]

ty·ing (tī′ing), *v.* ppr. of **tie.**

tyke (tīk), *n.* **1.** cur. **2.** *Colloq.* a mischievous or troublesome child. Also, **tike.** [< Scand. *tík* bitch]

Ty·ler (tī′lər), *n.* **John,** 1790–1862, tenth president of the United States, 1841–1845.

āge, cāre, fär; ēqual, tėrm; īce; ōpen, ôrder; půt, rüle, ūse; ŧħ, then; ə=a in about.

tym·pan·ic membrane (tim·pan′ik), eardrum.

tym·pa·nist (tim′pə·nist), *n.* member of an orchestra who plays a drum, cymbals, and other percussion instruments.

tym·pa·num (tim′pə·nəm), *n., pl.* -nums, -na (-nə). **1.** *Anat.* **a.** the eardrum. **b.** the middle ear, comprising that part of the ear situated in the recess behind the eardrum. **2.** a drum. **3.** *Archit.* **a.** space between the horizontal and sloping cornices of a pediment. **b.** space between an arch and the horizontal top of a door or window below. [< L, drum, < Gk. *tympanon.* Doublet of TIMBRE.] —**tym·pan·ic** (tim·pan′ik), *adj.*

Tyn·dale (tin′dəl), *n.* William, 1492?–1536, English religious martyr. He translated the New Testament and part of the Old Testament into English.

type (tīp), *n., v.,* **typed, typ·ing. 1.** a kind, class, or group having common characteristics: *some men prefer women of the blonde type.* **2.** a representative or typical specimen; likeness of something to come; example; model. **3.** the general form, style, or character of some kind, class, or group: *she is above the ordinary type.* **4.** figure, writing, or design on either side of a coin or medal. **5.** piece of metal or wood having on its upper surface a raised letter in reverse for use in printing. **6.** collection of such pieces. **7.** printed or typewritten letters. **8.** a blood type. —*v.* **1.** be a type of. **2.** find out the type of: *type a person's blood.* **3.** typewrite. [< L < Gk. *typos* dent, impression] —**Syn.** *n.* **2.** pattern, prototype, sign, emblem, token.

type·set·ter (tīp′set′ər), *n.* person or machine that sets type for printing. —**type′set′-ting,** *n., adj.*

type·write (tīp′rīt′), *v.,* -wrote, -writ·ten, -writ·ing. write with a typewriter. —**type′writ′-ing,** *n.* —**type′writ′ten,** *adj.*

type·writ·er (tīp′rīt′ər), *n. Am.* **1.** machine for making letters on paper. **2.** typist.

ty·phoid (tī′foid), *adj.* Also, **ty·phoi′dal. 1.** of or pertaining to typhoid fever. **2.** like typhus. —*n.* typhoid fever. [< *typhus*]

typhoid fever, an infectious, often fatal, fever with intestinal inflammation, caused by a germ taken into the body with food or drink. People can be inoculated against typhoid fever.

ty·phoon (tī·fün′), *n.* in the W Pacific, a violent storm; hurricane. [< Chinese *tai fung* big wind; infl. by Gk. *typhon* whirlwind] —**ty·phon·ic** (tī·fon′ik), *adj.*

ty·phus (tī′fəs), *n.* an acute infectious disease caused by germs carried by fleas, lice, etc. [< NL < Gk. *typhos* stupor, orig., smoke] —**ty′phous,** *adj.*

typ·i·cal (tip′ə·kəl), *adj.* **1.** being a type; representative: *a typical tourist.* **2.** characteristic; distinctive: *she has all the typical points of her mother's race.* —**typ′i·cal·ly,** *adv.* —**typ′i·cal-ness,** *n.* —**Syn. 1.** illustrative. **2.** indicative.

typ·i·fy (tip′ə·fī), *v.,* -fied, -fy·ing. **1.** be a symbol of. **2.** have the common characteristics of. Daniel Boone typifies the pioneer. **3.** indicate beforehand. —**typ′i·fi·ca′tion,** *n.* —**typ′i·fi′er,** *n.*

typ·ist (tīp′ist), *n.* person operating a typewriter; person who does typewriting as a regular occupation.

ty·pog·ra·pher (tī·pog′rə·fər), *n.* a printer.

ty·po·graph·ic (tī′pə·graf′ik), **ty·po-graph·i·cal** (-ə·kəl), *adj.* of or having to do with printing. *Catt* and *hoRse* contain typographical errors. —**ty′po·graph′i·cal·ly,** *adv.*

ty·pog·ra·phy (tī·pog′rə·fi), *n.* **1.** printing with types. **2.** arrangement, appearance, or style of printed matter.

ty·ran·ni·cal (ti·ran′ə·kəl; tī–), **ty·ran·nic** (-ik), *adj.* of or like a tyrant; arbitrary; cruel; unjust. [< *tyrannic* < L < Gk. *tyrannikos* < *tyrannos* tyrant] —**ty·ran′ni·cal·ly,** *adv.* —**ty·ran′ni·cal·ness,** *n.* —**Syn.** despotic, dictatorial, oppressive, severe.

tyr·an·nize (tir′ə·nīz), *v.,* -nized, -niz·ing. **1.** use power cruelly or unjustly. **2.** rule as a tyrant. **3.** rule cruelly; oppress. —**tyr′an·niz′er,** *n.* —**tyr′an·niz′ing·ly,** *adv.*

tyr·an·nous (tir′ə·nəs), *adj.* acting like a tyrant; cruel or unjust; arbitrary. —**tyr′an·nous-ly,** *adv.* —**tyr′an·nous·ness,** *n.*

tyr·an·ny (tir′ə·ni), *n., pl.* -nies. **1.** cruel or unjust use of power. **2.** a tyrannical act. **3.** government by an absolute ruler. **4.** state with such a government. —**Syn. 1.** despotism, oppression, harshness, severity.

ty·rant (tī′rənt), *n.* **1.** person who uses his power cruelly or unjustly. **2.** a cruel or unjust ruler; cruel master. **3.** an absolute ruler. Some tyrants of Greek cities were mild and just rulers. [< OF < L < Gk. *tyrannos* (def. 3)]

Tyre (tīr), *n.* an ancient seaport in S Phoenicia, noted for its wealth and wickedness. —**Tyr·i·an** (tir′i·ən), *adj., n.*

tyre (tīr), *n., v.,* **tyred, tyr·ing.** *Brit.* tire².

ty·ro (tī′rō), *n., pl.* -ros. beginner in learning anything; novice. Also, **tiro.** [< L *tiro* recruit]

Ty·rol (ti·rōl′; tī′rōl; tir′ol; tir′əl), *n.* Tirol. —**Ty·ro·lese** (tir′ə·lēz′; -lēs′), **Ty·ro·le·an** (ti·rō′li·ən), *adj., n.*

tzar (zär; tsär), *n.* czar.

tzar·e·vitch (zär′ə·vich; tsär′-), *n.* czarevitch.

tza·ri·na (zä·rē′nə; tsä-), *n.* czarina.

tzet·ze fly (tset′sē), or **tzetze,** *n.* tsetse fly.

U

U, u (ū), *n., pl.* **U's; u's. 1.** the 21st letter of the alphabet. **2.** anything shaped like a U.

U, *Chem.* uranium.

U.A.R., United Arab Republic.

UAW, U.A.W., United Automobile Workers.

u·biq·ui·tous (ū·bik′wə·təs), *adj.* being everywhere at the same time; present everywhere. [< *ubiquity*] —**u·biq′ui·tous·ly,** *adv.*

u·biq·ui·ty (ū·bik′wə·ti), *n.* **1.** being everywhere at the same time. **2.** ability to be everywhere at once. [< NL, < L *ubique* everywhere]

U-boat (ū′bōt′), *n.* a German submarine. [half-trans. of G *U-boot,* short for *untersee-boot* undersea boat]

u.c., *Printing.* upper case (capital letter[s]).

ud·der (ud′ər), *n.* the milk gland, esp. when baggy and with more than one teat, as in cows, goats, etc. [OE *üder*] —**ud′dered,** *adj.*

U·gan·da (ū·gan′də; ü·gän′dä), *n.* country in E Africa, a member of the British Commonwealth of Nations.

ug·ly (ug′li), *adj.,* -li·er, -li·est. **1.** very unpleasant to look at: *an ugly design, ugly furniture.* **2.** bad; disagreeable; offensive: *an ugly task.* **3.** likely to cause trouble; threatening; dangerous: *an ugly wound, ugly clouds.* **4.** *U.S. Colloq.* ill-natured; bad-tempered; quarrelsome. [< Scand. *uggligr* dreadful] —**ug′li·ly,** *adv.* —**ug′li·ness,** *n.* —**Syn. 1.** unsightly, uncomely, homely, repulsive, hideous.

U.K., United Kingdom.

u·kase (ū·kās′; ū′kās), *n.* **1.** formerly, an order of the ruler or government of Russia. **2.** any official proclamation or order. [< Russ, *ukaz*]

U·kraine (ū·krān′; ū′krān; ū·krīn′; ū′krīn), *n.* a republic of the Soviet Union, in the SW part. —**U·krain·i·an** (ū·krān′i·ən; ū·krīn′-), *adj., n.*

u·ku·le·le (ū′kə·lā′lē), *n. Am.* a small guitar having four strings. [< Hawaiian, orig., flea]

ul·cer (ul′sər), *n.* **1.** an open sore that discharges pus. **2.** a moral sore spot. [< L *ulcus*]

ul·cer·ate (ul′sər·āt), *v.,* -at·ed, -at·ing. affect or be affected with an ulcer; form an ulcer. —**ul′cer·a′tion,** *n.* —**ul′cer·a′tive,** *adj.*

ul·cer·ous (ul′sər·əs), *adj.* **1.** having an ulcer or ulcers. **2.** of an ulcer or ulcers.

ul·na (ul′nə), *n., pl.* -nae (-nē), -nas. **1.** the bone of the forearm on the side opposite the thumb. **2.** a corresponding bone in the foreleg of an animal. [< NL < L, elbow] —**ul′nar,** *adj.*

Ul·ster (ul'stər), *n.* **1.** a former province of Ireland, now divided between the Irish Republic and Northern Ireland. **2.** province in N Irish Republic. **3.** ulster, a long, loose, heavy overcoat.

ult., 1. ultimately. 2. ultimo; in the past month.

ul·te·ri·or (ul·tir'i·ər), *adj.* **1.** beyond what is seen or expressed; concealed; hidden. **2.** more distant; on the farther side. **3.** further; later. [< L, compar. of root of *ultra, ultro,* adv., beyond] —**ul·te'ri·or·ly,** *adv.*

ul·ti·mate (ul'tə·mit), *adj.* **1.** coming at the end; last possible; final: *the ultimate effects of the war.* **2.** fundamental; basic. **3.** greatest possible. —*n.* an ultimate point, result, fact, etc. [< Med.L, pp. of *ultimare* < Ital., bring to an end < L, come to an end < *ultimus* last] —**ul'ti·mate·ly,** *adv.* —**ul'ti·mate·ness,** *n.*

ultimate weapon, a weapon against which no effective defense exists or can be foreseen at the time of reference, esp. the ICBM.

ul·ti·ma·tum (ul'tə·mā'təm), *n., pl.* **-tums, -ta** (-tə). a final proposal or statement of conditions. [< NL, orig. neut. of Med.L *ultimatus* ULTIMATE]

ul·ti·mo (ul'tə·mō). *adj.* in or of last month. [< Med.L *ultimo* (*mense*) in the course of last (month)]

ul·tra (ul'trə), *adj.* beyond what is usual; very; excessive; extreme. [< L, beyond]

ultra-, *prefix.* **1.** beyond, as in *ultraviolet.* **2.** beyond what is usual; very; excessively, as in the following words:

ul'tra·af·fect'ed	ul'tra·in'ti·mate
ul'tra·am·bi'tious	ul'tra·len'ient
ul'tra·a·pol'o·get'ic	ul'tra·lib'er·al
ul'tra·bril'liant	ul'tra·loy'al
ul'tra·cer'e·mo'ni·ous	ul'tra·me·chan'i·cal
ul'tra·con'fi·dent	ul'tra·mod'ern
ul'tra·con·serv'a·tive	ul'tra·mod'est
ul'tra·cred'u·lous	ul'tra·per'fect
ul'tra·crit'i·cal	ul'tra·per·sua'sive
ul'tra·dem'o·crat'ic	ul'tra·proud'
ul'tra·dig'ni·fied	ul'tra·rad'i·cal
ul'tra·em·phat'ic	ul'tra·rap'id
ul'tra·ex·clu'sive	ul'tra·re·fined'
ul'tra·fan·tas'tic	ul'tra·re·li'gious
ul'tra·fash'ion·a·ble	ul'tra·trop'i·cal
ul'tra·for'mal	ul'tra·zeal'ous

ul·tra·ma·rine (ul'trə·mə·rēn'), *n.* **1.** a deep blue. **2.** a blue paint made from powdered lapis lazuli. **3.** an imitation of this. —*adj.* deep-blue.

ul·tra·son·ic (ul'trə·son'ik), *adj.* of or pertaining to sound waves beyond the limit of human audibility; supersonic.

ul·tra·vi·o·let (ul'trə·vi'ə·lit), *adj.* of or having to do with the invisible part of the spectrum just beyond the violet. Ultraviolet rays are present in sunlight, light from mercury-vapor lamps, etc.

ul·u·late (ūl'yə·lāt; ul'-), *v.,* **-lat·ed, -lat·ing.** howl, as a dog or wolf. [< L *ululat-,* pp. stem of *ululare* howl] —**ul·u·lant** (ūl'yə·lənt; ul'-), *adj.* —**ul'u·la'tion,** *n.*

U·lys·ses (ū·lis'ēz), *n.* Gk. Legend. the shrewdest of the Greek leaders in the Trojan War; Odysseus.

um·bel (um'bəl), *n. Bot.* a flower cluster in which stalks nearly equal in length spring from a common center and form a flat or slightly curved surface, as in parsley. [< L *umbella* parasol, dim. of *umbra* shade] —**um-**

Umbel

bel·lar (um'bəl·ər), **um·bel·late** (um'bəl·it; -āt), **um'bel·lat'ed,** *adj.* —**um'bel·late·ly,** *adv.*

um·ber (um'bər), *n.* **1.** an earth used in its natural state (**raw umber**) as a brown pigment, or after heating (**burnt umber**) as a reddish-brown pigment. **2.** a brown or reddish brown. —*adj.* brown or reddish-brown. [< Ital. (*terra di*) *ombra* (earth of) shade, but ? orig. < Ital. province *Umbria*]

um·bil·i·cal cord (um·bil'ə·kəl), cord connecting the fetus of a mammal with the placenta.

um·bil·i·cus (um·bil'ə·kəs; um'bə·lī'kəs), *n., pl.* **-ci** (-sī). navel. [< L, navel] —**um·bil'i·cal,** *adj.*

um·bra (um'brə), *n., pl.* **-brae** (-brē). **1.** *Astron.* a shadow of the earth or moon that completely hides the sun. **2.** shade; shadow. [< L]

um·brage (um'brij), *n.* **1.** suspicion that one has been slighted or injured; feeling offended; resentment. **2.** shade. **3.** foliage. [< F *ombrage,* ult. < L *umbra* shade] —**um·bra·geous** (um·brā'jəs), *adj.* —**Syn.** 1. irritation, pique.

um·brel·la (um·brel'ə), *n.* **1.** a light, folding frame covered with cloth, used as a protection against rain or sun. **2.** *Mil.* a barrage or screen of fighter aircraft to protect ground forces. [< Ital. *ombrella,* ult. < L *umbra* shade]

umbrella tree, *Am.* an American magnolia tree having long leaves in umbrellalike clusters.

u·mi·ak (ū'mi·ak), *n.* an open Eskimo boat. [< Eskimo]

um·laut (ùm'lout), *n.* **1.** change in vowel sound in the Germanic languages because of the influence of another vowel. **2.** the sign (··) used to indicate such a vowel, as in German *süss.* [< G, < *um* about + *laut* sound]

um·pire (um'pīr), *n., v.,* **-pired, -pir·ing.** —*n.* **1.** person who rules on the plays in a game. **2.** person chosen to settle a dispute. —*v.* **1.** act as umpire. **2.** act as umpire in. [earlier *a numpire* (taken as *an umpire*) < OF *nonper* not even, odd < *non* not (< L) + *per* equal < L *par*] —**um'pire·ship,** *n.* —**Syn.** 1. referee. 2. judge.

UMT, Universal Military Training (program).

UMW, U.M.W., United Mine Workers.

un-¹, *prefix.* not; the opposite of, as in *unfair, unjust, unequal.* [OE] ≻ **un-.** This dictionary lists hundreds of words at the bottom of the pages on which they would occur if placed in the main list, in which **un-** means *not.* Even so, **un-** is a prefix freely used in forming new words, and not all of the words in which it may be used can be shown here. See also **-in¹** and **a-¹** for usage notes.

un-², *prefix.* do the opposite of; do what will reverse the act, as in *undress, unlock, untie.* [OE *un-, on-*] ≻ **un-** is used freely to form verbs expressing the reversal of the action of the verb.

UN, U.N., United Nations.

un·a·ble (un·ā'bəl), *adj.* not able; lacking ability or power (*to*). —**Syn.** incapable, unfit.

un·ac·count·a·ble (un'ə·koun'tə·bəl), *adj.* **1.** that cannot be accounted for or explained. **2.** not responsible. —**un'ac·count'a·ble·ness,** *n.* —**un'ac·count'a·bly,** *adv.* —**Syn.** 1. inexplicable, incomprehensible.

un·ac·cus·tomed (un'ə·kus'təmd), *adj.* **1.** not accustomed. **2.** not familiar; unusual; strange. —**un'ac·cus'tomed·ness,** *n.*

un·ad·vised (un'əd·vizd'), *adj.* **1.** not advised; without advice. **2.** not prudent or discreet; rash. —**un·ad·vis·ed·ly** (un'əd·viz'id·li), *adv.* —**un'ad·vis'ed·ness,** *n.* —**Syn.** 2. imprudent, unwise.

un'a·bashed'	un'ac·a·dem'ic	un'ac·cred'it·ed	un'ad·mired'
un'a·bat'ed	un·ac'cent·ed	un'ac·cu'mu·lat'ed	un'ad·mit'ta·ble
un'a·bet'ted	un'ac·cen'tu·at'ed	un'ac·knowl'edged	un'a·dopt'a·ble
un'a·bid'ing	un'ac·cept'a·ble	un'ac·quaint'ed	un'a·dopt'ed
un'a·bid'ing·ly	un·ac·cli'mat·ed	un'ac·quit'ted	un'a·dored'
un'a·bridged'	un·ac·cli'ma·tized	un'a·dapt'a·ble	un'a·dorned'
un·ab·rupt'	un'ac·com'mo·dat'ing	un'a·dapt'ed	un'a·dul'ter·at'ed
un·ab'sent	un'ac·com'pa·nied	un'ad·journed'	un'ad·van·ta'geous
un'ab·solved'	un'ac·com'plished	un'ad·just'a·ble	un'aes·thet'ic
un'ab·sorbed'	un'ac·count'ed-for'	un'ad·just'ed	un'aes·thet'i·cal

āge, câre, fär; ēqual, tẽrm; īce; ōpen, ôrder; pùt, rūle, ūse; ŧħ, then; ə=a in about.

un·af·fect·ed[1] (un'ə·fek'tid), *adj.* not influenced. —Syn. unmoved, unimpressed.

un·af·fect·ed[2] (un'ə·fek'tid), *adj.* simple and natural; sincere. —un'af·fect'ed·ly, *adv.* —un'·af·fect'ed·ness, *n.*

un·A·mer·i·can (un'ə·mer'ə·kən), *adj.* not American; not characteristic of or proper to America; foreign or opposed to the American character, usages, standards, etc.

u·na·nim·i·ty (ū'nə·nim'ə·ti), *n.* complete accord or agreement. —Syn. unity, harmony.

u·nan·i·mous (ū·nan'ə·məs), *adj.* 1. in complete accord or agreement; agreed. 2. characterized by or showing complete accord: *a unanimous vote.* [< L *unanimus* < *unus* one + *animus* mind] —u·nan'i·mous·ly, *adv.* —u·nan'i·mous·ness, *n.*

un·an·swer·a·ble (un·an'sər·ə·bəl; -än'-), *adj.* 1. that cannot be answered. 2. that cannot be disproved. —un·an'swer·a·ble·ness, *n.* —un·an'swer·a·bly, *adv.*

un·an·swered (un·an'sərd; -än'-), *adj.* 1. not replied to. 2. not refuted: *an unanswered argument.* 3. not returned: *unanswered love.*

un·ap·proach·a·ble (un'ə·prōch'ə·bəl), *adj.* 1. very hard to approach; distant. 2. unrivaled; without an equal. —un'ap·proach'a·ble·ness, *n.* —un'ap·proach'a·bly, *adv.*

un·arm (un·ärm'), *v.* 1. disarm. 2. lay down one's weapons. —un·armed', *adj.*

un·as·sum·ing (un'ə·süm'ing), *adj.* modest. —un'as·sum'ing·ly, *adv.* —un'as·sum'ing·ness, *n.*

un·a·vail·ing (un'ə·vāl'ing), *adj.* not successful; useless. —un'a·vail'ing·ly, *adv.*

un·a·void·a·ble (un'ə·void'ə·bəl), *adj.* that cannot be avoided. —un'a·void'a·ble·ness, *n.* —un'a·void'a·bly, *adv.*

un·a·ware (un'ə·wâr'), *adj.* not aware; unconscious. —*adv.* without thought; unawares.

un·a·wares (un'ə·wârz'), *adv.* 1. without knowing. 2. without being expected; by surprise.

un·bal·ance (un·bal'əns), *n., v.,* -anced, -anc·ing. —*n.* lack of balance. —*v.* throw out of balance.

un·bal·anced (un·bal'ənst), *adj.* 1. not balanced. 2. not entirely sane.

un·bar (un·bär'), *v.,* -barred, -bar·ring. remove the bars from; unlock.

un·bear·a·ble (un·bâr'ə·bəl), *adj.* beyond endurance. —un·bear'a·ble·ness, *n.* —un·bear'a·bly, *adv.* —Syn. intolerable, insufferable.

un·be·com·ing (un'bi·kum'ing), *adj.* 1. not becoming; not appropriate: *unbecoming clothes.* 2. not fitting; not proper: *unbecoming behavior.* —un'be·com'ing·ly, *adv.* —un'be·com'ing·ness, *n.* —Syn. 1. unsuitable, inappropriate.

un·be·known (un'bi·nōn'), *adj. Colloq.* not known.

un·be·lief (un'bi·lēf'), *n.* lack of belief.

un·be·liev·er (un'bi·lēv'ər), *n.* 1. one who does not believe. 2. one who does not believe in a particular religion.

un·be·liev·ing (un'bi·lēv'ing), *adj.* not believing; doubting. —un'be·liev'ing·ly, *adv.* —un'be·liev'ing·ness, *n.* —Syn. skeptical, incredulous, suspicious, distrustful.

un·bend (un·bend'), *v.,* -bent or -bend·ed, -bend·ing. 1. straighten. 2. release from strain. 3. relax.

un·bend·ing (un·ben'ding), *adj.* 1. not bending or curving; rigid. 2. not yielding; firm: *an unbending attitude.* —*n.* relaxation. —un·bend'ing·ly, *adv.* —un·bend'ing·ness, *n.*

un·bi·ased, un·bi·assed (un·bī'əst), *adj.* not prejudiced; impartial; fair.

un·bid·den (un·bid'ən), *adj.* 1. not bidden; not invited. 2. not commanded.

un·bind (un·bīnd'), *v.,* -bound, -bind·ing. release from bonds or restraint; untie; unfasten.

un·blessed, un·blest (un·blest'), *adj.* 1. not blessed. 2. not holy. 3. unhappy.

un·blush·ing (un·blush'ing), *adj.* not blushing; shameless. —un·blush'ing·ly, *adv.*

un·bolt (un·bōlt'), *v.* draw back the bolts of (a door, etc.).

un·bolt·ed[1] (un·bōl'tid), *adj.* not fastened.

un·bolt·ed[2] (un·bōl'tid), *adj.* not sifted.

un·born (un·bôrn'), *adj.* not yet born; still to come; of the future: *unborn generations.*

un·bos·om (un·búz'əm; -bü'zəm), *v.* 1. reveal; disclose. 2. unbosom oneself, tell or reveal one's thoughts, feelings, secrets, etc. —un·bos'om·er, *n.*

un·bound·ed (un·boun'did), *adj.* 1. not limited; very great; boundless. 2. not kept within limits; not controlled. —un·bound'ed·ly, *adv.* —un·bound'ed·ness, *n.* —Syn. 1. infinite.

un·bowed (un·boud'), *adj.* 1. not bowed or bent. 2. not forced to yield or submit.

un·braid (un·brād'), *v.* separate the strands of.

un·bri·dled (un·brī'dəld), *adj.* 1. not having a bridle on. 2. not controlled; not restrained.

un·bro·ken (un·brō'kən), *adj.* 1. not broken; whole. 2. not interrupted; continuous. 3. not tamed. —un·bro'ken·ly, *adv.* —un·bro'ken·ness, *n.* —Syn. 1. entire, intact.

un·buck·le (un·buk'əl), *v.,* -led, -ling. 1. unfasten the buckle or buckles of. 2. unfasten.

un·bur·den (un·bėr'dən), *v.* 1. free from a burden. 2. relieve (one's mind or heart) by talking.

un·but·ton (un·but'ən), *v.* unfasten the button or buttons of.

un·cage (un·kāj'), *v.,* -caged, -cag·ing. 1. release from a cage. 2. release.

un·called-for (un·kôld'fôr'), *adj.* 1. not called for. 2. unnecessary and improper.

un'af·flict'ed	un'an·tic'i·pat'ed	un'as·sign'a·ble	un'be·liev'a·ble
un'af·front'ed	un'a·pol'o·get'ic	un'as·signed'	un·bend'a·ble
un'a·fraid'	un'ap·par'ent	un'as·sist'ed	un'be·trayed'
un·ag'gra·vat'ed	un'ap·peas'a·ble	un·at·tached'	un'be·trothed'
un·ag'gres'sive	un'ap·peased'	un'at·tain'a·ble	un'be·wailed'
un·ag'i·tat'ed	un·ap'pe·tiz'ing	un'at·tempt'ed	un·blam'a·ble
un·aid'ed	un'ap·plaud'ed	un'at·tend'ed	un·blamed'
un·aired'	un'ap·plied'	un'at·trac'tive	un·bleached'
un·a·larm'ing	un'ap·point'ed	un'aus·pi'cious	un·blem'ished
un'al·le'vi·at'ed	un'ap·pre'ci·at'ed	un·au·then'tic	un·blink'ing
un'al·lied'	un'ap·pre'ci·a'tive	un'au·then'ti·cat'ed	un·boiled'
un'al·low'a·ble	un'ap·proached'	un·au'thor·ized	un·both'ered
un·al'loyed'	un'ap·pro'pri·at'ed	un'a·vail'a·ble	un·bought'
un·al'pha·bet·ized	un'ap·proved'	un'a·venged'	un·bound'
un·al'ter·a·ble	un'ap·prov'ing	un'a·vowed'	un·braced'
un·al'ter·a·bly	un·apt'	un·awed'	un·branched'
un·al'tered	un·apt'ly	un·backed'	un·brand'ed
un·al'ter·ing	un·ar'mored	un·baked'	un·break'a·ble
un'am·big'u·ous	un'ar·rest'ed	un·band'aged	un·brib'a·ble
un'am·bi'tious	un·ar·tis'tic	un·band'ed	un·broth'er·ly
un·a'mi·a·ble	un'as·cer·tained'	un·bap·tized'	un·bruised'
un·am'pli·fied	un'a·shamed'	un·barbed'	un·bur'ied
un'a·mus'ing	un·asked'	un·bast'ed	un·burned'
un·an'chored	un·as'pi·rat'ed	un·beat'a·ble	un·burnt'
un·an'i·mat'ed	un·as·pir'ing	un·beat'en	un·busi'ness·like'
un'an·nounced'	un'as·sail'a·ble	un'be·fit'ting	un·but'toned
un'a·noint'ed	un'as·sert'ed	un'be·hold'en	un·can'celed

un·can·ny (un-kan′i), *adj.* strange and mysterious; weird. —**un·can′ni·ly**, *adv.* —**un·can′-ni·ness**, *n.*

un·cer·e·mo·ni·ous (un′ser-ə-mō′ni-əs), *adj.* not as courteous as would be expected; informal. —**un′cer·e·mo′ni·ous·ly**, *adv.* —**un′cer·e·mo′-ni·ous·ness**, *n.*

uncert., uncertain.

un·cer·tain (un-sėr′tən), *adj.* **1.** not sure; doubtful: *the election results were still uncertain.* **2.** not fixed: *the date was left uncertain.* **3.** not sure in mind; not decided: *be uncertain of one's facts.* **4.** likely to change; not reliable: *uncertain prospects.* **5.** not constant; varying: *an uncertain flicker of light.* **6.** vague; indefinite: *an uncertain shape.* —**un·cer′tain·ly**, *adv.* —**un·cer′tain·ness**, *n.* —Syn. **4.** capricious.

un·cer·tain·ty (un-sėr′tən·ti), *n., pl.* **-ties. 1.** doubt. **2.** something uncertain.

un·chain (un-chān′), *v.* let loose; set free.

un·change·a·ble (un-chān′jə-bəl), *adj.* that cannot be changed. —**un·change′a·ble·ness**, *n.* —**un·change′a·bly**, *adv.* —Syn. immutable, unalterable, invariable, permanent, constant.

un·char·i·ta·ble (un-char′ə-tə-bəl), *adj.* not generous; severe; harsh. —**un·char′i·ta·ble·ness**, *n.* —**un·char′i·ta·bly**, *adv.*

un·chaste (un-chāst′), *adj.* not chaste. —**un·chaste′ly**, *adv.* —**un·chas·ti·ty** (un-chas′tə·ti), *n.*

un·chris·tian (un-kris′chən), *adj.* **1.** not Christian. **2.** unworthy of Christians. —**un·chris·ti·an·i·ty** (un′kris·chi-an′ə·ti), *n.* —**un·chris′tian·like′**, *adj.* —**un·chris′tian·ly**, *adv.*

un·church (un-chėrch′), *v.* expel from a church; deprive of church rights and privileges.

un·ci·al (un′shi-əl; un′shəl), *n.* a kind of letter or writing used in old manuscripts. —*adj.* pertaining to such letters or writing. [< L, < *uncia* inch] —**un′ci·al·ly**, *adv.*

un·cir·cum·cised (un-sėr′kəm-sīzd), *adj.* **1.** not circumcised. **2.** not Jewish; Gentile. **3.** heathen. —**un′cir·cum·ci′sion**, *n.*

un·civ·il (un-siv′əl), *adj.* **1.** not civil; rude; impolite. **2.** not civilized. —**un·civ′il·ly**, *adv.* —**un·civ′il·ness**, *n.*

un·civ·i·lized (un-siv′ə·līzd), *adj.* not civilized; barbarous; savage.

un·clad (un-klad′), *adj.* not dressed; unclothed.

un·clasp (un-klasp′; -kläsp′), *v.* **1.** unfasten. **2.** release or be released from a clasp or grasp.

un·cle (ung′kəl), *n.* **1.** brother of one's father or mother. **2.** husband of one's aunt. **3.** *Colloq.* an elderly man. [< OF < L *avunculus* one's mother's brother]

un·clean (un-klēn′), *adj.* **1.** not clean; dirty; filthy. **2.** not pure morally; not chaste; evil. **3.** not ceremonially clean. —**un·clean′ness**, *n.*

un·clean·ly¹ (un-klen′li), *adj.* not cleanly; unclean. —**un·clean′li·ness**, *n.*

un·clean·ly² (un-klēn′li), *adv.* in an unclean manner.

Uncle Sam, *Am.* the government or people of the United States. [from the initials *U.S.*]

un·cloak (un-klōk′), *v.* **1.** remove the coat from. **2.** reveal; expose.

un·close (un-klōz′), *v.,* —**closed**, —**clos·ing.** open.

un·clothe (un-klōtʰ′), *v.,* —**clothed** or —**clad**, —**cloth·ing. 1.** strip of clothes; undress. **2.** lay bare; uncover.

un·co (ung′kō), *Scot.* —*adv.* remarkably; very; extremely. —*adj.* **1.** strange. **2.** remarkable. **3.** uncanny. [ult. var. of *uncouth*]

un·coil (un-koil′), *v.* unwind.

un·com·fort·a·ble (un-kumf′tə-bəl; -kum′-fər-tə-bəl), *adj.* **1.** not comfortable. **2.** uneasy. **3.** disagreeable; causing discomfort. —**un·com′-fort·a·ble·ness**, *n.* —**un·com′fort·a·bly**, *adv.*

un·com·mon (un-kom′ən), *adj.* **1.** rare; unusual. **2.** unusual in amount or degree. **3.** remarkable. —**un·com′mon·ly**, *adv.* —**un·com′-mon·ness**, *n.*

un·com·mu·ni·ca·tive (un′kə-mū′nə-kā′tiv; -kə·tiv), *adj.* not giving out any information, opinions, etc.; talking little; silent. —**un′com·mu′ni·ca′tive·ly**, *adv.* —**un′com·mu′ni·ca′tive·ness**, *n.* —Syn. reserved, reticent, taciturn.

un·com·pro·mis·ing (un·kom′prə-mīz′ing), *adj.* unyielding; firm. —**un·com′pro·mis′ing·ly**, *adv.*

un·con·cern (un′kən-sėrn′), *n.* lack of concern or interest; freedom from care or anxiety.

un·con·cerned (un′kən-sėrnd′), *adj.* not concerned; not interested; free from care or anxiety; indifferent. —**un·con·cern·ed·ly** (un′kən-sėr′nid-li), *adv.* —**un′con·cern′ed·ness**, *n.* —Syn. nonchalant, cool, apathetic.

un·con·di·tion·al (un′kən-dish′ən-əl; -dish′-nəl), *adj.* without conditions; absolute. —**un′-con·di′tion·al·ly**, *adv.* —**un′con·di′tion·al·ness**, *n.* —Syn. unqualified, unrestricted.

un·con·di·tioned (un′kən-dish′ənd), *adj.* **1.** without conditions; absolute. **2.** not learned; instinctive.

un·con·form·i·ty (un′kən-fôr′mə·ti), *n., pl.* **-ties. 1.** lack of agreement. **2.** a being inconsistent.

un·con·quer·a·ble (un-kong′kər-ə-bəl), *adj.* that cannot be conquered. —**un·con′quer·a·ble·ness**, *n.* —**un·con′quer·a·bly**, *adv.* —Syn. invincible, indomitable, insuperable.

un·con·scion·a·ble (un-kon′shən-ə-bəl), *adj.* **1.** not influenced or guided by conscience. **2.** unreasonable; very great. —**un·con′scion·a·ble·ness**, *n.* —**un·con′scion·a·bly**, *adv.*

un·con·scious (un-kon′shəs), *adj.* **1.** not conscious. **2.** not aware. **3.** not meant; not intended: *unconscious neglect.* —*n.* the unconscious, one's unconscious thoughts, desires, fears, etc. —**un·con′scious·ly**, *adv.* —**un·con′scious·ness**, *n.* —Syn. *adj.* **2.** oblivious, heedless, unmindful.

un·con·sti·tu·tion·al (un′kon-stə-tū′shən-əl; -tū′-), *adj.* contrary to the constitution. —**un′con·sti·tu′tion·al·i·ty**, *n.* —**un′con·sti·tu′tion·al·ly**, *adv.*

un·con·ven·tion·al (un′kən-ven′shən-əl; -vensh′nəl), *adj.* not bound by or conforming to

āge, cāre, fär; ēqual, tėrm; īce; ōpen, ôrder; put, rüle, ūse; tʰ, then; ə=a in about.

convention, rule, or precedent. —**un'con·ven'-tion·al'i·ty,** n. —**un'con·ven'tion·al·ly,** adv.

un·cork (un-kôrk'), v. pull the cork from.

un·count·ed (un-koun'tid), adj. **1.** not counted; not reckoned. **2.** very many; innumerable.

un·cou·ple (un-kup'əl), v., -pled, -pling. disconnect; unfasten.

un·couth (un-küth'), adj. **1.** awkward; clumsy; crude. **2.** strange and unpleasant. **3.** uncanny. [OE uncūth < un-¹ + cūth, pp. of cunnan know] —**un·couth'ly,** adv. —**un·couth'ness,** n.

un·cov·er (un-kuv'ər), v. **1.** remove the cover from. **2.** make known; reveal; expose. **3.** remove the hat, cap, etc., of. **4.** remove one's hat or cap in respect.

unc·tion (ungk'shən), n. **1.** an anointing with oil, ointment, or the like, for medical purposes or as a religious rite. **2.** the oil, ointment, or the like, used for anointing. **3.** something soothing or comforting: the unction of flattery. **4.** a soothing, sympathetic, and persuasive quality in speaking. **5.** fervor; earnestness. **6.** affected earnestness. [< L unctio < unguere anoint]

unc·tu·ous (ungk'chü-əs), adj. **1.** like an oil or ointment; oily; greasy. **2.** soothing, sympathetic, and persuasive. **3.** too smooth and oily: the salesman's unctuous manner. [< Med.L unctuosus, ult. < L unguere anoint] —**unc'tu·ous·ly,** adv. —**unc'tu·ous·ness,** n.

un·curl (un-kėrl'), v. straighten out.

un·daunt·ed (un-dôn'tid; -dän'-), adj. not afraid; not discouraged; fearless. —**un·daunt'ed·ly,** adv. —**un·daunt'ed·ness,** n.

un·de·ceive (un'di-sēv'), v., -ceived, -ceiving. free from error, mistake, or deception.

un·de·cid·ed (un'di-sīd'id), adj. **1.** not decided or settled. **2.** not having one's mind made up. —**un'de·cid'ed·ly,** adv. —**un'de·cid'ed·ness,** n. —Syn. **2.** irresolute, wavering.

un·de·fined (un'di-fīnd'), adj. **1.** not defined or explained. **2.** indefinite.

un·de·ni·a·ble (un'di·nī'ə·bəl), adj. **1.** not to be denied. **2.** unquestionably good; excellent. —**un'de·ni'a·ble·ness,** n. —**un'de·ni'a·bly,** adv.

un·de·nom·i·na·tion·al (un'di·nom'ə·nā'-shən·əl; -nāsh'nəl), adj. not connected with any particular religious sect.

un·der (un'dər), prep. **1.** below; beneath: under the table. **2.** below the surface of: under the ground. **3.** lower than; lower down than; not so high as: hit under the belt. **4.** less than: it will cost under ten dollars. **5.** lower in rank, dignity, etc.: a corporal is under a sergeant. **6.** during the rule, time, influence, etc., of: England under the four Georges. **7.** subject to the direction or guidance of: work under a famous scientist. **8.** in the position or condition of being affected by: under the new rules. **9.** with the favor or aid of: under protection. **10.** because of: under the circumstances. **11.** according to: under the law. **12.** represented by: under a new name. **13.** required or bound by: under obligation. **14.** in the class of: that book belongs under "Fiction." —adv. **1.** below or beneath something. **2.** below the surface: the swimmer went under. **3.** in or to a lower place or condition. —adj. lower in position, rank, degree, amount, price, etc.: the under layer. [OE]

under–, prefix. **1.** on the underside; to a lower position; from a lower position; below; beneath, as in:

underarch, v., n.
underarm, adj.
undercurve, v., n.
underdig, v.
underflow, v., n.
underlay, v., n.
undermentioned, adj.
underpin, v.
underpoint, n.

underprop, v.
underrun, v., n.
undersaw, v.
underspecified, adj.
undersupport, v., n.
underswell, v., n.
undervaulted, adj.
undervaulting, v.
underwash, v., n.

2. being beneath, worn beneath, as in:

underbeam, n.
underbed, n.
underbodice, n.
underbud, n.
undercloak, n.
underconsciousness, n.
undercrust, n.
underdrawers, n.
underface, n.
underfeathering, n.
underfeathers, n.
underflame, n.
underflannel, n.
underflooring, n.
underfrock, n.
underfur, n.

underjacket, n.
underpetticoat, n.
underseam, n.
undershield, n.
undershoe, n.
underskin, n.
underskirt, n.
undersleeve, n.
undersoil, n.
understem, n.
understrife, n.
undersuit, n.
undervalve, n.
undervest, n.
underwaist, n.
underwrap, n.

3. lower, as in:

underbelly, n.
underbranch, n.
underbridge, n.
undercellar, n.
underchamber, n.
underfloor, n.
underlife, n.
underlip, n.

underporch, n.
underregion, n.
underroom, n.
undersole, n.
underspring, n.
understratum, n.
understream, n.
undersurface, n.

4. lower in rank; subordinate, as in:

underadmiral, n.
underagent, n.
underbishop, n.
underbutler, n.
underchancellor, n.
underclerk, n.
underdeacon, n.
underfaculty, n.
underfeature, n.
underfootman, n.
undergeneral, n.
undergod, n.
underlieutenant, n.
undermaster, n.

underofficer, n.
underofficial, n.
underplan, n.
underplot, n.
underporter, n.
underpriest, n.
underservant, n.
undersheriff, n.
understeward, n.
underteacher, n.
undertenant, n.
undertutor, n.
underwarden, n.

5. not enough; insufficiently, as in:

underarmed, adj.
underbake, v.
underbred, adj.
undercapitalize, v.
underclad, adj.
underclothed, adj.
undercooked, adj.
underdevelop, v.
underdeveloped, adj.
underdone, adj.
underdressed, adj.
undereducated, adj.
underheat, v.
undernourish, v.

undernourishment, n.
underofficered, adj.
underpaid, adj.
underpopulate, v.
underproduce, v.
underrate, v.
underrigged, adj.
underripe, adj.
undersized, adj.
undersleep, v.
understress, v., n.
undersupply, v., n.
undertaxed, adj.
undertrained, adj.

6. below normal, as in:

underadjustment, n.
underconsumption, n.
underdevelopment, n.

underparticipation, n.
underpopulation, n.
underproduction, n.

un'con·vert'ed
un'con·vinced'
un'con·vinc'ing
un·cooked'
un·cooled'
un'co·ör'di·nat'ed
un·cor'dial
un·corked'
un'cor·rect'ed
un'cor·re·lat'ed
un'cor·rob'o·rat'ed
un'cor·rupt'ed
un·count'a·ble
un·court'ly
un'cre·at'ed

un·crit'i·cal
un·crit'i·ciz'a·ble
un·crowd'ed
un·crowned'
un·cul'ti·va·ble
un·cul'ti·vat'ed
un·cul'tured
un·curbed'
un·cured'
un·curled'
un'cur'rent
un'cur·tailed'
un'cur'tained
un·cut'
un·dam'aged

un·damped'
un·dat'ed
un·daugh'ter·ly
un·daz'zled
un'de·bat'a·ble
un'de·cayed'
un'de·ceiv'a·ble
un'de·ceived'
un'de·ci'pher·a·ble
un'de·ci'phered
un'de·clared'
un'de·clin'a·ble
un'de·clined'
un·dec'o·rat'ed
un'de·feat'a·ble

un'de·feat'ed
un'de·fend'ed
un'de·fen'si·ble
un'de·filed'
un'de·fin'a·ble
un'de·formed'
un'de·layed'
un'de·liv'ered
un·dem'o·crat'ic
un·dem'o·crat'i·cal·ly
un·de·mon'stra·ble
un·de·mon'stra·tive
un·de·nied'
un'de·pend'a·ble
un'de·pre'ci·at'ed

un·der·age (un′dər·āj′), *adj.* not of full age; of less than the usual age.

un·der·bid (un′dər·bid′), *v.*, –bid, –bid·ding. make a lower bid than. —**un′der·bid′der**, *n.*

un·der·brush (un′dər·brush′), *n. Am.* bushes, small trees, etc., growing under large trees in woods or forests.

un·der·charge (un′dər·chärj′), *v.*, –charged, –charg·ing. 1. charge (persons) less than the proper or fair price. 2. charge (so much) less than a proper price.

un·der·class·man (un′dər·klas′mən;–kläs′–), *n., pl.* –men. *Am.* freshman or sophomore.

un·der·clothes (un′dər·klōz′; –klōṭẖz′), *n.pl.* clothes worn under a suit or dress.

un·der·cov·er (un′dər·kuv′ər), *adj.* working or done in secret; secret.

un·der·cur·rent (un′dər·kėr′ənt), *n.* 1. current below the upper currents, or below the surface, of a body of water, air, etc. 2. an underlying tendency.

un·der·cut (un′dər·kut′), *v.*, –cut, –cut·ting. 1. cut under or beneath; cut away material from so as to leave a portion overhanging. 2. sell or work for less than (some other person).

un·der·dog (un′dər·dôg′; –dog′), *n. Am.* dog or person having the worst of an encounter.

un·der·es·ti·mate (*v.* un′dər·es′tə·māt; *n.* un′dər·es′tə·mit, –māt), *v.*, –mat·ed, –mat·ing, *n.* —*v.* estimate at too low a value, amount, rate, or the like. —*n.* an estimate that is too low. —**un′der·es′ti·ma′tion**, *n.*

un·der·ex·pose (un′dər·iks·pōz′), *v.*, –posed, –pos·ing. expose to light for too short a time. —**un·der·ex·po·sure** (un′dər·iks·pō′zhər), *n.*

un·der·feed (un′dər·fēd′), *v.*, –fed, –feed·ing. feed too little.

un·der·foot (un′dər·fût′), *adv.* 1. under one's foot or feet; underneath. 2. *Am.* in the way.

un·der·gar·ment (un′dər·gär′mənt), *n.* garment worn under a dress or suit.

un·der·go (un′dər·gō′), *v.*, –went, –gone, –go·ing. 1. go through; pass through; be subjected to. 2. endure; suffer.

un·der·grad·u·ate (un′dər·graj′ù·it), *n.* a student in a school, college, or university who has not received a degree for a course of study.

un·der·ground (*adv., adj.* un′dər·ground′; *n.* un′dər·ground′), *adv., adj.* 1. beneath the surface of the ground. 2. in or into secrecy or concealment. —*adj.* 1. being, working, or used beneath the surface of the ground. 2. secret. 3. resisting (tyrannical government, etc.) secretly. —*n.* 1. place or space beneath the surface of the ground. 2. *Esp. Brit.* an underground railroad; subway. 3. a secret organization, or grouping of such organizations, working to free a country from foreign domination or an autocratic régime.

underground railroad, *Am.* 1. railroad running below the surface of the earth. 2. a secret method of assisting the escape of fugitives.

un·der·growth (un′dər·grōth′), *n.* underbrush.

un·der·hand (un′dər·hand′), *adj.* Also, **un′der·hand′ed.** 1. not open or honest; secret; sly. 2. with the hand below the shoulder. —*adv.* 1. secretly; slyly. 2. with the hand below the shoulder: *pitch underhand.* —**un′der·hand′·ed·ly,** *adv.* —**un′der·hand′ed·ness,** *n.*

un·der·lie (un′dər·lī′), *v.*, –lay, –lain, –ly·ing. 1. lie under; be beneath. 2. be at the basis of; form the foundation of.

un·der·line (un′dər·līn′; un′dər·līn′), *v.*, –lined, –lin·ing. draw a line or lines under.

un·der·ling (un′dər·ling), *n.* usually disparagingly, a person of lower rank or position.

un·der·ly·ing (un′dər·lī′ing), *adj.* 1. lying under or beneath. 2. fundamental; basic; essential. —*v.* ppr. of **underlie.**

un·der·mine (un′dər·mīn′; un′dər·mīn′), *v.*, –mined, –min·ing. 1. make a passage or hole under; dig under. 2. wear away the foundations of. 3. weaken by secret or unfair means. 4. weaken or destroy gradually. —**un′der·min′er,** *n.*

un·der·neath (un′dər·nēth′), *prep.* beneath;

below: *sit underneath a tree, a cellar underneath a house.* —*adv.* beneath or below something: *someone was pushing underneath.* —*n.* the lower part or surface.

un·der·nour·ished (un′dər·nėr′isht), *adj.* not sufficiently nourished.

un·der·pass (un′dər·pas′; –päs′), *n. Am.* path underneath; road under railroad tracks or under another road.

un·der·pay (un′dər·pā′), *v.*, –paid, –pay·ing. pay too little.

un·der·pin·ning (un′dər·pin′ing), *n.* 1. the supports under a building. 2. a new foundation beneath a wall. 3. a support.

un·der·priv·i·leged (un′dər·priv′ə·lijd), *adj.* having fewer advantages than most people have, esp. because of poor economic or social status.

un·der·score (*v.* un′dər·skōr′, –skôr′; *n.* un′dər·skōr′, –skôr′), *v.*, –scored, –scor·ing, *n.* —*v.* underline. —*n.* an underscored line.

un·der·sea (*adj.* un′dər·sē′; *adv.* un′dər·sē′), *adj.* being, working, or used beneath the surface of the sea. —*adv.* Also, **underseas.** beneath or surface of the sea.

un·der·sec·re·tar·y (un′dər·sek′rə·ter′i), *n., pl.* –tar·ies. an assistant secretary, esp. of a government department. —**un′der·sec′re·tar′y·ship,** *n.*

un·der·sell (un′dər·sel′), *v.*, –sold, –sell·ing. sell things at a lower price than.

un·der·shirt (un′dər·shėrt′), *n.* shirt worn next to the skin under other clothing.

un·der·shot (un′dər·shot′), *adj.* 1. having the lower jaw projecting beyond the upper. 2. driven by water passing beneath.

un·der·side (un′dər·sīd′), *n.* the bottom side.

un·der·sign (un′dər·sīn′; un′dər·sīn′), *v.* sign one's name at the end of (a letter or document).

un·der·signed (un′dər·sīnd′), *n.* the undersigned, the person or persons signing a letter or document.

un·der·slung (un′dər·slung′; un′dər·slung′), *adj.* of vehicles, having the frame below the axles.

un·der·stand (un′dər·stand′), *v.*, –stood, –stand·ing. 1. get the meaning of: *now I understand the teacher's words.* 2. get the meaning: *people often listen but do not understand.* 3. grasp by the mind; comprehend; realize: *understand the nature of electricity.* 4. know how to deal with; know well; know: *a good teacher should understand children.* 5. be informed; learn: *I understand that he is leaving town.* 6. take as a fact; believe: *it is understood that you will come.* 7. take as meaning; take as meant: *what are we to understand from his words?* 8. *Gram.* supply in the mind. In "He hit the tree harder than I," the word *did* is understood after *I.* 9. understand each other, a. know each other's meaning and wishes. b. agree.

un·der·stand·a·ble (un′dər·stan′də·bəl), *adj.* able to be understood. —**un′der·stand′a·bil′i·ty,** *n.* —**un′der·stand′a·bly,** *adv.*

un·der·stand·ing (un′dər·stan′ding), *n.* 1. act of one that understands; comprehension; knowledge. 2. ability to learn and know; intelligence. 3. knowledge of each other's meaning and wishes: *come to an understanding.* —*adj.* that understands; intelligent. —**un′der·stand′·ing·ly,** *adv.*

un·der·state (un′dər·stāt′), *v.*, –stat·ed, –stat·ing. 1. state too weakly. 2. say less than the full truth about. —**un′der·state′ment,** *n.*

un·der·stud·y (un′dər·stud′i), *v.*, –stud·ied, –stud·y·ing, *n., pl.* –stud·ies. —*v.* learn (a part) in order to replace the regular performer when necessary. —*n.* person who can act as a substitute for an actor or actress.

un·der·take (un′dər·tāk′), *v.*, –took, –tak·en, –tak·ing. 1. set about; try; attempt. 2. agree to do; take upon oneself. 3. promise; guarantee.

un·der·tak·er (un′dər·tāk′ər *for 1;* un′dər·tāk′ər *for 2*), *n.* 1. person who undertakes something. 2. person whose business is preparing the dead for burial and taking charge of funerals.

un·der·tak·ing (un'dər·tāk'ing for 1 and 2; un'dər·tāk'ing for 3), n. **1.** something undertaken; task; enterprise. **2.** promise; guarantee. **3.** business of preparing the dead for burial and taking charge of funerals.

un·der·tone (un'dər·tōn'), n. **1.** a low or very quiet tone: talk in undertones. **2.** a subdued color; color seen through other colors. **3.** an underlying quality, condition, or element.

un·der·tow (un'dər·tō'), n. **1.** any strong current below the surface, moving in a direction different from that of the surface current. **2.** the backward flow from waves breaking on a beach.

un·der·val·ue (un'dər·val'ū), v., -ued, -u·ing. put too low a value on. —**un·der·val·u·a·tion** (un'dər·val'yū·ā'shən), n. —**Syn.** underrate, underestimate, depreciate.

un·der·wa·ter (un'dər·wô'tər; -wot'ər), adj. **1.** below the surface of the water. **2.** made for use under the water.

un·der·wear (un'dər·wâr'), n. clothing worn under one's outer clothes.

un·der·weight (adj. un'dər·wāt'; n. un'dər·wāt'), adj. having too little weight. —n. weight that is not up to standard.

un·der·went (un'dər·went'), v. pt. of undergo.

un·der·wood (un'dər·wud'), n. underbrush.

un·der·world (un'dər·wėrld'), n. **1.** the lower, degraded, or criminal part of human society. **2.** the lower world; Hades.

un·der·write (un'dər·rīt'; un'dər·rīt'), v., -wrote, -writ·ten, -writ·ing. **1.** sign (an insurance policy), thereby accepting the risk of insuring something against loss. **2.** insure (property) against loss. **3.** agree to buy (all the stocks or bonds of a certain issue that are not bought by the public). **4.** agree to meet the expense of. —un'der·writ'er, n.

un·de·sir·a·ble (un'di·zīr'ə·bəl), adj. objectionable; disagreeable. —n. an undesirable person or thing.

un·dis·ci·plined (un·dis'ə·plind), adj. not disciplined; without proper control; untrained. —Syn. wild, uncontrolled.

un·do (un·dü'), v., -did, -done, -do·ing. **1.** unfasten; untie. **2.** do away with; cause to be as if never done; spoil; destroy. **3.** bring to ruin. **4.** explain; solve. —un·do'er, n. —Syn. **1.** unloose.

un·do·ing (un·dü'ing), n. **1.** a doing away with; spoiling; destroying. **2.** cause of destruction or ruin.

un·doubt·ed (un·dout'id), adj. not doubted; accepted as true. —un·doubt'ed·ly, adv.

un·draw (un·drô'), v., -drew, -drawn, -draw·ing. draw back or away.

un·dress (v. un·dres'; n., adj. un'dres'), v. **1.**

take the clothes off; strip. **2.** take off one's clothes. —n. **1.** loose informal dress. **2.** ordinary clothes. —adj. of or pertaining to informal or ordinary clothes.

un·due (un·dü'; -dū'), adj. **1.** not fitting; not right; improper. **2.** too great; too much. **3.** not yet owing or payable. —Syn. **2.** excessive.

un·du·lant (un'dyə·lənt), adj. waving; wavy. —un'du·lan·cy, n.

un·du·late (v. un'dyə·lāt; adj. un'dyə·lit, -lāt), v., -lat·ed, -lat·ing, adj. —v. **1.** move in waves. **2.** have a wavy form or surface. —adj. having a waved form, surface, or margin; wavy. [< L undulatus diversified as with waves < unda wave] —un'du·lat'ing·ly, adv. —un'du·la'tion, n. —un·du·la·to·ry (un'dyə·lə·tô'ri; -tō'-), adj.

un·du·ly (un·dü'li; -dū'-), adv. **1.** improperly. **2.** excessively.

un·dy·ing (un·dī'ing), adj. deathless; immortal; eternal. —un·dy'ing·ly, adv. —un·dy'ing·ness, n.

un·earth (un·ėrth'), v. **1.** dig up. **2.** find out; discover: unearth a plot.

un·earth·ly (un·ėrth'li), adj. **1.** supernatural. **2.** strange; weird. **3.** Colloq. unnatural; extraordinary; preposterous. —un·earth'li·ness, n.

un·eas·y (un·ēz'i), adj., -eas·i·er, -eas·i·est. **1.** restless; disturbed; anxious. **2.** not comfortable. **3.** not easy in manner; awkward. —un·eas'i·ly, adv. —un·eas'i·ness, n.

un·em·ploy·a·ble (un'em·ploi'ə·bəl), adj. **1.** that cannot be employed. **2.** not fit to work.

un·em·ployed (un'em·ploid'), adj. not employed; not in use; having no work. —n. **the** unemployed, people out of work.

un·em·ploy·ment (un'em·ploi'mənt), n. lack of employment; being out of work.

un·e·qual (un·ē'kwəl), adj. **1.** not the same in amount, size, number, value, merit, rank, etc. **2.** not balanced; not well matched. **3.** not fair; one-sided: an unequal contest. **4.** not enough; not adequate: unequal to the task. **5.** not regular; not even; variable. —un·e'qual·ly, adv. —un·e'qual·ness, n.

un·e·qualed, esp. Brit. **un·e·qualled** (un·ē'kwəld), adj. not equaled; matchless.

un·e·quiv·o·cal (un'i·kwiv'ə·kəl), adj. clear; plain. —un'e·quiv'o·cal·ly, adv. —un'e·quiv'o·cal·ness, n.

un·err·ing (un·ėr'ing; -er'-), adj. making no mistakes; exactly right. —un·err'ing·ly, adv. —un·err'ing·ness, n. —Syn. infallible, certain.

U·NES·CO, U·nes·co, or **U.N.E.S.C.O.** (ū·nes'kō), n. the United Nations Educational, Scientific, and Cultural Organization, an independent organization related to and recognized by the UN as one of its specialized agencies.

---

un'de·scrib'a·ble
un'de·served'
un'de·serv'ing
un·des'ig·nat'ed
un'de·sign'ing
un'de·sired'
un'de·spair'ing
un'de·stroyed'
un'de·tach'a·ble
un'de·tect'ed
un'de·ter'mi·na·ble
un'de·ter'mined
un'de·terred'
un·de'vel·oped
un·de'vi·at'ing
un'di·ag·nosed'
un'dif·fer·en'ti·at'ed
un'di·gest'ed
un·dig'ni·fied
un·di·lut'ed
un'di·min'ished
un'di·min'ish·ing
un·dimmed'
un'dip·lo·mat'ic
un·di·rect'ed
un'dis·cerned'
un'dis·cern'i·ble
un'dis·cern'ing
un'dis·charged'
un'dis·closed'
un'dis·cour'aged

un'dis·cov'er·a·ble
un'dis·cov'ered
un'dis·crim'i·nat'ing
un·dis'guised'
un'dis·guis'ed·ly
un'dis·mayed'
un'dis·posed'
un·dis'put·ed
un'dis·so'ci·at'ed
un'dis·solved'
un·dis'tilled'
un'dis·tin'guish·a·ble
un'dis·tin'guished
un'dis·tin'guish·ing
un'dis·tort'ed
un'dis·tract'ed
un'dis·trib'ut·ed
un'dis·turbed'
un'di·ver'si·fied
un'di·vid'ed
un'di·vulged'
un'do·mes'tic
un'do·mes'ti·cat'ed
un·dom'i·nat'ed
un·dou'bled
un·doubt'ing
un·drained'
un·drape'
un·draped'
un·dreamed'

un·dream'ing
un·dreamt'
un·dressed'
un·dried'
un·drilled'
un·drink'a·ble
un·dumped'
un·du'ti·ful
un·dyed'
un·earned'
un·eat'a·ble
un·eat'en
un·e·clipsed'
un'e·co·nom'ic
un'e·co·nom'i·cal
un·ed'i·fied
un·ed'i·fy'ing
un·ed'u·ca·ble
un·ed'u·cat'ed
un·ef·faced'
un·e·lat'ed
un'e·lec'tri·fied
un·elf·e·vat'ed
un'e·lim'i·nat'ed
un'e·man'ci·pat'ed
un'em·balmed'
un'em·bar'rassed
un'em·bel'lished
un'em·brace'a·ble
un'e·mend'a·ble
un'e·mend'ed

un'e·mo'tion·al
un·em·phat'ic
un'en·closed'
un'en·coun'tered
un'en·cour'aged
un'en·cum'bered
un'en·dan'gered
un·end'ing
un·en·dorsed'
un·en·dur'a·ble
un·en·dur'ing
un·en·force'a·ble
un·en·forced'
un·en·gaged'
un·en·hanced'
un·en·joy'a·ble
un'en·light'ened
un·en·rolled'
un·en'ter·pris'ing
un'en·ter·tain'ing
un'en·thu'si·as'tic
un·en'vi·a·ble
un·en'vied
un·e·quipped'
un'e·rect'ed
un·es·cap'a·ble
un·es·sen'tial
un·es·teemed'
un·es'ti·mat'ed
un·eth'i·cal
un'e·val'u·at'ed

un·e·ven (un·ē′vən), *adj.* **1.** not level: *uneven ground.* **2.** not equal: *an uneven contest.* **3.** of a number, that cannot be divided by 2 without a remainder. —un·e′ven·ly, *adv.* —un·e′ven·ness, *n.* —Syn. 1. rough, rugged, jagged.

un·e·vent·ful (un′i·vent′fəl), *adj.* without important or striking occurrences. —un′e·vent′ful·ly, *adv.* —un′e·vent′ful·ness, *n.*

un·ex·am·pled (un′ig·zam′pəld; -zäm′-), *adj.* having no equal or like; without precedent or parallel; without anything like it.

un·ex·cep·tion·a·ble (un′ik·sep′shən·ə·bəl), *adj.* beyond criticism; wholly admirable. —un′·ex·cep′tion·a·ble·ness, *n.* —un′ex·cep′tion·a·bly, *adv.*

un·ex·cep·tion·al (un′ik·sep′shən·əl), *adj.* **1.** ordinary. **2.** admitting of no exception. —un′·ex·cep′tion·al·ly, *adv.*

un·ex·pect·ed (un′iks·pek′tid), *adj.* not expected. —un′ex·pect′ed·ly, *adv.* —un′ex·pect′·ed·ness, *n.* —Syn. unforeseen, unanticipated.

un·fail·ing (un·fāl′ing), *adj.* **1.** never failing; tireless; loyal. **2.** never running short; endless. **3.** sure; certain. —un·fail′ing·ly, *adv.* —un·fail′ing·ness, *n.*

un·fair (un·fār′), *adj.* not honest; unjust. —un·fair′ly, *adv.* —un·fair′ness, *n.* —Syn. partial, prejudiced, biased, one-sided.

un·faith·ful (un·fāth′fəl), *adj.* **1.** not faithful; not true to duty or one's promises; faithless. **2.** not accurate; not exact. **3.** guilty of adultery. —un·faith′ful·ly, *adv.* —un·faith′ful·ness, *n.* —Syn. 1. false, disloyal, inconstant.

un·fa·mil·iar (un′fə·mil′yər), *adj.* **1.** not well known; unusual; strange. **2.** not acquainted. —un·fa·mil·i·ar·i·ty (un′fə·mil′i·ar′ə·ti), *n.* —un′fa·mil′iar·ly, *adv.*

un·fas·ten (un·fas′ən; -fäs′-), *v.* undo; loose; open.

un·fa·vor·a·ble, *esp. Brit.* **un·fa·vour·a·ble** (un·fā′vər·ə·bəl; -fāv′rə-), *adj.* not favorable; adverse; harmful. —un·fa′vor·a·ble·ness, *esp. Brit.* un·fa′vour·a·ble·ness, *n.* —un·fa′vor·a·bly, *esp. Brit.* un·fa′vour·a·bly, *adv.*

un·feel·ing (un·fēl′ing), *adj.* **1.** hard-hearted; cruel. **2.** not able to feel. —un·feel′ing·ly, *adv.* —un·feel′ing·ness, *n.* —Syn. 1. unsympathetic.

un·feigned (un·fānd′), *adj.* sincere; real. —un·feign·ed·ly (un·fān′id·li), *adv.* —un·feign′ed·ness, *n.* —Syn. unaffected, genuine.

un·fin·ished (un·fin′isht), *adj.* **1.** not finished; not complete. **2.** without some special finish; not polished; rough.

un·fit (un·fit′), *adj., n., v.,* -fit·ted, -fit·ting. —*adj.* **1.** not fit; not suitable. **2.** not good enough; unqualified. **3.** not adapted. —*n.* the unfit, those who are unfit. —*v.* make unfit; spoil. —un·fit′ly, *adv.* —un·fit′ness, *n.* —Syn. 1. improper.

un·fix (un·fiks′), *v.* loosen; unfasten.

un·flag·ging (un·flag′ing), *adj.* not drooping or failing. —un·flag′ging·ly, *adv.*

un·fledged (un·flejd′), *adj.* **1.** too young to fly. **2.** undeveloped; immature.

un·flinch·ing (un·flin′ching), *adj.* not drawing back from difficulty, danger, or pain; firm; resolute. —un·flinch′ing·ly, *adv.*

un·fold (un·fōld′), *v.* **1.** open the folds of; spread out. **2.** reveal; show; explain. **3.** open; develop. —un·fold′er, *n.*

un·fore·seen (un′fōr·sēn′; -fōr-), *adj.* not known beforehand; unexpected.

un·for·get·ta·ble (un′fər·get′ə·bəl), *adj.* that can never be forgotten. —un′for·get′ta·bly, *adv.*

un·for·tu·nate (un·fôr′chə·nit), *adj.* **1.** not lucky; having bad luck. **2.** not suitable; not fitting. —*n.* an unfortunate person. —un·for′tu·nate·ly, *adv.* —un·for′tu·nate·ness, *n.*

un·found·ed (un·foun′did), *adj.* without foundation; baseless. —un·found′ed·ly, *adv.* —un·found′ed·ness, *n.*

un·fre·quent·ed (un′fri·kwen′tid), *adj.* not frequented; seldom visited; rarely used.

un·friend·ly (un·frend′li), *adj.* **1.** not friendly; hostile. **2.** not favorable. —*adv.* in an unfriendly manner. —un·friend′li·ness, *n.*

un·frock (un·frok′), *v.* deprive (a priest or minister) of his office.

un·furl (un·fėrl′), *v.* spread out; shake out; unfold: *unfurl a sail.*

un·gain·ly (un·gān′li), *adj.* awkward; clumsy. —un·gain′li·ness, *n.* —Syn. uncouth, ungraceful.

un·god·ly (un·god′li), *adj.* **1.** not religious; wicked; sinful. **2.** *Colloq.* very annoying; shocking. —un·god′li·ness, *n.*

un·gov·ern·a·ble (un·guv′ər·nə·bəl), *adj.* impossible to control; very hard to control or rule; unruly. —un·gov′ern·a·ble·ness, *n.* —un·gov′·ern·a·bly, *adv.*

un·grace·ful (un·grās′fəl), *adj.* not graceful; clumsy; awkward. —un·grace′ful·ly, *adv.* —un·grace′ful·ness, *n.*

un·gra·cious (un·grā′shəs), *adj.* **1.** not polite; rude. **2.** unpleasant; disagreeable. —un·gra′cious·ly, *adv.* —un·gra′cious·ness, *n.*

un·grate·ful (un·grāt′fəl), *adj.* **1.** not grateful; not thankful. **2.** unpleasant; disagreeable. —un·grate′ful·ly, *adv.* —un·grate′ful·ness, *n.*

un·ground·ed (un·groun′did), *adj.* without foundation; without reasons.

un·guard·ed (un·gär′did), *adj.* **1.** not protected. **2.** careless. —un·guard′ed·ly, *adv.* —un·guard′ed·ness, *n.*

un·guent (ung′gwənt), *n.* ointment for sores, burns, etc.; salve. [< L *unguentum* < *unguere* anoint] —un·guen·tar·y (ung′gwən·ter′i), *adj.*

un·gu·la (ung′gyə·lə), *n., pl.* -lae (-lē). **1.** hoof. **2.** nail; claw. **3.** the claw-shaped base of a petal. [< L, dim. of *unguis* nail, hoof] —un′gu·lar, *adj.*

un·gu·late (ung′gyə·lit; -lāt), *adj.* having hoofs; belonging to the group of animals having hoofs. —*n.* animal that has hoofs.

un′e·vict′ed | un·fad′ing | un·fit′ting | un·fur′nished
un′ex·ag′ger·at′ed | un·fal′ter·ing | un·fixed′ | un·gained′
un′ex·am′ined | un·fash′ion·a·ble | un·flat′tened | un·gal′lant
un′ex·celled′ | un·fash′ioned | un·flat′ter·ing | un·gar′nished
un′ex·change′a·ble | un·fas′tened | un·fla′vored | un·gath′ered
un′ex·cit′ing | un·fath′om·a·ble | un·flus′tered | un·gen′er·ous
un′ex·cused′ | un·fath′omed | un·forced′ | un·gen′er·ous·ly
un′ex·e·cut′ed | un·feared′ | un′fore·see′a·ble | un·gen′tle
un′ex·ert′ed | un·fear′ing | un·for·est′ed | un·gen′tle·man·ly
un′ex·haust′ed | un·fea′si·ble | un′for·get′ting | un·gift′ed
un′ex·pend′ed | un·feath′ered | un′for·giv′a·ble | un·gird′led
un′ex·pe′ri·enced | un·fed′ | un′for·giv′en | un·glazed′
un′ex·pired′ | un·fed′er·at′ed | un′for·giv′ing | un·glo′ri·fied
un′ex·plain′a·ble | un·felt′ | un′for·got′ten | un·gloved′
un′ex·plained′ | un·fem′i·nine | un·formed′ | un·gov′erned
un′ex·plod′ed | un·fenced′ | un·for′mu·lat′ed | un·grad′ed
un′ex·ploit′ed | un·fer·ment′ed | un·for′ti·fied | un′gram·mat′i·cal
un′ex·plored′ | un·fer′ti·lized | un·framed′ | un·grat′i·fied
un′ex·pressed′ | un·fet′tered | un·free′ | un·grouped′
un′ex·pres′sive | un·filed′ | un·freed′ | un·grudg′ing
un·ex′pur·gat′ed | un·fil′i·al | un·fre′quent | un·grudg′ing·ly
un′ex·tend′ed | un·filled′ | un·fre′quent·ly | un′guar·an·teed′
un′ex·tin′guished | un·fil′tered | un·fruit′ful | un·guess′a·ble
un·fad′ed | un·fired′ | un·ful·filled′ | un·guid′ed

un·hal·lowed (un·hal′ōd), *adj.* **1.** not made holy; not sacred. **2.** wicked.

un·hand (un·hand′), *v.* let go; take the hands from.

un·hand·y (un·han′di), *adj.* **1.** not easy to handle or manage. **2.** not skillful in using the hands. —**un·hand′i·ly**, *adv.* —**un·hand′i·ness**, *n.*

un·hap·py (un·hap′i), *adj.*, **-pi·er, -pi·est. 1.** sad; sorrowful. **2.** unlucky. **3.** not suitable. —**un·hap′pi·ly**, *adv.* —**un·hap′pi·ness**, *n.*

un·har·ness (un·här′nis), *v.* **1.** remove harness from (a horse, etc.); free from harness or gear. **2.** remove harness or gear. **3.** divest of armor.

un·health·ful (un·helth′fəl), *adj.* bad for the health. —**un·health′ful·ly**, *adv.* —**un·health′ful·ness**, *n.*

un·health·y (un·hel′thi), *adj.* **1.** not possessing good health; not well: *an unhealthy child.* **2.** characteristic of or resulting from poor health: *an unhealthy paleness.* **3.** hurtful to health; unwholesome: *an unhealthy climate.* **4.** morally harmful. —**un·health′i·ly**, *adv.* —**un·health′i·ness**, *n.* —**Syn. 1.** sickly, frail, ill, diseased. **3.** unsanitary, unhygienic.

un·heard (un·hėrd′), *adj.* **1.** not perceived by the ear. **2.** not given a hearing **3.** not heard of; unknown.

un·heard-of (un·hėrd′ov′; -uv′), *adj.* **1.** that was never heard of; unknown. **2.** such as was never known before; unprecedented.

un·hinge (un·hinj′), *v.*, **-hinged, -hing·ing. 1.** take (a door, etc.) off its hinges. **2.** remove the hinges from. **3.** separate from something; detach. **4.** unsettle; disorganize; upset.

un·hitch (un·hich′), *v.* unfasten.

un·ho·ly (un·hō′li), *adj.*, **-li·er, -li·est. 1.** not holy; wicked; sinful. **2.** *Colloq.* not seemly; fearful. —**un·ho′li·ly**, *adv.* —**un·ho′li·ness**, *n.*

un·hook (un·hů̇k′), *v.* **1.** loosen from a hook. **2.** undo by loosening a hook or hooks.

un·horse (un·hôrs′), *v.*, **-horsed, -hors·ing.** throw from a horse's back; cause to fall from a horse.

uni-, *word element.* one. [< L *unus* one]

u·ni·cam·er·al (ū′nə·kam′ər·əl), *adj.* of a lawmaking body, composed of only one group.

u·ni·cel·lu·lar (ū′nə·sel′yə·lər), *adj.* having one cell only. The amoeba is a unicellular animal.

u·ni·corn (ū′nə·kôrn), *n.* a mythical animal like a horse, but having a single long horn in the middle of its forehead. [< L, < *unus* one + *cornu* horn]

Unicorn

u·ni·fi·ca·tion (ū′nə·fə·kā′shən), *n.* **1.** formation into one unit; union. **2.** a making or being made more alike.

u·ni·form (ū′nə·fôrm), *adj.* **1.** always the same; not changing: *uniform temperature.* **2.** all alike; not varying: *bricks of uniform size.* **3.** regular; even: *a uniform pace.* —*n.* the distinctive clothes worn by the members of a group when on duty, by which they may be recognized as belonging to that group. Sol-

diers, policemen, and nurses wear uniforms. —*v. Am.* clothe or furnish with a uniform. [< L, < *unus* one + *forma* form] —**u′ni·form′-ly**, *adv.* —**u′ni·form′ness**, *n.*

u·ni·form·i·ty (ū′nə·fôr′mə·ti), *n.*, *pl.* **-ties.** uniform condition or character; sameness throughout.

u·ni·fy (ū′nə·fī), *v.*, **-fied, -fy·ing.** make or form into one; unite. [< LL, < L *unus* one + *facere* make] —**u′ni·fi′er**, *n.*

u·ni·lat·er·al (ū′nə·lat′ər·əl), *adj.* **1.** of, on, or affecting one side only. **2.** having all the parts arranged on one side of an axis; one-sided. **3.** *Law.* affecting one party or person only. **4.** concerned with or considering only one side of a matter. —**u′ni·lat′er·al·ly**, *adv.*

un·im·peach·a·ble (un′im·pēch′ə·bəl), *adj.* free from fault; blameless. —**un′im·peach′a·bly**, *adv.*

un·im·por·tant (un′im·pôr′tənt), *adj.* insignificant; trifling. —**un′im·por′tance**, *n.*

un·in·tel·li·gi·ble (un′in·tel′ə·jə·bəl), *adj.* that cannot be understood. —**un′in·tel′li·gi·bil′i·ty, un′in·tel′li·gi·ble·ness**, *n.* —**un′in·tel′li·gi·bly**, *adv.*

un·in·ter·rupt·ed (un′in·tə·rup′tid), *adj.* without interruption; continuous. —**un′in·ter·rupt′ed·ly**, *adv.*

un·ion (ūn′yən), *n.* **1.** a uniting or being united: *the United States was formed by the union of thirteen States.* **2.** group of people, states, etc., united for some special purpose: *the American colonies formed a union.* **3.** the Union, *Am.* the United States of America. **4.** a labor union; trade union. **5.** marriage. **6.** flag, or part of one, that is an emblem of union. The blue rectangle with stars in the American flag is the union. **7.** any of various devices for connecting parts of machinery or apparatus. [< L, < *unus* one] —**Syn. 2.** combination, consolidation, fusion, coalition, confederation.

un·ion·ism (ūn′yən·iz·əm), *n.* **1.** the principle of union. **2.** attachment to a union. **3.** system, principles, or methods of labor unions. —**un′-ion·ist**, *n.* —**un′ion·is′tic**, *adj.*

un·ion·ize (ūn′yən·īz), *v.*, **-ized, -iz·ing. 1.** form into a labor union. **2.** organize under a labor union. **3.** join in a labor union. —**un′ion·i·za′tion**, *n.*

union jack, 1. a small flag that is a symbol of union. **2. Union Jack,** the British national flag.

Union of India, former name of the republic of India, used during the period immediately following attainment of autonomy within the British Commonwealth of Nations.

Union of South Africa, former name of the Republic of South Africa.

Union of Soviet Socialist Republics, full name of the Soviet Union.

union shop, a factory or business firm in which most of the employees belong to a recognized labor union.

union suit, type of one-piece underwear.

u·nique (ū·nēk′), *adj.* **1.** having no like or equal; being the only one of its kind. **2.** rare; unusual. [< F < L *unicus*] —**u·nique′ly**, *adv.* —**u·nique′ness**, *n.* —**Syn. 1.** unmatched, single.

un·ham′pered	un·hes′i·tat′ing	un′im·ped′ed	un′in·hab′it·ed
un·hand′i·capped	un·hes′i·tat′ing·ly	un′im·pos′ing	un′in·hib′it·ed
un·hand′some	un·hin′dered	un′im·pressed′	un′i·ni′ti·at′ed
un·hand′some·ly	un·hon′ored	un′im·press′i·ble	un·in′jured
un·hanged′	un·hoped′-for′	un′im·pres′sion·a·ble	un′in·quir′ing
un·har′assed	un·housed′	un′im·pres′sive	un′in·spired′
un·har′dened	un·hur′ried	un′im·pris′oned	un′in·struct′ed
un·harmed′	un·hur′ry·ing	un′im·proved′	un·in′su·lat′ed
un′har·mo′ni·ous	un·hurt′	un′in·clud′ed	un·in′sured′
un·har′nessed	un·hurt′ful	un′in·cor′po·rat′ed	un′in·tel′li·gent
un·hatched′	un′hy·gi·en′ic	un′in·den′tured	un′in·tend′ed
un·healed′	un·hy′phen·at′ed	un′in·dexed′	un·in·ten′tion·al
un·heal′ing	un′i·de′al	un′in·dict′a·ble	un·in′ter·est·ed
un·heed′ed	un′i·den′ti·fied	un′in·dict′ed	un·in′ter·est·ing
un·heed′ful	un′id·i·o·mat′ic	un′in·fect′ed	un·in′ter·mit′tent
un·heed′ing	un·il·lu′mi·nat′ed	un′in·flam′ma·ble	un·in′ter·mit′ting
un·help′ful	un′i·mag′i·na·ble	un′in·flect′ed	un·in′tim·i·dat′ed
un·hemmed′	un′i·mag′i·na′tive	un′in·flu·enced	un·in′ven·tive
un·her′ald·ed	un′im·paired′	un′in·formed′	un·in′vit·ed
un′he·ro′ic	un′im·pas′sioned	un′in·hab′it·a·ble	un·in′vit·ing

u·ni·son (ū'nə·zən; -sən), *n.* **1.** agreement. **2.** agreement in pitch of two or more tones, voices, etc. [< Med.L *unisonus* sounding the same < L *unus* one + *sonus* sound]

u·nit (ū'nit), *n.* **1.** a single thing or person. **2.** any group of things or persons considered as one. **3.** one of the individuals or groups into which a whole can be analyzed. **4.** a standard quantity or amount. A foot is a unit of length. **5.** the smallest whole number; 1. [prob. < *unity*]

U·ni·tar·i·an (ū'nə·târ'i·ən), *n.* person who maintains that God exists as one being, in opposition to the doctrine of the Trinity. Unitarians accept the moral teachings of Jesus, but do not believe that he was divine. —*adj.* of or pertaining to Unitarians. —**U'ni·tar'i·an·ism,** *n.*

u·nite (ū·nīt'), *v.,* **u·nit·ed, u·nit·ing. 1.** join together; make one; join in action, interest, opinion, feeling, etc.; combine. **2.** become one; join in action, etc. [< L, < *unus* one] —**u·nit'er,** *n.* —**Syn. 1.** merge, consolidate, unify, couple, link. —**Ant. 1.** separate.

u·nit·ed (ū·nīt'id), *adj.* **1.** made one; joined; combined. **2.** pertaining to or produced by two or more. —**u·nit'ed·ly,** *adv.* —**u·nit'ed·ness,** *n.*

United Arab Republic, republic in NE Africa and W Asia, formed in 1958 by the joining together of Syria and Egypt.

United Kingdom, 1. kingdom composed of Great Britain and Northern Ireland, in NW Europe. **2.** Great Britain and Ireland from 1801 to 1922.

United Nations, 1. the nations that belong to a world-wide organization devoted to establishing world peace. **2.** this organization, in existence since Oct. 24, 1945. **3.** the Allies (def. 2).

United States, or **United States of America,** country in North America, extending from the Atlantic to the Pacific and from the Gulf of Mexico to Canada, with Alaska (the 49th State) lying W and NW of Canada, Hawaii (the 50th State) lying W in the Pacific, the District of Columbia, the territory of Puerto Rico and other possessions. *Abbrev.:* U.S.; U.S.A. ▶ **United States.** We live in *the* United States, and the article should be kept.

u·ni·ty (ū'nə·ti), *n., pl.* **-ties. 1.** oneness; being united. A circle has more unity than a row of dots. A nation has more unity than a group of tribes. **2.** union of parts forming a complex whole. **3.** harmony. **4.** the number one (1). **5.** oneness of effect; choice and arrangement of material (for a composition, book, picture, statue, etc.) to secure a single effect. **6.** the **unities,** the rules of action, time, and place that require a play to have one plot or course of events occurring on one day in one place. [< L, < *unus* one]

Univ., 1. Universalist. **2.** University.

U·NI·VAC (ū'nə·vak), *n. Trademark.* an electronic computing device which uses a binary numbering system. [< *Univ(ersal) A(utomatic) C(omputer)*]

u·ni·va·lent (ū'nə·vā'lənt; ū·niv'ə-), *adj.* having a valence of one. —**u'ni·va'lence,** *n.*

u·ni·ver·sal (ū'nə·vėr'səl), *adj.* **1.** of or for all; done, used, held, etc., by everybody. **2.** existing everywhere. **3.** covering a whole group of persons, things, cases, etc.; general. **4.** of or pertaining to the universe. **5.** adaptable to different sizes, angles, kinds of work, etc. —*n.* a proposition that asserts or denies something of every member of a class. —**u'ni·ver'sal·ness,** *n.*

U·ni·ver·sal·ist (ū'nə·vėr'səl·ist), *n. Am.* a member of a Protestant church holding the belief that all people will finally be saved. —**U'ni·ver'sal·ism,** *n.*

u·ni·ver·sal·i·ty (ū'nə·vėr·sal'ə·ti), *n., pl.* **-ties.** a being universal; universal character or range of knowledge.

u·ni·ver·sal·ly (ū'nə·vėr'səl·i), *adv.* **1.** in every instance; without exception. **2.** everywhere.

u·ni·verse (ū'nə·vėrs), *n.* all things; everything there is: *our world is but a small part of the universe.* [< L *universum,* orig. neut. adj., whole, turned into one < *unus* one + *vertere* turn]

u·ni·ver·si·ty (ū'nə·vėr'sə·ti), *n., pl.* **-ties.** institution of learning of the highest grade. A university usually has schools of law, medicine, teaching, business, etc., and in the United States, colleges for general instruction as well. [< AF < Med.L *universitas* corporation < L, < *unus* one + *versus.* See UNIVERSE.]

un·joint (un·joint'), *v.* disjoint.

un·just (un·just'), *adj.* not just; not fair. —**un·just'ly,** *adv.* —**un·just'ness,** *n.*

un·kempt (un·kempt'), *adj.* **1.** not combed. **2.** neglected; untidy. [< UN-¹ + OE *cembed* combed, pp. of *cemban* < *camb* comb] —**un·kempt'ness,** *n.*

un·kind (un·kīnd'), *adj.* harsh; cruel. —**un·kind'ly,** *adv.* —**un·kind'li·ness,** *n.* —**un·kind'ness,** *n.* —**Syn.** unsympathetic, ungracious.

un·known (un·nōn'), *adj.* **1.** not known. **2.** not familiar; strange. —**Syn. 1.** obscure, nameless, unrenowned.

un·lace (un·lās'), *v.,* **-laced, -lac·ing.** undo the laces of.

un·latch (un·lach'), *v.* unfasten or open by lifting a latch.

un·law·ful (un·lô'fəl), *adj.* **1.** contrary to the law; against the law; forbidden; illegal. **2.** illegitimate. —**un·law'ful·ly,** *adv.* —**un·law'ful·ness,** *n.*

un·learn (un·lėrn'), *v.* get rid of (ideas, habits, or tendencies); forget.

un·learn·ed (un·lėr'nid *for 1 and 3;* un·lėrnd' *for 2*), *adj.* **1.** not educated; ignorant. **2.** not learned; known without being learned. **3.** not showing education. —**un·learn'ed·ly,** *adv.*

un·leash (un·lēsh'), *v.* **1.** release from a leash. **2.** let loose: *unleash one's temper.*

un·leav·ened (un·lev'ənd), *adj.* not leavened. Unleavened bread is made without yeast.

un·less (ən·les'; un-), *conj.* if it were not that; if not: *we shall go unless it rains.* —*prep.* except. [< *on* + *less,* i.e., on a less condition (than)]

un·let·tered (un·let'ərd), *adj.* **1.** not educated. **2.** not able to read or write.

un·like (un·līk'), *adj.* not like; different: *the two problems are quite unlike.* —*prep.* different from: *act unlike others.* —**un·like'ness,** *n.* —**Syn.** *adj.* dissimilar, diverse.

un·like·li·hood (un·līk'li·hůd), *n.* improbability.

un·like·ly (un·līk'li), *adj.* **1.** not likely; not probable: *unlikely to succeed.* **2.** not likely to succeed: *an unlikely adventure.* —**un·like'li·ness,** *n.*

un·lim·ber (un·lim'bər), *v.* **1.** detach the limber or forepart of the carriage from (a gun). **2.** prepare for action.

un·lim·it·ed (un·lim'it·id), *adj.* **1.** without limits; boundless. **2.** not restricted. **3.** not definite. —**un·lim'it·ed·ly,** *adv.* —**un·lim'it·ed·ness,** *n.*

un·load (un·lōd'), *v.* **1.** remove (a load). **2.** take the load from. **3.** get rid of. **4.** remove powder, shot, etc., from (a gun). **5.** discharge a cargo: *the ship is unloading.* —**un·load'er,** *n.*

un·lock (un·lok'), *v.* **1.** open the lock of; open (anything firmly closed). **2.** disclose; reveal. **3.** become unlocked.

un·is'sued	un·know'a·ble	un·laud'a·ble	un·like'a·ble
un·jus'ti·fi'a·ble	un·know'ing	un·laun'dered	un·liked'
un·kept'	un·la'beled	un·leased'	un·lined'
un·killed'	un·lac'quered	un·led'	un·liq'ui·dat'ed
un·kin'dled	un·la'dy·like'	turn'li censed	un·lit'
un·king'ly	un·laid'	un·licked'	un·lit'er·ar'y
un·kissed'	un'la·ment'ed	un·light'ed	un·lit'tered
un·knight'ly	un·lat'ticed	un·lik'a·ble	un·lo'cat·ed

un·looked-for (un-lukt′fôr′), *adj.* unexpected; unforeseen.

un·loose (un-lūs′), **un·loos·en** (-lūs′ən), *v.,* -loosed, -loos·ing; -loos·ened, -loos·en·ing. let loose; set free; release.

un·love·ly (un-luv′li), *adj.* without beauty or charm; unpleasing in appearance; unpleasant; objectionable; disagreeable. —**un·love′li·ness,** *n.*

un·luck·y (un-luk′i), *adj.* not lucky; unfortunate; bringing bad luck. —**un·luck′i·ly,** *adv.* —**un·luck′i·ness,** *n.* —**Syn.** unsuccessful, ill-fated.

un·make (un-māk′), *v.,* -made, -mak·ing. undo; destroy; ruin. —**un·mak′er,** *n.*

un·man (un-man′), *v.,* -manned, -man·ning. 1. deprive of the qualities of a man. 2. weaken or break down the spirit of.

un·man·ly (un-man′li), *adj.* not manly; weak; cowardly. —**un·man′li·ness,** *n.*

un·man·ner·ly (un-man′ər·li), *adj.* having bad manners; discourteous. —*adv.* with bad manners; rudely. —**un·man′ner·li·ness,** *n.*

un·mask (un-mask′; -mäsk′), *v.* 1. remove a mask or disguise. 2. take off a mask or disguise from. 3. expose the true character of.

un·mean·ing (un-mēn′ing), *adj.* 1. without meaning: *unmeaning words.* 2. without sense; without expression: *an unmeaning stare.* —**un·mean′ing·ly,** *adv.* —**un·mean′ing·ness,** *n.*

un·men·tion·a·ble (un-men′shən·ə·bəl; -mensh′nə·bəl), *adj.* that cannot be mentioned; not fit to be spoken about. —**un·men′tion·a·ble·ness,** *n.*

un·mer·ci·ful (un-mèr′si·fəl), *adj.* having no mercy; showing no mercy. —**un·mer′ci·ful·ly,** *adv.* —**un·mer′ci·ful·ness,** *n.* —**Syn.** pitiless.

un·mis·tak·a·ble (un′mis·tāk′ə·bəl), *adj.* that cannot be mistaken or misunderstood; clear; plain; evident. —**un′mis·tak′a·ble·ness,** *n.* —**un′mis·tak′a·bly,** *adv.* —**Syn.** manifest.

un·mor·al (un-môr′əl; -mor′-), *adj.* neither moral nor immoral; not perceiving or involving right and wrong. —**un·mo·ral·i·ty** (un′mə·ral′-ə·ti), *n.* —**un·mor′al·ly,** *adv.*

un·muz·zle (un-muz′əl), *v.,* -zled, -zling. 1. remove a muzzle from (a dog, etc.). 2. free from restraint.

un·nat·u·ral (un-nach′ə·rəl; -nach′rəl), *adj.* not natural; not normal. —**un·nat′u·ral·ly,** *adv.* —**un·nat′u·ral·ness,** *n.* —**Syn.** irregular, artificial.

un·nec·es·sar·y (un-nes′ə·ser′i), *adj.* not necessary; needless. —**un·nec·es·sar·i·ly** (un·nes′-ə·ser′ə·li; *emphatic* un′nes·ə·sâr′ə·li), *adv.* —**un·nec′es·sar′i·ness,** *n.*

un·nerve (un-nèrv′), *v.,* -nerved, -nerv·ing. deprive of nerve, firmness, or self-control.

un·num·bered (un-num′bərd), *adj.* 1. not numbered; not counted. 2. too many to count.

un·oc·cu·pied (un-ok′yə·pīd), *adj.* vacant; idle.

un·or·gan·ized (un-ôr′gən·īzd), *adj.* 1. not formed into an organized or systematized whole. 2. *Am.* not organized into labor unions. 3. not being a living organism. An enzyme is an unorganized ferment.

un·pack (un-pak′), *v.* 1. take out (things packed in a box, trunk, etc.). 2. take things out of. 3. take out things packed. —**un·pack′er,** *n.*

un·pal·at·a·ble (un·pal′it·ə·bəl), *adj.* not agreeable to the taste; distasteful; unpleasant. —**un·pal′at·a·ble·ness,** *n.* —**un·pal′at·a·bly,** *adv.* —**Syn.** unappetizing, unsavory.

un·par·al·leled (un·par′ə·leld), *adj.* having no parallel; unequaled; matchless.

un·par·lia·men·ta·ry (un′pär·lə·men′tə·ri; -men′tri), *adj.* not in accordance with parliamentary practice. —**un′par·lia·men′ta·ri·ly,** *adv.* —**un′par·lia·men′ta·ri·ness,** *n.*

un·peo·ple (un·pē′pəl), *v.,* -pled, -pling. deprive of people. —**un·peo′pled,** *adj.*

un·pin (un·pin′), *v.,* -pinned, -pin·ning. take out a pin or pins from; unfasten.

un·pleas·ant (un-plez′ənt), *adj.* not pleasant; disagreeable. —**un·pleas′ant·ly,** *adv.* —**un·pleas′ant·ness,** *n.* —**Syn.** objectionable, obnoxious.

un·plumbed (un·plumd′), *adj.* 1. not measured; of unknown depth. 2. having no plumbing.

un·pop·u·lar (un·pop′yə·lər), *adj.* not generally liked; disliked. —**un·pop·u·lar·i·ty** (un′pop-yə·lar′ə·ti), *n.* —**un·pop′u·lar·ly,** *adv.*

un·prac·ti·cal (un·prak′tə·kəl), *adj.* imprac-

un·lov′a·ble	un·min′is·tered	un′ob·jec′tion·a·ble	un·penned′
un·loved′	un·mirth′ful	un·ob′li·gat′ed	un·pen′sioned
un·lov′ing	un·mit′i·gat′ed	un′o·blig′ing	un′per·ceived′
un·loy′al	un·mix′a·ble	un′o·bliged′	un′per·ceiv′ing
un·mag′ni·fied	un·mixed′	un′ob·scured′	un·perf′o·rat′ed
un·maid′en·ly	un·mixt′	un′ob·serv′a·ble	un·per′me·at′ed
un·mall′a·ble	un·mod′i·fied	un′ob·serv′ant	un′per·suad′ed
un·mailed′	un·mod′u·lat′ed	un′ob·served′	un′per·sua′sive
un·mal′le·a·ble	un·mold′ed	un′ob·serv′ing	un′per·turbed′
un·man′a·cled	un·mo·lest′ed	un′ob·struct′ed	un′pe·rused′
un·man′age·a·ble	un·mo′ti·vat′ed	un′ob·tain′a·ble	un′per·vert′ed
un·manned′	un·mot′tled	un′ob·tained′	un′phil·o·soph′ic
un′man·u·fac′tured	un·mount′ed	un′ob·tru′sive	un′phil·o·soph′i·cal
un·marked′	un·mourned′	un′ob·tru′sive·ly	un·pho′to·graphed
un·mar′ket·a·ble	un·mov′a·ble	un′ob·tru′sive·ness	un·picked′
un·mar′ket·ed	un·moved′	un′of·fend′ing	un·pierced′
un·mar′riage·a·ble	un·mov′ing	un·of′fered	un·pit′ied
un·mar′ried	un·mown′	un·of′fi·cered	un·pit′y·ing
un·mas′tered	un·mud′died	un·of′fi·cial	un·placed′
un·match′a·ble	un·muf′fled	un·oiled′	un·planned′
un·matched′	un·mu′si·cal	un·o′pen	un·plant′ed
un·meant′	un·mussed′	un·o′pened	un·plat′ted
un·meas′ured	un·mut′ed	un′op·posed′	un·played′
un′me·chan′i·cal	un·nam′a·ble	un′or·dained′	un·pleased′
un·me′di·at′ed	un·name′a·ble	un′o·rig′i·nal	un·pleas′ing
un·meet′a·ble	un·named′	un·or′tho·dox	un·pledged′
un·me·lo′di·ous	un·nat′u·ral·ized	un·os′si·fied	un·ploughed′
un·melt′a·ble	un·nav′i·ga·ble	un′os·ten·ta′tious	un·plowed′
un·melt′ed	un·nav′i·gat′ed	un·owned′	un′po·et′ic
un·mend′a·ble	un′ne·ces′si·tat′ed	un·paged′	un′po·et′i·cal
un·men′tion·a·bly	un·need′ed	un·paid′	un·po′lar·ized
un·men′tioned	un·need′ful	un·pained′	un·pol′ished
un·mer′it·ed	un′ne·go′tia·ble	un·paint′ed	un·pol′i·tic
un·me′tered	un·neigh′bor·ly	un·paired′	un·pol′lut′ed
un′me·thod′i·cal	un·notched′	un′par′a·phrased	un·pon′dered
un·mil′i·tant	un·not′ed	un·par′don·a·ble	un′por·tend′ed
un·mil′i·tar′y	un·no′tice·a·ble	un·par′doned	un′por·ten′tous
un·mind′ful	un·no′ticed	un·pas′teur·ized	un′por·tray′a·ble
un·mind′ful·ly	un·nu·mer′i·cal	un·pa′tri·ot′ic	un·pos′ing
un·min′gled	un′o·beyed′	un·paved′	un′pos·sessed′
		un·peace′ful	un·poured′

tical. —un'**prac·ti·cal'i·ty**, un·**prac'ti·cal·ness**, n. —un·**prac'ti·cal·ly**, adv.

un·prac·ticed, un·prac·tised (un-prakt'-tist), adj. 1. not skilled. 2. not used.

un·prec·e·dent·ed (un·pres'ə·den'tid), adj. having no precedent; never done before; never known before. —un·**prec'e·dent'ed·ly**, adv. —Syn. unexampled, new.

un·prej·u·diced (un-prej'ə-dist), adj. 1. without prejudice; impartial. 2. not impaired.

un·pre·tend·ing (un'pri·ten'ding), adj. unassuming; modest. —un'**pre·tend'ing·ly**, adv.

un·pre·ten·tious (un'pri·ten'shəs), adj. modest. —un'**pre·ten'tious·ly**, adv. —un'**pre·ten'tious·ness**, n.

un·prin·ci·pled (un·prin'sə·pəld), adj. lacking good moral principles; bad. —un·**prin'ci·pled·ness**, n.

un·print·a·ble (un·prin'tə·bəl), adj. not fit to be printed.

un·pro·fes·sion·al (un'prə·fesh'ən·əl; -fesh'-nəl), adj. 1. contrary to professional etiquette; unbecoming in members of a profession. 2. not pertaining to or connected with a profession. 3. not belonging to a profession. —un'**pro·fes'sion·al·ly**, adv.

un·pro·voked (un'prə·vōkt'), adj. without provocation. —un·**pro·vok·ed·ly** (un'prə·vōk'id·li), adv.

un·qual·i·fied (un·kwol'ə·fīd), adj. 1. not qualified; not fitted. 2. not modified, limited, or restricted in any way: unqualified praise. 3. complete; absolute: an unqualified failure. —un·**qual'i·fied·ly**, adv. —un·**qual'i·fied·ness**, n.

un·ques·tion·a·ble (un·kwes'chən·ə·bəl), adj. beyond dispute or doubt; certain. —un·**ques'tion·a·ble·ness**, n. —un·**ques'tion·a·bly**, adv.

un·qui·et (un·kwī'ət), adj. restless; disturbed; uneasy. —un·**qui'et·ly**, adv. —un·**qui'et·ness**, n.

un·quote (un·kwōt'), v., -quot·ed, -quot·ing, n. —v. end a quotation. —n. end of a quotation.

un·rav·el (un·rav'əl), v., -eled, -el·ing; esp. Brit. -elled, -el·ling. 1. separate the threads of;

pull apart. 2. come apart. 3. bring or come out of a tangled state: unravel a mystery.

un·read (un-red'), adj. 1. not read: an unread book. 2. not having read much: an unread person.

un·read·y (un-red'i), adj. 1. not ready; not prepared. 2. not prompt or quick. —un·**read'i·ly**, adv. —un·**read'i·ness**, n.

un·re·al (un-rē'əl), adj. imaginary; not real; not substantial; fanciful. —un·**re·al'i·ty** (un'ri·al'ə·ti), n. —un·**re'al·ly**, adv. —Syn. fictitious, visionary.

un·rea·son·a·ble (un·rē'zən·ə·bəl), adj. 1. not reasonable. 2. not moderate; excessive. —un·**rea'son·a·ble·ness**, n. —un·**rea'son·a·bly**, adv. —Syn. 1. irrational. 2. exorbitant.

un·rea·son·ing (un·rē'zən·ing; -rēz'ning), adj. not using reason; reasonless. —un·**rea'son·ing·ly**, adv.

un·reel (un-rēl'), v. unwind from a reel.

un·re·gen·er·ate (un'ri·jen'ər·it), adj. 1. not born again spiritually; not turned to the love of God. 2. wicked; bad. —un'**re·gen'er·ate·ly**, adv. —un'**re·gen'er·ate·ness**, n.

un·re·lent·ing (un'ri·len'ting), adj. 1. hardhearted; merciless. 2. not slackening or relaxing. —un'**re·lent'ing·ly**, adv. —un'**re·lent'ing·ness**, n. —Syn. 1. unyielding, obdurate, harsh.

un·re·li·a·ble (un'ri·lī'ə·bəl), adj. not reliable; not to be depended on. —un'**re·li·a·bil'i·ty**, un'**re·li'a·ble·ness**, n. —un'**re·li'a·bly**, adv. —Syn. uncertain, irresponsible.

un·re·li·gious (un'ri·lij'əs), adj. 1. irreligious. 2. nonreligious.

un·re·mit·ting (un'ri·mit'ing), adj. never stopping; not slackening; maintained steadily. —un'**re·mit'ting·ly**, adv. —un'**re·mit'ting·ness**, n. —Syn. unceasing, incessant, constant.

un·re·served (un'ri·zérvd'), adj. 1. frank; open. 2. not restricted; without reservation. —un'**re·serv·ed·ly** (un'ri·zér'vid·li), adv. —un'**re·serv'ed·ness**, n.

un·rest (un-rest'), n. 1. lack of ease and quiet; restlessness. 2. agitation or disturbance amount-

un' pre·cise'	un' pro·vok' ing	un·rec' og·niz' a·ble	un' re·peat' ed
un' pre·dict' a·ble	un·pruned'	un·rec' og·nized	un' re·pent' ant
un' pre·dict' ed	un·pub' lish·a·ble	un·rec' om·pensed	un' re·pent' ing
un' pre·med' i·tat' ed	un·pub' lished	un' rec·on·cil' a·ble	un' re·placed'
un' pre·pared'	un·pul' ver·ized	un·rec' on·ciled	un' re·port' ed
un' pre·pos·sess' ing	un·punched'	un' re·cord' a·ble	un' rep·re·sent' a·tive
un' pre·scribed'	un·punc' tu·al	un' re·cord' ed	un' rep·re·sent' ed
un·pressed'	un·pun' ish·a·ble	un' re·cov' er·a·ble	un' re·pressed'
un' pre·sumed'	un·pun' ished	un' re·cruit' ed	un' re·proached'
un' pre·sum' ing	un' pur·chas·a·ble	un' re·deemed'	un' re·proved'
un' pre·vail' ing	un·purged'	un' re·duced'	un' re·pu' di·at' ed
un' pre·vent' a·ble	un·pu' ri·fied	un' re·fined'	un' re·quest' ed
un·print' ed	un·pur' posed	un' re·flect' ing	un' re·quit' ed
un·priv' i·leged	un' pur·sued'	un' re·flect' ing·ly	un' re·signed'
un·prized'	un' pur·su' ing	un' re·flec' tive	un' re·sist' ant
un·pro' bat·ed	un·quail' ing	un' re·formed'	un' re·sist' ed
un·proc' tored	un·quak' ing	un' re·freshed'	un' re·sist' ing
un' pro·cur' a·ble	un·qual' i·fy' ing	un' re·fut' ed	un' re·solved'
un' pro·cured'	un' quar' an·tined	un' re·gard' ed	un' re·spond' ing
un' pro·duc' tive	un·quench' a·ble	un·reg' is·tered	un' re·spon' sive
un' pro·faned'	un·quenched'	un·reg' u·lat' ed	un' re·stored'
un' pro·fessed'	un·ques' tioned	un' re·hearsed'	un' re·strain' a·ble
un' pro·fess' ing	un·ques' tion·ing	un' re·lat' ed	un' re·strained'
un·prof' it·a·ble	un·quiv' er·ing	un' re·laxed'	un' re·strict' ed
un' pro·gres' sive	un·quot' a·ble	un' re·lax' ing	un' re·sumed'
un' pro·ject' ed	un·raised'	un' re·liev' a·ble	un' re·tard' ed
un·prom' is·ing	un·raked'	un' re·lieved'	un' re·ten' tive
un' pro·mot' ed	un·ran' somed	un·rem' e·died	un' re·trieved'
un·prompt' ed	un·rat' i·fied	un' re·mem' bered	un' re·turned'
un' pro·nounce' a·ble	un·razed'	un' re·mit' ted	un' re·vealed'
un' pro·nounced'	un·read' a·ble	un' re·moved'	un' re·venged'
un·proph' e·sied	un' re·al·is' tic	un' re·mu' ner·at' ed	un' re·versed'
un' pro·pi' tious	un·re' al·ized	un' re·mu' ner·a' tive	un' re·viewed'
un' pro·por' tioned	un·reaped'	un·ren' dered	un' re·vised'
un·propped'	un' rea' soned	un' re·nowned'	un' re·voked'
un' pros' per·ous	un' re·buked'	un·rent' a·ble	un' re·ward' ed
un' pro·tect' a·ble	un' re·ceipt' ed	un·rent' ed	un' re·ward' ing
un' pro·tect' ed	un' re·ceived'	un' re·paid'	un·rhymed'
un' pro·test' ed	un' re·cep' tive	un' re·paired'	un·rhyth' mic
un·proved'	un' re·claimed'	un' re·pealed'	un·rhyth' mi·cal
un·prov' en	un' re·clined'		un·rigged'
un' pro·vid' ed	un' re·clin' ing		un·right' ed

ing almost to rebellion. —**Syn. 1.** inquietude, uneasiness.

un·right·eous (un-rī'chəs), *adj.* wicked; sinful; unjust. —**un·right'eous·ly,** *adv.* —**un·right'eous·ness,** *n.*

un·ripe (un-rīp'), *adj.* not ripe; green. —**un·ripe'ness,** *n.*

un·ri·valed, *esp. Brit.* **un·ri·valled** (un-rī'vəld), *adj.* having no rival; without an equal.

un·roll (un-rōl'), *v.* **1.** open or spread out (something rolled). **2.** become opened or spread out. **3.** lay open; display. —**Syn. 1.** unfold, unfurl.

UNRRA (un'rə), United Nations Relief and Rehabilitation Administration.

un·ruf·fled (un-ruf'əld), *adj.* **1.** not ruffled; smooth. **2.** not disturbed; calm.

un·ru·ly (un-rü'li), *adj.* hard to rule or control; lawless. —**un·ru'li·ness,** *n.* —**Syn** disobedient, refractory, insubordinate, ungovernable.

un·sad·dle (un-sad'əl), *v.,* **-dled, -dling. 1.** take the saddle off (a horse). **2.** cause to fall from a horse.

un·safe (un-sāf'), *adj.* dangerous. —**un·safe'ly,** *adv.* —**un·safe'ness,** *n.* —**un·safe'ty,** *n.* —**Syn.** perilous, hazardous, precarious.

un·san·i·tar·y (un-san'ə-ter'i), *adj.* unhealthful. —**un·san'i·tar'i·ness,** *n.*

un·sa·vor·y, *esp. Brit.* **un·sa·vour·y** (un-sā'vər·i; -sāv'ri), *adj.* **1.** tasteless. **2.** unpleasant in taste or smell. **3.** morally unpleasant; offensive. —**un·sa'vor·i·ly,** *esp. Brit.* **un·sa'vour·i·ly,** *adv.* —**un·sa'vor·i·ness,** *esp. Brit.* **un·sa'vour·i·ness,** *n.*

un·say (un-sā'), *v.,* **-said, -say·ing.** take back (something said).

un·scathed (un-skātʰd'), *adj.* not harmed; uninjured.

un·sci·en·tif·ic (un'sī-ən-tif'ik), *adj.* **1.** not in accordance with the facts or principles of science. **2.** not acting in accordance with such facts or principles. —**un'sci·en·tif'i·cal·ly,** *adv.*

un·scram·ble (un-skram'bəl), *v.,* **-bled, -bling.** reduce from confusion to order; bring out of a scrambled condition.

un·screw (un-skrü'), *v.* **1.** take out the screw or screws from. **2.** loosen or take off by turning; untwist.

un·scru·pu·lous (un-skrü'pyə-ləs), *adj.* not careful about right or wrong; without principles or conscience. —**un·scru'pu·lous·ly,** *adv.* —**un·scru'pu·lous·ness,** *n.*

un·seal (un-sēl'), *v.* **1.** break or remove the seal of. **2.** open: *the threat unsealed her lips.*

un·search·a·ble (un-sér'chə-bəl), *adj.* not to be searched into; mysterious. —**un·search'a·ble·ness,** *n.* —**un·search'a·bly,** *adv.*

un·sea·son·a·ble (un-sē'zən-ə-bəl; -sēz'nə-bəl), *adj.* **1.** not suitable to the season. **2.** coming at the wrong time. —**un·sea'son·a·ble·ness,** *n.* —**un·sea'son·a·bly,** *adv.* —**Syn. 2.** inopportune, untimely.

un·seat (un-sēt'), *v.* **1.** displace from a seat. **2.** throw (a rider) from a saddle. **3.** remove from office.

un·seem·ly (un-sēm'li), *adj.* not seemly; not suitable; improper. —*adv.* improperly; unsuitably. —**un·seem'li·ness,** *n.*

un·seen (un-sēn'), *adj.* **1.** not seen. **2.** not visible. —**Syn. 1.** unnoticed, unobserved.

un·self·ish (un-sel'fish), *adj.* considerate of others; generous. —**un·self'ish·ly,** *adv.* —**un·self'ish·ness,** *n.* —**Syn.** charitable, liberal.

un·set·tle (un-set'əl), *v.,* **-tled, -tling.** make or become unstable; disturb; shake; weaken. —**un·set'tled,** *adj.* —**un·set'tled·ness,** *n.* —**Syn.** disorder, upset, disconcert.

un·sex (un-seks'), *v.* deprive of the attributes of one's sex, esp. to deprive of womanly character.

un·shack·le (un-shak'əl), *v.,* **-led, -ling.** remove shackles from; set free.

un·sheathe (un-shētʰ'), *v.,* **-sheathed, -sheath·ing.** draw (a sword, knife, or the like) from a sheath.

un·ship (un-ship'), *v.,* **-shipped, -ship·ping.** put off or take off from a ship.

un·shod (un-shod'), *adj.* without shoes.

un·sight·ly (un-sīt'li), *adj.* ugly or unpleasant to look at. —**un·sight'li·ness,** *n.*

un·skilled (un-skild'), *adj.* **1.** not skilled; not trained. **2.** not using skill.

un·skill·ful, un·skil·ful (un-skil'fəl), *adj.* awkward; clumsy. —**un·skill'ful·ly,** **un·skil'ful·ly,** *adv.* —**un·skill'ful·ness,** **un·skil'ful·ness,** *n.*

un·snap (un-snap'), *v.,* **-snapped, -snap·ping.** unfasten the snap or snaps of.

un·snarl (un-snärl'), *v.* untangle.

un·so·cia·ble (un-sō'shə-bəl), *adj.* not sociable; not associating easily with others. —**un'·so·cia·bil'i·ty, un·so'cia·ble·ness,** *n.* —**un·so'cia·bly,** *adv.*

un·so·phis·ti·cat·ed (un'sə-fis'tə-kāt'id), *adj.* simple; natural; artless. —**un'so·phis'ti·cat'ed·ness, un'so·phis'ti·ca'tion,** *n.*

un·sound (un-sound'), *adj.* **1.** not in good condition; not sound. **2.** not based on truth or fact. **3.** not deep; not restful; disturbed: *an unsound sleep.* —**un·sound'ly,** *adv.* —**un·sound'ness,** *n.*

un·spar·ing (un-spâr'ing), *adj.* **1.** very generous; liberal. **2.** not merciful; severe. —**un·spar'ing·ly,** *adv.* —**un·spar'ing·ness,** *n.*

---

un·right'ful
un·rip'ened
un'ro·man'tic
un·roped'
un·rubbed'
un·ruled'
un·rust'ed
un·said'
un·saint'ly
un·sal'a·ble
un·sal'a·ried
un·sale'a·ble
un·salt'ed
un·sanc'ti·fied
un·sanc'tioned
un·sapped'
un·sat'ti·at'ed
un'sat·is·fac'to·ry
un·sat'is·fi'a·ble
un·sat'is·fied
un·sat'is·fy'ing
un·sat'u·rat'ed
un·sav'a·ble
un·saved'
un·scal'a·ble
un·scaled'
un·scared'
un·scarred'
un·scent'ed

un·sched'uled
un·schol'ar·ly
un·schooled'
un·scorched'
un·scoured'
un·scraped'
un·scratched'
un·screened'
un·scrip'tur·al
un·scru'ti·nized
un·sculp'tured
un·seamed'
un·sea'soned
un·seat'ed
un·sea'wor'thy
un·se·cured'
un·see'ing
un·seg'ment·ed
un·seg're·gat'ed
un·seized'
un'se·lect'ed
un'se·lec'tive
un'sen·ti·men'tal
un·sep'a·rat'ed
un·served'
un·ser'vice·a·ble
un·set'
un·sev'ered
un·sewn'
un·shad'ed

un·shak'a·ble
un·shake'a·ble
un·shak'en
un·shamed'
un·shaped'
un·shape'ly
un·shared'
un·sharp'ened
un·shat'tered
un·shaved'
un·shav'en
un·shed'
un·shel'tered
un·shield'ed
un·shift'ing
un·shocked'
un·shorn'
un·short'ened
un·showed'
un·shown'
un·shrink'a·ble
un·shrink'ing
un·shuf'fled
un·shunned'
un·shunt'ed
un·sift'ed
un·sight'ed
un·signed'
un·si'lenced
un·sim'pli·fied

un·singed'
un·sink'a·ble
un·sis'ter·ly
un·sized'
un·slacked'
un·slaked'
un·slaugh'tered
un·sleep'ing
un·sliced'
un·smeared'
un·smil'ing
un·smooth'
un·smoothed'
un·smudged'
un·snagged'
un·so'cial
un·sof'tened
un·soiled'
un·sold'
un·sol'dier·ly
un'so·lic'it·ed
un'so·lic'it·ous
un'so·lic'i·fied
un·solv'a·ble
un·solved'
un·sort'ed
un·sought'
un·sound'ed
un·sowed'
un·sown'

un·speak·a·ble (un·spēk′ə·bəl), *adj.* **1.** that cannot be expressed in words. **2.** extremely bad; so bad that it is not spoken of. —**un·speak′a·bly,** *adv.*

un·sta·ble (un·stā′bəl), *adj.* **1.** not firmly fixed; easily moved, shaken, or overthrown. **2.** not constant; variable. **3.** *Chem.* easily decomposed; readily changing into other compounds. —**un·sta′ble·ness,** *n.* —**un·sta′bly,** *adv.* —**Syn. 1.** unsteady, insecure, unsettled, wavering.

unstable element, *Nuclear Physics.* a radioactive element which eventually changes into a radioactive isotope.

un·stead·y (un·sted′ĭ), *adj.* **1.** not steady; shaky. **2.** likely to change; not reliable. **3.** not regular in habits. —**un·stead′i·ly,** *adv.* —**un·stead′i·ness,** *n.*

un·stop (un·stop′), *v.,* **-stopped, -stop·ping. 1.** remove the stopper from (a bottle, etc.). **2.** free from any obstruction; open.

un·strap (un·strap′), *v.,* **-strapped, -strapping.** loosen the strap of (a trunk, box, etc.).

un·string (un·string′), *v.,* **-strung, -stringing. 1.** take off or loosen the string or strings of. **2.** take from a string. **3.** weaken the nerves of; make nervous.

un·strung (un·strung′), *adj.* nervous. —*v.* pt. and pp. of **unstring.**

un·stud·ied (un·stud′ĭd), *adj.* not planned ahead; natural.

un·sub·stan·tial (un′səb·stan′shəl), *adj.* flimsy; slight; unreal. —**un·sub·stan·ti·al·i·ty** (un′səb·stan′shi·al′ə·ti), *n.* —**un′sub·stan′tial·ly,** *adv.*

un·suit·a·ble (un·süt′ə·bəl), *adj.* not suitable; unfit. —**un′suit·a·bil′i·ty, un·suit′a·ble·ness,** *n.* —**un·suit′a·bly,** *adv.* —**Syn.** inappropriate, incongruous.

un·suit·ed (un·süt′ĭd), *adj.* unfit.

un·sung (un·sung′), *adj.* **1.** not sung. **2.** not honored in song or poetry.

un·tan·gle (un·tang′gəl), *v.,* **-gled, -gling. 1.** take the tangles out of; disentangle. **2.** straighten out or clear up (anything confused or perplexing).

un·taught (un·tôt′), *adj.* **1.** not educated. **2.** learned naturally.

un·thank·ful (un·thangk′fəl), *adj.* **1.** ungrateful. **2.** not appreciated; thankless. —**unthank′ful·ly,** *adv.* —**un·thank′ful·ness,** *n.*

un·think·ing (un·thingk′ing), *adj.* thoughtless; heedless; careless. —**un·think′ing·ly,** *adv.*

un·thought-of (un·thôt′ov′; -uv′), *adj.* not imagined or considered.

un·thread (un·thred′), *v.* **1.** take the thread out of. **2.** unravel. **3.** find one's way through.

un·ti·dy (un·tī′di), *adj.* not in order; not neat. —**un·ti′di·ly,** *adv.* —**un·ti′di·ness,** *n.* —**Syn.** disorderly, slovenly, littered.

un·tie (un·tī′), *v.,* **-tied, -ty·ing.** loosen; unfasten.

un·til (ən·til′; un-), *prep.* **1.** up to the time of: *wait until tomorrow.* **2.** before: *he did not go until night.* —*conj.* **1.** up to the time when: *he worked until the job was completed.* **2.** before: *he did not come until the meeting was half over.* **3.** to the degree or place that: *he worked until he was tired.* [ME, < Scand. *und* up to + *till*[1]] ≫ See **till**[1] for usage note.

un·time·ly (un·tīm′li), *adj.* at a wrong time or season: *snow in May is untimely.* —*adv.* too early; too soon. —**un·time′li·ness,** *n.*

un·tir·ing (un·tīr′ing), *adj.* tireless; unwearying. —**un·tir′ing·ly,** *adv.*

un·to (un′tü; un′tù), *prep. Archaic or Poetic.* **1.** to. **2.** until. [ME, < *un-* (see UNTIL) + *to*]

un·told (un·tōld′), *adj.* **1.** not told; not revealed. **2.** too many to be counted or numbered; very great: *untold numbers.*

un·touch·a·ble (un·tuch′ə·bəl), *adj.* **1.** that cannot be touched; out of reach. **2.** that must not be touched. —*n.* person of the lowest caste in India, whose touch supposedly defiles members of higher castes.

un·to·ward (un·tôrd′; -tōrd′), *adj.* **1.** unfavorable; unfortunate. **2.** perverse; stubborn; willful. —**un·to′ward·ly,** *adv.* —**un·to′ward·ness,** *n.* —**Syn. 1.** inconvenient, awkward. **2.** intractable, refractory, contrary.

un·tram·meled, *esp. Brit.* **un·trammelled** (un·tram′əld), *adj.* not hindered or restrained; free.

un·trod (un·trod′), *adj.* not trodden.

un·true (un·trü′), *adj.* **1.** false; incorrect. **2.** not faithful. **3.** not true to a standard or rule. —**un·true′ness,** *n.* —**un·tru′ly,** *adv.*

un·truss (un·trus′), *v.* **1.** unfasten. **2.** undress.

un·truth (un·trüth′), *n.* **1.** lack of truth; falsity. **2.** a lie; falsehood.

un·truth·ful (un·trüth′fəl), *adj.* not truthful; contrary to the truth. —**un·truth′ful·ly,** *adv.* —**un·truth′ful·ness,** *n.*

un·tu·tored (un·tü′tərd; -tū′-), *adj.* untaught.

---

un·spe′cial·ized	un·stressed′	un·sym′pa·thiz′ing	un·tinc′tured
un·spe′ci·fied	un·stri′at·ed	un′sys·tem·at′ic	un·tinged′
un·spec′u·la′tive	un·stuffed′	un·sys′tem·a·tized	un·tipped′
un·spent′	un′sub·dued′	un·tab′u·lat′ed	un·tired′
un·spiced′	un′sub·mis′sive	un·tact′ful	un·ti′tled
un·spilled′	un′sub·mit′ted	un·taint′ed	un·toil′ing
un·spir′it·u·al	un′sub·mit′ting	un·tak′en	un·torn′
un·splashed′	un·sub′si·dized	un·tal′ent·ed	un·to′taled
un·spoiled′	un′sub·stan′ti·at′ed	un·tam′a·ble	un·touched′
un·spoilt′	un′suc·cess′ful	un·tame′a·ble	un·trace′a·ble
un·spo′ken	un′suc·cess′ful·ly	un·tamed′	un·traced′
un·sports′man·like′	un·suf′fer·a·ble	un·tanned′	un·tracked′
un·spot′ted	un′sug·ges′tive	un·ta′pered	un·tract′a·ble
un·sprayed′	un·sul′lied	un·tapped′	un·trad′ed
un·sprin′kled	un′sup·port′a·ble	un·tar′nished	un·trained′
un·sprung′	un′sup·port′ed	un·tast′ed	un′trans·fer′a·ble
un·squeezed′	un′sup·pressed′	un·tax′a·ble	un′trans·ferred′
un·squelched′	un·sure′	un·taxed′	un′trans·lat′a·ble
un·stain′a·ble	un′sur·mount′a·ble	un·teach′a·ble	un′trans·lat′ed
un·stained′	un′sur·passed′	un·tech′ni·cal	un′trans·mit′ted
un·stamped′	un′sur·ren′dered	un·tem′pered	un′trans·port′ed
un·stand′ard·ized	un′sur·ren′der·ing	un·tend′a·ble	un′trans·posed′
un·starched′	un·sus·pect′ed	un·tend′ed	un·trapped′
un·stat′ed	un·sus·pect′ing	un·ter′ri·fied	un′trav′eled
un·states′man·like′	un·sus·pi′cious	un·test′ed	un′trav′ers·a·ble
un·ster′i·lized	un′sus·tain′a·ble	un·thanked′	un′trav′ersed
un·stiff′ened	un·sus·tained′	un·think′a·ble	un·trem′bling
un·stig′ma·tized	un·swayed′	un·thought′	un·tried′
un·stint′ed	un·sweet′ened	un·thought′ful	un·trimmed′
un·stitched′	un·swept′	un·thrift′y	un·trod′den
un·stop′pered	un·swerv′ing	un·till′a·ble	un·trou′bled
un·strained′	un·swol′len	un·tilled′	un·trust′wor′thy
un′stra·te′gic	un′sym·met′ri·cal	un·tilt′ed	un·tucked′
un·strat′i·fied	un′sym·pa·thet′ic		un·tun′a·ble

āge, câre, fär; ēqual, tėrm; īce; ōpen, ôrder; pùt, rüle, ūse; tħ, then; ə=a in about.

un·twine (un·twīn′), v., **-twined, -twin·ing.** untwist.

un·twist (un·twist′), v. **1.** undo or loosen something twisted; unravel. **2.** become untwisted.

un·used (un·ūzd′), adj. **1.** not used: *an unused room.* **2.** not accustomed: *hands unused to labor.* **3.** never having been used: *unused drinking cups.*

un·u·su·al (un·ū′zhủ·əl), adj. beyond the ordinary; not common; rare. —**un·u′su·al·ly,** adv. —**un·u′su·al·ness,** n. —**Syn.** strange, singular.

un·ut·ter·a·ble (un·ut′ər·ə·bəl), adj. that cannot be expressed; unspeakable. —**un·ut′ter·a·bly,** adv.

un·var·nished (un·vär′nisht), adj. **1.** not varnished. **2.** plain; unadorned: *the unvarnished truth.*

un·veil (un·vāl′), v. **1.** remove a veil from; disclose; reveal. **2.** remove a veil; reveal oneself; become unveiled.

un·war·rant·a·ble (un·wôr′ən·tə·bəl; -wor′-), adj. not justifiable; illegal; improper. —**un·war′rant·a·ble·ness,** n. —**un·war′rant·a·bly,** adv.

un·war·y (un·wãr′ĭ), adj. not cautious; not careful; unguarded. —**un·war′i·ly,** adv. —**un·war′i·ness,** n. —**Syn.** careless, indiscreet.

un·weave (un·wēv′), v., **-wove, -wo·ven, -weav·ing.** take apart (something woven).

un·well (un·wel′), adj. ill; sick.

un·wept (un·wept′), adj. **1.** not wept for. **2.** not shed: *unwept tears.*

un·whole·some (un·hōl′səm), adj. bad for the body or the mind; unhealthy. —**un·whole′some·ly,** adv. —**un·whole′some·ness,** n.

un·wield·y (un·wēl′di), adj. not easily handled or managed, because of size, shape, or weight; bulky and clumsy: *the unwieldy armor of knights.* —**un·wield′i·ly,** adv. —**un·wield′i·ness,** n. —**Syn.** unmanageable, cumbersome.

un·will·ing (un·wil′ing), adj. not willing; not consenting. —**un·will′ing·ly,** adv. —**un·will′ing·ness,** n. —**Syn.** reluctant, averse, loath.

un·wind (un·wīnd′), v., **-wound, -wind·ing. 1.** wind off; take from a spool, ball, etc. **2.** become unwound. **3.** disentangle.

un·wise (un·wīz′), adj. not wise; not showing good judgment; foolish. —**un·wise′ly,** adv. —**Syn.** imprudent, indiscreet.

un·wit·ting (un·wit′ing), adj. not knowing; unaware; unconscious; unintentional. —**un·wit′ting·ly,** adv.

un·wont·ed (un·wun′tid; -wōn′-), adj. **1.** not customary; not usual. **2.** not accustomed; not used. —**un·wont′ed·ly,** adv. —**un·wont′ed·ness,** n.

un·wor·thy (un·wėr′thǐ), adj. **1.** not worthy; not deserving. **2.** base; shameful. —**un·wor′thi·ly,** adv. —**un·wor′thi·ness,** n. —**Syn. 2.** ignoble, discreditable, mean.

un·wrap (un·rap′), v., **-wrapped, -wrap·ping. 1.** remove a wrapping from; open. **2.** become opened.

un·wrin·kle (un·ring′kəl), v., **-kled, -kling.** smooth the wrinkles from.

un·writ·ten (un·rit′ən), adj. **1.** not written. **2.** understood or customary, but not actually expressed in writing. **3.** not written on; blank.

unwritten law, 1. the common law. **2.** principle that a man has a right to receive lenient treatment if he kills a person who has seduced his wife or daughter.

un·yoke (un·yōk′), v., **-yoked, -yok·ing.** free from a yoke.

up (up), adv., prep., adj., n., v., **upped, up·ping.** —adv. **1.** from a lower to a higher place or condition; to, toward, or near the top: *up in a tree.* **2.** in a higher place or condition; on or at a higher level. **3.** from a smaller to a larger amount: *prices have gone up.* **4.** to or at any point, place, or condition that is considered higher: *up north.* **5.** above the horizon: *the sun is up.* **6.** in or into an erect position: *stand up.* **7.** out of bed: *get up.* **8.** thoroughly; completely; entirely: *the house burned up.* **9.** at an end; over: *his time is up.* **10.** in or into being or action: *don't stir up trouble.* **11.** in process of going on or happening: *what's up over there?* **12.** together: *add these up.* **13.** to or in an even position; not behind: *catch up in a race, keep up to the times.* **14.** well advanced or versed, as in a subject: *be up on mathematics.* **15.** in or into view, notice, or consideration: *bring up a new topic.* **16.** in or into a state of tightness, etc.: *shut him up in his cage.* **17.** into safe-keeping, storage, etc.; aside; by: *lay up supplies.* **18.** *Am.* at bat in baseball. **19.** *Golf.* ahead of an opponent by a specified number of holes. **20.** in tennis, etc., apiece; for each one. **21.** **up against,** *Colloq.* facing as a thing to be dealt with. **22. up to, a.** doing; about to do. **b.** equal to; capable of doing: *up to a task.* **c.** plotting; scheming: *what are you up to?* **d.** *Colloq.* before (a person) as a duty or task to be done. —prep. **1.** to or at a higher place on or in: *up a tree.* **2.** to, toward, or near the top of: *up the hill.* **3.** along; through: *she walked up the street.* **4.** toward or in the inner or upper part of: *we sailed up the river, he lives up state.* —adj. **1.** advanced; forward. **2.** moving upward; directed upward: *an up trend.* **3.** above the ground: *the wheat is up.* **4.** near; close. **5.** *Am.* at bat in baseball. **6. up and doing,** busy; active. —n. **1.** an upward movement, course, or slope. **2.** piece of good luck. —v. **1.** put up. **2.** get up. [OE *upp(e)*]

UP, U.P., United Press.

up·borne (up·bôrn′; -bōrn′), adj. borne up; raised aloft; supported.

up·braid (up·brād′), v. find fault with; blame; reprove. [OE *upbregdan* < *upp* up + *bregdan* weave, braid] —**up·braid′er,** n. —**Syn.** reproach, scold.

up·braid·ing (up·brād′ing), n. a severe reproof; scolding. —adj. full of reproach. —**up·braid′ing·ly,** adv.

up·bring·ing (up′bring′ing), n. care and training given to a child while growing up.

up·coun·try (up′kun′tri), *Am.* —n. the interior of a country. —adv. toward or in the interior of a country. —adj. remote from the coast or border; interior.

up·end (up·end′), v. set on end; stand on end. —**up·end′ed,** adj.

up·grade (n. up′grād′; adv., adj. up′grād′), *Am.* —n. **1.** an upward slope or incline. **2. on the upgrade,** rising; improving. —adj. uphill.

up·heav·al (up·hēv′əl), n. a heaving up; being heaved up.

up·heave (up·hēv′), v., **-heaved or -hove, -heav·ing. 1.** heave up; lift up. **2.** rise.

up·hill (up′hil′), adj. **1.** going or pointing up the slope of a hill; upward. **2.** difficult: *an uphill fight.* —adv. up the slope of a hill.

up·hold (up·hōld′), v., **-held, -hold·ing. 1.** keep from falling; support. **2.** give moral support to. **3.** sustain; approve; confirm: *the higher*

court upheld the lower court's decision. —up-hold′er, *n.*

up·hol·ster (up·hōl′stər), *v. Am.* provide (furniture) with coverings, cushions, springs, stuffing, etc. [ult. < *uphold*] **—up·hol′stered,** *adj.* **—up·hol′ster·er,** *n.*

up·hol·ster·y (up·hōl′stər·i; -stri), *n., pl.* **-ster·ies. 1.** coverings for furniture. **2.** curtains, cushions, carpets, and hangings. **3.** business of upholstering.

up·keep (up′kēp′), *n.* **1.** maintenance. **2.** cost of operating and repair.

up·land (up′lənd; -land′), *n.* high land. *—adj.* of high land; living or growing on high land.

up·lift (*v.* up·lift′; *n.* up′lift′), *v.* **1.** lift up; raise. **2.** exalt emotionally or spiritually. **3.** raise socially or morally. *—n. Am.* **1.** act of lifting up; elevation. **2.** emotional or spiritual exaltation. **3.** social or moral improvement or effort toward it. **—up·lift′er,** *n.* **—up·lift′ment,** *n.*

up·most (up′mōst), *adj.* uppermost.

up·on (ə·pon′; ə·pôn′), *prep.* on. [ME, < *up* + *on*] **▶ upon, on.** *Upon* is used as an equivalent of *on* in all its senses, with no added idea of ascent or elevation, and preferred in certain cases only for euphonic or metrical reasons.

up·per (up′ər), *adj.* **1.** higher: *the upper lip, the upper rows.* **2.** higher in rank, office, etc.; superior. **3.** more recent. *—n.* **1.** part of a shoe or boot above the sole. **2. on one's uppers,** *Am., Colloq.* **a.** with the soles of one's shoes worn out. **b.** very shabby or poor.

upper case, capital letters. **—up′per-case′,** *adj.*

up·per-class (up′ər·klas′; -kläs′), *adj.* **1.** of or pertaining to a superior class. **2.** in universities, schools, etc., of or pertaining to the junior and senior classes.

up·per·class·man (up′ər·klas′mən; -kläs′-), *n., pl.* **-men.** *Am.* junior or senior.

up·per·cut (up′ər·kut′), *n., v., -cut, -cut-ting. —n.* *Boxing.* a swinging blow directed upwards. *—v.* strike with an uppercut.

upper hand, the, control; advantage.

Upper House, Often **upper house.** the higher or more restricted house in a legislature, deliberative body, etc.

up·per·most (up′ər·mōst), *adj.* Also, **up′most. 1.** highest; topmost. **2.** having the most force or influence; most prominent. *—adv.* **1.** in the highest place. **2.** first.

Upper Vol·ta (vol′tə), a republic in W Africa N of Ghana, formerly part of French West Africa.

up·pish (up′ish), *adj. Colloq.* somewhat arrogant, self-assertive, or conceited. **—up′pish·ly,** *adv.* **—up′pish·ness,** *n.*

up·pi·ty (up′ə·ti), *adj. Am., Colloq.* uppish.

up·right (up′rīt′; up·rīt′), *adj.* **1.** standing up straight; erect. **2.** good; honest; righteous. *—adv.* straight up; in a vertical position. *—n.* **1.** a vertical part or piece. **2.** something upright, as a goal post or an upright piano. **—up′right′ly,** *adv.* **—up′right′ness,** *n.*

up·ris·ing (up′rīz′ing; up·rīz′-), *n.* **1.** revolt. **2.** an upward slope; ascent.

up·roar (up′rôr′; -rōr′), *n.* **1.** a noisy or violent disturbance. **2.** a loud or confused noise. [< Du. *oproer* insurrection, tumult; infl. by assoc. with *roar*] **—Syn. 1.** tumult, commotion.

up·roar·i·ous (up·rôr′i·əs; -rōr′-), *adj.* **1.** noisy and disorderly: *an uproarious crowd.* **2.** loud and confused: *uproarious laughter.* **—up-roar′i·ous·ly,** *adv.* **—up·roar′i·ous·ness,** *n.*

up·root (up·rüt′; -rüt′), *v.* **1.** tear up by the roots. **2.** remove completely. **—up·root′er,** *n.*

up·set (*v., adj.* up·set′; *n.* up′set′), *v., -set, -set·ting, n., adj. —v.* **1.** tip over; overturn: *upset a boat.* **2.** disturb greatly; disorder: *rain upset our plans for a picnic, the shock upset her nerves.* **3.** overthrow; defeat: *upset a will.* **4.** become upset. *—n.* **1.** a tipping over; overturn. **2.** a great disturbance; disorder. **3.** an overthrowing; defeat. *—adj.* **1.** tipped over; overturned. **2.** greatly disturbed; disordered. **—up-set′ter,** *n.* **—Syn.** *v.* **1.** invert, capsize.

up·shot (up′shot′), *n.* conclusion; climax; result. **—Syn.** outcome, issue.

up·side (up′sīd′), *n.* the upper side.

upside down, 1. having what should be on top at the bottom. **2.** in complete disorder: *the room was upside down.* **—up′side′-down′,** *adj.*

up·si·lon (ūp′sə·lon), *n.* the 20th letter (Υ, υ) of the Greek alphabet.

up·stage (up′stāj′), *adv.* toward or at the back of the stage. *—adj.* **1.** toward or at the back of the stage. **2.** *Colloq.* haughty; aloof; supercilious.

up·stairs (up′stārz′), *adv.* **1.** up the stairs. **2.** on an upper floor. **3.** *Colloq.* of aircraft, in the air, esp. at a high altitude. *—adj.* on an upper floor. *—n.* the upper story.

up·stand·ing (up·stan′ding), *adj.* **1.** standing up; erect. **2.** honorable.

up·start (up′stärt′), *n.* **1.** person who has suddenly risen from a humble position to wealth, power, or importance. **2.** an unpleasant, conceited, and self-assertive person.

up·state (up′stāt′), *Am. —adj.* of the more inland or northern part of a State. *—n.* the more inland or northern part of a State, used esp. in New York State. **—up′stat′er,** *n.*

up·stream (up′strēm′), *adv., adj.* against the current of a stream; up a stream.

up·swing (up′swing′), *n.* **1.** an upward swing; movement upward. **2.** marked improvement.

up·thrust (up′thrust′), *n.* **1.** an upward push. **2.** movement upward of part of the earth's crust.

up-to-date (up′tə·dāt′), *adj.* **1.** extending to the present time. **2.** keeping up with the times in style, ideas, etc.; modern. **—up′-to-date′-ness,** *n.*

up·town (up′toun′), *adv.* to or in the upper part of a town. *—adj.* **1.** in the upper part of a town. **2.** *Am.* of or pertaining to the fashionable or residential area of a city, town, etc. *—n. Am.* the fashionable or residential area of a city, town, etc.

up·turn (*v.* up·tėrn′; *n.* up′tėrn′), *v.* turn up. *—n.* an upward turn. **—up·turned′,** *adj.*

up·ward (up′wərd), *adv.* Also, **up′wards. 1.** toward a higher place. **2.** toward a higher or greater rank, amount, age, etc. **3.** above; more. **4. upward or upwards of,** more than. *—adj.* directed or moving toward a higher place; in a higher position. **—up′ward·ly,** *adv.*

u·rae·mi·a (yu·rē′mi·ə), *n.* uremia. **—u·rae′-mic,** *adj.*

U·ral Mountains (yur′əl), or **Urals,** *n.pl.* range or chain of mountains in the Soviet Union, between Europe and Asia.

u·ra·ni·um (yu·rā′ni·əm), *n. Chem.* a heavy, white, radioactive metallic element, U or Ur. The uranium isotope U^{235} can sustain efficient chain reaction and is for this reason used in the atomic bomb. [< NL, < *Uranus,* the planet]

U·ra·nus (yur′ə·nəs), *n.* **1.** *Gk. Myth.* the personification of heaven, the father of the Titans and the Cyclopes. **2.** *Astron.* one of the larger planets, seventh in order from the sun.

ur·ban (ėr′bən), *adj.* **1.** of or pertaining to cities or towns. **2.** living in cities. **3.** characteristic of cities. [< L *urbanus* < *urbs* city]

ur·bane (ėr·bān′), *adj.* **1.** courteous; refined; elegant. **2.** smoothly polite. [< L *urbanus,* orig., URBAN] **—ur·bane′ly,** *adv.* **—ur·bane′ness,** *n.*

ur·ban·i·ty (ėr·ban′ə·ti), *n., pl.* **-ties. 1.** courtesy; refinement; elegance. **2.** smooth politeness.

ur·ban·ize (ėr′bən·īz), *v.,* **-ized, -iz·ing.** render urban: *urbanize a district or its people.* **—ur′ban·i·za′tion,** *n.*

ur·chin (ėr′chən), *n.* **1.** a mischievous boy. **2.** a poor, ragged child. [< OF *irechon* < L *ericius* < *er* hedgehog]

-ure, *suffix.* **1.** act or fact of ——ing, as in *failure.* **2.** state of being ——ed, as in *pleasure.* **3.** result of ——ing, as in *enclosure.* **4.** thing that ——s, as in *legislature.* **5.** thing that is ——ed, as in *disclosure.* **6.** other special meanings, as in *procedure, sculpture, denture.* [< F *-ure* < L *-ura*]

āge, cāre, fär; ēqual, tėrm; īce; ōpen, ôrder; půt, rüle, ūse; tħ, then; ə=*a* in about.

u·re·a (yu̇·rē′ə; yu̇r′i·ə), *n. Chem.* a soluble crystalline solid, $CO(NH_2)_2$, present in the urine of mammals. Urea is frequently used in making adhesives and plastics. [< NL, ult. < Gk. *ouron* urine] —**u·re′al,** *adj.*

u·re·mi·a (yu̇·rē′mi·ə), *n.* a poisoned condition resulting from the accumulation in the blood of waste products that should normally be eliminated in the urine. Also, **uraemia.** [< NL, < Gk. *ouron* urine + *haima* blood] —**u·re′mic,** *adj.*

u·re·ter (yu̇·rē′tər; yu̇r′ə·tər), *n.* duct that carries urine from a kidney to the bladder. [< NL < Gk. *oureter,* ult. < *ouron* urine]

u·re·thra (yu̇·rē′thrə), *n., pl.* **-thrae** (-thrē), **-thras.** duct by which urine is discharged from the bladder. [< LL < Gk. *ourethra,* ult. < *ouron* urine] —**u·re′thral,** *adj.*

urge (ėrj), *v.,* **urged, urg·ing,** *n.* —*v.* 1. drive with force, threats, etc.; push forward with effort: *he urged his horse along.* 2. try to persuade with arguments; ask earnestly: *they urged him to stay.* 3. plead or argue earnestly for; recommend strongly: *motorists urged better roads.* 4. press upon the attention; refer to often and with emphasis: *urge a claim.* —*n.* 1. a driving force or impulse. 2. act of urging. [< L *urgere*] —**Syn.** *v.* 1. press, impel, incite, spur, goad. 2. importune, exhort.

ur·gen·cy (ėr′jən·si), *n., pl.* **-cies.** 1. urgent character; need for immediate action or attention: *a matter of great urgency.* 2. insistence.

ur·gent (ėr′jənt), *adj.* 1. demanding immediate action or attention; pressing; important. 2. insistent. —**ur′gent·ly,** *adv.* —**Syn.** 1. imperative, necessary. 2. importunate.

u·ric (yu̇r′ik), *adj.* of or pertaining to urine or urea.

uric acid, *Chem.* a solid white substance, $C_5H_4N_4O_3$, only slightly soluble in water, that is formed in the body as a waste product from proteins.

u·ri·nal (yu̇r′ə·nəl), *n.* 1. container for urine. 2. place for urinating.

u·ri·nal·y·sis (yu̇r′ə·nal′ə·sis), *n., pl.* **-ses** (-sēz). *Am.* analysis of a sample of urine.

u·ri·nar·y (yu̇r′ə·ner′i), *adj., n., pl.* **-nar·ies.** —*adj.* 1. of or pertaining to urine. 2. of or pertaining to the organs that secrete and discharge urine. —*n.* urinal.

u·ri·nate (yu̇r′ə·nāt), *v.,* **-nat·ed, -nat·ing.** discharge urine from the body. —**u′ri·na′tion,** *n.* —**u′ri·na′tive,** *adj.*

u·rine (yu̇r′ən), *n.* the fluid that is secreted by the kidneys, passes into the bladder, and is then discharged from the body. [< L *urina*]

urn (ėrn), *n.* 1. vase with a foot or pedestal, esp. one used to hold the ashes of the dead. 2. place of burial; grave; tomb. 3. a coffee pot or teapot with a faucet, used for making or serving coffee or tea at the table. [< L *urna*]

Coffee urn

u·ro·gen·i·tal (yu̇r′ō·jen′ə·təl), *adj.* noting or pertaining to the urinary and genital organs. [< *uro-* (< Gk. *ouron* urine) + *genital*]

u·ros·co·py (yu̇·ros′kə·pi), *n. Med.* examination of the urine as a means of diagnosis, etc.

Ur·sa Ma·jor (ėr′sə mā′jər), *gen.* **Ur·sae Ma·jo·ris** (ėr′sē mə·jô′ris; -jō′-), *Astron.* the northern constellation that includes the stars of the Big Dipper; the Great Bear. [< L]

Ur·sa Mi·nor (ėr′sə mī′nər), *gen.* **Ur·sae Mi·no·ris** (ėr′sē mi·nô′ris; -nō′-), *Astron.* the northern constellation that includes the stars of the Little Dipper; the Little Bear. [< L]

ur·sine (ėr′sīn; -sin), *adj.* of or pertaining to bears; bearlike. [< L, < *ursus* bear]

U·ru·guay (yu̇r′ə·gwā; -gwī), *n.* country in the SE part of South America. —**U′ru·guay′an,** *adj., n.*

us (us; *unstressed* əs), *pron.* the objective case of we: *Mother went with us.* [OE *ūs*]

U.S., *Am.* the United States.

U.S.A., 1. *Am.* the United States of America. 2.

Also, **USA.** *Am.* the United States Army. 3. the Union of South Africa.

us·a·ble (ūz′ə·bəl), *adj.* that can be used; fit for use. Also, **useable.** —**us′a·bil′i·ty, us′a·ble·ness,** *n.*

USAF, U.S.A.F., United States Air Force.

us·age (ūs′ij; ūz′-), *n.* 1. way or manner of using; treatment: *the car has had rough usage.* 2. a long-continued practice; customary use; habit; custom: *travelers should learn many of the usages of the countries they visit.* 3. the customary way of using words: *usage determines what is good English.*

USCG, U.S.C.G., United States Coast Guard.

use (*v.* ūz; *n.* ūs), *v.,* **used, us·ing,** *n.* —*v.* 1. put into action or service: *use a knife.* 2. act toward; treat: *use a dog cruelly.* 3. consume or expend by using: *we have used most of the amount.* 4. avail oneself of: *may I use your telephone?* 5. **used to, a.** accustomed to: *used to hardships.* **b.** was or were accustomed to; formerly did: *he used to come every day.* 6. use up, **a.** consume or expend entirely. **b.** *Colloq.* tire out; weary; exhaust. —*n.* 1. a using: *the use of tools.* 2. a being used: *methods long out of use.* 3. usefulness: *a thing of no practical use.* 4. purpose that a thing is used for: *find a new use for something.* 5. way of using: *poor use of a material.* 6. way of treating; treatment: *give a car rough use.* 7. need; occasion: *he had no further use for it.* 8. power, right, or privilege of using: *have the use of a boat for the summer.* 9. help, profit, or resulting good: *what's the use of talking?* 10. custom; habit; usage: *it was his use to rise early.* 11. *Law.* benefit or profit of property held by someone for the beneficiary. 12. **have no use for, a.** not need or want. **b.** *Am., Colloq.* dislike. 13. **in use,** being used. 14. **make use of,** use; employ. 15. **put to use,** use. [< OF *user* < VL *usare,* intensive of L *uti* use] —**us′er,** *n.* —**Syn.** *v.* 1. employ, utilize, apply. —*n.* 1. employment, application, service, utilization.

use·a·ble (ūz′ə·bəl), *adj.* usable. —**use′a·bil′i·ty, use′a·ble·ness,** *n.*

use·ful (ūs′fəl), *adj.* 1. of use; giving service; helpful. —**use′ful·ly,** *adv.* —**use′ful·ness,** *n.*

use·less (ūs′lis), *adj.* of no use; worthless. —**use′less·ly,** *adv.* —**use′less·ness,** *n.* —**Syn.** valueless, unavailing, futile, unprofitable.

U-shaped (ū′shāpt′), *adj.* having the shape of the letter U.

ush·er (ush′ər), *n.* 1. person who shows people to their seats in a church, theater, etc. 2. *Am.* a male friend of the bride or groom serving as an usher at a wedding. 3. *Brit.* an assistant teacher. —*v.* conduct; escort; show: *he ushered the visitors to the door.* [< AF < VL *ustiarius* doorkeeper < *ustium,* var. of L *ostium* door]

U.S.M., 1. United States Mail. 2. United States Marine.

USMC, U.S.M.C., United States Marine Corps.

USN, U.S.N., United States Navy.

USNG, U.S.N.G., United States National Guard.

U.S.S., 1. Also, **USS.** United States Ship, Steamer, or Steamship. 2. United States Senate.

U.S.S.R., USSR, Union of Soviet Socialist Republics.

u·su·al (ū′zhu̇·əl), *adj.* 1. in common use; ordinary; customary. 2. **as usual,** in the usual manner. [< LL *usualis,* ult. < *uti* use] —**u′su·al·ly,** *adv.* —**u′su·al·ness,** *n.* —**Syn.** 1. general, prevailing, conventional, accustomed. —**Ant.** 1. strange, exceptional, extraordinary.

u·su·rer (ū′zhə·rər), *n.* person who lends money at an extremely high or unlawful rate of interest. [< OF < LL *usurarius* < *usuria* USURY]

u·su·ri·ous (ū·zhu̇r′i·əs), *adj.* 1. taking extremely high or unlawful interest for the use of money. 2. of or having to do with usury. —**u·su′ri·ous·ly,** *adv.* —**u·su′ri·ous·ness,** *n.*

u·surp (ū·sėrp′; ū·zėrp′), *v.* seize and hold (power, position, authority, etc.) by force or without right. [< L *usurpare,* ult. < *usus* use + *rapere* seize] —**u·surp′er,** *n.* —**u·surp′ing·ly,** *adv.* —**Syn.** appropriate, arrogate, assume.

u·sur·pa·tion (ū'zər·pā'shən; ū'sər-), *n.* a usurping; the seizing and holding of the place or power of another by force or without right.

u·su·ry (ū'zhə·ri), *n., pl.* **-ries.** 1. the lending of money at an extremely high or unlawful rate of interest. 2. an extremely high or unlawful interest. [< Med.L *usuria,* ult. < *uti* use]

Ut., Utah.

U·tah (ū'tô; ū'tä), *n.* a Western State of the United States. *Capital:* Salt Lake City. *Abbrev.:* Ut. —**U'tah·an,** *adj., n.*

u·ten·sil (ū·ten'səl), *n.* 1. container or implement used for practical purposes. Pots, pans, kettles, and mops are kitchen utensils. 2. instrument or tool used for some special purpose. Pens and pencils are writing utensils. [< Med.L, < L *utensilis* useful < *uti* use]

u·ter·ine (ū'tər·in; -īn), *adj.* 1. of or pertaining to the uterus. 2. having the same mother, but a different father.

u·ter·us (ū'tər·əs), *n., pl.* **-ter·i** (-tər·ī). the part of the body in mammals that holds and nourishes the young till birth; womb. [< L]

U Thant (ü thant; thont), born 1909, Burmese statesman, Secretary General of the United Nations since 1962.

U·ti·ca (ū'tə·kə), *n.* city in C New York State.

u·til·i·tar·i·an (ū·til'ə·târ'i·ən), *adj.* 1. having to do with utility. 2. aiming at usefulness rather than beauty, style, etc. —*n.* adherent of utilitarianism.

u·til·i·tar·i·an·ism (ū·til'ə·târ'i·ən·iz'əm), *n.* 1. the doctrine or belief that the greatest good of the greatest number should be the purpose of human conduct. 2. the doctrine or belief that actions are good if they are useful.

u·til·i·ty (ū·til'ə·ti), *n., pl.* **-ties.** 1. usefulness; power to satisfy people's needs. 2. a useful thing. 3. company that performs a public service. Railroads, bus lines, gas and electric companies are utilities. [< L *utilitas,* ult. < *uti* use]

u·ti·lize (ū'tə·līz), *v.,* **-lized, -liz·ing.** make use of; put to some practical use. —**u'ti·liz'a·ble,** *adj.* —**u'ti·li·za'tion,** *n.* —**u'ti·liz'er,** *n.*

ut·most (ut'mōst), *adj.* 1. greatest possible; extreme: *the utmost effort.* 2. most distant; farthest: *the utmost part of the country.* —*n.* the most that is possible; extreme limit. Also, uttermost. [OE *ūtemest* < *ūte* outside + *-mest* -MOST]

U·to·pi·a (ū·tō'pi·ə), *n.* 1. an ideal commonwealth described in *Utopia* by Sir Thomas More. 2. Often, **utopia.** an ideal place or state with perfect laws. 3. Often, **utopia.** a visionary, impractical system of political or social perfection. [< NL, < Gk. *ou* not + *topos* place]

U·to·pi·an (ū·tō'pi·ən), *adj.* 1. of, pertaining to, or resembling Utopia. 2. Often, **utopian.** visionary; impractical. —*n.* 1. inhabitant of Utopia. 2. Often, **utopian.** an ardent but impractical reformer; idealist. —**u·to'pi·an·ism,** *n.*

U·trecht (ū'trekt), *n.* city in the C part of the Netherlands.

ut·ter[1] (ut'ər), *adj.* complete; total; absolute. [OE *ūtera* outer] —**ut'ter·ly,** *adv.* —**Syn.** entire, unqualified, sheer.

ut·ter[2] (ut'ər), *v.* 1. pronounce; speak: *the last words he uttered.* 2. make known; express: *utter one's thoughts.* 3. give; give out: *he uttered a cry of pain.* [ult. < OE *ūt* out] —**ut'ter·a·ble,** *adj.* —**ut'ter·er,** *n.* —**Syn.** 1. deliver, articulate.

ut·ter·ance (ut'ər·əns), *n.* 1. an uttering; expression in words or sounds: *the child gave utterance to his grief.* 2. way of speaking. 3. something uttered; a spoken word or words.

ut·ter·most (ut'ər·mōst), *adj., n.* utmost.

u·vu·la (ū'vyə·lə), *n., pl.* **-las, -lae** (-lē). *Anat.* the small piece of flesh hanging down from the soft palate in the back of the mouth. [< LL, dim. of L *uva,* orig., grape]

u·vu·lar (ū'vyə·lər), *adj.* 1. of or pertaining to the uvula. 2. *Phonet.* articulated at or near the uvula.

ux·o·ri·ous (uks·ô'ri·əs; -ō'-; ug·zô'-; -zō'-), *adj.* excessively or foolishly fond of one's wife. [< L, < *uxor* wife] —**ux·o'ri·ous·ly,** *adv.* —**ux·o'ri·ous·ness,** *n.*

Uz·bek (uz'bek), *n.* a constituent republic of the Soviet Union, in W Asia N of Afghanistan.

V

V, v (vē), *n., pl.* **V's; v's.** 1. the 22nd letter of the alphabet. 2. anything shaped like a V. 3. the Roman numeral for 5.

V, 1. *Chem.* vanadium. 2. Victory. 3. volt.

v., 1. see. [< L *vide*] 2. verb. 3. versus. 4. volt; voltage; volts. 5. volume. 6. von.

VA, V.A., Veterans' Administration.

Va., Virginia.

va·can·cy (vā'kən·si), *n., pl.* **-cies.** 1. state of being vacant; emptiness. 2. an unoccupied position: *a vacancy in a business.* 3. state of being or becoming unoccupied. 4. a room, space, or apartment for rent; empty space.

va·cant (vā'kənt), *adj.* 1. not occupied: *a vacant house.* 2. not filled; empty: *vacant space.* 3. without thought or intelligence: *a vacant smile.* 4. not being used: *vacant time.* [< L *vacans* being empty] —**va'cant·ly,** *adv.*

va·cate (vā'kāt), *v.,* **-cat·ed, -cat·ing.** 1. go away from and leave empty or unoccupied; make vacant. 2. leave. 3. make void; annul; cancel. [< L *vacatus* emptied]

va·ca·tion (vā·kā'shən), *Am.* —*n.* time of rest and freedom from work. —*v.* take a vacation. —**va·ca'tion·ist, va·ca'tion·er,** *n. Am.*

vac·ci·nate (vak'sə·nāt), *v.,* **-nat·ed, -nat·ing.** *Med.* 1. inoculate with vaccine as a protection against smallpox. 2. take similar measures against other diseases. —**vac'ci·na'tion,** *n.* —**vac'ci·na'tor,** *n.*

vac·cine (vak'sēn; -sin), *n.* 1. the germs causing cowpox, used for the protection of people against smallpox. 2. any preparation of disease germs, or the like, that is used for preventive inoculation. [< L *vaccinus* pertaining to cows < *vacca* cow]

vac·il·late (vas'ə·lāt), *v.,* **-lat·ed, -lat·ing.** 1. move first one way and then another; waver. 2. waver in mind or opinion. [< L, pp. of *vacillare*] —**vac'il·lat'ing,** *adj.* —**vac'il·lat'ing·ly,** *adv.* —**vac'il·la'tion,** *n.* —**vac·il·la·to·ry** (vas'ə·lə·tô'ri; -tō'-), *adj.* —**Syn.** 1. oscillate, sway.

va·cu·i·ty (va·kū'ə·ti), *n., pl.* **-ties.** 1. emptiness. 2. an empty space; vacuum. 3. lack of thought or intelligence. 4. something foolish or stupid.

vac·u·ole (vak'yū·ōl), *n.* 1. a tiny cavity in a living cell, containing fluid. 2. formerly, any very small cavity in organic tissue. [< F, < L *vacuus* empty]

vac·u·ous (vak'yū·əs), *adj.* 1. showing no thought or intelligence; foolish; stupid. 2. empty. [< L *vacuus*] —**vac'u·ous·ly,** *adv.* —**vac'u·ous·ness,** *n.*

vac·u·um (vak'yū·əm), *n., pl.* **vac·u·ums, vac·u·a** (vak'yū·ə), *v.* —*n.* 1. an empty space without even air in it. 2. space from which almost all air, gas, etc., has been removed. 3. an empty space; void. 4. *Am.* a vacuum cleaner. —*v. Colloq.* clean with a vacuum cleaner. [< L, neut. adj., empty]

vacuum bottle, bottle surrounded by a container, with a vacuum between, used to keep liquids hot or cold.

vacuum cleaner, apparatus for cleaning carpets, curtains, floors, etc., by suction.

vacuum pump, pump or device by which a partial vacuum can be produced.

vacuum tube, a sealed tube or bulb from which almost all the air has been removed, and into which electrodes from outside project. Vacuum tubes are used in radio sets to control the flow of electric currents.

va·de me·cum (vā'dē mē'kəm), 1. anything a person carries about with him because of its usefulness. 2. book for ready reference; manual; handbook. [< L, go with me]

vag·a·bond (vag'ə·bond), n. 1. an idle wanderer; tramp. 2. a good-for-nothing person; rascal. —adj. 1. wandering. 2. good-for-nothing; worthless. 3. moving hither and thither; drifting. [< OF < L vagabundus, ult. < vagus rambling] —vag'a·bond·ism, n. —Syn. n. 1. vagrant, nomad, hobo.

vag·a·bond·age (vag'ə·bon'dij), n. fact or state of being a vagabond; idle wandering.

va·gar·y (və·gãr'i; vā'gə·ri), n., pl. -gar·ies. 1. an odd fancy; extravagant notion: the vagaries of a dream. 2. odd action; caprice; freak: the vagaries of women's fashions. [prob. < L vagari wander < vagus roving] —va·gar'i·ous, adj.

va·gi·na (və·jī'nə), n., pl. -nas, -nae (-nē). 1. in female mammals, passage from the uterus to the vulva or external opening. 2. sheath; sheathlike part. [< L, orig., sheath] —vag·i·nal (vaj'ə·nəl; və·jī'nəl), adj.

va·gran·cy (vā'grən·si), n., pl. -cies. 1. a wandering idly from place to place without proper means, or ability to earn a living. 2. a wandering. 3. a vagrant act or idea.

va·grant (vā'grənt), n. an idle wanderer; tramp. —adj. 1. moving in no definite direction or course; wandering. 2. wandering without proper means of earning a living. 3. of or pertaining to a vagrant. [? alter. of AF wakerant, infl. by L vagari wander] —va'grant·ly, adv. —va'grant·ness, n.

vague (vāg), adj., va·guer, va·guest. 1. not definite: vague promises. 2. not clear; not distinct: vague forms. [< OF < L vagus wandering] —vague'ly, adv. —vague'ness, n. —Syn. 1. ambiguous. 2. obscure, hazy.

vain (vān), adj. 1. having too much pride in one's looks, ability, etc. 2. of no use; without effect or success; producing no good result: vain attempts. 3. of no value or importance; worthless; empty: a vain boast. 4. in vain, without effect; unsuccessfully. [< OF < L vanus] —vain'ly, adv. —vain'ness, n. —Syn. adj. 1. conceited, egotistical. 2. futile, ineffectual.

vain·glo·ri·ous (vān'glô'ri·əs; -glō'-), adj. excessively proud or boastful; extremely vain. —vain'glo'ri·ous·ly, adv. —vain'glo'ri·ous·ness, n. —Syn. vaunting, arrogant, conceited.

vain·glo·ry (vān'glô'ri; -glō'-), n. 1. an extreme pride in oneself; boastful vanity. 2. worthless pomp or show.

val·ance (val'əns), n. a short drapery over the top of a window. [? < derivative of OF valer to lower] —val'anced, adj.

vale[1] (vāl), n. Poetic. valley. [< OF val < L vallis]

va·le[2] (vā'lē; vä'lā), interj., n. Latin. good-by; farewell.

val·e·dic·tion (val'ə·dik'shən), n. a bidding farewell. [< L, < pp. stem of valedicere bid farewell < vale be well! + dicere say]

val·e·dic·to·ri·an (val'ə·dik·tô'ri·ən; -tō'-), n. Am. the student who gives the farewell address at the graduating exercises, often the student who ranks highest in his class.

val·e·dic·to·ry (val'ə·dik'tə·ri; -dik'tri), n., pl. -ries. —n. Am. a farewell address, esp. at the graduating exercises of a school or college. —adj. bidding farewell. [see VALEDICTION]

va·lence (vā'ləns), **va·len·cy** (-lən·si), n., pl. -lenc·es, -cies. Chem. combining capacity of an atom measured by a unit of hydrogen. The valence of hydrogen or chlorine is 1, of oxygen is 2, of aluminum is 3. [< L valentia strength < valere be strong]

Va·len·cia (və·len'shə; -shi·ə), n. seaport in E Spain.

val·en·tine (val'ən·tīn), n. 1. a greeting card or small gift sent on Valentine's Day, February 14. 2. a sweetheart chosen on this day.

Val·en·tine (val'ən·tīn), n. Saint, Christian martyr of the third century A.D.

Valentine's Day, Saint Valentine's Day, day on which valentines are exchanged, February 14.

va·le·ri·an (və·lir'i·ən), n. 1. a strong-smelling drug used to quiet the nerves. 2. the plant from whose root it is made. [< OF valeriane or Med.L valeriana < L Valerius, Roman gens name]

val·et (val'it; val'ā), n., v., -et·ed, -et·ing. —n. 1. servant who takes care of a man's clothes, helps him dress, etc. 2. a similar servant in a hotel who cleans or presses clothes. —v. serve as a valet. [< F, var. of OF vaslet VARLET] —val'et·less, adj.

val·e·tu·di·nar·i·an (val'ə·tü'də·nãr'i·ən; -tū'-), n. 1. an invalid. 2. person who thinks he is ill when he is not. —adj. 1. sickly. 2. thinking too much about health. [< L valetudinarius sickly < valetudo (good or bad) health < valere be strong] —val'e·tu'di·nar'i·an·ism, n.

Val·hal·la (val·hal'ə), n. Scand. Myth. hall of the god Odin where he receives the souls of the slain warrior heroes.

val·iant (val'yənt), adj. brave; courageous. [< OF < vaillant, ppr. of valoir be strong < L valere] —val'iant·ly, adv. —val'iant·ness, n.

val·id (val'id), adj. 1. supported by facts or authority; sound; true: a valid argument. 2. having legal force; legally binding. [< L validus strong] —val'id·ly, adv. —val'id·ness, n.

val·i·date (val'ə·dāt), v., -dat·ed, -dat·ing. 1. make or declare legally binding; give legal force to. 2. support by facts or authority; confirm. —val'i·da'tion, n.

va·lid·i·ty (və·lid'ə·ti), n., pl. -ties. 1. truth; soundness: the validity of an argument. 2. legal soundness or force. 3. effectiveness.

va·lise (və·lēs'), n. a traveling bag to hold clothes, etc. [< F < Ital. valigia]

Val·kyr·ie (val·kir'i), **Val·kyr** (val'kir), n. Scand. Myth. one of the handmaidens of Odin, who ride through the air and hover over battlefields, choosing the heroes who are to die in battle and afterward leading them to Valhalla. —Val·kyr'i·an, adj.

val·ley (val'i), n., pl. -leys. 1. a low land between hills or mountains. 2. a wide region drained by a great river system: the Mississippi valley. 3. any hollow or structure like a valley. [< OF valee < val vale < L vallis] —val'ley·like', adj. —Syn. 1. vale, dale, glen, dell.

Valley Forge, village in SE Pennsylvania, near which Washington and his army spent the winter of 1777-1778.

val·or, esp. Brit. **val·our** (val'ər), n. bravery; courage. [< LL, < L valere be strong] —val'or·ous, adj. —val'or·ous·ly, adv. —val'or·ous·ness, n.

val·or·i·za·tion (val'ər·ə·zā'shən), n. Am. the actual or attempted maintenance of certain prices for a commodity by a government.

val·or·ize (val'ər·īz), v., -ized, -iz·ing. 1. assign a value to. 2. regulate the price of by valorization.

Val·pa·rai·so (val'pə·rī'zo), n. seaport in C Chile.

valse (väls), n. French. waltz.

val·u·a·ble (val'yū·ə·bəl), adj. 1. having value; being worth something. 2. having great value. 3. that can have its value measured. —n. Usually, valuables. an article of value. —val'u·a·ble·ness, n. —val'u·a·bly, adv. —Syn. adj. 2. precious, expensive.

val·u·a·tion (val'yū·ā'shən), n. 1. value estimated or determined: the jeweler's valuation of the necklace was $10,000. 2. an estimating or determining of the value of something. —val'u·a'tion·al, adj.

val·ue (val'ū), n., v., -ued, -u·ing. —n. 1. worth; excellence; usefulness; importance: the value of education. 2. the real worth; proper price: he bought the house for less than its value. 3. power to buy: the value of the dollar has varied greatly. 4. estimated worth: he placed a value on his furniture. 5. an excellent buy; bargain. 6. meaning; effect; force: the value of a symbol. 7. number or amount represented by a symbol: the value of XIV is fourteen. 8. values, the established ideals of life. 9. Music. the relative length of a tone indicated by a note. 10. degree of lightness or darkness in a painting, etc. —v. 1. rate at a certain value or price; estimate the value of. 2. think highly of; regard highly: *value one's judgment.* [< OF, < pp. of *valoir* be worth < L *valere*] —**val'u·er**, *n.* —Syn. *v.* 2. esteem, prize.

val·ued (val'ūd), *adj.* 1. having its value estimated or determined. 2. regarded highly. 3. having the value specified.

val·ue·less (val'yù·lis), *adj.* without value; worthless. —**val'ue·less·ness**, *n.*

valve (valv), *n., v.,* **valved, valv·ing.** —*n.* 1. a movable part that controls the flow of a liquid, gas, etc., through a pipe by opening and closing the passage. A faucet is one kind of valve. 2. a membrane that works similarly. The valves of the heart control the flow of blood. 3. *Zool.* one of the parts of hinged shells like those of oysters and clams. 4. *Music.* device in wind instruments for changing the pitch of the tone by changing the direction and length of the column of air. Cornets and French horns have valves. —*v.* control the flow of (a liquid, gas, etc.) by a valve. [< L *valva* one of a pair of folding doors] —**valv'al,** *adj.* —**valve'less,** *adj.* —**valve'like',** *adj.*

val·vu·lar (val'vyə·lər), *adj.* 1. having to do with valves, esp. with the valves of the heart. 2. having the form of a valve. 3. furnished with valves; working by valves.

va·moose (va·müs'), **va·mose** (–mōs'), *v.,* –**moosed,** –**moos·ing;** –**mosed,** –**mos·ing.** *Am., Slang.* go away quickly. [< Sp. *vamos* let us go]

vamp¹ (vamp), *n.* 1. the upper front part of a shoe or boot. 2. piece or patch added to an old thing to make it look new. —*v.* 1. furnish with a vamp; repair with a new vamp. 2. patch up; make (an old thing) look new. [< OF *avanpie* < *avant* before < L *ab* from + *ante* before) + *pie* foot < L *pes*] —**vamp'er,** *n.*

vamp² (vamp), *Slang.* —*n.* an unscrupulous flirt. —*v.* flirt with. [< *vampire*] —**vamp'er,** *n.*

vam·pire (vam'pir), *n.* 1. a corpse supposed to come to life at night and suck the blood of people while they sleep. 2. person who preys ruthlessly on others. 3. woman who flirts with men to get money or to please her vanity. 4. Also, **vampire bat.** any of various South and Central American bats, including **true vampires,** a species which actually sucks the blood of animals and men. [< F < Hung. *vampir,* ? ult. < Turk. *uber* witch]

van¹ (van), *n.* the front part of an army, fleet, or other advancing group. [< *vanguard*]

van² (van), *n.* 1. a covered truck or wagon for moving furniture, etc. 2. *Brit.* a railroad baggage car. [< *caravan*]

va·na·di·um (va·nā'di·əm), *n. Chem.* a rare metallic element, V, used in making vanadium steel, a tough and durable steel.

Van Bu·ren (van byür'ən), Martin, 1782–1862, the eighth president of the United States, 1837–1841.

Van·cou·ver (van·kü'vər), *n.* 1. seaport in SW Canada. 2. island in the Pacific Ocean, just off the SW coast of Canada.

van·dal (van'dəl), *n.* 1. person who willfully or ignorantly destroys or damages beautiful or valuable things. 2. **Vandal,** member of a pair of Germanic tribe that ravaged Gaul, Spain, and N Africa. In 455 A.D. the Vandals took Rome. —*adj.* 1. destructive. 2. **Vandal,** of or having to do with the Vandals. —**van'dal·ism,** *n.*

Van Dyck, Van·dyke (van·dīk'), *n.* Sir Anthony, 1599–1641, Flemish painter who lived for some years in England.

van·dyke (van·dīk'), *n.* a short, pointed beard.

vane (vān), *n.* 1. a movable device that shows which way the wind is blowing. 2. blade of a windmill, blade of a ship's propeller, etc. 3. the flat, soft part of a feather. [OE *fana* banner] —**vaned** (vānd), *adj.* —**vane'less,** *adj.*

Vandyke beard

Van Gogh (van gō'; gôk'), Vincent. See Gogh.

van·guard (van'gärd'), *n.* 1. soldiers march-

ing ahead of the main part of an army to clear the way and guard against surprise. 2. the foremost or leading position. 3. leaders of a movement. [< OF *avangarde* < *avant* before (< L *ab* from + *ante* before) + *garde* GUARD]

va·nil·la (va·nil'ə), *n.* 1. a flavoring extract used in candy, ice cream, perfume, etc. 2. the tropical plant that yields the beans used in making this flavoring. 3. Also, **vanilla bean.** the bean itself. [< NL < Sp. *vainilla,* lit., little pod, ult. < L *vagina* sheath] —**va·nil'lic,** *adj.*

van·ish (van'ish), *v.* 1. disappear; disappear suddenly. 2. pass away; cease to be. [< OF *evaniss-,* ult. < L *evanescere* (< *ex-* out + *vanus* empty] —**van'ish·er,** *n.* —**van'ish·ing·ly,** *adv.*

van·i·ty (van'ə·ti), *n., pl.* –**ties.** 1. too much pride in one's looks, ability, etc.: *girlish vanity.* 2. lack of real value; worthlessness: *the vanity of wealth.* 3. a useless or worthless thing. 4. worthless pleasure or display. 5. a vanity case. 6. a dressing table with an attached mirror. [< OF < L, < *vanus* empty] —Syn. 1. conceit, egotism, self-esteem. —Ant. 1. humility.

vanity case, case containing a small mirror, powder, rouge, etc., carried by women.

van·quish (vang'kwish; van'–), *v.* conquer; defeat; overcome. [< OF *vencus,* pp. of *veintre* or < OF *vainquiss-,* both < L *vincere* conquer] —**van'quish·a·ble,** *adj.* —**van'quish·er,** *n.* —**van'quish·ment,** *n.*

van·tage (van'tij; vän'–), *n.* a better position or condition; advantage. [ult. < *advantage*]

vantage ground, position that gives one an advantage; favorable position.

van·ward (van'wərd), *adj., adv.* toward or in the front.

vap·id (vap'id), *adj.* without much life or flavor; tasteless; dull. [< L *vapidus*] —**va·pid'i·ty,** **vap'id·ness,** *n.* —**vap'id·ly,** *adv.*

va·por, *esp. Brit.* **va·pour** (vā'pər), *n.* 1. steam from boiling water; moisture in the air that can be seen; fog; mist. 2. a gas formed from a substance that is usually a liquid or a solid. 3. something without substance; empty fancy. 4. **the vapors,** *Archaic.* low spirits. —*v.* 1. pass off as vapor. 2. send out in vapor. 3. boast; swagger; brag. [< L] —**va'por·er,** *esp. Brit.* **va'pour·er,** *n.* —**va'por·ing·ly,** *esp. Brit.* **va'pour·ing·ly,** *adv.* —**va'por·ish,** *esp. Brit.* **va'pour·ish,** *adj.* —**va'por·less,** *esp. Brit.* **va'pour·less,** *adj.*

va·por·ize, *esp. Brit.* **va·pour·ize** (vā'pər·īz), *v.,* –**ized,** –**iz·ing.** change into vapor. —**va'por·iz'a·ble,** *esp. Brit.* **va'pour·iz'a·ble,** *adj.* —**va'por·i·za'tion,** *esp. Brit.* **va'pour·i·za'tion,** *n.* —**va'por·iz'er,** *esp. Brit.* **va'pour·iz'er,** *n.*

va·por·ous (vā'pər·əs), *adj.* 1. full of vapor; misty. 2. like vapor. 3. soon passing; worthless. —**va'por·ous·ly,** *adv.* —**va'por·ous·ness, va'por·os'i·ty,** *n.*

vapor trail, visible stream of moisture left by the engines of a jet plane flying at high altitude.

va·que·ro (vä·kār'ō), *n., pl.* –**ros.** *Am., S.W.* cowboy; herdsman. [< Sp., ult. < L *vacca* cow]

var., 1. variant. 2. variety. 3. various.

var·i·a·ble (vār'i·ə·bəl), *adj.* 1. apt to change; changeable; uncertain: *variable winds.* 2. that can be varied: *these curtain rods are of variable length.* 3. deviating from the strict biological type. —*n.* 1. a thing or quantity that varies. 2. in science, a quantity whose varying amounts are related to known facts or possibilities. 3. a shifting wind. —**var'i·a·bil'i·ty, var'i·a·ble·ness,** *n.* —**var'i·a·bly,** *adv.* —Syn. *adj.* 1. unsteady, unstable, fluctuating, wavering.

Vaquero

var·i·ance (vār'i·əns), *n.* 1. difference; discrepancy; deviation. 2. discord; dissension; quarrel. 3. a varying change.

var·i·ant (vār'i·ənt), *adj.* 1. varying; different: *"rime" is a variant spelling of "rhyme."* 2. variable; changing. —*n.* 1. a different form. 2. a different pronunciation or spelling of the same word.

var·i·a·tion (vâr′i·ā′shən), *n.* **1.** a varying in condition, degree, etc.; change. **2.** amount of change. **3.** a varied or changed form. **4.** *Music.* tune or theme repeated with changes. **5.** *Biol.* deviation of an animal or plant from type. —var′i·a′tion·al, *adj.*

var·i·col·ored, *esp. Brit.* **var·i·col·oured** (vâr′i·kul′ərd), *adj.* **1.** having various colors. **2.** divergent; varied.

var·i·cose (var′ə·kōs; vâr′-), *adj.* **1.** swollen or enlarged: *varicose veins.* **2.** pertaining to, affected with, or designed to remedy varicose veins. [< L *varicosus* < *varix* dilated vein] —var′i·cosed, *adj.* —var·i·cos·i·ty (var′ə·kos′ə·ti), var′i·cose·ness, *n.*

var·ied (vâr′id), *adj.* **1.** of or characterized by different kinds; having variety. **2.** changed; altered. —var′ied·ly, *adv.* —var′ied·ness, *n.*

var·i·e·gate (vâr′i·ə·gāt; -i·gāt), *v.,* -gat·ed, -gat·ing. **1.** vary in appearance; mark, spot, or streak with different colors. **2.** give variety to. [< L, pp. of *variegare*] —var′i·e·ga′tion, *n.* —var′i·e·ga′tor, *n.*

var·i·e·gat·ed (vâr′i·ə·gāt′id; -i·gāt′id), *adj.* **1.** varied in appearance; marked with different colors. Pansies are usually variegated. **2.** having variety.

va·ri·e·ty (və·rī′ə·ti), *n., pl.* -ties. **1.** lack of sameness; difference; variation. **2.** number of different kinds: *the store has a great variety of toys.* **3.** kind; sort: *all varieties of fortune.* **4.** a different form, phase, etc., of something. **5.** a division of a species. **6.** Also, **variety show,** *esp. Brit.* vaudeville.

va·ri·o·la (və·rī′ə·lə), *n.* smallpox. [< Med.L, < L *varius* various, spotted] —va·ri′o·lar, *adj.*

var·i·o·rum (vâr′i·ô′rəm; -ō′rəm), *n.* edition of a book that has the comments and notes of several editors, critics, etc. [< L (*cum notis*) *variorum* (with notes) of various people]

var·i·ous (vâr′i·əs), *adj.* **1.** differing from one another; different. **2.** several; many. **3.** varied; many-sided: *lives made various by learning.* **4.** varying; changeable. [< L *varius*] —var′i·ous·ly, *adv.* —var′i·ous·ness, *n.* —Syn. **1.** diverse, diversified.

var·let (vär′lit), *n. Archaic.* rascal. [< OF, var. of *vaslet,* orig., young man < Celtic]

var·mint (vär′mənt), *n. Dial.* **1.** vermin. **2.** an objectionable animal or person.

var·nish (vär′nish), *n.* **1.** a liquid that gives a smooth, glossy appearance to wood, metal, etc., made from resinous substances dissolved in oil or turpentine. **2.** the smooth, hard surface made by this liquid when dry. **3.** a glossy appearance. **4.** a false or deceiving appearance; pretense. —*v.* **1.** put varnish on. **2.** give a false or deceiving appearance to. [< OF *vernisser,* v., < *vernis,* n., ult. < Gk. *Berenice,* ancient city in Libya] —var′nish·er, *n.*

var·si·ty (vär′sə·ti), *n., pl.* -ties. the most important team in a given sport in a university, college, or school. [< (*uni*)*versity*]

var·y (vâr′i), *v.,* var·ied, var·y·ing. **1.** make or become different, as in form, degree, etc.; change: *the weather varies.* **2.** *Music.* repeat (a tune or theme) with changes and ornament. **3.** be different; differ: *the stars vary in brightness.* **4.** give variety to: *vary one's style of writing.* [< L, < *varius* various] —var′i·er, *n.* —var′y·ing·ly, *adv.* —Syn. **1.** alter, modify, diversify. **3.** disagree, deviate.

vas (vas), *n., pl.* **va·sa** (vā′sə). *Anat., Zool., Bot.* duct; vessel. [< L, vessel] —va·sal (vā′səl), *adj.*

vas·cu·lar (vas′kyə·lər), *adj. Biol.* pertaining to, made of, or provided with vessels that carry blood, sap, etc. [< NL *vascularis,* ult. < L *vas* vessel] —vas′cu·lar′i·ty, *n.* —vas′cu·lar·ly, *adv.*

vase (vās; vāz; *esp. Brit.* väz), *n.* a holder or container used for ornament or for holding flowers. [< F < L *vas* vessel] —vase′like′, *adj.*

Vas·e·line (vas′ə·lēn), *n. Am., Trademark.* name for certain petroleum products.

vas·o·mo·tor (vas′ō·mō′tər), *adj.* regulating the tension and size of blood vessels, as certain nerves. [< L *vas* vessel + E *motor,* adj.]

vas·sal (vas′əl), *n.* **1.** person who held land from a lord or superior, to whom in return he gave help in war or some other service. A great noble could be a vassal of the king and have many other men as his vassals. **2.** servant, follower, or slave. —*adj.* like a vassal; like that of a vassal. [< OF < Med.L *vassallus* < LL *vassus* < Celtic] —vas′sal·less, *adj.*

vas·sal·age (vas′əl·ij), *n.* **1.** the condition of being a vassal. **2.** the homage or service due from a vassal to his lord or superior. **3.** dependence; servitude. **4.** land held by a vassal.

vast (vast; väst), *adj.* very great; immense: *a billion dollars is a vast amount of money.* [< L *vastus*] —vast′ly, *adv.* —vast′ness, *n.* —Syn. tremendous, colossal, extensive.

vast·y (vas′ti; väs′-), *adj. Poetic.* vast.

vat (vat), *n., v.,* vat·ted, vat·ting. —*n.* a large container for liquids; tank: *a vat of dye.* —*v.* put into or treat in a vat. [OE *fæt*]

Vat·i·can (vat′ə·kən), *n.* **1.** collection of buildings grouped about the palace of the Pope, next to Saint Peter's Church in Rome. **2.** the government, office, or authority of the Pope.

Vatican City, an independent state inside the city of Rome, ruled by the Pope and including Saint Peter's Church and the Vatican.

vau·de·ville (vō′də·vil; vōd′vil), *n.* theatrical entertainment consisting of a variety of acts. Vaudeville consists of songs, dances, acrobatic feats, short plays, trained animals, etc. [< F, < *Vau de Vire,* valley in Normandy]

vault[1] (vôlt), *n.* **1.** an arched roof or ceiling; series of arches. **2.** an arched space or passage. **3.** something like an arched roof. **4.** Also, **vault of heaven.** the full extent of the sky. **5.** an underground cellar or storehouse. **6.** *Am.* place for storing valuable things and keeping them safe. Vaults are often made of steel. **7.** place for burial. —*v.* **1.** make in the form of a vault. **2.** cover with a vault. [< OF *vaulte,* ult. < L *volvere* roll] —vault′ed, *adj.* —vault′like′, *adj.*

vault[2] (vôlt), *v.* **1.** jump or leap over by using a pole or the hands. **2.** jump or leap. —*n.* such a jump. [< OF *volter,* ult. < L *volvere* roll] —vault′er, *n.*

vault·ing[1] (vôl′ting), *n.* **1.** a vaulted structure. **2.** vaults collectively.

vault·ing[2] (vôl′ting), *adj.* **1.** that vaults. **2.** overly aggressive; exaggerated: *vaulting ambition.*

vaunt (vônt; vänt), *v., n.* boast. [< F < LL *vanitare* < *vanus* vain] —vaunt′er, *n.* —vaunt′ing, *adj.* —vaunt′ing·ly, *adv.*

vb., verb; verbal.

V.C., **1.** Vice-Chairman. **2.** Vice-Chancellor. **3.** Victoria Cross.

V.D., VD, venereal disease.

V-Day, day marking the complete victory of the Allied Forces in World War II, Dec. 31, 1946.

veal (vēl), *n.* meat from a calf. [< OF *veel,* ult. < L *vitellus,* dim. of *vitulus* calf]

Veb·len (veb′lən), *n.* **Thorstein,** 1857–1929, American economist, teacher, and writer.

vec·tor (vek′tər), *n. Math.* **1.** quantity involving direction as well as magnitude. **2.** line representing both the direction and the magnitude of some force, etc. [< L, carrier, < *vehere* carry] —vec·to·ri·al (vek·tô′ri·əl; -tō′-), *adj.*

Ve·da (vā′də; vē′də), *n.* any or all of the four collections of sacred writings of the ancient Hindus. —Ve·da·ic (vi·dā′ik), Ve·dic (vā′dik; vē′-), *adj.* —Ve·da·ism (vā′də·iz·əm; vē′-), *n.*

V-E Day, date of the Allied victory in Europe in World War II, May 8, 1945.

Veep (vēp), *n. Slang.* **1.** Vice-president of the United States. **2.** veep, any vice-president.

veer (vir), *v.* change in direction; shift; turn: *the wind veered to the south.* —*n.* a shift; turn. [< F *virer*] —veer′ing·ly, *adv.*

Ve·ga (vē′gə), *n. Astron.* a bluish-white star of the first magnitude, in the northern skies.

veg·e·ta·ble (vej′tə·bəl; vej′ə·tə-), *n.* **1.** plant grown for food, as the cabbage, carrot, bean, etc. **2.** the part of such a plant that is eaten. **3.** any plant. —*adj.* **1.** of or pertaining to plants; like plants: *the vegetable kingdom.* **2.** consisting of or made from vegetables. [< OF, or < LL *vegetabilis* vivifying, refreshing < *vegetus* vigorous]

veg·e·tal (vej′ə·təl), *adj.* of or like plants. —**veg′e·tal′i·ty,** *n.*

veg·e·tar·i·an (vej′ə·târ′i·ən), *n.* person who eats vegetables but no meat. —*adj.* 1. devoted to or advocating vegetarianism. 2. eating vegetables but no meat. 3. containing no meat.

veg·e·tar·i·an·ism (vej′ə·târ′i·ən·iz′əm), *n.* practice or principle of eating vegetables but no meat.

veg·e·tate (vej′ə·tāt), *v.,* –tat·ed, –tat·ing. 1. grow as plants do. 2. live with very little action, thought, or feeling. [< L *vegetatus* enlivened < *vegetus* lively]

veg·e·ta·tion (vej′ə·tā′shən), *n.* 1. plant life; growing plants. 2. a vegetating; the growth of plants. —**veg′e·ta′tion·al,** *adj.*

veg·e·ta·tive (vej′ə·tā′tiv), *adj.* 1. growing as plants do. 2. of plants or plant life. 3. helping growth in plants: *vegetative mold.* 4. having very little action, thought, or feeling; vegetating. —**veg′e·ta′tive·ly,** *adv.* —**veg′e·ta′tive·ness,** *n.*

ve·he·ment (vē′ə·mənt), *adj.* 1. having or showing strong feeling; caused by strong feeling; eager; passionate. 2. forceful; violent. [< L *vehemens*] —**ve′he·mence, ve′he·men·cy,** *n.* —**ve′he·ment·ly,** *adv.* —Syn. 1. ardent, fervid.

ve·hi·cle (vē′ə·kəl), *n.* 1. a carriage, cart, wagon, automobile, sled, or any other conveyance used on land. 2. a means of carrying or conveying. Language is the vehicle of thought. 3. in painting, a liquid in which a pigment is applied to a surface. Linseed oil is a vehicle for paint. [< L *vehiculum* < *vehere* carry] —**ve·hic·u·lar** (vē·hik′yə·lər), *adj.*

veil (vāl), *n.* 1. piece of very thin material worn to protect or hide the face, or as an ornament. 2. piece of material worn so as to fall over the head and shoulders, as the headdress of a nun. 3. anything that covers or hides. 4. disguise; pretense. 5. take the veil, become a nun. —*v.* 1. cover with a veil. 2. cover; hide. [< OF < L *velum* covering. Doublet of VOILE.] —**veiled,** *adj.* —**veil′less,** *adj.* —**veil′like′,** *adj.* —Syn. *v.* 2. conceal, mask, screen.

veil·ing (vāl′ing), *n.* 1. a veil. 2. material for veils.

vein (vān), *n.* 1. one of the blood vessels or tubes that carry blood to the heart from all parts of the body. 2. *Bot.* one of the strands or bundles of vascular tissue forming the principal framework of a leaf. 3. *Zool.* rib of an insect's wing. 4. a crack or seam in rock filled with a different mineral: *a vein of copper.* 5. a special character or disposition; state of mind; mood: *a vein of cruelty, a joking vein.* —*v.* cover with veins; mark with veins. [< OF < L *vena*] —**veined,** *adj.* —**vein′less,** *adj.* —**vein′like′,** *adj.* —**vein′ous,** *adj.*

Veins:
A, of leaf; B, of insect's wing.

vein·ing (vān′ing), *n.* arrangement of veins.

ve·lar (vē′lər), *adj.* 1. of or pertaining to a velum. 2. *Phonet.* pronounced by the aid of the soft palate. *C* in *coo* has a velar sound, *c* in *cat* does not. —*n. Phonet.* a velar sound.

Ve·lás·quez (və·läs′kes), *n.* Diego Rodríguez de Silva y, 1599–1660, Spanish painter.

veld, veldt (velt; felt), *n.* open country in South Africa, having grass or bushes but few trees. [< Du., field]

vel·lum (vel′əm), *n.* 1. the finest kind of parchment, used for writing, binding books, etc. 2. paper or cloth imitating such parchment. [< OF *velin* < *veel* calf, VEAL]

ve·loc·i·pede (və·los′ə·pēd), *n.* 1. a child's tricycle. 2. an early kind of bicycle or tricycle. [< F, < L *velox* swift + *pes* foot]

Velocipede

ve·loc·i·ty (və·los′ə·ti), *n., pl.* –ties. 1. rapidity of motion; swiftness; quickness: *fly with the velocity of a bird.* 2. *Physics.* rate of motion; the change of position of a point per unit of time: *the velocity of light is about 186,000 miles per second.* [< L, < *velox* swift]

ve·lours, ve·lour (və·lùr′), *n. sing.* and *pl.* a fabric like velvet, made of silk, wool, or cotton, used for clothing, draperies, upholstery, etc. [< F, velvet, earlier *velous* < Pr., ult. < L *villus* shaggy hair]

ve·lum (vē′ləm), *n., pl.* –la (–lə). 1. *Biol.* a veillike membranous covering or partition. 2. *Anat.* the soft palate. [< L, covering]

ve·lure (və·lùr′), *n., v.,* –lured, –lur·ing. —*n.* 1. a soft material like velvet. 2. a soft pad used for smoothing silk hats. —*v.* smooth with a velure. [var. of *velour* velours VELOURS]

vel·vet (vel′vit), *n.* 1. cloth with a thick, soft pile, made of silk, rayon, cotton, or some combination of these. 2. something like velvet. 3. *Am., Slang.* clear profit or gain. —*adj.* 1. made of velvet. 2. like velvet. [< Med.L *velvetum,* ult. < L *villus* tuft of hair] —**vel′vet·ed,** *adj.* —**vel′vet·y, vel′vet·like′,** *adj.*

vel·vet·een (vel′və·tēn′), *n.* velvet made of cotton or of silk and cotton.

ve·nal (vē′nəl), *adj.* 1. willing to sell one's services or influence basely; open to bribes; corrupt. 2. influenced or obtained by bribery: *venal conduct.* [< L, < *venum* sale] —**ve·nal·i·ty** (vē·nal′ə·ti), *n.* —**ve′nal·ly,** *adv.*

ve·na·tion (vē·nā′shən), *n.* 1. arrangement of veins in a leaf or in an insect's wing. 2. these veins. —**ve·na′tion·al,** *adj.*

vend (vend), *v.* sell; peddle. [< L *vendere* < *venum dare* offer for sale]

vend·ee (ven·dē′), *n.* buyer.

vend·er, ven·dor (ven′dər), *n.* 1. seller, esp. a peddler. 2. Also, **vending machine.** machine from which one obtains candy, stamps, etc., when a coin is dropped in.

ven·det·ta (ven·det′ə), *n.* feud in which a murdered man's relatives try to kill the slayer or his relatives. [< Ital. < L *vindicta* revenge] —**ven·det′tist,** *n.*

vend·i·ble (ven′də·bəl), *adj.* salable. —*n.* a salable thing. —**vend′i·bil′i·ty, vend′i·ble·ness,** *n.* —**vend′i·bly,** *adv.*

ve·neer (və·nir′), *v.* 1. cover (wood) with a thin layer of finer wood or other material: *veneer a pine desk with mahogany.* 2. cover (anything) with a layer of something else to give an appearance of superior quality. —*n.* 1. a thin layer of wood or other material used in veneering. 2. surface appearance or show. [earlier *fineer* < G *furnir* < F *fournir* FURNISH] —**ve·neer′er,** *n.*

ven·er·a·ble (ven′ər·ə·bəl), *adj.* worthy of reverence; deserving respect because of age, character, or associations. —**ven′er·a·bil′i·ty, ven′er·a·ble·ness,** *n.* —**ven′er·a·bly,** *adv.*

ven·er·ate (ven′ər·āt), *v.,* –at·ed, –at·ing. regard with deep respect; revere. [< L *veneratus*] —**ven′er·a′tor,** *n.* —Syn. honor, esteem.

ven·er·a·tion (ven′ər·ā′shən), *n.* deep respect; reverence. —**ven′er·a·tive,** *adj.*

ve·ne·re·al (və·nir′i·əl), *adj.* 1. of or pertaining to sexual intercourse. 2. caused or transmitted by sexual intercourse: *a venereal disease.* 3. pertaining to diseases transmitted by sexual intercourse: *venereal remedies.* 4. infected with syphilis, gonorrhea, or other venereal disease. [< L *venereus* < *Venus* Venus]

ven·er·y¹ (ven′ər·i), *n.* gratification of sexual desire. [< L *Venus* Venus]

ven·er·y² (ven′ər·i), *n. Archaic.* hunting. [< OF *venerie,* ult. < L *venari* hunt]

Ve·ne·tian (və·nē′shən), *adj.* of Venice or its people. —*n.* native or inhabitant of Venice.

Venetian blind, a window blind made of many horizontal wooden slats that can be opened or closed to regulate the light, air, etc.

Ven·e·zue·la (ven′ə·zwē′lə; –zwā′–), *n.* country in the N part of South America. —**Ven′e·zue′lan,** *adj., n.*

venge·ance (ven′jəns), *n.* 1. punishment in return for a wrong; revenge. 2. with a vengeance, a. with great force or violence. b. extremely. **c.** much more than expected. [< OF, ult. < L *vindex* avenger] —**Syn. 1.** retribution.

venge·ful (venj′fəl), *adj.* feeling or showing a strong desire for vengeance. —**venge′ful·ly,** *adv.* —**venge′ful·ness,** *n.*

ve·ni·al (vē′ni·əl; vē′nyəl), *adj.* that can be forgiven; not very wrong; pardonable. [< L, < *venia* forgiveness] —**ve′ni·al′i·ty, ve′ni·al·ness,** *n.* —**ve′ni·al·ly,** *adv.*

Ven·ice (ven′is), *n.* **1.** city on the NE coast of Italy. Venice has many canals in place of streets. **2.** Gulf of, the N part of the Adriatic.

ve·ni·re (və·nī′rē), *n. Law.* writ by a sheriff summoning a person to serve on a jury. [< L, you may cause (him) to come]

ve·ni·re·man (və·nī′rē·mən), *n., pl.* —**men.** *Am., Law.* person summoned to serve on a jury by a writ of venire.

ven·i·son (ven′ə·zən; -sən), *n.* the flesh of a deer, used for food; deer meat. [< OF < L *venatio* hunting < *venari* hunt]

ve·ni, vi·di, vi·ci (vē′nī vī′dī vī′sī; wā′nē wē′dē wē′kē), *Latin.* I came, I saw, I conquered (a report of victory made by Julius Caesar to the Roman Senate).

ven·om (ven′əm), *n.* **1.** the poison of snakes, spiders, etc. **2.** spite; malice. [< OF *venin* < L *venenum* poison] —**ven′om·er,** *n.* —**ven′om·less,** *adj.* —**Syn. 2.** rancor, hate, malignity.

ven·om·ous (ven′əm·əs), *adj.* **1.** poisonous. Rattlesnakes are venomous. **2.** spiteful; malicious: *venomous words.* —**ven′om·ous·ly,** *adv.* —**ven′om·ous·ness,** *n.*

ve·nous (vē′nəs), *adj.* **1.** of, in, or pertaining to veins. **2.** having veins. —**ve′nous·ly,** *adv.* —**ve′nous·ness, ve·nos·i·ty** (vē·nos′ə·ti), *n.*

vent (vent), *n.* **1.** hole; opening, esp. one serving as an outlet. **2.** slit in a garment. **3.** a way out of something; outlet; expression: *her grief found vent in tears.* **4.** in automobiles, etc., a small window that can be opened for indirect ventilation. —*v.* **1.** relieve (oneself) by expressing something freely; give utterance to. **2.** make public. **3.** make a vent in. [< OF *fente* slit, ult. < L *findere*; infl. by F *vent* wind < L *ventus* and F *évent* < L *ex-* out + *ventus* wind] —**vent′er,** *n.* —**vent′less,** *adj.*

ven·ti·late (ven′tə·lāt), *v.,* —**lat·ed,** —**lat·ing. 1.** change the air in: *we ventilate a room by opening windows.* **2.** purify by fresh air: *the lungs ventilate the blood.* **3.** make known publicly; discuss openly. **4.** furnish with a vent or opening for the escape of air, gas, etc. [< L *ventilatus* fanned < *ventus* wind] —**ven·ti·la·ble** (ven′tə·lə·bəl), *adj.* —**ven′ti·la′tion,** *n.* —**ven′ti·la′tive,** *adj.*

ven·ti·la·tor (ven′tə·lā′tər), *n.* **1.** one who or that which ventilates. **2.** any apparatus or means for changing or improving the air.

ven·tral (ven′trəl), *adj.* **1.** of or pertaining to the belly; abdominal. **2.** *Zool.* of, pertaining to, or on the surface or part opposite the back. [< LL, < L *venter* belly] —**ven′tral·ly,** *adv.*

ven·tri·cle (ven′trə·kəl), *n.* either of the two lower chambers of the heart that receive blood and force it into the arteries. [< L *ventriculus,* dim. of *venter* belly] —**ven·tric·u·lar** (ven·trik′yə·lər), *adj.*

ven·tril·o·quism (ven·tril′ə·kwiz·əm), **ven·tril·o·quy** (-kwi), *n.* art or practice of speaking or uttering sounds with the lips nearly shut so that the voice may seem to come from some other source than the speaker. [< L *ventriloquus* ventriloquist < *venter* belly + *loqui* speak] —**ven·tri·lo·qui·al** (ven′trə·lō′kwi·əl), *adj.* —**ven′tri·lo′qui·al·ly,** *adv.* —**ven·tril′o·quist,** *n.* —**ven·tril′o·quis′tic,** *adj.*

ven·ture (ven′chər), *n., v.,* —**tured,** —**tur·ing.** —*n.* **1.** a risky or daring undertaking. **2.** speculation to make money. **3.** thing risked; stake. **4.** at a venture, at random; by chance. —*v.* **1.** expose to risk or danger: *he ventured his money in the new business.* **2.** run a risk; dare: *venture to say what one thinks.* **3.** dare to say or make: *venture an objection.* **4.** dare to come, go, or proceed: *venture from a hiding place.* [< earlier *aventure* ADVENTURE] —**ven′tur·er,** *n.* —**Syn. n. 1.** enterprise, adventure, risk.

ven·ture·some (ven′chər·səm), *adj.* **1.** inclined to take risks; rash; daring. **2.** hazardous. —**ven′ture·some·ly,** *adv.* —**ven′ture·some·ness,** *n.* —**Syn. 1.** adventurous, bold. —**Ant. 1.** timid.

ven·tur·ous (ven′chər·əs), *adj.* **1.** rash; daring; adventurous. **2.** risky; dangerous. —**ven′tur·ous·ly,** *adv.* —**ven′tur·ous·ness,** *n.*

ven·ue (ven′ū), *n. Law.* **1.** the place or neighborhood of a crime or cause of action. **2.** the place where the jury is gathered and the case tried. [< OF, coming, ult. < L *venire* come]

Ve·nus (vē′nəs), *n.* **1.** the Roman goddess of love and beauty. The Romans identified her with the Greek goddess Aphrodite. **2.** a very beautiful woman. **3.** *Astron.* the most brilliant planet, second in order from the sun.

Ve·nus's-fly·trap (vē′nəs·iz·flī′trap′), *n. Am.* a plant whose hairy leaves have two lobes at the end that fold together to trap and digest insects.

ve·ra·cious (və·rā′shəs), *adj.* **1.** truthful. **2.** true. [< L *verax* < *verus* true] —**ve·ra′cious·ly,** *adv.* —**ve·ra′cious·ness,** *n.*

ve·rac·i·ty (və·ras′ə·ti), *n., pl.* —**ties. 1.** truthfulness. **2.** truth. **3.** correctness; accuracy. [< Med.L, < L *verax* VERACIOUS]

Ver·a·cruz, Ver·a Cruz (ver′ə·krüz′), *n.* a principal seaport in SE Mexico.

ve·ran·da, ve·ran·dah (və·ran′də), *n.* a large porch along one or more sides of a house. [< Hind. and other Indian langs. < Pg. *varanda* railing] —**ve·ran′daed, ve·ran′dahed,** *adj.* —**ve·ran′da·less, ve·ran′dah·less,** *adj.*

verb (vėrb), *n. Gram.* word that tells what is or what is done; the part of speech that expresses action or being. *Do, go, come, be, sit, think, know,* and *eat* are verbs. [< L *verbum,* orig., word] —**verb′less,** *adj.* ➤ A verb is transitive when it is used with an object to complete its meaning: *They fought the whole gang.* A verb is intransitive when it does not have an object, when the recipient of the action is not named: *The choir will sing. They hid in the tall grass.* Many verbs are used in both constructions: *He wrote two books* (transitive). *She cannot write* (intransitive).

ver·bal (vėr′bəl), *adj.* **1.** in words; of words. **2.** expressed in spoken words; oral: *a verbal promise.* **3.** word for word; literal: *a verbal translation.* **4.** pertaining to or concerned with words only, rather than ideas, etc.: *make verbal changes in a manuscript.* **5.** *Gram.* **a.** pertaining to a verb. Two common verbal endings are -*ed* and -*ing.* **b.** derived from a verb: *a verbal noun.* —*n. Gram.* a noun, adjective, or other word derived from a verb. [< L, < *verbum* word, verb] —**ver′bal·ly,** *adv.* ➤ **verbal noun. 1.** FORM AND USE. A verbal noun (or gerund) is the form of the verb ending in -*ing* when used as a noun. It has the same form as the present participle but differs in use. Verbal noun: *Running a hotel appealed to him.* Participle: *Running around the corner, he ran into a cop.* [*Running* modifies *he.*] A verbal noun may take an object (as in *running a hotel*), and it may serve any of the functions of a noun: Subject: *Looking for an apartment always fascinated her.* Object: *He taught dancing.* Predicate noun: *Seeing is believing.* Adjective use: *a fishing boat* [a boat *for fishing,* not a boat *that* fishes]. When not in one of these constructions a verbal noun is related to the rest of the sentence by a preposition. **2.** PHRASES WITH VERBAL NOUNS. Verbal nouns are frequently used in phrases: *In coming to an agreement,* they had compromised on all points. It's the best thing *for coughing at night.* Misrelated: *In coming to an agreement,* a compromise had to be voted for. [The compromise did not come to the agreement, but *they* or some other word meaning the voters.] **3.** "THE" AND VERBAL NOUNS. In current style there is a tendency to use verbal nouns without *the* and with a direct object rather than an *of*-phrase. This emphasizes the verbal phase of the word and makes for economy and force: His chief amusement is *telling jokes.* [Rather than: His chief amusement is *the telling of jokes.*] ➤ See oral for another usage note.

ver·bal·ism (vėr′bəl·iz·əm), *n.* **1.** a verbal expression; word, phrase, etc. **2.** a stock phrase or formula in words with little meaning. **3.** too much attention to mere words. **4.** wordiness.

ver·bal·ist (vér′bəl·ist), *n.* **1.** person who is skilled in the use or choice of words. **2.** person who pays too much attention to mere words. **3.** a wordy person.

ver·bal·ize (vér′bəl·īz), *v.,* **-ized, -iz·ing. 1.** express in words. **2.** use too many words; be wordy. **3.** *Gram.* change (a noun, etc.) into a verb. —**ver′bal·i·za′-tion,** *n.* —**ver′bal·iz′er,** *n.*

ver·ba·tim (vér·bā′tim), *adv., adj.* word for word; in exactly the same words. [< Med.L, < L *verbum* word]

ver·be·na (vər·bē′nə), *n.* any of certain low-growing garden plants with elongated or flattened spikes of flowers having various colors. [< L, leafy branch]

Verbena

ver·bi·age (vér′bi·ij), *n.* use of too many words; abundance of useless words.

ver·bose (vér·bōs′), *adj.* using too many words; wordy. [< L, < *verbum* word] —**ver·bose′ly,** *adv.* —**ver·bose′ness,** **ver·bos·i·ty** (vér·bos′ə·ti), *n.* —**Ant.** terse, concise, succinct.

ver·bo·ten (fer·bō′tən), *adj.* forbidden by authority; prohibited. [< G]

ver·dan·cy (vér′dən·si), *n.* **1.** greenness. **2.** inexperience.

ver·dant (vér′dənt), *adj.* **1.** green. **2.** inexperienced. [< *verdure*] —**ver′dant·ly,** *adv.*

Verde (vérd), *n.* Cape, the most western point of Africa.

Ver·di (vâr′di), *n.* Giuseppe, 1813–1901, Italian composer.

ver·dict (vér′dikt), *n.* **1.** the decision of a jury. **2.** decision; judgment. [< AF *verdit* < *ver* true (< L *verus*) + *dit,* pp. of *dire* speak < L *dicere*]

ver·di·gris (vér′də·grēs; -gris), *n.* a green or bluish coating that forms on brass, copper, or bronze when exposed for long periods of time. [< OF *vert de grice,* lit., green of Greece]

Ver·dun (vər·dun′), *n.* town and fortifications in NE France, on the Meuse River.

ver·dure (vér′jər), *n.* **1.** a fresh greenness. **2.** a fresh growth of green grass, plants, or leaves. [< OF, ult. < L *viridis* green] —**ver′dured,** *adj.* —**ver′dure·less,** *adj.* —**ver′dur·ous,** *adj.* —**ver′-dur·ous·ness,** *n.*

verge[1] (vérj), *n., v.,* **verged, verg·ing.** —*n.* **1.** edge; rim; brink: *his business is on the verge of ruin.* **2.** a limiting belt, strip, or border of something. —*v.* be on the verge; border. [< OF < L *virga* staff]

verge[2] (vérj), *v.,* **verged, verg·ing.** tend; incline: *she was plump, verging toward fatness.* [< L *vergere*]

Ver·gil (vér′jəl), *n.* 70–19 B.C., Roman poet. Also, **Virgil.** —**Ver·gil′i·an,** *adj.*

ver·i·fi·a·ble (ver′ə·fī′ə·bəl), *adj.* that can be checked or tested and proved to be true. —**ver′-i·fi·a·bil′i·ty, ver′i·fi′a·ble·ness,** *n.*

ver·i·fi·ca·tion (ver′ə·fə·kā′shən), *n.* proof by evidence or testimony; confirmation. —**ver′-i·fi·ca′tive, ver·i·fi·ca·to·ry** (ver′ə·fə·kā′tə·ri), *adj.*

ver·i·fy (ver′ə·fī), *v.,* **-fied, -fy·ing. 1.** prove (something) to be true; confirm: *the driver's report of the accident was verified by eyewitnesses.* **2.** state to be true, esp. under oath. **3.** test the correctness of; check for accuracy. [< OF < Med.L, < L *verus* true + *facere* make] —**ver′i·fi′er,** *n.* —**Syn. 1.** substantiate, corroborate, authenticate.

ver·i·ly (ver′ə·li), *adv.* in truth; truly; really.

ver·i·sim·i·lar (ver′ə·sim′ə·lər), *adj.* appearing true or real; probable. —**ver′i·sim′i·lar·ly,** *adv.*

ver·i·si·mil·i·tude (ver′ə·sə·mil′ə·tūd; -tūd), *n.* **1.** appearance of truth or reality; probability. **2.** apparent truth. [< L, < *verus* true + *similis* like]

ver·i·ta·ble (ver′ə·tə·bəl), *adj.* true; real; ac-

tual. [< F, < *verité* VERITY] —**ver′i·ta·ble·ness,** *n.* —**ver′i·ta·bly,** *adv.*

ver·i·ty (ver′ə·ti), *n., pl.* **-ties. 1.** truth. **2.** a true statement or fact. **3.** reality. [< L, < *verus* true]

ver·juice (vér′jüs′), *n.* **1.** an acid liquor made from sour juice of crab apples, unripe grapes, etc. Verjuice was formerly used in cooking. **2.** sourness, as of temper or expression. [< OF, < *vert* green (< L *viridis*) + *jus* juice < L]

ver·mi·cel·li (vér′mə·sel′i; -chel′i), *n.* a mixture of flour and water, like macaroni and spaghetti, but made in long, slender, solid threads. [< Ital., lit., little worms, ult. < L *vermis* worm]

ver·mi·cide (vér′mə·sīd), *n.* any agent that kills worms, esp. a drug used to kill parasitic intestinal worms. —**ver′mi·cid′al,** *adj.*

ver·mi·form (vér′mə·fôrm), *adj.* shaped like a worm. [< Med.L, < L *vermis* worm + *forma* form]

vermiform appendix, a slender tube, closed at one end, growing out of the large intestine in the lower right-hand part of the abdomen. Appendicitis is inflammation of the vermiform appendix.

ver·mi·fuge (vér′mə·fūj), *n.* medicine to expel worms from the intestines. [< F, < L *vermis* worm + *fugare* cause to flee] —**ver·mif·u·gal** (vér·mif′yə·gəl), *adj.*

ver·mil·ion (vər·mil′yən), *n.* **1.** a bright red. **2.** a bright-red coloring matter. —*adj.* bright-red. [< OF *vermillion,* ult. < L *vermis* worm]

ver·min (vér′mən), *n., pl. or sing.* **1.** small animals that are troublesome or destructive. Fleas, lice, bedbugs, rats, and mice are vermin. **2.** *Brit.* animals or birds that destroy game, poultry, etc. **3.** a vile, worthless person or persons. [< OF, ult. < L *vermis* worm] —**ver′min·ous,** *adj.* —**ver′min·ous·ly,** *adv.* —**ver′min·ous·ness,** *n.*

Ver·mont (vər·mont′), *n.* a State forming the NW part of New England. *Capital:* Montpelier. *Abbrev.:* Vt. —**Ver·mont′er,** *n.* *Am.*

ver·mouth (vər·müth′; vér′müth), *n.* a white wine flavored with wormwood or other herbs and used as a liqueur or in cocktails. [< F < G *wermut(h)*]

ver·nac·u·lar (vər·nak′yə·lər), *n.* **1.** a native language; language used by the people of a certain country or place. **2.** everyday language; informal speech. **3.** language of a profession, trade, etc.: *the vernacular of the lawyers.* —*adj.* **1.** used by the people of a certain country, place, etc.; native: *English is our vernacular tongue.* **2.** of or in the native language, rather than a literary or learned language. [< L *vernaculus* domestic, native < *verna* home-born slave] —**ver·nac′u·lar·ly,** *adv.*

ver·nal (vér′nəl), *adj.* **1.** of spring; pertaining to spring: *vernal green, vernal flowers.* **2.** like spring; suggesting spring. **3.** youthful. [< L *vernalis* < *ver* spring] —**ver′nal·ly,** *adv.*

vernal equinox. See equinox.

Verne (vérn), *n.* Jules, 1828–1905, French writer of stories of adventure.

ver·ni·er (vér′ni·ər), or **vernier scale,** *n.* a small, movable scale for measuring a fractional part of one of the divisions of a fixed scale. [after P. Vernier, French mathematician]

Ver·o·nal (ver′ə·nəl; -nôl), *n. Trademark.* barbital.

ve·ron·i·ca (və·ron′ə·kə), *n.* **1.** a kind of plant or shrub with blue, purple, pink, or white flowers. **2.** cloth with a representation of Christ's face.

Ver·sailles (vâr·sī′; vər·sālz′), *n.* city in N France, near Paris. The treaty ending World War I was signed there on June 28, 1919.

ver·sa·tile (vér′sə·təl), *adj.* able to do many things well. [< L *versatilis* turning, ult. < *vertere* turn] —**ver′sa·tile·ly,** *adv.* —**ver′sa·til′i·ty, ver′sa·tile·ness,** *n.* —**Syn.** many-sided.

verse (vérs), *n.* **1.** poetry. **2.** a single line of poetry. **3.** a group of lines or short portion in poetry. **4.** poem. **5.** type of poetry; meter: *blank* *verse, iambic verse.* **6.** a short division of a chapter in the Bible. [< L *versus,* orig., row, furrow < *vertere* turn around] ➤ **verse.** A full line or more of verse quoted in a paper should be lined off and written exactly as it is in the original. It should be indented from the left margin and, if very short, far enough not to leave a conspicuous blank at its right.

versed (vėrst), *adj.* experienced; practiced; skilled: *a doctor should be well versed in medical theory.* —**Syn.** proficient, acquainted.

ver·si·cle (vėr′sə·kəl), *n.* one of a series of short sentences said or sung by the minister during services, to which the people make response. [< L *versiculus,* dim. of *versus* VERSE]

ver·si·fi·ca·tion (vėr′sə·fə·kā′shən), *n.* **1.** the making of verses. **2.** art or theory of making verses. **3.** form or style of poetry; metrical structure.

ver·si·fy (vėr′sə·fī), *v.,* **-fied, -fy·ing. 1.** write verses. **2.** tell in verse. **3.** turn (prose) into poetry. —**ver′si·fi′er,** *n.*

ver·sion (vėr′zhən; -shən), *n.* **1.** a translation from one language to another. **2.** one particular statement, account, or description: *this is my version of the quarrel.* [< L *versio,* orig., a turning < *vertere* turn] —**ver′sion·al,** *adj.*

vers li·bre (vâr lē′brə), French. free verse. —**vers li·brist** (vâr lē′brist).

verst (vėrst), *n.* a Russian measure of distance, equal to about 3500 feet. [< Russ. *versta*]

ver·sus (vėr′səs), *prep.* against. [< L, turned toward, pp. of *vertere* turn]

ver·te·bra (vėr′tə·brə), *n., pl.* **-brae** (-brē), **-bras.** *Anat., Zool.* one of the bones of the backbone. [< L, < *vertere* turn] —**ver′te·bral,** *adj.* —**ver′te·bral·ly,** *adv.*

Three vertebrae

ver·te·brate (vėr′tə·brāt; -brit), *n.* animal that has a backbone. Fishes, Amphibia, reptiles, birds, and mammals are vertebrates. —*adj.* having a backbone.

ver·tex (vėr′teks), *n., pl.* **-tex·es, -ti·ces** (-tə·sēz). **1.** the highest point; top. **2.** point opposite the base of a triangle, pyramid, etc. [< L, orig., whirl, < *vertere* turn] —**Syn. 1.** apex, summit.

ver·ti·cal (vėr′tə·kəl), *adj.* **1.** straight up and down; perpendicular to a level surface. A person standing up straight is in a vertical position. **2.** of or at the highest point; of the vertex. **3.** directly overhead; at the zenith. **4.** so organized as to include many or all stages in the production of some manufactured product: *a vertical union, vertical trusts.* **5.** of or pertaining to a vertex; opposite to the base: *a vertical angle.* —*n.* a vertical line, plane, circle, position, part, etc. —**ver′ti·cal′i·ty, ver′ti·cal·ness,** *n.* —**ver′ti·cal·ly,** *adv.* —**Ant.** *adj.* **1.** horizontal.

ver·tig·i·nous (vėr·tij′ə·nəs), *adj.* **1.** whirling; rotary. **2.** affected with vertigo; dizzy. **3.** of the nature of or pertaining to vertigo. —**ver·tig′i·nous·ly,** *adv.* —**ver·tig′i·nous·ness,** *n.*

ver·ti·go (vėr′tə·gō), *n., pl.* **ver·ti·goes, ver·tig·i·nes** (vėr·tij′ə·nēz). dizziness; giddiness. [< L, < *vertere* turn]

verve (vėrv), *n.* vigorous spirit; enthusiasm; energy; liveliness. [< F]

ver·y (ver′i), *adv., adj.,* **ver·i·er, ver·i·est.** —*adv.* **1.** much; greatly; extremely: *the sun is very hot.* **2.** absolutely; exactly: *he stood in the very same place for an hour.* —*adj.* **1.** same; identical: *the very people who used to love her hate her now.* **2.** even; mere; sheer: *the very thought of blood makes her sick, she wept from very joy.* **3.** real; true; genuine: *she seemed a very queen.* **4.** actual: *he was caught in the very act of stealing.* [< OF *verai,* ult. < L *verus* true] —**Syn.** *adv.* **1.** exceedingly, surpassingly, excessively. ➤ **very and past participles.** In formal English many people will not use *very* with a past participle in a phrasal verb (*he was very excited*)—because by rights *very* is an intensive, supposedly marking a high degree of a *quality,* as in *very happy,* and the verb function of the participle denotes an *action* rather than a quality. The formal locution would be: he was *very much* excited.

This distinction, however, is based purely on grammatical reasoning and users of colloquial and informal English often use *very* to modify such participles without any qualms: *I shall be very pleased to come, we shall be very delighted to have you.*

ves·i·cant (ves′ə·kənt), *adj.* producing a blister or blisters. —*n.* a vesicant agent or substance.

ves·i·cate (ves′ə·kāt), *v.,* **-cat·ed, -cat·ing.** cause blisters on; blister. —**ves′i·ca′tion,** *n.*

ves·i·ca·to·ry (ves′ə·kə·tô′ri; -tō′-; və·sik′-ə·tô′ri; -tō′-), *adj., n., pl.* **-ries.** vesicant.

ves·i·cle (ves′ə·kəl), *n.* a small bladder, cavity, sac, or cyst. A blister is a vesicle in the skin. [< L *vesicula,* dim. of *vesica* bladder, blister] —**ve·sic·u·lar** (və·sik′yə·lər), **ve·sic·u·late** (və·sik′yə·lit; -lāt), *adj.* —**ve·sic′u·lar·ly,** *adv.*

Ves·pa·sian (ves·pā′zhən), *n.* 9–79 A.D., Roman emperor 70–79 A.D.

ves·per (ves′pər), *n.* **1.** evening. **2.** Vesper, the evening star. **3.** an evening prayer, hymn, or service; evening bell. —*adj.* **1.** of evening. **2.** Sometimes, Vesper. of or pertaining to vespers. [< L]

ves·pers, Ves·pers (ves′pərz), *n.pl.* **1.** a church service held in the late afternoon or in the evening. **2.** the sixth of the canonical hours.

Ves·puc·ci (ves·pü′chi), *n.* Amerigo (*Americus Vespucius*), 1451–1512, Italian merchant, adventurer, and explorer. America is named for him.

ves·sel (ves′əl), *n.* **1.** a large boat; ship. **2.** airship. **3.** a hollow holder or container, as a cup, bowl, pitcher, bottle, barrel, tub, etc. **4.** *Biol.* tube carrying blood or other fluid. Veins and arteries are blood vessels. [< OF < L *vascellum,* double dim. of *vas* vessel]

vest (vest), *n.* **1.** a short, sleeveless garment worn by men under the coat. **2.** garment like this worn by women; the facing in a waist or coat made to look like a vest. **3.** undershirt. —*v.* **1.** clothe; robe; dress in vestments: *the vested priest stood before the altar.* **2.** furnish with powers, authority, rights, etc.: *Congress is vested with the power to declare war.* **3.** put in the possession or control of a person or persons: *the management of the hospital is vested in a board of trustees.* [< OF, ult. < L *vestis* garment] —**vest′less,** *adj.*

Ves·ta (ves′tə), *n. Roman Myth.* goddess of the hearth. A sacred fire was always kept burning in the temple of Vesta.

ves·tal (ves′təl), *n.* **1.** Also, **vestal virgin.** one of the virgins consecrated to Vesta whose duties included tending an undying fire in honor of Vesta at her temple in ancient Rome. **2.** virgin. **3.** nun. —*adj.* **1.** of or suitable for a vestal. **2.** pure; chaste.

vest·ed (ves′tid), *adj.* **1.** placed in the possession or control of a person or persons; fixed; settled: *vested rights.* **2.** clothed or robed, esp. in church garments: *a vested choir.*

vest·ee (ves·tē′), *n. Am.* a little vest used for ornament on a woman's dress.

ves·ti·bule (ves′tə·būl), *n.* **1.** passage or hall between the outer door and the inside of a building; antechamber. **2.** *Am.* the enclosed space at the end of a railroad passenger car. **3.** *Anat., Zool.* cavity of the body that leads to another cavity: *the vestibule of the ear.* [< L *vestibulum*] —**ves·tib·u·lar** (ves·tib′yə·lər), *adj.*

ves·tige (ves′tij), *n.* **1.** a slight remnant; trace. **2.** *Biol.* part, organ, etc., that is no longer fully developed or useful. *Obs.* footprint. [< F < L *vestigium* footprint]

ves·tig·i·al (ves·tij′i·əl), *adj.* **1.** remaining as a vestige of something that has disappeared. **2.** no longer fully developed or useful. —**ves·tig′i·al·ly,** *adv.*

vest·ment (vest′mənt), *n.* **1.** garment. **2.** garment worn by a clergyman in performing sacred duties. [< OF *vestement,* ult. < L *vestis* garment] —**vest′ment·al,** *adj.*

vest-pock·et (vest′pok′it), *adj.* able to fit into a vest pocket; very small.

ves·try (ves′tri), *n., pl.* **-tries. 1.** room in a

church, where vestments are kept. **2.** room in a church or an attached building, used for Sunday school, etc. **3.** in the Church of England and the Protestant Episcopal Church of America, a committee that helps manage church business.

ves·try·man (ves′trĭ·mən), *n.*, *pl.* **-men.** member of a committee that helps manage church business.

ves·ture (ves′chər), *n.* **1.** clothing; garments. **2.** covering. [< OF, ult. < L *vestis* garment] **—ves′tur·al,** *adj.*

Ve·su·vi·us (və·sü′vĭ·əs), *n.* Mount, an active volcano near Naples, Italy. **—Ve·su′vi·an,** *adj.*

vet[1] (vet), *n.* *Colloq.* veterinarian.

vet[2] (vet), *n.* *Am.*, *Colloq.* veteran.

vet., **1.** veteran. **2.** veterinarian; veterinary.

vetch (vech), *n.* vine or plant of the same family as the pea, grown as food for cattle and sheep. [< dial. OF < L *vicia*] **—vetch′like′,** *adj.*

vet·er·an (vet′ər·ən; vet′rən), *n.* **1.** person who has had much experience in war; old soldier or sailor. **2.** *Am.* person who has served in the armed forces. **3.** person who has had much experience in some position, occupation, etc. *—adj.* **1.** having had much experience in war. **2.** grown old in service; having had much experience. **3.** of, pertaining to, or characteristic of veterans. [< L *veteranus* < *vetus* old]

Veterans Day, Nov. 11, formerly Armistice Day. It was changed to Veterans Day by act of Congress in 1954.

vet·er·i·nar·i·an (vet′ər·ə·nâr′ĭ·ən; vet′ə·nâr′-), *n.* doctor or surgeon who treats animals.

vet·er·i·nar·y (vet′ər·ə·ner′ĭ; vet′ə·ner′ĭ), *adj.*, *n.*, *pl.* **-nar·ies.** *—adj.* pertaining to the medical or surgical treatment of animals. *—n.* veterinarian. [< L, < *veterinus* pertaining to domestic animals]

ve·to (vē′tō), *n.*, *pl.* **-toes,** *adj.*, *v.*, **-toed,** **-to·ing.** *—n.* **1.** the right of a president, governor, etc., to reject bills passed by a lawmaking body. **2.** the use of this right: *the governor's veto kept the bill from becoming a law.* **3.** statement of the reasons for disapproval of a bill passed by the legislature. **4.** power or right to prevent action through prohibition. **5.** refusal of consent; prohibition. *—adj.* having to do with a veto: *veto power.* *—v.* **1.** reject by a veto. **2.** refuse to consent to. [< L, I forbid] **—ve′to·er,** *n.* **—ve′to·less,** *adj.*

vex (veks), *v.* **1.** anger by trifles; annoy; provoke. **2.** disturb; trouble: *Cape Hatteras is much vexed by storms.* [< L *vexare*] **—vexed,** *adj.* **—vex·ed·ly** (vek′sĭd·lĭ), *adv.* **—vex′ed·ness,** *n.* **—vex′er,** *n.*

vex·a·tion (veks·ā′shən), *n.* **1.** a vexing or being vexed. **2.** thing that vexes. **—Syn. 1.** irritation, exasperation, annoyance, chagrin.

vex·a·tious (veks·ā′shəs), *adj.* vexing; annoying. **—vex·a′tious·ly,** *adv.* **—vex·a′tious·ness,** *n.*

Vi, *Chem.* Virginium.

V.I., Virgin Islands.

v.i., intransitive verb.

vi·a (vī′ə; vē′ə), *prep.* by way of; by a route that passes through. [< L, abl. of *via* way]

vi·a·ble (vī′ə·bəl), *adj.* able to keep alive. [< F, < *vie* life < L *vita*] **—vi′a·bil′i·ty,** *n.*

vi·a·duct (vī′ə·dukt), *n.* bridge for carrying a road or railroad over a valley, a part of a city, etc. [< L *via* road + *ductus* a leading; patterned on *aqueduct*]

vi·al (vī′əl), *n.* a small glass bottle for holding medicines or the like; bottle. [var. of *phial*]

vi·and (vī′ənd), *n.* **1.** article of food. **2.** viands, articles of choice food. [< OF *viande* < LL *vivenda* things for living < L, pl., to be lived]

vi·at·i·cum (vī·at′ĭ·kəm), *n.*, *pl.* **-ca** (-kə), **-cums.** **1.** Holy Communion given to a person dying or in danger of death. **2.** supplies or money for a journey. [< L, ult. < *via* road. Doublet of VOYAGE.]

vi·brant (vī′brənt), *adj.* **1.** vibrating. **2.** resounding; resonant. **3.** full of energy; vigorous. **4.** *Phonet.* voiced. [< L *vibrans* vibrating] **—vi′bran·cy,** *n.* **—vi′brant·ly,** *adv.*

vi·brate (vī′brāt), *v.*, **-brat·ed,** **-brat·ing.** **1.** move rapidly to and fro. **2.** cause to swing to and fro; set in motion. **3.** measure by moving to and fro: *a pendulum vibrates seconds.* **4.** be moved; quiver. **5.** thrill, as in emotional response. **6.** resound: *the clanging vibrated in his ears.* [< L *vibratus* shaken] **—Syn. 1.** swing, oscillate. **4.** tremble, shake, throb.

vi·bra·tile (vī′brə·til; -tĭl), *adj.* **1.** capable of vibrating or of being vibrated. **2.** having a vibratory motion. **3.** pertaining to vibration. **—vi′bra·til′i·ty,** *n.*

vi·bra·tion (vī·brā′shən), *n.* **1.** a rapid movement to and fro; quivering motion; tremor. **2.** a rapid or slow movement to and fro. **3.** motion back and forth across a position of equilibrium; one complete movement of this sort. **4.** the vibrating motion of a string or other sonorous body, producing musical sound. **—vi·bra′tion·al,** *adj.* **—vi·bra′tion·less,** *adj.*

vi·bra·tor (vī′brā·tər), *n.* **1.** one that vibrates. **2.** instrument causing vibration.

vi·bra·to·ry (vī′brə·tô′rĭ; -tō′-), *adj.* **1.** vibrating. **2.** pertaining to vibration. **3.** causing vibration. **4.** capable of vibration. **5.** consisting of vibration.

vi·bur·num (vī·bėr′nəm), *n.* **1.** any of several shrubs or small trees of the same family as the honeysuckle. **2.** the dried bark of certain species, used in medicine. [< L]

vic·ar (vik′ər), *n.* **1.** the minister of an English parish who is paid a salary by the receiver of tithes. **2.** clergyman in the Protestant Episcopal Church who has charge of one chapel in a parish. **3.** a Roman Catholic clergyman who represents the Pope or a bishop. **4.** person acting in place of another; representative. [< OF < L *vicarius.* Doublet of VICARIOUS.] **—vi·car·i·al** (vī·kâr′ĭ·əl; vĭ-), *adj.* **—vi·car′i·ate** (vī·kâr′ĭ·it; vĭ-), *n.* **vic′ar·ship,** *n.*

vic·ar·age (vik′ər·ij), *n.* **1.** residence of a vicar. **2.** position or duties of a vicar. **3.** salary paid to a vicar.

vic·ar-gen·er·al (vik′ər·jen′ər·əl; -jen′rəl), *n.*, *pl.* **vic·ars-gen·er·al. 1.** in the Roman Catholic Church, deputy of a bishop or an archbishop, assisting him in the government of the diocese. **2.** in the Church of England, an ecclesiastical officer, usually a layman, who assists a bishop or an archbishop.

vi·car·i·ous (vī·kâr′ĭ·əs; vĭ-), *adj.* **1.** done or suffered for others: *vicarious work.* **2.** felt by sharing in others' experience: *her son's successes gave her vicarious joy.* **3.** taking the place of another: *a vicarious agent.* **4.** delegated: *vicarious authority.* [< L *vicarius* < *vicis* (gen.) turn, substitution. Doublet of VICAR.] **—vi·car′i·ous·ly,** *adv.* **—vi·car′i·ous·ness,** *n.*

vice[1] (vīs), *n.* **1.** an evil habit or tendency. **2.** evil; wickedness. **3.** an undesirable habit; fault; defect, as in a horse. [< OF < L *vitium*] **—vice′less,** *adj.* **—Syn. 2.** sin, iniquity, depravity, corruption. ➤ See vise for usage note.

vice[2] (vīs), *n.*, *v.*, **viced, vic·ing.** *Esp. Brit.* vise.

vi·ce[3] (vī′sē), *prep.* instead of; in the place of. [< L, (abl.) turn, change]

vice-, *prefix.* substitute; deputy; subordinate, as in *vice-president, vice-admiral, vice-chairman, vice-chancellor.* [see VICE[3]]

vice-ad·mi·ral (vīs′ad′mə·rəl), *n.* a naval officer ranking next below an admiral and next above a rear admiral. **—vice′-ad′mi·ral·ty,** *n.*

vice-con·sul (vīs′kon′səl), *n.* person next in rank below a consul, who substitutes for the regular consul or acts as his assistant. **—vice′-con′sul·ship,** *n.*

vice-ge·ren·cy (vīs·jir′ən·sĭ), *n.*, *pl.* **-cies. 1.** position of vicegerent. **2.** territory governed by a vicegerent.

vice-ge·rent (vīs·jir′ənt), *n.* person exercising the powers or authority of another; deputy. *—adj.* acting in another's place. [< Med.L *vicegerens* < L *vice* instead (of) + *gerere* manage]

vice-pres·i·dent (vīs′prez′ə·dənt; -prez′-dənt), **vice president,** *n.* officer next in rank to the president, who takes the president's place when necessary. —**vice′-pres′i·den·cy,** n. —**vice-pres·i·den·tial** (vīs′prez-ə-den′shəl), adj.

vice·re·gal (vīs·rē′gəl), adj. of or pertaining to a viceroy. —**vice·re′gal·ly,** adv.

vice·re·gent (vīs′rē′jənt), n. person who takes the place of the regular regent whenever necessary. —**vice′-re′gen·cy,** n.

vice·roy (vīs′roi), n. person ruling a country or province as the deputy of the sovereign. [< F, < vice VICE³ + roi king < L rex] —**vice·roy′al,** adj. —**vice·roy′al·ty,** vice′roy·ship, n.

vi·ce ver·sa (vī′sə ver′sə; vīs), the other way round; conversely. [< L]

Vich·y (vish′i), n. 1. city in C France, the capital of unoccupied France, 1940–44. 2. Vichy water.

Vichy water, 1. a natural mineral water from springs at Vichy, France, containing sodium bicarbonate and other salts, used in the treatment of digestive disturbances, gout, etc. 2. a natural or artificial water of similar composition.

vi·cin·i·ty (və·sin′ə·ti), n., pl. **-ties. 1.** region near or about a place; neighborhood; surrounding district. 2. nearness in place; being close. [< L, < vicinus neighboring < vicus quarter, village]

vi·cious (vish′əs), adj. **1.** disposed to evil; wicked. 2. characterized by vice or immorality; depraved. 3. having bad habits or a bad disposition: a vicious horse. 4. not correct; having faults: vicious reasoning. 5. spiteful; malicious: vicious words. 6. Colloq. unpleasantly severe: a vicious headache. —**vi′cious·ly,** adv. —**vi′cious·ness,** n.

vicious circle, 1. two or more undesirable things each of which keeps causing the other. 2. false reasoning that uses one statement to prove a second statement when the first statement really depends on the second for proof.

vi·cis·si·tude (və·sis′ə·tüd; -tūd), n. 1. change in circumstances, fortune, etc.: the vicissitudes of life may suddenly make a rich man very poor. 2. change; variation. [< L vicissitudo < vicis (gen.) change] —**vi·cis′si·tu′di·nar′y,** adj.

Vicks·burg (viks′bèrg), n. city in W Mississippi, on the Mississippi River.

vic·tim (vik′təm), n. **1.** person or animal sacrificed, injured, or destroyed: victims of war, victims of an accident. 2. dupe: the victim of a swindler. 3. a person or animal killed as a sacrifice to a god. [< L victima]

vic·tim·ize (vik′təm·īz), v., **-ized, -iz·ing. 1.** make a victim of; cause to suffer. 2. cheat; swindle. —**vic′tim·iz′a·ble,** adj. —**vic′tim·i·za′tion,** n. —**vic′tim·iz′er,** n.

vic·tor (vik′tər), n. winner; conqueror. —adj. victorious. [< L, < vincere conquer]

Vic·to·ri·a (vik·tô′ri·ə; -tō′-), n. **1.** 1819–1901, queen of England 1837–1901. 2. capital of British Columbia. 3. state in SE Australia. 4. Lake, lake in E Africa. 5. victoria, a low, four-wheeled carriage with a folding top, a seat for two passengers, and a raised seat in front for the driver.

Victoria Cross, a Maltese cross awarded to British soldiers and sailors as a decoration for remarkable valor during battle.

Vic·to·ri·an (vik·tô′ri·ən; -tō′-), adj. **1.** of or pertaining to the time of Queen Victoria. 2. possessing characteristics attributed to Victorians, as prudishness, bigotry, etc. —n. person, esp. an author, who lived during the reign of Queen Victoria. —**Vic·to′ri·an·ism,** n.

vic·to·ri·ous (vik·tô′ri·əs; -tō′-), adj. **1.** having won a victory; conquering. 2. having to do with victory. —**vic·to′ri·ous·ly,** adv. —**vic·to′ri·ous·ness,** n.

vic·to·ry (vik′tə·ri; -tri), n., pl. **-ries.** defeat of an enemy or opponent; success in a contest. [< L victoria, ult. < vincere conquer] —**Syn.** triumph, conquest. —**Ant.** defeat, failure.

Vic·tro·la (vik·trō′lə), n. Am. **1.** Trademark. a kind of phonograph. 2. victrola, any phonograph.

vict·ual (vit′əl), n., v., **-ualed, -ual·ing;** esp. Brit. **-ualled, -ual·ling.** —n. Usually, victuals. Colloq. or Dial. food. —v. **1.** supply with food. 2. take on a supply of food: the ship will victual

before sailing. [< OF vitaille < L victualia, pl., ult. < vivere live] —**vict′ual·less,** adj.

vict·ual·er, esp. Brit. **vict·ual·ler** (vit′əl-ər), n. **1.** person who supplies food or provisions to a ship, an army, etc. 2. Esp. Brit. keeper of an inn, tavern, saloon, etc. 3. ship that carries provisions for other ships or for troops.

vi·cu·ña (vi·kün′yə; -kū′nə), n. **1.** a South American animal somewhat like a camel, having a soft, delicate wool. 2. Also, vicuña cloth. cloth made from this wool, or from some substitute. [< Sp. < Kechua < South American Indian lang.)]

Vicuña
(ab. 2 ½ ft. high at the shoulder)

vid., see.

vi·de (vī′dē), v. Latin. see.

vi·de in·fra (vī′dē in′frə), Latin. see below.

vi·de·li·cet (və·del′ə·set), adv. that is to say; to wit; namely. Viz. is the abbreviation of videlicet. [< L, for videre licet it is permissible to see] ► See viz. for usage note.

vid·e·o (vid′i·ō), adj. of or used in the transmission or reception of images, as in television. —n. television. [< L, I see]

vi·de su·pra (vī′dē sü′prə), Latin. see above.

vie (vī), v., vied, vy·ing. strive for superiority; contend in rivalry; compete. [< F envier challenge < L invitare invite]

Vi·en·na (vi·en′ə), n. capital of Austria, on the Danube River. —**Vi·en·nese** (vē′ə·nēz′; -nēs′), adj., n.

Vien·tiane (vyen·tyän′), n. administrative capital of Laos, in the C part.

Vi·et·cong (vē·et′công′; vē′et-; vē·et′cong′; vē′et-), n., **Viet Cong,** the Communist guerrilla force in Indochina.

Vi·et·minh (vē·et′min′; vē′et-), n., **Viet Minh,** the Communist party in Indochina.

Vi·et·nam, Vi·et-Nam (vē·et′näm′; vē′et-), n. country in SE Asia, divided in 1954 into North Vietnam, and South Vietnam. —**Vi·et·nam·ese,** Vi·et-Nam·ese (vē·et′näm·ēz′; -ēs′), adj., n.

view (vū), n. **1.** act of seeing; sight: our first view of the ocean. 2. power of seeing; range of the eye: a ship came into view. 3. thing seen; scene: the view from the mountain. 4. picture of some scene: various views of the mountains hung on the walls. 5. a mental picture; idea: a general view of the war. 6. way of looking at or considering a matter; opinion: what are your views on the subject? 7. aim; purpose: it is my view to leave tomorrow. 8. prospect; expectation: with no view of success. 9. in view, a. in sight. b. under consideration. c. as a purpose or intention. d. as a hope; as an expectation. 10. in view of, considering; because. 11. on view, to be seen; open for people to see. 12. with a view to, a. with the purpose or intention of. b. with a hope of; expecting. —v. **1.** see; look at: they viewed the scene with pleasure. 2. consider; regard: the plan was viewed favorably. [< AF, < OF veoir see < L videre] —**view′er,** n. —**Syn.** n. **1.** look, survey, inspection, scrutiny. 3. vista, panorama. 5. notion, conception, impression.

view·less (vū′lis), adj. **1.** that cannot be seen. 2. without views or opinions. —**view′less·ly,** adv.

view·point (vū′point′), n. **1.** place from which one looks at something. 2. attitude of mind; point of view.

vi·ges·i·mal (vī·jes′ə·məl), adj. **1.** twentieth. 2. in or by twenties. [< L vigesimus twentieth]

vig·il (vij′əl), n. **1.** a staying awake for some purpose; a watching; watch: all night the mother kept vigil over the sick child. 2. a night spent in prayer. 3. the day and night before a solemn church festival. 4. Often, vigils. devotions, prayers, services, etc., on the night before a religious festival. [< OF < L vigilia < vigil watchful]

vig·i·lance (vij′ə·ləns), n. **1.** watchfulness; alertness; caution: constant vigilance is necessary in order to avoid accidents in driving. 2. sleeplessness.

vigilance committee, Am. a self-appointed

and unauthorized committee of citizens to maintain order and punish criminals.

vig·i·lant (vij′ə·lənt), *adj.* **1.** watchful; alert. **2.** keenly attentive to detect danger; wary. [< L *vigilans* watching < *vigil* watchful] —**vig′i·lant·ly,** *adv.* —**vig′i·lant·ness,** *n.* —**Syn. 1.** observant, attentive. —**Ant. 1.** inattentive.

vig·i·lan·te (vij′ə·lan′tē), *n. Am.* member of a vigilance committee. [< Sp., VIGILANT] —**vig′i·lan′tism,** *n.*

vi·gnette (vin·yet′), *n., v.,* —**gnet·ted,** —**gnet·ting.** —*n.* **1.** a decorative design on a page of a book, esp. on the title page. **2.** a literary sketch; short verbal description. **3.** an engraving, drawing, photograph, or the like, that shades off gradually at the edge. —*v.* **1.** make a vignette of. **2.** finish (a photograph, picture, etc.) in the manner of a vignette. [< F, dim. of *vigne* VINE] —**vi·gnett′ist,** *n.*

vig·or, *esp. Brit.* **vig·our** (vig′ər), *n.* **1.** active strength or force. **2.** healthy energy or power. **3.** legal force; validity. [< OF < L]

vig·or·ous (vig′ər·əs), *adj.* full of vigor; strong and active; energetic; forceful. —**vig′or·ous·ly,** *adv.* —**vig′or·ous·ness,** *n.* —**Syn.** robust, sturdy, hardy. —**Ant.** frail.

Vi·king, vi·king (vī′king), *n.* one of the daring Scandinavian pirates who raided the coasts of Europe during the eighth, ninth, and tenth centuries A.D.

vile (vīl), *adj.,* **vil·er, vil·est. 1.** very bad: *vile weather.* **2.** highly objectionable; disgusting; obnoxious: *a vile smell.* **3.** evil; low; immoral: *vile language.* **4.** poor; mean; lowly: *the vile tasks of the kitchen.* [< OF < L *vilis* cheap] —**vile′ly,** *adv.* —**vile′ness,** *n.*

vil·i·fy (vil′ə·fī), *v.,* —**fied,** —**fy·ing.** make vile; speak evil of; revile; slander. [< LL, < L *vilis* vile + *facere* make] —**vil′i·fi·ca′tion,** *n.* —**vil′i·fi′er,** *n.* —**Syn.** disparage.

vil·la (vil′ə), *n.* a house in the country or suburbs, sometimes at the seashore. A villa is usually a large or elegant residence. [< Ital. < L] —**vil′la·like′,** *adj.*

vil·lage (vil′ij), *n.* **1.** group of houses, usually smaller than a town. **2.** the people of a village. [< OF, ult. < L *villa* country house] —**vil′lage·less,** *adj.*

vil·lag·er (vil′ij·ər), *n.* person who lives in a village.

vil·lain (vil′ən), *n.* **1.** a very wicked person; dangerous scoundrel. **2.** a playful name for a mischievous person. **3.** villein. [< OF < Med.L *villanus* farmhand < L *villa* country house] —**vil′lain·ess,** *n. fem.* —**Syn. 1.** miscreant, reprobate, malefactor.

vil·lain·ous (vil′ən·əs), *adj.* **1.** very wicked. **2.** extremely bad; vile. —**vil′lain·ous·ly,** *adv.* —**vil′lain·ous·ness,** *n.*

vil·lain·y (vil′ən·i), *n., pl.* —**lain·ies. 1.** great wickedness. **2.** a very wicked act; crime. —**Syn. 1.** baseness, rascality, infamy.

vil·lein (vil′ən), *n.* one of a class of half-free peasants in the Middle Ages. A villein was under the control of his lord, but in his relations with other men had the rights of a freeman. [var. of *villain*]

Vil·lon (vē·yôn′), *n.* François, 1431–1463?, French poet and vagabond.

Vil·na (vil′nə), *n.* city in E Lithuania. Also, Polish **Wilno.**

vim (vim), *n. Am.* force; energy; vigor. [< L, accus. of *vis* force]

vin·ai·grette (vin′ə·gret′), *n.* an ornamental bottle or box for smelling salts, etc. [< F, < *vinaigre* VINEGAR]

Vin·ci (vin′chi), *n.* Leonardo da. See da Vinci.

vin·ci·ble (vin′sə·bəl), *adj.* conquerable. [< L, < *vincere* conquer] —**vin′ci·bil′i·ty, vin′ci·ble·ness,** *n.*

vin·di·cate (vin′də·kāt), *v.,* —**cat·ed,** —**cat·ing. 1.** clear from suspicion, dishonor, hint, or charge of wrongdoing, etc.: *the verdict of "Not guilty" vindicated him.* **2.** defend successfully against opposition; uphold; justify: *the heir vindicated his claim to the fortune.* [< L *vindicatus* < *vin-*

dex defender] —**vin·di·ca·ble** (vin′də·kə·bəl), *adj.* —**vin′di·ca′tion,** *n.* —**vin·dic·a·tive** (vin·dik′ə·tiv; vin′də·kā′tiv), *adj.* —**vin′di·ca′tor,** *n.* —**vin·di·ca·to·ry** (vin′də·kə·tô′ri; -tō′-), *adj.*

vin·dic·tive (vin·dik′tiv), *adj.* feeling or showing a strong tendency toward revenge; bearing a grudge. —**vin·dic′tive·ly,** *adv.* —**vin·dic′tive·ness,** *n.* —**Syn.** revengeful, spiteful.

vine (vīn), *n.* **1.** plant with a long, slender stem, that grows along the ground or that climbs by attaching itself to a wall, tree, or other support. **2.** grapevine. [< OF < L *vinea* < *vinum* wine] —**vine′less,** *adj.* —**vine′like′,** *adj.*

vin·e·gar (vin′ə·gər), *n.* a sour liquid produced by the fermentation of cider, wine, etc., consisting largely of dilute, impure acetic acid. Vinegar is used in flavoring and preserving food. [< OF, < *vin* wine (< L *vinum*) + *egre* sour < L *acer*] —**vin′e·gar·ish, vin′e·gar·y,** *adj.*

vin·er·y (vīn′ər·i), *n., pl.* —**er·ies. 1.** vineyard. **2.** *Am.* vines collectively.

vine·yard (vin′yərd), *n.* place planted with grapevines. —**vine′yard·ed,** *adj.* —**vine′yard·ist,** *n. Am.*

vi·nous (vī′nəs), *adj.* **1.** of, like, or having to do with wine. **2.** caused by drinking wine. [< L, < *vinum* wine] —**vi·nos·i·ty** (vī·nos′ə·ti), *n.*

Vin·son (vin′sən), *n.* Frederick Moore, 1890–1953, chief justice of the U. S. Supreme Court, 1946–1953.

vin·tage (vin′tij), *n.* **1.** the wine from a certain crop of grapes. **2.** a year's crop of grapes. **3.** the gathering of grapes for making wine. **4.** Also, **vintage wine,** an unusually fine wine from the crop of a good year. **5.** *Colloq.* crop or output of anything at some particular time: *her old hat was of the vintage of 1930.* [< AF, alter. of OF *vendange* < L *vindemia* < *vinum* wine + *demere* take off; infl. by *vintner*]

vint·ner (vint′nər), *n. Esp. Brit.* dealer in wine. [earlier *vinter* < AF, ult. < L *vinum* wine]

vi·nyl (vī′nil; vin′il), *n. Chem.* the univalent radical CH_2:CH derived from ethylene. Thermoplastic resins are formed by polymerization of some vinyl compounds.

vi·ol (vī′əl), *n.* a stringed musical instrument played with a bow. [< F *viole*]

Boy playing a large viol

vi·o·la (vi·ō′lə; vī–), *n.* a musical instrument like a violin, but somewhat larger; a tenor or alto violin. [< Ital.]

vi·o·la·ble (vī′ə·lə·bəl), *adj.* that can be violated. —**vi′o·la·bil′i·ty, vi′o·la·ble·ness,** *n.* —**vi′o·la·bly,** *adv.*

vi·o·late (vī′ə·lāt), *v.,* —**lat·ed,** —**lat·ing. 1.** break (a law, rule, agreement, promise, etc.); act contrary to; fail to perform: *violate a law.* **2.** treat with disrespect or contempt: *he violated their beliefs.* **3.** break in upon; disturb: *violate one's privacy.* **4.** break through or pass by force or without right: *violate a boundary.* **5.** trespass on; infringe on: *violate the right of free speech.* **6.** use force against (a woman or girl); rape. [< L *violatus* < *vis* violence] —**vi′o·la′tive,** *adj.* —**vi′o·la′tor,** *n.* —**Syn. 2.** dishonor, desecrate, profane.

vi·o·la·tion (vī′ə·lā′shən), *n.* **1.** use of force; violence. **2.** a breaking (of a law, rule, agreement, promise, etc.). **3.** treatment (of a holy thing) with contempt. **4.** ravishment; rape. —**Syn. 2.** infringement, infraction, breach.

vi·o·lence (vī′ə·ləns), *n.* **1.** rough force in action: *he slammed the door with violence.* **2.** rough or harmful action or treatment. **3.** harm; injury: *it would do violence to her principles to work on Sunday.* **4.** unlawful use of force. **5.** strength of action, feeling, etc.

vi·o·lent (vī′ə·lənt), *adj.* **1.** acting or done with strong, rough force: *a violent blow.* **2.** caused by strong, rough force: *a violent death.* **3.** showing or caused by very strong feeling, action, etc.: *violent language.* **4.** severe; extreme; very great: *violent pain.* [< L *violentus* < *vis* force] —**vi′o-**

lent·ly, *adv.* —**Syn. 1.** fierce, furious. **3.** vehement, passionate.

vi·o·let (vī′ə·lit), *n.* **1.** any of various stemless or leafy-stemmed plants with purple, blue, yellow, or white flowers. **2.** the flower. **3.** a bluish purple. —*adj.* **1.** bluish-purple. **2.** having the scent of fragrant violets. [< OF *violete*, ult. < L *viola*] —**vi′o·let·like′,** *adj.*

violet rays, 1. the shortest rays of the spectrum that can be seen. **2.** ultraviolet rays.

vi·o·lin (vī′ə·lin′), *n.* **1.** the commonest musical instrument with four strings, held horizontally against the shoulder and played with a bow. **2.** any modern instrument of the same general class, as a viola or violoncello. **3.** in an orchestra, a violinist. [< Ital. *violino*, dim. of *viola* viol] —**vi′o·lin′less,** *adj.*

vi·o·lin·ist (vī′ə·lin′ist), *n.* person who plays the violin.

vi·ol·ist (vī′əl·ist), *n.* person who plays the viol.

vi·o·lon·cel·lo (vī′ə·lən·chel′ō; vē′ə-), *n., pl.* **-los.** *Music.* cello. [< Ital., ult. < *viola* viol] —**vi·o·lon·cel·list** (vī′ə·lən·chel′ist; vē′ə-), *n.*

VIP, V.I.P., *Colloq.* very important person.

vi·per (vī′pər), *n.* **1.** a thick-bodied poisonous snake with a pair of large perforated fangs. **2.** a spiteful, treacherous person. [< L *vipera* < *vivus* alive + *parere* bring forth] —**vi′per·ish,** **vi′per·like′,** *adj.*

vi·per·ous (vī′pər·əs), *adj.* **1.** of or pertaining to a viper or vipers. **2.** like a viper. **3.** spiteful; treacherous. —**vi′per·ous·ly,** *adv.*

vi·ra·go (və·rä′gō), *n., pl.* **-goes, -gos.** a violent, bad-tempered, or scolding woman. [< L, < *vir* man] —**vi·rag′i·nous** (və·raj′ə·nəs), *adj.*

vir·e·o (vir′i·ō), *n., pl.* **-e·os.** *Am.* **1.** a small, olive-green, insect-eating American songbird. **2.** any bird of the same family. [< L, kind of bird]

Vireo (ab. 6 in. long)

vi·res·cent (vī·res′ənt), *adj.* turning green; tending to a green color; greenish. [< L *virescens* turning green] —**vi·res′cence,** *n.*

Vir·gil (vér′jəl), *n.* Vergil. —**Vir·gil′i·an,** *adj.*

vir·gin (vér′jən), *n.* **1.** a maiden; unmarried woman. **2.** person who has not had sexual intercourse. **3.** the Virgin, the Virgin Mary. **4.** Virgin, Virgo. —*adj.* **1.** of or pertaining to a virgin; suitable for a virgin: *virgin modesty.* **2.** pure; spotless: *virgin snow.* **3.** being a virgin. **4.** not yet used: *virgin soil, a virgin forest.* **5.** not trained; with no experience; fresh; new. [< OF < L *virgo*]

vir·gin·al (vér′jən·əl), *adj.* of or suitable for a virgin; maidenly; pure. —*n.* a musical instrument like a small piano, but set in a box without legs. It was much used in the 16th and 17th centuries. [< L *virginalis* < *virgo* maiden] —**vir′gin·al·ly,** *adv.* —**vir′gin·al·ness,** *n.*

virgin birth, *Theol.* doctrine that Jesus was the son of God and was miraculously conceived by the Virgin Mary.

Vir·gin·ia (vər·jin′yə), *n.* a State in the E United States. *Capital:* Richmond. *Abbrev.:* Va. —**Vir·gin′ian,** *adj., n. Am.*

Virginia creeper, *Am.* a climbing plant having leaves with five leaflets and bluish-black berries; woodbine; American ivy.

Virginia reel, *Am.* a dance in which the partners form two lines facing each other and perform a number of dance steps.

Virgin Islands, 1. Also, Virgin Islands of the United States. group of islands in the West Indies that belong to the United States. The chief ones are St. John, St. Thomas, and St. Croix. **2.** Also, British Virgin Islands. group of islands E of Puerto Rico, part of the Leeward Islands colony of Great Britain.

vir·gin·i·ty (vər·jin′ə·ti), *n.* virgin condition; maidenhood.

vir·gin·i·um (vər·jin′i·əm), *n. Chem.* a rare metallic element, Vi. [< NL, after the state of *Virginia*]

Virgin Mary, the mother of Jesus.

Virgin Queen, Queen Elizabeth I of England.

Vir·go (vér′gō), *n., gen.* Vir·gi·nis (vér′jə·nis). *Astron.* **1.** the Virgin, a zodiacal constellation. **2.** the sixth sign of the zodiac.

vir·gule (vér′gūl), *n.* a slanting stroke (/) between two words indicating that the meaning of either word pertains, as in *and/or.* [< L *virgula* little rod]

vir·i·des·cent (vir′ə·des′ənt), *adj.* greenish. [< LL *viridescens* turning green < L *viridis* green] —**vir′i·des′cence,** *n.*

vir·ile (vir′əl), *adj.* **1.** manly; masculine. **2.** full of manly strength or masculine vigor. **3.** capable of procreation. **4.** vigorous; forceful. [< L, < *vir* man] —**vir′ile·ly,** *adv.*

vi·ril·i·ty (və·ril′ə·ti), *n., pl.* **-ties. 1.** manly strength; masculine vigor. **2.** power of procreation. **3.** vigor; forcefulness.

vir·tu (vėr·tü′; vėr′tü), *n.* **1.** excellence or merit in an object of art because of its workmanship, rarity, antiquity, or the like. **2.** (*pl. in use*). objects of art; choice curios. **3.** a taste for objects of art; knowledge of objects of art. [< Ital., excellence, < L *virtus* virtue. Doublet of virtue.]

vir·tu·al (vér′chü·əl), *adj.* being something in effect, though not so in name; actual; real. —**vir′tu·al′i·ty,** *n.*

vir·tu·al·ly (vér′chü·əl·i), *adv.* in effect, though not in name; actually; really.

vir·tue (vér′chü), *n.* **1.** moral excellence; goodness. **2.** a particular moral excellence: *kindness is a virtue.* **3.** a good quality: *he praised the virtues of the car.* **4.** chastity; purity. **5.** power to produce effects: *there is little virtue in that medicine.* **6.** by or in virtue of, relying on; because of; on account of. **7.** make a virtue of necessity, do willingly what must be done anyway. [< L *virtus* manliness < *vir* man. Doublet of virtu.] —**vir′tue·less,** *adj.* —**Syn. 1.** uprightness, integrity. **3.** merit.

vir·tu·os·i·ty (vér′chü·os′ə·ti), *n., pl.* **-ties.** character or skill of a virtuoso.

vir·tu·o·so (vér′chü·ō′sō), *n., pl.* **-sos, -si** (-sē). **1.** person skilled in the method of an art, esp. in playing a musical instrument. **2.** person who has a cultivated appreciation of artistic excellence. [< Ital., learned]

vir·tu·ous (vér′chü·əs), *adj.* **1.** good; moral; righteous. **2.** chaste; pure. —**vir′tu·ous·ly,** *adv.* —**vir′tu·ous·ness,** *n.* —**Syn. 1.** upright, worthy.

vir·u·lent (vir′yə·lənt; vir′ə-), *adj.* **1.** very poisonous or harmful; deadly. **2.** intensely bitter or spiteful; violently hostile. [< L, < *virus* poison] —**vir′u·lence,** **vir′u·len·cy,** *n.* —**vir′u·lent·ly,** *adv.* —**Syn. 1.** venomous, noxious.

vi·rus (vī′rəs), *n.* **1.** a poison produced in a person or animal suffering from an infectious disease. **2.** any of a group of disease-producing agents smaller than any known bacteria and dependent upon the living tissue of hosts for their reproduction and growth. **3.** corrupting influence. [< L, poison]

virus X, an infection or disease of uncertain nature, sometimes resembling influenza.

vis (vis), *n. Latin.* force.

vi·sa (vē′zə), *n., v.,* **-saed, -sa·ing.** —*n.* an official signature or endorsement upon a passport or document, showing that it has been examined and approved. —*v.* examine and sign. Also, visé. [< F, ult. < L *videre* see]

vis·age (viz′ij), *n.* **1.** face. **2.** appearance. [< OF, < *vis* face < L *visus* a look < *videre* see] —**vis′aged,** *adj.*

vis-à-vis (vē′zə·vē′), *adv., adj.* face to face; opposite: *we sat vis-à-vis.* [< F]

Visc., Viscount.

vis·cer·a (vis′ər·ə), *n.pl., sing.* **vis·cus** (vis′kəs). the soft inside parts of the body. The heart, stomach, liver, intestines, kidneys, etc., are viscera. [< L, pl. of *viscus*] —**vis′cer·al,** *adj.*

vis·cid (vis′id), *adj.* thick and sticky like heavy syrup or glue. [< LL, < L *viscum* bird lime] —**vis·cid′i·ty,** **vis′cid·ness,** *n.* —**vis′cid·ly,** *adv.*

vis·cose (vis′kōs), *n.* a plastic material prepared by treating cellulose with caustic soda and carbon bisulfide. Viscose is used in manufacturing artificial silk, in making a product resembling celluloid, for sizing, and for other purposes. [< L *viscosus* VISCOUS]

vis·cos·i·ty (vis·kos′ə·ti), *n., pl.* –ties. 1. viscous quality. 2. resistance of a fluid to the motion of its molecules among themselves.

vis·count (vī′kount), *n.* a nobleman ranking next below an earl or count and next above a baron. [< AF < OF *vis*– vice– + *conte* COUNT²] —**vis·count·cy** (vī′kount·si), **vis′count·y**, **vis′count·ship**, *n.*

vis·count·ess (vī′koun·tis), *n.* 1. wife or widow of a viscount. 2. woman holding in her own right a rank equivalent to that of a viscount.

vis·cous (vis′kəs), *adj.* 1. of a liquid, sticky; thick like syrup or glue. 2. of a solid, able to change its shape gradually under stress. [< L, < *viscum* bird lime] —**vis′cous·ly**, *adv.* —**vis′cous·ness**, *n.*

vise (vīs), *n., v.,* vised, vis·ing. —*n.* tool having two jaws moved by a screw, used to hold an object firmly while work is being done on it. —*v.* hold, press, or force with a vise. Also, *esp. Brit.* vice. [< OF *vis* screw < VL *vitium* < L *vitis* vine] —**vise′like′**, *adj.* ≯ vise, vice. The name of the tool is more commonly spelled with *s*, but both *vise* and *vice* are found, the latter chiefly in British usage. *Vice*, the quality of evil or undesirableness, is always *vice*, and the adjective is *vicious*.

vi·sé (vē′zā), *n., v.,* vi·séed or vi·sé′d, vi·sé·ing. visa.

Vish·nu (vish′nū), *n.* in Hindu religion, one of the three chief divinities, called "the Preserver."

vis·i·bil·i·ty (viz′ə·bil′ə·ti), *n., pl.* –ties. 1. condition or quality of being visible. 2. condition of light, atmosphere, etc., with reference to the distance at which things can be clearly seen.

vis·i·ble (viz′ə·bəl), *adj.* that can be seen: *the shore was barely visible through the fog, visible means of support.* [< L *visibilis* < *videre* see] —**vis′i·ble·ness**, *n.* —**vis′i·bly**, *adv.*

Vis·i·goth (viz′ī·goth), *n.* member of the western division of the Goths that plundered Rome in 410 A.D. and formed a monarchy in France and northern Spain about 418 A.D. —**Vis′i·goth′ic**, *adj.*

vi·sion (vizh′ən), *n.* 1. power of seeing; sense of sight. 2. a seeing; sight. 3. power of perceiving by the imagination or by clear thinking: *a prophet of great vision.* 4. something seen in the imagination, in a dream, in one's thoughts, etc. 5. phantom. 6. a very beautiful person, scene, etc. —*v.* see in, or as if in, a vision. [< L *visio* < *videre* see] —**vi′sion·al**, *adj.* —**vi′sion·al·ly**, *adv.* —**vi′sion·less**, *adj.*

vi·sion·ar·y (vizh′ən·er′i), *adj., n., pl.* –aries. —*adj.* 1. not practical; dreamy: *visionary plans.* 2. of or belonging to a vision; seen in a vision. 3. not actual; imaginary. —*n.* 1. person who is not practical; dreamer. 2. person who sees visions. —**vi′sion·ar′i·ness**, *n.* —Syn. *adj.* 1. fanciful. —Ant. *adj.* 1. practical.

vis·it (viz′it), *v.* 1. go or come to see: *visit New York.* 2. make a call on or stay with for social or other reasons: *visit one's aunt.* 3. pay a call; make a stay; be a guest: *visit in the country.* 4. go or come to see, to inspect, or to examine officially: *the inspector visited the factory.* 5. come upon; afflict: *he was visited by many troubles.* 6. send upon; inflict: *visit one's anger on someone.* 7. **visit with,** *Am., Colloq.* talk with. —*n.* 1. a visiting; a call from friendship, for purpose of inspection, for medical treatment, etc. 2. a stay or sojourn as a guest. 3. *Am., Colloq.* an informal talk; chat. [< L *visitare*, ult. < *videre* see] —**vis′it·a·ble**, *adj.*

vis·it·ant (viz′ə·tənt), *n.* 1. visitor; guest. 2. a migratory bird. —*adj.* visiting.

vis·it·a·tion (viz′ə·tā′shən), *n.* 1. act of visiting. 2. a visit for the purpose of making an official inspection or examination. Also, **Visitation.** visit of the Virgin Mary to Eliza-

beth, her cousin. Luke 1:39–56. 4. **Visitation,** a festival of the Roman Catholic Church, held July 2, in honor of this visit. 5. a punishment or reward sent by God. —**vis′it·a′tion·al**, *adj.*

visiting card, a calling card.

vis·i·tor (viz′ə·tər), *n.* person who visits or is visiting; guest. —**vis·i·to·ri·al** (viz′ə·tô′ri·əl; –tō′–), *adj.* —Syn. caller, visitant.

vi·sor (vī′zər), *n.* 1. the movable front part of a helmet, covering the face. 2. *Am.* the projecting brim of a cap, to protect the eyes from the sun. 3. mask. Also, **vizor.** [< AF *viser* < *vis* face, ult. < L *videre* see] —**vi′sored**, *adj.* —**vi′sor·less**, *adj.*

VISOR

vis·ta (vis′tə), *n.* 1. view seen through a narrow opening or passage. 2. such an opening or passage itself. 3. a mental view. [< Ital., ult. < L *videre* see] —**vis·taed** (vis′təd), *adj.* —**vis′ta·less**, *adj.*

Vis·tu·la (vis′chú·lə), *n.* river in Poland flowing from the Carpathians to the Baltic Sea.

vis·u·al (vizh′ú·əl), *adj.* 1. of sight; having to do with sight. 2. of or perceived by vision; having vision; done by vision. 3. that can be seen; visible. [< LL, < L *visus* sight < *videre* see] —**vis′u·al·ly**, *adv.*

visual aid, device or means for aiding the learning process through the sense of sight, as a chart, diagram, motion picture, etc.

vis·u·al·ize (vizh′ú·əl·īz), *v.,* –ized, –iz·ing. 1. form a mental picture of. 2. make visible. —**vis′u·al·i·za′tion**, *n.* —**vis′u·al·iz′er**, *n.*

vi·tal (vī′təl), *adj.* 1. of life; having to do with life: *vital statistics.* 2. having life; living. 3. necessary to life: *vital organs.* 4. very necessary; very important; essential. 5. causing death, failure, or ruin: *a vital wound.* 6. full of life and spirit; lively. —*n.* **vitals,** a. parts or organs necessary to life, as the heart, brain, or lungs. b. essential parts or features. [< L, < *vita* life] —**vi′tal·ly**, *adv.* —**vi′tal·ness**, *n.*

vi·tal·ism (vī′təl·iz·əm), *n.* doctrine that the behavior of a living organism is, at least in part, due to a vital principle that cannot possibly be explained by physics and chemistry. —**vi′tal·ist**, *n.* —**vi′tal·is′tic**, *adj.*

vi·tal·i·ty (vī·tal′ə·ti), *n., pl.* –ties. 1. a vital force; power to live. 2. power to endure and be active. 3. strength or vigor of mind or body.

vi·tal·ize (vī′təl·īz), *v.,* –ized, –iz·ing. 1. give life to. 2. put vitality into. —**vi′tal·i·za′tion**, *n.* —**vi′tal·iz′er**, *n.*

vi·ta·min, vi·ta·mine (vī′tə·min), *n.* any of certain special substances present in variable quantities in natural foodstuffs, required for the normal growth and nourishment of the body. Lack of vitamins in food causes such diseases as rickets and scurvy as well as general poor health. —*adj.* of or pertaining to vitamins. [< L *vita* life + E *amine* (< *ammonia*)] —**vi′ta·min′ic**, *adj.*

vitamin A, the fat-soluble vitamin found in milk, butter, cod-liver oil, egg yolk, liver, leafy green vegetables, etc., that increases the resistance of the body to infection and prevents night blindness. It exists in two known forms, A_1 and A_2.

vitamin B₁, thiamine.

vitamin B₂, riboflavin. Also, **vitamin G.**

vitamin B₆, pyridoxine.

vitamin B₁₂, a newly discovered crystalline liver extract, supposedly the pure anti-anemia factor of the liver.

vitamin B complex, group of different vitamins including vitamin B₁, vitamin B₂, vitamin B₆, etc., found in high concentration in yeast and liver.

vitamin C, the antiscorbutic vitamin, $C_6H_8O_6$, found esp. in citrus fruits; ascorbic acid.

vitamin D, the antirachitic vitamin found in cod-liver oil, milk, and egg yolk, that is necessary for the growth and health of bones and teeth. It exists in many related forms including D_1, D_2, D_3, and D_4.

vitamin E, vitamin found in wheat, lettuce, milk, etc., that is necessary for reproductive processes. Lack of vitamin E causes sterility.

vitamin G, vitamin B₂.

vi·ti·ate (vish′i·āt), v., -at·ed, -at·ing. 1. impair the quality of; spoil. 2. destroy the legal force or authority of. [< L, < *vitium* fault] —vi′-ti·at′ed, adj. —vi′ti·a′tion, n. —vi′ti·a′tor, n.

vit·i·cul·ture (vit′ə·kul′chər; vī′tə-), n. the cultivation of grapes. [< L *vitis* vine + E *culture*] —vit′i·cul′tur·al, adj. —vit′i·cul′tur·er, vit′i·cul′tur·ist, n.

vit·re·ous (vit′ri·əs), adj. 1. glassy; like glass. 2. pertaining to glass. [< L, < *vitrum* glass] —vit′re·ous·ly, adv. —vit′re·ous·ness, vit·ri·os·i·ty (vit′ri·os′ə·ti), n.

vitreous humor, *Anat.* the transparent, jelly-like substance that fills the eyeball in back of the lens.

vit·ri·form (vit′rə·fôrm), adj. having the structure or appearance of glass.

vit·ri·fy (vit′rə·fī), v., -fied, -fy·ing. change into glass or something like glass. [< F, < L *vitrum* glass + *facere* make] —vit′ri·fi′a·ble, adj. —vit′ri·fi′a·bil′i·ty, n. —vit′ri·fi·ca′tion, vit·ri·fac·tion (vit′rə·fak′shən), n.

vit·ri·ol (vit′ri·əl), n. 1. *Chem.* a. any of certain sulfates, as of copper (blue vitriol), of iron (green vitriol), and of zinc (white vitriol). b. sulfuric acid. Vitriol burns deeply and leaves very bad scars. 2. very sharp speech or severe criticism. [< Med.L *vitriolum*, ult. < L *vitrum* glass]

vit·ri·ol·ic (vit′ri·ol′ik), adj. 1. of, containing, or obtained from vitriol. 2. like vitriol. 3. bitterly severe; biting; sharp.

vi·tu·per·ate (vī·tū′pər·āt; -tū′-; vi-), v., -at·ed, -at·ing. find fault with in abusive words; revile. [< L *vituperatus* < *vitium* fault + *parare* prepare] —vi·tu′per·a′tion, n. —vi·tu′-per·a′tive, adj. —vi·tu′per·a′tive·ly, adv. —vi·tu′per·a′tor, n. —Syn. abuse, berate, upbraid.

vi·va (vē′və), interj. (long) live (the person or thing named). —n. shout of applause or good will. [< Ital.]

vi·va·cious (vī·vā′shəs; vi-), adj. lively; sprightly; animated; gay. [< L *vivax*] —vi·va′-cious·ly, adv. —vi·va′cious·ness, n.

vi·vac·i·ty (vī·vas′ə·ti; vi-), n., pl. -ties. liveliness; sprightliness; animation; gaiety. [< L, < *vivax* lively]

vi·var·i·um (vī·vār′i·əm), n., pl. -i·ums, -i·a (-i·ə). place where animals or plants are kept in, or under circumstances simulating, their natural state. [< L]

vi·va vo·ce (vī′və vō′sē), orally; oral. [< L, lit., by living voice]

vive (vēv), interj. *French.* (long) live (the person or thing named).

viv·id (viv′id), adj. 1. brilliant; strikingly bright: *dandelions are a vivid yellow.* 2. full of life; lively: *a vivid description.* 3. strong and distinct: *a vivid memory.* [< L *vividus*] —viv′id·ly, adv. —viv′id·ness, n. —Syn. 2. animated, spirited. —Ant. 1. dull. 2. lifeless. 3. vague.

viv·i·fy (viv′ə·fī), v., -fied, -fy·ing. 1. give life or vigor to. 2. enliven; make vivid. [< L, < *vivus* alive + *facere* make] —viv′i·fi·ca′tion, n. —viv′i·fi′er, n.

vi·vip·a·rous (vī·vip′ə·rəs), adj. bringing forth living young, rather than eggs. Dogs, cats, cows, and human beings are viviparous. [< L, < *vivus* alive + *parere* bring forth] —vi·vi·par·i·ty (viv′ə·par′ə·ti), vi·vip′a·rous·ness, n. —vi·vip′a·rous·ly, adv.

viv·i·sect (viv′ə·sekt; viv′ə·sekt′), v. 1. practice vivisection on. 2. practice vivisection.

viv·i·sec·tion (viv′ə·sek′shən), n. cutting into or experimenting on living animals for scientific study. [< L *vivus* alive + E *section*] —viv′i·sec′tion·al, adj. —viv′i·sec′tion·ist, n. —viv′i·sec′-tor, n.

vix·en (vik′sən), n. 1. a female fox. 2. a bad-tempered or quarrelsome woman. [OE *fyxen* < *fox* fox] —vix′en·ish, vix′en·like′, adj.

viz., namely. ➤ Viz. is the abbreviation of Latin *videlicet* (və·del′ə·set), to wit, namely. Viz. exists

only in the language of rather formal documents or reference works.

vi·zier, vi·zir (vi·zir′), n. a high official in Mohammedan countries; minister of state. [< Turk. < Ar. *wazīr*, orig., porter] —vi·zier·ate, vi·zir·ate (vi·zir′it; -āt); vi·zier′ship, vi·zir′-ship, n. —vi·zier′i·al, vi·zir′i·al, adj.

vi·zor (vī′zər), n. visor. —vi′zored, adj. —vi′zor·less, adj.

V-J Day, date of the Allied victory over Japan in World War II, August 14, 1945.

VL, Vulgar Latin.

Vlad·i·vos·tok (vlad′ə·vos·tok′; -vos′tok), n. seaport in the E Soviet Union in Asia.

V-Mail (vē′māl′), n. during World War II, a service using microfilm and reproductions to transmit letters to and from members of the U.S. armed forces overseas.

voc., *Gram.* vocative.

vocab., vocabulary.

vo·ca·ble (vō′kə·bəl), n. a word, esp. a word as heard or seen without consideration of its meaning. [< L *vocabulum* < *vocare* call]

vo·cab·u·lar·y (vō·kab′yə·ler′i), n., pl. -lar-ies. 1. stock of words used by a person, class of people, profession, etc. Reading will increase your vocabulary. 2. a collection or list of words, usually in alphabetical order and defined. [< Med.L *vocabularius* < L *vocabulum* VOCABLE] —Syn. 2. glossary, dictionary, lexicon.

vocabulary entry, 1. word, term, or item entered in a vocabulary. 2. in dictionaries, any word or phrase in alphabetical order and defined, or any related word listed for identification under the word from which it is derived.

vo·cal (vō′kəl), adj. 1. of, by, for, with, or pertaining to the voice: *vocal organs, vocal power.* 2. having a voice; giving forth sound. Men are vocal beings. 3. rendered by or intended for singing: *vocal music.* 4. aroused to speech; inclined to talk freely: *he became vocal with indignation.* [< L *vocalis* < *vox* voice. Doublet of VOWEL.] —vo·cal·i·ty (vō·kal′ə·ti), vo′cal-ness, n.

vocal cords, two pairs of membranes in the throat. The lower pair can be pulled tight and the passage of breath between them then causes them to vibrate, which produces the sound of voice.

vo·cal·ic (vō·kal′ik), adj. 1. of or like a vowel sound. 2. having many vowel sounds.

vo·cal·ist (vō′kəl·ist), n. singer.

vo·cal·ize (vō′kəl·īz), v., -ized, -iz·ing. 1. speak, sing, shout, etc. 2. make vocal; utter. 3. *Phonet.* a. change into a vowel; use as a vowel. Some people vocalize the r in *four.* b. utter with the voice, and not just with the breath. —vo′cal·i·za′tion, n. —vo′cal·iz′er, n. —vo′cal·ly, adv.

vocat., *Gram.* vocative.

vo·ca·tion (vō·kā′shən), n. 1. occupation; business; profession; trade. 2. an inner call or summons. [< L *vocatio*, lit., a calling < *vocare* call]

vo·ca·tion·al (vō·kā′shən·əl; -kāsh′nəl), adj. 1. having to do with some occupation, trade, etc. 2. *Am.* guiding or preparing for a business: *a vocational school.* —vo·ca′tion·al·ly, adv.

voc·a·tive (vok′ə·tiv), *Gram.* —adj. showing the person or thing spoken to. —n. 1. the vocative case. 2. a word in that case. [< L, < *vocare* call] —voc′a·tive·ly, adv.

vo·cif·er·ant (vō·sif′ər·ənt), adj. vociferating. —n. person who vociferates. —vo·cif′er·ance, n.

vo·cif·er·ate (vō·sif′ər·āt), v., -at·ed, -at·ing. cry out loudly or noisily; shout. [< L *vociferatus* < *vox* voice + *ferre* bear] —vo·cif′er·a′tion, n. —vo·cif′er·a′tor, n. —Syn. clamor, scream.

vo·cif·er·ous (vō·sif′ər·əs), adj. loud and noisy; shouting; clamoring: *a vociferous person, vociferous cheers.* [< L *vociferari* VOCIFERATE] —vo·cif′er·ous·ly, adv. —vo·cif′er·ous·ness, n.

vod·ka (vod′kə), n. a Russian intoxicating liquor. [< Russ., dim. of *voda* water]

vogue (vōg), n. 1. the fashion: *hoop skirts were in vogue many years ago.* 2. popularity; acceptance: *that song had a great vogue at one* *time.* [< F, a rowing, course, success < *voguer* float < Ital. *vogare*.]

voice (vois), *n., v.,* voiced, voic·ing. —*n.* 1. sound made through the mouth, esp. by people in speaking, singing, shouting, etc. 2. power to make sounds through the mouth. 3. anything like speech or song: *the voice of the wind.* 4. ability as a singer. 5. singer. 6. part of a piece of music for one kind of singer or instrument. 7. expression: *they gave voice to their joy.* 8. an expressed opinion, choice, wish, etc.: *his voice was for compromise.* 9. the right to express an opinion or choice: *we have no voice in the matter.* 10. *Gram.* a form of the verb that shows whether the subject is active or passive. 11. *Phonet.* sound uttered with vibration of the vocal cords, not with mere breath. 12. **in voice,** in condition to sing or speak well. 13. **lift up one's voice,** a. shout; yell. b. protest; complain. 14. **with one voice,** unanimously. —*v.* 1. express; utter. 2. *Phonet.* utter with a sound made by vibration of the vocal cords. *Z* and *v* are voiced; *s* and *f* are not. [< OF < L *vox*] —voiced, *adj.* —voic′er, *n.* ➤ voice: definition and forms. When the subject of a verb is the doer of the action or is in the condition named by its verb, the verb is in the active voice: the congregation *sang* "Abide with Me," they *will go* swimming, our side *had won,* Jimmy's father *gave* him a car, we *rested* an hour. When the subject of a verb receives the action, the verb is in the passive voice: "Abide with Me" *was sung* by the congregation, Jimmy *was given* a car by his father, the pit *was dug* fully eight feet deep, they *were caught.* The passive form is always a form of the verb *be* and a past participle:

	Active	Passive
PRESENT:	he asks (is asking)	he is asked (is being asked)
FUTURE:	he will ask	he will be asked
PERFECT:	he has asked	he has been asked
INFINITIVES:	to ask, to have asked	to be asked, to have been asked
PARTICIPLES:	asking	being asked

voice·less (vois′lis), *adj.* 1. having no voice; dumb; silent. 2. *Phonet.* spoken without vibration of the vocal cords. The consonants *p, t,* and *k* are voiceless. —voice′less·ly, *adv.* —voice′less·ness, *n.*

Voice of America, an international broadcasting service maintained by the U.S. government to implement U.S. foreign policy by giving overseas listeners a true picture of American life, culture, and aims.

void (void), *adj.* 1. without legal force or effect; not binding in law. 2. empty; vacant: *a void space.* 3. without effect; useless. 4. void of, devoid of; without; lacking. —*v.* 1. make of no force or effect in law. 2. empty out. —*n.* an empty space. [< OF *voide* < VL *vocitus,* ult. < var. of L *vacuus* empty] —void′a·ble, *adj.* —void′a·ble·ness, *n.* —void′er, *n.* —void′ly, *adv.* —void′ness, *n.* —Syn. 1. invalid, null. —*v.* 1. invalidate, nullify.

voile (voil), *n.* a very thin cloth with an open weave. [< F, orig., *veil.* Doublet of VEIL.]

vol., *pl.* vols. volume.

vo·lant (vō′lənt), *adj.* 1. flying; able to fly. 2. *Heraldry.* represented as flying. 3. nimble; quick. [< L *volans* flying]

vol·a·tile (vol′ə·təl), *adj.* 1. evaporating rapidly; changing into vapor easily: *gasoline is volatile.* 2. changing rapidly from one mood or interest; fickle; frivolous. 3. fleeting; transient. [< L *volatilis* flying < *volare* fly] —vol′a·til·i·ty, *n.* —vol′a·tile·ness, *n.*

vol·a·til·ize (vol′ə·təl·īz), *v.,* -ized, -iz·ing. change into vapor; evaporate. —vol′a·til·iz′a·ble, *adj.* —vol′a·til·i·za′tion, *n.* —vol′a·til·iz′er, *n.*

vol·can·ic (vol·kan′ik), *adj.* 1. of or caused by a volcano; having to do with volcanoes: *a volcanic eruption.* 2. characterized by the presence of volcanoes: *volcanic country.* 3. like a volcano; liable to break out violently: *a volcanic*

temper. —vol·can′i·cal·ly, *adv.* —vol·can·ic·i·ty (vol′kən·is′ə·ti), *n.*

vol·can·ism (vol′kən·iz·əm), *n.* phenomena connected with volcanoes and volcanic activity.

vol·ca·no (vol·kā′nō), *n., pl.* -noes, -nos. 1. an opening in the surface of the earth through which steam, ashes, and lava are expelled. 2. a cone-shaped hill or mountain around this opening, built up of material thus expelled. [< Ital. < L *Vulcanus* Vulcan]

Vol·ga (vol′gə), *n.* river flowing from W Soviet Union into the Caspian Sea.

Vol·go·grad (vol′gə·grad), *n.* city in SW Soviet Union. Formerly called **Stalingrad.**

vo·li·tion (vō·lish′ən), *n.* 1. act of willing: *the man went away by his own volition.* 2. power of willing: *the use of drugs has weakened his volition.* [< Med.L *volitio* < L *volo* I wish] —vo·li′tion·al, vo·li·tion·a·ry (vō·lish′ən·er′i), *adj.* —vo·li′tion·al·ly, *adv.* —Syn. 1. choice, preference, decision.

vol·ley (vol′i), *n., pl.* -leys, *v.,* -leyed, -ley·ing. —*n.* 1. shower of stones, bullets, arrows, words, oaths, etc. 2. the discharge of a number of guns at once. 3. *Tennis.* a. flight of a ball in play before touching the ground. b. the hitting or return of a ball before it touches the ground. —*v.* 1. discharge or be discharged in a volley. 2. hit or return (a tennis ball, etc.) before it touches the ground. [< F *volée* flight < *voler* fly < L *volare*] —vol′ley·er, *n.*

vol·ley·ball (vol′i·bôl′), *n. Am.* 1. game played with a large ball and a high net. The ball is hit with the hands back and forth over the net without letting it touch the ground. 2. the ball.

vol·plane (vol′plān′), *v.,* -planed, -plan·ing. glide toward the earth in an airplane without using motor power. [< F *vol plané* gliding flight]

volt (vōlt), *n. Elect.* the unit of electromotive force. One volt causes a current of one ampere to flow through a resistance of one ohm. [after A. *Volta,* physicist]

volt·age (vōl′tij), *n.* electromotive force expressed in volts. A current of high voltage is used in transmitting electric power over long distances.

vol·ta·ic (vol·tā′ik), *adj.* 1. producing an electric current by chemical action. 2. of or pertaining to electric currents produced by chemical action; galvanic.

Vol·taire (vol·tār′), *n.* François Marie Arouet de, 1694–1778, French political philosopher and author.

volt·am·e·ter (vol·tam′ə·tər), *n.* device for measuring the quantity of electricity passing through a conductor or for measuring the strength of a current. —volt·a·met·ric (vol′tə·met′rik), *adj.*

volt·me·ter (vōlt′mē′tər), *n.* instrument for measuring voltage.

vol·u·ble (vol′yə·bəl), *adj.* 1. tending to talk much; fond of talking. 2. having a smooth, rapid flow of words. [< L *volubilis,* orig., rolling < *volvere* roll] —vol′u·bil′i·ty, vol′u·ble·ness, *n.* —vol′u·bly, *adv.*

vol·ume (vol′yəm), *n.* 1. collection of printed or written sheets bound together to form a book. 2. book forming part of a set or series. 3. space occupied: *the storeroom has a volume of 400 cubic feet.* 4. amount; quantity: *volumes of smoke poured from the chimneys of the factory.* 5. amount of sound; fullness of tone. 6. **speak volumes,** express much; be full of meaning. [< OF < L *volumen* book roll, scroll < *volvere* roll] —vol′umed, *adj.* ➤ See book for usage note.

vol·u·met·ric (vol′yə·met′rik), **vol·u·met·ri·cal** (-rə·kəl), *adj.* of or having to do with measurement by volume. —vol′u·met′ri·cal·ly, *adv.* —vo·lu·me·try (və·lü′mə·tri), *n.*

vo·lu·mi·nous (və·lü′mə·nəs), *adj.* 1. forming, filling, or writing a large book or many books. 2. of great size; very bulky; large. —vo·lu′mi·nous·ly, *adv.* —vo·lu′mi·nous·ness, vo·lu·mi·nos·i·ty (və·lü′mə·nos′ə·ti), *n.*

vol·un·tar·y (vol′ən·ter′i), *adj., n., pl.* -tar-les. —*adj.* **1.** done, made, given, etc., of one's own free will; not forced or compelled: *a voluntary contribution.* **2.** acting of one's own free will or choice: *a voluntary substitute.* **3.** able to act of one's own free will: *a voluntary agent.* **4.** deliberately intended; done on purpose: *voluntary manslaughter.* **5.** controlled by the will. Talking is voluntary; breathing is only partly so. —*n.* **1.** anything done, made, given, etc., of one's own free will. **2.** an organ solo played before, during, or after a church service. [< L, < *voluntas* will] —**vol·un·tar·i·ly** (vol'ən·ter'ə·li; emphatic vol'ən·târ'ə·li), *adv.* —**vol'un·tar'i·ness,** *n.* —Syn. adj. **1.** unforced, unconstrained.

vol·un·teer (vol'ən·tir'), *n.* person who enters any service of his own free will, esp. military service. —*v.* **1.** offer one's services: *as soon as war was declared, many men volunteered.* **2.** offer of one's own free will: *he volunteered to do the job.* **3.** tell or say voluntarily: *she volunteered the information.* —*adj.* **1.** of or made up of volunteers: *a volunteer fire company.* **2.** serving as a volunteer: *a volunteer fireman.* **3.** voluntary. [< F *volontaire,* orig. adj., VOLUNTARY]

vo·lup·tu·ar·y (və·lup'chŭ·er'i), *n., pl.* **-ar·ies.** person who cares much for luxurious or sensual pleasures. [< L, < *voluptas* pleasure]

vo·lup·tu·ous (və·lup'chŭ·əs), *adj.* **1.** caring much for the pleasures of the senses. **2.** giving pleasure to the senses. [< L, < *voluptas* pleasure] —**vo·lup'tu·ous·ly,** *adv.* —**vo·lup'tu·ous·ness,** *n.*

vo·lute (və·lüt'), *adj.* rolled up; spiral. —*n.* **1.** a spiral or twisted thing or form. **2.** a spiral or scroll-like ornament in architecture. [< F, or < L *voluta,* fem. pp., rolled] —**vo·lut'ed,** *adj.* —**vo·lu'tion,** *n.*

Volute shell

vom·it (vom'it), *v.* **1.** throw up what has been eaten. **2.** throw up; throw out with force: *the chimneys vomited forth smoke.* **3.** come out with force or violence. —*n.* the substance thrown up from the stomach. [< AF, or < L *vomitus* spewed forth] —**vom'it·er,** *n.* —**vom'i·tive,** *adj.*

von (fôn; *English* von), *prep. German.* from; of. ➤ von is much used in German personal names, originally before names of places or estates, and later before family names, as an indication of nobility or rank.

voo·doo (vü'dü), *n., pl.* **-doos,** *adj. Am.* —*n.* **1.** mysterious rites, including magic and conjuration, originally African and still prevalent in the West Indies and the S United States. **2.** person who practices such rites. —*adj.* of or pertaining to such rites. [of African origin] —**voo'doo·ism,** *n. Am.* —**voo'doo·ist,** *n.* —**voo'doo·is'tic,** *adj.*

vo·ra·cious (və·rā'shəs), *adj.* **1.** eating much; greedy in eating; ravenous. **2.** very eager; unable to be satisfied. [< L *vorax* greedy] —**vo·ra'cious·ly,** *adv.* —**vo·rac·i·ty** (və·ras'ə·ti), **vo·ra'cious·ness,** *n.* —Syn. **1.** gluttonous. **2.** insatiable.

vor·tex (vôr'teks), *n., pl.* **-tex·es,** **-ti·ces** (-tə·sēz). **1.** a whirling mass of water, air, etc., that sucks in everything near it; whirlpool; whirlwind. **2.** whirl of activity or other situation from which it is hard to escape: *the vortex of war.* [< L, var. of *vertex* VERTEX] —**vor'ti·cal** (vôr'tə·kəl), *adj.* —**vor'ti·cal·ly,** *adv.*

Vosges Mountains (vōzh), a mountain range in E France.

vo·ta·ress (vō'tə·ris), **vo·tress** (-tris), *n.* a woman votary.

vo·ta·ry (vō'tə·ri), **vo·ta·rist** (-rist), *n., pl.* **-ries;** **-rists. 1.** person devoted to something; devotee. **2.** person bound by vows to a religious life. [< L *votum* vow]

vote (vōt), *n., v.,* **vot·ed,** **vot·ing.** —*n.* **1.** a formal expression of a wish or choice: *the person receiving the most votes is elected.* **2.** the right to give such an expression: *not everybody has a vote.* **3.** what is expressed or granted by a majority of voters. **4.** votes considered together: *the labor vote, the vote of the people.* **5.** voter. **6.** ticket; ballot. —*v.* **1.** give or cast a vote: *he voted for the Democrats.* **2.** support by one's

vote: *vote the Republican ticket.* **3.** pass, determine, or grant by a vote. **4.** declare, esp. by general consent. **5.** *Colloq.* suggest: *I vote that we go.* **6.** vote down, defeat by voting against. **7.** vote in, elect. [< L *votum* vow] —**vot'a·ble,** *adj.* —**vote'less,** *adj.*

vot·er (vōt'ər), *n.* **1.** person who votes. **2.** person who has the right to vote.

voting machine, *Am.* a mechanical device for registering and counting votes.

voting paper, *Brit.* ballot.

vo·tive (vō'tiv), *adj.* promised by a vow; done, given, etc., because of a vow. [< L, < *votum* vow] —**vo'tive·ly,** *adv.* —**vo'tive·ness,** *n.*

vouch (vouch), *v.* **1.** be responsible; give a guarantee. **2.** answer for; confirm; guarantee. **3.** sustain or uphold by, or as by, some practical proof. [< AF *voucher* < L *vocare* call]

vouch·er (vouch'ər), *n.* **1.** person or thing that vouches for something. **2.** a written evidence of payment; receipt.

vouch·safe (vouch·sāf'), *v.,* **-safed,** **-saf·ing.** be willing to grant or give; deign (to do or give). [orig. meaning "guarantee," to *vouch* for as *safe*] —**vouch·safe'ment,** *n.*

vow (vou), *n.* **1.** a solemn promise: *a vow of secrecy.* **2.** promise made to God: *a nun's vows.* **3.** take vows, become a member of a religious order. —*v.* **1.** make a vow. **2.** make a vow to do, give, get, etc. **3.** declare earnestly or emphatically. [< OF *vou* < L *votum* < *vovere* to vow] —**vow'er,** *n.* —**vow'less,** *adj.*

vow·el (vou'əl), *n.* **1.** *Phonet.* a voiced sound in the production of which the breath stream is relatively unimpeded. A vowel can form a syllable by itself, as the first syllable of *awful* (ô'fəl). **2.** *Gram.* a letter representing such a sound. A, e, i, o, and u are vowels. —*adj.* of or pertaining to a vowel. [< OF < L (*littera*) *vocalis* sounding (letter) < *vox* voice. Doublet of VOCAL.] —**vow'el·less,** *adj.*

vox (voks), *n., pl.* **vo·ces** (vō'sēz). voice; sound; word; expression.

vox po·pu·li (voks' pop'yǔ·lī), *Latin.* the voice or opinion of the people.

voy·age (voi'ij), *n., v.,* **-aged,** **-ag·ing.** —*n.* journey, esp. a long journey; passage or travel by water. —*v.* make or take a voyage. [< F < L *viaticum.* Doublet of VIATICUM.] —**voy'age·a·ble,** *adj.* —**voy'ag·er,** *n.* —Syn. *n.* cruise, sail.

vo·ya·geur (vwä·yä·zhœr'), *n., pl.* **-geurs** (-zhœr'). *Am.* a French Canadian or half-breed accustomed to travel on foot or by canoe through unsettled regions. [< F, ult. < *voyage* VOYAGE]

V.P., *or* **VP,** *or* **V. Pres.,** Vice-President.

vs., **1.** verse. **2.** versus.

v.s., see above. [< L *vide supra*]

V-shaped (vē'shāpt'), *adj.* shaped like the letter V.

Vt., Vermont.

v.t., transitive verb.

Vul·can (vul'kən), *n. Roman Myth.* god of fire and metalworking. —**Vul·ca·ni·an** (vul·kā'ni·ən), *adj.*

vul·can·ite (vul'kən·īt), *n.* a hard rubber obtained by treating India rubber with a large amount of sulfur and heating it, used for combs, for buttons, in electric insulation, etc.

vul·can·ize (vul'kən·īz), *v.,* **-ized,** **-iz·ing.** treat (rubber) with sulfur and heat to make it more elastic and durable. [< Vulcan] —**vul'can·i·za'tion,** *n.* —**vul'can·iz'er,** *n.*

vul·gar (vul'gər), *adj.* **1.** showing a lack of good breeding, manners, taste, etc.; not refined; coarse; low. **2.** common; in common use; ordinary. **3.** of the common people. [< L *vulgaris* < *vulgus* common people] —**vul'gar·ly,** *adv.* —**vul'gar·ness,** *n.* —Syn. **1.** inelegant. **3.** plebeian, lowborn, ignoble. —Ant. **1.** cultured, polite.

vul·gar·i·an (vul·gâr'i·ən), *n.* a vulgar person. **2.** a rich person who lacks good breeding, manners, taste, etc.

vul·gar·ism (vul'gər·iz·əm), *n.* **1.** word, phrase, or expression used only in ignorant or coarse speech. In "I disremember his name," *disremember* is a vulgarism. **2.** vulgar character or action; vulgarity. **3.** a vulgar expression.

vul·gar·i·ty (vul-gar′ə-ti), *n.*, *pl.* –ties. 1. lack of refinement; lack of good breeding, manners, taste, etc.; coarseness. 2. action, habit, speech, etc., showing vulgarity.

vul·gar·ize (vul′gər-īz), *v.*, –ized, –iz·ing. make vulgar. —**vul′gar·i·za′tion**, *n.* —**vul′gar·iz′er**, *n.*

Vulgar Latin, a popular form of Latin, the main source of French, Spanish, Italian, and Portuguese.

Vul·gate (vul′gāt), *n.* 1. the Latin translation of the Bible used by the Roman Catholic Church. The Vulgate was made in the fourth century A.D. 2. the **vulgate**, substandard speech.

vul·ner·a·bil·i·ty (vul′nər-ə-bil′ə-ti), *n.* vulnerable quality or condition.

vul·ner·a·ble (vul′nər-ə-bəl), *adj.* 1. capable of being wounded or injured; open to attack: *Achilles was vulnerable only in his heel.* 2.

sensitive to criticism, temptations, influences, etc.: *most people are vulnerable to ridicule.* 3. in the game of contract bridge, in the position where penalties and premiums are increased. [< LL *vulnerabilis* wounding, ult. < *vulnus* wound] —**vul′ner·a·ble·ness**, *n.* —**vul′ner·a·bly**, *adv.*

vul·pine (vul′pīn; –pin), *adj.* of or like a fox. [< L, < *vulpus* fox]

vul·ture (vul′chər), *n.* 1. a large bird of prey related to eagles, hawks, etc., that eats the flesh of dead animals. 2. a greedy, ruthless person. [< L *vultur*] —**vul′ture·like′**, *adj.* —**vul′tur·ous**, *adj.*

vul·va (vul′və), *n.*, *pl.* –vae (–vē), –vas. the external genital organs of the female. [< L, womb] —**vul′val**, **vul′var**, *adj.* —**vul·vi·form** (vul′və-fôrm), *adj.*

vy·ing (vī′ing), *v.* ppr. of vie. —*adj.* that vies. —**vy′ing·ly**, *adv.*

W, w (dub′əl-yù), *n.*, *pl.* **W's;** **w's.** the 23rd letter of the alphabet.

W, 1. *Chem.* tungsten. 2. watt. 3. west; western.

W., 1. Wednesday. 2. west; western.

w., 1. watt. 2. west; western. 3. wide.

WAAC, W.A.A.C., 1. *U.S.* the former name of the WAC. 2. *Brit.* Women's Army Auxiliary Corps.

Wa·bash (wô′bash), *n.* river flowing from W Ohio SW across Indiana into the Ohio River.

wab·ble (wob′əl), *v.*, –bled, –bling, *n.* wobble. —**wab′bler**, *n.* —**wab′bling**, *adj.* —**wab′bling·ly**, *adv.* —**wab′bly**, *adj.*

WAC, Wac (wak), *n.* *U.S.* member of the Women's Army Corps (WAC).

wack·y (wak′i), *adj.* *U.S. Slang.* unconventional in behavior; eccentric; crazy. Also, **whacky.**

wad (wod), *n.*, *v.*, **wad·ded**, **wad·ding.** —*n.* 1. a small, soft mass: *a wad of cotton.* 2. a tight roll; compact bundle or mass. 3. *Am., Colloq.* a roll of paper money. 4. *Am., Slang.* stock of money. —*v.* 1. make into a wad; press into a wad. 2. stuff with a wad. 3. pad. [< Med.L *wadda*, ? < L *bātin* lining] —**wad′der**, *n.*

wad·ding (wod′ing), *n.* a soft material for padding, stuffing, packing, etc., esp. carded cotton in sheets.

wad·dle (wod′əl), *v.*, –dled, –dling, *n.* —*v.* walk with short steps and an awkward swaying motion, as a duck does. —*n.* 1. act of waddling. 2. an awkward, swaying gait. [< *wade*] —**wad′dler**, *n.* —**wad′dling·ly**, *adv.*

wade (wād), *v.*, **wad·ed**, **wad·ing**, *n.* —*v.* 1. walk through water, snow, sand, mud, or anything that hinders free motion. 2. make one's way with difficulty: *wade through an uninteresting book.* 3. cross or pass through by wading. 4. **wade into**, *Am., Colloq.* attack or go to work upon vigorously. —*n.* act of wading. [OE *wadan* proceed] —**wad′er**, *n.*

wa·di, wa·dy (wä′di), *n.*, *pl.* –dis; –dies. 1. valley or ravine in Arabia, N Africa, etc., through which a stream flows during the rainy season. 2. stream or torrent running through such a ravine. [< Ar.]

WAF (waf), *n.* *U.S.* member of the Women's Air Force (WAF).

wa·fer (wā′fər), *n.* 1. a very thin cake or biscuit, sometimes flavored or sweetened. 2. the thin, round piece of unleavened bread used in Holy Communion in the Roman Catholic Church. 3. piece of sticky paper, dried paste, etc., used as a seal or fastening. [< AF *wafre* < Gmc.] —**wa′fer·like′**, *adj.*

wa·fer·y (wā′fər-i), *adj.* like a wafer.

waf·fle (wof′əl), *n.* *Am.* a batter cake cooked in a special griddle (**waffle iron**) that makes the cakes very thin in places. [< Du. *wafel*]

waft (waft; wäft), *v.* 1. carry over water or through air. 2. float. —*n.* 1. act of wafting. 2. a waving movement. 3. a breath or puff of air,

wind, etc. [< earlier *wafter* convoy ship < Du., LG *wachter* guard] —**waft′er**, *n.*

wag (wag), *v.*, **wagged**, **wag·ging**, *n.* —*v.* 1. move from side to side or up and down, esp. rapidly and repeatedly. 2. **wag the tongue**, talk; talk much. —*n.* 1. act of wagging; a wagging motion. 2. person who is fond of making jokes. [< Scand. *vagga* rock] —**wag′ger**, *n.*

wage (wāj), *n.*, *v.*, **waged**, **wag·ing.** —*n.* Usually, **wages** (*sometimes sing. in use*). a. amount paid for work: *his wages are $30 a week.* b. something given in return: *the wages of sin.* —*v.* carry on: *doctors wage war against disease.* [< OF *wagier* < Gmc. Doublet of GAGE¹.] —**wage′-less**, *adj.* —Syn. *n.* a. salary, pay, compensation, remuneration, stipend.

wage earner, wageworker.

wa·ger (wā′jər), *n.* 1. something staked on an uncertain event. 2. act of betting; bet. 3. **wager of battle**, the use of personal combat to decide which party in a dispute is right. —*v.* bet; gamble. [< AF *wageure* < OF *wage* pledge < Gmc.] —**wa′ger·er**, *n.*

wage·work·er (wāj′wėr′kər), *n.* *Am.* person who works for wages. —**wage′work′ing**, *n., adj.*

wag·ger·y (wag′ər-i), *n.*, *pl.* –ger·ies. 1. a joking. 2. joke.

wag·gish (wag′ish), *adj.* 1. fond of making jokes. 2. characteristic of a wag. —**wag′gish·ly**, *adv.* —**wag′gish·ness**, *n.*

wag·gle (wag′əl), *v.*, –gled, –gling, *n.* —*v.* move quickly and repeatedly from side to side; wag. —*n.* a waggling motion. —**wag′gling·ly**, *adv.*

Wag·ner (väg′nər), *n.* Richard, 1813–1883, German composer. —**Wag·ne·ri·an** (väg·nir′i-ən), *adj., n.*

wag·on, esp. *Brit.* **wag·gon** (wag′ən), *n.* 1. a four-wheeled vehicle, esp. one for carrying loads: *a milk wagon, a station wagon.* 2. *Brit.* a railroad freight car. 3. **on the wagon**, *Am., Slang.* not drinking alcoholic liquors. —*v.* convey by wagon. [< Du. *wagen*] —**wag′on·less**, esp. *Brit.* **wag′gon·less**, *adj.*

wag·on·er, esp. *Brit.* **wag·gon·er** (wag′ən-ər), *n.* person who drives a wagon.

wag·on·load, esp. *Brit.* **wag·gon·load** (wag′ən-lōd′), *n.* amount a wagon carries.

wagon train, *Am.* group of wagons moving along in a line one after another.

waif (wāf), *n.* 1. person without home or friends; homeless or neglected child. 2. anything without an owner; stray thing, animal, etc. [< AF, prob. < Scand.]

Wai·ki·ki (wī′kē-kē′), *n.* a bathing beach near Honolulu, Hawaii.

wail (wāl), *v.* 1. cry loud and long because of grief or pain. 2. lament; mourn. —*n.* 1. a long cry of grief or pain. 2. a sound like such a cry. [< Scand. *væla*] —**wail′er**, *n.* —**wail′ful**, *adj.* —**wail′ful·ly**, *adv.* —**wail′ing·ly**, *adv.*

āge, cāre, fär; ēqual, tėrm; īce; ōpen, ôrder; pùt, rüle, ūse; th, then; ə=a in about.

wain (wān), *n.* Archaic. wagon. [OE *wægn*]

wain·scot (wān′skət; -skot), *n.*, *v.*, -scot·ed, -scot·ing, *esp.* Brit. -scot·ted, -scot·ting. —*n.* 1. a lining of wood, usually in panels, on the walls of a room. 2. the lower part of the wall of a room when it is decorated differently from the upper part. —*v.* line with wood. [< MLG *wagenschot* < *wagen* wągon + *schot* partition]

wain·scot·ing, *esp.* Brit. **wain·scot·ting** (wān′skot-ing; -skot-), *n.* 1. wainscot. 2. material used for wainscots.

Wainscot (def. 2)

wain·wright (wān′rīt′), *n.* wagonmaker.

waist (wāst), *n.* 1. the part of the human body between the ribs and the hips. 2. waistline. 3. a garment or part of a garment covering the body from the neck or shoulders to the waistline. 4. the middle part. [< root of *wax²*] —*waist′less, adj.*

waist·band (wāst′band′), *n.* a band around the waist.

waist·coat (wāst′kōt′; wes′kət), *n.* Esp. Brit. a man's vest. —*waist′coat′ed, adj.*

waist·line (wāst′līn′), *n.* an imaginary line around the body at the smallest part of the waist.

wait (wāt), *v.* 1. stay or be inactive until someone comes or something happens: *let's wait in the shade.* 2. Colloq. delay or put off: *wait dinner for him.* 3. look forward; be expecting or ready: *wait for a train.* 4. be left undone; be put off: *that matter can wait until tomorrow.* 5. wait for: *wait one's chance.* 6. act as a servant; change plates, pass food, etc., at table. 7. serve. 8. wait on or upon, a. be a servant to; serve, esp. at the table. b. call on (a superior) to pay a respectful visit. c. go with; result from. —*n.* 1. act or time of waiting. 2. lie in wait, stay hidden ready to attack. [< OF *waitier,* orig., watch < Gmc.] —Syn. *v.* 1. tarry, linger, remain, abide.

wait·er (wāt′ər), *n.* 1. person who waits. 2. man who waits on table in a hotel or restaurant. 3. tray for carrying dishes. 4. dumbwaiter.

wait·ing (wāt′ing), *adj.* 1. that waits. 2. used to wait in. —*n.* 1. time that one waits. 2. in waiting, in attendance on a king, queen, prince, princess, etc.

waiting room, room at a railroad station, doctor's office, etc., for people to wait in.

wait·ress (wāt′ris), *n.* woman who waits on table in a dining room.

waive (wāv), *v.*, waived, waiv·ing. 1. give up (a right, claim, etc.); refrain from claiming or pressing; do without; relinquish. 2. put aside; defer. [< AF *weyver* abandon, prob. < Scand.] —Syn. 1. surrender, forgo, abandon.

waiv·er (wāv′ər), *n.* 1. a giving up of a right, claim, etc. 2. a written statement of this.

wake¹ (wāk), *v.*, waked or woke, waked or (Archaic and Dial.) wo·ken, wak·ing, *n.* —*v.* 1. stop sleeping: *wake up early in the morning, wake at seven every morning.* 2. cause to stop sleeping: *the noise of the traffic always wakes him, wake him up early.* 3. be awake; stay awake: *all his waking hours.* 4. become alive or active: *the flowers wake in the spring.* 5. make alive or active: *he needs some interest to wake him up.* —*n.* 1. a watching, esp. for some solemn purpose. 2. an all-night watch kept beside the body of a dead person. [OE *wacian*] —*wak′er, n.* —Syn. *v.* 1, 2. awake, waken, rouse, arouse.

wake² (wāk), *n.* 1. track left behind a moving ship. 2. track left behind any moving thing. 3. in the wake of, following; behind; after. [< MDu.]

wake·ful (wāk′fəl), *adj.* 1. not able to sleep. 2. without sleep. 3. watchful. —*wake′ful·ly, adv.* —*wake′ful·ness, n.*

Wake Island, a small island in the Pacific, about 2000 mi. W of Hawaii, belonging to the United States.

wak·en (wāk′ən), *v.* wake. [OE *wæcnan*] —*wak′en·er, n.*

wake-rob·in (wāk′rob′ən), *n.* Am. 1. trillium. 2. jack-in-the-pulpit.

wale (wāl), *n.*, *v.*, waled, wal·ing. —*n.* 1. a streak or ridge made on the skin by a stick or whip; welt. 2. a ridge in the weave of cloth. 3. texture of a cloth. —*v.* 1. mark with wales; raise wales on. 2. weave with ridges. [OE *walu*]

Wales (wālz), *n.* the division of Great Britain W of England; the land of the Welsh.

walk (wôk), *v.* 1. go on foot. In walking, a person always has one foot on the ground. 2. roam: *the ghost will walk tonight.* 3. go over, on, or through: *the captain walked the deck.* 4. make, put, drive, etc., by walking: *walk off a headache.* 5. go slowly: *walk, do not run.* 6. cause to walk: *the rider walked his horse.* 7. Am., Baseball. go to first base after the pitcher has thrown four balls. b. of a pitcher, give (a batter) a base on balls. 8. walk away from, progress much faster than. 9. walk off with, a. take; get; win. b. steal. 10. walk out, a. Am., Colloq. go on strike. b. leave suddenly. 11. walk out on, Am., Colloq. desert. —*n.* 1. act of walking, esp. walking for pleasure or exercise: *a walk in the country.* 2. distance to walk: *it is a long walk from here.* 3. manner of going on foot; gait. 4. place for walking; path; sidewalk; promenade. 5. a usual course; route. 6. way of living: *different walks of life.* 7. Am., Baseball. permitting a batter to reach first base on balls; pass. 8. an enclosed place; tract: *a poultry walk.* [OE *wealcan* roll] —*walk′er, n.* —Syn. *v.* 1. step, stride, saunter, march, tramp, hike, trudge, tread. —*n.* 1. stroll, hike, tramp, promenade.

walk·a·way (wôk′ə·wā′), *n.* Colloq. an easy victory.

walk·ie-talk·ie, walk·y-talk·y (wôk′i-tôk′i), *n.*, *pl.* -talk·ies. a small, portable receiving and transmitting set, used by the U.S. Army in World War II.

walking papers, Am., Colloq. dismissal from a position, etc.

walking stick, 1. Esp. Brit. cane. 2. any of various insects having a body like a stick.

walk·out (wôk′out′), *n.* Am., Colloq. strike of workers.

walk·o·ver (wôk′ō′vər), *n.* Colloq. an easy victory.

walk·up (wôk′up′), Am. —*n.* an apartment house or building having no elevator. —*adj.* not having an elevator.

wall (wôl), *n.* 1. side of a house, room, or other hollow thing. 2. structure of stone, brick, or other material built up to enclose, divide, support, or protect. 3. Often, walls. rampart. 4. something like a wall in looks or use. 5. drive or push to the wall, make desperate or helpless. 6. go to the wall, a. give way; be defeated. b. fail in business. —*v.* enclose, divide, protect, or fill with a wall, or as if with a wall. [< L *vallum*] —*walled, adj.* —*wall′·less, adj.* —*wall′·like′, adj.* —Syn. *n.* 2. partition.

wal·la·by (wol′ə·bi), *n.*, *pl.* -bies or (*esp. collectively*) -by. a kangaroo of the smaller sorts. Some wallabies are no larger than rabbits. [from native Australian name]

Wallaby

Wal·lace (wol′is; wôl′is), *n.* Henry Agard, 1888-1965, vice-president of the United States, 1941-1945.

wall·board (wôl′bôrd′; -bōrd′), *n.* an artificial board used instead of wooden boards or plaster to make or cover walls.

wal·let (wol′it; wôl′it), *n.* 1. Am. a small, flat leather case for carrying paper money, cards, etc., in one's pocket; folding pocketbook. 2. bag for carrying things when on a journey.

wall·eye (wôl′ī′), *n.* any of various fishes with large staring eyes.

wall·eyed (wôl′id′), *adj.* 1. having eyes that show much white and little color. 2. having both eyes turned away from the nose. 3. having large staring eyes. The pike is a walleyed fish. [< Scand. *vagl-eygr* < *vagl,* prob., beam in the eye + *auga* eye]

wall·flow·er (wôl′flou′ər), *n.* 1. Colloq. person who sits by the wall at a dance instead of dancing. 2. a perennial plant with sweet-smelling yellow, orange, or red flowers, found growing on walls, cliffs, etc.

Wal·loon (wo·lün′), *n.* **1.** one of a group of people inhabiting chiefly the S and SE parts of Belgium and adjacent regions in France. **2.** their language, the French dialect of Belgium. —*adj.* of or having to do with the Walloons or their language.

wal·lop (wol′əp), *Colloq.* —*v.* **1.** beat soundly; thrash. **2.** hit very hard. —*n.* a very hard blow. [< OF *waloper* GALLOP] —**wal′lop·er,** *n.* —**wal′lop·ing,** *n., adj.*

wal·low (wol′ō), *v.* **1.** roll about; flounder: *the pigs wallowed in the mud.* **2.** live contentedly in filth, wickedness, etc., like a beast. —*n.* **1.** act of wallowing. **2.** *Am.* place where animals wallow. [OE *wealwian* roll] —**wal′low·er,** *n.*

wall·pa·per (wôl′pā′pər), *n.* paper for covering walls. —*v.* put wallpaper on.

Wall Street, *Am.* **1.** street in downtown New York, the chief financial center of the United States. **2.** the money market or the financiers of the United States.

wal·nut (wôl′nut; -nət), *n.* **1.** a large, round, edible nut with a plain division between its two halves. **2.** the tree that it grows on. **3.** its wood. **4.** the brown color of polished walnut wood. [OE *wealhhnutu < wealh* foreign + *hnutu* nut]

Wal·pur·gis night (väl·pür′gis), the night of April 30th, when witches were supposed to hold revels with the devil.

wal·rus (wôl′rəs; wol′-), *n., pl.* **-rus·es** or (esp. collectively) **-rus.** a large sea animal of the arctic regions, resembling a seal but having long tusks. Walrus hide is made into leather for suitcases, bags, etc. [< Du. *walrus, walros < wal- (visch)* whale + *ros* horse]

Wal·ton (wôl′tən), *n.* Izaak, 1593–1683, English writer.

waltz (wôlts), *n.* **1.** a smooth, even, gliding dance in triple rhythm. **2.** music for it. —*v.* **1.** dance a waltz. **2.** move nimbly or quickly. [< G *walzer < walzen* roll] —**waltz′er,** *n.* —**waltz′like′,** *adj.*

wam·pum (wom′pəm; wôm′-), *n. Am.* **1.** beads made from shells, formerly used by American Indians as money and ornament. **2.** *Slang.* money. [< Algonquian]

wan (won), *adj.,* **wan·ner, wan·nest. 1.** pale in color or hue; pallid. **2.** looking worn or tired; faint; weak: *the sick boy's wan smile.* [OE *wann* dark] —**wan′ly,** *adv.* —**wan′ness,** *n.*

wand (wond), *n.* **1.** a slender stick or rod: *the magician waved his wand.* **2.** rod borne as a sign of office or authority; scepter. **3.** baton. [< Scand. *völndr*] —**wand′like′,** *adj.*

wan·der (won′dər), *v.* **1.** move here and there without any special purpose: *wander about the world.* **2.** go aimlessly over or through. **3.** go from the right way; stray: *wander off and become lost.* **4.** be delirious; be incoherent: *he wandered during his illness.* [OE *wandrian*] —**wan′der·er,** *n.* —**wan′der·ing·ly,** *adv.* —**Syn. 1.** ramble, roam, rove, range, meander.

wan·der·lust (won′dər·lust′), *n.* a strong desire to wander. [< G, < *wandern* wander + *lust* desire]

wane (wān), *v.,* **waned, wan·ing,** —*v.* **1.** become smaller; become smaller gradually: *the moon wanes after it has become full.* **2.** decline in power, influence, importance, etc. **3.** decline in strength, intensity, etc.: *the light of day wanes in the evening.* **4.** draw to a close: *summer wanes as autumn approaches.* —*n.* **1.** a waning. **2.** in or on the wane, waning. [OE *wanian*]

wan·gle (wang′gəl), *v.,* **-gled, -gling.** *Colloq.* **1.** manage to get by schemes, tricks, persuasion, etc. **2.** make one's way through difficulties. —**wan′gler,** *n.*

wan·nish (won′ish), *adj.* somewhat wan.

want (wont; wônt), *v.* **1.** wish for; wish: *he wants to become an engineer, he wants a new car.* **2.** be without; lack: *want judgment.* **3.** need: *plants want water.* **4.** fall short by: *the sum collected wants but a few dollars of the desired*

amount. **5.** need food, clothing, and shelter; be very poor. **6.** *Colloq.* ought; had better. **7.** want for, lack. —*n.* **1.** thing desired or needed; desire: *his wants are few.* **2.** a lack: *want of rain.* **3.** a need: *supply a long felt want.* **4.** a lack of food, clothing, or shelter; great poverty. [< Scand. *vanta*] —**want′er,** *n.* —**want′less,** *adj.* —**Syn. v. 1.** desire, crave. —*n.* **2.** deficiency, dearth, scarcity, insufficiency. **3.** requirement, necessity. **4.** destitution, privation, indigence, straits. —**Ant.** *n.* **2.** abundance, plenty. ≫ **want.** The formal and informal idiom with *want* is with an infinitive: Formal, informal: *I want you to get all you can from the year's work.* Substandard: *I want for you to get all you can from the year's work. I want that you should get all you can from the year's work.* Want is colloquial for *ought, had better: You want to review all the notes if you're going to pass his exam.*

want ad, *Am., Colloq.* a small notice in a newspaper stating that something is wanted, as an employee, an apartment, etc.; classified ad.

want·ing (won′ting; wôn′-), *adj.* **1.** lacking; missing: *one volume of the set is wanting.* **2.** not coming up to a standard or need: *weighed and found wanting.* —*prep.* without; less; minus: *a year wanting three days.*

wan·ton (won′tən), *adj.* **1.** reckless or disregardful of right, justice, humanity, etc.: *wanton cruelty.* **2.** done, shown, used, etc., maliciously or unjustifiably: *a wanton attack.* **3.** not moral; not chaste: *a wanton woman.* **4.** *Poetic.* frolicsome; playful. **5.** *Poetic.* not restrained. —*n.* a wanton person. —*v.* act in a wanton manner. [ME *wantowen* < OE *wan-* not (cf. WANE) + *togen* brought up, pp. of *tēon* bring] —**wan′ton·er,** *n.* —**wan′ton·ly,** *adv.* —**wan′ton·ness,** *n.* —**Syn. adj. 3.** dissolute, licentious.

wap·i·ti (wop′ə·ti), *n., pl.* **-tis** or (esp. collectively) **-ti.** a North American deer with long, slender antlers; the American elk. [< Algonquian]

war (wôr), *n., v.,* **warred, war·ring,** *adj.* —*n.* **1.** a fight carried on by armed force between nations or parts of a nation. **2.** fighting; strife; conflict. **3.** the occupation or art of fighting with weapons; military science. **4.** at war, taking part in a war. **5.** go to war, a. start a war. b. go as a soldier. —*v.* fight; make war. —*adj.* used in war; having to do with war; caused by war. [< OF *werre* < Gmc.] —**war′less,** *adj.* —**Syn.** *n.* **1.** warfare, hostilities.

War between the States, *Am.* the American Civil War, from 1861 to 1865.

war·ble (wôr′bəl), *v.,* **-bled, -bling,** *n.* —*v.* **1.** sing with trills, quavers, or melodious turns: *birds warbled in the trees.* **2.** make a sound like that of a bird warbling. **3.** *U.S.* yodel. —*n.* a warbling. [< OF *werbler* < Gmc.]

war·bler (wôr′blər), *n.* **1.** person, bird, etc., that warbles. **2.** *Am.* any of a large variety of small songbirds, often brightly colored.

war bride, bride of a soldier in wartime.

war cry, 1. word or phrase shouted in fighting; battle cry. **2.** a party cry in any contest.

ward (wôrd), *n.* **1.** person under the care of a guardian or of a court. **2.** a district of a city or town. **3.** a division of a hospital or prison. **4.** custody; prison. —*v.* **1.** *Archaic.* keep watch over; protect. **2.** ward off, keep away; turn aside. [OE *weardian* guard. Doublet of GUARD.]

Ward (wôrd), *n.* Artemus (*Charles Ferrar Browne*), 1834–1867, American humorist.

-ward, *suffix.* in the direction of; that is, moves, or faces toward; toward, as in *backward, heavenward, onward, seaward.* See also **-wards.** [OE *-weard*]

war dance, *Am.* dance of primitive tribes before going to war or to celebrate a victory.

ward·en (wôr′dən), *n.* **1.** keeper; guard: *a game warden.* **2.** the administrative head of a prison. **3.** the head of certain colleges, schools, etc. **4.** churchwarden. [< OF *wardein,* ult. < Gmc.] —**ward′en·ship,** *n.*

ward·er (wôr′dər), *n.* **1.** guard; watchman. **2.** warden; jailer. —**ward′er·ship,** *n.*

ward heeler, *Am., Colloq.* follower of a political boss, who goes around asking for votes, etc.

ward·robe (wôrd'rōb'), *n.* **1.** stock of clothes: *a spring wardrobe.* **2.** room, closet, or piece of furniture for holding clothes.

ward·room (wôrd'rüm'; -rúm'), *n.* the living and eating quarters for all the commissioned officers on a warship except the commanding officer.

-wards, *suffix.* in the direction of, as in *backwards, upwards.* See also **-ward.** ≻ **-wards.** Used originally and chiefly in adverbs.

ward·ship (wôrd'ship), *n.* **1.** guardianship, esp. over a minor or ward; custody. **2.** condition of being a ward.

ware (wãr), *n.* **1.** Usually, **wares.** a manufactured thing; article for sale: *the peddler sold his wares cheap.* **2.** pottery. Delft is a blue-and-white ware. [OE *waru*]

ware·house (wãr'hous'), *n., v.,* **-housed,** **-hous·ing.** *—n.* **1.** place where goods are kept; storehouse. **2.** *Esp. Brit.* a wholesale store or a large retail store. *—v.* store or put in a warehouse.

ware·house·man (wãr'hous'mən), *n., pl.* **-men.** man who owns or works in a warehouse.

war·fare (wôr'fãr'), *n.* war; fighting.

war game, a training exercise that imitates war. It may be an exercise on a map or maneuvers with actual troops, weapons, and equipment.

war·head (wôr'hed), *n.* the forward part of a torpedo, missile, etc., that contains the explosive.

war horse, 1. horse used in war. **2.** *Colloq.* person who has taken part in many battles, struggles, etc.

war·i·ly (wãr'ə·li), *adv.* cautiously; carefully.

war·i·ness (wãr'i·nis), *n.* caution; care.

war·like (wôr'līk'), *adj.* **1.** fit for war; ready for war; fond of war. **2.** threatening war: *a warlike speech.* **3.** of or having to do with war. **—war'like'ness,** *n.* **—Syn. 2.** belligerent, hostile. **3.** martial, military.

warm (wôrm), *adj.* **1.** more hot than cold; having heat; giving forth heat: *a warm fire.* **2.** of or at a moderately high temperature: *a warm climate.* **3.** having a feeling of heat: *be warm from running.* **4.** that makes or keeps warm: *a warm coat.* **5.** having or showing affection, enthusiasm, or zeal: *a warm welcome.* **6.** strongly attached; intimate: *warm friends.* **7.** easily excited: *a warm temper.* **8.** exciting; lively; brisk: *a warm dispute.* **9.** fresh and strong: *a warm scent.* **10.** *Colloq.* near what one is searching for. **11.** suggesting heat. Red, orange, and yellow are called warm colors. **12.** uncomfortable; unpleasant: *make things warm for a person.* *—v.* **1.** make or become warm: *warm a room.* **2.** make or become cheered, interested, friendly, or sympathetic: *warm one's heart.* **3. warm up,** practice or exercise for a few minutes before entering a game, contest, etc. [OE *wearm*] **—warm'er,** *n.* **—warm'ish,** *adj.* **—warm'ly,** *adv.* **—warm'ness,** *n.* **—Syn. adj. 5.** cordial, hearty, fervent, enthusiastic. **7.** fiery, peppery.

warm-blood·ed (wôrm'blud'id), *adj.* **1.** pertaining to animals, as mammals and birds, having warm blood and a body temperature from 98 degrees to 112 degrees. **2.** with much feeling; eager; ardent.

warm-heart·ed (wôrm'här'tid), *adj.* kind; sympathetic; friendly. **—warm'-heart'ed·ly,** *adv.* **—warm'-heart'ed·ness,** *n.*

warming pan, a covered pan with a long handle, formerly filled with hot coals and used to warm beds.

war·mon·ger (wôr'mung'gər; -mong'), *n.* one who is in favor of war or attempts to bring it about. **—war'mon'ger·ing,** *n., adj.*

warmth (wôrmth), *n.* **1.** being warm: *the warmth of the open fire.* **2.** moderate or gentle heat. **3.** liveliness of feelings or emotions; fervor. **4.** in painting, a glowing effect, as from the use of reds and yellows. **—Syn. 3.** zeal, ardor.

warn (wôrn), *v.* **1.** give notice to in advance; put on guard (against danger, evil, harm, etc.): *the clouds warned us of a storm.* **2.** give notice to; inform. **3.** give notice to to go, stay, etc.: *warn trespassers off.* [OE *warnian*] **—warn'er,** *n.* **—Syn. 1.** caution, admonish. **2.** apprise.

warn·ing (wôr'ning), *n.* something that warns; notice given in advance. *—adj.* that warns. **—warn'ing·ly,** *adv.* **—Syn. n.** admonition, advice.

warp (wôrp), *v.* **1.** bend or twist out of shape. **2.** mislead; pervert: *prejudice warps our judgment.* **3.** move (a ship, etc.) by ropes fastened to something fixed. *—n.* **1.** a bend or twist; distortion. **2.** rope used in moving a ship. **3.** the threads running lengthwise in a fabric: *the warp is crossed by the woof.* [OE *weorpan* to throw]

war paint, 1. *Am.* paint put on the face or body by savages before going to war. **2.** *Colloq.* full dress; ornaments.

war·path (wôr'path'; -päth'), *n. Am.* **1.** way taken by a fighting expedition of American Indians. **2. on the warpath, a.** ready for war. **b.** looking for a fight; angry.

war·plane (wôr'plān'), *n.* airplane used in war.

war·rant (wôr'ənt; wor'-), *n.* **1.** that which gives a right; authority: *he had no warrant for his action.* **2.** a written order giving authority for something: *a warrant to search the house.* **3.** a good and sufficient reason; promise; guarantee: *he had no warrant for his hopes.* **4.** a document certifying something, esp. to a purchaser. **5.** official certificate of appointment issued to a noncommissioned officer in the army or navy. *—v.* **1.** authorize: *the law warrants his arrest.* **2.** justify: *nothing can warrant such rudeness.* **3.** give one's word for; guarantee; promise: *the storekeeper warranted the quality of the coffee.* **4.** *Colloq.* declare positively; certify. [< OF *warant* < Gmc.] **—war'rant·a·ble,** *adj.* **—war'rant·a·ble·ness,** *n.* **—war'rant·a·bly,** *adv.* **—Syn. n. 1.** sanction, authorization. *—v.* **1.** sanction. **2.** assure. **4.** affirm, attest.

war·ran·tee (wôr'ən·tē'; wor'-), *n. Law.* person to whom a warranty is made.

war·rant·er (wôr'ən·tər; wor'-), *esp. Law* **war·ran·tor** (wôr'ən·tər, wor'-; wôr'ən·tôr', wor'-), *n.* person who warrants.

warrant officer, an army or navy officer who has received a certificate of appointment, but not a commission, ranking between commissioned officers and enlisted men.

war·ran·ty (wôr'ən·ti; wor'-), *n., pl.* **-ties. 1.** warrant; authority; justification. **2.** promise or pledge that something is what it is claimed to be; guarantee. [< OF *warantie.* See **WARRANT.**] Doublet of **GUARANTY.**]

war·ren (wôr'ən; wor'-), *n.* piece of ground filled with burrows, where rabbits live or are raised. [< AF *warenne* < Celtic]

War·ren (wôr'ən; wor'-), *n.* **Earl,** born 1891, chief justice of the U.S. Supreme Court since October 5, 1953.

war·ri·or (wôr'i·ər; wor'-), *n.* a fighting man; experienced soldier. **—war'ri·or·like',** *adj.*

war risk insurance, insurance issued by the U.S. government for members of the armed forces.

War·saw (wôr'sô), *n.* capital and largest city of Poland, in the E part.

war·ship (wôr'ship'), *n.* ship used in war.

wart (wôrt), *n.* **1.** a small, hard lump on the skin. **2.** a similar lump on a plant. [OE *wearte*]

wart hog, a wild hog of Africa that has two large tusks and two large wartlike growths on each side of its face.

war·time (wôr'tīm'), *n.* a time of war.

war whoop, *Am.* a war cry of American Indians.

war·y (wãr'i), *adj.,* **war·i·er, war·i·est. 1.** on one's guard against danger, deception, etc. **2.** cautious; careful. **3.** wary of, cautious about; careful about. [< *ware* watchful (OE *wær*)] **—Syn. 1.** alert, guarded, vigilant, watchful.

Wart hog (3 ft. high at the shoulder)

was (woz; wuz; *unstressed* wəz), *v.* the 1st and 3rd pers. sing., past indicative of **be:** *I was late.* [OE *wæs*]

wash (wosh; wôsh), *v.* 1. clean with water or other liquid: *wash clothes, wash one's face.* 2. make clean: *washed from sin.* 3. remove (dirt, stains, paint, etc.) by or as by the action of water: *wash a spot out.* 4. wash oneself: *wash for supper.* 5. wash clothes. 6. undergo washing without damage: *that cloth washes well.* 7. be carried along or away by water or other liquid: *the road washed out during the storm.* 8. carry (by a liquid): *washed ashore by the waves.* 9. wear (by water or any liquid): *the cliffs are being washed away by the waves.* 10. flow or beat with a lapping sound: *the waves washed upon the rocks.* 11. make wet: *a rose washed with dew.* 12. cover with a thin coating of color or of metal: *walls washed with blue.* 13. sift (earth, ore, etc.) by action of water to separate valuable material. 14. *Colloq.* stand being put to the proof: *patriotism that won't wash.* 15. wash one's hands of, renounce all interest in or responsibility for. —*n.* 1. a washing or being washed. 2. quantity of clothes washed or to be washed. 3. material carried and then dropped by water. 4. motion, rush, or sound of water: *wash of the waves.* 5. tract of land sometimes overflowed with water and sometimes left dry; fen, marsh, or bog. 6. liquid for a special use: *a hair wash.* 7. washy or weak liquid food. 8. waste liquid matter; liquid garbage. 9. a thin coating of color or metal. 10. earth, etc., from which gold or the like can be washed. 11. the rough or broken water left behind a moving ship. 12. disturbance in air made by an airplane or any of its parts. —*adj. Am.* that can be washed without damage. [OE *wascan*] —**Syn.** *v.* 1. cleanse, rinse. 4. bathe.

Wash., the State of Washington.

wash·a·ble (wosh′ə·bəl; wôsh′–), *adj.* that can be washed without damage: *washable silk.*

wash·board (wosh′bôrd; –bōrd′; wôsh′–), *n. Am.* a board having ridges on it, used for rubbing the dirt out of clothes.

wash·bowl (wosh′bōl′; wôsh′–); *Am.,* **wash·ba·sin** (–bā′sən), *n.* bowl for holding water to wash one's hands and face.

wash·cloth (wosh′klôth′; –kloth′; wôsh′–), *n.* a small cloth for washing oneself.

wash·day (wosh′dā′; wôsh′–), *n.* day when clothes are washed.

washed-out (wosht′out′; wôsht′–), *adj.* 1. lacking color; faded. 2. *Colloq.* lacking life, spirit, etc.

washed-up (wosht′up′; wôsht′–), *adj. Colloq.* 1. done with; through, esp. after having failed. 2. fatigued.

wash·er (wosh′ər; wôsh′–), *n.* 1. person who washes. 2. machine that washes. 3. a flat ring of metal, rubber, leather, etc., used with bolts or nuts, or to make joints tight.

wash·er·wom·an (wosh′ər·wûm′ən; wôsh′–), *n., pl.* –wom·en. woman whose work is washing clothes.

wash·ing (wosh′ing; wôsh′–), *n.* 1. a cleaning with water. 2. clothes, etc., washed or to be washed. 3. Sometimes, **washings. a.** liquid that has been used to wash something. **b.** matter removed in washing something. 4. matter carried away or deposited by a flow of water.

washing machine, machine that washes clothes, etc.

washing soda, sodium carbonate, used in washing.

Wash·ing·ton (wosh′ing·tən; wôsh′–), *n.* 1. capital of the United States, coextensive with the District of Columbia. 2. a Northwestern State of the United States, on the Pacific Coast. *Capital:* Olympia. *Abbrev.:* Wash. 3. Booker T(aliaferro), 1859?–1915, American Negro writer and educator. 4. George, 1732–1799, commander in chief of the American army in the Revolutionary War and the first president of the United States, 1789–1797.

Wash·ing·to·ni·an (wosh′ing·tō′ni·ən; wôsh′–), *n. Am.* native or inhabitant of Wash-

ington. —*adj.* of or having to do with Washington, D.C., or the State of Washington.

wash·out (wosh′out′; wôsh′–), *n. Am.* 1. a washing away of earth, a road, etc., by water. 2. the hole or break made by it. 3. *Slang.* failure; disappointment.

wash·rag (wosh′rag′; wôsh′–), *n. Am.* washcloth.

wash·room (wosh′rüm′; –rûm′; wôsh′–), *n. Am.* room where people can wash themselves.

wash·stand (wosh′stand′; wôsh′–), *n.* 1. bowl with pipes and faucets for running water to wash one's hands and face. 2. stand for holding a basin, pitcher, etc., for washing.

wash·tub (wosh′tub′; wôsh′–), *n.* tub used to wash or soak clothes in.

wash·wom·an (wosh′wûm′ən; wôsh′–), *n., pl.* –wom·en. washerwoman.

wash·y (wosh′i; wôsh′i), *adj.,* **wash·i·er, wash·i·est.** too much diluted; weak; watery.

wasp (wosp; wôsp), *n.* a kind of insect that has a slender body and a powerful sting. [OE *wæsp*] —**wasp′like′, wasp′y,** *adj.*

WASP, Wasp (wosp; wôsp), *n.* member of the Women's Air Force Service Pilots (WASP).

Wasp (ab. actual size)

wasp·ish (wos′pish; wôs′–), *adj.* 1. like a wasp; like that of a wasp. 2. bad-tempered; irritable. —**wasp′ish·ly,** *adv.* —**wasp′ish·ness,** *n.*

was·sail (wos′əl; was′–), *n.* 1. a drinking party; revel with drinking of healths. 2. spiced ale or other liquor drunk at a wassail. 3. a salutation meaning "Your health!" —*v.* 1. take part in a wassail; revel. 2. drink to the health of. —*interj.* "Your health!" [< Scand. *ves heill* be healthy!] —**was′sail·er,** *n.*

Was·ser·mann test (wos′ər·mən), **Wassermann reaction,** or **Wassermann,** *n.* test for syphilis, made on a sample of a person's blood or spinal fluid.

wast (wost), *v. Archaic or Poetic.* the 2nd pers. sing., past tense of **be.** "Thou wast" means "you were."

wast·age (wās′tij), *n.* 1. loss by use, wear, decay, leakage, etc.; waste. 2. amount wasted.

waste (wāst), *v.,* **wast·ed, wast·ing,** *n., adj.* —*v.* 1. make poor use of; spend uselessly; fail to get value from: *waste money.* 2. fail or neglect to use: *waste an opportunity.* 3. wear down little by little; destroy or lose gradually: *wasted by disease.* 4. become used up or worn down: *rocks waste under the action of water.* 5. damage greatly; destroy: *the soldiers wasted the enemy's fields.* 6. become emaciated or weak: *he wasted from disease.* 7. be put to a poor use or none: *the food wasted.* —*n.* 1. poor use; useless spending; failure to get the most out of something: *waste of money, time, etc.* 2. neglect, instead of use: *waste of opportunity.* 3. gradual destruction or decay: *waste and repair of bodily tissue.* 4. useless or worthless material; stuff to be thrown away: *garbage or sewage is waste.* 5. bare or wild land; desert; wilderness. 6. cotton or wool threads in bunches, used to wipe off oil, grease, etc. 7. go to waste, be wasted. —*adj.* 1. thrown away as useless or worthless. 2. left over; not used. 3. not cultivated; that is a desert or wilderness; bare; wild. 4. in a state of desolation or ruin. 5. lay waste, damage greatly; destroy; ravage. [< OF, ult. < L *vastus,* vast, waste, infl. by cognate Gmc. word] —**wast′er,** *n.* —**Syn.** *v.* 1. squander, dissipate. 3. diminish. 6. wither, decline. —*n.* 4. trash, rubbish, refuse. —*adj.* 1. rejected. 3. desolate, uninhabited. 4. devastated.

waste·bas·ket (wāst′bas′kit; –bäs′–), *n.* basket or other container for wastepaper.

waste·ful (wāst′fəl), *adj.* using or spending too much. —**waste′ful·ly,** *adv.* —**waste′ful·ness,** *n.*

waste·pa·per (wāst′pā′pər), **waste paper,** *n.* paper thrown away or to be thrown away as trash.

āge, cãre, fär; ēqual, tèrm; īce; ōpen, ôrder; pút, rüle, ūse; тн, then; ə=a in about.

waste pipe, pipe for carrying off waste water, etc.

wast·ing (wās′ting), adj. 1. laying waste; devastating. 2. gradually destructive to the body.

wast·rel (wās′trəl), n. 1. waster. 2. idler.

watch (woch; wôch), v. 1. look at; observe: *watch a play.* 2. look or wait with care and attention; be very careful: *watch for the approach of an enemy.* 3. look at or wait for with care and attention: *the police watched the prisoner.* 4. keep guard: *he watched throughout the night.* 5. keep guard over: *the dog watched the little boy.* 6. stay awake for some purpose: *the nurse watches with the sick.* 7. watch out, Am. be careful; be on guard. —n. 1. a careful looking; attitude of attention: *be on the watch for automobiles when you cross the street.* 2. a protecting; guarding: *a man keeps watch over the bank at night.* 3. person or persons kept to guard. 4. period of time for guarding. 5. wakefulness, esp. a staying awake for some purpose. 6. a spring-driven device for telling time, small enough to be carried in a pocket or worn on the wrist. 7. Naut. a. the time of duty of one part of a ship's crew. A watch usually lasts four hours. b. the part of a crew on duty at the same time. [OE *wœccan*] —watch′er, n.

watch·case (woch′kās′; wôch′-), n. the outer covering for the works of a watch.

watch·dog (woch′dôg′; -dog′; wôch′-), n. 1. dog kept to guard property. 2. a watchful guardian.

watch fire, fire kept burning at night in camps, etc.

watch·ful (woch′fəl; wôch′-), adj. watching carefully; on the lookout; wide-awake. —watch′ful·ly, adv. —watch′ful·ness, n. —Syn. vigilant, alert, attentive.

watch·mak·er (woch′māk′ər; wôch′-), n. man who makes and repairs watches. —watch′mak′ing, n.

watch·man (woch′mən; wôch′-), n., pl. -men. man who keeps watch; guard.

watch meeting, watch night, a church service on the last night of the year.

watch·tow·er (woch′tou′ər; wôch′-), n. tower from which a man watches for enemies, fires, ships, etc.

watch·word (woch′wėrd′; wôch′-), n. 1. a secret word that allows a person to pass a guard; password. 2. motto; slogan.

wa·ter (wô′tər; wot′ər), n. 1. liquid that constitutes rain, oceans, rivers, lakes, and ponds. Perfectly pure water is a transparent, colorless, tasteless, scentless compound of hydrogen and oxygen, H_2O, freezing at 32 degrees F. or 0 degrees C., and boiling at 212 degrees F. or 100 degrees C. 2. liquid from the body, as tears, sweat, saliva, urine, serum, etc. 3. any liquid preparation that suggests water: *rose water.* 4. body of water; sea, lake, river, etc. 5. water of a river, with reference to its relative height, etc.: *high or low water.* 6. a wavy marking on silk, metal, etc. 7. additional shares or securities issued without corresponding increase of capital or assets. 8. waters, a. flowing water. b. water moving in waves; the sea; the high sea. c. spring water; mineral water. 9. above water, out of trouble or difficulty. 10. back water, make a boat go backward. 11. by water, on a ship or boat. 12. hold water, stand the test; be true, dependable, effective, etc. 13. like water, very freely. 14. of the first water, of the highest degree. —v. 1. sprinkle or wet with water. 2. supply with water. 3. get or take in water. 4. fill with water; discharge water: *her eyes watered.* 5. weaken by adding water. 6. make a wavy marking on. 7. Am. increase (stock, etc.) by issue of additional shares or securities without a corresponding increase in capital or assets. [OE *wœter*] —wa′ter·er, n. —wa′ter·less, adj.

water bird, bird that swims or wades in water.

water boa, anaconda (def. 1).

wa·ter·borne (wô′tər·bôrn′; -bōrn′; wot′ər-), adj. 1. supported by water; floating. 2. conveyed by a boat or the like.

water buffalo, the buffalo of Asia and the Philippines.

Wa·ter·bur·y (wô′tər·ber′i; wot′ər-), n. city in W Connecticut.

Water Carrier, Aquarius.

water clock, instrument for measuring time by the flow of water.

water closet, toilet flushed by water.

water color, 1. paint mixed with water instead of oil. 2. a painting with water colors. 3. picture made with water colors. —wa′ter·col′or, adj. —wa′ter·col′or·ist, n.

wa·ter·cool (wô′tər·kül′; wot′ər-), v. cool by means of water circulating in a jacket or pipes. —wa′ter-cooled′, adj.

water cooler, any device for cooling water, or for cooling something by means of water.

wa·ter·course (wô′tər·kôrs′; -kōrs′; wot′ər-), n. 1. stream of water; river; brook. 2. channel for water.

wa·ter·craft (wô′tər·kraft′; -kräft′; wot′ər-), n. 1. skill in water sports, as boating, swimming, etc. 2. ship or ships; boat or boats.

water cress, a plant that grows in water, used for salad and as a garnish. —wa′ter-cress′, adj.

water cure, hydropathy.

wa·ter·fall (wô′tər·fôl′; wot′ər-), n. fall of water from a high place.

wa·ter·fowl (wô′tər·foul′; wot′ər-), n., pl. -fowls or (esp. collectively) -fowl. 1. a water bird. 2. water birds, esp. birds that swim.

water front, 1. land at the water's edge. 2. Am. the part of a city beside a river, lake, or harbor.

water gap, Am. gap in a mountain ridge through which a stream flows.

water gas, a gas used for lighting or fuel. Water gas is largely carbon monoxide and hydrogen, made by passing steam over very hot coal or coke.

water glass, wa·ter·glass (wô′tər·glas′; -gläs′; wot′ər-), n. 1. glass to hold water; tumbler. 2. gauge which indicates the level of water. 3. sodium or potassium silicate, a substance used esp. to coat eggs and keep them from spoiling.

water ice, Esp. Brit. a frozen mixture of fruit juice, sugar, and water; sherbet.

watering place, 1. Esp. Brit. resort with springs containing mineral water. 2. Esp. Brit. resort where there is bathing, boating, etc. 3. place where water may be obtained.

watering pot, can with a spout for sprinkling water on plants, etc.

water jacket, a casing with water in it, put around something to keep it cool or at a certain temperature.

water level, 1. the surface level of a body of water. 2. water line.

water lily, a water plant having flat, floating leaves and showy, fragrant flowers. The flowers of the common American water lily are white, or sometimes pink.

Common American water lily

water line, wa·ter·line (wô′tər·līn′; wot′ər-), n. Naut. 1. line where the surface of the water touches the side of a ship or boat. 2. any of several lines marked on a ship's hull to show the depth to which it sinks when unloaded, partly loaded, or fully loaded.

wa·ter·logged (wô′tər·lôgd′; -logd′; wot′ər-), adj. 1. so full of water that it will barely float. 2. thoroughly soaked with water.

Wa·ter·loo (wô′tər·lü; wô′tər·lü′), n. 1. the battle in which Napoleon was finally defeated in 1815. 2. any decisive or crushing defeat.

water main, a large pipe for carrying water.

wa·ter·man (wô′tər·mən; wot′ər-), n., pl. -men. 1. boatman. 2. oarsman. —wa′ter·man·ship′, n.

wa·ter·mark (wô′tər·märk′; wot′ər-), n. 1. a mark showing how high water has risen or how low it has fallen. 2. a faint design made in some kinds of paper. —v. put a watermark in.

wa·ter·mel·on (wô′tər·mel′ən; wot′ər-), n.

1. a large, juicy melon with red or pink pulp and a hard green rind. 2. vine bearing these melons.

water mill, mill whose machinery is run by water power.

water moccasin, *Am.* 1. a poisonous snake of the S United States that lives in swamps and along streams; the cottonmouth. 2. any of various similar but harmless snakes.

water of crystallization, *Chem.* water that is present in certain crystalline substances. When the water is removed by heating, the crystals break up into a powder.

water ouzel, any of various small birds related to the thrushes, that wade and dive in deep water for food.

Water ouzel (ab. 7 in. long)

water polo, game played with an inflated ball by two teams of swimmers.

water power, the power from flowing or falling water. It can be used to drive machinery and make electricity.

wa·ter·proof (wô′tər·prüf′; wot′ər-), *adj.* that will not let water through; resistant to water. —*n.* 1. a waterproof material. 2. a waterproof coat; raincoat. —*v.* make waterproof.

wa·ter·shed (wô′tər·shed′; wot′ər-), *n.* 1. ridge between the regions drained by two different river systems. 2. the region drained by one river system.

wa·ter·side (wô′tər·sīd′; wot′ər-), *n.* land along the sea, a lake, a river, etc.

wa·ter·soak (wô′tər·sōk′; wot′ər-), *v.* soak thoroughly with water.

water spaniel, a curly-haired dog that is often trained to swim out for wild ducks, geese, etc., that have been shot down by hunters.

wa·ter·spout (wô′tər·spout′; wot′ər-), *n.* 1. pipe which takes away or spouts water. 2. whirlwind over the ocean or a large lake. It looks like a column of water reaching upward to the clouds.

water sprite, sprite supposed to live in water.

water table, in engineering, etc., the level below which the ground is saturated with water.

wa·ter·tight (wô′tər·tīt′; wot′ər-), *adj.* 1. so tight that no water can get in or out: *the watertight compartments of a ship.* 2. leaving no opening for misunderstanding, criticism, etc.; perfect. —**wa′ter·tight′ness,** *n.*

water tower, 1. a big tower to hold water. 2. *Am.* a fire-extinguishing apparatus used to throw water on the upper parts of tall buildings.

water vapor, water in a gaseous state, esp. when below the boiling point and fairly diffused, as distinguished from steam.

wa·ter·way (wô′tər·wā′; wot′ər-), *n.* 1. river, canal, or other body of water that ships can go on. 2. channel for water.

water wheel, 1. wheel turned by water and used to do work. 2. wheel for raising water.

water wings, two waterproof bags filled with air and used to hold a person afloat while he is learning to swim.

wa·ter·works (wô′tər·werks′; wot′ər-), *n.pl.* (*often sing. in use*) 1. system of pipes, reservoirs, water towers, pumps, etc., for supplying a city or town with water. 2. pumping station.

wa·ter·worn (wô′tər·wôrn′; -wōrn′; wot′ər-), *adj.* worn or smoothed by the action of water.

wa·ter·y (wô′tər·i; wot′ər-), *adj.* 1. of water; connected with water. 2. full of water; wet: *a watery sky.* 3. tearful. 4. like water. 5. weak; thin; poor; pale: *a watery blue.* 6. in or under water: *a watery grave.* —**wa′ter·i·ness,** *n.*

watt (wot), *n.* a unit of electric power, equivalent to one joule per second. [after J. *Watt*]

Watt (wot), *n.* **James,** 1736–1819, Scottish engineer and inventor who perfected the steam engine.

watt·age (wot′ij), *n.* electric power expressed in watts. A flatiron that uses 5 amperes of current on a 110-volt circuit has a wattage of 550.

watt-hour (wot′our′), *n.* unit of electrical energy or work, equal to one watt maintained for one hour.

wat·tle (wot′əl), *n., v.,* **-tled, -tling.** —*n.* 1. Also, **wattles.** sticks interwoven with twigs or branches; framework of wicker. 2. the red fleshy hanging down from the throat of a chicken, turkey, etc. —*v.* 1. make (a fence, wall, roof, hut, etc.) of wattle. 2. twist or weave together (twigs, branches, etc.). 3. bind together with interwoven twigs, branches, etc. [OE *watul*] —**wat′tled,** *adj.*

Wattle of a turkey

watt·me·ter (wot′mē′tər), *n.* instrument for measuring in watts the power developed in an electric circuit.

wave (wāv), *n., v.,* **waved, wav·ing.** —*n.* 1. a moving ridge or swell of water. 2. any movement like this. 3. *Physics.* a movement of particles to and fro; vibration. 4. a swell, surge, or rush; increase of some emotion, influence, condition, etc.; outburst: *a cold wave, a wave of enthusiasm.* 5. a waving, esp. of something, as a signal. 6. a curve or series of curves. 7. a permanent wave. 8. *Poetic.* body of water; sea. —*v.* 1. move as waves do; move up and down or back and forth; sway. 2. have a wavelike form: *her hair waves naturally.* 3. give a wavelike form or pattern to. 4. signal or direct by waving: *she waved him away.* 5. shake in the air; brandish: *he waved the stick at them.* [OE *wafian*] —**wav′a·ble,** *adj.* —**wave′less,** *adj.* —**wave′like′,** *adj.* —**wav′er,** *n.* —Syn. *n.* 1. billow, breaker, whitecap. —*v.* 1. rock, fluctuate.

Wave, WAVE (wāv), *n.* member of the Waves, the Women's Reserve, U.S. Naval Reserve. [from initial letters of W(omen's) A(ppointed) V(olunteer) E(mergency) S(ervice)]

wave length, *Physics.* the distance between any particle of a medium through which waves are passing and the next particle that is in the same phase with it.

wave·let (wāv′lit), *n.* a little wave.

wa·ver (wā′vər), *v.* 1. move to and fro; flutter. 2. vary in intensity; flicker. 3. be undecided; hesitate. 4. become unsteady; begin to give way. —*n.* a wavering. [ult. < *wave*] —**wa′ver·er,** *n.* —**wa′ver·ing·ly,** *adv.* —**wa′ver·y,** *adj.*

wav·y (wāv′i), *adj.,* **wav·i·er, wav·i·est.** having waves; having many waves: *wavy hair, a wavy line.* —**wav′i·ly,** *adv.* —**wav′i·ness,** *n.*

wax[1] (waks), *n.* 1. a yellowish substance made by bees for constructing their honeycomb. 2. any substance like this. 3. wax in one's hands, person easy to influence and manage. —*v.* rub, stiffen, polish, etc., with wax. —*adj.* of wax. [OE *weax*] —**wax′er,** *n.* —**wax′like′,** *adj.*

wax[2] (waks), *v.,* **waxed, waxed** or (*Poetic*) **wax·en, wax·ing.** 1. grow bigger or greater; increase. 2. become: *the party waxed merry.* [OE *weaxan*]

wax bean, *Am.* a yellow string bean.

wax·en (wak′sən), *adj.* 1. made of wax. 2. like wax; smooth, soft, and pale.

wax myrtle, any of various shrubs or trees whose small berries are coated with wax. The bayberry is a wax myrtle.

wax paper, paper coated with paraffin.

wax·wing (waks′wing′), *n.* any of several small birds with a showy crest and red markings at the tips of the wings, as the cedarbird.

wax·work (waks′werk′), *n.* 1. figure or figures made of wax. 2. **waxworks** (*sing. in use*), exhibition of figures made of wax. —**wax′work′er,** *n.*

wax·y (wak′si), *adj.,* **wax·i·er, wax·i·est.** 1. made of or covered with wax; containing wax. 2. like wax. 3. pliable; yielding. —**wax′i·ness,** *n.*

way (wā), *n.* 1. manner; style: *reply in a polite way.* 2. a characteristic or habitual manner: *that is only his way.* 3. method; means: *new ways to prevent disease.* 4. point; feature; respect; detail: *a plan defective in several ways.* 5. direction: *look this way.* 6. motion along a course: *the guide led the way.* 7. distance: *the* *sun is a long way off.* **8.** road; path; street; course. **9.** space for passing or going ahead: *make way.* **10.** Often, **ways.** habit; custom. **11.** one's wish; will: *he wants his own way.* **12.** *Colloq.* condition; state: *that sick man is in a bad way.* **13.** movement; forward motion: *the ship slowly gathered way.* **14.** range of experience or notice: *the best idea that ever came my way.* **15.** course of life, action, or experience: *the way of the just.* **16.** ways, timbers on which a ship is built and launched. **17.** by the way, a. while coming or going. **b.** in that connection; incidentally. **18.** by way of, a. by the route of; through. **b.** as; for. **19.** come one's way, happen to one. **20.** give way, a. make way; retreat; yield. **b.** break down or fail. **c.** abandon oneself to emotion. **21.** go out of the way, make a special effort. **22.** have a way with one, be persuasive. **23.** in a way, to some extent. **24.** in the way, being an obstacle, hindrance, etc. **25.** make one's way, a. go. **b.** get ahead; succeed. **26.** make way, a. give space for passing or going ahead; make room. **b.** move forward. **27.** out of the way, a. so as not to be an obstacle, hindrance, etc. **b.** far from where most people live or go. **c.** unusual; strange. **d.** to death. **28.** under way, going on; in motion; in progress. *—adv. Colloq.* away. [OE *weg*] **—Syn.** *n.* **1.** mode, fashion. **2.** practice. **8.** route, highway, avenue, lane. **13.** progress, advance. ➤ **way, ways.** *Way* is colloquially and informally used for *away* (*way over across the valley*). *Way* is used in a number of colloquial idioms: *in a bad way, out our way, I don't see how she can act the way she does. Ways* is colloquially used for *way* in expressions like *a little ways* down the road.

way·bill (wā′bil′), *n. Am.* list of goods with a statement of where they are to go and how they are to get there.

way·far·er (wā′fâr′ər), *n.* traveler.

way·far·ing (wā′fâr′ing), *adj.* traveling.

way·lay (wā′lā′; wā′lā′), *v.,* **–laid,** **–lay·ing. 1.** lie in wait for; attack on the way: *Robin Hood waylaid travelers and robbed them.* **2.** stop (a person) on his way. **—way′lay′er,** *n.*

–ways, *suffix* forming adverbs showing direction or position, as in *edgeways, sideways,* or adverbs showing manner, as in *anyways, noways.* [< *way*]

way·side (wā′sīd′), *n.* edge of a road or path. *—adj.* along the edge of a road or path.

way station, *Am.* station between main stations on a railroad.

way train, *Am.* a railroad train that stops at all or most of the stations on its way.

way·ward (wā′wərd), *adj.* **1.** turning from the right way; disobedient; willful. **2.** irregular; unsteady. **—way′ward·ly,** *adv.* **—way′ward·ness,** *n.* **—Syn. 1.** perverse, stubborn, unruly, refractory.

W.C.T.U., *Am.* Woman's Christian Temperance Union.

we (wē; *unstressed* wi), *pron., pl. nom.; poss.,* **our** or **ours;** *obj.* **us.** the 1st pers. nom. pl. of **I.** [OE *wē*]. ➤ **we. 1.** Indefinite *we. We* is used as an indefinite pronoun in expressions like *we find, we sometimes feel,* and to avoid passive and impersonal constructions. **2.** Editorial *we.* In editorial columns and in some other regular departments of periodicals the writer refers to himself as *we.* In some instances the *we* refers to an editorial board that determines the opinions expressed but more often it is a convention. The usage has passed into familiar and informal writing, especially of a light tone. Used merely to avoid using *I, we* is usually conspicuous.

weak (wēk), *adj.* **1.** that can easily be broken, crushed, overcome, torn, etc.; not strong: *a weak foundation, weak defenses.* **2.** lacking bodily strength or health: *a weak constitution.* **3.** lacking power, authority, force, etc.: *a weak law.* **4.** lacking mental power: *a weak mind.* **5.** lacking moral strength or firmness; vacillating: *a weak character.* **6.** lacking or poor in amount, volume, loudness, taste, intensity, etc.: *a weak army, weak arguments.* **7.** wanting in logical or legal soundness: *a weak claim to the title.* **8.** lacking or poor in something specified: *a com-*

position weak in spelling. **9.** *Gram.* (of Germanic verbs) inflected by additions of consonants to the stem, not by vowel change. English weak verbs form the past tense and past participle by adding *–ed, –d,* or *–t.* **10.** *Phonet.* **a.** of a sound, not stressed. **b.** of an accent or stress, light; not strong. **11.** of a verse ending, having the metrical stress on a word or syllable which would not be stressed in natural speech. [< Scand. *veikr*] **—weak′ness,** *n.* **—Syn. 1.** fragile, soft, bending, pliant. **2.** frail, feeble, delicate. **5.** irresolute.

weak·en (wēk′ən), *v.* make or become weak or weaker. **—weak′en·er,** *n.* **—weak′en·ing·ly,** *adv.* **—Syn.** enfeeble, debilitate, exhaust, lessen, diminish.

weak·fish (wēk′fish′), *n., pl.* **–fish·es** or (*esp. collectively*) **–fish.** *Am.* a spiny-finned salt-water food fish with a tender mouth.

weak-kneed (wēk′nēd′), *adj.* **1.** having weak knees. **2.** yielding easily to opposition, intimidation, etc.

weak·ling (wēk′ling), *n.* a weak person or animal.

weak·ly (wēk′li), *adv., adj.,* **–li·er,** **–li·est.** *—adv.* in a weak manner. *—adj.* weak; feeble; sickly. **—weak′li·ness,** *n.*

weak-mind·ed (wēk′mīn′did), *adj.* **1.** having or showing little intelligence; feeble-minded. **2.** lacking firmness of mind. **—weak′-mind′ed·ness,** *n.*

weal[1] (wēl), *n. Archaic.* well-being; prosperity; happiness. [OE *wela*]

weal[2] (wēl), *n.* streak or ridge on the skin made by a stick or whip; welt.

weald (wēld), *n. Poetic.* open country. [OE, woods]

wealth (welth), *n.* **1.** much money or property; riches. **2.** all things that have money value. **3.** all things that have value. **4.** a large quantity; abundance: *a wealth of words.* [< *well*[1] or *weal*] **—Syn. 1.** prosperity, fortune. **4.** profusion.

wealth·y (wel′thi), *adj.,* **wealth·i·er,** **wealth·i·est. 1.** having wealth; rich. **2.** abundant; ample. **—wealth′i·ly,** *adv.* **—wealth′i·ness,** *n.*

wean (wēn), *v.* **1.** accustom (a child or young animal) to food other than its mother's milk. **2.** accustom (a person) to do without something; cause to turn away; detach. [OE *wenian*] **—wean′er,** *n.*

weap·on (wep′ən), *n.* any instrument used in fighting; means of attack or defense. Swords, arrows, guns, and claws are weapons. [OE *wǣpen*] **—weap′oned,** *adj.* **—weap′on·less,** *adj.*

weap·on·ry (wep′ən·ri), *n.* weapons collectively: *nuclear weaponry.*

wear (wâr), *v.,* **wore, worn, wear·ing,** *n.* *—v.* **1.** have on the body: *we wear clothes.* **2.** cause loss or damage to by using: *these shoes are worn out.* **3.** suffer loss or damage from being used: *his coat has worn to shreds.* **4.** make by rubbing, scraping, washing away, etc.: *walking wore a hole in my shoe.* **5.** tire; weary: *running wore him out.* **6.** last long; give good service: *this coat has worn well.* **7.** have; show: *the house wore an air of sadness.* **8.** pass or go gradually: *it became hotter as the day wore on.* **9.** of a ship, turn or be turned around by pointing the bow away from the wind. **10.** wear away, scrape, rub, or wash away. **11.** wear down, a. tire; weary. **b.** overcome by persistent effort. **c.** reduce in height. **12.** wear off, become less.*—n.* **1.** a wearing; a being worn: *clothing for summer wear.* **2.** things worn or to be worn; clothing: *the store sells children's wear.* **3.** gradual loss or damage caused by use: *the rug shows wear.* **4.** lasting quality; good service: *there is still wear in these shoes.* **5.** wear and tear, loss or damage caused by use. [OE *werian*] **—wear′a·ble,** *adj.* **—wear′-a·bil′i·ty, wear′a·ble·ness,** *n.* **—wear′er,** *n.*

wearing apparel, clothes.

wea·ri·some (wir′i·səm), *adj.* wearying; tiring; tiresome. **—wea′ri·some·ly,** *adv.* **—wea′ri·some·ness,** *n.* **—Syn.** fatiguing, tedious.

wea·ry (wir′i), *adj.,* **–ri·er, –ri·est,** *v.,* **–ried, –ry·ing.** *—adj.* **1.** tired: *weary feet, a weary brain.* **2.** causing fatigue; tiring: *a weary wait.* **3.** having one's patience, tolerance, or liking exhausted. —v. 1. make weary; tire. 2. become weary. 3. long: *she is wearying for home.* [OE *wērig*] —wea'ri·less, *adj.* —wea'ri·ly, *adv.* —wea'ri·ness, *n.* —wea'ry·ing·ly, *adv.* —Syn. *adj.* 1. fatigued, exhausted, fagged.

wea·sand (wē'zənd), *n. Archaic.* 1. windpipe. 2. throat. [OE *wāsend*]

wea·sel (wē'zəl), *n.* 1. a small, quick, sly animal with a long, slender body and short legs. Weasels feed on rats, birds, eggs, etc. 2. a cunning, sneaking person. [OE *weosule*]

Weasel (6 to 8 in. long, without the tail)

weath·er (weᵗʰ'ər), *n.* 1. condition of the atmosphere with respect to temperature, moisture, or other meteorological phenomena. 2. windy or stormy weather. 3. **keep one's weather eye open,** be on the lookout for possible danger or trouble. 4. **under the weather,** *Colloq.* sick; ailing. —v. 1. expose to the weather. 2. become discolored or worn by air, rain, sun, frost, etc. 3. go or come through safely: *the ship weathered the storm.* 4. sail to the windward of: *the ship weathered the cape.* —adj. 1. toward the wind; windward. 2. of the side exposed to the wind. [OE *weder*] —weath'ered, *adj.*

weath·er-beat·en (weᵗʰ'ər·bēt'ən), *adj.* worn or hardened by the wind, rain, and other forces of the weather.

weath·er·board (weᵗʰ'ər·bôrd'; -bōrd'), *n.* clapboard. —v. cover with weatherboards.

weath·er-bound (weᵗʰ'ər·bound'), *adj.* delayed by bad weather: *a weather-bound ship.*

Weather Bureau, *Am.* division of the United States Department of Commerce that records and forecasts the weather.

weath·er·cock (weᵗʰ'ər·kok'), *n.* a weather vane, esp. one in the shape of a cock.

weath·er·glass (weᵗʰ'ər·glas'; -gläs'), *n.* instrument to show the weather, as a barometer.

weath·er·ing (weᵗʰ'ər·ing), *n.* process by which rocks are decomposed by air, water, frost, etc.

weath·er·man (weᵗʰ'ər·man'), **weather man,** *n., pl.* -men. *Colloq.* man who forecasts the weather.

weath·er·proof (weᵗʰ'ər·prüf'), *adj.* protected against rain, snow, or wind; able to stand exposure to all kinds of weather. —v. make weatherproof.

weather station, installation where meteorological observations are made.

weather strip, *Am.* a narrow strip to fill or cover the space between a door or window and the casing, so as to keep out rain, snow, and wind.

weath·er-strip (weᵗʰ'ər·strip'), *v.,* -stripped, -strip·ping. *Am.* fit with weather strips.

weather stripping, *Am.* 1. a weather strip. 2. weather strips.

weather vane, device to show which way the wind is blowing.

weath·er·wise (weᵗʰ'ər·wīz'), *adj.* 1. skillful in forecasting the changes of the weather. 2. skillful in forecasting changes in opinion, etc.

weave (wēv), *v.,* **wove** or (*Rare*) **weaved,** **wo·ven** or **wove,** **weav·ing,** *n.* —v. 1. form (threads or strips) into a thing or fabric: *weave thread into cloth.* 2. make out of thread, etc.: *she is weaving a rug.* 3. combine into a whole: *the author wove three plots together into one story.* 4. make by combining parts: *the author wove a story from three plots.* 5. weave one's way, make one's way by twisting and turning. —n. method or pattern of weaving: *a cloth of coarse weave.* [OE *wefan*]

weav·er (wēv'ər), *n.* 1. person who weaves. 2. person whose work is weaving. 3. weaverbird.

weav·er·bird (wēv'ər·bėrd'), *n.* a bird of Asia and Africa, that builds an elaborately woven nest.

web (web), *n.* 1. something woven. 2. fabric of delicate, silken threads spun by a spider or by

the larvae of certain insects. 3. a whole piece of cloth made at one time. 4. anything like a web: *a web of lies, the web of life.* 5. the skin joining the toes of ducks, geese, and other swimming birds. [OE *webb*] —webbed, *adj.* —web'less, *adj.* —web'like', *adj.*

web·bing (web'ing), *n.* 1. cloth woven into strong strips, used in upholstery and for belts. 2. the plain foundation fabric left for protection at the edge of some rugs, etc. 3. skin joining the toes, as in a duck's feet.

web-foot (web'fut'), *n., pl.* -feet. foot in which the toes are joined by a web. —web'-foot'ed, *adj.*

Web·ster (web'stər), *n.* 1. Daniel, 1782–1852, American statesman and orator. 2. Noah, 1758–1843, American lexicographer.

web·ster (web'stər), *n. Archaic.* weaver.

web-toed (web'tōd'), *adj.* web-footed.

wed (wed), *v.,* **wed·ded, wed·ded** or **wed, wed·ding.** 1. marry. 2. unite. [OE *weddian*]

Wed., Wednesday.

wed·ded (wed'id), *adj.* 1. married. 2. united. 3. devoted.

wed·ding (wed'ing), *n.* 1. the marriage ceremony. 2. an anniversary of it. A **golden wedding** is the fiftieth anniversary of a marriage.

wedge (wej), *n., v.,* **wedged, wedg·ing.** —n. 1. piece of wood or metal with a tapering thin edge, used in splitting, separating, etc. 2. something shaped like a wedge or used like a wedge: *an entering wedge into society.* —v. 1. split or separate with a wedge. 2. fasten or tighten with a wedge. 3. thrust or pack in tightly; squeeze: *he wedged himself through the narrow window.* 4. force a way. [OE *wecg*] —wedge'like', wedg'y, *adj.*

Wedge splitting a log; wedge.

Wedg·wood (wej'wud'), or **Wedgwood ware,** *n.* type of pottery with tinted ground and white decoration in relief in designs patterned after Greek and Roman models. [after J. *Wedgwood*, potter]

wed·lock (wed'lok), *n.* married life; marriage. [OE *wedlāc* pledge < *wedd* pledge + -*lāc*, noun suffix]

Wednes·day (wenz'di; -dā), *n.* the fourth day of the week, following Tuesday.

wee (wē), *adj.,* **we·er, we·est.** very small; tiny. [from the phrase *a little wee* a little bit < OE *wǣg* weight]

weed (wēd), *n.* 1. a useless or troublesome plant; plant occurring in cultivated ground to the exclusion or injury of the desired crop. 2. *Colloq.* tobacco. 3. *Colloq.* cigar; cigarette. 4. a thin, ungainly person or animal. —v. 1. take weeds out of. 2. **weed out,** a. free from what is useless or worthless. b. remove as useless or worthless. [OE *wēod*] —weed'er, *n.* —weed'less, *adj.* —weed'like', *adj.*

weeds (wēdz), *n.pl.* mourning garments. [OE *wǣd*]

weed·y (wēd'i), *adj.,* **weed·i·er, weed·i·est.** 1. full of weeds. 2. of or like weeds. 3. thin and lanky; weak. —weed'i·ly, *adv.* —weed'i·ness, *n.*

week (wēk), *n.* 1. seven days, one after another. 2. the time from Sunday through Saturday. 3. the working days of a seven-day period. 4. **week in, week out,** week after week. [OE *wice*]

week·day (wēk'dā'), *n.* any day except Sunday. —adj. of or on a weekday.

week·end (wēk'end'), *n.* Saturday and Sunday as a time for recreation, visiting, etc. —adj. of or on a weekend. —v. spend a weekend. —week'end'er, *n.*

week·ly (wēk'li), *adj., adv., n., pl.* -lies. —adj. 1. of a week; for a week; lasting a week. 2. done or happening once a week. —adv. once each week; every week. —n. a newspaper or magazine published once a week.

ween (wēn), *v. Archaic.* think; suppose; believe; expect. [OE *wēnan*]

weep (wēp), *v.,* **wept, weep·ing,** *n.* —v. 1. shed tears; cry. 2. shed tears for; mourn. 3. let fall in drops; shed: *she wept bitter tears.* 4. be very damp; drip. 5. exude. —*n.* act or fact of weeping. [OE *wēpan*] —weep′er, *n.* —weep′y, *adj.* —Syn. *v.* 1. sob. 2. bewail.

weep·ing (wēp′ing), *adj.* 1. that weeps. 2. having thin, drooping branches: *a weeping willow.* —weep′ing·ly, *adv.*

wee·vil (wē′vəl), *n.* 1. a small beetle whose larvae destroy grain, nuts, cotton, fruit, etc. 2. any of various small insects that destroy stored grain. [OE *wifel*] —wee′-viled, wee′villed, *adj.* —wee′vil·y, wee′vil·ly, *adj.*

Weevil (line shows actual length)

weft (weft), *n.* woof. [OE, < *wefan* weave]

weigh (wā), *v.* 1. find the weight of: *weigh oneself.* 2. have as a measure by weight: *I weighed 110 pounds.* 3. measure by weight: *the grocer weighed out five pounds of butter.* 4. bend by weight; burden: *she is weighed down with many troubles.* 5. balance in the mind; consider carefully: *he weighed the idea before speaking.* 6. have importance or influence. 7. bear down: *the mistake weighed heavily upon his mind.* 8. lift up (an anchor). 9. **weigh down,** oppress; overburden. 10. **weigh in,** find out one's weight before a contest. 11. **weigh on,** be a burden to. 12. **weigh one's words,** think carefully before speaking and choose each word with care. [OE *wegan*] —weigh′a·ble, *adj.* —weigh′er, *n.*

weight (wāt), *n.* 1. how heavy a thing is; the amount a thing weighs: *the dog's weight is 50 pounds.* 2. quality that makes all things tend toward the center of the earth; heaviness: *gas has hardly any weight.* 3. system of units for expressing weight: *avoirdupois weight, troy weight.* 4. unit of such a system. 5. piece of metal having a specific weight, used in weighing things: *a pound weight.* 6. a heavy thing or mass: *a weight keeps the papers in place.* 7. load; burden: *the weight of responsibility.* 8. influence; importance; value: *an opinion of great weight.* 9. **by weight,** measured by weighing. 10. **pull one's weight,** do one's part or share. —*v.* 1. load down; burden. 2. add weight to; put weight on. [OE *wiht* < *wegan* weigh] —weight′-less, *adj.*

weight·y (wāt′i), *adj.,* **weight·i·er, weight·i·est.** 1. heavy. 2. burdensome: *weighty cares of state.* 3. important: *weighty negotiations.* 4. influential: *a weighty speaker.* 5. convincing: *weighty arguments.* —weight′i·ly, *adv.* —weight′i·ness, *n.* —Syn. 1. massive, ponderous. 3. momentous, serious, authoritative. —Ant. 1. light, feathery. 3. trivial, unimportant.

Wei·mar (vī′mär), *n.* city in W Germany.

weir (wir), *n.* 1. dam in a river. 2. fence of stakes or broken branches put in a stream or channel to catch fish. [OE *wer*]

weird (wird), *adj.* 1. unearthly; mysterious. 2. *Colloq.* odd; fantastic; queer. 3. having to do with fate or destiny. [OE *wyrd* fate] —weird′ly, *adv.* —weird′ness, *n.* —Syn. 1. uncanny, eerie.

welch (welch; welsh), *v.* welsh. —welch′er, *n.*

wel·come (wel′kəm), *interj., n., v.* —comed, —com·ing, *adj.* —*interj.* word of kindly greeting: *welcome home!* —*n.* 1. a kindly greeting. 2. a kind reception: *you will always have a welcome here.* —*v.* 1. greet kindly. 2. receive gladly. —*adj.* 1. gladly received; agreeable: *a welcome letter.* 2. gladly or freely permitted: *you are welcome to pick the flowers.* 3. free to enjoy courtesies, etc., without obligation (used in conventional response to thanks): *you are quite welcome.* [orig. meaning "agreeable guest," OE *wilcuma* < *wil*— (cf. *will* pleasure) + *cuma* comer] —wel′-come·less, *adj.* —wel′come·ly, *adv.* —wel′-come·ness, *n.* —wel′com·er, *n.*

weld (weld), *v.* 1. join together (metal, plastic, etc.) by hammering or pressing while soft and hot. 2. unite closely. 3. be welded or be capable of being welded. —*n.* 1. a welded joint. 2. a welding. [< *well²,* v.] —weld′a·ble, *adj.* —weld′er, *n.*

wel·fare (wel′fār′), *n.* health, happiness, and prosperity; being or doing well.

welfare state, state whose government pro-

vides for the welfare of its citizens, as through social security, unemployment insurance, etc.

welfare work, work done to improve the conditions of people who need help, as in a community, business, etc. —welfare worker.

wel·kin (wel′kən), *n.* Archaic. sky. [OE *wolcen* cloud]

well¹ (wel), *adv.,* **bet·ter, best,** *adj., interj.* —*adv.* 1. in a satisfactory, favorable, or advantageous manner; all right: *the job was well done.* 2. in a good manner; excellently: *he writes well.* 3. thoroughly; soundly: *shake well before using.* 4. to a considerable degree; much: *the fair brought in well over a hundred dollars.* 5. in detail; intimately: *he knows the subject well.* 6. fairly; reasonably; properly: *I couldn't very well refuse.* 7. sufficiently; adequately: *think well before you act.* 8. as well, a. also; besides. b. equally. 9. **as well as,** a. in addition to; besides. b. as much as. —*adj.* 1. satisfactory; good; right: *all is well with us.* 2. in good health: *I am very well.* 3. proper; advisable: *is it well to act so hastily?* 4. in a satisfactory position, condition, etc. —*interj.* expression used to show mild surprise, agreement, etc., or merely to fill in. [OE *wel*] —well′ness, *n.* —Syn. *adj.* 2. hale, sound, hearty. ▶ See **good** for usage note.

well² (wel), *n.* 1. hole dug or bored in the ground to get water, oil, gas, etc. 2. spring; fountain; source. 3. something like a well in shape or use: *the well of a fountain pen.* 4. shaft for stairs or elevator, extending vertically through the floors of a building. —*v.* spring; rise; gush. [OE *wella,* n., *wiellan,* v.]

we'll (wēl; *unstressed* wil), we shall; we will.

Wel·land Canal (wel′ənd), canal in Canada, between lakes Erie and Ontario.

well-ap·point·ed (wel′ə·poin′tid), *adj.* having good furnishings or equipment.

well-a·way (wel′ə·wā′), **well-a·day** (—dā′), *interj.* Archaic. alas!

well-bal·anced (wel′bal′ənst), *adj.* 1. rightly balanced, adjusted, or regulated. 2. sensible; sane.

well-be·haved (wel′bi·hāvd′), *adj.* showing good manners or conduct.

well-be·ing (wel′bē′ing), *n.* health and happiness; welfare.

well-born (wel′bôrn′), *adj.* belonging to a good family.

well-bred (wel′bred′), *adj.* well brought up; having or showing good manners.

well-con·tent (wel′kən·tent′), *adj.* highly pleased or satisfied.

well-dis·posed (wel′dis·pōzd′), *adj.* 1. rightly or properly disposed. 2. well-meaning. 3. favorably or kindly disposed.

well-do·ing (wel′dü′ing), *n.* doing right. —well′-do′er, *n.*

well-fa·vored, *esp. Brit.* **well-fa·voured** (wel′fā′vərd), *adj.* of pleasing appearance; good-looking.

well-fed (wel′fed′), *adj.* showing the result of good feeding; fat; plump.

well-fixed (wel′fixt′), *adj. Am., Colloq.* well-to-do.

well-found (wel′found′), *adj.* well supplied or equipped.

well-found·ed (wel′foun′did), *adj.* rightly or justly founded: *a well-founded faith in schools.*

well-groomed (wel′grümd′), *adj.* well cared for; neat and trim.

well-ground·ed (wel′groun′did), *adj.* 1. based on good reasons. 2. thoroughly instructed in the fundamental principles of a subject.

well-heeled (wel′hēld′), *adj. Slang.* wealthy.

well-in·formed (wel′in·fôrmd′), *adj.* 1. having reliable or full information on a subject. 2. having information on a wide variety of subjects.

Wel·ling·ton (wel′ing·tən), *n.* 1. 1st Duke of (*Arthur Wellesley*), 1769–1852, British general who defeated Napoleon at Waterloo. 2. capital of New Zealand, on North Island.

well-kept (wel′kept′), *adj.* well cared for; carefully tended.

well-known (wel′nōn′), *adj.* 1. clearly or

fully known. 2. familiar. 3. generally or widely known.

well-man·nered (wel′man′ərd), *adj.* having or showing good manners; polite; courteous.

well-mean·ing (wel′mēn′ing), *adj.* 1. having good intentions. 2. Also, **well-meant** (wel′-ment′). proceeding from good intentions.

well-nigh (wel′nī′), *adv.* very nearly; almost.

well-off (wel′ôf′; -of′), *adj.* 1. in a good condition or position. 2. fairly rich.

well-pre·served (wel′pri-zérvd′), *adj.* showing few signs of age.

well-read (wel′red′), *adj.* having read much; knowing a great deal about books and literature.

Wells (welz), *n.* H(erbert) G(eorge), 1866–1946, English novelist and writer.

well-spo·ken (wel′spō′kən), *adj.* 1. speaking well, fittingly, or pleasingly; polite in speech. 2. spoken well.

well·spring (wel′spring′), *n.* 1. fountainhead. 2. source, esp. of a supply that never fails.

well-suit·ed (wel′süt′id), *adj.* suitable; convenient.

well sweep, a tapering or weighted pole swung on a pivot and having a bucket hung on the smaller or lighter end.

well-thought-of (wel′thôt′ov′; -uv′), *adj.* having a very good reputation.

well-timed (wel′tīmd′), *adj.* timely.

well-to-do (wel′tə-dü′), *adj.* having enough money to live well; prosperous.

well-wish·er (wel′wish′ər), *n.* person who wishes well to a person, cause, etc.

well-worn (wel′wôrn′; -wōrn′), *adj.* 1. much worn by use. 2. used too much; trite; stale.

Welsh (welsh; welch), *adj.* of or pertaining to Wales, its people, or their Celtic language. —*n.* 1. the people of Wales. 2. their language.

welsh (welsh; welch), *v. Slang.* evade paying a bet or fulfilling an obligation. Also, **welch.** —**welsh′er,** *n.*

Welsh·man (welsh′mən; welch′-), *n., pl.* -men. native of Wales.

Welsh rabbit, mixture containing cheese, cooked and poured over toast.

Welsh rarebit, Welsh rabbit.

welt (welt), *n.* 1. a strip of leather between the upper part and the sole of a shoe. 2. the narrow border, trimming, etc., on the edge of a garment or upholstery. 3. *Colloq.* a streak or ridge made on the skin by a stick or whip. 4. *Colloq.* a heavy blow. —*v.* 1. put a welt on. 2. *Colloq.* beat severely. [ME *welte, walte*]

wel·ter (wel′tər), *v.* 1. roll or toss about; wallow. 2. lie soaked; be drenched. —*n.* 1. a rolling and tossing. 2. confusion; commotion. [< MDu., MLG *welteren*]

wel·ter·weight (wel′tər-wāt′), *n.* boxer or wrestler weighing between 135 and 147 pounds. [earlier *welter* (< *welt,* def. 2) + *weight*]

wen (wen), *n.* a harmless tumor of the skin. [OE *wenn*]

wench (wench), *n.* 1. girl or young woman. 2. a woman servant. [< *wenchel* child, OE *wencel*]

Wen·chow (wen′chou′), *n.* former name of Yungkia.

wend (wend), *v.,* **wend·ed** or (*Archaic*) **went, wend·ing.** 1. direct (one's way): *we wended our way home.* 2. go. [OE *wendan*]

went (went), *v.* pt. of **go:** *I went home.*

wept (wept), *v.* pt. and pp. of **weep.**

were (wér; *unstressed* wər), *v.* 1. pl. and 2nd pers. sing. past indicative of **be:** *the officers were obeyed by the soldiers.* 2. past subjunctive of **be:** *if I were rich, I would travel.* 3. **as it were,** as if it were; so to speak; in some way. [OE *wǣron*]

were·wolf, wer·wolf (wir′wûlf′), *n., pl.* -wolves (-wûlvz′). in folklore, a person who has been changed into a wolf; person who can change himself into a wolf. [OE *werwulf* < *wer* man + *wulf* wolf]

wert (wért; *unstressed* wərt), *v. Archaic.* were.

Wes·ley (wes′li; *esp. Brit.* wez′li), *n.* John, 1703–1791, English clergyman who founded the Methodist Church.

Wes·ley·an (wes′li·ən; *esp. Brit.* wez′li·ən), *n.* member of the church founded by John Wesley; Methodist. —*adj.* of or having to do with John Wesley or the Methodist Church.

Wes·sex (wes′iks), *n.* 1. an ancient kingdom in S England from 500? A.D. to 886 A.D. 2. a modern region corresponding to it.

west (west), *n.* 1. the direction of the sunset; the point of the compass to the left as one faces north. 2. Also, **West.** the part of any country toward the west. 3. **West,** *Am.* the western part of the United States. 4. **West. a.** countries in Europe and America as distinguished from those in Asia, esp. SE Asia. **b.** the non-Communist countries of Europe and America, including also Australia, New Zealand, Japan, etc. —*adj.* 1. lying toward or situated in the west. 2. originating in or coming from the west: *a west wind.* —*adv.* 1. toward the west. 2. in the west. [OE]

west·er·ly (wes′tər-li), *adj., adv.* 1. toward the west. 2. from the west. —**west′er·li·ness,** *n.*

west·ern (wes′tərn), *adj.* 1. toward the west. 2. from the west. 3. of or in the west. 4. **Western, a.** of or in the W part of the United States. **b.** of or in Europe and the Americas. **c.** of or in the Western Hemisphere. —*n. Am., Colloq.* story or motion picture dealing with life in the West, esp. cowboy life. —**west·ern·most** (wes′tərn-mōst′), *adj.*

Western Church, the part of the Catholic Church that acknowledges the Pope as its spiritual leader and follows the Latin Rite.

Western civilization, European and American civilization as contrasted with Oriental civilization.

West·ern·er (wes′tər-nər), *n.* 1. *Am.* person born or living in the W part of the United States. 2. westerner, native or inhabitant of the west.

Western Hemisphere, the half of the world that includes North and South America.

western union, western European union, alliance of the Benelux nations, France, and Great Britain.

West Germany, area of Germany under American, British, and French control after World War II, since 1949 a federal republic. Military occupation ended in 1955.

West Indies, islands between Florida and South America; Greater Antilles, Lesser Antilles, and the Bahamas. —**West Indian.**

West·ing·house (wes′ting·hous′), *n.* George, 1846–1914, American inventor.

West Irian (i·ri·än′), a part of Indonesia, in W New Guinea.

West·min·ster Abbey (west′min′stər), a church in London in which many English kings and famous men are buried.

West Point, *Am.* the training school for officers of the U.S. Army, in SE New York.

West Virginia, an Eastern State of the United States. *Capital:* Charleston. *Abbrev.:* W. Va. —**West Virginian,** *Am.*

west·ward (west′wərd), *adv.* Also, **west′wards.** toward the west. —*adj.* 1. toward the west. 2. west. —*n.* west.

west·ward·ly (west′wərd·li), *adj., adv.* 1. toward the west. 2. of winds, from the west.

wet (wet), *adj.,* **wet·ter, wet·test,** *v.,* **wet** or **wet·ted, wet·ting,** *n.* 1. covered or soaked with water or other liquid: *wet hands.* 2. watery; liquid: *wet paint.* 3. rainy: *a wet day.* 4. *Am.* having or favoring laws that permit making and selling of alcoholic drinks. 5. **be all wet,** *Am., Slang.* be quite wrong. —*v.* make or become wet. —*n.* 1. water or other liquid. 2. wetness; rain. 3. *Am., Colloq.* person who favors laws that permit making and selling of alcoholic drinks. [ME *wett,* pp. of *wete(n),* OE *wǣtan*] —**wet′ness,** *n.* —**wet′tish,** *adj.* —**Syn.** *adj.* 1. moist.

wet·back (wet′bak′), *n.* a Mexican who enters the U.S. illegally, esp. by swimming or wading across the Rio Grande. [< *wet* + *back*]

wet blanket, person or thing that has a discouraging or depressing effect.

wet cell, *Elect.* cell having a free-flowing electrolyte.

āge, cāre, fär; ēqual, tèrm; īce; ōpen, ôrder; pŭt, rüle, ūse; th̬, then; ə=a in about.

weth·er (weth'ər), *n.* a castrated male sheep. [OE]

wet nurse, woman employed to suckle the infant of another.

w.f., wf, *Printing.* wrong font.

whack (hwak), *n.* **1.** *Colloq.* a sharp, resounding blow. **2.** *Slang.* share. **3.** *Am., Slang.* trial or attempt. —*v. Colloq.* strike with a sharp, resounding blow. [? imit.] —**whack'er,** *n.*

whack·ing (hwak'ing), *adj. Colloq.* large; forcible.

whack·y (hwak'i), *adj.* wacky.

whale[1] (hwāl), *n., pl.* **whales** or (*esp.* collectively) **whale,** *v.,* **whaled, whal·ing.** —*n.* **1.** any of various fishlike mammals that are air-breathing and suckle their young. **2.** *Am., Colloq.* something very big, great, impressive, etc. —*v.* hunt and catch whales. [OE *hwæl*]

whale[2] (hwāl), *v.,* **whaled, whal·ing. 1.** beat; whip severely. **2.** *Colloq.* hit hard. [appar. var. of *wale*]

whale·back (hwāl'bak'), *n. Am.* a freight steamer having a rounded upper deck shaped like a whale's back.

whale·boat (hwāl'bōt'), *n.* a long, narrow rowboat, sharp at both ends.

whale·bone (hwāl'bōn'), *n.* **1.** an elastic, horny substance growing in place of teeth in the upper jaw of certain whales and forming a series of thin, parallel plates. **2.** a thin strip of this used for stiffening corsets, dresses, etc.

whal·er (hwāl'ər), *n.* **1.** person who hunts whales. **2.** ship used for whaling.

whal·ing (hwāl'ing), *n.* the hunting and killing of whales.

wharf (hwôrf), *n., pl.* **wharves** (hwôrvz), **wharfs.** platform built on the shore or out from the shore, beside which ships can load and unload. [OE *hwearf*] —**wharf'less,** *adj.*

wharf·age (hwôr'fij), *n.* **1.** the use of a wharf for mooring a ship, storing and handling goods, etc. **2.** the charge made for this. **3.** wharves.

Whar·ton (hwôr'tən), *n.* Edith, 1862–1937, American novelist.

what (hwot; hwut), *pron., pl.* **what,** *adj., adv., conj.* —*pron.* **1.** (as an interrogative pronoun) word used in asking questions about persons or things: *what is your name?, what if I did?* **2.** (as a relative pronoun) **a.** that which; those which; any that: *I know what you mean.* **b.** whatever; anything that: *do what you please.* **c.** the kind of thing or person that; such as: *the old man is not what he was.* **d.** something that: *but he left, and what is more surprising, he left early.* **3.** **and what not,** and all kinds of other things. **4.** **what for,** why. **5.** **what if,** what would happen if. **6.** **what's what,** *Colloq.* the true state of affairs. —*adj.* **1.** (as an interrogative adj.) word used in asking questions about persons or things: *what time is it?* **2.** (as a relative adj.) **a.** that which; those which: *put back what money is left.* **b.** whatever; any that: *take what supplies you will need.* **3.** word used to show surprise, doubt, anger, liking, etc., or to add emphasis: *what foolishness!* —*adv.* **1.** how much; how: *what does it matter?* **2.** partly: *what with the wind and what with the rain, our walk was spoiled.* **3.** word used to show surprise, doubt, anger, liking, etc., to add emphasis: *what happy times!* —*conj.* **1.** *Colloq.* as much as: *he helps me what he can.* **2. but what,** but that. [OE *hwæt*]

what·e'er (hwot·âr'; hwət-), *pron., adj. Poetic.* whatever.

what·ev·er (hwot·ev'ər; hwət-), *pron.* **1.** anything that: *do whatever you like.* **2.** any amount that: *he will give whatever you may need.* **3.** no matter what: *whatever happens, he is safe.* **4.** what, used emphatically in questions: *whatever do you mean?* —*adj.* **1.** any that: *take whatever books you like.* **2.** no matter what: *whatever excuse he makes will not be believed.* **3.** at all: *I see nothing whatever.*

what·not (hwot'not'; hwut-), *n.* stand with several shelves for books, ornaments, etc.

what·so·e'er (hwot'sō·âr'; hwut'-), *pron., adj. Poetic.* whatsoever.

what·so·ev·er (hwot'sō·ev'ər; hwut'-), *pron., adj.* whatever.

wheal (hwēl), *n.* a small burning or itching swelling on the skin. [cf. OE *hwelian* suppurate]

wheat (hwēt), *n.* **1.** the grain of a widely distributed cereal grass, used to make flour. **2.** the plant that it grows on. [OE *hwǣte*] —**wheat'en,** *adj.* —**wheat'less,** *adj.*

whee·dle (hwē'dəl), *v.,* **-dled, -dling. 1.** persuade by flattery, smooth words, caresses, etc.; coax. **2.** get by wheedling. [OE *wǣdlian* beg] —**whee'dler,** *n.* —**whee'dling,** *adj.* —**whee'dling·ly,** *adv.* —**Syn. 1.** cajole, blandish.

wheel (hwēl), *n.* **1.** a round frame turning on a pin or shaft in the center. **2.** any instrument, machine, apparatus, etc., shaped or moving like a wheel: *a spinning wheel, steering wheel.* **3.** anything resembling or suggesting a wheel in shape or movement: *the wheel of fortune.* **4.** *Am., Colloq.* a bicycle. **5.** any force thought of as moving or propelling: *the wheels of the government.* **6. wheels,** machinery. **7. at the wheel,** **a.** at the steering wheel. **b.** in control. **8. wheels within wheels,** complicated circumstances, motives, influences, etc. —*v.* **1.** turn: *he wheeled around suddenly.* **2.** move or perform in a curved or circular direction. **3.** move on wheels: *the workman was wheeling a load of bricks.* —*adj.* of, pertaining to, next to, or containing a wheel. [OE *hwēol*] —**wheeled,** *adj.* —**wheel'less,** *adj.*

wheel·bar·row (hwēl'bar'ō), *n.* frame with a wheel at one end and two handles at the other, used for carrying loads.

wheel·base (hwēl'bās'), **wheel base,** *n.* in automobiles, etc., the distance in inches between the centers of the front and rear axles.

wheel chair, chair mounted on wheels, used esp. by invalids.

wheel·er (hwēl'ər), *n.* **1.** person or thing that wheels. **2.** thing that has a wheel or wheels. **3.** a wheel horse.

wheel·er-deal·er (hwēl'ər·dēl'ər), *n. Am., Slang.* person who delights in bold financial undertakings.

wheel horse, 1. horse nearest to the wheels. **2.** *Am., Colloq.* person who works effectively.

wheel·wright (hwēl'rīt'), *n.* man whose work is making or repairing wheels, carriages, and wagons.

wheeze (hwēz), *v.,* **wheezed, wheez·ing,** *n.* —*v.* **1.** breathe with difficulty and a whistling sound. **2.** make a sound like this: *the old engine wheezed.* **3.** say with a wheeze. —*n.* **1.** a whistling sound caused by difficult breathing. **2.** actor's gag or joke. *Slang.* a trite saying, adage, or story. [? < Scand. *hvǣsa* hiss] —**wheez'er,** *n.* —**wheez'ing·ly,** *adv.* —**wheez'y,** *adj.* —**wheez'i·ly,** *adv.* —**wheez'i·ness,** *n.*

whelk (hwelk), *n.* a mollusk with a spiral shell, used for food in Europe. [OE *weoloc*]

whelm (hwelm), *v.* **1.** overwhelm. **2.** submerge. [akin to OE *-hwelfan,* as in *āhwelfan* cover over]

Whelk
(Shell 2 to
3 in. long)

whelp (hwelp), *n.* **1.** puppy or cub; young dog, wolf, bear, lion, tiger, etc. **2.** a good-for-nothing boy or young man. —*v.* give birth to (whelps). [OE *hwelp*]

when (hwen; *unstressed* hwən), *adv.* at what time: *when will you come?* —*conj.* **1.** at the time that: *rise when one's name is called.* **2.** at any time that: *he is impatient when he is kept waiting.* **3.** at which time; and then: *the dog growled till his master spoke, when he gave a joyful bark.* **4.** although: *you play when you should work.* —*pron.* what time; which time: *since when have you known?* —*n.* the time or occasion: *the when and where of an act.* [OE *hwænne*] ➤ **when.** When-clauses are used in colloquial and substandard English as equivalent to nouns: Substandard: *Welding is when two pieces of metal are heated and made into one.* Written: *Welding is heating two pieces of metal and making them one.*

when·as (hwen·az'; hwən-), *conj. Archaic.* when; while; whereas.

whence (hwens), *adv.* 1. from what place; from where: *whence do you come?* 2. from what source or cause; from what: *whence has he so much wisdom?* —*conj.* from what place, source, cause, etc.: *the country whence he came.* [ME *whennes* < OE *hwanone*]

whence·so·ev·er (hwens'sō-ev'ər), *conj.* from whatever place, source, or cause.

when·e'er (hwen-âr'; hwən-), *conj., adv.* Poetic. whenever.

when·ev·er (hwen-ev'ər), *conj., adv.* when; at whatever time; at any time that.

when·so·ev·er (hwen'sō-ev'ər), *conj., adv.* whenever; at whatever time.

where (hwâr), *adv.* 1. in what place; at what place: *where is he?* 2. to what place: *where are you going?* 3. from what place: *where did you get that story?* 4. in, at, or to which place: *find out where he is going, I don't know where he is.* 5. in, at, or to which: *the house where he was born, the place where he is going.* 6. in what way; in what respect: *where is the harm in trying?* 7. in what position, direction, circumstances, etc.: *where does he stand on the tariff?* —*n.* 1. what place: *where does he come from?* 2. place; scene. —*conj.* 1. in the place in which; at the place at which: *the book is where you left it.* 2. any place to which: *I will go where you go.* 3. in or at which place: *they came to the town, where they stayed for the night.* 4. in any place in which; at any place at which: *use the salve where the pain is felt.* 5. in the case, circumstances, respect, etc., in which: *some people worry where it does no good.* [OE *hwǣr*]

where·a·bouts (hwâr'ə-bouts'), *adv., conj.* where; near what place: *whereabouts can I find a doctor?, we did not know whereabouts we were.* —*n.* Also, **where'a·bout'.** place where a person or thing is: *do you know the whereabouts of the cottage?*

where·as (hwâr-az'), *conj.* 1. on the contrary; but; while: *some children like school, whereas others do not.* 2. considering that; since: *"Whereas the people of the colonies have been grieved and burdened with taxes," etc.* —*n.* document or statement beginning with "Whereas."

where·at (hwâr-at'), *adv., conj.* at what; at which.

where·by (hwâr-bī'), *adv., conj.* by what; by which.

wher·e'er (hwâr-âr'), *conj., adv.* Poetic. wherever.

where·fore (hwâr'fôr; -fōr), *adv.* 1. for what reason; why? 2. for which reason; therefore; so. —*conj.* for what reason; why. —*n.* reason.

where·from (hwâr-from'; -frum'), *adv.* whence.

where·in (hwâr-in'), *adv., conj.* in what; in which; how.

where·in·to (hwâr-in'tü; hwâr'in-tü'), *adv., conj.* into what; into which.

where·of (hwâr-ov'; -uv'), *adv., conj.* of what; of which; of whom.

where·on (hwâr-on'; -ôn'), *adv., conj.* on which; on what.

where·so·e'er (hwâr'sō-âr'), *conj., adv.* Poetic. wheresoever.

where·so·ev·er (hwâr'sō-ev'ər), *conj., adv.* wherever.

where·to (hwâr-tü'), *adv., conj.* 1. to what; to which; where. 2. for what purpose; why.

where·un·to (hwâr-un'tü; hwâr'un-tü'), *adv., conj.* Archaic. whereto.

where·up·on (hwâr'ə-pon'; -pôn'), *adv., conj.* 1. upon what; upon which. 2. at which; after which.

wher·ev·er (hwâr-ev'ər), *conj., adv.* where; to whatever place; in whatever place: *wherever are you going?, sit wherever you like, he will be happy wherever he lives.*

where·with (hwâr-with'; -with'), *adv., conj.* with what; with which. —*pron.* that with which: *"So shall I have wherewith to answer him."* —*n.* wherewithal.

where·with·al (*n.* hwâr'with-ôl; *adv.* hwâr'-with·ôl'), *n.* means, supplies, or money needed: *has she the wherewithal to pay for the trip?* —*adv.* wherewith.

wher·ry (hwer'i), *n., pl. -ries.* 1. a light, shallow rowboat for carrying passengers and goods on rivers. 2. a light rowboat for one person, used for racing. 3. Brit. a broad sailboat, used chiefly on rivers. —**wher'ry·man,** *n.*

whet (hwet), *v., whet·ted, whet·ting, n.* —*v.* 1. sharpen by rubbing: *whet a knife.* 2. make keen or eager; stimulate: *the smell of food whetted my appetite.* —*n.* act of whetting. [OE *hwettan*] —**whet'ter,** *n.*

wheth·er (hweth'ər), *conj.* 1. Whether is a conjunction expressing a choice or an alternative: *it matters little whether we go or stay, he does not know whether to work or play.* 2. either: *whether sick or well, she is always cheerful.* 3. if: *he asked whether he should finish the work.* 4. whether or no, in any case; no matter what happens. [OE *hwether*] ➤ See if for usage note.

whet·stone (hwet'stōn'), *n.* a stone for sharpening knives or tools.

whew (hwū), *interj., n.* exclamation of surprise, dismay, etc.

whey (hwā), *n.* the watery part of milk that separates from the curd when milk sours and becomes coagulated or when cheese is made. [OE *hwǣg*] —**whey'ey, whey'ish, whey'like',** *adj.*

which (hwich), *pron.* 1. word used in asking questions about persons or things: *which seems the best plan?* 2. word used in connecting a group of words with some word in the sentence: *read the book which you have.* 3. the one that; any that: *choose which you like.* 4. a thing that: *and, which is worse, you were late.* 5. which is which, which is one and which is the other. —*adj.* 1. word used in asking questions about persons or things: *which boy won the prize?, which books are yours?* 2. word used in connecting a group of words with some word in the sentence: *be careful which way you turn.* [OE *hwilc*]

which·ev·er (hwich-ev'ər), *pron., adj.* 1. any one that; any that: *take whichever you want.* 2. no matter which: *whichever side wins, I shall be satisfied.*

whiff (hwif), *n.* 1. a slight gust; puff: breath. 2. a slight smell; puff of air having an odor. 3. puff of tobacco smoke. —*v.* 1. blow; puff. 2. puff tobacco smoke from (a pipe, etc.); smoke. —**whiff'er,** *n.*

whif·fet (hwif'it), *n.* 1. U.S. Colloq. an insignificant person or thing. 2. a small dog.

whif·fle (hwif'əl), *v., -fled, -fling.* 1. blow in puffs or gusts. 2. veer; shift. 3. blow lightly; scatter. —**whif'fler,** *n.*

whif·fle·tree (hwif'əl-trē'), *n. Am.* the swinging bar of a carriage or wagon, to which the traces of a harness are fastened. Also, whipple-tree, singletree, swingletree.

Whig (hwig), *n.* 1. member of a former political party in Great Britain that favored reforms and progress. 2. *Am.* an American who favored the Revolution against England. 3. *Am.* member of a political party in the United States that was formed about 1834 in opposition to the Democratic Party. —*adj.* 1. composed of Whigs; having to do with Whigs; like Whigs. 2. being a Whig. —**Whig'gish,** *adj.* —**Whig'gish·ly,** *adv.* —**Whig'gish·ness,** *n.* —**Whig'gism,** *n.*

while (hwil), *n., conj., v., whiled, whil·ing.* —*n.* 1. time; space of time: *the postman came a while ago.* 2. Archaic. a particular time. 3. between whiles, at times; at intervals. 4. the while, during the time. 5. worth one's while, worth time, attention, or effort. —*conj.* 1. during the time that; in the time that; in the same time that: *while I was speaking he said nothing.* 2. as long as: *while the condition exists, it is a menace to everyone.* 3. in contrast with the fact that; although: *while I like the color of the hat, I do not like its shape.* —*v.* pass or spend in some easy, pleasant manner: *the children while away many afternoons on the beach.* [OE *hwil*]

whiles (hwilz), *Archaic or Dial.* —*adv.* 1. sometimes. 2. in the meantime. —*conj.* while.

whi·lom (hwī′ləm), *Archaic.* —*adj.* former. —*adv.* formerly; once. [OE *hwīlum* at times, dative pl. of *hwīl* while]

whilst (hwilst), *conj. Esp. Brit.* while.

whim (hwim), *n.* a sudden fancy or notion; freakish or capricious idea or desire.

whim·per (hwim′pər), *v.* 1. cry with low, broken, mournful sounds: *the sick child whimpered.* 2. complain in a weak way; whine. —*n.* a whimpering cry or sound. —**whim′per·er,** *n.* —**whim′per·ing,** *adj.* —**whim′per·ing·ly,** *adv.*

whim·si·cal (hwim′zə·kəl), *adj.* 1. having many odd notions or fancies; fanciful; odd. 2. full of whims. —**whim′si·cal′i·ty, whim′si·cal·ness,** *n.* —**whim′si·cal·ly,** *adv.* —**Syn.** 2. capricious, notional.

whim·sy, whim·sey (hwim′zi), *n., pl.* -**sies;** -**seys.** 1. an odd or fanciful notion. 2. odd or fanciful humor; quaintness. 3. something showing this. 4. whim.

whine (hwīn), *v.,* whined, whin·ing, *n.* —*v.* 1. make a low, complaining cry or sound. 2. complain in a peevish, childish way. —*n.* 1. a low, complaining cry or sound. 2. a peevish, childish complaint. [OE *hwīnan*] —**whin′er,** *n.* —**whin′ing,** *adj.* —**whin′ing·ly,** *adv.* —**whin′y,** *adj.*

whin·ny (hwin′i), *n., pl.* -**nies,** *v.,* -**nied,** -**nying.** —*n.* the sound that a horse makes. —*v.* make such a sound. [akin to *whine*]

whip (hwip), *n., v.,* whipped *or* whipt, whip·ping. —*n.* 1. thing to whip with, usually a stick with a lash at the end. 2. a whipping motion. 3. dessert made by beating cream, eggs, etc., into a froth. 4. member of a political party who controls and directs the other members in a lawmaking body. —*v.* 1. strike; beat; lash: *he whipped the horse.* 2. move, pull, or pull quickly and suddenly: *he whipped off his coat.* 3. *Am., Colloq.* defeat. 4. beat (cream, eggs, etc.) to a froth. 5. sew with stitches passing over and over an edge. 6. wind closely with thread or string; wind (cord, twine, or thread) around something. 7. fish upon: *whip a stream.* [cf. MDu., MLG *wippe* swing] —**whip′like′,** *adj.* —**whip′per,** *n.* —**Syn.** *n.* 1. scourge, switch. -*v.* 1. scourge, flog, thrash, switch.

whip·cord (hwip′kôrd′), *n.* 1. a strong, twisted cord, sometimes used for the lashes of whips. 2. a strong worsted cloth with diagonal ridges on it.

whip hand, 1. the hand that holds the whip in driving. 2. position of control; advantage.

whip·lash (hwip′lash′), *n.* lash of a whip.

whip·per·snap·per (hwip′ər·snap′ər), *n.* an insignificant person who thinks he is smart or important.

whip·pet (hwip′it), *n.* very swift dog that looks somewhat like a small greyhound, often used in racing. [< *whip* in sense of "move quickly"]

whip·ping (hwip′ing), *n.* 1. a beating; flogging. 2. arrangement of cord, twine, or the like, wound about a thing.

whipping boy, scapegoat.

whipping post, post to which lawbreakers are tied to be whipped.

whip·ple·tree (hwip′əl·trē′), *n.* whiffletree.

whip·poor·will (hwip′ər·wil′; hwip′ər·wil), *n. Am.* an American bird whose call sounds somewhat like its name. It is active at night or twilight. [imit.]

Whippoorwill
(9 to 10 in. long)

whip·saw (hwip′sô′), *n.* a long, narrow saw with its ends held in a frame. —*v. Am.* 1. cut with such a saw. 2. get the better of (a person) no matter what he does. —**whip′saw′er,** *n. Am.*

whip·stitch (hwip′stich′), *v.* sew with stitches passing over and over an edge. —*n.* stitch so made.

whip·stock (hwip′stok′), *n.* handle of a whip.

whir, whirr (hwér), *n., v.,* whirred, whir·ring. —*n.* a noise that sounds like whir-r-r. —*v.* move quickly with such a noise: *the motor whirs.* [cf. Dan. *hvirre* whirl]

whirl (hwérl), *v.* 1. turn or swing round and round; spin: *whirl a top.* 2. move round and round: *the sails of the windmill whirled.* 3. turn about or aside quickly: *he whirled from the push.* 4. move or carry quickly: *we were whirled away in an airplane.* 5. feel dizzy or confused. —*n.* 1. a whirling movement. 2. something that whirls. 3. dizzy or confused condition. 4. a short drive, run, walk, or the like. 5. a rapid round of happenings, parties, etc. [< Scand. *hvirfla < hverfa* turn] —**whirl′er,** *n.*

whirl·i·gig (hwér′li·gig′), *n.* 1. toy that whirls. 2. merry-go-round. 3. something that whirls round and round. [< *whirl + gig*]

whirl·pool (hwérl′pül′), *n.* 1. water whirling round and round rapidly and violently. 2. anything like a whirlpool.

whirl·wind (hwérl′wind′), *n.* 1. current of air whirling violently round and round; whirling windstorm. 2. anything like a whirlwind.

whirl·y·bird (hwér′li·bérd′), *n. Am., Slang.* a helicopter.

whish (hwish), *n.* a soft rushing sound; whiz; swish. —*v.* make this sound.

whisk[1] (hwisk), *v.* 1. sweep or brush (dust, crumbs, etc.) from a surface. 2. move quickly. 3. draw or snatch lightly and rapidly. —*n.* 1. a quick sweep. 2. a light, quick movement. [< Scand. (Sw.) *viska*]

whisk[2] (hwisk), *v.* beat or whip to a froth. [< n.] —*n.* 1. a whisk broom. 2. a wire beater for eggs, cream, etc. [< Scand. *visk* wisp]

whisk broom, a small broom for brushing clothes, etc.

whisk·er (hwis′kər), *n.* 1. Usually, **whiskers.** hair growing on a man's cheeks. 2. a single hair of a man's beard. 3. a long, stiff hair growing near the mouth of a cat, rat, etc. [< *whisk*[2]] —**whisk′ered,** *adj.* —**whisk′er·less,** *adj.*

whis·key, whis·ky (hwis′ki), *n., pl.* -**keys;** -**kies.** a strong alcoholic drink made from grain, as barley, rye, etc. Whiskey is about half alcohol. [ult. < Gaelic *uisgebeatha,* lit., water of life]

whis·per (hwis′pər), *v.* 1. speak very softly and low. 2. speak to in a whisper. 3. tell secretly or privately. 4. make a soft, rustling sound. 5. speak without vibration of the vocal cords. —*n.* 1. a very soft, low spoken sound. 2. something told secretly or privately. 3. a soft, rustling sound. 4. speech without vibration of the vocal cords. [OE *hwisprian*] —**whis′per·er,** *n.* —**whis′per·ing,** *n., adj.* —**whis′per·ing·ly,** *adv.*

whist[1] (hwist), *n.* a card game somewhat like bridge for two pairs of players. [alter. of *whisk*[1] infl. by *whist*[2]]

whist[2] (hwist), *interj.* hush! silence!

whis·tle (hwis′əl), *v.,* -**tled,** -**tling,** *n.* —*v.* 1. make a clear, shrill sound by forcible expulsion of the breath through a small opening made by contracting the lips. 2. make a similar sound by any means: *the engine whistled.* 3. blow or sound a whistle. 4. produce or utter by whistling: *whistle a tune.* 5. call, signal, or direct by a whistle. 6. move with a shrill sound: *the wind whistled around the house.* 7. whistle for, *Colloq.* go without; fail to get. —*n.* 1. the sound made by whistling. 2. an instrument for making whistling sounds. 3. wet one's whistle, *Colloq.* take a drink. [OE *hwistlian*] —**whis′tler,** *n.* —**whis′tling,** *n., adj.* —**whis′tling·ly,** *adv.*

Whis·tler (hwis′lər), *n.* James McNeill, 1834–1903, American painter and etcher. —**Whis·tle·ri·an** (hwis·lir′i·ən), *adj.*

whistle stop, *Am.* a small, insignificant railroad town.

whit (hwit), *n.* a very small bit: *the sick man is not a whit better.* [var. of OE *wiht* thing, wight]

white (hwīt), *n., adj.,* whit·er, whit·est. —*n.* 1. the color of snow or salt, opposite to black. 2. a white coloring matter. 3. **whites,** white clothing. 4. something white; white or colorless part: *the white of an egg, the whites of the eyes.* 5. a white person. —*adj.* 1. having the color of snow or salt; reflecting light without absorbing any of the rays composing it. 2. approaching this color. 3. pale. 4. light-colored: *white wines, white meat.* 5. having a light-colored skin; noting or pertaining to the Caucasian race. 6. silvery; gray: *white* *hair.* **7.** snowy: *a white winter.* **8.** blank: *white space.* **9.** spotless; pure; innocent. **10.** *Am., Colloq.* honorable; trustworthy; fair. **11.** *Esp. Poetic.* blond; fair. **12.** bleed white, use up or take away all of one's money, strength, etc. [OE *hwīt*] —**white′ly,** *adv.* —**white′ness,** *n.*

white ant, a pale-white insect; termite. White ants eat wood and are very destructive to buildings.

white·bait (hwīt′bāt′), *n., pl.* **–bait.** a young herring or sprat an inch or two long; very small fish used for food.

white·cap (hwīt′kap′), *n.* wave with a foaming white crest.

white clover, a kind of clover with white flowers, common in fields and lawns.

white coal, water used as a source of power.

white-col·lar (hwīt′kol′ər), *adj. Am.* of or pertaining to clerical, professional, or business work or workers.

white elephant, 1. anything that is expensive and troublesome to keep and take care of. **2.** any troublesome possession.

white feather, 1. symbol of cowardice. **2.** show the white feather, act like a coward.

white-fish (hwīt′fish′), *n., pl.* **–fish·es** or (*esp. collectively*) **–fish. 1.** a food fish with white or silvery sides, found in lakes and streams. **2.** any of various other whitish fish.

white flag, a plain white flag used as a sign of truce or surrender.

white gold, alloy of gold that looks much like platinum and is used for jewelry, commonly containing gold, nickel, copper, and zinc.

White·hall (hwīt′hôl′), *n.* **1.** an important street in London, where many government offices are located. **2.** the British government or its policies.

white heat, 1. extremely great heat at which things give off a dazzling white light. **2.** state of extremely great activity, excitement, or feeling.

white-hot (hwīt′hot′), *adj.* **1.** white with heat; extremely hot. **2.** very enthusiastic; excited; violent.

White House, The, *Am.* **1.** the official residence or "executive mansion" of the President of the United States, in Washington, D.C. **2.** *Colloq.* office, authority, opinion, etc., of the President of the United States.

white lead, a compound of lead used in making paint; basic carbonate of lead.

white lie, lie about some small matter; polite or harmless lie.

white-liv·ered (hwīt′liv′ərd), *adj.* **1.** cowardly. **2.** pale; unhealthy looking.

white matter, tissue of the brain, spinal cord, etc., that consists chiefly of nerve fibers.

White Mountains, range of the Appalachian Mountains in New Hampshire.

whit·en (hwīt′ən), *v.* make or become white. —**whit′en·er,** *n.* —Syn. bleach, blanch.

white oak, *Am.* **1.** oak of E North America having a light-gray or whitish bark and a hard, durable wood. **2.** any similar species of oak. **3.** the wood of any of these trees.

white pepper, spice made from husked dried pepper berries.

white pine, *Am.* **1.** a tall pine tree of E North America, valued for its soft, light wood. **2.** this wood, much used for building. **3.** any of various similar pines.

white poplar, *Am.* a poplar tree whose leaves have silvery-white down on the under surface.

white potato, *Am.* a very common variety of potato with a whitish inside; Irish potato.

white primary, *U.S.* a primary election held in some Southern States of the United States, in which only white persons are permitted to vote.

White Russia, 1. a Soviet republic in the W Soviet Union. **2.** region in W Russia including this republic and other nearby territory inhabited by the White Russians.

White Russian, 1. Russian living in the W part of the Soviet Union, N of the Ukraine. **2.** Russian who recognizes the former czarist government of Russia as the legal government of that country.

white sauce, sauce made of milk, butter, and flour cooked together.

White Sea, sea in N Soviet Union, part of the Arctic Ocean.

white slave, 1. a woman forced to be a prostitute. **2.** a white person held as a slave. —**white slaver.** —**white slavery.**

white-wash (hwīt′wosh′; -wôsh′), *n.* **1.** liquid for whitening walls, woodwork, etc., usually made of lime and water. **2.** the covering up of faults or mistakes. **3.** anything that covers up faults or mistakes. —*v.* **1.** whiten with whitewash. **2.** cover up the faults or mistakes of. **3.** *Am., Colloq.* defeat without a score for the loser. —**white′wash′er,** *n.*

whith·er (hwith′ər), *adv., conj.* to what place; to which place; where. [OE *hwider*]

whith·er·so·ev·er (hwith′ər·sō·ev′ər), *adv., conj.* wherever; to whatever place.

whit·ing¹ (hwīt′ing), *n., pl.* **–ings** or (*esp. collectively*) **–ing. 1.** a European fish like the cod. **2.** *Am.* the silver hake. **3.** any of several other food fishes. [var. of OE *hwītling*]

whit·ing² (hwīt′ing), *n.* a powdered white chalk, used in making putty, whitewash, and silver polish. [< *white*]

whit·ish (hwīt′ish), *adj.* somewhat white. —**whit′ish·ness,** *n.*

whit·low (hwīt′lō), *n.* abscess on a finger or toe, usually near the nail. [earlier *whitflaw,* prob. < *white* + *flaw*]

Whit·man (hwīt′mən), *n.* Walt, 1819–1892, American poet.

Whit·ney (hwīt′ni), *n.* **1.** Eli, 1765–1825, American who invented the cotton gin. **2.** Mount, peak of the Sierra Nevada mountains, in E California, the highest mountain in the United States.

Whit·sun (hwīt′sən), *adj.* of or pertaining to Whitsunday or Whitsuntide.

Whit·sun·day (hwīt′sun′di; –dā; hwīt′sən·dā′), *n.* the seventh Sunday after Easter; Pentecost. [< *white* + *Sunday*]

Whit·sun·tide (hwīt′sən·tīd′), **Whitsun Tide,** the week beginning with Whitsunday, esp. the first three days.

Whit·ti·er (hwīt′i·ər), *n.* John Greenleaf, 1807–1892, American poet.

whit·tle (hwīt′əl), *v.,* **–tled, –tling. 1.** cut shavings or chips from (wood, etc.) with a knife. **2.** shape by whittling; carve. **3.** whittle down or away, cut down little by little. [earlier *thwittle,* ult. < OE *thwītan* cut] —**whit′tler,** *n.*

whit·y (hwīt′i), *adj.* whitish.

whiz, whizz (hwiz), *n., v.,* whizzed, whizzing. —*n.* **1.** a humming or hissing sound. **2.** *Am., Slang.* a very clever person; expert. —*v.* make a humming or hissing sound; move or rush with such a sound: *an arrow whizzed past his head.* [imit.] —**whiz′zer,** *n.* —**whiz′zing·ly,** *adv.*

who (hü; *unstressed relative* ü), *pron., poss.* **whose,** *obj.* **whom. 1.** (as an interrogative pronoun) **a.** what person or persons: *who is your friend?, who told you?* **b.** what as to character, origin, importance: *who is the man in uniform?* **2.** (as a relative pronoun) **a.** word used in connecting a group of following words with some previous word in the sentence: *the girl who spoke is my best friend, we saw men who were working in the fields.* **b.** the person that; any person that; one that: *who is not for us is against us.* **3.** who's who, **a.** which is one person and which is the other. **b.** which people are important. [OE *hwā*] **➤ who, whom. 1.** *Who* refers to people, to personified objects (a ship, a country), and occasionally to animals: *They have three dogs, who always give us a big welcome.* **2.** In formal English *whom* is always used as the accusative form. In informal English when the *who* stands before a verb or preposition of which it is the object, *who* is the generally accepted form: *Who* [object of *introduce*] *do you introduce to whom* [object of the immediately preceding to]*? No matter who* [object of *meet*] *you*

meet, *the first thing you mention is the weather.*
3. When *who* is the subject of a verb separated from it by other words, the nominative is used: *He made a list of all the writers who* [subject of *were*] *he thought were important in the period.*
4. A verb of which *who* is the subject has the number of the antecedent of the *who: I'm one of the few people who don't* [antecedent *people*] *like to read many books. I'm one who doesn't* [antecedent *one*] *like to read books.*

whoa (hwō; wō), *interj.* stop!

who·dun·it (hü·dun'ĭt), *n. Slang.* story or motion picture dealing with crime and its detection.

who·ev·er (hü·ev'ər), *pron.* **1.** who; any person that: *whoever wants the book may have it.* **2.** no matter who: *whoever else goes hungry, he won't.*

whole (hōl), *adj.* **1.** having all its parts or elements; complete: *a whole set of dishes.* **2.** comprising the full quantity, amount, extent, number, etc.; entire: *a whole melon, a whole year.* **3.** being fully or entirely such: *a whole brother* [by both parents]. **4.** not injured, broken, or defective: *get out of a fight with a whole skin.* **5.** in one piece; undivided: *swallow a thing whole.* **6.** *Math.* not fractional; integral: *a whole number.* **7.** well; healthy. **8.** made out of whole cloth, *Am., Colloq.* entirely false or imaginary. —*n.* **1.** all of a thing; the total: *four quarters make a whole.* **2.** thing complete in itself. **3.** an entire group, collection, system, etc. **4.** as a whole, as one complete thing; altogether. **5.** on the whole, a. considering everything. b. for the most part. [OE *hāl*] —whole′ness, *n.* —Syn. *adj.* **1.** perfect, intact. **2.** total. **4.** unimpaired, uninjured, unbroken. **7.** hale, sound. —*n.* **1.** entirety, aggregate, sum. —Ant. *n.* **1.** portion, part.

whole-heart·ed (hōl′här′tĭd), *adj. Am.* earnest; sincere; hearty; cordial. —whole′-heart′ed·ly, *adv.* —whole′-heart′ed·ness, *n.*

whole note, *Music.* note indicating a tone to be given as much time as four quarter notes; semibreve.

whole number, integer, such as 2, 5, 15, 106, etc.

whole·sale (hōl′sāl′), *n., adj., adv., v.,* –saled, –sal·ing. —*n.* sale of goods in large quantities at a time, usually to retailers rather than to consumers directly. —*adj.* **1.** in large lots or quantities. **2.** selling in large quantities. **3.** broad and general; extensive and indiscriminate. —*adv.* in a wholesale manner. —*v.* **1.** sell in large quantities. **2.** be sold in large quantities. —whol′er, *n.* —whol′sal′er, *n.*

whole·some (hōl′səm), *adj.* **1.** good for the health; healthful: *a wholesome food.* **2.** healthy-looking; suggesting health: *a wholesome face.* **3.** good for the mind or morals; beneficial: *a wholesome book.* —whole′some·ly, *adv.* —whole′some·ness, *n.* —Syn. **1.** salubrious, nourishing.

whole step, whole tone, *Music.* an interval equal to one sixth of an octave, such as D to E.

whole-wheat (hōl′hwēt′), *adj.* made of the entire wheat kernel.

who'll (hül), who will; who shall.

whol·ly (hōl′ĭ), *adv.* to the whole amount or extent; completely; entirely; totally.

whom (hüm), *pron.* the objective case of *who.* ➤ See *who* for usage note.

whoop (hüp; hwüp), *n.* **1.** a loud cry or shout. **2.** cry of an owl, crane, etc.; hoot. **3.** the loud, gasping noise a person with whooping cough makes after a fit of coughing. —*v.* **1.** shout loudly. **2.** hoot. **3.** make a whooping noise. **4.** utter with a whoop or whoops. **5.** whoop it up, *Am., Slang.* make a noisy disturbance. [imit.]

whoop·ee (hwüp′ē; hwüp′ē), *Am., Slang.* —*interj.* a cry expressing merriment or excitement. —*n.* lively festivity.

whoop·ing cough (hüp′ĭng; hüp′–), an infectious disease of children, characterized by fits of coughing that end with a loud, gasping sound.

whooping crane, *Am.* a large white crane having a loud raucous cry.

whoosh (hwüsh), *Colloq.* —*n.* a muffled roar; rushing sound. —*v.* go with such a sound; rush.

whop·per (hwop′ər), *n. Colloq.* **1.** something very large. **2.** a big lie.

whop·ping (hwop′ĭng), *adj. Colloq.* very large; of its kind; huge.

whore (hōr; hôr), *n., v.,* whored, whor·ing. —*n.* prostitute. —*v.* **1.** act as a whore. **2.** have intercourse with whores. **3.** make a whore of; debauch. [OE *hōre*]

whorl (hwėrl; hwôrl), *n.* **1.** *Bot.* circle of leaves or flowers round a stem of a plant. **2.** *Zool.* one of the turns of a spiral shell. **3.** *Anat.* one of the turns in the cochlea of the ear. **4.** anything that circles or turns on or around something else. A person can be identified by the whorls of his fingerprints. [prob. var. of *whirl*] —whorled, *adj.*

Whorl of leaves

whor·tle·ber·ry (hwėr′təl·ber′ĭ), *n., pl.* –ries. *Am.* **1.** a small blackish berry much like the huckleberry. **2.** the shrub that it grows on. [< *whortle* (ult. < OE *horte* whortleberry) + *berry*]

whose (hüz), *pron.* the possessive case of *who* and of *which.*

who·so (hü′sō), *pron. Archaic.* whoever.

Shell showing whorls

who·so·ev·er (hü′sō·ev′ər), *pron.* whoever; anybody who.

why (hwī), *adv., n., pl.* whys, *interj.* —*adv.* **1.** for what cause, reason, or purpose: *why did you do it?, I don't know why I did it.* **2.** for which; because of which: *that is the reason why he failed.* **3.** the reason for which: *that is why he raised the question.* —*n.* cause; reason; purpose: *she tried to find out the whys and wherefores of his behavior.* —*interj.* expression used to show surprise, doubt, etc., or just to fill in. [OE *hwij,* instrumental case of *hwā* who and *hwæt* what]

W.I., West Indies; West Indian.

Wich·i·ta (wich′ə·tō), *n.* city in S Kansas, on the Arkansas River.

wick (wik), *n.* the part of an oil lamp or candle that is lighted. The oil or melted wax is drawn up the wick and burned. [OE *wēoce*] —wick′less, *adj.*

wick·ed (wik′ĭd), *adj.* **1.** bad; evil; sinful: *a wicked person.* **2.** mischievous; playfully sly: *a wicked smile.* **3.** dangerous; savage; vicious: *a wicked horse.* **4.** *Colloq.* unpleasant; severe: *a wicked task.* [< *wick* wicked, prob. ult. < OE *wicca* wizard] —wick′ed·ly, *adv.* —wick′ed·ness, *n.* —Syn. **1.** unrighteous, ungodly, immoral, corrupt, depraved, vile, infamous.

wick·er (wik′ər), *n.* **1.** a slender, easily bent branch or twig. **2.** twigs or branches woven together. Wicker is used in making baskets and furniture. —*adj.* **1.** made of wicker. **2.** covered with wicker. [< Scand. (dial. Sw.) *vikker* willow] —wick′ered, *adj.*

wick·er·work (wik′ər·wėrk′), *n.* **1.** twigs or branches woven together; wicker. **2.** objects made of wicker.

wick·et (wik′ĭt), *n.* **1.** a small door or gate. **2.** a small window or opening. **3.** gate by which a flow of water is regulated. **4.** turnstile in an entrance. **5.** *Croquet. Am.* a wire arch stuck in the ground to knock the ball through. **6.** *Cricket.* a. either of the two sets of sticks that one side tries to hit with the ball. b. the level space between these. c. one batsman's turn. [< AF, ult. < Scand.]

wick·et·keep·er (wik′ĭt·kēp′ər), *n. Cricket.* the player who stands behind the wicket.

wick·ing (wik′ĭng), *n.* material for wicks.

wide (wīd), *adj., wid·er, wid·est, adv., n.* —*adj.* **1.** filling more space from side to side than the usual thing of the same sort; not narrow; broad: *a wide street.* **2.** filling much space from side to side: *the wide ocean.* **3.** extending a certain distance from side to side: *a door three feet wide.* **4.** full; ample; roomy, as clothing. **5.** of great range: *wide reading.* **6.** far or fully open; distended: *stare with wide eyes.* **7.** far from a named point, object, target, etc.: *wide of the truth.* **8.** *Phonet.* uttered with a relatively wide opening of the vocal organs. —*adv.* **1.** to a great or relatively great extent from side to side: *wide apart.* **2.** over an extensive space or region: *far* *and* wide. 3. to the full extent; fully: *open your mouth wide.* 4. aside; astray: *the shot went wide.* —*n.* 1. a wide space or expanse. 2. that which goes wide. [OE *wīd*] —**wide′ly**, *adv.* —**wide′-ness**, *n.* —**wid′ish**, *adj.* —**Syn.** *adj.* 2. extensive, vast, spacious. —**Ant.** *adj.* 1, 2. narrow.

wide-a·wake (wīd′ə·wāk′), *adj.* 1. with the eyes wide open; fully awake. 2. alert; keen; knowing. —**wide′-a·wake′ness**, *n.*

wide-eyed (wīd′īd′), *adj.* with the eyes wide open.

wid·en (wīd′ən), *v.* make or become wide or wider. —**wid′en·er**, *n.*

wide-o·pen (wīd′ō′pən), *adj.* 1. opened as much as possible. 2. lax in the enforcement of laws, esp. those pertaining to the sale of liquor, gambling, and prostitution.

wide·spread (wīd′spred′), **wide·spread-ing** (-ing), *adj.* 1. spread widely. 2. spread over a wide space. 3. occurring in many places or among many persons far apart: *widespread revolt.*

widg·eon (wij′ən), *n., pl.* -eons or (esp. collectively) -eon. any of several kinds of fresh-water ducks, slightly larger than a teal; scaup duck. Also, **wigeon.**

wid·ow (wid′ō), *n.* 1. woman whose husband is dead and who has not married again. 2. *Cards.* an extra hand or part of a hand, such as a hand dealt to the table. —*v.* make a widow of. [OE *widuwe*] —**wid′ow·hood**, *n.*

wid·ow·er (wid′ō·ər), *n.* man whose wife is dead and who has not married again.

widow's mite, a small amount of money given cheerfully by a poor person.

width (width; witth), *n.* 1. how wide a thing is; distance across; breadth: *the room is 12 feet in width.* 2. piece of a certain width: *a width of cloth.*

width·ways (width′wāz′; witth′-), **width-wise** (-wīz′), *adv.* in the direction of the width.

wield (wēld), *v.* 1. hold and use; manage; control: *wield a sword, a pen, power, authority, etc.* 2. exercise authority; govern; rule. [OE *wieldan*] —**wield′a·ble**, *adj.* —**wield′er**, *n.* —**wield′y**, *adj.*

wie·ner (wē′nər), **wie·ner·wurst** (-wērst′), *n. Am.* a small, reddish sausage made of beef and pork mixed together; frankfurter. [< G, Viennese sausage]

wife (wīf), *n., pl.* **wives.** 1. a married woman. 2. *Archaic.* woman. 3. take to wife, marry. [OE *wīf*] —**wife′hood, wife′dom,** *n.* —**wife′less,** *adj.* —**wife′less·ness,** *n.*

wife·ly (wīf′li), *adj.,* -li·er, -li·est. of or like a wife; suitable for a wife.

wig (wig), *n., v.,* **wigged, wig·ging.** —*n.* an artificial covering of hair for the head. —*v.* 1. furnish with a wig or wigs. 2. *Esp. Brit. Colloq.* rebuke; scold. [< *periwig*] —**wigged,** *adj.* —**wig′-less,** *adj.* —**wig′like′,** *adj.*

Judge's wig

wig·eon (wij′ən), *n.* widgeon.

wig·gle (wig′əl), *v.,* -gled, -gling, *n.* —*v.* move with short, quick movements from side to side; wriggle. —*n.* 1. such a movement. 2. a line that wiggles. [cf. Du. *wiggelen*] —**wig′gly,** *adj.* —**Syn.** *v.* squirm, twist.

wig·gler (wig′lər), *n.* 1. person or thing that wiggles. 2. the larva of a mosquito.

wight (wīt), *n. Archaic or Dial.* a human being; person. [OE *wiht*]

Wight (wīt), *n.* Isle of, a small island S of England, in the English Channel; one of the British Isles.

wig·wag (wig′wag′), *v.,* -wagged, -wag·ging, *n.* —*v.* 1. move to and fro. 2. signal by movements of arms, flags, lights, etc.; according to a code. —*n.* 1. such signaling. 2. the message signaled. —**wig′wag′ger,** *n.*

wig·wam (wig′wom; -wôm), *n. Am.* a hut of poles covered with bark, mats, or skins, made by American Indians. [< Algonquian]

Wil·ber·force (wil′bər·fôrs; -fōrs), *n.* William, 1759–1833, English statesman and philan-

thropist who urged the abolition of the slave trade.

wild (wīld), *adj.* 1. living or growing in the forests or fields; not tamed; not cultivated: *a wild animal, a wild flower.* 2. with no people living in it: *wild land.* 3. not civilized; savage: *wild tribes.* 4. not checked; not restrained: *a wild rush for the ball.* 5. not in proper control or order: *wild hair.* 6. boisterous: *wild boys.* 7. dissipated: *he was wild in his youth.* 8. violently excited; frantic: *wild with rage.* 9. violent: *a wild storm.* 10. rash; crazy: *wild schemes.* 11. extreme; fantastic: *wild notions.* 12. *Colloq.* very eager. 13. far from the mark. 14. **run wild,** live or grow without restraint. —*n.* 1. an uncultivated or desolate region or tract; waste; desert. 2. wilds, wild country. —*adv.* in a wild manner; to a wild degree. [OE *wilde*] —**wild′ish,** *adj.* —**wild′ly,** *adv.* —**wild′ness,** *n.* —**Syn.** *adj.* 1. undomesticated. 2. uninhabited. 3. barbarous. 10. reckless. 11. queer, bizarre. 12. enthusiastic, excited. —**Ant.** *adj.* 1. tame, cultivated.

wild boar, a wild hog of Europe, S Asia, and N Africa.

wild carrot, a common weed with a thin woody root and lacy white flowers.

wild·cat (wīld′kat′), *n., adj., v.,* -cat·ted, -cat·ting. —*n.* 1. a lynx or other wild animal like a cat, but larger. 2. a fierce fighter. 3. *Am., Colloq.* locomotive and tender operating without other cars. 4. *Am.* well drilled for oil or gas in a region where none has hitherto been found. —*adj.* 1. *Am.* using very unsound business methods: *wildcat banking.* 2. speculative; reckless: *wildcat schemes.* 3. running without control or without a schedule: *a wildcat engine.* 4. *Am.* not authorized by proper union officials; precipitated by small groups or local unions: *a wildcat strike.* —*v. Am.* drill wells in regions not known to contain oil. —**wild′cat′ter,** *n. Am.* —**wild′cat′ting,** *n., adj. Am.*

Wilde (wīld), *n.* Oscar (Fingal O'Flahertie Wills), 1854–1900, British writer.

wil·de·beest (wil′də·bēst′), *n.* gnu. [< Du., wild beast]

wil·der·ness (wil′dər·nis), *n.* 1. a wild place; region with no people living in it. 2. a bewildering mass or collection: *a wilderness of streets.* [< ME *wilderne* wild, OE *wildēorn,* ult. < *wilde* wild + *dēor* animal] —**Syn.** 1. desert, waste.

wild-eyed (wīld′īd′), *adj.* having wild eyes; staring wildly or angrily.

wild·fire (wīld′fīr′), *n.* 1. fire hard to put out, formerly used in warfare. 2. like wildfire, very rapidly.

wild flower, 1. any flowering plant that grows in the woods, fields, etc.; uncultivated plant. 2. flower of such a plant.

wild fowl, birds, ordinarily hunted, such as wild ducks or geese, partridges, quail, etc.

wild-goose chase, useless search or attempt.

wild·life (wīld′līf′), *n.* wild animals and plants collectively, usually those native to an area.

wild oat, 1. *Am.* an oatlike grass growing as a weed in meadows, etc. 2. wild oats, youthful dissipation. 3. sow one's wild oats, indulge in youthful dissipation before settling down in life.

wild West, Wild West, *Am.* the western United States during pioneer days.

wild·wood (wīld′wŏŏd′), *n.* forest.

wile (wīl), *n., v.,* wiled, wil·ing. —*n.* 1. a trick to deceive; cunning way. 2. subtle trickery; slyness; craftiness. —*v.* 1. coax; lure; entice: *the sunshine wiled me from work.* 2. wile away, while away; pass easily or pleasantly. [OE *wigle* magic] —**Syn.** *n.* 1. artifice, stratagem, ruse.

wil·ful (wil′fəl), *adj.* willful. —**wil′ful·ly,** *adv.* —**wil′ful·ness,** *n.*

Wil·hel·mi·na I (wil′hel·mē′nə; wil′ə·mē′-nə), 1880–1962, queen of the Netherlands 1890–1948.

will[1] (wil; *unstressed* wəl), *auxiliary v., pres. indic. sing., 1st and 3rd pers.* will, *2nd* will or (*Archaic*) wilt, *3rd will, pl.* will; *pt. 1st* would, *2nd* would or (*Archaic*) wouldst, *3rd* would, *pl.* would; *pp.* would or (*Obs.*) wold; *imperative*

āge, câre, fär; ēqual, tėrm; īce; ōpen, ôrder; pùt, rüle, ūse; ᵺ, then; ə=*a* in about.

and infinitive lacking. **1.** am going to; is going to; are going to: *he will come tomorrow.* **2.** am willing to; is willing to; are willing to: *I will go if you do.* **3.** wish; desire: *we cannot always do as we will.* **4.** be able to; can: *the pail will hold four gallons.* **5.** must: *you will do it at once!* **6.** do often or usually: *she will read for hours at a time.* [OE *willan*] ➤ See **shall** for usage note.

will² (wil), *n., v.,* willed, will·ing. —*n.* **1.** the power of the mind to decide and do; deliberate control over thought and action: *strength of will.* **2.** purpose; determination: *the will to live.* **3.** wish; desire: *what is your will?* **4.** *Law.* **a.** a legal statement of a person's wishes about what shall be done with his property after he is dead. **b.** document containing such a statement. **5.** feeling toward another: *good will, ill will.* **6. at will,** whenever one wishes. **7. do the will of,** obey. **8. with a will,** with energy and determination. —*v.* **1.** decide by using power of the mind to decide and do; use the will: *she willed to keep awake.* **2.** influence or try to influence by deliberate control over thought and action: *she willed the person in front of her to turn around.* **3.** determine; decide: *fate has willed it otherwise.* **4.** give by a will: *will a house to someone.* [OE] —will′a·ble, *adj.* —will′er, *n.* —will′less, *adj.* —Syn. *n.* **2.** resolution, decision. **3.** inclination, preference, choice. —*v.* **3.** purpose, intend. **4.** bequeath.

willed (wild), *adj.* having a certain kind of will: *strong-willed.*

will·ful (wil′fəl), *adj.* **1.** wanting or taking one's own way; stubborn. **2.** done on purpose; intended: *willful murder, willful waste.* Also, **wilful.** —will′ful·ly, *adv.* —will′ful·ness, *n.* —Syn. **1.** obstinate, headstrong, perverse. **2.** deliberate, intentional.

Wil·liam I (wil′yəm), **1.** (*William the Conqueror*) 1027?–1087, duke of Normandy who conquered England at the battle of Hastings in 1066 and was king of England 1066–1087. **2.** 1797–1888, king of Prussia 1861–1888 and German emperor 1871–1888.

William II, 1. (*William Rufus*) 1056?–1100, king of England 1087–1100. **2.** 1859–1941, German emperor 1888–1918.

William III, (*William of Orange, Prince of Orange*) 1650–1702, king of England 1689–1702. He ruled with his wife Mary II from 1689 until her death in 1694.

Wil·liams (wil′yəmz), *n.* Roger, 1604?–1683, English clergyman who founded Rhode Island.

wil·lies (wil′iz), *n. Am., Colloq.* spell of nervousness.

will·ing (wil′ing), *adj.* **1.** ready; consenting. **2.** cheerfully ready. —will′ing·ly, *adv.* —will′ing·ness, *n.* —Syn. **1.** disposed, inclined.

will-o'-the-wisp (wil′ə·thə·wisp′), *n.* **1.** a moving light appearing at night over marshy places, caused by combustion of marsh gas. **2.** thing that deceives or misleads by luring on.

wil·low (wil′ō), *n.* **1.** tree or shrub with tough, slender branches and narrow leaves. **2.** its wood. The branches of most willows bend easily and are used to make furniture. —*adj.* made of willow. [ult. < OE *welig*] —wil′low·like′, *adj.*

wil·low·y (wil′ō·i), *adj.* **1.** like a willow; slender; supple; graceful. **2.** having many willows.

wil·ly-nil·ly (wil′i·nil′i), *adv.* willingly or not; with or against one's wishes. —*adj.* undecided. [< will I (*he, ye*), nill I (*he, ye*); nill not will, OE *nyllan* < *ne* not + *willan*]

Wil·ming·ton (wil′ming·tən), *n.* city in NE Delaware.

Wil·no (vil′nō), *n.* Polish name of Vilna.

Wil·son (wil′sən), *n.* **1.** (James) Harold, born 1916, British prime minister since 1964. **2.** (Thomas) Woodrow, 1856–1924, the 28th president of the United States, 1913–1921. **3.** Mount, peak in SW California; astronomical observatory.

Wilson Dam, a power dam across the Tennessee River in NW Alabama.

wilt¹ (wilt), *v.* **1.** become limp and drooping; wither. **2.** lose strength, vigor, assurance, etc. **3.** cause to wilt. —*n.* a wilting. [? alter. of *welk;* cf. MDu., MLG *welken*]

wilt² (wilt), *v. Archaic.* will.

Wil·ton (wil′tən), or **Wilton carpet,** *n.* a kind of velvety carpet.

wil·y (wil′i), *adj.,* wil·i·er, wil·i·est. using subtle tricks to deceive; crafty; cunning; sly. —wil′i·ly, *adv.* —wil′i·ness, *n.* —Syn. artful, subtle, designing, insidious.

Wim·ble·don (wim′bəl·dən), *n.* city in SE England, near London; international tennis matches.

wim·ple (wim′pəl), *n., v.,* -pled, -pling. —*n.* cloth for the head arranged in folds about the head, cheeks, chin, and neck, worn by nuns and formerly by other women. —*v.* **1.** cover or muffle with a wimple. **2.** ripple or cause to ripple. [OE *wimpel*]

Wimple

win (win), *v.,* won or (*Archaic*) wan, won, win·ning, *n.* —*v.* **1.** get victory or success, esp. by striving or effort: *the tortoise won in the end.* **2.** get victory or success in: *he won the race.* **3.** get by victory: *win a bet.* **4.** get by effort; gain: *win fame.* **5.** gain the favor of; persuade: *the speaker won his audience.* **6.** get the love of; persuade to marry. **7.** get to; reach, often by effort: *win the summit of a mountain.* —*n. Colloq.* act or fact of winning; success; victory. [OE *winnan*] —Syn. *v.* **4.** secure, obtain, earn, achieve, attain.

wince (wins), *v.,* winced, winc·ing, *n.* —*v.* draw back suddenly; flinch slightly. —*n.* act of wincing. [< var. of OF *guencir* < Gmc.] —winc′er, *n.* —Syn. *v.* shrink, recoil.

winch (winch), *n.* **1.** a machine for lifting or pulling, turned by a crank. **2.** handle of a revolving machine. [OE *wince*] —winch′er, *n.*

Win·ches·ter (win′ches′tər; -chis·tər), or **Winchester rifle,** *n. Trademark.* a kind of repeating rifle, first made and used about 1866.

wind¹ (*n.* wind, *Archaic and Poetic* wīnd; *v.* wind), *n., v.,* wind·ed, wind·ing. —*n.* **1.** air in motion. The wind varies in force from a slight breeze to a strong gale. **2.** a strong wind; gale. **3.** gas in the stomach or bowels. **4.** a wind instrument. **5.** air filled with some smell: *the deer got wind of the hunter and ran off.* **6.** power of breathing; breath: *a runner needs good wind.* **7.** empty, useless talk. **8.** winds, wind instruments. **9. get wind of,** find out about; get a hint of. **10. in the wind,** happening; about to happen; impending. **11. take the wind out of one's sails,** take away one's advantage, argument, etc., suddenly or unexpectedly. —*v.* **1.** expose to wind or air. **2.** follow by scent; smell. **3.** put out of breath; cause difficulty in breathing. **4.** let recover breath. [OE] —wind′less, *adj.* —Syn. *n.* **1.** breeze, zephyr. **2.** blast, hurricane, cyclone.

wind² (wind), *v.,* wound or (*Rare*) wind·ed, wind·ing, *n.* —*v.* **1.** move this way and that; move in a crooked way; change direction; turn: *a stream winding through the woods, we wound our way through the streets.* **2.** proceed in a roundabout or indirect manner: *wind into power.* **3.** make (one's way) by indirect or insidious procedure: *wind one's way into control.* **4.** introduce insidiously: *the spy wound herself into his confidence.* **5.** fold, wrap, or place about something: *the mother wound her arms about the child.* **6.** roll into a ball or on a spool: *wind yarn.* **7.** twist or turn around something: *the vine winds round a pole.* **8.** make (some machine) go by turning some part of it: *wind a clock.* **9.** be wound: *this clock winds easily.* **10. wind up, a.** end; settle; conclude. **b.** make the movements that a baseball pitcher does just before pitching the ball. **c.** roll or coil; wind completely. —*n.* a bend; turn; twist. [OE *windan*] —wind′a·ble, *adj.* —wind′er, *n.* —wind′ing·ly, *adv.* —Syn. *v.* **1.** curve, crook, twist, bend. **4.** insinuate.

wind·age (win′dij), *n.* **1.** power of the wind to turn a missile from its course. **2.** distance that a missile is turned from its course by the wind.

wind·bag (wind′bag′), *n.* **1.** bag full of wind. **2.** *Slang.* person who talks a great deal but does not say much.

Winch. Arrows show direction

wind·blown (wind'blōn'), *adj.* **1.** blown by the wind. **2.** with the hair cut short and brushed forward.

wind·borne (wind'bôrn'; –bōrn'), *adj.* carried by the wind, as pollen or seed.

wind·break (wind'brāk'), *n. Am.* shelter from the wind.

wind·break·er (wind'brāk'ər), *n. Am.* **1.** a short sports jacket of wool, leather, etc., having a tight-fitting band at the waist and cuffs, used for outdoor wear. **2.** Windbreaker, a trademark for this jacket.

wind·bro·ken (wind'brō'kən), *adj.* having the power of breathing injured; having the heaves.

wind·ed (win'did), *adj.* **1.** out of breath. **2.** having wind or breath (as specified): *short-winded.* **—wind'ed·ness,** *n.*

wind·fall (wind'fôl'), *n.* **1.** fruit blown down by the wind. **2.** an unexpected piece of good luck.

wind·ing (wīn'ding), *n.* **1.** act of one that winds. **2.** bend; turn. **3.** something that is wound or coiled. **—***adj.* bending; turning. **—wind'ing·ly,** *adv.*

winding sheet, shroud.

wind instrument, *Music.* instrument sounded by blowing air into it. Horns, flutes, and trombones are wind instruments.

wind·jam·mer (wind'jam'ər), *n. Am., Colloq.* **1.** a sailing ship. **2.** member of its crew.

wind·lass (wind'ləs), *n.* machine for pulling or lifting things; winch. [< ME *windel* (< *wind*[2]) + Scand. *āss* pole]

wind·mill (wind'mil'), *n.* **1.** a mill or machine operated by the wind. Windmills are mostly used to pump water. **2.** tilt at windmills, fight against an imaginary opponent; be a quixotic reformer.

Windmill for pumping water

win·dow (win'dō), *n.* **1.** an opening in the wall or roof of a building, boat, car, etc., to let in light or air. **2.** such an opening with the frame, panes of glass, etc., that fill it. **3.** any opening that suggests a window. **—***v.* furnish with windows. [< Scand. *vindauga* < *vindr* wind + *auga* eye] **—win'dowed,** *adj.* **—win'dow·less,** *adj.*

win·dow·pane (win'dō·pān'), *n.* piece of glass in a window.

window sash, frame for the glass in a window.

window seat, bench built into the wall of a room, under a window.

win·dow·shop (win'dō·shop'), *v.,* **–shopped, –shop·ping.** examine or gaze desirously at merchandise in store windows without buying. **—win'dow·shop'per,** *n.* **—win'dow·shop'ping,** *adj., n.*

window sill, piece of wood or stone across the bottom of a window.

wind·pipe (wind'pīp'), *n.* the passage from the throat to the lungs; trachea.

wind·row (wind'rō'), *n.* **1.** row of hay raked together to dry before being made into heaps. **2.** any similar row, as of sheaves of grain, made for the purpose of drying; row of dry leaves, dust, etc., swept together by wind or the like. **—***v.* arrange in a windrow or windrows. **—wind'row'er,** *n.*

wind·shield (wind'shēld'), *n. Am.* in an automobile, a sheet of glass above the dashboard to keep off the wind.

wind sleeve or **sock,** a cone-shaped sleeve mounted on a pole or the like, showing the direction of the wind.

Wind·sor (win'zər), *n.* **1.** Duke of, Edward VIII. **2.** the family name of the royal house of Great Britain since 1917. **3.** town in S England, where Windsor Castle, chief residence of British sovereigns, is located.

Windsor chair, a kind of comfortable wooden chair, with a spindle back and slanting legs.

Windsor tie, *Am.* a wide necktie of soft silk, tied in a loose bow.

wind·storm (wind'stôrm'), *n.* storm with much wind but little or no rain.

wind·up (wīnd'up'), *n.* **1.** a winding up. **2.** end; close; conclusion. **3.** *Baseball.* series of movements made by a pitcher just before pitching the ball.

wind·ward (wind'wərd; *Naut.* win'dərd), *adv.* toward the wind. **—***adj.* **1.** on the side toward the wind. **2.** in the direction from which the wind is blowing. **—***n.* **1.** the side toward the wind. **2.** direction from which the wind is blowing.

Wind·ward Islands (wind'wərd), the S part of the Lesser Antilles in the West Indies.

wind·y (win'di), *adj.,* **wind·i·er, wind·i·est. 1.** having much wind. **2.** made of wind; unsubstantial; empty: *windy talk.* **3.** talking a great deal; voluble. **4.** like wind. **5.** exposed to the wind. **6.** causing gas in the stomach or intestines. **—wind'i·ly,** *adv.* **—wind'i·ness,** *n.*

wine (wīn), *n., v.,* **wined, win·ing. —***n.* **1.** the juice of grapes after it has fermented and contains alcohol. **2.** the fermented juice of other fruits or plants: *currant wine, dandelion wine.* **3.** something that cheers or intoxicates as wine does. **4.** the color of red wine. **—***v.* entertain with wine. [ult. < L *vinum*] **—wine'less,** *adj.*

wine·bib·ber (wīn'bib'ər), *n.* person who drinks much wine. **—wine'bib'bing,** *n., adj.*

wine cellar, 1. cellar where wine is stored. **2.** wine stored there.

wine·col·ored (wīn'kul'ərd), *adj.* dark purplish-red.

wine gallon, the standard gallon of the United States; 231 cu. in.

wine·glass (wīn'glas'; –gläs'), *n.* a small drinking glass for wine.

wine·grow·er (wīn'grō'ər), *n.* person who raises grapes and makes wine. **—wine'grow'ing,** *n., adj.*

wine press or **presser, 1.** machine for pressing the juice from grapes. **2.** vat in which grapes are trodden in the process of making wine.

win·er·y (wīn'ər·i), *n., pl.* **–er·ies.** *Am.* place where wine is made.

Wine·sap, wine·sap (wīn'sap'), *n. Am.* a variety of red winter apple of the United States.

wine·skin (wīn'skin'), *n.* container made of the nearly complete skin of a goat, hog, etc., used in some countries for holding wine.

wing (wing), *n.* **1.** the part of a bird, insect, etc., by which it flies; corresponding part in a bird, insect, etc., that does not fly. **2.** anything like a wing in shape or use. **3.** one of the major lifting and supporting surfaces, or airfoils, of an airplane. **4.** *Humorous.* foreleg or arm. **5.** part of a building that sticks out sidewise from the main part. **6.** either of the spaces to the right or left of the stage in a theater. **7.** *U.S.* an administrative and tactical unit of the Air Force. **8.** *Mil.* that part of a military force to the right or left of the main body. **9. wings,** insignia awarded by the U.S. Air Force to men who have qualified as pilots, navigators, etc. **10.** part of an organization; faction: *the radicals of a political group are called the left wing.* **11.** flying; winged flight. **12. on the wing, a.** flying. **b.** moving; active; busy. **c.** going away. **13.** player whose position is on either side of the center in certain games. **14. take wing,** fly away. **15. under the wing of,** under the protection or sponsorship of. **—***v.* **1.** fly. **2.** fly through. **3.** supply with wings. **4.** able to fly; give speed to: *terror winged his steps.* **5.** wound in the wing or arm. **6. wing its way,** fly. [< Scand. *vængr*] **—wing'-less,** *adj.* **—wing'like',** *adj.*

wing case, either of the hardened front wings of certain insects.

wing chair, a comfortable upholstered chair with side pieces as high as the back.

winged (wingd, *esp. Poetic* wing'id *for 1 and 2;* wingd *for 3 and 4*), *adj.* **1.** having wings. **2.** moving as if on wings; swift; rapid. **3.** of birds.

āge, cāre, fär; ēqual, tėrm; īce; ōpen, ôrder; pùt, rüle, ūse; tħ, then; ə=a in about.

disabled in a wing. 4. *Colloq.* of persons, wounded in the arm or some other nonvital part.

wing·spread (wing′spred′), *n.* distance between the tips of the wings when they are spread.

wink (wingk), *v.* 1. close the eyes and open them again quickly. 2. close and open quickly. 3. close one eye and open it again as a hint or signal. 4. move or affect by winking: *wink back tears.* 5. flicker; twinkle: *the stars winked.* 6. wink at, pretend not to see. —*n.* 1. a winking. 2. a hint or signal given by winking. 3. a flickering; twinkle. 4. a very short time: *I didn't sleep a wink.* 5. forty winks, a short sleep; nap. [OE *wincian*]

wink·er (wingk′ər), *n.* 1. person or thing that winks. 2. *Colloq.* eyelash.

win·kle (wing′kəl), *n.* a sea snail used for food. [OE *wincle*, as in *pinewincle* periwinkle]

win·ner (win′ər), *n.* person or thing that wins.

win·ning (win′ing), *adj.* 1. that wins. 2. charming; attractive. —*n.* 1. act of one that wins. 2. Usually, **winnings.** what is won; money won. —**win′ning·ly,** *adv.*

Win·ni·peg (win′ə·peg), *n.* 1. city in S Canada. 2. Lake, lake in S Canada.

win·now (win′ō), *v.* 1. blow off the chaff from (grain); drive or blow away (chaff). 2. blow chaff from grain. 3. sort out; separate; sift. 4. fan (with wings); flap (wings). —*n.* 1. a winnowing. 2. device for winnowing grains, etc. [OE *windwian* < *wind* wind[1]] —**win′now·er,** *n.*

win·some (win′səm), *adj.* charming; attractive; pleasing. [OE *wynsum* < *wynn* joy] —**win′some·ly,** *adv.* —**win′some·ness,** *n.*

win·ter (win′tər), *n.* 1. the coldest of the four seasons; last season of the year. 2. the last period of life; period of decline, dreariness, or adversity. —*adj.* of, pertaining to, or characteristic of winter. —*v.* 1. pass the winter. 2. keep, feed, or manage during winter. [OE] —**win′ter·er,** *n.* —**win′ter·less,** *adj.*

win·ter·green (win′tər·grēn′), *n.* 1. *Am.* a small evergreen plant of North America with bright-red berries and aromatic leaves. An oil made from its leaves (**oil of wintergreen** or **wintergreen oil**) is used in medicine and candy. 2. this oil. 3. its flavor.

win·ter·ize (win′tər·īz), *v.,* **-ized, -iz·ing.** make (an automobile, etc.) ready for operation or use during the winter.

win·ter·kill (win′tər·kil′), *v. Am.* kill by or die from exposure to cold weather. —**win′ter·kill′ing,** *adj., n.*

winter solstice. See solstice.

win·ter·time (win′tər·tīm′), **win·ter·tide** (-tīd′), *n.* winter.

winter wheat, wheat planted in the autumn and ripening in the following spring or summer.

Win·throp (win′thrəp), *n.* 1. **John,** 1588–1649, governor of Massachusetts. 2. his son, **John,** 1606–1676, governor of Connecticut.

win·try (win′tri), **win·ter·y** (win′tər·i), *adj.,* **-tri·er, -tri·est;** **-ter·i·er, -ter·i·est.** of or pertaining to winter; like winter: *a wintry sky, a wintry manner.* —**win′tri·ly,** *adv.* —**win′tri·ness,** *n.*

win·y (wīn′i), *adj.* 1. of, pertaining to, or characteristic of wine. 2. tasting, smelling, or looking like wine. 3. affected by wine.

wipe (wīp), *v.,* **wiped, wip·ing,** *n.* —*v.* 1. rub with paper, cloth, etc., in order to clean or dry: *wipe the table.* 2. take (away, off, or out) by rubbing: *wipe away your tears.* 3. remove: *the rain wiped out the footprints.* 4. rub or draw (something) over a surface. 5. wipe out, remove, esp. by death; destroy completely. —*n.* 1. act of wiping. 2. *Colloq.* a sweeping stroke or blow. 3. *Slang.* handkerchief. [OE *wīpian*] —**wip′er,** *n.*

wire (wīr), *n., adj., v.,* **wired, wir·ing.** —*n.* 1. metal drawn out into a thread. 2. such metal as a material. 3. a long piece of such metal used for electrical transmission, as in electric lighting, telephones, etc. 4. telegraph: *he sent a message by wire.* 5. *Am., Colloq.* telegram. 6. get under the wire, *Am.* arrive or finish just before

it is too late. 7. pull wires, *Am., Colloq.* a. direct the actions of others secretly. b. use secret influence to accomplish one's purposes. —*adj.* made of or consisting of wire. —*v.* 1. furnish with wire: *wire a house for electricity.* 2. fasten with wire. 3. catch by a wire or wires. 4. *Am., Colloq.* telegraph: *wire a birthday greeting.* [OE *wīr*] —**wir′a·ble,** *adj.* —**wired,** *adj.* —**wire′-like′,** *adj.* —**wir′er,** *n.*

wire gauge, device for measuring the diameter of wire, the thickness of metal sheets, etc., usually a disk with different-sized notches in it.

wire-haired (wīr′hārd′), *adj.* having coarse, stiff hair: *a wire-haired fox terrier.*

wire·less (wīr′lis), *adj.* 1. having no wire; operated without wire or wires: *wireless telegraphy, wireless telephony.* 2. *Esp. Brit.* radio. —*n.* 1. radio. 2. message sent by radio. —*v. Esp. Brit.* send or transmit by radio. —**wire′less·ly,** *adv.*

wire·pho·to (wīr′fō′tō), *n.* 1. method for transmitting photographs by reproducing a facsimile through electric signals. 2. a photograph transmitted in this fashion.

wire puller, *Am., Colloq.* person who uses secret influence to accomplish his purposes.

wire pulling, *Am., Colloq.* the use of secret influence to accomplish a purpose.

wire recorder, device for recording sound magnetically on a fine steel wire, the sound impulses from the microphone being actuated by an electromagnet. The sounds are reproduced as the magnetized wire moves past a receiver.

wire recording, a reproduction of voices, music, etc., made on a wire recorder.

wire tapping, the making of a secret connection with telephone or telegraph wires to find out the messages sent over them. —**wire tapper.**

wir·ing (wīr′ing), *n.* system of wires to carry an electric current.

wir·y (wīr′i), *adj.,* **wir·i·er, wir·i·est.** 1. made of wire. 2. like wire. 3. lean, strong, and tough. —**wir′i·ly,** *adv.* —**wir′i·ness,** *n.*

wis (wis), *v. Archaic.* know. [< *iwis* certainly (taken as *I wis*), OE *gewiss*]

Wis., Wisc., Wisconsin.

Wis·con·sin (wis·kon′sən), *n.* a Middle Western State of the United States. *Capital:* Madison. *Abbrev.:* Wis. or Wisc.

wis·dom (wiz′dəm), *n.* 1. knowledge and good judgment based on experience; being wise. 2. wise conduct. 3. wise sayings or teachings. 4. scholarly knowledge. 5. something wise; wise act or saying. [OE *wisdōm* < *wis* wise] —**wis′dom·less,** *adj.* —**Syn.** 1. sagacity, sapience. 2. prudence, discretion. 4. learning, erudition, sapience.

wisdom tooth, the back tooth on either side of each jaw, ordinarily appearing between the ages of 17 and 25.

wise[1] (wīz), *adj.,* **wis·er, wis·est.** 1. having or showing knowledge and good judgment: *a wise judge, wise plans.* 2. having knowledge or information: *we are none the wiser for his explanations.* 3. learned; erudite. 4. *Slang.* cognizant; aware. [OE *wīs*] —**wise′ly,** *adv.* —**wise′ness,** *n.* —**Syn.** 1. sagacious, judicious, prudent, discreet, sensible, sapient, sage. —**Ant.** 1. foolish.

wise[2] (wīz), *n.* 1. way of proceeding; manner. 2. respect; degree: *in no wise.* [OE *wīse*]

-wise, *suffix.* 1. in a —— manner, as in *anywise* and *likewise.* 2. in a ——ing manner, as in *slantwise.* 3. in the characteristic way of a ——. *Clockwise* means in the way the hands of a clock go. 4. in the direction of the ——, as in *lengthwise.* 5. special meanings, as in *sidewise.* [< *wise*[2]]

wise·a·cre (wīz′ā′kər), *n.* person who thinks that he knows everything. [< MDu. *wijssegger* soothsayer < G]

wise·crack (wīz′krak′), *n., v. Am., Slang.* a snappy comeback; smart remark. —**wise′crack′er,** *n.*

wish (wish), *v.* 1. have a desire for; be glad to have, do, etc.; want: *wish aid, wish money.* 2. have or express a desire: *he wished for a new house.* 3. desire (something) for (someone); desire that (someone) shall be or have; have a hope for; express a hope for: *we wish all men health, I wish you a Happy New Year.* **4.** wish on, *Colloq.* pass on to; foist on. —*n.* **1.** a turning of the mind toward the doing, having, getting, etc., of something; desire or longing. **2.** expression of a wish. **3.** thing wished for: *the girl got her wish.* [OE *wȳscan*] —wish′er, *n.* —wish′-less, *adj.*

wish·bone (wish′bōn′), *n.* the forked bone in the front of the breastbone in poultry and other birds.

wish·ful (wish′fəl), *adj.* having or expressing a wish; desiring; desirous. —wish′ful·ly, *adv.* —wish′ful·ness, *n.*

wishful thinking, believing something to be true that one wishes or wants to be true.

wish·y-wash·y (wish′i·wosh′i; -wôsh′i), *adj.* **1.** thin and weak; watery. **2.** lacking in substantial qualities; feeble; inferior.

wisp (wisp), *n.* **1.** a small bundle; small bunch: *a wisp of hay.* **2.** a small tuft, lock, or portion of anything: *a wisp of smoke.* **3.** a little thing: *a wisp of a girl.* **4.** will-o′-the-wisp. **5.** a whisk broom. [cf. W Frisian *wisp*] —wisp′y, wisp′ish, wisp′like′, *adj.*

wist (wist), *v. Archaic.* pt. and pp. of **wit.**

wis·te·ri·a (wis·tir′i·ə), **wis·tar·i·a** (-tār′-i·ə), *n. Am.* a climbing shrub with large clusters of purple, yellow, or white flowers. [after C. *Wistar*, scientist]

wist·ful (wist′fəl), *adj.* **1.** longing; yearning. **2.** pensive; melancholy. —wist′ful·ly, *adv.* —wist′ful·ness, *n.*

wit[1] (wit), *n.* **1.** the power to perceive quickly and express cleverly ideas that are unusual, striking, and amusing. **2.** person with such power. **3.** understanding; mind; sense: *have wit enough to earn a living.* **4.** wits, mental faculties or senses: *out of one's wits with fright.* **5.** at one's wit's end, not knowing what to do or say. [OE *witt*] —Syn. **1.** humor. **3.** intelligence.

wit[2] (wit), *v.,* pres. 1st pers. wot, 2nd pers. wost, 3rd pers. wot, pl. wit; pt. and pp. wist; ppr. wit·ting. **1.** *Archaic.* know. **2. to wit,** that is to say; namely. [OE *witan*]

witch (wich), *n.* **1.** woman supposed to be under the influence of evil spirits and to have magic power. **2.** an ugly old woman. **3.** *Colloq.* a charming or fascinating girl or woman. —*v.* **1.** use the power of a witch on. **2.** charm; fascinate; bewitch. —*adj.* of a witch. [OE *wicce*] —witch′-like′, *adj.*

witch·craft (wich′kraft′; -kräft′), *n.* what a witch does or can do; magic power or influence.

witch doctor, medicine man, esp. among African tribes.

witch·er·y (wich′ər·i; wich′ri), *n., pl.* -er·ies. **1.** witchcraft; magic. **2.** charm; fascination.

witch hazel, *Am.* **1.** shrub of E North America that has yellow flowers in the fall or winter after the leaves have fallen. **2.** lotion for cooling and soothing the skin, made from the bark and leaves of this shrub.

witch hunt, *U.S. Slang.* persecuting or defaming (a person) to gain a political advantage.

witch·ing (wich′ing), *adj.* bewitching; magical; enchanting. —witch′ing·ly, *adv.*

with (with; with), *prep.* **1.** in the company of: *come with me.* **2.** among: *they will mix with the crowd.* **3.** having, wearing, carrying, etc.: *a man with brains, a telegram with bad news.* **4.** by means of; by using: *cut meat with a knife.* **5.** using; showing: *work with care.* **6.** as an addition to; added to: *do you want sugar with your tea?* **7.** in relation to: *they are friendly with us.* **8.** in regard to: *we are pleased with the house.* **9.** in proportion to: *their power increased with their number.* **10.** because of: *shake with cold.* **11.** in the keeping or service of: *leave the dog with me.* **12.** in the region, sphere, experience, opinion, or view of: *high taxes are unpopular with many people.* **13.** at the same time as: *with this battle the war ended.* **14.** in the same direction as: *shadows move with the sun.* **15.** on the side of; for: *I am with you on that question.* **16.**

from: *part with a thing.* **17.** against: *the English fought with the Germans.* **18.** receiving; having been allowed: *I went with his permission.* **19.** in spite of: *with all his weight he was not a strong man.* [OE, against]

with·al (with·ôl′; with-), *Archaic.* —*adv.* with it all; as well; besides; also. —*prep.* with.

with·draw (with·drô′; with-), *v.,* -drew, -drawn, -draw·ing. **1.** draw back or away: *withdraw one's hand from a hot stove.* **2.** take back; remove: *worn-out paper money is withdrawn from use by the government.* **3.** go away: *she withdrew from the room.* —with·draw′al, with·draw′ment, *n.* —with·draw′er, *n.* —Syn. **2.** recall, retract. **3.** leave, depart.

withe (with; with; with), *n.* **1.** a willow twig. **2.** any tough, easily bent twig suitable for binding things together. [OE *withthe*]

with·er (with′ər), *v.* **1.** lose or cause to lose freshness, vigor, etc.; dry up; shrivel. **2.** cause to feel ashamed or confused. [< *weather*] —with′er·ing·ly, *adv.*

with·ers (with′ərz), *n.pl.* the highest part of a horse's or other animal's back, behind the neck.

with·hold (with·hōld′; with-), *v.,* -held, -hold·ing. **1.** refuse to give: *withhold one's consent.* **2.** hold or keep back: *withhold soldiers from attack.* —with·hold′er, *n.* —with·hold′-ment, *n.*

with·in (with·in′; with-), *prep.* **1.** inside the limits of; not beyond: *within the city.* **2.** in or into the inner part of; inside of: *within the body, within a house.* **3.** at or to some amount or degree not exceeding: *come within a dollar of.* **4.** in the course or period of: *within one's lifetime.* **5.** not transgressing: *within reason, within the law.* —*adv.* **1.** in or into the inner part; inside: *they went within.* **2.** in the mind; inwardly: *keep one's thoughts within.*

with·out (with·out′; with-), *prep.* **1.** with no; not having; free from; lacking: *without a home, without food.* **2.** so as to omit, avoid, or neglect: *she walked past without noticing us.* **3.** free from; excluding: *without exception.* **4.** outside of; beyond: *without the city.* —*adv.* **1.** in or into a space outside: *stand without.* **2.** on the outside; outwardly: *they were waiting without.* **3.** lacking (something implied): *eat what is here or go without (food).* —*conj. Dial.* unless.

with·stand (with·stand′; with-), *v.,* -stood, -stand·ing. stand against; hold out against; oppose, esp. successfully. —Syn. resist, endure.

wit·less (wit′lis), *adj.* lacking sense; stupid; foolish. —wit′less·ly, *adv.* —wit′less·ness, *n.*

wit·ness (wit′nis), *n.* **1.** person or thing able to give evidence; person who saw something happen. **2.** person who swears to tell the truth in a court of law. **3.** evidence; testimony. **4.** person writing his name on a document to show that he saw the maker sign it. **5. bear witness,** be evidence; give evidence; testify. —*v.* **1.** see; perceive: *he witnessed the accident.* **2.** testify to; give evidence of. **3.** give evidence; testify. **4.** sign (a document) as a witness. [OE *witnes* knowledge < *witt*[1]] —wit′ness·er, *n.*

witness stand, *Am.* place where a witness stands or sits to give evidence in a law court.

wit·ti·cism (wit′ə·siz·əm), *n.* a witty remark. [< *witty*, on model of *criticism*]

wit·ting·ly (wit′ing·li), *adv.* knowingly.

wit·ty (wit′i), *adj.,* -ti·er, -ti·est. full of wit; clever and amusing. [OE *wittig*] —wit′ti·ly, *adv.* —wit′ti·ness, *n.* —Syn. facetious, droll.

wive (wīv), *v.,* wived, wiv·ing. **1.** marry a woman. **2.** take as a wife. [OE *wīfian*]

wives (wīvz), *n.* pl. of **wife.**

wiz·ard (wiz′ərd), *n.* **1.** man supposed to have magic power; sorcerer. **2.** conjurer; juggler. **3.** *Colloq.* a very clever person; expert. [ult. < *wise*[1]] —wiz′ard·like′, *adj.* —wiz′ard·ly, *adj.*

wiz·ard·ry (wiz′ərd·ri), *n.* magic; magic skill.

wiz·ened (wiz′ənd), *adj.* dried up; withered; shriveled. [pp. of *wizen*, OE *wisnian*]

wk., **1.** pl. wks. week. **2.** work.

w.l., wave length.

āge, cãre, fär; ēqual, tērm; īce; ōpen, ôrder; pút, rüle, ūse; th, then; ə=a in about.

WNW, W.N.W., between west and north-west.

wob·ble (wob′əl), v., –bled, –bling, n. —v. 1. move unsteadily from side to side; shake; tremble. 2. be uncertain, unsteady, or inconstant; waver. —n. a wobbling motion. Also, **wabble.** [cf. LG wabbeln] —**wob′bler,** n. —**wob′bling,** adj. —**wob′bling·ly,** adv. —**wob′bly,** adj.

Wo·den (wō′dən), n. the most important Anglo-Saxon god, corresponding to Odin in Norse mythology.

woe, wo (wō), n. great grief, trouble, or distress. —interj. an exclamation of grief, trouble, or distress. [OE wā, interj.] —**Syn.** n. sorrow.

woe·be·gone, wo·be·gone (wō′bi·gôn′; –gon′), adj. looking sad, sorrowful, or wretched.

woe·ful, wo·ful (wō′fəl), adj. 1. full of woe; sad; sorrowful; wretched. 2. pitiful. 3. of wretched quality. —**woe′ful·ly, wo′ful·ly,** adv. —**woe′ful·ness, wo′ful·ness,** n. —**Syn.** 1. mournful, distressed, miserable.

woke (wōk), v. pt. and pp. of wake[1].

wo·ken (wō′kən), v. Archaic and Dial. pp. of wake[1].

wold (wōld), n. high, rolling country, bare of woods. [OE weald a wood]

wolf (wŭlf), n., pl. wolves, v. —n. 1. a carnivorous wild animal somewhat like a dog, and belonging to the same family. 2. a cruel, greedy person. 3. Slang. man who possesses a special talent for and interest in enticing members of the opposite sex. —v. 1. hunt wolves. 2. eat greedily. [OE wulf] —**wolf′-ish,** adj. —**wolf′ish·ly,** adv. —**wolf′ish·ness,** n. —**wolf′like′,** adj.

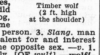

Timber wolf
(2 ft. high
at the shoulder)

Wolfe (wŭlf), n. Thomas, 1900–1938, American novelist.

wolf·hound (wŭlf′hound′), n. a large dog of any of various breeds once used in hunting wolves.

wol·fram (wŭl′frəm), n. 1. Chem. a metallic element, W, used in making steel and for electric lamp filaments; formerly called tungsten. It has stable and radioactive isotopes. 2. wolframite. [< G].

wolf·ram·ite (wŭl′frəm·īt), n. an ore consisting of compounds of wolfram with iron and manganese.

wolf′s-bane, wolfs·bane (wŭlfs′bān′), n. a poisonous plant with yellow flowers, a kind of aconite.

Wol·sey (wŭl′zi), n. Thomas, 1475?–1530, English cardinal and statesman.

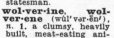

Wolverine (2 to 3 ft.
long, without the tail)

wol·ver·ine, wol·ver·ene (wŭl′vər·ēn′), n. 1. a clumsy, heavily built, meat-eating animal of northern regions, related to the weasel; glutton. 2. its fur. [earlier wolvering < wolf]

wolves (wŭlvz), n. pl. of wolf.

wom·an (wŭm′ən), n., pl. wom·en, adj. —n. 1. the adult human female. 2. women as a group; the average woman. 3. woman's nature. 4. a wife. 5. a female servant. —adj. of, pertaining to, or characteristic of women. [OE wīfman < wīf woman + man human being] —**wom′an·less,** adj. ➤ See man for discussion.

wom·an·hood (wŭm′ən·hud), n. 1. condition or time of being a woman. 2. character or qualities of a woman. 3. women as a group.

wom·an·ish (wŭm′ən·ish), adj. 1. characteristic of a woman. 2. imitating a woman. —**wom′an·ish·ly,** adv. —**wom′an·ish·ness,** n.

wom·an·kind (wŭm′ən·kīnd′), n. the female sex; women.

wom·an·like (wŭm′ən·līk′), adj. 1. like a woman; womanly. 2. suitable for a woman.

wom·an·ly (wŭm′ən·li), adj. 1. like a woman. 2. as a woman should be. 3. suitable for a woman. —**wom′an·li·ness,** n.

woman of the world, woman who knows people and customs, and is tolerant of both.

woman's rights, social, political, and legal rights for women, equal to those of men.

woman suffrage, 1. the political right of women to vote. 2. women's votes. —**wom′an-suf′frage,** adj. —**wom′an-suf′fra·gist,** n.

womb (wüm), n. 1. the organ of the body that holds and nourishes the young till birth; uterus. 2. place containing or producing anything. [OE wamb]

wom·bat (wom′bat), n. an Australian animal that looks like a small bear. A female wombat has a pouch for carrying her young. [< Australian lang.]

Wombat
(ab. 2½ ft. long)

wom·en (wim′ən), n., pl. of woman.

wom·en·folk (wim′ən·fōk′), **wom·en·folks** (–fōks′), n.pl. women.

won (wun), v. pt. and pp. of win.

won·der (wun′dər), n. 1. a strange and surprising thing or event: see the wonders of a city, it is a wonder he turned down the offer. 2. the feeling caused by what is strange and surprising: stare in open-mouthed wonder. —v. 1. feel wonder: wonder at a thing. 2. be surprised or astonished: I shouldn't wonder if he wins the prize. 3. be curious; be curious about; think about; wish to know: I wonder what happened. [OE wundor] —**won′der·er,** n. —**won′der·ing,** adj. —**won′der·ing·ly,** adv.

won·der·ful (wun′dər·fəl), adj. causing wonder; marvelous; remarkable. —**won′der·ful·ly,** adv. —**won′der·ful·ness,** n. —**Syn.** surprising, astonishing, extraordinary, phenomenal, curious.

won·der·land (wun′dər·land′), n. a land full of wonders.

won·der·ment (wun′dər·mənt), n. wonder; surprise.

won·drous (wun′drəs), adj. wonderful. —adv. wonderfully. —**won′drous·ly,** adv. —**won′-drous·ness,** n.

wont (wunt; wōnt), adj. accustomed. —n. custom; habit. [orig. pp., ult. < OE wunian be accustomed]

won't (wōnt; wunt), will not.

wont·ed (wun′tid; wōn′-), adj. accustomed; customary; usual. —**wont′ed·ly,** adv. —**wont′-ed·ness,** n

woo (wü), v. 1. make love to; seek to marry. 2. make love; court. 3. seek to win; try to get: woo fame. 4. try to persuade; urge. [OE wōgian] —**woo′er,** n. —**woo′ing·ly,** adv.

wood (wŭd), n. 1. the hard substance beneath the bark of trees and shrubs. 2. trees cut up for use. 3. thing made of wood. 4. cask; barrel; keg. 5. Music. a. a wooden wind instrument or such instruments collectively. b. woods, the wood winds of an orchestra. 6. Often, woods, a large number of growing trees; forest. —adj. made of wood. —v. 1. supply with wood; get wood for. 2. get supplies of wood. 3. plant with trees; reforest. [OE wudu] —**wood′ed,** adj. —**wood′less,** adj. ➤ Woods gives trouble because though plural in form it is really singular (or collective) in meaning. In informal and colloquial usage people speak of a woods. Formal usage keeps the word strictly plural or uses a wood.

wood alcohol, a poisonous, inflammable liquid often made by distilling wood; methyl alcohol. It is used as a solvent, fuel, etc.

wood·bine (wŭd′bīn′), n. 1. honeysuckle. 2. the Virginia creeper, a climbing vine with bluish-black berries. [OE wudu-bind(e) < wudu wood + binde wreathe]

American woodcock
(nearly 1 ft. long, including the long bill)

wood·chuck (wŭd′chuk′), n. Am. a North American marmot; the ground hog. Woodchucks grow fat in summer and sleep in their holes in the ground all winter. [< Algonquian; infl. by wood]

wood·cock (wŭd′kok′), n., pl. –cocks or

(*esp. collectively*) —**cock.** a small game bird with a long bill and short legs.

wood·craft (wŭd′kraft′; -kräft′), *n.* **1.** knowledge about how to get food and shelter in the woods; skill in hunting, trapping, finding one's way, etc. **2.** art of making things from wood. **3.** forestry. —**wood′crafts′man,** *n.*

wood·cut (wŭd′kut′), **wood block,** *n.* **1.** an engraved block of wood to print from. **2.** a print from such a block.

wood·cut·ter (wŭd′kut′ər), *n. Am.* man who cuts down trees or chops wood. —**wood′cut′ting,** *n. Am.*

wood·en (wŭd′ən), *adj.* **1.** made of wood. **2.** stiff; awkward. **3.** dull; stupid. —**wood′en·ly,** *adv.* —**wood′en·ness,** *n.*

wood engraving, 1. art or process of making woodcuts. **2.** a woodcut. —**wood engraver.**

wood·en·head·ed (wŭd′ən·hed′id), *adj. Colloq.* dull; stupid. —**wood′en·head′ed·ness,** *n.*

wooden horse, the Trojan horse.

wood·en·ware (wŭd′ən·wâr′), *n.* containers, utensils, etc., made of wood. Pails, tubs, and rolling pins are woodenware.

wood·land (*n.* wŭd′land′, -lənd; *adj.* wŭd′lənd), *n.* land covered with trees. —*adj.* of or in the woods; pertaining to woods.

wood·land·er (wŭd′lən·dər), *n.* person who lives in the woods.

wood·lark (wŭd′lärk′), *n.* a European lark closely related to the skylark.

wood·man (wŭd′mən), *n., pl.* -men. **1.** man who cuts down trees. **2.** person who lives in the woods.

wood note, a musical sound made by a bird or animal of the forest.

wood·peck·er (wŭd′pek′ər), *n.* a bird with a hard, pointed bill for pecking holes in trees to get insects.

wood·pile (wŭd′pīl′), *n.* pile of wood, esp. wood for fuel.

wood pulp, wood made into pulp for making paper.

Woodpecker (ab. 9 in. long)

wood·shed (wŭd′shed′), *n.* shed for storing wood.

woods·man (wŭdz′mən), *n., pl.* -men. **1.** man used to life in the woods and skilled in hunting, fishing, trapping, etc. **2.** lumberman.

wood sorrel, plant with sour juice and with leaves composed of three heart-shaped leaflets.

woods·y (wŭd′zi), *adj. Am.* of or like the woods.

wood tar, a dark, sticky substance obtained from wood by distillation.

wood thrush, *Am.* thrush common in the thickets and woods of eastern North America.

wood turning, the shaping of pieces of wood by using a lathe. —**wood turner.**

wood wind (wind), *Music.* **1.** wood winds, wooden wind instruments of an orchestra, as clarinets, bassoons, etc. **2.** any one of them. —**wood′-wind′,** *adj.*

wood·work (wŭd′wèrk′), *n.* things made of wood; wooden parts inside of a house, such as doors, stairs, moldings, and the like. —**wood′work′er,** *n.* —**wood′work′ing,** *n., adj.*

wood·worm (wŭd′wèrm′), *n.* worm or larva that is bred in wood or bores in wood.

wood·y (wŭd′i), *adj.,* wood·i·er, wood·i·est. **1.** having many trees; covered with trees. **2.** consisting of wood. **3.** like wood; like that of wood. —**wood′i·ness,** *n.*

woof (wŭf), *n.* **1.** the threads running from side to side across a woven fabric. See the picture under warp. **2.** fabric; cloth; texture. [OE *ōwef*]

woof·er (wŭf′ər), *n.* a loud-speaker designed esp. to reproduce low bass sounds.

wool (wŭl), *n.* **1.** the soft, curly hair or fur of sheep and some other animals. **2.** short, thick, curly hair. **3.** something like wool. **4.** yarn, cloth, or garments made of wool. **5. pull the wool over one's eyes,** *Am., Colloq.* deceive or trick one. —*adj.* made of wool. [OE *wull*]

wool·en, *esp. Brit.* **wool·len** (wŭl′ən), *adj.* **1.** made of wool. **2.** of or having to do with wool or

cloth made of wool. —*n.* **woolens,** cloth or clothing made of wool.

wool·gath·er·ing (wŭl′gath′ər·ing; -gath′-ring), *n.* absorption in thinking or daydreaming; absent-mindedness. —*adj.* inattentive; absent-minded; dreamy. —**wool′gath′er·er,** *n.*

wool·grow·er (wŭl′grō′ər), *n.* person who raises sheep for their wool. —**wool′grow′ing,** *n.*

wool·ly (wŭl′i), *adj.,* -li·er, -li·est, *n., pl.* -lies. —*adj.* Also, **wooly. 1.** consisting of wool. **2.** like wool. **3.** covered with wool or something like it. —*n.* **1.** *Am., W.* a sheep. **2.** *Colloq.* article of clothing made from wool. —**wool′li·ness,** *n.*

wool·sack (wŭl′sak′), *n.* **1.** bag of wool. **2.** cushion on which the Lord Chancellor sits in the British House of Lords. **3.** office of Lord Chancellor.

wool·y (wŭl′i), *adj.,* wool·i·er, wool·i·est. woolly. —**wool′i·ness,** *n.*

wooz·y (wüz′i; wŭz′i), *adj. Slang.* muddled.

Worces·ter (wŭs′tər), *n.* **1.** city in C Massachusetts. **2. Joseph Emerson,** 1784–1865, American lexicographer.

word (wèrd), *n.* **1.** a sound or a group of sounds that has meaning and is an independent unit of speech. We speak words when we talk. **2.** the writing or printing that stands for a word. *Bat, bet, bit, bot,* and *but* are words. **3.** a short talk: *may I have a word with you?* **4.** Often, **words.** speech: *honest in word and deed.* **5.** a brief expression: *a word of praise.* **6.** command; order: *his word was law.* **7.** signal: *the word for tonight is "the King."* **8.** promise: *the boy kept his word.* **9.** news: *no word has come from the battle front.* **10. words,** angry talk; quarrel; dispute. **11. words,** the text of a song as distinguished from the notes. **12. the Word, a.** Often, **the Word of God.** the Bible. **b.** the thought and will of God as shown by Christ. **13. by word of mouth,** by spoken words; orally. **14. in a word,** briefly. **15. word for word,** in the exact words. —*v.* put into words: *word a question.* [OE] —**word′less,** *adj.*

word·age (wèrd′ij), *n.* words collectively.

word·book (wèrd′bŭk′), *n.* **1.** list of words for some special purpose; dictionary; vocabulary. **2.** libretto.

word element, *Gram.* a form of a word (English or other) used for combining with other words or word elements, as *psycho-* (from Greek *psyche*) in *psychoanalysis;* combining form.

word·ing (wèr′ding), *n.* way of saying a thing; choice and use of words.

word of honor, a solemn promise.

word order, *Gram.* the grammatically meaningful sequence of words in a sentence, phrase, etc. In English the grammatical word order for statements is subject + verb + object, as in *John hit the ball, the ball hit John.*

Words·worth (wèrdz′wèrth; -wèrth), *n.* William, 1770–1850, English poet.

word·y (wèr′di), *adj.,* word·i·er, word·i·est. using too many words. —**word′i·ly,** *adv.* —**word′i·ness,** *n.* —**Syn.** verbose, prolix, long-winded. —**Ant.** terse, concise.

wore (wôr; wōr), *v.* pt. of **wear.**

work (wèrk), *n., v.,* worked or wrought, working, *adj.* —*n.* **1.** effort in doing or making something: *hard work.* **2.** something to do; occupation; employment: *he is out of work.* **3.** something made or done; result of effort: *a work of art.* **4.** that on which effort is put; task: *she did her work at a desk.* **5.** *Physics.* **a.** transference of energy from one body or system to another. **b.** that which is accomplished by a force when it acts through a distance. **6.** fortification. **7.** an engineering structure. **8. works** (*often sing. in use*), place for doing some kind of work; factory. **9. works,** the moving parts of a machine or device: *the works of a watch.* **10. works,** righteous deeds. **11. at work,** working. **12. make short work of,** do or get rid of quickly. —*v.* **1.** do work; labor: *most people must work for a living.* **2.** be employed: *he works at an airplane factory.* **3.** carry on operations in (districts, etc.): *the salesman worked the eastern States.* **4.** put effort on: *he worked his farm with success.* **5.** act;

operate, esp. effectively: *this pump will not work, the plan worked.* 6. put into operation; use; manage: *work a scheme.* 7. cause to do work: *he works his men long hours.* 8. treat or handle in making; knead; mix: *work dough.* 9. make, get, do, or bring about by effort: *he worked his way through college.* 10. move as if with effort: *his face worked.* 11. bring about; cause; do: *the plan worked harm.* 12. go slowly or with effort: *the ship worked to windward.* 13. come or become (up, round, loose, etc.): *the clay has worked up through the crushed stone on the tennis court, the window catch has worked loose.* 14. form; shape: *he worked a silver dollar into a bracelet.* 15. influence; persuade: *work men to one's will.* 16. move; stir; excite: *don't work yourself into a temper.* 17. solve: *work all the problems on the page.* 18. *Colloq.* flatter or trick (a person) to get something: *work a friend for a loan.* 19. ferment: *yeast makes beer work.* 20. make or decorate by needlework. 21. **work in,** put in. 22. **work off,** get rid of. 23. **work on** or **upon,** try to persuade or influence. 24. **work out,** a. plan; develop. b. solve; find out. c. use up. d. give exercise to; practice. e. accomplish. f. result. 25. **work up,** a. plan; develop. b. excite; stir up. —*adj.* of, for, or pertaining to work: *a work horse.* [OE *weorc*] —**work′a·bil′i·ty, work′a·ble·ness,** *n.* —**work′less,** *adj.* —**Syn.** *n.* 1. exertion, labor, toil, industry. 3. product, achievement, feat, deed. —*v.* 1. toil, drudge, strive. 5. perform. 6. execute. 11. accomplish, effect. 14. fashion, mold.

work·a·day (wėr′kə·dā′), *adj.* of working days; practical; commonplace; ordinary.

work·bench (wėrk′bench′), *n.* table at which a mechanic or artisan works.

work·book (wėrk′bŭk′), *n.* 1. book containing outlines for the study of some subject, questions to be answered, etc.; book in which a student does parts of his written work. 2. book containing rules for doing certain work. 3. book for notes of work planned or work done.

work·day (wėrk′dā′), **working day,** *n.* 1. day for work; day that is not Sunday or a holiday. 2. part of a day during which work is done. —*adj.* workaday.

work·er (wėr′kər), *n.* 1. person or thing that works. 2. bee, ant, wasp, or other insect that works for its community. —**work′er·less,** *adj.* —**Syn.** 1. laborer, toiler, artisan, craftsman.

work·house (wėrk′hous′), *n.* 1. *Am.* place where petty criminals are kept and made to work. 2. *Brit.* house where very poor people are lodged and set to work.

work·ing (wėr′king), *n.* 1. method or manner of work; operation; action. 2. act or process of working. 3. Usually, **workings.** parts of a mine, quarry, tunnel, etc., where work is being done. —*adj.* 1. that works. 2. used in working. 3. operating successfully. 4. used to operate with or by: *a working majority.*

work·man (wėrk′mən), **work·ing·man** (wėr′king·man′), *n.,* pl. **-men.** 1. worker. 2. man who works with his hands or with machines. —**work′man·ly,** *adj., adv.*

work·man·like (wėrk′mən·līk′), *adj.* skillful; well-done. —*adv.* skillfully.

work·man·ship (wėrk′mən·ship′), *n.* 1. the art or skill in a worker or his work. 2. quality or manner of work. 3. the work done.

work of art, a creative work, esp. in the arts, done or made with great skill, as a painting, statue, etc.

work·out (wėrk′out′), *n. Colloq.* 1. *Am.* exercise; practice. 2. trial; test.

work·peo·ple (wėrk′pē′pəl), *n.pl. Esp. Brit.* people who work, esp. those who work with their hands or with machines.

work·room (wėrk′rüm′; -rům′), *n.* room where work is done.

work·shop (wėrk′shop′), *n.* 1. shop where work is done. 2. course of study, discussion, etc., in a particular field: *a writers' workshop.*

work·ta·ble (wėrk′tā′bəl), *n.* 1. table at which one works. 2. table holding utensils and materials for work, such as one holding sewing materials.

work·wom·an (wėrk′wům′ən), *n.,* pl. **-women.** 1. a woman worker. 2. woman who works with her hands or with machines.

world (wėrld), *n.* 1. the earth. 2. a particular division of the earth: *the New World.* 3. the earth, with its inhabitants, affairs, etc., during a particular period: *the ancient world.* 4. any sphere, realm, or domain, with all that pertains to it: *the insect world.* 5. a particular class of mankind, with common interests, aims, etc.: *the world of fashion.* 6. all people; the human race; the public: *the whole world knows it.* 7. the things of this life and the people devoted to them: *man of the world.* 8. star; planet. 9. any time, condition, or place of life: *heaven is in the world to come.* 10. all things; everything; the universe. 11. any very great expanse: *the world of waters.* 12. a great deal; very much; large amount: *the rest did her a world of good.* 13. the course of affairs: *how goes the world with you?* 14. **come into the world,** be born. 15. **for all the world,** a. for any reason, no matter how great. b. in every respect; exactly. [OE *weorold*]

World Court, court made up of representatives of various nations and having the power to settle certain disputes between nations.

world island, *Geopolitics.* the land mass which constitutes Asia, Africa, and Europe.

world·ling (wėrld′ling), *n.* a worldly person.

world·ly (wėrld′li), *adj.,* **-li·er, -li·est,** *adv.* —*adj.* 1. of or pertaining to this world; not of heaven. 2. caring much for the interests and pleasures of this world. —*adv.* in a worldly manner. —**world′li·ness,** *n.* —**Syn.** *adj.* 1. earthly, mundane.

world·ly-mind·ed (wėrld′li·mīn′did), *adj.* caring much for the interests and pleasures of this world. —**world′ly-mind′ed·ness,** *n.*

world·ly-wise (wėrld′li·wīz′), *adj.* wise about the ways and affairs of this world.

world series, world's series, *Am., Baseball.* series of games played each fall between the winners of the two major league championships, to decide the professional championship of the United States.

World War, 1. Also, **World War I.** war in Europe, Asia, Africa, and elsewhere, from July 28, 1914 to Nov. 11, 1918. The United States, Great Britain, France, Russia, and their allies were on one side; Germany, Austria-Hungary, and their allies were on the other side. 2. Also, **World War II.** war from September 1, 1939 to August 14, 1945, beginning as a war between Great Britain, France, and Poland on one side and Germany on the other, ultimately involving most of the world. The chief conflict was between Great Britain, the United States, and Russia on one side and Germany, Italy, and Japan on the other.

world-wea·ry (wėrld′wir′i), *adj.* weary of this world; tired of living.

world-wide (wėrld′wīd′), *adj.* spread throughout the world. —**world′-wide′ly,** *adv.*

worm (wėrm), *n.* 1. any of numerous small, slender, crawling or creeping animals, usually soft-bodied and legless. 2. something like a worm in shape or movement, such as the thread of a screw. 3. **worms,** disease caused by worms in the body. —*v.* 1. move like a worm; crawl or creep like a worm. 2. work or get by persistent and secret means. 3. remove worms from. [OE *wyrm*] —**worm′er,** *n.* —**worm′less,** *adj.* —**worm′like′,** *adj.* —**worm′i·ness,** *n.*

worm-eat·en (wėrm′ēt′ən), *adj.* 1. eaten into by worms. 2. worn-out; worthless; out-of-date.

worm gear, 1. a worm wheel. 2. a worm wheel and an endless screw together. By a worm gear the rotary motion of one shaft can be transmitted to another shaft at right angles to it.

Worm gear

worm·hole (wėrm′hōl′), *n.* hole made by a worm. —**worm′holed′,** *adj.*

Worms (wėrmz; *Ger.* vôrms), *n.* city in W Germany, on the Rhine. At the **Diet of Worms,** in

1521, Martin Luther was asked to renounce his beliefs.

worm wheel, wheel with teeth that fit into a revolving screw.

worm·wood (wẽrm′wu̇d′), *n.* 1. a bitter plant used in medicine, absinthe, etc. 2. something bitter or extremely unpleasant. [< OE *wermōd,* infl. by *worm, wood*]

worn (wôrn; wōrn), *v.* pp. of **wear.** —*adj.* 1. damaged by use: *worn rugs.* 2. tired; wearied: *a worn face.*

worn-out (wôrn′out′; wōrn′-), *adj.* 1. used until no longer fit for use. 2. fatigued.

wor·ri·ment (wẽr′i·mənt), *n. Colloq.* 1. a worrying. 2. worry; anxiety.

wor·ri·some (wẽr′i·səm), *adj.* 1. causing worry. 2. inclined to worry. —**wor′ri·some·ly,** *adv.*

wor·ry (wẽr′i), *v.,* -ried, -ry·ing, *n., pl.* -ries. —*v.* 1. feel anxious or uneasy: *worry about one's job.* 2. cause to feel anxious or troubled: *the problem worried him.* 3. annoy; bother: *don't worry me with questions.* 4. seize and shake with the teeth; bite at; snap at. 5. do thus to animals or objects. 6. **worry along,** *Am.* manage somehow. —*n.* 1. a worrying. 2. anxiety; uneasiness; trouble; care: *worry kept her awake.* 3. cause of trouble or care: *a mother of sick children has many worries.* [OE *wyrgan* strangle] —**wor′ri·er,** *n.* —**wor′ry·less,** *adj.* —**wor′ry·ing·ly,** *adv.*

worse (wẽrs), *adj. (comparative of* **bad***).* 1. less well; more ill: *the patient is worse.* 2. less good; more evil. 3. more unfavorable. —*adv.* in a more severe or evil manner or degree: *it is raining worse than ever.* —*n.* that which is worse. [OE *wyrsa*]

wors·en (wẽr′sən), *v.* make or become worse.

wor·ship (wẽr′ship), *n., v.,* -shiped, -ship·ing; *esp. Brit.* -shipped, -ship·ping. —*n.* 1. great honor and respect: *the worship of God, hero worship.* 2. ceremonies or services in honor of God. 3. great love and admiration; adoration. 4. a title used in addressing certain magistrates. —*v.* 1. pay great honor and respect to. 2. take part in a religious service. 3. consider extremely precious; hold very dear; adore: *a miser worships money.* [OE *weorthscipe* < *weorth* worth + -*scipe* -ship] —**wor′ship·er,** *esp. Brit.* **wor′ship·per,** *n.* —**Syn.** *v.* 1. reverence. —*v.* 1. revere, venerate.

wor·ship·ful (wẽr′ship·fəl), *adj.* 1. honorable. 2. worshiping. —**wor′ship·ful·ly,** *adv.* —**wor′ship·ful·ness,** *n.*

worst (wẽrst), *adj. (superlative of* **bad***).* 1. least well; most ill. 2. least good; most evil. 3. most unfavorable. —*adv.* to an extreme degree of badness or evil. —*n.* 1. that which is worst. 2. at worst, under the least favorable circumstances. 3. **if worst comes to worst,** if the very worst thing happens. —*v.* beat; defeat: *the hero worsted his enemies.* [OE *wyrresta*]

wor·sted (wu̇s′tid), *n.* 1. a firmly twisted woolen thread or yarn. 2. cloth made from such thread or yarn. 3. a woolen yarn for knitting, crocheting, and needlework. —*adj.* made of worsted. [after *Worsted,* England (now *Worstead*)]

wort[1] (wẽrt), *n.* the liquid made from malt which later becomes beer, ale, or other liquor. [OE *wyrt*]

wort[2] (wẽrt), *n.* plant, herb, or vegetable. [OE *wyrt*]

worth (wẽrth), *adj.* 1. good or important enough for; deserving of: *the book is worth reading.* 2. equal in value to: *not worth a cent.* 3. having property that amounts to: *that man is worth millions.* —*n.* 1. merit; usefulness; importance: *show one's worth in a crisis.* 2. excellence of character or quality: *a man of worth.* 3. value: *you got your money's worth.* 4. a quantity of something of specified value: *a dollar's worth of sugar.* 5. property; wealth. [OE *weorth*]

worth·less (wẽrth′lis), *adj.* without worth; good-for-nothing; useless. —**worth′less·ly,** *adv.* —**worth′less·ness,** *n.* —**Syn.** valueless, trashy.

worth-while (wẽrth′hwīl′), *adj.* worth time, attention, or effort. —**worth′-while′ness,** *n.*

wor·thy (wẽr′tнi), *adj.,* -thi·er, -thi·est, *n., pl.* -thies. —*adj.* 1. having worth or merit. 2. deserving; meriting. 3. **worthy of,** a. deserving. b. having enough worth for. —*n.* person of great merit; admirable person. —**wor′thi·ly,** *adv.* —**wor′thi·ness,** *n.*

wot (wot), *v. Archaic.* know. [OE *wāt*]

would (wu̇d; *unstressed* wəd), *v.* 1. pt. of **will.** See **will** for ordinary uses. 2. *Would* has special uses: a. to express future time: *would he never go?* b. to express action done again and again: *the children would play for hours on the beach.* c. to express a wish: *would I were dead!* d. to make a statement or question less direct or blunt: *would that be fair?, would you help us, please?* e. to express conditions: *if he would only try, he could do it.* [OE *wolde*] ➤ **would.** See **shall** and **habitual** for usage notes. ➤ **would rather.** See **had** for usage note.

would-be (wu̇d′bē′), *adj.* 1. wishing or pretending to be. 2. intended to be.

wouldst (wu̇dst), *v. Archaic and Poetic.* would.

wound[1] (wu̇nd; *Archaic and Poetic* wound), *n.* 1. a hurt or injury caused by cutting, stabbing, shooting, etc. 2. any hurt or injury to feelings, reputation, etc. —*v.* 1. injure by cutting, stabbing, shooting, etc.; hurt. 2. injure in feelings, reputation, etc. [OE *wund*] —**wound′er,** *n.* —**wound′less,** *adj.*

wound[2] (wound), *v.* pt. and pp. of **wind**[2].

wove (wōv), *v.* pt. and pp. of **weave.**

wo·ven (wō′vən), *v.* pp. of **weave.**

wow (wou), *n. U.S. Slang.* an unqualified success; hit.

WPA, Works Progress Administration.

wrack (rak), *n.* 1. wreckage. 2. ruin; destruction. 3. seaweed cast ashore. [< MDu., MLG *wrak* wreck]

wraith (rāth), *n.* 1. ghost of a person seen before or soon after his death. 2. specter; ghost. [? < Scand. *vörthr* guardian] —**wraith′like′,** *adj.*

Wran·gel (rang′gəl), *n.* island in the Arctic Ocean just N of the Soviet Union in Asia, belonging to the Soviet Union.

wran·gle (rang′gəl), *v.,* -gled, -gling, *n.* —*v.* 1. dispute noisily; quarrel angrily. 2. argue. 3. *Am., W.* herd or tend (horses, etc.) on the range. —*n.* a noisy dispute; angry quarrel. [? < LG *wrangeln*] —**Syn.** *v.* 1. bicker, squabble, brawl.

wran·gler (rang′glər), *n.* 1. person who wrangles. 2. *Am., W.* herder in charge of horses. 3. *Brit.* person winning high honors in mathematics at Cambridge University.

wrap (rap), *v.,* wrapped or wrapt, wrap·ping, *n.* —*v.* 1. cover by winding or folding something around: *wrap oneself in a shawl.* 2. wind or fold around as a covering: *wrap a shawl around you.* 3. cover with paper and tie up or fasten. 4. cover; envelop; hide. 5. **wrapped up in,** a. devoted to; thinking mainly of. b. involved in; associated with. 6. **wrap up,** put on warm outer clothes. —*n.* Often, **wraps.** outer covering. Shawls, scarfs, coats, and furs are wraps.

wrap·per (rap′ər), *n.* 1. person or thing that wraps. 2. thing in which something is wrapped; covering; cover. 3. a long, loose garment.

wrap·ping (rap′ing), *n.* Usually, **wrappings.** paper, cloth, etc., in which something is wrapped.

wrath (rath; räth), *n.* 1. very great anger; rage. 2. vengeance; punishment. [OE *wrǣththu*] —**wrath′less,** *adj.* —**Syn.** 1. ire, fury, indignation, resentment.

wrath·ful (rath′fəl; räth′-), *adj.* feeling or showing wrath; very angry. —**wrath′ful·ly,** *adv.* —**wrath′ful·ness,** *n.* —**Syn.** irate, furious, raging, incensed.

wrath·y (rath′i; räth′-), *adj.,* wrath·i·er, wrath·i·est. wrathful. —**wrath′i·ly,** *adv.* —**wrath′i·ness,** *n.*

wreak (rēk), *v.* 1. give expression to; work off (feelings, desires, etc.). 2. inflict (vengeance, punishment, etc.). [OE *wrecan*] —**wreak′er,** *n.*

wreath (rēth), *n., pl.* wreaths (rēтнz). 1. a ring of flowers or leaves twisted together. 2. something suggesting a wreath. [OE *wrǣth*] —wreath′less, *adj.* —wreath′like′, *adj.*

wreathe (rēth), *v.*, wreathed, wreathed or (*Archaic*) wreath·en, wreath·ing. 1. make into a wreath; twist. 2. decorate or adorn with wreaths. 3. make a ring around; encircle. 4. envelop. 5. move in rings: *the smoke wreathed upward.* —wreath′er, *n.*

wreck (rek), *n.* 1. partial or total destruction of a ship, building, train, automobile, or airship. 2. destruction or serious injury. 3. what is left of anything that has been destroyed or much injured. 4. person who has lost his health or money. 5. goods cast up by the sea. —*v.* 1. cause the wreck of; destroy; ruin. 2. be wrecked; suffer serious injury. 3. cause to lose health or money. 4. act as wrecker. [< Scand.]

wreck·age (rek′ij), *n.* 1. what is left of a thing that has been wrecked. 2. a wrecking or being wrecked.

wreck·er (rek′ər), *n.* 1. person who causes wrecks. 2. person whose work is tearing down buildings. 3. person, car, train, or machine that removes wrecks. 4. person or ship that recovers wrecked or disabled ships or their cargoes.

wren (ren), *n.* any of a number of small songbirds with slender bills and short tails. [OE *wrenna*]

wrench (rench), *n.* 1. a violent twist or twisting pull. 2. injury caused by twisting. 3. grief; pain. 4. tool for turning nuts, bolts, etc. —*v.* 1. twist or pull violently. 2. injure by twisting: *he wrenched his back in falling from the horse.* 3. twist the meaning of. 4. affect distressingly. [OE *wrencan* twist] —Syn. *v.* 1. wring, wrest. 2. strain, sprain.

Pipe wrench

wrest (rest), *v.* 1. twist, pull, or tear away with force; wrench away. 2. take by force. 3. twist or turn from the proper meaning, use, etc. —*n.* 1. a wresting; forcible twist. 2. key for tuning a harp, piano, etc. [OE *wrǣstan*] —wrest′er, *n.*

wres·tle (res′əl), *v.*, -tled, -tling, *n.* —*v.* 1. try to throw or force (an opponent) to the ground. 2. contend with in wrestling, or as if in wrestling; struggle. —*n.* 1. a wrestling match. 2. struggle. [ult. < *wrest*] —wres′tler, *n.*

wres·tling (res′ling), *n.* sport or contest in which each of two opponents tries to throw or force the other to the ground. The rules for wrestling do not allow using the fists or certain holds on the body.

wretch (rech), *n.* 1. a very unfortunate or unhappy person. 2. a very bad person. [OE *wrecca* exile] —Syn. 2. scoundrel, villain, rogue.

wretch·ed (rech′id), *adj.* 1. very unfortunate or unhappy. 2. very unsatisfactory; miserable. 3. very bad. —wretch′ed·ly, *adv.* —wretch′ed·ness, *n.* —Syn. 1. distressed, dejected. 2. pitiful, shabby. 3. despicable, base, mean.

wrick (rik), *v.*, *n.* strain; sprain.

wrig·gle (rig′əl), *v.*, -gled, -gling, *n.* —*v.* 1. twist and turn. 2. move by twisting and turning. 3. make one's way by shifts and tricks: *wriggle out of a difficulty.* —*n.* a wriggling. [cf. Du. *wriggelen*] —wrig′gly, *adj.*

wrig·gler (rig′lər), *n.* 1. person who wriggles. 2. larva of a mosquito.

wright (rīt), *n.* (now usually in combinations) a maker of something, as in *wheelwright, playwright.* [OE *wryhta*, var. of *wyrhta* < *weorc* work]

Wright (rīt), *n.* Orville, 1871–1948, and Wilbur, 1867–1912, brothers who perfected the airplane and flew a motor-powered plane successfully in 1903 for the first time.

wring (ring), *v.*, wrung or (*Rare*) wringed, wring·ing, *n.* —*v.* 1. twist with force; squeeze hard: *wring clothes.* 2. force by twisting or squeezing: *wring water out of clothes.* 3. perform the action of wringing something: *I wash, and she wrings.* 4. clasp tightly: *wring another's hand in greeting.* 5. get by force, effort, or persuasion: *the old beggar could wring money from anyone by his sad story.* 6. cause pain, pity, etc.,

in: *their poverty wrung his heart.* 7. **wring out,** force (water, etc.) from by twisting or squeezing. —*n.* a twist; squeeze. [OE *wringan*]

wring·er (ring′ər), *n.* 1. one who wrings. 2. machine for squeezing water from clothes.

wrin·kle[1] (ring′kəl), *n.*, *v.*, -kled, -kling. —*n.* ridge; fold. —*v.* 1. make a wrinkle or wrinkles in: *he wrinkled his forehead.* 2. have wrinkles; acquire wrinkles: *these sleeves wrinkle.* [cf. OE *gewrinclod*, pp. winding] —wrin′kle·less, *adj.* —wrin′kly, *adj.* —Syn. *v.* 1. crease, crinkle.

wrin·kle[2] (ring′kəl), *n. Colloq.* a useful hint or idea; clever trick. [? special use of *wrinkle*[1]]

wrist (rist), *n.* 1. the joint connecting hand and arm; carpus. 2. a corresponding joint or part of the forelimb of an animal. 3. part of the arm between forearm and hand. [OE]

wrist·band (rist′band′; rist′bənd), *n.* the band of a sleeve fitting around the wrist.

wrist·let (rist′lit), *n.* 1. band worn around the wrist to keep it warm. 2. bracelet.

wrist pin, a stud or pin projecting from the side of a crank, wheel, or the like, and forming a means of attachment to a connecting rod.

writ (rit), *n.* 1. something written; piece of writing. The Bible is Holy Writ. 2. *Law.* a formal order directing a person to do or not to do something. —*v. Archaic.* pt. and pp. of **write.** [OE, < *writan* write]

write (rīt), *v.*, wrote or (*Archaic*) writ, written (rit′ən) or (*Archaic*) writ, writ·ing. 1. make letters, words, etc., with pen, pencil, chalk, etc. 2. mark with letters, words, etc.: *write a check.* 3. put down the letters, words, etc., of: *write a sentence.* 4. express in writing; give in writing; record. 5. make (books, stories, articles, poems, letters, etc.) by using written letters, words, etc.; compose. 6. be a writer: *her ambition was to write.* 7. write a letter. 8. write a letter to. 9. show plainly: *honesty is written on his face.* 10. **write down, a.** put into writing. **b.** put a lower value on. 11. **write off,** cancel. 12. **write out, a.** put into writing. **b.** write in full. 13. **write up, a.** write a description or account of. **b.** write in detail. [OE *writan*, orig., scratch]

write-in (rīt′in′), *n.* 1. the casting of a vote for someone whose name is not on the official ballot by writing his name in. 2. the name written in.

write-off (rīt′ôf′), *n.* deduction or cancellation, as of a tax.

writ·er (rīt′ər), *n.* 1. person who writes. 2. person whose profession or business is writing; author. —Syn. 1. penman, scribe.

write-up (rīt′up′), *n. Am., Colloq.* a written description or account.

writhe (rīth), *v.*, writhed, writhed or (*Obs. except Poetic*) writh·en (rith′ən), writh·ing, *n.* —*v.* 1. twist and turn. 2. suffer mentally; be very uncomfortable. —*n.* a writhing movement. [OE *writhan*] —writh′er, *n.* —writh′ing·ly, *adv.*

writ·ing (rīt′ing), *n.* 1. act of making letters, words, etc., with pen, pencil, etc. 2. written form: *put your ideas in writing.* 3. handwriting. 4. something written; letter, document, etc. 5. book, story, article, poem, etc. 6. profession or business of a person who writes. —*adj.* 1. that writes. 2. used in writing; used to write on.

Wro·cław (vrôts′läf), *n.* city in SW Poland, formerly part of Germany. German, Breslau.

wrong (rông; rong), *adj.* 1. not right; bad; unjust; unlawful: *it is wrong to tell lies.* 2. incorrect: *the wrong answer.* 3. unsuitable; improper: *the wrong clothes for the occasion.* 4. in a bad state or condition; out of order; amiss: *is something wrong with you?* 5. not meant to be seen; less or least important: *cloth often has a wrong side and a right side.* 6. **go wrong, a.** turn out badly. **b.** stop being good and become bad. —*adv.* in a wrong manner; in the wrong direction; badly. —*n.* 1. what is wrong; wrong thing or things: *two wrongs do not make a right.* 2. injustice; injury. 3. **in the wrong,** wrong. —*v.* do wrong to; treat unjustly; injure. [< Scand. (OSw.) *vranger* crooked] —wrong′er, *n.* —wrong′ful, *adj.* —wrong′ful·ly, *adv.* —wrong′ful·ness, *n.* —wrong′ly, *adv.* —wrong′ness, *n.* —Syn. *adj.* 1. evil, wicked, reprehensible. 2. inaccurate, erroneous, faulty.

3. inappropriate, unfit. *–n.* **1.** evil, sin, misdemeanor. *–v.* harm, maltreat, abuse, oppress.

wrong·do·er (rông′dü′ ər; rong′–), *n.* person who does wrong. **—wrong′do′ing,** *n.*

wrong-head·ed (rông′hed′id; rong′–), *adj.* **1.** wrong in judgment or opinion. **2.** stubborn even when wrong. **—wrong′-head′ed·ly,** *adv.* **—wrong′-head′ed·ness,** *n.*

wrote (rōt), *v.* pt. of write.

wroth (rôth; roth), *adj.* angry. [OE *wrāth*]

wrought (rôt), *v.* pt. and pp. of work. *—adj.* **1.** fashioned; made: *a well-wrought statue.* **2.** manufactured or treated; not in a raw state. **3.** formed with care; not rough or crude; ornamented. **4.** of metals, formed by hammering.

wrought iron, a tough form of iron with little carbon in it. Wrought iron will not break as easily as cast iron.

wrought-up (rôt′up′), *adj.* stirred up; excited.

wrung (rung), *v.* pt. and pp. of wring.

wry (rī), *adj.,* wri·er, wri·est. turned to one side; twisted: *she made a wry face to show her disgust.* [ult. < OE *wrigian* turn] **—wry′ly,** *adv.* **—wry′ness,** *n.*

WSW, W.S.W., between west and southwest.

wt., weight.

Wu·chang (wü′chäng′), *n.* city in E China, on the Yangtze River.

Wu·hsien (wü′shyen′), *n.* city in E China. Formerly, Soochow.

Wup·per·tal (vūp′ər·täl), *n.* city in W Germany.

Würt·tem·berg (wėr′təm·bérg; *Ger.* vyr′təm-berk), *n.* district in SW Germany.

W. Va., West Virginia.

Wy., Wyoming.

Wy·an·dotte (wī′ən·dot), *n. Am.* any of an American breed of medium-sized, hardy domestic fowls.

Wyc·liffe (wik′lif), *n.* **John,** 1320?–1384, English religious reformer who translated the Bible into English. **—Wyc·lif·fite, Wyc·lif·ite** (wik′-lif·īt), *adj., n.*

Wyo., Wyoming.

Wy·o·ming (wī·ō′ming), *n.* a Western State of the United States. *Capital:* Cheyenne. *Abbrev.:* Wyo. or Wy. **—Wy·o·ming·ite** (wī·ō′-ming·īt), *n.*

X

X, x (eks), *n., pl.* **X's; x's. 1.** the 24th letter of the alphabet. **2.** a term often used to designate a person, thing, agency, factor, or the like whose true name is unknown or withheld. **3.** anything shaped like an X. **4.** the Roman numeral for 10. **5.** an unknown quantity.

xan·thous (zan′thəs) , *adj.* yellow. [< Gk. *xanthos*]

Xa·vi·er (zā′vi·ər; zav′i–), *n.* **Saint Francis,** 1506–1552, Spanish Jesuit missionary.

X chromosome, chromosome related to femaleness. An egg containing two X chromosomes, one from each parent, develops into a female.

Xe, *Chem.* xenon.

xe·bec (zē′bek), *n.* a small, three-masted vessel of the Mediterranean. [< F, ult. < Ar. *shabbāk*]

xe·non (zē′non; zen′on), *n. Chem.* a heavy, colorless gas, Xe, that is chemically inactive. It is a rare element that occurs in the air in very small quantities. [< Gk., neut. adj., strange]

xen·o·pho·bi·a (zen′ ə·fō′bi·ə), *n.* hatred or fear of foreigners. [< NL, < Gk. *xenos* stranger + *phobos* fear]

Xen·o·phon (zen′ə·fən), *n.* 430?–355? B.C., Greek historian.

xe·ro·phyte (zir′ə·fīt), *n.* plant that loses very

little water and can grow in deserts or very dry ground, as cacti, sagebrush, etc. [< Gk. *xeros* dry + *phyton* plant]

Xerx·es (zėrk′sēz), *n.* 519?–465 B.C., king of ancient Persia 486?–465 B.C.

xi (sī; zī; ksē), *n.* the 14th letter (Ξ, ξ) of the Greek alphabet.

Xmas (kris′məs), *n.* Christmas.

X ray, 1. a ray with an extremely short wave length formed when cathode rays impinge upon a solid body (as the wall of a vacuum tube) that can penetrate opaque substances; a Roentgen ray. X rays are used to locate breaks in bones, bullets lodged in the body, etc., and to diagnose and treat certain diseases. **2.** a picture made by means of X rays.

X-ray (eks′rā′), *v.* examine, photograph, or treat with X rays. *—adj.* of, by, or pertaining to X rays.

xy·lem (zī′lem), *n. Bot.* the woody part of plants. [< G < Gk. *xylon* wood]

xy·lo·phone (zī′lə·fōn; zil′ə–), *n.* a musical instrument consisting of a row of wooden bars, sounded by striking them with small wooden hammers. [< Gk. *xylon* wood + *phone* sound] **—xy·lo·phon·ist** (zī′lə·fōn′ist; zī·lof′ə·nist; zī–), *n.*

Y

Y, y (wī), *n., pl.* **Y's; y's. 1.** the 25th letter of the alphabet. **2.** something resembling the letter Y in shape. **3.** an unknown quantity.

Y, *Chem.* yttrium. Also, Yt.

-y[1], *suffix.* **1.** full of, composed of, containing, having, or characterized by, as in *airy, cloudy, dewy, icy, juicy, watery.* **2.** somewhat, as in *chilly, salty, whity.* **3.** inclined to, as in *chatty, fidgety.* **4.** resembling; suggesting, as in *messy, sloppy, sugary, willowy.* **5.** In certain words, such as *paly, steepy, stilly, vasty,* the addition of *y* does not change the meaning. [OE *–ig*]

-y[2], *suffix.* small, as in *dolly;* used also to show kind feeling or intimacy, as in *aunty, Dicky.* [ME]

-y[3], *suffix.* **1.** state or quality, as in *jealousy, victory.* **2.** activity, as in *delivery, entreaty.* [< L *–ia,* Gk. *–ia,* F *–ie*]

yacht (yot), *n.* boat for pleasure trips or racing. *–v.* sail or race on a yacht. [< earlier Du. *jaght* < *jaghtschip* chasing ship] **—yacht′er,** *n.* **—nyami′,** *n., adj.*

yachts·man (yots′mən), *n., pl.* **-men.** person

who owns or sails a yacht. **—yachts′man·ship,** *n.*

yah (yä), *interj.* noise made to express derision, disgust, or impatience.

Ya·hoo (yä′hü; yä·hü′), *n.* **1.** in Swift's *Gulliver's Travels,* a brute in human shape who works for a race of intelligent horses. **2. yahoo,** a rough, coarse, or uncouth person.

Yah·weh, Yah·we (yä′wā), *n.* a name of God in the Hebrew text of the Old Testament, often used by writers on the religion of the Hebrews. Also, **Jahve, Jahveh.**

yak (yak), *n.* the long-haired ox of Tibet and C Asia. [< Tibetan *gyag*]

yam (yam), *n.* **1.** the starchy root of a vine grown for food in warm countries. **2.** the vine itself. **3.** *Am.* a kind of sweet potato. [< Sp. *iñame,* ult. < Senegalese *nyami* eat]

Yak (ab. 5 ft. tall)

Yang·tze, Yang·tse (yang′tsē′), *n.* river

flowing through C China into the China Sea, the longest river in China.

yank (yangk), *v., n. Colloq.* jerk.

Yank (yangk), *n., adj. Am., Slang.* Yankee.

Yan·kee (yang′ki), *n.* 1. *Am.* native of New England. 2. *Am.* native of any of the Northern States. 3. *Southern U.S.* a Northerner (usually in a contemptuous or hostile sense). 4. native or inhabitant of the United States. —*adj.* of or having to do with Yankees: *Yankee shrewdness.* [prob. ult. < Du. *Jan Kee* John Cheese (nickname), the *-s* being taken for pl. ending]

Yan·kee·dom (yang′ki·dəm), *n.* 1. *Am.* Yankees collectively. 2. region inhabited by Yankees.

Yankee Doo·dle (düʹdəl), *Am.* an American song, probably of English origin and taken over by the American soldiers in the Revolutionary War.

Yan·kee·ism (yang′ki·iz·əm), *n. Am.* 1. Yankee character or characteristics. 2. a Yankee peculiarity.

yap (yap), *n., v.,* yapped, yap·ping. —*n.* 1. a snappish bark; yelp. 2. *Slang.* snappish, noisy, or foolish talk. 3. *Slang.* a peevish or noisy person. —*v.* 1. bark snappishly; yelp. 2. *Slang.* talk snappishly, noisily, or foolishly. [imit.]

Yap (yäp; yap), *n.* one of the Caroline Islands in the W Pacific, now a U.S. cable station.

yard¹ (yärd), *n.* 1. piece of ground near or around a house, barn, school, etc. 2. piece of enclosed ground for some special purpose or business: *a chicken yard.* 3. space with tracks where railroad cars are stored, shifted around, etc. —*v.* put into or enclose in a yard. [OE *geard*]

yard² (yärd), *n.* 1. measure of length; 36 inches; 3 feet. 2. *Naut.* a long, slender beam or pole fastened across a mast, used to support a sail. [OE *gierd* rod]

YARDS

yard·age (yärʹdij), *n.* 1. length in yards. 2. amount measured in yards.

yard·arm (yärdʹärm′), *n. Naut.* either end of a long, slender beam or pole used to support a square sail.

yard·mas·ter (yärdʹmasʹtər; -mäsʹ-), *n. Am.* man in charge of a railroad yard.

yard·stick (yärdʹstik′), *n. Am.* 1. a stick one yard long, used for measuring. 2. any standard of judgment or comparison.

yarn (yärn), *n.* 1. any spun thread, esp. that prepared for weaving or knitting. 2. *Colloq.* tale; story. —*v. Colloq.* 1. tell stories. 2. converse; talk. [OE *gearn*]

yar·row (yarʹō), *n.* a common plant with finely divided leaves and flat clusters of white or pink flowers. [OE *gearwe*]

yat·a·ghan, yat·a·gan (yatʹə·gan; -gən), *n.* sword used by Mohammedans, having no guard for the hand and no crosspiece, but usually a large pommel. [< Turk.]

yaw (yô), *v.* 1. turn from a straight course; go unsteadily. 2. of an aircraft, turn from a straight course by a motion about its vertical axis. —*n.* such a movement.

yawl (yôl), *n.* 1. boat like a sloop with a second short mast set near the stern. 2. a ship's boat rowed by four or six oars. [< Du. *jol*]

yawn (yôn), *v.* 1. open the mouth wide because one is sleepy, tired, or bored. 2. open wide. 3. say with a yawn. —*n.* 1. a yawning. 2. an open space; opening; chasm. [OE *geonian*] —yawn′ing·ly, *adv.* —yawn′y, *adj.* —Syn. *v.* 1. gape.

yawp (yôp; yäp), *Dial.* or *Colloq.* —*v.* utter a loud, harsh cry. —*n.* such a cry. —yawp′er, *n.*

yaws (yôz), *n.pl.* a contagious disease of the tropics, characterized by sores on the skin. [< Carib]

Yb, *Chem.* ytterbium.

Y chromosome, chromosome related to maleness. An egg containing a Y chromosome develops into a male.

y·clept, y·cleped (i·kleptʹ), *adj. Archaic.* called; named; styled. [OE *geclipod* named]

yd., *pl.* **yds.** yard.

ye¹ (yē; *unstressed* yi), *pron. pl. Archaic.* you. [OE *gē*]

ye² (t͟hē; *incorrectly* yē), *definite article. Archaic.* the.

yea (yā), *adv.* 1. yes. 2. indeed; truly. —*n.* an affirmative vote or voter. [OE *gēa*]

yean (yēn), *v.* give birth to (a lamb or kid). [OE (assumed) *geēanian;* cf. *ēanian* yean, *geēan,* adj., pregnant]

yean·ling (yēnʹling), *n.* a lamb or kid.

year (yir), *n.* 1. 12 months or 365 days (366 every fourth year); January 1 to December 31; calendar year. 2. 12 months reckoned from any point. A fiscal year is a period of 12 months at the end of which the accounts of a government, business, or the like, are balanced. 3. the part of a year spent in a certain activity. A school year is from 8–10 months. 4. period of the earth's revolution around the sun. The solar or astronomical year is 365 days, 5 hours, 48 minutes, 46 seconds. 5. the time it takes for the apparent traveling of the sun from a given fixed star back to it again. The sidereal year is 20 minutes, 23 seconds longer than the solar year. 6. the time in which any planet completes its revolution round the sun. 7. years, a. age. b. a very long time. 8. year by year, with each succeeding year; as years go by. 9. year in, year out, always; continuously. [OE *gēar*]

year·book (yirʹbúk′), *n.* a book or report published every year.

year·ling (yirʹling; yèrʹ-), *n.* an animal one year old. —*adj.* 1. one year old: *a yearling colt.* 2. of a year's duration.

year·long (yirʹlông′; -long′), *adj.* 1. lasting for a year. 2. lasting for years.

year·ly (yirʹli), *adj.* 1. once a year; in every year. 2. lasting a year. 3. for a year. —*adv.* once a year; in every year.

yearn (yèrn), *v.* 1. feel a longing or desire; desire earnestly. 2. feel pity; have tender feelings. [OE *giernan*] —yearn′ful, *adj.* —yearn′ful·ly, *adv.*

yearn·ing (yèrʹning), *adj.* that yearns. —*n.* earnest or strong desire; longing. —yearn′ing·ly, *adv.*

yeast (yēst), *n.* 1. the substance used in raising bread, making beer, etc. Yeast consists of very small plants or cells that grow quickly in a liquid containing sugar. 2. a yeast plant or yeast cell. 3. Also, yeast cake. flour or meal mixed with this substance and pressed into small cakes. 4. influence, element, etc., that acts as a leaven. 5. foam; froth. [OE *gist*]

yeast·y (yēsʹti), *adj.* 1. of, containing, or resembling yeast. 2. frothy or foamy: *yeasty waves.* 3. light or trifling; frivolous.

Yeats (yāts), *n.* William Butler, 1865–1939, Irish writer of poems, plays, and essays.

yegg (yeg), *n. Am., Slang.* 1. burglar who robs safes. 2. any burglar.

yell (yel), *v.* 1. cry out with a strong, loud sound. 2. say with a yell. —*n.* 1. a strong, loud cry. 2. *Am.* a special shout or cheer used by a school or college. [OE *giellan*] —yell′er, *n.*

yel·low (yelʹō), *n.* 1. the color of gold, butter, or ripe lemons. 2. a yellow pigment or dye. 3. yolk of an egg. —*adj.* 1. having a yellow color. 2. having a yellowish skin. 3. jaundiced. 4. jealous; envious. 5. *Am., Colloq.* cowardly. 6. *Am.* sensational: *a yellow journal.* —*v.* turn yellow. [OE *geolu*] —yel′low·ish, *adj.* —yel′low·ly, *adv.* —yel′low·ness, *n.*

yel·low·bird (yelʹō·bėrd′), *n.* 1. *Am.* the goldfinch of America. 2. the yellow warbler of America. 3. any of various other yellow birds, such as an oriole of Europe.

yellow fever, *Am.* a dangerous, infectious tropical disease transmitted by the bite of a mosquito.

yel·low·ham·mer (yelʹō·hamʹər), *n.* 1. a European bird with a yellow head, neck, and breast. 2. *Am.* the flicker or golden-winged woodpecker of E North America.

yellow jack, *Am.* 1. yellow fever. 2. a yellow flag used as a signal of quarantine.

yellow jacket, *Am.* wasp or hornet marked with bright yellow.

yellow metal, 1. gold. 2. a yellowish alloy containing copper and zinc.

yellow peril, the alleged danger from the growth and activities of Japan or China.

yellow pine, *Am.* 1. a pine tree with yellowish wood. 2. its wood.

Yellow River, Hwang Ho.

Yellow Sea, part of the Pacific Ocean between NE China and Korea.

Yel·low·stone (yel′ō·stōn′), *n.* 1. Yellowstone National Park. 2. river flowing from NW Wyoming through Yellowstone National Park into the Missouri River in Montana.

Yellowstone National Park, a large park, mostly in NW Wyoming, famous for its scenery, hot springs, and geysers.

yellow warbler, a small American warbler. The male has yellow plumage streaked with brown.

yelp (yelp), *n.* the quick, sharp bark or cry of a dog, fox, etc. —*v.* 1. make such a bark or cry. 2. utter with a yelp. [OE *gielpan* boast] —**yelp′er,** *n.*

Yem·en (yem′ən), *n.* country in SW Arabia.

yen¹ (yen), *n., pl.* **yen.** unit of money of Japan, worth about ⅓ of a cent. [< Jap. < Chinese *yüan* round object]

yen² (yen), *n., v.,* **yenned, yen·ning.** *Am., Colloq.* —*n.* 1. a fanciful desire. 2. have a yen for, desire. —*v.* desire.

yeo·man (yō′mən), *n., pl.* **-men.** 1. *U.S. Navy.* a petty officer who performs clerical duties. 2. *Brit.* person who owns land, but not a large amount. 3. *Archaic.* a servant or attendant of a lord or king.

yeo·man·ly (yō′mən·li), *adj.* of or suitable for a yeoman; sturdy; honest. —*adv.* like a yeoman; bravely.

yeo·man·ry (yō′mən·ri), *n.* yeomen.

yeoman's service, yeoman service, good, useful service; faithful support or assistance.

yes (yes), *adv., n., pl.* **yes·es,** *v.,* **yessed, yes·sing.** —*adv.* 1. word used to express agreement, consent, or affirmation: *Will you go? Yes.* 2. and what is more; in addition to that: *it is good, yes, very good.* —*n.* an answer that agrees, consents, or affirms. —*v.* say yes. [OE *gēse* < *gēa* yea + *si* be it] ➤ **Yes** and **no** are adverbs. They may modify a sentence (*Yes, you're right*) or may have the value of a coördinate clause (*No; but you should have told me*) or they may stand as complete sentences (*"Do you really intend to go with him?" "Yes."*).

yes man, *Am., Slang.* person who habitually agrees with his employer, superior officer, party, etc., without criticism.

yes·ter·day (yes′tər·di; -dā), *n.* 1. the day before today. 2. the recent past. —*adv.* 1. on the day before today. 2. recently. [OE *geostrandæg* < *geostran* yesterday + *dæg* day]

yes·ter·year (yes′tər·yir′), *n., adv. Archaic* or *Poetic.* last year; the year before this.

yet (yet), *adv.* 1. up to the present time; thus far: *the work is not yet finished.* 2. now: *don't go yet, it was not yet dark.* 3. still; even now: *she is talking yet.* 4. sometime: *the thief will be caught yet.* 5. also; again: *yet once more I forbid you to go.* 6. moreover: *he won't do it for you nor yet for me.* 7. even: *the king spoke yet more harshly.* 8. nevertheless; however: *strange and yet true.* 9. as yet, up to now. —*conj.* nevertheless; however: *the work is good, yet it could be better.* [OE *giet(a)*] ➤ **Yet** is an adverb: *The books haven't come yet.* In formal English it is also used as a conjunction, or conjunctive adverb, equivalent to *but: His speech was almost unintelligible, yet for some unknown reason I enjoyed it.*

yew (ū), *n.* 1. an evergreen tree native to Europe and Asia. 2. the wood of this tree. [OE *iw*]

Yew

Yid·dish (yid′ish), *n.* a language which developed from a dialect of Middle High German, containing many Hebrew and Slavic words, and written in Hebrew characters. Yiddish is spoken mainly by Jews in or from Russia and C Europe. —*adj.* in or pertaining to Yiddish.

yield (yēld), *v.* 1. produce: *land yields crops.* 2. give forth by a natural process: *the fruit of a tree yields seeds.* 3. produce as profit or interest. 4. give; grant: *yield consent.* 5. give up; surrender: *yield a position to the enemy.* 6. give way: *the surface yielded under the weight.* 7. give place: *we yield to nobody in love of freedom.* —*n.* amount yielded; product. [OE *gieldan* pay] —**yield′a·ble,** *adj.* —**yield′er,** *n.* —Syn. *v.* 1. furnish, supply. 4. afford, confer. 5. relinquish, resign. —*n.* harvest, crop.

yield·ing (yēl′ding), *adj.* not resisting; submissive. —**yield′ing·ly,** *adv.* —**yield′ing·ness,** *n.* —Syn. compliant, flexible.

yip (yip), *v.,* **yipped, yip·ping,** *n. Am., Colloq.* —*v.* esp. of dogs, bark or yelp briskly. —*n.* a sharp barking sound. [imit.]

Y.M.C.A., Young Men's Christian Association.

Y.M.H.A., Young Men's Hebrew Association.

yo·del (yō′dəl), *v.,* **-deled, -del·ing;** *esp. Brit.* **-delled, -del·ling.** —*v.* sing with frequent changes from the ordinary voice to a forced shrill voice. —*n.* act or sound of yodeling. [< G *jodeln*] —**yo′del·er,** *esp. Brit.* **yo′del·ler,** *n.*

yo·dle (yō′dəl), *v.,* **-dled, -dling,** *n.* yodel. —**yo′dler,** *n.*

yo·ga, Yo·ga (yō′gə), *n.* system of Hindu religious philosophy that requires intense concentration and deep meditation upon the universal spirit. [< Hind. < Skt., union]

yo·gi (yō′gi), *n., pl.* **-gis.** person who practices or follows yoga. —**yo′gism,** *n.*

yo·gurt (yō′gərt), *n.* food made from whole or partly skimmed milk, curdled by means of bacteriological cultures.

yo-heave-ho (yō′hēv′hō′), *interj.* exclamation used by sailors in pulling or lifting together.

yoicks (yoiks), *interj.* Esp. *Brit.* cry used to urge on the hounds in fox hunting.

yoke (yōk), *n., v.,* **yoked, yok·ing.** —*n.* 1. a wooden frame to fasten two work animals together, usually consisting of a crosspiece with two bow-shaped pieces beneath. 2. pair fastened together by a yoke. 3. anything resembling a yoke in shape or use. 4. something that joins or unites; bond; tie. 5. something that holds people in slavery or submission. —*v.* 1. fasten by a yoke or harness: *yoke the horses.* 2. fasten to by a yoke or harness: *yoke the chariot.* 3. join; unite. [OE *geoc*]

Yoke on a pair of oxen

yoke·fel·low (yōk′fel′ō), **yoke·mate** (-māt′), *n.* 1. person joined or united with another in a task; partner. 2. husband or wife.

yo·kel (yō′kəl), *n.* a country fellow.

Yo·ko·ha·ma (yō′kə·hä′mə), *n.* seaport in SE Japan.

yolk (yōk; yōlk), *n.* 1. the yellow part of an egg. 2. fat or grease in sheep's wool. [OE *geolca* < *geolu* yellow] —**yolked,** *adj.* —**yolk′less,** *adj.* —**yolk′y,** *adj.*

Yom Kip·pur (yom kip′ər), the Day of Atonement, an annual Jewish fast day observed on the tenth day of the first month of the Jewish year.

yon (yon), **yond** (yond), *adj., adv. Archaic* or *Dial.* yonder. [OE *geon*]

yon·der (yon′dər), *adv.* within sight, but not near; over there: *away off yonder.* —*adj.* 1. situated over there; being within sight, but not near: *he lives in yonder cottage.* 2. farther; more distant: *the yonder side.* [ME]

Yon·kers (yong′kərz), *n.* city in SE New York State, just N of New York City.

yore (yôr; yōr), *n.* of yore, of long ago; in the past; formerly. —*adv. Obs.* long ago; years ago. [OE *geāra,* gen. pl. of *gēar* year]

āge, cāre, fär; ēqual, tėrm; īce; ōpen, ôrder; pủt, rüle, ūse; th, then; ə=a in about.

York (yôrk), *n.* **1.** the royal house of England from 1461 to 1485. Its emblem was a white rose. **2.** Yorkshire.

York·shire (yôrk'shir; –shər), *n.* county in N England; York.

Yorkshire pudding, a batter cake often served with roast beef.

Yorkshire terrier, any of an English breed of small, shaggy dogs.

Yo·sem·i·te (yō·sem'ə·tē), *n.* a very deep valley in E California with lofty and very beautiful falls (**Yosemite Falls**).

you (ū; *unstressed* yú, yə), *pron. pl. or sing.* **1.** the person or persons spoken to: *are you ready?* **2.** one; anybody: *you push this button to get a light.* [OE *ēow,* dative and accus. of *gē* ye¹] ➤ **You** is used as an indefinite pronoun (*It's a good book if you like detective stories; Then you must protect them from rats*) in speech and informal writing. Formal English would more often use *one* or a different construction. In substandard English and sometimes in familiar English *was* is used with *you* referring to one person. ➤ **you all.** In Southern American *you all,* contracted to *y'all,* is frequently used as the plural of *you,* as in some other regions *you folks* is used. It is also used when addressing one person regarded as one of a group, usually a family. It is sometimes asserted that *you all* is also used as a singular, addressing one. It apparently is occasionally used as a singular but this use is regarded by educated Southerners as an error.

young (yung), *adj.* **1.** in the early part of life or growth; not old: *a young child.* **2.** having the looks or qualities of youth or a young person: *she looks young for her age.* **3.** of youth; early: *one's young days.* **4.** not so old as another: *young Mr. Jones worked for his father.* **5.** in an early stage; not far advanced: *night was still young when they left.* **6.** without much experience or practice: *I was too young in the trade to be successful.* **7.** representing or advocating recent or progressive tendencies. —*n.* **1.** young ones. **2.** the young, young people. **3.** with young, pregnant. [OE *geong*] —**young'ish,** *adj.* —**young'ly,** *adv.* —**young'ness,** *n.* —*Syn. adj.* **1.** immature, undeveloped. —*Ant. adj.* **1.** old.

Young (yung), *n.* **Brigham,** 1801–1877, American Mormon leader.

young·ber·ry (yung'ber'i), *n., pl.* –ries. hybrid between a blackberry and dewberry, grown largely in SW United States.

young blood, youthful people; youthful energy, ideas, etc.

young·ling (yung'ling), *n.* **1.** a young person, animal, or plant. **2.** novice; beginner. —*adj.* young; youthful.

young·ster (yung'stər), *n.* **1.** child. **2.** a young person.

Youngs·town (yungz'toun), *n.* city in NE Ohio.

youn·ker (yung'kər), *n. Archaic or Colloq.* a young fellow. [< MDu. *jonckher jonchere* < *jonc* young + *here* lord, master]

your (yûr; *unstressed* yər), *pron. pl. or sing., possessive form* of **you.** **1.** belonging to you: *your book.* **2.** having to do with you: *your enemies.* **3.** that you know, esp. as a type; well-known; that you speak of; that is spoken of: *your real lover of music, your modern girl.* **4.** part of a title: *Your Lordship.* [OE *ēower,* gen. of *gē* ye¹]

yours (yûrz), *pron. sing. and pl., possessive form* of **you** (*used predicatively or with no noun*

following). **1.** belonging to or having to do with you: *this pencil is yours.* **2.** the one or ones belonging to or having to do with you: *where are yours?* **3.** at your service: *I remain yours to command.* **4.** of yours, belonging to you.

your·self (yûr·self'; yər–), *pron., pl.* –selves (–selvz'). **1.** the emphatic form of **you:** *you yourself know the story is not true.* **2.** the reflexive form of **you:** *you will hurt yourself.* **3.** your real self: *you aren't yourself today.*

yours truly, 1. phrase used at the end of a letter, before the signature. **2.** *Colloq.* I; me.

youth (ūth), *n., pl.* **youths** (ūths; ūthz) or (*collectively*) **youth. 1.** fact or quality of being young: *she keeps her youth well.* **2.** the time between childhood and manhood or womanhood. **3.** a young man. **4.** the first or early stage of anything; early period of growth or development: *during the youth of this country.* **5.** young people. [OE *geoguth*] —**youth'hood,** *n.*

youth·ful (ūth'fəl), *adj.* **1.** young. **2.** of youth; suitable for young people. **3.** having the looks or qualities of youth. —**youth'ful·ly,** *adv.* —**youth'ful·ness,** *n.* —*Syn.* **1.** immature, juvenile.

Yo·yo (yō'yō), *n., pl.* –yos. *Am., Trademark.* a small disk-shaped toy, which is spun out and reeled in by an attached string.

yowl (youl), *n.* a long, distressful, or dismal cry; howl. —*v.* howl. [imit.]

Y·pres (ē'pra), *n.* town in W Belgium. Many battles of World War I were fought there.

yr., 1. year; years. 2. your.

yrs., 1. years. 2. yours.

Yt, *Chem.* yttrium. Also, **Y.**

yt·ter·bi·um (i·tèr'bi·əm), *n.* a rare metallic element, Yb, belonging to the yttrium group. [< NL, ult. < *Ytterby,* Sweden] —**yt·ter'bic,** *adj.*

yt·tri·um (it'ri·əm), *n. Chem.* a rare metallic element, Y or Yt. Compounds of yttrium are used for incandescent gas mantles. [< NL, ult. < *Ytterby,* Sweden] —**yt'tric,** *adj.*

Yu·ca·tán (ū'kə·tän'; –tän'), *n.* peninsula of SE Mexico and part of Central America. —**Yu·ca·tec·an** (ū'kə·tek'ən), *adj., n.*

yuc·ca (yuk'ə), *n.* plant that has sword-shaped evergreen leaves and a cluster of large, white, lilylike flowers on a tall stalk. [< NL < Sp. *yuca*]

Yu·go·slav (ū'gō·släv'; –slav'), *n.* native or inhabitant of Yugoslavia. —*adj.* of or having to do with Yugoslavia or its people. Also, **Jugoslav, Jugo-Slav.** —Yu'go·slav'ic, *adj.*

Yucca

Yu·go·sla·vi·a (ū'gō·slä'vi·ə), *n.* country in SE Europe. Also, **Jugoslavia, Jugo-Slavia.** —**Yu'go·sla'vi·an,** *adj., n.*

Yu·kon (ū'kon), *n.* **1.** river flowing from NW Canada through C Alaska into Bering Sea. **2.** territory in NW Canada.

Yule (ūl), *n.* **1.** Christmas. **2.** the Christmas season. [OE *geōl*]

Yule log, a large log burned at Christmas.

Yule·tide (ūl'tīd'), *n.* Christmas time; the Christmas season.

Yung·kia (yúng'jyä'), *n.* seaport in E China. Formerly, **Wenchow.**

Y.W.C.A., Young Women's Christian Association.

Y.W.H.A., Young Women's Hebrew Association.

Z

Z, z (zē), *n., pl.* **Z's; z's.** the 26th and last letter of the alphabet.

Z, 1. *Chem.* atomic number. 2. zenith.

z., zone.

Za·greb (zä'greb), *n.* city in NW Yugoslavia.

zai·bat·su (zī·bät'sü), *n.pl. or sing.* the leading families of Japan, directing its industries.

Zam·be·zi (zam·bē'zi), *n.* river flowing from S Africa into the Indian Ocean.

Zam·bi·a (zam'bē·ə), *n.* country in SE Africa. Formerly called Northern Rhodesia.

za·ny (zā'ni), *n., pl.* –nies. **1.** fool. **2.** *Archaic.* clown. [< F < dial. Ital. *zanni,* orig. var. of *Giovanni* John]

Zan·zi·bar (zan'zə·bär), *n.* **1.** island near the E coast of Africa. **2.** country consisting of the island of Zanzibar and nearby smaller islands. Formerly a British protectorate; now joined in a federation, Tanzania, with Tanganyika.

Zar·a·thus·tra (zar'ə·thüs'trə), *n.* Zoroaster. **—Zar·a·thus·tri·an** (zar'ə·thüs'tri·ən), *adj., n.*

zeal (zēl), *n.* eager desire; earnest enthusiasm. [< L < Gk. *zelos*] **—Syn.** fervor, ardor.

Zea·land (zē'lənd), *n.* the largest island in Denmark, in the E part. Copenhagen is located on it.

zeal·ot (zel'ət), *n.* person who shows too much zeal; fanatic.

zeal·ot·ry (zel'ət·ri), *n.* too great zeal; fanaticism.

zeal·ous (zel'əs), *adj.* full of zeal; eager; earnest; enthusiastic. **—zeal'ous·ly**, *adv.* **—zeal'ous·ness,** *n.* **—Syn.** ardent, fervent, passionate. **—Ant.** apathetic, indifferent.

ze·bra (zē'brə), *n.* a wild animal like a horse but striped with dark bands on white. [< African lang.] **—ze·brine** (zē'brīn; -brin), *adj.*

ze·bu (zē'bū), *n.* an animal resembling an ox but with a large hump. The zebu is a domestic animal in Asia and E. Africa. [< F]

Zebu

Zech·a·ri·ah (zek'ə·rī'ə), *n.* **1.** prophet of Israel, in the sixth century B.C. **2.** book of the Old Testament written by him.

zed (zed), *n. Esp. Brit.* the letter Z, z. [< F *zède* < LL < Gk. *zeta*]

zee (zē), *n. Esp. U.S.* the letter Z, z.

Zee·brug·ge (zā'brüg'ə), *n.* seaport in NW Belgium.

Zeit·geist (tsīt'gīst'), *n. German.* characteristic thought or feeling of a period of time.

Zend (zend), *n.* the translation and explanation of the Zoroastrian Avesta. **—Zend'ic,** *adj.*

Zend-A·ves·ta (zend'ə·ves'tə), *n.* the sacred writings of the Zoroastrian religion.

ze·nith (zē'nith), *n.* **1.** the point in the heavens directly overhead. See the diagram under nadir. **2.** the highest point; culmination. [< OF or Med.L *senit* < Ar. *samt* (*ar-rās*) the way (over the head)] **—ze'nith·al,** *adj.* **—Syn. 2.** top, apex, summit.

Ze·no (zē'nō), *n.* 336?–264? B.C., Greek philosopher who founded the philosophy of Stoicism.

Zeph·a·ni·ah (zef'ə·nī'ə), *n.* **1.** a Hebrew prophet. **2.** a book of the Old Testament containing his prophecies.

zeph·yr (zef'ər), *n.* **1.** the west wind. **2.** any soft, gentle wind; mild breeze. **3.** Also, zephyr yarn or worsted. a fine, soft yarn or worsted. [< L < Gk. *zephyros*]

Zep·pe·lin, zep·pe·lin (zep'ə·lən; zep'lən), *n.* a large dirigible balloon shaped like a cigar. [after F. von *Zeppelin*, airship builder]

ze·ro (zir'ō), *n., pl.* -ros, -roes, *adj.* **—n. 1.** naught; 0. **2.** point marked with a zero on the scale of a thermometer, etc. **3.** temperature that corresponds to zero on the scale of a thermometer; complete absence of quantity; nothing. **4.** the lowest point: *his courage was at zero.* **—adj. 1.** of or at zero. **2.** not any; none at all. [< Ital. < Ar. *ṣifr* empty. Doublet of CIPHER.]

zero hour, time set for beginning an attack, etc.

zest (zest), *n.* **1.** keen enjoyment; relish: *a hungry man eats with zest.* **2.** a pleasant or exciting quality, flavor, etc.: *wit gives zest to conversation.* **—v.** give zest to. [< F *zeste* orange or lemon peel] **—zest'ful,** *adj.* **—zest'ful·ly,** *adv.* **—zest'ful·ness,** *n.* **—zest'less,** *adj.*

ze·ta (zā'tə; zē'tə), *n.* the sixth letter (Z, ζ) of the Greek alphabet.

Zeus (zūs), *n. Gk. Myth.* the ruler of gods and men, identified by the Romans with Jupiter.

Zhu·kov (zhü'kəf), *n.* Georgi K., born 1896, Soviet general, defense minister from 1955 to 1957.

zig·zag (zig'zag'), *adj., adv., v.,* -zagged, -zagging, *n.* **—adj., adv.** with short, sharp turns from one side to the other. **—v.** move in a zigzag way. **—n. 1.** a zigzag line or course. **2.** one of the short, sharp turns of a zigzag. [< F]

zinc (zingk), *n., v.,* zincked (zingkt), zinck·ing (zingk'ing); zinced, zinc·ing. **—n.** *Chem.* a bluish-white metal, Zn, very little affected by air and moisture. Zinc is used as a coating for iron, in mixture with other metals, as a roofing material, in electric batteries, in paint, and in medicine. **—v.** coat or cover with zinc. [< G *zink*] **—zinc·ic** (zingk'ik), **zinc'ous,** *adj.*

zinc ointment, salve containing zinc oxide, used esp. in treating skin disorders.

zinc oxide, an insoluble white powder, ZnO, used in making paint, rubber, glass, cosmetics, ointments, etc.

zing (zing), *n., interj.* a sharp humming sound. **—v.** make such a sound, esp. in going rapidly. [imit.]

zin·ni·a (zin'i·ə), *n.* a garden plant grown for its showy flowers of many colors. [< NL; named after J. G. *Zinn*, botanist]

Zi·on (zī'ən), *n.* **1.** hill in Jerusalem on which the royal palace and the temple were built. **2.** Israel; the people of Israel. **3.** heaven; the heavenly city. **4.** the church of God. Also, Sion.

Zi·on·ism (zī'ən·iz·əm), *n.* a plan or modern movement to colonize Jewish people in Palestine. **—Zi'on·ist,** *n.* **—Zi'on·is'tic,** *adj.*

zip (zip), *n., v.,* zipped, zip·ping. **—n. 1.** a sudden, brief hissing sound, as of a flying bullet. **2.** *Colloq.* energy or vim. **—v. 1.** make a sudden, brief hissing sound. **2.** *Am., Colloq.* proceed with energy. **3.** fasten or close with a zipper. [imit.]

ZIP code (zip), *Am.* a Post-Office code which assigns an identifying numeral to each zone of mail delivery. [< *Z*(one) *I*(mprovement) *P*(lan)]

zip·per (zip'ər), *n. Am.* **1.** a sliding fastener for clothing, shoes, etc. **2.** Zipper, a trademark for this fastening.

zip·py (zip'i), *adj.,* -pi·er, -pi·est. *Colloq.* full of energy; lively; gay.

zir·con (zèr'kon), *n.* a crystalline mineral, ZrSiO₄, that occurs in various forms and colors. Transparent zircon is used as a gem. [prob. < F < Ar. *zarqūn*]

zir·co·ni·um (zər·kō'ni·əm), *n. Chem.* a rare metallic element, Zr, used in alloys for wires, filaments, etc. **—zir·con·ic** (zər·kon'ik), *adj.*

zith·er (zith'ər), **zith·ern** (zith'ərn), *n.* a musical instrument having 30 to 40 strings, played with a plectrum and the fingers. [< G < L < Gk. *kithara.* Doublet of CITHARA and GUITAR.] **—zith'er·ist,** *n.*

Man playing a zither

zlo·ty (zlô'ti), *n., pl.* -tys or (*collectively*) -ty. **1.** a monetary unit of Poland, worth about ¼ of a cent (1950). **2.** a Polish nickel coin having this value.

Zn, *Chem.* zinc.

zo·di·ac (zō'di·ak), *n.* **1.** a belt of the heavens extending on both sides of the apparent yearly path of the sun. The zodiac is divided into 12 equal parts, called signs, named after 12 groups of stars, used in astrology. **3.** belt; circuit. [< L < Gk. *zoidiakos* (*kyklos*), lit., (circle) of animals, ult. < *zoion* animal] **—zo·di·a·cal** (zō·dī'ə·kəl), *adj.*

Zo·la (zō'lə), *n.* Emile, 1840–1902, French novelist.

zom·bi, zom·bie (zom'bi), *n., pl.* -bis, -bies. *Am.* **1.** a corpse brought back to life by supernatural agency. **2.** *Slang.* a very unintelligent and morbid appearing person. **3.** a strong alcoholic drink, usually of rum and brandy. [< Haitian Creole *zôbi* < African (Congo) *nsumbi* devil]

zon·al (zōn'əl), *adj.* **1.** of a zone; having to do with zones. **2.** divided into zones. **3.** of soils, manifesting influences of vegetation and climate as a result of the maturation of parent materials. **—zon'al·ly,** *adv.*

zone (zōn), *n.*, *v.*, **zoned, zon·ing.** —*n.* **1.** any of the five great divisions of the earth's surface, bounded by lines parallel to the equator. **2.** any region or area especially considered or set off: *a war zone.* **3.** area or district in a city or town under special restrictions as to building. **4.** in the U.S. parcel-post system, an area to all points within which the same rate of postage prevails for parcel-post shipments from a particular place. —*v.* **1.** divide into zones. **2.** be formed into zones. [< L. *zona* < Gk. *zone,* orig., girdle] —**zoned,** *adj.* —**zone′less,** *adj.*

zon·ing (zōn′ing), *n.* building restrictions in an area of a city or town.

zoo (zü), *n.* place where wild animals are kept and shown; zoological garden.

zoo–, *word element.* living being; animal, as in *zoology.* [< Gk., < *zoion* animal]

zo·o·ge·og·ra·phy (zō′ə·ji·og′rə·fi), *n.* study of the distribution of animals over the surface of the earth. —**zo′o·ge·og′ra·pher,** *n.* —**zo·o·ge·o·graph·ic** (zō′ə·jē′ə·graf′ik), **zo′o·ge′o·graph′i·cal,** *adj.* —**zo′o·ge′o·graph′i·cal·ly,** *adv.*

zo·og·ra·phy (zō·og′rə·fi), *n.* a complete description of animals and their habits; descriptive zoology. —**zo·og′ra·pher,** *n.* —**zo·o·graph·ic** (zō′ə·graf′ik), **zo′o·graph′i·cal,** *adj.*

zool., zoology.

zoological garden, zoo.

zo·ol·o·gy (zō·ol′ə·ji), *n.* **1.** the science of animals; the study of animals and animal life. Zoology deals with the form, structure, physiology, development, and classification of animals. It also includes study of special groups, as birds, insects, snakes, mammals, etc. **2.** the collective animal life of a particular region. —**zo′o·log·i·cal** (zō′ə·loj′ə·kəl), **zo′o·log′ic,** *adj.* —**zo′o·log′i·cal·ly,** *adv.* —**zo·ol′o·gist,** *n.*

zoom (züm), *v.* **1.** make a loud humming sound. **2.** move suddenly upward: *the airplane zoomed.* —*n.* a sudden upward flight. [imit.]

zo·o·phyte (zō′ə·fīt), *n.* animal that looks somewhat like a plant, such as a coral, sea anemone, etc. [< zoo– + Gk. *phyton* plant] —**zo·o·phyt·ic** (zō′ə·fit′ik), **zo′o·phyt′i·cal,** *adj.*

zoot suit (züt), *Am., Slang.* a man's suit with large shoulders, a long coat, and tight trouser cuffs.

Zo·ro·as·ter (zō′rō·as′tər; zō′–), *n.* Persian religious teacher who lived about 1000 B.C. Also,

Zarathustra. —**Zo·ro·as·tri·an** (zō′rō·as′tri·ən; zō′–), *adj., n.* —**Zo′ro·as′tri·an·ism,** *n.*

Zou·ave (zü·äv′; zwäv), *n.* **1.** soldier wearing an Oriental style of uniform. **2.** member of certain regiments in the French army, usually stationed in French territory in N Africa.

Zouave

zounds (zoundz), *interj.* *Archaic.* an oath expressing surprise or anger. [< *God's wounds!*]

Zr, *Chem.* zirconium.

zuc·chet·to (zü·ket′ō), *n., pl.* –**tos.** a small, round skullcap of varying colors, worn by Roman Catholic ecclesiastics. A priest wears black, a bishop violet, a cardinal red, and the Pope white. [< Ital.]

Zui·der Zee, Zuy·der Zee (zī′dər zē′), a shallow gulf in C Netherlands, now closed from the North Sea by a dike.

Zu·lu (zü′lü), *n., pl.* –**lus,** –**lu,** *adj.* —*n.* **1.** member of a warlike tribe in SE Africa. **2.** their language. —*adj.* of this tribe.

Zu·lu·land (zü′lü·land′), *n.* territory in NE Natal.

Zu·ñi (zün′yi; sün′–), *n., pl.* –**ñis,** –**ñi,** *adj.* —*n. Am.* member of a tribe of American Indians living in W New Mexico. —*adj.* of this tribe.

Zu·rich (zür′ik), *n.* city in N Switzerland.

zwie·back (tswē′bäk′; swē′–; swī′–; zwī′–), *n. Am.* a kind of bread cut into slices and toasted brown and crisp in an oven. [< G, < *zwie–* two + *backen* bake]

Zwing·li (tsving′li), *n.* Huldreich or Ulrich, 1484–1531, Swiss Protestant reformer. —**Zwing·li·an** (zwing′gli·ən; tsving′li·ən), *adj., n.* —**Zwing′li·an·ism,** *n.* —**Zwing′li·an·ist,** *adj., n.*

zy·gote (zī′gōt; zig′ōt), *n. Biol.* any cell formed by the union of two gametes (i.e., reproductive cells). A fertilized egg is a zygote. [< Gk. *zygotos* yoked < *zygon* yoke]

zy·mase (zī′mās), *n.* **1.** an enzyme in yeast that changes sugar into alcohol and carbon dioxide. **2.** any of a group of enzymes that change certain carbohydrates into CO_2 and H_2O when oxygen is present, or into CO_2 and alcohol or into lactic acid when no oxygen is present. [< F, < Gk. *zyme* leaven]

zy·mur·gy (zī′mėr·ji), *n.* branch of chemistry dealing with the processes of fermentation, as in brewing, etc. [< Gk. *zyme* leaven + *–ourgia* working]

COMPLETE PRONUNCIATION KEY

The pronunciation of each word is shown just after the word, in this way: **ab.bre.vi.ate** (ə.brē′vi.āt). The letters and signs used are pronounced as in the words below. The mark ′ is placed after a syllable with primary or strong accent, as in the example above. The mark ′ after a syllable shows a secondary or lighter accent, as in **ab.bre.vi.a.tion** (ə.brē′vi.ā′shən).

Some words, taken from foreign languages, are spoken with sounds that otherwise do not occur in English. Symbols for these sounds are given at the end of the table as "Foreign Sounds."

a	hat, cap	**i**	it, pin	**s**	say, yes
ā	age, face	**ī**	ice, five	**sh**	she, rush
ã	care, air			**t**	tell, it
ä	father, far	**j**	jam, enjoy	**th**	thin, both
		k	kind, seek	**t̶h̶**	then, smooth
b	bad, rob	**l**	land, coal		
ch	child, much	**m**	me, am	**u**	cup, son
d	did, red	**n**	no, in	**u̇**	put, book
		ng	long, bring	**ü**	rule, move
e	let, best	**o**	hot, rock	**ū**	use, music
ē	equal, see	**ō**	open, go		
ėr	term, learn	**ô**	order, all	**v**	very, save
		oi	oil, toy	**w**	will, woman
f	fat, if	**ou**	out, now	**y**	you, yet
g	go, bag			**z**	zero, breeze
h	he, how	**p**	pet, cup	**zh**	measure,
		r	run, try		seizure

ə occurs only in unaccented syllables and represents the sound of *a* in *a*bout, *e* in tak*e*n, *i* in penc*i*l, *o* in lem*o*n, and *u* in circ*u*s.

FOREIGN SOUNDS

Y as in French *lune*, German *süss*. Pronounce ē as in *equal* with the lips rounded for ü as in *rule*.

œ as in French *peu*, German *könig*. Pronounce ā as in *age* with the lips rounded for ō as in *open*.

N as in French *bon*. The N is not pronounced, but shows that the vowel before it is nasalized.

H as in German *ach*, Scottish *loch*. Pronounce k without closing the breath passage.